ULTIMATE COLLEGE GUIDE

#1 Comprehensive College Guide

by the Staff of *U.S.News & World Report*

Anne McGrath, Editor

Robert J. Morse, Director of Data Research

Samuel Flanigan, Deputy Director of Data Research

Margaret Mannix, Executive Editor

Brian Kelly, Series Editor

 sourcebooks

Published by Sourcebooks, Inc.
P.O. Box 4410
Naperville, Illinois 60567-4410
(630) 961-3900 FAX: (630) 961-2168
www.sourcebooks.com

Eighth Edition
Printed and bound in the United States of America
DR 10 9 8 7 6 5 4 3 2 1

Table of Contents

Introduction

In the coming months, you will be tackling the often overwhelming, frequently confusing, always anxiety-producing, and (we hope) ultimately rewarding task of selecting the right college and getting in. We may not be able to ease your worries completely, but we think the 2011 edition of the *Ultimate College Guide* will be a pretty big help on all other counts.

This book will lead you through each step of the process, from figuring out what you want in a college and researching which schools fill the bill to putting together a killer application and negotiating a financial aid package after you make it in. The exclusive Insider's Index, which begins on page 93, contains a rich assortment of data that you can use to compare colleges. The Ultimate College Directory, which begins on page 325, allows you to dig deep into the details.

The first step in the process is to figure out what you want your new life in college to be like. Chapter One, "How to Choose the Right School for You," will help you frame and find answers to such crucial questions as: What academic programs interest you, and just how tough do you want the coursework to be? Outside of class, how will you create a life that's full and fun? What sort of campus setting will make you feel at home?

The chapter goes on to examine a number of routes you might take, including big universities and small liberal arts colleges, public honors programs, women's colleges, and community colleges. It also offers tips on how to research your potential schools (how to use the Internet wisely as a source of information, for example) and how to make the most of a visit to campus.

In Chapter Two, you'll learn what admissions deans really care about when they start scrutinizing you. You'll find out why your straight As might not be as awesome as you think they are and why being a member of one or two clubs or sports teams might serve you better than having joined 10. You'll hear about the value of "hooks"—the special qualities that make you interesting in a crowded field—and how to sharpen yours. The information in this chapter will be of particular use to the younger brothers and sisters of this year's college applicants because building a truly impressive résumé by senior year takes planning—and time.

Chapters Three and Four cover the nuts and bolts of getting in: taking the college entrance exams and putting together your application. We help you think through the decision about which test to take—the SAT or ACT, or both—and how to prepare for the big day. If you decide that some test prep might be in order, your options range from expensive private coaching to free online tutorials. In Chapter Four, you'll find detailed instructions on how to write a winning essay, how to ask for and get effective letters of recommendation, and how to stay in touch with the admissions office without driving anyone crazy.

Should you apply using early decision? Maybe, because in many cases an early applicant stands a better chance of getting in. But there are good reasons not to, as well; for one thing, you won't have multiple financial aid offers to consider. On page 57, Joyce Slayton Mitchell, former director of college advising at Nightingale-Bamford School in New York City, discusses common mistakes families make when students apply to college.

The final chapter lays out everything you need to know—but probably don't realize you need to know—about financial aid and winning scholarships.

The fact that three or four colleges can come up with wildly different ideas of how much a family can afford to pay leaves many parents scratching their heads in frustration. This chapter describes how colleges arrive at their figures and all of the tools they have handy to plug the gap between what you're expected to pay and the cost of freshman year. You'll learn about federal sources of aid (Pell grants, Stafford and PLUS loans, and work-study programs), state aid programs, institutional awards (based on need, academic achievement, or a particular talent), and loans from private lenders. And in case you end up with a bottom line you can't live with, we'll teach you how to go back and successfully ask for more.

The Insider's Index will show you how your colleges stack up against the competition in areas of special interest to applicants. Take note of which schools have the best record of graduating their students, for example. Note which schools lose the most freshmen before sophomore year; when you're visiting, you might want to ask for an explanation. A look at the table on page 95 ("Schools that are the hardest and easiest to get into") will tell you whether your test scores, grade point average, and class standing put you in the ballpark or not.

Several of the tables should help you deal with money matters. The "Great deals at great schools" table on page 153, for example, features schools that give you the most for your money. To assemble the list, we factored in each school's *U.S. News* rank (which appears in its directory entry in this book) and the cost of attending after aid is taken into account. The higher the quality of the program and the lower the cost, the better the deal. Beginning on page 164, you can see the average size of each school's financial aid package, what proportion of the student body gets aid, and how much of the package comes in the form of grants and loans, on average. You can also see, beginning on page 157, how much debt the average graduate takes on.

The Ultimate College Directory provides detailed profiles of some 1,400 four-year accredited colleges and universities based on an exhaustive survey *U.S. News* sends out annually. The profiles contain the most up-to-date information on virtually everything from programs of study available, to the academic credentials of the most recently admitted class, to housing options and various aspects of extracurricular life. You'll get a sense of the demographic makeup of both the student body and the faculty; what sorts of services are available to disabled students; and information on tuition, room and board, and the specifics of financial aid.

As you do your research, remember that the choices you make will have a big impact on your quality of life for the next four years. Very likely, they'll influence your career path over the long term, too—and maybe the size of your paycheck. We hope that the leads you find in this guide will point you in the right direction.

Chapter One

How to Choose the Right School for You

You're about to make one of your first grown-up decisions, and it's going to be a tough one. From among the thousands of colleges in the country, you have to choose just a handful to apply to. You could take the easy way out, of course—you know, pick a school according to how well it did in the NCAA Final Four, or the one that has the most luxurious dorms, or just fall in with the driven seniors who will apply indiscriminately to most of the Ivies.

Or you can do the slightly harder work that will pay off for decades to come. You can take a long look in the mirror and ask yourself: Who *is* this person anyway? What does she want out of college? What kind of campus will make him feel at home? If you haven't worried too much about self-awareness before, then now's the time—before you make a huge, costly blooper and wind up unhappy.

What kinds of situations have made you feel academically and socially successful in high school? If you haven't been successful, why not? Which kinds of classes have you gotten the most out of? What sorts of people have you enjoyed hanging out with? Which activities have really been fun? How different from high school do you want your college experience to be?

Remember, you're aiming to find the school that best suits *you*—not your friends, not your teachers, and not your parents. This chapter will help you narrow the choices down to a manageable list of five to 10 places where you stand a great chance of being happy for the next four years. Your final list should include "reach" schools (schools that may be a bit too hard to get into), "probables" (schools where your qualifications are apt to get you in), and "safeties" (ones you can count on accepting you).

Don't skimp on the "safeties" category. As the competition to get into college has increased, lots of schools that have been thought of as safeties are suddenly awash in very strong applicants. One persuasive argument for applying to a couple of sure things is that many colleges and universities can get pretty generous with their scholarships when they want to nab candidates whose grades put them near the top of the applicant pool.

Questions to ask yourself

Here's a shocker: As many as one in every three first-year college students decides for some reason not to come back for sophomore year. Many of the students who drop out or transfer are those who didn't do their research and made a hasty decision the first time around. There's no need for you to find yourself among them if you ponder the following questions as you do your research.

What kinds of academic programs interest me?

First, ask yourself why you want to go to college at all. Are you looking for a chance to dig deep into your studies, to think big thoughts, and to discuss them late into the night over coffee with your intellectual friends? Or are you mostly after the training that will prepare you for a specific career? Somebody who

thinks of college as a time to burn the midnight oil exploring new lines of inquiry is apt to be happiest with a liberal arts education that will supply the general knowledge and critical thinking skills needed in any number of jobs. A preprofessional or more practice-oriented education, one with lots of internship opportunities, for example, might suit you better if you already know that you're headed for a career in, say, nursing, nuclear engineering, or graphic design.

But unless you have such a highly specialized career in mind, knowing what type of education you want (liberal arts or practice-oriented) isn't the same thing as knowing exactly what you want to study—nor should it be. College counselors and admissions officers say one of the most common mistakes high school students make when figuring out where to apply is that they worry too much about finding colleges strong in whatever field they think will be their major.

Partly, this is because *not* knowing what they want to study makes them anxious, especially when Aunt Martha, their parents' colleagues, and even the clerks at the local grocery store keep asking them where they're going to go and what they plan to study. Another reason is that with such a long list of colleges to consider, having an intended major to plug into an Internet search engine seems like an obvious and easy way to whittle the list down to size.

However, many students come to regret this overly simple strategy. The fact is, most undergrads change their minds about what they want to study at least once, and a good many switch majors two or three times. "We think that's a healthy thing," says William Hiss, vice president for external affairs at Bates College in Lewiston, Maine. "Some of the jobs young people today will do haven't even been invented yet."

Stay nimble. A better approach when you're not absolutely positive about your career direction is to look for schools that offer you flexibility. Let's say that you're interested in art. If you think it's definitely going to be your life's work, then you should consider a specialty school like the San Francisco Art Institute or the Maryland Institute College of Art in Baltimore. But if you think there's a possibility you'll want to do something else, you might want to pick a liberal arts college or a big university where art is one item in a rich menu of choices and where it's easy to get a taste of some other fare. A good rule of thumb, counselors say, is to identify three or four academic fields that excite you and find schools with strong departments in all of them.

Besides giving thought to what you might like to study, it's a good idea to check out how the learning happens. For example, freshmen often feel so lost in the crowd when they come to a big university that many schools now try to help new students connect with other students and faculty members right from the start. Instead of dumping newcomers all into large introductory lecture courses with 300 or 400 students, they might put each freshman into one small seminar of 15 or 20 that is taught by a professor rather than a graduate assistant.

Many of the larger institutions, including the University of Texas–Austin, the University of Maryland–College Park, and the University of Georgia–Athens, offer honors programs for their most capable undergraduates. These programs typically feature rigorous coursework in smaller-than-normal classes and intensive research with the possibility of a "senior capstone" project, like a thesis. At a small liberal arts college, as opposed to a large university, you're more apt to spend much of your time deep in class discussions, contributing to group projects, or working one-on-one with a professor on some kind of independent study.

Live and learn. On some campuses, students are grouped together in learning communities, sometimes called "living/learning communities." They might take two or more courses together and even live in the same dorm so that discussions can continue long after class ends. You're interested in science? Investigate the chances that you'll get to participate in an original research project with a faculty member supervising you. Whether or not you intend to stick with Spanish, you might want to check out the study abroad options. On some campuses, large numbers of students spend time

studying overseas because, in the era of globalization, it is good preparation for working in almost any kind of business. If you've enjoyed community service as a high school student, you might be happy at a college that makes service a class requirement—where architecture students might direct the renovation of a local day-care center, for example, or urban policy students might volunteer at inner-city nonprofit agencies.

Someone who's superfocused on preparing for

"Some of the jobs young people today will do haven't even been invented yet."

the job market might want to think about schools that emphasize internships or offer cooperative education. In co-op programs, undergrads in various fields—from marketing and engineering to communications and psychology—fit several terms of paid, professional work experience into their schedules. Alternating between full-time work and full-time study means that you can get a grasp of the theory in class before seeing it in action in the office. When you return to class, you can then hash over what worked and what didn't. Employers love to hire graduates of co-op programs because they often show up with already-honed communication skills and have had practice solving problems. They also have lots of experience operating in teams, which is how most people work these days. Meanwhile, the paychecks, which can total thousands of dollars a year, go a long way toward covering tuition. The trade-off is that you usually have to put in a fifth year of college and give up your summers from sophomore year until graduation to fit in all the coursework.

How challenging do I want school to be?

Lots of students these days are so determined to impress their friends and families that they automatically limit their list to the most selective colleges they can get into. They don't stop to think about how hard they want to study and how well they handle pressure. These are both important questions to

You can't choose the right school unless you know the answer, so get set to take a long look inward. Ask yourself these questions:

- **What do I want to get out of college?** Maybe you're after an intense but broad intellectual experience. Or perhaps you want training for a career in Web design.
- **What's my learning style?** Are you the hide-in-the-back-of-the-lecture-hall type? Or are you someone who thrives on being in the thick of the discussion?
- **How competitive am I?** You may struggle just to stay in the middle of the pack at a college where the whole freshman class consists of former high school stars.
- **What will I want to do with my time outside of class?** Volunteer at a homeless shelter? Hike in the mountains? Go shopping?
- **How important is diversity?** Perhaps you're pretty conservative but don't mind taking the heat from liberals, or maybe you're more relaxed when you're one of the crowd and everyone looks like you.
- **How independent am I?** Remember: A major reason students transfer is that they want to be closer to home.

ask yourself as you get ready to leave high school for the bigger world. Often, the answer hinges on where you fall now—and where you want to fall—in the academic pecking order. If you loved being at the top of the heap in high school, then you might get bummed out at a college where everybody was a valedictorian, too. You might find yourself pulling all-nighters on a regular basis just to stay in the middle of the pack. Rather than be miserable and stressed out for the next four years, it might be better to pick a somewhat less competitive school where you can get a good education but still stand out.

If, on the other hand, you're jazzed by competition and by people who can match you brilliant thought for brilliant thought, you might be happiest at a really tough school—as long as you come prepared to study and even to fight for resources. The best way to tell if a school has more of a collaborative or cutthroat culture is to ask its current students. Find out, for example, if team learning, in which five or six students work together and all receive the same grade, is common. This kind of learning is becoming more popular as schools look for ways to really engage students in their coursework. Or maybe you have to worry that somebody's going to destroy your science experiment when no one's looking. One New Jersey student ended up choosing the College of William and Mary in Virginia rather than a nearby university after a tour guide at the university let slip that during exam time, students sometimes ripped key pages out of books in the library. "I couldn't deal with a place that competitive," she says.

Will I be happier at a big university or a small liberal arts college?

Howard Payne University in Brownwood, Texas, has an enrollment of around 1,400 students. The population at the University of Texas–Austin, meanwhile, is about 39,000 undergrads, plus 11,000 graduate students. Many liberal arts colleges hold the line at a couple of thousand students; a midsize university might enroll 10,000 or so. It isn't necessarily true that small equals friendly and intimate and big means lost-in-the-shuffle, but a school's size will definitely make a difference in your college experience.

For one thing, size is usually a pretty good indicator of how much a college or university focuses on its undergraduates (at big universities, graduate students often get the attention of the best faculty members and first dibs on things like laboratory space). Smaller schools typically have smaller classes than large universities and fewer students per professor, so faculty members can be available for plenty of give-

and-take with undergraduates inside the classroom, during office hours, over coffee in the student center, and sometimes even in their homes. Students can get to know each other a lot more easily in a discussion-oriented class of 20 or 30 than in a huge lecture of 300 or 400 people. In smaller groups, they are more apt to collaborate on projects, and are more likely to be actively engaged in their coursework.

Even though many big schools are making an effort to do a better job of serving undergraduates with freshman seminars, learning communities, and other programs, it is still often true that first-year students find themselves lectured to by graduate assistants in one jam-packed auditorium after the next. You'll want to ask about average class sizes and a school's student-to-faculty ratio, which will give you some indication of how accessible professors will be.

Liberal arts colleges also tend to have many fewer graduate students than universities, if any. That means that students in the sciences, particularly, are likely to get a real crack at doing serious one-on-one research with the school's most accomplished professors. On university campuses, the Ph.D. candidates are going to take precedence, and the faculty stars might never actually work with undergrads.

On the other hand, the typical university offers a much wider variety of majors than most small colleges and many more courses to choose from, although space might be limited to those in the major. Moreover, in fields like science and engineering, where you want cutting-edge research to be reflected in your classwork, it can be a real advantage to be on a campus that is producing Ph.D.s. Many students cherish the freedom that comes along with being anonymous in a large crowd, and they'd rather learn by lecture than be put on the spot in a class discussion. After all, it's not so easy to skip class or to let your readings or papers slide when you're one of only a small number of students.

Are you looking for a community where the faces are mostly familiar and there's a sense of common identity? Do you want a place with such a multitude of people—and diverse groups of people—that you're constantly meeting someone new and different from you? A large school is bound to offer more social and extracurricular options than a small school. A look at the Howard Payne and University of Texas websites reveals that the smaller school has fewer than 40 clubs and organizations, compared with UT's 900-plus.

Small colleges often work hard to ensure that new students are all set to succeed on campus and that they're bonding with peers and professors. At a big school, you'll have to take charge of reaching out and forming new relationships, or you will risk being lost among the masses. Richard DiFeliciantonio, vice president for enrollment at Ursinus College, a liberal arts school in Pennsylvania, points to the lower graduation rates at big universities as a sign that such schools can be really rotten choices for even bright students who arrive without a clear direction and focus, because those students are likely to flounder when left completely to their own devices.

It will be up to you to stand up for yourself and to be insistent, to ask for face time with your professors, and to see the registrar when necessary to get a place in a required course. It will be up to you to find a group of students with whom you'll feel like you belong. One young woman who chose Pennsylvania State University (undergraduate student body: around 36,000) and loved it recalls that as soon as she arrived for freshman orientation, she began seeking out professors for chats and investigating a list of more than 600 clubs. She discovered student government, and, overall, had a great four years.

What kind of place will make me feel at home?

When you pick a college, you're also committing to where—not to mention how—you'll be spending almost all your time for the next four years. On the way from your dorm to the library, will you be walking by burned-out buildings on filthy streets or biking past ivy-covered brick buildings and perfect green quads? During your downtime, will you go snowboarding or snorkeling, apple picking or clothes shopping? Is hiking in the country your idea of a good time, or do you really enjoy exploring a city and diving into the club scene?

Many students, especially those who intend to study hard in college, never think about how weather and geography can be a boost or a downer, and how much both can affect their ability to turn out grade-A work. One graduate of a college in Connecticut holds the cloudy days and limited vistas at least partly accountable for her four years of undergraduate misery. Coming from Nevada, she'd known before enrolling that Connecticut was short on blue skies and mountain views, but she figured—wrongly—that the scenery wouldn't affect her mood much.

Obviously, the farther you go from home, the tougher (or more expensive) it will be to drop back in for the weekend. How badly do you want to stay in close contact with your family and hometown buddies? Some college counselors advise their clients to page through the calendar and count up the holidays or other dates that will be spent at home. How much will all these trips cost in time and fares? Research shows that well over half of all college freshmen attend a school within 100 miles of home.

Weigh the action. Think about how hectic you'd like the pace of life around the campus to be. One rural New Englander was dead set on going to New York University until she spent a summer there and found city life too stressful. She picked a small California college instead. On the other hand, one young man who chose the University of Wisconsin–Madison reports that shortly after classes started, he realized that the quiet setting was going to drive him nuts. Because he wanted to become a financial adviser eventually, he decided to transfer to NYU, where he could take advantage of Wall Street by snagging internships and summer jobs that would prepare him for his career.

Consider where you'll actually be living, too. Some colleges put most of their students in campus housing, and the lounges and rooms are where a whole lot of the fun happens. At other schools large numbers of students live in off-campus apartments or commute from home. You might like the freedom at a school like that—or you might really miss having the dorm experience.

One final point: local companies tend to recruit on campus, which means that many students end up settling near their college. Do you like your favorite school's location well enough to stick around after graduation? A major move might mean starting out your job search without a network of connections that can help open doors for you.

What will I want to do in my spare time?

Remember, you're moving your whole self to campus, not just your brains. What else really charges your batteries? There aren't too many athletes who get to be stars in college, but if you played lacrosse or field hockey seriously in high school, then you might find that there's a big hole in your week if you choose a school without an intramural program. If music or theater has always kept you busy in your off hours, what will you do if there's no drama club or singing groups? A school's website often includes lists and descriptions of student organizations, sometimes with e-mail links so you can send your questions to current members. Whether you end up at a small college or a university, belonging to an organization of students who share your interests is a great way to make lasting friends.

It's a good idea to talk with students who participate in the clubs or sports that interest you because you'll want to find out how active the club is and how hard it is to get off the sidelines and to be involved. There might be a jazz ensemble on paper, but maybe there's been no concert in three years. Maybe the drama club or the debate team is so filled with talented people that you'll mostly be sitting in the audience.

Will I fit in?

This question worries even the most confident high schoolers. Yes, you probably want college to be a much bigger and more exciting world than you're used to. And yes, you probably know that living in a diverse community is good preparation for real life. But feeling comfortable is important, too. If you're not, then chances are you won't feel able to freely speak up and express your views or to be as relaxed and socially content as you might be.

How much diversity is right for you? Think for a minute about your social life in high school. If you felt you had to blend in with the "in crowd" no matter what, then you probably should stick with schools where many of the students are like you, whether racially, economically, politically, or in their ideas of fun. On the other hand, if you were happy to go your own way or enjoyed the idea of being in a diverse community, then too much sameness may feel boring and suffocating.

Ease up, Mom and Dad

The following stories are true, but names have been omitted for obvious reasons:

- The day after their son was rejected by a highly selective college, Mom and Dad marched into his guidance counselor's office waving plane tickets. The counselor was instructed to jump on a plane and go straighten out the "mistake."
- One father called his daughter's counselor to read the essay he had written for her Ivy League application. The daughter rejected her father's version and wrote her own, only to learn later that Mom's "typing" was actually heavy editing.
- A parent called her alma mater with a question about the status of her son's application. An admissions officer called the son back with the answer, only to learn that the boy had no idea he'd applied to the school and had no desire to attend. The son withdrew his mother's application.

Are some parents overinvolved in their child's college search? You bet. "Parents, bite your tongues, go to your rooms, back off," advises Wylie Mitchell, dean of admissions at Bates College in Maine. A kid who spends freshman year at Mom's or Dad's top choice often spends sophomore year as a transfer student. "A lot of it is a self-fulfilling prophecy," says Karen Levin Coburn, coauthor of *Letting Go: A Parents' Guide to Understanding the College Years.* "If they come in with a chip on their shoulder, they probably won't seek out opportunities that make it a positive experience."

Letting the teenager take the lead leaves parents in an important supporting role. You can help develop a list of schools that all of you are comfortable with by making suggestions and by asking questions, rather than by dictating what you believe are the most acceptable five or 10. If your child insists that she wants a diverse, urban environment, then don't keep harping on the virtues of a small liberal arts college in the middle of nowhere. In fact, don't harp at all.

You should lay out any financial or geographical constraints up front, however. You need to be serious about the situation for your own sake as well as your child's. It can be devastating to a student who has his heart set on Harvard to hear in April that, despite a $16,000 award, the budget just won't bear it.

College visits require even more restraint. "Top off the tank and stand by," advises Howard Greene, a former admissions officer at Princeton who is now an independent educational consultant in Westport, Connecticut. James Sumner, former dean of admission and financial aid at Grinnell College in Iowa, recalls attempting to interview one young man whose father first refused to leave the room, then answered all of the questions himself. (The student didn't get in.)

Hands off the application essay as well. Admissions officers can easily distinguish between the writing of a 45-year-old and a 17-year-old, so "editing" is apt to backfire. Instead, plan on reviewing your child's application folder for mistakes or omissions. Once it has been sent, do not call, write, or e-mail the admissions office. All communication should come from the student.

In the end, if a thin envelope should drop through your mail slot, then the best course of action is to receive it philosophically and supportively, and to focus on where the student did get in. If you turn your child's great disappointment into your own, then he's apt to feel that he has failed you, too.

You might be happiest in a great big polyglot population—as long as you can belong to a club or a sports team with others who feel like kindred spirits.

Keep in mind that diversity means much more than the color of the faces you'll encounter. You'll also want to think about students' socioeconomic, political, religious, geographic, and educational backgrounds. How will you feel, as a public school graduate, if many of the kids you're living with graduated from prep school and come from families with tons of money? Or how will you feel as an atheist if a large number of other students share—and actively practice—a particular faith? Some students are looking for a chance to be among people with different perspectives; it allows them to test their own worldview and to expand or defend it.

Consider what's cool. Whether you'll feel at home on campus will also depend on the dominant culture, if there is one. What's considered cool to do outside of class? Investigate whether everybody heads off to fraternity parties on the weekend or is more apt to be marching at an antiglobalization rally. Or are students 20,000 strong in the football stadium? Maybe there's equal room for all three. Is it perfectly respectable to spend Friday nights at the library, or is it considered kind of nerdy? "We don't have football—we're chess champions," says Freeman Hrabowski, president of the University of Maryland–Baltimore County. "This is a place where it's cool to be smart." To get a fix on these aspects of diversity, it's a good idea to quiz as many current students as possible. The student newspaper and a calendar of events can also help you figure out what matters on campus.

Current students can also tell you how well a highly diverse population actually mixes in practice. Although large, urban schools and big state universities usually score best on diversity measures, sometimes they can also be the most fractured. Students find and hang around with other kids exactly like themselves. If you notice during your campus visit that the African-American students are sitting at one table in the dining hall, Koreans at another, and female lacrosse players at a third, then it's probably safe to assume that there's not a whole lot of mixing and mingling going on outside the cafeteria, either.

How important is prestige?

When college freshmen are asked to identify what factors made them choose their school, academic reputation usually tops the list. One obvious reason is that it is impressive to get into a name-brand college or university that everybody admires. But there's another reason, too. Many people r——ely on school reputation because they have so little actual knowledge of the colleges they're considering. A school's prestige is taken as a sign that it's really, really good.

Yes, there's a connection, and not just in the minds of parents. Employers also assume that prestigious schools do a good job of educating their future workers. Some leading companies recruit almost exclusively on elite campuses, and an Ivy League degree definitely can help you get your foot in the door when you're looking for your first job. Being surrounded by crowds of smart, talented students almost certainly means a higher level of discussion and debate than you would find at a less competitive institution. It also suggests you'll acquire a list of valuable contacts for later in life.

But prestige isn't the only or necessarily the best indicator of quality—particularly when it comes to figuring out which school is right for you. Many lesser-known colleges offer top-notch, tough programs with very strong records of sending students on to graduate school. The "top 10" lists of colleges whose graduates go on for Ph.D.s in various disciplines are sprinkled liberally with names like Reed College, Carleton, Oberlin, and Kalamazoo. While national acceptance rates to medical school hover around 50 percent, Knox College in Illinois gets nearly 80 percent of its applicants into med school, while Abilene Christian University placed more than 80 percent of its med school applicants over the past five years.

Ask for the stats. Most colleges keep statistics like these, and you should ask for them, as well as information on the kinds of alumni networking opportunities the schools offer and the kinds of jobs previous graduates have landed.

Will a degree from an Ivy guarantee you a bigger paycheck? Not necessarily. Consider the results of one study (headed by a Princeton economist, no less). When the researchers compared the earnings

If school is a struggle

It used to be that colleges simply rejected students with learning disabilities—or left them alone to sink or swim. These days, students who learn in nontraditional ways are finding that scores of schools are not only happy to take them, but will take pains to help them succeed. The key to getting help is to be "upfront and know what to ask for," says educational consultant Imy F. Wax, coauthor of the *K&W Guide to Colleges for Students with Learning Disabilities or Attention Deficit Disorder.*

First, you have to find a college whose policies match your needs, because approaches to serving learning-disabled students vary considerably from campus to campus. Many schools tend to limit their services to untimed tests in quiet rooms, plus the regular academic counseling that's offered to all students. Others add tutoring and training in time management. Some provide textbooks on tape to students who have a hard time reading; others send a paid note-taker to class with anyone who can't process a lecture. The services are usually free, but not always. Freshmen and sophomores in the University of Arizona's Strategic Alternative Learning Techniques program, for example, get a learning specialist, a writing program, and tutors for $2,450 a semester. Upperclassmen, who use the services less frequently, pay somewhat less.

Ironically, the one college in the country dedicated entirely to students with learning disabilities and ADHD (attention deficit hyperactivity disorder), two-year Landmark College in southern Vermont, refuses to provide note-takers or books on tape. Landmark, which receives two applications for every $54,200-per-year slot, prides itself instead on arming students with the skills and strategies necessary to pursue a rigorous liberal arts curriculum. Learning communities, a student-to-faculty ratio of 5 to 1, and a "master notebook" system (main ideas of a lecture or text go in one column and supporting details in another) help result in 92 percent of graduates transferring to four-year colleges.

To find out how welcoming a college is apt to be, call the admissions office and ask about programs for learning-disabled students. If your call is referred to an academic support office, a learning opportunities program, or another office that handles matters related to the Americans with Disabilities Act, and everyone seems eager to respond, then that's a good sign. (You'll want to dig for details about what kinds of support are available, though, because colleges can define services for learning-disabled students in very different ways.) If your questions to admissions are greeted by hemming and hawing, then the college may not, in fact, provide much in the way of services.

---

of students who were accepted to elite colleges but decided to attend lesser-known schools with the earnings of students who attended the elite schools, they found that the former group earned just as much as the latter. Why? It's the students that matter, not the school, say the economists. Students who are accepted by elite colleges aren't just smart; they are motivated, hardworking, and creative—traits that will help them get ahead regardless of where they actually go to school.

How should you use the *U.S. News* college rankings?

Each year, *U.S.News & World Report* surveys nearly 1,450 four-year colleges and universities in the country to gather information about their academic and extracurricular programs. The results of that survey are published in one form in this book (in the lengthy descriptions of each school that begin on page 330). They are also used to create a yearly ranking of schools that is published each sum-

An Ivy experience at half the cost?

St. Mary's College of Maryland and New College of Florida are both innovative small liberal arts schools that do well in the annual *U.S. News* college rankings. Both offer tough academic programs and generally small classes that attract some pretty impressive talent. But because they are public honors colleges within their state university systems, they're downright cheap compared to similar private colleges. A year's tuition, room, and board at St. Mary's runs around $24,000 for in-state students, and at New College, about $13,500.

The two schools are unusual in that they have their own separate campuses; the more typical public honors program is a "college within a college" on the grounds of State U, where students live in separate housing, attend accelerated classes, and do research that leads to a publishable paper or a thesis.

Often, honors students collect very generous scholarships. One recent computer science graduate of the University of Delaware, who focused his research on natural language processing and artificial intelligence, could have gone to the Massachusetts Institute of Technology, Harvard, Columbia, Cornell, or the University of Pennsylvania. But Delaware offered to fully cover the $70,000 cost of his four years there. Some 70 universities now offer honors programs as states fight to keep their best and brightest at home. Among them are the University of South Carolina, California State University–Fresno, Middle Tennessee State University, and Western Washington University.

Not surprisingly, these programs are breeding grounds for future graduate students. A recent survey found that 59 percent of St. Mary's alumni attend graduate school or professional school within five years of graduating. Some 10 percent of New College graduates have gone on to complete their Ph.D.s.

---

mer in a separate guide, "Best Colleges," available on newsstands, and on the *U.S. News* website (www.usnews.com). The rankings show how schools stack up against one another based on a number of quality measures, including the proportion of freshmen who return for sophomore year, the percentage of students who graduate within six years, average class size and student-to-faculty ratio, how much a school spends per student on instruction and research, and the capabilities of incoming students as measured by their class standing and test scores. *U.S. News* collects data on up to 16 of these indicators, crunches all the numbers, and ranks schools among their peer institutions.

Many guidance counselors and college admissions deans worry that high schoolers place too much importance on a school's numerical ranking in developing a list of colleges, arguing that it's impossible to reduce all of the intangibles that make a college a good fit to mere numbers. It's true that the ranking alone won't tell you what you need to know to make a decision, but the ranking tables are crammed with hard-to-gather information that allows you to compare schools on key characteristics that contribute to academic excellence. There hasn't been a whole lot of research done on how students pick colleges, but a couple of surveys of current students suggest that most applicants use rankings properly—as one piece of useful information about a school, not as the sole basis for a decision.

Mine the data. The best way to take advantage of the *U.S. News* rankings is to study the data for clues that will help you narrow your search. For instance, you can scan the column of SAT scores to figure out where you could be admitted—or even rise to the top of the applicant pool and possibly qualify for a merit scholarship. You can use the data on class size to get a sense of just how intimate the classroom experience will be—or how good the chances are that you can hide in the back of the room. You can check student-to-faculty ratios to see how much attention you're likely to get from professors outside of class, or look at the freshman retention rates to learn how hard schools work to keep students from dropping out. Perhaps you'll find a great candidate or two that you hadn't considered before, or even heard of. The rankings can be used to inform your thinking—they just won't provide an easy answer.

How safe will I be?

Universities have come to understand that they need to do a better job of protecting students from crime. Today, emergency phones and late-night buses or escorts are as common on campus as pizza boxes and laptops. Families can thank the federal government for the increased focus on security. The law now requires all schools receiving federal funding to report their statistics on how many and what kinds of crimes are committed on campus to the Department of Education and to publish the information in an annual report. Often, the information is available in the campus security area of the school's website. If you can't find it there, then call and ask for the latest report. By reading the local newspaper and asking the police for crime statistics, you can get a feel for what goes on in the world around the campus, too.

More specifically, you'll want to find out how secure the dorms are and whether outsiders have access to the library, fitness center, or student union. At the University of Maryland–Baltimore County, new dorms have been equipped with a video security system that requires visitors to stand in front of a camera before being buzzed in. The University of Pennsylvania has taken video technology to the campus perimeter, where it has installed a network of closed-circuit television cameras that keep an eye on the surrounding streets. Since the cameras were put in place, the school has seen an impressive drop in robberies and attempted robberies on campus. At the University of Delaware, students can read about incidents in a crime news box that pops up on the school's customized Web browser the day after they're reported. Depending on where you're looking, you might want to quiz officials about crisis policies and evacuation plans, too.

How much will it cost?

This is one of the first questions most parents are going to want an answer to, and it obviously has to be considered and discussed up front. But don't rule out a wonderful college just because it's expensive! If you're a desirable candidate, a school will usually do its best to meet your need with financial aid or, in some cases, scholarships based on your particular talents. Sometimes, a middle-income family with a highly qualified applicant is offered such a generous package that the pricey private school is actually less expensive than a $10,000 or $12,000 state university. Desirable students at or under the poverty line probably can count on having all their costs covered with a combination of federal, state, and college grants; student loans; and work-study. That said, Mom and Dad should talk about their financial limits early on. It can be crushing to be accepted by a first-choice school only to find out that it was never a real option. (For more on how to meet the costs of college, see Chapter Five.)

Where might I get the best deal?

Universities increasingly use money to attract the most talented applicants possible, so you'll definitely want to investigate schools where your qualifications put you among the cream of the applicant crop. The surest way to stand out is to have a grade point average and test scores that outshine the school's averages. "The institution will treat students at the top of the pecking order more generously," says Barry McCarty, former dean of enrollment services at Lafayette College in Easton, Pennsylvania.

Schools that draw most of their students from a single state or region and are trying to improve diversity on campus may be especially willing to shell out extra cash for students from far-flung places. "We'd like to see more out-of-state students apply," says Julie Rice Mallette, the director of scholarships and financial aid at North Carolina State University–Raleigh. On the other hand, sticking close to home can also save you money. Several states, including Georgia, Kentucky, South Carolina, New Mexico, and West Virginia, offer merit scholarships to state residents if they choose to attend a state school. Eligibility requirements vary by state, but the awards typically go to any student who has a record of achieving good grades. Those who qualify find that these programs generally cover the tuition at a state university and that the grants can be applied toward tuition at in-state private schools, too.

Is community college an option?

Here's a statistic that may surprise you: About 43 percent of all first-time college freshmen in the country go to a community college. Many of them will stop with a two-year associate's degree and join the workforce, but perhaps one third will continue on and graduate from a four-year college or university. Chances are they'll be well prepared to succeed once they transfer, and students who choose the two-plus-two option will almost certainly save money by starting out closer to home. They might even end up at a better four-year school than they would have as a freshman. "I was absolutely stoked!" says one young man of his transfer to the highly ranked and hard-to-get-into University of California–Berkeley. He had started out at his local community college after high school when every single one of his four-year choices turned him down.

Some high school graduates decide to attend a community college because they aren't yet academically ready for a four-year program or are not emotionally prepared to leave family and friends behind. Others want to keep the total cost of a four-year degree as low as possible. It has always been one mission of community colleges to prepare such students to continue successfully at state public universities. But now that two-year schools have been sprucing up their academic offerings to attract more competitive students, a growing number of their graduates have been using the two-year experience as a stepping stone to more selective private schools. Schools like Dickinson College in Carlisle, Pennsylvania; Washington University in St. Louis; New York University in New York City; Cornell University in Ithaca, New York; and Johns Hopkins University in Baltimore have launched scholarship programs for community college honors students. Some selective universities, including the University of Wisconsin–Madison, feature "dual enrollment" programs with local community colleges. Students

admitted to these programs are guaranteed a place at the partnering four-year school in their junior year if they complete an associate's degree.

At the same time, community colleges are revamping their course offerings to make them more challenging so that their grads are equipped for the greater rigors of a four-year school. Over the past 10 years, the number of two-year schools with honors programs has jumped by nearly 50 percent to more than 550, says Rod Risley, executive director of Phi Theta Kappa, a community college honors organization. Graduates of these programs speak highly of the small classes, dedicated teachers, and opportunities for one-on-one interaction with faculty members.

There's a pretty wide range of quality and mission among two-year colleges, so you'll have to choose carefully if this seems like the route for you. Some schools emphasize job training while others really concentrate on preparing students to continue a liberal arts education. Ask about transfer rates—and where graduates end up. Inquire whether the schools you're considering have any articulation agreements with public universities in your state. Such agreements spell out which community college classes will be accepted by the four-year school; they also signal whether successful transfers are a priority.

Once enrolled, don't specialize too much or choose a major. "We are looking for breadth and balance," says Jennifer Fondiller, dean of admissions at Barnard College in New York City. While four-year universities typically accept credits for most core courses, they often refuse to grant credit for upper-division courses or vocational classes. To avoid haggling later on, you will want to contact your prospective four-year schools as soon as possible during your freshman year, both to signal your interest and to find out which courses will transfer easily.

The right way to handle the research

Once you've figured out who you are and what type of school you want, it's time to start searching for the college that fits you best. Whittling the possibilities into a short list of the five or eight or 10 that you'll

When your back starts aching from too many hours in front of your computer, try curling up with a more traditional source of information: a book. We reviewed a shelf-load of selections on college admissions and found a number that are well worth your time.

- *Colleges That Change Lives* by Loren Pope (Penguin Books, 2006, $15). An advocate of a liberal arts education, Pope profiles 40 progressive, lesser-known schools that offer a first-class college experience.
- *Don't Miss Out* by Anna and Robert Leider (Octameron, 2009, $14). This is the flagship volume of an inexpensive but quality guidebook series that covers everything from campus visits to finding scholarships. Available at www.amazon.com or www.octameron.com.
- *Fiske Guide to Colleges 2011* by Edward B. Fiske (Sourcebooks, 2010, $23.99). Check out this guide for detailed, narrative descriptions of universities, including useful dates, such as when applications are due. There are also insider tidbits, like which school's students (Caltech's) hold an annual Pumpkin Drop (which involves immersing a gourd in liquid nitrogen and dropping it from the library's roof).
- *Financing College* by the editors of Kiplinger's Personal Finance (Kiplinger, 2005, $17.95). This comprehensive book reports on every aspect of paying for higher education, including how to invest college savings and what to do if you haven't put enough away.
- *The Insider's Guide to the Colleges, 2011* by the staff of the *Yale Daily News* (St. Martin's Griffin, 2010, $22.99). Editors and writers at Yale's student-run newspaper profile more than 320 top colleges. The style is chatty and informal, though the small type can be difficult to read.
- *Winning the Heart of the College Admissions Dean* by Joyce Slayton Mitchell (Ten Speed Press, 2005, $14.95). Mitchell, former director of college advising at the tony Nightingale-Bamford School in New York City, details the process of choosing and getting into your first-choice school.
- *You're Gonna Love This College Guide* by Marty Nemko (Barron's, 1999, $9.95). If you want just one easy-to-read volume covering the whole college admissions process, this is the book for you.
- *Writing a Successful College Application Essay* by George Ehrenhaft (Barron's, 2000, $10.95). This step-by-step guide helps students navigate their way through the application process and includes tips on how to choose an essay topic, write a draft, and make revisions.

apply to is going to take some serious digging—at least as much as your parents do when they buy a new house or car. You should plan on spending some time browsing through the college guides in your high school's guidance or college-counseling office, and contacting the schools that interest you to get their course catalogs and application materials.

Next, start talking to people. Assuming your guidance counselor isn't too overwhelmed by her workload to give you some quality time, you'll definitely want her input. You might also tell other adults who know you really well—family, friends, and teachers, for example—what it is you're looking for and which schools you've got on your list, and take their feedback into account. Later, you might want to ask the admissions office at your favorite schools for the names of a few recent graduates who wouldn't mind giving you their views. And you'll probably want to e-mail or talk to several current students to find out what they like (and don't) about their school.

You may be tempted to bag the college fairs because it's so much easier these days to check out schools on your computer, but it's smart to go anyway. Many colleges that want to enroll the most enthusiastic freshmen now keep track of how much interest their applicants show, and the fairs are a pretty painless way to make contact. They also offer a quick and easy way to meet admissions representatives from a variety of local and national schools at once and to pick up informational material. Perhaps you'll discover a college or two you hadn't yet thought of. Come armed with a list of fairly specific questions, or you're apt to get nothing more than a sales pitch.

Cultivate your counselor

If your guidance counselor is like most, he's probably too swamped for frequent chatty visits. While it might be tempting to work without your counselor's input, that's almost always a mistake. Your biggest college resource may be his connections. If he visits campuses regularly and invites lots of admissions officers to your high school, then he's probably very familiar with many colleges' strengths, weaknesses, unique qualities, and selectivity. Later in the process, it will be your counselor who writes your letters of recommendation. So introduce yourself, ask questions about colleges, and drop off a résumé that lists your recent accomplishments. Ask for leads on useful guidebooks and websites. Find out whether your school hosts workshops on college admissions. If so, then attend them all and sit in the front row.

You won't always want to take your counselor's advice, however. His judgments about your abilities might not be based on the most up-to-date, mature you—or he may not know you well enough to understand how your aspirations and determination might lead you someplace your grades alone won't. One Cincinnati girl remembers having had a really difficult freshman year in high school and being advised to steer clear of the toughest math and science courses from then on. By the time she had to sign up for junior-year courses, she knew she could handle Advanced Placement biology. She petitioned for the right, and won her case. In her senior year, she was accepted at Northwestern University.

Surf the Web

Virtually everybody applying to college nowadays uses the Web for at least some research—up from just 4 percent in 1996—and it's easy to see why. College websites are far snazzier and more sophisticated than they were even a few years ago, and they are jammed with information about courses, financial aid, extracurricular opportunities, and campus life. But surf with caution, advises Ken Hartman, executive director of the National Technology Institute for School Counselors in Cherry Hill, New Jersey. Much of what you'll find, he says, is the cyber equivalent of a glossy brochure.

To arrive at a list of candidate schools, start with a visit to one or two of the college search engines. One of the most extensive sites is www.collegeboard.com, which creates a list of potential schools based on your answers to questions about such factors as cost and geographic location. The search feature at www.usnews.com, the *U.S.News & World Report* site, also generates a customized roster of schools based on your preferences. The site features the annual rankings of colleges and universities produced by *U.S. News*, as well as a tool that permits you to rerank schools according to the criteria that matter most to you, such as student-to-faculty ratio, class size, or acceptance rate. Other search engines include Princeton Review's www.princetonreview.com and CollegeView's www.collegeview.com.

Once you've created a list of possible schools, you typically can click straight through to each college's home page—and to a wealth of good intelligence if you take the time to dig deep. Beyond course descriptions, you can find details about professors' research programs, their e-mail addresses, and possibly even student evaluations of their teaching abilities. A look at the registrar's pages might give you an idea of whether the most interesting classes have long waiting lists. By checking out the home pages of student organizations that intrigue you, and by going through back copies of the student newspaper, you can dig up all kinds of clues about life on campus (e.g., the state of race relations, the crime rate, or details about the fraternity and sorority scene). You can also take a virtual tour of the campus, from science labs to dining halls.

E-mail offers another way to get the facts you need. If you are an athlete, you might contact coaches at the college you are most eager to attend; one young man checked out crew teams by contacting coaches and ended up rowing for an Ivy League

Why choose a women's college? Views from the top

There are about 50 colleges for women in this country, compared with just a handful for men. What's the appeal? *U.S. News* asked the presidents of Smith College in Northampton, Massachusetts, and Barnard College in New York City to describe the benefits of the single-sex experience.

Carol Christ (Smith): Those who have taught in both co-ed and women's colleges know that women participate more actively in discussion in classes composed entirely of women. This difference is particularly important in male-dominated disciplines such as mathematics, science, and engineering. Studies have shown that women's high dropout rates from engineering programs, as well as from majors in math, chemistry, and physics, result from hostility from male peers and instructors. Such hostility obviously doesn't exist at Smith. Engineering students study with a faculty that is more than half female.

Our alumnae consistently tell us that Smith helped them develop intellectual self-confidence and authority, qualities that helped them markedly in their careers.

The many leadership roles open to women—in student government, in extracurricular organizations—provide the opportunity for women to develop into leaders accustomed to making a difference. To see this, you need only to look at our graduates. Smith alumnae include Gloria Steinem, founder of *Ms.* magazine; Shelly Lazarus, CEO of Ogilvy & Mather; Laura D'Andrea Tyson, the first woman to head the White House Council of Economic Advisors; Margaret Edson, winner of the 1999 Pulitzer Prize for drama; and Victoria Murden McClure, the first woman and first American to row solo across the Atlantic Ocean.

Judith Shapiro (Barnard, now former president): It is a hard sell to many young women. In fact, most applicants come to Barnard for a host of other reasons: academic quality, the combination of enjoying all the advantages of a liberal arts college plus the opportunities afforded by [partner school] Columbia, a large research university. And then, of course, there is New York. But the overwhelming majority of the students I have known really connect with this aspect of the institution's

identity, and come to see it as core to their experience and a highly positive force in their lives.

I often say that [the experience] prepares students exceptionally well for a world that may not be as friendly to women as Barnard, since they will assume that the problem is not with them but with the world—and even as they are savvy enough to adapt to it, they will also be working to change it. I believe that women's college graduates are far less likely to suffer from what one might call "the enemy within," all the things we do to sabotage ourselves through insecurity, because they have developed a strong sense of who they are and what they can do. Our graduates are strongly represented in fields like medicine, among women starting their own businesses, and at the top of various professions where men have dominated. Women's college graduates are hugely overrepresented among women who sit on the boards of *Fortune* 500 corporations and occupy high positions in the world of finance generally.

college. You might not have the nerve to approach a group of students on campus with your queries about how well they like their classes or whether minority students feel at home, but e-mail makes the asking easy. Many schools periodically open chat-room discussions where students who are interested can quiz counselors or other students.

Make the most of your visit

Someone who prefers to go his own way rather than joining the crowd may feel out of place at a school dominated by fraternities; sports fans may feel frustrated at a college with no school spirit. No matter how much your virtual visit tells you about a college, there's no substitute for a trip to campus if you want to get a real feel for how well you'll fit in. Besides, showing up for an admissions interview and campus visit is an important way to let the decision makers know that you're seriously interested. These days, many colleges are flooded with applications from superqualified students, and your level of interest—measured by visits, number of phone calls or e-mail exchanges, and contact with professors and coaches, for example—can influence whether you get a thumbs-up or thumbs-down if it comes to a vote between you and another equally qualified applicant.

The college tour should begin junior year if possible because you definitely want to be nosing around when classes are in session so you can sit in, observe the students in action, and talk to a professor or two. High school students themselves should make the interview appointments and sign up for the tours. "It looks bad to have your mother calling," says admissions consultant Katherine Cohen, author of *The Truth About Getting In* and *Rock Hard Apps: How to Write a Killer College Application.*

Overall, you'll probably want to see a number of colleges and universities of different sizes and types in urban, rural, or suburban locations. But cramming five or six schools into a two-day period will only prove to be an exercise in frustration. Not only will you not have time for a thorough check, but your head will be spinning by the time you head home. It is ideal to maintain a one-school-a-day policy.

Once on campus, be aware that your tour guide will present the school in the most favorable light.

Ask a few blunt questions. How serious a problem is crime? How big do the classes tend to be? How easy is it to get the classes you need? Does everybody head home on weekends? Then, since it can be tough to form your own impression with opinionated parents in tow, spend time wandering around alone. To learn about campus issues, read the college paper. Check out bulletin boards. Flyers—whether for keg parties or an Albanian film festival—can provide a useful glimpse into the social scene. Aspiring college athletes might hang out in the sports complex, while performers should see the stages or check out a rehearsal.

Parental prerogatives

Parents should view themselves primarily as chauffeurs whose job it is to get their child to an important meeting unfrazzled and on time. Once on campus, they should recede into the background. Many counselors advise parents to skip the tour altogether or to go on a separate one.

While formal interviews are no longer required at many schools, a scheduled talk with an admissions officer can provide a fine opportunity both to gain information and to impress the staff. Even if the talk feels really comfortable and informal, keep in mind that you're being judged the whole time on how enthusiastic you seem to be about the school and its programs as well as on your thoughtfulness, intelligence, and humor. Admissions officers don't mind at all if you ask pointed questions (Why do so many freshmen decide not to come back?), but you might want to save your queries about where to find the best weekend parties for your campus tour guide.

The college admissions office may be able to arrange for you to spend a night in a dorm, which is a great way to get a feel for what daily life is like. You'll find out pretty quickly whether the hallways are noisy with music and conversation, whether groups of students are congregating to watch TV, or if everybody's quietly studying behind closed doors. Spending this kind of relaxed time with students will give you a chance to ask questions like: What do you like and hate about this school? What are the classes like—and do professors or graduate students teach the introductory courses? How easy is it to get to know professors and to see them outside of class? What do students do for fun

Freshman year

Fall

- Buckle down early, since even your ninth-grade As (and Ds) will count in the eyes of college admissions counselors. Consider taking a study skills and time management class or workshop—and then put what you've learned to use.

- Explore clubs and activities in and outside of school that offer you the chance to develop your interests and abilities as well as your leadership skills. Consider volunteering in your community. Too often, students wait until junior or senior year and then hurriedly—and unconvincingly—pad their résumés. Colleges want to see passion and long-term commitment.

- Visit your guidance counselor early in the term to map out a four-year curriculum that will meet college entrance requirements and put you into the most challenging courses you can handle. If you expect to take Advanced Placement courses later, then you may need to sign up for prerequisites now.

- Look into National Collegiate Athletic Association requirements if you think you may want to participate in college sports. And consider whether your sports experience jibes with your college plans. Do schools that interest you need players in your sport?

- Research careers and talk to your parents about your interests and goals. Find opportunities to meet people working in fields that interest you.

Summer

- Those who are old enough to get a summer job may need to work and begin saving money for college. Others who are not old enough might take on volunteer work to gain experience or enroll in an enrichment course or summer camp at a college.

- Read for pleasure—and while you're at it, learn the unfamiliar words. Vocabulary skills come in very handy on the SAT.

Sophomore year

September

- Draw up a list of college majors that intrigue you and review your four-year course load with the majors in mind.

- Register for the PSAT or the practice ACT (the PLAN) if they are offered to sophomores at your school. These tests will prepare you for the SAT and the ACT and can help you identify weaknesses in time to address them.

October and November

- Take the PLAN, which measures your academic development. Or take the PSAT to practice for the SAT.

- College fairs are a great way to "see" many schools at once. Go to www.nacacnet.org, the website of the National Association for College Admission Counseling, to find the fairs nearest you.

December

- Discuss your test results with your guidance counselor and figure out how to make improvements where needed.

- Explore your reasons for going to college, which may have a huge bearing on where you belong.

April and May

- Talk to your guidance counselor and your parents about whether you should take summer-school classes to improve your grades, to fit in a needed course, or to investigate a subject that appeals to you. Look around, too, for a job or other constructive ways to spend your summer.

June

- Take the ACT or the June SAT Subject Tests, if appropriate. It's best to take the subject tests as soon as you complete biology or geometry, for example—even if that happens to be in ninth or tenth grade.

- Spend some time researching colleges.

Junior year

September

- Get serious about your schoolwork if you haven't already; junior-year grades are extremely important in the college admissions process, as is the rigor of your coursework.
- Attend college fairs, and gather information. If you are just beginning your college search, then click on "Best Colleges" at www.usnews.com for additional information on more than 1,900 schools and to link to the colleges' own websites.
- Talk with your parents about whether they plan to set limitations on where you can attend college. Knowing now how much your parents will contribute financially or whether they object to a campus far from home may affect your decision about where to apply.
- Start researching scholarships. You may find useful information in your school or public library and at www.finaid.org and www.fastaid.com. The *U.S. News* site features a scholarship search tool, too.
- If you hope to play for a college team, and perhaps qualify for an athletic scholarship, then introduce yourself to coaches at colleges you are considering. Also, ask your high school coach for advice.

October

- If you haven't already, take the PSAT to practice for the SAT and to qualify for scholarships offered by the National Merit Scholarship Corp.

December

- Review your test results with your counselor and consider taking an SAT preparation course or using test-prep software.

January and February

- Check with your schools to see if they prefer—or require—the ACT, the SAT, or neither. Most colleges will accept either test, and some counselors recommend taking both, since many students do better on one than on the other.

March

- Identify the characteristics of a college that mat-ter to you—size, location, cost, academic rigor, social environment, and diversity, to name a few. View college brochures in your counselor's office, or go online to search websites such as www.usnews.com or www.collegeview.com. You can also go to specific college sites.
- Work up a list of schools to visit during spring break (or in the fall) with your parents or a counselor who takes groups of students on tour. It's best to plan to be on campus while school is in session, so that you can visit classes and talk to students and professors.

April

- Register for June SAT or ACT tests if you plan to apply early.
- Try to line up a summer job that will give you experience in a field that interests you and that will sharpen your leadership skills.

May

- Take Advanced Placement tests if you are eligible.

Summer

- Send for college applications, and think about essay topics. Consider whom to ask for recommendations.
- Counselors advise entering senior year with three or four schools in mind that are apt to accept you, as well as one or two "reaches." If you haven't already been to campus, then visiting schools now or in the early fall will help you create a list. Map an itinerary, and set up admissions interviews.
- Compile a résumé of your activities, honors, leadership positions, and job experience. (There is a profile form on page 92 that will help you.) You'll need this information for college applications and scholarship forms.
- Continue to read extensively and work on your writing skills.
- Work if you can to save money and to gain experience.
- Talk honestly with your parents about how you will finance your college costs and how much they expect you to supply. Colleges typically expect freshmen to contribute about $1,500 to their own college costs.

Senior year

September

- Check your course list one more time. Are you missing credits required by schools you're applying to? Plan to work really hard this term because your first-quarter or first-semester grades will be included on your transcript.
- Ask colleges to send you their application materials. Begin to look for college applications online.
- Continue researching scholarships. Begin assembling documents for aid applications.
- Give out recommendation forms and stamped envelopes addressed to the colleges' admissions offices.
- If you plan to apply for early decision, then consider what effect that choice could have on financial aid.
- Review your final list of colleges with your counselor.
- As you schedule visits with admissions and financial aid advisers, think also about visiting with faculty members and students in the department that interests you.
- Register for the fall ACT and/or SAT.

October

- Request that your transcripts be sent to colleges.
- Mail early-action or early-decision applications.
- Take any tests for which you are registered. Have your test results sent to schools.

November

- Take the SAT Subject Test in Language with Listening (for Chinese, French, German, Japanese, Korean, and Spanish), if required by your colleges.
- Start writing your essays. If you applied for early decision, then notify the college about honors you have received since you submitted your application and ask your high school to send out a recent transcript.

December

- Mail applications, or turn them in at school.
- If you applied early decision and you were accepted, then withdraw regular applications from other schools.
- Start working with your parents on completing the Free Application for Federal Student Aid form. Apply at www.fafsa.ed.gov, or get forms from your high school or by calling (800) 433-3243.

January

- File all federal financial aid forms, and apply for state aid.
- Ask your school to send midyear grade reports to your colleges.
- Verify that all your application materials have been sent out.

February

- Check with colleges to make sure they have the documentation they require.

March

- Look for your decision letters this month and in April.
- Don't give in to "senioritis." Your college admission is contingent upon your final high school grades.

April

- Evaluate your financial aid offers. You'll have to make a decision about where to go and notify your college by May 1. You should then let other schools know you won't be coming.

June and summer

- Have your high school send your final transcript to the college you will be attending.
- Know when tuition and room-and-board payments are due.
- Notify the financial aid office if there have been any changes in your family's circumstances that might make you eligible for additional aid. (Perhaps one of your parents was laid off or there was a major illness in the family.)

Best colleges

Each year, *U.S.News & World Report* ranks more than 1,400 colleges and universities based on such measures of excellence as graduation and freshman retention rates, class size and student-to-faculty ratio, and the expert opinions of college presidents and deans. To see where your schools rank, check out the "Best Colleges" guidebook, available on newsstands, or go to www.usnews.com. Here are the schools that top the lists for 2011. Colleges whose ranks are identical are tied.

National Universities

Universities in this category offer a full range of undergraduate, master's, and Ph.D. programs, and emphasize faculty research.

1. Harvard University (MA)
1. Princeton University (NJ)
3. Yale University (CT)
4. Columbia University (NY)
5. Stanford University (CA)
5. University of Pennsylvania
7. California Institute of Technology
7. Massachusetts Inst. of Technology
9. Dartmouth College (NH)
9. Duke University (NC)
9. University of Chicago

National Liberal Arts Colleges

Liberal arts colleges focus almost entirely on undergraduate education and award more than half of their degrees in the liberal arts disciplines.

1. Williams College (MA)
2. Amherst College (MA)
3. Swarthmore College (PA)
4. Middlebury College (VT)
4. Wellesley College (MA)
6. Bowdoin College (ME)
6. Pomona College (CA)
8. Carleton College (MN)
9. Davidson College (NC)
9. Haverford College (PA)

Regional Universities

These schools offer a full range of undergraduate degrees and some master's programs but few, if any, doctoral programs.

North

1. Villanova University (PA)
2. Providence College (RI)
3. Loyola College in Maryland
4. Bentley University (MA)
4. College of New Jersey
4. Fairfield University (CT)

South

1. Rollins College (FL)
2. Elon University (NC)
3. James Madison University (VA)
3. Stetson University (FL)
5. Belmont University (TN)

Midwest

1. Creighton University (NE)
2. Butler University (IN)
3. Drake University (IA)
3. Xavier University (OH)
5. Valparaiso University (IN)

West

1. Trinity University (TX)
2. Santa Clara University (CA)
3. Loyola Marymount University (CA)
4. Gonzaga University (WA)
4. Mills College (CA)

Regional Colleges

These colleges focus on undergraduate education and offer degree programs in the liberal arts and in such professional fields as business, nursing, and education.

North

1. U.S. Coast Guard Academy (CT)
2. Cooper Union (NY)
3. U.S. Merchant Marine Academy (NY)
4. Messiah College (PA)
5. Elizabethtown College (PA)

South

1. Ouachita Baptist University (AR)
2. John Brown University (AR)
3. High Point University (NC)
4. Erskine College (SC)
5. Tuskegee University (AL)

Midwest

1. Taylor University (IN)
2. Marietta College (OH)
3. Dordt College (IA)
3. Ohio Northern University
5. Augustana College (SD)
5. Cedarville University (OH)

West

1. U.S. Air Force Academy (CO)
2. Master's College and Seminary (CA)
2. Oklahoma Baptist University
4. California Maritime Academy
5. Corban College (OR)

on the weekends? How much studying and partying goes on? After you've seen the college, it's a good idea to walk around the city or town to get a sense of what it would feel like to be a part of the larger community.

Every school will make an impression. But count on it: You'll forget a lot of the details by the time you need them. (Which school was it that had the great gym? The unbelievable drama department? The cute tour guide?) It's smart to write down your observations along the way. In April, after all those fat acceptance letters arrive, you're going to be the one weighing the candidates and making the decision.

Chapter Two

What Colleges Will Look For in You

Anybody who's heard the depressing stories of standout students rejected by every school (and of whole classfuls of valedictorians turned away by the Ivy League) might logically wonder how his own not-even-close-to-star-quality credentials will gain him a spot in any college. It's true that getting into highly ranked schools is harder than ever these days—and that a smaller proportion of applicants are making the cut even at places that used to be considered sure bets, or "safeties." And it's *really* hard, it seems, to make it to the end of the process with your sanity intact. Driven by anxiety and mistaken ideas about what admissions officers expect, too many teenagers treat high school as an endurance test these days, taking on more tough courses and activities than they can handle and leaving little time for friends or sleep. This single-minded focus often means "the battle is lost in terms of a healthy high school education," says Scott White, guidance supervisor at Montclair High School in New Jersey, who sees more students than ever suffering from anxiety, depression, anorexia, and panic attacks.

But it doesn't have to be this way. *U.S. News* asked several dozen counselors and admissions deans to describe what schools are looking for in applicants and how you can measure up without totally stressing out. The first thing to remember is that most schools still accept more than half of their applicants. And even if you're applying to more competitive colleges, you can greatly improve your chances by preparing early, pursuing your interests actively (but not confusing quality with quantity), and looking for the right fit.

First, consider what you're up against

Some students are so anxious about getting into college that they or their families are taking creative—even extreme—measures to gain an edge. For instance, there was the senior at a New York City high school who stole Bowdoin College's catalog from the guidance office so it wouldn't tempt her classmates to apply there. (She didn't get in.) There was the Miami teenager who checked the Federal Election Commission website to find out whether any admissions officers she'd be trying to impress had made political donations. Upon discovering that the Colby College interviewer had given money to the Republican Party, "I muted my leftist views," says the future government major. (Also a no-go.)

One determined father took a year off from work to run his daughter's get-into-college campaign; a mom used her daughter's e-mail address to contact prestigious colleges with impressively intelligent questions. Meanwhile, Katherine Cohen, a New York college consultant whose firm, IvyWise, collects up to $33,000 for each student it helps to select a college and get accepted, is booked for a year, with a waiting list. Some of her clients fly 2,000 miles to keep their appointments. Yet even she was surprised when a parent brought in a new assignment: a student who had only recently finished seventh grade.

The anxiety that makes applicants and their families take such bizarre steps can be blamed partly on the fact that so many kids are determined to land in the same small group of prestigious schools. The quality of the applicant pool is so strong at the University

of Pennsylvania, for example, that the admissions staff could easily fill a very impressive freshman class just with the students who don't quite make the grade, says Lee Stetson, former dean of admissions there. For the class entering in 2010, Penn received nearly 27,000 applications for about 2,400 spaces.

The simple truth is that there are more students than ever fighting for a limited number of spaces. The Department of Education predicts that the number of high school graduates will increase by 9 percent, to 3.4 million, between 2005 and the school year starting in 2018. Almost two thirds of the students graduating from high school today head directly to college, up from just half 20 years ago. The University of Wisconsin–Madison, for example, received over 50 percent more applications for 2009's entering class than it received in 1989. The University of Miami, dismissed not so long ago as "Suntan U," received 21,844 applications for the 2,006 spots in the class entering in 2009—more than double the number of a decade earlier. Colleges are making matters worse by marketing strenuously to the most talented students they can possibly attract. (Thus the pounds and pounds of material you may have already received in the mail.) The result tends to be that applications go way up—and the schools can be pickier.

Because the students who don't make the cut at the most elite colleges have taken their second or third choice, it's now harder to get into schools that have been less selective in the past. Muhlenberg College in Pennsylvania is now accepting about 48 percent of applicants, down from 74 percent in 1995. Brandeis's acceptance rate has dropped from 66 percent to 33 percent over that time, and the rate at Adelphi University in New York has dipped from 79 percent to 70 percent since 1997.

Some students have responded by applying to more schools; instead of five or eight applications, they're spending hundreds of dollars to send off 10 or 15. (Indeed, part of the increase in competition can be blamed on all these multiple applications.) But the real key, say the pros, is to apply to the right schools, understand what admissions people are really looking for, and—if you're reading this book before the last minute—start thinking well in

Yes, indeed, athletes do have an edge—as do trilingual students and gifted artists. Amherst College in Massachusetts, a Division III school that does not offer athletic scholarships, sets aside about 66 places in each freshman class of 465 for athletes who will participate in one or more of the 27 varsity sports, from women's field hockey to men's swimming. "There's no question that there's an advantage for a very limited number of 'impact' athletes," says Richard Nesbitt, director of admission at nearby Williams College, which fills about 66 spots every year with athletes who play 30 varsity sports. But at highly selective schools, grades and recommendations count very heavily, too. "It's hard to justify admitting a mediocre student when you're turning away superior kids," says Monica Inzer, former dean of undergraduate admission and student financial services at Babson College near Boston and now dean of admission and financial aid at Hamilton College in New York.

Athletes who can rise to the level of play at Division I powerhouse universities generally get more leeway when it comes to grades and test scores. While researching their book, *The Game of Life: College Sports and Educational Values*, William G. Bowen and James L. Shulman analyzed data from 30 colleges and found that the high-profile athletes at Division I schools (which can offer scholarships) have SAT scores 237 points lower than students at large; at liberal arts colleges, there is a 135-point gap. In his book *Intercollegiate Athletics and the American University*, former University of Michigan president James J. Duderstadt says that Division I coaches get "a certain number of 'no questions asked' admits, so that they can confidently go after the very top athletes."

How can the more typical athlete use a sport to his or her advantage? Pay attention to supply and demand. Which sports tend to have a shortage of college players? Which schools are launching teams or graduating players—or just added the only goalie they need? (You can find much of this sort of intelligence by scouring college websites.) Julie Browning, the dean of undergraduate enrollment at Rice University in Houston, recalls that the launch of a women's soccer team in 2001 created a need to recruit 13 players. When Babson added women's track, the school created immediate openings for a range of talent from shot-putters to distance runners. In general, Title IX legislation, meant to ensure gender equity in educational programs receiving federal funding, has led to a boom in women's athletics and a hearty appetite for players. "There are more programs in some sports than there are quality athletes," says Tracy Coyne, head coach of the women's lacrosse team at the University of Notre Dame.

If you think you've got the talent to make a college team, then you should be showcasing your skills at summer camps that draw college scouts; golfers and tennis players should be entering some tournaments. Ask your high school coach to contact college coaches on your behalf, and follow up with a letter and video highlights of your play. (While NCAA regulations prohibit coaches from approaching you until the summer before senior year, there's nothing stopping you from initiating the contact.) Coaches can't necessarily get you in, but they can have enormous pull with admissions. Once you've secured a spot on the "coach's list," Bowen and Shulman found, you've improved your chances for admission by as much as 50 percent.

advance about how you can become the strongest candidate possible. (Younger brothers and sisters, take note: Eighth-grade algebra is the essential first step toward Advanced Placement calculus.)

"You can't control who else is applying," says Nancy Hargrave Meislahn, dean of admission and financial aid at Wesleyan University in Connecticut. But you can make sure you find activities that allow you to stand out. And you can decide to always take the most challenging courses you can handle. Here are a few principles to keep in mind.

Grades don't matter the way you think

Guess what? Perfect As and a standing at the head of the class aren't as impressive as they used to be.

This may be hard to believe, given the scary headlines about how tough the competition is. And, in fact, it's true that your transcript, and what it shows about your four years in high school, is still the most important part of your application. But the numbers by themselves might just mean you've been given a big leg up by grade inflation, or that you've chosen easy courses with an eye toward snagging the top slot. Lots of high school administrators don't even bother calculating class rank for their seniors anymore because they don't believe rank gives a very accurate picture of what a student has actually achieved. So instead of focusing on your grade point average as a measure of your performance, the people in admissions are going to scour your transcript for signs that you've taken full advantage of all the intellectual opportunities your high school has to offer, that you're determined, and that you're maturing as a student.

How can they tell you've made the most of your school's resources? Your guidance counselor tucks in a detailed profile of your school with your recommendation letter. The profile, which you'll learn more about in Chapter Four, lists all the courses that you've been able to select from, so the people in admissions can see whether you've taken honors and Advanced Placement classes or have instead chosen the easiest possible path. If the school's curriculum wasn't all that challenging, then it probably won't be held against you—as long as your grades are good. On the other hand, a student in a competitive high school with 20-plus AP courses might be able to show lower grades without any penalty, but she had better also show a course load that reflects an effort to make the most of the curriculum.

Besides helping admissions staffers gauge what kind of student you are, the profiles allow them to better distinguish among candidates from schools that often differ wildly in resources and rigor. For example, they might decide to reject a class valedictorian from School A in favor of No. 100 at School B if the second school offers far more rigorous courses (on the assumption that No. 100 is more thoroughly prepared for college work).

This is not to suggest that you ought to be signing up for 10 AP courses. (See pages 27–28 for advice on planning your AP strategy.) But you definitely are going to be judged on whether your courses make sense, given your previous record. A student who took geometry in freshman year and has good grades in math might well be expected to be in AP calculus senior year. On the other hand, admissions officers probably wouldn't hold regular chemistry against a student who's always received only average grades in science.

A mediocre grade in a tough course is going to be looked at closely, so you'd better think carefully about what to do if you're struggling. The questionable grade might not hurt you at all if it's one C among mostly As, say, and you're obviously stretching yourself by taking the course. One high school student considered dropping AP calculus before receiving her first C ever during first semester of senior year. She stuck with the class after an admissions officer told her that he would rather see kids taking accelerated courses than getting straight As. Taken as a whole, her transcript showed a strong student rising to a challenge. If your transcript is not otherwise filled with As, then the grade could instead signal to admissions staffers that you're not quite ready to handle college-level work in the subject. In that case, you might be better off dropping down a level than scraping through an advanced course and finishing unprepared.

Suppose you're someone who floundered freshman year but settled in and succeeded as a junior. You probably won't be penalized for your early erratic performance if the overall direction of your high school record is upward. The people judging your application are looking for evidence of determination and personal growth as well as obvious ability. "We'll be very excited about a student who receives poor advising into the vocational track but who takes college prep courses out of sheer will," says Nancy Cable, former vice president and dean of admissions and financial aid at Davidson College in North Carolina who now holds a similar position at Bates College in Maine.

On the other hand, your grades might make you a hot prospect

One real benefit of looking for colleges that match your interests and abilities, as opposed to schools with a prestigious name and reputation, is that you're apt to discover that you're in demand. Many fine schools below the top ranks are eager to attract applicants whose qualifications will help boost the student-body profile. Even better, they're often willing to hand out generous merit awards to induce you to enroll. Ray Loewe, founder and president of College Money, a consulting firm in Marlton, New Jersey, that helps families figure out how to finance college, tells his student clients to search out schools where their grades and test scores will put them in the top quarter of the applicant pool. Not only will these students become "premium candidates," Loewe says, but "the money comes out on the table. A really sharp kid in the top 25 percent of incoming students has some real negotiating power."

The good news here is that your options beyond the most selective schools have never been stronger. A trickle-down of talent—students as well as profes-

sors—means that many less selective and lesser-known schools just keep getting better and more attractive. Taking advantage of the ultra-tight academic job market, these colleges are scooping up top-notch faculty members who haven't managed to get hired at more prestigious places. After aggressively recruiting talented professors, the University of Maryland–Baltimore County regularly sends its students off to graduate schools like the Massachusetts Institute of Technology, Stanford, and Oxford. In a

> *"A really sharp kid in the top 25 percent of incoming students has some real negotiating power."*

typical year, the top-ranked medical school at Johns Hopkins accepts applicants from many colleges without fancy reputations—places like Oakwood University in Alabama, Frostburg State University in Maryland, and the University of California–Irvine. While Ohio State was luring senior professors away from universities such as Berkeley and Tufts by building state-of-the-art research facilities, it also attracted students with higher ACT scores. The average has gone from 21.9 to 27.5 since 1987.

Any old AP courses won't do

Colleges send slightly mixed messages about what they want in terms of an AP record. At the same time that admissions officers say they expect applicants to be taking full advantage of challenging courses, they also worry that the academic content of the courses is being diluted. A 2002 report by the National Research Council contended that both AP classes and the fast-growing International Baccalaureate (IB) courses (a rigorous two-year curriculum of study intended to get students ready for college anywhere in the world) were often taught by poorly prepared teachers who stressed rote memorization rather than problem-solving and discussion. About the same time as the report came out, Harvard announced that college credit would be awarded only for perfect AP test scores of 5 because professors were complaining that students with lower scores weren't sufficiently prepared to move into advanced classes.

The best approach for college-bound students is to keep taking AP classes, but to pick them wisely. You'll be better off if you can show a strong background in core subjects (English, math, the basic sciences, history, and a foreign language), so concentrate your advanced coursework in those areas. Don't expect AP courses such as environmental science or art history, which some critics deride as "AP lite," to impress admissions officers unless you already have a solid grounding in the basics. And plan on taking the AP test, given in May. No matter what grade you earn in the class, not showing a score for the test—or showing a low score—may signal to administrators that the course wasn't all that advanced and that you didn't master college-level material.

The number of AP classes that admissions officials expect to see on your transcript varies widely. One or two will suffice at some schools, while the typical applicant to highly ranked Amherst College has four. Most high school students can't handle a full load of college-level courses in one year, so overdosing on APs may drive you crazy and leave colleges unimpressed. "If AP is truly demanding, it should not be possible to take five classes" over such a short period, says William Shain, former dean of undergraduate admissions at Vanderbilt University.

You need to love learning—not just getting As

As colleges are swamped these days with highly qualified applicants, one way they differentiate among prospects is to look for the spark that says, "I like to learn just for the fun of it." Students with this quality can be counted on to contribute to a school's intellectual life rather than doing little more than attending their required classes.

It may be that all the proof you need exists within your school experience. Perhaps you're a capable mathematician who decides to go to summer school so you can fit in an extra course. Maybe you're a science student passionately interested in the environment who participates in the science fair every year or researches an article for the school paper on the impact of a local highway project.

Or maybe you're interested in being a lawyer someday and you join the debate team to get practice arguing.

But many elite colleges are also noting how much effort goes into intellectual pursuits outside of the school day. Sometimes the opportunities are ready-made (a community college course that takes you to the next level in photography; a summer enrichment camp with a focus on astronomy or computer programming; a workshop on local artists and their paintings at your city's museum). Sometimes you have to create the opportunities yourself. If you love writing, you could volunteer to report on student life for your community newspaper. If history's your thing, you might start a summer business researching genealogies for local families.

Fancy internships or exotic field trips that seem to speak more about your family's money and connections than your love of learning won't dazzle the folks at the most prestigious schools anymore; too many students have friends and relatives who can find them a summer gig at a law firm. The secret is to find experiences that admissions officers can tell are clearly meaningful to you—because they make sense in the context of who you show yourself to be.

Don't simply be a joiner, do what you love

That advice—choose meaningful experiences—holds true when it comes to extracurricular activities, too. Why? It used to be that colleges wanted well-rounded students. Now, faced with growing piles of applications padded with indiscriminate club memberships, most selective schools aim to produce a well-rounded freshman class instead. "The embodiment at age 17 of a Renaissance person is difficult to find," says David Gould, a former admissions dean at Brandeis who now runs an independent counseling service in Concord, Massachusetts. "We realized we could accomplish the same thing with lots of different people."

The take-home message is that you should show a commitment to one or two of your burning interests and not simply join every club in school in a misguided effort to appear really active. What impresses the people who read applications is proof that an interest is a theme of your life, not just during school hours but outside, too. One young TV-sports addict started writing a sports column for his high school paper, coaching basketball in a poor neighborhood, and interning at an all-sports television channel, for example. A Wisconsin girl, a music lover, chose as her essay topic how practicing the piano had helped her develop discipline and confidence. Asked on her applications about community service, she described how she'd raised $1,600 for a missionary effort through her church by putting on two solo recitals. Her extracurricular activities included the school's jazz group, the wind ensemble, and the orchestra that accompanied the musicals. Along with her good grades and high SAT scores, the girl's passion for music proved irresistible to Northwestern, Marquette, Tufts—and the University of Chicago, where she enrolled.

It's important to keep in mind that while you don't want to appear to be a person who just racks up memberships, neither do you want to show a complete lack of versatility. Given a choice between a brilliant musician whose whole life is music and a brilliant musician who's also a key member of the diving team, many schools will prefer the multidimensional person.

Leaders tend to have an edge

Many colleges, especially selective ones with a surplus of desirable candidates, are looking for leadership talent: students who have the gumption and people skills to influence others and to make things happen. You may not be able to point to a class presidency (few can), but think about other achievements you can highlight. Chances are, if you've poured yourself into a couple of activities that really mean something to you, then it won't be hard to come up with evidence that you don't just sit back and wait for life to happen. Maybe your years of baseball have included several seasons assisting your brother's Little League coach. Maybe your gift with animals has inspired you to start a petsitting business, or to volunteer to help raise funds for the local pound. When colleges compare two applicants whose interests and academic qualifications are similar, such signs of initiative can make one an obvious pick.

Beach time doesn't count for much

Admissions deans don't look kindly on summers spent lazing at the beach, but otherwise they're surprisingly open-minded. If you need money, take that fast-food restaurant job, then try to make the experience as meaningful as you can. One student who worked in a mailroom ended up changing a computer program to make mail distribution more efficient, which helped lead to an acceptance at Williams College.

If you don't have to spend your whole summer at work, you might really benefit by investing some time in community service. Service is now such an integral part of the high school experience for so many students that many colleges have come to expect it and ask about it. Examining volunteer efforts can tell an admissions staffer a lot about the applicant's leadership abilities, imagination, and capacity to show compassion and concern for others. A superficial, one-time effort made for show won't do you any good—again, colleges are looking for commitment.

The sharper your "hook," the better

What many students don't realize when they start this whole process is that even near perfection might not be enough to win acceptance at selective schools. Although colleges hate to admit it, many target certain groups of applicants for admission—maybe because they want to increase the diversity of the student body or to expand the physics department, say, or to add women's ice hockey or a few potential future donors. Most people think of ethnic mix when the importance of diversity is discussed, but colleges want the population to reflect socioeconomic differences, too—and they don't want all their students to come from the same three or four cities. Applications from states with small populations such as Wyoming or Nevada sometimes get a second close read at colleges hoping to boast that their students come from all 50 states. Students in the targeted groups are described as having "hooks," attributes so attractive that they're likely to overcome even ho-hum grades.

At highly selective schools like Harvard, almost all slots go to kids with some hook, says Joyce Slayton Mitchell, author of *Winning the Heart of the College Admissions Dean*. "To have the freshman community they want," she explains, "colleges need musicians and athletes, leadership in student organizations and government, a certain percentage of alumni children, and minorities and international students. That's almost everybody." (For Mitchell's views on the biggest goofs applicants and their parents make during the college search process, see page 57.)

One way to find out where you might be needed is to call coaches, musical directors, and department chairs, for example, and ask what they're searching for this year. A baseball coach with too many catchers will probably tell you there won't be a place for another on the team, whereas a conductor desperate for bassoonists may demand you send in an audition sample—and more important, will tell the admissions committee if you seem promising.

During the time you spend online and on campus, you'll want to study up on the schools' personalities, too. That's because admissions people are looking for students who will be a good "fit," just as applicants are looking for a college that fits them (or should be, anyway). Some universities value initiative and the ability to take risks; Stanford judges all applicants on their "intellectual vitality." Pepperdine routinely turns down top-scoring students in favor of others who share the university's commitment to community service. In the end, success at this process hinges on your ability to offer something special that the college needs or wants.

Chapter Three

How to Ace the Big Exam

Have you ever had that nightmare where you're sitting in an empty classroom, No. 2 pencil in hand, feeling nauseated and totally unprepared to take any sort of test, when a faceless teacher places a copy of the SAT in front of you and shouts "go," right before the hands on the clock start speeding around and your mind goes absolutely blank? Then you wake up—thankfully—sweaty and screaming?

You're not alone. Students lose sleep about the SATs and ACTs for a reason: They matter. And there are lots of questions regarding how to proceed with standardized testing. For example, which of the two college entrance exams should you take in order to maximize your scoring potential? Is it worth shelling out big bucks for professional test prep or are you better off studying on your own? How important are the SAT and ACT writing sections to the admissions office?

It's essential to consider these issues, as standardized test scores are the second most important factor to admissions officers, right behind grades in academic courses, according to a survey by the National Association for College Admission Counseling, the professional organization of guidance counselors and admissions deans. And schools—the vast majority of which still require applicants to submit SAT or ACT scores—rely on the results for a range of important decisions.

For example, many large state institutions, including the University of Iowa and the University of Washington, plug scores into a formula along with grade point average to determine a cutoff number below which nobody gets in. Cleveland State University draws the line for entrance to its honors program at a combined SAT score of 1950 (out of a possible 2400) or an ACT of 30 (out of 36), while schools such as Howard University in Washington, D.C., Boston University, and the University of North Carolina–Greensboro, among dozens of others, hand out freshman scholarships based partly on test results.

But don't panic

The importance of admissions tests can be overstated at times. Many schools, particularly small liberal arts colleges that don't have to screen tens of thousands of applicants, look at SAT or ACT scores in the context of the entire application file; in other words, the scores are just one piece of the puzzle of who you are. Anybody who has been prepping frantically to retake the SAT for a third time in a last-ditch effort to gain a few more points should bear in mind that test scores seldom overshadow the transcript. When there's a mismatch between the two, admissions officers try to figure out why. Often, they give more weight to grades.

This works in favor of diligent and successful students and against underachievers whose test scores suggest brilliance but whose report cards hint at laziness. "If a student with a B in chemistry gets a 750 on the [SAT] subject test, I think, 'This kid knows how to take a test,'" but hasn't shown the sustained effort and mastery needed for a top mark, says William

Conley, dean of enrollment and academic services at Johns Hopkins University in Baltimore.

If you find yourself in this boat, about to be tossed overboard with no life preserver, you can use your application essay and interview to explain the discrepancy as best you can and to point out any achievements in other areas, such as sports or the arts, that make you a good pick anyway. You should also make sure the admissions staff understands that you've matured and plan to work harder in college. If you're particularly excited by a school's new biochemistry department or the stellar 18th-century Brit. Lit. faculty, for instance, then ask intelligent questions and make contact with students and professors. Your obvious enthusiasm for academic pursuits, new as it may be, may make admissions officers more willing to take a gamble on your application.

If you lean in the opposite direction, with low scores and a series of stellar report cards, use well-chosen teacher recommendations and the quality of your writing to convince admissions officers that your grades are the more accurate measure of your smarts and not the result of grade inflation at your high school. Ideally, of course, both your standardized exam results and your GPA will be high.

Here's the rest of what you need to know about the testing system—and how to turn the stuff of nightmares into a big, fat acceptance letter from the school of your dreams.

The SAT versus the ACT

Consider this question: To test best, should Joe take (A) the SAT, (B) the ACT, or (C) both of the above? High achievers gunning for top-tier schools often assume they have no choice but to select (A). In the college-crowded state of Massachusetts, for example, more than 80 percent of 2009's high school graduates took the SAT, while just 18 percent took the ACT, the college entrance test that dominates at many midwestern and southern high schools. Nationally, however, the latter is steadily closing the gap. In the graduating class of 2009, more than 1.5 million students sat for the SAT, but nearly 1.5 million took the ACT—a 25 percent increase since 2005.

Looking past the SAT

If you've taken both the SAT and the ACT and are disappointed with your lackluster results, don't despair. A growing number of the nation's four-year institutions leave standardized test scores out of admissions decisions for many freshman applicants. Among them are schools that give students the option of not submitting test scores, like Bates, Bowdoin (the first school to make the SAT optional, back in 1969), Connecticut College, Dickinson, and Mount Holyoke, and those, like the University of Texas, that admit in-state students near the top of their high school class regardless of SAT performance. The size of this entire cluster of schools has grown more than 60 percent in the last five years, according to the National Center for Fair and Open Testing, to about 850 institutions. For a list of schools surveyed by *U.S. News* that make the tests optional for some or all students, see Page 36. For additional choices, visit http://www.fairtest.org/university/optional.

Muhlenberg College, in Allentown, Pennsylvania, which made the SAT optional for the class entering in 1997, has a policy that is typical for test-optional schools. Applicants who decide not to submit their scores can now send in a graded paper and come to campus for an interview instead. If you choose this route, one of the best ways to impress admissions committees is to send in a transcript packed with challenging courses. Many administrators say they have found the strength of an applicant's high school curriculum, and how well he or she succeeded at taking advantage of it, to be highly reliable predictors of the applicant's college achievement. Showing Advanced Placement courses, plus high marks on the AP exams, gives you an edge—and, as a bonus, in many cases you will also receive college credit.

Among schools that still require the tests are a number that have de-emphasized their importance. In the past, applicants to the University of California–Berkeley whose grades and SAT scores fell below a numerical cutoff were removed from the pool before deliberations about admissions began. Now there's no cutoff. "When you have so many [qualified] students, you have to go deeper into academics," explains one admissions staffer. Other large schools that get a flood of applications from high achievers, such as the University of North Carolina–Chapel Hill, sort applicants by the numbers and then search for qualities that might override mediocre scores. All of these admissions policies are more equitable, say anti-testing advocates, as they don't penalize those who can't afford expensive prep courses.

Today, virtually all colleges accept both tests, and that means you can present the one that best shows your stuff. For instance, one young woman from Maryland worried that her combined score of 1100 (out of 1600) on the old SAT wouldn't make the grade at her top choice, the University of Michigan–Ann Arbor, and took the ACT as well. She scored a 28 (equal to approximately 1260 on the critical reading and math sections of the SAT) and enrolled at Michigan the next fall.

Why the variation in her scores? Historically, the two exams have assessed different things—the SAT measured raw aptitude while the ACT measures academic achievement in high school content areas. The SAT now is much more similar to the ACT, though differences remain. To gauge which exam is right for you, it helps to know the basic structure and content of each test.

According to a recent *U.S. News* survey of colleges and universities, these schools have decided not to require SAT or ACT scores from some or all of their applicants. Among them are several that have changed their policies in recent years following the brouhaha over the addition of the writing exam, like the College of the Holy Cross in Worcester, Massachusetts, and Lawrence University in Appleton, Wisconsin. You'll want to check with schools that interest you; some institutions recommend that scores be submitted even though they're not required, and some will consider test results if applicants want them to.

Adelphi University (NY)
Agnes Scott College (GA)
Alabama State University
Albright College (PA)
Allen University (SC)
Amer. Indian Coll. of the Assemblies of God (AZ)
Arkansas Baptist College
Art Center College of Design (CA)
Assumption College (MA)
Augustana College (IL)
Austin Peay State University (TN)
Baker College of Flint (MI)
Baldwin-Wallace College (OH)
Ball State University (IN)
Baptist Bible College (MO)
Bard College (NY)
Bard College at Simon's Rock (MA)
Bates College (ME)
Beacon College (FL)
Bellevue University (NE)
Belmont Abbey College (NC)
Bennett College (NC)
Bennington College (VT)
Berklee College of Music (MA)
Bethany Lutheran College (MN)
Black Hills State University (SD)
Boricua College (NY)
Boston Architectural College

Boston Conservatory
Bowdoin College (ME)
Brigham Young University–Hawaii
Burlington College (VT)
California College of the Arts
California Institute of the Arts
California State University–Bakersfield
California State University–East Bay
California State University–Los Angeles
California State University–Monterey Bay
California State University–Sacramento
California State University–San Marcos
California State University–Stanislaus
Calumet College of St. Joseph (IN)
Cambridge College (MA)
Cazenovia College (NY)
Chadron State College (NE)
Chatham University (PA)
Chester College of New England (NH)
Christopher Newport University (VA)
City University (WA)
Cleary University (MI)
Cleveland Institute of Music
Cogswell Polytechnical College (CA)
Colby College (ME)
College of New Rochelle (NY)
College of St. Mary (NE)
College of St. Thomas More (TX)
College of the Atlantic (ME)
College of the Holy Cross (MA)
Columbia College (IL)
Concordia College (AL)
Connecticut College
Cornish College of the Arts (WA)
CUNY–College of Staten Island
CUNY–Medgar Evers College
Curry College (MA)
Daemen College (NY)
Dalton State College (GA)
Davenport University (MI)
Denison University (OH)
Dickinson College (PA)

Dowling College (NY)

Drew University (NJ)

Edinboro University of Pennsylvania

Edward Waters College (FL)

Excelsior College (NY)

Fairfield University (CT)

Fashion Institute of Technology (NY)

Finlandia University (MI)

Fisher College (MA)

Florida Memorial University

Franklin and Marshall College (PA)

Franklin University (OH)

Furman University (SC)

George Mason University (VA)

Georgian Court University (NJ)

Gettysburg College (PA)

Goddard College (VT)

Golden Gate University (CA)

Goucher College (MD)

Grace Bible College (MI)

Granite State College (NH)

Gratz College (PA)

Great Basin College (NV)

Green Mountain College (VT)

Guilford College (NC)

Gustavus Adolphus College (MN)

Hampshire College (MA)

Hartwick College (NY)

Heritage University (WA)

Hilbert College (NY)

Hobart and William Smith Colleges (NY)

Hodges University (FL)

Hofstra University (NY)

Humboldt State University (CA)

Humphreys College (CA)

Huston-Tillotson University (TX)

Illinois College

Illinois Institute of Technology

John F. Kennedy University (CA)

Johnson and Wales University (RI)

Juilliard School (NY)

Juniata College (PA)

Kansas State University

Kendall College (IL)

Keuka College (NY)

King's College (PA)

Knox College (IL)

Lake Forest College (IL)

Lawrence University (WI)

Lebanon Valley College (PA)

Lees-McRae College (NC)

Lewis & Clark College (OR)

Lewis-Clark State College (ID)

Lincoln University (MO)

Lindsey Wilson College (KY)

Longy School of Music (MA)

Loras College (IA)

Lourdes College (OH)

Loyola University Maryland

Lyndon State College (VT)

Macon State College (GA)

Maharishi University of Management (IA)

Maine College of Art

Manhattan School of Music (NY)

Martin University (IN)

Marygrove College (MI)

Marylhurst University (OR)

Mercy College (NY)

Merrimack College (MA)

Messiah College (PA)

Metropolitan State University (MN)

Miles College (AL)

Milwaukee Institute of Art and Design

Missouri Baptist University

Missouri Western State University

Mitchell College (CT)

Montana State University–Northern

Montserrat College of Art (MA)

Morris College (SC)

Mountain State University (WV)

Mount Holyoke College (MA)

Mount Olive College (NC)

Muhlenberg College (PA)

Naropa University (CO)

National Hispanic University (CA)

National University (CA)

Nazareth College (NY)

Newbury College (MA)

New England College (NH)

New England Conservatory of Music (MA)

New School (NY)

North Carolina Wesleyan College

Northwest Missouri State University

Nyack College (NY)

Oakland University (MI)

Oklahoma Panhandle State University

Ottawa University (KS)

Pacific Northwest College of Art (OR)

Paul Smith's College (NY)

Peirce College (PA)

Pennsylvania College of Technology

Pikeville College (KY)

Pitzer College (CA)

Providence College (RI)

Purdue University–North Central (IN)

Ringling College of Art and Design (FL)

Rivier College (NH)

Robert Morris University (IL)

Rollins College (FL)

Russell Sage College (NY)

Sacred Heart University (CT)

Sage Colleges–Albany (NY)

Salisbury University (MD)

San Francisco Art Institute

San Francisco Conservatory of Music

San Francisco State University

San Jose State University (CA)

Sarah Lawrence College (NY)

Sewanee–University of the South (TN)

Shawnee State University (OH)

Sierra Nevada College (NV)

Smith College (MA)

Sojourner-Douglass College (MD)

Southern Nazarene University (OK)

Southwestern Christian College (TX)

St. Anselm College (NH)

Stetson University (FL)

St. John's College (MD)

St. John's College (NM)

St. Lawrence University (NY)

St. Michael's College (VT)

Stonehill College (MA)

SUNY College of Agriculture and Tech.–Cobleskill

SUNY College of Technology–Alfred

SUNY College of Technology–Delhi

SUNY College–Potsdam

SUNY Empire State College

Susquehanna University (PA)

Texas College

Texas Southern University

Texas Woman's University

Thomas Edison State College (NJ)

Thomas More College of Liberal Arts (NH)

Thomas University (GA)

Touro College (NY)

Trinity University (DC)

Union College (NY)

Union Institute and University (OH)

Unity College (ME)

University of Alaska–Anchorage

University of Alaska–Southeast

University of Arizona

University of Arkansas–Little Rock

University of Arkansas–Monticello

University of Great Falls (MT)

University of Hawaii–West Oahu

University of Houston–Downtown

University of Maine–Augusta

University of Maine–Farmington

University of Maine–Fort Kent

University of Maine–Presque Isle

University of Maryland–University College

University of Mississippi

University of Nevada–Las Vegas

University of Nevada–Reno

University of Northwestern Ohio

University of South Alabama

University of Texas–Brownsville

University of Texas–El Paso

University of the District of Columbia

University of Wisconsin–Parkside

University of Wisconsin–Whitewater

Upper Iowa University	Weber State University (UT)
Urbana University (OH)	Western Governors University (UT)
Ursinus College (PA)	Western New Mexico University
Utah Valley University	Western State College of Colorado
Utica College (NY)	Wheaton College (MA)
VanderCook College of Music (IL)	Whitworth University (WA)
Vermont Technical College	Wichita State University (KS)
Voorhees College (SC)	Wiley College (TX)
Wake Forest University (NC)	Wilmington University (DE)
Walsh College of Account. and Bus. Admin. (MI)	Wilson College (PA)
Warner Pacific College (OR)	Wittenberg University (OH)
Washington and Jefferson College (PA)	Worcester Polytechnic Institute (MA)

The SAT, designed to measure your academic preparedness (or how much knowledge you have actually mastered), has a maximum score of 2400. The exam takes an endurance-testing three hours and 45 minutes, and costs $45. First comes a short, hand-written, 25-minute essay. Sample query: "Novelty is too often mistaken for progress. Assignment: The statement above suggests that what is new and different is often confused with advancement. To what extent do you agree or disagree with this view?" The essay is scored by two readers and accounts for approximately 30 percent of the writing score. (See page 38 for more on the essay and how it's graded.) The rest of the writing section is in two parts, with 49 multiple-choice grammar and usage questions.

The 70-minute "Critical Reading" section consists of three parts, with 67 multiple-choice questions that include sentence completions and both long and short reading comprehension passages. The 70-minute math section, also in three parts, tests your knowledge of geometry, statistics, and Algebra II topics such as exponential growth, absolute value, and functional notation; it allows calculators and includes both multiple-choice and grid-in questions.

The SAT also includes a 25-minute experimental section (used to test new questions) that may have either additional reading, math, or multiple-choice writing questions. It does not count toward your score, but you won't know which part it is, so you'll have to take all the parts seriously. The test will end with writing questions, but otherwise the

content areas can come in any order.

SAT questions appear in order of difficulty, from easy to hard, and the style of the test can be tricky. Possible answers include lots of "distractors"—choices that are specifically meant to distract test-takers from the correct response. One SAT question, for example, asked for the antonym of "blue" (meaning "sad"); two colors, including "red," appeared as options to throw test-takers off. Students are penalized for wrong answers, which means that guessing isn't a good idea unless you can definitely eliminate one or more incorrect responses.

The ACT, on the other hand, is a roughly three-hour exam that costs $32 and measures academic preparation in four sections. English, which covers usage and mechanics like grammar and punctuation as well as rhetorical skills, takes 45 minutes. Mathematics, which includes questions on pre-algebra, algebra, geometry, and trigonometry, takes 60 minutes. Science, which measures your ability to design and interpret basic experiments, takes 35 minutes. Reading, in four subject areas, also takes 35 minutes. The 215 multiple-choice questions are presented in random order—simple and killer queries all mixed together from the start—and the style is considered more straightforward than the SAT. There is no penalty for wrong answers, so feel free to take your chances.

Test-takers choosing the ACT also have the option of adding a 30-minute essay that costs an additional $15 and will satisfy colleges that demand a writing score as part of your application. A sample query: "In some high schools, many teachers and parents have encouraged the school to adopt a dress code that sets guidelines for what students can wear in the school building. Some teachers and parents support a dress code because they think it will improve the learning environment in the school. Other teachers and parents do not support a dress code because they think it restricts the individual student's freedom of expression. In your opinion, should high schools adopt dress codes for students? In your essay, take a position on this question. You may write about either one of the two points of view given, or you may present a different point of view on this question. Use specific reasons and examples to support your position."

For the high school class of 2009, the average score on the SAT was 501 out of a possible 800 for the critical reading section, 515 for the math section, and 493 for the writing section. The mean ACT was 21.1 out of a top score of 36. Those who plan to be tested multiple times—or who fear they'll have to be—take note: Depending on the school, the SAT's new "Score Choice" policy will let you choose which test score you submit, just like the ACT.

To figure out which exam to take, you can buy review books for under $20 apiece and try a practice version of each test. Then compare your scores using a concordance table, which shows how SAT scores and ACT scores line up. (A sample is available at http://www.act.org/aap/concordance/.) You can also try the practice questions and tests at the SAT and ACT websites.

> "Holistic scoring has far less to do with [what your answer is] and far more to do with whether or not you develop your argument well."

If you perform substantially better on the practice SAT, then stick with that exam, or go ahead and take both and report the ACT score if it turns out to be a pleasant surprise. Keep in mind that many top-ranking colleges require two or three SAT Subject Tests in addition to the SAT Reasoning Test, but some, like Wesleyan University in Connecticut, will accept the ACT in lieu of all SATs. The upshot: Check with the colleges you think you want to apply to before deciding which tests to take.

How your SAT essay will be graded—and used

What happens to your brilliant ideas and exquisite phrasings once you've put the pencil down? Your essay will be trucked off to two members of an army of readers across the country who've been specially trained in the art of "holistic" scoring—in other words, absorbing and judging your prose in a couple minutes flat.

Each reader will give you a grade of 0 to 6, based on how convincingly you take a stand on an issue and prove your point. Your two scores will be combined for a composite of 0 to 12; if there is a discrepancy of more than one point between the two readers, then a more senior reader will make the call. This raw score then counts for about 30 percent of the total 200–800 writing score.

According to the College Board's scoring guidelines, a 0 means you completely failed to answer the question; a 6 means you've eloquently and effectively argued your case. "Holistic scoring has far less to do with [what your answer is] and far more to do with whether or not you develop your argument well," says Brian O'Reilly, executive director of SAT program relations for the College Board, which develops the test. "You can take either side of the issue and back up your argument with something you read in a textbook, novel, newspaper article, or even saw in a movie."

Believe it or not, as long as your essay is readable, errors in spelling, punctuation, and grammar will not be held against you—the multiple-choice portion of the new writing section will test your knowledge in those areas. And don't spend precious time trying to remember that the French Revolution started in 1789, since you will not be judged on how straight your facts are, either. "We don't want to penalize [students] on a writing assignment because they reference the wrong date historically or the wrong author of a literary work," explains O'Reilly, noting that this would be particularly unfair given that students who use personal experiences in an essay could make up stories that fit their argument. "What we're measuring is how well did they develop an argument."

Interestingly enough, a recent analysis of sample SAT essays and grades by a Massachusetts Institute of Technology professor found that the longer a student's answer, the better his or her score. Testing officials insist the correlation was expected. "In the process of developing a full, complete argument—bringing in supporting examples and explaining why they support your side of the argument—length is not unimportant," says O'Reilly. "On average, the longer essays do get higher scores because the student is saying more than his or her fellow student is saying in a short essay." But before you ramble on and on, be forewarned: College Board officials insist that length is not an automatic guarantee of 5 or 6. "There are plenty of examples of longer essays with lower scores," O'Reilly adds.

The readers, many of whom are English teachers experienced in grading the old SAT Subject Test in writing, understand that what you manage to piece together in 25 minutes will be substantially different from a paper handed in at school. "In a testing situation, we are taking a snapshot of a first draft," says Bernard Phelan, a Chicago-area educator and consultant, and a member of the committee that developed the writing section. To be sure that everyone's on the same wavelength, readers are assigned sample essays representing each point level from 0 to 6 and must come up with the right score for each on their own before they can proceed with grading real essays.

In general, says Agnes Yamada, professor emerita of English at California State University–Dominguez Hills and an experienced test-reader herself, the people scoring your essay will expect to get a clear sense of your direction—and to see that you actually move forward rather than jump around or get stuck. "At level 3, you often have papers that are so undeveloped that every sentence sounds like the beginning of a new essay," says Yamada. Or the writers just repeat themselves and fail to "advance the paper." Besides direction, she says, readers want "good details, good examples, and specificity." If human rights is the topic, for example, you might start by describing your position and listing the several people—Martin Luther King Jr., Elie Wiesel, Nelson Mandela—whose experiences and beliefs you will use to support it, then devote a paragraph to specifics about each that make your case. Suppose you decide that writing about your own life would prove your point. A narrative is completely acceptable—as long as your story is rich in details. "The writer has to remember that we are not familiar with his aunt or grandma," says Yamada.

Because the actual essays will not be included in the SAT score reports, college officials must decide whether to read them online. One tack many will take is to call up the essay when they feel a need to compare it with a polished application essay, which may have been produced as an English assignment, say, and carefully honed over a long period—or even written by a parent. Officials might download the essays of marginal applicants about whom more information is needed, or those by candidates for merit awards. "The short essay will represent the student's ability to think logically, to prepare ideas in draft form, and to demonstrate written communication skills," says Ann Wright, a veteran admissions official now with the College Board. "We've been trying to find more ways to evaluate students because they are starting to

"On average, the longer essays do get higher scores because the student is saying more than his or her fellow student is saying in a short essay."

look the same on paper," says Todd Rinehart, assistant vice chancellor for enrollment at the University of Denver, which has also decided to use the essay in admissions decisions, viewing it as a source of much-needed extra information.

The uncertainty surrounding colleges' use of the writing exams has exacerbated student confusion and concern, says Alan Crocker, former assistant headmaster and college adviser at the New Hampton School in New Hampshire. "It would be nice if there was some consistency in the use" of the relatively new tests, he says. But students shouldn't expend much effort trying to make sense of school policies, says Joyce Slayton Mitchell, who was formerly director of college advising at a private school in New York and is the author of *Winning the Heart of the College Admissions Dean.* "Build the strongest academic record you can build, document the local record with national SATs in as many areas as you can do well. Then see who wants a student just like you. No need to get into who wants what.... Do the best you can in as many areas as you can document."

Calculating how much prep you need

Once you decide which test to take, how much time and energy—not to mention money—should you devote to preparing for it? First, you'll need to figure out how important test scores are to the colleges you're interested in attending. Schools that have dropped the tests entirely as an entrance requirement reason that high school GPAs and writing samples are equal or even better predictors of success in college and that eliminating applicants solely on the basis of test scores penalizes the less affluent who can't afford any sort of fancy test prep. Others have unofficially decided to de-emphasize the importance of test scores in admissions deci-

"We've been trying to find more ways to evaluate students because they are starting to look the same on paper."

sions for the same reasons, though you probably won't know this when you apply.

The next step is to calculate how the test results you can expect to get would stack up against the scores of the college's entering freshmen. To get a sense of how you'll perform when the big day

comes, you'll need to look at your success on the PLAN test or the PSAT. The PLAN, which schools in the ACT-centric states administer to tenth graders (many of whom also choose to take the PSAT), mirrors the ACT: It is divided into English, math, reading, and science sections, and is graded on the same 36-point basis. The idea is that if you find you're weak in certain subject areas, you can tailor your course selection or study to get ready for the big test. The PSAT, which students usually take in their sophomore or junior year, closely reflects the SAT exam: The two hour and 10 minute test is divided into three sections—50 minutes apiece of math and critical reading, and 30 minutes of multiple-choice "writing skills" questions. Each section is scored on a 20-to-80 scale. The PSAT does not include a written essay, mostly because grading it is labor intensive, but high schools may assign a practice essay anyway.

Add your math, reading, and writing PSAT scores together, then tack on a zero. This will give you a number that should roughly approximate the combined score you'll earn on the SAT. Test prep of any sort, however, should give you a boost, and even just having the PSAT under your belt might help your performance on the SAT.

See where you stand

To get an idea of how your PLAN and/or PSAT results measure up against the scores of students who have been accepted at colleges you're interested in, take a look at the math and verbal SAT and ACT score ranges provided in each school's entry in the Ultimate College Directory. Although mean scores on the new 2400-point scale will not be available, experts in counseling, admissions, and testing note that your math and critical reading scores are exactly comparable to the old scores; thus, judging your combined scores in those two sections against the scores reported in a school's directory entry should give you a ballpark idea of where you stand. "Reading and writing are skills that usually overlap," adds the College Board's O'Reilly. "It's not universal—there will be differences—but, in general, most students will see their reading and writing scores be relatively similar, and so they can simply view writing scores in comparison to verbal scores at colleges as well."

If your predicted score is better than the scores of freshmen at schools you're applying to, you probably don't need to do exhaustive studying, except that you will certainly want to take several practice tests to familiarize yourself with the exam's format and pacing. "The new SAT isn't that much harder; it's just longer. You get pretty tired out after the third hour—and there's still more to go," says a student who took the exam, and whose concerns about time have been echoed by countless peers. Think of it this way: You don't want to tackle a marathon without doing some long runs beforehand. In addition, anybody who has been racing down the accelerated math track in high school should also spend some time dusting off those perhaps long-forgotten algebra and geometry skills.

If your practice test scores are only mediocre, you should absolutely prepare for the real exam more extensively, whether you study by yourself at home or pay for a coaching class. Says Robert Schaeffer, public education director of the National Center for Fair and Open Testing in Cambridge, Massachusetts, an organization that advocates standardized testing reform: "There's no human endeavor, from writing to tennis, that practice doesn't improve. Why should the SAT be any different?"

Studying on your own for the new SAT

Walk into any bookstore and you'll be confronted with shelves upon shelves of the latest-and-greatest SAT and ACT prep materials, from compilations of practice exams to tips on how to beat the system. Still, a good place to start is the source. The College Board develops the SAT, and its website, www.collegeboard. com, contains practice questions for all sections as well as a free downloadable practice test that comes with an explanation of correct answers. *The Official SAT Study Guide: Second Edition*, with 10 full-length exams, is another great resource at $21.99. In addition, the ACT student website, www.actstudent.org/ testprep/index.html, contains free sample questions,

test-taking tips, and links to official materials like *The Real ACT Prep Guide*, with three full-length exams and a price tag of $25.

The cast of test-prep characters

If you decide that your SAT or ACT score could use a boost from a professional, you've got plenty of test-prep options to choose from. In fact, teaching nervous teens to ace these tests has turned into a multibillion-dollar industry. A slew of new coaching services, from free online courses to $100-an-hour-and-up private tutors, have joined classroom kings Princeton Review and Kaplan in the business over the past few years. The range of choices means you can probably find a style and method of prep that will work best for you.

Some students need the stimulation and structure of a classroom, while others learn better when relaxed at home, cozying up to a computer. One of the big selling points of private tutoring and online courses is that you can learn at your own pace. But the latter route may not be a great idea for unmotivated students, and some parents are understandably wary of encouraging their kids to spend hours online where distractions, like instant messaging, are plentiful.

Both Kaplan and Princeton Review offer cram courses that review material likely to appear on the exams and teach key test-taking skills. For example, you'll learn guessing techniques and strategies, such as how to gauge when a problem isn't worth the time it will take to solve. But the courses don't come cheap. Kaplan's "Complete" SAT or ACT prep course, which includes 18 hours of classroom or online instruction, is $499, while a more comprehensive package with additional features is $999. Princeton Review has an 18-hour classroom course for $599 and an "Ultimate Classroom" course for $999 to $1,249, depending on location.

If you can't concentrate in a group and a higher price tag isn't an obstacle, then one-on-one help might be the right answer. Private tutoring at Kaplan costs between $1,000 and $4,000, depending on the number of hours, while Princeton Review offers a 24-hour package of individual tutoring that runs from $2,760 to $7,800, depending on location and tutor.

The online option

If you'd rather do your preparation by computer, possibilities abound—many of them free. SparkNotes, for example, features a free, fully searchable version of its *Guide to the New SAT*, which is sold in bookstores for $19.95, at www.sparknotes.com/testprep/books/newsat; you can also download free diagnostic tests and other tools, such as novels that include frequently tested vocabulary words. The website Number2.com offers free interactive ACT and SAT courses that teach you how to approach each type of question, let you practice at your own pace, and monitor your progress; these tutorials automatically adjust according to your skill level. Countless other sites provide various forms of help for free; just use your favorite search engine to find and take advantage of these services.

Not to be outdone, Kaplan and Princeton Review also offer a range of online course options that cost $99 and up, depending on content and duration. (In the latter's "LiveOnline" class, students can talk directly to their instructor with a specialized headset, included in the $599 cost.) The College Board's "Official SAT Online Course" contains specific lessons like "algebra and functions review" and over 600 practice questions, as well as 10 official practice tests, which you can take online or on paper—the latter being key to approximating real test-taking conditions—with detailed score and skills reports; a four-month subscription is $69.95.

How much will it help?

Both Kaplan and Princeton Review have historically asserted that students who take any of their pricey coaching courses typically see huge gains in their scores. But Princeton Review recently stopped claim-

---

"The new SAT isn't that much harder, it's just longer. You get pretty tired out after the third hour—and there's still more to go."

---

ing that its "Ultimate Classroom" course boosted SAT scores an average of 255 points, following a complaint by Kaplan to the National Advertising Division of the Council of Better Business Bureaus.

Both firms still say they guarantee higher scores and, under some circumstances, will refund the cost of the course if you don't show improvement.

Generally, however, independent research suggests that the gains from prep courses are fairly modest. While acknowledging that the research had limitations, and so far had not covered the revised and expanded SAT, a 2009 report by the National Association for College Admission Counseling said average gains from commercial coaching are "in the neighborhood of 30 points."

While it's impossible to predict whether taking a course will boost your scores enough to make the cost worthwhile, you might benefit more if you suffer from test anxiety, say guidance counselors. Indeed, much of what these classes are selling is confidence: There's less chance of going into the testing room and choking if you've been drilling and taking practice tests for weeks or months in advance. Also, students who had trouble with the math portions of the PSAT may profit quite a bit from prep programs, because math skills generally are easier to improve through coaching than verbal skills.

Check references

Before shelling out hundreds of dollars for any kind of course or tutor, do some investigative work, says Judi Robinovitz, a private education consultant who runs several learning centers in Florida and tutoring services in New York City. The best referrals are those from someone you trust who has had firsthand experience. You'll want to ask about the credentials of an outfit's instructors. Have they been teaching SAT prep for at least five years? Do they take the SAT themselves on a regular basis and continue to score in the top 5 percent of test-takers? Do they teach from real and recent College Board tests? A professional should be able to provide you with several student references, says Robinovitz. She also suggests auditing the first session of any class before you sign up to make sure it's a good fit.

Keeping it all in perspective

It's important not to get carried away with test prepping, especially during the all-important junior year, when your grades matter more than almost anything else. You don't want any obsessing about the SAT to distract you from more worthwhile pursuits, like paying attention to Dickens in AP English or truly grasping the origins of capitalism in history class. And remember that a higher-than-average score will not ensure that your dream schools will be clamoring to admit you, since most look at students holistically, judging the application and the person as a whole.

"We consider a student's best test scores," reads Harvard University's admissions website, "but it is generally our experience that taking tests more than twice offers diminishing returns." In addition, while academic preparation is key, don't underestimate the value of simple steps like getting a good night's sleep before the exam, eating a healthy breakfast that morning, and trying to stay calm throughout the entire process. Remember: Even a perfect 2400 or 36 is no magic guarantee of getting in, say admissions officers across the country. At the end of the day, scores are just one part of the package.

Chapter Four

Putting Together a Killer Application

You've sweated your way through the challenging courses and put your heart into drama club, student government, four seasons of lacrosse, and hours and hours at the local food bank. You've prepped for the SATs—and taken them twice—and tramped behind tour guides across more than a dozen campuses.

The hard work has only begun.

Now you've got to put all the facts, figures, and that special *je ne sais quoi* together in a package that will blow the minds of the admissions committee and nail you a place in next year's freshman class.

This is no small feat, given the competition. To ace this last, most crucial phase of admissions, you're going to have to give careful thought to each step of the application process. How do you write an essay that will grab a tired staffer who's been plowing through more than 30 a day for weeks? How can you get a recommendation from a teacher who will write as if he knows you, and not just serve up clichés? Is it better to be honest about that trouble you got into—even if it was ages ago in the ninth grade—or not? What do you stand to gain and lose by applying early decision? And how about when your alumni interviewer pressures you to divulge where else you're applying?

What follows are answers to all these questions and more, gleaned from admissions professionals who have judged hundreds of thousands of applicants before you.

Get great guidance

Here's why your high school guidance counselor should be your new best friend: Besides helping you zero in on a sensible list of schools, counselors can get you into any remaining classes you need, suggest which standardized test will best showcase your abilities, and write a recommendation that, come April, will help determine whether you receive fat envelopes or skinny ones.

In fact, your biggest college resource may be your counselor's connections, because she's probably well plugged in to the college admissions scene. Why does this matter to you? Admissions officers who know and trust her may call for the inside scoop—like who from your senior class are the best candidates. She'll be the one fielding phone calls about everything from a low grade on your transcript to a difficult disciplinary problem. And if that's not enough to convince you, suppose that—worst-case scenario—you wind up getting rejected everywhere you apply; a sympathetic counselor might plead your case to admissions officials at schools that still have open slots.

These are the kind of people you definitely want watching your back, so don't be shy about making the first move. You can be one of the few faces in the hall that your adviser recognizes if you pop into her office often to talk about college, extracurriculars, and the state of the world in general. If your counselor is too swamped for frequent chats, it's a good idea to drop off a résumé that lists your recent accomplishments for her files. "If students are going to brag to anyone, we're the people," says Risa Green, former codirector of college counseling at Milken Community High School in Los Angeles. She suggests handing over a portfolio of your best papers and creative projects, too. Be prepared to share any major personal problems. If one of your parents gets seriously ill and your grades slip as a result, your counselor can explain the situation in her recommendation.

One of your counselor's responsibilities is to send colleges a profile of your high school, which has a big impact on how admissions personnel view your application. The profile helps them determine how thoroughly you've taken advantage of available opportunities by describing the curriculum that you've chosen from, including all of the Advanced Placement, International Baccalaureate, and honors courses at your school. It explains the grading system and how class rank is calculated, and supplies a tally of the universities that accepted last year's seniors. Most profiles also describe the demographic makeup of the school and its community.

As a result, admissions officers can interpret your grades in light of what they know about your school's resources. The less challenging the school's curriculum, the higher an applicant's grades must be, for example. It's a good idea to look at your school's profile to see, for instance, whether it reports an average family income that far surpasses your parents' earnings. If so, you might ask your counselor to clarify the situation in the recommendation letter; the added insight will help explain why you're working after school instead of playing sports.

While lots of high schoolers get great counsel, many others have to navigate college admissions with little or no guidance. The numbers tell the story: Although the National Association for College Admission Counseling recommends that the student-to-counselor ratio in a school not exceed 100 to 1 (which already sounds pretty big), at some large public high schools the numbers push as high as 565 to 1. Not only do most counselors have too many students, they also have too many duties, including scheduling classes, finding resources for learning-disabled students, and dealing with troublemakers.

So what do you do if your counselor is permanently missing in action, resists all advances, or doesn't know enough about colleges to be helpful? Experts suggest trying to make an appointment with another counselor at your school—being sure to tell your own adviser that you're gathering information from as many people as possible so he or she doesn't get offended. Eventually you may be able to officially switch counselors, but it isn't easy. A student who argues that she's not getting a fair shake because

Does money matter?

It depends. Most colleges claim to keep a wall between admissions and financial aid, so checking the tiny box on an application that says you're going to be applying for assistance shouldn't influence the decision-making process at all. Still, Donald Heller, a Penn State professor of education and coauthor of several studies on financial aid, notes that relatively few schools—mostly the Ivies and a clutch of small, selective institutions like Amherst, Vassar, and Williams—are truly committed to a "need-blind" admissions policy that ignores a student's ability to pay, coupled with a promise to fully meet the need of every student admitted.

Most schools, says Heller, take a "need-aware" approach. In other words, stellar candidates will be admitted regardless of their financial status, but middling students are apt to be judged, in part, by how much they will cost the school. The result is that many applicants who might meet the standards for admission are rejected if the college knows it won't meet their need. Some schools admit a large percentage of their freshmen without considering whether they will need financial aid; from that point on, the class is filled out with those who can afford full tuition.

In the end, the only way to deal with this situation is to know what you're up against. Ask colleges up front about how their decisions are affected by need. Then use your application and any interviews to make yourself seem so valuable that the committee will want you no matter what.

---

an older sibling's bad behavior biased the counselor against the whole family may have a shot, but pleas based on personality clashes or alleged incompetence aren't normally approved. However, college admissions committees know that, for a variety of reasons, not everyone gets good advice or a fair recommendation. Says one admissions dean, "We try not to hold [a mediocre letter] against a candidate if the rest of the transcript is strong."

Look into hired help

You may find that you want to investigate outside counseling options as a way to lower your anxiety level a few notches. Counselors-for-hire will coach you on all the basics and more: picking appropriate high school courses and extracurricular activities, researching and selecting colleges to apply to, writing an engaging essay, preparing for your interviews, and applying for financial aid.

Qualified advisers abound these days, but they don't come cheap. At the high end are private educational consultants who sometimes start counseling students as early as the eighth or ninth grade, grooming them as desirable candidates and later helping them develop a list of schools and prepare applications. Their services usually cost from $700 to upwards of $2,200 a year. Less-personalized guidance is available, too, in seminars or online packages. If you are truly needy, you can turn to groups such as the Bottom Line in Boston, which counsels students for free. Many pricey consultants also do pro bono advising, so you may want to call several in your area, explain your situation, and ask if they can help or suggest some other options.

One motive shared by many families who use private counseling is the desire to keep Mom, Dad, and the kids from strangling one another during these often tense months. "Most parents come to us saying, 'I can't talk to my kids. They won't listen to me. I think it'll be much better coming from you,'" says one California adviser. As for students, they get to spill their guts to someone with a sympathetic ear. In fact, independent counselors often end up acting more like a therapist—a fair, unbiased person who will listen as you stress out about choosing a topic for your essay, then offer you advice, without screaming.

You can put away the white out

The Internet has put an end to typing and retyping—and erasing and retyping—the same information on dozens of forms. Today, most colleges and universities have their application forms online so that they can be filled out and printed or completed electronically. In addition to college-specific sites, you can log on to one of several that host hundreds of colleges' e-applications, such as www.collegenet.com and www.xap.com. In most cases, their services are free to applicants, although you still have to pay an application fee to the schools. Students can also go to www.commonapp.org for a generic form, called the Common Application, which is accepted by about 400 colleges and universities.

Just don't let the relative ease of applying electronically be your downfall, guidance counselors and admissions officers warn. Too often, students who would take care with a paper form hurry through the Internet version. If you decide to apply online, be sure to have a parent or teacher read over your essays before you hit the submit button. Print it out and read it through yourself, too. Keep a copy; Internet delivery is not infallible. Chasing down the mail carrier so you can white out that glaring spelling error you just remembered is—sadly or not—no longer an option.

No matter what kind of program you choose, be sure to check out a prospective counselor's qualifications first. Perhaps the most important question to ask any private consultant is: How much experience have you had? It's smart to expect at least five years as a high school guidance counselor or in college admissions, as well as membership in either the Independent Educational Consultants Association (703-591-4850) or the National Association for College Admission Counseling (800-822-6285). Ask for professional and client references—and call them.

Avoid inexperienced consultants who claim that their Ivy League degrees give them special insight into the admission process, consultants who promise entrance into prestigious schools before viewing your academic record, and independent counselors who have cantankerous relationships with guidance offices. Remember, you can't afford to alienate your high school counselor! He still writes the all-important recommendation, and colleges will still call him if they want to know more about you.

Pull the pieces together

By the time you're sitting down to fill in the blanks, there's not a whole lot you can do about your transcript, which, as the key part of your application, is going to get a thorough going-over. Besides demonstrating how well you've succeeded academically (your grades), the transcript shows whether you've challenged yourself or skated by (your course load) and, when studied alongside your standardized test scores, often hints at whether you're a consistent and hard worker or an underachiever. (For more on what the admissions office wants to see when it reviews your four-year history, see Chapter Two, "What Colleges Will Look For in You.")

Elsewhere in the application, the effort you put in now can greatly improve your odds. Here are some tips.

Hit the mark with your essay

Dante got it wrong. There is another circle of hell: writing the college essay, an exercise that can make or break your chances of being admitted. "Often [test] scores are in the same acceptable range, the kid's done well in the same classes everybody else has taken, and it's the essay we finally refer to," says former University of Chicago admissions dean Ted O'Neill.

How to compose the prose that will win you that coveted spot is, of course, what everybody hopes to learn from books like this one. Most start with the premise that essay writing is easy—if you just know the secrets. Well, it's not. Writing about yourself with imagination and the perfect balance of humility and pride is really, really difficult. To succeed, you'll have to start early, be willing to rewrite, and follow a few rules—some of which are quite simple.

Let's start with the easiest: Always answer the question. If it's "Why do you want to go to Kalamazoo College?" don't talk about your lifelong ambition to be a trapeze artist; address what's compelling about Kalamazoo. If a university asks, "If you could be a tree, what kind of tree would you be?" try to get into the spirit of things—and don't be snotty, no matter how inane the question might seem.

There's agreement among admissions deans that literary perfection is not necessary; they want an introduction to the real 17-year-old you. "Sometimes the least successful essays are so polished they don't reveal anything about the writer," says O'Neill. Chicago is renowned for its offbeat topics, which have included the significance of given names and the possible extraterrestrial origins of such features of modern life as the tax code. The answers, says O'Neill, can reveal a lot about a student's creativity and thought process.

Many other schools leave the topic open, and settling on a good one is the hardest part of the job for many seniors. If you have no idea where to begin, try taking the advice of Michael Thompson, former dean of admission and financial aid at the University of Southern California in Los Angeles, and tell your readers something they don't already know about you. "When a student writes to us that they work 30 hours a week and the money they make goes into the family income," he says, "then the fact that they weren't president of the chess club makes more sense." Some favorites that stick in admissions deans' memories:

- A reflection on race by a part-time cashier in a discount clothing store
- A deadpan appreciation of late-night TV game shows
- A young American Indian woman's recounting of moving from a big city in Utah back to the Navajo reservation
- A young man's reflection on having his right foot amputated at age 2, living with a prosthesis, and growing up to play three varsity sports

"Sometimes the least successful essays are so polished they don't reveal anything about the writer."

- An emotional essay about the torment a young woman went through after severely injuring her father in a skiing accident

Thompson warns that, though tempting, essays about adversity and how you surmounted it can be hard to pull off. The last thing you want to do is sound whiny. He advises focusing on the positive lessons learned. Do not under any circumstances write about breaking up with a boyfriend or girlfriend! A broken heart is one of the few topics admissions officers agree are off limits. If you still have no idea where to begin, try canvassing the people who know you best for their take on your three most compelling qualities, or ask them to help you recall a formative experience.

Once you've chosen a subject, use the KISS principle of writing: Keep It Super Simple. Take a single idea or event, and describe it in loving detail. One mistake college essayists often make is that they write an overview of their lives. A narrow focus is bound to offer your readers more interesting insights about what you think and who you are. Another rule that writers follow: Show, don't tell. Telling is making a statement like "I am a very passionate person." Oh, really? Says who? Show your readers how passionately you feel about, say, scuba diving, with details that put them on the water with

Tips for homeschoolers

What do you do for teacher recommendations if Dad did the teaching? How do you produce a class rank for the only kid in school? Each year, thousands of homeschooled students must jump through hoops to document their accomplishments for admissions officers.

Use your ingenuity and do some early strategic planning, advises Cafi Cohen, author of *And What About College? How Homeschooling Leads to Admissions to the Best Colleges and Universities*. Selective institutions like the University of Virginia and Stanford insist on a solid curriculum in certain subjects such as math and science, and are on the lookout for any extraordinary talent—musical, athletic, or oth-

erwise. Most schools also want evidence that a student educated alone interacts well with others, such as a history of participation in team sports or a local choir, for example. Some tips:

- *Establish an academic record.* Like many homeschooling parents, Cohen did not grade her homeschooled son, Jeff. When schools wanted a transcript, she awarded As in subjects she felt he had mastered—a tactic she explained up front to admissions officers. Jeff ended up getting a place at the U.S. Air Force Academy. Another alternative is to present a bibliography of what students have read for each course.
- *Take college classes.* College coursework indicates

achievement in much the same way that Advanced Placement courses do for regular applicants.
- *Test your knowledge.* College entrance exams carry extra weight because, as one dean put it, "We can't trust the grades." The University of Virginia, for one, urges homeschoolers to take five or six SAT Subject Tests, if possible.
- *Polish your portfolio.* Essays take on greater importance, too. Articulate why you've been homeschooled and what you've learned from various projects. Supporting evidence of intellectual vitality, like academic papers and samples of artwork, is also welcome.

you, like how thrilling it is to smell the salty air as the dive boat races toward the reef, how you're filled with anticipation and more than a little fear. Write about how your anxiety dissipates as you sink toward the sea floor, with only the crackle of snapping shrimp and the hiss of your own breathing for company. Caring passionately, it turns out, is one of the personal qualities that schools want most in applicants. Admissions officers don't expect every student to be a Renaissance boy or girl—captain of the soccer team, president of the student body, and a member of the French, history, and glee clubs. They want students who are excited about life and scholarship and who can express this—and thus, themselves—in writing.

However, a college essay is no place for the fancy words you memorized for the SATs; your audience wants to hear your thoughts in your own voice. If

your expostulation is transmogrified to mephitic pedantry, throw out the thesaurus and try again.

Get a glowing recommendation

The impact of recommendation letters is easy to underestimate, but that would be a big mistake. A 2009 survey of college admissions officers by the National Association for College Admission Counseling showed that nearly 60 percent considered recommendations from teachers to be important in their efforts to distinguish one qualified student from the next; a slightly higher percentage said recommendations from guidance counselors were important.

Most colleges require letters from your guidance counselor and one or two high school teachers. In a perfect world, the teachers would speak to your fabulous performance in the classroom and the counselor would carry on about your contributions to the school and your community. But overworked guidance counselors often don't know students well enough to give colleges much more than a school profile and your class rank. So it makes sense to approach teachers who can describe your place in the big picture—preferably somebody who has seen your best work academically over a period of time.

If you've been deeply involved in an organization in or outside of school, consider adding an extra letter from someone who knows you in that context. For example, if ballet is a major part of your life and you spend hours every day after school practicing pirouettes, it's probably a good idea to have the director of your ballet school—who can speak to your dedication, talent, and drive—write a letter on your behalf. Letters from alums (or a CEO or a senator, for that matter) can bolster your chances if they shed light on your abilities or personality, but only if they are written by someone who really knows you well. VIP recommendations that say merely that Jack or Jill mowed the lawn and seemed like a nice kid don't help, no matter who they come from.

Quantity should not be confused with quality. Emory University in Atlanta has a three-recommendation limit; most other schools say they rarely want more than four recommendations total—and definitely not the 14 that filled one recent applicant's folder at Wake Forest University in North Carolina.

Once you've found the right people to ask for letters, there's a lot you can do to make it easier for them to enthuse on your behalf. Obviously, it helps to approach teachers and counselors well before the letters are due; a month in advance of the deadline is a good rule of thumb. For students applying early decision or early action, this can mean asking teachers almost as soon as school starts in the fall. Be sure to come prepared with the appropriate forms along with stamped, preaddressed envelopes, and remember to check the privacy waiver. This reassures admissions officials that the evaluation is an honest one.

If you haven't spent much time recently with the teacher or counselor who will recommend you, make an appointment to talk over your high school accomplishments and your goals for college. You want to make sure your letter writers have something concrete to say, because shallow recommendations do little to further your cause. Ideally, your teacher or counselor will be able to point to specific stories or particular qualities and say this is a great kid "because"; that kind of insight can really make a difference in how admissions staffers view you. Talking yourself up isn't always the easiest job, but if you do your part, your teachers can often get information

> *"Recommendations can highlight things that you can't write about gracefully or talk about without seeming like an arrogant jerk."*

across that you'd never feel comfortable expressing in your essay or in interviews with admissions officials. "Sometimes it's obnoxious to do a real strong self-presentation," explains Charles Cogan, associate dean of admissions and director of international recruitment at Carleton College in Northfield, Minnesota. "Recommendations can highlight things that you can't write about gracefully or talk about without seeming like an arrogant jerk."

Stick in any relevant extras

So you're a rap-rock guitarist? A successful Internet entrepreneur? A published author? Students who have a special talent or an unusual accomplishment or personal quality that can be captured in a portfolio may want to send the evidence to the admissions office along with their application—particularly if they've received recognition from someone other than Mom. Such "hooks" can help you stand out in a field of outstanding applicants and sway opinion in your favor, even if other aspects of your application aren't top-notch.

Smaller colleges especially welcome extra information, including tapes or CDs, videos, and websites. "We really want to know as much about each candidate as possible," says Paula Mitchell, director of the U.S. office of higher education for the Council of International Schools. For example, one woman applying to Ithaca College sent slides of her paint-

Hello, you're in

If you can't take the pressure of filling out a slew of applications and then waiting months upon months to learn your fate, there is another answer. Getting accepted into Newbury College in Brookline, Massachusetts, and a number of other schools could take about as long as watching your favorite sitcom. Under these schools' "instant admissions" options, applicants meet with an admissions official who reviews their transcript and test scores, and asks them a few questions about their academic interests and extracurricular activities. Applicants then get a thumbs-up or a thumbs-down, usually within half an hour.

Virtually unheard of 20 years ago, "instant" or "on-site" admission has been adopted by a host of state schools over the past decade, including William Paterson University of New Jersey in Wayne and Virginia Tech in Blacksburg. Virginia Tech counselors travel to high schools, where the admissions decisions are made. Now, private colleges like Newbury are jumping on the bandwagon, too. For schools, the advantage of this quickie service is that accepted students are more likely to attend, perhaps because their admittance comes with a smile and a handshake. For their part, high school seniors get a big reduction in stress. While they may be accepted as early as the fall, they can usually wait until May to give the school an answer. Or they can just say yes on the spot.

Going with an instant-admission interview may or may not affect your chances of getting in. At Western Michigan University, the odds are equal whichever way you apply; Newbury has recently taken about 3 percent of instant-admission applicants and about 64 percent of the regular pool. It's a good idea to call ahead to ask what you need to bring to the interview. Newbury still requires a 250-word writing sample, for example; Western Michigan does not ask for a personal essay. Also be sure to practice your interview skills and topics with a guidance counselor or parent before the big day. If you got an F in sophomore English, you should be prepared to explain why and how you've improved. If you can't, you might flunk instant admissions, too.

---

ings to emphasize that, although she didn't plan on majoring in art, she devoted lots of time and energy to creating it. Many big state schools don't have the resources to examine your works of genius, however, so find out an institution's policy before dropping anything like this into the mail.

If your talent—as a leader in student politics, for example—can't easily be demonstrated in a portfolio, you might include a résumé instead. This way, you can add detail about what you've accomplished to the bare-bones list of activities on your application.

Don't tweak the truth

When you're staring down at that blank application form or empty computer screen, it can be tempting to embroider your qualifications or download an essay and call it your own. With the growing number of qualified students vying for spots at selective colleges, the urge to cheat on an application sometimes seizes even the most capable student. For example, one applicant some years ago to Pomona College in Claremont, California, seemed like a shoo-in. He was valedictorian of his class and scored well into the 1500s on his SAT. But there was something about his essay that seemed familiar to the assistant dean of admissions reading his application file. In fact, it was the third time that afternoon she had read the same work—from applicants scattered around the globe.

The essay, it turned out, was a sample posted on www.essayedge.com, a site that offers editing and writing tips for college essays. Bruce Poch, vice president for admissions at Pomona, returned the papers along with a copy of the EssayEdge sample. The valedictorian confessed to his school's headmaster and soon received a rejection letter in the mail.

Poch figures that the student, "who could have done the essay in his sleep," was simply too overwhelmed to bother—and it seems he's not alone. "You get a lot of students who feel they suffer disadvantages," says Rutgers University professor Donald McCabe, an authority on academic integrity issues, so they think they can "make the playing field more level."

Admissions officers warn that they read application folders very carefully and are good at catching this kind of fakery. "That's why we have bags under our eyes," quips Keith White, former associate director of enrollment management at the University of Wisconsin–Madison, who has seen several essays shared among siblings and friends. He says certain topics and word choices often tipped him off. He once noticed that two students from the same high school had described their relationships with their parents using words straight from an episode of the TV show *Friends*. When White compared the essays, he found them to be virtually identical. (In such cases, the UW admissions office asks for a written explanation of the similarities; the applicants rarely respond, and that is the end of the process.)

One desperate father wrote a glowing recommendation for his daughter, signed her guidance counselor's name, and sent it off to Notre Dame. After the university's assistant provost for enrollment smelled a rat—the letter and the student's transcript didn't seem to describe the same person—he phoned the guidance counselor, who knew nothing of the missive. Needless to say, the student did not go to Notre Dame.

Another red flag is a transcript and an essay that just don't jibe. "You say, 'Gee, this essay seems to have been written by Maya Angelou, but the transcript belongs to Willie Lumplump,'" says William Hiss, former admissions dean at Bates College, who is now vice president of external affairs there. More often, the transcript belongs to Junior and the essay is written or heavily edited by Mom and Dad. William Shain, former dean of undergraduate admissions at Vanderbilt and Bowdoin, says that

when he reads an essay that is implausible even for a very literary 17-year-old, "the essay ceases to have any impact, because you lose the natural charm of a high school senior." Remember, admissions people know what high school students sound like.

Most often, students embellish the truth, exaggerating a leadership role or their contributions on the soccer field. Spinning a bench-warming career into a star turn is a high-stakes move because admissions folks may contact your high school coach. Pomona's Poch recalls several applicants whose listed number of weekly hours spent on extracurricular activities exceeded what was possible given the number of waking hours in a week. If dance and community service are so much a part of your life, why haven't they been mentioned in your letters of recommendation? In four cases out of five, this sort of fudging backfires, experts warn. You probably won't actually be accused of dishonesty, but you definitely won't get in.

Deal wisely with admissions

This is a relationship you want to manage carefully. Here are a few pointers.

Stay in contact

Colleges want to know just how badly they're wanted, and it can sometimes help your chances to be really clear about your interest. Having a handle on which applicants will enroll if accepted helps schools prevent the expensive error of ending up with too many, or too few, freshmen come fall. As a result, many schools record your every contact with the campus. If you order a video tour of Emory, an admissions officer will note the request in your application folder; e-mails to Miami University in Oxford, Ohio, will be logged in a database. Most institutions naturally construe a campus visit as a sign of serious interest, so you should be sure to travel to the schools that top your list—and let the admissions office know you've stopped by.

But don't just call for the sake of calling. Every communication should have a point. Maybe you're updating the admissions staff on your latest achievements or searching for information that you really

April may be known as the cruelest month, but that's only because Harvard grad T. S. Eliot never had to sweat out May, June, and even July in today's wait-list wasteland. Many colleges are trimming acceptances and expanding their waiting lists to avoid over-enrolling students, which has meant crowded classes and housing crunches on hundreds of campuses. The result is a growing number of not-quite-yes-but-still-not-quite-no letters and masses of nervous high school grads come spring.

While no magical combination of grades or activities can propel borderline applicants over the top, there's plenty a stranded candidate can do to catch an admissions officer's eye again—starting with an expression of eagerness to attend. "It's e-mail; it's faxes saying, 'I'm still out here and I'm still interested,'" says Michael Steidel, admissions director at Carnegie Mellon University in Pittsburgh. "That's the message we want to hear."

If you're bound and determined to scale the walls of a highly selective school, you'll have a better shot if you give colleges information they don't already have, like updates on grades, new honors, academic awards, lessons learned doing additional community service, or even a letter of recommendation from a senior-year teacher. You should also alert colleges as soon as possible if you no longer need financial aid; funds get doled out early, making those who can pay their way much more attractive late in the game.

Sheer creativity can help, too. Carnegie Mellon's Steidel still keeps in his office a bottle that he received from one wait-listed candidate. The jug, covered with Life Savers candy, had a scroll inside that read: "SOS SOS SOS. I'm stranded here in South Carolina." It went on to detail how the applicant needed to be rescued by the admissions committee to fulfill her dream of becoming a cosmetic surgeon. "We loved it," recalls Steidel. "It was cute; it was innovative." And it won the girl a seat. Another memorable wait-list winner, from Hawaii, painted the seascape outside her window on a coconut—a scene she said she'd love to pine for from a dorm room in Pittsburgh. "When you know someone wants it that badly," Steidel says, "it does turn the committee's head."

can't find in brochures or on the website. Call to find out which professor you should talk to about opportunities in biochemistry research or to study abroad, for example. Then you might send the appropriate person an e-mail introducing yourself and your interests.

Will admissions officers think you're a pest if you check on your application? That depends on what you mean by "check." Trying to find out whether you've been accepted before decisions are released will almost certainly irritate whoever takes your call, but checking that your application is complete can stave off disaster. One high school student didn't realize until March of her senior year that the College Board hadn't sent her SAT scores to any of the schools she'd designated. She had to postpone college for a year and go through the whole process again. The second time around, she says, "I was that annoying person who called every single day." She ended up getting into all of the 12 schools to which she applied and going to Elon University.

Schedule an interview

You've heard about the "optional" college interview? Well, it really isn't so optional if you want to show commitment to the school. "All other things being equal, we are more inclined to admit a student if that student has interviewed," says William Caren, associate vice president for enrollment services at the State University of New York–Geneseo. (Most admissions officers will understand if applicants can't visit because the cost is too great or there is some other hardship.) The best way to shine, beyond looking clean and neatly dressed, is to show that you're passionate about your interests and equally passionate about attending the school. Practice speaking about your favorite classes and activities, experts say, and avoid one-word answers.

You'll definitely want to research the school thoroughly before the interview because no one will be impressed by a barrage of questions about statistics you could have found on the website. It is better to ask why students transfer, say, or if graduate assistants teach classes. The idea is to gather information that will help you decide whether it's the school for you, while astonishing the interviewer with your curiosity and thoughtful turn of mind. Brandeis, for one, rates students on a 1-to-5 scale on the basis of their intellectual curiosity and personal qualities. At other schools, admissions officers take notes during the session and review them with the admissions committee afterward. Making an extremely positive impression can push your application over the top.

'Fess up to bad behavior

One important job of the admissions office is to ferret out any bad apples. By probing applicants' disciplinary histories, colleges hope to avoid admitting nasty characters who might harm other students or cause legal headaches down the road. Youthful high jinks don't worry anyone much, but more serious charges like assault, drug dealing, or academic dishonesty will be closely scrutinized.

If you're asked, straight out, whether you've ever been arrested or suspended or expelled from high school, you should absolutely come clean. Getting caught in a lie will kill your chances of being admitted—and you might get kicked out if you've already been accepted. "If a student has falsified [his] answer [to the discipline question], I have no problem pulling the rug out from under them," says Christopher Gruber, dean of admission and financial aid at Davidson College in North Carolina. The likely leak-

ers? High school counselors who report infractions to colleges and teachers who inadvertently mention in a recommendation letter how much Steve has matured since he burned down the gym during sophomore year. Most private schools have policies to notify colleges of suspensions and expulsions. Public school counselors are hampered by state privacy laws, but they can hint at problems with vague phrases like "had difficulty last semester."

The key here is to demonstrate that your brush with authority led to personal growth. Writing a

---

"All other things being equal, we are more inclined to admit a student if that student has interviewed."

---

thoughtful explanation of what happened, to send along with your application, will help, but a special trip to campus to explain yourself in person may be in order if the infraction was serious. One Florida high schooler, who was expelled when marijuana was found in her car, arranged a meeting with officials from the New College of Florida in Sarasota to clarify what had happened. The student had already signed up for drug counseling and taken steps toward earning her GED. Joel Bauman, then dean of admissions and financial aid, was impressed. "She confronted the problem head-on and had done things to make up for it," says Bauman, who is now vice president of enrollment management at Westminster College in Utah. "That takes courage, integrity, and character." The student was admitted.

Keep your other colleges to yourself

This is one case where full disclosure may not be in your best interest. In fact, if you do answer the question "Where else are you applying?" you run the risk that the information will actually be used against you.

Sometimes there's an innocent reason for a college's nosiness. The staff may want to figure out what all your schools have in common (strong journalism programs, say), so as to better sell their institution to you. But in many cases, the goal is to guess how likely you are to actually attend if you get in. Colleges that are worried about boosting their "yield," or the fraction of admitted students who ultimately enroll, may reject or wait-list even the most outstanding candidates if they've also applied to more popular or more prestigious schools.

There are two places this issue may come up: on the application or in an interview. What to do? Some counselors suggest supplying the names of a few similarly competitive schools from your list or stating that you are still undecided. You can also leave the question blank on the application or declare yourself uncomfortable with the question in an interview. For the most part, colleges will let unanswered questions slide. "I respect a student who says they prefer not to answer," says Michael Frantz, vice president for enrollment and financial aid at Robert Morris University in Pennsylvania.

But don't be surprised if an interviewer pushes for an answer. One applicant says a Tufts University alumni interviewer asked four or five times what other schools he was applying to. He tried to evade the question, he says, but the man persisted, leaving him with a "sour aftertaste." Although he was admitted to Tufts, he ultimately enrolled at Harvard.

If you're learning disabled, say so

Students who have struggled with learning disabilities will inevitably wonder: to tell or not to tell? Most guidance counselors recommend honesty in this situation—at least if there are any red flags in your history that need explaining. A precipitous drop in English grades or poor test scores are likely to raise questions in an admissions committee. When there's no clear reason, colleges can be expected to reject a candidate who seemingly doesn't measure up. Plus, so many learning-disabled students today are reaching college age and choosing to apply that many schools are much more open to taking kids who learn in nontraditional ways—not to mention helping them succeed.

You can often gauge a college's attitudes before applying by phoning the admissions office and asking who coordinates services for learning-disabled students and what programs and accommodations the school offers. If your questions are met with silence, you may be better off looking elsewhere. (For more on what to seek in a college if you're learning disabled, see page 9.)

Consider early decision—but be careful

While Ivy League presidents and editorial writers continue to debate the pros and cons of early decision, the process (or the similar early action) is alive and well at more than 400 of the nation's four-year colleges and universities. Many admissions offices, in fact, accept a large proportion of each entering class early. The University of Pennsylvania, for instance, took 49 percent of the 2010-2011 freshman class from its early-applicant pool.

So high schoolers intent on getting into one of these schools have to ask themselves, "Should I put myself into that early group?" Three-quarters or more of seniors at some affluent high schools now are doing so, up from around a quarter a decade ago. If you join them, you promise to enroll if you're accepted, and you'll know by mid-December whether you've got a spot. (It used to be that early-decision candidates couldn't apply to more than one school. Revised guidelines from the National Association for College Admission Counseling now allow them to apply elsewhere as regular candidates, as long as they withdraw any pending applications if accepted by their first choice.)

You don't have to be a math major to figure out why so many students apply early. Their odds of getting in go up, sometimes a lot. "The admit rates look so good, it's hard not to be tempted by them," says Hector Martinez, director of college guidance at The Webb Schools in Claremont, California. Johns Hopkins University in Baltimore admitted 43 percent of its early-decision applicants in 2010, compared with 19 percent of the regular admission pool. Carleton College in Northfield, Minnesota, which has two early-decision deadlines, took 53 percent of its combined early pools and 30 percent of its regular applicants in 2009. Penn took 31 percent in the early round for 2010,

—by Joyce Slayton Mitchell, former director of college advising at Nightingale-Bamford School in New York City and the author of *Winning the Heart of the College Admissions Dean* (2005, Ten Speed Press, $14.95)

"The handwriting isn't the same throughout the application!" says Johnny's counselor to Johnny's mom. "It looks like you wrote most of it for him."

"But he is so busy with his classes, and soccer, and music, and the school newspaper!" Mom replies. "He has no time to be writing his college applications!"

"Yes, we give interviews. Ask Susie to give us a call before her campus visit."

"Oh, she won't have time to call—she's too busy with classes, and soccer, and music, and the school newspaper to be calling the colleges. I'll make the appointment for her."

"I've got 650s on my SATs, so my parents want me to spend the summer cramming in an SAT-prep program. I've got to get my scores up to get the college I want!"

When I would swap stories with my colleagues, I often heard of panicked parents and well-meaning students making these kinds of statements. In our experience,

here are the most common mistakes families make when applying to college—and how to avoid them.

Parents take the initiative, and that hurts the student

Nowadays, many colleges are so concerned about their image that they are choosing their freshman classes with a very close eye on their "yield" (the proportion of accepted students who actually choose to enroll). What this means for applicants is that enthusiasm about a school counts for a lot to the admissions dean, who wants to pick students who won't turn down an offer. But it's the student, not the parent, who has to show the interest.

When a parent or a hired consultant stands in, even if only to handle clerical chores, the youngster's image suffers more than you might imagine. The seniors who make it into Selective U are not only very busy, they're also the ones who can manage their academics, sports, music, theater, publications, student government, friends, and family—with sleep deprivation like they won't have again in their lives until they bring home a new baby—and still have the maturity to take charge of the college selection process and make a case for themselves. They need to be the ones making the phone calls to admissions, contacting

professors and coaches with questions, and thinking about and actually doing the writing on their applications. If parents think about it, they'll want their kids to take on this developmental task, which will help them get ready to leave home.

Raising test scores becomes an obsession

Yes, the higher your test scores, the better you'll feel. But test scores usually reflect the kind of curriculum you study and the grades you earn—it doesn't pay to try to eke out a gain at all costs!

Let's think about it. Deans are looking for interesting young people who are eager to learn, kids with great curiosity about the world. Does someone who studied vocab and took practice tests for two months, or every Saturday morning for the past year, sound like an interesting kid to you? No, she sounds like an ordinary kid from a fearful family. Harvard, Georgetown, Stanford, Northwestern, Rice, Amherst, and other top schools think nothing of turning down the applicant with the perfect SAT scores. As soon as a student is within a certain range of numbers, admissions deans want to know, "Who is this kid? What did she do last summer?"

When Fred Hargadon, the former dean of admission at Princeton, was asked by a mother what would be the best thing her son could do the summer before senior year to get into Princeton, his response was, "Pump gas!" He didn't literally mean that pumping gas would open the door. Rather, it's very important that applicants have experiences that lead to personal growth—not that the students fit some preconceived notion of the ideal applicant. A student might choose a summer of service to others, or sports, or reading, or ceramics, or starting a business, or cutting grass, or working in the supermarket. It matters less what he picks than that he learn something about himself and is able to express that learning in writing.

If the student is interesting enough, 650s on the SAT won't keep him out of any college in the country. And if he's not, no score will get him in.

Application questions aren't taken as seriously as the essay

I tried to instill in my students an appreciation for the importance of the application question: Why did you choose to apply to Duke? Admissions staffers want to know whether you understand the match between your personality and the college culture—and they are impressed when they discover that you do. You can imagine my chagrin when Eric Kaplan, associate secretary at Penn who also served as interim admissions director, called to say, "Joyce, I love this kid, but she wants to go to Duke!" I said to my students, "I should be able to take the name of the college out of your response and know what college you are talking about."

When you get to the essay, keep in mind that whatever questions you are asked, all of your colleges are after the same infor-

mation: an idea of what you've learned about yourself and the world from the opportunities you've been given. And they want it presented in the authentic voice of a 17-year-old.

If your essay is one of a couple thousand about the war in Afghanistan, the admissions officer's eyes will glaze over. If it is about one of the three Ds (divorce, depression, or drugs), chances are he will groan. If your essay is about God, love, injustice, or the purpose of life, it had better be funny! Bill Fitzsimmons, the admissions dean at Harvard, once told a group of counselors that a farm boy had chosen not to write about his work on the family farm because he thought, "Those big-time college deans wouldn't want to hear about anything so ordinary." In fact, they do. Think about it: The admissions deans won't know that you're interesting unless they know who you are. It's your job to tell them!

compared with 11 percent of regular applicants. (For a list of schools where applying early boosts your chances most, see page 103.)

Granted, these numbers can be attributed in part to the high grade point averages and test scores of many early applicants; applying early won't help at all if you aren't qualified. But there's no doubt that applying early decision gives many students an edge. Former Penn admissions dean Lee Stetson openly acknowledges that applicants there have a better chance of getting in early than they do during regular admissions. A study at Harvard's Kennedy School of Government confirmed that early applicants have a leg up at a number of top-ranking schools.

Still, applying early is by no means a good choice for everyone. For starters, if you're asking for financial aid—and particularly for merit aid that's handed out based on talent rather than need—it's best to apply to several places during the regular admissions cycle. This way, schools get to compete for you, and you can compare offers. Keep in mind that even when colleges do arrive at the same conclusion about how much aid you need, one may be more generous with its outright grants than another. Late bloomers, too, probably should not apply early, in order to leave more time to rack up achievements. A student with a mediocre GPA may be better served by a stellar fall semester than by applying early, which helps, but won't turn old Bs into As.

So who might benefit from taking the plunge? Strong students with a clear sense of what they want out of college—a cutting-edge art department, say—and who are sure that a given college is their first choice. Applicants whose parents are alums ("legacies," in admissions office parlance) and wealthy students also have lots of incentive to apply early, particularly if they lack some special quality or talent that would give them a boost during the regular round. Schools often court these applicants, whose families tend to make good donors and who turn into loyal alumni themselves, but they might give such students preference only during the early-admissions cycle.

Applying early just to get the work of filling out forms behind you is dangerous, because you risk binding acceptance to a school you wouldn't have picked with a couple of months' more thought. For many students, the idea of what's important in a college—an urban location or small size, for example—does a 180-degree turn between November, when early applications are due, and April, when most college-bound kids are weighing their options. Students who diligently identify their ideal school by the beginning of 12th grade pay a price, too, in time stolen from academics and extra-curriculars during the all-important junior year. Early applicants also take their standardized tests on a shorter timetable and lose the ability to show admissions officials their leadership and academic prowess as seniors.

If the binding commitment doesn't appeal to you but shortening that dreadful period of suspense does, consider applying "early action" if it's offered by your top-choice school. These plans generally don't give you the same edge in admissions, but they also don't require a promise to attend. Applicants are notified of their status in December but given until May to accept or reject an offer. Because early action is nonbinding, a student can test his or her chances at one or more early-action schools, see what happens, and still apply to additional colleges in the spring.

Once you're in, don't blow it

When that long-awaited acceptance letter arrives in the mail, you'll obviously want to celebrate—perhaps for the rest of senior year. But forsaking academics for an easy coast into prom week can have serious consequences.

Michele Hernandez, author of *A Is for Admission: The Insider's Guide to Getting into the Ivy League and Other Top Colleges*, points out that an offer of admission is contingent on successful completion of high school. Admissions personnel at most colleges will inspect your final transcript, and you're going to have to explain any big drop in grades in a written statement. The director of admissions reads these accounts and decides what action to take.

She'll probably be sympathetic if there's valid cause for a decline in academic performance—a serious illness in the family, say, or one particularly difficult math class. But genuine slackers do have to answer for their behavior. Summer school may be required, or you might be placed on academic probation for the first semester of freshman year. In the most extreme instances—a straight-A student inexplicably has a straight-D quarter, for example—acceptances can be revoked. In fact, Hernandez estimates that a few students a year are "de-admitted" from each of the more selective colleges. Less selective institutions are unlikely to turn errant students away entirely, though they may require corrective action.

Other symptoms of senioritis are of interest to the admissions staff, too, although they generally aren't evident in a transcript. Any criminal violations that come to light, like sexual assault or vandalism, will almost certainly result in a reevaluation of your admittance. So will episodes of cheating or frequent cutting of classes, which are often reported by guidance counselors or teachers.

Aside from fulfilling the "successful completion of senior year" bargain, there are other, more practical reasons to stay engaged in high school until the bittersweet end. Getting superior marks in the final semester is essential for those who have been put on wait lists, for one thing. Those in AP courses can't afford to slack off either, as a high score of 5 or even 4 on an exam often translates into college credit; this can save tuition and may allow you to opt out of an introductory lecture class and get straight into a more advanced seminar. Besides, if you keep working hard until the end of senior year, you'll be far less rusty when you start studying in the fall. Just remember, you'll still have two full months to celebrate after final grades are in hand.

Chapter Five

How to Find the Money to Pay for College

If fall is the season of teenage college dreams, spring is when the grown-ups wake up and face reality. The acceptance letters have come and it won't be long before the first check is due. And it might be a big one. Now what?

The sticker shock that families experience when faced with actually making tuition payments has been exacerbated in recent years by a struggling economy. Even as stock portfolios took a big hit, colleges and universities—confronted with depressed endowments, rising energy and health insurance costs, and shrinking state support—have been sharply jacking up tuition.

At the College of William and Mary in Williamsburg, Virginia, for example, tuition and fees for in-state students in 2010-2011 went up almost 10 percent to about $12,200 (nonresidents pay around $33,800). The corresponding rise was almost 9 percent for in-state students at the University of Iowa in Iowa City, where tuition and fees have jumped about one-third since 2005. Even the less-arresting percentage increases imposed by private schools translate into big dollars. How can parents possibly satisfy the tuition collectors as well as their starry-eyed children?

OK, take a deep breath. And remember that relatively few families have to come up with the staggering tuitions charged by the Ivy League and many other private institutions. In recent years, more than one in three U.S. undergrads have attended public four-year colleges or universities, and the average amount for in-state tuition and fees was just over $7,000 in 2009-2010, according to the College Board. (Another 40 percent or more attended two-year public colleges, which generally are substantially cheaper.) The upshot is that more than half of all full-time undergraduates at four-year institutions faced a bill of less than $9,000 in tuition and fees in 2009-2010, even before financial aid was considered. Only about a quarter overall were at schools costing $21,000 or more.

Granted, these statistics bring cold comfort to students who have their hearts set on high-priced private schools. But even those colleges don't etch their sticker prices in stone; they offer financial aid to roughly three-quarters of their students. And overall, about two-thirds of full-time undergrads get grants. The savvier you are about what financial aid is available and how it is doled out, the more likely it is that you'll get a share of the money. In the following pages, you'll learn how aid packages are calculated and put together, how to appeal a school's offer of aid if it seems too low, and how students can boost their chances of winning a merit scholarship (an award that's based on academic performance or some other talent, not on need). And if it turns out your family doesn't qualify for much—or any—free money, you'll be equipped to better manage the bills with information about low-cost loans, tax breaks available for college expenses, and employment options a student might consider.

How colleges figure out what you "need"

In a nutshell, you fill out a federal or maybe a college-specific form that asks a lot of questions about your income, assets, and expenses. The numbers are crunched, and out pops your "expected family contribution," or EFC in financial aid lingo. The difference between the cost of a year in college and your expected contribution is your "need," or the amount of aid you are eligible for.

Sounds straightforward enough. So why does it turn out that College A says you need so much less than College B? The experience of one upstate New York family is typical. While the federal government estimated that the family should be able to afford to pay $14,450 a year, Arizona State University judged that the family could pay $15,533, and Penn State expected the family to come up with $20,375.

The often-great differences between financial aid awards are one of the aspects of this process that puzzle and frustrate families the most. Colleges argue that it isn't such an easy matter to gauge a family's true need. Because of the fluctuating value of people's homes, the availability of financial tools like flexible home-equity credit lines, and the complicated finances of blended families, it's tough to figure out which moms and dads are really hard-pressed for cash and which ones simply don't want to sacrifice this year's Caribbean vacation.

What's more, aid officers argue, it's reasonable to expect families to have saved something for college, and to borrow if necessary, because education is an investment that pays off with much higher future earnings. So colleges make their own, and often quite different, judgments about what families have in the way of resources. Finally, aid officials look at their own school's "need" (that is, how badly they want you to attend based on your academic accomplishments or other talents) before deciding how much they'll actually award. Here's a detailed look at how the process works.

You start with the FAFSA...

The first exercise you must go through is filling out the Department of Education's Free Application for Federal Student Aid, or FAFSA. (The electronic form, which flags errors and missing data for you before you submit it, can be found at www.fafsa.ed.gov.)

The government applies a formula called the "federal methodology" to the numbers you supply on the FAFSA to determine your eligibility for a slice of the billions of dollars in federal grants and loans

Great deals at great schools

To determine which schools offer the best value, we use a formula that relates a school's academic quality, as indicated by its *U.S. News* ranking, to the net cost of attendance for a student who receives the average level of financial aid. The higher the quality of the program and the lower the cost, the better the deal. For more great values, see page 153.

National Universities

Universities in this category offer a full range of undergraduate, master's, and Ph.D. programs, and emphasize faculty research.

1. Yale University (CT)
2. Harvard University (MA)
3. Princeton University (NJ)
4. Massachusetts Institute of Technology
5. Stanford University (CA)
6. Columbia University (NY)
7. Dartmouth College (NH)
8. California Institute of Technology
9. Duke University (NC)
10. Cornell University (NY)

National Liberal Arts Colleges

Liberal arts colleges focus almost entirely on undergraduate education and award more than half of their degrees in the liberal arts disciplines.

1. Amherst College (MA)
2. Williams College (MA)
3. Wellesley College (MA)
4. Pomona College (CA)
5. Swarthmore College (PA)
6. Hamilton College (NY)
7. Grinnell College (IA)
8. Bowdoin College (ME)
9. Claremont McKenna College (CA)
10. University of Richmond (VA)

Regional Universities

These schools offer a full range of undergraduate degrees and some master's programs but few, if any, doctoral programs.

North
1. Villanova University (PA)
2. Rochester Institute of Technology (NY)
3. Alfred University (NY)
4. Bentley College (MA)
5. Providence College (RI)

South
1. Converse College (SC)
2. Rollins College (FL)
3. Stetson University (FL)
4. Mercer University (GA)
5. Harding University (AR)

Midwest
1. Creighton University (NE)
2. Aquinas College (MI)
3. University of Evansville (IN)
4. Valparaiso University (IN)
5. Bradley University (IL)

West
1. Trinity University (TX)
2. Mills College (CA)
3. Seattle Pacific University
4. Gonzaga University (WA)
5. Whitworth University (WA)

Regional Colleges

The regional colleges focus on undergraduate education and offer degree programs in the liberal arts and in such professional fields as business, nursing, and education.

North

1. Wilson College (PA)
2. Lebanon Valley College (PA)
3. Elmira College (NY)
4. Cazenovia College (NY)
5. Seton Hill University (PA)

Midwest

1. College of the Ozarks (MO)
2. Augustana College (SD)
3. Franklin College (IN)
4. Taylor University (IN)
5. Huntington University (IN)

South

1. Claflin University (SC)
2. Ouachita Baptist University (AR)
3. Alice Lloyd College (KY)
4. Milligan College (TN)
5. University of the Ozarks (AR)

West

1. University of Science and Arts of Oklahoma
2. Howard Payne University (TX)
3. Pacific Union College (CA)
4. Corban College (OR)
5. Master's College and Seminary (CA)

awarded each year. States use the results to award their own state aid, too. Most public universities use the FAFSA to construct your entire aid package, which may include grants or loans from the institution's own budget as well as the government money. How much you'll have to pay depends entirely on your own complex set of financial characteristics.

...and maybe the Profile

Applicants to several hundred of the country's most selective (and high-priced) private colleges face an additional and much more detailed aid form, the College Board's CSS/Profile application, which feeds into a far more sensitive "institutional methodology." The Profile form asks about home equity, for example, while the federal form does not, so a family might wind up with a considerably higher expected contribution. The Profile also asks about parental assets held in a sibling's name and does not account for business or investment losses, which can make a significant difference for some families.

Each college has its own way of calculating your expected family contribution. Many colleges and universities, for example, don't let parents deduct the cost of tuition for private elementary or secondary school from their resources, reasoning that private school-

ing is a matter of personal choice. Other schools may allow a generous deduction. One institution may expect contributions from both parents whether they're still married or not, while another won't.

You can file the Profile online at https://profile online.collegeboard.com/prf/index.jsp. The College Board charges applicants $25 to process the form, plus $16 for each additional college to which you have the profile sent. A fee waiver is available for students from families with low income and limited assets.

Then the college might fiddle...

Once all the formulas have been applied, financial aid officers have the right to use their discretion and adjust the bottom line. Even though the formulas say that your tax-deferred retirement assets won't count against you, for instance, some schools might trim your award if the family nest egg is huge. Or your award might get a boost if an aid officer makes adjustments for expenses that the forms don't ask about, like nursing home care for a family member. (Make sure you bring any such hidden costs to light by writing the college to explain unusual circumstances.)

Even if all of the colleges in your candidate pool somehow do agree on how much you should be able to afford, their financial aid packages may still vary in significant ways because of "preferential packaging." This means that colleges with a limited amount of aid to dole out are increasingly awarding more money to students they really want. One college might make outright grants a higher proportion of the total package, for instance, while a college less keen on snagging you might offer more of the award in the form of loans and work-study.

Basically, schools handing out money from their own coffers—as opposed to Uncle Sam's—can use the information from the FAFSA and Profile forms in any way they want. And they do, because they're often competing to get the same terrific students. Some colleges even apply the federal methodology to one student and the institutional methodology to another, driving "need" up or down by using whichever formula supports the school's assessment of a student's appeal. Home equity is a favorite tool. For a highly desirable student, information about family assets could come from the FAFSA, which ignores home equity. For a student who is less interesting, assets could be taken from the Profile form, which counts it.

...and you end up happy—or "gapped"

Many colleges pride themselves on "meeting full need," which means they come up with aid packages that fill the entire difference between each family's expected contribution and the cost of freshman year. (Of course, plenty of families don't agree that their need is being met when they realize just how much they're expected to contribute. "The big shocker is that the only place it looks like teachers make a fortune is on the FAFSA," says one dad whose wife is also a teacher. "It says you're good for $16,000 a year. I'm thinking, 'Wow!'") At Princeton University, which has one of the most generous aid policies in the nation and doesn't require students to take out any loans, the average grant for families with incomes of $60,000 to $80,000 will be $45,100 for the 2010-2011 school year, covering tuition plus a significant share of room and board. For families in the $120,000 to $140,000 income range, the average grant is $34,700, almost enough to cover tuition.

But more and more often when the aid budget is tight, the package doesn't come close to meeting full need, which means that the family has to come up with both the expected contribution and whatever the college doesn't cover. "Most schools don't have enough money," says Sandy Baum, a professor of economics at Skidmore College and an expert on financial aid. One school might leave a $3,000 gap, for example, while another might leave a $6,000 gap. (Instead of "gapping," some schools manage their financial aid budgets by practicing "need-con-

> "The big shocker is that the only place it looks like teachers make a fortune is on the FAFSA."

scious" or "need-aware" admissions, which means that the school considers ability to pay when deciding whether to admit some applicants. After 90 or 95 percent of the class is filled, the rest of the hopefuls, even if they're qualified, are likely to be rejected unless they don't need financial aid. Other schools use an "admit-deny" strategy. They admit all students regardless of their need but then decline to offer financial aid to the less qualified.)

Whatever the package, the initial offer is strictly conditional on a double-check of your financial information. The school will at least want corroborating tax information from the previous year. And many private schools and some public universities run all aid applicants through the "verification" mill, an audit-like process in which the college asks for tax returns, bank statements, and other paperwork that can back up your claims about income, assets, and expenses.

Since even schools with generous funds can run short, it's smart to file aid applications early. Your FAFSA ought to be in as soon as possible after January 1; due dates for other aid applications vary by school, but waiting until the last moment is a bad idea.

Finally, you weigh your offers

Once all of your aid letters are in hand, you have to make sense of their bottom lines. What will each school really cost you? The price tag includes tuition, fees, room, and board—the charges for which you will receive a bill from the college—plus books, personal expenses, and travel. To figure out how big a burden you'll have to assume, take the total cost and subtract the free money, which includes federal and state grants and institutional grants and scholarships. Then subtract the anticipated earnings from a work-study job, which is usually paid directly to the student and covers personal expenses. The remaining dollar figure is what you will have to pay, either up front or through loans. This should be your real point of comparison between aid packages.

Next, examine which type of loans (described in detail in the next section of this chapter) each college is offering you. Federally subsidized student loans, which are available to families with demonstrated financial need, offer extremely low interest rates and generous grace periods after graduation before interest accrues and repayments begin. Less desirable, but still often a good option, are unsubsidized loans for students and parents, which also carry low rates but begin accruing interest as soon as the loan is in your hands.

Finally, find out whether the aid will be renewed each year, and if it will be renewed in the same form. One young woman whose $20,000 in costs were completely covered by her large state university decided to transfer to another school after she discovered that $8,000 of her grant aid had been converted to loans for sophomore year.

Everything you need to know about the contents of your aid package

What's in an aid package? The first layer usually consists of whatever federal grants or loans you qualify for, plus possibly a work-study job. If you're eligible for aid from your state, that will come next. Then, if you still have need—which you might, because there are caps on how much federal and state aid each person can get—the school may award grants and possibly loans from its own funds.

Government giving

To qualify for any of the following, you must file the Free Application for Federal Student Aid (the FAFSA).

Pell grant. Students from families with modest household incomes (typically less than $45,000) may be awarded a federal Pell grant of up to $5,550 (as of the 2010-2011 award year) for each year of undergraduate study. This money, which comes from the federal budget, does not have to be repaid. Because need depends on family size and the number of family members in school as well as income, a student from a large family with a higher income might qualify, for instance. The key is the expected family contribution, which can be no higher than $5,273 for the year.

Federal Supplemental Educational Opportunity Grant. Exceptionally needy students—typically, they can't afford any family contribution at all—may qualify for an FSEOG in addition to a Pell grant. The amount ranges from $100 to $4,000 a year, depending on need and on the funding available at your school. FSEOG grants are an example of "campus-based" federal aid, which means that colleges apply each year to the Department of Education for funding, and the financial aid office determines how much each student receives.

Stafford loan. If you qualify for one of these low-rate loans based on need, your Stafford loan will be subsidized, which means that the federal government pays the interest on the loan while you're in school. You'll qualify if the total cost of attendance at your school exceeds your expected family contribution, plus any grants or merit awards. An unsubsidized Stafford loan, on which interest accrues while you're in school, is available to students regardless of need. You begin repaying your loan six months after you graduate or drop below half-time status, and you can choose from several repayment schedules, including the standard 10-year term, a longer term with lower payments, or payments that are based on your annual income.

In the past, Stafford loans were made either by the federal government or by private lenders. As of July 2010, all new federal student loans will be made directly by the U.S. Education Department. If you're a dependent, you can borrow up to $5,500 during your

Don't get scammed

The skyrocketing cost of higher education has a lot of people scrambling for money—including scam artists out to relieve you of your hard-earned funds. As you search for scholarships, steer clear of anybody who makes any of the following claims:

- *For a small fee, we'll do a search for you.* Some services charge a bundle for a search that you can do at little or no cost. With plenty of comprehensive, free scholarship searches available on the Web, there's no reason to pay for this service.
- *We guarantee you a scholarship or your money back.* In fact, even the most obscure scholarships are competitive; no legitimate organization will promise that you'll land an award. Any assurance by a scholarship search service that you'll get your money back if you're not satisfied with the results usually has many strings attached. You might be required, for instance, to show that you've been rejected for each scholarship suggested to you, even the ones that are obviously inappropriate.
- *You can't get this information anywhere else.* Scholarship providers spread the good news about their competitions widely because they are seeking a big pool of strong applicants. So "insider" or "exclusive" lists of awards mostly aren't.

---

freshman year, up to $6,500 during your sophomore year, and up to $7,500 in subsequent years, but no more than $31,000 overall for undergraduate study. Only a portion of these amounts may be in subsidized loans, however. Current rates are 6.8 percent for unsubsidized loans and 4.5 percent for subsidized loans; the latter will drop to 3.4 percent in July 2011. Independent students may borrow substantially larger amounts. There is also a net origination fee of 0.5 percent of the amount of the loan.

Perkins loan. Undergraduates may also qualify for a federal Perkins loan of up to $5,500 per year, depending on need and on the funds available at their school. The interest rate is a flat 5 percent for the life of the loan, there are no upfront fees, and the loan is repaid directly to the school. (Repayment rates are one of the variables that determine how much a school gets each year from the federal government to fund Perkins loans.)

Federal work-study. After a Stafford loan, a job subsidized by the federal work-study program is one of the most common components of a financial aid package. Some students turn up their noses at this form of "self-help," but a work-study job doesn't necessarily entail washing dishes in the campus cafeteria. Moreover, the pay can be competitive with off-campus employment. You might work 10 hours a week, for example, and earn at least minimum wage; pay usually ranges up to $12 an hour.

Financial aid departments set the standard amount for work-study awards based on their funding each year from the Department of Education. This funding is determined in part by the history of work-study earnings at the school. To some extent, colleges also factor in their philosophy about how many hours full-time students should work. At Rhodes College in Memphis, Tennessee, the standard work-study award is $1,600 a year, with work hours limited to 10 or 12 a week. At Colorado State University in Fort Collins, the average hourly pay is $9 and the typical work-study award is $2,500 for the year, with students working an average of 10 hours a week.

Job possibilities run the gamut from checkout at the library to lab research to staffing the office in the psych department. Increasingly, schools also are partnering with community organizations to create work-study positions that double as service—tutoring slots with the America Reads program, for example, or lifeguard jobs at the local Y. Once you've earned the full amount of your work-study award, the job officially ends, although sometimes an employer can continue your job and pay you from other funds.

It can be tempting to add hours by taking on a second job, but working too much may interfere with your studies. Surveys by the U.S. Education Department show that students who work more than 15 hours a week during the school year are less likely to complete their degrees than those who work up to 15 hours a week. Undergrads who work up to 15 hours a week also tend to have higher grade point

---

"Merit scholarships help to get the attention of exceptional students who might not otherwise look closely at us."

---

averages than those who put in more time.

Accepting a work-study job that is included in your aid package is not mandatory, and many students choose not to work at all or to work for an off-campus employer instead. The University of Wisconsin–Madison typically offers work-study jobs to about 10,000 students. About 40 percent accept when they sign off on their aid packages, but only about 60 percent of these students actually have earnings. (The rest presumably never take the next step of obtaining a work-study job; you do have to look for the work yourself.) At colleges in urban areas, in particular, you may be able to find better-paying work—or work that's more closely related to your field of study—outside of the work-study program. If you prefer not to work at all, the financial aid office might be able to replace your work-study award with a loan.

Don't be too quick to reject a work-study job in favor of an extra 50 cents an hour somewhere else. What many students don't realize is that what they make from work-study won't be counted next year in the calculation of their expected family contribution. But half of net earnings from other employment must go toward next year's family contribution.

In addition, on-campus bosses are often more willing than other employers to fit your work schedule around classes and exams. "If you're working for your academic department or the library and you ask for time off to work on a paper, generally they'll work with

you," says Joe Paul Case, director of financial aid at Amherst. That's less likely to happen at McDonald's. Another benefit of on-campus work: the chance to make connections with other students and faculty.

State grants and loans. Many states offer their own grants and loans to residents who attend school in state. Some of the money is awarded to students who show need, and some is given out to any student, regardless of family financial status, who keeps his or her grades up. To find out what your state offers, contact your state's higher education agency. (A listing is available at www.studentaid.ed.gov; click on "Funding Your Education," then scroll down to "State Aid.")

Aid from the college coffers

If a college determines that your financial need is $10,000 and federal and state aid covers $5,000, you're eligible for institutional aid to cover the remaining $5,000.

Need-based grants and loans. In the best-case scenario, you'd get a $5,000 grant from the school to make up the whole difference. Indeed, a student who is especially desirable to a college may get the whole amount covered, while a student who is fortunate to be admitted might receive a rather stingy grant. A school's generosity also depends on how much money it has to give away. While Princeton can afford to hand out grants only, less well-financed schools are likely to package a loan.

Merit money. Merit awards are granted by schools recruiting for some special talent or quality in applicants—high grades or test scores that will enhance the student body profile, for example, or chess-playing finesse, skills on trombone, or outstanding community service. You don't have to be needy to get one of these scholarships, just really attractive to the people making decisions. "Merit scholarships help to get the attention of exceptional students who might not otherwise look closely at us," says Ben Sandler, adjunct instructor and former financial aid director at Washington University in St. Louis.

While there's undeniable appeal in seeing just how prestigious a school you can get into, remember this: If you can earn admission to a top-ranked school, you also have the clout to win a merit scholarship at a very good school with a little less cachet. While it's a mistake to choose a college based entirely on cost, aiming for some merit money with a couple of your applications will give you more flexibility when the time comes to put down a deposit. Schools' goals naturally vary, so the kind of applicant they're willing to lavish aid on varies, too. Still, the quickest way to stand out is to have a grade point average and test scores that outshine the school's averages and put you in the top fifth or top quarter of the student body.

This focus on attracting students with merit aid, and the related trend of granting highly prized applicants more generous need-based financial aid packages, is most pronounced at second- and third-tier colleges. (Many of the most prestigious institutions don't offer merit scholarships.) One caveat is that merit awards don't always add much to your total package. That's because colleges anxious to make their aid money stretch as far as possible often substitute a merit scholarship for need-based aid you would have received otherwise. That's not so bad if the money is used to replace a work-study job or a loan. (Even better if the school uses the money to fill any gap between your official need and the school's aid package.) But the merit award may replace all or part of a need-based grant rather than add to your total haul.

How to negotiate for more aid—and win

Financial aid officers often deal with two kinds of disappointed parents: those who reasonably and convincingly make a case that they need more help, and those who rant and rave in frustration. If, in the end, you're bummed out by a puny package, you might find that aid officials have the power to make it grow—assuming you fall into the convincing camp.

These days, most aid administrators will readily hear an appeal. In fact, they pretty much expect to. "Everybody appeals after they get the initial award—I call it 'Let's Make a Deal,'" says Jim Stevenson, the retired director of financial aid at Rensselaer Polytechnic Institute in New York. The aid office doesn't increase every package, he says, but it makes a "fair number of adjustments" and has a fund for that purpose.

There is a certain etiquette to asking for more money. "I wouldn't say negotiate," says Kathy Ruby, dean of financial aid at St. Olaf College in Northfield, Minnesota. Ask her to reevaluate an aid offer, however, and you'll get another response entirely: "We've certainly been doing a lot more of that."

Walking into an aid office with a better offer in hand and a "match it" attitude won't garner you any sympathy, however. It's a great idea to tell schools that you've received alternative offers (Carnegie Mellon University in Pittsburgh, for example, explicitly encourages admitted students to send in aid packages from other institutions), but the key to success is giving the college a substantive reason to reconsider.

"If someone says, 'Well, I got this award from Emory, and their award is based on need, and your award is based on need, but it appears that you guys are way off in your assessment of what my need is,'" financial aid officials will be open to a second look, says Rodney Oto, the director of student financial services and associate dean of admissions at Carleton College, also in Northfield, Minnesota.

It may be that some of your family expenses are invisible on federal aid forms. Bates College in Lewiston, Maine, considers costs that families incur providing nursing home care for elderly parents, for instance, as well as changes in job status that may have happened after the forms were filed. Some aid officers say they might consider factoring in a younger sibling's upcoming class trip to Europe or, more commonly, the private high school tuition of a younger sibling, if it's clearly creating a hardship. To better the odds of getting the maximum award, follow these few ground rules:

- *Speak up.* Every family's finances are quirky in some way—there's an upcoming bonus that's a one-time event only, a bunch of pending hospital bills because of a sibling's serious illness, a business start-up or serious financial reversal. Let the aid office know about any anomalies; the more the office knows, the better.
- *Beat the application deadlines.* Sure, you don't have to have all of the verification information in until May 1. But that's what everybody else thinks, too. Dealing with a family's tangled

finances during crunch time puts tremendous pressure on overworked aid representatives. That's when mistakes happen.

- *Do your homework.* While aid staffers say they are happy to explain the logic behind an award, they hope you'll be prepared for the discussion. Review the forms that you filed and jot down any changes in your finances or any omissions. Provide any relevant new documentation to the aid office. Finally, calculate how much you can contribute to college costs, and be ready to justify the figures. If you're

---

"Everyone appeals after they get the initial award—I call it 'Let's Make a Deal.'"

---

comparing offers from different schools, consider the example of a Milwaukee mother who prepared a spreadsheet of the offers. It's smart to maintain a call log to verify whom you've been talking with, when, and what about.

- *Go to the top.* If you're not satisfied with what you're hearing from an aid representative, ask politely but firmly to speak with the director of financial aid. Most say their phone lines are open to anyone who makes a specific request.

Not all comers will be warmly received. Students with stellar grades and accomplished athletes, for example, tend to have a bit more bargaining power. Applicants to state schools tend to find less flexibility than at private universities. Families that hire a financial aid consultant to do their bargaining are apt to find the conversation over before it begins. Many schools refuse to deal with consultants on the grounds that doing so would violate the privacy of families.

Finally, it is best not to mistake financial aid officers for pushovers. "I've had people say to me, 'Well, look, we're paying for four cars,'" says Oto, recalling a particularly far-fetched plea. "That isn't going to fly."

Your other borrowing options

You've reviewed a college's aid offer a dozen times, pleaded with the financial aid officer, and even asked your wealthy great-aunt for money, and you still come up short. If you're willing to borrow to go the distance, here are some sources to tap.

The PLUS program

The Department of Education's PLUS loans are available to any creditworthy parent, regardless of need, and can be used to cover all costs of attending an accredited school. That means books and living expenses as well as tuition. As of 2010, the fixed interest rate for direct PLUS loans was 7.9 percent. There is also a loan origination fee of up to 4 percent. A rate reduction of 0.25 percent is offered to those who make their loan payments automatically through an electronic debit process. Interest is charged on a PLUS loan from the date of the first disbursement until the loan is paid in full, but payments can be deferred until six months after the student finishes school or drops below half-time status.

The program guarantees that all outstanding debts will be forgiven if the parent who signs the loan is permanently disabled or dies. And come tax time, families may be able to take a deduction on the interest paid.

Your home equity

Higher-income families may find that borrowing against their home makes more sense than taking out a PLUS loan. Many couples who don't qualify for the interest deduction because they earn too much can take a tax deduction for at least some of the interest on a second mortgage or home equity line of credit. A line of credit is usually the preferred option, even though rates are variable. Why? Second mortgages disburse the money in a lump sum, which means parents can end up paying interest on the costs of their child's senior year as early as the start of his or her freshman year.

Private lenders

Another borrowing option is a private student loan. These loans typically carry variable rates, and while the initial rates may be low, the long-term cost may

Extra help from Uncle Sam

Mostly, you're going to be writing big checks for the foreseeable future. But come April, parent and student taxpayers can get a little back from the Internal Revenue Service:

Tax credits

Two main credits for college expenses are available to parents: the American opportunity credit, which is an expanded version of the previous Hope credit, and the lifetime learning credit. The annual credits directly reduce tax, which means a $1,000 credit saves $1,000. The American opportunity credit, which applies to the 2010 tax year but could be renewed by Congress, is for 100 percent of the first $2,000 of tuition and related expenses and 25 percent of the next $2,000, for a maximum of $2,500. It can be claimed for the first four years of post-secondary education. The lifetime learning credit allows you to write off 20 percent of the first $10,000 in tuition and related expenses, so the most you can take is $2,000, but it can be claimed for any number of years. Parents putting more than one child through

school can claim an American opportunity credit for each child who qualifies but only $2,000 a year total in the lifetime learning credit. And you can only use one credit per student; you'll have to do the calculations to see which one works best. (Another modified version of the Hope credit may be available for students in Midwest disaster areas.)

Not everyone qualifies, however. For the American opportunity credit, married couples with more than $160,000 in adjusted gross income get a reduced credit, and those making more than $180,000 can't claim a credit at all. The income limits for single taxpayers are $80,000 and $90,000. Lifetime learning credits are reduced for couples making $100,000 to $120,000, and singles making $50,000 to $60,000, after which they are ineligible.

Tax deduction for tuition

An option for people who don't take a credit is to claim up to $4,000 of tuition and fees as a tax deduction. Unlike a credit, which reduces your tax, a deduction reduces the income upon which tax is figured. So for

someone in the 25 percent tax bracket, a $4,000 deduction saves $1,000. As of 2009, this benefit was available to people with incomes up to $160,000 on a joint return and $80,000 on a single return, though it was limited to $2,000 for couples making over $130,000 and singles making more than $65,000. Remember: You can't double-dip and take a credit and deduction for the same student.

Tax deduction for student loan interest

Interest on most personal loans isn't deductible, but up to $2,500 a year of interest is deductible on loans used for tuition, room and board, books, transportation, and other college expenses. (This doesn't apply to a loan from Grandma, by the way.) The amount of interest that was deductible for 2009 gradually phased out at incomes of $120,000 to $150,000 on a joint return and $60,000 to $75,000 on a single return. And remember, interest on a home equity loan is generally deductible no matter how the funds are used.

be more than that of PLUS or home equity loans. But some families prefer them because, in some cases, they offer parents the opportunity of eventually making the student entirely responsible for paying off the loan.

Your chosen college

Some colleges provide a list of private lenders that have served students satisfactorily in the

past, while offering no specific recommendations and noting that less expensive federal aid opportunities should be exhausted first. They also caution would-be borrowers to closely compare rates and other terms—variable interest rates can rise sharply—and note that such loans cannot be included under the federal consolidation program.

Weighing how much debt you can handle

As the cost of tuition keeps going up, so does the weight of the debt. At some institutions, graduates now leave campus with an average burden of $30,000. Most undergraduates misjudge how much they're going to owe—and how debt could affect their post-college plans—until late senior year, when aid offices provide exit counseling. Many students also are unfamiliar with their repayment options.

It's important to think now about how much debt you want to take on over four years and to make sure you stay on track. Financial aid experts advise visiting an aid officer periodically during college, beginning in January of freshman year, both to monitor how fast the loan amounts are piling up and to get some help in thinking ahead about how repaying the money will factor into your post-college plans.

Ask how much the monthly payments are likely to be on your existing and projected levels of debt, and compare that with your expected post-graduation income. Payments on $20,000 in Stafford loans at current rates over 10 years, for instance, would equal about $230 a month, a sizable chunk of an entry-level, $25,000 salary. (You can stretch repayment beyond the standard 10-year repayment schedule to lower the payment, but it will cost you additional interest.)

Credit card debt, too, lies in wait to trap unsuspecting borrowers. According to a study released by student loan agency Sallie Mae, 84 percent of undergraduates in 2008 had credit cards, with an average balance of almost $3,200. Half had four or more cards, which were often used for school expenses, including tuition. Seniors had average credit card debt of more than $4,100, the study found. These balances rack up interest at alarming rates and, unlike subsidized student loans, don't wait until graduation to grow. Keeping up with the monthly payments on an outsize balance will, at best, be a drag on your lifestyle. And not keeping up can really haunt you later. Late payments and delinquencies on a credit report can make it difficult to borrow for a car, a home, or graduate school. (Changes in law that took effect in 2010, however, make it more difficult for students and others under 21 to get a credit card without a cosigner, such as a parent, or proof that they can repay the debt.)

Beyond a bad credit report, some students face financial disaster. According to data collected for Harvard University's Consumer Bankruptcy Project by lead researcher Elizabeth Warren, a professor at the law school, and project director Deborah Thorne, of Ohio University, about 42,500 Americans under age 25 filed for bankruptcy in 2007. Although this was a drop from 2001, when the number exceeded 100,000, it also followed the 2005 bankruptcy law overhaul, which made the process much more difficult. "Young people may be juggling debt longer before they file for bankruptcy," the researchers wrote. "If that is the case, we can expect to see more bankruptcies on the horizon" as these

Looking for authoritative online sources of college aid information? Start here:

- *www.collegeboard.com*. A comprehensive site on college admissions and finances. Under the tab "Pay for college," you'll find a good financial aid calculator, plus debt calculators, a scholarship search, and a worksheet for comparing aid awards.
- *www.fastweb.com*. The leading free scholarship search service features a database of 1.3 million scholarships worth more than $3 billion.

- *www.finaid.org*. Devoted solely to college aid, this site covers scholarship, loan, and financial aid basics, with more detail as you drill down through the pages. Includes good tips on maximizing financial aid eligibility.
- *www.studentaid.ed.gov*. On this Department of Education site, you'll find a number of fact sheets, publications, and checklists, including a guide entitled "Funding Education Beyond High School: The Guide to Federal Student Aid," which provides details on Pell grants

and Stafford, Perkins, and PLUS loans.
- *www.usnews.com*. You'll find all the *U.S. News* college rankings and statistics here—plus, under "Find the Money," guidance on scholarships, loans, and other financial aid.
- *www.collegeanswer.com*. You can compare lenders and apply for student loans at this site, created by student loan giant Sallie Mae. You'll also find loan and financial aid calculators and a scholarship database.

people take on more debt to buy homes and raise families. In the last several years, bankruptcy filings overall have risen sharply.

How to find and win an outside scholarship or two

Suppose you don't qualify for any federal or college aid in the first place—or your appeal for more help falls on deaf ears. Thousands of other organizations stand ready to give money away, if only students ask; indeed, over the past several years, new scholarships have popped up like weeds. Some go to brainiacs, some to the best essayists, some to the student who lives in the right place or belongs to the right club. FastWeb, one of the first Internet scholarship search sites, has expanded its database from 180,000 awards in 1996 to more than 1.3 million today, worth a total of over $3 billion.

What can you do to collar some of this cash? First and foremost, apply for it. Online search engines, like those at www.usnews.com and www.fastweb.com, can locate a lot of potential awards fast.

You fill out a form about yourself—including every characteristic and hobby you can think of—and all of the relevant scholarships pop up. It's important to be detailed about your interests. One award found on CollegeNET (www.collegenet.com) is for water-skiers, while another is for people who play the recorder.

Don't rely solely on the Internet in your scholarship search, however. Many local scholarships handed out by 4-H clubs, churches, civic groups, and hospitals aren't listed online. Your high school's guidance office probably keeps a list of the possibilities close to home, and it's smart to just call around and ask about awards. College financial aid offices may also maintain listings of outside scholarships; sometimes they're posted online.

Once you've assembled the necessary application forms, take a deep breath and ... slow down. Spending time on an application will help produce impressive essays (be sure to get a parent's or teacher's critique). It's OK to file and reuse your essays on other applications, but you'll want to refine them as you go. The process gets easier with practice, says Ben Kaplan, who wrote *How to Go to College Almost for Free* and *The Scholarship Scouting Report: An Insider's Guide to America's Best Scholarships.* Kaplan's first scholarship application took about 16 hours to complete, but by the time his awards were approaching $90,000, he could finish some entries in as little as an hour. By his account, he graduated from Harvard debt-free, with virtually all costs covered by his two dozen-plus scholarships.

Maximizing the money

If you win a scholarship from an outside sponsor, whether it's the prestigious Intel Science Talent Search award or a prize from your local Elks club, you're likely to feel an impact on whatever financial aid you receive from your school. Often, outside awards, like merit awards, are used to replace a portion of your need-based aid. It used to be that colleges simply used the outside scholarship money to replace their own grants, which left the students no better off. Now, it's common for colleges to use at least half of an outside award to lower your loan burden, while the remainder goes to replace school-awarded grants. At the most generous schools, outside scholarships replace your loans first. If you still have scholarship money coming after the school loans are wiped out, the college will sub the remaining funds for its own grant awards. Some schools describe their scholarship policy on their websites, but most do not, which means you'll have to call your financial aid officer and ask him or her directly.

If you do discover that your school soaks up part of your scholarship by using it to replace grants you would otherwise receive, you can try to negotiate a better deal. Ask your scholarship provider to help you make your plea, because providers often have a lot of clout with financial aid officers. If the school upsets a parent or student with its policy, there's just one student and one tuition at stake. But schools risk a wealth of future funding when they displease a scholarship provider.

Military Options

Students considering military service, or who are military members or veterans, have several options to consider. Reserve Officers Training Corps pro-

grams, available at many colleges, offer scholarships up to full tuition, plus allowances for books and fees, and an annual stipend. Details vary among the Army, Navy, and Air Force ROTC programs, but scholarship recipients, who become commissioned officers, typically commit to four years of active-duty military service, followed by some duty as a reservist. In addition, educational benefits are available from the Department of Veterans Affairs under the GI Bill; in some cases, benefits can be transferred to a spouse or child. Detailed information is available at www.gibill.va.gov/.

Picking schools with aid in mind

No, you shouldn't opt for a school just because it's cheap. On the other hand, choosing colleges shrewdly can minimize your costs. One strategy, as we've noted, is to target a couple of schools with merit awards to hand out. Here are some additional tips.

Stay in state

Aside from the fact that tuition is cheaper for residents who attend public colleges, a number of states, including Kentucky, South Carolina, New Mexico, and West Virginia, offer good students (the requirements vary by state) scholarships if they attend a state school. Modeled on Georgia's HOPE scholarship, these programs typically cover tuition at State U, but the grants can be applied toward tuition at in-state private schools as well. So far, Georgia's effort to slow its brain drain is succeeding. The HOPE program is credited with helping the state retain many of its brightest students. It also has coincided with a rise in SAT scores and minority enrollments.

Apply to colleges in clusters

What do the California Institute of Technology, the Massachusetts Institute of Technology, and Rice University have in common? These schools all compete for the same students. Indeed, most schools have a serious rival or two.

Savvy applicants sometimes can take advantage of these rivalries if they apply to more than one school in a group. While it's a mistake to try to pit one financial aid officer against another, many school officials admit that if their offer is bettered by that of a rival, they're likely to take a second look at their own package. Dan Lundquist, former vice president for admissions and financial aid at Union College in Schenectady, New York, says that if a student he had admitted received a stronger need-based offer from another liberal arts college in New York, "we would want to discuss the differential and reasons behind it." Similarly, Lundquist would want to hear about an offer of merit aid from a rival. "We would give serious consideration to a non-need-based offer to help a student's family feel good about saying yes to Union," he says.

Go north

Canadian colleges are not necessarily the bargain they used to be for Americans, but they are an option. The cost of attending prominent Canadian schools such as McGill University in Montreal and the University of British Columbia in Vancouver ranges from about $22,000 to $35,000 (in U.S. dollars) a year. Competition can be fierce. The University of Toronto, where international students make up about 11 percent of the enrollment, had more than 60,000 applications this year for about 11,000 "first entry" spots. But think of it this way: As an American bringing some diversity to campus, you might have at least a slight edge.

Glossary

What does it mean if a college is "test-optional" or practices "gapping"? Here, you'll find a key to the large and specialized vocabulary of admissions and financial aid. If a term appears in boldface inside a definition, you can find its own entry elsewhere. Some of these terms are further explained in "How to Use the Directory" on page 326.

acceptance rate. The proportion of applicants admitted is one measure of how selective a college is. It gives you an idea of how much competition you'll face.

ACT. Most colleges and universities will accept either of two college admissions exams, the ACT Assessment or the **SAT**. The ACT tends to be the more popular of the two among students applying to many Midwestern and Southern institutions. It tests your knowledge in English, reading, mathematics, and science reasoning. The ACT is administered nationally five times a year, in October, December, February, April, and June. Many counselors advise students to take both the ACT and the SAT to see which one better shows off their capabilities.

admissions committee. Your application may be read by several people on this committee. It is typically made up of faculty and staff members, and sometimes alumni and students, who, along with admissions officers, help evaluate applications. The committee will review each component of your application, from test scores and transcripts to essays and letters of recommendation.

admissions interview. You probably won't have to sit for an interview with someone on the admissions staff, but it's a good idea. An interview lets you show how interested you are in a school, as well as how intelligent, humorous, and multitalented you are. Many schools use interviews as an opportunity to get to know and assess prospective students in a more personal way than the application alone allows. Interviews can be done on campus during your visit or by an alumnus in your area.

admit-deny. Schools whose financial aid budgets are stretched sometimes use what's known as an "admit-deny" strategy, admitting students who are academically qualified but offering them little or no aid even though they need it. Because these students often can't enroll, the strategy is typically used for marginal applicants.

Advanced Placement (AP) courses. Admissions staffers like to see some Advanced Placement entries on an applicant's transcript because these more rigorous courses indicate that the student has challenged himself and presumably can handle college-level work. AP tests are given nationwide in the late spring, usually during the first two weeks of May, and are scored on a scale of 1 to 5. If you get a "qualifying" grade on the AP Exam, colleges may give you credit for the course and you can move into an advanced class. A score of 3 may qualify for credit, but some schools demand a 4 or a 5.

aid. See **financial aid.**

alumna; alumnae. A female graduate or former student of a college or university; more than one female former student.

alumnus; alumni. A male graduate or former student of a college or university; more than one male former student (or a mixed-gender group).

application fee. This fee accompanies your application and typically runs $25 to $60 or more.

articulation agreement. If you're thinking about completing a year or two at a technical or **community college** before transferring to a four-year college or university, you should find out whether your community college has an articulation agreement with any colleges or universities. These arrangements smooth the transfer process because they define which community college credits will be honored by the four-year school; a two-year degree would typically satisfy the new college's lower-division general education requirements.

associate's degree. The two-year associate's degree in science awarded by a junior or **community college** might be career-oriented and lead to a job as a veterinary technician, dental hygienist, or legal secretary, for example. The more general associate's degree in arts often is the first part of a four-year bachelor's degree.

board scores. When someone brags about her board scores, she's telling you what she got on the **SAT** entrance exam or the **SAT Subject Tests**, which are administered by the College Board.

campus visit. You can narrow your choices by studying this book, attending **college fairs**, scouring websites, and collecting school catalogs, but you won't want to actually make a decision until you see the campus. This will give you the chance to talk to students, sit in on a class or two, get a taste of the cafeteria food, and perhaps spend a night in the dorm. Many counselors suggest visiting colleges of varying sizes and types, in urban and more rural locations, to get a feel for how schools differ. They also suggest that the student (not Mom or Dad) call admissions and schedule the visit.

class rank. Your class rank is determined by where your high school **grade point average (GPA)** sits among those of the rest of your class. Many high schools calculate a "weighted rank," which takes into account both your grades and how tough your courses were. Others figure a "straight rank," based strictly on grades. Some have stopped calculating class rank because they don't believe it gives a very accurate idea of achievement.

class size. The number of students in your college classes will determine to a large extent how the teaching and learning happens. An introductory economics course with 500 other students will be taught by lecture, probably supplemented by smaller group discussions led by graduate assistants, who will also grade your tests and papers. By contrast, a seminar on 18th-century British literature with only seven other students will center on class discussion and debate while offering students the chance to really get to know the professor. The college profiles in the directory section of this book contain information on class sizes at each school.

college catalog. Unlike a college's **view book**, a heavily illustrated first peek at a school, its catalog is an all-business publication that lists all classes offered, faculty members and their credentials, requirements for graduation, and detailed information on costs.

college entrance requirements. The admissions requirements set by a college or university vary from school to school, but typically include a minimum **GPA** or test scores and a certain number of courses in English, mathematics, social studies, science, and foreign language.

college fair. Here's your chance to meet with admissions representatives from a wide range of schools on the same day and ask about course offerings, admissions, and **financial aid** requirements. It may seem easier to stay home and browse the Web, but colleges want to know who's really, truly interested, and showing up is one way to demonstrate that. Be sure to complete the student information cards put out by each college you're considering so it's clear that you were there.

college-sponsored loan. A small number of schools offer their own loans to parents and students. Check each college's aid materials to see if such loans are available, and ask about interest rates.

community college. According to the American Association of Community Colleges, there are now more than 1,150 of these two-year post-secondary institutions that offer certificate programs and **associate's degrees**. Some students choose to spend a year or two at a community college, then transfer to a four-year college. It can be a great way to transition to life after high school if you aren't quite ready to take the full plunge—and a good way to save some tuition dollars even if you are. Many community colleges have **articulation agreements** with four-year schools that allow credits to transfer smoothly.

cooperative education. Colleges that offer a "co-op" program—particularly popular in business and technical fields—alternate a term in the classroom with time in the workforce. You learn the theory in class, then apply it on the job and, as a bonus, earn money and build connections and a résumé that can prove valuable upon graduation. The trade-off: You typically must put in a fifth year of college and several summers.

cost of attendance. The total amount it will cost a student to go to school for a year. The figure includes **tuition** and fees; **room and board** (or a housing and food allowance for off-campus students); and allowances for books, supplies, transportation, and miscellaneous expenses, including the rental or purchase of a personal computer.

counselor-for-hire. See **educational consultant.**

CSS/Profile. Several hundred of the country's most selective private colleges ask financial aid applicants to fill out this detailed form in addition to the federal aid application form, known as the **Free Application for Federal Student Aid (FAFSA).**

curriculum. A set of courses that make up a program. Many schools have a general curriculum, required of all students, that consists of courses in mathematics, English, science, and the humanities. Your major will also have a curriculum of required classes.

diversity. The mix of cultures and ethnic groups, as well as the variety of people from different religious and socioeconomic backgrounds, will have a big impact on the character of a school. Are you comfortable befriending and working with people unlike you, and who hold views different from your own? Or would you rather stick with students from your home state or your own religion? Statistics on the demographic breakdown of the student body appear in each college's directory profile.

double major. Specialization in two academic fields of study, or majors.

dual enrollment. A majority of states have adopted policies that encourage enrollment partnerships between high schools and colleges. These arrangements allow high school students to take courses that earn credit toward a high school diploma and a college degree at the same time.

early action. Under an early-action plan, you apply to college in the fall and get "action"—which is to say, a decision or deferral—on your application by December or January. You can apply to more than one school and have until May 1 to make your decision. Early action may be a good choice for someone who has narrowed the field to two or three schools and is anxious to be done with the waiting game.

early decision. A growing number of applicants opt for early decision because they want an edge over the competition. Colleges often accept a higher proportion of early-decision applicants than they do of those in the regular pool. But you have to be really sure about a school, because you're obligated to enroll if you're accepted and receive an adequate aid package. Early-decision applications are usually due in November, and you'll most likely get the decision within a month. The problem, say counselors, is that students may make hasty and poorly researched choices. Plus, they lose the opportunity to compare financial aid offers.

educational consultant. For a fee that usually ranges from several hundred to several thousand dollars, educational consultants guide juniors and seniors and their families through the process of selecting the right schools, getting ready for admissions tests and interviews, and preparing applications. If you choose to hire a consultant and are unable to find one by word of mouth, it's a good idea to interview several from among the membership of the Independent Educational Consultants Association (www. educationalconsulting.org) or the National Association for College Admission Counseling (www.nacacnet.org).

essay. Colleges typically require a personal statement on the application so the admissions staff can get behind the numbers and see how cogently and creatively you think, as well as how your experiences have contributed to your personal growth. You'll want to do a careful job, because when two candidates are equally qualified, the essay may tip the balance. If the topic is left up to you, counselors and deans alike advise that you write about a familiar subject (as opposed to a theme such as poverty or world peace) and that you spend time drafting and editing. It's a good idea to ask Mom and Dad for feedback and proofreading, but that's all they should do!

expected family contribution (EFC). This number, which appears on financial aid award letters, is the amount your family will be asked to contribute to the cost of your education. It is calculated based on the information you supplied about your income and assets on the **Free Application for Federal Student Aid (FAFSA)** and on a second form used by many private colleges, the **CSS/Profile**. Your EFC may vary quite a bit from college to college because schools interpret families' financial situations differently.

extracurricular activities. What life offers outside of class at college will probably have a big impact on your happiness, just as it did in high school. So when you're creating a list of schools, pay attention to whether you'll still be able to play lacrosse, write for the school paper, belong to the drama club (and actually have a shot at some stage time), or work for the local food bank. When you interview, you'll want to be able to talk about one or two activities that are particularly important to you.

FAFSA. See Free Application for Federal Student Aid.

Federal Family Education Loan Program (FFELP). This program, in which banks and other lenders received guaranteed federal subsidies to make student loans, was replaced in July 2010 by an expanded program of direct federal loans.

federal methodology. In calculating how much financial aid you are eligible for, the federal government takes the information you supply on the federal aid application form and feeds it into this formula to arrive at your expected contribution to the cost of college.

Federal Supplemental Educational Opportunity Grant (FSEOG). This federal grant, which can range from $100 to $4,000 per year, goes to exceptionally needy students whose families typically can't afford to contribute anything to college costs. To be considered for this grant, you must complete the **Free Application for Federal Student Aid (FAFSA).**

fifth-year program. Some schools have designed curricula that allow you to complete both a bachelor's degree and a master's degree in five years. This is usually accomplished through some accelerated coursework and an overlap of undergraduate and graduate classes. These programs usually require high levels of academic performance.

financial aid. A financial aid package usually consists of federal **Pell grants** and state grants, which don't have to be repaid; federal **Stafford** and **Perkins** loans for students, which do; and **work-study** programs. Colleges may add their own **grants** or **scholarships** as well. Financial aid amounts are based on the information you supply in your **Free Application for Federal Student Aid (FAFSA)** and other forms, but colleges may use **preferential packaging** as a way to recruit outstanding students—offering more in grants and less in loans than marginal candidates might receive.

financial aid adviser. If you apply for any type of **financial aid** from your school, you will be assigned a financial aid adviser on the staff who assembles your package and is available to help you plan your funding throughout your college years.

Ford Federal Direct Loan Program. Under this program, your student loans come directly from the federal government but may be administered by your college. They may be subsidized or unsubsidized.

fraternities/sororities. How strong an influence do these social societies have on campus life? A school where much of the social life revolves around frat parties and where many students choose to live in fraternity and sorority houses may feel inhospitable to someone who prefers not to participate—or just right to someone excited about Greek life.

Free Application for Federal Student Aid (FAFSA). This is the application you'll need to complete if you're applying for federal and state **grants**, **loans**, and **work-study**. The paper version of the FAFSA is available in your guidance office, public library, or the financial aid office of a local college. You can also have a paper copy of the FAFSA mailed to you by calling 800-433-3243. For additional information or to fill the form out online, visit www.fafsa.ed.gov.

freshman retention rate. The proportion of students who return to school for their sophomore year is a number worth looking at. If it's low, you'll want to find out why. Do students feel lost in the shuffle? Do their aid packages tend to shrink after freshman year? We've included each school's rate in its profile.

freshman seminar. Recognizing that a schedule full of large lecture classes makes it difficult for freshmen to connect with professors and peers, many schools make sure each first-year student has at least one enriching small-group class experience. The seminars are typically led by a faculty member, so students can form a bond with a professor earlier than they might otherwise.

full need. In financial aid parlance, colleges that "meet full need" are those that can provide enough in **grants**, **loans**, and **work-study** to fill the whole gap between what a family is expected to pay and the cost of a year in college.

gapping. Many schools' financial aid budgets are too strained to allow them to meet every student's **full need**. Instead, they may "gap" a family, or offer aid that is not sufficient to cover the difference between the **expected family contribution (EFC)** and the cost of college. This gap can be closed through outside scholarships and bigger parent loans. But it will be up to you to find them. Your **financial aid adviser** can offer guidance.

grade point average (GPA). Your grade point average is calculated using a formula that takes into account both your grades and the number of credits earned in each class. An A in a class worth two credits will not influence your GPA as much as an A in a class worth four credits. Some high schools calculate "weighted GPAs" by giving extra worth to grades in AP and honors classes. Sometimes, the GPA that colleges use is figured without grades in nonessential courses such as typing. It's a good idea to know the policies of both your high school and the colleges to which you'll apply. If your high school calculates **class rank**, colleges may consider your rank and your GPA.

graduate assistant. Freshmen at large universities are apt to be taught part of the time by graduate students who work as teaching assistants to faculty members. If you take a large lecture course, you will most likely take part in study sessions facilitated by graduate students, who may also grade your papers.

graduation rate. The proportion of students who have graduated within a certain time period; *U.S. News* uses a six-year graduation rate when calculating its annual rankings of colleges and universities. This number, available in the directory profiles, will give you some perspective on how students fare at a school. (The methodology is explained on Page 328.) If a school's graduation rate seems low, ask the admissions office to explain why. Do students transfer in great numbers? Is it hard to get into courses,

so students have to stay longer than they expected to get all of their credits?

grant. A form of financial aid that never has to be paid back. The federal **Pell grant** is an example.

honors colleges and programs. These programs take different forms, but their purpose is the same: to attract stellar students and give them the chance to do accelerated work in smaller-than-usual classes with respected faculty members. Some honors programs require a separate application; others offer a spot based on high school performance. At some schools, honors students are housed together so they engage with one another outside the classroom as well as in it. Typically, some sort of culminating project or thesis is required.

hook. Many applicants don't realize that admissions decisions are often heavily influenced by what skills or characteristics a certain school needs in a given year. It might want to add a women's soccer team, expand the biology department, or be able to boast a student body representing all 50 states. Your special qualities or talents are apt to put you high on some college's wish list. It's up to you to develop these "hooks" and convey them in your interviews and on your application.

indebtedness. As tuition rises, so does the amount students have to borrow. It's a good idea to talk regularly with the financial aid office during college about how your total indebtedness at graduation might affect your plans afterward. Many students underestimate how much they'll owe and how painful the payback will be on an entry-level salary.

in-state/out-of-state tuition. At private colleges, tuition costs are the same whether you're a resident of the state or not. At colleges and universities funded by taxpayers of a state, the tuition for an out-of-state student is generally far higher than what the in-state student pays.

institutional methodology. Colleges that use the **CSS/Profile** to calculate financial aid feed your family data into a formula that is more sensitive than the federal formula. It considers home equity as a resource, for example, while the federal methodology does not.

intercollegiate sports. Intercollegiate competition pits one college's team against another college's team.

interdisciplinary major. In an increasingly complex world, biologists studying the brain must understand chemistry and physics to make progress, and architects need to understand the environment to design buildings. As a result, college students today sometimes choose a field of study that crosses disciplines. Bioengineering draws from biology, physics, chemistry, and mathematics. Cognitive science combines linguistics, computer science, and psychology. If a school doesn't offer one of those types of majors, it might let you craft your own.

internship. Many colleges encourage or even require short stints in the workplace, on the theory that an internship in a field related to your studies gives you a chance to apply and reinforce what you've learned in class, gain hands-on experience, and build your résumé.

intramural sports. Rather than compete against teams from other colleges, members of an intramural sports team play against other teams from their school.

Ivy League. The term is now used as shorthand for eight of the country's most elite schools: Brown, Columbia, Cornell, Dartmouth, Harvard, the University of Pennsylvania, Princeton, and Yale. Technically, it is the name of the athletic league formed by the eight schools, with shared academic standards and eligibility requirements for athletes.

learning center. The campus learning center provides a wide variety of student services, from academic and career counseling to tutoring, test preparation, and study skills workshops. Check with your school to find out what types of services are available.

learning community, living/learning community. To ensure students are engaged in their studies and bonding with peers and professors, many schools have devised ways to keep the conversations going after class. Typically, students in a learning community take two or more linked courses as a small group and get to know one another especially well. In some cases, they also live and eat in the same residence halls.

lecture. Courses taught in a lecture format involve little classroom interaction and often have enrollments of a few hundred students. A professor gives the actual lectures, but he or she usually relies on graduate assistants to lead discussion groups and review sessions and to grade papers and exams.

legacy. Someone who is a legacy of a college has a close relative who also attended (usually a parent or grandparent). Some schools may give preferential consideration to these applicants, or perhaps a bit more scholarship aid, while others disregard legacy status entirely in the admissions process.

liberal arts college. These typically small, residential colleges emphasize undergraduate education and a curriculum centered on a broad set of courses as opposed to more specialized technical or professional training. These courses typically include language, literature, philosophy, history, and the natural sciences. Liberal arts colleges award more than half of their degrees in liberal arts disciplines.

loan. Money you receive that must be paid back. See **Perkins loan**, **PLUS loan**, **Stafford loan**, **college-sponsored loan**, and **private loan**.

major. Some students enter college having known since elementary school what their chosen field of study would be; others come to school without a clue as to which path they'll follow. Many students switch majors once or twice as they discover new interests. Usually, you declare your major as you enter junior year and are required to take a certain number of credits in the subject. Many students choose to **double major**, or major in two subjects. Some colleges offer **interdisciplinary majors**, such as American studies, which combine coursework from several fields.

merit awards or merit scholarships. In order to attract students with outstanding grades and test scores, many colleges award scholarships based not on financial need but on academic achievement. Scholarships are also given in recognition of other talents or accomplishments the college finds desirable, such as musical ability, athletic excellence, or community service.

National Association for College Admission Counseling (NACAC). The professional organization of admissions officers and college counselors.

National Association of Intercollegiate Athletics (NAIA). The NAIA is a voluntary association of nearly 300 mostly smaller colleges and universities in 14 regions. The NAIA conducts 23 national championship events in sports that include basketball, football, swimming, and tennis. The big intercollegiate sports powerhouses belong to the other athletic governing body, the **National Collegiate Athletic Association (NCAA)**.

National Collegiate Athletic Association (NCAA). The NCAA is a voluntary association of about 1,250 colleges, universities, athletic conferences, and sports organizations responsible for the administration of intercollegiate athletics. Member schools compete in three groups: Division I, Division II, and Division III. The organization administers 88 championships in 23 sports.

National Merit Scholarship Corp. This group administers two annual scholarship competitions: the National Merit Scholarship Program and the National Achievement Scholarship Program, which recognizes outstanding African-American students. High school students enter this competition by taking the PSAT/National Merit Scholarship Qualifying Test, usually during their junior year. Students whose scores and other academic standards qualify them as finalists are considered for scholarships. Other high scorers are recognized for their achievement.

need-based aid. Need-based financial aid is awarded to students whose family income, assets, and expenses—as indicated on the **Free Application for Federal Student Aid (FAFSA)**—demonstrate that they can't afford to pay the whole cost of college by themselves. Their need is the differ-

ence between the amount the family is expected to be able to pay (by each college's calculations) and the cost of a year in college. The aid package usually consists of a combination of **grants**, **loans**, and **work-study**.

need-blind admissions. When a school has a need-blind admissions policy, it judges all applications for admissions without regard to whether a student will need financial aid.

need-conscious or need-aware admissions. Schools that can't afford to meet every student's full need sometimes accept most of their students in a need-blind fashion, then make decisions about the final 5 or 10 percent of the incoming class based on ability to pay.

open admission. Under an open-admission policy, a school accepts all applicants who meet or exceed a certain standard. For example, an open-admissions standard may require a high school diploma and a minimum **grade point average**. Anyone who meets those requirements is virtually guaranteed admission. The policy is most often used by community colleges.

orientation. Sometime before classes start, you'll get a chance to spend time on campus forging connections with faculty members and your new classmates. Orientation activities vary widely from school to school. You might go out on a citywide scavenger hunt, take a backpacking or white-water rafting trip, tackle a community service project, or just attend a meeting or two.

Pell grant. These federal grants are awarded to the neediest undergraduate students as part of the financial aid package and do not have to be repaid. To be considered, you must fill out the **Free Application for Federal Student Aid (FAFSA)** form. Your eligibility depends on the size of your **expected family contribution**. It can be no higher than $5,273 for the year. Typically, Pell grants go to families with household incomes of less than $45,000 yearly. The grants are capped at $5,550 for undergraduate study in the 2010-2011 award year.

Perkins loan. Perkins loans, need-based loans of up to $5,500 per year, are awarded by the financial aid office. The interest rate is a flat 5 percent for the life of the loan, and you don't make any loan payments while in school or for a nine-month grace period afterward.

PLAN. The PLAN is a "pre-ACT" test typically administered in the fall of sophomore year of high school. It covers the same subject areas as the **ACT** (English, mathematics, reading, and science), making it a predictor of success on the **ACT**. It also includes an "interest inventory" to help students prepare for life after high school.

PLUS loan. What was formerly known as the federal Parent Loan for Undergraduate Students is available to any credit-worthy parent of a dependent student, regardless of need, and can be used to cover all costs of attending an accredited school. The PLUS loan lets parents borrow enough to cover any costs not already covered by the student's financial aid package, up to the full cost of attendance. The fixed interest rate is 7.9 percent. Parents interested in this type of loan should submit a completed PLUS application to the school's financial aid office.

preferential packaging. In order to shape their incoming classes and attract the most desirable students, some schools offer more attractive financial aid packages to more appealing students. A very talented applicant might receive almost all **grant** aid, for example, while a less outstanding contender might be offered a package equally split among grants, loans, and work-study.

private loan. A number of lenders and other financial institutions offer private education loans for parents and students. These loans usually carry a higher interest rate than the federal student or **PLUS loans**, and the student loans are not subsidized.

PSAT. The Preliminary SAT is a standardized test that offers practice for the SAT. It also gives you a chance to qualify for the **National Merit Scholarship Corp.**'s scholarship programs. The test measures verbal reasoning skills, critical reading skills, mathematical problem-solving skills, and writing skills. While it is designed to be taken during the junior year of high school, some students choose to take it sophomore year.

reach school. Looking only at your grades and scores, getting into a "reach" school is a long shot. On the other hand, maybe you've got a **hook** that will compensate. Most students like to include a reach school or two on their list of colleges as well as some that will probably accept them and a couple of **safety schools** that almost certainly will.

recommendation. Admissions and scholarship committees use letters of recommendation from guidance counselors and teachers to learn about the character and personality of each applicant. You want to seek recommendations from people who know you well enough to say something specific about you or your performance; clichés won't help your case.

rolling admissions. Schools that use rolling admissions evaluate and respond to applicants as the applications come in, rather than waiting until all applications have arrived. They continue accepting students until the class is full.

room and board. Room charges are for housing; board charges are for food service. These charges can vary depending on the student's choice of meal plan and type of campus housing.

safety school. You're very likely to make it into your safety schools because you exceed all of the entrance requirements and have grades and test scores that rise above the average. Because most schools are interested in improving the academic profile of their student body, many give out **merit scholarships** to induce their highly qualified applicants to enroll. Many students apply to a couple of safety schools in addition to their more desirable choices.

SAT Reasoning Test. The SAT college entrance exam takes 3 hours and 45 minutes and measures the critical reading, mathematical, and writing skills students have developed over time. The SAT is scored on a scale of 200-800 and is usually taken by high school juniors and seniors. The test is given seven times a year. Because many schools will accept either the SAT or the ACT, students often opt to take both and see which score is stronger. The total score possible on the SAT is 2400.

SAT Subject Test. The SAT Subject Tests are one-hour, mostly multiple-choice tests designed to measure how much students know about a particular academic subject and how well they can apply that knowledge. Some colleges and universities require applicants to submit SAT Subject Test results; others use them as an additional indicator of academic achievement or of where to place you in first-year classes. The tests are offered six times a year, and there are 20 specific subjects, including literature and languages.

scholarship. A scholarship is a form of funding that does not have to be repaid. Usually, scholarships are awarded based on academic, athletic, or other talent.

selectivity. Schools that receive 15 applications for each spot are much more selective than schools that receive only two. They accept a much smaller proportion of their applicant pool and have the luxury of taking only the most highly qualified students.

self-help aid. The part of the aid package that isn't just handed out, but requires some effort on your part—**loans** and **work-study**.

senior capstone. These culminating projects are generally completed over the course of your final year or semester at college under the guidance of a faculty adviser and might consist of an independent research project (like a thesis), a service-learning project, or an internship experience. You can expect to present a final project, paper, or presentation at the close of the year.

senioritis. Nope, it's not "inflammation of the senior." This affliction plagues some high school students who have heard they've been accepted by a college and are anticipating graduation. Symptoms include the inability or lack of motivation to continue working. Better fight it off, because colleges do look at those final transcripts and may require summer school if grades slip too much.

service learning. Schools that build service learning into the curriculum require volunteer work as a class assignment. Students get practical experience related to what they're studying and work on citizenship, too.

Stafford loan, subsidized. These need-based student loans have an ultralow interest rate, and the federal government pays the yearly interest while you're in school.

Stafford loan, unsubsidized: Students who don't demonstrate significant financial need can still take out a Stafford loan to help pay the family share of costs, but they'll be responsible for the interest on the loan that accrues while in school.

student-to-faculty ratio. This measure, which shows how many students are enrolled in a college or university per professor, gives a rough sense of the sort of contact you're apt to have with faculty members. The greater the number of students per professor, the harder it may be to get individual attention. Student-to-faculty ratios can be found in the profiles in this book.

test-optional school. In recent years, a number of schools dissatisfied with standardized tests as a predictor of performance have decided to stop requiring them in admissions decisions. A test-optional school does not require applicants to submit **SAT** or **ACT** scores, although students may choose to.

transcript. This all-important document shows the courses you've taken and the grades received. When it is studied alongside a profile of your high school that lists all courses available to you, admissions officers can get a sense of whether you've challenged yourself or chosen easier courses.

tuition. Tuition is what you pay to be educated at a college or university. It does not include what you pay for food, housing, or other expenses.

tuition discounting. Schools that give out lots of their own aid (on top of what Uncle Sam hands out) are often said to be discounting their tuition. Students receive different "discounts" depending on how badly the institution wants them.

view book. A college view book is often a prospective applicant's first introduction to a school. It typically contains general information on degree programs, gives a sense of the student-body profile, and describes the types of student clubs and organizations.

wait list. If you fit the admissions criteria for a particular school but miss the cut, you may be offered a place on the waiting list. If your heart is set on the school, be sure to keep your grades up, let the admissions office know about any new honors that come your way, and make sure it's clear that you're still interested. Wait-listed candidates are usually encouraged to make a deposit at another school to ensure they have a spot in the fall, though they'll forfeit the deposit if their first choice makes an offer.

work-study. Federal work-study money, which may be promised as part of a financial aid package, supports jobs for students with financial need. You can expect to work between eight and 20 hours a week, and earn at least minimum wage (maybe more, depending on the type of work and the skills required). Once you've earned the full amount of your work-study award, the job officially ends, although employers often find ways to keep valued workers on the payroll by tapping alternative funds. Your **financial aid adviser** can point you to work-study jobs.

yield. A college's yield is the proportion of admitted students who accept the offer and enroll. It's a number that colleges watch closely. For one thing, a high yield indicates that students really want to be at the school. Also, schools are concerned about ending up with too many or too few freshmen.

College Planner

With all the details and dates to remember, applying to college can be a major organizational challenge. This planner can help. You can copy this sheet and then fill one out for each school you're considering. Your comments will allow you to compare characteristics of different schools—and remind yourself of interesting facts down the line.

SCHOOL: _____

LOCATION	COMMENTS
Region	
Setting (urban, suburban, rural)	
Distance from home	
ACADEMICS	
Rigor of coursework	
Choice of majors	
Class size and student/faculty ratio	
Academic facilities	
Quality of professors	
Access to professors	
CAMPUS LIFE	
Size of student body	
Diversity of student body	
Student attitudes about the school	
Social life	
Extracurricular activities	
Housing options	
Atmosphere	
COSTS	
Affordability	
Access to grants/aid	
CAREER PREPARATION	
Range of internships	
Quality of career services	
OTHER FACTORS	

CAMPUS VISITS: QUESTIONS TO ASK

Once you've decided on a short list, it's extremely helpful to visit the campuses, if possible. You'll be overwhelmed with information, but don't forget to ask questions, too. Current students are one of the best candid sources of information. Talk to a few different ones, not just the tour guide. Consider these questions and add a few of your own.

SCHOOL: _____

QUESTIONS FOR STUDENTS: What do you like most about this college? What's the worst thing about it? _____

_____

What do you wish you had known when you were making your own decision? _____

_____

What are the students like here? _____

_____

What are the classes like? Lots of small discussion groups? Mostly large lectures? _____

_____

Do graduate students or professors teach introductory classes? _____

_____

How often in the past semester have you participated in class or met with a professor outside of class? _____

_____

Where do students study? Where do students hang out on campus? Off campus? On the weekend? _____

_____

How central are fraternities and sororities to campus social life? What about sports? _____

_____

QUESTIONS FOR ADMINISTRATORS: What percentage of students go on to graduate or professional schools? _____

_____

What percentage of students graduate in four years? What percentage of first-year students return the next year? _____

_____

What was the average tuition increase over the past five years? _____

_____

When must you declare a major? Can you design your own major? _____

_____

(If applicable) Can you take classes at other schools in the area? _____

_____

Who serves as a student's adviser? Do advisers change each year? _____

_____

What are the living options on campus? Off campus? _____

_____

What percentage of students study abroad at some point during their four years? _____

_____

Additional questions: _____

_____

_____

Contact information (names, phone numbers, e-mail addresses) for students and administrators I met: _____

_____

_____

_____

APPLICATION ORGANIZER

With this organizer you can always see at a glance what's done, what needs to be done, and when it has to happen. At the top of each column, write the name of the school you are applying to. Note the deadlines for the application and financial aid forms. Then just check off the squares as you complete each item for each school.

	1	2	3	4	5	6	7	8	9	10
SCHOOL NAMES										
APPLICATIONS										
Application deadline										
Application form completed	☐	☐	☐	☐	☐	☐	☐	☐	☐	☐
Essays completed	☐	☐	☐	☐	☐	☐	☐	☐	☐	☐
Application mailed or e-mailed	☐	☐	☐	☐	☐	☐	☐	☐	☐	☐
RECOMMENDATIONS										
Gave form to	☐	☐	☐	☐	☐	☐	☐	☐	☐	☐
Writer mailed form or returned it to me	☐	☐	☐	☐	☐	☐	☐	☐	☐	☐
Sent thank-you note	☐	☐	☐	☐	☐	☐	☐	☐	☐	☐
Gave form to	☐	☐	☐	☐	☐	☐	☐	☐	☐	☐
Writer mailed form or returned it to me	☐	☐	☐	☐	☐	☐	☐	☐	☐	☐
Sent thank-you note	☐	☐	☐	☐	☐	☐	☐	☐	☐	☐
Gave form to	☐	☐	☐	☐	☐	☐	☐	☐	☐	☐
Writer mailed form or returned it to me	☐	☐	☐	☐	☐	☐	☐	☐	☐	☐
Sent thank-you note	☐	☐	☐	☐	☐	☐	☐	☐	☐	☐
TRANSCRIPTS										
Gave transcript form to counselor	☐	☐	☐	☐	☐	☐	☐	☐	☐	☐
Form mailed	☐	☐	☐	☐	☐	☐	☐	☐	☐	☐
Gave midyear report form to counselor	☐	☐	☐	☐	☐	☐	☐	☐	☐	☐
Form mailed	☐	☐	☐	☐	☐	☐	☐	☐	☐	☐
TEST SCORES										
Requested that score reports be sent	☐	☐	☐	☐	☐	☐	☐	☐	☐	☐
SAT I	☐	☐	☐	☐	☐	☐	☐	☐	☐	☐
SAT II	☐	☐	☐	☐	☐	☐	☐	☐	☐	☐
ACT	☐	☐	☐	☐	☐	☐	☐	☐	☐	☐
AP exams	☐	☐	☐	☐	☐	☐	☐	☐	☐	☐
FINANCIAL AID FORMS										
Financial aid application deadline										
FAFSA form submitted	☐	☐	☐	☐	☐	☐	☐	☐	☐	☐
Completed Profile registration process	☐	☐	☐	☐	☐	☐	☐	☐	☐	☐
Profile form submitted	☐	☐	☐	☐	☐	☐	☐	☐	☐	☐
If needed, college's form submitted	☐	☐	☐	☐	☐	☐	☐	☐	☐	☐

MY PERSONAL PROFILE

Filling out a personal profile will help you complete the application process more quickly and easily. You can use it as a cheat sheet as you complete your college applications, and give copies (at least in some form) to the people who are writing your letters of recommendation. If you haven't thought of that perfect essay topic yet, a thoughtfully completed profile should give you some good ideas.

Name: _____   Phone number: _____

Address: _____   E-mail address: _____

High school counselor's name: _____   Phone number: _____

Colleges I'm applying to: _____

SCORES

SAT: _____   ACT: _____   High school GPA: _____

Verbal: _____   Multiple Choice: _____   AP (subject, score): _____

Math: _____   Writing Test: _____   AP (subject, score): _____

Writing: _____

Subject Tests: _____

HIGH SCHOOL COURSES (Attach a transcript.) List your favorite courses and a few words about why they interested you.

_____   _____
_____   _____
_____   _____

AWARDS List award, date received, and description.

_____   _____
_____   _____
_____   _____

ACTIVITIES Include jobs, volunteer work, and extracurricular activities. List the dates you participated and/or hours per week, and any leadership positions you held. On a separate sheet, you can summarize what you did and why it was meaningful.

_____   _____
_____   _____
_____   _____
_____   _____
_____   _____

PERSONAL INFO Are you the first member of your family to attend college? Did you have an extraordinary childhood? Do you breed show turtles for fun? Outside of individual awards, activities, and courses, what is most interesting about you? What makes you stand out as a college applicant? Using the space below, write down a few ideas, and continue brainstorming on a separate sheet.

_____
_____
_____
_____
_____

The U.S. News Insider's Index

How Do Your Schools Compare?

How to Use the Insider's Index

The Insider's Index will help you see how your schools stack up on key measures, from graduation rate to the size of their financial aid packages to the diversity of the student body. (See page vi in the Introduction for further discussion.) As you search for a particular college or university, you'll notice that the lists are organized by type of institution:

- National Universities, which offer a wide range of undergraduate majors as well as master's and doctoral degrees
- National Liberal Arts Colleges, which emphasize undergraduate education and award at least half of their degrees in the liberal arts disciplines

- Regional Universities, which offer a full range of undergraduate and master's programs but few, if any, doctoral programs
- Regional Colleges, which offer programs in the liberal arts (accounting for fewer than half of their degrees) and in professional fields such as business, nursing, and education

Schools that did not supply the necessary data do not appear in the tables. "N/A" means "not available."

Schools that are the hardest and easiest to get into

How much competition are you facing? In this table, colleges and universities are organized by how "selective" they are: that is, how picky they can be in choosing freshmen. Selectivity is determined by the test scores and high school class standing of applicants who enroll, plus the proportion of applicants who are accepted. Within each category, schools are ranked by their acceptance rate. SAT results are the combined math and critical reading scores; you can compare your scores on the math and critical reading sections of the test to get an idea of how well you fit a school's profile. All data are for the fall 2009 entering freshman class. The SAT and ACT percentile scores show the range within which half the students scored; 25 percent scored at or higher than the top end of the range, and 25 percent at or lower than the low end.

The hardest to get into

Most Selective Schools	Acceptance rate	SAT Critical Reading 25th–75th percentile	SAT Math 25th–75th percentile	SAT Composite 25th–75th percentile	ACT Composite 25th–75th percentile	High school class standing Top 10%	High school class standing Top 25%	Average high school GPA
National Universities								
Harvard University (MA)	7%	690-780	690-790	1380-1570	31-34	95%	100%	N/A
Stanford University (CA)	8%	660-760	680-780	1340-1540	30-34	91%	99%	N/A
Yale University (CT)	8%	700-800	700-780	1400-1580	30-34	96%	100%	N/A
Columbia University (NY)	10%	680-770	690-780	1370-1550	31-34	97%	99%	N/A
Princeton University (NJ)	10%	690-790	700-790	1390-1580	31-35	95%	100%	3.9
Brown University (RI)	11%	650-760	670-770	1320-1530	29-34	92%	99%	N/A
Massachusetts Institute of Technology	11%	650-760	720-800	1370-1560	32-35	95%	100%	N/A
Dartmouth College (NH)	13%	660-770	680-780	1340-1550	30-34	91%	99%	N/A
California Institute of Technology	15%	690-770	770-800	1460-1570	33-35	98%	100%	N/A
University of Pennsylvania	18%	660-750	690-780	1350-1530	30-34	96%	99%	3.8
Cornell University (NY)	19%	630-730	660-770	1290-1500	29-33	86%	98%	N/A
Duke University (NC)	19%	660-750	680-780	1340-1530	30-34	90%	97%	N/A
Georgetown University (DC)	20%	650-750	650-750	1300-1500	27-33	94%	99%	N/A
Vanderbilt University (TN)	20%	660-750	690-770	1350-1520	30-34	86%	97%	3.7
Rice University (TX)	22%	640-750	680-780	1320-1530	30-34	84%	94%	N/A
University of California–Berkeley	22%	590-710	640-760	1230-1470	27-32	98%	100%	N/A
University of California–Los Angeles	22%	570-680	600-730	1170-1410	24-31	97%	100%	4.0
Washington University in St. Louis	22%	680-750	710-780	1390-1530	32-34	96%	100%	N/A
University of Southern California	24%	620-710	650-740	1270-1450	29-32	86%	97%	3.7
Tulane University (LA)	26%	630-700	620-700	1250-1400	29-32	60%	88%	3.5
Johns Hopkins University (MD)	27%	630-730	670-770	1300-1500	29-33	83%	97%	3.7
Northwestern University (IL)	27%	670-750	690-780	1360-1530	31-33	90%	99%	N/A
Tufts University (MA)	27%	680-750	680-750	1360-1500	30-33	85%	98%	N/A
University of Chicago	27%	690-780	680-780	1370-1560	28-32	87%	97%	N/A
University of Notre Dame (IN)	29%	650-750	680-760	1330-1510	31-34	89%	97%	N/A
Boston College	30%	610-700	640-730	1250-1430	N/A	79%	95%	N/A
Emory University (GA)	30%	640-730	660-750	1300-1480	29-33	85%	98%	N/A
University of North Carolina–Chapel Hill	32%	590-700	620-710	1210-1410	26-31	80%	96%	4.0
University of Virginia	32%	600-710	630-730	1230-1440	27-32	89%	97%	4.0
Lehigh University (PA)	33%	590-630	630-710	1220-1340	N/A	93%	99%	N/A
College of William and Mary (VA)	34%	620-730	620-720	1240-1450	27-32	79%	98%	4.0
Carnegie Mellon University (PA)	36%	620-720	670-780	1290-1500	29-33	75%	93%	3.6
New York University	38%	610-710	600-720	1210-1430	27-31	64%	92%	3.6
University of California–San Diego	38%	540-660	610-720	1150-1380	24-30	100%	100%	4.0
Wake Forest University (NC)	38%	580-690	600-700	1180-1390	27-31	75%	89%	N/A
University of Rochester (NY)	39%	590-690	640-720	1230-1410	28-33	76%	91%	3.8
Brandeis University (MA)	40%	620-730	640-730	1260-1460	27-31	79%	97%	3.8
University of California–Irvine	44%	520-640	570-680	1090-1320	N/A	96%	100%	3.9
University of California–Davis	46%	520-640	560-680	1080-1320	24-30	100%	100%	3.9
University of California–Santa Barbara	48%	540-660	550-670	1090-1330	24-30	96%	98%	3.9
University of Michigan–Ann Arbor	50%	590-690	640-740	1230-1430	27-31	92%	99%	3.8
University of Tulsa (OK)	50%	570-700	560-690	1130-1390	25-32	71%	85%	3.8
Georgia Institute of Technology	59%	580-680	650-750	1230-1430	27-31	81%	95%	3.8
National Liberal Arts Colleges								
Amherst College (MA)	16%	660-760	650-770	1310-1530	30-34	85%	94%	N/A
Claremont McKenna College (CA)	16%	650-750	660-760	1310-1510	29-33	85%	99%	3.9
Pomona College (CA)	16%	710-780	690-770	1400-1550	31-34	92%	99%	N/A
Swarthmore College (PA)	17%	670-760	670-770	1340-1530	29-33	87%	99%	N/A
Bowdoin College (ME)	19%	660-750	660-750	1320-1500	30-33	82%	96%	N/A
Washington and Lee University (VA)	19%	660-740	660-730	1320-1470	29-32	81%	94%	N/A
Middlebury College (VT)	20%	638-730	650-740	1288-1470	30-33	87%	94%	N/A
Williams College (MA)	20%	660-770	650-760	1310-1530	30-34	88%	99%	N/A

Schools that are the hardest and easiest to get into

Most Selective Schools, continued

	Acceptance rate	SAT Critical Reading 25th–75th percentile	SAT Math 25th–75th percentile	SAT Composite 25th–75th percentile	ACT Composite 25th–75th percentile	High school class standing Top 10%	High school class standing Top 25%	Average high school GPA
Wesleyan University (CT)	22%	640-750	650-750	1290-1500	29-33	70%	90%	3.8
Haverford College (PA)	25%	660-740	640-740	1300-1480	N/A	94%	99%	N/A
Vassar College (NY)	25%	660-750	640-720	1300-1470	29-32	67%	95%	3.8
Davidson College (NC)	26%	630-730	630-710	1260-1440	28-32	82%	97%	4.0
Bates College (ME)	27%	620-700	640-710	1260-1410	29-31	63%	91%	N/A
Hamilton College (NY)	30%	660-740	650-730	1310-1470	28-31	80%	97%	N/A
Barnard College (NY)	31%	630-730	620-710	1250-1440	28-32	75%	93%	3.8
Carleton College (MN)	31%	660-760	660-740	1320-1500	29-33	78%	96%	N/A
Colgate University (NY)	32%	630-710	640-730	1270-1440	29-32	68%	91%	3.6
Bard College (NY)	33%	680-740	650-680	1330-1420	N/A	64%	95%	3.5
Scripps College (CA)	33%	640-730	620-700	1260-1430	27-32	69%	94%	4.0
Grinnell College (IA)	34%	600-730	620-730	1220-1460	28-32	65%	93%	N/A
Harvey Mudd College (CA)	34%	680-770	740-790	1420-1560	32-35	94%	100%	N/A
Oberlin College (OH)	34%	660-750	640-720	1300-1470	28-32	69%	90%	3.6
Wellesley College (MA)	35%	640-740	640-730	1280-1470	29-32	78%	96%	N/A
Whitman College (WA)	44%	630-730	610-700	1240-1430	28-32	67%	90%	3.8
Macalester College (MN)	46%	660-740	630-710	1290-1450	29-32	67%	92%	N/A

Regional Colleges (North)

	Acceptance rate	SAT Critical Reading 25th–75th percentile	SAT Math 25th–75th percentile	SAT Composite 25th–75th percentile	ACT Composite 25th–75th percentile	High school class standing Top 10%	High school class standing Top 25%	Average high school GPA
Cooper Union (NY)	7%	600-710	600-770	1200-1480	29-33	93%	98%	3.6

Regional Colleges (West)

	Acceptance rate	SAT Critical Reading 25th–75th percentile	SAT Math 25th–75th percentile	SAT Composite 25th–75th percentile	ACT Composite 25th–75th percentile	High school class standing Top 10%	High school class standing Top 25%	Average high school GPA
United States Air Force Academy (CO)	17%	600-680	630-700	1230-1380	28-32	52%	81%	3.9

More Selective Schools

National Universities

	Acceptance rate	SAT Critical Reading 25th–75th percentile	SAT Math 25th–75th percentile	SAT Composite 25th–75th percentile	ACT Composite 25th–75th percentile	High school class standing Top 10%	High school class standing Top 25%	Average high school GPA
Binghamton University–SUNY	33%	580-670	620-710	1200-1380	27-30	51%	84%	3.6
George Washington University (DC)	37%	600-690	600-690	1200-1380	27-30	67%	93%	N/A
SUNY–Stony Brook	40%	520-620	580-670	1100-1290	24-28	38%	72%	3.6
Northeastern University (MA)	41%	580-670	620-700	1200-1370	27-31	50%	81%	N/A
Pepperdine University (CA)	41%	550-660	560-680	1110-1340	26-30	45%	77%	3.7
University of Florida	42%	560-670	580-690	1140-1360	26-31	77%	93%	4.0
University of Maryland–College Park	42%	580-680	620-710	1200-1390	N/A	71%	91%	3.9
University of the Pacific (CA)	42%	510-640	540-680	1050-1320	23-30	42%	76%	3.5
Rensselaer Polytechnic Institute (NY)	43%	610-700	660-750	1270-1450	25-30	61%	90%	3.7
SUNY College of Environmental Science and Forestry	43%	530-620	540-640	1070-1260	23-27	39%	77%	3.8
University of Miami (FL)	44%	570-680	600-700	1170-1380	27-31	63%	87%	4.0
University of Texas–Austin	45%	530-660	570-700	1100-1360	24-30	77%	94%	N/A
University of Central Florida	47%	530-620	560-650	1090-1270	23-28	35%	77%	3.7
University of South Florida	48%	520-620	530-640	1050-1260	22-28	35%	67%	3.7
University of San Diego	49%	550-640	565-660	1115-1300	25-29	45%	80%	3.8
Baylor University (TX)	50%	530-640	550-650	1080-1290	23-29	40%	73%	N/A
Fordham University (NY)	50%	570-670	570-670	1140-1340	26-30	42%	78%	3.5
University of Connecticut	50%	550-640	570-670	1120-1310	24-29	44%	83%	N/A
University of Minnesota–Twin Cities	50%	520-670	600-710	1120-1380	24-29	43%	83%	N/A
Stevens Institute of Technology (NJ)	51%	550-650	620-710	1170-1360	24-29	58%	85%	3.8
Pennsylvania State University–University Park	52%	530-630	560-670	1090-1300	N/A	50%	86%	3.6
University at Buffalo–SUNY	52%	510-600	550-650	1060-1250	23-28	28%	65%	3.3
University of Texas–Dallas	52%	520-660	560-690	1080-1350	24-30	36%	70%	3.6
American University (DC)	53%	590-700	580-670	1170-1370	26-30	50%	83%	3.7
Southern Methodist University (TX)	53%	560-660	580-680	1140-1340	25-30	43%	73%	3.6
Boston University	54%	N/A	N/A	N/A	N/A	55%	87%	N/A
University of Georgia	54%	560-660	570-670	1130-1330	25-29	54%	89%	3.8
Drexel University (PA)	55%	540-630	570-670	1110-1300	23-28	30%	63%	N/A
Kansas State University	55%	N/A	N/A	N/A	N/A	22%	49%	3.4
North Carolina State University–Raleigh	55%	520-620	560-660	1080-1280	23-28	41%	83%	3.6
Polytechnic Institute of New York University (NY)	55%	560-640	630-720	1190-1360	26-32	36%	69%	3.4
University of Arkansas	56%	500-620	520-640	1020-1260	23-29	30%	60%	3.6
Hofstra University (NY)	57%	540-630	560-640	1100-1270	24-28	31%	59%	3.4
University of Alabama	57%	500-600	500-620	1000-1220	21-28	43%	56%	3.5
University of Delaware	57%	520-630	540-650	1060-1280	24-28	37%	74%	3.5
University of Wisconsin–Madison	57%	550-670	620-720	1170-1390	26-30	57%	91%	3.7
University of Washington	58%	530-650	570-680	1100-1330	24-30	86%	97%	3.7
Texas Christian University	59%	520-630	530-650	1050-1280	23-28	30%	61%	N/A

	Acceptance rate	SAT Critical Reading 25th–75th percentile	SAT Math 25th–75th percentile	SAT Composite 25th–75th percentile	ACT Composite 25th–75th percentile	High school class standing Top 10%	High school class standing Top 25%	Average high school GPA
University of Pittsburgh	59%	570-680	590-680	1160-1360	25-30	49%	86%	3.9
Illinois Institute of Technology	60%	540-670	630-723	1170-1393	25-31	41%	72%	N/A
Syracuse University (NY)	60%	510-620	540-650	1050-1270	23-28	39%	73%	3.6
Florida State University	61%	550-640	560-650	1110-1290	24-28	34%	61%	3.7
Rutgers, the State University of New Jersey–New Brunswick	61%	530-630	560-680	1090-1310	N/A	42%	80%	N/A
University of Missouri–Kansas City	62%	520-650	550-690	1070-1340	21-28	31%	58%	3.3
Clemson University (SC)	63%	550-640	580-670	1130-1310	25-30	45%	78%	3.8
Colorado School of Mines	63%	550-650	620-700	1170-1350	26-30	52%	85%	3.7
University of Illinois–Chicago	63%	460-630	510-660	970-1290	21-26	28%	62%	N/A
University of Nebraska–Lincoln	63%	510-670	530-680	1040-1350	22-29	27%	54%	N/A
Worcester Polytechnic Institute (MA)	63%	560-660	630-720	1190-1380	26-31	55%	88%	3.8
Yeshiva University (NY)	63%	550-690	550-680	1100-1370	22-28	51%	80%	3.5
Clark University (MA)	64%	550-650	530-640	1080-1290	24-29	34%	71%	3.5
University of California–Santa Cruz	64%	510-630	520-640	1030-1270	22-28	96%	100%	3.6
University of South Carolina	64%	530-640	560-650	1090-1290	24-29	27%	60%	3.9
University of Illinois–Urbana-Champaign	65%	540-660	660-770	1200-1430	26-31	58%	94%	N/A
Marquette University (WI)	66%	540-640	540-660	1080-1300	24-29	33%	65%	N/A
Texas A&M University–College Station	67%	530-640	570-670	1100-1310	24-30	50%	89%	N/A
University of Cincinnati	67%	490-610	520-640	1010-1250	22-27	22%	49%	3.4
University of Massachusetts–Amherst	67%	520-630	540-650	1060-1280	23-28	27%	67%	3.6
Virginia Tech	67%	540-640	570-670	1110-1310	N/A	44%	85%	N/A
Brigham Young University–Provo (UT)	69%	560-670	570-680	1130-1350	25-30	51%	83%	3.8
Louisiana State University–Baton Rouge	69%	510-630	540-650	1050-1280	23-28	25%	53%	3.5
Case Western Reserve University (OH)	70%	590-700	650-740	1240-1440	28-32	65%	87%	N/A
University of Denver	70%	540-640	550-650	1090-1290	24-29	45%	75%	3.7
St. Louis University	71%	540-650	540-670	1080-1320	24-30	39%	71%	3.7
University of Vermont	71%	540-640	550-640	1090-1280	24-28	29%	66%	N/A
Colorado State University	72%	500-610	510-640	1010-1250	22-27	22%	50%	3.6
University of Alabama–Huntsville	72%	500-630	520-640	1020-1270	22-28	34%	63%	3.6
Clarkson University (NY)	73%	500-610	560-660	1060-1270	23-27	34%	67%	3.5
Indiana University–Bloomington	73%	520-630	540-660	1060-1290	24-29	34%	71%	3.6
Michigan State University	73%	470-610	540-660	1010-1270	23-27	31%	70%	3.6
Michigan Technological University	73%	510-650	600-690	1110-1340	23-29	28%	60%	3.6
Purdue University–West Lafayette (IN)	73%	500-610	540-670	1040-1280	23-29	35%	70%	3.5
University of Dayton (OH)	73%	510-610	520-640	1030-1250	23-28	27%	58%	3.6
University of Tennessee	73%	510-640	530-650	1040-1290	24-29	39%	70%	3.8
DePaul University (IL)	74%	520-640	520-620	1040-1260	22-27	22%	51%	3.5
University of Kentucky	74%	490-610	490-640	980-1250	22-28	27%	56%	3.4
Ohio State University–Columbus	76%	540-650	580-690	1120-1340	25-30	49%	85%	N/A
Loyola University Chicago	78%	540-650	530-650	1070-1300	24-29	32%	67%	3.7
University of California–Riverside	78%	450-570	480-620	930-1190	19-25	94%	100%	3.5
Miami University–Oxford (OH)	79%	530-630	560-660	1090-1290	24-29	39%	74%	3.7
Auburn University (AL)	80%	520-640	540-660	1060-1300	23-29	40%	65%	3.7
University of Iowa	83%	500-640	560-690	1060-1330	23-28	23%	55%	3.6
University of Missouri	83%	530-650	530-650	1060-1300	23-28	25%	55%	N/A
Samford University (AL)	84%	520-645	520-650	1040-1295	21-28	44%	70%	3.7
University of Colorado–Boulder	84%	530-630	550-650	1080-1280	24-29	25%	58%	3.6
Iowa State University	85%	490-640	540-690	1030-1330	22-28	28%	62%	3.5
Oklahoma State University	86%	480-600	500-640	980-1240	22-27	27%	55%	3.5
University of Kansas	91%	N/A	N/A	N/A	22-27	27%	55%	3.4
Missouri University of Science & Technology	93%	550-670	610-700	1160-1370	25-31	43%	71%	3.6
University of Oklahoma	93%	510-640	530-660	1040-1300	23-29	34%	68%	3.6

National Liberal Arts Colleges

	Acceptance rate	SAT Critical Reading 25th–75th percentile	SAT Math 25th–75th percentile	SAT Composite 25th–75th percentile	ACT Composite 25th–75th percentile	High school class standing Top 10%	High school class standing Top 25%	Average high school GPA
United States Naval Academy (MD)	10%	550-660	590-690	1140-1350	N/A	56%	81%	N/A
United States Military Academy (NY)	15%	560-660	580-670	1140-1330	25-29	42%	70%	N/A
Berea College (KY)	19%	500-620	465-585	965-1205	21-26	26%	69%	3.4
Pitzer College (CA)	20%	608-693	588-680	1196-1373	26-30	47%	89%	3.8
Tougaloo College (MS)	25%	480-550	500-510	980-1060	24-28	N/A	N/A	3.0
Bucknell University (PA)	30%	600-680	630-720	1230-1400	27-31	59%	88%	3.5
Colorado College	32%	620-710	620-710	1240-1420	28-31	63%	87%	N/A
Colby College (ME)	34%	630-720	640-720	1270-1440	28-31	59%	89%	N/A
College of the Holy Cross (MA)	36%	600-680	610-690	1210-1370	26-30	66%	93%	3.8
Connecticut College	37%	610-700	610-690	1220-1390	25-30	56%	93%	N/A
Kenyon College (OH)	39%	630-720	600-680	1230-1400	28-32	56%	87%	3.8
St. Lawrence University (NY)	39%	570-640	570-650	1140-1290	26-29	41%	81%	3.5
University of Richmond (VA)	39%	580-670	590-680	1170-1350	26-30	58%	87%	N/A
Gettysburg College (PA)	40%	610-690	610-690	1220-1380	27-30	68%	86%	N/A
Reed College (OR)	41%	660-760	620-710	1280-1470	29-33	59%	86%	3.9

Schools that are the hardest and easiest to get into

More Selective Schools, continued

	Acceptance rate	SAT Critical Reading 25th–75th percentile	SAT Math 25th–75th percentile	SAT Composite 25th–75th percentile	ACT Composite 25th–75th percentile	High school class standing Top 10%	High school class standing Top 25%	Average high school GPA
Trinity College (CT)	41%	590-680	610-690	1200-1370	26-30	68%	93%	N/A
Union College (NY)	41%	590-670	620-700	1210-1370	27-30	58%	84%	3.6
Lafayette College (PA)	42%	570-670	600-710	1170-1380	26-30	59%	87%	3.5
Oglethorpe University (GA)	42%	550-650	510-630	1060-1280	23-27	24%	63%	3.6
Rhodes College (TN)	42%	570-680	580-700	1150-1380	26-N/A	57%	84%	3.8
Skidmore College (NY)	42%	570-680	580-670	1150-1350	26-30	39%	74%	.0
Washington and Jefferson College (PA)	42%	510-610	520-620	1030-1230	22-28	38%	71%	3.3
Occidental College (CA)	43%	600-700	600-680	1200-1380	28-32	63%	94%	3.6
Cornell College (IA)	44%	550-680	550-680	1100-1360	24-29	35%	57%	3.5
Muhlenberg College (PA)	45%	560-660	560-660	1120-1320	25-31	41%	84%	3.3
Agnes Scott College (GA)	46%	520-650	490-620	1010-1270	22-28	33%	66%	3.6
Smith College (MA)	47%	610-710	580-690	1190-1400	27-30	66%	94%	3.9
Franklin and Marshall College (PA)	48%	600-670	630-700	1230-1370	28-31	63%	86%	N/A
Bryn Mawr College (PA)	49%	600-700	580-680	1180-1380	26-30	61%	87%	N/A
Dickinson College (PA)	49%	600-690	590-680	1190-1370	26-30	37%	71%	N/A
Wabash College (IN)	49%	500-600	530-660	1030-1260	21-27	31%	70%	3.5
Denison University (OH)	50%	600-700	600-680	1200-1380	27-30	54%	85%	3.5
Asbury University (KY)	53%	510-650	490-630	1000-1280	21-27	32%	63%	3.6
New College of Florida	53%	630-730	590-680	1220-1410	27-30	49%	84%	4.0
Siena College (NY)	53%	500-600	530-630	1030-1230	22-27	28%	61%	N/A
Illinois Wesleyan University	54%	570-680	600-720	1170-1400	26-30	45%	81%	3.9
William Jewell College (MO)	55%	490-640	510-650	1000-1290	23-29	34%	68%	3.7
Hobart and William Smith Colleges (NY)	56%	570-650	580-650	1150-1310	25-30	41%	73%	3.4
Stonehill College (MA)	56%	550-630	570-650	1120-1280	24-28	50%	87%	3.5
St. Mary's College of Maryland	57%	580-690	550-650	1130-1340	24-29	47%	78%	3.8
St. Olaf College (MN)	57%	590-710	590-690	1180-1400	26-31	53%	82%	3.6
Ursinus College (PA)	57%	570-680	570-670	1140-1350	25-29	47%	77%	3.6
Mount Holyoke College (MA)	58%	610-730	600-720	1210-1450	27-31	62%	87%	3.7
Wofford College (SC)	58%	560-670	580-680	1140-1350	22-29	57%	87%	3.5
Birmingham-Southern College (AL)	59%	520-640	520-630	1040-1270	23-28	33%	58%	3.4
College of Wooster (OH)	59%	540-660	540-650	1080-1310	24-29	36%	74%	3.6
Salem College (NC)	59%	N/A	N/A	N/A	N/A	36%	67%	N/A
Wheaton College (MA)	59%	570-680	560-670	1130-1350	27-30	53%	83%	3.5
Christopher Newport University (VA)	60%	560-640	560-640	1120-1280	22-27	19%	57%	3.6
Willamette University (OR)	60%	560-670	560-650	1120-1320	25-30	49%	80%	3.7
Hanover College (IN)	61%	490-600	500-620	990-1220	22-28	32%	71%	3.6
College of Idaho (ID)	62%	440-575	460-595	900-1170	22-27	30%	64%	3.6
Hillsdale College (MI)	62%	640-730	570-670	1210-1400	26-30	52%	77%	3.7
Hampshire College (MA)	63%	600-710	530-660	1130-1370	25-29	27%	69%	3.5
Southwestern University (TX)	63%	570-680	570-670	1140-1350	25-30	49%	84%	N/A
University of Puget Sound (WA)	63%	570-680	560-660	1130-1340	25-30	31%	68%	3.5
Grove City College (PA)	64%	563-685	568-682	1131-1367	25-30	51%	85%	3.8
Ohio Wesleyan University	64%	520-660	520-660	1040-1320	23-29	38%	63%	3.5
Coe College (IA)	65%	540-640	530-630	1070-1270	23-28	27%	61%	3.7
Lewis & Clark College (OR)	65%	610-710	610-680	1220-1390	27-30	46%	81%	3.7
Allegheny College (PA)	66%	550-660	560-650	1110-1310	23-29	45%	76%	3.8
Bennington College (VT)	66%	620-720	560-640	1180-1360	26-31	31%	63%	3.5
DePauw University (IN)	66%	530-650	550-670	1080-1320	24-29	51%	82%	3.6
Berry College (GA)	67%	520-640	510-610	1030-1250	22-28	32%	66%	3.6
Lyon College (AR)	67%	460-620	480-590	940-1210	22-30	26%	56%	3.5
Furman University (SC)	68%	580-690	600-680	1180-1370	25-30	61%	86%	3.8
Sewanee–University of the South (TN)	68%	570-690	580-670	1150-1360	26-30	43%	67%	3.6
Centre College (KY)	69%	550-670	570-670	1120-1340	26-30	59%	84%	3.6
Lake Forest College (IL)	69%	N/A	N/A	N/A	23-28	38%	62%	3.5
Lawrence University (WI)	69%	590-730	600-710	1190-1440	27-31	38%	70%	3.6
Luther College (IA)	70%	500-640	530-670	1030-1310	23-29	35%	64%	3.6
Presbyterian College (SC)	70%	490-620	510-630	1000-1250	21-27	35%	69%	3.4
Wheaton College (IL)	71%	600-710	600-700	1200-1410	27-31	59%	83%	3.7
Juniata College (PA)	72%	550-650	550-660	1100-1310	N/A	41%	74%	3.8
Washington College (MD)	72%	520-620	510-610	1030-1230	22-29	30%	71%	3.4
Wittenberg University (OH)	72%	500-620	500-620	1000-1240	22-28	27%	50%	3.4
Augustana College (IL)	73%	N/A	N/A	N/A	23-29	35%	64%	N/A
Beloit College (WI)	73%	575-710	560-670	1135-1380	25-30	32%	69%	3.4
Kalamazoo College (MI)	73%	570-690	560-680	1130-1370	26-30	46%	84%	3.6
Central College (IA)	74%	470-670	480-650	950-1320	21-27	28%	54%	3.5
Drew University (NJ)	74%	510-630	500-618	1010-1248	21-27	38%	67%	3.3
Gustavus Adolphus College (MN)	74%	N/A	N/A	N/A	24-29	32%	82%	3.6
Knox College (IL)	74%	600-730	560-690	1160-1420	26-31	37%	67%	3.3

	Acceptance rate	SAT Critical Reading 25th–75th percentile	SAT Math 25th–75th percentile	SAT Composite 25th–75th percentile	ACT Composite 25th–75th percentile	High school class standing Top 10%	High school class standing Top 25%	Average high school GPA
Millsaps College (MS)	74%	510-640	520-640	1030-1280	23-29	33%	50%	3.5
University of Minnesota–Morris	74%	520-710	520-710	1040-1420	22-28	30%	56%	N/A
Alma College (MI)	75%	470-708	483-668	953-1376	21-27	30%	57%	3.5
Bethel College (KS)	75%	420-700	460-730	880-1430	21-29	36%	58%	3.6
College of the Atlantic (ME)	75%	620-690	510-620	1130-1310	21-27	26%	63%	3.5
Carroll College (MT)	76%	N/A	N/A	N/A	N/A	26%	59%	N/A
Earlham College (IN)	76%	560-690	530-640	1090-1330	24-29	31%	59%	3.5
Thomas Aquinas College (CA)	78%	610-730	550-640	1160-1370	25-30	50%	80%	3.7
Albion College (MI)	79%	530-660	560-670	1090-1330	22-28	27%	56%	3.5
Concordia College–Moorhead (MN)	79%	510-680	523-658	1033-1338	22-28	32%	66%	3.6
Georgetown College (KY)	79%	430-570	480-560	910-1130	21-26	31%	60%	3.4
Ripon College (WI)	79%	490-640	500-640	990-1280	22-27	28%	61%	3.4
Austin College (TX)	80%	560-680	570-670	1130-1350	24-26	41%	70%	3.6
Hendrix College (AR)	80%	580-700	560-680	1140-1380	27-32	49%	77%	3.8
Westmont College (CA)	80%	520-650	530-650	1050-1300	23-29	38%	66%	3.8
Transylvania University (KY)	81%	530-650	510-630	1040-1280	23-29	42%	69%	3.7
Houghton College (NY)	82%	520-660	510-640	1030-1300	22-29	36%	62%	3.6
Nebraska Wesleyan University	82%	N/A	N/A	N/A	23-27	25%	60%	N/A
Hope College (MI)	84%	540-670	520-660	1060-1330	23-29	34%	63%	3.7
St. John's University (MN)	84%	493-648	523-675	1016-1323	23-29	23%	58%	3.5
College of St. Benedict (MN)	85%	510-660	510-670	1020-1330	23-28	40%	76%	3.7
St. Mary's College (IN)	86%	510-620	510-600	1020-1220	23-28	38%	58%	3.7
Simpson College (IA)	89%	N/A	N/A	N/A	21-27	31%	61%	N/A
Calvin College (MI)	93%	520-670	550-660	1070-1330	23-29	29%	57%	3.6
Centenary College of Louisiana	93%	N/A	N/A	N/A	N/A	29%	58%	N/A

Regional Universities (North)

	Acceptance rate	SAT Critical Reading 25th–75th percentile	SAT Math 25th–75th percentile	SAT Composite 25th–75th percentile	ACT Composite 25th–75th percentile	High school class standing Top 10%	High school class standing Top 25%	Average high school GPA
CUNY–Baruch College	23%	490-590	560-670	1050-1260	N/A	34%	61%	3.1
CUNY–Hunter College	26%	510-610	520-620	1030-1230	N/A	23%	52%	3.1
SUNY–Geneseo	35%	610-700	630-690	1240-1390	28-30	56%	88%	3.8
Marist College (NY)	36%	520-620	540-640	1060-1260	23-28	27%	70%	3.4
Emerson College (MA)	42%	570-670	540-640	1110-1310	24-29	42%	77%	3.6
Bentley University (MA)	43%	540-630	600-680	1140-1310	25-28	38%	79%	N/A
College of New Jersey	46%	560-660	590-690	1150-1350	N/A	61%	92%	N/A
Villanova University (PA)	46%	580-680	620-710	1200-1390	28-31	58%	88%	3.8
Providence College (RI)	60%	530-630	530-640	1060-1270	23-28	37%	72%	3.4
Quinnipiac University (CT)	60%	550-610	570-620	1120-1230	24-29	28%	68%	3.4
Rochester Institute of Technology (NY)	61%	530-640	560-670	1090-1310	25-30	33%	67%	N/A
Fairfield University (CT)	65%	520-610	530-630	1050-1240	N/A	41%	78%	3.4
Loyola University Maryland	66%	530-630	540-640	1070-1270	24-28	31%	65%	3.4
Touro College (NY)	71%	530-650	510-620	1040-1270	22-26	67%	92%	3.6
Ithaca College (NY)	79%	530-630	530-640	1060-1270	N/A	27%	67%	N/A

Regional Universities (South)

	Acceptance rate	SAT Critical Reading 25th–75th percentile	SAT Math 25th–75th percentile	SAT Composite 25th–75th percentile	ACT Composite 25th–75th percentile	High school class standing Top 10%	High school class standing Top 25%	Average high school GPA
Elon University (NC)	48%	570-660	570-660	1140-1320	25-29	32%	70%	4.0
Christian Brothers University (TN)	49%	480-620	480-630	960-1250	21-26	29%	60%	3.6
Bellarmine University (KY)	53%	480-600	510-600	990-1200	22-27	23%	51%	3.5
Spring Hill College (AL)	55%	480-600	480-570	960-1170	21-26	27%	61%	3.5
Loyola University New Orleans	58%	570-670	550-660	1120-1330	24-29	29%	60%	3.7
University of North Carolina–Wilmington	58%	530-620	550-630	1080-1250	22-27	24%	62%	3.8
James Madison University (VA)	61%	520-610	530-630	1050-1240	22-27	28%	72%	3.8
Mississippi College	61%	450-600	470-600	920-1200	20-27	24%	50%	3.4
Mercer University (GA)	62%	540-630	550-640	1090-1270	24-29	43%	73%	3.7
Rollins College (FL)	62%	565-652	565-653	1130-1305	24-29	39%	65%	3.3
Lipscomb University (TN)	66%	500-620	490-610	990-1230	21-27	28%	51%	3.5
College of Charleston (SC)	70%	560-650	560-640	1120-1290	23-27	31%	68%	3.9
Harding University (AR)	73%	490-630	490-640	980-1270	21-28	28%	50%	3.5
Belmont University (TN)	77%	540-640	530-640	1070-1280	23-29	35%	68%	3.5
Union University (TN)	84%	510-660	510-630	1020-1290	23-30	35%	63%	N/A

Regional Universities (Midwest)

	Acceptance rate	SAT Critical Reading 25th–75th percentile	SAT Math 25th–75th percentile	SAT Composite 25th–75th percentile	ACT Composite 25th–75th percentile	High school class standing Top 10%	High school class standing Top 25%	Average high school GPA
Newman University (KS)	42%	430-530	420-570	850-1100	19-27	27%	52%	3.4
Lawrence Technological University (MI)	50%	N/A	N/A	N/A	21-27	26%	56%	3.3
Webster University (MO)	52%	520-640	490-630	1010-1270	21-28	24%	55%	3.4
University of Detroit Mercy	62%	N/A	N/A	N/A	21-26	27%	61%	3.4
Maryville University of St. Louis (MO)	66%	450-570	490-520	940-1090	22-27	26%	56%	3.5
St. Catherine University (MN)	67%	N/A	N/A	N/A	21-26	26%	60%	3.6
University of Michigan–Dearborn	67%	N/A	530-680	-	21-27	26%	60%	3.4

Schools that are the hardest and easiest to get into

More Selective Schools, continued	Acceptance rate	SAT Critical Reading 25th–75th percentile	SAT Math 25th–75th percentile	SAT Composite 25th–75th percentile	ACT Composite 25th–75th percentile	High school class standing Top 10%	High school class standing Top 25%	Average high school GPA
University of Wisconsin–Eau Claire	67%	520-640	520-670	1040-1310	23-26	29%	61%	N/A
University of Wisconsin–La Crosse	69%	510-650	530-660	1040-1310	23-27	30%	79%	3.6
Drury University (MO)	70%	N/A	N/A	N/A	22-28	35%	67%	3.7
Franciscan University of Steubenville (OH)	72%	540-650	500-630	1040-1280	23-28	31%	60%	3.7
Truman State University (MO)	72%	540-660	560-660	1100-1320	25-30	46%	95%	3.7
Xavier University (OH)	73%	530-620	510-610	1040-1230	23-28	24%	58%	3.5
Bradley University (IL)	74%	480-600	510-640	990-1240	22-27	26%	60%	3.6
Drake University (IA)	74%	510-640	530-660	1040-1300	24-29	38%	70%	3.6
Rockhurst University (MO)	76%	530-650	530-640	1060-1290	22-28	22%	57%	3.5
Butler University (IN)	79%	520-630	540-650	1060-1280	25-30	50%	79%	3.8
Bethel University (MN)	80%	513-678	510-668	1023-1346	21-28	31%	55%	3.5
Creighton University (NE)	82%	520-640	540-650	1060-1290	24-29	41%	73%	3.8
University of Evansville (IN)	86%	510-610	510-628	1020-1238	22-28	38%	70%	3.7
Valparaiso University (IN)	91%	480-630	500-620	980-1250	22-29	26%	58%	3.3

Regional Universities (West)

	Acceptance rate	SAT Critical Reading 25th–75th percentile	SAT Math 25th–75th percentile	SAT Composite 25th–75th percentile	ACT Composite 25th–75th percentile	High school class standing Top 10%	High school class standing Top 25%	Average high school GPA
California Polytechnic State University–San Luis Obispo	37%	530-630	570-670	1100-1300	24-29	48%	84%	3.8
Chapman University (CA)	56%	547-661	568-678	1115-1339	25-29	48%	90%	3.7
University of Portland (OR)	56%	530-640	550-650	1080-1290	N/A	43%	76%	3.6
Mills College (CA)	57%	530-650	500-600	1030-1250	22-27	44%	76%	3.7
Loyola Marymount University (CA)	59%	530-630	550-650	1080-1280	24-28	29%	65%	3.7
Santa Clara University (CA)	59%	550-660	570-680	1120-1340	26-30	37%	76%	3.5
Trinity University (TX)	59%	590-700	610-690	1200-1390	27-31	55%	86%	3.6
Seattle University	66%	520-640	520-640	1040-1280	23-29	30%	61%	3.6
LeTourneau University (TX)	70%	510-640	550-653	1060-1293	22-29	41%	67%	3.6
Gonzaga University (WA)	78%	530-640	550-650	1080-1290	24-29	38%	72%	3.7
New Mexico Institute of Mining and Technology	79%	530-650	570-680	1100-1330	23-28	36%	67%	3.6
Oklahoma City University	79%	490-600	480-590	970-1190	22-27	32%	59%	3.5
Regis University (CO)	80%	470-590	470-590	940-1180	21-27	30%	60%	3.5
Westminster College (UT)	82%	510-620	500-630	1010-1250	22-27	29%	60%	3.5
University of Dallas	92%	560-700	530-650	1090-1350	23-30	36%	58%	3.7

	Acceptance rate	SAT Critical Reading 25th–75th percentile	SAT Math 25th–75th percentile	SAT Composite 25th–75th percentile	ACT Composite 25th–75th percentile	High school class standing		Average high school GPA
						Top 10%	Top 25%	
Regional Colleges (North)								
United States Coast Guard Academy (CT)	25%	560-660	600-680	1160-1340	24-30	49%	83%	3.7
Messiah College (PA)	69%	510-620	510-640	1020-1260	23-28	35%	67%	3.7
Regional Colleges (South)								
Covenant College (GA)	60%	540-660	510-620	1050-1280	22-28	31%	56%	3.7
Ouachita Baptist University (AR)	67%	470-590	490-610	960-1200	21-27	34%	61%	3.5
Milligan College (TN)	68%	480-580	460-570	940-1150	20-25	37%	65%	3.6
John Brown University (AR)	73%	520-660	510-640	1030-1300	22-28	32%	60%	3.6
Regional Colleges (Midwest)								
Cedarville University (OH)	76%	530-650	530-640	1060-1290	23-29	32%	53%	3.6
Marietta College (OH)	76%	480-600	490-610	970-1210	21-27	32%	58%	3.5
Ohio Northern University	76%	510-630	560-650	1070-1280	23-29	42%	66%	3.6
Augustana College (SD)	81%	N/A	N/A	N/A	22-28	29%	61%	3.6
Taylor University (IN)	83%	500-650	510-640	1010-1290	24-31	41%	66%	3.6
Dordt College (IA)	84%	460-610	480-620	940-1230	22-27	35%	57%	3.5
Regional Colleges (West)								
Oklahoma Wesleyan University	71%	421-605	453-628	874-1233	19-27	25%	50%	3.3

Schools that are the hardest and easiest to get into

The easiest to get into

	Acceptance rate	SAT Critical Reading 25th–75th percentile	SAT Math 25th–75th percentile	SAT Composite 25th–75th percentile	ACT Composite 25th–75th percentile	High school class standing Top 10%	High school class standing Top 25%	Average high school GPA
National Liberal Arts Colleges								
Jarvis Christian College (TX)	23%	350-400	310-400	660-800	17-18	2%	6%	2.5
Bennett College (NC)	54%	350-450	320-420	670-870	14-18	3%	10%	2.4
Allen University (SC)	72%	N/A	N/A	N/A	N/A	9%	8%	N/A
Regional Universities (North)								
Cheyney University of Pennsylvania	50%	330-420	320-410	650-830	14-21	6%	15%	2.4
College of St. Joseph (VT)	78%	380-480	390-490	770-970	15-20	N/A	11%	N/A
Regional Universities (South)								
Fayetteville State University (NC)	69%	370-440	390-460	760-900	15-19	1%	12%	2.8
Regional Colleges (North)								
CUNY–York College	N/A	N/A	N/A	N/A	N/A	N/A	N/A	N/A
Becker College (MA)	78%	390-490	390-490	780-980	17-21	N/A	N/A	N/A
CUNY–New York City College of Technology	84%	N/A	N/A	N/A	N/A	N/A	N/A	N/A
Keystone College (PA)	95%	390-480	380-480	770-960	16-18	3%	11%	2.9
CUNY–Medgar Evers College	100%	340-440	330-430	670-870	N/A	N/A	N/A	2.1
Regional Colleges (South)								
Shaw University (NC)	37%	330-430	320-420	650-850	11-16	3%	12%	2.4
St. Augustine's College (NC)	49%	320-420	320-420	640-840	13-17	6%	7%	2.4
Elizabeth City State University (NC)	64%	360-460	370-470	730-930	15-18	1%	13%	2.8
Livingstone College (NC)	67%	330-420	320-420	650-840	13-16	5%	22%	2.2
Benedict College (SC)	70%	N/A	N/A	N/A	N/A	5%	16%	N/A
Virginia Union University	81%	N/A	N/A	N/A	N/A	N/A	N/A	2.3
St. Paul's College (VA)	99%	250-420	320-420	570-840	13-16	1%	2%	2.2
Regional Colleges (Midwest)								
Harris-Stowe State University (MO)	96%	N/A	N/A	N/A	14-17	2%	11%	2.3
Regional Colleges (West)								
Langston University (OK)	45%	N/A	N/A	N/A	13 - 19	2%	8%	2.5
St. Gregory's University (OK)	97%	N/A	N/A	N/A	N/A	2%	9%	N/A
Wiley College (TX)	98%	320-420	330-430	650-850	13-18	3%	9%	2.6

Where applying early may help you most—or not

Applying early can sometimes boost your chances of getting in. One study of 14 elite schools by Harvard researchers found that applying early decision conferred an advantage equivalent to an extra 100 points on the old SAT. Acceptance rates and the design of early plans can change from year to year; in this table, colleges are ranked by the size of the difference between their early and non-early acceptance rates for the class that entered in fall 2009. The difference in acceptance rates is figured using unrounded data.

Most Selective Schools

	Early decision and/or early action acceptance rate	Non-early acceptance rate	Difference in acceptance rate	Freshmen enrolled through early plans	Type of plan (early decision and/or early action)
National Universities					
Lehigh University (PA)	65%	30%	34%	46%	ED
Johns Hopkins University (MD)	50%	25%	25%	N/A	ED
College of William and Mary (VA)	53%	32%	22%	36%	ED
Cornell University (NY)	37%	17%	20%	39%	ED
University of Notre Dame (IN)	42%	23%	19%	48%	EA
Brandeis University (MA)	57%	39%	18%	31%	ED
Duke University (NC)	36%	18%	18%	31%	ED
Boston College	44%	27%	18%	33%	EA
University of Pennsylvania	31%	15%	16%	45%	ED
University of North Carolina–Chapel Hill	38%	23%	15%	78%	EA
Dartmouth College (NH)	26%	11%	15%	36%	ED
Columbia University (NY)	23%	8%	14%	45%	ED
Brown University (RI)	24%	10%	14%	N/A	ED
Rice University (TX)	35%	21%	14%	26%	ED
Tulane University (LA)	33%	20%	13%	68%	EA
Northwestern University (IL)	39%	26%	13%	27%	ED
California Institute of Technology	22%	13%	8%	33%	EA
Yale University (CT)	13%	6%	7%	46%	EA
Stanford University (CA)	13%	7%	6%	32%	EA
Emory University (GA)	35%	29%	5%	N/A	ED
Wake Forest University (NC)	42%	37%	5%	N/A	ED
New York University	39%	38%	1%	N/A	EA, ED
Massachusetts Institute of Technology	12%	10%	1%	35%	EA
University of Rochester (NY)	39%	39%	0%	25%	ED
Carnegie Mellon University (PA)	24%	37%	-13%	19%	ED
National Liberal Arts Colleges					
Oberlin College (OH)	65%	32%	33%	26%	ED
Whitman College (WA)	72%	42%	30%	30%	ED
Colgate University (NY)	56%	29%	26%	47%	ED
Washington and Lee University (VA)	43%	17%	26%	46%	ED
Davidson College (NC)	49%	23%	25%	45%	ED
Haverford College (PA)	49%	24%	25%	37%	ED
Wellesley College (MA)	59%	34%	25%	20%	ED
Carleton College (MN)	53%	28%	25%	39%	ED
Bates College (ME)	48%	24%	23%	N/A	ED
Barnard College (NY)	52%	29%	23%	32%	ED
Scripps College (CA)	54%	32%	22%	N/A	ED
Wesleyan University (CT)	41%	20%	21%	47%	ED
Vassar College (NY)	43%	23%	20%	39%	ED
Swarthmore College (PA)	33%	16%	18%	42%	ED
Williams College (MA)	36%	19%	17%	40%	ED
Grinnell College (IA)	48%	32%	15%	35%	ED
Hamilton College (NY)	42%	28%	14%	49%	ED
Claremont McKenna College (CA)	28%	15%	12%	35%	ED
Harvey Mudd College (CA)	46%	33%	12%	23%	ED
Bowdoin College (ME)	30%	18%	12%	41%	ED
Macalester College (MN)	53%	46%	7%	20%	ED
Regional Colleges (North)					
Cooper Union (NY)	13%	6%	7%	39%	ED

Where applying early may help you most—or not

More Selective Schools

	Early decision and/or early action acceptance rate	Non-early acceptance rate	Difference in acceptance rate	Freshmen enrolled through early plans	Type of plan (early decision and/or early action)
National Universities					
University of Arkansas	89%	32%	57%	65%	EA
SUNY College of Environmental Science and Forestry	83%	31%	52%	54%	EA
University of Connecticut	60%	32%	28%	81%	EA
University of Georgia	63%	36%	27%	78%	EA
University of Denver	85%	63%	22%	48%	EA
American University (DC)	73%	53%	21%	19%	ED
Miami University–Oxford (OH)	87%	66%	20%	73%	EA, ED
Illinois Institute of Technology	71%	51%	19%	N/A	EA, ED
Stevens Institute of Technology (NJ)	67%	48%	19%	44%	ED
Syracuse University (NY)	77%	59%	18%	18%	ED
Northeastern University (MA)	53%	36%	17%	45%	EA
Case Western Reserve University (OH)	82%	66%	17%	39%	EA
University of San Diego	61%	45%	16%	39%	EA
Clarkson University (NY)	88%	72%	15%	13%	ED
Binghamton University–SUNY	44%	30%	15%	37%	EA
George Washington University (DC)	47%	36%	12%	34%	ED
University of Colorado–Boulder	88%	80%	9%	60%	EA
Fordham University (NY)	55%	47%	8%	34%	EA
University of Miami (FL)	49%	41%	8%	57%	EA, ED
University of Massachusetts–Amherst	69%	66%	3%	31%	EA
Rensselaer Polytechnic Institute (NY)	39%	43%	-5%	27%	ED
University of Vermont	62%	74%	-12%	41%	EA
University of South Carolina	54%	69%	-15%	49%	EA
Virginia Tech	52%	69%	-17%	23%	ED
Hofstra University (NY)	48%	67%	-19%	41%	EA
National Liberal Arts Colleges					
Tougaloo College (MS)	100%	25%	75%	0%	EA
Dickinson College (PA)	85%	33%	53%	71%	EA, ED
St. Lawrence University (NY)	79%	37%	42%	31%	ED
Wittenberg University (OH)	88%	48%	41%	73%	EA, ED
College of Idaho (ID)	97%	57%	40%	25%	EA
College of the Holy Cross (MA)	73%	34%	40%	47%	ED
Presbyterian College (SC)	87%	48%	39%	71%	EA, ED
Connecticut College	71%	34%	36%	42%	ED
Pitzer College (CA)	55%	19%	36%	28%	ED
Bucknell University (PA)	62%	27%	35%	44%	ED
Gettysburg College (PA)	71%	37%	34%	43%	ED
St. Olaf College (MN)	88%	56%	33%	N/A	ED
Union College (NY)	72%	39%	33%	40%	ED
Denison University (OH)	81%	49%	32%	N/A	ED
Skidmore College (NY)	71%	40%	30%	41%	ED
Wofford College (SC)	80%	51%	29%	51%	ED
College of Wooster (OH)	88%	59%	29%	6%	EA, ED
University of Puget Sound (WA)	92%	63%	29%	14%	ED
University of Richmond (VA)	66%	38%	28%	27%	ED
Juniata College (PA)	83%	56%	28%	71%	EA, ED
Ursinus College (PA)	61%	34%	27%	88%	EA, ED
Beloit College (WI)	91%	64%	27%	42%	EA
Wheaton College (MA)	83%	58%	25%	29%	ED
Lawrence University (WI)	87%	62%	25%	36%	EA, ED
College of St. Benedict (MN)	91%	66%	24%	86%	EA
Occidental College (CA)	65%	43%	23%	8%	ED
St. Mary's College of Maryland	78%	55%	23%	34%	ED
Westmont College (CA)	93%	70%	22%	62%	EA
Kenyon College (OH)	59%	37%	22%	45%	ED

	Early decision and/or early action acceptance rate	Non-early acceptance rate	Difference in acceptance rate	Freshman enrolled through early plans	Type of plan (early decision and/or early action)
Knox College (IL)	87%	65%	22%	47%	EA
Lafayette College (PA)	62%	41%	21%	45%	ED
Drew University (NJ)	95%	74%	21%	7%	ED
Hampshire College (MA)	79%	58%	20%	36%	EA, ED
Willamette University (OR)	78%	58%	20%	8%	EA
Washington and Jefferson College (PA)	42%	23%	20%	97%	EA, ED
St. John's University (MN)	89%	72%	17%	75%	EA
Hobart and William Smith Colleges (NY)	72%	55%	17%	29%	ED
Colorado College	43%	26%	17%	63%	EA, ED
Hanover College (IN)	68%	52%	17%	63%	EA
Southwestern University (TX)	79%	63%	16%	N/A	EA, ED
Stonehill College (MA)	65%	52%	14%	48%	EA, ED
Wabash College (IN)	53%	40%	13%	61%	EA, ED
Reed College (OR)	51%	40%	12%	N/A	ED
Lewis & Clark College (OR)	74%	62%	11%	35%	EA
Albion College (MI)	83%	75%	8%	52%	EA
Earlham College (IN)	79%	72%	7%	49%	EA, ED
College of the Atlantic (ME)	79%	74%	5%	32%	ED
Washington College (MD)	76%	72%	5%	10%	EA, ED
Furman University (SC)	71%	67%	4%	34%	ED
Mount Holyoke College (MA)	61%	58%	4%	19%	ED
St. Mary's College (IN)	87%	86%	1%	18%	ED
Agnes Scott College (GA)	54%	44%	10%	22%	EA
Nebraska Wesleyan University	88%	79%	10%	52%	EA
Austin College (TX)	80%	79%	1%	42%	EA
Smith College (MA)	56%	47%	9%	23%	ED
Allegheny College (PA)	66%	66%	0%	9%	ED
Wheaton College (IL)	69%	74%	-5%	56%	EA
Grove City College (PA)	60%	65%	-5%	51%	ED
Cornell College (IA)	42%	49%	-6%	82%	EA, ED
Sewanee–University of the South (TN)	59%	69%	-10%	N/A	ED
Transylvania University (KY)	78%	88%	-10%	65%	EA
Rhodes College (TN)	31%	43%	-12%	20%	EA, ED
Kalamazoo College (MI)	66%	78%	-12%	56%	EA, ED
Bennington College (VT)	47%	68%	-21%	21%	EA, ED

Regional Universities (North)

Bentley University (MA)	62%	29%	34%	66%	EA, ED
Loyola University Maryland	81%	49%	32%	66%	EA
Emerson College (MA)	60%	36%	25%	51%	EA
Marist College (NY)	46%	26%	19%	67%	EA, ED
College of New Jersey	47%	46%	1%	9%	ED
Villanova University (PA)	45%	47%	-2%	31%	EA
Fairfield University (CT)	59%	70%	-11%	41%	EA

Regional Universities (South)

Elon University (NC)	80%	47%	33%	25%	EA, ED
Rollins College (FL)	76%	60%	16%	N/A	ED
College of Charleston (SC)	70%	69%	0%	56%	EA

Where applying early may help you most—or not

	Early decision and/or early action acceptance rate	Non-early acceptance rate	Difference in acceptance rate	Freshman enrolled through early plans	Type of plan (early decision and/or early action)
Regional Universities (Midwest)					
University of Evansville (IN)	92%	69%	22%	75%	EA
Valparaiso University (IN)	96%	88%	9%	43%	EA
Butler University (IN)	80%	77%	3%	79%	EA
Regional Universities (West)					
Seattle University	78%	61%	17%	42%	EA
Loyola Marymount University (CA)	71%	56%	15%	29%	EA
Mills College (CA)	68%	54%	15%	31%	EA
Santa Clara University (CA)	69%	56%	13%	33%	EA
Chapman University (CA)	64%	52%	12%	52%	EA
University of Dallas	96%	90%	6%	37%	EA
California Polytechnic State University–San Luis Obispo	23%	39%	-16%	N/A	ED
Regional Colleges (North)					
United States Coast Guard Academy (CT)	28%	22%	6%	50%	EA

Selective Schools

	Early decision and/or early action acceptance rate	Non-early acceptance rate	Difference in acceptance rate	Freshman enrolled through early plans	Type of plan (early decision and/or early action)
National Universities					
Howard University (DC)	72%	49%	23%	34%	EA, ED
University of Rhode Island	90%	71%	19%	68%	EA
Adelphi University (NY)	83%	65%	18%	33%	EA
University of Maryland–Baltimore County	82%	64%	17%	29%	EA
George Mason University (VA)	77%	60%	16%	27%	EA
Pace University (NY)	88%	74%	14%	30%	EA
Old Dominion University (VA)	75%	69%	5%	56%	EA
University of San Francisco	78%	69%	9%	28%	EA
George Fox University (OR)	62%	71%	-9%	27%	EA
University of New Hampshire	63%	78%	-15%	36%	EA
Duquesne University (PA)	60%	83%	-23%	28%	EA, ED
National Liberal Arts Colleges					
Gordon College (MA)	94%	57%	37%	42%	EA, ED
Morehouse College (GA)	100%	66%	34%	N/A	EA, ED
Russell Sage College (NY)	98%	70%	28%	34%	EA
Linfield College (OR)	98%	77%	22%	32%	EA
Spelman College (GA)	55%	33%	22%	58%	EA, ED
Purchase College–SUNY	47%	27%	20%	2%	ED
Wells College (NY)	77%	58%	19%	67%	EA, ED

	Early decision and/or early action acceptance rate	Non-early acceptance rate	Difference in acceptance rate	Freshman enrolled through early plans	Type of plan (early decision and/or early action)
Virginia Military Institute	68%	53%	15%	33%	ED
Guilford College (NC)	66%	53%	13%	69%	EA
Goucher College (MD)	80%	69%	11%	44%	EA
Massachusetts College of Liberal Arts	76%	69%	7%	22%	EA
Maryville College (TN)	77%	73%	5%	N/A	EA, ED
Moravian College (PA)	79%	75%	4%	N/A	ED
McDaniel College (MD)	80%	78%	2%	55%	EA
Hartwick College (NY)	92%	91%	1%	N/A	ED
St. Michael's College (VT)	77%	85%	-7%	45%	EA
Randolph-Macon College (VA)	56%	65%	-9%	68%	EA
Hollins University (VA)	66%	93%	-26%	16%	ED
Roanoke College (VA)	33%	70%	-37%	N/A	ED

Regional Universities (North)

	Early decision and/or early action acceptance rate	Non-early acceptance rate	Difference in acceptance rate	Freshman enrolled through early plans	Type of plan (early decision and/or early action)
Framingham State College (MA)	100%	62%	38%	20%	EA
SUNY–Fredonia	82%	49%	33%	7%	ED
La Salle University (PA)	83%	56%	27%	38%	EA
St. Joseph's University (PA)	92%	69%	22%	65%	EA
Assumption College (MA)	92%	72%	20%	43%	EA
College of St. Rose (NY)	80%	61%	19%	63%	EA
Bryant University (RI)	71%	52%	19%	25%	EA, ED
Le Moyne College (NY)	85%	67%	18%	6%	ED
Wheelock College (MA)	88%	71%	17%	34%	EA
SUNY–Plattsburgh	64%	48%	15%	4%	ED
Buffalo State College–SUNY	58%	43%	15%	4%	ED
Monmouth University (NJ)	70%	56%	14%	51%	EA
SUNY College–Oneonta	49%	36%	13%	39%	EA
Nazareth College (NY)	84%	71%	13%	60%	EA, ED
Manhattan College (NY)	76%	65%	11%	N/A	ED
Niagara University (NY)	88%	80%	8%	5%	EA
Mount St. Mary's University (MD)	90%	84%	6%	14%	EA
Salve Regina University (RI)	67%	63%	5%	41%	EA
Simmons College (MA)	57%	57%	-0%	59%	EA
St. John Fisher College (NY)	63%	65%	-2%	9%	ED
University of Massachusetts–Dartmouth	65%	68%	-4%	2%	EA
Springfield College (MA)	65%	69%	-4%	10%	ED
Wagner College (NY)	59%	70%	-11%	13%	ED
Rider University (NJ)	66%	77%	-12%	19%	EA, ED
Suffolk University (MA)	58%	92%	-34%	29%	EA

Regional Universities (South)

	Early decision and/or early action acceptance rate	Non-early acceptance rate	Difference in acceptance rate	Freshman enrolled through early plans	Type of plan (early decision and/or early action)
Stetson University (FL)	87%	53%	34%	4%	ED
Lynchburg College (VA)	51%	66%	-16%	N/A	ED
Hampton University (VA)	35%	54%	-19%	22%	EA
Western Carolina University (NC)	26%	50%	-24%	51%	EA
Georgia College & State University	39%	72%	-33%	15%	EA
Longwood University (VA)	44%	89%	-45%	24%	EA

Regional Universities (Midwest)

	Early decision and/or early action acceptance rate	Non-early acceptance rate	Difference in acceptance rate	Freshman enrolled through early plans	Type of plan (early decision and/or early action)
Hamline University (MN)	84%	69%	15%	44%	EA

Regional Universities (West)

	Early decision and/or early action acceptance rate	Non-early acceptance rate	Difference in acceptance rate	Freshman enrolled through early plans	Type of plan (early decision and/or early action)
Whitworth University (WA)	58%	50%	9%	47%	EA
Prescott College (AZ)	75%	81%	-6%	N/A	ED
Concordia University (CA)	53%	73%	-20%	41%	EA
St. Mary's College of California	62%	85%	-24%	22%	EA

Where applying early may help you most—or not

Selective Schools, continued

	Early decision and/or early action acceptance rate	Non-early acceptance rate	Difference in acceptance rate	Freshman enrolled through early plans	Type of plan (early decision and/or early action)
Regional Colleges (North)					
Maine Maritime Academy	96%	60%	36%	24%	ED
Champlain College (VT)	70%	79%	-9%	39%	ED
Elmira College (NY)	37%	81%	-44%	8%	ED
Regional Colleges (South)					
Flagler College (FL)	60%	39%	21%	N/A	ED
Florida Southern College	86%	69%	17%	11%	ED
High Point University (NC)	74%	68%	6%	74%	EA, ED
Regional Colleges (Midwest)					
Carthage College (WI)	72%	76%	-4%	22%	EA

Less Selective Schools

	Early decision and/or early action acceptance rate	Non-early acceptance rate	Difference in acceptance rate	Freshman enrolled through early plans	Type of plan (early decision and/or early action)
National Liberal Arts Colleges					
Bloomfield College (NJ)	64%	78%	-14%	6%	EA
Regional Universities (North)					
Sage Colleges–Albany (NY)	100%	62%	38%	8%	EA
Regional Colleges (North)					
Curry College (MA)	38%	76%	-38%	N/A	ED

Schools whose freshmen are least (and most) likely to return

As many as one in three first-year students doesn't make it back for sophomore year. The reasons run the gamut, of course, from family problems to loneliness to academic struggles to a lack of money. If schools you're considering have a low freshman retention rate, you'll want to ask the admissions office why. Some colleges do a great job of taking care of their freshmen; some don't. The retention rates shown below, from lowest to highest, are the average proportion of freshmen entering between 2005 and 2008 who returned the following fall. The freshman enrollment is for the fall 2009 entering class.

National Universities

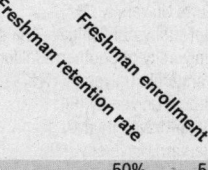

School	Freshman retention rate	Freshman enrollment
Golden Gate University (CA)	50%	5
University of Bridgeport (CT)	52%	440
Idaho State University	57%	1,906
Texas A&M University–Commerce	59%	574
Cleveland State University	61%	1,185
Texas A&M University–Kingsville	61%	1,086
Barry University (FL)	63%	648
Nova Southeastern University (FL)	64%	579
University of Texas–Arlington	64%	2,319
South Carolina State University	65%	723
Spalding University (KY)	65%	N/A
Indiana State University	67%	2,035
Morgan State University (MD)	67%	1,283
Indiana Univ.-Purdue Univ.–Indianapolis	68%	3,019
Portland State University (OR)	68%	1,675
Southern Illinois University–Carbondale	68%	2,450
Tennessee State University	68%	1,338
University of Akron (OH)	68%	4,252
University of Northern Colorado	68%	2,351
East Tennessee State University	69%	2,099
Immaculata University (PA)	69%	196
Regent University (VA)	69%	106
University of Texas–El Paso	69%	2,516
University of Toledo (OH)	69%	4,371
Wilmington University (DE)	69%	695
Clark Atlanta University	70%	703
Long Island Univ.–C.W. Post Campus (NY)	70%	855
University of Missouri–St. Louis	70%	525
Wichita State University (KS)	70%	1,390
Wright State University (OH)	70%	2,364
Texas Woman's University	71%	742
Trevecca Nazarene University (TN)	71%	244
University of Colorado–Denver	71%	1,053
Wayne State University (MI)	71%	3,046
Montana State University	72%	2,316
Oakland University (MI)	72%	2,466
Trinity International University (IL)	72%	156
University of Missouri–Kansas City	72%	1,004
University of Montana	72%	1,886
University of New Orleans	72%	1,259
University of Wisconsin–Milwaukee	72%	4,100
Jackson State University (MS)	73%	853
Louisiana Tech University	73%	1,507
North Carolina A&T State University	73%	1,898
Union Institute and University (OH)	73%	28
University of Hartford (CT)	73%	1,394
University of South Dakota	73%	1,118
University of Southern Mississippi	73%	1,602
Widener University (PA)	73%	720
Kent State University (OH)	74%	4,151
University of Louisiana–Lafayette	74%	2,606
University of Massachusetts–Boston	74%	987
University of Memphis	74%	2,256
University of Nevada–Las Vegas	74%	3,236

School	Freshman retention rate	Freshman enrollment
University of Wyoming	74%	1,594
Utah State University	74%	2,839
Western Michigan University	74%	3,193
Bowling Green State University (OH)	75%	3,163
Florida Atlantic University	75%	2,569
Florida Institute of Technology	75%	539
Indiana University of Pennsylvania	75%	3,008
Pace University (NY)	75%	1,672
St. Mary's University of Minnesota	75%	330
University of Alaska–Fairbanks	75%	1,008
University of West Florida	75%	1,110
New Mexico State University	76%	2,878
Northern Illinois University	76%	3,033
University of Idaho	76%	1,780
University of North Carolina–Greensboro	76%	2,511
University of North Texas	76%	3,327
Ball State University (IN)	77%	4,178
Central Michigan University	77%	3,691
East Carolina University (NC)	77%	N/A
Old Dominion University (VA)	77%	2,755
South Dakota State University	77%	2,135
University of Alabama–Huntsville	77%	802
University of New Mexico	77%	3,409
University of North Carolina–Charlotte	77%	3,187
University of North Dakota	77%	1,992
George Fox University (OR)	78%	413
Hofstra University (NY)	78%	1,568
Oral Roberts University (OK)	78%	498
St. John's University (NY)	78%	3,108
University of Alabama–Birmingham	78%	1,517
University of Hawaii–Manoa	78%	1,922
University of Houston	78%	3,295
University of Louisville (KY)	78%	2,478
University of Massachusetts–Lowell	78%	1,522
University of Nevada–Reno	78%	2,172
Adelphi University (NY)	79%	1,005
Georgia Southern University	79%	3,539
Kansas State University	79%	3,522
Oklahoma State University	79%	3,148
Pacific University (OR)	79%	349
University of Arizona	79%	6,966
University of Illinois–Chicago	79%	3,147
University of Kentucky	79%	4,153
University of Maine	79%	1,731
Andrews University (MI)	80%	377
Arizona State University	80%	9,344
Florida International University	80%	2,013
North Dakota State University	80%	2,459
Ohio University	80%	4,072
University of Kansas	80%	3,942
University of Mississippi	80%	2,576
University of Rhode Island	80%	3,055
West Virginia University	80%	4,589
Azusa Pacific University (CA)	81%	1,022

School	Freshman retention rate	Freshman enrollment
Catholic University of America (DC)	81%	814
New School (NY)	81%	1,152
University of La Verne (CA)	81%	333
University of Utah	81%	2,867
Colorado State University	82%	4,322
Florida A&M University	82%	2,444
Georgia State University	82%	2,934
Michigan Technological University	82%	1,160
New Jersey Institute of Technology	82%	994
Oregon State University	82%	3,436
Polytechnic Inst. of New York Univ. (NY)	82%	366
San Diego State University	82%	4,273
Texas Tech University	82%	4,586
University of Texas–Dallas	82%	1,343
Mississippi State University	83%	2,450
Seton Hall University (NJ)	83%	1,139
University of Arkansas	83%	2,919
University of Cincinnati	83%	3,647
University of Iowa	83%	4,063
University of Oregon	83%	3,839
University of San Francisco	83%	1,073
University of the Pacific (CA)	83%	894
Virginia Commonwealth University	83%	3,665
Washington State University	83%	3,668
Brigham Young University–Provo (UT)	84%	5,421
DePaul University (IL)	84%	2,531
Drexel University (PA)	84%	2,346
Illinois State University	84%	3,033
Iowa State University	84%	4,356
Louisiana State University–Baton Rouge	84%	4,789
Loyola University Chicago	84%	2,076
Samford University (AL)	84%	733
St. Louis University	84%	1,597
University at Albany–SUNY	84%	2,333
University of Colorado–Boulder	84%	5,555
University of Nebraska–Lincoln	84%	3,986
University of Oklahoma	84%	3,760
University of South Florida	84%	3,857
University of Tennessee	84%	3,717
Baylor University (TX)	85%	3,098
Biola University (CA)	85%	792
Clarkson University (NY)	85%	777
George Mason University (VA)	85%	2,656
Texas Christian University	85%	1,823
University of Alabama	85%	5,116
University of Central Florida	85%	6,397
University of Maryland–Baltimore County	85%	1,532
University of Massachusetts–Amherst	85%	4,124
University of Missouri	85%	5,593
University of Vermont	85%	2,619
Auburn University (AL)	86%	3,918
Colorado School of Mines	86%	880
Howard University (DC)	86%	1,598
Purdue University–West Lafayette (IN)	86%	6,171

Schools whose freshmen are least (and most) likely to return

National Universities, continued

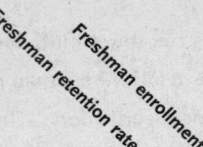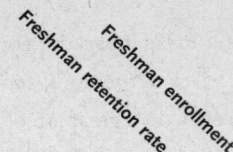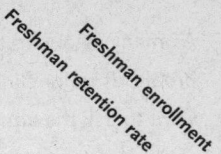

School	Freshman retention rate	Freshman enrollment
SUNY Coll. of Environ. Sci. and Forestry	86%	283
University of California–Riverside	86%	4,299
University of San Diego	86%	1,082
Duquesne University (PA)	87%	1,432
Illinois Institute of Technology	87%	459
Missouri University of Science & Tech.	87%	1,108
Rutgers–Newark	87%	914
Temple University (PA)	87%	4,203
University of Dayton (OH)	87%	1,707
University of Denver	87%	1,207
University of New Hampshire	87%	3,004
University of South Carolina	87%	3,917
University of Tulsa (OK)	87%	690
American University (DC)	88%	1,533
Southern Methodist University (TX)	88%	1,329
University at Buffalo–SUNY	88%	3,194
University of Minnesota–Twin Cities	88%	5,400
University of St. Thomas (MN)	88%	1,352
Clark University (MA)	89%	550
Florida State University	89%	5,967
Indiana University–Bloomington	89%	7,327
Pepperdine University (CA)	89%	766
SUNY–Stony Brook	89%	2,806
Tulane University (LA)	89%	1,502
University of California–Santa Cruz	89%	3,214
Binghamton University–SUNY	90%	2,123
Fordham University (NY)	90%	1,835
Marquette University (WI)	90%	1,952
Miami University–Oxford (OH)	90%	3,236
North Carolina State University–Raleigh	90%	4,638
Stevens Institute of Technology (NJ)	90%	561
University of Miami (FL)	90%	2,006
Boston University	91%	N/A
Case Western Reserve University (OH)	91%	966
Clemson University (SC)	91%	3,339
George Washington University (DC)	91%	2,592
Michigan State University	91%	7,416
Northeastern University (MA)	91%	2,833
Rutgers–New Brunswick	91%	5,835
Syracuse University (NY)	91%	3,261
University of California–Davis	91%	4,412
University of California–Santa Barbara	91%	4,583
University of Delaware	91%	4,223
University of Pittsburgh	91%	3,642
Virginia Tech	91%	5,050
Yeshiva University (NY)	91%	809
New York University	92%	4,998
Texas A&M University–College Station	92%	8,071
University of Texas–Austin	92%	7,243
Georgia Institute of Technology	93%	2,660
Ohio State University–Columbus	93%	6,739
Pennsylvania State Univ.–University Park	93%	6,560
Rensselaer Polytechnic Institute (NY)	93%	1,337
University of Connecticut	93%	3,221
University of Illinois–Urbana-Champaign	93%	6,991
University of Maryland–College Park	93%	4,202
University of Washington	93%	5,338
Worcester Polytechnic Institute (MA)	93%	925
Brandeis University (MA)	94%	781
Lehigh University (PA)	94%	1,193
University of California–Irvine	94%	4,030
University of California–San Diego	94%	3,749
University of Georgia	94%	4,684
University of Wisconsin–Madison	94%	5,680
Wake Forest University (NC)	94%	1,200
Boston College	95%	2,171
Carnegie Mellon University (PA)	95%	1,423
College of William and Mary (VA)	95%	1,395
Emory University (GA)	95%	1,315
University of Florida	95%	6,253
University of Rochester (NY)	95%	1,087
Cornell University (NY)	96%	3,181
Georgetown University (DC)	96%	1,555
Tufts University (MA)	96%	1,314
University of Michigan–Ann Arbor	96%	6,079
University of Southern California	96%	2,869
Vanderbilt University (TN)	96%	1,599
Brown University (RI)	97%	1,494
Duke University (NC)	97%	1,723
Harvard University (MA)	97%	1,663
Johns Hopkins University (MD)	97%	1,349
Northwestern University (IL)	97%	2,128
Rice University (TX)	97%	894
University of California–Berkeley	97%	4,356
University of California–Los Angeles	97%	4,472
University of North Carolina–Chapel Hill	97%	3,960
University of Virginia	97%	3,246
Washington University in St. Louis	97%	1,510
California Institute of Technology	98%	252
Dartmouth College (NH)	98%	1,094
Massachusetts Institute of Technology	98%	1,072
Princeton University (NJ)	98%	1,320
Stanford University (CA)	98%	1,694
University of Chicago	98%	1,336
University of Notre Dame (IN)	98%	2,064
University of Pennsylvania	98%	2,475
Columbia University (NY)	99%	1,419
Yale University (CT)	99%	1,307

National Liberal Arts Colleges

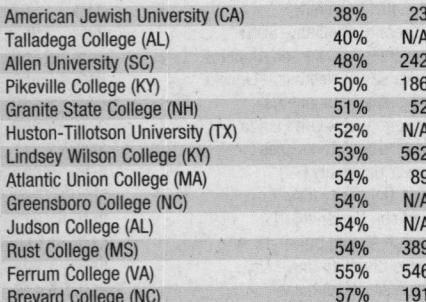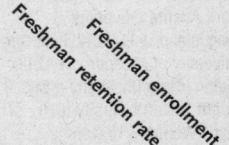

School	Freshman retention rate	Freshman enrollment
American Jewish University (CA)	38%	23
Talladega College (AL)	40%	N/A
Allen University (SC)	48%	242
Pikeville College (KY)	50%	186
Granite State College (NH)	51%	52
Huston-Tillotson University (TX)	52%	N/A
Lindsey Wilson College (KY)	53%	562
Atlantic Union College (MA)	54%	89
Greensboro College (NC)	54%	N/A
Judson College (AL)	54%	N/A
Rust College (MS)	54%	389
Ferrum College (VA)	55%	546
Brevard College (NC)	57%	191
Fort Lewis College (CO)	58%	802
Mesa State College (CO)	58%	1,602
Paine College (GA)	58%	274
Jarvis Christian College (TX)	59%	119
Thiel College (PA)	60%	272
University of Hawaii–West Oahu	60%	77
Burlington College (VT)	61%	24
Kentucky Wesleyan College	61%	227
Lambuth University (TN)	61%	N/A
Western State College of Colorado	61%	499
Dillard University (LA)	62%	326
Marymount Manhattan College (NY)	63%	516
University of Wisconsin–Parkside	63%	890
Colorado State University–Pueblo	64%	1,054
Huntingdon College (AL)	64%	237
Sterling College (KS)	64%	187
Franklin Pierce University (NH)	65%	388
Johnson C. Smith University (NC)	65%	282
Olivet College (MI)	65%	285
Peace College (NC)	65%	151
Pine Manor College (MA)	65%	142
St. Andrews Presbyterian College (NC)	65%	147
Carson-Newman College (TN)	66%	513
Green Mountain College (VT)	66%	221
Lane College (TN)	66%	692
Metropolitan State College of Denver	66%	2,205
Sierra Nevada College (NV)	66%	88
Bennett College (NC)	67%	232
Emory and Henry College (VA)	67%	291
Lyon College (AR)	67%	217
McPherson College (KS)	67%	137
University of Hawaii–Hilo	67%	N/A
University of Virginia–Wise	67%	406
Virginia Wesleyan College	67%	319
Bethany College (WV)	68%	283
Simpson University (CA)	68%	145
Texas Lutheran University	68%	346
Bloomfield College (NJ)	69%	483
Brigham Young University–Hawaii	69%	N/A
California State University–Monterey Bay	69%	949
Coastal Carolina University (SC)	69%	1,775
Evangel University (MO)	69%	432
North Greenville University (SC)	69%	494
Shimer College (IL)	69%	N/A
Stephens College (MO)	70%	269
Warren Wilson College (NC)	70%	N/A
Wingate University (NC)	70%	375
Hastings College (NE)	71%	332
Bryn Athyn Coll. of the New Church (PA)	72%	70
Concordia College (NY)	72%	N/A

	Freshman retention rate	Freshman enrollment
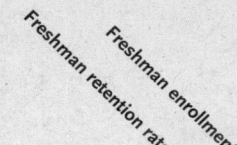		

College	Freshman retention rate	Freshman enrollment
Maryville College (TN)	72%	303
Northland College (WI)	72%	135
Randolph College (VA)	72%	135
Thomas More Coll. of Liberal Arts (NH)	72%	24
Tougaloo College (MS)	72%	234
Wesleyan College (GA)	72%	99
Bethel College (KS)	73%	92
Guilford College (NC)	73%	448
Hollins University (VA)	73%	198
Monmouth College (IL)	73%	440
University of Maine–Machias	73%	105
Albright College (PA)	74%	541
Bridgewater College (VA)	74%	497
Hartwick College (NY)	74%	402
Massachusetts College of Liberal Arts	74%	351
SUNY College–Old Westbury	74%	421
Wells College (NY)	74%	145
West Virginia Wesleyan College	74%	399
Albertus Magnus College (CT)	75%	168
Meredith College (NC)	75%	481
Randolph-Macon College (VA)	75%	362
University of Wisconsin–Green Bay	75%	1,046
Baker University (KS)	76%	257
Berry College (GA)	76%	569
Centenary College of Louisiana	76%	N/A
Clarke University (IA)	76%	148
Roanoke College (VA)	76%	560
Sweet Briar College (VA)	76%	157
Wisconsin Lutheran College	76%	202
Carroll College (MT)	77%	N/A
Doane College (NE)	77%	312
Fisk University (TN)	77%	92
Illinois College	77%	225
Merrimack College (MA)	77%	554
Birmingham-Southern College (AL)	78%	424
Eckerd College (FL)	78%	505
Millikin University (IL)	78%	542
Oglethorpe University (GA)	78%	232
Russell Sage College (NY)	78%	128
University of Mount Union (OH)	78%	578
Wartburg College (IA)	78%	480
Whittier College (CA)	78%	358
William Jewell College (MO)	78%	282
Wittenberg University (OH)	78%	488
Cedar Crest College (PA)	79%	196
College of Idaho (ID)	79%	306
Eastern Mennonite University (VA)	79%	219
Georgetown College (KY)	79%	378
Hampden-Sydney College (VA)	79%	295
Hiram College (OH)	79%	293
Lycoming College (PA)	79%	386
Millsaps College (MS)	79%	283
Alma College (MI)	80%	396
Central College (IA)	80%	443
Christopher Newport University (VA)	80%	1,213
Goucher College (MD)	80%	400
Lake Forest College (IL)	80%	355
Purchase College–SUNY	80%	694
University of North Carolina–Asheville	80%	641
Berea College (KY)	81%	392
Coe College (IA)	81%	325
Hampshire College (MA)	81%	373
Hanover College (IN)	81%	293
Nebraska Wesleyan University	81%	393
Ohio Wesleyan University	81%	498

	Freshman retention rate	Freshman enrollment
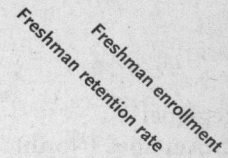		

College	Freshman retention rate	Freshman enrollment
Salem College (NC)	81%	N/A
Sarah Lawrence College (NY)	81%	365
Agnes Scott College (GA)	82%	237
Asbury University (KY)	82%	315
Concordia College–Moorhead (MN)	82%	726
Drew University (NJ)	82%	506
Linfield College (OR)	82%	423
Simpson College (IA)	82%	390
St. Norbert College (WI)	82%	545
Transylvania University (KY)	82%	283
Virginia Military Institute	82%	455
Westminster College (MO)	82%	311
Austin College (TX)	83%	413
College of the Atlantic (ME)	83%	76
Cornell College (IA)	83%	335
Earlham College (IN)	83%	292
Moravian College (PA)	83%	380
Washington College (MD)	83%	378
Goshen College (IN)	84%	238
Houghton College (NY)	84%	287
McDaniel College (MD)	84%	425
New College of Florida	84%	218
Presbyterian College (SC)	84%	364
Southwestern University (TX)	84%	375
Augustana College (IL)	85%	616
Beacon College (FL)	85%	28
Juniata College (PA)	85%	366
Lewis & Clark College (OR)	85%	498
Morehouse College (GA)	85%	655
St. Anselm College (NH)	85%	531
St. Mary's College (IN)	85%	435
St. Vincent College (PA)	85%	448
Thomas Aquinas College (CA)	85%	102
University of Puget Sound (WA)	85%	721
Albion College (MI)	86%	434
Bard College (NY)	86%	505
Bennington College (VT)	86%	197
Hobart and William Smith Colleges (NY)	86%	549
Luther College (IA)	86%	657
Ripon College (WI)	86%	249
Susquehanna University (PA)	86%	624
University of Minnesota–Morris	86%	405
Washington and Jefferson College (PA)	86%	393
Wheaton College (MA)	86%	424
Calvin College (MI)	87%	945
College of Wooster (OH)	87%	481
Gordon College (MA)	87%	382
Hendrix College (AR)	87%	412
Siena College (NY)	87%	783
Wabash College (IN)	87%	247
Westminster College (PA)	87%	451
Westmont College (CA)	87%	320
Willamette University (OR)	87%	541
Allegheny College (PA)	88%	583
Rhodes College (TN)	88%	432
Stonehill College (MA)	88%	684
Beloit College (WI)	89%	332
DePauw University (IN)	89%	717
Hillsdale College (MI)	89%	375
Hope College (MI)	89%	803
Reed College (OR)	89%	368
Sewanee–University of the South (TN)	89%	402
Spelman College (GA)	89%	553
St. Lawrence University (NY)	89%	580
St. Michael's College (VT)	89%	475

College	Freshman retention rate	Freshman enrollment
Ursinus College (PA)	89%	513
College of St. Benedict (MN)	90%	551
Connecticut College	90%	502
Denison University (OH)	90%	649
Gustavus Adolphus College (MN)	90%	620
Knox College (IL)	90%	359
Lawrence University (WI)	90%	352
St. John's University (MN)	90%	461
St. Mary's College of Maryland	90%	488
Wofford College (SC)	90%	392
Centre College (KY)	91%	333
Gettysburg College (PA)	91%	739
Kalamazoo College (MI)	91%	391
Pitzer College (CA)	91%	256
Smith College (MA)	91%	665
Trinity College (CT)	91%	573
United States Military Academy (NY)	91%	1,262
University of Richmond (VA)	91%	918
Dickinson College (PA)	92%	581
Franklin and Marshall College (PA)	92%	629
Furman University (SC)	92%	656
Grove City College (PA)	92%	633
Illinois Wesleyan University	92%	518
Mount Holyoke College (MA)	92%	574
Occidental College (CA)	92%	576
Scripps College (CA)	92%	203
Union College (NY)	92%	520
Bryn Mawr College (PA)	93%	362
Kenyon College (OH)	93%	469
Macalester College (MN)	93%	565
Muhlenberg College (PA)	93%	577
Principia College (IL)	93%	111
St. Olaf College (MN)	93%	778
Colby College (ME)	94%	480
Colgate University (NY)	94%	750
Grinnell College (IA)	94%	378
Harvey Mudd College (CA)	94%	207
Lafayette College (PA)	94%	616
Oberlin College (OH)	94%	806
Skidmore College (NY)	94%	664
Washington and Lee University (VA)	94%	472
Whitman College (WA)	94%	396
Barnard College (NY)	95%	577
Bates College (ME)	95%	469
Bucknell University (PA)	95%	920
College of the Holy Cross (MA)	95%	747
Colorado College	95%	526
Hamilton College (NY)	95%	466
Wellesley College (MA)	95%	589
Wesleyan University (CT)	95%	745
Wheaton College (IL)	95%	620
Claremont McKenna College (CA)	96%	282
Davidson College (NC)	96%	491
Haverford College (PA)	96%	323
Middlebury College (VT)	96%	603
Vassar College (NY)	96%	660
Carleton College (MN)	97%	529
Swarthmore College (PA)	97%	394
United States Naval Academy (MD)	97%	1,251
Williams College (MA)	97%	546
Amherst College (MA)	98%	467
Bowdoin College (ME)	98%	494
Pomona College (CA)	98%	390

Schools whose freshmen are least (and most) likely to return

Regional Universities (North)

School	Freshman retention rate	Freshman enrollment
Cambridge College (MA)	46%	99
Metropolitan College of New York	46%	126
University of the District of Columbia	55%	940
Mercy College (NY)	58%	926
Cheyney University of Pennsylvania	59%	607
Coppin State University (MD)	61%	610
Delaware State University	63%	757
Gratz College (PA)	63%	N/A
Dowling College (NY)	64%	544
Anna Maria College (MA)	65%	N/A
La Roche College (PA)	65%	193
University of Southern Maine	66%	924
American International College (MA)	67%	350
Chestnut Hill College (PA)	67%	273
Dominican College (NY)	67%	375
Sage Colleges–Albany (NY)	67%	105
University of Maryland–Eastern Shore	67%	921
Utica College (NY)	67%	565
Cabrini College (PA)	68%	359
Carlow University (PA)	69%	N/A
Castleton State College (VT)	69%	515
Lock Haven University of Pennsylvania	69%	1,202
SUNY Institute of Tech.–Utica/Rome	69%	203
Chatham University (PA)	70%	131
College of St. Joseph (VT)	70%	48
Husson University (ME)	70%	532
Lincoln University (PA)	70%	579
Medaille College (NY)	70%	402
Wheelock College (MA)	70%	191
Alvernia University (PA)	71%	328
Johnson and Wales University (RI)	71%	2,299
Mansfield University of Pennsylvania	71%	717
Mount St. Mary College (NY)	71%	478
Western Connecticut State University	71%	1,019
D'Youville College (NY)	72%	155
Daemen College (NY)	72%	402
Edinboro University of Pennsylvania	72%	1,440
Frostburg State University (MD)	72%	1,041
Lesley University (MA)	72%	385
Rosemont College (PA)	72%	177
Suffolk University (MA)	72%	1,254
Bowie State University (MD)	73%	642
Caldwell College (NJ)	73%	272
Clarion University of Pennsylvania	73%	1,449
Framingham State College (MA)	73%	724
Neumann University (PA)	73%	520
New Jersey City University	73%	763
New York Institute of Technology	73%	1,103
Point Park University (PA)	73%	530
Regis College (MA)	73%	N/A
Salem State College (MA)	73%	994
CUNY–John Jay College of Criminal Justice	74%	2,873
CUNY–Lehman College	74%	774
College of Mount St. Vincent (NY)	74%	390
Fairleigh Dickinson University (NJ)	74%	1,357
Georgian Court University (NJ)	74%	253
Rivier College (NH)	74%	236
SUNY College–Potsdam	74%	835
Shippensburg University of Pennsylvania	74%	1,679
Southern New Hampshire University	74%	471
St. Peter's College (NJ)	74%	539
St. Thomas Aquinas College (NY)	74%	295
Centenary College (NJ)	75%	271
College of Notre Dame of Maryland	75%	N/A
Eastern Connecticut State University	75%	981
Fitchburg State College (MA)	75%	783
Robert Morris University (PA)	75%	726
St. Joseph College (CT)	75%	184
University of Massachusetts–Dartmouth	75%	1,511
University of New Haven (CT)	75%	1,271
Waynesburg University (PA)	75%	386
Buffalo State College–SUNY	76%	1,524
Eastern University (PA)	76%	408
Manhattanville College (NY)	76%	492
Norwich University (VT)	76%	684
Philadelphia University	76%	720
Rhode Island College	76%	1,253
University of New England (ME)	76%	607
Western New England College (MA)	76%	689
Worcester State College (MA)	76%	695
Southern Connecticut State University	77%	1,244
Westfield State College (MA)	77%	1,140
William Paterson Univ. of New Jersey	77%	1,453
Arcadia University (PA)	78%	534
Bridgewater State College (MA)	78%	1,479
CUNY–Brooklyn College	78%	977
California University of Pennsylvania	78%	951
Central Connecticut State University	78%	1,288
East Stroudsburg Univ. of Pennsylvania	78%	1,358
Emmanuel College (MA)	78%	424
Gwynedd-Mercy College (PA)	78%	315
Kean University (NJ)	78%	1,548
King's College (PA)	78%	496
Kutztown University of Pennsylvania	78%	1,989
Monmouth University (NJ)	78%	998
Plymouth State University (NH)	78%	969
Salve Regina University (RI)	78%	505
St. Joseph's College (ME)	78%	N/A
Wilkes University (PA)	78%	532
Alfred University (NY)	79%	N/A
Holy Family University (PA)	79%	382
Keene State College (NH)	79%	1,188
Mercyhurst College (PA)	79%	669
Niagara University (NY)	79%	677
SUNY–Oswego	79%	1,391
Slippery Rock University of Pennsylvania	79%	1,545
Bloomsburg University of Pennsylvania	80%	2,040
CUNY–City College	80%	1,770
Hood College (MD)	80%	251
Marywood University (PA)	80%	473
Mount St. Mary's University (MD)	80%	465
SUNY–Plattsburgh	80%	1,066
Sacred Heart University (CT)	80%	909
St. Bonaventure University (NY)	80%	466
Touro College (NY)	80%	970
Wagner College (NY)	80%	519
CUNY–College of Staten Island	81%	2,685
College of St. Rose (NY)	81%	583
Gannon University (PA)	81%	660
Philadelphia Biblical University	81%	195
Rider University (NJ)	81%	1,026
Rutgers–Camden	81%	435
SUNY College–Cortland	81%	1,167
Salisbury University (MD)	81%	1,276
Assumption College (MA)	82%	515
Canisius College (NY)	82%	708
College of St. Elizabeth (NJ)	82%	N/A
DeSales University (PA)	82%	378
Millersville University of Pennsylvania	82%	1,333
Misericordia University (PA)	82%	381
Montclair State University (NJ)	82%	2,117
Richard Stockton College of New Jersey	82%	870
SUNY College–Oneonta	82%	1,109
Simmons College (MA)	82%	354
Springfield College (MA)	82%	580
Towson University (MD)	82%	2,405
CUNY–Hunter College	83%	2,028
La Salle University (PA)	83%	1,009
Molloy College (NY)	83%	420
Roberts Wesleyan College (NY)	83%	264
CUNY–Queens College	84%	1,712
College at Brockport–SUNY	84%	1,090
Le Moyne College (NY)	84%	608
Nazareth College (NY)	84%	492
Rowan University (NJ)	84%	1,602
St. Francis University (PA)	84%	433
St. John Fisher College (NY)	84%	558
Iona College (NY)	85%	792
SUNY–Fredonia	85%	1,108
West Chester University of Pennsylvania	85%	2,248
Ithaca College (NY)	86%	2,027
Manhattan College (NY)	86%	693
SUNY–New Paltz	86%	1,055
St. Joseph's University (PA)	87%	1,192
Bryant University (RI)	88%	751
Quinnipiac University (CT)	88%	1,587
Ramapo College of New Jersey	88%	937
CUNY–Baruch College	89%	1,442
Emerson College (MA)	89%	766
Fairfield University (CT)	89%	849
Rochester Institute of Technology (NY)	89%	2,611
Loyola University Maryland	90%	968
Marist College (NY)	90%	1,041
University of Scranton (PA)	90%	1,038
SUNY–Geneseo	91%	948
Providence College (RI)	92%	955
Bentley University (MA)	93%	949
College of New Jersey	95%	1,284
Villanova University (PA)	95%	1,643

Regional Universities (South)

	Freshman retention rate	Freshman enrollment
Hodges University (FL)	39%	287
Southern University–New Orleans	43%	437
Mountain State University (WV)	45%	762
University of Arkansas–Monticello	47%	795
Alabama State University	54%	1,221
Cumberland University (TN)	57%	201
Henderson State University (AR)	58%	643
Union College (KY)	58%	191
Auburn University–Montgomery (AL)	59%	872
Grambling State University (LA)	59%	931
Lincoln Memorial University (TN)	60%	N/A
Tusculum College (TN)	60%	N/A
Charleston Southern University (SC)	61%	658
Lynn University (FL)	61%	477
Louisiana State University–Shreveport	62%	N/A
Mississippi Valley State University	62%	415
Bethel College (TN)	63%	1,623
Alcorn State University (MS)	64%	464
Delta State University (MS)	64%	373
Jacksonville University (FL)	64%	669
University of Tennessee–Chattanooga	64%	2,209
Augusta State University (GA)	65%	N/A
Eastern Kentucky University	65%	2,564
Life University (GA)	65%	208
Mary Baldwin College (VA)	65%	227
Southeastern Louisiana University	65%	2,717
Columbia College (SC)	66%	219
Nicholls State University (LA)	66%	1,247
University of North Alabama	66%	1,068
Austin Peay State University (TN)	67%	1,645
Belhaven University (MS)	67%	191
Brenau University (GA)	67%	159
McNeese State University (LA)	67%	1,334
Southern Univ. and A&M College (LA)	67%	N/A
University of Louisiana–Monroe	67%	1,345
Francis Marion University (SC)	68%	794
Mississippi University for Women	68%	212
Northwestern State Univ. of Louisiana	68%	1,340
Pfeiffer University (NC)	68%	240
Southern Wesleyan University (SC)	68%	221
St. Thomas University (FL)	68%	238

	Freshman retention rate	Freshman enrollment
University of West Alabama	68%	310
Alabama Agricultural and Mech. Univ.	69%	1,050
Arkansas State University–Jonesboro	69%	1,725
Arkansas Tech University	69%	1,841
Columbus State University (GA)	69%	1,319
Georgia Southwestern State University	69%	490
Jacksonville State University (AL)	69%	1,252
Morehead State University (KY)	69%	1,260
Northern Kentucky University	69%	2,243
Piedmont College (GA)	69%	239
Shenandoah University (VA)	69%	435
University of North Carolina–Pembroke	69%	1,219
University of South Alabama	69%	1,841
Armstrong Atlantic State University (GA)	70%	1,091
Mississippi College	70%	466
Thomas More College (KY)	70%	312
Campbell University (NC)	71%	739
Marymount University (VA)	71%	390
Palm Beach Atlantic University (FL)	71%	422
St. Leo University (FL)	71%	489
University of Central Arkansas	71%	1,777
University of Tennessee–Martin	71%	1,394
Virginia State University	71%	1,204
Winthrop University (SC)	71%	1,060
Fayetteville State University (NC)	72%	762
Gardner-Webb University (NC)	72%	450
Lee University (TN)	72%	832
Lynchburg College (VA)	72%	593
Marshall University (WV)	72%	1,882
Troy University (AL)	72%	3,322
Valdosta State University (GA)	72%	2,467
Western Carolina University (NC)	72%	1,555
Converse College (SC)	73%	157
Freed-Hardeman University (TN)	73%	408
Murray State University (KY)	73%	1,391
Queens University of Charlotte (NC)	73%	316
Savannah State University (GA)	73%	916
Tennessee Technological University	73%	1,893
University of Mobile (AL)	73%	228
University of West Georgia	73%	2,033
Western Kentucky University	73%	3,387

	Freshman retention rate	Freshman enrollment
Liberty University (VA)	74%	5,005
North Carolina Central University	74%	1,358
University of Montevallo (AL)	74%	429
University of Tampa (FL)	74%	1,419
Wheeling Jesuit University (WV)	74%	264
William Carey University (MS)	74%	136
Embry-Riddle Aeronautical University (FL)	75%	862
Florida Gulf Coast University	75%	1,991
Kennesaw State University (GA)	75%	2,749
Xavier University of Louisiana	75%	765
Southern Polytechnic State Univ. (GA)	76%	539
Albany State University (GA)	77%	732
Lipscomb University (TN)	77%	600
Longwood University (VA)	77%	1,010
Loyola University New Orleans	77%	809
North Georgia College and State Univ.	77%	822
Radford University (VA)	77%	1,447
Christian Brothers University (TN)	78%	301
Hampton University (VA)	78%	1,039
Spring Hill College (AL)	79%	358
Stetson University (FL)	79%	502
University of North Florida	79%	2,227
Bellarmine University (KY)	80%	603
Belmont University (TN)	80%	991
Fort Valley State University (GA)	80%	998
Mercer University (GA)	80%	616
Harding University (AR)	81%	955
Middle Tennessee State University	81%	3,596
College of Charleston (SC)	82%	2,143
The Citadel (SC)	83%	591
Georgia College & State University	84%	1,204
University of Mary Washington (VA)	84%	963
Rollins College (FL)	85%	464
University of North Carolina–Wilmington	85%	1,949
Appalachian State University (NC)	86%	2,743
Union University (TN)	88%	532
Elon University (NC)	90%	1,291
James Madison University (VA)	92%	3,952

Regional Universities (Midwest)

	Freshman retention rate	Freshman enrollment
National-Louis University (IL)	49%	1
Chicago State University	55%	N/A
Friends University (KS)	56%	N/A
Missouri Baptist University	56%	N/A
University of Rio Grande (OH)	57%	488
Calumet College of St. Joseph (IN)	58%	156
Columbia College (MO)	61%	174
Indiana University Southeast	61%	1,094
Indiana Univ.-Purdue Univ.–Fort Wayne	61%	2,222
Ohio Dominican University	61%	283
Fontbonne University (MO)	62%	180
Park University (MO)	62%	205
Rockford College (IL)	62%	92
Indiana University–South Bend	63%	1,206
Roosevelt University (IL)	63%	597

	Freshman retention rate	Freshman enrollment
University of St. Mary (KS)	63%	129
Davenport University (MI)	64%	2,052
Newman University (KS)	64%	176
Purdue University–Calumet (IN)	64%	1,359
Siena Heights University (MI)	64%	208
Tiffin University (OH)	64%	673
Washburn University (KS)	64%	820
Aurora University (IL)	65%	N/A
Indiana University Northwest	65%	954
Silver Lake College (WI)	65%	30
University of Southern Indiana	65%	2,093
Columbia College (IL)	66%	N/A
Minot State University (ND)	66%	438
Northeastern Illinois University	66%	1,070
Upper Iowa University	66%	176

	Freshman retention rate	Freshman enrollment
Fort Hays State University (KS)	67%	N/A
Heidelberg University (OH)	67%	381
Lindenwood University (MO)	67%	1,105
Graceland University (IA)	68%	222
Southwest Minnesota State University	68%	461
Southwestern College (KS)	68%	119
University of Wisconsin–Superior	68%	369
Avila University (MO)	69%	118
Lawrence Technological University (MI)	69%	344
Minnesota State University–Moorhead	69%	1,055
Mount Mary College (WI)	69%	161
Saginaw Valley State University (MI)	69%	N/A
Wayne State College (NE)	69%	665
Bemidji State University (MN)	70%	810
Cornerstone University (MI)	70%	337

Schools whose freshmen are least (and most) likely to return

Regional Universities (Midwest), continued

	Freshman retention rate	Freshman enrollment
Ashland University (OH)	71%	622
Emporia State University (KS)	71%	677
Ferris State University (MI)	71%	2,242
MidAmerica Nazarene University (KS)	71%	196
Muskingum University (OH)	71%	473
Oakland City University (IN)	71%	320
University of St. Francis (IN)	71%	N/A
University of Wisconsin–Stout	71%	1,526
Concordia University–St. Paul (MN)	72%	184
Edgewood College (WI)	72%	287
Southeast Missouri State University	72%	1,805
Southern Illinois University–Edwardsville	72%	1,950
Southwest Baptist University (MO)	72%	N/A
St. Cloud State University (MN)	72%	2,390
University of Central Missouri	72%	1,504
University of Michigan–Flint	72%	768
University of Nebraska–Omaha	72%	1,816
Ursuline College (OH)	72%	95
Youngstown State University (OH)	72%	2,637
Alverno College (WI)	73%	244
Aquinas College (MI)	73%	402
Concordia University Chicago (IL)	73%	363
Lakeland College (WI)	73%	N/A
Northern Michigan University	73%	1,772
Olivet Nazarene University (IL)	73%	778
Spring Arbor University (MI)	73%	381
University of Illinois–Springfield	73%	288
University of Indianapolis	73%	743
University of Mary (ND)	73%	312
University of Wisconsin–River Falls	73%	1,337
Western Illinois University	73%	1,641
Winona State University (MN)	73%	1,813
Benedictine College (KS)	74%	428
College of Mount St. Joseph (OH)	74%	368
Eastern Michigan University	74%	2,277
Malone University (OH)	74%	481
Missouri State University	74%	2,655
North Park University (IL)	74%	364
Pittsburg State University (KS)	74%	864
St. Xavier University (IL)	74%	439
Capital University (OH)	75%	610
Marian University (WI)	75%	319
Otterbein College (OH)	75%	643
University of Wisconsin–Oshkosh	75%	1,898
University of Wisconsin–Platteville	75%	1,518
Anderson University (IN)	76%	552
Benedictine University (IL)	76%	445
Carroll University (WI)	76%	1,486
Mount Marty College (SD)	76%	116
St. Ambrose University (IA)	76%	577
University of Findlay (OH)	76%	642
University of St. Francis (IL)	76%	223
University of Wisconsin–Whitewater	76%	1,953
Viterbo University (WI)	76%	N/A
Walsh University (OH)	76%	489
University of Detroit Mercy	77%	552
University of Wisconsin–Stevens Point	77%	1,640
Minnesota State University–Mankato	78%	2,287
North Central College (IL)	78%	543
St. Catherine University (MN)	78%	414
William Woods University (MO)	78%	243
Concordia University Wisconsin	79%	471
Lewis University (IL)	79%	658
University of Michigan–Dearborn	79%	922
Webster University (MO)	79%	494
College of St. Scholastica (MN)	80%	536
Dominican University (IL)	80%	405
Eastern Illinois University	80%	1,654
Hamline University (MN)	80%	400
University of Minnesota–Duluth	80%	2,118
University of Nebraska–Kearney	80%	983
Cardinal Stritch University (WI)	81%	267
Indiana Wesleyan University	81%	762
Maryville University of St. Louis (MO)	81%	374
University of Evansville (IN)	81%	701
Augsburg College (MN)	82%	465
Drury University (MO)	82%	338
Baldwin-Wallace College (OH)	83%	755
Madonna University (MI)	83%	189
University of Northern Iowa	83%	1,946
University of Wisconsin–Eau Claire	83%	2,013
Elmhurst College (IL)	84%	587
Franciscan University of Steubenville (OH)	84%	445
Grand Valley State University (MI)	84%	3,727
Rockhurst University (MO)	84%	419
Valparaiso University (IN)	84%	671
Bethel University (MN)	85%	727
John Carroll University (OH)	85%	661
Truman State University (MO)	86%	1,342
Creighton University (NE)	87%	1,054
Drake University (IA)	87%	863
University of Wisconsin–La Crosse	87%	1,778
Xavier University (OH)	87%	1,183
Bradley University (IL)	88%	1,106
Butler University (IN)	88%	946

Regional Universities (West)

	Freshman retention rate	Freshman enrollment
New Mexico Highlands University	47%	398
Western New Mexico University	48%	466
University of Alaska–Southeast	55%	N/A
Cameron University (OK)	56%	1,150
Marylhurst University (OR)	56%	23
Eastern New Mexico University	57%	N/A
Angelo State University (TX)	58%	1,474
Southeastern Oklahoma State University	58%	669
University of Great Falls (MT)	58%	N/A
University of Texas–San Antonio	58%	4,883
Our Lady of the Lake University (TX)	59%	252
University of Texas of the Permian Basin	59%	398
Montana State University–Billings	60%	900
Naropa University (CO)	60%	45
Texas A&M University–Corpus Christi	60%	1,308
University of Central Oklahoma	61%	2,208
Texas Wesleyan University	62%	188
University of Mary Hardin-Baylor (TX)	62%	479
California State University–Dominguez Hills	63%	1,135
East Central University (OK)	64%	N/A
Lamar University (TX)	64%	1,485
Northeastern State University (OK)	64%	1,113
Southern Utah University	64%	1,316
Stephen F. Austin State University (TX)	64%	2,396
University of Texas–Brownsville	64%	2,060
University of Texas–Tyler	64%	596
Wayland Baptist University (TX)	64%	219
Eastern Oregon University	65%	473
Southwestern Oklahoma State University	65%	926
West Texas A&M University	65%	1,202
Boise State University (ID)	66%	2,194
Hardin-Simmons University (TX)	66%	409
La Sierra University (CA)	66%	348
Lubbock Christian University (TX)	66%	252
Southern Oregon University	66%	706
Texas A&M International University	66%	720
University of the Incarnate Word (TX)	66%	744
Chaminade University of Honolulu	67%	264
Hawaii Pacific University	67%	637
Western Oregon University	67%	1,013
Southern Nazarene University (OK)	68%	281
College of Santa Fe (NM)	69%	0
Hope International University (CA)	69%	113
Northwest Nazarene University (ID)	69%	277
University of Colorado–Colorado Springs	69%	1,097
University of St. Thomas (TX)	69%	287
Evergreen State College (WA)	70%	578
Holy Names University (CA)	70%	127
New Mexico Institute of Mining and Tech.	70%	255
Alaska Pacific University	71%	28
Dallas Baptist University	71%	351
Houston Baptist University	71%	554
Midwestern State University (TX)	71%	715
Oklahoma Christian University	71%	471
University of Alaska–Anchorage	71%	1,950
Weber State University (UT)	71%	2,377
Notre Dame de Namur University (CA)	72%	116
Prairie View A&M University (TX)	72%	1,589
Sam Houston State University (TX)	72%	2,170
University of Texas–Pan American	72%	2,882
California State University–Bakersfield	73%	1,061
California State University–San Marcos	73%	1,567
Fresno Pacific University (CA)	73%	174

Regional Universities (West), continued

	Freshman retention rate	Freshman enrollment
Walla Walla University (WA)	73%	311
California State University–Northridge	74%	4,203
Eastern Washington University	74%	1,469
LeTourneau University (TX)	74%	346
Mills College (CA)	74%	162
St. Martin's University (WA)	74%	180
Abilene Christian University (TX)	75%	983
California State University–East Bay	75%	1,445
California State University–Los Angeles	75%	2,019
Colorado Christian University	75%	N/A
Concordia University (CA)	75%	328
Humboldt State University (CA)	75%	1,385
Prescott College (AZ)	75%	72
Sonoma State University (CA)	75%	2,215
Dominican University of California	76%	289
San Francisco State University	76%	4,032
Central Washington University	77%	1,660
Mount St. Mary's College (CA)	77%	371
Texas State University–San Marcos	77%	3,667
University of the Southwest (NM)	77%	51
California State University–Sacramento	78%	2,726
Oklahoma City University	78%	404
Westminster College (UT)	78%	469
Woodbury University (CA)	78%	128
California Lutheran University	79%	464
California State University–Fullerton	79%	4,065
St. Mary's University of San Antonio (TX)	79%	531
California Baptist University	80%	576
San Jose State University (CA)	80%	2,764
California State University–Chico	81%	2,505
California State University–Fresno	81%	2,765
California State Univ.–San Bernardino	81%	2,017
St. Mary's College of California	81%	572
California State Polytechnic Univ.–Pomona	82%	2,914
California State University–Stanislaus	82%	966
University of Dallas	82%	320
Pacific Lutheran University (WA)	83%	716
Regis University (CO)	83%	375
St. Edward's University (TX)	84%	757
University of Redlands (CA)	84%	561
Point Loma Nazarene University (CA)	85%	535
Western Washington University	85%	2,688
California State University–Long Beach	86%	3,551
Seattle Pacific University	86%	682
University of Portland (OR)	86%	816
Chapman University (CA)	87%	1,032
Whitworth University (WA)	87%	555
Loyola Marymount University (CA)	88%	1,385
Seattle University	88%	734
Trinity University (TX)	89%	642
Cal. Poly. State Univ.–San Luis Obispo	90%	3,908
Gonzaga University (WA)	92%	1,239
Santa Clara University (CA)	93%	1,085
National University (CA)	100%	N/A

Regional Colleges (North)

	Freshman retention rate	Freshman enrollment
Sojourner-Douglass College (MD)	45%	N/A
Wesley College (DE)	50%	591
Fisher College (MA)	53%	N/A
University of Maine–Augusta	55%	589
Post University (CT)	57%	246
Southern Vermont College	58%	N/A
CUNY–Medgar Evers College	59%	1,378
New England College (NH)	60%	258
Mount Ida College (MA)	63%	434
University of Maine–Fort Kent	63%	125
Keystone College (PA)	64%	336
Mount Aloysius College (PA)	64%	360
Paul Smith's College (NY)	64%	N/A
Peirce College (PA)	64%	N/A
SUNY College of Technology–Delhi	64%	1,027
Thomas College (ME)	64%	N/A
Curry College (MA)	65%	623
Felician College (NJ)	65%	254
Lyndon State College (VT)	65%	N/A
Mitchell College (CT)	65%	260
Washington Adventist University (MD)	65%	144
Baptist Bible College and Seminary (PA)	66%	N/A
Keuka College (NY)	67%	253
Lasell College (MA)	67%	522
SUNY College of Technology–Alfred	67%	1,319
Cazenovia College (NY)	68%	272
Bay Path College (MA)	69%	152
CUNY–York College	69%	N/A
Pennsylvania College of Technology	69%	2,347
Wilson College (PA)	69%	103
Eastern Nazarene College (MA)	70%	190
Unity College (ME)	70%	N/A
Valley Forge Christian College (PA)	70%	N/A
Vermont Technical College	70%	254
University of Pittsburgh–Bradford	71%	420
Colby-Sawyer College (NH)	72%	N/A
Daniel Webster College (NH)	72%	N/A
SUNY Coll. of Agr. and Tech.–Cobleskill	73%	1,173
SUNY Maritime College	73%	355
University of Maine–Farmington	73%	519
Elmira College (NY)	74%	430
Seton Hill University (PA)	74%	299
University of Pittsburgh–Johnstown	74%	822
Delaware Valley College (PA)	75%	452
St. Francis College (NY)	75%	603
Vaughn Coll. of Aero. and Tech. (NY)	75%	262
Farmingdale State College–SUNY	76%	1,355
CUNY–New York City College of Tech.	78%	3,251
Champlain College (VT)	78%	545
York College of Pennsylvania	78%	1,102
Bard College at Simon's Rock (MA)	80%	179
Roger Williams University (RI)	80%	1,026
Stevenson University (MD)	80%	527
Endicott College (MA)	81%	561
St. Joseph's College New York	81%	689
Massachusetts Maritime Academy	82%	332
Lebanon Valley College (PA)	83%	378
Maine Maritime Academy	83%	242
Fashion Institute of Technology (NY)	85%	1,068
Messiah College (PA)	85%	698
Elizabethtown College (PA)	86%	568
United States Coast Guard Academy (CT)	89%	288
United States Merchant Marine Acad. (NY)	89%	291
Cooper Union (NY)	94%	193

Schools whose freshmen are least (and most) likely to return

Regional Colleges (South)

	Freshman retention rate	Freshman enrollment
LeMoyne-Owen College (TN)	44%	N/A
St. Paul's College (VA)	44%	157
Edward Waters College (FL)	45%	N/A
Victory University (TN)	45%	19
Chowan University (NC)	47%	N/A
Kentucky State University	51%	540
Livingstone College (NC)	51%	423
Morris College (SC)	52%	N/A
Our Lady of Holy Cross College (LA)	52%	79
Shaw University (NC)	55%	N/A
Brewton-Parker College (GA)	56%	N/A
North Carolina Wesleyan College	56%	305
Virginia Union University	56%	560
Benedict College (SC)	57%	N/A
Stillman College (AL)	57%	440
Averett University (VA)	59%	227
Belmont Abbey College (NC)	59%	401
Louisiana College	59%	254
Miles College (AL)	59%	N/A
University of Arkansas–Pine Bluff	59%	977
Faulkner University (AL)	60%	428
Newberry College (SC)	60%	345
Reinhardt University (GA)	60%	239
St. Augustine's College (NC)	60%	448
Clayton State University (GA)	61%	535
Southern Arkansas University	61%	619
Bluefield State College (WV)	62%	319
Brescia University (KY)	62%	122
Central Baptist College (AR)	62%	N/A
Mount Olive College (NC)	62%	N/A

	Freshman retention rate	Freshman enrollment
Tennessee Wesleyan College	62%	249
University of the Cumberlands (KY)	62%	N/A
West Virginia University–Parkersburg	62%	N/A
Williams Baptist College (AR)	62%	139
Alice Lloyd College (KY)	63%	172
Atlanta Christian College	63%	111
Davis and Elkins College (WV)	63%	235
Lander University (SC)	63%	N/A
Lees-McRae College (NC)	63%	N/A
Mars Hill College (NC)	63%	297
LaGrange College (GA)	64%	231
Ohio Valley University (WV)	64%	90
University of South Carolina–Upstate	64%	875
Bluefield College (VA)	65%	N/A
Emmanuel College (GA)	65%	164
Free Will Baptist Bible College (TN)	65%	61
Glenville State College (WV)	65%	325
Philander Smith College (AR)	65%	158
Clearwater Christian College (FL)	66%	157
Concord University (WV)	66%	611
Southeastern University (FL)	66%	569
Anderson University (SC)	67%	495
Campbellsville University (KY)	67%	518
Limestone College (SC)	67%	257
Methodist University (NC)	67%	490
Shepherd University (WV)	67%	801
Toccoa Falls College (GA)	67%	171
Tuskegee University (AL)	67%	689
University of Charleston (WV)	67%	273
Alderson-Broaddus College (WV)	68%	162

	Freshman retention rate	Freshman enrollment
Coker College (SC)	68%	192
Fairmont State University (WV)	68%	820
Midway College (KY)	68%	N/A
Shorter College (GA)	68%	333
University of South Carolina–Aiken	68%	689
Barton College (NC)	69%	230
Bethune-Cookman University (FL)	69%	2,047
Oakwood University (AL)	69%	N/A
University of the Ozarks (AR)	69%	152
Virginia Intermont College	69%	N/A
West Liberty University (WV)	69%	578
Blue Mountain College (MS)	70%	75
King College (TN)	70%	207
Lenoir-Rhyne University (NC)	70%	354
Southern Adventist University (TN)	70%	603
Catawba College (NC)	71%	308
Claflin University (SC)	71%	468
Warner University (FL)	72%	131
Erskine College (SC)	73%	182
Milligan College (TN)	73%	211
Winston-Salem State University (NC)	73%	795
Florida Southern College	74%	553
Covenant College (GA)	75%	277
Bryan College (TN)	76%	192
Elizabeth City State University (NC)	76%	664
Ouachita Baptist University (AR)	76%	390
Flagler College (FL)	77%	564
John Brown University (AR)	79%	306
High Point University (NC)	80%	1,030

Regional Colleges (Midwest)

	Freshman retention rate	Freshman enrollment
Chancellor University (OH)	38%	N/A
Harris-Stowe State University (MO)	44%	411
Central State University (OH)	53%	713
Iowa Wesleyan College	54%	N/A
Purdue University–North Central (IN)	54%	768
William Penn University (IA)	54%	N/A
Robert Morris University (IL)	55%	959
Bethany College (KS)	56%	182
Indiana University–Kokomo	56%	434
Kansas Wesleyan University	56%	N/A
Black Hills State University (SD)	57%	600
Peru State College (NE)	57%	235
Rochester College (MI)	57%	N/A
Shawnee State University (OH)	57%	1,130
Mayville State University (ND)	59%	147
Dana College (NE)	60%	174
Indiana University East	60%	400
Lourdes College (OH)	60%	129
MacMurray College (IL)	60%	96
Blackburn College (IL)	61%	146
Dickinson State University (ND)	61%	340
Wilberforce University (OH)	61%	N/A

	Freshman retention rate	Freshman enrollment
Central Christian College (KS)	62%	111
Central Methodist University (MO)	62%	260
College of St. Mary (NE)	62%	108
Missouri Southern State University	63%	858
Missouri Western State University	63%	1,192
Culver-Stockton College (MO)	64%	148
Midland Lutheran College (NE)	64%	113
Ottawa University (KS)	64%	N/A
Briar Cliff University (IA)	65%	223
Lake Superior State University (MI)	65%	884
Notre Dame College of Ohio	65%	344
St. Joseph's College (IN)	65%	231
University of Dubuque (IA)	65%	354
Waldorf College (IA)	65%	N/A
Defiance College (OH)	66%	216
Hannibal-LaGrange College (MO)	66%	187
Valley City State University (ND)	66%	155
Chadron State College (NE)	67%	422
Tabor College (KS)	67%	140
Trine University (IN)	67%	458
Wilmington College (OH)	67%	337
Lake Erie College (OH)	68%	388

	Freshman retention rate	Freshman enrollment
Northern State University (SD)	68%	329
University of Sioux Falls (SD)	68%	279
Buena Vista University (IA)	69%	273
Crown College (MN)	69%	149
Grand View University (IA)	69%	233
Greenville College (IL)	69%	253
Manchester College (IN)	69%	426
Union College (NE)	69%	117
University of Minnesota–Crookston	69%	285
Concordia University (MI)	70%	N/A
Dakota State University (SD)	70%	323
Grace Bible College (MI)	70%	N/A
Judson University (IL)	70%	174
North Central University (MN)	70%	296
Quincy University (IL)	70%	249
Franklin College (IN)	72%	325
York College (NE)	72%	117
Adrian College (MI)	73%	480
Maranatha Baptist Bible College (WI)	73%	198
Morningside College (IA)	73%	325
Mount Vernon Nazarene University (OH)	73%	303
Bluffton University (OH)	74%	257

Regional Colleges (Midwest), continued

	Freshman retention rate	Freshman enrollment
Huntington University (IN)	74%	260
Jamestown College (ND)	74%	239
Loras College (IA)	74%	414
Marian University (IN)	74%	330
Marietta College (OH)	74%	388
Trinity Christian College (IL)	74%	201
Milwaukee School of Engineering	75%	534
Carthage College (WI)	76%	722

	Freshman retention rate	Freshman enrollment
St. Mary-of-the-Woods College (IN)	76%	90
Concordia University (NE)	77%	288
Eureka College (IL)	77%	143
McKendree University (IL)	77%	307
Mount Mercy College (IA)	78%	150
Northwestern College (IA)	78%	331
Augustana College (SD)	79%	432
Bethel College (IN)	79%	309

	Freshman retention rate	Freshman enrollment
Grace College and Seminary (IN)	79%	229
Dordt College (IA)	81%	364
Northwestern College (MN)	81%	439
College of the Ozarks (MO)	82%	245
Ohio Northern University	83%	641
Cedarville University (OH)	84%	729
Taylor University (IN)	86%	486

Regional Colleges (West)

	Freshman retention rate	Freshman enrollment
Bacone College (OK)	39%	207
Utah Valley University	45%	N/A
Patten University (CA)	47%	N/A
Texas College	47%	224
Rogers State University (OK)	50%	849
Langston University (OK)	52%	889
Mid-America Christian University (OK)	52%	N/A
Dixie State College of Utah	53%	1,743
Oklahoma Panhandle State University	53%	297
Concordia University Texas	54%	222
Lewis-Clark State College (ID)	54%	635
Wiley College (TX)	56%	312
McMurry University (TX)	57%	320

	Freshman retention rate	Freshman enrollment
University of Houston–Downtown	57%	1,071
East Texas Baptist University	58%	279
St. Gregory's University (OK)	60%	N/A
Howard Payne University (TX)	61%	218
Northwest Christian University (OR)	62%	78
Southwestern Assemb. of God Univ. (TX)	63%	343
Rocky Mountain College (MT)	64%	234
Schreiner University (TX)	65%	290
Southwestern Adventist University (TX)	65%	N/A
Northwestern Oklahoma State University	66%	406
Oklahoma Wesleyan University	66%	128
Warner Pacific College (OR)	66%	101
Univ. of Science and Arts of Oklahoma	67%	187

	Freshman retention rate	Freshman enrollment
University of Montana–Western	68%	240
Northwest University (WA)	69%	N/A
Cogswell Polytechnical College (CA)	70%	21
Montana Tech of the Univ. of Montana	71%	490
Oregon Institute of Technology	71%	368
Corban University (OR)	72%	215
Vanguard Univ. of Southern California	72%	268
Oklahoma Baptist University	74%	368
Pacific Union College (CA)	75%	324
California Maritime Academy	77%	N/A
Master's College and Seminary (CA)	81%	177
United States Air Force Academy (CO)	87%	1,362

Schools whose students are most (and least) likely to graduate

Like retention rates, graduation rates can tell you something about how colleges serve their students: how good a job they do at providing the support and access to courses students need to complete their degrees. A low four-year graduation rate may also indicate a large population of part-time students or a significant cooperative education program, which can require five years or more. Below, we show the average proportion who graduate in six years or less for classes starting in 2000 through 2003, and the proportion who started in 2003 who earned a degree in four years.

National Universities

School	6-year graduation rate	4-year graduation rate
Harvard University (MA)	98%	88%
Yale University (CT)	97%	90%
Princeton University (NJ)	96%	90%
University of Notre Dame (IN)	96%	90%
Brown University (RI)	95%	86%
Stanford University (CA)	95%	79%
University of Pennsylvania	95%	88%
Columbia University (NY)	94%	87%
Dartmouth College (NH)	94%	85%
Duke University (NC)	94%	89%
Georgetown University (DC)	94%	85%
Northwestern University (IL)	94%	87%
Massachusetts Institute of Technology	93%	83%
Rice University (TX)	93%	83%
University of Virginia	93%	84%
Washington University in St. Louis	93%	84%
Cornell University (NY)	92%	85%
Boston College	91%	88%
College of William and Mary (VA)	91%	83%
Johns Hopkins University (MD)	91%	83%
Tufts University (MA)	91%	85%
University of Chicago	91%	86%
Vanderbilt University (TN)	90%	84%
California Institute of Technology	89%	73%
University of California–Berkeley	89%	66%
University of California–Los Angeles	89%	67%
Wake Forest University (NC)	89%	85%
Brandeis University (MA)	88%	84%
Emory University (GA)	88%	84%
University of Michigan–Ann Arbor	88%	73%
Carnegie Mellon University (PA)	86%	67%
University of Southern California	86%	72%
Lehigh University (PA)	85%	76%
Pennsylvania State Univ.–University Park	85%	62%
University of California–San Diego	85%	56%
University of North Carolina–Chapel Hill	85%	74%
New York University	84%	78%
Rensselaer Polytechnic Institute (NY)	82%	64%
Syracuse University (NY)	82%	73%
University of California–Santa Barbara	82%	66%
University of Illinois–Urbana-Champaign	82%	65%
Boston University	81%	N/A
Miami University–Oxford (OH)	81%	71%
University of California–Davis	81%	51%
University of California–Irvine	81%	58%
University of Florida	81%	58%
University of Maryland–College Park	81%	63%
University of Rochester (NY)	81%	69%
Binghamton University–SUNY	80%	70%
Case Western Reserve University (OH)	80%	63%
George Washington University (DC)	80%	76%
Pepperdine University (CA)	80%	73%
University of Wisconsin–Madison	80%	50%
Fordham University (NY)	79%	75%
University of Texas–Austin	79%	51%
Virginia Tech	79%	53%
Brigham Young University–Provo (UT)	78%	30%
Georgia Institute of Technology	78%	31%
Texas A&M University–College Station	78%	45%
University of Georgia	78%	51%
Worcester Polytechnic Institute (MA)	78%	67%
Yeshiva University (NY)	78%	45%
Clemson University (SC)	77%	50%
Marquette University (WI)	77%	60%
University of Dayton (OH)	77%	58%
University of Delaware	77%	61%
University of Miami (FL)	77%	67%
University of Washington	77%	54%
University of Connecticut	76%	61%
University of Pittsburgh	76%	57%
Clark University (MA)	75%	73%
Michigan State University	75%	49%
Rutgers–New Brunswick	75%	52%
University of San Diego	75%	66%
American University (DC)	74%	71%
Southern Methodist University (TX)	74%	62%
St. Louis University	74%	60%
Stevens Institute of Technology (NJ)	74%	30%
Tulane University (LA)	74%	60%
University of Denver	74%	58%
University of New Hampshire	74%	60%
Indiana University–Bloomington	73%	53%
Ohio State University–Columbus	73%	46%
Baylor University (TX)	72%	47%
Catholic University of America (DC)	72%	65%
Duquesne University (PA)	72%	61%
Samford University (AL)	72%	53%
University of California–Santa Cruz	72%	51%
University of St. Thomas (MN)	72%	56%
Clarkson University (NY)	71%	54%
University of Vermont	71%	57%
Biola University (CA)	70%	51%
Florida State University	70%	47%
North Carolina State University–Raleigh	70%	N/A
Ohio University	70%	48%
Purdue University–West Lafayette (IN)	70%	38%
Texas Christian University	70%	55%
Colorado School of Mines	69%	41%
Northeastern University (MA)	69%	N/A
University of Missouri	68%	43%
Illinois State University	67%	42%
Iowa State University	67%	35%
Loyola University Chicago	67%	48%
University of Colorado–Boulder	67%	41%
University of Iowa	67%	42%
University of Massachusetts–Amherst	67%	49%
University of San Francisco	67%	49%
University of the Pacific (CA)	67%	41%
Illinois Institute of Technology	66%	35%
SUNY Coll. of Environ. Sci. and Forestry	66%	48%
University of Oregon	66%	46%
University of South Carolina	66%	46%
University of Alabama	65%	38%
University of California–Riverside	65%	41%
University of Minnesota–Twin Cities	65%	45%
Washington State University	65%	40%
Auburn University (AL)	64%	37%
George Fox University (OR)	64%	54%
Howard University (DC)	64%	47%
Michigan Technological University	64%	22%
University at Albany–SUNY	64%	53%
Adelphi University (NY)	63%	52%
Azusa Pacific University (CA)	63%	55%
Colorado State University	63%	35%
DePaul University (IL)	63%	43%
Drexel University (PA)	63%	25%
University at Buffalo–SUNY	63%	42%
University of Nebraska–Lincoln	63%	25%
University of Tulsa (OK)	63%	44%
Missouri University of Science & Tech.	62%	25%
New School (NY)	62%	51%
Pacific University (OR)	62%	52%
SUNY–Stony Brook	62%	45%
Temple University (PA)	62%	40%
University of Oklahoma	62%	29%
Oregon State University	61%	27%
University of Central Florida	61%	34%
George Mason University (VA)	60%	39%
Rutgers–Newark	60%	34%
San Diego State University	60%	29%
Seton Hall University (NJ)	60%	50%
St. John's University (NY)	60%	38%
University of Kansas	60%	32%
University of Kentucky	60%	32%
University of Tennessee	60%	31%
Bowling Green State University (OH)	59%	34%
Kansas State University	59%	26%
Louisiana State University–Baton Rouge	59%	28%
Mississippi State University	59%	31%
Oklahoma State University	59%	31%
University of La Verne (CA)	59%	44%
University of Maine	59%	34%
University of Maryland–Baltimore County	59%	34%
Ball State University (IN)	58%	35%
Immaculata University (PA)	58%	57%
University of Arkansas	58%	34%
University of Rhode Island	58%	39%
University of Texas–Dallas	58%	43%
Central Michigan University	57%	21%
Florida Institute of Technology	57%	39%
St. Mary's University of Minnesota	57%	46%
Texas Tech University	57%	32%

	6-year graduation rate	4-year graduation rate
University of Arizona	57%	32%
Andrews University (MI)	56%	34%
Arizona State University	56%	30%
Pace University (NY)	56%	45%
University of Mississippi	56%	36%
West Virginia University	56%	32%
Widener University (PA)	56%	41%
East Carolina University (NC)	55%	N/A
Hofstra University (NY)	55%	41%
University of Idaho	55%	25%
University of Wyoming	55%	22%
New Jersey Institute of Technology	54%	17%
Oral Roberts University (OK)	54%	39%
South Dakota State University	54%	N/A
University of Cincinnati	54%	20%
University of North Dakota	54%	23%
Western Michigan University	54%	22%
Trinity International University (IL)	53%	38%
University of Hartford (CT)	53%	40%
University of Utah	53%	22%
University of North Carolina–Charlotte	52%	26%
University of North Carolina–Greensboro	52%	28%
Indiana University of Pennsylvania	51%	33%
Polytechnic Inst. of New York Univ. (NY)	51%	36%
University of Hawaii–Manoa	51%	16%
University of Illinois–Chicago	51%	N/A
Utah State University	51%	27%
Kent State University (OH)	50%	25%
North Dakota State University	50%	22%
Northern Illinois University	50%	23%
Old Dominion University (VA)	50%	23%
Montana State University	49%	19%
University of Massachusetts–Lowell	49%	28%

	6-year graduation rate	4-year graduation rate
University of Northern Colorado	49%	28%
University of South Florida	49%	21%
Florida International University	48%	20%
Georgia State University	48%	18%
Louisiana Tech University	48%	26%
Trevecca Nazarene University (TN)	48%	37%
University of Nevada–Reno	48%	13%
University of South Dakota	48%	22%
Virginia Commonwealth University	48%	25%
University of Alabama–Huntsville	46%	17%
University of Southern Mississippi	46%	21%
University of West Florida	46%	21%
Georgia Southern University	45%	17%
South Carolina State University	45%	13%
University of Louisville (KY)	45%	21%
University of North Texas	45%	19%
University of Toledo (OH)	45%	23%
Southern Illinois University–Carbondale	44%	24%
University of Missouri–Kansas City	44%	19%
University of New Mexico	44%	11%
Wright State University (OH)	44%	19%
Clark Atlanta University	43%	30%
Long Island Univ.–C.W. Post Campus (NY)	43%	25%
New Mexico State University	43%	13%
Oakland University (MI)	43%	12%
Texas Woman's University	43%	22%
University of Missouri–St. Louis	43%	21%
University of Wisconsin–Milwaukee	43%	15%
Union Institute and University (OH)	42%	21%
University of Houston	42%	12%
University of Montana	42%	20%
East Tennessee State University	41%	19%
Florida A&M University	41%	12%

	6-year graduation rate	4-year graduation rate
Indiana State University	41%	19%
Nova Southeastern University (FL)	41%	22%
University of Louisiana–Lafayette	41%	13%
Wilmington University (DE)	41%	17%
University of Nevada–Las Vegas	40%	12%
University of Texas–Arlington	40%	17%
North Carolina A&T State University	39%	18%
University of Bridgeport (CT)	39%	21%
University of Colorado–Denver	39%	17%
Wichita State University (KS)	39%	15%
Barry University (FL)	38%	N/A
Florida Atlantic University	38%	16%
Tennessee State University	38%	13%
University of Alabama–Birmingham	38%	17%
Jackson State University (MS)	37%	15%
University of Memphis	37%	14%
Morgan State University (MD)	36%	11%
Texas A&M University–Commerce	36%	22%
University of Akron (OH)	35%	11%
University of Massachusetts–Boston	35%	11%
Portland State University (OR)	34%	8%
Wayne State University (MI)	34%	10%
Indiana Univ.–Purdue Univ.–Indianapolis	32%	10%
Golden Gate University (CA)	30%	0%
Texas A&M University–Kingsville	30%	8%
University of Texas–El Paso	30%	5%
Cleveland State University	29%	7%
Idaho State University	29%	7%
Spalding University (KY)	29%	N/A
University of Alaska–Fairbanks	26%	11%
University of New Orleans	23%	5%
University of Arkansas–Little Rock	22%	N/A

National Liberal Arts Colleges

	6-year graduation rate	4-year graduation rate
Williams College (MA)	96%	93%
Amherst College (MA)	95%	85%
Pomona College (CA)	94%	89%
Carleton College (MN)	93%	89%
Haverford College (PA)	93%	88%
Middlebury College (VT)	93%	83%
Swarthmore College (PA)	93%	86%
Bowdoin College (ME)	92%	89%
College of the Holy Cross (MA)	92%	87%
Davidson College (NC)	92%	89%
Vassar College (NY)	92%	88%
Wellesley College (MA)	92%	84%
Wesleyan University (CT)	92%	88%
Claremont McKenna College (CA)	91%	87%
Bates College (ME)	90%	86%
Colgate University (NY)	90%	85%
Lafayette College (PA)	90%	86%
Barnard College (NY)	89%	83%
Bucknell University (PA)	89%	88%
Washington and Lee University (VA)	89%	88%
Whitman College (WA)	89%	81%
Colby College (ME)	88%	82%
Hamilton College (NY)	88%	83%
Harvey Mudd College (CA)	88%	79%

	6-year graduation rate	4-year graduation rate
Grinnell College (IA)	87%	78%
Wheaton College (IL)	87%	80%
Kenyon College (OH)	86%	85%
Macalester College (MN)	86%	82%
Smith College (MA)	86%	78%
St. Olaf College (MN)	86%	82%
Trinity College (CT)	86%	76%
Union College (NY)	86%	80%
United States Naval Academy (MD)	86%	89%
University of Richmond (VA)	86%	82%
Colorado College	85%	78%
Connecticut College	85%	83%
Furman University (SC)	85%	81%
Muhlenberg College (PA)	85%	79%
Oberlin College (OH)	84%	73%
Occidental College (CA)	84%	78%
Stonehill College (MA)	84%	80%
DePauw University (IN)	83%	79%
Dickinson College (PA)	83%	81%
Grove City College (PA)	83%	78%
Illinois Wesleyan University	83%	81%
Bryn Mawr College (PA)	82%	74%
Franklin and Marshall College (PA)	82%	79%
Gettysburg College (PA)	82%	78%

	6-year graduation rate	4-year graduation rate
Mount Holyoke College (MA)	82%	78%
Skidmore College (NY)	82%	82%
Susquehanna University (PA)	82%	80%
United States Military Academy (NY)	82%	80%
College of St. Benedict (MN)	81%	73%
Scripps College (CA)	81%	85%
St. John's University (MN)	81%	71%
Centre College (KY)	80%	79%
Denison University (OH)	80%	80%
Spelman College (GA)	80%	65%
Wofford College (SC)	80%	77%
Beloit College (WI)	79%	74%
Gustavus Adolphus College (MN)	79%	80%
Juniata College (PA)	79%	75%
Sewanee–University of the South (TN)	79%	75%
St. Mary's College of Maryland	79%	71%
St. Michael's College (VT)	79%	71%
Thomas Aquinas College (CA)	79%	71%
St. Lawrence University (NY)	78%	79%
Ursinus College (PA)	78%	79%
Wheaton College (MA)	78%	73%
Augustana College (IL)	77%	72%
Bard College (NY)	77%	71%
Hope College (MI)	77%	66%

Schools whose students are most (and least) likely to graduate

National Liberal Arts Colleges, continued

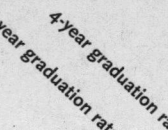
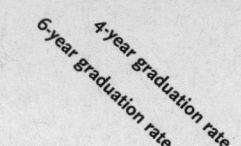
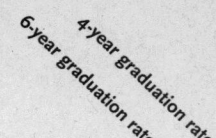

School	6-year graduation rate	4-year graduation rate
Kalamazoo College (MI)	77%	71%
Lawrence University (WI)	77%	60%
Reed College (OR)	77%	57%
Siena College (NY)	77%	68%
Westmont College (CA)	77%	75%
Willamette University (OR)	77%	71%
Austin College (TX)	76%	67%
Rhodes College (TN)	76%	75%
University of Puget Sound (WA)	76%	68%
Washington College (MD)	76%	75%
Westminster College (PA)	76%	59%
Calvin College (MI)	75%	55%
College of Wooster (OH)	75%	68%
Drew University (NJ)	75%	69%
Sarah Lawrence College (NY)	75%	64%
St. Mary's College (IN)	75%	73%
Allegheny College (PA)	74%	66%
Hobart and William Smith Colleges (NY)	74%	74%
Knox College (IL)	74%	66%
Luther College (IA)	74%	65%
Moravian College (PA)	74%	71%
Pitzer College (CA)	74%	70%
Principia College (IL)	74%	N/A
Ripon College (WI)	74%	60%
Southwestern University (TX)	74%	64%
Albion College (MI)	73%	63%
Gordon College (MA)	73%	64%
Earlham College (IN)	72%	60%
Lewis & Clark College (OR)	72%	69%
Linfield College (OR)	72%	64%
McDaniel College (MD)	72%	62%
St. Anselm College (NH)	72%	71%
St. Norbert College (WI)	72%	64%
St. Vincent College (PA)	72%	61%
Transylvania University (KY)	72%	67%
Virginia Military Institute	72%	64%
Houghton College (NY)	71%	61%
Presbyterian College (SC)	71%	63%
Washington and Jefferson College (PA)	71%	69%
Birmingham-Southern College (AL)	70%	63%
Coe College (IA)	70%	60%
Lycoming College (PA)	70%	67%
St. John's College (MD)	70%	N/A
Wabash College (IN)	70%	62%
Agnes Scott College (GA)	69%	60%
Alma College (MI)	69%	51%
Hillsdale College (MI)	69%	70%
Russell Sage College (NY)	69%	64%
Central College (IA)	68%	56%
Concordia College–Moorhead (MN)	68%	56%
Cornell College (IA)	68%	65%
Goucher College (MD)	68%	60%
Lake Forest College (IL)	68%	59%
Merrimack College (MA)	68%	60%
Nebraska Wesleyan University	68%	52%
Sweet Briar College (VA)	68%	59%
Asbury University (KY)	67%	57%
Clarke University (IA)	67%	48%
Doane College (NE)	67%	60%
Goshen College (IN)	67%	56%
Hendrix College (AR)	67%	59%
Millsaps College (MS)	67%	59%
Simpson College (IA)	67%	57%
Hampshire College (MA)	66%	53%
Hollins University (VA)	66%	60%
Monmouth College (IL)	66%	51%
Bethany College (WV)	65%	58%
Eastern Mennonite University (VA)	65%	48%
Hampden-Sydney College (VA)	65%	61%
Millikin University (IL)	65%	54%
Randolph College (VA)	65%	62%
Wartburg College (IA)	65%	61%
Beacon College (FL)	64%	50%
Ohio Wesleyan University	64%	51%
Roanoke College (VA)	64%	58%
University of Mount Union (OH)	64%	50%
William Jewell College (MO)	64%	51%
Wittenberg University (OH)	64%	58%
Berea College (KY)	63%	51%
College of Idaho (ID)	63%	55%
Hastings College (NE)	63%	55%
Wisconsin Lutheran College	63%	53%
Bridgewater College (VA)	62%	54%
Eckerd College (FL)	62%	58%
Hanover College (IN)	62%	58%
Hiram College (OH)	62%	64%
Meredith College (NC)	62%	44%
New College of Florida	62%	46%
Albright College (PA)	61%	55%
Berry College (GA)	61%	48%
College of the Atlantic (ME)	61%	48%
University of Minnesota–Morris	61%	45%
Westminster College (MO)	61%	40%
Carroll College (MT)	60%	N/A
Georgetown College (KY)	60%	49%
Granite State College (NH)	60%	43%
Morehouse College (GA)	60%	39%
Randolph-Macon College (VA)	60%	56%
Bennington College (VT)	59%	49%
Bethel College (KS)	59%	51%
Cedar Crest College (PA)	59%	45%
Guilford College (NC)	59%	48%
Illinois College	59%	50%
Oglethorpe University (GA)	59%	43%
Whittier College (CA)	59%	55%
Baker University (KS)	58%	36%
Centenary College of Louisiana	57%	N/A
Lyon College (AR)	57%	44%
Marlboro College (VT)	57%	N/A
University of North Carolina–Asheville	57%	29%
Emory and Henry College (VA)	56%	47%
Hartwick College (NY)	56%	44%
University of Hawaii–West Oahu	56%	20%
West Virginia Wesleyan College	56%	43%
American Jewish University (CA)	55%	37%
Carson-Newman College (TN)	55%	40%
Fisk University (TN)	55%	49%
Maryville College (TN)	55%	45%
Stephens College (MO)	55%	43%
Northland College (WI)	54%	50%
Shimer College (IL)	54%	N/A
Thomas More Coll. of Liberal Arts (NH)	54%	62%
University of Wisconsin–Green Bay	54%	25%
Wells College (NY)	54%	52%
Albertus Magnus College (CT)	53%	39%
Christopher Newport University (VA)	53%	39%
St. John's College (NM)	53%	N/A
Texas Lutheran University	53%	31%
Wesleyan College (GA)	53%	41%
Salem College (NC)	52%	N/A
Concordia College (NY)	51%	N/A
Huntingdon College (AL)	51%	35%
Massachusetts College of Liberal Arts	51%	38%
Wingate University (NC)	51%	42%
Purchase College–SUNY	50%	30%
Brigham Young University–Hawaii	49%	N/A
Warren Wilson College (NC)	48%	N/A
Franklin Pierce University (NH)	47%	33%
North Greenville University (SC)	47%	35%
Simpson University (CA)	47%	36%
Sterling College (KS)	47%	35%
Judson College (AL)	46%	N/A
Marymount Manhattan College (NY)	46%	39%
Coastal Carolina University (SC)	45%	22%
Evangel University (MO)	45%	32%
University of Virginia–Wise	45%	31%
St. Andrews Presbyterian College (NC)	44%	34%
Talladega College (AL)	44%	N/A
Tougaloo College (MS)	44%	24%
Virginia Wesleyan College	44%	35%
Kentucky Wesleyan College	42%	35%
Dillard University (LA)	41%	17%
Pine Manor College (MA)	41%	31%
Thiel College (PA)	41%	31%
University of Maine–Machias	41%	15%
Greensboro College (NC)	40%	N/A
Johnson C. Smith University (NC)	40%	26%
Lambuth University (TN)	40%	N/A
Bennett College (NC)	39%	28%
California State Univ.–Monterey Bay	39%	14%
University of Maine–Presque Isle	38%	N/A
Atlantic Union College (MA)	37%	N/A
Green Mountain College (VT)	37%	28%
McPherson College (KS)	37%	36%
Olivet College (MI)	36%	37%
SUNY College–Old Westbury	36%	18%
Western State College of Colorado	36%	20%
Baptist Bible College (MO)	35%	N/A
Peace College (NC)	35%	23%
Bloomfield College (NJ)	33%	11%
University of Hawaii–Hilo	33%	N/A
Colorado State University–Pueblo	32%	14%
Ferrum College (VA)	32%	23%
Fort Lewis College (CO)	32%	15%
Pikeville College (KY)	32%	18%
Brevard College (NC)	31%	23%
Lane College (TN)	31%	18%
Mesa State College (CO)	31%	10%
University of Wisconsin–Parkside	31%	8%
Paine College (GA)	29%	9%
Burlington College (VT)	27%	20%
Rust College (MS)	27%	18%
Lindsey Wilson College (KY)	26%	15%
Sierra Nevada College (NV)	26%	23%
West Virginia State University	26%	N/A
Bryn Athyn Coll. of the New Church (PA)	25%	22%
Metropolitan State College of Denver	22%	5%
Huston-Tillotson University (TX)	18%	N/A
Allen University (SC)	16%	9%
Jarvis Christian College (TX)	14%	9%
Martin University (IN)	11%	N/A

Regional Universities (North)

University	6-year graduation rate	4-year graduation rate
Villanova University (PA)	88%	82%
Providence College (RI)	87%	84%
Bentley University (MA)	85%	80%
College of New Jersey	85%	73%
Loyola University Maryland	83%	77%
Fairfield University (CT)	82%	83%
Marist College (NY)	80%	76%
SUNY–Geneseo	80%	64%
University of Scranton (PA)	80%	73%
Ithaca College (NY)	77%	71%
St. Joseph's University (PA)	77%	71%
Emerson College (MA)	75%	74%
Simmons College (MA)	74%	61%
Nazareth College (NY)	73%	62%
Quinnipiac University (CT)	73%	69%
Gwynedd-Mercy College (PA)	72%	50%
La Salle University (PA)	72%	61%
Le Moyne College (NY)	72%	61%
College of St. Rose (NY)	71%	53%
St. John Fisher College (NY)	71%	63%
Assumption College (MA)	70%	64%
Bryant University (RI)	70%	62%
Hood College (MD)	70%	61%
King's College (PA)	70%	63%
DeSales University (PA)	69%	63%
Manhattan College (NY)	69%	61%
Misericordia University (PA)	69%	66%
Ramapo College of New Jersey	69%	59%
St. Bonaventure University (NY)	69%	50%
Mount St. Mary's University (MD)	68%	70%
Salisbury University (MD)	68%	46%
Towson University (MD)	67%	46%
Alfred University (NY)	66%	N/A
Canisius College (NY)	66%	57%
Mercyhurst College (PA)	66%	57%
Richard Stockton College of New Jersey	66%	39%
Rowan University (NJ)	66%	43%
SUNY–New Paltz	66%	45%
Salve Regina University (RI)	66%	63%
Springfield College (MA)	66%	55%
Wagner College (NY)	66%	62%
College of St. Elizabeth (NJ)	65%	N/A
Marywood University (PA)	65%	55%
Sacred Heart University (CT)	65%	56%
Bloomsburg University of Pennsylvania	64%	41%
Gannon University (PA)	64%	46%
Millersville University of Pennsylvania	64%	36%
Molloy College (NY)	64%	36%
Niagara University (NY)	64%	59%
Rochester Institute of Technology (NY)	64%	28%
Shippensburg University of Pennsylvania	64%	45%
College of Notre Dame of Maryland	63%	57%
La Roche College (PA)	63%	34%
SUNY–Fredonia	63%	45%
West Chester University of Pennsylvania	63%	40%
Arcadia University (PA)	62%	53%
Eastern University (PA)	62%	58%
Roberts Wesleyan College (NY)	62%	55%
Rosemont College (PA)	62%	44%
Iona College (NY)	61%	50%
Montclair State University (NJ)	61%	30%
SUNY College–Cortland	61%	41%
St. Francis University (PA)	61%	57%
Anna Maria College (MA)	60%	N/A
College at Brockport–SUNY	60%	40%
Emmanuel College (MA)	60%	55%
Holy Family University (PA)	60%	48%
Manhattanville College (NY)	60%	53%
Monmouth University (NJ)	60%	40%
Wheelock College (MA)	60%	53%
Wilkes University (PA)	60%	50%
CUNY–Baruch College	59%	33%
Regis College (MA)	59%	N/A
Rider University (NJ)	59%	47%
Rutgers–Camden	59%	30%
SUNY College–Oneonta	59%	50%
St. Joseph's College (ME)	59%	N/A
Western New England College (MA)	59%	43%
Georgian Court University (NJ)	58%	24%
Philadelphia Biblical University	58%	19%
Touro College (NY)	58%	0%
Westfield State College (MA)	57%	42%
Keene State College (NH)	56%	36%
Philadelphia University	56%	43%
SUNY–Oswego	56%	40%
Slippery Rock University of Pennsylvania	56%	31%
Waynesburg University (PA)	56%	48%
Robert Morris University (PA)	55%	34%
SUNY–Plattsburgh	55%	43%
Alvernia University (PA)	54%	36%
Cabrini College (PA)	54%	47%
College of Mount St. Vincent (NY)	54%	40%
East Stroudsburg Univ. of Pennsylvania	54%	36%
Johnson and Wales University (RI)	54%	43%
Plymouth State University (NH)	54%	34%
CUNY–Queens College	53%	25%
Kutztown University of Pennsylvania	53%	30%
Lesley University (MA)	53%	38%
Lock Haven University of Pennsylvania	53%	29%
Mount St. Mary College (NY)	53%	39%
Rivier College (NH)	53%	41%
St. Joseph College (CT)	53%	31%
University of New England (ME)	53%	40%
Carlow University (PA)	52%	N/A
Clarion University of Pennsylvania	52%	40%
SUNY College–Potsdam	52%	37%
St. Thomas Aquinas College (NY)	52%	28%
Suffolk University (MA)	52%	36%
Bridgewater State College (MA)	51%	25%
California University of Pennsylvania	51%	30%
Chatham University (PA)	51%	51%
D'Youville College (NY)	51%	40%
Fitchburg State College (MA)	51%	24%
Neumann University (PA)	51%	N/A
Norwich University (VT)	51%	39%
Daemen College (NY)	50%	33%
SUNY Institute of Technology–Utica/Rome	50%	44%
Southern New Hampshire University	50%	49%
Caldwell College (NJ)	49%	29%
Centenary College (NJ)	49%	51%
Framingham State College (MA)	49%	33%
Frostburg State University (MD)	49%	25%
Utica College (NY)	49%	38%
William Paterson University of New Jersey	49%	21%
Chestnut Hill College (PA)	48%	35%
Eastern Connecticut State University	48%	32%
Point Park University (PA)	48%	41%
St. Peter's College (NJ)	48%	33%
CUNY–College of Staten Island	47%	23%
Edinboro University of Pennsylvania	47%	24%
Fairleigh Dickinson University (NJ)	47%	29%
Mansfield University of Pennsylvania	47%	28%
University of Massachusetts–Dartmouth	47%	32%
American International College (MA)	45%	32%
CUNY–Brooklyn College	45%	17%
Central Connecticut State University	45%	14%
Gratz College (PA)	45%	N/A
Rhode Island College	45%	15%
Buffalo State College–SUNY	44%	21%
Kean University (NJ)	44%	19%
University of New Haven (CT)	44%	39%
Castleton State College (VT)	43%	30%
Metropolitan College of New York	43%	N/A
New York Institute of Technology	43%	23%
Trinity University (DC)	43%	N/A
CUNY–John Jay Coll. of Criminal Justice	42%	23%
Medaille College (NY)	42%	50%
Worcester State College (MA)	42%	24%
Nyack College (NY)	41%	N/A
Sage Colleges–Albany (NY)	41%	28%
Salem State College (MA)	41%	13%
CUNY–Hunter College	40%	17%
College of St. Joseph (VT)	40%	27%
Dominican College (NY)	40%	19%
Husson University (ME)	40%	17%
Western Connecticut State University	39%	13%
Bowie State University (MD)	38%	13%
Dowling College (NY)	38%	16%
Lincoln University (PA)	38%	10%
Southern Connecticut State University	38%	12%
CUNY–City College	37%	4%
College of New Rochelle (NY)	36%	N/A
Delaware State University	36%	15%
Johnson State College (VT)	35%	N/A
University of Maryland–Eastern Shore	35%	18%
New Jersey City University	34%	7%
University of Southern Maine	34%	12%
CUNY–Lehman College	32%	11%
Gallaudet University (DC)	29%	N/A
Cheyney University of Pennsylvania	27%	N/A
Mercy College (NY)	27%	14%
Coppin State University (MD)	19%	5%
University of the District of Columbia	15%	N/A
SUNY Empire State College	14%	N/A
Univ. of Maryland–University College	12%	N/A

Schools whose students are most (and least) likely to graduate

Regional Universities (South)

School	6-year graduation rate	4-year graduation rate
James Madison University (VA)	81%	64%
University of Mary Washington (VA)	76%	67%
Elon University (NC)	75%	71%
The Citadel (SC)	70%	67%
Rollins College (FL)	68%	59%
University of North Carolina–Wilmington	67%	44%
Belmont University (TN)	65%	52%
Stetson University (FL)	65%	50%
Appalachian State University (NC)	63%	37%
Bellarmine University (KY)	63%	52%
Longwood University (VA)	63%	49%
Loyola University New Orleans	63%	48%
College of Charleston (SC)	62%	48%
Converse College (SC)	62%	64%
Spring Hill College (AL)	62%	50%
Union University (TN)	62%	N/A
Harding University (AR)	61%	38%
Embry-Riddle Aeronautical University (FL)	60%	29%
Queens University of Charlotte (NC)	60%	50%
Winthrop University (SC)	60%	37%
Mississippi College	59%	36%
Lipscomb University (TN)	58%	35%
Christian Brothers University (TN)	57%	39%
Radford University (VA)	57%	40%
Wheeling Jesuit University (WV)	57%	49%
Lynchburg College (VA)	56%	54%
Mercer University (GA)	56%	44%
University of Tampa (FL)	56%	44%
Freed-Hardeman University (TN)	55%	41%
Hampton University (VA)	54%	38%
Campbell University (NC)	53%	36%
Jacksonville University (FL)	52%	29%
Murray State University (KY)	52%	32%
Marymount University (VA)	51%	42%
Palm Beach Atlantic University (FL)	51%	41%
Pfeiffer University (NC)	51%	N/A
Brenau University (GA)	49%	32%
Gardner-Webb University (NC)	49%	35%
Lee University (TN)	49%	37%
North Georgia College and State Univ.	49%	24%
Western Carolina University (NC)	49%	26%
Western Kentucky University	49%	22%
Liberty University (VA)	48%	28%
Mary Baldwin College (VA)	48%	44%
Piedmont College (GA)	48%	34%
Shenandoah University (VA)	48%	33%
Tennessee Technological University	48%	22%
University of Mobile (AL)	48%	43%
North Carolina Central University	47%	19%
Southern Wesleyan University (SC)	47%	33%
University of Montevallo (AL)	46%	22%
University of North Florida	46%	23%
University of Tennessee–Martin	46%	24%
Columbia College (SC)	45%	33%
Delta State University (MS)	45%	17%
Georgia College & State University	45%	25%
Thomas More College (KY)	45%	28%
Albany State University (GA)	44%	N/A
Marshall University (WV)	44%	21%
Middle Tennessee State University	44%	N/A
Troy University (AL)	43%	19%
University of Central Arkansas	43%	22%
Xavier University of Louisiana	43%	N/A
Alcorn State University (MS)	42%	22%
Lincoln Memorial University (TN)	42%	N/A
St. Leo University (FL)	42%	24%
University of Tennessee–Chattanooga	42%	16%
Valdosta State University (GA)	42%	16%
Virginia State University	42%	25%
William Carey University (MS)	42%	37%
Belhaven University (MS)	41%	35%
Mississippi University for Women	41%	26%
Morehead State University (KY)	41%	16%
Tusculum College (TN)	41%	N/A
Francis Marion University (SC)	40%	20%
University of North Alabama	40%	18%
Arkansas State University–Jonesboro	39%	16%
Arkansas Tech University	39%	23%
Charleston Southern University (SC)	38%	19%
Eastern Kentucky University	37%	14%
Florida Gulf Coast University	37%	N/A
University of North Carolina–Pembroke	37%	23%
University of South Alabama	37%	13%
Fayetteville State University (NC)	36%	13%
McNeese State University (LA)	36%	12%
Northwestern State University of Louisiana	36%	18%
St. Thomas University (FL)	36%	28%
Cumberland University (TN)	35%	16%
Fort Valley State University (GA)	35%	13%
Georgia Southwestern State University	35%	15%
Jacksonville State University (AL)	35%	13%
Lynn University (FL)	35%	23%
University of West Georgia	35%	12%
Kennesaw State University (GA)	34%	10%
Mississippi Valley State University	34%	18%
Northern Kentucky University	34%	8%
Savannah State University (GA)	34%	13%
Alabama Agricultural and Mech. Univ.	33%	9%
Columbus State University (GA)	33%	11%
Grambling State University (LA)	33%	12%
Henderson State University (AR)	32%	17%
Hodges University (FL)	32%	N/A
Austin Peay State University (TN)	31%	13%
Nicholls State University (LA)	31%	13%
Norfolk State University (VA)	31%	N/A
Union College (KY)	31%	14%
Southeastern Louisiana University	30%	9%
University of Louisiana–Monroe	30%	11%
Southern University and A&M Coll. (LA)	29%	N/A
Auburn University–Montgomery (AL)	27%	11%
Bethel College (TN)	27%	N/A
Southern Polytechnic State Univ. (GA)	27%	7%
University of West Alabama	27%	N/A
Armstrong Atlantic State University (GA)	26%	7%
Alabama State University	25%	7%
University of Arkansas–Monticello	25%	N/A
Augusta State University (GA)	23%	N/A
Louisiana State University–Shreveport	21%	5%
Life University (GA)	14%	3%
Mountain State University (WV)	13%	3%
Southern University–New Orleans	8%	2%

Regional Universities (Midwest)

School	6-year graduation rate	4-year graduation rate
Xavier University (OH)	78%	68%
Bradley University (IL)	76%	52%
John Carroll University (OH)	76%	63%
Valparaiso University (IN)	76%	63%
Creighton University (NE)	75%	64%
Bethel University (MN)	74%	63%
Butler University (IN)	73%	57%
Drake University (IA)	73%	61%
Elmhurst College (IL)	70%	53%
Franciscan University of Steubenville (OH)	70%	63%
Indiana Wesleyan University	70%	55%
Baldwin-Wallace College (OH)	69%	50%
Truman State University (MO)	69%	47%
Dominican University (IL)	68%	60%
College of St. Scholastica (MN)	67%	62%
Hamline University (MN)	67%	58%
University of Wisconsin–La Crosse	66%	34%
University of Northern Iowa	65%	35%
Rockhurst University (MO)	64%	58%
Drury University (MO)	63%	55%
North Central College (IL)	63%	53%
Capital University (OH)	62%	52%
Cardinal Stritch University (WI)	62%	N/A
Concordia University Wisconsin	62%	32%
Maryville University of St. Louis (MO)	62%	51%
Otterbein College (OH)	62%	50%
University of Evansville (IN)	62%	52%
Webster University (MO)	62%	48%
St. Ambrose University (IA)	61%	53%
University of Wisconsin–Eau Claire	61%	25%
Ashland University (OH)	60%	46%
University of Illinois–Springfield	60%	47%
University of Wisconsin–Stevens Point	60%	20%
Eastern Illinois University	59%	30%
Spring Arbor University (MI)	59%	40%
St. Catherine University (MN)	59%	45%
University of St. Francis (IL)	59%	33%
Augsburg College (MN)	58%	37%
Benedictine University (IL)	58%	38%
Muskingum University (OH)	58%	40%
Carroll University (WI)	57%	N/A
Malone University (OH)	57%	44%
University of Nebraska–Kearney	57%	23%
Western Illinois University	57%	35%
Heidelberg University (OH)	56%	39%

School	6-year graduation rate	4-year graduation rate
Olivet Nazarene University (IL)	56%	44%
Anderson University (IN)	55%	44%
College of Mount St. Joseph (OH)	55%	36%
Grand Valley State University (MI)	55%	26%
Lewis University (IL)	55%	39%
St. Xavier University (IL)	55%	29%
University of Wisconsin–River Falls	55%	24%
Winona State University (MN)	55%	26%
Aquinas College (MI)	54%	33%
Benedictine College (KS)	54%	41%
MidAmerica Nazarene University (KS)	54%	40%
University of Findlay (OH)	54%	40%
University of Mary (ND)	54%	38%
University of Wisconsin–Whitewater	54%	25%
Walsh University (OH)	54%	51%
Fontbonne University (MO)	53%	31%
Missouri State University	53%	28%
North Park University (IL)	53%	34%
Northwest Missouri State University	53%	N/A
University of Detroit Mercy	53%	31%
University of Michigan–Dearborn	53%	18%
University of Wisconsin–Platteville	53%	18%
University of Indianapolis	52%	38%
University of Minnesota–Duluth	52%	26%
University of Wisconsin–Stout	52%	19%
Graceland University (IA)	51%	34%
Oakland City University (IN)	51%	42%
Pittsburg State University (KS)	51%	43%
University of Central Missouri	51%	24%
University of St. Francis (IN)	51%	N/A
Concordia University Chicago (IL)	50%	39%
Edgewood College (WI)	50%	27%
Minnesota State University–Mankato	50%	20%
Silver Lake College (WI)	50%	20%
Southeast Missouri State University	50%	24%
Southwest Baptist University (MO)	49%	N/A
Wayne State College (NE)	49%	27%
Aurora University (IL)	48%	N/A
Cornerstone University (MI)	48%	34%
Fort Hays State University (KS)	48%	N/A
Northern Michigan University	48%	18%
St. Cloud State University (MN)	48%	17%
University of Wisconsin–Oshkosh	48%	15%
Ursuline College (OH)	48%	30%
Concordia University–St. Paul (MN)	47%	35%
Marian University (WI)	47%	29%
Mount Marty College (SD)	47%	21%
Southwestern College (KS)	47%	29%
Viterbo University (WI)	47%	N/A
Bemidji State University (MN)	46%	23%
Lawrence Technological University (MI)	46%	18%
Washburn University (KS)	46%	21%
William Woods University (MO)	45%	41%
Columbia College (MO)	44%	31%
Emporia State University (KS)	44%	22%
Madonna University (MI)	44%	18%
Maharishi University of Management (IA)	44%	N/A
Ohio Dominican University	44%	30%
Lindenwood University (MO)	43%	28%
Minnesota State University–Moorhead	43%	20%
Newman University (KS)	43%	29%
Siena Heights University (MI)	43%	N/A
Southwest Minnesota State University	43%	24%
Southern Illinois University–Edwardsville	42%	16%
University of Nebraska–Omaha	42%	13%
Ferris State University (MI)	41%	23%
Missouri Baptist University	41%	N/A
University of St. Mary (KS)	41%	29%
Avila University (MO)	40%	22%
Lakeland College (WI)	40%	N/A
Mount Mary College (WI)	40%	20%
Rockford College (IL)	40%	29%
Upper Iowa University	40%	21%
Alverno College (WI)	39%	17%
Eastern Michigan University	39%	12%
Park University (MO)	39%	16%
Roosevelt University (IL)	39%	28%
University of Wisconsin–Superior	39%	20%
Friends University (KS)	38%	N/A
Tiffin University (OH)	38%	36%
University of Michigan–Flint	38%	14%
Youngstown State University (OH)	36%	11%
Saginaw Valley State University (MI)	35%	N/A
Columbia College (IL)	34%	N/A
University of Southern Indiana	34%	17%
Minot State University (ND)	31%	11%
Indiana University Southeast	29%	8%
Indiana University Northwest	26%	9%
Indiana University–South Bend	26%	7%
Lincoln University (MO)	25%	N/A
Indiana Univ.-Purdue Univ.–Fort Wayne	22%	6%
Purdue University–Calumet (IN)	22%	6%
University of Rio Grande (OH)	22%	N/A
Bellevue University (NE)	21%	N/A
Marygrove College (MI)	21%	N/A
Davenport University (MI)	20%	0%
Metropolitan State University (MN)	20%	N/A
Northeastern Illinois University	19%	3%
Calumet College of St. Joseph (IN)	17%	23%
Chicago State University	16%	N/A
National-Louis University (IL)	11%	N/A

Regional Universities (West)

School	6-year graduation rate	4-year graduation rate
Santa Clara University (CA)	85%	78%
Gonzaga University (WA)	81%	68%
Trinity University (TX)	79%	68%
Loyola Marymount University (CA)	77%	71%
Whitworth University (WA)	75%	61%
University of Portland (OR)	72%	68%
Cal. Polytechnic St. Univ.–San Luis Obispo	71%	25%
Seattle University	71%	52%
Point Loma Nazarene University (CA)	70%	62%
University of Redlands (CA)	69%	61%
Chapman University (CA)	68%	53%
Pacific Lutheran University (WA)	68%	59%
Seattle Pacific University	67%	60%
Western Washington University	67%	35%
California Lutheran University	65%	54%
University of Dallas	65%	62%
St. Mary's College of California	64%	50%
Mills College (CA)	63%	53%
Concordia University (CA)	61%	57%
Mount St. Mary's College (CA)	61%	50%
Regis University (CO)	61%	44%
Fresno Pacific University (CA)	60%	N/A
Evergreen State College (WA)	59%	43%
St. Edward's University (TX)	59%	44%
Abilene Christian University (TX)	58%	41%
St. Mary's University of San Antonio (TX)	58%	31%
California Baptist University	57%	45%
Westminster College (UT)	56%	42%
Notre Dame de Namur University (CA)	55%	48%
Texas State University–San Marcos	55%	24%
Central Washington University	54%	28%
Sonoma State University (CA)	54%	24%
California State University–Chico	53%	N/A
Dallas Baptist University	52%	38%
St. Martin's University (WA)	52%	35%
California State Poly. Univ.–Pomona	51%	15%
California State University–Long Beach	51%	13%
California State University–Stanislaus	51%	22%
Northwest Nazarene University (ID)	51%	37%
Oklahoma City University	51%	40%
Southern Nazarene University (OK)	51%	32%
California State University–Fullerton	50%	16%
California State Univ.–San Bernardino	50%	12%
Dominican University of California	50%	38%
University of St. Thomas (TX)	50%	30%
Woodbury University (CA)	50%	26%
Hardin-Simmons University (TX)	49%	29%
LeTourneau University (TX)	49%	29%
Walla Walla University (WA)	49%	21%
California State University–Fresno	48%	14%
Concordia University (OR)	48%	N/A
Eastern Washington University	48%	21%
Houston Baptist University	48%	24%
New Mexico Institute of Mining and Tech.	48%	21%
Oklahoma Christian University	45%	40%
San Francisco State University	45%	12%
University of the Southwest (NM)	45%	N/A
California State University–East Bay	44%	17%
Sam Houston State University (TX)	44%	21%
University of Colorado–Colorado Springs	44%	22%
University of Mary Hardin-Baylor (TX)	44%	30%
California State University–San Marcos	43%	14%
College of Santa Fe (NM)	43%	37%
Humboldt State University (CA)	43%	11%
Prescott College (AZ)	43%	10%
San Jose State University (CA)	43%	9%

Schools whose students are most (and least) likely to graduate

Regional Universities (West), continued

	6-year graduation rate	4-year graduation rate
Western Oregon University	43%	N/A
California State University–Sacramento	42%	18%
Lubbock Christian University (TX)	42%	28%
University of the Incarnate Word (TX)	42%	18%
Weber State University (UT)	42%	12%
California State University–Bakersfield	41%	13%
California State University–Northridge	41%	12%
Hawaii Pacific University	41%	23%
Naropa University (CO)	41%	19%
National University (CA)	41%	N/A
Southern Utah University	41%	23%
Tarleton State University (TX)	41%	N/A
Stephen F. Austin State University (TX)	40%	18%
Colorado Christian University	39%	N/A
Texas A&M University–Corpus Christi	39%	19%
Hope International University (CA)	38%	20%
Wayland Baptist University (TX)	38%	20%
West Texas A&M University	38%	N/A
Chaminade University of Honolulu	37%	21%

	6-year graduation rate	4-year graduation rate
Our Lady of the Lake University (TX)	37%	19%
Southern Oregon University	36%	N/A
Southwestern Oklahoma State University	36%	12%
Texas A&M International University	36%	19%
University of Central Oklahoma	36%	12%
University of Texas–Tyler	36%	15%
Alaska Pacific University	35%	29%
Prairie View A&M University (TX)	35%	8%
University of Texas–Pan American	35%	14%
East Central University (OK)	34%	N/A
Angelo State University (TX)	33%	15%
California State Univ.–Dominguez Hills	33%	5%
California State University–Los Angeles	33%	9%
Holy Names University (CA)	33%	26%
Lamar University (TX)	33%	9%
Adams State College (CO)	32%	N/A
University of Texas of the Permian Basin	32%	18%
La Sierra University (CA)	31%	14%
Midwestern State University (TX)	31%	10%

	6-year graduation rate	4-year graduation rate
Northeastern State University (OK)	31%	11%
Southeastern Oklahoma State University	31%	13%
Eastern New Mexico University	30%	N/A
Eastern Oregon University	30%	N/A
Marylhurst University (OR)	30%	13%
Montana State University–Billings	29%	14%
Texas Wesleyan University	28%	10%
University of Texas–San Antonio	28%	8%
Boise State University (ID)	27%	6%
Cameron University (OK)	25%	5%
University of Alaska–Anchorage	25%	9%
University of Great Falls (MT)	23%	N/A
New Mexico Highlands University	22%	N/A
Western New Mexico University	21%	N/A
Sul Ross State University (TX)	20%	N/A
University of Texas–Brownsville	17%	4%
University of Alaska–Southeast	14%	N/A
Heritage University (WA)	13%	N/A
Texas Southern University	12%	N/A

Regional Colleges (North)

	6-year graduation rate	4-year graduation rate
Cooper Union (NY)	85%	70%
Messiah College (PA)	77%	71%
United States Coast Guard Academy (CT)	76%	73%
United States Merchant Marine Acad. (NY)	74%	65%
College of Our Lady of the Elms (MA)	72%	N/A
Elizabethtown College (PA)	71%	66%
Lebanon Valley College (PA)	71%	68%
St. Joseph's College New York	71%	59%
Champlain College (VT)	66%	52%
Maine Maritime Academy	65%	44%
Endicott College (MA)	64%	68%
Elmira College (NY)	63%	63%
Massachusetts Maritime Academy	63%	51%
Stevenson University (MD)	62%	46%
University of Maine–Farmington	61%	46%
University of Pittsburgh–Johnstown	61%	42%
Colby-Sawyer College (NH)	60%	N/A
Roger Williams University (RI)	59%	51%
York College of Pennsylvania	59%	42%
Baptist Bible College and Seminary (PA)	57%	N/A
Geneva College (PA)	56%	N/A
Peirce College (PA)	56%	7%
Seton Hill University (PA)	56%	46%
Wilson College (PA)	55%	34%

	6-year graduation rate	4-year graduation rate
Fashion Institute of Technology (NY)	54%	N/A
SUNY Coll. of Agr. and Tech.–Cobleskill	54%	35%
St. Francis College (NY)	54%	17%
Vermont Technical College	53%	24%
Hilbert College (NY)	52%	N/A
SUNY Maritime College	52%	27%
Delaware Valley College (PA)	51%	37%
Thomas College (ME)	51%	N/A
Bay Path College (MA)	50%	N/A
Eastern Nazarene College (MA)	50%	32%
Curry College (MA)	48%	38%
Keuka College (NY)	48%	45%
Pennsylvania College of Technology	48%	40%
Valley Forge Christian College (PA)	48%	45%
Lasell College (MA)	47%	37%
Newbury College (MA)	46%	N/A
University of Pittsburgh–Bradford	45%	28%
Daniel Webster College (NH)	44%	N/A
New England College (NH)	44%	30%
Cazenovia College (NY)	43%	35%
SUNY College of Technology–Delhi	43%	23%
Becker College (MA)	42%	N/A
Southern Vermont College	42%	33%
Unity College (ME)	42%	N/A

	6-year graduation rate	4-year graduation rate
Vaughn Coll. of Aero. and Tech. (NY)	42%	31%
SUNY College of Technology–Alfred	40%	34%
University of Maine–Fort Kent	40%	21%
Keystone College (PA)	39%	N/A
Lyndon State College (VT)	39%	N/A
Mitchell College (CT)	37%	25%
Mount Aloysius College (PA)	37%	22%
Washington Adventist University (MD)	37%	13%
Wesley College (DE)	37%	19%
Paul Smith's College (NY)	36%	N/A
Felician College (NJ)	35%	15%
Farmingdale State College–SUNY	31%	14%
Mount Ida College (MA)	31%	24%
Post University (CT)	30%	21%
Bard College at Simon's Rock (MA)	28%	20%
CUNY–York College	25%	N/A
Boricua College (NY)	21%	N/A
Sojourner-Douglass College (MD)	21%	N/A
University of Maine–Augusta	15%	4%
CUNY–New York City College of Tech.	14%	6%
CUNY–Medgar Evers College	13%	0%
Fisher College (MA)	8%	N/A

Regional Colleges (South)

College	6-year graduation rate	4-year graduation rate
John Brown University (AR)	67%	53%
Thomas University (GA)	66%	13%
Erskine College (SC)	65%	63%
Covenant College (GA)	61%	47%
Flagler College (FL)	61%	49%
Ouachita Baptist University (AR)	60%	41%
Milligan College (TN)	59%	N/A
Bryan College (TN)	57%	45%
High Point University (NC)	56%	47%
Blue Mountain College (MS)	54%	40%
Florida Southern College	54%	38%
Claflin University (SC)	53%	29%
King College (TN)	53%	49%
Lenoir-Rhyne University (NC)	53%	40%
LaGrange College (GA)	52%	37%
Toccoa Falls College (GA)	51%	56%
Free Will Baptist Bible College (TN)	49%	29%
Ohio Valley University (WV)	49%	46%
Shorter College (GA)	49%	43%
Southern Adventist University (TN)	49%	22%
Davis and Elkins College (WV)	48%	35%
Coker College (SC)	47%	35%
Elizabeth City State University (NC)	47%	22%
Tuskegee University (AL)	47%	16%
Alderson-Broaddus College (WV)	46%	28%
Anderson University (SC)	46%	46%
Catawba College (NC)	46%	42%
Central Baptist College (AR)	46%	N/A
West Liberty University (WV)	45%	N/A
Newberry College (SC)	44%	31%
North Carolina Wesleyan College	44%	9%
Oakwood University (AL)	44%	N/A
Tennessee Wesleyan College	44%	33%
University of the Ozarks (AR)	44%	31%
Clearwater Christian College (FL)	43%	40%
Lander University (SC)	43%	N/A
Southeastern University (FL)	43%	33%
University of Charleston (WV)	43%	38%
Williams Baptist College (AR)	43%	41%
Fairmont State University (WV)	42%	14%
Louisiana College	42%	23%
Averett University (VA)	41%	34%
Brescia University (KY)	41%	26%
Winston-Salem State University (NC)	41%	14%
Shepherd University (WV)	40%	21%
University of the Cumberlands (KY)	40%	N/A
Barton College (NC)	39%	33%
Belmont Abbey College (NC)	39%	29%
Mars Hill College (NC)	39%	25%
University of South Carolina–Aiken	39%	17%
Bluefield College (VA)	38%	39%
Campbellsville University (KY)	38%	26%
Glenville State College (WV)	38%	16%
Methodist University (NC)	38%	15%
University of South Carolina–Upstate	38%	20%
Alice Lloyd College (KY)	37%	23%
Bethune-Cookman University (FL)	37%	16%
Limestone College (SC)	37%	21%
Emmanuel College (GA)	36%	29%
Reinhardt University (GA)	36%	31%
Concord University (WV)	35%	19%
Warner University (FL)	35%	21%
Miles College (AL)	34%	N/A
West Virginia University Institute of Tech.	34%	N/A
Florida Memorial University	33%	N/A
Morris College (SC)	33%	N/A
Southern Arkansas University	33%	13%
Montreat College (NC)	32%	N/A
Mount Olive College (NC)	31%	N/A
Our Lady of Holy Cross College (LA)	31%	0%
Shaw University (NC)	31%	17%
Atlanta Christian College	30%	N/A
Martin Methodist College (TN)	30%	N/A
St. Augustine's College (NC)	30%	N/A
Virginia Intermont College	30%	N/A
University of Arkansas–Pine Bluff	29%	6%
Voorhees College (SC)	29%	N/A
Benedict College (SC)	28%	N/A
Chowan University (NC)	28%	1%
Livingstone College (NC)	28%	11%
Virginia Union University	28%	N/A
Faulkner University (AL)	27%	12%
Aquinas College (TN)	26%	N/A
Arkansas Baptist College	26%	N/A
Brewton-Parker College (GA)	26%	N/A
Kentucky State University	26%	8%
Lees-McRae College (NC)	26%	N/A
Clayton State University (GA)	25%	12%
Bluefield State College (WV)	23%	11%
Concordia College (AL)	22%	N/A
Midway College (KY)	22%	N/A
LeMoyne-Owen College (TN)	21%	N/A
Philander Smith College (AR)	21%	4%
Stillman College (AL)	21%	14%
St. Paul's College (VA)	18%	N/A
Victory University (TN)	18%	16%
West Virginia University–Parkersburg	17%	N/A
Macon State College (GA)	13%	N/A
Edward Waters College (FL)	10%	N/A
Dalton State College (GA)	5%	N/A

Regional Colleges (Midwest)

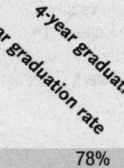

College	6-year graduation rate	4-year graduation rate
Taylor University (IN)	78%	71%
Cedarville University (OH)	70%	62%
Augustana College (SD)	66%	51%
Ohio Northern University	66%	45%
Loras College (IA)	64%	54%
Dordt College (IA)	63%	58%
Bethel College (IN)	61%	44%
Bluffton University (OH)	61%	56%
Concordia University (NE)	61%	39%
Huntington University (IN)	61%	54%
Mount Mercy College (IA)	61%	51%
Northwestern College (IA)	61%	53%
College of the Ozarks (MO)	60%	36%
Marietta College (OH)	60%	43%
McKendree University (IL)	60%	39%
Buena Vista University (IA)	59%	46%
Northwestern College (IA)	59%	45%
Trinity Christian College (IL)	59%	54%
Franklin College (IN)	57%	50%
Wilmington College (OH)	57%	50%
Carthage College (WI)	56%	51%
Grace College and Seminary (IN)	56%	50%
Midland Lutheran College (NE)	55%	43%
Milwaukee School of Engineering	55%	39%
St. Joseph's College (IN)	55%	52%
Tabor College (KS)	55%	55%
Judson University (IL)	53%	34%
Manchester College (IN)	53%	38%
College of St. Mary (NE)	52%	42%
Defiance College (OH)	52%	38%
Eureka College (IL)	52%	N/A
Mount Vernon Nazarene University (OH)	52%	37%
Crown College (MN)	51%	32%
St. Mary-of-the-Woods College (IN)	51%	54%
Union College (NE)	51%	27%
Greenville College (IL)	50%	38%
Maranatha Baptist Bible College (WI)	50%	32%
Briar Cliff University (IA)	49%	41%
Jamestown College (ND)	49%	31%
Marian University (IN)	49%	32%
Robert Morris University (IL)	49%	N/A
Trine University (IN)	49%	29%
Culver-Stockton College (MO)	48%	43%
Dakota State University (SD)	48%	18%
Dana College (NE)	48%	33%
MacMurray College (IL)	48%	30%
University of Sioux Falls (SD)	48%	28%
Adrian College (MI)	47%	46%
Hannibal-LaGrange College (MO)	47%	8%
Notre Dame College of Ohio	47%	36%
Quincy University (IL)	47%	31%
Morningside College (IA)	46%	39%
Valley City State University (ND)	46%	23%
Northern State University (SD)	45%	N/A
Chadron State College (NE)	44%	17%
Grand View University (IA)	44%	27%
Bethany Lutheran College (MN)	43%	N/A

Schools whose students are most (and least) likely to graduate

Regional Colleges (Midwest), continued

	6-year graduation rate	4-year graduation rate
University of Northwestern Ohio	43%	N/A
Bethany College (KS)	42%	24%
Blackburn College (IL)	42%	27%
Lake Erie College (OH)	42%	34%
University of Dubuque (IA)	42%	21%
Dakota Wesleyan University (SD)	41%	31%
North Central University (MN)	41%	N/A
York College (NE)	41%	18%
Central Methodist University (MO)	40%	27%
Concordia University (MI)	40%	N/A
Lake Superior State University (MI)	39%	N/A
Kendall College (IL)	38%	N/A
Grace Bible College (MI)	37%	N/A
Ottawa University (KS)	36%	N/A
Kansas Wesleyan University	35%	N/A
Lourdes College (OH)	35%	3%
Mayville State University (ND)	35%	19%
Central Christian College (KS)	34%	35%
Missouri Southern State University	34%	N/A
Rochester College (MI)	34%	N/A
Peru State College (NE)	33%	15%
University of Minnesota–Crookston	33%	21%
Urbana University (OH)	32%	N/A
Wilberforce University (OH)	32%	N/A
Dickinson State University (ND)	31%	11%
Missouri Western State University	28%	12%
Waldorf College (IA)	28%	N/A
Indiana University–Kokomo	27%	9%
Missouri Valley College	27%	N/A
Black Hills State University (SD)	26%	9%
Shawnee State University (OH)	26%	15%
Central State University (OH)	24%	8%
Finlandia University (MI)	23%	N/A
William Penn University (IA)	23%	N/A
Chancellor University (OH)	22%	N/A
Iowa Wesleyan College	22%	N/A
Harris-Stowe State University (MO)	20%	8%
Indiana University East	20%	9%
Purdue University–North Central (IN)	15%	6%
Baker College of Flint (MI)	11%	N/A
East-West University (IL)	11%	8%

Regional Colleges (West)

	6-year graduation rate	4-year graduation rate
United States Air Force Academy (CO)	79%	77%
California Maritime Academy	59%	N/A
Master's College and Seminary (CA)	58%	50%
Oklahoma Baptist University	57%	40%
Vanguard University of Southern California	52%	45%
Corban University (OR)	51%	46%
Brigham Young University–Idaho	49%	N/A
Northwest University (WA)	49%	43%
Rocky Mountain College (MT)	49%	32%
Pacific Union College (CA)	47%	38%
Cogswell Polytechnical College (CA)	44%	22%
Schreiner University (TX)	43%	26%
Southwestern Adventist University (TX)	43%	N/A
Warner Pacific College (OR)	43%	36%
McMurry University (TX)	42%	26%
Oklahoma Wesleyan University	41%	41%
Montana Tech of the Univ. of Montana	40%	16%
Oklahoma Panhandle State University	40%	23%
Oregon Institute of Technology	39%	20%
Howard Payne University (TX)	38%	26%
Humphreys College (CA)	38%	N/A
East Texas Baptist University	37%	27%
Northwest Christian University (OR)	36%	32%
Southwestern Assemb. of God Univ. (TX)	35%	29%
Concordia University Texas	33%	18%
Langston University (OK)	33%	6%
Bethany University (CA)	32%	N/A
Dixie State College of Utah	31%	28%
Northwestern Oklahoma State University	31%	16%
University of Montana–Western	31%	12%
Mid-America Christian University (OK)	29%	N/A
Amer. Ind. Coll. of the Assemb. of God (AZ)	28%	N/A
St. Gregory's University (OK)	28%	N/A
Univ. of Science and Arts of Oklahoma	28%	20%
Montana State University–Northern	27%	N/A
Rogers State University (OK)	26%	4%
Wiley College (TX)	26%	12%
Utah Valley University	24%	N/A
Lewis-Clark State College (ID)	23%	N/A
Texas College	20%	2%
National Hispanic University (CA)	19%	N/A
Patten University (CA)	16%	N/A
Bacone College (OK)	14%	4%
University of Houston–Downtown	14%	2%
Southwestern Christian College (TX)	6%	N/A

Schools with the most diverse student bodies

If you're looking for a campus culture that features a wealth of different student backgrounds, the *U.S. News* diversity index can point you to institutions with both a healthy proportion of minority students and a mix of different groups. The closer the index number is to 1.0, the more diverse the population and more likely you are to encounter undergraduates from a racial or ethnic group different from your own. All the data are for the 2009–2010 school year; around the top 40 percent of each category is shown.

National Universities

	Diversity index	Men	Women	American Indian	Asian	Black	Hispanic	White	International	Undergraduates from out of state	Average age of full-time students
Rutgers, the State University of New Jersey–Newark	0.74	47%	53%	0%	24%	19%	21%	34%	2%	3%	22
University of Houston	0.73	50%	50%	0%	22%	15%	24%	34%	4%	1%	22
Nova Southeastern University (FL)	0.70	28%	72%	0%	5%	27%	28%	35%	4%	18%	24
New Jersey Institute of Technology	0.69	79%	21%	1%	21%	10%	20%	44%	4%	4%	21
Polytechnic Institute of New York University (NY)	0.69	80%	20%	0%	30%	10%	12%	35%	12%	13%	20
St. John's University (NY)	0.69	45%	55%	0%	18%	18%	15%	45%	5%	23%	20
University of California–Riverside	0.69	48%	52%	0%	40%	8%	29%	21%	2%	1%	21
Andrews University (MI)	0.68	45%	55%	0%	11%	26%	12%	39%	12%	44%	21
Stanford University (CA)	0.68	51%	49%	3%	23%	10%	13%	44%	7%	54%	20
Massachusetts Institute of Technology	0.67	55%	45%	1%	26%	8%	13%	43%	9%	91%	20
University of Bridgeport (CT)	0.66	32%	68%	0%	3%	37%	15%	33%	11%	35%	22
University of Texas–Arlington	0.66	46%	54%	1%	12%	16%	19%	49%	4%	2%	23
Georgia State University	0.65	40%	60%	0%	12%	34%	7%	45%	2%	6%	23
Golden Gate University (CA)	0.65	43%	57%	0%	23%	10%	12%	50%	4%	6%	31
Texas Woman's University	0.65	8%	92%	1%	8%	21%	19%	50%	2%	1%	23
University of California–Los Angeles	0.65	44%	56%	0%	38%	4%	15%	38%	5%	5%	21
University of Illinois–Chicago	0.65	48%	52%	0%	22%	8%	18%	49%	1%	2%	21
University of California–Berkeley	0.64	47%	53%	1%	40%	4%	12%	38%	5%	7%	21
Barry University (FL)	0.63	31%	69%	0%	1%	20%	25%	48%	5%	N/A	N/A
University of California–Davis	0.63	44%	56%	1%	40%	3%	14%	41%	2%	2%	21
University of Nevada–Las Vegas	0.63	45%	55%	1%	18%	8%	17%	53%	3%	16%	22
University of New Mexico	0.63	44%	56%	7%	4%	3%	37%	48%	1%	9%	22
University of Southern California	0.63	50%	50%	1%	24%	6%	13%	46%	10%	35%	21
University of the Pacific (CA)	0.63	45%	55%	1%	35%	4%	12%	45%	4%	13%	20
Rice University (TX)	0.62	52%	48%	0%	21%	7%	12%	50%	9%	44%	20
San Diego State University	0.62	43%	57%	1%	15%	4%	26%	51%	3%	6%	22
University of California–San Diego	0.62	48%	52%	0%	44%	2%	13%	35%	7%	3%	21
University of San Francisco	0.62	37%	63%	1%	21%	5%	14%	50%	9%	26%	20
Rutgers–New Brunswick	0.61	52%	48%	0%	25%	8%	10%	55%	2%	7%	20
University of Maryland–Baltimore County	0.61	54%	46%	1%	21%	17%	4%	54%	4%	7%	21
University of Texas–Austin	0.61	49%	51%	0%	18%	5%	19%	53%	4%	4%	21
University of Texas–Dallas	0.61	55%	45%	1%	22%	7%	12%	54%	4%	3%	22
Columbia University (NY)	0.60	50%	50%	1%	15%	9%	11%	53%	10%	72%	20
Florida Atlantic University	0.60	42%	58%	0%	5%	18%	20%	54%	3%	4%	22
Union Institute and University (OH)	0.60	40%	60%	1%	2%	30%	13%	54%	0%	N/A	N/A
University of California–Irvine	0.60	47%	53%	0%	53%	2%	14%	28%	3%	2%	21
University of California–Santa Cruz	0.60	47%	53%	1%	22%	3%	18%	56%	0%	3%	22
University of La Verne (CA)	0.60	41%	59%	1%	4%	7%	39%	48%	1%	1%	20
University of Massachusetts–Boston	0.60	43%	57%	0%	13%	16%	9%	57%	4%	5%	23
University of California–Santa Barbara	0.59	46%	54%	1%	16%	3%	21%	57%	1%	3%	20
California Institute of Technology	0.58	62%	38%	0%	40%	1%	7%	40%	12%	65%	20
Carnegie Mellon University (PA)	0.58	58%	42%	1%	24%	5%	5%	49%	15%	79%	20
Duke University (NC)	0.58	51%	49%	0%	22%	10%	7%	55%	7%	83%	20
SUNY–Stony Brook	0.58	52%	48%	0%	23%	7%	9%	55%	7%	7%	21
Emory University (GA)	0.57	45%	55%	0%	22%	10%	4%	55%	8%	70%	20
New Mexico State University	0.57	45%	55%	4%	1%	3%	44%	43%	5%	18%	22
University of Miami (FL)	0.57	48%	52%	0%	5%	8%	24%	54%	9%	49%	20
Wayne State University (MI)	0.57	42%	58%	1%	7%	32%	3%	55%	3%	2%	22
Dartmouth College (NH)	0.56	51%	49%	4%	15%	8%	7%	59%	7%	95%	20
University of Pennsylvania	0.56	49%	51%	0%	19%	8%	6%	56%	10%	81%	20
University of Washington	0.56	48%	52%	1%	28%	3%	6%	55%	6%	12%	21
Harvard University (MA)	0.55	49%	51%	1%	17%	8%	7%	56%	11%	85%	20
Johns Hopkins University (MD)	0.55	50%	50%	0%	21%	7%	7%	57%	8%	86%	20
Trinity International University (IL)	0.55	43%	57%	0%	4%	23%	11%	61%	1%	40%	20
University of Florida	0.55	45%	55%	1%	9%	10%	16%	64%	1%	3%	21
Virginia Commonwealth University	0.55	43%	57%	1%	12%	20%	4%	61%	3%	7%	21
Yale University (CT)	0.55	50%	50%	1%	14%	9%	9%	58%	9%	94%	20

Schools with the most diverse student bodies

National Universities, continued

	Diversity index	Men	Women	American Indian	Asian	Black	Hispanic	White	International	Undergraduates from out of state	Average age of full-time students
Princeton University (NJ)	0.54	51%	49%	0%	16%	8%	8%	58%	10%	81%	20
University of Memphis	0.54	39%	61%	0%	3%	39%	2%	55%	1%	9%	23
University of South Florida	0.54	44%	56%	0%	7%	13%	15%	64%	1%	3%	22
Brown University (RI)	0.53	47%	53%	1%	16%	7%	9%	59%	9%	95%	20
George Mason University (VA)	0.53	47%	53%	0%	16%	8%	9%	63%	3%	10%	21
University of Maryland–College Park	0.53	53%	47%	0%	15%	12%	6%	64%	2%	24%	20
University of North Texas	0.53	46%	54%	1%	6%	14%	14%	63%	2%	N/A	21
New York University	0.52	39%	61%	0%	20%	4%	8%	60%	8%	65%	20
Pace University (NY)	0.52	40%	60%	0%	9%	11%	13%	62%	5%	31%	20
University of New Orleans	0.52	49%	51%	1%	6%	18%	7%	64%	4%	5%	22
Howard University (DC)	0.51	32%	68%	0%	0%	47%	0%	49%	3%	N/A	N/A
New School (NY)	0.51	29%	71%	0%	12%	5%	8%	51%	23%	66%	22
Northwestern University (IL)	0.51	48%	52%	0%	19%	6%	7%	62%	6%	N/A	N/A
Pepperdine University (CA)	0.51	45%	55%	1%	10%	7%	12%	65%	6%	43%	20
Regent University (VA)	0.51	34%	66%	1%	2%	26%	6%	64%	1%	56%	29
Seton Hall University (NJ)	0.51	42%	58%	0%	7%	14%	12%	65%	2%	25%	20
University of Chicago	0.51	51%	49%	0%	15%	6%	9%	61%	9%	77%	20
Florida International University	0.50	44%	56%	0%	3%	12%	65%	15%	5%	2%	21
Old Dominion University (VA)	0.50	45%	55%	1%	5%	24%	4%	65%	1%	7%	22
University of Arizona	0.50	48%	52%	3%	7%	4%	18%	65%	3%	30%	20
DePaul University (IL)	0.49	45%	55%	0%	8%	9%	13%	68%	1%	18%	21
Illinois Institute of Technology	0.49	71%	29%	1%	13%	4%	8%	57%	17%	32%	21
Texas A&M University–Commerce	0.49	38%	62%	1%	2%	19%	10%	67%	1%	3%	24
University of Central Florida	0.49	45%	55%	0%	6%	9%	15%	68%	1%	5%	21
Biola University (CA)	0.48	39%	61%	1%	12%	3%	13%	69%	2%	25%	19
Cornell University (NY)	0.48	51%	49%	0%	17%	5%	6%	63%	8%	64%	20
Temple University (PA)	0.48	47%	53%	0%	10%	16%	4%	67%	3%	20%	21
University of Alabama–Birmingham	0.48	42%	58%	0%	4%	26%	2%	65%	2%	6%	22
University of Colorado–Denver	0.48	44%	56%	1%	11%	5%	12%	66%	5%	5%	23
University of San Diego	0.48	43%	57%	2%	11%	3%	15%	66%	4%	37%	20
Arizona State University	0.47	49%	51%	2%	6%	5%	16%	68%	2%	20%	22
Azusa Pacific University (CA)	0.47	36%	64%	1%	8%	5%	15%	69%	2%	19%	20
Georgia Institute of Technology	0.47	70%	30%	0%	17%	6%	4%	66%	6%	27%	21
University of Alaska–Fairbanks	0.47	40%	60%	19%	3%	3%	4%	69%	2%	13%	23
University of Illinois–Urbana-Champaign	0.47	54%	46%	0%	13%	7%	7%	65%	8%	6%	21
University of North Carolina–Greensboro	0.47	33%	67%	0%	4%	23%	4%	69%	1%	6%	21
University of Southern Mississippi	0.47	39%	61%	0%	1%	30%	2%	66%	1%	12%	22
Cleveland State University	0.45	45%	55%	0%	3%	21%	4%	70%	2%	2%	24
Florida Institute of Technology	0.45	54%	46%	1%	2%	14%	7%	62%	14%	56%	20
Northern Illinois University	0.45	49%	51%	1%	6%	14%	8%	71%	1%	2%	N/A
Oral Roberts University (OK)	0.45	41%	59%	3%	2%	15%	6%	68%	7%	64%	21
Pacific University (OR)	0.45	35%	65%	1%	23%	1%	5%	68%	2%	47%	21
University of Hawaii–Manoa	0.45	46%	54%	1%	67%	1%	3%	24%	4%	23%	21
University of Missouri–Kansas City	0.45	42%	58%	1%	6%	15%	5%	70%	3%	26%	23

National Liberal Arts Colleges

	Diversity index	Men	Women	American Indian	Asian	Black	Hispanic	White	International	Undergraduates from out of state	Average age of full-time students
SUNY College–Old Westbury	0.70	41%	59%	1%	8%	33%	19%	39%	2%	2%	23
Bloomfield College (NJ)	0.63	35%	65%	0%	3%	50%	20%	26%	1%	5%	22
Pine Manor College (MA)	0.63	0%	100%	0%	4%	51%	16%	26%	3%	N/A	N/A
Swarthmore College (PA)	0.60	48%	52%	1%	16%	10%	11%	56%	7%	87%	20
Wellesley College (MA)	0.60	2%	98%	1%	26%	7%	8%	49%	10%	83%	20
Whittier College (CA)	0.60	47%	53%	1%	9%	6%	30%	54%	2%	24%	20
Albertus Magnus College (CT)	0.59	32%	68%	0%	1%	31%	12%	55%	0%	5%	29
Colorado State University–Pueblo	0.56	44%	56%	2%	3%	9%	25%	60%	1%	7%	23
Occidental College (CA)	0.56	44%	56%	1%	16%	6%	13%	62%	1%	53%	19
Pomona College (CA)	0.55	50%	50%	0%	14%	9%	11%	62%	4%	68%	20
Amherst College (MA)	0.54	50%	50%	0%	10%	11%	11%	60%	8%	89%	20
California State University–Monterey Bay	0.54	41%	59%	1%	6%	4%	26%	62%	1%	2%	22
Williams College (MA)	0.53	48%	52%	0%	12%	10%	10%	61%	7%	86%	20
Agnes Scott College (GA)	0.52	1%	99%	0%	4%	25%	5%	59%	7%	42%	20
Wesleyan College (GA)	0.52	2%	98%	0%	3%	24%	2%	49%	20%	15%	21

U.S.NEWS & WORLD REPORT

	Diversity index	Men	Women	American Indian	Asian	Black	Hispanic	White	International	Undergraduates from out of state	Average age of full-time students
Texas Lutheran University	0.51	48%	52%	0%	1%	10%	23%	64%	1%	4%	21
Oglethorpe University (GA)	0.50	40%	60%	0%	4%	23%	5%	64%	3%	N/A	N/A
Pitzer College (CA)	0.49	41%	59%	1%	8%	6%	15%	67%	3%	46%	20
Austin College (TX)	0.48	46%	54%	1%	15%	3%	10%	69%	2%	7%	20
Bowdoin College (ME)	0.48	49%	51%	1%	12%	6%	10%	68%	3%	88%	20
Ferrum College (VA)	0.48	51%	49%	1%	1%	31%	3%	64%	1%	12%	20
Barnard College (NY)	0.47	0%	100%	0%	16%	4%	9%	66%	5%	67%	20
Marymount Manhattan College (NY)	0.47	24%	76%	0%	3%	12%	14%	68%	3%	55%	20
Smith College (MA)	0.47	0%	100%	1%	13%	7%	7%	67%	6%	78%	20
University of Hawaii–West Oahu	0.47	29%	71%	0%	64%	2%	2%	29%	3%	2%	18
Harvey Mudd College (CA)	0.46	64%	36%	1%	20%	1%	7%	68%	3%	57%	20
Thomas Edison State College (NJ)	0.46	62%	38%	1%	3%	16%	8%	70%	1%	67%	N/A
Guilford College (NC)	0.45	41%	59%	1%	1%	25%	3%	69%	1%	34%	24
Mount Holyoke College (MA)	0.45	0%	100%	0%	10%	7%	6%	58%	20%	73%	21
Peace College (NC)	0.45	1%	99%	2%	2%	19%	5%	71%	1%	N/A	N/A
Wesleyan University (CT)	0.45	49%	51%	1%	10%	7%	9%	67%	7%	92%	20
Bryn Mawr College (PA)	0.44	0%	100%	0%	12%	6%	5%	66%	10%	84%	20
Scripps College (CA)	0.44	0%	100%	1%	13%	4%	9%	71%	2%	58%	20
Fort Lewis College (CO)	0.43	51%	49%	21%	1%	1%	5%	71%	1%	34%	22
Westmont College (CA)	0.43	38%	63%	2%	9%	3%	11%	74%	1%	31%	20
Drew University (NJ)	0.42	40%	60%	0%	6%	8%	10%	74%	2%	40%	20
Haverford College (PA)	0.42	45%	55%	0%	9%	8%	8%	73%	3%	86%	21
Vassar College (NY)	0.42	41%	59%	0%	11%	5%	7%	70%	6%	73%	20
Virginia Wesleyan College	0.42	37%	63%	0%	2%	21%	4%	73%	1%	22%	21
Claremont McKenna College (CA)	0.41	55%	45%	0%	12%	3%	9%	70%	6%	41%	20
Metropolitan State College of Denver	0.41	45%	55%	1%	4%	6%	14%	74%	1%	N/A	N/A
Berea College (KY)	0.40	41%	59%	1%	1%	18%	3%	70%	7%	57%	21
Grinnell College (IA)	0.40	47%	53%	1%	8%	6%	7%	67%	11%	86%	20
Purchase College–SUNY	0.39	44%	56%	0%	3%	7%	12%	76%	2%	19%	21
Randolph College (VA)	0.39	27%	73%	1%	2%	11%	6%	68%	12%	53%	20
Simpson University (CA)	0.39	37%	63%	2%	10%	4%	8%	77%	0%	14%	25
United States Military Academy (NY)	0.39	85%	15%	1%	7%	6%	9%	76%	1%	94%	20
University of Wisconsin–Parkside	0.39	45%	55%	0%	3%	10%	9%	76%	1%	9%	23
Carleton College (MN)	0.38	48%	52%	1%	10%	5%	6%	72%	7%	77%	20
McPherson College (KS)	0.38	56%	44%	3%	2%	10%	7%	77%	1%	5%	21
Reed College (OR)	0.38	45%	55%	1%	9%	3%	7%	73%	6%	87%	N/A
Southwestern University (TX)	0.38	38%	62%	1%	4%	3%	15%	77%	0%	7%	20
Macalester College (MN)	0.36	42%	58%	1%	9%	4%	4%	70%	12%	80%	20
Middlebury College (VT)	0.36	49%	51%	0%	9%	4%	5%	71%	10%	94%	20
Oberlin College (OH)	0.36	45%	55%	1%	7%	7%	5%	74%	6%	9%	20
United States Naval Academy (MD)	0.36	80%	20%	0%	4%	5%	12%	78%	1%	96%	20
Knox College (IL)	0.35	40%	60%	1%	7%	5%	5%	75%	7%	47%	19
Albright College (PA)	0.34	41%	59%	0%	1%	11%	6%	76%	6%	35%	20
University of Minnesota–Morris	0.34	43%	57%	12%	3%	3%	2%	77%	4%	12%	20
Whitman College (WA)	0.34	42%	58%	1%	11%	2%	6%	78%	2%	40%	20
Colgate University (NY)	0.33	47%	53%	1%	5%	6%	6%	77%	5%	67%	20
College of the Holy Cross (MA)	0.33	45%	55%	0%	6%	4%	8%	80%	1%	63%	20
Linfield College (OR)	0.33	43%	57%	2%	9%	2%	5%	77%	5%	45%	20
Skidmore College (NY)	0.33	40%	60%	1%	9%	4%	5%	78%	3%	67%	20
Trinity College (CT)	0.33	50%	50%	0%	6%	6%	6%	77%	5%	82%	20
Cedar Crest College (PA)	0.32	5%	95%	0%	3%	8%	7%	81%	1%	19%	N/A
Coastal Carolina University (SC)	0.32	47%	53%	0%	1%	15%	3%	80%	1%	49%	21
Hamilton College (NY)	0.32	47%	53%	1%	8%	4%	5%	78%	5%	67%	20
Hampshire College (MA)	0.32	40%	60%	1%	4%	4%	8%	78%	4%	82%	19
Lake Forest College (IL)	0.32	41%	59%	0%	4%	5%	7%	73%	11%	50%	20
St. Mary's College of Maryland	0.32	42%	58%	1%	4%	8%	4%	81%	2%	19%	20
University of Richmond (VA)	0.32	47%	53%	0%	5%	8%	4%	78%	5%	80%	20
Huntingdon College (AL)	0.31	48%	52%	0%	1%	16%	1%	81%	1%	13%	21
Millsaps College (MS)	0.31	50%	50%	0%	4%	11%	2%	81%	2%	52%	21
Stephens College (MO)	0.31	3%	97%	1%	1%	13%	3%	82%	0%	46%	21
University of Puget Sound (WA)	0.31	41%	59%	2%	10%	3%	4%	81%	1%	74%	20
Bates College (ME)	0.30	47%	53%	1%	7%	5%	4%	78%	6%	90%	20
Davidson College (NC)	0.30	49%	51%	1%	5%	7%	5%	80%	3%	78%	20
Lewis & Clark College (OR)	0.30	40%	60%	1%	7%	2%	5%	78%	6%	82%	20
Meredith College (NC)	0.30	0%	100%	1%	3%	11%	3%	82%	1%	9%	21
New College of Florida	0.30	38%	62%	1%	3%	2%	11%	83%	0%	22%	20
Olivet College (MI)	0.30	55%	45%	1%	0%	12%	3%	83%	0%	4%	19
Randolph-Macon College (VA)	0.30	47%	53%	1%	2%	11%	2%	81%	2%	32%	19
Sterling College (KS)	0.30	51%	49%	2%	1%	7%	7%	82%	1%	41%	20

Schools with the most diverse student bodies

National Liberal Arts Colleges, continued

	Diversity index	Men	Women	American Indian	Asian	Black	Hispanic	White	International	Undergraduates from out of state	Average age of full-time students
Union College (NY)	0.30	51%	49%	0%	7%	5%	5%	80%	3%	59%	20
Wingate University (NC)	0.30	46%	54%	1%	2%	10%	3%	79%	4%	28%	20
Bethel College (KS)	0.29	51%	49%	1%	2%	5%	7%	81%	3%	25%	21
Rhodes College (TN)	0.29	43%	57%	1%	5%	7%	2%	81%	4%	73%	20
Willamette University (OR)	0.29	44%	56%	1%	7%	2%	6%	83%	1%	68%	20
Colorado College	0.28	47%	53%	1%	6%	2%	7%	81%	4%	76%	20
Goucher College (MD)	0.28	32%	68%	1%	3%	8%	5%	83%	1%	72%	20
Lafayette College (PA)	0.28	53%	47%	0%	4%	5%	5%	78%	7%	76%	20
Mesa State College (CO)	0.28	43%	57%	2%	3%	2%	9%	84%	0%	10%	23
Birmingham-Southern College (AL)	0.27	50%	50%	1%	4%	8%	2%	85%	0%	39%	20
Christopher Newport University (VA)	0.27	44%	56%	1%	3%	8%	3%	84%	0%	7%	20
Colby College (ME)	0.27	46%	54%	1%	8%	3%	3%	80%	5%	87%	20
Connecticut College	0.27	39%	61%	0%	5%	4%	6%	81%	4%	85%	20
DePauw University (IN)	0.27	43%	57%	0%	3%	6%	4%	79%	7%	59%	20
Dickinson College (PA)	0.27	44%	56%	0%	4%	4%	5%	80%	6%	75%	20
Franklin and Marshall College (PA)	0.27	48%	52%	1%	4%	4%	5%	78%	8%	70%	20
Hollins University (VA)	0.27	1%	99%	1%	2%	8%	4%	82%	4%	44%	22
Millikin University (IL)	0.27	40%	60%	0%	1%	10%	3%	84%	1%	12%	21
Virginia Military Institute	0.27	92%	8%	0%	4%	6%	4%	84%	2%	40%	20
Wheaton College (IL)	0.27	50%	50%	0%	8%	4%	4%	83%	1%	76%	20

Regional Universities (North)

	Diversity index	Men	Women	American Indian	Asian	Black	Hispanic	White	International	Undergraduates from out of state	Average age of full-time students
St. Peter's College (NJ)	0.72	43%	57%	0%	11%	25%	28%	33%	3%	14%	21
CUNY–Baruch College	0.71	49%	51%	0%	32%	10%	16%	30%	12%	4%	22
CUNY–City College	0.71	49%	51%	0%	20%	23%	36%	11%	11%	8%	22
CUNY–Brooklyn College	0.70	40%	60%	0%	16%	25%	12%	41%	6%	1%	22
CUNY–Hunter College	0.70	33%	67%	0%	21%	12%	19%	39%	9%	4%	22
CUNY–John Jay College of Criminal Justice	0.70	43%	57%	0%	8%	23%	41%	25%	3%	4%	21
New Jersey City University	0.69	39%	61%	0%	7%	20%	35%	36%	1%	1%	20
Mercy College (NY)	0.68	33%	67%	0%	3%	27%	30%	39%	1%	5%	24
CUNY–Queens College	0.67	41%	59%	0%	23%	9%	18%	44%	6%	1%	N/A
College of Mount St. Vincent (NY)	0.66	25%	75%	0%	10%	12%	30%	48%	0%	11%	20
Cambridge College (MA)	0.65	30%	70%	0%	3%	29%	19%	48%	1%	4%	30
Kean University (NJ)	0.64	38%	62%	0%	7%	19%	21%	51%	2%	2%	22
CUNY–Lehman College	0.61	30%	70%	0%	5%	30%	51%	10%	4%	1%	24
Dominican College (NY)	0.60	32%	68%	0%	10%	11%	21%	56%	1%	29%	20
Rosemont College (PA)	0.60	20%	80%	0%	4%	46%	7%	42%	1%	21%	21
American International College (MA)	0.57	42%	58%	1%	3%	27%	9%	56%	4%	35%	23
University of Maryland–University College	0.57	44%	56%	1%	4%	32%	6%	56%	2%	39%	29
William Paterson University of New Jersey	0.56	45%	55%	0%	6%	14%	19%	60%	1%	2%	21
Fairleigh Dickinson University (NJ)	0.55	44%	56%	0%	5%	12%	19%	60%	4%	14%	21
Chestnut Hill College (PA)	0.54	31%	69%	0%	2%	38%	4%	56%	1%	22%	24
Montclair State University (NJ)	0.54	39%	61%	0%	6%	9%	20%	63%	2%	3%	22
Eastern University (PA)	0.52	31%	69%	0%	2%	21%	11%	64%	1%	42%	20
Metropolitan College of New York	0.52	29%	71%	1%	1%	63%	19%	13%	3%	N/A	N/A
Molloy College (NY)	0.52	22%	78%	0%	7%	15%	11%	65%	1%	0%	22
Rutgers, the State University of New Jersey–Camden	0.51	45%	55%	0%	8%	16%	9%	66%	1%	2%	21
Caldwell College (NJ)	0.50	34%	66%	1%	2%	12%	16%	61%	8%	17%	N/A
Touro College (NY)	0.50	31%	69%	0%	5%	16%	11%	68%	0%	N/A	N/A
College of Notre Dame of Maryland	0.48	6%	94%	0%	3%	29%	2%	64%	2%	14%	N/A
La Salle University (PA)	0.48	36%	64%	0%	4%	17%	9%	68%	1%	39%	20
Manhattanville College (NY)	0.47	35%	65%	0%	2%	8%	16%	61%	13%	38%	20
Frostburg State University (MD)	0.44	51%	49%	0%	2%	24%	3%	71%	0%	8%	21
Delaware State University	0.43	40%	60%	0%	1%	70%	2%	25%	1%	54%	20
New York Institute of Technology	0.42	62%	38%	0%	8%	7%	7%	69%	8%	11%	21
University of the District of Columbia	0.42	38%	62%	0%	3%	74%	6%	17%	0%	7%	30
SUNY Empire State College	0.41	40%	60%	1%	2%	14%	8%	71%	5%	6%	33
St. Joseph College (CT)	0.40	1%	99%	0%	2%	11%	10%	76%	0%	7%	21
Gwynedd-Mercy College (PA)	0.39	26%	74%	0%	2%	21%	1%	75%	0%	8%	24
College of New Jersey	0.38	41%	59%	0%	6%	6%	9%	77%	1%	6%	20
Point Park University (PA)	0.37	40%	60%	0%	1%	19%	2%	77%	1%	17%	22
CUNY–College of Staten Island	0.36	42%	58%	0%	6%	6%	8%	77%	3%	1%	21
Georgian Court University (NJ)	0.36	9%	91%	0%	2%	11%	8%	78%	0%	3%	23
Mount St. Mary College (NY)	0.36	25%	75%	0%	2%	7%	10%	79%	0%	13%	21
Philadelphia Biblical University	0.36	46%	54%	0%	4%	13%	4%	78%	1%	45%	23
Richard Stockton College of New Jersey	0.36	43%	57%	0%	6%	8%	7%	78%	0%	1%	22

	Diversity index	Men	Women	American Indian	Asian	Black	Hispanic	White	International	Undergraduates from out of state	Average age of full-time students
Southern Connecticut State University	0.36	37%	63%	0%	2%	13%	6%	78%	1%	6%	21
Suffolk University (MA)	0.36	44%	56%	0%	7%	4%	7%	71%	10%	32%	20
Ramapo College of New Jersey	0.35	42%	58%	0%	5%	5%	9%	79%	2%	5%	21
Rider University (NJ)	0.35	40%	60%	0%	3%	10%	6%	77%	3%	22%	20
Rowan University (NJ)	0.35	47%	53%	0%	3%	9%	7%	79%	1%	2%	21
SUNY–New Paltz	0.35	34%	66%	1%	4%	5%	10%	77%	3%	4%	21
Salem State College (MA)	0.35	38%	62%	0%	3%	9%	7%	77%	3%	3%	22
University of New Haven (CT)	0.35	50%	50%	0%	2%	9%	8%	78%	2%	48%	20
Wheelock College (MA)	0.35	9%	91%	1%	2%	9%	8%	80%	1%	34%	20
Buffalo State College–SUNY	0.34	41%	59%	0%	1%	13%	5%	79%	1%	1%	21
D'Youville College (NY)	0.34	26%	74%	1%	2%	11%	4%	73%	9%	5%	23
Sage Colleges–Albany (NY)	0.34	34%	66%	0%	2%	14%	4%	79%	0%	6%	21
St. Thomas Aquinas College (NY)	0.34	45%	55%	0%	4%	4%	12%	79%	1%	21%	20
Towson University (MD)	0.34	40%	60%	0%	4%	12%	3%	77%	3%	18%	21
Alvernia University (PA)	0.33	32%	68%	1%	2%	11%	6%	80%	1%	17%	21
Central Connecticut State University	0.33	51%	49%	0%	3%	8%	7%	81%	1%	5%	21
Dowling College (NY)	0.33	45%	55%	0%	2%	8%	9%	77%	4%	6%	21
Iona College (NY)	0.33	44%	56%	0%	2%	5%	12%	80%	1%	22%	19
Manhattan College (NY)	0.33	53%	47%	0%	3%	3%	12%	79%	2%	27%	20
Villanova University (PA)	0.33	50%	50%	0%	7%	5%	7%	78%	3%	76%	21
Johnson and Wales University (RI)	0.32	46%	54%	0%	2%	7%	6%	76%	8%	81%	18
Simmons College (MA)	0.32	0%	100%	0%	7%	6%	4%	80%	3%	39%	22
Western Connecticut State University	0.32	46%	54%	0%	3%	7%	8%	81%	0%	8%	21
Hood College (MD)	0.31	32%	68%	0%	2%	11%	4%	80%	2%	19%	21
Lincoln University (PA)	0.31	42%	58%	0%	0%	79%	0%	18%	2%	56%	20
Neumann University (PA)	0.31	35%	65%	0%	1%	13%	3%	80%	2%	28%	20
Springfield College (MA)	0.31	41%	59%	0%	0%	14%	4%	82%	0%	70%	21
Utica College (NY)	0.31	43%	57%	1%	2%	11%	4%	80%	2%	19%	20

Regional Universities (South)

	Diversity index	Men	Women	American Indian	Asian	Black	Hispanic	White	International	Undergraduates from out of state	Average age of full-time students
University of North Carolina–Pembroke	0.66	39%	61%	15%	2%	31%	4%	47%	2%	6%	22
Hodges University (FL)	0.61	31%	69%	0%	2%	17%	27%	54%	0%	4%	31
St. Thomas University (FL)	0.61	44%	56%	0%	1%	25%	48%	17%	9%	15%	24
Marymount University (VA)	0.57	28%	72%	0%	8%	15%	13%	55%	9%	40%	21
Christian Brothers University (TN)	0.55	44%	56%	0%	5%	34%	2%	57%	2%	16%	23
Columbus State University (GA)	0.55	40%	60%	1%	2%	34%	5%	58%	1%	14%	22
Life University (GA)	0.54	52%	48%	1%	4%	30%	6%	60%	N/A	N/A	N/A
Troy University (AL)	0.54	40%	60%	2%	1%	42%	3%	51%	2%	44%	28
Columbia College (SC)	0.53	2%	98%	1%	2%	42%	2%	52%	1%	N/A	N/A
Francis Marion University (SC)	0.53	32%	68%	1%	1%	48%	1%	49%	1%	4%	21
Mississippi University for Women	0.51	19%	81%	0%	1%	40%	1%	57%	1%	9%	24
Bethel College (TN)	0.50	41%	59%	0%	0%	37%	1%	59%	2%	N/A	N/A
Delta State University (MS)	0.50	39%	61%	0%	1%	39%	1%	58%	2%	10%	23
Loyola University New Orleans	0.50	43%	57%	1%	5%	14%	11%	66%	3%	48%	20
Northwestern State University of Louisiana	0.50	33%	67%	2%	1%	30%	2%	64%	1%	9%	22
Palm Beach Atlantic University (FL)	0.50	36%	64%	0%	1%	17%	14%	65%	2%	27%	24
Southern Polytechnic State University (GA)	0.50	81%	19%	0%	5%	20%	5%	63%	6%	2%	22
University of West Alabama	0.50	39%	61%	0%	1%	54%	1%	43%	1%	19%	22
Mercer University (GA)	0.49	31%	69%	0%	4%	26%	2%	64%	3%	20%	20
Auburn University–Montgomery (AL)	0.48	38%	62%	1%	2%	32%	1%	62%	3%	4%	22
Brenau University (GA)	0.48	0%	100%	0%	3%	21%	5%	64%	6%	8%	22
Georgia Southwestern State University	0.48	35%	65%	0%	1%	30%	2%	63%	3%	4%	22
Charleston Southern University (SC)	0.47	38%	62%	0%	1%	29%	3%	66%	1%	N/A	N/A
University of Arkansas–Monticello	0.47	41%	59%	1%	0%	33%	1%	64%	0%	11%	24
Valdosta State University (GA)	0.47	42%	58%	0%	1%	31%	1%	65%	2%	4%	22
William Carey University (MS)	0.47	27%	73%	0%	1%	31%	2%	63%	3%	20%	26
Jacksonville University (FL)	0.46	40%	60%	1%	3%	19%	6%	70%	2%	36%	22
Winthrop University (SC)	0.46	32%	68%	0%	2%	27%	2%	66%	2%	11%	21
Belhaven University (MS)	0.45	35%	65%	1%	2%	22%	3%	71%	1%	45%	22
Southern Wesleyan University (SC)	0.45	37%	63%	1%	0%	29%	2%	67%	1%	17%	31

Schools with the most diverse student bodies

Regional Universities (South), continued

	Diversity index	Men	Women	American Indian	Asian	Black	Hispanic	White	International	Undergraduates from out of state	Average age of full-time students
University of Louisiana–Monroe	0.45	37%	63%	0%	2%	28%	1%	68%	1%	7%	22
University of West Georgia	0.45	40%	60%	0%	1%	27%	2%	68%	1%	3%	21
Armstrong Atlantic State University (GA)	0.44	35%	65%	1%	2%	21%	4%	68%	4%	12%	23
Louisiana State University–Shreveport	0.44	38%	62%	1%	2%	24%	2%	70%	2%	N/A	N/A
Jacksonville State University (AL)	0.43	42%	58%	1%	1%	27%	1%	68%	3%	17%	23
Queens University of Charlotte (NC)	0.43	23%	77%	0%	2%	18%	5%	70%	5%	25%	22
Spring Hill College (AL)	0.43	38%	62%	1%	1%	18%	7%	72%	1%	52%	20
University of South Alabama	0.43	43%	57%	1%	3%	19%	2%	70%	4%	19%	N/A
Pfeiffer University (NC)	0.42	45%	55%	1%	1%	21%	3%	70%	4%	N/A	N/A
Mississippi College	0.41	40%	60%	0%	1%	25%	1%	70%	2%	18%	22
Mary Baldwin College (VA)	0.40	9%	91%	0%	2%	18%	4%	75%	1%	30%	19
St. Leo University (FL)	0.40	49%	51%	0%	1%	10%	11%	70%	8%	36%	20
University of Mobile (AL)	0.40	34%	66%	2%	0%	22%	1%	73%	2%	18%	24
University of North Florida	0.40	44%	56%	0%	6%	11%	7%	75%	1%	3%	22
Xavier University of Louisiana	0.40	28%	72%	0%	10%	74%	1%	13%	2%	51%	20
Embry-Riddle Aeronautical University (FL)	0.39	83%	17%	0%	6%	6%	8%	67%	13%	67%	21
Henderson State University (AR)	0.39	46%	54%	1%	1%	21%	2%	74%	2%	14%	21

Regional Universities (Midwest)

	Diversity index	Men	Women	American Indian	Asian	Black	Hispanic	White	International	Undergraduates from out of state	Average age of full-time students
Calumet College of St. Joseph (IN)	0.66	52%	48%	0%	1%	28%	25%	45%	0%	36%	N/A
Northeastern Illinois University	0.66	42%	58%	0%	10%	10%	30%	46%	4%	0%	24
National-Louis University (IL)	0.62	21%	79%	0%	2%	35%	14%	49%	0%	4%	N/A
Roosevelt University (IL)	0.59	34%	66%	0%	5%	20%	15%	58%	2%	14%	N/A
Park University (MO)	0.58	48%	52%	1%	2%	22%	15%	56%	3%	N/A	N/A
Alverno College (WI)	0.55	0%	100%	1%	5%	18%	13%	62%	1%	3%	24
Indiana University Northwest	0.54	32%	68%	0%	2%	21%	13%	63%	0%	1%	24
Purdue University–Calumet (IN)	0.54	45%	55%	0%	1%	19%	15%	61%	3%	11%	21
St. Xavier University (IL)	0.53	30%	70%	0%	3%	17%	14%	64%	0%	6%	21
Mount Mary College (WI)	0.52	4%	96%	1%	4%	22%	8%	65%	1%	4%	23
Dominican University (IL)	0.51	31%	69%	0%	2%	6%	26%	63%	2%	7%	21
Benedictine University (IL)	0.50	43%	57%	0%	14%	10%	7%	68%	1%	4%	25
Cardinal Stritch University (WI)	0.48	34%	66%	1%	2%	24%	4%	66%	3%	N/A	N/A
Fontbonne University (MO)	0.47	30%	70%	0%	1%	33%	2%	63%	2%	11%	26
Ohio Dominican University	0.44	40%	60%	0%	1%	26%	2%	70%	1%	3%	24
Ursuline College (OH)	0.44	9%	91%	0%	1%	26%	2%	70%	0%	2%	24
North Park University (IL)	0.43	39%	61%	0%	6%	8%	10%	72%	3%	32%	21
St. Catherine University (MN)	0.43	3%	97%	1%	10%	11%	3%	74%	1%	8%	21
Bellevue University (NE)	0.42	53%	47%	2%	2%	12%	8%	73%	2%	N/A	N/A
Concordia University Chicago (IL)	0.42	43%	57%	0%	2%	12%	13%	73%	1%	32%	21
Eastern Michigan University	0.42	43%	57%	1%	2%	21%	3%	72%	2%	8%	22
Lewis University (IL)	0.41	42%	58%	0%	4%	9%	11%	72%	3%	5%	22
University of Detroit Mercy	0.41	36%	64%	0%	2%	19%	4%	71%	4%	N/A	N/A
Davenport University (MI)	0.40	33%	67%	0%	2%	19%	3%	75%	0%	4%	31
Newman University (KS)	0.39	34%	66%	2%	4%	6%	10%	73%	5%	11%	24
University of St. Francis (IL)	0.39	33%	67%	0%	4%	7%	12%	76%	1%	5%	22
Tiffin University (OH)	0.38	44%	56%	0%	1%	19%	3%	74%	3%	29%	24
University of St. Mary (KS)	0.37	36%	64%	1%	1%	12%	8%	78%	0%	38%	24
Augsburg College (MN)	0.35	46%	54%	2%	6%	8%	3%	80%	1%	13%	24
University of Illinois–Springfield	0.35	45%	55%	1%	3%	13%	3%	78%	1%	9%	24
Upper Iowa University	0.35	39%	61%	0%	1%	14%	2%	68%	14%	42%	N/A
Avila University (MO)	0.34	34%	66%	1%	1%	11%	5%	76%	5%	28%	24
Concordia University–St. Paul (MN)	0.34	42%	58%	1%	7%	10%	2%	80%	0%	18%	22
Lawrence Technological University (MI)	0.34	77%	23%	0%	4%	13%	2%	75%	7%	2%	24
Madonna University (MI)	0.34	26%	74%	0%	2%	14%	3%	76%	5%	N/A	N/A
University of Michigan–Dearborn	0.34	48%	52%	0%	6%	11%	3%	79%	1%	0%	22
University of Michigan–Flint	0.34	39%	61%	1%	2%	14%	3%	79%	1%	2%	23
Webster University (MO)	0.33	41%	59%	0%	2%	12%	3%	72%	11%	21%	23
Youngstown State University (OH)	0.33	47%	53%	0%	1%	16%	2%	79%	1%	8%	23
Concordia University Wisconsin	0.32	36%	64%	1%	1%	14%	2%	80%	1%	27%	20
Creighton University (NE)	0.32	41%	59%	1%	10%	3%	4%	80%	2%	63%	20
Bradley University (IL)	0.30	46%	54%	0%	4%	8%	4%	83%	1%	11%	21
Elmhurst College (IL)	0.30	38%	62%	0%	4%	4%	8%	83%	1%	10%	20

	Diversity index	Men	Women	American Indian	Asian	Black	Hispanic	White	International	Undergraduates from out of state	Average age of full-time students
Graceland University (IA)	0.30	39%	61%	1%	2%	10%	3%	75%	9%	37%	20
Olivet Nazarene University (IL)	0.30	38%	62%	0%	1%	11%	4%	83%	0%	64%	20
Rockford College (IL)	0.30	40%	60%	0%	2%	8%	6%	83%	0%	10%	23
Southwestern College (KS)	0.30	52%	48%	2%	2%	8%	6%	82%	1%	34%	21
Xavier University (OH)	0.30	45%	55%	0%	2%	12%	3%	81%	1%	39%	20
Hamline University (MN)	0.29	44%	56%	1%	5%	7%	3%	81%	3%	17%	20
Eastern Illinois University	0.28	42%	58%	1%	1%	12%	3%	84%	0%	2%	21
MidAmerica Nazarene University (KS)	0.28	42%	58%	0%	1%	11%	4%	83%	2%	46%	25
Siena Heights University (MI)	0.28	42%	58%	0%	1%	11%	4%	83%	2%	5%	N/A
Southern Illinois University–Edwardsville	0.28	46%	54%	0%	2%	11%	2%	83%	1%	N/A	N/A
University of Indianapolis	0.28	33%	67%	0%	1%	11%	2%	80%	5%	11%	21
Western Illinois University	0.28	53%	47%	0%	1%	9%	5%	83%	1%	7%	22
Cornerstone University (MI)	0.27	41%	59%	0%	1%	10%	3%	85%	1%	20%	21
Indiana University–South Bend	0.27	39%	61%	0%	1%	8%	5%	83%	2%	4%	23
Rockhurst University (MO)	0.27	39%	61%	0%	3%	6%	6%	84%	1%	59%	20
Lindenwood University (MO)	0.26	44%	56%	0%	1%	10%	3%	76%	10%	24%	24
Oakland City University (IN)	0.26	45%	55%	0%	0%	12%	2%	85%	0%	N/A	N/A

Regional Universities (West)

	Diversity index	Men	Women	American Indian	Asian	Black	Hispanic	White	International	Undergraduates from out of state	Average age of full-time students
La Sierra University (CA)	0.73	44%	56%	1%	25%	9%	29%	25%	12%	14%	21
Houston Baptist University	0.72	35%	65%	0%	14%	20%	25%	37%	4%	3%	21
California State University–East Bay	0.71	40%	60%	0%	26%	12%	17%	38%	7%	1%	N/A
California State University–Dominguez Hills	0.70	34%	66%	0%	9%	27%	40%	22%	2%	1%	24
California State Polytechnic University–Pomona	0.69	57%	43%	0%	27%	3%	32%	33%	5%	2%	22
California State University–Long Beach	0.69	41%	59%	1%	24%	5%	29%	38%	4%	2%	22
California State University–Fullerton	0.68	42%	58%	0%	22%	3%	31%	40%	3%	1%	22
San Francisco State University	0.68	41%	59%	0%	28%	5%	18%	41%	7%	1%	22
San Jose State University (CA)	0.68	48%	52%	0%	34%	5%	19%	38%	4%	1%	22
California State University–Fresno	0.67	43%	57%	1%	16%	6%	35%	42%	1%	1%	22
California State University–San Bernardino	0.67	36%	64%	1%	8%	12%	40%	37%	3%	1%	23
Holy Names University (CA)	0.67	26%	74%	0%	9%	24%	18%	45%	4%	N/A	N/A
Mount St. Mary's College (CA)	0.67	8%	92%	0%	20%	9%	48%	22%	0%	2%	20
California State University–Northridge	0.66	43%	57%	0%	12%	8%	32%	42%	6%	4%	22
Hawaii Pacific University	0.65	42%	58%	2%	37%	7%	9%	39%	7%	25%	23
Notre Dame de Namur University (CA)	0.65	34%	66%	1%	15%	8%	25%	49%	2%	12%	21
California State University–Bakersfield	0.64	35%	65%	2%	7%	7%	39%	43%	2%	N/A	N/A
California State University–Los Angeles	0.64	40%	60%	0%	18%	7%	49%	20%	6%	6%	23
Dominican University of California	0.64	26%	74%	1%	24%	6%	17%	51%	2%	6%	21
University of St. Thomas (TX)	0.64	40%	60%	1%	12%	5%	34%	44%	4%	3%	21
University of Texas–San Antonio	0.64	50%	50%	0%	7%	9%	44%	37%	2%	2%	21
Woodbury University (CA)	0.63	48%	52%	0%	10%	5%	33%	42%	10%	N/A	23
California State University–Sacramento	0.62	43%	57%	1%	20%	7%	16%	54%	1%	1%	N/A
Texas Wesleyan University	0.62	35%	65%	1%	2%	20%	23%	52%	2%	6%	27
California State University–Stanislaus	0.61	35%	65%	1%	12%	3%	32%	50%	2%	1%	22
Loyola Marymount University (CA)	0.60	43%	57%	1%	13%	8%	19%	56%	3%	25%	20
Fresno Pacific University (CA)	0.58	34%	66%	1%	3%	6%	34%	53%	3%	N/A	N/A
Lamar University (TX)	0.58	40%	60%	0%	4%	32%	8%	56%	1%	2%	21
St. Mary's College of California	0.58	37%	63%	1%	11%	7%	20%	58%	2%	14%	20
Texas A&M University–Corpus Christi	0.58	41%	59%	1%	3%	5%	41%	48%	3%	3%	22
University of the Southwest (NM)	0.57	51%	49%	0%	2%	7%	38%	50%	3%	N/A	27
Western New Mexico University	0.57	40%	60%	2%	2%	4%	51%	39%	2%	11%	28
Cameron University (OK)	0.56	41%	59%	8%	3%	16%	8%	60%	4%	14%	25
Santa Clara University (CA)	0.56	47%	53%	1%	17%	4%	15%	60%	3%	39%	20
University of Texas of the Permian Basin	0.56	41%	59%	1%	1%	5%	43%	49%	1%	3%	23
Northeastern State University (OK)	0.55	40%	60%	30%	1%	6%	2%	59%	3%	4%	24
Seattle University	0.55	40%	60%	1%	19%	5%	8%	57%	10%	49%	21
University of the Incarnate Word (TX)	0.55	35%	65%	0%	3%	7%	57%	30%	3%	4%	22
California State University–San Marcos	0.54	39%	61%	1%	11%	3%	22%	62%	2%	1%	23
Southeastern Oklahoma State University	0.54	45%	55%	30%	1%	6%	3%	59%	2%	23%	24
St. Edward's University (TX)	0.54	41%	59%	1%	3%	5%	30%	58%	3%	7%	20

Schools with the most diverse student bodies

Regional Colleges (North)

	Diversity index	Men	Women	American Indian	Asian	Black	Hispanic	White	International	Undergraduates from out of state	Average age of full-time students
CUNY–New York City College of Technology	0.71	52%	48%	0%	16%	37%	27%	14%	6%	0%	22
Vaughn College of Aeronautics and Technology (NY)	0.71	88%	12%	1%	12%	21%	38%	26%	2%	8%	23
Washington Adventist University (MD)	0.62	34%	66%	0%	6%	52%	11%	31%	N/A	57%	N/A
Felician College (NJ)	0.57	23%	77%	0%	8%	12%	18%	59%	2%	N/A	N/A
Cooper Union (NY)	0.56	63%	37%	1%	19%	5%	8%	52%	15%	42%	21
St. Francis College (NY)	0.56	45%	55%	0%	4%	15%	15%	58%	7%	2%	20
Wesley College (DE)	0.54	45%	55%	1%	1%	35%	5%	58%	0%	66%	20
Peirce College (PA)	0.52	28%	72%	0%	1%	60%	5%	32%	2%	15%	33
Eastern Nazarene College (MA)	0.47	41%	59%	2%	2%	18%	7%	70%	1%	34%	20
Fashion Institute of Technology (NY)	0.42	16%	84%	0%	7%	6%	9%	66%	11%	30%	22
Post University (CT)	0.42	41%	59%	0%	1%	18%	7%	73%	1%	57%	26
Bay Path College (MA)	0.41	0%	100%	0%	2%	11%	11%	75%	0%	47%	N/A
St. Joseph's College New York	0.40	27%	73%	0%	2%	11%	10%	76%	0%	1%	22
SUNY College of Technology–Delhi	0.39	51%	49%	0%	2%	12%	8%	77%	1%	2%	21
Mitchell College (CT)	0.38	51%	49%	2%	1%	13%	8%	76%	1%	42%	20
Mount Ida College (MA)	0.37	35%	65%	0%	2%	12%	6%	74%	5%	39%	21
Valley Forge Christian College (PA)	0.37	48%	52%	0%	2%	10%	10%	77%	0%	N/A	N/A
SUNY Maritime College	0.36	90%	10%	0%	4%	6%	9%	74%	7%	27%	21
Stevenson University (MD)	0.36	30%	70%	1%	3%	17%	2%	78%	0%	8%	21

Regional Colleges (South)

	Diversity index	Men	Women	American Indian	Asian	Black	Hispanic	White	International	Undergraduates from out of state	Average age of full-time students
Southern Adventist University (TN)	0.55	44%	56%	0%	6%	11%	17%	60%	6%	69%	20
Warner University (FL)	0.53	43%	57%	0%	1%	23%	11%	63%	2%	10%	27
Atlanta Christian College	0.52	44%	56%	0%	0%	55%	4%	40%	1%	9%	N/A
Averett University (VA)	0.52	52%	48%	1%	1%	32%	3%	59%	4%	41%	N/A
Faulkner University (AL)	0.52	36%	64%	0%	0%	49%	1%	48%	1%	25%	30
North Carolina Wesleyan College	0.52	41%	59%	1%	1%	55%	1%	36%	6%	N/A	N/A
Clayton State University (GA)	0.50	30%	70%	0%	4%	63%	3%	28%	1%	2%	25
Belmont Abbey College (NC)	0.49	37%	63%	0%	2%	27%	5%	64%	3%	28%	28
Our Lady of Holy Cross College (LA)	0.48	19%	81%	1%	4%	21%	5%	69%	N/A	N/A	N/A
University of South Carolina–Upstate	0.48	36%	64%	0%	2%	27%	4%	66%	1%	4%	22
Southern Arkansas University	0.47	41%	59%	1%	1%	30%	2%	63%	4%	25%	22
Thomas University (GA)	0.47	29%	71%	1%	2%	24%	4%	65%	4%	N/A	N/A
University of South Carolina–Aiken	0.47	34%	66%	0%	1%	28%	3%	66%	1%	9%	22
Kentucky State University	0.46	42%	58%	0%	0%	64%	1%	34%	1%	41%	22
Barton College (NC)	0.44	28%	72%	1%	2%	26%	2%	69%	1%	14%	21
Newberry College (SC)	0.44	55%	45%	0%	1%	27%	2%	67%	3%	23%	20
Coker College (SC)	0.43	38%	62%	1%	0%	25%	2%	69%	3%	18%	20
Emmanuel College (GA)	0.43	46%	54%	0%	1%	21%	6%	71%	1%	22%	20
Methodist University (NC)	0.41	55%	45%	1%	1%	18%	5%	70%	4%	42%	23
LaGrange College (GA)	0.40	45%	55%	0%	1%	22%	2%	73%	2%	11%	22
Louisiana College	0.39	51%	49%	1%	2%	19%	2%	76%	0%	N/A	N/A
Bluefield College (VA)	0.38	41%	59%	0%	1%	20%	2%	75%	2%	N/A	N/A
Limestone College (SC)	0.38	58%	42%	0%	0%	20%	3%	76%	0%	45%	21
Southeastern University (FL)	0.38	42%	58%	0%	1%	9%	12%	77%	0%	39%	22
Mars Hill College (NC)	0.36	48%	52%	1%	2%	15%	3%	76%	3%	29%	20
Catawba College (NC)	0.34	48%	52%	0%	1%	18%	1%	78%	2%	23%	25
Victory University (TN)	0.33	25%	75%	0%	1%	79%	1%	18%	1%	7%	33
Elizabeth City State University (NC)	0.30	39%	61%	0%	0%	81%	1%	17%	1%	29%	22
Florida Southern College	0.30	43%	57%	1%	2%	6%	8%	80%	3%	25%	20
Shorter College (GA)	0.30	50%	50%	0%	1%	14%	2%	78%	5%	9%	21
Winston-Salem State University (NC)	0.30	30%	70%	0%	1%	81%	1%	16%	1%	11%	N/A
Blue Mountain College (MS)	0.29	32%	68%	0%	0%	15%	1%	83%	0%	12%	24
High Point University (NC)	0.29	37%	63%	0%	1%	13%	2%	82%	2%	69%	19
University of the Ozarks (AR)	0.29	49%	51%	3%	1%	5%	5%	69%	18%	29%	20
Anderson University (SC)	0.28	33%	67%	0%	1%	12%	2%	82%	2%	16%	21
Lenoir-Rhyne University (NC)	0.27	35%	65%	1%	2%	10%	2%	84%	2%	17%	21
Reinhardt University (GA)	0.27	39%	61%	0%	1%	9%	5%	85%	0%	22%	19
Bluefield State College (WV)	0.26	39%	61%	0%	0%	13%	1%	82%	3%	12%	26

Regional Colleges (Midwest)

	Diversity index	Men	Women	American Indian	Asian	Black	Hispanic	White	International	Undergraduates from out of state	Average age of full-time students
Robert Morris University (IL)	0.67	38%	62%	0%	2%	35%	23%	39%	1%	6%	24
Kendall College (IL)	0.55	30%	70%	0%	4%	18%	13%	60%	5%	N/A	N/A
McKendree University (IL)	0.55	45%	55%	0%	1%	13%	24%	60%	2%	32%	22
East-West University (IL)	0.46	40%	60%	0%	3%	60%	13%	7%	16%	N/A	N/A
College of St. Mary (NE)	0.38	0%	100%	1%	1%	12%	9%	76%	1%	10%	25
Notre Dame College of Ohio	0.38	42%	58%	0%	1%	21%	2%	76%	0%	4%	21
Marian University (IN)	0.37	36%	64%	0%	1%	18%	3%	77%	0%	7%	23
Lourdes College (OH)	0.36	20%	80%	0%	1%	16%	5%	78%	0%	8%	26
MacMurray College (IL)	0.36	37%	63%	0%	1%	16%	4%	78%	0%	12%	21
Central Christian College (KS)	0.35	51%	49%	2%	0%	14%	4%	77%	2%	58%	20
University of Dubuque (IA)	0.34	55%	45%	1%	2%	12%	4%	80%	1%	53%	N/A
Bethany College (KS)	0.33	50%	50%	1%	1%	10%	6%	77%	5%	51%	20
Briar Cliff University (IA)	0.32	44%	56%	2%	3%	7%	6%	82%	0%	39%	22
Bethel College (IN)	0.31	33%	67%	1%	1%	13%	3%	80%	2%	72%	24
Trinity Christian College (IL)	0.31	33%	67%	0%	2%	8%	7%	80%	2%	28%	21
Tabor College (KS)	0.30	50%	50%	1%	1%	7%	7%	83%	1%	44%	20
Union College (NE)	0.30	41%	59%	1%	3%	3%	8%	77%	7%	73%	21
York College (NE)	0.30	56%	44%	1%	1%	9%	5%	82%	5%	70%	20
St. Joseph's College (IN)	0.28	43%	57%	0%	1%	10%	5%	84%	1%	26%	21
Crown College (MN)	0.27	41%	59%	1%	8%	4%	3%	85%	0%	34%	21
Quincy University (IL)	0.27	44%	56%	0%	1%	10%	4%	84%	1%	27%	21
Grace College and Seminary (IN)	0.26	52%	48%	1%	1%	11%	2%	85%	1%	47%	21
Missouri Western State University	0.26	42%	58%	1%	1%	11%	2%	85%	0%	9%	24
Buena Vista University (IA)	0.25	49%	51%	0%	2%	6%	5%	83%	4%	24%	21
Culver-Stockton College (MO)	0.25	45%	55%	1%	1%	9%	2%	84%	3%	48%	20
Mayville State University (ND)	0.25	43%	57%	2%	1%	6%	4%	83%	3%	37%	N/A
Midland Lutheran College (NE)	0.25	43%	57%	0%	2%	8%	3%	85%	1%	N/A	N/A
Purdue University–North Central (IN)	0.25	43%	57%	1%	1%	7%	5%	86%	0%	2%	23
Dana College (NE)	0.24	54%	46%	1%	2%	6%	5%	86%	0%	40%	20
Defiance College (OH)	0.24	48%	52%	1%	1%	7%	4%	87%	0%	18%	21
Grand View University (IA)	0.24	38%	62%	0%	3%	7%	3%	86%	1%	8%	23
Judson University (IL)	0.24	43%	57%	0%	2%	4%	7%	83%	5%	26%	24
Greenville College (IL)	0.22	45%	55%	1%	1%	8%	3%	87%	2%	30%	24
Lake Erie College (OH)	0.22	47%	53%	0%	1%	9%	2%	87%	1%	18%	21
Lake Superior State University (MI)	0.22	49%	51%	9%	0%	1%	1%	80%	9%	3%	22
University of Minnesota–Crookston	0.22	50%	50%	1%	2%	5%	3%	81%	8%	34%	22

Regional Colleges (West)

	Diversity index	Men	Women	American Indian	Asian	Black	Hispanic	White	International	Undergraduates from out of state	Average age of full-time students
University of Houston–Downtown	0.71	38%	62%	0%	10%	28%	35%	22%	5%	1%	25
Bacone College (OK)	0.69	51%	49%	30%	0%	24%	5%	40%	0%	N/A	N/A
Pacific Union College (CA)	0.65	44%	56%	0%	24%	5%	20%	46%	6%	15%	21
Rogers State University (OK)	0.51	37%	63%	30%	2%	3%	2%	63%	1%	4%	24
McMurry University (TX)	0.50	49%	51%	1%	1%	16%	15%	66%	1%	4%	23
Concordia University Texas	0.49	42%	58%	1%	2%	11%	18%	68%	0%	5%	N/A
Oklahoma Panhandle State University	0.45	52%	48%	3%	1%	7%	16%	69%	4%	51%	21
Southwestern Assemblies of God University (TX)	0.45	50%	50%	1%	2%	9%	18%	70%	1%	N/A	N/A
Vanguard University of Southern California	0.45	38%	62%	2%	4%	4%	17%	71%	1%	14%	21
Cogswell Polytechnical College (CA)	0.44	84%	16%	0%	11%	4%	12%	70%	4%	13%	22
Schreiner University (TX)	0.43	44%	56%	2%	0%	4%	22%	72%	0%	0%	21
East Texas Baptist University	0.42	49%	51%	2%	1%	15%	8%	73%	1%	10%	21
California Maritime Academy	0.39	86%	14%	1%	11%	2%	8%	76%	1%	19%	26
Howard Payne University (TX)	0.39	52%	48%	1%	1%	7%	16%	75%	1%	1%	21
United States Air Force Academy (CO)	0.39	80%	20%	1%	8%	5%	8%	76%	1%	93%	20
University of Science and Arts of Oklahoma	0.39	35%	65%	11%	1%	5%	5%	73%	6%	8%	22
Oklahoma Baptist University	0.36	43%	57%	8%	1%	7%	4%	76%	4%	34%	20
Oklahoma Wesleyan University	0.33	40%	60%	10%	1%	5%	2%	79%	3%	42%	N/A
Northwest University (WA)	0.32	40%	60%	1%	7%	4%	6%	80%	2%	N/A	N/A
Master's College and Seminary (CA)	0.30	52%	48%	1%	5%	3%	8%	78%	5%	N/A	21
Northwestern Oklahoma State University	0.29	44%	56%	6%	1%	5%	4%	83%	2%	20%	22
Langston University (OK)	0.28	41%	59%	2%	1%	82%	1%	12%	2%	N/A	N/A
Texas College	0.28	55%	45%	0%	0%	83%	12%	3%	1%	17%	N/A
Oregon Institute of Technology	0.27	51%	49%	2%	6%	1%	5%	84%	1%	25%	N/A

Priciest private schools

The sticker price of a year at an elite private school may be a far cry from what most people actually pay, so it's a good idea not to rule out any favorites based just on price. Many high-priced institutions are generous with their financial aid. The schools are listed here by sticker price—the sum of tuition, fees, and room and board—for the 2009–2010 academic year. (Remember, though, some schools don't charge for tuition or room and board.) In addition, the table lists the average need-based financial aid package granted to undergraduates during 2009–2010. The typical aid package has three components: a need-based grant, need-based loans, and work-study. In order to qualify, students must file an annual aid application that demonstrates financial need. Expenses for 2010–2011 are provided in the directory when available.

National Universities

School	Tuition, fees, room and board	Average financial aid package
George Washington University (DC)	$52,355	$39,572
Boston College	$52,039	$30,968
New York University	$51,993	$23,900
Georgetown University (DC)	$51,918	$31,181
Columbia University (NY)	$51,544	$37,490
Vanderbilt University (TN)	$51,229	$41,954
Washington University in St. Louis	$51,193	$32,350
Johns Hopkins University (MD)	$51,190	$31,853
Tufts University (MA)	$51,088	$30,974
University of Chicago	$51,078	$36,915
Carnegie Mellon University (PA)	$50,758	$28,013
University of Southern California	$50,642	$35,593
Rensselaer Polytechnic Institute (NY)	$50,310	$32,065
Boston University	$50,288	N/A
Fordham University (NY)	$50,165	N/A
Northwestern University (IL)	$50,164	$30,080
Cornell University (NY)	$50,114	$36,812
Duke University (NC)	$50,090	$36,576
Stevens Institute of Technology (NJ)	$50,050	$27,104
University of Pennsylvania	$49,986	$33,060
Dartmouth College (NH)	$49,974	$38,449
University of Rochester (NY)	$49,890	$32,203
New School (NY)	$49,850	$25,345
Tulane University (LA)	$49,754	$35,519
Brandeis University (MA)	$49,554	$30,397
Stanford University (CA)	$49,344	$39,900
Massachusetts Institute of Technology	$49,142	$37,696
Brown University (RI)	$49,128	$34,586
Wake Forest University (NC)	$49,032	$32,965
Emory University (GA)	$48,932	$32,415
University of San Diego	$48,894	$28,993
Harvard University (MA)	$48,868	$40,234
University of Notre Dame (IN)	$48,845	$34,101
Lehigh University (PA)	$48,830	$33,008
Pepperdine University (CA)	$48,750	$34,721
Worcester Polytechnic Institute (MA)	$48,600	$25,306
Case Western Reserve University (OH)	$48,028	$33,478
American University (DC)	$47,903	$31,258
Northeastern University (MA)	$47,712	$19,325
Southern Methodist University (TX)	$47,606	$30,985
Yale University (CT)	$47,500	$39,270
Syracuse University (NY)	$47,300	$29,976
Princeton University (NJ)	$47,020	$36,495
University of Miami (FL)	$46,988	$30,640
University of San Francisco	$46,310	$26,830
University of Denver	$45,381	$28,632
California Institute of Technology	$45,339	$33,902
Drexel University (PA)	$44,515	N/A
Clarkson University (NY)	$44,028	$31,447
Catholic University of America (DC)	$44,024	$20,209
Pace University (NY)	$43,986	$28,055
Rice University (TX)	$43,287	$25,819
St. John's University (NY)	$43,180	$20,524
Widener University (PA)	$43,110	$23,048
University of the Pacific (CA)	$42,846	$29,320
Polytechnic Institute of New York University (NY)	$42,834	$26,211
Yeshiva University (NY)	$42,474	$27,297
Seton Hall University (NJ)	$42,170	N/A
Florida Institute of Technology	$42,150	$27,868
Clark University (MA)	$41,970	$25,904
Loyola University Chicago	$41,541	$27,092
Hofstra University (NY)	$41,460	$18,000
University of Hartford (CT)	$40,742	$22,400
St. Louis University	$40,242	$21,747
University of La Verne (CA)	$39,360	$24,932
Long Island University–C.W. Post Campus (NY)	$39,314	$14,500
Illinois Institute of Technology	$39,060	$24,602
Marquette University (WI)	$38,776	$21,428
Texas Christian University	$38,098	$20,647
Pacific University (OR)	$38,084	$23,485
DePaul University (IL)	$37,959	$20,459
Immaculata University (PA)	$37,460	$16,583
Baylor University (TX)	$37,124	$20,452
University of Dayton (OH)	$36,980	$25,054
University of Bridgeport (CT)	$36,545	$22,618
Biola University (CA)	$36,294	$33,123
University of St. Thomas (MN)	$36,246	$23,858
Azusa Pacific University (CA)	$36,064	N/A
Adelphi University (NY)	$35,800	$17,850
Duquesne University (PA)	$35,668	$20,623
Barry University (FL)	$35,400	$18,528
University of Tulsa (OK)	$35,356	$26,961
George Fox University (OR)	$34,500	$23,840
St. Mary's University of Minnesota	$31,800	$19,846
Trinity International University (IL)	$29,800	$20,273
Nova Southeastern University (FL)	$29,734	$16,863
Andrews University (MI)	$28,030	$23,932
Samford University (AL)	$27,044	$16,910
Oral Roberts University (OK)	$27,022	$17,820
Clark Atlanta University	$24,658	$5,876
Trevecca Nazarene University (TN)	$24,124	N/A
Howard University (DC)	$24,041	$11,133
Regent University (VA)	$23,500	N/A
Union Institute and University (OH)	$22,520	N/A
Spalding University (KY)	$20,700	N/A
Golden Gate University (CA)	$19,760	N/A
Brigham Young University–Provo (UT)	$11,130	$6,656
Wilmington University (DE)	$9,080	N/A

National Liberal Arts Colleges

	Tuition, fees, room and board	Average financial aid package
Sarah Lawrence College (NY)	$55,318	$29,576
Vassar College (NY)	$51,470	$37,512
Trinity College (CT)	$51,400	N/A
Bates College (ME)	$51,300	$33,852
Skidmore College (NY)	$51,196	$34,104
Bard College (NY)	$51,180	$34,643
Wesleyan University (CT)	$51,132	$37,187
Connecticut College	$51,115	$31,101
Harvey Mudd College (CA)	$51,037	$32,547
Claremont McKenna College (CA)	$51,035	$35,177
Haverford College (PA)	$50,975	$34,629
Barnard College (NY)	$50,969	$35,365
Colgate University (NY)	$50,940	$37,738
Bowdoin College (ME)	$50,900	$34,960
Bennington College (VT)	$50,860	$32,970
Middlebury College (VT)	$50,780	$33,345
Pitzer College (CA)	$50,770	$35,835
Hampshire College (MA)	$50,668	$35,310
Mount Holyoke College (MA)	$50,576	$33,399
Scripps College (CA)	$50,550	$34,330
Oberlin College (OH)	$50,484	$32,508
Union College (NY)	$50,439	$33,778
Franklin and Marshall College (PA)	$50,410	$29,613
Smith College (MA)	$50,380	$34,526
Bucknell University (PA)	$50,320	$25,500
Colby College (ME)	$50,320	$32,252
Lafayette College (PA)	$50,289	$34,061
Hobart and William Smith Colleges (NY)	$50,245	$29,433
Carleton College (MN)	$50,205	$34,141
Dickinson College (PA)	$50,194	$33,332
Bryn Mawr College (PA)	$50,034	$35,351
St. John's College (NM)	$49,996	N/A
St. John's College (MD)	$49,992	N/A
St. Lawrence University (NY)	$49,925	$35,989
Williams College (MA)	$49,880	$39,540
Hamilton College (NY)	$49,860	$36,305
Wellesley College (MA)	$49,848	$35,951
Occidental College (CA)	$49,702	$36,048
Reed College (OR)	$49,690	$33,090
Pomona College (CA)	$49,668	$35,416
Swarthmore College (PA)	$49,600	$35,342
Wheaton College (MA)	$49,440	$31,770
College of the Holy Cross (MA)	$49,342	$29,293
Amherst College (MA)	$49,078	$41,124
Washington and Lee University (VA)	$48,702	$37,052
Gettysburg College (PA)	$48,500	$31,030
University of Richmond (VA)	$48,490	$36,857
Drew University (NJ)	$48,385	$30,067
Kenyon College (OH)	$48,240	$31,610
Ursinus College (PA)	$47,920	$27,627
Colorado College	$47,102	$30,203
Macalester College (MN)	$46,942	$32,258
Whitman College (WA)	$46,200	$29,197
Furman University (SC)	$45,826	$28,079
Denison University (OH)	$45,720	$32,040
Muhlenberg College (PA)	$45,430	$23,370
Davidson College (NC)	$45,030	$24,121
Grinnell College (IA)	$45,012	$32,958
University of Puget Sound (WA)	$44,990	$27,595
Lewis & Clark College (OR)	$44,553	$27,618
Willamette University (OR)	$43,960	$29,387
Sewanee–University of the South (TN)	$43,932	$26,112
College of Wooster (OH)	$43,900	$27,955
Ohio Wesleyan University	$43,848	$28,014
Westmont College (CA)	$43,740	$24,129
St. Olaf College (MN)	$43,700	$26,401
Whittier College (CA)	$43,636	$33,257
Stonehill College (MA)	$43,450	$20,972
Goucher College (MD)	$43,393	$25,518
Wittenberg University (OH)	$42,962	$27,562
Marlboro College (VT)	$42,880	N/A
Washington College (MD)	$42,810	$21,084
Hartwick College (NY)	$42,405	$24,206
Earlham College (IN)	$42,324	$27,660
Lake Forest College (IL)	$42,212	$26,500
Allegheny College (PA)	$42,000	$27,087
DePauw University (IN)	$41,990	$28,224
Washington and Jefferson College (PA)	$41,820	$24,008
Illinois Wesleyan University	$41,758	$25,753
St. Anselm College (NH)	$41,755	$23,195
Lawrence University (WI)	$41,649	$26,155
College of the Atlantic (ME)	$41,550	$30,646
St. Michael's College (VT)	$41,495	$21,928
Susquehanna University (PA)	$41,250	$23,880
Eckerd College (FL)	$41,162	$27,743
Kalamazoo College (MI)	$40,419	N/A
Albright College (PA)	$40,370	$25,053
Rhodes College (TN)	$40,288	$31,373
Hampden-Sydney College (VA)	$40,257	$23,772
Beloit College (WI)	$40,248	$28,203
Juniata College (PA)	$40,200	$24,152
Merrimack College (MA)	$40,000	$15,668
Moravian College (PA)	$39,978	$23,421
Agnes Scott College (GA)	$39,955	$28,845
Sweet Briar College (VA)	$39,795	$18,064
Gustavus Adolphus College (MN)	$39,710	$23,652
Southwestern University (TX)	$39,530	$26,810
Roanoke College (VA)	$39,364	$24,772
Knox College (IL)	$39,075	$25,642
Centre College (KY)	$39,000	$25,091
St. Mary's College (IN)	$38,822	$22,125
Wofford College (SC)	$38,760	$28,954
Wells College (NY)	$38,680	$21,009
McDaniel College (MD)	$38,600	$24,842
College of St. Benedict (MN)	$38,566	$23,152
Albion College (MI)	$38,516	$24,776
Franklin Pierce University (NH)	$38,500	$18,733
Hollins University (VA)	$38,145	$22,059
Randolph College (VA)	$38,145	N/A
Randolph-Macon College (VA)	$38,073	$21,777
Lycoming College (PA)	$38,028	$23,264
Wabash College (IN)	$37,850	$27,083
Luther College (IA)	$37,670	$24,932
Russell Sage College (NY)	$37,660	N/A
Shimer College (IL)	$37,656	N/A
Cedar Crest College (PA)	$37,456	$21,570
St. John's University (MN)	$37,240	$22,414
Linfield College (OR)	$37,228	$19,168
Presbyterian College (SC)	$37,225	$29,765
Augustana College (IL)	$37,116	$25,819
Cornell College (IA)	$37,080	$25,535
Austin College (TX)	$36,940	$26,331
Oglethorpe University (GA)	$36,790	$26,500
Green Mountain College (VT)	$36,570	$19,464
Maryville College (TN)	$36,531	$26,285
Westminster College (PA)	$36,480	$23,163
Coe College (IA)	$36,420	$23,085
Hendrix College (AR)	$36,420	$22,498
Birmingham-Southern College (AL)	$36,345	$31,807
Hiram College (OH)	$36,115	N/A
Gordon College (MA)	$36,072	$19,311
Marymount Manhattan College (NY)	$35,530	$13,251
Millsaps College (MS)	$35,492	$24,659
Siena College (NY)	$35,215	$17,659

Priciest private schools

National Liberal Arts Colleges, continued

	Tuition, fees, room and board	Average financial aid package
Wartburg College (IA)	$35,065	$21,639
Guilford College (NC)	$35,010	$21,918
Virginia Wesleyan College	$34,860	$17,752
Alma College (MI)	$34,596	$23,085
Bridgewater College (VA)	$34,400	$21,596
Wheaton College (IL)	$34,290	$22,934
Hanover College (IN)	$34,250	$23,495
St. Vincent College (PA)	$34,230	$21,705
Millikin University (IL)	$34,211	$19,958
St. Norbert College (WI)	$34,024	$24,799
American Jewish University (CA)	$33,968	$24,500
Concordia College (NY)	$33,825	N/A
Stephens College (MO)	$33,480	$20,787
Central College (IA)	$33,378	$22,115
Eastern Mennonite University (VA)	$33,240	N/A
Emory and Henry College (VA)	$33,180	$23,244
Georgetown College (KY)	$33,110	$22,830
Greensboro College (NC)	$33,067	N/A
Transylvania University (KY)	$33,050	$21,670
Albertus Magnus College (CT)	$33,040	$10,828
Simpson College (IA)	$32,994	$25,103
Ripon College (WI)	$32,715	$22,365
Salem College (NC)	$32,590	N/A
Peace College (NC)	$32,383	$19,858
Sierra Nevada College (NV)	$32,332	$19,500
Morehouse College (GA)	$32,322	$12,425
Calvin College (MI)	$32,310	$17,931
Monmouth College (IL)	$32,250	$20,775
Concordia College–Moorhead (MN)	$32,035	$20,465
Warren Wilson College (NC)	$31,966	$21,323
Pine Manor College (MA)	$31,859	N/A
Berry College (GA)	$31,700	$20,606
Principia College (IL)	$31,680	$24,175
Meredith College (NC)	$31,510	$18,638
Houghton College (NY)	$31,440	$20,192
Thiel College (PA)	$31,378	$19,313
Bloomfield College (NJ)	$31,300	$16,544
Goshen College (IN)	$31,300	$17,727
University of Mount Union (OH)	$31,300	$19,313
William Jewell College (MO)	$31,300	$20,258
Ferrum College (VA)	$31,195	$19,884
Spelman College (GA)	$30,988	$15,439
Centenary College of Louisiana	$30,840	$19,140
Northland College (WI)	$30,786	N/A
Clarke University (IA)	$30,360	$19,614
Bethany College (WV)	$30,165	N/A
St. Andrews Presbyterian College (NC)	$29,952	$15,948
Thomas Aquinas College (CA)	$29,800	$19,294
West Virginia Wesleyan College	$29,680	$23,785
Carroll College (MT)	$29,574	N/A
Texas Lutheran University	$29,010	$18,482

	Tuition, fees, room and board	Average financial aid package
Illinois College	$28,900	$18,014
Brevard College (NC)	$28,650	$20,500
Wisconsin Lutheran College	$28,630	$17,521
Nebraska Wesleyan University	$28,542	$16,199
Wingate University (NC)	$28,190	$17,956
Baker University (KS)	$27,930	$9,417
Asbury University (KY)	$27,827	$17,794
Huntingdon College (AL)	$27,820	$14,949
Hastings College (NE)	$27,782	$16,744
Hillsdale College (MI)	$27,490	$14,046
Simpson University (CA)	$27,300	$19,486
College of Idaho (ID)	$27,228	$16,324
Doane College (NE)	$27,010	$17,462
Bethel College (KS)	$26,846	$21,569
Olivet College (MI)	$26,690	$17,155
Lambuth University (TN)	$26,585	N/A
Westminster College (MO)	$25,820	$17,676
Wesleyan College (GA)	$25,500	$16,980
Lyon College (AR)	$25,418	$17,498
McPherson College (KS)	$25,310	$20,033
Lindsey Wilson College (KY)	$25,150	$15,075
Fisk University (TN)	$25,120	$14,957
Carson-Newman College (TN)	$24,310	$15,747
Sterling College (KS)	$24,290	N/A
Thomas More College of Liberal Arts (NH)	$23,600	$13,172
Kentucky Wesleyan College	$23,310	$16,017
Dillard University (LA)	$22,090	N/A
Bennett College (NC)	$21,970	$12,120
Johnson C. Smith University (NC)	$21,886	$12,940
Evangel University (MO)	$21,730	$11,981
Atlantic Union College (MA)	$21,570	$12,049
Judson College (AL)	$20,860	N/A
Pikeville College (KY)	$20,535	$14,677
Burlington College (VT)	$20,424	$12,910
Grove City College (PA)	$19,414	$5,942
North Greenville University (SC)	$19,320	N/A
Baptist Bible College (MO)	$19,110	N/A
Bryn Athyn College of the New Church (PA)	$18,291	$14,592
Huston-Tillotson University (TX)	$18,124	N/A
Paine College (GA)	$17,542	N/A
Jarvis Christian College (TX)	$16,323	$11,020
College of St. Thomas More (TX)	$16,240	N/A
Tougaloo College (MS)	$16,040	$14,500
Allen University (SC)	$15,574	$10,149
Talladega College (AL)	$13,824	N/A
Lane College (TN)	$13,520	$3,304
Martin University (IN)	$13,520	N/A
Rust College (MS)	$10,630	$6,533
Brigham Young University–Hawaii	$8,380	N/A
Berea College (KY)	$6,644	$32,141
Hope College (MI)	$0	$22,419

Regional Universities (North)

	Tuition, fees, room and board	Average financial aid package
Loyola University Maryland	$48,890	$27,300
Fairfield University (CT)	$48,760	$27,082
Villanova University (PA)	$48,625	$26,967
Bentley University (MA)	$47,568	$29,415
Manhattanville College (NY)	$46,260	$26,779
St. Joseph's University (PA)	$45,665	$19,271
Quinnipiac University (CT)	$44,780	$19,785
Providence College (RI)	$44,480	$20,770
La Salle University (PA)	$43,850	$22,923
Ithaca College (NY)	$43,840	$28,273

	Tuition, fees, room and board	Average financial aid package
Simmons College (MA)	$43,500	$21,304
University of Scranton (PA)	$43,242	$22,585
Cabrini College (PA)	$42,368	$21,251
Wagner College (NY)	$42,280	$20,457
Bryant University (RI)	$42,258	$20,116
Emerson College (MA)	$42,198	$17,364
Sacred Heart University (CT)	$41,982	$18,782
Arcadia University (PA)	$41,940	$21,411
University of New Haven (CT)	$41,842	$19,495
Fairleigh Dickinson University (NJ)	$41,834	N/A

	Tuition, fees, room and board	Average financial aid package
Suffolk University (MA)	$41,752	$19,274
Emmanuel College (MA)	$41,315	$21,994
Regis College (MA)	$41,090	N/A
Salve Regina University (RI)	$40,950	$21,024
Lesley University (MA)	$40,783	$15,355
Assumption College (MA)	$40,241	$19,557
University of New England (ME)	$40,190	N/A
Canisius College (NY)	$40,068	$24,558
Western New England College (MA)	$39,796	$18,654
Rider University (NJ)	$39,780	$21,152
St. Joseph College (CT)	$39,639	$20,293
Wheelock College (MA)	$39,360	$20,806
Rochester Institute of Technology (NY)	$38,925	$22,500
Mount St. Mary's University (MD)	$38,898	$18,996
Iona College (NY)	$38,800	$18,067
Utica College (NY)	$38,134	$20,690
Marist College (NY)	$37,830	$15,387
Marywood University (PA)	$37,768	$22,222
St. Peter's College (NJ)	$37,724	$19,780
Hood College (MD)	$37,610	$21,899
Sage Colleges–Albany (NY)	$37,600	N/A
Wilkes University (PA)	$37,110	$20,291
Norwich University (VT)	$36,854	$22,182
DeSales University (PA)	$36,750	$17,336
Chatham University (PA)	$36,726	$15,515
Southern New Hampshire University	$36,618	N/A
Philadelphia University	$36,610	$21,048
Rosemont College (PA)	$36,530	$22,951
American International College (MA)	$36,430	$21,229
Alfred University (NY)	$36,420	$25,152
St. Joseph's College (ME)	$36,400	$20,192
College of Notre Dame of Maryland	$36,350	$19,708
Anna Maria College (MA)	$36,250	N/A
College of New Rochelle (NY)	$36,026	N/A
Springfield College (MA)	$35,990	$19,104
Centenary College (NJ)	$35,968	$17,867
College of St. Elizabeth (NJ)	$35,962	N/A
Chestnut Hill College (PA)	$35,900	$17,839
Le Moyne College (NY)	$35,770	$20,065
College of Mount St. Vincent (NY)	$35,610	N/A
King's College (PA)	$35,482	$18,300
Nazareth College (NY)	$35,440	$18,649
St. Bonaventure University (NY)	$35,085	$22,000
Niagara University (NY)	$34,950	$19,418
New York Institute of Technology	$34,660	$20,439
Caldwell College (NJ)	$34,600	N/A
Monmouth University (NJ)	$34,568	$17,601

	Tuition, fees, room and board	Average financial aid package
Rivier College (NH)	$34,478	$14,344
St. John Fisher College (NY)	$34,370	$17,795
St. Francis University (PA)	$34,271	$19,405
Misericordia University (PA)	$34,100	$16,738
Georgian Court University (NJ)	$33,876	$17,906
Mount St. Mary College (NY)	$33,514	$13,804
Gwynedd-Mercy College (PA)	$33,510	$14,187
Alvernia University (PA)	$33,445	$16,156
Dowling College (NY)	$33,050	$16,426
Mercyhurst College (PA)	$32,958	$19,803
Gannon University (PA)	$32,904	$19,802
Eastern University (PA)	$32,640	N/A
College of St. Rose (NY)	$32,546	$8,897
Holy Family University (PA)	$32,360	$16,005
Roberts Wesleyan College (NY)	$31,966	$17,513
Johnson and Wales University (RI)	$31,170	$15,772
St. Thomas Aquinas College (NY)	$31,150	$11,924
Neumann University (PA)	$31,078	$19,000
Dominican College (NY)	$31,070	$15,918
Robert Morris University (PA)	$30,930	$16,548
Daemen College (NY)	$30,660	N/A
Point Park University (PA)	$30,354	$15,767
Carlow University (PA)	$30,272	N/A
La Roche College (PA)	$30,196	$21,212
D'Youville College (NY)	$29,830	$15,796
Trinity University (DC)	$29,009	N/A
Cambridge College (MA)	$28,240	$8,184
Medaille College (NY)	$27,658	$24,000
Mercy College (NY)	$27,302	$12,855
Nyack College (NY)	$27,250	N/A
Philadelphia Biblical University	$26,722	$14,138
Metropolitan College of New York	$26,350	N/A
College of St. Joseph (VT)	$25,900	$17,669
Manhattan College (NY)	$25,805	$16,839
Touro College (NY)	$25,700	$12,200
Waynesburg University (PA)	$25,130	$12,864
Gratz College (PA)	$23,050	N/A
Molloy College (NY)	$20,960	$12,545
Gallaudet University (DC)	$20,886	N/A
Husson University (ME)	$19,984	$11,462
Goddard College (VT)	$13,628	$7,791
Molloy College (NY)	$19,635	$12,007
Husson University (ME)	$19,540	$10,019
Goddard College (VT)	$12,672	$6,356
Southeastern University (DC)	$12,210	N/A
Cambridge College (MA)	$8,280	$4,659

Regional Universities (South)

	Tuition, fees, room and board	Average financial aid package
Rollins College (FL)	$47,540	$33,763
Lynn University (FL)	$41,000	$20,853
Stetson University (FL)	$40,704	$27,435
Mercer University (GA)	$38,328	$30,024
Bellarmine University (KY)	$37,310	$23,927
Embry-Riddle Aeronautical University (FL)	$36,800	$15,246
Lynchburg College (VA)	$36,695	$20,193
Loyola University New Orleans	$36,520	$24,349
Spring Hill College (AL)	$35,180	$23,948
Jacksonville University (FL)	$34,360	$19,580
Elon University (NC)	$33,725	$18,939
Wheeling Jesuit University (WV)	$33,154	$21,466
Belmont University (TN)	$33,025	$11,966
Converse College (SC)	$32,990	$22,193

	Tuition, fees, room and board	Average financial aid package
Shenandoah University (VA)	$32,750	$15,545
Marymount University (VA)	$32,365	$15,574
Mary Baldwin College (VA)	$31,655	$19,749
Queens University of Charlotte (NC)	$30,966	$16,810
Palm Beach Atlantic University (FL)	$30,808	$20,405
University of Tampa (FL)	$30,778	$16,003
Christian Brothers University (TN)	$30,050	$19,826
Columbia College (SC)	$29,930	N/A
Brenau University (GA)	$29,128	$18,874
Campbell University (NC)	$28,740	$31,629
Thomas More College (KY)	$28,503	$14,988
Lipscomb University (TN)	$28,240	$16,409
St. Thomas University (FL)	$28,206	N/A
Gardner-Webb University (NC)	$27,980	$17,438

Priciest private schools

Regional Universities (South), continued

	Tuition, fees, room and board	Average financial aid package
Union University (TN)	$27,870	$19,643
Tusculum College (TN)	$27,265	N/A
Pfeiffer University (NC)	$27,143	N/A
Charleston Southern University (SC)	$26,670	N/A
Southern Wesleyan University (SC)	$26,500	$11,837
St. Leo University (FL)	$26,070	$16,532
Hampton University (VA)	$24,876	$4,545
Piedmont College (GA)	$24,000	$16,890
Cumberland University (TN)	$23,780	$14,386
Union College (KY)	$23,769	$19,623
Liberty University (VA)	$23,738	N/A
Belhaven University (MS)	$22,900	$14,653

	Tuition, fees, room and board	Average financial aid package
University of Mobile (AL)	$22,420	$12,998
Xavier University of Louisiana	$22,300	$16,797
Freed-Hardeman University (TN)	$21,390	$13,942
Lincoln Memorial University (TN)	$21,380	$16,166
Life University (GA)	$20,832	$9,750
Mississippi College	$19,940	$16,013
Harding University (AR)	$19,402	$11,146
Bethel College (TN)	$19,266	N/A
Lee University (TN)	$17,310	$10,108
Mountain State University (WV)	$14,666	$7,033
Hodges University (FL)	$14,180	$9,200
William Carey University (MS)	$13,750	$15,000

Regional Universities (Midwest)

	Tuition, fees, room and board	Average financial aid package
Butler University (IN)	$38,986	$20,922
Creighton University (NE)	$38,358	$25,003
Xavier University (OH)	$37,820	$17,748
Hamline University (MN)	$37,639	$22,477
University of Detroit Mercy	$37,510	$25,795
Capital University (OH)	$37,174	$23,895
John Carroll University (OH)	$37,170	$23,033
Valparaiso University (IN)	$36,280	$21,000
University of Evansville (IN)	$35,426	$22,537
North Central College (IL)	$35,295	$19,870
Elmhurst College (IL)	$35,204	$21,073
Augsburg College (MN)	$35,142	$18,744
Ashland University (OH)	$34,998	$23,254
Bethel University (MN)	$34,940	$20,421
Otterbein College (OH)	$34,926	N/A
College of St. Scholastica (MN)	$34,562	$21,625
University of Findlay (OH)	$34,328	$18,215
St. Catherine University (MN)	$33,758	$26,870
Concordia University–St. Paul (MN)	$33,650	$17,022
Drake University (IA)	$33,422	$20,813
Rockhurst University (MO)	$32,970	$25,772
St. Xavier University (IL)	$32,748	$19,878
Ohio Dominican University	$32,716	N/A
Dominican University (IL)	$32,320	$18,277
Lawrence Technological University (MI)	$32,311	$18,772
Roosevelt University (IL)	$32,108	$18,843
Bradley University (IL)	$31,874	$16,201
Lewis University (IL)	$31,340	$18,419
Columbia College (IL)	$31,320	N/A
Concordia University Chicago (IL)	$31,158	$17,219
Rockford College (IL)	$31,000	$17,247
Baldwin-Wallace College (OH)	$30,970	$19,838
Anderson University (IN)	$30,890	$20,553
St. Ambrose University (IA)	$30,845	$16,770
Ursuline College (OH)	$30,664	$14,705
University of St. Francis (IL)	$30,636	$18,171
Maharishi University of Management (IA)	$30,430	N/A
Webster University (MO)	$30,126	$22,542
Olivet Nazarene University (IL)	$29,990	$17,812
Carroll University (WI)	$29,960	$17,231
College of Mount St. Joseph (OH)	$29,952	$16,176
Heidelberg University (OH)	$29,714	$16,911

	Tuition, fees, room and board	Average financial aid package
Benedictine University (IL)	$29,350	$16,602
Walsh University (OH)	$29,350	$16,350
Aquinas College (MI)	$29,328	$21,533
University of Indianapolis	$29,210	$15,526
Maryville University of St. Louis (MO)	$29,204	$17,959
Concordia University Wisconsin	$28,916	$21,364
University of St. Francis (IN)	$28,510	N/A
Mount Mary College (WI)	$28,446	$16,132
Cardinal Stritch University (WI)	$28,390	N/A
Malone University (OH)	$28,180	$15,984
Edgewood College (WI)	$28,143	$16,399
Upper Iowa University	$27,996	$8,513
Muskingum University (OH)	$27,620	$17,950
Indiana Wesleyan University	$27,266	$15,739
Fontbonne University (MO)	$27,206	$10,972
Cornerstone University (MI)	$27,030	$18,623
Avila University (MO)	$27,000	$13,105
Silver Lake College (WI)	$26,960	$16,479
North Park University (IL)	$26,940	N/A
Graceland University (IA)	$26,870	$19,566
Viterbo University (WI)	$26,870	N/A
Spring Arbor University (MI)	$26,740	$22,445
Marian University (WI)	$26,540	$19,560
Franciscan University of Steubenville (OH)	$26,400	$12,549
Benedictine College (KS)	$26,300	$22,755
Siena Heights University (MI)	$26,280	N/A
University of Rio Grande (OH)	$26,060	$11,695
Drury University (MO)	$25,861	$7,985
Newman University (KS)	$25,856	$14,402
Aurora University (IL)	$25,818	N/A
Lakeland College (WI)	$25,748	N/A
Tiffin University (OH)	$25,715	$13,569
MidAmerica Nazarene University (KS)	$25,598	N/A
Alverno College (WI)	$25,578	$14,191
University of St. Mary (KS)	$25,550	N/A
Southwestern College (KS)	$25,430	$18,500
Missouri Baptist University	$24,950	N/A
Friends University (KS)	$24,900	N/A
Mount Marty College (SD)	$24,274	$18,937
William Woods University (MO)	$24,260	$14,901
Marygrove College (MI)	$23,310	N/A
Southwest Baptist University (MO)	$22,000	N/A

	Tuition, fees, room and board	Average financial aid package
Bellevue University (NE)	$21,876	N/A
Oakland City University (IN)	$21,638	N/A
Columbia College (MO)	$20,474	$11,935
Lindenwood University (MO)	$20,360	$5,855
Madonna University (MI)	$19,958	$8,902

	Tuition, fees, room and board	Average financial aid package
National-Louis University (IL)	$18,435	N/A
University of Mary (ND)	$17,520	N/A
Davenport University (MI)	$16,001	N/A
Calumet College of St. Joseph (IN)	$13,220	$11,510

Regional Universities (West)

	Tuition, fees, room and board	Average financial aid package
Chapman University (CA)	$49,596	$27,771
Loyola Marymount University (CA)	$48,679	$29,477
Mills College (CA)	$47,712	$30,185
Santa Clara University (CA)	$47,400	$23,774
Dominican University of California	$46,890	$21,904
St. Mary's College of California	$45,850	$25,104
University of Redlands (CA)	$44,366	$28,324
University of Portland (OR)	$40,406	$25,029
California Lutheran University	$39,320	$22,500
Regis University (CO)	$39,100	$15,333
Mount St. Mary's College (CA)	$38,510	$30,185
Trinity University (TX)	$38,462	$23,645
Notre Dame de Namur University (CA)	$38,410	$24,693
College of Santa Fe (NM)	$38,382	N/A
Seattle University	$38,145	$28,428
Gonzaga University (WA)	$37,651	$22,922
Woodbury University (CA)	$37,003	$19,622
Whitworth University (WA)	$36,770	$23,442
Pacific Lutheran University (WA)	$36,700	$27,906
Holy Names University (CA)	$36,660	$20,413
Seattle Pacific University	$36,354	$24,734
University of Dallas	$34,514	$20,940
Point Loma Nazarene University (CA)	$33,940	$18,695
Alaska Pacific University	$33,710	$15,100
St. Martin's University (WA)	$33,542	$18,279
Concordia University (CA)	$33,180	$24,529
St. Edward's University (TX)	$32,936	$20,039
Oklahoma City University	$32,700	$18,004
Westminster College (UT)	$32,002	$18,640
Naropa University (CO)	$31,998	$25,123
La Sierra University (CA)	$31,563	N/A
Prescott College (AZ)	$30,801	$13,099

	Tuition, fees, room and board	Average financial aid package
Fresno Pacific University (CA)	$30,078	$15,215
University of the Incarnate Word (TX)	$30,070	$15,618
Colorado Christian University	$29,950	N/A
Hope International University (CA)	$29,920	$14,609
Concordia University (OR)	$29,910	N/A
California Baptist University	$29,436	$8,651
University of St. Thomas (TX)	$29,230	$15,107
St. Mary's University of San Antonio (TX)	$28,966	$20,138
LeTourneau University (TX)	$28,360	$10,706
Northwest Nazarene University (ID)	$27,990	$16,918
Houston Baptist University	$27,805	$17,712
Abilene Christian University (TX)	$27,800	$13,841
Our Lady of the Lake University (TX)	$27,365	$22,500
Chaminade University of Honolulu	$27,280	N/A
Walla Walla University (WA)	$26,256	N/A
Hawaii Pacific University	$26,054	$14,529
University of Mary Hardin-Baylor (TX)	$26,000	$15,535
Hardin-Simmons University (TX)	$25,568	$16,930
City University (WA)	$24,895	N/A
University of Great Falls (MT)	$24,822	N/A
Texas Wesleyan University	$24,416	N/A
Southern Nazarene University (OK)	$24,154	N/A
Dallas Baptist University	$23,126	$13,557
Oklahoma Christian University	$22,356	$15,488
Lubbock Christian University (TX)	$20,236	$13,010
Heritage University (WA)	$19,680	N/A
University of the Southwest (NM)	$17,357	$3,877
Marylhurst University (OR)	$16,920	$11,390
John F. Kennedy University (CA)	$16,680	N/A
Wayland Baptist University (TX)	$16,256	$11,850
National University (CA)	$10,728	N/A

Regional Colleges (North)

	Tuition, fees, room and board	Average financial aid package
Bard College at Simon's Rock (MA)	$51,130	$33,639
Cooper Union (NY)	$46,300	$35,000
Elmira College (NY)	$45,600	$26,317
Colby-Sawyer College (NH)	$41,950	N/A
Roger Williams University (RI)	$40,990	$22,835
Curry College (MA)	$40,480	$18,475
Elizabethtown College (PA)	$39,950	$22,582
Lebanon Valley College (PA)	$38,570	$22,686
Daniel Webster College (NH)	$38,315	N/A
Delaware Valley College (PA)	$37,578	$19,249
Champlain College (VT)	$37,520	$15,071
Endicott College (MA)	$37,212	$16,827
Mitchell College (CT)	$37,175	N/A
New England College (NH)	$37,076	$23,584
Fisher College (MA)	$36,050	N/A
Wilson College (PA)	$36,000	$22,148

	Tuition, fees, room and board	Average financial aid package
Lasell College (MA)	$35,800	$20,097
College of Our Lady of the Elms (MA)	$35,706	N/A
Seton Hill University (PA)	$35,432	$21,411
Mount Ida College (MA)	$34,785	$15,105
Felician College (NJ)	$34,750	$18,560
Newbury College (MA)	$34,730	N/A
Messiah College (PA)	$34,580	$18,236
Bay Path College (MA)	$34,565	N/A
Becker College (MA)	$34,540	$10,070
Cazenovia College (NY)	$34,214	$20,838
Keuka College (NY)	$31,790	$16,576
Paul Smith's College (NY)	$31,010	$17,041
Stevenson University (MD)	$30,940	$14,124
St. Francis College (NY)	$30,100	$10,887
Eastern Nazarene College (MA)	$29,927	$20,974
Geneva College (PA)	$29,170	N/A

Priciest private schools

Regional Colleges (North), continued

	Tuition, fees, room and board	Average financial aid package
Thomas College (ME)	$28,850	N/A
Wesley College (DE)	$28,800	$16,500
Southern Vermont College	$27,720	N/A
Vaughn College of Aeronautics and Technology (NY)	$27,280	$20,950
Keystone College (PA)	$27,180	$22,554
Unity College (ME)	$26,520	N/A
Hilbert College (NY)	$25,690	N/A
Mount Aloysius College (PA)	$24,580	$11,300

	Tuition, fees, room and board	Average financial aid package
Baptist Bible College and Seminary (PA)	$22,820	$11,513
York College of Pennsylvania	$22,540	$10,915
Valley Forge Christian College (PA)	$22,248	$8,841
St. Joseph's College New York	$16,773	$10,449
Peirce College (PA)	$14,850	N/A
Boricua College (NY)	$9,500	N/A
Sojourner-Douglass College (MD)	$7,920	N/A

Regional Colleges (South)

	Tuition, fees, room and board	Average financial aid package
High Point University (NC)	$33,400	$10,995
Erskine College (SC)	$32,970	$20,694
Lenoir-Rhyne University (NC)	$32,740	N/A
University of Charleston (WV)	$32,700	N/A
Covenant College (GA)	$32,440	$18,697
Catawba College (NC)	$31,940	$18,422
Methodist University (NC)	$31,370	$15,164
Belmont Abbey College (NC)	$31,208	$13,151
Virginia Intermont College	$30,697	$15,499
Averett University (VA)	$30,042	$15,682
Florida Southern College	$29,995	$19,093
LaGrange College (GA)	$29,884	$17,664
Aquinas College (TN)	$29,822	N/A
North Carolina Wesleyan College	$29,440	N/A
King College (TN)	$29,298	$16,736
Lees-McRae College (NC)	$29,275	N/A
Newberry College (SC)	$29,220	$20,440
Alderson-Broaddus College (WV)	$28,656	$20,942
Mars Hill College (NC)	$28,134	N/A
Barton College (NC)	$27,660	$19,289
Milligan College (TN)	$27,510	$16,482
Davis and Elkins College (WV)	$27,250	$19,574
Montreat College (NC)	$27,217	$12,337
Anderson University (SC)	$26,532	$15,340
Chowan University (NC)	$26,330	N/A
Coker College (SC)	$26,098	$19,956
John Brown University (AR)	$25,756	$15,787
Campbellsville University (KY)	$25,350	$14,521
Limestone College (SC)	$25,100	$13,802
Martin Methodist College (TN)	$25,038	N/A
University of the Ozarks (AR)	$24,950	$18,877
Midway College (KY)	$24,800	N/A
Bluefield College (VA)	$24,726	$13,338
Tennessee Wesleyan College	$24,700	N/A
Brescia University (KY)	$24,130	$14,241
Ohio Valley University (WV)	$23,636	$12,250
Ouachita Baptist University (AR)	$23,469	$15,237
Tuskegee University (AL)	$23,460	$17,000
Bryan College (TN)	$23,214	$14,768
Shorter College (GA)	$23,170	$15,152

	Tuition, fees, room and board	Average financial aid package
Reinhardt University (GA)	$22,942	$11,498
Benedict College (SC)	$22,762	N/A
St. Augustine's College (NC)	$22,608	$1,778
Southeastern University (FL)	$22,566	$10,890
University of the Cumberlands (KY)	$22,484	N/A
Southern Adventist University (TN)	$22,192	$20,165
Warner University (FL)	$22,135	N/A
Brewton-Parker College (GA)	$21,713	N/A
Oakwood University (AL)	$21,594	N/A
Clearwater Christian College (FL)	$21,450	N/A
Claflin University (SC)	$21,411	$17,933
Toccoa Falls College (GA)	$21,162	N/A
Atlanta Christian College	$20,730	N/A
Bethune-Cookman University (FL)	$20,608	$13,046
Flagler College (FL)	$20,490	$17,705
Virginia Union University	$20,440	$10,921
Faulkner University (AL)	$20,260	N/A
Livingstone College (NC)	$20,000	$12,607
St. Paul's College (VA)	$19,870	$8,147
Stillman College (AL)	$19,798	$18,804
Mount Olive College (NC)	$19,316	N/A
Free Will Baptist Bible College (TN)	$19,234	$9,377
Florida Memorial University	$19,176	N/A
Shaw University (NC)	$18,896	N/A
Emmanuel College (GA)	$18,400	N/A
Thomas University (GA)	$17,592	N/A
Louisiana College	$16,980	$5,809
Williams Baptist College (AR)	$16,600	$12,992
Voorhees College (SC)	$16,478	N/A
Edward Waters College (FL)	$16,464	N/A
Central Baptist College (AR)	$16,450	N/A
Philander Smith College (AR)	$15,840	N/A
LeMoyne-Owen College (TN)	$15,168	N/A
Miles College (AL)	$15,164	N/A
Arkansas Baptist College	$14,416	N/A
Morris College (SC)	$14,287	N/A
Alice Lloyd College (KY)	$13,450	$10,395
Blue Mountain College (MS)	$12,420	$5,656
Concordia College (AL)	$11,370	N/A
Our Lady of Holy Cross College (LA)	$10,332	N/A

Regional Colleges (Midwest)

	Tuition, fees, room and board	Average financial aid package
Ohio Northern University	$40,146	$25,576
Carthage College (WI)	$36,000	$18,268
Milwaukee School of Engineering	$35,829	$17,687
Marietta College (OH)	$35,112	$24,875
Lake Erie College (OH)	$33,368	$19,991
Buena Vista University (IA)	$32,832	$24,136
Wilmington College (OH)	$32,558	N/A
Trine University (IN)	$32,500	$16,957
Loras College (IA)	$32,374	$16,558
Taylor University (IN)	$32,104	$18,002
Bluffton University (OH)	$32,014	$21,413
St. Joseph's College (IN)	$31,950	$21,891
Adrian College (MI)	$31,900	$21,057
Manchester College (IN)	$31,840	$21,729
Judson University (IL)	$31,700	N/A
Marian University (IN)	$31,512	N/A
St. Mary-of-the-Woods College (IN)	$31,510	$15,681
Defiance College (OH)	$30,645	$18,433
Northwestern College (MN)	$30,606	$16,842
Quincy University (IL)	$30,410	$20,172
Notre Dame College of Ohio	$30,334	N/A
Franklin College (IN)	$30,160	$17,703
Augustana College (SD)	$29,964	$19,740
Culver-Stockton College (MO)	$29,950	$20,481
McKendree University (IL)	$29,920	$17,718
Briar Cliff University (IA)	$29,298	$6,300
Robert Morris University (IL)	$29,145	$12,121
Mount Mercy College (IA)	$29,080	$16,094
Northwestern College (IA)	$28,825	$18,093
Morningside College (IA)	$28,760	$18,517
Midland Lutheran College (NE)	$28,596	N/A
College of St. Mary (NE)	$28,564	N/A
Huntington University (IN)	$28,470	$16,098
Trinity Christian College (IL)	$28,424	$12,219
Urbana University (OH)	$28,120	N/A
Concordia University (MI)	$28,096	$13,083
Dordt College (IA)	$28,090	$20,705
Grace College and Seminary (IN)	$27,980	N/A
Iowa Wesleyan College	$27,842	N/A
Dana College (NE)	$27,790	N/A

	Tuition, fees, room and board	Average financial aid package
University of Dubuque (IA)	$27,580	$18,833
Lincoln College (IL)	$27,500	N/A
Cedarville University (OH)	$27,458	$14,534
Bethel College (IN)	$27,228	$18,230
Greenville College (IL)	$27,198	$15,347
Crown College (MN)	$27,140	$15,394
Ottawa University (KS)	$26,946	N/A
Concordia University (NE)	$26,770	$17,208
Tabor College (KS)	$26,540	N/A
Waldorf College (IA)	$26,508	N/A
Mount Vernon Nazarene University (OH)	$26,220	$15,619
University of Sioux Falls (SD)	$26,210	N/A
Bethany Lutheran College (MN)	$26,050	N/A
Kansas Wesleyan University	$25,800	N/A
Grand View University (IA)	$25,766	$14,309
Dakota Wesleyan University (SD)	$25,470	$19,000
MacMurray College (IL)	$25,370	$24,166
Bethany College (KS)	$24,941	$20,598
Central Methodist University (MO)	$24,910	$15,394
Eureka College (IL)	$24,830	$11,105
Finlandia University (MI)	$24,410	N/A
William Penn University (IA)	$24,226	N/A
Union College (NE)	$23,320	$13,000
Central Christian College (KS)	$22,900	$14,480
Rochester College (MI)	$22,858	N/A
Missouri Valley College	$22,800	$14,600
College of the Ozarks (MO)	$21,990	$15,783
Hannibal-LaGrange College (MO)	$21,480	$9,792
Grace Bible College (MI)	$20,770	N/A
North Central University (MN)	$20,536	N/A
University of Northwestern Ohio	$20,150	N/A
York College (NE)	$19,940	$13,265
Blackburn College (IL)	$18,867	$13,873
Jamestown College (ND)	$18,392	$11,925
Wilberforce University (OH)	$18,170	N/A
Maranatha Baptist Bible College (WI)	$16,990	N/A
East-West University (IL)	$15,795	N/A
Lourdes College (OH)	$15,300	$9,732
Baker College of Flint (MI)	$9,645	N/A
Chancellor University (OH)	$7,800	N/A

Regional Colleges (West)

	Tuition, fees, room and board	Average financial aid package
Vanguard University of Southern California	$33,446	$18,766
Master's College and Seminary (CA)	$32,280	$18,028
Corban University (OR)	$30,844	$17,364
Pacific Union College (CA)	$30,729	$17,290
Northwest Christian University (OR)	$29,700	$19,146
Concordia University Texas	$29,000	$20,951
Cogswell Polytechnical College (CA)	$28,908	N/A
Northwest University (WA)	$28,718	$15,580
Rocky Mountain College (MT)	$26,496	$17,118
McMurry University (TX)	$25,962	$17,424
Bethany University (CA)	$25,700	N/A
Oklahoma Wesleyan University	$24,258	$11,318
Warner Pacific College (OR)	$23,756	$15,928
St. Gregory's University (OK)	$23,598	N/A
Southwestern Adventist University (TX)	$23,364	N/A

	Tuition, fees, room and board	Average financial aid package
Oklahoma Baptist University	$23,134	$13,131
Howard Payne University (TX)	$22,547	$15,273
East Texas Baptist University	$22,344	$14,327
Patten University (CA)	$20,530	$6,709
Humphreys College (CA)	$20,388	N/A
Mid-America Christian University (OK)	$19,040	N/A
Schreiner University (TX)	$18,731	$15,360
Western Governors University (UT)	$18,470	N/A
Texas College	$16,090	$9,402
Wiley College (TX)	$15,590	$14,701
American Indian College of the Assemblies of God (AZ)	$13,824	N/A
Southwestern Assemblies of God University (TX)	$12,900	$11,363
Southwestern Christian College (TX)	$10,510	N/A
Brigham Young University–Idaho	$8,066	N/A
National Hispanic University (CA)	$6,640	N/A

Cheapest public schools

Four out of five students attend public institutions, where the costs for in-state students run far below the headline-grabbing level. The schools are listed by in-state tuition and fees for the 2009–2010 academic year. Also provided is the 2009–2010 charge for room and board, as well as the tuition and fees for out-of-state students. (Not all schools offer housing, so in some cases no charges appear for room and board—though you'll still have living expenses, of course.) In addition, the table lists the average need-based financial aid package granted to undergraduates during 2009–2010. The typical aid package has three components: a need-based grant, need-based loans, and work-study. In order to qualify, students must file an annual aid application that demonstrates financial need. Expenses for 2010–2011 are provided in the directory when available.

National Universities

	Tuition, fees (in-state)	Tuition, fees (out-of-state)	Room and board	Average financial aid package
University of Wyoming	$3,686	$11,606	$8,006	$9,332
North Carolina A&T State University	$3,696	$13,138	$5,659	$11,899
San Diego State University	$3,754	$13,924	$11,485	$8,500
University of Louisiana–Lafayette	$4,004	$10,184	$4,630	$7,037
Florida A&M University	$4,130	$16,121	$7,814	$12,216
Florida International University	$4,168	$16,567	$11,946	N/A
Florida Atlantic University	$4,187	$4,187	$9,582	$8,271
University of West Florida	$4,210	$17,092	$6,900	N/A
University of North Carolina–Greensboro	$4,234	$15,995	$6,506	$9,204
University of New Orleans	$4,306	$11,702	$6,130	$8,014
University of Florida	$4,373	$23,744	$7,500	$13,448
University of North Carolina–Charlotte	$4,449	$15,061	$7,500	$8,642
East Carolina University (NC)	$4,477	$15,311	N/A	N/A
University of Central Florida	$4,526	$20,005	$8,540	$7,951
Florida State University	$4,566	$18,804	$8,000	$10,419
University of South Florida	$4,577	$15,386	$8,750	$8,470
Jackson State University (MS)	$4,634	$11,358	$5,693	N/A
University of Nevada–Reno	$4,756	$17,096	$10,595	$7,598
Louisiana Tech University	$4,776	$8,760	$5,178	$9,446
Utah State University	$4,828	$13,802	$4,900	$7,300
University of Idaho	$4,932	$15,012	$7,242	$12,076
Idaho State University	$4,968	$14,770	$5,050	N/A
University of Nevada–Las Vegas	$4,973	$17,313	$10,456	$9,706
New Mexico State University	$4,998	$15,150	$6,338	$7,539
University of Alabama–Birmingham	$5,096	$11,432	$8,142	$9,334
University of New Mexico	$5,101	$17,254	$7,746	N/A
University of Mississippi	$5,106	$13,050	$6,562	$7,677
Mississippi State University	$5,151	$13,021	$7,520	$10,551
Louisiana State University–Baton Rouge	$5,233	$14,383	$7,738	$11,518
University of Oklahoma	$5,245	$13,229	$7,598	$13,072
University of Southern Mississippi	$5,296	$12,946	$6,200	$9,117
West Virginia University	$5,304	$16,402	$7,528	$6,959
University of Alaska–Fairbanks	$5,398	$15,298	$6,630	$10,556
University of Northern Colorado	$5,451	$14,499	$8,370	$14,872
Wichita State University (KS)	$5,467	$13,501	$6,060	$7,278
Tennessee State University	$5,474	$17,552	$5,610	$8,464
Texas A&M University–Commerce	$5,500	$14,040	$6,890	$9,608
North Carolina State University–Raleigh	$5,527	$18,012	$7,966	$10,594
University of Montana	$5,533	$18,373	$6,611	$8,638
University of Arizona	$5,542	$18,676	$7,812	$10,021
University of North Carolina–Chapel Hill	$5,626	$23,514	$8,670	$12,860
Georgia Southern University	$5,640	$17,616	$7,900	$8,704
SUNY College of Environmental Science and Forestry	$5,793	$13,693	$12,460	$13,000
University of Utah	$5,804	$18,352	$6,240	$10,944
Texas A&M University–Kingsville	$5,981	$14,292	$5,900	N/A
Montana State University	$6,031	$17,607	$7,578	$10,268
Georgia State University	$6,056	$20,624	$11,178	$8,393
South Dakota State University	$6,155	$7,528	$5,668	$9,214
Oklahoma State University	$6,202	$16,556	$6,402	$10,788
University of Texas–El Paso	$6,224	$14,834	$8,343	$12,125
Colorado State University	$6,318	$22,240	$8,346	$10,051
University of Arkansas–Little Rock	$6,338	$14,798	$3,198	N/A
University of Colorado–Denver	$6,394	$19,366	$13,524	$8,804

	Tuition, fees (in-state)	Tuition, fees (out-of-state)	Room and board	Average financial aid package
North Dakota State University	$6,410	$15,509	$6,402	$4,652
SUNY–Stony Brook	$6,430	$14,330	$9,588	$11,124
University of Memphis	$6,458	$13,874	$7,350	$9,005
University of Arkansas	$6,460	$15,338	$7,807	$9,030
University of South Dakota	$6,468	$7,841	$5,787	$6,471
East Tennessee State University	$6,492	$18,570	$7,306	N/A
University of North Dakota	$6,513	$15,325	$5,472	$5,723
Arizona State University	$6,526	$19,629	$9,210	N/A
Morgan State University (MD)	$6,548	$15,418	$8,340	$17,329
Iowa State University	$6,651	$17,871	$7,277	$10,771
Texas Woman's University	$6,660	$15,000	$5,831	$7,813
Oregon State University	$6,727	$19,651	$8,352	$9,856
University at Albany–SUNY	$6,748	$14,648	$10,238	$9,649
Binghamton University–SUNY	$6,761	$14,661	$10,614	$11,940
Portland State University (OR)	$6,765	$21,198	$9,135	$9,343
University of Iowa	$6,824	$22,198	$8,004	$7,781
University of Tennessee	$6,850	$20,646	$6,652	$10,679
Kansas State University	$6,870	$17,577	$6,752	$10,655
University at Buffalo–SUNY	$6,935	$14,835	$10,092	$9,070
Auburn University (AL)	$6,972	$19,452	$8,972	$9,085
University of Nebraska–Lincoln	$7,000	$18,154	$7,630	$10,060
University of Alabama	$7,000	$19,200	$7,796	$9,506
University of Alabama–Huntsville	$7,161	$16,279	$7,208	$8,226
University of Hawaii–Manoa	$7,167	$19,215	$8,493	$8,703
Indiana University of Pennsylvania	$7,225	$15,557	$6,296	$8,991
Virginia Commonwealth University	$7,254	$20,926	$10,492	$9,365
University of North Texas	$7,300	$15,610	$6,534	$10,811
Old Dominion University (VA)	$7,318	$19,768	$7,868	$7,701
University of Kansas	$7,414	$18,097	$6,802	$10,014
Indiana State University	$7,426	$16,002	$7,463	$9,198
University of Oregon	$7,430	$23,720	$8,939	$9,168
Texas Tech University	$7,485	$15,795	$7,527	$10,578
Indiana University-Purdue University–Indianapolis	$7,523	$22,420	$7,944	$8,978
University of Georgia	$7,530	$25,740	$8,046	$9,509
Wright State University (OH)	$7,533	$14,595	$7,925	$9,177
Georgia Institute of Technology	$7,606	$25,816	$8,204	$10,933
University of Washington	$7,692	$24,367	$8,949	$11,550
Ball State University (IN)	$7,830	$20,398	$7,932	$9,450
University of Toledo (OH)	$7,927	$16,738	$8,656	$14,129
University of Colorado–Boulder	$7,932	$26,886	$10,378	$14,790
University of Wisconsin–Milwaukee	$7,988	$17,716	$8,800	$7,800
Cleveland State University	$8,020	$10,824	$9,230	$8,565
George Mason University (VA)	$8,024	$23,120	$7,970	$11,449
University of Maryland–College Park	$8,053	$23,990	$9,377	$9,481
University of Kentucky	$8,123	$16,678	$9,125	$8,831
Texas A&M University–College Station	$8,176	$22,606	$8,039	$14,658
University of Texas–Arlington	$8,186	$16,496	$6,097	$9,939
University of California–Los Angeles	$8,228	$29,897	$13,310	$17,008
University of Missouri–Kansas City	$8,273	$19,364	$9,560	$9,704
University of Wisconsin–Madison	$8,314	$23,063	$8,040	$11,141
University of Louisville (KY)	$8,348	$19,676	$7,126	$10,170
Western Michigan University	$8,382	$19,502	$7,784	$11,000
Kent State University (OH)	$8,430	$15,862	$7,940	$8,820
South Carolina State University	$8,462	$16,626	$8,262	N/A
University of Missouri	$8,467	$19,558	$8,100	$13,136
Washington State University	$8,488	$19,564	$8,164	$11,018
University of Houston	$8,496	$16,806	$7,164	$12,018
Missouri University of Science & Technology	$8,498	$19,589	$6,970	$13,362
University of California–Riverside	$8,508	$30,177	$10,900	$16,903
University of Missouri–St. Louis	$8,595	$19,686	$8,164	$8,707
Virginia Tech	$8,605	$21,878	$6,580	$11,642
Indiana University–Bloomington	$8,613	$26,160	$7,546	$10,440
Purdue University–West Lafayette (IN)	$8,638	$25,118	$8,640	$10,555
Wayne State University (MI)	$8,643	$18,412	$7,659	$15,020
Ohio State University–Columbus	$8,706	$22,278	$8,409	$10,725
University of Akron (OH)	$8,752	$18,000	$8,697	$7,641
University of California–Irvine	$8,775	$28,796	$10,655	$16,286
Oakland University (MI)	$8,783	$20,498	$7,350	$7,730
University of Maryland–Baltimore County	$8,872	$18,213	$9,303	$10,480
University of California–Santa Cruz	$8,890	$31,559	$13,641	$18,545
Ohio University	$8,907	$17,871	$10,275	$8,484
University of Texas–Austin	$8,930	$30,006	$9,602	$12,388

Cheapest public schools

National Universities, continued

	Tuition, fees (in-state)	Tuition, fees (out-of-state)	Room and board	Average financial aid package
University of California–Berkeley	$8,938	$31,655	$15,308	$18,322
University of California–Santa Barbara	$9,055	$30,724	$12,765	$17,380
Bowling Green State University (OH)	$9,060	$16,368	$7,670	$12,886
University of South Carolina	$9,156	$23,732	$7,328	$12,016
University of California–Davis	$9,364	$31,385	$12,361	$16,066
University of California–San Diego	$9,377	$24,621	$11,093	$18,560
University of Cincinnati	$9,399	$23,922	$9,702	$7,843
University of Delaware	$9,486	$23,186	$4,654	$12,675
University of Rhode Island	$9,528	$26,026	$10,334	$12,794
University of Maine	$9,626	$24,776	$8,348	$10,588
University of Virginia	$9,672	$31,672	$8,290	$20,202
University of Connecticut	$9,886	$25,486	$10,120	$12,238
Southern Illinois University–Carbondale	$10,096	$20,559	$7,673	$11,809
Central Michigan University	$10,170	$23,670	$7,896	$10,428
University of Texas–Dallas	$10,340	$23,730	$7,733	N/A
Illinois State University	$10,531	$16,561	$7,882	$11,678
University of Massachusetts–Boston	$10,611	$18,655	N/A	$12,369
University of Massachusetts–Lowell	$10,681	$17,794	$8,635	$12,300
Clemson University (SC)	$10,688	$24,998	$6,774	$10,911
College of William and Mary (VA)	$11,100	$30,902	$8,502	$14,220
Northern Illinois University	$11,276	$19,020	$8,112	$11,087
University of Minnesota–Twin Cities	$11,293	$15,293	$7,582	$13,189
Michigan Technological University	$11,348	$23,618	$8,121	$10,793
Rutgers, the State University of New Jersey–Newark	$11,414	$22,046	$11,155	$13,090
Michigan State University	$11,434	$27,832	$7,444	$10,620
University of Massachusetts–Amherst	$11,732	$19,955	$8,276	$14,606
University of Michigan–Ann Arbor	$11,738	$34,230	$8,590	$11,511
Temple University (PA)	$11,764	$21,044	$9,234	$15,577
Rutgers, the State University of New Jersey–New Brunswick	$11,886	$22,518	$10,676	$14,415
University of Illinois–Chicago	$12,034	$24,424	$10,480	$12,980
Colorado School of Mines	$12,244	$26,404	$8,120	$11,927
University of Illinois–Urbana-Champaign	$12,286	$26,070	$9,284	$12,614
Miami University–Oxford (OH)	$12,312	$26,670	$9,458	$11,374
University of New Hampshire	$12,743	$26,713	$8,874	$18,346
New Jersey Institute of Technology	$12,856	$22,600	$11,080	$13,059
University of Vermont	$13,554	$31,410	$8,996	$18,364
University of Pittsburgh	$14,154	$23,852	$8,900	$10,132
Pennsylvania State University–University Park	$14,416	$25,946	$8,790	$10,179

National Liberal Arts Colleges

	Tuition, fees (in-state)	Tuition, fees (out-of-state)	Room and board	Average financial aid package
United States Military Academy (NY)	$0	$0	$0	N/A
United States Naval Academy (MD)	$0	$0	$0	$0
Metropolitan State College of Denver	$3,639	$13,132	N/A	$7,774
University of North Carolina–Asheville	$4,411	$16,128	$6,890	$10,553
California State University–Monterey Bay	$4,512	$15,672	$8,290	$9,181
West Virginia State University	$4,524	$10,764	$6,070	N/A
Fort Lewis College (CO)	$4,646	$17,616	$7,444	$8,042
New College of Florida	$4,784	$26,386	$7,783	$13,282
Thomas Edison State College (NJ)	$4,798	$6,823	N/A	N/A
University of Hawaii–Hilo	$4,888	$14,392	$6,914	N/A
Colorado State University–Pueblo	$5,210	$15,602	$7,244	$8,512
Mesa State College (CO)	$5,374	$14,340	$7,507	$6,913
SUNY College–Old Westbury	$5,897	$13,797	$9,390	$7,115
Western State College of Colorado	$6,104	$13,260	$7,456	$9,500
Granite State College (NH)	$6,195	$6,555	$6,400	N/A
University of Wisconsin–Parkside	$6,280	$13,853	$6,252	N/A
Purchase College–SUNY	$6,475	$14,375	$10,270	$9,728
University of Wisconsin–Green Bay	$6,614	$14,187	$5,000	$10,169
University of Maine–Machias	$6,775	$17,515	$6,936	N/A
University of Maine–Presque Isle	$6,835	$15,985	$6,710	N/A

	Tuition, fees (in-state)	Tuition, fees (out-of-state)	Room and board	Average financial aid package
Massachusetts College of Liberal Arts	$6,875	$15,820	$7,868	$9,979
University of Virginia–Wise	$7,148	$19,276	$7,770	$9,212
Christopher Newport University (VA)	$8,250	$15,952	$9,040	$7,937
Coastal Carolina University (SC)	$8,950	$18,770	$7,200	$8,878
University of Minnesota–Morris	$10,716	$10,716	$7,050	$14,261
Virginia Military Institute	$11,190	$28,738	$6,792	$19,078
St. Mary's College of Maryland	$13,234	$24,627	$9,940	$6,500

Regional Universities (North)

	Tuition, fees (in-state)	Tuition, fees (out-of-state)	Room and board	Average financial aid package
CUNY–City College	$4,278	$8,918	$12,207	$10,085
CUNY–Hunter College	$4,399	$9,039	$11,755	$5,092
CUNY–Baruch College	$4,920	$12,770	N/A	$6,598
CUNY–John Jay College of Criminal Justice	$4,929	$12,779	N/A	$10,150
CUNY–Lehman College	$4,940	$10,300	$10,382	$4,002
CUNY–College of Staten Island	$4,978	$11,178	N/A	$7,520
CUNY–Brooklyn College	$5,031	$12,881	N/A	$6,100
CUNY–Queens College	$5,116	$10,476	$11,125	$7,500
SUNY Empire State College	$5,195	$13,095	N/A	N/A
University of Maryland–University College	$5,760	$12,216	N/A	$6,795
Buffalo State College–SUNY	$5,995	$13,895	$9,726	$9,450
SUNY Institute of Technology–Utica/Rome	$6,033	$13,933	$9,550	N/A
Bowie State University (MD)	$6,038	$16,476	$8,135	$8,114
SUNY–Plattsburgh	$6,080	$13,980	$8,574	$11,140
SUNY–New Paltz	$6,081	$13,981	$9,202	$9,023
University of Maryland–Eastern Shore	$6,082	$13,306	$7,230	$14,500
College at Brockport–SUNY	$6,108	$14,008	$9,200	$9,606
SUNY College–Potsdam	$6,170	$14,070	$9,630	$14,073
SUNY College–Oneonta	$6,185	$14,085	$8,900	$11,712
SUNY College–Cortland	$6,215	$14,115	$10,490	$11,858
SUNY–Fredonia	$6,258	$14,158	$9,330	$8,119
SUNY–Geneseo	$6,278	$14,178	$9,170	$8,041
University of the District of Columbia	$6,300	$12,300	$0	N/A
Rhode Island College	$6,408	$15,488	$8,818	$8,365
Delaware State University	$6,481	$13,742	$9,386	$11,526
Framingham State College (MA)	$6,540	$12,620	$8,148	$7,715
Bridgewater State College (MA)	$6,604	$12,744	$9,670	$7,621
Worcester State College (MA)	$6,605	$12,685	$9,067	$9,679
Salisbury University (MD)	$6,618	$15,114	$7,910	$7,027
SUNY–Oswego	$6,651	$14,551	$10,870	$10,744
Frostburg State University (MD)	$6,684	$16,880	$8,250	$8,927
Salem State College (MA)	$6,744	$12,884	$9,438	N/A
Fitchburg State College (MA)	$6,900	$12,980	$7,810	$8,645
Lock Haven University of Pennsylvania	$6,917	$12,955	$6,448	$8,394
Westfield State College (MA)	$7,016	$13,096	$8,240	$7,812
Bloomsburg University of Pennsylvania	$7,110	$15,546	$6,488	$11,899
Millersville University of Pennsylvania	$7,147	$15,479	$7,766	$8,124
University of Baltimore (MD)	$7,171	$20,677	N/A	N/A
West Chester University of Pennsylvania	$7,211	$15,543	$7,214	$7,648
Slippery Rock University of Pennsylvania	$7,235	$10,012	$8,322	$8,260
Edinboro University of Pennsylvania	$7,316	$10,094	$7,130	$7,473
Coppin State University (MD)	$7,355	$16,050	$9,966	N/A
Cheyney University of Pennsylvania	$7,360	$15,692	$8,038	N/A
Clarion University of Pennsylvania	$7,380	$12,934	$6,390	$8,210
East Stroudsburg University of Pennsylvania	$7,394	$15,726	$6,418	$5,933
Kutztown University of Pennsylvania	$7,397	$15,729	$7,698	$7,379
Central Connecticut State University	$7,414	$15,784	$9,122	$6,601
Towson University (MD)	$7,418	$18,232	$8,670	$9,182
Shippensburg University of Pennsylvania	$7,444	$15,776	$7,086	$7,738
Western Connecticut State University	$7,462	$15,832	$9,517	$8,090
Southern Connecticut State University	$7,578	$15,948	$9,469	$8,355
Mansfield University of Pennsylvania	$7,756	$16,088	$7,016	$2,694

Cheapest public schools

Regional Universities (North), continued

	Tuition, fees (in-state)	Tuition, fees (out-of-state)	Room and board	Average financial aid package
California University of Pennsylvania	$7,765	$11,099	$9,320	$9,093
Eastern Connecticut State University	$7,783	$16,183	$9,580	$8,000
University of Southern Maine	$8,174	$20,384	$8,762	$13,618
Lincoln University (PA)	$8,390	$12,390	$7,900	$10,678
Johnson State College (VT)	$8,716	$17,956	$7,808	N/A
Plymouth State University (NH)	$8,784	$17,027	$8,594	$9,403
Castleton State College (VT)	$8,820	$18,060	$7,808	N/A
Keene State College (NH)	$9,334	$17,504	$8,444	$8,603
Kean University (NJ)	$9,446	$14,081	$12,264	$9,810
Montclair State University (NJ)	$10,003	$16,636	$10,886	$9,153
University of Massachusetts–Dartmouth	$10,358	$17,040	$9,370	$13,949
William Paterson University of New Jersey	$10,838	$17,592	$10,280	$14,598
Richard Stockton College of New Jersey	$10,940	$16,623	$10,189	$15,435
Ramapo College of New Jersey	$11,188	$18,871	$11,240	$12,053
Rowan University (NJ)	$11,234	$18,308	$9,958	$8,793
Rutgers, the State University of New Jersey–Camden	$11,698	$22,330	$9,788	$12,413
College of New Jersey	$12,722	$21,408	$9,996	$10,088

Regional Universities (South)

	Tuition, fees (in-state)	Tuition, fees (out-of-state)	Room and board	Average financial aid package
Southern University–New Orleans	$3,161	$6,899	N/A	N/A
Fayetteville State University (NC)	$3,457	$13,800	$5,421	$9,796
McNeese State University (LA)	$3,587	$10,259	$5,770	N/A
Armstrong Atlantic State University (GA)	$3,604	$12,070	$6,048	$7,750
Augusta State University (GA)	$3,730	$13,018	$9,600	N/A
Louisiana State University–Shreveport	$3,733	$8,503	N/A	N/A
University of North Carolina–Pembroke	$3,736	$12,943	$5,740	$9,268
University of Louisiana–Monroe	$3,813	$10,070	$5,890	N/A
North Carolina Central University	$3,922	$13,991	$6,530	N/A
Northwestern State University of Louisiana	$3,932	$10,618	$6,682	$6,741
Southeastern Louisiana University	$3,932	$11,188	$6,450	N/A
Nicholls State University (LA)	$3,965	$10,433	$7,310	$7,415
University of South Alabama	$3,998	$7,996	N/A	N/A
Grambling State University (LA)	$4,016	$9,902	$7,168	$16,539
Southern University and A&M College (LA)	$4,132	$9,924	$5,666	N/A
University of North Florida	$4,193	$17,582	$9,982	$1,822
Columbus State University (GA)	$4,250	$13,548	$7,800	$8,161
Western Carolina University (NC)	$4,330	$13,927	$5,912	$8,681
Florida Gulf Coast University	$4,337	$18,869	$8,659	$7,231
Mississippi University for Women	$4,423	$12,051	$5,164	$8,408
Delta State University (MS)	$4,450	$11,520	$5,778	N/A
Appalachian State University (NC)	$4,491	$15,112	$6,400	$9,991
Alcorn State University (MS)	$4,498	$11,064	$5,384	$9,494
Alabama Agricultural and Mechanical University	$4,692	$8,640	$5,350	$8,642
University of North Carolina–Wilmington	$4,710	$15,592	$7,690	$9,078
University of Arkansas–Monticello	$4,750	$9,010	$4,080	N/A
Georgia Southwestern State University	$4,762	$16,376	$7,115	$7,655
Savannah State University (GA)	$4,774	$16,388	$5,958	N/A
Mississippi Valley State University	$4,877	$11,460	$5,081	N/A
Kennesaw State University (GA)	$4,942	$16,918	$4,977	$3,970
Fort Valley State University (GA)	$5,012	$16,626	$6,188	$4,400
North Georgia College and State University	$5,036	$16,650	$5,248	$8,400
Marshall University (WV)	$5,236	$12,482	$7,556	$9,498
University of West Georgia	$5,382	$17,358	$6,254	$8,224
Alabama State University	$5,460	$10,068	$4,600	N/A
Southern Polytechnic State University (GA)	$5,474	$18,594	$6,350	$3,678
University of Tennessee–Martin	$5,510	$16,790	$5,973	$11,491
Tennessee Technological University	$5,526	$17,126	$7,600	$7,954
University of West Alabama	$5,560	$10,620	$4,416	N/A
Arkansas Tech University	$5,610	$10,620	$5,156	$7,638
University of Tennessee–Chattanooga	$5,656	$16,954	$6,890	$9,853
Valdosta State University (GA)	$5,706	$13,617	$7,062	$8,550
Georgia College & State University	$5,738	$19,294	$8,228	$7,514
Austin Peay State University (TN)	$5,808	$17,736	$6,120	$8,513

	Tuition, fees (In-state)	Tuition, fees (out-of-state)	Room and board	Average financial aid package
Norfolk State University (VA)	$5,872	$17,931	$8,376	N/A
Auburn University–Montgomery (AL)	$5,925	$17,205	N/A	N/A
Murray State University (KY)	$5,976	$16,236	$6,562	$5,825
Middle Tennessee State University	$5,988	$17,916	$6,754	N/A
Morehead State University (KY)	$6,036	$15,096	$6,192	$9,447
University of North Alabama	$6,042	$11,052	$4,784	$4,993
Virginia State University	$6,174	$14,508	$8,050	N/A
Henderson State University (AR)	$6,204	$11,304	$4,964	$10,648
Jacksonville State University (AL)	$6,240	$12,480	$5,254	$6,563
Arkansas State University–Jonesboro	$6,370	$14,290	$6,256	$9,950
University of Central Arkansas	$6,698	$11,903	$4,880	N/A
Eastern Kentucky University	$6,772	$17,740	$6,500	$10,183
Northern Kentucky University	$6,792	$12,792	$5,698	N/A
Radford University (VA)	$6,904	$16,568	$6,970	$9,394
University of Montevallo (AL)	$7,010	$13,550	$4,440	$8,531
Troy University (AL)	$7,020	$13,196	$4,572	$4,485
Western Kentucky University	$7,200	$17,784	$6,351	$12,057
James Madison University (VA)	$7,244	$19,376	$7,690	$7,885
University of Mary Washington (VA)	$7,862	$19,590	$8,116	$9,800
Francis Marion University (SC)	$7,960	$15,585	$6,024	N/A
College of Charleston (SC)	$8,988	$21,846	$9,411	$12,882
Longwood University (VA)	$9,045	$18,150	$7,596	$10,118
The Citadel (SC)	$9,993	$23,227	$6,038	$15,434
Winthrop University (SC)	$11,606	$21,596	$6,530	$10,109

Regional Universities (Midwest)

	Tuition, fees (In-state)	Tuition, fees (out-of-state)	Room and board	Average financial aid package
Fort Hays State University (KS)	$2,946	$11,099	$6,560	N/A
Emporia State University (KS)	$4,374	$13,578	$6,146	$7,960
Pittsburg State University (KS)	$4,592	$13,116	$5,744	$9,900
Wayne State College (NE)	$4,805	$8,480	$5,280	$6,771
Lincoln University (MO)	$4,948	$8,716	$4,660	N/A
Minot State University (ND)	$5,410	$5,410	$5,822	$7,187
University of Southern Indiana	$5,474	$12,755	$6,700	$8,198
Metropolitan State University (MN)	$5,627	$11,173	N/A	N/A
University of Nebraska–Kearney	$5,635	$10,397	$6,830	$9,443
Indiana University Southeast	$5,890	$14,578	$8,860	$7,611
University of Nebraska–Omaha	$5,893	$15,471	$7,230	$2,458
Indiana University Northwest	$5,919	$15,024	N/A	$8,238
Indiana University–South Bend	$6,015	$15,712	$6,796	$7,902
Washburn University (KS)	$6,116	$13,766	$5,792	$8,748
Indiana University-Purdue University–Fort Wayne	$6,233	$14,829	$8,877	N/A
Southeast Missouri State University	$6,255	$10,890	$6,358	$8,384
Purdue University–Calumet (IN)	$6,308	$14,115	$7,073	$6,632
University of Wisconsin–River Falls	$6,390	$13,963	$6,372	$9,099
Minnesota State University–Mankato	$6,429	$12,861	$6,322	$8,130
University of Wisconsin–Platteville	$6,450	$14,400	$5,550	N/A
University of Wisconsin–Whitewater	$6,495	$14,068	$5,028	$7,957
University of Wisconsin–Stevens Point	$6,532	$14,105	$5,612	$8,284
University of Wisconsin–Oshkosh	$6,540	$14,900	$6,520	$5,350
University of Central Missouri	$6,585	$12,444	$6,320	$9,426
St. Cloud State University (MN)	$6,606	$13,234	$3,008	$14,317
Minnesota State University–Moorhead	$6,626	$6,626	$6,174	$8,172
University of Wisconsin–Eau Claire	$6,633	$14,206	$5,630	$8,587
University of Northern Iowa	$6,636	$14,900	$7,082	$8,243
Truman State University (MO)	$6,692	$11,543	$6,854	$9,996
University of Wisconsin–Superior	$6,736	$14,309	$5,285	N/A
Winona State University (MN)	$6,800	$11,540	$6,920	$6,728
Northwest Missouri State University	$6,911	$8,543	$7,408	N/A
Southwest Minnesota State University	$6,932	$6,932	$6,520	$8,541
Youngstown State University (OH)	$6,956	$12,629	$7,400	$8,308
Missouri State University	$6,972	$12,252	$5,952	$8,018

Cheapest public schools

Regional Universities (Midwest), continued

	Tuition, fees (in-state)	Tuition, fees (out-of-state)	Room and board	Average financial aid package
Bemidji State University (MN)	$6,996	$6,996	$6,024	$9,118
Northeastern Illinois University	$7,082	$12,722	$0	$8,362
Saginaw Valley State University (MI)	$7,312	$13,205	$7,487	N/A
Northern Michigan University	$7,454	$11,828	$7,846	$7,979
University of Wisconsin–La Crosse	$7,509	$15,082	$5,630	$6,397
University of Wisconsin–Stout	$7,658	$15,403	$5,196	$9,291
Chicago State University	$8,006	$13,922	$7,540	N/A
Eastern Michigan University	$8,069	$21,464	$7,352	$8,219
University of Michigan–Flint	$8,279	$15,793	$6,874	N/A
Southern Illinois University–Edwardsville	$8,336	$17,638	$7,430	$15,749
Grand Valley State University (MI)	$8,630	$12,944	$7,478	$8,485
Western Illinois University	$8,726	$11,954	$7,210	$9,261
University of Michigan–Dearborn	$8,809	$19,297	N/A	$8,515
University of Illinois–Springfield	$9,168	$18,318	$8,250	$10,929
Eastern Illinois University	$9,429	$23,769	$8,078	$8,912
Ferris State University (MI)	$9,480	$15,900	$8,940	$15,531
University of Minnesota–Duluth	$11,193	$13,193	$6,176	$11,087

Regional Universities (West)

	Tuition, fees (in-state)	Tuition, fees (out-of-state)	Room and board	Average financial aid package
New Mexico Highlands University	$2,761	$4,328	$7,555	N/A
California State University–Fullerton	$3,382	$14,542	$9,082	$12,421
Eastern New Mexico University	$3,552	$9,102	$5,374	N/A
Western New Mexico University	$3,589	$12,825	$7,750	$8,662
California State University–Long Beach	$3,698	$13,868	$10,832	$12,627
California State Polytechnic University–Pomona	$3,879	$14,049	$9,240	$10,874
California State University–Fresno	$4,000	$14,170	$7,577	$10,984
California State University–San Bernardino	$4,026	$12,954	$9,432	$10,373
Weber State University (UT)	$4,081	$11,547	$4,259	N/A
Cameron University (OK)	$4,110	$9,675	$7,969	$10,100
Southwestern Oklahoma State University	$4,110	$9,450	$4,100	$4,890
Northeastern State University (OK)	$4,155	$10,245	$4,966	$8,680
University of Central Oklahoma	$4,223	$10,652	$7,468	$7,378
Southern Utah University	$4,269	$12,847	$5,300	N/A
East Central University (OK)	$4,271	$10,286	$4,324	N/A
Southeastern Oklahoma State University	$4,316	$10,687	$4,650	$9,675
California State University–Bakersfield	$4,383	$11,199	$7,137	N/A
Sul Ross State University (TX)	$4,396	$11,044	$6,370	N/A
Adams State College (CO)	$4,454	$13,598	$7,220	N/A
University of Texas–Pan American	$4,560	$11,208	$5,230	N/A
New Mexico Institute of Mining and Technology	$4,607	$13,118	$5,702	$10,397
California State University–Los Angeles	$4,640	$15,800	$9,105	$11,144
California State University–Dominguez Hills	$4,645	$13,573	$9,970	$5,457
California State University–San Marcos	$4,650	$8,136	N/A	N/A
San Francisco State University	$4,740	$15,900	$10,904	$10,668
University of Alaska–Anchorage	$4,820	$14,720	$9,177	$10,055
California State University–Stanislaus	$4,840	$16,000	$7,669	$10,247
Boise State University (ID)	$4,864	$13,868	$5,602	$8,282
California State University–East Bay	$4,872	$13,800	$10,029	$10,000
University of Texas–Brownsville	$4,872	$12,074	$5,782	$8,685
University of Alaska–Southeast	$4,888	$14,788	$6,430	N/A
California State University–Sacramento	$4,900	$16,060	$9,472	$7,030
Tarleton State University (TX)	$4,909	$11,557	$6,591	N/A
California State University–Chico	$4,968	$15,138	$8,718	$12,447
Humboldt State University (CA)	$5,166	$14,094	$9,986	$10,984
Montana State University–Billings	$5,207	$10,555	$5,310	$8,806
Sonoma State University (CA)	$5,290	$13,426	$10,418	$9,782
University of Texas of the Permian Basin	$5,300	$13,730	$4,234	$7,384
San Jose State University (CA)	$5,423	$13,559	$10,438	$12,240
Evergreen State College (WA)	$5,647	$16,954	$8,052	$10,554
Texas A&M International University	$5,746	$14,176	$6,918	$9,248
Eastern Washington University	$5,872	$14,590	$7,073	$11,043
West Texas A&M University	$5,890	$14,200	$5,698	$8,425
University of Texas–Tyler	$6,042	$14,352	$7,340	N/A

	Tuition, fees (in-state)	Tuition, fees (out-of-state)	Room and board	Average financial aid package
Texas A&M University–Corpus Christi	$6,098	$14,408	$8,648	$9,277
Angelo State University (TX)	$6,138	$14,568	$7,256	$7,016
Western Washington University	$6,159	$17,190	$8,393	$11,001
California Polytechnic State University–San Luis Obispo	$6,198	$17,358	$9,623	$8,687
Midwestern State University (TX)	$6,226	$7,126	$5,770	$8,459
Southern Oregon University	$6,252	$19,914	$8,454	N/A
Prairie View A&M University (TX)	$6,320	$15,720	$7,100	N/A
Central Washington University	$6,363	$17,616	$8,460	$8,993
Texas Southern University	$6,401	$14,711	$8,706	$12,213
Eastern Oregon University	$6,456	$6,456	$7,435	$9,776
Sam Houston State University (TX)	$6,515	$14,825	$6,744	$4,340
Stephen F. Austin State University (TX)	$6,528	$14,958	$7,377	N/A
Western Oregon University	$6,576	$17,376	$8,208	$8,626
Lamar University (TX)	$6,607	$14,917	$6,290	$10,723
University of Colorado–Colorado Springs	$6,805	$16,924	$8,498	$8,396
Texas State University–San Marcos	$7,482	$15,792	$6,392	$13,634
University of Texas–San Antonio	$7,527	$15,837	$8,937	$8,412

Regional Colleges (North)

	Tuition, fees (in-state)	Tuition, fees (out-of-state)	Room and board	Average financial aid package
United States Merchant Marine Academy (NY)	N/A	N/A	N/A	$3,300
United States Coast Guard Academy (CT)	N/A	N/A	N/A	$0
Fashion Institute of Technology (NY)	$4,164	$11,592	$11,248	$11,288
CUNY–York College	$4,262	$8,902	N/A	N/A
CUNY–New York City College of Technology	$4,339	$11,139	N/A	$7,863
CUNY–Medgar Evers College	$4,982	$10,262	N/A	$3,721
Farmingdale State College–SUNY	$6,030	$13,930	$11,090	N/A
SUNY Maritime College	$6,090	$13,990	$9,930	$9,735
SUNY College of Agriculture and Technology–Cobleskill	$6,109	$14,009	$9,460	$7,134
University of Maine–Augusta	$6,110	$13,858	N/A	$10,766
Massachusetts Maritime Academy	$6,119	$18,758	$8,996	N/A
SUNY College of Technology–Delhi	$6,120	$14,020	$9,224	N/A
SUNY College of Technology–Alfred	$6,162	$14,062	$9,190	$12,452
University of Maine–Fort Kent	$6,803	$15,953	$7,080	$5,422
University of Maine–Farmington	$8,710	$17,094	$7,552	N/A
Lyndon State College (VT)	$8,820	$18,060	$7,808	N/A
Maine Maritime Academy	$10,105	$17,805	$8,450	$8,890
Vermont Technical College	$10,892	$19,940	$7,808	$8,152
University of Pittsburgh–Bradford	$11,722	$21,282	$7,480	$12,600
University of Pittsburgh–Johnstown	$11,754	$21,314	$7,370	$10,226
Pennsylvania College of Technology	$12,480	$15,630	$8,350	N/A

Regional Colleges (South)

	Tuition, fees (in-state)	Tuition, fees (out-of-state)	Room and board	Average financial aid package
Elizabeth City State University (NC)	$1,915	$6,439	$2,748	N/A
Macon State College (GA)	$2,304	$8,280	N/A	N/A
West Virginia University–Parkersburg	$2,844	$7,512	N/A	N/A
Dalton State College (GA)	$2,900	$10,382	$4,440	N/A
Winston-Salem State University (NC)	$3,522	$12,508	$6,924	$9,577
Louisiana State University–Alexandria	$3,562	$6,270	$6,410	N/A
Bluefield State College (WV)	$4,596	$9,000	N/A	$6,200
University of Arkansas–Fort Smith	$4,600	$10,000	$7,180	N/A
University of Arkansas–Pine Bluff	$4,706	$5,366	$3,310	N/A
Clayton State University (GA)	$4,858	$16,472	$8,078	$4,163
West Liberty University (WV)	$4,880	$11,950	$6,870	$8,023
Glenville State College (WV)	$4,888	$11,702	$6,460	$11,448

Cheapest public schools

Regional Colleges (South), continued

	Tuition, fees (in-state)	Tuition, fees (out-of-state)	Room and board	Average financial aid package
Fairmont State University (WV)	$4,952	$10,684	$6,400	$7,654
Concord University (WV)	$4,976	$11,052	$6,766	$9,562
West Virginia University Institute of Technology	$5,164	$13,264	$7,720	N/A
Shepherd University (WV)	$5,234	$13,574	$7,522	$10,791
Kentucky State University	$5,686	$14,058	$6,480	$8,529
Southern Arkansas University	$6,438	$9,078	$8,130	$7,679
University of South Carolina–Aiken	$7,950	$15,682	$6,400	$9,108
Lander University (SC)	$8,770	$16,570	$6,186	N/A
University of South Carolina–Upstate	$8,817	$17,459	$6,580	$9,335

Regional Colleges (Midwest)

	Tuition, fees (in-state)	Tuition, fees (out-of-state)	Room and board	Average financial aid package
Harris-Stowe State University (MO)	$4,336	$8,154	$7,860	N/A
Chadron State College (NE)	$4,730	$8,400	$4,900	N/A
Peru State College (NE)	$4,946	$4,946	$4,804	N/A
Missouri Southern State University	$5,026	$9,406	$5,020	$14,602
Dickinson State University (ND)	$5,249	$12,195	$4,494	$7,914
Central State University (OH)	$5,294	$11,806	$7,920	N/A
Missouri Western State University	$5,560	$9,688	$6,370	$7,432
Mayville State University (ND)	$5,793	$7,849	$4,488	$8,594
Indiana University East	$5,801	$14,957	N/A	$7,943
Indiana University–Kokomo	$5,838	$14,527	N/A	$7,733
Valley City State University (ND)	$5,924	$13,076	$4,726	$8,480
Northern State University (SD)	$6,063	$7,436	$5,700	$7,047
Shawnee State University (OH)	$6,132	$10,476	$8,148	N/A
Purdue University–North Central (IN)	$6,384	$15,057	N/A	$6,947
Black Hills State University (SD)	$6,641	$6,641	$5,523	N/A
Dakota State University (SD)	$6,872	$8,245	$4,818	$7,897
Lake Superior State University (MI)	$8,284	$16,468	$7,994	N/A
University of Minnesota–Crookston	$10,005	$10,005	$6,248	$11,016

Regional Colleges (West)

	Tuition, fees (in-state)	Tuition, fees (out-of-state)	Room and board	Average financial aid package
United States Air Force Academy (CO)	N/A	N/A	N/A	$0
Great Basin College (NV)	$2,010	$8,198	$4,790	N/A
Dixie State College of Utah	$3,145	$10,897	$3,948	N/A
University of Science and Arts of Oklahoma	$3,552	$8,448	$5,000	$9,044
Langston University (OK)	$3,827	$9,407	$7,040	$9,611
Utah Valley University	$4,048	$11,888	$8,670	N/A
Northwestern Oklahoma State University	$4,111	$10,141	$3,700	N/A
Rogers State University (OK)	$4,314	$10,178	$6,894	$8,004
Lewis-Clark State College (ID)	$4,596	$12,786	$7,530	$8,048
University of Montana–Western	$4,866	$13,050	$5,510	$3,282
University of Houston–Downtown	$5,000	$13,430	$4,300	$8,126
Montana State University–Northern	$5,080	$14,070	$8,000	N/A
Oklahoma Panhandle State University	$5,142	$10,482	$3,416	N/A
Montana Tech of the University of Montana	$6,005	$16,820	$6,602	$9,086
Oregon Institute of Technology	$6,570	$18,090	$8,245	$5,554
California Maritime Academy	$7,772	$14,588	$9,360	N/A

Best values: Great deals at great schools

To determine which schools offer the best value, *U.S. News* uses a formula that relates a school's academic quality to the net cost of attendance for a student who receives the average level of financial aid. The higher the quality of the program (as indicated by its *U.S. News* ranking) and the lower the cost, the better the deal. We considered only schools ranked in, or near, the top half of their peer groups. The methodology we used is described in detail below.

National Universities

		% receiving grants based on need ('09)	Average cost after receiving grants based on need ('09)	Average discount from total cost ('09)
1	Yale University (CT)	54%	$13,631	73%
2	Harvard University (MA)	60%	$14,380	72%
3	Princeton University (NJ)	59%	$15,792	69%
4	Massachusetts Institute of Technology	62%	$16,530	68%
5	Stanford University (CA)	49%	$16,479	69%
6	Columbia University (NY)	49%	$18,589	66%
7	Dartmouth College (NH)	53%	$18,539	66%
8	California Institute of Technology	55%	$19,899	60%
9	Duke University (NC)	41%	$19,920	63%
10	Cornell University (NY)	45%	$20,503	61%
11	Vanderbilt University (TN)	42%	$20,004	63%
12	University of Chicago	39%	$21,312	61%
13	Brown University (RI)	39%	$20,856	60%
14	University of North Carolina–Chapel Hill	39%	$17,388	51%
15	University of Pennsylvania	40%	$23,757	56%
16	Rice University (TX)	41%	$22,329	51%
17	University of Notre Dame (IN)	47%	$24,448	52%
18	Emory University (GA)	43%	$24,079	54%
19	Johns Hopkins University (MD)	40%	$25,710	52%
20	Brigham Young University–Provo (UT)	29%	$11,678	27%
21	Texas A&M University–College Station	65%	$19,259	45%
22	Northwestern University (IL)	41%	$27,167	50%
23	Washington University in St. Louis	41%	$27,081	51%
24	Georgetown University (DC)	37%	$25,190	54%
25	SUNY College of Environmental Science and Forestry	60%	$17,841	37%
26	University of California–San Diego	23%	$18,716	54%
27	University of Rochester (NY)	57%	$25,949	51%
28	North Carolina State University–Raleigh	48%	$15,042	49%
29	Lehigh University (PA)	44%	$23,332	54%
30	Tufts University (MA)	36%	$25,288	53%
31	Wake Forest University (NC)	35%	$25,609	51%
32	Brandeis University (MA)	48%	$26,264	50%
33	University of Virginia	27%	$23,389	46%
34	Pepperdine University (CA)	48%	$23,621	54%
35	Case Western Reserve University (OH)	62%	$28,685	44%
36	Rensselaer Polytechnic Institute (NY)	65%	$29,892	43%
37	Clarkson University (NY)	79%	$25,397	46%
38	Carnegie Mellon University (PA)	47%	$30,369	43%
39	University of Southern California	36%	$28,817	46%
40	University of the Pacific (CA)	66%	$25,482	46%
41	Clark University (MA)	55%	$23,015	47%
42	Missouri University of Science & Technology	68%	$19,802	34%
43	Boston College	37%	$27,639	49%
44	University of California–Riverside	33%	$18,869	59%
45	Worcester Polytechnic Institute (MA)	67%	$31,621	36%
46	Syracuse University (NY)	54%	$28,852	42%
47	Illinois Institute of Technology	62%	$24,949	42%
48	University of Miami (FL)	47%	$29,175	44%
49	Marquette University (WI)	58%	$26,612	35%
50	University of California–Irvine	25%	$23,612	46%

How we calculated the best values

To be considered, a university or college had to finish in, or near, the top half of its category in the *U.S. News* "Best Colleges 2011" rankings. The best values rankings were based on three variables:

1. Ratio of quality to price: A school's ranking—its overall score in the "Best Colleges" survey—was divided by the cost to a student receiving an average grant meeting financial need. The higher the ratio, the better the value.

2. Percentage of all undergraduates receiving grants meeting financial need during the 2009–2010 year.

3. Average discount: percentage of a school's 2009–2010 total costs (tuition, room and board, fees, books, and other expenses) covered by the average need-based grant to undergraduates. In the case of public institutions, 2009–2010 out-of-state tuition and percentage of out-of-state students receiving grants meeting need were used.

Overall rank was determined first by standardizing the scores achieved by every school in each of the three variables and weighting those scores. The first variable—the ratio of quality to price—accounted for 60 percent of the overall score; the percentage of all undergraduates receiving grants accounted for 25 percent; and the average discount accounted for 15 percent. The weighted scores for each school were totaled. The school with the highest total weighted points became No. 1 in its category. The scores for the other schools were then ranked in descending order.

Best values: Great deals at great schools

National Liberal Arts Colleges

		% receiving grants based on need ('09)	Average cost after receiving grants based on need ('09)	Average discount from total cost ('09)
1	Amherst College (MA)	57%	$13,077	75%
2	Williams College (MA)	52%	$14,678	72%
3	Wellesley College (MA)	60%	$18,884	64%
4	Pomona College (CA)	54%	$18,257	65%
5	Swarthmore College (PA)	49%	$18,411	65%
6	Hamilton College (NY)	41%	$16,158	69%
7	Grinnell College (IA)	63%	$19,715	59%
8	Bowdoin College (ME)	43%	$19,068	64%
9	Claremont McKenna College (CA)	44%	$18,759	65%
10	University of Richmond (VA)	46%	$17,126	66%
11	Vassar College (NY)	56%	$21,005	61%
12	Presbyterian College (SC)	68%	$14,589	65%
13	Smith College (MA)	60%	$21,986	58%
14	Virginia Military Institute	50%	$15,077	61%
15	Agnes Scott College (GA)	73%	$18,430	56%
16	Ripon College (WI)	84%	$17,315	51%
17	Haverford College (PA)	46%	$20,714	62%
18	Macalester College (MN)	67%	$22,131	55%
19	Middlebury College (VT)	49%	$23,062	56%
20	Wesleyan University (CT)	43%	$21,054	61%
21	Hanover College (IN)	76%	$17,236	53%
22	Wabash College (IN)	79%	$21,612	46%
23	Trinity College (CT)	39%	$18,482	65%
24	Mount Holyoke College (MA)	65%	$23,898	54%
25	Carleton College (MN)	56%	$24,371	53%
26	Centre College (KY)	59%	$19,759	52%
27	Cornell College (IA)	74%	$19,635	51%
28	Colgate University (NY)	35%	$19,669	63%
29	Wofford College (SC)	52%	$17,507	59%
30	Bryn Mawr College (PA)	57%	$22,557	57%
31	Harvey Mudd College (CA)	54%	$23,468	56%
32	Bates College (ME)	41%	$21,017	60%
33	Fisk University (TN)	88%	$19,092	39%
34	Beloit College (WI)	63%	$20,513	51%
35	Westminster College (PA)	83%	$20,067	48%
36	Scripps College (CA)	39%	$20,894	60%
37	Thomas Aquinas College (CA)	68%	$19,216	42%
38	Transylvania University (KY)	65%	$18,345	49%
39	Colby College (ME)	38%	$20,997	60%
40	Washington and Lee University (VA)	33%	$21,087	60%

Regional Universities (North)

		% receiving grants based on need ('09)	Average cost after receiving grants based on need ('09)	Average discount from total cost ('09)
1	Villanova University (PA)	42%	$28,974	43%
2	Rochester Institute of Technology (NY)	66%	$24,950	39%
3	Alfred University (NY)	82%	$20,756	47%
4	Bentley University (MA)	43%	$27,762	44%
5	Providence College (RI)	49%	$29,767	36%
6	Le Moyne College (NY)	85%	$22,798	41%
7	Ithaca College (NY)	67%	$28,013	40%
8	Hood College (MD)	81%	$22,366	45%
9	St. Bonaventure University (NY)	76%	$21,105	43%
10	Canisius College (NY)	75%	$23,556	43%
11	Fairfield University (CT)	49%	$31,502	40%
12	Loyola University Maryland	44%	$32,205	37%
13	University of Scranton (PA)	66%	$29,398	36%
14	College of Notre Dame of Maryland	81%	$23,229	41%
15	Gannon University (PA)	84%	$21,068	42%

Regional Universities (South)

		% receiving grants based on need ('09)	Average cost after receiving grants based on need ('09)	Average discount from total cost ('09)
1	Converse College (SC)	82%	$17,886	51%
2	Rollins College (FL)	46%	$23,819	54%
3	Stetson University (FL)	63%	$22,716	48%
4	Mercer University (GA)	71%	$21,971	47%
5	Harding University (AR)	52%	$16,003	31%
6	The Citadel (SC)	27%	$21,409	44%
7	Elon University (NC)	31%	$24,385	34%
8	Loyola University New Orleans	63%	$24,449	37%
9	Mississippi College	48%	$14,671	39%
10	Mary Baldwin College (VA)	78%	$18,651	45%
11	Spring Hill College (AL)	66%	$21,507	45%
12	Brenau University (GA)	73%	$18,184	44%
13	Freed-Hardeman University (TN)	75%	$16,891	38%
14	Lee University (TN)	56%	$13,647	36%
15	Queens University of Charlotte (NC)	65%	$21,665	37%

Regional Universities (Midwest)

		% receiving grants based on need ('09)	Average cost after receiving grants based on need ('09)	Average discount from total cost ('09)
1	Creighton University (NE)	49%	$22,661	46%
2	Aquinas College (MI)	82%	$12,363	61%
3	University of Evansville (IN)	71%	$19,288	50%
4	Valparaiso University (IN)	71%	$23,420	40%
5	Bradley University (IL)	68%	$22,582	36%
6	Muskingum University (OH)	82%	$15,980	47%
7	Drake University (IA)	56%	$23,922	37%
8	Butler University (IN)	63%	$26,036	38%
9	Baldwin-Wallace College (OH)	80%	$20,653	40%
10	Elmhurst College (IL)	67%	$20,850	45%
11	Indiana Wesleyan University	66%	$16,927	43%
12	Hamline University (MN)	78%	$23,747	40%
13	Dominican University (IL)	81%	$20,207	42%
14	Truman State University (MO)	18%	$19,122	18%
15	John Carroll University (OH)	55%	$24,361	39%

Regional Universities (West)

		% receiving grants based on need ('09)	Average cost after receiving grants based on need ('09)	Average discount from total cost ('09)
1	Trinity University (TX)	38%	$23,843	41%
2	Mills College (CA)	84%	$27,919	45%
3	Seattle Pacific University	67%	$20,012	50%
4	Gonzaga University (WA)	57%	$25,179	40%
5	Whitworth University (WA)	68%	$23,930	41%
6	University of Redlands (CA)	75%	$26,007	47%
7	St. Mary's University of San Antonio (TX)	77%	$20,354	41%
8	Pacific Lutheran University (WA)	70%	$24,381	39%
9	Seattle University	60%	$27,011	38%
10	Chapman University (CA)	61%	$28,720	46%
11	University of Dallas	61%	$23,979	40%
12	Abilene Christian University (TX)	65%	$22,148	31%
13	University of Portland (OR)	49%	$26,701	38%
14	Westminster College (UT)	60%	$21,570	39%
15	St. Mary's College of California	59%	$28,712	43%

Regional Colleges (North)

		% receiving grants based on need ('09)	Average cost after receiving grants based on need ('09)	Average discount from total cost ('09)
1	Wilson College (PA)	83%	$19,886	48%
2	Lebanon Valley College (PA)	80%	$22,513	46%
3	Elmira College (NY)	78%	$24,640	47%
4	Cazenovia College (NY)	85%	$19,892	45%
5	Seton Hill University (PA)	83%	$22,199	43%
6	Elizabethtown College (PA)	72%	$23,753	43%
7	Messiah College (PA)	71%	$24,890	34%
8	Keuka College (NY)	85%	$22,924	34%
9	Lasell College (MA)	78%	$24,534	38%
10	Delaware Valley College (PA)	78%	$25,743	36%

Regional Colleges (South)

		% receiving grants based on need ('09)	Average cost after receiving grants based on need ('09)	Average discount from total cost ('09)
1	Claflin University (SC)	94%	$11,863	57%
2	Ouachita Baptist University (AR)	56%	$15,012	44%
3	Alice Lloyd College (KY)	81%	$9,617	45%
4	Milligan College (TN)	77%	$17,193	44%
5	University of the Ozarks (AR)	58%	$15,722	47%
6	Shorter College (GA)	73%	$14,589	46%
7	Alderson-Broaddus College (WV)	91%	$15,929	50%
8	LaGrange College (GA)	80%	$20,417	39%
9	Erskine College (SC)	69%	$21,712	43%
10	Covenant College (GA)	59%	$20,636	41%

Best values: Great deals at great schools

Regional Colleges (Midwest)

		% receiving grants based on need ('09)	Average cost after receiving grants based on need ('09)	Average discount from total cost ('09)
1	College of the Ozarks (MO)	75%	$12,752	50%
2	Augustana College (SD)	69%	$17,443	46%
3	Franklin College (IN)	80%	$17,553	44%
4	Taylor University (IN)	59%	$20,747	41%
5	Huntington University (IN)	70%	$18,618	41%
6	Concordia University (NE)	77%	$16,634	44%
7	Dordt College (IA)	74%	$20,685	36%
8	Manchester College (IN)	78%	$17,664	49%
9	St. Joseph's College (IN)	86%	$19,094	44%
10	Bluffton University (OH)	86%	$20,522	42%

Regional Colleges (West)

		% receiving grants based on need ('09)	Average cost after receiving grants based on need ('09)	Average discount from total cost ('09)
1	University of Science and Arts of Oklahoma	41%	$7,936	57%
2	Howard Payne University (TX)	77%	$15,339	41%
3	Pacific Union College (CA)	97%	$21,009	41%
4	Corban University (OR)	83%	$21,049	40%
5	Master's College and Seminary (CA)	81%	$23,150	37%
6	Northwest University (WA)	76%	$20,341	36%
7	Oklahoma Wesleyan University	68%	$20,262	29%
8	Rocky Mountain College (MT)	46%	$18,537	39%
9	McMurry University (TX)	78%	$20,358	32%
10	University of Montana–Western	67%	$19,252	18%

Schools whose graduates have the most and least debt

How mired in debt will you be when you get your diploma? This table shows the percentage of 2009 graduates who took on debt and the average cumulative amount they borrowed. The data include loans taken out by students from the colleges themselves; from financial institutions; and from federal, state, and local governments. Parents' loans are not included.

National Universities

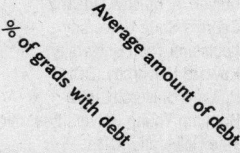
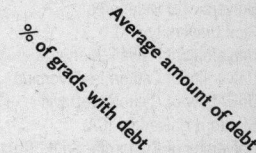

School	% of grads with debt	Average amount of debt
Oral Roberts University (OK)	45%	$49,007
Worcester Polytechnic Institute (MA)	74%	$44,340
Clark Atlanta University	94%	$41,979
American University (DC)	54%	$40,966
Florida Institute of Technology	69%	$40,630
Widener University (PA)	87%	$38,372
University of Dayton (OH)	66%	$37,517
Case Western Reserve Univ. (OH)	64%	$37,496
Nova Southeastern University (FL)	71%	$36,908
University of North Dakota	69%	$36,120
Barry University (FL)	66%	$35,880
Loyola University Chicago	77%	$35,526
Pace University (NY)	58%	$34,115
Andrews University (MI)	73%	$33,931
St. Louis University	64%	$33,747
New York University	59%	$33,487
Morgan State University (MD)	87%	$32,582
George Washington University (DC)	47%	$32,547
Texas Christian University	43%	$32,357
St. Mary's University of Minnesota	77%	$32,166
University of St. Thomas (MN)	67%	$32,132
Clarkson University (NY)	85%	$32,125
Marquette University (WI)	65%	$31,469
Lehigh University (PA)	54%	$31,123
Poly. Inst. of New York Univ. (NY)	74%	$31,035
Rensselaer Polytechnic Institute (NY)	71%	$30,838
University of Maine	77%	$30,824
University of New Hampshire	74%	$30,760
St. John's University (NY)	70%	$30,692
Iowa State University	71%	$30,411
New School (NY)	51%	$30,275
University of Southern California	45%	$30,097
University of Tulsa (OK)	48%	$30,086
Temple University (PA)	75%	$29,886
University of Hartford (CT)	75%	$29,869
Biola University (CA)	78%	$29,693
University of Alaska–Fairbanks	54%	$29,485
Carnegie Mellon University (PA)	50%	$29,456
Penn. State Univ.–University Park	68%	$28,680
Bowling Green State University (OH)	72%	$28,542
University of Notre Dame (IN)	57%	$28,371
Syracuse University (NY)	65%	$28,358
Adelphi University (NY)	69%	$28,307
Pepperdine University (CA)	58%	$28,299
University of San Diego	57%	$27,999
Pacific University (OR)	85%	$27,770
University of Vermont	63%	$27,696
Florida A&M University	81%	$27,662
Tulane University (LA)	47%	$27,522
University of Rochester (NY)	55%	$27,121
University of Toledo (OH)	71%	$27,066
Ind. Univ.–Purdue Univ.–Indianapolis	72%	$27,062
SUNY Coll. of Env. Sci. and Forestry	80%	$27,000
University of Denver	45%	$26,986
University of San Francisco	64%	$26,886
University of Michigan–Ann Arbor	46%	$26,819
Michigan Technological University	68%	$26,764
Kent State University (OH)	75%	$26,698
Central Michigan University	71%	$26,615
Miami University–Oxford (OH)	53%	$26,582
University of Minnesota–Twin Cities	63%	$26,516
Brandeis University (MA)	58%	$26,078
University of Cincinnati	69%	$25,878
Emory University (GA)	42%	$25,865
University of Missouri–St. Louis	65%	$25,776
Indiana University–Bloomington	54%	$25,522
University of La Verne (CA)	83%	$25,491
New Jersey Institute of Technology	39%	$25,408
Wright State University (OH)	73%	$25,357
Georgetown University (DC)	45%	$25,085
University of Alabama–Huntsville	26%	$24,938
North Dakota State University	81%	$24,833
George Fox University (OR)	83%	$24,624
University of Tennessee	47%	$24,593
Wake Forest University (NC)	38%	$24,561
University of Miami (FL)	55%	$24,396
University of Chicago	48%	$24,238
Missouri Univ. of Science & Tech.	83%	$24,235
Northern Illinois University	63%	$24,154
University of Alabama	52%	$23,964
Indiana State University	65%	$23,963
Purdue University–West Lafayette (IN)	54%	$23,924
Trinity International University (IL)	88%	$23,864
University of Massachusetts–Amherst	67%	$23,847
Tufts University (MA)	41%	$23,731
Mississippi State University	51%	$23,413
Georgia Institute of Technology	62%	$23,352
University of Memphis	29%	$23,342
New Mexico State University	51%	$23,262
Duke University (NC)	40%	$23,059
University of Kentucky	33%	$22,943
University of Mississippi	39%	$22,866
Virginia Commonwealth University	61%	$22,864
University of Iowa	61%	$22,684
Ball State University (IN)	67%	$22,598
University of Idaho	68%	$22,527
Colorado School of Mines	62%	$22,500
University of Rhode Island	72%	$22,500
University of Kansas	45%	$22,478
Portland State University (OR)	58%	$22,440
Texas Woman's University	57%	$22,293
Auburn University (AL)	40%	$22,232
University of Texas–Austin	50%	$22,102
Ohio University	66%	$22,095
University at Albany–SUNY	71%	$22,092
Virginia Tech	52%	$22,070
Cornell University (NY)	46%	$21,951
Clark University (MA)	86%	$21,925
Texas A&M University–Commerce	74%	$21,881
Johns Hopkins University (MD)	46%	$21,859
Brown University (RI)	41%	$21,858
University of South Carolina	46%	$21,755
University of Alabama–Birmingham	53%	$21,670
Yeshiva University (NY)	47%	$21,665
Montana State University	64%	$21,571
University of Wisconsin–Madison	50%	$21,552
College of William and Mary (VA)	38%	$21,544
University of Massachusetts–Lowell	73%	$21,542
University of Delaware	49%	$21,370
Southern Illinois Univ.–Carbondale	50%	$21,359
Oakland University (MI)	56%	$21,330
Texas A&M Univ.–College Station	54%	$21,276
University of Colorado–Denver	66%	$21,264
University of Connecticut	61%	$21,257
Univ. of Illinois–Urbana-Champaign	55%	$21,145
Texas Tech University	67%	$21,001
Northwestern University (IL)	48%	$20,802
Kansas State University	62%	$20,700
University of Missouri	57%	$20,689
University of Missouri–Kansas City	65%	$20,512
Wayne State University (MI)	57%	$20,507
Colorado State University	57%	$20,432
University of South Florida	52%	$20,266
University of Maryland–College Park	44%	$20,256
University of Montana	61%	$20,223
University of Arkansas	43%	$20,171
Southern Methodist University (TX)	32%	$20,146
Illinois State University	61%	$20,105
Western Michigan University	66%	$20,000
University of Virginia	34%	$19,939
University of Wisconsin–Milwaukee	67%	$19,830
Rutgers–New Brunswick	52%	$19,760
Michigan State University	44%	$19,696
Vanderbilt University (TN)	40%	$19,563
George Mason University (VA)	52%	$19,528
Boston College	49%	$19,514
Rutgers–Newark	55%	$19,500
Oklahoma State University	56%	$19,468
Florida State University	48%	$19,364
Univ. of Maryland–Baltimore County	50%	$19,353
University of Oregon	55%	$19,336
University of Massachusetts–Boston	67%	$19,327
University of Colorado–Boulder	42%	$19,211
University of Nebraska–Lincoln	60%	$19,128
Dartmouth College (NH)	48%	$19,081
DePaul University (IL)	64%	$19,072
North Carolina State Univ.–Raleigh	48%	$19,011
University of Akron (OH)	65%	$19,000
University of Southern Mississippi	64%	$18,878
University of Arizona	46%	$18,712
Georgia Southern University	65%	$18,618
Univ. of North Carolina–Greensboro	67%	$18,604
Clemson University (SC)	49%	$18,463
University of Illinois–Chicago	61%	$18,440
Ohio State University–Columbus	54%	$18,426
Louisiana State Univ.–Baton Rouge	41%	$18,118
University of Washington	49%	$17,800
University of Pennsylvania	41%	$17,787
Univ. of California–Santa Barbara	47%	$17,768
University of California–San Diego	51%	$17,679
University of Louisville (KY)	47%	$17,651
SUNY–Stony Brook	63%	$17,528
University of Texas–El Paso	64%	$17,346
Florida Atlantic University	47%	$17,338
University of Nevada–Las Vegas	37%	$17,256
Old Dominion University (VA)	81%	$17,250
University of Wyoming	50%	$17,084

Schools whose graduates have the most and least debt

National Universities, continued

	% of grads with debt	Average amount of debt
University of Central Florida	41%	$17,044
University of California–Los Angeles	46%	$16,824
University of Oklahoma	48%	$16,723
Rice University (TX)	31%	$16,716
University of Hawaii–Manoa	35%	$16,528
University of California–Riverside	62%	$16,398
University of California–Davis	51%	$16,222
Stanford University (CA)	36%	$16,219
University of California–Santa Cruz	53%	$16,024
University of Florida	41%	$15,932
University at Buffalo–SUNY	85%	$15,911

	% of grads with debt	Average amount of debt
University of Nevada–Reno	36%	$15,854
Wichita State University (KS)	57%	$15,769
Samford University (AL)	38%	$15,702
University of California–Irvine	48%	$15,529
University of Utah	40%	$15,201
University of Texas–Arlington	53%	$15,171
Massachusetts Institute of Tech.	45%	$15,043
Florida International University	39%	$14,901
University of Georgia	44%	$14,766
San Diego State University	44%	$14,700
Binghamton University–SUNY	49%	$14,560

	% of grads with debt	Average amount of debt
University of California–Berkeley	41%	$14,493
Univ. of North Carolina–Chapel Hill	29%	$14,262
University of New Orleans	16%	$13,623
Georgia State University	58%	$13,166
Louisiana Tech University	51%	$12,408
Howard University (DC)	81%	$12,000
Harvard University (MA)	38%	$10,871
Brigham Young University–Provo (UT)	24%	$10,730
Yale University (CT)	31%	$10,717
California Institute of Technology	42%	$8,218
Princeton University (NJ)	22%	$5,667

National Liberal Arts Colleges

	% of grads with debt	Average amount of debt
Franklin Pierce University (NH)	85%	$41,848
Whittier College (CA)	78%	$40,220
Green Mountain College (VT)	82%	$39,862
Atlantic Union College (MA)	83%	$38,328
Burlington College (VT)	80%	$38,198
Thiel College (PA)	92%	$37,783
Bennett College (NC)	98%	$37,667
St. Anselm College (NH)	75%	$36,823
Central College (IA)	86%	$36,068
Beacon College (FL)	12%	$35,000
Clarke University (IA)	90%	$34,386
Simpson College (IA)	92%	$34,354
Luther College (IA)	82%	$34,101
Hartwick College (NY)	74%	$32,800
Gordon College (MA)	81%	$32,405
Meredith College (NC)	76%	$32,300
Morehouse College (GA)	90%	$32,125
Albright College (PA)	83%	$31,845
St. Lawrence University (NY)	74%	$31,653
Alma College (MI)	74%	$31,476
Coastal Carolina University (SC)	77%	$31,472
Hobart and William Smith Coll. (NY)	79%	$30,970
Ohio Wesleyan University	74%	$30,954
Birmingham-Southern College (AL)	41%	$30,907
St. Michael's College (VT)	76%	$30,742
Concordia College–Moorhead (MN)	83%	$30,720
Coe College (IA)	83%	$30,665
Evangel University (MO)	77%	$30,506
Eckerd College (FL)	63%	$30,494
Albion College (MI)	55%	$30,149
St. Norbert College (WI)	72%	$30,001
Millsaps College (MS)	59%	$29,848
University of Puget Sound (WA)	63%	$29,514
Lycoming College (PA)	85%	$29,478
Bridgewater College (VA)	74%	$29,331
Lake Forest College (IL)	74%	$29,279
Texas Lutheran University	63%	$29,200
Wesleyan University (CT)	44%	$29,174
Stonehill College (MA)	73%	$29,163
Ferrum College (VA)	82%	$29,040
Wittenberg University (OH)	68%	$28,729
Washington College (MD)	58%	$28,727
Hope College (MI)	64%	$28,682
Calvin College (MI)	68%	$28,500
Millikin University (IL)	82%	$28,449
Wabash College (IN)	70%	$28,383
Houghton College (NY)	96%	$28,334

	% of grads with debt	Average amount of debt
Bloomfield College (NJ)	87%	$28,310
Westminster College (PA)	80%	$28,262
Siena College (NY)	77%	$28,200
Cornell College (IA)	72%	$27,990
Hanover College (IN)	67%	$27,807
Virginia Wesleyan College	80%	$27,658
Wingate University (NC)	75%	$27,616
Furman University (SC)	40%	$27,373
Fisk University (TN)	77%	$27,345
Gustavus Adolphus College (MN)	70%	$27,297
Linfield College (OR)	71%	$27,271
Wartburg College (IA)	81%	$27,225
Franklin and Marshall College (PA)	52%	$27,162
Randolph-Macon College (VA)	72%	$26,763
Metropolitan State College of Denver	61%	$26,635
Illinois Wesleyan University	56%	$26,458
Purchase College–SUNY	58%	$26,275
Asbury University (KY)	85%	$26,150
Bard College (NY)	52%	$26,131
Ripon College (WI)	76%	$26,073
Rhodes College (TN)	47%	$26,071
Roanoke College (VA)	66%	$25,932
Ursinus College (PA)	80%	$25,875
McPherson College (KS)	85%	$25,865
University of Minnesota–Morris	77%	$25,855
St. Olaf College (MN)	66%	$25,853
University of Mount Union (OH)	70%	$25,804
Westmont College (CA)	54%	$25,565
Wheaton College (MA)	53%	$25,540
St. Mary's College (IN)	72%	$25,531
Sweet Briar College (VA)	52%	$25,372
McDaniel College (MD)	63%	$25,325
College of Wooster (OH)	58%	$25,140
Lawrence University (WI)	76%	$25,049
Bethany College (WV)	90%	$25,000
Grove City College (PA)	45%	$24,895
Bethel College (KS)	79%	$24,858
Union College (NY)	61%	$24,739
Olivet College (MI)	87%	$24,690
Cedar Crest College (PA)	92%	$24,641
Monmouth College (IL)	81%	$24,476
Georgetown College (KY)	76%	$24,462
College of Idaho (ID)	67%	$24,237
DePauw University (IN)	48%	$24,210
Wells College (NY)	82%	$24,180
William Jewell College (MO)	75%	$24,102
Southwestern University (TX)	61%	$24,036

	% of grads with debt	Average amount of debt
Knox College (IL)	73%	$24,018
Hollins University (VA)	83%	$24,002
Merrimack College (MA)	66%	$24,000
Hampden-Sydney College (VA)	54%	$23,822
College of the Holy Cross (MA)	57%	$23,785
Earlham College (IN)	55%	$23,752
Willamette University (OR)	63%	$23,643
Juniata College (PA)	89%	$23,618
Washington and Lee University (VA)	31%	$23,615
Peace College (NC)	78%	$23,428
Presbyterian College (SC)	56%	$23,391
Gettysburg College (PA)	61%	$23,258
Dickinson College (PA)	55%	$23,224
Agnes Scott College (GA)	69%	$23,176
Guilford College (NC)	71%	$23,050
Mount Holyoke College (MA)	61%	$23,008
Washington and Jefferson Coll. (PA)	75%	$23,000
Stephens College (MO)	78%	$22,942
Bennington College (VT)	70%	$22,402
Maryville College (TN)	66%	$22,268
Wofford College (SC)	45%	$22,199
Connecticut College	34%	$22,038
Allen University (SC)	85%	$21,970
Nebraska Wesleyan University	78%	$21,931
Colby College (ME)	41%	$21,697
Smith College (MA)	62%	$21,573
University of Richmond (VA)	42%	$21,555
West Virginia Wesleyan College	71%	$21,502
Middlebury College (VT)	44%	$21,458
Hastings College (NE)	84%	$21,329
Illinois College	76%	$21,258
Thomas More Coll. of Liberal Arts (NH)	77%	$21,133
Wesleyan College (GA)	63%	$20,983
Kentucky Wesleyan College	89%	$20,906
Davidson College (NC)	38%	$20,858
Simpson University (CA)	83%	$20,855
Brevard College (NC)	59%	$20,770
Reed College (OR)	53%	$20,750
Lafayette College (PA)	47%	$20,745
Hampshire College (MA)	51%	$20,669
Muhlenberg College (PA)	83%	$20,602
Wheaton College (IL)	51%	$20,455
Pitzer College (CA)	45%	$20,448
Warren Wilson College (NC)	34%	$20,441
Wisconsin Lutheran College	73%	$20,340
Trinity College (CT)	42%	$20,174
College of the Atlantic (ME)	54%	$20,170

School	% of grads with debt	Average amount of debt
Bryn Mawr College (PA)	52%	$20,156
Westminster College (MO)	58%	$20,018
Kenyon College (OH)	58%	$19,934
Transylvania University (KY)	65%	$19,893
Lyon College (AR)	61%	$19,642
University of Wisconsin–Green Bay	71%	$19,636
Grinnell College (IA)	54%	$19,540
Hamilton College (NY)	46%	$19,466
Colgate University (NY)	30%	$19,202
Doane College (NE)	83%	$19,196
Emory and Henry College (VA)	65%	$19,168
Virginia Military Institute	34%	$19,046
St. Andrews Presbyterian Coll. (NC)	57%	$19,032
Johnson C. Smith University (NC)	81%	$19,000
Oberlin College (OH)	54%	$18,981
Vassar College (NY)	49%	$18,876
Mesa State College (CO)	43%	$18,834
Tougaloo College (MS)	80%	$18,806
Bucknell University (PA)	61%	$18,800
Sewanee–University of the South (TN)	38%	$18,717
Oglethorpe University (GA)	42%	$18,650
Carleton College (MN)	54%	$18,601
Jarvis Christian College (TX)	83%	$18,550
Goucher College (MD)	74%	$18,465
Bowdoin College (ME)	45%	$18,382
Skidmore College (NY)	51%	$18,303
Christopher Newport University (VA)	55%	$18,285
Pikeville College (KY)	76%	$18,103
Centenary College of Louisiana	58%	$18,100
North Greenville University (SC)	61%	$18,100
Hillsdale College (MI)	61%	$18,000
Whitman College (WA)	49%	$17,955
Bates College (ME)	38%	$17,945
Beloit College (WI)	69%	$17,909
Western State College of Colorado	75%	$17,750
Hendrix College (AR)	87%	$17,641
Occidental College (CA)	67%	$17,561
Berry College (GA)	82%	$17,502
Drew University (NJ)	61%	$17,444
Massachusetts Coll. of Liberal Arts	51%	$17,297
Macalester College (MN)	76%	$17,275
Sarah Lawrence College (NY)	52%	$17,246
Centre College (KY)	53%	$17,190
St. Mary's College of Maryland	70%	$17,125
SUNY College–Old Westbury	46%	$17,104
Lewis & Clark College (OR)	58%	$17,084
Goshen College (IN)	75%	$16,564
Haverford College (PA)	38%	$16,500
Sierra Nevada College (NV)	75%	$16,500
Harvey Mudd College (CA)	59%	$16,384
Colorado College	35%	$16,172
Marymount Manhattan College (NY)	84%	$15,988
Fort Lewis College (CO)	54%	$15,962
Swarthmore College (PA)	45%	$15,737
California State Univ.–Monterey Bay	63%	$15,254
Thomas Aquinas College (CA)	71%	$15,000
Principia College (IL)	64%	$14,963
New College of Florida	41%	$14,794
Barnard College (NY)	44%	$14,706
University of North Carolina–Asheville	50%	$14,596
Carson-Newman College (TN)	67%	$14,164
Spelman College (GA)	70%	$14,070
Huntingdon College (AL)	58%	$14,034
Wellesley College (MA)	56%	$13,324
Rust College (MS)	71%	$13,055
Bryn Athyn Col. of the New Church (PA)	57%	$12,729
University of Virginia–Wise	58%	$12,120
Pomona College (CA)	55%	$11,700
Amherst College (MA)	41%	$11,347
Scripps College (CA)	38%	$11,270
American Jewish University (CA)	75%	$9,800
Claremont McKenna College (CA)	30%	$9,259
Lane College (TN)	88%	$8,769
Berea College (KY)	79%	$8,133
Williams College (MA)	43%	$8,103

Regional Universities (North)

School	% of grads with debt	Average amount of debt
La Roche College (PA)	78%	$69,494
Simmons College (MA)	78%	$45,237
CUNY–John Jay Coll. of Crim. Justice	49%	$45,000
La Salle University (PA)	84%	$44,645
Wheelock College (MA)	96%	$43,319
St. Joseph's University (PA)	59%	$40,933
Neumann University (PA)	80%	$40,000
St. Joseph College (CT)	82%	$39,743
Springfield College (MA)	88%	$38,689
Bryant University (RI)	75%	$38,270
Wagner College (NY)	61%	$36,988
St. Bonaventure University (NY)	83%	$36,832
Rivier College (NH)	94%	$36,389
University of New Haven (CT)	86%	$36,272
Gwynedd-Mercy College (PA)	90%	$36,255
St. Joseph's College (ME)	87%	$36,071
Arcadia University (PA)	88%	$35,975
Utica College (NY)	86%	$35,534
Salve Regina University (RI)	81%	$35,394
Fairfield University (CT)	60%	$35,161
Robert Morris University (PA)	84%	$35,055
Rider University (NJ)	72%	$35,042
Nazareth College (NY)	90%	$35,010
Providence College (RI)	63%	$34,927
Wilkes University (PA)	87%	$34,775
Quinnipiac University (CT)	69%	$34,621
Alvernia University (PA)	94%	$34,062
College of Notre Dame of Maryland	72%	$33,882
Georgian Court University (NJ)	85%	$33,729
Canisius College (NY)	77%	$33,645
Misericordia University (PA)	78%	$33,641
Bentley University (MA)	64%	$33,073
Husson University (ME)	88%	$33,010
Mount St. Mary College (NY)	94%	$32,729
Philadelphia University	81%	$32,037
Holy Family University (PA)	82%	$31,855
Point Park University (PA)	83%	$31,656
Marywood University (PA)	94%	$31,471
D'Youville College (NY)	100%	$31,401
Gannon University (PA)	86%	$31,234
DeSales University (PA)	76%	$31,077
Villanova University (PA)	55%	$31,048
Dowling College (NY)	74%	$31,000
University of Scranton (PA)	75%	$30,920
King's College (PA)	84%	$30,843
Lincoln University (PA)	89%	$30,818
Cabrini College (PA)	81%	$30,633
College of St. Joseph (VT)	100%	$30,579
Roberts Wesleyan College (NY)	99%	$30,329
St. John Fisher College (NY)	84%	$30,281
Molloy College (NY)	77%	$29,823
Plymouth State University (NH)	82%	$29,709
Norwich University (VT)	87%	$29,473
College of St. Rose (NY)	84%	$29,391
Marist College (NY)	76%	$29,345
Mansfield University of Pennsylvania	81%	$28,937
Philadelphia Biblical University	97%	$28,214
Centenary College (NJ)	83%	$28,104
Richard Stockton Coll. of New Jersey	69%	$27,847
Keene State College (NH)	78%	$27,785
Sacred Heart University (CT)	96%	$27,500
Le Moyne College (NY)	84%	$27,483
Niagara University (NY)	78%	$27,215
Loyola University Maryland	72%	$26,855
Manhattan College (NY)	68%	$26,779
Alfred University (NY)	83%	$26,750
Mount St. Mary's University (MD)	67%	$26,160
College at Brockport–SUNY	81%	$26,095
Rowan University (NJ)	73%	$26,092
Western Connecticut State University	36%	$26,024
William Paterson Univ. of New Jersey	64%	$25,893
East Stroudsburg Univ. of Penn.	73%	$25,887
American International College (MA)	100%	$25,693
SUNY–Oswego	86%	$25,351
SUNY–Fredonia	86%	$25,101
Monmouth University (NJ)	73%	$25,000
College of New Jersey	58%	$24,801
Dominican College (NY)	97%	$24,690
Caldwell College (NJ)	87%	$24,500
West Chester Univ. of Pennsylvania	70%	$24,471
Assumption College (MA)	83%	$24,382
Montclair State University (NJ)	77%	$24,226
Iona College (NY)	68%	$24,213
Slippery Rock Univ. of Pennsylvania	81%	$23,879
California University of Pennsylvania	80%	$23,824
Manhattanville College (NY)	75%	$23,292
Eastern Connecticut State University	73%	$22,659
Mercyhurst College (PA)	76%	$22,630
Lock Haven Univ. of Pennsylvania	85%	$22,585
Rutgers–Camden	70%	$22,552
St. Francis University (PA)	85%	$22,500
Millersville University of Pennsylvania	72%	$22,479
Waynesburg University (PA)	87%	$22,000
Univ. of Massachusetts–Dartmouth	73%	$21,905
Goddard College (VT)	82%	$21,700
Edinboro University of Pennsylvania	46%	$21,518
Rosemont College (PA)	87%	$21,338
Bloomsburg Univ. of Pennsylvania	71%	$21,322
Shippensburg Univ. of Pennsylvania	74%	$21,163
SUNY–Plattsburgh	72%	$21,010
Medaille College (NY)	95%	$21,000
SUNY–Geneseo	63%	$21,000
Kutztown University of Pennsylvania	86%	$20,707
Fitchburg State College (MA)	67%	$19,902
Ramapo College of New Jersey	55%	$19,789
St. Peter's College (NJ)	68%	$19,744
Kean University (NJ)	68%	$19,698
SUNY College–Potsdam	80%	$19,220

Schools whose graduates have the most and least debt

Regional Universities (North), continued

	% of grads with debt	Average amount of debt
Central Connecticut State University	48%	$19,200
Framingham State College (MA)	65%	$19,000
Daemen College (NY)	90%	$18,910
Westfield State College (MA)	73%	$18,648
Rhode Island College	71%	$18,352
Buffalo State College–SUNY	71%	$18,350
Frostburg State University (MD)	64%	$18,255
Worcester State College (MA)	42%	$17,819

	% of grads with debt	Average amount of debt
Salisbury University (MD)	56%	$17,521
Hood College (MD)	64%	$17,382
Southern Connecticut State University	66%	$17,374
Bowie State University (MD)	66%	$17,198
CUNY–Brooklyn College	42%	$17,000
Lesley University (MA)	90%	$17,000
SUNY–New Paltz	66%	$16,823
CUNY–City College	31%	$16,821

	% of grads with debt	Average amount of debt
SUNY College–Oneonta	75%	$16,490
Emerson College (MA)	59%	$15,262
CUNY–Baruch College	37%	$14,676
CUNY–Queens College	41%	$14,000
CUNY–Lehman College	32%	$13,700
Towson University (MD)	23%	$13,245
CUNY–Hunter College	53%	$7,500
University of Maryland–Eastern Shore	89%	$5,290

Regional Universities (South)

	% of grads with debt	Average amount of debt
Campbell University (NC)	75%	$38,696
Fort Valley State University (GA)	98%	$34,190
Lynn University (FL)	43%	$34,075
Freed-Hardeman University (TN)	67%	$33,659
Mountain State University (WV)	81%	$33,218
Belhaven University (MS)	100%	$32,728
Alabama Agricultural and Mech. Univ.	82%	$32,024
Harding University (AR)	70%	$31,043
Lynchburg College (VA)	67%	$30,954
Stetson University (FL)	83%	$30,914
Grambling State University (LA)	57%	$30,112
Belmont University (TN)	57%	$29,268
Mercer University (GA)	58%	$29,065
Christian Brothers University (TN)	69%	$28,259
University of Tampa (FL)	62%	$28,129
Xavier University of Louisiana	88%	$27,586
Lee University (TN)	64%	$27,549
Southern Wesleyan University (SC)	85%	$26,923
Thomas More College (KY)	74%	$26,862
Francis Marion University (SC)	76%	$26,356
Wheeling Jesuit University (WV)	89%	$26,334
Mississippi College	73%	$26,323
Mary Baldwin College (VA)	74%	$25,665
University of North Alabama	64%	$24,500
Winthrop University (SC)	68%	$24,463
Union University (TN)	58%	$24,253
Union College (KY)	79%	$24,083
Morehead State University (KY)	69%	$24,045
St. Leo University (FL)	63%	$23,787

	% of grads with debt	Average amount of debt
Marymount University (VA)	76%	$22,946
Elon University (NC)	45%	$22,939
Palm Beach Atlantic University (FL)	68%	$22,443
Loyola University New Orleans	64%	$22,320
Rollins College (FL)	51%	$22,255
Spring Hill College (AL)	72%	$21,823
Northwestern State Univ. of Louisiana	68%	$21,773
Bellarmine University (KY)	69%	$21,639
Columbus State University (GA)	64%	$21,538
Florida Gulf Coast University	35%	$21,247
University of Tennessee–Martin	71%	$20,997
Cumberland University (TN)	69%	$20,973
Longwood University (VA)	62%	$20,855
Converse College (SC)	61%	$20,739
Georgia Southwestern State University	62%	$20,505
Fayetteville State University (NC)	63%	$20,185
Austin Peay State University (TN)	56%	$20,158
Queens University of Charlotte (NC)	79%	$20,108
College of Charleston (SC)	46%	$19,875
Delta State University (MS)	65%	$19,840
Marshall University (WV)	62%	$19,562
Lipscomb University (TN)	64%	$19,523
University of Tennessee–Chattanooga	65%	$19,456
Alcorn State University (MS)	50%	$19,290
Armstrong Atlantic State Univ. (GA)	49%	$19,000
Southeastern Louisiana University	60%	$18,947
Arkansas State University–Jonesboro	68%	$18,900
University of Mobile (AL)	25%	$18,840
Nicholls State University (LA)	56%	$18,822

	% of grads with debt	Average amount of debt
Radford University (VA)	59%	$18,817
Mississippi University for Women	64%	$18,363
James Madison University (VA)	51%	$18,183
Murray State University (KY)	65%	$18,000
Brenau University (GA)	64%	$17,999
Valdosta State University (GA)	65%	$17,840
Hodges University (FL)	78%	$17,600
Life University (GA)	60%	$17,600
William Carey University (MS)	85%	$17,500
Kennesaw State University (GA)	43%	$17,262
Piedmont College (GA)	71%	$16,986
University of Montevallo (AL)	54%	$16,581
Henderson State University (AR)	56%	$16,529
Southern Polytechnic State Univ. (GA)	50%	$16,280
Appalachian State University (NC)	55%	$16,153
Univ. of North Carolina–Wilmington	54%	$16,115
University of Mary Washington (VA)	57%	$16,000
Georgia College & State University	52%	$15,800
University of North Florida	41%	$15,619
Western Kentucky University	55%	$15,168
Tennessee Technological University	44%	$14,691
Eastern Kentucky University	66%	$12,588
Arkansas Tech University	51%	$12,562
The Citadel (SC)	43%	$11,927
Western Carolina University (NC)	51%	$11,609
Lincoln Memorial University (TN)	60%	$10,623
North Georgia Coll. and State Univ.	65%	$9,885

Regional Universities (Midwest)

	% of grads with debt	Average amount of debt
Lawrence Technological Univ. (MI)	73%	$42,723
College of St. Scholastica (MN)	81%	$40,401
Ashland University (OH)	82%	$36,545
Ursuline College (OH)	86%	$36,116
Heidelberg University (OH)	90%	$35,397
Drake University (IA)	71%	$34,919
Ferris State University (MI)	76%	$34,767
Hamline University (MN)	79%	$34,598
College of Mount St. Joseph (OH)	84%	$33,648
University of Findlay (OH)	89%	$33,266
St. Ambrose University (IA)	77%	$33,216
Creighton University (NE)	70%	$32,888
Concordia University–St. Paul (MN)	85%	$32,444

	% of grads with debt	Average amount of debt
Alverno College (WI)	83%	$32,142
Valparaiso University (IN)	73%	$31,783
Edgewood College (WI)	70%	$31,327
Bethel University (MN)	80%	$30,496
Butler University (IN)	64%	$30,470
Franciscan Univ. of Steubenville (OH)	79%	$30,180
Graceland University (IA)	89%	$29,924
University of Michigan–Dearborn	22%	$29,564
Augsburg College (MN)	93%	$28,988
John Carroll University (OH)	74%	$28,830
Olivet Nazarene University (IL)	77%	$28,473
Indiana University Northwest	68%	$28,403
Muskingum University (OH)	79%	$28,343

	% of grads with debt	Average amount of debt
Minnesota State Univ.–Moorhead	80%	$28,149
Southwestern College (KS)	86%	$27,973
University of Minnesota–Duluth	72%	$27,931
North Central College (IL)	72%	$27,285
Winona State University (MN)	74%	$27,190
Xavier University (OH)	66%	$27,098
University of Indianapolis	79%	$27,070
Carroll University (WI)	78%	$27,066
St. Xavier University (IL)	78%	$26,939
Indiana Wesleyan University	75%	$26,847
Concordia University Chicago (IL)	82%	$26,577
Tiffin University (OH)	82%	$26,345
Webster University (MO)	57%	$26,184

Regional Universities (Midwest), continued

	% of grads with debt	Average amount of debt
Spring Arbor University (MI)	86%	$26,077
Cornerstone University (MI)	83%	$26,025
Rockford College (IL)	100%	$25,844
Benedictine University (IL)	65%	$25,781
Fontbonne University (MO)	85%	$25,712
Minnesota State University–Mankato	82%	$25,667
Malone University (OH)	81%	$25,655
University of Evansville (IN)	72%	$25,598
Anderson University (IN)	84%	$25,401
Indiana University–South Bend	71%	$25,384
Concordia University Wisconsin	76%	$25,169
University of Wisconsin–Stout	78%	$25,134
Upper Iowa University	97%	$24,769
Marian University (WI)	96%	$24,595
Bemidji State University (MN)	80%	$24,474
St. Catherine University (MN)	96%	$24,400
St. Cloud State University (MN)	68%	$24,373
University of Northern Iowa	80%	$24,123
Northern Michigan University	67%	$24,074
Grand Valley State University (MI)	70%	$24,030
Newman University (KS)	77%	$23,996
Walsh University (OH)	92%	$23,446

	% of grads with debt	Average amount of debt
North Park University (IL)	72%	$23,343
Madonna University (MI)	59%	$23,323
Mount Marty College (SD)	79%	$22,699
Univ. of Wisconsin–Stevens Point	71%	$22,650
Indiana University Southeast	60%	$22,649
Calumet College of St. Joseph (IN)	80%	$22,524
University of Wisconsin–Superior	75%	$22,516
Eastern Michigan University	63%	$22,370
University of Wisconsin–La Crosse	65%	$21,998
Rockhurst University (MO)	79%	$21,950
Truman State University (MO)	52%	$21,858
Capital University (OH)	83%	$21,805
University of St. Francis (IL)	96%	$21,594
Mount Mary College (WI)	86%	$21,414
Dominican University (IL)	89%	$21,392
Emporia State University (KS)	68%	$21,158
University of Wisconsin–Oshkosh	64%	$21,000
University of Wisconsin–Whitewater	67%	$20,715
Southern Illinois Univ.–Edwardsville	44%	$20,603
Western Illinois University	68%	$20,550
Drury University (MO)	67%	$20,500
Lewis University (IL)	70%	$20,413

	% of grads with debt	Average amount of debt
Southeast Missouri State University	69%	$20,350
Benedictine College (KS)	75%	$20,078
Purdue University–Calumet (IN)	62%	$19,926
University of Wisconsin–Eau Claire	68%	$19,687
Minot State University (ND)	75%	$19,384
University of Nebraska–Kearney	73%	$19,160
William Woods University (MO)	75%	$18,997
Southwest Minnesota State University	82%	$18,830
Silver Lake College (WI)	88%	$18,706
Avila University (MO)	82%	$18,526
Pittsburg State University (KS)	67%	$18,516
Maryville University of St. Louis (MO)	73%	$18,341
Elmhurst College (IL)	90%	$18,329
University of Central Missouri	69%	$18,272
University of Rio Grande (OH)	76%	$18,146
Baldwin-Wallace College (OH)	67%	$17,716
Washburn University (KS)	66%	$17,031
Aquinas College (MI)	66%	$14,983
University of Illinois–Springfield	64%	$14,717
Columbia College (MO)	63%	$13,948
Eastern Illinois University	53%	$11,547
Northeastern Illinois University	16%	$10,903

Regional Universities (West)

	% of grads with debt	Average amount of debt
Woodbury University (CA)	91%	$47,059
Alaska Pacific University	94%	$42,392
Northwest Nazarene University (ID)	85%	$35,808
Abilene Christian University (TX)	71%	$35,453
Hardin-Simmons University (TX)	73%	$35,429
Texas Southern University	39%	$35,304
California Baptist University	89%	$34,650
Mount St. Mary's College (CA)	90%	$33,030
St. Mary's College of California	80%	$31,330
St. Edward's University (TX)	79%	$29,810
Point Loma Nazarene University (CA)	87%	$29,491
Loyola Marymount University (CA)	61%	$28,596
St. Martin's University (WA)	78%	$28,518
Marylhurst University (OR)	71%	$27,846
Hope International University (CA)	97%	$27,000
Seattle University	79%	$26,665
Oklahoma Christian University	76%	$26,612
Lubbock Christian University (TX)	79%	$26,320
Dominican University of California	84%	$26,176
Seattle Pacific University	70%	$25,799
Regis University (CO)	66%	$25,558
Wayland Baptist University (TX)	78%	$25,387
Western Oregon University	61%	$25,063
Gonzaga University (WA)	70%	$24,883
Pacific Lutheran University (WA)	72%	$24,639
University of Dallas	57%	$24,624
University of Redlands (CA)	70%	$24,218

	% of grads with debt	Average amount of debt
Northeastern State University (OK)	68%	$24,143
California Lutheran University	68%	$23,920
Chapman University (CA)	64%	$23,917
Santa Clara University (CA)	43%	$23,909
Naropa University (CO)	71%	$23,717
Boise State University (ID)	64%	$23,256
Montana State University–Billings	73%	$23,189
University of Texas–San Antonio	64%	$23,145
Concordia University (CA)	68%	$23,113
University of St. Thomas (TX)	71%	$22,857
St. Mary's Univ. of San Antonio (TX)	79%	$22,592
University of the Southwest (NM)	86%	$22,200
Our Lady of the Lake University (TX)	81%	$22,133
University of Alaska–Anchorage	49%	$22,043
Notre Dame de Namur University (CA)	82%	$21,758
Holy Names University (CA)	84%	$21,478
Univ. of Colorado–Colorado Springs	61%	$20,923
Southern Nazarene University (OK)	80%	$20,900
Westminster College (UT)	54%	$20,251
Texas State University–San Marcos	58%	$19,757
Midwestern State University (TX)	52%	$19,049
Texas A&M University–Corpus Christi	58%	$19,000
Fresno Pacific University (CA)	82%	$18,929
Whitworth University (WA)	68%	$18,801
Oklahoma City University	48%	$18,532
Univ. of Texas of the Permian Basin	64%	$18,507
Eastern Washington University	68%	$18,435

	% of grads with debt	Average amount of debt
Humboldt State University (CA)	66%	$17,668
Dallas Baptist University	79%	$17,214
Central Washington University	55%	$16,507
California State University–Stanislaus	25%	$16,500
Angelo State University (TX)	37%	$16,372
Sonoma State University (CA)	44%	$15,954
Western Washington University	50%	$15,929
San Francisco State University	39%	$15,684
Prescott College (AZ)	67%	$14,947
California State University–Fullerton	39%	$14,706
California State University–Northridge	39%	$14,691
California State University–East Bay	34%	$14,643
Evergreen State College (WA)	51%	$14,310
California State Poly. Univ.–Pomona	36%	$14,035
Texas A&M International University	68%	$13,746
University of Texas–Pan American	64%	$13,088
California State Univ.–Sacramento	35%	$12,473
San Jose State University (CA)	49%	$12,313
Lamar University (TX)	61%	$12,003
California State Univ.–Long Beach	43%	$10,927
California State University–Fresno	65%	$10,406
California State Univ.–Dominguez Hills	56%	$7,946
New Mexico Inst. of Mining and Tech.	90%	$7,894
Prairie View A&M University (TX)	78%	$7,890
Cameron University (OK)	35%	$7,500
Sam Houston State University (TX)	55%	$6,195
Western New Mexico University	40%	$5,500

Schools whose graduates have the most and least debt

Regional Colleges (North)

	% of grads with debt	Average amount of debt
Eastern Nazarene College (MA)	83%	$47,815
Mount Ida College (MA)	89%	$43,911
Valley Forge Christian College (PA)	96%	$42,894
Maine Maritime Academy	73%	$39,237
Lasell College (MA)	64%	$38,419
Curry College (MA)	78%	$38,374
Messiah College (PA)	76%	$33,867
Endicott College (MA)	69%	$33,783
Wilson College (PA)	87%	$33,673
New England College (NH)	77%	$33,466
Lebanon Valley College (PA)	82%	$33,348
Roger Williams University (RI)	79%	$32,586
Becker College (MA)	98%	$31,800
Mount Aloysius College (PA)	80%	$29,802
Elizabethtown College (PA)	85%	$29,178
York College of Pennsylvania	75%	$27,583
Elmira College (NY)	81%	$26,874
Delaware Valley College (PA)	63%	$26,350
Massachusetts Maritime Academy	77%	$26,037
Vermont Technical College	80%	$26,000
Wesley College (DE)	65%	$25,900
Seton Hill University (PA)	91%	$25,807
Keystone College (PA)	89%	$24,750
Fashion Institute of Technology (NY)	57%	$24,554
University of Pittsburgh–Johnstown	85%	$23,243
University of Pittsburgh–Bradford	82%	$21,683
Vaughn Coll. of Aero. and Tech. (NY)	78%	$21,432
St. Joseph's College New York	62%	$20,941
Stevenson University (MD)	65%	$20,779
Bard College at Simon's Rock (MA)	38%	$20,000
Peirce College (PA)	87%	$19,748
SUNY Col. of Agr. and Tech.–Cobleskill	66%	$19,627
Felician College (NJ)	62%	$17,026
Paul Smith's College (NY)	88%	$16,784
Keuka College (NY)	95%	$16,500
Cooper Union (NY)	33%	$12,700
Washington Adventist University (MD)	80%	$9,799
U.S. Merchant Marine Acad. (NY)	29%	$6,416

Regional Colleges (South)

	% of grads with debt	Average amount of debt
Methodist University (NC)	81%	$38,820
Kentucky State University	76%	$35,552
Claflin University (SC)	81%	$33,816
Tuskegee University (AL)	59%	$33,500
Livingstone College (NC)	99%	$33,236
University of South Carolina–Aiken	54%	$31,462
Averett University (VA)	67%	$30,943
Newberry College (SC)	86%	$30,693
Alderson-Broaddus College (WV)	98%	$29,613
Barton College (NC)	66%	$28,343
Davis and Elkins College (WV)	80%	$27,583
Bethune-Cookman University (FL)	96%	$27,103
Catawba College (NC)	73%	$25,506
Coker College (SC)	81%	$24,601
LaGrange College (GA)	75%	$24,561
Erskine College (SC)	66%	$24,058
Stillman College (AL)	96%	$23,000
Southern Adventist University (TN)	58%	$22,977
Shorter College (GA)	75%	$22,967
Florida Southern College	63%	$22,910
St. Paul's College (VA)	19%	$21,917
Victory University (TN)	58%	$21,505
Campbellsville University (KY)	90%	$21,500
University of South Carolina–Upstate	67%	$21,099
Belmont Abbey College (NC)	73%	$21,000
Limestone College (SC)	89%	$20,701
Shepherd University (WV)	65%	$20,053
Faulkner University (AL)	81%	$20,000
John Brown University (AR)	60%	$19,991
Milligan College (TN)	90%	$19,803
Glenville State College (WV)	77%	$19,722
Bluefield College (VA)	87%	$19,675
Bluefield State College (WV)	50%	$19,500
St. Augustine's College (NC)	91%	$19,347
Free Will Baptist Bible College (TN)	78%	$18,911
West Liberty University (WV)	82%	$18,910
University of the Ozarks (AR)	56%	$18,425
Montreat College (NC)	81%	$18,295
Flagler College (FL)	55%	$18,190
Southeastern University (FL)	100%	$17,044
Williams Baptist College (AR)	80%	$16,826
Anderson University (SC)	82%	$16,488
Virginia Intermont College	76%	$16,337
Blue Mountain College (MS)	80%	$16,300
King College (TN)	96%	$15,756
Southern Arkansas University	72%	$15,672
Covenant College (GA)	70%	$15,478
Bryan College (TN)	74%	$14,976
Ohio Valley University (WV)	93%	$14,976
Ouachita Baptist University (AR)	58%	$14,156
Concord University (WV)	86%	$14,030
Winston-Salem State University (NC)	92%	$12,560
High Point University (NC)	69%	$9,437
Alice Lloyd College (KY)	42%	$6,500

Regional Colleges (Midwest)

	grads with debt % of	Average amount of debt
Ohio Northern University	82%	$45,902
Buena Vista University (IA)	91%	$40,569
University of Dubuque (IA)	97%	$37,936
Morningside College (IA)	89%	$37,479
Milwaukee School of Engineering	94%	$35,722
Trinity Christian College (IL)	77%	$33,133
Crown College (MN)	88%	$31,804
Northwestern College (IA)	87%	$31,062
Mount Mercy College (IA)	94%	$30,233
Loras College (IA)	82%	$30,100
Dakota Wesleyan University (SD)	67%	$30,000
Mount Vernon Nazarene Univ. (OH)	85%	$29,761
Augustana College (SD)	76%	$29,531
Concordia University (MI)	93%	$29,354
Carthage College (WI)	80%	$29,075
St. Joseph's College (IN)	77%	$28,135
Grand View University (IA)	83%	$28,041
Huntington University (IN)	55%	$27,541
MacMurray College (IL)	94%	$27,524
Indiana University East	78%	$27,300

	grads with debt % of	Average amount of debt
Franklin College (IN)	85%	$26,903
Bluffton University (OH)	88%	$26,896
Robert Morris University (IL)	94%	$26,752
Cedarville University (OH)	67%	$26,672
Judson University (IL)	88%	$26,493
Northwestern College (MN)	84%	$26,259
University of Minnesota–Crookston	86%	$26,199
Mayville State University (ND)	90%	$25,931
Valley City State University (ND)	88%	$25,929
Jamestown College (ND)	84%	$25,717
St. Mary-of-the-Woods College (IN)	97%	$25,500
Defiance College (OH)	90%	$25,388
Indiana University–Kokomo	65%	$24,788
Greenville College (IL)	94%	$24,070
Culver-Stockton College (MO)	90%	$23,761
Central Methodist University (MO)	79%	$23,437
Dakota State University (SD)	80%	$23,368
Missouri Valley College	82%	$23,200
Union College (NE)	65%	$23,000
Taylor University (IN)	53%	$22,971

	grads with debt % of	Average amount of debt
Bethany College (KS)	84%	$22,699
Marietta College (OH)	87%	$22,623
York College (NE)	78%	$22,020
Concordia University (NE)	79%	$21,941
Quincy University (IL)	77%	$21,785
Central Christian College (KS)	73%	$21,500
University of Sioux Falls (SD)	78%	$21,332
Purdue University–North Central (IN)	75%	$20,859
Bethel College (IN)	75%	$20,800
Blackburn College (IL)	85%	$20,077
Dordt College (IA)	85%	$19,988
McKendree University (IL)	73%	$19,445
Trine University (IN)	81%	$19,334
Dickinson State University (ND)	78%	$18,852
Missouri Western State University	67%	$17,989
Adrian College (MI)	81%	$17,160
Manchester College (IN)	80%	$16,235
Eureka College (IL)	79%	$15,390
Missouri Southern State University	51%	$10,006

Regional Colleges (West)

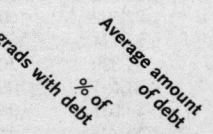

	grads with debt % of	Average amount of debt
Langston University (OK)	76%	$30,186
Master's College and Seminary (CA)	68%	$30,003
Concordia University Texas	65%	$30,000
Corban University (OR)	91%	$28,537
Howard Payne University (TX)	75%	$28,400
McMurry University (TX)	77%	$27,935
Oregon Institute of Technology	64%	$27,266
Vanguard Univ. of Southern California	77%	$26,435
Wiley College (TX)	89%	$24,906

	grads with debt % of	Average amount of debt
Rocky Mountain College (MT)	68%	$24,361
Northwest University (WA)	76%	$23,965
Montana Tech of the Univ. of Montana	85%	$23,000
Warner Pacific College (OR)	93%	$22,433
University of Montana–Western	82%	$22,009
Oklahoma Wesleyan University	98%	$21,891
Northwest Christian University (OR)	85%	$21,633
Oklahoma Baptist University	68%	$21,554
East Texas Baptist University	77%	$21,380

	grads with debt % of	Average amount of debt
Pacific Union College (CA)	70%	$19,000
Texas College	92%	$18,735
University of Houston–Downtown	75%	$16,204
Univ. of Sci. and Arts of Oklahoma	58%	$15,598
Rogers State University (OK)	55%	$11,880
Patten University (CA)	75%	$9,500
Northwestern Oklahoma State Univ.	49%	$9,381

Where the money is: Schools that award the most need-based aid

The schools at the top of this list handed out the largest need-based financial aid packages, on average, during the 2009–2010 school year. The typical aid package has three components: need-based grants, need-based loans, and work-study. In order to qualify, students must file an annual aid application that demonstrates financial need. The table also lists the percentage of undergraduates receiving a need-based aid package, the average need-based grant and loan awarded to undergraduates, and the average percentage of a student's demonstrated need that was met by the school during the 2009–2010 academic year. In addition, some colleges give out merit awards, which are based on academic ability or other talents and not on financial need. The table lists the percentage of undergraduates receiving such awards and the average amount of the award during 2009–2010.

National Universities	Average amount of aid package	% students receiving need-based package	Average need-based grant	Average need-based loan	Average % of need met	Average merit award	% students receiving merit awards
Vanderbilt University (TN)	$41,954	46%	$34,715	$526	99%	$20,506	9%
Harvard University (MA)	$40,234	60%	$37,620	$4,461	100%	$0	0%
Stanford University (CA)	$39,900	50%	$37,400	$2,700	100%	$3,600	12%
George Washington University (DC)	$39,572	43%	$27,633	$5,229	93%	$13,050	12%
Yale University (CT)	$39,270	54%	$37,639	$2,136	100%	N/A	N/A
Dartmouth College (NH)	$38,449	55%	$35,209	$3,340	100%	$450	0%
Massachusetts Institute of Technology	$37,696	63%	$35,470	$3,217	100%	N/A	N/A
Columbia University (NY)	$37,490	50%	$35,705	$2,541	100%	N/A	N/A
University of Chicago	$36,915	49%	$33,027	$5,074	100%	$13,208	11%
Cornell University (NY)	$36,812	46%	$31,911	$3,327	100%	N/A	N/A
Duke University (NC)	$36,576	42%	$33,810	$2,666	100%	$23,185	6%
Princeton University (NJ)	$36,495	59%	$34,828	$0	100%	N/A	N/A
University of Southern California	$35,593	40%	$24,801	$5,617	100%	$18,179	18%
Tulane University (LA)	$35,519	40%	$25,138	$7,945	92%	$21,207	39%
Pepperdine University (CA)	$34,721	53%	$27,829	$4,823	85%	$16,964	18%
Brown University (RI)	$34,586	44%	$31,474	$5,208	100%	$14,000	0%
University of Notre Dame (IN)	$34,101	49%	$26,847	$4,782	99%	$7,465	3%
California Institute of Technology	$33,902	55%	$30,069	$2,502	100%	$34,967	4%
Case Western Reserve University (OH)	$33,478	64%	$22,793	$7,474	87%	$18,930	19%
Biola University (CA)	$33,123	68%	$12,955	$1,339	70%	$14,829	10%
University of Pennsylvania	$33,060	43%	$30,043	$1,491	100%	N/A	N/A
Lehigh University (PA)	$33,008	45%	$27,718	$4,581	96%	$10,524	7%
Wake Forest University (NC)	$32,965	38%	$26,473	$11,305	99%	$13,864	9%
Emory University (GA)	$32,415	45%	$28,053	$4,333	100%	$21,345	6%
Washington University in St. Louis	$32,350	42%	$28,649	$6,193	100%	$7,865	15%
University of Rochester (NY)	$32,203	57%	$26,741	$4,808	96%	$9,508	31%
Rensselaer Polytechnic Institute (NY)	$32,065	65%	$22,268	$6,068	84%	$14,086	32%
Johns Hopkins University (MD)	$31,853	46%	$28,380	$4,530	98%	$27,360	1%
Clarkson University (NY)	$31,447	81%	$21,803	$5,218	87%	$14,547	10%
American University (DC)	$31,258	50%	$13,290	$4,838	87%	$18,412	17%
Georgetown University (DC)	$31,181	43%	$30,140	$4,492	100%	$0	0%
Southern Methodist University (TX)	$30,985	36%	$17,879	$3,433	88%	$14,240	35%
Tufts University (MA)	$30,974	41%	$28,112	$3,846	100%	$500	1%
Boston College	$30,968	42%	$26,500	$4,708	100%	$16,443	2%
University of Miami (FL)	$30,640	48%	$22,869	$5,078	82%	$18,529	20%
Brandeis University (MA)	$30,397	51%	$25,790	$5,085	81%	$23,564	12%
Northwestern University (IL)	$30,080	43%	$26,817	$4,625	100%	$2,521	5%
Syracuse University (NY)	$29,976	59%	$21,300	$7,225	86%	$9,130	14%
University of the Pacific (CA)	$29,320	69%	$22,044	$5,013	N/A	$9,534	14%
University of San Diego	$28,993	48%	$21,139	$8,037	74%	$13,385	16%
University of Denver	$28,632	43%	$23,435	$4,310	81%	$11,172	37%
Pace University (NY)	$28,055	74%	$23,607	$4,517	78%	$9,602	19%
Carnegie Mellon University (PA)	$28,013	49%	$22,789	$4,661	80%	$12,083	8%
Florida Institute of Technology	$27,868	61%	$19,004	$4,704	81%	$10,155	26%
Yeshiva University (NY)	$27,297	50%	$20,958	$6,043	87%	$18,644	11%
Stevens Institute of Technology (NJ)	$27,104	73%	$14,655	$4,841	72%	$13,102	11%
Loyola University Chicago	$27,092	73%	$16,380	$4,891	82%	$7,524	17%
University of Tulsa (OK)	$26,961	42%	$5,996	$4,211	85%	$13,567	37%
University of San Francisco	$26,830	59%	$21,762	$4,795	65%	$18,254	2%
Polytechnic Institute of New York University (NY)	$26,211	72%	$12,353	$4,683	89%	$18,428	21%
Clark University (MA)	$25,904	55%	$20,705	$3,288	94%	$13,013	34%
Rice University (TX)	$25,819	41%	$23,558	$3,722	100%	$16,015	12%
New School (NY)	$25,345	47%	$13,761	$11,085	65%	$11,267	3%

	Average amount of aid package	% students receiving need-based package	Average need-based grant	Average need-based loan	Average % of need met	Average merit award	% students receiving merit awards
Worcester Polytechnic Institute (MA)	$25,306	70%	$17,979	$6,836	70%	$15,384	28%
University of Dayton (OH)	$25,054	59%	$14,164	$7,402	100%	$6,328	40%
University of La Verne (CA)	$24,932	83%	$11,941	$4,884	60%	$15,146	11%
Illinois Institute of Technology	$24,602	63%	$18,411	$4,555	75%	$12,584	36%
Andrews University (MI)	$23,932	67%	$8,350	$4,663	86%	$5,853	31%
New York University	$23,900	49%	$16,870	$5,583	64%	$7,426	8%
University of St. Thomas (MN)	$23,858	58%	$15,779	$7,447	92%	$11,065	11%
George Fox University (OR)	$23,840	74%	$9,057	$3,633	89%	$7,163	6%
Pacific University (OR)	$23,485	80%	$14,309	$4,448	83%	$10,908	19%
Widener University (PA)	$23,048	80%	$8,804	$4,794	72%	$11,490	12%
University of Bridgeport (CT)	$22,618	79%	$8,420	$5,539	56%	$15,194	21%
University of Hartford (CT)	$22,400	78%	$8,365	$3,979	90%	$6,484	0%
St. Louis University	$21,747	55%	$15,711	$5,126	64%	$10,408	28%
Marquette University (WI)	$21,428	60%	$14,614	$5,440	78%	$8,138	24%
Texas Christian University	$20,647	42%	$17,440	$4,368	71%	$10,715	25%
Duquesne University (PA)	$20,623	70%	$12,312	$4,400	80%	$7,759	25%
St. John's University (NY)	$20,524	80%	$10,506	$6,601	62%	$10,463	5%
DePaul University (IL)	$20,459	63%	$14,428	$4,732	67%	$9,128	4%
Baylor University (TX)	$20,452	55%	$15,180	$3,169	67%	$8,805	31%
Trinity International University (IL)	$20,273	77%	$9,420	$4,810	96%	$4,591	7%
Catholic University of America (DC)	$20,209	58%	$15,576	$4,377	81%	$10,449	31%
University of Virginia	$20,202	30%	$14,772	$5,468	100%	$9,858	11%
St. Mary's University of Minnesota	$19,846	73%	$15,012	$4,884	76%	$9,361	25%
Northeastern University (MA)	$19,325	54%	$14,627	$4,910	59%	$9,139	23%
University of California–San Diego	$18,560	60%	$13,983	$5,833	86%	$9,419	3%
University of California–Santa Cruz	$18,545	53%	$13,735	$5,617	89%	$8,010	2%
Barry University (FL)	$18,528	81%	$6,975	$5,332	52%	$6,871	10%
University of Vermont	$18,364	59%	$14,576	$6,413	71%	$2,426	18%
University of New Hampshire	$18,346	59%	$3,223	$3,456	80%	$8,640	21%
University of California–Berkeley	$18,322	51%	$13,976	$5,215	87%	$5,984	5%
Hofstra University (NY)	$18,000	61%	$11,000	$5,000	56%	$10,000	19%
Adelphi University (NY)	$17,850	61%	$6,469	$4,509	38%	$8,353	64%
Oral Roberts University (OK)	$17,820	73%	$11,055	$5,621	72%	$8,811	18%
University of California–Santa Barbara	$17,380	50%	$13,876	$6,264	82%	$6,021	2%
Morgan State University (MD)	$17,329	74%	$3,832	$4,030	49%	$6,746	1%
University of California–Los Angeles	$17,008	53%	$13,302	$6,387	81%	$4,169	4%
Samford University (AL)	$16,910	42%	N/A	$4,672	71%	$6,515	19%
University of California–Riverside	$16,903	69%	$12,935	$5,991	84%	$7,687	1%
Nova Southeastern University (FL)	$16,863	76%	$6,287	$5,568	67%	$5,631	6%
Immaculata University (PA)	$16,583	70%	$2,749	$4,093	25%	$7,713	18%
University of California–Irvine	$16,286	53%	$13,035	$6,093	84%	$8,121	3%
University of California–Davis	$16,066	57%	$12,800	$5,140	82%	$5,879	4%
Temple University (PA)	$15,577	67%	$5,972	$4,184	84%	$8,528	12%
Wayne State University (MI)	$15,020	68%	$6,378	$4,150	83%	$5,483	10%
University of Northern Colorado	$14,872	51%	$6,877	$4,496	100%	$2,743	16%
University of Colorado–Boulder	$14,790	34%	$8,125	$6,796	92%	$6,707	26%
Texas A&M University–College Station	$14,658	37%	$8,953	$6,070	71%	$3,441	5%
University of Massachusetts–Amherst	$14,606	57%	$8,848	$4,383	88%	$2,835	5%
Long Island University–C.W. Post Campus (NY)	$14,500	66%	$5,800	$5,350	75%	$6,950	14%
Rutgers, the State University of New Jersey–New Brunswick	$14,415	56%	$11,354	$4,440	65%	$6,098	3%
College of William and Mary (VA)	$14,220	33%	N/A	$3,275	78%	$6,221	5%
University of Toledo (OH)	$14,129	67%	$6,514	$7,599	86%	$3,921	22%
University of Florida	$13,448	43%	$6,942	$4,196	85%	$4,700	47%
Missouri University of Science & Technology	$13,362	76%	$4,370	$5,640	44%	$4,889	12%
University of Minnesota–Twin Cities	$13,189	53%	$7,832	$6,073	83%	$5,020	13%
University of Missouri	$13,136	47%	$7,152	$4,441	84%	$3,531	17%
Rutgers, the State University of New Jersey–Newark	$13,090	68%	$10,680	$4,474	77%	$6,000	2%
University of Oklahoma	$13,072	57%	$4,453	$4,470	89%	$4,268	15%
New Jersey Institute of Technology	$13,059	67%	$11,735	$4,281	61%	$10,574	11%
SUNY College of Environmental Science and Forestry	$13,000	60%	$5,000	$6,750	100%	$2,500	6%
University of Illinois–Chicago	$12,980	65%	$11,628	$4,149	72%	$3,650	4%
Bowling Green State University (OH)	$12,886	62%	$6,327	$7,674	76%	$4,727	15%
University of North Carolina–Chapel Hill	$12,860	36%	$10,877	$3,990	100%	$5,348	14%
University of Rhode Island	$12,794	60%	$7,540	$5,499	57%	$5,057	3%
University of Delaware	$12,675	57%	$6,398	$7,543	76%	$5,965	20%
University of Illinois–Urbana-Champaign	$12,614	44%	$10,570	$4,473	70%	$3,359	11%
University of Texas–Austin	$12,388	44%	$8,822	$4,204	75%	N/A	5%
University of Massachusetts–Boston	$12,369	60%	$6,534	$5,965	95%	$3,539	4%
University of Massachusetts–Lowell	$12,300	58%	$5,934	$6,487	94%	$2,154	20%
University of Connecticut	$12,238	52%	$7,796	$4,204	68%	$6,280	8%
Florida A&M University	$12,216	75%	$5,077	$3,982	80%	$5,285	4%
University of Texas–El Paso	$12,125	N/A	$7,139	$6,549	84%	$2,396	N/A
University of Idaho	$12,076	62%	$4,365	$7,208	76%	$4,810	14%
University of Houston	$12,018	56%	$6,649	$6,908	76%	$4,544	2%

Where the money is: Schools that award the most need–based aid

National Universities, continued	Average amount of aid package	% students receiving need-based package	Average need-based grant	Average need-based loan	Average % of need met	Average merit award	% students receiving merit awards
University of South Carolina	$12,016	45%	$4,341	$3,922	76%	$6,688	38%
Binghamton University–SUNY	$11,940	46%	$6,643	$5,358	79%	$4,311	3%
Colorado School of Mines	$11,927	43%	$6,586	$5,041	68%	$4,633	21%
North Carolina A&T State University	$11,899	83%	$4,764	$1,967	84%	$18,563	11%
Southern Illinois University–Carbondale	$11,809	63%	$6,934	$4,121	95%	$6,359	9%
Illinois State University	$11,678	52%	$8,857	$7,103	79%	$3,231	2%
Virginia Tech	$11,642	40%	$6,329	$4,248	71%	$2,564	8%
University of Washington	$11,550	37%	$8,720	$2,850	79%	$4,430	3%
Louisiana State University–Baton Rouge	$11,518	35%	$8,505	$4,360	69%	$5,135	16%
University of Michigan–Ann Arbor	$11,511	46%	$9,529	$4,305	90%	$6,479	34%
George Mason University (VA)	$11,449	45%	$6,685	$4,454	71%	$6,171	2%
Miami University–Oxford (OH)	$11,374	43%	$6,359	$4,699	59%	$4,559	16%
University of Wisconsin–Madison	$11,141	36%	$5,850	$4,896	76%	$3,234	10%
Howard University (DC)	$11,133	81%	$3,356	$2,249	81%	$4,927	4%
SUNY–Stony Brook	$11,124	55%	$6,953	$4,545	71%	$3,599	7%
Northern Illinois University	$11,087	64%	$7,582	$4,278	65%	$912	0%
Washington State University	$11,018	52%	$8,197	$4,211	81%	$3,387	12%
Western Michigan University	$11,000	62%	$4,800	$4,000	85%	$3,500	12%
University of Utah	$10,944	41%	$5,317	$4,820	63%	$4,688	5%
Georgia Institute of Technology	$10,933	33%	$9,265	$4,532	72%	$4,368	5%
Clemson University (SC)	$10,911	43%	$4,714	$4,196	61%	$2,489	18%
University of North Texas	$10,811	50%	$6,245	$4,286	71%	$4,843	10%
Michigan Technological University	$10,793	63%	$5,167	$4,386	70%	$4,162	23%
Oklahoma State University	$10,788	50%	$6,022	$4,161	72%	$4,305	23%
Iowa State University	$10,771	52%	$5,560	$4,359	82%	$2,285	31%
Ohio State University–Columbus	$10,725	55%	$8,073	$4,671	57%	$4,645	20%
University of Tennessee	$10,679	50%	$3,104	$4,304	73%	$2,461	12%
Kansas State University	$10,655	50%	$4,188	$4,264	84%	$3,024	16%
Michigan State University	$10,620	48%	$8,420	$4,222	66%	$7,278	4%
North Carolina State University–Raleigh	$10,594	44%	$8,678	$2,806	84%	$5,293	4%
University of Maine	$10,588	77%	$6,826	$6,392	74%	$4,115	10%
Texas Tech University	$10,578	41%	$9,519	$5,394	59%	$4,973	18%
University of Alaska–Fairbanks	$10,556	43%	$5,339	$9,707	56%	$7,683	28%
Purdue University–West Lafayette (IN)	$10,555	46%	$8,738	$4,562	95%	$5,637	7%
Mississippi State University	$10,551	55%	$5,422	$3,641	67%	$2,829	20%
University of Maryland–Baltimore County	$10,480	46%	$7,723	$4,061	63%	$5,240	32%
Indiana University–Bloomington	$10,440	41%	$8,677	$4,322	89%	$5,708	22%
Central Michigan University	$10,428	54%	$4,768	$6,481	83%	$3,467	9%
Florida State University	$10,419	34%	$4,071	$3,648	76%	$2,254	6%
Montana State University	$10,268	48%	$4,530	$4,422	72%	$2,039	4%
Pennsylvania State University–University Park	$10,179	51%	$6,498	$4,638	57%	$3,262	6%
University of Louisville (KY)	$10,170	55%	$7,641	$4,024	65%	$6,948	14%
University of Pittsburgh	$10,132	55%	$8,321	$4,894	79%	$15,282	7%
University of Nebraska–Lincoln	$10,060	43%	$6,784	$4,016	86%	$5,325	8%
Colorado State University	$10,051	42%	$5,170	$6,525	74%	$3,371	9%
University of Arizona	$10,021	38%	$7,849	$4,325	64%	$5,064	25%
University of Kansas	$10,014	42%	$5,775	$3,664	53%	$3,234	10%
University of Texas–Arlington	$9,939	64%	$6,493	$4,162	73%	$5,050	2%
Oregon State University	$9,856	53%	$2,957	$3,936	62%	$3,994	0%
University of Nevada–Las Vegas	$9,706	48%	$5,123	$4,146	56%	$3,194	2%
University of Missouri–Kansas City	$9,704	65%	$6,675	$8,436	51%	$5,101	13%
University at Albany–SUNY	$9,649	58%	$6,398	$4,408	68%	$3,528	5%
Texas A&M University–Commerce	$9,608	69%	$7,113	$4,097	64%	$2,581	7%
University of Georgia	$9,509	32%	$7,953	$3,809	76%	$1,872	5%
University of Alabama	$9,506	39%	$6,419	$4,106	54%	$6,947	20%
University of Maryland–College Park	$9,481	38%	$6,950	$4,280	60%	$6,584	11%
Ball State University (IN)	$9,450	63%	$6,145	$4,170	60%	$5,062	6%
Louisiana Tech University	$9,446	46%	$7,171	$3,745	65%	$2,370	16%
Virginia Commonwealth University	$9,365	50%	$5,603	$4,414	60%	$6,229	4%
Portland State University (OR)	$9,343	61%	$6,302	$4,536	61%	$1,988	1%
University of Alabama–Birmingham	$9,334	51%	$5,063	$4,394	50%	$6,449	16%
University of Wyoming	$9,332	44%	$4,660	$3,446	44%	$4,751	40%
South Dakota State University	$9,214	76%	$4,340	$5,010	86%	$1,422	21%
University of North Carolina–Greensboro	$9,204	75%	$6,332	$4,010	59%	$2,349	4%
Indiana State University	$9,198	67%	$6,110	$3,755	80%	$4,820	10%
Wright State University (OH)	$9,177	68%	$6,113	$4,106	54%	$4,091	8%
University of Oregon	$9,168	41%	$6,321	$4,471	63%	$2,544	6%
University of Southern Mississippi	$9,117	63%	$3,982	$4,901	82%	$3,590	8%
Auburn University (AL)	$9,085	32%	$5,693	$4,434	57%	$4,908	14%
University at Buffalo–SUNY	$9,070	48%	$4,490	$4,305	65%	$3,335	5%

	Average amount of aid package	% students receiving need-based package	Average need-based grant	Average need-based loan	Average % of need met	Average merit award	% students receiving merit awards
University of Arkansas	$9,030	39%	$6,343	$4,306	64%	$5,315	17%
University of Memphis	$9,005	63%	$5,942	$4,360	70%	$7,945	16%
Indiana University of Pennsylvania	$8,991	66%	$5,035	$4,093	70%	$2,705	3%
Indiana University–Purdue University–Indianapolis	$8,978	65%	$6,925	$4,127	90%	$3,407	7%
University of Kentucky	$8,831	45%	$5,137	$4,011	83%	$5,451	19%
Kent State University (OH)	$8,820	64%	$6,152	$3,989	52%	$3,815	13%
University of Colorado–Denver	$8,804	54%	$2,189	$3,611	55%	$2,138	5%
University of Missouri–St. Louis	$8,707	67%	$5,815	$4,543	48%	$4,315	9%
Georgia Southern University	$8,704	57%	$6,494	$4,158	58%	$1,846	3%
University of Hawaii–Manoa	$8,703	42%	$6,561	$3,796	60%	$7,427	12%
University of North Carolina–Charlotte	$8,642	55%	$6,096	$3,724	74%	$2,427	1%
University of Montana	$8,638	57%	$3,899	$3,931	74%	$6,352	22%
Cleveland State University	$8,565	76%	$6,172	$4,157	49%	$4,242	5%
San Diego State University	$8,500	52%	$7,100	$4,100	73%	$1,800	5%
Ohio University	$8,484	55%	$7,145	$4,287	58%	$2,291	12%
University of South Florida	$8,470	53%	$4,999	$4,505	48%	$1,951	16%
Tennessee State University	$8,464	85%	$3,995	$4,197	70%	N/A	N/A
Georgia State University	$8,393	63%	$4,443	$5,341	12%	$3,503	1%
Florida Atlantic University	$8,271	51%	$6,358	$3,972	69%	$0	0%
University of Alabama–Huntsville	$8,226	49%	$5,372	$7,286	57%	$4,332	18%
University of New Orleans	$8,014	62%	$5,799	$3,925	59%	$1,627	4%
University of Central Florida	$7,951	42%	$4,640	$4,681	67%	$2,327	6%
University of Cincinnati	$7,843	57%	$5,883	$4,223	63%	$4,755	17%
Texas Woman's University	$7,813	62%	$7,592	$3,703	88%	$3,000	11%
University of Wisconsin–Milwaukee	$7,800	61%	$6,834	$4,348	52%	$3,217	0%
University of Iowa	$7,781	46%	$5,298	$4,102	65%	$3,279	15%
Oakland University (MI)	$7,730	54%	$4,985	$3,992	73%	$2,696	26%
Old Dominion University (VA)	$7,701	54%	$4,483	$4,063	74%	$3,441	2%
University of Mississippi	$7,677	44%	$6,278	$4,661	76%	$4,106	20%
University of Akron (OH)	$7,641	70%	$5,227	$3,973	52%	$3,802	8%
University of Nevada–Reno	$7,598	40%	$6,034	$4,310	59%	$2,880	38%
New Mexico State University	$7,539	56%	$5,125	$4,130	48%	$315	1%
Utah State University	$7,300	51%	$4,959	$4,080	63%	$2,500	3%
Wichita State University (KS)	$7,278	37%	$3,604	$4,729	50%	$1,704	21%
University of Louisiana–Lafayette	$7,037	47%	$5,320	$3,780	57%	$1,644	7%
West Virginia University	$6,959	49%	$5,266	$4,433	75%	$1,912	16%
Brigham Young University–Provo (UT)	$6,656	36%	$4,252	$4,374	44%	$3,188	27%
University of South Dakota	$6,471	35%	$3,846	$4,076	78%	$3,597	22%
Clark Atlanta University	$5,876	91%	$4,209	$2,429	20%	$9,577	0%
University of North Dakota	$5,723	73%	$2,892	$4,130	39%	$1,469	29%
North Dakota State University	$4,652	84%	$2,842	$3,672	51%	$1,601	30%

National Liberal Arts Colleges

	Average amount of aid package	% students receiving need-based package	Average need-based grant	Average need-based loan	Average % of need met	Average merit award	% students receiving merit awards
Amherst College (MA)	$41,124	58%	$39,451	$2,941	100%	$0	0%
Williams College (MA)	$39,540	52%	$37,783	$0	100%	$0	0%
Colgate University (NY)	$37,738	35%	$33,211	$4,505	100%	$0	0%
Vassar College (NY)	$37,512	56%	$33,155	$2,614	100%	$0	0%
Wesleyan University (CT)	$37,187	48%	$33,168	$4,069	100%	$46,085	2%
Washington and Lee University (VA)	$37,052	35%	$31,111	$3,700	100%	$27,499	9%
University of Richmond (VA)	$36,857	46%	$33,404	$3,032	100%	$19,879	14%
Hamilton College (NY)	$36,305	41%	$35,502	$3,835	100%	$22,205	2%
Occidental College (CA)	$36,048	55%	$28,994	$6,346	100%	$9,316	20%
St. Lawrence University (NY)	$35,989	62%	$26,987	$4,282	90%	$11,335	16%
Wellesley College (MA)	$35,951	62%	$34,014	$3,104	100%	$0	0%
Pitzer College (CA)	$35,835	40%	$30,356	$3,647	100%	$5,000	5%
Pomona College (CA)	$35,416	54%	$34,061	$0	100%	$0	0%
Barnard College (NY)	$35,365	44%	$30,538	$4,692	100%	$0	0%
Bryn Mawr College (PA)	$35,351	57%	$29,927	$5,018	100%	$15,438	2%
Swarthmore College (PA)	$35,342	49%	$33,859	$0	100%	$37,510	1%
Hampshire College (MA)	$35,310	59%	$28,085	$4,750	98%	$6,220	16%
Claremont McKenna College (CA)	$35,177	44%	$34,276	$0	100%	$12,591	7%
Bowdoin College (ME)	$34,960	43%	$33,832	N/A	100%	$1,000	4%
Bard College (NY)	$34,643	62%	$28,319	$4,501	92%	$13,098	2%
Haverford College (PA)	$34,629	48%	$33,093	$17,534	100%	N/A	0%

Where the money is: Schools that award the most need-based aid

National Liberal Arts Colleges, continued	Average amount of aid package	% students receiving need-based package	Average need-based grant	Average need-based loan	Average % of need met	Average merit award	% students receiving merit awards
Smith College (MA)	$34,526	63%	$30,971	$4,567	100%	$9,805	5%
Scripps College (CA)	$34,330	41%	$31,456	$2,614	100%	$18,671	8%
Carleton College (MN)	$34,141	56%	$27,989	$4,802	100%	$2,644	7%
Skidmore College (NY)	$34,104	44%	$28,524	$3,878	87%	$10,000	0%
Lafayette College (PA)	$34,061	46%	$28,697	$4,090	98%	$17,090	7%
Bates College (ME)	$33,852	43%	$31,083	$4,371	100%	N/A	N/A
Union College (NY)	$33,778	47%	$28,489	$4,007	99%	$10,002	16%
Mount Holyoke College (MA)	$33,399	68%	$28,578	$4,675	100%	$16,023	7%
Middlebury College (VT)	$33,345	49%	$29,918	$3,659	100%	$0	0%
Dickinson College (PA)	$33,332	52%	$27,318	$4,716	94%	$11,709	8%
Whittier College (CA)	$33,257	72%	$12,980	$10,564	87%	$14,448	21%
Reed College (OR)	$33,090	52%	$30,710	$4,234	100%	$0	0%
Bennington College (VT)	$32,970	69%	$28,738	$3,977	81%	$13,744	9%
Grinnell College (IA)	$32,958	64%	$27,997	$3,133	100%	$10,181	21%
Harvey Mudd College (CA)	$32,547	54%	$29,269	$5,052	100%	$11,375	23%
Oberlin College (OH)	$32,508	55%	$27,634	$4,776	100%	$11,812	26%
Macalester College (MN)	$32,258	67%	$27,111	$3,644	100%	$6,293	4%
Colby College (ME)	$32,252	38%	$31,423	$2,340	100%	$337	3%
Berea College (KY)	$32,141	100%	$29,964	$213	93%	$0	0%
Denison University (OH)	$32,040	46%	$26,112	$4,387	96%	$15,282	47%
Birmingham-Southern College (AL)	$31,807	53%	N/A	N/A	95%	$13,639	42%
Wheaton College (MA)	$31,770	56%	$25,214	$4,614	97%	$10,725	13%
Kenyon College (OH)	$31,610	42%	$28,583	$4,500	98%	$9,496	10%
Rhodes College (TN)	$31,373	47%	$20,727	$6,822	80%	$13,433	36%
Connecticut College	$31,101	45%	$29,616	$4,389	100%	$0	0%
Gettysburg College (PA)	$31,030	53%	$23,781	$5,851	100%	$10,713	14%
College of the Atlantic (ME)	$30,646	85%	$26,366	$4,830	96%	$0	0%
Colorado College	$30,203	37%	$28,207	$3,284	92%	$17,773	10%
Drew University (NJ)	$30,067	58%	$24,393	$4,923	80%	$11,697	37%
Beacon College (FL)	$30,000	67%	$20,000	$5,500	80%	$0	0%
Presbyterian College (SC)	$29,765	68%	$27,536	$4,111	88%	$13,050	28%
Franklin and Marshall College (PA)	$29,613	44%	$25,470	$4,569	93%	$10,748	12%
Sarah Lawrence College (NY)	$29,576	58%	$29,576	$3,465	92%	$0	0%
Hobart and William Smith Colleges (NY)	$29,433	75%	$24,984	$4,190	78%	$14,177	23%
Willamette University (OR)	$29,387	63%	$23,226	$4,334	89%	$11,727	32%
College of the Holy Cross (MA)	$29,293	54%	$27,089	$5,320	100%	$24,997	0%
Whitman College (WA)	$29,197	44%	$24,366	$4,361	94%	$10,686	29%
Wofford College (SC)	$28,954	56%	$24,703	$4,364	87%	$13,278	25%
Agnes Scott College (GA)	$28,845	74%	$23,525	$3,767	91%	$15,195	24%
DePauw University (IN)	$28,224	53%	$24,150	$3,870	90%	$15,637	45%
Beloit College (WI)	$28,203	64%	$21,235	$5,101	94%	$13,583	27%
Furman University (SC)	$28,079	47%	$24,782	$4,935	81%	$16,007	27%
Ohio Wesleyan University	$28,014	58%	$22,841	$5,378	85%	$16,509	39%
College of Wooster (OH)	$27,955	60%	$22,600	$4,550	86%	$15,642	35%
Eckerd College (FL)	$27,743	57%	$18,255	$4,807	87%	$10,777	32%
Earlham College (IN)	$27,660	58%	$19,870	$4,832	90%	$10,413	26%
Ursinus College (PA)	$27,627	69%	$23,120	$4,377	80%	$13,682	24%
Lewis & Clark College (OR)	$27,618	55%	$20,201	$4,408	85%	$10,371	13%
University of Puget Sound (WA)	$27,595	64%	$22,319	$5,357	82%	$8,809	25%
Wittenberg University (OH)	$27,562	73%	$21,660	$4,546	85%	$13,539	27%
Allegheny College (PA)	$27,087	69%	$20,179	$5,023	89%	$11,621	28%
Wabash College (IN)	$27,083	80%	$18,638	$5,319	96%	$16,398	17%
Southwestern University (TX)	$26,810	57%	$20,735	$5,728	90%	$12,688	32%
Lake Forest College (IL)	$26,500	76%	$23,300	$4,900	N/A	$12,400	17%
Oglethorpe University (GA)	$26,500	56%	$19,876	$6,326	86%	$12,291	27%
St. Olaf College (MN)	$26,401	66%	$21,228	$6,575	100%	$8,611	17%
Austin College (TX)	$26,331	61%	$19,001	$6,200	95%	$12,949	22%
Maryville College (TN)	$26,285	83%	$21,732	$3,459	87%	$15,380	12%
Lawrence University (WI)	$26,155	60%	$18,952	$5,540	92%	$12,417	31%
Sewanee–University of the South (TN)	$26,112	54%	$20,919	$4,234	95%	$14,376	25%
Augustana College (IL)	$25,819	69%	$15,738	$7,306	85%	$11,868	29%
Illinois Wesleyan University	$25,753	59%	$18,340	$5,313	97%	$11,861	30%
Knox College (IL)	$25,642	70%	$19,765	$5,062	90%	$10,845	20%
Cornell College (IA)	$25,535	74%	$20,545	$4,755	93%	$13,250	19%
Goucher College (MD)	$25,518	57%	$22,271	$4,250	80%	$12,129	20%
Bucknell University (PA)	$25,500	46%	$21,300	$5,400	95%	$11,907	4%
Simpson College (IA)	$25,103	86%	$16,915	$3,506	89%	$12,819	14%
Centre College (KY)	$25,091	59%	$21,641	$4,803	85%	$14,106	36%
Albright College (PA)	$25,053	82%	$19,406	$4,935	78%	$12,235	12%
Luther College (IA)	$24,932	69%	$17,454	$6,406	88%	$9,617	10%

	Average amount of aid package	% students receiving need-based package	Average need-based grant	Average need-based loan	Average % of need met	Average merit award	% students receiving merit awards
McDaniel College (MD)	$24,842	69%	$17,794	$4,879	97%	$12,939	22%
St. Norbert College (WI)	$24,799	68%	$19,152	$4,566	94%	$8,957	29%
Albion College (MI)	$24,776	65%	$19,748	$4,912	88%	$13,179	33%
Roanoke College (VA)	$24,772	67%	$19,058	$4,558	87%	$10,405	31%
Millsaps College (MS)	$24,659	58%	$18,969	$4,359	84%	$15,127	39%
American Jewish University (CA)	$24,500	95%	$9,809	$4,500	96%	$2,000	42%
Hartwick College (NY)	$24,206	74%	$19,972	$4,681	78%	$10,267	23%
Principia College (IL)	$24,175	70%	$20,119	$5,342	85%	$16,727	17%
Juniata College (PA)	$24,152	71%	$18,970	$4,865	83%	$13,879	28%
Westmont College (CA)	$24,129	62%	$19,229	$5,483	70%	$10,128	27%
Davidson College (NC)	$24,121	43%	$21,962	$3,250	100%	$17,182	14%
Washington and Jefferson College (PA)	$24,008	77%	$9,786	$4,809	79%	$10,736	19%
Susquehanna University (PA)	$23,880	68%	$19,015	$4,390	79%	$10,081	24%
West Virginia Wesleyan College	$23,785	76%	$18,591	$4,189	78%	$12,053	20%
Hampden-Sydney College (VA)	$23,772	52%	$18,945	$4,725	80%	$9,413	44%
Gustavus Adolphus College (MN)	$23,652	65%	$17,264	$4,812	90%	$7,352	32%
Hanover College (IN)	$23,495	76%	$19,414	$3,530	88%	$12,193	22%
Moravian College (PA)	$23,421	79%	$17,584	$4,706	79%	$9,240	14%
Muhlenberg College (PA)	$23,370	51%	$20,674	$4,388	93%	$9,228	26%
Lycoming College (PA)	$23,264	85%	$18,340	$4,760	78%	$10,852	12%
Emory and Henry College (VA)	$23,244	82%	$20,989	$4,283	86%	$11,497	19%
St. Anselm College (NH)	$23,195	72%	$16,967	$5,788	82%	$8,216	17%
Westminster College (PA)	$23,163	83%	$18,663	$4,312	83%	$12,701	16%
College of St. Benedict (MN)	$23,152	66%	$17,595	$4,405	88%	$10,821	29%
Alma College (MI)	$23,085	81%	$18,926	$4,829	84%	$11,882	19%
Coe College (IA)	$23,085	77%	$18,611	$5,054	82%	$16,112	21%
Wheaton College (IL)	$22,934	54%	$16,241	$4,803	84%	$5,397	16%
Georgetown College (KY)	$22,830	77%	$19,189	$4,622	83%	$13,990	22%
Hendrix College (AR)	$22,498	61%	$18,080	$4,919	83%	$14,775	38%
Hope College (MI)	$22,419	62%	$17,144	$4,612	84%	$7,532	26%
St. John's University (MN)	$22,414	59%	$17,654	$4,692	90%	$10,628	34%
Ripon College (WI)	$22,365	85%	$17,850	$4,378	89%	$10,587	17%
St. Mary's College (IN)	$22,125	69%	$15,340	$4,491	71%	$10,227	23%
Central College (IA)	$22,115	82%	$16,141	$4,643	84%	$10,799	18%
Hollins University (VA)	$22,059	79%	$16,471	$5,240	84%	$11,994	21%
St. Michael's College (VT)	$21,928	62%	$16,539	$5,270	77%	$8,180	28%
Guilford College (NC)	$21,918	73%	$8,113	$5,126	91%	$7,307	6%
Randolph-Macon College (VA)	$21,777	65%	$17,689	$4,627	79%	$10,726	33%
St. Vincent College (PA)	$21,705	77%	$16,506	$4,662	81%	$12,349	23%
Transylvania University (KY)	$21,670	65%	$17,805	$4,457	83%	$10,461	33%
Wartburg College (IA)	$21,639	79%	$17,076	$4,637	83%	$13,202	20%
Bridgewater College (VA)	$21,596	76%	$17,183	$4,923	79%	$9,887	24%
Cedar Crest College (PA)	$21,570	90%	$16,975	$4,628	76%	$8,626	10%
Bethel College (KS)	$21,569	81%	$5,291	$6,787	94%	$9,003	19%
Warren Wilson College (NC)	$21,323	63%	$12,522	$3,165	74%	$5,461	16%
Washington College (MD)	$21,084	55%	$18,614	$4,824	71%	$13,730	27%
Wells College (NY)	$21,009	83%	$16,271	$4,562	82%	$8,069	12%
Stonehill College (MA)	$20,972	67%	$16,617	$4,820	74%	$8,861	19%
Stephens College (MO)	$20,787	77%	$16,735	$4,334	78%	$8,629	23%
Monmouth College (IL)	$20,775	84%	$16,052	$4,085	84%	$10,425	16%
Berry College (GA)	$20,606	68%	$15,281	$3,833	83%	$9,206	28%
Brevard College (NC)	$20,500	72%	$14,200	$4,260	83%	$2,600	20%
Concordia College–Moorhead (MN)	$20,465	71%	$14,278	$4,708	76%	$9,005	19%
William Jewell College (MO)	$20,258	71%	$15,963	$5,335	79%	$9,994	16%
Houghton College (NY)	$20,192	82%	$14,050	$5,316	78%	$8,825	15%
McPherson College (KS)	$20,033	85%	$6,422	$5,184	88%	$9,344	14%
Millikin University (IL)	$19,958	79%	$8,811	$4,204	92%	$9,108	10%
Ferrum College (VA)	$19,884	88%	$14,425	$3,674	88%	$7,151	12%
Peace College (NC)	$19,858	81%	$15,690	$3,978	72%	$7,830	18%
Clarke University (IA)	$19,614	87%	$15,231	$4,670	88%	$15,566	11%
Sierra Nevada College (NV)	$19,500	68%	$16,500	$4,500	60%	$8,000	7%
Simpson University (CA)	$19,486	87%	$14,586	$4,655	75%	$6,785	13%
Green Mountain College (VT)	$19,464	79%	$15,201	$4,512	65%	$11,488	16%
Thiel College (PA)	$19,313	80%	$15,071	$4,548	71%	$7,810	11%
University of Mount Union (OH)	$19,313	79%	$13,935	$4,984	79%	$7,537	18%
Gordon College (MA)	$19,311	67%	$12,579	$7,043	75%	$9,343	24%
Thomas Aquinas College (CA)	$19,294	76%	$14,076	$3,729	100%	$0	0%
Linfield College (OR)	$19,168	69%	$9,252	$4,280	85%	$11,388	31%
Centenary College of Louisiana	$19,140	63%	$16,330	$3,998	81%	$10,442	26%
Virginia Military Institute	$19,078	45%	$16,888	$3,935	90%	$15,850	28%

Where the money is: Schools that award the most need—based aid

National Liberal Arts Colleges, continued	Average amount of aid package	% students receiving need-based package	Average need-based grant	Average need-based loan	Average % of need met	Average merit award	% students receiving merit awards
Franklin Pierce University (NH)	$18,733	74%	$14,047	$4,921	63%	$8,615	18%
Meredith College (NC)	$18,638	71%	$14,917	$4,250	78%	$6,790	8%
Texas Lutheran University	$18,482	73%	$13,472	$4,844	37%	$8,785	20%
Sweet Briar College (VA)	$18,064	67%	$15,960	$4,515	29%	$11,705	40%
Illinois College	$18,014	82%	$13,434	$4,660	89%	$8,805	17%
Wingate University (NC)	$17,956	72%	$7,832	$4,194	79%	$7,895	27%
Calvin College (MI)	$17,931	65%	$11,375	$6,270	78%	$4,509	29%
Asbury University (KY)	$17,794	74%	$11,682	$3,907	81%	$9,343	10%
Virginia Wesleyan College	$17,752	73%	$13,507	$7,228	68%	$7,171	18%
Goshen College (IN)	$17,727	74%	$14,462	$4,193	81%	$10,361	20%
Westminster College (MO)	$17,676	57%	$13,156	$3,849	80%	$9,144	41%
Siena College (NY)	$17,659	68%	$13,350	$4,510	73%	$9,154	12%
Wisconsin Lutheran College	$17,521	79%	$13,061	$4,070	83%	$8,774	18%
Lyon College (AR)	$17,498	75%	$13,015	$4,031	81%	$11,687	26%
Doane College (NE)	$17,462	79%	$13,506	$4,464	91%	$10,924	8%
Olivet College (MI)	$17,155	92%	$11,655	$4,554	82%	$10,450	12%
Wesleyan College (GA)	$16,980	67%	$13,510	$4,359	81%	$15,208	32%
Hastings College (NE)	$16,744	74%	$12,964	$4,747	76%	$8,671	23%
Bloomfield College (NJ)	$16,544	87%	$13,844	$8,289	56%	$9,892	9%
College of Idaho (ID)	$16,324	58%	$5,178	$4,415	88%	$11,583	35%
Nebraska Wesleyan University	$16,199	71%	$11,649	$4,636	71%	$6,800	28%
Kentucky Wesleyan College	$16,017	83%	$12,886	$4,078	78%	$8,955	16%
St. Andrews Presbyterian College (NC)	$15,948	75%	$11,765	$4,327	74%	$5,228	21%
Carson-Newman College (TN)	$15,747	79%	$11,740	$3,517	74%	$6,853	17%
Merrimack College (MA)	$15,668	61%	$9,868	$4,775	70%	$10,500	16%
Spelman College (GA)	$15,439	79%	$12,829	$4,307	47%	$0	0%
Lindsey Wilson College (KY)	$15,075	91%	$11,898	$4,234	N/A	$0	0%
Fisk University (TN)	$14,957	95%	$12,028	$4,387	71%	$0	0%
Huntingdon College (AL)	$14,949	70%	$12,025	$3,491	74%	$9,324	27%
Pikeville College (KY)	$14,677	93%	$11,834	$4,202	92%	N/A	0%
Bryn Athyn College of the New Church (PA)	$14,592	62%	$10,548	$2,977	92%	$3,531	8%
Tougaloo College (MS)	$14,500	93%	$2,500	$3,375	25%	$16,524	0%
University of Minnesota–Morris	$14,261	66%	$9,147	$6,633	83%	$3,589	16%
Hillsdale College (MI)	$14,046	47%	$6,900	$4,500	65%	$5,200	37%
New College of Florida	$13,282	45%	$9,844	$3,857	92%	$2,778	49%
Marymount Manhattan College (NY)	$13,251	62%	$9,454	$4,236	47%	$5,119	17%
Thomas More College of Liberal Arts (NH)	$13,172	69%	$9,794	$4,290	87%	$3,000	8%
Johnson C. Smith University (NC)	$12,940	91%	$8,759	$5,105	51%	$6,654	2%
Burlington College (VT)	$12,910	68%	$7,443	$5,518	52%	$0	0%
Morehouse College (GA)	$12,425	97%	$10,850	$5,500	64%	N/A	N/A
Bennett College (NC)	$12,120	91%	$9,326	$3,843	48%	$6,100	1%
Atlantic Union College (MA)	$12,049	81%	$6,876	$4,384	65%	$2,963	10%
Evangel University (MO)	$11,981	83%	$7,873	$4,392	56%	$3,381	9%
Jarvis Christian College (TX)	$11,020	100%	$6,957	$3,604	82%	$0	0%
Albertus Magnus College (CT)	$10,828	N/A	$7,146	$4,271	49%	$7,414	N/A
University of North Carolina–Asheville	$10,553	47%	$6,052	$3,920	85%	$3,401	5%
University of Wisconsin–Green Bay	$10,169	61%	$6,129	$5,117	86%	$2,255	1%
Allen University (SC)	$10,149	98%	$7,104	$3,342	59%	$2,000	0%
Massachusetts College of Liberal Arts	$9,979	67%	$5,367	$3,905	86%	$2,384	5%
Purchase College–SUNY	$9,728	56%	$6,001	$4,787	59%	$1,989	3%
Western State College of Colorado	$9,500	38%	$2,500	$5,300	40%	$1,700	22%
Baker University (KS)	$9,417	67%	$5,710	$4,278	85%	$11,488	13%
University of Virginia–Wise	$9,212	75%	$5,474	$3,168	74%	$3,456	8%
California State University–Monterey Bay	$9,181	51%	$7,782	$4,138	74%	$0	0%
Coastal Carolina University (SC)	$8,878	64%	$5,106	$8,033	51%	$10,946	17%
Colorado State University–Pueblo	$8,512	72%	$5,936	$3,235	58%	$2,556	6%
Fort Lewis College (CO)	$8,042	51%	$3,660	$3,835	71%	$1,241	12%
Christopher Newport University (VA)	$7,937	40%	$4,719	$3,849	72%	$961	6%
Metropolitan State College of Denver	$7,774	49%	$3,943	$4,174	59%	$991	17%
SUNY College–Old Westbury	$7,115	78%	$5,785	$2,561	44%	$0	0%
Mesa State College (CO)	$6,913	56%	$4,749	$3,721	59%	$1,938	8%
Rust College (MS)	$6,533	88%	$3,260	$3,873	89%	$#######	22%
St. Mary's College of Maryland	$6,500	44%	$4,000	$6,000	62%	$4,000	27%
Grove City College (PA)	$5,942	38%	$5,726	$0	50%	$2,369	13%
Excelsior College (NY)	$5,237	N/A	$2,235	$3,501	90%	N/A	N/A
Lane College (TN)	$3,304	95%	$1,730	$1,968	43%	$2,713	2%
United States Naval Academy (MD)	$0	0%	$0	$0	0%	$0	0%

Regional Universities (North)

	Average amount of aid package	% students receiving need-based package	Average need-based grant	Average need-based loan	Average % of need met	Average merit award	% students receiving merit awards
Bentley University (MA)	$29,415	51%	$21,991	$5,324	92%	$15,729	15%
Ithaca College (NY)	$28,273	69%	$18,579	$6,243	90%	$9,551	18%
Loyola University Maryland	$27,300	49%	$19,275	$5,875	97%	$14,190	10%
Fairfield University (CT)	$27,082	55%	$20,623	$4,671	85%	$13,813	6%
Villanova University (PA)	$26,967	48%	$22,101	$4,643	80%	$11,337	7%
Manhattanville College (NY)	$26,779	66%	$17,427	$4,523	96%	$18,753	28%
Alfred University (NY)	$25,152	83%	$18,114	$5,797	85%	$10,412	6%
Canisius College (NY)	$24,558	76%	$18,092	$4,228	81%	$13,797	20%
Medaille College (NY)	$24,000	96%	$8,030	$7,000	55%	$9,000	1%
Rosemont College (PA)	$22,951	93%	$19,749	$3,342	71%	$10,490	6%
La Salle University (PA)	$22,923	78%	$18,743	$4,577	76%	$12,962	17%
University of Scranton (PA)	$22,585	68%	$16,794	$4,590	74%	$9,932	16%
Rochester Institute of Technology (NY)	$22,500	72%	$16,000	$5,500	88%	$8,000	11%
Marywood University (PA)	$22,222	85%	$7,524	$5,211	81%	$10,678	14%
Norwich University (VT)	$22,182	73%	$18,150	$4,725	75%	$12,342	24%
St. Bonaventure University (NY)	$22,000	76%	$15,935	$4,600	79%	$10,307	22%
Emmanuel College (MA)	$21,994	79%	$15,747	$4,975	69%	$11,671	10%
Hood College (MD)	$21,899	82%	$18,444	$4,242	78%	$18,175	18%
Arcadia University (PA)	$21,411	88%	$17,923	$4,409	74%	$12,735	7%
Simmons College (MA)	$21,304	71%	$14,879	$5,140	64%	$8,520	19%
Cabrini College (PA)	$21,251	73%	$8,116	$4,657	71%	$10,454	24%
American International College (MA)	$21,229	88%	$17,033	$4,178	68%	$10,968	10%
La Roche College (PA)	$21,212	74%	$2,292	$2,596	90%	$4,803	7%
Rider University (NJ)	$21,152	70%	$15,320	$4,178	72%	$10,703	20%
Philadelphia University	$21,048	73%	$13,751	$5,277	72%	$5,137	27%
Salve Regina University (RI)	$21,024	72%	$16,603	$4,559	66%	$6,462	11%
Wheelock College (MA)	$20,806	84%	$15,922	$5,097	69%	$10,010	13%
Providence College (RI)	$20,770	55%	$17,013	$4,745	78%	$26,886	6%
Utica College (NY)	$20,690	91%	$7,886	$4,300	68%	$9,954	7%
Wagner College (NY)	$20,457	59%	$16,157	$4,643	73%	$12,072	31%
New York Institute of Technology	$20,439	51%	$6,796	$6,226	N/A	$11,506	10%
St. Joseph College (CT)	$20,293	85%	$15,867	$4,536	71%	$8,651	11%
Wilkes University (PA)	$20,291	83%	$14,948	$4,433	73%	$9,743	12%
St. Joseph's College (ME)	$20,192	83%	$13,447	$6,858	78%	$8,155	16%
Bryant University (RI)	$20,116	67%	$12,555	$4,521	66%	$12,455	12%
Le Moyne College (NY)	$20,065	85%	$15,652	$4,499	76%	$5,414	8%
Mercyhurst College (PA)	$19,803	71%	$10,956	$5,913	62%	$10,475	22%
Gannon University (PA)	$19,802	85%	$15,398	$4,180	79%	$8,170	9%
Quinnipiac University (CT)	$19,785	59%	$14,200	$4,476	65%	$9,748	14%
St. Peter's College (NJ)	$19,780	85%	$17,051	$3,805	68%	$14,670	11%
College of Notre Dame of Maryland	$19,708	84%	$15,921	$4,079	69%	$14,732	9%
Assumption College (MA)	$19,557	75%	$15,334	$4,723	71%	$9,517	19%
University of New Haven (CT)	$19,495	79%	$15,882	$4,129	65%	$9,607	12%
Niagara University (NY)	$19,418	71%	$15,144	$4,675	82%	$9,291	17%
St. Francis University (PA)	$19,405	93%	$16,230	$4,203	78%	$19,763	38%
Suffolk University (MA)	$19,274	61%	$11,574	$4,603	70%	$8,195	9%
St. Joseph's University (PA)	$19,271	50%	$14,947	$5,179	76%	$10,206	40%
Springfield College (MA)	$19,104	82%	$14,054	$4,509	75%	$5,783	11%
Neumann University (PA)	$19,000	90%	$15,000	$5,000	65%	N/A	N/A
Mount St. Mary's University (MD)	$18,996	66%	$14,784	$4,434	72%	$9,586	32%
Sacred Heart University (CT)	$18,782	69%	$14,508	$4,527	65%	$5,541	16%
Western New England College (MA)	$18,654	75%	$13,383	$4,775	67%	$9,625	12%
Nazareth College (NY)	$18,649	81%	$13,536	$4,922	73%	$14,045	17%
King's College (PA)	$18,300	80%	$14,278	$4,830	69%	$11,244	18%
Iona College (NY)	$18,067	75%	$5,153	$2,964	29%	$11,070	21%
Georgian Court University (NJ)	$17,906	86%	$14,262	$4,667	67%	$7,232	7%
Centenary College (NJ)	$17,867	48%	$13,118	$4,493	70%	$7,470	18%
Chestnut Hill College (PA)	$17,839	77%	$13,510	$5	71%	$5,837	1%
St. John Fisher College (NY)	$17,795	82%	$13,219	$4,594	81%	$7,634	16%
College of St. Joseph (VT)	$17,669	93%	$9,982	$4,212	83%	$2,406	5%
Monmouth University (NJ)	$17,601	65%	$12,348	$4,828	68%	$6,689	30%
Roberts Wesleyan College (NY)	$17,513	89%	$11,890	$5,450	69%	$4,707	9%
Emerson College (MA)	$17,364	56%	$15,028	$4,509	73%	$12,327	5%
DeSales University (PA)	$17,336	74%	$13,352	$4,287	68%	$8,494	15%
Manhattan College (NY)	$16,839	64%	$7,690	$4,369	67%	$8,126	33%
Misericordia University (PA)	$16,738	83%	$12,018	$8,612	71%	$6,835	9%
Robert Morris University (PA)	$16,548	77%	$10,397	$5,774	71%	$7,763	15%
Dowling College (NY)	$16,426	72%	$9,144	$4,406	94%	$5,478	7%
Alvernia University (PA)	$16,156	88%	$10,774	$5,593	66%	$6,749	8%
Holy Family University (PA)	$16,005	82%	$11,705	$4,351	71%	$8,093	8%
Dominican College (NY)	$15,918	91%	$10,619	$4,360	75%	$6,147	7%

Where the money is: Schools that award the most need–based aid

Regional Universities (North), continued

	Average amount of aid package	% students receiving need-based package	Average need-based grant	Average need-based loan	Average % of need met	Average merit award	% students receiving merit awards
D'Youville College (NY)	$15,796	91%	$10,534	$5,988	63%	$6,656	5%
Johnson and Wales University (RI)	$15,772	68%	$7,226	$5,297	68%	$4,618	17%
Point Park University (PA)	$15,767	81%	$10,080	$5,159	65%	$6,170	15%
Chatham University (PA)	$15,515	76%	$8,645	$9,265	66%	$13,107	4%
Richard Stockton College of New Jersey	$15,435	66%	$8,353	$4,569	70%	$6,019	20%
Marist College (NY)	$15,387	61%	$11,209	$5,931	62%	$7,101	25%
Lesley University (MA)	$15,355	71%	$14,014	$4,028	70%	$8,885	18%
William Paterson University of New Jersey	$14,598	65%	$8,850	$4,405	N/A	$6,271	5%
University of Maryland–Eastern Shore	$14,500	81%	$7,150	$4,950	84%	$2,875	6%
Rivier College (NH)	$14,344	82%	$10,255	$4,362	60%	$4,849	14%
Gwynedd-Mercy College (PA)	$14,187	74%	$11,605	$6,441	72%	$15,592	20%
Philadelphia Biblical University	$14,138	84%	$10,131	$4,955	66%	$6,421	5%
SUNY College–Potsdam	$14,073	65%	$5,956	$4,360	71%	$11,677	6%
University of Massachusetts–Dartmouth	$13,949	65%	$6,461	$7,223	90%	$2,251	17%
Mount St. Mary College (NY)	$13,804	77%	$10,089	$4,171	58%	$7,667	12%
University of Southern Maine	$13,618	82%	$5,518	$7,613	69%	$3,474	4%
Waynesburg University (PA)	$12,864	69%	$10,051	$3,877	76%	$7,094	7%
Mercy College (NY)	$12,855	82%	$8,544	$4,113	56%	$3,827	2%
Molloy College (NY)	$12,545	86%	$8,590	$5,598	53%	$6,352	7%
Rutgers, the State University of New Jersey–Camden	$12,413	72%	$10,049	$4,316	64%	$5,544	4%
Touro College (NY)	$12,200	98%	$3,600	$3,500	90%	$1,800	25%
Ramapo College of New Jersey	$12,053	45%	$10,678	$4,563	69%	$12,174	5%
St. Thomas Aquinas College (NY)	$11,924	64%	$9,369	$4,295	60%	$6,044	13%
Bloomsburg University of Pennsylvania	$11,899	80%	$5,822	$4,162	72%	$1,971	2%
SUNY College–Cortland	$11,858	59%	$4,673	$4,183	71%	$8,868	18%
SUNY College–Oneonta	$11,712	56%	$5,001	$4,486	63%	$2,000	19%
Delaware State University	$11,526	84%	$3,642	$3,494	70%	$9,784	12%
Husson University (ME)	$11,462	85%	$7,963	$4,076	73%	$3,687	6%
SUNY–Plattsburgh	$11,140	59%	$5,723	$6,897	90%	$6,268	28%
SUNY–Oswego	$10,744	64%	$4,642	$6,146	84%	$7,290	17%
Lincoln University (PA)	$10,678	87%	$5,249	$3,791	49%	$2,793	2%
CUNY–John Jay College of Criminal Justice	$10,150	77%	$3,175	$3,500	85%	$0	0%
College of New Jersey	$10,088	47%	N/A	$4,326	52%	$4,777	18%
CUNY–City College	$10,085	87%	$6,672	$3,774	81%	$2,630	4%
Kean University (NJ)	$9,810	62%	$7,731	$4,454	56%	$2,703	1%
Worcester State College (MA)	$9,679	49%	$4,391	$2,521	85%	$0	0%
College at Brockport–SUNY	$9,606	70%	$5,045	$4,605	74%	$4,245	3%
Buffalo State College–SUNY	$9,450	88%	$4,150	$3,902	66%	$2,200	4%
Plymouth State University (NH)	$9,403	60%	$5,042	$4,225	62%	$2,567	8%
Towson University (MD)	$9,182	45%	$7,429	$4,129	67%	$5,229	8%
Montclair State University (NJ)	$9,153	63%	$3,573	$4,154	60%	$6,473	2%
California University of Pennsylvania	$9,093	70%	$5,070	$3,860	92%	$2,747	13%
SUNY–New Paltz	$9,023	51%	$4,774	$4,287	59%	$1,591	1%
Frostburg State University (MD)	$8,927	56%	$6,538	$3,794	71%	$2,995	10%
College of St. Rose (NY)	$8,897	97%	$3,453	$2,346	8%	$2,104	9%
Rowan University (NJ)	$8,793	56%	$8,507	$4,303	81%	$3,927	8%
Fitchburg State College (MA)	$8,645	54%	$4,336	$3,679	93%	$1,292	2%
Keene State College (NH)	$8,603	52%	$5,091	$4,085	68%	$3,026	7%
New Jersey City University	$8,440	72%	$6,727	$4,280	59%	$4,982	1%
Lock Haven University of Pennsylvania	$8,394	72%	$6,304	$4,172	75%	$1,076	5%
Rhode Island College	$8,365	56%	$5,360	$3,759	75%	$1,819	2%
Southern Connecticut State University	$8,355	55%	$5,784	$3,731	79%	$3,677	4%
Slippery Rock University of Pennsylvania	$8,260	67%	$3,563	$3,863	67%	$7,241	18%
Clarion University of Pennsylvania	$8,210	71%	$5,943	$4,003	72%	$2,666	5%
Cambridge College (MA)	$8,184	81%	$5,308	$4,659	31%	$0	0%
Millersville University of Pennsylvania	$8,124	57%	$5,447	$4,099	77%	$3,002	2%
SUNY–Fredonia	$8,119	66%	$4,048	$4,306	65%	$2,051	7%
Bowie State University (MD)	$8,114	79%	$6,319	$4,001	48%	$159	2%
Western Connecticut State University	$8,090	68%	N/A	N/A	54%	$2,740	1%
SUNY–Geneseo	$8,041	44%	$4,018	$4,466	73%	$2,068	10%
Eastern Connecticut State University	$8,000	50%	$6,000	$4,273	56%	$3,470	0%
Westfield State College (MA)	$7,812	53%	$5,058	$3,955	73%	$4,695	1%
Goddard College (VT)	$7,791	61%	$4,590	$4,485	37%	$0	0%
Shippensburg University of Pennsylvania	$7,738	55%	$5,705	$3,844	69%	$3,969	8%
Framingham State College (MA)	$7,715	54%	$4,584	$4,196	81%	$2,290	2%
West Chester University of Pennsylvania	$7,648	53%	$5,289	$4,203	71%	$3,601	2%
Bridgewater State College (MA)	$7,621	61%	$4,505	$4,363	N/A	$6,492	1%
CUNY–College of Staten Island	$7,520	57%	$6,695	$4,143	60%	$1,545	5%
CUNY–Queens College	$7,500	78%	$4,800	$4,900	95%	$8,300	1%
Edinboro University of Pennsylvania	$7,473	75%	$3,080	$3,622	63%	$2,100	6%

	Average amount of aid package	% students receiving need-based package	Average need-based grant	Average need-based loan	Average % of need met	Average merit award	% students receiving merit awards
Kutztown University of Pennsylvania	$7,379	57%	$4,698	$4,048	58%	$2,071	4%
Salisbury University (MD)	$7,027	40%	$5,256	$3,764	60%	$2,225	8%
University of Maryland–University College	$6,795	59%	$3,978	$4,200	23%	N/A	N/A
Central Connecticut State University	$6,601	56%	$3,501	$3,988	63%	$2,781	1%
CUNY–Baruch College	$6,598	65%	$4,958	$5,000	76%	$4,600	1%
CUNY–Brooklyn College	$6,100	74%	$3,600	$3,500	99%	$1,700	11%
East Stroudsburg University of Pennsylvania	$5,933	43%	$4,312	$4,106	83%	$10,063	18%
CUNY–Hunter College	$5,092	55%	$4,141	$3,179	78%	$2,368	7%
CUNY–Lehman College	$4,002	81%	$1,455	$2,006	66%	$3,243	1%
Mansfield University of Pennsylvania	$2,694	85%	$2,404	$3,309	81%	$594	0%

Regional Universities (South)

	Average amount of aid package	% students receiving need-based package	Average need-based grant	Average need-based loan	Average % of need met	Average merit award	% students receiving merit awards
Rollins College (FL)	$33,763	47%	$28,226	$4,380	86%	$15,291	16%
Campbell University (NC)	$31,629	79%	$6,504	$3,998	80%	$4,961	25%
Mercer University (GA)	$30,024	71%	$19,558	$8,304	88%	$19,395	28%
Stetson University (FL)	$27,435	64%	$20,704	$4,877	81%	$12,241	28%
Loyola University New Orleans	$24,349	64%	$14,571	$4,390	82%	$15,906	34%
Spring Hill College (AL)	$23,948	70%	$17,473	$4,732	82%	$13,699	28%
Bellarmine University (KY)	$23,927	74%	$15,752	$4,112	77%	$16,198	24%
Converse College (SC)	$22,193	83%	$18,754	$4,989	82%	$13,251	16%
Wheeling Jesuit University (WV)	$21,466	80%	$6,559	$4,767	86%	$10,869	20%
Lynn University (FL)	$20,853	42%	$13,761	$5,643	60%	$11,381	22%
Palm Beach Atlantic University (FL)	$20,405	75%	$5,521	$4,242	63%	$5,946	9%
Lynchburg College (VA)	$20,193	69%	$16,607	$3,526	78%	$9,958	27%
Christian Brothers University (TN)	$19,826	75%	$7,004	$4,404	85%	$10,240	19%
Mary Baldwin College (VA)	$19,749	81%	$15,304	$4,885	77%	$10,768	6%
Union University (TN)	$19,643	72%	$5,479	$4,453	69%	$7,432	11%
Union College (KY)	$19,623	86%	$12,442	$7,501	80%	$10,421	8%
Jacksonville University (FL)	$19,580	71%	$15,432	$4,433	61%	$8,925	25%
Elon University (NC)	$18,939	34%	$12,840	$4,907	82%	$5,442	23%
Brenau University (GA)	$18,874	73%	$14,244	$4,319	73%	$10,492	18%
Gardner-Webb University (NC)	$17,438	52%	$8,412	$4,266	71%	$6,860	12%
Piedmont College (GA)	$16,890	65%	$2,696	$4,465	59%	$9,166	9%
Queens University of Charlotte (NC)	$16,810	65%	$12,901	$3,961	71%	$8,229	22%
Xavier University of Louisiana	$16,797	86%	$6,273	$4,811	14%	$8,511	3%
Grambling State University (LA)	$16,539	80%	$5,151	$3,397	73%	$2,501	3%
St. Leo University (FL)	$16,532	72%	$11,571	$4,111	76%	$7,217	2%
Lipscomb University (TN)	$16,409	62%	$6,819	$4,975	62%	$6,645	17%
Lincoln Memorial University (TN)	$16,166	86%	$11,463	$2,625	72%	$1,793	2%
Mississippi College	$16,013	62%	$9,484	$7,582	78%	$10,104	35%
University of Tampa (FL)	$16,003	55%	$5,644	$4,315	83%	$5,443	33%
Marymount University (VA)	$15,574	60%	$6,427	$4,337	67%	$9,553	20%
Shenandoah University (VA)	$15,545	67%	$5,000	$4,500	92%	$4,000	7%
The Citadel (SC)	$15,434	52%	$14,670	$4,171	71%	$15,830	7%
Embry-Riddle Aeronautical University (FL)	$15,246	61%	$9,085	$4,672	0%	$0	0%
William Carey University (MS)	$15,000	90%	$8,000	$7,000	90%	$7,400	13%
Thomas More College (KY)	$14,988	70%	$12,017	$4,073	70%	$12,022	15%
Belhaven University (MS)	$14,653	72%	$10,710	$4,342	61%	$6,318	10%
Cumberland University (TN)	$14,386	81%	$6,673	$4,068	61%	$4,636	50%
Freed-Hardeman University (TN)	$13,942	79%	$10,139	$4,188	66%	$6,191	17%
University of Mobile (AL)	$12,998	72%	$8,765	$5,505	59%	$5,830	7%
College of Charleston (SC)	$12,882	42%	$3,173	$4,008	63%	$11,423	12%
Western Kentucky University	$12,057	63%	$5,349	$3,826	31%	$5,052	8%
Belmont University (TN)	$11,966	52%	$5,881	$4,394	80%	$6,326	13%
Southern Wesleyan University (SC)	$11,837	46%	$9,305	$3,772	69%	$7,453	2%
University of Tennessee–Martin	$11,491	70%	$5,687	$3,886	78%	$5,229	20%
Harding University (AR)	$11,146	57%	$7,199	$4,520	68%	$5,370	11%
Henderson State University (AR)	$10,648	74%	N/A	$3,984	83%	$9,096	3%
Eastern Kentucky University	$10,183	63%	$5,949	$3,652	83%	$5,126	12%
Longwood University (VA)	$10,118	42%	$5,380	$5,504	85%	$3,941	6%
Winthrop University (SC)	$10,109	68%	$7,768	$4,281	59%	$7,376	13%
Lee University (TN)	$10,108	64%	$7,803	$4,189	58%	$6,235	17%
Appalachian State University (NC)	$9,991	41%	$6,611	$5,494	88%	$2,837	8%
Arkansas State University–Jonesboro	$9,950	73%	$5,875	$4,600	50%	$5,650	6%

Where the money is: Schools that award the most need-based aid

Regional Universities (South), continued

	Average amount of aid package	% students receiving need-based package	Average need-based grant	Average need-based loan	Average % of need met	Average merit award	% students receiving merit awards
University of Tennessee–Chattanooga	$9,853	59%	$4,320	$4,310	83%	$2,720	13%
University of Mary Washington (VA)	$9,800	27%	$6,200	$4,200	56%	$1,750	11%
Fayetteville State University (NC)	$9,796	83%	$5,971	$4,293	77%	$668	3%
Life University (GA)	$9,750	75%	$4,825	$500	1%	$1,000	0%
Marshall University (WV)	$9,498	56%	$6,177	$6,871	58%	$6,063	16%
Alcorn State University (MS)	$9,494	93%	$3,529	$4,033	90%	$2,470	21%
Morehead State University (KY)	$9,447	70%	$5,224	$3,657	74%	$6,526	13%
Radford University (VA)	$9,394	44%	$7,661	$3,694	83%	$3,895	2%
University of North Carolina–Pembroke	$9,268	73%	$6,566	$3,647	77%	$1,050	0%
Hodges University (FL)	$9,200	74%	$4,600	$4,300	74%	$260	4%
University of North Carolina–Wilmington	$9,078	45%	$6,030	$3,547	84%	$2,272	3%
Western Carolina University (NC)	$8,681	56%	$6,722	$4,390	81%	$1,799	5%
Alabama Agricultural and Mechanical University	$8,642	78%	$6,243	$4,265	14%	$3,665	1%
Valdosta State University (GA)	$8,550	63%	$6,092	$3,948	58%	$1,653	1%
University of Montevallo (AL)	$8,531	52%	$5,979	$3,880	67%	$5,370	17%
Austin Peay State University (TN)	$8,513	72%	$4,782	$4,422	N/A	$4,655	10%
Mississippi University for Women	$8,408	74%	$5,201	$4,494	63%	$4,732	16%
North Georgia College and State University	$8,400	38%	$2,000	$5,500	79%	$1,500	4%
University of West Georgia	$8,224	60%	$5,804	$3,980	60%	$1,532	3%
Columbus State University (GA)	$8,161	60%	$4,804	$3,993	72%	$1,514	3%
Tennessee Technological University	$7,954	55%	$4,182	$1,804	82%	$5,647	29%
James Madison University (VA)	$7,885	34%	$7,055	$4,189	51%	$3,056	1%
Armstrong Atlantic State University (GA)	$7,750	34%	$4,000	$4,500	82%	$3,000	19%
Georgia Southwestern State University	$7,655	66%	$4,323	$3,914	56%	$1,886	6%
Arkansas Tech University	$7,638	59%	$3,983	$3,743	75%	$6,920	17%
Georgia College & State University	$7,514	43%	$4,104	$4,057	34%	$1,197	1%
Nicholls State University (LA)	$7,415	46%	$4,482	$3,532	90%	$2,811	6%
Florida Gulf Coast University	$7,231	33%	$4,430	$5,272	62%	$3,869	4%
Mountain State University (WV)	$7,033	50%	$4,211	$4,592	48%	$4,214	0%
Northwestern State University of Louisiana	$6,741	60%	$4,672	$6,517	54%	$4,874	27%
Jacksonville State University (AL)	$6,563	78%	$3,878	$3,889	N/A	N/A	N/A
Murray State University (KY)	$5,825	56%	$2,738	$2,446	N/A	$2,306	35%
University of North Alabama	$4,993	43%	$3,819	$2,818	65%	$2,781	25%
Hampton University (VA)	$4,545	41%	$3,349	$3,214	41%	$8,442	3%
Troy University (AL)	$4,485	71%	N/A	$4,531	N/A	$3,927	12%
Fort Valley State University (GA)	$4,400	84%	N/A	N/A	82%	$1,776	0%
Kennesaw State University (GA)	$3,970	54%	$2,321	$2,115	24%	$1,087	19%
Southern Polytechnic State University (GA)	$3,678	50%	$3,739	$4,824	78%	$8,269	0%
University of North Florida	$1,822	45%	$1,500	$1,793	90%	$1,210	13%

Regional Universities (Midwest)

	Average amount of aid package	% students receiving need-based package	Average need-based grant	Average need-based loan	Average % of need met	Average merit award	% students receiving merit awards
St. Catherine University (MN)	$26,870	85%	$10,925	$4,610	83%	$7,170	6%
University of Detroit Mercy	$25,795	82%	$21,741	$3,636	86%	$10,224	12%
Rockhurst University (MO)	$25,772	77%	$8,021	$3,739	100%	$12,904	10%
Creighton University (NE)	$25,003	50%	$19,497	$6,649	91%	$11,594	27%
Capital University (OH)	$23,895	80%	$4,405	$5,242	21%	$12,963	19%
Ashland University (OH)	$23,254	82%	$15,366	$4,717	90%	$8,168	10%
John Carroll University (OH)	$23,033	55%	$15,809	$4,296	81%	$9,983	18%
Benedictine College (KS)	$22,755	73%	$12,418	$3,335	75%	$7,981	12%
Webster University (MO)	$22,542	68%	$7,033	$4,475	N/A	$8,343	17%
University of Evansville (IN)	$22,537	72%	$19,392	$4,615	83%	$12,866	21%
Hamline University (MN)	$22,477	79%	$16,092	$4,736	81%	$10,309	15%
Spring Arbor University (MI)	$22,445	86%	$12,196	$4,406	91%	$3,374	0%
College of St. Scholastica (MN)	$21,625	78%	$7,011	$4,381	77%	$10,496	8%
Aquinas College (MI)	$21,533	82%	$19,287	$2,216	88%	$11,267	21%
Concordia University Wisconsin	$21,364	81%	$10,948	$5,939	73%	$8,308	15%
Elmhurst College (IL)	$21,073	69%	$17,050	$4,575	78%	$10,816	6%
Valparaiso University (IN)	$21,000	72%	$15,700	$5,000	80%	$9,200	22%
Butler University (IN)	$20,922	66%	$15,800	$5,387	N/A	$11,674	22%
Drake University (IA)	$20,813	57%	$13,960	$4,951	82%	$10,664	36%
Anderson University (IN)	$20,553	81%	$13,414	$1,651	93%	$9,500	18%
Bethel University (MN)	$20,421	73%	$14,570	$4,601	79%	$5,888	23%

	Average amount of aid package	% students receiving need-based package	Average need-based grant	Average need-based loan	Average % of need met	Average merit award	% students receiving merit awards
St. Xavier University (IL)	$19,878	84%	$14,015	$4,626	80%	$9,765	15%
North Central College (IL)	$19,870	76%	$15,023	$4,531	76%	$10,390	20%
Baldwin-Wallace College (OH)	$19,838	80%	$13,687	$4,827	85%	$10,050	17%
Graceland University (IA)	$19,566	70%	$14,710	$4,891	80%	$10,029	23%
Marian University (WI)	$19,560	84%	$10,669	$6,758	91%	$4,931	11%
Mount Marty College (SD)	$18,937	90%	$7,508	$5,168	89%	$14,147	8%
Roosevelt University (IL)	$18,843	78%	$8,305	$7,600	75%	$5,330	15%
Lawrence Technological University (MI)	$18,772	65%	$10,957	$7,796	69%	$9,000	15%
Augsburg College (MN)	$18,744	82%	$14,459	$4,695	63%	$7,532	5%
Cornerstone University (MI)	$18,623	84%	$11,526	$4,352	85%	$6,113	15%
Southwestern College (KS)	$18,500	80%	$10,894	$5,630	88%	$7,914	18%
Lewis University (IL)	$18,419	72%	$8,954	$4,322	84%	$7,538	9%
Dominican University (IL)	$18,277	83%	$14,403	$4,132	74%	$7,912	12%
University of Findlay (OH)	$18,215	72%	$11,837	$4,755	67%	$11,300	11%
University of St. Francis (IL)	$18,171	81%	$7,816	$4,538	72%	$6,748	17%
Maryville University of St. Louis (MO)	$17,959	78%	$10,244	$4,021	70%	$6,609	19%
Muskingum University (OH)	$17,950	82%	$14,040	$4,055	80%	$5,114	15%
Olivet Nazarene University (IL)	$17,812	76%	$13,112	$4,419	82%	$10,134	24%
Xavier University (OH)	$17,748	60%	$12,753	$4,593	70%	$10,906	30%
Rockford College (IL)	$17,247	90%	$12,354	$4,706	68%	$8,620	9%
Carroll University (WI)	$17,231	80%	$12,726	$3,170	80%	$9,370	22%
Concordia University Chicago (IL)	$17,219	84%	$13,364	$4,077	76%	$10,057	15%
Concordia University–St. Paul (MN)	$17,022	71%	$13,962	$4,888	67%	$6,867	9%
Heidelberg University (OH)	$16,911	71%	$11,834	$4,602	79%	$8,359	10%
St. Ambrose University (IA)	$16,770	74%	$10,732	$4,713	26%	$7,158	23%
Benedictine University (IL)	$16,602	68%	$7,641	$4,394	N/A	$8,536	44%
Silver Lake College (WI)	$16,479	85%	$9,146	$4,388	66%	$6,602	5%
Edgewood College (WI)	$16,399	76%	$10,575	$5,296	53%	$3,910	15%
Walsh University (OH)	$16,350	70%	$6,334	$4,701	86%	$6,334	14%
Bradley University (IL)	$16,201	71%	$12,618	$4,608	69%	$7,764	28%
College of Mount St. Joseph (OH)	$16,176	82%	$12,251	$4,518	75%	$8,166	13%
Mount Mary College (WI)	$16,132	85%	$11,547	$4,493	68%	$5,355	13%
Malone University (OH)	$15,984	79%	$12,173	$4,520	72%	$6,959	10%
Southern Illinois University–Edwardsville	$15,749	63%	$9,606	$10,045	46%	$7,261	4%
Indiana Wesleyan University	$15,739	71%	$12,529	$4,203	74%	$5,450	20%
Ferris State University (MI)	$15,531	71%	$4,830	$4,292	84%	$3,690	10%
University of Indianapolis	$15,526	72%	$8,000	$4,174	70%	$7,138	45%
William Woods University (MO)	$14,901	70%	$11,340	$3,751	74%	$7,178	29%
Ursuline College (OH)	$14,705	87%	$10,414	$5,243	63%	$5,034	5%
Newman University (KS)	$14,402	81%	$4,872	$4,056	62%	$5,673	4%
St. Cloud State University (MN)	$14,317	44%	$4,801	$6,776	69%	$2,021	2%
Alverno College (WI)	$14,191	83%	$10,651	$4,088	N/A	$5,195	12%
Tiffin University (OH)	$13,569	90%	$5,747	$3,986	5%	$6,870	4%
Avila University (MO)	$13,105	68%	$7,852	$5,650	52%	$8,510	30%
Franciscan University of Steubenville (OH)	$12,549	68%	$8,177	$4,311	60%	$4,094	12%
Columbia College (MO)	$11,935	54%	$5,213	$3,956	54%	$7,566	12%
University of Rio Grande (OH)	$11,695	62%	N/A	$1,875	62%	$0	0%
Calumet College of St. Joseph (IN)	$11,510	77%	$7,300	$3,591	72%	$2,400	0%
University of Minnesota–Duluth	$11,087	58%	$6,432	$5,705	76%	$2,752	10%
Fontbonne University (MO)	$10,972	86%	$4,731	$3,430	74%	$6,584	7%
University of Illinois–Springfield	$10,929	66%	$7,928	$4,204	74%	$3,903	12%
Truman State University (MO)	$9,996	48%	$3,820	$3,516	83%	$2,332	17%
Pittsburg State University (KS)	$9,900	58%	$4,525	$3,889	75%	$2,450	8%
University of Nebraska–Kearney	$9,443	60%	$5,582	$3,512	80%	$2,200	12%
University of Central Missouri	$9,426	34%	$3,361	$4,543	90%	$8,345	14%
University of Wisconsin–Stout	$9,291	56%	$5,346	$4,207	90%	$1,707	3%
Western Illinois University	$9,261	65%	$7,479	$4,159	61%	$3,081	5%
Bemidji State University (MN)	$9,118	64%	$5,408	$3,726	72%	$9,121	16%
University of Wisconsin–River Falls	$9,099	56%	$1,934	$3,645	84%	$1,151	1%
Eastern Illinois University	$8,912	50%	$3,632	$4,136	67%	$3,934	4%
Madonna University (MI)	$8,902	N/A	$5,608	$4,229	40%	$3,827	N/A
Washburn University (KS)	$8,748	62%	$4,778	$4,295	39%	$1,888	15%
University of Wisconsin–Eau Claire	$8,587	47%	$5,368	$4,604	90%	$1,834	7%
Southwest Minnesota State University	$8,541	65%	$5,128	$3,946	57%	$349	15%
University of Michigan–Dearborn	$8,515	56%	$4,035	$4,330	33%	$3,256	44%
Upper Iowa University	$8,513	77%	$6,761	$3,991	52%	$9,184	4%
Grand Valley State University (MI)	$8,485	61%	$5,572	$4,542	61%	$3,384	8%
Southeast Missouri State University	$8,384	58%	$5,269	$3,836	70%	$4,227	15%
Northeastern Illinois University	$8,362	58%	$7,038	$4,477	48%	$3,063	3%
Youngstown State University (OH)	$8,308	75%	$5,546	$3,744	29%	$2,605	6%

Where the money is: Schools that award the most need–based aid

Regional Universities (Midwest), continued

	Average amount of aid package	% students receiving need-based package	Average need-based grant	Average need-based loan	Average % of need met	Average merit award	% students receiving merit awards
University of Wisconsin–Stevens Point	$8,284	54%	$6,568	$4,682	76%	$2,072	6%
University of Northern Iowa	$8,243	57%	$4,691	$4,261	65%	$2,959	14%
Indiana University Northwest	$8,238	67%	$6,334	$3,727	90%	$3,260	5%
Eastern Michigan University	$8,219	63%	$4,506	$4,310	54%	$4,037	10%
University of Southern Indiana	$8,198	60%	$4,433	$3,494	78%	$2,730	10%
Minnesota State University–Moorhead	$8,172	55%	$4,001	$4,307	N/A	N/A	N/A
Minnesota State University–Mankato	$8,130	52%	$5,236	$3,806	86%	$2,273	4%
Missouri State University	$8,018	56%	$5,132	$3,997	67%	$4,266	11%
Drury University (MO)	$7,985	95%	$6,990	$5,500	86%	$3,585	14%
Northern Michigan University	$7,979	57%	$4,624	$3,801	64%	$2,755	5%
Emporia State University (KS)	$7,960	60%	$5,258	$5,765	88%	$1,335	14%
University of Wisconsin–Whitewater	$7,957	53%	$5,220	$3,984	73%	$1,424	4%
Indiana University–South Bend	$7,902	68%	$6,266	$3,634	93%	$3,361	4%
Indiana University Southeast	$7,611	62%	$6,010	$3,793	92%	$1,482	5%
Minot State University (ND)	$7,187	54%	$3,988	$3,990	64%	$1,050	28%
Wayne State College (NE)	$6,771	67%	$3,797	$3,747	73%	$2,805	12%
Winona State University (MN)	$6,728	52%	$4,078	$4,045	44%	$2,557	12%
Purdue University–Calumet (IN)	$6,632	56%	$4,989	$3,355	12%	$2,370	5%
University of Wisconsin–La Crosse	$6,397	40%	$5,523	$3,817	81%	$1,524	2%
Lindenwood University (MO)	$5,855	64%	$3,662	$1,984	91%	$4,685	15%
University of Wisconsin–Oshkosh	$5,350	48%	$2,200	$3,750	33%	$390	5%
University of Nebraska–Omaha	$2,458	45%	$2,075	$3,251	N/A	$2,261	5%

Regional Universities (West)

	Average amount of aid package	% students receiving need-based package	Average need-based grant	Average need-based loan	Average % of need met	Average merit award	% students receiving merit awards
Mills College (CA)	$30,185	84%	$23,193	$6,515	85%	$14,955	8%
Mount St. Mary's College (CA)	$30,185	90%	N/A	N/A	93%	$9,821	3%
Loyola Marymount University (CA)	$29,477	57%	$19,354	$5,517	75%	$10,954	12%
Seattle University	$28,428	63%	$16,432	$4,766	77%	$5,402	0%
University of Redlands (CA)	$28,324	76%	$23,039	$6,122	66%	$12,888	12%
Pacific Lutheran University (WA)	$27,906	71%	$15,898	$9,067	86%	$11,635	24%
Chapman University (CA)	$27,771	62%	$24,076	$4,511	100%	$17,256	17%
Naropa University (CO)	$25,123	66%	$15,279	$9,226	88%	$0	0%
St. Mary's College of California	$25,104	76%	$21,692	$4,789	75%	$12,574	4%
University of Portland (OR)	$25,029	64%	$16,705	$4,824	83%	$11,193	26%
Seattle Pacific University	$24,734	68%	$20,131	$5,108	83%	$13,592	25%
Notre Dame de Namur University (CA)	$24,693	75%	$19,236	$4,980	70%	N/A	N/A
Concordia University (CA)	$24,529	67%	$12,705	$4,382	62%	$7,043	20%
Santa Clara University (CA)	$23,774	38%	$18,666	$4,461	67%	$11,557	26%
Trinity University (TX)	$23,645	39%	$16,619	$6,658	90%	$12,112	44%
Whitworth University (WA)	$23,442	71%	$16,353	$4,818	81%	$10,424	22%
Gonzaga University (WA)	$22,922	58%	$16,522	$5,312	83%	$10,029	37%
California Lutheran University	$22,500	64%	$16,300	$3,700	84%	$10,900	35%
Our Lady of the Lake University (TX)	$22,500	100%	$3,143	$3,300	82%	$17,180	4%
Dominican University of California	$21,904	77%	$17,736	$4,667	54%	$10,746	6%
University of Dallas	$20,940	62%	$16,235	$5,110	73%	$11,400	34%
Holy Names University (CA)	$20,413	92%	$17,912	$4,822	53%	$800	4%
St. Mary's University of San Antonio (TX)	$20,138	79%	$14,206	$6,124	76%	$7,292	25%
St. Edward's University (TX)	$20,039	64%	$11,815	$4,360	67%	$8,167	7%
Woodbury University (CA)	$19,622	88%	$15,051	$4,988	55%	$6,549	9%
Point Loma Nazarene University (CA)	$18,695	64%	$13,258	$5,785	68%	$6,256	19%
Westminster College (UT)	$18,640	60%	$13,657	$4,980	78%	$10,995	33%
St. Martin's University (WA)	$18,279	81%	$13,848	$3,883	77%	$6,990	17%
Oklahoma City University	$18,004	48%	$12,968	$4,862	78%	$9,942	17%
Houston Baptist University	$17,712	68%	$7,266	$1,263	83%	$3,749	5%
Hardin-Simmons University (TX)	$16,930	71%	$6,349	$4,113	69%	$6,983	28%
Northwest Nazarene University (ID)	$16,918	75%	$8,356	$3,436	84%	$5,566	24%
University of the Incarnate Word (TX)	$15,618	87%	$10,754	$4,576	64%	$6,908	5%
University of Mary Hardin-Baylor (TX)	$15,535	83%	$7,863	$4,203	62%	$4,686	9%
Oklahoma Christian University	$15,488	65%	$2,445	$3,889	55%	$3,935	22%
Regis University (CO)	$15,333	60%	$10,756	$2,226	54%	$10,411	24%
Fresno Pacific University (CA)	$15,215	72%	$8,667	$4,616	58%	N/A	N/A
University of St. Thomas (TX)	$15,107	59%	$11,859	$4,684	65%	$7,987	24%

	Average amount of aid package	% students receiving need-based package	Average need-based grant	Average need-based loan	Average % of need met	Average merit award	% students receiving merit awards
Alaska Pacific University	$15,100	77%	$7,900	$4,570	92%	$9,570	3%
Hope International University (CA)	$14,609	38%	$9,344	$5,005	39%	$7,477	1%
Hawaii Pacific University	$14,529	46%	$2,016	$6,501	77%	$4,402	52%
Abilene Christian University (TX)	$13,841	67%	$10,152	$4,228	67%	$6,690	14%
Texas State University–San Marcos	$13,634	52%	$6,374	$4,438	65%	$2,611	2%
Dallas Baptist University	$13,557	61%	$3,624	$3,991	64%	$7,088	18%
Prescott College (AZ)	$13,099	63%	$9,075	$4,589	47%	$5,467	22%
Lubbock Christian University (TX)	$13,010	73%	$9,089	$4,124	67%	$3,839	15%
California State University–Long Beach	$12,627	61%	$5,697	$3,455	83%	$2,247	6%
California State University–Chico	$12,447	46%	$8,292	$4,475	90%	$1,978	4%
California State University–Fullerton	$12,421	53%	$7,123	$4,124	51%	$6,277	8%
San Jose State University (CA)	$12,240	53%	$6,034	$5,280	85%	$3,405	1%
Texas Southern University	$12,213	89%	$5,822	$8,022	73%	$5,281	14%
Wayland Baptist University (TX)	$11,850	71%	$9,044	$3,665	73%	$7,202	20%
Marylhurst University (OR)	$11,390	49%	$8,638	$4,450	49%	$4,737	4%
California State University–Los Angeles	$11,144	75%	$8,862	$5,366	67%	$3,884	1%
Eastern Washington University	$11,043	55%	$5,875	$3,217	71%	$2,908	5%
Western Washington University	$11,001	41%	$7,788	$4,326	85%	$1,510	2%
California State University–Fresno	$10,984	62%	N/A	$4,086	72%	$3,310	1%
Humboldt State University (CA)	$10,984	59%	$8,560	$4,248	71%	$2,011	3%
California State Polytechnic University–Pomona	$10,874	51%	$8,815	$3,929	83%	$1,462	0%
Lamar University (TX)	$10,723	54%	N/A	N/A	54%	N/A	N/A
LeTourneau University (TX)	$10,706	77%	$8,618	$5,206	43%	$5,862	6%
San Francisco State University	$10,668	55%	$8,635	$3,245	64%	$2,799	1%
Evergreen State College (WA)	$10,554	56%	$7,978	$3,952	79%	$4,128	1%
New Mexico Institute of Mining and Technology	$10,397	44%	$6,463	$5,089	89%	$5,226	38%
California State University–San Bernardino	$10,373	71%	$7,810	$3,569	64%	$3,188	0%
California State University–Stanislaus	$10,247	81%	$6,103	$5,402	56%	$4,238	1%
Cameron University (OK)	$10,100	56%	$3,350	$4,500	82%	$500	11%
University of Alaska–Anchorage	$10,055	44%	$4,088	$4,042	73%	$2,932	3%
California State University–East Bay	$10,000	49%	$8,594	$7,120	53%	N/A	N/A
Sonoma State University (CA)	$9,782	41%	$8,889	$4,251	70%	$1,610	2%
Eastern Oregon University	$9,776	74%	$6,065	$3,443	57%	$852	1%
Southeastern Oklahoma State University	$9,675	70%	$1,575	$1,730	18%	$860	5%
Texas A&M University–Corpus Christi	$9,277	53%	$5,981	$4,280	60%	$2,173	3%
Texas A&M International University	$9,248	85%	$5,740	$4,014	70%	$3,450	4%
Central Washington University	$8,993	52%	$6,201	$4,052	70%	$710	0%
Montana State University–Billings	$8,806	59%	$4,392	$3,500	68%	$2,071	3%
California Polytechnic State University–San Luis Obispo	$8,687	31%	$2,390	$3,696	63%	$2,498	4%
University of Texas–Brownsville	$8,685	81%	$7,045	$3,845	59%	$3,577	2%
Northeastern State University (OK)	$8,680	57%	$5,245	$3,825	71%	$3,374	3%
Western New Mexico University	$8,662	76%	$4,412	$3,863	75%	$4,019	5%
California Baptist University	$8,651	69%	$4,677	$2,298	58%	$3,656	16%
Western Oregon University	$8,626	75%	$6,271	$3,969	67%	$2,159	7%
Midwestern State University (TX)	$8,459	51%	$5,885	$7,136	70%	$2,096	18%
West Texas A&M University	$8,425	53%	$5,623	$4,204	58%	$2,308	7%
University of Texas–San Antonio	$8,412	59%	$5,416	$4,027	53%	$1,742	4%
University of Colorado–Colorado Springs	$8,396	55%	$6,282	$4,160	53%	$1,506	4%
Boise State University (ID)	$8,282	67%	$4,453	$6,599	23%	$1,071	5%
University of Texas of the Permian Basin	$7,384	57%	$6,842	$3,540	81%	$2,460	13%
University of Central Oklahoma	$7,378	49%	$7,249	$4,339	67%	$5,549	54%
California State University–Sacramento	$7,030	77%	$5,716	$4,072	90%	$1,250	0%
Angelo State University (TX)	$7,016	62%	$4,534	$3,655	45%	$3,648	14%
California State University–Dominguez Hills	$5,457	63%	$4,310	$2,401	34%	$3,165	2%
Southwestern Oklahoma State University	$4,890	61%	$1,463	$1,677	89%	$491	33%
Sam Houston State University (TX)	$4,340	26%	$906	$189	31%	$321	6%
University of the Southwest (NM)	$3,877	86%	$2,534	$1,585	70%	$1,240	6%

Where the money is: Schools that award the most need–based aid

Regional Colleges (North)

	Average amount of aid package	% students receiving need-based package	Average need-based grant	Average need-based loan	Average % of need met	Average merit award	% students receiving merit awards
Cooper Union (NY)	$35,000	32%	$5,000	$3,100	92%	$35,000	68%
Bard College at Simon's Rock (MA)	$33,639	62%	$17,567	$4,644	68%	$14,929	15%
Elmira College (NY)	$26,317	78%	$22,110	$4,354	80%	$17,653	19%
New England College (NH)	$23,584	71%	$15,259	$8,253	81%	$10,846	23%
Roger Williams University (RI)	$22,835	58%	$12,815	$7,542	86%	$7,841	11%
Lebanon Valley College (PA)	$22,686	81%	$18,957	$4,705	82%	$12,717	15%
Elizabethtown College (PA)	$22,582	73%	$17,947	$4,438	82%	$11,974	21%
Keystone College (PA)	$22,554	93%	$20,719	$6,500	77%	$11,868	3%
Wilson College (PA)	$22,148	84%	$18,314	$4,344	78%	$12,357	14%
Seton Hill University (PA)	$21,411	83%	$16,733	$5,108	75%	$11,798	10%
Eastern Nazarene College (MA)	$20,974	66%	$8,326	$9,166	72%	$7,848	11%
Vaughn College of Aeronautics and Technology (NY)	$20,950	96%	$2,950	$1,750	85%	$2,200	27%
Cazenovia College (NY)	$20,838	85%	$16,422	$4,068	77%	$11,444	11%
Lasell College (MA)	$20,097	78%	$14,766	$7,221	89%	$7,742	9%
Delaware Valley College (PA)	$19,249	79%	$14,435	$4,371	68%	$10,096	20%
Felician College (NJ)	$18,560	78%	$12,359	$4,246	56%	$10,963	6%
Curry College (MA)	$18,475	69%	$12,322	$4,360	66%	$5,293	4%
Messiah College (PA)	$18,236	72%	$12,640	$4,803	69%	$9,283	26%
Paul Smith's College (NY)	$17,041	86%	$11,300	$5,401	75%	$5,802	8%
Endicott College (MA)	$16,827	60%	$9,103	$4,594	61%	$7,007	17%
Keuka College (NY)	$16,576	90%	$11,866	$5,811	74%	$9,185	7%
Wesley College (DE)	$16,500	91%	$7,755	$5,660	80%	$3,100	5%
Mount Ida College (MA)	$15,105	80%	$11,328	$4,063	58%	$4,236	17%
Champlain College (VT)	$15,071	61%	$7,691	$4,687	70%	$3,060	8%
Stevenson University (MD)	$14,124	68%	$10,967	$4,095	63%	$6,920	21%
University of Pittsburgh–Bradford	$12,600	89%	$5,520	$4,327	90%	$5,589	18%
SUNY College of Technology–Alfred	$12,452	79%	$5,248	$7,987	64%	$4,982	6%
Post University (CT)	$11,812	98%	$4,247	$4,075	69%	$0	0%
Baptist Bible College and Seminary (PA)	$11,513	96%	$3,870	$7,643	N/A	N/A	N/A
Mount Aloysius College (PA)	$11,300	97%	$2,000	$3,400	35%	$3,500	3%
Fashion Institute of Technology (NY)	$11,288	47%	$5,327	$4,292	66%	$1,641	2%
York College of Pennsylvania	$10,915	61%	$5,383	$5,961	70%	$3,717	11%
St. Francis College (NY)	$10,887	64%	$8,092	$4,314	52%	$6,917	4%
University of Maine–Augusta	$10,766	79%	$2,328	$3,452	73%	$1,260	1%
St. Joseph's College New York	$10,449	65%	$7,760	$4,265	69%	$6,856	14%
University of Pittsburgh–Johnstown	$10,226	73%	$5,373	$4,297	57%	$2,869	1%
Becker College (MA)	$10,070	34%	$7,189	$4,031	74%	$2,114	24%
SUNY Maritime College	$9,735	48%	$4,526	$4,576	53%	$2,611	3%
Maine Maritime Academy	$8,890	67%	$6,351	$4,370	35%	$3,373	6%
Valley Forge Christian College (PA)	$8,841	73%	$6,048	$3,980	44%	$2,283	20%
Vermont Technical College	$8,152	71%	$5,272	$3,484	68%	$4,632	2%
CUNY–New York City College of Technology	$7,863	77%	$7,501	$3,859	60%	$491	1%
SUNY College of Agriculture and Technology–Cobleskill	$7,134	74%	$4,848	$3,420	81%	$357	15%
University of Maine–Fort Kent	$5,422	57%	$2,756	$2,361	82%	$881	6%
CUNY–Medgar Evers College	$3,721	83%	$3,542	$1,621	N/A	N/A	N/A
United States Merchant Marine Academy (NY)	$3,300	19%	N/A	$1,393	90%	N/A	N/A
United States Coast Guard Academy (CT)	$0	N/A	$0	$0	100%	$0	N/A

Regional Colleges (South)

	Average amount of aid package	% students receiving need-based package	Average need-based grant	Average need-based loan	Average % of need met	Average merit award	% students receiving merit awards
Alderson-Broaddus College (WV)	$20,942	92%	$16,092	$4,981	81%	$8,196	7%
Erskine College (SC)	$20,694	69%	$16,158	$4,750	83%	$10,645	20%
Newberry College (SC)	$20,440	N/A	$16,969	$4,474	76%	$11,552	N/A
Southern Adventist University (TN)	$20,165	46%	$9,814	$4,793	77%	$5,408	27%
Coker College (SC)	$19,956	86%	$7,208	$4,258	89%	$7,228	13%
Davis and Elkins College (WV)	$19,574	79%	$4,797	$5,523	84%	$11,606	21%
Barton College (NC)	$19,289	84%	$6,134	$5,318	67%	$4,837	13%
Florida Southern College	$19,093	67%	$6,615	$4,228	71%	$9,903	11%
University of the Ozarks (AR)	$18,877	60%	$13,990	$10,173	77%	$16,569	32%
Stillman College (AL)	$18,804	96%	$6,000	$5,500	N/A	$6,489	6%
Covenant College (GA)	$18,697	61%	$14,104	$4,336	77%	$8,403	22%
Catawba College (NC)	$18,422	74%	$5,861	$4,026	70%	$5,405	9%
Claflin University (SC)	$17,933	98%	$15,698	$6,223	84%	$0	0%
Flagler College (FL)	$17,705	52%	$4,664	$4,151	61%	$1,731	7%
LaGrange College (GA)	$17,664	81%	$12,967	$4,268	75%	$10,356	13%
Tuskegee University (AL)	$17,000	81%	$1,500	$5,500	80%	$1,200	18%

	Average amount of aid package	% students receiving need-based package	Average need-based grant	Average need-based loan	Average % of need met	Average merit award	% students receiving merit awards
King College (TN)	$16,736	75%	$14,125	$4,773	69%	$8,610	7%
Milligan College (TN)	$16,482	79%	$13,301	$4,445	79%	$7,283	15%
John Brown University (AR)	$15,787	65%	$7,787	$4,330	50%	$6,308	14%
Averett University (VA)	$15,682	85%	$12,492	$3,747	75%	$7,934	14%
Virginia Intermont College	$15,499	85%	$11,767	$3,853	60%	$8,961	11%
Anderson University (SC)	$15,340	81%	$12,216	$4,339	72%	$8,064	17%
Ouachita Baptist University (AR)	$15,237	57%	$11,957	$2,289	73%	$8,000	39%
Methodist University (NC)	$15,164	87%	$7,810	$4,001	67%	$3,274	4%
Shorter College (GA)	$15,152	73%	$12,411	$3,588	71%	$4,845	16%
Bryan College (TN)	$14,768	75%	$8,587	$3,678	76%	$4,703	10%
Campbellsville University (KY)	$14,521	93%	$11,351	$3,785	74%	$5,340	6%
Brescia University (KY)	$14,241	97%	$5,772	$3,645	N/A	N/A	N/A
Limestone College (SC)	$13,802	81%	$11,174	$3,755	45%	$4,807	9%
Bluefield College (VA)	$13,338	85%	$9,042	$5,151	63%	$3,788	10%
Belmont Abbey College (NC)	$13,151	81%	$9,398	$4,073	56%	$10,008	18%
Bethune-Cookman University (FL)	$13,046	94%	$9,245	$4,659	52%	$8,636	3%
Williams Baptist College (AR)	$12,992	52%	$4,228	$3,611	0%	$0	0%
Livingstone College (NC)	$12,607	96%	$9,090	$3,685	55%	$3,785	2%
Montreat College (NC)	$12,337	87%	$8,571	$4,183	66%	$8,139	7%
Ohio Valley University (WV)	$12,250	76%	$9,162	$4,202	68%	$6,447	10%
Reinhardt University (GA)	$11,498	83%	$8,852	$3,547	53%	$4,835	14%
Glenville State College (WV)	$11,448	82%	$5,650	$3,663	76%	$2,089	4%
High Point University (NC)	$10,995	66%	$2,884	$5,082	56%	$2,117	21%
Virginia Union University	$10,921	84%	$5,371	$3,894	N/A	N/A	N/A
Southeastern University (FL)	$10,890	72%	$7,917	$4,048	55%	$3,224	11%
Shepherd University (WV)	$10,791	50%	$4,145	$3,888	84%	$8,775	23%
Alice Lloyd College (KY)	$10,395	82%	$7,833	$903	78%	$4,344	16%
Winston-Salem State University (NC)	$9,577	78%	$6,808	$3,827	73%	$6,146	2%
Concord University (WV)	$9,562	69%	$5,604	$3,604	99%	$3,345	8%
Free Will Baptist Bible College (TN)	$9,377	39%	$4,516	$4,467	49%	$3,263	61%
University of South Carolina–Upstate	$9,335	71%	$4,872	$4,045	57%	$1,920	2%
University of South Carolina–Aiken	$9,108	58%	$6,552	$4,254	69%	$5,686	22%
Kentucky State University	$8,529	76%	$5,405	$3,972	20%	$4,918	4%
St. Paul's College (VA)	$8,147	96%	$4,508	$1,337	57%	$0	0%
West Liberty University (WV)	$8,023	85%	$5,177	$4,311	N/A	N/A	N/A
Southern Arkansas University	$7,679	64%	$4,106	$3,692	100%	$5,891	13%
Fairmont State University (WV)	$7,654	67%	N/A	$3,635	N/A	$1,109	11%
Bluefield State College (WV)	$6,200	67%	$3,500	$3,600	70%	$1,400	26%
Louisiana College	$5,809	88%	$2,156	$2,850	34%	$1,050	88%
Blue Mountain College (MS)	$5,656	41%	$3,456	$6,000	48%	$8,445	11%
Victory University (TN)	$4,709	88%	$3,146	$2,226	47%	$0	0%
Clayton State University (GA)	$4,163	79%	$2,442	$1,901	35%	$745	3%
St. Augustine's College (NC)	$1,778	72%	$1,664	$2,183	50%	$1,984	2%

Regional Colleges (Midwest)

	Average amount of aid package	% students receiving need-based package	Average need-based grant	Average need-based loan	Average % of need met	Average merit award	% students receiving merit awards
Ohio Northern University	$25,576	78%	$19,373	$8,021	79%	$16,294	14%
Marietta College (OH)	$24,875	77%	$12,858	$3,755	93%	$8,636	18%
MacMurray College (IL)	$24,166	95%	$14,107	$10,059	93%	$9,212	3%
Buena Vista University (IA)	$24,136	87%	$9,415	$5,120	50%	$11,139	7%
St. Joseph's College (IN)	$21,891	87%	$14,856	$4,382	80%	$12,711	11%
Manchester College (IN)	$21,729	84%	$16,881	$6,024	92%	$10,470	9%
Bluffton University (OH)	$21,413	88%	$15,092	$4,878	89%	$8,315	11%
Adrian College (MI)	$21,057	81%	$9,754	$4,243	79%	$10,885	11%
Dordt College (IA)	$20,705	74%	$11,515	$5,437	88%	$11,435	20%
Bethany College (KS)	$20,598	81%	$7,399	$4,783	94%	$6,948	7%
Culver-Stockton College (MO)	$20,481	87%	$15,634	$4,939	79%	$11,829	13%
Quincy University (IL)	$20,172	80%	$15,730	$4,704	79%	$9,884	3%
Lake Erie College (OH)	$19,991	91%	$16,203	$4,238	69%	$10,714	8%
Augustana College (SD)	$19,740	69%	$14,921	$5,461	89%	$10,019	29%
Dakota Wesleyan University (SD)	$19,000	86%	$9,800	$4,300	70%	$11,000	7%
University of Dubuque (IA)	$18,833	89%	$12,769	$6,780	78%	$6,984	10%
Morningside College (IA)	$18,517	86%	$6,774	$4,665	81%	$166	14%

Where the money is: Schools that award the most need—based aid

Regional Colleges (Midwest), continued

	Average amount of aid package	% students receiving need-based package	Average need-based grant	Average need-based loan	Average % of need met	Average merit award	% students receiving merit awards
Defiance College (OH)	$18,433	93%	$6,007	$4,544	75%	$9,308	7%
Carthage College (WI)	$18,268	75%	$13,416	$4,266	65%	$9,564	23%
Bethel College (IN)	$18,230	80%	$8,140	$5,330	69%	$6,240	12%
Northwestern College (IA)	$18,093	77%	$7,043	$4,185	89%	$6,323	19%
Taylor University (IN)	$18,002	62%	$14,157	$4,542	79%	$6,520	23%
McKendree University (IL)	$17,718	77%	$14,101	$3,996	79%	$8,591	17%
Franklin College (IN)	$17,703	80%	$13,782	$4,665	80%	$8,013	19%
Milwaukee School of Engineering	$17,687	83%	$14,730	$3,246	67%	$9,724	17%
Concordia University (NE)	$17,208	77%	$13,086	$4,374	79%	$8,914	11%
Trine University (IN)	$16,957	71%	$4,373	$3,573	91%	$8,604	5%
Northwestern College (MN)	$16,842	82%	$12,088	$4,365	70%	$5,383	14%
Loras College (IA)	$16,558	76%	$8,276	$3,071	89%	$9,620	24%
Huntington University (IN)	$16,098	74%	$12,852	$4,495	72%	$7,555	16%
Mount Mercy College (IA)	$16,094	84%	$11,589	$4,952	72%	$8,107	14%
College of the Ozarks (MO)	$15,783	90%	$12,613	$0	82%	$10,299	10%
St. Mary-of-the-Woods College (IN)	$15,681	90%	$7,724	$4,131	77%	$6,236	10%
Mount Vernon Nazarene University (OH)	$15,619	70%	$9,344	$3,984	70%	$4,102	6%
Central Methodist University (MO)	$15,394	68%	$5,634	$4,022	64%	$9,190	10%
Crown College (MN)	$15,394	66%	$6,232	$4,364	61%	$7,375	9%
Greenville College (IL)	$15,347	87%	$11,629	$4,158	68%	$6,763	11%
Missouri Southern State University	$14,602	74%	$5,953	$4,283	55%	$4,122	9%
Missouri Valley College	$14,600	72%	$11,670	$3,250	83%	$10,900	27%
Cedarville University (OH)	$14,534	66%	$4,396	$6,372	42%	$14,395	21%
Central Christian College (KS)	$14,480	81%	$5,081	$5,083	70%	$6,110	21%
Grand View University (IA)	$14,309	82%	$11,883	$4,029	75%	$5,861	15%
Blackburn College (IL)	$13,873	83%	$11,209	$4,107	80%	$5,163	10%
York College (NE)	$13,265	85%	$9,266	$4,352	77%	$4,207	7%
Concordia University (MI)	$13,083	64%	$10,171	$4,149	48%	$6,218	11%
Union College (NE)	$13,000	74%	$3,000	$4,500	63%	$4,000	25%
Trinity Christian College (IL)	$12,219	86%	$4,120	$4,447	49%	$7,024	10%
Robert Morris University (IL)	$12,121	91%	$8,739	$4,482	45%	$6,819	3%
Jamestown College (ND)	$11,925	66%	$8,254	$4,270	78%	$4,784	29%
Eureka College (IL)	$11,105	72%	$7,062	$3,846	61%	$3,232	15%
University of Minnesota–Crookston	$11,016	68%	$7,088	$4,764	74%	$2,254	8%
Hannibal-LaGrange College (MO)	$9,792	67%	$7,356	$3,889	59%	$6,180	13%
Lourdes College (OH)	$9,732	85%	$6,590	$4,134	N/A	$0	0%
Mayville State University (ND)	$8,594	63%	$4,425	$3,916	66%	$878	46%
Valley City State University (ND)	$8,480	66%	$4,339	$3,891	76%	$1,761	45%
Indiana University East	$7,943	79%	$5,769	$3,684	95%	$1,275	4%
Dickinson State University (ND)	$7,914	46%	$4,257	$3,726	32%	$1,290	30%
Dakota State University (SD)	$7,897	68%	$4,756	$3,868	84%	$3,454	9%
Indiana University–Kokomo	$7,733	67%	$6,231	$3,671	92%	$1,237	4%
Missouri Western State University	$7,432	72%	$5,501	$3,581	62%	$4,162	8%
Northern State University (SD)	$7,047	64%	$3,574	$3,543	69%	$2,138	8%
Purdue University–North Central (IN)	$6,947	58%	$4,063	$3,872	40%	$1,362	1%
Briar Cliff University (IA)	$6,300	70%	$6,200	$4,775	78%	$11,550	30%

Regional Colleges (West)

	Average amount of aid package	% students receiving need-based package	Average need-based grant	Average need-based loan	Average % of need met	Average merit award	% students receiving merit awards
Concordia University Texas	$20,951	72%	$7,765	$3,934	82%	$8,386	12%
Northwest Christian University (OR)	$19,146	74%	$14,903	$4,290	79%	$6,099	10%
Vanguard University of Southern California	$18,766	79%	$9,347	$4,681	68%	$8,187	16%
Master's College and Seminary (CA)	$18,028	88%	$13,630	$5,232	70%	$6,381	7%
McMurry University (TX)	$17,424	84%	$9,646	$4,252	84%	$5,458	6%
Corban University (OR)	$17,364	83%	$13,897	$4,505	65%	$5,336	14%
Pacific Union College (CA)	$17,290	97%	$14,400	$3,488	44%	$3,444	32%
Rocky Mountain College (MT)	$17,118	73%	$11,959	$3,905	69%	$6,891	20%
Warner Pacific College (OR)	$15,928	90%	$5,436	$4,423	72%	$3,346	9%
Northwest University (WA)	$15,580	77%	$11,427	$3,791	71%	$6,632	15%
Schreiner University (TX)	$15,360	80%	$11,946	$3,409	74%	$7,041	18%
Howard Payne University (TX)	$15,273	78%	$10,858	$3,927	86%	$6,166	18%
Wiley College (TX)	$14,701	95%	$6,900	$7,500	95%	$9,015	4%
East Texas Baptist University	$14,327	83%	$6,247	$3,634	48%	$6,692	17%
Oklahoma Baptist University	$13,131	67%	$5,477	$4,882	70%	$2,704	17%
Southwestern Assemblies of God University (TX)	$11,363	93%	$7,475	$4,423	50%	$2,697	5%
Oklahoma Wesleyan University	$11,318	77%	$8,196	$4,099	63%	$5,404	8%
Langston University (OK)	$9,611	84%	$4,726	$3,791	64%	$3,890	15%
Texas College	$9,402	86%	$6,375	$3,304	58%	$3,099	3%
Montana Tech of the University of Montana	$9,086	54%	$4,425	$3,699	76%	$2,862	14%
University of Science and Arts of Oklahoma	$9,044	61%	$6,991	$3,085	72%	$1,872	13%
University of Houston–Downtown	$8,126	77%	$5,465	$3,819	49%	$2,669	2%
Lewis-Clark State College (ID)	$8,048	65%	$3,796	$3,918	10%	$2,758	11%
Rogers State University (OK)	$8,004	66%	$5,267	$3,748	54%	$2,836	3%
Patten University (CA)	$6,709	69%	$5,375	$3,704	26%	$4,875	4%
Oregon Institute of Technology	$5,554	84%	N/A	N/A	19%	$6,617	0%
University of Montana–Western	$3,282	87%	$2,980	$4,102	17%	$1,041	7%
United States Air Force Academy (CO)	$0	N/A	$0	$0	N/A	$0	N/A

Getting a late start? All is not lost

Midterms are over and your applications still aren't out. Here's a list of schools whose application deadlines are later in the year or that have "rolling" admissions, meaning they take applications until the freshman class is full. Schools are listed by application deadline for the academic year starting in the fall of 2011.

National Universities

School	Admission deadline
Brigham Young University–Provo (UT)	2/1
Colorado State University	2/1
DePaul University (IL)	2/1
Miami University–Oxford (OH)	2/1
North Carolina State University–Raleigh	2/1
Ohio State University–Columbus	2/1
Ohio University	2/1
Old Dominion University (VA)	2/1
Stevens Institute of Technology (NJ)	2/1
University of Connecticut	2/1
University of Maryland–Baltimore County	2/1
University of Michigan–Ann Arbor	2/1
University of New Hampshire	2/1
University of Rhode Island	2/1
University of Wisconsin–Madison	2/1
Worcester Polytechnic Institute (MA)	2/1
Catholic University of America (DC)	2/15
Howard University (DC)	2/15
Pace University (NY)	2/15
Texas Christian University	2/15
University of Kentucky	2/15
Yeshiva University (NY)	2/15
Drexel University (PA)	3/1
Georgia State University	3/1
Illinois State University	3/1
New Jersey Institute of Technology	3/1
Purdue University–West Lafayette (IN)	3/1
Temple University (PA)	3/1
University at Albany–SUNY	3/1
University of San Diego	3/1
University of South Florida	3/1
East Carolina University (NC)	3/15
Southern Methodist University (TX)	3/15
University of Arizona	4/1
University of Houston	4/1
University of Iowa	4/1
University of Kansas	4/1
University of Oklahoma	4/1
University of Utah	4/1
Louisiana State University–Baton Rouge	4/15
Clemson University (SC)	5/1
Colorado School of Mines	5/1
Florida Atlantic University	5/1
Florida International University	5/1
Georgia Southern University	5/1
Indiana University-Purdue University–Indianapolis	5/1
St. Mary's University of Minnesota	5/1
University of Central Florida	5/1
University of Hawaii–Manoa	5/1
University of Nebraska–Lincoln	5/1
Florida A&M University	5/15
South Carolina State University	5/31
Azusa Pacific University (CA)	6/1
Clark Atlanta University	6/1
University of Cincinnati	6/1
University of Massachusetts–Boston	6/1
University of West Florida	6/30
Duquesne University (PA)	7/1
Missouri University of Science & Technology	7/1
Tennessee State University	7/1

School	Admission deadline
University of Alaska–Fairbanks	7/1
University of Memphis	7/1
University of North Carolina–Charlotte	7/1
University of Texas–Dallas	7/1
University of Wisconsin–Milwaukee	7/1
Bowling Green State University (OH)	7/15
Texas Woman's University	7/15
University of Mississippi	7/20
Louisiana Tech University	7/31
Jackson State University (MS)	8/1
Kent State University (OH)	8/1
Northern Illinois University	8/1
Texas A&M University–Commerce	8/1
Texas Tech University	8/1
Trevecca Nazarene University (TN)	8/1
University of Arkansas	8/1
University of Idaho	8/1
University of North Carolina–Greensboro	8/1
University of North Texas	8/1
West Virginia University	8/1
Regent University (VA)	8/3
University of Akron (OH)	8/9
University of Wyoming	8/10
Ball State University (IN)	8/15
Indiana State University	8/15
Pacific University (OR)	8/15
University of Alabama–Huntsville	8/15
Cleveland State University	8/16
University of New Orleans	8/20
University of Missouri–St. Louis	8/23
University of Louisville (KY)	8/25
New Mexico State University	8/28
Adelphi University (NY)	rolling
Andrews University (MI)	rolling
Auburn University (AL)	rolling
Barry University (FL)	rolling
Baylor University (TX)	rolling
Binghamton University–SUNY	rolling
Biola University (CA)	rolling
Central Michigan University	rolling
East Tennessee State University	rolling
Florida Institute of Technology	rolling
George Fox University (OR)	rolling
Golden Gate University (CA)	rolling
Hofstra University (NY)	rolling
Idaho State University	rolling
Illinois Institute of Technology	rolling
Immaculata University (PA)	rolling
Indiana University of Pennsylvania	rolling
Indiana University–Bloomington	rolling
Iowa State University	rolling
Kansas State University	rolling
Long Island University–C.W. Post Campus (NY)	rolling
Loyola University Chicago	rolling
Michigan State University	rolling
Michigan Technological University	rolling
Mississippi State University	rolling
Montana State University	rolling
Morgan State University (MD)	rolling
New School (NY)	rolling

School	Admission deadline
North Carolina A&T State University	rolling
North Dakota State University	rolling
Nova Southeastern University (FL)	rolling
Oakland University (MI)	rolling
Oklahoma State University	rolling
Oral Roberts University (OK)	rolling
Pennsylvania State University–University Park	rolling
Polytechnic Institute of New York Univ. (NY)	rolling
Portland State University (OR)	rolling
Rutgers–New Brunswick	rolling
Rutgers–Newark	rolling
SUNY College of Environ. Science and Forestry	rolling
SUNY–Stony Brook	rolling
Samford University (AL)	rolling
Seton Hall University (NJ)	rolling
South Dakota State University	rolling
Southern Illinois University–Carbondale	rolling
Spalding University (KY)	rolling
St. John's University (NY)	rolling
Texas A&M University–Kingsville	rolling
Trinity International University (IL)	rolling
Union Institute and University (OH)	rolling
University at Buffalo–SUNY	rolling
University of Alabama	rolling
University of Alabama–Birmingham	rolling
University of Arkansas–Little Rock	rolling
University of Bridgeport (CT)	rolling
University of Colorado–Denver	rolling
University of Dayton (OH)	rolling
University of Hartford (CT)	rolling
University of La Verne (CA)	rolling
University of Louisiana–Lafayette	rolling
University of Maine	rolling
University of Massachusetts–Lowell	rolling
University of Minnesota–Twin Cities	rolling
University of Missouri	rolling
University of Missouri–Kansas City	rolling
University of Montana	rolling
University of Nevada–Las Vegas	rolling
University of Nevada–Reno	rolling
University of North Dakota	rolling
University of Northern Colorado	rolling
University of Pittsburgh	rolling
University of San Francisco	rolling
University of South Dakota	rolling
University of Southern Mississippi	rolling
University of St. Thomas (MN)	rolling
University of Texas–Arlington	rolling
University of Texas–El Paso	rolling
University of Toledo (OH)	rolling
University of Tulsa (OK)	rolling
Utah State University	rolling
Virginia Commonwealth University	rolling
Washington State University	rolling
Wayne State University (MI)	rolling
Wichita State University (KS)	rolling
Widener University (PA)	rolling
Wilmington University (DE)	rolling
Wright State University (OH)	rolling

National Liberal Arts Colleges

College	Admission deadline
Centre College (KY)	2/1
Cornell College (IA)	2/1
DePauw University (IN)	2/1
Dickinson College (PA)	2/1
Franklin and Marshall College (PA)	2/1
Gettysburg College (PA)	2/1
Goucher College (MD)	2/1
Grove City College (PA)	2/1
Hobart and William Smith Colleges (NY)	2/1
Kalamazoo College (MI)	2/1
Knox College (IL)	2/1
Lewis & Clark College (OR)	2/1
Merrimack College (MA)	2/1
Sewanee–University of the South (TN)	2/1
Spelman College (GA)	2/1
St. Lawrence University (NY)	2/1
St. Michael's College (VT)	2/1
Sweet Briar College (VA)	2/1
Transylvania University (KY)	2/1
Virginia Military Institute	2/1
Willamette University (OR)	2/1
Wofford College (SC)	2/1
Allegheny College (PA)	2/15
Brigham Young University–Hawaii	2/15
College of Wooster (OH)	2/15
College of the Atlantic (ME)	2/15
Drew University (NJ)	2/15
Earlham College (IN)	2/15
Hillsdale College (MI)	2/15
Marlboro College (VT)	2/15
McDaniel College (MD)	2/15
Morehouse College (GA)	2/15
Muhlenberg College (PA)	2/15
Siena College (NY)	2/15
University of North Carolina–Asheville	2/15
Ursinus College (PA)	2/15
United States Military Academy (NY)	2/28
Warren Wilson College (NC)	2/28
Christopher Newport University (VA)	3/1
Coe College (IA)	3/1
Hampden-Sydney College (VA)	3/1
Hanover College (IN)	3/1
Maryville College (TN)	3/1
Moravian College (PA)	3/1
Randolph-Macon College (VA)	3/1
St. Anselm College (NH)	3/1
Susquehanna University (PA)	3/1
Washington College (MD)	3/1
Washington and Jefferson College (PA)	3/1
Wells College (NY)	3/1
Juniata College (PA)	3/15
Roanoke College (VA)	3/15
University of Minnesota–Morris	3/15
Randolph College (VA)	4/1
St. Vincent College (PA)	4/1
New College of Florida	4/15
Berea College (KY)	4/30
Agnes Scott College (GA)	5/1
Austin College (TX)	5/1
Johnson C. Smith University (NC)	5/2
American Jewish University (CA)	5/31
Carroll College (MT)	6/1
Fisk University (TN)	6/1
Lycoming College (PA)	6/1
Wesleyan College (GA)	6/1
Western State College of Colorado	6/1
Presbyterian College (SC)	6/30
Bryn Athyn College of the New Church (PA)	7/1

College	Admission deadline
University of Hawaii–Hilo	7/1
Purchase College–SUNY	7/15
Berry College (GA)	7/23
Shimer College (IL)	7/31
Atlantic Union College (MA)	8/1
Bloomfield College (NJ)	8/1
Centenary College of Louisiana	8/1
College of Idaho (ID)	8/1
Colorado State University–Pueblo	8/1
Dillard University (LA)	8/1
Fort Lewis College (CO)	8/1
Georgetown College (KY)	8/1
Goshen College (IN)	8/1
Hendrix College (AR)	8/1
Huston-Tillotson University (TX)	8/1
Jarvis Christian College (TX)	8/1
Lane College (TN)	8/1
Metropolitan State College of Denver	8/1
Paine College (GA)	8/1
University of Hawaii–West Oahu	8/1
University of Wisconsin–Parkside	8/1
Carson-Newman College (TN)	8/8
Guilford College (NC)	8/10
West Virginia State University	8/10
Albertus Magnus College (CT)	8/15
Burlington College (VT)	8/15
Calvin College (MI)	8/15
Coastal Carolina University (SC)	8/15
Concordia College (NY)	8/15
Evangel University (MO)	8/15
Huntingdon College (AL)	8/15
Nebraska Wesleyan University	8/15
University of Maine–Machias	8/15
University of Virginia–Wise	8/15
William Jewell College (MO)	8/15
Pikeville College (KY)	8/16
Albion College (MI)	rolling
Albright College (PA)	rolling
Allen University (SC)	rolling
Alma College (MI)	rolling
Asbury University (KY)	rolling
Augustana College (IL)	rolling
Baker University (KS)	rolling
Beacon College (FL)	rolling
Bennett College (NC)	rolling
Bethany College (WV)	rolling
Bethel College (KS)	rolling
Birmingham-Southern College (AL)	rolling
Brevard College (NC)	rolling
Bridgewater College (VA)	rolling
Cedar Crest College (PA)	rolling
Central College (IA)	rolling
Clarke University (IA)	rolling
College of St. Benedict (MN)	rolling
Concordia College–Moorhead (MN)	rolling
Doane College (NE)	rolling
Eastern Mennonite University (VA)	rolling
Eckerd College (FL)	rolling
Emory and Henry College (VA)	rolling
Excelsior College (NY)	rolling
Ferrum College (VA)	rolling
Franklin Pierce University (NH)	rolling
Gordon College (MA)	rolling
Granite State College (NH)	rolling
Green Mountain College (VT)	rolling
Greensboro College (NC)	rolling
Gustavus Adolphus College (MN)	rolling
Hartwick College (NY)	rolling

College	Admission deadline
Hastings College (NE)	rolling
Hiram College (OH)	rolling
Hollins University (VA)	rolling
Hope College (MI)	rolling
Houghton College (NY)	rolling
Illinois College	rolling
Illinois Wesleyan University	rolling
Judson College (AL)	rolling
Kentucky Wesleyan College	rolling
Lake Forest College (IL)	rolling
Lambuth University (TN)	rolling
Lindsey Wilson College (KY)	rolling
Linfield College (OR)	rolling
Luther College (IA)	rolling
Lyon College (AR)	rolling
Martin University (IN)	rolling
Marymount Manhattan College (NY)	rolling
Massachusetts College of Liberal Arts	rolling
McPherson College (KS)	rolling
Meredith College (NC)	rolling
Mesa State College (CO)	rolling
Millikin University (IL)	rolling
Millsaps College (MS)	rolling
Monmouth College (IL)	rolling
North Greenville University (SC)	rolling
Northland College (WI)	rolling
Oglethorpe University (GA)	rolling
Ohio Wesleyan University	rolling
Olivet College (MI)	rolling
Peace College (NC)	rolling
Pine Manor College (MA)	rolling
Principia College (IL)	rolling
Ripon College (WI)	rolling
Russell Sage College (NY)	rolling
Rust College (MS)	rolling
SUNY College–Old Westbury	rolling
Salem College (NC)	rolling
Sierra Nevada College (NV)	rolling
Simpson College (IA)	rolling
Simpson University (CA)	rolling
Southwestern University (TX)	rolling
St. Andrews Presbyterian College (NC)	rolling
St. John's College (NM)	rolling
St. John's University (MN)	rolling
St. Mary's College (IN)	rolling
St. Norbert College (WI)	rolling
Stephens College (MO)	rolling
Sterling College (KS)	rolling
Talladega College (AL)	rolling
Texas Lutheran University	rolling
Thiel College (PA)	rolling
Thomas Aquinas College (CA)	rolling
Thomas Edison State College (NJ)	rolling
Thomas More College of Liberal Arts (NH)	rolling
Tougaloo College (MS)	rolling
University of Maine–Presque Isle	rolling
University of Mount Union (OH)	rolling
University of Wisconsin–Green Bay	rolling
Virginia Wesleyan College	rolling
Wabash College (IN)	rolling
Wartburg College (IA)	rolling
West Virginia Wesleyan College	rolling
Westminster College (MO)	rolling
Westmont College (CA)	rolling
Whittier College (CA)	rolling
Wingate University (NC)	rolling
Wisconsin Lutheran College	rolling
Wittenberg University (OH)	rolling

Getting a late start? All is not lost

Regional Universities (North)

Regional Universities (South)

	Admission deadline
College of Charleston (SC)	2/1
University of Mary Washington (VA)	2/1
University of North Carolina–Wilmington	2/1
Rollins College (FL)	2/15
Hampton University (VA)	3/1
Western Carolina University (NC)	3/1
Georgia College & State University	4/1
Virginia State University	5/1
Kennesaw State University (GA)	5/14
Norfolk State University (VA)	5/31
Grambling State University (LA)	6/1
Louisiana State University–Shreveport	6/1
University of West Georgia	6/1
Florida Gulf Coast University	6/2
University of North Florida	6/11
Valdosta State University (GA)	6/15
Armstrong Atlantic State University (GA)	6/29
Columbus State University (GA)	6/30
Albany State University (GA)	7/1
Fayetteville State University (NC)	7/1
Mercer University (GA)	7/1
North Georgia College and State University	7/1
Piedmont College (GA)	7/1
Savannah State University (GA)	7/1
Southern Polytechnic State University (GA)	7/1
Southern University and A&M College (LA)	7/1
Xavier University of Louisiana	7/1
Northwestern State University of Louisiana	7/6
Alabama Agricultural and Mechanical University	7/15
Henderson State University (AR)	7/15
Spring Hill College (AL)	7/15
Fort Valley State University (GA)	7/19
Georgia Southwestern State University	7/21
Austin Peay State University (TN)	7/23
Alabama State University	7/30
University of North Carolina–Pembroke	7/31
Belmont University (TN)	8/1
Columbia College (SC)	8/1
Delta State University (MS)	8/1

	Admission deadline
Eastern Kentucky University	8/1
Murray State University (KY)	8/1
Northern Kentucky University	8/1
Shenandoah University (VA)	8/1
Southeastern Louisiana University	8/1
Southern Wesleyan University (SC)	8/1
Tennessee Technological University	8/1
Thomas More College (KY)	8/1
University of Mobile (AL)	8/1
University of Montevallo (AL)	8/1
University of Tennessee–Chattanooga	8/1
University of Tennessee–Martin	8/1
Western Kentucky University	8/1
Bethel College (TN)	8/4
Bellarmine University (KY)	8/15
St. Leo University (FL)	8/15
Union University (TN)	8/15
Francis Marion University (SC)	8/17
University of South Alabama	8/22
Arkansas State University–Jonesboro	8/23
Alcorn State University (MS)	rolling
Appalachian State University (NC)	rolling
Arkansas Tech University	rolling
Auburn University–Montgomery (AL)	rolling
Augusta State University (GA)	rolling
Belhaven University (MS)	rolling
Brenau University (GA)	rolling
Campbell University (NC)	rolling
Charleston Southern University (SC)	rolling
Christian Brothers University (TN)	rolling
Converse College (SC)	rolling
Cumberland University (TN)	rolling
Embry-Riddle Aeronautical University (FL)	rolling
Freed-Hardeman University (TN)	rolling
Gardner-Webb University (NC)	rolling
Harding University (AR)	rolling
Hodges University (FL)	rolling
Jacksonville State University (AL)	rolling
Jacksonville University (FL)	rolling

	Admission deadline
Liberty University (VA)	rolling
Lincoln Memorial University (TN)	rolling
Lipscomb University (TN)	rolling
Longwood University (VA)	rolling
Loyola University New Orleans	rolling
Lynchburg College (VA)	rolling
Lynn University (FL)	rolling
Marshall University (WV)	rolling
Mary Baldwin College (VA)	rolling
Marymount University (VA)	rolling
McNeese State University (LA)	rolling
Middle Tennessee State University	rolling
Mississippi College	rolling
Mississippi University for Women	rolling
Mississippi Valley State University	rolling
Morehead State University (KY)	rolling
Mountain State University (WV)	rolling
Nicholls State University (LA)	rolling
North Carolina Central University	rolling
Palm Beach Atlantic University (FL)	rolling
Pfeiffer University (NC)	rolling
Queens University of Charlotte (NC)	rolling
Southern University–New Orleans	rolling
St. Thomas University (FL)	rolling
Stetson University (FL)	rolling
The Citadel (SC)	rolling
Troy University (AL)	rolling
Tusculum College (TN)	rolling
Union College (KY)	rolling
University of Arkansas–Monticello	rolling
University of Central Arkansas	rolling
University of Louisiana–Monroe	rolling
University of North Alabama	rolling
University of Tampa (FL)	rolling
University of West Alabama	rolling
Wheeling Jesuit University (WV)	rolling
William Carey University (MS)	rolling
Winthrop University (SC)	rolling

Regional Universities (Midwest)

	Admission deadline
John Carroll University (OH)	2/1
University of Evansville (IN)	2/1
Xavier University (OH)	2/1
Creighton University (NE)	2/15
Aurora University (IL)	5/1
Grand Valley State University (MI)	5/1
Southern Illinois University–Edwardsville	5/1
Western Illinois University	5/15
St. Cloud State University (MN)	6/1
Webster University (MO)	6/1
Anderson University (IN)	7/1
Malone University (OH)	7/1
North Park University (IL)	7/1
Northeastern Illinois University	7/1
Southeast Missouri State University	7/1
University of Findlay (OH)	7/1
Elmhurst College (IL)	7/15
Missouri State University	7/20
Butler University (IN)	8/1
Cardinal Stritch University (WI)	8/1

	Admission deadline
Concordia University Wisconsin	8/1
Drury University (MO)	8/1
Ferris State University (MI)	8/1
Indiana University-Purdue Univ.–Fort Wayne	8/1
Lincoln University (MO)	8/1
Marygrove College (MI)	8/1
MidAmerica Nazarene University (KS)	8/1
Minnesota State University–Moorhead	8/1
Muskingum University (OH)	8/1
Oakland City University (IN)	8/1
Park University (MO)	8/1
Spring Arbor University (MI)	8/1
University of Minnesota–Duluth	8/1
University of Nebraska–Omaha	8/1
University of St. Francis (IN)	8/1
University of St. Francis (IL)	8/1
University of Wisconsin–Whitewater	8/1
Washburn University (KS)	8/1
Columbia College (MO)	8/14
Edgewood College (WI)	8/14

	Admission deadline
Augsburg College (MN)	8/15
College of Mount St. Joseph (OH)	8/15
Cornerstone University (MI)	8/15
Maryville University of St. Louis (MO)	8/15
University of Northern Iowa	8/15
University of Southern Indiana	8/15
Valparaiso University (IN)	8/15
Walsh University (OH)	8/15
William Woods University (MO)	8/15
Youngstown State University (OH)	8/15
University of Central Missouri	8/19
Southwestern College (KS)	8/25
Mount Marty College (SD)	8/30
Alverno College (WI)	rolling
Aquinas College (MI)	rolling
Ashland University (OH)	rolling
Avila University (MO)	rolling
Baldwin-Wallace College (OH)	rolling
Bellevue University (NE)	rolling
Bemidji State University (MN)	rolling

Getting a late start? All is not lost

Regional Universities (Midwest), continued

	Admission deadline
Benedictine College (KS)	rolling
Benedictine University (IL)	rolling
Bethel University (MN)	rolling
Bradley University (IL)	rolling
Calumet College of St. Joseph (IN)	rolling
Capital University (OH)	rolling
Carroll University (WI)	rolling
Chicago State University	rolling
College of St. Scholastica (MN)	rolling
Columbia College (IL)	rolling
Concordia University Chicago (IL)	rolling
Concordia University–St. Paul (MN)	rolling
Davenport University (MI)	rolling
Dominican University (IL)	rolling
Drake University (IA)	rolling
Eastern Illinois University	rolling
Eastern Michigan University	rolling
Emporia State University (KS)	rolling
Fontbonne University (MO)	rolling
Fort Hays State University (KS)	rolling
Franciscan University of Steubenville (OH)	rolling
Friends University (KS)	rolling
Graceland University (IA)	rolling
Hamline University (MN)	rolling
Heidelberg University (OH)	rolling
Indiana University Northwest	rolling
Indiana University Southeast	rolling
Indiana University–South Bend	rolling
Indiana Wesleyan University	rolling

	Admission deadline
Lakeland College (WI)	rolling
Lawrence Technological University (MI)	rolling
Lewis University (IL)	rolling
Lindenwood University (MO)	rolling
Madonna University (MI)	rolling
Maharishi University of Management (IA)	rolling
Marian University (WI)	rolling
Metropolitan State University (MN)	rolling
Minnesota State University–Mankato	rolling
Minot State University (ND)	rolling
Missouri Baptist University	rolling
Mount Mary College (WI)	rolling
National-Louis University (IL)	rolling
Newman University (KS)	rolling
North Central College (IL)	rolling
Northern Michigan University	rolling
Northwest Missouri State University	rolling
Ohio Dominican University	rolling
Olivet Nazarene University (IL)	rolling
Otterbein College (OH)	rolling
Pittsburg State University (KS)	rolling
Purdue University–Calumet (IN)	rolling
Rockford College (IL)	rolling
Rockhurst University (MO)	rolling
Roosevelt University (IL)	rolling
Saginaw Valley State University (MI)	rolling
Siena Heights University (MI)	rolling
Silver Lake College (WI)	rolling
Southwest Baptist University (MO)	rolling

	Admission deadline
St. Ambrose University (IA)	rolling
St. Catherine University (MN)	rolling
St. Xavier University (IL)	rolling
Tiffin University (OH)	rolling
Truman State University (MO)	rolling
University of Detroit Mercy	rolling
University of Illinois–Springfield	rolling
University of Indianapolis	rolling
University of Mary (ND)	rolling
University of Michigan–Dearborn	rolling
University of Michigan–Flint	rolling
University of Nebraska–Kearney	rolling
University of Rio Grande (OH)	rolling
University of St. Mary (KS)	rolling
University of Wisconsin–Eau Claire	rolling
University of Wisconsin–La Crosse	rolling
University of Wisconsin–Oshkosh	rolling
University of Wisconsin–Platteville	rolling
University of Wisconsin–River Falls	rolling
University of Wisconsin–Stevens Point	rolling
University of Wisconsin–Stout	rolling
University of Wisconsin–Superior	rolling
Upper Iowa University	rolling
Ursuline College (OH)	rolling
Viterbo University (WI)	rolling
Wayne State College (NE)	rolling
Winona State University (MN)	rolling

Regional Universities (West)

	Admission deadline
Gonzaga University (WA)	2/1
Seattle Pacific University	2/1
St. Mary's College of California	2/1
Trinity University (TX)	2/1
University of Portland (OR)	2/1
Abilene Christian University (TX)	2/15
California State University–Bakersfield	3/1
California State University–Sacramento	3/1
Mills College (CA)	3/1
Western Washington University	3/1
Whitworth University (WA)	3/1
California Lutheran University	3/15
Central Washington University	4/1
St. Edward's University (TX)	5/1
Tarleton State University (TX)	5/1
Texas State University–San Marcos	5/1
University of St. Thomas (TX)	5/1
Prairie View A&M University (TX)	6/1
University of Redlands (CA)	6/1
Boise State University (ID)	6/30
Montana State University–Billings	7/1
Texas A&M International University	7/1
Texas A&M University–Corpus Christi	7/1
University of Alaska–Anchorage	7/1
University of Colorado–Colorado Springs	7/1
University of Dallas	7/1
University of Texas–Brownsville	7/1
University of Texas–San Antonio	7/1
Our Lady of the Lake University (TX)	7/15
University of Texas of the Permian Basin	7/15
Fresno Pacific University (CA)	7/31

	Admission deadline
Adams State College (CO)	8/1
Alaska Pacific University	8/1
Colorado Christian University	8/1
Lamar University (TX)	8/1
New Mexico Institute of Mining and Technology	8/1
Regis University (CO)	8/1
Sam Houston State University (TX)	8/1
Southern Utah University	8/1
Texas Southern University	8/1
Western New Mexico University	8/1
Southern Nazarene University (OK)	8/6
Midwestern State University (TX)	8/7
University of Texas–Pan American	8/11
Angelo State University (TX)	8/15
Eastern Washington University	8/15
Hawaii Pacific University	8/15
Holy Names University (CA)	8/15
Lubbock Christian University (TX)	8/15
Northwest Nazarene University (ID)	8/15
Prescott College (AZ)	8/15
Oklahoma City University	8/20
California Baptist University	rolling
California State University–Dominguez Hills	rolling
California State University–San Bernardino	rolling
Cameron University (OK)	rolling
Chaminade University of Honolulu	rolling
City University (WA)	rolling
College of Santa Fe (NM)	rolling
Concordia University (CA)	rolling
Concordia University (OR)	rolling
Dallas Baptist University	rolling

	Admission deadline
Dominican University of California	rolling
East Central University (OK)	rolling
Eastern New Mexico University	rolling
Evergreen State College (WA)	rolling
Hardin-Simmons University (TX)	rolling
Hope International University (CA)	rolling
Houston Baptist University	rolling
John F. Kennedy University (CA)	rolling
La Sierra University (CA)	rolling
LeTourneau University (TX)	rolling
Marylhurst University (OR)	rolling
Mount St. Mary's College (CA)	rolling
Naropa University (CO)	rolling
National University (CA)	rolling
New Mexico Highlands University	rolling
Northeastern State University (OK)	rolling
Notre Dame de Namur University (CA)	rolling
Oklahoma Christian University	rolling
Pacific Lutheran University (WA)	rolling
Point Loma Nazarene University (CA)	rolling
Seattle University	rolling
Southeastern Oklahoma State University	rolling
Southern Oregon University	rolling
Southwestern Oklahoma State University	rolling
St. Martin's University (WA)	rolling
St. Mary's University of San Antonio (TX)	rolling
Stephen F. Austin State University (TX)	rolling
Sul Ross State University (TX)	rolling
Texas Wesleyan University	rolling
University of Alaska–Southeast	rolling
University of Central Oklahoma	rolling

	Admission deadline			Admission deadline			Admission deadline
University of Mary Hardin-Baylor (TX)	rolling		Walla Walla University (WA)	rolling		Western Oregon University	rolling
University of Texas–Tyler	rolling		Wayland Baptist University (TX)	rolling		Westminster College (UT)	rolling
University of the Incarnate Word (TX)	rolling		Weber State University (UT)	rolling		Woodbury University (CA)	rolling
University of the Southwest (NM)	rolling		West Texas A&M University	rolling			

Regional Colleges (North)

	Admission deadline			Admission deadline			Admission deadline
Roger Williams University (RI)	2/1		Cazenovia College (NY)	rolling		Paul Smith's College (NY)	rolling
United States Coast Guard Academy (CT)	2/1		College of Our Lady of the Elms (MA)	rolling		Peirce College (PA)	rolling
Endicott College (MA)	2/15		Curry College (MA)	rolling		Post University (CT)	rolling
United States Merchant Marine Academy (NY)	3/1		Daniel Webster College (NH)	rolling		SUNY College of Agr. and Tech.–Cobleskill	rolling
Elmira College (NY)	3/15		Delaware Valley College (PA)	rolling		SUNY College of Technology–Alfred	rolling
Colby-Sawyer College (NH)	4/1		Eastern Nazarene College (MA)	rolling		SUNY College of Technology–Delhi	rolling
Wesley College (DE)	4/30		Elizabethtown College (PA)	rolling		SUNY Maritime College	rolling
CUNY–Medgar Evers College	5/3		Farmingdale State College–SUNY	rolling		Southern Vermont College	rolling
Maine Maritime Academy	5/31		Felician College (NJ)	rolling		St. Francis College (NY)	rolling
Pennsylvania College of Technology	7/1		Fisher College (MA)	rolling		St. Joseph's College New York	rolling
Unity College (ME)	7/1		Geneva College (PA)	rolling		Stevenson University (MD)	rolling
Keystone College (PA)	7/15		Keuka College (NY)	rolling		Thomas College (ME)	rolling
Washington Adventist University (MD)	8/1		Lasell College (MA)	rolling		University of Maine–Farmington	rolling
Baptist Bible College and Seminary (PA)	8/15		Lebanon Valley College (PA)	rolling		University of Maine–Fort Kent	rolling
Seton Hill University (PA)	8/15		Lyndon State College (VT)	rolling		University of Pittsburgh–Bradford	rolling
University of Maine–Augusta	8/31		Massachusetts Maritime Academy	rolling		University of Pittsburgh–Johnstown	rolling
Bard College at Simon's Rock (MA)	rolling		Messiah College (PA)	rolling		Valley Forge Christian College (PA)	rolling
Bay Path College (MA)	rolling		Mitchell College (CT)	rolling		Vaughn College of Aeronautics and Tech. (NY)	rolling
Becker College (MA)	rolling		Mount Aloysius College (PA)	rolling		Vermont Technical College	rolling
CUNY–New York City College of Technology	rolling		Mount Ida College (MA)	rolling		Wilson College (PA)	rolling
CUNY–York College	rolling		New England College (NH)	rolling		York College of Pennsylvania	rolling

Regional Colleges (South)

	Admission deadline			Admission deadline			Admission deadline
Flagler College (FL)	3/1		Milligan College (TN)	8/1		Bluefield College (VA)	rolling
Florida Southern College	3/1		Montreat College (NC)	8/1		Bluefield State College (WV)	rolling
Tuskegee University (AL)	3/15		University of South Carolina–Aiken	8/1		Brescia University (KY)	rolling
Winston-Salem State University (NC)	3/15		Virginia Union University	8/9		Brewton-Parker College (GA)	rolling
LeMoyne-Owen College (TN)	4/1		West Virginia University Institute of Technology	8/11		Bryan College (TN)	rolling
Alice Lloyd College (KY)	7/1		High Point University (NC)	8/15		Catawba College (NC)	rolling
Clayton State University (GA)	7/1		Lander University (SC)	8/15		Central Baptist College (AR)	rolling
Lees-McRae College (NC)	7/1		Louisiana College	8/15		Chowan University (NC)	rolling
Southeastern University (FL)	7/1		University of the Cumberlands (KY)	8/15		Claflin University (SC)	rolling
Averett University (VA)	7/15		Victory University (TN)	8/21		Clearwater Christian College (FL)	rolling
Our Lady of Holy Cross College (LA)	7/20		Alderson-Broaddus College (WV)	8/25		Concord University (WV)	rolling
Shaw University (NC)	7/30		Limestone College (SC)	8/26		Concordia College (AL)	rolling
Ohio Valley University (WV)	7/31		Southern Arkansas University	8/27		Covenant College (GA)	rolling
Atlanta Christian College	8/1		Tennessee Wesleyan College	8/31		Dalton State College (GA)	rolling
Belmont Abbey College (NC)	8/1		Anderson University (SC)	rolling		Davis and Elkins College (WV)	rolling
Campbellsville University (KY)	8/1		Arkansas Baptist College	rolling		Edward Waters College (FL)	rolling
Coker College (SC)	8/1		Barton College (NC)	rolling		Erskine College (SC)	rolling
Elizabeth City State University (NC)	8/1		Benedict College (SC)	rolling		Fairmont State University (WV)	rolling
Emmanuel College (GA)	8/1		Bethune-Cookman University (FL)	rolling		Faulkner University (AL)	rolling
Martin Methodist College (TN)	8/1		Blue Mountain College (MS)	rolling		Florida Memorial University	rolling

Getting a late start? All is not lost

Regional Colleges (South), continued

	Admission deadline
Free Will Baptist Bible College (TN)	rolling
Glenville State College (WV)	rolling
John Brown University (AR)	rolling
Kentucky State University	rolling
King College (TN)	rolling
LaGrange College (GA)	rolling
Lenoir-Rhyne University (NC)	rolling
Livingstone College (NC)	rolling
Mars Hill College (NC)	rolling
Methodist University (NC)	rolling
Midway College (KY)	rolling
Miles College (AL)	rolling
Morris College (SC)	rolling

	Admission deadline
Mount Olive College (NC)	rolling
Newberry College (SC)	rolling
North Carolina Wesleyan College	rolling
Oakwood University (AL)	rolling
Ouachita Baptist University (AR)	rolling
Philander Smith College (AR)	rolling
Reinhardt University (GA)	rolling
Shepherd University (WV)	rolling
Shorter College (GA)	rolling
St. Augustine's College (NC)	rolling
St. Paul's College (VA)	rolling
Stillman College (AL)	rolling
Thomas University (GA)	rolling

	Admission deadline
Toccoa Falls College (GA)	rolling
University of Arkansas–Pine Bluff	rolling
University of Charleston (WV)	rolling
University of South Carolina–Upstate	rolling
University of the Ozarks (AR)	rolling
Virginia Intermont College	rolling
Voorhees College (SC)	rolling
Warner University (FL)	rolling
West Liberty University (WV)	rolling
West Virginia University–Parkersburg	rolling
Williams Baptist College (AR)	rolling

Regional Colleges (Midwest)

	Admission deadline
College of the Ozarks (MO)	2/15
Grace College and Seminary (IN)	3/1
Marietta College (OH)	4/15
Missouri Western State University	5/1
North Central University (MN)	6/1
Wilberforce University (OH)	6/1
Black Hills State University (SD)	7/1
Mount Vernon Nazarene University (OH)	7/15
Central Christian College (KS)	8/1
Concordia University (NE)	8/1
Dordt College (IA)	8/1
Eureka College (IL)	8/1
Greenville College (IL)	8/1
Huntington University (IN)	8/1
Lake Erie College (OH)	8/1
Marian University (IN)	8/1
Northwestern College (MN)	8/1
Trine University (IN)	8/1
Wilmington College (OH)	8/1
Midland Lutheran College (NE)	8/7
Bluffton University (OH)	8/15
Grand View University (IA)	8/15
Lake Superior State University (MI)	8/15
Northwestern College (IA)	8/15
Ohio Northern University	8/15
University of Dubuque (IA)	8/15
Dakota Wesleyan University (SD)	8/25
Hannibal-LaGrange College (MO)	8/26
Trinity Christian College (IL)	8/31
York College (NE)	8/31
Adrian College (MI)	rolling
Augustana College (SD)	rolling

	Admission deadline
Bethany College (KS)	rolling
Bethel College (IN)	rolling
Blackburn College (IL)	rolling
Briar Cliff University (IA)	rolling
Buena Vista University (IA)	rolling
Carthage College (WI)	rolling
Cedarville University (OH)	rolling
Central Methodist University (MO)	rolling
Central State University (OH)	rolling
Chadron State College (NE)	rolling
Chancellor University (OH)	rolling
College of St. Mary (NE)	rolling
Concordia University (MI)	rolling
Crown College (MN)	rolling
Culver-Stockton College (MO)	rolling
Dakota State University (SD)	rolling
Dana College (NE)	rolling
Defiance College (OH)	rolling
Dickinson State University (ND)	rolling
East-West University (IL)	rolling
Finlandia University (MI)	rolling
Franklin College (IN)	rolling
Grace Bible College (MI)	rolling
Harris-Stowe State University (MO)	rolling
Indiana University East	rolling
Iowa Wesleyan College	rolling
Jamestown College (ND)	rolling
Judson University (IL)	rolling
Kansas Wesleyan University	rolling
Kendall College (IL)	rolling
Lincoln College (IL)	rolling
Loras College (IA)	rolling

	Admission deadline
Lourdes College (OH)	rolling
MacMurray College (IL)	rolling
Manchester College (IN)	rolling
Maranatha Baptist Bible College (WI)	rolling
Mayville State University (ND)	rolling
McKendree University (IL)	rolling
Milwaukee School of Engineering	rolling
Missouri Southern State University	rolling
Missouri Valley College	rolling
Morningside College (IA)	rolling
Mount Mercy College (IA)	rolling
Notre Dame College of Ohio	rolling
Ottawa University (KS)	rolling
Peru State College (NE)	rolling
Purdue University–North Central (IN)	rolling
Quincy University (IL)	rolling
Robert Morris University (IL)	rolling
Rochester College (MI)	rolling
Shawnee State University (OH)	rolling
St. Joseph's College (IN)	rolling
St. Mary-of-the-Woods College (IN)	rolling
Tabor College (KS)	rolling
Taylor University (IN)	rolling
Union College (NE)	rolling
University of Minnesota–Crookston	rolling
University of Sioux Falls (SD)	rolling
Urbana University (OH)	rolling
Valley City State University (ND)	rolling
Waldorf College (IA)	rolling
William Penn University (IA)	rolling

Regional Colleges (West)

College	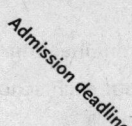Admission deadline
United States Air Force Academy (CO)	2/15
Cogswell Polytechnical College (CA)	5/1
Warner Pacific College (OR)	5/30
University of Houston–Downtown	6/1
Northwest University (WA)	7/15
Bethany University (CA)	7/31
Corban University (OR)	8/1
Oklahoma Baptist University	8/1
Schreiner University (TX)	8/1
McMurry University (TX)	8/15
Utah Valley University	8/15
East Texas Baptist University	8/17
Langston University (OK)	8/31
University of Science and Arts of Oklahoma	8/31

College	Admission deadline
Amer. Indian Coll.of the Assemblies of God (AZ)	rolling
Bacone College (OK)	rolling
California Maritime Academy	rolling
Concordia University Texas	rolling
Dixie State College of Utah	rolling
Howard Payne University (TX)	rolling
Humphreys College (CA)	rolling
Lewis-Clark State College (ID)	rolling
Master's College and Seminary (CA)	rolling
Mid-America Christian University (OK)	rolling
Montana State University–Northern	rolling
Montana Tech of the University of Montana	rolling
Northwest Christian University (OR)	rolling
Northwestern Oklahoma State University	rolling

College	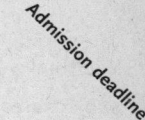Admission deadline
Oklahoma Panhandle State University	rolling
Oklahoma Wesleyan University	rolling
Pacific Union College (CA)	rolling
Patten University (CA)	rolling
Rocky Mountain College (MT)	rolling
Rogers State University (OK)	rolling
Southwestern Assemblies of God Univ. (TX)	rolling
St. Gregory's University (OK)	rolling
Texas College	rolling
University of Montana–Western	rolling
Vanguard University of Southern California	rolling
Western Governors University (UT)	rolling

Index to Major Fields of Study

You think you'd like to specialize in architectural engineering? Or possibly biblical studies? Use this list to find schools offering majors in subject areas of interest and then learn more about each school by studying its directory entry. For more specifics on programs offered, consult the schools' websites.

Accounting and Computer Science

Central Christian Coll. (KS)
Davenport Univ. (MI)
Houston Baptist Univ.
San Jose State Univ. (CA)
Schreiner Univ. (TX)
Simpson Coll. (IA)
Southern New Hampshire Univ.
St. Mary-of-the-Woods Coll. (IN)
Western Washington Univ.

Accounting and Related Services

Abilene Christian Univ. (TX)
Adelphi Univ. (NY)
Adrian Coll. (MI)
Alabama Agricultural and Mechanical Univ.
Alabama State Univ.
Alaska Pacific Univ.
Albany State Univ. (GA)
Albright Coll. (PA)
Alcorn State Univ. (MS)
Alderson-Broaddus Coll. (WV)
Alfred Univ. (NY)
Alma Coll. (MI)
Alvernia Univ. (PA)
American Univ. (DC)
Anderson Univ. (SC)
Anderson Univ. (IN)
Andrews Univ. (MI)
Angelo State Univ. (TX)
Anna Maria Coll. (MA)
Appalachian State Univ. (NC)
Aquinas Coll. (MI)
Arcadia Univ. (PA)
Arizona State Univ.
Arkansas State Univ.–Jonesboro
Arkansas Tech Univ.
Asbury Univ. (KY)
Ashland Univ. (OH)
Assumption Coll. (MA)
Auburn Univ. (AL)
Auburn Univ.–Montgomery (AL)
Augsburg Coll. (MN)
Augusta State Univ. (GA)
Augustana Coll. (IL)
Augustana Coll. (SD)
Aurora Univ. (IL)
Averett Univ. (VA)
Avila Univ. (MO)
Azusa Pacific Univ. (CA)
Babson Coll. (MA)
Baker Coll. of Flint (MI)
Baker Univ. (KS)
Baldwin-Wallace Coll. (OH)
Ball State Univ. (IN)

Barry Univ. (FL)
Barton Coll. (NC)
Baylor Univ. (TX)
Belhaven Univ. (MS)
Bellarmine Univ. (KY)
Bellevue Univ. (NE)
Belmont Abbey Coll. (NC)
Belmont Univ. (TN)
Bemidji State Univ. (MN)
Benedict Coll. (SC)
Benedictine Coll. (KS)
Benedictine Univ. (IL)
Bennett Coll. (NC)
Bentley Univ. (MA)
Berry Coll. (GA)
Bethany Coll. (WV)
Bethany Coll. (KS)
Bethel Coll. (IN)
Bethune-Cookman Univ. (FL)
Binghamton Univ.–SUNY
Biola Univ. (CA)
Black Hills State Univ. (SD)
Bloomfield Coll. (NJ)
Bloomsburg Univ. of Pennsylvania
Bluefield Coll. (VA)
Bluefield State Coll. (WV)
Bluffton Univ. (OH)
Boise State Univ. (ID)
Boston Univ.
Bowling Green State Univ. (OH)
Bradley Univ. (IL)
Brenau Univ. (GA)
Brescia Univ. (KY)
Brewton-Parker Coll. (GA)
Briar Cliff Univ. (IA)
Bridgewater State Coll. (MA)
Brigham Young Univ.–Hawaii
Brigham Young Univ.–Provo (UT)
Bryant Univ. (RI)
Bucknell Univ. (PA)
Buena Vista Univ. (IA)
Butler Univ. (IN)
Cabrini Coll. (PA)
Caldwell Coll. (NJ)
California Baptist Univ.
California Lutheran Univ.
California State Polytechnic Univ.–Pomona
California State Univ.–East Bay
California State Univ.–Fullerton
California State Univ.–Long Beach
California State Univ.–Sacramento
California State Univ.–San Marcos
California Univ. of Pennsylvania
Calumet Coll. of St. Joseph (IN)
Calvin Coll. (MI)
Cameron Univ. (OK)
Campbell Univ. (NC)
Campbellsville Univ. (KY)
Canisius Coll. (NY)

Capital Univ. (OH)
Cardinal Stritch Univ. (WI)
Carlow Univ. (PA)
Carroll Coll. (MT)
Carroll Univ. (WI)
Carson-Newman Coll. (TN)
Carthage Coll. (WI)
Case Western Reserve Univ. (OH)
Castleton State Coll. (VT)
Catawba Coll. (NC)
Catholic Univ. of America (DC)
Cazenovia Coll. (NY)
Cedar Crest Coll. (PA)
Cedarville Univ. (OH)
Centenary Coll. (NJ)
Centenary Coll. of Louisiana
Central Christian Coll. (KS)
Central Coll. (IA)
Central Connecticut State Univ.
Central Methodist Univ. (MO)
Central Michigan Univ.
Central State Univ. (OH)
Central Washington Univ.
Chaminade Univ. of Honolulu
Champlain Coll. (VT)
Chapman Univ. (CA)
Chatham Univ. (PA)
Chestnut Hill Coll. (PA)
Christopher Newport Univ. (VA)
City Univ. (WA)
Claremont McKenna Coll. (CA)
Clarion Univ. of Pennsylvania
Clark Atlanta Univ.
Clayton State Univ. (GA)
Clearwater Christian Coll. (FL)
Cleary Univ. (MI)
Clemson Univ. (SC)
Cleveland State Univ.
Coastal Carolina Univ. (SC)
Coe Coll. (IA)
Coll. at Brockport–SUNY
Coll. of Charleston (SC)
Coll. of Idaho (ID)
Coll. of Mount St. Joseph (OH)
Coll. of New Jersey
Coll. of Our Lady of the Elms (MA)
Coll. of Santa Fe (NM)
Coll. of St. Benedict (MN)
Coll. of St. Joseph (VT)
Coll. of St. Rose (NY)
Coll. of St. Scholastica (MN)
Coll. of the Holy Cross (MA)
Coll. of the Ozarks (MO)
Colorado Christian Univ.
Colorado State Univ.–Pueblo
Columbia Coll. (MO)
Columbia Coll. (SC)
Columbus State Univ. (GA)
Concordia Coll.–Moorhead (MN)
Concordia Univ. (NE)

Concordia Univ. Chicago (IL)
Concordia Univ. Wisconsin
Concordia Univ.–St. Paul (MN)
Converse Coll. (SC)
Corban Univ. (OR)
Cornerstone Univ. (MI)
Creighton Univ. (NE)
Culver-Stockton Coll. (MO)
Cumberland Univ. (TN)
CUNY–Baruch Coll.
CUNY–Brooklyn Coll.
CUNY–Coll. of Staten Island
CUNY–Hunter Coll.
CUNY–Lehman Coll.
CUNY–Medgar Evers Coll.
CUNY–York Coll.
D'Youville Coll. (NY)
Daemen Coll. (NY)
Dakota State Univ. (SD)
Dallas Baptist Univ.
Dana Coll. (NE)
Davenport Univ. (MI)
Davis and Elkins Coll. (WV)
Defiance Coll. (OH)
Delaware State Univ.
Delaware Valley Coll. (PA)
Delta State Univ. (MS)
DePaul Univ. (IL)
DeSales Univ. (PA)
Dickinson State Univ. (ND)
Dillard Univ. (LA)
Dominican Coll. (NY)
Dominican Univ. (IL)
Dordt Coll. (IA)
Dowling Coll. (NY)
Drake Univ. (IA)
Drury Univ. (MO)
Duquesne Univ. (PA)
East Carolina Univ. (NC)
East Central Univ. (OK)
East Tennessee State Univ.
East Texas Baptist Univ.
Eastern Connecticut State Univ.
Eastern Illinois Univ.
Eastern Kentucky Univ.
Eastern Mennonite Univ. (VA)
Eastern Michigan Univ.
Eastern Nazarene Coll. (MA)
Eastern New Mexico Univ.
Eastern Univ. (PA)
Eastern Washington Univ.
Edgewood Coll. (WI)
Edward Waters Coll. (FL)
Elizabeth City State Univ. (NC)
Elizabethtown Coll. (PA)
Elmhurst Coll. (IL)
Elmira Coll. (NY)
Elon Univ. (NC)
Emory and Henry Coll. (VA)
Emory Univ. (GA)

Emporia State Univ. (KS)
Eureka Coll. (IL)
Evangel Univ. (MO)
Excelsior Coll. (NY)
Fairleigh Dickinson Univ. (NJ)
Fairmont State Univ. (WV)
Fayetteville State Univ. (NC)
Ferris State Univ. (MI)
Ferrum Coll. (VA)
Fitchburg State Coll. (MA)
Flagler Coll. (FL)
Florida Atlantic Univ.
Florida Gulf Coast Univ.
Florida Institute of Technology
Florida International Univ.
Florida Southern Coll.
Florida State Univ.
Fordham Univ. (NY)
Fort Hays State Univ. (KS)
Fort Lewis Coll. (CO)
Fort Valley State Univ. (GA)
Francis Marion Univ. (SC)
Franciscan Univ. of Steubenville (OH)
Franklin Coll. (IN)
Franklin Pierce Univ. (NH)
Freed-Hardeman Univ. (TN)
Fresno Pacific Univ. (CA)
Friends Univ. (KS)
Frostburg State Univ. (MD)
Furman Univ. (SC)
Gallaudet Univ. (DC)
Gannon Univ. (PA)
Gardner-Webb Univ. (NC)
Geneva Coll. (PA)
George Fox Univ. (OR)
George Mason Univ. (VA)
George Washington Univ. (DC)
Georgetown Coll. (KY)
Georgetown Univ. (DC)
Georgia Coll. & State Univ.
Georgia Southern Univ.
Georgia Southwestern State Univ.
Georgia State Univ.
Georgian Court Univ. (NJ)
Golden Gate Univ. (CA)
Goldey Beacom Coll. (DE)
Gonzaga Univ. (WA)
Gordon Coll. (MA)
Goshen Coll. (IN)
Grace Coll. and Seminary (IN)
Graceland Univ. (IA)
Grambling State Univ. (LA)
Grand Valley State Univ. (MI)
Grand View Univ. (IA)
Greensboro Coll. (NC)
Greenville Coll. (IL)
Grove City Coll. (PA)
Guilford Coll. (NC)
Gustavus Adolphus Coll. (MN)

Gwynedd-Mercy Coll. (PA)
Hampton Univ. (VA)
Hardin-Simmons Univ. (TX)
Harding Univ. (AR)
Harris-Stowe State Univ. (MO)
Hartwick Coll. (NY)
Hawaii Pacific Univ.
Heidelberg Univ. (OH)
Henderson State Univ. (AR)
Hendrix Coll. (AR)
Heritage Univ. (WA)
High Point Univ. (NC)
Hillsdale Coll. (MI)
Hiram Coll. (OH)
Hodges Univ. (FL)
Hofstra Univ. (NY)
Holy Family Univ. (PA)
Hope Coll. (MI)
Houghton Coll. (NY)
Houston Baptist Univ.
Howard Payne Univ. (TX)
Howard Univ. (DC)
Humphreys Coll. (CA)
Huntingdon Coll. (AL)
Huntington Univ. (IN)
Husson Univ. (ME)
Idaho State Univ.
Illinois Coll.
Illinois State Univ.
Illinois Wesleyan Univ.
Immaculata Univ. (PA)
Indiana Institute of Technology
Indiana State Univ.
Indiana Univ. of Pennsylvania
Indiana Univ. Southeast
Indiana Univ.–Kokomo
Indiana Univ.–South Bend
Indiana Univ.-Purdue Univ.–Fort
 Wayne
Indiana Wesleyan Univ.
Iona Coll. (NY)
Iowa Wesleyan Coll.
Ithaca Coll. (NY)
Jackson State Univ. (MS)
Jacksonville State Univ. (AL)
Jacksonville Univ. (FL)
James Madison Univ. (VA)
Jamestown Coll. (ND)
John Brown Univ. (AR)
John Carroll Univ. (OH)
Johnson and Wales Univ. (RI)
Judson Univ. (IL)
Juniata Coll. (PA)
Kansas State Univ.
Kansas Wesleyan Univ.
Kean Univ. (NJ)
Kennesaw State Univ. (GA)
Kent State Univ. (OH)
Kentucky State Univ.
Kentucky Wesleyan Coll.
Kettering Univ. (MI)
Keuka Coll. (NY)
King's Coll. (PA)
Kutztown Univ. of Pennsylvania
La Roche Coll. (PA)
La Salle Univ. (PA)
La Sierra Univ. (CA)
LaGrange Coll. (GA)
Lake Erie Coll. (OH)
Lake Superior State Univ. (MI)
Lakeland Coll. (WI)

Lamar Univ. (TX)
Lambuth Univ. (TN)
Lasell Coll. (MA)
Le Moyne Coll. (NY)
Lebanon Valley Coll. (PA)
Lehigh Univ. (PA)
Lenoir-Rhyne Univ. (NC)
LeTourneau Univ. (TX)
Lewis Univ. (IL)
Lewis-Clark State Coll. (ID)
Liberty Univ. (VA)
Limestone Coll. (SC)
Lincoln Univ. (PA)
Lincoln Univ. (MO)
Lindenwood Univ. (MO)
Linfield Coll. (OR)
Lipscomb Univ. (TN)
Livingstone Coll. (NC)
Lock Haven Univ. of Pennsylvania
Long Island Univ.–C.W. Post
 Campus (NY)
Loras Coll. (IA)
Louisiana Coll.
Louisiana State Univ.–Baton Rouge
Louisiana State Univ.–Shreveport
Louisiana Tech Univ.
Lourdes Coll. (OH)
Loyola Marymount Univ. (CA)
Loyola Univ. Chicago
Loyola Univ. Maryland
Loyola Univ. New Orleans
Lubbock Christian Univ. (TX)
Luther Coll. (IA)
Lycoming Coll. (PA)
Lynchburg Coll. (VA)
Lyndon State Coll. (VT)
Lyon Coll. (AR)
MacMurray Coll. (IL)
Macon State Coll. (GA)
Madonna Univ. (MI)
Malone Univ. (OH)
Manchester Coll. (IN)
Manhattan Coll. (NY)
Mansfield Univ. of Pennsylvania
Maranatha Baptist Bible Coll. (WI)
Marian Univ. (IN)
Marian Univ. (WI)
Marietta Coll. (OH)
Marist Coll. (NY)
Marquette Univ. (WI)
Marshall Univ. (WV)
Martin Methodist Coll. (TN)
Martin Univ. (IN)
Marygrove Coll. (MI)
Maryville Univ. of St. Louis (MO)
Marywood Univ. (PA)
Master's Coll. and Seminary (CA)
McKendree Univ. (IL)
McNeese State Univ. (LA)
McPherson Coll. (KS)
Mercy Coll. (NY)
Mercyhurst Coll. (PA)
Meredith Coll. (NC)
Mesa State Coll. (CO)
Messiah Coll. (PA)
Methodist Univ. (NC)
Metropolitan State Coll. of Denver
Miami Univ.–Oxford (OH)
Michigan State Univ.
MidAmerica Nazarene Univ. (KS)
Middle Tennessee State Univ.

Midland Lutheran Coll. (NE)
Midwestern State Univ. (TX)
Miles Coll. (AL)
Milligan Coll. (TN)
Millikin Univ. (IL)
Millsaps Coll. (MS)
Minnesota State Univ.–Mankato
Minnesota State Univ.–Moorhead
Minot State Univ. (ND)
Misericordia Univ. (PA)
Mississippi Coll.
Mississippi State Univ.
Mississippi Univ. for Women
Mississippi Valley State Univ.
Missouri Baptist Univ.
Missouri Southern State Univ.
Missouri State Univ.
Missouri Valley Coll.
Missouri Western State Univ.
Molloy Coll. (NY)
Monmouth Coll. (IL)
Moravian Coll. (PA)
Morehead State Univ. (KY)
Morgan State Univ. (MD)
Morningside Coll. (IA)
Mount Aloysius Coll. (PA)
Mount Marty Coll. (SD)
Mount Mary Coll. (WI)
Mount Mercy Coll. (IA)
Mount St. Mary Coll. (NY)
Mount St. Mary's Univ. (MD)
Mount Vernon Nazarene Univ.
 (OH)
Muhlenberg Coll. (PA)
Murray State Univ. (KY)
Muskingum Univ. (OH)
National Univ. (CA)
National-Louis Univ. (IL)
Nazareth Coll. (NY)
Nebraska Wesleyan Univ.
Neumann Univ. (PA)
New Mexico Highlands Univ.
New Mexico State Univ.
New York Institute of Technology
New York Univ.
Niagara Univ. (NY)
Nicholls State Univ. (LA)
Nichols Coll. (MA)
Norfolk State Univ. (VA)
North Carolina A&T State Univ.
North Carolina Central Univ.
North Carolina State University–
 Raleigh
North Central Coll. (IL)
North Central Univ. (MN)
North Dakota State Univ.
North Georgia Coll. and State Univ.
North Greenville Univ. (SC)
Northeastern Illinois Univ.
Northeastern State Univ. (OK)
Northeastern Univ. (MA)
Northern Arizona Univ.
Northern Illinois Univ.
Northern Kentucky Univ.
Northern Michigan Univ.
Northern State Univ. (SD)
Northwest Christian Univ. (OR)
Northwest Missouri State Univ.
Northwest Nazarene Univ. (ID)
Northwestern Coll. (MN)
Northwestern Coll. (IA)

Northwestern Oklahoma State
 Univ.
Northwestern State Univ. of
 Louisiana
Northwood Univ. (MI)
Norwich Univ. (VT)
Notre Dame Coll. of Ohio
Nova Southeastern Univ. (FL)
Nyack Coll. (NY)
Oakland City Univ. (IN)
Oakland Univ. (MI)
Oakwood Univ. (AL)
Oglethorpe Univ. (GA)
Ohio Dominican Univ.
Ohio Northern Univ.
Ohio State Univ.–Columbus
Ohio Univ.
Ohio Valley Univ. (WV)
Ohio Wesleyan Univ.
Oklahoma Baptist Univ.
Oklahoma Christian Univ.
Oklahoma City Univ.
Oklahoma Panhandle State Univ.
Oklahoma State Univ.
Old Dominion Univ. (VA)
Oral Roberts Univ. (OK)
Oregon Institute of Technology
Otterbein Coll. (OH)
Ouachita Baptist Univ. (AR)
Our Lady of Holy Cross Coll. (LA)
Our Lady of the Lake Univ. (TX)
Pace Univ. (NY)
Paine Coll. (GA)
Palm Beach Atlantic Univ. (FL)
Park Univ. (MO)
Pennsylvania Coll. of Technology
Pennsylvania State Univ.–Univ. Park
Pepperdine Univ. (CA)
Peru State Coll. (NE)
Pfeiffer Univ. (NC)
Philadelphia Univ.
Pittsburg State Univ. (KS)
Plymouth State Univ. (NH)
Point Loma Nazarene Univ. (CA)
Point Park Univ. (PA)
Post Univ. (CT)
Prairie View A&M Univ. (TX)
Providence Coll. (RI)
Purdue Univ.–Calumet (IN)
Purdue Univ.–West Lafayette (IN)
Quincy Univ. (IL)
Quinnipiac Univ. (CT)
Radford Univ. (VA)
Ramapo Coll. of New Jersey
Randolph-Macon Coll. (VA)
Regis Univ. (CO)
Reinhardt Univ. (GA)
Rhode Island Coll.
Rhodes Coll. (TN)
Rider Univ. (NJ)
Robert Morris Univ. (PA)
Roberts Wesleyan Coll. (NY)
Rochester Coll. (MI)
Rochester Institute of Tech. (NY)
Rockford Coll. (IL)
Rocky Mountain Coll. (MT)
Roger Williams Univ. (RI)
Roosevelt Univ. (IL)
Rosemont Coll. (PA)
Rutgers, the State Univ. of New
 Jersey–Camden

Rutgers, the State Univ. of New
 Jersey–New Brunswick
Rutgers, the State Univ. of New
 Jersey–Newark
Sacred Heart Univ. (CT)
Sage Colleges–Albany (NY)
Saginaw Valley State Univ. (MI)
Salem Coll. (NC)
Salisbury Univ. (MD)
Salve Regina Univ. (RI)
Sam Houston State Univ. (TX)
Samford Univ. (AL)
San Diego State Univ.
Santa Clara Univ. (CA)
Savannah State Univ. (GA)
Schreiner Univ. (TX)
Scripps Coll. (CA)
Seattle Pacific Univ.
Seattle Univ.
Seton Hall Univ. (NJ)
Seton Hill Univ. (PA)
Shaw Univ. (NC)
Shawnee State Univ. (OH)
Shepherd Univ. (WV)
Shippensburg Univ. of Pennsylvania
Shorter Coll. (GA)
Siena Coll. (NY)
Silver Lake Coll. (WI)
Simpson Coll. (IA)
Simpson Univ. (CA)
Sojourner-Douglass Coll. (MD)
South Carolina State Univ.
Southeast Missouri State Univ.
Southeastern Louisiana Univ.
Southeastern Oklahoma State Univ.
Southeastern Univ. (FL)
Southern Adventist Univ. (TN)
Southern Arkansas Univ.
Southern Connecticut State Univ.
Southern Illinois Univ.–Carbondale
Southern Illinois Univ.–Edwardsville
Southern Methodist Univ. (TX)
Southern Nazarene Univ. (OK)
Southern New Hampshire Univ.
Southern Univ. and A&M Coll. (LA)
Southern Univ.–New Orleans
Southern Utah Univ.
Southern Wesleyan Univ. (SC)
Southwest Baptist Univ. (MO)
Southwest Minnesota State Univ.
Southwestern Adventist Univ. (TX)
Southwestern Coll. (KS)
Southwestern Univ. (TX)
Spalding Univ. (KY)
Spring Arbor Univ. (MI)
St. Ambrose Univ. (IA)
St. Anselm Coll. (NH)
St. Bonaventure Univ. (NY)
St. Catherine Univ. (MN)
St. Cloud State Univ. (MN)
St. Edward's Univ. (TX)
St. Francis Coll. (NY)
St. Francis Univ. (PA)
St. Gregory's Univ. (OK)
St. John Fisher Coll. (NY)
St. John's Univ. (MN)
St. John's Univ. (NY)
St. Joseph's Coll. (IN)
St. Joseph's Coll. (ME)
St. Joseph's Coll. New York
St. Joseph's Univ. (PA)

St. Leo Univ. (FL)
St. Martin's Univ. (WA)
St. Mary's Coll. (IN)
St. Mary's Coll. of California
St. Mary's Univ. of Minnesota
St. Mary's Univ. of San Antonio
(TX)
St. Mary-of-the-Woods Coll. (IN)
St. Michael's Coll. (VT)
St. Norbert Coll. (WI)
St. Paul's Coll. (VA)
St. Peter's Coll. (NJ)
St. Thomas Aquinas Coll. (NY)
St. Thomas Univ. (FL)
St. Vincent Coll. (PA)
St. Xavier Univ. (IL)
Stephen F. Austin State Univ. (TX)
Stephens Coll. (MO)
Stetson Univ. (FL)
Stevenson Univ. (MD)
Stonehill Coll. (MA)
Suffolk Univ. (MA)
Sul Ross State Univ. (TX)
SUNY Coll.–Old Westbury
SUNY Coll.–Oneonta
SUNY Empire State Coll.
SUNY Institute of Technology–
Utica/Rome
SUNY–Fredonia
SUNY–Geneseo
SUNY–Oswego
SUNY–Plattsburgh
Susquehanna Univ. (PA)
Syracuse Univ. (NY)
Tabor Coll. (KS)
Tarleton State Univ. (TX)
Taylor Univ. (IN)
Temple Univ. (PA)
Tennessee State Univ.
Tennessee Technological Univ.
Tennessee Wesleyan Coll.
Texas A&M International Univ.
Texas A&M Univ.–Coll. Station
Texas A&M Univ.–Commerce
Texas A&M Univ.–Corpus Christi
Texas A&M Univ.–Kingsville
Texas Christian Univ.
Texas Lutheran Univ.
Texas State Univ.–San Marcos
Texas Tech Univ.
Texas Wesleyan Univ.
Texas Woman's Univ.
Thiel Coll. (PA)
Thomas Coll. (ME)
Thomas Edison State Coll. (NJ)
Thomas More Coll. (KY)
Thomas Univ. (GA)
Tiffin Univ. (OH)
Tougaloo Coll. (MS)
Towson Univ. (MD)
Transylvania Univ. (KY)
Trevecca Nazarene Univ. (TN)
Trine Univ. (IN)
Trinity Christian Coll. (IL)
Trinity International Univ. (IL)
Trinity Univ. (DC)
Troy Univ. (AL)
Truman State Univ. (MO)
Tulane Univ. (LA)
Tuskegee Univ. (AL)
Union Coll. (KY)

Union Coll. (NE)
Union Univ. (TN)
Univ. at Albany–SUNY
Univ. of Akron (OH)
Univ. of Alabama
Univ. of Alabama–Birmingham
Univ. of Alabama–Huntsville
Univ. of Alaska–Anchorage
Univ. of Alaska–Fairbanks
Univ. of Alaska–Southeast
Univ. of Arizona
Univ. of Arkansas
Univ. of Arkansas–Little Rock
Univ. of Arkansas–Pine Bluff
Univ. of Central Arkansas
Univ. of Central Florida
Univ. of Central Missouri
Univ. of Central Oklahoma
Univ. of Charleston (WV)
Univ. of Connecticut
Univ. of Dayton (OH)
Univ. of Delaware
Univ. of Denver
Univ. of Detroit Mercy
Univ. of Dubuque (IA)
Univ. of Evansville (IN)
Univ. of Findlay (OH)
Univ. of Florida
Univ. of Georgia
Univ. of Great Falls (MT)
Univ. of Hartford (CT)
Univ. of Hawaii–Hilo
Univ. of Hawaii–Manoa
Univ. of Houston
Univ. of Houston–Downtown
Univ. of Illinois–Chicago
Univ. of Illinois–Springfield
Univ. of Illinois–Urbana-Champaign
Univ. of Indianapolis
Univ. of Iowa
Univ. of Kansas
Univ. of Kentucky
Univ. of La Verne (CA)
Univ. of Louisiana–Lafayette
Univ. of Louisiana–Monroe
Univ. of Louisville (KY)
Univ. of Maine
Univ. of Maine–Augusta
Univ. of Mary (ND)
Univ. of Mary Hardin-Baylor (TX)
Univ. of Maryland–Coll. Park
Univ. of Maryland–Eastern Shore
Univ. of Maryland–Univ. Coll.
Univ. of Massachusetts–Amherst
Univ. of Massachusetts–Dartmouth
Univ. of Memphis
Univ. of Miami (FL)
Univ. of Michigan–Dearborn
Univ. of Michigan–Flint
Univ. of Minnesota–Crookston
Univ. of Minnesota–Duluth
Univ. of Minnesota–Twin Cities
Univ. of Mississippi
Univ. of Missouri
Univ. of Missouri–Kansas City
Univ. of Missouri–St. Louis
Univ. of Montana
Univ. of Montevallo (AL)
Univ. of Mount Union (OH)
Univ. of Nebraska–Lincoln
Univ. of Nebraska–Omaha

Univ. of Nevada–Las Vegas
Univ. of Nevada–Reno
Univ. of New Hampshire
Univ. of New Haven (CT)
Univ. of New Orleans
Univ. of North Alabama
Univ. of North Carolina–Asheville
Univ. of North Carolina–Charlotte
Univ. of North Carolina–
Greensboro
Univ. of North Carolina–Pembroke
Univ. of North Carolina–
Wilmington
Univ. of North Dakota
Univ. of North Florida
Univ. of North Texas
Univ. of Northern Iowa
Univ. of Northwestern Ohio
Univ. of Notre Dame (IN)
Univ. of Oklahoma
Univ. of Oregon
Univ. of Pennsylvania
Univ. of Pittsburgh
Univ. of Pittsburgh–Bradford
Univ. of Pittsburgh–Johnstown
Univ. of Portland (OR)
Univ. of Redlands (CA)
Univ. of Rhode Island
Univ. of Richmond (VA)
Univ. of Rio Grande (OH)
Univ. of San Diego
Univ. of San Francisco
Univ. of Scranton (PA)
Univ. of Sioux Falls (SD)
Univ. of South Alabama
Univ. of South Carolina
Univ. of South Dakota
Univ. of South Florida
Univ. of Southern California
Univ. of Southern Indiana
Univ. of Southern Maine
Univ. of Southern Mississippi
Univ. of St. Francis (IL)
Univ. of St. Francis (IN)
Univ. of St. Mary (KS)
Univ. of St. Thomas (MN)
Univ. of St. Thomas (TX)
Univ. of Tennessee
Univ. of Tennessee–Chattanooga
Univ. of Tennessee–Martin
Univ. of Texas of the Permian Basin
Univ. of Texas–Austin
Univ. of Texas–Brownsville
Univ. of Texas–Dallas
Univ. of Texas–El Paso
Univ. of Texas–Pan American
Univ. of Texas–San Antonio
Univ. of Texas–Tyler
Univ. of the Cumberlands (KY)
Univ. of the District of Columbia
Univ. of the Ozarks (AR)
Univ. of Toledo (OH)
Univ. of Tulsa (OK)
Univ. of Utah
Univ. of Virginia–Wise
Univ. of Washington
Univ. of West Alabama
Univ. of West Florida
Univ. of West Georgia
Univ. of Wisconsin–Eau Claire
Univ. of Wisconsin–Green Bay

Univ. of Wisconsin–La Crosse
Univ. of Wisconsin–Madison
Univ. of Wisconsin–Milwaukee
Univ. of Wisconsin–Oshkosh
Univ. of Wisconsin–Platteville
Univ. of Wisconsin–River Falls
Univ. of Wisconsin–Stevens Point
Univ. of Wisconsin–Superior
Univ. of Wisconsin–Whitewater
Univ. of Wyoming
Upper Iowa Univ.
Urbana Univ. (OH)
Ursuline Coll. (OH)
Utah State Univ.
Utah Valley Univ.
Utica Coll. (NY)
Valdosta State Univ. (GA)
Valparaiso Univ. (IN)
Vanguard Univ. of Southern
California
Villanova Univ. (PA)
Virginia Commonwealth Univ.
Virginia State Univ.
Virginia Tech
Virginia Union Univ.
Viterbo Univ. (WI)
Voorhees Coll. (SC)
Wagner Coll. (NY)
Wake Forest Univ. (NC)
Walsh Coll. of Accountancy and
Business Administration (MI)
Walsh Univ. (OH)
Wartburg Coll. (IA)
Washburn Univ. (KS)
Washington Adventist Univ. (MD)
Washington and Jefferson Coll.
(PA)
Washington and Lee Univ. (VA)
Washington State Univ.
Washington Univ. in St. Louis
Wayne State Univ. (MI)
Waynesburg Univ. (PA)
Webber International Univ. (FL)
Weber State Univ. (UT)
Webster Univ. (MO)
Wesley Coll. (DE)
Wesleyan Coll. (GA)
West Chester Univ. of Pennsylvania
West Texas A&M Univ.
West Virginia Univ.
West Virginia Univ. Institute of
Technology
West Virginia Wesleyan Coll.
Western Carolina Univ. (NC)
Western Connecticut State Univ.
Western Illinois Univ.
Western Kentucky Univ.
Western Michigan Univ.
Western New England Coll. (MA)
Western New Mexico Univ.
Western State Coll. of Colorado
Western Washington Univ.
Westminster Coll. (UT)
Westminster Coll. (MO)
Westminster Coll. (PA)
Wheeling Jesuit Univ. (WV)
Whitworth Univ. (WA)
Wichita State Univ. (KS)
Widener Univ. (PA)
Wilberforce Univ. (OH)
Wiley Coll. (TX)

Wilkes Univ. (PA)
William Jewell Coll. (MO)
William Paterson Univ. of New
Jersey
William Woods Univ. (MO)
Wilmington Coll. (OH)
Wilmington Univ. (DE)
Wilson Coll. (PA)
Wingate Univ. (NC)
Winston-Salem State Univ. (NC)
Wofford Coll. (SC)
Woodbury Univ. (CA)
Wright State Univ. (OH)
Xavier Univ. (OH)
Yeshiva Univ. (NY)
York Coll. (NE)
York Coll. of Pennsylvania
Youngstown State Univ. (OH)

Advanced/Graduate Dentistry and Oral Sciences (Cert., M.S., Ph.D.)

Univ. of Florida
Univ. of Kentucky

Aerospace, Aeronautical, and Astronautical Engineering

Arizona State Univ.
Auburn Univ. (AL)
Bethel Coll. (IN)
Boston Univ.
California Institute of Technology
California Polytechnic State Univ.–
San Luis Obispo
California State Polytechnic Univ.–
Pomona
California State Univ.–Long Beach
Case Western Reserve Univ. (OH)
Clarkson Univ. (NY)
Cornell Univ. (NY)
Daniel Webster Coll. (NH)
Dowling Coll. (NY)
Embry-Riddle Aeronautical Univ.
(FL)
Florida Institute of Technology
Georgia Institute of Technology
Illinois Institute of Technology
Iowa State Univ.
Massachusetts Institute of
Technology
Mississippi State Univ.
Missouri Univ. of Science &
Technology
New Mexico State Univ.
North Carolina State Univ.–Raleigh
Ohio State Univ.–Columbus
Oklahoma State Univ.
Pennsylvania State Univ.–Univ. Park
Rensselaer Polytechnic Institute
(NY)
Rochester Institute of Technology
(NY)
San Diego State Univ.
San Jose State Univ. (CA)
St. Louis Univ.
Stanford Univ. (CA)
Syracuse Univ. (NY)

Texas A&M Univ.–Coll. Station
Tuskegee Univ. (AL)
United States Air Force Academy
  (CO)
United States Naval Academy (MD)
Univ. at Buffalo–SUNY
Univ. of Alabama
Univ. of Arizona
Univ. of California–Davis
Univ. of California–Irvine
Univ. of California–Los Angeles
Univ. of California–San Diego
Univ. of Central Florida
Univ. of Colorado–Boulder
Univ. of Florida
Univ. of Illinois–Urbana-Champaign
Univ. of Kansas
Univ. of Maryland–Coll. Park
Univ. of Miami (FL)
Univ. of Michigan–Ann Arbor
Univ. of Minnesota–Twin Cities
Univ. of Notre Dame (IN)
Univ. of Oklahoma
Univ. of Southern California
Univ. of Tennessee
Univ. of Texas–Arlington
Univ. of Texas–Austin
Univ. of Virginia
Univ. of Washington
Utah State Univ.
Virginia Tech
West Virginia Univ.
Western Michigan Univ.
Wichita State Univ. (KS)
Worcester Polytechnic Institute
  (MA)

African Languages, Literatures, and Linguistics

Univ. of California–Los Angeles
Univ. of Wisconsin–Madison

Agricultural and Domestic Animal Services

Averett Univ. (VA)
Bethany Coll. (WV)
Centenary Coll. (NJ)
Colorado State Univ.
Johnson and Wales Univ. (RI)
Lake Erie Coll. (OH)
Midway Coll. (KY)
North Dakota State Univ.
Otterbein Coll. (OH)
Post Univ. (CT)
Rocky Mountain Coll. (MT)
St. Mary-of-the-Woods Coll. (IN)
Texas A&M Univ.–Coll. Station
Univ. of Findlay (OH)
Univ. of Minnesota–Crookston
Univ. of New Hampshire
Vermont Technical Coll.
Virginia Intermont Coll.
West Texas A&M Univ.
William Woods Univ. (MO)
Wilson Coll. (PA)

Agricultural and Food Products Processing

Florida A&M Univ.
Kansas State Univ.
Ohio State Univ.–Columbus
Purdue Univ.–West Lafayette (IN)
Texas A&M Univ.–Coll. Station
Univ. of Florida

Agricultural Business and Management

Abilene Christian Univ. (TX)
Alabama Agricultural and
  Mechanical Univ.
Alcorn State Univ. (MS)
Arkansas State Univ.–Jonesboro
Arkansas Tech Univ.
Auburn Univ. (AL)
Bellarmine Univ. (KY)
Berea Coll. (KY)
Bethel Univ. (MN)
Boise State Univ. (ID)
Bradley Univ. (IL)
California Lutheran Univ.
California Polytechnic State Univ.–
  San Luis Obispo
California State Polytechnic Univ.–
  Pomona
California State Univ.–Chico
California State Univ.–Fresno
Cameron Univ. (OK)
Clemson Univ. (SC)
Cleveland State Univ.
Coll. of the Ozarks (MO)
Colorado State Univ.
Cornell Univ. (NY)
Delaware State Univ.
Delaware Valley Coll. (PA)
Dillard Univ. (LA)
Dordt Coll. (IA)
Drury Univ. (MO)
Eastern Kentucky Univ.
Eastern New Mexico Univ.
Eastern Oregon Univ.
Elmhurst Coll. (IL)
Faulkner Univ. (AL)
Florida A&M Univ.
Florida Southern Coll.
Fort Hays State Univ. (KS)
Fort Lewis Coll. (CO)
Fort Valley State Univ. (GA)
Francis Marion Univ. (SC)
Gettysburg Coll. (PA)
Hannibal-LaGrange Coll. (MO)
Hardin-Simmons Univ. (TX)
Hope Coll. (MI)
Illinois State Univ.
Iowa State Univ.
Johnson and Wales Univ. (RI)
Kansas State Univ.
Lake Erie Coll. (OH)
Lincoln Univ. (MO)
Louisiana State Univ.–Baton Rouge
Louisiana Tech Univ.
Lubbock Christian Univ. (TX)
Marymount Manhattan Coll. (NY)
McPherson Coll. (KS)
Michigan State Univ.
Middle Tennessee State Univ.

Mississippi State Univ.
Missouri State Univ.
Montana State Univ.
Neumann Univ. (PA)
New Mexico State Univ.
Nicholls State Univ. (LA)
North Carolina A&T State Univ.
North Carolina State Univ.–Raleigh
North Dakota State Univ.
Northwest Missouri State Univ.
Northwestern Oklahoma State
  Univ.
Ohio State Univ.–Columbus
Oklahoma State Univ.
Oregon State Univ.
Pennsylvania State Univ.–Univ. Park
Peru State Coll. (NE)
Purdue Univ.–West Lafayette (IN)
Regis Univ. (CO)
Rocky Mountain Coll. (MT)
Sam Houston State Univ. (TX)
San Diego State Univ.
Shippensburg Univ. of Pennsylvania
South Carolina State Univ.
South Dakota State Univ.
Southeast Missouri State Univ.
Southern Arkansas Univ.
Southern Illinois Univ.–Carbondale
Southern New Hampshire Univ.
Southern Univ. and A&M Coll. (LA)
Southwest Minnesota State Univ.
Southwestern Univ. (TX)
Stephen F. Austin State Univ. (TX)
Sul Ross State Univ. (TX)
SUNY Coll. of Agriculture and
  Technology–Cobleskill
SUNY–Plattsburgh
Tarleton State Univ. (TX)
Texas A&M Univ.–Coll. Station
Texas A&M Univ.–Commerce
Texas A&M Univ.–Kingsville
Texas Christian Univ.
Texas State Univ.–San Marcos
Texas Tech Univ.
Tufts Univ. (MA)
Tuskegee Univ. (AL)
Univ. of Arizona
Univ. of Arkansas
Univ. of Arkansas–Pine Bluff
Univ. of California–Davis
Univ. of Central Missouri
Univ. of Connecticut
Univ. of Delaware
Univ. of Florida
Univ. of Georgia
Univ. of Illinois–Urbana-Champaign
Univ. of Kentucky
Univ. of Louisiana–Monroe
Univ. of Maine
Univ. of Maryland–Coll. Park
Univ. of Maryland–Eastern Shore
Univ. of Minnesota–Crookston
Univ. of Minnesota–Twin Cities
Univ. of Missouri
Univ. of Nebraska–Kearney
Univ. of Nebraska–Lincoln
Univ. of Nevada–Reno
Univ. of New Hampshire
Univ. of South Dakota
Univ. of Tennessee
Univ. of Wisconsin–Madison

Univ. of Wisconsin–Platteville
Univ. of Wisconsin–River Falls
Univ. of Wyoming
Utah State Univ.
Vermont Technical Coll.
Virginia Tech
Washington State Univ.
West Texas A&M Univ.
West Virginia Univ.
Westminster Coll. (MO)

Agricultural Mechanization

California Polytechnic State Univ.–
  San Luis Obispo
Clemson Univ. (SC)
Coll. of the Ozarks (MO)
Florida A&M Univ.
Kansas State Univ.
Middle Tennessee State Univ.
Montana State Univ.
North Carolina State Univ.–Raleigh
North Dakota State Univ.
Pennsylvania State Univ.–Univ. Park
Sam Houston State Univ. (TX)
South Dakota State Univ.
Stephen F. Austin State Univ. (TX)
SUNY Coll. of Agriculture and
  Technology–Cobleskill
Tarleton State Univ. (TX)
Texas A&M Univ.–Kingsville
Univ. of Illinois–Urbana-Champaign
Univ. of Missouri
Univ. of Nebraska–Lincoln
Univ. of Wisconsin–River Falls
Washington State Univ.

Agricultural Production Operations

Angelo State Univ. (TX)
Auburn Univ. (AL)
Brigham Young Univ.–Provo (UT)
California State Polytechnic Univ.–
  Pomona
Cornell Univ. (NY)
Delaware Valley Coll. (PA)
Eastern Kentucky Univ.
Florida A&M Univ.
Lake Erie Coll. (OH)
Montana State Univ.–Northern
North Dakota State Univ.
Purdue Univ.–West Lafayette (IN)
Southern Nazarene Univ. (OK)
St. Mary-of-the-Woods Coll. (IN)
Stephen F. Austin State Univ. (TX)
Tarleton State Univ. (TX)
Texas A&M Univ.–Coll. Station
Unity Coll. (ME)
Univ. of Hawaii–Hilo
Univ. of Illinois–Urbana-Champaign
Univ. of Maine
Univ. of Minnesota–Crookston
Univ. of New England (ME)
Univ. of New Hampshire
Vermont Technical Coll.
Washington State Univ.

Agricultural Public Services

Kansas State Univ.
Michigan State Univ.
North Carolina State Univ.–Raleigh
North Dakota State Univ.
Oklahoma State Univ.
Pennsylvania State Univ.–Univ. Park
Purdue Univ.–West Lafayette (IN)
Tarleton State Univ. (TX)
Texas Tech Univ.
Univ. of Georgia
Univ. of Illinois–Urbana-Champaign
Univ. of Kentucky
Univ. of Missouri
Univ. of Nebraska–Lincoln
Univ. of Wisconsin–Madison
Univ. of Wyoming
Washington State Univ.

Agricultural/Biological Engineering and Bioengineering

Auburn Univ. (AL)
California Polytechnic State Univ.–
  San Luis Obispo
Cornell Univ. (NY)
Florida A&M Univ.
Iowa State Univ.
Kansas State Univ.
Michigan State Univ.
New Mexico State Univ.
North Carolina A&T State Univ.
North Carolina State Univ.–Raleigh
North Dakota State Univ.
Ohio State Univ.–Columbus
Oklahoma State Univ.
Pennsylvania State Univ.–Univ. Park
Rutgers, the State Univ. of New
  Jersey–New Brunswick
South Dakota State Univ.
Texas A&M Univ.–Coll. Station
Univ. of Arizona
Univ. of Arkansas
Univ. of California–Davis
Univ. of California–Los Angeles
Univ. of Florida
Univ. of Georgia
Univ. of Hawaii–Manoa
Univ. of Illinois–Urbana-Champaign
Univ. of Kentucky
Univ. of Maine
Univ. of Maryland–Coll. Park
Univ. of Minnesota–Twin Cities
Univ. of Missouri
Univ. of Nebraska–Lincoln
Univ. of Tennessee
Univ. of the Pacific (CA)
Univ. of Wisconsin–Madison
Utah State Univ.
Virginia Tech
Washington State Univ.

Agriculture, Agriculture Operations, and Related Sciences

Alabama Agricultural and
  Mechanical Univ.
California State Polytechnic Univ.–
  Pomona
California State Univ.–Fresno

California State Univ.–Stanislaus
Evergreen State Coll. (WA)
Michigan State Univ.
North Carolina A&T State Univ.
Ohio State Univ.–Columbus
Prescott Coll. (AZ)
Tennessee State Univ.
Texas A&M Univ.–Commerce
Univ. of Arizona
Univ. of Arkansas–Pine Bluff
Univ. of California–Davis
Univ. of Georgia
Univ. of Kentucky
Univ. of Massachusetts–Amherst

Air Transportation

Averett Univ. (VA)
Baylor Univ. (TX)
Bowling Green State Univ. (OH)
Bridgewater State Coll. (MA)
Central Washington Univ.
Coll. of the Ozarks (MO)
Daniel Webster Coll. (NH)
Delaware State Univ.
Delta State Univ. (MS)
Eastern Kentucky Univ.
Eastern Michigan Univ.
Elizabeth City State Univ. (NC)
Embry-Riddle Aeronautical Univ.
   (FL)
Farmingdale State Coll.–SUNY
Florida Institute of Technology
Geneva Coll. (PA)
Hampton Univ. (VA)
Henderson State Univ. (AR)
Indiana State Univ.
Jacksonville Univ. (FL)
Kansas State Univ.
Kent State Univ. (OH)
LeTourneau Univ. (TX)
Lewis Univ. (IL)
Liberty Univ. (VA)
Louisiana Tech Univ.
Marywood Univ. (PA)
Metropolitan State Coll. of Denver
Middle Tennessee State Univ.
Minnesota State Univ.–Mankato
Northern Michigan Univ.
Ohio State Univ.–Columbus
Ohio Univ.
Oklahoma State Univ.
Pacific Union Coll. (CA)
Park Univ. (MO)
Purdue Univ.–West Lafayette (IN)
Quincy Univ. (IL)
Robert Morris Univ. (PA)
Rocky Mountain Coll. (MT)
San Jose State Univ. (CA)
Southeastern Oklahoma State Univ.
Southern Illinois Univ.–Carbondale
Southern Nazarene Univ. (OK)
St. Cloud State Univ. (MN)
St. Louis Univ.
Tarleton State Univ. (TX)
Thomas Edison State Coll. (NJ)
Univ. of Alaska–Anchorage
Univ. of Central Missouri
Univ. of Dubuque (IA)
Univ. of Illinois–Urbana-Champaign
Univ. of Louisiana–Monroe

Univ. of Maryland–Eastern Shore
Univ. of Minnesota–Crookston
Univ. of Nebraska–Omaha
Univ. of North Dakota
Univ. of Oklahoma
Univ. of the District of Columbia
Utah State Univ.
Utah Valley Univ.
Vaughn Coll. of Aeronautics and
   Technology (NY)
Western Michigan Univ.
Westminster Coll. (UT)
Wilmington Univ. (DE)

Allied Health and Medical Assisting Services

Boise State Univ. (ID)
Coll. of St. Mary (NE)
Drury Univ. (MO)
Fairmont State Univ. (WV)
Fort Valley State Univ. (GA)
Medaille Coll. (NY)
Michigan State Univ.
Missouri State Univ.
Murray State Univ. (KY)
National-Louis Univ. (IL)
New York Institute of Technology
Newberry Coll. (SC)
North Dakota State Univ.
Northern Michigan Univ.
Ohio State Univ.–Columbus
Quinnipiac Univ. (CT)
Shawnee State Univ. (OH)
St. John's Univ. (NY)
Tennessee State Univ.
Thomas Edison State Coll. (NJ)
Univ. of Evansville (IN)
Univ. of Findlay (OH)
Univ. of Louisiana–Monroe
Univ. of Louisville (KY)
Univ. of Maryland–Coll. Park
Univ. of Maryland–Eastern Shore
Univ. of Nebraska–Lincoln
Vermont Technical Coll.
Washington Adventist Univ. (MD)
Wayne State Univ. (MI)
Wilson Coll. (PA)

Allied Health Diagnostic, Intervention, and Treatment Professions

Albion Coll. (MI)
Alcorn State Univ. (MS)
Alderson-Broaddus Coll. (WV)
Alfred Univ. (NY)
Alma Coll. (MI)
Alvernia Univ. (PA)
Anderson Univ. (IN)
Angelo State Univ. (TX)
Appalachian State Univ. (NC)
Aquinas Coll. (MI)
Arkansas State Univ.–Jonesboro
Armstrong Atlantic State Univ. (GA)
Augustana Coll. (SD)
Averett Univ. (VA)
Avila Univ. (MO)
Baldwin-Wallace Coll. (OH)
Ball State Univ. (IN)

Barry Univ. (FL)
Barton Coll. (NC)
Baylor Univ. (TX)
Bellarmine Univ. (KY)
Belmont Univ. (TN)
Benedictine Coll. (KS)
Benedictine Univ. (IL)
Bethel Coll. (KS)
Bethel Univ. (MN)
Bloomfield Coll. (NJ)
Bloomsburg Univ. of Pennsylvania
Bluefield State Coll. (WV)
Boise State Univ. (ID)
Boston Univ.
Bowling Green State Univ. (OH)
Briar Cliff Univ. (IA)
Bridgewater Coll. (VA)
Bridgewater State Coll. (MA)
Brigham Young Univ.–Provo (UT)
Buena Vista Univ. (IA)
Butler Univ. (IN)
California State Univ.–Long Beach
California State Univ.–Sacramento
California Univ. of Pennsylvania
Campbell Univ. (NC)
Canisius Coll. (NY)
Capital Univ. (OH)
Carlow Univ. (PA)
Carroll Univ. (WI)
Carson-Newman Coll. (TN)
Carthage Coll. (WI)
Cedarville Univ. (OH)
Central Connecticut State Univ.
Central Methodist Univ. (MO)
Central Michigan Univ.
Central Washington Univ.
Champlain Coll. (VT)
Chapman Univ. (CA)
Clarion Univ. of Pennsylvania
Coe Coll. (IA)
Colby-Sawyer Coll. (NH)
Coll. of Charleston (SC)
Coll. of Mount St. Joseph (OH)
Coll. of Notre Dame of Maryland
Concord Univ. (WV)
Concordia Univ. Chicago (IL)
Concordia Univ. Wisconsin
Culver-Stockton Coll. (MO)
Cumberland Univ. (TN)
CUNY–City Coll.
CUNY–Coll. of Staten Island
D'Youville Coll. (NY)
Daemen Coll. (NY)
Dakota State Univ. (SD)
Dakota Wesleyan Univ. (SD)
Defiance Coll. (OH)
Delta State Univ. (MS)
DePauw Univ. (IN)
DeSales Univ. (PA)
Dominican Coll. (NY)
Drexel Univ. (PA)
Drury Univ. (MO)
Duquesne Univ. (PA)
East Carolina Univ. (NC)
East Stroudsburg Univ. of
   Pennsylvania
East Texas Baptist Univ.
Eastern Kentucky Univ.
Eastern Michigan Univ.
Eastern Washington Univ.
Elon Univ. (NC)

Emory and Henry Coll. (VA)
Emory Univ. (GA)
Emporia State Univ. (KS)
Erskine Coll. (SC)
Eureka Coll. (IL)
Fairleigh Dickinson Univ. (NJ)
Florida Southern Coll.
Florida State Univ.
Fort Hays State Univ. (KS)
Fort Lewis Coll. (CO)
Franklin Coll. (IN)
Fresno Pacific Univ. (CA)
Frostburg State Univ. (MD)
Gannon Univ. (PA)
George Washington Univ. (DC)
Georgetown Coll. (KY)
Georgia Southern Univ.
Georgia State Univ.
Georgian Court Univ. (NJ)
Graceland Univ. (IA)
Grand Valley State Univ. (MI)
Greensboro Coll. (NC)
Guilford Coll. (NC)
Gustavus Adolphus Coll. (MN)
Gwynedd-Mercy Coll. (PA)
Hardin-Simmons Univ. (TX)
Harding Univ. (AR)
High Point Univ. (NC)
Hofstra Univ. (NY)
Holy Family Univ. (PA)
Hope Coll. (MI)
Howard Payne Univ. (TX)
Howard Univ. (DC)
Huntingdon Coll. (AL)
Idaho State Univ.
Illinois State Univ.
Indiana State Univ.
Indiana Univ. East
Indiana Univ. Northwest
Indiana Univ. of Pennsylvania
Indiana Univ.–Bloomington
Indiana Univ.–Kokomo
Indiana Univ.–Purdue Univ.–
   Indianapolis
Indiana Wesleyan Univ.
Ithaca Coll. (NY)
James Madison Univ. (VA)
Jamestown Coll. (ND)
John Brown Univ. (AR)
Kansas State Univ.
Kean Univ. (NJ)
Keene State Coll. (NH)
Kent State Univ. (OH)
King's Coll. (PA)
La Roche Coll. (PA)
Lake Superior State Univ. (MI)
Lasell Coll. (MA)
Lees-McRae Coll. (NC)
Lenoir-Rhyne Univ. (NC)
Lewis Univ. (IL)
Liberty Univ. (VA)
Limestone Coll. (SC)
Lincoln Memorial Univ. (TN)
Lindenwood Univ. (MO)
Linfield Coll. (OR)
Lipscomb Univ. (TN)
Long Island Univ.–C.W. Post
   Campus (NY)
Louisiana Coll.
Luther Coll. (IA)
Lynchburg Coll. (VA)

Madonna Univ. (MI)
Manchester Coll. (IN)
Mansfield Univ. of Pennsylvania
Marian Univ. (WI)
Marietta Coll. (OH)
Marist Coll. (NY)
Marquette Univ. (WI)
Marshall Univ. (WV)
Marywood Univ. (PA)
McKendree Univ. (IL)
McMurry Univ. (TX)
McNeese State Univ. (LA)
Merrimack Coll. (MA)
Messiah Coll. (PA)
Methodist Univ. (NC)
Miami Univ.–Oxford (OH)
Midwestern State Univ. (TX)
Millikin Univ. (IL)
Minnesota State Univ.–Mankato
Minnesota State Univ.–Moorhead
Minot State Univ. (ND)
Misericordia Univ. (PA)
Missouri State Univ.
Montana State Univ.–Billings
Montclair State Univ. (NJ)
Morehead State Univ. (KY)
Mount Aloysius Coll. (PA)
Mount Marty Coll. (SD)
Mountain State Univ. (WV)
National-Louis Univ. (IL)
Nebraska Wesleyan Univ.
New Mexico State Univ.
Newman Univ. (KS)
North Carolina Central Univ.
North Central Coll. (IL)
North Dakota State Univ.
North Georgia Coll. and State Univ.
North Park Univ. (IL)
Northeastern Univ. (MA)
Northern Arizona Univ.
Northern Kentucky Univ.
Northern Michigan Univ.
Northwestern State Univ. of
   Louisiana
Norwich Univ. (VT)
Nova Southeastern Univ. (FL)
Ohio Northern Univ.
Ohio State Univ.–Columbus
Ohio Univ.
Oklahoma State Univ.
Old Dominion Univ. (VA)
Olivet Nazarene Univ. (IL)
Oregon Institute of Technology
Otterbein Coll. (OH)
Ouachita Baptist Univ. (AR)
Pace Univ. (NY)
Palm Beach Atlantic Univ. (FL)
Park Univ. (MO)
Philadelphia Univ.
Plymouth State Univ. (NH)
Point Loma Nazarene Univ. (CA)
Purdue Univ.–West Lafayette (IN)
Quinnipiac Univ. (CT)
Ramapo Coll. of New Jersey
Regis Univ. (CO)
Rhode Island Coll.
Roanoke Coll. (VA)
Rochester Institute of Technology
   (NY)
Rocky Mountain Coll. (MT)
Roosevelt Univ. (IL)

Rutgers, the State Univ. of New
  Jersey–Newark
Sacred Heart Univ. (CT)
Saginaw Valley State Univ. (MI)
Salem State Coll. (MA)
Salisbury Univ. (MD)
Samford Univ. (AL)
Seattle Univ.
Seton Hill Univ. (PA)
Shaw Univ. (NC)
Shenandoah Univ. (VA)
Simpson Coll. (IA)
Slippery Rock Univ. of Pennsylvania
South Dakota State Univ.
Southeastern Louisiana Univ.
Southern Arkansas Univ.
Southern Illinois Univ.–Carbondale
Southern Nazarene Univ. (OK)
Southern Utah Univ.
Southwest Baptist Univ. (MO)
Southwestern Coll. (KS)
Springfield Coll. (MA)
St. Catherine Univ. (MN)
St. Cloud State Univ. (MN)
St. Francis Coll. (NY)
St. Francis Univ. (PA)
St. John's Univ. (NY)
St. Louis Univ.
St. Mary's Univ. of Minnesota
St. Vincent Coll. (PA)
Sterling Coll. (KS)
SUNY Coll.–Cortland
SUNY–Stony Brook
Tabor Coll. (KS)
Texas Christian Univ.
Texas Lutheran Univ.
Texas State Univ.–San Marcos
Thomas Edison State Coll. (NJ)
Touro Coll. (NY)
Towson Univ. (MD)
Trinity International Univ. (IL)
Troy Univ. (AL)
Tulane Univ. (LA)
Tusculum Coll. (TN)
Union Coll. (NE)
Union Univ. (TN)
Univ. at Buffalo–SUNY
Univ. of Akron (OH)
Univ. of Alabama
Univ. of Alabama–Birmingham
Univ. of Arkansas–Monticello
Univ. of Central Arkansas
Univ. of Central Florida
Univ. of Charleston (WV)
Univ. of Connecticut
Univ. of Delaware
Univ. of Evansville (IN)
Univ. of Findlay (OH)
Univ. of Florida
Univ. of Hartford (CT)
Univ. of Illinois–Urbana-Champaign
Univ. of Indianapolis
Univ. of Iowa
Univ. of Kansas
Univ. of Kentucky
Univ. of La Verne (CA)
Univ. of Louisiana–Lafayette
Univ. of Louisiana–Monroe
Univ. of Louisville (KY)
Univ. of Mary (ND)
Univ. of Mary Hardin-Baylor (TX)

Univ. of Maryland–Baltimore
  County
Univ. of Maryland–Eastern Shore
Univ. of Miami (FL)
Univ. of Michigan–Ann Arbor
Univ. of Michigan–Flint
Univ. of Minnesota–Duluth
Univ. of Minnesota–Twin Cities
Univ. of Missouri
Univ. of Mount Union (OH)
Univ. of Nebraska–Kearney
Univ. of Nebraska–Lincoln
Univ. of Nevada–Las Vegas
Univ. of New England (ME)
Univ. of New Hampshire
Univ. of New Mexico
Univ. of North Carolina–Chapel Hill
Univ. of North Carolina–Pembroke
Univ. of North Carolina–
  Wilmington
Univ. of North Dakota
Univ. of North Florida
Univ. of Northern Iowa
Univ. of Oklahoma
Univ. of Pittsburgh–Bradford
Univ. of Sioux Falls (SD)
Univ. of South Alabama
Univ. of South Carolina
Univ. of South Dakota
Univ. of South Florida
Univ. of Southern Indiana
Univ. of Southern Mississippi
Univ. of St. Francis (IL)
Univ. of St. Francis (IN)
Univ. of Tampa (FL)
Univ. of Texas–Arlington
Univ. of Texas–Austin
Univ. of Texas–Pan American
Univ. of the Incarnate Word (TX)
Univ. of Toledo (OH)
Univ. of Tulsa (OK)
Univ. of Vermont
Univ. of Washington
Univ. of West Alabama
Univ. of Wisconsin–Eau Claire
Univ. of Wisconsin–La Crosse
Univ. of Wisconsin–Madison
Univ. of Wisconsin–Oshkosh
Valdosta State Univ. (GA)
Vanguard Univ. of Southern
  California
Virginia Commonwealth Univ.
Wagner Coll. (NY)
Washburn Univ. (KS)
Washington Adventist Univ. (MD)
Washington State Univ.
Wayne State Coll. (NE)
Wayne State Univ. (MI)
Waynesburg Univ. (PA)
Weber State Univ. (UT)
West Chester Univ. of Pennsylvania
West Texas A&M Univ.
West Virginia Wesleyan Coll.
Western Carolina Univ. (NC)
Western Michigan Univ.
Wheeling Jesuit Univ. (WV)
Whitworth Univ. (WA)
Wichita State Univ. (KS)
William Woods Univ. (MO)
Wilmington Coll. (OH)
Wingate Univ. (NC)

Wright State Univ. (OH)
Xavier Univ. (OH)
York Coll. of Pennsylvania
Youngstown State Univ. (OH)

Alternative and Complementary Medicine and Medical Systems

Maharishi Univ. of Management
  (IA)

American Literature (United States and Canadian)

American Jewish Univ. (CA)
Ashland Univ. (OH)
Bennington Coll. (VT)
Creighton Univ. (NE)
CUNY–Baruch Coll.
Eastern Michigan Univ.
Eastern Nazarene Coll. (MA)
Harvard Univ. (MA)
Lawrence Univ. (WI)
Marlboro Coll. (VT)
Middlebury Coll. (VT)
New York Univ.
Tufts Univ. (MA)
Univ. of California–Los Angeles
Univ. of Pittsburgh–Johnstown
Univ. of Southern California

American Sign Language (ASL)

Arcadia Univ. (PA)
Augustana Coll. (SD)
Bethel Coll. (IN)
Columbia Coll. (IL)
Eastern Kentucky Univ.
Gallaudet Univ. (DC)
Gardner-Webb Univ. (NC)
Goshen Coll. (IN)
Idaho State Univ.
Indiana Univ.–Purdue Univ.–
  Indianapolis
Kent State Univ. (OH)
Madonna Univ. (MI)
Maryville Coll. (TN)
Mount Aloysius Coll. (PA)
North Central Univ. (MN)
Northeastern Univ. (MA)
Pacific Lutheran Univ. (WA)
Rochester Institute of Technology
  (NY)
St. Catherine Univ. (MN)
Univ. of Arkansas–Little Rock
Univ. of Louisville (KY)
Univ. of New Mexico
Univ. of Rochester (NY)
Valdosta State Univ. (GA)
Western Oregon Univ.

Animal Sciences

Abilene Christian Univ. (TX)
Alabama Agricultural and
  Mechanical Univ.
Alcorn State Univ. (MS)

Andrews Univ. (MI)
Angelo State Univ. (TX)
Arkansas State Univ.–Jonesboro
Auburn Univ. (AL)
Berry Coll. (GA)
California Polytechnic State Univ.–
  San Luis Obispo
California State Polytechnic Univ.–
  Pomona
Coll. of the Ozarks (MO)
Colorado State Univ.
Cornell Univ. (NY)
Delaware State Univ.
Delaware Valley Coll. (PA)
Dordt Coll. (IA)
Fort Valley State Univ. (GA)
Hardin-Simmons Univ. (TX)
Iowa State Univ.
Kansas State Univ.
Louisiana State Univ.–Baton Rouge
Louisiana Tech Univ.
Michigan State Univ.
Mississippi State Univ.
Missouri State Univ.
Montana State Univ.
New Mexico State Univ.
North Carolina A&T State Univ.
North Carolina State Univ.–Raleigh
North Dakota State Univ.
Northwest Missouri State Univ.
Ohio State Univ.–Columbus
Oklahoma Panhandle State Univ.
Oklahoma State Univ.
Oregon State Univ.
Pennsylvania State Univ.–Univ. Park
Rutgers, the State Univ. of New
  Jersey–New Brunswick
South Dakota State Univ.
Southeast Missouri State Univ.
Southern Illinois Univ.–Carbondale
Stephen F. Austin State Univ. (TX)
Sul Ross State Univ. (TX)
SUNY Coll. of Agriculture and
  Technology–Cobleskill
Tarleton State Univ. (TX)
Texas A&M Univ.–Coll. Station
Texas A&M Univ.–Commerce
Texas A&M Univ.–Kingsville
Texas State Univ.–San Marcos
Texas Tech Univ.
Tuskegee Univ. (AL)
Univ. of Arizona
Univ. of Arkansas
Univ. of California–Davis
Univ. of Connecticut
Univ. of Delaware
Univ. of Denver
Univ. of Findlay (OH)
Univ. of Florida
Univ. of Georgia
Univ. of Hawaii–Hilo
Univ. of Hawaii–Manoa
Univ. of Illinois–Urbana-Champaign
Univ. of Kentucky
Univ. of Maine
Univ. of Maryland–Coll. Park
Univ. of Maryland–Eastern Shore
Univ. of Massachusetts–Amherst
Univ. of Minnesota–Crookston
Univ. of Minnesota–Twin Cities
Univ. of Missouri

Univ. of Nebraska–Lincoln
Univ. of Nevada–Reno
Univ. of New Hampshire
Univ. of Rhode Island
Univ. of Tennessee
Univ. of Vermont
Univ. of Wisconsin–Madison
Univ. of Wisconsin–Platteville
Univ. of Wisconsin–River Falls
Univ. of Wyoming
Utah State Univ.
Vermont Technical Coll.
Virginia Tech
Washington State Univ.
West Texas A&M Univ.
West Virginia Univ.

Anthropology

Adelphi Univ. (NY)
Albion Coll. (MI)
Alma Coll. (MI)
American Univ. (DC)
Amherst Coll. (MA)
Appalachian State Univ. (NC)
Arizona State Univ.
Auburn Univ. (AL)
Ball State Univ. (IN)
Barnard Coll. (NY)
Bates Coll. (ME)
Baylor Univ. (TX)
Beloit Coll. (WI)
Bennington Coll. (VT)
Binghamton Univ.–SUNY
Biola Univ. (CA)
Bloomsburg Univ. of Pennsylvania
Boise State Univ. (ID)
Boston Univ.
Bowdoin Coll. (ME)
Brandeis Univ. (MA)
Bridgewater State Coll. (MA)
Brigham Young Univ.–Hawaii
Brigham Young University–Provo
  (UT)
Brown Univ. (RI)
Bryn Mawr Coll. (PA)
Bucknell Univ. (PA)
Buffalo State Coll.–SUNY
Butler Univ. (IN)
California State Polytechnic Univ.–
  Pomona
California State Univ.–Bakersfield
California State Univ.–Chico
California State Univ.–Dominguez
  Hills
California State Univ.–East Bay
California State Univ.–Fresno
California State Univ.–Fullerton
California State Univ.–Long Beach
California State Univ.–Los Angeles
California State Univ.–Northridge
California State Univ.–Sacramento
California State Univ.–San
  Bernardino
California State Univ.–Stanislaus
Canisius Coll. (NY)
Carnegie Mellon Univ. (PA)
Case Western Reserve Univ. (OH)
Catholic Univ. of America (DC)
Central Coll. (IA)
Central Connecticut State Univ.

Central Michigan Univ.
Central Washington Univ.
Clarion Univ. of Pennsylvania
Cleveland State Univ.
Colby Coll. (ME)
Colgate Univ. (NY)
Coll. at Brockport–SUNY
Coll. of Charleston (SC)
Coll. of Idaho (ID)
Coll. of the Holy Cross (MA)
Coll. of William and Mary (VA)
Coll. of Wooster (OH)
Colorado Coll.
Colorado State Univ.
Columbia Univ. (NY)
Connecticut Coll.
Cornell Coll. (IA)
Cornell Univ. (NY)
Creighton Univ. (NE)
CUNY–Brooklyn Coll.
CUNY–City Coll.
CUNY–Hunter Coll.
CUNY–Lehman Coll.
CUNY–Queens Coll.
CUNY–York Coll.
Dartmouth Coll. (NH)
Davidson Coll. (NC)
Denison Univ. (OH)
DePaul Univ. (IL)
DePauw Univ. (IN)
Dickinson Coll. (PA)
Drake Univ. (IA)
Drew Univ. (NJ)
Drexel Univ. (PA)
Duke Univ. (NC)
Earlham Coll. (IN)
East Carolina Univ. (NC)
Eastern Kentucky Univ.
Eastern Michigan Univ.
Eastern New Mexico Univ.
Eastern Washington Univ.
Eckerd Coll. (FL)
Edinboro Univ of Pennsylvania
Elizabethtown Coll. (PA)
Emory and Henry Coll. (VA)
Emory Univ. (GA)
Florida Atlantic Univ.
Florida State Univ.
Fordham Univ. (NY)
Fort Lewis Coll. (CO)
Franciscan Univ. of Steubenville
    (OH)
Franklin and Marshall Coll. (PA)
Franklin Pierce Univ. (NH)
George Mason Univ. (VA)
George Washington Univ. (DC)
Georgetown Univ. (DC)
Georgia Southern Univ.
Georgia State Univ.
Grand Valley State Univ. (MI)
Grinnell Coll. (IA)
Gustavus Adolphus Coll. (MN)
Hamilton Coll. (NY)
Hamline Univ. (MN)
Hampshire Coll. (MA)
Hanover Coll. (IN)
Hartwick Coll. (NY)
Harvard Univ. (MA)
Haverford Coll. (PA)
Hawaii Pacific Univ.
Heidelberg Univ. (OH)

Hobart and William Smith Colleges
    (NY)
Hofstra Univ. (NY)
Howard Univ. (DC)
Humboldt State Univ. (CA)
Idaho State Univ.
Illinois State Univ.
Illinois Wesleyan Univ.
Indiana State Univ.
Indiana Univ. of Pennsylvania
Indiana Univ.–Bloomington
Indiana Univ.-Purdue Univ.–Fort
    Wayne
Indiana Univ.-Purdue Univ.–
    Indianapolis
Iowa State Univ.
Ithaca Coll. (NY)
James Madison Univ. (VA)
Johns Hopkins Univ. (MD)
Johnson State Coll. (VT)
Juniata Coll. (PA)
Kansas State Univ.
Kennesaw State Univ. (GA)
Kent State Univ. (OH)
Kenyon Coll. (OH)
Kutztown Univ. of Pennsylvania
Lawrence Univ. (WI)
Lehigh Univ. (PA)
Lincoln Univ. (PA)
Linfield Coll. (OR)
Longwood Univ. (VA)
Louisiana State Univ.–Baton Rouge
Loyola Univ. Chicago
Luther Coll. (IA)
Macalester Coll. (MN)
Marlboro Coll. (VT)
Marquette Univ. (WI)
Marylhurst Univ. (OR)
Massachusetts Institute of
    Technology
Mercyhurst Coll. (PA)
Metropolitan State Coll. of Denver
Miami Univ.–Oxford (OH)
Michigan State Univ.
Michigan Technological Univ.
Middle Tennessee State Univ.
Millersville Univ. of Pennsylvania
Millsaps Coll. (MS)
Minnesota State Univ.–Mankato
Minnesota State Univ.–Moorhead
Mississippi State Univ.
Missouri State Univ.
Missouri Valley Coll.
Monmouth Univ. (NJ)
Montana State Univ.
Montclair State Univ. (NJ)
Mount Holyoke Coll. (MA)
Muhlenberg Coll. (PA)
Nazareth Coll. (NY)
New Mexico State Univ.
New York Univ.
North Carolina State Univ.–Raleigh
North Central Coll. (IL)
North Dakota State Univ.
North Park Univ. (IL)
Northeastern Illinois Univ.
Northeastern Univ. (MA)
Northern Arizona Univ.
Northern Illinois Univ.
Northern Kentucky Univ.
Northwestern Univ. (IL)

Oakland Univ. (MI)
Oberlin Coll. (OH)
Occidental Coll. (CA)
Ohio State Univ.–Columbus
Ohio Univ.
Oklahoma Baptist Univ.
Oregon State Univ.
Pacific Lutheran Univ. (WA)
Pacific Univ. (OR)
Pennsylvania State Univ.–Univ. Park
Pitzer Coll. (CA)
Pomona Coll. (CA)
Portland State Univ. (OR)
Prescott Coll. (AZ)
Princeton Univ. (NJ)
Principia Coll. (IL)
Purchase Coll.–SUNY
Purdue Univ.–West Lafayette (IN)
Radford Univ. (VA)
Reed Coll. (OR)
Rhode Island Coll.
Rhodes Coll. (TN)
Rice Univ. (TX)
Ripon Coll. (WI)
Roger Williams Univ. (RI)
Rollins Coll. (FL)
Rutgers, the State Univ. of New
    Jersey–New Brunswick
Rutgers, the State Univ. of New
    Jersey–Newark
Salve Regina Univ. (RI)
San Diego State Univ.
San Francisco State Univ.
San Jose State Univ. (CA)
Santa Clara Univ. (CA)
Scripps Coll. (CA)
Seattle Univ.
Seton Hall Univ. (NJ)
Sewanee–Univ. of the South (TN)
Skidmore Coll. (NY)
Smith Coll. (MA)
Sonoma State Univ. (CA)
Southeast Missouri State Univ.
Southern Illinois Univ.–Carbondale
Southern Illinois Univ.–Edwardsville
Southern Methodist Univ. (TX)
Southern Oregon Univ.
Southwestern Univ. (TX)
St. Cloud State Univ. (MN)
St. John Fisher Coll. (NY)
St. John's Univ. (NY)
St. Lawrence Univ. (NY)
St. Martin's Univ. (WA)
St. Mary's Coll. (IN)
St. Mary's Coll. of California
St. Mary's Coll. of Maryland
St. Michael's Coll. (VT)
St. Vincent Coll. (PA)
Stanford Univ. (CA)
SUNY Coll.–Cortland
SUNY Coll.–Oneonta
SUNY Coll.–Potsdam
SUNY–Fredonia
SUNY–Geneseo
SUNY–Oswego
SUNY–Plattsburgh
SUNY–Stony Brook
Syracuse Univ. (NY)
Texas A&M Univ.–Coll. Station
Texas A&M Univ.–Kingsville
Texas Christian Univ.

Texas State Univ.–San Marcos
Texas Tech Univ.
Thomas Edison State Coll. (NJ)
Tougaloo Coll. (MS)
Transylvania Univ. (KY)
Trinity Coll. (CT)
Truman State Univ. (MO)
Tufts Univ. (MA)
Tulane Univ. (LA)
Union Coll. (NY)
Univ. at Albany–SUNY
Univ. at Buffalo–SUNY
Univ. of Alabama
Univ. of Alabama–Birmingham
Univ. of Alaska–Anchorage
Univ. of Alaska–Fairbanks
Univ. of Arizona
Univ. of Arkansas
Univ. of California–Berkeley
Univ. of California–Davis
Univ. of California–Irvine
Univ. of California–Los Angeles
Univ. of California–Riverside
Univ. of California–San Diego
Univ. of California–Santa Barbara
Univ. of California–Santa Cruz
Univ. of Central Florida
Univ. of Central Missouri
Univ. of Chicago
Univ. of Colorado–Boulder
Univ. of Colorado–Colorado
    Springs
Univ. of Colorado–Denver
Univ. of Connecticut
Univ. of Delaware
Univ. of Denver
Univ. of Florida
Univ. of Georgia
Univ. of Hawaii–Hilo
Univ. of Hawaii–Manoa
Univ. of Houston
Univ. of Illinois–Chicago
Univ. of Illinois–Urbana-Champaign
Univ. of Indianapolis
Univ. of Iowa
Univ. of Kansas
Univ. of Kentucky
Univ. of La Verne (CA)
Univ. of Louisiana–Lafayette
Univ. of Louisville (KY)
Univ. of Maine
Univ. of Maine–Farmington
Univ. of Mary Washington (VA)
Univ. of Maryland–Baltimore
    County
Univ. of Maryland–Coll. Park
Univ. of Massachusetts–Amherst
Univ. of Massachusetts–Boston
Univ. of Massachusetts–Dartmouth
Univ. of Memphis
Univ. of Miami (FL)
Univ. of Michigan–Ann Arbor
Univ. of Michigan–Dearborn
Univ. of Michigan–Flint
Univ. of Minnesota–Duluth
Univ. of Minnesota–Morris
Univ. of Minnesota–Twin Cities
Univ. of Mississippi
Univ. of Missouri
Univ. of Missouri–St. Louis
Univ. of Montana

Univ. of Nebraska–Lincoln
Univ. of Nevada–Las Vegas
Univ. of Nevada–Reno
Univ. of New Hampshire
Univ. of New Mexico
Univ. of New Orleans
Univ. of North Carolina–Chapel Hill
Univ. of North Carolina–Charlotte
Univ. of North Carolina–
    Greensboro
Univ. of North Carolina–
    Wilmington
Univ. of North Dakota
Univ. of North Florida
Univ. of North Texas
Univ. of Northern Colorado
Univ. of Northern Iowa
Univ. of Notre Dame (IN)
Univ. of Oklahoma
Univ. of Oregon
Univ. of Pennsylvania
Univ. of Pittsburgh
Univ. of Redlands (CA)
Univ. of Rhode Island
Univ. of Richmond (VA)
Univ. of Rochester (NY)
Univ. of San Diego
Univ. of South Alabama
Univ. of South Carolina
Univ. of South Dakota
Univ. of South Florida
Univ. of Southern California
Univ. of Southern Mississippi
Univ. of Tennessee
Univ. of Texas–Arlington
Univ. of Texas–Austin
Univ. of Texas–El Paso
Univ. of Texas–Pan American
Univ. of Texas–San Antonio
Univ. of Toledo (OH)
Univ. of Tulsa (OK)
Univ. of Utah
Univ. of Vermont
Univ. of Virginia
Univ. of Washington
Univ. of West Florida
Univ. of West Georgia
Univ. of Wisconsin–Madison
Univ. of Wisconsin–Milwaukee
Univ. of Wisconsin–Oshkosh
Univ. of Wisconsin–Parkside
Univ. of Wyoming
Utah State Univ.
Vanderbilt Univ. (TN)
Vanguard Univ. of Southern
    California
Vassar Coll. (NY)
Virginia Commonwealth Univ.
Wagner Coll. (NY)
Wake Forest Univ. (NC)
Washburn Univ. (KS)
Washington and Lee Univ. (VA)
Washington Coll. (MD)
Washington State Univ.
Washington Univ. in St. Louis
Wayne State Univ. (MI)
Weber State Univ. (UT)
Webster Univ. (MO)
Wellesley Coll. (MA)
Wells Coll. (NY)
Wesleyan Univ. (CT)

West Chester Univ. of Pennsylvania
Western Carolina Univ. (NC)
Western Kentucky Univ.
Western Michigan Univ.
Western Oregon Univ.
Western State Coll. of Colorado
Western Washington Univ.
Westminster Coll. (MO)
Westminster Coll. (UT)
Wheaton Coll. (IL)
Wheaton Coll. (MA)
Whitman Coll. (WA)
Wichita State Univ. (KS)
Widener Univ. (PA)
Willamette Univ. (OR)
William Paterson Univ. of New
    Jersey
Williams Coll. (MA)
Wright State Univ. (OH)
Yale Univ. (CT)
Youngstown State Univ. (OH)

Apparel and Textiles

Appalachian State Univ. (NC)
Auburn Univ. (AL)
California State Polytechnic Univ.–
    Pomona
California State Univ.–Long Beach
Carson-Newman Coll. (TN)
Cheyney Univ. of Pennsylvania
Clemson Univ. (SC)
Coll. of the Ozarks (MO)
Colorado State Univ.
Concordia Coll.–Moorhead (MN)
Delaware State Univ.
East Carolina Univ. (NC)
Fashion Institute of Technology
    (NY)
Florida State Univ.
Fontbonne Univ. (MO)
Framingham State Coll. (MA)
Georgia Southern Univ.
Indiana State Univ.
Indiana Univ.–Bloomington
Kansas State Univ.
Kentucky State Univ.
Lambuth Univ. (TN)
Lasell Coll. (MA)
Lipscomb Univ. (TN)
Mars Hill Coll. (NC)
Marygrove Coll. (MI)
Miami Univ.–Oxford (OH)
Middle Tennessee State Univ.
Missouri State Univ.
New Mexico State Univ.
North Dakota State Univ.
Northern Illinois Univ.
Northwest Missouri State Univ.
Ohio State Univ.–Columbus
Ohio Univ.
Oregon State Univ.
Seattle Pacific Univ.
South Dakota State Univ.
Southern Illinois Univ.–Carbondale
St. Catherine Univ. (MN)
Stephens Coll. (MO)
SUNY Coll.–Oneonta
Syracuse Univ. (NY)
Texas Tech Univ.
Univ. of Akron (OH)

Univ. of Alabama
Univ. of Arkansas
Univ. of California–Davis
Univ. of Central Missouri
Univ. of Central Oklahoma
Univ. of Delaware
Univ. of Hawaii–Manoa
Univ. of Kentucky
Univ. of Minnesota–Twin Cities
Univ. of Missouri
Univ. of Nebraska–Lincoln
Univ. of North Carolina–
    Greensboro
Univ. of Northern Iowa
Univ. of Rhode Island
Univ. of Southern Mississippi
Univ. of Texas–Austin
Univ. of Wisconsin–Madison
Univ. of Wisconsin–Stout
Utah State Univ.
Washington State Univ.
Wayne State Univ. (MI)
Western Kentucky Univ.
Western Michigan Univ.

Applied Horticulture/ Horticultural Business Services

Andrews Univ. (MI)
Bethel Coll. (IN)
Brigham Young Univ.–Provo (UT)
California Polytechnic State Univ.–
    San Luis Obispo
California State Polytechnic Univ.–
    Pomona
Christopher Newport Univ. (VA)
Clemson Univ. (SC)
Coll. of the Ozarks (MO)
Colorado State Univ.
Cornell Univ. (NY)
Delaware Valley Coll. (PA)
Eastern Kentucky Univ.
Farmingdale State Coll.–SUNY
Ferrum Coll. (VA)
Florida Southern Coll.
Heritage Univ. (WA)
Iowa State Univ.
Mississippi State Univ.
New Mexico State Univ.
North Carolina State Univ.–Raleigh
North Dakota State Univ.
Ohio State Univ.–Columbus
Oklahoma State Univ.
Oregon State Univ.
Pennsylvania State Univ.–Univ. Park
Purdue Univ.–West Lafayette (IN)
South Dakota State Univ.
Tarleton State Univ. (TX)
Temple Univ. (PA)
Texas A&M Univ.–Coll. Station
Texas Tech Univ.
Thomas Edison State Coll. (NJ)
Unity Coll. (ME)
Univ. of Arkansas
Univ. of Delaware
Univ. of Florida
Univ. of Georgia
Univ. of Illinois–Urbana-Champaign
Univ. of Maine
Univ. of Minnesota–Crookston

Univ. of Nebraska–Lincoln
Univ. of Rhode Island
Univ. of Tennessee
Vermont Technical Coll.

Applied Mathematics

Alderson-Broaddus Coll. (WV)
American Univ. (DC)
Arizona State Univ.
Asbury Univ. (KY)
Auburn Univ. (AL)
Averett Univ. (VA)
Barnard Coll. (NY)
Baylor Univ. (TX)
Bloomfield Coll. (NJ)
Bowling Green State Univ. (OH)
Brescia Univ. (KY)
Brown Univ. (RI)
California Institute of Technology
California State Univ.–Fullerton
California State Univ.–Long Beach
Carnegie Mellon Univ. (PA)
Carroll Univ. (WI)
Case Western Reserve Univ. (OH)
Charleston Southern Univ. (SC)
Clarion Univ. of Pennsylvania
Clarkson Univ. (NY)
Coastal Carolina Univ. (SC)
Coll. of Idaho (ID)
Colorado School of Mines
Columbia Univ. (NY)
CUNY–Brooklyn Coll.
CUNY–City Coll.
CUNY–New York City Coll. of
    Technology
Farmingdale State Coll.–SUNY
Ferris State Univ. (MI)
Florida Institute of Technology
Florida International Univ.
Fresno Pacific Univ. (CA)
Geneva Coll. (PA)
George Washington Univ. (DC)
Georgia Institute of Technology
Gettysburg Coll. (PA)
Grand View Univ. (IA)
Hampden-Sydney Coll. (VA)
Harvard Univ. (MA)
Hawaii Pacific Univ.
Hillsdale Coll. (MI)
Hofstra Univ. (NY)
Humboldt State Univ. (CA)
Illinois Institute of Technology
Indiana Univ. of Pennsylvania
Indiana Univ.–South Bend
Indiana Univ.–Purdue Univ.–Fort
    Wayne
Iona Coll. (NY)
Jamestown Coll. (ND)
Johns Hopkins Univ. (MD)
Keene State Coll. (NH)
Kent State Univ. (OH)
Kettering Univ. (MI)
Knox Coll. (IL)
Loyola Marymount Univ. (CA)
Loyola Univ. Maryland
Lycoming Coll. (PA)
Mansfield Univ. of Pennsylvania
Marist Coll. (NY)
Marquette Univ. (WI)
Mary Baldwin Coll. (VA)

Maryville Univ. of St. Louis (MO)
Michigan State Univ.
Millikin Univ. (IL)
Missouri Southern State Univ.
Missouri Univ. of Science &
    Technology
National-Louis Univ. (IL)
New Jersey Institute of Technology
New Mexico Institute of Mining
    and Technology
North Carolina A&T State Univ.
North Carolina State Univ.–Raleigh
North Central Coll. (IL)
Northern Michigan Univ.
Northwestern Univ. (IL)
Oakland City Univ. (IN)
Oakwood Univ. (AL)
Ohio Univ.
Princeton Univ. (NJ)
Purdue Univ.–West Lafayette (IN)
Rice Univ. (TX)
Robert Morris Univ. (PA)
Rochester Institute of Technology
    (NY)
Rutgers, the State Univ. of New
    Jersey–Newark
Saginaw Valley State Univ. (MI)
Salem State Coll. (MA)
San Jose State Univ. (CA)
Siena Coll. (NY)
St. Mary's Coll. (IN)
Stanford Univ. (CA)
Stevenson Univ. (MD)
SUNY Institute of Technology–
    Utica/Rome
SUNY–Oswego
SUNY–Stony Brook
Taylor Univ. (IN)
Texas A&M Univ.–Coll. Station
Texas State Univ.–San Marcos
Tufts Univ. (MA)
Univ. at Albany–SUNY
Univ. of Akron (OH)
Univ. of Alaska–Fairbanks
Univ. of Arkansas–Pine Bluff
Univ. of California–Berkeley
Univ. of California–Davis
Univ. of California–Los Angeles
Univ. of California–San Diego
Univ. of California–Santa Barbara
Univ. of Colorado–Boulder
Univ. of Connecticut
Univ. of Dayton (OH)
Univ. of Evansville (IN)
Univ. of Houston
Univ. of Houston–Downtown
Univ. of Illinois–Urbana-Champaign
Univ. of Iowa
Univ. of Kentucky
Univ. of Massachusetts–Lowell
Univ. of Miami (FL)
Univ. of Michigan–Ann Arbor
Univ. of Michigan–Dearborn
Univ. of Nevada–Las Vegas
Univ. of New Hampshire
Univ. of New Haven (CT)
Univ. of North Carolina–Chapel Hill
Univ. of Northern Iowa
Univ. of Pittsburgh
Univ. of Pittsburgh–Bradford
Univ. of Richmond (VA)

Univ. of Rochester (NY)
Univ. of Sioux Falls (SD)
Univ. of South Carolina–Aiken
Univ. of South Carolina–Upstate
Univ. of Texas–Dallas
Univ. of Texas–El Paso
Univ. of the Pacific (CA)
Univ. of Tulsa (OK)
Univ. of Virginia
Univ. of Washington
Univ. of Wisconsin–Madison
Univ. of Wisconsin–Milwaukee
Univ. of Wisconsin–Stout
Univ. of Wyoming
Valdosta State Univ. (GA)
Washington State Univ.
Washington Univ. in St. Louis
Western Michigan Univ.
Western Washington Univ.
Whitman Coll. (WA)
Whitworth Univ. (WA)
Worcester Polytechnic Institute
    (MA)
Yale Univ. (CT)

Archaeology

Baylor Univ. (TX)
Boston Univ.
Bridgewater State Coll. (MA)
Brown Univ. (RI)
Coll. of Wooster (OH)
Columbia Univ. (NY)
Cornell Univ. (NY)
CUNY–Brooklyn Coll.
CUNY–Hunter Coll.
Dickinson Coll. (PA)
George Washington Univ. (DC)
Hamilton Coll. (NY)
Haverford Coll. (PA)
Hofstra Univ. (NY)
Oberlin Coll. (OH)
Pennsylvania State Univ.–Univ. Park
Southern Adventist Univ. (TN)
St. Mary's Coll. of California
Stanford Univ. (CA)
SUNY Coll.–Potsdam
Tufts Univ. (MA)
Univ. of California–San Diego
Univ. of Evansville (IN)
Univ. of Indianapolis
Univ. of Missouri
Univ. of Texas–Austin
Univ. of Wisconsin–La Crosse
Washington Univ. in St. Louis
Wesleyan Univ. (CT)
Western Washington Univ.
Wheaton Coll. (IL)
Yale Univ. (CT)

Architectural Engineering

Auburn Univ. (AL)
California Polytechnic State Univ.–
    San Luis Obispo
California State Univ.–Fresno
Illinois Institute of Technology
Kansas State Univ.
Milwaukee School of Engineering
Missouri Univ. of Science &
    Technology

North Carolina A&T State Univ.
Oklahoma State Univ.
Philadelphia Univ.
SUNY Coll. of Technology–Alfred
Tennessee State Univ.
Tufts Univ. (MA)
Univ. of Colorado–Boulder
Univ. of Kansas
Univ. of Miami (FL)
Univ. of Nebraska–Lincoln
Univ. of Nebraska–Omaha
Univ. of Oklahoma
Univ. of Texas–Austin
Univ. of Wyoming

Architectural Engineering Technologies/ Technicians

Bluefield State Coll. (WV)
Eastern Kentucky Univ.
Fairmont State Univ. (WV)
Farmingdale State Coll.–SUNY
Fitchburg State Coll. (MA)
Indiana State Univ.
Indiana Univ.-Purdue Univ.–
    Indianapolis
Louisiana Coll.
Northern Kentucky Univ.
Southern Polytechnic State Univ.
    (GA)
Texas Tech Univ.
Univ. of Central Missouri
Univ. of Hartford (CT)
Univ. of Southern Mississippi
Vermont Technical Coll.
Virginia Tech

Architectural History and Criticism

Brown Univ. (RI)
Carnegie Mellon Univ. (PA)
Catholic Univ. of America (DC)
Columbia Univ. (NY)
Cornell Univ. (NY)
Roger Williams Univ. (RI)
Savannah Coll. of Art and Design
    (GA)
Univ. of California–Santa Barbara
Univ. of Kansas

Architectural Technology/Technician

Carnegie Mellon Univ. (PA)
CUNY–Coll. of Staten Island
CUNY–New York City Coll. of
    Technology
Fitchburg State Coll. (MA)
Keene State Coll. (NH)
Vermont Technical Coll.
Washington Univ. in St. Louis

Architecture

Andrews Univ. (MI)
Arizona State Univ.
Auburn Univ. (AL)
Ball State Univ. (IN)
Barnard Coll. (NY)

Baylor Univ. (TX)
Bennington Coll. (VT)
Boston Architectural Coll.
California Coll. of the Arts
California Institute of Technology
California Polytechnic State Univ.–
    San Luis Obispo
California State Polytechnic Univ.–
    Pomona
Carnegie Mellon Univ. (PA)
Catholic Univ. of America (DC)
Clemson Univ. (SC)
Columbia Univ. (NY)
Connecticut Coll.
Cornell Univ. (NY)
CUNY–City Coll.
Drexel Univ. (PA)
Eastern Michigan Univ.
Florida A&M Univ.
Florida Atlantic Univ.
Florida International Univ.
Georgia Institute of Technology
Hampton Univ. (VA)
Howard Univ. (DC)
Illinois Institute of Technology
Iowa State Univ.
Judson Univ. (IL)
Kansas State Univ.
Keene State Coll. (NH)
Kent State Univ. (OH)
Lawrence Technological Univ. (MI)
Lehigh Univ. (PA)
Louisiana State Univ.–Baton Rouge
Massachusetts Institute of
    Technology
Miami Univ.–Oxford (OH)
Mississippi State Univ.
Montana State Univ.
Mount Holyoke Coll. (MA)
New Jersey Institute of Technology
New York Institute of Technology
North Carolina State Univ.–Raleigh
North Dakota State Univ.
Northeastern Univ. (MA)
Norwich Univ. (VT)
Ohio State Univ.–Columbus
Oklahoma State Univ.
Pennsylvania State Univ.–Univ. Park
Philadelphia Univ.
Portland State Univ. (OR)
Prairie View A&M Univ. (TX)
Pratt Institute (NY)
Princeton Univ. (NJ)
Rensselaer Polytechnic Institute
    (NY)
Rice Univ. (TX)
Roger Williams Univ. (RI)
Savannah Coll. of Art and Design
    (GA)
School of the Art Institute of
    Chicago
Smith Coll. (MA)
Southern California Institute of
    Architecture
Southern Illinois Univ.–Carbondale
Southern Polytechnic State Univ.
    (GA)
Southern Univ. and A&M Coll. (LA)
SUNY Coll. of Technology–Alfred
Syracuse Univ. (NY)
Temple Univ. (PA)

Texas A&M Univ.–Coll. Station
Texas Tech Univ.
Tulane Univ. (LA)
Tuskegee Univ. (AL)
Univ. at Buffalo–SUNY
Univ. of Arizona
Univ. of Arkansas
Univ. of California–Berkeley
Univ. of California–Los Angeles
Univ. of Detroit Mercy
Univ. of Florida
Univ. of Houston
Univ. of Idaho
Univ. of Illinois–Urbana-Champaign
Univ. of Kansas
Univ. of Kentucky
Univ. of Maryland–Coll. Park
Univ. of Maryland–Eastern Shore
Univ. of Miami (FL)
Univ. of Michigan–Ann Arbor
Univ. of Minnesota–Twin Cities
Univ. of Nebraska–Lincoln
Univ. of Nevada–Las Vegas
Univ. of New Mexico
Univ. of North Carolina–Charlotte
Univ. of Notre Dame (IN)
Univ. of Oklahoma
Univ. of Oregon
Univ. of Pennsylvania
Univ. of San Francisco
Univ. of Southern California
Univ. of Tennessee
Univ. of Texas–Arlington
Univ. of Texas–Austin
Univ. of Texas–San Antonio
Univ. of the District of Columbia
Univ. of Utah
Univ. of Virginia
Univ. of Washington
Univ. of Wisconsin–Milwaukee
Virginia Tech
Washington State Univ.
Washington Univ. in St. Louis
Wellesley Coll. (MA)
Woodbury Univ. (CA)
Yale Univ. (CT)

Architecture and Related Services

Carnegie Mellon Univ. (PA)
Catholic Univ. of America (DC)
Georgia Institute of Technology
Hampshire Coll. (MA)
Hobart and William Smith Colleges
    (NY)
La Roche Coll. (PA)
Lipscomb Univ. (TN)
Louisiana Tech Univ.
Metropolitan State Coll. of Denver
New York Institute of Technology
Olivet Nazarene Univ. (IL)
Philadelphia Univ.
Rensselaer Polytechnic Institute
    (NY)
SUNY Coll. of Technology–Delhi
Tulane Univ. (LA)
Univ. of Dallas
Univ. of Illinois–Chicago
Univ. of Louisiana–Lafayette
Univ. of Nevada–Las Vegas

Univ. of Utah
Univ. of Virginia
Vermont Technical Coll.

Area Studies

Adelphi Univ. (NY)
Adrian Coll. (MI)
Agnes Scott Coll. (GA)
Albion Coll. (MI)
Albright Coll. (PA)
American International Coll. (MA)
American Jewish Univ. (CA)
American Univ. (DC)
Amherst Coll. (MA)
Assumption Coll. (MA)
Augsburg Coll. (MN)
Augustana Coll. (IL)
Austin Coll. (TX)
Bard Coll. at Simon's Rock (MA)
Barnard Coll. (NY)
Bates Coll. (ME)
Baylor Univ. (TX)
Beloit Coll. (WI)
Bennington Coll. (VT)
Binghamton Univ.–SUNY
Boston Univ.
Bowdoin Coll. (ME)
Bowling Green State Univ. (OH)
Brandeis Univ. (MA)
Bridgewater State Coll. (MA)
Brigham Young Univ.–Hawaii
Brigham Young Univ.–Provo (UT)
Brown Univ. (RI)
Bryn Mawr Coll. (PA)
Bucknell Univ. (PA)
Burlington Coll. (VT)
Cabrini Coll. (PA)
Caldwell Coll. (NJ)
California State Univ.–Chico
California State Univ.–Dominguez
    Hills
California State Univ.–East Bay
California State Univ.–Fullerton
California State Univ.–Long Beach
California State Univ.–Los Angeles
California State Univ.–Sacramento
California State Univ.–San
    Bernardino
Calvin Coll. (MI)
Canisius Coll. (NY)
Carleton Coll. (MN)
Carnegie Mellon Univ. (PA)
Carroll Univ. (WI)
Carthage Coll. (WI)
Case Western Reserve Univ. (OH)
Cedarville Univ. (OH)
Centenary Coll. of Louisiana
Central Michigan Univ.
Central Washington Univ.
Claflin Univ. (SC)
Claremont McKenna Coll. (CA)
Coe Coll. (IA)
Colby Coll. (ME)
Colgate Univ. (NY)
Coll. of Charleston (SC)
Coll. of Santa Fe (NM)
Coll. of St. Elizabeth (NJ)
Coll. of St. Rose (NY)
Coll. of William and Mary (VA)
Coll. of Wooster (OH)

Colorado Coll.
Columbia Coll. (MO)
Columbia Univ. (NY)
Concordia Coll. (NY)
Connecticut Coll.
Cornell Coll. (IA)
Cornell Univ. (NY)
Creighton Univ. (NE)
Cumberland Univ. (TN)
CUNY–Brooklyn Coll.
CUNY–Coll. of Staten Island
CUNY–Hunter Coll.
CUNY–Lehman Coll.
CUNY–Queens Coll.
Dartmouth Coll. (NH)
Denison Univ. (OH)
DePaul Univ. (IL)
DePauw Univ. (IN)
Dickinson Coll. (PA)
Dominican Univ. (IL)
Drew Univ. (NJ)
Drexel Univ. (PA)
Duke Univ. (NC)
Earlham Coll. (IN)
Eastern Michigan Univ.
Eckerd Coll. (FL)
Elmhurst Coll. (IL)
Elmira Coll. (NY)
Emmanuel Coll. (MA)
Emory and Henry Coll. (VA)
Emory Univ. (GA)
Erskine Coll. (SC)
Fairfield Univ. (CT)
Flagler Coll. (FL)
Florida A&M Univ.
Florida International Univ.
Florida State Univ.
Fordham Univ. (NY)
Franklin and Marshall Coll. (PA)
Franklin Coll. (IN)
Franklin Pierce Univ. (NH)
Furman Univ. (SC)
Gannon Univ. (PA)
George Mason Univ. (VA)
George Washington Univ. (DC)
Georgetown Coll. (KY)
Georgetown Univ. (DC)
Georgia Southern Univ.
Georgia State Univ.
Gettysburg Coll. (PA)
Gonzaga Univ. (WA)
Goucher Coll. (MD)
Grand Valley State Univ. (MI)
Gustavus Adolphus Coll. (MN)
Hamilton Coll. (NY)
Hamline Univ. (MN)
Hampshire Coll. (MA)
Harding Univ. (AR)
Harvard Univ. (MA)
Haverford Coll. (PA)
Hendrix Coll. (AR)
Heritage Univ. (WA)
High Point Univ. (NC)
Hillsdale Coll. (MI)
Hobart and William Smith Colleges
    (NY)
Hofstra Univ. (NY)
Hollins Univ. (VA)
Hood Coll. (MD)
Hope Coll. (MI)
Howard Univ. (DC)

Idaho State Univ.
Illinois Wesleyan Univ.
Indiana Univ. Southeast
Iowa State Univ.
Ithaca Coll. (NY)
Johns Hopkins Univ. (MD)
Kalamazoo Coll. (MI)
Keene State Coll. (NH)
Kennesaw State Univ. (GA)
Kent State Univ. (OH)
Kenyon Coll. (OH)
Knox Coll. (IL)
La Salle Univ. (PA)
Lafayette Coll. (PA)
Lake Forest Coll. (IL)
Lawrence Univ. (WI)
Lebanon Valley Coll. (PA)
Lehigh Univ. (PA)
Lesley Univ. (MA)
Lewis & Clark Coll. (OR)
Lewis Univ. (IL)
Lindenwood Univ. (MO)
Lindsey Wilson Coll. (KY)
Linfield Coll. (OR)
Lipscomb Univ. (TN)
Loyola Marymount Univ. (CA)
Lycoming Coll. (PA)
Macalester Coll. (MN)
MacMurray Coll. (IL)
Madonna Univ. (MI)
Manhattanville Coll. (NY)
Marist Coll. (NY)
Marlboro Coll. (VT)
Mary Baldwin Coll. (VA)
Miami Univ.–Oxford (OH)
Michigan State Univ.
Middlebury Coll. (VT)
Millersville Univ. of Pennsylvania
Millikin Univ. (IL)
Mills Coll. (CA)
Millsaps Coll. (MS)
Minnesota State Univ.–Mankato
Minnesota State Univ.–Moorhead
Montreat Coll. (NC)
Mount Holyoke Coll. (MA)
Mount St. Mary's Coll. (CA)
Muhlenberg Coll. (PA)
Nazareth Coll. (NY)
New York Univ.
North Central Coll. (IL)
North Park Univ. (IL)
Northwestern Univ. (IL)
Nova Southeastern Univ. (FL)
Oakland Univ. (MI)
Oberlin Coll. (OH)
Occidental Coll. (CA)
Oglethorpe Univ. (GA)
Ohio State Univ.–Columbus
Ohio Univ.
Ohio Wesleyan Univ.
Oklahoma State Univ.
Old Dominion Univ. (VA)
Oregon State Univ.
Pace Univ. (NY)
Pacific Lutheran Univ. (WA)
Pennsylvania State Univ.–Univ. Park
Pepperdine Univ. (CA)
Pfeiffer Univ. (NC)
Pitzer Coll. (CA)
Pomona Coll. (CA)
Prescott Coll. (AZ)

Princeton Univ. (NJ)
Providence Coll. (RI)
Purdue Univ.–Calumet (IN)
Purdue Univ.–West Lafayette (IN)
Queens Univ. of Charlotte (NC)
Ramapo Coll. of New Jersey
Randolph Coll. (VA)
Reed Coll. (OR)
Rhode Island Coll.
Rhodes Coll. (TN)
Rice Univ. (TX)
Rider Univ. (NJ)
Ripon Coll. (WI)
Rollins Coll. (FL)
Roosevelt Univ. (IL)
Rutgers, the State Univ. of New
    Jersey–New Brunswick
Rutgers, the State Univ. of New
    Jersey–Newark
Salem Coll. (NC)
Salve Regina Univ. (RI)
Samford Univ. (AL)
San Diego State Univ.
San Francisco State Univ.
Scripps Coll. (CA)
Seattle Pacific Univ.
Seattle Univ.
Seton Hall Univ. (NJ)
Sewanee–Univ. of the South (TN)
Shenandoah Univ. (VA)
Siena Coll. (NY)
Simmons Coll. (MA)
Skidmore Coll. (NY)
Smith Coll. (MA)
Southern Methodist Univ. (TX)
Southern Nazarene Univ. (OK)
Southwestern Univ. (TX)
Springfield Coll. (MA)
St. Andrews Presbyterian Coll. (NC)
St. Cloud State Univ. (MN)
St. Edward's Univ. (TX)
St. Francis Coll. (NY)
St. John Fisher Coll. (NY)
St. John's Univ. (NY)
St. Joseph's Univ. (PA)
St. Lawrence Univ. (NY)
St. Louis Univ.
St. Mary's Coll. of California
St. Michael's Coll. (VT)
St. Olaf Coll. (MN)
St. Peter's Coll. (NJ)
Stanford Univ. (CA)
Stetson Univ. (FL)
Stonehill Coll. (MA)
Suffolk Univ. (MA)
SUNY Coll.–Old Westbury
SUNY Coll.–Oneonta
SUNY–Oswego
SUNY–Plattsburgh
SUNY–Stony Brook
Swarthmore Coll. (PA)
Syracuse Univ. (NY)
Temple Univ. (PA)
Tennessee Wesleyan Coll.
Texas A&M International Univ.
Texas A&M Univ.–Coll. Station
Texas Christian Univ.
Texas State Univ.–San Marcos
Texas Tech Univ.
Thomas More Coll. (KY)
Towson Univ. (MD)

Trinity Coll. (CT)
Trinity Univ. (DC)
Tufts Univ. (MA)
Tulane Univ. (LA)
Union Coll. (NY)
Univ. at Albany–SUNY
Univ. at Buffalo–SUNY
Univ. of Alabama
Univ. of Alaska–Fairbanks
Univ. of Arizona
Univ. of Arkansas
Univ. of California–Berkeley
Univ. of California–Davis
Univ. of California–Irvine
Univ. of California–Los Angeles
Univ. of California–Riverside
Univ. of California–San Diego
Univ. of California–Santa Barbara
Univ. of California–Santa Cruz
Univ. of Chicago
Univ. of Colorado–Boulder
Univ. of Connecticut
Univ. of Dayton (OH)
Univ. of Delaware
Univ. of Denver
Univ. of Florida
Univ. of Georgia
Univ. of Hawaii–Hilo
Univ. of Hawaii–Manoa
Univ. of Houston
Univ. of Illinois–Chicago
Univ. of Illinois–Urbana-Champaign
Univ. of Iowa
Univ. of Kansas
Univ. of Kentucky
Univ. of Mary Hardin-Baylor (TX)
Univ. of Mary Washington (VA)
Univ. of Maryland–Baltimore
    County
Univ. of Maryland–Coll. Park
Univ. of Maryland–Univ. Coll.
Univ. of Massachusetts–Amherst
Univ. of Massachusetts–Boston
Univ. of Massachusetts–Lowell
Univ. of Miami (FL)
Univ. of Michigan–Ann Arbor
Univ. of Michigan–Dearborn
Univ. of Minnesota–Duluth
Univ. of Minnesota–Morris
Univ. of Minnesota–Twin Cities
Univ. of Mississippi
Univ. of Missouri
Univ. of Missouri–Kansas City
Univ. of Mount Union (OH)
Univ. of Nebraska–Lincoln
Univ. of Nebraska–Omaha
Univ. of Nevada–Las Vegas
Univ. of New England (ME)
Univ. of New Hampshire
Univ. of New Mexico
Univ. of North Carolina–Chapel Hill
Univ. of North Carolina–Pembroke
Univ. of Northern Iowa
Univ. of Notre Dame (IN)
Univ. of Oregon
Univ. of Pennsylvania
Univ. of Pittsburgh–Johnstown
Univ. of Portland (OR)
Univ. of Puget Sound (WA)
Univ. of Redlands (CA)
Univ. of Rhode Island

Univ. of Richmond (VA)
Univ. of Rio Grande (OH)
Univ. of Rochester (NY)
Univ. of San Francisco
Univ. of South Carolina
Univ. of South Florida
Univ. of Southern California
Univ. of Southern Mississippi
Univ. of St. Francis (IN)
Univ. of St. Thomas (MN)
Univ. of Texas–Austin
Univ. of Texas–Dallas
Univ. of Texas–El Paso
Univ. of Texas–Pan American
Univ. of Texas–San Antonio
Univ. of Toledo (OH)
Univ. of Utah
Univ. of Vermont
Univ. of Virginia
Univ. of Washington
Univ. of Wisconsin–Eau Claire
Univ. of Wisconsin–Madison
Univ. of Wyoming
Ursinus Coll. (PA)
Ursuline Coll. (OH)
Utah State Univ.
Valparaiso Univ. (IN)
Vanderbilt Univ. (TN)
Vassar Coll. (NY)
Virginia Commonwealth Univ.
Virginia Wesleyan Coll.
Washington and Lee Univ. (VA)
Washington Coll. (MD)
Washington State Univ.
Washington Univ. in St. Louis
Wayne State Univ. (MI)
Wellesley Coll. (MA)
Wells Coll. (NY)
Wesley Coll. (DE)
Wesleyan Coll. (GA)
Wesleyan Univ. (CT)
West Chester Univ. of Pennsylvania
Western Connecticut State Univ.
Western Michigan Univ.
Western Washington Univ.
Westmont Coll. (CA)
Wheaton Coll. (MA)
Wheelock Coll. (MA)
Whitman Coll. (WA)
Whittier Coll. (CA)
Whitworth Univ. (WA)
Willamette Univ. (OR)
William Jewell Coll. (MO)
William Paterson Univ. of New
    Jersey
Williams Coll. (MA)
Wingate Univ. (NC)
Winston-Salem State Univ. (NC)
Wittenberg Univ. (OH)
Wright State Univ. (OH)
Yale Univ. (CT)
Youngstown State Univ. (OH)

Area, Ethnic, Cultural, and Gender Studies

Alfred Univ. (NY)
Azusa Pacific Univ. (CA)
Bethel Univ. (MN)
Binghamton Univ.–SUNY
Brandeis Univ. (MA)

Brown Univ. (RI)
Burlington Coll. (VT)
Carleton Coll. (MN)
Chatham Univ. (PA)
Christian Brothers Univ. (TN)
Columbia Coll. (IL)
Connecticut Coll.
CUNY–City Coll.
Dartmouth Coll. (NH)
Emmanuel Coll. (MA)
Evergreen State Coll. (WA)
Excelsior Coll. (NY)
Fort Lewis Coll. (CO)
Hanover Coll. (IN)
Hawaii Pacific Univ.
Hobart and William Smith Colleges
    (NY)
Humboldt State Univ. (CA)
Lafayette Coll. (PA)
Manhattanville Coll. (NY)
New York Univ.
Northwest Christian Univ. (OR)
Norwich Univ. (VT)
Pepperdine Univ. (CA)
Point Park Univ. (PA)
Prescott Coll. (AZ)
Sage Colleges–Albany (NY)
Savannah State Univ. (GA)
Siena Coll. (NY)
Skidmore Coll. (NY)
St. Mary's Coll. of California
Syracuse Univ. (NY)
Union Univ. (TN)
Univ. of California–Davis
Univ. of California–San Diego
Univ. of Denver
Univ. of Michigan–Ann Arbor
Univ. of North Carolina–Chapel Hill
Univ. of North Carolina–Charlotte
Univ. of Oregon
Univ. of Richmond (VA)
Univ. of Tennessee
Univ. of the Incarnate Word (TX)
Univ. of Wisconsin–Stevens Point
Williams Coll. (MA)

Astronomy and Astrophysics

Agnes Scott Coll. (GA)
Amherst Coll. (MA)
Barnard Coll. (NY)
Benedictine Coll. (KS)
Bennington Coll. (VT)
Boston Univ.
Brigham Young Univ.–Provo (UT)
Bryn Mawr Coll. (PA)
Buffalo State Coll.–SUNY
California Institute of Technology
California State Univ.–Los Angeles
California State Univ.–Northridge
Carnegie Mellon Univ. (PA)
Case Western Reserve Univ. (OH)
Central Michigan Univ.
Colgate Univ. (NY)
Columbia Univ. (NY)
Concordia Univ. Chicago (IL)
Connecticut Coll.
Cornell Univ. (NY)
Creighton Univ. (NE)
Denison Univ. (OH)

Drake Univ. (IA)
Eastern Univ. (PA)
Florida Institute of Technology
Franklin and Marshall Coll. (PA)
George Mason Univ. (VA)
Harvard Univ. (MA)
Haverford Coll. (PA)
Indiana Univ.–Bloomington
Lehigh Univ. (PA)
Lycoming Coll. (PA)
Marlboro Coll. (VT)
Michigan State Univ.
Minnesota State Univ.–Mankato
Mount Holyoke Coll. (MA)
New Mexico Institute of Mining
 and Technology
Northern Arizona Univ.
Northern Michigan Univ.
Ohio State Univ.–Columbus
Ohio Univ.
Ohio Wesleyan Univ.
Pennsylvania State Univ.–Univ. Park
Princeton Univ. (NJ)
Rice Univ. (TX)
Rutgers, the State Univ. of New
 Jersey–New Brunswick
San Diego State Univ.
Savannah State Univ. (GA)
Smith Coll. (MA)
SUNY–Stony Brook
Swarthmore Coll. (PA)
Texas A&M Univ.–Commerce
Texas Christian Univ.
Tufts Univ. (MA)
Union Coll. (NY)
Univ. of Arizona
Univ. of California–Berkeley
Univ. of California–Los Angeles
Univ. of California–San Diego
Univ. of Colorado–Boulder
Univ. of Florida
Univ. of Georgia
Univ. of Hawaii–Hilo
Univ. of Illinois–Urbana-Champaign
Univ. of Iowa
Univ. of Kansas
Univ. of Maryland–Coll. Park
Univ. of Massachusetts–Amherst
Univ. of Michigan–Ann Arbor
Univ. of Minnesota–Twin Cities
Univ. of New Hampshire
Univ. of New Mexico
Univ. of Oklahoma
Univ. of Southern California
Univ. of Texas–Austin
Univ. of Texas–El Paso
Univ. of Toledo (OH)
Univ. of Virginia
Univ. of Washington
Univ. of Wisconsin–Madison
Univ. of Wyoming
Valdosta State Univ. (GA)
Vassar Coll. (NY)
Wellesley Coll. (MA)
Wesleyan Univ. (CT)
Western Washington Univ.
Wheaton Coll. (MA)
Whitman Coll. (WA)
Williams Coll. (MA)
Yale Univ. (CT)
Youngstown State Univ. (OH)

Atmospheric Sciences and Meteorology

Central Michigan Univ.
Coll. at Brockport–SUNY
Cornell Univ. (NY)
Creighton Univ. (NE)
Embry-Riddle Aeronautical Univ.
 (FL)
Florida Institute of Technology
Florida State Univ.
Iowa State Univ.
Jackson State Univ. (MS)
Lyndon State Coll. (VT)
Metropolitan State Coll. of Denver
New Mexico Institute of Mining
 and Technology
North Carolina State Univ.–Raleigh
Northern Illinois Univ.
Northland Coll. (WI)
Ohio State Univ.–Columbus
Ohio Univ.
Pennsylvania State Univ.–Univ. Park
Plymouth State Univ. (NH)
Princeton Univ. (NJ)
Purdue Univ.–West Lafayette (IN)
Rutgers, the State Univ. of New
 Jersey–New Brunswick
San Jose State Univ. (CA)
St. Cloud State Univ. (MN)
St. Louis Univ.
SUNY Coll.–Oneonta
SUNY–Oswego
United States Air Force Academy
 (CO)
Univ. at Albany–SUNY
Univ. of Arizona
Univ. of California–Berkeley
Univ. of California–Davis
Univ. of California–Los Angeles
Univ. of Hawaii–Manoa
Univ. of Kansas
Univ. of Louisiana–Monroe
Univ. of Miami (FL)
Univ. of Michigan–Ann Arbor
Univ. of Missouri
Univ. of Nebraska–Lincoln
Univ. of North Carolina–Asheville
Univ. of North Dakota
Univ. of Oklahoma
Univ. of South Alabama
Univ. of the Incarnate Word (TX)
Univ. of Utah
Univ. of Washington
Univ. of Wisconsin–Madison
Univ. of Wisconsin–Milwaukee
Valparaiso Univ. (IN)
Western Connecticut State Univ.
Western Illinois Univ.

Audiovisual Communications Technologies/ Technicians

Alabama Agricultural and
 Mechanical Univ.
American Univ. (DC)
Asbury Univ. (KY)
Ashland Univ. (OH)
Butler Univ. (IN)

California State Univ.–Monterey Bay
Columbia Coll. (IL)
CUNY–Brooklyn Coll.
Eastern Michigan Univ.
Ferris State Univ. (MI)
Gannon Univ. (PA)
Gonzaga Univ. (WA)
Greenville Coll. (IL)
Hampshire Coll. (MA)
Ithaca Coll. (NY)
Johns Hopkins Univ. (MD)
Lebanon Valley Coll. (PA)
Liberty Univ. (VA)
Loyola Marymount Univ. (CA)
Malone Univ. (OH)
Michigan Technological Univ.
New York Univ.
Polytechnic Institute of New York
 Univ. (NY)
Rowan Univ. (NJ)
San Francisco State Univ.
Savannah Coll. of Art and Design
 (GA)
Southern Oregon Univ.
St. John's Univ. (NY)
Suffolk Univ. (MA)
SUNY–Fredonia
Syracuse Univ. (NY)
Texas State Univ.–San Marcos
Univ. of Arizona
Univ. of Georgia
York Coll. of Pennsylvania

Behavioral Sciences

Andrews Univ. (MI)
California Baptist Univ.
Carnegie Mellon Univ. (PA)
Columbia Coll. (SC)
Concordia Univ. (NE)
Concordia Univ. (CA)
Dakota Wesleyan Univ. (SD)
Drew Univ. (NJ)
George Fox Univ. (OR)
Grand Valley State Univ. (MI)
Granite State Coll. (NH)
Hampshire Coll. (MA)
Mercy Coll. (NY)
Mount Mary Coll. (WI)
National Univ. (CA)
Oglethorpe Univ. (GA)
Point Park Univ. (PA)
Rochester Coll. (MI)
San Jose State Univ. (CA)
Sterling Coll. (KS)
Tennessee Wesleyan Coll.
Trevecca Nazarene Univ. (TN)
United States Air Force Academy
 (CO)
Univ. of California–Santa Cruz
Univ. of Kansas
Univ. of Maine–Machias
Univ. of Maine–Presque Isle
Univ. of North Texas
Widener Univ. (PA)
Wilmington Univ. (DE)
Wilson Coll. (PA)
York Coll. of Pennsylvania

Bible/Biblical Studies

Abilene Christian Univ. (TX)
American Jewish Univ. (CA)
Anderson Univ. (IN)
Asbury Univ. (KY)
Atlanta Christian Coll.
Azusa Pacific Univ. (CA)
Bethany Univ. (CA)
Bethel Coll. (IN)
Bethel Univ. (MN)
Biola Univ. (CA)
Blue Mountain Coll. (MS)
Bryan Coll. (TN)
California Baptist Univ.
Calvin Coll. (MI)
Cedarville Univ. (OH)
Central Baptist Coll. (AR)
Central Christian Coll. (KS)
Clearwater Christian Coll. (FL)
Colorado Christian Univ.
Concordia Univ. Chicago (IL)
Concordia Univ. Wisconsin
Corban Univ. (OR)
Cornerstone Univ. (MI)
Covenant Coll. (GA)
East Texas Baptist Univ.
Eastern Mennonite Univ. (VA)
Eastern Nazarene Coll. (MA)
Eastern Univ. (PA)
Erskine Coll. (SC)
Faulkner Univ. (AL)
Freed-Hardeman Univ. (TN)
Fresno Pacific Univ. (CA)
Geneva Coll. (PA)
George Fox Univ. (OR)
Gordon Coll. (MA)
Grace Coll. and Seminary (IN)
Hannibal-LaGrange Coll. (MO)
Hardin-Simmons Univ. (TX)
Harding Univ. (AR)
Hope International Univ. (CA)
Houghton Coll. (NY)
Howard Payne Univ. (TX)
Huntington Univ. (IN)
Indiana Wesleyan Univ.
Judson Univ. (IL)
King Coll. (TN)
LeTourneau Univ. (TX)
Liberty Univ. (VA)
Lipscomb Univ. (TN)
Lubbock Christian Univ. (TX)
Malone Univ. (OH)
Maranatha Baptist Bible Coll. (WI)
Master's Coll. and Seminary (CA)
Messiah Coll. (PA)
Mid-Continent Univ. (KY)
MidAmerica Nazarene Univ. (KS)
Milligan Coll. (TN)
Montreat Coll. (NC)
North Central Univ. (MN)
North Park Univ. (IL)
Northwest Christian Univ. (OR)
Northwest Univ. (WA)
Northwestern Coll. (MN)
Nyack Coll. (NY)
Ohio Valley Univ. (WV)
Oklahoma Baptist Univ.
Oklahoma Christian Univ.
Oklahoma Wesleyan Univ.
Olivet Nazarene Univ. (IL)
Oral Roberts Univ. (OK)
Ouachita Baptist Univ. (AR)

Palm Beach Atlantic Univ. (FL)
Patten Univ. (CA)
Point Loma Nazarene Univ. (CA)
Rochester Coll. (MI)
Simpson Univ. (CA)
Southeastern Univ. (FL)
Southwest Baptist Univ. (MO)
Southwestern Assemblies of God
 Univ. (TX)
Spring Arbor Univ. (MI)
Taylor Univ. (IN)
Toccoa Falls Coll. (GA)
Trinity International Univ. (IL)
Union Coll. (NE)
Union Coll. (TN)
Univ. of Evansville (IN)
Univ. of Mary Hardin-Baylor (TX)
Vanguard Univ. of Southern
 California
Victory Univ. (TN)
Warner Univ. (FL)
Wheaton Coll. (IL)
William Carey Univ. (MS)
Williams Baptist Coll. (AR)
York Coll. (NE)

Bilingual, Multilingual, and Multicultural Education

Boise State Univ. (ID)
Boston Univ.
California State Univ.–Fullerton
California State Univ.–Sacramento
Calvin Coll. (MI)
Chicago State Univ.
Coll. of St. Scholastica (MN)
Concordia Univ.–St. Paul (MN)
CUNY–Lehman Coll.
Free Will Baptist Bible Coll. (TN)
Heritage Univ. (WA)
Houston Baptist Univ.
Loyola Univ. Chicago
Midwestern State Univ. (TX)
Monmouth Coll. (IL)
Mount Mary Coll. (WI)
Northeastern Illinois Univ.
SUNY Coll.–Old Westbury
Texas Christian Univ.
Texas Wesleyan Univ.
Univ. of California–Riverside
Univ. of Findlay (OH)
Washington State Univ.
Weber State Univ. (UT)
Western Illinois Univ.
Western Oregon Univ.

Biochemistry, Biophysics, and Molecular Biology

Abilene Christian Univ. (TX)
Adelphi Univ. (NY)
Agnes Scott Coll. (GA)
Albright Coll. (PA)
Allegheny Coll. (PA)
Alma Coll. (MI)
Alvernia Univ. (PA)
Alverno Coll. (WI)
American Univ. (DC)
Anderson Univ. (IN)
Andrews Univ. (MI)

Angelo State Univ. (TX)
Arizona State Univ.
Asbury Univ. (KY)
Ashland Univ. (OH)
Auburn Univ. (AL)
Austin Coll. (TX)
Baker Univ. (KS)
Barnard Coll. (NY)
Barry Univ. (FL)
Bates Coll. (ME)
Baylor Univ. (TX)
Bellarmine Univ. (KY)
Belmont Univ. (TN)
Beloit Coll. (WI)
Benedictine Coll. (KS)
Benedictine Univ. (IL)
Bethany Coll. (WV)
Binghamton Univ.–SUNY
Biola Univ. (CA)
Blackburn Coll. (IL)
Boston Univ.
Bowdoin Coll. (ME)
Bradley Univ. (IL)
Brandeis Univ. (MA)
Bridgewater State Coll. (MA)
Brigham Young Univ.–Hawaii
Brigham Young Univ.–Provo (UT)
Brown Univ. (RI)
Bucknell Univ. (PA)
California Lutheran Univ.
California Polytechnic State Univ.–
    San Luis Obispo
California State Univ.–Dominguez
    Hills
California State Univ.–East Bay
California State Univ.–Fullerton
California State Univ.–Long Beach
California State Univ.–Los Angeles
California State Univ.–Northridge
California State Univ.–Sacramento
California State Univ.–San Marcos
Calvin Coll. (MI)
Campbell Univ. (NC)
Capital Univ. (OH)
Carnegie Mellon Univ. (PA)
Carroll Univ. (WI)
Case Western Reserve Univ. (OH)
Catholic Univ. of America (DC)
Cedar Crest Coll. (PA)
Centenary Coll. of Louisiana
Central Connecticut State Univ.
Central Michigan Univ.
Centre Coll. (KY)
Charleston Southern Univ. (SC)
Chatham Univ. (PA)
Chestnut Hill Coll. (PA)
Claflin Univ. (SC)
Claremont McKenna Coll. (CA)
Clarion Univ. of Pennsylvania
Clark Univ. (MA)
Clarke Univ. (IA)
Clarkson Univ. (NY)
Clemson Univ. (SC)
Coe Coll. (IA)
Colby Coll. (ME)
Colgate Univ. (NY)
Coll. of Mount St. Joseph (OH)
Coll. of Mount St. Vincent (NY)
Coll. of St. Benedict (MN)
Coll. of St. Elizabeth (NJ)

Coll. of St. Rose (NY)
Coll. of St. Scholastica (MN)
Coll. of Wooster (OH)
Colorado Coll.
Colorado State Univ.
Columbia Univ. (NY)
Connecticut Coll.
Converse Coll. (SC)
Cornell Coll. (IA)
Cornell Univ. (NY)
CUNY–Coll. of Staten Island
CUNY–Lehman Coll.
Daemen Coll. (NY)
Dartmouth Coll. (NH)
Defiance Coll. (OH)
Denison Univ. (OH)
DePauw Univ. (IN)
Dickinson Coll. (PA)
Doane Coll. (NE)
Drake Univ. (IA)
Drew Univ. (NJ)
Duquesne Univ. (PA)
Earlham Coll. (IN)
East Carolina Univ. (NC)
East Central Univ. (OK)
East Stroudsburg Univ. of
    Pennsylvania
Eastern Connecticut State Univ.
Eastern Kentucky Univ.
Eastern Mennonite Univ. (VA)
Eastern Michigan Univ.
Eastern Nazarene Coll. (MA)
Eastern New Mexico Univ.
Eastern Oregon Univ.
Eastern Univ. (PA)
Eckerd Coll. (FL)
Elizabethtown Coll. (PA)
Elmhurst Coll. (IL)
Emmanuel Coll. (MA)
Emporia State Univ. (KS)
Fairleigh Dickinson Univ. (NJ)
Ferris State Univ. (MI)
Florida Institute of Technology
Florida State Univ.
Fort Lewis Coll. (CO)
Franklin and Marshall Coll. (PA)
Freed-Hardeman Univ. (TN)
Georgetown Univ. (DC)
Georgian Court Univ. (NJ)
Gettysburg Coll. (PA)
Goshen Coll. (IN)
Grand Valley State Univ. (MI)
Grinnell Coll. (IA)
Grove City Coll. (PA)
Gustavus Adolphus Coll. (MN)
Hamilton Coll. (NY)
Hamline Univ. (MN)
Hardin-Simmons Univ. (TX)
Harding Univ. (AR)
Hartwick Coll. (NY)
Harvard Univ. (MA)
Harvey Mudd Coll. (CA)
Heidelberg Univ. (OH)
Hendrix Coll. (AR)
Hiram Coll. (OH)
Hofstra Univ. (NY)
Holy Family Univ. (PA)
Hood Coll. (MD)
Houghton Coll. (NY)
Houston Baptist Univ.
Howard Univ. (DC)

Humboldt State Univ. (CA)
Huntingdon Coll. (AL)
Idaho State Univ.
Illinois Institute of Technology
Illinois State Univ.
Indiana Univ. East
Indiana Univ. of Pennsylvania
Indiana Univ.–Bloomington
Indiana Wesleyan Univ.
Iona Coll. (NY)
Iowa State Univ.
Ithaca Coll. (NY)
Jamestown Coll. (ND)
John Brown Univ. (AR)
Johns Hopkins Univ. (MD)
Juniata Coll. (PA)
Kansas State Univ.
Kennesaw State Univ. (GA)
Kenyon Coll. (OH)
Keuka Coll. (NY)
King Coll. (TN)
Knox Coll. (IL)
Kutztown Univ. of Pennsylvania
La Salle Univ. (PA)
La Sierra Univ. (CA)
Lafayette Coll. (PA)
LaGrange Coll. (GA)
Lakeland Coll. (WI)
Lawrence Technological Univ. (MI)
Lawrence Univ. (WI)
Le Moyne Coll. (NY)
Lebanon Valley Coll. (PA)
Lehigh Univ. (PA)
Lewis & Clark Coll. (OR)
Lewis Univ. (IL)
Liberty Univ. (VA)
Lipscomb Univ. (TN)
Loras Coll. (IA)
Louisiana State Univ.–Baton Rouge
Louisiana State Univ.–Shreveport
Loyola Marymount Univ. (CA)
Madonna Univ. (MI)
Manhattan Coll. (NY)
Manhattanville Coll. (NY)
Mansfield Univ. of Pennsylvania
Marietta Coll. (OH)
Marist Coll. (NY)
Marlboro Coll. (VT)
Marquette Univ. (WI)
Mary Baldwin Coll. (VA)
Maryville Coll. (TN)
McMurry Univ. (TX)
McPherson Coll. (KS)
Mercyhurst Coll. (PA)
Meredith Coll. (NC)
Merrimack Coll. (MA)
Messiah Coll. (PA)
Miami Univ.–Oxford (OH)
Michigan State Univ.
Michigan Technological Univ.
Middlebury Coll. (VT)
Millikin Univ. (IL)
Mills Coll. (CA)
Minnesota State Univ.–Mankato
Misericordia Univ. (PA)
Mississippi Coll.
Mississippi State Univ.
Missouri Southern State Univ.
Missouri Western State Univ.
Monmouth Coll. (IL)
Montclair State Univ. (NJ)

Moravian Coll. (PA)
Mount Holyoke Coll. (MA)
Mount St. Mary's Univ. (MD)
Muhlenberg Coll. (PA)
Muskingum Univ. (OH)
Nazareth Coll. (NY)
Nebraska Wesleyan Univ.
New Mexico State Univ.
New York Univ.
Newman Univ. (KS)
Niagara Univ. (NY)
North Carolina State Univ.–Raleigh
North Central Coll. (IL)
North Dakota State Univ.
Northeastern Univ. (MA)
Northern Arizona Univ.
Northern Michigan Univ.
Norwich Univ. (VT)
Notre Dame Coll. of Ohio
Notre Dame de Namur Univ. (CA)
Oakland Univ. (MI)
Oakwood Univ. (AL)
Oberlin Coll. (OH)
Occidental Coll. (CA)
Ohio Northern Univ.
Ohio State Univ.–Columbus
Ohio Wesleyan Univ.
Oklahoma Christian Univ.
Oklahoma City Univ.
Oklahoma State Univ.
Oklahoma Wesleyan Univ.
Old Dominion Univ. (VA)
Olivet Coll. (MI)
Oral Roberts Univ. (OK)
Oregon State Univ.
Otterbein Coll. (OH)
Pace Univ. (NY)
Pacific Union Coll. (CA)
Pacific Univ. (OR)
Pennsylvania State Univ.–Univ. Park
Pepperdine Univ. (CA)
Philadelphia Univ.
Pitzer Coll. (CA)
Point Loma Nazarene Univ. (CA)
Polytechnic Institute of New York
    Univ. (NY)
Pomona Coll. (CA)
Princeton Univ. (NJ)
Providence Coll. (RI)
Purdue Univ.–West Lafayette (IN)
Queens Univ. of Charlotte (NC)
Ramapo Coll. of New Jersey
Reed Coll. (OR)
Regis Coll. (MA)
Regis Univ. (CO)
Rensselaer Polytechnic Institute
    (NY)
Rice Univ. (TX)
Richard Stockton Coll. of New
    Jersey
Rider Univ. (NJ)
Roanoke Coll. (VA)
Roberts Wesleyan Coll. (NY)
Rochester Institute of Tech. (NY)
Rockford Coll. (IL)
Rockhurst Univ. (MO)
Rollins Coll. (FL)
Rosemont Coll. (PA)
Russell Sage Coll. (NY)
Rutgers, the State Univ. of New
    Jersey–New Brunswick

Sacred Heart Univ. (CT)
Saginaw Valley State Univ. (MI)
Samford Univ. (AL)
San Francisco State Univ.
Schreiner Univ. (TX)
Scripps Coll. (CA)
Seattle Pacific Univ.
Seattle Univ.
Seton Hall Univ. (NJ)
Seton Hill Univ. (PA)
Sewanee–Univ. of the South (TN)
Siena Coll. (NY)
Simmons Coll. (MA)
Simpson Coll. (IA)
Skidmore Coll. (NY)
Smith Coll. (MA)
Southern Adventist Univ. (TN)
Southern Methodist Univ. (TX)
Southern Nazarene Univ. (OK)
Southwestern Coll. (KS)
Spelman Coll. (GA)
Spring Arbor Univ. (MI)
Spring Hill Coll. (AL)
St. Anselm Coll. (NH)
St. Bonaventure Univ. (NY)
St. Cloud State Univ. (MN)
St. Edward's Univ. (TX)
St. Francis Univ. (PA)
St. John's Univ. (MN)
St. Joseph Coll. (CT)
St. Joseph's Coll. (IN)
St. Joseph's Univ. (PA)
St. Lawrence Univ. (NY)
St. Louis Univ.
St. Mary's Coll. of California
St. Mary's Coll. of Maryland
St. Mary's Univ. of Minnesota
St. Michael's Coll. (VT)
St. Peter's Coll. (NJ)
St. Vincent Coll. (PA)
Stetson Univ. (FL)
Stevens Institute of Technology
    (NJ)
Stonehill Coll. (MA)
Suffolk Univ. (MA)
SUNY Coll.–Potsdam
SUNY–Fredonia
SUNY–Geneseo
SUNY–Oswego
SUNY–Plattsburgh
SUNY–Stony Brook
Swarthmore Coll. (PA)
Syracuse Univ. (NY)
Tabor Coll. (KS)
Temple Univ. (PA)
Texas A&M Univ.–Coll. Station
Texas Christian Univ.
Texas Lutheran Univ.
Texas State Univ.–San Marcos
Texas Tech Univ.
Texas Wesleyan Univ.
Trinity Coll. (CT)
Trinity Univ. (DC)
Tulane Univ. (LA)
Union Coll. (NY)
Union Coll. (NE)
Univ. at Albany–SUNY
Univ. at Buffalo–SUNY
Univ. of Arizona
Univ. of California–Davis
Univ. of California–Irvine

Univ. of California–Los Angeles
Univ. of California–Riverside
Univ. of California–San Diego
Univ. of California–Santa Barbara
Univ. of California–Santa Cruz
Univ. of Chicago
Univ. of Colorado–Boulder
Univ. of Connecticut
Univ. of Dallas
Univ. of Dayton (OH)
Univ. of Delaware
Univ. of Denver
Univ. of Evansville (IN)
Univ. of Florida
Univ. of Georgia
Univ. of Hartford (CT)
Univ. of Houston
Univ. of Illinois–Chicago
Univ. of Illinois–Urbana-Champaign
Univ. of Iowa
Univ. of Kansas
Univ. of Kentucky
Univ. of Maine
Univ. of Maryland–Baltimore
    County
Univ. of Maryland–Coll. Park
Univ. of Massachusetts–Amherst
Univ. of Massachusetts–Boston
Univ. of Miami (FL)
Univ. of Michigan–Ann Arbor
Univ. of Michigan–Dearborn
Univ. of Michigan–Flint
Univ. of Minnesota–Duluth
Univ. of Minnesota–Twin Cities
Univ. of Missouri
Univ. of Missouri–St. Louis
Univ. of Mount Union (OH)
Univ. of Nebraska–Lincoln
Univ. of Nevada–Las Vegas
Univ. of Nevada–Reno
Univ. of New England (ME)
Univ. of New Hampshire
Univ. of New Mexico
Univ. of North Carolina–
    Greensboro
Univ. of North Texas
Univ. of Northern Iowa
Univ. of Notre Dame (IN)
Univ. of Oklahoma
Univ. of Oregon
Univ. of Pennsylvania
Univ. of Pittsburgh
Univ. of Puget Sound (WA)
Univ. of Redlands (CA)
Univ. of Richmond (VA)
Univ. of Scranton (PA)
Univ. of Southern California
Univ. of Southern Indiana
Univ. of St. Thomas (MN)
Univ. of Tampa (FL)
Univ. of Texas–Arlington
Univ. of Texas–Austin
Univ. of Texas–Dallas
Univ. of the Pacific (CA)
Univ. of Tulsa (OK)
Univ. of Vermont
Univ. of Washington
Univ. of Wisconsin–Eau Claire
Univ. of Wisconsin–La Crosse
Univ. of Wisconsin–Madison
Univ. of Wisconsin–Milwaukee

Univ. of Wisconsin–Parkside
Univ. of Wisconsin–Superior
Univ. of Wyoming
Valparaiso Univ. (IN)
Vanderbilt Univ. (TN)
Vassar Coll. (NY)
Villanova Univ. (PA)
Virginia Tech
Viterbo Univ. (WI)
Wartburg Coll. (IA)
Washburn Univ. (KS)
Washington Adventist Univ. (MD)
Washington and Jefferson Coll.
    (PA)
Washington and Lee Univ. (VA)
Washington State Univ.
Washington Univ. in St. Louis
Wells Coll. (NY)
Wesleyan Univ. (CT)
West Chester Univ. of Pennsylvania
Western Kentucky Univ.
Western Michigan Univ.
Western New England Coll. (MA)
Western Washington Univ.
Westminster Coll. (PA)
Wheaton Coll. (MA)
Whitman Coll. (WA)
Whittier Coll. (CA)
Widener Univ. (PA)
Wilkes Univ. (PA)
William Jewell Coll. (MO)
Winston-Salem State Univ. (NC)
Wisconsin Lutheran Coll.
Wittenberg Univ. (OH)
Worcester Polytechnic Institute
    (MA)
Yale Univ. (CT)

Bioethics/Medical Ethics

Brown Univ. (RI)

Biological and Biomedical Sciences

Alderson-Broaddus Coll. (WV)
Arcadia Univ. (PA)
Azusa Pacific Univ. (CA)
Beloit Coll. (WI)
Berea Coll. (KY)
Bethel Univ. (MN)
Brown Univ. (RI)
California State Univ.–Sacramento
Capital Univ. (OH)
Carlow Univ. (PA)
Carnegie Mellon Univ. (PA)
Central Michigan Univ.
Charleston Southern Univ. (SC)
Clemson Univ. (SC)
Cornell Univ. (NY)
CUNY–City Coll.
CUNY–Hunter Coll.
Dakota State Univ. (SD)
Davis and Elkins Coll. (WV)
Eastern Univ. (PA)
Emory Univ. (GA)
Erskine Coll. (SC)
Eureka Coll. (IL)
Fairleigh Dickinson Univ. (NJ)
Farmingdale State Coll.–SUNY
Florida Southern Coll.

Fresno Pacific Univ. (CA)
Frostburg State Univ. (MD)
Geneva Coll. (PA)
Guilford Coll. (NC)
Johns Hopkins Univ. (MD)
Kansas State Univ.
Kent State Univ. (OH)
LeTourneau Univ. (TX)
Maine Maritime Academy
Martin Univ. (IN)
Midland Lutheran Coll. (NE)
Northwest Missouri State Univ.
Norwich Univ. (VT)
Ohio State Univ.–Columbus
Oral Roberts Univ. (OK)
Park Univ. (MO)
Pennsylvania State Univ.–Univ. Park
Purdue Univ.–Calumet (IN)
Ramapo Coll. of New Jersey
Regis Univ. (CO)
Rensselaer Polytechnic Institute
    (NY)
Rochester Institute of Technology
    (NY)
Siena Coll. (NY)
Skidmore Coll. (NY)
Southwestern Univ. (TX)
Springfield Coll. (MA)
St. Lawrence Univ. (NY)
St. Mary's Coll. of California
SUNY–Fredonia
Swarthmore Coll. (PA)
Syracuse Univ. (NY)
Texas A&M Univ.–Coll. Station
Texas Wesleyan Univ.
Touro Coll. (NY)
Trevecca Nazarene Univ. (TN)
Union Coll. (NY)
Univ. at Albany–SUNY
Univ. at Buffalo–SUNY
Univ. of Florida
Univ. of Illinois–Urbana-Champaign
Univ. of Kansas
Univ. of Kentucky
Univ. of Maryland–Univ. Coll.
Univ. of Minnesota–Twin Cities
Univ. of Mississippi
Univ. of North Dakota
Ursuline Coll. (OH)
Wayland Baptist Univ. (TX)

Biological and Physical Sciences

Adelphi Univ. (NY)
Albertus Magnus Coll. (CT)
Alfred Univ. (NY)
Alma Coll. (MI)
Averett Univ. (VA)
Avila Univ. (MO)
Baldwin-Wallace Coll. (OH)
Bard Coll. (NY)
Benedictine Coll. (KS)
Benedictine Univ. (IL)
Bluefield State Coll. (WV)
Bowie State Univ. (MD)
Brevard Coll. (NC)
Buena Vista Univ. (IA)
California State Univ.–Dominguez
    Hills
California State Univ.–Fullerton

California State Univ.–Los Angeles
Cameron Univ. (OK)
Central Coll. (IA)
Central Michigan Univ.
Charleston Southern Univ. (SC)
Clarion Univ. of Pennsylvania
Clarke Univ. (IA)
Coll. of St. Benedict (MN)
Coll. of the Ozarks (MO)
Colorado Christian Univ.
Columbia Univ. (NY)
Concordia Univ. (MI)
Concordia Univ. Chicago (IL)
Covenant Coll. (GA)
CUNY–Baruch Coll.
CUNY–Lehman Coll.
Dallas Baptist Univ.
Delta State Univ. (MS)
Dominican Univ. (IL)
Dowling Coll. (NY)
Drexel Univ. (PA)
East Stroudsburg Univ. of
    Pennsylvania
Eastern Michigan Univ.
Eastern Nazarene Coll. (MA)
Edinboro Univ. of Pennsylvania
Elmira Coll. (NY)
Evergreen State Coll. (WA)
Fairleigh Dickinson Univ. (NJ)
Florida Institute of Technology
Fordham Univ. (NY)
Fort Hays State Univ. (KS)
Furman Univ. (SC)
George Washington Univ. (DC)
Georgetown Univ. (DC)
Grand Valley State Univ. (MI)
Heritage Univ. (WA)
Immaculata Univ. (PA)
Indiana Univ. East
Indiana Univ. of Pennsylvania
Indiana Univ.–Kokomo
Johns Hopkins Univ. (MD)
King's Coll. (PA)
Kutztown Univ. of Pennsylvania
Lawrence Univ. (WI)
Le Moyne Coll. (NY)
Lehigh Univ. (PA)
Lock Haven Univ. of Pennsylvania
Louisiana Coll.
Lyndon State Coll. (VT)
Manchester Coll. (IN)
Maryville Univ. of St. Louis (MO)
Michigan State Univ.
Middle Tennessee State Univ.
Mississippi State Univ.
Mount Mary Coll. (WI)
National-Louis Univ. (IL)
North Central Coll. (IL)
North Park Univ. (IL)
Northern Michigan Univ.
Northwestern Univ. (IL)
Olivet Coll. (MI)
Oral Roberts Univ. (OK)
Oregon State Univ.
Pacific Univ. (OR)
Pennsylvania State Univ.–Univ. Park
Ramapo Coll. of New Jersey
San Francisco State Univ.
Shimer Coll. (IL)
Southeastern Oklahoma State Univ.
Southern Arkansas Univ.

St. Andrews Presbyterian Coll. (NC)
St. Anselm Coll. (NH)
St. John's Univ. (MN)
St. Mary's Coll. of Maryland
St. Norbert Coll. (WI)
St. Peter's Coll. (NJ)
St. Thomas Aquinas Coll. (NY)
St. Xavier Univ. (IL)
Taylor Univ. (IN)
Texas A&M Univ.–Coll. Station
Texas Tech Univ.
Towson Univ. (MD)
Union Coll. (NY)
Univ. of Alabama–Birmingham
Univ. of Alaska–Anchorage
Univ. of Alaska–Fairbanks
Univ. of Arkansas–Monticello
Univ. of Central Arkansas
Univ. of Denver
Univ. of Georgia
Univ. of Houston
Univ. of Houston–Downtown
Univ. of Maine
Univ. of Massachusetts–Amherst
Univ. of Nevada–Las Vegas
Univ. of North Florida
Univ. of Northern Iowa
Univ. of Oregon
Univ. of Pittsburgh
Univ. of South Florida
Univ. of Southern Indiana
Univ. of St. Francis (IN)
Univ. of Texas of the Permian Basin
Univ. of Texas–El Paso
Univ. of Texas–Pan American
Univ. of Texas–San Antonio
Univ. of the Pacific (CA)
Univ. of West Alabama
Univ. of West Florida
Univ. of Wisconsin–Platteville
Univ. of Wisconsin–River Falls
Univ. of Wisconsin–Stevens Point
Univ. of Wisconsin–Superior
Urbana Univ. (OH)
Ursinus Coll. (PA)
Vanguard Univ. of Southern
    California
Virginia Commonwealth Univ.
Washington State Univ.
Waynesburg Univ. (PA)
Western Oregon Univ.
Western Washington Univ.
Worcester State Coll. (MA)

Biology

Abilene Christian Univ. (TX)
Adams State Coll. (CO)
Adelphi Univ. (NY)
Adrian Coll. (MI)
Agnes Scott Coll. (GA)
Alabama Agricultural and
    Mechanical Univ.
Alabama State Univ.
Albany State Univ. (GA)
Albertus Magnus Coll. (CT)
Albion Coll. (MI)
Albright Coll. (PA)
Alcorn State Univ. (MS)
Alderson-Broaddus Coll. (WV)
Alfred Univ. (NY)

Alice Lloyd Coll. (KY)
Allegheny Coll. (PA)
Allen Univ. (SC)
Alma Coll. (MI)
Alvernia Univ. (PA)
Alverno Coll. (WI)
American International Coll. (MA)
American Univ. (DC)
Amherst Coll. (MA)
Anderson Univ. (SC)
Anderson Univ. (IN)
Andrews Univ. (MI)
Angelo State Univ. (TX)
Appalachian State Univ. (NC)
Aquinas Coll. (MI)
Arcadia Univ. (PA)
Arizona State Univ.
Arkansas State Univ.–Jonesboro
Arkansas Tech Univ.
Armstrong Atlantic State Univ. (GA)
Asbury Univ. (KY)
Ashland Univ. (OH)
Assumption Coll. (MA)
Atlantic Union Coll. (MA)
Auburn Univ. (AL)
Auburn Univ.–Montgomery (AL)
Augsburg Coll. (MN)
Augusta State Univ. (GA)
Augustana Coll. (SD)
Augustana Coll. (IL)
Aurora Univ. (IL)
Austin Coll. (TX)
Austin Peay State Univ. (TN)
Averett Univ. (VA)
Avila Univ. (MO)
Azusa Pacific Univ. (CA)
Baker Univ. (KS)
Baldwin-Wallace Coll. (OH)
Ball State Univ. (IN)
Bard Coll. at Simon's Rock (MA)
Barnard Coll. (NY)
Barry Univ. (FL)
Barton Coll. (NC)
Bates Coll. (ME)
Bay Path Coll. (MA)
Baylor Univ. (TX)
Belhaven Univ. (MS)
Bellarmine Univ. (KY)
Bellevue Univ. (NE)
Belmont Abbey Coll. (NC)
Belmont Univ. (TN)
Beloit Coll. (WI)
Bemidji State Univ. (MN)
Benedict Coll. (SC)
Benedictine Coll. (KS)
Benedictine Univ. (IL)
Bennett Coll. (NC)
Bennington Coll. (VT)
Berea Coll. (KY)
Berry Coll. (GA)
Bethany Coll. (WV)
Bethany Coll. (KS)
Bethel Coll. (IN)
Bethel Coll. (TN)
Bethel Coll. (KS)
Bethel Univ. (MN)
Bethune-Cookman Univ. (FL)
Binghamton Univ.–SUNY
Biola Univ. (CA)
Birmingham-Southern Coll. (AL)
Black Hills State Univ. (SD)

Blackburn Coll. (IL)
Bloomfield Coll. (NJ)
Bloomsburg Univ. of Pennsylvania
Blue Mountain Coll. (MS)
Bluefield Coll. (VA)
Bluffton Univ. (OH)
Boise State Univ. (ID)
Boston Univ.
Bowdoin Coll. (ME)
Bowie State Univ. (MD)
Bowling Green State Univ. (OH)
Bradley Univ. (IL)
Brandeis Univ. (MA)
Brenau Univ. (GA)
Brescia Univ. (KY)
Brewton-Parker Coll. (GA)
Briar Cliff Univ. (IA)
Bridgewater Coll. (VA)
Bridgewater State Coll. (MA)
Brigham Young Univ.–Hawaii
Brigham Young Univ.–Provo (UT)
Brown Univ. (RI)
Bryn Athyn Coll. of the New Church
    (PA)
Bryn Mawr Coll. (PA)
Bucknell Univ. (PA)
Buena Vista Univ. (IA)
Buffalo State Coll.–SUNY
Butler Univ. (IN)
Cabrini Coll. (PA)
Caldwell Coll. (NJ)
California Baptist Univ.
California Institute of Technology
California Lutheran Univ.
California Polytechnic State Univ.–
    San Luis Obispo
California State Univ.–Bakersfield
California State Univ.–Chico
California State Univ.–Dominguez
    Hills
California State Univ.–East Bay
California State Univ.–Fresno
California State Univ.–Fullerton
California State Univ.–Long Beach
California State Univ.–Los Angeles
California State Univ.–Monterey Bay
California State Univ.–Northridge
California State Univ.–Sacramento
California State Univ.–San
    Bernardino
California State Univ.–San Marcos
California State Univ.–Stanislaus
California Univ. of Pennsylvania
Calvin Coll. (MI)
Cameron Univ. (OK)
Campbell Univ. (NC)
Campbellsville Univ. (KY)
Canisius Coll. (NY)
Capital Univ. (OH)
Cardinal Stritch Univ. (WI)
Carleton Coll. (MN)
Carlow Univ. (PA)
Carnegie Mellon Univ. (PA)
Carroll Coll. (MT)
Carroll Univ. (WI)
Carson-Newman Coll. (TN)
Carthage Coll. (WI)
Case Western Reserve Univ. (OH)
Castleton State Coll. (VT)
Catawba Coll. (NC)
Catholic Univ. of America (DC)

Cedar Crest Coll. (PA)
Cedarville Univ. (OH)
Centenary Coll. of Louisiana
Central Christian Coll. (KS)
Central Coll. (IA)
Central Connecticut State Univ.
Central Methodist Univ. (MO)
Central Michigan Univ.
Central State Univ. (OH)
Central Washington Univ.
Centre Coll. (KY)
Chadron State Coll. (NE)
Chaminade Univ. of Honolulu
Chapman Univ. (CA)
Charleston Southern Univ. (SC)
Chatham Univ. (PA)
Chestnut Hill Coll. (PA)
Cheyney Univ. of Pennsylvania
Chicago State Univ.
Chowan Univ. (NC)
Christian Brothers Univ. (TN)
Christopher Newport Univ. (VA)
Claflin Univ. (SC)
Claremont McKenna Coll. (CA)
Clarion Univ. of Pennsylvania
Clark Atlanta Univ.
Clark Univ. (MA)
Clarkson Univ. (NY)
Clayton State Univ. (GA)
Clearwater Christian Coll. (FL)
Cleveland State Univ.
Coastal Carolina Univ. (SC)
Coe Coll. (IA)
Coker Coll. (SC)
Colby Coll. (ME)
Colby-Sawyer Coll. (NH)
Colgate Univ. (NY)
Coll. at Brockport–SUNY
Coll. of Charleston (SC)
Coll. of Idaho (ID)
Coll. of Mount St. Joseph (OH)
Coll. of Mount St. Vincent (NY)
Coll. of New Jersey
Coll. of Notre Dame of Maryland
Coll. of Our Lady of the Elms (MA)
Coll. of St. Benedict (MN)
Coll. of St. Elizabeth (NJ)
Coll. of St. Mary (NE)
Coll. of St. Rose (NY)
Coll. of St. Scholastica (MN)
Coll. of the Holy Cross (MA)
Coll. of William and Mary (VA)
Coll. of Wooster (OH)
Colorado Christian Univ.
Colorado Coll.
Colorado State Univ.
Colorado State Univ.–Pueblo
Columbia Coll. (MO)
Columbia Coll. (SC)
Columbus State Univ. (GA)
Concord Univ. (WV)
Concordia Coll. (NY)
Concordia Coll.–Moorhead (MN)
Concordia Univ. (CA)
Concordia Univ. (MI)
Concordia Univ. (OR)
Concordia Univ. (NE)
Concordia Univ. Chicago (IL)
Concordia Univ. Texas
Concordia Univ. Wisconsin
Concordia Univ.–St. Paul (MN)

Connecticut Coll.
Converse Coll. (SC)
Coppin State Univ. (MD)
Cornell Coll. (IA)
Cornell Univ. (NY)
Cornerstone Univ. (MI)
Covenant Coll. (GA)
Creighton Univ. (NE)
Crown Coll. (MN)
Culver-Stockton Coll. (MO)
Cumberland Univ. (TN)
CUNY–Baruch Coll.
CUNY–Brooklyn Coll.
CUNY–City Coll.
CUNY–Coll. of Staten Island
CUNY–Hunter Coll.
CUNY–Lehman Coll.
CUNY–Medgar Evers Coll.
CUNY–Queens Coll.
CUNY–York Coll.
Curry Coll. (MA)
D'Youville Coll. (NY)
Daemen Coll. (NY)
Dakota Wesleyan Univ. (SD)
Dallas Baptist Univ.
Dana Coll. (NE)
Dartmouth Coll. (NH)
Davidson Coll. (NC)
Davis and Elkins Coll. (WV)
Defiance Coll. (OH)
Delaware State Univ.
Delaware Valley Coll. (PA)
Delta State Univ. (MS)
Denison Univ. (OH)
DePaul Univ. (IL)
DePauw Univ. (IN)
DeSales Univ. (PA)
Dickinson Coll. (PA)
Dickinson State Univ. (ND)
Dillard Univ. (LA)
Dixie State Coll. of Utah
Dominican Coll. (NY)
Dominican Univ. (IL)
Dominican Univ. of California
Dordt Coll. (IA)
Dowling Coll. (NY)
Drake Univ. (IA)
Drew Univ. (NJ)
Drexel Univ. (PA)
Drury Univ. (MO)
Duke Univ. (NC)
Duquesne Univ. (PA)
Earlham Coll. (IN)
East Carolina Univ. (NC)
East Central Univ. (OK)
East Stroudsburg Univ. of
    Pennsylvania
East Tennessee State Univ.
East Texas Baptist Univ.
Eastern Connecticut State Univ.
Eastern Illinois Univ.
Eastern Kentucky Univ.
Eastern Mennonite Univ. (VA)
Eastern Michigan Univ.
Eastern Nazarene Coll. (MA)
Eastern New Mexico Univ.
Eastern Oregon Univ.
Eastern Univ. (PA)
Eastern Washington Univ.
Eckerd Coll. (FL)
Edgewood Coll. (WI)

Edinboro Univ. of Pennsylvania
Edward Waters Coll. (FL)
Elizabeth City State Univ. (NC)
Elizabethtown Coll. (PA)
Elmhurst Coll. (IL)
Elmira Coll. (NY)
Elon Univ. (NC)
Emmanuel Coll. (MA)
Emmanuel Coll. (GA)
Emory and Henry Coll. (VA)
Emory Univ. (GA)
Emporia State Univ. (KS)
Erskine Coll. (SC)
Eureka Coll. (IL)
Evangel Univ. (MO)
Evergreen State Coll. (WA)
Excelsior Coll. (NY)
Fairfield Univ. (CT)
Fairleigh Dickinson Univ. (NJ)
Fairmont State Univ. (WV)
Fayetteville State Univ. (NC)
Felician Coll. (NJ)
Ferris State Univ. (MI)
Ferrum Coll. (VA)
Fisk Univ. (TN)
Fitchburg State Coll. (MA)
Florida Atlantic Univ.
Florida Institute of Technology
Florida International Univ.
Florida Memorial Univ.
Florida Southern Coll.
Florida State Univ.
Fontbonne Univ. (MO)
Fordham Univ. (NY)
Fort Hays State Univ. (KS)
Fort Lewis Coll. (CO)
Fort Valley State Univ. (GA)
Framingham State Coll. (MA)
Francis Marion Univ. (SC)
Franciscan Univ. of Steubenville
    (OH)
Franklin and Marshall Coll. (PA)
Franklin Coll. (IN)
Franklin Pierce Univ. (NH)
Freed-Hardeman Univ. (TN)
Fresno Pacific Univ. (CA)
Friends Univ. (KS)
Frostburg State Univ. (MD)
Furman Univ. (SC)
Gallaudet Univ. (DC)
Gannon Univ. (PA)
Gardner-Webb Univ. (NC)
Geneva Coll. (PA)
George Fox Univ. (OR)
George Mason Univ. (VA)
George Washington Univ. (DC)
Georgetown Coll. (KY)
Georgetown Univ. (DC)
Georgia Coll. & State Univ.
Georgia Institute of Technology
Georgia Southern Univ.
Georgia Southwestern State Univ.
Georgia State Univ.
Georgian Court Univ. (NJ)
Gettysburg Coll. (PA)
Glenville State Coll. (WV)
Gonzaga Univ. (WA)
Gordon Coll. (MA)
Goucher Coll. (MD)
Grace Coll. and Seminary (IN)
Graceland Univ. (IA)

Grambling State Univ. (LA)
Grand Valley State Univ. (MI)
Grand View Univ. (IA)
Green Mountain Coll. (VT)
Greensboro Coll. (NC)
Greenville Coll. (IL)
Grinnell Coll. (IA)
Grove City Coll. (PA)
Guilford Coll. (NC)
Gustavus Adolphus Coll. (MN)
Gwynedd-Mercy Coll. (PA)
Hamilton Coll. (NY)
Hamline Univ. (MN)
Hampden-Sydney Coll. (VA)
Hampshire Coll. (MA)
Hampton Univ. (VA)
Hannibal-LaGrange Coll. (MO)
Hanover Coll. (IN)
Hardin-Simmons Univ. (TX)
Harding Univ. (AR)
Hartwick Coll. (NY)
Harvard Univ. (MA)
Harvey Mudd Coll. (CA)
Haverford Coll. (PA)
Hawaii Pacific Univ.
Heidelberg Univ. (OH)
Henderson State Univ. (AR)
Hendrix Coll. (AR)
Heritage Univ. (WA)
High Point Univ. (NC)
Hillsdale Coll. (MI)
Hiram Coll. (OH)
Hobart and William Smith Colleges (NY)
Hofstra Univ. (NY)
Hollins Univ. (VA)
Holy Family Univ. (PA)
Holy Names Univ. (CA)
Hood Coll. (MD)
Hope Coll. (MI)
Houghton Coll. (NY)
Houston Baptist Univ.
Howard Payne Univ. (TX)
Howard Univ. (DC)
Humboldt State Univ. (CA)
Huntingdon Coll. (AL)
Huntington Univ. (IN)
Husson Univ. (ME)
Huston-Tillotson Univ. (TX)
Idaho State Univ.
Illinois Coll.
Illinois Institute of Technology
Illinois State Univ.
Illinois Wesleyan Univ.
Immaculata Univ. (PA)
Indiana State Univ.
Indiana Univ. Northwest
Indiana Univ. of Pennsylvania
Indiana Univ. Southeast
Indiana Univ.–Bloomington
Indiana Univ.–Kokomo
Indiana Univ.-Purdue Univ.–Fort Wayne
Indiana Univ.-Purdue Univ.– Indianapolis
Indiana Wesleyan Univ.
Iona Coll. (NY)
Iowa State Univ.
Iowa Wesleyan Coll.
Ithaca Coll. (NY)
Jackson State Univ. (MS)

Jacksonville State Univ. (AL)
Jacksonville Univ. (FL)
James Madison Univ. (VA)
Jamestown Coll. (ND)
Jarvis Christian Coll. (TX)
John Brown Univ. (AR)
John Carroll Univ. (OH)
Johns Hopkins Univ. (MD)
Johnson C. Smith Univ. (NC)
Johnson State Coll. (VT)
Judson Coll. (AL)
Judson Univ. (IL)
Juniata Coll. (PA)
Kalamazoo Coll. (MI)
Kansas State Univ.
Kansas Wesleyan Univ.
Kean Univ. (NJ)
Keene State Coll. (NH)
Kennesaw State Univ. (GA)
Kent State Univ. (OH)
Kentucky State Univ.
Kentucky Wesleyan Coll.
Kenyon Coll. (OH)
Keuka Coll. (NY)
King Coll. (TN)
King's Coll. (PA)
Knox Coll. (IL)
Kutztown Univ. of Pennsylvania
La Roche Coll. (PA)
La Salle Univ. (PA)
La Sierra Univ. (CA)
Lafayette Coll. (PA)
LaGrange Coll. (GA)
Lake Erie Coll. (OH)
Lake Forest Coll. (IL)
Lake Superior State Univ. (MI)
Lakeland Coll. (WI)
Lamar Univ. (TX)
Lambuth Univ. (TN)
Lander Univ. (SC)
Lane Coll. (TN)
Langston Univ. (OK)
Lawrence Univ. (WI)
Le Moyne Coll. (NY)
Lebanon Valley Coll. (PA)
Lees-McRae Coll. (NC)
Lehigh Univ. (PA)
LeMoyne-Owen Coll. (TN)
Lenoir-Rhyne Univ. (NC)
Lesley Univ. (MA)
LeTourneau Univ. (TX)
Lewis & Clark Coll. (OR)
Lewis Univ. (IL)
Lewis-Clark State Coll. (ID)
Liberty Univ. (VA)
Life Univ. (GA)
Limestone Coll. (SC)
Lincoln Memorial Univ. (TN)
Lincoln Univ. (PA)
Lincoln Univ. (MO)
Lindenwood Univ. (MO)
Lindsey Wilson Coll. (KY)
Linfield Coll. (OR)
Lipscomb Univ. (TN)
Livingstone Coll. (NC)
Lock Haven Univ. of Pennsylvania
Long Island Univ.–C.W. Post Campus (NY)
Longwood Univ. (VA)
Loras Coll. (IA)
Louisiana Coll.

Louisiana State Univ.–Baton Rouge
Louisiana Tech Univ.
Lourdes Coll. (OH)
Loyola Marymount Univ. (CA)
Loyola Univ. Chicago
Loyola Univ. Maryland
Loyola Univ. New Orleans
Lubbock Christian Univ. (TX)
Luther Coll. (IA)
Lycoming Coll. (PA)
Lynchburg Coll. (VA)
Lynn Univ. (FL)
Lyon Coll. (AR)
Macalester Coll. (MN)
MacMurray Coll. (IL)
Macon State Coll. (GA)
Madonna Univ. (MI)
Malone Univ. (OH)
Manchester Coll. (IN)
Manhattan Coll. (NY)
Manhattanville Coll. (NY)
Mansfield Univ. of Pennsylvania
Maranatha Baptist Bible Coll. (WI)
Marian Univ. (WI)
Marian Univ. (IN)
Marietta Coll. (OH)
Marist Coll. (NY)
Marlboro Coll. (VT)
Marquette Univ. (WI)
Mars Hill Coll. (NC)
Marshall Univ. (WV)
Martin Methodist Coll. (TN)
Martin Univ. (IN)
Mary Baldwin Coll. (VA)
Marygrove Coll. (MI)
Marymount Manhattan Coll. (NY)
Marymount Univ. (VA)
Maryville Coll. (TN)
Maryville Univ. of St. Louis (MO)
Marywood Univ. (PA)
Massachusetts Coll. of Liberal Arts
Massachusetts Institute of Technology
Master's Coll. and Seminary (CA)
Mayville State Univ. (ND)
McDaniel Coll. (MD)
McKendree Univ. (IL)
McMurry Univ. (TX)
McNeese State Univ. (LA)
McPherson Coll. (KS)
Medaille Coll. (NY)
Mercy Coll. (NY)
Mercyhurst Coll. (PA)
Meredith Coll. (NC)
Merrimack Coll. (MA)
Mesa State Coll. (CO)
Messiah Coll. (PA)
Methodist Univ. (NC)
Metropolitan State Coll. of Denver
Michigan State Univ.
Michigan Technological Univ.
MidAmerica Nazarene Univ. (KS)
Middle Tennessee State Univ.
Middlebury Coll. (VT)
Midland Lutheran Coll. (NE)
Midway Coll. (KY)
Midwestern State Univ. (TX)
Miles Coll. (AL)
Millersville Univ. of Pennsylvania
Milligan Coll. (TN)
Millikin Univ. (IL)

Mills Coll. (CA)
Millsaps Coll. (MS)
Minnesota State Univ.–Mankato
Minnesota State Univ.–Moorhead
Minot State Univ. (ND)
Misericordia Univ. (PA)
Mississippi Coll.
Mississippi State Univ.
Mississippi Univ. for Women
Mississippi Valley State Univ.
Missouri Southern State Univ.
Missouri State Univ.
Missouri Univ. of Science & Technology
Missouri Valley Coll.
Missouri Western State Univ.
Molloy Coll. (NY)
Monmouth Coll. (IL)
Monmouth Univ. (NJ)
Montana State Univ.
Montana State Univ.–Billings
Montana State Univ.–Northern
Montana Tech of the Univ. of Montana
Montclair State Univ. (NJ)
Montreat Coll. (NC)
Moravian Coll. (PA)
Morehead State Univ. (KY)
Morehouse Coll. (GA)
Morgan State Univ. (MD)
Morningside Coll. (IA)
Morris Coll. (SC)
Mount Aloysius Coll. (PA)
Mount Holyoke Coll. (MA)
Mount Ida Coll. (MA)
Mount Marty Coll. (SD)
Mount Mary Coll. (WI)
Mount Mercy Coll. (IA)
Mount Olive Coll. (NC)
Mount St. Mary Coll. (NY)
Mount St. Mary's Coll. (CA)
Mount St. Mary's Univ. (MD)
Mountain State Univ. (WV)
Muhlenberg Coll. (PA)
Murray State Univ. (KY)
Muskingum Univ. (OH)
National-Louis Univ. (IL)
Nazareth Coll. (NY)
Nebraska Wesleyan Univ.
Neumann Univ. (PA)
New Jersey City Univ.
New Jersey Institute of Technology
New Mexico Highlands Univ.
New Mexico Institute of Mining and Technology
New Mexico State Univ.
New York Institute of Technology
New York Univ.
Newberry Coll. (SC)
Newman Univ. (KS)
Niagara Univ. (NY)
Nicholls State Univ. (LA)
Norfolk State Univ. (VA)
North Carolina A&T State Univ.
North Carolina Central Univ.
North Carolina State Univ.–Raleigh
North Carolina Wesleyan Coll.
North Central Coll. (IL)
North Dakota State Univ.
North Georgia Coll. and State Univ.
North Greenville Univ. (SC)

North Park Univ. (IL)
Northeastern Illinois Univ.
Northeastern State Univ. (OK)
Northeastern Univ. (MA)
Northern Arizona Univ.
Northern Illinois Univ.
Northern Kentucky Univ.
Northern Michigan Univ.
Northern State Univ. (SD)
Northland Coll. (WI)
Northwest Nazarene Univ. (ID)
Northwestern Coll. (IA)
Northwestern Coll. (MN)
Northwestern Oklahoma State Univ.
Northwestern State Univ. of Louisiana
Northwestern Univ. (IL)
Norwich Univ. (VT)
Notre Dame Coll. of Ohio
Notre Dame de Namur Univ. (CA)
Nova Southeastern Univ. (FL)
Oakland City Univ. (IN)
Oakland Univ. (MI)
Oakwood Univ. (AL)
Oberlin Coll. (OH)
Occidental Coll. (CA)
Ohio Dominican Univ.
Ohio Northern Univ.
Ohio State Univ.–Columbus
Ohio Univ.
Ohio Wesleyan Univ.
Oklahoma Baptist Univ.
Oklahoma Christian Univ.
Oklahoma City Univ.
Oklahoma Panhandle State Univ.
Oklahoma State Univ.
Oklahoma Wesleyan Univ.
Old Dominion Univ. (VA)
Olivet Coll. (MI)
Olivet Nazarene Univ. (IL)
Oral Roberts Univ. (OK)
Oregon State Univ.
Otterbein Coll. (OH)
Ouachita Baptist Univ. (AR)
Our Lady of Holy Cross Coll. (LA)
Our Lady of the Lake Univ. (TX)
Pace Univ. (NY)
Pacific Lutheran Univ. (WA)
Pacific Union Coll. (CA)
Pacific Univ. (OR)
Paine Coll. (GA)
Palm Beach Atlantic Univ. (FL)
Park Univ. (MO)
Paul Smith's Coll. (NY)
Peace Coll. (NC)
Pennsylvania State Univ.–Univ. Park
Pepperdine Univ. (CA)
Peru State Coll. (NE)
Pfeiffer Univ. (NC)
Philadelphia Univ.
Philander Smith Coll. (AR)
Piedmont Coll. (GA)
Pikeville Coll. (KY)
Pine Manor Coll. (MA)
Pittsburg State Univ. (KS)
Pitzer Coll. (CA)
Plymouth State Univ. (NH)
Point Loma Nazarene Univ. (CA)
Point Park Univ. (PA)
Pomona Coll. (CA)

Portland State Univ. (OR)
Post Univ. (CT)
Prairie View A&M Univ. (TX)
Presbyterian Coll. (SC)
Prescott Coll. (AZ)
Principia Coll. (IL)
Providence Coll. (RI)
Purchase Coll.–SUNY
Purdue Univ.–Calumet (IN)
Purdue Univ.–North Central (IN)
Queens Univ. of Charlotte (NC)
Quincy Univ. (IL)
Quinnipiac Univ. (CT)
Radford Univ. (VA)
Ramapo Coll. of New Jersey
Randolph Coll. (VA)
Randolph-Macon Coll. (VA)
Reed Coll. (OR)
Regis Coll. (MA)
Regis Univ. (CO)
Reinhardt Univ. (GA)
Rensselaer Polytechnic Institute
    (NY)
Rhode Island Coll.
Rhodes Coll. (TN)
Rice Univ. (TX)
Richard Stockton Coll. of New
    Jersey
Rider Univ. (NJ)
Ripon Coll. (WI)
Rivier Coll. (NH)
Roanoke Coll. (VA)
Roberts Wesleyan Coll. (NY)
Rochester Institute of Technology
    (NY)
Rockford Coll. (IL)
Rockhurst Univ. (MO)
Rocky Mountain Coll. (MT)
Roger Williams Univ. (RI)
Rogers State Univ. (OK)
Rollins Coll. (FL)
Roosevelt Univ. (IL)
Rose-Hulman Institute of
    Technology (IN)
Rosemont Coll. (PA)
Russell Sage Coll. (NY)
Rust Coll. (MS)
Rutgers, the State Univ. of New
    Jersey–Camden
Rutgers, the State Univ. of New
    Jersey–New Brunswick
Rutgers, the State Univ. of New
    Jersey–Newark
Sacred Heart Univ. (CT)
Saginaw Valley State Univ. (MI)
Salem Coll. (NC)
Salem State Coll. (MA)
Salisbury Univ. (MD)
Salve Regina Univ. (RI)
Sam Houston State Univ. (TX)
Samford Univ. (AL)
San Diego State Univ.
San Francisco State Univ.
San Jose State Univ. (CA)
Santa Clara Univ. (CA)
Savannah State Univ. (GA)
Schreiner Univ. (TX)
Scripps Coll. (CA)
Seattle Pacific Univ.
Seattle Univ.
Seton Hall Univ. (NJ)

Seton Hill Univ. (PA)
Sewanee–Univ. of the South (TN)
Shaw Univ. (NC)
Shawnee State Univ. (OH)
Shenandoah Univ. (VA)
Shepherd Univ. (WV)
Shippensburg Univ. of Pennsylvania
Shorter Coll. (GA)
Siena Coll. (NY)
Sierra Nevada Coll. (NV)
Silver Lake Coll. (WI)
Simmons Coll. (MA)
Simpson Coll. (IA)
Skidmore Coll. (NY)
Slippery Rock Univ. of Pennsylvania
Smith Coll. (MA)
Sonoma State Univ. (CA)
South Carolina State Univ.
South Dakota State Univ.
Southeast Missouri State Univ.
Southeastern Louisiana Univ.
Southeastern Oklahoma State Univ.
Southeastern Univ. (FL)
Southern Adventist Univ. (TN)
Southern Arkansas Univ.
Southern Connecticut State Univ.
Southern Illinois Univ.–Carbondale
Southern Illinois Univ.–Edwardsville
Southern Methodist Univ. (TX)
Southern Nazarene Univ. (OK)
Southern Oregon Univ.
Southern Polytechnic State Univ.
    (GA)
Southern Univ. and A&M Coll. (LA)
Southern Univ.–New Orleans
Southern Utah Univ.
Southern Wesleyan Univ. (SC)
Southwest Baptist Univ. (MO)
Southwest Minnesota State Univ.
Southwestern Adventist Univ. (TX)
Southwestern Coll. (KS)
Southwestern Oklahoma State
    Univ.
Southwestern Univ. (TX)
Spelman Coll. (GA)
Spring Arbor Univ. (MI)
Spring Hill Coll. (AL)
Springfield Coll. (MA)
St. Ambrose Univ. (IA)
St. Andrews Presbyterian Coll. (NC)
St. Anselm Coll. (NH)
St. Augustine's Coll. (NC)
St. Bonaventure Univ. (NY)
St. Catherine Univ. (MN)
St. Cloud State Univ. (MN)
St. Edward's Univ. (TX)
St. Francis Coll. (NY)
St. Francis Univ. (PA)
St. John Fisher Coll. (NY)
St. John's Univ. (MN)
St. John's Univ. (NY)
St. Joseph Coll. (CT)
St. Joseph's Coll. (IN)
St. Joseph's Coll. (ME)
St. Joseph's Coll. New York
St. Joseph's Univ. (PA)
St. Lawrence Univ. (NY)
St. Leo Univ. (FL)
St. Louis Univ.
St. Martin's Univ. (WA)
St. Mary's Coll. (IN)

St. Mary's Coll. of California
St. Mary's Coll. of Maryland
St. Mary's Univ. of Minnesota
St. Mary's Univ. of San Antonio
    (TX)
St. Mary-of-the-Woods Coll. (IN)
St. Michael's Coll. (VT)
St. Norbert Coll. (WI)
St. Olaf Coll. (MN)
St. Peter's Coll. (NJ)
St. Thomas Aquinas Coll. (NY)
St. Thomas Univ. (FL)
St. Vincent Coll. (PA)
St. Xavier Univ. (IL)
Stanford Univ. (CA)
Stephen F. Austin State Univ. (TX)
Stephens Coll. (MO)
Sterling Coll. (KS)
Stetson Univ. (FL)
Stevenson Univ. (MD)
Stillman Coll. (AL)
Stonehill Coll. (MA)
Suffolk Univ. (MA)
Sul Ross State Univ. (TX)
SUNY Coll.–Cortland
SUNY Coll.–Old Westbury
SUNY Coll.–Oneonta
SUNY Coll.–Potsdam
SUNY–Fredonia
SUNY–Geneseo
SUNY–Oswego
SUNY–Plattsburgh
SUNY–Stony Brook
Susquehanna Univ. (PA)
Swarthmore Coll. (PA)
Syracuse Univ. (NY)
Tabor Coll. (KS)
Talladega Coll. (AL)
Tarleton State Univ. (TX)
Taylor Univ. (IN)
Temple Univ. (PA)
Tennessee State Univ.
Tennessee Technological Univ.
Tennessee Wesleyan Coll.
Texas A&M International Univ.
Texas A&M Univ.–Coll. Station
Texas A&M Univ.–Commerce
Texas A&M Univ.–Corpus Christi
Texas A&M Univ.–Kingsville
Texas Christian Univ.
Texas Coll.
Texas Lutheran Univ.
Texas State Univ.–San Marcos
Texas Tech Univ.
Texas Wesleyan Univ.
Texas Woman's Univ.
The Citadel (SC)
Thiel Coll. (PA)
Thomas Edison State Coll. (NJ)
Thomas More Coll. (KY)
Thomas More Coll. of Liberal Arts
    (NH)
Thomas Univ. (GA)
Toccoa Falls Coll. (GA)
Tougaloo Coll. (MS)
Touro Coll. (NY)
Towson Univ. (MD)
Transylvania Univ. (KY)
Trevecca Nazarene Univ. (TN)
Trine Univ. (IN)
Trinity Christian Coll. (IL)

Trinity Coll. (CT)
Trinity International Univ. (IL)
Trinity Univ. (DC)
Troy Univ. (AL)
Truman State Univ. (MO)
Tufts Univ. (MA)
Tulane Univ. (LA)
Tusculum Coll. (TN)
Union Coll. (NY)
Union Coll. (KY)
Union Coll. (NE)
Union Univ. (TN)
United States Air Force Academy
    (CO)
Univ. at Albany–SUNY
Univ. at Buffalo–SUNY
Univ. of Akron (OH)
Univ. of Alabama
Univ. of Alabama–Birmingham
Univ. of Alabama–Huntsville
Univ. of Alaska–Anchorage
Univ. of Alaska–Fairbanks
Univ. of Alaska–Southeast
Univ. of Arizona
Univ. of Arkansas
Univ. of Arkansas–Pine Bluff
Univ. of California–Berkeley
Univ. of California–Davis
Univ. of California–Irvine
Univ. of California–Los Angeles
Univ. of California–Riverside
Univ. of California–San Diego
Univ. of California–Santa Barbara
Univ. of California–Santa Cruz
Univ. of Central Arkansas
Univ. of Central Florida
Univ. of Central Missouri
Univ. of Central Oklahoma
Univ. of Charleston (WV)
Univ. of Chicago
Univ. of Colorado–Colorado
    Springs
Univ. of Colorado–Denver
Univ. of Connecticut
Univ. of Dallas
Univ. of Dayton (OH)
Univ. of Delaware
Univ. of Denver
Univ. of Detroit Mercy
Univ. of Dubuque (IA)
Univ. of Evansville (IN)
Univ. of Findlay (OH)
Univ. of Georgia
Univ. of Great Falls (MT)
Univ. of Hartford (CT)
Univ. of Hawaii–Hilo
Univ. of Hawaii–Manoa
Univ. of Houston
Univ. of Houston–Downtown
Univ. of Illinois–Chicago
Univ. of Illinois–Springfield
Univ. of Illinois–Urbana-Champaign
Univ. of Indianapolis
Univ. of Iowa
Univ. of Kansas
Univ. of Kentucky
Univ. of La Verne (CA)
Univ. of Louisiana–Lafayette
Univ. of Louisiana–Monroe
Univ. of Louisville (KY)
Univ. of Maine

Univ. of Maine–Augusta
Univ. of Maine–Farmington
Univ. of Maine–Fort Kent
Univ. of Maine–Machias
Univ. of Maine–Presque Isle
Univ. of Mary (ND)
Univ. of Mary Hardin-Baylor (TX)
Univ. of Mary Washington (VA)
Univ. of Maryland–Baltimore
    County
Univ. of Maryland–Coll. Park
Univ. of Maryland–Eastern Shore
Univ. of Massachusetts–Amherst
Univ. of Massachusetts–Boston
Univ of Massachusetts–Lowell
Univ. of Memphis
Univ. of Miami (FL)
Univ. of Michigan–Ann Arbor
Univ. of Michigan–Dearborn
Univ. of Michigan–Flint
Univ. of Minnesota–Duluth
Univ. of Minnesota–Morris
Univ. of Minnesota–Twin Cities
Univ. of Mississippi
Univ. of Missouri
Univ. of Missouri–Kansas City
Univ. of Missouri–St. Louis
Univ. of Mobile (AL)
Univ. of Montana
Univ. of Montevallo (AL)
Univ. of Mount Union (OH)
Univ. of Nebraska–Kearney
Univ. of Nebraska–Lincoln
Univ. of Nebraska–Omaha
Univ. of Nevada–Las Vegas
Univ. of Nevada–Reno
Univ. of New England (ME)
Univ. of New Hampshire
Univ. of New Haven (CT)
Univ. of New Mexico
Univ. of New Orleans
Univ. of North Alabama
Univ. of North Carolina–Asheville
Univ. of North Carolina–Chapel Hill
Univ. of North Carolina–Charlotte
Univ. of North Carolina–
    Greensboro
University of North Carolina–
    Pembroke
Univ. of North Carolina–
    Wilmington
Univ. of North Dakota
Univ. of North Florida
Univ. of North Texas
Univ. of Northern Colorado
Univ. of Northern Iowa
Univ. of Notre Dame (IN)
Univ. of Oregon
Univ. of Pennsylvania
Univ. of Pittsburgh
Univ. of Pittsburgh–Bradford
Univ. of Pittsburgh–Johnstown
Univ. of Portland (OR)
Univ. of Puget Sound (WA)
Univ. of Redlands (CA)
Univ. of Rhode Island
Univ. of Richmond (VA)
Univ. of Rio Grande (OH)
Univ. of Rochester (NY)
Univ. of San Diego
Univ. of San Francisco

Univ. of Science and Arts of
 Oklahoma
Univ. of Scranton (PA)
Univ. of Sioux Falls (SD)
Univ. of South Alabama
Univ. of South Carolina
Univ. of South Carolina–Aiken
Univ. of South Carolina–Upstate
Univ. of South Dakota
Univ. of South Florida
Univ. of Southern California
Univ. of Southern Indiana
Univ. of Southern Maine
Univ. of Southern Mississippi
Univ. of St. Francis (IL)
Univ. of St. Mary (KS)
Univ. of St. Thomas (MN)
Univ. of St. Thomas (TX)
Univ. of Tampa (FL)
Univ. of Tennessee
Univ. of Tennessee–Chattanooga
Univ. of Tennessee–Martin
Univ. of Texas of the Permian Basin
Univ. of Texas–Arlington
Univ. of Texas–Austin
Univ. of Texas–Brownsville
Univ. of Texas–Dallas
Univ. of Texas–El Paso
Univ. of Texas–Pan American
Univ. of Texas–San Antonio
Univ. of Texas–Tyler
Univ. of the Cumberlands (KY)
Univ. of the District of Columbia
Univ. of the Incarnate Word (TX)
Univ. of the Ozarks (AR)
Univ. of the Pacific (CA)
Univ. of the Southwest (NM)
Univ. of Toledo (OH)
Univ. of Tulsa (OK)
Univ. of Utah
Univ. of Vermont
Univ. of Virginia
Univ. of Virginia–Wise
Univ. of Washington
Univ. of West Alabama
Univ. of West Florida
Univ. of West Georgia
Univ. of Wisconsin–Eau Claire
Univ. of Wisconsin–Green Bay
Univ. of Wisconsin–La Crosse
Univ. of Wisconsin–Madison
Univ. of Wisconsin–Milwaukee
Univ. of Wisconsin–Oshkosh
Univ. of Wisconsin–Platteville
Univ. of Wisconsin–River Falls
Univ. of Wisconsin–Stevens Point
Univ. of Wisconsin–Superior
Univ. of Wisconsin–Whitewater
Univ. of Wyoming
Upper Iowa Univ.
Ursinus Coll. (PA)
Ursuline Coll. (OH)
Utah State Univ.
Utah Valley Univ.
Utica Coll. (NY)
Valdosta State Univ. (GA)
Valley City State Univ. (ND)
Valparaiso Univ. (IN)
Vanderbilt Univ. (TN)
Vanguard Univ. of Southern
 California

Vassar Coll. (NY)
Victory Univ. (TN)
Villanova Univ. (PA)
Virginia Commonwealth Univ.
Virginia Intermont Coll.
Virginia Military Institute
Virginia State Univ.
Virginia Tech
Virginia Union Univ.
Virginia Wesleyan Coll.
Viterbo Univ. (WI)
Voorhees Coll. (SC)
Wabash Coll. (IN)
Wagner Coll. (NY)
Wake Forest Univ. (NC)
Walsh Univ. (OH)
Warner Pacific Coll. (OR)
Warner Univ. (FL)
Warren Wilson Coll. (NC)
Wartburg Coll. (IA)
Washburn Univ. (KS)
Washington Adventist Univ. (MD)
Washington and Jefferson Coll.
 (PA)
Washington and Lee Univ. (VA)
Washington Coll. (MD)
Washington State Univ.
Washington Univ. in St. Louis
Wayland Baptist Univ. (TX)
Wayne State Coll. (NE)
Wayne State Univ. (MI)
Waynesburg Univ. (PA)
Webster Univ. (MO)
Wellesley Coll. (MA)
Wells Coll. (NY)
Wesley Coll. (DE)
Wesleyan Coll. (GA)
Wesleyan Univ. (CT)
West Chester Univ. of Pennsylvania
West Liberty Univ. (WV)
West Texas A&M Univ.
West Virginia State Univ.
West Virginia Univ.
West Virginia Univ. Institute of
 Technology
West Virginia Wesleyan Coll.
Western Carolina Univ. (NC)
Western Connecticut State Univ.
Western Illinois Univ.
Western Kentucky Univ.
Western Michigan Univ.
Western New England Coll. (MA)
Western New Mexico Univ.
Western Oregon Univ.
Western State Coll. of Colorado
Western Washington Univ.
Westfield State Coll. (MA)
Westminster Coll. (UT)
Westminster Coll. (PA)
Westminster Coll. (MO)
Westmont Coll. (CA)
Wheaton Coll. (IL)
Wheaton Coll. (MA)
Wheeling Jesuit Univ. (WV)
Whitman Coll. (WA)
Whittier Coll. (CA)
Whitworth Univ. (WA)
Wichita State Univ. (KS)
Widener Univ. (PA)
Wilberforce Univ. (OH)
Wiley Coll. (TX)

Wilkes Univ. (PA)
Willamette Univ. (OR)
William Carey Univ. (MS)
William Jewell Coll. (MO)
William Paterson Univ. of New
 Jersey
William Penn Univ. (IA)
William Woods Univ. (MO)
Williams Baptist Coll. (AR)
Williams Coll. (MA)
Wilmington Coll. (OH)
Wilson Coll. (PA)
Wingate Univ. (NC)
Winston-Salem State Univ. (NC)
Winthrop Univ. (SC)
Wisconsin Lutheran Coll.
Wittenberg Univ. (OH)
Wofford Coll. (SC)
Worcester Polytechnic Institute
 (MA)
Worcester State Coll. (MA)
Wright State Univ. (OH)
Xavier Univ. (OH)
Xavier Univ. of Louisiana
Yale Univ. (CT)
York Coll. (NE)
York Coll. of Pennsylvania
Youngstown State Univ. (OH)

Biology Technician/ Biotechnology Laboratory Technician

Florida Memorial Univ.
Gannon Univ. (PA)
Mansfield Univ. of Pennsylvania
Pennsylvania State Univ.–Univ. Park
Texas Wesleyan Univ.
Tusculum Coll. (TN)
Univ. of New Haven (CT)

Biomathematics and Bioinformatics

Baylor Univ. (TX)
Brigham Young Univ.–Provo (UT)
Brown Univ. (RI)
Canisius Coll. (NY)
Case Western Reserve Univ. (OH)
Cedar Crest Coll. (PA)
Claflin Univ. (SC)
Clark Univ. (MA)
Cornell Univ. (NY)
Davenport Univ. (MI)
Eastern Michigan Univ.
Emmanuel Coll. (MA)
Florida State Univ.
Gannon Univ. (PA)
Harvey Mudd Coll. (CA)
Indiana Univ.-Purdue Univ.–
 Indianapolis
La Sierra Univ. (CA)
Loyola Univ. Chicago
Michigan Technological Univ.
Ohio State Univ.–Columbus
Pacific Univ. (OR)
Ramapo Coll. of New Jersey
Rochester Institute of Tech. (NY)
Rockhurst Univ. (MO)
St. Edward's Univ. (TX)
St. Vincent Coll. (PA)

Tulane Univ. (LA)
Univ. at Buffalo–SUNY
Univ. of California–Los Angeles
Univ. of California–San Diego
Univ. of California–Santa Cruz
Univ. of Denver
Univ. of Maryland–Baltimore
 County
Univ. of Michigan–Ann Arbor
Univ. of Nebraska–Lincoln
Univ. of Nebraska–Omaha
Univ. of North Carolina–Chapel Hill
Univ. of Northern Iowa
Univ. of Pennsylvania
Univ. of Scranton (PA)
Univ. of St. Thomas (TX)
Univ. of Wisconsin–Parkside
Virginia Commonwealth Univ.

Biomedical/Medical Engineering

Alfred Univ. (NY)
Arizona State Univ.
Binghamton Univ.–SUNY
Boston Univ.
Brown Univ. (RI)
Bucknell Univ. (PA)
California Lutheran Univ.
Carnegie Mellon Univ. (PA)
Case Western Reserve Univ. (OH)
Catholic Univ. of America (DC)
Cedar Crest Coll. (PA)
Clemson Univ. (SC)
Coll. of New Jersey
Columbia Univ. (NY)
Cornell Univ. (NY)
CUNY–City Coll.
Drexel Univ. (PA)
Duke Univ. (NC)
Florida A&M Univ.
Florida International Univ.
George Washington Univ. (DC)
Georgia Institute of Technology
Hofstra Univ. (NY)
Illinois Institute of Technology
Indiana Institute of Technology
Indiana Univ.-Purdue Univ.–
 Indianapolis
Johns Hopkins Univ. (MD)
Kettering Univ. (MI)
Lawrence Technological Univ. (MI)
Lehigh Univ. (PA)
LeTourneau Univ. (TX)
Louisiana State Univ.–Baton Rouge
Louisiana Tech Univ.
Marquette Univ. (WI)
Massachusetts Institute of
 Technology
Michigan Technological Univ.
Milwaukee School of Engineering
Mississippi State Univ.
New Jersey Institute of Technology
North Carolina State Univ.–Raleigh
Northwestern Univ. (IL)
Ohio State Univ.–Columbus
Oral Roberts Univ. (OK)
Oregon State Univ.
Pennsylvania State Univ.–Univ. Park
Rensselaer Polytechnic Institute
 (NY)

Rice Univ. (TX)
Rochester Institute of Technology
 (NY)
Rose-Hulman Institute of
 Technology (IN)
Rutgers, the State Univ. of New
 Jersey–New Brunswick
St. Louis Univ.
Stanford Univ. (CA)
Stevens Institute of Technology
 (NJ)
SUNY–Stony Brook
Syracuse Univ. (NY)
Texas A&M Univ.–Coll. Station
Trinity Coll. (CT)
Tulane Univ. (LA)
Univ. of Akron (OH)
Univ. of Alabama–Birmingham
Univ. of California–Berkeley
Univ. of California–Davis
Univ. of California–Irvine
Univ. of California–Riverside
Univ. of Central Oklahoma
Univ. of Connecticut
Univ. of Florida
Univ. of Houston
Univ. of Illinois–Chicago
Univ. of Illinois–Urbana-Champaign
Univ. of Iowa
Univ. of Kentucky
Univ. of Louisville (KY)
Univ. of Memphis
Univ. of Miami (FL)
Univ. of Minnesota–Twin Cities
Univ. of Nebraska–Lincoln
Univ. of Pennsylvania
Univ. of Pittsburgh
Univ. of Rhode Island
Univ. of Rochester (NY)
Univ. of South Carolina
Univ. of Southern California
Univ. of Texas–Austin
Univ. of the Pacific (CA)
Univ. of Toledo (OH)
Univ. of Utah
Univ. of Virginia
Univ. of Washington
Univ. of Wisconsin–Madison
Vanderbilt Univ. (TN)
Virginia Commonwealth Univ.
Washington State Univ.
Washington Univ. in St. Louis
Western New England Coll. (MA)
Worcester Polytechnic Institute
 (MA)
Wright State Univ. (OH)
Yale Univ. (CT)

Biopsychology

Hiram Coll. (OH)
Simmons Coll. (MA)
Tufts Univ. (MA)
Univ. of California–Santa Barbara

Biotechnology

Brigham Young Univ.–Provo (UT)
California State Polytechnic Univ.–
 Pomona
California State Univ.–San Marcos

Calvin Coll. (MI)
Claflin Univ. (SC)
Coll. of Notre Dame of Maryland
CUNY–York Coll.
East Stroudsburg Univ. of
    Pennsylvania
Elizabethtown Coll. (PA)
Fayetteville State Univ. (NC)
Ferris State Univ. (MI)
Fitchburg State Coll. (MA)
Florida Gulf Coast Univ.
Fontbonne Univ. (MO)
James Madison Univ. (VA)
Kennesaw State Univ. (GA)
Kent State Univ. (OH)
Marywood Univ. (PA)
Minnesota State Univ.–Mankato
Missouri Southern State Univ.
Montana State Univ.
North Dakota State Univ.
Oregon State Univ.
Plymouth State Univ. (NH)
Point Park Univ. (PA)
Purdue Univ.–Calumet (IN)
Rochester Institute of Technology
    (NY)
Roosevelt Univ. (IL)
Rutgers, the State Univ. of New
    Jersey–New Brunswick
Sojourner-Douglass Coll. (MD)
Southeastern Oklahoma State Univ.
Stevenson Univ. (MD)
SUNY Coll. of Agriculture and
    Technology–Cobleskill
SUNY Coll. of Environmental
    Science and Forestry
Univ. at Buffalo–SUNY
Univ. of California–Davis
Univ. of California–Los Angeles
Univ. of Georgia
Univ. of Illinois–Urbana-Champaign
Univ. of Kentucky
Univ. of Nebraska–Omaha
Univ. of Nevada–Las Vegas
Univ. of Nevada–Reno
Univ. of Northern Iowa
Univ. of Wisconsin–River Falls
Ursuline Coll. (OH)
Washington State Univ.
West Texas A&M Univ.
William Paterson Univ. of New
    Jersey
Winston-Salem State Univ. (NC)
Worcester Polytechnic Institute
    (MA)
Worcester State Coll. (MA)

Botany/Plant Biology

Arizona State Univ.
Bennington Coll. (VT)
Brigham Young Univ.–Provo (UT)
California State Polytechnic Univ.–
    Pomona
California State Univ.–Long Beach
Colorado State Univ.
Connecticut Coll.
Cornell Univ. (NY)
Frostburg State Univ. (MD)
Humboldt State Univ. (CA)
Idaho State Univ.

Iowa State Univ.
Juniata Coll. (PA)
Kent State Univ. (OH)
Lawrence Univ. (WI)
Marlboro Coll. (VT)
Mars Hill Coll. (NC)
Methodist Univ. (NC)
Miami Univ.–Oxford (OH)
Michigan State Univ.
New Mexico State Univ.
North Carolina State Univ.–Raleigh
North Dakota State Univ.
Northern Arizona Univ.
Northern Michigan Univ.
Northwestern Oklahoma State
    Univ.
Ohio State Univ.–Columbus
Ohio Univ.
Ohio Wesleyan Univ.
Oklahoma State Univ.
Oregon State Univ.
Rutgers, the State Univ. of New
    Jersey–Newark
Southern Illinois Univ.–Carbondale
St. Xavier Univ. (IL)
Texas A&M Univ.–Coll. Station
Texas State Univ.–San Marcos
Univ. of Akron (OH)
Univ. of California–Berkeley
Univ. of California–Davis
Univ. of California–Irvine
Univ. of California–Los Angeles
Univ. of California–Riverside
Univ. of Florida
Univ. of Georgia
Univ. of Hawaii–Manoa
Univ. of Illinois–Urbana-Champaign
Univ. of Kentucky
Univ. of Maine
Univ. of Michigan–Ann Arbor
Univ. of Minnesota–Twin Cities
Univ. of Nebraska–Lincoln
Univ. of Nevada–Las Vegas
Univ. of New Hampshire
Univ. of Oklahoma
Univ. of Rhode Island
Univ. of Texas–Austin
Univ. of Vermont
Univ. of Washington
Univ. of Wisconsin–Madison
Univ. of Wisconsin–Superior
Univ. of Wyoming
Utah State Univ.
Washington State Univ.
Weber State Univ. (UT)
Western New Mexico Univ.
Western Washington Univ.

Building/Construction Finishing, Management, and Inspection

California State Univ.–Sacramento
Central Connecticut State Univ.
Drexel Univ. (PA)
Northern Michigan Univ.
Roger Williams Univ. (RI)
Southern Utah Univ.
SUNY Coll. of Technology–Alfred
Univ. of Minnesota–Twin Cities
Univ. of the District of Columbia

Weber State Univ. (UT)

Business Administration, Management, and Operations

Abilene Christian Univ. (TX)
Adams State Coll. (CO)
Adelphi Univ. (NY)
Adrian Coll. (MI)
Alabama Agricultural and
    Mechanical Univ.
Alabama State Univ.
Alaska Pacific Univ.
Albany State Univ. (GA)
Albertus Magnus Coll. (CT)
Albion Coll. (MI)
Albright Coll. (PA)
Alcorn State Univ. (MS)
Alderson-Broaddus Coll. (WV)
Alfred Univ. (NY)
Alice Lloyd Coll. (KY)
Allen Univ. (SC)
Alma Coll. (MI)
Alvernia Univ. (PA)
Alverno Coll. (WI)
American Jewish Univ. (CA)
American Univ. (DC)
Anderson Univ. (IN)
Anderson Univ. (SC)
Andrews Univ. (MI)
Angelo State Univ. (TX)
Anna Maria Coll. (MA)
Appalachian State Univ. (NC)
Aquinas Coll. (MI)
Arcadia Univ. (PA)
Arizona State Univ.
Arkansas State Univ.–Jonesboro
Arkansas Tech Univ.
Assumption Coll. (MA)
Atlanta Christian Coll.
Atlantic Union Coll. (MA)
Auburn Univ. (AL)
Auburn Univ.–Montgomery (AL)
Augusta State Univ. (GA)
Aurora Univ. (IL)
Austin Peay State Univ. (TN)
Averett Univ. (VA)
Babson Coll. (MA)
Baker Coll. of Flint (MI)
Baker Univ. (KS)
Baldwin-Wallace Coll. (OH)
Ball State Univ. (IN)
Barry Univ. (FL)
Barton Coll. (NC)
Bay Path Coll. (MA)
Baylor Univ. (TX)
Becker Coll. (MA)
Belhaven Coll. (MS)
Bellevue Univ. (NE)
Belmont Abbey Coll. (NC)
Beloit Coll. (WI)
Bemidji State Univ. (MN)
Benedictine Coll. (KS)
Benedictine Univ. (IL)
Bennett Coll. (NC)
Bentley Univ. (MA)
Berry Coll. (GA)
Bethel Coll. (IN)
Bethel Univ. (MN)
Bethune-Cookman Univ. (FL)

Binghamton Univ.–SUNY
Black Hills State Univ. (SD)
Bloomfield Coll. (NJ)
Bloomsburg Univ. of Pennsylvania
Blue Mountain Coll. (MS)
Bluefield Coll. (VA)
Bluefield State Coll. (WV)
Bluffton Univ. (OH)
Boise State Univ. (ID)
Boston Univ.
Bowie State Univ. (MD)
Bowling Green State Univ. (OH)
Bradley Univ. (IL)
Brenau Univ. (GA)
Brescia Univ. (KY)
Brevard Coll. (NC)
Brewton-Parker Coll. (GA)
Briar Cliff Univ. (IA)
Bridgewater Coll. (VA)
Bridgewater State Coll. (MA)
Brigham Young Univ.–Hawaii
Bryant Univ. (RI)
Bucknell Univ. (PA)
Cabrini Coll. (PA)
Caldwell Coll. (NJ)
California Baptist Univ.
California Lutheran Univ.
California Maritime Academy
California Polytechnic State Univ.–
    San Luis Obispo
California State Polytechnic Univ.–
    Pomona
California State Univ.–Bakersfield
California State Univ.–Chico
California State Univ.–East Bay
California State Univ.–Fresno
California State Univ.–Fullerton
California State Univ.–Los Angeles
California State Univ.–Northridge
California State Univ.–Sacramento
California State Univ.–San
    Bernardino
California State Univ.–San Marcos
California State Univ.–Stanislaus
California Univ. of Pennsylvania
Calumet Coll. of St. Joseph (IN)
Calvin Coll. (MI)
Cameron Univ. (OK)
Campbell Univ. (NC)
Campbellsville Univ. (KY)
Canisius Coll. (NY)
Capital Univ. (OH)
Cardinal Stritch Univ. (WI)
Carnegie Mellon Univ. (PA)
Carroll Coll. (MT)
Carroll Univ. (WI)
Carson-Newman Coll. (TN)
Carthage Coll. (WI)
Case Western Reserve Univ. (OH)
Castleton State Coll. (VT)
Catawba Coll. (NC)
Catholic Univ. of America (DC)
Cazenovia Coll. (NY)
Cedar Crest Coll. (PA)
Cedarville Univ. (OH)
Centenary Coll. (NJ)
Centenary Coll. of Louisiana
Central Baptist Coll. (AR)
Central Christian Coll. (KS)
Central Coll. (IA)
Central Connecticut State Univ.

Central Methodist Univ. (MO)
Central Michigan Univ.
Central Washington Univ.
Chadron State Coll. (NE)
Chaminade Univ. of Honolulu
Champlain Coll. (VT)
Chapman Univ. (CA)
Charleston Southern Univ. (SC)
Chatham Univ. (PA)
Chestnut Hill Coll. (PA)
Cheyney Univ. of Pennsylvania
Chicago State Univ.
Chowan Univ. (NC)
Christian Brothers Univ. (TN)
Christopher Newport Univ. (VA)
City Univ. (WA)
Claflin Univ. (SC)
Clarion Univ. of Pennsylvania
Clark Atlanta Univ.
Clark Univ. (MA)
Clarkson Univ. (NY)
Clayton State Univ. (GA)
Clearwater Christian Coll. (FL)
Cleary Univ. (MI)
Coastal Carolina Univ. (SC)
Coe Coll. (IA)
Coker Coll. (SC)
Colby-Sawyer Coll. (NH)
Coll. at Brockport–SUNY
Coll. of Charleston (SC)
Coll. of Idaho (ID)
Coll. of Mount St. Joseph (OH)
Coll. of Mount St. Vincent (NY)
Coll. of New Jersey
Coll. of Notre Dame of Maryland
Coll. of Santa Fe (NM)
Coll. of St. Benedict (MN)
Coll. of St. Elizabeth (NJ)
Coll. of St. Joseph (VT)
Coll. of St. Mary (NE)
Coll. of St. Rose (NY)
Coll. of St. Scholastica (MN)
Coll. of the Ozarks (MO)
Coll. of William and Mary (VA)
Colorado Christian Univ.
Colorado State Univ.
Columbia Coll. (SC)
Columbia Coll. (MO)
Concord Univ. (WV)
Concordia Coll. (AL)
Concordia Coll. (NY)
Concordia Coll.–Moorhead (MN)
Concordia Univ. (MI)
Concordia Univ. (OR)
Concordia Univ. (NE)
Concordia Univ. Chicago (IL)
Concordia Univ. Texas
Concordia Univ. Wisconsin
Concordia Univ.–St. Paul (MN)
Corban Univ. (OR)
Cornerstone Univ. (MI)
Creighton Univ. (NE)
Crown Coll. (MN)
Culver-Stockton Coll. (MO)
CUNY–Baruch Coll.
CUNY–Brooklyn Coll.
CUNY–City Coll.
CUNY–Lehman Coll.
CUNY–Medgar Evers Coll.
CUNY–New York City Coll. of
    Technology

CUNY–York Coll.
Curry Coll. (MA)
Daemen Coll. (NY)
Dakota State Univ. (SD)
Dallas Baptist Univ.
Dana Coll. (NE)
Daniel Webster Coll. (NH)
Davenport Univ. (MI)
Davis and Elkins Coll. (WV)
Defiance Coll. (OH)
Delaware State Univ.
Delaware Valley Coll. (PA)
Delta State Univ. (MS)
DePaul Univ. (IL)
Dickinson State Univ. (ND)
Dillard Univ. (LA)
Dixie State Coll. of Utah
Dominican Coll. (NY)
Dominican Univ. (IL)
Dominican Univ. of California
Dordt Coll. (IA)
Dowling Coll. (NY)
Drury Univ. (MO)
Duquesne Univ. (PA)
East Carolina Univ. (NC)
East Central Univ. (OK)
East Stroudsburg Univ. of
    Pennsylvania
East Tennessee State Univ.
Eastern Illinois Univ.
Eastern Kentucky Univ.
Eastern Mennonite Univ. (VA)
Eastern Michigan Univ.
Eastern Nazarene Coll. (MA)
Eastern New Mexico Univ.
Eastern Univ. (PA)
Eastern Washington Univ.
Eckerd Coll. (FL)
Edinboro Univ. of Pennsylvania
Edward Waters Coll. (FL)
Elizabeth City State Univ. (NC)
Elizabethtown Coll. (PA)
Elmhurst Coll. (IL)
Elmira Coll. (NY)
Elon Univ. (NC)
Embry-Riddle Aeronautical Univ.
    (FL)
Emmanuel Coll. (GA)
Emmanuel Coll. (MA)
Emory and Henry Coll. (VA)
Emory Univ. (GA)
Emporia State Univ. (KS)
Endicott Coll. (MA)
Erskine Coll. (SC)
Eureka Coll. (IL)
Evangel Univ. (MO)
Evergreen State Coll. (WA)
Excelsior Coll. (NY)
Fairfield Univ. (CT)
Fairleigh Dickinson Univ. (NJ)
Fairmont State Univ. (WV)
Farmingdale State Coll.–SUNY
Faulkner Univ. (AL)
Fayetteville State Univ. (NC)
Felician Coll. (NJ)
Ferris State Univ. (MI)
Ferrum Coll. (VA)
Fitchburg State Coll. (MA)
Flagler Coll. (FL)
Florida Atlantic Univ.
Florida Gulf Coast Univ.

Florida Institute of Technology
Florida International Univ.
Florida Southern Coll.
Florida State Univ.
Fontbonne Univ. (MO)
Fordham Univ. (NY)
Fort Hays State Univ. (KS)
Fort Lewis Coll. (CO)
Fort Valley State Univ. (GA)
Francis Marion Univ. (SC)
Franciscan Univ. of Steubenville
    (OH)
Franklin and Marshall Coll. (PA)
Franklin Pierce Univ. (NH)
Free Will Baptist Bible Coll. (TN)
Freed-Hardeman Univ. (TN)
Fresno Pacific Univ. (CA)
Friends Univ. (KS)
Frostburg State Univ. (MD)
Furman Univ. (SC)
Gallaudet Univ. (DC)
Gannon Univ. (PA)
Gardner-Webb Univ. (NC)
Geneva Coll. (PA)
George Fox Univ. (OR)
George Mason Univ. (VA)
George Washington Univ. (DC)
Georgetown Univ. (DC)
Georgia Coll. & State Univ.
Georgia Institute of Technology
Georgia Southern Univ.
Georgia Southwestern State Univ.
Georgia State Univ.
Georgian Court Univ. (NJ)
Gettysburg Coll. (PA)
Glenville State Coll. (WV)
Golden Gate Univ. (CA)
Goldey Beacom Coll. (DE)
Gonzaga Univ. (WA)
Gordon Coll. (MA)
Goucher Coll. (MD)
Grace Coll. and Seminary (IN)
Graceland Univ. (IA)
Grambling State Univ. (LA)
Grand Valley State Univ. (MI)
Granite State Coll. (NH)
Green Mountain Coll. (VT)
Greensboro Coll. (NC)
Greenville Coll. (IL)
Grove City Coll. (PA)
Guilford Coll. (NC)
Gustavus Adolphus Coll. (MN)
Gwynedd-Mercy Coll. (PA)
Hamline Univ. (MN)
Hampton Univ. (VA)
Hardin-Simmons Univ. (TX)
Harding Univ. (AR)
Harris-Stowe State Univ. (MO)
Hartwick Coll. (NY)
Hawaii Pacific Univ.
Heidelberg Univ. (OH)
Heritage Univ. (WA)
Hodges Univ. (FL)
Hofstra Univ. (NY)
Holy Family Univ. (PA)
Holy Names Univ. (CA)
Hood Coll. (MD)
Hope Coll. (MI)
Hope International Univ. (CA)
Houghton Coll. (NY)
Houston Baptist Univ.

Howard Univ. (DC)
Humboldt State Univ. (CA)
Humphreys Coll. (CA)
Huntingdon Coll. (AL)
Huntington Univ. (IN)
Husson Univ. (ME)
Idaho State Univ.
Illinois Institute of Technology
Illinois State Univ.
Immaculata Univ. (PA)
Indiana Institute of Technology
Indiana State Univ.
Indiana Univ. of Pennsylvania
Indiana Univ. Southeast
Indiana Univ.–Kokomo
Indiana Univ.–South Bend
Indiana Univ.-Purdue Univ.–Fort
    Wayne
Indiana Univ.-Purdue Univ.–
    Indianapolis
Indiana Wesleyan Univ.
Iona Coll. (NY)
Iowa State Univ.
Iowa Wesleyan Coll.
Ithaca Coll. (NY)
Jackson State Univ. (MS)
Jacksonville State Univ. (AL)
Jacksonville Univ. (FL)
James Madison Univ. (VA)
Jamestown Coll. (ND)
Jarvis Christian Coll. (TX)
John Brown Univ. (AR)
John Carroll Univ. (OH)
Johnson C. Smith Univ. (NC)
Judson Coll. (AL)
Judson Univ. (IL)
Juniata Coll. (PA)
Kansas State Univ.
Kansas Wesleyan Univ.
Kean Univ. (NJ)
Keene State Coll. (NH)
Kendall Coll. (IL)
Kennesaw State Univ. (GA)
Kent State Univ. (OH)
Kettering Univ. (MI)
Keuka Coll. (NY)
King Coll. (TN)
King's Coll. (PA)
Kutztown Univ. of Pennsylvania
La Roche Coll. (PA)
La Salle Univ. (PA)
La Sierra Univ. (CA)
LaGrange Coll. (GA)
Lake Superior State Univ. (MI)
Lakeland Coll. (WI)
Lambuth Univ. (TN)
Lander Univ. (SC)
Lane Coll. (TN)
Lasell Coll. (MA)
Lawrence Technological Univ. (MI)
Le Moyne Coll. (NY)
Lebanon Valley Coll. (PA)
Lees-McRae Coll. (NC)
Lehigh Univ. (PA)
LeMoyne-Owen Coll. (TN)
LeTourneau Univ. (TX)
Lewis Univ. (IL)
Lewis-Clark State Coll. (ID)
Liberty Univ. (VA)
Limestone Coll. (SC)
Lincoln Univ. (MO)

Lincoln Univ. (PA)
Lindenwood Univ. (MO)
Lindsey Wilson Coll. (KY)
Linfield Coll. (OR)
Lipscomb Univ. (TN)
Livingstone Coll. (NC)
Lock Haven Univ. of Pennsylvania
Long Island Univ.–C.W. Post
    Campus (NY)
Longwood Univ. (VA)
Loras Coll. (IA)
Louisiana Coll.
Louisiana State Univ.–Baton Rouge
Louisiana State Univ.–Shreveport
Louisiana Tech Univ.
Lourdes Coll. (OH)
Loyola Marymount Univ. (CA)
Loyola Univ. Chicago
Loyola Univ. New Orleans
Lubbock Christian Univ. (TX)
Luther Coll. (IA)
Lycoming Coll. (PA)
Lynchburg Coll. (VA)
Lyndon State Coll. (VT)
Lynn Univ. (FL)
Lyon Coll. (AR)
MacMurray Coll. (IL)
Macon State Coll. (GA)
Maharishi Univ. of Management
    (IA)
Malone Univ. (OH)
Manchester Coll. (IN)
Manhattan Coll. (NY)
Manhattanville Coll. (NY)
Mansfield Univ. of Pennsylvania
Marian Univ. (WI)
Marietta Coll. (OH)
Marist Coll. (NY)
Marquette Univ. (WI)
Mars Hill Coll. (NC)
Marshall Univ. (WV)
Martin Methodist Coll. (TN)
Martin Univ. (IN)
Mary Baldwin Coll. (VA)
Marygrove Coll. (MI)
Marylhurst Univ. (OR)
Marymount Manhattan Coll. (NY)
Marymount Univ. (VA)
Maryville Coll. (TN)
Maryville Univ. of St. Louis (MO)
Marywood Univ. (PA)
Massachusetts Coll. of Liberal Arts
Massachusetts Maritime Academy
Master's Coll. and Seminary (CA)
Mayville State Univ. (ND)
McDaniel Coll. (MD)
McKendree Univ. (IL)
McMurry Univ. (TX)
McNeese State Univ. (LA)
McPherson Coll. (KS)
Mercy Coll. (NY)
Mercyhurst Coll. (PA)
Meredith Coll. (NC)
Merrimack Coll. (MA)
Mesa State Coll. (CO)
Messiah Coll. (PA)
Methodist Univ. (NC)
Metropolitan State Coll. of Denver
Miami Univ.–Oxford (OH)
Michigan State Univ.
Michigan Technological Univ.

MidAmerica Nazarene Univ. (KS)
Middle Tennessee State Univ.
Midland Lutheran Coll. (NE)
Midwestern State Univ. (TX)
Miles Coll. (AL)
Millersville Univ. of Pennsylvania
Milligan Coll. (TN)
Millikin Univ. (IL)
Millsaps Coll. (MS)
Milwaukee School of Engineering
Minnesota State Univ.–Mankato
Minnesota State Univ.–Moorhead
Minot State Univ. (ND)
Misericordia Univ. (PA)
Mississippi Coll.
Mississippi State Univ.
Mississippi Univ. for Women
Mississippi Valley State Univ.
Missouri Baptist Univ.
Missouri Southern State Univ.
Missouri State Univ.
Missouri Univ. of Science &
    Technology
Missouri Valley Coll.
Missouri Western State Univ.
Mitchell Coll. (CT)
Molloy Coll. (NY)
Monmouth Coll. (IL)
Monmouth Univ. (NJ)
Montana State Univ.–Northern
Montclair State Univ. (NJ)
Montreat Coll. (NC)
Moravian Coll. (PA)
Morehead State Univ. (KY)
Morehouse Coll. (GA)
Morgan State Univ. (MD)
Morningside Coll. (IA)
Morris Coll. (SC)
Mount Aloysius Coll. (PA)
Mount Ida Coll. (MA)
Mount Marty Coll. (SD)
Mount Mary Coll. (WI)
Mount Mercy Coll. (IA)
Mount Olive Coll. (NC)
Mount St. Mary Coll. (NY)
Mount St. Mary's Coll. (CA)
Mount Vernon Nazarene Univ.
    (OH)
Mountain State Univ. (WV)
Muhlenberg Coll. (PA)
Murray State Univ. (KY)
National Univ. (CA)
National-Louis Univ. (IL)
Nazareth Coll. (NY)
Neumann Univ. (PA)
New England Coll. (NH)
New Jersey City Univ.
New Jersey Institute of Technology
New Mexico Highlands Univ.
New Mexico Institute of Mining
    and Technology
New Mexico State Univ.
New School (NY)
New York Institute of Technology
Newberry Coll. (SC)
Nicholls State Univ. (LA)
Nichols Coll. (MA)
North Carolina A&T State Univ.
North Carolina Central Univ.
North Carolina State Univ.–Raleigh
North Central Coll. (IL)

North Central Univ. (MN)
North Dakota State Univ.
North Georgia Coll. and State Univ.
North Greenville Univ. (SC)
North Park Univ. (IL)
Northeastern Illinois Univ.
Northeastern State Univ. (OK)
Northeastern Univ. (MA)
Northern Arizona Univ.
Northern Illinois Univ.
Northern Kentucky Univ.
Northern Michigan Univ.
Northern State Univ. (SD)
Northwest Christian Univ. (OR)
Northwest Missouri State Univ.
Northwest Nazarene Univ. (ID)
Northwestern Coll. (MN)
Northwestern Coll. (IA)
Northwestern Oklahoma State
    Univ.
Northwestern State Univ. of
    Louisiana
Northwood Univ. (MI)
Norwich Univ. (VT)
Notre Dame Coll. of Ohio
Notre Dame de Namur Univ. (CA)
Nova Southeastern Univ. (FL)
Nyack Coll. (NY)
Oakland City Univ. (IN)
Oakwood Univ. (AL)
Oglethorpe Univ. (GA)
Ohio Dominican Univ.
Ohio State Univ.–Columbus
Ohio Univ.
Ohio Valley Univ. (WV)
Oklahoma Christian Univ.
Oklahoma City Univ.
Oklahoma Panhandle State Univ.
Oklahoma State Univ.
Oklahoma Wesleyan Univ.
Old Dominion Univ. (VA)
Olivet Coll. (MI)
Oral Roberts Univ. (OK)
Oregon Institute of Technology
Oregon State Univ.
Otterbein Coll. (OH)
Ouachita Baptist Univ. (AR)
Our Lady of Holy Cross Coll. (LA)
Our Lady of the Lake Univ. (TX)
Pace Univ. (NY)
Pacific Lutheran Univ. (WA)
Pacific Univ. (OR)
Paine Coll. (GA)
Palm Beach Atlantic Univ. (FL)
Park Univ. (MO)
Patten Univ. (CA)
Peace Coll. (NC)
Peirce Coll. (PA)
Pennsylvania Coll. of Technology
Pepperdine Univ. (CA)
Peru State Coll. (NE)
Pfeiffer Univ. (NC)
Philadelphia Univ.
Philander Smith Coll. (AR)
Piedmont Coll. (GA)
Pikeville Coll. (KY)
Pine Manor Coll. (MA)
Pitzer Coll. (CA)
Plymouth State Univ. (NH)
Point Loma Nazarene Univ. (CA)
Point Park Univ. (PA)

Post Univ. (CT)
Prairie View A&M Univ. (TX)
Presbyterian Coll. (SC)
Prescott Coll. (AZ)
Principia Coll. (IL)
Providence Coll. (RI)
Purdue Univ.–Calumet (IN)
Purdue Univ.–North Central (IN)
Queens Univ. of Charlotte (NC)
Quincy Univ. (IL)
Quinnipiac Univ. (CT)
Radford Univ. (VA)
Ramapo Coll. of New Jersey
Regis Univ. (CO)
Rensselaer Polytechnic Institute
    (NY)
Rhode Island Coll.
Rhodes Coll. (TN)
Rice Univ. (TX)
Richard Stockton Coll. of New
    Jersey
Rider Univ. (NJ)
Ripon Coll. (WI)
Rivier Coll. (NH)
Roanoke Coll. (VA)
Robert Morris Univ. (PA)
Robert Morris Univ. (IL)
Roberts Wesleyan Coll. (NY)
Rochester Coll. (MI)
Rochester Institute of Technology
    (NY)
Rockford Coll. (IL)
Rockhurst Univ. (MO)
Rocky Mountain Coll. (MT)
Rogers State Univ. (OK)
Russell Sage Coll. (NY)
Rust Coll. (MS)
Rutgers, the State Univ. of New
    Jersey–Camden
Rutgers, the State Univ. of New
    Jersey–New Brunswick
Rutgers, the State Univ. of New
    Jersey–Newark
Sacred Heart Univ. (CT)
Sage Colleges–Albany (NY)
Saginaw Valley State Univ. (MI)
Salem Coll. (NC)
Salem State Coll. (MA)
Salisbury Univ. (MD)
Salve Regina Univ. (RI)
Sam Houston State Univ. (TX)
Samford Univ. (AL)
San Diego State Univ.
San Francisco State Univ.
San Jose State Univ. (CA)
Savannah State Univ. (GA)
Schreiner Univ. (TX)
Seattle Univ.
Seton Hall Univ. (NJ)
Seton Hill Univ. (PA)
Shaw Univ. (NC)
Shawnee State Univ. (OH)
Shenandoah Univ. (VA)
Shepherd Univ. (WV)
Shippensburg Univ. of Pennsylvania
Shorter Coll. (GA)
Sierra Nevada Coll. (NV)
Silver Lake Coll. (WI)
Simpson Univ. (CA)
Slippery Rock Univ. of Pennsylvania
Sojourner-Douglass Coll. (MD)

Sonoma State Univ. (CA)
South Carolina State Univ.
Southeast Missouri State Univ.
Southeastern Louisiana Univ.
Southeastern Oklahoma State Univ.
Southeastern Univ. (FL)
Southern Adventist Univ. (TN)
Southern Illinois Univ.–Carbondale
Southern Illinois Univ.–Edwardsville
Southern Methodist Univ. (TX)
Southern Nazarene Univ. (OK)
Southern New Hampshire Univ.
Southern Oregon Univ.
Southern Polytechnic State Univ.
    (GA)
Southern Univ. and A&M Coll. (LA)
Southern Univ.–New Orleans
Southern Utah Univ.
Southern Vermont Coll.
Southern Wesleyan Univ. (SC)
Southwest Baptist Univ. (MO)
Southwest Minnesota State Univ.
Southwestern Adventist Univ. (TX)
Southwestern Assemblies of God
    Univ. (TX)
Southwestern Coll. (KS)
Southwestern Oklahoma State
    Univ.
Spring Arbor Univ. (MI)
Spring Hill Coll. (AL)
Springfield Coll. (MA)
St. Ambrose Univ. (IA)
St. Andrews Presbyterian Coll. (NC)
St. Bonaventure Univ. (NY)
St. Catherine Univ. (MN)
St. Cloud State Univ. (MN)
St. Edward's Univ. (TX)
St. Francis Univ. (PA)
St. Gregory's Univ. (OK)
St. John Fisher Coll. (NY)
St. John's Univ. (MN)
St. John's Univ. (NY)
St. Joseph's Coll. (ME)
St. Joseph's Coll. New York
St. Joseph's Univ. (PA)
St. Leo Univ. (FL)
St. Louis Univ.
St. Martin's Univ. (WA)
St. Mary's Coll. (IN)
St. Mary's Univ. of Minnesota
St. Mary's Univ. of San Antonio
    (TX)
St. Mary-of-the-Woods Coll. (IN)
St. Michael's Coll. (VT)
St. Paul's Coll. (VA)
St. Peter's Coll. (NJ)
St. Thomas Aquinas Coll. (NY)
St. Thomas Univ. (FL)
St. Vincent Coll. (PA)
St. Xavier Univ. (IL)
Stephen F. Austin State Univ. (TX)
Stephens Coll. (MO)
Sterling Coll. (KS)
Stetson Univ. (FL)
Stevens Institute of Technology
    (NJ)
Stevenson Univ. (MD)
Stillman Coll. (AL)
Stonehill Coll. (MA)
Suffolk Univ. (MA)
Sul Ross State Univ. (TX)

SUNY Coll.–Old Westbury
SUNY Coll.–Potsdam
SUNY Empire State Coll.
SUNY Institute of Technology–
    Utica/Rome
SUNY–Fredonia
SUNY–Geneseo
SUNY–Oswego
SUNY–Stony Brook
Susquehanna Univ. (PA)
Syracuse Univ. (NY)
Tabor Coll. (KS)
Talladega Coll. (AL)
Tarleton State Univ. (TX)
Taylor Univ. (IN)
Temple Univ. (PA)
Tennessee State Univ.
Tennessee Technological Univ.
Tennessee Wesleyan Coll.
Texas A&M International Univ.
Texas A&M Univ.–Coll. Station
Texas A&M Univ.–Commerce
Texas A&M Univ.–Corpus Christi
Texas Christian Univ.
Texas Coll.
Texas Lutheran Univ.
Texas State Univ.–San Marcos
Texas Tech Univ.
Texas Wesleyan Univ.
Texas Woman's Univ.
The Citadel (SC)
Thiel Coll. (PA)
Thomas Edison State Coll. (NJ)
Thomas More Coll. (KY)
Thomas Univ. (GA)
Tiffin Univ. (OH)
Toccoa Falls Coll. (GA)
Tougaloo Coll. (MS)
Touro Coll. (NY)
Towson Univ. (MD)
Trevecca Nazarene Univ. (TN)
Trine Univ. (IN)
Trinity International Univ. (IL)
Trinity Univ. (DC)
Troy Univ. (AL)
Truman State Univ. (MO)
Tulane Univ. (LA)
Tusculum Coll. (TN)
Tuskegee Univ. (AL)
Union Coll. (KY)
Union Coll. (NE)
Union Univ. (TN)
United States Coast Guard
    Academy (CT)
Univ. at Albany–SUNY
Univ. at Buffalo–SUNY
Univ. of Akron (OH)
Univ. of Alabama
Univ. of Alabama–Birmingham
Univ. of Alabama–Huntsville
Univ. of Alaska–Anchorage
Univ. of Alaska–Fairbanks
Univ. of Alaska–Southeast
Univ. of Arizona
Univ. of Arkansas
Univ. of Arkansas–Little Rock
Univ. of Arkansas–Pine Bluff
Univ. of California–Berkeley
Univ. of California–Riverside
Univ. of Central Arkansas
Univ. of Central Florida

Univ. of Central Missouri
Univ. of Central Oklahoma
Univ. of Charleston (WV)
Univ. of Colorado–Boulder
Univ. of Colorado–Colorado
    Springs
Univ. of Colorado–Denver
Univ. of Connecticut
Univ. of Dallas
Univ. of Dayton (OH)
Univ. of Delaware
Univ. of Denver
Univ. of Dubuque (IA)
Univ. of Evansville (IN)
Univ. of Findlay (OH)
Univ. of Florida
Univ. of Georgia
Univ. of Great Falls (MT)
Univ. of Hartford (CT)
Univ. of Hawaii–Hilo
Univ. of Hawaii–Manoa
Univ. of Hawaii–West Oahu
Univ. of Houston
Univ. of Houston–Downtown
Univ. of Illinois–Springfield
Univ. of Illinois–Urbana-Champaign
Univ. of Indianapolis
Univ. of Iowa
Univ. of Kansas
Univ. of La Verne (CA)
Univ. of Louisiana–Lafayette
Univ. of Louisiana–Monroe
Univ. of Louisville (KY)
Univ. of Maine
Univ. of Maine–Augusta
Univ. of Maine–Fort Kent
Univ. of Mary (ND)
Univ. of Mary Hardin-Baylor (TX)
Univ. of Mary Washington (VA)
Univ. of Maryland–Coll. Park
Univ. of Maryland–Eastern Shore
Univ. of Maryland–Univ. Coll.
Univ. of Massachusetts–Amherst
Univ. of Massachusetts–Boston
Univ. of Massachusetts–Dartmouth
Univ. of Massachusetts–Lowell
Univ. of Memphis
Univ. of Miami (FL)
Univ. of Michigan–Ann Arbor
Univ. of Michigan–Dearborn
Univ. of Michigan–Flint
Univ. of Minnesota–Crookston
Univ. of Minnesota–Duluth
Univ. of Minnesota–Morris
Univ. of Minnesota–Twin Cities
Univ. of Mississippi
Univ. of Missouri–St. Louis
Univ. of Montana
Univ. of Montevallo (AL)
Univ. of Mount Union (OH)
Univ. of Nebraska–Kearney
Univ. of Nebraska–Lincoln
Univ. of Nebraska–Omaha
Univ. of Nevada–Las Vegas
Univ. of Nevada–Reno
Univ. of New England (ME)
Univ. of New Hampshire
Univ. of New Haven (CT)
Univ. of New Mexico
Univ. of New Orleans
Univ. of North Alabama

Univ. of North Carolina–Asheville
Univ. of North Carolina–Chapel Hill
Univ. of North Carolina–Charlotte
Univ. of North Carolina–
    Greensboro
Univ. of North Carolina–Pembroke
Univ. of North Carolina–
    Wilmington
Univ. of North Florida
Univ. of North Texas
Univ. of Northern Colorado
Univ. of Northern Iowa
Univ. of Northwestern Ohio
Univ. of Notre Dame (IN)
Univ. of Oklahoma
Univ. of Pennsylvania
Univ. of Pittsburgh
Univ. of Pittsburgh–Bradford
Univ. of Puget Sound (WA)
Univ. of Redlands (CA)
Univ. of Rhode Island
Univ. of Richmond (VA)
Univ. of Rio Grande (OH)
Univ. of San Diego
Univ. of San Francisco
Univ. of Science and Arts of
    Oklahoma
Univ. of Scranton (PA)
Univ. of Sioux Falls (SD)
Univ. of South Alabama
Univ. of South Carolina
Univ. of South Carolina–Aiken
Univ. of South Carolina–Upstate
Univ. of South Dakota
Univ. of South Florida
Univ. of Southern California
Univ. of Southern Indiana
Univ. of Southern Maine
Univ. of Southern Mississippi
Univ. of St. Francis (IN)
Univ. of St. Francis (IL)
Univ. of St. Mary (KS)
Univ. of St. Thomas (MN)
Univ. of St. Thomas (TX)
Univ. of Tampa (FL)
Univ. of Tennessee
Univ. of Tennessee–Martin
Univ. of Texas of the Permian Basin
Univ. of Texas–Arlington
Univ. of Texas–Austin
Univ. of Texas–Brownsville
Univ. of Texas–Dallas
Univ. of Texas–El Paso
Univ. of Texas–Pan American
Univ. of Texas–San Antonio
Univ. of Texas–Tyler
Univ. of the District of Columbia
Univ. of the Incarnate Word (TX)
Univ. of the Ozarks (AR)
Univ. of the Pacific (CA)
Univ. of Toledo (OH)
Univ. of Tulsa (OK)
Univ. of Utah
Univ. of Vermont
Univ. of Virginia–Wise
Univ. of Washington
Univ. of West Alabama
Univ. of West Florida
Univ. of West Georgia
Univ. of Wisconsin–Eau Claire
Univ. of Wisconsin–Green Bay

Univ. of Wisconsin–La Crosse
Univ. of Wisconsin–Madison
Univ. of Wisconsin–Milwaukee
Univ. of Wisconsin–Platteville
Univ. of Wisconsin–River Falls
Univ. of Wisconsin–Stevens Point
Univ. of Wisconsin–Stout
Univ. of Wisconsin–Superior
Univ. of Wisconsin–Whitewater
Univ. of Wyoming
Upper Iowa Univ.
Urbana Univ. (OH)
Ursuline Coll. (OH)
Utah State Univ.
Utah Valley Univ.
Utica Coll. (NY)
Valley City State Univ. (ND)
Vanguard Univ. of Southern
    California
Victory Univ. (TN)
Villanova Univ. (PA)
Virginia Commonwealth Univ.
Virginia Intermont Coll.
Virginia State Univ.
Virginia Tech
Viterbo Univ. (WI)
Voorhees Coll. (SC)
Wagner Coll. (NY)
Waldorf Coll. (IA)
Walsh Coll. of Accountancy and
    Business Administration (MI)
Walsh Univ. (OH)
Warner Pacific Coll. (OR)
Warner Univ. (FL)
Washburn Univ. (KS)
Washington and Lee Univ. (VA)
Washington Coll. (MD)
Washington State Univ.
Washington Univ. in St. Louis
Wayland Baptist Univ. (TX)
Wayne State Coll. (NE)
Wayne State Univ. (MI)
Waynesburg Univ. (PA)
Webber International Univ. (FL)
Weber State Univ. (UT)
Webster Univ. (MO)
Wells Coll. (NY)
Wesleyan Coll. (GA)
West Chester Univ. of Pennsylvania
West Liberty Univ. (WV)
West Texas A&M Univ.
West Virginia State Univ.
West Virginia Univ.
West Virginia Univ. Institute of
    Technology
West Virginia Univ.–Parkersburg
West Virginia Wesleyan Coll.
Western Carolina Univ. (NC)
Western Connecticut State Univ.
Western Governors Univ. (UT)
Western Illinois Univ.
Western Kentucky Univ.
Western Michigan Univ.
Western New England Coll. (MA)
Western New Mexico Univ.
Western State Coll. of Colorado
Western Washington Univ.
Westminster Coll. (UT)
Westminster Coll. (PA)
Wheeling Jesuit Univ. (WV)
Whittier Coll. (CA)

Whitworth Univ. (WA)
Wichita State Univ. (KS)
Widener Univ. (PA)
Wilberforce Univ. (OH)
Wiley Coll. (TX)
Wilkes Univ. (PA)
William Carey Univ. (MS)
William Jewell Coll. (MO)
William Paterson Univ. of New
    Jersey
William Woods Univ. (MO)
Williams Baptist Coll. (AR)
Wilmington Coll. (OH)
Wilmington Univ. (DE)
Wilson Coll. (PA)
Wingate Univ. (NC)
Winston-Salem State Univ. (NC)
Winthrop Univ. (SC)
Woodbury Univ. (CA)
Worcester Polytechnic Institute
    (MA)
Worcester State Coll. (MA)
Wright State Univ. (OH)
Xavier Univ. (OH)
Yeshiva Univ. (NY)
York Coll. (NE)
York Coll. of Pennsylvania
Youngstown State Univ. (OH)

Business Operations Support and Assistant Services

Alcorn State Univ. (MS)
Auburn Univ.–Montgomery (AL)
Baptist Bible Coll. and Seminary
    (PA)
Bellevue Univ. (NE)
Cedarville Univ. (OH)
Central Washington Univ.
Clearwater Christian Coll. (FL)
Concordia Coll.–Moorhead (MN)
CUNY–Lehman Coll.
Davenport Univ. (MI)
Delaware State Univ.
East Carolina Univ. (NC)
East Central Univ. (OK)
Eastern Oregon Univ.
Howard Payne Univ. (TX)
Humphreys Coll. (CA)
Idaho State Univ.
Lewis-Clark State Coll. (ID)
Lincoln Univ. (MO)
Mayville State Univ. (ND)
Midland Lutheran Coll. (NE)
Minot State Univ. (ND)
New York Institute of Technology
Northern Michigan Univ.
Northern State Univ. (SD)
Northwest Missouri State Univ.
Northwestern Oklahoma State
    Univ.
Roosevelt Univ. (IL)
Southeast Missouri State Univ.
Suffolk Univ. (MA)
Univ. of Central Oklahoma
Univ. of Rio Grande (OH)
Utah State Univ.
Valdosta State Univ. (GA)
Weber State Univ. (UT)

Business, Management, Marketing, and Related Support Services

Adelphi Univ. (NY)
Arcadia Univ. (PA)
Atlantic Union Coll. (MA)
Baylor Univ. (TX)
Bellevue Univ. (NE)
Belmont Abbey Coll. (NC)
Bentley Univ. (MA)
Boise State Univ. (ID)
Bowling Green State Univ. (OH)
Bridgewater State Coll. (MA)
Cabrini Coll. (PA)
California State Univ.–Dominguez
    Hills
California State Univ.–Long Beach
California State Univ.–Stanislaus
Campbellsville Univ. (KY)
Claflin Univ. (SC)
Cleary Univ. (MI)
Clemson Univ. (SC)
Columbus State Univ. (GA)
Dalton State Coll. (GA)
DePaul Univ. (IL)
DeSales Univ. (PA)
Dominican Univ. (IL)
Dominican Univ. of California
Dowling Coll. (NY)
Drake Univ. (IA)
Drexel Univ. (PA)
Duquesne Univ. (PA)
Eastern Nazarene Coll. (MA)
Eastern Univ. (PA)
Johnson and Wales Univ. (RI)
Johnson State Coll. (VT)
La Sierra Univ. (CA)
Long Island Univ.–C.W. Post
    Campus (NY)
Lourdes Coll. (OH)
Loyola Univ. Chicago
Marquette Univ. (WI)
Mercy Coll. (NY)
Messiah Coll. (PA)
Metropolitan State Coll. of Denver
Midland Lutheran Coll. (NE)
Misericordia Univ. (PA)
Missouri State Univ.
Missouri Univ. of Science &
    Technology
Morgan State Univ. (MD)
Nebraska Wesleyan Univ.
New York Institute of Technology
New York Univ.
North Carolina A&T State Univ.
Norwich Univ. (VT)
Nyack Coll. (NY)
Ohio Valley Univ. (WV)
Old Dominion Univ. (VA)
Oral Roberts Univ. (OK)
Park Univ. (MO)
Point Park Univ. (PA)
Polytechnic Institute of New York
    Univ. (NY)
Purdue Univ.–North Central (IN)
Rensselaer Polytechnic Institute
    (NY)
Rochester Coll. (MI)
Rochester Institute of Technology
    (NY)

Seton Hill Univ. (PA)
Skidmore Coll. (NY)
Southern Illinois Univ.–Carbondale
Southern New Hampshire Univ.
St. Vincent Coll. (PA)
SUNY Coll. of Agriculture and
    Technology–Cobleskill
SUNY Coll. of Technology–Delhi
SUNY–Fredonia
SUNY–Oswego
Syracuse Univ. (NY)
Texas Wesleyan Univ.
Touro Coll. (NY)
Trevecca Nazarene Univ. (TN)
Trinity International Univ. (IL)
Troy Univ. (AL)
Univ. of Central Missouri
Univ. of Denver
Univ. of Louisiana–Lafayette
Univ. of Nebraska–Lincoln
Univ. of Toledo (OH)
Univ. of Wisconsin–Stout
Ursuline Coll. (OH)
Western Michigan Univ.
Wheeling Jesuit Univ. (WV)
Wiley Coll. (TX)
Woodbury Univ. (CA)
Worcester Polytechnic Institute
    (MA)

Business/Commerce

Alabama Agricultural and
    Mechanical Univ.
Albright Coll. (PA)
American Jewish Univ. (CA)
American Univ. (DC)
Asbury Univ. (KY)
Auburn Univ.–Montgomery (AL)
Augustana Coll. (IL)
Augustana Coll. (SD)
Austin Coll. (TX)
Austin Peay State Univ. (TN)
Averett Univ. (VA)
Avila Univ. (MO)
Babson Coll. (MA)
Baker Univ. (KS)
Ball State Univ. (IN)
Baylor Univ. (TX)
Belhaven Univ. (MS)
Bellarmine Univ. (KY)
Bellevue Univ. (NE)
Belmont Univ. (TN)
Bentley Univ. (MA)
Berea Coll. (KY)
Bethel Coll. (KS)
Bethel Coll. (TN)
Biola Univ. (CA)
Black Hills State Univ. (SD)
Bloomsburg Univ. of Pennsylvania
Boise State Univ. (ID)
Bowling Green State Univ. (OH)
Brenau Univ. (GA)
Brigham Young Univ.–Provo (UT)
California Lutheran Univ.
California State Univ.–Dominguez
    Hills
California State Univ.–East Bay
California State Univ.–Monterey Bay
Campbellsville Univ. (KY)
Capital Univ. (OH)

Cardinal Stritch Univ. (WI)
Carlow Univ. (PA)
Carson-Newman Coll. (TN)
Catholic Univ. of America (DC)
Central Christian Coll. (KS)
Central Methodist Univ. (MO)
Central State Univ. (OH)
Clayton State Univ. (GA)
Coll. of Mount St. Vincent (NY)
Coll. of the Ozarks (MO)
Colorado State Univ.–Pueblo
Columbia Coll. (MO)
Concordia Univ. (OR)
Concordia Univ. (CA)
Concordia Univ. Chicago (IL)
Concordia Univ. Texas
Converse Coll. (SC)
Cornerstone Univ. (MI)
Covenant Coll. (GA)
Cumberland Univ. (TN)
CUNY–Baruch Coll.
CUNY–Coll. of Staten Island
D'Youville Coll. (NY)
Dakota Wesleyan Univ. (SD)
Davenport Univ. (MI)
Delta State Univ. (MS)
DePaul Univ. (IL)
Dickinson State Univ. (ND)
Dordt Coll. (IA)
Drexel Univ. (PA)
Duquesne Univ. (PA)
Earlham Coll. (IN)
East Texas Baptist Univ.
East-West Univ. (IL)
Eastern Connecticut State Univ.
Eastern Kentucky Univ.
Eastern Michigan Univ.
Eastern Oregon Univ.
Eckerd Coll. (FL)
Edgewood Coll. (WI)
Elmhurst Coll. (IL)
Emporia State Univ. (KS)
Excelsior Coll. (NY)
Ferrum Coll. (VA)
Fisk Univ. (TN)
Florida State Univ.
Fort Valley State Univ. (GA)
Framingham State Coll. (MA)
Franklin Coll. (IN)
Gallaudet Univ. (DC)
George Washington Univ. (DC)
Georgetown Coll. (KY)
Georgia Coll. & State Univ.
Georgia Southwestern State
    University
Grace Coll. and Seminary (IN)
Grand View Univ. (IA)
Harris-Stowe State Univ. (MO)
Hawaii Pacific Univ.
Henderson State Univ. (AR)
High Point Univ. (NC)
Hofstra Univ. (NY)
Hollins Univ. (VA)
Houston Baptist Univ.
Howard Payne Univ. (TX)
Huntington Univ. (IN)
Idaho State Univ.
Illinois Wesleyan Univ.
Indiana Univ. East
Indiana Univ.–Bloomington
Indiana Univ.–Kokomo

Indiana Univ.-Purdue Univ.–
    Indianapolis
Jacksonville Univ. (FL)
Juniata Coll. (PA)
Kansas State Univ.
Kentucky State Univ.
Kentucky Wesleyan Coll.
La Sierra Univ. (CA)
Lake Forest Coll. (IL)
Lamar Univ. (TX)
Lambuth Univ. (TN)
Lasell Coll. (MA)
Lenoir-Rhyne Univ. (NC)
Liberty Univ. (VA)
Life Univ. (GA)
Limestone Coll. (SC)
Lindenwood Univ. (MO)
Linfield Coll. (OR)
Loras Coll. (IA)
Louisiana Coll.
Loyola Univ. Maryland
Loyola Univ. New Orleans
Macon State Coll. (GA)
Madonna Univ. (MI)
Manhattan Coll. (NY)
Marian Univ. (WI)
Marian Univ. (IN)
Marygrove Coll. (MI)
Maryville Univ. of St. Louis (MO)
Massachusetts Institute of
    Technology
Mayville State Univ. (ND)
Medaille Coll. (NY)
Mercy Coll. (NY)
Mesa State Coll. (CO)
Miami Univ.–Oxford (OH)
Midway Coll. (KY)
Midwestern State Univ. (TX)
Milwaukee School of Engineering
Missouri State Univ.
Missouri Univ. of Science &
    Technology
Montana State Univ.
Montana State Univ.–Billings
Montana Tech of the Univ. of
    Montana
Mount Mercy Coll. (IA)
Mount St. Mary's Univ. (MD)
Murray State Univ. (KY)
Muskingum Univ. (OH)
Nebraska Wesleyan Univ.
New Mexico State Univ.
New York Univ.
Niagara Univ. (NY)
Norfolk State Univ. (VA)
Northern Arizona Univ.
Northern Kentucky Univ.
Northern Michigan Univ.
Northern State Univ. (SD)
Nova Southeastern Univ. (FL)
Oakland Univ. (MI)
Ohio State Univ.–Columbus
Ohio Valley Univ. (WV)
Oklahoma Wesleyan Univ.
Our Lady of the Lake Univ. (TX)
Pace Univ. (NY)
Paul Smith's Coll. (NY)
Pittsburg State Univ. (KS)
Pitzer Coll. (CA)
Plymouth State Univ. (NH)
Prescott Coll. (AZ)

Randolph Coll. (VA)
Regis Coll. (MA)
Reinhardt Univ. (GA)
Ripon Coll. (WI)
Roger Williams Univ. (RI)
Roosevelt Univ. (IL)
Rosemont Coll. (PA)
Saginaw Valley State Univ. (MI)
Sam Houston State Univ. (TX)
Schreiner Univ. (TX)
Seattle Pacific Univ.
Seattle Univ.
Shorter Coll. (GA)
Skidmore Coll. (NY)
Southern Arkansas Univ.
Southern Nazarene Univ. (OK)
Southern Oregon Univ.
Southwestern Assemblies of God
    Univ. (TX)
Southwestern Univ. (TX)
Spalding Univ. (KY)
St. Ambrose Univ. (IA)
St. Anselm Coll. (NH)
St. Cloud State Univ. (MN)
St. Joseph Coll. (CT)
St. Joseph's Coll. (IN)
St. Mary's Coll. of California
St. Mary's Univ. of Minnesota
St. Mary's Univ. of San Antonio
    (TX)
St. Mary-of-the-Woods Coll. (IN)
St. Norbert Coll. (WI)
St. Thomas Univ. (FL)
St. Vincent Coll. (PA)
Stephen F. Austin State Univ. (TX)
Stephens Coll. (MO)
Suffolk Univ. (MA)
Sul Ross State Univ. (TX)
SUNY Empire State Coll.
SUNY Maritime Coll.
SUNY–Plattsburgh
Tarleton State Univ. (TX)
Temple Univ. (PA)
Texas A&M Univ.–Commerce
Texas A&M Univ.–Corpus Christi
Texas A&M Univ.–Kingsville
Texas Lutheran Univ.
Texas Tech Univ.
Thomas More Coll. (KY)
Thomas Univ. (GA)
Transylvania Univ. (KY)
Trinity Christian Coll. (IL)
Trinity International Univ. (IL)
Troy Univ. (AL)
Tulane Univ. (LA)
Union Coll. (NE)
Union Institute and Univ. (OH)
Univ. of Alaska–Southeast
Univ. of Arizona
Univ. of Arkansas
Univ. of Baltimore (MD)
Univ. of Bridgeport (CT)
Univ. of Central Arkansas
Univ. of Central Florida
Univ. of Central Oklahoma
Univ. of Connecticut
Univ. of Denver
Univ. of Detroit Mercy
Univ. of Georgia
Univ. of Hawaii–Manoa
Univ. of Houston–Downtown

Univ. of Illinois–Urbana-Champaign
Univ. of Kansas
Univ. of Kentucky
Univ. of Maine
Univ. of Mary Hardin-Baylor (TX)
Univ. of Maryland–Coll. Park
Univ. of Maryland–Eastern Shore
Univ. of Michigan–Flint
Univ. of Mississippi
Univ. of Missouri
Univ. of Missouri–Kansas City
Univ. of Missouri–St. Louis
Univ. of Montana
Univ. of Nebraska–Omaha
Univ. of Nevada–Las Vegas
Univ. of New Hampshire
Univ. of North Dakota
Univ. of North Texas
Univ. of Notre Dame (IN)
Univ. of Oregon
Univ. of Pittsburgh–Johnstown
Univ. of Redlands (CA)
Univ. of Rhode Island
Univ. of South Alabama
Univ. of South Florida
Univ. of Southern Indiana
Univ. of Tennessee
Univ. of Tennessee–Chattanooga
Univ. of Texas–Austin
Univ. of Texas–Brownsville
Univ. of Texas–El Paso
Univ. of Texas–San Antonio
Univ. of the Cumberlands (KY)
Univ. of Toledo (OH)
Univ. of Tulsa (OK)
Univ. of Utah
Univ. of Virginia
Univ. of Washington
Univ. of Wisconsin–Platteville
Univ. of Wisconsin–Superior
Univ. of Wisconsin–Whitewater
Utah State Univ.
Valdosta State Univ. (GA)
Vanguard Univ. of Southern
    California
Vermont Technical Coll.
Villanova Univ. (PA)
Virginia Wesleyan Coll.
Wake Forest Univ. (NC)
Walsh Univ. (OH)
Wartburg Coll. (IA)
Washburn Univ. (KS)
Washington and Jefferson Coll.
    (PA)
Washington State Univ.
Wayne State Univ. (MI)
Waynesburg Univ. (PA)
Webber International Univ. (FL)
Webster Univ. (MO)
West Chester Univ. of Pennsylvania
West Texas A&M Univ.
West Virginia Univ. Institute of
    Technology
Western Michigan Univ.
Western New England Coll. (MA)
Western Oregon Univ.
Western State Coll. of Colorado
Western Washington Univ.
Westfield State Coll. (MA)
Westminster Coll. (UT)
Wittenberg Univ. (OH)

Worcester Polytechnic Institute
    (MA)
Xavier Univ. (OH)
York Coll. of Pennsylvania

Business/Corporate Communications

Aquinas Coll. (MI)
Arcadia Univ. (PA)
Babson Coll. (MA)
Bentley Univ. (MA)
Calvin Coll. (MI)
Chestnut Hill Coll. (PA)
Concordia Univ. (NE)
Concordia Univ.–St. Paul (MN)
CUNY–Baruch Coll.
Dana Coll. (NE)
Duquesne Univ. (PA)
Fort Hays State Univ. (KS)
Harding Univ. (AR)
Hawaii Pacific Univ.
Kentucky Wesleyan Coll.
Lindenwood Univ. (MO)
Mercy Coll. (NY)
Morningside Coll. (IA)
North Dakota State Univ.
Ohio Dominican Univ.
Otterbein Coll. (OH)
Pennsylvania Coll. of Technology
Point Loma Nazarene Univ. (CA)
Rochester Coll. (MI)
Rockhurst Univ. (MO)
Rosemont Coll. (PA)
Southwestern Coll. (KS)
Stevenson Univ. (MD)
Trinity Christian Coll. (IL)
Univ. of Houston
Univ. of Mary (ND)
Urbana Univ. (OH)
Walsh Univ. (OH)

Business/Managerial Economics

Albertus Magnus Coll. (CT)
Allegheny Coll. (PA)
Anderson Univ. (IN)
Andrews Univ. (MI)
Arkansas State Univ.–Jonesboro
Auburn Univ. (AL)
Auburn Univ.–Montgomery (AL)
Babson Coll. (MA)
Ball State Univ. (IN)
Baylor Univ. (TX)
Benedictine Univ. (IL)
Bentley Univ. (MA)
Bethel Coll. (IN)
Bloomsburg Univ. of Pennsylvania
Bowling Green State Univ. (OH)
Bradley Univ. (IL)
Buena Vista Univ. (IA)
California State Univ.–Fullerton
California State Univ.–Long Beach
Capital Univ. (OH)
Carnegie Mellon Univ. (PA)
Carson-Newman Coll. (TN)
Centenary Coll. of Louisiana
Central Christian Coll. (KS)
Chapman Univ. (CA)
Chatham Univ. (PA)

Christopher Newport Univ. (VA)
Clarion Univ. of Pennsylvania
Clemson Univ. (SC)
Cleveland State Univ.
Coastal Carolina Univ. (SC)
Coll. of the Ozarks (MO)
Coll. of Wooster (OH)
Colorado State Univ.–Pueblo
CUNY–Baruch Coll.
DePaul Univ. (IL)
Dominican Coll. (NY)
Drexel Univ. (PA)
Duquesne Univ. (PA)
East Tennessee State Univ.
Eastern Kentucky Univ.
Eastern Michigan Univ.
Emmanuel Coll. (MA)
Fairleigh Dickinson Univ. (NJ)
Fairmont State Univ. (WV)
Fayetteville State Univ. (NC)
Fort Lewis Coll. (CO)
Fort Valley State Univ. (GA)
Francis Marion Univ. (SC)
Georgia Coll. & State Univ.
Georgia Institute of Technology
Georgia Southern Univ.
Georgia State Univ.
Gordon Coll. (MA)
Grambling State Univ. (LA)
Hampden-Sydney Coll. (VA)
Hawaii Pacific Univ.
High Point Univ. (NC)
Hofstra Univ. (NY)
Hope Coll. (MI)
Houston Baptist Univ.
Huntington Univ. (IN)
Illinois Coll.
Indiana Univ. Southeast
Indiana Univ.-Purdue Univ.–Fort
    Wayne
Iowa State Univ.
Jackson State Univ. (MS)
Jacksonville Univ. (FL)
James Madison Univ. (VA)
John Carroll Univ. (OH)
Kennesaw State Univ. (GA)
Kent State Univ. (OH)
King Coll. (TN)
Kutztown Univ. of Pennsylvania
Lambuth Univ. (TN)
Lehigh Univ. (PA)
Limestone Coll. (SC)
Lincoln Univ. (MO)
Lipscomb Univ. (TN)
Long Island Univ.–C.W. Post
    Campus (NY)
Louisiana Coll.
Louisiana State Univ.–Baton Rouge
Louisiana State Univ.–Shreveport
Louisiana Tech Univ.
Loyola Univ. Chicago
Loyola Univ. New Orleans
Manhattan Coll. (NY)
Marian Univ. (WI)
Marquette Univ. (WI)
Marshall Univ. (WV)
Messiah Coll. (PA)
Miami Univ.–Oxford (OH)
Middle Tennessee State Univ.
Midland Lutheran Coll. (NE)
Millikin Univ. (IL)

Mills Coll. (CA)
Mississippi State Univ.
Missouri Southern State Univ.
Missouri Univ. of Science &
    Technology
Morehead State Univ. (KY)
New York Univ.
Nichols Coll. (MA)
North Carolina State Univ.–Raleigh
North Greenville Univ. (SC)
Northern Arizona Univ.
Northern Kentucky Univ.
Northern State Univ. (SD)
Northland Coll. (WI)
Northwest Missouri State Univ.
Northwood Univ. (MI)
Norwich Univ. (VT)
Oakland Univ. (MI)
Ohio State Univ.–Columbus
Ohio Univ.
Ohio Wesleyan Univ.
Oklahoma City Univ.
Oklahoma State Univ.
Oklahoma Wesleyan Univ.
Old Dominion Univ. (VA)
Park Univ. (MO)
Pennsylvania State Univ.–Univ. Park
Presbyterian Coll. (SC)
Purdue Univ.–Calumet (IN)
Randolph-Macon Coll. (VA)
Regis Univ. (CO)
Rhodes Coll. (TN)
Rider Univ. (NJ)
Robert Morris Univ. (PA)
Roosevelt Univ. (IL)
Rosemont Coll. (PA)
Sacred Heart Univ. (CT)
Saginaw Valley State Univ. (MI)
Sam Houston State Univ. (TX)
Samford Univ. (AL)
Santa Clara Univ. (CA)
Seattle Univ.
Seton Hall Univ. (NJ)
Shorter Coll. (GA)
South Carolina State Univ.
Southern Illinois Univ.–Carbondale
Southern Illinois Univ.–Edwardsville
Southern Univ. and A&M Coll. (LA)
St. Anselm Coll. (NH)
St. Joseph Coll. (CT)
St. Peter's Coll. (NJ)
Stephen F. Austin State Univ. (TX)
Stetson Univ. (FL)
SUNY Coll.–Oneonta
SUNY Coll.–Potsdam
SUNY–Plattsburgh
Taylor Univ. (IN)
Tennessee State Univ.
Texas A&M International Univ.
Texas A&M Univ.–Corpus Christi
Texas State Univ.–San Marcos
Texas Wesleyan Univ.
Tougaloo Coll. (MS)
Trinity Univ. (DC)
Tulane Univ. (LA)
Union Univ. (TN)
Univ. of Alabama
Univ. of Alabama–Birmingham
Univ. of Arizona
Univ. of Arkansas
Univ. of Arkansas–Little Rock

Univ. of California–Los Angeles
Univ. of California–Riverside
Univ. of California–Santa Cruz
Univ. of Central Florida
Univ. of Central Oklahoma
Univ. of Dayton (OH)
Univ. of Denver
Univ. of Evansville (IN)
Univ. of Georgia
Univ. of Indianapolis
Univ. of Iowa
Univ. of Kentucky
Univ. of Louisiana–Lafayette
Univ. of Louisiana–Monroe
Univ. of Louisville (KY)
Univ. of Maine
Univ. of Maine–Farmington
Univ. of Memphis
Univ. of Miami (FL)
Univ. of Mississippi
Univ. of Nebraska–Lincoln
Univ. of Nebraska–Omaha
Univ. of Nevada–Reno
Univ. of New Haven (CT)
Univ. of New Orleans
Univ. of North Alabama
Univ. of North Carolina–Charlotte
Univ. of North Carolina–
    Greensboro
Univ. of North Carolina–
    Wilmington
Univ. of North Dakota
Univ. of North Florida
Univ. of North Texas
Univ. of Oklahoma
Univ. of Pittsburgh–Johnstown
Univ. of Redlands (CA)
Univ. of San Diego
Univ. of South Carolina
Univ. of South Florida
Univ. of Southern Mississippi
Univ. of Tennessee
Univ. of Tennessee–Martin
Univ. of Texas of the Permian Basin
Univ. of Texas–Arlington
Univ. of Texas–El Paso
Univ. of Texas–San Antonio
Univ. of Texas–Tyler
Univ. of West Florida
Univ. of West Georgia
Univ. of Wisconsin–Whitewater
Univ. of Wyoming
Utica Coll. (NY)
Valdosta State Univ. (GA)
Villanova Univ. (PA)
Virginia Commonwealth Univ.
Virginia State Univ.
Virginia Tech
Warren Wilson Coll. (NC)
Washburn Univ. (KS)
Washington State Univ.
Washington Univ. in St. Louis
Weber State Univ. (UT)
West Chester Univ. of Pennsylvania
West Texas A&M Univ.
West Virginia Univ.
West Virginia Wesleyan Coll.
Western Illinois Univ.
Western Kentucky Univ.
Westminster Coll. (UT)
Wheaton Coll. (IL)

William Jewell Coll. (MO)
Wisconsin Lutheran Coll.
Wofford Coll. (SC)
Wright State Univ. (OH)
Xavier Univ. (OH)
York Coll. of Pennsylvania
Youngstown State Univ. (OH)

Carpenters

Northern Michigan Univ.

Cell/Cellular Biology and Anatomical Sciences

Beloit Coll. (WI)
Bennington Coll. (VT)
Berea Coll. (KY)
Bridgewater State Coll. (MA)
Bucknell Univ. (PA)
California State Univ.–Long Beach
Cedarville Univ. (OH)
Colby Coll. (ME)
Coll. of St. Rose (NY)
Dartmouth Coll. (NH)
Fort Lewis Coll. (CO)
Grand Valley State Univ. (MI)
Huntingdon Coll. (AL)
Johns Hopkins Univ. (MD)
Juniata Coll. (PA)
Lawrence Univ. (WI)
Mansfield Univ. of Pennsylvania
Marymount Univ. (VA)
Master's Coll. and Seminary (CA)
Methodist Univ. (NC)
Missouri State Univ.
Montana State Univ.
Northeastern State Univ. (OK)
Northern Arizona Univ.
Ohio State Univ.–Columbus
Ohio Univ.
Oklahoma City Univ.
Purdue Univ.–West Lafayette (IN)
Rensselaer Polytechnic Institute
    (NY)
Rutgers, the State Univ. of New
    Jersey–New Brunswick
San Diego State Univ.
Southwest Minnesota State Univ.
St. Cloud State Univ. (MN)
SUNY–Plattsburgh
Texas A&M Univ.–Coll. Station
Texas Tech Univ.
Tulane Univ. (LA)
Univ. of Arizona
Univ. of California–Berkeley
Univ. of California–Davis
Univ. of California–Irvine
Univ. of California–Los Angeles
Univ. of California–San Diego
Univ. of California–Santa Barbara
Univ. of California–Santa Cruz
Univ. of Colorado–Boulder
Univ. of Connecticut
Univ. of Georgia
Univ. of Illinois–Urbana-Champaign
Univ. of Kentucky
Univ. of Maine
Univ. of Michigan–Ann Arbor
Univ. of Minnesota–Duluth
Univ. of Minnesota–Twin Cities

Univ. of Nevada–Las Vegas
Univ. of Texas–Dallas
Univ. of Utah
Univ. of Wisconsin–Superior
Vanderbilt Univ. (TN)
Washington and Jefferson Coll.
    (PA)
Western Washington Univ.
William Jewell Coll. (MO)

Celtic Languages, Literatures, and Linguistics

Univ. of California–Berkeley

Ceramic Sciences and Engineering

Alfred Univ. (NY)
Clemson Univ. (SC)
Missouri Univ. of Science &
    Technology
Rutgers, the State Univ. of New
    Jersey–New Brunswick
Univ. of Illinois–Urbana-Champaign

Chemical Engineering

Arizona State Univ.
Auburn Univ. (AL)
Bethel Coll. (IN)
Brigham Young Univ.–Provo (UT)
Bucknell Univ. (PA)
California Institute of Technology
California State Polytechnic Univ.–
    Pomona
California State Univ.–Long Beach
Calvin Coll. (MI)
Carnegie Mellon Univ. (PA)
Case Western Reserve Univ. (OH)
Christian Brothers Univ. (TN)
Clarkson Univ. (NY)
Clemson Univ. (SC)
Cleveland State Univ.
Colorado School of Mines
Colorado State Univ.
Columbia Univ. (NY)
Cooper Union (NY)
Cornell Univ. (NY)
CUNY–City Coll.
Drexel Univ. (PA)
Florida A&M Univ.
Florida Institute of Technology
Florida International Univ.
Florida State Univ.
Gannon Univ. (PA)
Geneva Coll. (PA)
Georgia Institute of Technology
Hampton Univ. (VA)
Howard Univ. (DC)
Illinois Institute of Technology
Iowa State Univ.
Johns Hopkins Univ. (MD)
Kansas State Univ.
Lafayette Coll. (PA)
Lamar Univ. (TX)
Lehigh Univ. (PA)
Louisiana State Univ.–Baton Rouge
Louisiana Tech Univ.
Manhattan Coll. (NY)

Massachusetts Institute of
Technology
Miami Univ.–Oxford (OH)
Michigan State Univ.
Michigan Technological Univ.
Mississippi State Univ.
Missouri Univ. of Science &
Technology
Montana State Univ.
New Jersey Institute of Technology
New Mexico Institute of Mining
and Technology
New Mexico State Univ.
North Carolina A&T State Univ.
North Carolina State Univ.–Raleigh
Northeastern Univ. (MA)
Northwestern Univ. (IL)
Ohio State Univ.–Columbus
Ohio Univ.
Oklahoma State Univ.
Oregon State Univ.
Pennsylvania State Univ.–Univ. Park
Polytechnic Institute of New York
Univ. (NY)
Prairie View A&M Univ. (TX)
Princeton Univ. (NJ)
Rensselaer Polytechnic Institute
(NY)
Rice Univ. (TX)
Rose-Hulman Institute of
Technology (IN)
Rutgers, the State Univ. of New
Jersey–New Brunswick
San Jose State Univ. (CA)
South Dakota School of Mines and
Technology
Stanford Univ. (CA)
Stevens Institute of Technology
(NJ)
Syracuse Univ. (NY)
Tennessee Technological Univ.
Texas A&M Univ.–Coll. Station
Texas A&M Univ.–Kingsville
Texas Tech Univ.
Trine Univ. (IN)
Tufts Univ. (MA)
Tulane Univ. (LA)
Tuskegee Univ. (AL)
United States Military Academy
(NY)
Univ. at Buffalo–SUNY
Univ. of Akron (OH)
Univ. of Alabama
Univ. of Alabama–Huntsville
Univ. of Arizona
Univ. of Arkansas
Univ. of California–Berkeley
Univ. of California–Davis
Univ. of California–Irvine
Univ. of California–Los Angeles
Univ. of California–San Diego
Univ. of California–Santa Barbara
Univ. of Colorado–Boulder
Univ. of Connecticut
Univ. of Dayton (OH)
Univ. of Florida
Univ. of Georgia
Univ. of Houston
Univ. of Illinois–Chicago
Univ. of Illinois–Urbana-Champaign
Univ. of Iowa

Univ. of Kansas
Univ. of Kentucky
Univ. of Louisiana–Lafayette
Univ. of Louisville (KY)
Univ. of Maine
Univ. of Maryland–Baltimore
County
Univ. of Maryland–Coll. Park
Univ. of Massachusetts–Amherst
Univ. of Massachusetts–Lowell
Univ. of Michigan–Ann Arbor
Univ. of Minnesota–Duluth
Univ. of Minnesota–Twin Cities
Univ. of Mississippi
Univ. of Missouri
Univ. of Nebraska–Lincoln
Univ. of Nevada–Reno
Univ. of New Hampshire
Univ. of New Haven (CT)
Univ. of New Mexico
Univ. of North Dakota
Univ. of Notre Dame (IN)
Univ. of Oklahoma
Univ. of Pennsylvania
Univ. of Pittsburgh
Univ. of Rhode Island
Univ. of Rochester (NY)
Univ. of South Alabama
Univ. of South Carolina
Univ. of South Florida
Univ. of Southern California
Univ. of Tennessee
Univ. of Texas–Austin
Univ. of Toledo (OH)
Univ. of Tulsa (OK)
Univ. of Utah
Univ. of Virginia
Univ. of Washington
Univ. of Wisconsin–Madison
Univ. of Wyoming
Vanderbilt Univ. (TN)
Villanova Univ. (PA)
Virginia Commonwealth Univ.
Virginia Tech
Washington and Lee Univ. (VA)
Washington State Univ.
Washington Univ. in St. Louis
Wayne State Univ. (MI)
West Virginia Univ.
West Virginia Univ. Institute of
Technology
Western Michigan Univ.
Widener Univ. (PA)
Worcester Polytechnic Institute
(MA)
Yale Univ. (CT)
Youngstown State Univ. (OH)

Chemistry

Abilene Christian Univ. (TX)
Adams State Coll. (CO)
Adelphi Univ. (NY)
Adrian Coll. (MI)
Agnes Scott Coll. (GA)
Alabama Agricultural and
Mechanical Univ.
Alabama State Univ.
Albany State Univ. (GA)
Albertus Magnus Coll. (CT)
Albion Coll. (MI)

Albright Coll. (PA)
Alcorn State Univ. (MS)
Alderson-Broaddus Coll. (WV)
Allegheny Coll. (PA)
Allen Univ. (SC)
Alma Coll. (MI)
Alvernia Univ. (PA)
Alverno Coll. (WI)
American Univ. (DC)
Amherst Coll. (MA)
Anderson Univ. (IN)
Andrews Univ. (MI)
Angelo State Univ. (TX)
Anna Maria Coll. (MA)
Appalachian State Univ. (NC)
Aquinas Coll. (MI)
Arcadia Univ. (PA)
Arizona State Univ.
Arkansas State Univ.–Jonesboro
Arkansas Tech Univ.
Armstrong Atlantic State Univ. (GA)
Asbury Univ. (KY)
Ashland Univ. (OH)
Assumption Coll. (MA)
Auburn Univ. (AL)
Augsburg Coll. (MN)
Augusta State Univ. (GA)
Augustana Coll. (IL)
Austin Coll. (TX)
Austin Peay State Univ. (TN)
Averett Univ. (VA)
Avila Univ. (MO)
Azusa Pacific Univ. (CA)
Baker Univ. (KS)
Baldwin-Wallace Coll. (OH)
Ball State Univ. (IN)
Barnard Coll. (NY)
Barry Univ. (FL)
Barton Coll. (NC)
Bates Coll. (ME)
Baylor Univ. (TX)
Belhaven Univ. (MS)
Bellarmine Univ. (KY)
Belmont Univ. (TN)
Beloit Coll. (WI)
Benedict Coll. (SC)
Benedictine Coll. (KS)
Benedictine Univ. (IL)
Bennington Coll. (VT)
Berea Coll. (KY)
Berry Coll. (GA)
Bethany Coll. (KS)
Bethany Coll. (WV)
Bethel Coll. (IN)
Bethel Coll. (KS)
Bethel Univ. (MN)
Bethune-Cookman Univ. (FL)
Binghamton Univ.–SUNY
Black Hills State Univ. (SD)
Bloomfield Coll. (NJ)
Bloomsburg Univ. of Pennsylvania
Bluefield Coll. (VA)
Bluffton Univ. (OH)
Boise State Univ. (ID)
Boston Univ.
Bowdoin Coll. (ME)
Bowling Green State Univ. (OH)
Bradley Univ. (IL)
Brandeis Univ. (MA)
Brescia Univ. (KY)
Briar Cliff Univ. (IA)

Bridgewater Coll. (VA)
Bridgewater State Coll. (MA)
Brigham Young Univ.–Provo (UT)
Brown Univ. (RI)
Bryn Mawr Coll. (PA)
Bucknell Univ. (PA)
Buena Vista Univ. (IA)
Buffalo State Coll.–SUNY
Butler Univ. (IN)
Cabrini Coll. (PA)
Caldwell Coll. (NJ)
California Institute of Technology
California Lutheran Univ.
California Polytechnic State Univ.–
San Luis Obispo
California State Polytechnic Univ.–
Pomona
California State Univ.–Bakersfield
California State Univ.–Chico
California State Univ.–Dominguez
Hills
California State Univ.–East Bay
California State Univ.–Fresno
California State Univ.–Fullerton
California State Univ.–Long Beach
California State Univ.–Los Angeles
California State Univ.–Northridge
California State Univ.–Sacramento
California State Univ.–San
Bernardino
California State Univ.–San Marcos
California State Univ.–Stanislaus
California Univ. of Pennsylvania
Calvin Coll. (MI)
Cameron Univ. (OK)
Campbellsville Univ. (KY)
Canisius Coll. (NY)
Capital Univ. (OH)
Cardinal Stritch Univ. (WI)
Carleton Coll. (MN)
Carlow Univ. (PA)
Carnegie Mellon Univ. (PA)
Carroll Coll. (MT)
Carroll Univ. (WI)
Carson-Newman Coll. (TN)
Carthage Coll. (WI)
Case Western Reserve Univ. (OH)
Catawba Coll. (NC)
Catholic Univ. of America (DC)
Cedar Crest Coll. (PA)
Cedarville Univ. (OH)
Centenary Coll. of Louisiana
Central Christian Coll. (KS)
Central Coll. (IA)
Central Connecticut State Univ.
Central Methodist Univ. (MO)
Central Michigan Univ.
Central State Univ. (OH)
Central Washington Univ.
Centre Coll. (KY)
Chapman Univ. (CA)
Charleston Southern Univ. (SC)
Chatham Univ. (PA)
Chestnut Hill Coll. (PA)
Cheyney Univ. of Pennsylvania
Chicago State Univ.
Christian Brothers Univ. (TN)
Christopher Newport Univ. (VA)
Claflin Univ. (SC)
Claremont McKenna Coll. (CA)
Clarion Univ. of Pennsylvania

Clark Atlanta Univ.
Clark Univ. (MA)
Clarke Univ. (IA)
Clarkson Univ. (NY)
Clemson Univ. (SC)
Cleveland State Univ.
Coastal Carolina Univ. (SC)
Coe Coll. (IA)
Coker Coll. (SC)
Colby Coll. (ME)
Colgate Univ. (NY)
Coll. at Brockport–SUNY
Coll. of Charleston (SC)
Coll. of Idaho (ID)
Coll. of Mount St. Joseph (OH)
Coll. of Mount St. Vincent (NY)
Coll. of New Jersey
Coll. of Notre Dame of Maryland
Coll. of Our Lady of the Elms (MA)
Coll. of St. Benedict (MN)
Coll. of St. Elizabeth (NJ)
Coll. of St. Mary (NE)
Coll. of St. Rose (NY)
Coll. of St. Scholastica (MN)
Coll. of the Holy Cross (MA)
Coll. of the Ozarks (MO)
Coll. of William and Mary (VA)
Coll. of Wooster (OH)
Colorado Coll.
Colorado School of Mines
Colorado State Univ.
Colorado State Univ.–Pueblo
Columbia Coll. (MO)
Columbia Coll. (SC)
Columbia Univ. (NY)
Columbus State Univ. (GA)
Concord Univ. (WV)
Concordia Coll.–Moorhead (MN)
Concordia Univ. (NE)
Concordia Univ. (MI)
Concordia Univ. (CA)
Concordia Univ. Chicago (IL)
Concordia Univ.–St. Paul (MN)
Connecticut Coll.
Converse Coll. (SC)
Coppin State Univ. (MD)
Cornell Coll. (IA)
Cornell Univ. (NY)
Covenant Coll. (GA)
Creighton Univ. (NE)
CUNY–Brooklyn Coll.
CUNY–City Coll.
CUNY–Coll. of Staten Island
CUNY–Lehman Coll.
CUNY–Queens Coll.
CUNY–York Coll.
Dana Coll. (NE)
Dartmouth Coll. (NH)
Davidson Coll. (NC)
Davis and Elkins Coll. (WV)
Delaware State Univ.
Delaware Valley Coll. (PA)
Delta State Univ. (MS)
Denison Univ. (OH)
DePaul Univ. (IL)
DePauw Univ. (IN)
DeSales Univ. (PA)
Dickinson Coll. (PA)
Dickinson State Univ. (ND)
Dillard Univ. (LA)
Dominican Univ. (IL)

Dordt Coll. (IA)
Drake Univ. (IA)
Drew Univ. (NJ)
Drexel Univ. (PA)
Drury Univ. (MO)
Duke Univ. (NC)
Duquesne Univ. (PA)
Earlham Coll. (IN)
East Carolina Univ. (NC)
East Central Univ. (OK)
East Stroudsburg Univ. of Pennsylvania
East Tennessee State Univ.
East Texas Baptist Univ.
Eastern Illinois Univ.
Eastern Kentucky Univ.
Eastern Mennonite Univ. (VA)
Eastern Michigan Univ.
Eastern Nazarene Coll. (MA)
Eastern New Mexico Univ.
Eastern Oregon Univ.
Eastern Univ. (PA)
Eastern Washington Univ.
Eckerd Coll. (FL)
Edgewood Coll. (WI)
Edinboro Univ. of Pennsylvania
Elizabeth City State Univ. (NC)
Elizabethtown Coll. (PA)
Elmhurst Coll. (IL)
Elmira Coll. (NY)
Elon Univ. (NC)
Emmanuel Coll. (MA)
Emory and Henry Coll. (VA)
Emory Univ. (GA)
Emporia State Univ. (KS)
Erskine Coll. (SC)
Eureka Coll. (IL)
Excelsior Coll. (NY)
Fairfield Univ. (CT)
Fairleigh Dickinson Univ. (NJ)
Fairmont State Univ. (WV)
Fayetteville State Univ. (NC)
Ferris State Univ. (MI)
Ferrum Coll. (VA)
Fisk Univ. (TN)
Florida Atlantic Univ.
Florida Institute of Technology
Florida International Univ.
Florida Southern Coll.
Florida State Univ.
Fordham Univ. (NY)
Fort Hays State Univ. (KS)
Fort Lewis Coll. (CO)
Fort Valley State Univ. (GA)
Framingham State Coll. (MA)
Francis Marion Univ. (SC)
Franciscan Univ. of Steubenville (OH)
Franklin and Marshall Coll. (PA)
Franklin Coll. (IN)
Freed-Hardeman Univ. (TN)
Fresno Pacific Univ. (CA)
Friends Univ. (KS)
Frostburg State Univ. (MD)
Furman Univ. (SC)
Gallaudet Univ. (DC)
Gannon Univ. (PA)
Gardner-Webb Univ. (NC)
Geneva Coll. (PA)
George Fox Univ. (OR)
George Mason Univ. (VA)

George Washington Univ. (DC)
Georgetown Coll. (KY)
Georgetown Univ. (DC)
Georgia Coll. & State Univ.
Georgia Institute of Technology
Georgia Southern Univ.
Georgia Southwestern State Univ.
Georgia State Univ.
Georgian Court Univ. (NJ)
Gettysburg Coll. (PA)
Glenville State Coll. (WV)
Gonzaga Univ. (WA)
Gordon Coll. (MA)
Goshen Coll. (IN)
Goucher Coll. (MD)
Graceland Univ. (IA)
Grambling State Univ. (LA)
Grand Valley State Univ. (MI)
Greensboro Coll. (NC)
Greenville Coll. (IL)
Grinnell Coll. (IA)
Grove City Coll. (PA)
Guilford Coll. (NC)
Gustavus Adolphus Coll. (MN)
Hamilton Coll. (NY)
Hamline Univ. (MN)
Hampden-Sydney Coll. (VA)
Hampshire Coll. (MA)
Hampton Univ. (VA)
Hanover Coll. (IN)
Hardin-Simmons Univ. (TX)
Harding Univ. (AR)
Hartwick Coll. (NY)
Harvard Univ. (MA)
Harvey Mudd Coll. (CA)
Haverford Coll. (PA)
Heidelberg Univ. (OH)
Henderson State Univ. (AR)
Hendrix Coll. (AR)
Heritage Univ. (WA)
High Point Univ. (NC)
Hillsdale Coll. (MI)
Hiram Coll. (OH)
Hobart and William Smith Colleges (NY)
Hofstra Univ. (NY)
Hollins Univ. (VA)
Holy Family Univ. (PA)
Hood Coll. (MD)
Hope Coll. (MI)
Houghton Coll. (NY)
Houston Baptist Univ.
Howard Payne Univ. (TX)
Howard Univ. (DC)
Humboldt State Univ. (CA)
Huntingdon Coll. (AL)
Huntington Univ. (IN)
Husson Univ. (ME)
Huston-Tillotson Univ. (TX)
Idaho State Univ.
Illinois Coll.
Illinois Institute of Technology
Illinois State Univ.
Illinois Wesleyan Univ.
Immaculata Univ. (PA)
Indiana State Univ.
Indiana Univ. Northwest
Indiana Univ. of Pennsylvania
Indiana Univ. Southeast
Indiana Univ.–Bloomington
Indiana Univ.–Kokomo

Indiana Univ.–South Bend
Indiana Univ.-Purdue Univ.–Fort Wayne
Indiana Univ.-Purdue Univ.–Indianapolis
Indiana Wesleyan Univ.
Iona Coll. (NY)
Iowa State Univ.
Iowa Wesleyan Coll.
Ithaca Coll. (NY)
Jackson State Univ. (MS)
Jacksonville State Univ. (AL)
Jacksonville Univ. (FL)
James Madison Univ. (VA)
Jamestown Coll. (ND)
Jarvis Christian Coll. (TX)
John Brown Univ. (AR)
John Carroll Univ. (OH)
Johns Hopkins Univ. (MD)
Johnson C. Smith Univ. (NC)
Judson Coll. (AL)
Judson Univ. (IL)
Juniata Coll. (PA)
Kalamazoo Coll. (MI)
Kansas State Univ.
Kansas Wesleyan Univ.
Kean Univ. (NJ)
Keene State Coll. (NH)
Kennesaw State Univ. (GA)
Kent State Univ. (OH)
Kentucky State Univ.
Kentucky Wesleyan Coll.
Kenyon Coll. (OH)
Kettering Univ. (MI)
King Coll. (TN)
King's Coll. (PA)
Knox Coll. (IL)
Kutztown Univ. of Pennsylvania
La Roche Coll. (PA)
La Salle Univ. (PA)
La Sierra Univ. (CA)
Lafayette Coll. (PA)
LaGrange Coll. (GA)
Lake Forest Coll. (IL)
Lake Superior State Univ. (MI)
Lakeland Coll. (WI)
Lamar Univ. (TX)
Lambuth Univ. (TN)
Lander Univ. (SC)
Lane Coll. (TN)
Lawrence Technological Univ. (MI)
Lawrence Univ. (WI)
Le Moyne Coll. (NY)
Lebanon Valley Coll. (PA)
Lehigh Univ. (PA)
LeMoyne-Owen Coll. (TN)
Lenoir-Rhyne Univ. (NC)
LeTourneau Univ. (TX)
Lewis & Clark Coll. (OR)
Lewis Univ. (IL)
Lewis-Clark State Coll. (ID)
Limestone Coll. (SC)
Lincoln Memorial Univ. (TN)
Lincoln Univ. (MO)
Lincoln Univ. (PA)
Lindenwood Univ. (MO)
Linfield Coll. (OR)
Lipscomb Univ. (TN)
Lock Haven Univ. of Pennsylvania
Long Island Univ.–C.W. Post Campus (NY)

Longwood Univ. (VA)
Loras Coll. (IA)
Louisiana Coll.
Louisiana State Univ.–Baton Rouge
Louisiana State Univ.–Shreveport
Louisiana Tech Univ.
Loyola Marymount Univ. (CA)
Loyola Univ. Chicago
Loyola Univ. Maryland
Loyola Univ. New Orleans
Lubbock Christian Univ. (TX)
Luther Coll. (IA)
Lycoming Coll. (PA)
Lynchburg Coll. (VA)
Lyon Coll. (AR)
Macalester Coll. (MN)
Madonna Univ. (MI)
Malone Univ. (OH)
Manchester Coll. (IN)
Manhattan Coll. (NY)
Manhattanville Coll. (NY)
Mansfield Univ. of Pennsylvania
Marian Univ. (WI)
Marian Univ. (IN)
Marietta Coll. (OH)
Marist Coll. (NY)
Marquette Univ. (WI)
Mars Hill Coll. (NC)
Marshall Univ. (WV)
Martin Univ. (IN)
Mary Baldwin Coll. (VA)
Marygrove Coll. (MI)
Maryville Coll. (TN)
Maryville Univ. of St. Louis (MO)
Massachusetts Institute of Technology
Mayville State Univ. (ND)
McDaniel Coll. (MD)
McKendree Univ. (IL)
McMurry Univ. (TX)
McNeese State Univ. (LA)
McPherson Coll. (KS)
Mercer Univ. (GA)
Mercyhurst Coll. (PA)
Meredith Coll. (NC)
Merrimack Coll. (MA)
Messiah Coll. (PA)
Methodist Univ. (NC)
Metropolitan State Coll. of Denver
Miami Univ.–Oxford (OH)
Michigan State Univ.
Michigan Technological Univ.
MidAmerica Nazarene Univ. (KS)
Middle Tennessee State Univ.
Middlebury Coll. (VT)
Midway Coll. (KY)
Midwestern State Univ. (TX)
Miles Coll. (AL)
Millersville Univ. of Pennsylvania
Milligan Coll. (TN)
Millikin Univ. (IL)
Mills Coll. (CA)
Millsaps Coll. (MS)
Minnesota State Univ.–Mankato
Minnesota State Univ.–Moorhead
Minot State Univ. (ND)
Misericordia Univ. (PA)
Mississippi Coll.
Mississippi State Univ.
Mississippi Univ. for Women
Mississippi Valley State Univ.

Missouri Baptist Univ.
Missouri Southern State Univ.
Missouri Univ. of Science & Technology
Missouri Western State Univ.
Monmouth Coll. (IL)
Monmouth Univ. (NJ)
Montana State Univ.
Montana State Univ.–Billings
Montana Tech of the Univ. of Montana
Montclair State Univ. (NJ)
Moravian Coll. (PA)
Morehead State Univ. (KY)
Morehouse Coll. (GA)
Morgan State Univ. (MD)
Morningside Coll. (IA)
Mount Holyoke Coll. (MA)
Mount Marty Coll. (SD)
Mount Mary Coll. (WI)
Mount St. Mary Coll. (NY)
Mount St. Mary's Coll. (CA)
Mount St. Mary's Univ. (MD)
Mount Vernon Nazarene Univ. (OH)
Muhlenberg Coll. (PA)
Murray State Univ. (KY)
Muskingum Univ. (OH)
Nazareth Coll. (NY)
Nebraska Wesleyan Univ.
New Jersey City Univ.
New Jersey Institute of Technology
New Mexico Highlands Univ.
New Mexico Institute of Mining and Technology
New Mexico State Univ.
New York Institute of Technology
New York Univ.
Newberry Coll. (SC)
Niagara Univ. (NY)
Nicholls State Univ. (LA)
Norfolk State Univ. (VA)
North Carolina Central Univ.
North Carolina State Univ.–Raleigh
North Carolina Wesleyan Coll.
North Central Coll. (IL)
North Dakota State Univ.
North Georgia Coll. and State Univ.
North Park Univ. (IL)
Northeastern Illinois Univ.
Northeastern State Univ. (OK)
Northeastern Univ. (MA)
Northern Arizona Univ.
Northern Illinois Univ.
Northern Kentucky Univ.
Northern Michigan Univ.
Northern State Univ. (SD)
Northland Coll. (WI)
Northwest Missouri State Univ.
Northwest Nazarene Univ. (ID)
Northwestern Coll. (IA)
Northwestern Oklahoma State Univ.
Northwestern State Univ. of Louisiana
Northwestern Univ. (IL)
Norwich Univ. (VT)
Notre Dame Coll. of Ohio
Oakland Univ. (MI)
Oakwood Univ. (AL)
Oberlin Coll. (OH)

Occidental Coll. (CA)
Oglethorpe Univ. (GA)
Ohio Dominican Univ.
Ohio Northern Univ.
Ohio State Univ.–Columbus
Ohio Univ.
Ohio Wesleyan Univ.
Oklahoma Baptist Univ.
Oklahoma Christian Univ.
Oklahoma City Univ.
Oklahoma Panhandle State Univ.
Oklahoma State Univ.
Oklahoma Wesleyan Univ.
Old Dominion Univ. (VA)
Olivet Coll. (MI)
Olivet Nazarene Univ. (IL)
Oral Roberts Univ. (OK)
Oregon State Univ.
Otterbein Coll. (OH)
Ouachita Baptist Univ. (AR)
Our Lady of the Lake Univ. (TX)
Pace Univ. (NY)
Pacific Lutheran Univ. (WA)
Pacific Union Coll. (CA)
Pacific Univ. (OR)
Paine Coll. (GA)
Park Univ. (MO)
Pennsylvania State Univ.–Univ. Park
Pepperdine Univ. (CA)
Pfeiffer Univ. (NC)
Philadelphia Univ.
Philander Smith Coll. (AR)
Piedmont Coll. (GA)
Pikeville Coll. (KY)
Pittsburg State Univ. (KS)
Plymouth State Univ. (NH)
Point Loma Nazarene Univ. (CA)
Polytechnic Institute of New York
   Univ. (NY)
Pomona Coll. (CA)
Portland State Univ. (OR)
Prairie View A&M Univ. (TX)
Presbyterian Coll. (SC)
Princeton Univ. (NJ)
Principia Coll. (IL)
Providence Coll. (RI)
Purchase Coll.–SUNY
Purdue Univ.–Calumet (IN)
Quincy Univ. (IL)
Quinnipiac Univ. (CT)
Radford Univ. (VA)
Ramapo Coll. of New Jersey
Randolph Coll. (VA)
Randolph-Macon Coll. (VA)
Reed Coll. (OR)
Regis Univ. (CO)
Rensselaer Polytechnic Institute
   (NY)
Rhode Island Coll.
Rhodes Coll. (TN)
Rice Univ. (TX)
Richard Stockton Coll. of New
   Jersey
Rider Univ. (NJ)
Ripon Coll. (WI)
Roanoke Coll. (VA)
Roberts Wesleyan Coll. (NY)
Rochester Institute of Tech. (NY)
Rockford Coll. (IL)
Rockhurst Univ. (MO)
Rocky Mountain Coll. (MT)

Roger Williams Univ. (RI)
Rollins Coll. (FL)
Roosevelt Univ. (IL)
Rose-Hulman Institute of
   Technology (IN)
Rosemont Coll. (PA)
Russell Sage Coll. (NY)
Rust Coll. (MS)
Rutgers, the State Univ. of New
   Jersey–Camden
Rutgers, the State Univ. of New
   Jersey–New Brunswick
Rutgers, the State Univ. of New
   Jersey–Newark
Sacred Heart Univ. (CT)
Saginaw Valley State Univ. (MI)
Salem Coll. (NC)
Salem State Coll. (MA)
Salisbury Univ. (MD)
Salve Regina Univ. (RI)
Sam Houston State Univ. (TX)
Samford Univ. (AL)
San Diego State Univ.
San Francisco State Univ.
San Jose State Univ. (CA)
Santa Clara Univ. (CA)
Savannah State Univ. (GA)
Schreiner Univ. (TX)
Scripps Coll. (CA)
Seattle Pacific Univ.
Seattle Univ.
Seton Hall Univ. (NJ)
Seton Hill Univ. (PA)
Shaw Univ. (NC)
Shawnee State Univ. (OH)
Shenandoah Univ. (VA)
Shepherd Univ. (WV)
Shippensburg Univ. of Pennsylvania
Shorter Coll. (GA)
Siena Coll. (NY)
Simmons Coll. (MA)
Simpson Coll. (IA)
Skidmore Coll. (NY)
Slippery Rock Univ. of Pennsylvania
Smith Coll. (MA)
Sonoma State Univ. (CA)
South Carolina State Univ.
South Dakota School of Mines and
   Technology
South Dakota State Univ.
Southeast Missouri State Univ.
Southeastern Louisiana Univ.
Southeastern Oklahoma State Univ.
Southern Adventist Univ. (TN)
Southern Arkansas Univ.
Southern Connecticut State Univ.
Southern Illinois Univ.–Carbondale
Southern Illinois Univ.–Edwardsville
Southern Methodist Univ. (TX)
Southern Nazarene Univ. (OK)
Southern Oregon Univ.
Southern Univ. and A&M Coll. (LA)
Southern Univ.–New Orleans
Southern Utah Univ.
Southern Wesleyan Univ. (SC)
Southwest Baptist Univ. (MO)
Southwest Minnesota State Univ.
Southwestern Adventist Univ. (TX)
Southwestern Coll. (KS)
Southwestern Oklahoma State
   Univ.

Southwestern Univ. (TX)
Spelman Coll. (GA)
Spring Arbor Univ. (MI)
Spring Hill Coll. (AL)
Springfield Coll. (MA)
St. Ambrose Univ. (IA)
St. Andrews Presbyterian Coll. (NC)
St. Anselm Coll. (NH)
St. Augustine's Coll. (NC)
St. Bonaventure Univ. (NY)
St. Catherine Univ. (MN)
St. Cloud State Univ. (MN)
St. Edward's Univ. (TX)
St. Francis Coll. (NY)
St. Francis Univ. (PA)
St. Gregory's Univ. (OK)
St. John Fisher Coll. (NY)
St. John's Univ. (MN)
St. John's Univ. (NY)
St. Joseph Coll. (CT)
St. Joseph's Coll. (IN)
St. Joseph's Coll. (ME)
St. Joseph's Coll. New York
St. Joseph's Univ. (PA)
St. Lawrence Univ. (NY)
St. Louis Univ.
St. Martin's Univ. (WA)
St. Mary's Coll. (IN)
St. Mary's Coll. of California
St. Mary's Coll. of Maryland
St. Mary's Univ. of Minnesota
St. Mary's Univ. of San Antonio
   (TX)
St. Michael's Coll. (VT)
St. Norbert Coll. (WI)
St. Olaf Coll. (MN)
St. Peter's Coll. (NJ)
St. Vincent Coll. (PA)
St. Xavier Univ. (IL)
Stanford Univ. (CA)
Stephen F. Austin State Univ. (TX)
Sterling Coll. (KS)
Stetson Univ. (FL)
Stevens Institute of Technology
   (NJ)
Stevenson Univ. (MD)
Stonehill Coll. (MA)
Suffolk Univ. (MA)
Sul Ross State Univ. (TX)
SUNY Coll. of Environmental
   Science and Forestry
SUNY Coll.–Cortland
SUNY Coll.–Old Westbury
SUNY Coll.–Oneonta
SUNY Coll.–Potsdam
SUNY–Fredonia
SUNY–Geneseo
SUNY–Oswego
SUNY–Plattsburgh
SUNY–Stony Brook
Susquehanna Univ. (PA)
Swarthmore Coll. (PA)
Syracuse Univ. (NY)
Tabor Coll. (KS)
Talladega Coll. (AL)
Tarleton State Univ. (TX)
Taylor Univ. (IN)
Temple Univ. (PA)
Tennessee State Univ.
Tennessee Technological Univ.
Tennessee Wesleyan Coll.

Texas A&M International Univ.
Texas A&M Univ.–Coll. Station
Texas A&M Univ.–Commerce
Texas A&M Univ.–Corpus Christi
Texas A&M Univ.–Kingsville
Texas Christian Univ.
Texas Lutheran Univ.
Texas State Univ.–San Marcos
Texas Tech Univ.
Texas Wesleyan Univ.
Texas Woman's Univ.
The Citadel (SC)
Thiel Coll. (PA)
Thomas More Coll. (KY)
Touro Coll. (NY)
Towson Univ. (MD)
Transylvania Univ. (KY)
Trevecca Nazarene Univ. (TN)
Trine Univ. (IN)
Trinity Christian Coll. (IL)
Trinity Coll. (CT)
Trinity International Univ. (IL)
Trinity Univ. (DC)
Troy Univ. (AL)
Truman State Univ. (MO)
Tufts Univ. (MA)
Tulane Univ. (LA)
Union Coll. (KY)
Union Coll. (NE)
Union Coll. (NY)
Union Univ. (TN)
United States Air Force Academy
   (CO)
United States Naval Academy (MD)
Univ. at Albany–SUNY
Univ. at Buffalo–SUNY
Univ. of Akron (OH)
Univ. of Alabama
Univ. of Alabama–Birmingham
Univ. of Alabama–Huntsville
Univ. of Alaska–Anchorage
Univ. of Alaska–Fairbanks
Univ. of Arizona
Univ. of Arkansas
Univ. of Arkansas–Little Rock
Univ. of Arkansas–Monticello
Univ. of Arkansas–Pine Bluff
Univ. of California–Berkeley
Univ. of California–Davis
Univ. of California–Irvine
Univ. of California–Los Angeles
Univ. of California–Riverside
Univ. of California–San Diego
Univ. of California–Santa Barbara
Univ. of California–Santa Cruz
Univ. of Central Arkansas
Univ. of Central Florida
Univ. of Central Oklahoma
Univ. of Charleston (WV)
Univ. of Chicago
Univ. of Colorado–Boulder
Univ. of Colorado–Colorado
   Springs
Univ. of Colorado–Denver
Univ. of Connecticut
Univ. of Dallas
Univ. of Dayton (OH)
Univ. of Delaware
Univ. of Denver
Univ. of Detroit Mercy
Univ. of Evansville (IN)

Univ. of Florida
Univ. of Georgia
Univ. of Hartford (CT)
Univ. of Hawaii–Hilo
Univ. of Hawaii–Manoa
Univ. of Houston
Univ. of Houston–Downtown
Univ. of Illinois–Chicago
Univ. of Illinois–Springfield
Univ. of Illinois–Urbana-Champaign
Univ. of Indianapolis
Univ. of Iowa
Univ. of Kansas
Univ. of Kentucky
Univ. of La Verne (CA)
Univ. of Louisiana–Lafayette
Univ. of Louisiana–Monroe
Univ. of Louisville (KY)
Univ. of Maine
Univ. of Mary Hardin-Baylor (TX)
Univ. of Mary Washington (VA)
Univ. of Maryland–Baltimore
   County
Univ. of Maryland–Coll. Park
Univ. of Maryland–Eastern Shore
Univ. of Massachusetts–Amherst
Univ. of Massachusetts–Boston
Univ. of Massachusetts–Dartmouth
Univ. of Massachusetts–Lowell
Univ. of Memphis
Univ. of Miami (FL)
Univ. of Michigan–Ann Arbor
Univ. of Michigan–Dearborn
Univ. of Michigan–Flint
Univ. of Minnesota–Duluth
Univ. of Minnesota–Morris
Univ. of Minnesota–Twin Cities
Univ. of Mississippi
Univ. of Missouri
Univ. of Missouri–Kansas City
Univ. of Missouri–St. Louis
Univ. of Mobile (AL)
Univ. of Montana
Univ. of Montevallo (AL)
Univ. of Mount Union (OH)
Univ. of Nebraska–Kearney
Univ. of Nebraska–Lincoln
Univ. of Nebraska–Omaha
Univ. of Nevada–Las Vegas
Univ. of Nevada–Reno
Univ. of New England (ME)
Univ. of New Hampshire
Univ. of New Haven (CT)
Univ. of New Mexico
Univ. of New Orleans
Univ. of North Alabama
Univ. of North Carolina–Asheville
Univ. of North Carolina–Chapel Hill
Univ. of North Carolina–Charlotte
Univ. of North Carolina–
   Greensboro
Univ. of North Carolina–Pembroke
Univ. of North Carolina–
   Wilmington
Univ. of North Dakota
Univ. of North Florida
Univ. of North Texas
Univ. of Northern Colorado
Univ. of Northern Iowa
Univ. of Notre Dame (IN)
Univ. of Oklahoma

Univ. of Oregon
Univ. of Pennsylvania
Univ. of Pittsburgh
Univ. of Pittsburgh–Bradford
Univ. of Pittsburgh–Johnstown
Univ. of Portland (OR)
Univ. of Puget Sound (WA)
Univ. of Redlands (CA)
Univ. of Rhode Island
Univ. of Richmond (VA)
Univ. of Rochester (NY)
Univ. of San Diego
Univ. of San Francisco
Univ. of Science and Arts of
    Oklahoma
Univ. of Scranton (PA)
Univ. of Sioux Falls (SD)
Univ. of South Alabama
Univ. of South Carolina
Univ. of South Carolina–Aiken
Univ. of South Carolina–Upstate
Univ. of South Dakota
Univ. of South Florida
Univ. of Southern California
Univ. of Southern Indiana
Univ. of Southern Maine
Univ. of Southern Mississippi
Univ. of St. Francis (IN)
Univ. of St. Mary (KS)
Univ. of St. Thomas (MN)
Univ. of St. Thomas (TX)
Univ. of Tampa (FL)
Univ. of Tennessee
Univ. of Tennessee–Chattanooga
Univ. of Tennessee–Martin
Univ. of Texas of the Permian Basin
Univ. of Texas–Arlington
Univ. of Texas–Austin
Univ. of Texas–Brownsville
Univ. of Texas–Dallas
Univ. of Texas–El Paso
Univ. of Texas–Pan American
Univ. of Texas–San Antonio
Univ. of Texas–Tyler
Univ. of the Cumberlands (KY)
Univ. of the District of Columbia
Univ. of the Incarnate Word (TX)
Univ. of the Ozarks (AR)
Univ. of the Pacific (CA)
Univ. of Toledo (OH)
Univ. of Tulsa (OK)
Univ. of Utah
Univ. of Vermont
Univ. of Virginia
Univ. of Virginia–Wise
Univ. of Washington
Univ. of West Alabama
Univ. of West Florida
Univ. of West Georgia
Univ. of Wisconsin–Eau Claire
Univ. of Wisconsin–Green Bay
Univ. of Wisconsin–La Crosse
Univ. of Wisconsin–Madison
Univ. of Wisconsin–Milwaukee
Univ. of Wisconsin–Parkside
Univ. of Wisconsin–Platteville
Univ. of Wisconsin–River Falls
Univ. of Wisconsin–Stevens Point
Univ. of Wisconsin–Superior
Univ. of Wisconsin–Whitewater
Univ. of Wyoming

Upper Iowa Univ.
Ursinus Coll. (PA)
Utah State Univ.
Utah Valley Univ.
Utica Coll. (NY)
Valdosta State Univ. (GA)
Valley City State Univ. (ND)
Valparaiso Univ. (IN)
Vanderbilt Univ. (TN)
Vanguard Univ. of Southern
    California
Vassar Coll. (NY)
Villanova Univ. (PA)
Virginia Commonwealth Univ.
Virginia Military Institute
Virginia State Univ.
Virginia Tech
Virginia Wesleyan Coll.
Viterbo Univ. (WI)
Wabash Coll. (IN)
Wagner Coll. (NY)
Wake Forest Univ. (NC)
Walsh Univ. (OH)
Warren Wilson Coll. (NC)
Wartburg Coll. (IA)
Washburn Univ. (KS)
Washington Adventist Univ. (MD)
Washington and Jefferson Coll.
    (PA)
Washington and Lee Univ. (VA)
Washington Coll. (MD)
Washington State Univ.
Washington Univ. in St. Louis
Wayland Baptist Univ. (TX)
Wayne State Coll. (NE)
Wayne State Univ. (MI)
Waynesburg Univ. (PA)
Weber State Univ. (UT)
Wellesley Coll. (MA)
Wells Coll. (NY)
Wesleyan Coll. (GA)
Wesleyan Univ. (CT)
West Chester Univ. of Pennsylvania
West Liberty Univ. (WV)
West Texas A&M Univ.
West Virginia State Univ.
West Virginia Univ.
West Virginia Univ. Institute of
    Technology
West Virginia Wesleyan Coll.
Western Carolina Univ. (NC)
Western Connecticut State Univ.
Western Illinois Univ.
Western Kentucky Univ.
Western Michigan Univ.
Western New England Coll. (MA)
Western New Mexico Univ.
Western Oregon Univ.
Western State Coll. of Colorado
Western Washington Univ.
Westminster Coll. (PA)
Westminster Coll. (UT)
Westminster Coll. (MO)
Westmont Coll. (CA)
Wheaton Coll. (MA)
Wheaton Coll. (IL)
Wheeling Jesuit Univ. (WV)
Whitman Coll. (WA)
Whittier Coll. (CA)
Whitworth Univ. (WA)
Wichita State Univ. (KS)

Wiley Coll. (TX)
Wilkes Univ. (PA)
Willamette Univ. (OR)
William Carey Univ. (MS)
William Jewell Coll. (MO)
William Paterson Univ. of New
    Jersey
Williams Coll. (MA)
Wilmington Coll. (OH)
Wilson Coll. (PA)
Wingate Univ. (NC)
Winthrop Univ. (SC)
Wisconsin Lutheran Coll.
Wittenberg Univ. (OH)
Wofford Coll. (SC)
Worcester Polytechnic Institute
    (MA)
Worcester State Coll. (MA)
Wright State Univ. (OH)
Xavier Univ. (OH)
Yale Univ. (CT)
Yeshiva Univ. (NY)
York Coll. of Pennsylvania
Youngstown State Univ. (OH)

Chiropractic (D.C.)

D'Youville Coll. (NY)

City/Urban, Community, and Regional Planning

Alabama Agricultural and
    Mechanical Univ.
Appalachian State Univ. (NC)
Arizona State Univ.
Auburn Univ. (AL)
Ball State Univ. (IN)
Bridgewater State Coll. (MA)
California Polytechnic State Univ.–
    San Luis Obispo
California State Polytechnic Univ.–
    Pomona
California State Univ.–San
    Bernardino
Catholic Univ. of America (DC)
Cornell Univ. (NY)
East Carolina Univ. (NC)
Eastern Michigan Univ.
Eastern Washington Univ.
Florida Atlantic Univ.
Frostburg State Univ. (MD)
Grand Valley State Univ. (MI)
Indiana Univ. of Pennsylvania
Iowa State Univ.
Jackson State Univ. (MS)
Massachusetts Institute of
    Technology
Miami Univ.–Oxford (OH)
Michigan State Univ.
Missouri State Univ.
New Mexico State Univ.
New York Univ.
Ohio State Univ.–Columbus
Plymouth State Univ. (NH)
Savannah Coll. of Art and Design
    (GA)
Sojourner-Douglass Coll. (MD)
Stanford Univ. (CA)
Temple Univ. (PA)
Texas A&M Univ.–Coll. Station

Texas State Univ.–San Marcos
Univ. of Akron (OH)
Univ. of Arizona
Univ. of California–Davis
Univ. of Florida
Univ. of Illinois–Urbana-Champaign
Univ. of Iowa
Univ. of Miami (FL)
Univ. of Missouri–Kansas City
Univ. of Nebraska–Lincoln
Univ. of Nevada–Las Vegas
Univ. of New Hampshire
Univ. of North Texas
Univ. of San Francisco
Univ. of Virginia
Univ. of Washington
Washington State Univ.
Westfield State Coll. (MA)

Civil Engineering

Alabama Agricultural and
    Mechanical Univ.
Arizona State Univ.
Auburn Univ. (AL)
Bethel Coll. (IN)
Boise State Univ. (ID)
Bradley Univ. (IL)
Brigham Young Univ.–Provo (UT)
Bucknell Univ. (PA)
California Polytechnic State Univ.–
    San Luis Obispo
California State Polytechnic Univ.–
    Pomona
California State Univ.–Chico
California State Univ.–Fullerton
California State Univ.–Long Beach
California State Univ.–Los Angeles
California State Univ.–Sacramento
Calvin Coll. (MI)
Carnegie Mellon Univ. (PA)
Carroll Coll. (MT)
Case Western Reserve Univ. (OH)
Central State Univ. (OH)
Christian Brothers Univ. (TN)
Clarkson Univ. (NY)
Clemson Univ. (SC)
Cleveland State Univ.
Colorado School of Mines
Colorado State Univ.
Columbia Univ. (NY)
Cooper Union (NY)
Cornell Univ. (NY)
CUNY–City Coll.
Drexel Univ. (PA)
Duke Univ. (NC)
Embry-Riddle Aeronautical Univ.
    (FL)
Florida A&M Univ.
Florida Atlantic Univ.
Florida Institute of Technology
Florida International Univ.
Florida State Univ.
George Mason Univ. (VA)
George Washington Univ. (DC)
Georgia Institute of Technology
Gonzaga Univ. (WA)
Hofstra Univ. (NY)
Howard Univ. (DC)
Idaho State Univ.

Illinois Institute of Technology
Indiana Univ.-Purdue Univ.–Fort
    Wayne
Iowa State Univ.
Jackson State Univ. (MS)
Johns Hopkins Univ. (MD)
Johnson and Wales Univ. (RI)
Kansas State Univ.
Lafayette Coll. (PA)
Lamar Univ. (TX)
Lawrence Technological Univ. (MI)
Lehigh Univ. (PA)
Louisiana State Univ.–Baton Rouge
Louisiana Tech Univ.
Loyola Marymount Univ. (CA)
Manhattan Coll. (NY)
Marquette Univ. (WI)
Massachusetts Institute of
    Technology
Merrimack Coll. (MA)
Michigan State Univ.
Michigan Technological Univ.
Minnesota State Univ.–Mankato
Mississippi State Univ.
Missouri Univ. of Science &
    Technology
Montana State Univ.
Morgan State Univ. (MD)
New England Coll. (NH)
New Jersey Institute of Technology
New Mexico Institute of Mining
    and Technology
New Mexico State Univ.
North Carolina A&T State Univ.
North Carolina State Univ.–Raleigh
North Dakota State Univ.
Northeastern Univ. (MA)
Northern Arizona Univ.
Northwestern Univ. (IL)
Norwich Univ. (VT)
Ohio Northern Univ.
Ohio State Univ.–Columbus
Ohio Univ.
Oklahoma State Univ.
Old Dominion Univ. (VA)
Oregon Institute of Technology
Oregon State Univ.
Pennsylvania State Univ.–Univ. Park
Polytechnic Institute of New York
    Univ. (NY)
Portland State Univ. (OR)
Prairie View A&M Univ. (TX)
Princeton Univ. (NJ)
Rensselaer Polytechnic Institute
    (NY)
Rice Univ. (TX)
Rose-Hulman Institute of
    Technology (IN)
Rutgers, the State Univ. of New
    Jersey–New Brunswick
San Diego State Univ.
San Francisco State Univ.
San Jose State Univ. (CA)
Santa Clara Univ. (CA)
Savannah State Univ. (GA)
Seattle Univ.
South Dakota School of Mines and
    Technology
South Dakota State Univ.
Southern Illinois Univ.–Carbondale
Southern Illinois Univ.–Edwardsville

Southern Univ. and A&M Coll. (LA)
Southern Univ.–New Orleans
St. Martin's Univ. (WA)
Stanford Univ. (CA)
Stevens Institute of Technology
(NJ)
Syracuse Univ. (NY)
Temple Univ. (PA)
Tennessee State Univ.
Tennessee Technological Univ.
Texas A&M Univ.–Coll. Station
Texas A&M Univ.–Kingsville
Texas Tech Univ.
The Citadel (SC)
Trine Univ. (IN)
Tufts Univ. (MA)
Tulane Univ. (LA)
United States Air Force Academy
(CO)
United States Coast Guard
Academy (CT)
United States Military Academy
(NY)
Univ. at Buffalo–SUNY
Univ. of Akron (OH)
Univ. of Alabama
Univ. of Alabama–Birmingham
Univ. of Alabama–Huntsville
Univ. of Alaska–Anchorage
Univ. of Alaska–Fairbanks
Univ. of Arizona
Univ. of Arkansas
Univ. of California–Berkeley
Univ. of California–Davis
Univ. of California–Irvine
Univ. of California–Los Angeles
Univ. of California–San Diego
Univ. of Central Florida
Univ. of Central Missouri
Univ. of Colorado–Boulder
Univ. of Colorado–Denver
Univ. of Connecticut
Univ. of Dayton (OH)
Univ. of Detroit Mercy
Univ. of Evansville (IN)
Univ. of Florida
Univ. of Hartford (CT)
Univ. of Hawaii–Manoa
Univ. of Houston
Univ. of Illinois–Chicago
Univ. of Illinois–Urbana-Champaign
Univ. of Iowa
Univ. of Kansas
Univ. of Kentucky
Univ. of Louisiana–Lafayette
Univ. of Louisville (KY)
Univ. of Maine
Univ. of Maryland–Coll. Park
Univ. of Massachusetts–Amherst
Univ. of Massachusetts–Dartmouth
Univ. of Massachusetts–Lowell
Univ. of Memphis
Univ. of Miami (FL)
Univ. of Michigan–Ann Arbor
Univ. of Minnesota–Twin Cities
Univ. of Mississippi
Univ. of Missouri
Univ. of Missouri–Kansas City
Univ. of Missouri–St. Louis
Univ. of Nebraska–Lincoln
Univ. of Nebraska–Omaha

Univ. of Nevada–Las Vegas
Univ. of Nevada–Reno
Univ. of New Hampshire
Univ. of New Haven (CT)
Univ. of New Mexico
Univ. of New Orleans
Univ. of North Carolina–Charlotte
Univ. of North Dakota
Univ. of North Florida
Univ. of Notre Dame (IN)
Univ. of Oklahoma
Univ. of Pennsylvania
Univ. of Pittsburgh
Univ. of Portland (OR)
Univ. of Rhode Island
Univ. of South Alabama
Univ. of South Carolina
Univ. of South Florida
Univ. of Southern California
Univ. of Tennessee
Univ. of Texas–Arlington
Univ. of Texas–Austin
Univ. of Texas–El Paso
Univ. of Texas–San Antonio
Univ. of Texas–Tyler
Univ. of the District of Columbia
Univ. of the Pacific (CA)
Univ. of Toledo (OH)
Univ. of Utah
Univ. of Vermont
Univ. of Virginia
Univ. of Washington
Univ. of Wisconsin–Madison
Univ. of Wisconsin–Milwaukee
Univ. of Wisconsin–Platteville
Univ. of Wyoming
Utah State Univ.
Valparaiso Univ. (IN)
Vanderbilt Univ. (TN)
Villanova Univ. (PA)
Virginia Military Institute
Virginia Tech
Washington State Univ.
Washington Univ. in St. Louis
Wayne State Univ. (MI)
West Virginia Univ.
West Virginia Univ. Institute of
Technology
Western Kentucky Univ.
Western Michigan Univ.
Widener Univ. (PA)
Worcester Polytechnic Institute
(MA)
Youngstown State Univ. (OH)

Civil Engineering Technologies/ Technicians

Alabama Agricultural and
Mechanical Univ.
Bluefield State Coll. (WV)
Central Connecticut State Univ.
Colorado State Univ.–Pueblo
Fairleigh Dickinson Univ. (NJ)
Fairmont State Univ. (WV)
Florida A&M Univ.
Georgia Southern Univ.
Lincoln Univ. (MO)
Metropolitan State Coll. of Denver
Michigan Technological Univ.

Missouri Western State Univ.
Montana State Univ.–Northern
Murray State Univ. (KY)
Old Dominion Univ. (VA)
Pennsylvania Coll. of Technology
Point Park Univ. (PA)
Rochester Institute of Technology
(NY)
South Carolina State Univ.
Southern Polytechnic State Univ.
(GA)
SUNY Institute of Technology–
Utica/Rome
Thomas Edison State Coll. (NJ)
Univ. of Houston–Downtown
Univ. of Maine
Univ. of Maryland–Eastern Shore
Univ. of Massachusetts–Lowell
Univ. of North Carolina–Charlotte
Univ. of Pittsburgh–Johnstown
Univ. of Tennessee–Martin
Univ. of Toledo (OH)
Vermont Technical Coll.
Western Kentucky Univ.
Youngstown State Univ. (OH)

Classical and Ancient Studies

Agnes Scott Coll. (GA)
Bates Coll. (ME)
Boston Univ.
Bowdoin Coll. (ME)
Brown Univ. (RI)
Bryn Mawr Coll. (PA)
Calvin Coll. (MI)
Coll. of Wooster (OH)
Columbia Univ. (NY)
Furman Univ. (SC)
Georgia State Univ.
Hillsdale Coll. (MI)
Lawrence Univ. (WI)
Loyola Marymount Univ. (CA)
Lycoming Coll. (PA)
Michigan State Univ.
Mount Holyoke Coll. (MA)
Ohio Wesleyan Univ.
Randolph Coll. (VA)
Rice Univ. (TX)
Rutgers, the State Univ. of New
Jersey–Newark
Santa Clara Univ. (CA)
St. Olaf Coll. (MN)
Univ. of California–Berkeley
Univ. of California–Davis
Univ. of California–Irvine
Univ. of California–Los Angeles
Univ. of California–Riverside
Univ. of California–Santa Cruz
Univ. of Chicago
Univ. of Illinois–Chicago
Univ. of Iowa
Univ. of Kansas
Univ. of Maryland–Baltimore
County
Univ. of Minnesota–Twin Cities
Univ. of Mount Union (OH)
Univ. of Nebraska–Lincoln
Univ. of Oregon
Univ. of Richmond (VA)
Univ. of Texas–Austin

Vassar Coll. (NY)
Washington Univ. in St. Louis
Wellesley Coll. (MA)
Wheaton Coll. (MA)

Classics and Classical Languages, Literatures, and Linguistics

Agnes Scott Coll. (GA)
Amherst Coll. (MA)
Assumption Coll. (MA)
Augustana Coll. (IL)
Austin Coll. (TX)
Ball State Univ. (IN)
Barnard Coll. (NY)
Baylor Univ. (TX)
Belmont Univ. (TN)
Beloit Coll. (WI)
Berea Coll. (KY)
Binghamton Univ.–SUNY
Boston Univ.
Bowdoin Coll. (ME)
Bowling Green State Univ. (OH)
Brandeis Univ. (MA)
Brown Univ. (RI)
Bryn Mawr Coll. (PA)
Bucknell Univ. (PA)
Butler Univ. (IN)
California State Univ.–Long Beach
Calvin Coll. (MI)
Carleton Coll. (MN)
Carroll Coll. (MT)
Carthage Coll. (WI)
Case Western Reserve University
(OH)
Catholic Univ. of America (DC)
Centenary Coll. of Louisiana
Centre Coll. (KY)
Claremont McKenna Coll. (CA)
Clark Univ. (MA)
Colby Coll. (ME)
Colgate Univ. (NY)
Coll. of Charleston (SC)
Coll. of St. Benedict (MN)
Coll. of the Holy Cross (MA)
Coll. of William and Mary (VA)
Colorado Coll.
Columbia Univ. (NY)
Concordia Coll.–Moorhead (MN)
Concordia Univ. (MI)
Connecticut Coll.
Cornell Coll. (IA)
Cornell Univ. (NY)
Creighton Univ. (NE)
CUNY–Brooklyn Coll.
CUNY–Lehman Coll.
CUNY–Queens Coll.
Dartmouth Coll. (NH)
Davidson Coll. (NC)
Denison Univ. (OH)
DePauw Univ. (IN)
Dickinson Coll. (PA)
Drew Univ. (NJ)
Duke Univ. (NC)
Duquesne Univ. (PA)
Earlham Coll. (IN)
Emory Univ. (GA)
Evergreen State Coll. (WA)
Florida State Univ.
Fordham Univ. (NY)

Franciscan Univ. of Steubenville
(OH)
Franklin and Marshall Coll. (PA)
Furman Univ. (SC)
George Washington Univ. (DC)
Georgetown Univ. (DC)
Georgia State Univ.
Gettysburg Coll. (PA)
Grand Valley State Univ. (MI)
Grinnell Coll. (IA)
Gustavus Adolphus Coll. (MN)
Hampden-Sydney Coll. (VA)
Hanover Coll. (IN)
Harvard Univ. (MA)
Haverford Coll. (PA)
Hillsdale Coll. (MI)
Hiram Coll. (OH)
Hobart and William Smith Colleges
(NY)
Hofstra Univ. (NY)
Hollins Univ. (VA)
Hope Coll. (MI)
Howard Univ. (DC)
Illinois Wesleyan Univ.
Indiana Univ.–Bloomington
John Carroll Univ. (OH)
Johns Hopkins Univ. (MD)
Kent State Univ. (OH)
Kenyon Coll. (OH)
Knox Coll. (IL)
La Salle Univ. (PA)
Lawrence Univ. (WI)
Lehigh Univ. (PA)
Lenoir-Rhyne Univ. (NC)
Louisiana State Univ.–Baton Rouge
Loyola Marymount Univ. (CA)
Loyola Univ. Chicago
Loyola Univ. Maryland
Loyola Univ. New Orleans
Luther Coll. (IA)
Macalester Coll. (MN)
Manhattanville Coll. (NY)
Marquette Univ. (WI)
Mercer Univ. (GA)
Miami Univ.–Oxford (OH)
Michigan State Univ.
Middlebury Coll. (VT)
Millsaps Coll. (MS)
Missouri State Univ.
Monmouth Coll. (IL)
Montclair State Univ. (NJ)
Moravian Coll. (PA)
Mount Holyoke Coll. (MA)
New York Univ.
North Central Coll. (IL)
North Dakota State Univ.
Northwestern Univ. (IL)
Oberlin Coll. (OH)
Ohio State Univ.–Columbus
Ohio Univ.
Ohio Wesleyan Univ.
Pacific Lutheran Univ. (WA)
Pennsylvania State Univ.–Univ. Park
Pitzer Coll. (CA)
Pomona Coll. (CA)
Princeton Univ. (NJ)
Purdue Univ.–West Lafayette (IN)
Randolph Coll. (VA)
Randolph-Macon Coll. (VA)
Reed Coll. (OR)
Rhodes Coll. (TN)

Rice Univ. (TX)
Ripon Coll. (WI)
Rockford Coll. (IL)
Rollins Coll. (FL)
Rutgers, the State Univ. of New
    Jersey–New Brunswick
Salisbury Univ. (MD)
Samford Univ. (AL)
San Diego State Univ.
San Francisco State Univ.
Santa Clara Univ. (CA)
Seattle Pacific Univ.
Seton Hall Univ. (NJ)
Sewanee–Univ. of the South (TN)
Siena Coll. (NY)
Skidmore Coll. (NY)
Smith Coll. (MA)
Southern Illinois Univ.–Carbondale
Southwestern Univ. (TX)
St. Anselm Coll. (NH)
St. John's Univ. (MN)
St. Joseph Coll. (CT)
St. Joseph's Coll. (ME)
St. Joseph's Univ. (PA)
St. Louis Univ.
St. Mary's Coll. of California
St. Michael's Coll. (VT)
St. Olaf Coll. (MN)
St. Peter's Coll. (NJ)
Stanford Univ. (CA)
Swarthmore Coll. (PA)
Syracuse Univ. (NY)
Temple Univ. (PA)
Texas Tech Univ.
Transylvania Univ. (KY)
Trinity Coll. (CT)
Truman State Univ. (MO)
Tufts Univ. (MA)
Tulane Univ. (LA)
Union Coll. (NY)
Univ. at Albany–SUNY
Univ. at Buffalo–SUNY
Univ. of Akron (OH)
Univ. of Arizona
Univ. of Arkansas
Univ. of California–Berkeley
Univ. of California–Davis
Univ. of California–Irvine
Univ. of California–Los Angeles
Univ. of California–Riverside
Univ. of California–Santa Barbara
Univ. of Chicago
Univ. of Colorado–Boulder
Univ. of Connecticut
Univ. of Dallas
Univ. of Evansville (IN)
Univ. of Florida
Univ. of Georgia
Univ. of Hawaii–Manoa
Univ. of Houston
Univ. of Illinois–Chicago
Univ. of Illinois–Urbana-Champaign
Univ. of Iowa
Univ. of Kansas
Univ. of Kentucky
Univ. of Maine
Univ. of Mary Washington (VA)
Univ. of Maryland–Coll. Park
Univ. of Massachusetts–Amherst
Univ. of Massachusetts–Boston
Univ. of Michigan–Ann Arbor

Univ. of Minnesota–Twin Cities
Univ. of Mississippi
Univ. of Missouri
Univ. of Montana
Univ. of Nebraska–Lincoln
Univ. of New Hampshire
Univ. of New Mexico
Univ. of North Carolina–Asheville
Univ. of North Carolina–Chapel Hill
Univ. of North Carolina–
    Greensboro
Univ. of North Texas
Univ. of Notre Dame (IN)
Univ. of Oklahoma
Univ. of Oregon
Univ. of Pennsylvania
Univ. of Pittsburgh
Univ. of Puget Sound (WA)
Univ. of Rhode Island
Univ. of Richmond (VA)
Univ. of Rochester (NY)
Univ. of Scranton (PA)
Univ. of South Carolina
Univ. of South Florida
Univ. of Southern California
Univ. of St. Thomas (MN)
Univ. of Tennessee
Univ. of Texas–Austin
Univ. of Texas–San Antonio
Univ. of Utah
Univ. of Vermont
Univ. of Virginia
Univ. of Washington
Univ. of Wisconsin–Madison
Univ. of Wisconsin–Milwaukee
Ursinus Coll. (PA)
Valparaiso Univ. (IN)
Vanderbilt Univ. (TN)
Vassar Coll. (NY)
Villanova Univ. (PA)
Virginia Wesleyan Coll.
Wabash Coll. (IN)
Wake Forest Univ. (NC)
Washington and Lee Univ. (VA)
Washington Univ. in St. Louis
Wayne State Univ. (MI)
Wellesley Coll. (MA)
West Chester Univ. of Pennsylvania
Western Michigan Univ.
Wheaton Coll. (IL)
Wheaton Coll. (MA)
Whitman Coll. (WA)
Willamette Univ. (OR)
Williams Coll. (MA)
Wright State Univ. (OH)
Xavier Univ. (OH)
Yale Univ. (CT)
Yeshiva Univ. (NY)

Clinical Child Psychology

Eastern Nazarene Coll. (MA)

Clinical Psychology

Alabama Agricultural and
    Mechanical Univ.
Auburn Univ. (AL)
Averett Univ. (VA)
Eastern Michigan Univ.
Eastern Nazarene Coll. (MA)

Gallaudet Univ. (DC)
Husson Univ. (ME)
Indiana Univ. of Pennsylvania
Jackson State Univ. (MS)
Keene State Coll. (NH)
Liberty Univ. (VA)
Lincoln Univ. (PA)
Our Lady of the Lake Univ. (TX)
Pacific Univ. (OR)
Tufts Univ. (MA)
Univ. of Kentucky
Univ. of Michigan–Flint
Washington Adventist Univ. (MD)

Clinical/Medical Laboratory Science and Allied Professions

Gwynedd-Mercy Coll. (PA)
Lake Superior State Univ. (MI)
Union Coll. (NE)
Univ. of Washington
Univ. of Wisconsin–Oshkosh

Cognitive Psychology and Psycholinguistics

Averett Univ. (VA)
California State Univ.–Stanislaus
Northwestern Univ. (IL)
Occidental Coll. (CA)
Pomona Coll. (CA)
Rice Univ. (TX)
Univ. of California–Los Angeles
Univ. of California–San Diego
Univ. of Connecticut
Univ. of Georgia
Univ. of Kansas
Univ. of Michigan–Ann Arbor
Vanderbilt Univ. (TN)
Wellesley Coll. (MA)

Cognitive Science

Brown Univ. (RI)
Carnegie Mellon Univ. (PA)
Case Western Reserve Univ. (OH)
Central Michigan Univ.
Dartmouth Coll. (NH)
George Fox Univ. (OR)
Hampshire Coll. (MA)
Lawrence Univ. (WI)
Lehigh Univ. (PA)
Massachusetts Institute of
    Technology
Rice Univ. (TX)
SUNY–Oswego
Univ. of California–Berkeley
Univ. of California–Los Angeles
Univ. of Evansville (IN)
Univ. of Pennsylvania
Univ. of Richmond (VA)
Univ. of Texas–Dallas
Vassar Coll. (NY)
Wellesley Coll. (MA)
Yale Univ. (CT)

Communication and Media Studies

Adelphi Univ. (NY)

Adrian Coll. (MI)
Alabama State Univ.
Albion Coll. (MI)
Albright Coll. (PA)
Alcorn State Univ. (MS)
Alderson-Broaddus Coll. (WV)
Alfred Univ. (NY)
Allegheny Coll. (PA)
Alma Coll. (MI)
Alvernia Univ. (PA)
Alverno Coll. (WI)
American International Coll. (MA)
American Univ. (DC)
Anderson Univ. (IN)
Anderson Univ. (SC)
Andrews Univ. (MI)
Angelo State Univ. (TX)
Anna Maria Coll. (MA)
Aquinas Coll. (MI)
Arcadia Univ. (PA)
Arizona State Univ.
Ashland Univ. (OH)
Auburn Univ.–Montgomery (AL)
Augsburg Coll. (MN)
Augusta State Univ. (GA)
Augustana Coll. (SD)
Aurora Univ. (IL)
Austin Coll. (TX)
Austin Peay State Univ. (TN)
Avila Univ. (MO)
Azusa Pacific Univ. (CA)
Baker Univ. (KS)
Baldwin-Wallace Coll. (OH)
Baptist Bible Coll. and Seminary
    (PA)
Barry Univ. (FL)
Barton Coll. (NC)
Baylor Univ. (TX)
Belhaven Univ. (MS)
Bellarmine Univ. (KY)
Bellevue Univ. (NE)
Belmont Univ. (TN)
Bemidji State Univ. (MN)
Benedict Coll. (SC)
Benedictine Coll. (KS)
Benedictine Univ. (IL)
Bennett Coll. (NC)
Berea Coll. (KY)
Bethany Coll. (WV)
Bethel Coll. (IN)
Bethel Coll. (KS)
Bethel Univ. (MN)
Biola Univ. (CA)
Black Hills State Univ. (SD)
Blackburn Coll. (IL)
Bloomfield Coll. (NJ)
Bloomsburg Univ. of Pennsylvania
Bluefield Coll. (VA)
Bluffton Univ. (OH)
Boston Univ.
Bradley Univ. (IL)
Brenau Univ. (GA)
Brewton-Parker Coll. (GA)
Bridgewater Coll. (VA)
Brigham Young Univ.–Provo (UT)
Brown Univ. (RI)
Bryan Coll. (TN)
Buena Vista Univ. (IA)
Buffalo State Coll.–SUNY
Butler Univ. (IN)
Cabrini Coll. (PA)

Caldwell Coll. (NJ)
California Baptist Univ.
California Lutheran Univ.
California State Univ.–Bakersfield
California State Univ.–Chico
California State Univ.–Dominguez
    Hills
California State Univ.–East Bay
California State Univ.–Fullerton
California State Univ.–Long Beach
California State Univ.–Los Angeles
California State Univ.–Sacramento
California State Univ.–San
    Bernardino
California State Univ.–Stanislaus
California Univ. of Pennsylvania
Calumet Coll. of St. Joseph (IN)
Calvin Coll. (MI)
Campbell Univ. (NC)
Canisius Coll. (NY)
Capital Univ. (OH)
Cardinal Stritch Univ. (WI)
Carlow Univ. (PA)
Carnegie Mellon Univ. (PA)
Carroll Univ. (WI)
Carson-Newman Coll. (TN)
Carthage Coll. (WI)
Catawba Coll. (NC)
Catholic Univ. of America (DC)
Cazenovia Coll. (NY)
Cedarville Univ. (OH)
Centenary Coll. (NJ)
Centenary Coll. of Louisiana
Central Christian Coll. (KS)
Central Coll. (IA)
Central Methodist Univ. (MO)
Central Michigan Univ.
Central Washington Univ.
Chaminade Univ. of Honolulu
Champlain Coll. (VT)
Chapman Univ. (CA)
Chatham Univ. (PA)
Christopher Newport Univ. (VA)
Claflin Univ. (SC)
Clarion Univ. of Pennsylvania
Clark Atlanta Univ.
Clark Univ. (MA)
Clarke Univ. (IA)
Clayton State Univ. (GA)
Clearwater Christian Coll. (FL)
Clemson Univ. (SC)
Cleveland State Univ.
Coastal Carolina Univ. (SC)
Coe Coll. (IA)
Coker Coll. (SC)
Colby-Sawyer Coll. (NH)
Coll. at Brockport–SUNY
Coll. of Charleston (SC)
Coll. of Mount St. Joseph (OH)
Coll. of Mount St. Vincent (NY)
Coll. of Notre Dame of Maryland
Coll. of Our Lady of the Elms (MA)
Coll. of St. Elizabeth (NJ)
Coll. of St. Joseph (VT)
Coll. of St. Scholastica (MN)
Coll. of the Ozarks (MO)
Coll. of Wooster (OH)
Colorado Christian Univ.
Colorado State Univ.–Pueblo
Columbia Coll. (SC)
Columbia Coll. (MO)

Concordia Coll.–Moorhead (MN)
Concordia Univ. (NE)
Concordia Univ. (MI)
Concordia Univ. (CA)
Concordia Univ. Texas
Concordia Univ.–St. Paul (MN)
Corban Univ. (OR)
Cornell Univ. (NY)
Cornerstone Univ. (MI)
Creighton Univ. (NE)
Crown Coll. (MN)
CUNY–City Coll.
CUNY–Coll. of Staten Island
CUNY–Hunter Coll.
CUNY–Lehman Coll.
CUNY–Queens Coll.
Curry Coll. (MA)
Dakota Wesleyan Univ. (SD)
Dallas Baptist Univ.
Davis and Elkins Coll. (WV)
Defiance Coll. (OH)
Denison Univ. (OH)
DePaul Univ. (IL)
DePauw Univ. (IN)
Dickinson State Univ. (ND)
Dillard Univ. (LA)
Dominican Univ. (IL)
Dominican Univ. of California
Dordt Coll. (IA)
Dowling Coll. (NY)
Drury Univ. (MO)
Duquesne Univ. (PA)
East Carolina Univ. (NC)
East Central Univ. (OK)
East Stroudsburg Univ. of
    Pennsylvania
East Tennessee State Univ.
East Texas Baptist Univ.
Eastern Connecticut State Univ.
Eastern Kentucky Univ.
Eastern Mennonite Univ. (VA)
Eastern Michigan Univ.
Eastern New Mexico Univ.
Eastern Univ. (PA)
Eastern Washington Univ.
Eckerd Coll. (FL)
Edgewood Coll. (WI)
Edinboro Univ. of Pennsylvania
Edward Waters Coll. (FL)
Elizabeth City State Univ. (NC)
Elon Univ. (NC)
Embry-Riddle Aeronautical Univ.
    (FL)
Emmanuel Coll. (GA)
Emmanuel Coll. (MA)
Emory and Henry Coll. (VA)
Emporia State Univ. (KS)
Endicott Coll. (MA)
Eureka Coll. (IL)
Evangel Univ. (MO)
Evergreen State Coll. (WA)
Excelsior Coll. (NY)
Fairfield Univ. (CT)
Fairleigh Dickinson Univ. (NJ)
Fairmont State Univ. (WV)
Fayetteville State Univ. (NC)
Ferris State Univ. (MI)
Fitchburg State Coll. (MA)
Florida A&M Univ.
Florida Atlantic Univ.
Florida Institute of Technology

Florida International Univ.
Florida State Univ.
Fontbonne Univ. (MO)
Fordham Univ. (NY)
Fort Hays State Univ. (KS)
Fort Lewis Coll. (CO)
Francis Marion Univ. (SC)
Franciscan Univ. of Steubenville
    (OH)
Franklin Pierce Univ. (NH)
Freed-Hardeman Univ. (TN)
Fresno Pacific Univ. (CA)
Frostburg State Univ. (MD)
Furman Univ. (SC)
Gallaudet Univ. (DC)
Gardner-Webb Univ. (NC)
Geneva Coll. (PA)
George Fox Univ. (OR)
George Mason Univ. (VA)
George Washington Univ. (DC)
Georgetown Coll. (KY)
Georgia Southern Univ.
Georgian Court Univ. (NJ)
Gordon Coll. (MA)
Goucher Coll. (MD)
Grace Coll. and Seminary (IN)
Graceland Univ. (IA)
Grambling State Univ. (LA)
Grand Valley State Univ. (MI)
Grand View Univ. (IA)
Green Mountain Coll. (VT)
Greenville Coll. (IL)
Gustavus Adolphus Coll. (MN)
Hamilton Coll. (NY)
Hamline Univ. (MN)
Hampshire Coll. (MA)
Hannibal-LaGrange Coll. (MO)
Hanover Coll. (IN)
Hardin-Simmons Univ. (TX)
Harding Univ. (AR)
Hawaii Pacific Univ.
Heidelberg Univ. (OH)
High Point Univ. (NC)
Hilbert Coll. (NY)
Hiram Coll. (OH)
Hobart and William Smith Colleges
    (NY)
Hofstra Univ. (NY)
Hollins Univ. (VA)
Holy Family Univ. (PA)
Hood Coll. (MD)
Hope Coll. (MI)
Houghton Coll. (NY)
Houston Baptist Univ.
Howard Payne Univ. (TX)
Howard Univ. (DC)
Huntington Univ. (IN)
Idaho State Univ.
Illinois State Univ.
Indiana Institute of Technology
Indiana State Univ.
Indiana Univ. East
Indiana Univ. Northwest
Indiana Univ. of Pennsylvania
Indiana Univ.–Kokomo
Indiana Univ.–South Bend
Indiana Univ.-Purdue Univ.–Fort
    Wayne
Indiana Univ.-Purdue Univ.–
    Indianapolis
Indiana Wesleyan Univ.

Iona Coll. (NY)
Ithaca Coll. (NY)
Jackson State Univ. (MS)
Jacksonville Univ. (FL)
James Madison Univ. (VA)
Jamestown Coll. (ND)
John Carroll Univ. (OH)
Johnson C. Smith Univ. (NC)
Judson Univ. (IL)
Juniata Coll. (PA)
Kansas Wesleyan Univ.
Kean Univ. (NJ)
Keene State Coll. (NH)
Kennesaw State Univ. (GA)
Kent State Univ. (OH)
Kentucky Wesleyan Coll.
Keuka Coll. (NY)
King's Coll. (PA)
La Roche Coll. (PA)
La Salle Univ. (PA)
La Sierra Univ. (CA)
Lake Erie Coll. (OH)
Lake Forest Coll. (IL)
Lamar Univ. (TX)
Lambuth Univ. (TN)
Lane Coll. (TN)
Lawrence Technological Univ. (MI)
Le Moyne Coll. (NY)
Lees-McRae Coll. (NC)
Lenoir-Rhyne Univ. (NC)
Lewis & Clark Coll. (OR)
Lewis Univ. (IL)
Lewis-Clark State Coll. (ID)
Liberty Univ. (VA)
Lincoln Univ. (PA)
Lindenwood Univ. (MO)
Lindsey Wilson Coll. (KY)
Linfield Coll. (OR)
Lipscomb Univ. (TN)
Longwood Univ. (VA)
Loras Coll. (IA)
Louisiana Coll.
Louisiana State Univ.–Baton Rouge
Louisiana State Univ.–Shreveport
Loyola Univ. Chicago
Loyola Univ. Maryland
Loyola Univ. New Orleans
Lubbock Christian Univ. (TX)
Luther Coll. (IA)
Lycoming Coll. (PA)
Lynchburg Coll. (VA)
Lyndon State Coll. (VT)
Lynn Univ. (FL)
Macon State Coll. (GA)
Madonna Univ. (MI)
Manchester Coll. (IN)
Manhattan Coll. (NY)
Mansfield Univ. of Pennsylvania
Marian Univ. (IN)
Marian Univ. (WI)
Marietta Coll. (OH)
Marist Coll. (NY)
Marquette Univ. (WI)
Martin Univ. (IN)
Mary Baldwin Coll. (VA)
Marylhurst Univ. (OR)
Marymount Manhattan Coll. (NY)
Marymount Univ. (VA)
Maryville Univ. of St. Louis (MO)
Massachusetts Institute of
    Technology

McDaniel Coll. (MD)
McKendree Univ. (IL)
McNeese State Univ. (LA)
Medaille Coll. (NY)
Menlo Coll. (CA)
Mercyhurst Coll. (PA)
Meredith Coll. (NC)
Merrimack Coll. (MA)
Mesa State Coll. (CO)
Messiah Coll. (PA)
Methodist Univ. (NC)
Miami Univ.–Oxford (OH)
Michigan State Univ.
Michigan Technological Univ.
MidAmerica Nazarene Univ. (KS)
Middle Tennessee State Univ.
Midwestern State Univ. (TX)
Miles Coll. (AL)
Millersville Univ. of Pennsylvania
Milligan Coll. (TN)
Millikin Univ. (IL)
Mills Coll. (CA)
Minnesota State Univ.–Mankato
Minnesota State Univ.–Moorhead
Minot State Univ. (ND)
Misericordia Univ. (PA)
Mississippi Coll.
Mississippi State Univ.
Mississippi Univ. for Women
Missouri Baptist Univ.
Missouri Southern State Univ.
Missouri State Univ.
Missouri Valley Coll.
Mitchell Coll. (CT)
Molloy Coll. (NY)
Monmouth Univ. (NJ)
Montana State Univ.–Billings
Montana State Univ.–Northern
Montclair State Univ. (NJ)
Morehead State Univ. (KY)
Morehouse Coll. (GA)
Morgan State Univ. (MD)
Morningside Coll. (IA)
Mount Mary Coll. (WI)
Mount St. Mary Coll. (NY)
Mount St. Mary's Univ. (MD)
Muhlenberg Coll. (PA)
Muskingum Univ. (OH)
National Univ. (CA)
Nazareth Coll. (NY)
Nebraska Wesleyan Univ.
Neumann Univ. (PA)
New Jersey City Univ.
New Mexico Highlands Univ.
New School (NY)
New York Institute of Technology
New York Univ.
Newberry Coll. (SC)
Niagara Univ. (NY)
Nicholls State Univ. (LA)
North Carolina A&T State Univ.
North Carolina Central Univ.
North Carolina State Univ.–Raleigh
North Central Coll. (IL)
North Central Univ. (MN)
North Dakota State Univ.
North Greenville Univ. (SC)
North Park Univ. (IL)
Northeastern Illinois Univ.
Northeastern Univ. (MA)
Northern Arizona Univ.

Northern Illinois Univ.
Northern Michigan Univ.
Northwest Christian Univ. (OR)
Northwest Nazarene Univ. (ID)
Northwestern Coll. (MN)
Northwestern Oklahoma State
    Univ.
Northwestern Univ. (IL)
Notre Dame Coll. of Ohio
Notre Dame de Namur Univ. (CA)
Nova Southeastern Univ. (FL)
Nyack Coll. (NY)
Oakland Univ. (MI)
Oakwood Univ. (AL)
Ohio Dominican Univ.
Ohio Northern Univ.
Ohio State Univ.–Columbus
Ohio Univ.
Oklahoma Baptist Univ.
Oklahoma City Univ.
Oklahoma Wesleyan Univ.
Olivet Coll. (MI)
Oral Roberts Univ. (OK)
Oregon Institute of Technology
Oregon State Univ.
Otterbein Coll. (OH)
Ouachita Baptist Univ. (AR)
Our Lady of the Lake Univ. (TX)
Pace Univ. (NY)
Pacific Lutheran Univ. (WA)
Palm Beach Atlantic Univ. (FL)
Park Univ. (MO)
Peace Coll. (NC)
Pennsylvania State Univ.–Univ. Park
Pepperdine Univ. (CA)
Pfeiffer Univ. (NC)
Philadelphia Univ.
Piedmont Coll. (GA)
Pikeville Coll. (KY)
Pine Manor Coll. (MA)
Pittsburg State Univ. (KS)
Plymouth State Univ. (NH)
Point Loma Nazarene Univ. (CA)
Point Park Univ. (PA)
Pomona Coll. (CA)
Portland State Univ. (OR)
Prairie View A&M Univ. (TX)
Prescott Coll. (AZ)
Principia Coll. (IL)
Purchase Coll.–SUNY
Purdue Univ.–Calumet (IN)
Purdue Univ.–North Central (IN)
Queens Univ. of Charlotte (NC)
Radford Univ. (VA)
Ramapo Coll. of New Jersey
Randolph Coll. (VA)
Regent Univ. (VA)
Regis Coll. (MA)
Regis Univ. (CO)
Reinhardt Univ. (GA)
Rensselaer Polytechnic Institute
    (NY)
Rhode Island Coll.
Richard Stockton Coll. of New
    Jersey
Ripon Coll. (WI)
Robert Morris Univ. (PA)
Roberts Wesleyan Coll. (NY)
Rochester Coll. (MI)
Rochester Institute of Technology
    (NY)

Rockhurst Univ. (MO)
Rocky Mountain Coll. (MT)
Roger Williams Univ. (RI)
Rollins Coll. (FL)
Roosevelt Univ. (IL)
Rosemont Coll. (PA)
Russell Sage Coll. (NY)
Rutgers, the State Univ. of New
    Jersey–New Brunswick
Sacred Heart Univ. (CT)
Saginaw Valley State Univ. (MI)
Salem Coll. (NC)
Salisbury Univ. (MD)
Salve Regina Univ. (RI)
Samford Univ. (AL)
San Diego State Univ.
San Jose State Univ. (CA)
Santa Clara Univ. (CA)
Scripps Coll. (CA)
Seattle Pacific Univ.
Seattle Univ.
Seton Hall Univ. (NJ)
Seton Hill Univ. (PA)
Shaw Univ. (NC)
Shenandoah Univ. (VA)
Shepherd Univ. (WV)
Shorter Coll. (GA)
Simmons Coll. (MA)
Simpson Coll. (IA)
Simpson Univ. (CA)
Slippery Rock Univ. of Pennsylvania
Sonoma State Univ. (CA)
Southeast Missouri State Univ.
Southeastern Louisiana Univ.
Southeastern Oklahoma State Univ.
Southeastern Univ. (FL)
Southern Connecticut State Univ.
Southern Illinois Univ.–Edwardsville
Southern Nazarene Univ. (OK)
Southern New Hampshire Univ.
Southern Polytechnic State Univ.
    (GA)
Southern Univ. and A&M Coll. (LA)
Southern Utah Univ.
Southern Vermont Coll.
Southern Wesleyan Univ. (SC)
Southwest Baptist Univ. (MO)
Southwest Minnesota State Univ.
Southwestern Coll. (KS)
Southwestern Univ. (TX)
Spalding Univ. (KY)
Spring Arbor Univ. (MI)
Spring Hill Coll. (AL)
Springfield Coll. (MA)
St. Ambrose Univ. (IA)
St. Andrews Presbyterian Coll. (NC)
St. Catherine Univ. (MN)
St. Edward's Univ. (TX)
St. Francis Coll. (NY)
St. Francis Univ. (PA)
St. Gregory's Univ. (OK)
St. John Fisher Coll. (NY)
St. Joseph's Coll. (IN)
St. Joseph's Univ. (PA)
St. Leo Univ. (FL)
St. Louis Univ.
St. Mary's Coll. (IN)
St. Mary's Coll. of California
St. Mary's Univ. of San Antonio
    (TX)

St. Norbert Coll. (WI)
St. Peter's Coll. (NJ)
St. Thomas Aquinas Coll. (NY)
St. Thomas Univ. (FL)
St. Vincent Coll. (PA)
St. Xavier Univ. (IL)
Stanford Univ. (CA)
Stephens Coll. (MO)
Sterling Coll. (KS)
Stetson Univ. (FL)
Stonehill Coll. (MA)
Suffolk Univ. (MA)
SUNY Coll.–Cortland
SUNY Coll.–Old Westbury
SUNY Coll.–Oneonta
SUNY–Fredonia
SUNY–Oswego
SUNY–Plattsburgh
Susquehanna Univ. (PA)
Syracuse Univ. (NY)
Tabor Coll. (KS)
Talladega Coll. (AL)
Tarleton State Univ. (TX)
Taylor Univ. (IN)
Temple Univ. (PA)
Texas A&M International Univ.
Texas A&M Univ.–Corpus Christi
Texas A&M Univ.–Kingsville
Texas Christian Univ.
Texas Lutheran Univ.
Texas State Univ.–San Marcos
Texas Wesleyan Univ.
Thiel Coll. (PA)
Thomas Edison State Coll. (NJ)
Thomas More Coll. (KY)
Tiffin Univ. (OH)
Toccoa Falls Coll. (GA)
Towson Univ. (MD)
Trevecca Nazarene Univ. (TN)
Trine Univ. (IN)
Trinity Christian Coll. (IL)
Trinity International Univ. (IL)
Trinity Univ. (DC)
Truman State Univ. (MO)
Tulane Univ. (LA)
Tusculum Coll. (TN)
Union Coll. (NE)
Union Institute and Univ. (OH)
Univ. at Buffalo–SUNY
Univ. of Akron (OH)
Univ. of Alabama
Univ. of Alabama–Birmingham
Univ. of Alaska–Fairbanks
Univ. of Arkansas
Univ. of Arkansas–Little Rock
Univ. of California–Berkeley
Univ. of California–Los Angeles
Univ. of California–Santa Barbara
Univ. of Central Florida
Univ. of Central Missouri
Univ. of Central Oklahoma
Univ. of Colorado–Boulder
Univ. of Colorado–Colorado
    Springs
Univ. of Colorado–Denver
Univ. of Connecticut
Univ. of Dayton (OH)
Univ. of Denver
Univ. of Detroit Mercy
Univ. of Evansville (IN)
Univ. of Florida

Univ. of Hartford (CT)
Univ. of Hawaii–Hilo
Univ. of Hawaii–Manoa
Univ. of Houston
Univ. of Illinois–Chicago
Univ. of Illinois–Springfield
Univ. of Illinois–Urbana-Champaign
Univ. of Indianapolis
Univ. of Iowa
Univ. of Kentucky
Univ. of La Verne (CA)
Univ. of Louisiana–Lafayette
Univ. of Louisiana–Monroe
Univ. of Louisville (KY)
Univ. of Maine
Univ. of Mary (ND)
Univ. of Mary Hardin-Baylor (TX)
Univ. of Maryland–Baltimore
    County
Univ. of Maryland–Coll. Park
Univ. of Maryland–Univ. Coll.
Univ. of Massachusetts–Amherst
Univ. of Memphis
Univ. of Miami (FL)
Univ. of Michigan–Ann Arbor
Univ. of Michigan–Dearborn
Univ. of Michigan–Flint
Univ. of Minnesota–Crookston
Univ. of Minnesota–Duluth
Univ. of Missouri
Univ. of Missouri–St. Louis
Univ. of Montana
Univ. of Mount Union (OH)
Univ. of Nebraska–Lincoln
Univ. of Nebraska–Omaha
Univ. of Nevada–Las Vegas
Univ. of Nevada–Reno
Univ. of New Hampshire
Univ. of New Haven (CT)
Univ. of New Orleans
Univ. of North Carolina–Asheville
Univ. of North Carolina–Chapel Hill
Univ. of North Carolina–Charlotte
Univ. of North Carolina–
    Greensboro
Univ. of North Carolina–Pembroke
Univ. of North Carolina–
    Wilmington
Univ. of North Dakota
Univ. of North Florida
Univ. of Northern Colorado
Univ. of Northern Iowa
Univ. of Oklahoma
Univ. of Oregon
Univ. of Pennsylvania
Univ. of Pittsburgh
Univ. of Pittsburgh–Johnstown
Univ. of Portland (OR)
Univ. of Puget Sound (WA)
Univ. of Rhode Island
Univ. of Rio Grande (OH)
Univ. of San Diego
Univ. of San Francisco
Univ. of Science and Arts of
    Oklahoma
Univ. of Scranton (PA)
Univ. of Sioux Falls (SD)
Univ. of South Alabama
Univ. of South Carolina–Aiken
Univ. of South Carolina–Upstate
Univ. of South Dakota

Univ. of South Florida
Univ. of Southern California
Univ. of Southern Indiana
Univ. of Southern Maine
Univ. of Southern Mississippi
Univ. of St. Francis (IL)
Univ. of St. Francis (IN)
Univ. of St. Mary (KS)
Univ. of St. Thomas (MN)
Univ. of St. Thomas (TX)
Univ. of Tampa (FL)
Univ. of Tennessee
Univ. of Tennessee–Chattanooga
Univ. of Tennessee–Martin
Univ. of Texas of the Permian Basin
Univ. of Texas–Austin
Univ. of Texas–Brownsville
Univ. of Texas–El Paso
Univ. of Texas–Pan American
Univ. of Texas–San Antonio
Univ. of the Arts (PA)
Univ. of the Cumberlands (KY)
Univ. of the Incarnate Word (TX)
Univ. of the Ozarks (AR)
Univ. of the Pacific (CA)
Univ. of Toledo (OH)
Univ. of Tulsa (OK)
Univ. of Utah
Univ. of Virginia–Wise
Univ. of Washington
Univ. of West Florida
Univ. of Wisconsin–Eau Claire
Univ. of Wisconsin–La Crosse
Univ. of Wisconsin–Madison
Univ. of Wisconsin–Milwaukee
Univ. of Wisconsin–Oshkosh
Univ. of Wisconsin–Platteville
Univ. of Wisconsin–River Falls
Univ. of Wisconsin–Stevens Point
Univ. of Wisconsin–Superior
Univ. of Wyoming
Upper Iowa Univ.
Urbana Univ. (OH)
Ursinus Coll. (PA)
Utica Coll. (NY)
Valdosta State Univ. (GA)
Valley City State Univ. (ND)
Valparaiso Univ. (IN)
Vanderbilt Univ. (TN)
Vanguard Univ. of Southern
    California
Villanova Univ. (PA)
Virginia Commonwealth Univ.
Virginia State Univ.
Virginia Tech
Virginia Union Univ.
Wake Forest Univ. (NC)
Waldorf Coll. (IA)
Walsh Univ. (OH)
Warner Univ. (FL)
Wartburg Coll. (IA)
Washburn Univ. (KS)
Washington Adventist Univ. (MD)
Washington State Univ.
Wayland Baptist Univ. (TX)
Wayne State Coll. (NE)
Wayne State Univ. (MI)
Waynesburg Univ. (PA)
Weber State Univ. (UT)
Webster Univ. (MO)
Wesley Coll. (DE)

West Chester Univ. of Pennsylvania
West Liberty Univ. (WV)
West Virginia State Univ.
West Virginia Wesleyan Coll.
Western Carolina Univ. (NC)
Western Connecticut State Univ.
Western Illinois Univ.
Western Kentucky Univ.
Western Michigan Univ.
Western New England Coll. (MA)
Western State Coll. of Colorado
Western Washington Univ.
Westfield State Coll. (MA)
Westminster Coll. (PA)
Westminster Coll. (UT)
Westmont Coll. (CA)
Wheaton Coll. (IL)
Whitman Coll. (WA)
Whitworth Univ. (WA)
Wichita State Univ. (KS)
Widener Univ. (PA)
Wilberforce Univ. (OH)
Wiley Coll. (TX)
Wilkes Univ. (PA)
William Carey Univ. (MS)
William Jewell Coll. (MO)
William Paterson Univ. of New
    Jersey
Wilson Coll. (PA)
Wingate Univ. (NC)
Winston-Salem State Univ. (NC)
Winthrop Univ. (SC)
Wisconsin Lutheran Coll.
Wittenberg Univ. (OH)
Woodbury Univ. (CA)
Worcester State Coll. (MA)
Wright State Univ. (OH)
Yeshiva Univ. (NY)
York Coll. of Pennsylvania
Youngstown State Univ. (OH)

Communication Disorders Sciences and Services

Abilene Christian Univ. (TX)
Adelphi Univ. (NY)
Alabama Agricultural and
    Mechanical Univ.
Andrews Univ. (MI)
Appalachian State Univ. (NC)
Arizona State Univ.
Arkansas State Univ.–Jonesboro
Armstrong Atlantic State Univ. (GA)
Auburn Univ. (AL)
Augustana Coll. (SD)
Augustana Coll. (IL)
Baldwin-Wallace Coll. (OH)
Ball State Univ. (IN)
Baylor Univ. (TX)
Biola Univ. (CA)
Bloomsburg Univ. of Pennsylvania
Boston Univ.
Bowling Green State Univ. (OH)
Brescia Univ. (KY)
Bridgewater State Coll. (MA)
Brigham Young Univ.–Provo (UT)
Butler Univ. (IN)
California State Univ.–Chico
California State Univ.–East Bay
California State Univ.–Fresno

California State Univ.–Fullerton
California State Univ.–Long Beach
California State Univ.–Los Angeles
California State Univ.–Sacramento
California Univ. of Pennsylvania
Calvin Coll. (MI)
Case Western Reserve Univ. (OH)
Central Michigan Univ.
Clarion Univ. of Pennsylvania
Cleveland State Univ.
Coll. of Our Lady of the Elms (MA)
Coll. of St. Rose (NY)
Coll. of Wooster (OH)
Columbia Coll. (SC)
CUNY–Brooklyn Coll.
CUNY–Hunter Coll.
CUNY–Lehman Coll.
CUNY–Queens Coll.
Delta State Univ. (MS)
Duquesne Univ. (PA)
East Carolina Univ. (NC)
East Stroudsburg Univ. of
    Pennsylvania
Eastern Illinois Univ.
Eastern Kentucky Univ.
Eastern Michigan Univ.
Eastern New Mexico Univ.
Eastern Washington Univ.
Edinboro Univ. of Pennsylvania
Elmhurst Coll. (IL)
Elmira Coll. (NY)
Emerson Coll. (MA)
Florida State Univ.
Fontbonne Univ. (MO)
Fort Hays State Univ. (KS)
Geneva Coll. (PA)
George Washington Univ. (DC)
Grambling State Univ. (LA)
Hampton Univ. (VA)
Hardin-Simmons Univ. (TX)
Harding Univ. (AR)
Hofstra Univ. (NY)
Howard Univ. (DC)
Idaho State Univ.
Illinois State Univ.
Indiana State Univ.
Indiana Univ. of Pennsylvania
Indiana Univ.–Bloomington
Indiana Univ.-Purdue Univ.–Fort
    Wayne
Iona Coll. (NY)
Ithaca Coll. (NY)
Jackson State Univ. (MS)
James Madison Univ. (VA)
Kansas State Univ.
Kent State Univ. (OH)
La Salle Univ. (PA)
Lamar Univ. (TX)
Lambuth Univ. (TN)
Longwood Univ. (VA)
Louisiana State Univ.–Baton Rouge
Louisiana State Univ.–Shreveport
Louisiana Tech Univ.
Loyola Univ. Maryland
Maranatha Baptist Bible Coll. (WI)
Marquette Univ. (WI)
Marshall Univ. (WV)
Marymount Manhattan Coll. (NY)
Maryville Coll. (TN)
Marywood Univ. (PA)
Miami Univ.–Oxford (OH)

Michigan State Univ.
Minnesota State Univ.–Mankato
Minnesota State Univ.–Moorhead
Minot State Univ. (ND)
Misericordia Univ. (PA)
Mississippi Univ. for Women
Missouri State Univ.
Molloy Coll. (NY)
Murray State Univ. (KY)
Nazareth Coll. (NY)
New York Univ.
Nicholls State Univ. (LA)
Northeastern State Univ. (OK)
Northeastern Univ. (MA)
Northern Illinois Univ.
Northern Michigan Univ.
Northwestern Univ. (IL)
Ohio State Univ.–Columbus
Ohio Univ.
Oklahoma State Univ.
Old Dominion Univ. (VA)
Ouachita Baptist Univ. (AR)
Our Lady of the Lake Univ. (TX)
Pace Univ. (NY)
Pennsylvania State Univ.–Univ. Park
Portland State Univ. (OR)
Purdue Univ.–West Lafayette (IN)
Radford Univ. (VA)
Richard Stockton Coll. of New
    Jersey
Rockhurst Univ. (MO)
San Diego State Univ.
San Francisco State Univ.
San Jose State Univ. (CA)
Shaw Univ. (NC)
South Carolina State Univ.
Southeast Missouri State Univ.
Southeastern Louisiana Univ.
Southern Illinois Univ.–Carbondale
Southern Illinois Univ.–Edwardsville
Southern Univ. and A&M Coll. (LA)
St. Cloud State Univ. (MN)
St. John's Univ. (NY)
St. Louis Univ.
St. Xavier Univ. (IL)
Stephen F. Austin State Univ. (TX)
SUNY Coll.–Cortland
SUNY–Fredonia
SUNY–Geneseo
SUNY–Plattsburgh
Syracuse Univ. (NY)
Temple Univ. (PA)
Tennessee State Univ.
Texas A&M Univ.–Kingsville
Texas Christian Univ.
Texas State Univ.–San Marcos
Texas Woman's Univ.
Thiel Coll. (PA)
Towson Univ. (MD)
Truman State Univ. (MO)
Univ. at Buffalo–SUNY
Univ. of Akron (OH)
Univ. of Alabama
Univ. of Arizona
Univ. of Arkansas
Univ. of Central Arkansas
Univ. of Central Florida
Univ. of Central Missouri
Univ. of Central Oklahoma
Univ. of Colorado–Boulder
Univ. of Florida

Univ. of Georgia
Univ. of Hawaii–Manoa
Univ. of Houston
Univ. of Illinois–Urbana-Champaign
Univ. of Iowa
Univ. of Kansas
Univ. of Kentucky
Univ. of Louisiana–Lafayette
Univ. of Louisiana–Monroe
Univ. of Maine
Univ. of Maryland–Coll. Park
Univ. of Massachusetts–Amherst
Univ. of Michigan–Ann Arbor
Univ. of Minnesota–Duluth
Univ. of Minnesota–Twin Cities
Univ. of Mississippi
Univ. of Missouri
Univ. of Montevallo (AL)
Univ. of Nebraska–Kearney
Univ. of Nebraska–Lincoln
Univ. of Nevada–Reno
Univ. of New Hampshire
Univ. of New Mexico
Univ. of North Carolina–
    Greensboro
Univ. of North Dakota
Univ. of North Texas
Univ. of Northern Colorado
Univ. of Northern Iowa
Univ. of Oklahoma
Univ. of Oregon
Univ. of Pittsburgh
Univ. of Redlands (CA)
Univ. of Rhode Island
Univ. of Science and Arts of
    Oklahoma
Univ. of South Alabama
Univ. of South Dakota
Univ. of South Florida
Univ. of Southern Mississippi
Univ. of Tennessee
Univ. of Texas–Austin
Univ. of Texas–Dallas
Univ. of Texas–El Paso
Univ. of Texas–Pan American
Univ. of the District of Columbia
Univ. of the Pacific (CA)
Univ. of Toledo (OH)
Univ. of Tulsa (OK)
Univ. of Utah
Univ. of Vermont
Univ. of Virginia
Univ. of Washington
Univ. of West Georgia
Univ. of Wisconsin–Eau Claire
Univ. of Wisconsin–Madison
Univ. of Wisconsin–Milwaukee
Univ. of Wisconsin–River Falls
Univ. of Wisconsin–Stevens Point
Univ. of Wisconsin–Whitewater
Univ. of Wyoming
Utah State Univ.
Valdosta State Univ. (GA)
Washington State Univ.
Wayne State Univ. (MI)
West Chester Univ. of Pennsylvania
West Texas A&M Univ.
West Virginia Univ.
Western Carolina Univ. (NC)
Western Illinois Univ.
Western Michigan Univ.

Western Washington Univ.
Wichita State Univ. (KS)
Winthrop Univ. (SC)
Worcester State Coll. (MA)
Yeshiva Univ. (NY)

Communication, Journalism, and Related Programs

Abilene Christian Univ. (TX)
Albertus Magnus Coll. (CT)
Aquinas Coll. (MI)
Arkansas State Univ.–Jonesboro
Austin Univ. (TX)
Berry Coll. (GA)
Bethel Coll. (IN)
Bowling Green State Univ. (OH)
Bridgewater State Coll. (MA)
Bryant Univ. (RI)
Buena Vista Univ. (IA)
Carlow Univ. (PA)
Champlain Coll. (VT)
Chestnut Hill Coll. (PA)
Coll. of Santa Fe (NM)
Columbia Coll. (SC)
Concordia Univ. (NE)
Culver-Stockton Coll. (MO)
CUNY–Brooklyn Coll.
Elmhurst Coll. (IL)
Flagler Coll. (FL)
Fort Hays State Univ. (KS)
Friends Univ. (KS)
Hope Coll. (MI)
Humboldt State Univ. (CA)
Illinois Institute of Technology
Immaculata Univ. (PA)
Indiana Univ. Northwest
Ithaca Coll. (NY)
Judson Univ. (IL)
King Coll. (TN)
Lehigh Univ. (PA)
Madonna Univ. (MI)
Malone Univ. (OH)
Marquette Univ. (WI)
Mary Baldwin Coll. (VA)
Michigan Technological Univ.
Milwaukee School of Engineering
Mississippi Coll.
Mount St. Mary Coll. (NY)
New York Univ.
Norfolk State Univ. (VA)
Northern Arizona Univ.
Northwest Christian Univ. (OR)
Northwest Missouri State Univ.
Norwich Univ. (VT)
Ohio State Univ.–Columbus
Ohio Univ.
Oral Roberts Univ. (OK)
Pace Univ. (NY)
Pacific Univ. (OR)
Patten Univ. (CA)
Pennsylvania State Univ.–Univ. Park
Pepperdine Univ. (CA)
Polytechnic Institute of New York
    Univ. (NY)
Quincy Univ. (IL)
Rivier Coll. (NH)
Rochester Institute of Technology
    (NY)
San Diego State Univ.

St. Mary's Coll. of California
St. Mary's Univ. of San Antonio
    (TX)
SUNY Institute of Technology–
    Utica/Rome
SUNY–Fredonia
SUNY–Geneseo
Syracuse Univ. (NY)
Trevecca Nazarene Univ. (TN)
Trinity International Univ. (IL)
Tulane Univ. (LA)
Univ. of Central Missouri
Univ. of Evansville (IN)
Univ. of Findlay (OH)
Univ. of Miami (FL)
Univ. of Minnesota–Twin Cities
Univ. of Mississippi
Univ. of Missouri–Kansas City
Univ. of New England (ME)
Univ. of the Arts (PA)
Univ. of Wisconsin–Green Bay
Virginia Intermont Coll.
Virginia Wesleyan Coll.
Waldorf Coll. (IA)
Washington Univ. in St. Louis
Webster Univ. (MO)
Wesleyan Coll. (GA)
West Liberty Univ. (WV)
West Virginia Univ.
Western Michigan Univ.
Wingate Univ. (NC)
Wisconsin Lutheran Coll.

Communications Technologies/ Technicians and Support Services

Alverno Coll. (WI)
California State Univ.–Monterey Bay
Chestnut Hill Coll. (PA)
Fort Hays State Univ. (KS)
Framingham State Coll. (MA)
Hampton Univ. (VA)
Indiana Univ.–Bloomington
Touro Coll. (NY)
Univ. of Wisconsin–Platteville

Communications Technology/Technician

California State Univ.–Monterey Bay
Cedarville Univ. (OH)
Coll. of St. Rose (NY)
East Stroudsburg Univ. of
    Pennsylvania
Eastern Michigan Univ.
Lawrence Technological Univ. (MI)
Lesley Univ. (MA)
Lyndon State Coll. (VT)
Minot State Univ. (ND)
San Diego State Univ.
Southern Adventist Univ. (TN)
Suffolk Univ. (MA)
Texas A&M Univ.–Coll. Station
Univ. of Nebraska–Lincoln

Community Organization and Advocacy

Albertus Magnus Coll. (CT)

Alverno Coll. (WI)
Aquinas Coll. (MI)
Black Hills State Univ. (SD)
California State Univ.–Dominguez
	Hills
Central Michigan Univ.
Cornell Univ. (NY)
CUNY–John Jay Coll. of Criminal
	Justice
Delta State Univ. (MS)
Eastern Michigan Univ.
Elmira Coll. (NY)
Emory and Henry Coll. (VA)
Lynn Univ. (FL)
New Mexico State Univ.
New York Univ.
Northern State Univ. (SD)
Northwestern Univ. (IL)
Pace Univ. (NY)
Portland State Univ. (OR)
Prescott Coll. (AZ)
Providence Coll. (RI)
Southern Arkansas Univ.
Springfield Coll. (MA)
St. Leo Univ. (FL)
St. Martin's Univ. (WA)
St. Thomas Univ. (FL)
SUNY Empire State Coll.
Thomas Edison State Coll. (NJ)
Univ. of Alaska–Fairbanks
Univ. of Bridgeport (CT)
Univ. of Massachusetts–Boston
Univ. of New Mexico
Univ. of Tennessee
West Virginia Univ. Institute of
	Technology

Community Psychology

Clayton State Univ. (GA)
Mitchell Coll. (CT)
Montana State Univ.–Billings
National-Louis Univ. (IL)
New York Institute of Technology
North Georgia Coll. and State Univ.
Northwestern Univ. (IL)
Pikeville Coll. (KY)
Seton Hill Univ. (PA)
Southern Nazarene Univ. (OK)
Univ. of St. Mary (KS)
Walsh Univ. (OH)

Comparative Linguistics and Related Language Studies and Services

Albright Coll. (PA)
Arkansas Tech Univ.
Assumption Coll. (MA)
Auburn Univ.–Montgomery (AL)
Austin Peay State Univ. (TN)
Barnard Coll. (NY)
Baylor Univ. (TX)
Beloit Coll. (WI)
Benedict Coll. (SC)
Benedictine Univ. (IL)
Bennington Coll. (VT)
Binghamton Univ.–SUNY
Boise State Univ. (ID)
Boston Univ.
Brandeis Univ. (MA)

Brigham Young Univ.–Provo (UT)
Brown Univ. (RI)
Bryn Mawr Coll. (PA)
California Polytechnic State Univ.–
	San Luis Obispo
California State Univ.–Fresno
California State Univ.–Fullerton
California State Univ.–Long Beach
California State Univ.–Northridge
Cameron Univ. (OK)
Carnegie Mellon Univ. (PA)
Case Western Reserve Univ. (OH)
Centenary Coll. of Louisiana
Central Coll. (IA)
Central Washington Univ.
Clark Univ. (MA)
Cleveland State Univ.
Coll. of Mount St. Vincent (NY)
Coll. of Notre Dame of Maryland
Coll. of the Holy Cross (MA)
Coll. of William and Mary (VA)
Coll. of Wooster (OH)
Colorado Coll.
Colorado State Univ.
Colorado State Univ.–Pueblo
Columbia Univ. (NY)
Converse Coll. (SC)
Cornell Univ. (NY)
Crown Coll. (MN)
CUNY–Baruch Coll.
CUNY–Brooklyn Coll.
CUNY–City Coll.
CUNY–Hunter Coll.
CUNY–Lehman Coll.
CUNY–Queens Coll.
Dartmouth Coll. (NH)
Delta State Univ. (MS)
Dowling Coll. (NY)
Duke Univ. (NC)
Duquesne Univ. (PA)
Earlham Coll. (IN)
East Tennessee State Univ.
Eastern Illinois Univ.
Eastern Michigan Univ.
Eckerd Coll. (FL)
Elmira Coll. (NY)
Emporia State Univ. (KS)
Florida Atlantic Univ.
Fordham Univ. (NY)
Fort Hays State Univ. (KS)
Framingham State Coll. (MA)
Francis Marion Univ. (SC)
Frostburg State Univ. (MD)
Gallaudet Univ. (DC)
Gannon Univ. (PA)
George Mason Univ. (VA)
Georgetown Univ. (DC)
Georgia State Univ.
Gordon Coll. (MA)
Grace Coll. and Seminary (IN)
Graceland Univ. (IA)
Hamilton Coll. (NY)
Hampshire Coll. (MA)
Hartwick Coll. (NY)
Harvard Univ. (MA)
Haverford Coll. (PA)
Heidelberg Univ. (OH)
High Point Univ. (NC)
Hobart and William Smith Colleges
	(NY)
Hofstra Univ. (NY)

Indiana Univ. Northwest
Indiana Univ.–Bloomington
Iowa State Univ.
Jackson State Univ. (MS)
Jacksonville State Univ. (AL)
James Madison Univ. (VA)
Johns Hopkins Univ. (MD)
Judson Coll. (AL)
Juniata Coll. (PA)
Kansas State Univ.
Kenyon Coll. (OH)
King Coll. (TN)
Knox Coll. (IL)
Lambuth Univ. (TN)
Lawrence Univ. (WI)
Lewis & Clark Coll. (OR)
Long Island Univ.–C.W. Post
	Campus (NY)
Longwood Univ. (VA)
Louisiana Coll.
Louisiana State Univ.–Shreveport
Lycoming Coll. (PA)
Macalester Coll. (MN)
Manhattan Coll. (NY)
Marian Univ. (IN)
Marian Univ. (WI)
Marshall Univ. (WV)
Massachusetts Institute of
	Technology
Mercyhurst Coll. (PA)
Metropolitan State Coll. of Denver
Miami Univ.–Oxford (OH)
Michigan State Univ.
Middle Tennessee State Univ.
Mills Coll. (CA)
Minnesota State Univ.–Moorhead
Minot State Univ. (ND)
Mississippi Coll.
Mississippi State Univ.
Monmouth Univ. (NJ)
Montana State Univ.
Montclair State Univ. (NJ)
Nazareth Coll. (NY)
New Mexico State Univ.
New York Univ.
Newberry Coll. (SC)
Northeastern Univ. (MA)
Northern Arizona Univ.
Northwestern Univ. (IL)
Oakland Univ. (MI)
Ohio State Univ.–Columbus
Ohio Univ.
Old Dominion Univ. (VA)
Pace Univ. (NY)
Pacific Univ. (OR)
Pennsylvania State Univ.–Univ. Park
Pittsburg State Univ. (KS)
Pitzer Coll. (CA)
Portland State Univ. (OR)
Presbyterian Coll. (SC)
Princeton Univ. (NJ)
Purchase Coll.–SUNY
Quincy Univ. (IL)
Radford Univ. (VA)
Ramapo Coll. of New Jersey
Reed Coll. (OR)
Rice Univ. (TX)
Richard Stockton Coll. of New
	Jersey
Ripon Coll. (WI)
Roosevelt Univ. (IL)

Rosemont Coll. (PA)
Rutgers, the State Univ. of New
	Jersey–New Brunswick
Samford Univ. (AL)
San Diego State Univ.
San Francisco State Univ.
San Jose State Univ. (CA)
Seattle Pacific Univ.
Seton Hall Univ. (NJ)
Smith Coll. (MA)
South Carolina State Univ.
Southern Adventist Univ. (TN)
Southern Illinois Univ.–Carbondale
Southern Illinois Univ.–Edwardsville
Spelman Coll. (GA)
St. Ambrose Univ. (IA)
St. Cloud State Univ. (MN)
St. Lawrence Univ. (NY)
St. Louis Univ.
St. Mary's Coll. of Maryland
St. Peter's Coll. (NJ)
Stanford Univ. (CA)
Stonehill Coll. (MA)
Suffolk Univ. (MA)
SUNY–Geneseo
SUNY–Oswego
SUNY–Stony Brook
Swarthmore Coll. (PA)
Syracuse Univ. (NY)
Temple Univ. (PA)
Tennessee State Univ.
Thomas Edison State Coll. (NJ)
Truman State Univ. (MO)
Tufts Univ. (MA)
Tulane Univ. (LA)
Union Coll. (NY)
Univ. at Albany–SUNY
Univ. at Buffalo–SUNY
Univ. of Alabama
Univ. of Alabama–Birmingham
Univ. of Alabama–Huntsville
Univ. of Alaska–Anchorage
Univ. of Alaska–Fairbanks
Univ. of Arizona
Univ. of California–Berkeley
Univ. of California–Davis
Univ. of California–Irvine
Univ. of California–Los Angeles
Univ. of California–Riverside
Univ. of California–San Diego
Univ. of California–Santa Barbara
Univ. of California–Santa Cruz
Univ. of Central Florida
Univ. of Central Oklahoma
Univ. of Chicago
Univ. of Colorado–Boulder
Univ. of Connecticut
Univ. of Dayton (OH)
Univ. of Delaware
Univ. of Florida
Univ. of Georgia
Univ. of Hartford (CT)
Univ. of Hawaii–Hilo
Univ. of Illinois–Urbana-Champaign
Univ. of Iowa
Univ. of Kansas
Univ. of Kentucky
Univ. of La Verne (CA)
Univ. of Louisiana–Lafayette
Univ. of Maine
Univ. of Maine–Fort Kent

Univ. of Mary Washington (VA)
Univ. of Maryland–Baltimore
	County
Univ. of Maryland–Coll. Park
Univ. of Massachusetts–Amherst
Univ. of Massachusetts–Lowell
Univ. of Memphis
Univ. of Michigan–Ann Arbor
Univ. of Minnesota–Twin Cities
Univ. of Mississippi
Univ. of Missouri
Univ. of Montana
Univ. of Montevallo (AL)
Univ. of Nebraska–Lincoln
Univ. of Nevada–Las Vegas
Univ. of New Hampshire
Univ. of New Mexico
Univ. of North Alabama
Univ. of North Carolina–Chapel Hill
Univ. of North Dakota
Univ. of Northern Colorado
Univ. of Northern Iowa
Univ. of Oklahoma
Univ. of Oregon
Univ. of Pennsylvania
Univ. of Pittsburgh
Univ. of Rhode Island
Univ. of Rochester (NY)
Univ. of San Francisco
Univ. of South Alabama
Univ. of South Carolina
Univ. of Southern California
Univ. of Southern Maine
Univ. of Southern Mississippi
Univ. of Tennessee–Chattanooga
Univ. of Texas–Arlington
Univ. of Texas–Austin
Univ. of Texas–El Paso
Univ. of Texas–Tyler
Univ. of Toledo (OH)
Univ. of Utah
Univ. of Virginia
Univ. of Virginia–Wise
Univ. of Washington
Univ. of Wisconsin–Madison
Univ. of Wisconsin–Milwaukee
Univ. of Wisconsin–Platteville
Univ. of Wisconsin–River Falls
Virginia Commonwealth Univ.
Virginia Military Institute
Virginia Tech
Virginia Wesleyan Coll.
Washington and Lee Univ. (VA)
Washington Coll. (MD)
Washington State Univ.
Washington Univ. in St. Louis
Wayne State Coll. (NE)
Wayne State Univ. (MI)
Weber State Univ. (UT)
West Chester Univ. of Pennsylvania
West Virginia Univ.
Western Washington Univ.
Westmont Coll. (CA)
Wichita State Univ. (KS)
Willamette Univ. (OR)
William Woods Univ. (MO)
Williams Coll. (MA)
Winthrop Univ. (SC)
Yale Univ. (CT)
York Coll. of Pennsylvania
Youngstown State Univ. (OH)

Adelphi Univ. (NY)
Alabama Agricultural and
    Mechanical Univ.
Albany State Univ. (GA)
Albright Coll. (PA)
Alcorn State Univ. (MS)
Alvernia Univ. (PA)
Alverno Coll. (WI)
American International Coll. (MA)
Andrews Univ. (MI)
Angelo State Univ. (TX)
Aquinas Coll. (MI)
Arcadia Univ. (PA)
Arkansas State Univ.–Jonesboro
Arkansas Tech Univ.
Armstrong Atlantic State Univ. (GA)
Atlantic Union Coll. (MA)
Auburn Univ. (AL)
Augusta State Univ. (GA)
Augustana Coll. (SD)
Austin Peay State Univ. (TN)
Avila Univ. (MO)
Azusa Pacific Univ. (CA)
Babson Coll. (MA)
Ball State Univ. (IN)
Barton Coll. (NC)
Beacon Coll. (FL)
Belhaven Univ. (MS)
Bellarmine Univ. (KY)
Bellevue Univ. (NE)
Belmont Abbey Coll. (NC)
Belmont Univ. (TN)
Benedict Coll. (SC)
Benedictine Univ. (IL)
Bennett Coll. (NC)
Bentley Univ. (MA)
Bethel Coll. (IN)
Bethel Univ. (MN)
Binghamton Univ.–SUNY
Biola Univ. (CA)
Bloomfield Coll. (NJ)
Bloomsburg Univ. of Pennsylvania
Bluefield State Coll. (WV)
Bluffton Univ. (OH)
Boise State Univ. (ID)
Bowie State Univ. (MD)
Bowling Green State Univ. (OH)
Bradley Univ. (IL)
Brigham Young Univ.–Hawaii
Brigham Young Univ.–Provo (UT)
Brown Univ. (RI)
Bryan Coll. (TN)
Bryant Univ. (RI)
Butler Univ. (IN)
Cabrini Coll. (PA)
Caldwell Coll. (NJ)
California Lutheran Univ.
California State Polytechnic Univ.–
    Pomona
California State Univ.–Chico
California State Univ.–Fresno
California State Univ.–Los Angeles
California State Univ.–Monterey Bay
California State Univ.–Northridge
California State Univ.–Sacramento
California State Univ.–San
    Bernardino
California State Univ.–Stanislaus

California Univ. of Pennsylvania
Calumet Coll. of St. Joseph (IN)
Calvin Coll. (MI)
Campbellsville Univ. (KY)
Carroll Univ. (WI)
Carson-Newman Coll. (TN)
Carthage Coll. (WI)
Catawba Coll. (NC)
Cedar Crest Coll. (PA)
Cedarville Univ. (OH)
Central Connecticut State Univ.
Central Michigan Univ.
Central Washington Univ.
Chaminade Univ. of Honolulu
Chancellor Univ. (OH)
Chapman Univ. (CA)
Chestnut Hill Coll. (PA)
Cheyney Univ. of Pennsylvania
Christian Brothers Univ. (TN)
Clarion Univ. of Pennsylvania
Clark Atlanta Univ.
Clarke Univ. (IA)
Clayton State Univ. (GA)
Clemson Univ. (SC)
Cleveland State Univ.
Coastal Carolina Univ. (SC)
Coll. at Brockport–SUNY
Coll. of Charleston (SC)
Coll. of Mount St. Joseph (OH)
Coll. of New Jersey
Coll. of Notre Dame of Maryland
Coll. of Our Lady of the Elms (MA)
Coll. of Santa Fe (NM)
Coll. of St. Joseph (VT)
Coll. of St. Rose (NY)
Coll. of St. Scholastica (MN)
Coll. of the Holy Cross (MA)
Coll. of the Ozarks (MO)
Coll. of William and Mary (VA)
Colorado Christian Univ.
Colorado Coll.
Colorado School of Mines
Colorado State Univ.
Columbia Coll. (SC)
Columbia Coll. (MO)
Columbia Univ. (NY)
Concordia Coll.–Moorhead (MN)
Concordia Univ. Chicago (IL)
Converse Coll. (SC)
Coppin State Univ. (MD)
Cornell Univ. (NY)
Covenant Coll. (GA)
Cumberland Univ. (TN)
CUNY–Baruch Coll.
CUNY–Brooklyn Coll.
CUNY–City Coll.
CUNY–Hunter Coll.
CUNY–John Jay Coll. of Criminal
    Justice
CUNY–Lehman Coll.
CUNY–Queens Coll.
CUNY–York Coll.
Curry Coll. (MA)
Dakota State Univ. (SD)
Dallas Baptist Univ.
Davenport Univ. (MI)
Defiance Coll. (OH)
Delaware State Univ.
Denison Univ. (OH)
DePaul Univ. (IL)
DePauw Univ. (IN)

Dickinson Coll. (PA)
Dickinson State Univ. (ND)
Dixie State Coll. of Utah
Dominican Coll. (NY)
Dordt Coll. (IA)
Dowling Coll. (NY)
Drake Univ. (IA)
Drury Univ. (MO)
Duke Univ. (NC)
Earlham Coll. (IN)
East Stroudsburg Univ. of
    Pennsylvania
East Tennessee State Univ.
East-West Univ. (IL)
Eastern Illinois Univ.
Eastern Kentucky Univ.
Eastern Michigan Univ.
Eastern Nazarene Coll. (MA)
Eastern New Mexico Univ.
Eastern Oregon Univ.
Eastern Washington Univ.
Edgewood Coll. (WI)
Edinboro Univ. of Pennsylvania
Edward Waters Coll. (FL)
Elizabeth City State Univ. (NC)
Elmhurst Coll. (IL)
Elon Univ. (NC)
Emmanuel Coll. (GA)
Emory and Henry Coll. (VA)
Emory Univ. (GA)
Emporia State Univ. (KS)
Eureka Coll. (IL)
Evangel Univ. (MO)
Evergreen State Coll. (WA)
Excelsior Coll. (NY)
Fairfield Univ. (CT)
Fairleigh Dickinson Univ. (NJ)
Fairmont State Univ. (WV)
Faulkner Univ. (AL)
Felician Coll. (NJ)
Ferris State Univ. (MI)
Fitchburg State Coll. (MA)
Florida A&M Univ.
Florida Atlantic Univ.
Florida Gulf Coast Univ.
Florida International Univ.
Florida Memorial Univ.
Florida State Univ.
Fontbonne Univ. (MO)
Fordham Univ. (NY)
Fort Hays State Univ. (KS)
Fort Lewis Coll. (CO)
Fort Valley State Univ. (GA)
Framingham State Coll. (MA)
Francis Marion Univ. (SC)
Franciscan Univ. of Steubenville
    (OH)
Franklin Coll. (IN)
Freed-Hardeman Univ. (TN)
Friends Univ. (KS)
Frostburg State Univ. (MD)
Furman Univ. (SC)
Gallaudet Univ. (DC)
Gannon Univ. (PA)
Geneva Coll. (PA)
George Fox Univ. (OR)
George Mason Univ. (VA)
George Washington Univ. (DC)
Georgetown Coll. (KY)
Georgia Coll. & State Univ.
Georgia Institute of Technology

Georgia Southern Univ.
Georgia Southwestern State Univ.
Georgia State Univ.
Georgian Court Univ. (NJ)
Goldey Beacom Coll. (DE)
Gonzaga Univ. (WA)
Grace Coll. and Seminary (IN)
Grand Valley State Univ. (MI)
Grand View Univ. (IA)
Granite State Coll. (NH)
Grove City Coll. (PA)
Guilford Coll. (NC)
Gwynedd-Mercy Coll. (PA)
Hamilton Coll. (NY)
Hampden-Sydney Coll. (VA)
Hannibal-LaGrange Coll. (MO)
Hanover Coll. (IN)
Harding Univ. (AR)
Hartwick Coll. (NY)
Harvey Mudd Coll. (CA)
Haverford Coll. (PA)
Heidelberg Univ. (OH)
Henderson State Univ. (AR)
Hobart and William Smith Colleges
    (NY)
Hodges Univ. (FL)
Hofstra Univ. (NY)
Hope Coll. (MI)
Houghton Coll. (NY)
Humboldt State Univ. (CA)
Huntington Univ. (IN)
Huston-Tillotson Univ. (TX)
Idaho State Univ.
Illinois Institute of Technology
Illinois State Univ.
Indiana Institute of Technology
Indiana State Univ.
Indiana Univ. Northwest
Indiana Univ. of Pennsylvania
Indiana Univ.–Bloomington
Indiana Univ.–Kokomo
Indiana Univ.-Purdue Univ.–
    Indianapolis
Iowa State Univ.
Iowa Wesleyan Coll.
Ithaca Coll. (NY)
Jackson State Univ. (MS)
Jacksonville State Univ. (AL)
Jacksonville Univ. (FL)
James Madison Univ. (VA)
Jamestown Coll. (ND)
Jarvis Christian Coll. (TX)
Johns Hopkins Univ. (MD)
Johnson C. Smith Univ. (NC)
Juniata Coll. (PA)
Kalamazoo Coll. (MI)
Kansas State Univ.
Kansas Wesleyan Univ.
Kean Univ. (NJ)
Keene State Coll. (NH)
Kennesaw State Univ. (GA)
Kentucky State Univ.
Kentucky Wesleyan Coll.
Kettering Univ. (MI)
King's Coll. (PA)
Kutztown Univ. of Pennsylvania
La Roche Coll. (PA)
La Salle Univ. (PA)
La Sierra Univ. (CA)
Lafayette Coll. (PA)
LaGrange Coll. (GA)

Lake Superior State Univ. (MI)
Lamar Univ. (TX)
Lambuth Univ. (TN)
Lander Univ. (SC)
Lane Coll. (TN)
Lawrence Technological Univ. (MI)
LeMoyne-Owen Coll. (TN)
Lenoir-Rhyne Univ. (NC)
Lewis-Clark State Coll. (ID)
Liberty Univ. (VA)
Life Univ. (GA)
Limestone Coll. (SC)
Lincoln Memorial Univ. (TN)
Lincoln Univ. (PA)
Lindenwood Univ. (MO)
Lipscomb Univ. (TN)
Livingstone Coll. (NC)
Lock Haven Univ. of Pennsylvania
Long Island Univ.–C.W. Post
    Campus (NY)
Louisiana State Univ.–Shreveport
Loyola Marymount Univ. (CA)
Loyola Univ. Chicago
Lubbock Christian Univ. (TX)
Lycoming Coll. (PA)
Lynchburg Coll. (VA)
Lyndon State Coll. (VT)
Macalester Coll. (MN)
Macon State Coll. (GA)
Madonna Univ. (MI)
Manchester Coll. (IN)
Manhattan Coll. (NY)
Manhattanville Coll. (NY)
Marian Univ. (WI)
Marist Coll. (NY)
Marquette Univ. (WI)
Mary Baldwin Coll. (VA)
Marygrove Coll. (MI)
Marymount Univ. (VA)
Maryville Coll. (TN)
Massachusetts Coll. of Liberal Arts
Mayville State Univ. (ND)
McDaniel Coll. (MD)
McMurry Univ. (TX)
McPherson Coll. (KS)
Medaille Coll. (NY)
Mercyhurst Coll. (PA)
Meredith Coll. (NC)
Merrimack Coll. (MA)
Mesa State Coll. (CO)
Methodist Univ. (NC)
Miami Univ.–Oxford (OH)
Michigan State Univ.
Michigan Technological Univ.
Midland Lutheran Coll. (NE)
Midwestern State Univ. (TX)
Miles Coll. (AL)
Millersville Univ. of Pennsylvania
Milligan Coll. (TN)
Mills Coll. (CA)
Millsaps Coll. (MS)
Minnesota State Univ.–Mankato
Minnesota State Univ.–Moorhead
Minot State Univ. (ND)
Misericordia Univ. (PA)
Mississippi Coll.
Mississippi State Univ.
Mississippi Valley State Univ.
Missouri Baptist Univ.
Missouri Southern State Univ.
Missouri State Univ.

Missouri Univ. of Science & Technology
Missouri Valley Coll.
Missouri Western State Univ.
Molloy Coll. (NY)
Monmouth Coll. (IL)
Monmouth Univ. (NJ)
Montana State Univ.–Northern
Montclair State Univ. (NJ)
Montreat Coll. (NC)
Morehead State Univ. (KY)
Morehouse Coll. (GA)
Morgan State Univ. (MD)
Mount Aloysius Coll. (PA)
Mount Marty Coll. (SD)
Mount Olive Coll. (NC)
Mount St. Mary Coll. (NY)
Mount St. Mary's Univ. (MD)
Mountain State Univ. (WV)
Muhlenberg Coll. (PA)
Murray State Univ. (KY)
National Univ. (CA)
National-Louis Univ. (IL)
Neumann Univ. (PA)
New Jersey City Univ.
New Jersey Institute of Technology
New Mexico Highlands Univ.
New Mexico Institute of Mining and Technology
New Mexico State Univ.
New York Institute of Technology
New York Univ.
Niagara Univ. (NY)
Norfolk State Univ. (VA)
North Carolina Wesleyan Coll.
North Georgia Coll. and State Univ.
Northeastern Univ. (MA)
Northern Arizona Univ.
Northern Kentucky Univ.
Northern Michigan Univ.
Northern State Univ. (SD)
Northwest Christian Univ. (OR)
Northwest Missouri State Univ.
Northwestern Coll. (IA)
Northwestern Oklahoma State Univ.
Northwestern Univ. (IL)
Northwood Univ. (MI)
Norwich Univ. (VT)
Notre Dame de Namur Univ. (CA)
Nova Southeastern Univ. (FL)
Nyack Coll. (NY)
Oakland City Univ. (IN)
Oakland Univ. (MI)
Oberlin Coll. (OH)
Ohio State Univ.–Columbus
Ohio Univ.
Oklahoma Baptist Univ.
Oklahoma Christian Univ.
Oklahoma City Univ.
Oklahoma Panhandle State Univ.
Oklahoma State Univ.
Old Dominion Univ. (VA)
Olivet Coll. (MI)
Olivet Nazarene Univ. (IL)
Oral Roberts Univ. (OK)
Oregon Institute of Technology
Oregon State Univ.
Otterbein Coll. (OH)
Our Lady of the Lake Univ. (TX)
Pace Univ. (NY)

Pacific Lutheran Univ. (WA)
Park Univ. (MO)
Pennsylvania State Univ.–Univ. Park
Peru State Coll. (NE)
Pfeiffer Univ. (NC)
Pikeville Coll. (KY)
Pittsburg State Univ. (KS)
Plymouth State Univ. (NH)
Point Park Univ. (PA)
Polytechnic Institute of New York Univ. (NY)
Post Univ. (CT)
Prairie View A&M Univ. (TX)
Prescott Coll. (AZ)
Principia Coll. (IL)
Quinnipiac Univ. (CT)
Ramapo Coll. of New Jersey
Randolph-Macon Coll. (VA)
Regis Coll. (MA)
Regis Univ. (CO)
Rensselaer Polytechnic Institute (NY)
Rhode Island Coll.
Rice Univ. (TX)
Rider Univ. (NJ)
Ripon Coll. (WI)
Rivier Coll. (NH)
Robert Morris Univ. (IL)
Rochester Institute of Tech. (NY)
Rocky Mountain Coll. (MT)
Roger Williams Univ. (RI)
Rollins Coll. (FL)
Rutgers, the State Univ. of New Jersey–Camden
Rutgers, the State Univ. of New Jersey–New Brunswick
Rutgers, the State Univ. of New Jersey–Newark
Sacred Heart Univ. (CT)
Sage Colleges–Albany (NY)
Saginaw Valley State Univ. (MI)
Salem State Coll. (MA)
Salisbury Univ. (MD)
San Diego State Univ.
San Francisco State Univ.
Scripps Coll. (CA)
Seton Hall Univ. (NJ)
Sewanee–Univ. of the South (TN)
Shaw Univ. (NC)
Shepherd Univ. (WV)
Shippensburg Univ. of Pennsylvania
Shorter Coll. (GA)
Siena Coll. (NY)
Simmons Coll. (MA)
Simpson Coll. (IA)
Skidmore Coll. (NY)
Slippery Rock Univ. of Pennsylvania
Sojourner-Douglass Coll. (MD)
Sonoma State Univ. (CA)
South Carolina State Univ.
South Dakota School of Mines and Technology
South Dakota State Univ.
Southeast Missouri State Univ.
Southeastern Oklahoma State Univ.
Southern Arkansas Univ.
Southern Nazarene Univ. (OK)
Southern New Hampshire Univ.
Southern Oregon Univ.
Southern Polytechnic State Univ. (GA)

Southern Utah Univ.
Southwest Baptist Univ. (MO)
Southwest Minnesota State Univ.
Southwestern Coll. (KS)
Southwestern Oklahoma State Univ.
Southwestern Univ. (TX)
Spelman Coll. (GA)
Springfield Coll. (MA)
St. Augustine's Coll. (NC)
St. Cloud State Univ. (MN)
St. Edward's Univ. (TX)
St. Francis Coll. (NY)
St. John Fisher Coll. (NY)
St. John's Univ. (NY)
St. Joseph's Coll. (IN)
St. Joseph's Univ. (PA)
St. Louis Univ.
St. Mary's Coll. of California
St. Mary's Coll. of Maryland
St. Mary's Univ. of San Antonio (TX)
St. Mary-of-the-Woods Coll. (IN)
St. Peter's Coll. (NJ)
St. Thomas Aquinas Coll. (NY)
St. Thomas Univ. (FL)
St. Vincent Coll. (PA)
Stanford Univ. (CA)
Stephen F. Austin State Univ. (TX)
Sterling Coll. (KS)
Stetson Univ. (FL)
Stillman Coll. (AL)
Suffolk Univ. (MA)
Sul Ross State Univ. (TX)
SUNY Coll.–Old Westbury
SUNY Coll.–Potsdam
SUNY Institute of Technology–Utica/Rome
SUNY–Fredonia
SUNY–Oswego
SUNY–Plattsburgh
Susquehanna Univ. (PA)
Swarthmore Coll. (PA)
Syracuse Univ. (NY)
Taylor Univ. (IN)
Temple Univ. (PA)
Tennessee Wesleyan Coll.
Texas A&M International Univ.
Texas A&M Univ.–Coll. Station
Texas A&M Univ.–Commerce
Texas A&M Univ.–Corpus Christi
Texas A&M Univ.–Kingsville
Texas Christian Univ.
Texas Lutheran Univ.
Texas State Univ.–San Marcos
Texas Tech Univ.
Texas Wesleyan Univ.
Texas Woman's Univ.
The Citadel (SC)
Thiel Coll. (PA)
Thomas Coll. (ME)
Thomas More Coll. (KY)
Tiffin Univ. (OH)
Touro Coll. (NY)
Transylvania Univ. (KY)
Trevecca Nazarene Univ. (TN)
Trine Univ. (IN)
Trinity Univ. (DC)
Troy Univ. (AL)
Truman State Univ. (MO)
Tufts Univ. (MA)

Tulane Univ. (LA)
Tuskegee Univ. (AL)
Union Coll. (NY)
Union Coll. (KY)
Union Coll. (NE)
United States Naval Academy (MD)
Univ. at Albany–SUNY
Univ. of Alabama
Univ. of Alabama–Birmingham
Univ. of Alabama–Huntsville
Univ. of Alaska–Anchorage
Univ. of Alaska–Fairbanks
Univ. of Alaska–Southeast
Univ. of Arizona
Univ. of Arkansas
Univ. of Arkansas–Little Rock
Univ. of Arkansas–Pine Bluff
Univ. of Baltimore (MD)
Univ. of California–Davis
Univ. of California–Irvine
Univ. of Central Arkansas
Univ. of Central Florida
Univ. of Central Missouri
Univ. of Central Oklahoma
Univ. of Charleston (WV)
Univ. of Chicago
Univ. of Colorado–Colorado Springs
Univ. of Colorado–Denver
Univ. of Delaware
Univ. of Denver
Univ. of Detroit Mercy
Univ. of Dubuque (IA)
Univ. of Evansville (IN)
Univ. of Florida
Univ. of Great Falls (MT)
Univ. of Hartford (CT)
Univ. of Hawaii–Manoa
Univ. of Houston
Univ. of Houston–Downtown
Univ. of Illinois–Urbana-Champaign
Univ. of Iowa
Univ. of Kansas
Univ. of Kentucky
Univ. of La Verne (CA)
Univ. of Maine
Univ. of Maine–Augusta
Univ. of Maine–Fort Kent
Univ. of Mary Hardin-Baylor (TX)
Univ. of Mary Washington (VA)
Univ. of Maryland–Coll. Park
Univ. of Maryland–Eastern Shore
Univ. of Maryland–Univ. Coll.
Univ. of Massachusetts–Boston
Univ. of Michigan–Ann Arbor
Univ. of Michigan–Dearborn
Univ. of Michigan–Flint
Univ. of Mississippi
Univ. of Missouri
Univ. of Missouri–Kansas City
Univ. of Missouri–St. Louis
Univ. of Mobile (AL)
Univ. of Nebraska–Kearney
Univ. of Nebraska–Lincoln
Univ. of Nevada–Reno
Univ. of New Hampshire
Univ. of New Haven (CT)
Univ. of New Mexico
Univ. of North Alabama
Univ. of North Carolina–Pembroke
Univ. of North Dakota

Univ. of North Florida
Univ. of North Texas
Univ. of Northern Iowa
Univ. of Notre Dame (IN)
Univ. of Oregon
Univ. of Pittsburgh–Johnstown
Univ. of Portland (OR)
Univ. of Redlands (CA)
Univ. of Rhode Island
Univ. of Richmond (VA)
Univ. of San Francisco
Univ. of Sioux Falls (SD)
Univ. of South Alabama
Univ. of South Carolina
Univ. of South Carolina–Upstate
Univ. of South Dakota
Univ. of South Florida
Univ. of Southern California
Univ. of Southern Indiana
Univ. of Southern Mississippi
Univ. of St. Francis (IL)
Univ. of St. Mary (KS)
Univ. of St. Thomas (MN)
Univ. of Tampa (FL)
Univ. of Tennessee–Chattanooga
Univ. of Texas of the Permian Basin
Univ. of Texas–Austin
Univ. of Texas–Brownsville
Univ. of Texas–Dallas
Univ. of Texas–El Paso
Univ. of Texas–Pan American
Univ. of Texas–San Antonio
Univ. of Texas–Tyler
Univ. of the Cumberlands (KY)
Univ. of the District of Columbia
Univ. of the Incarnate Word (TX)
Univ. of Tulsa (OK)
Univ. of Virginia
Univ. of Virginia–Wise
Univ. of Washington
Univ. of West Florida
Univ. of West Georgia
Univ. of Wisconsin–Eau Claire
Univ. of Wisconsin–Green Bay
Univ. of Wisconsin–La Crosse
Univ. of Wisconsin–Madison
Univ. of Wisconsin–Milwaukee
Univ. of Wisconsin–Oshkosh
Univ. of Wisconsin–Platteville
Univ. of Wisconsin–River Falls
Univ. of Wisconsin–Stevens Point
Univ. of Wisconsin–Stout
Univ. of Wisconsin–Whitewater
Upper Iowa Univ.
Utah State Univ.
Utica Coll. (NY)
Valdosta State Univ. (GA)
Valley City State Univ. (ND)
Vanderbilt Univ. (TN)
Vassar Coll. (NY)
Vermont Technical Coll.
Villanova Univ. (PA)
Virginia Commonwealth Univ.
Virginia State Univ.
Virginia Tech
Virginia Union Univ.
Viterbo Univ. (WI)
Voorhees Coll. (SC)
Wake Forest Univ. (NC)
Waldorf Coll. (IA)
Wartburg Coll. (IA)

Washburn Univ. (KS)
Washington and Jefferson Coll. (PA)
Washington and Lee Univ. (VA)
Washington Coll. (MD)
Washington State Univ.
Wayne State Coll. (NE)
Wayne State Univ. (MI)
Waynesburg Univ. (PA)
Webber International Univ. (FL)
Weber State Univ. (UT)
Webster Univ. (MO)
Wells Coll. (NY)
Wesleyan Coll. (GA)
West Chester Univ. of Pennsylvania
West Texas A&M Univ.
West Virginia Univ.
West Virginia Univ. Institute of Technology
West Virginia Wesleyan Coll.
Western Connecticut State Univ.
Western Governors Univ. (UT)
Western Illinois Univ.
Western Kentucky Univ.
Western Michigan Univ.
Western New Mexico Univ.
Western Oregon Univ.
Western State Coll. of Colorado
Western Washington Univ.
Westminster Coll. (MO)
Westmont Coll. (CA)
Whitworth Univ. (WA)
Wichita State Univ. (KS)
Wilberforce Univ. (OH)
Wiley Coll. (TX)
Wilkes Univ. (PA)
Willamette Univ. (OR)
William Paterson Univ. of New Jersey
William Woods Univ. (MO)
Wilmington Univ. (DE)
Winston-Salem State Univ. (NC)
Winthrop Univ. (SC)
Yale Univ. (CT)
Yeshiva Univ. (NY)
York Coll. of Pennsylvania
Youngstown State Univ. (OH)

Computer and Information Sciences and Support Services

Bloomsburg Univ. of Pennsylvania
Cabrini Coll. (PA)
Champlain Coll. (VT)
Coll. at Brockport–SUNY
CUNY–Coll. of Staten Island
Delaware Valley Coll. (PA)
DePaul Univ. (IL)
Dowling Coll. (NY)
Elmhurst Coll. (IL)
Ferris State Univ. (MI)
Humboldt State Univ. (CA)
Indiana Institute of Technology
Indiana Univ. East
Indiana Univ. Southeast
Indiana Univ.-Purdue Univ.– Indianapolis
Indiana Wesleyan Univ.
Johnson and Wales Univ. (RI)

Johnson State Coll. (VT)
Lehigh Univ. (PA)
Mayville State Univ. (ND)
Missouri Univ. of Science & Technology
Mount Marty Coll. (SD)
New York Univ.
Norwich Univ. (VT)
Ohio State Univ.–Columbus
Park Univ. (MO)
Pepperdine Univ. (CA)
Purdue Univ.–North Central (IN)
Regis Coll. (MA)
Rensselaer Polytechnic Institute (NY)
Southern Adventist Univ. (TN)
Southern Nazarene Univ. (OK)
Southwestern Coll. (KS)
SUNY Coll. of Agriculture and Technology–Cobleskill
SUNY Coll. of Technology–Delhi
Syracuse Univ. (NY)
Taylor Univ. (IN)
Towson Univ. (MD)
Univ. of Findlay (OH)
Univ. of Michigan–Ann Arbor
Univ. of Notre Dame (IN)
Univ. of Pittsburgh
Univ. of Wisconsin–Milwaukee
Utah State Univ.
Valley City State Univ. (ND)
Vanguard Univ. of Southern California
Virginia Union Univ.
William Woods Univ. (MO)
Wilmington Univ. (DE)
Woodbury Univ. (CA)

Computer Engineering

Abilene Christian Univ. (TX)
Allegheny Coll. (PA)
Arizona State Univ.
Auburn Univ. (AL)
Bellarmine Univ. (KY)
Benedict Coll. (SC)
Bethel Coll. (IN)
Bethune-Cookman Univ. (FL)
Brigham Young Univ.–Provo (UT)
Bucknell Univ. (PA)
California Polytechnic State Univ.– San Luis Obispo
California State Polytechnic Univ.– Pomona
California State Univ.–Chico
California State Univ.–Fresno
California State Univ.–Fullerton
California State Univ.–Long Beach
California State Univ.–Sacramento
Capital Univ. (OH)
Carnegie Mellon Univ. (PA)
Carroll Univ. (WI)
Case Western Reserve Univ. (OH)
Cedarville Univ. (OH)
Champlain Coll. (VT)
Christopher Newport Univ. (VA)
Claflin Univ. (SC)
Clarkson Univ. (NY)
Clemson Univ. (SC)
Cleveland State Univ.
Coll. of New Jersey

Colorado State Univ.
Columbia Univ. (NY)
CUNY–City Coll.
Drexel Univ. (PA)
Eastern Nazarene Coll. (MA)
Elizabethtown Coll. (PA)
Embry-Riddle Aeronautical Univ. (FL)
Florida A&M Univ.
Florida Atlantic Univ.
Florida Institute of Technology
Florida International Univ.
Florida State Univ.
George Mason Univ. (VA)
George Washington Univ. (DC)
Georgia Institute of Technology
Grand Valley State Univ. (MI)
Harding Univ. (AR)
Hofstra Univ. (NY)
Howard Univ. (DC)
Illinois Institute of Technology
Indiana Institute of Technology
Indiana Univ.-Purdue Univ.–Fort Wayne
Indiana Univ.-Purdue Univ.– Indianapolis
Iowa State Univ.
Jackson State Univ. (MS)
Johns Hopkins Univ. (MD)
Johnson C. Smith Univ. (NC)
Kansas State Univ.
Kettering Univ. (MI)
Lake Superior State Univ. (MI)
Lawrence Technological Univ. (MI)
Lehigh Univ. (PA)
LeTourneau Univ. (TX)
Lipscomb Univ. (TN)
Louisiana State Univ.–Baton Rouge
Manhattan Coll. (NY)
Marquette Univ. (WI)
Miami Univ.–Oxford (OH)
Michigan State Univ.
Michigan Technological Univ.
Milwaukee School of Engineering
Minnesota State Univ.–Mankato
Mississippi State Univ.
Missouri Univ. of Science & Technology
Monmouth Univ. (NJ)
Montana State Univ.
Montana Tech of the Univ. of Montana
National Univ. (CA)
New Jersey Institute of Technology
North Carolina State Univ.–Raleigh
North Dakota State Univ.
Northeastern Univ. (MA)
Northwestern Univ. (IL)
Norwich Univ. (VT)
Oakland Univ. (MI)
Ohio Northern Univ.
Oklahoma Christian Univ.
Old Dominion Univ. (VA)
Oral Roberts Univ. (OK)
Oregon State Univ.
Pacific Lutheran Univ. (WA)
Pennsylvania State Univ.–Univ. Park
Polytechnic Institute of New York Univ. (NY)
Portland State Univ. (OR)
Princeton Univ. (NJ)

Purdue Univ.–Calumet (IN)
Rensselaer Polytechnic Institute (NY)
Rice Univ. (TX)
Robert Morris Univ. (PA)
Rochester Institute of Technology (NY)
Roger Williams Univ. (RI)
Rose-Hulman Institute of Technology (IN)
San Diego State Univ.
San Jose State Univ. (CA)
Santa Clara Univ. (CA)
Seattle Pacific Univ.
South Dakota School of Mines and Technology
South Dakota State Univ.
Southern Illinois Univ.–Carbondale
Southern Illinois Univ.–Edwardsville
Southern Methodist Univ. (TX)
Southern Polytechnic State Univ. (GA)
St. Cloud State Univ. (MN)
St. Mary's Univ. of Minnesota
St. Mary's Univ. of San Antonio (TX)
Stevens Institute of Technology (NJ)
Stonehill Coll. (MA)
Suffolk Univ. (MA)
SUNY Coll. of Technology–Alfred
SUNY–Stony Brook
Syracuse Univ. (NY)
Taylor Univ. (IN)
Tennessee Technological Univ.
Texas A&M Univ.–Coll. Station
Texas A&M Univ.–Kingsville
Texas Tech Univ.
Trine Univ. (IN)
Trinity Coll. (CT)
Tufts Univ. (MA)
Tulane Univ. (LA)
United States Air Force Academy (CO)
Univ. at Buffalo–SUNY
Univ. of Akron (OH)
Univ. of Alabama–Huntsville
Univ. of Alaska–Fairbanks
Univ. of Arizona
Univ. of Arkansas
Univ. of California–Davis
Univ. of California–Irvine
Univ. of California–Los Angeles
Univ. of California–Riverside
Univ. of California–San Diego
Univ. of California–Santa Barbara
Univ. of California–Santa Cruz
Univ. of Central Florida
Univ. of Colorado–Boulder
Univ. of Colorado–Colorado Springs
Univ. of Connecticut
Univ. of Dayton (OH)
Univ. of Denver
Univ. of Evansville (IN)
Univ. of Florida
Univ. of Georgia
Univ. of Hartford (CT)
Univ. of Houston
Univ. of Illinois–Chicago
Univ. of Illinois–Urbana-Champaign

Univ. of Indianapolis
Univ. of Iowa
Univ. of Kansas
Univ. of Kentucky
Univ. of Louisiana–Lafayette
Univ. of Louisville (KY)
Univ. of Maine
Univ. of Maryland–Baltimore County
Univ. of Maryland–Coll. Park
Univ. of Massachusetts–Amherst
Univ. of Massachusetts–Dartmouth
Univ. of Massachusetts–Lowell
Univ. of Memphis
Univ. of Miami (FL)
Univ. of Michigan–Ann Arbor
Univ. of Michigan–Dearborn
Univ. of Minnesota–Duluth
Univ. of Minnesota–Twin Cities
Univ. of Missouri
Univ. of Missouri–Kansas City
Univ. of Nebraska–Lincoln
Univ. of Nebraska–Omaha
Univ. of Nevada–Las Vegas
Univ. of Nevada–Reno
Univ. of New Hampshire
Univ. of New Haven (CT)
Univ. of New Mexico
Univ. of North Carolina–Charlotte
Univ. of North Texas
Univ. of Notre Dame (IN)
Univ. of Oklahoma
Univ. of Pennsylvania
Univ. of Pittsburgh
Univ. of Rhode Island
Univ. of Scranton (PA)
Univ. of South Alabama
Univ. of South Carolina
Univ. of South Florida
Univ. of Southern California
Univ. of Tennessee
Univ. of Texas–Arlington
Univ. of Texas–Dallas
Univ. of the Pacific (CA)
Univ. of Toledo (OH)
Univ. of Utah
Univ. of Virginia
Univ. of Virginia–Wise
Univ. of Washington
Univ. of West Florida
Univ. of Wisconsin–Madison
Univ. of Wisconsin–Platteville
Univ. of Wyoming
Utah State Univ.
Valparaiso Univ. (IN)
Vanderbilt Univ. (TN)
Villanova Univ. (PA)
Virginia Commonwealth Univ.
Virginia Military Institute
Virginia State Univ.
Virginia Tech
Washington State Univ.
Washington Univ. in St. Louis
West Virginia Univ.
Western Michigan Univ.
Wichita State Univ. (KS)
Wilberforce Univ. (OH)
Wright State Univ. (OH)
York Coll. of Pennsylvania

Computer Engineering Technologies/Technicians

Andrews Univ. (MI)
California State Polytechnic Univ.–Pomona
California State Univ.–Long Beach
California Univ. of Pennsylvania
Central Connecticut State Univ.
Central Michigan Univ.
Central Washington Univ.
Cogswell Polytechnical Coll. (CA)
CUNY–New York City Coll. of Technology
Eastern Kentucky Univ.
Eastern Michigan Univ.
Eastern Washington Univ.
Farmingdale State Coll.–SUNY
Florida Atlantic Univ.
Georgia Southwestern State Univ.
Indiana State Univ.
Indiana Univ.-Purdue Univ.–Fort Wayne
Indiana Univ.-Purdue Univ.–Indianapolis
LeTourneau Univ. (TX)
Martin Univ. (IN)
Minnesota State Univ.–Mankato
Missouri Western State Univ.
Montana State Univ.–Northern
Norfolk State Univ. (VA)
Northeastern Univ. (MA)
Northern Kentucky Univ.
Northern Michigan Univ.
Oregon Institute of Technology
Prairie View A&M Univ. (TX)
Purdue Univ.–West Lafayette (IN)
Rochester Institute of Technology (NY)
Shawnee State Univ. (OH)
Southern Polytechnic State Univ. (GA)
SUNY Institute of Technology–Utica/Rome
Thomas Edison State Coll. (NJ)
Univ. of California–Los Angeles
Univ. of Central Florida
Univ. of Dayton (OH)
Univ. of Hartford (CT)
Univ. of Houston
Univ. of Houston–Downtown
Univ. of Memphis
Univ. of Minnesota–Crookston
Univ. of Southern Mississippi
Utah State Univ.
Vermont Technical Coll.
Wayne State Univ. (MI)
Weber State Univ. (UT)

Computer Programming

Bellevue Univ. (NE)
Bloomfield Coll. (NJ)
California Lutheran Univ.
Calvin Coll. (MI)
Champlain Coll. (VT)
Charleston Southern Univ. (SC)
City Univ. (WA)
Clayton State Univ. (GA)
Cleary Univ. (MI)

CUNY–Coll. of Staten Island
Davenport Univ. (MI)
Farmingdale State Coll.–SUNY
Friends Univ. (KS)
Gannon Univ. (PA)
Grand Valley State Univ. (MI)
Grand View Univ. (IA)
Hardin-Simmons Univ. (TX)
Indiana Univ.–South Bend
Indiana Wesleyan Univ.
Johnson and Wales Univ. (RI)
Limestone Coll. (SC)
Marist Coll. (NY)
Minot State Univ. (ND)
Missouri Southern State Univ.
Missouri Univ. of Science & Technology
Morningside Coll. (IA)
Mount Marty Coll. (SD)
National Univ. (CA)
New Jersey City Univ.
New Mexico Institute of Mining and Technology
Northern Michigan Univ.
Northwest Christian Univ. (OR)
Pepperdine Univ. (CA)
Purdue Univ.–Calumet (IN)
Southeast Missouri State Univ.
Stevenson Univ. (MD)
SUNY Coll. of Technology–Alfred
SUNY Coll. of Technology–Delhi
Temple Univ. (PA)
Tufts Univ. (MA)
Univ. of Evansville (IN)
Univ. of Illinois–Urbana-Champaign
Univ. of Michigan–Dearborn
Vermont Technical Coll.
Western Michigan Univ.
Youngstown State Univ. (OH)

Computer Science

Abilene Christian Univ. (TX)
Alabama State Univ.
Albion Coll. (MI)
Alderson-Broaddus Coll. (WV)
Allegheny Coll. (PA)
Alma Coll. (MI)
American International Coll. (MA)
American Univ. (DC)
Amherst Coll. (MA)
Anderson Univ. (IN)
Appalachian State Univ. (NC)
Arizona State Univ.
Assumption Coll. (MA)
Atlantic Union Coll. (MA)
Augustana Coll. (SD)
Augustana Coll. (IL)
Aurora Univ. (IL)
Austin Coll. (TX)
Baker Univ. (KS)
Baldwin-Wallace Coll. (OH)
Barnard Coll. (NY)
Barry Univ. (FL)
Baylor Univ. (TX)
Bellevue Univ. (NE)
Beloit Coll. (WI)
Bemidji State Univ. (MN)
Benedict Coll. (SC)
Benedictine Coll. (KS)
Bennington Coll. (VT)

Berry Coll. (GA)
Bethany Coll. (WV)
Bethel Coll. (IN)
Bethel Coll. (KS)
Bethune-Cookman Univ. (FL)
Blackburn Coll. (IL)
Bloomsburg Univ. of Pennsylvania
Bluffton Univ. (OH)
Boston Univ.
Bowdoin Coll. (ME)
Bradley Univ. (IL)
Brandeis Univ. (MA)
Briar Cliff Univ. (IA)
Bridgewater Coll. (VA)
Bridgewater State Coll. (MA)
Brigham Young Univ.–Hawaii
Brigham Young Univ.–Provo (UT)
Brown Univ. (RI)
Bryn Mawr Coll. (PA)
Buena Vista Univ. (IA)
Caldwell Coll. (NJ)
California Institute of Technology
California Lutheran Univ.
California Polytechnic State Univ.–San Luis Obispo
California State Univ.–Bakersfield
California State Univ.–Chico
California State Univ.–Dominguez Hills
California State Univ.–East Bay
California State Univ.–Fullerton
California State Univ.–Long Beach
California State Univ.–Los Angeles
California State Univ.–Sacramento
California State Univ.–San Bernardino
California State Univ.–San Marcos
California State Univ.–Stanislaus
Calvin Coll. (MI)
Cameron Univ. (OK)
Campbell Univ. (NC)
Canisius Coll. (NY)
Capital Univ. (OH)
Cardinal Stritch Univ. (WI)
Carleton Coll. (MN)
Carnegie Mellon Univ. (PA)
Carson-Newman Coll. (TN)
Carthage Coll. (WI)
Case Western Reserve Univ. (OH)
Catholic Univ. of America (DC)
Cedarville Univ. (OH)
Central Coll. (IA)
Central Methodist Univ. (MO)
Central Michigan Univ.
Central State Univ. (OH)
Centre Coll. (KY)
Chapman Univ. (CA)
Charleston Southern Univ. (SC)
Chicago State Univ.
Christopher Newport Univ. (VA)
Claflin Univ. (SC)
Clarke Univ. (IA)
Clarkson Univ. (NY)
Clemson Univ. (SC)
Coe Coll. (IA)
Coker Coll. (SC)
Colby Coll. (ME)
Colgate Univ. (NY)
Coll. of Santa Fe (NM)
Coll. of St. Benedict (MN)

Coll. of St. Elizabeth (NJ)
Coll. of the Ozarks (MO)
Coll. of Wooster (OH)
Columbia Coll. (MO)
Columbia Univ. (NY)
Concordia Coll.–Moorhead (MN)
Concordia Univ. (NE)
Concordia Univ. Texas
Connecticut Coll.
Corban Univ. (OR)
Cornell Coll. (IA)
Cornerstone Univ. (MI)
Creighton Univ. (NE)
CUNY–Baruch Coll.
CUNY–Coll. of Staten Island
CUNY–Lehman Coll.
CUNY–York Coll.
Daniel Webster Coll. (NH)
Dartmouth Coll. (NH)
Davis and Elkins Coll. (WV)
Delaware State Univ.
Dominican Univ. (IL)
Drew Univ. (NJ)
Drexel Univ. (PA)
Drury Univ. (MO)
Duquesne Univ. (PA)
East Carolina Univ. (NC)
Eastern Kentucky Univ.
Eastern Mennonite Univ. (VA)
Eastern Michigan Univ.
Eastern Nazarene Coll. (MA)
Eckerd Coll. (FL)
Elizabethtown Coll. (PA)
Elmhurst Coll. (IL)
Elon Univ. (NC)
Embry-Riddle Aeronautical Univ. (FL)
Fairleigh Dickinson Univ. (NJ)
Fayetteville State Univ. (NC)
Fisk Univ. (TN)
Fitchburg State Coll. (MA)
Florida Institute of Technology
Franciscan Univ. of Steubenville (OH)
Franklin Coll. (IN)
Franklin Pierce Univ. (NH)
Furman Univ. (SC)
Gallaudet Univ. (DC)
Gardner-Webb Univ. (NC)
George Mason Univ. (VA)
Georgetown Univ. (DC)
Georgia Southwestern State Univ.
Georgia State Univ.
Gettysburg Coll. (PA)
Gordon Coll. (MA)
Goshen Coll. (IN)
Goucher Coll. (MD)
Graceland Univ. (IA)
Grambling State Univ. (LA)
Grinnell Coll. (IA)
Gustavus Adolphus Coll. (MN)
Hampshire Coll. (MA)
Hampton Univ. (VA)
Hannibal-LaGrange Coll. (MO)
Harding Univ. (AR)
Harvard Univ. (MA)
Hawaii Pacific Univ.
Heidelberg Univ. (OH)
Hendrix Coll. (AR)
Heritage Univ. (WA)
High Point Univ. (NC)

Hofstra Univ. (NY)
Hood Coll. (MD)
Houghton Coll. (NY)
Illinois Coll.
Illinois Institute of Technology
Illinois State Univ.
Illinois Wesleyan Univ.
Indiana Institute of Technology
Indiana Univ. Southeast
Indiana Univ.–South Bend
Indiana Univ.-Purdue Univ.–Fort Wayne
Iona Coll. (NY)
Jamestown Coll. (ND)
John Brown Univ. (AR)
John Carroll Univ. (OH)
Kettering Univ. (MI)
King's Coll. (PA)
Knox Coll. (IL)
La Roche Coll. (PA)
La Salle Univ. (PA)
La Sierra Univ. (CA)
Lake Forest Coll. (IL)
Lakeland Coll. (WI)
Lamar Univ. (TX)
Lawrence Technological Univ. (MI)
Lawrence Univ. (WI)
Lebanon Valley Coll. (PA)
Lehigh Univ. (PA)
LeTourneau Univ. (TX)
Lewis & Clark Coll. (OR)
Lewis Univ. (IL)
Lewis-Clark State Coll. (ID)
Limestone Coll. (SC)
Lindenwood Univ. (MO)
Linfield Coll. (OR)
Lipscomb Univ. (TN)
Lock Haven Univ. of Pennsylvania
Long Island Univ.–C.W. Post Campus (NY)
Longwood Univ. (VA)
Loras Coll. (IA)
Louisiana State Univ.–Baton Rouge
Louisiana State Univ.–Shreveport
Louisiana Tech Univ.
Loyola Univ. Maryland
Luther Coll. (IA)
Lyon Coll. (AR)
Maharishi Univ. of Management (IA)
Malone Univ. (OH)
Mansfield Univ. of Pennsylvania
Marietta Coll. (OH)
Marist Coll. (NY)
Marymount Univ. (VA)
Maryville Univ. of St. Louis (MO)
Massachusetts Institute of Technology
Master's Coll. and Seminary (CA)
McKendree Univ. (IL)
McNeese State Univ. (LA)
Meredith Coll. (NC)
Merrimack Coll. (MA)
Messiah Coll. (PA)
Metropolitan State Coll. of Denver
Miami Univ.–Oxford (OH)
Middle Tennessee State Univ.
Middlebury Coll. (VT)
Millikin Univ. (IL)
Minnesota State Univ.–Mankato
Minnesota State Univ.–Moorhead

Mississippi Coll.
Missouri Univ. of Science & Technology
Monmouth Coll. (IL)
Montana State Univ.
Montana Tech of the Univ. of Montana
Moravian Coll. (PA)
Mount Holyoke Coll. (MA)
Mount Marty Coll. (SD)
Mount Mary Coll. (WI)
Mount Mercy Coll. (IA)
Mount Vernon Nazarene Univ. (OH)
Mountain State Univ. (WV)
Muskingum Univ. (OH)
National Univ. (CA)
Nebraska Wesleyan Univ.
New Mexico Institute of Mining and Technology
New York Univ.
Niagara Univ. (NY)
Nicholls State Univ. (LA)
North Carolina A&T State Univ.
North Carolina Central Univ.
North Carolina State Univ.–Raleigh
North Central Coll. (IL)
North Dakota State Univ.
Northeastern Illinois Univ.
Northeastern State Univ. (OK)
Northern Arizona Univ.
Northern Illinois Univ.
Northern Michigan Univ.
Northwest Nazarene Univ. (ID)
Northwestern Coll. (IA)
Northwestern Univ. (IL)
Norwich Univ. (VT)
Notre Dame de Namur University (CA)
Nova Southeastern Univ. (FL)
Ohio Northern Univ.
Ohio Univ.
Ohio Wesleyan Univ.
Oklahoma Christian Univ.
Ouachita Baptist Univ. (AR)
Pace Univ. (NY)
Pacific Union Coll. (CA)
Pacific Univ. (OR)
Palm Beach Atlantic Univ. (FL)
Park Univ. (MO)
Philander Smith Coll. (AR)
Plymouth State Univ. (NH)
Point Loma Nazarene Univ. (CA)
Pomona Coll. (CA)
Portland State Univ. (OR)
Presbyterian Coll. (SC)
Providence Coll. (RI)
Purdue Univ.–Calumet (IN)
Purdue Univ.–West Lafayette (IN)
Quincy Univ. (IL)
Radford Univ. (VA)
Regis Univ. (CO)
Rhodes Coll. (TN)
Roanoke Coll. (VA)
Roberts Wesleyan Coll. (NY)
Rochester Institute of Technology (NY)
Rockford Coll. (IL)
Rockhurst Univ. (MO)
Rocky Mountain Coll. (MT)
Roosevelt Univ. (IL)

Rose-Hulman Institute of Technology (IN)
Rust Coll. (MS)
Sacred Heart Univ. (CT)
Sage Colleges–Albany (NY)
Samford Univ. (AL)
Seattle Univ.
Seton Hill Univ. (PA)
Shaw Univ. (NC)
Sierra Nevada Coll. (NV)
Silver Lake Coll. (WI)
Simmons Coll. (MA)
Simpson Coll. (IA)
Smith Coll. (MA)
Sonoma State Univ. (CA)
Southeastern Louisiana Univ.
Southeastern Oklahoma State Univ.
Southern Adventist Univ. (TN)
Southern Connecticut State Univ.
Southern Illinois Univ.–Carbondale
Southern Illinois Univ.–Edwardsville
Southern Methodist Univ. (TX)
Southern Polytechnic State Univ. (GA)
Southern Univ. and A&M Coll. (LA)
Southern Univ.–New Orleans
Southern Utah Univ.
Southwest Baptist Univ. (MO)
Southwest Minnesota State Univ.
Spring Arbor Univ. (MI)
St. Ambrose Univ. (IA)
St. Anselm Coll. (NH)
St. Bonaventure Univ. (NY)
St. Edward's Univ. (TX)
St. Francis Univ. (PA)
St. John's Univ. (MN)
St. Martin's Univ. (WA)
St. Mary's Univ. of Minnesota
St. Michael's Coll. (VT)
St. Norbert Coll. (WI)
St. Olaf Coll. (MN)
St. Thomas Univ. (FL)
St. Xavier Univ. (IL)
Stetson Univ. (FL)
Stevens Institute of Technology (NJ)
Stillman Coll. (AL)
Stonehill Coll. (MA)
Suffolk Univ. (MA)
SUNY Coll.–Oneonta
SUNY–Geneseo
SUNY–Stony Brook
Tabor Coll. (KS)
Talladega Coll. (AL)
Tennessee State Univ.
Tennessee Technological Univ.
Texas A&M Univ.–Kingsville
Texas Coll.
Thomas Edison State Coll. (NJ)
Trinity Christian Coll. (IL)
Trinity Coll. (CT)
Tufts Univ. (MA)
Tulane Univ. (LA)
Tuskegee Univ. (AL)
Union Coll. (NE)
Union Univ. (TN)
United States Air Force Academy (CO)
United States Military Academy (NY)
Univ. at Buffalo–SUNY

Univ. of Akron (OH)
Univ. of Alaska–Anchorage
Univ. of Alaska–Fairbanks
Univ. of California–Berkeley
Univ. of California–Irvine
Univ. of California–Riverside
Univ. of California–San Diego
Univ. of California–Santa Barbara
Univ. of California–Santa Cruz
Univ. of Colorado–Boulder
Univ. of Connecticut
Univ. of Dayton (OH)
Univ. of Denver
Univ. of Detroit Mercy
Univ. of Findlay (OH)
Univ. of Georgia
Univ. of Great Falls (MT)
Univ. of Hawaii–Hilo
Univ. of Hawaii–Manoa
Univ. of Illinois–Chicago
Univ. of Illinois–Springfield
Univ. of Illinois–Urbana-Champaign
Univ. of Indianapolis
Univ. of Louisiana–Lafayette
Univ. of Louisiana–Monroe
Univ. of Maine–Farmington
Univ. of Mary Hardin-Baylor (TX)
Univ. of Maryland–Baltimore County
Univ. of Maryland–Coll. Park
Univ. of Massachusetts–Amherst
Univ. of Massachusetts–Lowell
Univ. of Memphis
Univ. of Miami (FL)
Univ. of Michigan–Ann Arbor
Univ. of Michigan–Flint
Univ. of Minnesota–Duluth
Univ. of Minnesota–Morris
Univ. of Minnesota–Twin Cities
Univ. of Montana
Univ. of Mount Union (OH)
Univ. of Nebraska–Omaha
Univ. of Nevada–Las Vegas
Univ. of Nevada–Reno
Univ. of New Hampshire
Univ. of New Orleans
Univ. of North Carolina–Asheville
Univ. of North Carolina–Chapel Hill
Univ. of North Carolina–Charlotte
Univ. of North Carolina–Greensboro
Univ. of North Carolina–Pembroke
Univ. of North Carolina–Wilmington
Univ. of Northern Iowa
Univ. of Oklahoma
Univ. of Pittsburgh
Univ. of Pittsburgh–Bradford
Univ. of Puget Sound (WA)
Univ. of Rio Grande (OH)
Univ. of Rochester (NY)
Univ. of San Diego
Univ. of Science and Arts of Oklahoma
Univ. of Scranton (PA)
Univ. of Sioux Falls (SD)
Univ. of Southern Maine
Univ. of St. Francis (IL)
Univ. of St. Thomas (MN)
Univ. of Tennessee
Univ. of Tennessee–Martin

Univ. of Texas–Arlington
Univ. of Texas–Pan American
Univ. of the District of Columbia
Univ. of the Pacific (CA)
Univ. of the Southwest (NM)
Univ. of Tulsa (OK)
Univ. of Utah
Univ. of Vermont
Univ. of Washington
Univ. of Wisconsin–Superior
Univ. of Wyoming
Ursinus Coll. (PA)
Utah Valley Univ.
Valparaiso Univ. (IN)
Virginia Military Institute
Virginia State Univ.
Virginia Wesleyan Coll.
Wagner Coll. (NY)
Walsh Univ. (OH)
Washington Adventist Univ. (MD)
Washington State Univ.
Washington Univ. in St. Louis
Weber State Univ. (UT)
Wellesley Coll. (MA)
Wesleyan Univ. (CT)
West Virginia Univ.
West Virginia Wesleyan Coll.
Western Carolina Univ. (NC)
Western Michigan Univ.
Western New England Coll. (MA)
Westfield State Coll. (MA)
Westminster Coll. (UT)
Westminster Coll. (PA)
Wheaton Coll. (IL)
Wheaton Coll. (MA)
Wheeling Jesuit Univ. (WV)
Widener Univ. (PA)
Wilberforce Univ. (OH)
Wiley Coll. (TX)
William Jewell Coll. (MO)
Williams Coll. (MA)
Wilmington Coll. (OH)
Wingate Univ. (NC)
Winston-Salem State Univ. (NC)
Wittenberg Univ. (OH)
Worcester Polytechnic Institute (MA)
Worcester State Coll. (MA)
Wright State Univ. (OH)
Xavier Univ. (OH)
York Coll. of Pennsylvania
Youngstown State Univ. (OH)

Computer Software and Media Applications

Baker Univ. (KS)
Baldwin-Wallace Coll. (OH)
Bellevue Univ. (NE)
California State Univ.–Chico
Cameron Univ. (OK)
Champlain Coll. (VT)
City Univ. (WA)
Clarkson Univ. (NY)
Columbia Coll. (IL)
CUNY–Lehman Coll.
Dakota State Univ. (SD)
Dakota Wesleyan Univ. (SD)
Dana Coll. (NE)
Daniel Webster Coll. (NH)
Davenport Univ. (MI)

Dominican Univ. (IL)
Drexel Univ. (PA)
Duquesne Univ. (PA)
Elmhurst Coll. (IL)
Hampshire Coll. (MA)
Husson Univ. (ME)
Illinois Institute of Technology
Indiana Institute of Technology
Indiana Univ.–South Bend
Indiana Wesleyan Univ.
Iona Coll. (NY)
Jacksonville Univ. (FL)
La Salle Univ. (PA)
Lasell Coll. (MA)
Lewis Univ. (IL)
Limestone Coll. (SC)
Louisiana Coll.
Marist Coll. (NY)
Memphis Coll. of Art
Minot State Univ. (ND)
Montana Tech of the Univ. of Montana
Mount Mary Coll. (WI)
National Univ. (CA)
Northern Michigan Univ.
Purdue Univ.–Calumet (IN)
Purdue Univ.–West Lafayette (IN)
Rochester Institute of Technology (NY)
Savannah Coll. of Art and Design (GA)
Stetson Univ. (FL)
SUNY Coll.–Oneonta
Thomas More Coll. (KY)
Trevecca Nazarene Univ. (TN)
Union Univ. (TN)
Univ. of Denver
Univ. of Dubuque (IA)
Univ. of Mary Hardin-Baylor (TX)
Univ. of Miami (FL)
Univ. of North Carolina–Asheville
Univ. of Pennsylvania
Univ. of Tampa (FL)
Univ. of the Incarnate Word (TX)
Univ. of Wisconsin–Stevens Point

Computer Systems Analysis

Arkansas Tech Univ.
Baldwin-Wallace Coll. (OH)
Bellevue Univ. (NE)
California State Polytechnic Univ.–Pomona
Davenport Univ. (MI)
Eastern Mennonite Univ. (VA)
Husson Univ. (ME)
Kent State Univ. (OH)
Marshall Univ. (WV)
Miami Univ.–Oxford (OH)
Missouri Univ. of Science & Technology
New Jersey City Univ.
Pace Univ. (NY)
Pittsburg State Univ. (KS)
Purdue Univ.–Calumet (IN)
Saginaw Valley State Univ. (MI)
Seattle Pacific Univ.
Shippensburg Univ. of Pennsylvania
Tabor Coll. (KS)
Univ. of Denver

Univ. of Great Falls (MT)
Univ. of Houston
Univ. of North Dakota
Univ. of Vermont
Univ. of Wisconsin–Whitewater
Vermont Technical Coll.
Washburn Univ. (KS)

Computer Systems Networking and Telecommunications

Baldwin-Wallace Coll. (OH)
Bellevue Univ. (NE)
Bloomfield Coll. (NJ)
Boston Univ.
California State Univ.–East Bay
Champlain Coll. (VT)
City Univ. (WA)
Daniel Webster Coll. (NH)
Davenport Univ. (MI)
Harris-Stowe State Univ. (MO)
Holy Names Univ. (CA)
Illinois State Univ.
Indiana Institute of Technology
Iona Coll. (NY)
Kansas State Univ.
Kean Univ. (NJ)
Lake Superior State Univ. (MI)
Michigan Technological Univ.
Northeastern State Univ. (OK)
Northern Michigan Univ.
Purdue Univ.–West Lafayette (IN)
Rochester Institute of Technology (NY)
Roosevelt Univ. (IL)
Sage Colleges–Albany (NY)
St. Ambrose Univ. (IA)
SUNY Coll. of Technology–Alfred
Univ. of Akron (OH)
Univ. of Denver
Univ. of Minnesota–Duluth
Univ. of Minnesota–Twin Cities
Univ. of North Carolina–Greensboro
Univ. of Northern Iowa
Univ. of Oklahoma
Univ. of Pennsylvania
Univ. of Wisconsin–Stout
Weber State Univ. (UT)
Western Illinois Univ.
Widener Univ. (PA)

Computer/Information Technology Administration and Management

Albertus Magnus Coll. (CT)
Bellevue Univ. (NE)
Daniel Webster Coll. (NH)
Husson Univ. (ME)
Indiana Wesleyan Univ.
Master's Coll. and Seminary (CA)
McPherson Coll. (KS)
Missouri Univ. of Science & Technology
Oklahoma Baptist Univ.
Purdue Univ.–Calumet (IN)
Univ. of Great Falls (MT)
Widener Univ. (PA)

Construction Engineering

Bradley Univ. (IL)
Iowa State Univ.
National Univ. (CA)
North Carolina State Univ.–Raleigh
North Dakota State Univ.
Oregon State Univ.
Southern Polytechnic State Univ. (GA)
Univ. of Alabama
Univ. of Illinois–Urbana-Champaign

Construction Engineering Technologies

California State Univ.–Long Beach
Farmingdale State Coll.–SUNY

Construction Management

California State Univ.–Sacramento
Univ. of Washington

Construction Trades

Boise State Univ. (ID)
Tuskegee Univ. (AL)
Univ. of Maryland–Eastern Shore
Vermont Technical Coll.

Cosmetology and Related Personal Grooming Services

Northern Michigan Univ.

Counseling Psychology

Alabama Agricultural and Mechanical Univ.
Auburn Univ. (AL)
Baptist Bible Coll. and Seminary (PA)
Bellevue Univ. (NE)
Bethel Univ. (MN)
Chestnut Hill Coll. (PA)
Coker Coll. (SC)
Coll. of Santa Fe (NM)
Coppin State Univ. (MD)
Eastern Michigan Univ.
Eastern Washington Univ.
Emmanuel Coll. (MA)
Grace Coll. and Seminary (IN)
Jamestown Coll. (ND)
Kutztown Univ. of Pennsylvania
Lesley Univ. (MA)
Liberty Univ. (VA)
Martin Univ. (IN)
Methodist Univ. (NC)
Mid-Continent Univ. (KY)
Midwestern State Univ. (TX)
Morningside Coll. (IA)
North Central Univ. (MN)
Our Lady of Holy Cross Coll. (LA)
Pacific Univ. (OR)
Paine Coll. (GA)
Palm Beach Atlantic Univ. (FL)
Prescott Coll. (AZ)
Rochester Coll. (MI)

Sage Colleges–Albany (NY)
South Dakota State Univ.
Southern Nazarene Univ. (OK)
Southwestern Assemblies of God Univ. (TX)
St. Joseph Coll. (CT)
St. Xavier Univ. (IL)
Texas A&M Univ.–Commerce
Texas Wesleyan Univ.
Toccoa Falls Coll. (GA)
Univ. of Florida
Univ. of La Verne (CA)
Univ. of North Alabama
Univ. of North Texas
Wayne State Coll. (NE)
West Virginia Wesleyan Coll.
Western Washington Univ.

Crafts/Craft Design, Folk Art, and Artisanry

Bowling Green State Univ. (OH)
Bridgewater State Coll. (MA)
Brigham Young Univ.–Provo (UT)
Indiana Univ.-Purdue Univ.–Fort Wayne
Kent State Univ. (OH)
Kutztown Univ. of Pennsylvania
Massachusetts Coll. of Art and Design
Rochester Institute of Technology (NY)
Univ. of Illinois–Urbana-Champaign
Univ. of the Arts (PA)
Virginia Commonwealth Univ.

Creative Writing

Agnes Scott Coll. (GA)
Alderson-Broaddus Coll. (WV)
Allegheny Coll. (PA)
Arkansas Tech Univ.
Asbury Univ. (KY)
Ashland Univ. (OH)
Bard Coll. at Simon's Rock (MA)
Beloit Coll. (WI)
Benedictine Univ. (IL)
Bennington Coll. (VT)
Bluffton Univ. (OH)
Bowling Green State Univ. (OH)
Brandeis Univ. (MA)
Bridgewater State Coll. (MA)
Brown Univ. (RI)
Bucknell Univ. (PA)
California Coll. of the Arts
California State Univ.–Long Beach
California State Univ.–Sacramento
Capital Univ. (OH)
Cardinal Stritch Univ. (WI)
Carlow Univ. (PA)
Carnegie Mellon Univ. (PA)
Carroll Univ. (WI)
Central Michigan Univ.
Chapman Univ. (CA)
Chatham Univ. (PA)
Colby Coll. (ME)
Coll. of Idaho (ID)
Coll. of Santa Fe (NM)
Colorado Coll.
Colorado State Univ.
Columbia Coll. (IL)

Columbia Univ. (NY)
Concordia Coll.–Moorhead (MN)
Converse Coll. (SC)
Cornerstone Univ. (MI)
Creighton Univ. (NE)
CUNY–Baruch Coll.
CUNY–Brooklyn Coll.
CUNY–Lehman Coll.
Dartmouth Coll. (NH)
Denison Univ. (OH)
DePauw Univ. (IN)
Dickinson State Univ. (ND)
Drake Univ. (IA)
Drury Univ. (MO)
Eastern Michigan Univ.
Eastern Nazarene Coll. (MA)
Eastern Washington Univ.
Eckerd Coll. (FL)
Elon Univ. (NC)
Emerson Coll. (MA)
Emory and Henry Coll. (VA)
Emory Univ. (GA)
Fairleigh Dickinson Univ. (NJ)
Fitchburg State Coll. (MA)
Franklin and Marshall Coll. (PA)
Gallaudet Univ. (DC)
George Washington Univ. (DC)
Grand Valley State Univ. (MI)
Green Mountain Coll. (VT)
Hamilton Coll. (NY)
Hampshire Coll. (MA)
Hiram Coll. (OH)
Hofstra Univ. (NY)
Hollins Univ. (VA)
Houghton Coll. (NY)
Indiana Wesleyan Univ.
Ithaca Coll. (NY)
Johns Hopkins Univ. (MD)
Johnson State Coll. (VT)
Knox Coll. (IL)
Lewis-Clark State Coll. (ID)
Linfield Coll. (OR)
Loras Coll. (IA)
Loyola Univ. Maryland
Loyola Univ. New Orleans
Marlboro Coll. (VT)
Massachusetts Institute of Technology
McMurry Univ. (TX)
Methodist Univ. (NC)
Miami Univ.–Oxford (OH)
Millikin Univ. (IL)
Minnesota State Univ.–Mankato
Moravian Coll. (PA)
New School (NY)
North Central Coll. (IL)
Northern Michigan Univ.
Northwestern Univ. (IL)
Oberlin Coll. (OH)
Ohio Northern Univ.
Ohio Univ.
Ohio Wesleyan Univ.
Oklahoma Christian Univ.
Pacific Univ. (OR)
Pratt Institute (NY)
Prescott Coll. (AZ)
Purchase Coll.–SUNY
Purdue Univ.–West Lafayette (IN)
Queens Univ. of Charlotte (NC)
Randolph Coll. (VA)
Roger Williams Univ. (RI)

Savannah Coll. of Art and Design (GA)
School of the Art Institute of Chicago
Seattle Univ.
Seton Hill Univ. (PA)
Southeastern Oklahoma State Univ.
Southern Methodist Univ. (TX)
Southern New Hampshire Univ.
Southern Vermont Coll.
Southwest Minnesota State Univ.
St. Andrews Presbyterian Coll. (NC)
St. Cloud State Univ. (MN)
St. Joseph's Coll. (IN)
St. Leo Univ. (FL)
St. Mary's Coll. (IN)
St. Mary's Coll. of California
Stephen F. Austin State Univ. (TX)
Stephens Coll. (MO)
Suffolk Univ. (MA)
SUNY–Oswego
Susquehanna Univ. (PA)
Union Coll. (NE)
Univ. of Arizona
Univ. of California–Riverside
Univ. of Charleston (WV)
Univ. of Evansville (IN)
Univ. of Findlay (OH)
Univ. of Florida
Univ. of Houston
Univ. of Iowa
Univ. of Maine–Farmington
Univ. of Miami (FL)
Univ. of Michigan–Ann Arbor
Univ. of Mount Union (OH)
Univ. of Nebraska–Omaha
Univ. of North Carolina–Wilmington
Univ. of Pittsburgh
Univ. of Pittsburgh–Bradford
Univ. of Pittsburgh–Johnstown
Univ. of Redlands (CA)
Univ. of San Francisco
Univ. of Southern California
Univ. of St. Thomas (MN)
Univ. of Tampa (FL)
Univ. of Texas–El Paso
Valparaiso Univ. (IN)
Warren Wilson Coll. (NC)
Weber State Univ. (UT)
Wells Coll. (NY)
West Virginia Wesleyan Coll.
Western Michigan Univ.
Western New England Coll. (MA)
Western Washington Univ.
Wheeling Jesuit Univ. (WV)
Widener Univ. (PA)

Criminal Justice and Corrections

Adelphi Univ. (NY)
Adrian Coll. (MI)
Alabama State Univ.
Albany State Univ. (GA)
Albertus Magnus Coll. (CT)
Alcorn State Univ. (MS)
Alfred Univ. (NY)
Alvernia Univ. (PA)
American Univ. (DC)
Anderson Univ. (IN)

Anderson Univ. (SC)
Angelo State Univ. (TX)
Anna Maria Coll. (MA)
Appalachian State Univ. (NC)
Arizona State Univ.
Arkansas State Univ.–Jonesboro
Armstrong Atlantic State Univ. (GA)
Ashland Univ. (OH)
Auburn Univ.–Montgomery (AL)
Augusta State Univ. (GA)
Aurora Univ. (IL)
Austin Peay State Univ. (TN)
Averett Univ. (VA)
Baldwin-Wallace Coll. (OH)
Ball State Univ. (IN)
Barry Univ. (FL)
Barton Coll. (NC)
Bay Path Coll. (MA)
Baylor Univ. (TX)
Becker Coll. (MA)
Bellarmine Univ. (KY)
Bellevue Univ. (NE)
Bemidji State Univ. (MN)
Benedict Coll. (SC)
Bethany Coll. (KS)
Bethel Coll. (IN)
Bethune-Cookman Univ. (FL)
Bloomsburg Univ. of Pennsylvania
Bluefield Coll. (VA)
Bluefield State Coll. (WV)
Bluffton Univ. (OH)
Boise State Univ. (ID)
Bowling Green State Univ. (OH)
Bradley Univ. (IL)
Briar Cliff Univ. (IA)
Bridgewater State Coll. (MA)
Buena Vista Univ. (IA)
Buffalo State Coll.–SUNY
Butler Univ. (IN)
Caldwell Coll. (NJ)
California Baptist Univ.
California Lutheran Univ.
California State Univ.–Bakersfield
California State Univ.–Chico
California State Univ.–Dominguez
    Hills
California State Univ.–East Bay
California State Univ.–Fullerton
California State Univ.–Long Beach
California State Univ.–Los Angeles
California State Univ.–Sacramento
California State Univ.–San
    Bernardino
California State Univ.–Stanislaus
California Univ. of Pennsylvania
Calumet Coll. of St. Joseph (IN)
Campbell Univ. (NC)
Campbellsville Univ. (KY)
Canisius Coll. (NY)
Carroll Univ. (WI)
Carthage Coll. (WI)
Castleton State Coll. (VT)
Cedar Crest Coll. (PA)
Cedarville Univ. (OH)
Centenary Coll. (NJ)
Central Christian Coll. (KS)
Central Methodist Univ. (MO)
Central Washington Univ.
Chadron State Coll. (NE)
Chaminade Univ. of Honolulu
Champlain Coll. (VT)

Charleston Southern Univ. (SC)
Chatham Univ. (PA)
Chestnut Hill Coll. (PA)
Chicago State Univ.
Chowan Univ. (NC)
Claflin Univ. (SC)
Clarion Univ. of Pennsylvania
Clark Atlanta Univ.
Clayton State Univ. (GA)
Coker Coll. (SC)
Coll. at Brockport–SUNY
Coll. of New Jersey
Coll. of Santa Fe (NM)
Coll. of St. Rose (NY)
Coll. of the Ozarks (MO)
Columbia Coll. (MO)
Concordia Univ. (MI)
Concordia Univ. Texas
Coppin State Univ. (MD)
Culver-Stockton Coll. (MO)
Cumberland Univ. (TN)
CUNY–John Jay Coll. of Criminal
    Justice
Curry Coll. (MA)
Dakota Wesleyan Univ. (SD)
Dallas Baptist Univ.
Dana Coll. (NE)
Davenport Univ. (MI)
Defiance Coll. (OH)
Delaware Valley Coll. (PA)
Delta State Univ. (MS)
DeSales Univ. (PA)
Dillard Univ. (LA)
Drexel Univ. (PA)
Drury Univ. (MO)
East Carolina Univ. (NC)
East Central Univ. (OK)
East Tennessee State Univ.
Eastern Kentucky Univ.
Eastern Nazarene Coll. (MA)
Eastern New Mexico Univ.
Edgewood Coll. (WI)
Edinboro Univ. of Pennsylvania
Edward Waters Coll. (FL)
Elizabeth City State Univ. (NC)
Elmira Coll. (NY)
Emporia State Univ. (KS)
Endicott Coll. (MA)
Eureka Coll. (IL)
Excelsior Coll. (NY)
Fairleigh Dickinson Univ. (NJ)
Fairmont State Univ. (WV)
Farmingdale State Coll.–SUNY
Faulkner Univ. (AL)
Fayetteville State Univ. (NC)
Ferris State Univ. (MI)
Ferrum Coll. (VA)
Fitchburg State Coll. (MA)
Florida Atlantic Univ.
Florida Gulf Coast Univ.
Florida International Univ.
Florida State Univ.
Fort Hays State Univ. (KS)
Fort Valley State Univ. (GA)
Franklin Pierce Univ. (NH)
Friends Univ. (KS)
Frostburg State Univ. (MD)
Gannon Univ. (PA)
George Mason Univ. (VA)
George Washington Univ. (DC)
Georgia Coll. & State Univ.

Georgia Southern Univ.
Georgia State Univ.
Georgian Court Univ. (NJ)
Gonzaga Univ. (WA)
Grace Coll. and Seminary (IN)
Graceland Univ. (IA)
Grambling State Univ. (LA)
Grand Valley State Univ. (MI)
Grand View Univ. (IA)
Granite State Coll. (NH)
Greenville Coll. (IL)
Guilford Coll. (NC)
Gustavus Adolphus Coll. (MN)
Gwynedd-Mercy Coll. (PA)
Hamline Univ. (MN)
Hannibal-LaGrange Coll. (MO)
Hardin-Simmons Univ. (TX)
Harding Univ. (AR)
Harris-Stowe State Univ. (MO)
Hawaii Pacific Univ.
Heidelberg Univ. (OH)
High Point Univ. (NC)
Hilbert Coll. (NY)
Hodges Univ. (FL)
Hofstra Univ. (NY)
Holy Family Univ. (PA)
Howard Univ. (DC)
Husson Univ. (ME)
Huston-Tillotson Univ. (TX)
Illinois State Univ.
Immaculata Univ. (PA)
Indiana Institute of Technology
Indiana Univ. East
Indiana Univ. Northwest
Indiana Univ. Southeast
Indiana Univ.–Bloomington
Indiana Univ.–Kokomo
Indiana Univ.-Purdue Univ.–Fort
    Wayne
Indiana Univ.-Purdue Univ.–
    Indianapolis
Indiana Wesleyan Univ.
Iona Coll. (NY)
Jackson State Univ. (MS)
Jacksonville State Univ. (AL)
Jamestown Coll. (ND)
Johnson and Wales Univ. (RI)
Judson Univ. (IL)
Kansas Wesleyan Univ.
Kean Univ. (NJ)
Kennesaw State Univ. (GA)
Kent State Univ. (OH)
Kentucky State Univ.
Kentucky Wesleyan Coll.
Keuka Coll. (NY)
King Coll. (TN)
King's Coll. (PA)
Kutztown Univ. of Pennsylvania
La Roche Coll. (PA)
La Salle Univ. (PA)
Lake Superior State Univ. (MI)
Lakeland Coll. (WI)
Lamar Univ. (TX)
Lambuth Univ. (TN)
Lane Coll. (TN)
Langston Univ. (OK)
Lasell Coll. (MA)
LeMoyne-Owen Coll. (TN)
Lewis Univ. (IL)
Lewis-Clark State Coll. (ID)
Liberty Univ. (VA)

Limestone Coll. (SC)
Lincoln Univ. (PA)
Lincoln Univ. (MO)
Lindenwood Univ. (MO)
Lindsey Wilson Coll. (KY)
Livingstone Coll. (NC)
Lock Haven Univ. of Pennsylvania
Long Island Univ.–C.W. Post
    Campus (NY)
Longwood Univ. (VA)
Loras Coll. (IA)
Louisiana Coll.
Louisiana State Univ.–Shreveport
Lourdes Coll. (OH)
Loyola Univ. Chicago
Loyola Univ. New Orleans
Lubbock Christian Univ. (TX)
Lycoming Coll. (PA)
Lynn Univ. (FL)
MacMurray Coll. (IL)
Madonna Univ. (MI)
Mansfield Univ. of Pennsylvania
Marian Univ. (WI)
Marist Coll. (NY)
Marshall Univ. (WV)
Martin Univ. (IN)
Marymount Univ. (VA)
Marywood Univ. (PA)
McNeese State Univ. (LA)
Medaille Coll. (NY)
Mercy Coll. (NY)
Mercyhurst Coll. (PA)
Messiah Coll. (PA)
Methodist Univ. (NC)
Metropolitan State Coll. of Denver
Michigan State Univ.
Mid-America Christian Univ. (OK)
Middle Tennessee State Univ.
Midwestern State Univ. (TX)
Miles Coll. (AL)
Millikin Univ. (IL)
Minnesota State Univ.–Mankato
Minnesota State Univ.–Moorhead
Minot State Univ. (ND)
Mississippi Coll.
Mississippi Valley State Univ.
Missouri Baptist Univ.
Missouri State Univ.
Missouri Valley Coll.
Missouri Western State Univ.
Mitchell Coll. (CT)
Molloy Coll. (NY)
Monmouth Univ. (NJ)
Morris Coll. (SC)
Mount Aloysius Coll. (PA)
Mount Marty Coll. (SD)
Mount Mary Coll. (WI)
Mount Mercy Coll. (IA)
Mount Olive Coll. (NC)
Mount St. Mary's Univ. (MD)
Mount Vernon Nazarene Univ.
    (OH)
Mountain State Univ. (WV)
Murray State Univ. (KY)
Muskingum Univ. (OH)
National Univ. (CA)
Neumann Univ. (PA)
New Jersey City Univ.
New Mexico Highlands Univ.
New Mexico State Univ.
New York Institute of Technology

Niagara Univ. (NY)
Nichols Coll. (MA)
North Carolina Central Univ.
North Carolina Wesleyan Coll.
North Dakota State Univ.
North Georgia Coll. and State Univ.
Northeastern State Univ. (OK)
Northeastern Univ. (MA)
Northern Arizona Univ.
Northern Kentucky Univ.
Northern Michigan Univ.
Northwestern Coll. (MN)
Northwestern Oklahoma State
    Univ.
Northwestern State Univ. of
    Louisiana
Nova Southeastern Univ. (FL)
Oakland City Univ. (IN)
Ohio Dominican Univ.
Ohio Northern Univ.
Olivet Coll. (MI)
Olivet Nazarene Univ. (IL)
Our Lady of the Lake Univ. (TX)
Pace Univ. (NY)
Park Univ. (MO)
Pennsylvania State Univ.–Univ. Park
Pepperdine Univ. (CA)
Peru State Coll. (NE)
Pfeiffer Univ. (NC)
Piedmont Coll. (GA)
Pikeville Coll. (KY)
Pittsburg State Univ. (KS)
Plymouth State Univ. (NH)
Point Park Univ. (PA)
Post Univ. (CT)
Prairie View A&M Univ. (TX)
Purdue Univ.–Calumet (IN)
Purdue Univ.–West Lafayette (IN)
Quincy Univ. (IL)
Quinnipiac Univ. (CT)
Radford Univ. (VA)
Regis Univ. (CO)
Reinhardt Univ. (GA)
Rhode Island Coll.
Rivier Coll. (NH)
Roanoke Coll. (VA)
Roberts Wesleyan Coll. (NY)
Rochester Institute of Technology
    (NY)
Roger Williams Univ. (RI)
Roosevelt Univ. (IL)
Russell Sage Coll. (NY)
Rutgers, the State Univ. of New
    Jersey–Camden
Rutgers, the State Univ. of New
    Jersey–New Brunswick
Rutgers, the State Univ. of New
    Jersey–Newark
Sacred Heart Univ. (CT)
Sage Colleges–Albany (NY)
Saginaw Valley State Univ. (MI)
Salem State Coll. (MA)
Salve Regina Univ. (RI)
Sam Houston State Univ. (TX)
San Diego State Univ.
San Francisco State Univ.
San Jose State Univ. (CA)
Savannah State Univ. (GA)
Seattle Univ.
Seton Hall Univ. (NJ)
Seton Hill Univ. (PA)

Shaw Univ. (NC)
Shenandoah Univ. (VA)
Shippensburg Univ. of Pennsylvania
Simpson Coll. (IA)
Sonoma State Univ. (CA)
South Carolina State Univ.
Southeast Missouri State Univ.
Southeastern Louisiana Univ.
Southeastern Oklahoma State Univ.
Southeastern Univ. (FL)
Southern Arkansas Univ.
Southern Illinois Univ.–Carbondale
Southern Illinois Univ.–Edwardsville
Southern New Hampshire Univ.
Southern Oregon Univ.
Southern Univ. and A&M Coll. (LA)
Southern Univ.–New Orleans
Southern Utah Univ.
Southern Vermont Coll.
Southern Wesleyan Univ. (SC)
Southwest Baptist Univ. (MO)
Southwest Minnesota State Univ.
Southwestern Adventist Univ. (TX)
Southwestern Oklahoma State
    Univ.
Springfield Coll. (MA)
St. Ambrose Univ. (IA)
St. Augustine's Coll. (NC)
St. Catherine Univ. (MN)
St. Cloud State Univ. (MN)
St. Edward's Univ. (TX)
St. Francis Coll. (NY)
St. Francis Univ. (PA)
St. Gregory's Univ. (OK)
St. John's Univ. (NY)
St. Joseph's Coll. (ME)
St. Joseph's Coll. (IN)
St. Leo Univ. (FL)
St. Louis Univ.
St. Mary's Univ. of Minnesota
St. Paul's Coll. (VA)
St. Peter's Coll. (NJ)
St. Thomas Aquinas Coll. (NY)
St. Thomas Univ. (FL)
St. Xavier Univ. (IL)
Stephen F. Austin State Univ. (TX)
Stonehill Coll. (MA)
Suffolk Univ. (MA)
Sul Ross State Univ. (TX)
SUNY Coll.–Oneonta
SUNY Coll.–Potsdam
SUNY–Oswego
SUNY–Plattsburgh
Syracuse Univ. (NY)
Tarleton State Univ. (TX)
Temple Univ. (PA)
Tennessee State Univ.
Texas A&M International Univ.
Texas A&M Univ.–Commerce
Texas A&M Univ.–Corpus Christi
Texas A&M Univ.–Kingsville
Texas Christian Univ.
Texas State Univ.–San Marcos
Texas Wesleyan Univ.
Texas Woman's Univ.
The Citadel (SC)
Thomas Coll. (ME)
Thomas Edison State Coll. (NJ)
Thomas More Coll. (KY)
Thomas Univ. (GA)
Tiffin Univ. (OH)

Trine Univ. (IN)
Trinity Univ. (DC)
Troy Univ. (AL)
Truman State Univ. (MO)
Tulane Univ. (LA)
Union Institute and Univ. (OH)
Univ. of Akron (OH)
Univ. of Alabama
Univ. of Alabama–Birmingham
Univ. of Alaska–Anchorage
Univ. of Alaska–Fairbanks
Univ. of Arizona
Univ. of Arkansas
Univ. of Arkansas–Little Rock
Univ. of Arkansas–Monticello
Univ. of Arkansas–Pine Bluff
Univ. of Baltimore (MD)
Univ. of Central Florida
Univ. of Central Missouri
Univ. of Central Oklahoma
Univ. of Colorado–Colorado
    Springs
Univ. of Dayton (OH)
Univ. of Detroit Mercy
Univ. of Dubuque (IA)
Univ. of Findlay (OH)
Univ. of Georgia
Univ. of Great Falls (MT)
Univ. of Hartford (CT)
Univ. of Houston–Downtown
Univ. of Illinois–Chicago
Univ. of Illinois–Springfield
Univ. of Indianapolis
Univ. of Iowa
Univ. of Louisiana–Lafayette
Univ. of Louisiana–Monroe
Univ. of Louisville (KY)
Univ. of Maine–Augusta
Univ. of Maine–Presque Isle
Univ. of Mary (ND)
Univ. of Mary Hardin-Baylor (TX)
Univ. of Maryland–Eastern Shore
Univ. of Maryland–Univ. Coll.
Univ. of Massachusetts–Boston
Univ. of Massachusetts–Lowell
Univ. of Memphis
Univ. of Michigan–Dearborn
Univ. of Michigan–Flint
Univ. of Mississippi
Univ. of Missouri–Kansas City
Univ. of Nebraska–Kearney
Univ. of Nebraska–Omaha
Univ. of Nevada–Las Vegas
Univ. of New Haven (CT)
Univ. of New Mexico
Univ. of North Alabama
Univ. of North Carolina–Charlotte
Univ. of North Carolina–Pembroke
Univ. of North Carolina–
    Wilmington
Univ. of North Dakota
Univ. of North Florida
Univ. of North Texas
Univ. of Northern Colorado
Univ. of Pittsburgh
Univ. of Pittsburgh–Bradford
Univ. of Richmond (VA)
Univ. of Scranton (PA)
Univ. of Sioux Falls (SD)
Univ. of South Alabama
Univ. of South Carolina

Univ. of South Carolina–Upstate
Univ. of South Dakota
Univ. of Southern Mississippi
Univ. of Tampa (FL)
Univ. of Tennessee–Chattanooga
Univ. of Tennessee–Martin
Univ. of Texas of the Permian Basin
Univ. of Texas–Arlington
Univ. of Texas–Brownsville
Univ. of Texas–El Paso
Univ. of Texas–Pan American
Univ. of Texas–San Antonio
Univ. of Texas–Tyler
Univ. of the District of Columbia
Univ. of the Southwest (NM)
Univ. of Toledo (OH)
Univ. of Washington
Univ. of West Florida
Univ. of Wisconsin–Eau Claire
Univ. of Wisconsin–Milwaukee
Univ. of Wisconsin–Parkside
Univ. of Wisconsin–Platteville
Univ. of Wisconsin–Superior
Univ. of Wyoming
Urbana Univ. (OH)
Utah Valley Univ.
Utica Coll. (NY)
Valdosta State Univ. (GA)
Villanova Univ. (PA)
Virginia Commonwealth Univ.
Virginia Intermont Coll.
Virginia State Univ.
Virginia Union Univ.
Viterbo Univ. (WI)
Voorhees Coll. (SC)
Washburn Univ. (KS)
Washington State Univ.
Wayland Baptist Univ. (TX)
Wayne State Coll. (NE)
Wayne State Univ. (MI)
Waynesburg Univ. (PA)
Weber State Univ. (UT)
West Chester Univ. of Pennsylvania
West Liberty Univ. (WV)
West Texas A&M Univ.
West Virginia State Univ.
West Virginia Univ.
West Virginia Univ.–Parkersburg
West Virginia Wesleyan Coll.
Western Carolina Univ. (NC)
Western Connecticut State Univ.
Western Illinois Univ.
Western Michigan Univ.
Western New England Coll. (MA)
Western New Mexico Univ.
Western Oregon Univ.
Westfield State Coll. (MA)
Wheeling Jesuit Univ. (WV)
Wichita State Univ. (KS)
Widener Univ. (PA)
Wiley Coll. (TX)
Wilkes Univ. (PA)
William Woods Univ. (MO)
Wilmington Coll. (OH)
Wilmington Univ. (DE)
Winona State Univ. (MN)
Winston-Salem State Univ. (NC)
Worcester State Coll. (MA)
Xavier Univ. (OH)
York Coll. of Pennsylvania
Youngstown State Univ. (OH)

Criminology

Albright Coll. (PA)
Arcadia Univ. (PA)
Arkansas State Univ.–Jonesboro
Auburn Univ. (AL)
Buffalo State Coll.–SUNY
Cabrini Coll. (PA)
California State Univ.–Fresno
Cameron Univ. (OK)
Capital Univ. (OH)
Central Connecticut State Univ.
Coker Coll. (SC)
Coll. of Mount St. Joseph (OH)
Coll. of Notre Dame of Maryland
Coll. of the Ozarks (MO)
Columbus State Univ. (GA)
Concordia Univ. Chicago (IL)
Concordia Univ.–St. Paul (MN)
CUNY–John Jay Coll. of Criminal
    Justice
Davis and Elkins Coll. (WV)
Delaware State Univ.
Dominican Univ. (IL)
Drury Univ. (MO)
Eastern Michigan Univ.
Eastern Washington Univ.
Elizabethtown Coll. (PA)
Evangel Univ. (MO)
Florida Memorial Univ.
Florida Southern Coll.
Fort Lewis Coll. (CO)
Gallaudet Univ. (DC)
Holy Names Univ. (CA)
Indiana State Univ.
Indiana Univ. of Pennsylvania
Iowa Wesleyan Coll.
Johnson C. Smith Univ. (NC)
Judson Coll. (AL)
Juniata Coll. (PA)
Le Moyne Coll. (NY)
Lebanon Valley Coll. (PA)
Lees-McRae Coll. (NC)
Lindenwood Univ. (MO)
Longwood Univ. (VA)
Lycoming Coll. (PA)
Mansfield Univ. of Pennsylvania
Marquette Univ. (WI)
Marymount Univ. (VA)
Maryville Univ. of St. Louis (MO)
MidAmerica Nazarene Univ. (KS)
Midland Lutheran Coll. (NE)
Missouri Valley Coll.
Mount St. Mary's Univ. (MD)
New England Coll. (NH)
Niagara Univ. (NY)
North Carolina State Univ.–Raleigh
North Carolina Wesleyan Coll.
Northeastern Illinois Univ.
Ohio State Univ.–Columbus
Ohio Univ.
Old Dominion Univ. (VA)
Our Lady of Holy Cross Coll. (LA)
Paine Coll. (GA)
Purdue Univ.–Calumet (IN)
Richard Stockton Coll. of New
    Jersey
Russell Sage Coll. (NY)
San Diego State Univ.
Sojourner-Douglass Coll. (MD)
St. Anselm Coll. (NH)

St. Edward's Univ. (TX)
St. Joseph's Univ. (PA)
St. Martin's Univ. (WA)
St. Mary-of-the-Woods Coll. (IN)
Stonehill Coll. (MA)
Suffolk Univ. (MA)
SUNY Coll.–Cortland
SUNY Coll.–Old Westbury
Texas A&M Univ.–Commerce
Texas A&M Univ.–Kingsville
Thiel Coll. (PA)
Union Coll. (KY)
Univ. at Albany–SUNY
Univ. of Akron (OH)
Univ. of California–Irvine
Univ. of Delaware
Univ. of Denver
Univ. of Florida
Univ. of Great Falls (MT)
Univ. of Hawaii–Hilo
Univ. of La Verne (CA)
Univ. of Maryland–Coll. Park
Univ. of Massachusetts–Dartmouth
Univ. of Miami (FL)
Univ. of Minnesota–Duluth
Univ. of Minnesota–Twin Cities
Univ. of Missouri–St. Louis
Univ. of Nevada–Reno
Univ. of New Hampshire
Univ. of Northern Iowa
Univ. of South Florida
Univ. of Southern Maine
Univ. of St. Mary (KS)
Univ. of St. Thomas (MN)
Univ. of Tampa (FL)
Univ. of Texas of the Permian Basin
Univ. of Texas–Dallas
Univ. of Virginia–Wise
Univ. of West Georgia
Upper Iowa Univ.
Valparaiso Univ. (IN)
Virginia Wesleyan Coll.
Western Michigan Univ.

Culinary Arts and Related Services

Drexel Univ. (PA)
Johnson and Wales Univ. (RI)
Kendall Coll. (IL)
Madonna Univ. (MI)
Mississippi Univ. for Women
Mountain State Univ. (WV)
Nicholls State Univ. (LA)
Northern Michigan Univ.
Paul Smith's Coll. (NY)
Pennsylvania Coll. of Technology
Southern New Hampshire Univ.
Texas A&M Univ.–Kingsville
Thiel Coll. (PA)
Univ. of Alaska–Anchorage
Univ. of Nevada–Las Vegas
Univ. of New Hampshire

Curriculum and Instruction

Averett Univ. (VA)
Bethel Univ. (MN)
California State Univ.–Sacramento
Campbellsville Univ. (KY)

Colorado Christian Univ.
Coppin State Univ. (MD)
Eastern Michigan Univ.
Eastern Washington Univ.
Lake Erie Coll. (OH)
Lincoln Memorial Univ. (TN)
Midwestern State Univ. (TX)
Northern State Univ. (SD)
Our Lady of the Lake Univ. (TX)
South Dakota State Univ.
Southern Nazarene Univ. (OK)
Syracuse Univ. (NY)
Texas A&M Univ.–Coll. Station
Texas Wesleyan Univ.
Univ. of California–Riverside
Univ. of Florida
Univ. of Iowa
Univ. of Kentucky
Univ. of Nebraska–Lincoln
Univ. of Nevada–Las Vegas
Univ. of Redlands (CA)
Univ. of the Southwest (NM)
Univ. of Wisconsin–Oshkosh
Utah State Univ.
Washington State Univ.

Dance

Adelphi Univ. (NY)
Alma Coll. (MI)
Appalachian State Univ. (NC)
Arizona State Univ.
Ball State Univ. (IN)
Bard Coll. at Simon's Rock (MA)
Barnard Coll. (NY)
Belhaven Univ. (MS)
Beloit Coll. (WI)
Bennington Coll. (VT)
Boston Conservatory
Brenau Univ. (GA)
Brigham Young Univ.–Provo (UT)
Butler Univ. (IN)
California Institute of the Arts
California State Univ.–Fullerton
California State Univ.–Long Beach
California State Univ.–Sacramento
Carleton Coll. (MN)
Cedar Crest Coll. (PA)
Centenary Coll. of Louisiana
Chapman Univ. (CA)
Coker Coll. (SC)
Coll. at Brockport–SUNY
Colorado Coll.
Columbia Coll. (IL)
Columbia Coll. (SC)
Columbia Univ. (NY)
Connecticut Coll.
Cornell Univ. (NY)
Cornish Coll. of the Arts (WA)
CUNY–Hunter Coll.
CUNY–Lehman Coll.
CUNY–Queens Coll.
Denison Univ. (OH)
DeSales Univ. (PA)
Dominican Univ. of California
East Carolina Univ. (NC)
Eastern Michigan Univ.
Eastern Univ. (PA)
Elon Univ. (NC)
Emory Univ. (GA)
Florida International Univ.

Florida State Univ.
Fordham Univ. (NY)
Franklin and Marshall Coll. (PA)
Friends Univ. (KS)
Frostburg State Univ. (MD)
George Mason Univ. (VA)
George Washington Univ. (DC)
Goucher Coll. (MD)
Gustavus Adolphus Coll. (MN)
Hamilton Coll. (NY)
Hampshire Coll. (MA)
Hobart and William Smith Colleges (NY)
Hofstra Univ. (NY)
Hollins Univ. (VA)
Hope Coll. (MI)
Howard Univ. (DC)
Indiana Univ.–Bloomington
Jacksonville Univ. (FL)
Juilliard School (NY)
Keene State Coll. (NH)
Kent State Univ. (OH)
Kenyon Coll. (OH)
La Roche Coll. (PA)
Lamar Univ. (TX)
Lees-McRae Coll. (NC)
Lindenwood Univ. (MO)
Long Island Univ.–C.W. Post Campus (NY)
Loyola Marymount Univ. (CA)
Manhattanville Coll. (NY)
Marygrove Coll. (MI)
Marymount Manhattan Coll. (NY)
Mercyhurst Coll. (PA)
Meredith Coll. (NC)
Middlebury Coll. (VT)
Mills Coll. (CA)
Minnesota State Univ.–Mankato
Missouri State Univ.
Montclair State Univ. (NJ)
Mount Holyoke Coll. (MA)
Muhlenberg Coll. (PA)
New Jersey City Univ.
New Mexico State Univ.
New School (NY)
New York Univ.
Northwestern Univ. (IL)
Oberlin Coll. (OH)
Ohio State Univ.–Columbus
Ohio Univ.
Ohio Wesleyan Univ.
Oklahoma City Univ.
Oral Roberts Univ. (OK)
Palm Beach Atlantic Univ. (FL)
Pitzer Coll. (CA)
Point Park Univ. (PA)
Pomona Coll. (CA)
Prescott Coll. (AZ)
Purchase Coll.–SUNY
Radford Univ. (VA)
Randolph Coll. (VA)
Rhode Island Coll.
Roger Williams Univ. (RI)
Rutgers, the State Univ. of New Jersey–New Brunswick
Sam Houston State Univ. (TX)
San Diego State Univ.
San Francisco State Univ.
San Jose State Univ. (CA)
Scripps Coll. (CA)
Shenandoah Univ. (VA)

Skidmore Coll. (NY)
Slippery Rock Univ. of Pennsylvania
Smith Coll. (MA)
Southern Methodist Univ. (TX)
Southern Utah Univ.
Springfield Coll. (MA)
St. Gregory's Univ. (OK)
St. Mary's Coll. of California
St. Olaf Coll. (MN)
Stephen F. Austin State Univ. (TX)
Stephens Coll. (MO)
SUNY Coll.–Potsdam
Swarthmore Coll. (PA)
Temple Univ. (PA)
Texas Christian Univ.
Texas State Univ.–San Marcos
Texas Tech Univ.
Texas Woman's Univ.
Towson Univ. (MD)
Trinity Coll. (CT)
Tulane Univ. (LA)
Univ. at Buffalo–SUNY
Univ. of Akron (OH)
Univ. of Alabama
Univ. of Arizona
Univ. of California–Berkeley
Univ. of California–Irvine
Univ. of California–Riverside
Univ. of California–Santa Barbara
Univ. of Central Oklahoma
Univ. of Colorado–Boulder
Univ. of Florida
Univ. of Georgia
Univ. of Hartford (CT)
Univ. of Hawaii–Hilo
Univ. of Hawaii–Manoa
Univ. of Houston
Univ. of Illinois–Urbana-Champaign
Univ. of Iowa
Univ. of Kansas
Univ. of Maryland–Baltimore County
Univ. of Maryland–Coll. Park
Univ. of Massachusetts–Amherst
Univ. of Michigan–Ann Arbor
Univ. of Minnesota–Twin Cities
Univ. of Missouri–Kansas City
Univ. of Montana
Univ. of Nebraska–Lincoln
Univ. of Nevada–Las Vegas
Univ. of New Mexico
Univ. of North Carolina School of the Arts
Univ. of North Carolina–Charlotte
Univ. of North Carolina– Greensboro
Univ. of North Texas
Univ. of Oklahoma
Univ. of Oregon
Univ. of South Carolina
Univ. of South Florida
Univ. of Southern Mississippi
Univ. of Texas–Austin
Univ. of Texas–El Paso
Univ. of Texas–Pan American
Univ. of the Arts (PA)
Univ. of Utah
Univ. of Washington
Univ. of Wisconsin–Madison
Univ. of Wisconsin–Milwaukee
Ursinus Coll. (PA)

Utah State Univ.
Utah Valley Univ.
Valdosta State Univ. (GA)
Virginia Commonwealth Univ.
Virginia Intermont Coll.
Washington Univ. in St. Louis
Wayne State Univ. (MI)
Weber State Univ. (UT)
Webster Univ. (MO)
Wesleyan Univ. (CT)
West Texas A&M Univ.
Western Michigan Univ.
Western Oregon Univ.
Winthrop Univ. (SC)
Wright State Univ. (OH)

Data Entry/ Microcomputer Applications

Vermont Technical Coll.

Data Processing

Arkansas State Univ.–Jonesboro
Clayton State Univ. (GA)
CUNY–Brooklyn Coll.
Dominican Coll. (NY)
Indiana Univ.–Kokomo
Pace Univ. (NY)
Roosevelt Univ. (IL)
Stephen F. Austin State Univ. (TX)
Texas State Univ.–San Marcos
Univ. of Arkansas
Univ. of Southern Indiana
Univ. of Southern Mississippi
Utah Valley Univ.

Demography and Population Studies

Alfred Univ. (NY)
Bennett Coll. (NC)
Campbell Univ. (NC)
Chadron State Coll. (NE)
Concordia Coll.–Moorhead (MN)
CUNY–Hunter Coll.
Duke Univ. (NC)
Hampshire Coll. (MA)
Missouri State Univ.
North Carolina A&T State Univ.
Northern Arizona Univ.
Princeton Univ. (NJ)
Univ. of Central Missouri
Univ. of North Carolina–Pembroke
Western New Mexico Univ.

Dental Support Services and Allied Professions

Armstrong Atlantic State Univ. (GA)
Clayton State Univ. (GA)
Dixie State Coll. of Utah
East Tennessee State Univ.
Eastern Washington Univ.
Farmingdale State Coll.–SUNY
Idaho State Univ.
Indiana Univ.-Purdue Univ.– Indianapolis
Louisiana Coll.
Midwestern State Univ. (TX)

Minnesota State Univ.–Mankato
Mount Ida Coll. (MA)
Northern Arizona Univ.
Ohio State Univ.–Columbus
Old Dominion Univ. (VA)
Oregon Institute of Technology
Pennsylvania Coll. of Technology
Southern Illinois Univ.–Carbondale
Tennessee State Univ.
Texas Woman's Univ.
Thomas Edison State Coll. (NJ)
Univ. of Bridgeport (CT)
Univ. of Colorado–Denver
Univ. of Detroit Mercy
Univ. of Hawaii–Manoa
Univ. of Louisiana–Lafayette
Univ. of Louisiana–Monroe
Univ. of Louisville (KY)
Univ. of Maine–Augusta
Univ. of Maryland–Coll. Park
Univ. of Maryland–Eastern Shore
Univ. of Michigan–Ann Arbor
Univ. of Minnesota–Twin Cities
Univ. of Missouri–Kansas City
Univ. of New England (ME)
Univ. of New Haven (CT)
Univ. of New Mexico
Univ. of North Carolina–Chapel Hill
Univ. of Oklahoma
Univ. of Pittsburgh
Univ. of Rhode Island
Univ. of Southern California
Univ. of Southern Indiana
Univ. of Tennessee
Univ. of the Pacific (CA)
Univ. of Washington
Univ. of Wyoming
Vermont Technical Coll.
Virginia Commonwealth Univ.
Weber State Univ. (UT)
West Liberty Univ. (WV)
West Virginia Univ.
Western Kentucky Univ.
Wichita State Univ. (KS)

Dentistry (D.D.S., D.M.D.)

Ohio State Univ.–Columbus
Univ. of Florida
Univ. of Kentucky

Design and Applied Arts

Abilene Christian Univ. (TX)
Adrian Coll. (MI)
Albertus Magnus Coll. (CT)
Albright Coll. (PA)
Alma Coll. (MI)
Alverno Coll. (WI)
American Univ. (DC)
Anderson Univ. (IN)
Anderson Univ. (SC)
Andrews Univ. (MI)
Anna Maria Coll. (MA)
Appalachian State Univ. (NC)
Arcadia Univ. (PA)
Arizona State Univ.
Arkansas State Univ.–Jonesboro
Art Academy of Cincinnati
Art Center Coll. of Design (CA)

Ashland Univ. (OH)
Atlantic Union Coll. (MA)
Auburn Univ. (AL)
Augusta State Univ. (GA)
Baker Coll. of Flint (MI)
Baylor Univ. (TX)
Becker Coll. (MA)
Bellevue Univ. (NE)
Belmont Univ. (TN)
Bemidji State Univ. (MN)
Bennington Coll. (VT)
Bethel Coll. (IN)
Biola Univ. (CA)
Black Hills State Univ. (SD)
Boise State Univ. (ID)
Boston Univ.
Bowling Green State Univ. (OH)
Bradley Univ. (IL)
Brenau Univ. (GA)
Brescia Univ. (KY)
Briar Cliff Univ. (IA)
Bridgewater State Coll. (MA)
Brigham Young Univ.–Provo (UT)
Buena Vista Univ. (IA)
Buffalo State Coll.–SUNY
Cabrini Coll. (PA)
California Baptist Univ.
California Coll. of the Arts
California Institute of the Arts
California Polytechnic State Univ.–
    San Luis Obispo
California State Polytechnic Univ.–
    Pomona
California State Univ.–Chico
California State Univ.–Long Beach
California State Univ.–Sacramento
California Univ. of Pennsylvania
Campbell Univ. (NC)
Cardinal Stritch Univ. (WI)
Carlow Univ. (PA)
Carnegie Mellon Univ. (PA)
Carroll Univ. (WI)
Carson-Newman Coll. (TN)
Cazenovia Coll. (NY)
Cedarville Univ. (OH)
Centenary Coll. (NJ)
Central Connecticut State Univ.
Central Michigan Univ.
Central Washington Univ.
Chaminade Univ. of Honolulu
Chapman Univ. (CA)
Chatham Univ. (PA)
Chowan Univ. (NC)
Cleveland Institute of Art
Cogswell Polytechnical Coll. (CA)
Coker Coll. (SC)
Colby-Sawyer Coll. (NH)
Coll. for Creative Studies (MI)
Coll. of Mount St. Joseph (OH)
Coll. of New Jersey
Coll. of Santa Fe (NM)
Coll. of St. Rose (NY)
Coll. of the Ozarks (MO)
Coll. of Visual Arts (MN)
Colorado State Univ.
Columbia Coll. (MO)
Columbia Coll. (IL)
Columbus Coll. of Art and Design
    (OH)
Concord Univ. (WV)
Concordia Univ. (NE)

Concordia Univ. Wisconsin
Converse Coll. (SC)
Corcoran Coll. of Art and Design
    (DC)
Cornell Univ. (NY)
Cornish Coll. of the Arts (WA)
Creighton Univ. (NE)
CUNY–Baruch Coll.
CUNY–Lehman Coll.
CUNY–New York City Coll. of
    Technology
CUNY–Queens Coll.
Daemen Coll. (NY)
Defiance Coll. (OH)
DePaul Univ. (IL)
Dominican Univ. (IL)
Dominican Univ. of California
Dordt Coll. (IA)
Dowling Coll. (NY)
Drake Univ. (IA)
Drexel Univ. (PA)
Drury Univ. (MO)
Duke Univ. (NC)
East Carolina Univ. (NC)
East Stroudsburg Univ. of
    Pennsylvania
Eastern Kentucky Univ.
Eastern Michigan Univ.
Eastern Washington Univ.
Edgewood Coll. (WI)
Elizabeth City State Univ. (NC)
Elmhurst Coll. (IL)
Emmanuel Coll. (MA)
Emory and Henry Coll. (VA)
Endicott Coll. (MA)
Farmingdale State Coll.–SUNY
Fashion Institute of Technology
    (NY)
Ferris State Univ. (MI)
Fitchburg State Coll. (MA)
Flagler Coll. (FL)
Florida A&M Univ.
Florida International Univ.
Florida Southern Coll.
Florida State Univ.
Fort Valley State Univ. (GA)
Franklin Pierce Univ. (NH)
Freed-Hardeman Univ. (TN)
Gallaudet Univ. (DC)
George Washington Univ. (DC)
Georgia Institute of Technology
Georgia Southern Univ.
Georgia State Univ.
Grace Coll. and Seminary (IN)
Graceland Univ. (IA)
Grand Valley State Univ. (MI)
Grand View Univ. (IA)
Hampshire Coll. (MA)
Hardin-Simmons Univ. (TX)
Harding Univ. (AR)
High Point Univ. (NC)
Hofstra Univ. (NY)
Howard Univ. (DC)
Huntington Univ. (IN)
Indiana Univ. of Pennsylvania
Indiana Univ.–Bloomington
Indiana Univ.-Purdue Univ.–Fort
    Wayne
Iowa State Univ.
Iowa Wesleyan Coll.
Jacksonville Univ. (FL)

John Brown Univ. (AR)
Judson Univ. (IL)
Kansas City Art Institute (MO)
Kansas State Univ.
Kean Univ. (NJ)
Keene State Coll. (NH)
Kent State Univ. (OH)
Kutztown Univ. of Pennsylvania
La Roche Coll. (PA)
La Sierra Univ. (CA)
Laguna Coll. of Art and Design (CA)
Lambuth Univ. (TN)
Lawrence Technological Univ. (MI)
Lehigh Univ. (PA)
Liberty Univ. (VA)
Limestone Coll. (SC)
Lindenwood Univ. (MO)
Lipscomb Univ. (TN)
Louisiana Coll.
Louisiana Tech Univ.
Loyola Univ. New Orleans
Lyndon State Coll. (VT)
Lynn Univ. (FL)
Madonna Univ. (MI)
Maine Coll. of Art
Marian Univ. (IN)
Marian Univ. (WI)
Marietta Coll. (OH)
Marist Coll. (NY)
Maryland Institute Coll. of Art
Marylhurst Univ. (OR)
Marymount Univ. (VA)
Maryville Univ. of St. Louis (MO)
Marywood Univ. (PA)
Massachusetts Coll. of Art and
    Design
McMurry Univ. (TX)
Memphis Coll. of Art
Meredith Coll. (NC)
Methodist Univ. (NC)
Metropolitan State Coll. of Denver
Miami Univ.–Oxford (OH)
Michigan State Univ.
MidAmerica Nazarene Univ. (KS)
Middle Tennessee State Univ.
Midland Lutheran Coll. (NE)
Millikin Univ. (IL)
Milwaukee Institute of Art and
    Design
Minneapolis Coll. of Art and Design
Minnesota State Univ.–Moorhead
Mississippi Coll.
Missouri State Univ.
Missouri Western State Univ.
Monmouth Coll. (IL)
Montana State Univ.–Northern
Montclair State Univ. (NJ)
Montserrat Coll. of Art (MA)
Moore Coll. of Art and Design (PA)
Morningside Coll. (IA)
Mount Mary Coll. (WI)
Mount Mercy Coll. (IA)
Mount Vernon Nazarene Univ.
    (OH)
New England Coll. (NH)
New Mexico Highlands Univ.
New School (NY)
New York Institute of Technology
New York Univ.
North Carolina A&T State Univ.
North Carolina State Univ.–Raleigh

North Central Coll. (IL)
North Dakota State Univ.
North Georgia Coll. and State Univ.
Northeastern State Univ. (OK)
Northeastern Univ. (MA)
Northern Arizona Univ.
Northern Kentucky Univ.
Northern Michigan Univ.
Northwestern Coll. (MN)
Notre Dame de Namur Univ. (CA)
Oakland City Univ. (IN)
Ohio Dominican Univ.
Ohio State Univ.–Columbus
Ohio Univ.
Oklahoma Christian Univ.
Oklahoma City Univ.
Oregon State Univ.
Otis Coll. of Art and Design (CA)
Ouachita Baptist Univ. (AR)
Pacific Northwest Coll. of Art (OR)
Pacific Union Coll. (CA)
Palm Beach Atlantic Univ. (FL)
Park Univ. (MO)
Peace Coll. (NC)
Pennsylvania Coll. of Technology
Pennsylvania State Univ.–Univ. Park
Philadelphia Univ.
Pittsburg State Univ. (KS)
Point Loma Nazarene Univ. (CA)
Point Park Univ. (PA)
Prairie View A&M Univ. (TX)
Pratt Institute (NY)
Prescott Coll. (AZ)
Purchase Coll.–SUNY
Purdue Univ.–West Lafayette (IN)
Quincy Univ. (IL)
Quinnipiac Univ. (CT)
Radford Univ. (VA)
Regis Coll. (MA)
Rhode Island School of Design
Ringling Coll. of Art and Design
    (FL)
Rivier Coll. (NH)
Robert Morris Univ. (PA)
Robert Morris Univ. (IL)
Rochester Institute of Technology
    (NY)
Roger Williams Univ. (RI)
Sacred Heart Univ. (CT)
Sage Colleges–Albany (NY)
Saginaw Valley State Univ. (MI)
Salem Coll. (NC)
Sam Houston State Univ. (TX)
Samford Univ. (AL)
San Diego State Univ.
San Jose State Univ. (CA)
Savannah Coll. of Art and Design
    (GA)
School of the Art Institute of
    Chicago
Schreiner Univ. (TX)
Seattle Pacific Univ.
Seton Hall Univ. (NJ)
Seton Hill Univ. (PA)
Shawnee State Univ. (OH)
Simpson Coll. (IA)
South Dakota State Univ.
Southeastern Oklahoma State Univ.
Southern Adventist Univ. (TN)
Southern Illinois Univ.–Carbondale
Southern New Hampshire Univ.

Southern Utah Univ.
Southwest Baptist Univ. (MO)
Southwestern Oklahoma State
    Univ.
Spring Arbor Univ. (MI)
Spring Hill Coll. (AL)
Springfield Coll. (MA)
St. Ambrose Univ. (IA)
St. Catherine Univ. (MN)
St. Edward's Univ. (TX)
St. John's Univ. (NY)
St. Mary's Univ. of Minnesota
St. Mary-of-the-Woods Coll. (IN)
St. Norbert Coll. (WI)
St. Thomas Aquinas Coll. (NY)
St. Vincent Coll. (PA)
Stephens Coll. (MO)
Stevenson Univ. (MD)
Suffolk Univ. (MA)
SUNY–Fredonia
Susquehanna Univ. (PA)
Syracuse Univ. (NY)
Tabor Coll. (KS)
Taylor Univ. (IN)
Temple Univ. (PA)
Texas A&M Univ.–Commerce
Texas Christian Univ.
Texas State Univ.–San Marcos
Texas Tech Univ.
Texas Woman's Univ.
Truman State Univ. (MO)
Union Coll. (NE)
Univ. of Akron (OH)
Univ. of Alabama
Univ. of California–Davis
Univ. of California–Los Angeles
Univ. of Central Missouri
Univ. of Central Oklahoma
Univ. of Charleston (WV)
Univ. of Dayton (OH)
Univ. of Delaware
Univ. of Denver
Univ. of Evansville (IN)
Univ. of Florida
Univ. of Hartford (CT)
Univ. of Houston
Univ. of Illinois–Chicago
Univ. of Illinois–Urbana-Champaign
Univ. of Indianapolis
Univ. of Kansas
Univ. of Kentucky
Univ. of Louisiana–Lafayette
Univ. of Louisville (KY)
Univ. of Maryland–Eastern Shore
Univ. of Massachusetts–Amherst
Univ. of Massachusetts–Dartmouth
Univ. of Miami (FL)
Univ. of Michigan–Ann Arbor
Univ. of Michigan–Flint
Univ. of Minnesota–Duluth
Univ. of Minnesota–Twin Cities
Univ. of Missouri–St. Louis
Univ. of Montana
Univ. of New Haven (CT)
Univ. of North Carolina–
    Greensboro
Univ. of North Texas
Univ. of Northern Iowa
Univ. of Notre Dame (IN)
Univ. of Oklahoma
Univ. of Oregon

Univ. of San Francisco
Univ. of South Carolina–Upstate
Univ. of St. Francis (IN)
Univ. of Tampa (FL)
Univ. of Tennessee
Univ. of Texas–Austin
Univ. of Texas–El Paso
Univ. of Texas–Pan American
Univ. of the Arts (PA)
Univ. of the Incarnate Word (TX)
Univ. of the Pacific (CA)
Univ. of Wisconsin–Madison
Univ. of Wisconsin–Stevens Point
Univ. of Wisconsin–Stout
Upper Iowa Univ.
Ursuline Coll. (OH)
Utah State Univ.
Utah Valley Univ.
Valdosta State Univ. (GA)
Virginia Commonwealth Univ.
Virginia Tech
Viterbo Univ. (WI)
Wartburg Coll. (IA)
Washington Univ. in St. Louis
Wayne State Coll. (NE)
Waynesburg Univ. (PA)
Weber State Univ. (UT)
West Liberty Univ. (WV)
West Texas A&M Univ.
West Virginia Wesleyan Coll.
Western Carolina Univ. (NC)
Western Michigan Univ.
Western Washington Univ.
Wichita State Univ. (KS)
William Woods Univ. (MO)
Wilmington Univ. (DE)
Woodbury Univ. (CA)
York Coll. of Pennsylvania
Youngstown State Univ. (OH)

Developmental and Child Psychology

American Jewish Univ. (CA)
Bridgewater State Coll. (MA)
California Polytechnic State Univ.–
　San Luis Obispo
Colby-Sawyer Coll. (NH)
Eastern Nazarene Coll. (MA)
Eastern Washington Univ.
Eckerd Coll. (FL)
Emmanuel Coll. (MA)
Fitchburg State Coll. (MA)
Gallaudet Univ. (DC)
Keene State Coll. (NH)
LeTourneau Univ. (TX)
Liberty Univ. (VA)
Maryville Coll. (TN)
Mitchell Coll. (CT)
National-Louis Univ. (IL)
Peace Coll. (NC)
Prescott Coll. (AZ)
Rivier Coll. (NH)
Sonoma State Univ. (CA)
St. Mary's Coll. of California
Tufts Univ. (MA)
Univ. of Detroit Mercy
Univ. of Kansas
Univ. of Minnesota–Twin Cities
Univ. of Wisconsin–Green Bay
Utica Coll. (NY)

Vanderbilt Univ. (TN)
Warner Pacific Coll. (OR)
Western Washington Univ.
Whittier Coll. (CA)

Dietetics and Clinical Nutrition Services

Abilene Christian Univ. (TX)
Andrews Univ. (MI)
Ball State Univ. (IN)
Bowling Green State Univ. (OH)
Bradley Univ. (IL)
Brigham Young Univ.–Provo (UT)
Buffalo State Coll.–SUNY
California Polytechnic State Univ.–
　San Luis Obispo
California State Univ.–Chico
California State Univ.–San
　Bernardino
Case Western Reserve Univ. (OH)
Central Michigan Univ.
Cheyney Univ. of Pennsylvania
Coll. of St. Benedict (MN)
Coll. of St. Elizabeth (NJ)
Coll. of the Ozarks (MO)
D'Youville Coll. (NY)
Dominican Univ. (IL)
East Carolina Univ. (NC)
Eastern Kentucky Univ.
Eastern Michigan Univ.
Florida International Univ.
Florida State Univ.
Fontbonne Univ. (MO)
Gannon Univ. (PA)
Harding Univ. (AR)
Idaho State Univ.
Immaculata Univ. (PA)
Indiana Univ. of Pennsylvania
Iowa State Univ.
Kansas State Univ.
Keene State Coll. (NH)
La Salle Univ. (PA)
Life Univ. (GA)
Lipscomb Univ. (TN)
Louisiana State Univ.–Baton Rouge
Louisiana Tech Univ.
Loyola Univ. Chicago
Madonna Univ. (MI)
Mansfield Univ. of Pennsylvania
Marshall Univ. (WV)
Marywood Univ. (PA)
Meredith Coll. (NC)
Messiah Coll. (PA)
Miami Univ.–Oxford (OH)
Michigan State Univ.
Missouri State Univ.
Mount Mary Coll. (WI)
Nicholls State Univ. (LA)
North Dakota State Univ.
Northern Illinois Univ.
Northern Michigan Univ.
Ohio State Univ.–Columbus
Ohio Univ.
Olivet Nazarene Univ. (IL)
Ouachita Baptist Univ. (AR)
Point Loma Nazarene Univ. (CA)
Purdue Univ.–West Lafayette (IN)
Rochester Institute of Technology
　(NY)
Sage Colleges–Albany (NY)

Seton Hill Univ. (PA)
St. Catherine Univ. (MN)
St. John's Univ. (MN)
SUNY Coll.–Oneonta
Tarleton State Univ. (TX)
Texas Christian Univ.
Texas Tech Univ.
Texas Woman's Univ.
Univ. of Akron (OH)
Univ. of Alabama
Univ. of Central Missouri
Univ. of Connecticut
Univ. of Dayton (OH)
Univ. of Delaware
Univ. of Georgia
Univ. of Illinois–Chicago
Univ. of Illinois–Urbana-Champaign
Univ. of Louisiana–Lafayette
Univ. of Maryland–Coll. Park
Univ. of New Hampshire
Univ. of New Haven (CT)
Univ. of North Dakota
Univ. of Northern Colorado
Univ. of Pittsburgh
Univ. of Rhode Island
Univ. of Southern Mississippi
Univ. of Texas–Pan American
Univ. of Vermont
Univ. of Wisconsin–Stout
Viterbo Univ. (WI)
Wayne State Univ. (MI)
West Chester Univ. of Pennsylvania
Western Carolina Univ. (NC)
Western Michigan Univ.
Youngstown State Univ. (OH)

Drafting/Design Engineering Technologies/ Technicians

Eastern Michigan Univ.
Grambling State Univ. (LA)
Indiana Univ.-Purdue Univ.–
　Indianapolis
Lewis-Clark State Coll. (ID)
Missouri State Univ.
Montana State Univ.–Northern
Northern Michigan Univ.
Prairie View A&M Univ. (TX)
Southern Utah Univ.
Thomas Edison State Coll. (NJ)
Trine Univ. (IN)
Weber State Univ. (UT)

Drama/Theater Arts and Stagecraft

Abilene Christian Univ. (TX)
Adams State Coll. (CO)
Adelphi Univ. (NY)
Adrian Coll. (MI)
Agnes Scott Coll. (GA)
Alabama State Univ.
Albertus Magnus Coll. (CT)
Albion Coll. (MI)
Albright Coll. (PA)
Alfred Univ. (NY)
Allegheny Coll. (PA)
Alma Coll. (MI)
American Univ. (DC)

Amherst Coll. (MA)
Anderson Univ. (IN)
Anderson Univ. (SC)
Angelo State Univ. (TX)
Appalachian State Univ. (NC)
Aquinas Coll. (MI)
Arcadia Univ. (PA)
Arizona State Univ.
Arkansas State Univ.–Jonesboro
Armstrong Atlantic State Univ. (GA)
Asbury Univ. (KY)
Ashland Univ. (OH)
Auburn Univ. (AL)
Augsburg Coll. (MN)
Augustana Coll. (IL)
Augustana Coll. (SD)
Averett Univ. (VA)
Avila Univ. (MO)
Azusa Pacific Univ. (CA)
Baker Univ. (KS)
Baldwin-Wallace Coll. (OH)
Ball State Univ. (IN)
Bard Coll. at Simon's Rock (MA)
Barnard Coll. (NY)
Barry Univ. (FL)
Barton Coll. (NC)
Bates Coll. (ME)
Baylor Univ. (TX)
Belhaven Univ. (MS)
Bellevue Univ. (NE)
Belmont Univ. (TN)
Beloit Coll. (WI)
Bemidji State Univ. (MN)
Benedictine Coll. (KS)
Bennington Coll. (VT)
Berea Coll. (KY)
Berklee Coll. of Music (MA)
Berry Coll. (GA)
Bethany Coll. (WV)
Bethany Univ. (CA)
Bethel Coll. (IN)
Bethel Univ. (MN)
Binghamton Univ.–SUNY
Bloomsburg Univ. of Pennsylvania
Bluefield Coll. (VA)
Boise State Univ. (ID)
Boston Univ.
Bowdoin Coll. (ME)
Bowling Green State Univ. (OH)
Bradley Univ. (IL)
Brandeis Univ. (MA)
Brenau Univ. (GA)
Brevard Coll. (NC)
Briar Cliff Univ. (IA)
Bridgewater State Coll. (MA)
Brigham Young Univ.–Provo (UT)
Brown Univ. (RI)
Bucknell Univ. (PA)
Buena Vista Univ. (IA)
Buffalo State Coll.–SUNY
Burlington Coll. (VT)
Butler Univ. (IN)
Caldwell Coll. (NJ)
California Baptist Univ.
California Institute of the Arts
California Lutheran Univ.
California Polytechnic State Univ.–
　San Luis Obispo
California State Polytechnic Univ.–
　Pomona
California State Univ.–Bakersfield

California State Univ.–Chico
California State Univ.–Dominguez
　Hills
California State Univ.–East Bay
California State Univ.–Fresno
California State Univ.–Fullerton
California State Univ.–Long Beach
California State Univ.–Los Angeles
California State Univ.–Northridge
California State Univ.–Sacramento
California State Univ.–San
　Bernardino
California State Univ.–San Marcos
California State Univ.–Stanislaus
California Univ. of Pennsylvania
Calvin Coll. (MI)
Cameron Univ. (OK)
Campbell Univ. (NC)
Campbellsville Univ. (KY)
Capital Univ. (OH)
Cardinal Stritch Univ. (WI)
Carleton Coll. (MN)
Carnegie Mellon Univ. (PA)
Carroll Coll. (MT)
Carroll Univ. (WI)
Carthage Coll. (WI)
Case Western Reserve Univ. (OH)
Castleton State Coll. (VT)
Catawba Coll. (NC)
Catholic Univ. of America (DC)
Cedar Crest Coll. (PA)
Cedarville Univ. (OH)
Centenary Coll. of Louisiana
Central Christian Coll. (KS)
Central Coll. (IA)
Central Connecticut State Univ.
Central Methodist Univ. (MO)
Central Michigan Univ.
Central Washington Univ.
Centre Coll. (KY)
Chadron State Coll. (NE)
Chapman Univ. (CA)
Charleston Southern Univ. (SC)
Chatham Univ. (PA)
Cheyney Univ. of Pennsylvania
Christopher Newport Univ. (VA)
Claremont McKenna Coll. (CA)
Clarion Univ. of Pennsylvania
Clark Univ. (MA)
Cleveland State Univ.
Coastal Carolina Univ. (SC)
Coe Coll. (IA)
Coker Coll. (SC)
Colby Coll. (ME)
Colgate Univ. (NY)
Coll. at Brockport–SUNY
Coll. of Charleston (SC)
Coll. of Idaho (ID)
Coll. of Santa Fe (NM)
Coll. of St. Benedict (MN)
Coll. of the Holy Cross (MA)
Coll. of the Ozarks (MO)
Coll. of William and Mary (VA)
Colorado Christian Univ.
Colorado Coll.
Colorado State Univ.
Columbia Coll. (IL)
Columbia Univ. (NY)
Columbus State Univ. (GA)
Concordia Coll.–Moorhead (MN)
Concordia Univ. (CA)

Concordia Univ. (NE)
Concordia Univ. (MI)
Concordia Univ.–St. Paul (MN)
Connecticut Coll.
Converse Coll. (SC)
Cornell Coll. (IA)
Cornell Univ. (NY)
Cornish Coll. of the Arts (WA)
Covenant Coll. (GA)
Creighton Univ. (NE)
Culver-Stockton Coll. (MO)
Cumberland Univ. (TN)
CUNY–Brooklyn Coll.
CUNY–City Coll.
CUNY–Coll. of Staten Island
CUNY–Hunter Coll.
CUNY–Lehman Coll.
CUNY–New York City Coll. of
    Technology
CUNY–Queens Coll.
Dartmouth Coll. (NH)
Davidson Coll. (NC)
Davis and Elkins Coll. (WV)
Denison Univ. (OH)
DePaul Univ. (IL)
DePauw Univ. (IN)
DeSales Univ. (PA)
Dickinson Coll. (PA)
Dickinson State Univ. (ND)
Dillard Univ. (LA)
Dominican Univ. (IL)
Dordt Coll. (IA)
Drake Univ. (IA)
Drew Univ. (NJ)
Drexel Univ. (PA)
Drury Univ. (MO)
Duke Univ. (NC)
Duquesne Univ. (PA)
Earlham Coll. (IN)
East Carolina Univ. (NC)
East Stroudsburg Univ. of
    Pennsylvania
East Texas Baptist Univ.
Eastern Illinois Univ.
Eastern Kentucky Univ.
Eastern Mennonite Univ. (VA)
Eastern Michigan Univ.
Eastern Nazarene Coll. (MA)
Eastern New Mexico Univ.
Eastern Oregon Univ.
Eastern Washington Univ.
Eckerd Coll. (FL)
Edinboro Univ. of Pennsylvania
Elizabethtown Coll. (PA)
Elmhurst Coll. (IL)
Elmira Coll. (NY)
Elon Univ. (NC)
Emerson Coll. (MA)
Emory and Henry Coll. (VA)
Emory Univ. (GA)
Emporia State Univ. (KS)
Eureka Coll. (IL)
Evangel Univ. (MO)
Evergreen State Coll. (WA)
Fairleigh Dickinson Univ. (NJ)
Fairmont State Univ. (WV)
Ferrum Coll. (VA)
Fisk Univ. (TN)
Fitchburg State Coll. (MA)
Flagler Coll. (FL)
Florida A&M Univ.

Florida Atlantic Univ.
Florida International Univ.
Florida Southern Coll.
Florida State Univ.
Fontbonne Univ. (MO)
Fordham Univ. (NY)
Fort Lewis Coll. (CO)
Francis Marion Univ. (SC)
Franciscan Univ. of Steubenville
    (OH)
Franklin and Marshall Coll. (PA)
Franklin Coll. (IN)
Franklin Pierce Univ. (NH)
Freed-Hardeman Univ. (TN)
Fresno Pacific Univ. (CA)
Friends Univ. (KS)
Frostburg State Univ. (MD)
Furman Univ. (SC)
Gallaudet Univ. (DC)
Gannon Univ. (PA)
Gardner-Webb Univ. (NC)
George Fox Univ. (OR)
George Mason Univ. (VA)
George Washington Univ. (DC)
Georgetown Coll. (KY)
Georgia Coll. & State Univ.
Georgia Southern Univ.
Georgia Southwestern State Univ.
Georgia State Univ.
Gettysburg Coll. (PA)
Gonzaga Univ. (WA)
Gordon Coll. (MA)
Goshen Coll. (IN)
Goucher Coll. (MD)
Graceland Univ. (IA)
Grand Valley State Univ. (MI)
Grand View Coll. (IA)
Greensboro Coll. (NC)
Greenville Coll. (IL)
Grinnell Coll. (IA)
Guilford Coll. (NC)
Gustavus Adolphus Coll. (MN)
Hamilton Coll. (NY)
Hamline Univ. (MN)
Hampshire Coll. (MA)
Hampton Univ. (VA)
Hannibal-LaGrange Coll. (MO)
Hanover Coll. (IN)
Hardin-Simmons Univ. (TX)
Harding Univ. (AR)
Hartwick Coll. (NY)
Heidelberg Univ. (OH)
Henderson State Univ. (AR)
Hendrix Coll. (AR)
High Point Univ. (NC)
Hillsdale Coll. (MI)
Hiram Coll. (OH)
Hofstra Univ. (NY)
Hollins Univ. (VA)
Hope Coll. (MI)
Howard Univ. (DC)
Humboldt State Univ. (CA)
Huntington Univ. (IN)
Idaho State Univ.
Illinois State Univ.
Illinois Wesleyan Univ.
Indiana State Univ.
Indiana Univ. Northwest
Indiana Univ. of Pennsylvania
Indiana Univ. Southeast
Indiana Univ.–Bloomington

Indiana Univ.–South Bend
Indiana Univ.-Purdue Univ.–Fort
    Wayne
Iona Coll. (NY)
Ithaca Coll. (NY)
Jacksonville State Univ. (AL)
Jacksonville Univ. (FL)
James Madison Univ. (VA)
Jamestown Coll. (ND)
Johnson State Coll. (VT)
Juilliard School (NY)
Juniata Coll. (PA)
Kalamazoo Coll. (MI)
Kansas State Univ.
Kansas Wesleyan Univ.
Kean Univ. (NJ)
Keene State Coll. (NH)
Kennesaw State Univ. (GA)
Kent State Univ. (OH)
Kenyon Coll. (OH)
King's Coll. (PA)
Knox Coll. (IL)
Kutztown Univ. of Pennsylvania
LaGrange Coll. (GA)
Lake Erie Coll. (OH)
Lamar Univ. (TX)
Lambuth Univ. (TN)
Langston Univ. (OK)
Lawrence Univ. (WI)
Le Moyne Coll. (NY)
Lees-McRae Coll. (NC)
Lehigh Univ. (PA)
Lenoir-Rhyne Univ. (NC)
Lewis & Clark Coll. (OR)
Liberty Univ. (VA)
Limestone Coll. (SC)
Lindenwood Univ. (MO)
Linfield Coll. (OR)
Lipscomb Univ. (TN)
Lock Haven Univ. of Pennsylvania
Long Island Univ.–C.W. Post
    Campus (NY)
Louisiana Coll.
Louisiana State Univ.–Baton Rouge
Loyola Marymount Univ. (CA)
Loyola Univ. Chicago
Loyola Univ. New Orleans
Luther Coll. (IA)
Lycoming Coll. (PA)
Lynchburg Coll. (VA)
Lyon Coll. (AR)
Macalester Coll. (MN)
Manhattanville Coll. (NY)
Marietta Coll. (OH)
Marquette Univ. (WI)
Mars Hill Coll. (NC)
Mary Baldwin Coll. (VA)
Marymount Manhattan Coll. (NY)
Maryville Coll. (TN)
Marywood Univ. (PA)
McDaniel Coll. (MD)
McKendree Univ. (IL)
McMurry Univ. (TX)
McNeese State Univ. (LA)
McPherson Coll. (KS)
Mercer Univ. (GA)
Meredith Coll. (NC)
Mesa State Coll. (CO)
Messiah Coll. (PA)
Methodist Univ. (NC)
Miami Univ.–Oxford (OH)

Michigan State Univ.
Michigan Technological Univ.
MidAmerica Nazarene Univ. (KS)
Middle Tennessee State Univ.
Middlebury Coll. (VT)
Midland Lutheran Coll. (NE)
Midwestern State Univ. (TX)
Millikin Univ. (IL)
Millsaps Coll. (MS)
Minnesota State Univ.–Mankato
Minnesota State Univ.–Moorhead
Minot State Univ. (ND)
Missouri Southern State Univ.
Missouri State Univ.
Missouri Valley Coll.
Molloy Coll. (NY)
Monmouth Univ. (NJ)
Montana State Univ.–Billings
Montclair State Univ. (NJ)
Morehead State Univ. (KY)
Morehouse Coll. (GA)
Morgan State Univ. (MD)
Morningside Coll. (IA)
Mount Holyoke Coll. (MA)
Mount Vernon Nazarene Univ.
    (OH)
Muhlenberg Coll. (PA)
Murray State Univ. (KY)
National-Louis Univ. (IL)
Nazareth Coll. (NY)
Nebraska Wesleyan Univ.
New England Coll. (NH)
New Jersey City Univ.
New Mexico State Univ.
New School (NY)
New York Univ.
Newberry Coll. (SC)
North Carolina A&T State Univ.
North Carolina Central Univ.
North Carolina Wesleyan Coll.
North Central Coll. (IL)
North Central Univ. (MN)
North Dakota State Univ.
North Greenville Univ. (SC)
Northeastern State Univ. (OK)
Northeastern Univ. (MA)
Northern Arizona Univ.
Northern Illinois Univ.
Northern Kentucky Univ.
Northern Michigan Univ.
Northwest Missouri State Univ.
Northwestern Coll. (MN)
Northwestern Coll. (IA)
Northwestern State Univ. of
    Louisiana
Northwestern Univ. (IL)
Notre Dame de Namur Univ. (CA)
Oakland Univ. (MI)
Oberlin Coll. (OH)
Occidental Coll. (CA)
Oglethorpe Univ. (GA)
Ohio State Univ.–Columbus
Ohio Univ.
Ohio Wesleyan Univ.
Oklahoma Baptist Univ.
Oklahoma Christian Univ.
Oklahoma City Univ.
Oklahoma State Univ.
Old Dominion Univ. (VA)
Olivet Coll. (MI)
Ouachita Baptist Univ. (AR)

Our Lady of the Lake Univ. (TX)
Pace Univ. (NY)
Pacific Lutheran Univ. (WA)
Pacific Univ. (OR)
Paine Coll. (GA)
Palm Beach Atlantic Univ. (FL)
Pennsylvania State Univ.–Univ. Park
Pepperdine Univ. (CA)
Piedmont Coll. (GA)
Pitzer Coll. (CA)
Plymouth State Univ. (NH)
Point Loma Nazarene Univ. (CA)
Point Park Univ. (PA)
Pomona Coll. (CA)
Portland State Univ. (OR)
Prairie View A&M Univ. (TX)
Presbyterian Coll. (SC)
Prescott Coll. (AZ)
Principia Coll. (IL)
Purchase Coll.–SUNY
Purdue Univ.–West Lafayette (IN)
Quinnipiac Univ. (CT)
Radford Univ. (VA)
Ramapo Coll. of New Jersey
Randolph Coll. (VA)
Randolph-Macon Coll. (VA)
Reed Coll. (OR)
Regis Coll. (MA)
Rhode Island Coll.
Rhodes Coll. (TN)
Ripon Coll. (WI)
Roanoke Coll. (VA)
Rockford Coll. (IL)
Rocky Mountain Coll. (MT)
Roger Williams Univ. (RI)
Rollins Coll. (FL)
Roosevelt Univ. (IL)
Russell Sage Coll. (NY)
Rutgers, the State Univ. of New
    Jersey–Camden
Rutgers, the State Univ. of New
    Jersey–New Brunswick
Rutgers, the State Univ. of New
    Jersey–Newark
Saginaw Valley State Univ. (MI)
Salem State Coll. (MA)
Salisbury Univ. (MD)
Salve Regina Univ. (RI)
Sam Houston State Univ. (TX)
Samford Univ. (AL)
San Diego State Univ.
San Francisco State Univ.
San Jose State Univ. (CA)
Santa Clara Univ. (CA)
Savannah Coll. of Art and Design
    (GA)
Schreiner Univ. (TX)
Scripps Coll. (CA)
Seattle Pacific Univ.
Seattle Univ.
Seton Hill Univ. (PA)
Sewanee–Univ. of the South (TN)
Shaw Univ. (NC)
Shenandoah Univ. (VA)
Shorter Coll. (GA)
Siena Coll. (NY)
Simpson Coll. (IA)
Skidmore Coll. (NY)
Slippery Rock Univ. of Pennsylvania
Smith Coll. (MA)
Sonoma State Univ. (CA)

South Carolina State Univ.
Southeast Missouri State Univ.
Southeastern Oklahoma State Univ.
Southeastern Univ. (FL)
Southern Arkansas Univ.
Southern Connecticut State Univ.
Southern Illinois Univ.–Carbondale
Southern Illinois Univ.–Edwardsville
Southern Methodist Univ. (TX)
Southern Oregon Univ.
Southern Univ. and A&M Coll. (LA)
Southern Utah Univ.
Southwest Baptist Univ. (MO)
Southwest Minnesota State Univ.
Southwestern Coll. (KS)
Southwestern Univ. (TX)
Spelman Coll. (GA)
Spring Hill Coll. (AL)
St. Ambrose Univ. (IA)
St. Bonaventure Univ. (NY)
St. Catherine Univ. (MN)
St. Cloud State Univ. (MN)
St. Edward's Univ. (TX)
St. John's Univ. (MN)
St. Joseph's Coll. (IN)
St. Lawrence Univ. (NY)
St. Louis Univ.
St. Martin's Univ. (WA)
St. Mary's Coll. (IN)
St. Mary's Coll. of California
St. Mary's Coll. of Maryland
St. Mary's Univ. of Minnesota
St. Mary-of-the-Woods Coll. (IN)
St. Michael's Coll. (VT)
St. Olaf Coll. (MN)
St. Vincent Coll. (PA)
Stanford Univ. (CA)
Stephen F. Austin State Univ. (TX)
Stephens Coll. (MO)
Sterling Coll. (KS)
Stetson Univ. (FL)
Suffolk Univ. (MA)
Sul Ross State Univ. (TX)
SUNY Coll.–Oneonta
SUNY Coll.–Potsdam
SUNY–Fredonia
SUNY–Geneseo
SUNY–Oswego
SUNY–Plattsburgh
SUNY–Stony Brook
Susquehanna Univ. (PA)
Swarthmore Coll. (PA)
Syracuse Univ. (NY)
Tarleton State Univ. (TX)
Taylor Univ. (IN)
Temple Univ. (PA)
Tennessee State Univ.
Texas A&M Univ.–Coll. Station
Texas A&M Univ.–Commerce
Texas A&M Univ.–Corpus Christi
Texas A&M Univ.–Kingsville
Texas Christian Univ.
Texas Lutheran Univ.
Texas State Univ.–San Marcos
Texas Tech Univ.
Texas Wesleyan Univ.
Texas Woman's Univ.
Thomas Edison State Coll. (NJ)
Thomas More Coll. (KY)
Towson Univ. (MD)
Transylvania Univ. (KY)

Trevecca Nazarene Univ. (TN)
Trinity Coll. (CT)
Truman State Univ. (MO)
Tufts Univ. (MA)
Tulane Univ. (LA)
Union Coll. (KY)
Univ. at Albany–SUNY
Univ. at Buffalo–SUNY
Univ. of Akron (OH)
Univ. of Alabama
Univ. of Alaska–Anchorage
Univ. of Alaska–Fairbanks
Univ. of Arizona
Univ. of Arkansas
Univ. of Arkansas–Little Rock
Univ. of California–Berkeley
Univ. of California–Davis
Univ. of California–Irvine
Univ. of California–Los Angeles
Univ. of California–Riverside
Univ. of California–Santa Barbara
Univ. of California–Santa Cruz
Univ. of Central Arkansas
Univ. of Central Florida
Univ. of Central Missouri
Univ. of Central Oklahoma
Univ. of Colorado–Boulder
Univ. of Colorado–Denver
Univ. of Connecticut
Univ. of Dallas
Univ. of Dayton (OH)
Univ. of Delaware
Univ. of Denver
Univ. of Detroit Mercy
Univ. of Evansville (IN)
Univ. of Findlay (OH)
Univ. of Florida
Univ. of Georgia
Univ. of Hartford (CT)
Univ. of Hawaii–Hilo
Univ. of Hawaii–Manoa
Univ. of Houston
Univ. of Illinois–Chicago
Univ. of Illinois–Urbana-Champaign
Univ. of Indianapolis
Univ. of Iowa
Univ. of Kansas
Univ. of Kentucky
Univ. of La Verne (CA)
Univ. of Louisville (KY)
Univ. of Maine
Univ. of Maine–Farmington
Univ. of Mary Hardin-Baylor (TX)
Univ. of Maryland–Baltimore
    County
Univ. of Maryland–Coll. Park
Univ. of Massachusetts–Amherst
Univ. of Massachusetts–Boston
Univ. of Memphis
Univ. of Miami (FL)
Univ. of Michigan–Ann Arbor
Univ. of Michigan–Flint
Univ. of Minnesota–Duluth
Univ. of Minnesota–Morris
Univ. of Minnesota–Twin Cities
Univ. of Mississippi
Univ. of Missouri
Univ. of Missouri–Kansas City
Univ. of Missouri–St. Louis
Univ. of Montana
Univ. of Montevallo (AL)

Univ. of Mount Union (OH)
Univ. of Nebraska–Kearney
Univ. of Nebraska–Lincoln
Univ. of Nebraska–Omaha
Univ. of Nevada–Las Vegas
Univ. of Nevada–Reno
Univ. of New Mexico
Univ. of North Carolina School of
    the Arts
Univ. of North Carolina–Asheville
Univ. of North Carolina–Chapel Hill
Univ. of North Carolina–Charlotte
Univ. of North Carolina–
    Greensboro
Univ. of North Carolina–Pembroke
Univ. of North Carolina–
    Wilmington
Univ. of North Dakota
Univ. of North Texas
Univ. of Northern Colorado
Univ. of Northern Iowa
Univ. of Notre Dame (IN)
Univ. of Oklahoma
Univ. of Oregon
Univ. of Pennsylvania
Univ. of Pittsburgh
Univ. of Pittsburgh–Johnstown
Univ. of Portland (OR)
Univ. of Puget Sound (WA)
Univ. of Redlands (CA)
Univ. of Rhode Island
Univ. of Richmond (VA)
Univ. of San Diego
Univ. of Science and Arts of
    Oklahoma
Univ. of Scranton (PA)
Univ. of South Alabama
Univ. of South Carolina
Univ. of South Dakota
Univ. of South Florida
Univ. of Southern California
Univ. of Southern Indiana
Univ. of Southern Mississippi
Univ. of St. Mary (KS)
Univ. of St. Thomas (MN)
Univ. of St. Thomas (TX)
Univ. of Tennessee
Univ. of Tennessee–Chattanooga
Univ. of Texas–Arlington
Univ. of Texas–Austin
Univ. of Texas–El Paso
Univ. of Texas–Pan American
Univ. of Texas–Tyler
Univ. of the Arts (PA)
Univ. of the Cumberlands (KY)
Univ. of the District of Columbia
Univ. of the Incarnate Word (TX)
Univ. of the Ozarks (AR)
Univ. of the Pacific (CA)
Univ. of Toledo (OH)
Univ. of Tulsa (OK)
Univ. of Utah
Univ. of Vermont
Univ. of Virginia
Univ. of Virginia–Wise
Univ. of Washington
Univ. of West Florida
Univ. of West Georgia
Univ. of Wisconsin–Eau Claire
Univ. of Wisconsin–Green Bay
Univ. of Wisconsin–La Crosse

Univ. of Wisconsin–Madison
Univ. of Wisconsin–Milwaukee
Univ. of Wisconsin–River Falls
Univ. of Wisconsin–Stevens Point
Univ. of Wisconsin–Superior
Univ. of Wisconsin–Whitewater
Univ. of Wyoming
Ursinus Coll. (PA)
Utah State Univ.
Valparaiso Univ. (IN)
Vanderbilt Univ. (TN)
Vanguard Univ. of Southern
    California
Vassar Coll. (NY)
Virginia Commonwealth Univ.
Virginia Intermont Coll.
Virginia Tech
Virginia Wesleyan Coll.
Viterbo Univ. (WI)
Wabash Coll. (IN)
Wagner Coll. (NY)
Wake Forest Univ. (NC)
Waldorf Coll. (IA)
Wartburg Coll. (IA)
Washburn Univ. (KS)
Washington and Jefferson Coll.
    (PA)
Washington and Lee Univ. (VA)
Washington Coll. (MD)
Washington State Univ.
Washington Univ. in St. Louis
Wayland Baptist Univ. (TX)
Wayne State Coll. (NE)
Wayne State Univ. (MI)
Weber State Univ. (UT)
Webster Univ. (MO)
Wellesley Coll. (MA)
Wesleyan Coll. (GA)
Wesleyan Univ. (CT)
West Chester Univ. of Pennsylvania
West Texas A&M Univ.
West Virginia Univ.
West Virginia Wesleyan Coll.
Western Carolina Univ. (NC)
Western Connecticut State Univ.
Western Illinois Univ.
Western Kentucky Univ.
Western Michigan Univ.
Western Oregon Univ.
Western State Coll. of Colorado
Western Washington Univ.
Westminster Coll. (UT)
Westminster Coll. (PA)
Westmont Coll. (CA)
Wheaton Coll. (MA)
Whitman Coll. (WA)
Whittier Coll. (CA)
Whitworth Univ. (WA)
Wichita State Univ. (KS)
Wilkes Univ. (PA)
Willamette Univ. (OR)
William Carey Univ. (MS)
William Jewell Coll. (MO)
William Woods Univ. (MO)
Williams Coll. (MA)
Wilmington Coll. (OH)
Winona State Univ. (MN)
Winthrop Univ. (SC)
Wisconsin Lutheran Coll.
Wofford Coll. (SC)
Wright State Univ. (OH)

Yale Univ. (CT)
York Coll. of Pennsylvania
Youngstown State Univ. (OH)

East Asian Languages, Literatures, and Linguistics

Arizona State Univ.
Ball State Univ. (IN)
Bates Coll. (ME)
Beloit Coll. (WI)
Bennington Coll. (VT)
Brigham Young Univ.–Provo (UT)
California State Univ.–Fullerton
California State Univ.–Los Angeles
Carnegie Mellon Univ. (PA)
Central Washington Univ.
Colgate Univ. (NY)
Columbia Univ. (NY)
Connecticut Coll.
CUNY–Hunter Coll.
Dartmouth Coll. (NH)
Eastern Michigan Univ.
Elizabethtown Coll. (PA)
Emory Univ. (GA)
George Washington Univ. (DC)
Georgetown Univ. (DC)
Gettysburg Coll. (PA)
Grinnell Coll. (IA)
Gustavus Adolphus Coll. (MN)
Hamilton Coll. (NY)
Hollins Univ. (VA)
Indiana Univ.–Bloomington
La Salle Univ. (PA)
Lawrence Univ. (WI)
Linfield Coll. (OR)
Macalester Coll. (MN)
Michigan State Univ.
Middlebury Coll. (VT)
North Central Coll. (IL)
Northwestern Univ. (IL)
Ohio State Univ.–Columbus
Pacific Lutheran Univ. (WA)
Pacific Univ. (OR)
Pennsylvania State Univ.–Univ. Park
Pomona Coll. (CA)
Purdue Univ.–West Lafayette (IN)
Reed Coll. (OR)
Rutgers, the State Univ. of New
    Jersey–New Brunswick
San Diego State Univ.
San Francisco State Univ.
San Jose State Univ. (CA)
Scripps Coll. (CA)
Smith Coll. (MA)
Stanford Univ. (CA)
Swarthmore Coll. (PA)
Trinity Coll. (CT)
Tufts Univ. (MA)
United States Naval Academy (MD)
Univ. of Alaska–Fairbanks
Univ. of California–Berkeley
Univ. of California–Davis
Univ. of California–Irvine
Univ. of California–Los Angeles
Univ. of California–Santa Barbara
Univ. of Colorado–Boulder
Univ. of Findlay (OH)
Univ. of Florida
Univ. of Georgia

Univ. of Hawaii–Hilo
Univ. of Hawaii–Manoa
Univ. of Illinois–Urbana-Champaign
Univ. of Iowa
Univ. of Kansas
Univ. of Maryland–Coll. Park
Univ. of Massachusetts–Amherst
Univ. of Minnesota–Twin Cities
Univ. of Montana
Univ. of Mount Union (OH)
Univ. of North Carolina–Charlotte
Univ. of Notre Dame (IN)
Univ. of Oklahoma
Univ. of Oregon
Univ. of Pennsylvania
Univ. of Pittsburgh
Univ. of Rochester (NY)
Univ. of San Francisco
Univ. of Southern California
Univ. of St. Thomas (MN)
Univ. of Texas–Austin
Univ. of the Pacific (CA)
Univ. of Utah
Univ. of Washington
Univ. of Wisconsin–Madison
Vassar Coll. (NY)
Wake Forest Univ. (NC)
Washington and Lee Univ. (VA)
Washington Univ. in St. Louis
Wellesley Coll. (MA)
Williams Coll. (MA)
Wofford Coll. (SC)
Yale Univ. (CT)

Ecology, Evolution, Systematics, and Population Biology

Alabama State Univ.
Alaska Pacific Univ.
Appalachian State Univ. (NC)
Arizona State Univ.
Arkansas Tech Univ.
Auburn Univ. (AL)
Averett Univ. (VA)
Bemidji State Univ. (MN)
Bennington Coll. (VT)
Bethel Coll. (IN)
Blackburn Coll. (IL)
Brevard Coll. (NC)
Bridgewater State Coll. (MA)
Brigham Young Univ.–Provo (UT)
Brown Univ. (RI)
California Polytechnic State Univ.–
    San Luis Obispo
California State Polytechnic Univ.–
    Pomona
California State Univ.–East Bay
California State Univ.–Long Beach
California State Univ.–Sacramento
California State Univ.–San Marcos
Case Western Reserve Univ. (OH)
Cedar Crest Coll. (PA)
Central Methodist Univ. (MO)
Clarkson Univ. (NY)
Coastal Carolina Univ. (SC)
Coe Coll. (IA)
Colby Coll. (ME)
Coll. of Charleston (SC)
Coll. of Santa Fe (NM)
Columbia Univ. (NY)

Concordia Coll. (NY)
Connecticut Coll.
Cornell Univ. (NY)
Cornerstone Univ. (MI)
Dartmouth Coll. (NH)
DeSales Univ. (PA)
Dowling Coll. (NY)
East Stroudsburg Univ. of
    Pennsylvania
Eastern Kentucky Univ.
Eastern Michigan Univ.
Eastern Nazarene Coll. (MA)
Eckerd Coll. (FL)
Elizabethtown Coll. (PA)
Fairleigh Dickinson Univ. (NJ)
Ferris State Univ. (MI)
Fitchburg State Coll. (MA)
Florida Institute of Technology
Florida International Univ.
Fort Lewis Coll. (CO)
Friends Univ. (KS)
Georgetown Coll. (KY)
Greenville Coll. (IL)
Hamline Univ. (MN)
Hawaii Pacific Univ.
Humboldt State Univ. (CA)
Idaho State Univ.
Illinois Coll.
Iona Coll. (NY)
Iowa State Univ.
Jacksonville Univ. (FL)
Johns Hopkins Univ. (MD)
Juniata Coll. (PA)
Lawrence Univ. (WI)
Lehigh Univ. (PA)
Lindenwood Univ. (MO)
Mansfield Univ. of Pennsylvania
Master's Coll. and Seminary (CA)
Michigan State Univ.
Missouri Southern State Univ.
Missouri Univ. of Science &
    Technology
Molloy Coll. (NY)
Monmouth Coll. (IL)
Monmouth Univ. (NJ)
Moravian Coll. (PA)
Morehead State Univ. (KY)
Nazareth Coll. (NY)
New Mexico State Univ.
Northeastern State Univ. (OK)
Northern Arizona Univ.
Northern Michigan Univ.
Northwest Missouri State Univ.
Northwestern Univ. (IL)
Nova Southeastern Univ. (FL)
Ohio State Univ.–Columbus
Olivet Nazarene Univ. (IL)
Oral Roberts Univ. (OK)
Philadelphia Univ.
Plymouth State Univ. (NH)
Prescott Coll. (AZ)
Princeton Univ. (NJ)
Queens Univ. of Charlotte (NC)
Rice Univ. (TX)
Richard Stockton Coll. of New
    Jersey
Rollins Coll. (FL)
Rutgers, the State Univ. of New
    Jersey–New Brunswick
Salisbury Univ. (MD)
Samford Univ. (AL)

San Diego State Univ.
Savannah State Univ. (GA)
Siena Coll. (NY)
Simpson Coll. (IA)
Slippery Rock Univ. of Pennsylvania
Southern Nazarene Univ. (OK)
Southwestern Coll. (KS)
St. Anselm Coll. (NH)
St. Francis Univ. (PA)
St. Gregory's Univ. (OK)
St. Joseph's Coll. (ME)
St. Mary's Univ. of Minnesota
Stetson Univ. (FL)
Suffolk Univ. (MA)
SUNY Coll. of Environmental
    Science and Forestry
SUNY Coll.–Oneonta
SUNY Maritime Coll.
Susquehanna Univ. (PA)
Taylor Univ. (IN)
Tennessee Technological Univ.
Texas State Univ.–San Marcos
Troy Univ. (AL)
Tufts Univ. (MA)
Tulane Univ. (LA)
United States Coast Guard
    Academy (CT)
Unity Coll. (ME)
Univ. of Akron (OH)
Univ. of Alabama
Univ. of Alaska–Southeast
Univ. of Arizona
Univ. of California–Davis
Univ. of California–Irvine
Univ. of California–Los Angeles
Univ. of California–Riverside
Univ. of California–San Diego
Univ. of California–Santa Barbara
Univ. of California–Santa Cruz
Univ. of Charleston (WV)
Univ. of Colorado–Boulder
Univ. of Connecticut
Univ. of Dayton (OH)
Univ. of Denver
Univ. of Florida
Univ. of Georgia
Univ. of Hawaii–Hilo
Univ. of Hawaii–Manoa
Univ. of La Verne (CA)
Univ. of Louisiana–Lafayette
Univ. of Maine
Univ. of Maine–Machias
Univ. of Maryland–Coll. Park
Univ. of Maryland–Eastern Shore
Univ. of Massachusetts–Dartmouth
Univ. of Miami (FL)
Univ. of Michigan–Ann Arbor
Univ. of Michigan–Flint
Univ. of Minnesota–Twin Cities
Univ. of Mount Union (OH)
Univ. of Nevada–Las Vegas
Univ. of Nevada–Reno
Univ. of New England (ME)
Univ. of New Haven (CT)
Univ. of North Alabama
Univ. of North Carolina–
    Wilmington
Univ. of Northern Iowa
Univ. of Oregon
Univ. of Pittsburgh
Univ. of Rhode Island

Univ. of San Diego
Univ. of South Carolina
Univ. of Southern Mississippi
Univ. of Tampa (FL)
Univ. of Texas–Austin
Univ. of Virginia–Wise
Univ. of West Alabama
Univ. of West Florida
Univ. of Wisconsin–Madison
Univ. of Wisconsin–Superior
Ursuline Coll. (OH)
Washington Coll. (MD)
Waynesburg Univ. (PA)
Western Washington Univ.
William Jewell Coll. (MO)
Wingate Univ. (NC)

Economics

Adelphi Univ. (NY)
Adrian Coll. (MI)
Agnes Scott Coll. (GA)
Alabama Agricultural and
    Mechanical Univ.
Albion Coll. (MI)
Albright Coll. (PA)
Alcorn State Univ. (MS)
Alfred Univ. (NY)
Allegheny Coll. (PA)
Alma Coll. (MI)
American Jewish Univ. (CA)
American Univ. (DC)
Amherst Coll. (MA)
Appalachian State Univ. (NC)
Aquinas Coll. (MI)
Arizona State Univ.
Arkansas State Univ.–Jonesboro
Arkansas Tech Univ.
Armstrong Atlantic State Univ. (GA)
Ashland Univ. (OH)
Assumption Coll. (MA)
Auburn Univ. (AL)
Augsburg Coll. (MN)
Augustana Coll. (IL)
Augustana Coll. (SD)
Austin Coll. (TX)
Babson Coll. (MA)
Baker Univ. (KS)
Baldwin-Wallace Coll. (OH)
Ball State Univ. (IN)
Barnard Coll. (NY)
Barry Univ. (FL)
Barton Coll. (NC)
Bates Coll. (ME)
Bellarmine Univ. (KY)
Belmont Abbey Coll. (NC)
Belmont Univ. (TN)
Beloit Coll. (WI)
Bemidji State Univ. (MN)
Benedict Coll. (SC)
Benedictine Coll. (KS)
Benedictine Univ. (IL)
Berea Coll. (KY)
Berry Coll. (GA)
Bethany Coll. (WV)
Bethel Univ. (MN)
Binghamton Univ.–SUNY
Bloomfield Coll. (NJ)
Bloomsburg Univ. of Pennsylvania
Bluffton Univ. (OH)
Boise State Univ. (ID)

Boston Univ.
Bowdoin Coll. (ME)
Bowling Green State Univ. (OH)
Bradley Univ. (IL)
Brandeis Univ. (MA)
Bridgewater Coll. (VA)
Bridgewater State Coll. (MA)
Brigham Young Univ.–Provo (UT)
Brown Univ. (RI)
Bryant Univ. (RI)
Bryn Mawr Coll. (PA)
Bucknell Univ. (PA)
Buffalo State Coll.–SUNY
Butler Univ. (IN)
California Institute of Technology
California Lutheran Univ.
California Polytechnic State Univ.–
    San Luis Obispo
California State Polytechnic Univ.–
    Pomona
California State Univ.–Bakersfield
California State Univ.–Chico
California State Univ.–Dominguez
    Hills
California State Univ.–East Bay
California State Univ.–Fresno
California State Univ.–Fullerton
California State Univ.–Long Beach
California State Univ.–Los Angeles
California State Univ.–Northridge
California State Univ.–Sacramento
California State Univ.–San
    Bernardino
California State Univ.–San Marcos
California State Univ.–Stanislaus
Calvin Coll. (MI)
Campbell Univ. (NC)
Canisius Coll. (NY)
Capital Univ. (OH)
Carleton Coll. (MN)
Carnegie Mellon Univ. (PA)
Carson-Newman Coll. (TN)
Carthage Coll. (WI)
Case Western Reserve Univ. (OH)
Catholic Univ. of America (DC)
Centenary Coll. of Louisiana
Central Coll. (IA)
Central Connecticut State Univ.
Central Michigan Univ.
Central State Univ. (OH)
Central Washington Univ.
Centre Coll. (KY)
Charleston Southern Univ. (SC)
Chatham Univ. (PA)
Cheyney Univ. of Pennsylvania
Chicago State Univ.
Claremont McKenna Coll. (CA)
Clarion Univ. of Pennsylvania
Clark Atlanta Univ.
Clark Univ. (MA)
Cleveland State Univ.
Coe Coll. (IA)
Colby Coll. (ME)
Colgate Univ. (NY)
Coll. of Charleston (SC)
Coll. of Idaho (ID)
Coll. of Mount St. Vincent (NY)
Coll. of New Jersey
Coll. of Notre Dame of Maryland
Coll. of St. Benedict (MN)
Coll. of St. Elizabeth (NJ)

Coll. of St. Scholastica (MN)
Coll. of the Holy Cross (MA)
Coll. of William and Mary (VA)
Coll. of Wooster (OH)
Colorado Coll.
Colorado School of Mines
Colorado State Univ.
Columbia Univ. (NY)
Concordia Coll.–Moorhead (MN)
Concordia Univ. Wisconsin
Connecticut Coll.
Converse Coll. (SC)
Cornell Coll. (IA)
Cornell Univ. (NY)
Covenant Coll. (GA)
Creighton Univ. (NE)
CUNY–Baruch Coll.
CUNY–Brooklyn Coll.
CUNY–City Coll.
CUNY–Coll. of Staten Island
CUNY–Hunter Coll.
CUNY–Lehman Coll.
CUNY–Queens Coll.
CUNY–York Coll.
Dartmouth Coll. (NH)
Davidson Coll. (NC)
Davis and Elkins Coll. (WV)
Denison Univ. (OH)
DePaul Univ. (IL)
DePauw Univ. (IN)
Dickinson Coll. (PA)
Dillard Univ. (LA)
Dominican Coll. (NY)
Dominican Univ. (IL)
Dowling Coll. (NY)
Drake Univ. (IA)
Drew Univ. (NJ)
Drury Univ. (MO)
Duke Univ. (NC)
Duquesne Univ. (PA)
Earlham Coll. (IN)
East Carolina Univ. (NC)
East Stroudsburg Univ. of
    Pennsylvania
East Tennessee State Univ.
Eastern Connecticut State Univ.
Eastern Illinois Univ.
Eastern Kentucky Univ.
Eastern Mennonite Univ. (VA)
Eastern Michigan Univ.
Eastern Univ. (PA)
Eastern Washington Univ.
Eckerd Coll. (FL)
Edgewood Coll. (WI)
Edinboro Univ. of Pennsylvania
Elizabethtown Coll. (PA)
Elmhurst Coll. (IL)
Elmira Coll. (NY)
Elon Univ. (NC)
Emory and Henry Coll. (VA)
Emory Univ. (GA)
Emporia State Univ. (KS)
Excelsior Coll. (NY)
Fairfield Univ. (CT)
Fairleigh Dickinson Univ. (NJ)
Farmingdale State Coll.–SUNY
Fayetteville State Univ. (NC)
Fitchburg State Coll. (MA)
Florida Atlantic Univ.
Florida International Univ.
Florida Southern Coll.

Florida State Univ.
Fordham Univ. (NY)
Fort Hays State Univ. (KS)
Fort Lewis Coll. (CO)
Framingham State Coll. (MA)
Francis Marion Univ. (SC)
Franciscan Univ. of Steubenville
    (OH)
Franklin and Marshall Coll. (PA)
Franklin Coll. (IN)
Frostburg State Univ. (MD)
Furman Univ. (SC)
Gallaudet Univ. (DC)
George Fox Univ. (OR)
George Mason Univ. (VA)
George Washington Univ. (DC)
Georgetown Coll. (KY)
Georgetown Univ. (DC)
Georgia Southern Univ.
Georgia State Univ.
Gettysburg Coll. (PA)
Gonzaga Univ. (WA)
Gordon Coll. (MA)
Goucher Coll. (MD)
Graceland Univ. (IA)
Grand Valley State Univ. (MI)
Grinnell Coll. (IA)
Grove City Coll. (PA)
Guilford Coll. (NC)
Gustavus Adolphus Coll. (MN)
Hamilton Coll. (NY)
Hamline Univ. (MN)
Hampden-Sydney Coll. (VA)
Hampshire Coll. (MA)
Hampton Univ. (VA)
Hanover Coll. (IN)
Hardin-Simmons Univ. (TX)
Harding Univ. (AR)
Hartwick Coll. (NY)
Harvard Univ. (MA)
Haverford Coll. (PA)
Hawaii Pacific Univ.
Heidelberg Univ. (OH)
Hendrix Coll. (AR)
Hillsdale Coll. (MI)
Hiram Coll. (OH)
Hobart and William Smith Colleges
    (NY)
Hofstra Univ. (NY)
Hollins Univ. (VA)
Holy Family Univ. (PA)
Hood Coll. (MD)
Hope Coll. (MI)
Howard Univ. (DC)
Humboldt State Univ. (CA)
Idaho State Univ.
Illinois Coll.
Illinois State Univ.
Illinois Wesleyan Univ.
Immaculata Univ. (PA)
Indiana State Univ.
Indiana Univ. Northwest
Indiana Univ. of Pennsylvania
Indiana Univ.–Bloomington
Indiana Univ.–Kokomo
Indiana Univ.–South Bend
Indiana Univ.-Purdue Univ.–Fort
    Wayne
Indiana Univ.-Purdue Univ.–
    Indianapolis
Indiana Wesleyan Univ.

Iona Coll. (NY)
Iowa State Univ.
Ithaca Coll. (NY)
Jacksonville State Univ. (AL)
Jacksonville Univ. (FL)
James Madison Univ. (VA)
Jamestown Coll. (ND)
John Carroll Univ. (OH)
Johns Hopkins Univ. (MD)
Johnson C. Smith Univ. (NC)
Juniata Coll. (PA)
Kalamazoo Coll. (MI)
Kansas State Univ.
Kean Univ. (NJ)
Keene State Coll. (NH)
Kenyon Coll. (OH)
King's Coll. (PA)
Knox Coll. (IL)
Kutztown Univ. of Pennsylvania
La Salle Univ. (PA)
Lafayette Coll. (PA)
Lake Forest Coll. (IL)
Lamar Univ. (TX)
Lawrence Univ. (WI)
Le Moyne Coll. (NY)
Lebanon Valley Coll. (PA)
Lenoir-Rhyne Univ. (NC)
Lewis & Clark Coll. (OR)
Lewis Univ. (IL)
Limestone Coll. (SC)
Lincoln Univ. (PA)
Linfield Coll. (OR)
Lock Haven Univ. of Pennsylvania
Long Island Univ.–C.W. Post
    Campus (NY)
Longwood Univ. (VA)
Loras Coll. (IA)
Louisiana Coll.
Louisiana State Univ.–Baton Rouge
Loyola Marymount Univ. (CA)
Loyola Univ. Maryland
Luther Coll. (IA)
Lycoming Coll. (PA)
Lynchburg Coll. (VA)
Lyon Coll. (AR)
Macalester Coll. (MN)
Manchester Coll. (IN)
Manhattan Coll. (NY)
Manhattanville Coll. (NY)
Mansfield Univ. of Pennsylvania
Marian Univ. (IN)
Marietta Coll. (OH)
Marist Coll. (NY)
Marlboro Coll. (VT)
Marquette Univ. (WI)
Marshall Univ. (WV)
Mary Baldwin Coll. (VA)
Marymount Univ. (VA)
Maryville Coll. (TN)
Massachusetts Institute of
    Technology
McDaniel Coll. (MD)
McKendree Univ. (IL)
Meredith Coll. (NC)
Merrimack Coll. (MA)
Messiah Coll. (PA)
Metropolitan State Coll. of Denver
Miami Univ.–Oxford (OH)
Michigan State Univ.
Michigan Technological Univ.
Middle Tennessee State Univ.

Middlebury Coll. (VT)
Midwestern State Univ. (TX)
Millersville Univ. of Pennsylvania
Mills Coll. (CA)
Millsaps Coll. (MS)
Minnesota State Univ.–Mankato
Minnesota State Univ.–Moorhead
Minot State Univ. (ND)
Mississippi State Univ.
Missouri State Univ.
Missouri Univ. of Science &
    Technology
Missouri Valley Coll.
Missouri Western State Univ.
Montana State Univ.
Montclair State Univ. (NJ)
Moravian Coll. (PA)
Morehouse Coll. (GA)
Mount Holyoke Coll. (MA)
Mount St. Mary's Univ. (MD)
Muhlenberg Coll. (PA)
Murray State Univ. (KY)
Muskingum Univ. (OH)
Nazareth Coll. (NY)
Nebraska Wesleyan Univ.
New Jersey City Univ.
New Mexico State Univ.
New York Institute of Technology
New York Univ.
North Carolina A&T State Univ.
North Central Coll. (IL)
North Dakota State Univ.
North Park Univ. (IL)
Northeastern Illinois Univ.
Northeastern Univ. (MA)
Northern Arizona Univ.
Northern Illinois Univ.
Northern Michigan Univ.
Northern State Univ. (SD)
Northland Coll. (WI)
Northwest Missouri State Univ.
Northwestern Coll. (IA)
Northwestern Univ. (IL)
Norwich Univ. (VT)
Oakland Univ. (MI)
Oberlin Coll. (OH)
Occidental Coll. (CA)
Oglethorpe Univ. (GA)
Ohio Dominican Univ.
Ohio State Univ.–Columbus
Ohio Univ.
Ohio Wesleyan Univ.
Oklahoma State Univ.
Old Dominion Univ. (VA)
Olivet Nazarene Univ. (IL)
Oregon State Univ.
Otterbein Coll. (OH)
Pace Univ. (NY)
Pacific Lutheran Univ. (WA)
Pacific Univ. (OR)
Park Univ. (MO)
Pennsylvania State Univ.–Univ. Park
Pepperdine Univ. (CA)
Pfeiffer Univ. (NC)
Pittsburg State Univ. (KS)
Pitzer Coll. (CA)
Point Loma Nazarene Univ. (CA)
Pomona Coll. (CA)
Portland State Univ. (OR)
Prairie View A&M Univ. (TX)
Princeton Univ. (NJ)

Principia Coll. (IL)
Providence Coll. (RI)
Purchase Coll.–SUNY
Quinnipiac Univ. (CT)
Radford Univ. (VA)
Ramapo Coll. of New Jersey
Randolph Coll. (VA)
Randolph-Macon Coll. (VA)
Reed Coll. (OR)
Regis Univ. (CO)
Rensselaer Polytechnic Institute
    (NY)
Rhode Island Coll.
Rhodes Coll. (TN)
Rice Univ. (TX)
Richard Stockton Coll. of New
    Jersey
Rider Univ. (NJ)
Ripon Coll. (WI)
Roanoke Coll. (VA)
Robert Morris Univ. (PA)
Rochester Institute of Technology
    (NY)
Rockford Coll. (IL)
Rockhurst Univ. (MO)
Rocky Mountain Coll. (MT)
Rollins Coll. (FL)
Roosevelt Univ. (IL)
Rose-Hulman Institute of
    Technology (IN)
Rosemont Coll. (PA)
Rutgers, the State Univ. of New
    Jersey–Camden
Rutgers, the State Univ. of New
    Jersey–New Brunswick
Rutgers, the State Univ. of New
    Jersey–Newark
Sacred Heart Univ. (CT)
Saginaw Valley State Univ. (MI)
Salem Coll. (NC)
Salem State Coll. (MA)
Salisbury Univ. (MD)
Salve Regina Univ. (RI)
Sam Houston State Univ. (TX)
San Diego State Univ.
San Francisco State Univ.
San Jose State Univ. (CA)
Santa Clara Univ. (CA)
Scripps Coll. (CA)
Seattle Pacific Univ.
Seattle Univ.
Seton Hall Univ. (NJ)
Seton Hill Univ. (PA)
Sewanee–Univ. of the South (TN)
Shepherd Univ. (WV)
Shippensburg Univ. of Pennsylvania
Siena Coll. (NY)
Simmons Coll. (MA)
Simpson Coll. (IA)
Skidmore Coll. (NY)
Slippery Rock Univ. of Pennsylvania
Smith Coll. (MA)
Sonoma State Univ. (CA)
South Dakota State Univ.
Southeast Missouri State Univ.
Southern Illinois Univ.–Carbondale
Southern Illinois Univ.–Edwardsville
Southern Methodist Univ. (TX)
Southern New Hampshire Univ.
Southern Oregon Univ.
Southern Utah Univ.

Southwestern Coll. (KS)
Southwestern Univ. (TX)
Spelman Coll. (GA)
St. Ambrose Univ. (IA)
St. Catherine Univ. (MN)
St. Cloud State Univ. (MN)
St. Edward's Univ. (TX)
St. Francis Coll. (NY)
St. Francis Univ. (PA)
St. John Fisher Coll. (NY)
St. John's Univ. (MN)
St. John's Univ. (NY)
St. Joseph Coll. (CT)
St. Joseph's Coll. (IN)
St. Joseph's Univ. (PA)
St. Lawrence Univ. (NY)
St. Louis Univ.
St. Mary's Coll. (IN)
St. Mary's Coll. of California
St. Mary's Coll. of Maryland
St. Mary's Univ. of San Antonio
    (TX)
St. Michael's Coll. (VT)
St. Norbert Coll. (WI)
St. Olaf Coll. (MN)
St. Peter's Coll. (NJ)
St. Vincent Coll. (PA)
Stanford Univ. (CA)
Stephen F. Austin State Univ. (TX)
Stetson Univ. (FL)
Stonehill Coll. (MA)
Suffolk Univ. (MA)
SUNY Coll.–Cortland
SUNY Coll.–Oneonta
SUNY Coll.–Potsdam
SUNY–Fredonia
SUNY–Geneseo
SUNY–Oswego
SUNY–Plattsburgh
SUNY–Stony Brook
Susquehanna Univ. (PA)
Swarthmore Coll. (PA)
Syracuse Univ. (NY)
Tarleton State Univ. (TX)
Temple Univ. (PA)
Tennessee Technological Univ.
Texas A&M Univ.–Coll. Station
Texas A&M Univ.–Commerce
Texas A&M Univ.–Corpus Christi
Texas Christian Univ.
Texas Lutheran Univ.
Texas State Univ.–San Marcos
Texas Tech Univ.
Thomas Edison State Coll. (NJ)
Thomas More Coll. (KY)
Tougaloo Coll. (MS)
Touro Coll. (NY)
Towson Univ. (MD)
Transylvania Univ. (KY)
Trinity Coll. (CT)
Trinity Univ. (DC)
Truman State Univ. (MO)
Tufts Univ. (MA)
Tulane Univ. (LA)
Tuskegee Univ. (AL)
Union Coll. (NY)
Union Univ. (TN)
United States Air Force Academy
    (CO)
United States Naval Academy (MD)
Univ. at Albany–SUNY

Univ. at Buffalo–SUNY
Univ. of Akron (OH)
Univ. of Alaska–Anchorage
Univ. of Alaska–Fairbanks
Univ. of Arizona
Univ. of Arkansas
Univ. of California–Berkeley
Univ. of California–Davis
Univ. of California–Irvine
Univ. of California–Los Angeles
Univ. of California–Riverside
Univ. of California–San Diego
Univ. of California–Santa Barbara
Univ. of California–Santa Cruz
Univ. of Central Arkansas
Univ. of Central Florida
Univ. of Central Missouri
Univ. of Central Oklahoma
Univ. of Chicago
Univ. of Colorado–Boulder
Univ. of Colorado–Colorado
    Springs
Univ. of Colorado–Denver
Univ. of Connecticut
Univ. of Dallas
Univ. of Dayton (OH)
Univ. of Delaware
Univ. of Denver
Univ. of Detroit Mercy
Univ. of Evansville (IN)
Univ. of Findlay (OH)
Univ. of Florida
Univ. of Georgia
Univ. of Hartford (CT)
Univ. of Hawaii–Hilo
Univ. of Hawaii–Manoa
Univ. of Houston
Univ. of Illinois–Chicago
Univ. of Illinois–Springfield
Univ. of Illinois–Urbana-Champaign
Univ. of Iowa
Univ. of Kansas
Univ. of Kentucky
Univ. of La Verne (CA)
Univ. of Louisville (KY)
Univ. of Maine
Univ. of Mary Washington (VA)
Univ. of Maryland–Baltimore
    County
Univ. of Maryland–Coll. Park
Univ. of Massachusetts–Amherst
Univ. of Massachusetts–Boston
Univ. of Massachusetts–Dartmouth
Univ. of Massachusetts–Lowell
Univ. of Memphis
Univ. of Miami (FL)
Univ. of Michigan–Ann Arbor
Univ. of Michigan–Dearborn
Univ. of Michigan–Flint
Univ. of Minnesota–Duluth
Univ. of Minnesota–Morris
Univ. of Minnesota–Twin Cities
Univ. of Mississippi
Univ. of Missouri
Univ. of Missouri–Kansas City
Univ. of Missouri–St. Louis
Univ. of Montana
Univ. of Mount Union (OH)
Univ. of Nebraska–Kearney
Univ. of Nebraska–Lincoln
Univ. of Nevada–Las Vegas

Univ. of Nevada–Reno
Univ. of New Hampshire
Univ. of New Mexico
Univ. of New Orleans
Univ. of North Carolina–Asheville
Univ. of North Carolina–Chapel Hill
Univ. of North Carolina–Charlotte
Univ. of North Carolina–
    Greensboro
Univ. of North Carolina–
    Wilmington
Univ. of North Dakota
Univ. of North Florida
Univ. of North Texas
Univ. of Northern Colorado
Univ. of Northern Iowa
Univ. of Notre Dame (IN)
Univ. of Oklahoma
Univ. of Oregon
Univ. of Pennsylvania
Univ. of Pittsburgh
Univ. of Pittsburgh–Bradford
Univ. of Pittsburgh–Johnstown
Univ. of Puget Sound (WA)
Univ. of Redlands (CA)
Univ. of Rhode Island
Univ. of Richmond (VA)
Univ. of Rochester (NY)
Univ. of San Diego
Univ. of San Francisco
Univ. of Science and Arts of
    Oklahoma
Univ. of Scranton (PA)
Univ. of South Carolina
Univ. of South Dakota
Univ. of South Florida
Univ. of Southern California
Univ. of Southern Indiana
Univ. of Southern Maine
Univ. of St. Thomas (MN)
Univ. of St. Thomas (TX)
Univ. of Tampa (FL)
Univ. of Tennessee
Univ. of Tennessee–Martin
Univ. of Texas–Arlington
Univ. of Texas–Austin
Univ. of Texas–Dallas
Univ. of Texas–Pan American
Univ. of the District of Columbia
Univ. of the Ozarks (AR)
Univ. of the Pacific (CA)
Univ. of Toledo (OH)
Univ. of Tulsa (OK)
Univ. of Utah
Univ. of Vermont
Univ. of Virginia
Univ. of Virginia–Wise
Univ. of Washington
Univ. of West Florida
Univ. of West Georgia
Univ. of Wisconsin–Eau Claire
Univ. of Wisconsin–Green Bay
Univ. of Wisconsin–La Crosse
Univ. of Wisconsin–Madison
Univ. of Wisconsin–Milwaukee
Univ. of Wisconsin–Oshkosh
Univ. of Wisconsin–Parkside
Univ. of Wisconsin–Platteville
Univ. of Wisconsin–River Falls
Univ. of Wisconsin–Stevens Point
Univ. of Wisconsin–Superior

Univ. of Wisconsin–Whitewater
Ursinus Coll. (PA)
Utah State Univ.
Utica Coll. (NY)
Valparaiso Univ. (IN)
Vanderbilt Univ. (TN)
Vassar Coll. (NY)
Virginia Military Institute
Virginia Tech
Wabash Coll. (IN)
Wagner Coll. (NY)
Wake Forest Univ. (NC)
Wartburg Coll. (IA)
Washburn Univ. (KS)
Washington and Jefferson Coll.
    (PA)
Washington and Lee Univ. (VA)
Washington Coll. (MD)
Washington State Univ.
Washington Univ. in St. Louis
Wayne State Univ. (MI)
Webster Univ. (MO)
Wellesley Coll. (MA)
Wells Coll. (NY)
Wesleyan Coll. (GA)
Wesleyan Univ. (CT)
West Texas A&M Univ.
West Virginia State Univ.
West Virginia Univ.
West Virginia Wesleyan Coll.
Western Connecticut State Univ.
Western Illinois Univ.
Western Kentucky Univ.
Western Michigan Univ.
Western New England Coll. (MA)
Western Oregon Univ.
Western State Coll. of Colorado
Western Washington Univ.
Westfield State Coll. (MA)
Westminster Coll. (PA)
Westminster Coll. (MO)
Westmont Coll. (CA)
Wheaton Coll. (IL)
Wheaton Coll. (MA)
Whitman Coll. (WA)
Whittier Coll. (CA)
Whitworth Univ. (WA)
Wichita State Univ. (KS)
Widener Univ. (PA)
Willamette Univ. (OR)
William Paterson Univ. of New
    Jersey
Williams Coll. (MA)
Winston-Salem State University
    (NC)
Winthrop Univ. (SC)
Wittenberg Univ. (OH)
Wofford Coll. (SC)
Worcester Polytechnic Institute
    (MA)
Worcester State Coll. (MA)
Wright State Univ. (OH)
Xavier Univ. (OH)
Yale Univ. (CT)
Yeshiva Univ. (NY)
Youngstown State Univ. (OH)

Education

Adelphi Univ. (NY)
Adrian Coll. (MI)

Alabama Agricultural and
    Mechanical Univ.
Albany State Univ. (GA)
Albertus Magnus Coll. (CT)
Alice Lloyd Coll. (KY)
Allegheny Coll. (PA)
Allen Univ. (SC)
Alma Coll. (MI)
Alverno Coll. (WI)
Anderson Univ. (IN)
Arcadia Univ. (PA)
Ashland Univ. (OH)
Auburn Univ. (AL)
Augsburg Coll. (MN)
Augustana Coll. (SD)
Baldwin-Wallace Coll. (OH)
Barton Coll. (NC)
Bay Path Coll. (MA)
Belhaven Univ. (MS)
Belmont Abbey Coll. (NC)
Belmont Univ. (TN)
Beloit Coll. (WI)
Benedict Coll. (SC)
Bennington Coll. (VT)
Berea Coll. (KY)
Bethany Coll. (KS)
Bethany Coll. (WV)
Bethel Coll. (IN)
Bethel Coll. (TN)
Bethel Univ. (MN)
Bethune-Cookman Univ. (FL)
Bloomfield Coll. (NJ)
Bluefield Coll. (VA)
Bowling Green State Univ. (OH)
Brevard Coll. (NC)
Brewton-Parker Coll. (GA)
Brown Univ. (RI)
Bryn Athyn Coll. of the New Church
    (PA)
Bucknell Univ. (PA)
Cabrini Coll. (PA)
California Baptist Univ.
California State Polytechnic Univ.–
    Pomona
California State Univ.–Fullerton
California State Univ.–Monterey Bay
California State Univ.–San
    Bernardino
California Univ. of Pennsylvania
Calumet Coll. of St. Joseph (IN)
Calvin Coll. (MI)
Capital Univ. (OH)
Cardinal Stritch Univ. (WI)
Carroll Univ. (WI)
Carson-Newman Coll. (TN)
Case Western Reserve Univ. (OH)
Castleton State Coll. (VT)
Catawba Coll. (NC)
Catholic Univ. of America (DC)
Centenary Coll. of Louisiana
Central Baptist Coll. (AR)
Central State Univ. (OH)
Charleston Southern Univ. (SC)
Clarke Univ. (IA)
Cleveland State Univ.
Coker Coll. (SC)
Colgate Univ. (NY)
Coll. of Wooster (OH)
Columbia Univ. (NY)
Concordia Coll. (NY)
Concordia Univ. (NE)

Concordia Univ. (OR)
Concordia Univ. Chicago (IL)
Concordia Univ.–St. Paul (MN)
Converse Coll. (SC)
Cornell Univ. (NY)
Cornerstone Univ. (MI)
Crown Coll. (MN)
Culver-Stockton Coll. (MO)
Cumberland Univ. (TN)
CUNY–City Coll.
CUNY–Lehman Coll.
Curry Coll. (MA)
D'Youville Coll. (NY)
Dallas Baptist Univ.
Defiance Coll. (OH)
Denison Univ. (OH)
Dowling Coll. (NY)
Drury Univ. (MO)
Duke Univ. (NC)
Duquesne Univ. (PA)
East Texas Baptist Univ.
Eastern Nazarene Coll. (MA)
Eastern Washington Univ.
Edgewood Coll. (WI)
Elmhurst Coll. (IL)
Elmira Coll. (NY)
Emory Univ. (GA)
Endicott Coll. (MA)
Eureka Coll. (IL)
Ferris State Univ. (MI)
Fitchburg State Coll. (MA)
Florida Memorial Univ.
Florida Southern Coll.
Fordham Univ. (NY)
Furman Univ. (SC)
Gallaudet Univ. (DC)
Gannon Univ. (PA)
George Washington Univ. (DC)
Georgia Southern Univ.
Goddard Coll. (VT)
Grace Coll. and Seminary (IN)
Graceland Univ. (IA)
Hampshire Coll. (MA)
Hardin-Simmons Univ. (TX)
Heidelberg Univ. (OH)
Heritage Univ. (WA)
High Point Univ. (NC)
Hiram Coll. (OH)
Houston Baptist Univ.
Howard Payne Univ. (TX)
Humboldt State Univ. (CA)
Huntington Univ. (IN)
Huston-Tillotson Univ. (TX)
Illinois Wesleyan Univ.
Jackson State Univ. (MS)
Jacksonville Univ. (FL)
Jarvis Christian Coll. (TX)
Johnson and Wales Univ. (RI)
Juniata Coll. (PA)
Kent State Univ. (OH)
King Coll. (TN)
Knox Coll. (IL)
Lake Forest Coll. (IL)
Lakeland Coll. (WI)
Lamar Univ. (TX)
Lasell Coll. (MA)
Lees-McRae Coll. (NC)
Limestone Coll. (SC)
Lincoln Memorial Univ. (TN)
Lincoln Univ. (PA)
Lindenwood Univ. (MO)

Lipscomb Univ. (TN)
Louisiana Coll.
Louisiana Tech Univ.
Macon State Coll. (GA)
Madonna Univ. (MI)
Manchester Coll. (IN)
Manhattanville Coll. (NY)
Mansfield Univ. of Pennsylvania
Marietta Coll. (OH)
Martin Univ. (IN)
Maryville Coll. (TN)
Massachusetts Coll. of Liberal Arts
Michigan State Univ.
Midwestern State Univ. (TX)
Millikin Univ. (IL)
Millsaps Coll. (MS)
Mississippi Coll.
Mississippi Valley State Univ.
Missouri Baptist Univ.
Missouri Univ. of Science & Technology
Missouri Valley Coll.
Mitchell Coll. (CT)
Monmouth Coll. (IL)
Monmouth Univ. (NJ)
Morehouse Coll. (GA)
Morningside Coll. (IA)
Mount Holyoke Coll. (MA)
Mount Mary Coll. (WI)
Mount St. Mary's Coll. (CA)
Mountain State Univ. (WV)
Newberry Coll. (SC)
Niagara Univ. (NY)
Nichols Coll. (MA)
North Carolina State Univ.–Raleigh
Northern Arizona Univ.
Northern Michigan Univ.
Northern State Univ. (SD)
Northland Coll. (WI)
Northwestern Coll. (IA)
Northwestern Oklahoma State Univ.
Northwestern Univ. (IL)
Nova Southeastern Univ. (FL)
Ohio Northern Univ.
Ohio State Univ.–Columbus
Oklahoma Baptist Univ.
Oklahoma Christian Univ.
Oklahoma City Univ.
Oklahoma State Univ.
Olivet Coll. (MI)
Oregon State Univ.
Our Lady of Holy Cross Coll. (LA)
Our Lady of the Lake Univ. (TX)
Pace Univ. (NY)
Pacific Lutheran Univ. (WA)
Palm Beach Atlantic Univ. (FL)
Park Univ. (MO)
Peru State Coll. (NE)
Point Loma Nazarene Univ. (CA)
Pratt Institute (NY)
Prescott Coll. (AZ)
Principia Coll. (IL)
Randolph Coll. (VA)
Regent Univ. (VA)
Regis Univ. (CO)
Ripon Coll. (WI)
Rockford Coll. (IL)
Roger Williams Univ. (RI)
Roosevelt Univ. (IL)
Salem State Coll. (MA)

San Jose State Univ. (CA)
Schreiner Univ. (TX)
Shaw Univ. (NC)
Shawnee State Univ. (OH)
Shepherd Univ. (WV)
Simmons Coll. (MA)
Simpson Coll. (IA)
Smith Coll. (MA)
Southeastern Univ. (FL)
Southern Adventist Univ. (TN)
Southern Nazarene Univ. (OK)
Southern New Hampshire Univ.
Southern Wesleyan Univ. (SC)
Southwest Minnesota State Univ.
Southwestern Univ. (TX)
Spalding Univ. (KY)
Spelman Coll. (GA)
Springfield Coll. (MA)
St. Andrews Presbyterian Coll. (NC)
St. John Fisher Coll. (NY)
St. Joseph Coll. (CT)
St. Joseph's Univ. (PA)
St. Mary-of-the-Woods Coll. (IN)
Suffolk Univ. (MA)
SUNY Coll.–Potsdam
SUNY Empire State Coll.
SUNY–Oswego
Swarthmore Coll. (PA)
Syracuse Univ. (NY)
Tabor Coll. (KS)
Tarleton State Univ. (TX)
Texas Christian Univ.
Texas Wesleyan Univ.
Thomas More Coll. (KY)
Thomas Univ. (GA)
Trinity Christian Coll. (IL)
Trinity Coll. (CT)
Tusculum Coll. (TN)
Tuskegee Univ. (AL)
Union Coll. (KY)
Union Institute and Univ. (OH)
Unity Coll. (ME)
Univ. of Alaska–Fairbanks
Univ. of Alaska–Southeast
Univ. of California–Riverside
Univ. of Central Missouri
Univ. of Charleston (WV)
Univ. of Dayton (OH)
Univ. of Evansville (IN)
Univ. of Findlay (OH)
Univ. of Great Falls (MT)
Univ. of Iowa
Univ. of La Verne (CA)
Univ. of Maine
Univ. of Maryland–Coll. Park
Univ. of Maryland–Eastern Shore
Univ. of Massachusetts–Amherst
Univ. of Michigan–Ann Arbor
Univ. of Michigan–Dearborn
Univ. of Michigan–Flint
Univ. of Minnesota–Morris
Univ. of Minnesota–Twin Cities
Univ. of Mississippi
Univ. of Missouri
Univ. of Missouri–Kansas City
Univ. of Missouri–St. Louis
Univ. of Montana
Univ. of Montevallo (AL)
Univ. of Nebraska–Lincoln
Univ. of Nevada–Las Vegas
Univ. of New England (ME)

Univ. of Oregon
Univ. of Pennsylvania
Univ. of Redlands (CA)
Univ. of Southern California
Univ. of St. Francis (IL)
Univ. of St. Mary (KS)
Univ. of Tennessee–Chattanooga
Univ. of the District of Columbia
Univ. of the Pacific (CA)
Univ. of Toledo (OH)
Univ. of Tulsa (OK)
Univ. of Utah
Univ. of Vermont
Univ. of Wisconsin–Green Bay
Univ. of Wisconsin–Milwaukee
Upper Iowa Univ.
Vanderbilt Univ. (TN)
Vanguard Univ. of Southern California
Vassar Coll. (NY)
Victory Univ. (TN)
Virginia Intermont Coll.
Wake Forest Univ. (NC)
Waldorf Coll. (IA)
Walsh Univ. (OH)
Washburn Univ. (KS)
Washington and Jefferson Coll. (PA)
Washington State Univ.
Washington Univ. in St. Louis
Wayland Baptist Univ. (TX)
Webster Univ. (MO)
Wellesley Coll. (MA)
Wesley Coll. (DE)
West Virginia Wesleyan Coll.
Western Michigan Univ.
Western Oregon Univ.
Western State Coll. of Colorado
Wheaton Coll. (IL)
Widener Univ. (PA)
William Paterson Univ. of New Jersey
William Woods Univ. (MO)
Wilmington Coll. (OH)
Wilmington Univ. (DE)
Wisconsin Lutheran Coll.
Xavier Univ. (OH)
Yeshiva Univ. (NY)
York Coll. of Pennsylvania
Youngstown State Univ. (OH)

Educational Administration and Supervision

Alabama Agricultural and Mechanical Univ.
Auburn Univ. (AL)
Bellarmine Univ. (KY)
Bethel Univ. (MN)
California State Univ.–Fullerton
California State Univ.–Sacramento
California State Univ.–San Bernardino
Carthage Coll. (WI)
Cazenovia Coll. (NY)
Centenary Coll. of Louisiana
Charleston Southern Univ. (SC)
Clarion Univ. of Pennsylvania
CUNY–Lehman Coll.
D'Youville Coll. (NY)

Eastern Michigan Univ.
Eastern Washington Univ.
Elizabeth City State Univ. (NC)
Fayetteville State Univ. (NC)
Gallaudet Univ. (DC)
Georgia Southern Univ.
Harding Univ. (AR)
Harris-Stowe State Univ. (MO)
Indiana Univ.–South Bend
Jackson State Univ. (MS)
Jacksonville State Univ. (AL)
LeTourneau Univ. (TX)
Lincoln Memorial Univ. (TN)
Lynn Univ. (FL)
Marshall Univ. (WV)
Maryville Univ. of St. Louis (MO)
North Georgia Coll. and State Univ.
Northern Michigan Univ.
Ohio State Univ.–Columbus
Our Lady of the Lake Univ. (TX)
Pacific Lutheran Univ. (WA)
Pennsylvania State Univ.–Univ. Park
Philander Smith Coll. (AR)
Point Loma Nazarene Univ. (CA)
Regis Univ. (CO)
Sage Colleges–Albany (NY)
South Dakota State Univ.
Southern Nazarene Univ. (OK)
Springfield Coll. (MA)
St. Mary's Univ. of San Antonio (TX)
SUNY Coll.–Cortland
Syracuse Univ. (NY)
Texas A&M Univ.–Coll. Station
Union Coll. (NE)
Univ. of Arkansas–Monticello
Univ. of California–Riverside
Univ. of Florida
Univ. of Iowa
Univ. of Kentucky
Univ. of La Verne (CA)
Univ. of Montevallo (AL)
Univ. of Nebraska–Lincoln
Univ. of Nevada–Las Vegas
Univ. of North Alabama
Univ. of Redlands (CA)
Univ. of the Southwest (NM)
Univ. of Wisconsin–Milwaukee
Univ. of Wisconsin–Oshkosh
Univ. of Wisconsin–River Falls
Washington State Univ.
West Liberty Univ. (WV)
Western Washington Univ.
York Coll. of Pennsylvania

Educational Assessment, Evaluation, and Research

Eastern Michigan Univ.
Midwestern State Univ. (TX)
Univ. of Florida
Univ. of Iowa
Univ. of Kentucky
Univ. of Nebraska–Lincoln
Univ. of the Southwest (NM)
Washington State Univ.

Educational Psychology

Alcorn State Univ. (MS)
Eastern Michigan Univ.

Marymount Univ. (VA)
Mississippi State Univ.
Shenandoah Univ. (VA)
Univ. of Florida
Univ. of Georgia
Univ. of Kentucky
Univ. of Nebraska–Lincoln
Univ. of Pittsburgh
Utah State Univ.

Educational/Instructional Media Design

Auburn Univ. (AL)
Bellevue Univ. (NE)
California State Univ.–Chico
California State Univ.–Fullerton
California State Univ.–Sacramento
Chestnut Hill Coll. (PA)
Clarke Univ. (IA)
Eastern Michigan Univ.
Eastern Washington Univ.
Georgia Southern Univ.
Jackson State Univ. (MS)
Jacksonville State Univ. (AL)
Kutztown Univ. of Pennsylvania
LeTourneau Univ. (TX)
St. Cloud State Univ. (MN)
Syracuse Univ. (NY)
Univ. of Iowa
Western Governors Univ. (UT)
Western Illinois Univ.
Western Oregon Univ.

Electrical Engineering Technologies/Technicians

Alabama Agricultural and
    Mechanical Univ.
Andrews Univ. (MI)
Bluefield State Coll. (WV)
Boston Univ.
Bowling Green State Univ. (OH)
Bradley Univ. (IL)
Buffalo State Coll.–SUNY
California State Polytechnic Univ.–
    Pomona
California State Univ.–Long Beach
California Univ. of Pennsylvania
Central Michigan Univ.
Central Washington Univ.
Cleveland State Univ.
Cogswell Polytechnical Coll. (CA)
Colorado State Univ.–Pueblo
CUNY–New York City Coll. of
    Technology
East-West Univ. (IL)
Eastern Michigan Univ.
Embry-Riddle Aeronautical Univ.
    (FL)
Fairleigh Dickinson Univ. (NJ)
Fairmont State Univ. (WV)
Farmingdale State Coll.–SUNY
Ferris State Univ. (MI)
Fitchburg State Coll. (MA)
Florida A&M Univ.
Fort Valley State Univ. (GA)
Georgia Southern Univ.
Grambling State Univ. (LA)
Indiana State Univ.

Indiana Univ.–South Bend
Indiana Univ.-Purdue Univ.–Fort
    Wayne
Indiana Univ.-Purdue Univ.–
    Indianapolis
Jacksonville State Univ. (AL)
Johnson and Wales Univ. (RI)
Kean Univ. (NJ)
LeTourneau Univ. (TX)
Louisiana Tech Univ.
Michigan Technological Univ.
Milwaukee School of Engineering
Minnesota State Univ.–Mankato
Missouri Western State Univ.
Montana State Univ.
Morehead State Univ. (KY)
New York Institute of Technology
Norfolk State Univ. (VA)
North Carolina A&T State Univ.
Northeastern Univ. (MA)
Northern Kentucky Univ.
Northern Michigan Univ.
Northwestern State Univ. of
    Louisiana
Oklahoma State Univ.
Old Dominion Univ. (VA)
Oregon Institute of Technology
Pittsburg State Univ. (KS)
Point Park Univ. (PA)
Portland State Univ. (OR)
Prairie View A&M Univ. (TX)
Purdue Univ.–Calumet (IN)
Rochester Institute of Technology
    (NY)
Roosevelt Univ. (IL)
Savannah State Univ. (GA)
South Carolina State Univ.
South Dakota State Univ.
Southern Illinois Univ.–Carbondale
Southern Polytechnic State Univ.
    (GA)
Southern Univ. and A&M Coll. (LA)
St. John's Univ. (NY)
SUNY Institute of Technology–
    Utica/Rome
Texas A&M Univ.–Coll. Station
Texas Tech Univ.
Thomas Edison State Coll. (NJ)
Troy Univ. (AL)
Univ. of Akron (OH)
Univ. of Arkansas–Little Rock
Univ. of Central Florida
Univ. of Dayton (OH)
Univ. of Hartford (CT)
Univ. of Houston
Univ. of Maine
Univ. of Massachusetts–Lowell
Univ. of Memphis
Univ. of Nebraska–Lincoln
Univ. of North Carolina–Charlotte
Univ. of North Texas
Univ. of Pittsburgh–Johnstown
Univ. of Southern Mississippi
Univ. of Tennessee–Martin
Univ. of Texas–Brownsville
Univ. of the District of Columbia
Vaughn Coll. of Aeronautics and
    Technology (NY)
Vermont Technical Coll.
Virginia State Univ.
Wayne State Univ. (MI)

Western Carolina Univ. (NC)
Western Kentucky Univ.
Western Washington Univ.
Wichita State Univ. (KS)
Youngstown State Univ. (OH)

Electrical, Electronics, and Communications Engineering

California State Univ.–Sacramento
Christian Brothers Univ. (TN)
Clarkson Univ. (NY)
Clemson Univ. (SC)
Cogswell Polytechnical Coll. (CA)
Colorado School of Mines
CUNY–City Coll.
Grove City Coll. (PA)
Hampton Univ. (VA)
Howard Univ. (DC)
Indiana Institute of Technology
Kettering Univ. (MI)
Lafayette Coll. (PA)
Lake Superior State Univ. (MI)
Miami Univ.–Oxford (OH)
Missouri Univ. of Science &
    Technology
Morgan State Univ. (MD)
Oklahoma Christian Univ.
Purdue Univ.–Calumet (IN)
Rice Univ. (TX)
South Dakota School of Mines and
    Technology
SUNY Maritime Coll.
Tennessee State Univ.
Texas A&M Univ.–Kingsville
Trine Univ. (IN)
Tufts Univ. (MA)
Tuskegee Univ. (AL)
United States Military Acad. (NY)
Univ. of California–San Diego
Univ. of California–Santa Barbara
Univ. of California–Santa Cruz
Univ. of Portland (OR)
Univ. of Texas–Dallas
Univ. of Texas–El Paso
Univ. of Washington
Vanderbilt Univ. (TN)
Widener Univ. (PA)

Electrical/Electronics Maintenance and Repair Technology

Lewis-Clark State Coll. (ID)
Northern Michigan Univ.

Electromechanical Instrumentation and Maintenance Technologies/Technicians

Alcorn State Univ. (MS)
Bowling Green State Univ. (OH)
Buffalo State Coll.–SUNY
Excelsior Coll. (NY)
Hampshire Coll. (MA)
Indiana State Univ.
Indiana Univ.-Purdue Univ.–
    Indianapolis

Keene State Coll. (NH)
Michigan Technological Univ.
Murray State Univ. (KY)
New York Institute of Technology
Northern Michigan Univ.
Suffolk Univ. (MA)
Texas A&M Univ.–Corpus Christi
Thomas Edison State Coll. (NJ)
Univ. of Northern Iowa
Univ. of Toledo (OH)
Vermont Technical Coll.
Wayne State Univ. (MI)

Engineering

Abilene Christian Univ. (TX)
Alfred Univ. (NY)
Andrews Univ. (MI)
Arcadia Univ. (PA)
Arizona State Univ.
Arkansas State Univ.–Jonesboro
Auburn Univ. (AL)
Augustana Coll. (IL)
Ball State Univ. (IN)
Bates Coll. (ME)
Baylor Univ. (TX)
Beloit Coll. (WI)
Bethel Coll. (IN)
Binghamton Univ.–SUNY
Brown Univ. (RI)
California Baptist Univ.
California Institute of Technology
California Polytechnic State Univ.–
    San Luis Obispo
California State Polytechnic Univ.–
    Pomona
California State Univ.–Chico
California State Univ.–Fresno
California State Univ.–Fullerton
California State Univ.–Long Beach
California State Univ.–Los Angeles
Calvin Coll. (MI)
Carnegie Mellon Univ. (PA)
Case Western Reserve University
    (OH)
Catholic Univ. of America (DC)
Charleston Southern Univ. (SC)
Christian Brothers Univ. (TN)
Claremont McKenna Coll. (CA)
Clark Atlanta Univ.
Clarkson Univ. (NY)
Cogswell Polytechnical Coll. (CA)
Coll. of Idaho (ID)
Coll. of Notre Dame of Maryland
Colorado School of Mines
Colorado State Univ.–Pueblo
Concordia Univ. (MI)
Cornell Univ. (NY)
CUNY–City Coll.
CUNY–Coll. of Staten Island
Dartmouth Coll. (NH)
Dickinson Coll. (PA)
Dordt Coll. (IA)
Dowling Coll. (NY)
Drexel Univ. (PA)
East Carolina Univ. (NC)
Eastern Illinois Univ.
Eastern Michigan Univ.
Eastern Nazarene Coll. (MA)
Elizabethtown Coll. (PA)
Elon Univ. (NC)

Embry-Riddle Aeronautical Univ.
    (FL)
Florida Institute of Technology
Fort Lewis Coll. (CO)
Geneva Coll. (PA)
George Fox Univ. (OR)
George Washington Univ. (DC)
Gonzaga Univ. (WA)
Harvey Mudd Coll. (CA)
Hope Coll. (MI)
Idaho State Univ.
Illinois Coll.
Indiana Univ.-Purdue Univ.–
    Indianapolis
Iowa State Univ.
Jackson State Univ. (MS)
John Brown Univ. (AR)
Johns Hopkins Univ. (MD)
Johnson and Wales Univ. (RI)
Juniata Coll. (PA)
Kent State Univ. (OH)
Kentucky State Univ.
Lafayette Coll. (PA)
Lehigh Univ. (PA)
LeTourneau Univ. (TX)
Lincoln Univ. (PA)
Lipscomb Univ. (TN)
Livingstone Coll. (NC)
Louisiana Coll.
Louisiana Tech Univ.
Loyola Marymount Univ. (CA)
Loyola Univ. Maryland
Lubbock Christian Univ. (TX)
Madonna Univ. (MI)
Manchester Coll. (IN)
Marquette Univ. (WI)
Maryville Coll. (TN)
Maryville Univ. of St. Louis (MO)
Massachusetts Maritime Academy
McNeese State Univ. (LA)
Messiah Coll. (PA)
Miami Univ.–Oxford (OH)
Michigan State Univ.
Michigan Technological Univ.
Midwestern State Univ. (TX)
Mills Coll. (CA)
Milwaukee School of Engineering
Mississippi State Univ.
Missouri Univ. of Science &
    Technology
Monmouth Coll. (IL)
Montana State Univ.
Montana Tech of the Univ. of
    Montana
Moravian Coll. (PA)
Morehouse Coll. (GA)
Mount Holyoke Coll. (MA)
National Univ. (CA)
New Mexico Highlands Univ.
New York Institute of Technology
Norfolk State Univ. (VA)
North Carolina State Univ.–Raleigh
Northeastern Univ. (MA)
Northern Arizona Univ.
Northwestern Univ. (IL)
Oakland Univ. (MI)
Oberlin Coll. (OH)
Ohio State Univ.–Columbus
Oral Roberts Univ. (OK)
Park Univ. (MO)
Pfeiffer Univ. (NC)

Philadelphia Univ.
Purdue Univ.–Calumet (IN)
Rensselaer Polytechnic Institute (NY)
Robert Morris Univ. (PA)
Rochester Institute of Technology (NY)
Roger Williams Univ. (RI)
Rose-Hulman Institute of Technology (IN)
San Jose State Univ. (CA)
Santa Clara Univ. (CA)
Schreiner Univ. (TX)
Smith Coll. (MA)
South Dakota State Univ.
Southwestern Oklahoma State Univ.
Spelman Coll. (GA)
Spring Hill Coll. (AL)
St. Anselm Coll. (NH)
St. Cloud State Univ. (MN)
St. Francis Univ. (PA)
St. Mary's Univ. of San Antonio (TX)
St. Michael's Coll. (VT)
St. Vincent Coll. (PA)
Stanford Univ. (CA)
Stevens Institute of Technology (NJ)
SUNY Coll. of Environmental Science and Forestry
SUNY Maritime Coll.
SUNY–Stony Brook
Swarthmore Coll. (PA)
Syracuse Univ. (NY)
Tarleton State Univ. (TX)
Temple Univ. (PA)
Texas Christian Univ.
Texas Tech Univ.
Thiel Coll. (PA)
Transylvania Univ. (KY)
Trinity Coll. (CT)
Trinity Univ. (DC)
Tufts Univ. (MA)
Tulane Univ. (LA)
United States Air Force Academy (CO)
United States Military Academy (NY)
United States Naval Academy (MD)
Univ. at Buffalo–SUNY
Univ. of Akron (OH)
Univ. of Alabama–Huntsville
Univ. of Alaska–Fairbanks
Univ. of Arizona
Univ. of California–Irvine
Univ. of Dallas
Univ. of Denver
Univ. of Georgia
Univ. of Hartford (CT)
Univ. of Illinois–Urbana-Champaign
Univ. of Iowa
Univ. of Kentucky
Univ. of Louisville (KY)
Univ. of Maine
Univ. of Maryland–Baltimore County
Univ. of Maryland–Coll. Park
Univ. of Maryland–Eastern Shore
Univ. of Massachusetts–Amherst
Univ. of Michigan–Ann Arbor

Univ. of Michigan–Dearborn
Univ. of Mississippi
Univ. of Nebraska–Lincoln
Univ. of Nevada–Las Vegas
Univ. of New Hampshire
Univ. of New Haven (CT)
Univ. of North Carolina–Asheville
Univ. of Oklahoma
Univ. of Pennsylvania
Univ. of Pittsburgh
Univ. of Pittsburgh–Bradford
Univ. of Portland (OR)
Univ. of Rhode Island
Univ. of Rochester (NY)
Univ. of South Florida
Univ. of Southern California
Univ. of Southern Indiana
Univ. of Tennessee–Chattanooga
Univ. of Tennessee–Martin
Univ. of the Incarnate Word (TX)
Univ. of the Pacific (CA)
Univ. of Toledo (OH)
Univ. of Tulsa (OK)
Univ. of Utah
Univ. of Washington
Ursinus Coll. (PA)
Vanderbilt Univ. (TN)
Villanova Univ. (PA)
Wake Forest Univ. (NC)
Washington State Univ.
Washington Univ. in St. Louis
Wesleyan Coll. (GA)
West Virginia Univ. Institute of Technology
Western Michigan Univ.
Wheaton Coll. (IL)
Widener Univ. (PA)
Worcester Polytechnic Institute (MA)
Yeshiva Univ. (NY)
Youngstown State Univ. (OH)

Engineering Mechanics

Columbia Univ. (NY)
Johns Hopkins Univ. (MD)
Lehigh Univ. (PA)
Lipscomb Univ. (TN)
Michigan State Univ.
Missouri Univ. of Science & Technology
New Mexico Institute of Mining and Technology
Northern Michigan Univ.
Ohio State Univ.–Columbus
United States Air Force Academy (CO)
Univ. of California–San Diego
Univ. of Florida
Univ. of Illinois–Urbana-Champaign
Univ. of Nebraska–Lincoln
Univ. of Wisconsin–Madison
Virginia Tech

Engineering Physics

Abilene Christian Univ. (TX)
Arkansas Tech Univ.
Barnard Coll. (NY)
Belmont Univ. (TN)
Bradley Univ. (IL)

Brown Univ. (RI)
Case Western Reserve Univ. (OH)
Christian Brothers Univ. (TN)
Colorado School of Mines
Connecticut Coll.
Cornell Univ. (NY)
Dartmouth Coll. (NH)
Eastern Michigan Univ.
Eastern Nazarene Coll. (MA)
Elizabethtown Coll. (PA)
Elon Univ. (NC)
Embry-Riddle Aeronautical Univ. (FL)
Fordham Univ. (NY)
Fort Lewis Coll. (CO)
Hope Coll. (MI)
Humboldt State Univ. (CA)
John Carroll Univ. (OH)
Juniata Coll. (PA)
Lehigh Univ. (PA)
Loras Coll. (IA)
Loyola Marymount Univ. (CA)
Miami Univ.–Oxford (OH)
Mississippi Coll.
Morgan State Univ. (MD)
Morningside Coll. (IA)
Murray State Univ. (KY)
New Mexico State Univ.
North Carolina A&T State Univ.
Northeastern State Univ. (OK)
Northern Arizona Univ.
Northwest Nazarene Univ. (ID)
Oakland Univ. (MI)
Ohio State Univ.–Columbus
Oklahoma Christian Univ.
Oral Roberts Univ. (OK)
Oregon State Univ.
Ouachita Baptist Univ. (AR)
Point Loma Nazarene Univ. (CA)
Providence Coll. (RI)
Purdue Univ.–Calumet (IN)
Randolph Coll. (VA)
Rensselaer Polytechnic Institute (NY)
Rose-Hulman Institute of Technology (IN)
Samford Univ. (AL)
Santa Clara Univ. (CA)
South Dakota State Univ.
Southeast Missouri State Univ.
Southwestern Coll. (KS)
Southwestern Oklahoma State Univ.
Spring Arbor Univ. (MI)
St. Ambrose Univ. (IA)
St. Mary's Univ. of Minnesota
Stevens Institute of Technology (NJ)
Syracuse Univ. (NY)
Tarleton State Univ. (TX)
Taylor Univ. (IN)
Texas Tech Univ.
Tufts Univ. (MA)
Union Univ. (TN)
Univ. at Buffalo–SUNY
Univ. of Arizona
Univ. of California–Berkeley
Univ. of California–San Diego
Univ. of Colorado–Boulder
Univ. of Connecticut
Univ. of Illinois–Chicago

Univ. of Illinois–Urbana-Champaign
Univ. of Kansas
Univ. of Maine
Univ. of Massachusetts–Boston
Univ. of Michigan–Ann Arbor
Univ. of Nebraska–Omaha
Univ. of Nevada–Reno
Univ. of Northern Iowa
Univ. of Oklahoma
Univ. of Pittsburgh
Univ. of Tennessee
Univ. of Texas–Brownsville
Univ. of the Pacific (CA)
Univ. of Tulsa (OK)
Univ. of Wisconsin–Madison
Univ. of Wisconsin–Platteville
Washington and Lee Univ. (VA)
West Virginia Univ. Institute of Technology
Westmont Coll. (CA)
Worcester Polytechnic Institute (MA)
Wright State Univ. (OH)
Yale Univ. (CT)

Engineering Science

Abilene Christian Univ. (TX)
Bethel Univ. (MN)
California State Univ.–Fullerton
Coll. of New Jersey
Colorado State Univ.
Dordt Coll. (IA)
Harvard Univ. (MA)
Hofstra Univ. (NY)
Iowa State Univ.
King Coll. (TN)
Lipscomb Univ. (TN)
Merrimack Coll. (MA)
New Jersey Institute of Technology
Northwestern Univ. (IL)
Pennsylvania State Univ.–Univ. Park
Principia Coll. (IL)
Rutgers, the State Univ. of New Jersey–New Brunswick
Seattle Pacific Univ.
Southern Utah Univ.
St. Mary's Univ. of San Antonio (TX)
Tufts Univ. (MA)
Tulane Univ. (LA)
Univ. of California–Berkeley
Univ. of California–San Diego
Univ. of Florida
Univ. of Miami (FL)
Univ. of Michigan–Ann Arbor
Univ. of Michigan–Flint
Univ. of New Mexico
Univ. of Pittsburgh–Bradford
Univ. of Rochester (NY)
Univ. of Tennessee
Univ. of Virginia
Wartburg Coll. (IA)
Washington State Univ.
West Virginia Univ. Institute of Technology
West Virginia Univ.–Parkersburg
Yale Univ. (CT)

Engineering Technologies/Technicians

Arkansas State Univ.–Jonesboro
Ball State Univ. (IN)
Bowling Green State Univ. (OH)
California State Polytechnic Univ.–Pomona
East Carolina Univ. (NC)
Eastern Washington Univ.
Elizabeth City State Univ. (NC)
Excelsior Coll. (NY)
Georgia Southern Univ.
Jacksonville State Univ. (AL)
LeTourneau Univ. (TX)
Maine Maritime Academy
Missouri State Univ.
New York Institute of Technology
North Carolina A&T State Univ.
Old Dominion Univ. (VA)
Pittsburg State Univ. (KS)
Rochester Institute of Technology (NY)
Rogers State Univ. (OK)
St. Cloud State Univ. (MN)
Thomas Edison State Coll. (NJ)
Univ. of Central Missouri
Univ. of Florida
Univ. of Hartford (CT)
Univ. of Maryland–Eastern Shore
Univ. of Northern Iowa
Univ. of Southern Indiana
Univ. of West Alabama
Vaughn Coll. of Aeronautics and Technology (NY)
Virginia State Univ.
Western Michigan Univ.

Engineering Technology

Austin Peay State Univ. (TN)
Berry Coll. (GA)
California Maritime Academy
California State Univ.–Long Beach
California Univ. of Pennsylvania
Cameron Univ. (OK)
Columbia Univ. (NY)
East Tennessee State Univ.
Eastern Michigan Univ.
Eastern New Mexico Univ.
Kansas State Univ.
Lawrence Technological Univ. (MI)
McNeese State Univ. (LA)
Michigan Technological Univ.
Mountain State Univ. (WV)
New Jersey Institute of Technology
New Mexico State Univ.
Northern Illinois Univ.
Southern Illinois Univ.–Carbondale
Southern Polytechnic State Univ. (GA)
Texas A&M Univ.–Coll. Station
Texas State Univ.–San Marcos
Univ. of North Texas
Univ. of West Florida
Univ. of Wisconsin–Stout
Vermont Technical Coll.
Western Carolina Univ. (NC)
Youngstown State Univ. (OH)

CUNY–Lehman Coll.
CUNY–Medgar Evers Coll.
CUNY–Queens Coll.
CUNY–York Coll.
Curry Coll. (MA)
D'Youville Coll. (NY)
Daemen Coll. (NY)
Dakota Wesleyan Univ. (SD)
Dallas Baptist Univ.
Dana Coll. (NE)
Dartmouth Coll. (NH)
Davidson Coll. (NC)
Davis and Elkins Coll. (WV)
Delaware Valley Coll. (PA)
Delta State Univ. (MS)
Denison Univ. (OH)
DePaul Univ. (IL)
DePauw Univ. (IN)
DeSales Univ. (PA)
Dickinson Coll. (PA)
Dickinson State Univ. (ND)
Dixie State Coll. of Utah
Dominican Coll. (NY)
Dominican Univ. (IL)
Dominican Univ. of California
Dordt Coll. (IA)
Dowling Coll. (NY)
Drake Univ. (IA)
Drew Univ. (NJ)
Drury Univ. (MO)
Duke Univ. (NC)
Duquesne Univ. (PA)
Earlham Coll. (IN)
East Carolina Univ. (NC)
East Stroudsburg Univ. of
    Pennsylvania
East Tennessee State Univ.
East Texas Baptist Univ.
East-West Univ. (IL)
Eastern Connecticut State Univ.
Eastern Illinois Univ.
Eastern Kentucky Univ.
Eastern Mennonite Univ. (VA)
Eastern Michigan Univ.
Eastern Nazarene Coll. (MA)
Eastern New Mexico Univ.
Eastern Oregon Univ.
Eastern Washington Univ.
Eckerd Coll. (FL)
Edgewood Coll. (WI)
Edinboro Univ. of Pennsylvania
Elizabeth City State Univ. (NC)
Elizabethtown Coll. (PA)
Elmhurst Coll. (IL)
Elmira Coll. (NY)
Elon Univ. (NC)
Emmanuel Coll. (MA)
Emmanuel Coll. (GA)
Emory and Henry Coll. (VA)
Emory Univ. (GA)
Emporia State Univ. (KS)
Endicott Coll. (MA)
Erskine Coll. (SC)
Eureka Coll. (IL)
Evangel Univ. (MO)
Evergreen State Coll. (WA)
Fairfield Univ. (CT)
Fairleigh Dickinson Univ. (NJ)
Fairmont State Univ. (WV)
Faulkner Univ. (AL)
Fayetteville State Univ. (NC)

Ferrum Coll. (VA)
Fisk Univ. (TN)
Fitchburg State Coll. (MA)
Flagler Coll. (FL)
Florida Atlantic Univ.
Florida International Univ.
Florida Southern Coll.
Florida State Univ.
Fontbonne Univ. (MO)
Fordham Univ. (NY)
Fort Hays State Univ. (KS)
Fort Lewis Coll. (CO)
Fort Valley State Univ. (GA)
Framingham State Coll. (MA)
Francis Marion Univ. (SC)
Franciscan Univ. of Steubenville
    (OH)
Franklin and Marshall Coll. (PA)
Franklin Coll. (IN)
Franklin Pierce Univ. (NH)
Free Will Baptist Bible Coll. (TN)
Freed-Hardeman Univ. (TN)
Fresno Pacific Univ. (CA)
Friends Univ. (KS)
Frostburg State Univ. (MD)
Gallaudet Univ. (DC)
Gardner-Webb Univ. (NC)
Geneva Coll. (PA)
George Fox Univ. (OR)
George Mason Univ. (VA)
George Washington Univ. (DC)
Georgetown Coll. (KY)
Georgetown Univ. (DC)
Georgia Coll. & State Univ.
Georgia Southern Univ.
Georgia State Univ.
Georgian Court Univ. (NJ)
Gettysburg Coll. (PA)
Glenville State Coll. (WV)
Gonzaga Univ. (WA)
Gordon Coll. (MA)
Goshen Coll. (IN)
Goucher Coll. (MD)
Grace Coll. and Seminary (IN)
Graceland Univ. (IA)
Grambling State Univ. (LA)
Grand Valley State Univ. (MI)
Grand View Univ. (IA)
Green Mountain Coll. (VT)
Greensboro Coll. (NC)
Greenville Coll. (IL)
Grinnell Coll. (IA)
Grove City Coll. (PA)
Guilford Coll. (NC)
Gustavus Adolphus Coll. (MN)
Hamline Univ. (MN)
Hampden-Sydney Coll. (VA)
Hampshire Coll. (MA)
Hampton Univ. (VA)
Hannibal-LaGrange Coll. (MO)
Hanover Coll. (IN)
Hardin-Simmons Univ. (TX)
Harding Univ. (AR)
Hartwick Coll. (NY)
Harvard Univ. (MA)
Haverford Coll. (PA)
Hawaii Pacific Univ.
Henderson State Univ. (AR)
Hendrix Coll. (AR)
Heritage Univ. (WA)
High Point Univ. (NC)

Hilbert Coll. (NY)
Hiram Coll. (OH)
Hobart and William Smith Colleges
    (NY)
Hofstra Univ. (NY)
Hollins Univ. (VA)
Holy Family Univ. (PA)
Holy Names Univ. (CA)
Hood Coll. (MD)
Hope Coll. (MI)
Houghton Coll. (NY)
Houston Baptist Univ.
Howard Payne Univ. (TX)
Howard Univ. (DC)
Humboldt State Univ. (CA)
Huntingdon Coll. (AL)
Huntington Univ. (IN)
Huston-Tillotson Univ. (TX)
Idaho State Univ.
Illinois Coll.
Illinois State Univ.
Illinois Wesleyan Univ.
Immaculata Univ. (PA)
Indiana State Univ.
Indiana Univ. East
Indiana Univ. Northwest
Indiana Univ. of Pennsylvania
Indiana Univ. Southeast
Indiana Univ.–Bloomington
Indiana Univ.–Kokomo
Indiana Univ.–South Bend
Indiana Univ.-Purdue Univ.–Fort
    Wayne
Indiana Univ.-Purdue Univ.–
    Indianapolis
Indiana Wesleyan Univ.
Iona Coll. (NY)
Iowa State Univ.
Iowa Wesleyan Coll.
Ithaca Coll. (NY)
Jackson State Univ. (MS)
Jacksonville State Univ. (AL)
James Madison Univ. (VA)
Jamestown Coll. (ND)
Jarvis Christian Coll. (TX)
John Brown Univ. (AR)
John Carroll Univ. (OH)
Johns Hopkins Univ. (MD)
Johnson C. Smith Univ. (NC)
Johnson State Coll. (VT)
Judson Coll. (AL)
Judson Univ. (IL)
Juniata Coll. (PA)
Kalamazoo Coll. (MI)
Kansas State Univ.
Kansas Wesleyan Univ.
Kean Univ. (NJ)
Keene State Coll. (NH)
Kennesaw State Univ. (GA)
Kent State Univ. (OH)
Kentucky State Univ.
Kentucky Wesleyan Coll.
Kenyon Coll. (OH)
Keuka Coll. (NY)
King Coll. (TN)
King's Coll. (PA)
Knox Coll. (IL)
Kutztown Univ. of Pennsylvania
La Roche Coll. (PA)
La Salle Univ. (PA)
La Sierra Univ. (CA)

Lafayette Coll. (PA)
LaGrange Coll. (GA)
Lake Superior State Univ. (MI)
Lakeland Coll. (WI)
Lamar Univ. (TX)
Lambuth Univ. (TN)
Lander Univ. (SC)
Lane Coll. (TN)
Langston Univ. (OK)
Lawrence Univ. (WI)
Le Moyne Coll. (NY)
Lebanon Valley Coll. (PA)
Lees-McRae Coll. (NC)
Lehigh Univ. (PA)
LeMoyne-Owen Coll. (TN)
Lenoir-Rhyne Univ. (NC)
LeTourneau Univ. (TX)
Lewis & Clark Coll. (OR)
Lewis-Clark State Coll. (ID)
Liberty Univ. (VA)
Limestone Coll. (SC)
Lincoln Memorial Univ. (TN)
Lincoln Univ. (MO)
Lincoln Univ. (PA)
Lindenwood Univ. (MO)
Lindsey Wilson Coll. (KY)
Linfield Coll. (OR)
Lipscomb Univ. (TN)
Livingstone Coll. (NC)
Lock Haven Univ. of Pennsylvania
Long Island Univ.–C.W. Post
    Campus (NY)
Loras Coll. (IA)
Louisiana Coll.
Louisiana State Univ.–Baton Rouge
Louisiana State Univ.–Shreveport
Louisiana Tech Univ.
Lourdes Coll. (OH)
Loyola Marymount Univ. (CA)
Loyola Univ. Chicago
Loyola Univ. Maryland
Loyola Univ. New Orleans
Lubbock Christian Univ. (TX)
Luther Coll. (IA)
Lycoming Coll. (PA)
Lynchburg Coll. (VA)
Lyon Coll. (AR)
Macalester Coll. (MN)
MacMurray Coll. (IL)
Macon State Coll. (GA)
Madonna Univ. (MI)
Maharishi Univ. of Management
    (IA)
Malone Univ. (OH)
Manchester Coll. (IN)
Manhattan Coll. (NY)
Manhattanville Coll. (NY)
Mansfield Univ. of Pennsylvania
Maranatha Baptist Bible Coll. (WI)
Marian Univ. (WI)
Marian Univ. (IN)
Marietta Coll. (OH)
Marist Coll. (NY)
Marquette Univ. (WI)
Mars Hill Coll. (NC)
Marshall Univ. (WV)
Martin Methodist Coll. (TN)
Martin Univ. (IN)
Mary Baldwin Coll. (VA)
Marygrove Coll. (MI)
Marylhurst Univ. (OR)

Marymount Manhattan Coll. (NY)
Marymount Univ. (VA)
Maryville Coll. (TN)
Maryville Univ. of St. Louis (MO)
Marywood Univ. (PA)
Massachusetts Coll. of Liberal Arts
Massachusetts Institute of
    Technology
Master's Coll. and Seminary (CA)
Mayville State Univ. (ND)
McDaniel Coll. (MD)
McKendree Univ. (IL)
McMurry Univ. (TX)
McNeese State Univ. (LA)
McPherson Coll. (KS)
Medaille Coll. (NY)
Mercyhurst Coll. (PA)
Meredith Coll. (NC)
Merrimack Coll. (MA)
Mesa State Coll. (CO)
Messiah Coll. (PA)
Methodist Univ. (NC)
Metropolitan State Coll. of Denver
Miami Univ.–Oxford (OH)
Michigan State Univ.
MidAmerica Nazarene Univ. (KS)
Middle Tennessee State Univ.
Middlebury Coll. (VT)
Midland Lutheran Coll. (NE)
Midway Coll. (KY)
Midwestern State Univ. (TX)
Miles Coll. (AL)
Millersville Univ. of Pennsylvania
Milligan Coll. (TN)
Millikin Univ. (IL)
Mills Coll. (CA)
Millsaps Coll. (MS)
Minnesota State Univ.–Mankato
Minnesota State Univ.–Moorhead
Minot State Univ. (ND)
Misericordia Univ. (PA)
Mississippi Coll.
Mississippi State Univ.
Mississippi Univ. for Women
Mississippi Valley State Univ.
Missouri Baptist Univ.
Missouri Southern State Univ.
Missouri State Univ.
Missouri Univ. of Science &
    Technology
Missouri Valley Coll.
Missouri Western State Univ.
Molloy Coll. (NY)
Monmouth Univ. (NJ)
Montana State Univ.
Montana State Univ.–Billings
Montana State Univ.–Northern
Montclair State Univ. (NJ)
Montreat Coll. (NC)
Moravian Coll. (PA)
Morehead State Univ. (KY)
Morehouse Coll. (GA)
Morningside Coll. (IA)
Morris Coll. (SC)
Mount Aloysius Coll. (PA)
Mount Marty Coll. (SD)
Mount Mary Coll. (WI)
Mount Mercy Coll. (IA)
Mount Olive Coll. (NC)
Mount St. Mary Coll. (NY)
Mount St. Mary's Coll. (CA)

Mount St. Mary's Univ. (MD)
Muhlenberg Coll. (PA)
Murray State Univ. (KY)
Muskingum Univ. (OH)
National Univ. (CA)
National-Louis Univ. (IL)
Nazareth Coll. (NY)
Nebraska Wesleyan Univ.
Neumann Univ. (PA)
New Jersey City Univ.
New Mexico Highlands Univ.
New Mexico State Univ.
New York Institute of Technology
New York Univ.
Newberry Coll. (SC)
Nicholls State Univ. (LA)
Nichols Coll. (MA)
Norfolk State Univ. (VA)
North Carolina A&T State Univ.
North Carolina Central Univ.
North Carolina State Univ.–Raleigh
North Carolina Wesleyan Coll.
North Central Coll. (IL)
North Central Univ. (MN)
North Dakota State Univ.
North Georgia Coll. and State Univ.
North Greenville Univ. (SC)
North Park Univ. (IL)
Northeastern Illinois Univ.
Northeastern Univ. (MA)
Northern Arizona Univ.
Northern Illinois Univ.
Northern Kentucky Univ.
Northern Michigan Univ.
Northern State Univ. (SD)
Northwest Missouri State Univ.
Northwest Nazarene Univ. (ID)
Northwest Univ. (WA)
Northwestern Coll. (IA)
Northwestern Coll. (MN)
Northwestern Oklahoma State
     Univ.
Northwestern State Univ. of
     Louisiana
Northwestern Univ. (IL)
Norwich Univ. (VT)
Notre Dame Coll. of Ohio
Notre Dame de Namur Univ. (CA)
Nova Southeastern Univ. (FL)
Nyack Coll. (NY)
Oakland City Univ. (IN)
Oakland Univ. (MI)
Oakwood Univ. (AL)
Oberlin Coll. (OH)
Ohio Dominican Univ.
Ohio State Univ.–Columbus
Ohio Univ.
Ohio Wesleyan Univ.
Oklahoma Baptist Univ.
Oklahoma Christian Univ.
Oklahoma City Univ.
Oklahoma Panhandle State Univ.
Oklahoma State Univ.
Oklahoma Wesleyan Univ.
Old Dominion Univ. (VA)
Olivet Coll. (MI)
Olivet Nazarene Univ. (IL)
Oregon State Univ.
Otterbein Coll. (OH)
Ouachita Baptist Univ. (AR)
Our Lady of Holy Cross Coll. (LA)

Our Lady of the Lake Univ. (TX)
Pace Univ. (NY)
Pacific Lutheran Univ. (WA)
Pacific Union Coll. (CA)
Pacific Univ. (OR)
Paine Coll. (GA)
Palm Beach Atlantic Univ. (FL)
Park Univ. (MO)
Peace Coll. (NC)
Pennsylvania State Univ.–Univ. Park
Pepperdine Univ. (CA)
Peru State Coll. (NE)
Pfeiffer Univ. (NC)
Philander Smith Coll. (AR)
Piedmont Coll. (GA)
Pikeville Coll. (KY)
Pine Manor Coll. (MA)
Pittsburg State Univ. (KS)
Pitzer Coll. (CA)
Plymouth State Univ. (NH)
Point Loma Nazarene Univ. (CA)
Point Park Univ. (PA)
Pomona Coll. (CA)
Post Univ. (CT)
Prairie View A&M Univ. (TX)
Presbyterian Coll. (SC)
Prescott Coll. (AZ)
Princeton Univ. (NJ)
Principia Coll. (IL)
Providence Coll. (RI)
Purchase Coll.–SUNY
Purdue Univ.–Calumet (IN)
Purdue Univ.–North Central (IN)
Purdue Univ.–West Lafayette (IN)
Queens Univ. of Charlotte (NC)
Quincy Univ. (IL)
Quinnipiac Univ. (CT)
Radford Univ. (VA)
Randolph Coll. (VA)
Randolph-Macon Coll. (VA)
Reed Coll. (OR)
Regent Univ. (VA)
Regis Coll. (MA)
Regis Univ. (CO)
Reinhardt Univ. (GA)
Rhode Island Coll.
Rhodes Coll. (TN)
Richard Stockton Coll. of New
     Jersey
Rider Univ. (NJ)
Ripon Coll. (WI)
Rivier Coll. (NH)
Roanoke Coll. (VA)
Robert Morris Univ. (PA)
Roberts Wesleyan Coll. (NY)
Rochester Coll. (MI)
Rockford Coll. (IL)
Rockhurst Univ. (MO)
Rocky Mountain Coll. (MT)
Roger Williams Univ. (RI)
Rollins Coll. (FL)
Roosevelt Univ. (IL)
Rosemont Coll. (PA)
Russell Sage Coll. (NY)
Rutgers, the State Univ. of New
     Jersey–Camden
Rutgers, the State Univ. of New
     Jersey–New Brunswick
Rutgers, the State Univ. of New
     Jersey–Newark
Sacred Heart Univ. (CT)

Saginaw Valley State Univ. (MI)
Salem Coll. (NC)
Salem State Coll. (MA)
Salisbury Univ. (MD)
Salve Regina Univ. (RI)
Sam Houston State Univ. (TX)
Samford Univ. (AL)
San Diego State Univ.
San Francisco State Univ.
San Jose State Univ. (CA)
Santa Clara Univ. (CA)
Savannah State Univ. (GA)
Schreiner Univ. (TX)
Seattle Pacific Univ.
Seattle Univ.
Seton Hall Univ. (NJ)
Seton Hill Univ. (PA)
Sewanee–Univ. of the South (TN)
Shaw Univ. (NC)
Shawnee State Univ. (OH)
Shenandoah Univ. (VA)
Shepherd Univ. (WV)
Shippensburg Univ. of Pennsylvania
Shorter Coll. (GA)
Siena Coll. (NY)
Sierra Nevada Coll. (NV)
Silver Lake Coll. (WI)
Simmons Coll. (MA)
Simpson Coll. (IA)
Simpson Univ. (CA)
Skidmore Coll. (NY)
Slippery Rock Univ. of Pennsylvania
Smith Coll. (MA)
Sonoma State Univ. (CA)
South Carolina State Univ.
South Dakota State Univ.
Southeast Missouri State Univ.
Southeastern Louisiana Univ.
Southeastern Oklahoma State Univ.
Southeastern Univ. (FL)
Southern Adventist Univ. (TN)
Southern Arkansas Univ.
Southern Illinois Univ.–Carbondale
Southern Illinois Univ.–Edwardsville
Southern Methodist Univ. (TX)
Southern Nazarene Univ. (OK)
Southern New Hampshire Univ.
Southern Oregon Univ.
Southern Univ. and A&M Coll. (LA)
Southern Univ.–New Orleans
Southern Utah Univ.
Southern Vermont Coll.
Southern Wesleyan Univ. (SC)
Southwest Baptist Univ. (MO)
Southwest Minnesota State Univ.
Southwestern Adventist Univ. (TX)
Southwestern Coll. (KS)
Southwestern Oklahoma State
     Univ.
Southwestern Univ. (TX)
Spelman Coll. (GA)
Spring Arbor Univ. (MI)
Spring Hill Coll. (AL)
Springfield Coll. (MA)
St. Ambrose Univ. (IA)
St. Andrews Presbyterian Coll. (NC)
St. Anselm Coll. (NH)
St. Augustine's Coll. (NC)
St. Catherine Univ. (MN)
St. Cloud State Univ. (MN)
St. Edward's Univ. (TX)

St. Francis Coll. (NY)
St. Francis Univ. (PA)
St. Gregory's Univ. (OK)
St. John Fisher Coll. (NY)
St. John's Univ. (NY)
St. John's Univ. (MN)
St. Joseph Coll. (CT)
St. Joseph's Coll. (ME)
St. Joseph's Coll. (IN)
St. Joseph's Coll. New York
St. Joseph's Univ. (PA)
St. Leo Univ. (FL)
St. Louis Univ.
St. Martin's Univ. (WA)
St. Mary's Coll. of California
St. Mary's Coll. of Maryland
St. Mary's Univ. of Minnesota
St. Mary's Univ. of San Antonio
     (TX)
St. Mary-of-the-Woods Coll. (IN)
St. Norbert Coll. (WI)
St. Olaf Coll. (MN)
St. Peter's Coll. (NJ)
St. Thomas Aquinas Coll. (NY)
St. Thomas Univ. (FL)
St. Vincent Coll. (PA)
St. Xavier Univ. (IL)
Stanford Univ. (CA)
Stephen F. Austin State Univ. (TX)
Stephens Coll. (MO)
Sterling Coll. (KS)
Stetson Univ. (FL)
Stevenson Univ. (MD)
Stillman Coll. (AL)
Stonehill Coll. (MA)
Suffolk Univ. (MA)
Sul Ross State Univ. (TX)
SUNY Coll.–Cortland
SUNY Coll.–Oneonta
SUNY Coll.–Potsdam
SUNY–Geneseo
SUNY–Oswego
SUNY–Plattsburgh
SUNY–Stony Brook
Susquehanna Univ. (PA)
Swarthmore Coll. (PA)
Syracuse Univ. (NY)
Tabor Coll. (KS)
Talladega Coll. (AL)
Tarleton State Univ. (TX)
Taylor Univ. (IN)
Temple Univ. (PA)
Tennessee State Univ.
Tennessee Technological Univ.
Tennessee Wesleyan Coll.
Texas A&M International Univ.
Texas A&M Univ.–Coll. Station
Texas A&M Univ.–Commerce
Texas A&M University–Corpus
     Christi
Texas Christian Univ.
Texas Coll.
Texas Lutheran Univ.
Texas State Univ.–San Marcos
Texas Tech Univ.
Texas Wesleyan Univ.
Texas Woman's Univ.
The Citadel (SC)
Thiel Coll. (PA)
Thomas Edison State Coll. (NJ)
Thomas More Coll. (KY)

Thomas More Coll. of Liberal Arts
     (NH)
Tiffin Univ. (OH)
Toccoa Falls Coll. (GA)
Tougaloo Coll. (MS)
Touro Coll. (NY)
Towson Univ. (MD)
Transylvania Univ. (KY)
Trevecca Nazarene Univ. (TN)
Trine Univ. (IN)
Trinity Christian Coll. (IL)
Trinity Coll. (CT)
Trinity International Univ. (IL)
Trinity Univ. (DC)
Troy Univ. (AL)
Truman State Univ. (MO)
Tulane Univ. (LA)
Tusculum Coll. (TN)
Tuskegee Univ. (AL)
Union Coll. (NY)
Union Coll. (KY)
Union Coll. (NE)
Union Univ. (TN)
United States Air Force Academy
     (CO)
United States Naval Academy (MD)
Univ. at Albany–SUNY
Univ. at Buffalo–SUNY
Univ. of Akron (OH)
Univ. of Alabama
Univ. of Alabama–Birmingham
Univ. of Alabama–Huntsville
Univ. of Alaska–Anchorage
Univ. of Alaska–Fairbanks
Univ. of Alaska–Southeast
Univ. of Arizona
Univ. of Arkansas
Univ. of Arkansas–Little Rock
Univ. of Arkansas–Pine Bluff
Univ. of Baltimore (MD)
Univ. of California–Berkeley
Univ. of California–Davis
Univ. of California–Irvine
Univ. of California–Los Angeles
Univ. of California–Riverside
Univ. of California–San Diego
Univ. of Central Arkansas
Univ. of Central Florida
Univ. of Central Missouri
Univ. of Central Oklahoma
Univ. of Charleston (WV)
Univ. of Chicago
Univ. of Colorado–Boulder
Univ. of Colorado–Colorado
     Springs
Univ. of Colorado–Denver
Univ. of Connecticut
Univ. of Dallas
Univ. of Dayton (OH)
Univ. of Delaware
Univ. of Denver
Univ. of Dubuque (IA)
Univ. of Evansville (IN)
Univ. of Findlay (OH)
Univ. of Florida
Univ. of Georgia
Univ. of Great Falls (MT)
Univ. of Hartford (CT)
Univ. of Hawaii–Hilo
Univ. of Hawaii–Manoa
Univ. of Houston

Univ. of Houston–Downtown
Univ. of Illinois–Chicago
Univ. of Illinois–Springfield
Univ. of Illinois–Urbana-Champaign
Univ. of Indianapolis
Univ. of Iowa
Univ. of Kansas
Univ. of Kentucky
Univ. of La Verne (CA)
Univ. of Louisiana–Lafayette
Univ. of Louisville (KY)
Univ. of Maine
Univ. of Maine–Farmington
Univ. of Maine–Fort Kent
Univ. of Maine–Machias
Univ. of Mary (ND)
Univ. of Mary Hardin-Baylor (TX)
Univ. of Mary Washington (VA)
Univ. of Maryland–Baltimore
    County
Univ. of Maryland–Coll. Park
Univ. of Maryland–Eastern Shore
Univ. of Maryland–Univ. Coll.
Univ. of Massachusetts–Amherst
Univ. of Massachusetts–Boston
Univ. of Massachusetts–Lowell
Univ. of Memphis
Univ. of Miami (FL)
Univ. of Michigan–Ann Arbor
Univ. of Michigan–Dearborn
Univ. of Michigan–Flint
Univ. of Minnesota–Duluth
Univ. of Minnesota–Twin Cities
Univ. of Mississippi
Univ. of Missouri
Univ. of Missouri–Kansas City
Univ. of Missouri–St. Louis
Univ. of Mobile (AL)
Univ. of Montana
Univ. of Montevallo (AL)
Univ. of Mount Union (OH)
Univ. of Nebraska–Kearney
Univ. of Nebraska–Lincoln
Univ. of Nebraska–Omaha
Univ. of Nevada–Las Vegas
Univ. of Nevada–Reno
Univ. of New England (ME)
Univ. of New Hampshire
Univ. of New Haven (CT)
Univ. of New Mexico
Univ. of New Orleans
Univ. of North Alabama
Univ. of North Carolina–Asheville
Univ. of North Carolina–Chapel Hill
Univ. of North Carolina–Charlotte
Univ. of North Carolina–
    Greensboro
Univ. of North Carolina–Pembroke
Univ. of North Carolina–
    Wilmington
Univ. of North Dakota
Univ. of North Florida
Univ. of North Texas
Univ. of Northern Colorado
Univ. of Northern Iowa
Univ. of Notre Dame (IN)
Univ. of Oklahoma
Univ. of Oregon
Univ. of Pennsylvania
Univ. of Pittsburgh–Bradford
Univ. of Portland (OR)

Univ. of Puget Sound (WA)
Univ. of Redlands (CA)
Univ. of Rhode Island
Univ. of Richmond (VA)
Univ. of Rio Grande (OH)
Univ. of Rochester (NY)
Univ. of San Diego
Univ. of San Francisco
Univ. of Science and Arts of
    Oklahoma
Univ. of Sioux Falls (SD)
Univ. of South Alabama
Univ. of South Carolina
Univ. of South Carolina–Aiken
Univ. of South Dakota
Univ. of South Florida
Univ. of Southern California
Univ. of Southern Indiana
Univ. of Southern Maine
Univ. of Southern Mississippi
Univ. of St. Francis (IN)
Univ. of St. Francis (IL)
Univ. of St. Mary (KS)
Univ. of St. Thomas (TX)
Univ. of St. Thomas (MN)
Univ. of Tampa (FL)
Univ. of Tennessee
Univ. of Tennessee–Chattanooga
Univ. of Tennessee–Martin
Univ. of Texas of the Permian Basin
Univ. of Texas–Arlington
Univ. of Texas–Austin
Univ. of Texas–Brownsville
Univ. of Texas–Pan American
Univ. of Texas–San Antonio
Univ. of Texas–Tyler
Univ. of the Cumberlands (KY)
Univ. of the District of Columbia
Univ. of the Incarnate Word (TX)
Univ. of the Ozarks (AR)
Univ. of the Pacific (CA)
Univ. of the Southwest (NM)
Univ. of Toledo (OH)
Univ. of Tulsa (OK)
Univ. of Utah
Univ. of Vermont
Univ. of Virginia
Univ. of Virginia–Wise
Univ. of Washington
Univ. of West Alabama
Univ. of West Florida
Univ. of West Georgia
Univ. of Wisconsin–Eau Claire
Univ. of Wisconsin–Green Bay
Univ. of Wisconsin–La Crosse
Univ. of Wisconsin–Madison
Univ. of Wisconsin–Milwaukee
Univ. of Wisconsin–Platteville
Univ. of Wisconsin–River Falls
Univ. of Wisconsin–Stevens Point
Univ. of Wisconsin–Whitewater
Univ. of Wyoming
Urbana Univ. (OH)
Ursinus Coll. (PA)
Ursuline Coll. (OH)
Utah State Univ.
Utah Valley Univ.
Utica Coll. (NY)
Valdosta State Univ. (GA)
Valley City State Univ. (ND)
Valparaiso Univ. (IN)

Vanderbilt Univ. (TN)
Vanguard Univ. of Southern Cal.
Vassar Coll. (NY)
Victory Univ. (TN)
Villanova Univ. (PA)
Virginia Commonwealth Univ.
Virginia Intermont Coll.
Virginia Military Institute
Virginia State Univ.
Virginia Tech
Virginia Wesleyan Coll.
Viterbo Univ. (WI)
Wabash Coll. (IN)
Wagner Coll. (NY)
Wake Forest Univ. (NC)
Waldorf Coll. (IA)
Walsh Univ. (OH)
Warner Pacific Coll. (OR)
Warner Univ. (FL)
Warren Wilson Coll. (NC)
Wartburg Coll. (IA)
Washington Adventist Univ. (MD)
Washington and Jefferson Coll.
    (PA)
Washington and Lee Univ. (VA)
Washington Coll. (MD)
Washington State Univ.
Washington Univ. in St. Louis
Wayland Baptist Univ. (TX)
Wayne State Coll. (NE)
Wayne State Univ. (MI)
Waynesburg Univ. (PA)
Weber State Univ. (UT)
Webster Univ. (MO)
Wells Coll. (NY)
Wesley Coll. (DE)
Wesleyan Coll. (GA)
West Chester Univ. of Pennsylvania
West Liberty Univ. (WV)
West Texas A&M Univ.
West Virginia Univ.
West Virginia Wesleyan Coll.
Western Carolina Univ. (NC)
Western Connecticut State Univ.
Western Illinois Univ.
Western Kentucky Univ.
Western Michigan Univ.
Western New England Coll. (MA)
Western New Mexico Univ.
Western Oregon Univ.
Western State Coll. of Colorado
Western Washington Univ.
Westfield State Coll. (MA)
Westminster Coll. (UT)
Westminster Coll. (PA)
Westminster Coll. (MO)
Westmont Coll. (CA)
Wheaton Coll. (MA)
Wheaton Coll. (IL)
Wheeling Jesuit Univ. (WV)
Whitman Coll. (WA)
Whittier Coll. (CA)
Whitworth Univ. (WA)
Wichita State Univ. (KS)
Wiley Coll. (TX)
Wilkes Univ. (PA)
Willamette Univ. (OR)
William Carey Univ. (MS)
William Jewell Coll. (MO)
William Paterson Univ. of New
    Jersey

William Woods Univ. (MO)
Williams Coll. (MA)
Wilmington Coll. (OH)
Wilson Coll. (PA)
Wingate Univ. (NC)
Winston-Salem State Univ. (NC)
Winthrop Univ. (SC)
Wisconsin Lutheran Coll.
Wittenberg Univ. (OH)
Wofford Coll. (SC)
Worcester State Coll. (MA)
Wright State Univ. (OH)
Xavier Univ. (OH)
Yale Univ. (CT)
York Coll. (NE)
York Coll. of Pennsylvania
Youngstown State Univ. (OH)

English Language and Literature/Letters

Bard Coll. (NY)
Beloit Coll. (WI)
Binghamton Univ.–SUNY
Boise State Univ. (ID)
Burlington Coll. (VT)
California State Univ.–East Bay
California State Univ.–Long Beach
Columbia Coll. (SC)
CUNY–Coll. of Staten Island
D'Youville Coll. (NY)
Dakota State Univ. (SD)
Drexel Univ. (PA)
Duke Univ. (NC)
Duquesne Univ. (PA)
Eastern Univ. (PA)
Edward Waters Coll. (FL)
Emmanuel Coll. (MA)
Ferris State Univ. (MI)
Florida Southern Coll.
Hannibal-LaGrange Coll. (MO)
Harvard Univ. (MA)
Hillsdale Coll. (MI)
Hofstra Univ. (NY)
Houston Baptist Univ.
Johns Hopkins Univ. (MD)
Lindenwood Univ. (MO)
Milligan Coll. (TN)
Mills Coll. (CA)
Monmouth Coll. (IL)
Northern Arizona Univ.
Ohio Wesleyan Univ.
Rust Coll. (MS)
Skidmore Coll. (NY)
Southeastern Univ. (FL)
Southwest Baptist Univ. (MO)
Spring Arbor Univ. (MI)
Spring Hill Coll. (AL)
St. Gregory's Univ. (OK)
St. Leo Univ. (FL)
St. Mary's Coll. of California
SUNY Coll.–Old Westbury
SUNY Empire State Coll.
Unity Coll. (ME)
Univ. of California–San Diego
Univ. of Findlay (OH)
Univ. of Iowa
Univ. of La Verne (CA)
Univ. of Maine–Augusta
Univ. of Pennsylvania
Univ. of Southern California

Viterbo Univ. (WI)
Washington Univ. in St. Louis
Western Kentucky Univ.
Whitman Coll. (WA)
Wilberforce Univ. (OH)
Williams Coll. (MA)
Yale Univ. (CT)

English Literature (British and Commonwealth)

Bennington Coll. (VT)
Creighton Univ. (NE)
CUNY–Baruch Coll.
CUNY–Hunter Coll.
Eastern Nazarene Coll. (MA)
Elmira Coll. (NY)
Emory Univ. (GA)
Excelsior Coll. (NY)
Gannon Univ. (PA)
Hofstra Univ. (NY)
Indiana Univ.-Purdue Univ.–Fort
    Wayne
Lawrence Univ. (WI)
Marian Univ. (WI)
Marlboro Coll. (VT)
Mills Coll. (CA)
New York Univ.
Ohio Northern Univ.
Oral Roberts Univ. (OK)
St. Mary's Coll. (IN)
Syracuse Univ. (NY)
Tufts Univ. (MA)
Univ. of California–San Diego
Univ. of Miami (FL)
Univ. of New Hampshire
Univ. of Pittsburgh
Univ. of Redlands (CA)

Entrepreneurial and Small Business Operations

Alaska Pacific Univ.
Babson Coll. (MA)
Ball State Univ. (IN)
Baylor Univ. (TX)
Belmont Univ. (TN)
Black Hills State Univ. (SD)
Boston Univ.
Bradley Univ. (IL)
Buena Vista Univ. (IA)
California State Univ.–Fullerton
Canisius Coll. (NY)
Central Christian Coll. (KS)
Central Michigan Univ.
Cleary Univ. (MI)
Davenport Univ. (MI)
Dickinson State Univ. (ND)
Drake Univ. (IA)
Duquesne Univ. (PA)
Eastern Michigan Univ.
Fairleigh Dickinson Univ. (NJ)
Ferris State Univ. (MI)
Gallaudet Univ. (DC)
Grove City Coll. (PA)
Hampton Univ. (VA)
Hawaii Pacific Univ.
High Point Univ. (NC)
Hofstra Univ. (NY)
Houston Baptist Univ.

Huntington Univ. (IN)
Husson Univ. (ME)
Indiana Wesleyan Univ.
Jackson State Univ. (MS)
Juniata Coll. (PA)
Lasell Coll. (MA)
Lewis-Clark State Coll. (ID)
Lindenwood Univ. (MO)
Lyndon State Coll. (VT)
Marquette Univ. (WI)
Messiah Coll. (PA)
Middle Tennessee State Univ.
Millikin Univ. (IL)
Mitchell Coll. (CT)
Mountain State Univ. (WV)
North Central Coll. (IL)
Northeastern State Univ. (OK)
Northeastern Univ. (MA)
Northern Kentucky Univ.
Northern Michigan Univ.
Northwood Univ. (MI)
Oregon Institute of Technology
Pace Univ. (NY)
Palm Beach Atlantic Univ. (FL)
Pepperdine Univ. (CA)
Purdue Univ.–Calumet (IN)
Reinhardt Univ. (GA)
Rider Univ. (NJ)
Seton Hill Univ. (PA)
Shaw Univ. (NC)
Sierra Nevada Coll. (NV)
South Dakota State Univ.
Southern Polytechnic State Univ.
    (GA)
Southwestern Coll. (KS)
St. Cloud State Univ. (MN)
St. Edward's Univ. (TX)
St. Leo Univ. (FL)
St. Mary's Univ. of San Antonio
    (TX)
Stetson Univ. (FL)
Suffolk Univ. (MA)
Syracuse Univ. (NY)
Temple Univ. (PA)
Thomas Edison State Coll. (NJ)
Trine Univ. (IN)
Union Coll. (NE)
Univ. of Arizona
Univ. of Dayton (OH)
Univ. of Hartford (CT)
Univ. of Illinois–Chicago
Univ. of Illinois–Urbana-Champaign
Univ. of Indianapolis
Univ. of Iowa
Univ. of Louisiana–Monroe
Univ. of Massachusetts–Lowell
Univ. of Miami (FL)
Univ. of Nevada–Las Vegas
Univ. of New Hampshire
Univ. of New Orleans
Univ. of Pittsburgh–Bradford
Univ. of Rio Grande (OH)
Univ. of San Francisco
Univ. of St. Thomas (MN)
Univ. of Toledo (OH)
Univ. of Utah
Univ. of Vermont
Univ. of Washington
Virginia Union Univ.
Washington Adventist Univ. (MD)
Washington State Univ.

Washington Univ. in St. Louis
Waynesburg Univ. (PA)
Wichita State Univ. (KS)
Wilkes Univ. (PA)
Xavier Univ. (OH)
York Coll. of Pennsylvania

Environmental Control Technologies/Technicians

Appalachian State Univ. (NC)
California State Univ.–Long Beach
Davis and Elkins Coll. (WV)
Eastern Kentucky Univ.
Fairmont State Univ. (WV)
Ferris State Univ. (MI)
Fitchburg State Coll. (MA)
Florida International Univ.
Jackson State Univ. (MS)
Mesa State Coll. (CO)
Middle Tennessee State Univ.
Montana State Univ.–Northern
Murray State Univ. (KY)
New York Institute of Technology
North Carolina State Univ.–Raleigh
Northern Michigan Univ.
Oregon Institute of Technology
Pennsylvania Coll. of Technology
Rochester Institute of Technology
    (NY)
Shawnee State Univ. (OH)
Thomas Edison State Coll. (NJ)
Univ. of Central Missouri
Univ. of Findlay (OH)
Univ. of South Carolina–Upstate
Vermont Technical Coll.
Western Kentucky Univ.

Environmental Design

Auburn Univ. (AL)
Ball State Univ. (IN)
Binghamton Univ.–SUNY
Boston Architectural Coll.
Bowling Green State Univ. (OH)
Cornell Univ. (NY)
Lawrence Technological Univ. (MI)
Miami Univ.–Oxford (OH)
Montana State Univ.
Morgan State Univ. (MD)
New School (NY)
North Carolina State Univ.–Raleigh
North Dakota State Univ.
Otis Coll. of Art and Design (CA)
Rutgers, the State Univ. of New
    Jersey–New Brunswick
Texas A&M Univ.–Coll. Station
Univ. at Buffalo–SUNY
Univ. of California–Davis
Univ. of California–Irvine
Univ. of Colorado–Boulder
Univ. of Houston
Univ. of Massachusetts–Amherst
Univ. of Memphis
Univ. of Michigan–Ann Arbor
Univ. of Minnesota–Twin Cities
Univ. of New Mexico
Univ. of Oklahoma
Univ. of Pennsylvania
Univ. of Texas–Arlington

Environmental Psychology

Embry-Riddle Aeronautical Univ.
    (FL)
Prescott Coll. (AZ)

Environmental/ Environmental Health Engineering

Bradley Univ. (IL)
California Polytechnic State Univ.–
    San Luis Obispo
Clarkson Univ. (NY)
Colorado School of Mines
Colorado State Univ.
Columbia Univ. (NY)
Cornell Univ. (NY)
Drexel Univ. (PA)
Florida International Univ.
Gannon Univ. (PA)
Georgia Institute of Technology
Hofstra Univ. (NY)
Humboldt State Univ. (CA)
Johns Hopkins Univ. (MD)
Lehigh Univ. (PA)
Louisiana State Univ.–Baton Rouge
Manhattan Coll. (NY)
Marquette Univ. (WI)
Massachusetts Institute of
    Technology
Michigan Technological Univ.
Missouri Univ. of Science &
    Technology
Montana Tech of the Univ. of
    Montana
New Jersey Institute of Technology
New Mexico Institute of Mining
    and Technology
North Carolina State Univ.–Raleigh
Northeastern State Univ. (OK)
Northern Arizona Univ.
Northwestern Univ. (IL)
Old Dominion Univ. (VA)
Oregon State Univ.
Pennsylvania State Univ.–Univ. Park
Rensselaer Polytechnic Institute
    (NY)
Rice Univ. (TX)
Roger Williams Univ. (RI)
San Diego State Univ.
Southern Methodist Univ. (TX)
Stanford Univ. (CA)
Stevens Institute of Technology
    (NJ)
Suffolk Univ. (MA)
Syracuse Univ. (NY)
Taylor Univ. (IN)
Temple Univ. (PA)
Texas A&M Univ.–Kingsville
Texas Tech Univ.
Tufts Univ. (MA)
Tulane Univ. (LA)
United States Air Force Academy
    (CO)
United States Military Academy
    (NY)
Univ. at Buffalo–SUNY
Univ. of California–Berkeley
Univ. of California–Irvine

Univ. of California–Riverside
Univ. of California–San Diego
Univ. of Central Florida
Univ. of Colorado–Boulder
Univ. of Connecticut
Univ. of Florida
Univ. of Georgia
Univ. of Illinois–Urbana-Champaign
Univ. of Miami (FL)
Univ. of Michigan–Ann Arbor
Univ. of Nebraska–Lincoln
Univ. of Nevada–Reno
Univ. of New Hampshire
Univ. of North Dakota
Univ. of Notre Dame (IN)
Univ. of Oklahoma
Univ. of Pennsylvania
Univ. of Southern California
Univ. of Vermont
Univ. of Wisconsin–Platteville
Utah State Univ.
Washington State Univ.
Wilkes Univ. (PA)
Worcester Polytechnic Institute
    (MA)
Yale Univ. (CT)

Ethnic, Cultural Minority, and Gender Studies

Agnes Scott Coll. (GA)
Albion Coll. (MI)
Albright Coll. (PA)
Allegheny Coll. (PA)
American Univ. (DC)
Amherst Coll. (MA)
Arizona State Univ.
Augsburg Coll. (MN)
Ball State Univ. (IN)
Barnard Coll. (NY)
Bates Coll. (ME)
Beloit Coll. (WI)
Bennington Coll. (VT)
Berea Coll. (KY)
Binghamton Univ.–SUNY
Black Hills State Univ. (SD)
Boise State Univ. (ID)
Bowdoin Coll. (ME)
Bowling Green State Univ. (OH)
Brandeis Univ. (MA)
Brown Univ. (RI)
Bucknell Univ. (PA)
Burlington Coll. (VT)
California State Polytechnic Univ.–
    Pomona
California State Univ.–Chico
California State Univ.–Dominguez
    Hills
California State Univ.–East Bay
California State Univ.–Fresno
California State Univ.–Fullerton
California State Univ.–Long Beach
California State Univ.–Los Angeles
California State Univ.–Monterey Bay
California State Univ.–Northridge
California State Univ.–Sacramento
California State Univ.–San Marcos
Carleton Coll. (MN)
Carnegie Mellon Univ. (PA)
Case Western Reserve Univ. (OH)
Central Michigan Univ.

Chatham Univ. (PA)
Chicago State Univ.
Claflin Univ. (SC)
Claremont McKenna Coll. (CA)
Clark Univ. (MA)
Cleveland State Univ.
Coe Coll. (IA)
Colby Coll. (ME)
Colgate Univ. (NY)
Coll. at Brockport–SUNY
Coll. of New Jersey
Coll. of St. Benedict (MN)
Coll. of St. Rose (NY)
Coll. of William and Mary (VA)
Coll. of Wooster (OH)
Colorado Coll.
Columbia Univ. (NY)
Connecticut Coll.
Cornell Coll. (IA)
Cornell Univ. (NY)
Creighton Univ. (NE)
CUNY–Brooklyn Coll.
CUNY–Coll. of Staten Island
CUNY–Hunter Coll.
CUNY–Lehman Coll.
CUNY–Queens Coll.
CUNY–York Coll.
Dartmouth Coll. (NH)
Denison Univ. (OH)
DePaul Univ. (IL)
DePauw Univ. (IN)
Dickinson Coll. (PA)
Dominican Univ. (IL)
Dominican Univ. of California
Drew Univ. (NJ)
Duke Univ. (NC)
Earlham Coll. (IN)
East Carolina Univ. (NC)
East Central Univ. (OK)
Eastern Illinois Univ.
Eastern Michigan Univ.
Eastern Washington Univ.
Eckerd Coll. (FL)
Emory Univ. (GA)
Evergreen State Coll. (WA)
Florida A&M Univ.
Florida International Univ.
Florida State Univ.
Fordham Univ. (NY)
Fort Lewis Coll. (CO)
Fresno Pacific Univ. (CA)
Furman Univ. (SC)
Gallaudet Univ. (DC)
George Washington Univ. (DC)
Georgetown Univ. (DC)
Georgia State Univ.
Goucher Coll. (MD)
Guilford Coll. (NC)
Gustavus Adolphus Coll. (MN)
Hamilton Coll. (NY)
Hamline Univ. (MN)
Hampshire Coll. (MA)
Hanover Coll. (IN)
Harvard Univ. (MA)
Hobart and William Smith Colleges
    (NY)
Hofstra Univ. (NY)
Hollins Univ. (VA)
Hope Coll. (MI)
Houghton Coll. (NY)
Howard Univ. (DC)

Humboldt State Univ. (CA)
Illinois Wesleyan Univ.
Indiana State Univ.
Indiana Univ. Northwest
Indiana Univ.–South Bend
Indiana Univ.–Purdue Univ.–Fort Wayne
Iowa State Univ.
Johns Hopkins Univ. (MD)
Kansas State Univ.
Kent State Univ. (OH)
Kenyon Coll. (OH)
Knox Coll. (IL)
Lawrence Univ. (WI)
Lehigh Univ. (PA)
Lincoln Univ. (PA)
Louisiana State Univ.–Baton Rouge
Loyola Marymount Univ. (CA)
Luther Coll. (IA)
Macalester Coll. (MN)
Martin Univ. (IN)
Meredith Coll. (NC)
Metropolitan State Coll. of Denver
Miami Univ.–Oxford (OH)
Michigan State Univ.
Middlebury Coll. (VT)
Mills Coll. (CA)
Minnesota State Univ.–Mankato
Minnesota State Univ.–Moorhead
Montclair State Univ. (NJ)
Morehouse Coll. (GA)
Morgan State Univ. (MD)
Mount Holyoke Coll. (MA)
Nebraska Wesleyan Univ.
New Mexico State Univ.
New York Univ.
North Carolina State Univ.–Raleigh
North Dakota State Univ.
North Park Univ. (IL)
Northeastern Illinois Univ.
Northeastern State Univ. (OK)
Northeastern Univ. (MA)
Northern Arizona Univ.
Northwestern Univ. (IL)
Oakland Univ. (MI)
Oberlin Coll. (OH)
Occidental Coll. (CA)
Ohio State Univ.–Columbus
Ohio Univ.
Ohio Wesleyan Univ.
Old Dominion Univ. (VA)
Oregon State Univ.
Our Lady of the Lake Univ. (TX)
Pace Univ. (NY)
Pacific Lutheran Univ. (WA)
Pennsylvania State Univ.–Univ. Park
Pitzer Coll. (CA)
Pomona Coll. (CA)
Portland State Univ. (OR)
Prescott Coll. (AZ)
Purchase Coll.–SUNY
Purdue Univ.–West Lafayette (IN)
Randolph-Macon Coll. (VA)
Regis Univ. (CO)
Rhode Island Coll.
Rice Univ. (TX)
Roosevelt Univ. (IL)
Rosemont Coll. (PA)
Russell Sage Coll. (NY)
Rutgers, the State Univ. of New Jersey–Camden

Rutgers, the State Univ. of New Jersey–New Brunswick
Rutgers, the State Univ. of New Jersey–Newark
San Diego State Univ.
San Francisco State Univ.
San Jose State Univ. (CA)
Scripps Coll. (CA)
Seton Hall Univ. (NJ)
Simmons Coll. (MA)
Skidmore Coll. (NY)
Smith Coll. (MA)
Sonoma State Univ. (CA)
Southern Adventist Univ. (TN)
Southern Methodist Univ. (TX)
Southwestern Univ. (TX)
Spelman Coll. (GA)
St. Bonaventure Univ. (NY)
St. Catherine Univ. (MN)
St. Cloud State Univ. (MN)
St. Francis Coll. (NY)
St. John's Univ. (MN)
St. Louis Univ.
St. Mary's Coll. of California
St. Olaf Coll. (MN)
Stanford Univ. (CA)
Stonehill Coll. (MA)
Suffolk Univ. (MA)
Sul Ross State Univ. (TX)
SUNY Coll.–Cortland
SUNY Coll.–Potsdam
SUNY–Geneseo
SUNY–Oswego
SUNY–Plattsburgh
SUNY–Stony Brook
Syracuse Univ. (NY)
Talladega Coll. (AL)
Temple Univ. (PA)
Tennessee State Univ.
Towson Univ. (MD)
Trinity Coll. (CT)
Tufts Univ. (MA)
Tulane Univ. (LA)
Univ. at Albany–SUNY
Univ. at Buffalo–SUNY
Univ. of Alabama–Birmingham
Univ. of Alaska–Fairbanks
Univ. of Arizona
Univ. of California–Berkeley
Univ. of California–Davis
Univ. of California–Irvine
Univ. of California–Los Angeles
Univ. of California–Riverside
Univ. of California–San Diego
Univ. of California–Santa Barbara
Univ. of California–Santa Cruz
Univ. of Central Arkansas
Univ. of Central Missouri
Univ. of Chicago
Univ. of Colorado–Boulder
Univ. of Connecticut
Univ. of Dayton (OH)
Univ. of Delaware
Univ. of Denver
Univ. of Florida
Univ. of Georgia
Univ. of Hartford (CT)
Univ. of Hawaii–Manoa
Univ. of Illinois–Chicago
Univ. of Illinois–Urbana-Champaign
Univ. of Iowa

Univ. of Kansas
Univ. of Louisville (KY)
Univ. of Maine
Univ. of Maine–Farmington
Univ. of Maryland–Baltimore County
Univ. of Maryland–Coll. Park
Univ. of Maryland–Eastern Shore
Univ. of Massachusetts–Amherst
Univ. of Massachusetts–Boston
Univ. of Memphis
Univ. of Miami (FL)
Univ. of Michigan–Ann Arbor
Univ. of Michigan–Dearborn
Univ. of Michigan–Flint
Univ. of Minnesota–Duluth
Univ. of Minnesota–Morris
Univ. of Minnesota–Twin Cities
Univ. of Mississippi
Univ. of Montana
Univ. of Nebraska–Lincoln
Univ. of Nebraska–Omaha
Univ. of Nevada–Las Vegas
Univ. of Nevada–Reno
Univ. of New Hampshire
Univ. of New Mexico
Univ. of New Orleans
Univ. of North Carolina–Asheville
Univ. of North Carolina–Chapel Hill
Univ. of North Carolina–Charlotte
Univ. of North Carolina–Greensboro
Univ. of North Carolina–Pembroke
Univ. of North Dakota
Univ. of Northern Colorado
Univ. of Oklahoma
Univ. of Oregon
Univ. of Pennsylvania
Univ. of Pittsburgh
Univ. of Redlands (CA)
Univ. of Rhode Island
Univ. of Richmond (VA)
Univ. of Rochester (NY)
Univ. of Science and Arts of Oklahoma
Univ. of South Carolina
Univ. of South Dakota
Univ. of South Florida
Univ. of Southern California
Univ. of Southern Maine
Univ. of St. Thomas (MN)
Univ. of Texas–Austin
Univ. of Texas–Dallas
Univ. of Texas–El Paso
Univ. of Texas–Pan American
Univ. of Texas–San Antonio
Univ. of the Incarnate Word (TX)
Univ. of Toledo (OH)
Univ. of Utah
Univ. of Vermont
Univ. of Virginia
Univ. of Washington
Univ. of Wisconsin–Eau Claire
Univ. of Wisconsin–Madison
Univ. of Wisconsin–Milwaukee
Univ. of Wisconsin–Whitewater
Univ. of Wyoming
Vanderbilt Univ. (TN)
Vassar Coll. (NY)
Virginia Commonwealth Univ.
Virginia Wesleyan Coll.

Warren Wilson Coll. (NC)
Washington State Univ.
Washington Univ. in St. Louis
Wayne State Univ. (MI)
Wellesley Coll. (MA)
Wells Coll. (NY)
Wesleyan Univ. (CT)
West Chester Univ. of Pennsylvania
Western Illinois Univ.
Western Michigan Univ.
Wheaton Coll. (MA)
Whitman Coll. (WA)
Wichita State Univ. (KS)
Willamette Univ. (OR)
William Paterson Univ. of New Jersey
Williams Coll. (MA)
Wright State Univ. (OH)
Yale Univ. (CT)
Youngstown State Univ. (OH)

Experimental Psychology

American Jewish Univ. (CA)
Eastern Nazarene Coll. (MA)
Keene State Coll. (NH)
Millikin Univ. (IL)
Moravian Coll. (PA)
Paine Coll. (GA)
Tufts Univ. (MA)
Univ. of Kentucky
Univ. of Rochester (NY)
Univ. of South Carolina

Family and Consumer Economics and Related Studies

Arizona State Univ.
Brigham Young Univ.–Provo (UT)
Buffalo State Coll.–SUNY
California State Polytechnic Univ.–Pomona
Concordia Coll.–Moorhead (MN)
Cornell Univ. (NY)
Indiana Univ. of Pennsylvania
Iowa State Univ.
Louisiana Tech Univ.
Middle Tennessee State Univ.
Oakwood Univ. (AL)
Ohio State Univ.–Columbus
Ohio Univ.
South Dakota State Univ.
St. Joseph Coll. (CT)
Syracuse Univ. (NY)
Tennessee State Univ.
Univ. of Akron (OH)
Univ. of Alabama
Univ. of Arizona
Univ. of Delaware
Univ. of Georgia
Univ. of Hawaii–Manoa
Univ. of Illinois–Urbana-Champaign
Univ. of Kentucky
Univ. of Minnesota–Twin Cities
Univ. of Missouri
Univ. of Nebraska–Kearney
Univ. of Nebraska–Lincoln
Univ. of Tennessee
Univ. of Utah
Univ. of Wisconsin–Madison

Utah State Univ.
Virginia State Univ.
Weber State Univ. (UT)

Family and Consumer Sciences/Human Sciences

Alabama Agricultural and Mechanical Univ.
Alcorn State Univ. (MS)
Ashland Univ. (OH)
Ball State Univ. (IN)
Baylor Univ. (TX)
Berea Coll. (KY)
Bluffton Univ. (OH)
Boise State Univ. (ID)
Bradley Univ. (IL)
Bridgewater Coll. (VA)
Brigham Young Univ.–Provo (UT)
California Polytechnic State Univ.–San Luis Obispo
California State Univ.–Fresno
California State Univ.–Long Beach
California State Univ.–Los Angeles
California State Univ.–Northridge
California State Univ.–Sacramento
Cameron Univ. (OK)
Campbell Univ. (NC)
Central Washington Univ.
Chadron State Coll. (NE)
Cheyney Univ. of Pennsylvania
Coll. of the Ozarks (MO)
Colorado State Univ.
Concordia Coll.–Moorhead (MN)
Cornell Univ. (NY)
CUNY–Lehman Coll.
CUNY–Queens Coll.
Delta State Univ. (MS)
East Tennessee State Univ.
Eastern Illinois Univ.
Eastern Kentucky Univ.
Eastern New Mexico Univ.
Fairmont State Univ. (WV)
Florida State Univ.
Framingham State Coll. (MA)
Gallaudet Univ. (DC)
George Fox Univ. (OR)
Grambling State Univ. (LA)
Harding Univ. (AR)
Henderson State Univ. (AR)
Idaho State Univ.
Illinois State Univ.
Indiana State Univ.
Indiana Univ. of Pennsylvania
Jacksonville State Univ. (AL)
Kansas State Univ.
Lambuth Univ. (TN)
Liberty Univ. (VA)
Lipscomb Univ. (TN)
Louisiana State Univ.–Baton Rouge
Madonna Univ. (MI)
Marshall Univ. (WV)
Master's Coll. and Seminary (CA)
McNeese State Univ. (LA)
Mercyhurst Coll. (PA)
Meredith Coll. (NC)
Michigan State Univ.
Minnesota State Univ.–Mankato
Mississippi State Univ.
Montana State Univ.

Montclair State Univ. (NJ)
Morehead State Univ. (KY)
New Jersey City Univ.
New Mexico Highlands Univ.
New Mexico State Univ.
Nicholls State Univ. (LA)
Norfolk State Univ. (VA)
North Carolina A&T State Univ.
North Carolina Central Univ.
Northeastern State Univ. (OK)
Northwestern Oklahoma State
    Univ.
Northwestern State Univ. of
    Louisiana
Ohio State Univ.–Columbus
Oklahoma Baptist Univ.
Oklahoma Christian Univ.
Oklahoma State Univ.
Oregon State Univ.
Pittsburg State Univ. (KS)
Point Loma Nazarene Univ. (CA)
Prairie View A&M Univ. (TX)
Purdue Univ.–Calumet (IN)
Sam Houston State Univ. (TX)
San Francisco State Univ.
Seattle Pacific Univ.
Seton Hill Univ. (PA)
South Carolina State Univ.
Southeast Missouri State Univ.
Southeastern Louisiana Univ.
Southern Univ. and A&M Coll. (LA)
Southern Utah Univ.
Stephen F. Austin State Univ. (TX)
SUNY Coll.–Oneonta
Tarleton State Univ. (TX)
Texas State Univ.–San Marcos
Texas Tech Univ.
Texas Woman's Univ.
Univ. of Alabama
Univ. of Arkansas
Univ. of Arkansas–Pine Bluff
Univ. of Central Arkansas
Univ. of Central Missouri
Univ. of Central Oklahoma
Univ. of Delaware
Univ. of Houston
Univ. of Louisiana–Monroe
Univ. of Maryland–Eastern Shore
Univ. of Mississippi
Univ. of Montevallo (AL)
Univ. of Nebraska–Lincoln
Univ. of New Mexico
Univ. of North Alabama
Univ. of Southern Mississippi
Univ. of Tennessee–Chattanooga
Univ. of Tennessee–Martin
Univ. of Texas–Austin
Univ. of Wisconsin–Madison
Univ. of Wyoming
Utah State Univ.
Washington State Univ.
Wayne State Coll. (NE)
West Virginia Univ.
Western Illinois Univ.
Youngstown State Univ. (OH)

Family and Consumer Sciences/Human Sciences Business Services

Ashland Univ. (OH)
Bradley Univ. (IL)
California State Univ.–Long Beach
Eastern Kentucky Univ.
Lasell Coll. (MA)
Madonna Univ. (MI)
Northwestern Oklahoma State
    Univ.
Our Lady of the Lake Univ. (TX)
San Jose State Univ. (CA)
Univ. of Georgia
Univ. of Houston
Univ. of Illinois–Urbana-Champaign
Univ. of Wisconsin–Eau Claire
Univ. of Wisconsin–Madison
Virginia Tech

Family Psychology

Corban Univ. (OR)
Walsh Univ. (OH)

Film/Video and Photographic Arts

American Univ. (DC)
Arcadia Univ. (PA)
Arizona State Univ.
Art Academy of Cincinnati
Art Center Coll. of Design (CA)
Baldwin-Wallace Coll. (OH)
Bard Coll. at Simon's Rock (MA)
Barnard Coll. (NY)
Barry Univ. (FL)
Bellevue Univ. (NE)
Bennington Coll. (VT)
Berklee Coll. of Music (MA)
Bethel Coll. (IN)
Binghamton Univ.–SUNY
Biola Univ. (CA)
Boston Univ.
Bowling Green State Univ. (OH)
Bradley Univ. (IL)
Briar Cliff Univ. (IA)
Bridgewater State Coll. (MA)
Brigham Young Univ.–Provo (UT)
Buffalo State Coll.–SUNY
Burlington Coll. (VT)
California Coll. of the Arts
California Institute of the Arts
California State Univ.–Long Beach
California State Univ.–Sacramento
Calvin Coll. (MI)
Cardinal Stritch Univ. (WI)
Carleton Coll. (MN)
Carlow Univ. (PA)
Carroll Univ. (WI)
Carson-Newman Coll. (TN)
Cazenovia Coll. (NY)
Central Washington Univ.
Chapman Univ. (CA)
Chatham Univ. (PA)
Claremont McKenna Coll. (CA)
Clark Univ. (MA)
Cleveland Institute of Art
Coker Coll. (SC)
Coll. for Creative Studies (MI)
Coll. of Santa Fe (NM)
Coll. of Visual Arts (MN)
Colorado Coll.
Columbia Coll. (MO)

Columbia Coll. (IL)
Columbia Univ. (NY)
Columbus Coll. of Art and Design
    (OH)
Connecticut Coll.
Corcoran Coll. of Art and Design
    (DC)
Cornell Univ. (NY)
CUNY–Brooklyn Coll.
CUNY–Coll. of Staten Island
CUNY–Hunter Coll.
CUNY–Queens Coll.
Dartmouth Coll. (NH)
Denison Univ. (OH)
DePauw Univ. (IN)
DeSales Univ. (PA)
Dominican Univ. (IL)
Drexel Univ. (PA)
Eastern Mennonite Univ. (VA)
Eastern Michigan Univ.
Eastern New Mexico Univ.
Eastern Washington Univ.
Emerson Coll. (MA)
Emory Univ. (GA)
Evergreen State Coll. (WA)
Fairleigh Dickinson Univ. (NJ)
Ferris State Univ. (MI)
Fitchburg State Coll. (MA)
Florida State Univ.
George Fox Univ. (OR)
Georgia State Univ.
Grand Valley State Univ. (MI)
Hampshire Coll. (MA)
Hofstra Univ. (NY)
Hollins Univ. (VA)
Howard Univ. (DC)
Huntington Univ. (IN)
Indiana Univ.–South Bend
Indiana Univ.-Purdue Univ.–Fort
    Wayne
Ithaca Coll. (NY)
Kansas City Art Institute (MO)
Kean Univ. (NJ)
Keene State Coll. (NH)
La Roche Coll. (PA)
Long Island Univ.–C.W. Post
    Campus (NY)
Louisiana Tech Univ.
Loyola Marymount Univ. (CA)
Maine Coll. of Art
Maryland Institute Coll. of Art
Marywood Univ. (PA)
Massachusetts Coll. of Art and
    Design
Middlebury Coll. (VT)
Milwaukee Institute of Art and
    Design
Minneapolis Coll. of Art and Design
Minnesota State Univ.–Moorhead
Missouri State Univ.
Montana State Univ.
Montserrat Coll. of Art (MA)
Moore Coll. of Art and Design (PA)
Morningside Coll. (IA)
Mount Holyoke Coll. (MA)
Mountain State Univ. (WV)
Muhlenberg Coll. (PA)
National Univ. (CA)
New Jersey City Univ.
New Mexico Highlands Univ.
New School (NY)

New York Univ.
Northern Arizona Univ.
Northern Michigan Univ.
Oakland Univ. (MI)
Ohio State Univ.–Columbus
Ohio Univ.
Oklahoma City Univ.
Otis Coll. of Art and Design (CA)
Pace Univ. (NY)
Pacific Northwest Coll. of Art (OR)
Pacific Union Coll. (CA)
Palm Beach Atlantic Univ. (FL)
Pennsylvania State Univ.–Univ. Park
Pitzer Coll. (CA)
Point Park Univ. (PA)
Prescott Coll. (AZ)
Providence Coll. (RI)
Purchase Coll.–SUNY
Rhode Island Coll.
Rhode Island School of Design
Ringling Coll. of Art and Design
    (FL)
Rochester Institute of Technology
    (NY)
Sage Colleges–Albany (NY)
Sam Houston State Univ. (TX)
San Francisco Art Institute
San Francisco State Univ.
San Jose State Univ. (CA)
Savannah Coll. of Art and Design
    (GA)
School of the Art Institute of
    Chicago
Shawnee State Univ. (OH)
Smith Coll. (MA)
Southern Adventist Univ. (TN)
Southern Illinois Univ.–Carbondale
Southern Methodist Univ. (TX)
Spring Arbor Univ. (MI)
St. Augustine's Coll. (NC)
St. Cloud State Univ. (MN)
St. Edward's Univ. (TX)
St. John's Univ. (NY)
St. Mary's Coll. of Maryland
Stanford Univ. (CA)
Suffolk Univ. (MA)
SUNY–Fredonia
SUNY–Oswego
Swarthmore Coll. (PA)
Syracuse Univ. (NY)
Temple Univ. (PA)
Texas A&M Univ.–Commerce
Texas Christian Univ.
Thomas Edison State Coll. (NJ)
Tulane Univ. (LA)
Univ. at Buffalo–SUNY
Univ. of Akron (OH)
Univ. of California–Berkeley
Univ. of California–Davis
Univ. of California–Irvine
Univ. of California–Los Angeles
Univ. of California–Riverside
Univ. of California–Santa Barbara
Univ. of California–Santa Cruz
Univ. of Central Arkansas
Univ. of Central Florida
Univ. of Central Missouri
Univ. of Chicago
Univ. of Colorado–Boulder
Univ. of Dayton (OH)
Univ. of Georgia

Univ. of Hartford (CT)
Univ. of Houston
Univ. of Illinois–Chicago
Univ. of Illinois–Urbana-Champaign
Univ. of Iowa
Univ. of Massachusetts–Dartmouth
Univ. of Miami (FL)
Univ. of Michigan–Ann Arbor
Univ. of Minnesota–Twin Cities
Univ. of Missouri–St. Louis
Univ. of Montana
Univ. of Nebraska–Lincoln
Univ. of Nevada–Las Vegas
Univ. of New Mexico
Univ. of North Carolina School of
    the Arts
Univ. of North Carolina–
    Wilmington
Univ. of North Texas
Univ. of Oklahoma
Univ. of Oregon
Univ. of Pennsylvania
Univ. of Pittsburgh
Univ. of Rhode Island
Univ. of Rochester (NY)
Univ. of South Carolina
Univ. of Southern California
Univ. of the Arts (PA)
Univ. of Toledo (OH)
Univ. of Tulsa (OK)
Univ. of Utah
Univ. of Vermont
Univ. of Wisconsin–Milwaukee
Vanguard Univ. of Southern
    California
Vassar Coll. (NY)
Virginia Commonwealth Univ.
Virginia Intermont Coll.
Washington Univ. in St. Louis
Wayne State Univ. (MI)
Weber State Univ. (UT)
Webster Univ. (MO)
Wellesley Coll. (MA)
Wesleyan Univ. (CT)
Western Michigan Univ.
Western Washington Univ.
Whitman Coll. (WA)
Wilmington Univ. (DE)
Woodbury Univ. (CA)
Wright State Univ. (OH)
Yale Univ. (CT)
Youngstown State Univ. (OH)

Finance and Financial Management Services

Abilene Christian Univ. (TX)
Adelphi Univ. (NY)
Alabama Agricultural and
    Mechanical Univ.
Alabama State Univ.
Alfred Univ. (NY)
Alma Coll. (MI)
American Univ. (DC)
Anderson Univ. (SC)
Anderson Univ. (IN)
Andrews Univ. (MI)
Angelo State Univ. (TX)
Appalachian State Univ. (NC)
Arcadia Univ. (PA)
Arizona State Univ.

Arkansas State Univ.–Jonesboro
Ashland Univ. (OH)
Auburn Univ. (AL)
Auburn Univ.–Montgomery (AL)
Augsburg Coll. (MN)
Augusta State Univ. (GA)
Aurora Univ. (IL)
Averett Univ. (VA)
Avila Univ. (MO)
Azusa Pacific Univ. (CA)
Babson Coll. (MA)
Baldwin-Wallace Coll. (OH)
Ball State Univ. (IN)
Baylor Univ. (TX)
Belmont Univ. (TN)
Benedictine Univ. (IL)
Bentley Univ. (MA)
Berry Coll. (GA)
Bethel Coll. (IN)
Boise State Univ. (ID)
Boston Univ.
Bowling Green State Univ. (OH)
Bradley Univ. (IL)
Bridgewater State Coll. (MA)
Bryant Univ. (RI)
Buena Vista Univ. (IA)
Butler Univ. (IN)
Cabrini Coll. (PA)
California State Polytechnic Univ.–
 Pomona
California State Univ.–Fullerton
California State Univ.–Long Beach
California State Univ.–Sacramento
Canisius Coll. (NY)
Capital Univ. (OH)
Carroll Univ. (WI)
Catholic Univ. of America (DC)
Cedarville Univ. (OH)
Centenary Coll. of Louisiana
Central Connecticut State Univ.
Central Methodist Univ. (MO)
Central Michigan Univ.
Christopher Newport Univ. (VA)
Clarion Univ. of Pennsylvania
Clarkson Univ. (NY)
Cleary Univ. (MI)
Clemson Univ. (SC)
Cleveland State Univ.
Coastal Carolina Univ. (SC)
Coll. at Brockport–SUNY
Coll. of William and Mary (VA)
Columbia Coll. (MO)
Columbus State Univ. (GA)
Concordia Coll.–Moorhead (MN)
Concordia Univ. Wisconsin
Concordia Univ.–St. Paul (MN)
Creighton Univ. (NE)
Culver-Stockton Coll. (MO)
CUNY–Baruch Coll.
CUNY–Queens Coll.
Dakota State Univ. (SD)
Dallas Baptist Univ.
Davenport Univ. (MI)
Delaware State Univ.
Delta State Univ. (MS)
DePaul Univ. (IL)
DeSales Univ. (PA)
Dominican Coll. (NY)
Dowling Coll. (NY)
Drake Univ. (IA)
Duquesne Univ. (PA)

East Carolina Univ. (NC)
East Tennessee State Univ.
Eastern Illinois Univ.
Eastern Kentucky Univ.
Eastern Michigan Univ.
Eastern Washington Univ.
Elmhurst Coll. (IL)
Evangel Univ. (MO)
Excelsior Coll. (NY)
Fairmont State Univ. (WV)
Fayetteville State Univ. (NC)
Ferris State Univ. (MI)
Fitchburg State Coll. (MA)
Florida Atlantic Univ.
Florida Gulf Coast Univ.
Florida International Univ.
Florida Southern Coll.
Florida State Univ.
Fort Hays State Univ. (KS)
Fort Lewis Coll. (CO)
Francis Marion Univ. (SC)
Franklin Pierce Univ. (NH)
Freed-Hardeman Univ. (TN)
Gannon Univ. (PA)
Gardner-Webb Univ. (NC)
George Mason Univ. (VA)
George Washington Univ. (DC)
Georgetown Univ. (DC)
Georgia Southern Univ.
Georgia Southwestern State Univ.
Georgia State Univ.
Goldey Beacom Coll. (DE)
Gordon Coll. (MA)
Grace Coll. and Seminary (IN)
Grand Valley State Univ. (MI)
Grove City Coll. (PA)
Gwynedd-Mercy Coll. (PA)
Hampton Univ. (VA)
Hardin-Simmons Univ. (TX)
Hawaii Pacific Univ.
High Point Univ. (NC)
Hillsdale Coll. (MI)
Hofstra Univ. (NY)
Holy Family Univ. (PA)
Houston Baptist Univ.
Howard Univ. (DC)
Huntington Univ. (IN)
Husson Univ. (ME)
Idaho State Univ.
Illinois Coll.
Illinois State Univ.
Immaculata Univ. (PA)
Indiana State Univ.
Indiana Univ. of Pennsylvania
Indiana Univ. Southeast
Indiana Univ.–Kokomo
Indiana Univ.–South Bend
Indiana Univ.-Purdue Univ.–Fort
 Wayne
Indiana Wesleyan Univ.
Iona Coll. (NY)
Iowa State Univ.
Jackson State Univ. (MS)
Jacksonville State Univ. (AL)
Jacksonville Univ. (FL)
James Madison Univ. (VA)
Jamestown Coll. (ND)
John Carroll Univ. (OH)
Johnson and Wales Univ. (RI)
Juniata Coll. (PA)
Kansas State Univ.

Kean Univ. (NJ)
Kennesaw State Univ. (GA)
Kent State Univ. (OH)
King's Coll. (PA)
Kutztown Univ. of Pennsylvania
La Roche Coll. (PA)
La Salle Univ. (PA)
La Sierra Univ. (CA)
Lake Superior State Univ. (MI)
Lamar Univ. (TX)
Lasell Coll. (MA)
Le Moyne Coll. (NY)
Lehigh Univ. (PA)
Lenoir-Rhyne Univ. (NC)
LeTourneau Univ. (TX)
Lincoln Univ. (PA)
Lindenwood Univ. (MO)
Linfield Coll. (OR)
Lipscomb Univ. (TN)
Long Island Univ.–C.W. Post
 Campus (NY)
Loras Coll. (IA)
Louisiana Coll.
Louisiana State Univ.–Baton Rouge
Louisiana State Univ.–Shreveport
Louisiana Tech Univ.
Loyola Univ. Chicago
Loyola Univ. New Orleans
Lynchburg Coll. (VA)
Madonna Univ. (MI)
Manchester Coll. (IN)
Manhattan Coll. (NY)
Manhattanville Coll. (NY)
Marian Univ. (IN)
Marquette Univ. (WI)
Marshall Univ. (WV)
Marywood Univ. (PA)
Master's Coll. and Seminary (CA)
McNeese State Univ. (LA)
Mercy Coll. (NY)
Methodist Univ. (NC)
Metropolitan State Coll. of Denver
Miami Univ.–Oxford (OH)
Michigan State Univ.
Middle Tennessee State Univ.
Midwestern State Univ. (TX)
Millikin Univ. (IL)
Minnesota State Univ.–Mankato
Minnesota State Univ.–Moorhead
Minot State Univ. (ND)
Mississippi State Univ.
Missouri Southern State Univ.
Missouri State Univ.
Missouri Univ. of Science &
 Technology
Missouri Western State Univ.
Morehead State Univ. (KY)
Morgan State Univ. (MD)
Morningside Coll. (IA)
Mount Vernon Nazarene Univ.
 (OH)
Mountain State Univ. (WV)
Muhlenberg Coll. (PA)
Murray State Univ. (KY)
National Univ. (CA)
New Mexico Highlands Univ.
New Mexico State Univ.
New York Institute of Technology
New York Univ.
Nicholls State Univ. (LA)
Nichols Coll. (MA)

North Carolina A&T State Univ.
North Central Coll. (IL)
North Georgia Coll. and State Univ.
Northeastern Illinois Univ.
Northeastern State Univ. (OK)
Northeastern Univ. (MA)
Northern Arizona Univ.
Northern Illinois Univ.
Northern Kentucky Univ.
Northern Michigan Univ.
Northern State Univ. (SD)
Northwest Missouri State Univ.
Northwestern Coll. (MN)
Northwestern Oklahoma State
 Univ.
Northwood Univ. (MI)
Nova Southeastern Univ. (FL)
Oakland Univ. (MI)
Oakwood Univ. (AL)
Ohio Dominican Univ.
Ohio State Univ.–Columbus
Ohio Univ.
Oklahoma Baptist Univ.
Oklahoma City Univ.
Oklahoma State Univ.
Old Dominion Univ. (VA)
Olivet Coll. (MI)
Oral Roberts Univ. (OK)
Our Lady of the Lake Univ. (TX)
Pace Univ. (NY)
Park Univ. (MO)
Pennsylvania State Univ.–Univ. Park
Pepperdine Univ. (CA)
Philadelphia Univ.
Pittsburg State Univ. (KS)
Post Univ. (CT)
Prairie View A&M Univ. (TX)
Princeton Univ. (NJ)
Providence Coll. (RI)
Purdue Univ.–West Lafayette (IN)
Quincy Univ. (IL)
Quinnipiac Univ. (CT)
Radford Univ. (VA)
Regis Univ. (CO)
Rhode Island Coll.
Rider Univ. (NJ)
Robert Morris Univ. (PA)
Rochester Institute of Technology
 (NY)
Roger Williams Univ. (RI)
Roosevelt Univ. (IL)
Rutgers, the State Univ. of New
 Jersey–Camden
Rutgers, the State Univ. of New
 Jersey–New Brunswick
Rutgers, the State Univ. of New
 Jersey–Newark
Sacred Heart Univ. (CT)
Saginaw Valley State Univ. (MI)
Salisbury Univ. (MD)
Salve Regina Univ. (RI)
Sam Houston State Univ. (TX)
San Diego State Univ.
Santa Clara Univ. (CA)
Schreiner Univ. (TX)
Seattle Univ.
Seton Hall Univ. (NJ)
Seton Hill Univ. (PA)
Shippensburg Univ. of Pennsylvania
Siena Coll. (NY)
Southeast Missouri State Univ.

Southeastern Louisiana Univ.
Southeastern Oklahoma State Univ.
Southeastern Univ. (FL)
Southern Adventist Univ. (TN)
Southern Connecticut State Univ.
Southern Illinois Univ.–Carbondale
Southern Methodist Univ. (TX)
Southern Nazarene Univ. (OK)
Southern Univ. and A&M Coll. (LA)
Southern Utah Univ.
Southwest Minnesota State Univ.
Southwestern Coll. (KS)
St. Ambrose Univ. (IA)
St. Anselm Coll. (NH)
St. Bonaventure Univ. (NY)
St. Cloud State Univ. (MN)
St. Edward's Univ. (TX)
St. Francis Univ. (PA)
St. John Fisher Coll. (NY)
St. John's Univ. (NY)
St. Joseph's Coll. (ME)
St. Joseph's Univ. (PA)
St. Mary's Coll. of California
St. Mary's Univ. of San Antonio
 (TX)
St. Thomas Aquinas Coll. (NY)
St. Thomas Univ. (FL)
St. Vincent Coll. (PA)
St. Xavier Univ. (IL)
Stephen F. Austin State Univ. (TX)
Stetson Univ. (FL)
Stonehill Coll. (MA)
Suffolk Univ. (MA)
Sul Ross State Univ. (TX)
SUNY Coll. of Technology–Alfred
SUNY Coll.–Old Westbury
SUNY Institute of Technology–
 Utica/Rome
SUNY–Oswego
Syracuse Univ. (NY)
Talladega Coll. (AL)
Tarleton State Univ. (TX)
Taylor Univ. (IN)
Temple Univ. (PA)
Tennessee Technological Univ.
Tennessee Wesleyan Coll.
Texas A&M International Univ.
Texas A&M Univ.–Coll. Station
Texas A&M Univ.–Commerce
Texas A&M Univ.–Corpus Christi
Texas A&M Univ.–Kingsville
Texas Christian Univ.
Texas State Univ.–San Marcos
Texas Tech Univ.
Thomas Coll. (ME)
Thomas Edison State Coll. (NJ)
Tiffin Univ. (OH)
Trine Univ. (IN)
Troy Univ. (AL)
Tulane Univ. (LA)
Tuskegee Univ. (AL)
Union Coll. (NE)
Univ. of Akron (OH)
Univ. of Alabama
Univ. of Alabama–Birmingham
Univ. of Alabama–Huntsville
Univ. of Alaska–Anchorage
Univ. of Arizona
Univ. of Arkansas
Univ. of Arkansas–Little Rock
Univ. of Central Arkansas

Univ. of Central Florida
Univ. of Central Missouri
Univ. of Central Oklahoma
Univ. of Charleston (WV)
Univ. of Connecticut
Univ. of Dayton (OH)
Univ. of Delaware
Univ. of Denver
Univ. of Evansville (IN)
Univ. of Findlay (OH)
Univ. of Florida
Univ. of Georgia
Univ. of Hartford (CT)
Univ. of Hawaii–Hilo
Univ. of Hawaii–Manoa
Univ. of Houston
Univ. of Houston–Downtown
Univ. of Illinois–Chicago
Univ. of Illinois–Urbana-Champaign
Univ. of Indianapolis
Univ. of Iowa
Univ. of Kansas
Univ. of Kentucky
Univ. of Louisiana–Lafayette
Univ. of Louisiana–Monroe
Univ. of Louisville (KY)
Univ. of Maine
Univ. of Maine–Augusta
Univ. of Mary Hardin-Baylor (TX)
Univ. of Maryland–Coll. Park
Univ. of Maryland–Univ. Coll.
Univ. of Massachusetts–Amherst
Univ. of Massachusetts–Dartmouth
Univ. of Memphis
Univ. of Miami (FL)
Univ. of Michigan–Dearborn
Univ. of Michigan–Flint
Univ. of Minnesota–Duluth
Univ. of Minnesota–Twin Cities
Univ. of Mississippi
Univ. of Montana
Univ. of Montevallo (AL)
Univ. of Nebraska–Lincoln
Univ. of Nebraska–Omaha
Univ. of Nevada–Las Vegas
Univ. of Nevada–Reno
Univ. of New Hampshire
Univ. of New Haven (CT)
Univ. of New Orleans
Univ. of North Alabama
Univ. of North Carolina–Charlotte
Univ. of North Carolina–
  Greensboro
Univ. of North Carolina–
  Wilmington
Univ. of North Dakota
Univ. of North Florida
Univ. of North Texas
Univ. of Northern Iowa
Univ. of Notre Dame (IN)
Univ. of Oklahoma
Univ. of Pennsylvania
Univ. of Pittsburgh
Univ. of Pittsburgh–Johnstown
Univ. of Portland (OR)
Univ. of Rhode Island
Univ. of Rio Grande (OH)
Univ. of San Diego
Univ. of San Francisco
Univ. of Scranton (PA)
Univ. of South Alabama

Univ. of South Carolina
Univ. of South Dakota
Univ. of South Florida
Univ. of Southern Indiana
Univ. of Southern Mississippi
Univ. of St. Francis (IL)
Univ. of St. Thomas (TX)
Univ. of St. Thomas (MN)
Univ. of Tampa (FL)
Univ. of Tennessee
Univ. of Texas of the Permian Basin
Univ. of Texas–Arlington
Univ. of Texas–Austin
Univ. of Texas–Brownsville
Univ. of Texas–Dallas
Univ. of Texas–El Paso
Univ. of Texas–Pan American
Univ. of Texas–San Antonio
Univ. of Texas–Tyler
Univ. of the District of Columbia
Univ. of Toledo (OH)
Univ. of Tulsa (OK)
Univ. of Utah
Univ. of Washington
Univ. of West Florida
Univ. of West Georgia
Univ. of Wisconsin–Eau Claire
Univ. of Wisconsin–La Crosse
Univ. of Wisconsin–Madison
Univ. of Wisconsin–Milwaukee
Univ. of Wisconsin–Oshkosh
Univ. of Wisconsin–Superior
Univ. of Wisconsin–Whitewater
Univ. of Wyoming
Utah State Univ.
Valdosta State Univ. (GA)
Valparaiso Univ. (IN)
Vanguard Univ. of Southern
  California
Villanova Univ. (PA)
Virginia Commonwealth Univ.
Virginia Tech
Virginia Union Univ.
Wagner Coll. (NY)
Wake Forest Univ. (NC)
Waldorf Coll. (IA)
Walsh Coll. of Accountancy and
  Business Administration (MI)
Walsh Univ. (OH)
Washburn Univ. (KS)
Washington Adventist Univ. (MD)
Washington State Univ.
Washington Univ. in St. Louis
Wayne State Univ. (MI)
Waynesburg Univ. (PA)
Webber International Univ. (FL)
Weber State Univ. (UT)
West Chester Univ. of Pennsylvania
West Texas A&M Univ.
West Virginia Univ.
West Virginia Wesleyan Coll.
Western Carolina Univ. (NC)
Western Connecticut State Univ.
Western Illinois Univ.
Western Kentucky Univ.
Western Michigan Univ.
Western New England Coll. (MA)
Western Washington Univ.
Westminster Coll. (UT)
Wichita State Univ. (KS)
Widener Univ. (PA)

Williams Baptist Coll. (AR)
Wingate Univ. (NC)
Wofford Coll. (SC)
Wright State Univ. (OH)
Xavier Univ. (OH)
York Coll. of Pennsylvania
Youngstown State Univ. (OH)

Fine and Studio Art

Abilene Christian Univ. (TX)
Adams State Coll. (CO)
Adelphi Univ. (NY)
Adrian Coll. (MI)
Agnes Scott Coll. (GA)
Alabama Agricultural and
  Mechanical Univ.
Alabama State Univ.
Albany State Univ. (GA)
Albertus Magnus Coll. (CT)
Albion Coll. (MI)
Albright Coll. (PA)
Alderson-Broaddus Coll. (WV)
Alfred Univ. (NY)
Allegheny Coll. (PA)
Alma Coll. (MI)
Alverno Coll. (WI)
American Univ. (DC)
Amherst Coll. (MA)
Anderson Univ. (SC)
Anderson Univ. (IN)
Andrews Univ. (MI)
Angelo State Univ. (TX)
Anna Maria Coll. (MA)
Appalachian State Univ. (NC)
Aquinas Coll. (MI)
Arcadia Univ. (PA)
Arizona State Univ.
Arkansas State Univ.–Jonesboro
Arkansas Tech Univ.
Armstrong Atlantic State Univ. (GA)
Art Academy of Cincinnati
Art Center Coll. of Design (CA)
Asbury Univ. (KY)
Atlantic Union Coll. (MA)
Auburn Univ. (AL)
Auburn Univ.–Montgomery (AL)
Augsburg Coll. (MN)
Augustana Coll. (SD)
Augustana Coll. (IL)
Austin Coll. (TX)
Austin Peay State Univ. (TN)
Averett Univ. (VA)
Avila Univ. (MO)
Azusa Pacific Univ. (CA)
Baker Coll. of Flint (MI)
Baker Univ. (KS)
Baldwin-Wallace Coll. (OH)
Ball State Univ. (IN)
Bard Coll. (NY)
Bard Coll. at Simon's Rock (MA)
Barnard Coll. (NY)
Barry Univ. (FL)
Barton Coll. (NC)
Bates Coll. (ME)
Baylor Univ. (TX)
Belhaven Univ. (MS)
Bellarmine Univ. (KY)
Bellevue Univ. (NE)
Belmont Univ. (TN)
Beloit Coll. (WI)

Bemidji State Univ. (MN)
Benedict Coll. (SC)
Benedictine Coll. (KS)
Benedictine Univ. (IL)
Bennington Coll. (VT)
Berea Coll. (KY)
Berry Coll. (GA)
Bethany Coll. (WV)
Bethany Coll. (KS)
Bethel Coll. (KS)
Bethel Coll. (IN)
Bethel Univ. (MN)
Binghamton Univ.–SUNY
Biola Univ. (CA)
Black Hills State Univ. (SD)
Bloomsburg Univ. of Pennsylvania
Bluefield Coll. (VA)
Bluffton Univ. (OH)
Boise State Univ. (ID)
Boston Univ.
Bowdoin Coll. (ME)
Bowie State Univ. (MD)
Bowling Green State Univ. (OH)
Bradley Univ. (IL)
Brandeis Univ. (MA)
Brenau Univ. (GA)
Brescia Univ. (KY)
Brevard Coll. (NC)
Briar Cliff Univ. (IA)
Bridgewater Coll. (VA)
Bridgewater State Coll. (MA)
Brigham Young Univ.–Hawaii
Brigham Young Univ.–Provo (UT)
Brown Univ. (RI)
Bryn Mawr Coll. (PA)
Bucknell Univ. (PA)
Buena Vista Univ. (IA)
Buffalo State Coll.–SUNY
Burlington Coll. (VT)
Butler Univ. (IN)
Cabrini Coll. (PA)
Caldwell Coll. (NJ)
California Baptist Univ.
California Coll. of the Arts
California Institute of the Arts
California Lutheran Univ.
California Polytechnic State Univ.–
  San Luis Obispo
California State Polytechnic Univ.–
  Pomona
California State Univ.–Bakersfield
California State Univ.–Chico
California State Univ.–Dominguez
  Hills
California State Univ.–East Bay
California State Univ.–Fresno
California State Univ.–Fullerton
California State Univ.–Long Beach
California State Univ.–Los Angeles
California State Univ.–Northridge
California State Univ.–Sacramento
California State Univ.–San
  Bernardino
California State Univ.–Stanislaus
California Univ. of Pennsylvania
Calvin Coll. (MI)
Cameron Univ. (OK)
Campbell Univ. (NC)
Campbellsville Univ. (KY)
Canisius Coll. (NY)
Capital Univ. (OH)

Cardinal Stritch Univ. (WI)
Carleton Coll. (MN)
Carlow Univ. (PA)
Carnegie Mellon Univ. (PA)
Carroll Univ. (WI)
Carson-Newman Coll. (TN)
Carthage Coll. (WI)
Case Western Reserve Univ. (OH)
Castleton State Coll. (VT)
Catholic Univ. of America (DC)
Cazenovia Coll. (NY)
Cedar Crest Coll. (PA)
Cedarville Univ. (OH)
Centenary Coll. of Louisiana
Central Coll. (IA)
Central Connecticut State Univ.
Central Michigan Univ.
Central State Univ. (OH)
Central Washington Univ.
Centre Coll. (KY)
Chadron State Coll. (NE)
Champlain Coll. (VT)
Chapman Univ. (CA)
Chatham Univ. (PA)
Cheyney Univ. of Pennsylvania
Chicago State Univ.
Chowan Univ. (NC)
Christopher Newport Univ. (VA)
Claflin Univ. (SC)
Clarion Univ. of Pennsylvania
Clark Atlanta Univ.
Clark Univ. (MA)
Clemson Univ. (SC)
Cleveland Institute of Art
Cleveland State Univ.
Coastal Carolina Univ. (SC)
Coe Coll. (IA)
Coker Coll. (SC)
Colby Coll. (ME)
Colby-Sawyer Coll. (NH)
Colgate Univ. (NY)
Coll. at Brockport–SUNY
Coll. for Creative Studies (MI)
Coll. of Charleston (SC)
Coll. of Idaho (ID)
Coll. of Mount St. Joseph (OH)
Coll. of New Jersey
Coll. of Notre Dame of Maryland
Coll. of Our Lady of the Elms (MA)
Coll. of Santa Fe (NM)
Coll. of St. Benedict (MN)
Coll. of St. Elizabeth (NJ)
Coll. of St. Mary (NE)
Coll. of St. Rose (NY)
Coll. of the Holy Cross (MA)
Coll. of the Ozarks (MO)
Coll. of Visual Arts (MN)
Coll. of William and Mary (VA)
Coll. of Wooster (OH)
Colorado Christian Univ.
Colorado Coll.
Colorado State Univ.
Colorado State Univ.–Pueblo
Columbia Coll. (MO)
Columbia Coll. (SC)
Columbia Coll. (IL)
Columbia Univ. (NY)
Columbus Coll. of Art and Design
  (OH)
Columbus State Univ. (GA)
Concord Univ. (WV)

Concordia Coll. (NY)
Concordia Coll.–Moorhead (MN)
Concordia Univ. (MI)
Concordia Univ. (NE)
Concordia Univ. (CA)
Concordia Univ. Wisconsin
Concordia Univ.–St. Paul (MN)
Connecticut Coll.
Converse Coll. (SC)
Cooper Union (NY)
Corcoran Coll. of Art and Design (DC)
Cornell Coll. (IA)
Cornell Univ. (NY)
Cornish Coll. of the Arts (WA)
Covenant Coll. (GA)
Creighton Univ. (NE)
Culver-Stockton Coll. (MO)
Cumberland Univ. (TN)
CUNY–Baruch Coll.
CUNY–Brooklyn Coll.
CUNY–City Coll.
CUNY–Coll. of Staten Island
CUNY–Hunter Coll.
CUNY–Lehman Coll.
CUNY–Queens Coll.
CUNY–York Coll.
Curry Coll. (MA)
Daemen Coll. (NY)
Dakota Wesleyan Univ. (SD)
Dallas Baptist Univ.
Dana Coll. (NE)
Dartmouth Coll. (NH)
Davidson Coll. (NC)
Davis and Elkins Coll. (WV)
Defiance Coll. (OH)
Delaware State Univ.
Denison Univ. (OH)
DePaul Univ. (IL)
DePauw Univ. (IN)
Dickinson Coll. (PA)
Dickinson State Univ. (ND)
Dillard Univ. (LA)
Dominican Univ. (IL)
Dominican Univ. of California
Dordt Coll. (IA)
Dowling Coll. (NY)
Drake Univ. (IA)
Drew Univ. (NJ)
Drury Univ. (MO)
Duke Univ. (NC)
Duquesne Univ. (PA)
Earlham Coll. (IN)
East Carolina Univ. (NC)
East Central Univ. (OK)
East Tennessee State Univ.
Eastern Connecticut State Univ.
Eastern Illinois Univ.
Eastern Kentucky Univ.
Eastern Mennonite Univ. (VA)
Eastern Michigan Univ.
Eastern New Mexico Univ.
Eastern Oregon Univ.
Eastern Univ. (PA)
Eastern Washington Univ.
Eckerd Coll. (FL)
Edgewood Coll. (WI)
Edinboro Univ. of Pennsylvania
Elizabeth City State Univ. (NC)
Elizabethtown Coll. (PA)
Elmhurst Coll. (IL)

Elmira Coll. (NY)
Elon Univ. (NC)
Emmanuel Coll. (MA)
Emory and Henry Coll. (VA)
Emory Univ. (GA)
Emporia State Univ. (KS)
Endicott Coll. (MA)
Erskine Coll. (SC)
Eureka Coll. (IL)
Evangel Univ. (MO)
Evergreen State Coll. (WA)
Fairfield Univ. (CT)
Fashion Institute of Technology (NY)
Felician Coll. (NJ)
Ferris State Univ. (MI)
Ferrum Coll. (VA)
Flagler Coll. (FL)
Florida A&M Univ.
Florida Atlantic Univ.
Florida International Univ.
Florida Southern Coll.
Florida State Univ.
Fontbonne Univ. (MO)
Fordham Univ. (NY)
Fort Hays State Univ. (KS)
Fort Lewis Coll. (CO)
Framingham State Coll. (MA)
Francis Marion Univ. (SC)
Franklin and Marshall Coll. (PA)
Franklin Pierce Univ. (NH)
Freed-Hardeman Univ. (TN)
Fresno Pacific Univ. (CA)
Friends Univ. (KS)
Furman Univ. (SC)
Gallaudet Univ. (DC)
Gardner-Webb Univ. (NC)
George Fox Univ. (OR)
George Mason Univ. (VA)
George Washington Univ. (DC)
Georgetown Coll. (KY)
Georgetown Univ. (DC)
Georgia Coll. & State Univ.
Georgia Southern Univ.
Georgia Southwestern State Univ.
Georgia State Univ.
Georgian Court Univ. (NJ)
Gettysburg Coll. (PA)
Gonzaga Univ. (WA)
Gordon Coll. (MA)
Goshen Coll. (IN)
Goucher Coll. (MD)
Grace Coll. and Seminary (IN)
Graceland Univ. (IA)
Grambling State Univ. (LA)
Grand Valley State Univ. (MI)
Grand View Univ. (IA)
Green Mountain Coll. (VT)
Greensboro Coll. (NC)
Greenville Coll. (IL)
Grinnell Coll. (IA)
Guilford Coll. (NC)
Gustavus Adolphus Coll. (MN)
Hamilton Coll. (NY)
Hamline Univ. (MN)
Hampshire Coll. (MA)
Hampton Univ. (VA)
Hannibal-LaGrange Coll. (MO)
Hanover Coll. (IN)
Hardin-Simmons Univ. (TX)
Harding Univ. (AR)

Hartwick Coll. (NY)
Harvard Univ. (MA)
Haverford Coll. (PA)
Henderson State Univ. (AR)
Hendrix Coll. (AR)
High Point Univ. (NC)
Hillsdale Coll. (MI)
Hiram Coll. (OH)
Hobart and William Smith Colleges (NY)
Hofstra Univ. (NY)
Hollins Univ. (VA)
Holy Family Univ. (PA)
Hood Coll. (MD)
Hope Coll. (MI)
Houghton Coll. (NY)
Houston Baptist Univ.
Howard Payne Univ. (TX)
Howard Univ. (DC)
Humboldt State Univ. (CA)
Huntingdon Coll. (AL)
Huntington Univ. (IN)
Idaho State Univ.
Illinois Coll.
Illinois State Univ.
Illinois Wesleyan Univ.
Indiana State Univ.
Indiana Univ. East
Indiana Univ. Northwest
Indiana Univ. of Pennsylvania
Indiana Univ. Southeast
Indiana Univ.–Bloomington
Indiana Univ.–South Bend
Indiana Univ.-Purdue Univ.–Fort Wayne
Indiana Univ.-Purdue Univ.–Indianapolis
Indiana Wesleyan Univ.
Iowa Wesleyan Coll.
Ithaca Coll. (NY)
Jacksonville State Univ. (AL)
Jacksonville Univ. (FL)
James Madison Univ. (VA)
Jamestown Coll. (ND)
John Carroll Univ. (OH)
Johns Hopkins Univ. (MD)
Johnson State Coll. (VT)
Judson Univ. (IL)
Juniata Coll. (PA)
Kalamazoo Coll. (MI)
Kansas City Art Institute (MO)
Kansas State Univ.
Kean Univ. (NJ)
Keene State Coll. (NH)
Kennesaw State Univ. (GA)
Kent State Univ. (OH)
Kentucky State Univ.
Kentucky Wesleyan Coll.
Kenyon Coll. (OH)
Knox Coll. (IL)
Kutztown Univ. of Pennsylvania
La Salle Univ. (PA)
La Sierra Univ. (CA)
Lafayette Coll. (PA)
Laguna Coll. of Art and Design (CA)
Lake Erie Coll. (OH)
Lake Forest Coll. (IL)
Lake Superior State Univ. (MI)
Lambuth Univ. (TN)
Lander Univ. (SC)
Lawrence Univ. (WI)

Lebanon Valley Coll. (PA)
Lehigh Univ. (PA)
LeMoyne-Owen Coll. (TN)
Lesley Univ. (MA)
Lewis & Clark Coll. (OR)
Lewis Univ. (IL)
Limestone Coll. (SC)
Lincoln Univ. (MO)
Lincoln Univ. (PA)
Lindenwood Univ. (MO)
Lindsey Wilson Coll. (KY)
Linfield Coll. (OR)
Lipscomb Univ. (TN)
Lock Haven Univ. of Pennsylvania
Long Island Univ.–C.W. Post Campus (NY)
Loras Coll. (IA)
Louisiana Coll.
Louisiana State Univ.–Baton Rouge
Louisiana State Univ.–Shreveport
Louisiana Tech Univ.
Lourdes Coll. (OH)
Loyola Marymount Univ. (CA)
Loyola Univ. Chicago
Loyola Univ. Maryland
Loyola Univ. New Orleans
Luther Coll. (IA)
Lycoming Coll. (PA)
Lynchburg Coll. (VA)
Lyon Coll. (AR)
Macalester Coll. (MN)
MacMurray Coll. (IL)
Madonna Univ. (MI)
Maine Coll. of Art
Malone Univ. (OH)
Manchester Coll. (IN)
Manhattanville Coll. (NY)
Mansfield Univ. of Pennsylvania
Marian Univ. (WI)
Marian Univ. (IN)
Marietta Coll. (OH)
Marist Coll. (NY)
Mars Hill Coll. (NC)
Marshall Univ. (WV)
Mary Baldwin Coll. (VA)
Marygrove Coll. (MI)
Maryland Institute Coll. of Art
Marylhurst Univ. (OR)
Marymount Manhattan Coll. (NY)
Marymount Univ. (VA)
Maryville Coll. (TN)
Maryville Univ. of St. Louis (MO)
Marywood Univ. (PA)
Massachusetts Coll. of Art and Design
Massachusetts Coll. of Liberal Arts
McDaniel Coll. (MD)
McKendree Univ. (IL)
McMurry Univ. (TX)
McNeese State Univ. (LA)
McPherson Coll. (KS)
Memphis Coll. of Art
Mercer Univ. (GA)
Mercyhurst Coll. (PA)
Meredith Coll. (NC)
Merrimack Coll. (MA)
Mesa State Coll. (CO)
Messiah Coll. (PA)
Methodist Univ. (NC)
Metropolitan State Coll. of Denver
Miami Univ.–Oxford (OH)

Michigan State Univ.
Middle Tennessee State Univ.
Middlebury Coll. (VT)
Midland Lutheran Coll. (NE)
Midwestern State Univ. (TX)
Millersville Univ. of Pennsylvania
Millikin Univ. (IL)
Mills Coll. (CA)
Millsaps Coll. (MS)
Milwaukee Institute of Art and Design
Minneapolis Coll. of Art and Design
Minnesota State Univ.–Mankato
Minnesota State Univ.–Moorhead
Minot State Univ. (ND)
Mississippi Coll.
Missouri Southern State Univ.
Missouri State Univ.
Missouri Valley Coll.
Missouri Western State Univ.
Molloy Coll. (NY)
Monmouth Univ. (NJ)
Montana State Univ.
Montana State Univ.–Billings
Montclair State Univ. (NJ)
Montserrat Coll. of Art (MA)
Moore Coll. of Art and Design (PA)
Moravian Coll. (PA)
Morehead State Univ. (KY)
Morehouse Coll. (GA)
Morgan State Univ. (MD)
Morningside Coll. (IA)
Mount Holyoke Coll. (MA)
Mount Mary Coll. (WI)
Mount Mercy Coll. (IA)
Mount St. Mary's Coll. (CA)
Mount Vernon Nazarene Univ. (OH)
Muhlenberg Coll. (PA)
Murray State Univ. (KY)
Muskingum Univ. (OH)
National-Louis Univ. (IL)
Nazareth Coll. (NY)
Nebraska Wesleyan Univ.
New England Coll. (NH)
New Jersey City Univ.
New Mexico Highlands Univ.
New Mexico State Univ.
New School (NY)
New York Institute of Technology
New York Univ.
Newberry Coll. (SC)
Newman Univ. (KS)
Nicholls State Univ. (LA)
Norfolk State Univ. (VA)
North Carolina A&T State Univ.
North Carolina Central Univ.
North Carolina State Univ.–Raleigh
North Central Coll. (IL)
North Dakota State Univ.
North Georgia Coll. and State Univ.
North Park Univ. (IL)
Northeastern Illinois Univ.
Northeastern State Univ. (OK)
Northeastern Univ. (MA)
Northern Arizona Univ.
Northern Illinois Univ.
Northern Kentucky Univ.
Northern Michigan Univ.
Northern State Univ. (SD)
Northland Coll. (WI)

Northwest Missouri State Univ.
Northwest Nazarene Univ. (ID)
Northwestern Coll. (IA)
Northwestern Coll. (MN)
Northwestern Oklahoma State
    Univ.
Northwestern State Univ. of
    Louisiana
Northwestern Univ. (IL)
Notre Dame Coll. of Ohio
Notre Dame de Namur University
    (CA)
Oakland City Univ. (IN)
Oakland Univ. (MI)
Oberlin Coll. (OH)
Occidental Coll. (CA)
Oglethorpe Univ. (GA)
Ohio Dominican Univ.
Ohio Northern Univ.
Ohio State Univ.–Columbus
Ohio Univ.
Ohio Wesleyan Univ.
Oklahoma Baptist Univ.
Oklahoma State Univ.
Old Dominion Univ. (VA)
Olivet Coll. (MI)
Olivet Nazarene Univ. (IL)
Oregon State Univ.
Otis Coll. of Art and Design (CA)
Ouachita Baptist Univ. (AR)
Our Lady of the Lake Univ. (TX)
Pace Univ. (NY)
Pacific Lutheran Univ. (WA)
Pacific Northwest Coll. of Art (OR)
Pacific Union Coll. (CA)
Pacific Univ. (OR)
Palm Beach Atlantic Univ. (FL)
Park Univ. (MO)
Pennsylvania State Univ.–Univ. Park
Pepperdine Univ. (CA)
Pfeiffer Univ. (NC)
Philadelphia Univ.
Piedmont Coll. (GA)
Pikeville Coll. (KY)
Pine Manor Coll. (MA)
Pittsburg State Univ. (KS)
Pitzer Coll. (CA)
Plymouth State Univ. (NH)
Point Loma Nazarene Univ. (CA)
Pomona Coll. (CA)
Portland State Univ. (OR)
Pratt Institute (NY)
Presbyterian Coll. (SC)
Prescott Coll. (AZ)
Princeton Univ. (NJ)
Principia Coll. (IL)
Providence Coll. (RI)
Purchase Coll.–SUNY
Purdue Univ.–West Lafayette (IN)
Queens Univ. of Charlotte (NC)
Radford Univ. (VA)
Ramapo Coll. of New Jersey
Randolph Coll. (VA)
Randolph-Macon Coll. (VA)
Reed Coll. (OR)
Reinhardt Univ. (GA)
Rhode Island Coll.
Rhode Island School of Design
Rhodes Coll. (TN)
Rice Univ. (TX)
Rider Univ. (NJ)

Ringling Coll. of Art and Design
    (FL)
Ripon Coll. (WI)
Rivier Coll. (NH)
Roanoke Coll. (VA)
Roberts Wesleyan Coll. (NY)
Rochester Institute of Technology
    (NY)
Rockford Coll. (IL)
Rocky Mountain Coll. (MT)
Roger Williams Univ. (RI)
Rollins Coll. (FL)
Roosevelt Univ. (IL)
Rosemont Coll. (PA)
Rutgers, the State Univ. of New
    Jersey–Camden
Rutgers, the State Univ. of New
    Jersey–New Brunswick
Rutgers, the State Univ. of New
    Jersey–Newark
Sacred Heart Univ. (CT)
Sage Colleges–Albany (NY)
Saginaw Valley State Univ. (MI)
Salem Coll. (NC)
Salisbury Univ. (MD)
Salve Regina Univ. (RI)
Sam Houston State Univ. (TX)
Samford Univ. (AL)
San Diego State Univ.
San Francisco Art Institute
San Francisco State Univ.
San Jose State Univ. (CA)
Santa Clara Univ. (CA)
Savannah Coll. of Art and Design
    (GA)
School of the Art Institute of
    Chicago
Scripps Coll. (CA)
Seattle Pacific Univ.
Seattle Univ.
Seton Hall Univ. (NJ)
Seton Hill Univ. (PA)
Sewanee–Univ. of the South (TN)
Shawnee State Univ. (OH)
Shenandoah Univ. (VA)
Shepherd Univ. (WV)
Shippensburg Univ. of Pennsylvania
Shorter Coll. (GA)
Sierra Nevada Coll. (NV)
Silver Lake Coll. (WI)
Simmons Coll. (MA)
Simpson Coll. (IA)
Skidmore Coll. (NY)
Slippery Rock Univ. of Pennsylvania
Smith Coll. (MA)
Sonoma State Univ. (CA)
South Carolina State Univ.
Southeast Missouri State Univ.
Southeastern Louisiana Univ.
Southeastern Oklahoma State Univ.
Southern Adventist Univ. (TN)
Southern Arkansas Univ.
Southern Connecticut State Univ.
Southern Illinois Univ.–Carbondale
Southern Illinois Univ.–Edwardsville
Southern Methodist Univ. (TX)
Southern Oregon Univ.
Southern Univ. and A&M Coll. (LA)
Southern Univ.–New Orleans
Southern Utah Univ.
Southwest Baptist Univ. (MO)

Southwest Minnesota State Univ.
Southwestern Adventist Univ. (TX)
Southwestern Univ. (TX)
Spelman Coll. (GA)
Spring Arbor Univ. (MI)
Spring Hill Coll. (AL)
Springfield Coll. (MA)
St. Ambrose Univ. (IA)
St. Andrews Presbyterian Coll. (NC)
St. Anselm Coll. (NH)
St. Catherine Univ. (MN)
St. Cloud State Univ. (MN)
St. Edward's Univ. (TX)
St. Gregory's Univ. (OK)
St. John's Univ. (NY)
St. John's Univ. (MN)
St. Joseph Coll. (CT)
St. Joseph's Coll. (IN)
St. Lawrence Univ. (NY)
St. Louis Univ.
St. Mary's Coll. (IN)
St. Mary's Coll. of California
St. Mary's Coll. of Maryland
St. Mary's Univ. of Minnesota
St. Mary-of-the-Woods Coll. (IN)
St. Michael's Coll. (VT)
St. Norbert Coll. (WI)
St. Olaf Coll. (MN)
St. Peter's Coll. (NJ)
St. Thomas Aquinas Coll. (NY)
St. Vincent Coll. (PA)
St. Xavier Univ. (IL)
Stanford Univ. (CA)
Stephen F. Austin State Univ. (TX)
Sterling Coll. (KS)
Stetson Univ. (FL)
Stevens Institute of Tech. (NJ)
Stillman Coll. (AL)
Stonehill Coll. (MA)
Suffolk Univ. (MA)
Sul Ross State Univ. (TX)
SUNY Coll.–Cortland
SUNY Coll.–Oneonta
SUNY Coll.–Potsdam
SUNY Empire State Coll.
SUNY–Fredonia
SUNY–Oswego
SUNY–Plattsburgh
SUNY–Stony Brook
Susquehanna Univ. (PA)
Swarthmore Coll. (PA)
Syracuse Univ. (NY)
Tarleton State Univ. (TX)
Taylor Univ. (IN)
Temple Univ. (PA)
Tennessee State Univ.
Tennessee Technological Univ.
Texas A&M Univ.–Commerce
Texas A&M Univ.–Corpus Christi
Texas A&M Univ.–Kingsville
Texas Christian Univ.
Texas Coll.
Texas Lutheran Univ.
Texas State Univ.–San Marcos
Texas Tech Univ.
Texas Wesleyan Univ.
Texas Woman's Univ.
Thomas Edison State Coll. (NJ)
Thomas More Coll. (KY)
Tiffin Univ. (OH)
Towson Univ. (MD)

Transylvania Univ. (KY)
Trinity Christian Coll. (IL)
Trinity Coll. (CT)
Trinity Univ. (DC)
Troy Univ. (AL)
Truman State Univ. (MO)
Tufts Univ. (MA)
Tulane Univ. (LA)
Union Coll. (NY)
Union Coll. (NE)
Union Univ. (TN)
Univ. at Albany–SUNY
Univ. at Buffalo–SUNY
Univ. of Akron (OH)
Univ. of Alabama
Univ. of Alabama–Birmingham
Univ. of Alabama–Huntsville
Univ. of Alaska–Anchorage
Univ. of Alaska–Fairbanks
Univ. of Arizona
Univ. of Arkansas
Univ. of Arkansas–Little Rock
Univ. of Arkansas–Pine Bluff
Univ. of California–Berkeley
Univ. of California–Davis
Univ. of California–Irvine
Univ. of California–Los Angeles
Univ. of California–Riverside
Univ. of California–Santa Barbara
Univ. of California–Santa Cruz
Univ. of Central Arkansas
Univ. of Central Florida
Univ. of Central Missouri
Univ. of Central Oklahoma
Univ. of Charleston (WV)
Univ. of Chicago
Univ. of Colorado–Boulder
Univ. of Colorado–Denver
Univ. of Connecticut
Univ. of Dallas
Univ. of Dayton (OH)
Univ. of Delaware
Univ. of Denver
Univ. of Evansville (IN)
Univ. of Findlay (OH)
Univ. of Florida
Univ. of Georgia
Univ. of Great Falls (MT)
Univ. of Hartford (CT)
Univ. of Hawaii–Hilo
Univ. of Hawaii–Manoa
Univ. of Houston
Univ. of Illinois–Chicago
Univ. of Illinois–Springfield
Univ. of Illinois–Urbana-Champaign
Univ. of Indianapolis
Univ. of Iowa
Univ. of Kansas
Univ. of Kentucky
Univ. of La Verne (CA)
Univ. of Louisiana–Lafayette
Univ. of Louisiana–Monroe
Univ. of Louisville (KY)
Univ. of Maine
Univ. of Maine–Augusta
Univ. of Maine–Farmington
Univ. of Maine–Presque Isle
Univ. of Mary Hardin-Baylor (TX)
Univ. of Mary Washington (VA)
Univ. of Maryland–Baltimore
    County

Univ. of Maryland–Coll. Park
Univ. of Massachusetts–Amherst
Univ. of Massachusetts–Boston
Univ. of Massachusetts–Dartmouth
Univ. of Massachusetts–Lowell
Univ. of Memphis
Univ. of Miami (FL)
Univ. of Michigan–Ann Arbor
Univ. of Michigan–Dearborn
Univ. of Michigan–Flint
Univ. of Minnesota–Duluth
Univ. of Minnesota–Morris
Univ. of Minnesota–Twin Cities
Univ. of Mississippi
Univ. of Missouri
Univ. of Missouri–Kansas City
Univ. of Missouri–St. Louis
Univ. of Montana
Univ. of Montevallo (AL)
Univ. of Mount Union (OH)
Univ. of Nebraska–Kearney
Univ. of Nebraska–Lincoln
Univ. of Nebraska–Omaha
Univ. of Nevada–Las Vegas
Univ. of Nevada–Reno
Univ. of New Hampshire
Univ. of New Haven (CT)
Univ. of New Mexico
Univ. of New Orleans
Univ. of North Alabama
Univ. of North Carolina–Asheville
Univ. of North Carolina–Chapel Hill
Univ. of North Carolina–Charlotte
Univ. of North Carolina–
    Greensboro
Univ. of North Carolina–Pembroke
Univ. of North Carolina–
    Wilmington
Univ. of North Dakota
Univ. of North Florida
Univ. of North Texas
Univ. of Northern Colorado
Univ. of Northern Iowa
Univ. of Notre Dame (IN)
Univ. of Oklahoma
Univ. of Oregon
Univ. of Pennsylvania
Univ. of Pittsburgh
Univ. of Puget Sound (WA)
Univ. of Redlands (CA)
Univ. of Rhode Island
Univ. of Richmond (VA)
Univ. of Rio Grande (OH)
Univ. of Rochester (NY)
Univ. of San Diego
Univ. of San Francisco
Univ. of Science and Arts of
    Oklahoma
Univ. of Sioux Falls (SD)
Univ. of South Alabama
Univ. of South Carolina
Univ. of South Carolina–Aiken
Univ. of South Dakota
Univ. of South Florida
Univ. of Southern California
Univ. of Southern Indiana
Univ. of Southern Maine
Univ. of St. Francis (IN)
Univ. of St. Mary (KS)
Univ. of St. Thomas (MN)
Univ. of St. Thomas (TX)

Univ. of Tampa (FL)
Univ. of Tennessee
Univ. of Tennessee–Chattanooga
Univ. of Texas of the Permian Basin
Univ. of Texas–Arlington
Univ. of Texas–Austin
Univ. of Texas–Brownsville
Univ. of Texas–Dallas
Univ. of Texas–El Paso
Univ. of Texas–Pan American
Univ. of Texas–San Antonio
Univ. of Texas–Tyler
Univ. of the Arts (PA)
Univ. of the Cumberlands (KY)
Univ. of the District of Columbia
Univ. of the Incarnate Word (TX)
Univ. of the Ozarks (AR)
Univ. of the Pacific (CA)
Univ. of Toledo (OH)
Univ. of Tulsa (OK)
Univ. of Utah
Univ. of Vermont
Univ. of Virginia
Univ. of Virginia–Wise
Univ. of Washington
Univ. of West Florida
Univ. of West Georgia
Univ. of Wisconsin–Eau Claire
Univ. of Wisconsin–Green Bay
Univ. of Wisconsin–La Crosse
Univ. of Wisconsin–Madison
Univ. of Wisconsin–Milwaukee
Univ. of Wisconsin–Platteville
Univ. of Wisconsin–River Falls
Univ. of Wisconsin–Stevens Point
Univ. of Wisconsin–Superior
Univ. of Wisconsin–Whitewater
Univ. of Wyoming
Ursinus Coll. (PA)
Ursuline Coll. (OH)
Utah State Univ.
Valdosta State Univ. (GA)
Valley City State Univ. (ND)
Valparaiso Univ. (IN)
Vanderbilt Univ. (TN)
Vassar Coll. (NY)
Villanova Univ. (PA)
Virginia Commonwealth Univ.
Virginia Intermont Coll.
Virginia Tech
Virginia Wesleyan Coll.
Viterbo Univ. (WI)
Wabash Coll. (IN)
Wagner Coll. (NY)
Wake Forest Univ. (NC)
Warren Wilson Coll. (NC)
Wartburg Coll. (IA)
Washburn Univ. (KS)
Washington and Jefferson Coll.
  (PA)
Washington and Lee Univ. (VA)
Washington Coll. (MD)
Washington State Univ.
Washington Univ. in St. Louis
Wayland Baptist Univ. (TX)
Wayne State Coll. (NE)
Wayne State Univ. (MI)
Waynesburg Univ. (PA)
Weber State Univ. (UT)
Webster Univ. (MO)
Wellesley Coll. (MA)

Wells Coll. (NY)
Wesleyan Coll. (GA)
Wesleyan Univ. (CT)
West Chester Univ. of Pennsylvania
West Texas A&M Univ.
West Virginia Univ.
West Virginia Wesleyan Coll.
Western Carolina Univ. (NC)
Western Connecticut State Univ.
Western Illinois Univ.
Western Kentucky Univ.
Western Michigan Univ.
Western New Mexico Univ.
Western Oregon Univ.
Western State Coll. of Colorado
Western Washington Univ.
Westfield State Coll. (MA)
Westminster Coll. (PA)
Westminster Coll. (UT)
Westmont Coll. (CA)
Wheaton Coll. (IL)
Wheaton Coll. (MA)
Whitman Coll. (WA)
Whittier Coll. (CA)
Whitworth Univ. (WA)
Wichita State Univ. (KS)
Willamette Univ. (OR)
William Carey Univ. (MS)
William Jewell Coll. (MO)
William Paterson Univ. of New
  Jersey
William Woods Univ. (MO)
Williams Baptist Coll. (AR)
Williams Coll. (MA)
Wilmington Coll. (OH)
Wilson Coll. (PA)
Wingate Univ. (NC)
Winston-Salem State Univ. (NC)
Winthrop Univ. (SC)
Wisconsin Lutheran Coll.
Wittenberg Univ. (OH)
Wofford Coll. (SC)
Wright State Univ. (OH)
Xavier Univ. (OH)
Yale Univ. (CT)
York Coll. of Pennsylvania
Youngstown State Univ. (OH)

Fire Protection

Anna Maria Coll. (MA)
California State Univ.–Los Angeles
Cogswell Polytechnical Coll. (CA)
Colorado State Univ.
Eastern Kentucky Univ.
Eastern Oregon Univ.
Holy Family Univ. (PA)
Lake Superior State Univ. (MI)
Lewis-Clark State Coll. (ID)
Lindenwood Univ. (MO)
Madonna Univ. (MI)
Oklahoma State Univ.
Park Univ. (MO)
Providence Coll. (RI)
Salem State Coll. (MA)
Southern Illinois Univ.–Carbondale
Thomas Edison State Coll. (NJ)
Univ. of Akron (OH)
Univ. of Florida
Univ. of Maryland–Univ. Coll.
Univ. of Nebraska–Lincoln

Univ. of New Haven (CT)
Univ. of North Carolina–Charlotte
Univ. of the District of Columbia
Utah Valley Univ.
Western Oregon Univ.

Fishing and Fisheries Sciences and Management

Colorado State Univ.
Humboldt State Univ. (CA)
Northland Coll. (WI)
Ohio State Univ.–Columbus
Oregon State Univ.
Purdue Univ.–West Lafayette (IN)
SUNY Coll. of Agriculture and
  Technology–Cobleskill
Texas A&M Univ.–Coll. Station
Texas Tech Univ.
Univ. of Alaska–Fairbanks
Univ. of Arkansas–Pine Bluff
Univ. of California–Davis
Univ. of Florida
Univ. of Georgia
Univ. of Michigan–Ann Arbor
Univ. of Minnesota–Twin Cities
Univ. of Rhode Island
Univ. of Washington
Valley City State Univ. (ND)

Food Science and Technology

California State Polytechnic Univ.–
  Pomona
Tarleton State Univ. (TX)

Foods, Nutrition, and Related Services

Alcorn State Univ. (MS)
Andrews Univ. (MI)
Appalachian State Univ. (NC)
Ashland Univ. (OH)
Ball State Univ. (IN)
Baylor Univ. (TX)
Benedictine Univ. (IL)
Bluffton Univ. (OH)
Bowling Green State Univ. (OH)
Bridgewater Coll. (VA)
California State Polytechnic Univ.–
  Pomona
California State Univ.–Los Angeles
Campbell Univ. (NC)
Carson-Newman Coll. (TN)
Case Western Reserve Univ. (OH)
Cedar Crest Coll. (PA)
Central Michigan Univ.
Central Washington Univ.
Coll. of the Ozarks (MO)
Colorado State Univ.
Concordia Coll.–Moorhead (MN)
Cornell Univ. (NY)
CUNY–Hunter Coll.
CUNY–Lehman Coll.
Delaware State Univ.
Dominican Univ. (IL)
Eastern Kentucky Univ.
Eastern Michigan Univ.
Eastern Washington Univ.

Fort Valley State Univ. (GA)
Framingham State Coll. (MA)
Georgia Southern Univ.
Georgia State Univ.
Indiana State Univ.
Indiana Univ. of Pennsylvania
Iowa State Univ.
James Madison Univ. (VA)
Johnson and Wales Univ. (RI)
Kansas State Univ.
Kent State Univ. (OH)
Lambuth Univ. (TN)
Lipscomb Univ. (TN)
Long Island Univ.–C.W. Post
  Campus (NY)
Madonna Univ. (MI)
Mansfield Univ. of Pennsylvania
Marygrove Coll. (MI)
Middle Tennessee State Univ.
Montclair State Univ. (NJ)
Morgan State Univ. (MD)
Murray State Univ. (KY)
New Mexico State Univ.
New York Univ.
North Carolina A&T State Univ.
North Dakota State Univ.
Northeastern State Univ. (OK)
Northern Michigan Univ.
Northwest Missouri State Univ.
Ohio State Univ.–Columbus
Ohio Univ.
Oklahoma State Univ.
Oregon State Univ.
Pennsylvania State Univ.–Univ. Park
Pepperdine Univ. (CA)
Point Loma Nazarene Univ. (CA)
Prairie View A&M Univ. (TX)
Radford Univ. (VA)
Rochester Institute of Technology
  (NY)
Sam Houston State Univ. (TX)
Samford Univ. (AL)
San Diego State Univ.
San Francisco State Univ.
Seattle Pacific Univ.
South Carolina State Univ.
South Dakota State Univ.
Southern Illinois Univ.–Carbondale
St. Catherine Univ. (MN)
St. Louis Univ.
Stephen F. Austin State Univ. (TX)
SUNY Coll.–Oneonta
SUNY–Plattsburgh
Syracuse Univ. (NY)
Tarleton State Univ. (TX)
Texas A&M Univ.–Coll. Station
Texas State Univ.–San Marcos
Texas Tech Univ.
Texas Woman's Univ.
Univ. of Arkansas
Univ. of California–Davis
Univ. of Dayton (OH)
Univ. of Georgia
Univ. of Houston
Univ. of Illinois–Urbana-Champaign
Univ. of Kentucky
Univ. of Maine
Univ. of Maryland–Coll. Park
Univ. of Massachusetts–Amherst
Univ. of Missouri
Univ. of Nebraska–Lincoln

Univ. of Nevada–Reno
Univ. of New Hampshire
Univ. of New Mexico
Univ. of North Carolina–Chapel Hill
Univ. of North Carolina–
  Greensboro
Univ. of Rhode Island
Univ. of Tennessee
Univ. of Texas–Austin
Univ. of the District of Columbia
Univ. of Wisconsin–Stout
Utah State Univ.
Virginia Tech
Washington State Univ.
Wayne State Univ. (MI)
Weber State Univ. (UT)
Western Michigan Univ.
Winthrop Univ. (SC)
Youngstown State Univ. (OH)

Foreign Languages, Literatures, and Linguistics

Andrews Univ. (MI)
Arcadia Univ. (PA)
Clark Atlanta Univ.
Edinboro Univ. of Pennsylvania
Evergreen State Coll. (WA)
Excelsior Coll. (NY)
Harvard Univ. (MA)
Hobart and William Smith Colleges
  (NY)
Hood Coll. (MD)
Indiana State Univ.
Indiana Univ. of Pennsylvania
John Carroll Univ. (OH)
Kennesaw State Univ. (GA)
Keuka Coll. (NY)
Mississippi Coll.
New York Univ.
Purdue Univ.–Calumet (IN)
Scripps Coll. (CA)
Southern Illinois Univ.–Carbondale
Southern Oregon Univ.
St. Mary's Coll. of California
St. Thomas Aquinas Coll. (NY)
Univ. of Alaska–Fairbanks
Univ. of California–Berkeley
Univ. of California–Riverside
Univ. of California–San Diego
Univ. of Findlay (OH)
Univ. of Scranton (PA)
Wingate Univ. (NC)

Forensic Psychology

Bay Path Coll. (MA)
Florida Institute of Technology
Lake Erie Coll. (OH)
St. Ambrose Univ. (IA)
St. Andrews Presbyterian Coll. (NC)
Tiffin Univ. (OH)

Forest Engineering

Oregon State Univ.
Univ. of Maine
Univ. of Washington

Forestry

Alabama Agricultural and
   Mechanical Univ.
Albright Coll. (PA)
Auburn Univ. (AL)
Baylor Univ. (TX)
California Polytechnic State Univ.–
   San Luis Obispo
Clemson Univ. (SC)
Colorado State Univ.
Davis and Elkins Coll. (WV)
Elizabethtown Coll. (PA)
High Point Univ. (NC)
Humboldt State Univ. (CA)
Iowa State Univ.
Louisiana State Univ.–Baton Rouge
Louisiana Tech Univ.
Miami Univ.–Oxford (OH)
Michigan State Univ.
Michigan Technological Univ.
Mississippi State Univ.
New Mexico Highlands Univ.
North Carolina State Univ.–Raleigh
Northern Arizona Univ.
Northland Coll. (WI)
Ohio State Univ.–Columbus
Oklahoma State Univ.
Oregon State Univ.
Pennsylvania State Univ.–Univ. Park
Sewanee–Univ. of the South (TN)
Southern Illinois Univ.–Carbondale
Southern Univ. and A&M Coll. (LA)
St. Francis Univ. (PA)
Stephen F. Austin State Univ. (TX)
SUNY Coll. of Environmental
   Science and Forestry
Texas A&M Univ.–Coll. Station
Thomas Edison State Coll. (NJ)
Unity Coll. (ME)
Univ. of Arkansas–Monticello
Univ. of California–Berkeley
Univ. of California–Davis
Univ. of Florida
Univ. of Georgia
Univ. of Illinois–Urbana-Champaign
Univ. of Kentucky
Univ. of Maine
Univ. of Maryland–Eastern Shore
Univ. of Massachusetts–Amherst
Univ. of Minnesota–Twin Cities
Univ. of Missouri
Univ. of Montana
Univ. of Nevada–Reno
Univ. of New Hampshire
Univ. of Tennessee
Univ. of Vermont
Univ. of Washington
Univ. of Wisconsin–Madison
Univ. of Wisconsin–Stevens Point
Utah State Univ.
Virginia Tech
Washington State Univ.
West Virginia Univ.

Funeral Service and Mortuary Science

Eastern Michigan Univ.
Gannon Univ. (PA)
Lindenwood Univ. (MO)
Point Park Univ. (PA)
Southern Illinois Univ.–Carbondale

St. John's Univ. (NY)
Thiel Coll. (PA)
Univ. of Central Oklahoma
Univ. of Minnesota–Twin Cities
Wayne State Univ. (MI)

General Sales, Merchandising, and Related Marketing Operations

Anna Maria Coll. (MA)
Aurora Univ. (IL)
Babson Coll. (MA)
Baylor Univ. (TX)
Bradley Univ. (IL)
Central Methodist Univ. (MO)
Central Michigan Univ.
CUNY–Baruch Coll.
Dowling Coll. (NY)
Eastern Michigan Univ.
Fordham Univ. (NY)
Franklin Pierce Univ. (NH)
Harding Univ. (AR)
High Point Univ. (NC)
Johnson and Wales Univ. (RI)
Kennesaw State Univ. (GA)
Keuka Coll. (NY)
Lindenwood Univ. (MO)
Michigan State Univ.
Oral Roberts Univ. (OK)
Our Lady of Holy Cross Coll. (LA)
Purdue Univ.–Calumet (IN)
Rochester Institute of Technology
   (NY)
Seton Hill Univ. (PA)
Simmons Coll. (MA)
Southern Adventist Univ. (TN)
Southern New Hampshire Univ.
St. Catherine Univ. (MN)
St. Joseph's Univ. (PA)
St. Mary's Univ. of Minnesota
Stephens Coll. (MO)
Syracuse Univ. (NY)
Texas A&M Univ.–Coll. Station
Tuskegee Univ. (AL)
Univ. of Akron (OH)
Univ. of Houston
Univ. of Illinois–Urbana-Champaign
Univ. of Memphis
Univ. of Minnesota–Twin Cities
Univ. of North Dakota
Univ. of North Texas
Univ. of Pennsylvania
Univ. of South Carolina
Univ. of Texas–San Antonio
Univ. of Texas–Tyler
Univ. of Wisconsin–Stout
Weber State Univ. (UT)
West Chester Univ. of Pennsylvania
William Paterson Univ. of New
   Jersey
Youngstown State Univ. (OH)

Genetics

Cedar Crest Coll. (PA)
Clemson Univ. (SC)
Cornell Univ. (NY)
Eastern Nazarene Coll. (MA)
Iowa State Univ.

Lawrence Univ. (WI)
Marlboro Coll. (VT)
Missouri Southern State Univ.
Ohio State Univ.–Columbus
Ohio Wesleyan Univ.
Purdue Univ.–West Lafayette (IN)
Rutgers, the State Univ. of New
   Jersey–New Brunswick
SUNY Coll.–Oneonta
Tulane Univ. (LA)
Univ. of California–Davis
Univ. of California–Irvine
Univ. of Georgia
Univ. of Michigan–Ann Arbor
Univ. of Wisconsin–Madison
Washington State Univ.
Western Kentucky Univ.

Geography and Cartography

Appalachian State Univ. (NC)
Aquinas Coll. (MI)
Arizona State Univ.
Arkansas State Univ.–Jonesboro
Auburn Univ. (AL)
Augustana Coll. (IL)
Ball State Univ. (IN)
Bemidji State Univ. (MN)
Binghamton Univ.–SUNY
Bloomsburg Univ. of Pennsylvania
Boston Univ.
Bowling Green State Univ. (OH)
Bridgewater State Coll. (MA)
Brigham Young Univ.–Provo (UT)
Bucknell Univ. (PA)
California State Polytechnic Univ.–
   Pomona
California State Univ.–Chico
California State Univ.–Dominguez
   Hills
California State Univ.–East Bay
California State Univ.–Fresno
California State Univ.–Fullerton
California State Univ.–Long Beach
California State Univ.–Los Angeles
California State Univ.–Northridge
California State Univ.–Sacramento
California State Univ.–San
   Bernardino
California State Univ.–Stanislaus
California Univ. of Pennsylvania
Calvin Coll. (MI)
Carthage Coll. (WI)
Central Connecticut State Univ.
Central Michigan Univ.
Central Washington Univ.
Cheyney Univ. of Pennsylvania
Chicago State Univ.
Clark Univ. (MA)
Colgate Univ. (NY)
Concord Univ. (WV)
Concordia Univ. (NE)
Concordia Univ. Chicago (IL)
CUNY–Hunter Coll.
CUNY–Lehman Coll.
Dartmouth Coll. (NH)
Denison Univ. (OH)
DePaul Univ. (IL)
East Carolina Univ. (NC)
East Central Univ. (OK)

East Stroudsburg Univ. of
   Pennsylvania
East Tennessee State Univ.
Eastern Illinois Univ.
Eastern Kentucky Univ.
Eastern Michigan Univ.
Eastern Washington Univ.
Edinboro Univ. of Pennsylvania
Elmhurst Coll. (IL)
Elon Univ. (NC)
Emory and Henry Coll. (VA)
Excelsior Coll. (NY)
Fayetteville State Univ. (NC)
Fitchburg State Coll. (MA)
Florida Atlantic Univ.
Florida International Univ.
Florida State Univ.
Fort Hays State Univ. (KS)
Framingham State Coll. (MA)
Frostburg State Univ. (MD)
George Mason Univ. (VA)
George Washington Univ. (DC)
Georgia Southern Univ.
Georgia State Univ.
Grand Valley State Univ. (MI)
Gustavus Adolphus Coll. (MN)
Hofstra Univ. (NY)
Humboldt State Univ. (CA)
Illinois State Univ.
Indiana State Univ.
Indiana Univ. of Pennsylvania
Indiana Univ. Southeast
Indiana Univ.–Bloomington
Indiana Univ.-Purdue Univ.–
   Indianapolis
Jacksonville State Univ. (AL)
Jacksonville Univ. (FL)
James Madison Univ. (VA)
Johns Hopkins Univ. (MD)
Kansas State Univ.
Keene State Coll. (NH)
Kennesaw State Univ. (GA)
Kent State Univ. (OH)
Kutztown Univ. of Pennsylvania
Lock Haven Univ. of Pennsylvania
Long Island Univ.–C.W. Post
   Campus (NY)
Louisiana State Univ.–Baton Rouge
Louisiana State Univ.–Shreveport
Louisiana Tech Univ.
Macalester Coll. (MN)
Mansfield Univ. of Pennsylvania
Marshall Univ. (WV)
Miami Univ.–Oxford (OH)
Michigan State Univ.
Middlebury Coll. (VT)
Millersville Univ. of Pennsylvania
Minnesota State Univ.–Mankato
Missouri State Univ.
Montclair State Univ. (NJ)
Morehead State Univ. (KY)
Mount Holyoke Coll. (MA)
New Mexico State Univ.
North Carolina Central Univ.
Northeastern Illinois Univ.
Northeastern State Univ. (OK)
Northern Arizona Univ.
Northern Illinois Univ.
Northern Kentucky Univ.
Northern Michigan Univ.
Northwest Missouri State Univ.

Northwestern Univ. (IL)
Ohio State Univ.–Columbus
Ohio Univ.
Ohio Wesleyan Univ.
Oklahoma State Univ.
Old Dominion Univ. (VA)
Olivet Nazarene Univ. (IL)
Oregon State Univ.
Pennsylvania State Univ.–Univ. Park
Pittsburg State Univ. (KS)
Portland State Univ. (OR)
Prairie View A&M Univ. (TX)
Prescott Coll. (AZ)
Radford Univ. (VA)
Rhode Island Coll.
Roosevelt Univ. (IL)
Rutgers, the State Univ. of New
   Jersey–New Brunswick
Salem State Coll. (MA)
Salisbury Univ. (MD)
Sam Houston State Univ. (TX)
Samford Univ. (AL)
San Diego State Univ.
San Francisco State Univ.
San Jose State Univ. (CA)
Shippensburg Univ. of Pennsylvania
Simpson Coll. (IA)
Slippery Rock Univ. of Pennsylvania
Sonoma State Univ. (CA)
South Dakota State Univ.
Southern Illinois Univ.–Carbondale
Southern Illinois Univ.–Edwardsville
Southern Oregon Univ.
St. Cloud State Univ. (MN)
Stephen F. Austin State Univ. (TX)
Stetson Univ. (FL)
SUNY Coll.–Cortland
SUNY Coll.–Oneonta
SUNY–Geneseo
SUNY–Plattsburgh
Syracuse Univ. (NY)
Taylor Univ. (IN)
Texas A&M Univ.–Coll. Station
Texas A&M Univ.–Commerce
Texas A&M Univ.–Corpus Christi
Texas A&M Univ.–Kingsville
Texas Christian Univ.
Texas State Univ.–San Marcos
Texas Tech Univ.
Towson Univ. (MD)
United States Air Force Academy
   (CO)
Univ. at Albany–SUNY
Univ. at Buffalo–SUNY
Univ. of Akron (OH)
Univ. of Alabama
Univ. of Alaska–Fairbanks
Univ. of Arizona
Univ. of Arkansas
Univ. of California–Berkeley
Univ. of California–Los Angeles
Univ. of California–Riverside
Univ. of California–Santa Barbara
Univ. of Central Arkansas
Univ. of Central Missouri
Univ. of Central Oklahoma
Univ. of Chicago
Univ. of Colorado–Boulder
Univ. of Colorado–Colorado
   Springs
Univ. of Colorado–Denver

Univ. of Connecticut
Univ. of Delaware
Univ. of Denver
Univ. of Florida
Univ. of Georgia
Univ. of Hawaii–Hilo
Univ. of Hawaii–Manoa
Univ. of Illinois–Urbana-Champaign
Univ. of Iowa
Univ. of Kansas
Univ. of Kentucky
Univ. of Louisville (KY)
Univ. of Maine–Farmington
Univ. of Mary Washington (VA)
Univ. of Maryland–Baltimore
County
Univ. of Maryland–Coll. Park
Univ. of Massachusetts–Amherst
Univ. of Massachusetts–Boston
Univ. of Memphis
Univ. of Miami (FL)
Univ. of Michigan–Ann Arbor
Univ. of Minnesota–Duluth
Univ. of Minnesota–Twin Cities
Univ. of Missouri
Univ. of Missouri–Kansas City
Univ. of Montana
Univ. of Nebraska–Kearney
Univ. of Nebraska–Lincoln
Univ. of Nebraska–Omaha
Univ. of Nevada–Reno
Univ. of New Hampshire
Univ. of New Mexico
Univ. of New Orleans
Univ. of North Alabama
Univ. of North Carolina–Chapel Hill
Univ. of North Carolina–Charlotte
Univ. of North Carolina–
Greensboro
Univ. of North Carolina–
Wilmington
Univ. of North Dakota
Univ. of North Texas
Univ. of Northern Colorado
Univ. of Northern Iowa
Univ. of Oklahoma
Univ. of Oregon
Univ. of Pittsburgh–Johnstown
Univ. of South Alabama
Univ. of South Carolina
Univ. of South Florida
Univ. of Southern California
Univ. of Southern Mississippi
Univ. of St. Thomas (MN)
Univ. of Tennessee
Univ. of Texas–Austin
Univ. of Texas–Dallas
Univ. of Texas–San Antonio
Univ. of Toledo (OH)
Univ. of Utah
Univ. of Vermont
Univ. of Washington
Univ. of West Georgia
Univ. of Wisconsin–Eau Claire
Univ. of Wisconsin–La Crosse
Univ. of Wisconsin–Madison
Univ. of Wisconsin–Milwaukee
Univ. of Wisconsin–Oshkosh
Univ. of Wisconsin–Parkside
Univ. of Wisconsin–Platteville
Univ. of Wisconsin–River Falls

Univ. of Wisconsin–Stevens Point
Univ. of Wisconsin–Whitewater
Univ. of Wyoming
Utah State Univ.
Valparaiso Univ. (IN)
Vassar Coll. (NY)
Virginia Tech
Wayne State Coll. (NE)
Wayne State Univ. (MI)
Weber State Univ. (UT)
West Chester Univ. of Pennsylvania
West Texas A&M Univ.
West Virginia Univ.
Western Carolina Univ. (NC)
Western Illinois Univ.
Western Kentucky Univ.
Western Michigan Univ.
Western Oregon Univ.
Western State Coll. of Colorado
Western Washington Univ.
William Paterson Univ. of New
Jersey
Wittenberg Univ. (OH)
Worcester State Coll. (MA)
Wright State Univ. (OH)
Youngstown State Univ. (OH)

Geological and Earth Sciences/Geosciences

Adams State Coll. (CO)
Adrian Coll. (MI)
Albion Coll. (MI)
Alfred Univ. (NY)
Allegheny Coll. (PA)
Amherst Coll. (MA)
Appalachian State Univ. (NC)
Arizona State Univ.
Arkansas Tech Univ.
Ashland Univ. (OH)
Auburn Univ. (AL)
Augustana Coll. (IL)
Austin Peay State Univ. (TN)
Ball State Univ. (IN)
Bates Coll. (ME)
Baylor Univ. (TX)
Beloit Coll. (WI)
Binghamton Univ.–SUNY
Bloomsburg Univ. of Pennsylvania
Boise State Univ. (ID)
Boston Univ.
Bowdoin Coll. (ME)
Bowling Green State Univ. (OH)
Bradley Univ. (IL)
Bridgewater State Coll. (MA)
Brigham Young Univ.–Provo (UT)
Brown Univ. (RI)
Bryn Mawr Coll. (PA)
Bucknell Univ. (PA)
California Institute of Technology
California Lutheran Univ.
California Polytechnic State Univ.–
San Luis Obispo
California State Polytechnic Univ.–
Pomona
California State Univ.–Bakersfield
California State Univ.–Chico
California State Univ.–Dominguez
Hills
California State Univ.–East Bay
California State Univ.–Fresno

California State Univ.–Fullerton
California State Univ.–Long Beach
California State Univ.–Los Angeles
California State Univ.–Northridge
California State Univ.–Sacramento
California State Univ.–San
Bernardino
California State Univ.–Stanislaus
California Univ. of Pennsylvania
Calvin Coll. (MI)
Carleton Coll. (MN)
Case Western Reserve Univ. (OH)
Castleton State Coll. (VT)
Centenary Coll. of Louisiana
Central Connecticut State Univ.
Central Michigan Univ.
Central State Univ. (OH)
Central Washington Univ.
Clarion Univ. of Pennsylvania
Cleveland State Univ.
Colby Coll. (ME)
Colgate Univ. (NY)
Coll. at Brockport–SUNY
Coll. of Charleston (SC)
Coll. of William and Mary (VA)
Coll. of Wooster (OH)
Colorado Coll.
Colorado School of Mines
Colorado State Univ.
Columbia Univ. (NY)
Columbus State Univ. (GA)
Cornell Coll. (IA)
Cornell Univ. (NY)
CUNY–Brooklyn Coll.
CUNY–City Coll.
CUNY–Lehman Coll.
CUNY–Queens Coll.
CUNY–York Coll.
Dartmouth Coll. (NH)
Denison Univ. (OH)
DePauw Univ. (IN)
Dickinson Coll. (PA)
Duke Univ. (NC)
Earlham Coll. (IN)
East Carolina Univ. (NC)
East Stroudsburg Univ. of
Pennsylvania
Eastern Connecticut State Univ.
Eastern Illinois Univ.
Eastern Kentucky Univ.
Eastern Michigan Univ.
Eastern New Mexico Univ.
Eastern Washington Univ.
Edinboro Univ. of Pennsylvania
Elizabeth City State Univ. (NC)
Elmira Coll. (NY)
Emporia State Univ. (KS)
Excelsior Coll. (NY)
Florida Atlantic Univ.
Florida Institute of Technology
Florida International Univ.
Florida State Univ.
Fort Hays State Univ. (KS)
Fort Lewis Coll. (CO)
Franklin and Marshall Coll. (PA)
Furman Univ. (SC)
George Mason Univ. (VA)
Georgia Institute of Technology
Georgia Southern Univ.
Georgia Southwestern State Univ.
Georgia State Univ.

Grand Valley State Univ. (MI)
Guilford Coll. (NC)
Gustavus Adolphus Coll. (MN)
Hamilton Coll. (NY)
Hampshire Coll. (MA)
Hanover Coll. (IN)
Hardin-Simmons Univ. (TX)
Hartwick Coll. (NY)
Harvard Univ. (MA)
Haverford Coll. (PA)
Hawaii Pacific Univ.
Heidelberg Univ. (OH)
Hofstra Univ. (NY)
Hope Coll. (MI)
Humboldt State Univ. (CA)
Idaho State Univ.
Illinois State Univ.
Indiana State Univ.
Indiana Univ. Northwest
Indiana Univ. of Pennsylvania
Indiana Univ.–Bloomington
Indiana Univ.-Purdue Univ.–Fort
Wayne
Indiana Univ.-Purdue Univ.–
Indianapolis
Iowa State Univ.
James Madison Univ. (VA)
Johns Hopkins Univ. (MD)
Juniata Coll. (PA)
Kansas State Univ.
Kean Univ. (NJ)
Keene State Coll. (NH)
Kent State Univ. (OH)
Kutztown Univ. of Pennsylvania
La Salle Univ. (PA)
Lafayette Coll. (PA)
Lake Superior State Univ. (MI)
Lamar Univ. (TX)
Lawrence Univ. (WI)
Lehigh Univ. (PA)
Lock Haven Univ. of Pennsylvania
Long Island Univ.–C.W. Post
Campus (NY)
Louisiana State Univ.–Baton Rouge
Macalester Coll. (MN)
Marietta Coll. (OH)
Marshall Univ. (WV)
Massachusetts Institute of
Technology
Mercyhurst Coll. (PA)
Miami Univ.–Oxford (OH)
Michigan State Univ.
Michigan Technological Univ.
Middle Tennessee State Univ.
Middlebury Coll. (VT)
Midwestern State Univ. (TX)
Millersville Univ. of Pennsylvania
Millsaps Coll. (MS)
Minnesota State Univ.–Mankato
Minnesota State Univ.–Moorhead
Minot State Univ. (ND)
Mississippi State Univ.
Missouri State Univ.
Missouri Univ. of Science &
Technology
Montana State Univ.
Montclair State Univ. (NJ)
Moravian Coll. (PA)
Morehead State Univ. (KY)
Mount Holyoke Coll. (MA)
Murray State Univ. (KY)

Muskingum Univ. (OH)
National Univ. (CA)
New Jersey City Univ.
New Mexico Highlands Univ.
New Mexico Institute of Mining
and Technology
New Mexico State Univ.
North Carolina State Univ.–Raleigh
North Dakota State Univ.
Northeastern Illinois Univ.
Northeastern Univ. (MA)
Northern Arizona Univ.
Northern Illinois Univ.
Northern Kentucky Univ.
Northern Michigan Univ.
Northwest Missouri State Univ.
Northwestern Univ. (IL)
Norwich Univ. (VT)
Oberlin Coll. (OH)
Occidental Coll. (CA)
Ohio State Univ.–Columbus
Ohio Univ.
Ohio Wesleyan Univ.
Oklahoma State Univ.
Old Dominion Univ. (VA)
Olivet Nazarene Univ. (IL)
Oregon State Univ.
Pace Univ. (NY)
Pacific Lutheran Univ. (WA)
Pennsylvania State Univ.–Univ. Park
Pomona Coll. (CA)
Portland State Univ. (OR)
Prescott Coll. (AZ)
Princeton Univ. (NJ)
Radford Univ. (VA)
Rensselaer Polytechnic Institute
(NY)
Rice Univ. (TX)
Richard Stockton Coll. of New
Jersey
Rider Univ. (NJ)
Rocky Mountain Coll. (MT)
Rutgers, the State Univ. of New
Jersey–New Brunswick
Rutgers, the State Univ. of New
Jersey–Newark
Salem State Coll. (MA)
Salisbury Univ. (MD)
San Diego State Univ.
San Francisco State Univ.
San Jose State Univ. (CA)
Scripps Coll. (CA)
Sewanee–Univ. of the South (TN)
Shippensburg Univ. of Pennsylvania
Simpson Coll. (IA)
Skidmore Coll. (NY)
Slippery Rock Univ. of Pennsylvania
Smith Coll. (MA)
Sonoma State Univ. (CA)
South Dakota School of Mines and
Technology
Southern Connecticut State Univ.
Southern Illinois University–
Carbondale
Southern Methodist Univ. (TX)
Southern Oregon Univ.
Southern Utah Univ.
Southwestern Adventist Univ. (TX)
St. Cloud State Univ. (MN)
St. Lawrence Univ. (NY)
St. Louis Univ.

St. Mary's Univ. of San Antonio (TX)
St. Norbert Coll. (WI)
Stanford Univ. (CA)
Stephen F. Austin State Univ. (TX)
Sul Ross State Univ. (TX)
SUNY Coll.–Cortland
SUNY Coll.–Oneonta
SUNY Coll.–Potsdam
SUNY–Fredonia
SUNY–Geneseo
SUNY–Oswego
SUNY–Plattsburgh
SUNY–Stony Brook
Susquehanna Univ. (PA)
Syracuse Univ. (NY)
Tarleton State Univ. (TX)
Taylor Univ. (IN)
Temple Univ. (PA)
Tennessee Technological Univ.
Texas A&M Univ.–Coll. Station
Texas A&M Univ.–Corpus Christi
Texas A&M Univ.–Kingsville
Texas Christian Univ.
Texas Tech Univ.
Towson Univ. (MD)
Tufts Univ. (MA)
Tulane Univ. (LA)
Union Coll. (NY)
United States Naval Academy (MD)
Univ. at Albany–SUNY
Univ. at Buffalo–SUNY
Univ. of Akron (OH)
Univ. of Alabama
Univ. of Alaska–Fairbanks
Univ. of Arizona
Univ. of Arkansas
Univ. of California–Berkeley
Univ. of California–Davis
Univ. of California–Irvine
Univ. of California–Los Angeles
Univ. of California–Riverside
Univ. of California–San Diego
Univ. of California–Santa Barbara
Univ. of California–Santa Cruz
Univ. of Chicago
Univ. of Colorado–Boulder
Univ. of Connecticut
Univ. of Dayton (OH)
Univ. of Delaware
Univ. of Florida
Univ. of Georgia
Univ. of Hawaii–Hilo
Univ. of Hawaii–Manoa
Univ. of Houston
Univ. of Illinois–Chicago
Univ. of Illinois–Urbana-Champaign
Univ. of Indianapolis
Univ. of Iowa
Univ. of Kansas
Univ. of Kentucky
Univ. of Louisiana–Lafayette
Univ. of Maine
Univ. of Maine–Farmington
Univ. of Maine–Presque Isle
Univ. of Maryland–Coll. Park
Univ. of Massachusetts–Amherst
Univ. of Memphis
Univ. of Miami (FL)
Univ. of Michigan–Ann Arbor
Univ. of Michigan–Dearborn

Univ. of Minnesota–Duluth
Univ. of Minnesota–Morris
Univ. of Minnesota–Twin Cities
Univ. of Mississippi
Univ. of Missouri
Univ. of Missouri–Kansas City
Univ. of Montana
Univ. of Mount Union (OH)
Univ. of Nebraska–Lincoln
Univ. of Nebraska–Omaha
Univ. of Nevada–Las Vegas
Univ. of Nevada–Reno
Univ. of New Hampshire
Univ. of New Mexico
Univ. of New Orleans
Univ. of North Carolina–Chapel Hill
Univ. of North Carolina–Charlotte
Univ. of North Carolina–Wilmington
Univ. of North Dakota
Univ. of North Texas
Univ. of Northern Colorado
Univ. of Northern Iowa
Univ. of Oklahoma
Univ. of Oregon
Univ. of Pennsylvania
Univ. of Pittsburgh
Univ. of Pittsburgh–Bradford
Univ. of Pittsburgh–Johnstown
Univ. of Puget Sound (WA)
Univ. of Rhode Island
Univ. of Rochester (NY)
Univ. of South Alabama
Univ. of South Carolina
Univ. of South Dakota
Univ. of South Florida
Univ. of Southern California
Univ. of Southern Indiana
Univ. of Southern Maine
Univ. of Southern Mississippi
Univ. of St. Thomas (MN)
Univ. of Tennessee
Univ. of Tennessee–Chattanooga
Univ. of Tennessee–Martin
Univ. of Texas of the Permian Basin
Univ. of Texas–Arlington
Univ. of Texas–Austin
Univ. of Texas–Dallas
Univ. of Texas–El Paso
Univ. of Texas–San Antonio
Univ. of the Pacific (CA)
Univ. of Toledo (OH)
Univ. of Tulsa (OK)
Univ. of Utah
Univ. of Vermont
Univ. of Washington
Univ. of West Florida
Univ. of West Georgia
Univ. of Wisconsin–Eau Claire
Univ. of Wisconsin–Green Bay
Univ. of Wisconsin–Madison
Univ. of Wisconsin–Milwaukee
Univ. of Wisconsin–Parkside
Univ. of Wisconsin–River Falls
Univ. of Wyoming
Utah State Univ.
Utah Valley Univ.
Valparaiso Univ. (IN)
Vanderbilt Univ. (TN)
Vassar Coll. (NY)
Virginia Tech

Washington and Lee Univ. (VA)
Washington State Univ.
Washington Univ. in St. Louis
Wayne State Univ. (MI)
Weber State Univ. (UT)
Wellesley Coll. (MA)
West Chester Univ. of Pennsylvania
West Texas A&M Univ.
West Virginia Univ.
Western Carolina Univ. (NC)
Western Connecticut State Univ.
Western Illinois Univ.
Western Kentucky Univ.
Western Michigan Univ.
Western Oregon Univ.
Western State Coll. of Colorado
Western Washington Univ.
Wheaton Coll. (IL)
Whitman Coll. (WA)
Wichita State Univ. (KS)
Wilkes Univ. (PA)
Williams Coll. (MA)
Wittenberg Univ. (OH)
Wright State Univ. (OH)
Yale Univ. (CT)
Youngstown State Univ. (OH)

Geological/Geophysical Engineering

Colorado School of Mines
Michigan Technological Univ.
Missouri Univ. of Science & Technology
Montana Tech of the Univ. of Montana
New Jersey Institute of Technology
Rutgers, the State Univ. of New Jersey–Newark
South Dakota School of Mines and Technology
Univ. of Alaska–Fairbanks
Univ. of Arizona
Univ. of California–Berkeley
Univ. of California–Los Angeles
Univ. of Michigan–Ann Arbor
Univ. of Minnesota–Twin Cities
Univ. of Mississippi
Univ. of Nevada–Reno
Univ. of North Dakota
Univ. of Rochester (NY)
Univ. of Utah
Univ. of Wisconsin–Madison

Germanic Languages, Literatures, and Linguistics

Adrian Coll. (MI)
Albion Coll. (MI)
Alfred Univ. (NY)
Allegheny Coll. (PA)
Alma Coll. (MI)
American Univ. (DC)
Amherst Coll. (MA)
Angelo State Univ. (TX)
Aquinas Coll. (MI)
Arizona State Univ.
Auburn Univ. (AL)
Augsburg Coll. (MN)
Augustana Coll. (SD)

Augustana Coll. (IL)
Austin Coll. (TX)
Baker Univ. (KS)
Baldwin-Wallace Coll. (OH)
Ball State Univ. (IN)
Barnard Coll. (NY)
Bates Coll. (ME)
Baylor Univ. (TX)
Belmont Univ. (TN)
Beloit Coll. (WI)
Bemidji State Univ. (MN)
Berea Coll. (KY)
Berry Coll. (GA)
Bethany Coll. (WV)
Bethel Coll. (KS)
Binghamton Univ.–SUNY
Bloomsburg Univ. of Pennsylvania
Boise State Univ. (ID)
Boston Univ.
Bowdoin Coll. (ME)
Bowling Green State Univ. (OH)
Bradley Univ. (IL)
Brandeis Univ. (MA)
Brigham Young Univ.–Provo (UT)
Brown Univ. (RI)
Bryn Mawr Coll. (PA)
Bucknell Univ. (PA)
Butler Univ. (IN)
California Lutheran Univ.
California State Univ.–Chico
California State Univ.–Fullerton
California State Univ.–Long Beach
California State Univ.–Northridge
California State Univ.–Sacramento
Calvin Coll. (MI)
Canisius Coll. (NY)
Carleton Coll. (MN)
Carnegie Mellon Univ. (PA)
Carson-Newman Coll. (TN)
Carthage Coll. (WI)
Case Western Reserve Univ. (OH)
Catholic Univ. of America (DC)
Centenary Coll. of Louisiana
Central Coll. (IA)
Central Connecticut State Univ.
Central Michigan Univ.
Central Washington Univ.
Centre Coll. (KY)
Christopher Newport Univ. (VA)
Claremont McKenna Coll. (CA)
Cleveland State Univ.
Coe Coll. (IA)
Colby Coll. (ME)
Colgate Univ. (NY)
Coll. of Charleston (SC)
Coll. of St. Benedict (MN)
Coll. of the Holy Cross (MA)
Coll. of the Ozarks (MO)
Coll. of William and Mary (VA)
Coll. of Wooster (OH)
Colorado Coll.
Columbia Univ. (NY)
Concordia Coll.–Moorhead (MN)
Concordia Univ. Wisconsin
Connecticut Coll.
Converse Coll. (SC)
Cornell Coll. (IA)
Cornell Univ. (NY)
Creighton Univ. (NE)
CUNY–Hunter Coll.
CUNY–Lehman Coll.

CUNY–Queens Coll.
Dartmouth Coll. (NH)
Davidson Coll. (NC)
Denison Univ. (OH)
DePaul Univ. (IL)
DePauw Univ. (IN)
Dickinson Coll. (PA)
Dordt Coll. (IA)
Drew Univ. (NJ)
Drury Univ. (MO)
Duke Univ. (NC)
Earlham Coll. (IN)
East Carolina Univ. (NC)
Eastern Michigan Univ.
Eckerd Coll. (FL)
Edinboro Univ. of Pennsylvania
Elizabethtown Coll. (PA)
Elmhurst Coll. (IL)
Emory Univ. (GA)
Fairfield Univ. (CT)
Florida Atlantic Univ.
Florida International Univ.
Florida State Univ.
Fordham Univ. (NY)
Franciscan Univ. of Steubenville (OH)
Franklin and Marshall Coll. (PA)
Furman Univ. (SC)
Georgetown Coll. (KY)
Georgetown Univ. (DC)
Georgia Southern Univ.
Georgia State Univ.
Gettysburg Coll. (PA)
Gordon Coll. (MA)
Grace Coll. and Seminary (IN)
Graceland Univ. (IA)
Grand Valley State Univ. (MI)
Grinnell Coll. (IA)
Guilford Coll. (NC)
Gustavus Adolphus Coll. (MN)
Hamilton Coll. (NY)
Hamline Univ. (MN)
Hampden-Sydney Coll. (VA)
Hanover Coll. (IN)
Harvard Univ. (MA)
Haverford Coll. (PA)
Heidelberg Univ. (OH)
Hendrix Coll. (AR)
Hillsdale Coll. (MI)
Hofstra Univ. (NY)
Hood Coll. (MD)
Hope Coll. (MI)
Howard Univ. (DC)
Humboldt State Univ. (CA)
Idaho State Univ.
Illinois Coll.
Illinois State Univ.
Illinois Wesleyan Univ.
Immaculata Univ. (PA)
Indiana State Univ.
Indiana Univ. of Pennsylvania
Indiana Univ.–Bloomington
Indiana Univ.–South Bend
Indiana Univ.-Purdue Univ.–Fort Wayne
Indiana Univ.-Purdue Univ.–Indianapolis
Iowa State Univ.
Ithaca Coll. (NY)
Jamestown Coll. (ND)
John Carroll Univ. (OH)

Johns Hopkins Univ. (MD)
Juniata Coll. (PA)
Kalamazoo Coll. (MI)
Kent State Univ. (OH)
Kenyon Coll. (OH)
Knox Coll. (IL)
Kutztown Univ. of Pennsylvania
La Salle Univ. (PA)
Lafayette Coll. (PA)
Lakeland Coll. (WI)
Lawrence Univ. (WI)
Lebanon Valley Coll. (PA)
Lehigh Univ. (PA)
Lenoir-Rhyne Univ. (NC)
Lewis & Clark Coll. (OR)
Linfield Coll. (OR)
Lipscomb Univ. (TN)
Lock Haven Univ. of Pennsylvania
Louisiana State Univ.–Baton Rouge
Loyola Univ. Chicago
Loyola Univ. Maryland
Luther Coll. (IA)
Lycoming Coll. (PA)
Macalester Coll. (MN)
Mansfield Univ. of Pennsylvania
Marquette Univ. (WI)
McDaniel Coll. (MD)
Mercer Univ. (GA)
Messiah Coll. (PA)
Miami Univ.–Oxford (OH)
Michigan State Univ.
Middlebury Coll. (VT)
Millersville Univ. of Pennsylvania
Millsaps Coll. (MS)
Minnesota State Univ.–Mankato
Minot State Univ. (ND)
Missouri Southern State Univ.
Moravian Coll. (PA)
Mount St. Mary's Univ. (MD)
Muhlenberg Coll. (PA)
Murray State Univ. (KY)
Muskingum Univ. (OH)
Nazareth Coll. (NY)
Nebraska Wesleyan Univ.
New York Univ.
Newberry Coll. (SC)
North Central Coll. (IL)
North Park Univ. (IL)
Northeastern Univ. (MA)
Northern Arizona Univ.
Northern Illinois Univ.
Northern State Univ. (SD)
Northwestern Univ. (IL)
Oakland Univ. (MI)
Oberlin Coll. (OH)
Ohio Northern Univ.
Ohio State Univ.–Columbus
Ohio Univ.
Ohio Wesleyan Univ.
Oklahoma Baptist Univ.
Oklahoma City Univ.
Oklahoma State Univ.
Oral Roberts Univ. (OK)
Oregon State Univ.
Pacific Lutheran Univ. (WA)
Pacific Univ. (OR)
Pennsylvania State Univ.–Univ. Park
Pepperdine Univ. (CA)
Pomona Coll. (CA)
Presbyterian Coll. (SC)
Princeton Univ. (NJ)

Purdue Univ.–Calumet (IN)
Randolph-Macon Coll. (VA)
Reed Coll. (OR)
Rhodes Coll. (TN)
Rice Univ. (TX)
Rider Univ. (NJ)
Ripon Coll. (WI)
Rosemont Coll. (PA)
Rutgers, the State Univ. of New
    Jersey–Camden
Rutgers, the State Univ. of New
    Jersey–New Brunswick
Rutgers, the State Univ. of New
    Jersey–Newark
Salem Coll. (NC)
Sam Houston State Univ. (TX)
Samford Univ. (AL)
San Diego State Univ.
San Francisco State Univ.
San Jose State Univ. (CA)
Santa Clara Univ. (CA)
Scripps Coll. (CA)
Seattle Pacific Univ.
Seattle Univ.
Sewanee–Univ. of the South (TN)
Simpson Coll. (IA)
Skidmore Coll. (NY)
Smith Coll. (MA)
South Dakota State Univ.
Southeast Missouri State Univ.
Southern Connecticut State Univ.
Southern Illinois Univ.–Carbondale
Southern Methodist Univ. (TX)
Southern Utah Univ.
Southwestern Univ. (TX)
St. Ambrose Univ. (IA)
St. Cloud State Univ. (MN)
St. John Fisher Coll. (NY)
St. John's Univ. (MN)
St. Joseph's Univ. (PA)
St. Lawrence Univ. (NY)
St. Louis Univ.
St. Norbert Coll. (WI)
St. Olaf Coll. (MN)
St. Peter's Coll. (NJ)
Stanford Univ. (CA)
Stetson Univ. (FL)
Suffolk Univ. (MA)
SUNY–Fredonia
SUNY–Oswego
SUNY–Stony Brook
Susquehanna Univ. (PA)
Swarthmore Coll. (PA)
Syracuse Univ. (NY)
Temple Univ. (PA)
Texas A&M Univ.–Coll. Station
Texas State Univ.–San Marcos
Texas Tech Univ.
The Citadel (SC)
Towson Univ. (MD)
Trinity Coll. (CT)
Truman State Univ. (MO)
Tufts Univ. (MA)
Tulane Univ. (LA)
Union Coll. (NE)
Univ. at Buffalo–SUNY
Univ. of Arizona
Univ. of Arkansas
Univ. of Arkansas–Little Rock
Univ. of California–Berkeley
Univ. of California–Davis

Univ. of California–Irvine
Univ. of California–Los Angeles
Univ. of California–San Diego
Univ. of California–Santa Barbara
Univ. of Central Missouri
Univ. of Chicago
Univ. of Colorado–Boulder
Univ. of Connecticut
Univ. of Dallas
Univ. of Dayton (OH)
Univ. of Denver
Univ. of Evansville (IN)
Univ. of Florida
Univ. of Georgia
Univ. of Hawaii–Manoa
Univ. of Houston
Univ. of Illinois–Urbana-Champaign
Univ. of Indianapolis
Univ. of Iowa
Univ. of Kansas
Univ. of Kentucky
Univ. of La Verne (CA)
Univ. of Louisville (KY)
Univ. of Maine
Univ. of Maryland–Coll. Park
Univ. of Massachusetts–Amherst
Univ. of Massachusetts–Boston
Univ. of Miami (FL)
Univ. of Michigan–Ann Arbor
Univ. of Minnesota–Morris
Univ. of Minnesota–Twin Cities
Univ. of Mississippi
Univ. of Missouri
Univ. of Missouri–Kansas City
Univ. of Missouri–St. Louis
Univ. of Montana
Univ. of Mount Union (OH)
Univ. of Nebraska–Kearney
Univ. of Nebraska–Lincoln
Univ. of Nebraska–Omaha
Univ. of Nevada–Las Vegas
Univ. of Nevada–Reno
Univ. of New Hampshire
Univ. of New Mexico
Univ. of North Carolina–Asheville
Univ. of North Carolina–Chapel Hill
Univ. of North Carolina–Charlotte
Univ. of North Carolina–
    Greensboro
Univ. of North Carolina–
    Wilmington
Univ. of North Dakota
Univ. of North Texas
Univ. of Northern Iowa
Univ. of Notre Dame (IN)
Univ. of Oklahoma
Univ. of Oregon
Univ. of Pennsylvania
Univ. of Pittsburgh
Univ. of Portland (OR)
Univ. of Puget Sound (WA)
Univ. of Redlands (CA)
Univ. of Rhode Island
Univ. of Richmond (VA)
Univ. of Rochester (NY)
Univ. of Scranton (PA)
Univ. of South Carolina
Univ. of South Dakota
Univ. of South Florida
Univ. of Southern California
Univ. of Southern Indiana

Univ. of St. Thomas (MN)
Univ. of Tennessee
Univ. of Texas–Arlington
Univ. of Texas–Austin
Univ. of Texas–San Antonio
Univ. of the Pacific (CA)
Univ. of Toledo (OH)
Univ. of Tulsa (OK)
Univ. of Utah
Univ. of Vermont
Univ. of Virginia
Univ. of Washington
Univ. of West Georgia
Univ. of Wisconsin–Eau Claire
Univ. of Wisconsin–Green Bay
Univ. of Wisconsin–La Crosse
Univ. of Wisconsin–Madison
Univ. of Wisconsin–Milwaukee
Univ. of Wisconsin–Parkside
Univ. of Wisconsin–Stevens Point
Univ. of Wisconsin–Whitewater
Univ. of Wyoming
Ursinus Coll. (PA)
Utah State Univ.
Valparaiso Univ. (IN)
Vanderbilt Univ. (TN)
Vassar Coll. (NY)
Villanova Univ. (PA)
Virginia Wesleyan Coll.
Wabash Coll. (IN)
Wake Forest Univ. (NC)
Wartburg Coll. (IA)
Washburn Univ. (KS)
Washington and Jefferson Coll.
    (PA)
Washington and Lee Univ. (VA)
Washington Coll. (MD)
Washington State Univ.
Washington Univ. in St. Louis
Wayne State Univ. (MI)
Weber State Univ. (UT)
Webster Univ. (MO)
Wellesley Coll. (MA)
Wells Coll. (NY)
West Chester Univ. of Pennsylvania
Western Carolina Univ. (NC)
Western Kentucky Univ.
Western Michigan Univ.
Western Oregon Univ.
Western Washington Univ.
Westminster Coll. (PA)
Wheaton Coll. (IL)
Wheaton Coll. (MA)
Whitman Coll. (WA)
Willamette Univ. (OR)
Williams Coll. (MA)
Wittenberg Univ. (OH)
Wofford Coll. (SC)
Wright State Univ. (OH)
Xavier Univ. (OH)
Yale Univ. (CT)
Youngstown State Univ. (OH)

Gerontology

Alfred Univ. (NY)
Alma Coll. (MI)
Barton Coll. (NC)
Bethel Univ. (MN)
Bethune-Cookman Univ. (FL)
Bowling Green State Univ. (OH)

California State Univ.–Fullerton
California State Univ.–Sacramento
California Univ. of Pennsylvania
Case Western Reserve Univ. (OH)
Central Washington Univ.
Dominican Univ. (IL)
Eastern Michigan Univ.
Edward Waters Coll. (FL)
Ithaca Coll. (NY)
Kansas State Univ.
Lander Univ. (SC)
Lindenwood Univ. (MO)
Madonna Univ. (MI)
Miami Univ.–Oxford (OH)
Minnesota State Univ.–Moorhead
Missouri State Univ.
Molloy Coll. (NY)
Roosevelt Univ. (IL)
San Diego State Univ.
Springfield Coll. (MA)
St. Ambrose Univ. (IA)
Stephen F. Austin State Univ. (TX)
Thomas Edison State Coll. (NJ)
Univ. of Kentucky
Univ. of La Verne (CA)
Univ. of Massachusetts–Boston
Univ. of Nebraska–Omaha
Univ. of Nevada–Las Vegas
Univ. of North Texas
Univ. of Northern Iowa
Univ. of South Alabama
Univ. of South Florida
Univ. of Southern California
Washburn Univ. (KS)
Wichita State Univ. (KS)
Winston-Salem State Univ. (NC)

Graphic Communications

American Univ. (DC)
Arkansas State Univ.–Jonesboro
Bellevue Univ. (NE)
Bennington Coll. (VT)
Bradley Univ. (IL)
Brigham Young Univ.–Provo (UT)
California State Univ.–Long Beach
Carroll Univ. (WI)
Carthage Coll. (WI)
Chowan Univ. (NC)
Clemson Univ. (SC)
Coll. of the Ozarks (MO)
Columbia Coll. (IL)
East Tennessee State Univ.
Eastern Kentucky Univ.
Eastern Washington Univ.
Fairmont State Univ. (WV)
Fashion Institute of Technology
    (NY)
Ferris State Univ. (MI)
Georgia Southern Univ.
Grand View Univ. (IA)
Kean Univ. (NJ)
Lewis-Clark State Coll. (ID)
Louisiana Coll.
Loyola Marymount Univ. (CA)
Minneapolis Coll. of Art and Design
Mount Marty Coll. (SD)
Murray State Univ. (KY)
North Central Coll. (IL)
Northwestern Coll. (MN)
Otis Coll. of Art and Design (CA)

Pennsylvania Coll. of Technology
Philadelphia Univ.
Pittsburg State Univ. (KS)
Point Loma Nazarene Univ. (CA)
Purdue Univ.–Calumet (IN)
Ringling Coll. of Art and Design (FL)
Rochester Institute of Technology (NY)
Savannah Coll. of Art and Design (GA)
Southern Nazarene Univ. (OK)
Texas A&M Univ.–Commerce
Texas State Univ.–San Marcos
Touro Coll. (NY)
Univ. of Central Missouri
Univ. of Findlay (OH)
Univ. of Miami (FL)
Univ. of Northern Iowa
Univ. of Wisconsin–Stout
West Virginia Univ. Institute of Technology
Western Illinois Univ.

Health and Medical Administrative Services

Alabama State Univ.
Alaska Pacific Univ.
Alfred Univ. (NY)
Anderson Univ. (SC)
Andrews Univ. (MI)
Appalachian State Univ. (NC)
Arcadia Univ. (PA)
Arkansas Tech Univ.
Auburn Univ. (AL)
Barry Univ. (FL)
Bellevue Univ. (NE)
Bemidji State Univ. (MN)
Benedictine Univ. (IL)
Black Hills State Univ. (SD)
Boise State Univ. (ID)
Bowling Green State Univ. (OH)
Brandeis Univ. (MA)
Brenau Univ. (GA)
Brescia Univ. (KY)
Burlington Coll. (VT)
California State Univ.–Long Beach
California State Univ.–Los Angeles
California State Univ.–San Bernardino
Calumet Coll. of St. Joseph (IN)
Carson-Newman Coll. (TN)
Catawba Coll. (NC)
Central Michigan Univ.
Chestnut Hill Coll. (PA)
Cheyney Univ. of Pennsylvania
Chicago State Univ.
Clark Atlanta Univ.
Clayton State Univ. (GA)
Coll. of St. Mary (NE)
Coll. of St. Scholastica (MN)
Concordia Coll.–Moorhead (MN)
Cornell Univ. (NY)
Creighton Univ. (NE)
CUNY–Lehman Coll.
CUNY–New York City Coll. of Technology
Dakota State Univ. (SD)
Dallas Baptist Univ.
Davenport Univ. (MI)

Dominican Coll. (NY)
Drexel Univ. (PA)
Duquesne Univ. (PA)
East Carolina Univ. (NC)
East Central Univ. (OK)
Eastern Kentucky Univ.
Eastern Michigan Univ.
Eastern Washington Univ.
Elmhurst Coll. (IL)
Elon Univ. (NC)
Ferris State Univ. (MI)
Florida Atlantic Univ.
Florida International Univ.
Freed-Hardeman Univ. (TN)
George Washington Univ. (DC)
Georgetown Univ. (DC)
Georgia Southern Univ.
Graceland Univ. (IA)
Gwynedd-Mercy Coll. (PA)
Harding Univ. (AR)
Hodges Univ. (FL)
Howard Payne Univ. (TX)
Howard Univ. (DC)
Idaho State Univ.
Illinois State Univ.
Immaculata Univ. (PA)
Indiana Institute of Technology
Indiana Univ. East
Indiana Univ.–Bloomington
Indiana Univ.-Purdue Univ.–Fort Wayne
Indiana Univ.-Purdue Univ.– Indianapolis
Iona Coll. (NY)
Ithaca Coll. (NY)
Jackson State Univ. (MS)
James Madison Univ. (VA)
Johnson and Wales Univ. (RI)
Kean Univ. (NJ)
Lamar Univ. (TX)
Lebanon Valley Coll. (PA)
Lewis-Clark State Coll. (ID)
Lindenwood Univ. (MO)
Long Island Univ.–C.W. Post Campus (NY)
Louisiana Tech Univ.
Lynn Univ. (FL)
Macon State Coll. (GA)
Madonna Univ. (MI)
Manchester Coll. (IN)
Mary Baldwin Coll. (VA)
Marywood Univ. (PA)
Methodist Univ. (NC)
Midway Coll. (KY)
Minnesota State Univ.–Moorhead
Misericordia Univ. (PA)
Missouri Southern State Univ.
Molloy Coll. (NY)
Montana State Univ.–Billings
Mount Mercy Coll. (IA)
National-Louis Univ. (IL)
New England Coll. (NH)
Norfolk State Univ. (VA)
North Greenville Univ. (SC)
Northeastern State Univ. (OK)
Northern Michigan Univ.
Northwestern Oklahoma State Univ.
Ohio State Univ.–Columbus
Ohio Univ.
Oklahoma Panhandle State Univ.

Olivet Nazarene Univ. (IL)
Oregon State Univ.
Our Lady of the Lake Univ. (TX)
Pennsylvania Coll. of Technology
Pennsylvania State Univ.–Univ. Park
Pepperdine Univ. (CA)
Pfeiffer Univ. (NC)
Prescott Coll. (AZ)
Providence Coll. (RI)
Regis Univ. (CO)
Rhode Island Coll.
Robert Morris Univ. (PA)
Roosevelt Univ. (IL)
San Francisco State Univ.
Shawnee State Univ. (OH)
Shippensburg Univ. of Pennsylvania
Sojourner-Douglass Coll. (MD)
Southern Adventist Univ. (TN)
Southern Illinois Univ.–Carbondale
Southwestern Oklahoma State Univ.
Spring Arbor Univ. (MI)
Springfield Coll. (MA)
St. Catherine Univ. (MN)
St. John's Univ. (NY)
St. Joseph's Coll. New York
St. Joseph's Univ. (PA)
St. Leo Univ. (FL)
St. Louis Univ.
St. Mary's Coll. of California
St. Peter's Coll. (NJ)
St. Thomas Univ. (FL)
Stephens Coll. (MO)
Stonehill Coll. (MA)
SUNY Institute of Technology– Utica/Rome
SUNY–Fredonia
Syracuse Univ. (NY)
Temple Univ. (PA)
Tennessee State Univ.
Texas State Univ.–San Marcos
Thomas Edison State Coll. (NJ)
Touro Coll. (NY)
Tulane Univ. (LA)
Univ. of Alabama
Univ. of Alabama–Birmingham
Univ. of Central Florida
Univ. of Central Oklahoma
Univ. of Connecticut
Univ. of Evansville (IN)
Univ. of Florida
Univ. of Illinois–Chicago
Univ. of Kansas
Univ. of Kentucky
Univ. of La Verne (CA)
Univ. of Louisiana–Lafayette
Univ. of Louisville (KY)
Univ. of Maryland–Baltimore County
Univ. of Michigan–Dearborn
Univ. of Michigan–Flint
Univ. of Minnesota–Crookston
Univ. of Minnesota–Twin Cities
Univ. of Nebraska–Omaha
Univ. of Nevada–Las Vegas
Univ. of New England (ME)
Univ. of New Hampshire
Univ. of North Carolina–Chapel Hill
Univ. of Northern Colorado
Univ. of Northwestern Ohio
Univ. of Pennsylvania

Univ. of Pittsburgh
Univ. of Rhode Island
Univ. of South Dakota
Univ. of St. Francis (IN)
Univ. of St. Francis (IL)
Univ. of Tennessee
Univ. of Texas–El Paso
Univ. of Toledo (OH)
Univ. of Washington
Univ. of Wisconsin–Eau Claire
Univ. of Wisconsin–Milwaukee
Ursuline Coll. (OH)
Utica Coll. (NY)
Washington Adventist Univ. (MD)
Washington State Univ.
Weber State Univ. (UT)
West Chester Univ. of Pennsylvania
Western Carolina Univ. (NC)
Western Illinois Univ.
Western Kentucky Univ.
Western Michigan Univ.
Wheeling Jesuit Univ. (WV)
Wichita State Univ. (KS)
Wilberforce Univ. (OH)
York Coll. of Pennsylvania
Youngstown State Univ. (OH)

Health and Physical Education/Fitness

Abilene Christian Univ. (TX)
Adams State Coll. (CO)
Adrian Coll. (MI)
Albany State Univ. (GA)
Albion Coll. (MI)
Alderson-Broaddus Coll. (WV)
Alice Lloyd Coll. (KY)
Alma Coll. (MI)
Alvernia Univ. (PA)
American Univ. (DC)
Anderson Univ. (SC)
Anderson Univ. (IN)
Angelo State Univ. (TX)
Appalachian State Univ. (NC)
Aquinas Coll. (MI)
Arizona State Univ.
Arkansas State Univ.–Jonesboro
Asbury Univ. (KY)
Augustana Coll. (SD)
Austin Peay State Univ. (TN)
Averett Univ. (VA)
Avila Univ. (MO)
Baker Univ. (KS)
Baldwin-Wallace Coll. (OH)
Ball State Univ. (IN)
Barry Univ. (FL)
Barton Coll. (NC)
Baylor Univ. (TX)
Belhaven Univ. (MS)
Belmont Univ. (TN)
Bemidji State Univ. (MN)
Bethel Coll. (KS)
Bethel Coll. (IN)
Bethel Univ. (MN)
Black Hills State Univ. (SD)
Bloomsburg Univ. of Pennsylvania
Blue Mountain Coll. (MS)
Bluefield Coll. (VA)
Bluffton Univ. (OH)
Boise State Univ. (ID)
Bowling Green State Univ. (OH)

Brevard Coll. (NC)
Brewton-Parker Coll. (GA)
Briar Cliff Univ. (IA)
Bridgewater Coll. (VA)
Bridgewater State Coll. (MA)
Brigham Young Univ.–Hawaii
Brigham Young Univ.–Provo (UT)
Bryan Coll. (TN)
Buena Vista Univ. (IA)
Cabrini Coll. (PA)
California Baptist Univ.
California Lutheran Univ.
California Polytechnic State Univ.– San Luis Obispo
California State Polytechnic Univ.– Pomona
California State Univ.–Chico
California State Univ.–Dominguez Hills
California State Univ.–Fullerton
California State Univ.–Long Beach
California State Univ.–Sacramento
California State Univ.–San Bernardino
California State Univ.–Stanislaus
California Univ. of Pennsylvania
Calvin Coll. (MI)
Campbell Univ. (NC)
Campbellsville Univ. (KY)
Capital Univ. (OH)
Carroll Coll. (MT)
Carroll Univ. (WI)
Carson-Newman Coll. (TN)
Carthage Coll. (WI)
Castleton State Coll. (VT)
Catawba Coll. (NC)
Cedarville Univ. (OH)
Centenary Coll. of Louisiana
Central Christian Coll. (KS)
Central Coll. (IA)
Central Michigan Univ.
Central Washington Univ.
Charleston Southern Univ. (SC)
Chatham Univ. (PA)
Chowan Univ. (NC)
Claflin Univ. (SC)
Clearwater Christian Coll. (FL)
Cleveland State Univ.
Coastal Carolina Univ. (SC)
Coker Coll. (SC)
Colby-Sawyer Coll. (NH)
Coll. of Idaho (ID)
Coll. of the Ozarks (MO)
Coll. of William and Mary (VA)
Colorado Christian Univ.
Colorado Coll.
Colorado State Univ.
Colorado State Univ.–Pueblo
Columbia Coll. (MO)
Concordia Coll.–Moorhead (MN)
Concordia Univ. (MI)
Concordia Univ. (NE)
Concordia Univ. (CA)
Concordia Univ. (OR)
Concordia Univ. Texas
Concordia Univ. Wisconsin
Concordia Univ.–St. Paul (MN)
Coppin State Univ. (MD)
Corban Univ. (OR)
Cornell Coll. (IA)
Cornerstone Univ. (MI)

Creighton Univ. (NE)
Crown Coll. (MN)
Cumberland Univ. (TN)
CUNY–Brooklyn Coll.
CUNY–Lehman Coll.
CUNY–Queens Coll.
Dakota State Univ. (SD)
Dakota Wesleyan Univ. (SD)
Dana Coll. (NE)
Davis and Elkins Coll. (WV)
Defiance Coll. (OH)
Delaware State Univ.
DePauw Univ. (IN)
DeSales Univ. (PA)
Doane Coll. (NE)
Dominican Coll. (NY)
Dordt Coll. (IA)
Drexel Univ. (PA)
Drury Univ. (MO)
East Carolina Univ. (NC)
East Stroudsburg Univ. of
    Pennsylvania
East Tennessee State Univ.
East Texas Baptist Univ.
Eastern Connecticut State Univ.
Eastern Mennonite Univ. (VA)
Eastern Michigan Univ.
Eastern Nazarene Coll. (MA)
Eastern New Mexico Univ.
Eastern Univ. (PA)
Eastern Washington Univ.
Edinboro Univ. of Pennsylvania
Elmhurst Coll. (IL)
Elon Univ. (NC)
Emmanuel Coll. (GA)
Emory and Henry Coll. (VA)
Endicott Coll. (MA)
Erskine Coll. (SC)
Eureka Coll. (IL)
Evangel Univ. (MO)
Faulkner Univ. (AL)
Ferrum Coll. (VA)
Fitchburg State Coll. (MA)
Flagler Coll. (FL)
Florida Atlantic Univ.
Florida Gulf Coast Univ.
Florida International Univ.
Florida Southern Coll.
Fontbonne Univ. (MO)
Fort Lewis Coll. (CO)
Franklin Pierce Univ. (NH)
Free Will Baptist Bible Coll. (TN)
Freed-Hardeman Univ. (TN)
Fresno Pacific Univ. (CA)
Friends Univ. (KS)
Frostburg State Univ. (MD)
Furman Univ. (SC)
Gannon Univ. (PA)
Gardner-Webb Univ. (NC)
George Fox Univ. (OR)
George Mason Univ. (VA)
Georgetown Coll. (KY)
Georgia Southern Univ.
Georgia State Univ.
Gordon Coll. (MA)
Grace Coll. and Seminary (IN)
Graceland Univ. (IA)
Grand Valley State Univ. (MI)
Greensboro Coll. (NC)
Greenville Coll. (IL)
Guilford Coll. (NC)

Gustavus Adolphus Coll. (MN)
Hamline Univ. (MN)
Hampton Univ. (VA)
Hanover Coll. (IN)
Hardin-Simmons Univ. (TX)
Harding Univ. (AR)
Heidelberg Univ. (OH)
Hendrix Coll. (AR)
High Point Univ. (NC)
Hofstra Univ. (NY)
Holy Family Univ. (PA)
Hope Coll. (MI)
Houghton Coll. (NY)
Houston Baptist Univ.
Howard Payne Univ. (TX)
Huntingdon Coll. (AL)
Huntington Univ. (IN)
Illinois Coll.
Illinois State Univ.
Immaculata Univ. (PA)
Indiana Institute of Technology
Indiana Univ. of Pennsylvania
Indiana Wesleyan Univ.
Iowa State Univ.
Iowa Wesleyan Coll.
Ithaca Coll. (NY)
Jacksonville Univ. (FL)
James Madison Univ. (VA)
John Brown Univ. (AR)
Johnson C. Smith Univ. (NC)
Judson Univ. (IL)
Kansas State Univ.
Kansas Wesleyan Univ.
Keene State Coll. (NH)
Kennesaw State Univ. (GA)
Kent State Univ. (OH)
Kentucky Wesleyan Coll.
La Sierra Univ. (CA)
Lake Superior State Univ. (MI)
Lambuth Univ. (TN)
Lander Univ. (SC)
Lasell Coll. (MA)
Lenoir-Rhyne Univ. (NC)
LeTourneau Univ. (TX)
Lewis Univ. (IL)
Lewis-Clark State Coll. (ID)
Liberty Univ. (VA)
Limestone Coll. (SC)
Lincoln Memorial Univ. (TN)
Lincoln Univ. (MO)
Lincoln Univ. (PA)
Lindenwood Univ. (MO)
Linfield Coll. (OR)
Lipscomb Univ. (TN)
Livingstone Coll. (NC)
Lock Haven Univ. of Pennsylvania
Longwood Univ. (VA)
Loras Coll. (IA)
Louisiana Coll.
Louisiana Tech Univ.
Lubbock Christian Univ. (TX)
Luther Coll. (IA)
Lynchburg Coll. (VA)
MacMurray Coll. (IL)
Malone Univ. (OH)
Marian Univ. (WI)
Marian Univ. (IN)
Martin Methodist Coll. (TN)
Marymount Univ. (VA)
Maryville Coll. (TN)
Marywood Univ. (PA)

Master's Coll. and Seminary (CA)
Mayville State Univ. (ND)
McDaniel Coll. (MD)
McNeese State Univ. (LA)
McPherson Coll. (KS)
Medaille Coll. (NY)
Meredith Coll. (NC)
Mesa State Coll. (CO)
Messiah Coll. (PA)
Methodist Univ. (NC)
Miami Univ.–Oxford (OH)
Michigan State Univ.
Michigan Technological Univ.
Middle Tennessee State Univ.
Midland Lutheran Coll. (NE)
Midwestern State Univ. (TX)
Milligan Coll. (TN)
Millikin Univ. (IL)
Minnesota State Univ.–Mankato
Minnesota State Univ.–Moorhead
Minot State Univ. (ND)
Misericordia Univ. (PA)
Mississippi Coll.
Mississippi Univ. for Women
Missouri Baptist Univ.
Missouri Southern State Univ.
Missouri Western State Univ.
Mitchell Coll. (CT)
Montana State Univ.
Montana State Univ.–Billings
Montana State Univ.–Northern
Morehead State Univ. (KY)
Morehouse Coll. (GA)
Mount Marty Coll. (SD)
Mount St. Mary's Univ. (MD)
Mount Vernon Nazarene Univ.
    (OH)
Murray State Univ. (KY)
Nebraska Wesleyan Univ.
Neumann Univ. (PA)
Newberry Coll. (SC)
Nichols Coll. (MA)
Norfolk State Univ. (VA)
North Carolina A&T State Univ.
North Carolina Central Univ.
North Carolina State Univ.–Raleigh
North Carolina Wesleyan Coll.
North Central Coll. (IL)
North Dakota State Univ.
North Greenville Univ. (SC)
North Park Univ. (IL)
Northeastern Illinois Univ.
Northeastern State Univ. (OK)
Northern Arizona Univ.
Northern Kentucky Univ.
Northern Michigan Univ.
Northern State Univ. (SD)
Northwest Nazarene Univ. (ID)
Northwestern Coll. (IA)
Northwestern Coll. (MN)
Northwestern State Univ. of
    Louisiana
Northwood Univ. (MI)
Notre Dame de Namur Univ. (CA)
Nova Southeastern Univ. (FL)
Occidental Coll. (CA)
Ohio Dominican Univ.
Ohio Northern Univ.
Ohio State Univ.–Columbus
Ohio Univ.
Ohio Wesleyan Univ.

Oklahoma Baptist Univ.
Oklahoma Christian Univ.
Oklahoma Panhandle State Univ.
Oklahoma Wesleyan Univ.
Olivet Coll. (MI)
Olivet Nazarene Univ. (IL)
Oregon State Univ.
Otterbein Coll. (OH)
Ouachita Baptist Univ. (AR)
Pacific Lutheran Univ. (WA)
Pacific Union Coll. (CA)
Pacific Univ. (OR)
Palm Beach Atlantic Univ. (FL)
Pennsylvania State Univ.–Univ. Park
Pepperdine Univ. (CA)
Pfeiffer Univ. (NC)
Plymouth State Univ. (NH)
Point Loma Nazarene Univ. (CA)
Portland State Univ. (OR)
Prairie View A&M Univ. (TX)
Principia Coll. (IL)
Purdue Univ.–Calumet (IN)
Purdue Univ.–West Lafayette (IN)
Quincy Univ. (IL)
Randolph Coll. (VA)
Rice Univ. (TX)
Ripon Coll. (WI)
Roanoke Coll. (VA)
Robert Morris Univ. (PA)
Rocky Mountain Coll. (MT)
Sacred Heart Univ. (CT)
Saginaw Valley State Univ. (MI)
Salisbury Univ. (MD)
Sam Houston State Univ. (TX)
Samford Univ. (AL)
San Jose State Univ. (CA)
Schreiner Univ. (TX)
Seattle Pacific Univ.
Seton Hall Univ. (NJ)
Shaw Univ. (NC)
Shawnee State Univ. (OH)
Shippensburg Univ. of Pennsylvania
Shorter Coll. (GA)
Simpson Coll. (IA)
Skidmore Coll. (NY)
Slippery Rock Univ. of Pennsylvania
Sonoma State Univ. (CA)
South Carolina State Univ.
South Dakota State Univ.
Southeast Missouri State Univ.
Southeastern Oklahoma State Univ.
Southern Adventist Univ. (TN)
Southern Arkansas Univ.
Southern Connecticut State Univ.
Southern Illinois Univ.–Edwardsville
Southern Nazarene Univ. (OK)
Southern New Hampshire Univ.
Southern Wesleyan Univ. (SC)
Southwest Baptist Univ. (MO)
Southwest Minnesota State Univ.
Southwestern Coll. (KS)
Southwestern Oklahoma State
    Univ.
Spring Arbor Univ. (MI)
Springfield Coll. (MA)
St. Andrews Presbyterian Coll. (NC)
St. Augustine's Coll. (NC)
St. Catherine Univ. (MN)
St. Cloud State Univ. (MN)
St. Edward's Univ. (TX)
St. John Fisher Coll. (NY)

St. John's Univ. (NY)
St. Joseph's Coll. (ME)
St. Leo Univ. (FL)
St. Louis Univ.
St. Mary's Coll. of California
St. Mary's Univ. of San Antonio
    (TX)
St. Olaf Coll. (MN)
St. Thomas Univ. (FL)
Stephen F. Austin State Univ. (TX)
Sterling Coll. (KS)
Stetson Univ. (FL)
Stillman Coll. (AL)
Sul Ross State Univ. (TX)
SUNY Coll.–Cortland
Tabor Coll. (KS)
Tarleton State Univ. (TX)
Taylor Univ. (IN)
Tennessee State Univ.
Tennessee Technological Univ.
Tennessee Wesleyan Coll.
Texas A&M International Univ.
Texas A&M Univ.–Coll. Station
Texas A&M Univ.–Commerce
Texas A&M Univ.–Corpus Christi
Texas A&M Univ.–Kingsville
Texas Christian Univ.
Texas Coll.
Texas Lutheran Univ.
Texas State Univ.–San Marcos
Texas Tech Univ.
Texas Wesleyan Univ.
Texas Woman's Univ.
Thomas Coll. (ME)
Thomas More Coll. (KY)
Tiffin Univ. (OH)
Towson Univ. (MD)
Transylvania Univ. (KY)
Trevecca Nazarene Univ. (TN)
Trine Univ. (IN)
Trinity Christian Coll. (IL)
Troy Univ. (AL)
Truman State Univ. (MO)
Tulane Univ. (LA)
Tusculum Coll. (TN)
Union Coll. (KY)
Union Coll. (NE)
Union Univ. (TN)
Univ. at Buffalo–SUNY
Univ. of Akron (OH)
Univ. of Arkansas
Univ. of Arkansas–Monticello
Univ. of Central Arkansas
Univ. of Charleston (WV)
Univ. of Dayton (OH)
Univ. of Delaware
Univ. of Dubuque (IA)
Univ. of Evansville (IN)
Univ. of Findlay (OH)
Univ. of Florida
Univ. of Georgia
Univ. of Great Falls (MT)
Univ. of Hawaii–Hilo
Univ. of Hawaii–Manoa
Univ. of Houston
Univ. of Illinois–Chicago
Univ. of Illinois–Urbana-Champaign
Univ. of Indianapolis
Univ. of Iowa
Univ. of Kansas
Univ. of Kentucky

Univ. of Louisville (KY)
Univ. of Maine–Presque Isle
Univ. of Mary (ND)
Univ. of Mary Hardin-Baylor (TX)
Univ. of Maryland–Coll. Park
Univ. of Maryland–Eastern Shore
Univ. of Massachusetts–Amherst
Univ. of Memphis
Univ. of Miami (FL)
Univ. of Michigan–Ann Arbor
Univ. of Minnesota–Crookston
Univ. of Minnesota–Duluth
Univ. of Minnesota–Twin Cities
Univ. of Mississippi
Univ. of Montevallo (AL)
Univ. of Mount Union (OH)
Univ. of Nebraska–Kearney
Univ. of Nevada–Las Vegas
Univ. of New England (ME)
Univ. of New Hampshire
Univ. of North Carolina–Chapel Hill
Univ. of North Carolina–Charlotte
Univ. of North Carolina–
   Greensboro
Univ. of North Carolina–Pembroke
Univ. of North Carolina–
   Wilmington
Univ. of North Texas
Univ. of Northern Colorado
Univ. of Northern Iowa
Univ. of Oklahoma
Univ. of Pittsburgh–Bradford
Univ. of Puget Sound (WA)
Univ. of Rio Grande (OH)
Univ. of San Francisco
Univ. of Science and Arts of
   Oklahoma
Univ. of Scranton (PA)
Univ. of Sioux Falls (SD)
Univ. of South Carolina
Univ. of South Carolina–Aiken
Univ. of Southern California
Univ. of Southern Indiana
Univ. of Southern Maine
Univ. of Southern Mississippi
Univ. of St. Mary (KS)
Univ. of St. Thomas (MN)
Univ. of Tennessee
Univ. of Tennessee–Chattanooga
Univ. of Tennessee–Martin
Univ. of Texas of the Permian Basin
Univ. of Texas–Arlington
Univ. of Texas–Austin
Univ. of Texas–Brownsville
Univ. of Texas–El Paso
Univ. of Texas–Pan American
Univ. of Texas–San Antonio
Univ. of Texas–Tyler
Univ. of the Cumberlands (KY)
Univ. of the District of Columbia
Univ. of the Incarnate Word (TX)
Univ. of the Pacific (CA)
Univ. of Toledo (OH)
Univ. of Tulsa (OK)
Univ. of Utah
Univ. of Vermont
Univ. of West Florida
Univ. of Wisconsin–Eau Claire
Univ. of Wisconsin–La Crosse
Univ. of Wisconsin–Madison
Univ. of Wisconsin–Milwaukee

Univ. of Wisconsin–Parkside
Univ. of Wisconsin–Stevens Point
Univ. of Wyoming
Upper Iowa Univ.
Urbana Univ. (OH)
Ursinus Coll. (PA)
Utah Valley Univ.
Valdosta State Univ. (GA)
Valley City State Univ. (ND)
Valparaiso Univ. (IN)
Vanguard Univ. of Southern
   California
Virginia Intermont Coll.
Voorhees Coll. (SC)
Wake Forest Univ. (NC)
Walla Walla Univ. (WA)
Walsh Univ. (OH)
Warner Pacific Coll. (OR)
Warner Univ. (FL)
Wartburg Coll. (IA)
Washburn Univ. (KS)
Washington Adventist Univ. (MD)
Washington State Univ.
Wayne State Coll. (NE)
Wesley Coll. (DE)
West Chester Univ. of Pennsylvania
West Liberty Univ. (WV)
West Texas A&M Univ.
West Virginia Univ.
West Virginia Wesleyan Coll.
Western Carolina Univ. (NC)
Western Illinois Univ.
Western Michigan Univ.
Western New England Coll. (MA)
Western New Mexico Univ.
Western Washington Univ.
Westfield State Coll. (MA)
Westmont Coll. (CA)
Wheaton Coll. (IL)
Wichita State Univ. (KS)
Willamette Univ. (OR)
William Carey Univ. (MS)
William Woods Univ. (MO)
Wilmington Coll. (OH)
Wilmington Univ. (DE)
Wilson Coll. (PA)
Wingate Univ. (NC)
Winston-Salem State Univ. (NC)
Winthrop Univ. (SC)
Xavier Univ. (OH)
York Coll. of Pennsylvania
Youngstown State Univ. (OH)

Health Professions and Related Clinical Sciences

Albertus Magnus Coll. (CT)
Alcorn State Univ. (MS)
Armstrong Atlantic State Univ. (GA)
Baldwin-Wallace Coll. (OH)
Boise State Univ. (ID)
Boston Univ.
Bowling Green State Univ. (OH)
California State Univ.–Dominguez
   Hills
California State Univ.–Fresno
California State Univ.–Fullerton
California State Univ.–Los Angeles
California State Univ.–Northridge
Campbell Univ. (NC)
Carlow Univ. (PA)

Clark Atlanta Univ.
Coll. at Brockport–SUNY
CUNY–Brooklyn Coll.
CUNY–Hunter Coll.
Curry Coll. (MA)
Dowling Coll. (NY)
East Tennessee State Univ.
Eastern Nazarene Coll. (MA)
Edward Waters Coll. (FL)
Emmanuel Coll. (GA)
Excelsior Coll. (NY)
Gannon Univ. (PA)
George Mason Univ. (VA)
Georgetown Univ. (DC)
Goddard Coll. (VT)
Gwynedd-Mercy Coll. (PA)
Hofstra Univ. (NY)
Howard Univ. (DC)
Kalamazoo Coll. (MI)
Keuka Coll. (NY)
King's Coll. (PA)
Lock Haven Univ. of Pennsylvania
Long Island Univ.–C.W. Post
   Campus (NY)
Marquette Univ. (WI)
Mars Hill Coll. (NC)
Maryville Coll. (TN)
Misericordia Univ. (PA)
Molloy Coll. (NY)
Montana State Univ.–Northern
Nazareth Coll. (NY)
New Jersey City Univ.
New York Institute of Technology
Northern Arizona Univ.
Nova Southeastern Univ. (FL)
Oakland Univ. (MI)
Ohio State Univ.–Columbus
Old Dominion Univ. (VA)
Oral Roberts Univ. (OK)
Pennsylvania Coll. of Technology
Point Park Univ. (PA)
Purdue Univ.–West Lafayette (IN)
Quinnipiac Univ. (CT)
Rochester Institute of Technology
   (NY)
San Diego State Univ.
San Francisco State Univ.
Southeastern Louisiana Univ.
Southwestern Oklahoma State
   Univ.
Southwestern Univ. (TX)
Springfield Coll. (MA)
St. Francis Coll. (NY)
St. Joseph's Coll. New York
St. Joseph's Univ. (PA)
St. Mary's Coll. of California
St. Mary-of-the-Woods Coll. (IN)
SUNY Coll.–Cortland
SUNY Coll.–Potsdam
SUNY–Stony Brook
Syracuse Univ. (NY)
Thomas Edison State Coll. (NJ)
Towson Univ. (MD)
Trinity International Univ. (IL)
Tulane Univ. (LA)
Union Coll. (NE)
Union Institute and Univ. (OH)
Univ. of Alabama
Univ. of Alabama–Birmingham
Univ. of Alaska–Anchorage
Univ. of Arkansas

Univ. of Central Arkansas
Univ. of Colorado–Colorado
   Springs
Univ. of Dallas
Univ. of Findlay (OH)
Univ. of Maryland–Baltimore
   County
Univ. of Miami (FL)
Univ. of Missouri
Univ. of Nevada–Las Vegas
Univ. of North Carolina–
   Wilmington
Univ. of Northern Iowa
Univ. of Pittsburgh
Univ. of Scranton (PA)
Univ. of Southern Indiana
Univ. of Southern Maine
Univ. of St. Francis (IN)
Univ. of Tennessee–Martin
Univ. of Texas–El Paso
Univ. of Wisconsin–Stevens Point
Waldorf Coll. (IA)
Wayne State Univ. (MI)
William Carey Univ. (MS)
Worcester State Coll. (MA)
Youngstown State Univ. (OH)

Health Psychology

Bridgewater State Coll. (MA)
Marquette Univ. (WI)
Prescott Coll. (AZ)

Health Services/Allied Health/Health Sciences

Alderson-Broaddus Coll. (WV)
Anna Maria Coll. (MA)
California State Univ.–Chico
California State Univ.–East Bay
California State Univ.–Monterey Bay
California State Univ.–San
   Bernardino
Centenary Coll. of Louisiana
Central Christian Coll. (KS)
Chicago State Univ.
Coll. of Idaho (ID)
Coll. of St. Scholastica (MN)
Corban Univ. (OR)
Covenant Coll. (GA)
CUNY–Lehman Coll.
Daemen Coll. (NY)
Emmanuel Coll. (MA)
Evergreen State Coll. (WA)
Felician Coll. (NJ)
Ferrum Coll. (VA)
Florida Atlantic Univ.
Florida Gulf Coast Univ.
Florida International Univ.
Gardner-Webb Univ. (NC)
Geneva Coll. (PA)
Graceland Univ. (IA)
Grand Valley State Univ. (MI)
Greensboro Coll. (NC)
Hendrix Coll. (AR)
Idaho State Univ.
Ithaca Coll. (NY)
Lebanon Valley Coll. (PA)
Liberty Univ. (VA)
Long Island Univ.–C.W. Post
   Campus (NY)

Marietta Coll. (OH)
Marywood Univ. (PA)
Mercyhurst Coll. (PA)
Merrimack Coll. (MA)
Metropolitan State Coll. of Denver
Monmouth Univ. (NJ)
Montclair State Univ. (NJ)
Nicholls State Univ. (LA)
Northern Kentucky Univ.
Pacific Univ. (OR)
Philadelphia Univ.
Quinnipiac Univ. (CT)
Sam Houston State Univ. (TX)
San Jose State Univ. (CA)
Southwestern Oklahoma State
   Univ.
St. Joseph's Univ. (PA)
Stephen F. Austin State Univ. (TX)
Stetson Univ. (FL)
Texas State Univ.–San Marcos
Texas Tech Univ.
Texas Woman's Univ.
Thomas Edison State Coll. (NJ)
Trevecca Nazarene Univ. (TN)
Truman State Univ. (MO)
Union Coll. (NE)
Univ. of Arizona
Univ. of Central Florida
Univ. of Florida
Univ. of Hartford (CT)
Univ. of Houston
Univ. of Michigan–Flint
Univ. of Minnesota–Crookston
Univ. of Mobile (AL)
Univ. of New England (ME)
Univ. of North Florida
Univ. of North Texas
Univ. of Northern Colorado
Univ. of Oklahoma
Univ. of Southern Mississippi
Univ. of Texas–Austin
Univ. of Texas–Brownsville
Univ. of Texas–Pan American
Univ. of Texas–San Antonio
Univ. of Utah
Univ. of West Florida
Univ. of Wyoming
Ursuline Coll. (OH)
Utica Coll. (NY)
Viterbo Univ. (WI)
Washburn Univ. (KS)
Widener Univ. (PA)

Health/Medical Preparatory Programs

Abilene Christian Univ. (TX)
Adrian Coll. (MI)
Allegheny Coll. (PA)
Alma Coll. (MI)
American International Coll. (MA)
Andrews Univ. (MI)
Arcadia Univ. (PA)
Asbury Univ. (KY)
Augustana Coll. (IL)
Augustana Coll. (SD)
Aurora Univ. (IL)
Austin Peay State Univ. (TN)
Averett Univ. (VA)
Avila Univ. (MO)
Azusa Pacific Univ. (CA)

Ball State Univ. (IN)
Baylor Univ. (TX)
Becker Coll. (MA)
Benedictine Univ. (IL)
Bennington Coll. (VT)
Bethel Coll. (IN)
Bluffton Univ. (OH)
Boise State Univ. (ID)
Brevard Coll. (NC)
California Baptist Univ.
Calvin Coll. (MI)
Carroll Coll. (MT)
Carroll Univ. (WI)
Cedarville Univ. (OH)
Chadron State Coll. (NE)
Charleston Southern Univ. (SC)
Clearwater Christian Coll. (FL)
Coll. of Charleston (SC)
Coll. of Idaho (ID)
Coll. of the Ozarks (MO)
Concordia Coll.–Moorhead (MN)
Concordia Univ. (MI)
Concordia Univ. (NE)
Cornerstone Univ. (MI)
Defiance Coll. (OH)
Delaware State Univ.
DeSales Univ. (PA)
Dordt Coll. (IA)
Drexel Univ. (PA)
Duquesne Univ. (PA)
Earlham Coll. (IN)
Eastern Mennonite Univ. (VA)
Eastern Michigan Univ.
Eastern Nazarene Coll. (MA)
Elmhurst Coll. (IL)
Farmingdale State Coll.–SUNY
Ferrum Coll. (VA)
Furman Univ. (SC)
Gannon Univ. (PA)
Geneva Coll. (PA)
Graceland Univ. (IA)
Grand Valley State Univ. (MI)
Guilford Coll. (NC)
Hardin-Simmons Univ. (TX)
Harding Univ. (AR)
Hartwick Coll. (NY)
Hawaii Pacific Univ.
Hodges Univ. (FL)
Hofstra Univ. (NY)
Howard Payne Univ. (TX)
Humboldt State Univ. (CA)
Huntington Univ. (IN)
Immaculata Univ. (PA)
Indiana Univ.-Purdue Univ.–Fort
  Wayne
Indiana Wesleyan Univ.
Iowa Wesleyan Coll.
Jarvis Christian Coll. (TX)
Juniata Coll. (PA)
Kansas State Univ.
Kent State Univ. (OH)
Lehigh Univ. (PA)
Lenoir-Rhyne Univ. (NC)
Lewis Univ. (IL)
Limestone Coll. (SC)
Lincoln Memorial Univ. (TN)
Lindenwood Univ. (MO)
Lipscomb Univ. (TN)
Lock Haven Univ. of Pennsylvania
Louisiana Coll.
Louisiana State Univ.–Shreveport

MacMurray Coll. (IL)
Madonna Univ. (MI)
Manchester Coll. (IN)
Mansfield Univ. of Pennsylvania
Marian Univ. (IN)
Maryville Univ. of St. Louis (MO)
Meredith Coll. (NC)
Michigan State Univ.
Midwestern State Univ. (TX)
Millikin Univ. (IL)
Minnesota State Univ.–Moorhead
Mississippi Coll.
Missouri Southern State Univ.
Missouri Univ. of Science &
  Technology
Monmouth Coll. (IL)
Montana State Univ.
Mount Mary Coll. (WI)
New York Institute of Technology
North Park Univ. (IL)
Northeastern State Univ. (OK)
Northern Arizona Univ.
Northern Illinois Univ.
Northern Michigan Univ.
Northwest Missouri State Univ.
Northwestern Univ. (IL)
Notre Dame Coll. of Ohio
Notre Dame de Namur Univ. (CA)
Ohio State Univ.–Columbus
Ohio Wesleyan Univ.
Oklahoma Baptist Univ.
Oklahoma State Univ.
Olivet Nazarene Univ. (IL)
Oral Roberts Univ. (OK)
Oregon Institute of Technology
Ouachita Baptist Univ. (AR)
Palm Beach Atlantic Univ. (FL)
Pennsylvania State Univ.–Univ. Park
Pfeiffer Univ. (NC)
Philadelphia Univ.
Purdue Univ.–West Lafayette (IN)
Rensselaer Polytechnic Institute
  (NY)
Rochester Institute of Technology
  (NY)
Roosevelt Univ. (IL)
Sacred Heart Univ. (CT)
Saginaw Valley State Univ. (MI)
Samford Univ. (AL)
Shawnee State Univ. (OH)
Simpson Coll. (IA)
Slippery Rock Univ. of Pennsylvania
Southeastern Univ. (FL)
Southern Nazarene Univ. (OK)
Southern Wesleyan Univ. (SC)
St. Francis Coll. (NY)
St. Gregory's Univ. (OK)
St. Mary-of-the-Woods Coll. (IN)
St. Thomas Univ. (FL)
St. Xavier Univ. (IL)
SUNY Coll.–Oneonta
Tarleton State Univ. (TX)
Tennessee Wesleyan Coll.
Texas A&M Univ.–Coll. Station
Texas Wesleyan Univ.
Trine Univ. (IN)
Trinity International Univ. (IL)
Tusculum Coll. (TN)
Union Univ. (TN)
Univ. of Akron (OH)
Univ. of Arizona

Univ. of Arkansas
Univ. of California–Riverside
Univ. of Connecticut
Univ. of Dayton (OH)
Univ. of Evansville (IN)
Univ. of Findlay (OH)
Univ. of Hawaii–Hilo
Univ. of Illinois–Chicago
Univ. of Illinois–Urbana-Champaign
Univ. of Iowa
Univ. of Louisville (KY)
Univ. of Maryland–Coll. Park
Univ. of Maryland–Eastern Shore
Univ. of Massachusetts–Amherst
Univ. of Miami (FL)
Univ. of Michigan–Flint
Univ. of Nebraska–Lincoln
Univ. of Nevada–Las Vegas
Univ. of Nevada–Reno
Univ. of New Mexico
Univ. of Notre Dame (IN)
Univ. of Pittsburgh–Johnstown
Univ. of South Alabama
Univ. of St. Francis (IN)
Univ. of St. Thomas (MN)
Univ. of the Ozarks (AR)
Univ. of Tulsa (OK)
Univ. of Wisconsin–Madison
Univ. of Wisconsin–Milwaukee
Utah State Univ.
Utica Coll. (NY)
Valley City State Univ. (ND)
Virginia Intermont Coll.
Walsh Univ. (OH)
Washburn Univ. (KS)
Washington State Univ.
West Chester Univ. of Pennsylvania
West Virginia Wesleyan Coll.
Westminster Coll. (UT)
Widener Univ. (PA)
Winona State Univ. (MN)
York Coll. of Pennsylvania
Youngstown State Univ. (OH)

HVAC and Refrigeration Maintenance Technology/Technician (HAC, HACR, HVAC, HVACR)

Lewis-Clark State Coll. (ID)
Northern Michigan Univ.

Heavy/Industrial Equipment Maintenance Technologies

Ferris State Univ. (MI)
Northern Michigan Univ.
San Francisco State Univ.

Historic Preservation and Conservation

Coll. of Charleston (SC)
Eastern Michigan Univ.
Goucher Coll. (MD)
Northwestern State Univ. of
  Louisiana
Roger Williams Univ. (RI)
Salve Regina Univ. (RI)

Savannah Coll. of Art and Design
  (GA)
Univ. of Delaware
Univ. of Kentucky
Univ. of Mary Washington (VA)
Ursuline Coll. (OH)

History

Abilene Christian Univ. (TX)
Adelphi Univ. (NY)
Adrian Coll. (MI)
Alabama State Univ.
Albany State Univ. (GA)
Albertus Magnus Coll. (CT)
Albion Coll. (MI)
Albright Coll. (PA)
Alcorn State Univ. (MS)
Alderson-Broaddus Coll. (WV)
Alfred Univ. (NY)
Allegheny Coll. (PA)
Alma Coll. (MI)
Alvernia Univ. (PA)
Alverno Coll. (WI)
American Jewish Univ. (CA)
American Univ. (DC)
Amherst Coll. (MA)
Anderson Univ. (IN)
Anderson Univ. (SC)
Angelo State Univ. (TX)
Anna Maria Coll. (MA)
Appalachian State Univ. (NC)
Aquinas Coll. (MI)
Arcadia Univ. (PA)
Arizona State Univ.
Arkansas State Univ.–Jonesboro
Arkansas Tech Univ.
Armstrong Atlantic State Univ. (GA)
Asbury Univ. (KY)
Ashland Univ. (OH)
Assumption Coll. (MA)
Atlantic Union Coll. (MA)
Auburn Univ. (AL)
Auburn Univ.–Montgomery (AL)
Augusta State Univ. (GA)
Augustana Coll. (SD)
Augustana Coll. (IL)
Aurora Univ. (IL)
Austin Coll. (TX)
Austin Peay State Univ. (TN)
Averett Univ. (VA)
Avila Univ. (MO)
Azusa Pacific Univ. (CA)
Babson Coll. (MA)
Baker Univ. (KS)
Baldwin-Wallace Coll. (OH)
Ball State Univ. (IN)
Bard Coll. at Simon's Rock (MA)
Barnard Coll. (NY)
Barry Univ. (FL)
Barton Coll. (NC)
Bates Coll. (ME)
Baylor Univ. (TX)
Belhaven Univ. (MS)
Bellarmine Univ. (KY)
Bellevue Univ. (NE)
Belmont Abbey Coll. (NC)
Belmont Univ. (TN)
Beloit Coll. (WI)
Bemidji State Univ. (MN)
Benedict Coll. (SC)

Benedictine Coll. (KS)
Bennington Coll. (VT)
Bentley Univ. (MA)
Berea Coll. (KY)
Berry Coll. (GA)
Bethany Coll. (WV)
Bethany Coll. (KS)
Bethel Coll. (TN)
Bethel Coll. (KS)
Bethel Univ. (MN)
Bethune-Cookman Univ. (FL)
Binghamton Univ.–SUNY
Biola Univ. (CA)
Black Hills State Univ. (SD)
Bloomfield Coll. (NJ)
Bloomsburg Univ. of Pennsylvania
Blue Mountain Coll. (MS)
Bluefield Coll. (VA)
Bluffton Univ. (OH)
Boise State Univ. (ID)
Bowie State Univ. (MD)
Bowling Green State Univ. (OH)
Bradley Univ. (IL)
Brenau Univ. (GA)
Brescia Univ. (KY)
Brevard Coll. (NC)
Brewton-Parker Coll. (GA)
Bridgewater Coll. (VA)
Bridgewater State Coll. (MA)
Brigham Young Univ.–Hawaii
Brigham Young Univ.–Provo (UT)
Brown Univ. (RI)
Bryan Coll. (TN)
Bryant Univ. (RI)
Bryn Athyn Coll. of the New Church
  (PA)
Bryn Mawr Coll. (PA)
Bucknell Univ. (PA)
Buena Vista Univ. (IA)
Buffalo State Coll.–SUNY
Butler Univ. (IN)
Cabrini Coll. (PA)
California Baptist Univ.
California Institute of Technology
California Lutheran Univ.
California Polytechnic State Univ.–
  San Luis Obispo
California State Polytechnic Univ.–
  Pomona
California State Univ.–Chico
California State Univ.–East Bay
California State Univ.–Fresno
California State Univ.–Fullerton
California State Univ.–Long Beach
California State Univ.–Los Angeles
California State Univ.–Monterey Bay
California State Univ.–Northridge
California State Univ.–Sacramento
California State Univ.–San
  Bernardino
California State Univ.–Stanislaus
California Univ. of Pennsylvania
Calvin Coll. (MI)
Cameron Univ. (OK)
Campbellsville Univ. (KY)
Canisius Coll. (NY)
Capital Univ. (OH)
Carleton Coll. (MN)
Carlow Univ. (PA)
Carnegie Mellon Univ. (PA)
Carroll Univ. (WI)

Carson-Newman Coll. (TN)
Carthage Coll. (WI)
Case Western Reserve Univ. (OH)
Castleton State Coll. (VT)
Catawba Coll. (NC)
Catholic Univ. of America (DC)
Cedar Crest Coll. (PA)
Cedarville Univ. (OH)
Centenary Coll. (NJ)
Centenary Coll. of Louisiana
Central Christian Coll. (KS)
Central Coll. (IA)
Central Connecticut State Univ.
Central Methodist Univ. (MO)
Central Michigan Univ.
Central State Univ. (OH)
Central Washington Univ.
Centre Coll. (KY)
Chadron State Coll. (NE)
Chaminade Univ. of Honolulu
Chapman Univ. (CA)
Chatham Univ. (PA)
Chestnut Hill Coll. (PA)
Chicago State Univ.
Chowan Univ. (NC)
Christopher Newport Univ. (VA)
Claflin Univ. (SC)
Claremont McKenna Coll. (CA)
Clarion Univ. of Pennsylvania
Clark Atlanta Univ.
Clark Univ. (MA)
Clarkson Univ. (NY)
Clayton State Univ. (GA)
Clearwater Christian Coll. (FL)
Clemson Univ. (SC)
Cleveland State Univ.
Coastal Carolina Univ. (SC)
Coe Coll. (IA)
Coker Coll. (SC)
Colby Coll. (ME)
Colgate Univ. (NY)
Coll. at Brockport–SUNY
Coll. of Charleston (SC)
Coll. of Idaho (ID)
Coll. of Mount St. Joseph (OH)
Coll. of Mount St. Vincent (NY)
Coll. of New Jersey
Coll. of Notre Dame of Maryland
Coll. of Our Lady of the Elms (MA)
Coll. of St. Benedict (MN)
Coll. of St. Elizabeth (NJ)
Coll. of St. Rose (NY)
Coll. of St. Scholastica (MN)
Coll. of the Holy Cross (MA)
Coll. of the Ozarks (MO)
Coll. of William and Mary (VA)
Colorado Christian Univ.
Colorado Coll.
Colorado State Univ.
Colorado State Univ.–Pueblo
Columbia Coll. (MO)
Columbia Coll. (SC)
Columbia Univ. (NY)
Concord Univ. (WV)
Concordia Coll. (NY)
Concordia Coll.–Moorhead (MN)
Concordia Univ. (CA)
Concordia Univ. (OR)
Concordia Univ. (NE)
Concordia Univ. (MI)
Concordia Univ. Chicago (IL)

Concordia Univ. Texas
Concordia Univ.–St. Paul (MN)
Connecticut Coll.
Converse Coll. (SC)
Cornell Coll. (IA)
Cornell Univ. (NY)
Cornerstone Univ. (MI)
Covenant Coll. (GA)
Creighton Univ. (NE)
Crown Coll. (MN)
Culver-Stockton Coll. (MO)
Cumberland Univ. (TN)
CUNY–Baruch Coll.
CUNY–Brooklyn Coll.
CUNY–City Coll.
CUNY–Coll. of Staten Island
CUNY–Hunter Coll.
CUNY–Lehman Coll.
CUNY–Queens Coll.
CUNY–York Coll.
D'Youville Coll. (NY)
Daemen Coll. (NY)
Dakota Wesleyan Univ. (SD)
Dana Coll. (NE)
Dartmouth Coll. (NH)
Davidson Coll. (NC)
Davis and Elkins Coll. (WV)
Defiance Coll. (OH)
Delta State Univ. (MS)
Denison Univ. (OH)
DePauw Univ. (IN)
DeSales Univ. (PA)
Dickinson Coll. (PA)
Dickinson State Univ. (ND)
Dillard Univ. (LA)
Dominican Coll. (NY)
Dominican Univ. (IL)
Dominican Univ. of California
Dordt Coll. (IA)
Dowling Coll. (NY)
Drake Univ. (IA)
Drew Univ. (NJ)
Drexel Univ. (PA)
Duke Univ. (NC)
Duquesne Univ. (PA)
Earlham Coll. (IN)
East Carolina Univ. (NC)
East Central Univ. (OK)
East Stroudsburg Univ. of
    Pennsylvania
East Tennessee State Univ.
East Texas Baptist Univ.
Eastern Connecticut State Univ.
Eastern Illinois Univ.
Eastern Kentucky Univ.
Eastern Mennonite Univ. (VA)
Eastern Michigan Univ.
Eastern Nazarene Coll. (MA)
Eastern New Mexico Univ.
Eastern Oregon Univ.
Eastern Univ. (PA)
Eastern Washington Univ.
Eckerd Coll. (FL)
Edgewood Coll. (WI)
Edinboro Univ. of Pennsylvania
Elizabeth City State Univ. (NC)
Elmhurst Coll. (IL)
Elmira Coll. (NY)
Elon Univ. (NC)
Emmanuel Coll. (GA)
Emmanuel Coll. (MA)

Emory and Henry Coll. (VA)
Emory Univ. (GA)
Emporia State Univ. (KS)
Erskine Coll. (SC)
Eureka Coll. (IL)
Evangel Univ. (MO)
Excelsior Coll. (NY)
Fairfield Univ. (CT)
Fairleigh Dickinson Univ. (NJ)
Fairmont State Univ. (WV)
Fayetteville State Univ. (NC)
Felician Coll. (NJ)
Ferris State Univ. (MI)
Ferrum Coll. (VA)
Fisk Univ. (TN)
Fitchburg State Coll. (MA)
Flagler Coll. (FL)
Florida Atlantic Univ.
Florida International Univ.
Florida Southern Coll.
Florida State Univ.
Fontbonne Univ. (MO)
Fordham Univ. (NY)
Fort Hays State Univ. (KS)
Fort Lewis Coll. (CO)
Fort Valley State Univ. (GA)
Framingham State Coll. (MA)
Francis Marion Univ. (SC)
Franciscan Univ. of Steubenville
    (OH)
Franklin and Marshall Coll. (PA)
Franklin Coll. (IN)
Franklin Pierce Univ. (NH)
Free Will Baptist Bible Coll. (TN)
Freed-Hardeman Univ. (TN)
Fresno Pacific Univ. (CA)
Friends Univ. (KS)
Frostburg State Univ. (MD)
Furman Univ. (SC)
Gallaudet Univ. (DC)
Gannon Univ. (PA)
Gardner-Webb Univ. (NC)
Geneva Coll. (PA)
George Fox Univ. (OR)
George Mason Univ. (VA)
George Washington Univ. (DC)
Georgetown Coll. (KY)
Georgetown Univ. (DC)
Georgia Coll. & State Univ.
Georgia Institute of Technology
Georgia Southern Univ.
Georgia Southwestern State Univ.
Georgia State Univ.
Georgian Court Univ. (NJ)
Gettysburg Coll. (PA)
Glenville State Coll. (WV)
Gonzaga Univ. (WA)
Gordon Coll. (MA)
Goshen Coll. (IN)
Goucher Coll. (MD)
Graceland Univ. (IA)
Grambling State Univ. (LA)
Grand Valley State Univ. (MI)
Green Mountain Coll. (VT)
Greensboro Coll. (NC)
Greenville Coll. (IL)
Grinnell Coll. (IA)
Grove City Coll. (PA)
Guilford Coll. (NC)
Gustavus Adolphus Coll. (MN)
Gwynedd-Mercy Coll. (PA)

Hamilton Coll. (NY)
Hamline Univ. (MN)
Hampden-Sydney Coll. (VA)
Hampshire Coll. (MA)
Hampton Univ. (VA)
Hardin-Simmons Univ. (TX)
Harding Univ. (AR)
Hartwick Coll. (NY)
Harvard Univ. (MA)
Haverford Coll. (PA)
Henderson State Univ. (AR)
Hendrix Coll. (AR)
High Point Univ. (NC)
Hobart and William Smith Colleges
    (NY)
Hofstra Univ. (NY)
Hollins Univ. (VA)
Holy Family Univ. (PA)
Holy Names Univ. (CA)
Hood Coll. (MD)
Hope Coll. (MI)
Houghton Coll. (NY)
Houston Baptist Univ.
Howard Payne Univ. (TX)
Humboldt State Univ. (CA)
Huntingdon Coll. (AL)
Huntington Univ. (IN)
Huston-Tillotson Univ. (TX)
Idaho State Univ.
Illinois Coll.
Illinois State Univ.
Illinois Wesleyan Univ.
Immaculata Univ. (PA)
Indiana State Univ.
Indiana Univ. East
Indiana Univ. Northwest
Indiana Univ. of Pennsylvania
Indiana Univ. Southeast
Indiana Univ.–Bloomington
Indiana Univ.–South Bend
Indiana Univ.–Purdue Univ.–Fort
    Wayne
Indiana Univ.–Purdue Univ.–
    Indianapolis
Indiana Wesleyan Univ.
Iona Coll. (NY)
Iowa State Univ.
Iowa Wesleyan Coll.
Ithaca Coll. (NY)
Jackson State Univ. (MS)
Jacksonville State Univ. (AL)
Jacksonville Univ. (FL)
James Madison Univ. (VA)
Jamestown Coll. (ND)
Jarvis Christian Coll. (TX)
John Brown Univ. (AR)
John Carroll Univ. (OH)
Johns Hopkins Univ. (MD)
Johnson C. Smith Univ. (NC)
Johnson State Coll. (VT)
Judson Coll. (AL)
Judson Univ. (IL)
Juniata Coll. (PA)
Kalamazoo Coll. (MI)
Kansas State Univ.
Kansas Wesleyan Univ.
Kean Univ. (NJ)
Keene State Coll. (NH)
Kennesaw State Univ. (GA)
Kent State Univ. (OH)
Kentucky State Univ.

Kentucky Wesleyan Coll.
Kenyon Coll. (OH)
King Coll. (TN)
King's Coll. (PA)
Knox Coll. (IL)
Kutztown Univ. of Pennsylvania
La Roche Coll. (PA)
La Salle Univ. (PA)
La Sierra Univ. (CA)
Lafayette Coll. (PA)
LaGrange Coll. (GA)
Lake Erie Coll. (OH)
Lake Forest Coll. (IL)
Lake Superior State Univ. (MI)
Lakeland Coll. (WI)
Lamar Univ. (TX)
Lambuth Univ. (TN)
Lander Univ. (SC)
Lane Coll. (TN)
Langston Univ. (OK)
Lasell Coll. (MA)
Le Moyne Coll. (NY)
Lebanon Valley Coll. (PA)
Lees-McRae Coll. (NC)
Lehigh Univ. (PA)
LeMoyne-Owen Coll. (TN)
Lenoir-Rhyne Univ. (NC)
LeTourneau Univ. (TX)
Lewis & Clark Coll. (OR)
Liberty Univ. (VA)
Limestone Coll. (SC)
Lincoln Memorial Univ. (TN)
Lincoln Univ. (PA)
Lindenwood Univ. (MO)
Lindsey Wilson Coll. (KY)
Linfield Coll. (OR)
Lipscomb Univ. (TN)
Livingstone Coll. (NC)
Lock Haven Univ. of Pennsylvania
Long Island Univ.–C.W. Post
    Campus (NY)
Loras Coll. (IA)
Louisiana Coll.
Louisiana State Univ.–Baton Rouge
Louisiana State Univ.–Shreveport
Louisiana Tech Univ.
Lourdes Coll. (OH)
Loyola Marymount Univ. (CA)
Loyola Univ. Chicago
Loyola Univ. Maryland
Loyola Univ. New Orleans
Lubbock Christian Univ. (TX)
Luther Coll. (IA)
Lycoming Coll. (PA)
Lynchburg Coll. (VA)
Lyon Coll. (AR)
Macalester Coll. (MN)
MacMurray Coll. (IL)
Macon State Coll. (GA)
Madonna Univ. (MI)
Malone Univ. (OH)
Manchester Coll. (IN)
Manhattan Coll. (NY)
Manhattanville Coll. (NY)
Mansfield Univ. of Pennsylvania
Marian Univ. (WI)
Marian Univ. (IN)
Marietta Coll. (OH)
Marist Coll. (NY)
Marlboro Coll. (VT)
Marquette Univ. (WI)

Union Coll. (NY)
Union Coll. (NE)
Union Coll. (KY)
Union Univ. (TN)
United States Air Force Academy (CO)
United States Naval Academy (MD)
Univ. at Albany–SUNY
Univ. at Buffalo–SUNY
Univ. of Akron (OH)
Univ. of Alabama
Univ. of Alabama–Birmingham
Univ. of Alabama–Huntsville
Univ. of Alaska–Anchorage
Univ. of Alaska–Fairbanks
Univ. of Arizona
Univ. of Arkansas
Univ. of Arkansas–Little Rock
Univ. of Arkansas–Pine Bluff
Univ. of Baltimore (MD)
Univ. of California–Berkeley
Univ. of California–Davis
Univ. of California–Irvine
Univ. of California–Los Angeles
Univ. of California–Riverside
Univ. of California–San Diego
Univ. of Central Arkansas
Univ. of Central Florida
Univ. of Central Missouri
Univ. of Central Oklahoma
Univ. of Charleston (WV)
Univ. of Chicago
Univ. of Colorado–Boulder
Univ. of Colorado–Colorado Springs
Univ. of Colorado–Denver
Univ. of Connecticut
Univ. of Dallas
Univ. of Dayton (OH)
Univ. of Delaware
Univ. of Denver
Univ. of Evansville (IN)
Univ. of Findlay (OH)
Univ. of Florida
Univ. of Georgia
Univ. of Great Falls (MT)
Univ. of Hawaii–Hilo
Univ. of Hawaii–Manoa
Univ. of Houston
Univ. of Houston–Downtown
Univ. of Illinois–Chicago
Univ. of Illinois–Springfield
Univ. of Illinois–Urbana-Champaign
Univ. of Indianapolis
Univ. of Iowa
Univ. of Kansas
Univ. of Kentucky
Univ. of La Verne (CA)
Univ. of Louisiana–Lafayette
Univ. of Louisiana–Monroe
Univ. of Louisville (KY)
Univ. of Maine
Univ. of Maine–Farmington
Univ. of Maine–Fort Kent
Univ. of Maine–Machias
Univ. of Mary (ND)
Univ. of Mary Hardin-Baylor (TX)
Univ. of Maryland–Baltimore County
Univ. of Maryland–Coll. Park
Univ. of Maryland–Eastern Shore

Univ. of Maryland–Univ. Coll.
Univ. of Massachusetts–Amherst
Univ. of Massachusetts–Boston
Univ. of Massachusetts–Lowell
Univ. of Memphis
Univ. of Miami (FL)
Univ. of Michigan–Ann Arbor
Univ. of Michigan–Dearborn
Univ. of Michigan–Flint
Univ. of Minnesota–Duluth
Univ. of Minnesota–Morris
Univ. of Minnesota–Twin Cities
Univ. of Mississippi
Univ. of Missouri
Univ. of Missouri–Kansas City
Univ. of Missouri–St. Louis
Univ. of Mobile (AL)
Univ. of Montana
Univ. of Montevallo (AL)
Univ. of Mount Union (OH)
Univ. of Nebraska–Kearney
Univ. of Nebraska–Lincoln
Univ. of Nebraska–Omaha
Univ. of Nevada–Las Vegas
Univ. of Nevada–Reno
Univ. of New England (ME)
Univ. of New Hampshire
Univ. of New Haven (CT)
Univ. of New Mexico
Univ. of New Orleans
Univ. of North Alabama
Univ. of North Carolina–Asheville
Univ. of North Carolina–Chapel Hill
Univ. of North Carolina–Charlotte
Univ. of North Carolina–Greensboro
Univ. of North Carolina–Pembroke
Univ. of North Carolina–Wilmington
Univ. of North Dakota
Univ. of North Florida
Univ. of North Texas
Univ. of Northern Colorado
Univ. of Northern Iowa
Univ. of Notre Dame (IN)
Univ. of Oklahoma
Univ. of Oregon
Univ. of Pennsylvania
Univ. of Pittsburgh
Univ. of Pittsburgh–Johnstown
Univ. of Portland (OR)
Univ. of Puget Sound (WA)
Univ. of Redlands (CA)
Univ. of Rhode Island
Univ. of Richmond (VA)
Univ. of Rochester (NY)
Univ. of San Diego
Univ. of San Francisco
Univ. of Science and Arts of Oklahoma
Univ. of Scranton (PA)
Univ. of Sioux Falls (SD)
Univ. of South Alabama
Univ. of South Carolina
Univ. of South Carolina–Aiken
Univ. of South Dakota
Univ. of South Florida
Univ. of Southern California
Univ. of Southern Indiana
Univ. of Southern Mississippi
Univ. of St. Francis (IL)

Univ. of St. Francis (IN)
Univ. of St. Mary (KS)
Univ. of St. Thomas (TX)
Univ. of St. Thomas (MN)
Univ. of Tampa (FL)
Univ. of Tennessee
Univ. of Tennessee–Chattanooga
Univ. of Tennessee–Martin
Univ. of Texas of the Permian Basin
Univ. of Texas–Arlington
Univ. of Texas–Austin
Univ. of Texas–Brownsville
Univ. of Texas–El Paso
Univ. of Texas–Pan American
Univ. of Texas–San Antonio
Univ. of Texas–Tyler
Univ. of the Cumberlands (KY)
Univ. of the District of Columbia
Univ. of the Incarnate Word (TX)
Univ. of the Ozarks (AR)
Univ. of the Pacific (CA)
Univ. of the Southwest (NM)
Univ. of Toledo (OH)
Univ. of Tulsa (OK)
Univ. of Utah
Univ. of Vermont
Univ. of Virginia
Univ. of Virginia–Wise
Univ. of Washington
Univ. of West Alabama
Univ. of West Florida
Univ. of West Georgia
Univ. of Wisconsin–Eau Claire
Univ. of Wisconsin–Green Bay
Univ. of Wisconsin–La Crosse
Univ. of Wisconsin–Madison
Univ. of Wisconsin–Milwaukee
Univ. of Wisconsin–Oshkosh
Univ. of Wisconsin–Platteville
Univ. of Wisconsin–River Falls
Univ. of Wisconsin–Stevens Point
Univ. of Wisconsin–Superior
Univ. of Wisconsin–Whitewater
Univ. of Wyoming
Urbana Univ. (OH)
Ursinus Coll. (PA)
Ursuline Coll. (OH)
Utah Valley Univ.
Utica Coll. (NY)
Valdosta State Univ. (GA)
Valley City State Univ. (ND)
Valparaiso Univ. (IN)
Vanderbilt Univ. (TN)
Vanguard Univ. of Southern California
Vassar Coll. (NY)
Victory Univ. (TN)
Villanova Univ. (PA)
Virginia Commonwealth Univ.
Virginia Intermont Coll.
Virginia Military Institute
Virginia State Univ.
Virginia Tech
Virginia Wesleyan Coll.
Wabash Coll. (IN)
Wagner Coll. (NY)
Wake Forest Univ. (NC)
Waldorf Coll. (IA)
Walsh Univ. (OH)
Warner Pacific Coll. (OR)
Warner Univ. (FL)

Warren Wilson Coll. (NC)
Wartburg Coll. (IA)
Washburn Univ. (KS)
Washington Adventist Univ. (MD)
Washington and Jefferson Coll. (PA)
Washington and Lee Univ. (VA)
Washington Coll. (MD)
Washington State Univ.
Washington Univ. in St. Louis
Wayland Baptist Univ. (TX)
Wayne State Coll. (NE)
Wayne State Univ. (MI)
Waynesburg Univ. (PA)
Webster Univ. (MO)
Wellesley Coll. (MA)
Wells Coll. (NY)
Wesley Coll. (DE)
Wesleyan Coll. (GA)
Wesleyan Univ. (CT)
West Chester Univ. of Pennsylvania
West Liberty Univ. (WV)
West Virginia State Univ.
West Virginia Univ.
West Virginia Wesleyan Coll.
Western Carolina Univ. (NC)
Western Connecticut State Univ.
Western Illinois Univ.
Western Kentucky Univ.
Western Michigan Univ.
Western New England Coll. (MA)
Western New Mexico Univ.
Western Oregon Univ.
Western State Coll. of Colorado
Western Washington Univ.
Westfield State Coll. (MA)
Westminster Coll. (MO)
Westminster Coll. (PA)
Westminster Coll. (UT)
Westmont Coll. (CA)
Wheaton Coll. (IL)
Wheaton Coll. (MA)
Wheeling Jesuit Univ. (WV)
Whitman Coll. (WA)
Whittier Coll. (CA)
Whitworth Univ. (WA)
Wichita State Univ. (KS)
Wiley Coll. (TX)
Wilkes Univ. (PA)
Willamette Univ. (OR)
William Carey Univ. (MS)
William Jewell Coll. (MO)
William Paterson Univ. of NJ
William Woods Univ. (MO)
Williams Coll. (MA)
Wilmington Coll. (OH)
Winston-Salem State Univ. (NC)
Winthrop Univ. (SC)
Wisconsin Lutheran Coll.
Wittenberg Univ. (OH)
Wofford Coll. (SC)
Woodbury Univ. (CA)
Worcester State Coll. (MA)
Wright State Univ. (OH)
Xavier Univ. (OH)
Yale Univ. (CT)
Yeshiva Univ. (NY)
York Coll. of Pennsylvania
Youngstown State Univ. (OH)

Hospitality Administration/ Management

Appalachian State Univ. (NC)
Arkansas State Univ.–Jonesboro
Arkansas Tech Univ.
Ashland Univ. (OH)
Auburn Univ. (AL)
Bethune-Cookman Univ. (FL)
Black Hills State Univ. (SD)
Boston Univ.
Bowling Green State Univ. (OH)
Brigham Young Univ.–Hawaii
Buffalo State Coll.–SUNY
California State Polytechnic Univ.–Pomona
Campbell Univ. (NC)
Central Michigan Univ.
Champlain Coll. (VT)
Cheyney Univ. of Pennsylvania
Clark Atlanta Univ.
Clemson Univ. (SC)
Coastal Carolina Univ. (SC)
Coll. of Charleston (SC)
Coll. of St. Joseph (VT)
Coll. of the Ozarks (MO)
Colorado State Univ.
Columbia Coll. (MO)
Concord Univ. (WV)
Concordia Univ. (MI)
Cornell Univ. (NY)
CUNY–New York City Coll. of Technology
Davis and Elkins Coll. (WV)
Delaware State Univ.
Delta State Univ. (MS)
Dowling Coll. (NY)
Drexel Univ. (PA)
East Carolina Univ. (NC)
East Stroudsburg Univ. of Pennsylvania
Eastern Kentucky Univ.
Eastern Michigan Univ.
Edward Waters Coll. (FL)
Endicott Coll. (MA)
Excelsior Coll. (NY)
Fairleigh Dickinson Univ. (NJ)
Fairmont State Univ. (WV)
Ferris State Univ. (MI)
Florida Atlantic Univ.
Florida Gulf Coast Univ.
Florida International Univ.
Florida State Univ.
George Washington Univ. (DC)
Georgia Southern Univ.
Georgia State Univ.
Grand Valley State Univ. (MI)
Green Mountain Coll. (VT)
Harris-Stowe State Univ. (MO)
Hawaii Pacific Univ.
Howard Univ. (DC)
Husson Univ. (ME)
Indiana Institute of Technology
Indiana Univ. of Pennsylvania
Indiana Univ.-Purdue Univ.–Fort Wayne
Indiana Univ.-Purdue Univ.–Indianapolis
Iowa State Univ.
James Madison Univ. (VA)

Johnson and Wales Univ. (RI)
Johnson State Coll. (VT)
Kansas State Univ.
Kendall Coll. (IL)
Keuka Coll. (NY)
Lakeland Coll. (WI)
Lasell Coll. (MA)
Lewis-Clark State Coll. (ID)
Lindenwood Univ. (MO)
Lynn Univ. (FL)
Madonna Univ. (MI)
Mansfield Univ. of Pennsylvania
Marywood Univ. (PA)
Mercyhurst Coll. (PA)
Methodist Univ. (NC)
Metropolitan State Coll. of Denver
Michigan State Univ.
Missouri State Univ.
Morgan State Univ. (MD)
Mount Ida Coll. (MA)
Mountain State Univ. (WV)
New Mexico State Univ.
New York Institute of Technology
Niagara Univ. (NY)
North Carolina Central Univ.
North Dakota State Univ.
Northeastern State Univ. (OK)
Northern Arizona Univ.
Northern Michigan Univ.
Northwestern State Univ. of
    Louisiana
Northwood Univ. (MI)
Ohio State Univ.–Columbus
Oklahoma State Univ.
Pace Univ. (NY)
Pennsylvania State Univ.–Univ. Park
Purdue Univ.–West Lafayette (IN)
Robert Morris Univ. (PA)
Rochester Institute of Technology
    (NY)
Roosevelt Univ. (IL)
Rutgers, the State Univ. of New
    Jersey–Camden
San Diego State Univ.
San Francisco State Univ.
Seton Hill Univ. (PA)
Sierra Nevada Coll. (NV)
South Dakota State Univ.
Southern New Hampshire Univ.
Southern Utah Univ.
Southwest Minnesota State Univ.
St. John's Univ. (NY)
St. Leo Univ. (FL)
St. Thomas Univ. (FL)
Stephen F. Austin State Univ. (TX)
SUNY–Plattsburgh
Tennessee State Univ.
Texas A&M International Univ.
Texas A&M Univ.–Coll. Station
Texas Tech Univ.
Thomas Edison State Coll. (NJ)
Tiffin Univ. (OH)
Tougaloo Coll. (MS)
Tuskegee Univ. (AL)
Univ. of Akron (OH)
Univ. of Alabama
Univ. of Central Florida
Univ. of Central Missouri
Univ. of Central Oklahoma
Univ. of Delaware
Univ. of Denver

Univ. of Findlay (OH)
Univ. of Hawaii–Manoa
Univ. of Houston
Univ. of Illinois–Urbana-Champaign
Univ. of Kentucky
Univ. of Louisiana–Lafayette
Univ. of Maryland–Eastern Shore
Univ. of Massachusetts–Amherst
Univ. of Memphis
Univ. of Minnesota–Crookston
Univ. of Missouri
Univ. of Nebraska–Lincoln
Univ. of Nevada–Las Vegas
Univ. of New Hampshire
Univ. of New Haven (CT)
Univ. of New Orleans
Univ. of North Carolina–
    Greensboro
Univ. of North Texas
Univ. of Pittsburgh–Bradford
Univ. of San Francisco
Univ. of South Carolina
Univ. of South Florida
Univ. of Southern Mississippi
Univ. of Tennessee
Univ. of Texas–San Antonio
Univ. of West Florida
Univ. of Wisconsin–Stout
Utah Valley Univ.
Virginia State Univ.
Virginia Tech
Viterbo Univ. (WI)
Washington State Univ.
Webber International Univ. (FL)
Western Carolina Univ. (NC)
Western Kentucky Univ.
Widener Univ. (PA)
Wiley Coll. (TX)
Youngstown State Univ. (OH)

Housing and Human Environments

CUNY–New York City Coll. of
    Technology
Eastern Kentucky Univ.
Eastern Michigan Univ.
Iowa State Univ.
Lasell Coll. (MA)
Miami Univ.–Oxford (OH)
Missouri State Univ.
Ohio Univ.
Oklahoma State Univ.
Oregon State Univ.
Univ. of Akron (OH)
Univ. of Arkansas
Univ. of Georgia
Univ. of Minnesota–Twin Cities
Univ. of Missouri
Univ. of Nevada–Reno
Utah State Univ.

Human Development, Family Studies, and Related Services

Abilene Christian Univ. (TX)
Alcorn State Univ. (MS)
Alderson-Broaddus Coll. (WV)
Anderson Univ. (IN)
Andrews Univ. (MI)

Appalachian State Univ. (NC)
Auburn Univ. (AL)
Baker Coll. of Flint (MI)
Ball State Univ. (IN)
Baylor Univ. (TX)
Bennington Coll. (VT)
Boston Coll.
Bowling Green State Univ. (OH)
California State Univ.–Bakersfield
California State Univ.–East Bay
California State Univ.–Long Beach
California State Univ.–San
    Bernardino
California State Univ.–San Marcos
Carson-Newman Coll. (TN)
Central Michigan Univ.
Chestnut Hill Coll. (PA)
Coll. of the Ozarks (MO)
Colorado State Univ.
Columbia Coll. (SC)
Concordia Univ. (NE)
Concordia Univ. (MI)
Concordia Univ.–St. Paul (MN)
Connecticut Coll.
Cornell Univ. (NY)
Cornerstone Univ. (MI)
CUNY–York Coll.
DeSales Univ. (PA)
East Carolina Univ. (NC)
East Tennessee State Univ.
Eastern Kentucky Univ.
Eastern Michigan Univ.
Eastern Washington Univ.
Ferris State Univ. (MI)
Florida State Univ.
Freed-Hardeman Univ. (TN)
Gallaudet Univ. (DC)
Georgia Southern Univ.
Georgia State Univ.
Hope International Univ. (CA)
Houston Baptist Univ.
Howard Univ. (DC)
Indiana State Univ.
Indiana Univ. of Pennsylvania
Iowa State Univ.
John Brown Univ. (AR)
Kansas State Univ.
Kent State Univ. (OH)
Kentucky State Univ.
Lasell Coll. (MA)
Lesley Univ. (MA)
Lewis-Clark State Coll. (ID)
Liberty Univ. (VA)
Lipscomb Univ. (TN)
Louisiana Tech Univ.
Lubbock Christian Univ. (TX)
Madonna Univ. (MI)
Mayville State Univ. (ND)
Meredith Coll. (NC)
Messiah Coll. (PA)
Miami Univ.–Oxford (OH)
Michigan State Univ.
Mills Coll. (CA)
Mississippi Univ. for Women
Missouri Baptist Univ.
Missouri State Univ.
Mitchell Coll. (CT)
Murray State Univ. (KY)
New Mexico State Univ.
North Carolina A&T State Univ.
North Dakota State Univ.

Northern Illinois Univ.
Northern Michigan Univ.
Northwest Missouri State Univ.
Oakwood Univ. (AL)
Ohio State Univ.–Columbus
Ohio Univ.
Oklahoma Baptist Univ.
Oklahoma Christian Univ.
Oklahoma State Univ.
Oregon State Univ.
Pennsylvania State Univ.–Univ. Park
Point Loma Nazarene Univ. (CA)
Prescott Coll. (AZ)
Purdue Univ.–Calumet (IN)
Purdue Univ.–West Lafayette (IN)
Quinnipiac Univ. (CT)
Samford Univ. (AL)
San Diego State Univ.
Seattle Pacific Univ.
Seton Hill Univ. (PA)
Sojourner-Douglass Coll. (MD)
South Dakota State Univ.
Southern Adventist Univ. (TN)
Southern Nazarene Univ. (OK)
Southern New Hampshire Univ.
Spring Arbor Univ. (MI)
St. Bonaventure Univ. (NY)
St. Joseph Coll. (CT)
St. Joseph's Coll. New York
St. Olaf Coll. (MN)
Stephen F. Austin State Univ. (TX)
Stevenson Univ. (MD)
SUNY Coll. of Agriculture and
    Technology–Cobleskill
SUNY Coll.–Oneonta
SUNY–Plattsburgh
Syracuse Univ. (NY)
Texas State Univ.–San Marcos
Texas Tech Univ.
Texas Woman's Univ.
Thomas Edison State Coll. (NJ)
Univ. of Akron (OH)
Univ. of Alabama
Univ. of Alaska–Anchorage
Univ. of Alaska–Fairbanks
Univ. of Arizona
Univ. of Arkansas
Univ. of Arkansas–Pine Bluff
Univ. of California–Davis
Univ. of California–San Diego
Univ. of Central Oklahoma
Univ. of Connecticut
Univ. of Delaware
Univ. of Florida
Univ. of Georgia
Univ. of Houston
Univ. of Illinois–Urbana-Champaign
Univ. of Kentucky
Univ. of La Verne (CA)
Univ. of Louisiana–Lafayette
Univ. of Maine
Univ. of Maryland–Coll. Park
Univ. of Missouri
Univ. of Nebraska–Lincoln
Univ. of Nevada–Reno
Univ. of New Hampshire
Univ. of New Mexico
Univ. of North Carolina–Charlotte
Univ. of North Carolina–
    Greensboro
Univ. of North Texas

Univ. of Northern Colorado
Univ. of Northern Iowa
Univ. of Rhode Island
Univ. of Scranton (PA)
Univ. of Southern Mississippi
Univ. of St. Mary (KS)
Univ. of Tennessee
Univ. of Texas of the Permian Basin
Univ. of Texas–Arlington
Univ. of Texas–Austin
Univ. of the Incarnate Word (TX)
Univ. of Utah
Univ. of Vermont
Univ. of Wisconsin–Madison
Univ. of Wisconsin–Stout
Utah State Univ.
Valparaiso Univ. (IN)
Virginia Tech
Warner Pacific Coll. (OR)
Washington State Univ.
Wayne State Coll. (NE)
Wayne State Univ. (MI)
Weber State Univ. (UT)
West Virginia Univ.
Western Michigan Univ.
Western Washington Univ.
Wheelock Coll. (MA)
Youngstown State Univ. (OH)

Human Resources Management and Services

Arcadia Univ. (PA)
Bellevue Univ. (NE)
California State Polytechnic Univ.–
    Pomona
Converse Coll. (SC)
Gwynedd-Mercy Coll. (PA)
Huntington Univ. (IN)
Lewis Univ. (IL)
New School (NY)
North Park Univ. (IL)
Northeastern Illinois Univ.
Oakland City Univ. (IN)
Otterbein Coll. (OH)
St. Mary-of-the-Woods Coll. (IN)
Texas A&M Univ.–Commerce
Thomas Coll. (ME)
Trinity International Univ. (IL)
Univ. of Central Oklahoma
Wright State Univ. (OH)
York Coll. (NE)

Human Services

Alaska Pacific Univ.
Anna Maria Coll. (MA)
Bard Coll. at Simon's Rock (MA)
Beacon Coll. (FL)
Bellevue Univ. (NE)
Bethel Coll. (TN)
Burlington Coll. (VT)
California State Univ.–Fullerton
California State Univ.–Monterey Bay
California State Univ.–Sacramento
California State Univ.–San
    Bernardino
Calumet Coll. of St. Joseph (IN)
Cazenovia Coll. (NY)
Central Washington Univ.

Chestnut Hill Coll. (PA)
Coll. of Notre Dame of Maryland
Coll. of St. Joseph (VT)
Coll. of St. Mary (NE)
Columbia Coll. (MO)
Concordia Univ.–St. Paul (MN)
Coppin State Univ. (MD)
CUNY–New York City Coll. of
  Technology
Dakota Wesleyan Univ. (SD)
East Central Univ. (OK)
Elmhurst Coll. (IL)
Elon Univ. (NC)
Fitchburg State Coll. (MA)
Florida Gulf Coast Univ.
Fontbonne Univ. (MO)
Geneva Coll. (PA)
Grand View Univ. (IA)
Gwynedd-Mercy Coll. (PA)
Hannibal-LaGrange Coll. (MO)
Hawaii Pacific Univ.
High Point Univ. (NC)
Holy Names Univ. (CA)
Iowa Wesleyan Coll.
Judson Univ. (IL)
Kennesaw State Univ. (GA)
Kentucky Wesleyan Coll.
La Roche Coll. (PA)
Lake Superior State Univ. (MI)
Lasell Coll. (MA)
Lenoir-Rhyne Univ. (NC)
Lesley Univ. (MA)
Lewis Univ. (IL)
Lincoln Univ. (PA)
Lindsey Wilson Coll. (KY)
Loyola Univ. Chicago
Macon State Coll. (GA)
Martin Methodist Coll. (TN)
Medaille Coll. (NY)
Millikin Univ. (IL)
Missouri Baptist Univ.
Missouri Valley Coll.
Montreat Coll. (NC)
Mount Ida Coll. (MA)
Mount St. Mary Coll. (NY)
Northeastern Univ. (MA)
Northwest Christian Univ. (OR)
Notre Dame de Namur Univ. (CA)
Pfeiffer Univ. (NC)
Post Univ. (CT)
Quincy Univ. (IL)
Seton Hill Univ. (PA)
Sojourner-Douglass Coll. (MD)
Southern Wesleyan Univ. (SC)
Southwest Baptist Univ. (MO)
Spelman Coll. (GA)
St. John's Univ. (NY)
St. Mary's Univ. of Minnesota
St. Mary-of-the-Woods Coll. (IN)
Tennessee Wesleyan Coll.
Thomas Edison State Coll. (NJ)
Tiffin Univ. (OH)
Touro Coll. (NY)
Univ. of Baltimore (MD)
Univ. of Detroit Mercy
Univ. of Maine–Presque Isle
Univ. of Massachusetts–Boston
Univ. of Minnesota–Morris
Univ. of Northern Colorado
Univ. of Oregon
Univ. of Tennessee–Chattanooga

Univ. of the Southwest (NM)
Univ. of Wisconsin–Oshkosh
Villanova Univ. (PA)
Waynesburg Univ. (PA)
William Woods Univ. (MO)
Wingate Univ. (NC)

Industrial and Organizational Psychology

Abilene Christian Univ. (TX)
Albright Coll. (PA)
Alvernia Univ. (PA)
Averett Univ. (VA)
Bloomfield Coll. (NJ)
Bridgewater State Coll. (MA)
Coll. of Santa Fe (NM)
Corban Univ. (OR)
CUNY–Baruch Coll.
East Texas Baptist Univ.
Fitchburg State Coll. (MA)
Georgia Institute of Technology
Holy Family Univ. (PA)
Ithaca Coll. (NY)
Lincoln Univ. (PA)
Madonna Univ. (MI)
Marymount Univ. (VA)
Maryville Univ. of St. Louis (MO)
Marywood Univ. (PA)
Middle Tennessee State Univ.
Missouri Univ. of Science &
  Technology
Morningside Coll. (IA)
Nebraska Wesleyan Univ.
Northwest Missouri State Univ.
Pepperdine Univ. (CA)
Point Loma Nazarene Univ. (CA)
Southern Adventist Univ. (TN)
St. Joseph's Univ. (PA)
St. Mary's Coll. of California
St. Xavier Univ. (IL)
Texas Wesleyan Univ.
Tiffin Univ. (OH)
Washington Univ. in St. Louis

Industrial Engineering

Andrews Univ. (MI)
Arizona State Univ.
Auburn Univ. (AL)
Bethel Coll. (IN)
Binghamton Univ.–SUNY
Bradley Univ. (IL)
California Polytechnic State Univ.–
  San Luis Obispo
California State Polytechnic Univ.–
  Pomona
California State Univ.–Fresno
California State Univ.–Long Beach
Cleveland State Univ.
Colorado State Univ.–Pueblo
Columbia Univ. (NY)
Elizabethtown Coll. (PA)
Florida A&M Univ.
Florida State Univ.
Gannon Univ. (PA)
George Washington Univ. (DC)
Georgia Institute of Technology
Hofstra Univ. (NY)
Indiana Institute of Technology

Iowa State Univ.
Kansas State Univ.
Kent State Univ. (OH)
Kettering Univ. (MI)
Lamar Univ. (TX)
Lehigh Univ. (PA)
Louisiana State Univ.–Baton Rouge
Louisiana Tech Univ.
Milwaukee School of Engineering
Mississippi State Univ.
Missouri Univ. of Science &
  Technology
Montana State Univ.
Morgan State Univ. (MD)
New Jersey Institute of Technology
New Mexico State Univ.
North Carolina A&T State Univ.
North Carolina State Univ.–Raleigh
North Dakota State Univ.
Northeastern Univ. (MA)
Northern Illinois Univ.
Northern Michigan Univ.
Northwestern Univ. (IL)
Ohio State Univ.–Columbus
Ohio Univ.
Oklahoma State Univ.
Oregon State Univ.
Pennsylvania State Univ.–Univ. Park
Philadelphia Univ.
Rensselaer Polytechnic Institute
  (NY)
Rochester Institute of Technology
  (NY)
Roosevelt Univ. (IL)
Rutgers, the State Univ. of New
  Jersey–New Brunswick
San Jose State Univ. (CA)
South Dakota School of Mines and
  Technology
Southern Illinois Univ.–Edwardsville
St. Ambrose Univ. (IA)
St. Mary's Univ. of San Antonio
  (TX)
Stanford Univ. (CA)
Tennessee Technological Univ.
Texas A&M Univ.–Coll. Station
Texas State Univ.–San Marcos
Texas Tech Univ.
Trine Univ. (IN)
Univ. at Buffalo–SUNY
Univ. of Alabama–Huntsville
Univ. of Alaska–Fairbanks
Univ. of Arizona
Univ. of Arkansas
Univ. of Central Florida
Univ. of Connecticut
Univ. of Houston
Univ. of Illinois–Chicago
Univ. of Illinois–Urbana-Champaign
Univ. of Iowa
Univ. of Louisville (KY)
Univ. of Massachusetts–Amherst
Univ. of Miami (FL)
Univ. of Michigan–Ann Arbor
Univ. of Michigan–Dearborn
Univ. of Minnesota–Crookston
Univ. of Minnesota–Duluth
Univ. of Minnesota–Twin Cities
Univ. of Missouri
Univ. of Nebraska–Lincoln
Univ. of Oklahoma

Univ. of Pittsburgh
Univ. of Rhode Island
Univ. of San Diego
Univ. of South Florida
Univ. of Southern California
Univ. of Southern Maine
Univ. of Tennessee
Univ. of Texas–Arlington
Univ. of Texas–El Paso
Univ. of Texas–Pan American
Univ. of Toledo (OH)
Univ. of Vermont
Univ. of Washington
Univ. of Wisconsin–Madison
Univ. of Wisconsin–Platteville
Utah State Univ.
Virginia Tech
Washington State Univ.
Wayne State Univ. (MI)
West Virginia Univ.
Western Michigan Univ.
Western New England Coll. (MA)
Wichita State Univ. (KS)
Worcester Polytechnic Institute
  (MA)
Youngstown State Univ. (OH)

Industrial Production Technologies/ Technicians

Alabama Agricultural and
  Mechanical Univ.
Alcorn State Univ. (MS)
Andrews Univ. (MI)
Baker Coll. of Flint (MI)
Ball State Univ. (IN)
Bemidji State Univ. (MN)
Berea Coll. (KY)
Black Hills State Univ. (SD)
Bowling Green State Univ. (OH)
Bradley Univ. (IL)
Buffalo State Coll.–SUNY
California State Univ.–Long Beach
California Univ. of Pennsylvania
Central Connecticut State Univ.
Central Michigan Univ.
Central State Univ. (OH)
Central Washington Univ.
Chadron State Coll. (NE)
Clarion Univ. of Pennsylvania
Clemson Univ. (SC)
East Carolina Univ. (NC)
Eastern Illinois Univ.
Eastern Kentucky Univ.
Eastern Michigan Univ.
Elizabeth City State Univ. (NC)
Farmingdale State Coll.–SUNY
Ferris State Univ. (MI)
Fitchburg State Coll. (MA)
Florida A&M Univ.
Georgia Southern Univ.
Humboldt State Univ. (CA)
Illinois State Univ.
Indiana State Univ.
Indiana Univ.–South Bend
Indiana Univ.–Purdue Univ.–Fort
  Wayne
Jackson State Univ. (MS)
Jacksonville State Univ. (AL)
Kean Univ. (NJ)

Lamar Univ. (TX)
Lawrence Technological Univ. (MI)
LeTourneau Univ. (TX)
Lewis-Clark State Coll. (ID)
Metropolitan State Coll. of Denver
Michigan Technological Univ.
Middle Tennessee State Univ.
Midwestern State Univ. (TX)
Millersville Univ. of Pennsylvania
Minnesota State Univ.–Mankato
Minnesota State Univ.–Moorhead
Mississippi State Univ.
Mississippi Valley State Univ.
Missouri State Univ.
Montana State Univ.–Northern
Morehead State Univ. (KY)
Murray State Univ. (KY)
North Carolina A&T State Univ.
Northern Illinois Univ.
Northern Kentucky Univ.
Northern Michigan Univ.
Northwest Missouri State Univ.
Northwestern State Univ. of
  Louisiana
Ohio Northern Univ.
Ohio Univ.
Oklahoma Panhandle State Univ.
Oregon Institute of Technology
Pennsylvania Coll. of Technology
Pittsburg State Univ. (KS)
Prairie View A&M Univ. (TX)
Purdue Univ.–Calumet (IN)
Purdue Univ.–North Central (IN)
Purdue Univ.–West Lafayette (IN)
Rochester Institute of Technology
  (NY)
Saginaw Valley State Univ. (MI)
Sam Houston State Univ. (TX)
Shawnee State Univ. (OH)
South Carolina State Univ.
South Dakota State Univ.
Southeast Missouri State Univ.
Southeastern Louisiana Univ.
Southern Arkansas Univ.
Southern Illinois Univ.–Carbondale
Southern Polytechnic State Univ.
  (GA)
Southern Univ.–New Orleans
Southern Utah Univ.
Southwestern Oklahoma State
  Univ.
St. Mary's Univ. of Minnesota
Sul Ross State Univ. (TX)
SUNY Coll. of Technology–Alfred
SUNY Institute of Technology–
  Utica/Rome
Tarleton State Univ. (TX)
Tennessee Technological Univ.
Texas A&M Univ.–Coll. Station
Texas A&M Univ.–Commerce
Texas A&M Univ.–Kingsville
Texas State Univ.–San Marcos
Thomas Edison State Coll. (NJ)
Univ. of Akron (OH)
Univ. of Arkansas–Pine Bluff
Univ. of Central Missouri
Univ. of Dayton (OH)
Univ. of Houston
Univ. of Louisiana–Lafayette
Univ. of Massachusetts–Lowell
Univ. of Memphis

Univ. of Minnesota–Crookston
Univ. of North Carolina–Charlotte
Univ. of North Dakota
Univ. of North Texas
Univ. of Northern Iowa
Univ. of Rio Grande (OH)
Univ. of Southern Mississippi
Univ. of Texas of the Permian Basin
Univ. of Texas–Brownsville
Univ. of Texas–Tyler
Univ. of West Alabama
Univ. of Wisconsin–Platteville
Univ. of Wisconsin–Stout
Utah State Univ.
Valdosta State Univ. (GA)
Wayne State Coll. (NE)
Wayne State Univ. (MI)
Weber State Univ. (UT)
West Texas A&M Univ.
Western Carolina Univ. (NC)
Western Illinois Univ.
Western Kentucky Univ.
Western Washington Univ.
William Penn Univ. (IA)

Information Science/ Studies

Adelphi Univ. (NY)
Alabama State Univ.
Albany State Univ. (GA)
Albright Coll. (PA)
American Univ. (DC)
Anderson Univ. (IN)
Armstrong Atlantic State Univ. (GA)
Averett Univ. (VA)
Babson Coll. (MA)
Baker Univ. (KS)
Barry Univ. (FL)
Bemidji State Univ. (MN)
Benedictine Univ. (IL)
Bethune-Cookman Univ. (FL)
Binghamton Univ.–SUNY
Bluffton Univ. (OH)
Boise State Univ. (ID)
Bradley Univ. (IL)
Brewton-Parker Coll. (GA)
Brigham Young Univ.–Hawaii
Buffalo State Coll.–SUNY
Butler Univ. (IN)
California State Univ.–Fullerton
California State Univ.–Sacramento
Carlow Univ. (PA)
Carnegie Mellon Univ. (PA)
Carroll Univ. (WI)
Cedar Crest Coll. (PA)
Central Coll. (IA)
Central Michigan Univ.
Chadron State Coll. (NE)
Christopher Newport Univ. (VA)
Clarion Univ. of Pennsylvania
Clayton State Univ. (GA)
Clearwater Christian Coll. (FL)
Coll. of Charleston (SC)
Coll. of Notre Dame of Maryland
Colorado State Univ.
Colorado State Univ.–Pueblo
Concord Univ. (WV)
CUNY–Baruch Coll.
CUNY–Coll. of Staten Island
CUNY–Lehman Coll.

CUNY–New York City Coll. of Technology
Dakota State Univ. (SD)
Davenport Univ. (MI)
Davis and Elkins Coll. (WV)
Delaware State Univ.
DePaul Univ. (IL)
DeSales Univ. (PA)
Dominican Univ. (IL)
Dordt Coll. (IA)
Drexel Univ. (PA)
Eastern Connecticut State Univ.
Eastern Kentucky Univ.
Eastern Michigan Univ.
Elizabethtown Coll. (PA)
Elmhurst Coll. (IL)
Elmira Coll. (NY)
Emporia State Univ. (KS)
Excelsior Coll. (NY)
Ferrum Coll. (VA)
Florida Institute of Technology
Fordham Univ. (NY)
Fort Valley State Univ. (GA)
Franklin Pierce Univ. (NH)
Frostburg State Univ. (MD)
Gallaudet Univ. (DC)
George Washington Univ. (DC)
Georgia Southern Univ.
Golden Gate Univ. (CA)
Grambling State Univ. (LA)
Grand Valley State Univ. (MI)
Guilford Coll. (NC)
Harris-Stowe State Univ. (MO)
High Point Univ. (NC)
Howard Payne Univ. (TX)
Idaho State Univ.
Immaculata Univ. (PA)
Indiana Univ.-Purdue Univ.–Fort Wayne
Jacksonville Univ. (FL)
James Madison Univ. (VA)
John Carroll Univ. (OH)
Johns Hopkins Univ. (MD)
Johnson and Wales Univ. (RI)
Kansas State Univ.
Kennesaw State Univ. (GA)
Lehigh Univ. (PA)
Lenoir-Rhyne Univ. (NC)
LeTourneau Univ. (TX)
Lincoln Univ. (MO)
Mansfield Univ. of Pennsylvania
Marist Coll. (NY)
Marymount Univ. (VA)
McKendree Univ. (IL)
Messiah Coll. (PA)
Minnesota State Univ.–Mankato
Minot State Univ. (ND)
Missouri Univ. of Science & Technology
Missouri Western State Univ.
Molloy Coll. (NY)
Murray State Univ. (KY)
Nazareth Coll. (NY)
Nebraska Wesleyan Univ.
New Jersey Institute of Technology
New Mexico Highlands Univ.
Niagara Univ. (NY)
North Carolina Central Univ.
North Georgia Coll. and State Univ.
Northeastern Univ. (MA)
Northern Kentucky Univ.

Northwestern Coll. (IA)
Northwestern State Univ. of Louisiana
Northwestern Univ. (IL)
Norwich Univ. (VT)
Oakwood Univ. (AL)
Ohio Dominican Univ.
Oklahoma Baptist Univ.
Oklahoma Christian Univ.
Oklahoma Wesleyan Univ.
Olivet Nazarene Univ. (IL)
Pace Univ. (NY)
Peirce Coll. (PA)
Pennsylvania State Univ.–Univ. Park
Philadelphia Univ.
Polytechnic Institute of New York Univ. (NY)
Prairie View A&M Univ. (TX)
Queens Univ. of Charlotte (NC)
Quincy Univ. (IL)
Quinnipiac Univ. (CT)
Radford Univ. (VA)
Ramapo Coll. of New Jersey
Regis Coll. (MA)
Regis Univ. (CO)
Richard Stockton Coll. of New Jersey
Roanoke Coll. (VA)
Robert Morris Univ. (PA)
Rochester Institute of Technology (NY)
Rutgers, the State Univ. of New Jersey–New Brunswick
Rutgers, the State Univ. of New Jersey–Newark
Salisbury Univ. (MD)
Salve Regina Univ. (RI)
San Diego State Univ.
Savannah State Univ. (GA)
Silver Lake Coll. (WI)
Southern Illinois Univ.–Carbondale
Southern Methodist Univ. (TX)
Southern Nazarene Univ. (OK)
Southern Utah Univ.
St. Ambrose Univ. (IA)
St. Catherine Univ. (MN)
St. Francis Univ. (PA)
St. Joseph's Coll. New York
St. Joseph's Univ. (PA)
St. Mary's Univ. of Minnesota
St. Michael's Coll. (VT)
St. Peter's Coll. (NJ)
Suffolk Univ. (MA)
SUNY Coll.–Old Westbury
SUNY Institute of Technology–Utica/Rome
SUNY–Oswego
SUNY–Stony Brook
Susquehanna Univ. (PA)
Syracuse Univ. (NY)
Taylor Univ. (IN)
Texas A&M Univ.–Commerce
Texas Christian Univ.
Texas Lutheran Univ.
Tiffin Univ. (OH)
Towson Univ. (MD)
Trinity Christian Coll. (IL)
Univ. at Albany–SUNY
Univ. at Buffalo–SUNY
Univ. of Arkansas–Little Rock
Univ. of California–Irvine

Univ. of California–Riverside
Univ. of Dayton (OH)
Univ. of Hartford (CT)
Univ. of Houston
Univ. of Illinois–Chicago
Univ. of Maine
Univ. of Mary (ND)
Univ. of Mary Hardin-Baylor (TX)
Univ. of Maryland–Baltimore County
Univ. of Maryland–Coll. Park
Univ. of Maryland–Univ. Coll.
Univ. of Massachusetts–Lowell
Univ. of Miami (FL)
Univ. of Michigan–Flint
Univ. of Mount Union (OH)
Univ. of New Haven (CT)
Univ. of North Carolina–Chapel Hill
Univ. of North Texas
Univ. of Oklahoma
Univ. of Pittsburgh
Univ. of Redlands (CA)
Univ. of San Francisco
Univ. of Scranton (PA)
Univ. of South Florida
Univ. of Texas of the Permian Basin
Univ. of Texas–Brownsville
Univ. of the District of Columbia
Univ. of the Pacific (CA)
Univ. of Toledo (OH)
Univ. of Tulsa (OK)
Urbana Univ. (OH)
Utah State Univ.
Valdosta State Univ. (GA)
Villanova Univ. (PA)
Virginia Commonwealth Univ.
Washington Adventist Univ. (MD)
Wayne State Coll. (NE)
Wayne State Univ. (MI)
Weber State Univ. (UT)
Western New England Coll. (MA)
Western Oregon Univ.
Westminster Coll. (PA)
Widener Univ. (PA)
Wilkes Univ. (PA)
William Jewell Coll. (MO)
York Coll. of Pennsylvania

Insurance

Appalachian State Univ. (NC)
Baylor Univ. (TX)
Bradley Univ. (IL)
California State Univ.–Sacramento
Delta State Univ. (MS)
Eastern Kentucky Univ.
Excelsior Coll. (NY)
Florida International Univ.
Florida State Univ.
Gannon Univ. (PA)
Georgia State Univ.
Howard Univ. (DC)
Illinois State Univ.
Illinois Wesleyan Univ.
Indiana State Univ.
Martin Univ. (IN)
Mississippi State Univ.
Missouri State Univ.
Ohio State Univ.–Columbus
Olivet Coll. (MI)
Roosevelt Univ. (IL)

St. John's Univ. (NY)
Temple Univ. (PA)
Univ. of Central Arkansas
Univ. of Connecticut
Univ. of Florida
Univ. of Georgia
Univ. of Hartford (CT)
Univ. of Illinois–Urbana-Champaign
Univ. of Louisiana–Lafayette
Univ. of Minnesota–Twin Cities
Univ. of Mississippi
Univ. of North Texas
Univ. of Pennsylvania
Univ. of South Carolina
Univ. of Wisconsin–Madison
Washington State Univ.

Intercultural/ Multicultural and Diversity Studies

Blackburn Coll. (IL)
Brigham Young Univ.–Hawaii
California Baptist Univ.
Covenant Coll. (GA)
Elmhurst Coll. (IL)
Evergreen State Coll. (WA)
Hampshire Coll. (MA)
Indiana Wesleyan Univ.
Ithaca Coll. (NY)
Johns Hopkins Univ. (MD)
Judson Univ. (IL)
Lawrence Univ. (WI)
Macalester Coll. (MN)
Nyack Coll. (NY)
St. Catherine Univ. (MN)
Univ. of San Diego
Wofford Coll. (SC)

Interior Architecture

Arizona State Univ.
Auburn Univ. (AL)
Boston Architectural Coll.
Bowling Green State Univ. (OH)
California State Univ.–Sacramento
Central Michigan Univ.
Chatham Univ. (PA)
Cooper Union (NY)
Indiana State Univ.
Kansas State Univ.
La Roche Coll. (PA)
Lawrence Technological Univ. (MI)
Louisiana State Univ.–Baton Rouge
Louisiana Tech Univ.
Miami Univ.–Oxford (OH)
Philadelphia Univ.
Sam Houston State Univ. (TX)
School of the Art Institute of Chicago
Stephen F. Austin State Univ. (TX)
Syracuse Univ. (NY)
Texas Tech Univ.
Univ. of Central Missouri
Univ. of Houston
Univ. of Louisiana–Lafayette
Univ. of Mississippi
Univ. of Nebraska–Lincoln
Univ. of Nevada–Las Vegas
Univ. of New Haven (CT)
Univ. of North Texas

Univ. of Oregon
Univ. of Southern Mississippi
Univ. of Texas–San Antonio
Woodbury Univ. (CA)

International Agriculture

Bridgewater Coll. (VA)
California State Polytechnic Univ.–
 Pomona
Colgate Univ. (NY)
Cornell Univ. (NY)
Eastern Mennonite Univ. (VA)
Iona Coll. (NY)
Iowa State Univ.
Lewis Univ. (IL)
Southern Connecticut State Univ.
Tarleton State Univ. (TX)
Univ. of California–Davis
Univ. of Illinois–Urbana-Champaign
Univ. of Memphis
Univ. of Minnesota–Morris
Univ. of Pittsburgh–Bradford
Univ. of Southern Maine
Univ. of Wisconsin–Superior
Utah State Univ.
Wesleyan Univ. (CT)
Wittenberg Univ. (OH)

International Business

Adrian Coll. (MI)
Alma Coll. (MI)
Alverno Coll. (WI)
American Univ. (DC)
Angelo State Univ. (TX)
Appalachian State Univ. (NC)
Aquinas Coll. (MI)
Arkansas State Univ.–Jonesboro
Assumption Coll. (MA)
Auburn Univ. (AL)
Avila Univ. (MO)
Azusa Pacific Univ. (CA)
Babson Coll. (MA)
Baker Univ. (KS)
Barry Univ. (FL)
Baylor Univ. (TX)
Bellarmine Univ. (KY)
Bellevue Univ. (NE)
Belmont Abbey Coll. (NC)
Benedictine Univ. (IL)
Bethel Coll. (IN)
Bethune-Cookman Univ. (FL)
Boise State Univ. (ID)
Bowling Green State Univ. (OH)
Bradley Univ. (IL)
Bridgewater State Coll. (MA)
Brigham Young Univ.–Hawaii
Bryant Univ. (RI)
Buena Vista Univ. (IA)
Butler Univ. (IN)
Caldwell Coll. (NJ)
California State Polytechnic Univ.–
 Pomona
California State Univ.–Fullerton
California State Univ.–Long Beach
California State Univ.–Sacramento
Campbell Univ. (NC)
Canisius Coll. (NY)
Cardinal Stritch Univ. (WI)
Carson-Newman Coll. (TN)

Catholic Univ. of America (DC)
Cedarville Univ. (OH)
Central Coll. (IA)
Central Connecticut State Univ.
Central Methodist Univ. (MO)
Central Michigan Univ.
Champlain Coll. (VT)
Chatham Univ. (PA)
Chestnut Hill Coll. (PA)
Clemson Univ. (SC)
Coll. at Brockport–SUNY
Coll. of Charleston (SC)
Coll. of Idaho (ID)
Coll. of Santa Fe (NM)
Coll. of the Ozarks (MO)
Columbia Coll. (MO)
Concordia Univ. Wisconsin
Converse Coll. (SC)
Cornell Coll. (IA)
Creighton Univ. (NE)
CUNY–Queens Coll.
D'Youville Coll. (NY)
Davenport Univ. (MI)
Davis and Elkins Coll. (WV)
Dickinson Coll. (PA)
Dominican Coll. (NY)
Dominican Univ. (IL)
Dowling Coll. (NY)
Drake Univ. (IA)
Drury Univ. (MO)
Duquesne Univ. (PA)
Eastern Mennonite Univ. (VA)
Eastern Michigan Univ.
Eastern Univ. (PA)
Eckerd Coll. (FL)
Elizabethtown Coll. (PA)
Elmhurst Coll. (IL)
Emory and Henry Coll. (VA)
Excelsior Coll. (NY)
Fashion Institute of Technology
 (NY)
Ferris State Univ. (MI)
Fitchburg State Coll. (MA)
Florida Atlantic Univ.
Florida International Univ.
Florida Southern Coll.
Florida State Univ.
Fort Lewis Coll. (CO)
Fresno Pacific Univ. (CA)
Gannon Univ. (PA)
George Washington Univ. (DC)
Georgetown Univ. (DC)
Georgia Coll. & State Univ.
Golden Gate Univ. (CA)
Goldey Beacom Coll. (DE)
Grace Coll. and Seminary (IN)
Graceland Univ. (IA)
Grand Valley State Univ. (MI)
Gustavus Adolphus Coll. (MN)
Gwynedd-Mercy Coll. (PA)
Hamline Univ. (MN)
Harding Univ. (AR)
Hawaii Pacific Univ.
High Point Univ. (NC)
Hillsdale Coll. (MI)
Hofstra Univ. (NY)
Holy Family Univ. (PA)
Howard Univ. (DC)
Husson Univ. (ME)
Illinois State Univ.
Illinois Wesleyan Univ.

Indiana Univ. of Pennsylvania
Iona Coll. (NY)
Iowa State Univ.
Jacksonville Univ. (FL)
James Madison Univ. (VA)
Jamestown Coll. (ND)
John Brown Univ. (AR)
Johnson and Wales Univ. (RI)
Juniata Coll. (PA)
King's Coll. (PA)
Kutztown Univ. of Pennsylvania
La Roche Coll. (PA)
Lake Erie Coll. (OH)
Lake Superior State Univ. (MI)
Lakeland Coll. (WI)
Lambuth Univ. (TN)
Lasell Coll. (MA)
Lenoir-Rhyne Univ. (NC)
LeTourneau Univ. (TX)
Lindenwood Univ. (MO)
Linfield Coll. (OR)
Long Island Univ.–C.W. Post
 Campus (NY)
Louisiana State Univ.–Baton Rouge
Loyola Univ. Chicago
Loyola Univ. New Orleans
Lynchburg Coll. (VA)
Madonna Univ. (MI)
Maine Maritime Academy
Manchester Coll. (IN)
Manhattan Coll. (NY)
Mansfield Univ. of Pennsylvania
Marietta Coll. (OH)
Marquette Univ. (WI)
Marygrove Coll. (MI)
Maryville Coll. (TN)
Marywood Coll. (PA)
Mercyhurst Coll. (PA)
Messiah Coll. (PA)
MidAmerica Nazarene Univ. (KS)
Midwestern State Univ. (TX)
Millikin Univ. (IL)
Milwaukee School of Engineering
Minnesota State Univ.–Mankato
Minnesota State Univ.–Moorhead
Minot State Univ. (ND)
Missouri Southern State Univ.
Monmouth Coll. (IL)
Monmouth Univ. (NJ)
Moravian Coll. (PA)
Morningside Coll. (IA)
Mount Vernon Nazarene Univ.
 (OH)
Murray State Univ. (KY)
Muskingum Univ. (OH)
Nebraska Wesleyan Univ.
Neumann Univ. (PA)
New Mexico State Univ.
New York Institute of Technology
New York Univ.
North Central Coll. (IL)
North Greenville Univ. (SC)
North Park Univ. (IL)
Northeastern State Univ. (OK)
Northeastern Univ. (MA)
Northern State Univ. (SD)
Northwest Missouri State Univ.
Northwestern Coll. (MN)
Northwood Univ. (MI)
Ohio Dominican Univ.
Ohio Northern Univ.

Ohio State Univ.–Columbus
Ohio Univ.
Ohio Wesleyan Univ.
Oklahoma Baptist Univ.
Oklahoma State Univ.
Old Dominion Univ. (VA)
Oral Roberts Univ. (OK)
Our Lady of the Lake Univ. (TX)
Pace Univ. (NY)
Paine Coll. (GA)
Palm Beach Atlantic Univ. (FL)
Pepperdine Univ. (CA)
Pfeiffer Univ. (NC)
Philadelphia Univ.
Pittsburg State Univ. (KS)
Post Univ. (CT)
Quinnipiac Univ. (CT)
Ramapo Coll. of New Jersey
Regent Univ. (VA)
Rider Univ. (NJ)
Rochester Institute of Technology
 (NY)
Roger Williams Univ. (RI)
Rollins Coll. (FL)
Sacred Heart Univ. (CT)
Saginaw Valley State Univ. (MI)
Salem Coll. (NC)
Sam Houston State Univ. (TX)
Samford Univ. (AL)
San Diego State Univ.
Savannah State Univ. (GA)
Schreiner Univ. (TX)
Seattle Univ.
Seton Hill Univ. (PA)
Shaw Univ. (NC)
Southeastern Univ. (FL)
Southern Adventist Univ. (TN)
Southern New Hampshire Univ.
St. Ambrose Univ. (IA)
St. Anselm Coll. (NH)
St. Cloud State Univ. (MN)
St. Edward's Univ. (TX)
St. Francis Univ. (PA)
St. Joseph's Coll. (ME)
St. Joseph's Univ. (PA)
St. Leo Univ. (FL)
St. Mary's Coll. of California
St. Mary's Univ. of Minnesota
St. Mary's Univ. of San Antonio
 (TX)
St. Norbert Coll. (WI)
St. Peter's Coll. (NJ)
St. Thomas Univ. (FL)
St. Vincent Coll. (PA)
St. Xavier Univ. (IL)
Stephen F. Austin State Univ. (TX)
Stetson Univ. (FL)
Stonehill Coll. (MA)
Suffolk Univ. (MA)
SUNY Maritime Coll.
Taylor Univ. (IN)
Temple Univ. (PA)
Texas A&M Univ.–Kingsville
Texas Christian Univ.
Texas Tech Univ.
Texas Wesleyan Univ.
Thomas Coll. (ME)
Thomas Edison State Coll. (NJ)
Tiffin Univ. (OH)
Trinity International Univ. (IL)
Tulane Univ. (LA)

Union Coll. (NE)
Union Univ. (TN)
Univ. of Akron (OH)
Univ. of Arkansas
Univ. of Arkansas–Little Rock
Univ. of Dayton (OH)
Univ. of Denver
Univ. of Evansville (IN)
Univ. of Findlay (OH)
Univ. of Georgia
Univ. of Hawaii–Manoa
Univ. of Houston–Downtown
Univ. of Indianapolis
Univ. of Iowa
Univ. of La Verne (CA)
Univ. of Maryland–Coll. Park
Univ. of Maryland–Univ. Coll.
Univ. of Memphis
Univ. of Miami (FL)
Univ. of Minnesota–Twin Cities
Univ. of Mississippi
Univ. of Montana
Univ. of Mount Union (OH)
Univ. of Nebraska–Lincoln
Univ. of Nevada–Las Vegas
Univ. of Nevada–Reno
Univ. of New Haven (CT)
Univ. of North Carolina–Charlotte
Univ. of North Carolina–
 Greensboro
Univ. of North Florida
Univ. of Pennsylvania
Univ. of Portland (OR)
Univ. of Rhode Island
Univ. of Rio Grande (OH)
Univ. of San Francisco
Univ. of Scranton (PA)
Univ. of South Carolina
Univ. of South Florida
Univ. of St. Mary (KS)
Univ. of St. Thomas (MN)
Univ. of Tampa (FL)
Univ. of Texas–Arlington
Univ. of Texas–Pan American
Univ. of Texas–San Antonio
Univ. of Toledo (OH)
Univ. of Tulsa (OK)
Univ. of Wisconsin–La Crosse
Univ. of Wisconsin–Madison
Univ. of Wisconsin–Superior
Valparaiso Univ. (IN)
Vanguard Univ. of Southern
 California
Villanova Univ. (PA)
Virginia Intermont Coll.
Wagner Coll. (NY)
Washington Adventist Univ. (MD)
Washington and Jefferson Coll.
 (PA)
Washington State Univ.
Washington Univ. in St. Louis
Webber International Univ. (FL)
Wesley Coll. (DE)
Wesleyan Coll. (GA)
West Virginia Wesleyan Coll.
Western Carolina Univ. (NC)
Western Washington Univ.
Westminster Coll. (UT)
Westminster Coll. (PA)
Whitworth Univ. (WA)
Wichita State Univ. (KS)

Widener Univ. (PA)
William Jewell Coll. (MO)
Wofford Coll. (SC)
Wright State Univ. (OH)
Xavier Univ. (OH)

International Relations and Affairs

Agnes Scott Coll. (GA)
Allegheny Coll. (PA)
Alverno Coll. (WI)
American Jewish Univ. (CA)
American Univ. (DC)
Aquinas Coll. (MI)
Arcadia Univ. (PA)
Ashland Univ. (OH)
Augustana Coll. (SD)
Austin Coll. (TX)
Baylor Univ. (TX)
Beloit Coll. (WI)
Benedictine Univ. (IL)
Bennington Coll. (VT)
Berry Coll. (GA)
Bethany Coll. (WV)
Bethel Univ. (MN)
Bethune-Cookman Univ. (FL)
Binghamton Univ.–SUNY
Boston Univ.
Bowling Green State Univ. (OH)
Bradley Univ. (IL)
Brenau Univ. (GA)
Bridgewater Coll. (VA)
Bridgewater State Coll. (MA)
Brigham Young Univ.–Provo (UT)
Brown Univ. (RI)
Bucknell Univ. (PA)
Butler Univ. (IN)
California State Univ.–Chico
California State Univ.–East Bay
California State Univ.–Sacramento
California State Univ.–San
  Bernardino
Calvin Coll. (MI)
Canisius Coll. (NY)
Capital Univ. (OH)
Carleton Coll. (MN)
Carnegie Mellon Univ. (PA)
Carroll Coll. (MT)
Carroll Univ. (WI)
Case Western Reserve Univ. (OH)
Centenary Coll. (NJ)
Central Michigan Univ.
Chaminade Univ. of Honolulu
Chatham Univ. (PA)
Claremont McKenna Coll. (CA)
Clark Univ. (MA)
Cleveland State Univ.
Colgate Univ. (NY)
Coll. at Brockport–SUNY
Coll. of New Jersey
Coll. of Notre Dame of Maryland
Coll. of William and Mary (VA)
Coll. of Wooster (OH)
Connecticut Coll.
Cornell Coll. (IA)
Creighton Univ. (NE)
CUNY–City Coll.
CUNY–Coll. of Staten Island
CUNY–Hunter Coll.
Denison Univ. (OH)

DePaul Univ. (IL)
Dickinson Coll. (PA)
Dominican Univ. (IL)
Drake Univ. (IA)
Drury Univ. (MO)
Duquesne Univ. (PA)
Eastern Washington Univ.
Eckerd Coll. (FL)
Edgewood Coll. (WI)
Elmira Coll. (NY)
Endicott Coll. (MA)
Fairfield Univ. (CT)
Fairleigh Dickinson Univ. (NJ)
Ferrum Coll. (VA)
Florida International Univ.
Florida State Univ.
Fordham Univ. (NY)
Francis Marion Univ. (SC)
Frostburg State Univ. (MD)
George Mason Univ. (VA)
George Washington Univ. (DC)
Georgetown Univ. (DC)
Georgia Institute of Technology
Georgia Southern Univ.
Gonzaga Univ. (WA)
Gordon Coll. (MA)
Goucher Coll. (MD)
Graceland Univ. (IA)
Grand Valley State Univ. (MI)
Guilford Coll. (NC)
Hawaii Pacific Univ.
Hendrix Coll. (AR)
Hobart and William Smith Colleges
  (NY)
Holy Names Univ. (CA)
Houghton Coll. (NY)
Idaho State Univ.
Immaculata Univ. (PA)
Indiana Univ. of Pennsylvania
Indiana Univ. Southeast
Indiana Wesleyan Univ.
Jacksonville Univ. (FL)
James Madison Univ. (VA)
Johns Hopkins Univ. (MD)
Juniata Coll. (PA)
Kennesaw State Univ. (GA)
Kent State Univ. (OH)
Knox Coll. (IL)
La Roche Coll. (PA)
Lafayette Coll. (PA)
Lake Forest Coll. (IL)
Lambuth Univ. (TN)
Lees-McRae Coll. (NC)
Lehigh Univ. (PA)
Lewis & Clark Coll. (OR)
Lincoln Univ. (PA)
Lindenwood Univ. (MO)
Lock Haven Univ. of Pennsylvania
Long Island Univ.–C.W. Post
  Campus (NY)
Loyola Univ. Chicago
Lynchburg Coll. (VA)
Lynn Univ. (FL)
Manhattan Coll. (NY)
Mars Hill Coll. (NC)
Marshall Univ. (WV)
Mary Baldwin Coll. (VA)
Marymount Manhattan Coll. (NY)
Maryville Univ. (TN)
McKendree Univ. (IL)
Methodist Univ. (NC)

Miami Univ.–Oxford (OH)
Michigan State Univ.
Middle Tennessee State Univ.
Middlebury Coll. (VT)
Millikin Univ. (IL)
Mills Coll. (CA)
Minnesota State Univ.–Mankato
Missouri Southern State Univ.
Morehouse Coll. (GA)
Morningside Coll. (IA)
Mount Holyoke Coll. (MA)
Mount Mary Coll. (WI)
Mount St. Mary's Univ. (MD)
Muhlenberg Coll. (PA)
Murray State Univ. (KY)
Muskingum Univ. (OH)
Nazareth Coll. (NY)
New York Univ.
Newberry Coll. (SC)
North Central Coll. (IL)
North Park Univ. (IL)
Northeastern Univ. (MA)
Northern Arizona Univ.
Northern Kentucky Univ.
Northern Michigan Univ.
Northwest Nazarene Univ. (ID)
Northwestern Univ. (IL)
Norwich Univ. (VT)
Nova Southeastern Univ. (FL)
Occidental Coll. (CA)
Oglethorpe Univ. (GA)
Ohio Northern Univ.
Ohio State Univ.–Columbus
Ohio Wesleyan Univ.
Old Dominion Univ. (VA)
Oral Roberts Univ. (OK)
Otterbein Coll. (OH)
Pacific Univ. (OR)
Pennsylvania State Univ.–Univ. Park
Point Park Univ. (PA)
Pomona Coll. (CA)
Portland State Univ. (OR)
Queens Univ. of Charlotte (NC)
Reed Coll. (OR)
Regis Coll. (MA)
Rhodes Coll. (TN)
Rider Univ. (NJ)
Roanoke Coll. (VA)
Rochester Institute of Technology
  (NY)
Rockford Coll. (IL)
Rollins Coll. (FL)
Roosevelt Univ. (IL)
Salem Coll. (NC)
Samford Univ. (AL)
San Diego State Univ.
San Francisco State Univ.
Scripps Coll. (CA)
Seton Hall Univ. (NJ)
Seton Hill Univ. (PA)
Shaw Univ. (NC)
Shawnee State Univ. (OH)
Simmons Coll. (MA)
Simpson Coll. (IA)
Skidmore Coll. (NY)
Sonoma State Univ. (CA)
Southern Methodist Univ. (TX)
Southern Nazarene Univ. (OK)
Southern Oregon Univ.
Southern Polytechnic State Univ.
  (GA)

Southwestern Univ. (TX)
Spring Hill Coll. (AL)
St. Anselm Coll. (NH)
St. Catherine Univ. (MN)
St. Cloud State Univ. (MN)
St. John Fisher Coll. (NY)
St. Joseph Coll. (CT)
St. Joseph's Coll. (IN)
St. Joseph's Univ. (PA)
St. Leo Univ. (FL)
St. Louis Univ.
St. Mary's Univ. of San Antonio
  (TX)
St. Norbert Coll. (WI)
St. Xavier Univ. (IL)
Stanford Univ. (CA)
Stetson Univ. (FL)
Stonehill Coll. (MA)
Suffolk Univ. (MA)
SUNY Coll.–Cortland
SUNY–Geneseo
SUNY–Oswego
Susquehanna Univ. (PA)
Syracuse Univ. (NY)
Taylor Univ. (IN)
Texas A&M Univ.–Commerce
Texas Christian Univ.
Texas State Univ.–San Marcos
Texas Wesleyan Univ.
Thomas More Coll. (KY)
Tiffin Univ. (OH)
Towson Univ. (MD)
Trinity Univ. (DC)
Tufts Univ. (MA)
Tulane Univ. (LA)
Union Coll. (NE)
Univ. of Akron (OH)
Univ. of Alabama
Univ. of Arkansas
Univ. of California–Davis
Univ. of California–Riverside
Univ. of Chicago
Univ. of Delaware
Univ. of Denver
Univ. of Evansville (IN)
Univ. of Florida
Univ. of Georgia
Univ. of Indianapolis
Univ. of Kansas
Univ. of Kentucky
Univ. of La Verne (CA)
Univ. of Maine
Univ. of Mary Washington (VA)
Univ. of Memphis
Univ. of Miami (FL)
Univ. of Minnesota–Duluth
Univ. of Minnesota–Twin Cities
Univ. of Mississippi
Univ. of Mount Union (OH)
Univ. of Nebraska–Kearney
Univ. of Nebraska–Lincoln
Univ. of Nevada–Reno
Univ. of New Hampshire
Univ. of Pennsylvania
Univ. of Redlands (CA)
Univ. of Richmond (VA)
Univ. of San Diego
Univ. of Scranton (PA)
Univ. of South Carolina
Univ. of South Florida
Univ. of Southern California

Univ. of Southern Indiana
Univ. of St. Mary (KS)
Univ. of St. Thomas (MN)
Univ. of Tennessee–Martin
Univ. of the Pacific (CA)
Univ. of Toledo (OH)
Univ. of Virginia
Univ. of West Florida
Univ. of West Georgia
Univ. of Wisconsin–Parkside
Univ. of Wisconsin–Whitewater
Univ. of Wyoming
Ursinus Coll. (PA)
Utica Coll. (NY)
Valparaiso Univ. (IN)
Vassar Coll. (NY)
Virginia Military Institute
Virginia Tech
Wagner Coll. (NY)
Wartburg Coll. (IA)
Washington Coll. (MD)
Washington Univ. in St. Louis
Webster Univ. (MO)
Wellesley Coll. (MA)
Wells Coll. (NY)
Wesleyan Coll. (GA)
West Virginia Wesleyan Coll.
Westminster Coll. (PA)
Westminster Coll. (MO)
Wheaton Coll. (MA)
Wheaton Coll. (IL)
Wheeling Jesuit Univ. (WV)
Widener Univ. (PA)
Wilkes Univ. (PA)
William Jewell Coll. (MO)
William Woods Univ. (MO)
Wilson Coll. (PA)
Worcester Polytechnic Institute
  (MA)
Xavier Univ. (OH)

International/Global Studies

Assumption Coll. (MA)
Bethel Coll. (IN)
Brandeis Univ. (MA)
Clark Univ. (MA)
Elon Univ. (NC)
Hampshire Coll. (MA)
Hanover Coll. (IN)
High Point Univ. (NC)
Lawrence Univ. (WI)
National Univ. (CA)
Oglethorpe Univ. (GA)
Russell Sage Coll. (NY)
Shorter Coll. (GA)
Simpson Coll. (IA)
St. Lawrence Univ. (NY)
SUNY Coll.–Oneonta
Univ. of California–San Diego
Univ. of California–Santa Barbara
Wright State Univ. (OH)

Iranian/Persian Languages, Literatures, and Linguistics

Univ. of Texas–Austin

Journalism

Abilene Christian Univ. (TX)
Adrian Coll. (MI)
Albany State Univ. (GA)
Allegheny Coll. (PA)
American Jewish Univ. (CA)
American Univ. (DC)
Anderson Univ. (SC)
Andrews Univ. (MI)
Angelo State Univ. (TX)
Appalachian State Univ. (NC)
Arcadia Univ. (PA)
Arizona State Univ.
Arkansas State Univ.–Jonesboro
Arkansas Tech Univ.
Asbury Univ. (KY)
Ashland Univ. (OH)
Auburn Univ. (AL)
Augustana Coll. (SD)
Averett Univ. (VA)
Ball State Univ. (IN)
Barry Univ. (FL)
Baylor Univ. (TX)
Belmont Univ. (TN)
Bennington Coll. (VT)
Bethel Univ. (MN)
Bethune-Cookman Univ. (FL)
Biola Univ. (CA)
Boston Univ.
Bowie State Univ. (MD)
Bowling Green State Univ. (OH)
Bradley Univ. (IL)
Briar Cliff Univ. (IA)
Brigham Young Univ.–Provo (UT)
Butler Univ. (IN)
California Baptist Univ.
California Lutheran Univ.
California Polytechnic State Univ.–
    San Luis Obispo
California State Univ.–Chico
California State Univ.–Fullerton
California State Univ.–Long Beach
California State Univ.–Monterey Bay
California State Univ.–Northridge
California State Univ.–Sacramento
Campbell Univ. (NC)
Campbellsville Univ. (KY)
Carroll Univ. (WI)
Carson-Newman Coll. (TN)
Central Michigan Univ.
Central State Univ. (OH)
Central Washington Univ.
Champlain Coll. (VT)
Chapman Univ. (CA)
Chatham Univ. (PA)
Clarke Univ. (IA)
Coll. at Brockport–SUNY
Coll. of St. Joseph (VT)
Coll. of the Ozarks (MO)
Colorado State Univ.
Columbia Coll. (IL)
Columbia Coll. (SC)
Concordia Coll.–Moorhead (MN)
Concordia Univ. (NE)
Concordia Univ. (MI)
Corban Univ. (OR)
Corcoran Coll. of Art and Design
    (DC)
Cornerstone Univ. (MI)
Creighton Univ. (NE)
CUNY–Baruch Coll.
CUNY–Brooklyn Coll.

CUNY–Lehman Coll.
Dana Coll. (NE)
Delaware State Univ.
Delta State Univ. (MS)
Doane Coll. (NE)
Dominican Univ. (IL)
Dordt Coll. (IA)
Drake Univ. (IA)
Drury Univ. (MO)
Duquesne Univ. (PA)
East Carolina Univ. (NC)
Eastern Illinois Univ.
Eastern Kentucky Univ.
Eastern Michigan Univ.
Eastern Nazarene Coll. (MA)
Edinboro Univ. of Pennsylvania
Edward Waters Coll. (FL)
Elon Univ. (NC)
Emerson Coll. (MA)
Evangel Univ. (MO)
Fitchburg State Coll. (MA)
Florida A&M Univ.
Florida Southern Coll.
Fort Valley State Univ. (GA)
Franklin Coll. (IN)
Freed-Hardeman Univ. (TN)
Gannon Univ. (PA)
Gardner-Webb Univ. (NC)
George Mason Univ. (VA)
George Washington Univ. (DC)
Georgia Coll. & State Univ.
Georgia Southern Univ.
Georgia State Univ.
Gonzaga Univ. (WA)
Grace Coll. and Seminary (IN)
Grand Valley State Univ. (MI)
Grand View Univ. (IA)
Hampton Univ. (VA)
Hardin-Simmons Univ. (TX)
Harding Univ. (AR)
Hawaii Pacific Univ.
Heidelberg Univ. (OH)
Henderson State Univ. (AR)
Hillsdale Coll. (MI)
Hofstra Univ. (NY)
Howard Univ. (DC)
Humboldt State Univ. (CA)
Huntington Univ. (IN)
Illinois Institute of Technology
Illinois State Univ.
Indiana State Univ.
Indiana Univ. Northwest
Indiana Univ. of Pennsylvania
Indiana Univ. Southeast
Indiana Univ.–South Bend
Indiana Univ.–Purdue Univ.–
    Indianapolis
Iona Coll. (NY)
Iowa State Univ.
Ithaca Coll. (NY)
John Brown Univ. (AR)
Johnson State Coll. (VT)
Kansas State Univ.
Keene State Coll. (NH)
Kent State Univ. (OH)
Lake Erie Coll. (OH)
Langston Univ. (OK)
Lehigh Univ. (PA)
Liberty Univ. (VA)
Lincoln Univ. (PA)
Lincoln Univ. (MO)

Lindenwood Univ. (MO)
Lipscomb Univ. (TN)
Lock Haven Univ. of Pennsylvania
Long Island Univ.–C.W. Post
    Campus (NY)
Louisiana Coll.
Louisiana Tech Univ.
Loyola Univ. Chicago
Lyndon State Coll. (VT)
Madonna Univ. (MI)
Mansfield Univ. of Pennsylvania
Marian Univ. (WI)
Marietta Coll. (OH)
Marist Coll. (NY)
Marquette Univ. (WI)
Marshall Univ. (WV)
Master's Coll. and Seminary (CA)
Messiah Coll. (PA)
Methodist Univ. (NC)
Metropolitan State Coll. of Denver
Miami Univ.–Oxford (OH)
Michigan State Univ.
Midland Lutheran Coll. (NE)
Missouri State Univ.
Morningside Coll. (IA)
Morris Coll. (SC)
Mount Vernon Nazarene Univ.
    (OH)
Murray State Univ. (KY)
Muskingum Univ. (OH)
New Mexico State Univ.
New York Univ.
Norfolk State Univ. (VA)
North Carolina A&T State Univ.
North Central Coll. (IL)
North Central Univ. (MN)
North Greenville Univ. (SC)
Northeastern State Univ. (OK)
Northeastern Univ. (MA)
Northern Arizona Univ.
Northern Illinois Univ.
Northern Kentucky Univ.
Northern Michigan Univ.
Northwestern Coll. (MN)
Northwestern Coll. (IA)
Northwestern State Univ. of
    Louisiana
Northwestern Univ. (IL)
Oakland Univ. (MI)
Ohio Northern Univ.
Ohio State Univ.–Columbus
Ohio Univ.
Ohio Wesleyan Univ.
Oklahoma Baptist Univ.
Oklahoma Christian Univ.
Oklahoma State Univ.
Olivet Coll. (MI)
Olivet Nazarene Univ. (IL)
Oral Roberts Univ. (OK)
Otterbein Coll. (OH)
Our Lady of the Lake Univ. (TX)
Paine Coll. (GA)
Palm Beach Atlantic Univ. (FL)
Pennsylvania State Univ.–Univ. Park
Pepperdine Univ. (CA)
Pfeiffer Univ. (NC)
Point Loma Nazarene Univ. (CA)
Point Park Univ. (PA)
Prescott Coll. (AZ)
Purchase Coll.–SUNY
Purdue Univ.–West Lafayette (IN)

Queens Univ. of Charlotte (NC)
Radford Univ. (VA)
Rider Univ. (NJ)
Rivier Coll. (NH)
Rochester Institute of Technology
    (NY)
Roosevelt Univ. (IL)
Rust Coll. (MS)
Rutgers, the State Univ. of New
    Jersey–New Brunswick
Rutgers, the State Univ. of New
    Jersey–Newark
Sam Houston State Univ. (TX)
Samford Univ. (AL)
San Diego State Univ.
San Francisco State Univ.
San Jose State Univ. (CA)
Savannah State Univ. (GA)
Seattle Univ.
Seton Hill Univ. (PA)
Shippensburg Univ. of Pennsylvania
Simpson Coll. (IA)
South Dakota State Univ.
Southeastern Univ. (FL)
Southern Adventist Univ. (TN)
Southern Arkansas Univ.
Southern Connecticut State Univ.
Southern Illinois Univ.–Carbondale
Southern Nazarene Univ. (OK)
Southern Oregon Univ.
Southern Univ.–New Orleans
Southwestern Adventist Univ. (TX)
Spring Arbor Univ. (MI)
St. Ambrose Univ. (IA)
St. Bonaventure Univ. (NY)
St. Gregory's Univ. (OK)
St. John's Univ. (NY)
St. Joseph's Coll. (ME)
St. Mary's Univ. of Minnesota
St. Mary-of-the-Woods Coll. (IN)
St. Michael's Coll. (VT)
Stephen F. Austin State Univ. (TX)
Stephens Coll. (MO)
Stillman Coll. (AL)
Suffolk Univ. (MA)
SUNY–Oswego
SUNY–Plattsburgh
SUNY–Stony Brook
Syracuse Univ. (NY)
Temple Univ. (PA)
Tennessee Technological Univ.
Texas A&M Univ.–Coll. Station
Texas A&M Univ.–Commerce
Texas Christian Univ.
Texas State Univ.–San Marcos
Texas Tech Univ.
Texas Wesleyan Univ.
Thomas Edison State Coll. (NJ)
Tougaloo Coll. (MS)
Troy Univ. (AL)
Union Coll. (NE)
Union Univ. (TN)
Univ. at Albany–SUNY
Univ. of Akron (OH)
Univ. of Alabama
Univ. of Alaska–Anchorage
Univ. of Alaska–Fairbanks
Univ. of Arizona
Univ. of Arkansas
Univ. of Arkansas–Little Rock
Univ. of Arkansas–Pine Bluff

Univ. of California–Irvine
Univ. of Central Arkansas
Univ. of Central Florida
Univ. of Central Missouri
Univ. of Central Oklahoma
Univ. of Colorado–Boulder
Univ. of Connecticut
Univ. of Dayton (OH)
Univ. of Denver
Univ. of Findlay (OH)
Univ. of Florida
Univ. of Georgia
Univ. of Hawaii–Manoa
Univ. of Houston
Univ. of Illinois–Urbana-Champaign
Univ. of Iowa
Univ. of Kansas
Univ. of Kentucky
Univ. of La Verne (CA)
Univ. of Maine
Univ. of Maryland–Coll. Park
Univ. of Massachusetts–Amherst
Univ. of Memphis
Univ. of Miami (FL)
Univ. of Michigan–Ann Arbor
Univ. of Minnesota–Twin Cities
Univ. of Mississippi
Univ. of Montana
Univ. of Nebraska–Kearney
Univ. of Nebraska–Lincoln
Univ. of Nebraska–Omaha
Univ. of Nevada–Las Vegas
Univ. of Nevada–Reno
Univ. of New Hampshire
Univ. of New Mexico
Univ. of North Texas
Univ. of Northern Colorado
Univ. of Oklahoma
Univ. of Oregon
Univ. of Pittsburgh–Johnstown
Univ. of Rhode Island
Univ. of Richmond (VA)
Univ. of Rio Grande (OH)
Univ. of South Carolina
Univ. of Southern California
Univ. of Southern Indiana
Univ. of Southern Mississippi
Univ. of St. Thomas (MN)
Univ. of Tennessee
Univ. of Texas–Arlington
Univ. of Texas–Austin
Univ. of Texas–Pan American
Univ. of Texas–Tyler
Univ. of Washington
Univ. of West Georgia
Univ. of Wisconsin–Eau Claire
Univ. of Wisconsin–Madison
Univ. of Wisconsin–Oshkosh
Univ. of Wisconsin–River Falls
Univ. of Wisconsin–Superior
Univ. of Wisconsin–Whitewater
Univ. of Wyoming
Utah State Univ.
Utica Coll. (NY)
Valparaiso Univ. (IN)
Waldorf Coll. (IA)
Washington Adventist Univ. (MD)
Washington and Lee Univ. (VA)
Wayne State Univ. (MI)
Weber State Univ. (UT)
Webster Univ. (MO)

West Texas A&M Univ.
West Virginia Univ.
Western Illinois Univ.
Western Kentucky Univ.
Western Michigan Univ.
Western Washington Univ.
Whitworth Univ. (WA)
Widener Univ. (PA)
William Woods Univ. (MO)
Youngstown State Univ. (OH)

Landscape Architecture

Arizona State Univ.
Auburn Univ. (AL)
Ball State Univ. (IN)
Boston Architectural Coll.
California Polytechnic State Univ.–
    San Luis Obispo
California State Polytechnic Univ.–
    Pomona
Clemson Univ. (SC)
Colorado State Univ.
Cornell Univ. (NY)
CUNY–City Coll.
Florida International Univ.
Iowa State Univ.
Kansas State Univ.
Louisiana State Univ.–Baton Rouge
Michigan State Univ.
Mississippi State Univ.
North Carolina A&T State Univ.
North Carolina State Univ.–Raleigh
North Dakota State Univ.
Ohio State Univ.–Columbus
Oklahoma State Univ.
Philadelphia Univ.
SUNY Coll. of Environmental
    Science and Forestry
Temple Univ. (PA)
Texas A&M Univ.–Coll. Station
Texas Tech Univ.
Univ. of Arkansas
Univ. of California–Berkeley
Univ. of California–Davis
Univ. of Connecticut
Univ. of Florida
Univ. of Georgia
Univ. of Illinois–Urbana-Champaign
Univ. of Kentucky
Univ. of Maine
Univ. of Maryland–Coll. Park
Univ. of Massachusetts–Amherst
Univ. of Michigan–Ann Arbor
Univ. of Nebraska–Lincoln
Univ. of Nevada–Las Vegas
Univ. of Oregon
Univ. of Rhode Island
Univ. of Southern California
Univ. of Washington
Univ. of Wisconsin–Madison
Utah State Univ.
Virginia Tech
Washington State Univ.
West Virginia Univ.

Law (LL.B., J.D.)

Loyola Univ. New Orleans
North Carolina Central Univ.
Ohio Northern Univ.

Ohio State Univ.–Columbus
Quinnipiac Univ. (CT)
Roger Williams Univ. (RI)
Texas Wesleyan Univ.
Tulane Univ. (LA)
Univ. of Florida
Univ. of Kentucky
Univ. of La Verne (CA)
Univ. of Nebraska–Lincoln
Univ. of Nevada–Las Vegas

Legal Professions and Studies

Armstrong Atlantic State Univ. (GA)
Ball State Univ. (IN)
Becker Coll. (MA)
Coll. of Our Lady of the Elms (MA)
Drake Univ. (IA)
Hodges Univ. (FL)
Johnson and Wales Univ. (RI)
Madonna Univ. (MI)
Pennsylvania Coll. of Technology
Post Univ. (CT)
Quinnipiac Univ. (CT)
Ramapo Coll. of New Jersey
St. Augustine's Coll. (NC)
St. Joseph's Univ. (PA)
Syracuse Univ. (NY)
Tulane Univ. (LA)
United States Military Academy
    (NY)
Univ. of Dallas
Univ. of Findlay (OH)
Univ. of Illinois–Springfield
Univ. of Massachusetts–Boston
Univ. of Nebraska–Lincoln
Univ. of Pennsylvania
Univ. of Tulsa (OK)
William Woods Univ. (MO)

Legal Research and Advanced Professional Studies (Post-LL.B./J.D.)

Arcadia Univ. (PA)
Grambling State Univ. (LA)
James Madison Univ. (VA)
Ohio State Univ.–Columbus
Univ. of Florida

Legal Support Services

Anna Maria Coll. (MA)
Avila Univ. (MO)
Bay Path Coll. (MA)
Bentley Univ. (MA)
Burlington Coll. (VT)
Calumet Coll. of St. Joseph (IN)
Champlain Coll. (VT)
Chancellor Univ. (OH)
Clarion Univ. of Pennsylvania
Coll. of Mount St. Joseph (OH)
Coll. of Our Lady of the Elms (MA)
CUNY–New York City Coll. of
    Technology
Davenport Univ. (MI)
Drury Univ. (MO)
East Central Univ. (OK)
Eastern Kentucky Univ.
Eastern Michigan Univ.

Florida Gulf Coast Univ.
Gannon Univ. (PA)
Grambling State Univ. (LA)
Hilbert Coll. (NY)
Husson Univ. (ME)
Johnson and Wales Univ. (RI)
Kent State Univ. (OH)
Lake Superior State Univ. (MI)
Lewis-Clark State Coll. (ID)
Lock Haven Univ. of Pennsylvania
Madonna Univ. (MI)
Marymount Univ. (VA)
Maryville Univ. of St. Louis (MO)
Minnesota State Univ.–Moorhead
Mississippi Coll.
Mississippi Univ. for Women
Morehead State Univ. (KY)
Mountain State Univ. (WV)
Northeastern State Univ. (OK)
Northern Michigan Univ.
Nova Southeastern Univ. (FL)
Peirce Coll. (PA)
Roger Williams Univ. (RI)
Roosevelt Univ. (IL)
Sage Colleges–Albany (NY)
Shawnee State Univ. (OH)
Southern Illinois Univ.–Carbondale
St. Mary-of-the-Woods Coll. (IN)
Stephen F. Austin State Univ. (TX)
Stevenson Univ. (MD)
Suffolk Univ. (MA)
Texas A&M Univ.–Commerce
Texas Woman's Univ.
Thomas Edison State Coll. (NJ)
Tulane Univ. (LA)
Univ. of Central Florida
Univ. of Detroit Mercy
Univ. of Great Falls (MT)
Univ. of Mississippi
Univ. of Southern Mississippi
Univ. of Tennessee–Chattanooga
Univ. of Toledo (OH)
Univ. of West Florida
Ursuline Coll. (OH)
Utah Valley Univ.
Valdosta State Univ. (GA)
Virginia Intermont Coll.
Washburn Univ. (KS)
Wesley Coll. (DE)
William Jewell Coll. (MO)
William Woods Univ. (MO)

Liberal Arts and Sciences Studies, and Humanities

Abilene Christian Univ. (TX)
Adams State Coll. (CO)
Adelphi Univ. (NY)
Alaska Pacific Univ.
Albertus Magnus Coll. (CT)
Albion Coll. (MI)
Alcorn State Univ. (MS)
Alderson-Broaddus Coll. (WV)
Alfred Univ. (NY)
Allen Univ. (SC)
Alma Coll. (MI)
Alvernia Univ. (PA)
Alverno Coll. (WI)
American Jewish Univ. (CA)
American Univ. (DC)
Anderson Univ. (IN)

Andrews Univ. (MI)
Angelo State Univ. (TX)
Anna Maria Coll. (MA)
Appalachian State Univ. (NC)
Aquinas Coll. (MI)
Arcadia Univ. (PA)
Arizona State Univ.
Arkansas State Univ.–Jonesboro
Arkansas Tech Univ.
Armstrong Atlantic State Univ. (GA)
Atlantic Union Coll. (MA)
Auburn Univ.–Montgomery (AL)
Augustana Coll. (SD)
Aurora Univ. (IL)
Austin Peay State Univ. (TN)
Averett Univ. (VA)
Avila Univ. (MO)
Azusa Pacific Univ. (CA)
Ball State Univ. (IN)
Barry Univ. (FL)
Barton Coll. (NC)
Bay Path Coll. (MA)
Baylor Univ. (TX)
Becker Coll. (MA)
Belhaven Univ. (MS)
Bellarmine Univ. (KY)
Bellevue Univ. (NE)
Belmont Abbey Coll. (NC)
Belmont Univ. (TN)
Bemidji State Univ. (MN)
Benedictine Univ. (IL)
Bennington Coll. (VT)
Bentley Univ. (MA)
Bethel Coll. (IN)
Bethel Coll. (TN)
Bethel Univ. (MN)
Bethune-Cookman Univ. (FL)
Binghamton Univ.–SUNY
Biola Univ. (CA)
Bluefield State Coll. (WV)
Bowling Green State Univ. (OH)
Bradley Univ. (IL)
Brenau Univ. (GA)
Brescia Univ. (KY)
Brewton-Parker Coll. (GA)
Bridgewater Coll. (VA)
Brigham Young Univ.–Hawaii
Brigham Young Univ.–Provo (UT)
Bryan Coll. (TN)
Bryant Univ. (RI)
Bucknell Univ. (PA)
Buffalo State Coll.–SUNY
Burlington Coll. (VT)
Butler Univ. (IN)
Cabrini Coll. (PA)
California Baptist Univ.
California Institute of Technology
California Lutheran Univ.
California Polytechnic State Univ.–
    San Luis Obispo
California State Univ.–Bakersfield
California State Univ.–Chico
California State Univ.–Dominguez
    Hills
California State Univ.–East Bay
California State Univ.–Fresno
California State Univ.–Fullerton
California State Univ.–Long Beach
California State Univ.–Los Angeles
California State Univ.–Monterey Bay
California State Univ.–Northridge

California State Univ.–Sacramento
California State Univ.–San
    Bernardino
California State Univ.–San Marcos
California State Univ.–Stanislaus
California Univ. of Pennsylvania
Calumet Coll. of St. Joseph (IN)
Calvin Coll. (MI)
Campbellsville Univ. (KY)
Canisius Coll. (NY)
Carlow Univ. (PA)
Carnegie Mellon Univ. (PA)
Carson-Newman Coll. (TN)
Carthage Coll. (WI)
Catholic Univ. of America (DC)
Cazenovia Coll. (NY)
Cedar Crest Coll. (PA)
Centenary Coll. (NJ)
Centenary Coll. of Louisiana
Central Christian Coll. (KS)
Central Coll. (IA)
Central Michigan Univ.
Central Washington Univ.
Chadron State Coll. (NE)
Champlain Coll. (VT)
Chapman Univ. (CA)
Charleston Southern Univ. (SC)
Chestnut Hill Coll. (PA)
Chicago State Univ.
Chowan Univ. (NC)
Christian Brothers Univ. (TN)
Clarion Univ. of Pennsylvania
Clark Atlanta Univ.
Clarkson Univ. (NY)
Clayton State Univ. (GA)
Clearwater Christian Coll. (FL)
Cleveland State Univ.
Coastal Carolina Univ. (SC)
Colgate Univ. (NY)
Coll. of Idaho (ID)
Coll. of Mount St. Joseph (OH)
Coll. of Mount St. Vincent (NY)
Coll. of Notre Dame of Maryland
Coll. of Our Lady of the Elms (MA)
Coll. of Santa Fe (NM)
Coll. of St. Benedict (MN)
Coll. of St. Joseph (VT)
Coll. of St. Mary (NE)
Coll. of St. Rose (NY)
Coll. of St. Scholastica (MN)
Coll. of St. Thomas More (TX)
Colorado Christian Univ.
Colorado Coll.
Colorado State Univ.
Colorado State Univ.–Pueblo
Columbia Coll. (IL)
Columbia Coll. (SC)
Concord Univ. (WV)
Concordia Coll. (NY)
Concordia Univ. (OR)
Concordia Univ. (CA)
Concordia Univ. Chicago (IL)
Concordia Univ. Texas
Concordia Univ. Wisconsin
Corban Univ. (OR)
Cornell Coll. (IA)
Cornell Univ. (NY)
Crown Coll. (MN)
Cumberland Univ. (TN)
CUNY–Baruch Coll.
CUNY–Brooklyn Coll.

CUNY–City Coll.
CUNY–Coll. of Staten Island
CUNY–Hunter Coll.
CUNY–Lehman Coll.
CUNY–York Coll.
Curry Coll. (MA)
D'Youville Coll. (NY)
Dakota Wesleyan Univ. (SD)
Dallas Baptist Univ.
Dartmouth Coll. (NH)
Delta State Univ. (MS)
DePaul Univ. (IL)
DeSales Univ. (PA)
Dickinson State Univ. (ND)
Dominican Coll. (NY)
Dominican Univ. (IL)
Dominican Univ. of California
Dordt Coll. (IA)
Dowling Coll. (NY)
Drake Univ. (IA)
Drexel Univ. (PA)
Drury Univ. (MO)
Duquesne Univ. (PA)
East Carolina Univ. (NC)
East Central Univ. (OK)
East Stroudsburg Univ. of
    Pennsylvania
East Tennessee State Univ.
East Texas Baptist Univ.
East-West Univ. (IL)
Eastern Connecticut State Univ.
Eastern Illinois Univ.
Eastern Kentucky Univ.
Eastern Mennonite Univ. (VA)
Eastern Michigan Univ.
Eastern Nazarene Coll. (MA)
Eastern New Mexico Univ.
Eastern Oregon Univ.
Eastern Washington Univ.
Eckerd Coll. (FL)
Edinboro Univ. of Pennsylvania
Elmhurst Coll. (IL)
Elmira Coll. (NY)
Emporia State Univ. (KS)
Endicott Coll. (MA)
Eureka Coll. (IL)
Evergreen State Coll. (WA)
Excelsior Coll. (NY)
Fairfield Univ. (CT)
Fairleigh Dickinson Univ. (NJ)
Faulkner Univ. (AL)
Felician Coll. (NJ)
Ferrum Coll. (VA)
Fitchburg State Coll. (MA)
Flagler Coll. (FL)
Florida Atlantic Univ.
Florida Gulf Coast Univ.
Florida Institute of Technology
Florida International Univ.
Florida State Univ.
Fontbonne Univ. (MO)
Fordham Univ. (NY)
Fort Hays State Univ. (KS)
Fort Lewis Coll. (CO)
Framingham State Coll. (MA)
Francis Marion Univ. (SC)
Franciscan Univ. of Steubenville
    (OH)
Franklin Pierce Univ. (NH)
Fresno Pacific Univ. (CA)
Friends Univ. (KS)

Frostburg State Univ. (MD)
Gannon Univ. (PA)
George Mason Univ. (VA)
George Washington Univ. (DC)
Georgetown Coll. (KY)
Georgetown Univ. (DC)
Georgia Coll. & State Univ.
Georgia Southern Univ.
Georgian Court Univ. (NJ)
Glenville State Coll. (WV)
Goddard Coll. (VT)
Gonzaga Univ. (WA)
Graceland Univ. (IA)
Grand Valley State Univ. (MI)
Grand View Univ. (IA)
Granite State Coll. (NH)
Green Mountain Coll. (VT)
Greenville Coll. (IL)
Hampden-Sydney Coll. (VA)
Hannibal-LaGrange Coll. (MO)
Harding Univ. (AR)
Harvard Univ. (MA)
Haverford Coll. (PA)
Hawaii Pacific Univ.
Henderson State Univ. (AR)
Heritage Univ. (WA)
Hilbert Coll. (NY)
Hobart and William Smith Colleges
    (NY)
Hofstra Univ. (NY)
Holy Family Univ. (PA)
Holy Names Univ. (CA)
Hope Coll. (MI)
Houghton Coll. (NY)
Houston Baptist Univ.
Howard Payne Univ. (TX)
Humboldt State Univ. (CA)
Idaho State Univ.
Illinois State Univ.
Indiana Institute of Technology
Indiana State Univ.
Indiana Univ. East
Indiana Univ. Northwest
Indiana Univ. of Pennsylvania
Indiana Univ. Southeast
Indiana Univ.–Bloomington
Indiana Univ.–Kokomo
Indiana Univ.–South Bend
Indiana Univ.-Purdue Univ.–Fort
    Wayne
Indiana Univ.-Purdue Univ.–
    Indianapolis
Indiana Wesleyan Univ.
Iona Coll. (NY)
Iowa State Univ.
Iowa Wesleyan Coll.
Ithaca Coll. (NY)
Jacksonville State Univ. (AL)
Jacksonville Univ. (FL)
James Madison Univ. (VA)
John Carroll Univ. (OH)
Johns Hopkins Univ. (MD)
Johnson C. Smith Univ. (NC)
Johnson State Coll. (VT)
Juniata Coll. (PA)
Kalamazoo Coll. (MI)
Kansas State Univ.
Kean Univ. (NJ)
Keene State Coll. (NH)
Kent State Univ. (OH)
Kentucky State Univ.

Keuka Coll. (NY)
Knox Coll. (IL)
Kutztown Univ. of Pennsylvania
La Roche Coll. (PA)
La Sierra Univ. (CA)
LaGrange Coll. (GA)
Lake Forest Coll. (IL)
Lake Superior State Univ. (MI)
Lambuth Univ. (TN)
Lander Univ. (SC)
Lasell Coll. (MA)
Lawrence Technological Univ. (MI)
LeMoyne-Owen Coll. (TN)
Lenoir-Rhyne Univ. (NC)
Lesley Univ. (MA)
Lewis & Clark Coll. (OR)
Liberty Univ. (VA)
Limestone Coll. (SC)
Lincoln Memorial Univ. (TN)
Lincoln Univ. (MO)
Lindenwood Univ. (MO)
Lindsey Wilson Coll. (KY)
Lipscomb Univ. (TN)
Lock Haven Univ. of Pennsylvania
Long Island Univ.–C.W. Post
    Campus (NY)
Longwood Univ. (VA)
Loras Coll. (IA)
Louisiana Coll.
Louisiana State Univ.–Baton Rouge
Louisiana State Univ.–Shreveport
Louisiana Tech Univ.
Loyola Marymount Univ. (CA)
Loyola Univ. Chicago
Lubbock Christian Univ. (TX)
Lynn Univ. (FL)
Macalester Coll. (MN)
MacMurray Coll. (IL)
Madonna Univ. (MI)
Malone Univ. (OH)
Manhattan Coll. (NY)
Manhattanville Coll. (NY)
Mansfield Univ. of Pennsylvania
Maranatha Baptist Bible Coll. (WI)
Marian Univ. (WI)
Marist Coll. (NY)
Marlboro Coll. (VT)
Marshall Univ. (WV)
Martin Univ. (IN)
Marylhurst Univ. (OR)
Marymount Manhattan Coll. (NY)
Marymount Univ. (VA)
Maryville Univ. of St. Louis (MO)
Massachusetts Institute of
    Technology
Master's Coll. and Seminary (CA)
Mayville State Univ. (ND)
McKendree Univ. (IL)
McNeese State Univ. (LA)
Medaille Coll. (NY)
Mercyhurst Coll. (PA)
Merrimack Coll. (MA)
Mesa State Coll. (CO)
Messiah Coll. (PA)
Michigan State Univ.
Michigan Technological Univ.
Middle Tennessee State Univ.
Middlebury Coll. (VT)
Midwestern State Univ. (TX)
Milligan Coll. (TN)
Mills Coll. (CA)

Minnesota State Univ.–Mankato
Minot State Univ. (ND)
Misericordia Univ. (PA)
Mississippi Coll.
Mississippi State Univ.
Missouri State Univ.
Missouri Valley Coll.
Mitchell Coll. (CT)
Molloy Coll. (NY)
Montana State Univ.
Montana State Univ.–Billings
Montana State Univ.–Northern
Montana Tech of the Univ. of
    Montana
Montclair State Univ. (NJ)
Morehead State Univ. (KY)
Morris Coll. (SC)
Mount Aloysius Coll. (PA)
Mount Ida Coll. (MA)
Mount Marty Coll. (SD)
Mount Mary Coll. (WI)
Mount St. Mary's Coll. (CA)
Mountain State Univ. (WV)
Murray State Univ. (KY)
Muskingum Univ. (OH)
National Univ. (CA)
Neumann Univ. (PA)
New Coll. of Florida
New Mexico Institute of Mining
    and Technology
New Mexico State Univ.
New School (NY)
New York Univ.
Nicholls State Univ. (LA)
North Carolina State Univ.–Raleigh
North Central Coll. (IL)
North Dakota State Univ.
Northeastern State Univ. (OK)
Northeastern Univ. (MA)
Northern Arizona Univ.
Northern Illinois Univ.
Northern Kentucky Univ.
Northern Michigan Univ.
Northern State Univ. (SD)
Northland Coll. (WI)
Northwest Christian Univ. (OR)
Northwest Missouri State Univ.
Northwest Nazarene Univ. (ID)
Northwest Univ. (WA)
Northwestern Coll. (IA)
Northwestern Oklahoma State
    Univ.
Northwestern State Univ. of
    Louisiana
Northwestern Univ. (IL)
Notre Dame de Namur Univ. (CA)
Nova Southeastern Univ. (FL)
Nyack Coll. (NY)
Oakland City Univ. (IN)
Oakland Univ. (MI)
Oakwood Univ. (AL)
Ohio Dominican Univ.
Ohio State Univ.–Columbus
Ohio Univ.
Ohio Valley Univ. (WV)
Ohio Wesleyan Univ.
Oklahoma Baptist Univ.
Oklahoma Christian Univ.
Oklahoma City Univ.
Oklahoma Panhandle State Univ.
Oklahoma State Univ.

Olivet Coll. (MI)
Olivet Nazarene Univ. (IL)
Oral Roberts Univ. (OK)
Oregon State Univ.
Otterbein Coll. (OH)
Our Lady of Holy Cross Coll. (LA)
Our Lady of the Lake Univ. (TX)
Pace Univ. (NY)
Pacific Union Coll. (CA)
Pacific Univ. (OR)
Palm Beach Atlantic Univ. (FL)
Park Univ. (MO)
Patten Univ. (CA)
Paul Smith's Coll. (NY)
Peace Coll. (NC)
Pennsylvania State Univ.–Univ. Park
Pepperdine Univ. (CA)
Peru State Coll. (NE)
Pfeiffer Univ. (NC)
Pine Manor Coll. (MA)
Pittsburg State Univ. (KS)
Plymouth State Univ. (NH)
Point Loma Nazarene Univ. (CA)
Point Park Univ. (PA)
Polytechnic Institute of New York
    Univ. (NY)
Post Univ. (CT)
Prescott Coll. (AZ)
Providence Coll. (RI)
Purdue Univ.–North Central (IN)
Purdue Univ.–West Lafayette (IN)
Quincy Univ. (IL)
Quinnipiac Univ. (CT)
Ramapo Coll. of New Jersey
Regis Coll. (MA)
Regis Univ. (CO)
Reinhardt Univ. (GA)
Rhode Island Coll.
Richard Stockton Coll. of New
    Jersey
Rider Univ. (NJ)
Rivier Coll. (NH)
Roberts Wesleyan Coll. (NY)
Roger Williams Univ. (RI)
Rogers State Univ. (OK)
Roosevelt Univ. (IL)
Rosemont Coll. (PA)
Rutgers, the State Univ. of New
    Jersey–Camden
Sacred Heart Univ. (CT)
Sage Colleges–Albany (NY)
Salem State Coll. (MA)
Salisbury Univ. (MD)
Salve Regina Univ. (RI)
Samford Univ. (AL)
San Diego State Univ.
San Francisco State Univ.
San Jose State Univ. (CA)
Santa Clara Univ. (CA)
Schreiner Univ. (TX)
Seattle Pacific Univ.
Seattle Univ.
Seton Hall Univ. (NJ)
Seton Hill Univ. (PA)
Shaw Univ. (NC)
Shawnee State Univ. (OH)
Shenandoah Univ. (VA)
Shimer Coll. (IL)
Shorter Coll. (GA)
Sierra Nevada Coll. (NV)
Simpson Univ. (CA)

Skidmore Coll. (NY)
Sonoma State Univ. (CA)
South Dakota State Univ.
Southeast Missouri State Univ.
Southeastern Louisiana Univ.
Southeastern Oklahoma State Univ.
Southern Arkansas Univ.
Southern Connecticut State Univ.
Southern Illinois Univ.–Carbondale
Southern Illinois Univ.–Edwardsville
Southern Methodist Univ. (TX)
Southern Nazarene Univ. (OK)
Southern New Hampshire Univ.
Southern Univ.–New Orleans
Southern Vermont Coll.
Southwest Baptist Univ. (MO)
Southwest Minnesota State Univ.
Southwestern Adventist Univ. (TX)
Southwestern Assemblies of God
    Univ. (TX)
Southwestern Coll. (KS)
Southwestern Univ. (TX)
Spalding Univ. (KY)
Spring Hill Coll. (AL)
Springfield Coll. (MA)
St. Andrews Presbyterian Coll. (NC)
St. Anselm Coll. (NH)
St. Cloud State Univ. (MN)
St. Edward's Univ. (TX)
St. Francis Coll. (NY)
St. Gregory's Univ. (OK)
St. John Fisher Coll. (NY)
St. John's Univ. (NY)
St. John's Univ. (MN)
St. Joseph Coll. (CT)
St. Joseph's Coll. New York
St. Joseph's Univ. (PA)
St. Louis Univ.
St. Martin's Univ. (WA)
St. Mary's Coll. (IN)
St. Mary's Coll. of California
St. Mary-of-the-Woods Coll. (IN)
St. Norbert Coll. (WI)
St. Olaf Coll. (MN)
St. Peter's Coll. (NJ)
St. Thomas Aquinas Coll. (NY)
St. Thomas Univ. (FL)
St. Vincent Coll. (PA)
St. Xavier Univ. (IL)
Stephen F. Austin State Univ. (TX)
Stetson Univ. (FL)
Stevens Institute of Technology
    (NJ)
Suffolk Univ. (MA)
SUNY Coll.–Old Westbury
SUNY Empire State Coll.
SUNY Institute of Technology–
    Utica/Rome
SUNY–Fredonia
SUNY–Oswego
SUNY–Plattsburgh
SUNY–Stony Brook
Syracuse Univ. (NY)
Tabor Coll. (KS)
Tarleton State Univ. (TX)
Temple Univ. (PA)
Tennessee State Univ.
Texas Christian Univ.
Texas Coll.
Texas Tech Univ.
Texas Woman's Univ.

Thomas Aquinas Coll. (CA)
Thomas Edison State Coll. (NJ)
Thomas More Coll. (KY)
Thomas Univ. (GA)
Tiffin Univ. (OH)
Tougaloo Coll. (MS)
Touro Coll. (NY)
Transylvania Univ. (KY)
Trine Univ. (IN)
Trinity International Univ. (IL)
Trinity Univ. (DC)
Troy Univ. (AL)
Tulane Univ. (LA)
Union Coll. (NY)
Union Coll. (NE)
Union Institute and Univ. (OH)
United States Air Force Academy
    (CO)
Unity Coll. (ME)
Univ. at Albany–SUNY
Univ. at Buffalo–SUNY
Univ. of Akron (OH)
Univ. of Alaska–Anchorage
Univ. of Alaska–Fairbanks
Univ. of Alaska–Southeast
Univ. of Arizona
Univ. of Arkansas–Little Rock
Univ. of Arkansas–Pine Bluff
Univ. of Baltimore (MD)
Univ. of Bridgeport (CT)
Univ. of California–Irvine
Univ. of California–Riverside
Univ. of Central Florida
Univ. of Central Missouri
Univ. of Central Oklahoma
Univ. of Charleston (WV)
Univ. of Chicago
Univ. of Colorado–Boulder
Univ. of Connecticut
Univ. of Dayton (OH)
Univ. of Delaware
Univ. of Detroit Mercy
Univ. of Evansville (IN)
Univ. of Georgia
Univ. of Hartford (CT)
Univ. of Hawaii–Manoa
Univ. of Hawaii–West Oahu
Univ. of Houston–Downtown
Univ. of Illinois–Chicago
Univ. of Illinois–Springfield
Univ. of Illinois–Urbana-Champaign
Univ. of Indianapolis
Univ. of Iowa
Univ. of Kansas
Univ. of Kentucky
Univ. of La Verne (CA)
Univ. of Louisiana–Lafayette
Univ. of Louisiana–Monroe
Univ. of Louisville (KY)
Univ. of Maine
Univ. of Maine–Farmington
Univ. of Maine–Fort Kent
Univ. of Maine–Machias
Univ. of Maine–Presque Isle
Univ. of Mary (ND)
Univ. of Mary Hardin-Baylor (TX)
Univ. of Mary Washington (VA)
Univ. of Maryland–Eastern Shore
Univ. of Maryland–Univ. Coll.
Univ. of Massachusetts–Amherst
Univ. of Massachusetts–Lowell

Univ. of Memphis
Univ. of Miami (FL)
Univ. of Michigan–Ann Arbor
Univ. of Michigan–Dearborn
Univ. of Michigan–Flint
Univ. of Minnesota–Morris
Univ. of Mississippi
Univ. of Missouri
Univ. of Missouri–Kansas City
Univ. of Missouri–St. Louis
Univ. of Montana
Univ. of Montana–Western
Univ. of Nebraska–Kearney
Univ. of Nebraska–Lincoln
Univ. of Nebraska–Omaha
Univ. of Nevada–Las Vegas
Univ. of Nevada–Reno
Univ. of New England (ME)
Univ. of New Hampshire
Univ. of New Haven (CT)
Univ. of New Mexico
Univ. of New Orleans
Univ. of North Alabama
Univ. of North Carolina–Asheville
Univ. of North Carolina–Chapel Hill
Univ. of North Carolina–
    Greensboro
Univ. of North Dakota
Univ. of North Florida
Univ. of North Texas
Univ. of Northern Iowa
Univ. of Notre Dame (IN)
Univ. of Oklahoma
Univ. of Oregon
Univ. of Pennsylvania
Univ. of Pittsburgh
Univ. of Pittsburgh–Johnstown
Univ. of Redlands (CA)
Univ. of Rhode Island
Univ. of Richmond (VA)
Univ. of Rochester (NY)
Univ. of San Diego
Univ. of San Francisco
Univ. of Scranton (PA)
Univ. of Sioux Falls (SD)
Univ. of South Alabama
Univ. of South Carolina
Univ. of South Carolina–Upstate
Univ. of South Dakota
Univ. of South Florida
Univ. of Southern California
Univ. of Southern Indiana
Univ. of Southern Maine
Univ. of St. Francis (IL)
Univ. of St. Francis (IN)
Univ. of St. Mary (KS)
Univ. of St. Thomas (TX)
Univ. of St. Thomas (MN)
Univ. of Tampa (FL)
Univ. of Tennessee–Chattanooga
Univ. of Texas of the Permian Basin
Univ. of Texas–Austin
Univ. of Texas–Dallas
Univ. of Texas–Pan American
Univ. of Texas–San Antonio
Univ. of Texas–Tyler
Univ. of the Cumberlands (KY)
Univ. of the Ozarks (AR)
Univ. of the Pacific (CA)
Univ. of the Southwest (NM)
Univ. of Toledo (OH)

Univ. of Tulsa (OK)
Univ. of Utah
Univ. of Vermont
Univ. of Virginia
Univ. of Virginia–Wise
Univ. of Washington
Univ. of West Florida
Univ. of Wisconsin–Green Bay
Univ. of Wisconsin–Milwaukee
Univ. of Wisconsin–Parkside
Univ. of Wisconsin–River Falls
Univ. of Wisconsin–Stevens Point
Univ. of Wisconsin–Superior
Univ. of Wisconsin–Whitewater
Univ. of Wyoming
Urbana Univ. (OH)
Ursuline Coll. (OH)
Utah State Univ.
Utica Coll. (NY)
Valdosta State Univ. (GA)
Vanguard Univ. of Southern
    California
Vassar Coll. (NY)
Victory Univ. (TN)
Villanova Univ. (PA)
Virginia Intermont Coll.
Virginia State Univ.
Virginia Tech
Virginia Wesleyan Coll.
Viterbo Univ. (WI)
Waldorf Coll. (IA)
Warner Pacific Coll. (OR)
Warren Wilson Coll. (NC)
Washburn Univ. (KS)
Washington Adventist Univ. (MD)
Washington Coll. (MD)
Washington State Univ.
Washington Univ. in St. Louis
Wells Coll. (NY)
Wesley Coll. (DE)
Wesleyan Coll. (GA)
West Chester Univ. of Pennsylvania
West Liberty Univ. (WV)
West Texas A&M Univ.
West Virginia State Univ.
West Virginia Univ.
West Virginia Univ. Institute of
    Technology
West Virginia Univ.–Parkersburg
Western Carolina Univ. (NC)
Western Connecticut State Univ.
Western Illinois Univ.
Western Kentucky Univ.
Western Michigan Univ.
Western New England Coll. (MA)
Western New Mexico Univ.
Western Oregon Univ.
Western Washington Univ.
Westfield State Coll. (MA)
Westmont Coll. (CA)
Wheeling Jesuit Univ. (WV)
Wheelock Coll. (MA)
Whittier Coll. (CA)
Whitworth Univ. (WA)
Wichita State Univ. (KS)
Wilkes Univ. (PA)
Willamette Univ. (OR)
William Carey Univ. (MS)
William Jewell Coll. (MO)
Williams Baptist Coll. (AR)
Wilmington Coll. (OH)

Wilmington Univ. (DE)
Wingate Univ. (NC)
Winston-Salem State Univ. (NC)
Wittenberg Univ. (OH)
Wofford Coll. (SC)
Worcester Polytechnic Institute
    (MA)
Wright State Univ. (OH)
Xavier Univ. (OH)
Yale Univ. (CT)
York Coll. (NE)
York Coll. of Pennsylvania
Youngstown State Univ. (OH)

Library Science

Syracuse Univ. (NY)
Univ. of Washington

Library Science/ Librarianship

Ball State Univ. (IN)
Chadron State Coll. (NE)
Clarion Univ. of Pennsylvania
Kutztown Univ. of Pennsylvania
Miami Univ.–Oxford (OH)
Northwestern Oklahoma State
    Univ.
Our Lady of the Lake Univ. (TX)
Syracuse Univ. (NY)
Univ. of Kentucky
Univ. of Maine–Augusta
Univ. of Nebraska–Omaha
Univ. of Southern Mississippi

Management Information Systems and Services

Albany State Univ. (GA)
Albertus Magnus Coll. (CT)
American Univ. (DC)
Anderson Univ. (SC)
Andrews Univ. (MI)
Angelo State Univ. (TX)
Anna Maria Coll. (MA)
Appalachian State Univ. (NC)
Arcadia Univ. (PA)
Arizona State Univ.
Ashland Univ. (OH)
Auburn Univ. (AL)
Auburn Univ.–Montgomery (AL)
Augsburg Coll. (MN)
Augusta State Univ. (GA)
Aurora Univ. (IL)
Avila Univ. (MO)
Azusa Pacific Univ. (CA)
Babson Coll. (MA)
Baker Coll. of Flint (MI)
Baker Univ. (KS)
Ball State Univ. (IN)
Barry Univ. (FL)
Baylor Univ. (TX)
Bellevue Univ. (NE)
Belmont Univ. (TN)
Biola Univ. (CA)
Boston Univ.
Bowling Green State Univ. (OH)
Bradley Univ. (IL)
Bridgewater Coll. (VA)

Bridgewater State Coll. (MA)
Brigham Young Univ.–Provo (UT)
Buena Vista Univ. (IA)
Cabrini Coll. (PA)
California State Univ.–Long Beach
California State Univ.–Sacramento
Calumet Coll. of St. Joseph (IN)
Calvin Coll. (MI)
Campbell Univ. (NC)
Canisius Coll. (NY)
Cardinal Stritch Univ. (WI)
Carroll Univ. (WI)
Catholic Univ. of America (DC)
Cedarville Univ. (OH)
Central Baptist Coll. (AR)
Central Connecticut State Univ.
Central Michigan Univ.
Chatham Univ. (PA)
City Univ. (WA)
Claflin Univ. (SC)
Clarkson Univ. (NY)
Clayton State Univ. (GA)
Cleary Univ. (MI)
Cleveland State Univ.
Coll. of Santa Fe (NM)
Colorado Christian Univ.
Columbia Coll. (MO)
Columbus State Univ. (GA)
Concordia Coll.–Moorhead (MN)
Concordia Univ. (NE)
Concordia Univ.–St. Paul (MN)
Corban Univ. (OR)
Cornerstone Univ. (MI)
Creighton Univ. (NE)
Culver-Stockton Coll. (MO)
CUNY–Baruch Coll.
Dallas Baptist Univ.
Dalton State Coll. (GA)
Dana Coll. (NE)
Daniel Webster Coll. (NH)
Davis and Elkins Coll. (WV)
Delaware Valley Coll. (PA)
Delta State Univ. (MS)
DeSales Univ. (PA)
Dominican Coll. (NY)
Drake Univ. (IA)
Duquesne Univ. (PA)
East Carolina Univ. (NC)
East Texas Baptist Univ.
Eastern Kentucky Univ.
Eastern Michigan Univ.
Eastern New Mexico Univ.
Eastern Univ. (PA)
Eastern Washington Univ.
Edgewood Coll. (WI)
Eureka Coll. (IL)
Excelsior Coll. (NY)
Fairmont State Univ. (WV)
Fayetteville State Univ. (NC)
Florida Atlantic Univ.
Florida Gulf Coast Univ.
Florida Institute of Technology
Florida International Univ.
Florida Southern Coll.
Florida State Univ.
Fort Lewis Coll. (CO)
Framingham State Coll. (MA)
Francis Marion Univ. (SC)
Freed-Hardeman Univ. (TN)
Fresno Pacific Univ. (CA)
Friends Univ. (KS)

Gallaudet Univ. (DC)
Gannon Univ. (PA)
Gardner-Webb Univ. (NC)
George Fox Univ. (OR)
George Mason Univ. (VA)
Georgetown Univ. (DC)
Georgia Southern Univ.
Georgia Southwestern State Univ.
Grace Coll. and Seminary (IN)
Graceland Univ. (IA)
Greenville Coll. (IL)
Hawaii Pacific Univ.
Henderson State Univ. (AR)
High Point Univ. (NC)
Hofstra Univ. (NY)
Holy Family Univ. (PA)
Houston Baptist Univ.
Howard Univ. (DC)
Humphreys Coll. (CA)
Illinois Coll.
Indiana State Univ.
Indiana Univ. of Pennsylvania
Indiana Univ. Southeast
Indiana Wesleyan Univ.
Iona Coll. (NY)
Iowa State Univ.
Jamestown Coll. (ND)
John Carroll Univ. (OH)
Judson Univ. (IL)
Juniata Coll. (PA)
Kettering Univ. (MI)
La Salle Univ. (PA)
La Sierra Univ. (CA)
Lake Erie Coll. (OH)
Lamar Univ. (TX)
Lambuth Univ. (TN)
Lasell Coll. (MA)
Le Moyne Coll. (NY)
Lenoir-Rhyne Univ. (NC)
LeTourneau Univ. (TX)
Lewis Univ. (IL)
Liberty Univ. (VA)
Lindenwood Univ. (MO)
Long Island Univ.–C.W. Post
    Campus (NY)
Loras Coll. (IA)
Louisiana Tech Univ.
Loyola Univ. Chicago
Luther Coll. (IA)
Macon State Coll. (GA)
Madonna Univ. (MI)
Maranatha Baptist Bible Coll. (WI)
Maryville Univ. of St. Louis (MO)
Master's Coll. and Seminary (CA)
Mesa State Coll. (CO)
Metropolitan State Coll. of Denver
Miami Univ.–Oxford (OH)
Mid-America Christian Univ. (OK)
Middle Tennessee State Univ.
Midland Lutheran Coll. (NE)
Midwestern State Univ. (TX)
Millikin Univ. (IL)
Milwaukee School of Engineering
Minot State Univ. (ND)
Misericordia Univ. (PA)
Mississippi State Univ.
Missouri Southern State Univ.
Missouri State Univ.
Missouri Univ. of Science &
    Technology
Monmouth Coll. (IL)

Montana Tech of the Univ. of
    Montana
Morehead State Univ. (KY)
Mount St. Mary's Univ. (MD)
Muhlenberg Coll. (PA)
Murray State Univ. (KY)
National-Louis Univ. (IL)
New Mexico Highlands Univ.
New York Institute of Technology
Nicholls State Univ. (LA)
Nichols Coll. (MA)
North Central Coll. (IL)
North Dakota State Univ.
North Park Univ. (IL)
Northeastern State Univ. (OK)
Northeastern Univ. (MA)
Northern Arizona Univ.
Northern Kentucky Univ.
Northern Michigan Univ.
Northern State Univ. (SD)
Northwest Christian Univ. (OR)
Northwest Missouri State Univ.
Northwestern Coll. (MN)
Northwood Univ. (MI)
Notre Dame Coll. of Ohio
Oakland City Univ. (IN)
Oakland Univ. (MI)
Ohio State Univ.–Columbus
Ohio Univ.
Oklahoma State Univ.
Oklahoma Wesleyan Univ.
Old Dominion Univ. (VA)
Oral Roberts Univ. (OK)
Oregon Institute of Technology
Our Lady of the Lake Univ. (TX)
Paine Coll. (GA)
Park Univ. (MO)
Pennsylvania State Univ.–Univ. Park
Pfeiffer Univ. (NC)
Point Loma Nazarene Univ. (CA)
Prairie View A&M Univ. (TX)
Purdue Univ.–Calumet (IN)
Reinhardt Univ. (GA)
Rhode Island Coll.
Rivier Coll. (NH)
Robert Morris Univ. (PA)
Rochester Institute of Technology
    (NY)
Rocky Mountain Coll. (MT)
Roger Williams Univ. (RI)
Rutgers, the State Univ. of New
    Jersey–Newark
Sage Colleges–Albany (NY)
Sam Houston State Univ. (TX)
Santa Clara Univ. (CA)
Schreiner Univ. (TX)
Seton Hall Univ. (NJ)
Seton Hill Univ. (PA)
Shawnee State Univ. (OH)
Simmons Coll. (MA)
Simpson Univ. (CA)
Sojourner-Douglass Coll. (MD)
Southeastern Univ. (FL)
Southern Adventist Univ. (TN)
Southern Connecticut State Univ.
Southern Illinois Univ.–Edwardsville
Southern New Hampshire Univ.
Southern Univ. and A&M Coll. (LA)
Southwestern Coll. (KS)
Spring Arbor Univ. (MI)
St. Bonaventure Univ. (NY)

St. Catherine Univ. (MN)
St. Cloud State Univ. (MN)
St. Gregory's Univ. (OK)
St. John's Univ. (NY)
St. Joseph's Coll. (IN)
St. Joseph's Univ. (PA)
St. Leo Univ. (FL)
St. Louis Univ.
St. Mary's Coll. (IN)
St. Mary's Univ. of San Antonio
    (TX)
St. Paul's Coll. (VA)
St. Xavier Univ. (IL)
Stetson Univ. (FL)
Stevens Institute of Technology
    (NJ)
Suffolk Univ. (MA)
Tarleton State Univ. (TX)
Temple Univ. (PA)
Texas A&M International Univ.
Texas A&M Univ.–Commerce
Texas A&M Univ.–Corpus Christi
Texas State Univ.–San Marcos
Texas Tech Univ.
Texas Wesleyan Univ.
Thiel Coll. (PA)
Thomas Edison State Coll. (NJ)
Touro Coll. (NY)
Trevecca Nazarene Univ. (TN)
Trine Univ. (IN)
Tulane Univ. (LA)
Univ. of Akron (OH)
Univ. of Alabama
Univ. of Alabama–Birmingham
Univ. of Alabama–Huntsville
Univ. of Alaska–Anchorage
Univ. of Arizona
Univ. of Arkansas–Little Rock
Univ. of Central Arkansas
Univ. of Central Florida
Univ. of Connecticut
Univ. of Dayton (OH)
Univ. of Denver
Univ. of Georgia
Univ. of Hartford (CT)
Univ. of Hawaii–Manoa
Univ. of Houston
Univ. of Houston–Downtown
Univ. of Illinois–Urbana-Champaign
Univ. of Indianapolis
Univ. of Kansas
Univ. of Louisiana–Lafayette
Univ. of Louisiana–Monroe
Univ. of Louisville (KY)
Univ. of Maine
Univ. of Mary Hardin-Baylor (TX)
Univ. of Massachusetts–Dartmouth
Univ. of Memphis
Univ. of Michigan–Dearborn
Univ. of Minnesota–Crookston
Univ. of Minnesota–Duluth
Univ. of Minnesota–Twin Cities
Univ. of Mississippi
Univ. of Missouri–St. Louis
Univ. of Montana
Univ. of Montevallo (AL)
Univ. of Nebraska–Omaha
Univ. of Nevada–Las Vegas
Univ. of Nevada–Reno
Univ. of New Orleans
Univ. of North Alabama

Univ. of North Carolina–Charlotte
Univ. of North Carolina–
    Wilmington
Univ. of North Texas
Univ. of Northern Iowa
Univ. of Notre Dame (IN)
Univ. of Oklahoma
Univ. of Pennsylvania
Univ. of Puget Sound (WA)
Univ. of Redlands (CA)
Univ. of Rhode Island
Univ. of Rio Grande (OH)
Univ. of San Francisco
Univ. of South Florida
Univ. of Southern Mississippi
Univ. of St. Thomas (TX)
Univ. of Tennessee–Martin
Univ. of Texas–Arlington
Univ. of Texas–Austin
Univ. of Texas–El Paso
Univ. of Texas–Pan American
Univ. of Texas–San Antonio
Univ. of Toledo (OH)
Univ. of Tulsa (OK)
Univ. of Utah
Univ. of Washington
Univ. of West Alabama
Univ. of West Florida
Univ. of West Georgia
Univ. of Wisconsin–Eau Claire
Univ. of Wisconsin–Green Bay
Univ. of Wisconsin–La Crosse
Univ. of Wisconsin–Madison
Univ. of Wisconsin–Milwaukee
Univ. of Wisconsin–Oshkosh
Univ. of Wisconsin–Parkside
Univ. of Wisconsin–Superior
Univ. of Wyoming
Upper Iowa Univ.
Ursuline Coll. (OH)
Villanova Univ. (PA)
Viterbo Univ. (WI)
Walsh Univ. (OH)
Washington State Univ.
Wayne State Univ. (MI)
Weber State Univ. (UT)
West Liberty Univ. (WV)
West Texas A&M Univ.
West Virginia Univ.
West Virginia Univ. Institute of
    Technology
Western Carolina Univ. (NC)
Western Connecticut State Univ.
Western Illinois Univ.
Western Kentucky Univ.
Western Michigan Univ.
Western New England Coll. (MA)
Western New Mexico Univ.
Western State Coll. of Colorado
Western Washington Univ.
Westminster Coll. (MO)
Westminster Coll. (UT)
Wichita State Univ. (KS)
Widener Univ. (PA)
Wilmington Univ. (DE)
Worcester Polytechnic Institute
    (MA)
Wright State Univ. (OH)
Xavier Univ. (OH)
York Coll. (NE)
York Coll. of Pennsylvania

Youngstown State Univ. (OH)

Management Sciences and Quantitative Methods

Arcadia Univ. (PA)
Aurora Univ. (IL)
Averett Univ. (VA)
Babson Coll. (MA)
Ball State Univ. (IN)
Bellarmine Univ. (KY)
Bellevue Univ. (NE)
Belmont Univ. (TN)
Boston Univ.
Bradley Univ. (IL)
Brigham Young Univ.–Provo (UT)
Bryant Univ. (RI)
Butler Univ. (IN)
Caldwell Coll. (NJ)
Carroll Univ. (WI)
Central Michigan Univ.
Central Washington Univ.
Christopher Newport Univ. (VA)
Cleveland State Univ.
Colorado Christian Univ.
Columbus State Univ. (GA)
Concordia Univ. Wisconsin
Cumberland Univ. (TN)
CUNY–Baruch Coll.
CUNY–Queens Coll.
Dalton State Coll. (GA)
Delaware State Univ.
Drake Univ. (IA)
Duquesne Univ. (PA)
Eastern Illinois Univ.
Eastern Michigan Univ.
Elizabethtown Coll. (PA)
Elmhurst Coll. (IL)
Fitchburg State Coll. (MA)
Florida State Univ.
Fordham Univ. (NY)
Georgia Coll. & State Univ.
Georgia State Univ.
Grand Valley State Univ. (MI)
Gwynedd-Mercy Coll. (PA)
Hampton Univ. (VA)
Hardin-Simmons Univ. (TX)
High Point Univ. (NC)
Hofstra Univ. (NY)
Illinois State Univ.
Indiana State Univ.
Indiana Univ. Northwest
Indiana Univ. Southeast
Iowa State Univ.
John Brown Univ. (AR)
La Roche Coll. (PA)
Lamar Univ. (TX)
Lasell Coll. (MA)
Lebanon Valley Coll. (PA)
Lehigh Univ. (PA)
Lincoln Univ. (PA)
Lindenwood Univ. (MO)
Louisiana State Univ.–Baton Rouge
Lourdes Coll. (OH)
Madonna Univ. (MI)
Manhattan Coll. (NY)
Maryville Univ. of St. Louis (MO)
McKendree Univ. (IL)
Miami Univ.–Oxford (OH)
Mount Ida Coll. (MA)

Mount Vernon Nazarene Univ. (OH)
National Univ. (CA)
National-Louis Univ. (IL)
North Central Coll. (IL)
North Greenville Univ. (SC)
Northeastern State Univ. (OK)
Northern Illinois Univ.
Northern Michigan Univ.
Northwestern Coll. (IA)
Ohio Northern Univ.
Ohio State Univ.–Columbus
Ohio Univ.
Oklahoma Baptist Univ.
Oklahoma Christian Univ.
Oral Roberts Univ. (OK)
Pace Univ. (NY)
Pennsylvania State Univ.–Univ. Park
Purdue Univ.–West Lafayette (IN)
Quincy Univ. (IL)
Regis Univ. (CO)
Rider Univ. (NJ)
Robert Morris Univ. (PA)
Rocky Mountain Coll. (MT)
Roosevelt Univ. (IL)
Rutgers, the State Univ. of New Jersey–New Brunswick
Salve Regina Univ. (RI)
Shippensburg Univ. of Pennsylvania
Simmons Coll. (MA)
Southern Adventist Univ. (TN)
Southern Connecticut State Univ.
Southern Illinois Univ.–Carbondale
Southern Methodist Univ. (TX)
Southwest Minnesota State Univ.
St. Ambrose Univ. (IA)
St. Bonaventure Univ. (NY)
St. Francis Univ. (PA)
St. Gregory's Univ. (OK)
St. John's Univ. (NY)
St. Joseph's Univ. (PA)
St. Leo Univ. (FL)
St. Louis Univ.
Stetson Univ. (FL)
Temple Univ. (PA)
Texas A&M Univ.–Kingsville
Texas Christian Univ.
Troy Univ. (AL)
Tulane Univ. (LA)
Tuskegee Univ. (AL)
Union Coll. (KY)
United States Air Force Academy (CO)
Univ. of Alabama
Univ. of Central Florida
Univ. of Central Missouri
Univ. of Central Oklahoma
Univ. of Connecticut
Univ. of Denver
Univ. of Florida
Univ. of Illinois–Chicago
Univ. of Illinois–Urbana-Champaign
Univ. of Iowa
Univ. of Kentucky
Univ. of Mary (ND)
Univ. of Maryland–Coll. Park
Univ. of Michigan–Flint
Univ. of Nebraska–Lincoln
Univ. of Nevada–Las Vegas
Univ. of Nevada–Reno
Univ. of Northern Iowa

Univ. of Oklahoma
Univ. of Pennsylvania
Univ. of San Francisco
Univ. of South Carolina
Univ. of Texas–San Antonio
Univ. of the Ozarks (AR)
Univ. of Toledo (OH)
Univ. of Wisconsin–Madison
Univ. of Wisconsin–Milwaukee
Univ. of Wyoming
Valparaiso Univ. (IN)
Virginia Tech
Wake Forest Univ. (NC)
Washington State Univ.
Western Michigan Univ.
Western New Mexico Univ.
Westminster Coll. (UT)
Worcester Polytechnic Institute (MA)
Wright State Univ. (OH)
Xavier Univ. (OH)

Manufacturing Engineering

Boston Univ.
Bradley Univ. (IL)
Brigham Young Univ.–Provo (UT)
California Polytechnic State Univ.–San Luis Obispo
California State Polytechnic Univ.–Pomona
Central Michigan Univ.
Central State Univ. (OH)
Cleveland State Univ.
Grand Valley State Univ. (MI)
Hofstra Univ. (NY)
Kettering Univ. (MI)
Marquette Univ. (WI)
Miami Univ.–Oxford (OH)
Missouri Univ. of Science & Technology
New Jersey Institute of Technology
North Carolina A&T State Univ.
North Dakota State Univ.
Northwestern Univ. (IL)
Oregon State Univ.
Robert Morris Univ. (PA)
Rochester Institute of Tech. (NY)
Southern Illinois Univ.–Edwardsville
Stanford Univ. (CA)
Texas State Univ.–San Marcos
Univ. of California–Berkeley
Univ. of Detroit Mercy
Univ. of Hartford (CT)
Univ. of Illinois–Urbana-Champaign
Univ. of Kentucky
Univ. of Louisville (KY)
Univ. of Miami (FL)
Univ. of Michigan–Dearborn
Univ. of Nebraska–Lincoln
Univ. of Southern Maine
Univ. of Wisconsin–Milwaukee
Univ. of Wisconsin–Stout
Utah State Univ.
Virginia State Univ.
Washington State Univ.
Western Michigan Univ.
Wichita State Univ. (KS)
Worcester Polytechnic Institute (MA)

Marine Transportation

California Maritime Academy
Humboldt State Univ. (CA)
Maine Maritime Academy
Massachusetts Maritime Academy
SUNY Maritime Coll.
United States Merchant Marine Academy (NY)

Marketing

Abilene Christian Univ. (TX)
Adrian Coll. (MI)
Alabama Agricultural and Mechanical Univ.
Alabama State Univ.
Albany State Univ. (GA)
Alderson-Broaddus Coll. (WV)
Alfred Univ. (NY)
Alma Coll. (MI)
Alvernia Univ. (PA)
American Univ. (DC)
Anderson Univ. (IN)
Andrews Univ. (MI)
Angelo State Univ. (TX)
Appalachian State Univ. (NC)
Arcadia Univ. (PA)
Arizona State Univ.
Arkansas State Univ.–Jonesboro
Assumption Coll. (MA)
Auburn Univ. (AL)
Augsburg Coll. (MN)
Augusta State Univ. (GA)
Aurora Univ. (IL)
Averett Univ. (VA)
Avila Univ. (MO)
Azusa Pacific Univ. (CA)
Babson Coll. (MA)
Baker Coll. of Flint (MI)
Baldwin-Wallace Coll. (OH)
Ball State Univ. (IN)
Barry Univ. (FL)
Baylor Univ. (TX)
Bellevue Univ. (NE)
Belmont Univ. (TN)
Benedict Coll. (SC)
Benedictine Univ. (IL)
Bentley Univ. (MA)
Berry Coll. (GA)
Biola Univ. (CA)
Black Hills State Univ. (SD)
Bloomfield Coll. (NJ)
Boise State Univ. (ID)
Boston Univ.
Bowling Green State Univ. (OH)
Bradley Univ. (IL)
Brenau Univ. (GA)
Bridgewater State Coll. (MA)
Bryant Univ. (RI)
Buena Vista Univ. (IA)
Butler Univ. (IN)
Cabrini Coll. (PA)
Caldwell Coll. (NJ)
California State Polytechnic Univ.–Pomona
California State Univ.–Fullerton
California State Univ.–Long Beach
California State Univ.–Sacramento
Canisius Coll. (NY)
Capital Univ. (OH)

Cardinal Stritch Univ. (WI)
Carlow Univ. (PA)
Carroll Univ. (WI)
Carthage Coll. (WI)
Catholic Univ. of America (DC)
Cedar Crest Coll. (PA)
Cedarville Univ. (OH)
Central Baptist Coll. (AR)
Central Connecticut State Univ.
Central Michigan Univ.
Champlain Coll. (VT)
Chatham Univ. (PA)
Chestnut Hill Coll. (PA)
Christopher Newport Univ. (VA)
City Univ. (WA)
Claflin Univ. (SC)
Clarion Univ. of Pennsylvania
Clark Atlanta Univ.
Clarkson Univ. (NY)
Clayton State Univ. (GA)
Cleary Univ. (MI)
Clemson Univ. (SC)
Cleveland State Univ.
Coastal Carolina Univ. (SC)
Coll. at Brockport–SUNY
Coll. of St. Scholastica (MN)
Coll. of the Ozarks (MO)
Columbia Coll. (IL)
Columbia Coll. (MO)
Columbus State Univ. (GA)
Concordia Univ.–St. Paul (MN)
Cornerstone Univ. (MI)
Creighton Univ. (NE)
Cumberland Univ. (TN)
CUNY–York Coll.
Dakota State Univ. (SD)
Dallas Baptist Univ.
Dalton State Coll. (GA)
Daniel Webster Coll. (NH)
Davenport Univ. (MI)
Davis and Elkins Coll. (WV)
Delaware State Univ.
Delaware Valley Coll. (PA)
Delta State Univ. (MS)
DePaul Univ. (IL)
DeSales Univ. (PA)
Dominican Coll. (NY)
Dominican Univ. (IL)
Drake Univ. (IA)
Duquesne Univ. (PA)
East Carolina Univ. (NC)
East Tennessee State Univ.
Eastern Illinois Univ.
Eastern Kentucky Univ.
Eastern Michigan Univ.
Eastern Univ. (PA)
Eastern Washington Univ.
Elmhurst Coll. (IL)
Emerson Coll. (MA)
Emporia State Univ. (KS)
Evangel Univ. (MO)
Excelsior Coll. (NY)
Fairfield Univ. (CT)
Fairleigh Dickinson Univ. (NJ)
Fairmont State Univ. (WV)
Fashion Institute of Technology (NY)
Felician Coll. (NJ)
Ferris State Univ. (MI)
Fitchburg State Coll. (MA)
Florida Atlantic Univ.

Florida Gulf Coast Univ.
Florida International Univ.
Florida Southern Coll.
Florida State Univ.
Fort Hays State Univ. (KS)
Fort Lewis Coll. (CO)
Fort Valley State Univ. (GA)
Francis Marion Univ. (SC)
Freed-Hardeman Univ. (TN)
Fresno Pacific Univ. (CA)
Friends Univ. (KS)
Gannon Univ. (PA)
Gardner-Webb Univ. (NC)
George Mason Univ. (VA)
George Washington Univ. (DC)
Georgetown Univ. (DC)
Georgia Coll. & State Univ.
Georgia Southern Univ.
Georgia Southwestern State Univ.
Georgia State Univ.
Golden Gate Univ. (CA)
Goldey Beacom Coll. (DE)
Grace Coll. and Seminary (IN)
Grambling State Univ. (LA)
Grand Valley State Univ. (MI)
Greenville Coll. (IL)
Grove City Coll. (PA)
Gwynedd-Mercy Coll. (PA)
Hampton Univ. (VA)
Hanover Coll. (IN)
Hardin-Simmons Univ. (TX)
Harding Univ. (AR)
Hawaii Pacific Univ.
High Point Univ. (NC)
Hillsdale Coll. (MI)
Hofstra Univ. (NY)
Houston Baptist Univ.
Howard Univ. (DC)
Husson Univ. (ME)
Idaho State Univ.
Illinois State Univ.
Indiana State Univ.
Indiana Univ. of Pennsylvania
Indiana Univ. Southeast
Indiana Univ.–Kokomo
Indiana Univ.–South Bend
Indiana Univ.-Purdue Univ.–Fort
    Wayne
Indiana Wesleyan Univ.
Iona Coll. (NY)
Iowa State Univ.
Jackson State Univ. (MS)
Jacksonville State Univ. (AL)
Jacksonville Univ. (FL)
James Madison Univ. (VA)
Jamestown Coll. (ND)
John Brown Univ. (AR)
John Carroll Univ. (OH)
Johnson and Wales Univ. (RI)
Juniata Coll. (PA)
Kansas State Univ.
Kean Univ. (NJ)
Kennesaw State Univ. (GA)
Kent State Univ. (OH)
Kentucky State Univ.
Kettering Univ. (MI)
King's Coll. (PA)
Kutztown Univ. of Pennsylvania
La Roche Coll. (PA)
La Salle Univ. (PA)
Lake Erie Coll. (OH)

Lake Superior State Univ. (MI)
Lakeland Coll. (WI)
Lamar Univ. (TX)
Lambuth Univ. (TN)
Lasell Coll. (MA)
Le Moyne Coll. (NY)
Lehigh Univ. (PA)
Lenoir-Rhyne Univ. (NC)
LeTourneau Univ. (TX)
Lewis Univ. (IL)
Limestone Coll. (SC)
Lindenwood Univ. (MO)
Lipscomb Univ. (TN)
Long Island Univ.–C.W. Post
    Campus (NY)
Loras Coll. (IA)
Louisiana Coll.
Louisiana State Univ.–Baton Rouge
Louisiana State Univ.–Shreveport
Louisiana Tech Univ.
Lourdes Coll. (OH)
Loyola Univ. Chicago
Loyola Univ. New Orleans
Lynchburg Coll. (VA)
MacMurray Coll. (IL)
Macon State Coll. (GA)
Madonna Univ. (MI)
Manhattan Coll. (NY)
Mansfield Univ. of Pennsylvania
Maranatha Baptist Bible Coll. (WI)
Marian Univ. (WI)
Marian Univ. (IN)
Marietta Coll. (OH)
Marquette Univ. (WI)
Marshall Univ. (WV)
Martin Univ. (IN)
Maryville Univ. of St. Louis (MO)
Marywood Univ. (PA)
McKendree Univ. (IL)
McNeese State Univ. (LA)
Messiah Coll. (PA)
Methodist Univ. (NC)
Miami Univ.–Oxford (OH)
Michigan State Univ.
MidAmerica Nazarene Univ. (KS)
Middle Tennessee State Univ.
Midwestern State Univ. (TX)
Millikin Univ. (IL)
Minnesota State Univ.–Mankato
Minnesota State Univ.–Moorhead
Minot State Univ. (ND)
Misericordia Univ. (PA)
Mississippi Coll.
Mississippi State Univ.
Missouri Baptist Univ.
Missouri Southern State Univ.
Missouri Western State Univ.
Mitchell Coll. (CT)
Morehead State Univ. (KY)
Morgan State Univ. (MD)
Morningside Coll. (IA)
Mount Mercy Coll. (IA)
Mount Vernon Nazarene Univ.
    (OH)
Murray State Univ. (KY)
Neumann Univ. (PA)
New Mexico Highlands Univ.
New Mexico State Univ.
New York Institute of Technology
Nicholls State Univ. (LA)
Nichols Coll. (MA)

North Central Coll. (IL)
North Georgia Coll. and State Univ.
North Greenville Univ. (SC)
Northeastern Illinois Univ.
Northeastern State Univ. (OK)
Northeastern Univ. (MA)
Northern Arizona Univ.
Northern Illinois Univ.
Northern Kentucky Univ.
Northern Michigan Univ.
Northern State Univ. (SD)
Northwest Missouri State Univ.
Northwestern Coll. (MN)
Northwood Univ. (MI)
Notre Dame Coll. of Ohio
Nova Southeastern Univ. (FL)
Oakland Univ. (MI)
Ohio State Univ.–Columbus
Ohio Univ.
Ohio Valley Univ. (WV)
Oklahoma Baptist Univ.
Oklahoma Christian Univ.
Oklahoma City Univ.
Oklahoma State Univ.
Oklahoma Wesleyan Univ.
Old Dominion Univ. (VA)
Olivet Coll. (MI)
Oregon Institute of Technology
Our Lady of the Lake Univ. (TX)
Pace Univ. (NY)
Paine Coll. (GA)
Palm Beach Atlantic Univ. (FL)
Park Univ. (MO)
Pennsylvania State Univ.–Univ. Park
Pepperdine Univ. (CA)
Philadelphia Univ.
Pittsburg State Univ. (KS)
Plymouth State Univ. (NH)
Point Park Univ. (PA)
Post Univ. (CT)
Prairie View A&M Univ. (TX)
Providence Coll. (RI)
Purdue Univ.–Calumet (IN)
Purdue Univ.–West Lafayette (IN)
Quincy Univ. (IL)
Radford Univ. (VA)
Regis Univ. (CO)
Rhode Island Coll.
Rider Univ. (NJ)
Robert Morris Univ. (PA)
Rochester Coll. (MI)
Rochester Institute of Technology
    (NY)
Roger Williams Univ. (RI)
Rutgers, the State Univ. of New
    Jersey–Camden
Rutgers, the State Univ. of New
    Jersey–New Brunswick
Rutgers, the State Univ. of New
    Jersey–Newark
Saginaw Valley State Univ. (MI)
Salisbury Univ. (MD)
Salve Regina Univ. (RI)
Sam Houston State Univ. (TX)
Santa Clara Univ. (CA)
Schreiner Univ. (TX)
Seattle Univ.
Seton Hall Univ. (NJ)
Seton Hill Univ. (PA)
Shippensburg Univ. of Pennsylvania
Siena Coll. (NY)

Simpson Coll. (IA)
South Carolina State Univ.
Southeast Missouri State Univ.
Southeastern Louisiana Univ.
Southeastern Oklahoma State Univ.
Southeastern Univ. (FL)
Southern Adventist Univ. (TN)
Southern Connecticut State Univ.
Southern Illinois Univ.–Carbondale
Southern Methodist Univ. (TX)
Southern Nazarene Univ. (OK)
Southern New Hampshire Univ.
Southern Univ. and A&M Coll. (LA)
Southern Utah Univ.
Southwest Minnesota State Univ.
Southwestern Adventist Univ. (TX)
Southwestern Coll. (KS)
St. Ambrose Univ. (IA)
St. Bonaventure Univ. (NY)
St. Cloud State Univ. (MN)
St. Edward's Univ. (TX)
St. Francis Univ. (PA)
St. Gregory's Univ. (OK)
St. John's Univ. (NY)
St. Joseph's Coll. (ME)
St. Joseph's Univ. (PA)
St. Leo Univ. (FL)
St. Mary's Coll. of California
St. Mary's Univ. of Minnesota
St. Mary's Univ. of San Antonio
    (TX)
St. Mary-of-the-Woods Coll. (IN)
St. Paul's Coll. (VA)
St. Peter's Coll. (NJ)
St. Thomas Aquinas Coll. (NY)
St. Vincent Coll. (PA)
St. Xavier Univ. (IL)
Stephen F. Austin State Univ. (TX)
Stephens Coll. (MO)
Stetson Univ. (FL)
Stonehill Coll. (MA)
Suffolk Univ. (MA)
SUNY Coll.–Old Westbury
SUNY–Oswego
Syracuse Univ. (NY)
Talladega Coll. (AL)
Tarleton State Univ. (TX)
Taylor Univ. (IN)
Temple Univ. (PA)
Tennessee Technological Univ.
Texas A&M Univ.–Coll. Station
Texas A&M Univ.–Commerce
Texas A&M Univ.–Corpus Christi
Texas A&M Univ.–Kingsville
Texas Christian Univ.
Texas State Univ.–San Marcos
Texas Tech Univ.
Texas Wesleyan Univ.
Texas Woman's Univ.
Thomas Coll. (ME)
Thomas Edison State Coll. (NJ)
Tiffin Univ. (OH)
Trevecca Nazarene Univ. (TN)
Trine Univ. (IN)
Trinity International Univ. (IL)
Troy Univ. (AL)
Tulane Univ. (LA)
Union Coll. (KY)
Union Coll. (NE)
Union Univ. (TN)
Univ. of Akron (OH)

Univ. of Alabama
Univ. of Alabama–Birmingham
Univ. of Alabama–Huntsville
Univ. of Alaska–Anchorage
Univ. of Alaska–Southeast
Univ. of Arkansas
Univ. of Arkansas–Little Rock
Univ. of Central Arkansas
Univ. of Central Florida
Univ. of Central Oklahoma
Univ. of Connecticut
Univ. of Dayton (OH)
Univ. of Delaware
Univ. of Denver
Univ. of Evansville (IN)
Univ. of Findlay (OH)
Univ. of Florida
Univ. of Georgia
Univ. of Hartford (CT)
Univ. of Hawaii–Hilo
Univ. of Hawaii–Manoa
Univ. of Houston
Univ. of Houston–Downtown
Univ. of Illinois–Chicago
Univ. of Illinois–Urbana-Champaign
Univ. of Indianapolis
Univ. of Iowa
Univ. of Kansas
Univ. of Kentucky
Univ. of Louisiana–Lafayette
Univ. of Louisiana–Monroe
Univ. of Louisville (KY)
Univ. of Mary Hardin-Baylor (TX)
Univ. of Maryland–Coll. Park
Univ. of Maryland–Univ. Coll.
Univ. of Massachusetts–Amherst
Univ. of Massachusetts–Dartmouth
Univ. of Memphis
Univ. of Miami (FL)
Univ. of Michigan–Dearborn
Univ. of Michigan–Flint
Univ. of Minnesota–Crookston
Univ. of Minnesota–Duluth
Univ. of Minnesota–Twin Cities
Univ. of Mississippi
Univ. of Montana
Univ. of Montevallo (AL)
Univ. of Nebraska–Lincoln
Univ. of Nebraska–Omaha
Univ. of Nevada–Las Vegas
Univ. of Nevada–Reno
Univ. of New Haven (CT)
Univ. of New Orleans
Univ. of North Alabama
Univ. of North Carolina–Charlotte
Univ. of North Carolina–
    Wilmington
Univ. of North Dakota
Univ. of North Florida
Univ. of North Texas
Univ. of Northern Iowa
Univ. of Notre Dame (IN)
Univ. of Oklahoma
Univ. of Pennsylvania
Univ. of Pittsburgh
Univ. of Portland (OR)
Univ. of Rhode Island
Univ. of Rio Grande (OH)
Univ. of San Diego
Univ. of San Francisco
Univ. of Scranton (PA)

Univ. of South Alabama
Univ. of South Carolina
Univ. of South Florida
Univ. of Southern Indiana
Univ. of Southern Mississippi
Univ. of St. Francis (IL)
Univ. of St. Thomas (TX)
Univ. of St. Thomas (MN)
Univ. of Tampa (FL)
Univ. of Tennessee
Univ. of Tennessee–Chattanooga
Univ. of Tennessee–Martin
Univ. of Texas of the Permian Basin
Univ. of Texas–Arlington
Univ. of Texas–Austin
Univ. of Texas–Brownsville
Univ. of Texas–El Paso
Univ. of Texas–Pan American
Univ. of Texas–San Antonio
Univ. of Texas–Tyler
Univ. of the District of Columbia
Univ. of the Ozarks (AR)
Univ. of the Southwest (NM)
Univ. of Toledo (OH)
Univ. of Tulsa (OK)
Univ. of Utah
Univ. of Washington
Univ. of West Florida
Univ. of West Georgia
Univ. of Wisconsin–Eau Claire
Univ. of Wisconsin–La Crosse
Univ. of Wisconsin–Madison
Univ. of Wisconsin–Milwaukee
Univ. of Wisconsin–Oshkosh
Univ. of Wisconsin–Superior
Univ. of Wisconsin–Whitewater
Univ. of Wyoming
Upper Iowa Univ.
Urbana Univ. (OH)
Ursuline Coll. (OH)
Utah State Univ.
Valdosta State Univ. (GA)
Valparaiso Univ. (IN)
Vanguard Univ. of Southern
    California
Villanova Univ. (PA)
Virginia Commonwealth Univ.
Virginia Intermont Coll.
Virginia State Univ.
Virginia Union Univ.
Viterbo Univ. (WI)
Wagner Coll. (NY)
Walsh Coll. of Accountancy and
    Business Administration (MI)
Walsh Univ. (OH)
Washburn Univ. (KS)
Washington Adventist Univ. (MD)
Washington State Univ.
Washington Univ. in St. Louis
Wayne State Univ. (MI)
Waynesburg Univ. (PA)
Webber International Univ. (FL)
Weber State Univ. (UT)
Wesley Coll. (DE)
West Texas A&M Univ.
West Virginia Univ.
West Virginia Wesleyan Coll.
Western Carolina Univ. (NC)
Western Connecticut State Univ.
Western Illinois Univ.
Western Kentucky Univ.

Western Michigan Univ.
Western New England Coll. (MA)
Western New Mexico Univ.
Western Washington Univ.
Westminster Coll. (UT)
Wheeling Jesuit Univ. (WV)
Whitworth Univ. (WA)
Wichita State Univ. (KS)
Widener Univ. (PA)
Wilberforce Univ. (OH)
Wilmington Univ. (DE)
Wingate Univ. (NC)
Woodbury Univ. (CA)
Wright State Univ. (OH)
Xavier Univ. (OH)
York Coll. of Pennsylvania
Youngstown State Univ. (OH)

Mason/Masonry

Northwestern Oklahoma State
    Univ.

Materials Engineering

Alfred Univ. (NY)
Arizona State Univ.
Auburn Univ. (AL)
California Polytechnic State Univ.–
    San Luis Obispo
California State Polytechnic Univ.–
    Pomona
California State Univ.–Long Beach
Columbia Univ. (NY)
Cornell Univ. (NY)
Drexel Univ. (PA)
Georgia Institute of Technology
Illinois Institute of Technology
Iowa State Univ.
Johns Hopkins Univ. (MD)
Lehigh Univ. (PA)
Massachusetts Institute of
    Technology
Michigan Technological Univ.
Missouri Univ. of Science &
    Technology
New Mexico Institute of Mining
    and Technology
North Carolina State Univ.–Raleigh
Northwestern Univ. (IL)
Ohio State Univ.–Columbus
Rensselaer Polytechnic Institute
    (NY)
Rice Univ. (TX)
Stevens Institute of Technology
    (NJ)
Univ. of Alabama–Birmingham
Univ. of California–Davis
Univ. of California–Irvine
Univ. of California–Los Angeles
Univ. of Connecticut
Univ. of Florida
Univ. of Illinois–Urbana-Champaign
Univ. of Iowa
Univ. of Kentucky
Univ. of Maryland–Coll. Park
Univ. of Minnesota–Twin Cities
Univ. of Nevada–Reno
Univ. of New Hampshire
Univ. of Pennsylvania
Univ. of Pittsburgh

Univ. of Tennessee
Univ. of Utah
Univ. of Washington
Univ. of Wisconsin–Madison
Univ. of Wisconsin–Milwaukee
Virginia Tech
Washington State Univ.
Winona State Univ. (MN)
Worcester Polytechnic Institute
    (MA)
Wright State Univ. (OH)
Youngstown State Univ. (OH)

Materials Science

Alfred Univ. (NY)
Carnegie Mellon Univ. (PA)
Case Western Reserve Univ. (OH)
Columbia Univ. (NY)
Michigan State Univ.
Northwestern Univ. (IL)
Pennsylvania State Univ.–Univ. Park
Stevens Institute of Technology
    (NJ)
Temple Univ. (PA)
Univ. of Arizona
Univ. of California–Berkeley
Univ. of California–Los Angeles
Univ. of Connecticut
Univ. of Illinois–Urbana-Champaign
Univ. of Michigan–Ann Arbor
Univ. of New Hampshire
Washington State Univ.
Wright State Univ. (OH)

Mathematics

Abilene Christian Univ. (TX)
Adams State Coll. (CO)
Adelphi Univ. (NY)
Adrian Coll. (MI)
Agnes Scott Coll. (GA)
Alabama Agricultural and
    Mechanical Univ.
Alabama State Univ.
Albany State Univ. (GA)
Albertus Magnus Coll. (CT)
Albion Coll. (MI)
Albright Coll. (PA)
Alcorn State Univ. (MS)
Alfred Univ. (NY)
Allegheny Coll. (PA)
Allen Univ. (SC)
Alma Coll. (MI)
Alvernia Univ. (PA)
Alverno Coll. (WI)
American International Coll. (MA)
American Univ. (DC)
Amherst Coll. (MA)
Anderson Univ. (IN)
Anderson Univ. (SC)
Andrews Univ. (MI)
Angelo State Univ. (TX)
Anna Maria Coll. (MA)
Appalachian State Univ. (NC)
Aquinas Coll. (MI)
Arcadia Univ. (PA)
Arizona State Univ.
Arkansas State Univ.–Jonesboro
Arkansas Tech Univ.
Armstrong Atlantic State Univ. (GA)

Asbury Univ. (KY)
Ashland Univ. (OH)
Assumption Coll. (MA)
Atlantic Union Coll. (MA)
Auburn Univ. (AL)
Auburn Univ.–Montgomery (AL)
Augsburg Coll. (MN)
Augusta State Univ. (GA)
Augustana Coll. (SD)
Augustana Coll. (IL)
Aurora Univ. (IL)
Austin Coll. (TX)
Austin Peay State Univ. (TN)
Averett Univ. (VA)
Avila Univ. (MO)
Azusa Pacific Univ. (CA)
Baker Univ. (KS)
Baldwin-Wallace Coll. (OH)
Ball State Univ. (IN)
Bard Coll. at Simon's Rock (MA)
Barnard Coll. (NY)
Barry Univ. (FL)
Barton Coll. (NC)
Bates Coll. (ME)
Baylor Univ. (TX)
Belhaven Univ. (MS)
Bellarmine Univ. (KY)
Belmont Univ. (TN)
Beloit Coll. (WI)
Bemidji State Univ. (MN)
Benedict Coll. (SC)
Benedictine Coll. (KS)
Benedictine Univ. (IL)
Bennett Coll. (NC)
Bennington Coll. (VT)
Bentley Univ. (MA)
Berea Coll. (KY)
Berry Coll. (GA)
Bethany Coll. (WV)
Bethany Coll. (KS)
Bethel Coll. (KS)
Bethel Coll. (TN)
Bethel Coll. (IN)
Bethel Univ. (MN)
Bethune-Cookman Univ. (FL)
Binghamton Univ.–SUNY
Biola Univ. (CA)
Black Hills State Univ. (SD)
Blackburn Coll. (IL)
Bloomfield Coll. (NJ)
Bloomsburg Univ. of Pennsylvania
Blue Mountain Coll. (MS)
Bluefield Coll. (VA)
Bluffton Univ. (OH)
Boise State Univ. (ID)
Boston Univ.
Bowdoin Coll. (ME)
Bowie State Univ. (MD)
Bowling Green State Univ. (OH)
Bradley Univ. (IL)
Brandeis Univ. (MA)
Brevard Coll. (NC)
Brewton-Parker Coll. (GA)
Briar Cliff Univ. (IA)
Bridgewater Coll. (VA)
Bridgewater State Coll. (MA)
Brigham Young Univ.–Hawaii
Brigham Young Univ.–Provo (UT)
Brown Univ. (RI)
Bryant Univ. (RI)
Bryn Mawr Coll. (PA)

Bucknell Univ. (PA)
Buena Vista Univ. (IA)
Buffalo State Coll.–SUNY
Butler Univ. (IN)
Cabrini Coll. (PA)
Caldwell Coll. (NJ)
California Baptist Univ.
California Institute of Technology
California Lutheran Univ.
California Polytechnic State Univ.–
    San Luis Obispo
California State Polytechnic Univ.–
    Pomona
California State Univ.–Bakersfield
California State Univ.–Chico
California State Univ.–Dominguez
    Hills
California State Univ.–East Bay
California State Univ.–Fresno
California State Univ.–Fullerton
California State Univ.–Long Beach
California State Univ.–Los Angeles
California State Univ.–Northridge
California State Univ.–Sacramento
California State Univ.–San
    Bernardino
California State Univ.–San Marcos
California State Univ.–Stanislaus
California Univ. of Pennsylvania
Calvin Coll. (MI)
Cameron Univ. (OK)
Campbell Univ. (NC)
Campbellsville Univ. (KY)
Capital Univ. (OH)
Cardinal Stritch Univ. (WI)
Carleton Coll. (MN)
Carlow Univ. (PA)
Carroll Coll. (MT)
Carroll Univ. (WI)
Carson-Newman Coll. (TN)
Carthage Coll. (WI)
Case Western Reserve Univ. (OH)
Catawba Coll. (NC)
Catholic Univ. of America (DC)
Cedar Crest Coll. (PA)
Cedarville Univ. (OH)
Centenary Coll. (NJ)
Centenary Coll. of Louisiana
Central Christian Coll. (KS)
Central Coll. (IA)
Central Connecticut State Univ.
Central Methodist Univ. (MO)
Central Michigan Univ.
Central State Univ. (OH)
Central Washington Univ.
Centre Coll. (KY)
Chadron State Coll. (NE)
Chapman Univ. (CA)
Charleston Southern Univ. (SC)
Chatham Univ. (PA)
Chestnut Hill Coll. (PA)
Cheyney Univ. of Pennsylvania
Chicago State Univ.
Chowan Univ. (NC)
Christian Brothers Univ. (TN)
Christopher Newport Univ. (VA)
Claflin Univ. (SC)
Claremont McKenna Coll. (CA)
Clarion Univ. of Pennsylvania
Clark Atlanta Univ.
Clark Univ. (MA)

Clarke Univ. (IA)
Clarkson Univ. (NY)
Clayton State Univ. (GA)
Clearwater Christian Coll. (FL)
Clemson Univ. (SC)
Cleveland State Univ.
Coe Coll. (IA)
Coker Coll. (SC)
Colby Coll. (ME)
Colgate Univ. (NY)
Coll. at Brockport–SUNY
Coll. of Charleston (SC)
Coll. of Idaho (ID)
Coll. of Mount St. Joseph (OH)
Coll. of Mount St. Vincent (NY)
Coll. of New Jersey
Coll. of Notre Dame of Maryland
Coll. of Our Lady of the Elms (MA)
Coll. of St. Benedict (MN)
Coll. of St. Elizabeth (NJ)
Coll. of St. Mary (NE)
Coll. of St. Rose (NY)
Coll. of St. Scholastica (MN)
Coll. of the Holy Cross (MA)
Coll. of the Ozarks (MO)
Coll. of William and Mary (VA)
Coll. of Wooster (OH)
Colorado Christian Univ.
Colorado Coll.
Colorado State Univ.
Colorado State Univ.–Pueblo
Columbia Coll. (SC)
Columbia Coll. (MO)
Columbia Univ. (NY)
Columbus State Univ. (GA)
Concord Univ. (WV)
Concordia Coll. (NY)
Concordia Coll.–Moorhead (MN)
Concordia Univ. (CA)
Concordia Univ. (MI)
Concordia Univ. (NE)
Concordia Univ. Chicago (IL)
Concordia Univ. Texas
Concordia Univ. Wisconsin
Concordia Univ.–St. Paul (MN)
Connecticut Coll.
Converse Coll. (SC)
Coppin State Univ. (MD)
Corban Univ. (OR)
Cornell Coll. (IA)
Cornell Univ. (NY)
Covenant Coll. (GA)
Creighton Univ. (NE)
Culver-Stockton Coll. (MO)
Cumberland Univ. (TN)
CUNY–Baruch Coll.
CUNY–Brooklyn Coll.
CUNY–City Coll.
CUNY–Coll. of Staten Island
CUNY–Hunter Coll.
CUNY–Lehman Coll.
CUNY–Medgar Evers Coll.
CUNY–Queens Coll.
CUNY–York Coll.
Daemen Coll. (NY)
Dakota Wesleyan Univ. (SD)
Dallas Baptist Univ.
Dana Coll. (NE)
Dartmouth Coll. (NH)
Davidson Coll. (NC)
Davis and Elkins Coll. (WV)

Defiance Coll. (OH)
Delaware State Univ.
Delaware Valley Coll. (PA)
Delta State Univ. (MS)
Denison Univ. (OH)
DePaul Univ. (IL)
DePauw Univ. (IN)
DeSales Univ. (PA)
Dickinson Coll. (PA)
Dickinson State Univ. (ND)
Dillard Univ. (LA)
Dominican Coll. (NY)
Dominican Univ. (IL)
Dordt Coll. (IA)
Dowling Coll. (NY)
Drake Univ. (IA)
Drew Univ. (NJ)
Drexel Univ. (PA)
Drury Univ. (MO)
Duke Univ. (NC)
Duquesne Univ. (PA)
Earlham Coll. (IN)
East Carolina Univ. (NC)
East Central Univ. (OK)
East Stroudsburg Univ. of
    Pennsylvania
East Tennessee State Univ.
East Texas Baptist Univ.
East-West Univ. (IL)
Eastern Connecticut State Univ.
Eastern Illinois Univ.
Eastern Kentucky Univ.
Eastern Mennonite Univ. (VA)
Eastern Michigan Univ.
Eastern Nazarene Coll. (MA)
Eastern New Mexico Univ.
Eastern Oregon Univ.
Eastern Univ. (PA)
Eastern Washington Univ.
Eckerd Coll. (FL)
Edgewood Coll. (WI)
Edinboro Univ. of Pennsylvania
Edward Waters Coll. (FL)
Elizabeth City State Univ. (NC)
Elizabethtown Coll. (PA)
Elmhurst Coll. (IL)
Elmira Coll. (NY)
Elon Univ. (NC)
Emmanuel Coll. (GA)
Emmanuel Coll. (MA)
Emory and Henry Coll. (VA)
Emory Univ. (GA)
Emporia State Univ. (KS)
Erskine Coll. (SC)
Eureka Coll. (IL)
Evangel Univ. (MO)
Excelsior Coll. (NY)
Fairfield Univ. (CT)
Fairleigh Dickinson Univ. (NJ)
Fairmont State Univ. (WV)
Faulkner Univ. (AL)
Fayetteville State Univ. (NC)
Felician Coll. (NJ)
Ferris State Univ. (MI)
Ferrum Coll. (VA)
Fitchburg State Coll. (MA)
Florida Atlantic Univ.
Florida Institute of Technology
Florida International Univ.
Florida Memorial Univ.
Florida Southern Coll.

Florida State Univ.
Fontbonne Univ. (MO)
Fordham Univ. (NY)
Fort Hays State Univ. (KS)
Fort Lewis Coll. (CO)
Fort Valley State Univ. (GA)
Framingham State Coll. (MA)
Francis Marion Univ. (SC)
Franciscan Univ. of Steubenville
    (OH)
Franklin and Marshall Coll. (PA)
Franklin Coll. (IN)
Franklin Pierce Univ. (NH)
Freed-Hardeman Univ. (TN)
Fresno Pacific Univ. (CA)
Friends Univ. (KS)
Frostburg State Univ. (MD)
Furman Univ. (SC)
Gallaudet Univ. (DC)
Gannon Univ. (PA)
Gardner-Webb Univ. (NC)
George Fox Univ. (OR)
George Mason Univ. (VA)
George Washington Univ. (DC)
Georgetown Coll. (KY)
Georgetown Univ. (DC)
Georgia Coll. & State Univ.
Georgia Southern Univ.
Georgia Southwestern State Univ.
Georgia State Univ.
Georgian Court Univ. (NJ)
Gettysburg Coll. (PA)
Gonzaga Univ. (WA)
Gordon Coll. (MA)
Goshen Coll. (IN)
Goucher Coll. (MD)
Grace Coll. and Seminary (IN)
Graceland Univ. (IA)
Grambling State Univ. (LA)
Grand Valley State Univ. (MI)
Greensboro Coll. (NC)
Greenville Coll. (IL)
Grinnell Coll. (IA)
Grove City Coll. (PA)
Guilford Coll. (NC)
Gustavus Adolphus Coll. (MN)
Gwynedd-Mercy Coll. (PA)
Hamilton Coll. (NY)
Hamline Univ. (MN)
Hampden-Sydney Coll. (VA)
Hampshire Coll. (MA)
Hampton Univ. (VA)
Hannibal-LaGrange Coll. (MO)
Hanover Coll. (IN)
Hardin-Simmons Univ. (TX)
Harding Univ. (AR)
Hartwick Coll. (NY)
Harvard Univ. (MA)
Harvey Mudd Coll. (CA)
Haverford Coll. (PA)
Heidelberg Univ. (OH)
Henderson State Univ. (AR)
Hendrix Coll. (AR)
Heritage Univ. (WA)
High Point Univ. (NC)
Hillsdale Coll. (MI)
Hiram Coll. (OH)
Hobart and William Smith Colleges
    (NY)
Hofstra Univ. (NY)
Holy Family Univ. (PA)

Hood Coll. (MD)
Hope Coll. (MI)
Houghton Coll. (NY)
Houston Baptist Univ.
Howard Payne Univ. (TX)
Howard Univ. (DC)
Humboldt State Univ. (CA)
Huntingdon Coll. (AL)
Huntington Univ. (IN)
Huston-Tillotson Univ. (TX)
Idaho State Univ.
Illinois Coll.
Illinois State Univ.
Illinois Wesleyan Univ.
Immaculata Univ. (PA)
Indiana State Univ.
Indiana Univ. East
Indiana Univ. Northwest
Indiana Univ. of Pennsylvania
Indiana Univ. Southeast
Indiana Univ.–Bloomington
Indiana Univ.–Kokomo
Indiana Univ.–South Bend
Indiana Univ.-Purdue Univ.–Fort
    Wayne
Indiana Univ.-Purdue Univ.–
    Indianapolis
Indiana Wesleyan Univ.
Iona Coll. (NY)
Iowa State Univ.
Iowa Wesleyan Coll.
Ithaca Coll. (NY)
Jackson State Univ. (MS)
Jacksonville State Univ. (AL)
Jacksonville Univ. (FL)
James Madison Univ. (VA)
Jamestown Coll. (ND)
Jarvis Christian Coll. (TX)
John Brown Univ. (AR)
John Carroll Univ. (OH)
Johns Hopkins Univ. (MD)
Johnson C. Smith Univ. (NC)
Judson Coll. (AL)
Judson Univ. (IL)
Juniata Coll. (PA)
Kalamazoo Coll. (MI)
Kansas State Univ.
Kansas Wesleyan Univ.
Kean Univ. (NJ)
Keene State Coll. (NH)
Kennesaw State Univ. (GA)
Kent State Univ. (OH)
Kentucky State Univ.
Kentucky Wesleyan Coll.
Kenyon Coll. (OH)
Keuka Coll. (NY)
King Coll. (TN)
King's Coll. (PA)
Knox Coll. (IL)
Kutztown Univ. of Pennsylvania
La Roche Coll. (PA)
La Salle Univ. (PA)
La Sierra Univ. (CA)
Lafayette Coll. (PA)
LaGrange Coll. (GA)
Lake Erie Coll. (OH)
Lake Forest Coll. (IL)
Lakeland Coll. (WI)
Lamar Univ. (TX)
Lambuth Univ. (TN)
Lander Univ. (SC)

Lane Coll. (TN)
Langston Univ. (OK)
Lawrence Technological Univ. (MI)
Lawrence Univ. (WI)
Le Moyne Coll. (NY)
Lebanon Valley Coll. (PA)
Lehigh Univ. (PA)
LeMoyne-Owen Coll. (TN)
Lenoir-Rhyne Univ. (NC)
Lesley Univ. (MA)
LeTourneau Univ. (TX)
Lewis & Clark Coll. (OR)
Lewis Univ. (IL)
Lewis-Clark State Coll. (ID)
Liberty Univ. (VA)
Limestone Coll. (SC)
Lincoln Memorial Univ. (TN)
Lincoln Univ. (PA)
Lincoln Univ. (MO)
Lindenwood Univ. (MO)
Lindsey Wilson Coll. (KY)
Linfield Coll. (OR)
Lipscomb Univ. (TN)
Livingstone Coll. (NC)
Lock Haven Univ. of Pennsylvania
Long Island Univ.–C.W. Post
    Campus (NY)
Longwood Univ. (VA)
Loras Coll. (IA)
Louisiana Coll.
Louisiana State Univ.–Baton Rouge
Louisiana State Univ.–Shreveport
Louisiana Tech Univ.
Loyola Marymount Univ. (CA)
Loyola Univ. Chicago
Loyola Univ. New Orleans
Lubbock Christian Univ. (TX)
Luther Coll. (IA)
Lycoming Coll. (PA)
Lynchburg Coll. (VA)
Lyon Coll. (AR)
Macalester Coll. (MN)
Macon State Coll. (GA)
Madonna Univ. (MI)
Maharishi Univ. of Management
    (IA)
Malone Univ. (OH)
Manchester Coll. (IN)
Manhattan Coll. (NY)
Manhattanville Coll. (NY)
Mansfield Univ. of Pennsylvania
Marian Univ. (WI)
Marian Univ. (IN)
Marietta Coll. (OH)
Marist Coll. (NY)
Marquette Univ. (WI)
Mars Hill Coll. (NC)
Marshall Univ. (WV)
Martin Univ. (IN)
Mary Baldwin Coll. (VA)
Marygrove Coll. (MI)
Marymount Univ. (VA)
Maryville Coll. (TN)
Maryville Univ. of St. Louis (MO)
Marywood Univ. (PA)
Massachusetts Coll. of Liberal Arts
Massachusetts Institute of
    Technology
Master's Coll. and Seminary (CA)
Mayville State Univ. (ND)
McDaniel Coll. (MD)

McKendree Univ. (IL)
McMurry Univ. (TX)
McNeese State Univ. (LA)
McPherson Coll. (KS)
Mercy Coll. (NY)
Mercyhurst Coll. (PA)
Meredith Coll. (NC)
Merrimack Coll. (MA)
Mesa State Coll. (CO)
Messiah Coll. (PA)
Methodist Univ. (NC)
Metropolitan State Coll. of Denver
Miami Univ.–Oxford (OH)
Michigan State Univ.
Michigan Technological Univ.
MidAmerica Nazarene Univ. (KS)
Middle Tennessee State Univ.
Middlebury Coll. (VT)
Midland Lutheran Coll. (NE)
Midway Coll. (KY)
Midwestern State Univ. (TX)
Miles Coll. (AL)
Millersville Univ. of Pennsylvania
Milligan Coll. (TN)
Millikin Univ. (IL)
Mills Coll. (CA)
Millsaps Coll. (MS)
Minnesota State Univ.–Mankato
Minnesota State Univ.–Moorhead
Misericordia Univ. (PA)
Mississippi Coll.
Mississippi State Univ.
Mississippi Univ. for Women
Mississippi Valley State Univ.
Missouri Baptist Univ.
Missouri Southern State Univ.
Missouri State Univ.
Missouri Univ. of Science & Technology
Missouri Valley Coll.
Missouri Western State Univ.
Molloy Coll. (NY)
Monmouth Coll. (IL)
Monmouth Univ. (NJ)
Montana State Univ.
Montana State Univ.–Billings
Montana Tech of the Univ. of Montana
Montclair State Univ. (NJ)
Moravian Coll. (PA)
Morehead State Univ. (KY)
Morehouse Coll. (GA)
Morgan State Univ. (MD)
Morningside Coll. (IA)
Morris Coll. (SC)
Mount Holyoke Coll. (MA)
Mount Marty Coll. (SD)
Mount Mary Coll. (WI)
Mount Mercy Coll. (IA)
Mount Olive Coll. (NC)
Mount St. Mary Coll. (NY)
Mount St. Mary's Coll. (CA)
Mount St. Mary's Univ. (MD)
Mount Vernon Nazarene Univ. (OH)
Muhlenberg Coll. (PA)
Murray State Univ. (KY)
Muskingum Univ. (OH)
National Univ. (CA)
Nazareth Coll. (NY)
Nebraska Wesleyan Univ.

New England Coll. (NH)
New Jersey City Univ.
New Mexico Highlands Univ.
New Mexico Institute of Mining and Technology
New Mexico State Univ.
New York Univ.
Newberry Coll. (SC)
Newman Univ. (KS)
Niagara Univ. (NY)
Nicholls State Univ. (LA)
Nichols Coll. (MA)
Norfolk State Univ. (VA)
North Carolina A&T State Univ.
North Carolina Central Univ.
North Carolina State Univ.–Raleigh
North Carolina Wesleyan Coll.
North Central Coll. (IL)
North Dakota State Univ.
North Georgia Coll. and State Univ.
North Greenville Univ. (SC)
North Park Univ. (IL)
Northeastern Illinois Univ.
Northeastern State Univ. (OK)
Northeastern Univ. (MA)
Northern Arizona Univ.
Northern Illinois Univ.
Northern Kentucky Univ.
Northern Michigan Univ.
Northern State Univ. (SD)
Northland Coll. (WI)
Northwest Missouri State Univ.
Northwest Univ. (WA)
Northwestern Coll. (MN)
Northwestern Coll. (IA)
Northwestern Oklahoma State Univ.
Northwestern State Univ. of Louisiana
Northwestern Univ. (IL)
Norwich Univ. (VT)
Notre Dame Coll. of Ohio
Nyack Coll. (NY)
Oakland Univ. (MI)
Oakwood Univ. (AL)
Oberlin Coll. (OH)
Occidental Coll. (CA)
Oglethorpe Univ. (GA)
Ohio Dominican Univ.
Ohio Northern Univ.
Ohio State Univ.–Columbus
Ohio Univ.
Ohio Wesleyan Univ.
Oklahoma Baptist Univ.
Oklahoma Christian Univ.
Oklahoma City Univ.
Oklahoma Panhandle State Univ.
Oklahoma State Univ.
Oklahoma Wesleyan Univ.
Old Dominion Univ. (VA)
Olivet Coll. (MI)
Olivet Nazarene Univ. (IL)
Oral Roberts Univ. (OK)
Oregon State Univ.
Otterbein Coll. (OH)
Ouachita Baptist Univ. (AR)
Our Lady of the Lake Univ. (TX)
Pace Univ. (NY)
Pacific Lutheran Univ. (WA)
Pacific Union Coll. (CA)
Pacific Univ. (OR)

Paine Coll. (GA)
Palm Beach Atlantic Univ. (FL)
Pennsylvania State Univ.–Univ. Park
Pepperdine Univ. (CA)
Peru State Coll. (NE)
Pfeiffer Univ. (NC)
Philander Smith Coll. (AR)
Pikeville Coll. (KY)
Pittsburg State Univ. (KS)
Pitzer Coll. (CA)
Plymouth State Univ. (NH)
Point Loma Nazarene Univ. (CA)
Polytechnic Institute of New York Univ. (NY)
Pomona Coll. (CA)
Prairie View A&M Univ. (TX)
Presbyterian Coll. (SC)
Prescott Coll. (AZ)
Princeton Univ. (NJ)
Principia Coll. (IL)
Providence Coll. (RI)
Purchase Coll.–SUNY
Purdue Univ.–Calumet (IN)
Queens Univ. of Charlotte (NC)
Quincy Univ. (IL)
Quinnipiac Univ. (CT)
Radford Univ. (VA)
Ramapo Coll. of New Jersey
Randolph Coll. (VA)
Randolph-Macon Coll. (VA)
Reed Coll. (OR)
Regis Univ. (CO)
Reinhardt Univ. (GA)
Rensselaer Polytechnic Institute (NY)
Rhode Island Coll.
Rhodes Coll. (TN)
Rice Univ. (TX)
Richard Stockton Coll. of New Jersey
Rider Univ. (NJ)
Ripon Coll. (WI)
Rivier Coll. (NH)
Roanoke Coll. (VA)
Roberts Wesleyan Coll. (NY)
Rockford Coll. (IL)
Rockhurst Univ. (MO)
Rocky Mountain Coll. (MT)
Roger Williams Univ. (RI)
Rollins Coll. (FL)
Roosevelt Univ. (IL)
Rose-Hulman Institute of Technology (IN)
Rosemont Coll. (PA)
Russell Sage Coll. (NY)
Rust Coll. (MS)
Rutgers, the State Univ. of New Jersey–Camden
Rutgers, the State Univ. of New Jersey–New Brunswick
Rutgers, the State Univ. of New Jersey–Newark
Sacred Heart Univ. (CT)
Saginaw Valley State Univ. (MI)
Salem Coll. (NC)
Salem State Coll. (MA)
Salisbury Univ. (MD)
Salve Regina Univ. (RI)
Sam Houston State Univ. (TX)
Samford Univ. (AL)
San Diego State Univ.

San Francisco State Univ.
San Jose State Univ. (CA)
Santa Clara Univ. (CA)
Savannah State Univ. (GA)
Schreiner Univ. (TX)
Scripps Coll. (CA)
Seattle Pacific Univ.
Seattle Univ.
Seton Hall Univ. (NJ)
Seton Hill Univ. (PA)
Sewanee–Univ. of the South (TN)
Shaw Univ. (NC)
Shawnee State Univ. (OH)
Shenandoah Univ. (VA)
Shepherd Univ. (WV)
Shippensburg Univ. of Pennsylvania
Shorter Coll. (GA)
Siena Coll. (NY)
Silver Lake Coll. (WI)
Simmons Coll. (MA)
Simpson Coll. (IA)
Simpson Univ. (CA)
Skidmore Coll. (NY)
Slippery Rock Univ. of Pennsylvania
Smith Coll. (MA)
Sonoma State Univ. (CA)
South Carolina State Univ.
South Dakota School of Mines and Technology
South Dakota State Univ.
Southeast Missouri State Univ.
Southeastern Louisiana Univ.
Southeastern Oklahoma State Univ.
Southeastern Univ. (FL)
Southern Adventist Univ. (TN)
Southern Arkansas Univ.
Southern Connecticut State Univ.
Southern Illinois Univ.–Carbondale
Southern Illinois Univ.–Edwardsville
Southern Methodist Univ. (TX)
Southern Nazarene Univ. (OK)
Southern Polytechnic State Univ. (GA)
Southern Univ. and A&M Coll. (LA)
Southern Univ.–New Orleans
Southern Utah Univ.
Southern Wesleyan Univ. (SC)
Southwest Baptist Univ. (MO)
Southwest Minnesota State Univ.
Southwestern Adventist Univ. (TX)
Southwestern Coll. (KS)
Southwestern Oklahoma State Univ.
Southwestern Univ. (TX)
Spelman Coll. (GA)
Spring Arbor Univ. (MI)
Spring Hill Coll. (AL)
Springfield Coll. (MA)
St. Ambrose Univ. (IA)
St. Andrews Presbyterian Coll. (NC)
St. Anselm Coll. (NH)
St. Augustine's Coll. (NC)
St. Bonaventure Univ. (NY)
St. Catherine Univ. (MN)
St. Cloud State Univ. (MN)
St. Edward's Univ. (TX)
St. Francis Coll. (NY)
St. Francis Univ. (PA)
St. Gregory's Univ. (OK)
St. John Fisher Coll. (NY)
St. John's Univ. (MN)

St. John's Univ. (NY)
St. Joseph Coll. (CT)
St. Joseph's Coll. (ME)
St. Joseph's Coll. (IN)
St. Joseph's Coll. New York
St. Joseph's Univ. (PA)
St. Lawrence Univ. (NY)
St. Leo Univ. (FL)
St. Louis Univ.
St. Martin's Univ. (WA)
St. Mary's Coll. (IN)
St. Mary's Coll. of California
St. Mary's Coll. of Maryland
St. Mary's Univ. of Minnesota
St. Mary's Univ. of San Antonio (TX)
St. Mary-of-the-Woods Coll. (IN)
St. Michael's Coll. (VT)
St. Norbert Coll. (WI)
St. Olaf Coll. (MN)
St. Peter's Coll. (NJ)
St. Vincent Coll. (PA)
St. Xavier Univ. (IL)
Stanford Univ. (CA)
Stephen F. Austin State Univ. (TX)
Sterling Coll. (KS)
Stetson Univ. (FL)
Stevens Institute of Technology (NJ)
Stillman Coll. (AL)
Stonehill Coll. (MA)
Suffolk Univ. (MA)
Sul Ross State Univ. (TX)
SUNY Coll.–Cortland
SUNY Coll.–Old Westbury
SUNY Coll.–Oneonta
SUNY Coll.–Potsdam
SUNY–Fredonia
SUNY–Geneseo
SUNY–Oswego
SUNY–Plattsburgh
SUNY–Stony Brook
Susquehanna Univ. (PA)
Swarthmore Coll. (PA)
Syracuse Univ. (NY)
Tabor Coll. (KS)
Talladega Coll. (AL)
Tarleton State Univ. (TX)
Taylor Univ. (IN)
Temple Univ. (PA)
Tennessee State Univ.
Tennessee Technological Univ.
Tennessee Wesleyan Coll.
Texas A&M International Univ.
Texas A&M Univ.–Coll. Station
Texas A&M Univ.–Commerce
Texas A&M Univ.–Corpus Christi
Texas A&M Univ.–Kingsville
Texas Christian Univ.
Texas Coll.
Texas Lutheran Univ.
Texas State Univ.–San Marcos
Texas Tech Univ.
Texas Wesleyan Univ.
Texas Woman's Univ.
The Citadel (SC)
Thiel Coll. (PA)
Thomas Edison State Coll. (NJ)
Thomas More Coll. (KY)
Touro Coll. (NY)
Towson Univ. (MD)

Transylvania Univ. (KY)
Trevecca Nazarene Univ. (TN)
Trine Univ. (IN)
Trinity Christian Coll. (IL)
Trinity Coll. (CT)
Trinity International Univ. (IL)
Trinity Univ. (DC)
Troy Univ. (AL)
Truman State Univ. (MO)
Tufts Univ. (MA)
Tulane Univ. (LA)
Tusculum Coll. (TN)
Tuskegee Univ. (AL)
Union Coll. (KY)
Union Coll. (NE)
Union Coll. (NY)
Union Univ. (TN)
United States Military Academy (NY)
United States Naval Academy (MD)
Univ. at Albany–SUNY
Univ. at Buffalo–SUNY
Univ. of Akron (OH)
Univ. of Alabama
Univ. of Alabama–Birmingham
Univ. of Alabama–Huntsville
Univ. of Alaska–Anchorage
Univ. of Alaska–Fairbanks
Univ. of Alaska–Southeast
Univ. of Arizona
Univ. of Arkansas
Univ. of Arkansas–Little Rock
Univ. of Arkansas–Pine Bluff
Univ. of California–Berkeley
Univ. of California–Davis
Univ. of California–Irvine
Univ. of California–Los Angeles
Univ. of California–Riverside
Univ. of California–San Diego
Univ. of California–Santa Barbara
Univ. of California–Santa Cruz
Univ. of Central Arkansas
Univ. of Central Florida
Univ. of Central Missouri
Univ. of Central Oklahoma
Univ. of Chicago
Univ. of Cincinnati
Univ. of Colorado–Boulder
Univ. of Colorado–Colorado Springs
Univ. of Colorado–Denver
Univ. of Connecticut
Univ. of Dallas
Univ. of Dayton (OH)
Univ. of Delaware
Univ. of Denver
Univ. of Detroit Mercy
Univ. of Evansville (IN)
Univ. of Findlay (OH)
Univ. of Florida
Univ. of Georgia
Univ. of Great Falls (MT)
Univ. of Hartford (CT)
Univ. of Hawaii–Hilo
Univ. of Hawaii–Manoa
Univ. of Houston
Univ. of Idaho
Univ. of Illinois–Chicago
Univ. of Illinois–Springfield
Univ. of Illinois–Urbana-Champaign
Univ. of Indianapolis

Univ. of Iowa
Univ. of Kansas
Univ. of Kentucky
Univ. of La Verne (CA)
Univ. of Louisiana–Lafayette
Univ. of Louisiana–Monroe
Univ. of Louisville (KY)
Univ. of Maine
Univ. of Maine–Farmington
Univ. of Mary (ND)
Univ. of Mary Hardin-Baylor (TX)
Univ. of Mary Washington (VA)
Univ. of Maryland–Baltimore County
Univ. of Maryland–Coll. Park
Univ. of Maryland–Eastern Shore
Univ. of Massachusetts–Amherst
Univ. of Massachusetts–Boston
Univ. of Massachusetts–Lowell
Univ. of Memphis
Univ. of Miami (FL)
Univ. of Michigan–Ann Arbor
Univ. of Michigan–Dearborn
Univ. of Michigan–Flint
Univ. of Minnesota–Duluth
Univ. of Minnesota–Morris
Univ. of Minnesota–Twin Cities
Univ. of Mississippi
Univ. of Missouri
Univ. of Missouri–Kansas City
Univ. of Missouri–St. Louis
Univ. of Mobile (AL)
Univ. of Montana
Univ. of Montevallo (AL)
Univ. of Mount Union (OH)
Univ. of Nebraska–Kearney
Univ. of Nebraska–Lincoln
Univ. of Nebraska–Omaha
Univ. of Nevada–Las Vegas
Univ. of Nevada–Reno
Univ. of New England (ME)
Univ. of New Hampshire
Univ. of New Haven (CT)
Univ. of New Mexico
Univ. of New Orleans
Univ. of North Alabama
Univ. of North Carolina–Asheville
Univ. of North Carolina–Chapel Hill
Univ. of North Carolina–Greensboro
Univ. of North Carolina–Pembroke
Univ. of North Carolina–Wilmington
Univ. of North Dakota
Univ. of North Florida
Univ. of North Texas
Univ. of Northern Colorado
Univ. of Northern Iowa
Univ. of Notre Dame (IN)
Univ. of Oklahoma
Univ. of Oregon
Univ. of Pennsylvania
Univ. of Pittsburgh
Univ. of Pittsburgh–Johnstown
Univ. of Portland (OR)
Univ. of Puget Sound (WA)
Univ. of Redlands (CA)
Univ. of Rhode Island
Univ. of Richmond (VA)
Univ. of Rio Grande (OH)
Univ. of Rochester (NY)

Univ. of San Diego
Univ. of San Francisco
Univ. of Science and Arts of Oklahoma
Univ. of Scranton (PA)
Univ. of Sioux Falls (SD)
Univ. of South Carolina
Univ. of South Carolina–Upstate
Univ. of South Dakota
Univ. of South Florida
Univ. of Southern California
Univ. of Southern Indiana
Univ. of Southern Maine
Univ. of Southern Mississippi
Univ. of St. Francis (IN)
Univ. of St. Francis (IL)
Univ. of St. Mary (KS)
Univ. of St. Thomas (TX)
Univ. of St. Thomas (MN)
Univ. of Tampa (FL)
Univ. of Tennessee
Univ. of Tennessee–Chattanooga
Univ. of Tennessee–Martin
Univ. of Texas of the Permian Basin
Univ. of Texas–Arlington
Univ. of Texas–Austin
Univ. of Texas–Brownsville
Univ. of Texas–Dallas
Univ. of Texas–El Paso
Univ. of Texas–Pan American
Univ. of Texas–San Antonio
Univ. of Texas–Tyler
Univ. of the Cumberlands (KY)
Univ. of the District of Columbia
Univ. of the Incarnate Word (TX)
Univ. of the Ozarks (AR)
Univ. of the Pacific (CA)
Univ. of the Southwest (NM)
Univ. of Toledo (OH)
Univ. of Tulsa (OK)
Univ. of Utah
Univ. of Vermont
Univ. of Virginia
Univ. of Virginia–Wise
Univ. of Washington
Univ. of West Alabama
Univ. of West Florida
Univ. of West Georgia
Univ. of Wisconsin–Eau Claire
Univ. of Wisconsin–Green Bay
Univ. of Wisconsin–La Crosse
Univ. of Wisconsin–Madison
Univ. of Wisconsin–Milwaukee
Univ. of Wisconsin–Oshkosh
Univ. of Wisconsin–Parkside
Univ. of Wisconsin–Platteville
Univ. of Wisconsin–River Falls
Univ. of Wisconsin–Stevens Point
Univ. of Wisconsin–Superior
Univ. of Wisconsin–Whitewater
Univ. of Wyoming
Upper Iowa Univ.
Urbana Univ. (OH)
Ursinus Coll. (PA)
Ursuline Coll. (OH)
Utah State Univ.
Utah Valley Univ.
Utica Coll. (NY)
Valdosta State Univ. (GA)
Valley City State Univ. (ND)
Valparaiso Univ. (IN)

Vanderbilt Univ. (TN)
Vanguard Univ. of Southern California
Vassar Coll. (NY)
Villanova Univ. (PA)
Virginia Commonwealth Univ.
Virginia Military Institute
Virginia State Univ.
Virginia Tech
Virginia Wesleyan Coll.
Viterbo Univ. (WI)
Voorhees Coll. (SC)
Wabash Coll. (IN)
Wagner Coll. (NY)
Wake Forest Univ. (NC)
Walsh Univ. (OH)
Warren Wilson Coll. (NC)
Wartburg Coll. (IA)
Washburn Univ. (KS)
Washington Adventist Univ. (MD)
Washington and Jefferson Coll. (PA)
Washington and Lee Univ. (VA)
Washington Coll. (MD)
Washington State Univ.
Washington Univ. in St. Louis
Wayland Baptist Univ. (TX)
Wayne State Coll. (NE)
Wayne State Univ. (MI)
Waynesburg Univ. (PA)
Weber State Univ. (UT)
Webster Univ. (MO)
Wellesley Coll. (MA)
Wells Coll. (NY)
Wesleyan Coll. (GA)
Wesleyan Univ. (CT)
West Chester Univ. of Pennsylvania
West Liberty Univ. (WV)
West Texas A&M Univ.
West Virginia State Univ.
West Virginia Univ.
West Virginia Univ. Institute of Technology
Western Carolina Univ. (NC)
Western Connecticut State Univ.
Western Illinois Univ.
Western Kentucky Univ.
Western Michigan Univ.
Western New England Coll. (MA)
Western New Mexico Univ.
Western Oregon Univ.
Western State Coll. of Colorado
Western Washington Univ.
Westfield State Coll. (MA)
Westminster Coll. (PA)
Westminster Coll. (MO)
Westminster Coll. (UT)
Westmont Coll. (CA)
Wheaton Coll. (MA)
Wheaton Coll. (IL)
Wheeling Jesuit Univ. (WV)
Whitman Coll. (WA)
Whittier Coll. (CA)
Whitworth Univ. (WA)
Wichita State Univ. (KS)
Widener Univ. (PA)
Wiley Coll. (TX)
Wilkes Univ. (PA)
Willamette Univ. (OR)
William Carey Univ. (MS)
William Jewell Coll. (MO)

William Paterson Univ. of New Jersey
William Woods Univ. (MO)
Williams Coll. (MA)
Wilmington Coll. (OH)
Wilson Coll. (PA)
Wingate Univ. (NC)
Winston-Salem State Univ. (NC)
Winthrop Univ. (SC)
Wisconsin Lutheran Coll.
Wittenberg Univ. (OH)
Wofford Coll. (SC)
Worcester Polytechnic Institute (MA)
Worcester State Coll. (MA)
Wright State Univ. (OH)
Xavier Univ. (OH)
Yale Univ. (CT)
Yeshiva Univ. (NY)
York Coll. of Pennsylvania
Youngstown State Univ. (OH)

Mathematics and Computer Science

Alfred Univ. (NY)
Anderson Univ. (IN)
Augustana Coll. (IL)
Belhaven Univ. (MS)
Bennington Coll. (VT)
Bethel Coll. (IN)
Boston Univ.
Bowdoin Coll. (ME)
Brescia Univ. (KY)
Brown Univ. (RI)
Central Coll. (IA)
Central Michigan Univ.
Chestnut Hill Coll. (PA)
Colby Coll. (ME)
Colgate Univ. (NY)
Coll. of St. Benedict (MN)
Colorado Coll.
Concordia Univ. Chicago (IL)
Delaware State Univ.
Dominican Univ. (IL)
Drew Univ. (NJ)
Eastern Illinois Univ.
Eastern Michigan Univ.
Eastern Nazarene Coll. (MA)
Friends Univ. (KS)
Furman Univ. (SC)
Gonzaga Univ. (WA)
Goshen Coll. (IN)
Hampden-Sydney Coll. (VA)
Harvey Mudd Coll. (CA)
Hofstra Univ. (NY)
Immaculata Univ. (PA)
Indiana Univ.-Purdue Univ.–Fort Wayne
Ithaca Coll. (NY)
Keene State Coll. (NH)
Lake Superior State Univ. (MI)
Lawrence Technological Univ. (MI)
Lawrence Univ. (WI)
LeTourneau Univ. (TX)
Loyola Univ. Chicago
Mary Baldwin Coll. (VA)
Maryville Coll. (TN)
Massachusetts Institute of Technology
Newberry Coll. (SC)

Oakwood Univ. (AL)
Oglethorpe Univ. (GA)
Paine Coll. (GA)
Pepperdine Univ. (CA)
Pfeiffer Univ. (NC)
San Diego State Univ.
Santa Clara Univ. (CA)
Springfield Coll. (MA)
St. Gregory's Univ. (OK)
St. John's Univ. (MN)
St. Lawrence Univ. (NY)
St. Mary's Coll. (IN)
St. Mary's Coll. of California
St. Mary's Univ. of Minnesota
Stanford Univ. (CA)
Stevens Institute of Technology
    (NJ)
Swarthmore Coll. (PA)
Touro Coll. (NY)
Tusculum Coll. (TN)
United States Air Force Academy
    (CO)
Univ. of Illinois–Chicago
Univ. of Illinois–Urbana-Champaign
Univ. of Michigan–Dearborn
Univ. of Oregon
Univ. of South Carolina–Aiken
Univ. of St. Francis (IL)
Western Oregon Univ.
Wheaton Coll. (MA)
Whitman Coll. (WA)
Wingate Univ. (NC)
Yale Univ. (CT)

Mathematics and Statistics

Anderson Univ. (IN)
Asbury Univ. (KY)
Canisius Coll. (NY)
Carnegie Mellon Univ. (PA)
Dakota State Univ. (SD)
Evergreen State Coll. (WA)
Fresno Pacific Univ. (CA)
Hofstra Univ. (NY)
Indiana Univ. of Pennsylvania
Ithaca Coll. (NY)
Lycoming Coll. (PA)
Missouri Univ. of Science &
    Technology
New York Univ.
Northwestern Univ. (IL)
Ohio State Univ.–Columbus
Ohio Univ.
Oregon State Univ.
Seattle Pacific Univ.
Siena Coll. (NY)
St. Joseph's Coll. New York
St. Mary's Coll. of California
SUNY–Fredonia
Taylor Univ. (IN)
Tulane Univ. (LA)
United States Coast Guard
    Academy (CT)
Univ. at Albany–SUNY
Univ. of Miami (FL)
Univ. of Missouri–Kansas City
Univ. of Nebraska–Lincoln
Univ. of Pittsburgh
Univ. of Rochester (NY)
Univ. of South Alabama

Univ. of Tennessee
William Jewell Coll. (MO)

Mechanical Engineering

Alabama Agricultural and
    Mechanical Univ.
Alfred Univ. (NY)
Arizona State Univ.
Arkansas Tech Univ.
Auburn Univ. (AL)
Baker Coll. of Flint (MI)
Baylor Univ. (TX)
Bethel Coll. (IN)
Binghamton Univ.–SUNY
Boise State Univ. (ID)
Boston Univ.
Bradley Univ. (IL)
Brigham Young Univ.–Provo (UT)
Bucknell Univ. (PA)
California Baptist Univ.
California Institute of Technology
California Maritime Academy
California Polytechnic State Univ.–
    San Luis Obispo
California State Polytechnic Univ.–
    Pomona
California State Univ.–Chico
California State Univ.–Fresno
California State Univ.–Fullerton
California State Univ.–Long Beach
California State Univ.–Los Angeles
California State Univ.–Sacramento
Calvin Coll. (MI)
Carnegie Mellon Univ. (PA)
Case Western Reserve Univ. (OH)
Catholic Univ. of America (DC)
Cedarville Univ. (OH)
Central Connecticut State Univ.
Central Michigan Univ.
Central Washington Univ.
Christian Brothers Univ. (TN)
Clarkson Univ. (NY)
Clemson Univ. (SC)
Cleveland State Univ.
Coll. of New Jersey
Colorado School of Mines
Colorado State Univ.
Columbia Univ. (NY)
Cooper Union (NY)
Cornell Univ. (NY)
CUNY–City Coll.
Daniel Webster Coll. (NH)
Dordt Coll. (IA)
Drexel Univ. (PA)
Duke Univ. (NC)
Embry-Riddle Aeronautical Univ.
    (FL)
Fairfield Univ. (CT)
Florida A&M Univ.
Florida Atlantic Univ.
Florida Institute of Technology
Florida International Univ.
Florida State Univ.
Gannon Univ. (PA)
George Washington Univ. (DC)
Georgia Institute of Technology
Gonzaga Univ. (WA)
Grand Valley State Univ. (MI)
Grove City Coll. (PA)
Harding Univ. (AR)

Hofstra Univ. (NY)
Howard Univ. (DC)
Idaho State Univ.
Illinois Institute of Technology
Indiana Institute of Technology
Indiana Univ.-Purdue Univ.–Fort
    Wayne
Indiana Univ.-Purdue Univ.–
    Indianapolis
Iowa State Univ.
Johns Hopkins Univ. (MD)
Kansas State Univ.
Kettering Univ. (MI)
Lafayette Coll. (PA)
Lake Superior State Univ. (MI)
Lamar Univ. (TX)
Lawrence Technological Univ. (MI)
Lehigh Univ. (PA)
LeTourneau Univ. (TX)
Louisiana State Univ.–Baton Rouge
Louisiana Tech Univ.
Loyola Marymount Univ. (CA)
Manhattan Coll. (NY)
Marquette Univ. (WI)
Massachusetts Institute of
    Technology
Miami Univ.–Oxford (OH)
Michigan State Univ.
Michigan Technological Univ.
Midwestern State Univ. (TX)
Milwaukee School of Engineering
Minnesota State University–
    Mankato
Mississippi State Univ.
Missouri Univ. of Science &
    Technology
Montana State Univ.
New Jersey Institute of Technology
New Mexico Institute of Mining
    and Technology
New Mexico State Univ.
New York Institute of Technology
North Carolina A&T State Univ.
North Carolina State Univ.–Raleigh
North Dakota State Univ.
Northeastern Univ. (MA)
Northern Arizona Univ.
Northern Illinois Univ.
Northern Michigan Univ.
Northwestern Univ. (IL)
Norwich Univ. (VT)
Oakland Univ. (MI)
Ohio Northern Univ.
Ohio State Univ.–Columbus
Ohio Univ.
Oklahoma Christian Univ.
Oklahoma State Univ.
Old Dominion Univ. (VA)
Oral Roberts Univ. (OK)
Oregon State Univ.
Pennsylvania State Univ.–Univ. Park
Philadelphia Univ.
Polytechnic Institute of New York
    Univ. (NY)
Portland State Univ. (OR)
Prairie View A&M Univ. (TX)
Princeton Univ. (NJ)
Purdue Univ.–Calumet (IN)
Rensselaer Polytechnic Institute
    (NY)
Rice Univ. (TX)

Rochester Institute of Technology
    (NY)
Rose-Hulman Institute of
    Technology (IN)
Rutgers, the State Univ. of New
    Jersey–New Brunswick
Saginaw Valley State Univ. (MI)
San Diego State Univ.
San Francisco State Univ.
San Jose State Univ. (CA)
Santa Clara Univ. (CA)
Seattle Univ.
South Dakota School of Mines and
    Technology
South Dakota State Univ.
Southern Illinois Univ.–Carbondale
Southern Illinois Univ.–Edwardsville
Southern Univ. and A&M Coll. (LA)
St. Cloud State Univ. (MN)
St. Louis Univ.
St. Martin's Univ. (WA)
Stanford Univ. (CA)
Stevens Institute of Technology
    (NJ)
SUNY Coll. of Technology–Alfred
SUNY Maritime Coll.
SUNY–Stony Brook
Syracuse Univ. (NY)
Temple Univ. (PA)
Tennessee State Univ.
Tennessee Technological Univ.
Texas A&M Univ.–Kingsville
Texas Tech Univ.
Trine Univ. (IN)
Trinity Coll. (CT)
Tufts Univ. (MA)
Tulane Univ. (LA)
Tuskegee Univ. (AL)
Union Coll. (NY)
Union Univ. (TN)
United States Air Force Academy
    (CO)
United States Coast Guard
    Academy (CT)
United States Military Academy
    (NY)
United States Naval Academy (MD)
Univ. at Buffalo–SUNY
Univ. of Akron (OH)
Univ. of Alabama
Univ. of Alabama–Birmingham
Univ. of Alabama–Huntsville
Univ. of Alaska–Fairbanks
Univ. of Arizona
Univ. of Arkansas
Univ. of California–Berkeley
Univ. of California–Davis
Univ. of California–Irvine
Univ. of California–Los Angeles
Univ. of California–Riverside
Univ. of California–San Diego
Univ. of California–Santa Barbara
Univ. of Central Florida
Univ. of Colorado–Boulder
Univ. of Colorado–Colorado
    Springs
Univ. of Colorado–Denver
Univ. of Connecticut
Univ. of Dayton (OH)
Univ. of Denver
Univ. of Detroit Mercy

Univ. of Evansville (IN)
Univ. of Florida
Univ. of Hartford (CT)
Univ. of Hawaii–Manoa
Univ. of Houston
Univ. of Illinois–Chicago
Univ. of Illinois–Urbana-Champaign
Univ. of Indianapolis
Univ. of Iowa
Univ. of Kansas
Univ. of Kentucky
Univ. of Louisiana–Lafayette
Univ. of Louisville (KY)
Univ. of Maine
Univ. of Maryland–Baltimore
    County
Univ. of Maryland–Coll. Park
Univ. of Massachusetts–Amherst
Univ. of Massachusetts–Dartmouth
Univ. of Massachusetts–Lowell
Univ. of Memphis
Univ. of Miami (FL)
Univ. of Michigan–Ann Arbor
Univ. of Michigan–Dearborn
Univ. of Minnesota–Duluth
Univ. of Minnesota–Twin Cities
Univ. of Mississippi
Univ. of Missouri
Univ. of Missouri–Kansas City
Univ. of Missouri–St. Louis
Univ. of Nebraska–Lincoln
Univ. of Nevada–Las Vegas
Univ. of Nevada–Reno
Univ. of New Hampshire
Univ. of New Haven (CT)
Univ. of New Mexico
Univ. of New Orleans
Univ. of North Carolina–Charlotte
Univ. of North Dakota
Univ. of North Florida
Univ. of Notre Dame (IN)
Univ. of Oklahoma
Univ. of Pennsylvania
Univ. of Pittsburgh
Univ. of Portland (OR)
Univ. of Rhode Island
Univ. of Rochester (NY)
Univ. of San Diego
Univ. of South Alabama
Univ. of South Carolina
Univ. of South Florida
Univ. of Southern California
Univ. of St. Thomas (MN)
Univ. of Tennessee
Univ. of Tennessee–Chattanooga
Univ. of Texas–Arlington
Univ. of Texas–Austin
Univ. of Texas–El Paso
Univ. of Texas–Pan American
Univ. of Texas–San Antonio
Univ. of Texas–Tyler
Univ. of the District of Columbia
Univ. of the Pacific (CA)
Univ. of Toledo (OH)
Univ. of Tulsa (OK)
Univ. of Utah
Univ. of Vermont
Univ. of Virginia
Univ. of Washington
Univ. of Wisconsin–Madison
Univ. of Wisconsin–Milwaukee

Univ. of Wisconsin–Platteville
Univ. of Wyoming
Utah State Univ.
Valparaiso Univ. (IN)
Vanderbilt Univ. (TN)
Villanova Univ. (PA)
Virginia Commonwealth Univ.
Virginia Military Institute
Virginia Tech
Washington State Univ.
Washington Univ. in St. Louis
Wayne State Univ. (MI)
Weber State Univ. (UT)
West Texas A&M Univ.
West Virginia Univ.
West Virginia Univ. Institute of
    Technology
Western Kentucky Univ.
Western Michigan Univ.
Western New England Coll. (MA)
Wichita State Univ. (KS)
Widener Univ. (PA)
Wilkes Univ. (PA)
Worcester Polytechnic Institute
    (MA)
Wright State Univ. (OH)
Yale Univ. (CT)
York Coll. of Pennsylvania
Youngstown State Univ. (OH)

Mechanical-Engineering-Related Technologies/Technicians

Alabama Agricultural and
    Mechanical Univ.
Andrews Univ. (MI)
Bluefield State Coll. (WV)
Bowling Green State Univ. (OH)
Buffalo State Coll.–SUNY
California State Univ.–Sacramento
Central Connecticut State Univ.
Central Michigan Univ.
Central Washington Univ.
Cleveland State Univ.
Colorado State Univ.–Pueblo
Eastern Michigan Univ.
Eastern Washington Univ.
Embry-Riddle Aeronautical Univ.
    (FL)
Fairleigh Dickinson Univ. (NJ)
Fairmont State Univ. (WV)
Farmingdale State Coll.–SUNY
Ferris State Univ. (MI)
Georgia Southern Univ.
Indiana State Univ.
Indiana Univ.–South Bend
Indiana Univ.–Purdue Univ.–Fort
    Wayne
Indiana Univ.–Purdue Univ.–
    Indianapolis
Johnson and Wales Univ. (RI)
LeTourneau Univ. (TX)
Lincoln Univ. (MO)
McPherson Coll. (KS)
Metropolitan State Coll. of Denver
Michigan Technological Univ.
Milwaukee School of Engineering
Minnesota State Univ.–Mankato
Missouri State Univ.
Montana State Univ.

New York Institute of Technology
Norfolk State Univ. (VA)
Northeastern Univ. (MA)
Oklahoma State Univ.
Old Dominion Univ. (VA)
Oregon Institute of Technology
Pennsylvania Coll. of Technology
Pittsburg State Univ. (KS)
Point Park Univ. (PA)
Prairie View A&M Univ. (TX)
Purdue Univ.–Calumet (IN)
Purdue Univ.–North Central (IN)
Purdue Univ.–West Lafayette (IN)
Rochester Institute of Technology
    (NY)
Savannah State Univ. (GA)
South Carolina State Univ.
Southern Illinois Univ.–Carbondale
Southern Polytechnic State Univ.
    (GA)
St. Louis Univ.
SUNY Institute of Technology–
    Utica/Rome
Syracuse Univ. (NY)
Tennessee State Univ.
Texas A&M Univ.–Coll. Station
Texas A&M Univ.–Corpus Christi
Texas Tech Univ.
Thomas Edison State Coll. (NJ)
Univ. of Akron (OH)
Univ. of Arkansas–Little Rock
Univ. of Central Florida
Univ. of Central Missouri
Univ. of Dayton (OH)
Univ. of Hartford (CT)
Univ. of Houston
Univ. of Houston–Downtown
Univ. of Maine
Univ. of Massachusetts–Lowell
Univ. of North Carolina–Charlotte
Univ. of North Texas
Univ. of Pittsburgh–Johnstown
Univ. of Tennessee–Martin
Univ. of Texas–Brownsville
Univ. of Toledo (OH)
Utah State Univ.
Vermont Technical Coll.
Virginia State Univ.
Wayne State Univ. (MI)
Weber State Univ. (UT)
Western Michigan Univ.
William Penn Univ. (IA)
Youngstown State Univ. (OH)

Mechanics and Repairers

Boise State Univ. (ID)
Lewis-Clark State Coll. (ID)

Medical Clinical Sciences/Graduate Medical Studies

Ohio State Univ.–Columbus

Medical Illustration and Informatics

Alma Coll. (MI)
Cleveland Institute of Art
Iowa State Univ.

Montana Tech of the Univ. of
    Montana
Rochester Institute of Technology
    (NY)

Medicine (M.D.)

Ohio State Univ.–Columbus
Tulane Univ. (LA)
Univ. of Florida
Univ. of Kentucky
Univ. of Washington

Medieval and Renaissance Studies

Barnard Coll. (NY)
Brown Univ. (RI)
Catholic Univ. of America (DC)
Coll. of William and Mary (VA)
Connecticut Coll.
Dickinson Coll. (PA)
Duke Univ. (NC)
Hanover Coll. (IN)
Mount Holyoke Coll. (MA)
Ohio State Univ.–Columbus
Ohio Wesleyan Univ.
Pennsylvania State Univ.–Univ. Park
Rice Univ. (TX)
Rutgers, the State Univ. of New
    Jersey–New Brunswick
Smith Coll. (MA)
Southern Methodist Univ. (TX)
Swarthmore Coll. (PA)
Tulane Univ. (LA)
Univ. at Albany–SUNY
Univ. of California–Davis
Univ. of California–Santa Barbara
Univ. of Chicago
Univ. of Iowa
Univ. of Michigan–Ann Arbor
Univ. of Nebraska–Lincoln
Univ. of Notre Dame (IN)
Univ. of Oregon
Univ. of Toledo (OH)
Vassar Coll. (NY)
Washington and Lee Univ. (VA)
Wesleyan Univ. (CT)
Yale Univ. (CT)

Mental and Social Health Services and Allied Professions

Alvernia Univ. (PA)
Bemidji State Univ. (MN)
Bethany Univ. (CA)
Bethel Univ. (MN)
California State Univ.–Sacramento
Central Washington Univ.
Clarion Univ. of Pennsylvania
Clark Atlanta Univ.
Dominican Univ. (IL)
Drexel Univ. (PA)
Eastern Kentucky Univ.
Eastern Washington Univ.
Edgewood Coll. (WI)
Franciscan Univ. of Steubenville
    (OH)
Graceland Univ. (IA)
Harding Univ. (AR)

Hilbert Coll. (NY)
Indiana State Univ.
Indiana Univ.-Purdue Univ.–Fort
    Wayne
Indiana Wesleyan Univ.
James Madison Univ. (VA)
John Brown Univ. (AR)
Keene State Coll. (NH)
Marymount Univ. (VA)
Minnesota State Univ.–Mankato
Minnesota State Univ.–Moorhead
Minot State Univ. (ND)
Missouri Valley Coll.
Montana State Univ.–Northern
Morris Coll. (SC)
Mount Olive Coll. (NC)
New Mexico Highlands Univ.
New Mexico State Univ.
Northern Illinois Univ.
Northern Kentucky Univ.
Northwestern State Univ. of
    Louisiana
Ohio Univ.
Old Dominion Univ. (VA)
Palm Beach Atlantic Univ. (FL)
Pennsylvania Coll. of Technology
Roger Williams Univ. (RI)
Seton Hill Univ. (PA)
Sojourner-Douglass Coll. (MD)
Southern Nazarene Univ. (OK)
St. Cloud State Univ. (MN)
St. John Fisher Coll. (NY)
Texas A&M Univ.–Coll. Station
Texas A&M Univ.–Commerce
Thomas Edison State Coll. (NJ)
Univ. of Central Arkansas
Univ. of Florida
Univ. of Kansas
Univ. of La Verne (CA)
Univ. of Maine–Augusta
Univ. of Mary (ND)
Univ. of Nebraska–Lincoln
Univ. of Nebraska–Omaha
Univ. of Pennsylvania
Univ. of South Dakota
Univ. of St. Thomas (MN)
Univ. of Texas–Pan American
Univ. of Texas–Tyler
Univ. of the Cumberlands (KY)
Univ. of Toledo (OH)
Univ. of West Florida
Washburn Univ. (KS)
Western Connecticut State Univ.
Western Kentucky Univ.
Western Michigan Univ.
Western New Mexico Univ.
Western Washington Univ.
Youngstown State Univ. (OH)

Metallurgical Engineering

Colorado School of Mines
Missouri Univ. of Science &
    Technology
South Dakota School of Mines and
    Technology
Univ. of Texas–El Paso
Univ. of Washington

Microbiological Sciences and Immunology

Arizona State Univ.
Auburn Univ. (AL)
Bowling Green State Univ. (OH)
Brigham Young Univ.–Provo (UT)
California Polytechnic State Univ.–
    San Luis Obispo
California State Polytechnic Univ.–
    Pomona
California State Univ.–Chico
California State Univ.–Fresno
California State Univ.–Long Beach
California State Univ.–Los Angeles
California State Univ.–Sacramento
Central Michigan Univ.
Colorado State Univ.
Cornell Univ. (NY)
Humboldt State Univ. (CA)
Idaho State Univ.
Indiana Univ.–Bloomington
Iowa State Univ.
Juniata Coll. (PA)
Kansas State Univ.
Lawrence Univ. (WI)
Louisiana State Univ.–Baton Rouge
Miami Univ.–Oxford (OH)
Michigan State Univ.
Mississippi State Univ.
Mississippi Univ. for Women
Montana State Univ.
New Mexico State Univ.
North Carolina State Univ.–Raleigh
North Dakota State Univ.
Northern Arizona Univ.
Northern Michigan Univ.
Ohio State Univ.–Columbus
Ohio Univ.
Ohio Wesleyan Univ.
Oklahoma State Univ.
Oregon State Univ.
Pennsylvania State Univ.–Univ. Park
Purdue Univ.–West Lafayette (IN)
Quinnipiac Univ. (CT)
Rutgers, the State Univ. of New
    Jersey–New Brunswick
San Diego State Univ.
South Dakota State Univ.
Southern Illinois Univ.–Carbondale
Texas A&M Univ.–Coll. Station
Texas State Univ.–San Marcos
Texas Tech Univ.
Tulane Univ. (LA)
Univ. of Akron (OH)
Univ. of Alabama
Univ. of Arizona
Univ. of California–Berkeley
Univ. of California–Davis
Univ. of California–Los Angeles
Univ. of California–San Diego
Univ. of California–Santa Barbara
Univ. of Central Florida
Univ. of Florida
Univ. of Georgia
Univ. of Hawaii–Manoa
Univ. of Houston–Downtown
Univ. of Illinois–Urbana-Champaign
Univ. of Iowa
Univ. of Kansas
Univ. of Kentucky
Univ. of Louisiana–Lafayette
Univ. of Maine
Univ. of Maryland–Coll. Park

Univ. of Massachusetts–Amherst
Univ. of Miami (FL)
Univ. of Michigan–Ann Arbor
Univ. of Michigan–Dearborn
Univ. of Minnesota–Twin Cities
Univ. of Missouri
Univ. of Montana
Univ. of Nevada–Las Vegas
Univ. of New Hampshire
Univ. of Northern Iowa
Univ. of Oklahoma
Univ. of Pittsburgh
Univ. of Rhode Island
Univ. of South Florida
Univ. of Texas–Arlington
Univ. of Texas–Austin
Univ. of Texas–El Paso
Univ. of Vermont
Univ. of Washington
Univ. of Wisconsin–La Crosse
Univ. of Wisconsin–Madison
Univ. of Wisconsin–Oshkosh
Univ. of Wyoming
Utah State Univ.
Wagner Coll. (NY)
Washington State Univ.
Weber State Univ. (UT)

Middle/Near Eastern and Semitic Languages, Literatures, and Linguistics

Asbury Univ. (KY)
Baylor Univ. (TX)
Binghamton Univ.–SUNY
Brandeis Univ. (MA)
Brigham Young Univ.–Provo (UT)
Calvin Coll. (MI)
Columbia Univ. (NY)
Concordia Univ. (MI)
Concordia Univ. Wisconsin
Cornerstone Univ. (MI)
CUNY–Hunter Coll.
CUNY–Lehman Coll.
CUNY–Queens Coll.
Dartmouth Coll. (NH)
Georgetown Univ. (DC)
Hofstra Univ. (NY)
Indiana Univ.–Bloomington
Lawrence Univ. (WI)
Loyola Marymount Univ. (CA)
Lubbock Christian Univ. (TX)
Luther Coll. (IA)
Master's Coll. and Seminary (CA)
Mid-Continent Univ. (KY)
New York Univ.
Ohio State Univ.–Columbus
Temple Univ. (PA)
Touro Coll. (NY)
Union Univ. (TN)
United States Naval Academy (MD)
Univ. of California–Los Angeles
Univ. of Chicago
Univ. of Illinois–Urbana-Champaign
Univ. of Michigan–Ann Arbor
Univ. of Minnesota–Twin Cities
Univ. of Notre Dame (IN)
Univ. of Pennsylvania
Univ. of Texas–Austin
Univ. of Washington

Univ. of Wisconsin–Madison
Univ. of Wisconsin–Milwaukee
Washington Univ. in St. Louis
Wayne State Univ. (MI)
Yale Univ. (CT)
Yeshiva Univ. (NY)

Military Technologies

Eastern Washington Univ.

Mining and Mineral Engineering

Colorado School of Mines
Missouri Univ. of Science & Technology
Montana Tech of the Univ. of Montana
New Mexico Institute of Mining and Technology
Pennsylvania State Univ.–Univ. Park
South Dakota School of Mines and Technology
Southern Illinois Univ.–Carbondale
Univ. of Arizona
Univ. of Kentucky
Univ. of Nevada–Reno
Univ. of Utah
Virginia Tech
West Virginia Univ.

Mining and Petroleum Technologies/ Technicians

Bluefield State Coll. (WV)
Nicholls State Univ. (LA)
Univ. of Alaska–Fairbanks
Univ. of Pittsburgh–Bradford

Missions/Missionary Studies and Missiology

Abilene Christian Univ. (TX)
Asbury Univ. (KY)
Bethany Univ. (CA)
Bethel Coll. (IN)
Biola Univ. (CA)
California Baptist Univ.
Cedarville Univ. (OH)
Central Baptist Coll. (AR)
Central Christian Coll. (KS)
Concordia Univ. Wisconsin
Concordia Univ.–St. Paul (MN)
Corban Univ. (OR)
Cornerstone Univ. (MI)
Covenant Coll. (GA)
Crown Coll. (MN)
East Texas Baptist Univ.
Eastern Univ. (PA)
Free Will Baptist Bible Coll. (TN)
Hardin-Simmons Univ. (TX)
Harding Univ. (AR)
Hope International Univ. (CA)
Huntington Univ. (IN)
John Brown Univ. (AR)
King Coll. (TN)
LeTourneau Univ. (TX)
Liberty Univ. (VA)
Lipscomb Univ. (TN)

Lubbock Christian Univ. (TX)
Maranatha Baptist Bible Coll. (WI)
Master's Coll. and Seminary (CA)
Mid-Continent Univ. (KY)
MidAmerica Nazarene Univ. (KS)
North Central Univ. (MN)
North Greenville Univ. (SC)
Northwest Univ. (WA)
Northwestern Coll. (MN)
Nyack Coll. (NY)
Oklahoma Baptist Univ.
Oklahoma Christian Univ.
Oklahoma Wesleyan Univ.
Oral Roberts Univ. (OK)
Ouachita Baptist Univ. (AR)
Palm Beach Atlantic Univ. (FL)
Patten Univ. (CA)
Pfeiffer Univ. (NC)
Rochester Coll. (MI)
Simpson Univ. (CA)
Southeastern Univ. (FL)
Southern Nazarene Univ. (OK)
Southwest Baptist Univ. (MO)
Southwestern Assemblies of God Univ. (TX)
Spring Arbor Univ. (MI)
Toccoa Falls Coll. (GA)
Vanguard Univ. of Southern California
Williams Baptist Coll. (AR)

Modern Greek Language and Literature

Boston Univ.
Butler Univ. (IN)
Columbia Univ. (NY)
CUNY–Queens Coll.
Lawrence Univ. (WI)
Mercer Univ. (GA)
New York Univ.
Ohio State Univ.–Columbus
St. Louis Univ.
Univ. of New Hampshire
Wellesley Coll. (MA)
Wright State Univ. (OH)
Yale Univ. (CT)

Movement and Mind-Body Therapies and Education

Texas Christian Univ.
Univ. of Vermont

Multi/Interdisciplinary Studies

Abilene Christian Univ. (TX)
Adelphi Univ. (NY)
Albright Coll. (PA)
Alfred Univ. (NY)
Allegheny Coll. (PA)
Alverno Coll. (WI)
Amherst Coll. (MA)
Angelo State Univ. (TX)
Arizona State Univ.
Arkansas Tech Univ.
Austin Coll. (TX)
Austin Peay State Univ. (TN)
Baldwin-Wallace Coll. (OH)

Bard Coll. (NY)
Bates Coll. (ME)
Baylor Univ. (TX)
Bellarmine Univ. (KY)
Beloit Coll. (WI)
Bennett Coll. (NC)
Bentley Univ. (MA)
Berea Coll. (KY)
Berry Coll. (GA)
Bethany Coll. (WV)
Bethel Univ. (MN)
Binghamton Univ.–SUNY
Blackburn Coll. (IL)
Bloomfield Coll. (NJ)
Bluffton Univ. (OH)
Boise State Univ. (ID)
Bowdoin Coll. (ME)
Bowling Green State Univ. (OH)
Brandeis Univ. (MA)
Brescia Univ. (KY)
Brevard Coll. (NC)
Brown Univ. (RI)
Bryn Athyn Coll. of the New Church (PA)
Bucknell Univ. (PA)
Buena Vista Univ. (IA)
Buffalo State Coll.–SUNY
Burlington Coll. (VT)
Caldwell Coll. (NJ)
California State Univ.–Chico
California State Univ.–Dominguez Hills
California State Univ.–Fresno
California State Univ.–Long Beach
California State Univ.–Los Angeles
California State Univ.–Northridge
California State Univ.–Sacramento
California State Univ.–San Bernardino
California State Univ.–Stanislaus
Cameron Univ. (OK)
Capital Univ. (OH)
Central Coll. (IA)
Central Connecticut State Univ.
Central Methodist Univ. (MO)
Central Washington Univ.
Chaminade Univ. of Honolulu
Chestnut Hill Coll. (PA)
Chowan Univ. (NC)
Christian Brothers Univ. (TN)
Christopher Newport Univ. (VA)
Claremont McKenna Coll. (CA)
Clark Univ. (MA)
Clearwater Christian Coll. (FL)
Cleveland State Univ.
Coll. of Idaho (ID)
Coll. of Notre Dame of Maryland
Coll. of Our Lady of the Elms (MA)
Coll. of Santa Fe (NM)
Coll. of St. Benedict (MN)
Coll. of St. Elizabeth (NJ)
Coll. of the Atlantic (ME)
Coll. of the Holy Cross (MA)
Coll. of William and Mary (VA)
Colorado Coll.
Columbia Coll. (MO)
Columbia Coll. (SC)
Columbia Coll. (IL)
Concord Univ. (WV)
Connecticut Coll.
Cornell Univ. (NY)

Cornerstone Univ. (MI)
Covenant Coll. (GA)
CUNY–Hunter Coll.
Curry Coll. (MA)
Dana Coll. (NE)
Dartmouth Coll. (NH)
Davidson Coll. (NC)
Delta State Univ. (MS)
Dickinson Coll. (PA)
Dickinson State Univ. (ND)
Drake Univ. (IA)
Duke Univ. (NC)
Earlham Coll. (IN)
East Tennessee State Univ.
East-West Univ. (IL)
Eastern Connecticut State Univ.
Eastern Illinois Univ.
Eastern Mennonite Univ. (VA)
Eastern Michigan Univ.
Eastern New Mexico Univ.
Eastern Oregon Univ.
Eastern Washington Univ.
Edgewood Coll. (WI)
Edward Waters Coll. (FL)
Elmhurst Coll. (IL)
Emmanuel Coll. (MA)
Emporia State Univ. (KS)
Eureka Coll. (IL)
Evergreen State Coll. (WA)
Fairfield Univ. (CT)
Fairleigh Dickinson Univ. (NJ)
Farmingdale State Coll.–SUNY
Florida Institute of Technology
Fordham Univ. (NY)
Fort Lewis Coll. (CO)
Franklin and Marshall Coll. (PA)
Freed-Hardeman Univ. (TN)
Frostburg State Univ. (MD)
Gannon Univ. (PA)
George Fox Univ. (OR)
George Washington Univ. (DC)
Georgetown Coll. (KY)
Georgia Institute of Technology
Gettysburg Coll. (PA)
Glenville State Coll. (WV)
Goddard Coll. (VT)
Gonzaga Univ. (WA)
Goucher Coll. (MD)
Granite State Coll. (NH)
Green Mountain Coll. (VT)
Greenville Coll. (IL)
Grinnell Coll. (IA)
Gustavus Adolphus Coll. (MN)
Hampshire Coll. (MA)
Hartwick Coll. (NY)
Haverford Coll. (PA)
Hawaii Pacific Univ.
Hendrix Coll. (AR)
Heritage Univ. (WA)
Hodges Univ. (FL)
Hofstra Univ. (NY)
Hood Coll. (MD)
Hope Coll. (MI)
Humboldt State Univ. (CA)
Huntingdon Coll. (AL)
Idaho State Univ.
Illinois Coll.
Illinois Institute of Technology
Illinois Wesleyan Univ.
Immaculata Univ. (PA)
Indiana Univ. Northwest

Indiana Univ.–Bloomington
Indiana Univ.-Purdue Univ.–
    Indianapolis
Iowa State Univ.
Ithaca Coll. (NY)
Jackson State Univ. (MS)
John Brown Univ. (AR)
Johns Hopkins Univ. (MD)
Judson Univ. (IL)
Juniata Coll. (PA)
Kalamazoo Coll. (MI)
Keene State Coll. (NH)
Kennesaw State Univ. (GA)
Kentucky Wesleyan Coll.
King Coll. (TN)
Lafayette Coll. (PA)
Lane Coll. (TN)
Lawrence Univ. (WI)
Lebanon Valley Coll. (PA)
Lees-McRae Coll. (NC)
LeTourneau Univ. (TX)
Lewis-Clark State Coll. (ID)
Liberty Univ. (VA)
Long Island Univ.–C.W. Post
    Campus (NY)
Louisiana Coll.
Lourdes Coll. (OH)
Loyola Marymount Univ. (CA)
Loyola Univ. Maryland
Luther Coll. (IA)
Lycoming Coll. (PA)
Maharishi Univ. of Management
    (IA)
Marian Univ. (WI)
Marquette Univ. (WI)
Marshall Univ. (WV)
Mary Baldwin Coll. (VA)
Marylhurst Univ. (OR)
Maryville Coll. (TN)
Massachusetts Coll. of Liberal Arts
McDaniel Coll. (MD)
McPherson Coll. (KS)
Mercyhurst Coll. (PA)
Messiah Coll. (PA)
Metropolitan State Coll. of Denver
Miami Univ.–Oxford (OH)
Middle Tennessee State Univ.
Middlebury Coll. (VT)
Midwestern State Univ. (TX)
Millikin Univ. (IL)
Mills Coll. (CA)
Millsaps Coll. (MS)
Minnesota State Univ.–Moorhead
Misericordia Univ. (PA)
Mississippi State Univ.
Missouri Baptist Univ.
Missouri Western State Univ.
Montana State Univ.
Montana State Univ.–Billings
Montclair State Univ. (NJ)
Moravian Coll. (PA)
Mount Holyoke Coll. (MA)
Mount Mercy Coll. (IA)
Mount St. Mary Coll. (NY)
Mount St. Mary's Univ. (MD)
Mountain State Univ. (WV)
Muskingum Univ. (OH)
New York Institute of Technology
Norfolk State Univ. (VA)
North Carolina Wesleyan Coll.
North Central Coll. (IL)

North Dakota State Univ.
North Greenville Univ. (SC)
Northern Arizona Univ.
Northwest Christian Univ. (OR)
Northwestern Coll. (MN)
Northwestern Univ. (IL)
Oberlin Coll. (OH)
Ohio State Univ.–Columbus
Ohio Wesleyan Univ.
Old Dominion Univ. (VA)
Olivet Coll. (MI)
Oral Roberts Univ. (OK)
Oregon State Univ.
Pace Univ. (NY)
Pacific Lutheran Univ. (WA)
Palm Beach Atlantic Univ. (FL)
Park Univ. (MO)
Pfeiffer Univ. (NC)
Piedmont Coll. (GA)
Pikeville Coll. (KY)
Pittsburg State Univ. (KS)
Plymouth State Univ. (NH)
Pomona Coll. (CA)
Prairie View A&M Univ. (TX)
Princeton Univ. (NJ)
Providence Coll. (RI)
Purchase Coll.–SUNY
Quinnipiac Univ. (CT)
Radford Univ. (VA)
Randolph Coll. (VA)
Reed Coll. (OR)
Regis Coll. (MA)
Regis Univ. (CO)
Rhode Island Coll.
Rhodes Coll. (TN)
Rivier Coll. (NH)
Robert Morris Univ. (PA)
Rochester Coll. (MI)
Rochester Institute of Technology
    (NY)
Rockford Coll. (IL)
Rocky Mountain Coll. (MT)
Rollins Coll. (FL)
Rutgers, the State Univ. of New
    Jersey–Camden
Rutgers, the State Univ. of New
    Jersey–New Brunswick
Rutgers, the State Univ. of New
    Jersey–Newark
Saginaw Valley State Univ. (MI)
Sam Houston State Univ. (TX)
San Diego State Univ.
San Francisco State Univ.
Santa Clara Univ. (CA)
Shippensburg Univ. of Pennsylvania
Siena Coll. (NY)
Simmons Coll. (MA)
Sonoma State Univ. (CA)
South Dakota School of Mines and
    Technology
Southeast Missouri State Univ.
Southern Adventist Univ. (TN)
Southern Arkansas Univ.
Southern Illinois Univ.–Carbondale
Southern Methodist Univ. (TX)
Southern Oregon Univ.
Southern Utah Univ.
Southwest Baptist Univ. (MO)
Southwestern Oklahoma State
    Univ.
Southwestern Univ. (TX)

Spring Hill Coll. (AL)
St. Ambrose Univ. (IA)
St. Edward's Univ. (TX)
St. John's Univ. (MN)
St. Mary's Coll. (IN)
St. Mary's Coll. of California
St. Mary's Coll. of Maryland
St. Mary's Univ. of Minnesota
St. Mary's Univ. of San Antonio
    (TX)
St. Olaf Coll. (MN)
St. Peter's Coll. (NJ)
Stephen F. Austin State Univ. (TX)
Sterling Coll. (KS)
Stevenson Univ. (MD)
Stillman Coll. (AL)
Stonehill Coll. (MA)
Sul Ross State Univ. (TX)
SUNY Coll.–Potsdam
SUNY Empire State Coll.
SUNY–Stony Brook
Tarleton State Univ. (TX)
Taylor Univ. (IN)
Tennessee Wesleyan Coll.
Texas A&M International Univ.
Texas A&M Univ.–Coll. Station
Texas A&M Univ.–Commerce
Texas A&M Univ.–Corpus Christi
Texas State Univ.–San Marcos
Texas Tech Univ.
Texas Wesleyan Univ.
Texas Woman's Univ.
Tiffin Univ. (OH)
Tulane Univ. (LA)
Tusculum Coll. (TN)
Univ. at Buffalo–SUNY
Univ. of Akron (OH)
Univ. of Alabama
Univ. of Alaska–Anchorage
Univ. of Alaska–Fairbanks
Univ. of Arizona
Univ. of California–Berkeley
Univ. of California–Davis
Univ. of California–Irvine
Univ. of California–Riverside
Univ. of Central Arkansas
Univ. of Colorado–Boulder
Univ. of Colorado–Colorado
    Springs
Univ. of Colorado–Denver
Univ. of Connecticut
Univ. of Dallas
Univ. of Delaware
Univ. of Denver
Univ. of Evansville (IN)
Univ. of Florida
Univ. of Hartford (CT)
Univ. of Houston
Univ. of Houston–Downtown
Univ. of Kentucky
Univ. of Maine–Farmington
Univ. of Mary Washington (VA)
Univ. of Maryland–Baltimore
    County
Univ. of Maryland–Coll. Park
Univ. of Maryland–Eastern Shore
Univ. of Maryland–Univ. Coll.
Univ. of Massachusetts–Amherst
Univ. of Massachusetts–Boston
Univ. of Memphis
Univ. of Michigan–Dearborn

Univ. of Michigan–Flint
Univ. of Minnesota–Crookston
Univ. of Minnesota–Duluth
Univ. of Minnesota–Twin Cities
Univ. of Missouri
Univ. of Missouri–Kansas City
Univ. of Missouri–St. Louis
Univ. of Montana
Univ. of Montana–Western
Univ. of Nebraska–Omaha
Univ. of Nevada–Las Vegas
Univ. of North Dakota
Univ. of North Texas
Univ. of Northern Colorado
Univ. of Puget Sound (WA)
Univ. of Redlands (CA)
Univ. of Richmond (VA)
Univ. of South Florida
Univ. of Southern California
Univ. of St. Francis (IL)
Univ. of St. Thomas (MN)
Univ. of Tennessee
Univ. of Tennessee–Martin
Univ. of Texas of the Permian Basin
Univ. of Texas–Arlington
Univ. of Texas–Austin
Univ. of Texas–Brownsville
Univ. of Texas–Dallas
Univ. of Texas–El Paso
Univ. of Texas–San Antonio
Univ. of Texas–Tyler
Univ. of the Arts (PA)
Univ. of Toledo (OH)
Univ. of Virginia
Univ. of Virginia–Wise
Univ. of Washington
Univ. of Wisconsin–Green Bay
Univ. of Wisconsin–Madison
Univ. of Wisconsin–Milwaukee
Univ. of Wisconsin–Platteville
Univ. of Wisconsin–Stevens Point
Univ. of Wisconsin–Superior
Univ. of Wisconsin–Whitewater
Univ. of Wyoming
Ursuline Coll. (OH)
Utah State Univ.
Utah Valley Univ.
Valley City State Univ. (ND)
Valparaiso Univ. (IN)
Vanderbilt Univ. (TN)
Vassar Coll. (NY)
Virginia Commonwealth Univ.
Virginia State Univ.
Viterbo Univ. (WI)
Washington and Jefferson Coll.
    (PA)
Washington and Lee Univ. (VA)
Washington Coll. (MD)
Washington State Univ.
Washington Univ. in St. Louis
Wayne State Coll. (NE)
Wayne State Univ. (MI)
Waynesburg Univ. (PA)
Wesleyan Coll. (GA)
West Liberty Univ. (WV)
West Texas A&M Univ.
West Virginia Univ.
West Virginia Univ. Institute of
    Technology
Western Kentucky Univ.
Western Michigan Univ.

Western Oregon Univ.
Western Washington Univ.
Wheaton Coll. (MA)
Wheaton Coll. (IL)
Wheeling Jesuit Univ. (WV)
Widener Univ. (PA)
Wilkes Univ. (PA)
William Jewell Coll. (MO)
William Woods Univ. (MO)
Wisconsin Lutheran Coll.
Worcester Polytechnic Institute
    (MA)
Yale Univ. (CT)

Museology/Museum Studies

Baylor Univ. (TX)
Juniata Coll. (PA)
Regis Coll. (MA)
Texas A&M Univ.–Coll. Station
Tusculum Coll. (TN)
Univ. of Florida
Univ. of Iowa
Univ. of Nebraska–Lincoln

Music

Abilene Christian Univ. (TX)
Adams State Coll. (CO)
Adelphi Univ. (NY)
Adrian Coll. (MI)
Agnes Scott Coll. (GA)
Alabama State Univ.
Albany State Univ. (GA)
Albion Coll. (MI)
Albright Coll. (PA)
Alcorn State Univ. (MS)
Alderson-Broaddus Coll. (WV)
Allegheny Coll. (PA)
Allen Univ. (SC)
Alma Coll. (MI)
Alverno Coll. (WI)
American Univ. (DC)
Amherst Coll. (MA)
Anderson Univ. (SC)
Anderson Univ. (IN)
Andrews Univ. (MI)
Angelo State Univ. (TX)
Anna Maria Coll. (MA)
Appalachian State Univ. (NC)
Aquinas Coll. (MI)
Arizona State Univ.
Arkansas State Univ.–Jonesboro
Arkansas Tech Univ.
Armstrong Atlantic State Univ. (GA)
Asbury Univ. (KY)
Atlanta Christian Coll.
Atlantic Union Coll. (MA)
Auburn Univ. (AL)
Augusta State Univ. (GA)
Augustana Coll. (IL)
Austin Coll. (TX)
Austin Peay State Univ. (TN)
Averett Univ. (VA)
Avila Univ. (MO)
Azusa Pacific Univ. (CA)
Baker Coll. of Flint (MI)
Baker Univ. (KS)
Baldwin-Wallace Coll. (OH)
Ball State Univ. (IN)

Bard Coll. at Simon's Rock (MA)
Barnard Coll. (NY)
Barry Univ. (FL)
Bates Coll. (ME)
Baylor Univ. (TX)
Bellarmine Univ. (KY)
Belmont Univ. (TN)
Beloit Coll. (WI)
Bemidji State Univ. (MN)
Benedictine Coll. (KS)
Benedictine Univ. (IL)
Bennington Coll. (VT)
Berea Coll. (KY)
Berklee Coll. of Music (MA)
Berry Coll. (GA)
Bethany Coll. (WV)
Bethany Coll. (KS)
Bethany Univ. (CA)
Bethel Coll. (KS)
Bethel Coll. (IN)
Bethel Univ. (MN)
Bethune-Cookman Univ. (FL)
Binghamton Univ.–SUNY
Biola Univ. (CA)
Black Hills State Univ. (SD)
Bloomsburg University of
   Pennsylvania
Blue Mountain Coll. (MS)
Bluefield Coll. (VA)
Bluffton Univ. (OH)
Boise State Univ. (ID)
Boston Conservatory
Boston Univ.
Bowdoin Coll. (ME)
Bowling Green State Univ. (OH)
Bradley Univ. (IL)
Brandeis Univ. (MA)
Brenau Univ. (GA)
Brevard Coll. (NC)
Brewton-Parker Coll. (GA)
Briar Cliff Univ. (IA)
Bridgewater Coll. (VA)
Bridgewater State Coll. (MA)
Brigham Young Univ.–Hawaii
Brigham Young Univ.–Provo (UT)
Brown Univ. (RI)
Bryan Coll. (TN)
Bryn Mawr Coll. (PA)
Bucknell Univ. (PA)
Buena Vista Univ. (IA)
Buffalo State Coll.–SUNY
Butler Univ. (IN)
Caldwell Coll. (NJ)
California Baptist Univ.
California Institute of the Arts
California Lutheran Univ.
California Polytechnic State Univ.–
   San Luis Obispo
California State Polytechnic Univ.–
   Pomona
California State Univ.–Bakersfield
California State Univ.–Chico
California State Univ.–Dominguez
   Hills
California State Univ.–East Bay
California State Univ.–Fresno
California State Univ.–Fullerton
California State Univ.–Long Beach
California State Univ.–Los Angeles
California State Univ.–Northridge
California State Univ.–Sacramento

California State Univ.–San
   Bernardino
California State Univ.–San Marcos
California State Univ.–Stanislaus
Calvin Coll. (MI)
Cameron Univ. (OK)
Campbell Univ. (NC)
Campbellsville Univ. (KY)
Canisius Coll. (NY)
Capital Univ. (OH)
Cardinal Stritch Univ. (WI)
Carleton Coll. (MN)
Carnegie Mellon Univ. (PA)
Carroll Univ. (WI)
Carson-Newman Coll. (TN)
Carthage Coll. (WI)
Case Western Reserve Univ. (OH)
Castleton State Coll. (VT)
Catholic Univ. of America (DC)
Cedar Crest Coll. (PA)
Cedarville Univ. (OH)
Centenary Coll. of Louisiana
Central Christian Coll. (KS)
Central Coll. (IA)
Central Connecticut State Univ.
Central Methodist Univ. (MO)
Central Michigan Univ.
Central State Univ. (OH)
Central Washington Univ.
Centre Coll. (KY)
Chadron State Coll. (NE)
Chapman Univ. (CA)
Charleston Southern Univ. (SC)
Chatham Univ. (PA)
Chestnut Hill Coll. (PA)
Cheyney Univ. of Pennsylvania
Chicago State Univ.
Chowan Univ. (NC)
Christopher Newport Univ. (VA)
Claflin Univ. (SC)
Clarion Univ. of Pennsylvania
Clark Atlanta Univ.
Clark Univ. (MA)
Clayton State Univ. (GA)
Clearwater Christian Coll. (FL)
Cleveland Institute of Music
Cleveland State Univ.
Coastal Carolina Univ. (SC)
Coe Coll. (IA)
Coker Coll. (SC)
Colby Coll. (ME)
Colgate Univ. (NY)
Coll. of Charleston (SC)
Coll. of Idaho (ID)
Coll. of Mount St. Joseph (OH)
Coll. of New Jersey
Coll. of Santa Fe (NM)
Coll. of St. Benedict (MN)
Coll. of St. Elizabeth (NJ)
Coll. of St. Rose (NY)
Coll. of St. Scholastica (MN)
Coll. of the Holy Cross (MA)
Coll. of the Ozarks (MO)
Coll. of William and Mary (VA)
Coll. of Wooster (OH)
Colorado Christian Univ.
Colorado Coll.
Colorado State Univ.
Colorado State Univ.–Pueblo
Columbia Coll. (SC)
Columbia Coll. (IL)

Columbia Univ. (NY)
Columbus State Univ. (GA)
Concordia Coll. (NY)
Concordia Coll.–Moorhead (MN)
Concordia Univ. (MI)
Concordia Univ. (CA)
Concordia Univ. (NE)
Concordia Univ. Wisconsin
Concordia Univ.–St. Paul (MN)
Connecticut Coll.
Converse Coll. (SC)
Corban Univ. (OR)
Cornell Coll. (IA)
Cornell Univ. (NY)
Cornerstone Univ. (MI)
Cornish Coll. of the Arts (WA)
Covenant Coll. (GA)
Creighton Univ. (NE)
Crown Coll. (MN)
Culver-Stockton Coll. (MO)
Cumberland Univ. (TN)
CUNY–Baruch Coll.
CUNY–Brooklyn Coll.
CUNY–City Coll.
CUNY–Coll. of Staten Island
CUNY–Hunter Coll.
CUNY–Lehman Coll.
CUNY–Queens Coll.
Curtis Institute of Music (PA)
Dakota Wesleyan Univ. (SD)
Dallas Baptist Univ.
Dana Coll. (NE)
Dartmouth Coll. (NH)
Davidson Coll. (NC)
Davis and Elkins Coll. (WV)
Delaware State Univ.
Delta State Univ. (MS)
Denison Univ. (OH)
DePaul Univ. (IL)
DePauw Univ. (IN)
Dickinson Coll. (PA)
Dickinson State Univ. (ND)
Dillard Univ. (LA)
Dominican Univ. (IL)
Dominican Univ. of California
Dordt Coll. (IA)
Dowling Coll. (NY)
Drake Univ. (IA)
Drew Univ. (NJ)
Drexel Univ. (PA)
Drury Univ. (MO)
Duke Univ. (NC)
Duquesne Univ. (PA)
Earlham Coll. (IN)
East Carolina Univ. (NC)
East Central Univ. (OK)
East Tennessee State Univ.
East Texas Baptist Univ.
Eastern Illinois Univ.
Eastern Kentucky Univ.
Eastern Mennonite Univ. (VA)
Eastern Michigan Univ.
Eastern Nazarene Coll. (MA)
Eastern New Mexico Univ.
Eastern Oregon Univ.
Eastern Univ. (PA)
Eastern Washington Univ.
Eckerd Coll. (FL)
Edgewood Coll. (WI)
Edinboro Univ. of Pennsylvania
Edward Waters Coll. (FL)

Elizabeth City State Univ. (NC)
Elizabethtown Coll. (PA)
Elmhurst Coll. (IL)
Elmira Coll. (NY)
Elon Univ. (NC)
Emmanuel Coll. (GA)
Emory and Henry Coll. (VA)
Emory Univ. (GA)
Emporia State Univ. (KS)
Erskine Coll. (SC)
Eureka Coll. (IL)
Evangel Univ. (MO)
Excelsior Coll. (NY)
Faulkner Univ. (AL)
Fayetteville State Univ. (NC)
Ferris State Univ. (MI)
Florida A&M Univ.
Florida Atlantic Univ.
Florida International Univ.
Florida Southern Coll.
Florida State Univ.
Fordham Univ. (NY)
Fort Hays State Univ. (KS)
Fort Lewis Coll. (CO)
Franklin and Marshall Coll. (PA)
Franklin Pierce Univ. (NH)
Free Will Baptist Bible Coll. (TN)
Freed-Hardeman Univ. (TN)
Fresno Pacific Univ. (CA)
Friends Univ. (KS)
Frostburg State Univ. (MD)
Furman Univ. (SC)
Geneva Coll. (PA)
George Fox Univ. (OR)
George Mason Univ. (VA)
George Washington Univ. (DC)
Georgetown Coll. (KY)
Georgia Coll. & State Univ.
Georgia Southern Univ.
Georgia Southwestern State Univ.
Georgia State Univ.
Georgian Court Univ. (NJ)
Gettysburg Coll. (PA)
Gonzaga Univ. (WA)
Gordon Coll. (MA)
Goshen Coll. (IN)
Goucher Coll. (MD)
Grace Coll. and Seminary (IN)
Graceland Univ. (IA)
Grambling State Univ. (LA)
Grand Valley State Univ. (MI)
Greensboro Coll. (NC)
Greenville Coll. (IL)
Grinnell Coll. (IA)
Grove City Coll. (PA)
Guilford Coll. (NC)
Gustavus Adolphus Coll. (MN)
Hamilton Coll. (NY)
Hamline Univ. (MN)
Hampshire Coll. (MA)
Hampton Univ. (VA)
Hannibal-LaGrange Coll. (MO)
Hanover Coll. (IN)
Hardin-Simmons Univ. (TX)
Harding Univ. (AR)
Hartwick Coll. (NY)
Harvard Univ. (MA)
Haverford Coll. (PA)
Heidelberg Univ. (OH)
Henderson State Univ. (AR)
Hendrix Coll. (AR)

High Point Univ. (NC)
Hillsdale Coll. (MI)
Hiram Coll. (OH)
Hobart and William Smith Colleges
   (NY)
Hofstra Univ. (NY)
Hollins Univ. (VA)
Holy Names Univ. (CA)
Hood Coll. (MD)
Hope Coll. (MI)
Houghton Coll. (NY)
Howard Payne Univ. (TX)
Howard Univ. (DC)
Humboldt State Univ. (CA)
Huntingdon Coll. (AL)
Huntington Univ. (IN)
Huston-Tillotson Univ. (TX)
Idaho State Univ.
Illinois Coll.
Illinois State Univ.
Illinois Wesleyan Univ.
Immaculata Univ. (PA)
Indiana State Univ.
Indiana Univ. of Pennsylvania
Indiana Univ. Southeast
Indiana Univ.–Bloomington
Indiana Univ.–South Bend
Indiana Univ.-Purdue Univ.–Fort
   Wayne
Indiana Wesleyan Univ.
Iowa Wesleyan Coll.
Ithaca Coll. (NY)
Jackson State Univ. (MS)
Jacksonville State Univ. (AL)
Jacksonville Univ. (FL)
James Madison Univ. (VA)
Jamestown Coll. (ND)
John Brown Univ. (AR)
Johns Hopkins Univ. (MD)
Johnson C. Smith Univ. (NC)
Johnson State Coll. (VT)
Judson Univ. (IL)
Juilliard School (NY)
Kalamazoo Coll. (MI)
Kansas State Univ.
Kean Univ. (NJ)
Keene State Coll. (NH)
Kennesaw State Univ. (GA)
Kent State Univ. (OH)
Kentucky State Univ.
Kentucky Wesleyan Coll.
Kenyon Coll. (OH)
Knox Coll. (IL)
Kutztown Univ. of Pennsylvania
La Salle Univ. (PA)
La Sierra Univ. (CA)
Lafayette Coll. (PA)
LaGrange Coll. (GA)
Lake Forest Coll. (IL)
Lakeland Coll. (WI)
Lamar Univ. (TX)
Lambuth Univ. (TN)
Lander Univ. (SC)
Lane Coll. (TN)
Lawrence Univ. (WI)
Lebanon Valley Coll. (PA)
Lehigh Univ. (PA)
LeMoyne-Owen Coll. (TN)
Lenoir-Rhyne Univ. (NC)
Lewis & Clark Coll. (OR)
Lewis Univ. (IL)

Liberty Univ. (VA)
Limestone Coll. (SC)
Lincoln Univ. (PA)
Lindenwood Univ. (MO)
Linfield Coll. (OR)
Lipscomb Univ. (TN)
Livingstone Coll. (NC)
Lock Haven Univ. of Pennsylvania
Long Island Univ.–C.W. Post
    Campus (NY)
Longy School of Music (MA)
Loras Coll. (IA)
Louisiana Coll.
Louisiana State Univ.–Baton Rouge
Louisiana Tech Univ.
Loyola Marymount Univ. (CA)
Loyola Univ. Chicago
Loyola Univ. New Orleans
Lubbock Christian Univ. (TX)
Luther Coll. (IA)
Lycoming Coll. (PA)
Lynchburg Coll. (VA)
Lynn Univ. (FL)
Lyon Coll. (AR)
Macalester Coll. (MN)
Madonna Univ. (MI)
Malone Univ. (OH)
Manchester Coll. (IN)
Manhattan School of Music (NY)
Manhattanville Coll. (NY)
Mansfield Univ. of Pennsylvania
Maranatha Baptist Bible Coll. (WI)
Marian Univ. (WI)
Marian Univ. (IN)
Marietta Coll. (OH)
Mars Hill Coll. (NC)
Martin Univ. (IN)
Mary Baldwin Coll. (VA)
Marygrove Coll. (MI)
Marylhurst Univ. (OR)
Maryville Coll. (TN)
Marywood Univ. (PA)
Massachusetts Institute of
    Technology
Master's Coll. and Seminary (CA)
McDaniel Coll. (MD)
McKendree Univ. (IL)
McMurry Univ. (TX)
McNeese State Univ. (LA)
McPherson Coll. (KS)
Mercer Univ. (GA)
Mercyhurst Coll. (PA)
Meredith Coll. (NC)
Mesa State Coll. (CO)
Messiah Coll. (PA)
Methodist Univ. (NC)
Metropolitan State Coll. of Denver
Miami Univ.–Oxford (OH)
Michigan State Univ.
Middle Tennessee State Univ.
Middlebury Coll. (VT)
Midland Lutheran Coll. (NE)
Midwestern State Univ. (TX)
Miles Coll. (AL)
Millersville Univ. of Pennsylvania
Milligan Coll. (TN)
Millikin Univ. (IL)
Mills Coll. (CA)
Millsaps Coll. (MS)
Minnesota State Univ.–Mankato
Minnesota State Univ.–Moorhead

Minot State Univ. (ND)
Mississippi Coll.
Mississippi Univ. for Women
Mississippi Valley State Univ.
Missouri Baptist Univ.
Missouri Southern State Univ.
Missouri State Univ.
Molloy Coll. (NY)
Monmouth Coll. (IL)
Monmouth Univ. (NJ)
Montana State Univ.
Montana State Univ.–Billings
Montclair State Univ. (NJ)
Montreat Coll. (NC)
Moravian Coll. (PA)
Morehead State Univ. (KY)
Morehouse Coll. (GA)
Morgan State Univ. (MD)
Morningside Coll. (IA)
Mount Holyoke Coll. (MA)
Mount Marty Coll. (SD)
Mount Mercy Coll. (IA)
Mount St. Mary's Coll. (CA)
Mount Vernon Nazarene Univ.
    (OH)
Muhlenberg Coll. (PA)
Murray State Univ. (KY)
Muskingum Univ. (OH)
Nazareth Coll. (NY)
Nebraska Wesleyan Univ.
New England Conservatory of
    Music (MA)
New Jersey City Univ.
New Mexico Highlands Univ.
New Mexico State Univ.
New School (NY)
New York Univ.
Newberry Coll. (SC)
Nicholls State Univ. (LA)
Norfolk State Univ. (VA)
North Carolina A&T State Univ.
North Carolina Central Univ.
North Central Coll. (IL)
North Central Univ. (MN)
North Dakota State Univ.
North Georgia Coll. and State Univ.
North Greenville Univ. (SC)
North Park Univ. (IL)
Northeastern Illinois Univ.
Northeastern State Univ. (OK)
Northeastern Univ. (MA)
Northern Arizona Univ.
Northern Illinois Univ.
Northern Kentucky Univ.
Northern Michigan Univ.
Northern State Univ. (SD)
Northland Coll. (WI)
Northwest Christian Univ. (OR)
Northwest Missouri State Univ.
Northwest Nazarene Univ. (ID)
Northwestern Coll. (IA)
Northwestern Coll. (MN)
Northwestern Oklahoma State
    Univ.
Northwestern State Univ. of
    Louisiana
Northwestern Univ. (IL)
Notre Dame de Namur Univ. (CA)
Nyack Coll. (NY)
Oakland Univ. (MI)
Oakwood Univ. (AL)

Oberlin Coll. (OH)
Occidental Coll. (CA)
Ohio Northern Univ.
Ohio State Univ.–Columbus
Ohio Univ.
Ohio Wesleyan Univ.
Oklahoma Baptist Univ.
Oklahoma Christian Univ.
Oklahoma City Univ.
Oklahoma State Univ.
Oklahoma Wesleyan Univ.
Old Dominion Univ. (VA)
Olivet Coll. (MI)
Olivet Nazarene Univ. (IL)
Oregon State Univ.
Ouachita Baptist Univ. (AR)
Our Lady of the Lake Univ. (TX)
Pacific Lutheran Univ. (WA)
Pacific Union Coll. (CA)
Pacific Univ. (OR)
Paine Coll. (GA)
Palm Beach Atlantic Univ. (FL)
Patten Univ. (CA)
Peace Coll. (NC)
Pennsylvania State Univ.–Univ. Park
Pepperdine Univ. (CA)
Pfeiffer Univ. (NC)
Philander Smith Coll. (AR)
Piedmont Coll. (GA)
Pittsburg State Univ. (KS)
Plymouth State Univ. (NH)
Point Loma Nazarene Univ. (CA)
Pomona Coll. (CA)
Portland State Univ. (OR)
Prairie View A&M Univ. (TX)
Presbyterian Coll. (SC)
Prescott Coll. (AZ)
Princeton Univ. (NJ)
Principia Coll. (IL)
Providence Coll. (RI)
Purchase Coll.–SUNY
Queens Univ. of Charlotte (NC)
Quincy Univ. (IL)
Radford Univ. (VA)
Ramapo Coll. of New Jersey
Randolph Coll. (VA)
Randolph-Macon Coll. (VA)
Reed Coll. (OR)
Reinhardt Univ. (GA)
Rhode Island Coll.
Rhodes Coll. (TN)
Rice Univ. (TX)
Rider Univ. (NJ)
Ripon Coll. (WI)
Roanoke Coll. (VA)
Roberts Wesleyan Coll. (NY)
Rochester Coll. (MI)
Rockford Coll. (IL)
Rocky Mountain Coll. (MT)
Rollins Coll. (FL)
Roosevelt Univ. (IL)
Rust Coll. (MS)
Rutgers, the State Univ. of New
    Jersey–Camden
Rutgers, the State Univ. of New
    Jersey–New Brunswick
Rutgers, the State Univ. of New
    Jersey–Newark
Saginaw Valley State Univ. (MI)
Salem Coll. (NC)
Salisbury Univ. (MD)

Salve Regina Univ. (RI)
Sam Houston State Univ. (TX)
Samford Univ. (AL)
San Diego State Univ.
San Francisco Conservatory of
    Music
San Francisco State Univ.
San Jose State Univ. (CA)
Santa Clara Univ. (CA)
Savannah State Univ. (GA)
Schreiner Univ. (TX)
Scripps Coll. (CA)
Seattle Pacific Univ.
Seton Hall Univ. (NJ)
Seton Hill Univ. (PA)
Sewanee–Univ. of the South (TN)
Shaw Univ. (NC)
Shenandoah Univ. (VA)
Shepherd Univ. (WV)
Shorter Coll. (GA)
Silver Lake Coll. (WI)
Simmons Coll. (MA)
Simpson Coll. (IA)
Simpson Univ. (CA)
Skidmore Coll. (NY)
Slippery Rock Univ. of Pennsylvania
Smith Coll. (MA)
Sonoma State Univ. (CA)
South Carolina State Univ.
South Dakota State Univ.
Southeast Missouri State Univ.
Southeastern Louisiana Univ.
Southeastern Oklahoma State Univ.
Southeastern Univ. (FL)
Southern Adventist Univ. (TN)
Southern Arkansas Univ.
Southern Connecticut State Univ.
Southern Illinois Univ.–Carbondale
Southern Illinois Univ.–Edwardsville
Southern Methodist Univ. (TX)
Southern Nazarene Univ. (OK)
Southern Oregon Univ.
Southern Univ. and A&M Coll. (LA)
Southern Utah Univ.
Southern Wesleyan Univ. (SC)
Southwest Baptist Univ. (MO)
Southwest Minnesota State Univ.
Southwestern Adventist Univ. (TX)
Southwestern Assemblies of God
    Univ. (TX)
Southwestern Coll. (KS)
Southwestern Oklahoma State
    Univ.
Southwestern Univ. (TX)
Spelman Coll. (GA)
Spring Arbor Univ. (MI)
St. Ambrose Univ. (IA)
St. Augustine's Coll. (NC)
St. Catherine Univ. (MN)
St. Cloud State Univ. (MN)
St. John's Univ. (MN)
St. Joseph's Coll. (IN)
St. Lawrence Univ. (NY)
St. Louis Univ.
St. Martin's Univ. (WA)
St. Mary's Coll. (IN)
St. Mary's Coll. of California
St. Mary's Coll. of Maryland
St. Mary's Univ. of Minnesota
St. Mary's Univ. of San Antonio
    (TX)

St. Mary-of-the-Woods Coll. (IN)
St. Michael's Coll. (VT)
St. Norbert Coll. (WI)
St. Olaf Coll. (MN)
St. Vincent Coll. (PA)
St. Xavier Univ. (IL)
Stanford Univ. (CA)
Stephen F. Austin State Univ. (TX)
Sterling Coll. (KS)
Stetson Univ. (FL)
Stevens Institute of Technology
    (NJ)
Stillman Coll. (AL)
Sul Ross State Univ. (TX)
SUNY Coll.–Cortland
SUNY Coll.–Oneonta
SUNY Coll.–Potsdam
SUNY–Fredonia
SUNY–Geneseo
SUNY–Oswego
SUNY–Plattsburgh
SUNY–Stony Brook
Susquehanna Univ. (PA)
Swarthmore Coll. (PA)
Syracuse Univ. (NY)
Tabor Coll. (KS)
Talladega Coll. (AL)
Tarleton State Univ. (TX)
Taylor Univ. (IN)
Temple Univ. (PA)
Tennessee State Univ.
Tennessee Technological Univ.
Tennessee Wesleyan Coll.
Texas A&M International Univ.
Texas A&M Univ.–Coll. Station
Texas A&M Univ.–Commerce
Texas A&M Univ.–Corpus Christi
Texas A&M Univ.–Kingsville
Texas Christian Univ.
Texas Coll.
Texas Lutheran Univ.
Texas State Univ.–San Marcos
Texas Tech Univ.
Texas Wesleyan Univ.
Texas Woman's Univ.
Thomas Edison State Coll. (NJ)
Toccoa Falls Coll. (GA)
Towson Univ. (MD)
Transylvania Univ. (KY)
Trevecca Nazarene Univ. (TN)
Trinity Christian Coll. (IL)
Trinity Coll. (CT)
Trinity International Univ. (IL)
Troy Univ. (AL)
Truman State Univ. (MO)
Tufts Univ. (MA)
Tulane Univ. (LA)
Union Coll. (NE)
Union Univ. (TN)
Univ. at Albany–SUNY
Univ. at Buffalo–SUNY
Univ. of Akron (OH)
Univ. of Alabama
Univ. of Alabama–Birmingham
Univ. of Alabama–Huntsville
Univ. of Alaska–Anchorage
Univ. of Alaska–Fairbanks
Univ. of Arizona
Univ. of Arkansas
Univ. of Arkansas–Little Rock
Univ. of Arkansas–Monticello

Univ. of Arkansas–Pine Bluff
Univ. of California–Berkeley
Univ. of California–Irvine
Univ. of California–Los Angeles
Univ. of California–Riverside
Univ. of California–Santa Barbara
Univ. of California–Santa Cruz
Univ. of Central Arkansas
Univ. of Central Florida
Univ. of Central Missouri
Univ. of Central Oklahoma
Univ. of Charleston (WV)
Univ. of Chicago
Univ. of Colorado–Boulder
Univ. of Colorado–Denver
Univ. of Connecticut
Univ. of Dayton (OH)
Univ. of Delaware
Univ. of Denver
Univ. of Evansville (IN)
Univ. of Florida
Univ. of Georgia
Univ. of Hartford (CT)
Univ. of Hawaii–Hilo
Univ. of Hawaii–Manoa
Univ. of Houston
Univ. of Illinois–Chicago
Univ. of Illinois–Urbana-Champaign
Univ. of Indianapolis
Univ. of Iowa
Univ. of Kansas
Univ. of Kentucky
Univ. of La Verne (CA)
Univ. of Louisiana–Lafayette
Univ. of Louisiana–Monroe
Univ. of Louisville (KY)
Univ. of Maine
Univ. of Maine–Augusta
Univ. of Maine–Farmington
Univ. of Mary (ND)
Univ. of Mary Hardin-Baylor (TX)
Univ. of Mary Washington (VA)
Univ. of Maryland–Baltimore
    County
Univ. of Maryland–Coll. Park
Univ. of Massachusetts–Amherst
Univ. of Massachusetts–Boston
Univ. of Massachusetts–Dartmouth
Univ. of Massachusetts–Lowell
Univ. of Memphis
Univ. of Miami (FL)
Univ. of Michigan–Ann Arbor
Univ. of Michigan–Flint
Univ. of Minnesota–Duluth
Univ. of Minnesota–Morris
Univ. of Minnesota–Twin Cities
Univ. of Mississippi
Univ. of Missouri
Univ. of Missouri–Kansas City
Univ. of Missouri–St. Louis
Univ. of Montana
Univ. of Montevallo (AL)
Univ. of Mount Union (OH)
Univ. of Nebraska–Kearney
Univ. of Nebraska–Lincoln
Univ. of Nebraska–Omaha
Univ. of Nevada–Las Vegas
Univ. of Nevada–Reno
Univ. of New Hampshire
Univ. of New Haven (CT)
Univ. of New Mexico

Univ. of New Orleans
Univ. of North Alabama
Univ. of North Carolina School of
    the Arts
Univ. of North Carolina–Asheville
Univ. of North Carolina–Chapel Hill
Univ. of North Carolina–Charlotte
Univ. of North Carolina–
    Greensboro
Univ. of North Carolina–Pembroke
Univ. of North Carolina–
    Wilmington
Univ. of North Dakota
Univ. of North Florida
Univ. of North Texas
Univ. of Northern Colorado
Univ. of Northern Iowa
Univ. of Notre Dame (IN)
Univ. of Oklahoma
Univ. of Oregon
Univ. of Pennsylvania
Univ. of Pittsburgh
Univ. of Portland (OR)
Univ. of Puget Sound (WA)
Univ. of Redlands (CA)
Univ. of Rhode Island
Univ. of Richmond (VA)
Univ. of Rochester (NY)
Univ. of San Diego
Univ. of Science and Arts of
    Oklahoma
Univ. of Sioux Falls (SD)
Univ. of South Alabama
Univ. of South Carolina
Univ. of South Dakota
Univ. of South Florida
Univ. of Southern California
Univ. of Southern Maine
Univ. of Southern Mississippi
Univ. of St. Francis (IL)
Univ. of St. Francis (IN)
Univ. of St. Thomas (TX)
Univ. of St. Thomas (MN)
Univ. of Tampa (FL)
Univ. of Tennessee
Univ. of Tennessee–Chattanooga
Univ. of Tennessee–Martin
Univ. of Texas–Arlington
Univ. of Texas–Austin
Univ. of Texas–Brownsville
Univ. of Texas–El Paso
Univ. of Texas–Pan American
Univ. of Texas–San Antonio
Univ. of Texas–Tyler
Univ. of the Arts (PA)
Univ. of the Cumberlands (KY)
Univ. of the District of Columbia
Univ. of the Incarnate Word (TX)
Univ. of the Ozarks (AR)
Univ. of the Pacific (CA)
Univ. of Toledo (OH)
Univ. of Tulsa (OK)
Univ. of Utah
Univ. of Vermont
Univ. of Virginia
Univ. of Washington
Univ. of West Florida
Univ. of West Georgia
Univ. of Wisconsin–Eau Claire
Univ. of Wisconsin–Green Bay
Univ. of Wisconsin–La Crosse

Univ. of Wisconsin–Madison
Univ. of Wisconsin–Milwaukee
Univ. of Wisconsin–Platteville
Univ. of Wisconsin–River Falls
Univ. of Wisconsin–Stevens Point
Univ. of Wisconsin–Superior
Univ. of Wisconsin–Whitewater
Univ. of Wyoming
Utah State Univ.
Valdosta State Univ. (GA)
Valley City State Univ. (ND)
Valparaiso Univ. (IN)
Vanderbilt Univ. (TN)
Vanguard Univ. of Southern
    California
Vassar Coll. (NY)
Virginia Commonwealth Univ.
Virginia State Univ.
Virginia Tech
Virginia Wesleyan Coll.
Viterbo Univ. (WI)
Wabash Coll. (IN)
Wagner Coll. (NY)
Wake Forest Univ. (NC)
Waldorf Coll. (IA)
Warner Pacific Coll. (OR)
Wartburg Coll. (IA)
Washburn Univ. (KS)
Washington Adventist Univ. (MD)
Washington and Jefferson Coll.
    (PA)
Washington and Lee Univ. (VA)
Washington Coll. (MD)
Washington State Univ.
Washington Univ. in St. Louis
Wayland Baptist Univ. (TX)
Wayne State Coll. (NE)
Wayne State Univ. (MI)
Weber State Univ. (UT)
Webster Univ. (MO)
Wellesley Coll. (MA)
Wesleyan Coll. (GA)
Wesleyan Univ. (CT)
West Chester Univ. of Pennsylvania
West Texas A&M Univ.
West Virginia Univ.
West Virginia Wesleyan Coll.
Western Carolina Univ. (NC)
Western Connecticut State Univ.
Western Illinois Univ.
Western Kentucky Univ.
Western Michigan Univ.
Western New Mexico Univ.
Western Oregon Univ.
Western State Coll. of Colorado
Western Washington Univ.
Westfield State Coll. (MA)
Westminster Coll. (PA)
Westmont Coll. (CA)
Wheaton Coll. (MA)
Wheaton Coll. (IL)
Whitman Coll. (WA)
Whittier Coll. (CA)
Whitworth Univ. (WA)
Wichita State Univ. (KS)
Wilberforce Univ. (OH)
Wiley Coll. (TX)
Wilkes Univ. (PA)
Willamette Univ. (OR)
William Carey Univ. (MS)
William Jewell Coll. (MO)

William Paterson Univ. of New
    Jersey
Williams Coll. (MA)
Wingate Univ. (NC)
Winston-Salem State Univ. (NC)
Winthrop Univ. (SC)
Wisconsin Lutheran Coll.
Wittenberg Univ. (OH)
Wright State Univ. (OH)
Xavier Univ. (OH)
Yale Univ. (CT)
Yeshiva Univ. (NY)
York Coll. (NE)
York Coll. of Pennsylvania
Youngstown State Univ. (OH)

Natural Resources and Conservation

California Polytechnic State Univ.–
    San Luis Obispo
California State Univ.–Sacramento
DePaul Univ. (IL)
Humboldt State Univ. (CA)
Pennsylvania State Univ.–Univ. Park
Prescott Coll. (AZ)
Springfield Coll. (MA)
Sul Ross State Univ. (TX)
Univ. of Alaska–Fairbanks
Univ. of California–Davis
Univ. of Louisiana–Lafayette
Univ. of Michigan–Flint
Univ. of Washington
Univ. of Wisconsin–Platteville
Univ. of Wisconsin–Stevens Point
Utah State Univ.

Natural Resources Conservation and Research

Abilene Christian Univ. (TX)
Adelphi Univ. (NY)
Adrian Coll. (MI)
Alaska Pacific Univ.
Albright Coll. (PA)
Alderson-Broaddus Coll. (WV)
Alfred Univ. (NY)
Allegheny Coll. (PA)
Alverno Coll. (WI)
American Univ. (DC)
Andrews Univ. (MI)
Anna Maria Coll. (MA)
Aquinas Coll. (MI)
Assumption Coll. (MA)
Auburn Univ. (AL)
Augustana Coll. (IL)
Aurora Univ. (IL)
Austin Coll. (TX)
Averett Univ. (VA)
Ball State Univ. (IN)
Bard Coll. at Simon's Rock (MA)
Barnard Coll. (NY)
Barry Univ. (FL)
Barton Coll. (NC)
Bates Coll. (ME)
Baylor Univ. (TX)
Beloit Coll. (WI)
Bemidji State Univ. (MN)
Benedictine Univ. (IL)
Bennington Coll. (VT)

Berry Coll. (GA)
Bethany Coll. (WV)
Bethel Univ. (MN)
Boston Univ.
Bowdoin Coll. (ME)
Bradley Univ. (IL)
Brevard Coll. (NC)
Brewton-Parker Coll. (GA)
Briar Cliff Univ. (IA)
Bridgewater Coll. (VA)
Brown Univ. (RI)
Bucknell Univ. (PA)
California Lutheran Univ.
California State Univ.–Chico
California State Univ.–Dominguez
    Hills
California State Univ.–East Bay
California State Univ.–Long Beach
California State Univ.–Monterey Bay
California State Univ.–Sacramento
California State Univ.–San
    Bernardino
California Univ. of Pennsylvania
Calvin Coll. (MI)
Canisius Coll. (NY)
Capital Univ. (OH)
Carlow Univ. (PA)
Carroll Coll. (MT)
Carroll Univ. (WI)
Carthage Coll. (WI)
Case Western Reserve Univ. (OH)
Catawba Coll. (NC)
Cazenovia Coll. (NY)
Central Coll. (IA)
Central Methodist Univ. (MO)
Central Michigan Univ.
Chatham Univ. (PA)
Chestnut Hill Coll. (PA)
Christopher Newport Univ. (VA)
Claflin Univ. (SC)
Claremont McKenna Coll. (CA)
Clarion Univ. of Pennsylvania
Clark Univ. (MA)
Clemson Univ. (SC)
Cleveland State Univ.
Colby Coll. (ME)
Colby-Sawyer Coll. (NH)
Colgate Univ. (NY)
Coll. at Brockport–SUNY
Coll. of Idaho (ID)
Coll. of Santa Fe (NM)
Coll. of St. Benedict (MN)
Coll. of St. Rose (NY)
Colorado Coll.
Colorado State Univ.
Columbia Coll. (MO)
Columbia Univ. (NY)
Concordia Univ. (OR)
Concordia Univ. Texas
Concordia Univ. Wisconsin
Cornell Coll. (IA)
Cornell Univ. (NY)
Creighton Univ. (NE)
CUNY–Brooklyn Coll.
CUNY–Medgar Evers Coll.
CUNY–Queens Coll.
Curry Coll. (MA)
Dartmouth Coll. (NH)
Delaware State Univ.
Denison Univ. (OH)
DePauw Univ. (IN)

Dickinson Coll. (PA)
Dominican Univ. (IL)
Dordt Coll. (IA)
Drake Univ. (IA)
Drexel Univ. (PA)
Drury Univ. (MO)
Duke Univ. (NC)
Duquesne Univ. (PA)
Earlham Coll. (IN)
Eastern Kentucky Univ.
Eastern Mennonite Univ. (VA)
Eastern Nazarene Coll. (MA)
Eastern Univ. (PA)
Eastern Washington Univ.
Eckerd Coll. (FL)
Edinboro Univ. of Pennsylvania
Elon Univ. (NC)
Emmanuel Coll. (MA)
Emory and Henry Coll. (VA)
Emory Univ. (GA)
Endicott Coll. (MA)
Eureka Coll. (IL)
Evergreen State Coll. (WA)
Fairleigh Dickinson Univ. (NJ)
Ferrum Coll. (VA)
Florida A&M Univ.
Florida Institute of Technology
Florida International Univ.
Franklin and Marshall Coll. (PA)
Franklin Pierce Univ. (NH)
Fresno Pacific Univ. (CA)
Frostburg State Univ. (MD)
Gannon Univ. (PA)
Georgia Coll. & State Univ.
Georgia State Univ.
Gettysburg Coll. (PA)
Goshen Coll. (IN)
Grand Valley State Univ. (MI)
Green Mountain Coll. (VT)
Guilford Coll. (NC)
Gustavus Adolphus Coll. (MN)
Hamline Univ. (MN)
Hampshire Coll. (MA)
Hampton Univ. (VA)
Hardin-Simmons Univ. (TX)
Harvard Univ. (MA)
Hawaii Pacific Univ.
Hendrix Coll. (AR)
Heritage Univ. (WA)
Hiram Coll. (OH)
Hobart and William Smith Colleges
     (NY)
Hofstra Univ. (NY)
Hollins Univ. (VA)
Hood Coll. (MD)
Hope Coll. (MI)
Humboldt State Univ. (CA)
Huntington Univ. (IN)
Illinois Wesleyan Univ.
Immaculata Univ. (PA)
Indiana Univ. East
Indiana Univ.–South Bend
Indiana Univ.-Purdue Univ.–
     Indianapolis
Iowa State Univ.
Ithaca Coll. (NY)
Jackson State Univ. (MS)
John Brown Univ. (AR)
Johnson State Coll. (VT)
Juniata Coll. (PA)
Keene State Coll. (NH)

Kent State Univ. (OH)
King's Coll. (PA)
Knox Coll. (IL)
Kutztown Univ. of Pennsylvania
La Salle Univ. (PA)
Lake Forest Coll. (IL)
Lake Superior State Univ. (MI)
Lamar Univ. (TX)
Lambuth Univ. (TN)
Lander Univ. (SC)
Lawrence Univ. (WI)
Lees-McRae Coll. (NC)
Lehigh Univ. (PA)
Lenoir-Rhyne Univ. (NC)
Lesley Univ. (MA)
Lewis & Clark Coll. (OR)
Lewis Univ. (IL)
Lincoln Memorial Univ. (TN)
Lincoln Univ. (PA)
Linfield Coll. (OR)
Lipscomb Univ. (TN)
Louisiana State Univ.–Baton Rouge
Louisiana State Univ.–Shreveport
Louisiana Tech Univ.
Lourdes Coll. (OH)
Loyola Univ. Chicago
Luther Coll. (IA)
Lynchburg Coll. (VA)
Lyon Coll. (AR)
Macalester Coll. (MN)
Madonna Univ. (MI)
Maharishi Univ. of Management
     (IA)
Manchester Coll. (IN)
Marietta Coll. (OH)
Marist Coll. (NY)
Marshall Univ. (WV)
Marylhurst Univ. (OR)
Marymount Univ. (VA)
Maryville Coll. (TN)
Maryville Univ. of St. Louis (MO)
Marywood Univ. (PA)
Massachusetts Coll. of Liberal Arts
Massachusetts Maritime Academy
McDaniel Coll. (MD)
McNeese State Univ. (LA)
Mercer Univ. (GA)
Meredith Coll. (NC)
Merrimack Coll. (MA)
Mesa State Coll. (CO)
Messiah Coll. (PA)
Miami Univ.–Oxford (OH)
Michigan State Univ.
Michigan Technological Univ.
Middlebury Coll. (VT)
Midwestern State Univ. (TX)
Miles Coll. (AL)
Mills Coll. (CA)
Minnesota State Univ.–Mankato
Mitchell Coll. (CT)
Montana State Univ.
Montana State Univ.–Billings
Montreat Coll. (NC)
Moravian Coll. (PA)
Mount Holyoke Coll. (MA)
Muhlenberg Coll. (PA)
Neumann Univ. (PA)
New England Coll. (NH)
New Jersey Institute of Technology
New Mexico Highlands Univ.
New Mexico State Univ.

North Carolina Central Univ.
North Carolina State Univ.–Raleigh
North Carolina Wesleyan Coll.
North Dakota State Univ.
Northeastern Illinois Univ.
Northeastern State Univ. (OK)
Northeastern Univ. (MA)
Northern Arizona Univ.
Northern Kentucky Univ.
Northern Michigan Univ.
Northland Coll. (WI)
Northwest Univ. (WA)
Northwestern Univ. (IL)
Nova Southeastern Univ. (FL)
Oberlin Coll. (OH)
Occidental Coll. (CA)
Ohio Northern Univ.
Ohio State Univ.–Columbus
Ohio Wesleyan Univ.
Oklahoma State Univ.
Olivet Coll. (MI)
Oregon Institute of Technology
Oregon State Univ.
Otterbein Coll. (OH)
Pace Univ. (NY)
Pacific Lutheran Univ. (WA)
Pacific Univ. (OR)
Paine Coll. (GA)
Paul Smith's Coll. (NY)
Pennsylvania State Univ.–Univ. Park
Pfeiffer Univ. (NC)
Philadelphia Univ.
Pitzer Coll. (CA)
Point Park Univ. (PA)
Pomona Coll. (CA)
Portland State Univ. (OR)
Post Univ. (CT)
Prescott Coll. (AZ)
Principia Coll. (IL)
Purdue Univ.–West Lafayette (IN)
Ramapo Coll. of New Jersey
Randolph Coll. (VA)
Randolph-Macon Coll. (VA)
Richard Stockton Coll. of New
     Jersey
Rider Univ. (NJ)
Ripon Coll. (WI)
Roanoke Coll. (VA)
Robert Morris Univ. (PA)
Rochester Institute of Technology
     (NY)
Rocky Mountain Coll. (MT)
Roosevelt Univ. (IL)
Rosemont Coll. (PA)
Russell Sage Coll. (NY)
Rutgers, the State Univ. of New
     Jersey–Camden
Rutgers, the State Univ. of New
     Jersey–New Brunswick
Rutgers, the State Univ. of New
     Jersey–Newark
Salisbury Univ. (MD)
Sam Houston State Univ. (TX)
Samford Univ. (AL)
San Diego State Univ.
San Francisco State Univ.
San Jose State Univ. (CA)
Santa Clara Univ. (CA)
Scripps Coll. (CA)
Seattle Univ.
Seton Hall Univ. (NJ)

Sewanee–Univ. of the South (TN)
Shaw Univ. (NC)
Shenandoah Univ. (VA)
Shepherd Univ. (WV)
Shippensburg Univ. of Pennsylvania
Shorter Coll. (GA)
Simmons Coll. (MA)
Simpson Coll. (IA)
Skidmore Coll. (NY)
Slippery Rock Univ. of Pennsylvania
Sonoma State Univ. (CA)
South Dakota State Univ.
Southeast Missouri State Univ.
Southeastern Oklahoma State Univ.
Southern Methodist Univ. (TX)
Southern New Hampshire Univ.
Southern Oregon Univ.
Southwest Minnesota State Univ.
Spelman Coll. (GA)
St. Bonaventure Univ. (NY)
St. Cloud State Univ. (MN)
St. Edward's Univ. (TX)
St. Francis Univ. (PA)
St. John's Univ. (MN)
St. John's Univ. (NY)
St. Joseph's Coll. (ME)
St. Joseph's Univ. (PA)
St. Leo Univ. (FL)
St. Louis Univ.
St. Mary's Coll. of California
St. Michael's Coll. (VT)
St. Norbert Coll. (WI)
St. Olaf Coll. (MN)
St. Vincent Coll. (PA)
Stanford Univ. (CA)
Stephen F. Austin State Univ. (TX)
Stetson Univ. (FL)
Suffolk Univ. (MA)
SUNY Coll. of Environmental
     Science and Forestry
SUNY Coll.–Oneonta
SUNY Coll.–Potsdam
SUNY–Plattsburgh
SUNY–Stony Brook
Taylor Univ. (IN)
Temple Univ. (PA)
Tennessee Wesleyan Coll.
Texas A&M International Univ.
Texas A&M Univ.–Coll. Station
Texas A&M Univ.–Corpus Christi
Texas Christian Univ.
Texas State Univ.–San Marcos
Texas Tech Univ.
Thiel Coll. (PA)
Thomas Edison State Coll. (NJ)
Thomas More Coll. (KY)
Thomas Univ. (GA)
Trine Univ. (IN)
Trinity Coll. (CT)
Trinity Univ. (DC)
Troy Univ. (AL)
Tulane Univ. (LA)
Tusculum Coll. (TN)
Unity Coll. (ME)
Univ. at Albany–SUNY
Univ. of Alabama
Univ. of Alaska–Southeast
Univ. of Arizona
Univ. of Arkansas
Univ. of California–Berkeley
Univ. of California–Davis

Univ. of California–Riverside
Univ. of California–Santa Barbara
Univ. of California–Santa Cruz
Univ. of Central Arkansas
Univ. of Charleston (WV)
Univ. of Chicago
Univ. of Colorado–Boulder
Univ. of Connecticut
Univ. of Delaware
Univ. of Denver
Univ. of Dubuque (IA)
Univ. of Evansville (IN)
Univ. of Florida
Univ. of Georgia
Univ. of Hawaii–Manoa
Univ. of Houston
Univ. of Illinois–Urbana-Champaign
Univ. of Indianapolis
Univ. of Iowa
Univ. of Kansas
Univ. of Kentucky
Univ. of La Verne (CA)
Univ. of Maine
Univ. of Maine–Farmington
Univ. of Maine–Fort Kent
Univ. of Maine–Machias
Univ. of Maine–Presque Isle
Univ. of Maryland–Baltimore
     County
Univ. of Maryland–Coll. Park
Univ. of Maryland–Univ. Coll.
Univ. of Massachusetts–Amherst
Univ. of Michigan–Ann Arbor
Univ. of Michigan–Dearborn
Univ. of Michigan–Flint
Univ. of Minnesota–Crookston
Univ. of Minnesota–Duluth
Univ. of Minnesota–Twin Cities
Univ. of Missouri
Univ. of Missouri–Kansas City
Univ. of Montana
Univ. of Nebraska–Lincoln
Univ. of Nebraska–Omaha
Univ. of Nevada–Las Vegas
Univ. of Nevada–Reno
Univ. of New England (ME)
Univ. of New Hampshire
Univ. of New Mexico
Univ. of New Orleans
Univ. of North Carolina–Asheville
Univ. of North Carolina–Chapel Hill
Univ. of North Carolina–Pembroke
Univ. of North Carolina–
     Wilmington
Univ. of Northern Iowa
Univ. of Notre Dame (IN)
Univ. of Oklahoma
Univ. of Oregon
Univ. of Pennsylvania
Univ. of Pittsburgh–Johnstown
Univ. of Portland (OR)
Univ. of Redlands (CA)
Univ. of Rhode Island
Univ. of Richmond (VA)
Univ. of Rio Grande (OH)
Univ. of Rochester (NY)
Univ. of San Francisco
Univ. of South Florida
Univ. of Southern California
Univ. of Southern Maine
Univ. of St. Francis (IL)

Univ. of St. Francis (IN)
Univ. of St. Thomas (MN)
Univ. of St. Thomas (TX)
Univ. of Tampa (FL)
Univ. of Tennessee–Chattanooga
Univ. of Texas of the Permian Basin
Univ. of Texas–Brownsville
Univ. of Texas–El Paso
Univ. of Texas–San Antonio
Univ. of the District of Columbia
Univ. of the Incarnate Word (TX)
Univ. of the Ozarks (AR)
Univ. of the Pacific (CA)
Univ. of Toledo (OH)
Univ. of Tulsa (OK)
Univ. of Utah
Univ. of Vermont
Univ. of Virginia
Univ. of Washington
Univ. of West Florida
Univ. of West Georgia
Univ. of Wisconsin–Green Bay
Univ. of Wisconsin–Milwaukee
Univ. of Wisconsin–River Falls
Univ. of Wisconsin–Stevens Point
Univ. of Wyoming
Upper Iowa Univ.
Ursinus Coll. (PA)
Valdosta State Univ. (GA)
Valparaiso Univ. (IN)
Vassar Coll. (NY)
Virginia Commonwealth Univ.
Virginia Intermont Coll.
Virginia Tech
Virginia Wesleyan Coll.
Washington and Jefferson Coll.
   (PA)
Washington and Lee Univ. (VA)
Washington Coll. (MD)
Washington State Univ.
Washington Univ. in St. Louis
Wayne State Univ. (MI)
Webster Univ. (MO)
Wellesley Coll. (MA)
Wells Coll. (NY)
Wesleyan Coll. (GA)
Wesleyan Univ. (CT)
West Texas A&M Univ.
West Virginia Wesleyan Coll.
Western Carolina Univ. (NC)
Western Michigan Univ.
Western State Coll. of Colorado
Western Washington Univ.
Westfield State Coll. (MA)
Westminster Coll. (PA)
Westminster Coll. (MO)
Wheaton Coll. (MA)
Wheaton Coll. (IL)
Whittier Coll. (CA)
Willamette Univ. (OR)
William Paterson Univ. of New
   Jersey
Wilson Coll. (PA)
Winthrop Univ. (SC)
Yale Univ. (CT)
Youngstown State Univ. (OH)

Natural Resources Management and Policy

Alaska Pacific Univ.

Angelo State Univ. (TX)
Bowling Green State Univ. (OH)
California State Univ.–Bakersfield
Carnegie Mellon Univ. (PA)
Charleston Southern Univ. (SC)
Colorado State Univ.
Drury Univ. (MO)
Elmhurst Coll. (IL)
Glenville State Coll. (WV)
Heidelberg Univ. (OH)
Humboldt State Univ. (CA)
Louisiana State Univ.–Baton Rouge
Mansfield Univ. of Pennsylvania
Michigan State Univ.
Montana State Univ.
New Mexico Highlands Univ.
North Carolina State Univ.–Raleigh
North Dakota State Univ.
Northern Michigan Univ.
Northland Coll. (WI)
Nova Southeastern Univ. (FL)
Ohio State Univ.–Columbus
Oregon State Univ.
Prescott Coll. (AZ)
Roanoke Coll. (VA)
Rochester Institute of Technology
   (NY)
Rutgers, the State Univ. of New
   Jersey–New Brunswick
Sewanee–Univ. of the South (TN)
South Dakota State Univ.
St. Norbert Coll. (WI)
St. Vincent Coll. (PA)
SUNY Coll. of Environmental
   Science and Forestry
Texas State Univ.–San Marcos
Tulane Univ. (LA)
Tuskegee Univ. (AL)
Unity Coll. (ME)
Univ. of Arizona
Univ. of California–Berkeley
Univ. of California–Davis
Univ. of Delaware
Univ. of Hawaii–Manoa
Univ. of Illinois–Urbana-Champaign
Univ. of Maine
Univ. of Maine–Farmington
Univ. of Massachusetts–Amherst
Univ. of Michigan–Ann Arbor
Univ. of Minnesota–Twin Cities
Univ. of Nebraska–Lincoln
Univ. of Nevada–Reno
Univ. of New Hampshire
Univ. of Rhode Island
Univ. of Tennessee–Martin
Univ. of Vermont
Univ. of Wisconsin–River Falls
Washington State Univ.
Western Carolina Univ. (NC)
Xavier Univ. (OH)

Natural Sciences

Bethel Coll. (KS)
Blue Mountain Coll. (MS)
California State Univ.–San
   Bernardino
Calvin Coll. (MI)
Carthage Coll. (WI)
Case Western Reserve Univ. (OH)
Central Christian Coll. (KS)

Central Washington Univ.
Christian Brothers Univ. (TN)
Colgate Univ. (NY)
Coll. of Mount St. Joseph (OH)
Colorado State Univ.
Covenant Coll. (GA)
Daemen Coll. (NY)
Dominican Univ. (IL)
Eastern Nazarene Coll. (MA)
Edgewood Coll. (WI)
Evergreen State Coll. (WA)
Georgian Court Univ. (NJ)
Hofstra Univ. (NY)
Houghton Coll. (NY)
Johns Hopkins Univ. (MD)
Johnson C. Smith Univ. (NC)
Juniata Coll. (PA)
Lawrence Univ. (WI)
Lewis-Clark State Coll. (ID)
Loyola Marymount Univ. (CA)
Madonna Univ. (MI)
Marygrove Coll. (MI)
Muhlenberg Coll. (PA)
National Univ. (CA)
Oklahoma Baptist Univ.
Our Lady of the Lake Univ. (TX)
Park Univ. (MO)
Pepperdine Univ. (CA)
Spelman Coll. (GA)
St. Gregory's Univ. (OK)
SUNY–Geneseo
Tabor Coll. (KS)
Thomas Edison State Coll. (NJ)
Univ. of Maine
Univ. of Nebraska–Omaha
Univ. of New Hampshire
Univ. of Pennsylvania
Univ. of Puget Sound (WA)
Univ. of Science and Arts of
   Oklahoma
Virginia Wesleyan Coll.
Xavier Univ. (OH)

Naval Architecture and Marine Engineering

Maine Maritime Academy
SUNY Maritime Coll.
United States Coast Guard
   Academy (CT)
United States Merchant Marine
   Academy (NY)
United States Naval Academy (MD)
Univ. of Michigan–Ann Arbor
Univ. of New Orleans
Univ. of Wisconsin–Madison
Webb Institute (NY)

Neuroscience

Allegheny Coll. (PA)
Amherst Coll. (MA)
Baldwin-Wallace Coll. (OH)
Barnard Coll. (NY)
Bates Coll. (ME)
Baylor Univ. (TX)
Bowdoin Coll. (ME)
Bowling Green State Univ. (OH)
Brandeis Univ. (MA)
Brigham Young Univ.–Provo (UT)
Brown Univ. (RI)

Bucknell Univ. (PA)
Carthage Coll. (WI)
Centenary Coll. of Louisiana
Central Michigan Univ.
Claremont McKenna Coll. (CA)
Colby Coll. (ME)
Colgate Univ. (NY)
Coll. of William and Mary (VA)
Colorado Coll.
Columbia Univ. (NY)
Connecticut Coll.
Cornell Univ. (NY)
CUNY–Queens Coll.
Dickinson Coll. (PA)
Drake Univ. (IA)
Drew Univ. (NJ)
Emmanuel Coll. (MA)
Fairfield Univ. (CT)
Franklin and Marshall Coll. (PA)
Furman Univ. (SC)
Hampshire Coll. (MA)
Johns Hopkins Univ. (MD)
Kenyon Coll. (OH)
King Coll. (TN)
King's Coll. (PA)
Knox Coll. (IL)
Lafayette Coll. (PA)
Lawrence Univ. (WI)
Macalester Coll. (MN)
Massachusetts Institute of
   Technology
Mount Holyoke Coll. (MA)
Muskingum Univ. (OH)
New York Univ.
Northeastern Univ. (MA)
Northwestern Univ. (IL)
Oberlin Coll. (OH)
Ohio State Univ.–Columbus
Ohio Wesleyan Univ.
Pomona Coll. (CA)
Smith Coll. (MA)
St. Andrews Presbyterian Coll. (NC)
St. Lawrence Univ. (NY)
Texas Christian Univ.
Tulane Univ. (LA)
Union Coll. (NY)
Univ. of California–Irvine
Univ. of California–Los Angeles
Univ. of California–Riverside
Univ. of California–San Diego
Univ. of California–Santa Cruz
Univ. of Evansville (IN)
Univ. of Illinois–Chicago
Univ. of Miami (FL)
Univ. of Michigan–Ann Arbor
Univ. of Minnesota–Twin Cities
Univ. of Mount Union (OH)
Univ. of Pennsylvania
Univ. of Pittsburgh
Univ. of Scranton (PA)
Univ. of Southern California
Univ. of Texas–Dallas
Ursinus Coll. (PA)
Vanderbilt Univ. (TN)
Washington and Lee Univ. (VA)
Washington State Univ.
Wellesley Coll. (MA)
Westminster Coll. (PA)

Nonprofessional General Legal Studies (Undergraduate)

Abilene Christian Univ. (TX)
Allegheny Coll. (PA)
Alma Coll. (MI)
Amherst Coll. (MA)
Anna Maria Coll. (MA)
Arizona State Univ.
Babson Coll. (MA)
Ball State Univ. (IN)
Barry Univ. (FL)
Bay Path Coll. (MA)
Benedictine Univ. (IL)
Bennington Coll. (VT)
Bethel Coll. (IN)
Bowling Green State Univ. (OH)
Brenau Univ. (GA)
Brevard Coll. (NC)
Bridgewater State Coll. (MA)
Burlington Coll. (VT)
California Lutheran Univ.
Calumet Coll. of St. Joseph (IN)
Calvin Coll. (MI)
Campbell Univ. (NC)
Carroll Coll. (MT)
Catawba Coll. (NC)
Cedarville Univ. (OH)
Central Christian Coll. (KS)
Chapman Univ. (CA)
Charleston Southern Univ. (SC)
Claremont McKenna Coll. (CA)
Clearwater Christian Coll. (FL)
Coll. of St. Mary (NE)
Coll. of the Ozarks (MO)
Coll. of William and Mary (VA)
Concordia Univ. (NE)
Concordia Univ. (MI)
Corban Univ. (OR)
Cornerstone Univ. (MI)
Creighton Univ. (NE)
Crown Coll. (MN)
Defiance Coll. (OH)
DeSales Univ. (PA)
Dickinson Coll. (PA)
Dillard Univ. (LA)
Dominican Coll. (NY)
Drury Univ. (MO)
Eastern Michigan Univ.
Eastern Nazarene Coll. (MA)
Elizabethtown Coll. (PA)
Emmanuel Coll. (GA)
Fontbonne Univ. (MO)
Franciscan Univ. of Steubenville
   (OH)
Gannon Univ. (PA)
Geneva Coll. (PA)
Georgia State Univ.
Grand Valley State Univ. (MI)
Hamline Univ. (MN)
Hampshire Coll. (MA)
Hardin-Simmons Univ. (TX)
Harding Univ. (AR)
Hofstra Univ. (NY)
Hood Coll. (MD)
Howard Payne Univ. (TX)
Huntington Univ. (IN)
Iowa Wesleyan Coll.
Ithaca Coll. (NY)
Juniata Coll. (PA)

Lake Erie Coll. (OH)
Lambuth Univ. (TN)
Lasell Coll. (MA)
Lawrence Univ. (WI)
Liberty Univ. (VA)
Limestone Coll. (SC)
Lindenwood Univ. (MO)
Lipscomb Univ. (TN)
Louisiana Coll.
MacMurray Coll. (IL)
Madonna Univ. (MI)
Mansfield Univ. of Pennsylvania
Marlboro Coll. (VT)
Maryville Univ. of St. Louis (MO)
Master's Coll. and Seminary (CA)
Mercy Coll. (NY)
Michigan State Univ.
Midwestern State Univ. (TX)
Millikin Univ. (IL)
Minnesota State Univ.–Mankato
Minnesota State Univ.–Moorhead
Mississippi Coll.
Missouri Univ. of Science &
    Technology
Mitchell Coll. (CT)
Monmouth Coll. (IL)
Mount Mary Coll. (WI)
National Univ. (CA)
New England Coll. (NH)
Northern Arizona Univ.
Northern Michigan Univ.
Northwestern Univ. (IL)
Notre Dame Coll. of Ohio
Nova Southeastern Univ. (FL)
Oberlin Coll. (OH)
Ohio State Univ.–Columbus
Ohio Wesleyan Univ.
Oklahoma Baptist Univ.
Oklahoma Christian Univ.
Oklahoma Wesleyan Univ.
Oral Roberts Univ. (OK)
Ouachita Baptist Univ. (AR)
Pacific Lutheran Univ. (WA)
Palm Beach Atlantic Univ. (FL)
Park Univ. (MO)
Pfeiffer Univ. (NC)
Philadelphia Univ.
Point Park Univ. (PA)
Regis Univ. (CO)
Rensselaer Polytechnic Institute
    (NY)
Rochester Institute of Technology
    (NY)
Roger Williams Univ. (RI)
Sacred Heart Univ. (CT)
Sage Colleges–Albany (NY)
Schreiner Univ. (TX)
Simpson Coll. (IA)
Southwestern Adventist Univ. (TX)
Spelman Coll. (GA)
St. Ambrose Univ. (IA)
St. Augustine's Coll. (NC)
St. Bonaventure Univ. (NY)
St. Francis Univ. (PA)
St. Gregory's Univ. (OK)
St. John's Univ. (NY)
St. Joseph's Univ. (PA)
Stephens Coll. (MO)
Suffolk Univ. (MA)
SUNY Coll.–Oneonta
Temple Univ. (PA)

Texas Wesleyan Univ.
Thiel Coll. (PA)
Thomas More Coll. (KY)
Toccoa Falls Coll. (GA)
Tougaloo Coll. (MS)
Trinity International Univ. (IL)
United States Air Force Academy
    (CO)
Univ. of Baltimore (MD)
Univ. of California–Berkeley
Univ. of California–Riverside
Univ. of California–Santa Barbara
Univ. of California–Santa Cruz
Univ. of Dayton (OH)
Univ. of Denver
Univ. of Evansville (IN)
Univ. of Illinois–Urbana-Champaign
Univ. of Iowa
Univ. of La Verne (CA)
Univ. of Maryland–Coll. Park
Univ. of Maryland–Eastern Shore
Univ. of Maryland–Univ. Coll.
Univ. of Massachusetts–Amherst
Univ. of Miami (FL)
Univ. of Nevada–Las Vegas
Univ. of New Haven (CT)
Univ. of Pittsburgh
Univ. of Pittsburgh–Johnstown
Univ. of St. Thomas (MN)
Univ. of Toledo (OH)
Univ. of Wisconsin–Madison
Univ. of Wisconsin–Superior
Utah State Univ.
Vanguard Univ. of Southern
    California
Victory Univ. (TN)
Virginia Intermont Coll.
Washburn Univ. (KS)
Webber International Univ. (FL)
Webster Univ. (MO)
West Texas A&M Univ.
West Virginia Wesleyan Coll.
Western New England Coll. (MA)
Westminster Coll. (UT)
Widener Univ. (PA)
William Woods Univ. (MO)
Wilmington Univ. (DE)
Winona State Univ. (MN)
York Coll. of Pennsylvania
Youngstown State Univ. (OH)

Nuclear and Industrial Radiologic Technologies/ Technicians

Univ. of North Texas

Nuclear Engineering

Georgia Institute of Technology
Idaho State Univ.
Massachusetts Institute of
    Technology
Missouri Univ. of Science &
    Technology
North Carolina State Univ.–Raleigh
Ohio State Univ.–Columbus
Oregon State Univ.
Pennsylvania State Univ.–Univ. Park
Rensselaer Polytechnic Institute
    (NY)

South Carolina State Univ.
Texas A&M Univ.–Coll. Station
United States Military Academy
    (NY)
Univ. of California–Berkeley
Univ. of Florida
Univ. of Illinois–Urbana-Champaign
Univ. of Michigan–Ann Arbor
Univ. of New Mexico
Univ. of Tennessee
Univ. of Wisconsin–Madison

Nuclear Engineering Technologies/ Technicians

Excelsior Coll. (NY)
Thomas Edison State Coll. (NJ)

Nursing

Abilene Christian Univ. (TX)
Adelphi Univ. (NY)
Albany State Univ. (GA)
Alcorn State Univ. (MS)
Alderson-Broaddus Coll. (WV)
Alvernia Univ. (PA)
Alverno Coll. (WI)
American International Coll. (MA)
Anderson Univ. (IN)
Andrews Univ. (MI)
Angelo State Univ. (TX)
Anna Maria Coll. (MA)
Appalachian State Univ. (NC)
Arkansas State Univ.–Jonesboro
Arkansas Tech Univ.
Armstrong Atlantic State Univ. (GA)
Atlantic Union Coll. (MA)
Auburn Univ. (AL)
Auburn Univ.–Montgomery (AL)
Augsburg Coll. (MN)
Augustana Coll. (SD)
Aurora Univ. (IL)
Austin Peay State Univ. (TN)
Avila Univ. (MO)
Azusa Pacific Univ. (CA)
Baker Univ. (KS)
Ball State Univ. (IN)
Barry Univ. (FL)
Barton Coll. (NC)
Baylor Univ. (TX)
Bellarmine Univ. (KY)
Belmont Univ. (TN)
Bemidji State Univ. (MN)
Benedictine Univ. (IL)
Berea Coll. (KY)
Berry Coll. (GA)
Bethel Coll. (KS)
Bethel Coll. (IN)
Bethel Univ. (MN)
Bethune-Cookman Univ. (FL)
Binghamton Univ.–SUNY
Biola Univ. (CA)
Bloomfield Coll. (NJ)
Bloomsburg Univ. of Pennsylvania
Bluefield State Coll. (WV)
Boise State Univ. (ID)
Boston Coll.
Bowie State Univ. (MD)
Bowling Green State Univ. (OH)
Bradley Univ. (IL)

Brenau Univ. (GA)
Briar Cliff Univ. (IA)
Brigham Young Univ.–Provo (UT)
California Baptist Univ.
California State Univ.–Bakersfield
California State Univ.–Chico
California State Univ.–Dominguez
    Hills
California State Univ.–East Bay
California State Univ.–Fresno
California State Univ.–Fullerton
California State Univ.–Long Beach
California State Univ.–Los Angeles
California State Univ.–Northridge
California State Univ.–Sacramento
California State Univ.–San
    Bernardino
California State Univ.–Stanislaus
California Univ. of Pennsylvania
Calvin Coll. (MI)
Capital Univ. (OH)
Carlow Univ. (PA)
Carroll Coll. (MT)
Carroll Univ. (WI)
Carson-Newman Coll. (TN)
Case Western Reserve Univ. (OH)
Catholic Univ. of America (DC)
Cedar Crest Coll. (PA)
Cedarville Univ. (OH)
Central Connecticut State Univ.
Central Methodist Univ. (MO)
Charleston Southern Univ. (SC)
Chatham Univ. (PA)
Chicago State Univ.
Clarion Univ. of Pennsylvania
Clayton State Univ. (GA)
Clemson Univ. (SC)
Cleveland State Univ.
Colby-Sawyer Coll. (NH)
Coll. at Brockport–SUNY
Coll. of Mount St. Joseph (OH)
Coll. of Mount St. Vincent (NY)
Coll. of New Jersey
Coll. of Notre Dame of Maryland
Coll. of Our Lady of the Elms (MA)
Coll. of St. Benedict (MN)
Coll. of St. Elizabeth (NJ)
Coll. of St. Mary (NE)
Coll. of St. Scholastica (MN)
Coll. of the Ozarks (MO)
Colorado State Univ.–Pueblo
Columbus State Univ. (GA)
Concordia Coll.–Moorhead (MN)
Concordia Univ. (OR)
Concordia Univ. Chicago (IL)
Concordia Univ. Wisconsin
Coppin State Univ. (MD)
Crown Coll. (MN)
Culver-Stockton Coll. (MO)
Cumberland Univ. (TN)
CUNY–City Coll.
CUNY–Coll. of Staten Island
CUNY–Hunter Coll.
CUNY–Lehman Coll.
CUNY–Medgar Evers Coll.
CUNY–York Coll.
Curry Coll. (MA)
D'Youville Coll. (NY)
Daemen Coll. (NY)
Dakota Wesleyan Univ. (SD)
Davenport Univ. (MI)

Delaware State Univ.
Delta State Univ. (MS)
DePaul Univ. (IL)
DeSales Univ. (PA)
Dickinson State Univ. (ND)
Dixie State Coll. of Utah
Dominican Coll. (NY)
Dominican Univ. (IL)
Dominican Univ. of California
Drexel Univ. (PA)
Duquesne Univ. (PA)
East Carolina Univ. (NC)
East Central Univ. (OK)
East Stroudsburg Univ. of
    Pennsylvania
East Tennessee State Univ.
East Texas Baptist Univ.
Eastern Kentucky Univ.
Eastern Mennonite Univ. (VA)
Eastern Michigan Univ.
Eastern New Mexico Univ.
Eastern Oregon Univ.
Eastern Univ. (PA)
Eastern Washington Univ.
Edgewood Coll. (WI)
Edinboro Univ. of Pennsylvania
Elmhurst Coll. (IL)
Elmira Coll. (NY)
Emmanuel Coll. (MA)
Emory Univ. (GA)
Emporia State Univ. (KS)
Endicott Coll. (MA)
Evangel Univ. (MO)
Excelsior Coll. (NY)
Fairfield Univ. (CT)
Fairleigh Dickinson Univ. (NJ)
Fairmont State Univ. (WV)
Farmingdale State Coll.–SUNY
Felician Coll. (NJ)
Ferris State Univ. (MI)
Fitchburg State Coll. (MA)
Florida Atlantic Univ.
Florida Gulf Coast Univ.
Florida International Univ.
Florida Southern Coll.
Florida State Univ.
Fort Hays State Univ. (KS)
Framingham State Coll. (MA)
Francis Marion Univ. (SC)
Franciscan Univ. of Steubenville
    (OH)
Gannon Univ. (PA)
Gardner-Webb Univ. (NC)
George Fox Univ. (OR)
George Mason Univ. (VA)
Georgetown Univ. (DC)
Georgia Coll. & State Univ.
Georgia Southern Univ.
Georgia Southwestern State Univ.
Georgia State Univ.
Glenville State Coll. (WV)
Gonzaga Univ. (WA)
Goshen Coll. (IN)
Graceland Univ. (IA)
Grambling State Univ. (LA)
Grand Valley State Univ. (MI)
Grand View Univ. (IA)
Gustavus Adolphus Coll. (MN)
Gwynedd-Mercy Coll. (PA)
Hampton Univ. (VA)
Hannibal-LaGrange Coll. (MO)

Hardin-Simmons Univ. (TX)
Harding Univ. (AR)
Hartwick Coll. (NY)
Hawaii Pacific Univ.
Henderson State Univ. (AR)
Holy Family Univ. (PA)
Holy Names Univ. (CA)
Hope Coll. (MI)
Houston Baptist Univ.
Howard Univ. (DC)
Humboldt State Univ. (CA)
Huntington Univ. (IN)
Husson Univ. (ME)
Idaho State Univ.
Illinois State Univ.
Illinois Wesleyan Univ.
Immaculata Univ. (PA)
Indiana State Univ.
Indiana Univ. East
Indiana Univ. Northwest
Indiana Univ. of Pennsylvania
Indiana Univ. Southeast
Indiana Univ.–Bloomington
Indiana Univ.–Kokomo
Indiana Univ.-Purdue Univ.–Fort
    Wayne
Indiana Univ.-Purdue Univ.–
    Indianapolis
Indiana Wesleyan Univ.
Iowa Wesleyan Coll.
Jacksonville State Univ. (AL)
Jacksonville Univ. (FL)
James Madison Univ. (VA)
Jamestown Coll. (ND)
Kansas Wesleyan Univ.
Kean Univ. (NJ)
Kennesaw State Univ. (GA)
Kent State Univ. (OH)
Kentucky State Univ.
Keuka Coll. (NY)
King Coll. (TN)
Kutztown Univ. of Pennsylvania
La Roche Coll. (PA)
La Salle Univ. (PA)
LaGrange Coll. (GA)
Lake Superior State Univ. (MI)
Lamar Univ. (TX)
Lander Univ. (SC)
Le Moyne Coll. (NY)
Lees-McRae Coll. (NC)
Lenoir-Rhyne Univ. (NC)
Lewis Univ. (IL)
Lewis-Clark State Coll. (ID)
Liberty Univ. (VA)
Lincoln Memorial Univ. (TN)
Lincoln Univ. (MO)
Lipscomb Univ. (TN)
Long Island Univ.–C.W. Post
    Campus (NY)
Louisiana Coll.
Lourdes Coll. (OH)
Loyola Univ. Chicago
Loyola Univ. New Orleans
Lubbock Christian Univ. (TX)
Luther Coll. (IA)
Lynchburg Coll. (VA)
MacMurray Coll. (IL)
Macon State Coll. (GA)
Madonna Univ. (MI)
Malone Univ. (OH)
Mansfield Univ. of Pennsylvania

Maranatha Baptist Bible Coll. (WI)
Marian Univ. (WI)
Marian Univ. (IN)
Marquette Univ. (WI)
Marshall Univ. (WV)
Marymount Univ. (VA)
Maryville Univ. of St. Louis (MO)
Marywood Univ. (PA)
McKendree Univ. (IL)
McMurry Univ. (TX)
McNeese State Univ. (LA)
Mesa State Coll. (CO)
Messiah Coll. (PA)
Metropolitan State Coll. of Denver
Miami Univ.–Oxford (OH)
Michigan State Univ.
MidAmerica Nazarene Univ. (KS)
Middle Tennessee State Univ.
Midland Lutheran Coll. (NE)
Midway Coll. (KY)
Midwestern State Univ. (TX)
Millersville Univ. of Pennsylvania
Milligan Coll. (TN)
Millikin Univ. (IL)
Milwaukee School of Engineering
Minnesota State Univ.–Mankato
Minnesota State Univ.–Moorhead
Minot State Univ. (ND)
Misericordia Univ. (PA)
Mississippi Coll.
Mississippi Univ. for Women
Missouri Southern State Univ.
Missouri State Univ.
Missouri Western State Univ.
Molloy Coll. (NY)
Monmouth Univ. (NJ)
Montana State Univ.
Montana State Univ.–Northern
Montana Tech of the Univ. of
    Montana
Moravian Coll. (PA)
Morehead State Univ. (KY)
Morningside Coll. (IA)
Mount Aloysius Coll. (PA)
Mount Marty Coll. (SD)
Mount Mary Coll. (WI)
Mount Mercy Coll. (IA)
Mount St. Mary Coll. (NY)
Mount St. Mary's Coll. (CA)
Mountain State Univ. (WV)
Murray State Univ. (KY)
National Univ. (CA)
Nazareth Coll. (NY)
Nebraska Wesleyan Univ.
Neumann Univ. (PA)
New Jersey City Univ.
New Mexico State Univ.
New York Institute of Technology
New York Univ.
Newman Univ. (KS)
Niagara Univ. (NY)
Nicholls State Univ. (LA)
Norfolk State Univ. (VA)
North Carolina A&T State Univ.
North Carolina Central Univ.
North Dakota State Univ.
North Georgia Coll. and State Univ.
North Park Univ. (IL)
Northeastern State Univ. (OK)
Northeastern Univ. (MA)
Northern Arizona Univ.

Northern Illinois Univ.
Northern Kentucky Univ.
Northern Michigan Univ.
Northwest Nazarene Univ. (ID)
Northwest Univ. (WA)
Northwestern Coll. (IA)
Northwestern Oklahoma State
    Univ.
Northwestern State Univ. of
    Louisiana
Norwich Univ. (VT)
Notre Dame Coll. of Ohio
Nova Southeastern Univ. (FL)
Oakland Univ. (MI)
Oakwood Univ. (AL)
Ohio Northern Univ.
Ohio State Univ.–Columbus
Ohio Univ.
Oklahoma Baptist Univ.
Oklahoma Christian Univ.
Oklahoma City Univ.
Oklahoma Panhandle State Univ.
Oklahoma Wesleyan Univ.
Old Dominion Univ. (VA)
Oral Roberts Univ. (OK)
Oregon Institute of Technology
Otterbein Coll. (OH)
Pace Univ. (NY)
Pacific Lutheran Univ. (WA)
Pacific Union Coll. (CA)
Palm Beach Atlantic Univ. (FL)
Pennsylvania Coll. of Technology
Pennsylvania State Univ.–Univ. Park
Pittsburg State Univ. (KS)
Point Loma Nazarene Univ. (CA)
Prairie View A&M Univ. (TX)
Purdue Univ.–Calumet (IN)
Purdue Univ.–North Central (IN)
Queens Univ. of Charlotte (NC)
Quincy Univ. (IL)
Quinnipiac Univ. (CT)
Radford Univ. (VA)
Ramapo Coll. of New Jersey
Regis Coll. (MA)
Regis Univ. (CO)
Rhode Island Coll.
Richard Stockton Coll. of New
    Jersey
Rivier Coll. (NH)
Robert Morris Univ. (PA)
Roberts Wesleyan Coll. (NY)
Rockford Coll. (IL)
Rockhurst Univ. (MO)
Russell Sage Coll. (NY)
Rutgers, the State Univ. of New
    Jersey–Camden
Rutgers, the State Univ. of New
    Jersey–Newark
Sacred Heart Univ. (CT)
Sage Colleges–Albany (NY)
Saginaw Valley State Univ. (MI)
Salem State Coll. (MA)
Salisbury Univ. (MD)
Salve Regina Univ. (RI)
Samford Univ. (AL)
San Diego State Univ.
San Francisco State Univ.
San Jose State Univ. (CA)
Seattle Pacific Univ.
Seattle Univ.
Seton Hall Univ. (NJ)

Shawnee State Univ. (OH)
Shenandoah Univ. (VA)
Shepherd Univ. (WV)
Silver Lake Coll. (WI)
Simmons Coll. (MA)
Slippery Rock Univ. of Pennsylvania
Sonoma State Univ. (CA)
South Carolina State Univ.
South Dakota State Univ.
Southeast Missouri State Univ.
Southeastern Louisiana Univ.
Southern Adventist Univ. (TN)
Southern Arkansas Univ.
Southern Connecticut State Univ.
Southern Illinois Univ.–Edwardsville
Southern Nazarene Univ. (OK)
Southern Univ. and A&M Coll. (LA)
Southern Utah Univ.
Southern Vermont Coll.
Southwest Baptist Univ. (MO)
Southwestern Coll. (KS)
Southwestern Oklahoma State
    Univ.
Spalding Univ. (KY)
Spring Arbor Univ. (MI)
Spring Hill Coll. (AL)
St. Ambrose Univ. (IA)
St. Anselm Coll. (NH)
St. Catherine Univ. (MN)
St. Cloud State Univ. (MN)
St. Francis Coll. (NY)
St. Francis Univ. (PA)
St. John Fisher Coll. (NY)
St. John's Univ. (MN)
St. Joseph Coll. (CT)
St. Joseph's Coll. (ME)
St. Joseph's Coll. (IN)
St. Joseph's Coll. New York
St. Louis Univ.
St. Mary's Coll. (IN)
St. Olaf Coll. (MN)
St. Peter's Coll. (NJ)
St. Xavier Univ. (IL)
Stephen F. Austin State Univ. (TX)
Stevenson Univ. (MD)
Stillman Coll. (AL)
SUNY Institute of Technology–
    Utica/Rome
SUNY–Plattsburgh
SUNY–Stony Brook
Tabor Coll. (KS)
Tarleton State Univ. (TX)
Temple Univ. (PA)
Tennessee State Univ.
Tennessee Technological Univ.
Tennessee Wesleyan Coll.
Texas A&M International Univ.
Texas A&M Univ.–Corpus Christi
Texas Christian Univ.
Texas Wesleyan Univ.
Texas Woman's Univ.
Thomas Edison State Coll. (NJ)
Thomas More Coll. (KY)
Thomas Univ. (GA)
Towson Univ. (MD)
Trevecca Nazarene Univ. (TN)
Trinity Christian Coll. (IL)
Troy Univ. (AL)
Truman State Univ. (MO)
Tuskegee Univ. (AL)
Union Coll. (NE)

Union Univ. (TN)
Univ. at Buffalo–SUNY
Univ. of Akron (OH)
Univ. of Alabama
Univ. of Alabama–Birmingham
Univ. of Alabama–Huntsville
Univ. of Alaska–Anchorage
Univ. of Arizona
Univ. of Arkansas
Univ. of Arkansas–Monticello
Univ. of Arkansas–Pine Bluff
Univ. of California–Los Angeles
Univ. of Central Arkansas
Univ. of Central Florida
Univ. of Central Missouri
Univ. of Central Oklahoma
Univ. of Charleston (WV)
Univ. of Colorado–Colorado
    Springs
Univ. of Colorado–Denver
Univ. of Connecticut
Univ. of Delaware
Univ. of Detroit Mercy
Univ. of Dubuque (IA)
Univ. of Evansville (IN)
Univ. of Findlay (OH)
Univ. of Florida
Univ. of Hartford (CT)
Univ. of Hawaii–Hilo
Univ. of Hawaii–Manoa
Univ. of Illinois–Chicago
Univ. of Indianapolis
Univ. of Iowa
Univ. of Kansas
Univ. of Kentucky
Univ. of Louisiana–Lafayette
Univ. of Louisiana–Monroe
Univ. of Louisville (KY)
Univ. of Maine
Univ. of Maine–Fort Kent
Univ. of Mary (ND)
Univ. of Mary Hardin-Baylor (TX)
Univ. of Maryland–Coll. Park
Univ. of Maryland–Eastern Shore
Univ. of Massachusetts–Amherst
Univ. of Massachusetts–Boston
Univ. of Massachusetts–Dartmouth
Univ. of Massachusetts–Lowell
Univ. of Memphis
Univ. of Miami (FL)
Univ. of Michigan–Ann Arbor
Univ. of Michigan–Flint
Univ. of Minnesota–Twin Cities
Univ. of Missouri
Univ. of Missouri–Kansas City
Univ. of Missouri–St. Louis
Univ. of Nevada–Las Vegas
Univ. of Nevada–Reno
Univ. of New England (ME)
Univ. of New Hampshire
Univ. of New Mexico
Univ. of North Alabama
Univ. of North Carolina–Chapel Hill
Univ. of North Carolina–Charlotte
Univ. of North Carolina–
    Greensboro
Univ. of North Carolina–Pembroke
Univ. of North Carolina–
    Wilmington
Univ. of North Dakota
Univ. of North Florida

Univ. of Northern Colorado
Univ. of Oklahoma
Univ. of Pennsylvania
Univ. of Pittsburgh
Univ. of Pittsburgh–Bradford
Univ. of Portland (OR)
Univ. of Rhode Island
Univ. of Rio Grande (OH)
Univ. of Rochester (NY)
Univ. of San Diego
Univ. of San Francisco
Univ. of Scranton (PA)
Univ. of South Alabama
Univ. of South Carolina
Univ. of South Carolina–Aiken
Univ. of South Carolina–Upstate
Univ. of South Florida
Univ. of Southern Indiana
Univ. of Southern Maine
Univ. of Southern Mississippi
Univ. of St. Francis (IL)
Univ. of St. Francis (IN)
Univ. of St. Mary (KS)
Univ. of Tampa (FL)
Univ. of Tennessee
Univ. of Tennessee–Chattanooga
Univ. of Tennessee–Martin
Univ. of Texas–Arlington
Univ. of Texas–Austin
Univ. of Texas–Brownsville
Univ. of Texas–El Paso
Univ. of Texas–Pan American
Univ. of Texas–Tyler
Univ. of the District of Columbia
Univ. of the Incarnate Word (TX)
Univ. of Toledo (OH)
Univ. of Tulsa (OK)
Univ. of Utah
Univ. of Vermont
Univ. of Virginia
Univ. of Washington
Univ. of West Florida
Univ. of West Georgia
Univ. of Wisconsin–Eau Claire
Univ. of Wisconsin–Green Bay
Univ. of Wisconsin–Madison
Univ. of Wisconsin–Milwaukee
Univ. of Wisconsin–Oshkosh
Univ. of Wisconsin–Parkside
Univ. of Wyoming
Urbana Univ. (OH)
Ursuline Coll. (OH)
Utah Valley Univ.
Utica Coll. (NY)
Valdosta State Univ. (GA)
Valparaiso Univ. (IN)
Vanguard Univ. of Southern
    California
Vermont Technical Coll.
Villanova Univ. (PA)
Virginia Commonwealth Univ.
Virginia State Univ.
Viterbo Univ. (WI)
Wagner Coll. (NY)
Walla Walla Univ. (WA)
Walsh Univ. (OH)
Washburn Univ. (KS)
Washington Adventist Univ. (MD)
Washington State Univ.
Wayne State Univ. (MI)
Waynesburg Univ. (PA)

Weber State Univ. (UT)
Webster Univ. (MO)
Wesley Coll. (DE)
West Chester Univ. of Pennsylvania
West Liberty Univ. (WV)
West Texas A&M Univ.
West Virginia Univ.
West Virginia Univ. Institute of
    Technology
West Virginia Univ.–Parkersburg
West Virginia Wesleyan Coll.
Western Carolina Univ. (NC)
Western Connecticut State Univ.
Western Kentucky Univ.
Western Michigan Univ.
Western New Mexico Univ.
Westminster Coll. (UT)
Wheaton Coll. (IL)
Wheeling Jesuit Univ. (WV)
Whitworth Univ. (WA)
Wichita State Univ. (KS)
Widener Univ. (PA)
Wilkes Univ. (PA)
William Carey Univ. (MS)
William Jewell Coll. (MO)
William Paterson Univ. of New
    Jersey
Wilmington Univ. (DE)
Winona State Univ. (MN)
Winston-Salem State Univ. (NC)
Worcester State Coll. (MA)
Wright State Univ. (OH)
Xavier Univ. (OH)
York Coll. of Pennsylvania
Youngstown State Univ. (OH)

Nutrition Sciences

Auburn Univ. (AL)
Boston Univ.
Brigham Young Univ.–Provo (UT)
Case Western Reserve Univ. (OH)
Coll. of St. Benedict (MN)
Cornell Univ. (NY)
Drexel Univ. (PA)
Howard Univ. (DC)
Life Univ. (GA)
Long Island Univ.–C.W. Post
    Campus (NY)
Michigan State Univ.
North Carolina State Univ.–Raleigh
Purdue Univ.–West Lafayette (IN)
Russell Sage Coll. (NY)
Rutgers, the State Univ. of New
    Jersey–New Brunswick
San Jose State Univ. (CA)
Simmons Coll. (MA)
St. John's Univ. (MN)
Texas Woman's Univ.
Tulane Univ. (LA)
Univ. of Arizona
Univ. of California–Berkeley
Univ. of California–Davis
Univ. of Connecticut
Univ. of Delaware
Univ. of Hawaii–Manoa
Univ. of Kentucky
Univ. of Maine
Univ. of Michigan–Ann Arbor
Univ. of Minnesota–Twin Cities
Univ. of Nebraska–Lincoln

Univ. of Nevada–Las Vegas
Univ. of North Carolina–
    Greensboro
Univ. of Oklahoma
Univ. of the Incarnate Word (TX)
Univ. of Vermont
Univ. of Wisconsin–Green Bay
Univ. of Wisconsin–Madison
Washington State Univ.

Ocean Engineering

Florida Atlantic Univ.
Florida Institute of Technology
Massachusetts Institute of
    Technology
Texas A&M Univ.–Coll. Station
United States Naval Academy (MD)
Univ. of Florida
Univ. of New Hampshire
Univ. of Rhode Island

Operations Research

Carnegie Mellon Univ. (PA)
Columbia Univ. (NY)
Cornell Univ. (NY)
CUNY–Baruch Coll.
New York Univ.
Princeton Univ. (NJ)
Syracuse Univ. (NY)
United States Air Force Academy
    (CO)
United States Military Academy
    (NY)
Univ. of California–Berkeley
Univ. of Illinois–Urbana-Champaign

Ophthalmic and Optometric Support Services and Allied Professions

Excelsior Coll. (NY)
Lindenwood Univ. (MO)

Optometry (O.D.)

Gannon Univ. (PA)
Indiana Univ.–Bloomington
Ohio State Univ.–Columbus
Univ. of California–Berkeley

Parks, Recreation, and Leisure Facilities Management

Alabama State Univ.
Alderson-Broaddus Coll. (WV)
American International Coll. (MA)
Appalachian State Univ. (NC)
Arkansas Tech Univ.
Asbury Univ. (KY)
Bluffton Univ. (OH)
California Univ. of Pennsylvania
Carroll Univ. (WI)
Central Christian Coll. (KS)
Central Methodist Univ. (MO)
Central Michigan Univ.
Central Washington Univ.
Cheyney Univ. of Pennsylvania

Chicago State Univ.
Coll. of the Ozarks (MO)
Colorado State Univ.
Cumberland Univ. (TN)
East Carolina Univ. (NC)
East Stroudsburg Univ. of
    Pennsylvania
Eastern Illinois Univ.
Eastern Kentucky Univ.
Eastern Michigan Univ.
Eastern Washington Univ.
Elmhurst Coll. (IL)
Ferris State Univ. (MI)
Florida International Univ.
Florida State Univ.
Gallaudet Univ. (DC)
Georgia Southern Univ.
Hannibal-LaGrange Coll. (MO)
Henderson State Univ. (AR)
High Point Univ. (NC)
Huntington Univ. (IN)
Illinois State Univ.
Indiana Institute of Technology
Indiana State Univ.
Johnson and Wales Univ. (RI)
Johnson State Coll. (VT)
Kansas State Univ.
Kean Univ. (NJ)
Kent State Univ. (OH)
Lock Haven Univ. of Pennsylvania
Lyndon State Coll. (VT)
Lynn Univ. (FL)
Marshall Univ. (WV)
Michigan State Univ.
Middle Tennessee State Univ.
Midland Lutheran Coll. (NE)
Minnesota State Univ.–Mankato
Missouri Valley Coll.
Missouri Western State Univ.
Morris Coll. (SC)
Mount Marty Coll. (SD)
Murray State Univ. (KY)
New Mexico Highlands Univ.
New Mexico State Univ.
New York Univ.
North Carolina A&T State Univ.
North Carolina Central Univ.
North Carolina State Univ.–Raleigh
Northern Michigan Univ.
Northwest Missouri State Univ.
Oklahoma Baptist Univ.
Old Dominion Univ. (VA)
Pennsylvania State Univ.–Univ. Park
Prairie View A&M Univ. (TX)
San Jose State Univ. (CA)
Savannah State Univ. (GA)
Slippery Rock Univ. of Pennsylvania
South Dakota State Univ.
Southwestern Oklahoma State
    Univ.
Springfield Coll. (MA)
St. Joseph's Coll. New York
St. Thomas Aquinas Coll. (NY)
Stephen F. Austin State Univ. (TX)
Texas A&M Univ.–Coll. Station
Texas State Univ.–San Marcos
Trine Univ. (IN)
Union Coll. (KY)
Unity Coll. (ME)
Univ. of Connecticut
Univ. of Delaware

Univ. of Florida
Univ. of Hawaii–Hilo
Univ. of Maine
Univ. of Maine–Machias
Univ. of Maine–Presque Isle
Univ. of Minnesota–Duluth
Univ. of Minnesota–Twin Cities
Univ. of Mississippi
Univ. of Montana
Univ. of North Carolina–Chapel Hill
Univ. of North Carolina–Pembroke
Univ. of North Carolina–
    Wilmington
Univ. of North Dakota
Univ. of North Texas
Univ. of Northern Colorado
Univ. of St. Francis (IL)
Univ. of Tennessee
Univ. of Vermont
Univ. of West Georgia
Univ. of Wisconsin–La Crosse
Univ. of Wisconsin–Madison
Webber International Univ. (FL)
West Virginia Univ.
Western Carolina Univ. (NC)
Western Illinois Univ.
Western Kentucky Univ.
York Coll. of Pennsylvania

Parks, Recreation, and Leisure Studies

Alaska Pacific Univ.
Alcorn State Univ. (MS)
Aquinas Coll. (MI)
Arizona State Univ.
Atlantic Union Coll. (MA)
Aurora Univ. (IL)
Benedict Coll. (SC)
Black Hills State Univ. (SD)
Bowling Green State Univ. (OH)
Brevard Coll. (NC)
Bridgewater State Coll. (MA)
Brigham Young Univ.–Provo (UT)
California Polytechnic State Univ.–
    San Luis Obispo
California State Univ.–Chico
California State Univ.–Dominguez
    Hills
California State Univ.–East Bay
California State Univ.–Fresno
California State Univ.–Long Beach
California State Univ.–Northridge
California State Univ.–Sacramento
Calvin Coll. (MI)
Carson-Newman Coll. (TN)
Catawba Coll. (NC)
Central Michigan Univ.
Central State Univ. (OH)
Coll. of St. Joseph (VT)
Davis and Elkins Coll. (WV)
Eastern Washington Univ.
Emporia State Univ. (KS)
Ferrum Coll. (VA)
Fort Lewis Coll. (CO)
Frostburg State Univ. (MD)
Gallaudet Univ. (DC)
Georgia Coll. & State Univ.
Georgia Southern Univ.
Gordon Coll. (MA)
Graceland Univ. (IA)

Grambling State Univ. (LA)
Grand Valley State Univ. (MI)
Green Mountain Coll. (VT)
Greenville Coll. (IL)
Houghton Coll. (NY)
Howard Payne Univ. (TX)
Huntingdon Coll. (AL)
Huntington Univ. (IN)
Huston-Tillotson Univ. (TX)
Indiana Univ. Northwest
Indiana Univ.–Bloomington
Ithaca Coll. (NY)
Jacksonville State Univ. (AL)
Kutztown Univ. of Pennsylvania
Lake Superior State Univ. (MI)
Mars Hill Coll. (NC)
Maryville Coll. (TN)
Messiah Coll. (PA)
Metropolitan State Coll. of Denver
Missouri State Univ.
Montreat Coll. (NC)
Mount Olive Coll. (NC)
Mountain State Univ. (WV)
New Mexico Highlands Univ.
Newberry Coll. (SC)
North Dakota State Univ.
Northern Arizona Univ.
Northern Michigan Univ.
Ohio Univ.
Oklahoma Baptist Univ.
Oklahoma State Univ.
Oregon State Univ.
Radford Univ. (VA)
San Diego State Univ.
San Francisco State Univ.
Shaw Univ. (NC)
Shepherd Univ. (WV)
South Dakota State Univ.
Southeast Missouri State Univ.
Southern Connecticut State Univ.
Southern Illinois Univ.–Carbondale
Southwest Baptist Univ. (MO)
Spring Arbor Univ. (MI)
Springfield Coll. (MA)
St. Cloud State Univ. (MN)
SUNY Coll.–Cortland
Temple Univ. (PA)
Texas A&M Univ.–Coll. Station
Thomas Edison State Coll. (NJ)
Towson Univ. (MD)
Unity Coll. (ME)
Univ. of Arkansas
Univ. of Arkansas–Pine Bluff
Univ. of Central Missouri
Univ. of Illinois–Urbana-Champaign
Univ. of Iowa
Univ. of Maine–Presque Isle
Univ. of Mary Hardin-Baylor (TX)
Univ. of Michigan–Ann Arbor
Univ. of Minnesota–Twin Cities
Univ. of Mississippi
Univ. of Missouri
Univ. of Nebraska–Kearney
Univ. of Nebraska–Omaha
Univ. of Nevada–Las Vegas
Univ. of New Hampshire
Univ. of North Carolina–
    Greensboro
Univ. of Northern Iowa
Univ. of South Alabama
Univ. of South Dakota

Univ. of Southern Mississippi
Univ. of Toledo (OH)
Univ. of Utah
Utah State Univ.
Virginia Commonwealth Univ.
Virginia Wesleyan Coll.
Washington State Univ.
West Virginia State Univ.
Western Michigan Univ.
Western State Coll. of Colorado
Western Washington Univ.
William Jewell Coll. (MO)
Wingate Univ. (NC)
York Coll. of Pennsylvania

Parks, Recreation, Leisure, and Fitness Studies

Becker Coll. (MA)
Brigham Young Univ.–Provo (UT)
Chadron State Coll. (NE)
Coker Coll. (SC)
Coll. at Brockport–SUNY
Culver-Stockton Coll. (MO)
Elon Univ. (NC)
Franklin Coll. (IN)
Howard Univ. (DC)
Huntington Univ. (IN)
Madonna Univ. (MI)
Malone Univ. (OH)
North Greenville Univ. (SC)
Pittsburg State Univ. (KS)
Plymouth State Univ. (NH)
Prescott Coll. (AZ)
Southern Adventist Univ. (TN)
Southern Nazarene Univ. (OK)
Southern Wesleyan Univ. (SC)
Springfield Coll. (MA)
St. Edward's Univ. (TX)
Trinity Christian Coll. (IL)
Univ. of Central Missouri
Univ. of Maryland–Eastern Shore
Univ. of North Alabama
Urbana Univ. (OH)
Utah State Univ.

Pastoral Counseling and Specialized Ministries

Abilene Christian Univ. (TX)
Anna Maria Coll. (MA)
Asbury Univ. (KY)
Augsburg Coll. (MN)
Bethany Univ. (CA)
Bethel Coll. (IN)
Bethel Univ. (MN)
Bluffton Univ. (OH)
Brescia Univ. (KY)
Cedarville Univ. (OH)
Central Christian Coll. (KS)
Charleston Southern Univ. (SC)
Clearwater Christian Coll. (FL)
Coll. of Mount St. Joseph (OH)
Colorado Christian Univ.
Concordia Univ. (NE)
Corban Univ. (OR)
Cornerstone Univ. (MI)
Crown Coll. (MN)
Dallas Baptist Univ.
Dominican Univ. (IL)

Dordt Coll. (IA)
East Texas Baptist Univ.
Eastern Nazarene Coll. (MA)
Eastern Univ. (PA)
Free Will Baptist Bible Coll. (TN)
George Fox Univ. (OR)
Gordon Coll. (MA)
Grace Coll. and Seminary (IN)
Greenville Coll. (IL)
Hardin-Simmons Univ. (TX)
Harding Univ. (AR)
Hope International Univ. (CA)
Howard Payne Univ. (TX)
Huntington Univ. (IN)
Indiana Wesleyan Univ.
John Brown Univ. (AR)
Judson Univ. (IL)
LeTourneau Univ. (TX)
Liberty Univ. (VA)
Lindenwood Univ. (MO)
Lipscomb Univ. (TN)
Lubbock Christian Univ. (TX)
MacMurray Coll. (IL)
Madonna Univ. (MI)
Malone Univ. (OH)
Maranatha Baptist Bible Coll. (WI)
Master's Coll. and Seminary (CA)
MidAmerica Nazarene Univ. (KS)
Midland Lutheran Coll. (NE)
Mount Vernon Nazarene Univ.
    (OH)
North Central Univ. (MN)
North Park Univ. (IL)
Northwest Univ. (WA)
Northwestern Coll. (MN)
Northwestern Coll. (IA)
Notre Dame Coll. of Ohio
Ohio Northern Univ.
Oklahoma Baptist Univ.
Oklahoma Christian Univ.
Oklahoma City Univ.
Oklahoma Wesleyan Univ.
Olivet Nazarene Univ. (IL)
Oral Roberts Univ. (OK)
Ouachita Baptist Univ. (AR)
Patten Univ. (CA)
Pfeiffer Univ. (NC)
Rochester Coll. (MI)
Simpson Univ. (CA)
Southeastern Univ. (FL)
Southern Adventist Univ. (TN)
Southern Nazarene Univ. (OK)
Southwest Baptist Univ. (MO)
Southwestern Assemblies of God
    Univ. (TX)
Spring Arbor Univ. (MI)
St. Gregory's Univ. (OK)
St. Joseph's Coll. (IN)
St. Mary's Univ. of Minnesota
Tabor Coll. (KS)
Texas Lutheran Univ.
Toccoa Falls Coll. (GA)
Trinity International Univ. (IL)
Union Coll. (NE)
Union Univ. (TN)
Univ. of Mary Hardin-Baylor (TX)
Univ. of Sioux Falls (SD)
Univ. of St. Mary (KS)
Univ. of St. Thomas (TX)
Ursuline Coll. (OH)
Valparaiso Univ. (IN)

Vanguard Univ. of Southern Cal.
Victory Univ. (TN)
Warner Pacific Coll. (OR)
York Coll. (NE)

Peace Studies and Conflict Resolution

Bennington Coll. (VT)
Bethel Univ. (MN)
California State Univ.–Dominguez
    Hills
California State Univ.–Long Beach
Chapman Univ. (CA)
Clarke Univ. (IA)
Colgate Univ. (NY)
Coll. of St. Benedict (MN)
Creighton Univ. (NE)
DePauw Univ. (IN)
Earlham Coll. (IN)
Eastern Mennonite Univ. (VA)
George Mason Univ. (VA)
Goshen Coll. (IN)
Goucher Coll. (MD)
Guilford Coll. (NC)
Gustavus Adolphus Coll. (MN)
Hamline Univ. (MN)
Hampshire Coll. (MA)
Juniata Coll. (PA)
Kent State Univ. (OH)
Le Moyne Coll. (NY)
Manchester Coll. (IN)
Manhattan Coll. (NY)
Nazareth Coll. (NY)
Prescott Coll. (AZ)
Salisbury Univ. (MD)
Siena Coll. (NY)
St. John's Univ. (MN)
Tufts Univ. (MA)
Univ. of California–Berkeley
Univ. of North Carolina–Chapel Hill
Univ. of St. Thomas (MN)
Valparaiso Univ. (IN)
Wellesley Coll. (MA)

Personal and Culinary Services

Kendall Coll. (IL)

Petroleum Engineering

Colorado School of Mines
Louisiana State Univ.–Baton Rouge
Marietta Coll. (OH)
Missouri Univ. of Science &
    Technology
Montana Tech of the Univ. of
    Montana
New Mexico Institute of Mining
    and Technology
Pennsylvania State Univ.–Univ. Park
Stanford Univ. (CA)
Texas A&M Univ.–Coll. Station
Texas A&M Univ.–Kingsville
Texas Tech Univ.
Univ. of Alaska–Fairbanks
Univ. of Kansas
Univ. of Louisiana–Lafayette
Univ. of Oklahoma
Univ. of Texas–Austin

Univ. of Tulsa (OK)
Univ. of Wyoming
West Virginia Univ.

Pharmacy, Pharmaceutical Sciences, and Administration

Gannon Univ. (PA)
Univ. of Missouri–Kansas City

Philosophy

Adelphi Univ. (NY)
Adrian Coll. (MI)
Agnes Scott Coll. (GA)
Albion Coll. (MI)
Albright Coll. (PA)
Alfred Univ. (NY)
Allegheny Coll. (PA)
Alma Coll. (MI)
Alvernia Univ. (PA)
Alverno Coll. (WI)
American International Coll. (MA)
American Univ. (DC)
Amherst Coll. (MA)
Anderson Univ. (IN)
Appalachian State Univ. (NC)
Aquinas Coll. (MI)
Arizona State Univ.
Arkansas State Univ.–Jonesboro
Asbury Univ. (KY)
Ashland Univ. (OH)
Assumption Coll. (MA)
Auburn Univ. (AL)
Augsburg Coll. (MN)
Augustana Coll. (SD)
Augustana Coll. (IL)
Austin Coll. (TX)
Austin Peay State Univ. (TN)
Azusa Pacific Univ. (CA)
Babson Coll. (MA)
Baker Univ. (KS)
Baldwin-Wallace Coll. (OH)
Ball State Univ. (IN)
Barnard Coll. (NY)
Barry Univ. (FL)
Bates Coll. (ME)
Baylor Univ. (TX)
Belhaven Univ. (MS)
Bellarmine Univ. (KY)
Belmont Abbey Coll. (NC)
Belmont Univ. (TN)
Beloit Coll. (WI)
Bemidji State Univ. (MN)
Benedictine Coll. (KS)
Benedictine Univ. (IL)
Bennington Coll. (VT)
Bentley Univ. (MA)
Berea Coll. (KY)
Bethel Coll. (IN)
Bethel Univ. (MN)
Binghamton Univ.–SUNY
Biola Univ. (CA)
Bloomfield Coll. (NJ)
Bloomsburg Univ. of Pennsylvania
Boise State Univ. (ID)
Boston Univ.
Bowdoin Coll. (ME)
Bowling Green State Univ. (OH)
Bradley Univ. (IL)

Brandeis Univ. (MA)
Bridgewater State Coll. (MA)
Brigham Young Univ.–Provo (UT)
Brown Univ. (RI)
Bryn Mawr Coll. (PA)
Bucknell Univ. (PA)
Buffalo State Coll.–SUNY
Butler Univ. (IN)
Cabrini Coll. (PA)
California Baptist Univ.
California Lutheran Univ.
California Polytechnic State Univ.–
San Luis Obispo
California State Polytechnic Univ.–
Pomona
California State Univ.–Bakersfield
California State Univ.–Chico
California State Univ.–Dominguez
Hills
California State Univ.–East Bay
California State Univ.–Fresno
California State Univ.–Fullerton
California State Univ.–Long Beach
California State Univ.–Los Angeles
California State Univ.–Monterey Bay
California State Univ.–Northridge
California State Univ.–Sacramento
California State Univ.–San
Bernardino
California State Univ.–Stanislaus
California Univ. of Pennsylvania
Calvin Coll. (MI)
Canisius Coll. (NY)
Capital Univ. (OH)
Carleton Coll. (MN)
Carlow Univ. (PA)
Carnegie Mellon Univ. (PA)
Carroll Coll. (MT)
Carson-Newman Coll. (TN)
Carthage Coll. (WI)
Case Western Reserve Univ. (OH)
Catholic Univ. of America (DC)
Cedarville Univ. (OH)
Centenary Coll. of Louisiana
Central Coll. (IA)
Central Connecticut State Univ.
Central Methodist Univ. (MO)
Central Michigan Univ.
Central Washington Univ.
Centre Coll. (KY)
Chaminade Univ. of Honolulu
Chapman Univ. (CA)
Christopher Newport Univ. (VA)
Claremont McKenna Coll. (CA)
Clarion Univ. of Pennsylvania
Clark Atlanta Univ.
Clark Univ. (MA)
Clarke Univ. (IA)
Clemson Univ. (SC)
Cleveland State Univ.
Coastal Carolina Univ. (SC)
Coe Coll. (IA)
Colby Coll. (ME)
Colgate Univ. (NY)
Coll. at Brockport–SUNY
Coll. of Charleston (SC)
Coll. of Idaho (ID)
Coll. of Mount St. Vincent (NY)
Coll. of New Jersey
Coll. of Notre Dame of Maryland
Coll. of St. Benedict (MN)

Coll. of St. Elizabeth (NJ)
Coll. of the Holy Cross (MA)
Coll. of William and Mary (VA)
Coll. of Wooster (OH)
Colorado Coll.
Colorado State Univ.
Columbia Univ. (NY)
Concordia Coll.–Moorhead (MN)
Concordia Univ. (MI)
Connecticut Coll.
Cornell Coll. (IA)
Cornell Univ. (NY)
Cornerstone Univ. (MI)
Covenant Coll. (GA)
Creighton Univ. (NE)
CUNY–Baruch Coll.
CUNY–Brooklyn Coll.
CUNY–City Coll.
CUNY–Coll. of Staten Island
CUNY–Hunter Coll.
CUNY–Lehman Coll.
CUNY–Queens Coll.
Curry Coll. (MA)
D'Youville Coll. (NY)
Dallas Baptist Univ.
Dartmouth Coll. (NH)
Davidson Coll. (NC)
Denison Univ. (OH)
DePaul Univ. (IL)
DePauw Univ. (IN)
DeSales Univ. (PA)
Dickinson Coll. (PA)
Dominican Univ. (IL)
Dordt Coll. (IA)
Dowling Coll. (NY)
Drake Univ. (IA)
Drew Univ. (NJ)
Drury Univ. (MO)
Duke Univ. (NC)
Duquesne Univ. (PA)
Earlham Coll. (IN)
East Carolina Univ. (NC)
East Stroudsburg Univ. of
Pennsylvania
East Tennessee State Univ.
Eastern Illinois Univ.
Eastern Kentucky Univ.
Eastern Michigan Univ.
Eastern Washington Univ.
Eckerd Coll. (FL)
Edinboro Univ. of Pennsylvania
Elizabethtown Coll. (PA)
Elmhurst Coll. (IL)
Elon Univ. (NC)
Emory and Henry Coll. (VA)
Emory Univ. (GA)
Erskine Coll. (SC)
Evangel Univ. (MO)
Excelsior Coll. (NY)
Fairfield Univ. (CT)
Fairleigh Dickinson Univ. (NJ)
Ferrum Coll. (VA)
Florida Atlantic Univ.
Florida International Univ.
Florida Southern Coll.
Florida State Univ.
Fordham Univ. (NY)
Fort Hays State Univ. (KS)
Fort Lewis Coll. (CO)
Franciscan Univ. of Steubenville
(OH)

Franklin and Marshall Coll. (PA)
Franklin Coll. (IN)
Freed-Hardeman Univ. (TN)
Fresno Pacific Univ. (CA)
Frostburg State Univ. (MD)
Furman Univ. (SC)
Gallaudet Univ. (DC)
Gannon Univ. (PA)
Geneva Coll. (PA)
George Fox Univ. (OR)
George Mason Univ. (VA)
George Washington Univ. (DC)
Georgetown Coll. (KY)
Georgetown Univ. (DC)
Georgia Coll. & State Univ.
Georgia Southern Univ.
Georgia State Univ.
Gettysburg Coll. (PA)
Gonzaga Univ. (WA)
Gordon Coll. (MA)
Goucher Coll. (MD)
Grand Valley State Univ. (MI)
Green Mountain Coll. (VT)
Greenville Coll. (IL)
Grinnell Coll. (IA)
Grove City Coll. (PA)
Guilford Coll. (NC)
Gustavus Adolphus Coll. (MN)
Hamilton Coll. (NY)
Hamline Univ. (MN)
Hampden-Sydney Coll. (VA)
Hampshire Coll. (MA)
Hanover Coll. (IN)
Hardin-Simmons Univ. (TX)
Hartwick Coll. (NY)
Harvard Univ. (MA)
Haverford Coll. (PA)
Heidelberg Univ. (OH)
Hendrix Coll. (AR)
High Point Univ. (NC)
Hillsdale Coll. (MI)
Hiram Coll. (OH)
Hobart and William Smith Colleges
(NY)
Hofstra Univ. (NY)
Hollins Univ. (VA)
Holy Names Univ. (CA)
Hood Coll. (MD)
Hope Coll. (MI)
Houghton Coll. (NY)
Howard Payne Univ. (TX)
Howard Univ. (DC)
Humboldt State Univ. (CA)
Huntington Univ. (IN)
Idaho State Univ.
Illinois Coll.
Illinois State Univ.
Illinois Wesleyan Univ.
Indiana State Univ.
Indiana Univ. Northwest
Indiana Univ. of Pennsylvania
Indiana Univ.–Bloomington
Indiana Univ.–South Bend
Indiana Univ.-Purdue Univ.–Fort
Wayne
Indiana Univ.-Purdue Univ.–
Indianapolis
Iona Coll. (NY)
Iowa State Univ.
Ithaca Coll. (NY)
Jacksonville Univ. (FL)

John Carroll Univ. (OH)
Johns Hopkins Univ. (MD)
Juniata Coll. (PA)
Kalamazoo Coll. (MI)
Kansas State Univ.
Kent State Univ. (OH)
Kenyon Coll. (OH)
King's Coll. (PA)
Knox Coll. (IL)
Kutztown Univ. of Pennsylvania
La Salle Univ. (PA)
Lafayette Coll. (PA)
Lake Forest Coll. (IL)
Lambuth Univ. (TN)
Lawrence Univ. (WI)
Le Moyne Coll. (NY)
Lebanon Valley Coll. (PA)
Lehigh Univ. (PA)
Lenoir-Rhyne Univ. (NC)
Lewis & Clark Coll. (OR)
Lewis Univ. (IL)
Liberty Univ. (VA)
Lincoln Univ. (PA)
Lindenwood Univ. (MO)
Linfield Coll. (OR)
Lipscomb Univ. (TN)
Lock Haven Univ. of Pennsylvania
Long Island Univ.–C.W. Post
Campus (NY)
Loras Coll. (IA)
Louisiana State Univ.–Baton Rouge
Loyola Marymount Univ. (CA)
Loyola Univ. Chicago
Loyola Univ. Maryland
Loyola Univ. New Orleans
Luther Coll. (IA)
Lycoming Coll. (PA)
Lynchburg Coll. (VA)
Macalester Coll. (MN)
MacMurray Coll. (IL)
Madonna Univ. (MI)
Malone Univ. (OH)
Manchester Coll. (IN)
Manhattan Coll. (NY)
Manhattanville Coll. (NY)
Mansfield Univ. of Pennsylvania
Marian Univ. (IN)
Marist Coll. (NY)
Mary Baldwin Coll. (VA)
Marymount Univ. (VA)
Massachusetts Coll. of Liberal Arts
Massachusetts Institute of
Technology
McDaniel Coll. (MD)
McKendree Univ. (IL)
McPherson Coll. (KS)
Mercy Coll. (NY)
Mercyhurst Coll. (PA)
Merrimack Coll. (MA)
Messiah Coll. (PA)
Metropolitan State Coll. of Denver
Miami Univ.–Oxford (OH)
Michigan State Univ.
Middle Tennessee State Univ.
Middlebury Coll. (VT)
Millersville Univ. of Pennsylvania
Millikin Univ. (IL)
Mills Coll. (CA)
Millsaps Coll. (MS)
Minnesota State Univ.–Mankato
Minnesota State Univ.–Moorhead

Misericordia Univ. (PA)
Mississippi State Univ.
Missouri State Univ.
Missouri Univ. of Science &
Technology
Molloy Coll. (NY)
Monmouth Coll. (IL)
Montana State Univ.
Montclair State Univ. (NJ)
Moravian Coll. (PA)
Morehead State Univ. (KY)
Morehouse Coll. (GA)
Morningside Coll. (IA)
Mount Holyoke Coll. (MA)
Mount Mary Coll. (WI)
Mount St. Mary's Coll. (CA)
Mount St. Mary's Univ. (MD)
Mount Vernon Nazarene Univ.
(OH)
Muhlenberg Coll. (PA)
Murray State Univ. (KY)
Nazareth Coll. (NY)
Nebraska Wesleyan Univ.
New England Coll. (NH)
New Jersey City Univ.
New Mexico State Univ.
New School (NY)
New York Univ.
Niagara Univ. (NY)
North Carolina State Univ.–Raleigh
North Central Coll. (IL)
North Dakota State Univ.
North Park Univ. (IL)
Northeastern Illinois Univ.
Northeastern Univ. (MA)
Northern Arizona Univ.
Northern Illinois Univ.
Northern Kentucky Univ.
Northern Michigan Univ.
Northland Coll. (WI)
Northwest Missouri State Univ.
Northwest Nazarene Univ. (ID)
Northwestern Coll. (IA)
Northwestern Univ. (IL)
Notre Dame de Namur Univ. (CA)
Nyack Coll. (NY)
Oakland Univ. (MI)
Oberlin Coll. (OH)
Occidental Coll. (CA)
Oglethorpe Univ. (GA)
Ohio Dominican Univ.
Ohio Northern Univ.
Ohio State Univ.–Columbus
Ohio Univ.
Ohio Wesleyan Univ.
Oklahoma Baptist Univ.
Oklahoma City Univ.
Oklahoma State Univ.
Old Dominion Univ. (VA)
Oregon State Univ.
Otterbein Coll. (OH)
Ouachita Baptist Univ. (AR)
Our Lady of the Lake Univ. (TX)
Pacific Lutheran Univ. (WA)
Pacific Univ. (OR)
Paine Coll. (GA)
Palm Beach Atlantic Univ. (FL)
Pennsylvania State Univ.–Univ. Park
Pepperdine Univ. (CA)
Plymouth State Univ. (NH)
Point Loma Nazarene Univ. (CA)

Pomona Coll. (CA)
Portland State Univ. (OR)
Presbyterian Coll. (SC)
Princeton Univ. (NJ)
Principia Coll. (IL)
Providence Coll. (RI)
Purchase Coll.–SUNY
Purdue Univ.–Calumet (IN)
Randolph Coll. (VA)
Randolph-Macon Coll. (VA)
Reed Coll. (OR)
Regis Univ. (CO)
Rensselaer Polytechnic Institute
  (NY)
Rhode Island Coll.
Rhodes Coll. (TN)
Rice Univ. (TX)
Rider Univ. (NJ)
Ripon Coll. (WI)
Roanoke Coll. (VA)
Rockford Coll. (IL)
Rockhurst Univ. (MO)
Roger Williams Univ. (RI)
Rollins Coll. (FL)
Roosevelt Univ. (IL)
Rosemont Coll. (PA)
Rutgers, the State Univ. of New
  Jersey–Camden
Rutgers, the State Univ. of New
  Jersey–New Brunswick
Rutgers, the State Univ. of New
  Jersey–Newark
Sacred Heart Univ. (CT)
Salem Coll. (NC)
Salisbury Univ. (MD)
Salve Regina Univ. (RI)
Sam Houston State Univ. (TX)
Samford Univ. (AL)
San Diego State Univ.
San Francisco State Univ.
San Jose State Univ. (CA)
Santa Clara Univ. (CA)
Scripps Coll. (CA)
Seattle Pacific Univ.
Seattle Univ.
Seton Hall Univ. (NJ)
Sewanee–Univ. of the South (TN)
Siena Coll. (NY)
Simmons Coll. (MA)
Simpson Coll. (IA)
Skidmore Coll. (NY)
Slippery Rock Univ. of Pennsylvania
Smith Coll. (MA)
Sonoma State Univ. (CA)
Southeast Missouri State Univ.
Southern Connecticut State Univ.
Southern Illinois Univ.–Carbondale
Southern Illinois Univ.–Edwardsville
Southern Methodist Univ. (TX)
Southern Nazarene Univ. (OK)
Southwest Minnesota State Univ.
Southwestern Univ. (TX)
Spelman Coll. (GA)
Spring Arbor Univ. (MI)
Spring Hill Coll. (AL)
St. Ambrose Univ. (IA)
St. Andrews Presbyterian Coll. (NC)
St. Anselm Coll. (NH)
St. Bonaventure Univ. (NY)
St. Catherine Univ. (MN)
St. Cloud State Univ. (MN)

St. Edward's Univ. (TX)
St. Francis Coll. (NY)
St. Francis Univ. (PA)
St. Gregory's Univ. (OK)
St. John Fisher Coll. (NY)
St. John's Univ. (MN)
St. John's Univ. (NY)
St. Joseph Coll. (CT)
St. Joseph's Coll. (IN)
St. Joseph's Coll. (ME)
St. Joseph's Univ. (PA)
St. Lawrence Univ. (NY)
St. Louis Univ.
St. Mary's Coll. (IN)
St. Mary's Coll. of California
St. Mary's Coll. of Maryland
St. Mary's Univ. of Minnesota
St. Mary's Univ. of San Antonio
  (TX)
St. Norbert Coll. (WI)
St. Olaf Coll. (MN)
St. Peter's Coll. (NJ)
St. Vincent Coll. (PA)
St. Xavier Univ. (IL)
Stanford Univ. (CA)
Stephen F. Austin State Univ. (TX)
Stetson Univ. (FL)
Stonehill Coll. (MA)
Suffolk Univ. (MA)
SUNY Coll.–Cortland
SUNY Coll.–Oneonta
SUNY Coll.–Potsdam
SUNY–Fredonia
SUNY–Geneseo
SUNY–Oswego
SUNY–Plattsburgh
SUNY–Stony Brook
Susquehanna Univ. (PA)
Swarthmore Coll. (PA)
Syracuse Univ. (NY)
Tabor Coll. (KS)
Taylor Univ. (IN)
Temple Univ. (PA)
Texas A&M Univ.–Coll. Station
Texas Christian Univ.
Texas Lutheran Univ.
Texas State Univ.–San Marcos
Texas Tech Univ.
Thiel Coll. (PA)
Thomas Edison State Coll. (NJ)
Thomas More Coll. (KY)
Thomas More Coll. of Liberal Arts
  (NH)
Touro Coll. (NY)
Towson Univ. (MD)
Transylvania Univ. (KY)
Trinity Christian Coll. (IL)
Trinity Coll. (CT)
Trinity International Univ. (IL)
Tufts Univ. (MA)
Tulane Univ. (LA)
Union Coll. (NY)
Union Univ. (TN)
Univ. at Albany–SUNY
Univ. at Buffalo–SUNY
Univ. of Akron (OH)
Univ. of Alabama
Univ. of Alabama–Birmingham
Univ. of Alabama–Huntsville
Univ. of Alaska–Anchorage
Univ. of Alaska–Fairbanks

Univ. of Arizona
Univ. of Arkansas
Univ. of Arkansas–Little Rock
Univ. of California–Berkeley
Univ. of California–Davis
Univ. of California–Irvine
Univ. of California–Los Angeles
Univ. of California–Riverside
Univ. of California–San Diego
Univ. of California–Santa Barbara
Univ. of California–Santa Cruz
Univ. of Central Arkansas
Univ. of Central Florida
Univ. of Central Oklahoma
Univ. of Chicago
Univ. of Colorado–Boulder
Univ. of Colorado–Colorado
  Springs
Univ. of Colorado–Denver
Univ. of Connecticut
Univ. of Dallas
Univ. of Dayton (OH)
Univ. of Delaware
Univ. of Denver
Univ. of Detroit Mercy
Univ. of Dubuque (IA)
Univ. of Evansville (IN)
Univ. of Findlay (OH)
Univ. of Florida
Univ. of Georgia
Univ. of Hartford (CT)
Univ. of Hawaii–Hilo
Univ. of Hawaii–Manoa
Univ. of Houston
Univ. of Houston–Downtown
Univ. of Illinois–Chicago
Univ. of Illinois–Springfield
Univ. of Illinois–Urbana-Champaign
Univ. of Indianapolis
Univ. of Iowa
Univ. of Kansas
Univ. of Kentucky
Univ. of La Verne (CA)
Univ. of Louisiana–Lafayette
Univ. of Louisville (KY)
Univ. of Maine
Univ. of Maryland–Baltimore
  County
Univ. of Maryland–Coll. Park
Univ. of Massachusetts–Amherst
Univ. of Massachusetts–Boston
Univ. of Massachusetts–Lowell
Univ. of Memphis
Univ. of Miami (FL)
Univ. of Michigan–Ann Arbor
Univ. of Michigan–Dearborn
Univ. of Michigan–Flint
Univ. of Minnesota–Duluth
Univ. of Minnesota–Morris
Univ. of Minnesota–Twin Cities
Univ. of Mississippi
Univ. of Missouri
Univ. of Missouri–Kansas City
Univ. of Missouri–St. Louis
Univ. of Montana
Univ. of Mount Union (OH)
Univ. of Nebraska–Kearney
Univ. of Nebraska–Lincoln
Univ. of Nebraska–Omaha
Univ. of Nevada–Las Vegas
Univ. of Nevada–Reno

Univ. of New Hampshire
Univ. of New Mexico
Univ. of New Orleans
Univ. of North Carolina–Asheville
Univ. of North Carolina–Chapel Hill
Univ. of North Carolina–Charlotte
Univ. of North Carolina–
  Greensboro
Univ. of North Dakota
Univ. of North Florida
Univ. of North Texas
Univ. of Northern Colorado
Univ. of Northern Iowa
Univ. of Notre Dame (IN)
Univ. of Oklahoma
Univ. of Oregon
Univ. of Pennsylvania
Univ. of Pittsburgh
Univ. of Portland (OR)
Univ. of Puget Sound (WA)
Univ. of Redlands (CA)
Univ. of Rhode Island
Univ. of Richmond (VA)
Univ. of Rochester (NY)
Univ. of San Diego
Univ. of San Francisco
Univ. of Scranton (PA)
Univ. of South Alabama
Univ. of South Carolina
Univ. of South Dakota
Univ. of South Florida
Univ. of Southern California
Univ. of Southern Indiana
Univ. of Southern Maine
Univ. of Southern Mississippi
Univ. of St. Francis (IN)
Univ. of St. Thomas (MN)
Univ. of St. Thomas (TX)
Univ. of Tennessee
Univ. of Tennessee–Martin
Univ. of Texas–Arlington
Univ. of Texas–Austin
Univ. of Texas–El Paso
Univ. of Texas–Pan American
Univ. of Texas–San Antonio
Univ. of the Cumberlands (KY)
Univ. of the Incarnate Word (TX)
Univ. of the Pacific (CA)
Univ. of Toledo (OH)
Univ. of Tulsa (OK)
Univ. of Utah
Univ. of Vermont
Univ. of Virginia
Univ. of Washington
Univ. of West Florida
Univ. of West Georgia
Univ. of Wisconsin–Eau Claire
Univ. of Wisconsin–Green Bay
Univ. of Wisconsin–La Crosse
Univ. of Wisconsin–Madison
Univ. of Wisconsin–Milwaukee
Univ. of Wisconsin–Oshkosh
Univ. of Wisconsin–Parkside
Univ. of Wisconsin–Platteville
Univ. of Wisconsin–Stevens Point
Univ. of Wyoming
Ursinus Coll. (PA)
Ursuline Coll. (OH)
Utah State Univ.
Utah Valley Univ.
Utica Coll. (NY)

Valdosta State Univ. (GA)
Valparaiso Univ. (IN)
Vanderbilt Univ. (TN)
Vassar Coll. (NY)
Villanova Univ. (PA)
Virginia Commonwealth Univ.
Virginia Tech
Virginia Wesleyan Coll.
Wabash Coll. (IN)
Wagner Coll. (NY)
Wake Forest Univ. (NC)
Walsh Univ. (OH)
Warren Wilson Coll. (NC)
Wartburg Coll. (IA)
Washburn Univ. (KS)
Washington and Jefferson Coll.
  (PA)
Washington and Lee Univ. (VA)
Washington Coll. (MD)
Washington State Univ.
Washington Univ. in St. Louis
Wayne State Univ. (MI)
Webster Univ. (MO)
Wellesley Coll. (MA)
Wesleyan Coll. (GA)
Wesleyan Univ. (CT)
West Chester Univ. of Pennsylvania
West Virginia Univ.
West Virginia Wesleyan Coll.
Western Carolina Univ. (NC)
Western Illinois Univ.
Western Kentucky Univ.
Western Michigan Univ.
Western New England Coll. (MA)
Western Oregon Univ.
Western State Coll. of Colorado
Western Washington Univ.
Westminster Coll. (PA)
Westminster Coll. (UT)
Westminster Coll. (MO)
Westmont Coll. (CA)
Wheaton Coll. (MA)
Wheaton Coll. (IL)
Wheeling Jesuit Univ. (WV)
Whitman Coll. (WA)
Whittier Coll. (CA)
Whitworth Univ. (WA)
Wichita State Univ. (KS)
Wilkes Univ. (PA)
Willamette Univ. (OR)
William Jewell Coll. (MO)
William Paterson Univ. of New
  Jersey
Williams Coll. (MA)
Wingate Univ. (NC)
Wisconsin Lutheran Coll.
Wittenberg Univ. (OH)
Wofford Coll. (SC)
Wright State Univ. (OH)
Xavier Univ. (OH)
Yale Univ. (CT)
Yeshiva Univ. (NY)
Youngstown State Univ. (OH)

Philosophy and Religious Studies

Alderson-Broaddus Coll. (WV)
Appalachian State Univ. (NC)
Barton Coll. (NC)
Bellarmine Univ. (KY)

Benedictine Coll. (KS)
Berry Coll. (GA)
Bethel Coll. (IN)
Bethune-Cookman Univ. (FL)
Bridgewater Coll. (VA)
Buena Vista Univ. (IA)
Butler Univ. (IN)
Campbell Univ. (NC)
Claflin Univ. (SC)
Colgate Univ. (NY)
Coll. of the Ozarks (MO)
Columbia Coll. (MO)
Covenant Coll. (GA)
Eastern Mennonite Univ. (VA)
Elmira Coll. (NY)
Eureka Coll. (IL)
Fisk Univ. (TN)
Flagler Coll. (FL)
Graceland Univ. (IA)
Hendrix Coll. (AR)
Indiana Univ. Southeast
Indiana Wesleyan Univ.
Ithaca Coll. (NY)
James Madison Univ. (VA)
Jamestown Coll. (ND)
Juniata Coll. (PA)
Kean Univ. (NJ)
Lambuth Coll. (TN)
Louisiana Coll.
Lyon Coll. (AR)
Marquette Univ. (WI)
Mary Baldwin Coll. (VA)
Marymount Manhattan Coll. (NY)
Midland Lutheran Coll. (NE)
Muskingum Univ. (OH)
Newman Univ. (KS)
Northwest Nazarene Univ. (ID)
Ohio Northern Univ.
Pace Univ. (NY)
Pepperdine Univ. (CA)
Philander Smith Coll. (AR)
Point Loma Nazarene Univ. (CA)
Queens Univ. of Charlotte (NC)
Quincy Univ. (IL)
Radford Univ. (VA)
Richard Stockton Coll. of New
    Jersey
Roberts Wesleyan Coll. (NY)
Rocky Mountain Coll. (MT)
Samford Univ. (AL)
Shaw Univ. (NC)
Southwestern Coll. (KS)
St. John's Univ. (NY)
St. Joseph's Coll. (IN)
St. Mary's Coll. of California
St. Thomas Aquinas Coll. (NY)
Sterling Coll. (KS)
SUNY Coll.–Old Westbury
Syracuse Univ. (NY)
Toccoa Falls Coll. (GA)
Truman State Univ. (MO)
Union Univ. (TN)
Univ. of Denver
Univ. of La Verne (CA)
Univ. of Maine–Farmington
Univ. of Mary Washington (VA)
Univ. of North Carolina–Pembroke
Univ. of North Carolina–
    Wilmington
Univ. of Notre Dame (IN)
Univ. of Sioux Falls (SD)

Univ. of Tennessee–Chattanooga
Univ. of the Ozarks (AR)
Urbana Univ. (OH)
Vanderbilt Univ. (TN)
Viterbo Univ. (WI)
Wells Coll. (NY)
Wheaton Coll. (MA)
William Jewell Coll. (MO)
Wilson Coll. (PA)
Winthrop Univ. (SC)

Physical Science Technologies/Technicians

Dakota State Univ. (SD)
Marian Univ. (IN)
Missouri State Univ.
Univ. of Alaska–Anchorage

Physical Sciences

Alfred Univ. (NY)
Arkansas Tech Univ.
Asbury Univ. (KY)
Auburn Univ.–Montgomery (AL)
Azusa Pacific Univ. (CA)
Baldwin-Wallace Coll. (OH)
Bennington Coll. (VT)
Biola Univ. (CA)
Black Hills State Univ. (SD)
California Institute of Technology
California Polytechnic State Univ.–
    San Luis Obispo
California State Univ.–Fresno
California State Univ.–Sacramento
California State Univ.–Stanislaus
California Univ. of Pennsylvania
Central Baptist Coll. (AR)
Central Connecticut State Univ.
Charleston Southern Univ. (SC)
Clarion Univ. of Pennsylvania
Colgate Univ. (NY)
Columbia Univ. (NY)
Concordia Univ. (NE)
Concordia Univ. Chicago (IL)
Cornell Coll. (IA)
Covenant Coll. (GA)
CUNY–John Jay Coll. of Criminal
    Justice
Dakota State Univ. (SD)
Defiance Coll. (OH)
East Stroudsburg Univ. of
    Pennsylvania
Eastern Michigan Univ.
Emporia State Univ. (KS)
Evangel Univ. (MO)
Evergreen State Coll. (WA)
Florida Institute of Technology
Fort Hays State Univ. (KS)
Freed-Hardeman Univ. (TN)
Frostburg State Univ. (MD)
Grace Coll. and Seminary (IN)
Graceland Univ. (IA)
Grand View Univ. (IA)
Hampshire Coll. (MA)
Hobart and William Smith Colleges
    (NY)
Humboldt State Univ. (CA)
Indiana Univ.–Kokomo
Johns Hopkins Univ. (MD)

Juniata Coll. (PA)
Kansas State Univ.
Keuka Coll. (NY)
La Sierra Univ. (CA)
Langston Univ. (OK)
Lawrence Univ. (WI)
Lincoln Univ. (PA)
Linfield Coll. (OR)
Loras Coll. (IA)
Marian Univ. (IN)
Marlboro Coll. (VT)
Mesa State Coll. (CO)
Michigan State Univ.
Minot State Univ. (ND)
Mississippi Univ. for Women
Missouri Univ. of Science &
    Technology
Montana Tech of the Univ. of
    Montana
Muhlenberg Coll. (PA)
Northern Arizona Univ.
Northland Coll. (WI)
Northwest Nazarene Univ. (ID)
Oklahoma Wesleyan Univ.
Olivet Nazarene Univ. (IL)
Oral Roberts Univ. (OK)
Otterbein Coll. (OH)
Pacific Univ. (OR)
Pitzer Coll. (CA)
Ripon Coll. (WI)
Roberts Wesleyan Coll. (NY)
Rochester Institute of Technology
    (NY)
San Diego State Univ.
Seattle Univ.
Southern Nazarene Univ. (OK)
Southwestern Univ. (TX)
Spring Arbor Univ. (MI)
St. Ambrose Univ. (IA)
St. Francis Univ. (PA)
St. John's Univ. (NY)
St. Joseph Coll. (CT)
St. Mary's Coll. of California
St. Michael's Coll. (VT)
Suffolk Univ. (MA)
SUNY Empire State Coll.
SUNY–Stony Brook
Texas A&M International Univ.
Texas A&M Univ.–Coll. Station
Trinity Univ. (DC)
Troy Univ. (AL)
Tusculum Coll. (TN)
United States Naval Academy (MD)
Univ. at Albany–SUNY
Univ. of Alaska–Anchorage
Univ. of California–Berkeley
Univ. of California–Davis
Univ. of California–Riverside
Univ. of Dayton (OH)
Univ. of Hartford (CT)
Univ. of Mary Washington (VA)
Univ. of Maryland–Coll. Park
Univ. of Massachusetts–Lowell
Univ. of Michigan–Flint
Univ. of North Alabama
Univ. of North Carolina–Chapel Hill
Univ. of Pittsburgh
Univ. of Pittsburgh–Bradford
Univ. of Rio Grande (OH)
Univ. of San Francisco
Univ. of Southern California

Univ. of Southern Maine
Univ. of St. Francis (IN)
Univ. of Texas–El Paso
Univ. of the Ozarks (AR)
Univ. of Utah
Univ. of Wyoming
Utah State Univ.
Villanova Univ. (PA)
Warner Pacific Coll. (OR)
Washburn Univ. (KS)
Washington State Univ.
Wayland Baptist Univ. (TX)
Western New Mexico Univ.
Westfield State Coll. (MA)
Wheeling Jesuit Univ. (WV)
Williams Coll. (MA)
Xavier Univ. (OH)

Physics

Abilene Christian Univ. (TX)
Adelphi Univ. (NY)
Adrian Coll. (MI)
Agnes Scott Coll. (GA)
Alabama Agricultural and
    Mechanical Univ.
Alabama State Univ.
Albion Coll. (MI)
Albright Coll. (PA)
Alfred Univ. (NY)
Allegheny Coll. (PA)
Alma Coll. (MI)
American Univ. (DC)
Amherst Coll. (MA)
Anderson Univ. (IN)
Andrews Univ. (MI)
Angelo State Univ. (TX)
Appalachian State Univ. (NC)
Arizona State Univ.
Arkansas State Univ.–Jonesboro
Armstrong Atlantic State Univ. (GA)
Ashland Univ. (OH)
Auburn Univ. (AL)
Augsburg Coll. (MN)
Augusta State Univ. (GA)
Augustana Coll. (IL)
Austin Coll. (TX)
Austin Peay State Univ. (TN)
Baker Univ. (KS)
Baldwin-Wallace Coll. (OH)
Ball State Univ. (IN)
Barnard Coll. (NY)
Bates Coll. (ME)
Baylor Univ. (TX)
Belmont Univ. (TN)
Beloit Coll. (WI)
Benedict Coll. (SC)
Benedictine Coll. (KS)
Benedictine Univ. (IL)
Bennington Coll. (VT)
Berea Coll. (KY)
Berry Coll. (GA)
Bethany Coll. (WV)
Bethel Coll. (IN)
Bethel Coll. (KS)
Bethel Univ. (MN)
Bethune-Cookman Univ. (FL)
Binghamton Univ.–SUNY
Bloomsburg Univ. of Pennsylvania
Bluffton Univ. (OH)
Boise State Univ. (ID)

Boston Univ.
Bowdoin Coll. (ME)
Bowling Green State Univ. (OH)
Bradley Univ. (IL)
Brandeis Univ. (MA)
Bridgewater Coll. (VA)
Bridgewater State Coll. (MA)
Brigham Young Univ.–Provo (UT)
Brown Univ. (RI)
Bryn Mawr Coll. (PA)
Bucknell Univ. (PA)
Buena Vista Univ. (IA)
Buffalo State Coll.–SUNY
Butler Univ. (IN)
California Institute of Technology
California Lutheran Univ.
California Polytechnic State Univ.–
    San Luis Obispo
California State Polytechnic Univ.–
    Pomona
California State Univ.–Bakersfield
California State Univ.–Chico
California State Univ.–Dominguez
    Hills
California State Univ.–East Bay
California State Univ.–Fresno
California State Univ.–Fullerton
California State Univ.–Long Beach
California State Univ.–Los Angeles
California State Univ.–Northridge
California State Univ.–Sacramento
California State Univ.–San
    Bernardino
California State Univ.–Stanislaus
California Univ. of Pennsylvania
Calvin Coll. (MI)
Cameron Univ. (OK)
Campbellsville Univ. (KY)
Canisius Coll. (NY)
Carleton Coll. (MN)
Carnegie Mellon Univ. (PA)
Carthage Coll. (WI)
Case Western Reserve Univ. (OH)
Catholic Univ. of America (DC)
Cedarville Univ. (OH)
Centenary Coll. of Louisiana
Central Coll. (IA)
Central Connecticut State Univ.
Central Methodist Univ. (MO)
Central Michigan Univ.
Central Washington Univ.
Centre Coll. (KY)
Chadron State Coll. (NE)
Chatham Univ. (PA)
Chicago State Univ.
Christian Brothers Univ. (TN)
Christopher Newport Univ. (VA)
Claremont McKenna Coll. (CA)
Clarion Univ. of Pennsylvania
Clark Atlanta Univ.
Clark Univ. (MA)
Clarke Univ. (IA)
Clarkson Univ. (NY)
Clemson Univ. (SC)
Cleveland State Univ.
Coastal Carolina Univ. (SC)
Coe Coll. (IA)
Colby Coll. (ME)
Colgate Univ. (NY)
Coll. at Brockport–SUNY
Coll. of Charleston (SC)

Coll. of Idaho (ID)
Coll. of New Jersey
Coll. of Notre Dame of Maryland
Coll. of St. Benedict (MN)
Coll. of the Holy Cross (MA)
Coll. of William and Mary (VA)
Coll. of Wooster (OH)
Colorado Coll.
Colorado State Univ.
Colorado State Univ.–Pueblo
Columbia Univ. (NY)
Concordia Coll.–Moorhead (MN)
Concordia Univ. (MI)
Connecticut Coll.
Cornell Coll. (IA)
Cornell Univ. (NY)
Covenant Coll. (GA)
Creighton Univ. (NE)
CUNY–Brooklyn Coll.
CUNY–Coll. of Staten Island
CUNY–Hunter Coll.
CUNY–Lehman Coll.
CUNY–Queens Coll.
CUNY–York Coll.
Dartmouth Coll. (NH)
Davidson Coll. (NC)
Delaware State Univ.
Denison Univ. (OH)
DePaul Univ. (IL)
DePauw Univ. (IN)
Dickinson Coll. (PA)
Dillard Univ. (LA)
Dordt Coll. (IA)
Drake Univ. (IA)
Drew Univ. (NJ)
Drexel Univ. (PA)
Drury Univ. (MO)
Duke Univ. (NC)
Duquesne Univ. (PA)
Earlham Coll. (IN)
East Carolina Univ. (NC)
East Central Univ. (OK)
East Stroudsburg Univ. of
    Pennsylvania
East Tennessee State Univ.
Eastern Illinois Univ.
Eastern Kentucky Univ.
Eastern Michigan Univ.
Eastern Nazarene Coll. (MA)
Eastern New Mexico Univ.
Eastern Oregon Univ.
Eastern Washington Univ.
Eckerd Coll. (FL)
Edinboro Univ. of Pennsylvania
Elizabeth City State Univ. (NC)
Elizabethtown Coll. (PA)
Elmhurst Coll. (IL)
Elon Univ. (NC)
Embry-Riddle Aeronautical Univ.
    (FL)
Emory and Henry Coll. (VA)
Emory Univ. (GA)
Emporia State Univ. (KS)
Erskine Coll. (SC)
Excelsior Coll. (NY)
Fairfield Univ. (CT)
Fisk Univ. (TN)
Florida Atlantic Univ.
Florida Institute of Technology
Florida International Univ.
Florida State Univ.

Fordham Univ. (NY)
Fort Hays State Univ. (KS)
Fort Lewis Coll. (CO)
Francis Marion Univ. (SC)
Franklin and Marshall Coll. (PA)
Frostburg State Univ. (MD)
Furman Univ. (SC)
Gallaudet Univ. (DC)
Geneva Coll. (PA)
George Mason Univ. (VA)
George Washington Univ. (DC)
Georgetown Coll. (KY)
Georgetown Univ. (DC)
Georgia Institute of Technology
Georgia Southern Univ.
Georgia State Univ.
Georgian Court Univ. (NJ)
Gettysburg Coll. (PA)
Gonzaga Univ. (WA)
Gordon Coll. (MA)
Goshen Coll. (IN)
Goucher Coll. (MD)
Grambling State Univ. (LA)
Grand Valley State Univ. (MI)
Greenville Coll. (IL)
Grinnell Coll. (IA)
Grove City Coll. (PA)
Guilford Coll. (NC)
Gustavus Adolphus Coll. (MN)
Hamilton Coll. (NY)
Hamline Univ. (MN)
Hampden-Sydney Coll. (VA)
Hampshire Coll. (MA)
Hampton Univ. (VA)
Hanover Coll. (IN)
Hardin-Simmons Univ. (TX)
Harding Univ. (AR)
Hartwick Coll. (NY)
Harvard Univ. (MA)
Harvey Mudd Coll. (CA)
Haverford Coll. (PA)
Heidelberg Univ. (OH)
Henderson State Univ. (AR)
Hendrix Coll. (AR)
Hillsdale Coll. (MI)
Hiram Coll. (OH)
Hobart and William Smith Colleges
    (NY)
Hofstra Univ. (NY)
Hollins Univ. (VA)
Hope Coll. (MI)
Houghton Coll. (NY)
Houston Baptist Univ.
Howard Univ. (DC)
Humboldt State Univ. (CA)
Huntington Univ. (IN)
Idaho State Univ.
Illinois Coll.
Illinois Institute of Technology
Illinois State Univ.
Illinois Wesleyan Univ.
Indiana State Univ.
Indiana Univ. of Pennsylvania
Indiana Univ.–Bloomington
Indiana Univ.–Purdue Univ.–Fort
    Wayne
Indiana Univ.-Purdue Univ.–
    Indianapolis
Iona Coll. (NY)
Iowa State Univ.
Ithaca Coll. (NY)

Jackson State Univ. (MS)
Jacksonville Univ. (FL)
James Madison Univ. (VA)
John Carroll Univ. (OH)
Johns Hopkins Univ. (MD)
Juniata Coll. (PA)
Kalamazoo Coll. (MI)
Kansas State Univ.
Kent State Univ. (OH)
Kentucky Wesleyan Coll.
Kenyon Coll. (OH)
Kettering Univ. (MI)
King Coll. (TN)
Knox Coll. (IL)
Kutztown Univ. of Pennsylvania
La Salle Univ. (PA)
Lafayette Coll. (PA)
Lake Forest Coll. (IL)
Lamar Univ. (TX)
Lane Coll. (TN)
Langston Univ. (OK)
Lawrence Technological Univ. (MI)
Lawrence Univ. (WI)
Le Moyne Coll. (NY)
Lebanon Valley Coll. (PA)
Lehigh Univ. (PA)
Lenoir-Rhyne Univ. (NC)
Lewis & Clark Coll. (OR)
Lewis Univ. (IL)
Lincoln Univ. (PA)
Lincoln Univ. (MO)
Linfield Coll. (OR)
Lipscomb Univ. (TN)
Lock Haven Univ. of Pennsylvania
Long Island Univ.–C.W. Post
    Campus (NY)
Longwood Univ. (VA)
Louisiana State Univ.–Baton Rouge
Louisiana State Univ.–Shreveport
Louisiana Tech Univ.
Loyola Marymount Univ. (CA)
Loyola Univ. Chicago
Loyola Univ. Maryland
Luther Coll. (IA)
Lycoming Coll. (PA)
Lynchburg Coll. (VA)
Macalester Coll. (MN)
Manchester Coll. (IN)
Manhattan Coll. (NY)
Manhattanville Coll. (NY)
Mansfield Univ. of Pennsylvania
Marian Univ. (IN)
Marietta Coll. (OH)
Marquette Univ. (WI)
Marshall Univ. (WV)
Mary Baldwin Coll. (VA)
Maryville Coll. (TN)
Massachusetts Coll. of Liberal Arts
Massachusetts Institute of
    Technology
McDaniel Coll. (MD)
McMurry Univ. (TX)
McNeese State Univ. (LA)
Mercer Univ. (GA)
Merrimack Coll. (MA)
Messiah Coll. (PA)
Metropolitan State Coll. of Denver
Miami Univ.–Oxford (OH)
Michigan State Univ.
Michigan Technological Univ.
Middle Tennessee State Univ.

Middlebury Coll. (VT)
Midwestern State Univ. (TX)
Millersville Univ. of Pennsylvania
Millikin Univ. (IL)
Millsaps Coll. (MS)
Minnesota State Univ.–Mankato
Minnesota State Univ.–Moorhead
Minot State Univ. (ND)
Mississippi Coll.
Mississippi State Univ.
Missouri Southern State Univ.
Missouri State Univ.
Missouri Univ. of Science &
    Technology
Monmouth Coll. (IL)
Montana State Univ.
Montclair State Univ. (NJ)
Moravian Coll. (PA)
Morehead State Univ. (KY)
Morehouse Coll. (GA)
Morgan State Univ. (MD)
Morningside Coll. (IA)
Mount Holyoke Coll. (MA)
Muhlenberg Coll. (PA)
Murray State Univ. (KY)
Muskingum Univ. (OH)
Nebraska Wesleyan Univ.
New Jersey City Univ.
New Jersey Institute of Technology
New Mexico Highlands Univ.
New Mexico Institute of Mining
    and Technology
New Mexico State Univ.
New York Institute of Technology
New York Univ.
Norfolk State Univ. (VA)
North Carolina A&T State Univ.
North Carolina Central Univ.
North Carolina State Univ.–Raleigh
North Central Coll. (IL)
North Dakota State Univ.
North Georgia Coll. and State Univ.
North Park Univ. (IL)
Northeastern Illinois Univ.
Northeastern Univ. (MA)
Northern Arizona Univ.
Northern Illinois Univ.
Northern Kentucky Univ.
Northern Michigan Univ.
Northland Coll. (WI)
Northwest Missouri State Univ.
Northwest Nazarene Univ. (ID)
Northwestern Oklahoma State
    Univ.
Northwestern State Univ. of
    Louisiana
Northwestern Univ. (IL)
Norwich Univ. (VT)
Oakland Univ. (MI)
Oberlin Coll. (OH)
Occidental Coll. (CA)
Oglethorpe Univ. (GA)
Ohio Northern Univ.
Ohio State Univ.–Columbus
Ohio Univ.
Ohio Wesleyan Univ.
Oklahoma Baptist Univ.
Oklahoma City Univ.
Oklahoma State Univ.
Old Dominion Univ. (VA)
Oral Roberts Univ. (OK)

Oregon State Univ.
Otterbein Coll. (OH)
Ouachita Baptist Univ. (AR)
Pace Univ. (NY)
Pacific Lutheran Univ. (WA)
Pacific Union Coll. (CA)
Pacific Univ. (OR)
Pennsylvania State Univ.–Univ. Park
Pepperdine Univ. (CA)
Pittsburg State Univ. (KS)
Point Loma Nazarene Univ. (CA)
Polytechnic Institute of New York
    Univ. (NY)
Pomona Coll. (CA)
Portland State Univ. (OR)
Prairie View A&M Univ. (TX)
Presbyterian Coll. (SC)
Princeton Univ. (NJ)
Principia Coll. (IL)
Purdue Univ.–Calumet (IN)
Radford Univ. (VA)
Ramapo Coll. of New Jersey
Randolph Coll. (VA)
Randolph-Macon Coll. (VA)
Reed Coll. (OR)
Rensselaer Polytechnic Institute
    (NY)
Rhode Island Coll.
Rhodes Coll. (TN)
Rice Univ. (TX)
Richard Stockton Coll. of New
    Jersey
Rider Univ. (NJ)
Ripon Coll. (WI)
Roanoke Coll. (VA)
Rochester Institute of Technology
    (NY)
Rockhurst Univ. (MO)
Rollins Coll. (FL)
Roosevelt Univ. (IL)
Rose-Hulman Institute of
    Technology (IN)
Rutgers, the State Univ. of New
    Jersey–Camden
Rutgers, the State Univ. of New
    Jersey–New Brunswick
Rutgers, the State Univ. of New
    Jersey–Newark
Saginaw Valley State Univ. (MI)
Salisbury Univ. (MD)
Sam Houston State Univ. (TX)
Samford Univ. (AL)
San Diego State Univ.
San Francisco State Univ.
San Jose State Univ. (CA)
Santa Clara Univ. (CA)
Scripps Coll. (CA)
Seattle Pacific Univ.
Seattle Univ.
Seton Hall Univ. (NJ)
Seton Hill Univ. (PA)
Sewanee–Univ. of the South (TN)
Shaw Univ. (NC)
Shippensburg Univ. of Pennsylvania
Siena Coll. (NY)
Simmons Coll. (MA)
Simpson Coll. (IA)
Skidmore Coll. (NY)
Slippery Rock Univ. of Pennsylvania
Smith Coll. (MA)
Sonoma State Univ. (CA)

South Carolina State Univ.
South Dakota School of Mines and
  Technology
South Dakota State Univ.
Southeast Missouri State Univ.
Southeastern Louisiana Univ.
Southern Adventist Univ. (TN)
Southern Arkansas Univ.
Southern Connecticut State Univ.
Southern Illinois Univ.–Carbondale
Southern Illinois Univ.–Edwardsville
Southern Methodist Univ. (TX)
Southern Nazarene Univ. (OK)
Southern Oregon Univ.
Southern Polytechnic State Univ.
  (GA)
Southern Univ. and A&M Coll. (LA)
Southern Univ.–New Orleans
Southwestern Adventist Univ. (TX)
Southwestern Coll. (KS)
Southwestern Oklahoma State
  Univ.
Southwestern Univ. (TX)
Spelman Coll. (GA)
Spring Arbor Univ. (MI)
St. Ambrose Univ. (IA)
St. Anselm Coll. (NH)
St. Bonaventure Univ. (NY)
St. Catherine Univ. (MN)
St. Cloud State Univ. (MN)
St. John Fisher Coll. (NY)
St. John's Univ. (MN)
St. John's Univ. (NY)
St. Joseph's Univ. (PA)
St. Lawrence Univ. (NY)
St. Louis Univ.
St. Mary's Coll. of California
St. Mary's Coll. of Maryland
St. Mary's Univ. of San Antonio
  (TX)
St. Michael's Coll. (VT)
St. Norbert Coll. (WI)
St. Olaf Coll. (MN)
St. Peter's Coll. (NJ)
St. Vincent Coll. (PA)
Stanford Univ. (CA)
Stephen F. Austin State Univ. (TX)
Stetson Univ. (FL)
Stevens Institute of Technology
  (NJ)
Suffolk Univ. (MA)
SUNY Coll.–Cortland
SUNY Coll.–Oneonta
SUNY Coll.–Potsdam
SUNY–Fredonia
SUNY–Geneseo
SUNY–Oswego
SUNY–Plattsburgh
SUNY–Stony Brook
Susquehanna Univ. (PA)
Swarthmore Coll. (PA)
Syracuse Univ. (NY)
Talladega Coll. (AL)
Tarleton State Univ. (TX)
Taylor Univ. (IN)
Temple Univ. (PA)
Tennessee State Univ.
Tennessee Technological Univ.
Texas A&M Univ.–Coll. Station
Texas A&M Univ.–Commerce
Texas A&M Univ.–Kingsville

Texas Christian Univ.
Texas Lutheran Univ.
Texas State Univ.–San Marcos
Texas Tech Univ.
The Citadel (SC)
Thiel Coll. (PA)
Thomas More Coll. (KY)
Towson Univ. (MD)
Transylvania Univ. (KY)
Trevecca Nazarene Univ. (TN)
Trinity Coll. (CT)
Truman State Univ. (MO)
Tufts Univ. (MA)
Tulane Univ. (LA)
Tuskegee Univ. (AL)
Union Coll. (NY)
Union Coll. (NE)
Union Univ. (TN)
United States Air Force Academy
  (CO)
United States Naval Academy (MD)
Univ. at Albany–SUNY
Univ. at Buffalo–SUNY
Univ. of Akron (OH)
Univ. of Alabama
Univ. of Alabama–Birmingham
Univ. of Alabama–Huntsville
Univ. of Alaska–Fairbanks
Univ. of Arizona
Univ. of Arkansas
Univ. of Arkansas–Little Rock
Univ. of Arkansas–Pine Bluff
Univ. of California–Berkeley
Univ. of California–Davis
Univ. of California–Irvine
Univ. of California–Los Angeles
Univ. of California–Riverside
Univ. of California–San Diego
Univ. of California–Santa Barbara
Univ. of California–Santa Cruz
Univ. of Central Arkansas
Univ. of Central Florida
Univ. of Central Oklahoma
Univ. of Chicago
Univ. of Colorado–Boulder
Univ. of Colorado–Colorado
  Springs
Univ. of Colorado–Denver
Univ. of Connecticut
Univ. of Dallas
Univ. of Dayton (OH)
Univ. of Delaware
Univ. of Denver
Univ. of Evansville (IN)
Univ. of Florida
Univ. of Georgia
Univ. of Hartford (CT)
Univ. of Hawaii–Hilo
Univ. of Hawaii–Manoa
Univ. of Houston
Univ. of Houston–Downtown
Univ. of Illinois–Chicago
Univ. of Illinois–Urbana-Champaign
Univ. of Indianapolis
Univ. of Iowa
Univ. of Kansas
Univ. of Kentucky
Univ. of La Verne (CA)
Univ. of Louisiana–Lafayette
Univ. of Louisville (KY)
Univ. of Maine

Univ. of Mary Washington (VA)
Univ. of Maryland–Baltimore
  County
Univ. of Maryland–Coll. Park
Univ. of Massachusetts–Amherst
Univ. of Massachusetts–Boston
Univ. of Massachusetts–Dartmouth
Univ. of Massachusetts–Lowell
Univ. of Memphis
Univ. of Miami (FL)
Univ. of Michigan–Ann Arbor
Univ. of Michigan–Dearborn
Univ. of Michigan–Flint
Univ. of Minnesota–Duluth
Univ. of Minnesota–Morris
Univ. of Minnesota–Twin Cities
Univ. of Mississippi
Univ. of Missouri
Univ. of Missouri–Kansas City
Univ. of Missouri–St. Louis
Univ. of Montana
Univ. of Mount Union (OH)
Univ. of Nebraska–Kearney
Univ. of Nebraska–Lincoln
Univ. of Nebraska–Omaha
Univ. of Nevada–Las Vegas
Univ. of Nevada–Reno
Univ. of New Hampshire
Univ. of New Mexico
Univ. of New Orleans
Univ. of North Alabama
Univ. of North Carolina–Asheville
Univ. of North Carolina–Chapel Hill
Univ. of North Carolina–Charlotte
Univ. of North Carolina–
  Greensboro
Univ. of North Carolina–Pembroke
Univ. of North Carolina–
  Wilmington
Univ. of North Dakota
Univ. of North Florida
Univ. of North Texas
Univ. of Northern Colorado
Univ. of Northern Iowa
Univ. of Notre Dame (IN)
Univ. of Oklahoma
Univ. of Oregon
Univ. of Pennsylvania
Univ. of Pittsburgh
Univ. of Portland (OR)
Univ. of Puget Sound (WA)
Univ. of Redlands (CA)
Univ. of Rhode Island
Univ. of Richmond (VA)
Univ. of Rochester (NY)
Univ. of San Diego
Univ. of San Francisco
Univ. of Science and Arts of
  Oklahoma
Univ. of Scranton (PA)
Univ. of South Alabama
Univ. of South Carolina
Univ. of South Dakota
Univ. of South Florida
Univ. of Southern California
Univ. of Southern Mississippi
Univ. of St. Thomas (MN)
Univ. of Tennessee
Univ. of Tennessee–Chattanooga
Univ. of Texas–Arlington
Univ. of Texas–Austin

Univ. of Texas–Brownsville
Univ. of Texas–Dallas
Univ. of Texas–El Paso
Univ. of Texas–Pan American
Univ. of Texas–San Antonio
Univ. of the Cumberlands (KY)
Univ. of the District of Columbia
Univ. of the Pacific (CA)
Univ. of Toledo (OH)
Univ. of Tulsa (OK)
Univ. of Utah
Univ. of Vermont
Univ. of Virginia
Univ. of Washington
Univ. of West Florida
Univ. of West Georgia
Univ. of Wisconsin–Eau Claire
Univ. of Wisconsin–La Crosse
Univ. of Wisconsin–Madison
Univ. of Wisconsin–Milwaukee
Univ. of Wisconsin–Parkside
Univ. of Wisconsin–River Falls
Univ. of Wisconsin–Stevens Point
Univ. of Wisconsin–Whitewater
Univ. of Wyoming
Ursinus Coll. (PA)
Utah State Univ.
Utah Valley Univ.
Utica Coll. (NY)
Valdosta State Univ. (GA)
Valparaiso Univ. (IN)
Vanderbilt Univ. (TN)
Vassar Coll. (NY)
Villanova Univ. (PA)
Virginia Commonwealth Univ.
Virginia Military Institute
Virginia State Univ.
Virginia Tech
Wabash Coll. (IN)
Wagner Coll. (NY)
Wake Forest Univ. (NC)
Wartburg Coll. (IA)
Washburn Univ. (KS)
Washington and Jefferson Coll.
  (PA)
Washington and Lee Univ. (VA)
Washington Coll. (MD)
Washington State Univ.
Washington Univ. in St. Louis
Wayne State Univ. (MI)
Weber State Univ. (UT)
Wellesley Coll. (MA)
Wells Coll. (NY)
Wesleyan Coll. (GA)
Wesleyan Univ. (CT)
West Chester Univ. of Pennsylvania
West Texas A&M Univ.
West Virginia Univ.
West Virginia Wesleyan Coll.
Western Illinois Univ.
Western Kentucky Univ.
Western Michigan Univ.
Western Washington Univ.
Westminster Coll. (MO)
Westminster Coll. (UT)
Westmont Coll. (CA)
Wheaton Coll. (MA)
Wheaton Coll. (IL)
Wheeling Jesuit Univ. (WV)
Whitman Coll. (WA)
Whittier Coll. (CA)

Whitworth Univ. (WA)
Wichita State Univ. (KS)
Willamette Univ. (OR)
William Jewell Coll. (MO)
Williams Coll. (MA)
Wittenberg Univ. (OH)
Wofford Coll. (SC)
Worcester Polytechnic Institute
  (MA)
Wright State Univ. (OH)
Xavier Univ. (OH)
Yale Univ. (CT)
Yeshiva Univ. (NY)
York Coll. of Pennsylvania
Youngstown State Univ. (OH)

Physiological Psychology/Psychobiology

Albright Coll. (PA)
Averett Univ. (VA)
Centre Coll. (KY)
Coll. of William and Mary (VA)
Earlham Coll. (IN)
Florida Atlantic Univ.
Holy Names Univ. (CA)
Lebanon Valley Coll. (PA)
Lincoln Univ. (PA)
Lynchburg Coll. (VA)
Medaille Coll. (NY)
Mills Coll. (CA)
Northwest Missouri State Univ.
Occidental Coll. (CA)
Pepperdine Univ. (CA)
Quinnipiac Univ. (CT)
St. Mary's Coll. of California
Swarthmore Coll. (PA)
Univ. of California–Los Angeles
Univ. of California–Santa Cruz
Univ. of Colorado–Denver
Univ. of Miami (FL)
Univ. of New England (ME)
Wheaton Coll. (MA)
Wilson Coll. (PA)
York Coll. (NE)

Physiology, Pathology, and Related Sciences

Augustana Coll. (SD)
Baldwin-Wallace Coll. (OH)
Baylor Univ. (TX)
Berry Coll. (GA)
Black Hills State Univ. (SD)
Boise State Univ. (ID)
Boston Univ.
Brigham Young Univ.–Provo (UT)
California State Univ.–Long Beach
Central Christian Coll. (KS)
Chapman Univ. (CA)
Colby Coll. (ME)
Coll. of St. Scholastica (MN)
Concordia Univ. Chicago (IL)
Denison Univ. (OH)
East Carolina Univ. (NC)
Eastern Michigan Univ.
Fitchburg State Coll. (MA)
Gettysburg Coll. (PA)
Gonzaga Univ. (WA)
Hamilton Coll. (NY)

Hiram Coll. (OH)
Huntington Univ. (IN)
Indiana Wesleyan Univ.
Lafayette Coll. (PA)
Lasell Coll. (MA)
Life Univ. (GA)
Lynchburg Coll. (VA)
Manchester Coll. (IN)
Marquette Univ. (WI)
Metropolitan State Coll. of Denver
Miami Univ.–Oxford (OH)
Michigan State Univ.
North Park Univ. (IL)
Northern Arizona Univ.
Northern Michigan Univ.
Northwest Christian Univ. (OR)
Ohio Northern Univ.
Ohio State Univ.–Columbus
Oklahoma State Univ.
Olivet Nazarene Univ. (IL)
Oral Roberts Univ. (OK)
Regis Univ. (CO)
Sacred Heart Univ. (CT)
San Diego State Univ.
Southern Illinois Univ.–Carbondale
Thiel Coll. (PA)
Tulane Univ. (LA)
Univ. of Arizona
Univ. of California–Davis
Univ. of California–Los Angeles
Univ. of California–Santa Barbara
Univ. of Colorado–Boulder
Univ. of Connecticut
Univ. of Delaware
Univ. of Illinois–Urbana-Champaign
Univ. of Kentucky
Univ. of Maine
Univ. of Miami (FL)
Univ. of Minnesota–Twin Cities
Univ. of North Carolina–Chapel Hill
Univ. of Oregon
Univ. of Washington
Utah State Univ.
West Virginia Univ.
Westminster Coll. (UT)

Plant Sciences

Alabama Agricultural and
    Mechanical Univ.
Alcorn State Univ. (MS)
Arkansas State Univ.–Jonesboro
Auburn Univ. (AL)
California Polytechnic State Univ.–
    San Luis Obispo
California State Polytechnic Univ.–
    Pomona
Chadron State Coll. (NE)
Coll. of the Ozarks (MO)
Colorado State Univ.
Cornell Univ. (NY)
Delaware State Univ.
Delaware Valley Coll. (PA)
Dordt Coll. (IA)
Eastern Kentucky Univ.
Eastern Oregon Univ.
Florida Southern Coll.
Hardin-Simmons Univ. (TX)
Humboldt State Univ. (CA)
Iowa State Univ.
Kansas State Univ.

Louisiana State Univ.–Baton Rouge
Michigan State Univ.
Mississippi State Univ.
Missouri State Univ.
Montana State Univ.
New Mexico State Univ.
North Carolina State Univ.–Raleigh
North Dakota State Univ.
Northwest Missouri State Univ.
Ohio State Univ.–Columbus
Oklahoma Panhandle State Univ.
Oklahoma State Univ.
Oregon State Univ.
Pennsylvania State Univ.–Univ. Park
Rutgers, the State Univ. of New
    Jersey–New Brunswick
South Dakota State Univ.
Southeast Missouri State Univ.
Southeastern Louisiana Univ.
Southern Illinois Univ.–Carbondale
Stephen F. Austin State Univ. (TX)
SUNY Coll. of Agriculture and
    Technology–Cobleskill
Tarleton State Univ. (TX)
Texas A&M Univ.–Coll. Station
Texas A&M Univ.–Commerce
Texas A&M Univ.–Kingsville
Texas Tech Univ.
Tuskegee Univ. (AL)
Univ. of Arizona
Univ. of Arkansas
Univ. of California–Davis
Univ. of Connecticut
Univ. of Delaware
Univ. of Florida
Univ. of Hawaii–Hilo
Univ. of Hawaii–Manoa
Univ. of Illinois–Urbana-Champaign
Univ. of Kentucky
Univ. of Maine
Univ. of Massachusetts–Amherst
Univ. of Minnesota–Crookston
Univ. of Minnesota–Twin Cities
Univ. of Missouri
Univ. of Nebraska–Lincoln
Univ. of Nevada–Reno
Univ. of New Hampshire
Univ. of Tennessee
Univ. of Vermont
Univ. of Wisconsin–Madison
Univ. of Wisconsin–Platteville
Univ. of Wisconsin–River Falls
Univ. of Wyoming
Utah State Univ.
Virginia Tech
Washington State Univ.
West Texas A&M Univ.
West Virginia Univ.

Podiatric Medicine/ Podiatry (D.P.M.)

Gannon Univ. (PA)

Political Science and Government

Agnes Scott Coll. (GA)
American Jewish Univ. (CA)
Arcadia Univ. (PA)
Assumption Coll. (MA)

Augsburg Coll. (MN)
Belhaven Univ. (MS)
Bemidji State Univ. (MN)
Benedict Coll. (SC)
Benedictine Coll. (KS)
Benedictine Univ. (IL)
Biola Univ. (CA)
Bowdoin Coll. (ME)
Bowie State Univ. (MD)
Brandeis Univ. (MA)
Bryan Coll. (TN)
California Lutheran Univ.
California State Polytechnic Univ.–
    Pomona
California State Univ.–Sacramento
California State Univ.–San Marcos
Clark Univ. (MA)
Clarkson Univ. (NY)
Clayton State Univ. (GA)
Coe Coll. (IA)
Columbus State Univ. (GA)
Concord Univ. (WV)
Concordia Univ. (CA)
Denison Univ. (OH)
Dillard Univ. (LA)
East Central Univ. (OK)
Elizabethtown Coll. (PA)
Emory and Henry Coll. (VA)
Furman Univ. (SC)
Greensboro Coll. (NC)
Grinnell Coll. (IA)
Grove City Coll. (PA)
Hamilton Coll. (NY)
Hampshire Coll. (MA)
Hanover Coll. (IN)
High Point Univ. (NC)
Hillsdale Coll. (MI)
Hiram Coll. (OH)
Hollins Univ. (VA)
Huston-Tillotson Univ. (TX)
Indiana Univ.–South Bend
Johnson State Coll. (VT)
La Salle Univ. (PA)
Lake Forest Coll. (IL)
Lawrence Univ. (WI)
Lewis Univ. (IL)
Manchester Coll. (IN)
Manhattan Coll. (NY)
Manhattanville Coll. (NY)
Marlboro Coll. (VT)
Marymount Manhattan Coll. (NY)
Methodist Univ. (NC)
Mount St. Mary's Univ. (MD)
North Carolina Wesleyan Coll.
North Park Univ. (IL)
Northland Coll. (WI)
Northwest Univ. (WA)
Norwich Univ. (VT)
Occidental Coll. (CA)
Oglethorpe Univ. (GA)
Oklahoma City Univ.
Olivet Nazarene Univ. (IL)
Otterbein Coll. (OH)
Pitzer Coll. (CA)
Principia Coll. (IL)
Purchase Coll.–SUNY
Queens Univ. of Charlotte (NC)
Randolph Coll. (VA)
Rice Univ. (TX)
Ripon Coll. (WI)
Russell Sage Coll. (NY)

Scripps Coll. (CA)
Sewanee–Univ. of the South (TN)
Shepherd Univ. (WV)
Simmons Coll. (MA)
Southern New Hampshire Univ.
Southern Univ.–New Orleans
Spelman Coll. (GA)
Spring Arbor Univ. (MI)
St. Bonaventure Univ. (NY)
St. Lawrence Univ. (NY)
St. Martin's Univ. (WA)
St. Mary's Univ. of Minnesota
St. Mary-of-the-Woods Coll. (IN)
Stephens Coll. (MO)
SUNY Coll.–Oneonta
Texas A&M Univ.–Kingsville
Thiel Coll. (PA)
Thomas Coll. (ME)
Thomas More Coll. of Liberal Arts
    (NH)
Towson Univ. (MD)
Truman State Univ. (MO)
Univ. of California–Santa Barbara
Univ. of Chicago
Univ. of Louisville (KY)
Univ. of Massachusetts–Dartmouth
Univ. of Portland (OR)
Univ. of South Carolina–Upstate
Univ. of St. Thomas (MN)
Univ. of Tennessee–Martin
Univ. of Washington
Univ. of Wisconsin–Whitewater
Wabash Coll. (IN)
Wellesley Coll. (MA)
Western State Coll. of Colorado
Westminster Coll. (MO)
Yeshiva Univ. (NY)

Polymer/Plastics Engineering

Case Western Reserve Univ. (OH)
Kettering Univ. (MI)
Stevens Institute of Technology
    (NJ)
Univ. of Akron (OH)
Univ. of Illinois–Urbana-Champaign
Univ. of Massachusetts–Lowell

Precision Metalworking

Lewis-Clark State Coll. (ID)
Northern Michigan Univ.
Utah State Univ.

Precision Production Trades

Boise State Univ. (ID)

Psychology

Abilene Christian Univ. (TX)
Adams State Coll. (CO)
Adelphi Univ. (NY)
Adrian Coll. (MI)
Alabama Agricultural and
    Mechanical Univ.
Alabama State Univ.
Alaska Pacific Univ.
Albany State Univ. (GA)

Albertus Magnus Coll. (CT)
Albion Coll. (MI)
Albright Coll. (PA)
Alcorn State Univ. (MS)
Alderson-Broaddus Coll. (WV)
Alfred Univ. (NY)
Allegheny Coll. (PA)
Alma Coll. (MI)
Alvernia Univ. (PA)
Alverno Coll. (WI)
American Jewish Univ. (CA)
American Univ. (DC)
Amherst Coll. (MA)
Anderson Univ. (IN)
Anderson Univ. (SC)
Andrews Univ. (MI)
Angelo State Univ. (TX)
Anna Maria Coll. (MA)
Appalachian State Univ. (NC)
Aquinas Coll. (MI)
Arcadia Univ. (PA)
Arizona State Univ.
Arkansas State Univ.–Jonesboro
Arkansas Tech Univ.
Armstrong Atlantic State Univ. (GA)
Asbury Univ. (KY)
Ashland Univ. (OH)
Assumption Coll. (MA)
Atlanta Christian Coll.
Atlantic Union Coll. (MA)
Auburn Univ. (AL)
Auburn Univ.–Montgomery (AL)
Augusta State Univ. (GA)
Augustana Coll. (IL)
Augustana Coll. (SD)
Aurora Univ. (IL)
Austin Coll. (TX)
Austin Peay State Univ. (TN)
Avila Univ. (MO)
Azusa Pacific Univ. (CA)
Baker Univ. (KS)
Baldwin-Wallace Coll. (OH)
Ball State Univ. (IN)
Bard Coll. at Simon's Rock (MA)
Barnard Coll. (NY)
Barry Univ. (FL)
Barton Coll. (NC)
Bates Coll. (ME)
Bay Path Coll. (MA)
Baylor Univ. (TX)
Becker Coll. (MA)
Belhaven Univ. (MS)
Bellarmine Univ. (KY)
Bellevue Univ. (NE)
Belmont Abbey Coll. (NC)
Belmont Univ. (TN)
Beloit Coll. (WI)
Bemidji State Univ. (MN)
Benedictine Coll. (KS)
Benedictine Univ. (IL)
Bennett Coll. (NC)
Bennington Coll. (VT)
Berea Coll. (KY)
Berry Coll. (GA)
Bethany Coll. (KS)
Bethany Coll. (WV)
Bethel Coll. (KS)
Bethel Coll. (TN)
Bethel Univ. (MN)
Bethune-Cookman Univ. (FL)
Binghamton Univ.–SUNY

Biola Univ. (CA)
Black Hills State Univ. (SD)
Bloomfield Coll. (NJ)
Bloomsburg Univ. of Pennsylvania
Blue Mountain Coll. (MS)
Bluefield Coll. (VA)
Bluffton Univ. (OH)
Boise State Univ. (ID)
Bowie State Univ. (MD)
Bowling Green State Univ. (OH)
Bradley Univ. (IL)
Brenau Univ. (GA)
Brescia Univ. (KY)
Brevard Coll. (NC)
Brewton-Parker Coll. (GA)
Briar Cliff Univ. (IA)
Bridgewater Coll. (VA)
Bridgewater State Coll. (MA)
Brigham Young Univ.–Hawaii
Brigham Young Univ.–Provo (UT)
Brown Univ. (RI)
Bryan Coll. (TN)
Bryant Univ. (RI)
Bryn Mawr Coll. (PA)
Bucknell Univ. (PA)
Buena Vista Univ. (IA)
Buffalo State Coll.–SUNY
Burlington Coll. (VT)
Butler Univ. (IN)
Cabrini Coll. (PA)
California Baptist Univ.
California Lutheran Univ.
California Polytechnic State Univ.–
    San Luis Obispo
California State Polytechnic Univ.–
    Pomona
California State Univ.–Chico
California State Univ.–Dominguez
    Hills
California State Univ.–East Bay
California State Univ.–Fresno
California State Univ.–Fullerton
California State Univ.–Long Beach
California State Univ.–Los Angeles
California State Univ.–Northridge
California State Univ.–Sacramento
California State Univ.–San
    Bernardino
California State Univ.–Stanislaus
California Univ. of Pennsylvania
Calumet Coll. of St. Joseph (IN)
Calvin Coll. (MI)
Cameron Univ. (OK)
Campbell Univ. (NC)
Campbellsville Univ. (KY)
Canisius Coll. (NY)
Capital Univ. (OH)
Cardinal Stritch Univ. (WI)
Carleton Coll. (MN)
Carlow Univ. (PA)
Carnegie Mellon Univ. (PA)
Carroll Univ. (WI)
Carson-Newman Coll. (TN)
Carthage Coll. (WI)
Case Western Reserve Univ. (OH)
Castleton State Coll. (VT)
Catawba Coll. (NC)
Catholic Univ. of America (DC)
Cazenovia Coll. (NY)
Cedar Crest Coll. (PA)
Cedarville Univ. (OH)

Centenary Coll. (NJ)
Centenary Coll. of Louisiana
Central Christian Coll. (KS)
Central Coll. (IA)
Central Connecticut State Univ.
Central Methodist Univ. (MO)
Central Michigan Univ.
Central State Univ. (OH)
Central Washington Univ.
Centre Coll. (KY)
Chadron State Coll. (NE)
Chaminade Univ. of Honolulu
Champlain Coll. (VT)
Chapman Univ. (CA)
Charleston Southern Univ. (SC)
Chatham Univ. (PA)
Chestnut Hill Coll. (PA)
Cheyney Univ. of Pennsylvania
Chicago State Univ.
Chowan Univ. (NC)
Christian Brothers Univ. (TN)
Christopher Newport Univ. (VA)
City Univ. (WA)
Claremont McKenna Coll. (CA)
Clarion Univ. of Pennsylvania
Clark Atlanta Univ.
Clark Univ. (MA)
Clarke Univ. (IA)
Clarkson Univ. (NY)
Clearwater Christian Coll. (FL)
Clemson Univ. (SC)
Cleveland State Univ.
Coastal Carolina Univ. (SC)
Coker Coll. (SC)
Colby Coll. (ME)
Colby-Sawyer Coll. (NH)
Colgate Univ. (NY)
Coll. at Brockport–SUNY
Coll. of Charleston (SC)
Coll. of Idaho (ID)
Coll. of Mount St. Joseph (OH)
Coll. of Mount St. Vincent (NY)
Coll. of New Jersey
Coll. of Notre Dame of Maryland
Coll. of Santa Fe (NM)
Coll. of St. Benedict (MN)
Coll. of St. Elizabeth (NJ)
Coll. of St. Joseph (VT)
Coll. of St. Mary (NE)
Coll. of St. Rose (NY)
Coll. of St. Scholastica (MN)
Coll. of the Holy Cross (MA)
Coll. of the Ozarks (MO)
Coll. of William and Mary (VA)
Colorado Christian Univ.
Colorado Coll.
Colorado State Univ.
Colorado State Univ.–Pueblo
Columbia Coll. (MO)
Columbia Coll. (SC)
Columbia Univ. (NY)
Concord Univ. (WV)
Concordia Coll.–Moorhead (MN)
Concordia Univ. (NE)
Concordia Univ. (OR)
Concordia Univ. (MI)
Concordia Univ. Chicago (IL)
Concordia Univ.–St. Paul (MN)
Connecticut Coll.
Converse Coll. (SC)
Corban Univ. (OR)

Cornell Coll. (IA)
Cornell Univ. (NY)
Cornerstone Univ. (MI)
Covenant Coll. (GA)
Creighton Univ. (NE)
Crown Coll. (MN)
Culver-Stockton Coll. (MO)
Cumberland Univ. (TN)
CUNY–Baruch Coll.
CUNY–Brooklyn Coll.
CUNY–City Coll.
CUNY–Coll. of Staten Island
CUNY–Hunter Coll.
CUNY–John Jay Coll. of Criminal
    Justice
CUNY–Lehman Coll.
CUNY–Medgar Evers Coll.
CUNY–Queens Coll.
CUNY–York Coll.
Curry Coll. (MA)
D'Youville Coll. (NY)
Daemen Coll. (NY)
Dakota Wesleyan Univ. (SD)
Dallas Baptist Univ.
Dana Coll. (NE)
Daniel Webster Coll. (NH)
Dartmouth Coll. (NH)
Davidson Coll. (NC)
Davis and Elkins Coll. (WV)
Defiance Coll. (OH)
Delaware State Univ.
Delta State Univ. (MS)
Denison Univ. (OH)
DePaul Univ. (IL)
DePauw Univ. (IN)
DeSales Univ. (PA)
Dickinson Coll. (PA)
Dickinson State Univ. (ND)
Dillard Univ. (LA)
Dominican Coll. (NY)
Dominican Univ. (IL)
Dominican Univ. of California
Dordt Coll. (IA)
Dowling Coll. (NY)
Drake Univ. (IA)
Drew Univ. (NJ)
Drexel Univ. (PA)
Drury Univ. (MO)
Duke Univ. (NC)
Duquesne Univ. (PA)
Earlham Coll. (IN)
East Carolina Univ. (NC)
East Stroudsburg Univ. of
    Pennsylvania
East Tennessee State Univ.
East Texas Baptist Univ.
Eastern Connecticut State Univ.
Eastern Illinois Univ.
Eastern Kentucky Univ.
Eastern Mennonite Univ. (VA)
Eastern Michigan Univ.
Eastern Nazarene Coll. (MA)
Eastern New Mexico Univ.
Eastern Oregon Univ.
Eastern Univ. (PA)
Eastern Washington Univ.
Eckerd Coll. (FL)
Edgewood Coll. (WI)
Edinboro Univ. of Pennsylvania
Edward Waters Coll. (FL)
Elizabeth City State Univ. (NC)

Elmhurst Coll. (IL)
Elmira Coll. (NY)
Elon Univ. (NC)
Emmanuel Coll. (MA)
Emmanuel Coll. (GA)
Emory and Henry Coll. (VA)
Emory Univ. (GA)
Emporia State Univ. (KS)
Endicott Coll. (MA)
Erskine Coll. (SC)
Eureka Coll. (IL)
Evangel Univ. (MO)
Evergreen State Coll. (WA)
Excelsior Coll. (NY)
Fairfield Univ. (CT)
Fairleigh Dickinson Univ. (NJ)
Fairmont State Univ. (WV)
Farmingdale State Coll.–SUNY
Faulkner Univ. (AL)
Fayetteville State Univ. (NC)
Ferris State Univ. (MI)
Ferrum Coll. (VA)
Fisk Univ. (TN)
Fitchburg State Coll. (MA)
Flagler Coll. (FL)
Florida Atlantic Univ.
Florida Institute of Technology
Florida International Univ.
Florida Southern Coll.
Florida State Univ.
Fontbonne Univ. (MO)
Fordham Univ. (NY)
Fort Hays State Univ. (KS)
Fort Lewis Coll. (CO)
Fort Valley State Univ. (GA)
Framingham State Coll. (MA)
Francis Marion Univ. (SC)
Franciscan Univ. of Steubenville
    (OH)
Franklin and Marshall Coll. (PA)
Franklin Coll. (IN)
Franklin Pierce Univ. (NH)
Free Will Baptist Bible Coll. (TN)
Freed-Hardeman Univ. (TN)
Fresno Pacific Univ. (CA)
Friends Univ. (KS)
Frostburg State Univ. (MD)
Gallaudet Univ. (DC)
Gannon Univ. (PA)
Gardner-Webb Univ. (NC)
George Fox Univ. (OR)
George Mason Univ. (VA)
George Washington Univ. (DC)
Georgetown Coll. (KY)
Georgetown Univ. (DC)
Georgia Coll. & State Univ.
Georgia Southern Univ.
Georgia Southwestern State Univ.
Georgia State Univ.
Georgian Court Univ. (NJ)
Gettysburg Coll. (PA)
Goddard Coll. (VT)
Gonzaga Univ. (WA)
Gordon Coll. (MA)
Goucher Coll. (MD)
Grace Coll. and Seminary (IN)
Graceland Univ. (IA)
Grambling State Univ. (LA)
Grand Valley State Univ. (MI)
Grand View Univ. (IA)
Green Mountain Coll. (VT)

Greensboro Coll. (NC)
Greenville Coll. (IL)
Grinnell Coll. (IA)
Guilford Coll. (NC)
Gustavus Adolphus Coll. (MN)
Gwynedd-Mercy Coll. (PA)
Hamline Univ. (MN)
Hampden-Sydney Coll. (VA)
Hampshire Coll. (MA)
Hannibal-LaGrange Coll. (MO)
Hardin-Simmons Univ. (TX)
Harding Univ. (AR)
Hartwick Coll. (NY)
Harvard Univ. (MA)
Haverford Coll. (PA)
Hawaii Pacific Univ.
Heidelberg Univ. (OH)
Henderson State Univ. (AR)
Hendrix Coll. (AR)
Heritage Univ. (WA)
High Point Univ. (NC)
Hilbert Coll. (NY)
Hobart and William Smith Colleges
    (NY)
Hodges Univ. (FL)
Hofstra Univ. (NY)
Hollins Univ. (VA)
Holy Family Univ. (PA)
Holy Names Univ. (CA)
Hood Coll. (MD)
Hope Coll. (MI)
Hope International Univ. (CA)
Houghton Coll. (NY)
Houston Baptist Univ.
Howard Payne Univ. (TX)
Howard Univ. (DC)
Humboldt State Univ. (CA)
Huntingdon Coll. (AL)
Huntington Univ. (IN)
Huston-Tillotson Univ. (TX)
Idaho State Univ.
Illinois Coll.
Illinois Institute of Technology
Illinois State Univ.
Illinois Wesleyan Univ.
Immaculata Univ. (PA)
Indiana Institute of Technology
Indiana State Univ.
Indiana Univ. East
Indiana Univ. Northwest
Indiana Univ. of Pennsylvania
Indiana Univ. Southeast
Indiana Univ.–Bloomington
Indiana Univ.–Kokomo
Indiana Univ.–South Bend
Indiana Univ.-Purdue Univ.–Fort
    Wayne
Indiana Univ.-Purdue Univ.–
    Indianapolis
Indiana Wesleyan Univ.
Iona Coll. (NY)
Iowa State Univ.
Iowa Wesleyan Coll.
Ithaca Coll. (NY)
Jackson State Univ. (MS)
Jacksonville State Univ. (AL)
Jacksonville Univ. (FL)
James Madison Univ. (VA)
John Carroll Univ. (OH)
Johns Hopkins Univ. (MD)
Johnson C. Smith Univ. (NC)

Johnson State Coll. (VT)
Judson Coll. (AL)
Judson Univ. (IL)
Juniata Coll. (PA)
Kalamazoo Coll. (MI)
Kansas State Univ.
Kansas Wesleyan Univ.
Kean Univ. (NJ)
Keene State Coll. (NH)
Kennesaw State Univ. (GA)
Kent State Univ. (OH)
Kentucky State Univ.
Kentucky Wesleyan Coll.
Kenyon Coll. (OH)
Keuka Coll. (NY)
King Coll. (TN)
King's Coll. (PA)
Knox Coll. (IL)
Kutztown Univ. of Pennsylvania
La Roche Coll. (PA)
La Salle Univ. (PA)
La Sierra Univ. (CA)
Lafayette Coll. (PA)
LaGrange Coll. (GA)
Lake Erie Coll. (OH)
Lake Forest Coll. (IL)
Lake Superior State Univ. (MI)
Lakeland Coll. (WI)
Lambuth Univ. (TN)
Lasell Coll. (MA)
Lawrence Technological Univ. (MI)
Le Moyne Coll. (NY)
Lebanon Valley Coll. (PA)
Lees-McRae Coll. (NC)
Lehigh Univ. (PA)
Lenoir-Rhyne Univ. (NC)
LeTourneau Univ. (TX)
Lewis & Clark Coll. (OR)
Lewis-Clark State Coll. (ID)
Liberty Univ. (VA)
Life Univ. (GA)
Limestone Coll. (SC)
Lincoln Memorial Univ. (TN)
Lincoln Univ. (PA)
Lincoln Univ. (MO)
Lindenwood Univ. (MO)
Lindsey Wilson Coll. (KY)
Linfield Coll. (OR)
Lipscomb Univ. (TN)
Livingstone Coll. (NC)
Lock Haven Univ. of Pennsylvania
Long Island Univ.–C.W. Post
    Campus (NY)
Loras Coll. (IA)
Louisiana Coll.
Louisiana State Univ.–Baton Rouge
Louisiana State Univ.–Shreveport
Louisiana Tech Univ.
Lourdes Coll. (OH)
Loyola Marymount Univ. (CA)
Loyola Univ. Chicago
Loyola Univ. Maryland
Loyola Univ. New Orleans
Lubbock Christian Univ. (TX)
Luther Coll. (IA)
Lycoming Coll. (PA)
Lynchburg Coll. (VA)
Lynn Univ. (FL)
Lyon Coll. (AR)
Macalester Coll. (MN)
MacMurray Coll. (IL)

Madonna Univ. (MI)
Malone Univ. (OH)
Manchester Coll. (IN)
Manhattan Coll. (NY)
Manhattanville Coll. (NY)
Mansfield Univ. of Pennsylvania
Marian Univ. (IN)
Marian Univ. (WI)
Marietta Coll. (OH)
Marist Coll. (NY)
Marquette Univ. (WI)
Mars Hill Coll. (NC)
Marshall Univ. (WV)
Martin Methodist Coll. (TN)
Martin Univ. (IN)
Mary Baldwin Coll. (VA)
Marygrove Coll. (MI)
Marylhurst Univ. (OR)
Marymount Manhattan Coll. (NY)
Marymount Univ. (VA)
Maryville Coll. (TN)
Maryville Univ. of St. Louis (MO)
Marywood Univ. (PA)
Massachusetts Coll. of Liberal Arts
Mayville State Univ. (ND)
McDaniel Coll. (MD)
McKendree Univ. (IL)
McMurry Univ. (TX)
McNeese State Univ. (LA)
McPherson Coll. (KS)
Medaille Coll. (NY)
Mercy Coll. (NY)
Mercyhurst Coll. (PA)
Meredith Coll. (NC)
Merrimack Coll. (MA)
Mesa State Coll. (CO)
Messiah Coll. (PA)
Methodist Univ. (NC)
Metropolitan State Coll. of Denver
Miami Univ.–Oxford (OH)
Michigan State Univ.
Michigan Technological Univ.
MidAmerica Nazarene Univ. (KS)
Middle Tennessee State Univ.
Middlebury Coll. (VT)
Midland Lutheran Coll. (NE)
Midway Coll. (KY)
Midwestern State Univ. (TX)
Millersville Univ. of Pennsylvania
Milligan Coll. (TN)
Millikin Univ. (IL)
Mills Coll. (CA)
Millsaps Coll. (MS)
Minnesota State Univ.–Mankato
Minnesota State Univ.–Moorhead
Minot State Univ. (ND)
Misericordia Univ. (PA)
Mississippi Coll.
Mississippi State Univ.
Mississippi Univ. for Women
Missouri Baptist Univ.
Missouri Southern State Univ.
Missouri State Univ.
Missouri Univ. of Science &
    Technology
Missouri Valley Coll.
Missouri Western State Univ.
Mitchell Coll. (CT)
Molloy Coll. (NY)
Monmouth Coll. (IL)
Monmouth Univ. (NJ)

Montana State Univ.
Montana State Univ.–Billings
Montclair State Univ. (NJ)
Moravian Coll. (PA)
Morehead State Univ. (KY)
Morehouse Coll. (GA)
Morningside Coll. (IA)
Mount Aloysius Coll. (PA)
Mount Holyoke Coll. (MA)
Mount Marty Coll. (SD)
Mount Mary Coll. (WI)
Mount Mercy Coll. (IA)
Mount Olive Coll. (NC)
Mount St. Mary Coll. (NY)
Mount St. Mary's Coll. (CA)
Mount St. Mary's Univ. (MD)
Mountain State Univ. (WV)
Muhlenberg Coll. (PA)
Murray State Univ. (KY)
Muskingum Univ. (OH)
National Univ. (CA)
National-Louis Univ. (IL)
Nazareth Coll. (NY)
Nebraska Wesleyan Univ.
Neumann Univ. (PA)
New England Coll. (NH)
New Jersey City Univ.
New Mexico Highlands Univ.
New Mexico Institute of Mining
    and Technology
New Mexico State Univ.
New York Institute of Technology
New York Univ.
Newberry Coll. (SC)
Newman Univ. (KS)
Niagara Univ. (NY)
Nicholls State Univ. (LA)
Nichols Coll. (MA)
Norfolk State Univ. (VA)
North Carolina A&T State Univ.
North Carolina Central Univ.
North Carolina State Univ.–Raleigh
North Carolina Wesleyan Coll.
North Central Coll. (IL)
North Dakota State Univ.
North Georgia Coll. and State Univ.
North Greenville Univ. (SC)
North Park Univ. (IL)
Northeastern State Univ. (OK)
Northeastern Univ. (MA)
Northern Arizona Univ.
Northern Illinois Univ.
Northern Kentucky Univ.
Northern Michigan Univ.
Northern State Univ. (SD)
Northland Coll. (WI)
Northwest Christian Univ. (OR)
Northwest Missouri State Univ.
Northwest Nazarene Univ. (ID)
Northwestern Coll. (IA)
Northwestern Coll. (MN)
Northwestern Oklahoma State
    Univ.
Northwestern State Univ. of
    Louisiana
Northwestern Univ. (IL)
Norwich Univ. (VT)
Notre Dame Coll. of Ohio
Notre Dame de Namur Univ. (CA)
Nova Southeastern Univ. (FL)
Nyack Coll. (NY)

Oakland Univ. (MI)
Oakwood Univ. (AL)
Oberlin Coll. (OH)
Occidental Coll. (CA)
Ohio Dominican Univ.
Ohio Northern Univ.
Ohio State Univ.–Columbus
Ohio Univ.
Ohio Valley Univ. (WV)
Ohio Wesleyan Univ.
Oklahoma Baptist Univ.
Oklahoma Christian Univ.
Oklahoma Panhandle State Univ.
Oklahoma State Univ.
Oklahoma Wesleyan Univ.
Old Dominion Univ. (VA)
Olivet Coll. (MI)
Olivet Nazarene Univ. (IL)
Oral Roberts Univ. (OK)
Oregon Institute of Technology
Oregon State Univ.
Otterbein Coll. (OH)
Ouachita Baptist Univ. (AR)
Our Lady of the Lake Univ. (TX)
Pace Univ. (NY)
Pacific Lutheran Univ. (WA)
Pacific Univ. (OR)
Paine Coll. (GA)
Palm Beach Atlantic Univ. (FL)
Park Univ. (MO)
Patten Univ. (CA)
Peace Coll. (NC)
Pennsylvania State Univ.–Univ. Park
Pepperdine Univ. (CA)
Peru State Coll. (NE)
Pfeiffer Univ. (NC)
Philadelphia Univ.
Philander Smith Coll. (AR)
Piedmont Coll. (GA)
Pikeville Coll. (KY)
Pine Manor Coll. (MA)
Pittsburg State Univ. (KS)
Pitzer Coll. (CA)
Plymouth State Univ. (NH)
Point Loma Nazarene Univ. (CA)
Point Park Univ. (PA)
Pomona Coll. (CA)
Post Univ. (CT)
Prairie View A&M Univ. (TX)
Presbyterian Coll. (SC)
Prescott Coll. (AZ)
Princeton Univ. (NJ)
Providence Coll. (RI)
Purchase Coll.–SUNY
Purdue Univ.–Calumet (IN)
Purdue Univ.–West Lafayette (IN)
Queens Univ. of Charlotte (NC)
Quincy Univ. (IL)
Quinnipiac Univ. (CT)
Radford Univ. (VA)
Ramapo Coll. of New Jersey
Randolph Coll. (VA)
Randolph-Macon Coll. (VA)
Reed Coll. (OR)
Regent Univ. (VA)
Regis Coll. (MA)
Regis Univ. (CO)
Reinhardt Univ. (GA)
Rensselaer Polytechnic Institute
    (NY)
Rhode Island Coll.

Rhodes Coll. (TN)
Rice Univ. (TX)
Richard Stockton Coll. of New
    Jersey
Rider Univ. (NJ)
Ripon Coll. (WI)
Rivier Coll. (NH)
Roanoke Coll. (VA)
Robert Morris Univ. (PA)
Roberts Wesleyan Coll. (NY)
Rochester Coll. (MI)
Rochester Institute of Technology
    (NY)
Rockford Coll. (IL)
Rockhurst Univ. (MO)
Rocky Mountain Coll. (MT)
Roger Williams Univ. (RI)
Rollins Coll. (FL)
Roosevelt Univ. (IL)
Rosemont Coll. (PA)
Russell Sage Coll. (NY)
Rutgers, the State Univ. of New
    Jersey–Camden
Rutgers, the State Univ. of New
    Jersey–New Brunswick
Rutgers, the State Univ. of New
    Jersey–Newark
Sacred Heart Univ. (CT)
Sage Colleges–Albany (NY)
Saginaw Valley State Univ. (MI)
Salem Coll. (NC)
Salem State Coll. (MA)
Salisbury Univ. (MD)
Salve Regina Univ. (RI)
Sam Houston State Univ. (TX)
Samford Univ. (AL)
San Diego State Univ.
San Francisco State Univ.
San Jose State Univ. (CA)
Santa Clara Univ. (CA)
Schreiner Univ. (TX)
Seattle Pacific Univ.
Seattle Univ.
Seton Hall Univ. (NJ)
Seton Hill Univ. (PA)
Shaw Univ. (NC)
Shawnee State Univ. (OH)
Shenandoah Univ. (VA)
Shippensburg Univ. of Pennsylvania
Shorter Coll. (GA)
Siena Coll. (NY)
Sierra Nevada Coll. (NV)
Silver Lake Coll. (WI)
Simmons Coll. (MA)
Simpson Univ. (CA)
Skidmore Coll. (NY)
Slippery Rock Univ. of Pennsylvania
Smith Coll. (MA)
Sonoma State Univ. (CA)
South Carolina State Univ.
South Dakota State Univ.
Southeast Missouri State Univ.
Southeastern Louisiana Univ.
Southeastern Oklahoma State Univ.
Southeastern Univ. (FL)
Southern Adventist Univ. (TN)
Southern Arkansas Univ.
Southern Illinois Univ.–Carbondale
Southern Illinois Univ.–Edwardsville
Southern Methodist Univ. (TX)
Southern Nazarene Univ. (OK)

Southern New Hampshire Univ.
Southern Oregon Univ.
Southern Univ. and A&M Coll. (LA)
Southern Univ.–New Orleans
Southern Utah Univ.
Southern Vermont Coll.
Southern Wesleyan Univ. (SC)
Southwest Baptist Univ. (MO)
Southwest Minnesota State Univ.
Southwestern Assemblies of God
    Univ. (TX)
Southwestern Coll. (KS)
Southwestern Oklahoma State
    Univ.
Southwestern Univ. (TX)
Spalding Univ. (KY)
Spring Arbor Univ. (MI)
Spring Hill Coll. (AL)
Springfield Coll. (MA)
St. Ambrose Univ. (IA)
St. Andrews Presbyterian Coll. (NC)
St. Anselm Coll. (NH)
St. Augustine's Coll. (NC)
St. Catherine Univ. (MN)
St. Cloud State Univ. (MN)
St. Edward's Univ. (TX)
St. Francis Coll. (NY)
St. Gregory's Univ. (OK)
St. John Fisher Coll. (NY)
St. John's Univ. (NY)
St. John's Univ. (MN)
St. Joseph Coll. (CT)
St. Joseph's Coll. (ME)
St. Joseph's Coll. (IN)
St. Joseph's Coll. New York
St. Joseph's Univ. (PA)
St. Lawrence Univ. (NY)
St. Leo Univ. (FL)
St. Louis Univ.
St. Martin's Univ. (WA)
St. Mary's Coll. (IN)
St. Mary's Coll. of California
St. Mary's Coll. of Maryland
St. Mary's Univ. of Minnesota
St. Mary's Univ. of San Antonio
    (TX)
St. Mary-of-the-Woods Coll. (IN)
St. Michael's Coll. (VT)
St. Norbert Coll. (WI)
St. Olaf Coll. (MN)
St. Peter's Coll. (NJ)
St. Thomas Aquinas Coll. (NY)
St. Thomas Univ. (FL)
St. Vincent Coll. (PA)
St. Xavier Univ. (IL)
Stanford Univ. (CA)
Stephen F. Austin State Univ. (TX)
Stetson Univ. (FL)
Stevenson Univ. (MD)
Stonehill Coll. (MA)
Suffolk Univ. (MA)
Sul Ross State Univ. (TX)
SUNY Coll.–Cortland
SUNY Coll.–Old Westbury
SUNY Coll.–Potsdam
SUNY Empire State Coll.
SUNY Institute of Technology–
    Utica/Rome
SUNY–Fredonia
SUNY–Geneseo
SUNY–Oswego

SUNY–Plattsburgh
SUNY–Stony Brook
Susquehanna Univ. (PA)
Swarthmore Coll. (PA)
Syracuse Univ. (NY)
Tabor Coll. (KS)
Tarleton State Univ. (TX)
Taylor Univ. (IN)
Temple Univ. (PA)
Tennessee State Univ.
Tennessee Technological Univ.
Tennessee Wesleyan Coll.
Texas A&M International Univ.
Texas A&M Univ.–Coll. Station
Texas A&M Univ.–Commerce
Texas A&M Univ.–Corpus Christi
Texas A&M Univ.–Kingsville
Texas Christian Univ.
Texas Lutheran Univ.
Texas State Univ.–San Marcos
Texas Tech Univ.
Texas Wesleyan Univ.
Texas Woman's Univ.
The Citadel (SC)
Thiel Coll. (PA)
Thomas Coll. (ME)
Thomas Edison State Coll. (NJ)
Thomas More Coll. (KY)
Tiffin Univ. (OH)
Tougaloo Coll. (MS)
Touro Coll. (NY)
Towson Univ. (MD)
Transylvania Univ. (KY)
Trevecca Nazarene Univ. (TN)
Trine Univ. (IN)
Trinity Christian Coll. (IL)
Trinity Coll. (CT)
Trinity International Univ. (IL)
Trinity Univ. (DC)
Troy Univ. (AL)
Truman State Univ. (MO)
Tufts Univ. (MA)
Tulane Univ. (LA)
Tusculum Coll. (TN)
Union Coll. (NY)
Union Coll. (NE)
Union Coll. (KY)
Union Institute and Univ. (OH)
Union Univ. (TN)
Univ. at Albany–SUNY
Univ. at Buffalo–SUNY
Univ. of Akron (OH)
Univ. of Alabama
Univ. of Alabama–Birmingham
Univ. of Alabama–Huntsville
Univ. of Alaska–Anchorage
Univ. of Alaska–Fairbanks
Univ. of Arizona
Univ. of Arkansas
Univ. of Arkansas–Little Rock
Univ. of Arkansas–Pine Bluff
Univ. of Baltimore (MD)
Univ. of Bridgeport (CT)
Univ. of California–Berkeley
Univ. of California–Davis
Univ. of California–Irvine
Univ. of California–Los Angeles
Univ. of California–Riverside
Univ. of California–San Diego
Univ. of Central Arkansas
Univ. of Central Florida

Univ. of Central Missouri
Univ. of Central Oklahoma
Univ. of Charleston (WV)
Univ. of Chicago
Univ. of Colorado–Boulder
Univ. of Colorado–Colorado
    Springs
Univ. of Colorado–Denver
Univ. of Connecticut
Univ. of Dallas
Univ. of Dayton (OH)
Univ. of Denver
Univ. of Detroit Mercy
Univ. of Evansville (IN)
Univ. of Findlay (OH)
Univ. of Florida
Univ. of Georgia
Univ. of Hartford (CT)
Univ. of Hawaii–Hilo
Univ. of Hawaii–Manoa
Univ. of Houston
Univ. of Houston–Downtown
Univ. of Illinois–Chicago
Univ. of Illinois–Springfield
Univ. of Illinois–Urbana-Champaign
Univ. of Indianapolis
Univ. of Iowa
Univ. of Kansas
Univ. of Kentucky
Univ. of La Verne (CA)
Univ. of Louisiana–Lafayette
Univ. of Louisiana–Monroe
Univ. of Louisville (KY)
Univ. of Maine
Univ. of Maine–Farmington
Univ. of Maine–Presque Isle
Univ. of Mary (ND)
Univ. of Mary Hardin-Baylor (TX)
Univ. of Mary Washington (VA)
Univ. of Maryland–Baltimore
    County
Univ. of Maryland–Coll. Park
Univ. of Maryland–Univ. Coll.
Univ. of Massachusetts–Amherst
Univ. of Massachusetts–Boston
Univ. of Massachusetts–Lowell
Univ. of Memphis
Univ. of Miami (FL)
Univ. of Michigan–Ann Arbor
Univ. of Michigan–Dearborn
Univ. of Michigan–Flint
Univ. of Minnesota–Duluth
Univ. of Minnesota–Morris
Univ. of Minnesota–Twin Cities
Univ. of Mississippi
Univ. of Missouri
Univ. of Missouri–Kansas City
Univ. of Missouri–St. Louis
Univ. of Mobile (AL)
Univ. of Montevallo (AL)
Univ. of Mount Union (OH)
Univ. of Nebraska–Kearney
Univ. of Nebraska–Lincoln
Univ. of Nebraska–Omaha
Univ. of Nevada–Las Vegas
Univ. of Nevada–Reno
Univ. of New England (ME)
Univ. of New Hampshire
Univ. of New Haven (CT)
Univ. of New Mexico
Univ. of New Orleans

Univ. of North Alabama
Univ. of North Carolina–Asheville
Univ. of North Carolina–Chapel Hill
Univ. of North Carolina–Charlotte
Univ. of North Carolina–
    Greensboro
Univ. of North Carolina–Pembroke
Univ. of North Carolina–
    Wilmington
Univ. of North Dakota
Univ. of North Florida
Univ. of North Texas
Univ. of Northern Colorado
Univ. of Northern Iowa
Univ. of Notre Dame (IN)
Univ. of Oklahoma
Univ. of Oregon
Univ. of Pennsylvania
Univ. of Pittsburgh
Univ. of Pittsburgh–Bradford
Univ. of Pittsburgh–Johnstown
Univ. of Portland (OR)
Univ. of Puget Sound (WA)
Univ. of Redlands (CA)
Univ. of Rhode Island
Univ. of Richmond (VA)
Univ. of Rio Grande (OH)
Univ. of Rochester (NY)
Univ. of San Diego
Univ. of San Francisco
Univ. of Science and Arts of
    Oklahoma
Univ. of Scranton (PA)
Univ. of Sioux Falls (SD)
Univ. of South Alabama
Univ. of South Carolina–Aiken
Univ. of South Carolina–Upstate
Univ. of South Dakota
Univ. of South Florida
Univ. of Southern California
Univ. of Southern Indiana
Univ. of Southern Maine
Univ. of Southern Mississippi
Univ. of St. Francis (IN)
Univ. of St. Francis (IL)
Univ. of St. Mary (KS)
Univ. of St. Thomas (TX)
Univ. of Tampa (FL)
Univ. of Tennessee
Univ. of Tennessee–Chattanooga
Univ. of Tennessee–Martin
Univ. of Texas of the Permian Basin
Univ. of Texas–Arlington
Univ. of Texas–Austin
Univ. of Texas–Brownsville
Univ. of Texas–Dallas
Univ. of Texas–El Paso
Univ. of Texas–Pan American
Univ. of Texas–San Antonio
Univ. of Texas–Tyler
Univ. of the Cumberlands (KY)
Univ. of the District of Columbia
Univ. of the Incarnate Word (TX)
Univ. of the Ozarks (AR)
Univ. of the Pacific (CA)
Univ. of the Southwest (NM)
Univ. of Toledo (OH)
Univ. of Tulsa (OK)
Univ. of Utah
Univ. of Vermont
Univ. of Virginia

Univ. of Virginia–Wise
Univ. of Washington
Univ. of West Alabama
Univ. of West Florida
Univ. of West Georgia
Univ. of Wisconsin–Eau Claire
Univ. of Wisconsin–Green Bay
Univ. of Wisconsin–La Crosse
Univ. of Wisconsin–Madison
Univ. of Wisconsin–Milwaukee
Univ. of Wisconsin–Oshkosh
Univ. of Wisconsin–Platteville
Univ. of Wisconsin–River Falls
Univ. of Wisconsin–Stevens Point
Univ. of Wisconsin–Stout
Univ. of Wisconsin–Superior
Univ. of Wisconsin–Whitewater
Univ. of Wyoming
Upper Iowa Univ.
Urbana Univ. (OH)
Ursinus Coll. (PA)
Ursuline Coll. (OH)
Utah State Univ.
Utah Valley Univ.
Utica Coll. (NY)
Valdosta State Univ. (GA)
Valley City State Univ. (ND)
Valparaiso Univ. (IN)
Vanderbilt Univ. (TN)
Vanguard Univ. of Southern
    California
Vassar Coll. (NY)
Victory Univ. (TN)
Villanova Univ. (PA)
Virginia Commonwealth Univ.
Virginia Intermont Coll.
Virginia Military Institute
Virginia State Univ.
Virginia Tech
Virginia Wesleyan Coll.
Viterbo Univ. (WI)
Wabash Coll. (IN)
Wagner Coll. (NY)
Wake Forest Univ. (NC)
Walsh Univ. (OH)
Warner Univ. (FL)
Warren Wilson Coll. (NC)
Wartburg Coll. (IA)
Washburn Univ. (KS)
Washington Adventist Univ. (MD)
Washington and Jefferson Coll.
    (PA)
Washington and Lee Univ. (VA)
Washington Coll. (MD)
Washington State Univ.
Washington Univ. in St. Louis
Wayland Baptist Univ. (TX)
Wayne State Coll. (NE)
Wayne State Univ. (MI)
Waynesburg Univ. (PA)
Weber State Univ. (UT)
Webster Univ. (MO)
Wells Coll. (NY)
Wesley Coll. (DE)
Wesleyan Coll. (GA)
West Chester Univ. of Pennsylvania
West Liberty Univ. (WV)
West Texas A&M Univ.
West Virginia State Univ.
West Virginia Univ.
West Virginia Wesleyan Coll.

Western Carolina Univ. (NC)
Western Connecticut State Univ.
Western Illinois Univ.
Western Kentucky Univ.
Western Michigan Univ.
Western New England Coll. (MA)
Western New Mexico Univ.
Western Oregon Univ.
Western State Coll. of Colorado
Western Washington Univ.
Westfield State Coll. (MA)
Westminster Coll. (UT)
Westminster Coll. (PA)
Westminster Coll. (MO)
Westmont Coll. (CA)
Wheaton Coll. (MA)
Wheaton Coll. (IL)
Wheeling Jesuit Univ. (WV)
Whitman Coll. (WA)
Whittier Coll. (CA)
Whitworth Univ. (WA)
Wichita State Univ. (KS)
Wilberforce Univ. (OH)
Wilkes Univ. (PA)
Willamette Univ. (OR)
William Carey Univ. (MS)
William Jewell Coll. (MO)
William Paterson Univ. of New Jersey
William Woods Univ. (MO)
Williams Coll. (MA)
Wilmington Coll. (OH)
Wilmington Univ. (DE)
Wingate Univ. (NC)
Winthrop Univ. (SC)
Wisconsin Lutheran Coll.
Wittenberg Univ. (OH)
Wofford Coll. (SC)
Woodbury Univ. (CA)
Worcester State Coll. (MA)
Wright State Univ. (OH)
Xavier Univ. (OH)
Yale Univ. (CT)
Yeshiva Univ. (NY)
York Coll. of Pennsylvania
Youngstown State Univ. (OH)

Psychometrics and Quantitative Psychology

North Dakota State Univ.

Public Administration

Alfred Univ. (NY)
Auburn Univ. (AL)
Augustana Coll. (IL)
Barry Univ. (FL)
Baylor Univ. (TX)
Bowling Green State Univ. (OH)
Buena Vista Univ. (IA)
California State Univ.–Bakersfield
California State Univ.–Chico
California State Univ.–Dominguez Hills
California State Univ.–Fresno
California State Univ.–Fullerton
California State Univ.–Sacramento
California State Univ.–San Bernardino
Calvin Coll. (MI)

Campbell Univ. (NC)
Capital Univ. (OH)
Carroll Coll. (MT)
Cedarville Univ. (OH)
Central Methodist Univ. (MO)
Chancellor Univ. (OH)
Cleveland State Univ.
Coll. of Santa Fe (NM)
Concordia Univ. (MI)
Cornell Univ. (NY)
CUNY–Baruch Coll.
CUNY–John Jay Coll. of Criminal Justice
CUNY–Medgar Evers Coll.
Dallas Baptist Univ.
Eastern Michigan Univ.
Eastern Washington Univ.
Elon Univ. (NC)
Ferris State Univ. (MI)
Florida Atlantic Univ.
Florida International Univ.
Florida Memorial Univ.
George Mason Univ. (VA)
Georgia Southern Univ.
Grambling State Univ. (LA)
Grand Valley State Univ. (MI)
Hampton Univ. (VA)
Harding Univ. (AR)
Harris-Stowe State Univ. (MO)
Hawaii Pacific Univ.
Henderson State Univ. (AR)
Indiana Univ. East
Indiana Univ. Northwest
Indiana Univ.–Bloomington
Indiana Univ.–Kokomo
Indiana Univ.–South Bend
Indiana Univ.-Purdue Univ.–Fort Wayne
Indiana Univ.-Purdue Univ.–Indianapolis
Iowa State Univ.
Jackson State Univ. (MS)
Jacksonville State Univ. (AL)
James Madison Univ. (VA)
Juniata Coll. (PA)
Kean Univ. (NJ)
Kentucky State Univ.
Kentucky Wesleyan Coll.
Kutztown Univ. of Pennsylvania
La Salle Univ. (PA)
Lewis Univ. (IL)
Lewis-Clark State Coll. (ID)
Lincoln Univ. (MO)
Lincoln Univ. (PA)
Lindenwood Univ. (MO)
Lipscomb Univ. (TN)
Long Island Univ.–C.W. Post Campus (NY)
Louisiana Coll.
Miami Univ.–Oxford (OH)
Michigan State Univ.
Mississippi Valley State Univ.
Missouri State Univ.
Murray State Univ. (KY)
New York Univ.
North Georgia Coll. and State Univ.
Northern Michigan Univ.
Northwest Missouri State Univ.
Oakland Univ. (MI)
Ohio State Univ.–Columbus
Park Univ. (MO)

Plymouth State Univ. (NH)
Point Park Univ. (PA)
Princeton Univ. (NJ)
Rhode Island Coll.
Roosevelt Univ. (IL)
Sage Colleges–Albany (NY)
Saginaw Valley State Univ. (MI)
Samford Univ. (AL)
San Diego State Univ.
Seattle Univ.
Shaw Univ. (NC)
Shenandoah Univ. (VA)
Shippensburg Univ. of Pennsylvania
Silver Lake Coll. (WI)
Sojourner-Douglass Coll. (MD)
Southern New Hampshire Univ.
Southwest Minnesota State Univ.
St. Ambrose Univ. (IA)
St. Cloud State Univ. (MN)
St. Francis Univ. (PA)
St. John's Univ. (NY)
St. Joseph's Univ. (PA)
St. Mary's Univ. of San Antonio (TX)
Stephen F. Austin State Univ. (TX)
Stonehill Coll. (MA)
Suffolk Univ. (MA)
Syracuse Univ. (NY)
Talladega Coll. (AL)
Texas State Univ.–San Marcos
Texas Woman's Univ.
Thomas Edison State Coll. (NJ)
Union Institute and Univ. (OH)
Univ. of Arizona
Univ. of Arkansas
Univ. of California–Riverside
Univ. of Central Arkansas
Univ. of Central Florida
Univ. of Denver
Univ. of Evansville (IN)
Univ. of Hawaii–West Oahu
Univ. of Kansas
Univ. of Kentucky
Univ. of La Verne (CA)
Univ. of Maine
Univ. of Maine–Augusta
Univ. of Massachusetts–Boston
Univ. of Michigan–Flint
Univ. of Missouri–St. Louis
Univ. of Nevada–Las Vegas
Univ. of New Haven (CT)
Univ. of North Carolina–Pembroke
Univ. of North Dakota
Univ. of North Texas
Univ. of Northern Iowa
Univ. of Oklahoma
Univ. of Oregon
Univ. of Pittsburgh
Univ. of San Francisco
Univ. of Southern California
Univ. of St. Thomas (MN)
Univ. of Tennessee
Univ. of Texas–Dallas
Univ. of Wisconsin–La Crosse
Univ. of Wisconsin–Stevens Point
Univ. of Wisconsin–Superior
Univ. of Wisconsin–Whitewater
Virginia Intermont Coll.
Virginia State Univ.
Washburn Univ. (KS)
Wayne State Univ. (MI)

Waynesburg Univ. (PA)
Wells Coll. (NY)
West Texas A&M Univ.
Western Carolina Univ. (NC)
Western Michigan Univ.
Western New Mexico Univ.
Western Oregon Univ.
York Coll. of Pennsylvania
Youngstown State Univ. (OH)

Public Administration and Social Service Professions

Cleveland State Univ.
Columbia Coll. (SC)
Eastern Michigan Univ.
Eastern Oregon Univ.
Elmira Coll. (NY)
Jacksonville State Univ. (AL)
Merrimack Coll. (MA)
Milligan Coll. (TN)
Mountain State Univ. (WV)
New York Univ.
Ohio Wesleyan Univ.
Pfeiffer Univ. (NC)
Quincy Univ. (IL)
Roosevelt Univ. (IL)
Samford Univ. (AL)
Seattle Univ.
Syracuse Univ. (NY)
Troy Univ. (AL)
Univ. at Albany–SUNY
Virginia Wesleyan Coll.

Public Health

Appalachian State Univ. (NC)
Baker Coll. of Flint (MI)
Bard Coll. at Simon's Rock (MA)
Bloomsburg Univ. of Pennsylvania
Boise State Univ. (ID)
Bowling Green State Univ. (OH)
Brown Univ. (RI)
California State Univ.–Long Beach
California State Univ.–Northridge
California State Univ.–Sacramento
Central Michigan Univ.
Central Washington Univ.
Chicago State Univ.
Coastal Carolina Univ. (SC)
Colorado State Univ.
Concordia Univ. (OR)
CUNY–York Coll.
D'Youville Coll. (NY)
Delaware State Univ.
Dickinson State Univ. (ND)
East Carolina Univ. (NC)
East Central Univ. (OK)
East Stroudsburg Univ. of Pennsylvania
East Tennessee State Univ.
Eastern Kentucky Univ.
Eastern Michigan Univ.
Eastern Washington Univ.
Elizabethtown Coll. (PA)
Emporia State Univ. (KS)
Georgetown Univ. (DC)
Georgia Southern Univ.
Grand Valley State Univ. (MI)
Harris-Stowe State Univ. (MO)

Hofstra Univ. (NY)
Illinois State Univ.
Indiana State Univ.
Indiana Univ. of Pennsylvania
Indiana Univ.–Bloomington
Indiana Univ.-Purdue Univ.–Fort Wayne
Indiana Univ.-Purdue Univ.–Indianapolis
Iowa Wesleyan Coll.
Ithaca Coll. (NY)
Jackson State Univ. (MS)
Johns Hopkins Univ. (MD)
Liberty Univ. (VA)
Louisiana State Univ.–Shreveport
Lynchburg Coll. (VA)
Malone Univ. (OH)
Mississippi Valley State Univ.
Missouri Southern State Univ.
Montana State Univ.–Northern
Montana Tech of the Univ. of Montana
Mountain State Univ. (WV)
New Mexico State Univ.
New York Univ.
North Carolina A&T State Univ.
North Carolina Central Univ.
Northern Arizona Univ.
Northwest Christian Univ. (OR)
Oakland Univ. (MI)
Ohio State Univ.–Columbus
Ohio Univ.
Oklahoma State Univ.
Old Dominion Univ. (VA)
Oregon State Univ.
Plymouth State Univ. (NH)
Purdue Univ.–West Lafayette (IN)
Quinnipiac Univ. (CT)
Richard Stockton Coll. of New Jersey
Robert Morris Univ. (PA)
Rutgers, the State Univ. of New Jersey–New Brunswick
Sage Colleges–Albany (NY)
Slippery Rock Univ. of Pennsylvania
Southeastern Louisiana Univ.
Southern Connecticut State Univ.
St. Cloud State Univ. (MN)
Temple Univ. (PA)
Tennessee State Univ.
Thomas Edison State Coll. (NJ)
Tulane Univ. (LA)
Univ. of Arkansas–Little Rock
Univ. of California–Berkeley
Univ. of Florida
Univ. of Georgia
Univ. of Illinois–Urbana-Champaign
Univ. of Kentucky
Univ. of Maine–Farmington
Univ. of Michigan–Flint
Univ. of Nevada–Las Vegas
Univ. of New Hampshire
Univ. of North Carolina–Asheville
Univ. of North Carolina–Chapel Hill
Univ. of North Carolina–Greensboro
Univ. of North Carolina–Pembroke
Univ. of Northern Colorado
Univ. of Scranton (PA)
Univ. of Southern California
Univ. of Southern Maine

Southwest Baptist Univ. (MO)
Univ. of Central Missouri
Univ. of Houston–Downtown
Univ. of New Haven (CT)
Univ. of North Dakota
Univ. of Texas–Tyler
Univ. of Wisconsin–Whitewater
Utah State Univ.

Radio, Television, and Digital Communication

Abilene Christian Univ. (TX)
American Univ. (DC)
Appalachian State Univ. (NC)
Arizona State Univ.
Arkansas State Univ.–Jonesboro
Ashland Univ. (OH)
Auburn Univ. (AL)
Ball State Univ. (IN)
Barry Univ. (FL)
Baylor Univ. (TX)
Belmont Univ. (TN)
Biola Univ. (CA)
Bowie State Univ. (MD)
Bradley Univ. (IL)
Butler Univ. (IN)
California Baptist Univ.
California State Univ.–Dominguez
    Hills
California State Univ.–Fullerton
California State Univ.–Los Angeles
California State Univ.–Northridge
California State Univ.–Sacramento
Calvin Coll. (MI)
Campbell Univ. (NC)
Campbellsville Univ. (KY)
Canisius Coll. (NY)
Capital Univ. (OH)
Cedarville Univ. (OH)
Central Michigan Univ.
Central State Univ. (OH)
Chicago State Univ.
Coll. of Notre Dame of Maryland
Coll. of the Ozarks (MO)
Columbia Coll. (IL)
Corcoran Coll. of Art and Design
    (DC)
Cornerstone Univ. (MI)
CUNY–Brooklyn Coll.
CUNY–City Coll.
Delaware State Univ.
Dixie State Coll. of Utah
Dordt Coll. (IA)
Drake Univ. (IA)
Eastern Kentucky Univ.
Eastern Mennonite Univ. (VA)
Eastern Nazarene Coll. (MA)
Emerson Coll. (MA)
Fitchburg State Coll. (MA)
Florida A&M Univ.
Florida Atlantic Univ.
George Washington Univ. (DC)
Georgia Institute of Technology
Georgia Southern Univ.
Grand Valley State Univ. (MI)
Grand View Univ. (IA)
Hampshire Coll. (MA)
Hardin-Simmons Univ. (TX)
Harding Univ. (AR)
Hawaii Pacific Univ.

Heidelberg Univ. (OH)
Hofstra Univ. (NY)
Holy Names Univ. (CA)
Howard Payne Univ. (TX)
Howard Univ. (DC)
Humboldt State Univ. (CA)
Huntington Univ. (IN)
Indiana State Univ.
Indiana Univ.-Purdue Univ.–
    Indianapolis
Iona Coll. (NY)
Ithaca Coll. (NY)
Jacksonville State Univ. (AL)
John Brown Univ. (AR)
Juniata Coll. (PA)
Kent State Univ. (OH)
Kutztown Univ. of Pennsylvania
Lasell Coll. (MA)
Lebanon Valley Coll. (PA)
LeTourneau Univ. (TX)
Long Island Univ.–C.W. Post
    Campus (NY)
Lyndon State Coll. (VT)
Madonna Univ. (MI)
Mansfield Univ. of Pennsylvania
Marietta Coll. (OH)
Marist Coll. (NY)
Marywood Univ. (PA)
Master's Coll. and Seminary (CA)
McPherson Coll. (KS)
Messiah Coll. (PA)
Michigan State Univ.
Minot State Univ. (ND)
Missouri State Univ.
Montclair State Univ. (NJ)
Morningside Coll. (IA)
Murray State Univ. (KY)
National Univ. (CA)
New York Institute of Technology
New York Univ.
North Carolina A&T State Univ.
North Central Coll. (IL)
North Dakota State Univ.
Northern Arizona Univ.
Northern Kentucky Univ.
Northern Michigan Univ.
Northwest Missouri State Univ.
Northwestern Coll. (IA)
Northwestern Coll. (MN)
Northwestern Univ. (IL)
Ohio Univ.
Oklahoma Christian Univ.
Oral Roberts Univ. (OK)
Otterbein Coll. (OH)
Palm Beach Atlantic Univ. (FL)
Pepperdine Univ. (CA)
Philadelphia Univ.
Prescott Coll. (AZ)
Purdue Univ.–Calumet (IN)
Roosevelt Univ. (IL)
Sage Colleges–Albany (NY)
Sam Houston State Univ. (TX)
San Diego State Univ.
San Jose State Univ. (CA)
Savannah Coll. of Art and Design
    (GA)
Southern Illinois Univ.–Carbondale
Southern Methodist Univ. (TX)
Southern New Hampshire Univ.
Southern Oregon Univ.
Southwest Minnesota State Univ.

St. Ambrose Univ. (IA)
St. Edward's Univ. (TX)
St. Joseph's Coll. (ME)
St. Mary-of-the-Woods Coll. (IN)
Stephen F. Austin State Univ. (TX)
Stephens Coll. (MO)
SUNY–Fredonia
SUNY–Oswego
Syracuse Univ. (NY)
Temple Univ. (PA)
Texas A&M Univ.–Commerce
Texas Christian Univ.
Texas State Univ.–San Marcos
Texas Tech Univ.
Texas Wesleyan Univ.
Towson Univ. (MD)
Trevecca Nazarene Univ. (TN)
Troy Univ. (AL)
Univ. of Akron (OH)
Univ. of Alabama
Univ. of Arkansas–Little Rock
Univ. of Central Florida
Univ. of Central Missouri
Univ. of Dayton (OH)
Univ. of Denver
Univ. of Florida
Univ. of Houston
Univ. of Kentucky
Univ. of La Verne (CA)
Univ. of Miami (FL)
Univ. of Michigan–Ann Arbor
Univ. of Montana
Univ. of Montevallo (AL)
Univ. of New Hampshire
Univ. of North Texas
Univ. of Northern Iowa
Univ. of Oregon
Univ. of Scranton (PA)
Univ. of South Carolina
Univ. of Southern Indiana
Univ. of Southern Mississippi
Univ. of Tampa (FL)
Univ. of Tennessee
Univ. of Texas–Arlington
Univ. of Texas–Austin
Univ. of Wisconsin–Oshkosh
Utah Valley Univ.
Valparaiso Univ. (IN)
Vanguard Univ. of Southern
    California
Waldorf Coll. (IA)
Washington State Univ.
Wayne State Univ. (MI)
Weber State Univ. (UT)
Western Illinois Univ.
Western Kentucky Univ.
Western Michigan Univ.
Westminster Coll. (PA)
Wilkes Univ. (PA)
William Jewell Coll. (MO)
William Woods Univ. (MO)
Xavier Univ. (OH)
York Coll. of Pennsylvania
Youngstown State Univ. (OH)

Real Estate

Angelo State Univ. (TX)
Baylor Univ. (TX)
California State Univ.–Sacramento
Clarion Univ. of Pennsylvania

CUNY–Baruch Coll.
CUNY–Lehman Coll.
Eastern Kentucky Univ.
Florida Atlantic Univ.
Florida International Univ.
Florida State Univ.
Georgia State Univ.
La Roche Coll. (PA)
Marquette Univ. (WI)
Marylhurst Univ. (OR)
Mississippi State Univ.
Morehead State Univ. (KY)
New Mexico State Univ.
New York Univ.
Ohio State Univ.–Columbus
St. Cloud State Univ. (MN)
Temple Univ. (PA)
Texas Christian Univ.
Thomas Edison State Coll. (NJ)
Univ. of Central Oklahoma
Univ. of Connecticut
Univ. of Denver
Univ. of Florida
Univ. of Georgia
Univ. of Illinois–Urbana-Champaign
Univ. of Mississippi
Univ. of Nebraska–Omaha
Univ. of Nevada–Las Vegas
Univ. of North Texas
Univ. of Northern Iowa
Univ. of Pennsylvania
Univ. of South Carolina
Univ. of St. Thomas (MN)
Univ. of Texas–Arlington
Univ. of West Georgia
Univ. of Wisconsin–Madison
Washington State Univ.
Weber State Univ. (UT)

Rehabilitation and Therapeutic Professions

Alabama State Univ.
Alcorn State Univ. (MS)
Alderson-Broaddus Coll. (WV)
Alvernia Univ. (PA)
Alverno Coll. (WI)
Anna Maria Coll. (MA)
Appalachian State Univ. (NC)
Arizona State Univ.
Arkansas Tech Univ.
Assumption Coll. (MA)
Baker Coll. of Flint (MI)
Baldwin-Wallace Coll. (OH)
Barry Univ. (FL)
Bay Path Coll. (MA)
Bellarmine Univ. (KY)
Boston Univ.
Bowling Green State Univ. (OH)
Brenau Univ. (GA)
Bridgewater State Coll. (MA)
California State Univ.–Long Beach
California State Univ.–Los Angeles
California State Univ.–Sacramento
California State Univ.–San
    Bernardino
Calvin Coll. (MI)
Capital Univ. (OH)
Carlow Univ. (PA)
Cedar Crest Coll. (PA)
Central Michigan Univ.

Chapman Univ. (CA)
Charleston Southern Univ. (SC)
Chicago State Univ.
Cleveland State Univ.
Coll. of Santa Fe (NM)
Coll. of Wooster (OH)
CUNY–Lehman Coll.
CUNY–York Coll.
D'Youville Coll. (NY)
Daemen Coll. (NY)
Dominican Coll. (NY)
Dominican Univ. (IL)
Dominican Univ. of California
Duquesne Univ. (PA)
East Carolina Univ. (NC)
East Stroudsburg Univ. of
    Pennsylvania
Eastern Kentucky Univ.
Eastern Michigan Univ.
Eastern Washington Univ.
Edgewood Coll. (WI)
Elizabethtown Coll. (PA)
Emmanuel Coll. (MA)
Emporia State Univ. (KS)
Endicott Coll. (MA)
Eureka Coll. (IL)
Florida Gulf Coast Univ.
Florida International Univ.
Florida State Univ.
Fresno Pacific Univ. (CA)
Gallaudet Univ. (DC)
Gannon Univ. (PA)
Georgia Coll. & State Univ.
Green Mountain Coll. (VT)
Harding Univ. (AR)
Hilbert Coll. (NY)
Howard Univ. (DC)
Huntington Univ. (IN)
Illinois Coll.
Immaculata Univ. (PA)
Indiana Institute of Technology
Indiana Univ. East
Indiana Univ. Northwest
Indiana Univ.–Bloomington
Indiana Univ.–Kokomo
Indiana Univ.-Purdue Univ.–Fort
    Wayne
Indiana Wesleyan Univ.
Ithaca Coll. (NY)
Jackson State Univ. (MS)
Keuka Coll. (NY)
Lenoir-Rhyne Univ. (NC)
Lesley Univ. (MA)
Lincoln Univ. (PA)
Long Island Univ.–C.W. Post
    Campus (NY)
Longwood Univ. (VA)
Louisiana Coll.
Loyola Marymount Univ. (CA)
Loyola Univ. New Orleans
Marian Univ. (WI)
Marygrove Coll. (MI)
Marylhurst Univ. (OR)
Maryville Univ. of St. Louis (MO)
Marywood Univ. (PA)
Master's Coll. and Seminary (CA)
McKendree Univ. (IL)
Mercyhurst Coll. (PA)
Messiah Coll. (PA)
Michigan State Univ.
Midwestern State Univ. (TX)

Millikin Univ. (IL)
Misericordia Univ. (PA)
Mississippi Univ. for Women
Montana State Univ.–Billings
Montclair State Univ. (NJ)
Moravian Coll. (PA)
Mount Aloysius Coll. (PA)
Mount Mary Coll. (WI)
Nazareth Coll. (NY)
New York Institute of Technology
Newman Univ. (KS)
North Georgia Coll. and State Univ.
Northeastern Univ. (MA)
Northern Illinois Univ.
Northwest Nazarene Univ. (ID)
Oakland Univ. (MI)
Ohio State Univ.–Columbus
Oral Roberts Univ. (OK)
Pennsylvania State Univ.–Univ. Park
Prescott Coll. (AZ)
Queens Univ. of Charlotte (NC)
Quinnipiac Univ. (CT)
Regis Univ. (CO)
Russell Sage Coll. (NY)
Sage Colleges–Albany (NY)
Salem State Coll. (MA)
Sam Houston State Univ. (TX)
San Jose State Univ. (CA)
Seton Hill Univ. (PA)
Shaw Univ. (NC)
Shenandoah Univ. (VA)
Slippery Rock Univ. of Pennsylvania
Southern Adventist Univ. (TN)
Southern Illinois Univ.–Carbondale
Southern Methodist Univ. (TX)
Southern Univ. and A&M Coll. (LA)
Spalding Univ. (KY)
Spring Hill Coll. (AL)
Springfield Coll. (MA)
St. Ambrose Univ. (IA)
St. Andrews Presbyterian Coll. (NC)
St. Catherine Univ. (MN)
St. Francis Univ. (PA)
St. Louis Univ.
St. Mary's Univ. of Minnesota
St. Mary-of-the-Woods Coll. (IN)
St. Vincent Coll. (PA)
Stephen F. Austin State Univ. (TX)
Temple Univ. (PA)
Tennessee State Univ.
Texas Woman's Univ.
Thomas Univ. (GA)
Touro Coll. (NY)
Towson Univ. (MD)
Troy Univ. (AL)
Tuskegee Univ. (AL)
Unity Coll. (ME)
Univ. at Buffalo–SUNY
Univ. of Akron (OH)
Univ. of Arkansas–Little Rock
Univ. of Arkansas–Pine Bluff
Univ. of Central Missouri
Univ. of Connecticut
Univ. of Dayton (OH)
Univ. of Evansville (IN)
Univ. of Findlay (OH)
Univ. of Florida
Univ. of Georgia
Univ. of Hartford (CT)
Univ. of Illinois–Urbana-Champaign
Univ. of Indianapolis

Univ. of Iowa
Univ. of Kansas
Univ. of Kentucky
Univ. of Louisville (KY)
Univ. of Maine–Farmington
Univ. of Maryland–Coll. Park
Univ. of Maryland–Eastern Shore
Univ. of Massachusetts–Lowell
Univ. of Miami (FL)
Univ. of Michigan–Flint
Univ. of Minnesota–Twin Cities
Univ. of Missouri
Univ. of Nevada–Las Vegas
Univ. of New Hampshire
Univ. of North Carolina–
　　Wilmington
Univ. of North Dakota
Univ. of North Texas
Univ. of Northern Colorado
Univ. of Pittsburgh
Univ. of Pittsburgh–Bradford
Univ. of Scranton (PA)
Univ. of Southern California
Univ. of Southern Indiana
Univ. of Southern Maine
Univ. of Tennessee
Univ. of Texas–El Paso
Univ. of Texas–Pan American
Univ. of the Incarnate Word (TX)
Univ. of the Pacific (CA)
Univ. of Toledo (OH)
Univ. of Utah
Univ. of Washington
Univ. of Wisconsin–Eau Claire
Univ. of Wisconsin–La Crosse
Univ. of Wisconsin–Madison
Univ. of Wisconsin–Milwaukee
Univ. of Wisconsin–Stout
Univ. of Wisconsin–Superior
Utah State Univ.
Utica Coll. (NY)
Wartburg Coll. (IA)
Wayne State Univ. (MI)
West Texas A&M Univ.
Western Carolina Univ. (NC)
Western Michigan Univ.
Western New Mexico Univ.
Western Oregon Univ.
Western Washington Univ.
Wheeling Jesuit Univ. (WV)
Wilberforce Univ. (OH)
William Carey Univ. (MS)
Wilson Coll. (PA)
Winston-Salem State Univ. (NC)
Worcester State Coll. (MA)
Wright State Univ. (OH)
York Coll. of Pennsylvania

Religion/Religious Studies

Adrian Coll. (MI)
Agnes Scott Coll. (GA)
Albion Coll. (MI)
Albright Coll. (PA)
Allegheny Coll. (PA)
Allen Univ. (SC)
Alma Coll. (MI)
Alverno Coll. (WI)
American Jewish Univ. (CA)
American Univ. (DC)

Amherst Coll. (MA)
Anderson Univ. (SC)
Anderson Univ. (IN)
Andrews Univ. (MI)
Appalachian State Univ. (NC)
Aquinas Coll. (MI)
Arizona State Univ.
Ashland Univ. (OH)
Atlantic Union Coll. (MA)
Augsburg Coll. (MN)
Augustana Coll. (SD)
Augustana Coll. (IL)
Aurora Univ. (IL)
Austin Coll. (TX)
Averett Univ. (VA)
Avila Univ. (MO)
Baker Univ. (KS)
Baldwin-Wallace Coll. (OH)
Ball State Univ. (IN)
Barnard Coll. (NY)
Bates Coll. (ME)
Baylor Univ. (TX)
Belhaven Univ. (MS)
Belmont Univ. (TN)
Beloit Coll. (WI)
Benedictine Coll. (KS)
Berea Coll. (KY)
Bethany Coll. (WV)
Bethel Coll. (KS)
Bethel Coll. (IN)
Binghamton Univ.–SUNY
Biola Univ. (CA)
Bloomfield Coll. (NJ)
Bluefield Coll. (VA)
Bluffton Univ. (OH)
Boston Univ.
Bowdoin Coll. (ME)
Bradley Univ. (IL)
Brevard Coll. (NC)
Brewton-Parker Coll. (GA)
Brown Univ. (RI)
Bryan Coll. (TN)
Bryn Athyn Coll. of the New Church
　　(PA)
Bryn Mawr Coll. (PA)
Bucknell Univ. (PA)
Butler Univ. (IN)
Cabrini Coll. (PA)
California Baptist Univ.
California Lutheran Univ.
California State Univ.–Bakersfield
California State Univ.–Chico
California State Univ.–Fullerton
California State Univ.–Long Beach
California State Univ.–Northridge
California State Univ.–Sacramento
Calumet Coll. of St. Joseph (IN)
Calvin Coll. (MI)
Canisius Coll. (NY)
Capital Univ. (OH)
Cardinal Stritch Univ. (WI)
Carleton Coll. (MN)
Carroll Univ. (WI)
Carson-Newman Coll. (TN)
Carthage Coll. (WI)
Case Western Reserve Univ. (OH)
Catawba Coll. (NC)
Catholic Univ. of America (DC)
Centenary Coll. of Louisiana
Central Christian Coll. (KS)
Central Coll. (IA)

Central Methodist Univ. (MO)
Central Michigan Univ.
Central Washington Univ.
Centre Coll. (KY)
Chaminade Univ. of Honolulu
Chapman Univ. (CA)
Charleston Southern Univ. (SC)
Chowan Univ. (NC)
Claremont McKenna Coll. (CA)
Clarke Univ. (IA)
Cleveland State Univ.
Coe Coll. (IA)
Colby Coll. (ME)
Colgate Univ. (NY)
Coll. of Charleston (SC)
Coll. of Idaho (ID)
Coll. of Mount St. Joseph (OH)
Coll. of Mount St. Vincent (NY)
Coll. of Notre Dame of Maryland
Coll. of Santa Fe (NM)
Coll. of St. Rose (NY)
Coll. of St. Scholastica (MN)
Coll. of the Holy Cross (MA)
Coll. of William and Mary (VA)
Coll. of Wooster (OH)
Colorado Coll.
Columbia Coll. (SC)
Columbia Univ. (NY)
Concordia Coll. (NY)
Concordia Coll.–Moorhead (MN)
Concordia Univ. (CA)
Concordia Univ. (MI)
Connecticut Coll.
Converse Coll. (SC)
Cornell Coll. (IA)
Cornell Univ. (NY)
Cornerstone Univ. (MI)
Creighton Univ. (NE)
Culver-Stockton Coll. (MO)
CUNY–Brooklyn Coll.
CUNY–Hunter Coll.
CUNY–Lehman Coll.
CUNY–Queens Coll.
Daemen Coll. (NY)
Dakota Wesleyan Univ. (SD)
Dana Coll. (NE)
Dartmouth Coll. (NH)
Davidson Coll. (NC)
Davis and Elkins Coll. (WV)
Defiance Coll. (OH)
Denison Univ. (OH)
DePaul Univ. (IL)
DePauw Univ. (IN)
Dickinson Coll. (PA)
Dominican Univ. (IL)
Dominican Univ. of California
Drake Univ. (IA)
Drew Univ. (NJ)
Drury Univ. (MO)
Duke Univ. (NC)
Earlham Coll. (IN)
East Texas Baptist Univ.
Eastern Nazarene Coll. (MA)
Eastern New Mexico Univ.
Eckerd Coll. (FL)
Edgewood Coll. (WI)
Elizabethtown Coll. (PA)
Elmhurst Coll. (IL)
Elon Univ. (NC)
Emmanuel Coll. (MA)
Emory and Henry Coll. (VA)

Emory Univ. (GA)
Erskine Coll. (SC)
Evangel Univ. (MO)
Fairfield Univ. (CT)
Ferrum Coll. (VA)
Florida Atlantic Univ.
Florida International Univ.
Florida Southern Coll.
Florida State Univ.
Fordham Univ. (NY)
Franklin and Marshall Coll. (PA)
Franklin Coll. (IN)
Friends Univ. (KS)
Furman Univ. (SC)
Gallaudet Univ. (DC)
Gardner-Webb Univ. (NC)
George Fox Univ. (OR)
George Mason Univ. (VA)
George Washington Univ. (DC)
Georgetown Coll. (KY)
Georgetown Univ. (DC)
Georgia State Univ.
Georgian Court Univ. (NJ)
Gettysburg Coll. (PA)
Gonzaga Univ. (WA)
Goshen Coll. (IN)
Goucher Coll. (MD)
Graceland Univ. (IA)
Grand View Univ. (IA)
Gratz Coll. (PA)
Greensboro Coll. (NC)
Greenville Coll. (IL)
Grinnell Coll. (IA)
Grove City Coll. (PA)
Guilford Coll. (NC)
Gustavus Adolphus Coll. (MN)
Hamilton Coll. (NY)
Hamline Univ. (MN)
Hampden-Sydney Coll. (VA)
Hampshire Coll. (MA)
Hanover Coll. (IN)
Hartwick Coll. (NY)
Harvard Univ. (MA)
Haverford Coll. (PA)
Heidelberg Univ. (OH)
Hendrix Coll. (AR)
High Point Univ. (NC)
Hillsdale Coll. (MI)
Hiram Coll. (OH)
Hobart and William Smith Colleges
　　(NY)
Hofstra Univ. (NY)
Hollins Univ. (VA)
Holy Family Univ. (PA)
Holy Names Univ. (CA)
Hood Coll. (MD)
Hope Coll. (MI)
Houghton Coll. (NY)
Houston Baptist Univ.
Howard Payne Univ. (TX)
Humboldt State Univ. (CA)
Huntingdon Coll. (AL)
Huntington Univ. (IN)
Illinois Coll.
Illinois Wesleyan Univ.
Indiana Univ. of Pennsylvania
Indiana Univ.–Bloomington
Indiana Univ.–South Bend
Indiana Univ.-Purdue Univ.–
　　Indianapolis
Iona Coll. (NY)

Iowa State Univ.
Iowa Wesleyan Coll.
Jarvis Christian Coll. (TX)
John Carroll Univ. (OH)
Judson Coll. (AL)
Juniata Coll. (PA)
Kalamazoo Coll. (MI)
Kansas Wesleyan Univ.
Kentucky Wesleyan Coll.
Kenyon Coll. (OH)
La Roche Coll. (PA)
La Salle Univ. (PA)
La Sierra Univ. (CA)
Lafayette Coll. (PA)
LaGrange Coll. (GA)
Lakeland Coll. (WI)
Lambuth Univ. (TN)
Lane Coll. (TN)
Lawrence Univ. (WI)
Le Moyne Coll. (NY)
Lebanon Valley Coll. (PA)
Lees-McRae Coll. (NC)
Lehigh Univ. (PA)
Lenoir-Rhyne Univ. (NC)
Lewis & Clark Coll. (OR)
Liberty Univ. (VA)
Lincoln Univ. (PA)
Lindenwood Univ. (MO)
Lindsey Wilson Coll. (KY)
Linfield Coll. (OR)
Loras Coll. (IA)
Lourdes Coll. (OH)
Loyola Univ. Maryland
Loyola Univ. New Orleans
Luther Coll. (IA)
Lycoming Coll. (PA)
Lynchburg Coll. (VA)
Macalester Coll. (MN)
MacMurray Coll. (IL)
Madonna Univ. (MI)
Manchester Coll. (IN)
Manhattan Coll. (NY)
Manhattanville Coll. (NY)
Marian Univ. (IN)
Mars Hill Coll. (NC)
Martin Univ. (IN)
Marygrove Coll. (MI)
Marylhurst Univ. (OR)
Marymount Univ. (VA)
Maryville Coll. (TN)
Marywood Univ. (PA)
McDaniel Coll. (MD)
McKendree Univ. (IL)
McMurry Univ. (TX)
Mercyhurst Coll. (PA)
Meredith Coll. (NC)
Merrimack Coll. (MA)
Messiah Coll. (PA)
Methodist Univ. (NC)
Miami Univ.–Oxford (OH)
Michigan State Univ.
MidAmerica Nazarene Univ. (KS)
Middlebury Coll. (VT)
Millsaps Coll. (MS)
Mississippi Coll.
Missouri Baptist Univ.
Missouri State Univ.
Molloy Coll. (NY)
Monmouth Coll. (IL)
Montclair State Univ. (NJ)
Moravian Coll. (PA)

Morehead State Univ. (KY)
Morehouse Coll. (GA)
Morningside Coll. (IA)
Mount Holyoke Coll. (MA)
Mount Marty Coll. (SD)
Mount Mary Coll. (WI)
Mount Mercy Coll. (IA)
Mount Olive Coll. (NC)
Mount St. Mary's Coll. (CA)
Mount Vernon Nazarene Univ.
   (OH)
Muhlenberg Coll. (PA)
Muskingum Univ. (OH)
Nazareth Coll. (NY)
Nebraska Wesleyan Univ.
New School (NY)
New York Univ.
Niagara Univ. (NY)
North Carolina State Univ.–Raleigh
North Carolina Wesleyan Coll.
North Central Coll. (IL)
North Greenville Univ. (SC)
Northern Arizona Univ.
Northland Coll. (WI)
Northwestern Coll. (IA)
Northwestern Univ. (IL)
Notre Dame de Namur Univ. (CA)
Nyack Coll. (NY)
Oakland City Univ. (IN)
Oakwood Univ. (AL)
Oberlin Coll. (OH)
Occidental Coll. (CA)
Ohio Northern Univ.
Ohio State Univ.–Columbus
Ohio Univ.
Ohio Wesleyan Univ.
Oklahoma Baptist Univ.
Oklahoma City Univ.
Oklahoma Wesleyan Univ.
Olivet Nazarene Univ. (IL)
Otterbein Coll. (OH)
Our Lady of the Lake Univ. (TX)
Pacific Lutheran Univ. (WA)
Pacific Union Coll. (CA)
Paine Coll. (GA)
Palm Beach Atlantic Univ. (FL)
Pennsylvania State Univ.–Univ. Park
Pepperdine Univ. (CA)
Pfeiffer Univ. (NC)
Pikeville Coll. (KY)
Point Loma Nazarene Univ. (CA)
Pomona Coll. (CA)
Presbyterian Coll. (SC)
Prescott Coll. (AZ)
Princeton Univ. (NJ)
Principia Coll. (IL)
Purdue Univ.–West Lafayette (IN)
Randolph Coll. (VA)
Randolph-Macon Coll. (VA)
Reed Coll. (OR)
Reinhardt Univ. (GA)
Rhodes Coll. (TN)
Rice Univ. (TX)
Ripon Coll. (WI)
Roanoke Coll. (VA)
Rockhurst Univ. (MO)
Rollins Coll. (FL)
Rosemont Coll. (PA)
Rutgers, the State Univ. of New
   Jersey–New Brunswick
Sacred Heart Univ. (CT)

Salem Coll. (NC)
Salve Regina Univ. (RI)
Samford Univ. (AL)
San Diego State Univ.
San Jose State Univ. (CA)
Santa Clara Univ. (CA)
Schreiner Univ. (TX)
Scripps Coll. (CA)
Seattle Univ.
Seton Hall Univ. (NJ)
Seton Hill Univ. (PA)
Sewanee–Univ. of the South (TN)
Shenandoah Univ. (VA)
Shorter Coll. (GA)
Siena Coll. (NY)
Simpson Coll. (IA)
Simpson Univ. (CA)
Skidmore Coll. (NY)
Smith Coll. (MA)
Southern Adventist Univ. (TN)
Southern Methodist Univ. (TX)
Southern Wesleyan Univ. (SC)
Southwestern Adventist Univ. (TX)
Southwestern Univ. (TX)
Spelman Coll. (GA)
Spring Arbor Univ. (MI)
St. Andrews Presbyterian Coll. (NC)
St. Francis Coll. (NY)
St. Francis Univ. (PA)
St. Gregory's Univ. (OK)
St. John Fisher Coll. (NY)
St. Joseph Coll. (CT)
St. Joseph's Univ. (PA)
St. Lawrence Univ. (NY)
St. Martin's Univ. (WA)
St. Mary's Coll. (IN)
St. Mary's Coll. of California
St. Mary's Coll. of Maryland
St. Norbert Coll. (WI)
St. Olaf Coll. (MN)
St. Paul's Coll. (VA)
St. Peter's Coll. (NJ)
St. Thomas Univ. (FL)
St. Xavier Univ. (IL)
Stanford Univ. (CA)
Stetson Univ. (FL)
Stonehill Coll. (MA)
SUNY–Stony Brook
Susquehanna Univ. (PA)
Swarthmore Coll. (PA)
Syracuse Univ. (NY)
Tabor Coll. (KS)
Temple Univ. (PA)
Tennessee Wesleyan Coll.
Texas Christian Univ.
Texas Coll.
Texas Wesleyan Univ.
Thiel Coll. (PA)
Thomas Edison State Coll. (NJ)
Thomas More Coll. (KY)
Touro Coll. (NY)
Transylvania Univ. (KY)
Trevecca Nazarene Univ. (TN)
Trinity Coll. (CT)
Tufts Univ. (MA)
Tulane Univ. (LA)
Union Coll. (NE)
Union Coll. (KY)
Union Univ. (TN)
Univ. at Albany–SUNY
Univ. of Alabama

Univ. of Arizona
Univ. of California–Berkeley
Univ. of California–Davis
Univ. of California–Los Angeles
Univ. of California–Riverside
Univ. of California–Santa Barbara
Univ. of Central Arkansas
Univ. of Colorado–Boulder
Univ. of Dayton (OH)
Univ. of Denver
Univ. of Detroit Mercy
Univ. of Dubuque (IA)
Univ. of Evansville (IN)
Univ. of Findlay (OH)
Univ. of Florida
Univ. of Georgia
Univ. of Hartford (CT)
Univ. of Hawaii–Hilo
Univ. of Hawaii–Manoa
Univ. of Illinois–Urbana-Champaign
Univ. of Indianapolis
Univ. of Iowa
Univ. of Kansas
Univ. of La Verne (CA)
Univ. of Mary (ND)
Univ. of Mary Hardin-Baylor (TX)
Univ. of Maryland–Coll. Park
Univ. of Massachusetts–Amherst
Univ. of Miami (FL)
Univ. of Michigan–Ann Arbor
Univ. of Minnesota–Twin Cities
Univ. of Missouri
Univ. of Mobile (AL)
Univ. of Mount Union (OH)
Univ. of Nebraska–Omaha
Univ. of New Mexico
Univ. of North Carolina–Asheville
Univ. of North Carolina–Chapel Hill
Univ. of North Carolina–Charlotte
Univ. of North Carolina–
   Greensboro
Univ. of North Dakota
Univ. of Northern Iowa
Univ. of Oklahoma
Univ. of Oregon
Univ. of Pennsylvania
Univ. of Pittsburgh
Univ. of Puget Sound (WA)
Univ. of Redlands (CA)
Univ. of Richmond (VA)
Univ. of Rochester (NY)
Univ. of San Diego
Univ. of San Francisco
Univ. of Scranton (PA)
Univ. of South Carolina
Univ. of South Florida
Univ. of Southern California
Univ. of Southern Mississippi
Univ. of St. Francis (IN)
Univ. of St. Thomas (MN)
Univ. of Tennessee
Univ. of Texas–Austin
Univ. of the Cumberlands (KY)
Univ. of the Incarnate Word (TX)
Univ. of the Pacific (CA)
Univ. of Toledo (OH)
Univ. of Tulsa (OK)
Univ. of Vermont
Univ. of Virginia
Univ. of Washington
Univ. of West Florida

Univ. of Wisconsin–Eau Claire
Univ. of Wisconsin–Madison
Univ. of Wisconsin–Milwaukee
Univ. of Wisconsin–Oshkosh
Ursuline Coll. (OH)
Vanguard Univ. of Southern
   California
Vassar Coll. (NY)
Villanova Univ. (PA)
Virginia Commonwealth Univ.
Virginia Intermont Coll.
Virginia Union Univ.
Virginia Wesleyan Coll.
Viterbo Univ. (WI)
Wabash Coll. (IN)
Wake Forest Univ. (NC)
Warner Pacific Coll. (OR)
Warren Wilson Coll. (NC)
Wartburg Coll. (IA)
Washburn Univ. (KS)
Washington and Lee Univ. (VA)
Washington State Univ.
Washington Univ. in St. Louis
Wayland Baptist Univ. (TX)
Webster Univ. (MO)
Wellesley Coll. (MA)
Wells Coll. (NY)
Wesleyan Coll. (GA)
Wesleyan Univ. (CT)
West Chester Univ. of Pennsylvania
West Virginia Wesleyan Coll.
Western Kentucky Univ.
Western Michigan Univ.
Westminster Coll. (PA)
Westminster Coll. (MO)
Westmont Coll. (CA)
Wheaton Coll. (MA)
Whitman Coll. (WA)
Whittier Coll. (CA)
Whitworth Univ. (WA)
Willamette Univ. (OR)
William Jewell Coll. (MO)
Williams Coll. (MA)
Wingate Univ. (NC)
Wittenberg Univ. (OH)
Wofford Coll. (SC)
Wright State Univ. (OH)
Xavier Univ. (OH)
Yale Univ. (CT)
Yeshiva Univ. (NY)
Youngstown State Univ. (OH)

Religious Education

American Jewish Univ. (CA)
Asbury Univ. (KY)
Azusa Pacific Univ. (CA)
Bethel Coll. (IN)
Biola Univ. (CA)
Bryan Coll. (TN)
Campbellsville Univ. (KY)
Carthage Coll. (WI)
Cedarville Univ. (OH)
Coll. of Mount St. Joseph (OH)
Columbia Coll. (SC)
Concordia Univ. (MI)
Concordia Univ. (NE)
Concordia Univ. (OR)
Concordia Univ. Texas
Concordia Univ.–St. Paul (MN)
Corban Univ. (OR)

Cornerstone Univ. (MI)
Crown Coll. (MN)
Dallas Baptist Univ.
Davis and Elkins Coll. (WV)
East Texas Baptist Univ.
Eastern Nazarene Coll. (MA)
Erskine Coll. (SC)
Franciscan Univ. of Steubenville (OH)
Free Will Baptist Bible Coll. (TN)
Harding Univ. (AR)
Houghton Coll. (NY)
Howard Payne Univ. (TX)
Huntington Univ. (IN)
Indiana Wesleyan Univ.
La Roche Coll. (PA)
LaGrange Coll. (GA)
Liberty Univ. (VA)
Louisiana Coll.
Loyola Univ. Chicago
Malone Univ. (OH)
Marian Univ. (IN)
Master's Coll. and Seminary (CA)
Mercyhurst Coll. (PA)
Messiah Coll. (PA)
Mid-Continent Univ. (KY)
MidAmerica Nazarene Univ. (KS)
Missouri Baptist Univ.
Morris Coll. (SC)
Mount Mary Coll. (WI)
Mountain State Univ. (WV)
North Park Univ. (IL)
Northwestern Coll. (IA)
Nyack Coll. (NY)
Oklahoma Christian Univ.
Olivet Nazarene Univ. (IL)
Oral Roberts Univ. (OK)
Patten Univ. (CA)
Pfeiffer Univ. (NC)
Regis Univ. (CO)
Seattle Pacific Univ.
Seton Hall Univ. (NJ)
Simpson Univ. (CA)
Southern Adventist Univ. (TN)
Southern Nazarene Univ. (OK)
Southwest Baptist Univ. (MO)
Southwestern Assemblies of God Univ. (TX)
St. Edward's Univ. (TX)
St. Mary's Univ. of Minnesota
St. Vincent Coll. (PA)
Sterling Coll. (KS)
Taylor Univ. (IN)
Texas Wesleyan Univ.
Toccoa Falls Coll. (GA)
Union Coll. (NE)
Univ. of California–San Diego
Univ. of the Cumberlands (KY)
Vanguard Univ. of Southern Cal.
Washington Adventist Univ. (MD)
Wayland Baptist Univ. (TX)
West Virginia Wesleyan Coll.
Westminster Coll. (PA)
Wheaton Coll. (IL)
Wheeling Jesuit Univ. (WV)
Williams Baptist Coll. (AR)

Religious/Sacred Music

Anderson Univ. (SC)
Anderson Univ. (IN)

Aquinas Coll. (MI)
Baylor Univ. (TX)
Bethel Coll. (IN)
Bethel Univ. (MN)
Biola Univ. (CA)
Bluefield Coll. (VA)
Calvin Coll. (MI)
Campbellsville Univ. (KY)
Carson-Newman Coll. (TN)
Cedarville Univ. (OH)
Central Baptist Coll. (AR)
Central Christian Coll. (KS)
Charleston Southern Univ. (SC)
Clearwater Christian Coll. (FL)
Coll. of the Ozarks (MO)
Concordia Coll. (NY)
Concordia Univ. (NE)
Concordia Univ. (MI)
Concordia Univ. Texas
Concordia Univ.–St. Paul (MN)
Corban Univ. (OR)
Crown Coll. (MN)
Dordt Coll. (IA)
East Texas Baptist Univ.
Eastern Nazarene Coll. (MA)
Emmanuel Coll. (GA)
Franciscan Univ. of Steubenville (OH)
Free Will Baptist Bible Coll. (TN)
Furman Univ. (SC)
Hannibal-LaGrange Coll. (MO)
Hardin-Simmons Univ. (TX)
Hope International Univ. (CA)
Howard Payne Univ. (TX)
Huntington Univ. (IN)
Indiana Wesleyan Univ.
Jacksonville Univ. (FL)
John Brown Univ. (AR)
Judson Univ. (IL)
Lambuth Univ. (TN)
Lenoir-Rhyne Univ. (NC)
Liberty Univ. (VA)
Lincoln Univ. (MO)
Louisiana Coll.
Malone Univ. (OH)
Maranatha Baptist Bible Coll. (WI)
Marian Univ. (IN)
MidAmerica Nazarene Univ. (KS)
Mississippi Coll.
Missouri Baptist Univ.
Newberry Coll. (SC)
North Central Univ. (MN)
North Greenville Univ. (SC)
Northwest Univ. (WA)
Nyack Coll. (NY)
Oklahoma City Univ.
Oklahoma Wesleyan Univ.
Oral Roberts Univ. (OK)
Ouachita Baptist Univ. (AR)
Palm Beach Atlantic Univ. (FL)
Pfeiffer Univ. (NC)
Point Loma Nazarene Univ. (CA)
Presbyterian Coll. (SC)
Rider Univ. (NJ)
Samford Univ. (AL)
Seton Hill Univ. (PA)
Shorter Coll. (GA)
Southern Nazarene Univ. (OK)
Southwest Baptist Univ. (MO)
Southwestern Assemblies of God Univ. (TX)

Susquehanna Univ. (PA)
Texas Christian Univ.
Toccoa Falls Coll. (GA)
Trevecca Nazarene Univ. (TN)
Union Univ. (TN)
Univ. of Mary Hardin-Baylor (TX)
Warner Univ. (FL)
Wartburg Coll. (IA)
Wayland Baptist Univ. (TX)
William Carey Univ. (MS)
William Jewell Coll. (MO)

Romance Languages, Literatures, and Linguistics

Abilene Christian Univ. (TX)
Adams State Coll. (CO)
Adelphi Univ. (NY)
Adrian Coll. (MI)
Agnes Scott Coll. (GA)
Albany State Univ. (GA)
Albertus Magnus Coll. (CT)
Albion Coll. (MI)
Albright Coll. (PA)
Alfred Univ. (NY)
Allegheny Coll. (PA)
Alma Coll. (MI)
American International Coll. (MA)
American Univ. (DC)
Amherst Coll. (MA)
Anderson Univ. (IN)
Anderson Univ. (SC)
Andrews Univ. (MI)
Angelo State Univ. (TX)
Anna Maria Coll. (MA)
Appalachian State Univ. (NC)
Aquinas Coll. (MI)
Arcadia Univ. (PA)
Arizona State Univ.
Arkansas State Univ.–Jonesboro
Armstrong Atlantic State Univ. (GA)
Asbury Univ. (KY)
Assumption Coll. (MA)
Auburn Univ. (AL)
Augsburg Coll. (MN)
Augusta State Univ. (GA)
Augustana Coll. (SD)
Augustana Coll. (IL)
Aurora Univ. (IL)
Austin Coll. (TX)
Austin Peay State Univ. (TN)
Azusa Pacific Univ. (CA)
Baker Univ. (KS)
Baldwin-Wallace Coll. (OH)
Ball State Univ. (IN)
Barnard Coll. (NY)
Barry Univ. (FL)
Barton Coll. (NC)
Bates Coll. (ME)
Baylor Univ. (TX)
Belmont Univ. (TN)
Beloit Coll. (WI)
Bemidji State Univ. (MN)
Benedictine Coll. (KS)
Benedictine Univ. (IL)
Bennington Coll. (VT)
Berea Coll. (KY)
Berry Coll. (GA)
Bethany Coll. (WV)
Bethel Coll. (KS)

Bethel Univ. (MN)
Binghamton Univ.–SUNY
Biola Univ. (CA)
Black Hills State Univ. (SD)
Bloomsburg Univ. of Pennsylvania
Blue Mountain Coll. (MS)
Bluffton Univ. (OH)
Boise State Univ. (ID)
Boston Univ.
Bowdoin Coll. (ME)
Bowling Green State Univ. (OH)
Bradley Univ. (IL)
Brandeis Univ. (MA)
Brescia Univ. (KY)
Briar Cliff Univ. (IA)
Bridgewater Coll. (VA)
Bridgewater State Coll. (MA)
Brigham Young Univ.–Provo (UT)
Brown Univ. (RI)
Bryan Coll. (TN)
Bryn Mawr Coll. (PA)
Bucknell Univ. (PA)
Buena Vista Univ. (IA)
Buffalo State Coll.–SUNY
Butler Univ. (IN)
Cabrini Coll. (PA)
Caldwell Coll. (NJ)
California Baptist Univ.
California Lutheran Univ.
California State Polytechnic Univ.– Pomona
California State Univ.–Bakersfield
California State Univ.–Chico
California State Univ.–Dominguez Hills
California State Univ.–East Bay
California State Univ.–Fresno
California State Univ.–Fullerton
California State Univ.–Long Beach
California State Univ.–Los Angeles
California State Univ.–Northridge
California State Univ.–Sacramento
California State Univ.–San Bernardino
California State Univ.–San Marcos
California State Univ.–Stanislaus
California Univ. of Pennsylvania
Calvin Coll. (MI)
Campbell Univ. (NC)
Canisius Coll. (NY)
Capital Univ. (OH)
Cardinal Stritch Univ. (WI)
Carleton Coll. (MN)
Carlow Univ. (PA)
Carnegie Mellon Univ. (PA)
Carroll Coll. (MT)
Carroll Univ. (WI)
Carson-Newman Coll. (TN)
Carthage Coll. (WI)
Case Western Reserve Univ. (OH)
Catawba Coll. (NC)
Catholic Univ. of America (DC)
Cedar Crest Coll. (PA)
Cedarville Univ. (OH)
Centenary Coll. of Louisiana
Central Coll. (IA)
Central Connecticut State Univ.
Central Methodist Univ. (MO)
Central Michigan Univ.
Central Washington Univ.
Centre Coll. (KY)

Chadron State Coll. (NE)
Chapman Univ. (CA)
Charleston Southern Univ. (SC)
Chatham Univ. (PA)
Chestnut Hill Coll. (PA)
Cheyney Univ. of Pennsylvania
Chicago State Univ.
Christopher Newport Univ. (VA)
Claremont McKenna Coll. (CA)
Clarion Univ. of Pennsylvania
Clark Univ. (MA)
Clarke Univ. (IA)
Cleveland State Univ.
Coastal Carolina Univ. (SC)
Coe Coll. (IA)
Coker Coll. (SC)
Colby Coll. (ME)
Colgate Univ. (NY)
Coll. at Brockport–SUNY
Coll. of Charleston (SC)
Coll. of Idaho (ID)
Coll. of Mount St. Vincent (NY)
Coll. of New Jersey
Coll. of Notre Dame of Maryland
Coll. of Our Lady of the Elms (MA)
Coll. of St. Benedict (MN)
Coll. of St. Elizabeth (NJ)
Coll. of St. Rose (NY)
Coll. of the Holy Cross (MA)
Coll. of the Ozarks (MO)
Coll. of William and Mary (VA)
Coll. of Wooster (OH)
Colorado Coll.
Columbia Coll. (SC)
Columbia Univ. (NY)
Columbus State Univ. (GA)
Concordia Coll.–Moorhead (MN)
Concordia Univ. (MI)
Concordia Univ. (NE)
Concordia Univ. Wisconsin
Connecticut Coll.
Converse Coll. (SC)
Cornell Coll. (IA)
Cornell Univ. (NY)
Creighton Univ. (NE)
CUNY–Baruch Coll.
CUNY–Brooklyn Coll.
CUNY–Coll. of Staten Island
CUNY–Hunter Coll.
CUNY–Lehman Coll.
CUNY–Queens Coll.
CUNY–York Coll.
Daemen Coll. (NY)
Dakota Wesleyan Univ. (SD)
Dana Coll. (NE)
Dartmouth Coll. (NH)
Davidson Coll. (NC)
Davis and Elkins Coll. (WV)
Denison Univ. (OH)
DePaul Univ. (IL)
DePauw Univ. (IN)
DeSales Univ. (PA)
Dickinson Coll. (PA)
Dickinson State Univ. (ND)
Dominican Coll. (NY)
Dominican Univ. (IL)
Dordt Coll. (IA)
Drew Univ. (NJ)
Drury Univ. (MO)
Duke Univ. (NC)
Duquesne Univ. (PA)

Earlham Coll. (IN)
East Carolina Univ. (NC)
East Stroudsburg Univ. of
    Pennsylvania
East Texas Baptist Univ.
Eastern Connecticut State Univ.
Eastern Kentucky Univ.
Eastern Mennonite Univ. (VA)
Eastern Michigan Univ.
Eastern New Mexico Univ.
Eastern Univ. (PA)
Eastern Washington Univ.
Eckerd Coll. (FL)
Edgewood Coll. (WI)
Edinboro Univ. of Pennsylvania
Elizabethtown Coll. (PA)
Elmhurst Coll. (IL)
Elon Univ. (NC)
Emmanuel Coll. (MA)
Emory and Henry Coll. (VA)
Emory Univ. (GA)
Erskine Coll. (SC)
Evangel Univ. (MO)
Fairfield Univ. (CT)
Fairleigh Dickinson Univ. (NJ)
Fayetteville State Univ. (NC)
Ferrum Coll. (VA)
Fisk Univ. (TN)
Flagler Coll. (FL)
Florida Atlantic Univ.
Florida International Univ.
Florida Southern Coll.
Florida State Univ.
Fordham Univ. (NY)
Fort Lewis Coll. (CO)
Franciscan Univ. of Steubenville
    (OH)
Franklin and Marshall Coll. (PA)
Franklin Coll. (IN)
Fresno Pacific Univ. (CA)
Friends Univ. (KS)
Furman Univ. (SC)
Gallaudet Univ. (DC)
Gardner-Webb Univ. (NC)
George Fox Univ. (OR)
George Washington Univ. (DC)
Georgetown Coll. (KY)
Georgetown Univ. (DC)
Georgia Coll. & State Univ.
Georgia Southern Univ.
Georgia State Univ.
Georgian Court Univ. (NJ)
Gettysburg Coll. (PA)
Gonzaga Univ. (WA)
Gordon Coll. (MA)
Goshen Coll. (IN)
Goucher Coll. (MD)
Grace Coll. and Seminary (IN)
Graceland Univ. (IA)
Grambling State Univ. (LA)
Grand Valley State Univ. (MI)
Greensboro Coll. (NC)
Greenville Coll. (IL)
Grinnell Coll. (IA)
Guilford Coll. (NC)
Gustavus Adolphus Coll. (MN)
Hamilton Coll. (NY)
Hamline Univ. (MN)
Hampden-Sydney Coll. (VA)
Hampshire Coll. (MA)
Hampton Univ. (VA)

Hanover Coll. (IN)
Hardin-Simmons Univ. (TX)
Harding Univ. (AR)
Harvard Univ. (MA)
Haverford Coll. (PA)
Heidelberg Univ. (OH)
Henderson State Univ. (AR)
Hendrix Coll. (AR)
High Point Univ. (NC)
Hillsdale Coll. (MI)
Hiram Coll. (OH)
Hofstra Univ. (NY)
Hollins Univ. (VA)
Holy Family Univ. (PA)
Holy Names Univ. (CA)
Hood Coll. (MD)
Hope Coll. (MI)
Houghton Coll. (NY)
Houston Baptist Univ.
Howard Payne Univ. (TX)
Howard Univ. (DC)
Humboldt State Univ. (CA)
Huntington Univ. (IN)
Idaho State Univ.
Illinois Coll.
Illinois State Univ.
Illinois Wesleyan Univ.
Immaculata Univ. (PA)
Indiana State Univ.
Indiana Univ. Northwest
Indiana Univ. of Pennsylvania
Indiana Univ. Southeast
Indiana Univ.–Bloomington
Indiana Univ.–South Bend
Indiana Univ.-Purdue Univ.–Fort
    Wayne
Indiana Univ.-Purdue Univ.–
    Indianapolis
Indiana Wesleyan Univ.
Iona Coll. (NY)
Iowa State Univ.
Ithaca Coll. (NY)
Jacksonville Univ. (FL)
Jamestown Coll. (ND)
John Brown Univ. (AR)
John Carroll Univ. (OH)
Johns Hopkins Univ. (MD)
Johnson C. Smith Univ. (NC)
Juniata Coll. (PA)
Kalamazoo Coll. (MI)
Kean Univ. (NJ)
Keene State Coll. (NH)
Kent State Univ. (OH)
Kentucky Wesleyan Coll.
Kenyon Coll. (OH)
King Coll. (TN)
King's Coll. (PA)
Knox Coll. (IL)
Kutztown Univ. of Pennsylvania
La Salle Univ. (PA)
La Sierra Univ. (CA)
Lafayette Coll. (PA)
LaGrange Coll. (GA)
Lake Forest Coll. (IL)
Lake Superior State Univ. (MI)
Lakeland Coll. (WI)
Lamar Univ. (TX)
Lander Univ. (SC)
Lane Coll. (TN)
Lawrence Univ. (WI)
Le Moyne Coll. (NY)

Lebanon Valley Coll. (PA)
Lehigh Univ. (PA)
Lenoir-Rhyne Univ. (NC)
Lewis & Clark Coll. (OR)
Liberty Univ. (VA)
Lincoln Univ. (PA)
Lincoln Univ. (MO)
Lindenwood Univ. (MO)
Linfield Coll. (OR)
Lipscomb Univ. (TN)
Lock Haven Univ. of Pennsylvania
Long Island Univ.–C.W. Post
    Campus (NY)
Loras Coll. (IA)
Louisiana Coll.
Louisiana State Univ.–Baton Rouge
Louisiana State Univ.–Shreveport
Louisiana Tech Univ.
Loyola Marymount Univ. (CA)
Loyola Univ. Chicago
Loyola Univ. Maryland
Loyola Univ. New Orleans
Luther Coll. (IA)
Lycoming Coll. (PA)
Lynchburg Coll. (VA)
Lyon Coll. (AR)
Macalester Coll. (MN)
MacMurray Coll. (IL)
Madonna Univ. (MI)
Malone Univ. (OH)
Manchester Coll. (IN)
Manhattan Coll. (NY)
Manhattanville Coll. (NY)
Mansfield Univ. of Pennsylvania
Marian Univ. (WI)
Marietta Coll. (OH)
Marist Coll. (NY)
Marquette Univ. (WI)
Mars Hill Coll. (NC)
Martin Univ. (IN)
Mary Baldwin Coll. (VA)
Maryville Coll. (TN)
Marywood Univ. (PA)
McDaniel Coll. (MD)
McMurry Univ. (TX)
McNeese State Univ. (LA)
McPherson Coll. (KS)
Mercer Univ. (GA)
Mercy Coll. (NY)
Meredith Coll. (NC)
Merrimack Coll. (MA)
Mesa State Coll. (CO)
Messiah Coll. (PA)
Methodist Univ. (NC)
Metropolitan State Coll. of Denver
Miami Univ.–Oxford (OH)
Michigan State Univ.
Middlebury Coll. (VT)
Midland Lutheran Coll. (NE)
Midwestern State Univ. (TX)
Millersville Univ. of Pennsylvania
Millikin Univ. (IL)
Mills Coll. (CA)
Millsaps Coll. (MS)
Minnesota State Univ.–Mankato
Minnesota State Univ.–Moorhead
Minot State Univ. (ND)
Mississippi Coll.
Mississippi Univ. for Women
Missouri Southern State Univ.
Missouri State Univ.

Missouri Western State Univ.
Molloy Coll. (NY)
Monmouth Coll. (IL)
Montana State Univ.–Billings
Montclair State Univ. (NJ)
Moravian Coll. (PA)
Morehead State Univ. (KY)
Morehouse Coll. (GA)
Morningside Coll. (IA)
Mount Holyoke Coll. (MA)
Mount Mary Coll. (WI)
Mount St. Mary Coll. (NY)
Mount St. Mary's Coll. (CA)
Mount St. Mary's Univ. (MD)
Mount Vernon Nazarene Univ.
    (OH)
Muhlenberg Coll. (PA)
Murray State Univ. (KY)
Muskingum Univ. (OH)
Nazareth Coll. (NY)
Nebraska Wesleyan Univ.
New Jersey City Univ.
New Mexico Highlands Univ.
New York Univ.
Newberry Coll. (SC)
Niagara Univ. (NY)
Nicholls State Univ. (LA)
North Carolina A&T State Univ.
North Carolina Central Univ.
North Carolina State Univ.–Raleigh
North Central Coll. (IL)
North Dakota State Univ.
North Georgia Coll. and State Univ.
North Park Univ. (IL)
Northeastern Illinois Univ.
Northeastern State Univ. (OK)
Northeastern Univ. (MA)
Northern Arizona Univ.
Northern Illinois Univ.
Northern Kentucky Univ.
Northern Michigan Univ.
Northern State Univ. (SD)
Northwest Missouri State Univ.
Northwest Nazarene Univ. (ID)
Northwestern Coll. (IA)
Northwestern Oklahoma State
    Univ.
Northwestern Univ. (IL)
Oakland Univ. (MI)
Oakwood Univ. (AL)
Oberlin Coll. (OH)
Occidental Coll. (CA)
Ohio Northern Univ.
Ohio State Univ.–Columbus
Ohio Univ.
Ohio Wesleyan Univ.
Oklahoma Baptist Univ.
Oklahoma Christian Univ.
Oklahoma City Univ.
Oklahoma State Univ.
Olivet Nazarene Univ. (IL)
Oral Roberts Univ. (OK)
Oregon State Univ.
Otterbein Coll. (OH)
Ouachita Baptist Univ. (AR)
Our Lady of the Lake Univ. (TX)
Pace Univ. (NY)
Pacific Lutheran Univ. (WA)
Pacific Union Coll. (CA)
Pacific Univ. (OR)
Park Univ. (MO)

Peace Coll. (NC)
Pennsylvania State Univ.–Univ. Park
Pepperdine Univ. (CA)
Piedmont Coll. (GA)
Pitzer Coll. (CA)
Plymouth State Univ. (NH)
Point Loma Nazarene Univ. (CA)
Pomona Coll. (CA)
Prairie View A&M Univ. (TX)
Presbyterian Coll. (SC)
Prescott Coll. (AZ)
Princeton Univ. (NJ)
Providence Coll. (RI)
Purdue Univ.–Calumet (IN)
Purdue Univ.–West Lafayette (IN)
Queens Univ. of Charlotte (NC)
Quinnipiac Univ. (CT)
Ramapo Coll. of New Jersey
Randolph Coll. (VA)
Randolph-Macon Coll. (VA)
Reed Coll. (OR)
Regis Coll. (MA)
Regis Univ. (CO)
Rhode Island Coll.
Rhodes Coll. (TN)
Rice Univ. (TX)
Rider Univ. (NJ)
Ripon Coll. (WI)
Rivier Coll. (NH)
Roanoke Coll. (VA)
Rockford Coll. (IL)
Rockhurst Univ. (MO)
Rollins Coll. (FL)
Roosevelt Univ. (IL)
Rosemont Coll. (PA)
Russell Sage Coll. (NY)
Rutgers, the State Univ. of New
    Jersey–Camden
Rutgers, the State Univ. of New
    Jersey–New Brunswick
Rutgers, the State Univ. of New
    Jersey–Newark
Sacred Heart Univ. (CT)
Saginaw Valley State Univ. (MI)
Salem Coll. (NC)
Salem State Coll. (MA)
Salisbury Univ. (MD)
Salve Regina Univ. (RI)
Sam Houston State Univ. (TX)
Samford Univ. (AL)
San Diego State Univ.
San Francisco State Univ.
San Jose State Univ. (CA)
Santa Clara Univ. (CA)
Scripps Coll. (CA)
Seattle Pacific Univ.
Seattle Univ.
Seton Hall Univ. (NJ)
Seton Hill Univ. (PA)
Sewanee–Univ. of the South (TN)
Shaw Univ. (NC)
Shenandoah Univ. (VA)
Shepherd Univ. (WV)
Shippensburg Univ. of Pennsylvania
Shorter Coll. (GA)
Siena Coll. (NY)
Simmons Coll. (MA)
Simpson Coll. (IA)
Skidmore Coll. (NY)
Slippery Rock Univ. of Pennsylvania
Smith Coll. (MA)

Sonoma State Univ. (CA)
South Dakota State Univ.
Southeast Missouri State Univ.
Southeastern Louisiana Univ.
Southeastern Oklahoma State Univ.
Southern Adventist Univ. (TN)
Southern Arkansas Univ.
Southern Connecticut State Univ.
Southern Illinois Univ.–Carbondale
Southern Methodist Univ. (TX)
Southern Nazarene Univ. (OK)
Southern Oregon Univ.
Southern Univ. and A&M Coll. (LA)
Southern Univ.–New Orleans
Southern Utah Univ.
Southwest Baptist Univ. (MO)
Southwest Minnesota State Univ.
Southwestern Adventist Univ. (TX)
Southwestern Oklahoma State
   Univ.
Southwestern Univ. (TX)
Spring Arbor Univ. (MI)
Spring Hill Coll. (AL)
St. Ambrose Univ. (IA)
St. Anselm Coll. (NH)
St. Bonaventure Univ. (NY)
St. Catherine Univ. (MN)
St. Cloud State Univ. (MN)
St. Edward's Univ. (TX)
St. Francis Coll. (NY)
St. Francis Univ. (PA)
St. John Fisher Coll. (NY)
St. John's Univ. (MN)
St. John's Univ. (NY)
St. Joseph Coll. (CT)
St. Joseph's Coll. New York
St. Joseph's Univ. (PA)
St. Lawrence Univ. (NY)
St. Louis Univ.
St. Mary's Coll. (IN)
St. Mary's Coll. of California
St. Mary's Univ. of Minnesota
St. Mary's Univ. of San Antonio
   (TX)
St. Michael's Coll. (VT)
St. Norbert Coll. (WI)
St. Olaf Coll. (MN)
St. Peter's Coll. (NJ)
St. Thomas Aquinas Coll. (NY)
St. Vincent Coll. (PA)
St. Xavier Univ. (IL)
Stanford Univ. (CA)
Stephen F. Austin State Univ. (TX)
Stetson Univ. (FL)
Suffolk Univ. (MA)
Sul Ross State Univ. (TX)
SUNY Coll.–Cortland
SUNY Coll.–Old Westbury
SUNY Coll.–Oneonta
SUNY Coll.–Potsdam
SUNY–Fredonia
SUNY–Geneseo
SUNY–Oswego
SUNY–Plattsburgh
SUNY–Stony Brook
Susquehanna Univ. (PA)
Swarthmore Coll. (PA)
Syracuse Univ. (NY)
Talladega Coll. (AL)
Tarleton State Univ. (TX)
Taylor Univ. (IN)

Temple Univ. (PA)
Texas A&M International Univ.
Texas A&M Univ.–Coll. Station
Texas A&M Univ.–Corpus Christi
Texas A&M Univ.–Kingsville
Texas Christian Univ.
Texas Lutheran Univ.
Texas State Univ.–San Marcos
Texas Tech Univ.
Texas Wesleyan Univ.
The Citadel (SC)
Thomas More Coll. (KY)
Towson Univ. (MD)
Transylvania Univ. (KY)
Trinity Christian Coll. (IL)
Trinity Coll. (CT)
Truman State Univ. (MO)
Tufts Univ. (MA)
Tulane Univ. (LA)
Union Coll. (NE)
Union Univ. (TN)
Univ. at Albany–SUNY
Univ. at Buffalo–SUNY
Univ. of Akron (OH)
Univ. of Alabama
Univ. of Arizona
Univ. of Arkansas
Univ. of Arkansas–Little Rock
Univ. of California–Berkeley
Univ. of California–Davis
Univ. of California–Irvine
Univ. of California–Los Angeles
Univ. of California–Riverside
Univ. of California–San Diego
Univ. of California–Santa Barbara
Univ. of Central Arkansas
Univ. of Central Florida
Univ. of Central Missouri
Univ. of Chicago
Univ. of Colorado–Boulder
Univ. of Colorado–Colorado
   Springs
Univ. of Colorado–Denver
Univ. of Connecticut
Univ. of Dallas
Univ. of Dayton (OH)
Univ. of Denver
Univ. of Evansville (IN)
Univ. of Findlay (OH)
Univ. of Florida
Univ. of Georgia
Univ. of Hawaii–Manoa
Univ. of Houston
Univ. of Houston–Downtown
Univ. of Illinois–Chicago
Univ. of Illinois–Urbana-Champaign
Univ. of Indianapolis
Univ. of Iowa
Univ. of Kansas
Univ. of Kentucky
Univ. of La Verne (CA)
Univ. of Louisiana–Monroe
Univ. of Louisville (KY)
Univ. of Maine
Univ. of Maine–Presque Isle
Univ. of Mary Hardin-Baylor (TX)
Univ. of Maryland–Coll. Park
Univ. of Massachusetts–Amherst
Univ. of Massachusetts–Boston
Univ. of Massachusetts–Dartmouth
Univ. of Miami (FL)

Univ. of Michigan–Ann Arbor
Univ. of Michigan–Dearborn
Univ. of Michigan–Flint
Univ. of Minnesota–Duluth
Univ. of Minnesota–Morris
Univ. of Minnesota–Twin Cities
Univ. of Mississippi
Univ. of Missouri
Univ. of Missouri–Kansas City
Univ. of Missouri–St. Louis
Univ. of Montana
Univ. of Mount Union (OH)
Univ. of Nebraska–Kearney
Univ. of Nebraska–Lincoln
Univ. of Nebraska–Omaha
Univ. of Nevada–Las Vegas
Univ. of Nevada–Reno
Univ. of New Hampshire
Univ. of New Mexico
Univ. of New Orleans
Univ. of North Carolina–Asheville
Univ. of North Carolina–Chapel Hill
Univ. of North Carolina–Charlotte
Univ. of North Carolina–
   Greensboro
Univ. of North Carolina–Pembroke
Univ. of North Carolina–
   Wilmington
Univ. of North Dakota
Univ. of North Florida
Univ. of North Texas
Univ. of Northern Colorado
Univ. of Northern Iowa
Univ. of Notre Dame (IN)
Univ. of Oklahoma
Univ. of Oregon
Univ. of Pennsylvania
Univ. of Pittsburgh
Univ. of Portland (OR)
Univ. of Puget Sound (WA)
Univ. of Redlands (CA)
Univ. of Rhode Island
Univ. of Richmond (VA)
Univ. of Rochester (NY)
Univ. of San Diego
Univ. of San Francisco
Univ. of Scranton (PA)
Univ. of Sioux Falls (SD)
Univ. of South Carolina
Univ. of South Carolina–Upstate
Univ. of South Dakota
Univ. of South Florida
Univ. of Southern California
Univ. of Southern Indiana
Univ. of Southern Maine
Univ. of St. Thomas (TX)
Univ. of St. Thomas (MN)
Univ. of Tampa (FL)
Univ. of Tennessee
Univ. of Tennessee–Martin
Univ. of Texas of the Permian Basin
Univ. of Texas–Arlington
Univ. of Texas–Austin
Univ. of Texas–Brownsville
Univ. of Texas–El Paso
Univ. of Texas–Pan American
Univ. of Texas–San Antonio
Univ. of Texas–Tyler
Univ. of the District of Columbia
Univ. of the Incarnate Word (TX)
Univ. of the Pacific (CA)

Univ. of Toledo (OH)
Univ. of Tulsa (OK)
Univ. of Utah
Univ. of Vermont
Univ. of Virginia
Univ. of Virginia–Wise
Univ. of Washington
Univ. of West Georgia
Univ. of Wisconsin–Eau Claire
Univ. of Wisconsin–Green Bay
Univ. of Wisconsin–La Crosse
Univ. of Wisconsin–Madison
Univ. of Wisconsin–Milwaukee
Univ. of Wisconsin–Parkside
Univ. of Wisconsin–Stevens Point
Univ. of Wisconsin–Whitewater
Univ. of Wyoming
Ursinus Coll. (PA)
Utah State Univ.
Utah Valley Univ.
Valdosta State Univ. (GA)
Valley City State Univ. (ND)
Valparaiso Univ. (IN)
Vanderbilt Univ. (TN)
Vanguard Univ. of Southern
   California
Vassar Coll. (NY)
Villanova Univ. (PA)
Virginia Wesleyan Coll.
Viterbo Univ. (WI)
Wabash Coll. (IN)
Wagner Coll. (NY)
Wake Forest Univ. (NC)
Walsh Univ. (OH)
Warren Wilson Coll. (NC)
Wartburg Coll. (IA)
Washburn Univ. (KS)
Washington and Jefferson Coll.
   (PA)
Washington and Lee Univ. (VA)
Washington Coll. (MD)
Washington State Univ.
Washington Univ. in St. Louis
Wayland Baptist Univ. (TX)
Wayne State Coll. (NE)
Wayne State Univ. (MI)
Weber State Univ. (UT)
Webster Univ. (MO)
Wellesley Coll. (MA)
Wells Coll. (NY)
Wesleyan Coll. (GA)
Wesleyan Univ. (CT)
West Chester Univ. of Pennsylvania
West Texas A&M Univ.
Western Carolina Univ. (NC)
Western Connecticut State Univ.
Western Illinois Univ.
Western Kentucky Univ.
Western Michigan Univ.
Western New Mexico Univ.
Western Oregon Univ.
Western State Coll. of Colorado
Western Washington Univ.
Westminster Coll. (PA)
Westminster Coll. (MO)
Westmont Coll. (CA)
Wheaton Coll. (IL)
Wheeling Jesuit Univ. (WV)
Whitman Coll. (WA)
Whittier Coll. (CA)
Whitworth Univ. (WA)

Widener Univ. (PA)
Wilkes Univ. (PA)
Willamette Univ. (OR)
William Jewell Coll. (MO)
William Paterson Univ. of New
   Jersey
Williams Coll. (MA)
Wilmington Coll. (OH)
Wilson Coll. (PA)
Wingate Univ. (NC)
Winston-Salem State Univ. (NC)
Wisconsin Lutheran Coll.
Wittenberg Univ. (OH)
Wofford Coll. (SC)
Worcester State Coll. (MA)
Wright State Univ. (OH)
Xavier Univ. (OH)
Yale Univ. (CT)
Yeshiva Univ. (NY)
York Coll. of Pennsylvania
Youngstown State Univ. (OH)

School Psychology

Eastern Washington Univ.
Gallaudet Univ. (DC)
Georgia Southern Univ.
Northern Michigan Univ.
Texas Wesleyan Univ.
Univ. of Florida
Univ. of Wisconsin–River Falls

Science Technologies/ Technicians

Bridgewater State Coll. (MA)
Carlow Univ. (PA)
Charleston Southern Univ. (SC)
Edward Waters Coll. (FL)
Humboldt State Univ. (CA)
Indiana Wesleyan Univ.
Kean Univ. (NJ)
Madonna Univ. (MI)
Northern Arizona Univ.
Univ. of Alaska–Anchorage
Univ. of Virginia–Wise
Univ. of Wisconsin–Stout

Science, Technology, and Society

Beloit Coll. (WI)
Brown Univ. (RI)
Butler Univ. (IN)
Carnegie Mellon Univ. (PA)
Clark Univ. (MA)
Colby Coll. (ME)
Cornell Univ. (NY)
Eastern Michigan Univ.
Georgetown Univ. (DC)
Georgia Institute of Technology
Hampshire Coll. (MA)
James Madison Univ. (VA)
La Salle Univ. (PA)
Lehigh Univ. (PA)
Massachusetts Institute of
   Technology
Michigan State Univ.
New Jersey Institute of Technology
New School (NY)
North Carolina State Univ.–Raleigh

Northwestern Univ. (IL)
Pomona Coll. (CA)
Prescott Coll. (AZ)
Rutgers, the State Univ. of New Jersey–Newark
Scripps Coll. (CA)
Slippery Rock Univ. of Pennsylvania
St. Cloud State Univ. (MN)
Stanford Univ. (CA)
Univ. of California–Davis
Univ. of Denver
Univ. of Puget Sound (WA)
Vassar Coll. (NY)
Wesleyan Univ. (CT)
Willamette Univ. (OR)
Worcester Polytechnic Institute (MA)

Security and Protective Services

Arkansas Tech Univ.
Eastern Michigan Univ.
Embry-Riddle Aeronautical Univ. (FL)
La Roche Coll. (PA)
North Dakota State Univ.
Point Park Univ. (PA)
Thomas Edison State Coll. (NJ)
Tiffin Univ. (OH)
Virginia Commonwealth Univ.
Western Illinois Univ.

Slavic, Baltic and Albanian Languages, Literatures, and Linguistics

American Univ. (DC)
Amherst Coll. (MA)
Arizona State Univ.
Barnard Coll. (NY)
Bates Coll. (ME)
Baylor Univ. (TX)
Beloit Coll. (WI)
Boston Univ.
Bowdoin Coll. (ME)
Bowling Green State Univ. (OH)
Brandeis Univ. (MA)
Brigham Young Univ.–Provo (UT)
Brown Univ. (RI)
Bryn Mawr Coll. (PA)
Bucknell Univ. (PA)
Carleton Coll. (MN)
Central Washington Univ.
Colby Coll. (ME)
Colgate Univ. (NY)
Coll. of the Holy Cross (MA)
Colorado Coll.
Columbia Univ. (NY)
Concordia Coll.–Moorhead (MN)
Connecticut Coll.
Cornell Coll. (IA)
Cornell Univ. (NY)
CUNY–Brooklyn Coll.
CUNY–Hunter Coll.
CUNY–Lehman Coll.
CUNY–Queens Coll.
Dartmouth Coll. (NH)
Dickinson Coll. (PA)
Duke Univ. (NC)

Emory Univ. (GA)
Ferrum Coll. (VA)
Florida State Univ.
Fordham Univ. (NY)
George Washington Univ. (DC)
Georgetown Univ. (DC)
Goucher Coll. (MD)
Grinnell Coll. (IA)
Harvard Univ. (MA)
Haverford Coll. (PA)
Hofstra Univ. (NY)
Howard Univ. (DC)
Indiana Univ.–Bloomington
Juniata Coll. (PA)
Kent State Univ. (OH)
Kutztown Univ. of Pennsylvania
La Salle Univ. (PA)
Lawrence Univ. (WI)
Macalester Coll. (MN)
Madonna Univ. (MI)
Miami Univ.–Oxford (OH)
Michigan State Univ.
Middlebury Coll. (VT)
New York Univ.
Northern Illinois Univ.
Northwestern Univ. (IL)
Oberlin Coll. (OH)
Ohio State Univ.–Columbus
Ohio Univ.
Oklahoma State Univ.
Oral Roberts Univ. (OK)
Ouachita Baptist Univ. (AR)
Pennsylvania State Univ.–Univ. Park
Pomona Coll. (CA)
Princeton Univ. (NJ)
Purdue Univ.–West Lafayette (IN)
Reed Coll. (OR)
Rice Univ. (TX)
Rider Univ. (NJ)
Rutgers, the State Univ. of New Jersey–New Brunswick
Salisbury Univ. (MD)
San Diego State Univ.
San Francisco State Univ.
Scripps Coll. (CA)
Seattle Pacific Univ.
Sewanee–Univ. of the South (TN)
Smith Coll. (MA)
St. Louis Univ.
St. Olaf Coll. (MN)
Stanford Univ. (CA)
SUNY–Oswego
SUNY–Stony Brook
Swarthmore Coll. (PA)
Syracuse Univ. (NY)
Temple Univ. (PA)
Trinity Coll. (CT)
Truman State Univ. (MO)
Tufts Univ. (MA)
Tulane Univ. (LA)
Univ. at Albany–SUNY
Univ. of Arizona
Univ. of California–Berkeley
Univ. of California–Davis
Univ. of California–Irvine
Univ. of California–Los Angeles
Univ. of California–San Diego
Univ. of California–Santa Barbara
Univ. of Chicago
Univ. of Denver
Univ. of Florida

Univ. of Georgia
Univ. of Hawaii–Manoa
Univ. of Illinois–Chicago
Univ. of Illinois–Urbana-Champaign
Univ. of Iowa
Univ. of Kansas
Univ. of Kentucky
Univ. of Maryland–Coll. Park
Univ. of Massachusetts–Boston
Univ. of Michigan–Ann Arbor
Univ. of Minnesota–Twin Cities
Univ. of Missouri
Univ. of Montana
Univ. of Nebraska–Lincoln
Univ. of New Hampshire
Univ. of New Mexico
Univ. of North Carolina–Chapel Hill
Univ. of Northern Iowa
Univ. of Notre Dame (IN)
Univ. of Oklahoma
Univ. of Oregon
Univ. of Pennsylvania
Univ. of Pittsburgh
Univ. of Rochester (NY)
Univ. of South Carolina
Univ. of South Florida
Univ. of Southern California
Univ. of Tennessee
Univ. of Texas–Arlington
Univ. of Texas–Austin
Univ. of Utah
Univ. of Vermont
Univ. of Virginia
Univ. of Washington
Univ. of Wisconsin–Madison
Univ. of Wisconsin–Milwaukee
Univ. of Wyoming
Vanderbilt Univ. (TN)
Vassar Coll. (NY)
Wake Forest Univ. (NC)
Washington State Univ.
Wayne State Univ. (MI)
Wellesley Coll. (MA)
Wesleyan Univ. (CT)
West Chester Univ. of Pennsylvania
Wheaton Coll. (MA)
Williams Coll. (MA)
Yale Univ. (CT)

Social and Philosophical Foundations of Education

Eastern Michigan Univ.
Eastern Washington Univ.
Goddard Coll. (VT)
Northwestern Univ. (IL)
Univ. of Florida
Univ. of Iowa
Univ. of Kentucky

Social Psychology

Atlantic Union Coll. (MA)
Bellevue Univ. (NE)
Bennington Coll. (VT)
Clarion Univ. of Pennsylvania
Eastern Nazarene Coll. (MA)
Florida Atlantic Univ.
Hannibal-LaGrange Coll. (MO)
Marymount Univ. (VA)

Maryville Univ. of St. Louis (MO)
Northwest Missouri State Univ.
Notre Dame de Namur Univ. (CA)
Paine Coll. (GA)
Park Univ. (MO)
Prescott Coll. (AZ)
St. Mary's Coll. of California
Trinity Univ. (DC)
Tufts Univ. (MA)
Univ. of California–Irvine
Walsh Univ. (OH)
Western Michigan Univ.

Social Sciences

Abilene Christian Univ. (TX)
Adams State Coll. (CO)
Adelphi Univ. (NY)
Agnes Scott Coll. (GA)
Albertus Magnus Coll. (CT)
Albright Coll. (PA)
Alice Lloyd Coll. (KY)
Allen Univ. (SC)
Alma Coll. (MI)
Alvernia Univ. (PA)
Alverno Coll. (WI)
American Jewish Univ. (CA)
Anna Maria Coll. (MA)
Aquinas Coll. (MI)
Asbury Univ. (KY)
Atlantic Union Coll. (MA)
Azusa Pacific Univ. (CA)
Bard Coll. (NY)
Bard Coll. at Simon's Rock (MA)
Belhaven Univ. (MS)
Bemidji State Univ. (MN)
Benedictine Coll. (KS)
Benedictine Univ. (IL)
Bennington Coll. (VT)
Berry Coll. (GA)
Bethel Univ. (MN)
Binghamton Univ.–SUNY
Biola Univ. (CA)
Black Hills State Univ. (SD)
Bloomsburg University of Pennsylvania
Blue Mountain Coll. (MS)
Bluefield Coll. (VA)
Bluefield State Coll. (WV)
Bluffton Univ. (OH)
Boise State Univ. (ID)
Bowie State Univ. (MD)
Brescia Univ. (KY)
Brewton-Parker Coll. (GA)
Briar Cliff Univ. (IA)
Brown Univ. (RI)
Bryant Univ. (RI)
Buena Vista Univ. (IA)
Buffalo State Coll.–SUNY
Burlington Coll. (VT)
California Lutheran Univ.
California Polytechnic State Univ.–San Luis Obispo
California State Polytechnic Univ.–Pomona
California State Univ.–Chico
California State Univ.–Fresno
California State Univ.–Los Angeles
California State Univ.–Monterey Bay
California State Univ.–Northridge
California State Univ.–Sacramento

California State Univ.–San Bernardino
California State Univ.–Stanislaus
California Univ. of Pennsylvania
Calumet Coll. of St. Joseph (IN)
Calvin Coll. (MI)
Campbell Univ. (NC)
Campbellsville Univ. (KY)
Canisius Coll. (NY)
Carleton Coll. (MN)
Carnegie Mellon Univ. (PA)
Carthage Coll. (WI)
Castleton State Coll. (VT)
Central Baptist Coll. (AR)
Central Christian Coll. (KS)
Central Coll. (IA)
Central Connecticut State Univ.
Central Michigan Univ.
Central Washington Univ.
Centre Coll. (KY)
Chaminade Univ. of Honolulu
Charleston Southern Univ. (SC)
Cheyney Univ. of Pennsylvania
Clarion Univ. of Pennsylvania
Clark Univ. (MA)
Cleveland State Univ.
Colby-Sawyer Coll. (NH)
Colgate Univ. (NY)
Coll. of St. Benedict (MN)
Coll. of St. Scholastica (MN)
Colorado Christian Univ.
Colorado Coll.
Colorado State Univ.–Pueblo
Columbia Coll. (SC)
Concordia Coll. (NY)
Concordia Univ. (MI)
Concordia Univ. Texas
Connecticut Coll.
Corban Univ. (OR)
Cornell Univ. (NY)
Covenant Coll. (GA)
CUNY–City Coll.
CUNY–Coll. of Staten Island
CUNY–Queens Coll.
Curry Coll. (MA)
Dana Coll. (NE)
Daniel Webster Coll. (NH)
Delta State Univ. (MS)
DePaul Univ. (IL)
Dickinson State Univ. (ND)
Dominican Coll. (NY)
Dominican Univ. (IL)
Dordt Coll. (IA)
Dowling Coll. (NY)
East Stroudsburg Univ. of Pennsylvania
East Texas Baptist Univ.
Eastern Mennonite Univ. (VA)
Eastern Michigan Univ.
Eastern New Mexico Univ.
Eastern Oregon Univ.
Edgewood Coll. (WI)
Edinboro Univ. of Pennsylvania
Elmira Coll. (NY)
Emporia State Univ. (KS)
Eureka Coll. (IL)
Evangel Univ. (MO)
Evergreen State Coll. (WA)
Ferrum Coll. (VA)
Florida Atlantic Univ.
Florida Southern Coll.

Florida State Univ.
Fordham Univ. (NY)
Fresno Pacific Univ. (CA)
Friends Univ. (KS)
Frostburg State Univ. (MD)
Gannon Univ. (PA)
Gardner-Webb Univ. (NC)
Georgetown Univ. (DC)
Georgia Southwestern State Univ.
Gettysburg Coll. (PA)
Glenville State Coll. (WV)
Graceland Univ. (IA)
Grand Valley State Univ. (MI)
Green Mountain Coll. (VT)
Greensboro Coll. (NC)
Hamline Univ. (MN)
Hampshire Coll. (MA)
Harding Univ. (AR)
Harvard Univ. (MA)
Hawaii Pacific Univ.
Hobart and William Smith Colleges (NY)
Hofstra Univ. (NY)
Hope Coll. (MI)
Hope International Univ. (CA)
Howard Payne Univ. (TX)
Humboldt State Univ. (CA)
Indiana Univ. of Pennsylvania
Indiana Univ.–Bloomington
Indiana Univ.–Kokomo
Ithaca Coll. (NY)
James Madison Univ. (VA)
Jamestown Coll. (ND)
John Brown Univ. (AR)
Johns Hopkins Univ. (MD)
Johnson C. Smith Univ. (NC)
Juniata Coll. (PA)
Kalamazoo Coll. (MI)
Kansas State Univ.
Keene State Coll. (NH)
Kentucky State Univ.
Keuka Coll. (NY)
King Coll. (TN)
Knox Coll. (IL)
Kutztown Univ. of Pennsylvania
La Sierra Univ. (CA)
Lafayette Coll. (PA)
Lake Forest Coll. (IL)
Lake Superior State Univ. (MI)
Lasell Coll. (MA)
Lehigh Univ. (PA)
LeMoyne-Owen Coll. (TN)
Lenoir-Rhyne Univ. (NC)
LeTourneau Univ. (TX)
Lewis-Clark State Coll. (ID)
Liberty Univ. (VA)
Lindsey Wilson Coll. (KY)
Livingstone Coll. (NC)
Lock Haven Univ. of Pennsylvania
Long Island Univ.–C.W. Post Campus (NY)
Louisiana Coll.
Loyola Univ. Maryland
Loyola Univ. New Orleans
Lynchburg Coll. (VA)
MacMurray Coll. (IL)
Madonna Univ. (MI)
Manhattan Coll. (NY)
Marygrove Coll. (MI)
Marylhurst Univ. (OR)
Marywood Univ. (PA)

Mayville State Univ. (ND)
McKendree Univ. (IL)
Mesa State Coll. (CO)
Metropolitan State Coll. of Denver
Michigan State Univ.
Michigan Technological Univ.
Mid-Continent Univ. (KY)
Midland Lutheran Coll. (NE)
Miles Coll. (AL)
Millersville Univ. of Pennsylvania
Mills Coll. (CA)
Minnesota State Univ.–Mankato
Minot State Univ. (ND)
Mississippi Univ. for Women
Mississippi Valley State Univ.
Missouri Baptist Univ.
Monmouth Univ. (NJ)
Morehead State Univ. (KY)
Mount Aloysius Coll. (PA)
Mount Holyoke Coll. (MA)
Mount Marty Coll. (SD)
Mount Mary Coll. (WI)
Mount St. Mary Coll. (NY)
Mount St. Mary's Coll. (CA)
Mount St. Mary's Univ. (MD)
Muhlenberg Coll. (PA)
National-Louis Univ. (IL)
Nazareth Coll. (NY)
New Jersey City Univ.
New Mexico Highlands Univ.
New York Institute of Technology
New York Univ.
North Central Coll. (IL)
North Dakota State Univ.
North Georgia Coll. and State Univ.
North Park Univ. (IL)
Northern Arizona Univ.
Northern Illinois Univ.
Northern Kentucky Univ.
Northern Michigan Univ.
Northwest Christian Univ. (OR)
Northwestern Univ. (IL)
Notre Dame de Namur Univ. (CA)
Nyack Coll. (NY)
Oakland City Univ. (IN)
Oakland Univ. (MI)
Oglethorpe Univ. (GA)
Ohio State Univ.–Columbus
Oklahoma Panhandle State Univ.
Oklahoma Wesleyan Univ.
Olivet Coll. (MI)
Olivet Nazarene Univ. (IL)
Oral Roberts Univ. (OK)
Ouachita Baptist Univ. (AR)
Our Lady of Holy Cross Coll. (LA)
Pace Univ. (NY)
Pacific Union Coll. (CA)
Pikeville Coll. (KY)
Plymouth State Univ. (NH)
Point Loma Nazarene Univ. (CA)
Point Park Univ. (PA)
Portland State Univ. (OR)
Prescott Coll. (AZ)
Providence Coll. (RI)
Purchase Coll.–SUNY
Purdue Univ.–North Central (IN)
Quinnipiac Univ. (CT)
Radford Univ. (VA)
Regis Univ. (CO)
Rensselaer Polytechnic Institute (NY)

Rhode Island Coll.
Robert Morris Univ. (PA)
Roberts Wesleyan Coll. (NY)
Rockford Coll. (IL)
Roger Williams Univ. (RI)
Rogers State Univ. (OK)
Roosevelt Univ. (IL)
Rosemont Coll. (PA)
Rust Coll. (MS)
Rutgers, the State Univ. of New Jersey–New Brunswick
Sage Colleges–Albany (NY)
Sam Houston State Univ. (TX)
San Diego State Univ.
San Francisco State Univ.
San Jose State Univ. (CA)
Shawnee State Univ. (OH)
Shimer Coll. (IL)
Simpson Univ. (CA)
Skidmore Coll. (NY)
Sonoma State Univ. (CA)
South Carolina State Univ.
Southern Arkansas Univ.
Southern Illinois Univ.–Carbondale
Southern Methodist Univ. (TX)
Southern New Hampshire Univ.
Southern Oregon Univ.
Southern Wesleyan Univ. (SC)
Southwestern Assemblies of God Univ. (TX)
Spalding Univ. (KY)
Spring Arbor Univ. (MI)
Spring Hill Coll. (AL)
Springfield Coll. (MA)
St. Augustine's Coll. (NC)
St. Catherine Univ. (MN)
St. Cloud State Univ. (MN)
St. Gregory's Univ. (OK)
St. John's Univ. (NY)
St. John's Univ. (MN)
St. Joseph Coll. (CT)
St. Joseph's Coll. New York
St. Martin's Univ. (WA)
St. Mary's Coll. of California
St. Mary's Univ. of Minnesota
St. Mary-of-the-Woods Coll. (IN)
St. Peter's Coll. (NJ)
St. Thomas Aquinas Coll. (NY)
St. Xavier Univ. (IL)
Stetson Univ. (FL)
Stevens Institute of Technology (NJ)
Suffolk Univ. (MA)
Sul Ross State Univ. (TX)
SUNY Coll.–Old Westbury
SUNY Empire State Coll.
SUNY–Stony Brook
Swarthmore Coll. (PA)
Syracuse Univ. (NY)
Tabor Coll. (KS)
Talladega Coll. (AL)
Texas A&M International Univ.
Texas A&M Univ.–Coll. Station
Texas A&M Univ.–Commerce
Texas Wesleyan Univ.
Thomas Edison State Coll. (NJ)
Touro Coll. (NY)
Towson Univ. (MD)
Transylvania Univ. (KY)
Trevecca Nazarene Univ. (TN)
Trine Univ. (IN)

Trinity International Univ. (IL)
Trinity Univ. (DC)
Troy Univ. (AL)
Tulane Univ. (LA)
Union Coll. (NE)
Union Coll. (NY)
Union Institute and Univ. (OH)
Union Univ. (TN)
United States Air Force Academy (CO)
Univ. of Akron (OH)
Univ. of Alabama–Birmingham
Univ. of Alaska–Southeast
Univ. of California–Berkeley
Univ. of California–Irvine
Univ. of California–Riverside
Univ. of California–San Diego
Univ. of Central Florida
Univ. of Chicago
Univ. of Denver
Univ. of Findlay (OH)
Univ. of Hartford (CT)
Univ. of Hawaii–West Oahu
Univ. of Houston–Downtown
Univ. of Illinois–Springfield
Univ. of Iowa
Univ. of Kentucky
Univ. of La Verne (CA)
Univ. of Maine–Augusta
Univ. of Maine–Fort Kent
Univ. of Maine–Presque Isle
Univ. of Mary (ND)
Univ. of Maryland–Univ. Coll.
Univ. of Massachusetts–Amherst
Univ. of Massachusetts–Boston
Univ. of Michigan–Ann Arbor
Univ. of Michigan–Dearborn
Univ. of Michigan–Flint
Univ. of Minnesota–Morris
Univ. of Mobile (AL)
Univ. of Montevallo (AL)
Univ. of Nevada–Las Vegas
Univ. of North Alabama
Univ. of North Dakota
Univ. of North Texas
Univ. of Northern Colorado
Univ. of Oregon
Univ. of Pennsylvania
Univ. of Pittsburgh
Univ. of Pittsburgh–Bradford
Univ. of Pittsburgh–Johnstown
Univ. of Rhode Island
Univ. of Rio Grande (OH)
Univ. of Rochester (NY)
Univ. of Sioux Falls (SD)
Univ. of South Florida
Univ. of Southern Indiana
Univ. of Southern Maine
Univ. of St. Thomas (MN)
Univ. of Tampa (FL)
Univ. of Tennessee–Chattanooga
Univ. of Texas–Pan American
Univ. of Texas–San Antonio
Univ. of the Pacific (CA)
Univ. of the Southwest (NM)
Univ. of Utah
Univ. of Washington
Univ. of West Florida
Univ. of Wisconsin–Green Bay
Univ. of Wisconsin–Platteville
Univ. of Wisconsin–River Falls

Univ. of Wisconsin–Stevens Point
Univ. of Wisconsin–Superior
Univ. of Wisconsin–Whitewater
Univ. of Wyoming
Upper Iowa Univ.
Ursinus Coll. (PA)
Utah State Univ.
Valley City State Univ. (ND)
Vanderbilt Univ. (TN)
Vanguard Univ. of Southern California
Vassar Coll. (NY)
Villanova Univ. (PA)
Virginia Wesleyan Coll.
Viterbo Univ. (WI)
Walsh Univ. (OH)
Warner Univ. (FL)
Washington State Univ.
Washington Univ. in St. Louis
Wayland Baptist Univ. (TX)
Wayne State Coll. (NE)
Wayne State Univ. (MI)
Waynesburg Univ. (PA)
Webster Univ. (MO)
West Liberty Univ. (WV)
West Texas A&M Univ.
Western Carolina Univ. (NC)
Western Connecticut State Univ.
Western Kentucky Univ.
Western Michigan Univ.
Western New Mexico Univ.
Western Oregon Univ.
Western State Coll. of Colorado
Western Washington Univ.
Westminster Coll. (UT)
Westmont Coll. (CA)
William Carey Univ. (MS)
William Penn Univ. (IA)
Williams Coll. (MA)
Wilson Coll. (PA)
Wisconsin Lutheran Coll.
Wright State Univ. (OH)
York Coll. of Pennsylvania
Youngstown State Univ. (OH)

Social Work

Abilene Christian Univ. (TX)
Adelphi Univ. (NY)
Adrian Coll. (MI)
Alabama Agricultural and Mechanical Univ.
Alabama State Univ.
Albany State Univ. (GA)
Alvernia Univ. (PA)
Anderson Univ. (IN)
Andrews Univ. (MI)
Anna Maria Coll. (MA)
Appalachian State Univ. (NC)
Arkansas State Univ.–Jonesboro
Asbury Univ. (KY)
Ashland Univ. (OH)
Atlantic Union Coll. (MA)
Auburn Univ. (AL)
Augsburg Coll. (MN)
Augusta State Univ. (GA)
Aurora Univ. (IL)
Austin Peay State Univ. (TN)
Avila Univ. (MO)
Azusa Pacific Univ. (CA)
Ball State Univ. (IN)

Barry Univ. (FL)
Barton Coll. (NC)
Baylor Univ. (TX)
Bellevue Univ. (NE)
Belmont Univ. (TN)
Bemidji State Univ. (MN)
Benedict Coll. (SC)
Bennett Coll. (NC)
Bethany Coll. (WV)
Bethany Coll. (KS)
Bethel Coll. (KS)
Bethel Univ. (MN)
Bloomsburg Univ. of Pennsylvania
Bluffton Univ. (OH)
Boise State Univ. (ID)
Bowie State Univ. (MD)
Bowling Green State Univ. (OH)
Bradley Univ. (IL)
Brescia Univ. (KY)
Briar Cliff Univ. (IA)
Bridgewater State Coll. (MA)
Brigham Young Univ.–Hawaii
Brigham Young Univ.–Provo (UT)
Buena Vista Univ. (IA)
Buffalo State Coll.–SUNY
Cabrini Coll. (PA)
California State Univ.–Chico
California State Univ.–Fresno
California State Univ.–Long Beach
California State Univ.–Los Angeles
California State Univ.–Sacramento
California State Univ.–San
    Bernardino
California Univ. of Pennsylvania
Calvin Coll. (MI)
Campbell Univ. (NC)
Campbellsville Univ. (KY)
Capital Univ. (OH)
Carlow Univ. (PA)
Carthage Coll. (WI)
Castleton State Coll. (VT)
Catholic Univ. of America (DC)
Cazenovia Coll. (NY)
Cedar Crest Coll. (PA)
Cedarville Univ. (OH)
Central Connecticut State Univ.
Central Michigan Univ.
Central State Univ. (OH)
Chadron State Coll. (NE)
Champlain Coll. (VT)
Chapman Univ. (CA)
Chatham Univ. (PA)
Christopher Newport Univ. (VA)
Clark Atlanta Univ.
Clarke Univ. (IA)
Cleveland State Univ.
Coker Coll. (SC)
Coll. at Brockport–SUNY
Coll. of Mount St. Joseph (OH)
Coll. of Our Lady of the Elms (MA)
Coll. of St. Benedict (MN)
Coll. of St. Rose (NY)
Coll. of St. Scholastica (MN)
Coll. of the Ozarks (MO)
Colorado State Univ.
Colorado State Univ.–Pueblo
Columbia Coll. (SC)
Concord Univ. (WV)
Concordia Coll. (NY)
Concordia Coll.–Moorhead (MN)
Concordia Univ. (OR)

Concordia Univ. Chicago (IL)
Concordia Univ. Wisconsin
Coppin State Univ. (MD)
Cornerstone Univ. (MI)
Creighton Univ. (NE)
CUNY–Coll. of Staten Island
CUNY–Lehman Coll.
CUNY–York Coll.
Daemen Coll. (NY)
Dalton State Coll. (GA)
Dana Coll. (NE)
Defiance Coll. (OH)
Delaware State Univ.
Delta State Univ. (MS)
Dillard Univ. (LA)
Dominican Coll. (NY)
Dordt Coll. (IA)
East Carolina Univ. (NC)
East Central Univ. (OK)
East Tennessee State Univ.
Eastern Connecticut State Univ.
Eastern Kentucky Univ.
Eastern Mennonite Univ. (VA)
Eastern Michigan Univ.
Eastern Nazarene Coll. (MA)
Eastern New Mexico Univ.
Eastern Univ. (PA)
Eastern Washington Univ.
Edinboro Univ. of Pennsylvania
Elizabeth City State Univ. (NC)
Elizabethtown Coll. (PA)
Ferris State Univ. (MI)
Ferrum Coll. (VA)
Florida Atlantic Univ.
Florida International Univ.
Florida State Univ.
Fordham Univ. (NY)
Fort Hays State Univ. (KS)
Fort Valley State Univ. (GA)
Franciscan Univ. of Steubenville
    (OH)
Franklin Pierce Univ. (NH)
Freed-Hardeman Univ. (TN)
Fresno Pacific Univ. (CA)
Frostburg State Univ. (MD)
Gallaudet Univ. (DC)
Gannon Univ. (PA)
George Fox Univ. (OR)
George Mason Univ. (VA)
Georgia State Univ.
Georgian Court Univ. (NJ)
Gordon Coll. (MA)
Goshen Coll. (IN)
Grace Coll. and Seminary (IN)
Graceland Univ. (IA)
Grambling State Univ. (LA)
Grand Valley State Univ. (MI)
Greenville Coll. (IL)
Gwynedd-Mercy Coll. (PA)
Hannibal-LaGrange Coll. (MO)
Hardin-Simmons Univ. (TX)
Harding Univ. (AR)
Hawaii Pacific Univ.
Henderson State Univ. (AR)
Heritage Univ. (WA)
Holy Family Univ. (PA)
Hood Coll. (MD)
Hope Coll. (MI)
Humboldt State Univ. (CA)
Huntington Univ. (IN)
Idaho State Univ.

Illinois State Univ.
Indiana State Univ.
Indiana Univ. East
Indiana Univ.–Kokomo
Indiana Univ.–South Bend
Indiana Univ.–Purdue Univ.–
    Indianapolis
Indiana Wesleyan Univ.
Iona Coll. (NY)
Jackson State Univ. (MS)
Jacksonville State Univ. (AL)
James Madison Univ. (VA)
Johnson C. Smith Univ. (NC)
Juniata Coll. (PA)
Kansas State Univ.
Kean Univ. (NJ)
Kentucky State Univ.
Keuka Coll. (NY)
Kutztown Univ. of Pennsylvania
La Salle Univ. (PA)
La Sierra Univ. (CA)
LeMoyne-Owen Coll. (TN)
Lewis Univ. (IL)
Limestone Coll. (SC)
Lincoln Memorial Univ. (TN)
Lindenwood Univ. (MO)
Lipscomb Univ. (TN)
Livingstone Coll. (NC)
Lock Haven Univ. of Pennsylvania
Long Island Univ.–C.W. Post
    Campus (NY)
Longwood Univ. (VA)
Loras Coll. (IA)
Louisiana Coll.
Lourdes Coll. (OH)
Loyola Univ. Chicago
Lubbock Christian Univ. (TX)
Luther Coll. (IA)
MacMurray Coll. (IL)
Madonna Univ. (MI)
Malone Univ. (OH)
Manchester Coll. (IN)
Mansfield Univ. of Pennsylvania
Marian Univ. (WI)
Marist Coll. (NY)
Marquette Univ. (WI)
Mars Hill Coll. (NC)
Marshall Univ. (WV)
Mary Baldwin Coll. (VA)
Marygrove Coll. (MI)
Marywood Univ. (PA)
McDaniel Coll. (MD)
Mercy Coll. (NY)
Mercyhurst Coll. (PA)
Meredith Coll. (NC)
Messiah Coll. (PA)
Methodist Univ. (NC)
Metropolitan State Coll. of Denver
Miami Univ.–Oxford (OH)
Michigan State Univ.
Middle Tennessee State Univ.
Midwestern State Univ. (TX)
Miles Coll. (AL)
Millersville Univ. of Pennsylvania
Millikin Univ. (IL)
Minnesota State Univ.–Mankato
Minnesota State Univ.–Moorhead
Minot State Univ. (ND)
Misericordia Univ. (PA)
Mississippi Coll.
Mississippi State Univ.

Mississippi Valley State Univ.
Missouri State Univ.
Missouri Western State Univ.
Molloy Coll. (NY)
Monmouth Univ. (NJ)
Morehead State Univ. (KY)
Mount Mary Coll. (WI)
Mount St. Mary's Coll. (CA)
Mount Vernon Nazarene Univ.
    (OH)
Mountain State Univ. (WV)
Murray State Univ. (KY)
National-Louis Univ. (IL)
Nazareth Coll. (NY)
Nebraska Wesleyan Univ.
New Mexico State Univ.
New York Univ.
Norfolk State Univ. (VA)
North Carolina A&T State Univ.
North Carolina Central Univ.
North Carolina State Univ.–Raleigh
Northeastern Illinois Univ.
Northern Arizona Univ.
Northern Kentucky Univ.
Northern Michigan Univ.
Northern State Univ. (SD)
Northwest Nazarene Univ. (ID)
Northwestern Coll. (IA)
Northwestern Oklahoma State
    Univ.
Northwestern State Univ. of
    Louisiana
Nyack Coll. (NY)
Oakwood Univ. (AL)
Oglethorpe Univ. (GA)
Ohio Dominican Univ.
Ohio State Univ.–Columbus
Ohio Univ.
Olivet Nazarene Univ. (IL)
Oral Roberts Univ. (OK)
Our Lady of the Lake Univ. (TX)
Pacific Lutheran Univ. (WA)
Pacific Union Coll. (CA)
Pacific Univ. (OR)
Philander Smith Coll. (AR)
Pittsburg State Univ. (KS)
Plymouth State Univ. (NH)
Point Loma Nazarene Univ. (CA)
Prairie View A&M Univ. (TX)
Providence Coll. (RI)
Purdue Univ.–West Lafayette (IN)
Quincy Univ. (IL)
Radford Univ. (VA)
Ramapo Coll. of New Jersey
Regis Coll. (MA)
Rhode Island Coll.
Richard Stockton Coll. of New
    Jersey
Roberts Wesleyan Coll. (NY)
Rust Coll. (MS)
Rutgers, the State Univ. of New
    Jersey–Camden
Rutgers, the State Univ. of New
    Jersey–New Brunswick
Rutgers, the State Univ. of New
    Jersey–Newark
Sacred Heart Univ. (CT)
Saginaw Valley State Univ. (MI)
Salem State Coll. (MA)
Salisbury Univ. (MD)
Salve Regina Univ. (RI)

San Diego State Univ.
San Francisco State Univ.
San Jose State Univ. (CA)
Savannah State Univ. (GA)
Seattle Univ.
Seton Hall Univ. (NJ)
Seton Hill Univ. (PA)
Shaw Univ. (NC)
Shepherd Univ. (WV)
Shippensburg Univ. of Pennsylvania
Siena Coll. (NY)
Skidmore Coll. (NY)
Slippery Rock Univ. of Pennsylvania
Sojourner-Douglass Coll. (MD)
South Carolina State Univ.
Southeast Missouri State Univ.
Southeastern Louisiana Univ.
Southeastern Univ. (FL)
Southern Adventist Univ. (TN)
Southern Arkansas Univ.
Southern Connecticut State Univ.
Southern Illinois Univ.–Carbondale
Southern Illinois Univ.–Edwardsville
Southern Univ. and A&M Coll. (LA)
Southern Univ.–New Orleans
Southwest Minnesota State Univ.
Southwestern Adventist Univ. (TX)
Southwestern Oklahoma State
    Univ.
Spalding Univ. (KY)
Spring Arbor Univ. (MI)
Springfield Coll. (MA)
St. Catherine Univ. (MN)
St. Cloud State Univ. (MN)
St. Edward's Univ. (TX)
St. Francis Univ. (PA)
St. John's Univ. (MN)
St. Joseph Coll. (CT)
St. Joseph's Coll. (IN)
St. Leo Univ. (FL)
St. Louis Univ.
St. Mary's Coll. (IN)
St. Olaf Coll. (MN)
Stephen F. Austin State Univ. (TX)
SUNY–Fredonia
SUNY–Plattsburgh
SUNY–Stony Brook
Syracuse Univ. (NY)
Tarleton State Univ. (TX)
Taylor Univ. (IN)
Temple Univ. (PA)
Tennessee State Univ.
Texas A&M International Univ.
Texas A&M Univ.–Commerce
Texas A&M Univ.–Kingsville
Texas Christian Univ.
Texas Coll.
Texas State Univ.–San Marcos
Texas Tech Univ.
Texas Woman's Univ.
Thomas Univ. (GA)
Trevecca Nazarene Univ. (TN)
Trinity Christian Coll. (IL)
Troy Univ. (AL)
Tulane Univ. (LA)
Tuskegee Univ. (AL)
Union Coll. (NE)
Union Coll. (KY)
Union Institute and Univ. (OH)
Union Univ. (TN)
Univ. at Albany–SUNY

Univ. of Akron (OH)
Univ. of Alabama
Univ. of Alabama–Birmingham
Univ. of Alaska–Anchorage
Univ. of Alaska–Fairbanks
Univ. of Arkansas
Univ. of Arkansas–Little Rock
Univ. of Arkansas–Monticello
Univ. of Arkansas–Pine Bluff
Univ. of California–Berkeley
Univ. of Central Florida
Univ. of Central Missouri
Univ. of Detroit Mercy
Univ. of Findlay (OH)
Univ. of Georgia
Univ. of Hawaii–Manoa
Univ. of Illinois–Chicago
Univ. of Illinois–Springfield
Univ. of Indianapolis
Univ. of Iowa
Univ. of Kansas
Univ. of Kentucky
Univ. of Louisiana–Monroe
Univ. of Maine
Univ. of Maine–Presque Isle
Univ. of Mary (ND)
Univ. of Mary Hardin-Baylor (TX)
Univ. of Maryland–Baltimore
    County
Univ. of Memphis
Univ. of Michigan–Flint
Univ. of Mississippi
Univ. of Missouri
Univ. of Missouri–St. Louis
Univ. of Montana
Univ. of Montevallo (AL)
Univ. of Nebraska–Kearney
Univ. of Nebraska–Omaha
Univ. of Nevada–Las Vegas
Univ. of Nevada–Reno
Univ. of New Hampshire
Univ. of North Alabama
Univ. of North Carolina–Charlotte
Univ. of North Carolina–
    Greensboro
Univ. of North Carolina–Pembroke
Univ. of North Carolina–
    Wilmington
Univ. of North Dakota
Univ. of North Texas
Univ. of Northern Iowa
Univ. of Oklahoma
Univ. of Pittsburgh
Univ. of Portland (OR)
Univ. of Rio Grande (OH)
Univ. of Sioux Falls (SD)
Univ. of South Alabama
Univ. of South Florida
Univ. of Southern Indiana
Univ. of Southern Maine
Univ. of Southern Mississippi
Univ. of St. Francis (IL)
Univ. of St. Francis (IN)
Univ. of St. Thomas (MN)
Univ. of Tennessee
Univ. of Tennessee–Martin
Univ. of Texas of the Permian Basin
Univ. of Texas–Arlington
Univ. of Texas–Austin
Univ. of Texas–El Paso
Univ. of Texas–Pan American

Univ. of the Cumberlands (KY)
Univ. of the District of Columbia
Univ. of Toledo (OH)
Univ. of Utah
Univ. of Vermont
Univ. of Washington
Univ. of West Florida
Univ. of Wisconsin–Eau Claire
Univ. of Wisconsin–Madison
Univ. of Wisconsin–Milwaukee
Univ. of Wisconsin–Oshkosh
Univ. of Wisconsin–River Falls
Univ. of Wisconsin–Superior
Univ. of Wisconsin–Whitewater
Univ. of Wyoming
Ursuline Coll. (OH)
Utah State Univ.
Valparaiso Univ. (IN)
Virginia Commonwealth Univ.
Virginia Intermont Coll.
Virginia State Univ.
Virginia Union Univ.
Viterbo Univ. (WI)
Warner Pacific Coll. (OR)
Warner Univ. (FL)
Warren Wilson Coll. (NC)
Wartburg Coll. (IA)
Washburn Univ. (KS)
Wayne State Univ. (MI)
Weber State Univ. (UT)
West Chester Univ. of Pennsylvania
West Texas A&M Univ.
West Virginia State Univ.
West Virginia Univ.
Western Carolina Univ. (NC)
Western Connecticut State Univ.
Western Illinois Univ.
Western Kentucky Univ.
Western Michigan Univ.
Western New England Coll. (MA)
Western New Mexico Univ.
Westfield State Coll. (MA)
Wheelock Coll. (MA)
Whittier Coll. (CA)
Wichita State Univ. (KS)
Widener Univ. (PA)
Wilberforce Univ. (OH)
William Woods Univ. (MO)
Wilmington Coll. (OH)
Winston-Salem State Univ. (NC)
Winthrop Univ. (SC)
Wright State Univ. (OH)
Xavier Univ. (OH)
Youngstown State Univ. (OH)

Sociology

Abilene Christian Univ. (TX)
Adams State Coll. (CO)
Adelphi Univ. (NY)
Adrian Coll. (MI)
Alabama Agricultural and
    Mechanical Univ.
Alabama State Univ.
Albany State Univ. (GA)
Albertus Magnus Coll. (CT)
Albion Coll. (MI)
Albright Coll. (PA)
Alcorn State Univ. (MS)
Alfred Univ. (NY)
Alma Coll. (MI)

Alverno Coll. (WI)
American Univ. (DC)
Amherst Coll. (MA)
Anderson Univ. (IN)
Andrews Univ. (MI)
Angelo State Univ. (TX)
Anna Maria Coll. (MA)
Appalachian State Univ. (NC)
Aquinas Coll. (MI)
Arcadia Univ. (PA)
Arizona State Univ.
Arkansas State Univ.–Jonesboro
Arkansas Tech Univ.
Asbury Univ. (KY)
Ashland Univ. (OH)
Assumption Coll. (MA)
Auburn Univ. (AL)
Auburn Univ.–Montgomery (AL)
Augsburg Coll. (MN)
Augusta State Univ. (GA)
Augustana Coll. (IL)
Augustana Coll. (SD)
Aurora Univ. (IL)
Austin Coll. (TX)
Austin Peay State Univ. (TN)
Averett Univ. (VA)
Avila Univ. (MO)
Azusa Pacific Univ. (CA)
Baker Univ. (KS)
Baldwin-Wallace Coll. (OH)
Ball State Univ. (IN)
Barnard Coll. (NY)
Barry Univ. (FL)
Bates Coll. (ME)
Baylor Univ. (TX)
Bellarmine Univ. (KY)
Bellevue Univ. (NE)
Belmont Abbey Coll. (NC)
Belmont Univ. (TN)
Beloit Coll. (WI)
Bemidji State Univ. (MN)
Benedict Coll. (SC)
Benedictine Coll. (KS)
Benedictine Univ. (IL)
Bennett Coll. (NC)
Bennington Coll. (VT)
Berea Coll. (KY)
Bethel Coll. (IN)
Bethune-Cookman Univ. (FL)
Binghamton Univ.–SUNY
Biola Univ. (CA)
Black Hills State Univ. (SD)
Bloomfield Coll. (NJ)
Bloomsburg Univ. of Pennsylvania
Bluffton Univ. (OH)
Boise State Univ. (ID)
Boston Univ.
Bowdoin Coll. (ME)
Bowie State Univ. (MD)
Bowling Green State Univ. (OH)
Bradley Univ. (IL)
Brandeis Univ. (MA)
Brewton-Parker Coll. (GA)
Briar Cliff Univ. (IA)
Bridgewater Coll. (VA)
Bridgewater State Coll. (MA)
Brigham Young Univ.–Provo (UT)
Brown Univ. (RI)
Bryn Mawr Coll. (PA)
Bucknell Univ. (PA)
Buena Vista Univ. (IA)

Butler Univ. (IN)
Cabrini Coll. (PA)
Caldwell Coll. (NJ)
California Baptist Univ.
California Lutheran Univ.
California State Polytechnic Univ.–
    Pomona
California State Univ.–Bakersfield
California State Univ.–Chico
California State Univ.–Dominguez
    Hills
California State Univ.–East Bay
California State Univ.–Fresno
California State Univ.–Fullerton
California State Univ.–Long Beach
California State Univ.–Los Angeles
California State Univ.–Northridge
California State Univ.–Sacramento
California State Univ.–San
    Bernardino
California State Univ.–San Marcos
California State Univ.–Stanislaus
Calvin Coll. (MI)
Cameron Univ. (OK)
Campbellsville Univ. (KY)
Canisius Coll. (NY)
Capital Univ. (OH)
Carlow Univ. (PA)
Carroll Coll. (MT)
Carroll Univ. (WI)
Carson-Newman Coll. (TN)
Carthage Coll. (WI)
Case Western Reserve Univ. (OH)
Castleton State Coll. (VT)
Catawba Coll. (NC)
Catholic Univ. of America (DC)
Cedarville Univ. (OH)
Centenary Coll. (NJ)
Centenary Coll. of Louisiana
Central Christian Coll. (KS)
Central Coll. (IA)
Central Connecticut State Univ.
Central Methodist Univ. (MO)
Central Michigan Univ.
Central State Univ. (OH)
Central Washington Univ.
Chadron State Coll. (NE)
Chapman Univ. (CA)
Charleston Southern Univ. (SC)
Chestnut Hill Coll. (PA)
Chicago State Univ.
Christopher Newport Univ. (VA)
Claflin Univ. (SC)
Clarion Univ. of Pennsylvania
Clark Atlanta Univ.
Clark Univ. (MA)
Clarke Univ. (IA)
Clarkson Univ. (NY)
Cleveland State Univ.
Coastal Carolina Univ. (SC)
Coe Coll. (IA)
Coker Coll. (SC)
Colby Coll. (ME)
Colgate Univ. (NY)
Coll. at Brockport–SUNY
Coll. of Charleston (SC)
Coll. of Idaho (ID)
Coll. of Mount St. Joseph (OH)
Coll. of Mount St. Vincent (NY)
Coll. of New Jersey
Coll. of Our Lady of the Elms (MA)

Coll. of St. Benedict (MN)
Coll. of St. Elizabeth (NJ)
Coll. of St. Rose (NY)
Coll. of the Holy Cross (MA)
Coll. of the Ozarks (MO)
Coll. of William and Mary (VA)
Coll. of Wooster (OH)
Colorado Coll.
Colorado State Univ.
Colorado State Univ.–Pueblo
Columbia Coll. (MO)
Columbia Univ. (NY)
Columbus State Univ. (GA)
Concord Univ. (WV)
Concordia Coll.–Moorhead (MN)
Concordia Univ. (MI)
Concordia Univ. Chicago (IL)
Concordia Univ.–St. Paul (MN)
Connecticut Coll.
Cornell Coll. (IA)
Cornell Univ. (NY)
Cornerstone Univ. (MI)
Covenant Coll. (GA)
Creighton Univ. (NE)
Cumberland Univ. (TN)
CUNY–Baruch Coll.
CUNY–Brooklyn Coll.
CUNY–City Coll.
CUNY–Hunter Coll.
CUNY–Lehman Coll.
CUNY–Queens Coll.
CUNY–York Coll.
Curry Coll. (MA)
D'Youville Coll. (NY)
Dakota Wesleyan Univ. (SD)
Dallas Baptist Univ.
Dartmouth Coll. (NH)
Davidson Coll. (NC)
Davis and Elkins Coll. (WV)
Delaware State Univ.
Denison Univ. (OH)
DePaul Univ. (IL)
DePauw Univ. (IN)
Dickinson Coll. (PA)
Dillard Univ. (LA)
Dominican Univ. (IL)
Dowling Coll. (NY)
Drake Univ. (IA)
Drew Univ. (NJ)
Drexel Univ. (PA)
Drury Univ. (MO)
Duke Univ. (NC)
Duquesne Univ. (PA)
Earlham Coll. (IN)
East Carolina Univ. (NC)
East Central Univ. (OK)
East Stroudsburg Univ. of
    Pennsylvania
East Tennessee State Univ.
East Texas Baptist Univ.
Eastern Connecticut State Univ.
Eastern Illinois Univ.
Eastern Kentucky Univ.
Eastern Mennonite Univ. (VA)
Eastern Michigan Univ.
Eastern Nazarene Coll. (MA)
Eastern New Mexico Univ.
Eastern Univ. (PA)
Eckerd Coll. (FL)
Edgewood Coll. (WI)
Edinboro Univ. of Pennsylvania

Edward Waters Coll. (FL)
Elizabeth City State Univ. (NC)
Elizabethtown Coll. (PA)
Elmhurst Coll. (IL)
Elon Univ. (NC)
Emmanuel Coll. (MA)
Emory and Henry Coll. (VA)
Emory Univ. (GA)
Emporia State Univ. (KS)
Evangel Univ. (MO)
Evergreen State Coll. (WA)
Excelsior Coll. (NY)
Fairfield Univ. (CT)
Fairleigh Dickinson Univ. (NJ)
Fairmont State Univ. (WV)
Fayetteville State Univ. (NC)
Ferris State Univ. (MI)
Fisk Univ. (TN)
Fitchburg State Coll. (MA)
Flagler Coll. (FL)
Florida Atlantic Univ.
Florida International Univ.
Florida Memorial Univ.
Florida Southern Coll.
Florida State Univ.
Fordham Univ. (NY)
Fort Hays State Univ. (KS)
Fort Lewis Coll. (CO)
Framingham State Coll. (MA)
Francis Marion Univ. (SC)
Franciscan Univ. of Steubenville (OH)
Franklin and Marshall Coll. (PA)
Franklin Coll. (IN)
Franklin Pierce Univ. (NH)
Fresno Pacific Univ. (CA)
Friends Univ. (KS)
Furman Univ. (SC)
Gallaudet Univ. (DC)
Gardner-Webb Univ. (NC)
Geneva Coll. (PA)
George Fox Univ. (OR)
George Mason Univ. (VA)
George Washington Univ. (DC)
Georgetown Coll. (KY)
Georgetown Univ. (DC)
Georgia Coll. & State Univ.
Georgia Southern Univ.
Georgia State Univ.
Georgian Court Univ. (NJ)
Gettysburg Coll. (PA)
Gonzaga Univ. (WA)
Gordon Coll. (MA)
Goshen Coll. (IN)
Goucher Coll. (MD)
Grace Coll. and Seminary (IN)
Graceland Univ. (IA)
Grambling State Univ. (LA)
Greensboro Coll. (NC)
Greenville Coll. (IL)
Grinnell Coll. (IA)
Grove City Coll. (PA)
Guilford Coll. (NC)
Gustavus Adolphus Coll. (MN)
Gwynedd-Mercy Coll. (PA)
Hamilton Coll. (NY)
Hamline Univ. (MN)
Hampshire Coll. (MA)
Hampton Univ. (VA)
Hanover Coll. (IN)
Hardin-Simmons Univ. (TX)

Hartwick Coll. (NY)
Harvard Univ. (MA)
Haverford Coll. (PA)
Hawaii Pacific Univ.
Henderson State Univ. (AR)
Hendrix Coll. (AR)
High Point Univ. (NC)
Hillsdale Coll. (MI)
Hiram Coll. (OH)
Hobart and William Smith Colleges (NY)
Hofstra Univ. (NY)
Hollins Univ. (VA)
Holy Family Univ. (PA)
Holy Names Univ. (CA)
Hood Coll. (MD)
Hope Coll. (MI)
Houghton Coll. (NY)
Houston Baptist Univ.
Howard Payne Univ. (TX)
Howard Univ. (DC)
Humboldt State Univ. (CA)
Huntington Univ. (IN)
Huston-Tillotson Univ. (TX)
Idaho State Univ.
Illinois Coll.
Illinois State Univ.
Illinois Wesleyan Univ.
Immaculata Univ. (PA)
Indiana State Univ.
Indiana Univ. East
Indiana Univ. Northwest
Indiana Univ. of Pennsylvania
Indiana Univ. Southeast
Indiana Univ.–Bloomington
Indiana Univ.–Kokomo
Indiana Univ.–South Bend
Indiana Univ.-Purdue Univ.–Fort Wayne
Indiana Univ.-Purdue Univ.–Indianapolis
Indiana Wesleyan Univ.
Iona Coll. (NY)
Iowa State Univ.
Iowa Wesleyan Coll.
Ithaca Coll. (NY)
Jackson State Univ. (MS)
Jacksonville State Univ. (AL)
Jacksonville Univ. (FL)
James Madison Univ. (VA)
Jarvis Christian Coll. (TX)
John Carroll Univ. (OH)
Johns Hopkins Univ. (MD)
Judson Univ. (IL)
Juniata Coll. (PA)
Kalamazoo Coll. (MI)
Kansas State Univ.
Kansas Wesleyan Univ.
Kean Univ. (NJ)
Keene State Coll. (NH)
Kennesaw State Univ. (GA)
Kent State Univ. (OH)
Kentucky State Univ.
Kentucky Wesleyan Coll.
Kenyon Coll. (OH)
Keuka Coll. (NY)
King's Coll. (PA)
Kutztown Univ. of Pennsylvania
La Roche Coll. (PA)
La Salle Univ. (PA)
LaGrange Coll. (GA)

Lake Forest Coll. (IL)
Lake Superior State Univ. (MI)
Lakeland Coll. (WI)
Lamar Univ. (TX)
Lambuth Univ. (TN)
Lander Univ. (SC)
Lane Coll. (TN)
Lasell Coll. (MA)
Le Moyne Coll. (NY)
Lebanon Valley Coll. (PA)
Lees-McRae Coll. (NC)
Lehigh Univ. (PA)
LeMoyne-Owen Coll. (TN)
Lenoir-Rhyne Univ. (NC)
Lewis & Clark Coll. (OR)
Lincoln Univ. (PA)
Lincoln Univ. (MO)
Lindenwood Univ. (MO)
Linfield Coll. (OR)
Livingstone Coll. (NC)
Lock Haven Univ. of Pennsylvania
Long Island Univ.–C.W. Post Campus (NY)
Longwood Univ. (VA)
Loras Coll. (IA)
Louisiana Coll.
Louisiana State Univ.–Baton Rouge
Louisiana State Univ.–Shreveport
Louisiana Tech Univ.
Lourdes Coll. (OH)
Loyola Marymount Univ. (CA)
Loyola Univ. Chicago
Loyola Univ. Maryland
Loyola Univ. New Orleans
Luther Coll. (IA)
Lycoming Coll. (PA)
Lynchburg Coll. (VA)
Macalester Coll. (MN)
Manchester Coll. (IN)
Manhattan Coll. (NY)
Manhattanville Coll. (NY)
Mansfield Univ. of Pennsylvania
Marian Univ. (IN)
Marlboro Coll. (VT)
Marquette Univ. (WI)
Mars Hill Coll. (NC)
Marshall Univ. (WV)
Martin Univ. (IN)
Mary Baldwin Coll. (VA)
Marylhurst Univ. (OR)
Marymount Manhattan Coll. (NY)
Marymount Univ. (VA)
Maryville Coll. (TN)
Maryville Univ. of St. Louis (MO)
Massachusetts Coll. of Liberal Arts
McDaniel Coll. (MD)
McKendree Univ. (IL)
McMurry Univ. (TX)
McNeese State Univ. (LA)
McPherson Coll. (KS)
Mercyhurst Coll. (PA)
Meredith Coll. (NC)
Merrimack Coll. (MA)
Mesa State Coll. (CO)
Messiah Coll. (PA)
Methodist Univ. (NC)
Metropolitan State Coll. of Denver
Miami Univ.–Oxford (OH)
Michigan State Univ.
MidAmerica Nazarene Univ. (KS)
Middle Tennessee State Univ.

Middlebury Coll. (VT)
Midland Lutheran Coll. (NE)
Midwestern State Univ. (TX)
Millersville Univ. of Pennsylvania
Milligan Coll. (TN)
Millikin Univ. (IL)
Mills Coll. (CA)
Millsaps Coll. (MS)
Minnesota State Univ.–Mankato
Minnesota State Univ.–Moorhead
Minot State Univ. (ND)
Mississippi Coll.
Mississippi State Univ.
Mississippi Valley State Univ.
Missouri Southern State Univ.
Missouri State Univ.
Missouri Valley Coll.
Molloy Coll. (NY)
Monmouth Coll. (IL)
Monmouth Univ. (NJ)
Montana State Univ.
Montana State Univ.–Billings
Montclair State Univ. (NJ)
Moravian Coll. (PA)
Morehead State Univ. (KY)
Morehouse Coll. (GA)
Morgan State Univ. (MD)
Morris Coll. (SC)
Mount Holyoke Coll. (MA)
Mount Mercy Coll. (IA)
Mount St. Mary Coll. (NY)
Mount St. Mary's Coll. (CA)
Mount St. Mary's Univ. (MD)
Mount Vernon Nazarene Univ. (OH)
Muhlenberg Coll. (PA)
Murray State Univ. (KY)
Muskingum Univ. (OH)
Nazareth Coll. (NY)
Nebraska Wesleyan Univ.
New England Coll. (NH)
New Jersey City Univ.
New Mexico State Univ.
New York Institute of Technology
New York Univ.
Newberry Coll. (SC)
Newman Univ. (KS)
Niagara Univ. (NY)
Nicholls State Univ. (LA)
Norfolk State Univ. (VA)
North Carolina A&T State Univ.
North Carolina Central Univ.
North Carolina State Univ.–Raleigh
North Carolina Wesleyan Coll.
North Central Coll. (IL)
North Dakota State Univ.
North Georgia Coll. and State Univ.
North Park Univ. (IL)
Northeastern Illinois Univ.
Northeastern State Univ. (OK)
Northeastern Univ. (MA)
Northern Arizona Univ.
Northern Illinois Univ.
Northern Kentucky Univ.
Northern Michigan Univ.
Northern State Univ. (SD)
Northland Coll. (WI)
Northwest Missouri State Univ.
Northwestern Coll. (IA)
Northwestern State Univ. of Louisiana

Northwestern Univ. (IL)
Notre Dame de Namur Univ. (CA)
Oakland City Univ. (IN)
Oakland Univ. (MI)
Oberlin Coll. (OH)
Occidental Coll. (CA)
Oglethorpe Univ. (GA)
Ohio Dominican Univ.
Ohio Northern Univ.
Ohio State Univ.–Columbus
Ohio Univ.
Ohio Wesleyan Univ.
Oklahoma Baptist Univ.
Oklahoma City Univ.
Oklahoma State Univ.
Old Dominion Univ. (VA)
Olivet Coll. (MI)
Olivet Nazarene Univ. (IL)
Oral Roberts Univ. (OK)
Oregon State Univ.
Otterbein Coll. (OH)
Ouachita Baptist Univ. (AR)
Our Lady of the Lake Univ. (TX)
Pacific Lutheran Univ. (WA)
Pacific Univ. (OR)
Paine Coll. (GA)
Park Univ. (MO)
Pennsylvania State Univ.–Univ. Park
Pepperdine Univ. (CA)
Pfeiffer Univ. (NC)
Philander Smith Coll. (AR)
Piedmont Coll. (GA)
Pikeville Coll. (KY)
Pittsburg State Univ. (KS)
Pitzer Coll. (CA)
Point Loma Nazarene Univ. (CA)
Pomona Coll. (CA)
Portland State Univ. (OR)
Post Univ. (CT)
Prairie View A&M Univ. (TX)
Presbyterian Coll. (SC)
Princeton Univ. (NJ)
Principia Coll. (IL)
Providence Coll. (RI)
Purdue Univ.–Calumet (IN)
Quinnipiac Univ. (CT)
Radford Univ. (VA)
Ramapo Coll. of New Jersey
Randolph Coll. (VA)
Randolph-Macon Coll. (VA)
Reed Coll. (OR)
Regis Coll. (MA)
Regis Univ. (CO)
Reinhardt Univ. (GA)
Rhode Island Coll.
Rhodes Coll. (TN)
Rice Univ. (TX)
Richard Stockton Coll. of New Jersey
Rider Univ. (NJ)
Ripon Coll. (WI)
Rivier Coll. (NH)
Roanoke Coll. (VA)
Roberts Wesleyan Coll. (NY)
Rockhurst Univ. (MO)
Rocky Mountain Coll. (MT)
Roger Williams Univ. (RI)
Rollins Coll. (FL)
Roosevelt Univ. (IL)
Rosemont Coll. (PA)
Russell Sage Coll. (NY)

Rust Coll. (MS)
Rutgers, the State Univ. of New Jersey–Camden
Rutgers, the State Univ. of New Jersey–New Brunswick
Rutgers, the State Univ. of New Jersey–Newark
Sacred Heart Univ. (CT)
Saginaw Valley State Univ. (MI)
Salem Coll. (NC)
Salem State Coll. (MA)
Salisbury Univ. (MD)
Salve Regina Univ. (RI)
Sam Houston State Univ. (TX)
Samford Univ. (AL)
San Diego State Univ.
San Francisco State Univ.
Santa Clara Univ. (CA)
Savannah State Univ. (GA)
Scripps Coll. (CA)
Seattle Pacific Univ.
Seattle Univ.
Seton Hall Univ. (NJ)
Seton Hill Univ. (PA)
Shaw Univ. (NC)
Shawnee State Univ. (OH)
Shenandoah Univ. (VA)
Shepherd Univ. (WV)
Shippensburg Univ. of Pennsylvania
Shorter Coll. (GA)
Siena Coll. (NY)
Simmons Coll. (MA)
Simpson Coll. (IA)
Skidmore Coll. (NY)
Slippery Rock Univ. of Pennsylvania
Smith Coll. (MA)
Sojourner-Douglass Coll. (MD)
Sonoma State Univ. (CA)
South Carolina State Univ.
South Dakota State Univ.
Southeastern Louisiana Univ.
Southeastern Oklahoma State Univ.
Southern Arkansas Univ.
Southern Illinois Univ.–Carbondale
Southern Illinois Univ.–Edwardsville
Southern Methodist Univ. (TX)
Southern Nazarene Univ. (OK)
Southern Oregon Univ.
Southern Univ. and A&M Coll. (LA)
Southern Univ.–New Orleans
Southern Utah Univ.
Southwest Baptist Univ. (MO)
Southwest Minnesota State Univ.
Southwestern Univ. (TX)
Spelman Coll. (GA)
Spring Arbor Univ. (MI)
Spring Hill Coll. (AL)
Springfield Coll. (MA)
St. Ambrose Univ. (IA)
St. Anselm Coll. (NH)
St. Bonaventure Univ. (NY)
St. Catherine Univ. (MN)
St. Cloud State Univ. (MN)
St. Edward's Univ. (TX)
St. Francis Coll. (NY)
St. Francis Univ. (PA)
St. Gregory's Univ. (OK)
St. John Fisher Coll. (NY)
St. John's Univ. (NY)
St. John's Univ. (MN)
St. Joseph Coll. (CT)

St. Joseph's Coll. (ME)
St. Joseph's Coll. (IN)
St. Joseph's Univ. (PA)
St. Lawrence Univ. (NY)
St. Leo Univ. (FL)
St. Louis Univ.
St. Mary's Coll. (IN)
St. Mary's Coll. of California
St. Mary's Coll. of Maryland
St. Mary's Univ. of Minnesota
St. Mary's Univ. of San Antonio (TX)
St. Michael's Coll. (VT)
St. Norbert Coll. (WI)
St. Olaf Coll. (MN)
St. Peter's Coll. (NJ)
St. Vincent Coll. (PA)
St. Xavier Univ. (IL)
Stanford Univ. (CA)
Stephen F. Austin State Univ. (TX)
Stetson Univ. (FL)
Stonehill Coll. (MA)
Suffolk Univ. (MA)
SUNY Coll.–Cortland
SUNY Coll.–Old Westbury
SUNY Coll.–Oneonta
SUNY Coll.–Potsdam
SUNY Institute of Technology–Utica/Rome
SUNY–Fredonia
SUNY–Geneseo
SUNY–Oswego
SUNY–Plattsburgh
SUNY–Stony Brook
Susquehanna Univ. (PA)
Syracuse Univ. (NY)
Tabor Coll. (KS)
Talladega Coll. (AL)
Tarleton State Univ. (TX)
Taylor Univ. (IN)
Temple Univ. (PA)
Tennessee State Univ.
Tennessee Technological Univ.
Texas A&M International Univ.
Texas A&M Univ.–Coll. Station
Texas A&M Univ.–Commerce
Texas A&M Univ.–Corpus Christi
Texas A&M Univ.–Kingsville
Texas Christian Univ.
Texas Coll.
Texas Lutheran Univ.
Texas State Univ.–San Marcos
Texas Tech Univ.
Texas Wesleyan Univ.
Texas Woman's Univ.
Thiel Coll. (PA)
Thomas Edison State Coll. (NJ)
Thomas More Coll. (KY)
Tougaloo Coll. (MS)
Touro Coll. (NY)
Transylvania Univ. (KY)
Trinity Christian Coll. (IL)
Trinity Coll. (CT)
Trinity Univ. (DC)
Troy Univ. (AL)
Truman State Univ. (MO)
Tufts Univ. (MA)
Tulane Univ. (LA)
Tuskegee Univ. (AL)
Union Coll. (KY)
Union Coll. (NY)

Union Univ. (TN)
Univ. at Albany–SUNY
Univ. at Buffalo–SUNY
Univ. of Akron (OH)
Univ. of Alabama
Univ. of Alabama–Birmingham
Univ. of Alabama–Huntsville
Univ. of Alaska–Anchorage
Univ. of Alaska–Fairbanks
Univ. of Arizona
Univ. of Arkansas
Univ. of Arkansas–Little Rock
Univ. of Arkansas–Pine Bluff
Univ. of California–Berkeley
Univ. of California–Davis
Univ. of California–Irvine
Univ. of California–Los Angeles
Univ. of California–Riverside
Univ. of California–San Diego
Univ. of California–Santa Barbara
Univ. of California–Santa Cruz
Univ. of Central Arkansas
Univ. of Central Florida
Univ. of Central Missouri
Univ. of Central Oklahoma
Univ. of Chicago
Univ. of Colorado–Boulder
Univ. of Colorado–Colorado Springs
Univ. of Colorado–Denver
Univ. of Connecticut
Univ. of Dayton (OH)
Univ. of Delaware
Univ. of Denver
Univ. of Detroit Mercy
Univ. of Dubuque (IA)
Univ. of Evansville (IN)
Univ. of Findlay (OH)
Univ. of Florida
Univ. of Georgia
Univ. of Great Falls (MT)
Univ. of Hartford (CT)
Univ. of Hawaii–Hilo
Univ. of Hawaii–Manoa
Univ. of Houston
Univ. of Houston–Downtown
Univ. of Illinois–Chicago
Univ. of Illinois–Urbana-Champaign
Univ. of Indianapolis
Univ. of Iowa
Univ. of Kansas
Univ. of Kentucky
Univ. of La Verne (CA)
Univ. of Louisiana–Lafayette
Univ. of Louisiana–Monroe
Univ. of Louisville (KY)
Univ. of Maine
Univ. of Maine–Presque Isle
Univ. of Mary Hardin-Baylor (TX)
Univ. of Mary Washington (VA)
Univ. of Maryland–Baltimore County
Univ. of Maryland–Coll. Park
Univ. of Maryland–Eastern Shore
Univ. of Massachusetts–Amherst
Univ. of Massachusetts–Boston
Univ. of Massachusetts–Dartmouth
Univ. of Massachusetts–Lowell
Univ. of Memphis
Univ. of Miami (FL)
Univ. of Michigan–Ann Arbor

Univ. of Michigan–Dearborn
Univ. of Michigan–Flint
Univ. of Minnesota–Duluth
Univ. of Minnesota–Morris
Univ. of Minnesota–Twin Cities
Univ. of Mississippi
Univ. of Missouri
Univ. of Missouri–Kansas City
Univ. of Missouri–St. Louis
Univ. of Montana
Univ. of Montevallo (AL)
Univ. of Mount Union (OH)
Univ. of Nebraska–Kearney
Univ. of Nebraska–Lincoln
Univ. of Nebraska–Omaha
Univ. of Nevada–Las Vegas
Univ. of Nevada–Reno
Univ. of New England (ME)
Univ. of New Hampshire
Univ. of New Mexico
Univ. of New Orleans
Univ. of North Alabama
Univ. of North Carolina–Asheville
Univ. of North Carolina–Chapel Hill
Univ. of North Carolina–Charlotte
Univ. of North Carolina–Greensboro
Univ. of North Carolina–Pembroke
Univ. of North Carolina–Wilmington
Univ. of North Dakota
Univ. of North Florida
Univ. of North Texas
Univ. of Northern Colorado
Univ. of Northern Iowa
Univ. of Notre Dame (IN)
Univ. of Oklahoma
Univ. of Oregon
Univ. of Pennsylvania
Univ. of Pittsburgh
Univ. of Pittsburgh–Bradford
Univ. of Pittsburgh–Johnstown
Univ. of Portland (OR)
Univ. of Puget Sound (WA)
Univ. of Redlands (CA)
Univ. of Rhode Island
Univ. of Richmond (VA)
Univ. of San Diego
Univ. of San Francisco
Univ. of Science and Arts of Oklahoma
Univ. of Scranton (PA)
Univ. of Sioux Falls (SD)
Univ. of South Alabama
Univ. of South Carolina
Univ. of South Carolina–Aiken
Univ. of South Carolina–Upstate
Univ. of South Dakota
Univ. of South Florida
Univ. of Southern California
Univ. of Southern Indiana
Univ. of Southern Maine
Univ. of Southern Mississippi
Univ. of St. Francis (IN)
Univ. of St. Mary (KS)
Univ. of St. Thomas (MN)
Univ. of Tampa (FL)
Univ. of Tennessee
Univ. of Tennessee–Martin
Univ. of Texas of the Permian Basin
Univ. of Texas–Austin

Univ. of Texas–Brownsville
Univ. of Texas–Dallas
Univ. of Texas–El Paso
Univ. of Texas–Pan American
Univ. of Texas–San Antonio
Univ. of Texas–Tyler
Univ. of the District of Columbia
Univ. of the Incarnate Word (TX)
Univ. of the Ozarks (AR)
Univ. of the Pacific (CA)
Univ. of Toledo (OH)
Univ. of Tulsa (OK)
Univ. of Utah
Univ. of Vermont
Univ. of Virginia
Univ. of Virginia–Wise
Univ. of Washington
Univ. of West Alabama
Univ. of West Florida
Univ. of West Georgia
Univ. of Wisconsin–La Crosse
Univ. of Wisconsin–Madison
Univ. of Wisconsin–Milwaukee
Univ. of Wisconsin–Parkside
Univ. of Wisconsin–River Falls
Univ. of Wisconsin–Stevens Point
Univ. of Wisconsin–Superior
Univ. of Wisconsin–Whitewater
Univ. of Wyoming
Urbana Univ. (OH)
Ursuline Coll. (OH)
Utah State Univ.
Utica Coll. (NY)
Valdosta State Univ. (GA)
Valparaiso Univ. (IN)
Vanderbilt Univ. (TN)
Vanguard Univ. of Southern California
Vassar Coll. (NY)
Villanova Univ. (PA)
Virginia Commonwealth Univ.
Virginia State Univ.
Virginia Tech
Virginia Wesleyan Coll.
Viterbo Univ. (WI)
Voorhees Coll. (SC)
Wagner Coll. (NY)
Wake Forest Univ. (NC)
Walsh Univ. (OH)
Wartburg Coll. (IA)
Washburn Univ. (KS)
Washington and Jefferson Coll. (PA)
Washington and Lee Univ. (VA)
Washington Coll. (MD)
Washington State Univ.
Wayne State Coll. (NE)
Wayne State Univ. (MI)
Weber State Univ. (UT)
Webster Univ. (MO)
Wellesley Coll. (MA)
Wells Coll. (NY)
Wesleyan Univ. (CT)
West Chester Univ. of Pennsylvania
West Texas A&M Univ.
West Virginia State Univ.
West Virginia Univ.
West Virginia Wesleyan Coll.
Western Carolina Univ. (NC)
Western Connecticut State Univ.
Western Illinois Univ.

Western Kentucky Univ.
Western Michigan Univ.
Western New England Coll. (MA)
Western New Mexico Univ.
Western Oregon Univ.
Western State Coll. of Colorado
Western Washington Univ.
Westfield State Coll. (MA)
Westminster Coll. (PA)
Westminster Coll. (UT)
Westminster Coll. (MO)
Westmont Coll. (CA)
Wheaton Coll. (IL)
Wheaton Coll. (MA)
Whitman Coll. (WA)
Whittier Coll. (CA)
Whitworth Univ. (WA)
Wichita State Univ. (KS)
Widener Univ. (PA)
Wilberforce Univ. (OH)
Wiley Coll. (TX)
Wilkes Univ. (PA)
Willamette Univ. (OR)
William Paterson Univ. of New
    Jersey
Williams Coll. (MA)
Wingate Univ. (NC)
Winston-Salem State Univ. (NC)
Winthrop Univ. (SC)
Wittenberg Univ. (OH)
Wofford Coll. (SC)
Worcester State Coll. (MA)
Wright State Univ. (OH)
Xavier Univ. (OH)
Yale Univ. (CT)
Yeshiva Univ. (NY)
York Coll. of Pennsylvania
Youngstown State Univ. (OH)

Soil Sciences

Brigham Young Univ.–Provo (UT)
California Polytechnic State Univ.–
    San Luis Obispo
California State Polytechnic Univ.–
    Pomona
Colorado State Univ.
Humboldt State Univ. (CA)
Michigan State Univ.
New Mexico State Univ.
North Dakota State Univ.
Ohio State Univ.–Columbus
Oklahoma State Univ.
Pennsylvania State Univ.–Univ. Park
Purdue Univ.–West Lafayette (IN)
Texas A&M Univ.–Coll. Station
Tuskegee Univ. (AL)
Univ. of Arizona
Univ. of California–Davis
Univ. of Delaware
Univ. of Florida
Univ. of Hawaii–Manoa
Univ. of Kentucky
Univ. of Maine
Univ. of Nebraska–Lincoln
Univ. of Rhode Island
Univ. of Tennessee
Univ. of Wisconsin–Madison
Utah State Univ.
Washington State Univ.

South Asian Languages, Literatures, and Linguistics

Univ. of Chicago

Southeast Asian and Australasian/Pacific Languages, Literatures, and Linguistics

Univ. of Chicago
Univ. of Hawaii–Manoa

Special Education and Teaching

Benedictine Univ. (IL)
Boston Univ.
Cazenovia Coll. (NY)
Cedar Crest Coll. (PA)
Cheyney Univ. of Pennsylvania
Clemson Univ. (SC)
Coll. of St. Joseph (VT)
Columbus State Univ. (GA)
Coppin State Univ. (MD)
CUNY–Lehman Coll.
East Central Univ. (OK)
Felician Coll. (NJ)
Fisk Univ. (TN)
Greensboro Coll. (NC)
Gwynedd-Mercy Coll. (PA)
Longwood Univ. (VA)
Marygrove Coll. (MI)
Mount Vernon Nazarene Univ.
    (OH)
Northeastern Illinois Univ.
Oklahoma Christian Univ.
Prescott Coll. (AZ)
Seattle Pacific Univ.
Simmons Coll. (MA)
Southern Connecticut State Univ.
Spring Arbor Univ. (MI)
St. Bonaventure Univ. (NY)
St. Martin's Univ. (WA)
St. Mary-of-the-Woods Coll. (IN)
Touro Coll. (NY)
Tusculum Coll. (TN)
Univ. of Great Falls (MT)
Univ. of Wisconsin–Oshkosh
Westfield State Coll. (MA)
Wheelock Coll. (MA)
Widener Univ. (PA)

Specialized Sales, Merchandising, and Marketing Operations

Ashland Univ. (OH)
Baylor Univ. (TX)
Bluffton Univ. (OH)
Bowling Green State Univ. (OH)
Brenau Univ. (GA)
California State Polytechnic Univ.–
    Pomona
Cazenovia Coll. (NY)
Centenary Coll. (NJ)
Central Connecticut State Univ.
Central Michigan Univ.
Central Washington Univ.
Clark Atlanta Univ.

Concord Univ. (WV)
Dominican Univ. (IL)
Eastern Kentucky Univ.
Eastern Michigan Univ.
Fashion Institute of Technology
    (NY)
Ferris State Univ. (MI)
Gannon Univ. (PA)
Grand Valley State Univ. (MI)
Harding Univ. (AR)
Howard Univ. (DC)
Immaculata Univ. (PA)
Indiana Univ. of Pennsylvania
Johnson and Wales Univ. (RI)
Kent State Univ. (OH)
Lambuth Univ. (TN)
Lasell Coll. (MA)
Liberty Univ. (VA)
Lipscomb Univ. (TN)
Louisiana State Univ.–Baton Rouge
Marist Coll. (NY)
Marymount Univ. (VA)
Meredith Coll. (NC)
Mount Ida Coll. (MA)
Mount Mary Coll. (WI)
Niagara Univ. (NY)
Northern Arizona Univ.
Northwood Univ. (MI)
Olivet Nazarene Univ. (IL)
Philadelphia Univ.
Purdue Univ.–Calumet (IN)
Purdue Univ.–West Lafayette (IN)
St. Catherine Univ. (MN)
St. Joseph's Univ. (PA)
St. Xavier Univ. (IL)
Stephen F. Austin State Univ. (TX)
Stephens Coll. (MO)
SUNY Coll. of Technology–Delhi
Texas Christian Univ.
Texas State Univ.–San Marcos
Texas Tech Univ.
Texas Woman's Univ.
Univ. of Arizona
Univ. of Central Missouri
Univ. of Central Oklahoma
Univ. of Georgia
Univ. of Louisiana–Lafayette
Univ. of Massachusetts–Amherst
Univ. of North Texas
Univ. of Rhode Island
Ursuline Coll. (OH)
Utah State Univ.
Western Carolina Univ. (NC)
Western Michigan Univ.
Woodbury Univ. (CA)
Youngstown State Univ. (OH)

Speech and Rhetorical Studies

American Jewish Univ. (CA)
Ashland Univ. (OH)
Dillard Univ. (LA)
Hillsdale Coll. (MI)
Huntington Univ. (IN)
Missouri Valley Coll.
Northwestern Oklahoma State
    Univ.
Oglethorpe Univ. (GA)
Olivet Nazarene Univ. (IL)
Simpson Coll. (IA)

Texas A&M Univ.–Commerce
Univ. of Minnesota–Morris
Univ. of Washington

Statistics

American Univ. (DC)
Appalachian State Univ. (NC)
Auburn Univ. (AL)
Babson Coll. (MA)
Barnard Coll. (NY)
Bowling Green State Univ. (OH)
Brown Univ. (RI)
California Polytechnic State Univ.–
    San Luis Obispo
California State Univ.–East Bay
California State Univ.–Fullerton
Carnegie Mellon Univ. (PA)
Case Western Reserve Univ. (OH)
Central Michigan Univ.
Columbia Univ. (NY)
CUNY–Baruch Coll.
CUNY–Hunter Coll.
Eastern Kentucky Univ.
Eastern Michigan Univ.
Florida International Univ.
Florida State Univ.
George Washington Univ. (DC)
Grace Coll. and Seminary (IN)
Grand Valley State Univ. (MI)
Harvard Univ. (MA)
Howard Univ. (DC)
Indiana Univ.-Purdue Univ.–Fort
    Wayne
Iowa State Univ.
Kansas State Univ.
Lehigh Univ. (PA)
Loyola Univ. Chicago
Luther Coll. (IA)
Master's Coll. and Seminary (CA)
Miami Univ.–Oxford (OH)
Michigan State Univ.
Mount Holyoke Coll. (MA)
New Mexico Institute of Mining
    and Technology
North Carolina State Univ.–Raleigh
North Dakota State Univ.
Northwest Missouri State Univ.
Northwestern Univ. (IL)
Oakland Univ. (MI)
Ohio Northern Univ.
Ohio State Univ.–Columbus
Oklahoma State Univ.
Pennsylvania State Univ.–Univ. Park
Rice Univ. (TX)
Rochester Institute of Technology
    (NY)
Roosevelt Univ. (IL)
Rutgers, the State Univ. of New
    Jersey–New Brunswick
San Diego State Univ.
Southern Methodist Univ. (TX)
St. Cloud State Univ. (MN)
Stanford Univ. (CA)
SUNY Coll.–Oneonta
Texas A&M Univ.–Coll. Station
Tulane Univ. (LA)
Univ. of Akron (OH)
Univ. of California–Berkeley
Univ. of California–Davis
Univ. of California–Los Angeles

Univ. of California–Riverside
Univ. of California–Santa Barbara
Univ. of Central Florida
Univ. of Connecticut
Univ. of Florida
Univ. of Georgia
Univ. of Illinois–Chicago
Univ. of Illinois–Urbana-Champaign
Univ. of Iowa
Univ. of Kentucky
Univ. of Maryland–Baltimore
    County
Univ. of Miami (FL)
Univ. of Michigan–Ann Arbor
Univ. of Minnesota–Morris
Univ. of Minnesota–Twin Cities
Univ. of Missouri
Univ. of Nebraska–Lincoln
Univ. of Nevada–Las Vegas
Univ. of New Mexico
Univ. of North Carolina–
    Wilmington
Univ. of North Florida
Univ. of Pennsylvania
Univ. of Pittsburgh
Univ. of Rochester (NY)
Univ. of South Carolina
Univ. of South Florida
Univ. of Tennessee
Univ. of Texas–Dallas
Univ. of Texas–El Paso
Univ. of Texas–San Antonio
Univ. of Vermont
Univ. of Washington
Univ. of Wisconsin–Madison
Univ. of Wyoming
Utah State Univ.
Valparaiso Univ. (IN)
Virginia Tech
Western Michigan Univ.
Worcester Polytechnic Institute
    (MA)

Student Counseling and Personnel Services

Auburn Univ. (AL)
Bellevue Univ. (NE)
Buena Vista Univ. (IA)
California State Univ.–Fullerton
California State Univ.–Sacramento
California State Univ.–San
    Bernardino
Carthage Coll. (WI)
CUNY–Lehman Coll.
Eastern Michigan Univ.
Eastern Washington Univ.
Gallaudet Univ. (DC)
Georgia Southern Univ.
Goddard Coll. (VT)
Harding Univ. (AR)
Husson Univ. (ME)
Indiana Univ.–Bloomington
Jackson State Univ. (MS)
Kutztown Univ. of Pennsylvania
Lincoln Memorial Univ. (TN)
Loyola Univ. New Orleans
MacMurray Coll. (IL)
Marshall Univ. (WV)
Northern Michigan Univ.
Northern State Univ. (SD)

Sage Colleges–Albany (NY)
Samford Univ. (AL)
Springfield Coll. (MA)
Stephens Coll. (MO)
Syracuse Univ. (NY)
Univ. of Florida
Univ. of Iowa
Univ. of Kentucky
Univ. of La Verne (CA)
Univ. of Montevallo (AL)
Univ. of Nevada–Las Vegas
Univ. of North Alabama
Univ. of North Carolina–Pembroke
Univ. of Redlands (CA)
Univ. of the Southwest (NM)
Univ. of Wisconsin–Oshkosh
Univ. of Wisconsin–River Falls
Washington State Univ.
Western Washington Univ.

Surveying Engineering

California State Univ.–Fresno
Michigan Technological Univ.
Purdue Univ.–West Lafayette (IN)
Univ. of Arkansas–Monticello
Univ. of Maine

Systems Engineering

California State Univ.–Fullerton
Case Western Reserve Univ. (OH)
Fairfield Univ. (CT)
Florida International Univ.
George Mason Univ. (VA)
Howard Univ. (DC)
Maine Maritime Academy
Missouri Univ. of Science & Technology
Oakland Univ. (MI)
Providence Coll. (RI)
Stanford Univ. (CA)
Stevens Institute of Technology (NJ)
United States Merchant Marine Academy (NY)
United States Military Academy (NY)
United States Naval Academy (MD)
Univ. of Arizona
Univ. of Arkansas–Little Rock
Univ. of Florida
Univ. of Maine
Univ. of Pennsylvania
Univ. of Virginia
Washington Univ. in St. Louis

Systems Science and Theory

Carnegie Mellon Univ. (PA)
Indiana Univ.–Bloomington
Marshall Univ. (WV)
Providence Coll. (RI)
Stanford Univ. (CA)
Wheeling Jesuit Univ. (WV)
Worcester Polytechnic Institute (MA)

Taxation

California State Univ.–Fullerton
Grand Valley State Univ. (MI)
Suffolk Univ. (MA)

Teacher Education and Professional Development

Abilene Christian Univ. (TX)
Adelphi Univ. (NY)
Adrian Coll. (MI)
Alabama Agricultural and Mechanical Univ.
Alabama State Univ.
Alaska Pacific Univ.
Albany State Univ. (GA)
Albion Coll. (MI)
Albright Coll. (PA)
Alcorn State Univ. (MS)
Alderson-Broaddus Coll. (WV)
Alfred Univ. (NY)
Allen Univ. (SC)
Alma Coll. (MI)
Alvernia Univ. (PA)
Alverno Coll. (WI)
American Indian Coll. of the Assemblies of God (AZ)
American Univ. (DC)
Anderson Univ. (SC)
Anderson Univ. (IN)
Andrews Univ. (MI)
Anna Maria Coll. (MA)
Appalachian State Univ. (NC)
Aquinas Coll. (MI)
Arcadia Univ. (PA)
Arizona State Univ.
Arkansas State Univ.–Jonesboro
Arkansas Tech Univ.
Armstrong Atlantic State Univ. (GA)
Asbury Univ. (KY)
Ashland Univ. (OH)
Atlanta Christian Coll.
Atlantic Union Coll. (MA)
Auburn Univ. (AL)
Auburn Univ.–Montgomery (AL)
Augsburg Coll. (MN)
Augusta State Univ. (GA)
Augustana Coll. (SD)
Augustana Coll. (IL)
Aurora Univ. (IL)
Austin Coll. (TX)
Austin Peay State Univ. (TN)
Averett Univ. (VA)
Avila Univ. (MO)
Azusa Pacific Univ. (CA)
Baker Univ. (KS)
Baldwin-Wallace Coll. (OH)
Ball State Univ. (IN)
Barry Univ. (FL)
Barton Coll. (NC)
Baylor Univ. (TX)
Bellarmine Univ. (KY)
Bellevue Univ. (NE)
Belmont Abbey Coll. (NC)
Belmont Univ. (TN)
Bemidji State Univ. (MN)
Benedict Coll. (SC)
Benedictine Coll. (KS)
Benedictine Univ. (IL)
Bennett Coll. (NC)
Bennington Coll. (VT)

Berea Coll. (KY)
Berry Coll. (GA)
Bethany Coll. (WV)
Bethany Coll. (KS)
Bethany Univ. (CA)
Bethel Coll. (KS)
Bethel Coll. (IN)
Bethel Univ. (MN)
Bethune-Cookman Univ. (FL)
Biola Univ. (CA)
Black Hills State Univ. (SD)
Blackburn Coll. (IL)
Bloomsburg Univ. of Pennsylvania
Blue Mountain Coll. (MS)
Bluefield Coll. (VA)
Bluefield State Coll. (WV)
Bluffton Univ. (OH)
Boise State Univ. (ID)
Boston Univ.
Bowie State Univ. (MD)
Bowling Green State Univ. (OH)
Bradley Univ. (IL)
Brenau Univ. (GA)
Brescia Univ. (KY)
Brevard Coll. (NC)
Brewton-Parker Coll. (GA)
Briar Cliff Univ. (IA)
Bridgewater Coll. (VA)
Bridgewater State Coll. (MA)
Brigham Young Univ.–Hawaii
Brigham Young Univ.–Provo (UT)
Bryan Coll. (TN)
Bucknell Univ. (PA)
Buena Vista Univ. (IA)
Buffalo State Coll.–SUNY
Butler Univ. (IN)
Cabrini Coll. (PA)
California Baptist Univ.
California Polytechnic State Univ.–San Luis Obispo
California State Polytechnic Univ.–Pomona
California State Univ.–Bakersfield
California State Univ.–Chico
California State Univ.–Dominguez Hills
California State Univ.–Fresno
California State Univ.–Fullerton
California State Univ.–Long Beach
California State Univ.–Los Angeles
California State Univ.–Monterey Bay
California State Univ.–Northridge
California State Univ.–Sacramento
California State Univ.–San Bernardino
California State Univ.–Stanislaus
California Univ. of Pennsylvania
Calumet Coll. of St. Joseph (IN)
Calvin Coll. (MI)
Cameron Univ. (OK)
Campbell Univ. (NC)
Campbellsville Univ. (KY)
Canisius Coll. (NY)
Capital Univ. (OH)
Cardinal Stritch Univ. (WI)
Carlow Univ. (PA)
Carroll Coll. (MT)
Carroll Univ. (WI)
Carson-Newman Coll. (TN)
Carthage Coll. (WI)
Case Western Reserve Univ. (OH)

Catholic Univ. of America (DC)
Cazenovia Coll. (NY)
Cedar Crest Coll. (PA)
Cedarville Univ. (OH)
Centenary Coll. of Louisiana
Central Baptist Coll. (AR)
Central Coll. (IA)
Central Connecticut State Univ.
Central Methodist Univ. (MO)
Central Michigan Univ.
Central State Univ. (OH)
Central Washington Univ.
Centre Coll. (KY)
Chadron State Coll. (NE)
Chaminade Univ. of Honolulu
Champlain Coll. (VT)
Chapman Univ. (CA)
Charleston Southern Univ. (SC)
Chatham Univ. (PA)
Chestnut Hill Coll. (PA)
Cheyney Univ. of Pennsylvania
Chicago State Univ.
Chowan Univ. (NC)
City Univ. (WA)
Claflin Univ. (SC)
Clarion Univ. of Pennsylvania
Clark Atlanta Univ.
Clarke Univ. (IA)
Clayton State Univ. (GA)
Clearwater Christian Coll. (FL)
Clemson Univ. (SC)
Cleveland State Univ.
Coastal Carolina Univ. (SC)
Coe Coll. (IA)
Coker Coll. (SC)
Colby-Sawyer Coll. (NH)
Coll. at Brockport–SUNY
Coll. of Charleston (SC)
Coll. of Idaho (ID)
Coll. of Mount St. Joseph (OH)
Coll. of New Jersey
Coll. of Notre Dame of Maryland
Coll. of Our Lady of the Elms (MA)
Coll. of Santa Fe (NM)
Coll. of St. Benedict (MN)
Coll. of St. Elizabeth (NJ)
Coll. of St. Joseph (VT)
Coll. of St. Mary (NE)
Coll. of St. Rose (NY)
Coll. of St. Scholastica (MN)
Coll. of the Ozarks (MO)
Coll. of Wooster (OH)
Colorado Christian Univ.
Colorado State Univ.
Columbia Coll. (IL)
Columbia Coll. (SC)
Columbus State Univ. (GA)
Concord Univ. (WV)
Concordia Coll. (AL)
Concordia Coll. (NY)
Concordia Coll.–Moorhead (MN)
Concordia Univ. (OR)
Concordia Univ. (NE)
Concordia Univ. (MI)
Concordia Univ. Chicago (IL)
Concordia Univ. Texas
Concordia Univ. Wisconsin
Concordia Univ.–St. Paul (MN)
Connecticut Coll.
Converse Coll. (SC)
Coppin State Univ. (MD)

Corban Univ. (OR)
Corcoran Coll. of Art and Design (DC)
Cornell Coll. (IA)
Cornell Univ. (NY)
Cornerstone Univ. (MI)
Covenant Coll. (GA)
Creighton Univ. (NE)
Crown Coll. (MN)
Culver-Stockton Coll. (MO)
Cumberland Univ. (TN)
CUNY–Brooklyn Coll.
CUNY–City Coll.
CUNY–Coll. of Staten Island
CUNY–Hunter Coll.
CUNY–Lehman Coll.
CUNY–Medgar Evers Coll.
CUNY–New York City Coll. of Technology
CUNY–Queens Coll.
CUNY–York Coll.
Curry Coll. (MA)
D'Youville Coll. (NY)
Daemen Coll. (NY)
Dakota State Univ. (SD)
Dakota Wesleyan Univ. (SD)
Dallas Baptist Univ.
Dalton State Coll. (GA)
Dana Coll. (NE)
Davis and Elkins Coll. (WV)
Defiance Coll. (OH)
Delaware State Univ.
Delaware Valley Coll. (PA)
Delta State Univ. (MS)
Denison Univ. (OH)
DePaul Univ. (IL)
DePauw Univ. (IN)
DeSales Univ. (PA)
Dickinson State Univ. (ND)
Dixie State Coll. of Utah
Dominican Coll. (NY)
Dominican Univ. of California
Dordt Coll. (IA)
Dowling Coll. (NY)
Drake Univ. (IA)
Drexel Univ. (PA)
Drury Univ. (MO)
Duquesne Univ. (PA)
East Carolina Univ. (NC)
East Central Univ. (OK)
East Stroudsburg Univ. of Pennsylvania
East Texas Baptist Univ.
Eastern Connecticut State Univ.
Eastern Illinois Univ.
Eastern Kentucky Univ.
Eastern Mennonite Univ. (VA)
Eastern Michigan Univ.
Eastern Nazarene Coll. (MA)
Eastern New Mexico Univ.
Eastern Oregon Univ.
Eastern Univ. (PA)
Eastern Washington Univ.
Edgewood Coll. (WI)
Edinboro Univ. of Pennsylvania
Edward Waters Coll. (FL)
Elizabeth City State Univ. (NC)
Elizabethtown Coll. (PA)
Elmhurst Coll. (IL)
Elmira Coll. (NY)
Elon Univ. (NC)

Emmanuel Coll. (GA)
Emmanuel Coll. (MA)
Emory and Henry Coll. (VA)
Emporia State Univ. (KS)
Endicott Coll. (MA)
Erskine Coll. (SC)
Eureka Coll. (IL)
Evangel Univ. (MO)
Fairmont State Univ. (WV)
Faulkner Univ. (AL)
Fayetteville State Univ. (NC)
Felician Coll. (NJ)
Ferris State Univ. (MI)
Fitchburg State Coll. (MA)
Flagler Coll. (FL)
Florida A&M Univ.
Florida Atlantic Univ.
Florida Gulf Coast Univ.
Florida Institute of Technology
Florida International Univ.
Florida Southern Coll.
Florida State Univ.
Fontbonne Univ. (MO)
Fordham Univ. (NY)
Fort Hays State Univ. (KS)
Fort Lewis Coll. (CO)
Fort Valley State Univ. (GA)
Framingham State Coll. (MA)
Francis Marion Univ. (SC)
Franciscan Univ. of Steubenville (OH)
Franklin Coll. (IN)
Free Will Baptist Bible Coll. (TN)
Fresno Pacific Univ. (CA)
Friends Univ. (KS)
Frostburg State Univ. (MD)
Furman Univ. (SC)
Gallaudet Univ. (DC)
Gannon Univ. (PA)
Gardner-Webb Univ. (NC)
Geneva Coll. (PA)
George Fox Univ. (OR)
George Mason Univ. (VA)
George Washington Univ. (DC)
Georgetown Coll. (KY)
Georgia Coll. & State Univ.
Georgia Southern Univ.
Georgia Southwestern State Univ.
Georgia State Univ.
Georgian Court Univ. (NJ)
Gettysburg Coll. (PA)
Glenville State Coll. (WV)
Goddard Coll. (VT)
Gonzaga Univ. (WA)
Gordon Coll. (MA)
Goshen Coll. (IN)
Goucher Coll. (MD)
Grace Coll. and Seminary (IN)
Graceland Univ. (IA)
Grambling State Univ. (LA)
Grand Valley State Univ. (MI)
Grand View Univ. (IA)
Granite State Coll. (NH)
Green Mountain Coll. (VT)
Greensboro Coll. (NC)
Greenville Coll. (IL)
Grove City Coll. (PA)
Guilford Coll. (NC)
Gustavus Adolphus Coll. (MN)
Gwynedd-Mercy Coll. (PA)
Hannibal-LaGrange Coll. (MO)

Hardin-Simmons Univ. (TX)
Harding Univ. (AR)
Harris-Stowe State Univ. (MO)
Hartwick Coll. (NY)
Heidelberg Univ. (OH)
Henderson State Univ. (AR)
Hendrix Coll. (AR)
Heritage Univ. (WA)
High Point Univ. (NC)
Hillsdale Coll. (MI)
Hiram Coll. (OH)
Hofstra Univ. (NY)
Holy Family Univ. (PA)
Hood Coll. (MD)
Hope Coll. (MI)
Hope International Univ. (CA)
Houghton Coll. (NY)
Houston Baptist Univ.
Howard Payne Univ. (TX)
Howard Univ. (DC)
Humboldt State Univ. (CA)
Huntingdon Coll. (AL)
Huntington Univ. (IN)
Husson Univ. (ME)
Idaho State Univ.
Illinois Coll.
Illinois State Univ.
Illinois Wesleyan Univ.
Immaculata Univ. (PA)
Indiana Institute of Technology
Indiana State Univ.
Indiana Univ. East
Indiana Univ. Northwest
Indiana Univ. of Pennsylvania
Indiana Univ. Southeast
Indiana Univ.–Bloomington
Indiana Univ.–Kokomo
Indiana Univ.–South Bend
Indiana Univ.-Purdue Univ.–Fort Wayne
Indiana Univ.-Purdue Univ.–Indianapolis
Indiana Wesleyan Univ.
Iona Coll. (NY)
Iowa State Univ.
Iowa Wesleyan Coll.
Ithaca Coll. (NY)
Jackson State Univ. (MS)
Jacksonville State Univ. (AL)
Jacksonville Univ. (FL)
James Madison Univ. (VA)
Jamestown Coll. (ND)
John Brown Univ. (AR)
John Carroll Univ. (OH)
Johns Hopkins Univ. (MD)
Johnson and Wales Univ. (RI)
Johnson C. Smith Univ. (NC)
Johnson State Coll. (VT)
Judson Coll. (AL)
Judson Univ. (IL)
Juniata Coll. (PA)
Kansas State Univ.
Kansas Wesleyan Univ.
Kean Univ. (NJ)
Keene State Coll. (NH)
Kendall Coll. (IL)
Kennesaw State Univ. (GA)
Kent State Univ. (OH)
Kentucky State Univ.
Kentucky Wesleyan Coll.
Keuka Coll. (NY)

King Coll. (TN)
King's Coll. (PA)
Kutztown Univ. of Pennsylvania
La Roche Coll. (PA)
La Salle Univ. (PA)
La Sierra Univ. (CA)
LaGrange Coll. (GA)
Lake Erie Coll. (OH)
Lake Superior State Univ. (MI)
Lakeland Coll. (WI)
Lamar Univ. (TX)
Lambuth Univ. (TN)
Lander Univ. (SC)
Lane Coll. (TN)
Langston Univ. (OK)
Lasell Coll. (MA)
Lawrence Univ. (WI)
Lebanon Valley Coll. (PA)
Lees-McRae Coll. (NC)
LeMoyne-Owen Coll. (TN)
Lenoir-Rhyne Univ. (NC)
Lesley Univ. (MA)
LeTourneau Univ. (TX)
Lewis Univ. (IL)
Lewis-Clark State Coll. (ID)
Liberty Univ. (VA)
Limestone Coll. (SC)
Lincoln Memorial Univ. (TN)
Lincoln Univ. (MO)
Lincoln Univ. (PA)
Lindenwood Univ. (MO)
Lindsey Wilson Coll. (KY)
Linfield Coll. (OR)
Lipscomb Univ. (TN)
Livingstone Coll. (NC)
Lock Haven Univ. of Pennsylvania
Long Island Univ.–C.W. Post Campus (NY)
Longwood Univ. (VA)
Loras Coll. (IA)
Louisiana Coll.
Louisiana State Univ.–Baton Rouge
Louisiana State Univ.–Shreveport
Louisiana Tech Univ.
Lourdes Coll. (OH)
Loyola Univ. Chicago
Loyola Univ. Maryland
Lubbock Christian Univ. (TX)
Luther Coll. (IA)
Lynchburg Coll. (VA)
Lyndon State Coll. (VT)
Lynn Univ. (FL)
Lyon Coll. (AR)
MacMurray Coll. (IL)
Macon State Coll. (GA)
Madonna Univ. (MI)
Maharishi Univ. of Management (IA)
Malone Univ. (OH)
Manchester Coll. (IN)
Manhattan Coll. (NY)
Mansfield Univ. of Pennsylvania
Maranatha Baptist Bible Coll. (WI)
Marian Univ. (IN)
Marian Univ. (WI)
Marietta Coll. (OH)
Marist Coll. (NY)
Marquette Univ. (WI)
Mars Hill Coll. (NC)
Marshall Univ. (WV)
Martin Methodist Coll. (TN)

Martin Univ. (IN)
Marygrove Coll. (MI)
Maryland Institute Coll. of Art
Maryville Coll. (TN)
Maryville Univ. of St. Louis (MO)
Marywood Univ. (PA)
Massachusetts Coll. of Art and Design
Master's Coll. and Seminary (CA)
Mayville State Univ. (ND)
McKendree Univ. (IL)
McMurry Univ. (TX)
McNeese State Univ. (LA)
McPherson Coll. (KS)
Medaille Coll. (NY)
Mercyhurst Coll. (PA)
Meredith Coll. (NC)
Messiah Coll. (PA)
Methodist Univ. (NC)
Metropolitan State Coll. of Denver
Miami Univ.–Oxford (OH)
Michigan State Univ.
Michigan Technological Univ.
Mid-America Christian Univ. (OK)
Mid-Continent Univ. (KY)
MidAmerica Nazarene Univ. (KS)
Middle Tennessee State Univ.
Midland Lutheran Coll. (NE)
Midway Coll. (KY)
Midwestern State Univ. (TX)
Miles Coll. (AL)
Millersville Univ. of Pennsylvania
Milligan Coll. (TN)
Millikin Univ. (IL)
Minnesota State Univ.–Mankato
Minnesota State University–Moorhead
Minot State Univ. (ND)
Misericordia Univ. (PA)
Mississippi Coll.
Mississippi State Univ.
Mississippi Univ. for Women
Mississippi Valley State Univ.
Missouri Baptist Univ.
Missouri Southern State Univ.
Missouri State Univ.
Missouri Univ. of Science & Technology
Missouri Valley Coll.
Missouri Western State Univ.
Mitchell Coll. (CT)
Molloy Coll. (NY)
Monmouth Coll. (IL)
Montana State Univ.
Montana State Univ.–Billings
Montana State Univ.–Northern
Montclair State Univ. (NJ)
Montreat Coll. (NC)
Moravian Coll. (PA)
Morehead State Univ. (KY)
Morgan State Univ. (MD)
Morningside Coll. (IA)
Morris Coll. (SC)
Mount Aloysius Coll. (PA)
Mount Ida Coll. (MA)
Mount Marty Coll. (SD)
Mount Mary Coll. (WI)
Mount Mercy Coll. (IA)
Mount Olive Coll. (NC)
Mount St. Mary Coll. (NY)
Mount St. Mary's Univ. (MD)

Mount Vernon Nazarene Univ. (OH)
Murray State Univ. (KY)
Muskingum Univ. (OH)
National Univ. (CA)
National-Louis Univ. (IL)
Nazareth Coll. (NY)
Nebraska Wesleyan Univ.
Neumann Univ. (PA)
New England Coll. (NH)
New Jersey City Univ.
New Mexico Highlands Univ.
New Mexico State Univ.
New York Institute of Technology
New York Univ.
Newberry Coll. (SC)
Newman Univ. (KS)
Niagara Univ. (NY)
Nicholls State Univ. (LA)
Norfolk State Univ. (VA)
North Carolina A&T State Univ.
North Carolina Central Univ.
North Carolina State Univ.–Raleigh
North Carolina Wesleyan Coll.
North Central Coll. (IL)
North Central Univ. (MN)
North Dakota State Univ.
North Georgia Coll. and State Univ.
North Greenville Univ. (SC)
North Park Univ. (IL)
Northeastern Illinois Univ.
Northeastern State Univ. (OK)
Northeastern Univ. (MA)
Northern Arizona Univ.
Northern Illinois Univ.
Northern Kentucky Univ.
Northern Michigan Univ.
Northern State Univ. (SD)
Northland Coll. (WI)
Northwest Christian Univ. (OR)
Northwest Missouri State Univ.
Northwest Nazarene Univ. (ID)
Northwest Univ. (WA)
Northwestern Coll. (IA)
Northwestern Coll. (MN)
Northwestern Oklahoma State Univ.
Northwestern State Univ. of Louisiana
Northwestern Univ. (IL)
Notre Dame Coll. of Ohio
Nova Southeastern Univ. (FL)
Nyack Coll. (NY)
Oakland City Univ. (IN)
Oakland Univ. (MI)
Oakwood Univ. (AL)
Oberlin Coll. (OH)
Ohio Dominican Univ.
Ohio Northern Univ.
Ohio State Univ.–Columbus
Ohio Univ.
Ohio Valley Univ. (WV)
Ohio Wesleyan Univ.
Oklahoma Baptist Univ.
Oklahoma Christian Univ.
Oklahoma City Univ.
Oklahoma Panhandle State Univ.
Oklahoma State Univ.
Oklahoma Wesleyan Univ.
Old Dominion Univ. (VA)
Olivet Coll. (MI)

Olivet Nazarene Univ. (IL)
Oral Roberts Univ. (OK)
Ouachita Baptist Univ. (AR)
Our Lady of the Lake Univ. (TX)
Pace Univ. (NY)
Pacific Lutheran Univ. (WA)
Pacific Union Coll. (CA)
Paine Coll. (GA)
Palm Beach Atlantic Univ. (FL)
Park Univ. (MO)
Patten Univ. (CA)
Pennsylvania State Univ.–Univ. Park
Pepperdine Univ. (CA)
Peru State Coll. (NE)
Pfeiffer Univ. (NC)
Philander Smith Coll. (AR)
Piedmont Coll. (GA)
Pikeville Coll. (KY)
Pittsburg State Univ. (KS)
Plymouth State Univ. (NH)
Point Loma Nazarene Univ. (CA)
Point Park Univ. (PA)
Presbyterian Coll. (SC)
Prescott Coll. (AZ)
Providence Coll. (RI)
Purdue Univ.–Calumet (IN)
Purdue Univ.–North Central (IN)
Purdue Univ.–West Lafayette (IN)
Queens Univ. of Charlotte (NC)
Quincy Univ. (IL)
Radford Univ. (VA)
Regis Coll. (MA)
Regis Univ. (CO)
Reinhardt Univ. (GA)
Rhode Island Coll.
Richard Stockton Coll. of New Jersey
Rider Univ. (NJ)
Rivier Coll. (NH)
Robert Morris Univ. (PA)
Roberts Wesleyan Coll. (NY)
Rochester Coll. (MI)
Rockford Coll. (IL)
Rockhurst Univ. (MO)
Rocky Mountain Coll. (MT)
Roger Williams Univ. (RI)
Rollins Coll. (FL)
Roosevelt Univ. (IL)
Russell Sage Coll. (NY)
Rust Coll. (MS)
Rutgers, the State Univ. of New Jersey–New Brunswick
Sage Colleges–Albany (NY)
Saginaw Valley State Univ. (MI)
Salem State Coll. (MA)
Salisbury Univ. (MD)
Salve Regina Univ. (RI)
Sam Houston State Univ. (TX)
Samford Univ. (AL)
San Diego State Univ.
San Francisco State Univ.
San Jose State Univ. (CA)
School of the Art Institute of Chicago
Schreiner Univ. (TX)
Seattle Pacific Univ.
Seton Hall Univ. (NJ)
Seton Hill Univ. (PA)
Shaw Univ. (NC)
Shawnee State Univ. (OH)
Shenandoah Univ. (VA)

Shippensburg Univ. of Pennsylvania
Shorter Coll. (GA)
Siena Coll. (NY)
Silver Lake Coll. (WI)
Simpson Univ. (CA)
Skidmore Coll. (NY)
Slippery Rock Univ. of Pennsylvania
Sonoma State Univ. (CA)
South Carolina State Univ.
South Dakota State Univ.
Southeast Missouri State Univ.
Southeastern Louisiana Univ.
Southeastern Oklahoma State Univ.
Southeastern Univ. (FL)
Southern Adventist Univ. (TN)
Southern Arkansas Univ.
Southern Connecticut State Univ.
Southern Illinois Univ.–Carbondale
Southern Illinois Univ.–Edwardsville
Southern Methodist Univ. (TX)
Southern Nazarene Univ. (OK)
Southern New Hampshire Univ.
Southern Oregon Univ.
Southern Univ. and A&M Coll. (LA)
Southern Univ.–New Orleans
Southern Utah Univ.
Southern Wesleyan Univ. (SC)
Southwest Baptist Univ. (MO)
Southwest Minnesota State Univ.
Southwestern Coll. (KS)
Southwestern Oklahoma State Univ.
Southwestern Univ. (TX)
Spalding Univ. (KY)
Spring Arbor Univ. (MI)
Spring Hill Coll. (AL)
Springfield Coll. (MA)
St. Ambrose Univ. (IA)
St. Andrews Presbyterian Coll. (NC)
St. Augustine's Coll. (NC)
St. Bonaventure Univ. (NY)
St. Catherine Univ. (MN)
St. Cloud State Univ. (MN)
St. Edward's Univ. (TX)
St. Francis Coll. (NY)
St. Francis Univ. (PA)
St. Gregory's Univ. (OK)
St. John Fisher Coll. (NY)
St. John's Univ. (NY)
St. John's Univ. (MN)
St. Joseph's Coll. (ME)
St. Joseph's Coll. (IN)
St. Joseph's Coll. New York
St. Joseph's Univ. (PA)
St. Leo Univ. (FL)
St. Louis Univ.
St. Martin's Univ. (WA)
St. Mary's Coll. (IN)
St. Mary's Univ. of Minnesota
St. Mary's Univ. of San Antonio (TX)
St. Mary-of-the-Woods Coll. (IN)
St. Michael's Coll. (VT)
St. Norbert Coll. (WI)
St. Olaf Coll. (MN)
St. Peter's Coll. (NJ)
St. Thomas Aquinas Coll. (NY)
St. Thomas Univ. (FL)
St. Vincent Coll. (PA)
St. Xavier Univ. (IL)
Stephens Coll. (MO)

Sterling Coll. (KS)
Stetson Univ. (FL)
Stevenson Univ. (MD)
Stillman Coll. (AL)
Stonehill Coll. (MA)
SUNY Coll.–Cortland
SUNY Coll.–Old Westbury
SUNY Coll.–Oneonta
SUNY Coll.–Potsdam
SUNY–Fredonia
SUNY–Geneseo
SUNY–Oswego
SUNY–Plattsburgh
Susquehanna Univ. (PA)
Syracuse Univ. (NY)
Tabor Coll. (KS)
Talladega Coll. (AL)
Taylor Univ. (IN)
Temple Univ. (PA)
Tennessee State Univ.
Tennessee Technological Univ.
Tennessee Wesleyan Coll.
Texas A&M Univ.–Kingsville
Texas Christian Univ.
Texas Coll.
Texas Lutheran Univ.
Texas Wesleyan Univ.
The Citadel (SC)
Thiel Coll. (PA)
Thomas Coll. (ME)
Thomas More Coll. (KY)
Thomas Univ. (GA)
Toccoa Falls Coll. (GA)
Tougaloo Coll. (MS)
Towson Univ. (MD)
Transylvania Univ. (KY)
Trevecca Nazarene Univ. (TN)
Trine Univ. (IN)
Trinity Christian Coll. (IL)
Trinity International Univ. (IL)
Trinity Univ. (DC)
Troy Univ. (AL)
Tufts Univ. (MA)
Tusculum Coll. (TN)
Tuskegee Univ. (AL)
Union Coll. (NE)
Union Coll. (KY)
Union Institute and Univ. (OH)
Union Univ. (TN)
Univ. at Albany–SUNY
Univ. of Akron (OH)
Univ. of Alabama
Univ. of Alabama–Birmingham
Univ. of Alabama–Huntsville
Univ. of Alaska–Anchorage
Univ. of Alaska–Fairbanks
Univ. of Alaska–Southeast
Univ. of Arizona
Univ. of Arkansas
Univ. of Arkansas–Little Rock
Univ. of Arkansas–Monticello
Univ. of Arkansas–Pine Bluff
Univ. of California–Riverside
Univ. of Central Arkansas
Univ. of Central Florida
Univ. of Central Missouri
Univ. of Central Oklahoma
Univ. of Charleston (WV)
Univ. of Colorado–Boulder
Univ. of Connecticut
Univ. of Dallas

Univ. of Dayton (OH)
Univ. of Delaware
Univ. of Denver
Univ. of Detroit Mercy
Univ. of Dubuque (IA)
Univ. of Evansville (IN)
Univ. of Findlay (OH)
Univ. of Florida
Univ. of Georgia
Univ. of Great Falls (MT)
Univ. of Hartford (CT)
Univ. of Hawaii–Hilo
Univ. of Hawaii–Manoa
Univ. of Hawaii–West Oahu
Univ. of Illinois–Chicago
Univ. of Illinois–Urbana-Champaign
Univ. of Indianapolis
Univ. of Iowa
Univ. of Kansas
Univ. of Kentucky
Univ. of La Verne (CA)
Univ. of Louisiana–Lafayette
Univ. of Louisiana–Monroe
Univ. of Louisville (KY)
Univ. of Maine
Univ. of Maine–Farmington
Univ. of Maine–Fort Kent
Univ. of Maine–Machias
Univ. of Maine–Presque Isle
Univ. of Mary (ND)
Univ. of Mary Hardin-Baylor (TX)
Univ. of Maryland–Coll. Park
Univ. of Maryland–Eastern Shore
Univ. of Massachusetts–Dartmouth
Univ. of Massachusetts–Lowell
Univ. of Memphis
Univ. of Miami (FL)
Univ. of Michigan–Ann Arbor
Univ. of Michigan–Dearborn
Univ. of Michigan–Flint
Univ. of Minnesota–Crookston
Univ. of Minnesota–Duluth
Univ. of Minnesota–Morris
Univ. of Minnesota–Twin Cities
Univ. of Mississippi
Univ. of Missouri
Univ. of Missouri–Kansas City
Univ. of Missouri–St. Louis
Univ. of Mobile (AL)
Univ. of Montana
Univ. of Montana–Western
Univ. of Montevallo (AL)
Univ. of Mount Union (OH)
Univ. of Nebraska–Kearney
Univ. of Nebraska–Lincoln
Univ. of Nebraska–Omaha
Univ. of Nevada–Las Vegas
Univ. of Nevada–Reno
Univ. of New England (ME)
Univ. of New Hampshire
Univ. of New Mexico
Univ. of New Orleans
Univ. of North Alabama
Univ. of North Carolina–Chapel Hill
Univ. of North Carolina–Charlotte
Univ. of North Carolina–Greensboro
Univ. of North Carolina–Pembroke
Univ. of North Carolina–Wilmington
Univ. of North Dakota

Univ. of North Florida
Univ. of Northern Colorado
Univ. of Northern Iowa
Univ. of Notre Dame (IN)
Univ. of Oklahoma
Univ. of Oregon
Univ. of Pennsylvania
Univ. of Pittsburgh
Univ. of Pittsburgh–Bradford
Univ. of Pittsburgh–Johnstown
Univ. of Portland (OR)
Univ. of Puget Sound (WA)
Univ. of Redlands (CA)
Univ. of Rhode Island
Univ. of Rio Grande (OH)
Univ. of Rochester (NY)
Univ. of Science and Arts of Oklahoma
Univ. of Scranton (PA)
Univ. of Sioux Falls (SD)
Univ. of South Alabama
Univ. of South Carolina
Univ. of South Carolina–Aiken
Univ. of South Carolina–Upstate
Univ. of South Dakota
Univ. of South Florida
Univ. of Southern California
Univ. of Southern Indiana
Univ. of Southern Maine
Univ. of Southern Mississippi
Univ. of St. Francis (IN)
Univ. of St. Francis (IL)
Univ. of St. Thomas (TX)
Univ. of St. Thomas (MN)
Univ. of Tampa (FL)
Univ. of Tennessee
Univ. of Tennessee–Martin
Univ. of the Arts (PA)
Univ. of the Cumberlands (KY)
Univ. of the District of Columbia
Univ. of the Incarnate Word (TX)
Univ. of the Ozarks (AR)
Univ. of the Pacific (CA)
Univ. of the Southwest (NM)
Univ. of Toledo (OH)
Univ. of Tulsa (OK)
Univ. of Utah
Univ. of Vermont
Univ. of Virginia
Univ. of West Alabama
Univ. of West Florida
Univ. of West Georgia
Univ. of Wisconsin–Eau Claire
Univ. of Wisconsin–La Crosse
Univ. of Wisconsin–Madison
Univ. of Wisconsin–Milwaukee
Univ. of Wisconsin–Oshkosh
Univ. of Wisconsin–Platteville
Univ. of Wisconsin–River Falls
Univ. of Wisconsin–Stevens Point
Univ. of Wisconsin–Stout
Univ. of Wisconsin–Superior
Univ. of Wisconsin–Whitewater
Univ. of Wyoming
Upper Iowa Univ.
Urbana Univ. (OH)
Ursuline Coll. (OH)
Utah State Univ.
Utah Valley Univ.
Valdosta State Univ. (GA)
Valley City State Univ. (ND)

Valparaiso Univ. (IN)
Vanderbilt Univ. (TN)
VanderCook Coll. of Music (IL)
Vanguard Univ. of Southern
  California
Victory Univ. (TN)
Villanova Univ. (PA)
Virginia Commonwealth Univ.
Virginia Intermont Coll.
Virginia State Univ.
Virginia Tech
Virginia Union Univ.
Virginia Wesleyan Coll.
Viterbo Univ. (WI)
Wagner Coll. (NY)
Wake Forest Univ. (NC)
Waldorf Coll. (IA)
Walsh Univ. (OH)
Warner Pacific Coll. (OR)
Warner Univ. (FL)
Wartburg Coll. (IA)
Washburn Univ. (KS)
Washington Adventist Univ. (MD)
Washington and Jefferson Coll.
  (PA)
Washington State Univ.
Washington Univ. in St. Louis
Wayland Baptist Univ. (TX)
Wayne State Coll. (NE)
Wayne State Univ. (MI)
Waynesburg Univ. (PA)
Weber State Univ. (UT)
Webster Univ. (MO)
Wesleyan Coll. (GA)
West Chester Univ. of Pennsylvania
West Liberty Univ. (WV)
West Virginia State Univ.
West Virginia Univ.
West Virginia Univ. Institute of
  Technology
West Virginia Univ.–Parkersburg
West Virginia Wesleyan Coll.
Western Carolina Univ. (NC)
Western Connecticut State Univ.
Western Governors Univ. (UT)
Western Illinois Univ.
Western Kentucky Univ.
Western Michigan Univ.
Western New England Coll. (MA)
Western New Mexico Univ.
Western Oregon Univ.
Western Washington Univ.
Westfield State Coll. (MA)
Westminster Coll. (MO)
Westminster Coll. (UT)
Westminster Coll. (PA)
Wheaton Coll. (IL)
Wheeling Jesuit Univ. (WV)
Wheelock Coll. (MA)
Whittier Coll. (CA)
Whitworth Univ. (WA)
Wichita State Univ. (KS)
Widener Univ. (PA)
Wiley Coll. (TX)
Wilkes Univ. (PA)
William Carey Univ. (MS)
William Jewell Coll. (MO)
William Paterson Univ. of New
  Jersey
William Penn Univ. (IA)
William Woods Univ. (MO)

Williams Baptist Coll. (AR)
Wilmington Univ. (DE)
Wilson Coll. (PA)
Wingate Univ. (NC)
Winston-Salem State Univ. (NC)
Winthrop Univ. (SC)
Wisconsin Lutheran Coll.
Wittenberg Univ. (OH)
Worcester State Coll. (MA)
Wright State Univ. (OH)
Xavier Univ. (OH)
York Coll. (NE)
York Coll. of Pennsylvania
Youngstown State Univ. (OH)

Teaching Assistants/ Aides

Tougaloo Coll. (MS)
Univ. of Central Oklahoma

Teaching English or French as a Second or Foreign Language

Bethel Univ. (MN)
Brigham Young Univ.–Hawaii
California State Univ.–Sacramento
Carnegie Mellon Univ. (PA)
Carroll Coll. (MT)
Cedarville Univ. (OH)
Coll. of Our Lady of the Elms (MA)
Concordia Univ. (NE)
Concordia Univ.–St. Paul (MN)
Cornerstone Univ. (MI)
CUNY–Queens Coll.
D'Youville Coll. (NY)
Eastern Michigan Univ.
Eastern Washington Univ.
Goshen Coll. (IN)
Hawaii Pacific Univ.
Heritage Univ. (WA)
Howard Payne Univ. (TX)
Indiana Wesleyan Univ.
Liberty Univ. (VA)
Master's Coll. and Seminary (CA)
Northern State Univ. (SD)
Northwest Univ. (WA)
Northwestern Coll. (MN)
Nyack Coll. (NY)
Oklahoma Christian Univ.
Salisbury Univ. (MD)
SUNY–Oswego
Texas Wesleyan Univ.
Union Univ. (TN)
Univ. of Evansville (IN)
Univ. of Findlay (OH)
Univ. of Nebraska–Lincoln
Univ. of Northern Iowa
Univ. of Wisconsin–Oshkosh
Univ. of Wisconsin–River Falls
Washington State Univ.

Technical and Business Writing

Allegheny Coll. (PA)
Auburn Univ. (AL)
Bowling Green State Univ. (OH)
Carlow Univ. (PA)
Carnegie Mellon Univ. (PA)

Cedarville Univ. (OH)
Coker Coll. (SC)
Coll. of Santa Fe (NM)
Dominican Univ. (IL)
Drexel Univ. (PA)
Eastern Michigan Univ.
Farmingdale State Coll.–SUNY
Ferris State Univ. (MI)
Grand Valley State Univ. (MI)
Indiana Univ.-Purdue Univ.–Fort
  Wayne
James Madison Univ. (VA)
Kutztown Univ. of Pennsylvania
Madonna Univ. (MI)
Maryville Coll. (TN)
Miami Univ.–Oxford (OH)
Michigan State Univ.
Missouri State Univ.
Montana Tech of the Univ. of
  Montana
Mount Mary Coll. (WI)
New Jersey Institute of Technology
New Mexico Institute of Mining
  and Technology
Northern Michigan Univ.
Ohio Northern Univ.
St. Mary-of-the-Woods Coll. (IN)
Univ. of Findlay (OH)
Univ. of Hartford (CT)
Univ. of Houston–Downtown
Univ. of Texas–San Antonio
Univ. of Washington
Univ. of Wisconsin–Stout
Valparaiso Univ. (IN)
Weber State Univ. (UT)
Winthrop Univ. (SC)
Worcester Polytechnic Institute
  (MA)
York Coll. of Pennsylvania
Youngstown State Univ. (OH)

Textile Sciences and Engineering

Auburn Univ. (AL)
Georgia Institute of Technology
North Carolina State Univ.–Raleigh
Philadelphia Univ.
Univ. of Massachusetts–Dartmouth

Theological and Ministerial Studies

Alma Coll. (MI)
Alvernia Univ. (PA)
American Indian Coll. of the
  Assemblies of God (AZ)
American Jewish Univ. (CA)
Anderson Univ. (IN)
Andrews Univ. (MI)
Anna Maria Coll. (MA)
Assumption Coll. (MA)
Atlantic Union Coll. (MA)
Azusa Pacific Univ. (CA)
Barry Univ. (FL)
Bellarmine Univ. (KY)
Belmont Abbey Coll. (NC)
Bethany Coll. (KS)
Bethany Univ. (CA)
Bethel Coll. (IN)
Biola Univ. (CA)

Bluefield Coll. (VA)
Boston Univ.
Brescia Univ. (KY)
Brewton-Parker Coll. (GA)
Briar Cliff Univ. (IA)
Calvin Coll. (MI)
Campbell Univ. (NC)
Carlow Univ. (PA)
Carroll Coll. (MT)
Carson-Newman Coll. (TN)
Cedarville Univ. (OH)
Central Christian Coll. (KS)
Clearwater Christian Coll. (FL)
Coll. of Our Lady of the Elms (MA)
Coll. of St. Benedict (MN)
Coll. of St. Elizabeth (NJ)
Concordia Univ. (NE)
Concordia Univ. (OR)
Concordia Univ. (MI)
Concordia Univ. (CA)
Concordia Univ. Chicago (IL)
Concordia Univ. Wisconsin
Concordia Univ.–St. Paul (MN)
Corban Univ. (OR)
Crown Coll. (MN)
Defiance Coll. (OH)
DeSales Univ. (PA)
Dominican Univ. (IL)
Dordt Coll. (IA)
Duquesne Univ. (PA)
East Texas Baptist Univ.
Eastern Mennonite Univ. (VA)
Eastern Univ. (PA)
Elmhurst Coll. (IL)
Emmanuel Coll. (GA)
Franciscan Univ. of Steubenville
  (OH)
Free Will Baptist Bible Coll. (TN)
Gannon Univ. (PA)
Grove City Coll. (PA)
Hanover Coll. (IN)
Hardin-Simmons Univ. (TX)
Harding Univ. (AR)
Hope International Univ. (CA)
Howard Payne Univ. (TX)
Huntington Univ. (IN)
Immaculata Univ. (PA)
Indiana Wesleyan Univ.
Iowa Wesleyan Coll.
John Brown Univ. (AR)
Juniata Coll. (PA)
King's Coll. (PA)
Livingstone Coll. (NC)
Louisiana Coll.
Loyola Marymount Univ. (CA)
Loyola Univ. Chicago
Madonna Univ. (MI)
Maranatha Baptist Bible Coll. (WI)
Marian Univ. (IN)
Marquette Univ. (WI)
Master's Coll. and Seminary (CA)
Morris Coll. (SC)
Mount Olive Coll. (NC)
Mount St. Mary's Univ. (MD)
Mount Vernon Nazarene Univ.
  (OH)
Newman Univ. (KS)
Northwest Christian Univ. (OR)
Northwest Nazarene Univ. (ID)
Northwest Univ. (WA)
Northwestern Coll. (MN)

Notre Dame Coll. of Ohio
Nyack Coll. (NY)
Oakwood Univ. (AL)
Ohio Dominican Univ.
Ohio Wesleyan Univ.
Oklahoma Wesleyan Univ.
Olivet Nazarene Univ. (IL)
Oral Roberts Univ. (OK)
Ouachita Baptist Univ. (AR)
Palm Beach Atlantic Univ. (FL)
Point Loma Nazarene Univ. (CA)
Providence Coll. (RI)
Regent Univ. (VA)
Regis Univ. (CO)
Roanoke Coll. (VA)
Roberts Wesleyan Coll. (NY)
Seattle Pacific Univ.
Shorter Coll. (GA)
Silver Lake Coll. (WI)
Southeastern Univ. (FL)
Southern Adventist Univ. (TN)
Southern Nazarene Univ. (OK)
Southwest Baptist Univ. (MO)
Southwestern Adventist Univ. (TX)
Spring Arbor Univ. (MI)
Spring Hill Coll. (AL)
St. Ambrose Univ. (IA)
St. Anselm Coll. (NH)
St. Bonaventure Univ. (NY)
St. Catherine Univ. (MN)
St. Gregory's Univ. (OK)
St. John's Univ. (MN)
St. Joseph's Coll. (ME)
St. Leo Univ. (FL)
St. Louis Univ.
St. Mary's Univ. of Minnesota
St. Mary's Univ. of San Antonio
  (TX)
St. Mary-of-the-Woods Coll. (IN)
St. Vincent Coll. (PA)
St. Xavier Univ. (IL)
Tabor Coll. (KS)
Tennessee Wesleyan Coll.
Texas Lutheran Univ.
Toccoa Falls Coll. (GA)
Trevecca Nazarene Univ. (TN)
Trinity Christian Coll. (IL)
Trinity International Univ. (IL)
Union Coll. (NE)
Union Univ. (TN)
Univ. of Chicago
Univ. of Dallas
Univ. of Great Falls (MT)
Univ. of Mary (ND)
Univ. of Mary Hardin-Baylor (TX)
Univ. of Notre Dame (IN)
Univ. of Portland (OR)
Univ. of San Francisco
Univ. of Sioux Falls (SD)
Univ. of St. Francis (IL)
Univ. of St. Francis (IN)
Univ. of St. Mary (KS)
Univ. of St. Thomas (TX)
Univ. of St. Thomas (MN)
Valparaiso Univ. (IN)
Vanguard Univ. of Southern
  California
Viterbo Univ. (WI)
Walsh Univ. (OH)
Warner Pacific Coll. (OR)
Warner Univ. (FL)

Washington Adventist Univ. (MD)
Wheeling Jesuit Univ. (WV)
Williams Baptist Coll. (AR)
Wisconsin Lutheran Coll.
Xavier Univ. (OH)

Theology and Religious Vocations

Abilene Christian Univ. (TX)
Bethel Univ. (MN)
Campbellsville Univ. (KY)
King Coll. (TN)
LeTourneau Univ. (TX)
Loyola Univ. New Orleans
Lubbock Christian Univ. (TX)
Marquette Univ. (WI)
Martin Methodist Coll. (TN)
Missouri Valley Coll.
Nyack Coll. (NY)
Oklahoma Wesleyan Univ.
Oral Roberts Univ. (OK)
Patten Univ. (CA)
Simpson Univ. (CA)
Southeastern Univ. (FL)
Southern Nazarene Univ. (OK)
Southwestern Assemblies of God
    Univ. (TX)
St. Edward's Univ. (TX)
Trinity Christian Coll. (IL)
Union Univ. (TN)
Univ. of St. Thomas (TX)
Univ. of Washington
Wayland Baptist Univ. (TX)

Transportation and Materials Moving

Dowling Coll. (NY)
SUNY Maritime Coll.
Syracuse Univ. (NY)

Turkic, Ural-Altaic, Caucasian, and Central Asian Languages, Literatures, and Lingustics

Univ. of Texas–Austin

Urban Studies/Affairs

Aquinas Coll. (MI)
Ball State Univ. (IN)
Barnard Coll. (NY)
Boston Univ.
Brown Univ. (RI)
Bryn Mawr Coll. (PA)
Buffalo State Coll.–SUNY
Butler Univ. (IN)
California State Univ.–Dominguez
    Hills
Canisius Coll. (NY)
Cleveland State Univ.
Coll. of Charleston (SC)
Coll. of Wooster (OH)
Columbia Univ. (NY)
Connecticut Coll.
CUNY–Hunter Coll.
CUNY–Queens Coll.
DePaul Univ. (IL)

Dillard Univ. (LA)
Eastern Nazarene Coll. (MA)
Elmhurst Coll. (IL)
Evergreen State Coll. (WA)
Fordham Univ. (NY)
Furman Univ. (SC)
Georgia State Univ.
Hamline Univ. (MN)
Hampshire Coll. (MA)
Harris-Stowe State Univ. (MO)
Hobart and William Smith Colleges
    (NY)
Indiana Univ.–South Bend
Jackson State Univ. (MS)
Lehigh Univ. (PA)
Lipscomb Univ. (TN)
Loyola Marymount Univ. (CA)
Manhattan Coll. (NY)
Minnesota State Univ.–Mankato
Morehouse Coll. (GA)
Mount Mercy Coll. (IA)
New York Univ.
North Central Univ. (MN)
Northeastern Univ. (MA)
Northwestern Univ. (IL)
Occidental Coll. (CA)
Ohio Univ.
Ohio Wesleyan Univ.
Rhodes Coll. (TN)
Roosevelt Univ. (IL)
Rutgers, the State Univ. of New
    Jersey–Camden
Rutgers, the State Univ. of New
    Jersey–New Brunswick
San Diego State Univ.
San Francisco State Univ.
St. Cloud State Univ. (MN)
St. Louis Univ.
St. Peter's Coll. (NJ)
Stanford Univ. (CA)
Temple Univ. (PA)
Texas A&M International Univ.
Trinity Coll. (CT)
Univ. at Albany–SUNY
Univ. of California–Berkeley
Univ. of California–San Diego
Univ. of Connecticut
Univ. of Illinois–Chicago
Univ. of Minnesota–Duluth
Univ. of Minnesota–Twin Cities
Univ. of Missouri–Kansas City
Univ. of Nebraska–Omaha
Univ. of New Orleans
Univ. of Pennsylvania
Univ. of Pittsburgh
Univ. of Richmond (VA)
Univ. of Texas–Austin
Univ. of the District of Columbia
Univ. of Utah
Univ. of Washington
Univ. of Wisconsin–Green Bay
Vassar Coll. (NY)
Virginia Commonwealth Univ.
Worcester State Coll. (MA)
Wright State Univ. (OH)

Vehicle Maintenance and Repair Technologies

Andrews Univ. (MI)
Coll. of the Ozarks (MO)

Embry-Riddle Aeronautical Univ.
    (FL)
Hampton Univ. (VA)
Kansas State Univ.
Lewis-Clark State Coll. (ID)
Montana State Univ.–Northern
Northern Michigan Univ.
Pennsylvania Coll. of Technology
Southern Illinois Univ.–Carbondale
Thomas Edison State Coll. (NJ)
Univ. of Alaska–Anchorage
Utah State Univ.
Vaughn Coll. of Aeronautics and
    Technology (NY)
Western Michigan Univ.

Veterinary Biomedical and Clinical Sciences (Cert., M.S., Ph.D.)

Auburn Univ. (AL)
Ohio State Univ.–Columbus
Univ. of Florida
Univ. of Kentucky
Washington State Univ.

Veterinary Medicine (D.V.M.)

Auburn Univ. (AL)
Clemson Univ. (SC)
Cornell Univ. (NY)
Ohio State Univ.–Columbus
Univ. of Florida
Univ. of Minnesota–Twin Cities
Washington State Univ.

Visual and Performing Arts

Adelphi Univ. (NY)
Alma Coll. (MI)
Assumption Coll. (MA)
Baldwin-Wallace Coll. (OH)
Ball State Univ. (IN)
Bard Coll. at Simon's Rock (MA)
Bennington Coll. (VT)
Berklee Coll. of Music (MA)
Bethany Coll. (WV)
Bloomfield Coll. (NJ)
Bluefield Coll. (VA)
Boston Conservatory
Brigham Young Univ.–Hawaii
California Coll. of the Arts
California Institute of the Arts
California State Polytechnic Univ.–
    Pomona
California State Univ.–Monterey Bay
California State Univ.–Sacramento
Calumet Coll. of St. Joseph (IN)
Carthage Coll. (WI)
Cazenovia Coll. (NY)
Cedar Crest Coll. (PA)
Centenary Coll. of Louisiana
Central Christian Coll. (KS)
Central Michigan Univ.
Cogswell Polytechnical Coll. (CA)
Coll. for Creative Studies (MI)
Concordia Univ. (NE)
Concordia Univ. Chicago (IL)
Coppin State Univ. (MD)

Cornell Coll. (IA)
Covenant Coll. (GA)
Dana Coll. (NE)
Delta State Univ. (MS)
Dominican Univ. (IL)
East Stroudsburg Univ. of
    Pennsylvania
Edgewood Coll. (WI)
Elmira Coll. (NY)
Evergreen State Coll. (WA)
Fairleigh Dickinson Univ. (NJ)
Fayetteville State Univ. (NC)
Ferrum Coll. (VA)
Fisk Univ. (TN)
Friends Univ. (KS)
Frostburg State Univ. (MD)
Gallaudet Univ. (DC)
Gannon Univ. (PA)
George Mason Univ. (VA)
George Washington Univ. (DC)
Green Mountain Coll. (VT)
Hampden-Sydney Coll. (VA)
Hampshire Coll. (MA)
Harvard Univ. (MA)
Haverford Coll. (PA)
Heritage Univ. (WA)
Hofstra Univ. (NY)
Howard Univ. (DC)
Huntington Univ. (IN)
Illinois Coll.
Illinois State Univ.
Illinois Wesleyan Univ.
Indiana Univ. of Pennsylvania
Iowa State Univ.
Ithaca Coll. (NY)
Jackson State Univ. (MS)
Judson Coll. (AL)
Kansas Wesleyan Univ.
Kent State Univ. (OH)
King Coll. (TN)
Kutztown Univ. of Pennsylvania
LaGrange Coll. (GA)
Lamar Univ. (TX)
Lambuth Univ. (TN)
Langston Univ. (OK)
Lawrence Univ. (WI)
Lincoln Memorial Univ. (TN)
Lindenwood Univ. (MO)
Longwood Univ. (VA)
Loras Coll. (IA)
Maharishi Univ. of Management
    (IA)
Mary Baldwin Coll. (VA)
Marywood Univ. (PA)
Massachusetts Coll. of Liberal Arts
Medaille Coll. (NY)
Mesa State Coll. (CO)
Milligan Coll. (TN)
Millikin Univ. (IL)
Mississippi State Univ.
Mississippi Univ. for Women
Mississippi Valley State Univ.
Missouri State Univ.
Molloy Coll. (NY)
Montana State Univ.–Billings
Mount Olive Coll. (NC)
Mount St. Mary's Univ. (MD)
Nebraska Wesleyan Univ.
New Mexico Highlands Univ.
New Mexico State Univ.
New York Univ.

Niagara Univ. (NY)
Northwestern Univ. (IL)
Oakland Univ. (MI)
Oberlin Coll. (OH)
Ohio State Univ.–Columbus
Oklahoma Baptist Univ.
Oregon State Univ.
Pacific Lutheran Univ. (WA)
Pennsylvania State Univ.–Univ. Park
Pepperdine Univ. (CA)
Pitzer Coll. (CA)
Pratt Institute (NY)
Prescott Coll. (AZ)
Providence Coll. (RI)
Purchase Coll.–SUNY
Purdue University–West Lafayette
    (IN)
Ramapo Coll. of New Jersey
Regis Univ. (CO)
Rensselaer Polytechnic Institute
    (NY)
Rhode Island School of Design
Rice Univ. (TX)
Richard Stockton Coll. of New
    Jersey
Roger Williams Univ. (RI)
Salem State Coll. (MA)
Samford Univ. (AL)
School of the Art Institute of
    Chicago
Seattle Univ.
Seton Hall Univ. (NJ)
Shenandoah Univ. (VA)
Siena Coll. (NY)
Sonoma State Univ. (CA)
South Dakota State Univ.
Southeast Missouri State Univ.
Southeastern Univ. (FL)
Southwestern Oklahoma State
    Univ.
Southwestern Univ. (TX)
St. Andrews Presbyterian College
    (NC)
St. Augustine's Coll. (NC)
St. Gregory's Univ. (OK)
St. Joseph Coll. (CT)
St. Joseph's Univ. (PA)
St. Mary's Coll. of California
St. Peter's Coll. (NJ)
Stevenson Univ. (MD)
Suffolk Univ. (MA)
SUNY Coll.–Cortland
SUNY Coll.–Old Westbury
SUNY Coll.–Potsdam
SUNY–Fredonia
Swarthmore Coll. (PA)
Syracuse Univ. (NY)
Texas Lutheran Univ.
Texas Wesleyan Univ.
Thomas More Coll. (KY)
Tulane Univ. (LA)
Tusculum Coll. (TN)
Univ. of Alabama–Birmingham
Univ. of Arkansas–Monticello
Univ. of California–Los Angeles
Univ. of California–San Diego
Univ. of Colorado–Colorado
    Springs
Univ. of Hartford (CT)
Univ. of Louisiana–Lafayette
Univ. of Maine–Machias

Univ. of Mary Washington (VA)
Univ. of Maryland–Baltimore County
Univ. of Miami (FL)
Univ. of Minnesota–Duluth
Univ. of Mississippi
Univ. of Montana
Univ. of New Hampshire
Univ. of Oklahoma
Univ. of Pennsylvania
Univ. of Pittsburgh–Bradford
Univ. of San Francisco
Univ. of South Florida
Univ. of Southern Maine
Univ. of Southern Mississippi
Univ. of St. Francis (IL)
Univ. of Tampa (FL)
Univ. of Tennessee–Martin
Univ. of Texas–Austin
Univ. of Texas–Dallas
Univ. of the Arts (PA)
Univ. of Utah
Univ of Wisconsin–Green Bay
Univ. of Wisconsin–Superior
Valdosta State Univ. (GA)
Virginia State Univ.
Viterbo Univ. (WI)
Washburn Univ. (KS)
Waynesburg Univ. (PA)
Wells Coll. (NY)
West Virginia Univ.
Western Kentucky Univ.
Western Oregon Univ.
Western Washington Univ.
Wheaton Coll. (IL)
Wheelock Coll. (MA)
Wichita State Univ. (KS)
Wittenberg Univ. (OH)
York Coll. of Pennsylvania
Youngstown State Univ. (OH)

Wildlife and Wildlands Science and Management

Arkansas State Univ.–Jonesboro
Auburn Univ. (AL)
Brigham Young Univ.–Provo (UT)
Colorado State Univ.
Delaware Valley Coll. (PA)
Eastern Kentucky Univ.
Eastern New Mexico Univ.
Frostburg State Univ. (MD)
Humboldt State Univ. (CA)
Lake Superior State Univ. (MI)
Lincoln Memorial Univ. (TN)
McNeese State Univ. (LA)
Michigan State Univ.
Michigan Technological Univ.
Mississippi State Univ.
Missouri State Univ.
Murray State Univ. (KY)
New Mexico State Univ.
Northland Coll. (WI)
Northwest Missouri State Univ.
Prescott Coll. (AZ)
South Dakota State Univ.
Stephen F. Austin State Univ. (TX)
SUNY Coll. of Agriculture and Technology–Cobleskill
Tarleton State Univ. (TX)
Tennessee Technological Univ.
Texas A&M Univ.–Coll. Station
Texas A&M Univ.–Kingsville
Texas Tech Univ.
Unity Coll. (ME)
Univ. of Alaska–Fairbanks
Univ. of Arizona
Univ. of Arkansas–Monticello
Univ. of California–Davis
Univ. of Delaware

Univ. of Florida
Univ. of Georgia
Univ. of Illinois–Urbana-Champaign
Univ. of Maine
Univ. of Massachusetts–Amherst
Univ. of Michigan–Ann Arbor
Univ. of Montana
Univ. of Nevada–Reno
Univ. of New Hampshire
Univ. of Rhode Island
Univ. of Washington
Univ. of Wisconsin–Madison
Univ. of Wisconsin–Stevens Point
Utah State Univ.
Washington State Univ.
West Texas A&M Univ.
West Virginia Univ.
Western New Mexico Univ.

Woodworking

Ferris State Univ. (MI)
Rochester Institute of Technology (NY)

Work and Family Studies

Ashland Univ. (OH)
Indiana Univ.–South Bend
Portland State Univ. (OR)
Texas Tech Univ.
Union Univ. (TN)
Ursuline Coll. (OH)

Zoology/Animal Biology

Auburn Univ. (AL)
Baker Univ. (KS)
Bennington Coll. (VT)
Bucknell Univ. (PA)

California State Polytechnic Univ.–Pomona
California State Univ.–Long Beach
Carroll Univ. (WI)
Clemson Univ. (SC)
Colorado State Univ.
Cornell Univ. (NY)
Delaware Valley Coll. (PA)
Friends Univ. (KS)
Humboldt State Univ. (CA)
Idaho State Univ.
Iowa State Univ.
Juniata Coll. (PA)
Kansas State Univ.
Kent State Univ. (OH)
Kentucky Wesleyan Coll.
Lawrence Univ. (WI)
Malone Univ. (OH)
Mars Hill Coll. (NC)
Methodist Univ. (NC)
Miami Univ.–Oxford (OH)
Michigan State Univ.
North Carolina State Univ.–Raleigh
North Dakota State Univ.
Northern Arizona Univ.
Northern Michigan Univ.
Northland Coll. (WI)
Northwestern Oklahoma State Univ.
Ohio State Univ.–Columbus
Ohio Univ.
Ohio Wesleyan Univ.
Oklahoma State Univ.
Olivet Nazarene Univ. (IL)
Oregon State Univ.
Prescott Coll. (AZ)
Purdue Univ.–West Lafayette (IN)
Rutgers, the State Univ. of New Jersey–Newark
San Diego State Univ.

Southeast Missouri State Univ.
Southern Illinois Univ.–Carbondale
SUNY–Oswego
Tarleton State Univ. (TX)
Texas A&M Univ.–Coll. Station
Texas State Univ.–San Marcos
Texas Tech Univ.
Texas Woman's Univ.
Tulane Univ. (LA)
Unity Coll. (ME)
Univ. of Akron (OH)
Univ. of California–Davis
Univ. of California–Riverside
Univ. of California–San Diego
Univ. of California–Santa Barbara
Univ. of Connecticut
Univ. of Delaware
Univ. of Florida
Univ. of Georgia
Univ. of Hawaii–Manoa
Univ. of Illinois–Urbana-Champaign
Univ. of Kentucky
Univ. of Maine
Univ. of Michigan–Ann Arbor
Univ. of Michigan–Flint
Univ. of Minnesota–Twin Cities
Univ. of Nebraska–Lincoln
Univ. of New Hampshire
Univ. of Oklahoma
Univ. of Rhode Island
Univ. of Texas–Austin
Univ. of Vermont
Univ. of Washington
Univ. of Wisconsin–Madison
Univ. of Wyoming
Utah State Univ.
Washington State Univ.
Weber State Univ. (UT)
Western New Mexico Univ.
Western Washington Univ.

U.S.News
& World Report

Ultimate
College
Directory

How to Use the Directory

In the following pages, you'll find exhaustive profiles of the more than 1,400 colleges and universities *U.S. News* surveys each year. The directory is organized by state, and schools are presented alphabetically within each state. The online version of the directory at www.usnews.com allows you to do a customized search of our database. Want to know which liberal arts colleges with no more than 2,000 students offer anthropology and are located within 100 miles of your home? Enter those criteria and pull up a list.

The vital statistics shown in each directory entry are explained below. The vital statistics and other data are as of July 11, 2010, and were collected from the schools themselves during 2010. If a college did not supply the data requested, the information either does not appear or is marked as "N/A" for "not available." If a school did not return the full *U.S. News* questionnaire, only limited information appears in its write-up. In some cases, data reported in previous years were used if current-year data were unavailable.

Addresses and essential stats

This section supplies the basics: college name and address, whether the institution is public or private, year founded, religious affiliation, and contact information. Use the admissions office phone number or e-mail address to request information or an application. Visit the school's website to research its programs, take a virtual tour, or submit an application.

- **Selectivity:** How competitive is the admissions process at the schools you are considering? Schools are designated "Most selective," "More selective," "Selective," "Less selective," or "Least selective" based on a formula that accounts for enrollees' test scores and class standing, and the school's acceptance rate (the percentage of applicants who are accepted). Since all of these factors are considered, a school that enrolls a high percentage of its applicants may still be considered selective if the students are of a high academic caliber.
- **Expenses:** Figures cited for tuition (including any required fees) are for the 2010–2011 academic

year. For public schools, we list both in-state and out-of-state tuition. If data for the 2010–2011 academic year are not available, we provide figures for 2009–2010 or, in some cases, the school's estimate for 2010–2011.

- **SAT critical reading/math or ACT score (25th/75th percentile):** The SAT or ACT composite scores shown represent the range within which half the students scored; 25 percent of students scored at or below the lower end of the range, and 25 percent scored at or above the upper end of the range. If no range was available, an average score was provided.
- **Rank in the 2011 edition of *U.S. News*'s "Best Colleges":** The school's rank indicates where it sits among its peers in the 2011 ranking of colleges and universities published by *U.S. News* at www.usnews.com and in its annual guide "Best Colleges." You'll see the school's rank, followed by the category of institution it falls into. The categories are National Universities, National Liberal Arts Colleges, Regional Universities, and Regional Colleges. The regional schools are divided by location: North, South, Midwest, and West. Colleges and universities in the top 75 percent of their categories are ranked numerically. Others are listed alphabetically as the Second Tier. You cannot compare the ranks of institutions in different categories because schools are assessed only against their peers. Schools that specialize in business, engineering, and art are labeled as such, but are not ranked; nor are those schools that don't use the SAT or ACT test in admission decisions, schools with fewer than 200 students, or schools with a high percentage of older or part-time students.
- **Acceptance rate:** The percentage of applicants accepted, a measure of how hard the school is to get into, is provided for the class entering in fall 2009.

Student body stats

What will your classmates be like? This section supplies the breakdown of full-time and part-time undergraduate students, the male and female enrollments, the ethnic makeup of the student body, and the percentage of students from countries other than the United States. In addition, a breakdown is given where reported of the percentage of students with various religious preferences. All figures are for the 2009–2010 academic year. Note that students who did not identify themselves as members of any demographic group are classified by schools as "White" and that numbers may not add up to 100 percent because of rounding.

Admissions facts and figures

Along with contact information for the admissions office, all of the application deadlines for fall 2011 admission—regular decision, early decision, and early action—are provided. You'll find out whether there is a date by which you must accept or turn down an offer, what the application fee is, and whether admission can be deferred. A school with rolling admissions makes decisions as applications are received, accepting students until the class has been filled. If the "common application" is accepted, the school is one of about 400 that recognize the standard application form distributed by the National Association of Secondary School Principals. For schools that allow you to apply online, the URL is provided.

Admissions requirements/recommendations: The high school academic courses required or recommended of applicants are noted. The number of required units stands alone, and the number of recommended units is enclosed in parentheses—e.g., English: 3 (4). If the information was unavailable, it does not appear. The section also tells you whether the school requires SAT or ACT scores or uses them in admissions decisions. Be aware that a school may consider SAT or ACT scores if they are available even if it does not require them for admission. Finally, information is provided on whether campus visits, admissions interviews, and off-campus interviews are available or recommended.

Factors that count in admissions decisions: Various academic and nonacademic factors that are—or might be—considered in admission decisions are rated on their relative importance: "Very important," "Important," "Considered," and "Not considered."

Overlap schools: Up to five schools are provided whose applicant pools have the greatest overlap with the school's own applicant pool.

Admissions statistics for the fall 2009 entering class: A look at the admissions statistics for the fall 2009 entering class will tell you the proportion of all applicants who were accepted, as well as the proportion of early-decision and early-action applicants who got in, compared to the acceptance rate for non-early applicants. You'll find how many of the freshmen enrolled were men, how many were women, and how many were from out of state. You will see statistics on how many students were put on the waiting list and how many of those students eventually enrolled.

Credentials of fall 2009 freshmen: For freshmen who submitted their high school class standing when they applied, you will see how many ranked among the top 10 percent of their high school class, in the top quarter, and in the top half. We supply the average high school grade point average of the 2009 freshmen, the percentage submitting SAT and ACT scores, and, for both tests, the range within which half the students scored. The 25th/75th percentiles shown tell you that 25 percent of students scored at or below the lower end of the range and 25 percent scored at or above the upper end.

Academics

Academic calendar: This tells you whether the school year operates on a traditional semester schedule or a different type of schedule, such as trimesters or 4-1-4.

Degrees offered: A list of what types of degrees the school offers is provided.

Most popular majors: Here you will find a list of the five most popular majors among 2009 graduates with a bachelor's degree (and the percentage of students who majored in each).

Majors offered: Undergraduate majors offered are listed here by main field of study. For a more specific idea of majors offered, consult the index of majors that begins on page 190. When a school did not submit information about its majors, *U.S. News* obtained the data from the U.S. Department of Education.

Course requirements: For graduation, does the school require a general education or core curriculum, a minor, physical education, or religion/theology courses? Areas of required coursework are listed.

Pre-professional programs: A list of pre-professional programs offered. If the information was not available, this section does not appear.

Special academic programs (% participating): A list of special academic programs offered. If the information was not available, this section does not appear.

Teacher certification offered in: Information on teacher certification offered by the school. If the information was not available, this section does not appear.

Cooperative education programs: A list of cooperative education programs offered. If the information was not available, this section does not appear.

Reserve Officers Training Corps (ROTC): This section indicates whether the school offers Army, Navy, or Air Force ROTC programs on campus or at a cooperating institution. If the information was not available, this section does not appear.

Faculty and instruction: Information on faculty includes the number of full-time and part-time professors and the breakdown of men, women, and minorities. You can also see what percentage have earned a Ph.D. or other terminal degree in their field. The student-to-faculty ratio is provided. Class-size figures tell you the percentage of classes during the fall 2009 term that had fewer than 20 students, the percentage with 20 to 49 students, and the percentage with 50 or more. (Labs and discussion sections are excluded.)

Advanced Placement and International Baccalaureate credit: If Advanced Placement (AP) and International Baccalaureate (IB) courses can be used for college credit or placement, that information is listed, along with the accepted AP scores.

Graduation and freshman retention rate: Two key numbers that applicants should consider are a school's freshman retention rate and its graduation rate. The freshman retention rate tells you the average proportion of the freshmen who started in 2005 through 2008 and returned the following fall. The graduation rates show the proportion starting college

in 2003 who earned a degree in four years and in five years. We also show the average proportion of graduates who earned a degree in six years or less for classes starting in 2000 through 2003. Because these data were collected in different years, the percentage of students who graduate in six years may be lower than the percentage who graduate in four or five years.

Graduate study: You can see the proportion of students who pursue further study immediately upon graduation, within one year, and within five years. Additionally, we provide a breakdown of the proportion of graduates who pursue further study in business, law, medicine, dentistry, engineering, theology (or the seminary), education, arts and sciences, and veterinary medicine, if those subject areas apply and the information was available.

Costs and financial aid

Expenses: One statistic you will surely want to know is the sticker price: tuition, room, board, and required fees. We provide figures for the 2010–2011 academic year. For public schools, we list both in-state and out-of-state tuition. If data for the 2010–2011 academic year were not available, we provide figures for 2009–2010 or, in some cases, the school's estimate for 2010–2011. We also provide estimates of the cost of books and supplies, transportation, and personal expenses.

Financial aid information: Anyone planning on applying for financial aid for the fall of 2011 will find the necessary deadlines as well as any priority filing dates. The data on financial aid packages are for those awarded to undergraduates during the 2009–2010 school year and include the percentage of undergraduates who applied for aid; the percentage determined by the school to have financial need; and the percentage whose need was fully met by an aid package that excluded parent or other private loans. In addition, we give the average financial aid package (including grants, loans, and jobs) and the proportion of students awarded a package; the average amount of gift aid (scholarships or grants) and the proportion awarded such aid; the average amount of self-help aid (work study or loans) and the proportion awarded such aid; and the average need-based student loan. Among students who received need-based aid, what percentage of their need was met, on average? Among students who were awarded aid based only on merit, what was the average amount and the proportion awarded such merit aid? What was the average athletic scholarship awarded and the proportion receiving such an award?

Debt burden: This section informs you what the average debt was for the students in the Class of 2009 who borrowed money to finance their education and the proportion of students who borrowed.

Campus life and extracurricular activities

Housing: What types of college-owned, -operated, or -affiliated housing are available for undergraduates on campus, and what percentage of students live there? Is housing available for married students? What percentage live in college-owned or -operated housing? These questions are answered in this section.

Student employment: Find out what proportion of undergraduates worked on campus during the 2009–2010 academic year and how much undergraduates can expect to earn per year from part-time, on-campus work.

Clubs and organizations: A sense of the extracurricular opportunities on campus can be gleaned from a list of major clubs and organizations, the numbers of fraternities and sororities and the proportion of undergraduates who are members, and the percentage of students who spend their weekends on campus.

2009–2010 sports program: This section includes information about the school's intercollegiate varsity sports program. Is the school a member of either the National Collegiate Athletic Association (NCAA) or the National Association of Intercollegiate Athletics (NAIA)? During the 2009–2010 year, how many intercollegiate varsity sports—and which ones—were played by men and women? When a school did not submit its sports data, *U.S. News* attempted to compile the information from the websites of the NCAA, the NAIA, or the school itself; in some cases, the information we supply may not be complete.

Services and facilities

Basic services: In this section, you'll find out what sorts of student services are offered, such as counseling, remedial assistance, and career placement.

Services for learning-disabled students: Find out if the school offers a separate structured program for learning-disabled students with separate admissions and additional fees, as well as how many undergraduates are either enrolled in a learning-disabled program or are otherwise receiving services. Services offered to learning-disabled students are listed.

Library: This section gives an idea of the size of the library's collection.

Information and technology resources: Are students required to lease or own a computer? How many computers does the school have for students to use? Does the school have a wireless network and, if so, approximately how many users can be accommodated? What proportion of college housing is wired for high-speed Internet access?

Campus security: A list of security services offered.

Transfer and international students

Transfer students: Students thinking of transferring can quickly find out when to apply and whether applicants need a minimum number of credits. We provide the number of transfer applications received for fall 2009, the number of transfer applicants offered admission, and the number who enrolled.

International students: We note how many undergraduates come from other countries and how many countries are represented. Minimum and average TOEFL scores are also listed, if they are available.

Alabama

Alabama Agricultural and Mech. Univ.

- **Address:** PO Box 1357, Normal, AL 35762
- **Website:** http://www.aamu.edu
- **Public**
- **Enrollment:** 4,153 full-time; 343 part-time

KEY STATS

✔ **U.S News College Ranking:** second tier, Regional Universities (South)
✔ **ACT Score (25th/75th percentile):** 16-19
✔ **Tuition:** 2009-2010: $4,692 in state, $8,640 out of state
  Selectivity: Less selective   **Room/board:** $5,350
  Acceptance rate: 47%   **Average debt:** $32,024
  Student/faculty ratio: 14/1   **Proportion who borrowed:** 82%

UNDERGRADUATE STUDENT BODY STATS

2009-2010 enrollment: 4,153 full-time; 343 part-time. Men: 48%; women: 52%. **Ethnic makeup:** African American: 96%; White: 3%; International: 1%.

ADMISSIONS FACTS AND FIGURES

Phone: (256) 372-5245. **Email:** admissions@aamu.edu. **Website:** http://www.aamu.edu. **Application deadlines for fall 2011:** Regular decision: July 15. Early decision: Not offered. Early action: Not offered. Admission can be deferred. **Application fee:** $25. **To apply online, go to:** http://www.aamu.edu/admissions/APPLY_ONLINE_NOW.aspx. **Admissions requirements/recommendations:** High school units required (recommended): English: 4; Mathematics: 4; Science: 2. Tests: The college uses SAT or ACT scores in admissions decisions. ACT required. Campus visit: Recommended. Admissions interview: Neither required nor recommended. Off-campus interview: Not available. **Factors that count in admissions decisions:** *Academic:* Secondary school record: Important. Class rank: Considered. Letters of recommendation: Important. Standardized test scores: Very Important. Essay: Considered. *Nonacademic:* Interview: Not Considered. Extracurricular activities: Considered. Talent/ability: Not Considered. Character/personal qualities: Considered. Alumni/ae relationship: Not Considered. Geographical residence: Not Considered. State residency: Important. Religious affiliation/commitment: Not Considered. Minority status: Considered. Volunteer work: Not Considered. Work experience: Not Considered. **Admissions statistics for the fall 2009 entering class:** Total applicants: 5,697. Total accepted: 2,696. Freshmen enrolled: 1,050; 41% were from out of state. Overall acceptance rate: 47%. **First-year students who submitted SAT scores:** 10%. Scores (25/75 percentile): Critical Reading: 400-470, Math: 380-470, Combined: 780-940. **First-year students submitting ACT scores:** 73%. Scores (25/75 percentile): English: 15-20, Math: 15-18, Composite: 16-19.

ACADEMICS

Year founded: 1875. **Academic calendar:** Semester. **Degrees offered:** bachelor's, master's, doctorate. **Most popular majors:** 23% business, management, marketing, and related support services, 12% biological and biomedical sciences, 12% education, 8% engineering, 6% social sciences. **Major fields of study:** agriculture, agriculture operations, and related sciences; architecture and related services; biological and biomedical sciences; business, management, marketing, and related support services; communications technologies/technicians and support services; computer and information sciences and support services; education; engineering; engineering technologies/technicians; English language and literature/letters; family and consumer sciences/human sciences; health professions and related clinical sciences; mathematics and statistics; natural resources and conservation; physical sciences; psychology; public administration and social service professions; social sciences; visual and performing arts. **Areas of required coursework:** arts/fine arts, humanities, computer literacy, mathematics, English (including composition), philosophy, foreign languages, sciences (biological or physical), history, social science. **Pre-professional programs:** pre-medicine. **Special academic programs:** accelerated program, cooperative (work-study plan) program, distance learning, double major, dual enrollment, exchange student program (domestic), honors program, independent study, intern-

ships, study abroad, teacher certificate program, weekend college. **Teacher certification offered in:** early childhood, special education, elementary, secondary. **Cooperative education programs:** agriculture, business, computer science, education, engineering, social/behavioral science. **Reserve Officers Training Corps (ROTC):** Army ROTC: Offered on campus. **Faculty and instruction (2009-2010):** Total instructional faculty: 311 full-time, 73 part-time (57% men; 43% women; 74% minorities). Full-time faculty with Ph.D. or other terminal degree: 45%. Student/faculty ratio: 14/1. Classes of fewer than 20 students: 49%; of 20 to 49 students: 47%; of 50 or more students: 4%. **Freshmen returning for sophomore year:** 69%. **Graduation rates:** Four-year: 9%; five-year: 23%; six-year: 33%. **Graduate study:** 40% of students pursue further study immediately upon graduation. Fields in which graduates pursue further study: Master of Business Administration (MBA), 17%; law, 5%; medicine, 5%; education, 36%; arts and sciences, 37%.

COSTS AND FINANCIAL AID

Financial aid office: (256) 372-5400. **Expenses (2009-2010):** Tuition and fees 2009-2010: $4,692 in state, $8,640 out of state; room/board: $5,350. **Financial aid:** Priority filing date for institution's financial aid form: February 1; deadline: July 15. In 2009-2010, 89% of undergraduates applied for financial aid. Of those, 79% were determined to have financial need; 14% had their need fully met. Average financial aid package (proportion receiving): $8,642 (78%). Average amount of gift aid, such as scholarships or grants (proportion receiving): $6,243 (66%). Average amount of self-help aid, such as work study or loans (proportion receiving): $2,553 (3%). Average need-based loan (excluding PLUS or other private loans): $4,265. Among students who received need-based aid, the average percentage of need met: 14%. Among students who received aid based on merit, the average award (and the proportion receiving): $3,665 (1%). The average athletic scholarship (and the proportion receiving): $7,700 (0%). Average amount of debt of borrowers graduating in 2009: $32,024. Proportion who borrowed: 82%.

CAMPUS LIFE AND EXTRACURRICULAR ACTIVITIES

Campus housing available (% using): women's dorms (20%), men's dorms (22%), other housing options (50%). Students who live in college-owned, operated, or affiliated housing: 47%. Average per-year earnings: $5,000. **Clubs and organizations:** Number of student organizations: 8. Activities include: choral groups, concert band, dance, drama/theater, jazz band, marching band, music ensembles, pep band, radio station, student government, student newspaper, television station, yearbook. Number of fraternities: 4; sororities: 4. **Sports program (2009-2010):** Member of NCAA I. *Men's intercollegiate varsity sports:* baseball, basketball, football, golf, soccer, tennis, track and field (indoor), track and field (outdoor), volleyball. *Women's intercollegiate varsity sports:* basketball, bowling, golf, soccer, softball, tennis, track and field (indoor), track and field (outdoor), volleyball.

SERVICES AND FACILITIES

Basic services: nonremedial tutoring, placement service, day care, health service, health insurance. **Remedial assistance:** reading, math, writing. **Counseling services:** minority student, career, military, older student, psychological. **For learning-disabled students:** Services include: remedial math, remedial English, remedial reading, tutors. **Library:** Number of titles: 597,969; number of current serial subscriptions: 1,151. **Information technology resources:** Students are not required to lease or own a computer. School has a wireless network. Approximate number of users that can be accommodated: 3,000. Proportion of college-owned housing units wired for high-speed internet access: 100%. **Campus safety:** Security services offered: late-night transport/escort service, 24-hour emergency telephones, lighted pathways/sidewalks, controlled dormitory access (key, security card, etc).

TRANSFER AND INTERNATIONAL STUDENTS

Transfer students: May apply for admission for the following academic terms: Fall, Spring, Summer. Applicants do not need a minimum number of credits to apply. For fall 2009: Transfer applications received: 301. Transfer applicants offered admission: 238. Transfer applicants enrolled: 237. **International students:** Number of foreign undergraduates: 38 (1% of student body). Minimum TOEFL score required: 500 (paper); 213 (computer).

Alabama State University

- **Address:** 915 S. Jackson Street, Montgomery, AL 36101
- **Website:** http://www.alasu.edu
- **Public**
- **Enrollment:** 4,216 full-time; 422 part-time

KEY STATS

✔ **U.S News College Ranking:** Unranked, Regional Universities (South)
✔ **ACT Score (25th/75th percentile):** 13-17
✔ **Tuition:** 2009-2010: $5,460 in state, $10,068 out of state

Selectivity: N/A	**Room/board:** $4,600
Acceptance rate: 44%	**Average debt:** N/A
Student/faculty ratio: N/A	**Proportion who borrowed:** N/A

UNDERGRADUATE STUDENT BODY STATS

2009-2010 enrollment: 4,216 full-time; 422 part-time. Men: 40%; women: 60%. **Ethnic makeup:** African American: 98%; White: 2%.

ADMISSIONS FACTS AND FIGURES

Phone: (334) 229-4291. **Email:** mpettway@alasu.edu. **Website:** http://www.alasu.edu. **Application deadlines for fall 2011:** Regular decision: July 30. Early decision: Not offered. Early action: Not offered. Admission can be deferred. **Application fee:** $25. **To apply online, go to:** http://www.alasu.edu/Admissions/. **Admissions requirements/recommendations:** High school units required (recommended): English: 4 (3); Mathematics: 3 (2); Science: 3 (2); Foreign language: 1 (2); Social studies: 3 (2); History: 0; Academic electives: 0; Total units: 15 (11). Tests: The college does not use SAT or ACT scores in admissions decisions. Neither SAT nor ACT required. For admission to the fall 2011 entering class, the school will accept: ACT with or without writing accepted. Campus visit: Recommended. Admissions interview: Recommended. Off-campus interview: May not be arranged. **Factors that count in admissions decisions:** *Academic:* Secondary school record: Important. Class rank: Not Considered. Letters of recommendation: Not Considered. Standardized test scores: Important. Essay: Not Considered. *Nonacademic:* Interview: Not Considered. Extracurricular activities: Not Considered. Talent/ability: Not Considered. Character/personal qualities: Not Considered. Alumni/ae relationship: Not Considered. Geographical residence: Not Considered. State residency: Not Considered. Religious affiliation/commitment: Not Considered. Minority status: Not Considered. Volunteer work: Not Considered. Work experience: Not Considered. **Admissions statistics for the fall 2009 entering class:** Total applicants: 8,229. Total accepted: 3,598. Freshmen enrolled: 1,221; Overall acceptance rate: 44%. **Credentials of fall 2009 freshmen:** 2% ranked in the top 10 percent of their high school class; 9% were in the top 25 percent; 29% were in the top half. (Proportion submitting class standing: 59%.) **Average high school grade point average:** 2.9. **First-year students who submitted SAT scores:** 26%. Scores (25/75 percentile): Critical Reading: 360-440, Math: 320-420, Combined: 680-860. **First-year students submitting ACT scores:** 87%. Scores (25/75 percentile): English: 14-16, Math: 12-18, Composite: 13-17.

ACADEMICS

Year founded: 1867. **Academic calendar:** Semester. **Degrees offered:** bachelor's, post-bachelor's certificate, master's, post-master's certificate, doctorate. **Major fields of study:** biological and biomedical sciences; business, management, marketing, and related support services; communication, journalism, and related programs; computer and information sciences and support services; education; English language and literature/letters; health professions and related clinical sciences; history; mathematics and statistics; parks, recreation, leisure, and fitness studies; physical sciences; psychology; public administration and social service professions; security and protective services; social sciences; visual and performing arts. **Areas of required coursework:** arts/fine arts, humanities, computer literacy, mathematics, English (including composition), sciences (biological or physical), history, social science, other. **Special academic programs:** cooperative (work-study plan) program, cross-registration, double major, honors program, independent study, internships, teacher certificate program. **Teacher certification offered in:** early childhood, special education, elementary, secondary. **Cooperative education programs:** art, business, computer science, education, humanities, natural science, social/behavioral science, vocational arts. **Reserve Officers Training Corps (ROTC):** Army ROTC: Offered at cooperating institution; Air Force ROTC: Offered on campus. **Advanced Placement and International Baccalaureate credit:** AP tests may be used for: Credit and/or placement. Scores accepted: 4, 5. **Freshmen returning for sophomore year:** 54%. **Graduation rates:** Four-year: 7%; five-year: 18%; six-year: 25%.

COSTS AND FINANCIAL AID

Financial aid office: (334) 229-4323. **Expenses (2009-2010):** Tuition and fees 2009-2010: $5,460 in state, $10,068 out of state; room/board: $4,600. Estimated books and supplies: $1,000; transportation: $1,164; personal expenses: $1,380. **Financial aid:** Priority filing date for institution's financial aid form: April 1.

CAMPUS LIFE AND EXTRACURRICULAR ACTIVITIES

Campus housing available (% using): women's dorms (55%), men's dorms (39%), special housing for disabled students, special housing for international students, other housing options (6%). **Student employment:** During the 2009-2010 academic year, 10% of undergraduates worked on campus. Average per-year earnings: $4,017. **Clubs and organizations:** Number of student organizations: 64. Activities include: choral groups, concert band, dance, drama/theater, jazz band, marching band, music ensembles, musical theater, pep band, radio station, student government, student newspaper, yearbook. Number of fraternities: 5; sororities: 4. Average proportion of students who stay on campus on weekends: 70%. **Sports program (2009-2010):** Member of NCAA I. *Men's intercollegiate varsity sports:* baseball, basketball, cross country, football, golf, tennis, track and field (indoor), track and field (outdoor). *Women's intercollegiate varsity sports:* basketball, bowling, cross country, golf, soccer, softball, tennis, track and field (indoor), track and field (outdoor), volleyball.

SERVICES AND FACILITIES

Basic services: nonremedial tutoring, placement service, health service, health insurance. **Remedial assistance:** reading, math, writing, study skills. **Counseling services:** minority student, career, military, personal, veteran student, academic, older student, psychological, birth control. **For learning-disabled students:** School does not offer a structured program with separate admission and additional fees. Services include: remedial math, remedial English, remedial reading, tape recorders, untimed tests, note-taking services, oral tests, learning center, extended time for tests, tutors. **Library:** Number of titles: 422,452; number of current serial subscriptions: 2,120. **Information technology resources:** Students are not required to lease or own a computer. Number of campus computers available to all students: 550. School has a wireless network. Approximate number of users that can be accommodated: 1,200. Proportion of college-owned housing units wired for high-speed internet access: 100%. **Campus safety:** Security services offered: 24-hour foot-and-vehicle patrols, late-night transport/escort service, 24-hour emergency telephones, controlled dormitory access (key, security card, etc).

TRANSFER AND INTERNATIONAL STUDENTS

Transfer students: May apply for admission for the following academic terms: Fall, Spring, Summer. Applicants need a minimum number of credits to apply. For fall 2009: Transfer applications received: 937. Transfer applicants offered admission: 241. Transfer applicants enrolled: 211. **International students:** Number of foreign undergraduates: 21. Number of countries represented: 6. Minimum TOEFL score required: 500 (paper); 173 (computer).

Auburn University

- **Address:** 202 Martin Hall, Auburn University, AL 36849
- **Website:** http://www.auburn.edu
- **Public**
- **Enrollment:** 18,387 full-time; 1,539 part-time

KEY STATS

✔ **U.S News College Ranking:** 85, National Universities
✔ **ACT Score (25th/75th percentile):** 23-29
✔ **Tuition:** 2010-2011: $7,900 in state, $21,916 out of state

Selectivity: More selective	**Room/board:** $9,630
Acceptance rate: 80%	**Average debt:** $22,232
Student/faculty ratio: 18/1	**Proportion who borrowed:** 40%

UNDERGRADUATE STUDENT BODY STATS

2009-2010 enrollment: 18,387 full-time; 1,539 part-time. Men: 52%; women: 48%. **Ethnic makeup:** African American: 8%; American-Indian: 1%; Asian American: 2%; Hispanic: 2%; White: 87%; International: 1%.

ADMISSIONS FACTS AND FIGURES

Phone: (334) 844-6425. **Email:** admissions@auburn.edu. **Website:** http://www.auburn.edu. **Application deadlines for fall 2011:** Regular decision: Rolling. Early decision: Not offered. Early action: Send application by: February 1; Decision sent by: October 15. Admission cannot be deferred. **Application fee:** $50. **To apply online, go to:** http://www.auburn.edu/admissions. **Admissions requirements/recommendations:** High school units required (recommended): English: 4 (4); Mathematics: 3 (3); Science: 2 (3); Foreign language: 0 (1); Social studies: 3 (4); History: 0 (0); Academic electives: 0 (0); Total units: 12 (15). Tests: The college uses SAT or ACT scores in admissions decisions. Either SAT or ACT required. For admission to the fall 2011 entering class, the school will accept: ACT with writing required. Campus visit: Recommended. Admissions interview: Neither required nor recommended. Off-campus interview: May be arranged. **Factors that count in admissions decisions:** *Academic:* Secondary school record: Important. Class rank: Considered. Letters of recommendation: Considered. Standardized test scores: Very Important. Essay: Very Important. *Nonacademic:* Interview: Not Considered. Extracurricular activities: Important. Talent/ability: Important. Character/personal qualities: Important. Alumni/ae relationship: Important. Geographical residence: Important. State residency: Important. Religious affiliation/commitment: Not Considered. Minority status: Not Considered. Volunteer work: Important. Work experience: Important. **Other schools with the greatest overlap in applicants:** Clemson University; Georgia Institute of Technology; University of Alabama; University of Florida; University of Georgia. **Admissions statistics for the fall 2009 entering class:** Total applicants: 14,862. Total accepted: 11,816. Freshmen enrolled: 3,918; 43% were from out of state. Accepted through early-decision or early-action plans: 43%. Overall acceptance rate: 80%. **Credentials of fall 2009 freshmen:** 40% ranked in the top 10 percent of their high school class; 65% were in the top 25 percent; 91% were in the top half. (Proportion submitting class standing: 68%.) **Average high school grade point average:** 3.7. **First-year students who submitted SAT scores:** 22%. Scores (25/75 percentile): Critical Reading: 520-640, Math: 540-660, Combined: 1060-1300. **First-year students submitting ACT scores:** 78%. Scores (25/75 percentile): English: 24-30, Math: 22-28, Composite: 23-29.

ACADEMICS

Year founded: 1856. **Academic calendar:** Semester. **Degrees offered:** bachelor's, master's, post-master's certificate, doctorate. **Most popular majors:** 24% business, management, marketing, and related support services, 13% engineering, 10% education, 6% biological and biomedical sciences, 6% social sciences. **Major fields of study:** agriculture, agriculture operations, and related sciences; architecture and related services; biological and biomedical sciences; business, management, marketing, and related support services; communication, journalism, and related programs; computer and information sciences and support services; education; engineering; English language and literature/letters; family and consumer sciences/human sciences; foreign languages, literatures, and linguistics; health professions and related clinical sciences; history; mathematics and statistics; multi/interdisciplinary studies; natural resources and conservation; philosophy and religious studies; physical sciences; psychology; public administration and social service professions; social sciences; visual and performing arts. **Areas of required coursework:** arts/fine arts, humanities, computer literacy, mathematics, English (including composition), philosophy, sciences (biological or physical), history, social science. **Pre-professional programs:** pre-law, pre-dentistry, pre-medicine, pre-veterinary science, pre-optometry, pre-pharmacy. **Special academic programs (% participation):** accelerated program, cooperative (work-study plan) program (2%), distance learning (5%), double major (2%), dual enrollment, English as a Second Language (ESL), honors program (5%), independent study (18%), internships (52%), liberal arts/career combination, study abroad (12%), teacher certificate program (7%). **Teacher certification offered in:** early childhood, special education, elementary, vo-tech, adult education, secondary, bilingual/bicultural. **Cooperative education programs:** agriculture, art, business, computer science, engineering, home economics, humanities, natural science, social/behavioral science, technologies, other. **Reserve Officers Training Corps (ROTC):** Army ROTC: Offered on campus; Navy ROTC: Offered on campus; Air Force ROTC: Offered on campus. **Faculty and instruction (2009-2010):** Total instructional faculty: 1,184 full-time, 159 part-time (66% men; 34% women; 15% minorities). Full-time faculty with Ph.D. or other terminal degree: 93%. Student/faculty ratio: 18/1. Classes of fewer than 20 students: 25%; of 20 to 49 students: 59%; of 50 or more students: 16%. **Advanced Placement and International Baccalaureate credit:** AP tests may be used for: Placement only. Scores accepted: 3, 4, 5. International Baccalaureate exams may be used for: Placement only. **Freshmen returning for sophomore**

year: 86%. **Graduation rates:** Four-year: 37%; five-year: 61%; six-year: 67%. **Graduate study:** Fields in which graduates pursue further study: Master of Business Administration (MBA), 18%; law, 7%; medicine, 16%; dentistry, 2%; engineering, 12%; theology (or the seminary), 3%; education, 18%; arts and sciences, 23%; veterinary medicine, 1%.

COSTS AND FINANCIAL AID

Financial aid office: (334) 844-4634. **Expenses (2010-2011):** Tuition and fees 2010-2011: $7,900 in state, $21,916 out of state; room/board: $9,630. Estimated books and supplies: $1,100; transportation: $2,346; personal expenses: $2,510. **Financial aid:** Priority filing date for institution's financial aid form: March 1. In 2009-2010, 55% of undergraduates applied for financial aid. Of those, 32% were determined to have financial need; 18% had their need fully met. Average financial aid package (proportion receiving): $9,085 (32%). Average amount of gift aid, such as scholarships or grants (proportion receiving): $5,693 (23%). Average amount of self-help aid, such as work study or loans (proportion receiving): $4,625 (27%). Average need-based loan (excluding PLUS or other private loans): $4,434. Among students who received need-based aid, the average percentage of need met: 57%. Among students who received aid based on merit, the average award (and the proportion receiving): $4,908 (14%). The average athletic scholarship (and the proportion receiving): $18,485 (2%). Average amount of debt of borrowers graduating in 2009: $22,232. Proportion who borrowed: 40%.

CAMPUS LIFE AND EXTRACURRICULAR ACTIVITIES

Campus housing available (% using): coed dorms (30%), women's dorms (20%), fraternity housing, apartment for single students (21%), special housing for disabled students (1%), other housing options (28%). Students who live in college-owned, operated, or affiliated housing: 19%. **Student employment:** During the 2009-2010 academic year, 13% of undergraduates worked on campus. Average per-year earnings: $4,500. **Clubs and organizations:** Number of student organizations: 250. Activities include: campus ministries, choral groups, concert band, dance, drama/theater, international student organization, jazz band, literary magazine, marching band, music ensembles, musical theater, opera, pep band, radio station, student government, student newspaper, student film society, symphony orchestra, television station, yearbook. Number of fraternities: 31; sororities: 20. Proportion of men in fraternities: 21%; of women in sororities: 31%. Average proportion of students who stay on campus on weekends: 70%. **Sports program (2009-2010):** Member of NCAA I. *Men's intercollegiate varsity sports:* baseball, basketball, cross country, football, golf, swimming, tennis, track and field (outdoor). *Women's intercollegiate varsity sports:* basketball, cross country, equestrian, golf, gymnastics, soccer, softball, swimming, tennis, track and field (outdoor), volleyball.

SERVICES AND FACILITIES

Basic services: nonremedial tutoring, women's center, placement service, health service, health insurance. **Counseling services:** minority student, career, military, personal, veteran student, academic, older student, psychological, birth control, religious, other. **For learning-disabled students:** School does not offer a structured program with separate admission and additional fees. Total undergraduates in learning-disabled program or receiving services: 445. Services include: reading machines, tape recorders, diagnostic testing service, note-taking services, oral tests, learning center, readers, extended time for tests, tutors, priority registration, priority seating, texts on tape, exams on tape or computer, other testing accommodations, other. **Library:** Number of titles: 3,697,283; number of current serial subscriptions: 39,318. **Information technology resources:** Students are not required to lease or own a computer. Number of campus computers available to all students: 1,722. School has a wireless network. Approximate number of users that can be accommodated: 15,000. Proportion of college-owned housing units wired for high-speed internet access: 0%. **Campus safety:** Security services offered: 24-hour foot-and-vehicle patrols, late-night transport/escort service, 24-hour emergency telephones, lighted pathways/sidewalks, controlled dormitory access (key, security card, etc).

TRANSFER AND INTERNATIONAL STUDENTS

Transfer students: May apply for admission for the following academic terms: Fall, Spring, Summer. Applicants need a minimum number of credits to apply. For fall 2009: Transfer applications received: 2,938. Transfer applicants offered admission: 2,088. Transfer applicants enrolled: 1,337. **International students:** Number of foreign undergraduates: 123 (1% of student body). Number of countries represented: 39. Minimum TOEFL score required: 550 (paper); 79 (computer). Average TOEFL score: 580 (paper).

Auburn University—Montgomery

- **Address:** PO Box 244023, Montgomery, AL 36124
- **Website:** http://www.aum.edu
- **Public**
- **Enrollment:** 3,140 full-time; 1,538 part-time

KEY STATS

✔ **U.S News College Ranking:** 74, Regional Universities (South)
✔ **ACT Score (25th/75th percentile):** 18-23
✔ **Tuition:** 2009-2010: $5,925 in state, $17,205 out of state

Selectivity: Selective	**Room/board:** N/A
Acceptance rate: 95%	**Average debt:** N/A
Student/faculty ratio: 18/1	**Proportion who borrowed:** N/A

UNDERGRADUATE STUDENT BODY STATS

2009-2010 enrollment: 3,140 full-time; 1,538 part-time. Men: 38%; women: 62%. **Ethnic makeup:** African American: 32%; American-Indian: 1%; Asian American: 2%; Hispanic: 1%; White: 62%; International: 3%.

ADMISSIONS FACTS AND FIGURES

Phone: (334) 244-3611. **Email:** vsamuel@aum.edu. **Website:** http://www.aum.edu. **Application deadlines for fall 2011:** Regular decision: Rolling. Early decision: Not offered. Early action: Not offered. Admission can be deferred. **Application fee:** $25. **To apply online, go to:** http://www.aum.edu/admission. **Admissions requirements/recommendations:** High school units required (recommended): English: 3 (4); Mathematics: 3 (4); Science: 2 (4); Foreign language: 2 (2); Social studies: 2 (2); History: 2 (2); Academic electives: 2 (2); Total units: 16. **Tests:** The college uses SAT or ACT scores in admissions decisions. ACT required. For admission to the fall 2011 entering class, the school will accept: ACT with or without writing accepted. Campus visit: Recommended. Admissions interview: Recommended. Off-campus interview: May be arranged. **Factors that count in admissions decisions:** *Academic:* Secondary school record: Very Important. Class rank: Very Important. Letters of recommendation: Considered. Standardized test scores: Very Important. Essay: Not Considered. *Nonacademic:* Interview: Not Considered. Extracurricular activities: Considered. Talent/ability: Not Considered. Character/personal qualities: Not Considered. Alumni/ae relationship: Considered. Geographical residence: Considered. State residency: Considered. Religious affiliation/commitment: Not Considered. Minority status: Not Considered. Volunteer work: Not Considered. Work experience: Not Considered. **Admissions statistics for the fall 2009 entering class:** Total applicants: 1,409. Total accepted: 1,339. Freshmen enrolled: 872; 6% were from out of state. Overall acceptance rate: 95%. **Credentials of fall 2009 freshmen:** 14% ranked in the top 10 percent of their high school class; 36% were in the top 25 percent; 67% were in the top half. (Proportion submitting class standing: 62%.) **First-year students submitting ACT scores:** 80%. Scores (25/75 percentile): English: 18-24, Math: 16-22, Composite: 18-23.

ACADEMICS

Year founded: 1967. **Academic calendar:** Semester. **Degrees offered:** bachelor's, master's, post-master's certificate, doctorate. **Most popular majors:** 33% business, management, marketing, and related support services, 13% education, 11% health professions and related clinical sciences, 10% biological and biomedical sciences, 4% security and protective services. **Major fields of study:** biological and biomedical sciences; business, management, marketing, and related support services; communication, journalism, and related programs; education; English language and literature/letters; foreign languages, literatures, and linguistics; health professions and related clinical sciences; history; liberal arts and sciences studies, and humanities; mathematics and statistics; physical sciences; psychology; security and protective services; social sciences; visual and performing arts. **Areas of required coursework:** mathematics, English (including composition), sciences (biological or physical), history, social science. **Pre-professional programs:** pre-law, pre-dentistry, pre-medicine, pre-veterinary science, pre-optometry, pre-pharmacy, other. **Special academic programs:** accelerated program, cooperative (work-study plan) program, cross-registration, distance learning, double major, dual enrollment, English as a Second Language (ESL), honors program, independent study, internships, liberal arts/career combination, study abroad, teacher certificate program, weekend college. **Teacher certification offered in:** early childhood, special education, elementary, secondary. **Cooperative education programs:** business, computer science, education, engineering, health professions, natural science, social/behavioral science, other. **Reserve Officers Training Corps (ROTC):** Army ROTC: Offered on campus; Air Force ROTC: Offered at cooperating institution (Alabama State University). **Faculty and instruction (2009-2010):** Total instructional faculty: 187 full-time, 121 part-time (50% men; 50% women; 17% minorities). Student/faculty ratio: 18/1. Classes of fewer than 20 students: 45%; of 20 to 49 students: 53%; of 50 or more students: 3%. **Advanced Placement and International Baccalaureate credit:** AP tests may be used for: Placement only. International Baccalaureate exams may be used for: Placement only. **Freshmen returning for sophomore year:** 59%. **Graduation rates:** Four-year: 11%; five-year: 22%; six-year: 27%.

COSTS AND FINANCIAL AID

Financial aid office: (334) 244-3571. **Expenses (2009-2010):** Tuition and fees 2009-2010: $5,925 in state, $17,205 out of state. Estimated books and supplies: $900; transportation: $1,530; personal expenses: $1,170. **Financial aid:** Priority filing date for institution's financial aid form: March 1. 33% had their need fully met. Average amount of gift aid, such as scholarships or grants (proportion receiving): $4,610 (N/A). Average need-based loan (excluding PLUS or other private loans): $4,241.

CAMPUS LIFE AND EXTRACURRICULAR ACTIVITIES

Campus housing available: coed dorms, apartments for married students, apartment for single students, special housing for disabled students. Students who live in college-owned, operated, or affiliated housing: 12%. Activities include: campus ministries, choral groups, dance, drama/theater, international student organization, musical theater, student government, student newspaper, student film society. Number of fraternities: 3; sororities: 7. Proportion of men in fraternities: 2%; of women in sororities: 3%. Average proportion of students who stay on campus on weekends: 60%. **Sports program (2009-2010):** Member of NAIA. *Men's intercollegiate varsity sports:* baseball, basketball, soccer, tennis. *Women's intercollegiate varsity sports:* basketball, soccer, softball, tennis.

SERVICES AND FACILITIES

Basic services: placement service, health service. **Remedial assistance:** reading, math, writing. **Counseling services:** career, military, personal, academic, birth control. **For learning-disabled students:** School does not offer a structured program with separate admission and additional fees. Total undergraduates in learning-disabled program or receiving services: 196. Services include: remedial math, remedial English, reading machines, remedial reading, tape recorders, note-taking services, oral tests, learning center, readers, extended time for tests, tutors, early syllabus, priority registration, priority seating, substitution of courses, texts on tape, exams on tape or computer, other testing accommodations, other. **Library:** Number of titles: 367,620; number of current serial subscriptions: 726. **Information technology resources:** Students are not required to lease or own a computer. Number of campus computers available to all students: 674. School has a wireless network. Approximate number of users that can be accommodated: 2,250. Proportion of college-owned housing units wired for high-speed internet access: 100%. **Campus safety:** Security services offered: 24-hour foot-and-vehicle patrols, late-night transport/escort service, 24-hour emergency telephones, lighted pathways/sidewalks, student patrols, controlled dormitory access (key, security card, etc).

TRANSFER AND INTERNATIONAL STUDENTS

Transfer students: May apply for admission for the following academic terms: Fall, Spring, Summer. Applicants need a minimum number of credits to apply. For fall 2009: Transfer applications received: 574. Transfer applicants offered admission: 509. Transfer applicants enrolled: 332. **International students:** Number of foreign undergraduates: 118 (3% of student body). Number of countries represented: 27. Minimum TOEFL score required: 500 (paper); 61 (computer).

Birmingham-Southern College

- **Address:** 900 Arkadelphia Road, Birmingham, AL 35254
- **Website:** http://www.bsc.edu
- **Private; Religious affiliation:** United Methodist
- **Enrollment:** 1,472 full-time; 36 part-time

KEY STATS

✔ **U.S News College Ranking:** 93, National Liberal Arts Colleges
✔ **ACT Score (25th/75th percentile):** 23-28
✔ **Tuition:** 2010-2011: $27,890

Selectivity: More selective	**Room/board:** $9,910
Acceptance rate: 59%	**Average debt:** $30,907
Student/faculty ratio: 12/1	**Proportion who borrowed:** 41%

UNDERGRADUATE STUDENT BODY STATS

2009-2010 enrollment: 1,472 full-time; 36 part-time. Men: 50%; women: 50%. **Ethnic makeup:** African American: 8%; American-Indian: 1%; Asian American: 4%; Hispanic: 2%; White: 85%. **Religious preference:** Roman Catholic: 12%; Protestant: 40%; Jewish: 1%; Hindu: 1%; No preference: 14%; United Methodist: 23%; Other: 9%.

ADMISSIONS FACTS AND FIGURES

Phone: (205) 226-4696. **Email:** admission@bsc.edu. **Website:** http://www.bsc.edu. **Application deadlines for fall 2011:** Regular decision: Rolling. Early decision: Not offered. Early action: Not offered. Admission can be deferred. **Application fee:** $40. **To apply online, go to:** https://www.bsc-now.org/secure/10163/preview_app.asp?wcc=FWA. **Admissions requirements/recommendations:** High school units required (recommended): English: 4; Mathematics: (4); Science: (4); Foreign language: (2); Social studies: (2); History: (2); Academic electives: (10); Total units: 16. Tests: The college uses SAT or ACT scores in admissions decisions. Either SAT or ACT required. For admission to the fall 2011 entering class, the school will accept: ACT with writing recommended. Campus visit: Recommended. Admissions interview: Recommended. Off-campus interview: Not available. **Factors that count in admissions decisions: Academic:** Secondary school record: Very Important. Class rank: Not Considered. Letters of recommendation: Very Important. Standardized test scores: Very Important. Essay: Very Important. *Nonacademic:* Interview: Considered. Extracurricular activities: Considered. Talent/ability: Considered. Character/personal qualities: Important. Alumni/ae relationship: Not Considered. Geographical residence: Not Considered. State residency: Not Considered. Religious affiliation/commitment: Not Considered. Minority status: Not Considered. Volunteer work: Considered. Work experience: Considered. **Other schools with the greatest overlap in applicants:** Auburn University; Millsaps College; Rhodes College; Sewanee–University of the South; University of Alabama. **Admissions statistics for the fall 2009 entering class:** Total applicants: 2,536. Total accepted: 1,486. Freshmen enrolled: 424; 41% were from out of state. Overall acceptance rate: 59%. **Size of waiting list:** 0 applicants; enrolled from waiting list: 0. **Credentials of fall 2009 freshmen:** 33% ranked in the top 10 percent of their high school class; 58% were in the top 25 percent; 84% were in the top half. (Proportion submitting class standing: 62%.) **Average high school grade point average:** 3.4. **First-year students who submitted SAT scores:** 45%. Scores (25/75 percentile): Critical Reading: 520-640, Math: 520-630, Combined: 1040-1270. **First-year students submitting ACT scores:** 86%. Scores (25/75 percentile): English: 22-28, Math: 23-31, Composite: 23-28.

ACADEMICS

Year founded: 1856. **Academic calendar:** 4-1-4. **Degrees offered:** bachelor's, master's. **Most popular majors:** 18% business administration and management, 11% biology/biological sciences, 9% English language and literature, 7% psychology, 6% accounting. **Major fields of study:** biological and biomedical sciences; computer and information sciences and support services; education; engineering; engineering technologies/technicians; English language and literature/letters; foreign languages, literatures, and linguistics; health professions and related clinical sciences; mathematics and statistics; multi/interdisciplinary studies; philosophy and religious studies; physical sciences; psychology; science technologies/technicians; social sciences; theology and religious vocations; visual and performing arts. **Areas of required coursework:** arts/fine arts, humanities, computer literacy, mathematics, English (including composition), philosophy, foreign languages, sciences (biological or physical), history, social science. **Pre-professional programs:** pre-law, pre-dentistry, pre-medicine, pre-theology, pre-veterinary science, pre-optometry, pre-pharmacy, other. **Special academic programs (% participation):** cross-registration

(3%), double major (1%), dual enrollment, exchange student program (domestic), honors program (8%), independent study (16%), internships (15%), student-designed major (1%), study abroad (1%), teacher certificate program (1%). **Teacher certification offered in:** special education, elementary, secondary. **Reserve Officers Training Corps (ROTC):** Army ROTC: Offered at cooperating institution (University of Alabama–Birmingham); Air Force ROTC: Offered at cooperating institution (Samford University). **Faculty and instruction (2009-2010):** Total instructional faculty: 111 full-time, 32 part-time (55% men; 45% women; 1% minorities). Full-time faculty with Ph.D. or other terminal degree: 91%. Student/faculty ratio: 12/1. Classes of fewer than 20 students: 63%; of 20 to 49 students: 37%; of 50 or more students: 1%. **Advanced Placement and International Baccalaureate credit:** AP tests may be used for: Placement only. Scores accepted: 4, 5. International Baccalaureate exams may be used for: Placement only. **Freshmen returning for sophomore year:** 78%. **Graduation rates:** Four-year: 63%; five-year: 70%; six-year: 72%. **Graduate study:** 48% of students pursue further study immediately upon graduation; 40% within one year. Fields in which graduates pursue further study: Master of Business Administration (MBA), 13%; law, 18%; medicine, 24%; dentistry, 2%; engineering, 6%; theology (or the seminary), 5%; education, 7%; arts and sciences, 24%; veterinary medicine, 1%.

COSTS AND FINANCIAL AID

Financial aid office: (205) 226-4688. **Expenses (2010-2011):** Tuition and fees 2010-2011: $27,890; room/board: $9,910. Estimated books and supplies: $1,200; transportation: $1,310; personal expenses: $1,700. **Financial aid:** Priority filing date for institution's financial aid form: March 1. In 2009-2010, 64% of undergraduates applied for financial aid. Of those, 53% were determined to have financial need; 47% had their need fully met. Average financial aid package (proportion receiving): $31,807 (53%). Average amount of gift aid, such as scholarships or grants (proportion receiving): N/A (44%). Average amount of self-help aid, such as work study or loans (proportion receiving): N/A (42%). Among students who received need-based aid, the average percentage of need met: 95%. Among students who received aid based on merit, the average award (and the proportion receiving): $13,639 (42%). The average athletic scholarship (and the proportion receiving): $24,590 (1%). Average amount of debt of borrowers graduating in 2009: $30,907. Proportion who borrowed: 41%.

CAMPUS LIFE AND EXTRACURRICULAR ACTIVITIES

Campus housing available (% using): women's dorms (33%), men's dorms (28%), sorority housing (4%), fraternity housing (10%), apartments for married students, apartment for single students (25%), special housing for disabled students. Students who live in college-owned, operated, or affiliated housing: 84%. **Student employment:** During the 2009-2010 academic year, 0% of undergraduates worked on campus. **Clubs and organizations:** Number of student organizations: 70. Activities include: campus ministries, choral groups, concert band, dance, drama/theater, international student organization, jazz band, literary magazine, marching band, music ensembles, musical theater, opera, pep band, student government, student newspaper, yearbook. Number of fraternities: 6; sororities: 6. Proportion of men in fraternities: 37%; of women in sororities: 46%. Average proportion of students who stay on campus on weekends: 75%. **Sports program (2009-2010):** Member of NCAA III. *Men's intercollegiate varsity sports:* baseball, basketball, cross country, football, golf, lacrosse, soccer, tennis, track and field (indoor), track and field (outdoor). *Women's intercollegiate varsity sports:* basketball, cross country, golf, lacrosse, rifle, soccer, softball, tennis, track and field (indoor), track and field (outdoor), volleyball.

SERVICES AND FACILITIES

Basic services: nonremedial tutoring, health service, health insurance, other. **Counseling services:** minority student, career, personal, academic, psychological, religious. **For learning-disabled students:** School does not offer a structured program with separate admission and additional fees. Services include: tape recorders, untimed tests, note-taking services, oral tests, learning center, extended time for tests, tutors, priority seating, texts on tape, typist/scribe, other testing accommodations. **Library:** Number of titles: 311,516; number of current serial subscriptions: 1,804. **Information technology resources:** Students are not required to lease or own a computer. Number of campus computers available to all students: 300. School has a wireless network. Approximate number of users that can be accommodated: 1,400. Proportion of college-owned housing units wired for high-speed internet access: 100%. **Campus safety:** Security services offered: 24-hour foot-and-vehicle patrols, late-night transport/escort service, 24-hour emergency telephones, lighted pathways/sidewalks, controlled dormitory access (key, security card, etc).

Transfer students: May apply for admission for the following academic terms: Fall, Winter, Spring, Summer. Applicants do not need a minimum number of credits to apply. For fall 2009: Transfer applications received: 104. Transfer applicants offered admission: 53. Transfer applicants enrolled: 38. **International students:** Number of foreign undergraduates: 1. Number of countries represented: 16. Minimum TOEFL score required: 500 (paper); 173 (computer). Average TOEFL score: 91 (paper).

Concordia College

- **Address:** 1804 Green Street, Selma, AL 36703-3323
- **Website:** http://www.concordiaselma.edu/
- **Private; Religious affiliation:** Lutheran
- **Enrollment:** 510 full-time; 58 part-time

KEY STATS

✔ **U.S News College Ranking:** 69, Regional Colleges (South)
✔ **SAT or ACT Score (25th/75th percentile):** N/A
✔ **Tuition:** 2009-2010: $7,670

Selectivity: Less selective	**Room/board:** $3,700
Acceptance rate: N/A	**Average debt:** N/A
Student/faculty ratio: N/A	**Proportion who borrowed:** N/A

UNDERGRADUATE STUDENT BODY STATS

2009-2010 enrollment: 510 full-time; 58 part-time. Men: 57%; women: 43%. **Ethnic makeup:** African American: 93%; Hispanic: 1%; White: 4%; International: 2%. **Religious preference:** Roman Catholic: 2%; Protestant: 51%; Unknown: 22%; Lutheran: 5%; Other: 20%.

ADMISSIONS FACTS AND FIGURES

Phone: (334) 874-5700. **Email:** admission@concordiaselma.edu. **Website:** http://www.concordiaselma.edu/. **Application deadlines for fall 2011:** Regular decision: Rolling; decision sent by August 15. Early decision: Not offered. Early action: Not offered. Admission cannot be deferred. **Application fee:** $10. **To apply online, go to:** http://www.faithwebsites.com/concordiaselma/onlapp.cfm#. **Admissions requirements/recommendations:** High school units required (recommended): English: 4 (4); Mathematics: 4 (4); Science: 4 (4); Foreign language: 0 (2); Social studies: 2 (2); History: 4 (4); Total units: 20 (22). Tests: The college uses SAT or ACT scores in admissions decisions. Neither SAT nor ACT required. For admission to the fall 2011 entering class, the school will accept: ACT with or without writing accepted. Campus visit: Neither required nor recommended. Admissions interview: Neither required nor recommended. **Factors that count in admissions decisions:** *Academic:* Secondary school record: Important. Class rank: Considered. Letters of recommendation: Considered. Standardized test scores: Important. Essay: Not Considered. *Nonacademic:* Interview: Considered. Extracurricular activities: Considered. Talent/ability: Important. Character/personal qualities: Very Important. Alumni/ae relationship: Important. Geographical residence: Considered. State residency: Considered. Religious affiliation/commitment: Considered. Minority status: Considered. Volunteer work: Considered. Work experience: Considered. **Other schools with the greatest overlap in applicants:** Alabama State University; Concordia University; Florida Christian College; Selma University; Stillman College. **Admissions statistics for the fall 2009 entering class:** Freshmen enrolled: 133; 32% were from out of state. **Size of waiting list:** 0 applicants; enrolled from waiting list: 0.

ACADEMICS

Year founded: 1922. **Academic calendar:** Semester. **Degrees offered:** associate, bachelor's. **Major fields of study:** business, management, marketing, and related support services; education. **Areas of required coursework:** arts/fine arts, humanities, computer literacy, mathematics, English (including composition), foreign languages, sciences (biological or physical), history, social science, other. **Pre-professional programs:** pre-theology. **Special academic programs (% participation):** cooperative (work-study plan) program (10%), independent study (15%), internships (99%), teacher certificate program (6%). **Teacher certification offered in:** early childhood, elementary. **Reserve Officers Training Corps (ROTC):** Army ROTC: Offered on campus. **Advanced Placement and International Baccalaureate credit:** AP tests may be used for: Placement only. Scores accepted: 4, 5. **Graduation rates:** Six-year: 22%. **Graduate study:** 6% of students pursue further study immediately upon graduation; 15% within one year; 30% within five years. Fields in which graduates pursue further study: Master of Business Administration (MBA), 3%; education, 35%.

COSTS AND FINANCIAL AID

Financial aid office: (334) 874-5700. **Expenses (2009-2010):** Tuition and fees 2009-2010: $7,670; room/board: $3,700. Estimated books and supplies: $1,200; transportation: $1,800; personal expenses: $1,200. **Financial aid:** Priority filing date for institution's financial aid form: May 15.

CAMPUS LIFE AND EXTRACURRICULAR ACTIVITIES

Campus housing available (% using): women's dorms (12%), men's dorms (26%). Students who live in college-owned, operated, or affiliated housing: 38%. **Student employment:** During the 2009-2010 academic year, 20% of undergraduates worked on campus. Average per-year earnings: $600. **Clubs and organizations:** Number of student organizations: 12. Activities include: choral groups, drama/theater, international student organization, marching band, music ensembles, student government, student newspaper. Number of fraternities: 0; sororities: 0. Average proportion of students who stay on campus on weekends: 21%. **Sports program (2009-2010):** *Men's intercollegiate varsity sports:* baseball, basketball, football, soccer. *Women's intercollegiate varsity sports:* basketball, softball.

SERVICES AND FACILITIES

Basic services: nonremedial tutoring, placement service. **Remedial assistance:** reading, math, writing, study skills. **Counseling services:** career, personal, academic, religious. **For learning-disabled students:** School does not offer a structured program with separate admission and additional fees. Total undergraduates in learning-disabled program or receiving services: 2. Services include: remedial math, remedial English, remedial reading, untimed tests, note-taking services, oral tests, readers, extended time for tests, tutors, exams on tape or computer. **Library:** Number of titles: 65,700; number of current serial subscriptions: 202. **Information technology resources:** Students are not required to lease or own a computer. Number of campus computers available to all students: 175. School has a wireless network. Proportion of college-owned housing units wired for high-speed internet access: 50%. **Campus safety:** Security services offered: 24-hour foot-and-vehicle patrols, lighted pathways/sidewalks, student patrols, controlled dormitory access (key, security card, etc).

TRANSFER AND INTERNATIONAL STUDENTS

Transfer students: May apply for admission for the following academic terms: Fall, Spring, Summer. Applicants need a minimum number of credits to apply. For fall 2009: Transfer applicants enrolled: 12. **International students:** Number of foreign undergraduates: 12 (2% of student body). Number of countries represented: 6. Minimum TOEFL score required: 500 (paper); 173 (computer).

Faulkner University

- **Address:** 5345 Atlanta Highway, Montgomery, AL 36109
- **Website:** http://www.faulkner.edu
- **Private; Religious affiliation:** Church of Christ
- **Enrollment:** 2,081 full-time; 681 part-time

KEY STATS

✔ **U.S News College Ranking:** 64, Regional Colleges (South)
✔ **ACT Score (25th/75th percentile):** 18-22
✔ **Tuition:** 2010-2011: $15,010

Selectivity: Selective	**Room/board:** $6,500
Acceptance rate: 58%	**Average debt:** $20,000
Student/faculty ratio: 14/1	**Proportion who borrowed:** 81%

UNDERGRADUATE STUDENT BODY STATS

2009-2010 enrollment: 2,081 full-time; 681 part-time. Men: 36%; women: 64%. **Ethnic makeup:** African American: 49%; Hispanic: 1%; White: 48%; International: 1%. **Religious preference:** Roman Catholic: 3%; Protestant: 31%; No preference: 32%; Unknown: 3%; Church of Christ: 18%.

ADMISSIONS FACTS AND FIGURES

Phone: (334) 386-7200. **Email:** kmock@faulkner.edu. **Website:** http://www.faulkner.edu. **Application deadlines for fall 2011:** Regular decision: Rolling. Early decision: Not offered. Early action: Not offered. Admission cannot be deferred. **Application fee:** $10. **To apply online, go to:** http://www.faulkner.

edu/admissions/undergraduate/application/apply.asp. **Admissions requirements/recommendations:** High school units required (recommended): English: 3 (4); Mathematics: 3 (4); Science: 3 (4); Foreign language: 0 (1); Social studies: 0 (2); History: 3 (2); Academic electives: 0; Total units: 15 (18). Tests: The college uses SAT or ACT scores in admissions decisions. Either SAT or ACT required. For admission to the fall 2011 entering class, the school will accept: ACT with or without writing accepted. Campus visit: Recommended. Admissions interview: Recommended. Off-campus interview: May be arranged. **Factors that count in admissions decisions:** *Academic:* Secondary school record: Very Important. Class rank: Important. Letters of recommendation: Very Important. Standardized test scores: Very Important. Essay: Important. *Nonacademic:* Interview: Very Important. Extracurricular activities: Very Important. Talent/ability: Important. Character/personal qualities: Very Important. Alumni/ae relationship: Very Important. Geographical residence: Considered. State residency: Not Considered. Religious affiliation/commitment: Very Important. Minority status: Not Considered. Volunteer work: Important. Work experience: Important. **Other schools with the greatest overlap in applicants:** Auburn University; Auburn University–Montgomery; Freed-Hardeman University; Harding University; Lipscomb University. **Admissions statistics for the fall 2009 entering class:** Total applicants: 999. Total accepted: 582. Freshmen enrolled: 428; 30% were from out of state. Overall acceptance rate: 58%. **Credentials of fall 2009 freshmen:** 10% ranked in the top 10 percent of their high school class; 20% were in the top 25 percent; 60% were in the top half. (Proportion submitting class standing: 30%.) **Average high school grade point average:** 2.5. **First-year students who submitted SAT scores:** 24%. Scores (25/75 percentile): Critical Reading: 440-570, Math: 440-530, Combined: 880-1100. **First-year students submitting ACT scores:** 83%. Scores (25/75 percentile): English: N/A, Math: N/A, Composite: 18-22.

ACADEMICS

Year founded: 1942. **Academic calendar:** Semester. **Degrees offered:** certificate, associate, bachelor's, post-bachelor's certificate, master's, doctorate. **Major fields of study:** agriculture, agriculture operations, and related sciences; business, management, marketing, and related support services; computer and information sciences and support services; education; English language and literature/letters; liberal arts and sciences studies, and humanities; mathematics and statistics; parks, recreation, leisure, and fitness studies; psychology; security and protective services; theology and religious vocations; visual and performing arts. **Areas of required coursework:** arts/fine arts, humanities, computer literacy, mathematics, English (including composition), philosophy, sciences (biological or physical), history, social science, other. **Pre-professional programs:** pre-law, pre-dentistry, pre-medicine, pre-veterinary science, pre-optometry, pre-pharmacy, other. **Special academic programs (% participation):** accelerated program (26%), cross-registration (3%), distance learning (3%), double major (3%), dual enrollment (1%), English as a Second Language (ESL), honors program (5%), independent study (3%), internships (100%), study abroad (2%), teacher certificate program (5%). **Teacher certification offered in:** elementary, middle/junior high, secondary. **Reserve Officers Training Corps (ROTC):** Army ROTC: Offered at cooperating institution (Auburn University–Montgomery); Air Force ROTC: Offered at cooperating institution (Alabama State University). **Faculty and instruction (2009-2010):** Total instructional faculty: 99 full-time, 190 part-time (56% men; 44% women; 18% minorities). Full-time faculty with Ph.D. or other terminal degree: 80%. Student/faculty ratio: 14/1. Classes of fewer than 20 students: 52%; of 20 to 49 students: 42%; of 50 or more students: 6%. **Advanced Placement and International Baccalaureate credit:** AP tests may be used for: Credit only. Scores accepted: 3, 4, 5. International Baccalaureate exams may be used for: Credit only. **Freshmen returning for sophomore year:** 60%. **Graduation rates:** Four-year: 12%; five-year: 35%; six-year: 27%. **Graduate study:** 22% of students pursue further study immediately upon graduation; 5% within one year; 5% within five years. Fields in which graduates pursue further study: Master of Business Administration (MBA), 30%; law, 24%; medicine, 1%; engineering, 3%; theology (or the seminary), 10%; education, 10%; arts and sciences, 25%; veterinary medicine, 1%.

COSTS AND FINANCIAL AID

Financial aid office: (334) 386-7195. **Expenses (2010-2011):** Tuition and fees 2010-2011: $15,010; room/board: $6,500. Estimated books and supplies: $1,600; transportation: $1,700; personal expenses: $1,350. **Financial aid:** Priority filing date for institution's financial aid form: May 1; deadline: August 1. Average amount of debt of borrowers graduating in 2009: $20,000. Proportion who borrowed: 81%.

CAMPUS LIFE AND EXTRACURRICULAR ACTIVITIES

Campus housing available (% using): women's dorms (26%), men's dorms (46%), apartment for single students (28%), special housing for disabled students (0%). Students who live in college-owned, operated, or affiliated housing: 25%. **Student employment:** During the 2009-2010 academic year, 5% of undergraduates worked on campus. Average per-year earnings: $1,627. **Clubs and organizations:** Number of student organizations: 12. Activities include: campus ministries, choral groups, drama/theater, jazz band, literary magazine, music ensembles, musical theater, pep band, student government, student newspaper, student film society, yearbook. Number of fraternities: 5; sororities: 5. Proportion of men in fraternities: 30%; of women in sororities: 30%. Average proportion of students who stay on campus on weekends: 70%. **Sports program (2009-2010):** Member of NAIA. *Men's intercollegiate varsity sports:* baseball, basketball, football, golf, soccer. *Women's intercollegiate varsity sports:* soccer, softball, volleyball.

SERVICES AND FACILITIES

Basic services: nonremedial tutoring, placement service, health service, health insurance. **Remedial assistance:** reading, math, writing, study skills. **Counseling services:** minority student, career, personal, veteran student, academic, older student, psychological, religious. **For learning-disabled students:** School does not offer a structured program with separate admission and additional fees. Services include: remedial math, remedial English, reading machines, remedial reading, tape recorders, untimed tests, notetaking services, oral tests, learning center, readers, extended time for tests, tutors, early syllabus, priority registration, priority seating, texts on tape, exams on tape or computer, other testing accommodations, other. **Library:** Number of titles: 225,000; number of current serial subscriptions: 4,695. **Information technology resources:** Students are not required to lease or own a computer. Number of campus computers available to all students: 417. School has a wireless network. Approximate number of users that can be accommodated: 1,000. Proportion of college-owned housing units wired for high-speed internet access: 100%. **Campus safety:** Security services offered: 24-hour foot-and-vehicle patrols, late-night transport/escort service, lighted pathways/sidewalks, student patrols, controlled dormitory access (key, security card, etc).

TRANSFER AND INTERNATIONAL STUDENTS

Transfer students: May apply for admission for the following academic terms: Fall, Spring, Summer. Applicants need a minimum number of credits to apply. For fall 2009: Transfer applications received: 450. Transfer applicants offered admission: 370. Transfer applicants enrolled: 289. **International students:** Number of foreign undergraduates: 23 (1% of student body). Number of countries represented: 21. Minimum TOEFL score required: 500 (paper); 61 (computer). Average TOEFL score: 450 (paper).

Huntingdon College

- **Address:** 1500 E. Fairview Avenue, Montgomery, AL 36106-2148
- **Website:** http://www.huntingdon.edu
- **Private; Religious affiliation:** Methodist
- **Enrollment:** 857 full-time; 218 part-time

KEY STATS

✔ **U.S News College Ranking:** second tier, National Liberal Arts Colleges
✔ **ACT Score (25th/75th percentile):** 19-24
✔ **Tuition:** 2009-2010: $20,320

Selectivity: Selective	**Room/board:** $7,500
Acceptance rate: 67%	**Average debt:** $14,034
Student/faculty ratio: 13/1	**Proportion who borrowed:** 58%

UNDERGRADUATE STUDENT BODY STATS

2009-2010 enrollment: 857 full-time; 218 part-time. Men: 48%; women: 52%. **Ethnic makeup:** African American: 16%; Asian American: 1%; Hispanic: 1%; White: 81%; International: 1%. **Religious preference:** Roman Catholic: 4%; Protestant: 1%; No preference: 21%; Unknown: 6%; Methodist: 24%; Baptist: 27%; Other: 17%.

ADMISSIONS FACTS AND FIGURES

Phone: (334) 833-4497. **Email:** admiss@huntingdon.edu. **Website:** http://www.huntingdon.edu. **Application deadlines for fall 2011:** Regular decision: August 15. Early decision: Not offered. Early action: Not offered. Admission can be deferred. **To apply online, go to:** http://www.huntingdon.

edu/admissions/apply_now. **Admissions requirements/recommendations:** High school units required (recommended): English: (4); Mathematics: (3); Science: (2); Foreign language: (2); Social studies: (3); Total units: (14). Tests: The college uses SAT or ACT scores in admissions decisions. Either SAT or ACT required. For admission to the fall 2011 entering class, the school will accept: ACT with or without writing accepted. Campus visit: Recommended. Admissions interview: Recommended. Off-campus interview: May be arranged. **Factors that count in admissions decisions:** *Academic:* Secondary school record: Important. Class rank: Considered. Letters of recommendation: Considered. Standardized test scores: Very Important. Essay: Considered. *Nonacademic:* Interview: Considered. Extracurricular activities: Not Considered. Talent/ability: Not Considered. Character/personal qualities: Not Considered. Alumni/ae relationship: Not Considered. Geographical residence: Not Considered. State residency: Not Considered. Religious affiliation/commitment: Not Considered. Minority status: Not Considered. Volunteer work: Not Considered. Work experience: Not Considered. **Other schools with the greatest overlap in applicants:** Auburn University; Auburn University–Montgomery; Birmingham-Southern College; Troy University; University of Alabama. **Admissions statistics for the fall 2009 entering class:** Total applicants: 1,138. Total accepted: 757. Freshmen enrolled: 237; 14% were from out of state. Overall acceptance rate: 67%. **Credentials of fall 2009 freshmen:** 14% ranked in the top 10 percent of their high school class; 36% were in the top 25 percent; 75% were in the top half. (Proportion submitting class standing: 71%.) **Average high school grade point average:** 3.3. **First-year students who submitted SAT scores:** 14%. Scores (25/75 percentile): Critical Reading: 450-610, Math: 430-560, Combined: 880-1170. **First-year students submitting ACT scores:** 95%. Scores (25/75 percentile): English: 17-24, Math: 20-25, Composite: 19-24.

ACADEMICS
Year founded: 1854. **Academic calendar:** Semester. **Degrees offered:** bachelor's. **Most popular majors:** 44% business/commerce, 11% biology, 8% health and physical education/fitness, 6% elementary education and teaching, 5% religion/religious studies. **Major fields of study:** biological and biomedical sciences; business, management, marketing, and related support services; education; English language and literature/letters; health professions and related clinical sciences; history; mathematics and statistics; multi/interdisciplinary studies; parks, recreation, leisure, and fitness studies; philosophy and religious studies; physical sciences; psychology; social sciences; visual and performing arts. **Areas of required coursework:** arts/fine arts, computer literacy, mathematics, English (including composition), sciences (biological or physical), history, social science, other. **Pre-professional programs:** pre-law, pre-dentistry, pre-medicine, pre-theology, pre-veterinary science, pre-optometry, pre-pharmacy, other. **Special academic programs (% participation):** cross-registration (5.85%), double major (5.85%), honors program (1.95%), independent study (30.2%), internships (18%), student-designed major (0%), study abroad (1%), teacher certificate program (5.85%), other (79%). **Teacher certification offered in:** elementary, middle/junior high, secondary. **Reserve Officers Training Corps (ROTC):** Army ROTC: Offered at cooperating institution (Auburn University–Montgomery); Air Force ROTC: Offered at cooperating institution (Alabama State University). **Faculty and instruction (2009-2010):** Total instructional faculty: 45 full-time, 75 part-time (63% men; 38% women; 12% minorities). Full-time faculty with Ph.D. or other terminal degree: 89%. Student/faculty ratio: 13/1. Classes of fewer than 20 students: 63%; of 20 to 49 students: 37%; of 50 or more students: 1%. **Advanced Placement and International Baccalaureate credit:** AP tests may be used for: Credit and/or placement. Scores accepted: 3, 4, 5. International Baccalaureate exams may be used for: Credit only. **Freshmen returning for sophomore year:** 64%. **Graduation rates:** Four-year: 35%; five-year: 45%; six-year: 46%. **Graduate study:** 55% of students pursue further study immediately upon graduation; 56% within one year. Fields in which graduates pursue further study: Master of Business Administration (MBA), 12%; law, 5%; medicine, 16%; dentistry, 1%; theology (or the seminary), 9%; education, 8%; arts and sciences, 20%; veterinary medicine, 1%.

COSTS AND FINANCIAL AID
Financial aid office: (334) 833-4519. **Expenses (2009-2010):** Tuition and fees 2009-2010: $20,320; room/board: $7,500. Estimated books and supplies: $1,000; transportation: $800; personal expenses: $900. **Financial aid:** Priority filing date for institution's financial aid form: April 15. In 2009-2010, 81% of undergraduates applied for financial aid. Of those, 70% were determined to have financial need; 19% had their need fully met. Average financial aid package (proportion receiving): $14,949 (70%). Average amount of gift aid, such as scholarships or grants (proportion

receiving): $12,025 (69%). Average amount of self-help aid, such as work study or loans (proportion receiving): $3,948 (55%). Average need-based loan (excluding PLUS or other private loans): $3,491. Among students who received need-based aid, the average percentage of need met: 74%. Among students who received aid based on merit, the average award (and the proportion receiving): $9,324 (27%). The average athletic scholarship (and the proportion receiving): $0 (0%). Average amount of debt of borrowers graduating in 2009: $14,034. Proportion who borrowed: 58%.

CAMPUS LIFE AND EXTRACURRICULAR ACTIVITIES
Campus housing available (% using): coed dorms (61%), women's dorms (19%), men's dorms (20%), special housing for disabled students (0%). Students who live in college-owned, operated, or affiliated housing: 41%. **Student employment:** During the 2009-2010 academic year, 2% of undergraduates worked on campus. Average per-year earnings: $1,500. **Clubs and organizations:** Number of student organizations: 50. Activities include: campus ministries, choral groups, concert band, dance, drama/theater, international student organization, literary magazine, marching band, model UN, music ensembles, pep band, student government, student newspaper, yearbook. Number of fraternities: 4; sororities: 4. Proportion of men in fraternities: 17%; of women in sororities: 20%. Average proportion of students who stay on campus on weekends: 79%. **Sports program (2009-2010):** Member of NCAA III. *Men's intercollegiate varsity sports:* baseball, basketball, cross country, football, golf, soccer, tennis. *Women's intercollegiate varsity sports:* basketball, cross country, golf, soccer, softball, tennis, volleyball.

SERVICES AND FACILITIES
Basic services: nonremedial tutoring, women's center, placement service, health service, health insurance. **Remedial assistance:** reading, math, writing, study skills. **Counseling services:** career, personal, academic, birth control, religious. **For learning-disabled students:** School does not offer a structured program with separate admission and additional fees. Total undergraduates in learning-disabled program or receiving services: 41. Services include: remedial English, tape recorders, untimed tests, note-taking services, oral tests, learning center, readers, extended time for tests, tutors, priority seating, exams on tape or computer, other testing accommodations. **Library:** Number of titles: 108,415; number of current serial subscriptions: 231. **Information technology resources:** Students are required to lease or own a computer. Number of campus computers available to all students: 13. School has a wireless network. Approximate number of users that can be accommodated: 280. Proportion of college-owned housing units wired for high-speed internet access: 100%. **Campus safety:** Security services offered: 24-hour foot-and-vehicle patrols, late-night transport/escort service, 24-hour emergency telephones, lighted pathways/sidewalks, student patrols, controlled dormitory access (key, security card, etc).

TRANSFER AND INTERNATIONAL STUDENTS
Transfer students: May apply for admission for the following academic terms: Fall, Spring, Summer. Applicants do not need a minimum number of credits to apply. For fall 2009: Transfer applications received: 316. Transfer applicants offered admission: 164. Transfer applicants enrolled: 122. **International students:** Number of foreign undergraduates: 8 (1% of student body). Number of countries represented: 10. Minimum TOEFL score required: 500 (paper); 173 (computer).

Jacksonville State University

- **Address:** 700 Pelham Road N, Jacksonville, AL 36265-1602
- **Website:** http://www.jsu.edu
- **Public**
- **Enrollment:** 5,957 full-time; 1,927 part-time

KEY STATS
✔ **U.S News College Ranking:** 83, Regional Universities (South)
✔ **ACT Score (25th/75th percentile):** 17-22
✔ **Tuition:** 2009-2010: $6,240 in state, $12,480 out of state

Selectivity: Selective	**Room/board:** $5,254
Acceptance rate: 88%	**Average debt:** N/A
Student/faculty ratio: 20/1	**Proportion who borrowed:** N/A

UNDERGRADUATE STUDENT BODY STATS

2009-2010 enrollment: 5,957 full-time; 1,927 part-time. Men: 42%; women: 58%. **Ethnic makeup:** African American: 27%; American-Indian: 1%; Asian American: 1%; Hispanic: 1%; White: 68%; International: 3%.

ADMISSIONS FACTS AND FIGURES

Phone: (256) 782-5268. **Email:** info@jsu.edu. **Website:** http://www.jsu.edu. **Application deadlines for fall 2011:** Regular decision: Rolling. Early decision: Not offered. Early action: Not offered. Admission can be deferred. **Application fee:** $30. **To apply online, go to:** http://www.jsu.edu/depart/undergraduate/. **Admissions requirements/recommendations:** Tests: The college uses SAT or ACT scores in admissions decisions. Either SAT or ACT required. For admission to the fall 2011 entering class, the school will accept: ACT with or without writing accepted. Campus visit: Recommended. Admissions interview: Neither required nor recommended. Off-campus interview: Not available. **Factors that count in admissions decisions:** *Academic:* Secondary school record: Very Important. Class rank: Not Considered. Letters of recommendation: Not Considered. Standardized test scores: Very Important. Essay: Not Considered. *Nonacademic:* Interview: Not Considered. Extracurricular activities: Not Considered. Talent/ability: Not Considered. Character/personal qualities: Not Considered. Alumni/ae relationship: Not Considered. Geographical residence: Not Considered. State residency: Not Considered. Religious affiliation/commitment: Not Considered. Minority status: Not Considered. Volunteer work: Not Considered. Work experience: Not Considered. **Other schools with the greatest overlap in applicants:** Auburn University; Auburn University–Montgomery; Troy University; University of Alabama–Birmingham; University of Alabama–Huntsville. **Admissions statistics for the fall 2009 entering class:** Total applicants: 2,919. Total accepted: 2,559. Freshmen enrolled: 1,252; 25% were from out of state. Overall acceptance rate: 88%. **Credentials of fall 2009 freshmen:** 12% ranked in the top 10 percent of their high school class; 33% were in the top 25 percent; 63% were in the top half. (Proportion submitting class standing: 77%.) **Average high school grade point average:** 3.0. **First-year students who submitted SAT scores:** 19%. Scores (25/75 percentile): Critical Reading: 400-510, Math: 400-500, Combined: 800-1010. **First-year students submitting ACT scores:** 86%. Scores (25/75 percentile): English: 16-21, Math: 16-23, Composite: 17-22.

ACADEMICS

Year founded: 1883. **Academic calendar:** Semester. **Degrees offered:** bachelor's, master's, post-master's certificate. **Most popular majors:** 18% nursing/registered nurse training (R.N., A.S.N., B.S.N., M.S.N.), 16% elementary education and teaching, 15% business administration and management, 7% criminal justice/safety studies, 7% social work. **Major fields of study:** biological and biomedical sciences; business, management, marketing, and related support services; communication, journalism, and related programs; computer and information sciences and support services; education; engineering technologies/technicians; English language and literature/letters; family and consumer sciences/human sciences; foreign languages, literatures, and linguistics; health professions and related clinical sciences; history; liberal arts and sciences studies, and humanities; mathematics and statistics; parks, recreation, leisure, and fitness studies; physical sciences; psychology; public administration and social service professions; security and protective services; social sciences; visual and performing arts. **Areas of required coursework:** arts/fine arts, humanities, computer literacy, mathematics, English (including composition), sciences (biological or physical), history, social science. **Pre-professional programs:** pre-law, pre-medicine. **Special academic programs:** accelerated program, cooperative (work-study plan) program, cross-registration, distance learning, double major, dual enrollment, English as a Second Language (ESL), honors program, independent study, internships, liberal arts/career combination, study abroad, teacher certificate program, weekend college. **Teacher certification offered in:** early childhood, special education, elementary, secondary. **Cooperative education programs:** art, business, computer science, engineering, technologies, vocational arts. **Reserve Officers Training Corps (ROTC):** Army ROTC: Offered on campus. **Faculty and instruction (2009-2010):** Total instructional faculty: 322 full-time, 141 part-time (48% men; 52% women; 10% minorities). Full-time faculty with Ph.D. or other terminal degree: 64%. Student/faculty ratio: 20/1. Classes of fewer than 20 students: 38%; of 20 to 49 students: 56%; of 50 or more students: 6%. **Freshmen returning for sophomore year:** 69%. **Graduation rates:** Four-year: 13%; five-year: 28%; six-year: 35%.

COSTS AND FINANCIAL AID

Financial aid office: (256) 782-5006. **Expenses (2009-2010):** Tuition and fees 2009-2010: $6,240 in state, $12,480 out of state; room/board: $5,254. Estimated books and supplies: $1,204; transportation: $1,750; personal expenses: $3,178. **Financial aid:** Priority filing date for institution's financial aid form: March 15. In 2009-2010, 80% of undergraduates applied for financial aid. Of those, 78% were determined to have financial need; Average financial aid package (proportion receiving): $6,563 (78%). Average amount of gift aid, such as scholarships or grants (proportion receiving): $3,878 (42%). Average amount of self-help aid, such as work study or loans (proportion receiving): $4,020 (53%). Average need-based loan (excluding PLUS or other private loans): $3,889.

CAMPUS LIFE AND EXTRACURRICULAR ACTIVITIES

Campus housing available (% using): coed dorms (46%), women's dorms (21%), men's dorms (11%), fraternity housing (1%), apartments for married students (2%), apartment for single students (15%), special housing for disabled students (1%), special housing for international students (3%). Students who live in college-owned, operated, or affiliated housing: 22%. **Student employment:** During the 2009-2010 academic year, 11% of undergraduates worked on campus. Average per-year earnings: $3,600. **Clubs and organizations:** Number of student organizations: 90. Activities include: choral groups, concert band, dance, drama/theater, jazz band, literary magazine, marching band, music ensembles, musical theater, opera, pep band, radio station, student government, student newspaper, student film society, symphony orchestra, television station, yearbook. Number of fraternities: 11; sororities: 8. Proportion of men in fraternities: 10%; of women in sororities: 10%. Average proportion of students who stay on campus on weekends: 25%. **Sports program (2009-2010):** Member of NCAA I. *Men's intercollegiate varsity sports:* baseball, basketball, football, golf, rifle, tennis. *Women's intercollegiate varsity sports:* basketball, golf, rifle, soccer, softball, tennis.

SERVICES AND FACILITIES

Basic services: nonremedial tutoring, placement service, day care, health service. **Remedial assistance:** reading, math, writing, study skills. **Counseling services:** minority student, career, military, personal, veteran student, academic, psychological, birth control. **For learning-disabled students:** School does not offer a structured program with separate admission and additional fees. Total undergraduates in learning-disabled program or receiving services: 71. Services include: remedial math, remedial English, remedial reading, tape recorders, other special classes, note-taking services, oral tests, learning center, readers, extended time for tests, tutors, priority registration, priority seating, other testing accommodations. **Library:** Number of titles: 703,600; number of current serial subscriptions: 32,728. **Information technology resources:** Students are not required to lease or own a computer. Number of campus computers available to all students: 636. School has a wireless network. Proportion of college-owned housing units wired for high-speed internet access: 75%. **Campus safety:** Security services offered: 24-hour foot-and-vehicle patrols, late-night transport/escort service, 24-hour emergency telephones, lighted pathways/sidewalks, controlled dormitory access (key, security card, etc).

TRANSFER AND INTERNATIONAL STUDENTS

Transfer students: May apply for admission for the following academic terms: Fall, Spring, Summer. Applicants need a minimum number of credits to apply. For fall 2009: Transfer applications received: 1,281. Transfer applicants offered admission: 1,017. Transfer applicants enrolled: 671. **International students:** Number of foreign undergraduates: 173 (3% of student body). Number of countries represented: 73. Minimum TOEFL score required: 500 (paper); 173 (computer).

Judson College

- **Address:** 302 Bibb Street, Marion, AL 36756
- **Website:** http://www.judson.edu/
- **Private; Religious affiliation:** Baptist
- **Enrollment:** N/A

KEY STATS

✔ **U.S News College Ranking:** second tier, National Liberal Arts Colleges
✔ **SAT or ACT Score (25th/75th percentile):** N/A
✔ **Tuition:** 2009-2010: $12,890

Selectivity: Selective	**Room/board:** $7,970
Acceptance rate: N/A	**Average debt:** N/A
Student/faculty ratio: N/A	**Proportion who borrowed:** N/A

Miles College

- **Address:** PO Box 3800, Birmingham, AL 35208
- **Website:** http://www.miles.edu
- **Private; Religious affiliation:** Christian Methodist Episcopal Church
- **Enrollment:** N/A

KEY STATS

✔ **U.S News College Ranking:** second tier, Regional Colleges (South)
✔ **SAT or ACT Score (25th/75th percentile):** N/A
✔ **Tuition:** 2009-2010: $9,164

Selectivity: Less selective	**Room/board:** $6,000
Acceptance rate: N/A	**Average debt:** N/A
Student/faculty ratio: N/A	**Proportion who borrowed:** N/A

Oakwood University

- **Address:** 7000 Adventist Boulevard, Huntsville, AL 35896
- **Website:** http://www.oakwood.edu
- **Private; Religious affiliation:** Seventh-day Adventist
- **Enrollment:** N/A

KEY STATS

✔ **U.S News College Ranking:** 31, Regional Colleges (South)
✔ **ACT Score (25th/75th percentile):** 16-21
✔ **Tuition:** 2010-2011: $14,248

Selectivity: Less selective	**Room/board:** $7,988
Acceptance rate: 56%	**Average debt:** N/A
Student/faculty ratio: N/A	**Proportion who borrowed:** N/A

Samford University

- **Address:** 800 Lakeshore Drive, Birmingham, AL 35229
- **Website:** http://www.samford.edu
- **Private; Religious affiliation:** Baptist
- **Enrollment:** 2,702 full-time; 206 part-time

KEY STATS

✔ **U.S News College Ranking:** 104, National Universities
✔ **ACT Score (25th/75th percentile):** 21-28
✔ **Tuition:** 2010-2011: $21,942

Selectivity: More selective	**Room/board:** $7,024
Acceptance rate: 84%	**Average debt:** $15,702
Student/faculty ratio: 12/1	**Proportion who borrowed:** 38%

UNDERGRADUATE STUDENT BODY STATS

2009-2010 enrollment: 2,702 full-time; 206 part-time. Men: 36%; women: 64%. **Ethnic makeup:** African American: 7%; Asian American: 1%; Hispanic: 1%; White: 90%. **Religious preference:** Roman Catholic: 5%; Unknown: 14%; Baptist: 43%; Other: 26%.

ADMISSIONS FACTS AND FIGURES

Phone: (800) 888-7218. **Email:** admiss@samford.edu. **Website:** http://www.samford.edu. **Application deadlines for fall 2011:** Regular decision: Rolling. Early decision: Not offered. Early action: Not offered. Admission can be deferred. **Application fee:** $35. **To apply online, go to:** http://samford.gotoextinguisher.com/application/login/. **Admissions requirements/recommendations:** High school units required (recommended): English: 4; Mathematics: 3; Science: 2; Foreign language: 2; History: 2; Total units: 13. Tests: The college uses SAT or ACT scores in admissions decisions. Either SAT or ACT required. For admission to the fall 2011 entering class, the school will accept: ACT with or without writing accepted. Campus visit: Recommended. Admissions interview: Recommended. Off-campus interview: May be arranged. **Factors that count in admissions decisions:** *Academic:* Secondary school record: Very Important. Class rank: Important. Letters of recommendation: Important. Standardized test scores: Very Important. Essay: Important. *Nonacademic:* Interview: Considered. Extracurricular activities: Considered. Talent/ability: Considered. Character/personal qualities:

Considered. Alumni/ae relationship: Considered. Geographical residence: Considered. State residency: Considered. Religious affiliation/commitment: Not Considered. Minority status: Considered. Volunteer work: Considered. Work experience: Not Considered. **Other schools with the greatest overlap in applicants:** Auburn University; Birmingham-Southern College; Furman University; University of Alabama; University of Georgia. **Admissions statistics for the fall 2009 entering class:** Total applicants: 2,288. Total accepted: 1,911. Freshmen enrolled: 733; 64% were from out of state. Overall acceptance rate: 84%. **Credentials of fall 2009 freshmen:** 44% ranked in the top 10 percent of their high school class; 70% were in the top 25 percent; 87% were in the top half. (Proportion submitting class standing: 48%.) **Average high school grade point average:** 3.7. **First-year students who submitted SAT scores:** 44%. Scores (25/75 percentile): Critical Reading: 520-645, Math: 520-650, Combined: 1040-1295. **First-year students submitting ACT scores:** 85%. Scores (25/75 percentile): English: 22-28, Math: 23-31, Composite: 21-28.

ACADEMICS

Year founded: 1841. **Academic calendar:** 4-1-4. **Degrees offered:** certificate, associate, terminal-associate, bachelor's, post-bachelor's certificate, master's, post-master's certificate, doctorate. **Most popular majors:** 19% business, management, marketing, and related support services, 14% health professions and related clinical sciences, 11% visual and performing arts, 9% biological and biomedical sciences, 7% communication, journalism, and related programs. **Major fields of study:** area, ethnic, cultural, and gender studies; biological and biomedical sciences; business, management, marketing, and related support services; communication, journalism, and related programs; computer and information sciences and support services; education; engineering; English language and literature/letters; family and consumer sciences/human sciences; foreign languages, literatures, and linguistics; health professions and related clinical sciences; history; liberal arts and sciences studies, and humanities; mathematics and statistics; natural resources and conservation; parks, recreation, leisure, and fitness studies; philosophy and religious studies; physical sciences; psychology; public administration and social service professions; social sciences; theology and religious vocations; visual and performing arts. **Areas of required coursework:** arts/fine arts, humanities, mathematics, English (including composition), foreign languages, sciences (biological or physical), history, social science, other. **Pre-professional programs:** pre-law, pre-dentistry, pre-medicine, pre-veterinary science, pre-optometry, pre-pharmacy. **Special academic programs:** accelerated program, cooperative (work-study plan) program, cross-registration, distance learning, double major, dual enrollment, exchange student program (domestic), honors program, independent study, internships, study abroad, teacher certificate program, weekend college. **Teacher certification offered in:** early childhood, special education, elementary, secondary. **Cooperative education programs:** art, business, computer science, health professions, humanities, natural science. **Reserve Officers Training Corps (ROTC):** Army ROTC: Offered at cooperating institution (University of Alabama–Birmingham); Air Force ROTC: Offered on campus. **Faculty and instruction (2009-2010):** Total instructional faculty: 282 full-time, 137 part-time (55% men; 45% women; 8% minorities). Full-time faculty with Ph.D. or other terminal degree: 95%. Student/faculty ratio: 12/1. Classes of fewer than 20 students: 65%; of 20 to 49 students: 33%; of 50 or more students: 2%. **Advanced Placement and International Baccalaureate credit:** AP tests may be used for: Credit only. International Baccalaureate exams may be used for: Credit only. **Freshmen returning for sophomore year:** 84%. **Graduation rates:** Four-year: 53%; five-year: 69%; six-year: 74%.

COSTS AND FINANCIAL AID

Financial aid office: (205) 726-2905. **Expenses (2010-2011):** Tuition and fees 2010-2011: $21,942; room/board: $7,024. Estimated books and supplies: $1,200; transportation: $1,200; personal expenses: $3,005. **Financial aid:** Priority filing date for institution's financial aid form: March 1. In 2009-2010, 61% of undergraduates applied for financial aid. Of those, 42% were determined to have financial need; 27% had their need fully met. Average financial aid package (proportion receiving): $16,910 (42%). Average amount of gift aid, such as scholarships or grants (proportion receiving): N/A (39%). Average amount of self-help aid, such as work study or loans (proportion receiving): $6,558 (35%). Average need-based loan (excluding PLUS or other private loans): $4,672. Among students who received need-based aid, the average percentage of need met: 71%. Among students who received aid based on merit, the average award (and the proportion receiving): $6,515 (19%). The average athletic scholarship (and the proportion receiving): $18,632 (2%). Average amount of debt of borrowers graduating in 2009: $15,702. Proportion who borrowed: 38%.

CAMPUS LIFE AND EXTRACURRICULAR ACTIVITIES

Campus housing available (% using): women's dorms (65%), men's dorms (35%), sorority housing, fraternity housing, apartment for single students, special housing for international students. Students who live in college-owned, operated, or affiliated housing: 67%. **Student employment:** During the 2009-2010 academic year, 20% of undergraduates worked on campus. Average per-year earnings: $1,000. **Clubs and organizations:** Number of student organizations: 115. Activities include: campus ministries, choral groups, concert band, dance, drama/theater, international student organization, jazz band, literary magazine, marching band, model UN, music ensembles, musical theater, radio station, student government, student newspaper, symphony orchestra, television station, yearbook. Number of fraternities: 4; sororities: 7. Proportion of men in fraternities: 21%; of women in sororities: 29%. **Sports program (2009-2010):** Member of NCAA I. **Men's intercollegiate varsity sports:** baseball, basketball, cross country, football, golf, tennis, track and field (indoor), track and field (outdoor). **Women's intercollegiate varsity sports:** basketball, cross country, golf, soccer, softball, tennis, track and field (indoor), track and field (outdoor), volleyball.

SERVICES AND FACILITIES

Basic services: nonremedial tutoring, placement service, health service, health insurance, other. **Counseling services:** minority student, career, personal, academic, older student, religious. **For learning-disabled students:** School does not offer a structured program with separate admission and additional fees. Total undergraduates in learning-disabled program or receiving services: 47. Services include: reading machines, tape recorders, note-taking services, oral tests, learning center, readers, extended time for tests, tutors, priority registration, priority seating, substitution of courses, texts on tape, typist/scribe, exams on tape or computer, other testing accommodations, other. **Library:** Number of titles: 447,861; number of current serial subscriptions: 38,965. **Information technology resources:** Students are not required to lease or own a computer. Number of campus computers available to all students: 533. School has a wireless network. Proportion of college-owned housing units wired for high-speed internet access: 100%. **Campus safety:** Security services offered: 24-hour foot-and-vehicle patrols, late-night transport/escort service, 24-hour emergency telephones, lighted pathways/sidewalks, controlled dormitory access (key, security card, etc).

TRANSFER AND INTERNATIONAL STUDENTS

Transfer students: May apply for admission for the following academic terms: Fall, Winter, Spring, Summer. Applicants need a minimum number of credits to apply. For fall 2009: Transfer applications received: 255. Transfer applicants offered admission: 163. Transfer applicants enrolled: 120. **International students:** Number of foreign undergraduates: 14. Number of countries represented: 8. Minimum TOEFL score required: 550 (paper); 213 (computer).

Spring Hill College

- **Address:** 4000 Dauphin Street, Mobile, AL 36608
- **Website:** http://www.shc.edu
- **Private; Religious affiliation:** Catholic
- **Enrollment:** 1,184 full-time; 126 part-time

KEY STATS

✔ **U.S News College Ranking:** 17, Regional Universities (South)
✔ **ACT Score (25th/75th percentile):** 21-26
✔ **Tuition:** 2010-2011: $26,730

Selectivity: More selective	**Room/board:** $10,250
Acceptance rate: 55%	**Average debt:** $21,823
Student/faculty ratio: 13/1	**Proportion who borrowed:** 72%

UNDERGRADUATE STUDENT BODY STATS

2009-2010 enrollment: 1,184 full-time; 126 part-time. Men: 38%; women: 62%. **Ethnic makeup:** African American: 18%; American-Indian: 1%; Asian American: 1%; Hispanic: 7%; White: 72%; International: 1%. **Religious preference:** Protestant: 30%; No preference: 2%; Unknown: 16%; Catholic: 52%.

ADMISSIONS FACTS AND FIGURES

Phone: (251) 380-3030. **Email:** admit@shc.edu. **Website:** http://www.shc.edu. **Application deadlines for fall 2011:** Regular decision: July 15. Early decision: Not offered. Early action: Not offered. Admission can be deferred. **Application fee:** $25. **To apply online, go to:** http://www.shc.edu/admis-

sion/apply. **Admissions requirements/recommendations:** High school units required (recommended): English: (4); Mathematics: (3); Science: (3); Foreign language: (2); Social studies: (2); History: (1); Academic electives: (1); Total units: (16). Tests: The college uses SAT or ACT scores in admissions decisions. Either SAT or ACT required. For admission to the fall 2011 entering class, the school will accept: ACT with writing recommended. Campus visit: Recommended. Admissions interview: Recommended. Off-campus interview: May be arranged. **Factors that count in admissions decisions:** *Academic:* Secondary school record: Very Important. Class rank: Important. Letters of recommendation: Important. Standardized test scores: Very Important. Essay: Considered. *Nonacademic:* Interview: Important. Extracurricular activities: Considered. Talent/ability: Considered. Character/personal qualities: Considered. Alumni/ae relationship: Considered. Geographical residence: Not Considered. State residency: Not Considered. Religious affiliation/commitment: Not Considered. Minority status: Not Considered. Volunteer work: Considered. Work experience: Not Considered. **Other schools with the greatest overlap in applicants:** Auburn University; Louisiana State University–Baton Rouge; Loyola University New Orleans; University of Alabama; University of South Alabama. **Admissions statistics for the fall 2009 entering class:** Total applicants: 4,249. Total accepted: 2,338. Freshmen enrolled: 358; 57% were from out of state. Overall acceptance rate: 55%. **Credentials of fall 2009 freshmen:** 27% ranked in the top 10 percent of their high school class; 61% were in the top 25 percent; 86% were in the top half. (Proportion submitting class standing: 70%.) **Average high school grade point average:** 3.5. **First-year students who submitted SAT scores:** 29%. Scores (25/75 percentile): Critical Reading: 480-600, Math: 480-570, Combined: 960-1170. **First-year students submitting ACT scores:** 92%. Scores (25/75 percentile): English: 22-28, Math: 20-25, Composite: 21-26.

ACADEMICS

Year founded: 1830. **Academic calendar:** Semester. **Degrees offered:** certificate, bachelor's, post-bachelor's certificate, master's, post-master's certificate. **Most popular majors:** 32% business, management, marketing, and related support services, 10% biological and biomedical sciences, 7% communication, journalism, and related programs, 6% theology and religious vocations, 5% psychology. **Major fields of study:** biological and biomedical sciences; business, management, marketing, and related support services; communication, journalism, and related programs; education; engineering; English language and literature/letters; foreign languages, literatures, and linguistics; health professions and related clinical sciences; history; liberal arts and sciences studies, and humanities; mathematics and statistics; multi/interdisciplinary studies; philosophy and religious studies; physical sciences; psychology; social sciences; theology and religious vocations; visual and performing arts. **Areas of required coursework:** arts/fine arts, mathematics, English (including composition), philosophy, foreign languages, sciences (biological or physical), history, social science, other. **Pre-professional programs:** pre-law, pre-dentistry, pre-medicine, pre-veterinary science, pre-optometry. **Special academic programs (% participation):** accelerated program (1%), distance learning (9%), double major (11%), dual enrollment, honors program (12%), independent study (25%), internships (36%), student-designed major (5%), study abroad, teacher certificate program (4%). **Teacher certification offered in:** early childhood, elementary, secondary. **Reserve Officers Training Corps (ROTC):** Army ROTC: Offered at cooperating institution (University of South Alabama); Air Force ROTC: Offered at cooperating institution (University of South Alabama). **Faculty and instruction (2009-2010):** Total instructional faculty: 82 full-time, 51 part-time (52% men; 48% women; 7% minorities). Full-time faculty with Ph.D. or other terminal degree: 85%. Student/faculty ratio: 13/1. Classes of fewer than 20 students: 49%; of 20 to 49 students: 50%; of 50 or more students: 1%. **Advanced Placement and International Baccalaureate credit:** AP tests may be used for: Credit and/or placement. Scores accepted: 3, 4, 5. International Baccalaureate exams may be used for: Credit and/or placement. **Freshmen returning for sophomore year:** 79%. **Graduation rates:** Four-year: 50%; five-year: 60%; six-year: 62%. **Graduate study:** 33% of students pursue further study immediately upon graduation. Fields in which graduates pursue further study: Master of Business Administration (MBA), 10%; law, 16%; medicine, 14%; education, 9%.

COSTS AND FINANCIAL AID

Financial aid office: (251) 380-3460. **Expenses (2010-2011):** Tuition and fees 2010-2011: $26,730; room/board: $10,250. Estimated books and supplies: $1,500; transportation: $1,700; personal expenses: $2,900. **Financial aid:** Priority filing date for institution's financial aid form: March 1. In 2009-2010, 81% of undergraduates applied for financial aid. Of those, 70% were determined to have financial need; 26% had their need fully met. Average financial aid package (proportion receiving): $23,948 (70%). Average amount of gift aid, such as scholarships or grants (proportion receiving): $17,473 (66%). Average amount of self-help aid, such as work study or loans (proportion receiving): $5,188 (56%). Average need-based loan (excluding PLUS or other private loans): $4,732. Among students who received need-based aid, the average percentage of need met: 82%. Among students who received aid based on merit, the average award (and the proportion receiving): $13,699 (28%). The average athletic scholarship (and the proportion receiving): $5,446 (8%). Average amount of debt of borrowers graduating in 2009: $21,823. Proportion who borrowed: 72%.

CAMPUS LIFE AND EXTRACURRICULAR ACTIVITIES

Campus housing available (% using): coed dorms (65%), women's dorms (11%), men's dorms (9%), apartment for single students (15%). Students who live in college-owned, operated, or affiliated housing: 73%. **Student employment:** During the 2009-2010 academic year, 5% of undergraduates worked on campus. Average per-year earnings: $1,070. **Clubs and organizations:** Number of student organizations: 66. Activities include: campus ministries, choral groups, dance, drama/theater, literary magazine, student government, student newspaper, yearbook. Number of fraternities: 3; sororities: 5. Proportion of men in fraternities: 13%; of women in sororities: 22%. Average proportion of students who stay on campus on weekends: 75%. **Sports program (2009-2010):** Member of NAIA. *Men's intercollegiate varsity sports:* baseball, basketball, cross country, golf, soccer, tennis. *Women's intercollegiate varsity sports:* basketball, cross country, golf, soccer, softball, tennis, volleyball.

SERVICES AND FACILITIES

Basic services: nonremedial tutoring, placement service, health service. **Remedial assistance:** study skills. **Counseling services:** minority student, career, personal, veteran student, academic, older student, psychological, religious. **For learning-disabled students:** School does not offer a structured program with separate admission and additional fees. Total undergraduates in learning-disabled program or receiving services: 62. Services include: remedial math, remedial English, remedial reading, tape recorders, other special classes, readers, extended time for tests, tutors, priority seating, substitution of courses, typist/scribe, exams on tape or computer, other testing accommodations. **Library:** Number of titles: 195,914; number of current serial subscriptions: 833. **Information technology resources:** Students are not required to lease or own a computer. Number of campus computers available to all students: 194. School has a wireless network. Approximate number of users that can be accommodated: 500. Proportion of college-owned housing units wired for high-speed internet access: 100%. **Campus safety:** Security services offered: 24-hour foot-and-vehicle patrols, late-night transport/escort service, 24-hour emergency telephones, lighted pathways/sidewalks, student patrols, controlled dormitory access (key, security card, etc).

TRANSFER AND INTERNATIONAL STUDENTS

Transfer students: May apply for admission for the following academic terms: Fall, Spring, Summer. Applicants do not need a minimum number of credits to apply. For fall 2009: Transfer applications received: 126. Transfer applicants offered admission: 41. Transfer applicants enrolled: 25. **International students:** Number of foreign undergraduates: 10 (1% of student body). Number of countries represented: 5. Minimum TOEFL score required: 550 (paper); 213 (computer).

Stillman College

- **Address:** PO Box 1430, 3600 Stillman Boulevard, Tuscaloosa, AL 35403
- **Website:** http://www.stillman.edu
- **Private; Religious affiliation:** Presbyterian Church (USA)
- **Enrollment:** 1,013 full-time; 28 part-time

KEY STATS

✔ **U.S News College Ranking:** 48, Regional Colleges (South)
✔ **ACT Score (25th/75th percentile):** 16-19
✔ **Tuition:** 2010-2011: $13,890

Selectivity: Less selective	**Room/board:** $6,526
Acceptance rate: 44%	**Average debt:** $23,000
Student/faculty ratio: 19/1	**Proportion who borrowed:** 96%

UNDERGRADUATE STUDENT BODY STATS

2009-2010 enrollment: 1,013 full-time; 28 part-time. Men: 43%; women: 57%. **Ethnic makeup:** African American: 87%; White: 12%. **Religious preference:** Protestant: 98%; Other: 2%.

ADMISSIONS FACTS AND FIGURES

Phone: (205) 366-8837. **Email:** admissions@stillman.edu. **Website:** http://www.stillman.edu. **Application deadlines for fall 2011:** Regular decision: Rolling. Early decision: Send application by: July 2; Decision sent by: July 6. Early action: Not offered. Admission can be deferred. **Application fee:** $15. **To apply online, go to:** http://www.stillman.edu/admissions/ApplyOnline/Admissions_form.asp. **Admissions requirements/recommendations:** High school units required (recommended): English: 4 (4); Mathematics: 1 (1); Science: 1 (1); Foreign language: 0 (0); Social studies: 0 (0); History: 1 (1); Academic electives: 16 (16); Total units: 24 (24). Tests: The college uses SAT or ACT scores in admissions decisions. Either SAT or ACT required. For admission to the fall 2011 entering class, the school will accept: ACT with or without writing accepted. Campus visit: Recommended. Admissions interview: Recommended. Off-campus interview: May be arranged. **Factors that count in admissions decisions:** *Academic:* Secondary school record: Very Important. Class rank: Very Important. Letters of recommendation: Very Important. Standardized test scores: Very Important. Essay: Very Important. *Nonacademic:* Interview: Important. Extracurricular activities: Important. Talent/ability: Considered. Character/personal qualities: Very Important. Alumni/ae relationship: Not Considered. Geographical residence: Not Considered. State residency: Not Considered. Religious affiliation/commitment: Not Considered. Minority status: Not Considered. Volunteer work: Considered. Work experience: Not Considered. **Other schools with the greatest overlap in applicants:** Alabama Agricultural and Mechanical University; Alabama State University; Spelman College; Troy University; University of Alabama–Birmingham. **Admissions statistics for the fall 2009 entering class:** Total applicants: 5,909. Total accepted: 2,580. Freshmen enrolled: 440; 44% were from out of state. Overall acceptance rate: 44%. Non-early acceptance rate: 44%. **Size of waiting list:** 0 applicants; enrolled from waiting list: 0. **Credentials of fall 2009 freshmen:** 12% ranked in the top 10 percent of their high school class; 26% were in the top 25 percent; 56% were in the top half. (Proportion submitting class standing: 69%.) **Average high school grade point average:** 2.8. **First-year students who submitted SAT scores:** 21%. Scores (25/75 percentile): Critical Reading: 380-450, Math: 370-470, Combined: 750-920. **First-year students submitting ACT scores:** 79%. Scores (25/75 percentile): English: 15-20, Math: 15-18, Composite: 16-19.

ACADEMICS

Year founded: 1876. **Academic calendar:** Semester. **Degrees offered:** bachelor's. **Most popular majors:** 32% biology/biological sciences, 25% business administration, management, and operations, 13% history, 10% elementary education and teaching, 8% English language and literature. **Major fields of study:** biological and biomedical sciences; business, management, marketing, and related support services; communication, journalism, and related programs; computer and information sciences and support services; education; English language and literature/letters; health professions and related clinical sciences; history; mathematics and statistics; multi/interdisciplinary studies; parks, recreation, leisure, and fitness studies; philosophy and religious studies; visual and performing arts. **Areas of required coursework:** humanities, computer literacy, mathematics, English (including composition), philosophy, sciences (biological or physical), history, social science, other. **Pre-professional programs:** pre-law, pre-medicine, pre-theology. **Special academic programs (% participation):** cooperative (work-study plan) program (15%), cross-registration (2%), double major (2%), honors program (2%), independent study (3%), internships (5%), liberal arts/career combination (3%), teacher certificate program (10%). **Teacher certification offered in:** elementary, secondary. **Cooperative education programs:** business, education, health professions, natural science, social/behavioral science. **Reserve Officers Training Corps (ROTC):** Army ROTC: Offered at cooperating institution; Air Force ROTC: Offered at cooperating institution. **Faculty and instruction (2009-2010):** Total instructional faculty: 53 full-time, 2 part-time (44% men; 56% women; 47% minorities). Full-time faculty with Ph.D. or other terminal degree: 83%. Student/faculty ratio: 19/1. Classes of fewer than 20 students: 47%; of 20 to 49 students: 40%; of 50 or more students: 12%. **Advanced Placement and International Baccalaureate credit:** AP tests may be used for: Placement only. **Freshmen returning for sophomore year:** 57%. **Graduation rates:** Four-year: 14%; five-year: 18%; six-year: 21%. **Graduate study:** 20% of students pursue further study immediately upon graduation; 20% within one year; 25% within five years. Fields in which graduates pursue further study: Master of Business Administration (MBA),

75%; law, 5%; medicine, 1%; theology (or the seminary), 1%; education, 15%; arts and sciences, 3%.

COSTS AND FINANCIAL AID
Financial aid office: (205) 366-8817. **Expenses (2010-2011):** Tuition and fees 2010-2011: $13,890; room/board: $6,526. Estimated books and supplies: $1,200; transportation: $1,000; personal expenses: $1,200. **Financial aid:** Priority filing date for institution's financial aid form: March 1; deadline: June 1. In 2009-2010, 100% of undergraduates applied for financial aid. Of those, 94% were determined to have financial need; 56% had their need fully met. Average financial aid package (proportion receiving): $18,804 (96%). Average amount of gift aid, such as scholarships or grants (proportion receiving): $6,000 (50%). Average amount of self-help aid, such as work study or loans (proportion receiving): $5,500 (96%). Average need-based loan (excluding PLUS or other private loans): $5,500. Among students who received aid based on merit, the average award (and the proportion receiving): $6,489 (6%). The average athletic scholarship (and the proportion receiving): $7,849 (1%). Average amount of debt of borrowers graduating in 2009: $23,000. Proportion who borrowed: 96%.

CAMPUS LIFE AND EXTRACURRICULAR ACTIVITIES
Campus housing available (% using): women's dorms (55%), men's dorms (45%). Students who live in college-owned, operated, or affiliated housing: 1%. **Student employment:** During the 2009-2010 academic year, 2% of undergraduates worked on campus. Average per-year earnings: $1,200. **Clubs and organizations:** Number of student organizations: 21. Activities include: choral groups, concert band, dance, drama/theater, international student organization, jazz band, literary magazine, marching band, music ensembles, pep band, student government, student newspaper, symphony orchestra, yearbook. Number of fraternities: 4; sororities: 4. Average proportion of students who stay on campus on weekends: 60%. **Sports program (2009-2010):** Member of NCAA II. *Men's intercollegiate varsity sports:* baseball, basketball, cross country, football, tennis, track and field (outdoor). *Women's intercollegiate varsity sports:* basketball, cross country, softball, tennis, track and field (outdoor), volleyball.

SERVICES AND FACILITIES
Basic services: nonremedial tutoring, placement service, health service, health insurance. **Remedial assistance:** reading, math, writing, study skills. **Counseling services:** minority student, career, personal, academic, older student, psychological, religious. **For learning-disabled students:** School does not offer a structured program with separate admission and additional fees. Total undergraduates in learning-disabled program or receiving services: 3. Services include: remedial math, remedial English, reading machines, tape recorders, untimed tests, oral tests, readers, extended time for tests, tutors, priority seating. **Library:** Number of titles: 117,500; number of current serial subscriptions: 6,300. **Information technology resources:** Students are required to lease or own a computer. Number of campus computers available to all students: 1,050. School has a wireless network. Approximate number of users that can be accommodated: 1,500. Proportion of college-owned housing units wired for high-speed internet access: 100%. **Campus safety:** Security services offered: 24-hour foot-and-vehicle patrols, lighted pathways/sidewalks, controlled dormitory access (key, security card, etc).

TRANSFER AND INTERNATIONAL STUDENTS
Transfer students: May apply for admission for the following academic terms: Fall, Spring, Summer. Applicants need a minimum number of credits to apply. For fall 2009: Transfer applications received: 206. Transfer applicants offered admission: 76. Transfer applicants enrolled: 48. **International students:** Number of foreign undergraduates: 0. Number of countries represented: 0. Minimum TOEFL score required: 550 (paper).

Talladega College

■ **Address:** 627 W. Battle Street, Talladega, AL 35160
■ **Website:** http://www.talladega.edu
■ **Private; Religious affiliation:** United Church of Christ
■ **Enrollment:** N/A

KEY STATS
✔ **U.S News College Ranking:** second tier, National Liberal Arts Colleges
✔ **SAT or ACT Score (25th/75th percentile):** N/A
✔ **Tuition:** 2009-2010: $8,940
  Selectivity: Selective   **Room/board:** $4,884
  Acceptance rate: 43%   **Average debt:** N/A
  Student/faculty ratio: N/A   **Proportion who borrowed:** N/A

Troy University

■ **Address:** University Avenue, Troy, AL 36082
■ **Website:** http://www.troy.edu/
■ **Public**
■ **Enrollment:** 11,070 full-time; 11,141 part-time

KEY STATS
✔ **U.S News College Ranking:** 65, Regional Universities (South)
✔ **ACT Score (25th/75th percentile):** 18-23
✔ **Tuition:** 2009-2010: $7,020 in state, $13,196 out of state
  Selectivity: Selective   **Room/board:** $4,572
  Acceptance rate: 66%   **Average debt:** N/A
  Student/faculty ratio: 21/1   **Proportion who borrowed:** N/A

UNDERGRADUATE STUDENT BODY STATS
2009-2010 enrollment: 11,070 full-time; 11,141 part-time. Men: 40%; women: 60%. **Ethnic makeup:** African American: 42%; American-Indian: 2%; Asian American: 1%; Hispanic: 3%; White: 51%; International: 2%.

ADMISSIONS FACTS AND FIGURES
Phone: (334) 670-3179. **Email:** admit@troy.edu. **Website:** http://www.troy.edu/. **Application deadlines for fall 2011:** Regular decision: Rolling. Early decision: Not offered. Early action: Not offered. Admission can be deferred. **Application fee:** $30. **To apply online, go to:** http://www.troy.edu/application/. **Admissions requirements/recommendations:** High school units required (recommended): English: 4; Mathematics: 4; Science: 4; Foreign language: (2); Social studies: 4; Total units: 18. Tests: The college uses SAT or ACT scores in admissions decisions. Either SAT or ACT required. For admission to the fall 2011 entering class, the school will accept: ACT with or without writing accepted. Campus visit: Recommended. Admissions interview: Recommended. Off-campus interview: Not available. **Factors that count in admissions decisions:** *Academic:* Secondary school record: Very Important. Class rank: Not Considered. Letters of recommendation: Considered. Standardized test scores: Very Important. Essay: Considered. *Nonacademic:* Interview: Considered. Extracurricular activities: Considered. Talent/ability: Considered. Character/personal qualities: Considered. Alumni/ae relationship: Considered. Geographical residence: Not Considered. State residency: Not Considered. Religious affiliation/commitment: Not Considered. Minority status: Not Considered. Volunteer work: Not Considered. Work experience: Not Considered. **Other schools with the greatest overlap in applicants:** Auburn University; Auburn University–Montgomery; University of Alabama; University of Maryland–University College; University of Phoenix. **Admissions statistics for the fall 2009 entering class:** Total applicants: 6,413. Total accepted: 4,246. Freshmen enrolled: 3,322; 31% were from out of state. Overall acceptance rate: 66%. **Credentials of fall 2009 freshmen:** 16% ranked in the top 10 percent of their high school class; 45% were in the top 25 percent; 80% were in the top half. (Proportion submitting class standing: 31%.) **First-year students submitting ACT scores:** 50%. Scores (25/75 percentile): English: 16-22, Math: 17-24, Composite: 18-23.

ACADEMICS
Year founded: 1887. **Academic calendar:** Semester. **Degrees offered:** associate, bachelor's, master's, post-master's certificate. **Most popular majors:** 40% business, management, marketing, and related support services, 14%

security and protective services, 12% psychology, 8% education, 8% social sciences. **Major fields of study:** biological and biomedical sciences; business, management, marketing, and related support services; communication, journalism, and related programs; computer and information sciences and support services; education; engineering technologies/technicians; English language and literature/letters; health professions and related clinical sciences; history; liberal arts and sciences studies, and humanities; mathematics and statistics; natural resources and conservation; parks, recreation, leisure, and fitness studies; physical sciences; psychology; public administration and social service professions; security and protective services; social sciences; visual and performing arts. **Areas of required coursework:** arts/fine arts, humanities, computer literacy, mathematics, English (including composition), sciences (biological or physical), history. **Pre-professional programs:** pre-law, pre-dentistry, pre-medicine, pre-theology, pre-veterinary science, pre-optometry, pre-pharmacy, other. **Special academic programs:** accelerated program, cross-registration, distance learning, double major, dual enrollment, English as a Second Language (ESL), honors program, independent study, internships, study abroad, teacher certificate program, weekend college. **Teacher certification offered in:** early childhood, special education, elementary, middle/junior high, adult education, secondary. **Reserve Officers Training Corps (ROTC):** Army ROTC: Offered on campus; Air Force ROTC: Offered on campus. **Faculty and instruction (2009-2010):** Total instructional faculty: 516 full-time, 995 part-time (52% men; 48% women; 17% minorities). Full-time faculty with Ph.D. or other terminal degree: 67%. Student/faculty ratio: 21/1. **Advanced Placement and International Baccalaureate credit:** AP tests may be used for: Placement only. Scores accepted: 3. **Freshmen returning for sophomore year:** 72%. **Graduation rates:** Four-year: 19%; five-year: 33%; six-year: 43%.

COSTS AND FINANCIAL AID

Financial aid office: (334) 670-3186. **Expenses (2009-2010):** Tuition and fees 2009-2010: $7,020 in state, $13,196 out of state; room/board: $4,572. Estimated books and supplies: $1,062; transportation: $2,502; personal expenses: $2,376. **Financial aid:** Priority filing date for institution's financial aid form: March 1. In 2009-2010, 71% of undergraduates applied for financial aid. Of those, 71% were determined to have financial need; Average financial aid package (proportion receiving): $4,485 (71%). Average amount of gift aid, such as scholarships or grants (proportion receiving): N/A (50%). Average amount of self-help aid, such as work study or loans (proportion receiving): $2,801 (71%). Average need-based loan (excluding PLUS or other private loans): $4,531. Among students who received aid based on merit, the average award (and the proportion receiving): $3,927 (12%). The average athletic scholarship (and the proportion receiving): $5,067 (1%).

CAMPUS LIFE AND EXTRACURRICULAR ACTIVITIES

Campus housing available (% using): coed dorms (7%), women's dorms (26%), men's dorms (24%), sorority housing (3%), fraternity housing (1%), apartments for married students (2%), apartment for single students (28%), special housing for international students (7%), other housing options (2%). Students who live in college-owned, operated, or affiliated housing: 30%. **Student employment:** During the 2009-2010 academic year, 3% of undergraduates worked on campus. Average per-year earnings: $2,300. **Clubs and organizations:** Number of student organizations: 150. Activities include: choral groups, concert band, dance, drama/theater, international student organization, jazz band, marching band, music ensembles, musical theater, opera, pep band, radio station, student government, student newspaper, symphony orchestra, television station, yearbook. Number of fraternities: 13; sororities: 9. **Sports program (2009-2010):** Member of NCAA I. *Men's intercollegiate varsity sports:* baseball, basketball, cross country, football, golf, tennis, track and field (outdoor). *Women's intercollegiate varsity sports:* basketball, golf, crew (lightweight), soccer, tennis, track and field (outdoor), volleyball.

SERVICES AND FACILITIES

Basic services: nonremedial tutoring, placement service, day care, health service, health insurance. **Remedial assistance:** reading, math, writing, study skills. **Counseling services:** minority student, career, military, personal, veteran student, academic, older student, psychological, birth control, religious. **For learning-disabled students:** School does not offer a structured program with separate admission and additional fees. Total undergraduates in learning-disabled program or receiving services: 162. Services include: remedial math, remedial English, tape recorders, note-taking services, oral tests, readers, extended time for tests, tutors, priority registration, priority seating, texts on tape, typist/scribe, exams on tape or computer, other. **Library:** Number of titles: 571,152; number of current serial subscriptions: 3,309. **Information technology resources:** Students are not required to lease

or own a computer. Number of campus computers available to all students: 1,570. School has a wireless network. Approximate number of users that can be accommodated: 1,206. Proportion of college-owned housing units wired for high-speed internet access: 95%. **Campus safety:** Security services offered: 24-hour foot-and-vehicle patrols, late-night transport/escort service, 24-hour emergency telephones, lighted pathways/sidewalks, student patrols, controlled dormitory access (key, security card, etc).

TRANSFER AND INTERNATIONAL STUDENTS

Transfer students: May apply for admission for the following academic terms: Fall, Spring, Summer. Applicants need a minimum number of credits to apply. For fall 2009: Transfer applications received: 4,974. Transfer applicants offered admission: 3,200. Transfer applicants enrolled: 2,392. **International students:** Number of foreign undergraduates: 423 (2% of student body). Minimum TOEFL score required: 500 (paper); 175 (computer).

Tuskegee University

- ■ **Address:** PO Box 1239, Tuskegee, AL 36088
- ■ **Website:** http://www.tuskegee.edu
- ■ **Private**
- ■ **Enrollment:** 2,419 full-time; 56 part-time

KEY STATS

✔ **U.S News College Ranking:** 5, Regional Colleges (South)
✔ **ACT Score (25th/75th percentile):** 17-21
✔ **Tuition:** 2010-2011: $16,820

Selectivity: Selective	**Room/board:** $7,570
Acceptance rate: 58%	**Average debt:** $33,500
Student/faculty ratio: 12/1	**Proportion who borrowed:** 59%

UNDERGRADUATE STUDENT BODY STATS

2009-2010 enrollment: 2,419 full-time; 56 part-time. Men: 43%; women: 57%. **Ethnic makeup:** African American: 88%; White: 11%; International: 1%.

ADMISSIONS FACTS AND FIGURES

Phone: (334) 727-8500. **Email:** admiweb@tusk.edu. **Website:** http://www.tuskegee.edu. **Application deadlines for fall 2011:** Regular decision: March 15. Early decision: Not offered. Early action: Not offered. Admission can be deferred. **Application fee:** $25. **Admissions requirements/recommendations:** High school units required (recommended): English: 4 (4); Mathematics: 3 (3); Science: 2 (2); Foreign language: 0 (0); Social studies: 3 (3); Academic electives: 4 (4); Total units: 16 (16). Tests: The college uses SAT or ACT scores in admissions decisions. Either SAT or ACT required. For admission to the fall 2011 entering class, the school will accept: ACT with or without writing accepted. Campus visit: Recommended. Admissions interview: Neither required nor recommended. Off-campus interview: May be arranged. **Factors that count in admissions decisions:** *Academic:* Secondary school record: Very Important. Class rank: Considered. Letters of recommendation: Considered. Standardized test scores: Important. Essay: Considered. *Nonacademic:* Interview: Not Considered. Extracurricular activities: Considered. Talent/ability: Considered. Character/personal qualities: Important. Alumni/ae relationship: Considered. State residency: Considered. Religious affiliation/commitment: Not Considered. Minority status: Considered. Volunteer work: Important. Work experience: Considered. **Other schools with the greatest overlap in applicants:** Alabama State University; Alcorn State University; Alcorn State University; Benedict College; Benedict College; Bennett College; Bennett College; Clark Atlanta University; Clark Atlanta University. **Admissions statistics for the fall 2009 entering class:** Total applicants: 2,692. Total accepted: 1,560. Freshmen enrolled: 689; 73% were from out of state. Overall acceptance rate: 58%. **Size of waiting list:** 0 applicants; enrolled from waiting list: 0. **Credentials of fall 2009 freshmen:** 20% ranked in the top 10 percent of their high school class; 59% were in the top 25 percent; 100% were in the top half. (Proportion submitting class standing: 100%.) **First-year students who submitted SAT scores:** 52%. Scores (25/75 percentile): Critical Reading: 390-490, Math: 390-480, Combined: 780-970. **First-year students submitting ACT scores:** 64%. Scores (25/75 percentile): English: N/A, Math: N/A, Composite: 17-21.

ACADEMICS

Year founded: 1881. **Academic calendar:** Semester. **Degrees offered:** bachelor's, master's, doctorate. **Most popular majors:** 16% engineering, 16% sales, distribution, and marketing operations, 13% biology/biological sciences, 10% psychology, 7% animal sciences. **Major fields of study:** agriculture, agriculture operations, and related sciences; architecture and related services; business, management, marketing, and related support services; computer and information sciences and support services; construction trades; education; engineering; English language and literature/letters; health professions and related clinical sciences; history; mathematics and statistics; natural resources and conservation; physical sciences; psychology; public administration and social service professions; social sciences. **Areas of required coursework:** arts/fine arts, mathematics, English (including composition), foreign languages, sciences (biological or physical), history, social science. **Pre-professional programs:** pre-dentistry, pre-medicine, pre-veterinary science. **Special academic programs (% participation):** cooperative (work-study plan) program (40%), double major (10%), honors program (10%), independent study, internships (20%), liberal arts/career combination, teacher certificate program. **Teacher certification offered in:** early childhood, special education, elementary. **Cooperative education programs:** agriculture, business, computer science, education, engineering, health professions. **Reserve Officers Training Corps (ROTC):** Army ROTC: Offered on campus; Air Force ROTC: Offered on campus. **Faculty and instruction (2009-2010):** Total instructional faculty: 267 full-time, 11 part-time (66% men; 34% women; 74% minorities). Full-time faculty with Ph.D. or other terminal degree: 82%. Student/faculty ratio: 12/1. Classes of fewer than 20 students: 55%; of 20 to 49 students: 35%; of 50 or more students: 10%. **Advanced Placement and International Baccalaureate credit:** AP tests may be used for: Placement only. Scores accepted: 3. **Freshmen returning for sophomore year:** 67%. **Graduation rates:** Four-year: 16%; five-year: 33%; six-year: 47%. **Graduate study:** 21% of students pursue further study immediately upon graduation; 45% within one year; 50% within five years. Fields in which graduates pursue further study: Master of Business Administration (MBA), 6%; law, 4%; medicine, 11%; dentistry, 2%; engineering, 16%; theology (or the seminary), 2%; education, 4%; arts and sciences, 2%; veterinary medicine, 13%.

COSTS AND FINANCIAL AID

Financial aid office: (334) 727-8201. **Expenses (2010-2011):** Tuition and fees 2010-2011: $16,820; room/board: $7,570. Estimated books and supplies: $1,165; transportation: $1,798; personal expenses: $1,887. **Financial aid:** Priority filing date for institution's financial aid form: March 31; deadline: March 31. In 2009-2010, 82% of undergraduates applied for financial aid. Of those, 81% were determined to have financial need; Average financial aid package (proportion receiving): $17,000 (81%). Average amount of gift aid, such as scholarships or grants (proportion receiving): $1,500 (33%). Average amount of self-help aid, such as work study or loans (proportion receiving): $2,610 (81%). Average need-based loan (excluding PLUS or other private loans): $5,500. Among students who received need-based aid, the average percentage of need met: 80%. Among students who received aid based on merit, the average award (and the proportion receiving): $1,200 (18%). The average athletic scholarship (and the proportion receiving): $4,500 (1%). Average amount of debt of borrowers graduating in 2009: $33,500. Proportion who borrowed: 59%.

CAMPUS LIFE AND EXTRACURRICULAR ACTIVITIES

Campus housing available (% using): women's dorms (14%), men's dorms (12%), apartments for married students (10%), apartment for single students (15%). Students who live in college-owned, operated, or affiliated housing: 55%. Average per-year earnings: $1,540. Activities include: campus ministries, choral groups, drama/theater, international student organization, marching band, music ensembles, student government, student newspaper, student film society, yearbook. Number of fraternities: 8; sororities: 4. Proportion of men in fraternities: 6%; of women in sororities: 5%. Average proportion of students who stay on campus on weekends: 75%. **Sports program (2009-2010):** Member of NCAA II. *Men's intercollegiate varsity sports:* baseball, basketball, cross country, football, tennis, track and field (outdoor). *Women's intercollegiate varsity sports:* basketball, cross country, softball, tennis, track and field (outdoor), volleyball.

SERVICES AND FACILITIES

Basic services: placement service, day care, health service, health insurance. **Remedial assistance:** reading, math, writing, study skills. **Counseling services:** minority student, career, personal, veteran student, academic, birth control, religious. **For learning-disabled students:** School does not offer a structured program with separate admission and additional fees. Services include: remedial math, remedial English, remedial reading, diagnostic testing service, learning center. **Library:** Number of titles: 310,000; number of current serial subscriptions: 53,000. **Information technology resources:** Students are not required to lease or own a computer. Number of campus computers available to all students: 1,600. School has a wireless network. Proportion of college-owned housing units wired for high-speed internet access: 100%. **Campus safety:** Security services offered: 24-hour foot-and-vehicle patrols, late-night transport/escort service, 24-hour emergency telephones, lighted pathways/sidewalks, controlled dormitory access (key, security card, etc).

TRANSFER AND INTERNATIONAL STUDENTS

Transfer students: May apply for admission for the following academic terms: Fall, Spring, Summer. Applicants do not need a minimum number of credits to apply. For fall 2009: Transfer applications received: 602. Transfer applicants offered admission: 331. Transfer applicants enrolled: 149. **International students:** Number of foreign undergraduates: 34 (1% of student body). Minimum TOEFL score required: 500 (paper); 69 (computer).

University of Alabama

- **Address:** Box 870100, Tuscaloosa, AL 35487-0100
- **Website:** http://www.ua.edu
- **Public**
- **Enrollment:** 21,738 full-time; 1,962 part-time

KEY STATS

- ✔ **U.S News College Ranking:** 79, National Universities
- ✔ **ACT Score (25th/75th percentile):** 21-28
- ✔ **Tuition:** 2009-2010: $7,000 in state, $19,200 out of state

Selectivity: More selective	**Room/board:** $7,796
Acceptance rate: 57%	**Average debt:** $23,964
Student/faculty ratio: 20/1	**Proportion who borrowed:** 52%

UNDERGRADUATE STUDENT BODY STATS

2009-2010 enrollment: 21,738 full-time; 1,962 part-time. Men: 48%; women: 52%. **Ethnic makeup:** African American: 12%; American-Indian: 1%; Asian American: 1%; Hispanic: 2%; White: 83%; International: 1%. **Religious preference:** Roman Catholic: 9%; Protestant: 41%; Jewish: 1%; No preference: 19%; Unknown: 16%; Other: 14%.

ADMISSIONS FACTS AND FIGURES

Phone: (205) 348-5666. **Email:** admissions@ua.edu. **Website:** http://www.ua.edu. **Application deadlines for fall 2011:** Regular decision: Rolling. Early decision: Not offered. Early action: Not offered. Admission cannot be deferred. **Application fee:** $40. **To apply online, go to:** http://apply.ua.edu/. **Admissions requirements/recommendations:** High school units required (recommended): English: 4 (4); Mathematics: 3 (3); Science: 3 (3); Foreign language: 1 (1); Social studies: 4 (4); History: 1 (1); Academic electives: 5 (3); Total units: 15 (15). Tests: The college uses SAT or ACT scores in admissions decisions. Either SAT or ACT required. For admission to the fall 2011 entering class, the school will accept: ACT with writing required. Campus visit: Recommended. Admissions interview: Neither required nor recommended. Off-campus interview: May be arranged. **Factors that count in admissions decisions:** *Academic:* Secondary school record: Very Important. Class rank: Important. Letters of recommendation: Considered. Standardized test scores: Very Important. Essay: Considered. *Nonacademic:* Interview: Considered. Extracurricular activities: Considered. Talent/ability: Considered. Character/personal qualities: Considered. Alumni/ae relationship: Considered. Geographical residence: Not Considered. State residency: Not Considered. Religious affiliation/commitment: Not Considered. Minority status: Not Considered. Volunteer work: Considered. Work experience: Considered. **Other schools with the greatest overlap in applicants:** Auburn University; University of Alabama–Birmingham; University of Georgia; University of Mississippi; University of Tennessee. **Admissions statistics for the fall 2009 entering class:** Total applicants: 19,518. Total accepted: 11,194. Freshmen enrolled: 5,116; 38% were from out of state. Overall acceptance rate: 57%. **Credentials of fall 2009 freshmen:** 43% ranked in the top 10 percent of their high school class; 56% were in the top 25 percent; 79% were in the top half. (Proportion submitting class standing: 72%.) **Average high school grade point average:** 3.5. **First-year students who submitted SAT scores:** 19%. Scores (25/75 percentile): Critical Reading: 500-

600, Math: 500-620, Combined: 1000-1220. **First-year students submitting ACT scores:** 79%. Scores (25/75 percentile): English: 22-30, Math: 20-27, Composite: 21-28.

ACADEMICS

Year founded: 1831. **Academic calendar:** Semester. **Degrees offered:** bachelor's, master's, post-master's certificate, doctorate. **Most popular majors:** 27% business, management, marketing, and related support services, 11% communication, journalism, and related programs, 9% health professions and related clinical sciences, 8% family and consumer sciences/human sciences, 7% education. **Major fields of study:** area, ethnic, cultural, and gender studies; biological and biomedical sciences; business, management, marketing, and related support services; communication, journalism, and related programs; computer and information sciences and support services; education; engineering; English language and literature/letters; family and consumer sciences/human sciences; foreign languages, literatures, and linguistics; health professions and related clinical sciences; history; mathematics and statistics; multi/interdisciplinary studies; natural resources and conservation; philosophy and religious studies; physical sciences; psychology; public administration and social service professions; security and protective services; social sciences; visual and performing arts. **Areas of required coursework:** arts/fine arts, humanities, computer literacy, mathematics, English (including composition), philosophy, foreign languages, sciences (biological or physical), history, social science. **Pre-professional programs:** pre-law, pre-dentistry, pre-medicine, pre-veterinary science, pre-optometry, pre-pharmacy, other. **Special academic programs (% participation):** accelerated program (0%), cooperative (work-study plan) program (3.7%), cross-registration (0%), distance learning (56.8%), double major (5.7%), dual enrollment (0%), English as a Second Language (ESL) (.4%), exchange student program (domestic) (.1%), external degree program (1%), honors program (14.3%), independent study (28.5%), internships (19.4%), liberal arts/career combination, student-designed major (2.6%), study abroad (5.6%), teacher certificate program (7.3%), weekend college (3%). **Teacher certification offered in:** early childhood, special education, elementary, middle/junior high, secondary, bilingual/bicultural. **Cooperative education programs:** art, business, computer science, engineering, health professions, home economics, humanities, natural science, social/behavioral science, technologies. **Reserve Officers Training Corps (ROTC):** Army ROTC: Offered on campus; Air Force ROTC: Offered on campus. **Faculty and instruction (2009-2010):** Total instructional faculty: 1,068 full-time, 369 part-time (56% men; 44% women; 14% minorities). Full-time faculty with Ph.D. or other terminal degree: 88%. Student/faculty ratio: 20/1. Classes of fewer than 20 students: 43%; of 20 to 49 students: 41%; of 50 or more students: 16%. **Advanced Placement and International Baccalaureate credit:** AP tests may be used for: Credit and/or placement. Scores accepted: 3, 4, 5. International Baccalaureate exams may be used for: Credit and/or placement. **Freshmen returning for sophomore year:** 85%. **Graduation rates:** Four-year: 38%; five-year: 60%; six-year: 66%. **Graduate study:** 24% of students pursue further study within one year. Fields in which graduates pursue further study: law, 8%; medicine, 7%; theology (or the seminary), 2%.

COSTS AND FINANCIAL AID

Financial aid office: (205) 348-2976. **Expenses (2009-2010):** Tuition and fees 2009-2010: $7,000 in state, $19,200 out of state; room/board: $7,796. Estimated books and supplies: $1,100; transportation: $1,165; personal expenses: $1,900. **Financial aid:** Priority filing date for institution's financial aid form: March 1. In 2009-2010, 52% of undergraduates applied for financial aid. Of those, 39% were determined to have financial need; 14% had their need fully met. Average financial aid package (proportion receiving): $9,506 (39%). Average amount of gift aid, such as scholarships or grants (proportion receiving): $6,419 (28%). Average amount of self-help aid, such as work study or loans (proportion receiving): $4,265 (34%). Average need-based loan (excluding PLUS or other private loans): $4,106. Among students who received need-based aid, the average percentage of need met: 54%. Among students who received aid based on merit, the average award (and the proportion receiving): $6,947 (20%). The average athletic scholarship (and the proportion receiving): $20,345 (2%). Average amount of debt of borrowers graduating in 2009: $23,964. Proportion who borrowed: 52%.

CAMPUS LIFE AND EXTRACURRICULAR ACTIVITIES

Campus housing available (% using): coed dorms (66%), women's dorms (15%), men's dorms (7%), sorority housing (6%), fraternity housing (5%), apartments for married students (1%), apartment for single students (0%), special housing for disabled students (0%), other housing options (0%). Students who live in college-owned, operated, or affiliated housing: 29%. **Student employment:** During the 2009-2010 academic year, 28% of

undergraduates worked on campus. Average per-year earnings: $3,200. **Clubs and organizations:** Number of student organizations: 389. Activities include: campus ministries, choral groups, concert band, dance, drama/theater, international student organization, jazz band, literary magazine, marching band, model UN, music ensembles, musical theater, opera, pep band, radio station, student government, student newspaper, student film society, symphony orchestra, television station, yearbook. Number of fraternities: 30; sororities: 23. Proportion of men in fraternities: 22%; of women in sororities: 30%. Average proportion of students who stay on campus on weekends: 66%. **Sports program (2009-2010):** Member of NCAA I. **Men's intercollegiate varsity sports:** baseball, basketball, cross country, football, golf, swimming, tennis, track and field (indoor), track and field (outdoor). **Women's intercollegiate varsity sports:** basketball, crew (heavyweight), cross country, golf, gymnastics, soccer, softball, swimming, tennis, track and field (indoor), track and field (outdoor), volleyball.

SERVICES AND FACILITIES

Basic services: nonremedial tutoring, women's center, placement service, day care, health service, health insurance. **Remedial assistance:** reading, math, writing, study skills, other. **Counseling services:** minority student, career, military, personal, veteran student, academic, older student, psychological, birth control, religious. **For learning-disabled students:** School does not offer a structured program with separate admission and additional fees. Total undergraduates in learning-disabled program or receiving services: 429. Services include: remedial math, reading machines, diagnostic testing service, note-taking services, oral tests, learning center, extended time for tests, tutors, priority registration, priority seating, substitution of courses, texts on tape, typist/scribe, exams on tape or computer, other testing accommodations, other. **Library:** Number of titles: 3,313,998; number of current serial subscriptions: 79,938. **Information technology resources:** Students are not required to lease or own a computer. Number of campus computers available to all students: 2,500. School has a wireless network. Approximate number of users that can be accommodated: 8,000. Proportion of college-owned housing units wired for high-speed internet access: 100%. **Campus safety:** Security services offered: 24-hour foot-and-vehicle patrols, late-night transport/escort service, 24-hour emergency telephones, lighted pathways/sidewalks, controlled dormitory access (key, security card, etc).

TRANSFER AND INTERNATIONAL STUDENTS

Transfer students: May apply for admission for the following academic terms: Fall, Spring, Summer. Applicants need a minimum number of credits to apply. For fall 2009: Transfer applications received: 2,506. Transfer applicants offered admission: 2,083. Transfer applicants enrolled: 1,187. **International students:** Number of foreign undergraduates: 204 (1% of student body). Number of countries represented: 66. Minimum TOEFL score required: 500 (paper); 61 (computer). Average TOEFL score: 520 (paper).

University of Alabama–Birmingham

- **Address:** 1530 Third Avenue S, Birmingham, AL 35294
- **Website:** http://www.uab.edu
- **Public**
- **Enrollment:** 7,938 full-time; 2,708 part-time

KEY STATS

✔ **U.S News College Ranking:** 151, National Universities
✔ **ACT Score (25th/75th percentile):** 21-27
✔ **Tuition:** 2009-2010: $5,096 in state, $11,432 out of state

Selectivity: Selective	**Room/board:** $8,142
Acceptance rate: 84%	**Average debt:** $21,670
Student/faculty ratio: 17/1	**Proportion who borrowed:** 53%

UNDERGRADUATE STUDENT BODY STATS

2009-2010 enrollment: 7,938 full-time; 2,708 part-time. Men: 42%; women: 58%. **Ethnic makeup:** African American: 26%; Asian American: 4%; Hispanic: 2%; White: 65%; International: 2%.

ADMISSIONS FACTS AND FIGURES

Phone: (205) 934-8221. **Email:** undergradadmit@uab.edu. **Website:** http://www.uab.edu. **Application deadlines for fall 2011:** Regular decision: Rolling. Early decision: Not offered. Early action: Not offered. Admission can be deferred. **Application fee:** $35. **To apply online, go to:** http://www.uab.edu/apply. **Admissions requirements/recommendations:** High school units required (recommended): English: 4 (4); Mathematics: 3 (3); Science: 3 (3); Foreign language: 1 (1); Social studies: 3 (3); Academic electives: 3 (3); Total units: 17 (17). Tests: The college uses SAT or ACT scores in admissions decisions. Either SAT or ACT required. For admission to the fall 2011 entering class, the school will accept: ACT with or without writing accepted. Campus visit: Neither required nor recommended. Admissions interview: Neither required nor recommended. Off-campus interview: May be arranged. **Factors that count in admissions decisions: Academic:** Secondary school record: Very Important. Class rank: Not Considered. Letters of recommendation: Not Considered. Standardized test scores: Very Important. Essay: Not Considered. **Nonacademic:** Interview: Not Considered. Extracurricular activities: Not Considered. Talent/ability: Not Considered. Character/personal qualities: Not Considered. Alumni/ae relationship: Not Considered. Geographical residence: Not Considered. State residency: Not Considered. Religious affiliation/commitment: Not Considered. Minority status: Not Considered. Volunteer work: Not Considered. Work experience: Not Considered. **Other schools with the greatest overlap in applicants:** Auburn University; University of Alabama; University of Alabama–Huntsville. **Admissions statistics for the fall 2009 entering class:** Total applicants: 4,418. Total accepted: 3,692. Freshmen enrolled: 1,517; 8% were from out of state. Overall acceptance rate: 84%. **Credentials of fall 2009 freshmen:** 27% ranked in the top 10 percent of their high school class; 55% were in the top 25 percent; 77% were in the top half. (Proportion submitting class standing: 73%.) **Average high school grade point average:** 3.5. **First-year students who submitted SAT scores:** 6%. **First-year students submitting ACT scores:** 93%. Scores (25/75 percentile): English: 21-28, Math: 19-26, Composite: 21-27.

ACADEMICS

Year founded: 1969. **Academic calendar:** Semester. **Degrees offered:** certificate, bachelor's, post-bachelor's certificate, master's, post-master's certificate, doctorate. **Most popular majors:** 19% health professions and related clinical sciences, 16% business, management, marketing, and related support services, 10% education, 8% psychology, 7% biological and biomedical sciences. **Major fields of study:** area, ethnic, cultural, and gender studies; biological and biomedical sciences; business, management, marketing, and related support services; communication, journalism, and related programs; computer and information sciences and support services; education; engineering; English language and literature/letters; foreign languages, literatures, and linguistics; health professions and related clinical sciences; history; mathematics and statistics; multi/interdisciplinary studies; philosophy and religious studies; physical sciences; psychology; public administration and social service professions; security and protective services; social sciences; visual and performing arts. **Areas of required coursework:** arts/fine arts, computer literacy, mathematics, English (including composition), philosophy, foreign languages, sciences (biological or physical), history, social science, other. **Pre-professional programs:** pre-law, pre-dentistry, pre-medicine, pre-optometry, other. **Special academic programs:** accelerated program, cooperative (work-study plan) program, cross-registration, distance learning, double major, dual enrollment, English as a Second Language (ESL), honors program, independent study, internships, student-designed major, study abroad, teacher certificate program. **Teacher certification offered in:** early childhood, special education, elementary, middle/junior high, secondary. **Cooperative education programs:** art, business, computer science, engineering, health professions, humanities, natural science, social/behavioral science. **Reserve Officers Training Corps (ROTC):** Army ROTC: Offered on campus; Air Force ROTC: Offered at cooperating institution (Samford University). **Faculty and instruction (2009-2010):** Total instructional faculty: 833 full-time, 81 part-time (56% men; 44% women; 20% minorities). Full-time faculty with Ph.D. or other terminal degree: 86%. Student/faculty ratio: 17/1. Classes of fewer than 20 students: 40%; of 20 to 49 students: 45%; of 50 or more students: 15%. **Advanced Placement and International Baccalaureate credit:** AP tests may be used for: Credit only. Scores accepted: 3, 4, 5. International Baccalaureate exams may be used for: Credit only. **Freshmen returning for sophomore year:** 78%. **Graduation rates:** Four-year: 17%; five-year: 32%; six-year: 39%.

COSTS AND FINANCIAL AID

Financial aid office: (205) 934-8223. **Expenses (2009-2010):** Tuition and fees 2009-2010: $5,096 in state, $11,432 out of state; room/board: $8,142. Estimated books and supplies: $1,000; transportation: $2,050; personal expenses: $2,000. **Financial aid:** Priority filing date for institution's financial aid form: March 1. In 2009-2010, 66% of undergraduates applied for financial aid. Of those, 53% were determined to have financial need; 15% had their need fully met. Average financial aid package (proportion receiving): $9,334 (51%). Average amount of gift aid, such as scholarships or grants

(proportion receiving): $5,063 (33%). Average amount of self-help aid, such as work study or loans (proportion receiving): $4,777 (42%). Average need-based loan (excluding PLUS or other private loans): $4,394. Among students who received need-based aid, the average percentage of need met: 50%. Among students who received aid based on merit, the average award (and the proportion receiving): $6,449 (16%). The average athletic scholarship (and the proportion receiving): $16,659 (4%). Average amount of debt of borrowers graduating in 2009: $21,670. Proportion who borrowed: 53%.

CAMPUS LIFE AND EXTRACURRICULAR ACTIVITIES

Campus housing available (% using): coed dorms (100%), apartments for married students, apartment for single students, special housing for disabled students (0%), special housing for international students. Students who live in college-owned, operated, or affiliated housing: 20%. **Clubs and organizations:** Number of student organizations: 200. Activities include: campus ministries, choral groups, concert band, dance, drama/theater, international student organization, jazz band, literary magazine, marching band, music ensembles, musical theater, opera, pep band, radio station, student government, student newspaper. Number of fraternities: 6; sororities: 7. Proportion of men in fraternities: 6%; of women in sororities: 6%. **Sports program (2009-2010):** Member of NCAA I. **Men's intercollegiate varsity sports:** baseball, basketball, football, golf, rifle, soccer, tennis. **Women's intercollegiate varsity sports:** basketball, cross country, golf, rifle, soccer, softball, sync swimming, tennis, track and field (indoor), track and field (outdoor), volleyball.

SERVICES AND FACILITIES

Basic services: nonremedial tutoring, women's center, placement service, day care, health service, health insurance. **Remedial assistance:** reading, math, writing, study skills. **Counseling services:** career, personal, veteran student, academic. **For learning-disabled students:** School does not offer a structured program with separate admission and additional fees. Services include: remedial math, remedial English, reading machines, tape recorders, note-taking services, oral tests, readers, extended time for tests, priority registration, priority seating, texts on tape, other testing accommodations. **Library:** Number of titles: 1,365,041; number of current serial subscriptions: 67,902. **Information technology resources:** Students are not required to lease or own a computer. School has a wireless network. Proportion of college-owned housing units wired for high-speed internet access: 100%. **Campus safety:** Security services offered: 24-hour foot-and-vehicle patrols, late-night transport/escort service, 24-hour emergency telephones, lighted pathways/sidewalks, controlled dormitory access (key, security card, etc).

TRANSFER AND INTERNATIONAL STUDENTS

Transfer students: May apply for admission for the following academic terms: Fall, Spring, Summer. Applicants need a minimum number of credits to apply. For fall 2009: Transfer applications received: 1,997. Transfer applicants offered admission: 1,694. Transfer applicants enrolled: 1,064. **International students:** Number of foreign undergraduates: 218 (2% of student body). Number of countries represented: 65. Minimum TOEFL score required: 500 (paper); 173 (computer).

University of Alabama–Huntsville

- **Address:** 301 Sparkman Drive, Huntsville, AL 35899
- **Website:** http://www.uah.edu
- **Public**
- **Enrollment:** 4,640 full-time; 1,479 part-time

KEY STATS
✔ **U.S News College Ranking:** 179, National Universities
✔ **ACT Score (25th/75th percentile):** 22-28
✔ **Tuition:** 2009-2010: $7,161 in state, $16,279 out of state
Selectivity: More selective **Room/board:** $7,208
Acceptance rate: 72% **Average debt:** $24,938
Student/faculty ratio: 17/1 **Proportion who borrowed:** 26%

UNDERGRADUATE STUDENT BODY STATS
2009-2010 enrollment: 4,640 full-time; 1,479 part-time. Men: 53%; women: 47%. **Ethnic makeup:** African American: 15%; American-Indian: 2%; Asian American: 3%; Hispanic: 2%; White: 75%; International: 3%.

ADMISSIONS FACTS AND FIGURES

Phone: (256) 824-6070. **Email:** admitme@uah.edu. **Website:** http://www.uah.edu. **Application deadlines for fall 2011:** Regular decision: August 15. Early decision: Not offered. Early action: Not offered. Admission can be deferred. **Application fee:** $30. **To apply online, go to:** http://www.uah.edu/main/uah/applynow.php. **Admissions requirements/recommendations:** High school units required (recommended): English: 4 (4); Mathematics: 3 (4); Science: 3 (4); Foreign language: 0 (2); Social studies: 4 (4); Academic electives: 6 (6); Total units: 20 (20). Tests: The college uses SAT or ACT scores in admissions decisions. Either SAT or ACT required. For admission to the fall 2011 entering class, the school will accept: ACT with or without writing accepted. Campus visit: Recommended. Admissions interview: Neither required nor recommended. Off-campus interview: Not available. **Factors that count in admissions decisions:** *Academic:* Secondary school record: Very Important. Class rank: Considered. Letters of recommendation: Considered. Standardized test scores: Very Important. Essay: Considered. *Nonacademic:* Interview: Not Considered. Extracurricular activities: Not Considered. Talent/ability: Not Considered. Character/personal qualities: Not Considered. Alumni/ae relationship: Not Considered. Geographical residence: Not Considered. State residency: Not Considered. Religious affiliation/commitment: Not Considered. Minority status: Not Considered. Volunteer work: Not Considered. Work experience: Not Considered. **Other schools with the greatest overlap in applicants:** Auburn University; Jacksonville State University; University of Alabama; University of Alabama–Birmingham; University of North Alabama. **Admissions statistics for the fall 2009 entering class:** Total applicants: 1,924. Total accepted: 1,387. Freshmen enrolled: 802; 15% were from out of state. Overall acceptance rate: 72%. **Credentials of fall 2009 freshmen:** 34% ranked in the top 10 percent of their high school class; 63% were in the top 25 percent; 85% were in the top half. (Proportion submitting class standing: 24%.) **Average high school grade point average:** 3.6. **First-year students who submitted SAT scores:** 21%. Scores (25/75 percentile): Critical Reading: 500-630, Math: 520-640, Combined: 1020-1270. **First-year students submitting ACT scores:** 92%. Scores (25/75 percentile): English: 22-29, Math: 21-27, Composite: 22-28.

ACADEMICS

Year founded: 1950. **Academic calendar:** Semester. **Degrees offered:** bachelor's, post-bachelor's certificate, master's, post-master's certificate, doctorate. **Major fields of study:** biological and biomedical sciences; business, management, marketing, and related support services; computer and information sciences and support services; education; engineering; English language and literature/letters; foreign languages, literatures, and linguistics; health professions and related clinical sciences; history; mathematics and statistics; philosophy and religious studies; physical sciences; psychology; social sciences; visual and performing arts. **Areas of required coursework:** arts/fine arts, humanities, computer literacy, mathematics, English (including composition), sciences (biological or physical), history, social science. **Preprofessional programs:** pre-law, pre-dentistry, pre-medicine, pre-veterinary science, pre-optometry, pre-pharmacy, other. **Special academic programs (% participation):** cooperative (work-study plan) program (11.5%), cross-registration, distance learning (7.1%), double major (3.7%), dual enrollment (2.5%), English as a Second Language (ESL) (2.4%), honors program (5%), independent study, internships (14.3%), liberal arts/career combination (1.4%), study abroad (.6%), teacher certificate program (4.2%), other (1%). **Teacher certification offered in:** special education, elementary, middle/junior high, secondary. **Cooperative education programs:** art, business, computer science, education, engineering, health professions, humanities, natural science, social/behavioral science, technologies. **Reserve Officers Training Corps (ROTC):** Army ROTC: Offered at cooperating institution (Alabama Agricultural and Mechanical University). **Faculty and instruction (2009-2010):** Total instructional faculty: 303 full-time, 154 part-time (59% men; 41% women; 17% minorities). Full-time faculty with Ph.D. or other terminal degree: 90%. Student/faculty ratio: 17/1. Classes of fewer than 20 students: 40%; of 20 to 49 students: 46%; of 50 or more students: 14%. **Advanced Placement and International Baccalaureate credit:** AP tests may be used for: Credit and/or placement. Scores accepted: 2, 3, 4, 5. International Baccalaureate exams may be used for: Credit and/or placement. **Freshmen returning for sophomore year:** 77%. **Graduation rates:** Four-year: 17%; five-year: 39%; six-year: 48%. **Graduate study:** 28% of students pursue further study immediately upon graduation. Fields in which graduates pursue further study: Master of Business Administration (MBA), 29%; medicine, 4%; engineering, 21%; education, 13%; arts and sciences, 33%.

COSTS AND FINANCIAL AID

Financial aid office: (256) 824-6241. **Expenses (2009-2010):** Tuition and fees 2009-2010: $7,161 in state, $16,279 out of state; room/board: $7,208. Estimated books and supplies: $1,542; transportation: $2,067; personal expenses: $1,928. **Financial aid:** Priority filing date for institution's financial aid form: April 1; deadline: July 31. In 2009-2010, 80% of undergraduates applied for financial aid. Of those, 49% were determined to have financial need; 9% had their need fully met. Average financial aid package (proportion receiving): $8,226 (49%). Average amount of gift aid, such as scholarships or grants (proportion receiving): $5,372 (37%). Average amount of self-help aid, such as work study or loans (proportion receiving): $7,452 (44%). Average need-based loan (excluding PLUS or other private loans): $7,286. Among students who received need-based aid, the average percentage of need met: 57%. Among students who received aid based on merit, the average award (and the proportion receiving): $4,332 (18%). The average athletic scholarship (and the proportion receiving): $8,096 (4%). Average amount of debt of borrowers graduating in 2009: $24,938. Proportion who borrowed: 26%.

CAMPUS LIFE AND EXTRACURRICULAR ACTIVITIES

Campus housing available (% using): coed dorms (80%), sorority housing (1%), fraternity housing (1%), apartments for married students (1%), apartment for single students (1%), special housing for disabled students (1%), other housing options (1%). Students who live in college-owned, operated, or affiliated housing: 20%. **Student employment:** During the 2009-2010 academic year, 10% of undergraduates worked on campus. Average per-year earnings: $6,708. **Clubs and organizations:** Number of student organizations: 53. Activities include: campus ministries, choral groups, concert band, dance, drama/theater, international student organization, jazz band, literary magazine, model UN, music ensembles, pep band, student government, student newspaper. Number of fraternities: 7; sororities: 4. Proportion of men in fraternities: 5%; of women in sororities: 7%. Average proportion of students who stay on campus on weekends: 55%. **Sports program (2009-2010):** Member of NCAA II. *Men's intercollegiate varsity sports:* baseball, basketball, cross country, ice hockey, soccer, tennis, track and field (indoor), track and field (outdoor). *Women's intercollegiate varsity sports:* basketball, cross country, soccer, softball, tennis, track and field (indoor), track and field (outdoor), volleyball.

SERVICES AND FACILITIES

Basic services: nonremedial tutoring, placement service, day care, health service, health insurance, other. **Remedial assistance:** reading, math, writing, study skills. **Counseling services:** minority student, career, military, personal, veteran student, academic, older student, psychological, birth control, religious. **For learning-disabled students:** School does not offer a structured program with separate admission and additional fees. Total undergraduates in learning-disabled program or receiving services: 122. Services include: remedial math, remedial English, reading machines, remedial reading, tape recorders, videotaped classes, untimed tests, note-taking services, oral tests, learning center, readers, extended time for tests, tutors, priority seating, texts on tape, typist/scribe, other testing accommodations. **Library:** Number of titles: 323,637; number of current serial subscriptions: 27,481. **Information technology resources:** Students are not required to lease or own a computer. Number of campus computers available to all students: 1,206. School has a wireless network. Approximate number of users that can be accommodated: 1,500. Proportion of college-owned housing units wired for high-speed internet access: 100%. **Campus safety:** Security services offered: 24-hour foot-and-vehicle patrols, late-night transport/escort service, 24-hour emergency telephones, lighted pathways/sidewalks, controlled dormitory access (key, security card, etc).

TRANSFER AND INTERNATIONAL STUDENTS

Transfer students: May apply for admission for the following academic terms: Fall, Spring, Summer. Applicants need a minimum number of credits to apply. For fall 2009: Transfer applications received: 1,574. Transfer applicants offered admission: 1,175. Transfer applicants enrolled: 758. **International students:** Number of foreign undergraduates: 184 (3% of student body). Number of countries represented: 45. Minimum TOEFL score required: 500 (paper); 173 (computer). Average TOEFL score: 526 (paper).

University of Mobile

- **Address:** 5735 College Parkway, Mobile, AL 36613-2842
- **Website:** http://www.umobile.edu
- **Private; Religious affiliation:** Baptist
- **Enrollment:** 1,257 full-time; 160 part-time

KEY STATS

✔ **U.S News College Ranking:** 59, Regional Universities (South)
✔ **ACT Score (25th/75th percentile):** 19-25
✔ **Tuition:** 2010-2011: $16,120

Selectivity: Selective	**Room/board:** $7,780
Acceptance rate: 78%	**Average debt:** $18,840
Student/faculty ratio: 12/1	**Proportion who borrowed:** 25%

UNDERGRADUATE STUDENT BODY STATS

2009-2010 enrollment: 1,257 full-time; 160 part-time. Men: 34%; women: 66%. **Ethnic makeup:** African American: 22%; American-Indian: 2%; Hispanic: 1%; White: 73%; International: 2%. **Religious preference:** Baptist: 66%; Other: 34%.

ADMISSIONS FACTS AND FIGURES

Phone: (251) 442-2273. **Email:** adminfo@umobile.edu. **Website:** http://www.umobile.edu. **Application deadlines for fall 2011:** Regular decision: August 1. Early decision: Not offered. Early action: Not offered. Admission can be deferred. **Application fee:** $50. **To apply online, go to:** http://www.umobile.edu/admissions/admapply.asp. **Admissions requirements/recommendations:** High school units required (recommended): English: (4); Mathematics: (3); Foreign language: (2); Social studies: (3); Total units: (22). Tests: The college uses SAT or ACT scores in admissions decisions. Either SAT or ACT required. For admission to the fall 2011 entering class, the school will accept: ACT with or without writing accepted. Campus visit: Recommended. Admissions interview: Neither required nor recommended. Off-campus interview: May be arranged. **Factors that count in admissions decisions:** *Academic:* Secondary school record: Considered. Class rank: Considered. Letters of recommendation: Considered. Standardized test scores: Very Important. Essay: Not Considered. *Nonacademic:* Interview: Not Considered. Extracurricular activities: Considered. Talent/ability: Considered. Character/personal qualities: Considered. Alumni/ae relationship: Not Considered. Geographical residence: Not Considered. State residency: Not Considered. Religious affiliation/commitment: Not Considered. Minority status: Not Considered. Volunteer work: Not Considered. Work experience: Not Considered. **Other schools with the greatest overlap in applicants:** Faulkner University; Spring Hill College; University of South Alabama. **Admissions statistics for the fall 2009 entering class:** Total applicants: 796. Total accepted: 618. Freshmen enrolled: 228; 29% were from out of state. Overall acceptance rate: 78%. **Credentials of fall 2009 freshmen:** 27% ranked in the top 10 percent of their high school class; 55% were in the top 25 percent; 79% were in the top half. (Proportion submitting class standing: 59%.) **Average high school grade point average:** 3.3. **First-year students who submitted SAT scores:** 16%. Scores (25/75 percentile): Critical Reading: 470-590, Math: 430-540, Combined: 900-1130. **First-year students submitting ACT scores:** 85%. Scores (25/75 percentile): English: 20-26, Math: 17-24, Composite: 19-25.

ACADEMICS

Year founded: 1961. **Academic calendar:** Semester. **Degrees offered:** associate, bachelor's, master's. **Most popular majors:** 21% business, management, marketing, and related support services, 20% education, 16% health professions and related clinical sciences, 12% philosophy and religious studies, 8% liberal arts and sciences studies, and humanities. **Major fields of study:** biological and biomedical sciences; business, management, marketing, and related support services; communication, journalism, and related programs; computer and information sciences and support services; education; English language and literature/letters; health professions and related clinical sciences; history; mathematics and statistics; multi/interdisciplinary studies; philosophy and religious studies; physical sciences; psychology; social sciences; visual and performing arts. **Areas of required coursework:** arts/fine arts, humanities, computer literacy, mathematics, English (including composition), sciences (biological or physical), history, social science, other. **Pre-professional programs:** pre-law, pre-dentistry, pre-medicine, pre-veterinary science, pre-pharmacy, other. **Special academic programs:** accelerated program, double major, dual enrollment, honors program, independent study, internships, teacher certificate program. **Teacher certifica-**

tion offered in: early childhood, elementary, middle/junior high, secondary. **Reserve Officers Training Corps (ROTC):** Army ROTC: Offered at cooperating institution (University of South Alabama); Air Force ROTC: Offered at cooperating institution (University of South Alabama). **Faculty and instruction (2009-2010):** Total instructional faculty: 84 full-time, 78 part-time (52% men; 48% women; 8% minorities). Full-time faculty with Ph.D. or other terminal degree: 61%. Student/faculty ratio: 12/1. Classes of fewer than 20 students: 54%; of 20 to 49 students: 46%; of 50 or more students: 0%. **Advanced Placement and International Baccalaureate credit:** AP tests may be used for: Credit only. Scores accepted: 3, 4, 5. International Baccalaureate exams may be used for: Credit only. **Freshmen returning for sophomore year:** 73%. **Graduation rates:** Four-year: 43%; five-year: 58%; six-year: 48%. **Graduate study:** 14% of students pursue further study immediately upon graduation; 5% within one year; 5% within five years. Fields in which graduates pursue further study: Master of Business Administration (MBA), 25%; law, 5%; medicine, 5%; theology (or the seminary), 20%; education, 25%; arts and sciences, 20%.

COSTS AND FINANCIAL AID

Financial aid office: (251) 442-2385. **Expenses (2010-2011):** Tuition and fees 2010-2011: $16,120; room/board: $7,780. Estimated books and supplies: $1,500; transportation: $1,100; personal expenses: $1,700. **Financial aid:** In 2009-2010, 76% of undergraduates applied for financial aid. Of those, 76% were determined to have financial need; Average financial aid package (proportion receiving): $12,998 (72%). Average amount of gift aid, such as scholarships or grants (proportion receiving): $8,765 (71%). Average amount of self-help aid, such as work study or loans (proportion receiving): $4,785 (60%). Average need-based loan (excluding PLUS or other private loans): $5,505. Among students who received need-based aid, the average percentage of need met: 59%. Among students who received aid based on merit, the average award (and the proportion receiving): $5,830 (7%). The average athletic scholarship (and the proportion receiving): $10,556 (2%). Average amount of debt of borrowers graduating in 2009: $18,840. Proportion who borrowed: 25%.

CAMPUS LIFE AND EXTRACURRICULAR ACTIVITIES

Campus housing available (% using): women's dorms (60%), men's dorms (40%). Students who live in college-owned, operated, or affiliated housing: 39%. **Student employment:** During the 2009-2010 academic year, 3% of undergraduates worked on campus. Average per-year earnings: $1,800. **Clubs and organizations:** Number of student organizations: 33. Activities include: campus ministries, choral groups, concert band, jazz band, music ensembles, musical theater, opera, pep band, student government, symphony orchestra. Number of fraternities: 0; sororities: 0. Average proportion of students who stay on campus on weekends: 30%. **Sports program (2009-2010):** Member of NAIA. *Men's intercollegiate varsity sports:* baseball, basketball, cross country, golf, soccer, tennis. *Women's intercollegiate varsity sports:* basketball, cross country, golf, soccer, softball, tennis, volleyball.

SERVICES AND FACILITIES

Basic services: nonremedial tutoring, health service, health insurance. **Remedial assistance:** reading, math, writing, study skills. **Counseling services:** career, military, personal, veteran student, academic, older student, religious. **For learning-disabled students:** School does not offer a structured program with separate admission and additional fees. Services include: remedial math, remedial English, remedial reading, tape recorders, untimed tests, oral tests, learning center, extended time for tests, priority seating. **Library:** Number of titles: 69,508; number of current serial subscriptions: 323. **Information technology resources:** Students are not required to lease or own a computer. Number of campus computers available to all students: 120. School has a wireless network. Approximate number of users that can be accommodated: 100. Proportion of college-owned housing units wired for high-speed internet access: 100%. **Campus safety:** Security services offered: 24-hour foot-and-vehicle patrols, lighted pathways/sidewalks, controlled dormitory access (key, security card, etc).

TRANSFER AND INTERNATIONAL STUDENTS

Transfer students: May apply for admission for the following academic terms: Fall, Spring, Summer. Applicants do not need a minimum number of credits to apply. For fall 2009: Transfer applications received: 386. Transfer applicants offered admission: 299. Transfer applicants enrolled: 157. **International students:** Number of foreign undergraduates: 22 (2% of student body). Minimum TOEFL score required: 500 (paper); 173 (computer). Average TOEFL score: 500 (paper).

University of Montevallo

- **Address:** Station 6030, Montevallo, AL 35115
- **Website:** http://www.montevallo.edu
- **Public**
- **Enrollment:** 2,275 full-time; 296 part-time

KEY STATS

✔ **U.S News College Ranking:** 40, Regional Universities (South)
✔ **ACT Score (25th/75th percentile):** 20-26
✔ **Tuition:** 2009-2010: $7,010 in state, $13,550 out of state
  Selectivity: Selective   **Room/board:** $4,440
  Acceptance rate: 72%   **Average debt:** $16,581
  Student/faculty ratio: 16/1 **Proportion who borrowed:** 54%

UNDERGRADUATE STUDENT BODY STATS

2009-2010 enrollment: 2,275 full-time; 296 part-time. Men: 33%; women: 67%. **Ethnic makeup:** African American: 10%; American-Indian: 1%; Asian American: 5%; Hispanic: 2%; White: 80%; International: 2%.

ADMISSIONS FACTS AND FIGURES

Phone: (205) 665-6030. **Email:** admissions@um.montevallo.edu. **Website:** http://www.montevallo.edu. **Application deadlines for fall 2011:** Regular decision: August 1. Early decision: Not offered. Early action: Not offered. Admission can be deferred. **Application fee:** $25. **To apply online, go to:** https://bansss.montevallo.edu:1444/pls/PROD/bwskalog.P_DispLoginNon. **Admissions requirements/recommendations:** High school units required (recommended): English: 4; Mathematics: 2 (3); Science: 2 (3); Foreign language: (2); Social studies: 2 (2); History: 2; Academic electives: 4; Total units: 16. Tests: The college uses SAT or ACT scores in admissions decisions. Either SAT or ACT required. For admission to the fall 2011 entering class, the school will accept: ACT with or without writing accepted. Campus visit: Recommended. Admissions interview: Recommended. Off-campus interview: May be arranged. **Factors that count in admissions decisions:** *Academic:* Secondary school record: Very Important. Class rank: Considered. Letters of recommendation: Considered. Standardized test scores: Very Important. Essay: Not Considered. *Nonacademic:* Interview: Considered. Extracurricular activities: Considered. Talent/ability: Considered. Character/personal qualities: Considered. Alumni/ae relationship: Considered. Geographical residence: Not Considered. State residency: Not Considered. Religious affiliation/commitment: Not Considered. Minority status: Not Considered. Volunteer work: Not Considered. Work experience: Considered. **Other schools with the greatest overlap in applicants:** Auburn University; Samford University; Troy University; University of Alabama; University of Alabama–Birmingham. **Admissions statistics for the fall 2009 entering class:** Total applicants: 1,350. Total accepted: 976. Freshmen enrolled: 429; 4% were from out of state. Overall acceptance rate: 72%. **First-year students who submitted SAT scores:** 4%. **First-year students submitting ACT scores:** 91%. Scores (25/75 percentile): English: 20-28, Math: 18-24, Composite: 20-26.

ACADEMICS

Year founded: 1896. **Academic calendar:** Semester. **Degrees offered:** bachelor's, master's, post-master's certificate. **Most popular majors:** 17% business, management, marketing, and related support services, 14% visual and performing arts, 11% family and consumer sciences/human sciences, 10% education, 7% English language and literature/letters. **Major fields of study:** biological and biomedical sciences; business, management, marketing, and related support services; communication, journalism, and related programs; education; English language and literature/letters; family and consumer sciences/human sciences; foreign languages, literatures, and linguistics; health professions and related clinical sciences; history; mathematics and statistics; parks, recreation, leisure, and fitness studies; physical sciences; psychology; public administration and social service professions; social sciences; visual and performing arts. **Areas of required coursework:** arts/fine arts, humanities, computer literacy, mathematics, English (including composition), philosophy, foreign languages, sciences (biological or physical), history, social science, other. **Pre-professional programs:** pre-law, pre-dentistry, pre-medicine, pre-optometry, pre-pharmacy, other. **Special academic programs:** accelerated program, cross-registration, double major, dual enrollment, honors program, independent study, internships, study abroad, teacher certificate program. **Teacher certification offered in:** early childhood, special education, elementary, vo-tech, middle/junior high, secondary. **Cooperative education programs:** business, computer science,

engineering. **Reserve Officers Training Corps (ROTC):** Army ROTC: Offered at cooperating institution (University of Alabama–Birmingham); Air Force ROTC: Offered at cooperating institution (Samford University). **Faculty and instruction (2009-2010):** Total instructional faculty: 137 full-time, 80 part-time (41% men; 59% women; 11% minorities). Full-time faculty with Ph.D. or other terminal degree: 94%. Student/faculty ratio: 16/1. Classes of fewer than 20 students: 52%; of 20 to 49 students: 47%; of 50 or more students: 0%. **Advanced Placement and International Baccalaureate credit:** AP tests may be used for: Credit only. Scores accepted: 3, 4, 5. International Baccalaureate exams may be used for: Credit only. **Freshmen returning for sophomore year:** 74%. **Graduation rates:** Four-year: 22%; five-year: 40%; six-year: 46%.

COSTS AND FINANCIAL AID

Financial aid office: (205) 665-6050. **Expenses (2009-2010):** Tuition and fees 2009-2010: $7,010 in state, $13,550 out of state; room/board: $4,440. Estimated books and supplies: $1,000; transportation: $1,400; personal expenses: $2,050. **Financial aid:** Priority filing date for institution's financial aid form: April 1. In 2009-2010, 68% of undergraduates applied for financial aid. Of those, 52% were determined to have financial need; 29% had their need fully met. Average financial aid package (proportion receiving): $8,531 (52%). Average amount of gift aid, such as scholarships or grants (proportion receiving): $5,979 (43%). Average amount of self-help aid, such as work study or loans (proportion receiving): $4,013 (44%). Average need-based loan (excluding PLUS or other private loans): $3,880. Among students who received need-based aid, the average percentage of need met: 67%. Among students who received aid based on merit, the average award (and the proportion receiving): $5,370 (17%). The average athletic scholarship (and the proportion receiving): $8,766 (4%). Average amount of debt of borrowers graduating in 2009: $16,581. Proportion who borrowed: 54%.

CAMPUS LIFE AND EXTRACURRICULAR ACTIVITIES

Campus housing available (% using): coed dorms, women's dorms (70%), men's dorms (30%), sorority housing, fraternity housing, apartments for married students, apartment for single students, special housing for disabled students. Students who live in college-owned, operated, or affiliated housing: 43%. **Student employment:** During the 2009-2010 academic year, 10% of undergraduates worked on campus. Average per-year earnings: $5,655. **Clubs and organizations:** Number of student organizations: 93. Activities include: campus ministries, choral groups, concert band, dance, drama/theater, international student organization, jazz band, literary magazine, model UN, music ensembles, musical theater, pep band, student government, student newspaper, television station, yearbook. Number of fraternities: 7; sororities: 8. Proportion of men in fraternities: 23%; of women in sororities: 18%. Average proportion of students who stay on campus on weekends: 30%. **Sports program (2009-2010):** Member of NCAA II. *Men's intercollegiate varsity sports:* baseball, basketball, golf, soccer. *Women's intercollegiate varsity sports:* basketball, cross country, golf, soccer, tennis, volleyball.

SERVICES AND FACILITIES

Basic services: nonremedial tutoring, placement service, health service. **Remedial assistance:** reading, math, writing, study skills. **Counseling services:** minority student, career, personal, academic, older student, birth control. **For learning-disabled students:** School does not offer a structured program with separate admission and additional fees. Total undergraduates in learning-disabled program or receiving services: 67. Services include: tape recorders, note-taking services, learning center, readers, extended time for tests, tutors, early syllabus, priority registration, priority seating, texts on tape, typist/scribe, exams on tape or computer, other testing accommodations, other. **Library:** Number of titles: 265,877; number of current serial subscriptions: 635. **Information technology resources:** Students are not required to lease or own a computer. Number of campus computers available to all students: 340. School has a wireless network. Approximate number of users that can be accommodated: 2,000. Proportion of college-owned housing units wired for high-speed internet access: 100%. **Campus safety:** Security services offered: 24-hour foot-and-vehicle patrols, late-night transport/escort service, 24-hour emergency telephones, lighted pathways/sidewalks, controlled dormitory access (key, security card, etc).

TRANSFER AND INTERNATIONAL STUDENTS

Transfer students: May apply for admission for the following academic terms: Fall, Spring, Summer. Applicants need a minimum number of credits to apply. For fall 2009: Transfer applications received: 490. Transfer applicants offered admission: 327. Transfer applicants enrolled: 192. **International students:** Number of foreign undergraduates: 62 (2% of stu-

dent body). Number of countries represented: 21. Minimum TOEFL score required: 525 (paper); 195 (computer). Average TOEFL score: 525 (paper).

University of North Alabama

- **Address:** UNA Box 5121, Florence, AL 35632
- **Website:** http://www.una.edu
- **Public**
- **Enrollment:** 5,023 full-time; 1,172 part-time

....

KEY STATS

✔ **U.S News College Ranking:** 66, Regional Universities (South)

✔ **ACT Score (25th/75th percentile):** 18-24

✔ **Tuition:** 2009-2010: $6,042 in state, $11,052 out of state

Selectivity: Selective
Acceptance rate: 82%
Student/faculty ratio: 19/1

Room/board: $4,784
Average debt: $24,500
Proportion who borrowed: 64%

UNDERGRADUATE STUDENT BODY STATS

2009-2010 enrollment: 5,023 full-time; 1,172 part-time. Men: 43%; women: 57%. **Ethnic makeup:** African American: 13%; American-Indian: 1%; Hispanic: 2%; White: 77%; International: 6%.

ADMISSIONS FACTS AND FIGURES

Phone: (256) 765-4608. **Email:** admissions@una.edu. **Website:** http://www.una.edu. **Application deadlines for fall 2011:** Regular decision: Rolling. Early decision: Not offered. Early action: Not offered. Admission can be deferred. **Application fee:** $25. **To apply online, go to:** https://www.applyweb.com/aw?una. **Admissions requirements/recommendations:** High school units required (recommended): English: 4; Mathematics: 2; Science: 2; Foreign language: 2; Social studies: 3; Total units: 13. Tests: The college uses SAT or ACT scores in admissions decisions. Either SAT or ACT required. For admission to the fall 2011 entering class, the school will accept: ACT with or without writing accepted. Campus visit: Recommended. Admissions interview: Recommended. Off-campus interview: May be arranged. **Factors that count in admissions decisions:** *Academic:* Secondary school record: Important. Class rank: Very Important. Letters of recommendation: Not Considered. Standardized test scores: Very Important. Essay: Not Considered. *Nonacademic:* Interview: Not Considered. Extracurricular activities: Not Considered. Talent/ability: Not Considered. Character/personal qualities: Important. Alumni/ae relationship: Not Considered. Geographical residence: Not Considered. State residency: Not Considered. Religious affiliation/commitment: Not Considered. Minority status: Not Considered. Volunteer work: Not Considered. Work experience: Not Considered. **Other schools with the greatest overlap in applicants:** Auburn University; University of Alabama; University of Alabama–Huntsville; University of Montevallo. **Admissions statistics for the fall 2009 entering class:** Total applicants: 2,583. Total accepted: 2,128. Freshmen enrolled: 1,068; 11% were from out of state. Overall acceptance rate: 82%. **Credentials of fall 2009 freshmen:** 28% ranked in the top 10 percent of their high school class; 43% were in the top 25 percent; 75% were in the top half. (Proportion submitting class standing: 88%.) **Average high school grade point average:** 2.9. **First-year students who submitted SAT scores:** 2%. Scores (25/75 percentile): Critical Reading: 400-485, Math: 370-530, Combined: 770-1015. **First-year students submitting ACT scores:** 96%. Scores (25/75 percentile): English: 18-25, Math: 17-23, Composite: 18-24.

ACADEMICS

Year founded: 1830. **Academic calendar:** Semester. **Degrees offered:** bachelor's, master's, post-master's certificate. **Most popular majors:** 27% business, management, marketing, and related support services, 17% health professions and related clinical sciences, 10% English language and literature/letters, 10% education, 6% social sciences. **Major fields of study:** biological and biomedical sciences; business, management, marketing, and related support services; computer and information sciences and support services; education; English language and literature/letters; family and consumer sciences/human sciences; foreign languages, literatures, and linguistics; health professions and related clinical sciences; history; liberal arts and sciences studies, and humanities; mathematics and statistics; parks, recreation, leisure, and fitness studies; physical sciences; psychology; public administration and social service professions; security and protective services; social sciences; visual and performing arts. **Areas of required coursework:** arts/fine arts, humanities, computer literacy, mathematics, English

(including composition), foreign languages, sciences (biological or physical), history, social science. **Pre-professional programs:** pre-law, pre-dentistry, pre-medicine, pre-theology, pre-veterinary science, pre-optometry, pre-pharmacy, other. **Special academic programs:** accelerated program, cooperative (work-study plan) program, distance learning, double major, dual enrollment, English as a Second Language (ESL), honors program, independent study, internships, student-designed major, study abroad, teacher certificate program, weekend college. **Teacher certification offered in:** special education, elementary, secondary. **Cooperative education programs:** business, technologies. **Reserve Officers Training Corps (ROTC):** Army ROTC: Offered on campus. **Faculty and instruction (2009-2010):** Total instructional faculty: 254 full-time, 121 part-time (53% men; 47% women; 9% minorities). Full-time faculty with Ph.D. or other terminal degree: 78%. Student/faculty ratio: 19/1. Classes of fewer than 20 students: 38%; of 20 to 49 students: 58%; of 50 or more students: 4%. **Advanced Placement and International Baccalaureate credit:** AP tests may be used for: Credit only. Scores accepted: 3, 4, 5. **Freshmen returning for sophomore year:** 66%. **Graduation rates:** Four-year: 18%; five-year: 34%; six-year: 40%.

COSTS AND FINANCIAL AID

Financial aid office: (256) 765-4278. **Expenses (2009-2010):** Tuition and fees 2009-2010: $6,042 in state, $11,052 out of state; room/board: $4,784. Estimated books and supplies: $1,300. **Financial aid:** Priority filing date for institution's financial aid form: April 1. In 2009-2010, 72% of undergraduates applied for financial aid. Of those, 44% were determined to have financial need; 45% had their need fully met. Average financial aid package (proportion receiving): $4,993 (43%). Average amount of gift aid, such as scholarships or grants (proportion receiving): $3,819 (29%). Average amount of self-help aid, such as work study or loans (proportion receiving): $2,958 (34%). Average need-based loan (excluding PLUS or other private loans): $2,818. Among students who received need-based aid, the average percentage of need met: 65%. Among students who received aid based on merit, the average award (and the proportion receiving): $2,781 (25%). The average athletic scholarship (and the proportion receiving): $4,432 (5%). Average amount of debt of borrowers graduating in 2009: $24,500. Proportion who borrowed: 64%.

CAMPUS LIFE AND EXTRACURRICULAR ACTIVITIES

Campus housing available (% using): coed dorms (31%), women's dorms (28%), men's dorms (25%), apartments for married students (9%), apartment for single students (7%). Students who live in college-owned, operated, or affiliated housing: 19%. **Clubs and organizations:** Number of student organizations: 226. Activities include: campus ministries, choral groups, concert band, drama/theater, international student organization, jazz band, literary magazine, marching band, music ensembles, musical theater, pep band, radio station, student government, student newspaper, student film society, symphony orchestra, yearbook. Number of fraternities: 9; sororities: 7. Proportion of men in fraternities: 5%; of women in sororities: 6%. Average proportion of students who stay on campus on weekends: 30%. **Sports program (2009-2010):** Member of NCAA II. *Men's intercollegiate varsity sports:* baseball, basketball, cross country, football, golf, tennis. *Women's intercollegiate varsity sports:* basketball, cross country, soccer, softball, tennis, volleyball.

SERVICES AND FACILITIES

Basic services: nonremedial tutoring, women's center, placement service, day care, health service. **Remedial assistance:** reading, math, writing, study skills, other. **Counseling services:** minority student, career, academic, older student, psychological, birth control, other. **For learning-disabled students:** School does not offer a structured program with separate admission and additional fees. Services include: remedial math, remedial English, remedial reading, tape recorders, untimed tests, note-taking services, oral tests, learning center, readers, extended time for tests, tutors, other. **Library:** Number of titles: 393,457; number of current serial subscriptions: 3,742. **Information technology resources:** Students are not required to lease or own a computer. Number of campus computers available to all students: 800. School has a wireless network. Approximate number of users that can be accommodated: 1,000. Proportion of college-owned housing units wired for high-speed internet access: 100%. **Campus safety:** Security services offered: 24-hour foot-and-vehicle patrols, late-night transport/escort service, 24-hour emergency telephones, lighted pathways/sidewalks, student patrols, controlled dormitory access (key, security card, etc.).

TRANSFER AND INTERNATIONAL STUDENTS

Transfer students: May apply for admission for the following academic terms: Fall, Spring, Summer. Applicants need a minimum number of cred-

its to apply. For fall 2009: Transfer applications received: 1,140. Transfer applicants offered admission: 920. Transfer applicants enrolled: 678. **International students:** Number of foreign undergraduates: 336 (6% of student body). Number of countries represented: 58. Minimum TOEFL score required: 500 (paper); 173 (computer). Average TOEFL score: 530 (paper).

University of South Alabama

- **Address:** 307 University Boulevard, Mobile, AL 36688-0002
- **Website:** http://www.southalabama.edu
- **Public**
- **Enrollment:** 8,527 full-time; 2,881 part-time

KEY STATS

✔ **U.S News College Ranking:** 52, Regional Universities (South)
✔ **ACT Score (25th/75th percentile):** 18-24
✔ **Tuition:** 2009-2010: $3,998 in state, $7,996 out of state

Selectivity: Selective	**Room/board:** N/A
Acceptance rate: 90%	**Average debt:** N/A
Student/faculty ratio: 23/1	**Proportion who borrowed:** N/A

UNDERGRADUATE STUDENT BODY STATS

2009-2010 enrollment: 8,527 full-time; 2,881 part-time. Men: 43%; women: 57%. **Ethnic makeup:** African American: 19%; American-Indian: 1%; Asian American: 3%; Hispanic: 2%; White: 70%; International: 4%. **Religious preference:** Roman Catholic: 12%; Protestant: 41%; Jewish: 1%; No preference: 2%; Unknown: 37%; Other: 7%.

ADMISSIONS FACTS AND FIGURES

Phone: (251) 460-6141. **Email:** admiss@usouthal.edu. **Website:** http://www.southalabama.edu. **Application deadlines for fall 2011:** Regular decision: August 22. Early decision: Not offered. Early action: Not offered. Admission can be deferred. **Application fee:** $35. **To apply online, go to:** http://www.southalabama.edu/admissions/apply.html. **Admissions requirements/recommendations:** High school units required (recommended): English: (4); Mathematics: (3); Science: (3); Social studies: (3); Academic electives: (3); Total units: (16). Tests: The college uses SAT or ACT scores in admissions decisions. Neither SAT nor ACT required. For admission to the fall 2011 entering class, the school will accept: ACT with or without writing accepted. Campus visit: Neither required nor recommended. Admissions interview: Neither required nor recommended. Off-campus interview: May be arranged. **Factors that count in admissions decisions:** *Academic:* Secondary school record: Very Important. Standardized test scores: Very Important. **Admissions statistics for the fall 2009 entering class:** Total applicants: 4,050. Total accepted: 3,631. Freshmen enrolled: 1,841; Overall acceptance rate: 90%. **First-year students who submitted SAT scores:** 8%. Scores (25/75 percentile): Critical Reading: 440-560, Math: 430-550, Combined: 870-1110. **First-year students submitting ACT scores:** 87%. Scores (25/75 percentile): English: 18-25, Math: 17-24, Composite: 18-24.

ACADEMICS

Year founded: 1963. **Academic calendar:** Semester. **Degrees offered:** certificate, bachelor's, post-bachelor's certificate, master's, post-master's certificate, doctorate. **Major fields of study:** biological and biomedical sciences; business, management, marketing, and related support services; communication, journalism, and related programs; computer and information sciences and support services; education; engineering; English language and literature/letters; foreign languages, literatures, and linguistics; health professions and related clinical sciences; history; liberal arts and sciences studies, and humanities; mathematics and statistics; multi/interdisciplinary studies; parks, recreation, leisure, and fitness studies; philosophy and religious studies; physical sciences; psychology; public administration and social service professions; security and protective services; social sciences; visual and performing arts. **Areas of required coursework:** arts/fine arts, humanities, computer literacy, mathematics, English (including composition), sciences (biological or physical), history, social science. **Preprofessional programs:** pre-law, pre-dentistry, pre-medicine, pre-veterinary science, pre-optometry, pre-pharmacy. **Special academic programs:** accelerated program, cooperative (work-study plan) program, distance learning, double major, dual enrollment, English as a Second Language (ESL), honors program, independent study, internships, student-designed major, study abroad, teacher certificate program, weekend college. **Teacher certification offered in:** early childhood, special education, elementary, middle/junior

high, secondary. **Cooperative education programs:** art, business, computer science, education, engineering, humanities, natural science, social/behavioral science. **Reserve Officers Training Corps (ROTC):** Army ROTC: Offered on campus; Air Force ROTC: Offered on campus. **Faculty and instruction (2009-2010):** Total instructional faculty: 517 full-time, 320 part-time (47% men; 53% women; 12% minorities). Full-time faculty with Ph.D. or other terminal degree: 73%. Student/faculty ratio: 23/1. Classes of fewer than 20 students: 41%; of 20 to 49 students: 52%; of 50 or more students: 7%. **Advanced Placement and International Baccalaureate credit:** AP tests may be used for: Placement only. Scores accepted: 3. **Freshmen returning for sophomore year:** 69%. **Graduation rates:** Four-year: 13%; five-year: 28%; six-year: 37%.

COSTS AND FINANCIAL AID

Financial aid office: (251) 460-6231. **Expenses (2009-2010):** Tuition and fees 2009-2010: $3,998 in state, $7,996 out of state. Estimated books and supplies: $1,200; transportation: $504; personal expenses: $1,950. **Financial aid:** Priority filing date for institution's financial aid form: May 1.

CAMPUS LIFE AND EXTRACURRICULAR ACTIVITIES

Campus housing available: coed dorms, sorority housing, fraternity housing, apartments for married students, apartment for single students, special housing for disabled students. Students who live in college-owned, operated, or affiliated housing: 19%. **Clubs and organizations:** Number of student organizations: 200. Activities include: campus ministries, choral groups, concert band, dance, drama/theater, jazz band, literary magazine, marching band, music ensembles, musical theater, student government, student newspaper, student film society, television station. Number of fraternities: 9; sororities: 10. **Sports program (2009-2010):** Member of NCAA I. **Men's intercollegiate varsity sports:** baseball, basketball, cross country, golf, track and field (indoor). **Women's intercollegiate varsity sports:** basketball, cross country, golf, track and field (indoor), volleyball.

SERVICES AND FACILITIES

Basic services: nonremedial tutoring, placement service, health service, health insurance. **Remedial assistance:** reading, math, writing, study skills. **Counseling services:** minority student, career, military, personal, veteran student, academic, older student, psychological. **For learning-disabled students:** School does not offer a structured program with separate admission and additional fees. Services include: remedial math, remedial English, reading machines, remedial reading, tape recorders, diagnostic testing service, untimed tests, note-taking services, oral tests, learning center, readers, extended time for tests, tutors. **Library:** Number of titles: 1,576,995; number of current serial subscriptions: 1,244. **Information technology resources:** Students are not required to lease or own a computer. Proportion of college-owned housing units wired for high-speed internet access: 100%. **Campus safety:** Security services offered: 24-hour foot-and-vehicle patrols, late-night transport/escort service, 24-hour emergency telephones, lighted pathways/sidewalks, controlled dormitory access (key, security card, etc).

TRANSFER AND INTERNATIONAL STUDENTS

Transfer students: May apply for admission for the following academic terms: Fall, Spring, Summer. Applicants do not need a minimum number of credits to apply. For fall 2009: Transfer applications received: 2,282. Transfer applicants offered admission: 1,861. Transfer applicants enrolled: 1,186. **International students:** Number of foreign undergraduates: 483 (4% of student body). Number of countries represented: 100. Minimum TOEFL score required: 500 (paper); 173 (computer). Average TOEFL score: 580 (paper).

University of West Alabama

- **Address:** Station 4, Livingston, AL 35470
- **Website:** http://www.uwa.edu
- **Public**
- **Enrollment:** 1,541 full-time; 404 part-time

KEY STATS

✔ **U.S News College Ranking:** second tier, Regional Universities (South)
✔ **ACT Score (25th/75th percentile):** 18-34
✔ **Tuition:** 2009-2010: $5,560 in state, $10,620 out of state

Selectivity: Selective	Room/board: $4,416
Acceptance rate: 61%	Average debt: N/A
Student/faculty ratio: 19/1	Proportion who borrowed: N/A

UNDERGRADUATE STUDENT BODY STATS

2009-2010 enrollment: 1,541 full-time; 404 part-time. Men: 39%; women: 61%. **Ethnic makeup:** African American: 54%; Asian American: 1%; Hispanic: 1%; White: 43%; International: 1%.

ADMISSIONS FACTS AND FIGURES

Phone: (205) 652-3578. **Email:** admissions@uwa.edu. **Website:** http://www.uwa.edu. **Application deadlines for fall 2011:** Regular decision: Rolling. Early decision: Not offered. Early action: Not offered. Admission can be deferred. **Application fee:** $50. **To apply online, go to:** http://admissions.uwa.edu/applications.htm. **Admissions requirements/recommendations:** High school units required (recommended): English: 3; Mathematics: 3; Science: 3; Foreign language: 0; Social studies: 3; History: 0; Academic electives: 3; Total units: 15. Tests: The college uses SAT or ACT scores in admissions decisions. Either SAT or ACT required. For admission to the fall 2011 entering class, the school will accept: ACT with or without writing accepted. Campus visit: Recommended. Admissions interview: Neither required nor recommended. Off-campus interview: Not available. **Factors that count in admissions decisions:** *Academic:* Secondary school record: Very Important. Class rank: Not Considered. Letters of recommendation: Not Considered. Standardized test scores: Very Important. Essay: Not Considered. *Nonacademic:* Interview: Not Considered. Extracurricular activities: Not Considered. Talent/ability: Not Considered. Character/personal qualities: Not Considered. Alumni/ae relationship: Not Considered. Geographical residence: Not Considered. State residency: Not Considered. Religious affiliation/commitment: Not Considered. Minority status: Not Considered. Volunteer work: Not Considered. Work experience: Not Considered. **Other schools with the greatest overlap in applicants:** Auburn University; University of Alabama; University of South Alabama. **Admissions statistics for the fall 2009 entering class:** Total applicants: 690. Total accepted: 424. Freshmen enrolled: 310; 19% were from out of state. Overall acceptance rate: 61%. **First-year students submitting ACT scores:** 100%. Scores (25/75 percentile): English: 16-34, Math: 18-35, Composite: 18-34.

ACADEMICS

Year founded: 1835. **Academic calendar:** Semester. **Degrees offered:** associate, bachelor's, master's. **Most popular majors:** 15% adult and continuing education and teaching, 11% physical education teaching and coaching, 10% business administration and management, 8% English language and literature, 8% biology/biological sciences. **Major fields of study:** biological and biomedical sciences; business, management, marketing, and related support services; education; engineering technologies/technicians; English language and literature/letters; health professions and related clinical sciences; history; mathematics and statistics; multi/interdisciplinary studies; physical sciences; psychology; social sciences. **Areas of required coursework:** arts/fine arts, humanities, mathematics, English (including composition), sciences (biological or physical), history, social science. **Special academic programs:** accelerated program, cooperative (work-study plan) program, distance learning, double major, dual enrollment, honors program, independent study, internships, teacher certificate program. **Teacher certification offered in:** early childhood, special education, elementary, middle/junior high, secondary. **Reserve Officers Training Corps (ROTC):** Air Force ROTC: Offered at cooperating institution (University of Alabama). **Faculty and instruction (2009-2010):** Total instructional faculty: 116 full-time, 131 part-time (42% men; 58% women; 12% minorities). Full-time faculty with Ph.D. or other terminal degree: 79%. Student/faculty ratio: 19/1. Classes of fewer than 20 students: 58%; of 20 to 49 students: 39%; of 50 or more students: 3%. **Advanced Placement and International Baccalaureate credit:** AP tests may be used for: Placement only. Scores accepted: 3, 4, 5. **Freshmen returning for sophomore year:** 68%. **Graduation rates:** Six-year: 27%.

COSTS AND FINANCIAL AID

Financial aid office: (205) 652-3576. **Expenses (2009-2010):** Tuition and fees 2009-2010: $5,560 in state, $10,620 out of state; room/board: $4,416. Estimated transportation: $900; personal expenses: $1,200. **Financial aid:** Priority filing date for institution's financial aid form: April 1.

CAMPUS LIFE AND EXTRACURRICULAR ACTIVITIES

Campus housing available (% using): coed dorms (45%), women's dorms (20%), men's dorms (25%), apartment for single students (10%). Students who live in college-owned, operated, or affiliated housing: 35%. **Student employment:** During the 2009-2010 academic year, 6% of undergraduates worked on campus. Average per-year earnings: $1,500. **Clubs and organizations:** Number of student organizations: 85. Activities include: campus ministries, choral groups, concert band, dance, drama/theater, international student organization, marching band, student government, student newspaper, television station, yearbook. Number of fraternities: 12; sororities: 6. Proportion of men in fraternities: 2%; of women in sororities: 2%. Average proportion of students who stay on campus on weekends: 45%. **Sports program (2009-2010):** Member of NCAA II. *Men's intercollegiate varsity sports:* baseball, basketball, cross country, football, tennis, track and field (outdoor). *Women's intercollegiate varsity sports:* basketball, cross country, softball, tennis, track and field (outdoor), volleyball.

SERVICES AND FACILITIES

Basic services: nonremedial tutoring, placement service, day care, health service. **Remedial assistance:** reading, math, writing, study skills. **Counseling services:** career, personal, academic, psychological. **For learning-disabled students:** School does not offer a structured program with separate admission and additional fees. Total undergraduates in learning-disabled program or receiving services: 22. Services include: remedial math, remedial English, remedial reading, tape recorders, diagnostic testing service, untimed tests, note-taking services, oral tests, learning center, readers, extended time for tests, tutors, priority registration, priority seating. **Library:** Number of titles: 171,191; number of current serial subscriptions: 6,000. **Information technology resources:** Students are not required to lease or own a computer. Number of campus computers available to all students: 350. School has a wireless network. Approximate number of users that can be accommodated: 1,000. Proportion of college-owned housing units wired for high-speed internet access: 100%. **Campus safety:** Security services offered: 24-hour foot-and-vehicle patrols, lighted pathways/sidewalks, controlled dormitory access (key, security card, etc).

TRANSFER AND INTERNATIONAL STUDENTS

Transfer students: May apply for admission for the following academic terms: Fall, Winter, Spring, Summer. Applicants do not need a minimum number of credits to apply. For fall 2009: Transfer applications received: 455. Transfer applicants offered admission: 300. Transfer applicants enrolled: 253. **International students:** Number of foreign undergraduates: 9 (1% of student body). Number of countries represented: 10. Minimum TOEFL score required: 500 (paper); 175 (computer). Average TOEFL score: 550 (paper).

Alaska

Alaska Pacific University

- **Address:** 4101 University Drive, Anchorage, AK 99508-3051
- **Website:** http://www.alaskapacific.edu
- **Private; Religious affiliation:** Methodist
- **Enrollment:** 301 full-time; 233 part-time

KEY STATS
- ✔ **U.S News College Ranking:** 56, Regional Universities (West)
- ✔ **SAT Score (25th/75th percentile):** 960-1180
- ✔ **Tuition:** 2010-2011: $26,360

Selectivity: Selective	**Room/board:** $9,300
Acceptance rate: 34%	**Average debt:** $42,392
Student/faculty ratio: 8/1	**Proportion who borrowed:** 94%

UNDERGRADUATE STUDENT BODY STATS
2009-2010 enrollment: 301 full-time; 233 part-time. Men: 33%; women: 67%. **Ethnic makeup:** African American: 4%; American-Indian: 17%; Asian American: 2%; Hispanic: 5%; White: 72%.

ADMISSIONS FACTS AND FIGURES
Phone: (800) 252-7528. **Email:** admissions@alaskapacific.edu. **Website:** http://www.alaskapacific.edu. **Application deadlines for fall 2011:** Regular decision: August 1. Early decision: Not offered. Early action: Not offered. Admission can be deferred. **Application fee:** $25. **To apply online, go to:** https://apply.alaskapacific.edu/. **Admissions requirements/recommendations:** High school units required (recommended): English: 4 (4); Mathematics: 3 (3); Science: 2 (2); Foreign language: 2 (2); Social studies: 1 (1); History: 1 (1); Total units: 14 (10). Tests: The college uses SAT or ACT scores in admissions decisions. Either SAT or ACT required. For admission to the fall 2011 entering class, the school will accept: ACT with or without writing accepted. Campus visit: Recommended. Admissions interview: Recommended. Off-campus interview: May be arranged. **Factors that count in admissions decisions:** *Academic:* Secondary school record: Very Important. Class rank: Not Considered. Letters of recommendation: Important. Standardized test scores: Important. Essay: Very Important. *Nonacademic:* Interview: Not Considered. Extracurricular activities: Considered. Talent/ability: Considered. Character/personal qualities: Not Considered. Alumni/ae relationship: Important. Geographical residence: Not Considered. State residency: Not Considered. Religious affiliation/commitment: Not Considered. Minority status: Not Considered. Volunteer work: Considered. Work experience: Considered. **Other schools with the greatest overlap in applicants:** Lewis-Clark State College; Portland State University; Prescott College; University of Alaska–Anchorage; Western Washington University. **Admissions statistics for the fall 2009 entering class:** Total applicants: 1,569. Total accepted: 529. Freshmen enrolled: 28; 75% were from out of state. Overall acceptance rate: 34%. **Credentials of fall 2009 freshmen:** 20% ranked in the top 10 percent of their high school class; 48% were in the top 25 percent; 84% were in the top half. (Proportion submitting class standing: 89%.) **Average high school grade point average:** 3.5. **First-year students who submitted SAT scores:** 79%. Scores (25/75 p ercentile): Critical Reading: 480-590, Math: 480-590, Combined: 960-1180. **First-year students submitting ACT scores:** 32%. Scores (25/75 percentile): English: 19-22, Math: 20-24, Composite: 21-25.

ACADEMICS
Year founded: 1957. **Academic calendar:** Semester. **Degrees offered:** certificate, associate, terminal-associate, bachelor's, post-bachelor's certificate, master's. **Most popular majors:** 16% parks, recreation, and leisure studies, 15% business administration and management, 11% environmental science, 9% elementary education and teaching, 9% psychology. **Major fields of study:** biological and biomedical sciences; business, management, marketing, and related support services; education; health professions and related clinical sciences; liberal arts and sciences studies, and humanities; natural resources and conservation; parks, recreation, leisure, and fitness studies; psychology; public administration and social service professions.

Areas of required coursework: humanities, mathematics, English (including composition), foreign languages, sciences (biological or physical), social science, other. **Pre-professional programs:** pre-law. **Special academic programs (% participation):** distance learning (13%), double major (0%), exchange student program (domestic) (0%), independent study (47%), internships (60%), teacher certificate program (9%). **Teacher certification offered in:** elementary, vo-tech, middle/junior high. **Reserve Officers Training Corps (ROTC):** Air Force ROTC: Offered at cooperating institution (University of Alaska–Anchorage). **Faculty and instruction (2009-2010):** Total instructional faculty: 50 full-time, 46 part-time (42% men; 58% women; 3% minorities). Full-time faculty with Ph.D. or other terminal degree: 64%. Student/faculty ratio: 8/1. Classes of fewer than 20 students: 96%; of 20 to 49 students: 4%. **Advanced Placement and International Baccalaureate credit:** AP tests may be used for: Credit only. Scores accepted: 3, 4, 5. International Baccalaureate exams may be used for: Credit only. **Freshmen returning for sophomore year:** 71%. **Graduation rates:** Four-year: 29%; five-year: 42%; six-year: 35%.

COSTS AND FINANCIAL AID
Financial aid office: (907) 564-8341. **Expenses (2010-2011):** Tuition and fees 2010-2011: $26,360; room/board: $9,300. Estimated books and supplies: $1,000; transportation: $2,000; personal expenses: $1,000. **Financial aid:** Priority filing date for institution's financial aid form: April 15. In 2009-2010, 85% of undergraduates applied for financial aid. Of those, 78% were determined to have financial need; 28% had their need fully met. Average financial aid package (proportion receiving): $15,100 (77%). Average amount of gift aid, such as scholarships or grants (proportion receiving): $7,900 (43%). Average amount of self-help aid, such as work study or loans (proportion receiving): $5,320 (72%). Average need-based loan (excluding PLUS or other private loans): $4,570. Among students who received need-based aid, the average percentage of need met: 92%. Among students who received aid based on merit, the average award (and the proportion receiving): $9,570 (3%). The average athletic scholarship (and the proportion receiving): $4,000 (0%). Average amount of debt of borrowers graduating in 2009: $42,392. Proportion who borrowed: 94%.

CAMPUS LIFE AND EXTRACURRICULAR ACTIVITIES
Campus housing available (% using): coed dorms (100%). Students who live in college-owned, operated, or affiliated housing: 26%. **Student employment:** During the 2009-2010 academic year, 50% of undergraduates worked on campus. Average per-year earnings: $5,120. **Clubs and organizations:** Number of student organizations: 15. Activities include: drama/theater, literary magazine, music ensembles, student government, student newspaper, yearbook. Number of fraternities: 0; sororities: 0. Average proportion of students who stay on campus on weekends: 98%. **Sports program (2009-2010):** *Men's intercollegiate varsity sports:* skiing (nordic). *Women's intercollegiate varsity sports:* skiing (nordic).

SERVICES AND FACILITIES
Basic services: health insurance. **Remedial assistance:** reading, math, writing. **Counseling services:** minority student, career, personal, academic, psychological, religious. **For learning-disabled students:** School does not offer a structured program with separate admission and additional fees. Services include: remedial math, remedial English, remedial reading, tape recorders, untimed tests, note-taking services, extended time for tests, tutors, other. **Library:** Number of titles: 945,948; number of current serial subscriptions: 5,877. **Information technology resources:** Students are not required to lease or own a computer. Number of campus computers available to all students: 105. School has a wireless network. Approximate number of users that can be accommodated: 15,000. Proportion of college-owned housing units wired for high-speed internet access: 100%. **Campus safety:** Security services offered: late-night transport/escort service, 24-hour emergency telephones, lighted pathways/sidewalks, controlled dormitory access (key, security card, etc).

TRANSFER AND INTERNATIONAL STUDENTS
Transfer students: May apply for admission for the following academic terms: Fall, Spring, Summer. Applicants need a minimum number

of credits to apply. For fall 2009: Transfer applications received: 169. Transfer applicants offered admission: 88. Transfer applicants enrolled: 81. **International students:** Number of foreign undergraduates: 1. Number of countries represented: 3. Minimum TOEFL score required: 550 (paper); 79 (computer). Average TOEFL score: 572 (paper).

University of Alaska–Anchorage

- **Address:** 3211 Providence Drive, Anchorage, AK 99508
- **Website:** http://www.uaa.alaska.edu
- **Public**
- **Enrollment:** 7,641 full-time; 9,214 part-time

KEY STATS

✔ **U.S News College Ranking:** 75, Regional Universities (West)

✔ **SAT Score (25th/75th percentile):** 850-1100

✔ **Tuition:** 2010-2011: $5,786 in state, $16,376 out of state

Selectivity: Less selective	**Room/board:** $9,177
Acceptance rate: 77%	**Average debt:** $22,043
Student/faculty ratio: 19/1	**Proportion who borrowed:** 49%

UNDERGRADUATE STUDENT BODY STATS

2009-2010 enrollment: 7,641 full-time; 9,214 part-time. Men: 41%; women: 59%. **Ethnic makeup:** African American: 3%; American-Indian: 10%; Asian American: 8%; Hispanic: 5%; White: 73%; International: 1%.

ADMISSIONS FACTS AND FIGURES

Phone: (907) 786-1480. **Email:** enroll@uaa.alaska.edu. **Website:** http://www.uaa.alaska.edu. **Application deadlines for fall 2011:** Regular decision: July 1. Early decision: Not offered. Early action: Not offered. Admission can be deferred. **Application fee:** $50. **To apply online, go to:** http://www.uaa.alaska.edu/admissions/requirements/index.cfm. **Admissions requirements/recommendations:** High school units required (recommended): English: 4 (4); Mathematics: 2 (2); Science: 3 (3); Foreign language: 1 (1); Social studies: 3 (3); History: 1 (1). Tests: The college uses SAT or ACT scores in admissions decisions. Neither SAT nor ACT required. For admission to the fall 2011 entering class, the school will accept: ACT with or without writing accepted. Campus visit: Recommended. Admissions interview: Neither required nor recommended. Off-campus interview: Not available. **Factors that count in admissions decisions:** *Academic:* Secondary school record: Very Important. Class rank: Considered. Letters of recommendation: Not Considered. Standardized test scores: Considered. Essay: Not Considered. *Nonacademic:* Interview: Not Considered. Extracurricular activities: Not Considered. Talent/ability: Considered. Character/personal qualities: Not Considered. Alumni/ae relationship: Not Considered. Geographical residence: Not Considered. State residency: Not Considered. Religious affiliation/commitment: Not Considered. Minority status: Not Considered. Volunteer work: Not Considered. Work experience: Not Considered. **Admissions statistics for the fall 2009 entering class:** Total applicants: 4,217. Total accepted: 3,244. Freshmen enrolled: 1,950; 6% were from out of state. Overall acceptance rate: 77%. **Credentials of fall 2009 freshmen:** 9% ranked in the top 10 percent of their high school class; 29% were in the top 25 percent; 57% were in the top half. (Proportion submitting class standing: 75%.) **First-year students who submitted SAT scores:** 40%. Scores (25/75 percentile): Critical Reading: 430-540, Math: 420-560, Combined: 850-1100. **First-year students submitting ACT scores:** 17%. Scores (25/75 percentile): English: N/A, Math: N/A, Composite: 17-24.

ACADEMICS

Year founded: 1954. **Academic calendar:** Semester. **Degrees offered:** certificate, associate, bachelor's, post-bachelor's certificate, master's, post-master's certificate. **Most popular majors:** 19% business administration and management, 16% health professions and related clinical sciences, 8% psychology, 6% education, 6% social sciences. **Major fields of study:** biological and biomedical sciences; business, management, marketing, and related support services; communication, journalism, and related programs; computer and information sciences and support services; education; engineering; English language and literature/letters; family and consumer sciences/human sciences; foreign languages, literatures, and linguistics; health professions and related clinical sciences; history; liberal arts and sciences studies, and humanities; mathematics and statistics; mechanic and repair technologies/technicians; multi/interdisciplinary studies; personal and culinary services; philosophy and religious studies; physical sciences; psychology; public

administration and social service professions; science technologies/technicians; security and protective services; social sciences; transportation and materials moving; visual and performing arts. **Areas of required coursework:** arts/fine arts, humanities, computer literacy, mathematics, English (including composition), sciences (biological or physical), history, social science, other. **Pre-professional programs:** pre-medicine. **Special academic programs:** cooperative (work-study plan) program, cross-registration, distance learning, double major, dual enrollment, English as a Second Language (ESL), exchange student program (domestic), honors program, independent study, internships, liberal arts/career combination, student-designed major, study abroad, teacher certificate program. **Teacher certification offered in:** early childhood, special education, elementary, middle/junior high, adult education, secondary, bilingual/bicultural. **Cooperative education programs:** art, business, computer science, education, engineering, health professions, humanities, natural science, social/behavioral science, technologies, vocational arts. **Reserve Officers Training Corps (ROTC):** Army ROTC: Offered on campus; Air Force ROTC: Offered on campus. **Faculty and instruction (2009-2010):** Total instructional faculty: 617 full-time, 661 part-time (45% men; 55% women; 10% minorities). Full-time faculty with Ph.D. or other terminal degree: 52%. Student/faculty ratio: 19/1. Classes of fewer than 20 students: 53%; of 20 to 49 students: 43%; of 50 or more students: 4%. **Advanced Placement and International Baccalaureate credit:** AP tests may be used for: Placement only. Scores accepted: 3, 4, 5. **Freshmen returning for sophomore year:** 71%. **Graduation rates:** Four-year: 9%; five-year: 20%; six-year: 25%.

COSTS AND FINANCIAL AID

Financial aid office: (907) 786-1586. **Expenses (2010-2011):** Tuition and fees 2010-2011: $5,786 in state, $16,376 out of state; room/board: $9,177. Estimated books and supplies: $1,194; transportation: $2,340; personal expenses: $1,499. **Financial aid:** Priority filing date for institution's financial aid form: April 1. In 2009-2010, 64% of undergraduates applied for financial aid. Of those, 47% were determined to have financial need; 16% had their need fully met. Average financial aid package (proportion receiving): $10,055 (44%). Average amount of gift aid, such as scholarships or grants (proportion receiving): $4,088 (31%). Average amount of self-help aid, such as work study or loans (proportion receiving): $5,967 (44%). Average need-based loan (excluding PLUS or other private loans): $4,042. Among students who received need-based aid, the average percentage of need met: 73%. Among students who received aid based on merit, the average award (and the proportion receiving): $2,932 (3%). The average athletic scholarship (and the proportion receiving): $13,182 (2%). Average amount of debt of borrowers graduating in 2009: $22,043. Proportion who borrowed: 49%.

CAMPUS LIFE AND EXTRACURRICULAR ACTIVITIES

Campus housing available (% using): coed dorms (32%), apartment for single students (41%), special housing for disabled students (2%), other housing options (25%). **Clubs and organizations:** Number of student organizations: 82. Activities include: campus ministries, choral groups, dance, drama/theater, international student organization, jazz band, literary magazine, model UN, music ensembles, musical theater, radio station, student government, student newspaper. Number of fraternities: 1; sororities: 2. **Sports program (2009-2010):** Member of NCAA II. *Men's intercollegiate varsity sports:* basketball, cross country, ice hockey, skiing (nordic), skiing (alpine), track and field (indoor), track and field (outdoor). *Women's intercollegiate varsity sports:* basketball, cross country, gymnastics, skiing (nordic), skiing (alpine), track and field (indoor), track and field (outdoor), volleyball.

SERVICES AND FACILITIES

Basic services: placement service, day care, health service. **Remedial assistance:** reading, math, writing, study skills. **Counseling services:** minority student, career, military, veteran student, academic, psychological, birth control. **For learning-disabled students:** School does not offer a structured program with separate admission and additional fees. Services include: remedial math, remedial English, reading machines, remedial reading, tape recorders, videotaped classes, note-taking services, oral tests, learning center, readers, extended time for tests, tutors, priority registration, priority seating, substitution of courses, texts on tape, typist/scribe, exams on tape or computer, other testing accommodations, other. **Library:** Number of titles: 958,063; number of current serial subscriptions: 4,611. **Information technology resources:** Students are not required to lease or own a computer. Number of campus computers available to all students: 860. School has a wireless network. Approximate number of users that can be accommodated: 7,500. Proportion of college-owned housing units wired for high-speed internet access: 100%. **Campus safety:** Security services offered: 24-hour foot-and-vehicle patrols, late-night transport/escort service, 24-hour emergency telephones, lighted pathways/sidewalks, student patrols, controlled dormitory access (key, security card, etc).

TRANSFER AND INTERNATIONAL STUDENTS

Transfer students: May apply for admission for the following academic terms: Fall, Spring, Summer. Applicants need a minimum number of credits to apply. For fall 2009: Transfer applications received: 2,144. Transfer applicants offered admission: 1,521. Transfer applicants enrolled: 1,015. **International students:** Number of foreign undergraduates: 110 (1% of student body). Number of countries represented: 41. Minimum TOEFL score required: 450 (paper); 133 (computer).

University of Alaska–Fairbanks

- **Address:** PO Box 757500, Fairbanks, AK 99775-7500
- **Website:** http://www.uaf.edu
- **Public**
- **Enrollment:** 3,639 full-time; 4,338 part-time

KEY STATS

✔ **U.S News College Ranking:** second tier, National Universities
✔ **SAT Score (25th/75th percentile):** 880-1190
✔ **Tuition:** 2010-2011: $5,668 in state, $16,258 out of state

Selectivity: Selective	**Room/board:** $6,800
Acceptance rate: 74%	**Average debt:** $29,485
Student/faculty ratio: 12/1	**Proportion who borrowed:** 54%

UNDERGRADUATE STUDENT BODY STATS

2009-2010 enrollment: 3,639 full-time; 4,338 part-time. Men: 40%; women: 60%. **Ethnic makeup:** African American: 3%; American-Indian: 19%; Asian American: 3%; Hispanic: 4%; White: 69%; International: 2%.

ADMISSIONS FACTS AND FIGURES

Phone: (800) 478-1823. **Email:** fyapply@uaf.edu. **Website:** http://www.uaf.edu. **Application deadlines for fall 2011:** Regular decision: July 1. Early decision: Not offered. Early action: Not offered. Admission can be deferred. **Application fee:** $50. **To apply online, go to:** http://www.uaf.edu/admissions/apply/index.html. **Admissions requirements/recommendations:** High school units required (recommended): English: 4; Mathematics: 3; Science: 3; Foreign language: (2); Social studies: 3; Total units: 16. Tests: The college uses SAT or ACT scores in admissions decisions. Either SAT or ACT required. For admission to the fall 2011 entering class, the school will accept: ACT with or without writing accepted. Campus visit: Neither required nor recommended. Admissions interview: Neither required nor recommended. Off-campus interview: Not available. **Factors that count in admissions decisions:** *Academic:* Secondary school record: Not Considered. Class rank: Not Considered. Letters of recommendation: Not Considered. Standardized test scores: Very Important. Essay: Not Considered. *Nonacademic:* Interview: Not Considered. Extracurricular activities: Not Considered. Talent/ability: Not Considered. Character/personal qualities: Not Considered. Alumni/ae relationship: Not Considered. Geographical residence: Not Considered. State residency: Not Considered. Religious affiliation/commitment: Not Considered. Minority status: Not Considered. Volunteer work: Not Considered. Work experience: Not Considered. **Other schools with the greatest overlap in applicants:** Montana State University; Oregon State University; University of Montana; University of Nevada–Reno; Western Washington University. **Admissions statistics for the fall 2009 entering class:** Total applicants: 2,030. Total accepted: 1,507. Freshmen enrolled: 1,008; 8% were from out of state. Overall acceptance rate: 74%. **Credentials of fall 2009 freshmen:** 15% ranked in the top 10 percent of their high school class; 34% were in the top 25 percent; 65% were in the top half. (Proportion submitting class standing: 60%.) **Average high school grade point average:** 3.2. **First-year students who submitted SAT scores:** 52%. Scores (25/75 percentile): Critical Reading: 450-600, Math: 430-590, Combined: 880-1190. **First-year students submitting ACT scores:** 48%. Scores (25/75 percentile): English: 17-25, Math: 16-24, Composite: 18-25.

ACADEMICS

Year founded: 1917. **Academic calendar:** Semester. **Degrees offered:** certificate, associate, transfer-associate, terminal-associate, bachelor's, post-bachelor's certificate, master's, doctorate. **Most popular majors:** 10% business, management, marketing, and related support services; 10% engineering,

9% biological and biomedical sciences, 9% psychology, 8% social sciences. **Major fields of study:** area, ethnic, cultural, and gender studies; biological and biomedical sciences; business, management, marketing, and related support services; communication, journalism, and related programs; computer and information sciences and support services; education; engineering; engineering technologies/technicians; English language and literature/letters; family and consumer sciences/human sciences; foreign languages, literatures, and linguistics; history; liberal arts and sciences studies, and humanities; mathematics and statistics; multi/interdisciplinary studies; natural resources and conservation; philosophy and religious studies; physical sciences; psychology; public administration and social service professions; security and protective services; social sciences; visual and performing arts. **Areas of required coursework:** arts/fine arts, humanities, mathematics, English (including composition), philosophy, sciences (biological or physical), history, social science, other. **Pre-professional programs:** pre-law, pre-dentistry, pre-medicine, pre-veterinary science, pre-pharmacy, other. **Special academic programs (% participation):** cooperative (work-study plan) program (7.8%), distance learning (82.7%), double major (6%), dual enrollment (2.4%), exchange student program (domestic), external degree program, honors program (8%), independent study (11.4%), internships, student-designed major (2.6%), study abroad, teacher certificate program (0%). **Teacher certification offered in:** elementary, secondary. **Cooperative education programs:** agriculture, art, business, computer science, education, engineering, health professions, humanities, natural science, social/behavioral science, technologies, vocational arts, other. **Reserve Officers Training Corps (ROTC):** Army ROTC: Offered on campus. **Faculty and instruction (2009-2010):** Total instructional faculty: 341 full-time, 708 part-time (56% men; 44% women). Full-time faculty with Ph.D. or other terminal degree: 55%. Student/faculty ratio: 12/1. Classes of fewer than 20 students: 62%; of 20 to 49 students: 34%; of 50 or more students: 4%. **Advanced Placement and International Baccalaureate credit:** AP tests may be used for: Credit and/or placement. Scores accepted: 3, 4, 5. International Baccalaureate exams may be used for: Credit and/or placement. **Freshmen returning for sophomore year:** 75%. **Graduation rates:** Four-year: 11%; five-year: 26%; six-year: 33%. **Graduate study:** 45% of students pursue further study within one year. Fields in which graduates pursue further study: Master of Business Administration (MBA), 11%; law, 2%; medicine, 18%; engineering, 8%; education, 15%; arts and sciences, 29%; veterinary medicine, 1%.

COSTS AND FINANCIAL AID

Financial aid office: (907) 474-7256. **Expenses (2010-2011):** Tuition and fees 2010-2011: $5,668 in state, $16,258 out of state; room/board: $6,800. Estimated books and supplies: $1,300; transportation: $432; personal expenses: $2,070. **Financial aid:** Priority filing date for institution's financial aid form: February 15; deadline: July 1. In 2009-2010, 68% of undergraduates applied for financial aid. Of those, 44% were determined to have financial need; 40% had their need fully met. Average financial aid package (proportion receiving): $10,556 (43%). Average amount of gift aid, such as scholarships or grants (proportion receiving): $5,339 (31%). Average amount of self-help aid, such as work study or loans (proportion receiving): $9,801 (32%). Average need-based loan (excluding PLUS or other private loans): $9,707. Among students who received need-based aid, the average percentage of need met: 56%. Among students who received aid based on merit, the average award (and the proportion receiving): $7,683 (28%). The average athletic scholarship (and the proportion receiving): $9,908 (3%). Average amount of debt of borrowers graduating in 2009: $29,485. Proportion who borrowed: 54%.

CAMPUS LIFE AND EXTRACURRICULAR ACTIVITIES

Campus housing available (% using): coed dorms (75%), apartments for married students (4%), apartment for single students (18%), special housing for disabled students (1%), special housing for international students (1%), other housing options (1%). Students who live in college-owned, operated, or affiliated housing: 25%. **Student employment:** During the 2009-2010 academic year, 14% of undergraduates worked on campus. Average per-year earnings: $4,760. **Clubs and organizations:** Number of student organizations: 110. Activities include: campus ministries, choral groups, concert band, dance, drama/theater, international student organization, jazz band, literary magazine, model UN, music ensembles, pep band, radio station, student government, student newspaper, symphony orchestra, television station. Number of fraternities: 1; sororities: 1. **Sports program (2009-2010):** Member of NCAA II. *Men's intercollegiate varsity sports:* basketball, cross country, ice hockey, skiing (nordic), rifle. *Women's intercollegiate varsity sports:* basketball, cross country, skiing (nordic), rifle, swimming, volleyball.

SERVICES AND FACILITIES

Basic services: nonremedial tutoring, women's center, placement service, health service, health insurance, other. **Remedial assistance:** reading, math, writing, study skills, other. **Counseling services:** minority student, career, military, personal, veteran student, academic, psychological, birth control. **For learning-disabled students:** School does not offer a structured program with separate admission and additional fees. Services include: reading machines, tape recorders, note-taking services, oral tests, readers, extended time for tests, early syllabus, priority registration, priority seating, texts on tape, typist/scribe, exams on tape or computer, other testing accommodations, other. **Library:** Number of titles: 859,637; number of current serial subscriptions: 52,262. **Information technology resources:** Students are not required to lease or own a computer. Number of campus computers available to all students: 125. School has a wireless network. Approximate number of users that can be accommodated: 5,000. Proportion of college-owned housing units wired for high-speed internet access: 100%. **Campus safety:** Security services offered: 24-hour foot-and-vehicle patrols, late-night transport/escort service, 24-hour emergency telephones, lighted pathways/sidewalks, controlled dormitory access (key, security card, etc).

TRANSFER AND INTERNATIONAL STUDENTS

Transfer students: May apply for admission for the following academic terms: Fall, Spring, Summer. Applicants need a minimum number of credits to apply. For fall 2009: Transfer applications received: 892. Transfer applicants offered admission: 702. Transfer applicants enrolled: 460. **International students:** Number of foreign undergraduates: 113 (2% of student body). Number of countries represented: 26. Minimum TOEFL score required: 550 (paper); 80 (computer).

University of Alaska–Southeast

- **Address:** 11120 Glacier Highway, Juneau, AK 99801
- **Website:** http://www.uas.alaska.edu
- **Public**
- **Enrollment:** N/A

KEY STATS
- ✔ **U.S News College Ranking:** Unranked, Regional Universities (West)
- ✔ **SAT or ACT Score (25th/75th percentile):** N/A
- ✔ **Tuition:** 2009-2010: $4,888 in state, $14,788 out of state

Selectivity: N/A	Room/board: $6,430
Acceptance rate: N/A	Average debt: N/A
Student/faculty ratio: N/A	Proportion who borrowed: N/A

Arizona

Amer. Indian Coll. of the Assemb. of God

- **Address:** 10020 N. 15th Avenue, Phoenix, AZ 85021-2199
- **Website:** http://www.aicag.edu
- **Private; Religious affiliation:** Assemblies of God
- **Enrollment:** N/A

....

KEY STATS

✔ **U.S News College Ranking:** Unranked, Regional Colleges (West)
✔ **SAT or ACT Score (25th/75th percentile):** N/A
✔ **Tuition:** 2009-2010: $7,974

Selectivity: N/A	**Room/board:** $5,850
Acceptance rate: N/A	**Average debt:** N/A
Student/faculty ratio: N/A	**Proportion who borrowed:** N/A

Arizona State University

- **Address:** Tempe, AZ 85287
- **Website:** http://www.asu.edu
- **Public**
- **Enrollment:** 45,597 full-time; 8,680 part-time

....

KEY STATS

✔ **U.S News College Ranking:** 143, National Universities
✔ **SAT Score (25th/75th percentile):** 950-1210
✔ **Tuition:** 2010-2011: $7,661 in state, $20,596 out of state

Selectivity: Selective	**Room/board:** $9,706
Acceptance rate: 91%	**Average debt:** N/A
Student/faculty ratio: 23/1	**Proportion who borrowed:** N/A

UNDERGRADUATE STUDENT BODY STATS

2009-2010 enrollment: 45,597 full-time; 8,680 part-time. Men: 49%; women: 51%. **Ethnic makeup:** African American: 5%; American-Indian: 2%; Asian American: 6%; Hispanic: 16%; White: 68%; International: 2%.

ADMISSIONS FACTS AND FIGURES

Phone: (480) 965-7788. **Email:** admissions@asu.edu. **Website:** http://www.asu.edu. **Application deadlines for fall 2011:** Early decision: Not offered. Early action: Not offered. Admission cannot be deferred. **Application fee:** $55. **To apply online, go to:** http://students.asu.edu/undergraduate-admission. **Admissions requirements/recommendations:** High school units required (recommended): English: 4; Mathematics: 4; Science: 3; Foreign language: 2; Social studies: 1; History: 1; Total units: 16. Tests: The college uses SAT or ACT scores in admissions decisions. Either SAT or ACT required. For admission to the fall 2011 entering class, the school will accept: ACT with or without writing accepted. Campus visit: Recommended. Admissions interview: Neither required nor recommended. Off-campus interview: Not available. **Factors that count in admissions decisions:** *Academic:* Secondary school record: Not Considered. Class rank: Very Important. Letters of recommendation: Not Considered. Standardized test scores: Very Important. Essay: Not Considered. *Nonacademic:* Interview: Not Considered. Extracurricular activities: Not Considered. Talent/ability: Not Considered. Character/personal qualities: Not Considered. Alumni/ae relationship: Not Considered. Geographical residence: Not Considered. State residency: Important. Religious affiliation/commitment: Not Considered. Minority status: Not Considered. Volunteer work: Not Considered. Work experience: Not Considered. **Other schools with the greatest overlap in applicants:** Northern Arizona University; San Diego State University; University of Arizona; University of California–Los Angeles; University of Southern California. **Admissions statistics for the fall 2009 entering class:** Total applicants: 28,304. Total accepted: 25,616. Freshmen enrolled: 9,344; 29% were from out of state. Overall acceptance rate: 91%. **Credentials of fall 2009 freshmen:** 31% ranked in the top 10 percent of their high school

class; 57% were in the top 25 percent; 84% were in the top half. (Proportion submitting class standing: 75%.) **Average high school grade point average:** 3.4. **First-year students who submitted SAT scores:** 74%. Scores (25/75 percentile): Critical Reading: 470-590, Math: 480-620, Combined: 950-1210. **First-year students submitting ACT scores:** 39%. Scores (25/75 percentile): English: 20-26, Math: 20-27, Composite: 20-26.

ACADEMICS

Year founded: 1885. **Academic calendar:** Semester. **Degrees offered:** bachelor's, post-bachelor's certificate, master's, post-master's certificate, doctorate. **Most popular majors:** 17% business, management, marketing, and related support services, 9% education, 9% multi/interdisciplinary studies, 8% social sciences, 7% communication, journalism, and related programs. **Major fields of study:** architecture and related services; area, ethnic, cultural, and gender studies; biological and biomedical sciences; business, management, marketing, and related support services; communication, journalism, and related programs; computer and information sciences and support services; education; engineering; English language and literature/letters; family and consumer sciences/human sciences; foreign languages, literatures, and linguistics; health professions and related clinical sciences; history; legal professions and studies; liberal arts and sciences studies, and humanities; mathematics and statistics; multi/interdisciplinary studies; parks, recreation, leisure, and fitness studies; philosophy and religious studies; physical sciences; psychology; security and protective services; social sciences; visual and performing arts. **Areas of required coursework:** arts/fine arts, humanities, computer literacy, mathematics, English (including composition), foreign languages, sciences (biological or physical), history, social science. **Pre-professional programs:** pre-law, pre-dentistry, pre-medicine, pre-theology, pre-optometry, pre-pharmacy, other. **Special academic programs:** accelerated program, cooperative (work-study plan) program, distance learning, double major, exchange student program (domestic), honors program, independent study, internships, study abroad, teacher certificate program. **Teacher certification offered in:** early childhood, special education, elementary, middle/junior high, secondary, bilingual/bicultural. **Cooperative education programs:** business, engineering. **Reserve Officers Training Corps (ROTC):** Army ROTC: Offered on campus; Air Force ROTC: Offered on campus. **Faculty and instruction (2009-2010):** Total instructional faculty: 2,492 full-time, 237 part-time (58% men; 42% women; 20% minorities). Full-time faculty with Ph.D. or other terminal degree: 85%. Student/faculty ratio: 23/1. Classes of fewer than 20 students: 38%; of 20 to 49 students: 45%; of 50 or more students: 17%. **Advanced Placement and International Baccalaureate credit:** AP tests may be used for: Credit only. Scores accepted: 3, 4, 5. International Baccalaureate exams may be used for: Credit only. **Freshmen returning for sophomore year:** 80%. **Graduation rates:** Four-year: 30%; five-year: 50%; six-year: 56%. **Graduate study:** Fields in which graduates pursue further study: Master of Business Administration (MBA), 21%; law, 9%; medicine, 7%; dentistry, 1%; engineering, 6%; education, 20%; arts and sciences, 27%; veterinary medicine, 1%.

COSTS AND FINANCIAL AID

Financial aid office: (480) 965-3355. **Expenses (2010-2011):** Tuition and fees 2010-2011: $7,661 in state, $20,596 out of state; room/board: $9,706. Estimated books and supplies: $1,290; transportation: $550; personal expenses: $2,200. **Financial aid:** Priority filing date for institution's financial aid form: March 1.

CAMPUS LIFE AND EXTRACURRICULAR ACTIVITIES

Campus housing available: coed dorms, sorority housing, fraternity housing, apartments for married students, apartment for single students, other housing options. Students who live in college-owned, operated, or affiliated housing: 20%. **Clubs and organizations:** Number of student organizations: 675. Activities include: campus ministries, choral groups, concert band, dance, drama/theater, international student organization, jazz band, literary magazine, marching band, model UN, music ensembles, musical theater, opera, pep band, radio station, student government, student newspaper, student film society, symphony orchestra, television station. Number of fraternities: 31; sororities: 23. Proportion of men in fraternities: 6%; of women in sororities: 6%. **Sports program (2009-2010):** Member of NCAA I. *Men's* intercollegiate varsity sports: baseball, basketball, cross country, football, golf, swimming, track and field (indoor), track and field (outdoor), wrestling. Women's intercollegiate varsity sports: basketball, cross country, golf, gymnastics, soccer, softball, swimming, tennis, track and field (indoor), track and field (outdoor), volleyball, water polo.

SERVICES AND FACILITIES

Basic services: nonremedial tutoring, women's center, placement service, day care, health service, health insurance. Counseling services: minority student, career, military, personal, veteran student, academic, older student, psychological, birth control, religious. For learning-disabled students: School does not offer a structured program with separate admission and additional fees. Total undergraduates in learning-disabled program or receiving services: 259. Services include: reading machines, note-taking services, oral tests, readers, extended time for tests, tutors, priority registration, substitution of courses, texts on tape, exams on tape or computer, other testing accommodations, other. Library: Number of titles: 4,393,156; number of current serial subscriptions: 95,515. Information technology resources: Students are not required to lease or own a computer. Number of campus computers available to all students: 4,200. School has a wireless network. Approximate number of users that can be accommodated: 84,000. Proportion of college-owned housing units wired for high-speed internet access: 100%. Campus safety: Security services offered: 24-hour foot-and-vehicle patrols, late-night transport/escort service, 24-hour emergency telephones, lighted pathways/sidewalks, controlled dormitory access (key, security card, etc).

TRANSFER AND INTERNATIONAL STUDENTS

Transfer students: May apply for admission for the following academic terms: Fall, Winter, Spring, Summer. Applicants do not need a minimum number of credits to apply. For fall 2009: Transfer applications received: 9,893. Transfer applicants offered admission: 8,348. Transfer applicants enrolled: 5,388. International students: Number of foreign undergraduates: 1220 (2% of student body). Number of countries represented: 101. Minimum TOEFL score required: 500 (paper); 173 (computer).

Prescott College

- **Address:** 220 Grove Avenue, Prescott, AZ 86301
- **Website:** http://www.prescott.edu/
- **Private**
- **Enrollment:** 634 full-time; 127 part-time

KEY STATS

- ✔ **U.S News College Ranking:** 62, Regional Universities (West)
- ✔ **SAT Score (25th/75th percentile):** 1000-1230
- ✔ **Tuition:** 2010-2011: $27,265

Selectivity: Selective	**Room/board:** $6,000
Acceptance rate: 81%	**Average debt:** $14,947
Student/faculty ratio: 8/1	**Proportion who borrowed:** 67%

UNDERGRADUATE STUDENT BODY STATS

2009-2010 enrollment: 634 full-time; 127 part-time. Men: 42%; women: 58%. Ethnic makeup: African American: 2%; American-Indian: 2%; Asian American: 1%; Hispanic: 7%; White: 88%; International: 1%.

ADMISSIONS FACTS AND FIGURES

Phone: (877) 350-2100. Email: admissions@prescott.edu. Website: http://www.prescott.edu/. Application deadlines for fall 2011: Regular decision: August 15. Early decision: Send application by: December 1; Decision sent by: December 15. Early action: Not offered. Admission can be deferred. Application fee: $25. To apply online, go to: http://www.prescott.edu/apply/index.html. Admissions requirements/recommendations: High school units required (recommended): English: 4 (4); Mathematics: 3 (3); Science: 2 (2); Foreign language: 1 (1); Social studies: 3 (3); History: 2 (2); Academic electives: 0 (0); Total units: 16 (16). Tests: The college uses SAT or ACT scores in admissions decisions. Either SAT or ACT required. For admission to the fall 2011 entering class, the school will accept: ACT with or without writing accepted. Campus visit: Recommended. Admissions interview: Recommended. Off-campus interview: May be arranged. Factors that count in admissions decisions: Academic: Secondary school record: Very Important. Class rank: Not Considered. Letters of recommendation: Very Important. Standardized test scores: Important. Essay: Very Important. Nonacademic: Interview: Important. Extracurricular activities: Important.

Talent/ability: Important. Character/personal qualities: Important. Alumni/ae relationship: Not Considered. Geographical residence: Not Considered. State residency: Not Considered. Religious affiliation/commitment: Not Considered. Minority status: Not Considered. Volunteer work: Important. Work experience: Important. Other schools with the greatest overlap in applicants: College of the Atlantic; Earlham College; Green Mountain College; Hampshire College; Reed College. Admissions statistics for the fall 2009 entering class: Total applicants: 342. Total accepted: 278. Freshmen enrolled: 72; 86% were from out of state. Overall acceptance rate: 81%. Early-decision acceptance rate: 75%. Non-early acceptance rate: 81%. Credentials of fall 2009 freshmen: 11% ranked in the top 10 percent of their high school class; 32% were in the top 25 percent; 57% were in the top half. (Proportion submitting class standing: 50%.) First-year students who submitted SAT scores: 38%. Scores (25/75 percentile): Critical Reading: 530-650, Math: 470-580, Combined: 1000-1230. First-year students submitting ACT scores: 31%. Scores (25/75 percentile): English: 21-29, Math: 17-26, Composite: 19-27.

ACADEMICS

Year founded: 1966. Academic calendar: Semester. Degrees offered: bachelor's, post-bachelor's certificate, master's, post-master's certificate, doctorate. Most popular majors: 38% education, 14% psychology, 10% natural resources and conservation, 8% military technologies, 7% public administration and social service professions. Major fields of study: agriculture, agriculture operations, and related sciences; area, ethnic, cultural, and gender studies; biological and biomedical sciences; business, management, marketing, and related support services; communication, journalism, and related programs; computer and information sciences and support services; education; English language and literature/letters; family and consumer sciences/human sciences; foreign languages, literatures, and linguistics; health professions and related clinical sciences; history; liberal arts and sciences studies, and humanities; library science; mathematics and statistics; multi/interdisciplinary studies; natural resources and conservation; parks, recreation, leisure, and fitness studies; philosophy and religious studies; physical sciences; psychology; public administration and social service professions; social sciences; visual and performing arts. Areas of required coursework: mathematics, English (including composition). Special academic programs: cross-registration, double major, exchange student program (domestic), external degree program, independent study, internships, liberal arts/career combination, student-designed major, study abroad, teacher certificate program, other. Teacher certification offered in: early childhood, special education, elementary, secondary, bilingual/bicultural. Cooperative education programs: other. Faculty instruction (2009-2010): Total instructional faculty: 69 full-time, 52 part-time (47% men; 53% women; 8% minorities). Full-time faculty with Ph.D. or other terminal degree: 75%. Student/faculty ratio: 8/1. Advanced Placement and International Baccalaureate credit: AP tests may be used for: Credit and/or placement. Scores accepted: 4, 5. International Baccalaureate exams may be used for: Credit and/or placement. Freshmen returning for sophomore year: 75%. Graduation rates: Four-year: 10%; five-year: 39%; six-year: 43%. Graduate study: 43% of students pursue further study within five years.

COSTS AND FINANCIAL AID

Financial aid office: (928) 350-1111. Expenses (2010-2011): Tuition and fees 2010-2011: $27,265; room/board: $6,000. Estimated books and supplies: $624; transportation: $2,290; personal expenses: $1,248. Financial aid: Priority filing date for institution's financial aid form: March 1. In 2009-2010, 70% of undergraduates applied for financial aid. Of those, 63% were determined to have financial need; 6% had their need fully met. Average financial aid package (proportion receiving): $13,099 (63%). Average amount of gift aid, such as scholarships or grants (proportion receiving): $9,075 (57%). Average amount of self-help aid, such as work study or loans (proportion receiving): $4,963 (61%). Average need-based loan (excluding PLUS or other private loans): $4,589. Among students who received need-based aid, the average percentage of need met: 47%. Among students who received aid based on merit, the average award (and the proportion receiving): $5,467 (22%). The average athletic scholarship (and the proportion receiving): $0 (0%). Average amount of debt of borrowers graduating in 2009: $14,947. Proportion who borrowed: 67%.

CAMPUS LIFE AND EXTRACURRICULAR ACTIVITIES

Campus housing available (% using): coed dorms (100%). Students who live in college-owned, operated, or affiliated housing: 4%. Clubs and organizations: Number of student organizations: 7. Activities include: dance, drama/theater, international student organization, literary magazine, radio station, student government, student newspaper, student film society. Number of fraternities: o; sororities: o. Average proportion of students who stay on campus on weekends: 3%.

SERVICES AND FACILITIES
Basic services: nonremedial tutoring, health insurance. **Remedial assistance:** reading, math, writing, study skills. **Counseling services:** career, personal, academic, psychological. **For learning-disabled students:** School does not offer a structured program with separate admission and additional fees. Services include: tape recorders, untimed tests, note-taking services, readers, extended time for tests, tutors, priority seating, texts on tape, other testing accommodations, other. **Library:** Number of titles: 33,302; number of current serial subscriptions: 242. **Information technology resources:** Students are not required to lease or own a computer. Number of campus computers available to all students: 72. School has a wireless network. Approximate number of users that can be accommodated: 250. Proportion of college-owned housing units wired for high-speed internet access: 100%. **Campus safety:** Security services offered: late-night transport/escort service, lighted pathways/sidewalks, controlled dormitory access (key, security card, etc).

TRANSFER AND INTERNATIONAL STUDENTS
Transfer students: May apply for admission for the following academic terms: Fall, Spring. Applicants do not need a minimum number of credits to apply. For fall 2009: Transfer applications received: 293. Transfer applicants offered admission: 247. Transfer applicants enrolled: 146. **International students:** Number of foreign undergraduates: 8 (1% of student body). Number of countries represented: 3. Minimum TOEFL score required: 500 (paper); 173 (computer). Average TOEFL score: 600 (paper).

University of Arizona

- **Address:** PO Box 210066, Tucson, AZ 85721-0066
- **Website:** http://www.arizona.edu
- **Public**
- **Enrollment:** 27,103 full-time; 3,243 part-time

KEY STATS
✔ **U.S News College Ranking:** 120, National Universities
✔ **SAT Score (25th/75th percentile):** 950-1220
✔ **Tuition:** 2010-2011: $6,845 in state, $22,254 out of state
Selectivity: Selective   **Room/board:** $8,614
Acceptance rate: 78%   **Average debt:** $18,712
Student/faculty ratio: 20/1   **Proportion who borrowed:** 46%

UNDERGRADUATE STUDENT BODY STATS
2009-2010 enrollment: 27,103 full-time; 3,243 part-time. Men: 48%; women: 52%. **Ethnic makeup:** African American: 4%; American-Indian: 3%; Asian American: 7%; Hispanic: 18%; White: 65%; International: 3%.

ADMISSIONS FACTS AND FIGURES
Phone: (520) 621-3237. **Email:** appinfo@arizona.edu. **Website:** http://www.arizona.edu. **Application deadlines for fall 2011:** Regular decision: April 1. Early decision: Not offered. Early action: Not offered. Admission cannot be deferred. **Application fee:** $50. **To apply online, go to:** http://www.admissions.arizona.edu. **Admissions requirements/recommendations:** High school units required (recommended): English: 4 (4); Mathematics: 3 (3); Science: 3 (3); Foreign language: 2 (2); Social studies: 1 (2); History: 1 (1); Total units: 16 (16). Tests: The college uses SAT or ACT scores in admissions decisions. Neither SAT nor ACT required. For admission to the fall 2011 entering class, the school will accept: ACT with or without writing accepted. Campus visit: Neither required nor recommended. Admissions interview: Neither required nor recommended. Off-campus interview: May be arranged. **Factors that count in admissions decisions:** *Academic:* Secondary school record: Very Important. Class rank: Considered. Letters of recommendation: Considered. Standardized test scores: Considered. Essay: Considered. *Nonacademic:* Interview: Considered. Extracurricular activities: Considered. Talent/ability: Considered. Character/personal qualities: Considered. Alumni/ae relationship: Not Considered. Geographical residence: Considered. State residency: Considered. Religious affiliation/commitment: Not Considered. Minority status: Considered. Volunteer work: Considered. Work experience: Considered. **Other schools with the greatest overlap in applicants:** Arizona State University; Northern Arizona University; San Diego State University; University of California–Irvine; University of California–San Diego. **Admissions statistics for the fall 2009 entering class:** Total applicants: 24,625. Total accepted: 19,207. Freshmen enrolled: 6,966; 39% were from out of state. Overall acceptance rate: 78%. **Credentials of fall 2009 freshmen:** 34% ranked in the top 10 percent of their high school class; 62% were in the top 25 percent; 88% were in the top half. (Proportion submitting class standing: 55%.) **Average high school grade point average:** 3.4. **First-year students who submitted SAT scores:** 76%. Scores (25/75 percentile): Critical Reading: 460-600, Math: 490-620, Combined: 950-1220. **First-year students submitting ACT scores:** 42%. Scores (25/75 percentile): English: N/A, Math: N/A, Composite: 21-27.

ACADEMICS
Year founded: 1885. **Academic calendar:** Semester. **Degrees offered:** bachelor's, post-bachelor's certificate, master's, doctorate. **Most popular majors:** 13% business, management, marketing, and related support services, 10% biological and biomedical sciences, 10% social sciences, 8% communication, journalism, and related programs, 8% psychology. **Major fields of study:** agriculture, agriculture operations, and related sciences; architecture and related services; area, ethnic, cultural, and gender studies; biological and biomedical sciences; business, management, marketing, and related support services; communication, journalism, and related programs; communications technologies/technicians and support services; computer and information sciences and support services; education; engineering; engineering technologies/technicians; English language and literature/letters; family and consumer sciences/human sciences; foreign languages, literatures, and linguistics; health professions and related clinical sciences; history; liberal arts and sciences studies, and humanities; mathematics and statistics; multi/interdisciplinary studies; natural resources and conservation; philosophy and religious studies; physical sciences; psychology; public administration and social service professions; security and protective services; social sciences; visual and performing arts. **Areas of required coursework:** arts/fine arts, humanities, mathematics, English (including composition), foreign languages, sciences (biological or physical), social science. **Pre-professional programs:** pre-law, pre-medicine, pre-veterinary science, pre-pharmacy. **Special academic programs:** accelerated program, cooperative (work-study plan) program, cross-registration, distance learning, double major, dual enrollment, English as a Second Language (ESL), exchange student program (domestic), external degree program, honors program, independent study, internships, study abroad, teacher certificate program, weekend college. **Teacher certification offered in:** special education, elementary, secondary, bilingual/bicultural. **Cooperative education programs:** agriculture. **Reserve Officers Training Corps (ROTC):** Army ROTC: Offered on campus; Navy ROTC: Offered on campus; Air Force ROTC: Offered on campus. **Faculty and instruction (2009-2010):** Total instructional faculty: 1,546 full-time, 407 part-time (62% men; 38% women; 16% minorities). Full-time faculty with Ph.D. or other terminal degree: 91%. Student/faculty ratio: 20/1. Classes of fewer than 20 students: 39%; of 20 to 49 students: 49%; of 50 or more students: 12%. **Advanced Placement and International Baccalaureate credit:** AP tests may be used for: Placement only. Scores accepted: 4, 5. International Baccalaureate exams may be used for: Placement only. **Freshmen returning for sophomore year:** 79%. **Graduation rates:** Four-year: 32%; five-year: 53%; six-year: 58%.

COSTS AND FINANCIAL AID
Financial aid office: (520) 621-5200. **Expenses (2010-2011):** Tuition and fees 2010-2011: $6,845 in state, $22,254 out of state; room/board: $8,614. Estimated books and supplies: $1,000; transportation: $1,682; personal expenses: $2,368. **Financial aid:** Priority filing date for institution's financial aid form: March 1. In 2009-2010, 64% of undergraduates applied for financial aid. Of those, 39% were determined to have financial need; 10% had their need fully met. Average financial aid package (proportion receiving): $10,021 (38%). Average amount of gift aid, such as scholarships or grants (proportion receiving): $7,849 (34%). Average amount of self-help aid, such as work study or loans (proportion receiving): $4,406 (25%). Average need-based loan (excluding PLUS or other private loans): $4,325. Among students who received need-based aid, the average percentage of need met: 64%. Among students who received aid based on merit, the average award (and the proportion receiving): $5,064 (25%). The average athletic scholarship (and the proportion receiving): $12,770 (1%). Average amount of debt of borrowers graduating in 2009: $18,712. Proportion who borrowed: 46%.

CAMPUS LIFE AND EXTRACURRICULAR ACTIVITIES
Campus housing available: coed dorms, women's dorms, sorority housing, fraternity housing, apartment for single students, special housing for disabled students, special housing for international students. Students who live in college-owned, operated, or affiliated housing: 20%. **Clubs and orga-**

nizations: Number of student organizations: 442. Activities include: campus ministries, choral groups, concert band, dance, drama/theater, international student organization, jazz band, literary magazine, marching band, model UN, music ensembles, musical theater, opera, pep band, radio station, student government, student newspaper, symphony orchestra, television station, yearbook. Number of fraternities: 29; sororities: 21. Proportion of men in fraternities: 10%; of women in sororities: 11%. **Sports program (2009-2010):** Member of NCAA I. *Men's intercollegiate varsity sports:* baseball, basketball, cross country, football, golf, gymnastics, soccer, swimming, tennis, track and field (indoor), track and field (outdoor). *Women's intercollegiate varsity sports:* basketball, cross country, golf, gymnastics, soccer, softball, swimming, tennis, track and field (indoor), track and field (outdoor), volleyball.

SERVICES AND FACILITIES

Basic services: nonremedial tutoring, women's center, placement service, health service, health insurance. **Counseling services:** minority student, career, military, personal, veteran student, academic, psychological, birth control. **For learning-disabled students:** School does not offer a structured program with separate admission and additional fees. Services include: remedial math, remedial English, reading machines, tape recorders, note-taking services, learning center, readers, extended time for tests, tutors, texts on tape, other testing accommodations. **Library:** Number of titles: 5,401,783; number of current serial subscriptions: 63,017. **Information technology resources:** Students are not required to lease or own a computer. Number of campus computers available to all students: 3,400. School has a wireless network. Proportion of college-owned housing units wired for high-speed internet access: 100%. **Campus safety:** Security services offered: 24-hour foot-and-vehicle patrols, late-night transport/escort service, 24-hour emergency telephones, lighted pathways/sidewalks, controlled dormitory access (key, security card, etc).

TRANSFER AND INTERNATIONAL STUDENTS

Transfer students: May apply for admission for the following academic terms: Fall, Spring, Summer. Applicants need a minimum number of credits to apply. For fall 2009: Transfer applications received: 4,633. Transfer applicants offered admission: 2,962. Transfer applicants enrolled: 1,912. **International students:** Number of foreign undergraduates: 978 (3% of student body). Number of countries represented: 122. Minimum TOEFL score required: 500 (paper); 173 (computer). Average TOEFL score: 590 (paper).

Arkansas

Arkansas Baptist College

- **Address:** 1600 Bishop Street, Little Rock, AR 72202
- **Website:** http://www.arkansasbaptist.edu/
- **Private; Religious affiliation:** Baptist
- **Enrollment:** N/A

KEY STATS
- ✔ **U.S News College Ranking:** Unranked, Regional Colleges (South)
- ✔ **SAT or ACT Score (25th/75th percentile):** N/A
- ✔ **Tuition:** 2009-2010: $7,018

Selectivity: N/A	Room/board: $7,398
Acceptance rate: N/A	Average debt: N/A
Student/faculty ratio: N/A	Proportion who borrowed: N/A

Arkansas State University–Jonesboro

- **Address:** PO Box 600, State University, AR 72467
- **Website:** http://www.astate.edu
- **Public**
- **Enrollment:** 7,732 full-time; 2,292 part-time

KEY STATS
- ✔ **U.S News College Ranking:** 58, Regional Universities (South)
- ✔ **ACT Score (25th/75th percentile):** 18-24
- ✔ **Tuition:** 2009-2010: $6,370 in state, $14,290 out of state

Selectivity: Selective	Room/board: $6,256
Acceptance rate: 77%	Average debt: $18,900
Student/faculty ratio: 17/1	Proportion who borrowed: 68%

UNDERGRADUATE STUDENT BODY STATS
2009-2010 enrollment: 7,732 full-time; 2,292 part-time. Men: 42%; women: 58%. **Ethnic makeup:** African American: 18%; American-Indian: 1%; Asian American: 1%; Hispanic: 1%; White: 77%; International: 2%.

ADMISSIONS FACTS AND FIGURES
Phone: (870) 972-3024. **Email:** admissions@astate.edu. **Website:** http://www.astate.edu. **Application deadlines for fall 2011:** Regular decision: August 23. Early decision: Not offered. Early action: Not offered. Admission can be deferred. **Application fee:** $15. **To apply online, go to:** http://www2.astate.edu/a/student-affairs/admissions/apply-now/. **Admissions requirements/recommendations:** High school units required (recommended): English: 4 (4); Mathematics: 4 (4); Science: 3 (3); Foreign language: 2 (2); Social studies: 1 (1); History: 2 (2); Total units: 16 (16). Tests: The college uses SAT or ACT scores in admissions decisions. Either SAT or ACT required. For admission to the fall 2011 entering class, the school will accept: ACT with or without writing accepted. Campus visit: Recommended. Admissions interview: Neither required nor recommended. Off-campus interview: Not available. **Factors that count in admissions decisions:** *Academic:* Secondary school record: Very Important. Class rank: Considered. Letters of recommendation: Considered. Standardized test scores: Very Important. Essay: Not Considered. *Nonacademic:* Interview: Not Considered. Extracurricular activities: Not Considered. Talent/ability: Considered. Character/personal qualities: Not Considered. Alumni/ae relationship: Not Considered. Geographical residence: Not Considered. State residency: Not Considered. Religious affiliation/commitment: Not Considered. Minority status: Not Considered. Volunteer work: Not Considered. Work experience: Not Considered. **Other schools with the greatest overlap in applicants:** University of Arkansas; University of Arkansas–Little Rock; University of Central Arkansas; University of Memphis; University of Mississippi. **Admissions statistics for the fall 2009 entering class:** Total applicants: 4,118. Total accepted: 3,156. Freshmen enrolled: 1,725; 14% were from out of state. Overall acceptance rate: 77%. **Credentials of fall 2009 freshmen:** 20% ranked

in the top 10 percent of their high school class; 40% were in the top 25 percent; 66% were in the top half. (Proportion submitting class standing: 51%.) **Average high school grade point average:** 3.2. **First-year students who submitted SAT scores:** 2%. Scores (25/75 percentile): Critical Reading: 410-540, Math: 440-570, Combined: 850-1110. **First-year students submitting ACT scores:** 90%. Scores (25/75 percentile): English: 18-25, Math: 17-24, Composite: 18-24.

ACADEMICS
Year founded: 1909. **Academic calendar:** Semester. **Degrees offered:** associate, bachelor's, post-bachelor's certificate, master's, post-master's certificate, doctorate. **Most popular majors:** 18% business, management, marketing, and related support services, 18% education, 14% health professions and related clinical sciences, 7% liberal arts and sciences studies, and humanities, 6% communication, journalism, and related programs. **Major fields of study:** agriculture, agriculture operations, and related sciences; biological and biomedical sciences; business, management, marketing, and related support services; communication, journalism, and related programs; communications technologies/technicians and support services; computer and information sciences and support services; education; engineering; engineering technologies/technicians; English language and literature/letters; foreign languages, literatures, and linguistics; health professions and related clinical sciences; history; liberal arts and sciences studies, and humanities; mathematics and statistics; natural resources and conservation; parks, recreation, leisure, and fitness studies; philosophy and religious studies; physical sciences; psychology; public administration and social service professions; security and protective services; social sciences; visual and performing arts. **Areas of required coursework:** arts/fine arts, humanities, mathematics, English (including composition), philosophy, sciences (biological or physical), history, social science, other. **Pre-professional programs:** pre-law, pre-dentistry, pre-medicine, pre-veterinary science, pre-pharmacy, other. **Special academic programs (% participation):** accelerated program (2%), distance learning (7%), double major (2%), dual enrollment (2%), English as a Second Language (ESL) (1%), exchange student program (domestic) (1%), honors program (6%), independent study (12%), internships (2%), study abroad (1%), teacher certificate program (9%). **Teacher certification offered in:** early childhood, special education, elementary, vo-tech, middle/junior high, adult education, secondary, bilingual/bicultural. **Reserve Officers Training Corps (ROTC):** Army ROTC: Offered on campus. **Faculty and instruction (2009-2010):** Total instructional faculty: 482 full-time, 172 part-time (46% men; 54% women; 15% minorities). Full-time faculty with Ph.D. or other terminal degree: 63%. Student/faculty ratio: 17/1. Classes of fewer than 20 students: 37%; of 20 to 49 students: 57%; of 50 or more students: 6%. **Advanced Placement and International Baccalaureate credit:** AP tests may be used for: Credit only. Scores accepted: 3, 4, 5. **Freshmen returning for sophomore year:** 69%. **Graduation rates:** Four-year: 16%; five-year: 30%; six-year: 39%. **Graduate study:** 10% of students pursue further study immediately upon graduation; 22% within one year; 35% within five years. Fields in which graduates pursue further study: Master of Business Administration (MBA), 20%; law, 1%; medicine, 25%; dentistry, 1%; engineering, 3%; education, 35%; arts and sciences, 14%; veterinary medicine, 1%.

COSTS AND FINANCIAL AID
Financial aid office: (870) 972-2310. **Expenses (2009-2010):** Tuition and fees 2009-2010: $6,370 in state, $14,290 out of state; room/board: $6,256. Estimated books and supplies: $1,000 personal expenses: $3,800. **Financial aid:** Priority filing date for institution's financial aid form: February 15; deadline: July 1. In 2009-2010, 94% of undergraduates applied for financial aid. Of those, 75% were determined to have financial need; 24% had their need fully met. Average financial aid package (proportion receiving): $9,950 (73%). Average amount of gift aid, such as scholarships or grants (proportion receiving): $5,875 (62%). Average amount of self-help aid, such as work study or loans (proportion receiving): $2,700 (56%). Average need-based loan (excluding PLUS or other private loans): $4,600. Among students who received need-based aid, the average percentage of need met: 50%. Among students who received aid based on merit, the average award (and the proportion receiving): $5,650 (6%). The average athletic scholarship (and the

proportion receiving): $8,865 (3%). Average amount of debt of borrowers graduating in 2009: $18,900. Proportion who borrowed: 68%.

CAMPUS LIFE AND EXTRACURRICULAR ACTIVITIES

Campus housing available (% using): coed dorms (52%), women's dorms (10%), men's dorms (12%), fraternity housing (1%), apartments for married students (6%), apartment for single students (18%), other housing options (1%). Students who live in college-owned, operated, or affiliated housing: 24%. **Student employment:** During the 2009-2010 academic year, 5% of undergraduates worked on campus. Average per-year earnings: $4,176. **Clubs and organizations:** Number of student organizations: 107. Activities include: campus ministries, choral groups, concert band, dance, drama/theater, international student organization, jazz band, marching band, model UN, music ensembles, musical theater, opera, pep band, radio station, student government, student newspaper, symphony orchestra, television station, yearbook. Number of fraternities: 9; sororities: 7. Proportion of men in fraternities: 12%; of women in sororities: 7%. Average proportion of students who stay on campus on weekends: 7%. **Sports program (2009-2010):** Member of NCAA I. *Men's intercollegiate varsity sports:* baseball, basketball, cross country, football, golf, track and field (indoor), track and field (outdoor). *Women's intercollegiate varsity sports:* basketball, bowling, cross country, golf, soccer, tennis, track and field (indoor), track and field (outdoor), volleyball.

SERVICES AND FACILITIES

Basic services: nonremedial tutoring, placement service, day care, health service, other. **Remedial assistance:** reading, math, writing, study skills, other. **Counseling services:** career, military, personal, veteran student, academic, older student, psychological. **For learning-disabled students:** School does not offer a structured program with separate admission and additional fees. Total undergraduates in learning-disabled program or receiving services: 158. Services include: remedial math, remedial English, reading machines, remedial reading, tape recorders, other special classes, videotaped classes, note-taking services, oral tests, learning center, readers, extended time for tests, tutors, priority registration, priority seating, substitution of courses, texts on tape, typist/scribe, exams on tape or computer, take home exams, other testing accommodations, waiver of foreign language degree requirement, waiver of math degree requirement, other. **Library:** Number of titles: 631,161; number of current serial subscriptions: 3,595. **Information technology resources:** Students are not required to lease or own a computer. Number of campus computers available to all students: 510. School has a wireless network. Approximate number of users that can be accommodated: 4,000. Proportion of college-owned housing units wired for high-speed internet access: 100%. **Campus safety:** Security services offered: 24-hour foot-and-vehicle patrols, late-night transport/escort service, 24-hour emergency telephones, lighted pathways/sidewalks, student patrols, controlled dormitory access (key, security card, etc).

TRANSFER AND INTERNATIONAL STUDENTS

Transfer students: May apply for admission for the following academic terms: Fall, Spring, Summer. Applicants need a minimum number of credits to apply. For fall 2009: Transfer applications received: 1,543. Transfer applicants offered admission: 1,260. Transfer applicants enrolled: 880. **International students:** Number of foreign undergraduates: 215 (2% of student body). Number of countries represented: 44. Minimum TOEFL score required: 500 (paper); 61 (computer). Average TOEFL score: 537 (paper).

Arkansas Tech University

- Address: 1509 N. Boulder Avenue, Russellville, AR 72801-2222
- Website: http://www.atu.edu
- Public
- Enrollment: 6,377 full-time; 1,876 part-time

KEY STATS

✔ **U.S News College Ranking:** 87, Regional Universities (South)
✔ **ACT Score (25th/75th percentile):** 20-26
✔ **Tuition:** 2009-2010: $5,610 in state, $10,620 out of state

Selectivity: Selective	**Room/board:** $5,156
Acceptance rate: 94%	**Average debt:** $12,562
Student/faculty ratio: 18/1	**Proportion who borrowed:** 51%

UNDERGRADUATE STUDENT BODY STATS

2009-2010 enrollment: 6,377 full-time; 1,876 part-time. Men: 47%; women: 53%. **Ethnic makeup:** African American: 5%; American-Indian: 2%; Asian American: 2%; Hispanic: 4%; White: 85%; International: 3%.

ADMISSIONS FACTS AND FIGURES

Phone: (479) 968-0343. **Email:** tech.enroll@atu.edu. **Website:** http://www.atu.edu. **Application deadlines for fall 2011:** Regular decision: Rolling. Early decision: Not offered. Early action: Not offered. Admission can be deferred. **To apply online, go to:** http://admissions.atu.edu. **Admissions requirements/recommendations:** High school units required (recommended): English: (4); Mathematics: 4 (0); Science: (3); Foreign language: (2); Social studies: (3); History: (0); Academic electives: (4); Total units: 4 (21). Tests: The college uses SAT or ACT scores in admissions decisions. Either SAT or ACT required. For admission to the fall 2011 entering class, the school will accept: ACT with or without writing accepted. Campus visit: Recommended. Admissions interview: Neither required nor recommended. Off-campus interview: May be arranged. **Factors that count in admissions decisions: *Academic:*** Secondary school record: Important. Class rank: Not Considered. Letters of recommendation: Not Considered. Standardized test scores: Very Important. Essay: Not Considered. ***Nonacademic:*** Interview: Not Considered. Extracurricular activities: Not Considered. Talent/ability: Not Considered. Character/personal qualities: Not Considered. Alumni/ae relationship: Not Considered. Geographical residence: Not Considered. State residency: Not Considered. Religious affiliation/commitment: Not Considered. Minority status: Not Considered. Volunteer work: Not Considered. Work experience: Not Considered. **Other schools with the greatest overlap in applicants:** University of Arkansas; University of Central Arkansas. **Admissions statistics for the fall 2009 entering class:** Total applicants: 3,304. Total accepted: 3,095. Freshmen enrolled: 1,841; 3% were from out of state. Overall acceptance rate: 94%. **Credentials of fall 2009 freshmen:** 19% ranked in the top 10 percent of their high school class; 45% were in the top 25 percent; 71% were in the top half. (Proportion submitting class standing: 82%.) **Average high school grade point average:** 3.2. **First-year students who submitted SAT scores:** 1%. Scores (25/75 percentile): Critical Reading: 370-530, Math: 460-620, Combined: 830-1150. **First-year students submitting ACT scores:** 79%. Scores (25/75 percentile): English: 19-26, Math: 20-27, Composite: 20-26.

ACADEMICS

Year founded: 1909. **Academic calendar:** Semester. **Degrees offered:** certificate, associate, terminal-associate, bachelor's, master's, post-master's certificate. **Most popular majors:** 9% early childhood education and teaching, 9% nursing/registered nurse training (R.N., A.S.N., B.S.N., M.S.N.), 8% business administration and management, 5% history, 5% multi/interdisciplinary studies. **Major fields of study:** agriculture, agriculture operations, and related sciences; biological and biomedical sciences; business, management, marketing, and related support services; communication, journalism, and related programs; computer and information sciences and support services; education; engineering; English language and literature/letters; foreign languages, literatures, and linguistics; health professions and related clinical sciences; history; liberal arts and sciences studies, and humanities; mathematics and statistics; multi/interdisciplinary studies; parks, recreation, leisure, and fitness studies; physical sciences; psychology; security and protective services; social sciences; visual and performing arts. **Areas of required coursework:** arts/fine arts, humanities, computer literacy, mathematics, English (including composition), philosophy, sciences (biological or physical), history, social science, other. **Pre-professional programs:** pre-law, pre-dentistry, pre-medicine, pre-pharmacy. **Special academic programs:** distance learning, double major, dual enrollment, English as a Second Language (ESL), honors program, independent study, internships, study abroad, teacher certificate program. **Teacher certification offered in:** early childhood, elementary, middle/junior high, secondary, bilingual/bicultural. **Reserve Officers Training Corps (ROTC):** Army ROTC: Offered at cooperating institution (University of Central Arkansas). **Faculty and instruction (2009-2010):** Total instructional faculty: 293 full-time, 163 part-time (48% men; 52% women; 7% minorities). Full-time faculty with Ph.D. or other terminal degree: 63%. Student/faculty ratio: 18/1. Classes of fewer than 20 students: 32%; of 20 to 49 students: 60%; of 50 or more students: 8%. **Advanced Placement and International Baccalaureate credit:** International Baccalaureate exams may be used for: Credit and/or placement. **Freshmen returning for sophomore year:** 69%. **Graduation rates:** Four-year: 23%; five-year: 37%; six-year: 39%.

COSTS AND FINANCIAL AID

Financial aid office: (479) 968-0399. **Expenses (2009-2010):** Tuition and fees 2009-2010: $5,610 in state, $10,620 out of state; room/board: $5,156. Estimated books and supplies: $1,380 personal expenses: $2,498. **Financial aid:** Priority filing date for institution's financial aid form: April 15. In 2009-2010, 74% of undergraduates applied for financial aid. Of those, 61% were determined to have financial need; 24% had their need fully met. Average financial aid package (proportion receiving): $7,638 (59%). Average amount of gift aid, such as scholarships or grants (proportion receiving): $3,983 (48%). Average amount of self-help aid, such as work study or loans (proportion receiving): $3,801 (42%). Average need-based loan (excluding PLUS or other private loans): $3,743. Among students who received need-based aid, the average percentage of need met: 75%. Among students who received aid based on merit, the average award (and the proportion receiving): $6,920 (17%). The average athletic scholarship (and the proportion receiving): $5,175 (4%). Average amount of debt of borrowers graduating in 2009: $12,562. Proportion who borrowed: 51%.

CAMPUS LIFE AND EXTRACURRICULAR ACTIVITIES

Campus housing available: coed dorms, women's dorms, men's dorms, sorority housing, apartment for single students. Students who live in college-owned, operated, or affiliated housing: 33%. **Clubs and organizations:** Number of student organizations: 130. Activities include: campus ministries, choral groups, concert band, dance, drama/theater, international student organization, jazz band, literary magazine, marching band, music ensembles, musical theater, pep band, radio station, student government, student newspaper, symphony orchestra, television station. Number of fraternities: 7; sororities: 3. Proportion of men in fraternities: 5%; of women in sororities: 5%. **Sports program (2009-2010):** Member of NCAA II. *Men's intercollegiate varsity sports:* baseball, basketball, football, golf. *Women's intercollegiate varsity sports:* basketball, cross country, golf, softball, tennis, volleyball.

SERVICES AND FACILITIES

Basic services: nonremedial tutoring, placement service, health service, health insurance. **Remedial assistance:** reading, math, writing, other. **Counseling services:** minority student, career, personal, academic, older student, psychological. **For learning-disabled students:** School does not offer a structured program with separate admission and additional fees. Services include: remedial math, remedial English, reading machines, remedial reading, tape recorders, untimed tests, note-taking services, oral tests, readers, extended time for tests, tutors, priority seating, proofreading services, texts on tape, typist/scribe, exams on tape or computer, other testing accommodations. **Library:** Number of titles: 289,158; number of current serial subscriptions: 829. **Information technology resources:** Students are not required to lease or own a computer. Number of campus computers available to all students: 1,250. School has a wireless network. Proportion of college-owned housing units wired for high-speed internet access: 100%. **Campus safety:** Security services offered: 24-hour foot-and-vehicle patrols, late-night transport/escort service, 24-hour emergency telephones, lighted pathways/sidewalks, student patrols, controlled dormitory access (key, security card, etc).

TRANSFER AND INTERNATIONAL STUDENTS

Transfer students: May apply for admission for the following academic terms: Fall, Spring, Summer. Applicants do not need a minimum number of credits to apply. For fall 2009: Transfer applications received: 803. Transfer applicants offered admission: 759. Transfer applicants enrolled: 382. **International students:** Number of foreign undergraduates: 205 (3% of student body). Number of countries represented: 32. Minimum TOEFL score required: 500 (paper); 173 (computer).

Central Baptist College

- **Address:** 1501 College Avenue, Conway, AR 72032
- **Website:** http://www.cbc.edu
- **Private; Religious affiliation:** Baptist Missionary Association of America
- **Enrollment:** N/A

KEY STATS

✔ **U.S News College Ranking:** second tier, Regional Colleges (South)
✔ **SAT or ACT Score (25th/75th percentile):** N/A
✔ **Tuition:** 2009-2010: $9,950

Selectivity: Less selective	**Room/board:** $6,500
Acceptance rate: 82%	**Average debt:** N/A
Student/faculty ratio: N/A	**Proportion who borrowed:** N/A

Harding University

- **Address:** 915 E. Market Avenue, Searcy, AR 72149
- **Website:** http://www.harding.edu
- **Private; Religious affiliation:** Church of Christ
- **Enrollment:** 3,828 full-time; 258 part-time

KEY STATS

✔ **U.S News College Ranking:** 20, Regional Universities (South)
✔ **ACT Score (25th/75th percentile):** 21-28
✔ **Tuition:** 2010-2011: $14,040

Selectivity: More selective	**Room/board:** $5,922
Acceptance rate: 73%	**Average debt:** $31,043
Student/faculty ratio: 17/1	**Proportion who borrowed:** 70%

UNDERGRADUATE STUDENT BODY STATS

2009-2010 enrollment: 3,828 full-time; 258 part-time. Men: 47%; women: 53%. **Ethnic makeup:** African American: 4%; American-Indian: 1%; Asian American: 1%; Hispanic: 2%; White: 86%; International: 6%.

ADMISSIONS FACTS AND FIGURES

Phone: (800) 477-4407. **Email:** admissions@harding.edu. **Website:** http://www.harding.edu. **Application deadlines for fall 2011:** Regular decision: Rolling. Early decision: Not offered. Early action: Send application by: November 15; Decision sent by: N/A. Admission can be deferred. **Application fee:** $40. **To apply online, go to:** https://www.applyweb.com/apply/harding/menu.html. **Admissions requirements/recommendations:** High school units required (recommended): English: 4 (4); Mathematics: 3 (4); Science: 2 (4); Foreign language: (2); Social studies: 3 (4); Academic electives: 3 (2); Total units: 15 (20). Tests: The college uses SAT or ACT scores in admissions decisions. Either SAT or ACT required. For admission to the fall 2011 entering class, the school will accept: ACT with or without writing accepted. Campus visit: Recommended. Admissions interview: Recommended. Off-campus interview: May be arranged. **Factors that count in admissions decisions:** *Academic:* Secondary school record: Very Important. Class rank: Important. Letters of recommendation: Very Important. Standardized test scores: Very Important. Essay: Considered. *Nonacademic:* Interview: Very Important. Extracurricular activities: Considered. Talent/ability: Important. Character/personal qualities: Very Important. Alumni/ae relationship: Considered. Geographical residence: Considered. State residency: Considered. Religious affiliation/commitment: Not Considered. Minority status: Not Considered. Volunteer work: Considered. Work experience: Considered. **Other schools with the greatest overlap in applicants:** Abilene Christian University; Arkansas State University–Jonesboro; Texas A&M University–College Station; University of Arkansas; University of Tennessee. **Admissions statistics for the fall 2009 entering class:** Total applicants: 1,970. Total accepted: 1,430. Freshmen enrolled: 955; 75% were from out of state. Overall acceptance rate: 73%. Non-early acceptance rate: 73%. **Size of waiting list:** 0 applicants; enrolled from waiting list: 0. **Credentials of fall 2009 freshmen:** 28% ranked in the top 10 percent of their high school class; 50% were in the top 25 percent; 79% were in the top half. (Proportion submitting class standing: 76%.) **Average high school grade point average:** 3.5. **First-year students who submitted SAT scores:** 39%. Scores (25/75 percentile): Critical Reading: 490-630, Math: 490-640, Combined: 980-1270. **First-year students submitting**

ACT scores: 79%. Scores (25/75 percentile): English: 21-29, Math: 20-27, Composite: 21-28.

ACADEMICS

Year founded: 1924. **Academic calendar:** Semester. **Degrees offered:** certificate, bachelor's, master's, post-master's certificate, doctorate. **Most popular majors:** 21% business, management, marketing, and related support services, 14% education, 14% health professions and related clinical sciences, 8% liberal arts and sciences studies, and humanities, 5% theology and religious vocations. **Major fields of study:** area, ethnic, cultural, and gender studies; biological and biomedical sciences; business, management, marketing, and related support services; communication, journalism, and related programs; computer and information sciences and support services; education; engineering; English language and literature/letters; family and consumer sciences/human sciences; foreign languages, literatures, and linguistics; health professions and related clinical sciences; history; legal professions and studies; liberal arts and sciences studies, and humanities; mathematics and statistics; multi/interdisciplinary studies; parks, recreation, leisure, and fitness studies; physical sciences; psychology; public administration and social service professions; security and protective services; social sciences; theology and religious vocations; visual and performing arts. **Areas of required coursework:** arts/fine arts, humanities, mathematics, English (including composition), sciences (biological or physical), history, social science, other. **Pre-professional programs:** pre-law, pre-dentistry, pre-medicine, pre-veterinary science, pre-optometry, pre-pharmacy. **Special academic programs (% participation):** cooperative (work-study plan) program (8%), distance learning, double major (8%), dual enrollment, English as a Second Language (ESL), honors program (29%), independent study (22%), internships (29%), study abroad (37%), teacher certificate program (13%). **Teacher certification offered in:** early childhood, special education, elementary, middle/junior high, secondary, bilingual/bicultural. **Cooperative education programs:** art, business, computer science, education, engineering, health professions, home economics, humanities, natural science, social/behavioral science. **Faculty and instruction (2009-2010):** Total instructional faculty: 248 full-time, 199 part-time (66% men; 34% women; 3% minorities). Full-time faculty with Ph.D. or other terminal degree: 67%. Student/faculty ratio: 17/1. Classes of fewer than 20 students: 50%; of 20 to 49 students: 42%; of 50 or more students: 8%. **Advanced Placement and International Baccalaureate credit:** AP tests may be used for: Credit and/or placement. Scores accepted: 3, 4, 5. International Baccalaureate exams may be used for: Credit and/or placement. **Freshmen returning for sophomore year:** 81%. **Graduation rates:** Four-year: 38%; five-year: 57%; six-year: 61%. **Graduate study:** 35% of students pursue further study immediately upon graduation; 40% within one year. Fields in which graduates pursue further study: Master of Business Administration (MBA), 16%; law, 4%; medicine, 6%; dentistry, 3%; engineering, 2%; theology (or the seminary), 9%; education, 14%.

COSTS AND FINANCIAL AID

Financial aid office: (501) 279-5278. **Expenses (2010-2011):** Tuition and fees 2010-2011: $14,040; room/board: $5,922. Estimated books and supplies: $900; transportation: $1,300; personal expenses: $1,300. **Financial aid:** Priority filing date for institution's financial aid form: April 15. In 2009-2010, 73% of undergraduates applied for financial aid. Of those, 58% were determined to have financial need; 23% had their need fully met. Average financial aid package (proportion receiving): $11,146 (57%). Average amount of gift aid, such as scholarships or grants (proportion receiving): $7,199 (52%). Average amount of self-help aid, such as work study or loans (proportion receiving): $4,734 (45%). Average need-based loan (excluding PLUS or other private loans): $4,520. Among students who received need-based aid, the average percentage of need met: 68%. Among students who received aid based on merit, the average award (and the proportion receiving): $5,370 (11%). The average athletic scholarship (and the proportion receiving): $8,365 (4%). Average amount of debt of borrowers graduating in 2009: $31,043. Proportion who borrowed: 70%.

CAMPUS LIFE AND EXTRACURRICULAR ACTIVITIES

Campus housing available (% using): women's dorms (51%), men's dorms (39%), apartments for married students (4%), apartment for single students (6%), special housing for disabled students. Students who live in college-owned, operated, or affiliated housing: 77%. **Student employment:** During the 2009-2010 academic year, 27% of undergraduates worked on campus. Average per-year earnings: $1,275. **Clubs and organizations:** Number of student organizations: 100. Activities include: campus ministries, choral groups, concert band, drama/theater, jazz band, marching band, music ensembles, pep band, radio station, student government, student news-

paper, television station, yearbook. Number of fraternities: 14; sororities: 15. Proportion of men in fraternities: 34%; of women in sororities: 38%. Average proportion of students who stay on campus on weekends: 75%. **Sports program (2009-2010):** Member of NCAA II. *Men's intercollegiate varsity sports:* baseball, basketball, cross country, football, golf, soccer, tennis, track and field (outdoor). *Women's intercollegiate varsity sports:* basketball, cross country, golf, soccer, tennis, track and field (outdoor), volleyball.

SERVICES AND FACILITIES

Basic services: nonremedial tutoring, placement service, health service. **Remedial assistance:** reading, math, writing, study skills. **Counseling services:** minority student, career, personal, academic, psychological, religious. **For learning-disabled students:** School does not offer a structured program with separate admission and additional fees. Services include: remedial math, remedial English, reading machines, remedial reading, tape recorders, other special classes, diagnostic testing service, note-taking services, oral tests, readers, extended time for tests, tutors, early syllabus, priority registration, priority seating, texts on tape, exams on tape or computer, other. **Library:** Number of titles: 176,517; number of current serial subscriptions: 30,847. **Information technology resources:** Students are not required to lease or own a computer. Number of campus computers available to all students: 470. School has a wireless network. Approximate number of users that can be accommodated: 4,000. Proportion of college-owned housing units wired for high-speed internet access: 100%. **Campus safety:** Security services offered: 24-hour foot-and-vehicle patrols, late-night transport/escort service, 24-hour emergency telephones, lighted pathways/sidewalks, student patrols, controlled dormitory access (key, security card, etc).

TRANSFER AND INTERNATIONAL STUDENTS

Transfer students: May apply for admission for the following academic terms: Fall, Spring, Summer. Applicants need a minimum number of credits to apply. For fall 2009: Transfer applications received: 303. Transfer applicants offered admission: 236. Transfer applicants enrolled: 183. **International students:** Number of foreign undergraduates: 229 (6% of student body). Number of countries represented: 48. Minimum TOEFL score required: 550 (paper); 79 (computer).

Henderson State University

- **Address:** 1100 Henderson Street, Arkadelphia, AR 71999-0001
- **Website:** http://www.getreddie.com
- **Public**
- **Enrollment:** 2,767 full-time; 340 part-time

KEY STATS
✔ **U.S News College Ranking:** 78, Regional Universities (South)
✔ **ACT Score (25th/75th percentile):** 19-25
✔ **Tuition:** 2010-2011: $6,444 in state, $11,784 out of state

Selectivity: Selective	**Room/board:** $5,014
Acceptance rate: 65%	**Average debt:** $16,529
Student/faculty ratio: 18/1	**Proportion who borrowed:** 56%

UNDERGRADUATE STUDENT BODY STATS

2009-2010 enrollment: 2,767 full-time; 340 part-time. Men: 46%; women: 54%. **Ethnic makeup:** African American: 21%; American-Indian: 1%; Asian American: 1%; Hispanic: 2%; White: 74%; International: 2%.

ADMISSIONS FACTS AND FIGURES

Phone: (870) 230-5028. **Email:** admissions@hsu.edu. **Website:** http://www.getreddie.com. **Application deadlines for fall 2011:** Regular decision: July 15. Early decision: Not offered. Early action: Not offered. Admission can be deferred. **Application fee:** None. **To apply online, go to:** http://www.hsu.edu/form.aspx?ekfrm=37716. **Admissions requirements/recommendations:** High school units required (recommended): English: 4 (4); Mathematics: 4 (4); Science: 3 (3); Foreign language: 0 (2); Social studies: 2 (2); History: 1 (1); Academic electives: 0 (3); Total units: 14 (22). Tests: The college uses SAT or ACT scores in admissions decisions. Either SAT or ACT required. For admission to the fall 2011 entering class, the school will accept: ACT with or without writing accepted. Campus visit: Recommended. Admissions interview: Neither required nor recommended. Off-campus interview: Not available. **Factors that count in admissions decisions:** *Academic:* Secondary school record: Very Important. Class rank: Considered. Letters of recommendation: Considered. Standardized test scores: Very Important. Essay:

Considered. *Nonacademic:* Interview: Considered. Extracurricular activities: Not Considered. Talent/ability: Not Considered. Character/personal qualities: Considered. Alumni/ae relationship: Not Considered. Geographical residence: Not Considered. State residency: Not Considered. Religious affiliation/commitment: Not Considered. Minority status: Not Considered. Volunteer work: Not Considered. Work experience: Not Considered. **Other schools with the greatest overlap in applicants:** Arkansas State University–Jonesboro; Arkansas Tech University; Southern Arkansas University; University of Arkansas; University of Central Arkansas. **Admissions statistics for the fall 2009 entering class:** Total applicants: 2,555. Total accepted: 1,659. Freshmen enrolled: 643; 16% were from out of state. Overall acceptance rate: 65%. **Size of waiting list:** 0 applicants; enrolled from waiting list: 0. **Credentials of fall 2009 freshmen:** 17% ranked in the top 10 percent of their high school class; 42% were in the top 25 percent; 76% were in the top half. (Proportion submitting class standing: 95%.) **Average high school grade point average:** 3.2. **First-year students who submitted SAT scores:** 6%. **First-year students submitting ACT scores:** 94%. Scores (25/75 percentile): English: 18-25, Math: 19-26, Composite: 19-25.

ACADEMICS
Year founded: 1890. **Academic calendar:** Semester. **Degrees offered:** associate, bachelor's, master's. **Most popular majors:** 23% education, 14% business, management, marketing, and related support services, 10% health professions and related clinical sciences, 6% liberal arts and sciences studies, and humanities, 5% psychology. **Major fields of study:** biological and biomedical sciences; business, management, marketing, and related support services; communication, journalism, and related programs; computer and information sciences and support services; education; English language and literature/letters; family and consumer sciences/human sciences; foreign languages, literatures, and linguistics; health professions and related clinical sciences; history; liberal arts and sciences studies, and humanities; mathematics and statistics; parks, recreation, leisure, and fitness studies; physical sciences; psychology; public administration and social service professions; social sciences; transportation and materials moving; visual and performing arts. **Areas of required coursework:** arts/fine arts, humanities, mathematics, English (including composition), sciences (biological or physical), history, social science, other. **Pre-professional programs:** pre-law, pre-dentistry, pre-medicine, pre-optometry, pre-pharmacy. **Special academic programs:** cross-registration, honors program, internships, liberal arts/career combination, teacher certificate program. **Teacher certification offered in:** early childhood, special education, elementary, middle/junior high, secondary. **Reserve Officers Training Corps (ROTC):** Army ROTC: Offered on campus. **Faculty and instruction (2009-2010):** Total instructional faculty: 170 full-time, 64 part-time (51% men; 49% women; 14% minorities). Full-time faculty with Ph.D. or other terminal degree: 68%. Student/faculty ratio: 18/1. Classes of fewer than 20 students: 60%; of 20 to 49 students: 39%; of 50 or more students: 1%. **Freshmen returning for sophomore year:** 58%. **Graduation rates:** Four-year: 17%; five-year: 28%; six-year: 32%.

COSTS AND FINANCIAL AID
Financial aid office: (870) 230-5148. **Expenses (2010-2011):** Tuition and fees 2010-2011: $6,444 in state, $11,784 out of state; room/board: $5,014. **Financial aid:** Priority filing date for institution's financial aid form: June 1; deadline: June 1. In 2009-2010, 89% of undergraduates applied for financial aid. Of those, 75% were determined to have financial need; 1% had their need fully met. Average financial aid package (proportion receiving): $10,648 (74%). Average amount of gift aid, such as scholarships or grants (proportion receiving): N/A (51%). Average amount of self-help aid, such as work study or loans (proportion receiving): $7,822 (45%). Average need-based loan (excluding PLUS or other private loans): $3,984. Among students who received need-based aid, the average percentage of need met: 83%. Among students who received aid based on merit, the average award (and the proportion receiving): $9,096 (3%). The average athletic scholarship (and the proportion receiving): $4,434 (0%). Average amount of debt of borrowers graduating in 2009: $16,529. Proportion who borrowed: 56%.

CAMPUS LIFE AND EXTRACURRICULAR ACTIVITIES
Campus housing available (% using): coed dorms (31%), women's dorms (28%), men's dorms (32%), special housing for international students (3%), other housing options (6%). Students who live in college-owned, operated, or affiliated housing: 45%. **Clubs and organizations:** Number of student organizations: 109. Activities include: choral groups, concert band, dance, drama/theater, jazz band, literary magazine, marching band, music ensembles, radio station, student government, student newspaper, television station, yearbook. Number of fraternities: 9; sororities: 6. Average proportion of students who stay on campus on weekends: 25%. **Sports program (2009-**

2010): Member of NCAA II. *Men's intercollegiate varsity sports:* baseball, basketball, cross country, football, golf, swimming. *Women's intercollegiate varsity sports:* basketball, cross country, golf, softball, swimming, tennis, volleyball.

SERVICES AND FACILITIES
Basic services: nonremedial tutoring, health service. **Remedial assistance:** reading, math, writing. **Counseling services:** career, veteran student, academic, psychological. **For learning-disabled students:** School does not offer a structured program with separate admission and additional fees. Services include: tape recorders, untimed tests, note-taking services, readers, tutors, texts on tape. **Library:** Number of titles: 258,443; number of current serial subscriptions: 1,474. **Information technology resources:** Students are not required to lease or own a computer. Number of campus computers available to all students: 350. School has a wireless network. Approximate number of users that can be accommodated: 500. Proportion of college-owned housing units wired for high-speed internet access: 100%. **Campus safety:** Security services offered: 24-hour foot-and-vehicle patrols, 24-hour emergency telephones, lighted pathways/sidewalks, controlled dormitory access (key, security card, etc).

TRANSFER AND INTERNATIONAL STUDENTS
Transfer students: May apply for admission for the following academic terms: Fall, Spring, Summer. Applicants need a minimum number of credits to apply. For fall 2009: Transfer applications received: 761. Transfer applicants offered admission: 448. Transfer applicants enrolled: 334. **International students:** Number of foreign undergraduates: 58 (2% of student body). Number of countries represented: 26. Minimum TOEFL score required: 500 (paper); 173 (computer).

Hendrix College

- **Address:** 1600 Washington Avenue, Conway, AR 72032
- **Website:** http://www.hendrix.edu
- **Private; Religious affiliation:** United Methodist
- **Enrollment:** 1,442 full-time; 14 part-time

KEY STATS
✔ **U.S News College Ranking:** 81, National Liberal Arts Colleges
✔ **ACT Score (25th/75th percentile):** 27-32
✔ **Tuition:** 2010-2011: $29,380

Selectivity: More selective	**Room/board:** $9,086
Acceptance rate: 80%	**Average debt:** $17,641
Student/faculty ratio: 13/1	**Proportion who borrowed:** 87%

UNDERGRADUATE STUDENT BODY STATS
2009-2010 enrollment: 1,442 full-time; 14 part-time. Men: 44%; women: 56%. **Ethnic makeup:** African American: 3%; American-Indian: 1%; Asian American: 3%; Hispanic: 4%; White: 86%; International: 3%. **Religious preference:** Roman Catholic: 8%; Protestant: 25%; Jewish: 1%; No preference: 4%; Unknown: 46%; United Methodist: 14%; Other: 2%.

ADMISSIONS FACTS AND FIGURES
Phone: (800) 277-9017. **Email:** adm@hendrix.edu. **Website:** http://www.hendrix.edu. **Application deadlines for fall 2011:** Regular decision: August 1. Early decision: Not offered. Early action: Not offered. Admission can be deferred. **Application fee:** $40. **To apply online, go to:** http://www.hendrix.edu/admission/admission.aspx?id=93. **Admissions requirements/recommendations:** High school units required (recommended): English: 4 (4); Mathematics: 3 (3); Science: 2 (2); Foreign language: 2 (2); Social studies: 3 (3); History: 0 (0); Academic electives: 0 (0); Total units: 14 (14). Tests: The college uses SAT or ACT scores in admissions decisions. Either SAT or ACT required. For admission to the fall 2011 entering class, the school will accept: ACT with or without writing accepted. Campus visit: Recommended. Admissions interview: Recommended. Off-campus interview: May be arranged. **Factors that count in admissions decisions: Academic:** Secondary school record: Very Important. Class rank: Important. Letters of recommendation: Important. Standardized test scores: Very Important. Essay: Very Important. *Nonacademic:* Interview: Important. Extracurricular activities: Important. Talent/ability: Considered. Character/personal qualities: Important. Alumni/ae relationship: Not Considered. Geographical residence: Not Considered. State residency: Not Considered. Religious affiliation/commitment: Not Considered. Minority status: Considered. Volunteer

work: Considered. Work experience: Not Considered. **Other schools with the greatest overlap in applicants:** Rhodes College; Southwestern University; Trinity University; University of Arkansas; University of Central Arkansas. **Admissions statistics for the fall 2009 entering class:** Total applicants: 1,627. Total accepted: 1,305. Freshmen enrolled: 412; 52% were from out of state. Overall acceptance rate: 80%. **Size of waiting list:** 36 applicants; enrolled from waiting list: 26. **Credentials of fall 2009 freshmen:** 49% ranked in the top 10 percent of their high school class; 77% were in the top 25 percent; 95% were in the top half. (Proportion submitting class standing: 75%.) **Average high school grade point average:** 3.8. **First-year students who submitted SAT scores:** 58%. Scores (25/75 percentile): Critical Reading: 580-700, Math: 560-680, Combined: 1140-1380. **First-year students submitting ACT scores:** 80%. Scores (25/75 percentile): English: 28-34, Math: 25-30, Composite: 27-32.

ACADEMICS

Year founded: 1876. **Academic calendar:** Semester. **Degrees offered:** bachelor's, master's. **Most popular majors:** 28% social sciences, 13% biological and biomedical sciences, 11% psychology, 7% philosophy and religious studies, 7% visual and performing arts. **Major fields of study:** area, ethnic, cultural, and gender studies; biological and biomedical sciences; business, management, marketing, and related support services; computer and information sciences and support services; education; English language and literature/letters; foreign languages, literatures, and linguistics; health professions and related clinical sciences; history; mathematics and statistics; multi/interdisciplinary studies; natural resources and conservation; parks, recreation, leisure, and fitness studies; philosophy and religious studies; physical sciences; psychology; social sciences; visual and performing arts. **Areas of required coursework:** arts/fine arts, humanities, mathematics, English (including composition), philosophy, foreign languages, sciences (biological or physical), history, social science, other. **Pre-professional programs:** pre-law, pre-dentistry, pre-medicine, pre-theology, pre-veterinary science, pre-pharmacy, other. **Special academic programs (% participation):** cooperative (work-study plan) program, double major (9%), independent study (25%), internships (14%), student-designed major (5%), study abroad (34%), teacher certificate program (2%). **Teacher certification offered in:** elementary, secondary. **Cooperative education programs:** engineering. **Reserve Officers Training Corps (ROTC):** Army ROTC: Offered at cooperating institution (University of Central Arkansas). **Faculty and instruction (2009-2010):** Total instructional faculty: 102 full-time, 33 part-time (57% men; 43% women; 9% minorities). Full-time faculty with Ph.D. or other terminal degree: 95%. Student/faculty ratio: 13/1. Classes of fewer than 20 students: 60%; of 20 to 49 students: 39%; of 50 or more students: 1%. **Advanced Placement and International Baccalaureate credit:** AP tests may be used for: Credit and/or placement. Scores accepted: 4, 5. International Baccalaureate exams may be used for: Credit and/or placement. **Freshmen returning for sophomore year:** 87%. **Graduation rates:** Four-year: 59%; five-year: 64%; six-year: 66%. **Graduate study:** 0% of students pursue further study immediately upon graduation; 55% within one year; 0% within five years. Fields in which graduates pursue further study: Master of Business Administration (MBA), 1%; law, 5%; medicine, 5%; education, 1%; arts and sciences, 42%.

COSTS AND FINANCIAL AID

Financial aid office: (501) 450-1368. **Expenses (2010-2011):** Tuition and fees 2010-2011: $29,380; room/board: $9,086. Estimated books and supplies: $900; transportation: $900; personal expenses: $1,928. **Financial aid:** Priority filing date for institution's financial aid form: February 15. In 2009-2010, 79% of undergraduates applied for financial aid. Of those, 61% were determined to have financial need; 38% had their need fully met. Average financial aid package (proportion receiving): $22,498 (61%). Average amount of gift aid, such as scholarships or grants (proportion receiving): $18,080 (61%). Average amount of self-help aid, such as work study or loans (proportion receiving): $6,195 (44%). Average need-based loan (excluding PLUS or other private loans): $4,919. Among students who received need-based aid, the average percentage of need met: 83%. Among students who received aid based on merit, the average award (and the proportion receiving): $14,775 (38%). The average athletic scholarship (and the proportion receiving): $0 (0%). Average amount of debt of borrowers graduating in 2009: $17,641. Proportion who borrowed: 87%.

CAMPUS LIFE AND EXTRACURRICULAR ACTIVITIES

Campus housing available (% using): coed dorms (13%), women's dorms (25%), men's dorms (22%), apartment for single students (31%), other housing options (7%). Students who live in college-owned, operated, or affiliated housing: 86%. **Student employment:** During the 2009-2010 academic year, 17% of undergraduates worked on campus. Average per-year earnings:

$1,100. **Clubs and organizations:** Number of student organizations: 80. Activities include: campus ministries, choral groups, concert band, dance, drama/theater, international student organization, jazz band, literary magazine, model UN, music ensembles, musical theater, pep band, radio station, student government, student newspaper, student film society, symphony orchestra, yearbook. Number of fraternities: 0; sororities: 0. Average proportion of students who stay on campus on weekends: 80%. **Sports program (2009-2010):** Member of NCAA III. **Men's intercollegiate varsity sports:** baseball, basketball, cross country, golf, lacrosse, soccer, swimming, tennis, track and field (outdoor). **Women's intercollegiate varsity sports:** basketball, cross country, field hockey, golf, soccer, softball, swimming, tennis, track and field (outdoor), volleyball.

SERVICES AND FACILITIES

Basic services: nonremedial tutoring, placement service, health service, health insurance. **Counseling services:** minority student, career, military, personal, veteran student, academic, older student, psychological, birth control, religious, other. **For learning-disabled students:** School does not offer a structured program with separate admission and additional fees. Total undergraduates in learning-disabled program or receiving services: 74. Services include: tape recorders, note-taking services, extended time for tests, tutors, priority seating, other testing accommodations. **Library:** Number of titles: 226,242; number of current serial subscriptions: 35,524. **Information technology resources:** Students are not required to lease or own a computer. Number of campus computers available to all students: 75. School has a wireless network. Approximate number of users that can be accommodated: 1,000. Proportion of college-owned housing units wired for high-speed internet access: 100%. **Campus safety:** Security services offered: 24-hour foot-and-vehicle patrols, late-night transport/escort service, 24-hour emergency telephones, lighted pathways/sidewalks, controlled dormitory access (key, security card, etc).

TRANSFER AND INTERNATIONAL STUDENTS

Transfer students: May apply for admission for the following academic terms: Fall, Spring. Applicants need a minimum number of credits to apply. For fall 2009: Transfer applications received: 55. Transfer applicants offered admission: 30. Transfer applicants enrolled: 9. **International students:** Number of foreign undergraduates: 45 (3% of student body). Number of countries represented: 13. Minimum TOEFL score required: 550 (paper); 79 (computer). Average TOEFL score: 556 (paper).

John Brown University

- **Address:** 2000 W. University Street, Siloam Springs, AR 72761
- **Website:** http://www.jbu.edu
- **Private; Religious affiliation:** interdenominational
- **Enrollment:** 1,365 full-time; 348 part-time

KEY STATS

✔ **U.S News College Ranking:** 2, Regional Colleges (South)
✔ **ACT Score (25th/75th percentile):** 22-28
✔ **Tuition:** 2010-2011: $19,730
  Selectivity: More selective   **Room/board:** $7,186
  Acceptance rate: 73%   **Average debt:** $19,991
  Student/faculty ratio: 13/1   **Proportion who borrowed:** 60%

UNDERGRADUATE STUDENT BODY STATS

2009-2010 enrollment: 1,365 full-time; 348 part-time. Men: 44%; women: 56%. **Ethnic makeup:** African American: 1%; American-Indian: 2%; Asian American: 1%; Hispanic: 3%; White: 83%; International: 9%. **Religious preference:** Roman Catholic: 2%; Protestant: 87%; Unknown: 11%.

ADMISSIONS FACTS AND FIGURES

Phone: (877) 528-4636. **Email:** jbuinfo@jbu.edu. **Website:** http://www.jbu.edu. **Application deadlines for fall 2011:** Regular decision: Rolling. Early decision: Not offered. Early action: Not offered. Admission can be deferred. **Application fee:** $25. **To apply online, go to:** http://www.jbu.edu/apply. **Admissions requirements/recommendations:** High school units required (recommended): English: 4 (4); Mathematics: 3 (3); Science: 2 (2); Foreign language: 2 (2); Social studies: 2 (2); History: 1 (1); Total units: 14 (15). Tests: The college uses SAT or ACT scores in admissions decisions. Either SAT or ACT required. For admission to the fall 2011 entering class, the school will accept: ACT with or without writing accepted. Campus visit: Recommended.

Admissions interview: Recommended. Off-campus interview: May be arranged. **Factors that count in admissions decisions:** *Academic:* Secondary school record: Considered. Class rank: Important. Letters of recommendation: Very Important. Standardized test scores: Very Important. Essay: Important. *Nonacademic:* Interview: Important. Extracurricular activities: Considered. Talent/ability: Considered. Character/personal qualities: Important. Alumni/ae relationship: Considered. Geographical residence: Not Considered. State residency: Not Considered. Religious affiliation/commitment: Important. Minority status: Not Considered. Volunteer work: Not Considered. Work experience: Not Considered. **Other schools with the greatest overlap in applicants:** Arkansas Tech University; Oklahoma Baptist University; Ouachita Baptist University; University of Arkansas; University of Central Arkansas. **Admissions statistics for the fall 2009 entering class:** Total applicants: 846. Total accepted: 616. Freshmen enrolled: 306; 70% were from out of state. Overall acceptance rate: 73%. **Credentials of fall 2009 freshmen:** 32% ranked in the top 10 percent of their high school class; 60% were in the top 25 percent; 83% were in the top half. (Proportion submitting class standing: 47%.) **Average high school grade point average:** 3.6. **First-year students who submitted SAT scores:** 40%. Scores (25/75 percentile): Critical Reading: 520-660, Math: 510-640, Combined: 1030-1300. **First-year students submitting ACT scores:** 90%. Scores (25/75 percentile): English: 22-29, Math: 20-27, Composite: 22-28.

ACADEMICS

Year founded: 1919. **Academic calendar:** Semester. **Degrees offered:** associate, bachelor's, master's. **Most popular majors:** 50% business, management, marketing, and related support services, 9% education, 7% theology and religious vocations, 7% visual and performing arts, 6% communication, journalism, and related programs. **Major fields of study:** biological and biomedical sciences; business, management, marketing, and related support services; communication, journalism, and related programs; computer and information sciences and support services; education; engineering; English language and literature/letters; family and consumer sciences/human sciences; foreign languages, literatures, and linguistics; health professions and related clinical sciences; history; mathematics and statistics; multi/interdisciplinary studies; natural resources and conservation; parks, recreation, leisure, and fitness studies; physical sciences; social sciences; theology and religious vocations; visual and performing arts. **Areas of required coursework:** arts/fine arts, humanities, mathematics, English (including composition), philosophy, foreign languages, sciences (biological or physical), history, social science, other. **Pre-professional programs:** pre-law, pre-dentistry, pre-medicine, pre-theology, pre-veterinary science, pre-optometry, pre-pharmacy. **Special academic programs (% participation):** distance learning (13%), double major (7%), dual enrollment (2%), English as a Second Language (ESL) (5%), honors program (14%), independent study (34%), internships (67%), liberal arts/career combination (2%), student-designed major (0%), study abroad (12%), teacher certificate program (6%). **Teacher certification offered in:** early childhood, middle/junior high, secondary. **Reserve Officers Training Corps (ROTC):** Army ROTC: Offered at cooperating institution (University of Arkansas); Air Force ROTC: Offered at cooperating institution (University of Arkansas). **Faculty and instruction (2009-2010):** Total instructional faculty: 75 full-time, 55 part-time (69% men; 31% women; 6% minorities). Full-time faculty with Ph.D. or other terminal degree: 72%. Student/faculty ratio: 13/1. Classes of fewer than 20 students: 51%; of 20 to 49 students: 49%; of 50 or more students: 0%. **Advanced Placement and International Baccalaureate credit:** AP tests may be used for: Credit and/or placement. Scores accepted: 3, 4, 5. International Baccalaureate exams may be used for: Credit only. **Freshmen returning for sophomore year:** 79%. **Graduation rates:** Four-year: 53%; five-year: 63%; six-year: 67%. **Graduate study:** 31% of students pursue further study immediately upon graduation. Fields in which graduates pursue further study: Master of Business Administration (MBA), 14%; law, 3%; medicine, 9%; engineering, 8%; theology (or the seminary), 14%; education, 6%; arts and sciences, 13%.

COSTS AND FINANCIAL AID

Financial aid office: (479) 524-7115. **Expenses (2010-2011):** Tuition and fees 2010-2011: $19,730; room/board: $7,186. Estimated books and supplies: $600; transportation: $1,500; personal expenses: $1,500. **Financial aid:** Priority filing date for institution's financial aid form: March 1. In 2009-2010, 75% of undergraduates applied for financial aid. Of those, 66% were determined to have financial need; 4% had their need fully met. Average financial aid package (proportion receiving): $15,787 (65%). Average amount of gift aid, such as scholarships or grants (proportion receiving): $7,787 (58%). Average amount of self-help aid, such as work study or loans (proportion receiving): $4,809 (52%). Average need-based loan (excluding

PLUS or other private loans): $4,330. Among students who received need-based aid, the average percentage of need met: 50%. Among students who received aid based on merit, the average award (and the proportion receiving): $6,308 (14%). The average athletic scholarship (and the proportion receiving): $15,108 (4%). Average amount of debt of borrowers graduating in 2009: $19,991. Proportion who borrowed: 60%.

CAMPUS LIFE AND EXTRACURRICULAR ACTIVITIES

Campus housing available (% using): coed dorms (38%), women's dorms (25%), men's dorms (22%), other housing options (15%). Students who live in college-owned, operated, or affiliated housing: 71%. **Student employment:** During the 2009-2010 academic year, 13% of undergraduates worked on campus. Average per-year earnings: $1,856. **Clubs and organizations:** Number of student organizations: 45. Activities include: campus ministries, choral groups, dance, drama/theater, international student organization, jazz band, literary magazine, music ensembles, musical theater, pep band, radio station, student government, student newspaper, student film society, yearbook. Number of fraternities: 0; sororities: 0. Average proportion of students who stay on campus on weekends: 65%. **Sports program (2009-2010):** Member of NAIA. *Men's intercollegiate varsity sports:* basketball, golf, soccer, tennis. *Women's intercollegiate varsity sports:* basketball, soccer, tennis, volleyball.

SERVICES AND FACILITIES

Basic services: nonremedial tutoring, other. **Remedial assistance:** reading, math, writing, study skills. **Counseling services:** minority student, career, personal, academic, older student, psychological, religious. **For learning-disabled students:** School does not offer a structured program with separate admission and additional fees. Total undergraduates in learning-disabled program or receiving services: 14. Services include: tape recorders, note-taking services, oral tests, readers, extended time for tests, tutors, early syllabus, priority seating, texts on tape, other testing accommodations, other. **Library:** Number of titles: 106,283; number of current serial subscriptions: 7,319. **Information technology resources:** Students are not required to lease or own a computer. Number of campus computers available to all students: 223. School has a wireless network. Approximate number of users that can be accommodated: 1,500. Proportion of college-owned housing units wired for high-speed internet access: 100%. **Campus safety:** Security services offered: 24-hour foot-and-vehicle patrols, late-night transport/escort service, lighted pathways/sidewalks, student patrols, controlled dormitory access (key, security card, etc).

TRANSFER AND INTERNATIONAL STUDENTS

Transfer students: May apply for admission for the following academic terms: Fall, Spring. Applicants do not need a minimum number of credits to apply. For fall 2009: Transfer applications received: 217. Transfer applicants offered admission: 133. Transfer applicants enrolled: 65. **International students:** Number of foreign undergraduates: 115 (9% of student body). Number of countries represented: 45. Minimum TOEFL score required: 500 (paper); 173 (computer).

Lyon College

- **Address:** PO Box 2317, Batesville, AR 72503-2317
- **Website:** http://www.lyon.edu
- **Private; Religious affiliation:** Presbyterian
- **Enrollment:** 580 full-time; 34 part-time

KEY STATS

✔ **U.S News College Ranking:** 144, National Liberal Arts Colleges
✔ **ACT Score (25th/75th percentile):** 22-30
✔ **Tuition:** 2010-2011: $19,214

Selectivity: More selective	**Room/board:** $7,340
Acceptance rate: 67%	**Average debt:** $19,642
Student/faculty ratio: 13/1	**Proportion who borrowed:** 61%

UNDERGRADUATE STUDENT BODY STATS

2009-2010 enrollment: 580 full-time; 34 part-time. Men: 45%; women: 55%. **Ethnic makeup:** African American: 4%; American-Indian: 1%; Asian American: 1%; Hispanic: 3%; White: 89%; International: 2%. **Religious preference:** Roman Catholic: 9%; Protestant: 59%; No preference: 27%; Presbyterian: 5%.

ADMISSIONS FACTS AND FIGURES

Phone: (800) 423-2542. **Email:** admissions@lyon.edu. **Website:** http://www.lyon.edu. **Application deadlines for fall 2011:** Regular decision: Rolling. Early decision: Not offered. Early action: Send application by: October 31; Decision sent by: November 15. Admission can be deferred. **Application fee:** $25. **To apply online, go to:** http://www.lyon.edu/admission/application-form.aspx. **Admissions requirements/recommendations:** High school units required (recommended): English: 4 (4); Mathematics: 3 (4); Science: 3 (4); Foreign language: 2 (2); Social studies: 1 (1); History: 2 (2); Academic electives: 1 (1); Total units: 16 (18). Tests: The college uses SAT or ACT scores in admissions decisions. Either SAT or ACT required. For admission to the fall 2011 entering class, the school will accept: ACT with or without writing accepted. Campus visit: Recommended. Admissions interview: Recommended. Off-campus interview: May be arranged. **Factors that count in admissions decisions:** *Academic:* Secondary school record: Important. Class rank: Considered. Letters of recommendation: Considered. Standardized test scores: Very Important. Essay: Considered. *Nonacademic:* Interview: Considered. Extracurricular activities: Considered. Talent/ability: Considered. Character/personal qualities: Considered. Alumni/ae relationship: Not Considered. Geographical residence: Not Considered. State residency: Not Considered. Religious affiliation/commitment: Not Considered. Minority status: Not Considered. Volunteer work: Considered. Work experience: Considered. **Other schools with the greatest overlap in applicants:** Arkansas State University–Jonesboro; Arkansas Tech University; Hendrix College; University of Arkansas; University of Central Arkansas. **Admissions statistics for the fall 2009 entering class:** Total applicants: 1,110. Total accepted: 749. Freshmen enrolled: 217; Overall acceptance rate: 67%. Non-early acceptance rate: 67%. **Credentials of fall 2009 freshmen:** 26% ranked in the top 10 percent of their high school class; 56% were in the top 25 percent; 84% were in the top half. (Proportion submitting class standing: 61%.) **Average high school grade point average:** 3.5. **First-year students who submitted SAT scores:** 17%. Scores (25/75 percentile): Critical Reading: 460-620, Math: 480-590, Combined: 940-1210. **First-year students submitting ACT scores:** 92%. Scores (25/75 percentile): English: 22-29, Math: 21-26, Composite: 22-30.

ACADEMICS

Year founded: 1872. **Academic calendar:** Semester. **Degrees offered:** bachelor's. **Most popular majors:** 27% business administration and management, 21% biology/biological sciences, 16% psychology, 10% English language and literature, 7% visual and performing arts. **Major fields of study:** biological and biomedical sciences; business, management, marketing, and related support services; computer and information sciences and support services; education; English language and literature/letters; foreign languages, literatures, and linguistics; history; mathematics and statistics; natural resources and conservation; philosophy and religious studies; physical sciences; psychology; social sciences; visual and performing arts. **Areas of required coursework:** arts/fine arts, humanities, mathematics, English (including composition), philosophy, foreign languages, sciences (biological or physical), history, social science, other. **Pre-professional programs:** pre-law, pre-dentistry, pre-medicine, pre-theology, pre-veterinary science, pre-optometry, pre-pharmacy, other. **Special academic programs (% participation):** accelerated program (0%), cross-registration (23%), double major (20%), dual enrollment (0%), internships (52%), student-designed major (18%), study abroad (30%), teacher certificate program (17%). **Teacher certification offered in:** early childhood, elementary, secondary. **Faculty and instruction (2009-2010):** Total instructional faculty: 40 full-time, 16 part-time (63% men; 38% women; 9% minorities). Full-time faculty with Ph.D. or other terminal degree: 88%. Student/faculty ratio: 13/1. Classes of fewer than 20 students: 76%; of 20 to 49 students: 24%. **Advanced Placement and International Baccalaureate credit:** AP tests may be used for: Credit only. Scores accepted: 3, 4, 5. International Baccalaureate exams may be used for: Credit only. **Freshmen returning for sophomore year:** 67%. **Graduation rates:** Four-year: 44%; five-year: 45%; six-year: 46%. **Graduate study:** 38% of students pursue further study immediately upon graduation; 39% within one year; 44% within five years. Fields in which graduates pursue further study: Master of Business Administration (MBA), 18%; law, 7%; medicine, 6%; dentistry, 1%; education, 4%; arts and sciences, 24%; veterinary medicine, 1%.

COSTS AND FINANCIAL AID

Financial aid office: (870) 698-4257. **Expenses (2010-2011):** Tuition and fees 2010-2011: $19,214; room/board: $7,340. Estimated books and supplies: $1,000; transportation: $1,000; personal expenses: $1,000. **Financial aid:** Priority filing date for institution's financial aid form: March 15. In 2009-2010, 87% of undergraduates applied for financial aid. Of those, 75% were determined to have financial need; 18% had their need fully met. Average financial aid package (proportion receiving): $17,498 (75%). Average amount of gift aid, such as scholarships or grants (proportion receiving): $13,015 (75%). Average amount of self-help aid, such as work study or loans (proportion receiving): $4,483 (55%). Average need-based loan (excluding PLUS or other private loans): $4,031. Among students who received need-based aid, the average percentage of need met: 81%. Among students who received aid based on merit, the average award (and the proportion receiving): $11,687 (26%). The average athletic scholarship (and the proportion receiving): $10,189 (11%). Average amount of debt of borrowers graduating in 2009: $19,642. Proportion who borrowed: 61%.

CAMPUS LIFE AND EXTRACURRICULAR ACTIVITIES

Campus housing available (% using): coed dorms (20%), women's dorms (28%), men's dorms (26%), apartment for single students (25%), other housing options (1%). **Student employment:** During the 2009-2010 academic year, 15% of undergraduates worked on campus. Average per-year earnings: $1,400. **Clubs and organizations:** Number of student organizations: 44. Activities include: campus ministries, choral groups, concert band, dance, drama/theater, international student organization, literary magazine, model UN, music ensembles, student government, student newspaper, yearbook. Number of fraternities: 3; sororities: 2. Average proportion of students who stay on campus on weekends: 60%. **Sports program (2009-2010):** Member of NAIA. *Men's intercollegiate varsity sports:* baseball, basketball, cross country, golf, soccer. *Women's intercollegiate varsity sports:* basketball, cross country, golf, soccer, softball, volleyball.

SERVICES AND FACILITIES

Basic services: nonremedial tutoring, placement service, health service, health insurance. **Counseling services:** minority student, career, personal, academic, psychological. **For learning-disabled students:** School does not offer a structured program with separate admission and additional fees. Total undergraduates in learning-disabled program or receiving services: 15. Services include: tape recorders, untimed tests, oral tests, readers, extended time for tests, other testing accommodations, other. **Library:** Number of titles: 148,184; number of current serial subscriptions: 434. **Information technology resources:** Students are not required to lease or own a computer. Number of campus computers available to all students: 110. School has a wireless network. Approximate number of users that can be accommodated: 250. Proportion of college-owned housing units wired for high-speed internet access: 100%. **Campus safety:** Security services offered: 24-hour foot-and-vehicle patrols, late-night transport/escort service, 24-hour emergency telephones, lighted pathways/sidewalks, controlled dormitory access (key, security card, etc).

TRANSFER AND INTERNATIONAL STUDENTS

Transfer students: May apply for admission for the following academic terms: Fall, Spring. Applicants do not need a minimum number of credits to apply. For fall 2009: Transfer applications received: 201. Transfer applicants offered admission: 115. Transfer applicants enrolled: 80. **International students:** Number of foreign undergraduates: 13 (2% of student body). Number of countries represented: 11. Minimum TOEFL score required: 550 (paper); 213 (computer).

Ouachita Baptist University

- **Address:** 410 Ouachita, Arkadelphia, AR 71998
- **Website:** http://www.obu.edu
- **Private; Religious affiliation:** Arkansas Baptist State Convention
- **Enrollment:** 1,416 full-time; 31 part-time

KEY STATS

✔ **U.S News College Ranking:** 1, Regional Colleges (South)
✔ **ACT Score (25th/75th percentile):** 21-27
✔ **Tuition:** 2010-2011: $18,815

Selectivity: More selective	**Room/board:** $5,840
Acceptance rate: 67%	**Average debt:** $14,156
Student/faculty ratio: 11/1	**Proportion who borrowed:** 58%

UNDERGRADUATE STUDENT BODY STATS

2009-2010 enrollment: 1,416 full-time; 31 part-time. Men: 47%; women: 53%. **Ethnic makeup:** African American: 7%; American-Indian: 1%; Asian American: 1%; Hispanic: 2%; White: 86%; International: 3%. **Religious**

preference: Roman Catholic: 2%; Protestant: 8%; Unknown: 14%; Arkansas Baptist State Convention: 76%.

ADMISSIONS FACTS AND FIGURES

Phone: (870) 245-5110. **Email:** admissions@obu.edu. **Website:** http://www.obu.edu. **Application deadlines for fall 2011:** Regular decision: Rolling. Early decision: Not offered. Early action: Not offered. Admission can be deferred. **To apply online, go to:** https://omega.obu.edu/public/obuapv45.pgm. **Admissions requirements/recommendations:** High school units required (recommended): English: 4 (4); Mathematics: 2 (3); Science: 2 (3); Foreign language: (2); Social studies: 1 (1); History: 2 (2); Total units: 15 (19). Tests: The college uses SAT or ACT scores in admissions decisions. Either SAT or ACT required. For admission to the fall 2011 entering class, the school will accept: ACT with or without writing accepted. Campus visit: Recommended. Admissions interview: Recommended. Off-campus interview: May be arranged. **Factors that count in admissions decisions:** *Academic:* Secondary school record: Very Important. Class rank: Not Considered. Letters of recommendation: Considered. Standardized test scores: Very Important. Essay: Not Considered. *Nonacademic:* Interview: Not Considered. Extracurricular activities: Not Considered. Talent/ability: Considered. Character/personal qualities: Considered. Alumni/ae relationship: Not Considered. Geographical residence: Not Considered. State residency: Not Considered. Religious affiliation/commitment: Not Considered. Minority status: Not Considered. Volunteer work: Not Considered. Work experience: Not Considered. **Other schools with the greatest overlap in applicants:** Baylor University; Henderson State University; Texas A&M University–College Station; University of Arkansas; University of Central Arkansas. **Admissions statistics for the fall 2009 entering class:** Total applicants: 1,592. Total accepted: 1,061. Freshmen enrolled: 390; 47% were from out of state. Overall acceptance rate: 67%. **Credentials of fall 2009 freshmen:** 34% ranked in the top 10 percent of their high school class; 61% were in the top 25 percent; 84% were in the top half. (Proportion submitting class standing: 70%.) **Average high school grade point average:** 3.5. **First-year students who submitted SAT scores:** 39%. Scores (25/75 percentile): Critical Reading: 470-590, Math: 490-610, Combined: 960-1200. **First-year students submitting ACT scores:** 78%. Scores (25/75 percentile): English: 21-29, Math: 19-27, Composite: 21-27.

ACADEMICS

Year founded: 1886. **Academic calendar:** Semester. **Degrees offered:** bachelor's. **Most popular majors:** 14% business, management, marketing, and related support services, 14% theology and religious vocations, 11% visual and performing arts, 9% biological and biomedical sciences, 8% communication, journalism, and related programs. **Major fields of study:** biological and biomedical sciences; business, management, marketing, and related support services; communication, journalism, and related programs; computer and information sciences and support services; education; engineering; English language and literature/letters; foreign languages, literatures, and linguistics; health professions and related clinical sciences; history; legal professions and studies; mathematics and statistics; parks, recreation, leisure, and fitness studies; philosophy and religious studies; physical sciences; psychology; social sciences; theology and religious vocations; visual and performing arts. **Areas of required coursework:** arts/fine arts, humanities, mathematics, English (including composition), philosophy, foreign languages, sciences (biological or physical), history, social science, other. **Pre-professional programs:** pre-law, pre-dentistry, pre-medicine, pre-veterinary science, pre-optometry, pre-pharmacy, other. **Special academic programs (% participation):** cross-registration (8%), double major (15%), English as a Second Language (ESL) (1%), honors program (12%), internships (10%), study abroad (6%), teacher certificate program (6%). **Teacher certification offered in:** early childhood, middle/junior high, secondary. **Reserve Officers Training Corps (ROTC):** Army ROTC: Offered on campus. **Faculty and instruction (2009-2010):** Total instructional faculty: 114 full-time, 35 part-time (58% men; 42% women; 2% minorities). Full-time faculty with Ph.D. or other terminal degree: 80%. Student/faculty ratio: 11/1. Classes of fewer than 20 students: 58%; of 20 to 49 students: 42%; of 50 or more students: 0%. **Advanced Placement and International Baccalaureate credit:** AP tests may be used for: Placement only. Scores accepted: 4. International Baccalaureate exams may be used for: Credit and/or placement. **Freshmen returning for sophomore year:** 76%. **Graduation rates:** Four-year: 41%; five-year: 52%; six-year: 60%. **Graduate study:** 40% of students pursue further study immediately upon graduation; 45% within one year; 50% within five years. Fields in which graduates pursue further study: Master of Business Administration (MBA), 10%; law, 8%; medicine, 6%; dentistry, 2%; engineering, 2%; theology (or the seminary), 6%; education, 5%; arts and sciences, 10%; veterinary medicine, 1%.

COSTS AND FINANCIAL AID

Financial aid office: (870) 245-5570. **Expenses (2010-2011):** Tuition and fees 2010-2011: $18,815; room/board: $5,840. Estimated books and supplies: $1,000; transportation: $1,000; personal expenses: $1,500. **Financial aid:** Priority filing date for institution's financial aid form: January 15; deadline: June 1. In 2009-2010, 69% of undergraduates applied for financial aid. Of those, 57% were determined to have financial need; 30% had their need fully met. Average financial aid package (proportion receiving): $15,237 (57%). Average amount of gift aid, such as scholarships or grants (proportion receiving): $11,957 (56%). Average amount of self-help aid, such as work study or loans (proportion receiving): $3,133 (42%). Average need-based loan (excluding PLUS or other private loans): $2,289. Among students who received need-based aid, the average percentage of need met: 73%. Among students who received aid based on merit, the average award (and the proportion receiving): $8,000 (39%). The average athletic scholarship (and the proportion receiving): $9,521 (7%). Average amount of debt of borrowers graduating in 2009: $14,156. Proportion who borrowed: 58%.

CAMPUS LIFE AND EXTRACURRICULAR ACTIVITIES

Campus housing available (% using): women's dorms (47%), men's dorms (41%), apartments for married students (1%), apartment for single students (11%). Students who live in college-owned, operated, or affiliated housing: 90%. **Clubs and organizations:** Number of student organizations: 33. Activities include: campus ministries, choral groups, concert band, dance, drama/theater, international student organization, jazz band, literary magazine, marching band, model UN, music ensembles, musical theater, opera, pep band, student government, student newspaper, student film society, yearbook. Number of fraternities: 5; sororities: 5. Proportion of men in fraternities: 15%; of women in sororities: 20%. Average proportion of students who stay on campus on weekends: 50%. **Sports program (2009-2010):** Member of NCAA II. *Men's intercollegiate varsity sports:* baseball, basketball, football, golf, soccer, swimming, tennis, wrestling. *Women's intercollegiate varsity sports:* basketball, cross country, golf, soccer, softball, swimming, tennis, volleyball.

SERVICES AND FACILITIES

Basic services: nonremedial tutoring, placement service, health service, health insurance. **Remedial assistance:** reading, math, study skills. **Counseling services:** minority student, career, military, personal, veteran student, academic, religious. **For learning-disabled students:** School does not offer a structured program with separate admission and additional fees. Total undergraduates in learning-disabled program or receiving services: 26. Services include: remedial math, remedial English, reading machines, remedial reading, tape recorders, other special classes, videotaped classes, note-taking services, oral tests, readers, extended time for tests, tutors. **Library:** Number of titles: 789,788; number of current serial subscriptions: 751. **Information technology resources:** Students are not required to lease or own a computer. Number of campus computers available to all students: 250. School has a wireless network. Approximate number of users that can be accommodated: 750. Proportion of college-owned housing units wired for high-speed internet access: 100%. **Campus safety:** Security services offered: 24-hour foot-and-vehicle patrols, 24-hour emergency telephones, lighted pathways/sidewalks, controlled dormitory access (key, security card, etc).

TRANSFER AND INTERNATIONAL STUDENTS

Transfer students: May apply for admission for the following academic terms: Fall, Spring, Summer. Applicants need a minimum number of credits to apply. For fall 2009: Transfer applications received: 174. Transfer applicants offered admission: 104. Transfer applicants enrolled: 56. **International students:** Number of foreign undergraduates: 42 (3% of student body). Number of countries represented: 23. Minimum TOEFL score required: 550 (paper); 213 (computer). Average TOEFL score: 700 (paper).

Philander Smith College

- **Address:** 900 W. Daisy Bates Drive, Little Rock, AR 72202-3718
- **Website:** http://www.philander.edu
- **Private; Religious affiliation:** United Methodist
- **Enrollment:** 596 full-time; 72 part-time

KEY STATS

✔ **U.S News College Ranking:** 71, Regional Colleges (South)
✔ **ACT Score (25th/75th percentile):** 16-22
✔ **Tuition:** 2009-2010: $9,000

Selectivity: Less selective	**Room/board:** $6,840
Acceptance rate: 69%	**Average debt:** N/A
Student/faculty ratio: 10/1	**Proportion who borrowed:** N/A

UNDERGRADUATE STUDENT BODY STATS

2009-2010 enrollment: 596 full-time; 72 part-time. Men: 37%; women: 63%. **Ethnic makeup:** African American: 95%; Hispanic: 1%; White: 1%; International: 3%. **Religious preference:** Roman Catholic: 1%; Protestant: 52%; No preference: 6%; Unknown: 25%; United Methodist: 4%; Non Denominational: 7%; Other: 5%.

ADMISSIONS FACTS AND FIGURES

Phone: (501) 370-5221. **Email:** admissions@philander.edu. **Website:** http://www.philander.edu. **Application deadlines for fall 2011:** Regular decision: Rolling. Early decision: Not offered. Early action: Not offered. Admission can be deferred. **Application fee:** $25. **Admissions requirements/recommendations:** High school units required (recommended): English: 3 (3); Mathematics: 3 (3); Science: 3 (3); Foreign language: 2 (2); Social studies: 2 (2). Tests: The college uses SAT or ACT scores in admissions decisions. Either SAT or ACT required. Campus visit: Recommended. Admissions interview: Neither required nor recommended. Off-campus interview: May be arranged. **Factors that count in admissions decisions:** *Academic:* Letters of recommendation: Considered. Standardized test scores: Very Important. Essay: Considered. *Nonacademic:* Interview: Considered. **Other schools with the greatest overlap in applicants:** Arkansas State University–Jonesboro; University of Arkansas–Little Rock; University of Arkansas–Pine Bluff; University of Central Arkansas. **Admissions statistics for the fall 2009 entering class:** Total applicants: 1,714. Total accepted: 1,187. Freshmen enrolled: 158; Overall acceptance rate: 69%. **Credentials of fall 2009 freshmen:** 16% ranked in the top 10 percent of their high school class; 29% were in the top 25 percent; 58% were in the top half. (Proportion submitting class standing: 80%.) **Average high school grade point average:** 2.9. **First-year students who submitted SAT scores:** 12%. Scores (25/75 percentile): Critical Reading: 400-480, Math: 410-500, Combined: 810-980. **First-year students submitting ACT scores:** 85%. Scores (25/75 percentile): English: 15-22, Math: 16-20, Composite: 16-22.

ACADEMICS

Year founded: 1877. **Academic calendar:** Semester. **Degrees offered:** bachelor's. **Most popular majors:** 28% business administration and management, 13% business administration, management, and operations, 10% biology/biological sciences, 7% psychology, 7% social work. **Major fields of study:** biological and biomedical sciences; business, management, marketing, and related support services; computer and information sciences and support services; education; English language and literature/letters; mathematics and statistics; philosophy and religious studies; physical sciences; psychology; public administration and social service professions; social sciences; visual and performing arts. **Areas of required coursework:** arts/fine arts, humanities, computer literacy, mathematics, English (including composition), philosophy, foreign languages, sciences (biological or physical), history, social science. **Pre-professional programs:** pre-medicine. **Special academic programs (% participation):** accelerated program (15%), double major (0%), independent study (15%), internships, study abroad (0%), teacher certificate program (4%), weekend college (10%). **Teacher certification offered in:** early childhood, vo-tech, middle/junior high. **Reserve Officers Training Corps (ROTC):** Army ROTC: Offered at cooperating institution. **Faculty and instruction (2009-2010):** Total instructional faculty: 48 full-time, 37 part-time (52% men; 48% women; 80% minorities). Full-time faculty with Ph.D. or other terminal degree: 52%. Student/faculty ratio: 10/1. Classes of fewer than 20 students: 72%; of 20 to 49 students: 28%. **Advanced Placement and International Baccalaureate credit:** AP tests may be used for: Credit and/or placement. **Freshmen returning for sophomore year:** 65%. **Graduation rates:**

Four-year: 4%; five-year: 15%; six-year: 21%. **Graduate study:** 28% of students pursue further study immediately upon graduation.

COSTS AND FINANCIAL AID

Financial aid office: (501) 370-5350. **Expenses (2009-2010):** Tuition and fees 2009-2010: $9,000; room/board: $6,840. Estimated books and supplies: $1,000; transportation: $1,484; personal expenses: $1,554. **Financial aid:** Priority filing date for institution's financial aid form: March 1.

CAMPUS LIFE AND EXTRACURRICULAR ACTIVITIES

Campus housing available (% using): coed dorms (100%). Students who live in college-owned, operated, or affiliated housing: 44%. **Student employment:** During the 2009-2010 academic year, 7% of undergraduates worked on campus. Average per-year earnings: $3,000. **Clubs and organizations:** Number of student organizations: 10. Activities include: choral groups, drama/theater, music ensembles, musical theater, opera, pep band, student government, student newspaper, yearbook. Number of fraternities: 3; sororities: 3. Proportion of men in fraternities: 5%; of women in sororities: 5%. **Sports program (2009-2010):** Member of NAIA. *Men's intercollegiate varsity sports:* basketball. *Women's intercollegiate varsity sports:* basketball, volleyball.

SERVICES AND FACILITIES

Basic services: nonremedial tutoring, placement service, health service, health insurance. **Remedial assistance:** reading, math, writing, study skills. **Counseling services:** career, personal, veteran student, academic, psychological, religious. **For learning-disabled students:** School does not offer a structured program with separate admission and additional fees. Services include: remedial math, remedial English, remedial reading, oral tests, extended time for tests, tutors, priority seating. **Library:** Number of titles: 71,100; number of current serial subscriptions: 296. **Information technology resources:** Students are not required to lease or own a computer. School has a wireless network. Proportion of college-owned housing units wired for high-speed internet access: 100%. **Campus safety:** Security services offered: 24-hour foot-and-vehicle patrols, controlled dormitory access (key, security card, etc).

TRANSFER AND INTERNATIONAL STUDENTS

Transfer students: May apply for admission for the following academic terms: Fall, Spring, Summer. Applicants need a minimum number of credits to apply. **International students:** Number of foreign undergraduates: 21 (3% of student body). Number of countries represented: 9. Minimum TOEFL score required: 500 (paper); 173 (computer). Average TOEFL score: 500 (paper).

Southern Arkansas University

- **Address:** Box 9392, Magnolia, AR 71754-9392
- **Website:** http://www.saumag.edu
- **Public**
- **Enrollment:** 2,385 full-time; 391 part-time

KEY STATS

✔ **U.S News College Ranking:** 57, Regional Colleges (South)
✔ **ACT Score (25th/75th percentile):** 18-24
✔ **Tuition:** 2009-2010: $6,438 in state, $9,078 out of state

Selectivity: Selective	**Room/board:** $8,130
Acceptance rate: 74%	**Average debt:** $15,672
Student/faculty ratio: 16/1	**Proportion who borrowed:** 72%

UNDERGRADUATE STUDENT BODY STATS

2009-2010 enrollment: 2,385 full-time; 391 part-time. Men: 41%; women: 59%. **Ethnic makeup:** African American: 30%; American-Indian: 1%; Asian American: 1%; Hispanic: 2%; White: 63%; International: 4%. **Religious preference:** Roman Catholic: 2%; Protestant: 81%; Hindu: 2%; No preference: 8%; Other: 7%.

ADMISSIONS FACTS AND FIGURES

Phone: (870) 235-4040. **Email:** muleriders@saumag.edu. **Website:** http://www.saumag.edu. **Application deadlines for fall 2011:** Regular decision: August 27. Early decision: Not offered. Early action: Not offered. Admission can be deferred. **Application fee:** None. **To apply online, go to:** http://admissions.southernarkansasuniversity.info/apply/. **Admissions requirements/**

recommendations: High school units required (recommended): English: 4; Mathematics: 4; Science: 3; Foreign language: (2); Social studies: 3; Total units: 17 (2). Tests: The college uses SAT or ACT scores in admissions decisions. Either SAT or ACT required. For admission to the fall 2011 entering class, the school will accept: ACT with or without writing accepted. Campus visit: Recommended. Admissions interview: Neither required nor recommended. Off-campus interview: May be arranged. **Factors that count in admissions decisions:** *Academic:* Secondary school record: Considered. Class rank: Considered. Letters of recommendation: Not Considered. Standardized test scores: Very Important. Essay: Not Considered. *Nonacademic:* Interview: Not Considered. Extracurricular activities: Not Considered. Talent/ability: Not Considered. Character/personal qualities: Not Considered. Alumni/ae relationship: Not Considered. Geographical residence: Not Considered. State residency: Not Considered. Religious affiliation/commitment: Not Considered. Minority status: Not Considered. Volunteer work: Not Considered. Work experience: Not Considered. **Other schools with the greatest overlap in applicants:** Arkansas Tech University; Henderson State University; Louisiana Tech University; University of Arkansas–Monticello; University of Central Arkansas. **Admissions statistics for the fall 2009 entering class:** Total applicants: 2,024. Total accepted: 1,493. Freshmen enrolled: 619; 23% were from out of state. Overall acceptance rate: 74%. **Credentials of fall 2009 freshmen:** 17% ranked in the top 10 percent of their high school class; 41% were in the top 25 percent; 68% were in the top half. (Proportion submitting class standing: 76%.) **Average high school grade point average:** 3.1. **First-year students who submitted SAT scores:** 6%. Scores (25/75 percentile): Critical Reading: 410-540, Math: 470-560, Combined: 880-1100. **First-year students submitting ACT scores:** 98%. Scores (25/75 percentile): English: 18-25, Math: 17-24, Composite: 18-24.

ACADEMICS

Year founded: 1909. **Academic calendar:** Semester. **Degrees offered:** associate, bachelor's, master's. **Most popular majors:** 25% business, management, marketing, and related support services, 21% education, 9% multi/interdisciplinary studies, 7% biological and biomedical sciences, 7% mathematics and statistics. **Major fields of study:** agriculture, agriculture operations, and related sciences; biological and biomedical sciences; business, management, marketing, and related support services; communication, journalism, and related programs; computer and information sciences and support services; education; engineering technologies/technicians; English language and literature/letters; foreign languages, literatures, and linguistics; health professions and related clinical sciences; history; liberal arts and sciences studies, and humanities; mathematics and statistics; multi/interdisciplinary studies; parks, recreation, leisure, and fitness studies; physical sciences; psychology; public administration and social service professions; security and protective services; social sciences; visual and performing arts. **Areas of required coursework:** arts/fine arts, humanities, computer literacy, mathematics, English (including composition), philosophy, foreign languages, sciences (biological or physical), history, social science. **Pre-professional programs:** pre-law, pre-dentistry, pre-medicine, pre-veterinary science, pre-optometry, pre-pharmacy, other. **Special academic programs (% participation):** distance learning (3.9%), double major (3.9%), dual enrollment (3.5%), honors program (3.5%), independent study (5.3%), internships (10.2%), study abroad (.2%), teacher certificate program (16.4%), weekend college. **Teacher certification offered in:** early childhood, special education, elementary, middle/junior high, secondary, bilingual/bicultural. **Faculty and instruction (2009-2010):** Total instructional faculty: 157 full-time, 55 part-time (52% men; 48% women; 15% minorities). Full-time faculty with Ph.D. or other terminal degree: 55%. Student/faculty ratio: 16/1. Classes of fewer than 20 students: %; of 20 to 49 students: %; of 50 or more students: %. **Advanced Placement and International Baccalaureate credit:** International Baccalaureate exams may be used for: Placement only. **Freshmen returning for sophomore year:** 61%. **Graduation rates:** Four-year: 13%; five-year: 25%; six-year: 33%.

COSTS AND FINANCIAL AID

Financial aid office: (870) 235-4023. **Expenses (2009-2010):** Tuition and fees 2009-2010: $6,438 in state, $9,078 out of state; room/board: $8,130. Estimated books and supplies: $1,000; transportation: $1,802; personal expenses: $2,332. **Financial aid:** Priority filing date for institution's financial aid form: July 1. In 2009-2010, 87% of undergraduates applied for financial aid. Of those, 78% were determined to have financial need; 67% had their need fully met. Average financial aid package (proportion receiving): $7,679 (64%). Average amount of gift aid, such as scholarships or grants (proportion receiving): $4,106 (46%). Average amount of self-help aid, such as work study or loans (proportion receiving): $4,922 (58%). Average need-based loan (excluding PLUS or other private loans): $3,692. Among students who received need-based aid, the average percentage of need met:

100%. Among students who received aid based on merit, the average award (and the proportion receiving): $5,891 (13%). The average athletic scholarship (and the proportion receiving): $4,986 (8%). Average amount of debt of borrowers graduating in 2009: $15,672. Proportion who borrowed: 72%.

CAMPUS LIFE AND EXTRACURRICULAR ACTIVITIES

Campus housing available (% using): coed dorms (54%), women's dorms (14%), men's dorms (13%), apartments for married students (1%), apartment for single students (18%). Students who live in college-owned, operated, or affiliated housing: 45%. **Student employment:** During the 2009-2010 academic year, 7% of undergraduates worked on campus. Average per-year earnings: $2,372. **Clubs and organizations:** Number of student organizations: 113. Activities include: campus ministries, choral groups, concert band, drama/theater, international student organization, jazz band, marching band, music ensembles, pep band, radio station, student government, student newspaper, yearbook. Number of fraternities: 8; sororities: 7. Proportion of men in fraternities: 1%; Average proportion of students who stay on campus on weekends: 20%. **Sports program (2009-2010):** Member of NCAA II. *Men's intercollegiate varsity sports:* baseball, basketball, cross country, football, golf, track and field (outdoor). *Women's intercollegiate varsity sports:* basketball, cross country, golf, softball, tennis, track and field (outdoor), volleyball.

SERVICES AND FACILITIES

Basic services: nonremedial tutoring, placement service, health service, health insurance, other. **Remedial assistance:** reading, math, writing. **Counseling services:** minority student, career, personal, veteran student, academic, older student, psychological. **For learning-disabled students:** School does not offer a structured program with separate admission and additional fees. Services include: remedial math, remedial English, remedial reading, tape recorders, note-taking services, readers, extended time for tests, tutors, priority seating, texts on tape, other testing accommodations. **Library:** Number of titles: 151,166; number of current serial subscriptions: 1,065. **Information technology resources:** Students are not required to lease or own a computer. Number of campus computers available to all students: 199. School has a wireless network. Approximate number of users that can be accommodated: 1,000. Proportion of college-owned housing units wired for high-speed internet access: 100%. **Campus safety:** Security services offered: 24-hour foot-and-vehicle patrols, late-night transport/escort service, 24-hour emergency telephones, lighted pathways/sidewalks, student patrols, controlled dormitory access (key, security card, etc).

TRANSFER AND INTERNATIONAL STUDENTS

Transfer students: May apply for admission for the following academic terms: Fall, Spring, Summer. Applicants need a minimum number of credits to apply. For fall 2009: Transfer applications received: 633. Transfer applicants offered admission: 363. Transfer applicants enrolled: 252. **International students:** Number of foreign undergraduates: 96 (4% of student body). Number of countries represented: 31. Minimum TOEFL score required: 500 (paper); 61 (computer). Average TOEFL score: 510 (paper).

University of Arkansas

- **Address:** 232 Silas Hunt Hall, Fayetteville, AR 72701
- **Website:** http://www.uark.edu
- **Public**
- **Enrollment:** 13,783 full-time; 2,052 part-time

KEY STATS

✔ **U.S News College Ranking:** 132, National Universities
✔ **ACT Score (25th/75th percentile):** 23-29
✔ **Tuition:** 2010-2011: $6,768 in state, $16,000 out of state
  Selectivity: More selective   **Room/board:** $8,042
  Acceptance rate: 56%   **Average debt:** $20,171
  Student/faculty ratio: 17/1   **Proportion who borrowed:** 43%

UNDERGRADUATE STUDENT BODY STATS

2009-2010 enrollment: 13,783 full-time; 2,052 part-time. Men: 52%; women: 48%. **Ethnic makeup:** African American: 5%; American-Indian: 2%; Asian American: 3%; Hispanic: 4%; White: 84%; International: 3%.

ADMISSIONS FACTS AND FIGURES

Phone: (800) 377-8632. **Email:** uofa@uark.edu. **Website:** http://www.uark.edu. **Application deadlines for fall 2011:** Regular decision: August 1. Early decision: Not offered. Early action: Send application by: November 15; Decision sent by: December 15. Admission cannot be deferred. **Application fee:** $40. **To apply online, go to:** http://admissions.uark.edu/app/. **Admissions requirements/recommendations:** High school units required (recommended): English: 4; Mathematics: 4; Science: 3; Foreign language: (2); Social studies: 3; Academic electives: 2; Total units: 16. Tests: The college uses SAT or ACT scores in admissions decisions. Either SAT or ACT required. For admission to the fall 2011 entering class, the school will accept: ACT with or without writing accepted. Campus visit: Recommended. Admissions interview: Recommended. Off-campus interview: May be arranged. **Factors that count in admissions decisions:** *Academic:* Secondary school record: Very Important. Class rank: Very Important. Letters of recommendation: Considered. Standardized test scores: Very Important. Essay: Considered. *Nonacademic:* Interview: Not Considered. Extracurricular activities: Considered. Talent/ability: Considered. Character/personal qualities: Considered. Alumni/ae relationship: Considered. Geographical residence: Considered. State residency: Considered. Religious affiliation/commitment: Not Considered. Minority status: Considered. Volunteer work: Considered. Work experience: Considered. **Other schools with the greatest overlap in applicants:** Missouri State University; Oklahoma State University; University of Oklahoma; University of Texas–Austin; University of Tulsa. **Admissions statistics for the fall 2009 entering class:** Total applicants: 12,035. Total accepted: 6,751. Freshmen enrolled: 2,919; 36% were from out of state. Accepted through early-decision or early-action plans: 65%. Overall acceptance rate: 56%. Non-early acceptance rate: 32%. **Credentials of fall 2009 freshmen:** 30% ranked in the top 10 percent of their high school class; 60% were in the top 25 percent; 89% were in the top half. (Proportion submitting class standing: 77%.) **Average high school grade point average:** 3.6. **First-year students who submitted SAT scores:** 27%. Scores (25/75 percentile): Critical Reading: 500-620, Math: 520-640, Combined: 1020-1260. **First-year students submitting ACT scores:** 92%. Scores (25/75 percentile): English: 22-28, Math: 22-30, Composite: 23-29.

ACADEMICS

Year founded: 1871. **Academic calendar:** Semester. **Degrees offered:** bachelor's, post-bachelor's certificate, master's, post-master's certificate, doctorate. **Most popular majors:** 24% business, management, marketing, and related support services, 9% engineering, 7% communication, journalism, and related programs, 7% social sciences, 6% education. **Major fields of study:** agriculture, agriculture operations, and related sciences; architecture and related services; area, ethnic, cultural, and gender studies; biological and biomedical sciences; business, management, marketing, and related support services; communication, journalism, and related programs; computer and information sciences and support services; education; engineering; English language and literature/letters; family and consumer sciences/human sciences; foreign languages, literatures, and linguistics; health professions and related clinical sciences; history; mathematics and statistics; natural resources and conservation; parks, recreation, leisure, and fitness studies; philosophy and religious studies; physical sciences; psychology; public administration and social service professions; security and protective services; social sciences; visual and performing arts. **Areas of required coursework:** arts/fine arts, humanities, mathematics, English (including composition), philosophy, foreign languages, sciences (biological or physical), history, social science. **Pre-professional programs:** pre-law, pre-dentistry, pre-medicine, pre-veterinary science, pre-optometry, pre-pharmacy, other. **Special academic programs (% participation):** accelerated program, cooperative (work-study plan) program (8.8%), distance learning (49.3%), double major (8.5%), dual enrollment, English as a Second Language (ESL), honors program (24.1%), independent study (25.3%), internships (30.9%), liberal arts/career combination, student-designed major, study abroad (16.8%), teacher certificate program. **Teacher certification offered in:** early childhood, special education, elementary, vo-tech, middle/junior high, adult education, secondary, bilingual/bicultural. **Cooperative education programs:** agriculture, art, business, computer science, engineering, home economics, humanities, natural science, social/behavioral science, technologies. **Reserve Officers Training Corps (ROTC):** Army ROTC: Offered on campus; Air Force ROTC: Offered on campus. **Faculty and instruction (2009-2010):** Total instructional faculty: 897 full-time, 86 part-time (66% men; 34% women; 12% minorities). Full-time faculty with Ph.D. or other terminal degree: 89%. Student/faculty ratio: 17/1. Classes of fewer than 20 students: 31%; of 20 to 49 students: 52%; of 50 or more students: 17%. **Advanced Placement and International Baccalaureate credit:** AP tests may be used for: Credit and/or placement. Scores accepted: 2, 3, 4, 5. International Baccalaureate exams

may be used for: Credit only. **Freshmen returning for sophomore year:** 83%. **Graduation rates:** Four-year: 34%; five-year: 55%; six-year: 59%. **Graduate study:** 34% of students pursue further study immediately upon graduation. Fields in which graduates pursue further study: Master of Business Administration (MBA), 20%; law, 15%; medicine, 12%; dentistry, 4%; engineering, 10%; education, 20%; arts and sciences, 10%.

COSTS AND FINANCIAL AID

Financial aid office: (479) 575-3806. **Expenses (2010-2011):** Tuition and fees 2010-2011: $6,768 in state, $16,000 out of state; room/board: $8,042. Estimated books and supplies: $1,162; transportation: $1,430; personal expenses: $2,088. **Financial aid:** Priority filing date for institution's financial aid form: March 15. In 2009-2010, 55% of undergraduates applied for financial aid. Of those, 41% were determined to have financial need; 18% had their need fully met. Average financial aid package (proportion receiving): $9,030 (39%). Average amount of gift aid, such as scholarships or grants (proportion receiving): $6,343 (30%). Average amount of self-help aid, such as work study or loans (proportion receiving): $4,834 (32%). Average need-based loan (excluding PLUS or other private loans): $4,306. Among students who received need-based aid, the average percentage of need met: 64%. Among students who received aid based on merit, the average award (and the proportion receiving): $5,315 (17%). The average athletic scholarship (and the proportion receiving): $7,808 (3%). Average amount of debt of borrowers graduating in 2009: $20,171. Proportion who borrowed: 43%.

CAMPUS LIFE AND EXTRACURRICULAR ACTIVITIES

Campus housing available (% using): coed dorms (50%), women's dorms (9%), sorority housing (10%), fraternity housing (9%), apartment for single students (3%), special housing for disabled students (1%), special housing for international students (2%), other housing options (16%). Students who live in college-owned, operated, or affiliated housing: 29%. **Student employment:** During the 2009-2010 academic year, 13% of undergraduates worked on campus. Average per-year earnings: $5,220. **Clubs and organizations:** Number of student organizations: 335. Activities include: campus ministries, choral groups, concert band, dance, drama/theater, international student organization, jazz band, literary magazine, marching band, music ensembles, musical theater, opera, pep band, radio station, student government, student newspaper, student film society, symphony orchestra, television station, yearbook. Number of fraternities: 16; sororities: 11. Proportion of men in fraternities: 17%; of women in sororities: 23%. Average proportion of students who stay on campus on weekends: 74%. **Sports program (2009-2010):** Member of NCAA I. *Men's intercollegiate varsity sports:* baseball, basketball, cross country, football, golf, tennis, track and field (indoor), track and field (outdoor). *Women's intercollegiate varsity sports:* basketball, cross country, golf, gymnastics, soccer, softball, swimming, tennis, track and field (indoor), track and field (outdoor), volleyball.

SERVICES AND FACILITIES

Basic services: nonremedial tutoring, placement service, day care, health service, health insurance, other. **Remedial assistance:** reading, math, writing, study skills. **Counseling services:** minority student, career, military, personal, veteran student, academic, older student, psychological, birth control, religious. **For learning-disabled students:** School does not offer a structured program with separate admission and additional fees. Total undergraduates in learning-disabled program or receiving services: 160. Services include: remedial math, remedial English, remedial reading, tape recorders, diagnostic testing service, note-taking services, learning center, readers, extended time for tests, tutors, priority registration, priority seating, other testing accommodations, other. **Library:** Number of titles: 1,903,122; number of current serial subscriptions: 26,130. **Information technology resources:** Students are not required to lease or own a computer. Number of campus computers available to all students: 3,014. School has a wireless network. Approximate number of users that can be accommodated: 9,816. Proportion of college-owned housing units wired for high-speed internet access: 100%. **Campus safety:** Security services offered: 24-hour foot-and-vehicle patrols, late-night transport/escort service, 24-hour emergency telephones, lighted pathways/sidewalks, student patrols, controlled dormitory access (key, security card, etc).

TRANSFER AND INTERNATIONAL STUDENTS

Transfer students: May apply for admission for the following academic terms: Fall, Spring, Summer. Applicants need a minimum number of credits to apply. For fall 2009: Transfer applications received: 3,150. Transfer applicants offered admission: 1,962. Transfer applicants enrolled: 1,320. **International students:** Number of foreign undergraduates: 452 (3% of stu-

dent body). Number of countries represented: 83. Minimum TOEFL score required: 550 (paper); 79 (computer). Average TOEFL score: 590 (paper).

University of Arkansas—Fort Smith

- **Address:** 520 Grand Avenue, PO Box 3649, Fort Smith, AR 72913-3649
- **Website:** http://www.uafortsmith.edu/Home/Index
- **Public**
- **Enrollment:** N/A

KEY STATS

✔ **U.S News College Ranking:** second tier, Regional Colleges (South)
✔ **SAT or ACT Score (25th/75th percentile):** N/A
✔ **Tuition:** 2009-2010: $4,600 in state, $10,000 out of state

Selectivity: Less selective	**Room/board:** $7,180
Acceptance rate: N/A	**Average debt:** N/A
Student/faculty ratio: N/A	**Proportion who borrowed:** N/A

University of Arkansas—Little Rock

- **Address:** 2801 S. University Avenue, Little Rock, AR 72204-1099
- **Website:** http://www.ualr.edu
- **Public**
- **Enrollment:** N/A

KEY STATS

✔ **U.S News College Ranking:** second tier, National Universities
✔ **SAT or ACT Score (25th/75th percentile):** N/A
✔ **Tuition:** 2009-2010: $6,338 in state, $14,798 out of state

Selectivity: Selective	**Room/board:** $3,198
Acceptance rate: N/A	**Average debt:** N/A
Student/faculty ratio: N/A	**Proportion who borrowed:** N/A

University of Arkansas—Monticello

- **Address:** UAM Box 3478, Monticello, AR 71656
- **Website:** http://www.uamont.edu
- **Public**
- **Enrollment:** 2,481 full-time; 882 part-time

KEY STATS

✔ **U.S News College Ranking:** Unranked, Regional Universities (South)
✔ **SAT or ACT Score (25th/75th percentile):** N/A
✔ **Tuition:** 2009-2010: $4,750 in state, $9,010 out of state

Selectivity: N/A	**Room/board:** $4,080
Acceptance rate: 50%	**Average debt:** N/A
Student/faculty ratio: 16/1	**Proportion who borrowed:** N/A

UNDERGRADUATE STUDENT BODY STATS

2009-2010 enrollment: 2,481 full-time; 882 part-time. Men: 41%; women: 59%. **Ethnic makeup:** African American: 33%; American-Indian: 1%; Hispanic: 1%; White: 64%.

ADMISSIONS FACTS AND FIGURES

Phone: (870) 460-1026. **Email:** admissions@uamont.edu. **Website:** http://www.uamont.edu. **Application deadlines for fall 2011:** Regular decision: Rolling. Early decision: Not offered. Early action: Not offered. Admission cannot be deferred. **To apply online, go to:** https://www.uamont.edu/forms/admissions/admissionsform2.asp. **Admissions requirements/recommendations:** High school units required (recommended): English: (4); Mathematics: (4); Science: (3); Social studies: (3); Total units: (14). Tests: The college does not use SAT or ACT scores in admissions decisions. Neither SAT nor ACT required. Campus visit: Recommended. Admissions interview: Neither required nor recommended. **Other schools with the greatest overlap in applicants:** Southern Arkansas University; University of Arkansas—Little Rock; University of Arkansas—Pine Bluff. **Admissions statistics for the fall 2009 entering class:** Total applicants: 1,998. Total accepted:

999. Freshmen enrolled: 795; 10% were from out of state. Overall acceptance rate: 50%. **Average high school grade point average:** 2.8.

ACADEMICS

Year founded: 1910. **Academic calendar:** Semester. **Degrees offered:** certificate, associate, bachelor's, post-bachelor's certificate, master's. **Most popular majors:** 27% business administration and management, 10% nursing/registered nurse training (R.N., A.S.N., B.S.N., M.S.N.), 8% education, 8% psychology, 7% agriculture, agriculture operations, and related sciences. **Major fields of study:** agriculture, agriculture operations, and related sciences; biological and biomedical sciences; business, management, marketing, and related support services; education; engineering; English language and literature/letters; health professions and related clinical sciences; history; mathematics and statistics; multi/interdisciplinary studies; natural resources and conservation; parks, recreation, leisure, and fitness studies; physical sciences; psychology; public administration and social service professions; security and protective services; social sciences; visual and performing arts. **Areas of required coursework:** arts/fine arts, humanities, mathematics, English (including composition), sciences (biological or physical), history, social science. **Pre-professional programs:** pre-law, pre-medicine, pre-veterinary science, pre-pharmacy. **Special academic programs:** cooperative (work-study plan) program, cross-registration, distance learning, double major, independent study, internships, teacher certificate program. **Teacher certification offered in:** early childhood, middle/junior high, secondary. **Reserve Officers Training Corps (ROTC):** Army ROTC: Offered on campus. **Faculty and instruction (2009-2010):** Total instructional faculty: 153 full-time, 63 part-time (50% men; 50% women; 12% minorities). Full-time faculty with Ph.D. or other terminal degree: 50%. Student/faculty ratio: 16/1. Classes of fewer than 20 students: 58%; of 20 to 49 students: 39%; of 50 or more students: 3%. **Advanced Placement and International Baccalaureate credit:** AP tests may be used for: Credit only. Scores accepted: 3, 4, 5. International Baccalaureate exams may be used for: Placement only. **Freshmen returning for sophomore year:** 47%. **Graduation rates:** Six-year: 25%.

COSTS AND FINANCIAL AID

Financial aid office: (870) 460-1050. **Expenses (2009-2010):** Tuition and fees 2009-2010: $4,750 in state, $9,010 out of state; room/board: $4,080. Estimated books and supplies: $800.

CAMPUS LIFE AND EXTRACURRICULAR ACTIVITIES

Campus housing available (% using): coed dorms (17%), women's dorms (26%), men's dorms (30%), apartments for married students (5%), apartment for single students (21%). Students who live in college-owned, operated, or affiliated housing: 22%. **Clubs and organizations:** Number of student organizations: 61. Activities include: campus ministries, choral groups, concert band, jazz band, literary magazine, marching band, music ensembles, musical theater, student government, student newspaper, yearbook. Number of fraternities: 7; sororities: 5. Proportion of men in fraternities: 8%; of women in sororities: 9%. Average proportion of students who stay on campus on weekends: 20%. **Sports program (2009-2010):** Member of NCAA II. *Men's intercollegiate varsity sports:* baseball, basketball, cross country, football, golf. *Women's intercollegiate varsity sports:* basketball, softball, volleyball.

SERVICES AND FACILITIES

Basic services: nonremedial tutoring, placement service, health service. **Remedial assistance:** reading, math, writing. **Counseling services:** career, academic. **For learning-disabled students:** School does not offer a structured program with separate admission and additional fees. Services include: remedial math, remedial English, remedial reading, tape recorders, videotaped classes, untimed tests, note-taking services, oral tests, readers, extended time for tests, tutors, priority registration, priority seating, texts on tape, other testing accommodations. **Library:** Number of titles: 241,822; number of current serial subscriptions: 1,140. **Information technology resources:** Students are not required to lease or own a computer. School has a wireless network. Proportion of college-owned housing units wired for high-speed internet access: 95%. **Campus safety:** Security services offered: 24-hour foot-and-vehicle patrols, 24-hour emergency telephones, lighted pathways/sidewalks, controlled dormitory access (key, security card, etc).

TRANSFER AND INTERNATIONAL STUDENTS

Transfer students: May apply for admission for the following academic terms: Fall, Spring, Summer. Applicants do not need a minimum number of credits to apply. For fall 2009: Transfer applications received: 553. Transfer applicants offered admission: 260. Transfer applicants enrolled:

230. **International students:** Number of foreign undergraduates: 5. Minimum TOEFL score required: 500 (paper); 173 (computer).

University of Arkansas–Pine Bluff

- ■ **Address:** 1200 N. University Drive, Pine Bluff, AR 71601
- ■ **Website:** http://www.uapb.edu/
- ■ **Public**
- ■ **Enrollment:** 3,313 full-time; 338 part-time

KEY STATS

✔ **U.S News College Ranking:** 60, Regional Colleges (South)
✔ **ACT Score (25th/75th percentile):** 14-18
✔ **Tuition:** 2009-2010: $4,706 in state, $5,366 out of state

Selectivity: Less selective	**Room/board:** $3,310
Acceptance rate: 33%	**Average debt:** N/A
Student/faculty ratio: 17/1	**Proportion who borrowed:** N/A

UNDERGRADUATE STUDENT BODY STATS

2009-2010 enrollment: 3,313 full-time; 338 part-time. Men: 42%; women: 58%. **Ethnic makeup:** African American: 95%; White: 3%; International: 1%.

ADMISSIONS FACTS AND FIGURES

Phone: (870) 575-8492. **Email:** jones_m@uapb.edu. **Website:** http://www.uapb.edu/. **Application deadlines for fall 2011:** Regular decision: Rolling. Early decision: Not offered. Early action: Not offered. Admission can be deferred. **To apply online, go to:** https://uapbactive.uapb.edu/apply. **Admissions requirements/recommendations:** High school units required (recommended) English: 4; Mathematics: 3; Science: 3; Foreign language: 2; Social studies: 1; History: 2; Academic electives: 4; Total units: 21. Tests: The college uses SAT or ACT scores in admissions decisions. Either SAT or ACT required. For admission to the fall 2011 entering class, the school will accept: ACT with or without writing accepted. Campus visit: Recommended. Admissions interview: Recommended. Off-campus interview: May be arranged. **Factors that count in admissions decisions:** *Academic:* Secondary school record: Very Important. Class rank: Not Considered. Letters of recommendation: Not Considered. Standardized test scores: Very Important. Essay: Not Considered. *Nonacademic:* Interview: Not Considered. Extracurricular activities: Not Considered. Talent/ability: Not Considered. Character/personal qualities: Not Considered. Alumni/ae relationship: Not Considered. Geographical residence: Not Considered. State residency: Not Considered. Religious affiliation/commitment: Not Considered. Minority status: Not Considered. Volunteer work: Not Considered. Work experience: Not Considered. **Admissions statistics for the fall 2009 entering class:** Total applicants: 4,792. Total accepted: 1,568. Freshmen enrolled: 977; 45% were from out of state. Overall acceptance rate: 33%. **Credentials of fall 2009 freshmen:** 12% ranked in the top 10 percent of their high school class; 27% were in the top 25 percent. **First-year students who submitted SAT scores:** 5%. Scores (25/75 percentile): Critical Reading: 370-490, Math: 360-480, Combined: 730-970. **First-year students submitting ACT scores:** 95%. Scores (25/75 percentile): English: 12-18, Math: 15-17, Composite: 14-18.

ACADEMICS

Year founded: 1873. **Academic calendar:** Semester. **Degrees offered:** certificate, associate, bachelor's, master's. **Most popular majors:** 14% business administration and management, 9% criminal justice/safety studies, 9% family and consumer sciences/human sciences, 7% general studies, 6% nursing/registered nurse training (R.N., A.S.N.; B.S.N., M.S.N.). **Major fields of study:** agriculture, agriculture operations, and related sciences; biological and biomedical sciences; business, management, marketing, and related support services; communication, journalism, and related programs; computer and information sciences and support services; education; engineering technologies/technicians; English language and literature/letters; family and consumer sciences/human sciences; health professions and related clinical sciences; history; liberal arts and sciences studies, and humanities; mathematics and statistics; natural resources and conservation; parks, recreation, leisure, and fitness studies; physical sciences; psychology; public administration and social service professions; security and protective services; social sciences; visual and performing arts. **Areas of required coursework:** arts/fine arts, humanities, mathematics, English (including composition), philosophy, foreign languages, sciences (biological or physical), history, social science. **Pre-professional programs:** pre-law, pre-dentistry, pre-medicine, pre-pharmacy. **Special academic programs:**

cooperative (work-study plan) program, cross-registration, distance learning, double major, dual enrollment, honors program, independent study, internships, teacher certificate program. **Teacher certification offered in:** early childhood, special education, middle/junior high, secondary. **Cooperative education programs:** agriculture, art, business, computer science, education, home economics, social/behavioral science. **Reserve Officers Training Corps (ROTC):** Army ROTC: Offered on campus. **Faculty and instruction (2009-2010):** Total instructional faculty: 173 full-time, 85 part-time (53% men; 47% women; 77% minorities). Full-time faculty with Ph.D. or other terminal degree: 61%. Student/faculty ratio: 17/1. Classes of fewer than 20 students: 42%; of 20 to 49 students: 53%; of 50 or more students: 5%. **Advanced Placement and International Baccalaureate credit:** AP tests may be used for: Credit only. **Freshmen returning for sophomore year:** 59%. **Graduation rates:** Four-year: 6%; five-year: 17%; six-year: 29%.

COSTS AND FINANCIAL AID

Financial aid office: (870) 575-8302. **Expenses (2009-2010):** Tuition and fees 2009-2010: $4,706 in state, $5,366 out of state; room/board: $3,310. **Financial aid:** Priority filing date for institution's financial aid form: April 1.

CAMPUS LIFE AND EXTRACURRICULAR ACTIVITIES

Campus housing available (% using): women's dorms (52%), men's dorms (48%). Students who live in college-owned, operated, or affiliated housing: 45%. **Student employment:** During the 2009-2010 academic year, 1% of undergraduates worked on campus. **Clubs and organizations:** Number of student organizations: 94. Activities include: campus ministries, choral groups, concert band, drama/theater, international student organization, jazz band, marching band, music ensembles, pep band, radio station, student government, student newspaper, symphony orchestra, television station, yearbook. Number of fraternities: 4; sororities: 4. **Sports program (2009-2010):** Member of NCAA I. *Men's intercollegiate varsity sports:* baseball, basketball, cross country, football, golf, tennis, track and field (indoor), track and field (outdoor). *Women's intercollegiate varsity sports:* basketball, bowling, cross country, golf, soccer, softball, tennis, track and field (indoor), track and field (outdoor), volleyball.

SERVICES AND FACILITIES

Basic services: placement service, health service. **Remedial assistance:** reading, math. **Counseling services:** career, academic. **For learning-disabled students:** School does not offer a structured program with separate admission and additional fees. Services include: remedial math, remedial English, remedial reading, note-taking services, learning center, readers, tutors. **Library:** Number of titles: 184,995; number of current serial subscriptions: 743. **Information technology resources:** Students are not required to lease or own a computer. Number of campus computers available to all students: 800. School has a wireless network. Approximate number of users that can be accommodated: 65,000. Proportion of college-owned housing units wired for high-speed internet access: 100%. **Campus safety:** Security services offered: 24-hour emergency telephones.

TRANSFER AND INTERNATIONAL STUDENTS

Transfer students: May apply for admission for the following academic terms: Fall, Spring, Summer. Applicants need a minimum number of credits to apply. For fall 2009: Transfer applications received: 541. Transfer applicants offered admission: 273. Transfer applicants enrolled: 188. **International students:** Number of foreign undergraduates: 43 (1% of student body). Number of countries represented: 20. Minimum TOEFL score required: 500 (paper); 173 (computer). Average TOEFL score: 520 (paper).

University of Central Arkansas

- ■ **Address:** 201 Donaghey Avenue, Conway, AR 72035
- ■ **Website:** http://www.uca.edu
- ■ **Public**
- ■ **Enrollment:** 8,507 full-time; 1,639 part-time

KEY STATS

✔ **U.S News College Ranking:** 47, Regional Universities (South)
✔ **ACT Score (25th/75th percentile):** 20-27
✔ **Tuition:** 2009-2010: $6,698 in state, $11,903 out of state

Selectivity: Selective	**Room/board:** $4,880
Acceptance rate: 94%	**Average debt:** N/A
Student/faculty ratio: 18/1	**Proportion who borrowed:** N/A

UNDERGRADUATE STUDENT BODY STATS

2009-2010 enrollment: 8,507 full-time; 1,639 part-time. Men: 44%; women: 56%. **Ethnic makeup:** African American: 17%; American-Indian: 1%; Asian American: 2%; Hispanic: 2%; White: 74%; International: 4%.

ADMISSIONS FACTS AND FIGURES

Phone: (501) 450-3128. **Email:** admissions@uca.edu. **Website:** http://www.uca.edu. **Application deadlines for fall 2011:** Regular decision: Rolling. Early decision: Not offered. Early action: Not offered. Admission can be deferred. **To apply online, go to:** http://www.uca.edu/admissions/apply-here.php. **Admissions requirements/recommendations:** High school units required (recommended): English: (4); Mathematics: (4); Science: (3); Social studies: (1); History: (2); Academic electives: (10); Total units: (24). Tests: The college uses SAT or ACT scores in admissions decisions. Either SAT or ACT required. For admission to the fall 2011 entering class, the school will accept: ACT with or without writing accepted. Campus visit: Recommended. Admissions interview: Neither required nor recommended. Off-campus interview: Not available. **Factors that count in admissions decisions:** *Academic:* Secondary school record: Not Considered. Class rank: Important. Letters of recommendation: Not Considered. Standardized test scores: Very Important. Essay: Not Considered. *Nonacademic:* Interview: Not Considered. Extracurricular activities: Not Considered. Talent/ability: Not Considered. Character/personal qualities: Not Considered. Alumni/ae relationship: Not Considered. Geographical residence: Not Considered. State residency: Not Considered. Religious affiliation/commitment: Not Considered. Minority status: Not Considered. Volunteer work: Not Considered. Work experience: Not Considered. **Other schools with the greatest overlap in applicants:** Arkansas State University–Jonesboro; Arkansas Tech University; Hendrix College; University of Arkansas; University of Arkansas–Little Rock. **Admissions statistics for the fall 2009 entering class:** Total applicants: 3,821. Total accepted: 3,595. Freshmen enrolled: 1,777; 7% were from out of state. Overall acceptance rate: 94%. **Credentials of fall 2009 freshmen:** 23% ranked in the top 10 percent of their high school class; 50% were in the top 25 percent; 79% were in the top half. (Proportion submitting class standing: 78%.) **Average high school grade point average:** 3.3. **First-year students submitting ACT scores:** 95%. Scores (25/75 percentile): English: 18-26, Math: 20-28, Composite: 20-27.

ACADEMICS

Year founded: 1907. **Academic calendar:** Semester. **Degrees offered:** certificate, associate, bachelor's, post-bachelor's certificate, master's, post-master's certificate, doctorate. **Most popular majors:** 5% health professions and related clinical sciences, 4% family and consumer sciences/human sciences, 4% kindergarten/preschool education and teaching, 4% nursing/registered nurse training (R.N., A.S.N., B.S.N., M.S.N.), 3% accounting. **Major fields of study:** area, ethnic, cultural, and gender studies; biological and biomedical sciences; business, management, marketing, and related support services; communication, journalism, and related programs; computer and information sciences and support services; education; English language and literature/letters; family and consumer sciences/human sciences; foreign languages, literatures, and linguistics; health professions and related clinical sciences; history; mathematics and statistics; multi/interdisciplinary studies; natural resources and conservation; parks, recreation, leisure, and fitness studies; philosophy and religious studies; physical sciences; psychology; public administration and social service professions; social sciences; visual and performing arts. **Areas of required coursework:** arts/fine arts, humanities, mathematics, English (including composition), sciences (biological or physical), history. **Pre-professional programs:** pre-law, pre-dentistry, pre-medicine, pre-veterinary science, pre-optometry, pre-pharmacy, other. **Special academic programs:** accelerated program, cooperative (work-study plan) program, distance learning, double major, dual enrollment, English as a Second Language (ESL), honors program, independent study, internships, liberal arts/career combination, study abroad, teacher certificate program, other. **Teacher certification offered in:** early childhood, special education, elementary, vo-tech, middle/junior high, secondary, bilingual/bicultural. **Cooperative education programs:** art, business, computer science, home economics, humanities, natural science, social/behavioral science. **Reserve Officers Training Corps (ROTC):** Army ROTC: Offered on campus. **Faculty and instruction (2009-2010):** Total instructional faculty: 512 full-time, 199 part-time (46% men; 54% women; 8% minorities). Full-time faculty with Ph.D. or other terminal degree: 66%. Student/faculty ratio: 18/1. Classes of fewer than 20 students: 52%; of 20 to 49 students: 46%; of 50 or more students: 2%. **Advanced Placement and International Baccalaureate credit:** AP tests may be used for: Credit only. Scores accepted: 3, 4, 5. International Baccalaureate exams may be used for: Credit only. **Freshmen returning for**

sophomore year: 71%. **Graduation rates:** Four-year: 22%; five-year: 35%; six-year: 43%.

COSTS AND FINANCIAL AID

Financial aid office: (501) 450-3140. **Expenses (2009-2010):** Tuition and fees 2009-2010: $6,698 in state, $11,903 out of state; room/board: $4,880. Estimated books and supplies: $1,000; transportation: $3,100; personal expenses: $2,360. **Financial aid:** Priority filing date for institution's financial aid form: February 15; deadline: September 1.

CAMPUS LIFE AND EXTRACURRICULAR ACTIVITIES

Campus housing available (% using): coed dorms (42%), women's dorms (11%), men's dorms (4%), fraternity housing (0%), apartments for married students (1%), apartment for single students (33%), special housing for disabled students (1%), special housing for international students (8%), other housing options (0%). Students who live in college-owned, operated, or affiliated housing: 35%. **Clubs and organizations:** Number of student organizations: 144. Activities include: campus ministries, choral groups, concert band, dance, drama/theater, international student organization, jazz band, literary magazine, marching band, model UN, music ensembles, pep band, radio station, student government, student newspaper, student film society, symphony orchestra, television station, yearbook. Number of fraternities: 12; sororities: 8. Proportion of men in fraternities: 10%; of women in sororities: 10%. Average proportion of students who stay on campus on weekends: 25%. **Sports program (2009-2010):** Member of NCAA I. *Men's intercollegiate varsity sports:* baseball, basketball, cross country, football, golf, soccer, track and field (indoor), track and field (outdoor). *Women's intercollegiate varsity sports:* basketball, cross country, golf, soccer, softball, tennis, track and field (indoor), track and field (outdoor), volleyball.

SERVICES AND FACILITIES

Basic services: nonremedial tutoring, women's center, placement service, day care, health service, health insurance. **Remedial assistance:** reading, math, writing, study skills. **Counseling services:** minority student, career, military, personal, veteran student, academic, older student, psychological, birth control, religious. **For learning-disabled students:** School does not offer a structured program with separate admission and additional fees. Services include: remedial math, remedial English, reading machines, remedial reading, tape recorders, note-taking services, oral tests, readers, extended time for tests, priority registration, priority seating, texts on tape, other testing accommodations, other. **Library:** Number of titles: 591,874; number of current serial subscriptions: 24,822. **Information technology resources:** Students are not required to lease or own a computer. Number of campus computers available to all students: 574. School has a wireless network. Approximate number of users that can be accommodated: 4,000. Proportion of college-owned housing units wired for high-speed internet access: 100%. **Campus safety:** Security services offered: 24-hour foot-and-vehicle patrols, late-night transport/escort service, 24-hour emergency telephones, lighted pathways/sidewalks, controlled dormitory access (key, security card, etc).

TRANSFER AND INTERNATIONAL STUDENTS

Transfer students: May apply for admission for the following academic terms: Fall, Winter, Spring, Summer. Applicants do not need a minimum number of credits to apply. For fall 2009: Transfer applications received: 801. Transfer applicants offered admission: 747. Transfer applicants enrolled: 500. **International students:** Number of foreign undergraduates: 359 (4% of student body). Number of countries represented: 66. Minimum TOEFL score required: 500 (paper); 173 (computer).

University of the Ozarks

- **Address:** 415 N. College Avenue, Clarksville, AR 72830
- **Website:** http://www.ozarks.edu
- **Private; Religious affiliation:** Presbyterian
- **Enrollment:** 590 full-time; 35 part-time

KEY STATS

✔ **U.S News College Ranking:** 13, Regional Colleges (South)
✔ **ACT Score (25th/75th percentile):** 19-25
✔ **Tuition:** 2010-2011: $20,530

Selectivity: Selective	**Room/board:** $6,300
Acceptance rate: 89%	**Average debt:** $18,425
Student/faculty ratio: 10/1	**Proportion who borrowed:** 56%

UNDERGRADUATE STUDENT BODY STATS

2009-2010 enrollment: 590 full-time; 35 part-time. Men: 49%; women: 51%. **Ethnic makeup:** African American: 5%; American-Indian: 3%; Asian American: 1%; Hispanic: 5%; White: 69%; International: 18%. **Religious preference:** Roman Catholic: 17%; Protestant: 56%; Buddhist: 1%; No preference: 18%; Presbyterian: 6%; Other: 2%.

ADMISSIONS FACTS AND FIGURES

Phone: (479) 979-1227. **Email:** admiss@ozarks.edu. **Website:** http://www.ozarks.edu. **Application deadlines for fall 2011:** Regular decision: Rolling. Early decision: Not offered. Early action: Not offered. Admission can be deferred. **Application fee:** $30. **To apply online, go to:** http://admissions.ozarks.edu/secure/forms/apply/default.aspx. **Admissions requirements/recommendations:** High school units required (recommended): English: 4 (4); Mathematics: 4 (4); Science: 3 (3); Foreign language: 2 (2); Social studies: 1 (1); History: 2 (2); Total units: 18 (18). Tests: The college uses SAT or ACT scores in admissions decisions. Either SAT or ACT required. For admission to the fall 2011 entering class, the school will accept: ACT with or without writing accepted. Campus visit: Recommended. Admissions interview: Recommended. Off-campus interview: Not available. **Factors that count in admissions decisions:** *Academic:* Secondary school record: Considered. Class rank: Not Considered. Letters of recommendation: Considered. Standardized test scores: Important. Essay: Considered. *Nonacademic:* Interview: Considered. Extracurricular activities: Considered. Talent/ability: Considered. Character/personal qualities: Considered. Alumni/ae relationship: Considered. Geographical residence: Not Considered. State residency: Not Considered. Religious affiliation/commitment: Not Considered. Minority status: Not Considered. Volunteer work: Considered. Work experience: Considered. **Other schools with the greatest overlap in applicants:** Arkansas Tech University; Ouachita Baptist University; University of Arkansas; University of Central Arkansas; University of Texas–Dallas. **Admissions statistics for the fall 2009 entering class:** Total applicants: 596. Total accepted: 530. Freshmen enrolled: 152; 36% were from out of state. Overall acceptance rate: 89%. **Credentials of fall 2009 freshmen:** 14% ranked in the top 10 percent of their high school class; 41% were in the top 25 percent; 75% were in the top half. (Proportion submitting class standing: 80%.) **Average high school grade point average:** 3.4. **First-year students who submitted SAT scores:** 27%. Scores (25/75 percentile): Critical Reading: 430-530, Math: 460-560, Combined: 890-1090. **First-year students submitting ACT scores:** 81%. Scores (25/75 percentile): English: 18-25, Math: 18-25, Composite: 19-25.

ACADEMICS

Year founded: 1834. **Academic calendar:** Semester. **Degrees offered:** bachelor's. **Most popular majors:** 35% business, management, marketing, and related support services, 13% social sciences, 10% education, 9% communication, journalism, and related programs, 9% visual and performing arts. **Major fields of study:** biological and biomedical sciences; business, management, marketing, and related support services; communication, journalism, and related programs; education; English language and literature/letters; health professions and related clinical sciences; history; liberal arts and sciences studies, and humanities; mathematics and statistics; natural resources and conservation; philosophy and religious studies; physical sciences; psychology; social sciences; visual and performing arts. **Areas of required coursework:** arts/fine arts, humanities, mathematics, English (including composition), philosophy, sciences (biological or physical), history, social science, other. **Pre-professional programs:** pre-law, pre-dentistry, pre-medicine, pre-veterinary science, pre-pharmacy, other. **Special academic programs (% participation):** cooperative (work-study plan) program (8%), double major (11%), dual enrollment (4%), independent study (3%), internships, liberal arts/career combination (10%), study abroad (5%), teacher certificate program (13%). **Teacher certification offered in:** early childhood, special education, elementary, middle/junior high, secondary. **Cooperative education programs:** business. **Faculty and instruction (2009-2010):** Total instructional faculty: 47 full-time, 34 part-time (60% men; 40% women; 5% minorities). Full-time faculty with Ph.D. or other terminal degree: 79%. Student/faculty ratio: 10/1. Classes of fewer than 20 students: 79%; of 20 to 49 students: 21%. **Advanced Placement and International Baccalaureate credit:** AP tests may be used for: Credit only. Scores accepted: 4. International Baccalaureate exams may be used for: Credit only. **Freshmen returning for sophomore year:** 69%. **Graduation rates:** Four-year: 31%; five-year: 39%; six-year: 44%. **Graduate study:** 25% of students pursue further study immediately upon graduation. Fields in which graduates pursue further study: Master of Business Administration (MBA), 25%; law, 10%; medicine, 10%; engineering, 2%; education, 10%; arts and sciences, 43%.

COSTS AND FINANCIAL AID

Financial aid office: (479) 979-1221. **Expenses (2010-2011):** Tuition and fees 2010-2011: $20,530; room/board: $6,300. Estimated books and supplies: $800; transportation: $1,061; personal expenses: $2,901. **Financial aid:** Priority filing date for institution's financial aid form: February 15. In 2009-2010, 66% of undergraduates applied for financial aid. Of those, 60% were determined to have financial need; 18% had their need fully met. Average financial aid package (proportion receiving): $18,877 (60%). Average amount of gift aid, such as scholarships or grants (proportion receiving): $13,990 (58%). Average amount of self-help aid, such as work study or loans (proportion receiving): $8,992 (51%). Average need-based loan (excluding PLUS or other private loans): $10,173. Among students who received need-based aid, the average percentage of need met: 77%. Among students who received aid based on merit, the average award (and the proportion receiving): $16,569 (32%). Average amount of debt of borrowers graduating in 2009: $18,425. Proportion who borrowed: 56%.

CAMPUS LIFE AND EXTRACURRICULAR ACTIVITIES

Campus housing available (% using): coed dorms (71%), women's dorms (13%), apartments for married students (3%), apartment for single students (13%). Students who live in college-owned, operated, or affiliated housing: 65%. **Student employment:** During the 2009-2010 academic year, 38% of undergraduates worked on campus. Average per-year earnings: $950. **Clubs and organizations:** Number of student organizations: 40. Activities include: campus ministries, choral groups, drama/theater, international student organization, literary magazine, radio station, student government, student newspaper, television station, yearbook. Number of fraternities: 0; sororities: 0. Average proportion of students who stay on campus on weekends: 50%. **Sports program (2009-2010):** Member of NCAA III. *Men's intercollegiate varsity sports:* baseball, basketball, cross country, soccer, tennis. *Women's intercollegiate varsity sports:* basketball, cross country, soccer, softball, tennis.

SERVICES AND FACILITIES

Basic services: nonremedial tutoring, placement service, health service. **Remedial assistance:** reading, math, writing, study skills. **Counseling services:** minority student, career, personal, academic, psychological, religious. **For learning-disabled students:** School does not offer a structured program with separate admission and additional fees. Services include: remedial math, remedial English, reading machines, remedial reading, tape recorders, other special classes, diagnostic testing service, note-taking services, oral tests, learning center, readers, extended time for tests, tutors, priority registration, texts on tape, other. **Library:** Number of titles: 105,348; number of current serial subscriptions: 300. **Information technology resources:** Students are not required to lease or own a computer. Number of campus computers available to all students: 150. School has a wireless network. Approximate number of users that can be accommodated: 200. Proportion of college-owned housing units wired for high-speed internet access: 100%. **Campus safety:** Security services offered: 24-hour foot-and-vehicle patrols, late-night transport/escort service, 24-hour emergency telephones, lighted pathways/sidewalks, controlled dormitory access (key, security card, etc).

TRANSFER AND INTERNATIONAL STUDENTS

Transfer students: May apply for admission for the following academic terms: Fall, Spring. Applicants do not need a minimum number of credits to apply. For fall 2009: Transfer applicants enrolled: 19. **International students:** Number of foreign undergraduates: 109 (18% of student body). Number of countries represented: 18. Minimum TOEFL score required: 500 (paper); 173 (computer). Average TOEFL score: 620 (paper).

Williams Baptist College

- **Address:** PO Box 3727, Walnut Ridge, AR 72476
- **Website:** http://www.williamsbaptistcollege.com
- **Private; Religious affiliation:** Southern Baptist Convention
- **Enrollment:** 503 full-time; 110 part-time

KEY STATS

✔ **U.S News College Ranking:** 62, Regional Colleges (South)
✔ **ACT Score (25th/75th percentile):** 19-23
✔ **Tuition:** 2010-2011: $12,020

Selectivity: Selective	**Room/board:** $5,400
Acceptance rate: 64%	**Average debt:** $16,826
Student/faculty ratio: 16/1	**Proportion who borrowed:** 80%

UNDERGRADUATE STUDENT BODY STATS

2009-2010 enrollment: 503 full-time; 110 part-time. Men: 44%; women: 56%. **Ethnic makeup:** African American: 2%; American-Indian: 1%; White: 96%; International: 1%. **Religious preference:** Roman Catholic: 2%; Protestant: 45%; Southern Baptist Convention: 47%; Other: 6%.

ADMISSIONS FACTS AND FIGURES

Phone: (800) 722-4434. **Email:** admissions@wbcoll.edu. **Website:** http://www.williamsbaptistcollege.com. **Application deadlines for fall 2011:** Regular decision: Rolling. Early decision: Not offered. Early action: Not offered. Admission cannot be deferred. **Application fee:** $20. **To apply online, go to:** http://www.williamsbaptistcollege.com/admissions/apply.php. **Admissions requirements/recommendations:** High school units required (recommended): English: (4); Mathematics: (4); Science: (3); Foreign language: (2); Social studies: (1); History: (2). **Tests:** The college uses SAT or ACT scores in admissions decisions. Either SAT or ACT required. For admission to the fall 2011 entering class, the school will accept: ACT with or without writing accepted. Campus visit: Recommended. Admissions interview: Recommended. Off-campus interview: May be arranged. **Factors that count in admissions decisions:** *Academic:* Secondary school record: Very Important. Class rank: Important. Letters of recommendation: Considered. Standardized test scores: Very Important. Essay: Considered. *Nonacademic:* Interview: Important. Extracurricular activities: Considered. Talent/ability: Important. Character/personal qualities: Important. Alumni/ae relationship: Not Considered. Geographical residence: Not Considered. State residency: Not Considered. Religious affiliation/commitment: Not Considered. Minority status: Not Considered. Volunteer work: Considered. Work experience: Not Considered. **Admissions statistics for the fall 2009 entering class:** Total applicants: 550. Total accepted: 353. Freshmen enrolled: 139; 85% were from out of state. Overall acceptance rate: 64%. **Average high school grade point average:** 3.3.

ACADEMICS

Year founded: 1941. **Academic calendar:** Semester. **Degrees offered:** associate, bachelor's. **Most popular majors:** 46% education, 15% theology and religious vocations, 14% psychology, 9% business administration and management. **Major fields of study:** agriculture, agriculture operations, and related sciences; biological and biomedical sciences; business, management, marketing, and related support services; computer and information sciences and support services; education; history; liberal arts and sciences studies, and humanities; psychology; theology and religious vocations; visual and performing arts. **Areas of required coursework:** arts/fine arts, humanities, computer literacy, mathematics, English (including composition), philosophy, foreign languages, sciences (biological or physical), history, social science, other. **Pre-professional programs:** pre-law, pre-dentistry, pre-medicine, pre-veterinary science, pre-pharmacy, other. **Special academic programs:** double major, internships, study abroad. **Teacher certification offered in:** early childhood, elementary, middle/junior high, secondary. **Reserve**

Officers Training Corps (ROTC): Army ROTC: Offered at cooperating institution. **Faculty and instruction (2009-2010):** Total instructional faculty: 30 full-time, 15 part-time (51% men; 49% women; 2% minorities). Full-time faculty with Ph.D. or other terminal degree: 57%. Student/faculty ratio: 16/1. Classes of fewer than 20 students: 50%; of 20 to 49 students: 50%. **Advanced Placement and International Baccalaureate credit:** International Baccalaureate exams may be used for: Credit and/or placement. **Freshmen returning for sophomore year:** 62%. **Graduation rates:** Four-year: 41%; five-year: 53%; six-year: 43%. **Graduate study:** 40% of students pursue further study immediately upon graduation; 50% within one year.

COSTS AND FINANCIAL AID

Financial aid office: (870) 759-4112. **Expenses (2010-2011):** Tuition and fees 2010-2011: $12,020; room/board: $5,400. Estimated books and supplies: $1,116; transportation: $1,140; personal expenses: $1,300. **Financial aid:** Priority filing date for institution's financial aid form: May 3. In 2009-2010, 82% of undergraduates applied for financial aid. Of those, 52% were determined to have financial need; Average financial aid package (proportion receiving): $12,992 (52%). Average amount of gift aid, such as scholarships or grants (proportion receiving): $4,228 (63%). Average amount of self-help aid, such as work study or loans (proportion receiving): $4,167 (66%). Average need-based loan (excluding PLUS or other private loans): $3,611. Among students who received aid based on merit, the average award (and the proportion receiving): $0 (0%). The average athletic scholarship (and the proportion receiving): $4,323 (29%). Average amount of debt of borrowers graduating in 2009: $16,826. Proportion who borrowed: 80%.

CAMPUS LIFE AND EXTRACURRICULAR ACTIVITIES

Campus housing available (% using): women's dorms (44%), men's dorms (39%), apartments for married students (8%), apartment for single students (9%). Students who live in college-owned, operated, or affiliated housing: 69%. **Clubs and organizations:** Number of student organizations: 30. Activities include: campus ministries, choral groups, drama/theater, international student organization, jazz band, literary magazine, student government. Number of fraternities: 0; sororities: 0. Average proportion of students who stay on campus on weekends: 35%. **Sports program (2009-2010):** Member of NAIA. *Men's intercollegiate varsity sports:* baseball, basketball, soccer. *Women's intercollegiate varsity sports:* basketball, softball, volleyball.

SERVICES AND FACILITIES

Basic services: nonremedial tutoring, placement service, health service. **Remedial assistance:** reading, math, writing, study skills. **Counseling services:** career, personal, academic, psychological, religious. **For learning-disabled students:** School does not offer a structured program with separate admission and additional fees. Services include: remedial math, tape recorders, other special classes, untimed tests, note-taking services, oral tests, learning center, readers, extended time for tests, tutors, priority seating. **Library:** Number of titles: 68,347; number of current serial subscriptions: 191. **Information technology resources:** Students are not required to lease or own a computer. Number of campus computers available to all students: 70. School does not have a wireless network. Proportion of college-owned housing units wired for high-speed internet access: 85%. **Campus safety:** Security services offered: 24-hour foot-and-vehicle patrols, 24-hour emergency telephones, lighted pathways/sidewalks, student patrols, controlled dormitory access (key, security card, etc).

TRANSFER AND INTERNATIONAL STUDENTS

Transfer students: May apply for admission for the following academic terms: Fall, Spring, Summer. Applicants do not need a minimum number of credits to apply. For fall 2009: Transfer applications received: 103. Transfer applicants offered admission: 57. Transfer applicants enrolled: 50. **International students:** Number of foreign undergraduates: 3 (1% of student body). Number of countries represented: 3. Minimum TOEFL score required: 500 (paper).

California

American Jewish University

- **Address:** 15600 Mulholland Drive, Los Angeles, CA 90077
- **Website:** http://www.ajula.edu
- **Private; Religious affiliation:** Jewish
- **Enrollment:** 107 full-time; 7 part-time

KEY STATS

- ✔ **U.S News College Ranking:** Unranked, National Liberal Arts Colleges
- ✔ **SAT Score (25th/75th percentile):** 875-1030
- ✔ **Tuition:** 2010-2011: $24,712

Selectivity: N/A	**Room/board:** $11,777
Acceptance rate: 96%	**Average debt:** $9,800
Student/faculty ratio: 4/1	**Proportion who borrowed:** 75%

UNDERGRADUATE STUDENT BODY STATS

2009-2010 enrollment: 107 full-time; 7 part-time. Men: 46%; women: 54%. **Ethnic makeup:** African American: 4%; American-Indian: 2%; Asian American: 1%; Hispanic: 5%; White: 87%; International: 2%. **Religious preference:** Roman Catholic: 2%; Unknown: 42%; Jewish: 55%; Baptist: 1%.

ADMISSIONS FACTS AND FIGURES

Phone: (310) 440-1247. **Email:** admissions@ajula.edu. **Website:** http://www.ajula.edu. **Application deadlines for fall 2011:** Regular decision: May 31. Early decision: Not offered. Early action: Not offered. Admission can be deferred. **Application fee:** $35. **To apply online, go to:** http://www.ajula.edu/apply. **Admissions requirements/recommendations:** Tests: The college uses SAT or ACT scores in admissions decisions. Either SAT or ACT required. For admission to the fall 2011 entering class, the school will accept: ACT with or without writing accepted. Campus visit: Recommended. Admissions interview: Recommended. Off-campus interview: May be arranged. **Factors that count in admissions decisions:** *Academic:* Secondary school record: Considered. Class rank: Considered. Letters of recommendation: Very Important. Standardized test scores: Important. Essay: Very Important. *Nonacademic:* Interview: Very Important. Extracurricular activities: Very Important. Talent/ability: Very Important. Character/personal qualities: Very Important. Alumni/ae relationship: Considered. Geographical residence: Considered. State residency: Considered. Religious affiliation/commitment: Considered. Minority status: Not Considered. Volunteer work: Very Important. Work experience: Considered. **Other schools with the greatest overlap in applicants:** Brandeis University; California State University–Northridge; Indiana State University; University of California–Los Angeles; University of Southern California. **Admissions statistics for the fall 2009 entering class:** Total applicants: 49. Total accepted: 47. Freshmen enrolled: 23; 48% were from out of state. Overall acceptance rate: 96%. **Credentials of fall 2009 freshmen:** 29% ranked in the top 10 percent of their high school class; 11% were in the top 25 percent; 45% were in the top half. (Proportion submitting class standing: 22%.) **Average high school grade point average:** 3.1. **First-year students who submitted SAT scores:** 78%. Scores (25/75 percentile): Critical Reading: 450-530, Math: 425-500, Combined: 875-1030. **First-year students submitting ACT scores:** 26%. Scores (25/75 percentile): English: 18-22, Math: 16-17, Composite: 18-20.

ACADEMICS

Year founded: 1941. **Academic calendar:** Semester. **Degrees offered:** bachelor's, master's. **Most popular majors:** 30% business, management, marketing, and related support services, 30% social sciences, 15% psychology, 11% biological and biomedical sciences, 7% philosophy and religious studies. **Major fields of study:** area, ethnic, cultural, and gender studies; biological and biomedical sciences; business, management, marketing, and related support services; communication, journalism, and related programs; English language and literature/letters; history; liberal arts and sciences studies, and humanities; philosophy and religious studies; psychology; social sciences; theology and religious vocations. **Areas of required coursework:** arts/fine arts, mathematics, English (including composition), sciences (biological or physical), other. **Pre-professional programs:** pre-law, pre-den-

tistry, pre-medicine, pre-theology, pre-pharmacy. **Special academic programs (% participation):** cross-registration (0%), double major (15%), independent study (38%), internships (31%), student-designed major (8%), study abroad (8%). **Faculty and instruction (2009-2010):** Total instructional faculty: 13 full-time, 67 part-time (51% men; 49% women). Full-time faculty with Ph.D. or other terminal degree: 92%. Student/faculty ratio: 4/1. Classes of fewer than 20 students: 100%; of 20 to 49 students: 0%; of 50 or more students: 0%. **Advanced Placement and International Baccalaureate credit:** AP tests may be used for: Credit only. Scores accepted: 4, 5. **Freshmen returning for sophomore year:** 38%. **Graduation rates:** Four-year: 37%; five-year: 37%; six-year: 55%.

COSTS AND FINANCIAL AID

Financial aid office: (310) 476-9777. **Expenses (2010-2011):** Tuition and fees 2010-2011: $24,712; room/board: $11,777. Estimated books and supplies: $1,638; transportation: $792; personal expenses: $2,250. **Financial aid:** Priority filing date for institution's financial aid form: March 2. In 2009-2010, 95% of undergraduates applied for financial aid. Of those, 95% were determined to have financial need; 96% had their need fully met. Average financial aid package (proportion receiving): $24,500 (95%). Average amount of gift aid, such as scholarships or grants (proportion receiving): $9,809 (38%). Average amount of self-help aid, such as work study or loans (proportion receiving): $7,382 (95%). Average need-based loan (excluding PLUS or other private loans): $4,500. Among students who received need-based aid, the average percentage of need met: 96%. Among students who received aid based on merit, the average award (and the proportion receiving): $2,000 (42%). Average amount of debt of borrowers graduating in 2009: $9,800. Proportion who borrowed: 75%.

CAMPUS LIFE AND EXTRACURRICULAR ACTIVITIES

Campus housing available (% using): coed dorms (88%), apartments for married students (5%), apartment for single students (5%), special housing for disabled students (2%). Students who live in college-owned, operated, or affiliated housing: 60%. **Student employment:** During the 2009-2010 academic year, 5% of undergraduates worked on campus. **Clubs and organizations:** Number of student organizations: 15. Activities include: choral groups, drama/theater, literary magazine, model UN, student government, student newspaper. Number of fraternities: 0; sororities: 0. Average proportion of students who stay on campus on weekends: 20%.

SERVICES AND FACILITIES

Basic services: health service, health insurance. **Counseling services:** career, personal, academic, psychological, religious. **For learning-disabled students:** School does not offer a structured program with separate admission and additional fees. Total undergraduates in learning-disabled program or receiving services: 14. Services include: tape recorders, untimed tests, note-taking services, oral tests, readers, extended time for tests, exams on tape or computer, other testing accommodations. **Library:** Number of titles: 120,000; number of current serial subscriptions: 135. **Information technology resources:** Students are not required to lease or own a computer. Number of campus computers available to all students: 38. School has a wireless network. Approximate number of users that can be accommodated: 100. Proportion of college-owned housing units wired for high-speed internet access: 100%. **Campus safety:** Security services offered: 24-hour foot-and-vehicle patrols, 24-hour emergency telephones, lighted pathways/sidewalks, controlled dormitory access (key, security card, etc).

TRANSFER AND INTERNATIONAL STUDENTS

Transfer students: May apply for admission for the following academic terms: Fall, Spring. Applicants need a minimum number of credits to apply. For fall 2009: Transfer applications received: 35. Transfer applicants offered admission: 32. Transfer applicants enrolled: 21. **International students:** Number of foreign undergraduates: 2 (2% of student body). Number of countries represented: 1. Minimum TOEFL score required: 530 (paper); 75 (computer).

Art Center College of Design

- **Address:** 1700 Lida Street, Pasadena, CA 91103
- **Website:** http://www.artcenter.edu
- **Private**
- **Enrollment:** 1,294 full-time; 478 part-time

KEY STATS
- ✔ **U.S News College Ranking:** Unranked Specialty School–Fine Arts
- ✔ **SAT Score:** 1105
- ✔ **Tuition:** 2009-2010: $31,576

Selectivity: N/A	Room/board: N/A
Acceptance rate: 66%	Average debt: N/A
Student/faculty ratio: 10/1	Proportion who borrowed: N/A

UNDERGRADUATE STUDENT BODY STATS
2009-2010 enrollment: 1,294 full-time; 478 part-time. Men: 56%; women: 44%.

ADMISSIONS FACTS AND FIGURES
Phone: (626) 396-2373. **Email:** admissions@artcenter.edu. **Website:** http://www.artcenter.edu. **Application deadlines for fall 2011:** Regular decision: Rolling. Early decision: Not offered. Early action: Not offered. Admission can be deferred. **Application fee:** $50. **To apply online, go to:** https://www.applyweb.com/apply/accd/. **Admissions requirements/recommendations:** High school units required (recommended): English: 0 (0); Mathematics: 0 (0); Science: 0 (0); Foreign language: 0 (0); Social studies: 0 (0); History: 0 (0); Academic electives: 0 (0); Total units: 0 (0). Tests: The college uses SAT or ACT scores in admissions decisions. Neither SAT nor ACT required. For admission to the fall 2011 entering class, the school will accept: ACT with writing recommended. Campus visit: Recommended. Admissions interview: Recommended. Off-campus interview: Not available. **Factors that count in admissions decisions:** *Academic:* Secondary school record: Very Important. Class rank: Important. Letters of recommendation: Considered. Standardized test scores: Considered. Essay: Very Important. *Nonacademic:* Interview: Considered. Extracurricular activities: Important. Talent/ability: Very Important. Character/personal qualities: Important. Alumni/ae relationship: Not Considered. Geographical residence: Not Considered. State residency: Not Considered. Religious affiliation/commitment: Not Considered. Minority status: Considered. Volunteer work: Important. Work experience: Important. **Other schools with the greatest overlap in applicants:** California Institute of the Arts; Otis College of Art and Design; Pratt Institute; Rhode Island School of Design; University of California–Los Angeles. **Admissions statistics for the fall 2009 entering class:** Total applicants: 742. Total accepted: 492. Freshmen enrolled: 308; 36% were from out of state. Overall acceptance rate: 66%. **Size of waiting list:** 0 applicants; enrolled from waiting list: 0. **Credentials of fall 2009 freshmen:** 20% ranked in the top 10 percent of their high school class; 25% were in the top 25 percent. **Average high school grade point average:** 3.1. **First-year students who submitted SAT scores:** 23%. **First-year students submitting ACT scores:** 3%. Scores (25/75 percentile): English: N/A, Math: N/A, Composite: N/A.

ACADEMICS
Year founded: 1930. **Academic calendar:** Trimester. **Degrees offered:** bachelor's, master's. **Most popular majors:** 100% visual and performing arts. **Major fields of study:** visual and performing arts. **Areas of required coursework:** arts/fine arts, humanities, computer literacy, mathematics, English (including composition), philosophy, sciences (biological or physical), history, social science. **Special academic programs (% participation):** cross-registration (3%), English as a Second Language (ESL) (4%), independent study (20%), internships (16%). **Faculty and instruction (2009-2010):** Total instructional faculty: 84 full-time, 262 part-time (73% men; 27% women; 18% minorities). Full-time faculty with Ph.D. or other terminal degree: 46%. Student/faculty ratio: 10/1. **Advanced Placement and International Baccalaureate credit:** AP tests may be used for: Credit only. Scores accepted: 4, 5. International Baccalaureate exams may be used for: Credit only. **Freshmen returning for sophomore year:** 87%. **Graduation rates:** Six-year: 88%.

COSTS AND FINANCIAL AID
Financial aid office: (626) 396-2215. **Expenses (2009-2010):** Tuition and fees 2009-2010: $31,576. **Financial aid:** Priority filing date for institution's financial aid form: March 1.

CAMPUS LIFE AND EXTRACURRICULAR ACTIVITIES
Students who live in college-owned, operated, or affiliated housing: 0%. **Student employment:** During the 2009-2010 academic year, 25% of undergraduates worked on campus. Average per-year earnings: $1,670. **Clubs and organizations:** Number of student organizations: 15. Activities include: student government. Number of fraternities: 0; sororities: 0.

SERVICES AND FACILITIES
Basic services: placement service, health insurance, other. **Remedial assistance:** reading, writing, study skills, other. **Counseling services:** career, personal, academic, psychological, other. **For learning-disabled students:** School does not offer a structured program with separate admission and additional fees. Total undergraduates in learning-disabled program or receiving services: 11. Services include: remedial English, reading machines, tape recorders, other special classes, untimed tests, note-taking services, special bookstore section, oral tests, readers, extended time for tests, tutors, early syllabus, priority registration, priority seating, substitution of courses, texts on tape, typist/scribe, exams on tape or computer, other testing accommodations, other. **Library:** Number of titles: 92,000; number of current serial subscriptions: 382. **Information technology resources:** Students are not required to lease or own a computer. Number of campus computers available to all students: 240. School has a wireless network. Approximate number of users that can be accommodated: 1,100. **Campus safety:** Security services offered: 24-hour foot-and-vehicle patrols, late-night transport/escort service, 24-hour emergency telephones, lighted pathways/sidewalks.

TRANSFER AND INTERNATIONAL STUDENTS
Transfer students: May apply for admission for the following academic terms: Fall, Spring, Summer. Applicants do not need a minimum number of credits to apply. For fall 2009: Transfer applications received: 45. Transfer applicants offered admission: 30. Transfer applicants enrolled: 24. **International students:** Number of countries represented: 25. Minimum TOEFL score required: 550 (paper); 80 (computer). Average TOEFL score: 565 (paper).

Azusa Pacific University

- **Address:** 901 E. Alosta Avenue, Azusa, CA 91702
- **Website:** http://www.apu.edu
- **Private; Religious affiliation:** Christian interdenominational
- **Enrollment:** 4,163 full-time; 711 part-time

KEY STATS
- ✔ **U.S News College Ranking:** 167, National Universities
- ✔ **SAT Score (25th/75th percentile):** 970-1190
- ✔ **Tuition:** 2010-2011: $28,800

Selectivity: Selective	Room/board: $8,398
Acceptance rate: 59%	Average debt: N/A
Student/faculty ratio: 12/1	Proportion who borrowed: N/A

UNDERGRADUATE STUDENT BODY STATS
2009-2010 enrollment: 4,163 full-time; 711 part-time. Men: 36%; women: 64%. **Ethnic makeup:** African American: 5%; American-Indian: 1%; Asian American: 8%; Hispanic: 15%; White: 69%; International: 2%. **Religious preference:** Roman Catholic: 8%; Protestant: 1%; No preference: 1%; Unknown: 2%; Christian interdenominational: 84%; Other: 1%.

ADMISSIONS FACTS AND FIGURES
Phone: (800) 825-5278. **Email:** admissions@apu.edu. **Website:** http://www.apu.edu. **Application deadlines for fall 2011:** Regular decision: June 1; decision sent by April 1. Early decision: Not offered. Early action: Send application by: November 15; Decision sent by: January 15. Admission can be deferred. **Application fee:** $45. **To apply online, go to:** https://www.apuadmissions.org/secure/9092/preview_app.asp?wcc=az2. **Admissions requirements/recommendations:** High school units required (recommended): English: (4); Mathematics: (3); Science: (2); Foreign language: (3); Social studies: (1); History: (2). Tests: The college uses SAT or ACT scores in admissions decisions. Either SAT or ACT required. For admission to the fall 2011 entering class, the school will accept: ACT with or without writing accepted. Campus visit: Neither required nor recommended. Admissions interview: Neither required nor recommended. Off-campus interview: Not available. **Factors that count in admissions decisions:** *Academic:* Secondary school record: Considered. Class rank: Very Important. Letters of recom-

mendation: Very Important. Standardized test scores: Very Important. Essay: Very Important. **Nonacademic:** Interview: Considered. Extracurricular activities: Considered. Talent/ability: Considered. Character/personal qualities: Important. Alumni/ae relationship: Considered. Geographical residence: Not Considered. State residency: Important. Religious affiliation/commitment: Not Considered. Minority status: Considered. Volunteer work: Considered. Work experience: Considered. **Other schools with the greatest overlap in applicants:** Biola University; California State University–Long Beach; Point Loma Nazarene University; University of California–Los Angeles; Westmont College. **Admissions statistics for the fall 2009 entering class:** Total applicants: 5,262. Total accepted: 3,090. Freshmen enrolled: 1,022; 27% were from out of state. Overall acceptance rate: 59%. Non-early acceptance rate: 59%. **Credentials of fall 2009 freshmen:** 32% ranked in the top 10 percent of their high school class; 63% were in the top 25 percent; 88% were in the top half. (Proportion submitting class standing: 63%.) **First-year students who submitted SAT scores:** 86%. Scores (25/75 percentile): Critical Reading: 490-590, Math: 480-600, Combined: 970-1190. **First-year students submitting ACT scores:** 38%. Scores (25/75 percentile): English: N/A, Math: N/A, Composite: 21-27.

ACADEMICS

Year founded: 1899. **Academic calendar:** Semester. **Degrees offered:** bachelor's, master's, doctorate. **Most popular majors:** 20% business, management, marketing, and related support services, 19% liberal arts and sciences studies, and humanities, 17% health professions and related clinical sciences, 8% communication, journalism, and related programs, 5% psychology. **Major fields of study:** area, ethnic, cultural, and gender studies; biological and biomedical sciences; business, management, marketing, and related support services; communication, journalism, and related programs; computer and information sciences and support services; education; English language and literature/letters; foreign languages, literatures, and linguistics; health professions and related clinical sciences; history; liberal arts and sciences studies, and humanities; mathematics and statistics; philosophy and religious studies; physical sciences; psychology; public administration and social service professions; social sciences; theology and religious vocations; visual and performing arts. **Areas of required coursework:** arts/fine arts, humanities, mathematics, English (including composition), philosophy, foreign languages, sciences (biological or physical), history, social science. **Pre-professional programs:** pre-law, other. **Special academic programs:** accelerated program, cooperative (work-study plan) program, distance learning, double major, English as a Second Language (ESL), exchange student program (domestic), honors program, independent study, internships, study abroad, teacher certificate program. **Teacher certification offered in:** special education, elementary, secondary. **Reserve Officers Training Corps (ROTC):** Army ROTC: Offered at cooperating institution. **Faculty and instruction (2009-2010):** Total instructional faculty: 339 full-time, 36 part-time (53% men; 47% women; 21% minorities). Full-time faculty with Ph.D. or other terminal degree: 74%. Student/faculty ratio: 12/1. Classes of fewer than 20 students: 64%; of 20 to 49 students: 34%; of 50 or more students: 2%. **Advanced Placement and International Baccalaureate credit:** AP tests may be used for: Credit only. Scores accepted: 3, 4, 5. International Baccalaureate exams may be used for: Credit only. **Freshmen returning for sophomore year:** 81%. **Graduation rates:** Four-year: 55%; five-year: 64%; six-year: 67%.

COSTS AND FINANCIAL AID

Financial aid office: (626) 815-6000. **Expenses (2010-2011):** Tuition and fees 2010-2011: $28,800; room/board: $8,398. Estimated books and supplies: $1,620; transportation: $730; personal expenses: $2,250. **Financial aid:** Priority filing date for institution's financial aid form: March 2; deadline: July 1.

CAMPUS LIFE AND EXTRACURRICULAR ACTIVITIES

Campus housing available (% using): coed dorms (34%), women's dorms (7%), men's dorms (5%), apartment for single students (54%). Students who live in college-owned, operated, or affiliated housing: 61%. **Student employment:** During the 2009-2010 academic year, 30% of undergraduates worked on campus. Average per-year earnings: $4,000. **Clubs and organizations:** Number of student organizations: 32. Activities include: choral groups, concert band, drama/theater, jazz band, marching band, music ensembles, musical theater, opera, pep band, radio station, student government, student newspaper, symphony orchestra, television station, yearbook. Number of fraternities: 0; sororities: 0. **Sports program (2009-2010):** Member of NAIA. **Men's intercollegiate varsity sports:** baseball, basketball, cross country, football, soccer, tennis, track and field (outdoor). **Women's**

intercollegiate varsity sports: basketball, cross country, soccer, softball, swimming, tennis, track and field (outdoor).

SERVICES AND FACILITIES

Basic services: nonremedial tutoring, women's center, health service, health insurance. **Remedial assistance:** reading, math, writing. **Counseling services:** minority student, career, personal, academic, psychological, religious, other. **For learning-disabled students:** School does not offer a structured program with separate admission and additional fees. Services include: remedial math, remedial reading, note-taking services, learning center, extended time for tests, tutors, other. **Library:** Number of titles: 185,708; number of current serial subscriptions: 14,031. **Information technology resources:** Students are not required to lease or own a computer. Number of campus computers available to all students: 456. School has a wireless network. Approximate number of users that can be accommodated: 8,000. Proportion of college-owned housing units wired for high-speed internet access: 100%. **Campus safety:** Security services offered: 24-hour foot-and-vehicle patrols, late-night transport/escort service, 24-hour emergency telephones, lighted pathways/sidewalks, controlled dormitory access (key, security card, etc).

TRANSFER AND INTERNATIONAL STUDENTS

Transfer students: May apply for admission for the following academic terms: Fall, Spring. Applicants need a minimum number of credits to apply. For fall 2009: Transfer applications received: 1,514. Transfer applicants offered admission: 768. Transfer applicants enrolled: 363. **International students:** Number of foreign undergraduates: 94 (2% of student body). Number of countries represented: 29. Minimum TOEFL score required: 500 (paper); 173 (computer). Average TOEFL score: 500 (paper).

Bethany University

- **Address:** 800 Bethany Drive, Scotts Valley, CA 95066
- **Website:** http://www.bethany.edu
- **Private; Religious affiliation:** Assemblies of God
- **Enrollment:** N/A

KEY STATS

✔ **U.S News College Ranking:** 24, Regional Colleges (West)
✔ **SAT Score (25th/75th percentile):** 740-1020
✔ **Tuition:** 2009-2010: $18,250

Selectivity: Less selective	**Room/board:** $7,450
Acceptance rate: 70%	**Average debt:** N/A
Student/faculty ratio: N/A	**Proportion who borrowed:** N/A

Biola University

- **Address:** 13800 Biola Avenue, La Mirada, CA 90639-0001
- **Website:** http://www.biola.edu
- **Private; Religious affiliation:** Christian, Interdenominational
- **Enrollment:** 3,591 full-time; 345 part-time

KEY STATS

✔ **U.S News College Ranking:** 170, National Universities
✔ **SAT Score (25th/75th percentile):** 980-1230
✔ **Tuition:** 2010-2011: $28,852

Selectivity: Selective	**Room/board:** $8,820
Acceptance rate: 82%	**Average debt:** $29,693
Student/faculty ratio: 17/1	**Proportion who borrowed:** 78%

UNDERGRADUATE STUDENT BODY STATS

2009-2010 enrollment: 3,591 full-time; 345 part-time. Men: 39%; women: 61%. **Ethnic makeup:** African American: 3%; American-Indian: 1%; Asian American: 12%; Hispanic: 13%; White: 69%; International: 2%. **Religious preference:** Protestant: 96%; Christian, Interdenominational: 4%.

ADMISSIONS FACTS AND FIGURES

Phone: (562) 903-4752. **Email:** admissions@biola.edu. **Website:** http://www.biola.edu. **Application deadlines for fall 2011:** Regular decision: Rolling; decision sent by April 1. Early decision: Not offered. Early action: Send application by: December 1; Decision sent by: February 15. Admission can be deferred. **Application fee:** $45. **To apply online, go to:** http://www. biola.edu/applynow. **Admissions requirements/recommendations:** High school units required (recommended): English: 0 (4); Mathematics: 0 (3); Science: 0 (3); Foreign language: 0 (4); Social studies: 0 (2); History: 0 (1); Academic electives: 0 (1); Total units: 0 (15). Tests: The college uses SAT or ACT scores in admissions decisions. Either SAT or ACT required. For admission to the fall 2011 entering class, the school will accept: ACT with or without writing accepted. Campus visit: Recommended. Admissions interview: Recommended. Off-campus interview: May be arranged. **Factors that count in admissions decisions:** *Academic:* Secondary school record: Important. Class rank: Considered. Letters of recommendation: Important. Standardized test scores: Very Important. Essay: Very Important. *Nonacademic:* Interview: Considered. Extracurricular activities: Considered. Talent/ability: Considered. Character/personal qualities: Important. Alumni/ae relationship: Considered. Geographical residence: Not Considered. State residency: Not Considered. Religious affiliation/commitment: Very Important. Minority status: Not Considered. Volunteer work: Considered. Work experience: Not Considered. **Other schools with the greatest overlap in applicants:** Azusa Pacific University; Master's College and Seminary; Point Loma Nazarene University; Vanguard University of Southern California; Westmont College. **Admissions statistics for the fall 2009 entering class:** Total applicants: 2,681. Total accepted: 2,186. Freshmen enrolled: 792; 26% were from out of state. Overall acceptance rate: 82%. Non-early acceptance rate: 82%. **Credentials of fall 2009 freshmen:** 33% ranked in the top 10 percent of their high school class; 64% were in the top 25 percent; 89% were in the top half. (Proportion submitting class standing: 44%.) **Average high school grade point average:** 3.5. **First-year students who submitted SAT scores:** 77%. Scores (25/75 percentile): Critical Reading: 500-620, Math: 480-610, Combined: 980-1230. **First-year students submitting ACT scores:** 29%. Scores (25/75 percentile): English: 21-28, Math: N/A, Composite: 21-27.

ACADEMICS

Year founded: 1908. **Academic calendar:** 4-1-4. **Degrees offered:** certificate, bachelor's, post-bachelor's certificate, master's, post-master's certificate, doctorate. **Most popular majors:** 19% business, management, marketing, and related support services, 16% theology and religious vocations, 15% communication, journalism, and related programs, 12% psychology, 7% social sciences. **Major fields of study:** biological and biomedical sciences; business, management, marketing, and related support services; communication, journalism, and related programs; computer and information sciences and support services; education; engineering; English language and literature/letters; foreign languages, literatures, and linguistics; health professions and related clinical sciences; history; liberal arts and sciences studies, and humanities; mathematics and statistics; philosophy and religious studies; physical sciences; psychology; social sciences; theology and religious vocations; visual and performing arts. **Areas of required coursework:** arts/fine arts, mathematics, English (including composition), philosophy, foreign languages, sciences (biological or physical), history, social science, other. **Pre-professional programs:** pre-law, pre-dentistry, pre-medicine, pre-theology, pre-veterinary science, pre-optometry, pre-pharmacy. **Special academic programs (% participation):** double major (1%), English as a Second Language (ESL) (1%), exchange student program (domestic) (3%), honors program (7%), independent study (1%), internships (61%), student-designed major (1%), study abroad (11%), teacher certificate program (5%). **Teacher certification offered in:** elementary, secondary. **Cooperative education programs:** engineering. **Reserve Officers Training Corps (ROTC):** Army ROTC: Offered at cooperating institution (California State University–Fullerton); Air Force ROTC: Offered at cooperating institution (University of Southern California). **Faculty and instruction (2009-2010):** Total instructional faculty: 221 full-time, 225 part-time (64% men; 36% women; 16% minorities). Full-time faculty with Ph.D. or other terminal degree: 74%. Student/faculty ratio: 17/1. Classes of fewer than 20 students: 47%; of 20 to 49 students: 48%; of 50 or more students: 5%. **Advanced Placement and International Baccalaureate credit:** AP tests may be used for: Placement only. Scores accepted: 3, 4, 5. International Baccalaureate exams may be used for: Placement only. **Freshmen returning for sophomore year:** 85%. **Graduation rates:** Four-year: 51%; five-year: 69%; six-year: 71%. **Graduate study:** 19% of students pursue further study immediately upon graduation; 20% within one year; 31% within five years. Fields in which graduates pursue further study: Master of Business Administration (MBA), 13%; law, 1%; medicine, 2%; engineering, 1%; theology (or the seminary), 21%; education, 16%; arts and sciences, 23%.

COSTS AND FINANCIAL AID

Financial aid office: (562) 903-4742. **Expenses (2010-2011):** Tuition and fees 2010-2011: $28,852; room/board: $8,820. Estimated books and supplies: $1,620; transportation: $729; personal expenses: $2,250. **Financial aid:** In 2009-2010, 77% of undergraduates applied for financial aid. Of those, 68% were determined to have financial need; 100% had their need fully met. Average financial aid package (proportion receiving): $33,123 (68%). Average amount of gift aid, such as scholarships or grants (proportion receiving): $12,955 (56%). Average amount of self-help aid, such as work study or loans (proportion receiving): $6,688 (66%). Average need-based loan (excluding PLUS or other private loans): $1,339. Among students who received need-based aid, the average percentage of need met: 70%. Among students who received aid based on merit, the average award (and the proportion receiving): $14,829 (10%). The average athletic scholarship (and the proportion receiving): $9,708 (2%). Average amount of debt of borrowers graduating in 2009: $29,693. Proportion who borrowed: 78%.

CAMPUS LIFE AND EXTRACURRICULAR ACTIVITIES

Campus housing available (% using): women's dorms (45%), men's dorms (28%), apartments for married students, apartment for single students (12%), special housing for disabled students (1%), other housing options (14%). Students who live in college-owned, operated, or affiliated housing: 69%. **Student employment:** During the 2009-2010 academic year, 35% of undergraduates worked on campus. Average per-year earnings: $3,000. **Clubs and organizations:** Number of student organizations: 37. Activities include: campus ministries, choral groups, concert band, dance, drama/theater, international student organization, jazz band, literary magazine, music ensembles, musical theater, opera, radio station, student government, student newspaper, student film society, symphony orchestra, television station, yearbook. Number of fraternities: 0; sororities: 0. **Sports program (2009-2010):** Member of NAIA. *Men's intercollegiate varsity sports:* baseball, basketball, cross country, soccer, swimming, tennis, track and field (outdoor). *Women's intercollegiate varsity sports:* basketball, cross country, soccer, softball, swimming, tennis, track and field (outdoor), volleyball.

SERVICES AND FACILITIES

Basic services: nonremedial tutoring, health service, health insurance. **Remedial assistance:** reading, writing, study skills. **Counseling services:** minority student, career, military, personal, veteran student, academic, older student, psychological, birth control, religious, other. **For learning-disabled students:** School does not offer a structured program with separate admission and additional fees. Services include: reading machines, tape recorders, diagnostic testing service, untimed tests, note-taking services, oral tests, learning center, readers, extended time for tests, tutors, priority registration, priority seating, texts on tape, other testing accommodations. **Library:** Number of titles: 233,865; number of current serial subscriptions: 39,000. **Information technology resources:** Students are not required to lease or own a computer. Number of campus computers available to all students: 165. School has a wireless network. Proportion of college-owned housing units wired for high-speed internet access: 100%. **Campus safety:** Security services offered: 24-hour foot-and-vehicle patrols, late-night transport/escort service, 24-hour emergency telephones, lighted pathways/sidewalks, student patrols, controlled dormitory access (key, security card, etc).

TRANSFER AND INTERNATIONAL STUDENTS

Transfer students: May apply for admission for the following academic terms: Fall, Winter, Spring, Summer. Applicants need a minimum number of credits to apply. For fall 2009: Transfer applications received: 748. Transfer applicants offered admission: 562. Transfer applicants enrolled: 269. **International students:** Number of foreign undergraduates: 91 (2% of student body). Minimum TOEFL score required: 500 (paper); 173 (computer). Average TOEFL score: 589 (paper).

California Baptist University

- Address: 8432 Magnolia Avenue, Riverside, CA 92504
- Website: http://www.calbaptist.edu
- Private; Religious affiliation: California Southern Baptist Convention
- Enrollment: 2,773 full-time; 449 part-time

KEY STATS

✔ U.S News College Ranking: 48, Regional Universities (West)
✔ SAT Score (25th/75th percentile): 890-1130
✔ Tuition: 2010-2011: $24,654

Selectivity: Selective	Room/board: $6,950
Acceptance rate: 74%	Average debt: $34,650
Student/faculty ratio: 18/1	Proportion who borrowed: 89%

UNDERGRADUATE STUDENT BODY STATS

2009-2010 enrollment: 2,773 full-time; 449 part-time. Men: 39%; women: 61%. **Ethnic makeup:** African American: 7%; American-Indian: 1%; Asian American: 4%; Hispanic: 19%; White: 65%; International: 4%. **Religious preference:** Roman Catholic: 7%; Protestant: 48%; Unknown: 14%; California Southern Baptist Convention: 25%; Other: 6%.

ADMISSIONS FACTS AND FIGURES

Phone: (877) 228-8866. **Email:** admissions@calbaptist.edu. **Website:** http://www.calbaptist.edu. **Application deadlines for fall 2011:** Regular decision: Rolling. Early decision: Not offered. Early action: Send application by: December 15; Decision sent by: January 31. Admission can be deferred. **Application fee:** $45. **To apply online, go to:** http://www.calbaptist.edu/apply/. **Admissions requirements/recommendations:** High school units required (recommended): English: 4 (4); Mathematics: 3 (4); Science: 2 (3); Foreign language: 2 (3); Social studies: 2 (2); History: 2 (2); Academic electives: (3); Total units: 15 (19). Tests: The college uses SAT or ACT scores in admissions decisions. Either SAT or ACT required. For admission to the fall 2011 entering class, the school will accept: ACT with or without writing accepted. Campus visit: Recommended. Admissions interview: Recommended. Off-campus interview: May be arranged. **Factors that count in admissions decisions: *Academic:*** Secondary school record: Very Important. Class rank: Considered. Letters of recommendation: Very Important. Standardized test scores: Very Important. Essay: Very Important. ***Nonacademic:*** Interview: Not Considered. Extracurricular activities: Considered. Talent/ability: Considered. Character/personal qualities: Very Important. Alumni/ae relationship: Not Considered. Geographical residence: Not Considered. State residency: Not Considered. Religious affiliation/commitment: Not Considered. Minority status: Not Considered. Volunteer work: Considered. Work experience: Not Considered. **Other schools with the greatest overlap in applicants:** Azusa Pacific University; Biola University; California State University–San Bernardino; Point Loma Nazarene University; Vanguard University of Southern California. **Admissions statistics for the fall 2009 entering class:** Total applicants: 1,734. Total accepted: 1,280. Freshmen enrolled: 576; 10% were from out of state. Overall acceptance rate: 74%. Non-early acceptance rate: 74%. **Credentials of fall 2009 freshmen:** 16% ranked in the top 10 percent of their high school class; 43% were in the top 25 percent; 78% were in the top half. (Proportion submitting class standing: 72%.) **Average high school grade point average:** 3.4. **First-year students who submitted SAT scores:** 69%. Scores (25/75 percentile): Critical Reading: 450-570, Math: 440-560, Combined: 890-1130. **First-year students submitting ACT scores:** 31%. Scores (25/75 percentile): English: 18-24, Math: 17-24, Composite: 19-24.

ACADEMICS

Year founded: 1950. **Academic calendar:** Semester. **Degrees offered:** bachelor's, master's. **Most popular majors:** 19% liberal arts and sciences/liberal studies, 18% business/commerce, 8% chiropractic (D.C.), 8% psychology, 7% parks, recreation, and leisure studies. **Major fields of study:** biological and biomedical sciences; business, management, marketing, and related support services; communication, journalism, and related programs; education; engineering; English language and literature/letters; foreign languages, literatures, and linguistics; health professions and related clinical sciences; history; liberal arts and sciences studies, and humanities; mathematics and statistics; multi/interdisciplinary studies; parks, recreation, leisure, and fitness studies; philosophy and religious studies; psychology; security and protective services; social sciences; theology and religious vocations; visual and performing arts. **Areas of required coursework:** arts/fine arts, humanities, computer literacy, mathematics, English (including

composition), philosophy, sciences (biological or physical), history, social science. **Pre-professional programs:** pre-law, pre-dentistry, pre-medicine, pre-theology, other. **Special academic programs (% participation):** accelerated program (15%), distance learning (3%), double major (1%), English as a Second Language (ESL) (1%), exchange student program (domestic) (1%), honors program (1%), internships (2%), study abroad (10%), teacher certificate program (11%), weekend college (6%). **Teacher certification offered in:** early childhood, special education, elementary, middle/junior high, secondary, bilingual/bicultural. **Reserve Officers Training Corps (ROTC):** Army ROTC: Offered on campus; Air Force ROTC: Offered at cooperating institution (California State University–San Bernardino). **Faculty and instruction (2009-2010):** Total instructional faculty: 164 full-time, 176 part-time (54% men; 46% women; 19% minorities). Full-time faculty with Ph.D. or other terminal degree: 53%. Student/faculty ratio: 18/1. Classes of fewer than 20 students: 49%; of 20 to 49 students: 45%; of 50 or more students: 6%. **Advanced Placement and International Baccalaureate credit:** AP tests may be used for: Placement only. Scores accepted: 3. International Baccalaureate exams may be used for: Placement only. **Freshmen returning for sophomore year:** 80%. **Graduation rates:** Four-year: 45%; five-year: 56%; six-year: 57%. **Graduate study:** 52% of students pursue further study immediately upon graduation; 38% within one year; 72% within five years. Fields in which graduates pursue further study: Master of Business Administration (MBA), 10%; law, 1%; medicine, 2%; dentistry, 1%; engineering, 3%; theology (or the seminary), 21%; education, 28%; arts and sciences, 9%.

COSTS AND FINANCIAL AID

Financial aid office: (951) 343-4236. **Expenses (2010-2011):** Tuition and fees 2010-2011: $24,654; room/board: $6,950. Estimated books and supplies: $1,620; transportation: $730; personal expenses: $2,250. **Financial aid:** Priority filing date for institution's financial aid form: March 2. In 2009-2010, 94% of undergraduates applied for financial aid. Of those, 69% were determined to have financial need; 85% had their need fully met. Average financial aid package (proportion receiving): $8,651 (69%). Average amount of gift aid, such as scholarships or grants (proportion receiving): $4,677 (57%). Average amount of self-help aid, such as work study or loans (proportion receiving): $2,313 (55%). Average need-based loan (excluding PLUS or other private loans): $2,298. Among students who received need-based aid, the average percentage of need met: 58%. Among students who received aid based on merit, the average award (and the proportion receiving): $3,656 (16%). The average athletic scholarship (and the proportion receiving): $4,688 (15%). Average amount of debt of borrowers graduating in 2009: $34,650. Proportion who borrowed: 89%.

CAMPUS LIFE AND EXTRACURRICULAR ACTIVITIES

Campus housing available (% using): women's dorms (15%), men's dorms (9%), other housing options (76%). Students who live in college-owned, operated, or affiliated housing: 52%. **Student employment:** During the 2009-2010 academic year, 23% of undergraduates worked on campus. Average per-year earnings: $2,700. **Clubs and organizations:** Number of student organizations: 31. Activities include: campus ministries, choral groups, concert band, drama/theater, international student organization, jazz band, music ensembles, musical theater, pep band, student government, student newspaper, symphony orchestra, yearbook. Number of fraternities: 0; sororities: 0. Average proportion of students who stay on campus on weekends: 50%. **Sports program (2009-2010):** Member of NAIA. *Men's intercollegiate varsity sports:* baseball, basketball, cross country, golf, soccer, swimming, track and field (outdoor), volleyball, water polo, wrestling. *Women's intercollegiate varsity sports:* basketball, cross country, golf, soccer, softball, swimming, track and field (outdoor), volleyball, water polo.

SERVICES AND FACILITIES

Basic services: nonremedial tutoring, placement service. **Remedial assistance:** reading, math, writing, study skills. **Counseling services:** career, military, personal, veteran student, academic, psychological, religious. **For learning-disabled students:** School does not offer a structured program with separate admission and additional fees. Services include: remedial English, tape recorders, note-taking services, oral tests, learning center, readers, extended time for tests, tutors, priority registration, priority seating, substitution of courses, texts on tape, other testing accommodations. **Library:** Number of titles: 203,175; number of current serial subscriptions: 16,712. **Information technology resources:** Students are not required to lease or own a computer. Number of campus computers available to all students: 279. School has a wireless network. Approximate number of users that can be accommodated: 2,000. Proportion of college-owned housing units wired for high-speed internet access: 100%. **Campus safety:** Security services offered: 24-hour foot-and-vehicle patrols, late-night transport/escort service, 24-hour

emergency telephones, lighted pathways/sidewalks, controlled dormitory access (key, security card, etc).

TRANSFER AND INTERNATIONAL STUDENTS
Transfer students: May apply for admission for the following academic terms: Fall, Spring, Summer. Applicants need a minimum number of credits to apply. For fall 2009: Transfer applications received: 636. Transfer applicants offered admission: 460. Transfer applicants enrolled: 308. **International students:** Number of foreign undergraduates: 121 (4% of student body). Number of countries represented: 26. Minimum TOEFL score required: 500 (paper); 153 (computer).

California College of the Arts

- **Address:** 1111 Eighth Street, San Francisco, CA 94107
- **Website:** http://www.cca.edu
- **Private**
- **Enrollment:** 1,289 full-time; 115 part-time

KEY STATS
✔ **U.S News College Ranking:** Unranked Specialty School–Fine Arts
✔ **SAT Score (25th/75th percentile):** 940-1240
✔ **Tuition:** 2010-2011: $35,222

Selectivity: N/A	**Room/board:** $7,000
Acceptance rate: 76%	**Average debt:** $29,508
Student/faculty ratio: 9/1	**Proportion who borrowed:** 69%

UNDERGRADUATE STUDENT BODY STATS
2009-2010 enrollment: 1,289 full-time; 115 part-time. Men: 39%; women: 61%. **Ethnic makeup:** African American: 4%; American-Indian: 1%; Asian American: 17%; Hispanic: 11%; White: 57%; International: 9%.

ADMISSIONS FACTS AND FIGURES
Phone: (800) 447-1278. **Email:** enroll@cca.edu. **Website:** http://www.cca.edu. **Application deadlines for fall 2011:** Regular decision: Rolling. Early decision: Not offered. Early action: Not offered. Admission can be deferred. **Application fee:** $60. **To apply online, go to:** https://apply.embark.com/Ugrad/CCA/50/. **Admissions requirements/recommendations:** Tests: The college uses SAT or ACT scores in admissions decisions. Neither SAT nor ACT required. For admission to the fall 2011 entering class, the school will accept: ACT with or without writing accepted. Campus visit: Recommended. Admissions interview: Recommended. Off-campus interview: May be arranged. **Factors that count in admissions decisions:** *Academic:* Secondary school record: Considered. Class rank: Not Considered. Letters of recommendation: Important. Standardized test scores: Considered. Essay: Very Important. *Nonacademic:* Interview: Considered. Extracurricular activities: Considered. Talent/ability: Very Important. Character/personal qualities: Considered. Alumni/ae relationship: Considered. Geographical residence: Not Considered. State residency: Not Considered. Religious affiliation/commitment: Not Considered. Minority status: Considered. Volunteer work: Considered. Work experience: Considered. **Other schools with the greatest overlap in applicants:** California Institute of the Arts; Maryland Institute College of Art; Pratt Institute; Rhode Island School of Design; School of the Art Institute of Chicago. **Admissions statistics for the fall 2009 entering class:** Total applicants: 1,181. Total accepted: 893. Freshmen enrolled: 212; 37% were from out of state. Overall acceptance rate: 76%. **Average high school grade point average:** 3.2. **First-year students who submitted SAT scores:** 72%. Scores (25/75 percentile): Critical Reading: 460-630, Math: 480-610, Combined: 940-1240. **First-year students submitting ACT scores:** 12%. Scores (25/75 percentile): English: 19-27, Math: 18-25, Composite: 20-26.

ACADEMICS
Year founded: 1907. **Academic calendar:** Semester. **Degrees offered:** bachelor's, master's. **Most popular majors:** 12% architecture (B.Arch., B.A./B.S., M.Arch., M.A./M.S., Ph.D.), 11% painting, 9% graphic design, 9% industrial design, 7% illustration. **Major fields of study:** architecture and related services; English language and literature/letters; visual and performing arts. **Areas of required coursework:** arts/fine arts, humanities, computer literacy, mathematics, English (including composition), philosophy, sciences (biological or physical), history, social science, other. **Special academic programs (% participation):** cross-registration (1%), double major (1%), English as a Second Language (ESL) (4%), exchange student program (domestic) (1%),

independent study (18%), internships (38%), student-designed major (7%), study abroad (17%). **Faculty and instruction (2009-2010):** Total instructional faculty: 82 full-time, 425 part-time (55% men; 45% women; 18% minorities). Full-time faculty with Ph.D. or other terminal degree: 73%. Student/faculty ratio: 9/1. Classes of fewer than 20 students: 89%; of 20 to 49 students: 11%; of 50 or more students: 0%. **Advanced Placement and International Baccalaureate credit:** AP tests may be used for: Credit and/or placement. Scores accepted: 3, 4, 5. International Baccalaureate exams may be used for: Credit and/or placement. **Freshmen returning for sophomore year:** 73%. **Graduation rates:** Four-year: 27%; five-year: 47%; six-year: 57%. **Graduate study:** 20% of students pursue further study immediately upon graduation; 41% within one year; 41% within five years. Fields in which graduates pursue further study: Master of Business Administration (MBA), 4%; medicine, 3%; engineering, 1%; theology (or the seminary), 1%; education, 9%; arts and sciences, 82%.

COSTS AND FINANCIAL AID
Financial aid office: (415) 703-9573. **Expenses (2010-2011):** Tuition and fees 2010-2011: $35,222; room/board: $7,000. Estimated books and supplies: $1,500; transportation: $1,250; personal expenses: $2,200. **Financial aid:** Priority filing date for institution's financial aid form: March 1. In 2009-2010, 73% of undergraduates applied for financial aid. Of those, 68% were determined to have financial need; 5% had their need fully met. Average financial aid package (proportion receiving): $22,702 (68%). Average amount of gift aid, such as scholarships or grants (proportion receiving): $17,858 (64%). Average amount of self-help aid, such as work study or loans (proportion receiving): $5,012 (66%). Average need-based loan (excluding PLUS or other private loans): $4,632. Among students who received need-based aid, the average percentage of need met: 58%. Among students who received aid based on merit, the average award (and the proportion receiving): $7,212 (13%). The average athletic scholarship (and the proportion receiving): $0 (0%). Average amount of debt of borrowers graduating in 2009: $29,508. Proportion who borrowed: 69%.

CAMPUS LIFE AND EXTRACURRICULAR ACTIVITIES
Campus housing available (% using): coed dorms (87%), apartment for single students (13%), special housing for disabled students, other housing options. Students who live in college-owned, operated, or affiliated housing: 19%. **Student employment:** During the 2009-2010 academic year, 23% of undergraduates worked on campus. Average per-year earnings: $2,182. **Clubs and organizations:** Number of student organizations: 25. Activities include: international student organization, literary magazine, student government, student film society. Number of fraternities: 1; sororities: 0. Average proportion of students who stay on campus on weekends: 15%.

SERVICES AND FACILITIES
Basic services: nonremedial tutoring, placement service, health insurance. **Remedial assistance:** reading, math, writing, study skills. **Counseling services:** career, personal, academic, psychological. **For learning-disabled students:** School does not offer a structured program with separate admission and additional fees. Total undergraduates in learning-disabled program or receiving services: 70. Services include: remedial English, reading machines, remedial reading, tape recorders, videotaped classes, untimed tests, note-taking services, oral tests, learning center, readers, extended time for tests, tutors, early syllabus, priority registration, priority seating, proofreading services, texts on tape, exams on tape or computer, take home exams, other testing accommodations. **Library:** Number of titles: 76,579; number of current serial subscriptions: 244. **Information technology resources:** Students are not required to lease or own a computer. Number of campus computers available to all students: 260. School has a wireless network. Proportion of college-owned housing units wired for high-speed internet access: 100%. **Campus safety:** Security services offered: 24-hour foot-and-vehicle patrols, late-night transport/escort service, 24-hour emergency telephones, lighted pathways/sidewalks, controlled dormitory access (key, security card, etc).

TRANSFER AND INTERNATIONAL STUDENTS
Transfer students: May apply for admission for the following academic terms: Fall, Spring. Applicants do not need a minimum number of credits to apply. For fall 2009: Transfer applications received: 603. Transfer applicants offered admission: 451. Transfer applicants enrolled: 183. **International students:** Number of foreign undergraduates: 127 (9% of student body). Number of countries represented: 36. Minimum TOEFL score required: 550 (paper); 213 (computer). Average TOEFL score: 550 (paper).

California Institute of Technology

- **Address:** 1200 E. California Boulevard, Pasadena, CA 91125
- **Website:** http://www.caltech.edu
- **Private**
- **Enrollment:** 951 full-time

KEY STATS

✔ **U.S News College Ranking:** 7, National Universities
✔ **SAT Score (25th/75th percentile):** 1460-1570
✔ **Tuition:** 2010-2011: $36,282

Selectivity: Most selective	**Room/board:** $11,397
Acceptance rate: 15%	**Average debt:** $8,218
Student/faculty ratio: 3/1	**Proportion who borrowed:** 42%

UNDERGRADUATE STUDENT BODY STATS

2009-2010 enrollment: 951 full-time. Men: 62%; women: 38%. **Ethnic makeup:** African American: 1%; Asian American: 40%; Hispanic: 7%; White: 40%; International: 12%.

ADMISSIONS FACTS AND FIGURES

Phone: (626) 395-6341. **Email:** ugadmissions@caltech.edu. **Website:** http://www.caltech.edu. **Application deadlines for fall 2011:** Regular decision: January 1; decision sent by April 1. Early decision: Not offered. Early action: Send application by: November 1; Decision sent by: December 15. Admission can be deferred. **Application fee:** $60. **To apply online, go to:** http://admissions.caltech.edu/admissions/applying. **Admissions requirements/recommendations:** High school units required (recommended): English: 3 (4); Mathematics: 4; Science: 2 (4); Foreign language: (3); Social studies: 1 (3); History: 1 (1). Tests: The college uses SAT or ACT scores in admissions decisions. Either SAT or ACT required. For admission to the fall 2011 entering class, the school will accept: ACT with or without writing accepted. Campus visit: Neither required nor recommended. Admissions interview: Neither required nor recommended. Off-campus interview: Not available. **Factors that count in admissions decisions:** *Academic:* Secondary school record: Very Important. Class rank: Important. Letters of recommendation: Important. Standardized test scores: Important. Essay: Important. *Nonacademic:* Interview: Not Considered. Extracurricular activities: Important. Talent/ability: Considered. Character/personal qualities: Important. Alumni/ae relationship: Considered. Geographical residence: Not Considered. State residency: Not Considered. Religious affiliation/commitment: Not Considered. Minority status: Considered. Volunteer work: Considered. Work experience: Considered. **Other schools with the greatest overlap in applicants:** Harvard University; Massachusetts Institute of Technology; Princeton University; Stanford University. **Admissions statistics for the fall 2009 entering class:** Total applicants: 4,413. Total accepted: 674. Freshmen enrolled: 252; 65% were from out of state. Accepted through early-decision or early-action plans: 33%. Overall acceptance rate: 15%. Non-early acceptance rate: 13%. **Size of waiting list:** 623 applicants; enrolled from waiting list: 0. **Credentials of fall 2009 freshmen:** 98% ranked in the top 10 percent of their high school class; 100% were in the top 25 percent; 100% were in the top half. (Proportion submitting class standing: 51%.) **First-year students who submitted SAT scores:** 97%. Scores (25/75 percentile): Critical Reading: 690-770, Math: 770-800, Combined: 1460-1570. **First-year students submitting ACT scores:** 35%. Scores (25/75 percentile): English: 33-35, Math: 34-36, Composite: 33-35.

ACADEMICS

Year founded: 1891. **Academic calendar:** Quarter. **Degrees offered:** bachelor's, master's, post-master's certificate, doctorate. **Most popular majors:** 34% engineering, 29% physical sciences, 14% mathematics and statistics, 13% biological and biomedical sciences, 9% computer and information sciences and support services. **Major fields of study:** architecture and related services; biological and biomedical sciences; computer and information sciences and support services; engineering; history; liberal arts and sciences studies, and humanities; mathematics and statistics; physical sciences; social sciences. **Areas of required coursework:** humanities, mathematics, sciences (biological or physical), social science. **Special academic programs:** cooperative (work-study plan) program, cross-registration, double major, English as a Second Language (ESL), exchange student program (domestic), independent study, liberal arts/career combination, student-designed major, study abroad. **Cooperative education programs:** other. **Reserve Officers Training Corps (ROTC):** Army ROTC: Offered at cooperating institution (University of Southern California); Air Force ROTC: Offered at cooperat-

ing institution (University of Southern California). **Faculty and instruction (2009-2010):** Total instructional faculty: 311 full-time, 32 part-time (82% men; 18% women; 14% minorities). Full-time faculty with Ph.D. or other terminal degree: 97%. Student/faculty ratio: 3/1. Classes of fewer than 20 students: 64%; of 20 to 49 students: 27%; of 50 or more students: 9%. **Freshmen returning for sophomore year:** 98%. **Graduation rates:** Four-year: 73%; five-year: 85%; six-year: 89%. **Graduate study:** 49% of students pursue further study immediately upon graduation. Fields in which graduates pursue further study: law, 1%; medicine, 10%; engineering, 25%; arts and sciences, 64%.

COSTS AND FINANCIAL AID

Financial aid office: (626) 395-6280. **Expenses (2010-2011):** Tuition and fees 2010-2011: $36,282; room/board: $11,397. Estimated books and supplies: $1,323 personal expenses: $3,387. **Financial aid:** Priority filing date for institution's financial aid form: February 1. In 2009-2010, 59% of undergraduates applied for financial aid. Of those, 55% were determined to have financial need; 100% had their need fully met. Average financial aid package (proportion receiving): $33,902 (55%). Average amount of gift aid, such as scholarships or grants (proportion receiving): $30,069 (55%). Average amount of self-help aid, such as work study or loans (proportion receiving): $4,919 (39%). Average need-based loan (excluding PLUS or other private loans): $2,502. Among students who received need-based aid, the average percentage of need met: 100%. Among students who received aid based on merit, the average award (and the proportion receiving): $34,967 (4%). The average athletic scholarship (and the proportion receiving): $0 (0%). Average amount of debt of borrowers graduating in 2009: $8,218. Proportion who borrowed: 42%.

CAMPUS LIFE AND EXTRACURRICULAR ACTIVITIES

Campus housing available (% using): coed dorms (83%), apartments for married students (1%), special housing for disabled students (1%), other housing options (15%). Students who live in college-owned, operated, or affiliated housing: 95%. **Student employment:** During the 2009-2010 academic year, 25% of undergraduates worked on campus. **Clubs and organizations:** Number of student organizations: 100. Activities include: choral groups, concert band, dance, drama/theater, international student organization, jazz band, literary magazine, music ensembles, musical theater, opera, pep band, student government, student newspaper, student film society, symphony orchestra, yearbook. Number of fraternities: 0; sororities: 0. Average proportion of students who stay on campus on weekends: 90%. **Sports program (2009-2010):** Member of NCAA III. *Men's intercollegiate varsity sports:* baseball, basketball, cross country, fencing, soccer, swimming, tennis, track and field (outdoor), water polo. *Women's intercollegiate varsity sports:* basketball, cross country, fencing, swimming, tennis, track and field (outdoor), volleyball, water polo.

SERVICES AND FACILITIES

Basic services: nonremedial tutoring, women's center, health service, health insurance. **Counseling services:** minority student, career, personal, academic, older student, psychological, birth control, religious. **For learning-disabled students:** School does not offer a structured program with separate admission and additional fees. Services include: tape recorders, diagnostic testing service, untimed tests, note-taking services, oral tests, readers, extended time for tests, tutors, texts on tape. **Library:** Number of titles: 614,879; number of current serial subscriptions: 3,298. **Information technology resources:** Students are not required to lease or own a computer. Number of campus computers available to all students: 56. School has a wireless network. Approximate number of users that can be accommodated: 10,000. Proportion of college-owned housing units wired for high-speed internet access: 100%. **Campus safety:** Security services offered: 24-hour foot-and-vehicle patrols, late-night transport/escort service, 24-hour emergency telephones, lighted pathways/sidewalks, controlled dormitory access (key, security card, etc).

TRANSFER AND INTERNATIONAL STUDENTS

Transfer students: May apply for admission for the following academic terms: Fall. Applicants need a minimum number of credits to apply. For fall 2009: Transfer applications received: 133. Transfer applicants offered admission: 6. Transfer applicants enrolled: 4. **International students:** Number of foreign undergraduates: 111 (12% of student body). Number of countries represented: 33.

California Institute of the Arts

■ **Address:** 24700 McBean Parkway, Valencia, CA 91355
■ **Website:** http://www.calarts.edu
■ **Private**
■ **Enrollment:** 882 full-time; 6 part-time

KEY STATS

✔ **U.S News College Ranking:** Unranked Specialty School–Fine Arts
✔ **SAT or ACT Score (25th/75th percentile):** N/A
✔ **Tuition:** 2010-2011: $36,742

Selectivity: N/A	**Room/board:** $9,293
Acceptance rate: 33%	**Average debt:** $38,349
Student/faculty ratio: 7/1	**Proportion who borrowed:** 67%

UNDERGRADUATE STUDENT BODY STATS

2009-2010 enrollment: 882 full-time; 6 part-time. Men: 51%; women: 49%. **Ethnic makeup:** African American: 8%; American-Indian: 1%; Asian American: 12%; Hispanic: 12%; White: 59%; International: 8%.

ADMISSIONS FACTS AND FIGURES

Phone: (661) 255-1050. **Email:** admiss@calarts.edu. **Website:** http://www.calarts.edu. **Application deadlines for fall 2011:** Regular decision: January 5. Early decision: Not offered. Early action: Not offered. Admission cannot be deferred. **Application fee:** $70. **Admissions requirements/recommendations:** High school units required (recommended): English: (4); Mathematics: (3); Science: (3); Foreign language: (2); Social studies: (3); Academic electives: (2). Tests: The college does not use SAT or ACT scores in admissions decisions. Neither SAT nor ACT required. Campus visit: Recommended. Admissions interview: Recommended. Off-campus interview: Not available. **Factors that count in admissions decisions:** *Academic:* Secondary school record: Considered. Class rank: Not Considered. Letters of recommendation: Important. Standardized test scores: Not Considered. Essay: Very Important. *Nonacademic:* Interview: Considered. Extracurricular activities: Important. Talent/ability: Very Important. Character/personal qualities: Considered. Alumni/ae relationship: Not Considered. Geographical residence: Not Considered. State residency: Not Considered. Religious affiliation/commitment: Not Considered. Minority status: Not Considered. Volunteer work: Not Considered. Work experience: Not Considered. **Other schools with the greatest overlap in applicants:** Juilliard School; New York University; Rhode Island School of Design; School of the Art Institute of Chicago; University of Southern California. **Admissions statistics for the fall 2009 entering class:** Total applicants: 1,186. Total accepted: 397. Freshmen enrolled: 160; 47% were from out of state. Overall acceptance rate: 33%. **Size of waiting list:** 209 applicants; enrolled from waiting list: 60.

ACADEMICS

Year founded: 1961. **Academic calendar:** Semester. **Degrees offered:** certificate, bachelor's, master's. **Most popular majors:** 28% film/cinema studies, 26% fine and studio art, 20% drama/theater arts and stagecraft, 14% music, 7% dance. **Major fields of study:** visual and performing arts. **Areas of required coursework:** arts/fine arts, humanities, mathematics, English (including composition), social science. **Special academic programs:** independent study, internships, student-designed major, study abroad. **Faculty and instruction (2009-2010):** Total instructional faculty: 160 full-time, 143 part-time (62% men; 38% women; 18% minorities). Full-time faculty with Ph.D. or other terminal degree: 68%. Student/faculty ratio: 7/1. Classes of fewer than 20 students: 78%; of 20 to 49 students: 21%; of 50 or more students: 2%. **Advanced Placement and International Baccalaureate credit:** AP tests may be used for: Credit only. Scores accepted: 3, 4, 5. International Baccalaureate exams may be used for: Credit only. **Freshmen returning for sophomore year:** 79%. **Graduation rates:** Four-year: 53%; five-year: 60%; six-year: 60%.

COSTS AND FINANCIAL AID

Financial aid office: (661) 253-7869. **Expenses (2010-2011):** Tuition and fees 2010-2011: $36,742; room/board: $9,293. Estimated books and supplies: $1,900; transportation: $1,338; personal expenses: $1,700. **Financial aid:** Priority filing date for institution's financial aid form: March 2. In 2009-2010, 81% of undergraduates applied for financial aid. Of those, 68% were determined to have financial need; 5% had their need fully met. Average financial aid package (proportion receiving): $30,252 (67%). Average amount of gift aid, such as scholarships or grants (proportion receiving): $15,035 (64%). Average amount of self-help aid, such as work study or loans

(proportion receiving): $6,247 (61%). Average need-based loan (excluding PLUS or other private loans): $5,249. Among students who received need-based aid, the average percentage of need met: 77%. Among students who received aid based on merit, the average award (and the proportion receiving): $5,085 (9%). The average athletic scholarship (and the proportion receiving): $0 (0%). Average amount of debt of borrowers graduating in 2009: $38,349. Proportion who borrowed: 67%.

CAMPUS LIFE AND EXTRACURRICULAR ACTIVITIES

Campus housing available (% using): coed dorms (40%), other housing options (60%). Students who live in college-owned, operated, or affiliated housing: 33%. **Clubs and organizations:** Number of student organizations: 9. Activities include: choral groups, dance, drama/theater, jazz band, literary magazine, music ensembles, opera, radio station, student government, student newspaper, student film society, television station. Number of fraternities: 0; sororities: 0. Average proportion of students who stay on campus on weekends: 80%.

SERVICES AND FACILITIES

Basic services: health service, health insurance. **Remedial assistance:** writing, study skills. **Counseling services:** career, personal, psychological, birth control. **For learning-disabled students:** School does not offer a structured program with separate admission and additional fees. Services include: reading machines, tape recorders, untimed tests, note-taking services, oral tests, learning center, readers, extended time for tests, tutors, early syllabus, priority seating, substitution of courses, texts on tape, typist/scribe, exams on tape or computer, take home exams, other testing accommodations, other. **Library:** Number of titles: 194,361; number of current serial subscriptions: 463. **Information technology resources:** Students are not required to lease or own a computer. Number of campus computers available to all students: 250. School has a wireless network. Approximate number of users that can be accommodated: 2,500. Proportion of college-owned housing units wired for high-speed internet access: 100%. **Campus safety:** Security services offered: 24-hour foot-and-vehicle patrols, 24-hour emergency telephones, lighted pathways/sidewalks, controlled dormitory access (key, security card, etc).

TRANSFER AND INTERNATIONAL STUDENTS

Transfer students: May apply for admission for the following academic terms: Fall, Spring. Applicants do not need a minimum number of credits to apply. For fall 2009: Transfer applications received: 806. Transfer applicants offered admission: 217. Transfer applicants enrolled: 86. **International students:** Number of foreign undergraduates: 70 (8% of student body). Number of countries represented: 31. Minimum TOEFL score required: 550 (paper); 213 (computer). Average TOEFL score: 634 (paper).

California Lutheran University

■ **Address:** 60 W. Olsen Road, Thousand Oaks, CA 91360
■ **Website:** http://www.clunet.edu
■ **Private; Religious affiliation:** Lutheran
■ **Enrollment:** 2,276 full-time; 76 part-time

KEY STATS

✔ **U.S News College Ranking:** 18, Regional Universities (West)
✔ **SAT Score (25th/75th percentile):** 1010-1190
✔ **Tuition:** 2010-2011: $31,000

Selectivity: Selective	**Room/board:** $10,580
Acceptance rate: 62%	**Average debt:** $23,920
Student/faculty ratio: 15/1	**Proportion who borrowed:** 68%

UNDERGRADUATE STUDENT BODY STATS

2009-2010 enrollment: 2,276 full-time; 76 part-time. Men: 39%; women: 61%. **Ethnic makeup:** African American: 4%; American-Indian: 1%; Asian American: 5%; Hispanic: 16%; White: 70%; International: 4%. **Religious preference:** Roman Catholic: 22%; Protestant: 23%; Jewish: 1%; No preference: 5%; Unknown: 30%; Lutheran: 17%; Mormon: 1%; Other: 1%.

ADMISSIONS FACTS AND FIGURES

Phone: (877) 258-3678. **Email:** CLUADM@clunet.edu. **Website:** http://www.clunet.edu. **Application deadlines for fall 2011:** Regular decision: March 15. Early decision: Not offered. Early action: Not offered. Admission can be deferred. **Application fee:** $45. **To apply online, go to:** http://www.callutheran.edu/admission/undergraduate/apply/apply_online.php. **Admissions requirements/recommendations:** High school units required (recommended): English: 4; Mathematics: 3; Science: 3; Foreign language: 2; Social studies: 2. Tests: The college uses SAT or ACT scores in admissions decisions. Either SAT or ACT required. For admission to the fall 2011 entering class, the school will accept: ACT with or without writing accepted. Campus visit: Recommended. Admissions interview: Recommended. Off-campus interview: May be arranged. **Factors that count in admissions decisions:** *Academic:* Secondary school record: Very Important. Class rank: Important. Letters of recommendation: Very Important. Standardized test scores: Very Important. Essay: Very Important. *Nonacademic:* Interview: Considered. Extracurricular activities: Important. Talent/ability: Important. Character/personal qualities: Considered. Alumni/ae relationship: Considered. Geographical residence: Considered. State residency: Considered. Religious affiliation/commitment: Considered. Minority status: Considered. Volunteer work: Considered. Work experience: Considered. **Other schools with the greatest overlap in applicants:** Chapman University; San Diego State University; University of California–Santa Barbara; University of San Diego; University of the Pacific. **Admissions statistics for the fall 2009 entering class:** Total applicants: 3,665. Total accepted: 2,281. Freshmen enrolled: 464; 26% were from out of state. Overall acceptance rate: 62%. **Size of waiting list:** 224 applicants; enrolled from waiting list: 87. **Credentials of fall 2009 freshmen:** 34% ranked in the top 10 percent of their high school class; 69% were in the top 25 percent; 92% were in the top half. (Proportion submitting class standing: 49%.) **Average high school grade point average:** 3.6. **First-year students who submitted SAT scores:** 90%. Scores (25/75 percentile): Critical Reading: 500-580, Math: 510-610, Combined: 1010-1190. **First-year students submitting ACT scores:** 39%. Scores (25/75 percentile): English: 21-28, Math: 20-27, Composite: 22-26.

ACADEMICS

Year founded: 1959. **Academic calendar:** Semester. **Degrees offered:** certificate, bachelor's, post-bachelor's certificate, master's, post-master's certificate. **Most popular majors:** 30% business, management, marketing, and related support services, 14% communication, journalism, and related programs, 7% liberal arts and sciences studies, and humanities, 7% social sciences, 6% psychology. **Major fields of study:** agriculture, agriculture operations, and related sciences; biological and biomedical sciences; business, management, marketing, and related support services; communication, journalism, and related programs; computer and information sciences and support services; engineering; English language and literature/letters; foreign languages, literatures, and linguistics; history; legal professions and studies; liberal arts and sciences studies, and humanities; mathematics and statistics; natural resources and conservation; parks, recreation, leisure, and fitness studies; philosophy and religious studies; physical sciences; psychology; security and protective services; social sciences; visual and performing arts. **Areas of required coursework:** arts/fine arts, humanities, computer literacy, mathematics, English (including composition), philosophy, foreign languages, sciences (biological or physical), history, social science, other. **Pre-professional programs:** pre-law, pre-dentistry, pre-medicine, pre-theology, pre-veterinary science, pre-pharmacy. **Special academic programs (% participation):** accelerated program (18%), cooperative (work-study plan) program (40%), double major (7%), dual enrollment, exchange student program (domestic) (5%), honors program (10%), independent study (21%), internships (32%), student-designed major (1%), study abroad (8%), teacher certificate program. **Teacher certification offered in:** special education, elementary, middle/junior high, secondary, bilingual/bicultural. **Cooperative education programs:** art, business, computer science, engineering, humanities, natural science, social/behavioral science, other. **Reserve Officers Training Corps (ROTC):** Army ROTC: Offered at cooperating institution (University of California–Santa Barbara); Air Force ROTC: Offered at cooperating institution (University of California–Los Angeles). **Faculty and instruction (2009-2010):** Total instructional faculty: 144 full-time, 180 part-time (51% men; 49% women; 17% minorities). Full-time faculty with Ph.D. or other terminal degree: 86%. Student/faculty ratio: 15/1. Classes of fewer than 20 students: 60%; of 20 to 49 students: 38%; of 50 or more students: 2%. **Advanced Placement and International Baccalaureate credit:** AP tests may be used for: Placement only. Scores accepted: 4, 5. International Baccalaureate exams may be used for: Credit only. **Freshmen returning for sophomore year:** 79%. **Graduation rates:** Four-year: 54%; five-year: 60%; six-year: 65%. **Graduate study:** 31% of students pursue further study immediately upon graduation; 37% within one year. Fields in which graduates pursue further study: Master of Business Administration (MBA), 11%; law, 8%; medicine, 4%; dentistry, 4%; theology (or the seminary), 2%; education, 31%; arts and sciences, 41%; veterinary medicine, 18%.

COSTS AND FINANCIAL AID

Financial aid office: (805) 493-3115. **Expenses (2010-2011):** Tuition and fees 2010-2011: $31,000; room/board: $10,580. Estimated books and supplies: $1,504; transportation: $729; personal expenses: $2,379. **Financial aid:** Priority filing date for institution's financial aid form: March 1. In 2009-2010, 97% of undergraduates applied for financial aid. Of those, 64% were determined to have financial need; 20% had their need fully met. Average financial aid package (proportion receiving): $22,500 (64%). Average amount of gift aid, such as scholarships or grants (proportion receiving): $16,300 (61%). Average amount of self-help aid, such as work study or loans (proportion receiving): $4,860 (63%). Average need-based loan (excluding PLUS or other private loans): $3,700. Among students who received need-based aid, the average percentage of need met: 84%. Among students who received aid based on merit, the average award (and the proportion receiving): $10,900 (35%). Average amount of debt of borrowers graduating in 2009: $23,920. Proportion who borrowed: 68%.

CAMPUS LIFE AND EXTRACURRICULAR ACTIVITIES

Campus housing available (% using): coed dorms (62%), apartment for single students (36%), special housing for disabled students (1%). Students who live in college-owned, operated, or affiliated housing: 61%. **Student employment:** During the 2009-2010 academic year, 18% of undergraduates worked on campus. Average per-year earnings: $2,500. **Clubs and organizations:** Number of student organizations: 70. Activities include: campus ministries, choral groups, concert band, dance, drama/theater, international student organization, jazz band, literary magazine, model UN, music ensembles, musical theater, opera, pep band, radio station, student government, student newspaper, student film society, symphony orchestra, television station. Number of fraternities: 0; sororities: 0. Average proportion of students who stay on campus on weekends: 60%. **Sports program (2009-2010):** Member of NCAA III. *Men's intercollegiate varsity sports:* baseball, basketball, cross country, football, golf, soccer, swimming, tennis, track and field (outdoor), water polo. *Women's intercollegiate varsity sports:* basketball, cross country, soccer, softball, swimming, tennis, track and field (outdoor), volleyball, water polo.

SERVICES AND FACILITIES

Basic services: nonremedial tutoring, women's center, placement service, health service, health insurance. **Remedial assistance:** reading, math, writing, study skills. **Counseling services:** minority student, career, military, personal, veteran student, academic, older student, psychological, birth control, religious. **For learning-disabled students:** School does not offer a structured program with separate admission and additional fees. Total undergraduates in learning-disabled program or receiving services: 34. Services include: reading machines, tape recorders, note-taking services, oral tests, learning center, readers, extended time for tests, tutors, early syllabus, priority registration, priority seating, texts on tape, typist/scribe, exams on tape or computer, other testing accommodations. **Library:** Number of titles: 130,402; number of current serial subscriptions: 500. **Information technology resources:** Students are not required to lease or own a computer. Number of campus computers available to all students: 334. School has a wireless network. Approximate number of users that can be accommodated: 3,000. Proportion of college-owned housing units wired for high-speed internet access: 100%. **Campus safety:** Security services offered: 24-hour foot-and-vehicle patrols, late-night transport/escort service, 24-hour emergency telephones, lighted pathways/sidewalks, student patrols, controlled dormitory access (key, security card, etc.).

TRANSFER AND INTERNATIONAL STUDENTS

Transfer students: May apply for admission for the following academic terms: Fall, Spring. Applicants need a minimum number of credits to apply. For fall 2009: Transfer applications received: 586. Transfer applicants offered admission: 352. Transfer applicants enrolled: 214. **International students:** Number of foreign undergraduates: 90 (4% of student body). Number of countries represented: 20. Minimum TOEFL score required: 560 (paper); 79 (computer). Average TOEFL score: 580 (paper).

California Maritime Academy

- **Address:** 200 Maritime Academy Drive, Vallejo, CA 94590-8181
- **Website:** http://www.csum.edu
- **Public**
- **Enrollment:** 823 full-time

KEY STATS
✔ **U.S News College Ranking:** 4, Regional Colleges (West)
✔ **ACT Score:** 23
✔ **Tuition:** 2009-2010: $7,772 in state, $14,588 out of state
  Selectivity: Selective **Room/board:** $9,360
  Acceptance rate: 73% **Average debt:** N/A
  Student/faculty ratio: N/A **Proportion who borrowed:** N/A

UNDERGRADUATE STUDENT BODY STATS
2009-2010 enrollment: 823 full-time. Men: 86%; women: 14%. **Ethnic makeup:** African American: 2%; American-Indian: 1%; Asian American: 11%; Hispanic: 8%; White: 76%; International: 1%.

ADMISSIONS FACTS AND FIGURES
Phone: (800) 561-1945. **Email:** admission@csum.edu. **Website:** http://www.csum.edu. **Application deadlines for fall 2011:** Regular decision: Rolling. Early decision: Not offered. Early action: Not offered. Admission cannot be deferred. **Application fee:** $55. **To apply online, go to:** http://www.csumentor.edu/admissionapp/undergrad_apply.asp. **Admissions requirements/recommendations:** High school units required (recommended): English: 40; Mathematics: 30; Science: 20; Foreign language: 20; Social studies: 10; History: 10; Academic electives: 10. Tests: The college uses SAT or ACT scores in admissions decisions. Either SAT or ACT required. For admission to the fall 2011 entering class, the school will accept: ACT with or without writing accepted. Campus visit: Recommended. Admissions interview: Neither required nor recommended. Off-campus interview: Not available. **Factors that count in admissions decisions:** *Academic:* Secondary school record: Considered. Class rank: Not Considered. Letters of recommendation: Considered. Standardized test scores: Very Important. Essay: Not Considered. *Nonacademic:* Interview: Not Considered. Extracurricular activities: Considered. Talent/ability: Considered. Character/personal qualities: Considered. Alumni/ae relationship: Considered. Geographical residence: Considered. State residency: Considered. Religious affiliation/commitment: Not Considered. Minority status: Not Considered. Volunteer work: Not Considered. Work experience: Not Considered. **Other schools with the greatest overlap in applicants:** California Polytechnic State University–San Luis Obispo; San Diego State University; San Jose State University; University of California–Berkeley; University of California–Davis. **Admissions statistics for the fall 2009 entering class:** Total applicants: 908. Total accepted: 667. 17% were from out of state. Overall acceptance rate: 73%. **Credentials of fall 2009 freshmen:** 9% ranked in the top 25 percent of their high school class.

ACADEMICS
Year founded: 1929. **Academic calendar:** Semester. **Degrees offered:** bachelor's. **Most popular majors:** 44% marine transportation, 23% mechanical-engineering-related technologies/technicians, 15% mechanical engineering, 9% international relations and affairs, 6% business administration, management, and operations. **Major fields of study:** business, management, marketing, and related support services; engineering; engineering technologies/technicians; transportation and materials moving. **Areas of required coursework:** arts/fine arts, humanities, computer literacy, mathematics, English (including composition), philosophy, foreign languages, sciences (biological or physical), history, social science. **Special academic programs (% participation):** cooperative (work-study plan) program (100%), internships (100%), study abroad (100%), other (100%). **Cooperative education programs:** business, engineering, technologies. **Reserve Officers Training Corps (ROTC):** Navy ROTC: Offered at cooperating institution (University of California–Berkeley). **Advanced Placement and International Baccalaureate credit:** AP tests may be used for: Placement only. Scores accepted: 3, 4, 5. International Baccalaureate exams may be used for: Placement only. **Freshmen returning for sophomore year:** 77%. **Graduation rates:** Six-year: 59%. **Graduate study:** 2% of students pursue further study immediately upon graduation; 10% within five years.

COSTS AND FINANCIAL AID
Financial aid office: (707) 654-1275. **Expenses (2009-2010):** Tuition and fees 2009-2010: $7,772 in state, $14,588 out of state; room/board: $9,360.

Estimated books and supplies: $1,734; transportation: $1,182; personal expenses: $2,928.

CAMPUS LIFE AND EXTRACURRICULAR ACTIVITIES
Campus housing available (% using): coed dorms (90%), other housing options (10%). Students who live in college-owned, operated, or affiliated housing: 85%. **Student employment:** During the 2009-2010 academic year, 15% of undergraduates worked on campus. Average per-year earnings: $600. Activities include: choral groups, dance, jazz band, student government, yearbook. Average proportion of students who stay on campus on weekends: 70%. **Sports program (2009-2010):** Member of NAIA.

SERVICES AND FACILITIES
Basic services: nonremedial tutoring, placement service, health service, health insurance. **Remedial assistance:** math, writing. **Counseling services:** career, veteran student, academic, psychological, birth control. **For learning-disabled students:** School does not offer a structured program with separate admission and additional fees. Services include: remedial math, remedial English, reading machines, tape recorders, note-taking services, learning center, extended time for tests, tutors, other testing accommodations. **Information technology resources:** Students are not required to lease or own a computer. Number of campus computers available to all students: 120. School has a wireless network. Proportion of college-owned housing units wired for high-speed internet access: 100%. **Campus safety:** Security services offered: 24-hour foot-and-vehicle patrols, late-night transport/escort service, 24-hour emergency telephones, lighted pathways/sidewalks, student patrols, controlled dormitory access (key, security card, etc).

TRANSFER AND INTERNATIONAL STUDENTS
Transfer students: May apply for admission for the following academic terms: Fall. Applicants do not need a minimum number of credits to apply. For fall 2009: Transfer applications received: 319. Transfer applicants offered admission: 208. Transfer applicants enrolled: 89. **International students:** Number of foreign undergraduates: 9 (1% of student body). Minimum TOEFL score required: 550 (paper); 213 (computer).

Cal Poly State Univ.–San Luis Obispo

- **Address:** 1 Grand Avenue, San Luis Obispo, CA 93407
- **Website:** http://www.calpoly.edu
- **Public**
- **Enrollment:** 17,623 full-time; 679 part-time

KEY STATS
✔ **U.S News College Ranking:** 6, Regional Universities (West)
✔ **SAT Score (25th/75th percentile):** 1100-1300
✔ **Tuition:** 2009-2010: $6,198 in state, $17,358 out of state
  Selectivity: More selective **Room/board:** $9,623
  Acceptance rate: 37% **Average debt:** N/A
  Student/faculty ratio: 19/1 **Proportion who borrowed:** N/A

UNDERGRADUATE STUDENT BODY STATS
2009-2010 enrollment: 17,623 full-time; 679 part-time. Men: 56%; women: 44%. **Ethnic makeup:** African American: 1%; American-Indian: 1%; Asian American: 11%; Hispanic: 12%; White: 75%; International: 1%.

ADMISSIONS FACTS AND FIGURES
Phone: (805) 756-2311. **Email:** admissions@calpoly.edu. **Website:** http://www.calpoly.edu. **Application deadlines for fall 2011:** Regular decision: November 30; decision sent by April 1. Early decision: Send application by: October 31; Decision sent by: December 15. Early action: Not offered. Admission cannot be deferred. **Application fee:** $55. **To apply online, go to:** http://www.ess.calpoly.edu/_admiss/. **Admissions requirements/recommendations:** High school units required (recommended): English: 4 (5); Mathematics: 3 (4); Science: 3 (4); Foreign language: 2 (3); Social studies: 2 (2); History: 1 (1); Academic electives: 1; Total units: 15 (22). Tests: The college uses SAT or ACT scores in admissions decisions. Either SAT or ACT required. For admission to the fall 2011 entering class, the school will accept: ACT with or without writing accepted. Campus visit: Neither required nor recommended. Admissions interview: Neither required nor recommended. Off-campus interview: Not available. **Factors that count in admissions decisions:** *Academic:* Secondary school record: Very Important. Class rank: Not Considered. Letters of recommendation: Not Considered.

Standardized test scores: Very Important. Essay: Not Considered. *Nonacademic:* Interview: Not Considered. Extracurricular activities: Considered. Talent/ability: Considered. Character/personal qualities: Not Considered. Alumni/ae relationship: Not Considered. Geographical residence: Considered. State residency: Not Considered. Religious affiliation/commitment: Not Considered. Minority status: Not Considered. Volunteer work: Considered. Work experience: Considered. **Admissions statistics for the fall 2009 entering class:** Total applicants: 31,489. Total accepted: 11,737. Freshmen enrolled: 3,908; 7% were from out of state. Overall acceptance rate: 37%. Early-decision acceptance rate: 23%. Non-early acceptance rate: 39%. **Size of waiting list:** 425 applicants; enrolled from waiting list: 33. **Credentials of fall 2009 freshmen:** 48% ranked in the top 10 percent of their high school class; 84% were in the top 25 percent; 98% were in the top half. (Proportion submitting class standing: 56%.) **Average high school grade point average:** 3.8. **First-year students who submitted SAT scores:** 94%. Scores (25/75 percentile): Critical Reading: 530-630, Math: 570-670, Combined: 1100-1300. **First-year students submitting ACT scores:** 59%. Scores (25/75 percentile): English: 23-29, Math: 25-31, Composite: 24-29.

ACADEMICS

Year founded: 1901. **Academic calendar:** Quarter. **Degrees offered:** bachelor's, master's. **Most popular majors:** 17% business administration and management, 5% agricultural business and management, 5% civil engineering, 5% mechanical engineering, 4% architecture (B.Arch., B.A./B.S., M.Arch., M.A./M.S., Ph.D.). **Major fields of study:** agriculture, agriculture operations, and related sciences; architecture and related services; biological and biomedical sciences; business, management, marketing, and related support services; communication, journalism, and related programs; computer and information sciences and support services; education; engineering; English language and literature/letters; family and consumer sciences/human sciences; foreign languages, literatures, and linguistics; health professions and related clinical sciences; history; liberal arts and sciences studies, and humanities; mathematics and statistics; natural resources and conservation; parks, recreation, leisure, and fitness studies; philosophy and religious studies; physical sciences; psychology; social sciences; visual and performing arts. **Areas of required coursework:** arts/fine arts, humanities, mathematics, English (including composition), philosophy, sciences (biological or physical), history, social science, other. **Special academic programs:** cooperative (work-study plan) program, distance learning, double major, English as a Second Language (ESL), exchange student program (domestic), honors program, internships, liberal arts/career combination, study abroad, teacher certificate program. **Teacher certification offered in:** special education, elementary, middle/junior high, secondary, bilingual/bicultural. **Cooperative education programs:** agriculture, art, business, computer science, engineering, natural science, social/behavioral science, other. **Reserve Officers Training Corps (ROTC):** Army ROTC: Offered on campus. **Faculty and instruction (2009-2010):** Total instructional faculty: 824 full-time, 411 part-time (64% men; 36% women). Full-time faculty with Ph.D. or other terminal degree: 82%. Student/faculty ratio: 19/1. Classes of fewer than 20 students: 15%; of 20 to 49 students: 72%; of 50 or more students: 13%. **Advanced Placement and International Baccalaureate credit:** AP tests may be used for: Credit only. Scores accepted: 3, 4, 5. International Baccalaureate exams may be used for: Credit only. **Freshmen returning for sophomore year:** 90%. **Graduation rates:** Four-year: 25%; five-year: 63%; six-year: 71%.

COSTS AND FINANCIAL AID

Financial aid office: (805) 756-2927. **Expenses (2009-2010):** Tuition and fees 2009-2010: $6,198 in state, $17,358 out of state; room/board: $9,623. Estimated books and supplies: $1,638; transportation: $1,062; personal expenses: $2,205. **Financial aid:** Priority filing date for institution's financial aid form: March 2. In 2009-2010, 50% of undergraduates applied for financial aid. Of those, 33% were determined to have financial need; 12% had their need fully met. Average financial aid package (proportion receiving): $8,687 (31%). Average amount of gift aid, such as scholarships or grants (proportion receiving): $2,390 (24%). Average amount of self-help aid, such as work study or loans (proportion receiving): $3,650 (23%). Average need-based loan (excluding PLUS or other private loans): $3,696. Among students who received need-based aid, the average percentage of need met: 63%. Among students who received aid based on merit, the average award (and the proportion receiving): $2,498 (4%). The average athletic scholarship (and the proportion receiving): $3,234 (2%).

CAMPUS LIFE AND EXTRACURRICULAR ACTIVITIES

Campus housing available (% using): coed dorms (45%), apartment for single students (55%), special housing for disabled students. Students who live in college-owned, operated, or affiliated housing: 35%. **Clubs and organi-** **zations:** Number of student organizations: 400. Activities include: campus ministries, choral groups, concert band, dance, drama/theater, international student organization, jazz band, literary magazine, marching band, model UN, music ensembles, musical theater, opera, pep band, radio station, student government, student newspaper, symphony orchestra, television station. Number of fraternities: 23; sororities: 14. Average proportion of students who stay on campus on weekends: 100%. **Sports program (2009-2010):** Member of NCAA I. *Men's intercollegiate varsity sports:* baseball, basketball, cross country, football, golf, soccer, swimming, tennis, track and field (outdoor), wrestling. *Women's intercollegiate varsity sports:* basketball, cross country, golf, soccer, softball, swimming, tennis, track and field (outdoor), volleyball.

SERVICES AND FACILITIES

Basic services: nonremedial tutoring, women's center, placement service, day care, health service, health insurance. **Remedial assistance:** reading, math, writing, study skills. **Counseling services:** career, personal, academic, psychological, birth control. **For learning-disabled students:** School does not offer a structured program with separate admission and additional fees. Services include: reading machines, note-taking services, readers, extended time for tests, texts on tape, other testing accommodations. **Library:** Number of titles: 607,317; number of current serial subscriptions: 24,413. **Information technology resources:** Students are not required to lease or own a computer. Number of campus computers available to all students: 360. School has a wireless network. Approximate number of users that can be accommodated: 4,000. Proportion of college-owned housing units wired for high-speed internet access: 100%. **Campus safety:** Security services offered: 24-hour foot-and-vehicle patrols, late-night transport/escort service, 24-hour emergency telephones, lighted pathways/sidewalks, student patrols, controlled dormitory access (key, security card, etc).

TRANSFER AND INTERNATIONAL STUDENTS

Transfer students: May apply for admission for the following academic terms: Fall. Applicants do not need a minimum number of credits to apply. For fall 2009: Transfer applications received: 5,185. Transfer applicants offered admission: 1,174. Transfer applicants enrolled: 716. **International students:** Number of foreign undergraduates: 145 (1% of student body). Minimum TOEFL score required: 550 (paper); 80 (computer).

California State Polytechnic Univ.—Pomona

- **Address:** 3801 W. Temple Avenue, Pomona, CA 91768-2557
- **Website:** http://www.csupomona.edu
- **Public**
- **Enrollment:** 16,641 full-time; 3,495 part-time

KEY STATS

✔ **U.S News College Ranking:** 32, Regional Universities (West)
✔ **SAT Score (25th/75th percentile):** 920-1170
✔ **Tuition:** 2010-2011: $4,551 in state, $15,711 out of state

Selectivity: Selective	**Room/board:** $9,570
Acceptance rate: 61%	**Average debt:** $14,035
Student/faculty ratio: 25/1	**Proportion who borrowed:** 36%

UNDERGRADUATE STUDENT BODY STATS

2009-2010 enrollment: 16,641 full-time; 3,495 part-time. Men: 57%; women: 43%. **Ethnic makeup:** African American: 3%; Asian American: 27%; Hispanic: 32%; White: 33%; International: 5%.

ADMISSIONS FACTS AND FIGURES

Phone: (909) 869-3210. **Email:** admissions@csupomona.edu. **Website:** http://www.csupomona.edu. **Application deadlines for fall 2011:** Regular decision: November 30. Early decision: Not offered. Early action: Not offered. Admission cannot be deferred. **Application fee:** $55. **To apply online, go to:** http://www.csumentor.edu/. **Admissions requirements/recommendations:** High school units required (recommended): English: 4; Mathematics: 3 (4); Science: 2; Foreign language: 2; Social studies: 1; History: 1; Academic electives: 1; Total units: 15. Tests: The college uses SAT or ACT scores in admissions decisions. Either SAT or ACT required. For admission to the fall 2011 entering class, the school will accept: ACT with or without writing accepted. Campus visit: Recommended. Admissions interview: Neither required nor recommended. Off-campus interview: May be arranged. **Factors that count in admissions decisions:** *Academic:* Secondary school record: Very Important. Class rank: Not Considered. Letters of recommendation: Not Considered. Standardized test scores: Very Important. Essay: Not Considered. **Nonacademic:** Interview: Not Considered. Extracurricular activities: Not Considered. Talent/ability: Not Considered. Character/personal qualities: Not Considered. Alumni/ae relationship: Not Considered. Geographical residence: Not Considered. State residency: Not Considered. Religious affiliation/commitment: Not Considered. Minority status: Not Considered. Volunteer work: Not Considered. Work experience: Not Considered. **Other schools with the greatest overlap in applicants:** California Polytechnic State University–San Luis Obispo; California State University–Fullerton; California State University–Long Beach; University of California–Irvine; University of California–Los Angeles. **Admissions statistics for the fall 2009 entering class:** Total applicants: 20,759. Total accepted: 12,731. Freshmen enrolled: 2,914; 1% were from out of state. Overall acceptance rate: 61%. **Average high school grade point average:** 3.4. **First-year students who submitted SAT scores:** 95%. Scores (25/75 percentile): Critical Reading: 450-560, Math: 470-610, Combined: 920-1170. **First-year students submitting ACT scores:** 27%. Scores (25/75 percentile): English: 19-25, Math: 20-27, Composite: 19-25.

ACADEMICS

Year founded: 1938. **Academic calendar:** Quarter. **Degrees offered:** bachelor's, master's. **Most popular majors:** 33% business, management, marketing, and related support services, 17% engineering, 5% biological and biomedical sciences, 5% social sciences, 4% architecture and related services. **Major fields of study:** agriculture, agriculture operations, and related sciences; architecture and related services; area, ethnic, cultural, and gender studies; biological and biomedical sciences; business, management, marketing, and related support services; communication, journalism, and related programs; computer and information sciences and support services; education; engineering; engineering technologies/technicians; English language and literature/letters; family and consumer sciences/human sciences; foreign languages, literatures, and linguistics; history; liberal arts and sciences studies, and humanities; mathematics and statistics; parks, recreation, leisure, and fitness studies; philosophy and religious studies; physical sciences; psychology; public administration and social service professions; social sciences; visual and performing arts. **Areas of required coursework:** arts/fine arts, humanities, computer literacy, mathematics, English (including composition), philosophy, foreign languages, sciences (biological or physical), history, social science. **Pre-professional programs:** pre-dentistry, pre-medicine, pre-veterinary science, pre-pharmacy. **Special academic programs:** cooperative (work-study plan) program, cross-registration, double major, dual enrollment, English as a Second Language (ESL), exchange student program (domestic), external degree program, honors program, internships, study abroad, teacher certificate program, other. **Teacher certification offered in:** special education, elementary, middle/junior high, secondary, bilingual/bicultural. **Cooperative education programs:** agriculture, art, business, computer science, education, engineering, natural science, social/behavioral science. **Reserve Officers Training Corps (ROTC):** Army ROTC: Offered on campus. **Faculty and instruction (2009-2010):** Total instructional faculty: 565 full-time, 455 part-time (61% men; 39% women; 32% minorities). Student/faculty ratio: 25/1. Classes of fewer than 20 students: 10%; of 20 to 49 students: 76%; of 50 or more students: 14%. **Advanced Placement and International Baccalaureate credit:** AP tests may be used for: Credit only. Scores accepted: 3, 4, 5. International Baccalaureate exams may be used for: Credit only. **Freshmen returning for sophomore year:** 82%. **Graduation rates:** Four-year: 15%; five-year: 41%; six-year: 51%.

COSTS AND FINANCIAL AID

Financial aid office: (909) 869-3700. **Expenses (2010-2011):** Tuition and fees 2010-2011: $4,551 in state, $15,711 out of state; room/board: $9,570. Estimated books and supplies: $1,500; transportation: $711; personal expenses: $1,575. **Financial aid:** Priority filing date for institution's financial aid form: March 2. In 2009-2010, 66% of undergraduates applied for financial aid. Of those, 56% were determined to have financial need; 31% had their need fully met. Average financial aid package (proportion receiving): $10,874 (51%). Average amount of gift aid, such as scholarships or grants (proportion receiving): $8,815 (42%). Average amount of self-help aid, such as work study or loans (proportion receiving): $3,977 (46%). Average need-based loan (excluding PLUS or other private loans): $3,929. Among students who received need-based aid, the average percentage of need met: 83%. Among students who received aid based on merit, the average award (and the proportion receiving): $1,462 (0%). The average athletic scholarship (and the proportion receiving): $3,499 (1%). Average amount of debt of borrowers graduating in 2009: $14,035. Proportion who borrowed: 36%.

CAMPUS LIFE AND EXTRACURRICULAR ACTIVITIES

Campus housing available: coed dorms, apartment for single students, special housing for disabled students, other housing options. Students who live in college-owned, operated, or affiliated housing: 9%. **Student employment:** During the 2009-2010 academic year, 10% of undergraduates worked on campus. Average per-year earnings: $2,000. **Clubs and organizations:** Number of student organizations: 280. Activities include: campus ministries, choral groups, concert band, dance, drama/theater, international student organization, jazz band, music ensembles, musical theater, opera, pep band, radio station, student government, student newspaper, symphony orchestra, television station. Number of fraternities: 12; sororities: 8. Proportion of men in fraternities: 2%; of women in sororities: 1%. Average proportion of students who stay on campus on weekends: 60%. **Sports program (2009-2010):** Member of NCAA II. **Men's intercollegiate varsity sports:** baseball, basketball, cross country, soccer, track and field (outdoor). **Women's intercollegiate varsity sports:** basketball, cross country, soccer, track and field (outdoor), volleyball.

SERVICES AND FACILITIES

Basic services: nonremedial tutoring, women's center, day care, health service, health insurance. **Remedial assistance:** reading, math, writing, study skills. **Counseling services:** minority student, career, military, personal, veteran student, academic, older student, psychological, birth control, religious. **For learning-disabled students:** School does not offer a structured program with separate admission and additional fees. Services include: reading machines, tape recorders, note-taking services, oral tests, learning center, extended time for tests, priority registration, other testing accommodations, other. **Library:** Number of titles: 670,580; number of current serial subscriptions: 6,883. **Information technology resources:** Students are not required to lease or own a computer. Number of campus computers available to all students: 1,225. School has a wireless network. Approximate number of users that can be accommodated: 600. Proportion of college-owned housing units wired for high-speed internet access: 100%. **Campus safety:** Security services offered: 24-hour foot-and-vehicle patrols, late-night transport/escort service, 24-hour emergency telephones, lighted pathways/sidewalks, student patrols, controlled dormitory access (key, security card, etc).

TRANSFER AND INTERNATIONAL STUDENTS

Transfer students: May apply for admission for the following academic terms: Fall, Winter, Spring. Applicants need a minimum number of credits to apply. For fall 2009: Transfer applications received: 5,289. Transfer applicants offered admission: 3,832. Transfer applicants enrolled: 1,567. **International students:** Number of foreign undergraduates: 984 (5% of student body). Number of countries represented: 40. Minimum TOEFL score required: 525 (paper); 195 (computer).

California State University–Bakersfield

- **Address:** 9001 Stockdale Highway, Bakersfield, CA 93311
- **Website:** http://www.csub.edu
- **Public**
- **Enrollment:** 5,540 full-time; 954 part-time

KEY STATS

✔ **U.S News College Ranking:** second tier, Regional Universities (West)
✔ **SAT Score (25th/75th percentile):** 780-1020
✔ **Tuition:** 2009-2010: $4,383 in state, $11,199 out of state

Selectivity: Less selective	**Room/board:** $7,137
Acceptance rate: 70%	**Average debt:** N/A
Student/faculty ratio: 22/1	**Proportion who borrowed:** N/A

UNDERGRADUATE STUDENT BODY STATS

2009-2010 enrollment: 5,540 full-time; 954 part-time. Men: 35%; women: 65%. **Ethnic makeup:** African American: 7%; American-Indian: 2%; Asian American: 7%; Hispanic: 39%; White: 43%; International: 2%.

ADMISSIONS FACTS AND FIGURES

Phone: (661) 654-3036. **Email:** admissions@csub.edu. **Website:** http://www.csub.edu. **Application deadlines for fall 2011:** Regular decision: March 1. Early decision: Not offered. Early action: Not offered. Admission can be deferred. **Application fee:** $55. **To apply online, go to:** http://www.csumentor.edu. **Admissions requirements/recommendations:** High school units required (recommended): English: 4; Mathematics: 3; Science: 2; Foreign language: 2; Social studies: 1; History: 1; Academic electives: 1; Total units: 15. Tests: The college uses SAT or ACT scores in admissions decisions. Neither SAT nor ACT required. For admission to the fall 2011 entering class, the school will accept: ACT with or without writing accepted. Campus visit: Neither required nor recommended. Admissions interview: Neither required nor recommended. Off-campus interview: Not available. **Factors that count in admissions decisions: *Academic:*** Secondary school record: Very Important. Class rank: Not Considered. Letters of recommendation: Not Considered. Standardized test scores: Important. Essay: Not Considered. ***Nonacademic:*** Interview: Not Considered. Extracurricular activities: Not Considered. Talent/ability: Not Considered. Character/personal qualities: Not Considered. Alumni/ae relationship: Not Considered. Geographical residence: Not Considered. State residency: Important. Religious affiliation/commitment: Not Considered. Minority status: Not Considered. Volunteer work: Not Considered. Work experience: Not Considered. **Other schools with the greatest overlap in applicants:** California State University–Fresno; California State University–Los Angeles; California State University–Northridge. **Admissions statistics for the fall 2009 entering class:** Total applicants: 4,303. Total accepted: 2,994. Freshmen enrolled: 1,061; Overall acceptance rate: 70%. **Average high school grade point average:** 3.0. **First-year students who submitted SAT scores:** 74%. Scores (25/75 percentile): Critical Reading: 390-500, Math: 390-520, Combined: 780-1020. **First-year students submitting ACT scores:** 26%. Scores (25/75 percentile): English: 14-21, Math: 16-22, Composite: 16-21.

ACADEMICS

Year founded: 1970. **Academic calendar:** Quarter. **Degrees offered:** bachelor's, master's. **Major fields of study:** biological and biomedical sciences; business, management, marketing, and related support services; communication, journalism, and related programs; computer and information sciences and support services; education; English language and literature/letters; family and consumer sciences/human sciences; foreign languages, literatures, and linguistics; health professions and related clinical sciences; history; liberal arts and sciences studies, and humanities; mathematics and statistics; natural resources and conservation; philosophy and religious studies; physical sciences; psychology; public administration and social service professions; security and protective services; social sciences; visual and performing arts. **Areas of required coursework:** arts/fine arts, humanities, computer literacy, mathematics, English (including composition), philosophy, foreign languages, sciences (biological or physical), history, social science, other. **Special academic programs:** accelerated program, cooperative (work-study plan) program, cross-registration, double major, dual enrollment, English as a Second Language (ESL), exchange student program (domestic), external degree program, honors program, independent study, internships, student-designed major, study abroad, teacher certificate program. **Teacher certification offered in:** early childhood, special education, elementary, middle/junior high, secondary, bilingual/bicultural. **Faculty and instruction (2009-2010):** Total instructional faculty: 284 full-time, 157 part-time (47% men; 53% women; 26% minorities). Full-time faculty with Ph.D. or other terminal degree: 66%. Student/faculty ratio: 22/1. Classes of fewer than 20 students: 29%; of 20 to 49 students: 62%; of 50 or more students: 9%. **Advanced Placement and International Baccalaureate credit:** AP tests may be used for: Placement only. Scores accepted: 3, 4, 5. **Freshmen returning for sophomore year:** 73%. **Graduation rates:** Four-year: 13%; five-year: 30%; six-year: 41%.

COSTS AND FINANCIAL AID

Financial aid office: (661) 654-3016. **Expenses (2009-2010):** Tuition and fees 2009-2010: $4,383 in state, $11,199 out of state; room/board: $7,137. Estimated books and supplies: $1,638; transportation: $1,032; personal expenses: $2,562.

CAMPUS LIFE AND EXTRACURRICULAR ACTIVITIES

Campus housing available: coed dorms, special housing for disabled students, other housing options. Activities include: campus ministries, choral groups, concert band, dance, drama/theater, international student organization, literary magazine, model UN, student government, student newspaper. Number of fraternities: 5; sororities: 6. **Sports program (2009-2010):** Member of NCAA II.

SERVICES AND FACILITIES

Basic services: nonremedial tutoring, placement service, day care, health service. **Counseling services:** minority student, career, personal, academic, older student, psychological, birth control. **For learning-disabled students:** School offers a structured program with separate admission and additional fees. Services include: remedial math, remedial English, reading machines, tape recorders, videotaped classes, diagnostic testing service, untimed tests, note-taking services, oral tests, readers, extended time for tests, tutors. **Library:** Number of titles: 450,874; number of current serial subscriptions: 3,168. **Information technology resources:** Students are not required to lease or own a computer. Number of campus computers available to all students: 196. School has a wireless network. Approximate number of users that can be accommodated: 500. Proportion of college-owned housing units wired for high-speed internet access: 100%. **Campus safety:** Security services offered: 24-hour foot-and-vehicle patrols, late-night transport/escort service, 24-hour emergency telephones, lighted pathways/sidewalks, student patrols, controlled dormitory access (key, security card, etc).

TRANSFER AND INTERNATIONAL STUDENTS

Transfer students: May apply for admission for the following academic terms: Fall, Winter, Spring, Summer. Applicants do not need a minimum number of credits to apply. For fall 2009: Transfer applications received: 2,230. Transfer applicants offered admission: 1,250. Transfer applicants enrolled: 876. **International students:** Number of foreign undergraduates: 109 (2% of student body). Minimum TOEFL score required: 500 (paper); 173 (computer).

California State University–Chico

- **Address:** 400 W. First Street, Chico, CA 95929-0722
- **Website:** http://www.csuchico.edu
- **Public**
- **Enrollment:** 14,334 full-time; 1,283 part-time

KEY STATS

✔ **U.S News College Ranking:** 30, Regional Universities (West)
✔ **SAT Score (25th/75th percentile):** 910-1120
✔ **Tuition:** 2010-2011: $6,296 in state, $17,456 out of state

Selectivity: Selective	**Room/board:** $9,404
Acceptance rate: 88%	**Average debt:** N/A
Student/faculty ratio: 23/1	**Proportion who borrowed:** N/A

UNDERGRADUATE STUDENT BODY STATS

2009-2010 enrollment: 14,334 full-time; 1,283 part-time. Men: 49%; women: 51%. **Ethnic makeup:** African American: 2%; American-Indian: 1%; Asian American: 5%; Hispanic: 14%; White: 75%; International: 3%.

ADMISSIONS FACTS AND FIGURES

Phone: (800) 542-4426. **Email:** info@csuchico.edu. **Website:** http://www.csuchico.edu. **Application deadlines for fall 2011:** Regular decision: November 30; decision sent by March 1. Early decision: Not offered. Early action: Not offered. Admission can be deferred. **Application fee:** $55. **To apply online, go to:** http://www.csumentor.edu. **Admissions requirements/recommendations:** High school units required (recommended): English: 4; Mathematics: 3; Science: 2; Foreign language: 2; Social studies: 2; History: 0; Academic electives: 1; Total units: 15. Tests: The college uses SAT or ACT scores in admissions decisions. Either SAT or ACT required. For admission to the fall 2011 entering class, the school will accept: ACT with or without writing accepted. Campus visit: Recommended. Admissions interview: Neither required nor recommended. Off-campus interview: Not available. **Factors that count in admissions decisions: *Academic:*** Secondary school record: Not Considered. Class rank: Not Considered. Letters of recommendation: Not Considered. Standardized test scores: Very Important. Essay: Not Considered. ***Nonacademic:*** Interview: Not Considered. Extracurricular activities: Not Considered. Talent/ability: Not Considered. Character/personal qualities: Not Considered. Alumni/ae relationship: Not Considered. Geographical residence: Important. State residency: Important. Religious affiliation/commitment: Not Considered. Minority status: Not Considered. Volunteer work: Not Considered. Work experience: Not Considered. **Other schools with the greatest overlap in applicants:** California Polytechnic State University–San Luis Obispo; California State University–Long Beach; San Diego State University; University of California–Davis; University of California–Santa Barbara. **Admissions statistics for the fall 2009 entering class:** Total applicants: 12,881. Total accepted: 11,298. Freshmen enrolled: 2,505; 2% were from out of state. Overall acceptance rate: 88%. **Credentials of fall 2009 freshmen:** 35% ranked in the top 10 percent of their high school class; 76% were in the top 25 percent; 100% were in the top half. (Proportion submitting class standing: 50%.) **Average high school grade point average:** 3.1. **First-year students who submitted SAT scores:**

89%. Scores (25/75 percentile): Critical Reading: 450-550, Math: 460-570, Combined: 910-1120. **First-year students submitting ACT scores:** 34%. Scores (25/75 percentile): English: 18-24, Math: 19-25, Composite: 19-24.

ACADEMICS

Year founded: 1887. **Academic calendar:** Semester. **Degrees offered:** certificate, bachelor's, post-bachelor's certificate, master's, post-master's certificate. **Most popular majors:** 16% business, management, marketing, and related support services, 9% social sciences, 8% parks, recreation, leisure, and fitness studies, 8% visual and performing arts, 7% health professions and related clinical sciences. **Major fields of study:** agriculture, agriculture operations, and related sciences; area, ethnic, cultural, and gender studies; biological and biomedical sciences; business, management, marketing, and related support services; communication, journalism, and related programs; computer and information sciences and support services; education; engineering; engineering technologies/technicians; English language and literature/letters; foreign languages, literatures, and linguistics; health professions and related clinical sciences; history; liberal arts and sciences studies, and humanities; mathematics and statistics; multi/interdisciplinary studies; natural resources and conservation; parks, recreation, leisure, and fitness studies; philosophy and religious studies; physical sciences; psychology; public administration and social service professions; security and protective services; social sciences; visual and performing arts. **Areas of required coursework:** arts/fine arts, humanities, computer literacy, mathematics, English (including composition), philosophy, sciences (biological or physical), history, social science. **Pre-professional programs:** pre-law, pre-dentistry, pre-medicine, pre-theology, pre-veterinary science, pre-optometry, pre-pharmacy, other. **Special academic programs:** cooperative (work-study plan) program, cross-registration, distance learning, double major, dual enrollment, English as a Second Language (ESL), exchange student program (domestic), external degree program, honors program, independent study, internships, student-designed major, study abroad, teacher certificate program. **Teacher certification offered in:** early childhood, special education, elementary, middle/junior high, secondary, bilingual/bicultural. **Cooperative education programs:** agriculture, art, business, computer science, education, engineering, health professions, humanities, natural science, social/behavioral science, technologies. **Faculty and instruction (2009-2010):** Total instructional faculty: 504 full-time, 379 part-time (54% men; 46% women; 15% minorities). Full-time faculty with Ph.D. or other terminal degree: 83%. Student/faculty ratio: 23/1. Classes of fewer than 20 students: 26%; of 20 to 49 students: 61%; of 50 or more students: 13%. **Advanced Placement and International Baccalaureate credit:** AP tests may be used for: Credit and/or placement. Scores accepted: 3, 4, 5. International Baccalaureate exams may be used for: Credit and/or placement. **Freshmen returning for sophomore year:** 81%. **Graduation rates:** Six-year: 53%. **Graduate study:** 21% of students pursue further study immediately upon graduation.

COSTS AND FINANCIAL AID

Financial aid office: (530) 898-6451. **Expenses (2010-2011):** Tuition and fees 2010-2011: $6,296 in state, $17,456 out of state; room/board: $9,404. Estimated books and supplies: $1,656; transportation: $950; personal expenses: $1,950. **Financial aid:** Priority filing date for institution's financial aid form: March 2. In 2009-2010, 58% of undergraduates applied for financial aid. Of those, 47% were determined to have financial need; 15% had their need fully met. Average financial aid package (proportion receiving): $12,447 (46%). Average amount of gift aid, such as scholarships or grants (proportion receiving): $8,292 (36%). Average amount of self-help aid, such as work study or loans (proportion receiving): $5,507 (37%). Average need-based loan (excluding PLUS or other private loans): $4,475. Among students who received need-based aid, the average percentage of need met: 90%. Among students who received aid based on merit, the average award (and the proportion receiving): $1,978 (4%). The average athletic scholarship (and the proportion receiving): $2,873 (1%).

CAMPUS LIFE AND EXTRACURRICULAR ACTIVITIES

Campus housing available: coed dorms, apartment for single students, special housing for disabled students, special housing for international students, other housing options. Students who live in college-owned, operated, or affiliated housing: 1%. **Student employment:** During the 2009-2010 academic year, 9% of undergraduates worked on campus. Average per-year earnings: $2,875. **Clubs and organizations:** Number of student organizations: 243. Activities include: choral groups, concert band, dance, drama/theater, jazz band, literary magazine, music ensembles, musical theater, opera, pep band, radio station, student government, student newspaper, student film society, symphony orchestra, yearbook. Number of fraternities: 13; sororities: 11. Proportion of men in fraternities: 1%; of women in sororities:

1%. **Sports program (2009-2010):** Member of NCAA II. *Men's intercollegiate varsity sports:* baseball, basketball, cross country, golf, soccer, track and field (outdoor). *Women's intercollegiate varsity sports:* basketball, cross country, golf, soccer, softball, track and field (outdoor), volleyball.

SERVICES AND FACILITIES

Basic services: nonremedial tutoring, women's center, placement service, day care, health service, health insurance, other. **Remedial assistance:** math, writing, study skills. **Counseling services:** minority student, career, personal, veteran student, academic, older student, psychological, birth control. **For learning-disabled students:** School does not offer a structured program with separate admission and additional fees. Services include: remedial English, reading machines, tape recorders, other special classes, videotaped classes, diagnostic testing service, note-taking services, oral tests, learning center, readers, extended time for tests, tutors, early syllabus, priority registration, priority seating, texts on tape, typist/scribe, exams on tape or computer, other testing accommodations, other. **Library:** Number of titles: 942,304; number of current serial subscriptions: 22,000. **Information technology resources:** Students are not required to lease or own a computer. Number of campus computers available to all students: 1,212. School has a wireless network. Approximate number of users that can be accommodated: 10,000. Proportion of college-owned housing units wired for high-speed internet access: 100%. **Campus safety:** Security services offered: 24-hour foot-and-vehicle patrols, late-night transport/escort service, 24-hour emergency telephones, lighted pathways/sidewalks, student patrols, controlled dormitory access (key, security card, etc).

TRANSFER AND INTERNATIONAL STUDENTS

Transfer students: May apply for admission for the following academic terms: Fall, Spring. Applicants need a minimum number of credits to apply. For fall 2009: Transfer applications received: 3,792. Transfer applicants offered admission: 2,789. Transfer applicants enrolled: 1,367. **International students:** Number of foreign undergraduates: 410 (3% of student body). Number of countries represented: 33. Minimum TOEFL score required: 500 (paper); 173 (computer). Average TOEFL score: 535 (paper).

California State Univ.–Dominguez Hills

- **Address:** 1000 E. Victoria Street, Carson, CA 90747
- **Website:** http://www.csudh.edu
- **Public**
- **Enrollment:** 6,746 full-time; 4,134 part-time

KEY STATS

✔ **U.S News College Ranking:** second tier, Regional Universities (West)
✔ **SAT Score (25th/75th percentile):** 730-930
✔ **Tuition:** 2009-2010: $4,645 in state, $13,573 out of state

Selectivity: Less selective	**Room/board:** $9,970
Acceptance rate: 84%	**Average debt:** $7,946
Student/faculty ratio: 23/1	**Proportion who borrowed:** 56%

UNDERGRADUATE STUDENT BODY STATS

2009-2010 enrollment: 6,746 full-time; 4,134 part-time. Men: 34%; women: 66%. **Ethnic makeup:** African American: 27%; Asian American: 9%; Hispanic: 40%; White: 22%; International: 2%.

ADMISSIONS FACTS AND FIGURES

Phone: (310) 243-3300. **Email:** info@csudh.edu. **Website:** http://www.csudh.edu. **Application deadlines for fall 2011:** Regular decision: Rolling. Early decision: Not offered. Early action: Not offered. Admission cannot be deferred. **Application fee:** $55. **To apply online, go to:** http://www.csumentor.edu/AdmissionApp/. **Admissions requirements/recommendations:** High school units required (recommended): English: 4 (4); Mathematics: 3 (3); Science: 2 (2); Foreign language: 2 (2); Social studies: 2 (2); History: 1 (2); Academic electives: 1 (1); Total units: 15 (15). Tests: The college uses SAT or ACT scores in admissions decisions. Either SAT or ACT required. For admission to the fall 2011 entering class, the school will accept: ACT with or without writing accepted. Campus visit: Recommended. Admissions interview: Neither required nor recommended. Off-campus interview: Not available. **Factors that count in admissions decisions:** *Academic:* Secondary school record: Not Considered. Class rank: Not Considered. Letters of recommendation: Not Considered. Standardized test scores: Considered. Essay: Not Considered. *Nonacademic:* Interview: Not Considered.

Extracurricular activities: Not Considered. Talent/ability: Not Considered. Character/personal qualities: Not Considered. Alumni/ae relationship: Not Considered. Geographical residence: Not Considered. State residency: Not Considered. Religious affiliation/commitment: Not Considered. Minority status: Not Considered. Volunteer work: Not Considered. Work experience: Not Considered. **Other schools with the greatest overlap in applicants:** California State Polytechnic University–Pomona; California State University–Fullerton; California State University–Long Beach; California State University–Los Angeles; California State University–Northridge. **Admissions statistics for the fall 2009 entering class:** Total applicants: 6,790. Total accepted: 5,737. Freshmen enrolled: 1,135; 1% were from out of state. Overall acceptance rate: 84%. **Average high school grade point average:** 3.0. **First-year students who submitted SAT scores:** 73%. Scores (25/75 percentile): Critical Reading: 370-460, Math: 360-470, Combined: 730-930. **First-year students submitting ACT scores:** 24%. Scores (25/75 percentile): English: 13-19, Math: 15-18, Composite: 15-19.

ACADEMICS

Year founded: 1960. **Academic calendar:** Semester. **Degrees offered:** bachelor's, post-bachelor's certificate, master's, post-master's certificate. **Most popular majors:** 23% business, management, marketing, and related support services, 14% liberal arts and sciences studies, and humanities, 13% health professions and related clinical sciences, 9% social sciences, 7% psychology. **Major fields of study:** area, ethnic, cultural, and gender studies; biological and biomedical sciences; business, management, marketing, and related support services; communication, journalism, and related programs; computer and information sciences and support services; education; engineering technologies/technicians; English language and literature/letters; foreign languages, literatures, and linguistics; health professions and related clinical sciences; liberal arts and sciences studies, and humanities; mathematics and statistics; multi/interdisciplinary studies; natural resources and conservation; parks, recreation, leisure, and fitness studies; philosophy and religious studies; physical sciences; psychology; public administration and social service professions; security and protective services; social sciences; visual and performing arts. **Areas of required coursework:** arts/fine arts, humanities, mathematics, English (including composition), philosophy, sciences (biological or physical), history, social science, other. **Preprofessional programs:** pre-law, pre-dentistry, pre-medicine, pre-veterinary science, pre-optometry, pre-pharmacy, other. **Special academic programs (% participation):** accelerated program, cross-registration (.7%), distance learning (10.2%), double major (2.7%), dual enrollment (0%), external degree program (.2%), honors program, internships, student-designed major (.1%), study abroad, teacher certificate program (21.5%), weekend college (0%). **Teacher certification offered in:** special education, elementary, adult education, secondary, bilingual/bicultural. **Reserve Officers Training Corps (ROTC):** Army ROTC: Offered on campus; Air Force ROTC: Offered at cooperating institution (University of California–Los Angeles). **Faculty and instruction (2009-2010):** Total instructional faculty: 318 full-time, 392 part-time (46% men; 54% women; 17% minorities). Full-time faculty with Ph.D. or other terminal degree: 88%. Student/faculty ratio: 23/1. Classes of fewer than 20 students: 20%; of 20 to 49 students: 62%; of 50 or more students: 18%. **Advanced Placement and International Baccalaureate credit:** AP tests may be used for: Credit and/or placement. Scores accepted: 3, 4, 5. **Freshmen returning for sophomore year:** 63%. **Graduation rates:** Four-year: 5%; five-year: 25%; six-year: 33%.

COSTS AND FINANCIAL AID

Financial aid office: (310) 243-3691. **Expenses (2009-2010):** Tuition and fees 2009-2010: $4,645 in state, $13,573 out of state; room/board: $9,970. Estimated books and supplies: $1,300; transportation: $963; personal expenses: $2,700. **Financial aid:** Priority filing date for institution's financial aid form: March 2. In 2009-2010, 69% of undergraduates applied for financial aid. Of those, 66% were determined to have financial need; 2% had their need fully met. Average financial aid package (proportion receiving): $5,457 (63%). Average amount of gift aid, such as scholarships or grants (proportion receiving): $4,310 (52%). Average amount of self-help aid, such as work study or loans (proportion receiving): $1,957 (2%). Average need-based loan (excluding PLUS or other private loans): $2,401. Among students who received need-based aid, the average percentage of need met: 34%. Among students who received aid based on merit, the average award (and the proportion receiving): $3,165 (2%). The average athletic scholarship (and the proportion receiving): $2,966 (0%). Average amount of debt of borrowers graduating in 2009: $7,946. Proportion who borrowed: 56%.

CAMPUS LIFE AND EXTRACURRICULAR ACTIVITIES

Campus housing available (% using): apartments for married students (0%), apartment for single students (95%), special housing for disabled students (5%). Students who live in college-owned, operated, or affiliated housing: 5%. **Student employment:** During the 2009-2010 academic year, 9% of undergraduates worked on campus. Average per-year earnings: $5,040. **Clubs and organizations:** Number of student organizations: 70. Activities include: choral groups, concert band, dance, drama/theater, jazz band, literary magazine, music ensembles, musical theater, radio station, student government, student newspaper, television station. Number of fraternities: 8; sororities: 8. Proportion of men in fraternities: 1%; of women in sororities: 1%. Average proportion of students who stay on campus on weekends: 85%. **Sports program (2009-2010):** Member of NCAA II. **Men's intercollegiate varsity sports:** baseball, basketball, golf, soccer. **Women's intercollegiate varsity sports:** basketball, cross country, soccer, softball, track and field (outdoor), volleyball.

SERVICES AND FACILITIES

Basic services: nonremedial tutoring, women's center, placement service, day care, health service, health insurance. **Remedial assistance:** reading, math, writing, study skills. **Counseling services:** minority student, career, personal, veteran student, older student, psychological. **For learning-disabled students:** School does not offer a structured program with separate admission and additional fees. Total undergraduates in learning-disabled program or receiving services: 284. Services include: remedial math, remedial English, reading machines, tape recorders, diagnostic testing service, note-taking services, learning center, readers, extended time for tests, tutors, priority registration, priority seating, texts on tape, other testing accommodations. **Library:** Number of titles: 442,893; number of current serial subscriptions: 673. **Information technology resources:** Students are not required to lease or own a computer. Number of campus computers available to all students: 217. School has a wireless network. Approximate number of users that can be accommodated: 5,000. Proportion of college-owned housing units wired for high-speed internet access: 0%. **Campus safety:** Security services offered: 24-hour foot-and-vehicle patrols, late-night transport/escort service, 24-hour emergency telephones, lighted pathways/sidewalks, controlled dormitory access (key, security card, etc).

TRANSFER AND INTERNATIONAL STUDENTS

Transfer students: May apply for admission for the following academic terms: Fall, Spring, Summer. Applicants need a minimum number of credits to apply. For fall 2009: Transfer applications received: 5,379. Transfer applicants offered admission: 5,055. Transfer applicants enrolled: 2,494. **International students:** Number of foreign undergraduates: 208 (2% of student body). Number of countries represented: 38. Minimum TOEFL score required: 550 (paper); 80 (computer).

California State University–East Bay

- **Address:** 25800 Carlos Bee Boulevard, Hayward, CA 94542
- **Website:** http://www.csueastbay.edu
- **Public**
- **Enrollment:** 9,493 full-time; 1,836 part-time

KEY STATS

✔ **U.S News College Ranking:** second tier, Regional Universities (West)
✔ **SAT Score (25th/75th percentile):** 800-1030
✔ **Tuition:** 2010-2011: $4,872 in state, $13,800 out of state

Selectivity: Less selective	**Room/board:** N/A
Acceptance rate: 73%	**Average debt:** $14,643
Student/faculty ratio: N/A	**Proportion who borrowed:** 34%

UNDERGRADUATE STUDENT BODY STATS

2009-2010 enrollment: 9,493 full-time; 1,836 part-time. Men: 40%; women: 60%. **Ethnic makeup:** African American: 12%; Asian American: 26%; Hispanic: 17%; White: 38%; International: 7%.

ADMISSIONS FACTS AND FIGURES

Phone: (510) 885-2784. **Email:** admissions@csueastbay.edu. **Website:** http://www.csueastbay.edu. **Application deadlines for fall 2011:** Regular decision: November 30. Early decision: Not offered. Early action: Not offered. Admission cannot be deferred. **Application fee:** $55. **To apply online, go to:** http://www.csumentor.edu. **Admissions requirements/recom-**

mendations: High school units required (recommended): English: 4 (4); Mathematics: 3 (4); Science: 2 (2); Foreign language: 2 (2); Social studies: 0 (0); History: 2 (2); Academic electives: 1 (0); Total units: 15 (15). Tests: The college uses SAT or ACT scores in admissions decisions. Neither SAT nor ACT required. For admission to the fall 2011 entering class, the school will accept: ACT with or without writing accepted. Campus visit: Recommended. Admissions interview: Neither required nor recommended. Off-campus interview: Not available. **Factors that count in admissions decisions:** *Academic:* Secondary school record: Very Important. Class rank: Not Considered. Letters of recommendation: Considered. Standardized test scores: Very Important. Essay: Not Considered. *Nonacademic:* Interview: Not Considered. Extracurricular activities: Not Considered. Talent/ability: Considered. Character/personal qualities: Not Considered. Alumni/ae relationship: Not Considered. Geographical residence: Not Considered. State residency: Considered. Religious affiliation/commitment: Not Considered. Minority status: Not Considered. Volunteer work: Not Considered. Work experience: Not Considered. **Other schools with the greatest overlap in applicants:** California State University–Sacramento; San Francisco State University; San Jose State University. **Admissions statistics for the fall 2009 entering class:** Total applicants: 8,722. Total accepted: 6,388. Freshmen enrolled: 1,445; 1% were from out of state. Overall acceptance rate: 73%. **First-year students who submitted SAT scores:** 88%. Scores (25/75 percentile): Critical Reading: 400-510, Math: 400-520, Combined: 800-1030. **First-year students submitting ACT scores:** 21%. Scores (25/75 percentile): English: 15-21, Math: 16-22, Composite: 16-22.

ACADEMICS

Year founded: 1957. **Academic calendar:** Quarter. **Degrees offered:** certificate, bachelor's, post-bachelor's certificate, master's. **Most popular majors:** 28% business administration and management, 9% liberal arts and sciences/liberal studies, 6% psychology, 6% sociology, 5% health services/allied health/health sciences. **Major fields of study:** area, ethnic, cultural, and gender studies; biological and biomedical sciences; business, management, marketing, and related support services; communication, journalism, and related programs; computer and information sciences and support services; English language and literature/letters; family and consumer sciences/human sciences; foreign languages, literatures, and linguistics; health professions and related clinical sciences; history; liberal arts and sciences studies, and humanities; mathematics and statistics; natural resources and conservation; parks, recreation, leisure, and fitness studies; philosophy and religious studies; physical sciences; psychology; security and protective services; social sciences; visual and performing arts. **Areas of required coursework:** arts/fine arts, humanities, mathematics, English (including composition), sciences (biological or physical), history, social science. **Pre-professional programs:** pre-law, pre-dentistry, pre-medicine, pre-veterinary science, pre-optometry, pre-pharmacy. **Special academic programs (% participation):** cooperative (work-study plan) program (3%), cross-registration, distance learning, double major (2%), exchange student program (domestic), independent study (9%), internships (4%), student-designed major (1%), study abroad. **Teacher certification offered in:** special education, elementary, middle/junior high, secondary, bilingual/bicultural. **Cooperative education programs:** art, business, computer science, health professions, humanities, natural science, social/behavioral science. **Faculty and instruction (2009-2010):** Total instructional faculty: 366 full-time, 454 part-time (45% men; 55% women; 29% minorities). Classes of fewer than 20 students: 17%; of 20 to 49 students: 63%; of 50 or more students: 20%. **Advanced Placement and International Baccalaureate credit:** AP tests may be used for: Placement only. Scores accepted: 3, 4, 5. International Baccalaureate exams may be used for: Placement only. **Freshmen returning for sophomore year:** 75%. **Graduation rates:** Four-year: 17%; five-year: 39%; six-year: 44%.

COSTS AND FINANCIAL AID

Financial aid office: (510) 885-2784. **Expenses (2010-2011):** Tuition and fees 2010-2011: $4,872 in state, $13,800 out of state. Estimated books and supplies: $1,734; transportation: $1,182; personal expenses: $3,120. **Financial aid:** Priority filing date for institution's financial aid form: March 2. In 2009-2010, 53% of undergraduates applied for financial aid. Of those, 51% were determined to have financial need; 2% had their need fully met. Average financial aid package (proportion receiving): $10,000 (49%). Average amount of gift aid, such as scholarships or grants (proportion receiving): $8,594 (40%). Average amount of self-help aid, such as work study or loans (proportion receiving): $7,039 (31%). Average need-based loan (excluding PLUS or other private loans): $7,120. Among students who received need-based aid, the average percentage of need met: 53%. Average amount of debt of borrowers graduating in 2009: $14,643. Proportion who borrowed: 34%.

CAMPUS LIFE AND EXTRACURRICULAR ACTIVITIES

Campus housing available (% using): coed dorms (80%), apartment for single students (5%), special housing for international students (15%). **Clubs and organizations:** Number of student organizations: 89. Activities include: choral groups, concert band, dance, drama/theater, jazz band, literary magazine, music ensembles, musical theater, opera, pep band, radio station, student government, student newspaper, symphony orchestra, television station. Number of fraternities: 9; sororities: 8. Average proportion of students who stay on campus on weekends: 2%. **Sports program (2009-2010):** Member of NCAA III. *Men's intercollegiate varsity sports:* baseball, basketball, cross country, soccer, track and field (outdoor). *Women's intercollegiate varsity sports:* basketball, cross country, soccer, softball, swimming, track and field (outdoor), water polo.

SERVICES AND FACILITIES

Basic services: nonremedial tutoring, placement service, day care, health service, health insurance. **Remedial assistance:** reading, math, writing, study skills. **Counseling services:** career, personal, veteran student, academic, psychological. **For learning-disabled students:** School does not offer a structured program with separate admission and additional fees. Services include: remedial math, remedial English, tape recorders, untimed tests, note-taking services, learning center, readers, extended time for tests, tutors, priority seating. **Library:** Number of titles: 908,577; number of current serial subscriptions: 2,210. **Information technology resources:** Students are not required to lease or own a computer. School has a wireless network. Proportion of college-owned housing units wired for high-speed internet access: 100%. **Campus safety:** Security services offered: 24-hour foot-and-vehicle patrols, late-night transport/escort service, 24-hour emergency telephones, lighted pathways/sidewalks, controlled dormitory access (key, security card, etc).

TRANSFER AND INTERNATIONAL STUDENTS

Transfer students: May apply for admission for the following academic terms: Fall, Winter, Spring. Applicants need a minimum number of credits to apply. For fall 2009: Transfer applications received: 6,290. Transfer applicants offered admission: 1,632. Transfer applicants enrolled: 2,000. **International students:** Number of foreign undergraduates: 757 (7% of student body). Minimum TOEFL score required: 525 (paper); 197 (computer).

California State University–Fresno

- **Address:** 5150 N. Maple, Fresno, CA 93740
- **Website:** http://www.csufresno.edu
- **Public**
- **Enrollment:** 15,420 full-time; 2,796 part-time

KEY STATS

✔ **U.S News College Ranking:** 44, Regional Universities (West)
✔ **SAT Score (25th/75th percentile):** 820-1060
✔ **Tuition:** 2010-2011: $4,672 in state, $15,832 out of state

Selectivity: Selective	Room/board: $7,846
Acceptance rate: 72%	Average debt: $10,406
Student/faculty ratio: 20/1	Proportion who borrowed: 65%

UNDERGRADUATE STUDENT BODY STATS

2009-2010 enrollment: 15,420 full-time; 2,796 part-time. Men: 43%; women: 57%. **Ethnic makeup:** African American: 6%; American-Indian: 1%; Asian American: 16%; Hispanic: 35%; White: 42%; International: 1%.

ADMISSIONS FACTS AND FIGURES

Phone: (559) 278-2261. **Email:** vivian_franco@csufresno.edu. **Website:** http://www.csufresno.edu. **Application deadlines for fall 2011:** Regular decision: January 15; decision sent by March 15. Early decision: Not offered. Early action: Not offered. Admission cannot be deferred. **Application fee:** $55. **To apply online, go to:** http://www.csumentor.edu/admissionapp/undergrad_apply.asp. **Admissions requirements/recommendations:** High school units required (recommended): English: 4 (0); Mathematics: 3 (1); Science: 2 (1); Foreign language: 2 (0); Social studies: 1 (0); History: 1 (0); Academic electives: 1 (1); Total units: 15 (3). Tests: The college uses SAT or ACT scores in admissions decisions. Either SAT or ACT required. For admission to the fall 2011 entering class, the school will accept: ACT with or without writing accepted. Campus visit: Recommended. Admissions interview: Neither required nor recommended. Off-campus interview:

Not available. **Factors that count in admissions decisions:** *Academic:* Secondary school record: Very Important. Class rank: Very Important. Letters of recommendation: Not Considered. Standardized test scores: Very Important. Essay: Not Considered. *Nonacademic:* Interview: Not Considered. Extracurricular activities: Not Considered. Talent/ability: Not Considered. Character/personal qualities: Not Considered. Alumni/ae relationship: Not Considered. Geographical residence: Considered. State residency: Important. Religious affiliation/commitment: Not Considered. Minority status: Not Considered. Volunteer work: Not Considered. Work experience: Not Considered. **Other schools with the greatest overlap in applicants:** California State University–Long Beach; California State University–Sacramento; San Diego State University; San Francisco State University; San Jose State University. **Admissions statistics for the fall 2009 entering class:** Total applicants: 14,025. Total accepted: 10,090. Freshmen enrolled: 2,765; Overall acceptance rate: 72%. **Size of waiting list:** 400 applicants; enrolled from waiting list: 30. **Credentials of fall 2009 freshmen:** 15% ranked in the top 10 percent of their high school class; 80% were in the top 25 percent; 99% were in the top half. (Proportion submitting class standing: 99%.) **Average high school grade point average:** 3.3. **First-year students who submitted SAT scores:** 90%. Scores (25/75 percentile): Critical Reading: 400-520, Math: 420-540, Combined: 820-1060. **First-year students submitting ACT scores:** 29%. Scores (25/75 percentile): English: 15-22, Math: 17-23, Composite: 17-22.

ACADEMICS

Year founded: 1911. **Academic calendar:** Semester. **Degrees offered:** certificate, bachelor's, post-bachelor's certificate, master's, post-master's certificate, doctorate. **Most popular majors:** 17% business, management, marketing, and related support services; 11% health professions and related clinical sciences, 11% social sciences, 10% liberal arts and sciences studies, and humanities, 6% psychology. **Major fields of study:** agriculture, agriculture operations, and related sciences; area, ethnic, cultural, and gender studies; biological and biomedical sciences; business, management, marketing, and related support services; computer and information sciences and support services; education; engineering; English language and literature/letters; family and consumer sciences/human sciences; foreign languages, literatures, and linguistics; health professions and related clinical sciences; history; liberal arts and sciences studies, and humanities; mathematics and statistics; multi/interdisciplinary studies; parks, recreation, leisure, and fitness studies; philosophy and religious studies; physical sciences; psychology; public administration and social service professions; social sciences; visual and performing arts. **Areas of required coursework:** arts/fine arts, humanities, computer literacy, mathematics, English (including composition), philosophy, foreign languages, sciences (biological or physical), history, social science, other. **Pre-professional programs:** pre-law, pre-dentistry, pre-medicine, pre-veterinary science, pre-optometry, pre-pharmacy, other. **Special academic programs (% participation):** accelerated program, cooperative (work-study plan) program (5.8%), cross-registration, distance learning (64%), double major (2.2%), dual enrollment, English as a Second Language (ESL) (1%), exchange student program (domestic), honors program (1.4%), independent study (13%), internships (8%), student-designed major (1%), study abroad, teacher certificate program (8.4%), other. **Teacher certification offered in:** early childhood, special education, elementary, middle/junior high, secondary, bilingual/bicultural. **Cooperative education programs:** agriculture, business, education, engineering, health professions, social/behavioral science, other. **Reserve Officers Training Corps (ROTC):** Army ROTC: Offered on campus; Air Force ROTC: Offered on campus. **Faculty and instruction (2009-2010):** Total instructional faculty: 658 full-time, 461 part-time (54% men; 46% women; 30% minorities). Full-time faculty with Ph.D. or other terminal degree: 85%. Student/faculty ratio: 20/1. Classes of fewer than 20 students: 16%; of 20 to 49 students: 73%; of 50 or more students: 10%. **Advanced Placement and International Baccalaureate credit:** AP tests may be used for: Credit and/or placement. Scores accepted: 3, 4, 5. International Baccalaureate exams may be used for: Credit only. **Freshmen returning for sophomore year:** 81%. **Graduation rates:** Four-year: 14%; five-year: 37%; six-year: 48%. **Graduate study:** 18% of students pursue further study within one year.

COSTS AND FINANCIAL AID

Financial aid office: (559) 278-2182. **Expenses (2010-2011):** Tuition and fees 2010-2011: $4,672 in state, $15,832 out of state; room/board: $7,846. Estimated books and supplies: $1,224; transportation: $754; personal expenses: $2,052. **Financial aid:** Priority filing date for institution's financial aid form: March 1; deadline: March 3. In 2009-2010, 72% of undergraduates applied for financial aid. Of those, 65% were determined to have financial need; 13% had their need fully met. Average financial aid package

(proportion receiving): $10,984 (62%). Average amount of gift aid, such as scholarships or grants (proportion receiving): N/A (51%). Average amount of self-help aid, such as work study or loans (proportion receiving): $3,875 (52%). Average need-based loan (excluding PLUS or other private loans): $4,086. Among students who received need-based aid, the average percentage of need met: 72%. Among students who received aid based on merit, the average award (and the proportion receiving): $3,310 (1%). The average athletic scholarship (and the proportion receiving): $11,673 (2%). Average amount of debt of borrowers graduating in 2009: $10,406. Proportion who borrowed: 65%.

CAMPUS LIFE AND EXTRACURRICULAR ACTIVITIES

Campus housing available (% using): coed dorms (31%), women's dorms (21%), men's dorms (18%), sorority housing (13%), fraternity housing (13%), special housing for disabled students (3%), special housing for international students (1%). Students who live in college-owned, operated, or affiliated housing: 6%. **Clubs and organizations:** Number of student organizations: 250. Activities include: campus ministries, choral groups, concert band, dance, drama/theater, international student organization, jazz band, literary magazine, marching band, music ensembles, musical theater, pep band, radio station, student government, student newspaper, symphony orchestra, television station, yearbook. Number of fraternities: 21; sororities: 20. Proportion of men in fraternities: 4%; of women in sororities: 3%. Average proportion of students who stay on campus on weekends: 70%. **Sports program (2009-2010):** Member of NCAA I.

SERVICES AND FACILITIES

Basic services: nonremedial tutoring, women's center, placement service, day care, health service, health insurance, other. **Remedial assistance:** reading, math, writing, study skills, other. **Counseling services:** minority student, career, military, personal, veteran student, academic, older student, psychological, birth control, other. **For learning-disabled students:** School does not offer a structured program with separate admission and additional fees. Services include: remedial math, remedial English, reading machines, tape recorders, diagnostic testing service, note-taking services, oral tests, learning center, readers, extended time for tests, tutors, early syllabus, priority registration, priority seating, substitution of courses, texts on tape, typist/scribe, exams on tape or computer, other testing accommodations, other. **Library:** Number of titles: 1,087,645; number of current serial subscriptions: 19,552. **Information technology resources:** Students are required to lease or own a computer. Number of campus computers available to all students: 1,316. School has a wireless network. Approximate number of users that can be accommodated: 15,000. Proportion of college-owned housing units wired for high-speed internet access: 100%. **Campus safety:** Security services offered: 24-hour foot-and-vehicle patrols, 24-hour emergency telephones, lighted pathways/sidewalks, student patrols, controlled dormitory access (key, security card, etc).

TRANSFER AND INTERNATIONAL STUDENTS

Transfer students: May apply for admission for the following academic terms: Fall, Spring. Applicants need a minimum number of credits to apply. For fall 2009: Transfer applications received: 4,105. Transfer applicants offered admission: 2,452. Transfer applicants enrolled: 1,571. **International students:** Number of foreign undergraduates: 264 (1% of student body). Number of countries represented: 49. Minimum TOEFL score required: 500 (paper); 173 (computer). Average TOEFL score: 563 (paper).

California State University–Fullerton

- **Address:** 800 N. State College Boulevard, Fullerton, CA 92834
- **Website:** http://www.fullerton.edu
- **Public**
- **Enrollment:** 22,962 full-time; 7,775 part-time

KEY STATS
✔ **U.S News College Ranking:** 37, Regional Universities (West)
✔ **SAT Score (25th/75th percentile):** 890-1110
✔ **Tuition:** 2010-2011: $4,662 in state, $15,822 out of state

Selectivity: Selective	**Room/board:** $9,632
Acceptance rate: 55%	**Average debt:** $14,706
Student/faculty ratio: 26/1	**Proportion who borrowed:** 39%

UNDERGRADUATE STUDENT BODY STATS

2009-2010 enrollment: 22,962 full-time; 7,775 part-time. Men: 42%; women: 58%. **Ethnic makeup:** African American: 3%; Asian American: 22%; Hispanic: 31%; White: 40%; International: 3%.

ADMISSIONS FACTS AND FIGURES

Phone: (657) 278-2371. **Email:** admissions@fullerton.edu. **Website:** http://www.fullerton.edu. **Application deadlines for fall 2011:** Regular decision: November 30. Early decision: Not offered. Early action: Not offered. Admission cannot be deferred. **Application fee:** $55. **To apply online, go to:** http://www.calstate.edu. **Admissions requirements/recommendations:** High school units required (recommended): English: 4 (4); Mathematics: 3 (3); Science: 2 (2); Foreign language: 2 (3); Social studies: 1 (1); History: 1 (1); Academic electives: 1 (1); Total units: 15 (16). Tests: The college uses SAT or ACT scores in admissions decisions. SAT required. For admission to the fall 2011 entering class, the school will accept: ACT with writing recommended. Campus visit: Recommended. Admissions interview: Neither required nor recommended. Off-campus interview: Not available. **Factors that count in admissions decisions:** *Academic:* Secondary school record: Not Considered. Class rank: Not Considered. Letters of recommendation: Not Considered. Standardized test scores: Very Important. Essay: Not Considered. *Nonacademic:* Interview: Not Considered. Extracurricular activities: Not Considered. Talent/ability: Not Considered. Character/personal qualities: Not Considered. Alumni/ae relationship: Not Considered. Geographical residence: Important. State residency: Very Important. Religious affiliation/commitment: Not Considered. Minority status: Not Considered. Volunteer work: Not Considered. Work experience: Not Considered. **Other schools with the greatest overlap in applicants:** California State Polytechnic University–Pomona; California State University–Long Beach; University of California–Irvine; University of California–Los Angeles; University of Southern California. **Admissions statistics for the fall 2009 entering class:** Total applicants: 30,612. Total accepted: 16,865. Freshmen enrolled: 4,065; 1% were from out of state. Overall acceptance rate: 55%. **Credentials of fall 2009 freshmen:** 17% ranked in the top 10 percent of their high school class; 53% were in the top 25 percent; 90% were in the top half. (Proportion submitting class standing: 56%.) **Average high school grade point average:** 3.3. **First-year students who submitted SAT scores:** 95%. Scores (25/75 percentile): Critical Reading: 440-540, Math: 450-570, Combined: 890-1110. **First-year students submitting ACT scores:** 28%. Scores (25/75 percentile): English: 17-24, Math: 18-25, Composite: 18-23.

ACADEMICS

Year founded: 1957. **Academic calendar:** Semester. **Degrees offered:** bachelor's, post-bachelor's certificate, master's, post-master's certificate. **Most popular majors:** 26% business, management, marketing, and related support services, 14% communication, journalism, and related programs, 6% education, 6% social sciences, 6% visual and performing arts. **Major fields of study:** area, ethnic, cultural, and gender studies; biological and biomedical sciences; business, management, marketing, and related support services; communication, journalism, and related programs; computer and information sciences and support services; education; engineering; English language and literature/letters; foreign languages, literatures, and linguistics; health professions and related clinical sciences; history; liberal arts and sciences studies, and humanities; mathematics and statistics; multi/interdisciplinary studies; parks, recreation, leisure, and fitness studies; philosophy and religious studies; physical sciences; psychology; public administration and social service professions; security and protective services; social sciences; visual and performing arts. **Areas of required coursework:** arts/fine arts, humanities, mathematics, English (including composition), philosophy, sciences (biological or physical), history, social science. **Special academic programs:** cooperative (work-study plan) program, distance learning, double major, honors program, independent study, internships, study abroad, teacher certificate program, other. **Teacher certification offered in:** early childhood, special education, elementary, middle/junior high, secondary, bilingual/bicultural. **Cooperative education programs:** art, business, computer science, engineering, natural science. **Reserve Officers Training Corps (ROTC):** Army ROTC: Offered on campus. **Faculty and instruction (2009-2010):** Total instructional faculty: 867 full-time, 748 part-time (51% men; 49% women; 26% minorities). Full-time faculty with Ph.D. or other terminal degree: 82%. Student/faculty ratio: 26/1. Classes of fewer than 20 students: 18%; of 20 to 49 students: 69%; of 50 or more students: 13%. **Advanced Placement and International Baccalaureate credit:** AP tests may be used for: Credit and/or placement. Scores accepted: 3, 4, 5. International Baccalaureate exams may be used for: Credit and/or placement. **Freshmen**

returning for sophomore year: 79%. **Graduation rates:** Four-year: 16%; five-year: 41%; six-year: 50%.

COSTS AND FINANCIAL AID

Financial aid office: (714) 278-3128. **Expenses (2010-2011):** Tuition and fees 2010-2011: $4,662 in state, $15,822 out of state; room/board: $9,632. Estimated books and supplies: $1,620; transportation: $1,100; personal expenses: $2,800. **Financial aid:** Priority filing date for institution's financial aid form: March 2. In 2009-2010, 64% of undergraduates applied for financial aid. Of those, 48% were determined to have financial need; 51% had their need fully met. Average financial aid package (proportion receiving): $12,421 (53%). Average amount of gift aid, such as scholarships or grants (proportion receiving): $7,123 (48%). Average amount of self-help aid, such as work study or loans (proportion receiving): $4,056 (51%). Average need-based loan (excluding PLUS or other private loans): $4,124. Among students who received need-based aid, the average percentage of need met: 51%. Among students who received aid based on merit, the average award (and the proportion receiving): $6,277 (8%). The average athletic scholarship (and the proportion receiving): $7,222 (1%). Average amount of debt of borrowers graduating in 2009: $14,706. Proportion who borrowed: 39%.

CAMPUS LIFE AND EXTRACURRICULAR ACTIVITIES

Campus housing available (% using): sorority housing (2%), fraternity housing (2%), apartment for single students (96%). Students who live in college-owned, operated, or affiliated housing: 3%. Average per-year earnings: $6,000. **Clubs and organizations:** Number of student organizations: 297. Activities include: choral groups, concert band, dance, drama/theater, international student organization, jazz band, model UN, music ensembles, musical theater, radio station, student government, student newspaper, symphony orchestra. Number of fraternities: 18; sororities: 9. Proportion of men in fraternities: 9%; of women in sororities: 8%. Average proportion of students who stay on campus on weekends: 2%. **Sports program (2009-2010):** Member of NCAA I. *Men's intercollegiate varsity sports:* baseball, basketball, cross country, golf, soccer, track and field (outdoor), wrestling. *Women's intercollegiate varsity sports:* basketball, cross country, golf, gymnastics, soccer, softball, tennis, track and field (outdoor), volleyball.

SERVICES AND FACILITIES

Basic services: nonremedial tutoring, women's center, placement service, day care, health service, health insurance. **Remedial assistance:** reading, math, writing, study skills. **Counseling services:** minority student, career, military, personal, veteran student, academic, older student, psychological, birth control. **For learning-disabled students:** School does not offer a structured program with separate admission and additional fees. Services include: remedial math, remedial English, tape recorders, diagnostic testing service, untimed tests, note-taking services, learning center, readers, extended time for tests, tutors, other testing accommodations. **Library:** Number of titles: 1,282,517; number of current serial subscriptions: 11,383. **Information technology resources:** Students are not required to lease or own a computer. Number of campus computers available to all students: 2,000. School has a wireless network. Proportion of college-owned housing units wired for high-speed internet access: 100%. **Campus safety:** Security services offered: 24-hour foot-and-vehicle patrols, late-night transport/escort service, 24-hour emergency telephones, lighted pathways/sidewalks, student patrols, controlled dormitory access (key, security card, etc).

TRANSFER AND INTERNATIONAL STUDENTS

Transfer students: May apply for admission for the following academic terms: Fall, Spring. Applicants need a minimum number of credits to apply. For fall 2009: Transfer applications received: 13,041. Transfer applicants offered admission: 5,955. Transfer applicants enrolled: 3,800. **International students:** Number of foreign undergraduates: 1065 (3% of student body). Minimum TOEFL score required: 500 (paper); 173 (computer). Average TOEFL score: 563 (paper).

California State University–Long Beach

- **Address:** 1250 Bellflower Boulevard, Long Beach, CA 90840
- **Website:** http://www.csulb.edu
- **Public**
- **Enrollment:** 23,695 full-time; 5,531 part-time

KEY STATS

✔ **U.S News College Ranking:** 24, Regional Universities (West)

✔ **SAT Score (25th/75th percentile):** 900-1150

✔ **Tuition:** 2010-2011: $4,606 in state, $15,766 out of state

Selectivity: Selective	**Room/board:** $11,038
Acceptance rate: 32%	**Average debt:** $10,927
Student/faculty ratio: 21/1	**Proportion who borrowed:** 43%

UNDERGRADUATE STUDENT BODY STATS

2009-2010 enrollment: 23,695 full-time; 5,531 part-time. Men: 41%; women: 59%. **Ethnic makeup:** African American: 5%; American-Indian: 1%; Asian American: 24%; Hispanic: 29%; White: 38%; International: 4%.

ADMISSIONS FACTS AND FIGURES

Phone: (562) 985-5471. **Website:** http://www.csulb.edu. **Application deadlines for fall 2011:** Regular decision: November 30. Early decision: Not offered. Early action: Not offered. Admission cannot be deferred. **Application fee:** $55. **To apply online, go to:** http://www.csumentor.edu. **Admissions requirements/recommendations:** High school units required (recommended): English: 4 (4); Mathematics: 3 (3); Science: 2 (2); Foreign language: 2 (2); Social studies: 1 (1); History: 1 (1); Academic electives: 1 (1); Total units: 15 (15). Tests: The college uses SAT or ACT scores in admissions decisions. Either SAT or ACT required. For admission to the fall 2011 entering class, the school will accept: ACT with or without writing accepted. Campus visit: Neither required nor recommended. Admissions interview: Neither required nor recommended. Off-campus interview: Not available. **Factors that count in admissions decisions:** *Academic:* Secondary school record: Very Important. Class rank: Not Considered. Letters of recommendation: Considered. Standardized test scores: Very Important. Essay: Considered. *Nonacademic:* Interview: Not Considered. Extracurricular activities: Considered. Talent/ability: Important. Character/personal qualities: Considered. Alumni/ae relationship: Not Considered. Geographical residence: Very Important. State residency: Very Important. Religious affiliation/commitment: Not Considered. Minority status: Not Considered. Volunteer work: Considered. Work experience: Considered. **Other schools with the greatest overlap in applicants:** California State University–Fullerton; San Diego State University; University of California–Irvine; University of California–Riverside; University of California–Santa Barbara. **Admissions statistics for the fall 2009 entering class:** Total applicants: 45,771. Total accepted: 14,543. Freshmen enrolled: 3,551; 1% were from out of state. Overall acceptance rate: 32%. **Credentials of fall 2009 freshmen:** 84% ranked in the top 25 percent of their high school class; 100% were in the top half. (Proportion submitting class standing: 69%.) **Average high school grade point average:** 3.4. **First-year students who submitted SAT scores:** 95%. Scores (25/75 percentile): Critical Reading: 440-560, Math: 460-590, Combined: 900-1150. **First-year students submitting ACT scores:** 33%. Scores (25/75 percentile): English: 18-25, Math: 17-24, Composite: 18-24.

ACADEMICS

Year founded: 1949. **Academic calendar:** Semester. **Degrees offered:** bachelor's, post-bachelor's certificate, master's. **Most popular majors:** 6% psychology, 5% liberal arts and sciences/liberal studies, 5% speech and rhetorical studies, 5% trade and industrial teacher education, 5% finance. **Major fields of study:** area, ethnic, cultural, and gender studies; biological and biomedical sciences; business, management, marketing, and related support services; communication, journalism, and related programs; communications technologies/technicians and support services; computer and information sciences and support services; education; engineering; engineering technologies/technicians; English language and literature/letters; family and consumer sciences/human sciences; foreign languages, literatures, and linguistics; health professions and related clinical sciences; history; liberal arts and sciences studies, and humanities; mathematics and statistics; multi/interdisciplinary studies; natural resources and conservation; parks, recreation, leisure, and fitness studies; philosophy and religious studies; physical sciences; psychology; public administration and social service professions; security and protective services; social sciences; visual and performing arts.

Areas of required coursework: arts/fine arts, humanities, mathematics, English (including composition), sciences (biological or physical), history, social science. **Pre-professional programs:** pre-law, pre-dentistry, pre-medicine, pre-veterinary science, pre-optometry, pre-pharmacy. **Special academic programs:** accelerated program, cross-registration, distance learning, double major, dual enrollment, English as a Second Language (ESL), honors program, independent study, internships, student-designed major, study abroad, teacher certificate program. **Teacher certification offered in:** early childhood, special education, elementary, vo-tech, middle/junior high, adult education, secondary, bilingual/bicultural. **Cooperative education programs:** art, business, computer science, education, engineering, health professions, humanities, natural science, social/behavioral science, technologies, other. **Reserve Officers Training Corps (ROTC):** Army ROTC: Offered on campus. **Faculty and instruction (2009-2010):** Total instructional faculty: 1,021 full-time, 963 part-time (50% men; 50% women; 28% minorities). Full-time faculty with Ph.D. or other terminal degree: 85%. Student/faculty ratio: 21/1. Classes of fewer than 20 students: 23%; of 20 to 49 students: 66%; of 50 or more students: 12%. **Advanced Placement and International Baccalaureate credit:** AP tests may be used for: Credit and/or placement. Scores accepted: 3, 4, 5. International Baccalaureate exams may be used for: Credit and/or placement. **Freshmen returning for sophomore year:** 86%. **Graduation rates:** Four-year: 13%; five-year: 13%; six-year: 51%.

COSTS AND FINANCIAL AID

Financial aid office: (562) 985-8403. **Expenses (2010-2011):** Tuition and fees 2010-2011: $4,606 in state, $15,766 out of state; room/board: $11,038. Estimated books and supplies: $1,620; transportation: $1,140; personal expenses: $2,067. **Financial aid:** Priority filing date for institution's financial aid form: March 2. In 2009-2010, 76% of undergraduates applied for financial aid. Of those, 72% were determined to have financial need; 49% had their need fully met. Average financial aid package (proportion receiving): $12,627 (61%). Average amount of gift aid, such as scholarships or grants (proportion receiving): $5,697 (49%). Average amount of self-help aid, such as work study or loans (proportion receiving): $3,573 (58%). Average need-based loan (excluding PLUS or other private loans): $3,455. Among students who received need-based aid, the average percentage of need met: 83%. Among students who received aid based on merit, the average award (and the proportion receiving): $2,247 (6%). The average athletic scholarship (and the proportion receiving): $6,074 (1%). Average amount of debt of borrowers graduating in 2009: $10,927. Proportion who borrowed: 43%.

CAMPUS LIFE AND EXTRACURRICULAR ACTIVITIES

Campus housing available: coed dorms, special housing for international students. Students who live in college-owned, operated, or affiliated housing: 7%. **Clubs and organizations:** Number of student organizations: 235. Activities include: choral groups, concert band, dance, drama/theater, jazz band, literary magazine, music ensembles, musical theater, opera, radio station, student government, student newspaper, student film society, symphony orchestra, television station, yearbook. Number of fraternities: 17; sororities: 14. Proportion of men in fraternities: 4%; of women in sororities: 4%. Average proportion of students who stay on campus on weekends: 50%. **Sports program (2009-2010):** Member of NCAA I.

SERVICES AND FACILITIES

Basic services: nonremedial tutoring, women's center, placement service, day care, health service, health insurance. **Remedial assistance:** reading, math, writing, study skills. **Counseling services:** career, personal, veteran student, academic, older student, psychological, birth control, religious. **For learning-disabled students:** School does not offer a structured program with separate admission and additional fees. Services include: remedial math, remedial English, reading machines, tape recorders, diagnostic testing service, untimed tests, note-taking services, oral tests, learning center, readers, extended time for tests, tutors, priority registration, priority seating, texts on tape, other testing accommodations, other. **Library:** Number of titles: 1,749,431; number of current serial subscriptions: 35,860. **Information technology resources:** Students are not required to lease or own a computer. Number of campus computers available to all students: 2,026. School does not have a wireless network. **Campus safety:** Security services offered: 24-hour foot-and-vehicle patrols, late-night transport/escort service, 24-hour emergency telephones, lighted pathways/sidewalks, controlled dormitory access (key, security card, etc).

TRANSFER AND INTERNATIONAL STUDENTS

Transfer students: May apply for admission for the following academic terms: Fall, Spring. Applicants need a minimum number of credits to apply. For fall 2009: Transfer applications received: 14,691. Transfer applicants offered admission: 3,651. Transfer applicants enrolled: 2,077. **International students:** Number of foreign undergraduates: 1252 (4% of student body). Minimum TOEFL score required: 500 (paper); 173 (computer).

California State University–Los Angeles

■ **Address:** 5151 State University Drive, Los Angeles, CA 90032
■ **Website:** http://www.calstatela.edu
■ **Public**
■ **Enrollment:** 11,751 full-time; 3,983 part-time

KEY STATS

✔ **U.S News College Ranking:** second tier, Regional Universities (West)
✔ **SAT Score (25th/75th percentile):** 730-990
✔ **Tuition:** 2010-2011: $4,701 in state, $15,861 out of state

Selectivity: Less selective	**Room/board:** $9,105
Acceptance rate: 68%	**Average debt:** N/A
Student/faculty ratio: 22/1	**Proportion who borrowed:** N/A

UNDERGRADUATE STUDENT BODY STATS

2009-2010 enrollment: 11,751 full-time; 3,983 part-time. Men: 40%; women: 60%. **Ethnic makeup:** African American: 7%; Asian American: 18%; Hispanic: 49%; White: 20%; International: 6%.

ADMISSIONS FACTS AND FIGURES

Phone: (323) 343-3901. **Email:** admission@calstatela.edu. **Website:** http://www.calstatela.edu. **Application deadlines for fall 2011:** Regular decision: November 30. Early decision: Not offered. Early action: Not offered. Admission cannot be deferred. **Application fee:** $55. **To apply online, go to:** http://www.csumentor.edu. **Admissions requirements/recommendations:** High school units required (recommended): English: 4 (4); Mathematics: 3 (3); Science: 2 (2); Foreign language: 2 (2); Social studies: 1 (1); History: 1 (1); Academic electives: 1 (1); Total units: 15 (15). Tests: The college uses SAT or ACT scores in admissions decisions. Neither SAT nor ACT required. For admission to the fall 2011 entering class, the school will accept: ACT with or without writing accepted. Campus visit: Neither required nor recommended. Admissions interview: Neither required nor recommended. Off-campus interview: Not available. **Factors that count in admissions decisions:** *Academic:* Secondary school record: Very Important. Class rank: Not Considered. Letters of recommendation: Not Considered. Standardized test scores: Very Important. Essay: Not Considered. *Nonacademic:* Interview: Not Considered. Extracurricular activities: Not Considered. Talent/ability: Not Considered. Character/personal qualities: Not Considered. Alumni/ae relationship: Not Considered. Geographical residence: Not Considered. State residency: Important. Religious affiliation/commitment: Not Considered. Minority status: Not Considered. Volunteer work: Not Considered. Work experience: Not Considered. **Admissions statistics for the fall 2009 entering class:** Total applicants: 21,365. Total accepted: 14,536. Freshmen enrolled: 2,019; 3% were from out of state. Overall acceptance rate: 68%. **Credentials of fall 2009 freshmen:** 3% ranked in the top 25 percent of their high school class; 100% were in the top half. (Proportion submitting class standing: 93%.) **Average high school grade point average:** 3.1. **First-year students who submitted SAT scores:** 88%. Scores (25/75 percentile): Critical Reading: 350-500, Math: 380-490, Combined: 730-990. **First-year students submitting ACT scores:** 26%. Scores (25/75 percentile): English: 13-20, Math: 16-21, Composite: 15-20.

ACADEMICS

Year founded: 1947. **Academic calendar:** Quarter. **Degrees offered:** certificate, bachelor's, post-bachelor's certificate, master's, doctorate. **Most popular majors:** 25% business, management, marketing, and related support services, 8% health professions and related clinical sciences, 8% public administration and social service professions, 8% social sciences, 7% security and protective services. **Major fields of study:** area, ethnic, cultural, and gender studies; biological and biomedical sciences; business, management, marketing, and related support services; communication, journalism, and related programs; computer and information sciences and support services; education; engineering; engineering technologies/technicians; English language and literature/letters; family and consumer sciences/human sciences; foreign languages, literatures, and linguistics; health professions and related clinical sciences; history; liberal arts and sciences studies, and humanities; mathematics and statistics; multi/interdisciplinary studies; philosophy and religious studies; physical sciences; psychology; public administration and

social service professions; security and protective services; social sciences; visual and performing arts. **Areas of required coursework:** arts/fine arts, humanities, computer literacy, mathematics, English (including composition), philosophy, sciences (biological or physical), history, social science. **Pre-professional programs:** other. **Special academic programs:** accelerated program, cooperative (work-study plan) program, cross-registration, distance learning, double major, dual enrollment, English as a Second Language (ESL), exchange student program (domestic), honors program, independent study, internships, student-designed major, study abroad, teacher certificate program. **Teacher certification offered in:** early childhood, special education, elementary, secondary, bilingual/bicultural. **Cooperative education programs:** art, business, computer science, engineering, health professions, natural science, social/behavioral science, technologies. **Reserve Officers Training Corps (ROTC):** Army ROTC: Offered at cooperating institution; Air Force ROTC: Offered at cooperating institution. **Faculty and instruction (2009-2010):** Total instructional faculty: 580 full-time, 458 part-time (52% men; 48% women; 39% minorities). Full-time faculty with Ph.D. or other terminal degree: 7%. Student/faculty ratio: 22/1. Classes of fewer than 20 students: 32%; of 20 to 49 students: 62%; of 50 or more students: 6%. **Advanced Placement and International Baccalaureate credit:** AP tests may be used for: Credit only. Scores accepted: 3, 4, 5. International Baccalaureate exams may be used for: Credit only. **Freshmen returning for sophomore year:** 75%. **Graduation rates:** Four-year: 9%; five-year: 25%; six-year: 33%.

COSTS AND FINANCIAL AID

Financial aid office: (323) 343-1784. **Expenses (2010-2011):** Tuition and fees 2010-2011: $4,701 in state, $15,861 out of state; room/board: $9,105. Estimated books and supplies: $1,620; transportation: $1,140; personal expenses: $2,898. **Financial aid:** Priority filing date for institution's financial aid form: March 2. In 2009-2010, 79% of undergraduates applied for financial aid. Of those, 75% were determined to have financial need; 14% had their need fully met. Average financial aid package (proportion receiving): $11,144 (75%). Average amount of gift aid, such as scholarships or grants (proportion receiving): $8,862 (63%). Average amount of self-help aid, such as work study or loans (proportion receiving): $5,455 (52%). Average need-based loan (excluding PLUS or other private loans): $5,366. Among students who received need-based aid, the average percentage of need met: 67%. Among students who received aid based on merit, the average award (and the proportion receiving): $3,884 (1%). The average athletic scholarship (and the proportion receiving): $7,312 (0%).

CAMPUS LIFE AND EXTRACURRICULAR ACTIVITIES

Campus housing available (% using): apartment for single students (90%), special housing for disabled students (1%), special housing for international students (9%). Students who live in college-owned, operated, or affiliated housing: 6%. **Student employment:** During the 2009-2010 academic year, 3% of undergraduates worked on campus. Average per-year earnings: $7,200. **Clubs and organizations:** Number of student organizations: 109. Activities include: choral groups, dance, drama/theater, jazz band, literary magazine, music ensembles, musical theater, opera, student government, student newspaper, student film society, symphony orchestra, yearbook. Number of fraternities: 7; sororities: 4. Proportion of men in fraternities: 1%; of women in sororities: 1%. **Sports program (2009-2010):** Member of NCAA II. *Men's intercollegiate varsity sports:* baseball, basketball, soccer, track and field (indoor), track and field (outdoor). *Women's intercollegiate varsity sports:* basketball, cross country, soccer, tennis, track and field (indoor), track and field (outdoor), volleyball.

SERVICES AND FACILITIES

Basic services: nonremedial tutoring, women's center, placement service, day care, health service, health insurance. **Remedial assistance:** reading, math, writing, study skills. **Counseling services:** minority student, career, personal, veteran student, academic, psychological, birth control. **For learning-disabled students:** School does not offer a structured program with separate admission and additional fees. Services include: remedial math, remedial English, reading machines, remedial reading, tape recorders, diagnostic testing service, note-taking services, oral tests, learning center, readers, extended time for tests, tutors, priority registration, priority seating, texts on tape, other testing accommodations. **Library:** Number of titles: 2,066,739; number of current serial subscriptions: 648. **Information technology resources:** Students are not required to lease or own a computer. Number of campus computers available to all students: 1,500. School has a wireless network. Approximate number of users that can be accommodated: 0. Proportion of college-owned housing units wired for high-speed internet access: 100%. **Campus safety:** Security services offered: 24-hour foot-and-vehicle patrols, late-night transport/escort service, 24-hour emergency telephones, lighted pathways/sidewalks, student patrols.

TRANSFER AND INTERNATIONAL STUDENTS

Transfer students: May apply for admission for the following academic terms: Fall, Winter, Spring, Summer. Applicants need a minimum number of credits to apply. For fall 2009: Transfer applications received: 9,729. Transfer applicants offered admission: 2,098. Transfer applicants enrolled: 1,826. **International students:** Number of foreign undergraduates: 886 (6% of student body). Number of countries represented: 88. Minimum TOEFL score required: 500 (paper); 173 (computer).

California State University—Monterey Bay

- **Address:** 100 Campus Center, Seaside, CA 93955-8001
- **Website:** http://www.csumb.edu
- **Public**
- **Enrollment:** 3,933 full-time; 345 part-time

....

KEY STATS

✔ **U.S News College Ranking:** second tier, National Liberal Arts Colleges
✔ **SAT Score (25th/75th percentile):** 880-1110
✔ **Tuition:** 2009-2010: $4,512 in state, $15,672 out of state

Selectivity: Less selective	**Room/board:** $8,290
Acceptance rate: 82%	**Average debt:** $15,254
Student/faculty ratio: 27/1	**Proportion who borrowed:** 63%

UNDERGRADUATE STUDENT BODY STATS

2009-2010 enrollment: 3,933 full-time; 345 part-time. Men: 41%; women: 59%. **Ethnic makeup:** African American: 4%; American-Indian: 1%; Asian American: 6%; Hispanic: 26%; White: 62%; International: 1%.

ADMISSIONS FACTS AND FIGURES

Phone: (831) 582-5100. **Email:** admissions@csumb.edu. **Website:** http://www.csumb.edu. **Application deadlines for fall 2011:** Regular decision: November 30. Early decision: Not offered. Early action: Not offered. Admission can be deferred. **Application fee:** $55. **To apply online, go to:** http://www.csumentor.edu/admissionapp/undergrad_apply.asp. **Admissions requirements/recommendations:** High school units required (recommended): English: 4 (0); Mathematics: 3 (0); Science: 2 (0); Foreign language: 2 (0); Social studies: 1 (0); History: 1 (0); Academic electives: 1 (0); Total units: 15 (0). Tests: The college uses SAT or ACT scores in admissions decisions. Neither SAT nor ACT required. For admission to the fall 2011 entering class, the school will accept: ACT with or without writing accepted. Campus visit: Recommended. Admissions interview: Neither required nor recommended. Off-campus interview: Not available. **Factors that count in admissions decisions:** *Academic:* Secondary school record: Important. Class rank: Not Considered. Letters of recommendation: Considered. Standardized test scores: Important. Essay: Not Considered. *Nonacademic:* Interview: Not Considered. Extracurricular activities: Not Considered. Talent/ability: Not Considered. Character/personal qualities: Not Considered. Alumni/ae relationship: Not Considered. Geographical residence: Not Considered. State residency: Considered. Religious affiliation/commitment: Not Considered. Minority status: Not Considered. Volunteer work: Not Considered. Work experience: Not Considered. **Admissions statistics for the fall 2009 entering class:** Total applicants: 9,938. Total accepted: 8,099. Freshmen enrolled: 949; 1% were from out of state. Overall acceptance rate: 82%. Size of waiting list: 250 applicants; enrolled from waiting list: 110. **Credentials of fall 2009 freshmen:** 9% ranked in the top 10 percent of their high school class; 34% were in the top 25 percent; 78% were in the top half. (Proportion submitting class standing: 68%.) **Average high school grade point average:** 3.1. **First-year students who submitted SAT scores:** 94%. Scores (25/75 percentile): Critical Reading: 440-550, Math: 440-560, Combined: 880-1110. **First-year students submitting ACT scores:** 33%. Scores (25/75 percentile): English: 17-24, Math: 17-24, Composite: 18-24.

ACADEMICS

Year founded: 1994. **Academic calendar:** Semester. **Degrees offered:** bachelor's, master's. **Most popular majors:** 18% business administration and management, 15% humanities/humanistic studies, 10% liberal arts and sciences/liberal studies, 8% social sciences, 7% health and physical education. **Major fields of study:** area, ethnic, cultural, and gender studies; biological and biomedical sciences; business, management, marketing, and related

support services; communication, journalism, and related programs; communications technologies/technicians and support services; computer and information sciences and support services; education; English language and literature/letters; family and consumer sciences/human sciences; foreign languages, literatures, and linguistics; health professions and related clinical sciences; history; liberal arts and sciences studies, and humanities; multi/interdisciplinary studies; natural resources and conservation; philosophy and religious studies; physical sciences; public administration and social service professions; science technologies/technicians; social sciences; visual and performing arts. **Areas of required coursework:** arts/fine arts, humanities, computer literacy, mathematics, English (including composition), foreign languages, sciences (biological or physical), history, social science, other. **Special academic programs (% participation):** cross-registration, distance learning (67%), double major (2%), exchange student program (domestic) (0%), independent study (19%), internships, student-designed major (4%), study abroad (0%), teacher certificate program (7%), other (100%). **Teacher certification offered in:** special education, elementary, middle/junior high, secondary, bilingual/bicultural. **Faculty and instruction (2009-2010):** Total instructional faculty: 114 full-time, 163 part-time (47% men; 53% women; 33% minorities). Full-time faculty with Ph.D. or other terminal degree: 89%. Student/faculty ratio: 27/1. Classes of fewer than 20 students: 18%; of 20 to 49 students: 73%; of 50 or more students: 9%. **Advanced Placement and International Baccalaureate credit:** AP tests may be used for: Credit only. Scores accepted: 3, 4, 5. International Baccalaureate exams may be used for: Credit only. **Freshmen returning for sophomore year:** 69%. **Graduation rates:** Four-year: 14%; five-year: 37%; six-year: 41%.

COSTS AND FINANCIAL AID

Financial aid office: (831) 582-5100. **Expenses (2009-2010):** Tuition and fees 2009-2010: $4,512 in state, $15,672 out of state; room/board: $8,290. Estimated books and supplies: $1,386; transportation: $812; personal expenses: $2,520. **Financial aid:** Priority filing date for institution's financial aid form: March 2. In 2009-2010, 72% of undergraduates applied for financial aid. Of those, 56% were determined to have financial need; 17% had their need fully met. Average financial aid package (proportion receiving): $9,181 (51%). Average amount of gift aid, such as scholarships or grants (proportion receiving): $7,782 (40%). Average amount of self-help aid, such as work study or loans (proportion receiving): $4,180 (35%). Average need-based loan (excluding PLUS or other private loans): $4,138. Among students who received need-based aid, the average percentage of need met: 74%. Among students who received aid based on merit, the average award (and the proportion receiving): $0 (0%). The average athletic scholarship (and the proportion receiving): $2,190 (3%). Average amount of debt of borrowers graduating in 2009: $15,254. Proportion who borrowed: 63%.

CAMPUS LIFE AND EXTRACURRICULAR ACTIVITIES

Campus housing available (% using): coed dorms (71%), apartments for married students (24%), apartment for single students (5%), special housing for disabled students, special housing for international students, other housing options. Students who live in college-owned, operated, or affiliated housing: 54%. **Student employment:** During the 2009-2010 academic year, 8% of undergraduates worked on campus. Average per-year earnings: $5,440. **Clubs and organizations:** Number of student organizations: 71. Activities include: campus ministries, choral groups, concert band, dance, drama/theater, international student organization, jazz band, literary magazine, model UN, music ensembles, radio station, student government, student newspaper. Number of fraternities: 4; sororities: 7. Proportion of men in fraternities: 3%; of women in sororities: 3%. **Sports program (2009-2010):** Member of NCAA II. *Men's intercollegiate varsity sports:* baseball, basketball, cross country, golf, soccer. *Women's intercollegiate varsity sports:* basketball, cross country, golf, soccer, softball, volleyball, water polo.

SERVICES AND FACILITIES

Basic services: day care, health service. **Remedial assistance:** reading, math, writing. **Counseling services:** minority student, career, personal, veteran student, academic, older student, psychological, birth control. **For learning-disabled students:** School does not offer a structured program with separate admission and additional fees. Total undergraduates in learning-disabled program or receiving services: 78. Services include: remedial math, remedial English, reading machines, tape recorders, note-taking services, learning center, extended time for tests, tutors, priority registration, texts on tape, other testing accommodations. **Library:** Number of titles: 79,352; number of current serial subscriptions: 44,895. **Information technology resources:** Students are not required to lease or own a computer. Number of campus computers available to all students: 980. School has a wireless network. Approximate number of users that can be accommodated: 3,270. Proportion

of college-owned housing units wired for high-speed internet access: 100%.
Campus safety: Security services offered: 24-hour foot-and-vehicle patrols, late-night transport/escort service, 24-hour emergency telephones, lighted pathways/sidewalks, student patrols, controlled dormitory access (key, security card, etc).

TRANSFER AND INTERNATIONAL STUDENTS

Transfer students: May apply for admission for the following academic terms: Fall, Spring. Applicants need a minimum number of credits to apply. For fall 2009: Transfer applications received: 2,193. Transfer applicants offered admission: 1,735. Transfer applicants enrolled: 595. **International students:** Number of foreign undergraduates: 34 (1% of student body). Number of countries represented: 24. Minimum TOEFL score required: 500 (paper); 16 (computer). Average TOEFL score: 519 (paper).

California State University—Northridge

- **Address:** 18111 Nordhoff Street, Northridge, CA 91330
- **Website:** http://www.csun.edu
- **Public**
- **Enrollment:** 21,738 full-time; 7,537 part-time

KEY STATS
✔ **U.S News College Ranking:** 77, Regional Universities (West)
✔ **SAT Score (25th/75th percentile):** 810-1060
✔ **Tuition:** 2010-2011: $3,702 in state, $18,888 out of state

Selectivity: Less selective	**Room/board:** $10,872
Acceptance rate: 73%	**Average debt:** $14,691
Student/faculty ratio: 24/1	**Proportion who borrowed:** 39%

UNDERGRADUATE STUDENT BODY STATS
2009-2010 enrollment: 21,738 full-time; 7,537 part-time. Men: 43%; women: 57%. **Ethnic makeup:** African American: 8%; Asian American: 12%; Hispanic: 32%; White: 42%; International: 6%.

ADMISSIONS FACTS AND FIGURES
Phone: (818) 677-3700. **Email:** admissions.records@csun.edu. **Website:** http://www.csun.edu. **Application deadlines for fall 2011:** Regular decision: November 30. Early decision: Not offered. Early action: Not offered. Admission cannot be deferred. **Application fee:** $55. **To apply online, go to:** http://www.csumentor.edu/. **Admissions requirements/recommendations:** High school units required (recommended): English: 4; Mathematics: 3; Science: 2; Foreign language: 2; Social studies: 1; History: 1; Academic electives: 1; Total units: 15. Tests: The college uses SAT or ACT scores in admissions decisions. Either SAT or ACT required. Campus visit: Recommended. Admissions interview: Neither required nor recommended. Off-campus interview: Not available. **Factors that count in admissions decisions:** *Academic:* Secondary school record: Very Important. Class rank: Not Considered. Letters of recommendation: Not Considered. Standardized test scores: Very Important. Essay: Not Considered. *Nonacademic:* Interview: Not Considered. Extracurricular activities: Not Considered. Talent/ability: Not Considered. Character/personal qualities: Not Considered. Alumni/ae relationship: Not Considered. Geographical residence: Considered. State residency: Considered. Religious affiliation/commitment: Not Considered. Minority status: Not Considered. Volunteer work: Not Considered. Work experience: Not Considered. **Admissions statistics for the fall 2009 entering class:** Total applicants: 20,657. Total accepted: 14,984. Freshmen enrolled: 4,203; 2% were from out of state. Overall acceptance rate: 73%. **First-year students who submitted SAT scores:** 79%. Scores (25/75 percentile): Critical Reading: 410-520, Math: 400-540, Combined: 810-1060. **First-year students submitting ACT scores:** 22%. Scores (25/75 percentile): English: N/A, Math: N/A, Composite: 16-22.

ACADEMICS
Year founded: 1958. **Academic calendar:** Semester. **Degrees offered:** bachelor's, master's. **Most popular majors:** 21% business, management, marketing, and related support services, 14% social sciences, 9% communication, journalism, and related programs, 9% communications technologies/technicians and support services, 9% psychology. **Major fields of study:** area, ethnic, cultural, and gender studies; biological and biomedical sciences; business, management, marketing, and related support services; communication, journalism, and related programs; computer and information sciences and support services; education; English language and literature/

letters; family and consumer sciences/human sciences; foreign languages, literatures, and linguistics; health professions and related clinical sciences; history; liberal arts and sciences studies, and humanities; mathematics and statistics; multi/interdisciplinary studies; parks, recreation, leisure, and fitness studies; philosophy and religious studies; physical sciences; psychology; social sciences; visual and performing arts. **Areas of required coursework:** humanities, computer literacy, mathematics, English (including composition), foreign languages, sciences (biological or physical), history, social science, other. **Special academic programs:** cross-registration, distance learning, double major, dual enrollment, English as a Second Language (ESL), exchange student program (domestic), independent study, internships, student-designed major, study abroad, teacher certificate program, other. **Teacher certification offered in:** special education, elementary, secondary, bilingual/bicultural. **Reserve Officers Training Corps (ROTC):** Army ROTC: Offered at cooperating institution (University of California–Los Angeles); Air Force ROTC: Offered at cooperating institution (University of California–Los Angeles). **Faculty and instruction (2009-2010):** Total instructional faculty: N/A. Student/faculty ratio: 24/1. Classes of fewer than 20 students: 11%; of 20 to 49 students: 76%; of 50 or more students: 12%. **Freshmen returning for sophomore year:** 74%. **Graduation rates:** Four-year: 12%; five-year: 33%; six-year: 41%.

COSTS AND FINANCIAL AID
Financial aid office: (818) 677-4085. **Expenses (2010-2011):** Tuition and fees 2010-2011: $3,702 in state, $18,888 out of state; room/board: $10,872. Estimated books and supplies: $1,638; transportation: $1,210; personal expenses: $3,920. **Financial aid:** Priority filing date for institution's financial aid form: March 2. Average amount of debt of borrowers graduating in 2009: $14,691. Proportion who borrowed: 39%.

CAMPUS LIFE AND EXTRACURRICULAR ACTIVITIES
Campus housing available: sorority housing, fraternity housing, apartment for single students, other housing options. Activities include: choral groups, concert band, dance, drama/theater, jazz band, music ensembles, musical theater, radio station, student government, student newspaper. **Sports program (2009-2010):** Member of NCAA I. *Men's intercollegiate varsity sports:* baseball, basketball, golf, soccer, swimming, track and field (outdoor), volleyball. *Women's intercollegiate varsity sports:* basketball, golf, soccer, softball, swimming, tennis, track and field (outdoor), volleyball, water polo.

SERVICES AND FACILITIES
For learning-disabled students: Services include: reading machines, tape recorders, note-taking services, oral tests, readers, priority registration, texts on tape, other testing accommodations. **Library:** Number of titles: 1,369,375; number of current serial subscriptions: 1,696. **Information technology resources:** Students are not required to lease or own a computer. Number of campus computers available to all students: 723.

TRANSFER AND INTERNATIONAL STUDENTS
Transfer students: May apply for admission for the following academic terms: Fall, Spring. Applicants do not need a minimum number of credits to apply. For fall 2009: Transfer applications received: 10,425. Transfer applicants offered admission: 5,999. Transfer applicants enrolled: 3,706. **International students:** Number of foreign undergraduates: 1714 (6% of student body). Minimum TOEFL score required: 500 (paper); 173 (computer).

California State University—Sacramento

- **Address:** 6000 J Street, Sacramento, CA 95819
- **Website:** http://www.csus.edu
- **Public**
- **Enrollment:** 19,824 full-time; 4,564 part-time

KEY STATS
✔ **U.S News College Ranking:** 62, Regional Universities (West)
✔ **SAT Score (25th/75th percentile):** 840-1080
✔ **Tuition:** 2009-2010: $4,900 in state, $16,060 out of state

Selectivity: Less selective	**Room/board:** $9,472
Acceptance rate: 80%	**Average debt:** $12,473
Student/faculty ratio: 26/1	**Proportion who borrowed:** 35%

UNDERGRADUATE STUDENT BODY STATS

2009-2010 enrollment: 19,824 full-time; 4,564 part-time. Men: 43%; women: 57%. **Ethnic makeup:** African American: 7%; American-Indian: 1%; Asian American: 20%; Hispanic: 16%; White: 54%; International: 1%.

ADMISSIONS FACTS AND FIGURES

Phone: (916) 278-3901. **Email:** admissions@csus.edu. **Website:** http://www.csus.edu. **Application deadlines for fall 2011:** Regular decision: March 1. Early decision: Not offered. Early action: Send application by: November 30; Decision sent by: November 1. Admission can be deferred. **Application fee:** $55. **To apply online, go to:** http://www.csumentor.edu. **Admissions requirements/recommendations:** High school units required (recommended): English: 4; Mathematics: 3; Science: 2; Foreign language: 2; Social studies: 1; History: 1; Academic electives: 1; Total units: 15. Tests: The college uses SAT or ACT scores in admissions decisions. Neither SAT nor ACT required. For admission to the fall 2011 entering class, the school will accept: ACT with or without writing accepted. Campus visit: Recommended. Admissions interview: Neither required nor recommended. **Factors that count in admissions decisions:** *Academic:* Secondary school record: Not Considered. Class rank: Not Considered. Letters of recommendation: Not Considered. Standardized test scores: Considered. Essay: Not Considered. *Nonacademic:* Interview: Not Considered. Extracurricular activities: Not Considered. Talent/ability: Not Considered. Character/personal qualities: Not Considered. Alumni/ae relationship: Not Considered. Geographical residence: Not Considered. State residency: Considered. Religious affiliation/commitment: Not Considered. Minority status: Not Considered. Volunteer work: Not Considered. Work experience: Not Considered. **Admissions statistics for the fall 2009 entering class:** Total applicants: 14,460. Total accepted: 11,570. Freshmen enrolled: 2,726; 1% were from out of state. Overall acceptance rate: 80%. Non-early acceptance rate: 80%. **First-year students who submitted SAT scores:** 80%. Scores (25/75 percentile): Critical Reading: 410-530, Math: 430-550, Combined: 840-1080. **First-year students submitting ACT scores:** 20%. Scores (25/75 percentile): English: 17-24, Math: 16-22, Composite: 17-23.

ACADEMICS

Year founded: 1947. **Academic calendar:** Semester. **Degrees offered:** bachelor's, master's, doctorate. **Major fields of study:** architecture and related services; area, ethnic, cultural, and gender studies; biological and biomedical sciences; business, management, marketing, and related support services; communication, journalism, and related programs; computer and information sciences and support services; construction trades; education; engineering; engineering technologies/technicians; English language and literature/letters; family and consumer sciences/human sciences; foreign languages, literatures, and linguistics; health professions and related clinical sciences; history; liberal arts and sciences studies, and humanities; mathematics and statistics; multi/interdisciplinary studies; natural resources and conservation; parks, recreation, leisure, and fitness studies; philosophy and religious studies; physical sciences; psychology; public administration and social service professions; security and protective services; social sciences; visual and performing arts. **Areas of required coursework:** arts/fine arts, humanities, mathematics, English (including composition), foreign languages, sciences (biological or physical), history, social science, other. **Special academic programs:** accelerated program, cooperative (work-study plan) program, cross-registration, distance learning, double major, dual enrollment, English as a Second Language (ESL), honors program, independent study, internships, student-designed major, study abroad, teacher certificate program. **Teacher certification offered in:** early childhood, special education, elementary, bilingual/bicultural. **Cooperative education programs:** art, business, computer science, education, engineering, health professions, humanities, natural science, social/behavioral science, technologies. **Reserve Officers Training Corps (ROTC):** Army ROTC: Offered at cooperating institution (University of California–Davis); Air Force ROTC: Offered on campus. **Faculty and instruction (2009-2010):** Total instructional faculty: 688 full-time, 818 part-time (51% men; 49% women; 23% minorities). Full-time faculty with Ph.D. or other terminal degree: 85%. Student/faculty ratio: 26/1. Classes of fewer than 20 students: 18%; of 20 to 49 students: 64%; of 50 or more students: 18%. **Advanced Placement and International Baccalaureate credit:** AP tests may be used for: Placement only. Scores accepted: 3, 4, 5. International Baccalaureate exams may be used for: Placement only. **Freshmen returning for sophomore year:** 78%. **Graduation rates:** Four-year: 18%; five-year: 38%; six-year: 42%.

COSTS AND FINANCIAL AID

Financial aid office: (916) 278-6554. **Expenses (2009-2010):** Tuition and fees 2009-2010: $4,900 in state, $16,060 out of state; room/board: $9,472.

Estimated books and supplies: $1,656 personal expenses: $3,856. **Financial aid:** Priority filing date for institution's financial aid form: March 2. In 2009-2010, 91% of undergraduates applied for financial aid. Of those, 85% were determined to have financial need; 11% had their need fully met. Average financial aid package (proportion receiving): $7,030 (77%). Average amount of gift aid, such as scholarships or grants (proportion receiving): $5,716 (52%). Average amount of self-help aid, such as work study or loans (proportion receiving): $4,078 (38%). Average need-based loan (excluding PLUS or other private loans): $4,072. Among students who received need-based aid, the average percentage of need met: 90%. Among students who received aid based on merit, the average award (and the proportion receiving): $1,250 (0%). Average amount of debt of borrowers graduating in 2009: $12,473. Proportion who borrowed: 35%.

CAMPUS LIFE AND EXTRACURRICULAR ACTIVITIES

Campus housing available: coed dorms, apartments for married students, apartment for single students, special housing for disabled students, special housing for international students, other housing options. Students who live in college-owned, operated, or affiliated housing: 5%. **Clubs and organizations:** Number of student organizations: 250. Activities include: concert band, dance, drama/theater, international student organization, marching band, music ensembles, musical theater, opera, pep band, radio station, student government, student newspaper. Number of fraternities: 20; sororities: 19. Proportion of men in fraternities: 7%; of women in sororities: 5%. Average proportion of students who stay on campus on weekends: 40%. **Sports program (2009-2010):** Member of NCAA I. *Men's intercollegiate varsity sports:* baseball, basketball, football, golf, soccer, tennis, track and field (outdoor). *Women's intercollegiate varsity sports:* basketball, crew (heavyweight), golf, gymnastics, crew (lightweight), soccer, softball, tennis, track and field (outdoor), volleyball.

SERVICES AND FACILITIES

Basic services: nonremedial tutoring, women's center, placement service, day care, health service, health insurance. **Remedial assistance:** reading, math, writing, study skills. **Counseling services:** career, personal, veteran student, academic, older student, psychological, birth control, other. **For learning-disabled students:** School does not offer a structured program with separate admission and additional fees. Services include: remedial math, remedial English, tape recorders, diagnostic testing service, note-taking services, learning center, readers, tutors, other testing accommodations, other. **Library:** Number of titles: 1,390,629; number of current serial subscriptions: 2,171. **Information technology resources:** Students are not required to lease or own a computer. Number of campus computers available to all students: 800. School has a wireless network. Proportion of college-owned housing units wired for high-speed internet access: 100%. **Campus safety:** Security services offered: 24-hour foot-and-vehicle patrols, late-night transport/escort service, 24-hour emergency telephones, lighted pathways/sidewalks, student patrols, controlled dormitory access (key, security card, etc).

TRANSFER AND INTERNATIONAL STUDENTS

Transfer students: May apply for admission for the following academic terms: Fall, Spring. Applicants need a minimum number of credits to apply. For fall 2009: Transfer applications received: 9,685. Transfer applicants offered admission: 7,558. Transfer applicants enrolled: 3,771. **International students:** Number of foreign undergraduates: 281 (1% of student body). Number of countries represented: 122. Minimum TOEFL score required: 550 (paper); 213 (computer).

California State University–San Bernardino

- **Address:** 5500 University Parkway, San Bernardino, CA 92407
- **Website:** http://www.csusb.edu
- **Public**
- **Enrollment:** 12,298 full-time; 2,118 part-time

KEY STATS

✔ **U.S News College Ranking:** 62, Regional Universities (West)
✔ **SAT Score (25th/75th percentile):** 800-1000
✔ **Tuition:** 2009-2010: $4,026 in state, $12,954 out of state

Selectivity: Less selective	**Room/board:** $9,432
Acceptance rate: 64%	**Average debt:** N/A
Student/faculty ratio: 21/1	**Proportion who borrowed:** N/A

UNDERGRADUATE STUDENT BODY STATS

2009-2010 enrollment: 12,298 full-time; 2,118 part-time. Men: 36%; women: 64%. **Ethnic makeup:** African American: 12%; American-Indian: 1%; Asian American: 8%; Hispanic: 40%; White: 37%; International: 3%.

ADMISSIONS FACTS AND FIGURES

Phone: (909) 537-5188. **Email:** moreinfo@csusb.edu. **Website:** http://www.csusb.edu. **Application deadlines for fall 2011:** Regular decision: Rolling. Early decision: Not offered. Early action: Send application by: N/A; Decision sent by: N/A. Admission can be deferred. **Application fee:** $55. **To apply online, go to:** http://www.csumentor.edu. **Admissions requirements/recommendations:** High school units required (recommended): English: 4 (4); Mathematics: 3 (3); Science: 2 (2); Foreign language: 2 (2); Social studies: 1 (1); History: 1 (1); Academic electives: 1 (1); Total units: 15 (15). Tests: The college uses SAT or ACT scores in admissions decisions. Either SAT or ACT required. For admission to the fall 2011 entering class, the school will accept: ACT with or without writing accepted. Campus visit: Recommended. Admissions interview: Neither required nor recommended. Off-campus interview: Not available. **Factors that count in admissions decisions:** *Academic:* Secondary school record: Not Considered. Class rank: Not Considered. Letters of recommendation: Very Important. Standardized test scores: Very Important. Essay: Not Considered. *Nonacademic:* Interview: Not Considered. Extracurricular activities: Not Considered. Talent/ability: Not Considered. Character/personal qualities: Not Considered. Alumni/ae relationship: Not Considered. Geographical residence: Considered. State residency: Not Considered. Religious affiliation/commitment: Not Considered. Minority status: Not Considered. Volunteer work: Not Considered. Work experience: Not Considered. **Other schools with the greatest overlap in applicants:** California State University–Fullerton; California State University–Los Angeles; University of California–Riverside. **Admissions statistics for the fall 2009 entering class:** Total applicants: 12,333. Total accepted: 7,914. Freshmen enrolled: 2,017; 1% were from out of state. Overall acceptance rate: 64%. Non-early acceptance rate: 64%. **Credentials of fall 2009 freshmen:** (Proportion submitting class standing: 99%.) **Average high school grade point average:** 3.1. **First-year students who submitted SAT scores:** 93%. Scores (25/75 percentile): Critical Reading: 400-500; Math: 400-500, Combined: 800-1000. **First-year students submitting ACT scores:** 30%. Scores (25/75 percentile): English: 16-21, Math: 15-21, Composite: 16-21.

ACADEMICS

Year founded: 1962. **Academic calendar:** Quarter. **Degrees offered:** bachelor's, master's, doctorate. **Most popular majors:** 25% liberal arts and sciences studies, and humanities, 23% business, management, marketing, and related support services, 10% psychology, 6% health professions and related clinical sciences, 6% security and protective services. **Major fields of study:** architecture and related services; area, ethnic, cultural, and gender studies; biological and biomedical sciences; business, management, marketing, and related support services; communication, journalism, and related programs; computer and information sciences and support services; education; English language and literature/letters; family and consumer sciences/human sciences; foreign languages, literatures, and linguistics; health professions and related clinical sciences; history; liberal arts and sciences studies, and humanities; mathematics and statistics; multi/interdisciplinary studies; natural resources and conservation; parks, recreation, leisure, and fitness studies; philosophy and religious studies; physical sciences; psychology; public administration and social service professions; security and protective services; social sciences; visual and performing arts. **Areas of required coursework:** arts/fine arts, humanities, computer literacy, mathematics, English (including composition), philosophy, foreign languages, sciences (biological or physical), history, social science, other. **Pre-professional programs:** pre-law, pre-dentistry, pre-medicine, pre-veterinary science, pre-pharmacy, other. **Special academic programs:** accelerated program, cooperative (work-study plan) program, cross-registration, distance learning, double major, dual enrollment, exchange student program (domestic), honors program, independent study, internships, study abroad, teacher certificate program. **Teacher certification offered in:** early childhood, special education, elementary, vo-tech, middle/junior high, secondary, bilingual/bicultural. **Reserve Officers Training Corps (ROTC):** Army ROTC: Offered on campus; Air Force ROTC: Offered on campus. **Faculty and instruction (2009-2010):** Total instructional faculty: 471 full-time, 424 part-time (51% men; 49% women; 28% minorities). Student/faculty ratio: 21/1. Classes of fewer than 20 students: 15%; of 20 to 49 students: 64%; of 50 or more students: 21%. **Freshmen returning for sophomore year:** 81%. **Graduation rates:** Four-year: 12%; five-year: 33%; six-year: 50%.

COSTS AND FINANCIAL AID

Financial aid office: (909) 537-7800. **Expenses (2009-2010):** Tuition and fees 2009-2010: $4,026 in state, $12,954 out of state; room/board: $9,432. Estimated books and supplies: $1,638; transportation: $1,041; personal expenses: $2,133. **Financial aid:** Priority filing date for institution's financial aid form: March 2. In 2009-2010, 79% of undergraduates applied for financial aid. Of those, 72% were determined to have financial need; 6% had their need fully met. Average financial aid package (proportion receiving): $10,373 (71%). Average amount of gift aid, such as scholarships or grants (proportion receiving): $7,810 (59%). Average amount of self-help aid, such as work study or loans (proportion receiving): $3,717 (70%). Average need-based loan (excluding PLUS or other private loans): $3,569. Among students who received need-based aid, the average percentage of need met: 64%. Among students who received aid based on merit, the average award (and the proportion receiving): $3,188 (0%). The average athletic scholarship (and the proportion receiving): $9,359 (1%).

CAMPUS LIFE AND EXTRACURRICULAR ACTIVITIES

Campus housing available: coed dorms, women's dorms, apartment for single students. Students who live in college-owned, operated, or affiliated housing: 10%. **Clubs and organizations:** Number of student organizations: 100. Activities include: campus ministries, choral groups, dance, drama/theater, international student organization, jazz band, model UN, music ensembles, musical theater, radio station, student government, student newspaper, television station. Number of fraternities: 9; sororities: 8. Proportion of men in fraternities: 3%; of women in sororities: 4%. Average proportion of students who stay on campus on weekends: 20%. **Sports program (2009-2010):** Member of NCAA II. *Men's intercollegiate varsity sports:* baseball, basketball, golf, soccer. *Women's intercollegiate varsity sports:* basketball, cross country, soccer, softball, tennis, volleyball, water polo.

SERVICES AND FACILITIES

Basic services: nonremedial tutoring, women's center, day care, health service, health insurance. **Remedial assistance:** math, writing. **Counseling services:** minority student, career, personal, veteran student, academic, older student, psychological, birth control. **For learning-disabled students:** School does not offer a structured program with separate admission and additional fees. Services include: remedial math, remedial English, reading machines, remedial reading, tape recorders, other special classes, diagnostic testing service, note-taking services, oral tests, learning center, readers, extended time for tests, tutors, priority registration, priority seating, texts on tape, other testing accommodations. **Library:** Number of titles: 123,728; number of current serial subscriptions: 806,072. **Information technology resources:** Students are not required to lease or own a computer. Number of campus computers available to all students: 1,500. School has a wireless network. Proportion of college-owned housing units wired for high-speed internet access: 99%. **Campus safety:** Security services offered: 24-hour foot-and-vehicle patrols, late-night transport/escort service, 24-hour emergency telephones, lighted pathways/sidewalks, student patrols, controlled dormitory access (key, security card, etc).

TRANSFER AND INTERNATIONAL STUDENTS

Transfer students: May apply for admission for the following academic terms: Fall, Winter, Spring, Summer. Applicants do not need a minimum number of credits to apply. For fall 2009: Transfer applications received: 5,995. Transfer applicants offered admission: 3,671. Transfer applicants enrolled: 1,977. **International students:** Number of foreign undergraduates: 385 (3% of student body). Number of countries represented: 46. Minimum TOEFL score required: 500 (paper); 173 (computer). Average TOEFL score: 500 (paper).

California State University—San Marcos

- **Address:** 333 S. Twin Oaks Valley Road, San Marcos, CA 92096-0001
- **Website:** http://www.csusm.edu
- **Public**
- **Enrollment:** 6,125 full-time; 2,602 part-time

KEY STATS

✔ **U.S News College Ranking:** 84, Regional Universities (West)
✔ **SAT Score (25th/75th percentile):** 860-1070
✔ **Tuition:** 2009-2010: $4,650 in state, $8,136 out of state

Selectivity: Less selective	Room/board: N/A
Acceptance rate: 71%	Average debt: N/A
Student/faculty ratio: 25/1	Proportion who borrowed: N/A

UNDERGRADUATE STUDENT BODY STATS

2009-2010 enrollment: 6,125 full-time; 2,602 part-time. Men: 39%; women: 61%. **Ethnic makeup:** African American: 3%; American-Indian: 1%; Asian American: 11%; Hispanic: 22%; White: 62%; International: 2%.

ADMISSIONS FACTS AND FIGURES

Phone: (760) 750-4848. **Email:** apply@csusm.edu. **Website:** http://www.csusm.edu. **Application deadlines for fall 2011:** Early decision: Not offered. Early action: Not offered. Admission cannot be deferred. **Application fee:** $55. **To apply online, go to:** http://www.csumentor.edu/AdmissionApp/. **Admissions requirements/recommendations:** High school units required (recommended): English: 4 (4); Mathematics: 3 (4); Science: 2 (2); Foreign language: 2 (2); Social studies: 2 (2); History: 0 (0); Academic electives: 1 (1); Total units: 15 (16). Tests: The college uses SAT or ACT scores in admissions decisions. Neither SAT nor ACT required. Campus visit: Recommended. Admissions interview: Neither required nor recommended. Off-campus interview: Not available. **Factors that count in admissions decisions:** *Academic:* Secondary school record: Very Important. Class rank: Not Considered. Letters of recommendation: Not Considered. Standardized test scores: Very Important. Essay: Not Considered. *Nonacademic:* Interview: Not Considered. Extracurricular activities: Not Considered. Talent/ability: Not Considered. Character/personal qualities: Not Considered. Alumni/ae relationship: Not Considered. Geographical residence: Considered. State residency: Considered. Religious affiliation/commitment: Not Considered. Minority status: Not Considered. Volunteer work: Not Considered. Work experience: Not Considered. **Admissions statistics for the fall 2009 entering class:** Total applicants: 9,734. Total accepted: 6,953. Freshmen enrolled: 1,567; 1% were from out of state. Overall acceptance rate: 71%. **Size of waiting list:** 1295 applicants; enrolled from waiting list: 0. **Average high school grade point average:** 3.2. **First-year students who submitted SAT scores:** 95%. Scores (25/75 percentile): Critical Reading: 430-530, Math: 430-540, Combined: 860-1070. **First-year students submitting ACT scores:** 30%. Scores (25/75 percentile): English: N/A, Math: N/A, Composite: N/A.

ACADEMICS

Year founded: 1989. **Academic calendar:** Semester. **Degrees offered:** bachelor's, master's. **Major fields of study:** area, ethnic, cultural, and gender studies; biological and biomedical sciences; business, management, marketing, and related support services; communication, journalism, and related programs; computer and information sciences and support services; English language and literature/letters; family and consumer sciences/human sciences; foreign languages, literatures, and linguistics; history; liberal arts and sciences studies, and humanities; mathematics and statistics; multi/interdisciplinary studies; physical sciences; psychology; social sciences; visual and performing arts. **Areas of required coursework:** humanities, computer literacy, mathematics, English (including composition), foreign languages, sciences (biological or physical), history, social science, other. **Special academic programs:** cross-registration, distance learning, double major, dual enrollment, English as a Second Language (ESL), independent study, internships, student-designed major, study abroad, teacher certificate program, weekend college, other. **Reserve Officers Training Corps (ROTC):** Army ROTC: Offered at cooperating institution (San Diego State University); Navy ROTC: Offered at cooperating institution (San Diego State University); Air Force ROTC: Offered at cooperating institution (San Diego State University). **Faculty and instruction (2009-2010):** Total instructional faculty: 202 full-time, 311 part-time. Student/faculty ratio: 25/1. Classes of fewer than 20 students: 15%; of 20 to 49 students: 70%; of 50 or more students: 14%. **Freshmen returning for sophomore year:** 73%. **Graduation rates:** Four-year: 14%; five-year: 33%; six-year: 43%.

COSTS AND FINANCIAL AID

Financial aid office: (760) 750-4850. **Expenses (2009-2010):** Tuition and fees 2009-2010: $4,650 in state, $8,136 out of state. Estimated books and supplies: $1,639; transportation: $1,250; personal expenses: $2,820. **Financial aid:** Priority filing date for institution's financial aid form: March 2.

CAMPUS LIFE AND EXTRACURRICULAR ACTIVITIES

Campus housing available: apartment for single students, special housing for disabled students, special housing for international students, other housing options. Students who live in college-owned, operated, or affiliated housing: 6%. Activities include: choral groups, dance, drama/theater, music ensembles, student newspaper. Number of fraternities: 2; sororities: 2. **Sports program (2009-2010):** Member of NAIA. *Men's intercollegiate varsity sports:* baseball, golf, soccer, track and field (outdoor). *Women's intercollegiate varsity sports:* golf, soccer, softball, track and field (outdoor).

SERVICES AND FACILITIES

Basic services: women's center, placement service, day care, health service. **Remedial assistance:** reading, math, writing, study skills. **Counseling services:** minority student, career, veteran student, birth control. **For learning-disabled students:** School does not offer a structured program with separate admission and additional fees. **Library:** Number of titles: 326,393; number of current serial subscriptions: 3,747. **Information technology resources:** Students are not required to lease or own a computer. Number of campus computers available to all students: 1,400. School has a wireless network. **Campus safety:** Security services offered: 24-hour emergency telephones, lighted pathways/sidewalks, controlled dormitory access (key, security card, etc).

TRANSFER AND INTERNATIONAL STUDENTS

Transfer students: May apply for admission for the following academic terms: Fall, Spring. Applicants need a minimum number of credits to apply. For fall 2009: Transfer applications received: 6,359. Transfer applicants offered admission: 2,860. Transfer applicants enrolled: 1,631. **International students:** Number of foreign undergraduates: 85 (2% of student body).

California State University—Stanislaus

- **Address:** 1 University Circle, Turlock, CA 95382
- **Website:** http://www.csustan.edu
- **Public**
- **Enrollment:** 4,889 full-time; 2,198 part-time

KEY STATS

✔ **U.S News College Ranking:** 48, Regional Universities (West)
✔ **SAT Score (25th/75th percentile):** 830-1060
✔ **Tuition:** 2010-2011: $5,242 in state, $16,402 out of state

Selectivity: Selective	Room/board: $7,993
Acceptance rate: 37%	Average debt: $16,500
Student/faculty ratio: 21/1	Proportion who borrowed: 25%

UNDERGRADUATE STUDENT BODY STATS

2009-2010 enrollment: 4,889 full-time; 2,198 part-time. Men: 35%; women: 65%. **Ethnic makeup:** African American: 3%; American-Indian: 1%; Asian American: 12%; Hispanic: 32%; White: 50%; International: 2%.

ADMISSIONS FACTS AND FIGURES

Phone: (209) 667-3152. **Email:** Outreach_Help_Desk@csustan.edu. **Website:** http://www.csustan.edu. **Application deadlines for fall 2011:** Regular decision: November 30. Early decision: Not offered. Early action: Not offered. Admission cannot be deferred. **Application fee:** $55. **To apply online, go to:** http://www.csumentor.edu/admissionApp. **Admissions requirements/recommendations:** High school units required (recommended): English: 4; Mathematics: 3; Science: 2; Foreign language: 2; Social studies: 1; History: 1; Academic electives: 1; Total units: 15. Tests: The college uses SAT or ACT scores in admissions decisions. Neither SAT nor ACT required. For admission to the fall 2011 entering class, the school will accept ACT with or without writing accepted. Campus visit: Recommended. Admissions interview: Neither required nor recommended. Off-campus interview: May be arranged. **Factors that count in admissions decisions:** *Academic:* Secondary school record: Very Important. Class rank: Important. Letters of recommendation: Not Considered. Standardized test scores: Very Important. Essay:

Not Considered. *Nonacademic:* Interview: Not Considered. Extracurricular activities: Not Considered. Talent/ability: Not Considered. Character/personal qualities: Not Considered. Alumni/ae relationship: Not Considered. Geographical residence: Not Considered. State residency: Not Considered. Religious affiliation/commitment: Not Considered. Minority status: Not Considered. Volunteer work: Not Considered. Work experience: Not Considered. **Admissions statistics for the fall 2009 entering class:** Total applicants: 4,421. Total accepted: 1,618. Freshmen enrolled: 966; 0% were from out of state. Overall acceptance rate: 37%. **Average high school grade point average:** 3.2. **First-year students who submitted SAT scores:** 72%. Scores (25/75 percentile): Critical Reading: 410-520, Math: 420-540, Combined: 830-1060. **First-year students submitting ACT scores:** 34%. Scores (25/75 percentile): English: 16-22, Math: 17-23, Composite: 17-22.

ACADEMICS

Year founded: 1957. **Academic calendar:** 4-1-4. **Degrees offered:** bachelor's, post-bachelor's certificate, master's, post-master's certificate. **Most popular majors:** 23% business administration and management, 13% liberal arts and sciences/liberal studies, 12% social sciences, 10% psychology, 8% criminal justice/safety studies. **Major fields of study:** agriculture, agriculture operations, and related sciences; biological and biomedical sciences; business, management, marketing, and related support services; communication, journalism, and related programs; computer and information sciences and support services; education; English language and literature/letters; foreign languages, literatures, and linguistics; health professions and related clinical sciences; history; liberal arts and sciences studies, and humanities; mathematics and statistics; multi/interdisciplinary studies; parks, recreation, leisure, and fitness studies; philosophy and religious studies; physical sciences; psychology; security and protective services; social sciences; visual and performing arts. **Areas of required coursework:** arts/fine arts, humanities, computer literacy, mathematics, English (including composition), philosophy, sciences (biological or physical), history, social science, other. **Pre-professional programs:** pre-law, pre-dentistry, pre-medicine, pre-veterinary science, pre-optometry, pre-pharmacy, other. **Special academic programs:** accelerated program, cooperative (work-study plan) program, distance learning, double major, dual enrollment, English as a Second Language (ESL), honors program, independent study, internships, liberal arts/career combination, student-designed major, study abroad, teacher certificate program. **Teacher certification offered in:** special education, elementary, secondary, bilingual/bicultural. **Cooperative education programs:** art, business, computer science, education, engineering, health professions, humanities, social/behavioral science. **Faculty and instruction (2009-2010):** Total instructional faculty: 279 full-time, 111 part-time (53% men; 47% women; 21% minorities). Full-time faculty with Ph.D. or other terminal degree: 87%. Student/faculty ratio: 21/1. Classes of fewer than 20 students: 20%; of 20 to 49 students: 66%; of 50 or more students: 13%. **Advanced Placement and International Baccalaureate credit:** AP tests may be used for: Credit only. Scores accepted: 3. International Baccalaureate exams may be used for: Credit only. **Freshmen returning for sophomore year:** 82%. **Graduation rates:** Four-year: 22%; five-year: 44%; six-year: 51%. **Graduate study:** 54% of students pursue further study immediately upon graduation; 32% within one year; 14% within five years. Fields in which graduates pursue further study: Master of Business Administration (MBA), 10%; law, 7%; medicine, 6%; education, 38%; arts and sciences, 33%.

COSTS AND FINANCIAL AID

Financial aid office: (209) 667-3336. **Expenses (2010-2011):** Tuition and fees 2010-2011: $5,242 in state, $16,402 out of state; room/board: $7,993. Estimated books and supplies: $1,650; transportation: $900; personal expenses: $2,410. **Financial aid:** Priority filing date for institution's financial aid form: March 2. In 2009-2010, 91% of undergraduates applied for financial aid. Of those, 83% were determined to have financial need; 4% had their need fully met. Average financial aid package (proportion receiving): $10,247 (81%). Average amount of gift aid, such as scholarships or grants (proportion receiving): $6,103 (65%). Average amount of self-help aid, such as work study or loans (proportion receiving): $5,972 (64%). Average need-based loan (excluding PLUS or other private loans): $5,402. Among students who received need-based aid, the average percentage of need met: 56%. Among students who received aid based on merit, the average award (and the proportion receiving): $4,238 (1%). The average athletic scholarship (and the proportion receiving): $1,455 (3%). Average amount of debt of borrowers graduating in 2009: $16,500. Proportion who borrowed: 25%.

CAMPUS LIFE AND EXTRACURRICULAR ACTIVITIES

Campus housing available: coed dorms, apartment for single students, other housing options. Students who live in college-owned, operated, or affili-ated housing: 8%. **Student employment:** During the 2009-2010 academic year, 10% of undergraduates worked on campus. **Clubs and organizations:** Number of student organizations: 80. Activities include: choral groups, concert band, dance, drama/theater, international student organization, jazz band, model UN, music ensembles, musical theater, opera, radio station, student government, student newspaper, symphony orchestra. Number of fraternities: 5; sororities: 8. Proportion of men in fraternities: 6%; of women in sororities: 5%. Average proportion of students who stay on campus on weekends: 30%. **Sports program (2009-2010):** Member of NCAA II. *Men's intercollegiate varsity sports:* baseball, basketball, cross country, golf, soccer, track and field (indoor), track and field (outdoor). *Women's intercollegiate varsity sports:* basketball, cross country, soccer, softball, tennis, track and field (indoor), volleyball.

SERVICES AND FACILITIES

Basic services: nonremedial tutoring, women's center, placement service, day care, health service, health insurance. **Remedial assistance:** reading, math, writing, study skills. **Counseling services:** minority student, career, military, personal, veteran student, academic, older student, psychological, birth control. **For learning-disabled students:** School does not offer a structured program with separate admission and additional fees. Total undergraduates in learning-disabled program or receiving services: 80. Services include: remedial math, remedial English, reading machines, tape recorders, note-taking services, readers, extended time for tests, tutors, priority registration, priority seating, texts on tape, other testing accommodations. **Library:** Number of titles: 372,636; number of current serial subscriptions: 841. **Information technology resources:** Students are not required to lease or own a computer. Number of campus computers available to all students: 201. School has a wireless network. Approximate number of users that can be accommodated: 100. Proportion of college-owned housing units wired for high-speed internet access: 100%. **Campus safety:** Security services offered: 24-hour foot-and-vehicle patrols, late-night transport/escort service, 24-hour emergency telephones, lighted pathways/sidewalks, student patrols, controlled dormitory access (key, security card, etc).

TRANSFER AND INTERNATIONAL STUDENTS

Transfer students: May apply for admission for the following academic terms: Fall, Winter, Spring, Summer. Applicants need a minimum number of credits to apply. For fall 2009: Transfer applications received: 2,407. Transfer applicants offered admission: 1,407. Transfer applicants enrolled: 845. **International students:** Number of foreign undergraduates: 107 (2% of student body). Number of countries represented: 30. Minimum TOEFL score required: 500 (paper); 173 (computer). Average TOEFL score: 578 (paper).

Chapman University

- **Address:** 1 University Drive, Orange, CA 92866
- **Website:** http://www.chapman.edu
- **Private; Religious affiliation:** Christian Church (Disciples of Christ)
- **Enrollment:** 4,264 full-time; 212 part-time

KEY STATS

✔ **U.S News College Ranking:** 8, Regional Universities (West)
✔ **SAT Score (25th/75th percentile):** 1115-1339
✔ **Tuition:** 2010-2011: $38,524

Selectivity: More selective	**Room/board:** $12,957
Acceptance rate: 56%	**Average debt:** $23,917
Student/faculty ratio: 14/1	**Proportion who borrowed:** 64%

UNDERGRADUATE STUDENT BODY STATS

2009-2010 enrollment: 4,264 full-time; 212 part-time. Men: 42%; women: 58%. **Ethnic makeup:** African American: 2%; American-Indian: 1%; Asian American: 9%; Hispanic: 10%; White: 76%; International: 3%. **Religious preference:** Roman Catholic: 24%; Protestant: 36%; Jewish: 6%; Muslim: 1%; Hindu: 1%; Buddhist: 1%; No preference: 7%; Unknown: 20%; Christian Church (Disciples of Christ): 2%; Christian Eastern Orthodox: 1%; Other: 1%.

ADMISSIONS FACTS AND FIGURES

Phone: (888) 282-7759. **Email:** admit@chapman.edu. **Website:** http://www.chapman.edu. **Application deadlines for fall 2011:** Regular decision: January 15. Early decision: Not offered. Early action: Send application by: November

15; Decision sent by: January 10. Admission cannot be deferred. **Application fee:** $60. **To apply online, go to:** http://www.chapman.edu/admission/commonApp/. **Admissions requirements/recommendations:** High school units required (recommended): English: 2 (4); Mathematics: 2 (3); Science: 2 (3); Foreign language: 2 (3); Social studies: 3 (4); Total units: 11 (17). Tests: The college uses SAT or ACT scores in admissions decisions. Either SAT or ACT required. For admission to the fall 2011 entering class, the school will accept: ACT with writing required. Campus visit: Recommended. Admissions interview: Recommended. Off-campus interview: May be arranged. **Factors that count in admissions decisions:** *Academic:* Secondary school record: Very Important. Class rank: Very Important. Letters of recommendation: Considered. Standardized test scores: Very Important. Essay: Very Important. *Nonacademic:* Interview: Not Considered. Extracurricular activities: Important. Talent/ability: Important. Character/personal qualities: Very Important. Alumni/ae relationship: Considered. Geographical residence: Considered. State residency: Not Considered. Religious affiliation/commitment: Not Considered. Minority status: Considered. Volunteer work: Important. Work experience: Considered. **Other schools with the greatest overlap in applicants:** Loyola Marymount University; Santa Clara University; University of California–Irvine; University of San Diego; University of Southern California. **Admissions statistics for the fall 2009 entering class:** Total applicants: 6,159. Total accepted: 3,468. Freshmen enrolled: 1,032; 37% were from out of state. Accepted through early-decision or early-action plans: 52%. Overall acceptance rate: 56%. Non-early acceptance rate: 52%. **Size of waiting list:** 456 applicants; enrolled from waiting list: 86. **Credentials of fall 2009 freshmen:** 48% ranked in the top 10 percent of their high school class; 90% were in the top 25 percent; 99% were in the top half. (Proportion submitting class standing: 31%.) **Average high school grade point average:** 3.7. **First-year students who submitted SAT scores:** 76%. Scores (25/75 percentile): Critical Reading: 547-661, Math: 568-678, Combined: 1115-1339. **First-year students submitting ACT scores:** 40%. Scores (25/75 percentile): English: 25-31, Math: 24-29, Composite: 25-29.

ACADEMICS

Year founded: 1861. **Academic calendar:** 4-1-4. **Degrees offered:** bachelor's, post-bachelor's certificate, master's, doctorate. **Most popular majors:** 21% business administration and management, 9% cinematography and film/video production, 7% communication studies/speech communication and rhetoric, 7% public relations/image management, 5% psychology. **Major fields of study:** biological and biomedical sciences; business, management, marketing, and related support services; communication, journalism, and related programs; computer and information sciences and support services; education; English language and literature/letters; foreign languages, literatures, and linguistics; health professions and related clinical sciences; history; legal professions and studies; liberal arts and sciences studies, and humanities; mathematics and statistics; multi/interdisciplinary studies; philosophy and religious studies; physical sciences; psychology; public administration and social service professions; social sciences; visual and performing arts. **Areas of required coursework:** arts/fine arts, humanities, mathematics, English (including composition), foreign languages, sciences (biological or physical), social science, other. **Pre-professional programs:** pre-dentistry, pre-medicine, pre-veterinary science. **Special academic programs (% participation):** distance learning (8%), double major (6%), English as a Second Language (ESL) (1%), honors program (3%), independent study (17%), internships (29%), student-designed major (.3%), study abroad (18%), teacher certificate program (1%). **Teacher certification offered in:** special education, elementary, secondary, bilingual/bicultural. **Reserve Officers Training Corps (ROTC):** Army ROTC: Offered at cooperating institution (California State Polytechnic University–Pomona); Air Force ROTC: Offered at cooperating institution (Loyola Marymount University). **Faculty and instruction (2009-2010):** Total instructional faculty: 349 full-time, 297 part-time (62% men; 38% women). Full-time faculty with Ph.D. or other terminal degree: 91%. Student/faculty ratio: 14/1. Classes of fewer than 20 students: 41%; of 20 to 49 students: 58%; of 50 or more students: 1%. **Advanced Placement and International Baccalaureate credit:** AP tests may be used for: Credit and/or placement. Scores accepted: 3, 4, 5. International Baccalaureate exams may be used for: Credit and/or placement. **Freshmen returning for sophomore year:** 87%. **Graduation rates:** Four-year: 53%; five-year: 69%; six-year: 68%. **Graduate study:** 32% of students pursue further study within one year. Fields in which graduates pursue further study: Master of Business Administration (MBA), 9%; law, 16%.

COSTS AND FINANCIAL AID

Financial aid office: (714) 997-6741. **Expenses (2010-2011):** Tuition and fees 2010-2011: $38,524; room/board: $12,957. Estimated books and supplies: $1,300; transportation: $400; personal expenses: $1,500. **Financial aid:** Priority filing date for institution's financial aid form: March 2. In 2009-2010, 89% of undergrads applied for financial aid. Of those, 62% were determined to have financial need; 100% had their need fully met. Average financial aid package (proportion receiving): $27,771 (62%). Average amount of gift aid, such as scholarships or grants (proportion receiving): $24,076 (61%). Average amount of self-help aid, such as work study or loans (proportion receiving): $6,729 (54%). Average need-based loan (excluding PLUS or other private loans): $4,511. Among students who received need-based aid, the average percentage of need met: 100%. Among students who received aid based on merit, the average award (and the proportion receiving): $17,256 (17%). The average athletic scholarship (and the proportion receiving): $0 (0%). Average amount of debt of borrowers graduating in 2009: $23,917. Proportion who borrowed: 64%.

CAMPUS LIFE AND EXTRACURRICULAR ACTIVITIES

Campus housing available (% using): coed dorms (88%), apartments for married students, apartment for single students (11%), special housing for disabled students, other housing options (1%). Students who live in college-owned, operated, or affiliated housing: 41%. **Student employment:** During the 2009-2010 academic year, 19% of undergraduates worked on campus. Average per-year earnings: $940. **Clubs and organizations:** Number of student organizations: 94. Activities include: campus ministries, choral groups, concert band, dance, drama/theater, international student organization, jazz band, literary magazine, model UN, music ensembles, musical theater, opera, pep band, radio station, student government, student newspaper, student film society, symphony orchestra, yearbook. Number of fraternities: 6; sororities: 6. Proportion of men in fraternities: 26%; of women in sororities: 30%. **Sports program (2009-2010):** Member of NCAA III. *Men's intercollegiate varsity sports:* baseball, basketball, cross country, football, golf, soccer, tennis, water polo. *Women's intercollegiate varsity sports:* basketball, crew (heavyweight), cross country, soccer, softball, swimming, tennis, track and field (outdoor), volleyball, water polo.

SERVICES AND FACILITIES

Basic services: nonremedial tutoring, day care, health service, health insurance. **Remedial assistance:** reading, math, writing, study skills. **Counseling services:** career, personal, veteran student, academic, older student, psychological, birth control, religious. **For learning-disabled students:** School does not offer a structured program with separate admission and additional fees. Total undergraduates in learning-disabled program or receiving services: 228. Services include: remedial math, tape recorders, note-taking services, oral tests, learning center, readers, extended time for tests, tutors, priority registration. **Library:** Number of titles: 249,503; number of current serial subscriptions: 51,534. **Information technology resources:** Students are not required to lease or own a computer. Number of campus computers available to all students: 775. School has a wireless network. Approximate number of users that can be accommodated: 37,000. Proportion of college-owned housing units wired for high-speed internet access: 100%. **Campus safety:** Security services offered: 24-hour foot-and-vehicle patrols, late-night transport/escort service, 24-hour emergency telephones, lighted pathways/sidewalks, controlled dormitory access (key, security card, etc).

TRANSFER AND INTERNATIONAL STUDENTS

Transfer students: May apply for admission for the following academic terms: Fall, Spring. Applicants need a minimum number of credits to apply. For fall 2009: Transfer applications received: 1,108. Transfer applicants offered admission: 626. Transfer applicants enrolled: 313. **International students:** Number of foreign undergraduates: 115 (3% of student body). Number of countries represented: 45. Minimum TOEFL score required: 550 (paper); 80 (computer). Average TOEFL score: 618 (paper).

Claremont McKenna College

- **Address:** 500 E. 9th Street, Claremont, CA 91711
- **Website:** http://www.claremontmckenna.edu
- **Private**
- **Enrollment:** 1,216 full-time; 1 part-time

KEY STATS

✔ **U.S News College Ranking:** 11, National Liberal Arts Colleges
✔ **SAT Score (25th/75th percentile):** 1310-1510
✔ **Tuition:** 2010-2011: $40,230

Selectivity: Most selective
Acceptance rate: 16%
Student/faculty ratio: 9/1
Room/board: $13,000
Average debt: $9,259
Proportion who borrowed: 30%

UNDERGRADUATE STUDENT BODY STATS

2009-2010 enrollment: 1,216 full-time; 1 part-time. Men: 55%; women: 45%. **Ethnic makeup:** African American: 3%; Asian American: 12%; Hispanic: 9%; White: 70%; International: 6%. **Religious preference:** Roman Catholic: 18%; Protestant: 30%; Jewish: 11%; Muslim: 2%; Hindu: 3%; Buddhist: 2%; No preference: 34%.

ADMISSIONS FACTS AND FIGURES

Phone: (909) 621-8088. **Email:** admission@claremontmckenna.edu. **Website:** http://www.claremontmckenna.edu. **Application deadlines for fall 2011:** Regular decision: January 2; decision sent by April 1. Early decision: Send application by: November 15; Decision sent by: December 15. Early action: Not offered. Admission can be deferred. **Application fee:** $60. **To apply online, go to:** http://www.commonapp.org. **Admissions requirements/ recommendations:** High school units required (recommended): English: 4 (4); Mathematics: 3 (4); Science: 2 (3); Foreign language: 3 (3); Social studies: 1 (2); History: 1 (1); Academic electives: 0 (0); Total units: 16 (20). Tests: The college uses SAT or ACT scores in admissions decisions. Either SAT or ACT required. For admission to the fall 2011 entering class, the school will accept: ACT with writing required. Campus visit: Recommended. Admissions interview: Recommended. Off-campus interview: May be arranged. **Factors that count in admissions decisions:** *Academic:* Secondary school record: Very Important. Class rank: Very Important. Letters of recommendation: Very Important. Standardized test scores: Very Important. Essay: Very Important. *Nonacademic:* Interview: Important. Extracurricular activities: Very Important. Talent/ability: Very Important. Character/ personal qualities: Very Important. Alumni/ae relationship: Important. Geographical residence: Important. State residency: Not Considered. Religious affiliation/commitment: Not Considered. Minority status: Considered. Volunteer work: Important. Work experience: Important. **Other schools with the greatest overlap in applicants:** Georgetown University; Pomona College; Stanford University; University of California–Berkeley; University of California–Los Angeles. **Admissions statistics for the fall 2009 entering class:** Total applicants: 4,276. Total accepted: 697. Freshmen enrolled: 282; 40% were from out of state. Accepted through early-decision or early-action plans: 35%. Overall acceptance rate: 16%. Early-decision acceptance rate: 28%. Non-early acceptance rate: 15%. **Size of waiting list:** 850 applicants; enrolled from waiting list: 24. **Credentials of fall 2009 freshmen:** 85% ranked in the top 10 percent of their high school class; 99% were in the top 25 percent; 100% were in the top half. (Proportion submitting class standing: 53%.) **Average high school grade point average:** 3.9. **First-year students who submitted SAT scores:** 83%. Scores (25/75 percentile): Critical Reading: 650-750, Math: 660-760, Combined: 1310-1510. **First-year students submitting ACT scores:** 45%. Scores (25/75 percentile): English: 29-33, Math: 29-33, Composite: 29-33.

ACADEMICS

Year founded: 1946. **Academic calendar:** Semester. **Degrees offered:** bachelor's, master's. **Most popular majors:** 34% economics, 19% political science and government, 17% psychology, 8% accounting, 8% international relations and affairs. **Major fields of study:** area, ethnic, cultural, and gender studies; biological and biomedical sciences; business, management, marketing, and related support services; engineering; engineering technologies/ technicians; English language and literature/letters; foreign languages, literatures, and linguistics; history; legal professions and studies; mathematics and statistics; multi/interdisciplinary studies; natural resources and conservation; philosophy and religious studies; physical sciences; psychology; social sciences; visual and performing arts. **Areas of required coursework:** humanities, mathematics, English (including composition), philosophy,

foreign languages, sciences (biological or physical), history, social science, other. **Special academic programs (% participation):** cross-registration (99%), double major (5%), exchange student program (domestic) (0%), independent study (13%), internships (31.2%), student-designed major (0%), study abroad (46.5%). **Reserve Officers Training Corps (ROTC):** Army ROTC: Offered on campus; Air Force ROTC: Offered at cooperating institution. **Faculty and instruction (2009-2010):** Total instructional faculty: 128 full-time, 21 part-time (68% men; 32% women; 19% minorities). Full-time faculty with Ph.D. or other terminal degree: 98%. Student/faculty ratio: 9/1. Classes of fewer than 20 students: 76%; of 20 to 49 students: 23%; of 50 or more students: 1%. **Advanced Placement and International Baccalaureate credit:** AP tests may be used for: Credit and/or placement. Scores accepted: 4, 5. International Baccalaureate exams may be used for: Credit and/or placement. **Freshmen returning for sophomore year:** 96%. **Graduation rates:** Four-year: 87%; five-year: 92%; six-year: 93%. **Graduate study:** 20% of students pursue further study immediately upon graduation; 40% within one year; 75% within five years. Fields in which graduates pursue further study: Master of Business Administration (MBA), 15%; law, 15%; medicine, 15%; dentistry, 1%; engineering, 2%; education, 2%; arts and sciences, 50%.

COSTS AND FINANCIAL AID

Financial aid office: (909) 621-8356. **Expenses (2010-2011):** Tuition and fees 2010-2011: $40,230; room/board: $13,000. Estimated books and supplies: $900; transportation: $0; personal expenses: $1,100. **Financial aid:** Priority filing date for institution's financial aid form: February 1; deadline: February 1. In 2009-2010, 50% of undergraduates applied for financial aid. Of those, 44% were determined to have financial need; 100% had their need fully met. Average financial aid package (proportion receiving): $35,177 (44%). Average amount of gift aid, such as scholarships or grants (proportion receiving): $34,276 (44%). Average amount of self-help aid, such as work study or loans (proportion receiving): $1,338 (36%). Average need-based loan (excluding PLUS or other private loans): $0. Among students who received need-based aid, the average percentage of need met: 100%. Among students who received aid based on merit, the average award (and the proportion receiving): $12,591 (7%). The average athletic scholarship (and the proportion receiving): $0 (0%). Average amount of debt of borrowers graduating in 2009: $9,259. Proportion who borrowed: 30%.

CAMPUS LIFE AND EXTRACURRICULAR ACTIVITIES

Campus housing available (% using): coed dorms (87%), apartment for single students (13%), special housing for disabled students (0%), other housing options (0%). Students who live in college-owned, operated, or affiliated housing: 98%. **Student employment:** During the 2009-2010 academic year, 40% of undergraduates worked on campus. Average per-year earnings: $1,600. **Clubs and organizations:** Number of student organizations: 110. Activities include: choral groups, dance, drama/theater, literary magazine, model UN, music ensembles, musical theater, radio station, student government, student newspaper, yearbook. Number of fraternities: 0; sororities: 0. Average proportion of students who stay on campus on weekends: 90%. **Sports program (2009-2010):** Member of NCAA III. *Men's intercollegiate varsity sports:* baseball, basketball, cross country, football, golf, soccer, swimming, tennis, track and field (outdoor), water polo. *Women's intercollegiate varsity sports:* basketball, cross country, golf, lacrosse, soccer, softball, swimming, tennis, track and field (outdoor), volleyball, water polo.

SERVICES AND FACILITIES

Basic services: nonremedial tutoring, women's center, placement service, health service, health insurance. **Remedial assistance:** writing. **Counseling services:** minority student, career, military, personal, academic, psychological, birth control, religious, other. **For learning-disabled students:** School does not offer a structured program with separate admission and additional fees. Total undergraduates in learning-disabled program or receiving services: 45. Services include: tape recorders, untimed tests, note-taking services, learning center, extended time for tests, tutors, priority seating, substitution of courses, exams on tape or computer, other testing accommodations, waiver of foreign language degree requirement, waiver of math degree requirement, other. **Library:** Number of titles: 2,618,747; number of current serial subscriptions: 47,450. **Information technology resources:** Students are not required to lease or own a computer. Number of campus computers available to all students: 220. School has a wireless network. Approximate number of users that can be accommodated: 2,120. Proportion of college-owned housing units wired for high-speed internet access: 100%. **Campus safety:** Security services offered: 24-hour foot-and-vehicle patrols, late-night transport/escort service, 24-hour emergency telephones, lighted pathways/sidewalks, controlled dormitory access (key, security card, etc).

TRANSFER AND INTERNATIONAL STUDENTS

Transfer students: May apply for admission for the following academic terms: Fall, Spring. Applicants do not need a minimum number of credits to apply. For fall 2009: Transfer applications received: 295. Transfer applicants offered admission: 33. Transfer applicants enrolled: 25. **International students:** Number of foreign undergraduates: 73 (6% of student body). Number of countries represented: 27. Minimum TOEFL score required: 600 (paper); 250 (computer). Average TOEFL score: 645 (paper).

Cogswell Polytechnical College

- **Address:** 1175 Bordeaux Drive, Sunnyvale, CA 94089-9772
- **Website:** http://www.cogswell.edu
- **Private**
- **Enrollment:** 113 full-time; 86 part-time

KEY STATS

✔ **U.S News College Ranking:** Unranked, Regional Colleges (West)
✔ **SAT Score (25th/75th percentile):** 970-1310
✔ **Tuition:** 2009-2010: $18,036

Selectivity: N/A	**Room/board:** $10,872
Acceptance rate: 94%	**Average debt:** N/A
Student/faculty ratio: 6/1	**Proportion who borrowed:** N/A

UNDERGRADUATE STUDENT BODY STATS

2009-2010 enrollment: 113 full-time; 86 part-time. Men: 84%; women: 16%. **Ethnic makeup:** African American: 4%; Asian American: 11%; Hispanic: 12%; White: 70%; International: 4%.

ADMISSIONS FACTS AND FIGURES

Phone: (408) 541-0100. **Email:** info@cogswell.edu. **Website:** http://www.cogswell.edu. **Application deadlines for fall 2011:** Regular decision: May 1. Early decision: Not offered. Early action: Not offered. Admission can be deferred. **Application fee:** $55. **Admissions requirements/recommendations:** High school units required (recommended): English: 3; Mathematics: 3; Science: 1; Total units: 7 (2). Tests: The college uses SAT or ACT scores in admissions decisions. Neither SAT nor ACT required. For admission to the fall 2011 entering class, the school will accept: ACT with or without writing accepted. Campus visit: Recommended. Admissions interview: Recommended. Off-campus interview: May be arranged. **Factors that count in admissions decisions:** *Academic:* Secondary school record: Not Considered. Class rank: Not Considered. Letters of recommendation: Important. Standardized test scores: Considered. Essay: Important. *Nonacademic:* Interview: Considered. Extracurricular activities: Not Considered. Talent/ability: Very Important. Character/personal qualities: Not Considered. Alumni/ae relationship: Not Considered. Geographical residence: Not Considered. State residency: Not Considered. Religious affiliation/commitment: Not Considered. Minority status: Not Considered. Volunteer work: Not Considered. Work experience: Considered. **Admissions statistics for the fall 2009 entering class:** Total applicants: 32. Total accepted: 30. Freshmen enrolled: 21; 14% were from out of state. Overall acceptance rate: 94%. **First-year students who submitted SAT scores:** 38%. Scores (25/75 percentile): Critical Reading: 550-650, Math: 420-660, Combined: 970-1310. **First-year students submitting ACT scores:** 9%. Scores (25/75 percentile): English: N/A, Math: N/A, Composite: 21-32.

ACADEMICS

Year founded: 1887. **Academic calendar:** Semester. **Degrees offered:** bachelor's. **Major fields of study:** engineering; engineering technologies/technicians; security and protective services; visual and performing arts. **Areas of required coursework:** arts/fine arts, humanities, computer literacy, mathematics, English (including composition), sciences (biological or physical), history, social science. **Special academic programs (% participation):** distance learning (37%), other (63%). **Faculty and instruction (2009-2010):** Total instructional faculty: 10 full-time, 31 part-time (80% men; 20% women; 0% minorities). Full-time faculty with Ph.D. or other terminal degree: 60%. Student/faculty ratio: 6/1. Classes of fewer than 20 students: 99%; of 20 to 49 students: 1%. **Advanced Placement and International Baccalaureate credit:** International Baccalaureate exams may be used for: Credit only. **Freshmen returning for sophomore year:** 70%. **Graduation rates:** Four-year: 22%; five-year: 33%; six-year: 44%.

COSTS AND FINANCIAL AID

Financial aid office: (408) 541-0100. **Expenses (2009-2010):** Tuition and fees 2009-2010: $18,036; room/board: $10,872. Estimated books and supplies: $1,638. **Financial aid:** Priority filing date for institution's financial aid form: March 2.

CAMPUS LIFE AND EXTRACURRICULAR ACTIVITIES

Campus housing available (% using): apartment for single students (100%). Students who live in college-owned, operated, or affiliated housing: 24%. **Student employment:** During the 2009-2010 academic year, 5% of undergraduates worked on campus. Average per-year earnings: $5,120. Activities include: radio station, student government. Number of fraternities: 0; sororities: 0. Average proportion of students who stay on campus on weekends: 1%.

SERVICES AND FACILITIES

Counseling services: academic. **Library:** Number of titles: 10,174; number of current serial subscriptions: 53. **Information technology resources:** Students are not required to lease or own a computer. Number of campus computers available to all students: 224. School has a wireless network. Approximate number of users that can be accommodated: 50. **Campus safety:** Security services offered: 24-hour emergency telephones, lighted pathways/sidewalks, controlled dormitory access (key, security card, etc).

TRANSFER AND INTERNATIONAL STUDENTS

Transfer students: May apply for admission for the following academic terms: Fall, Spring, Summer. Applicants need a minimum number of credits to apply. For fall 2009: Transfer applications received: 36. Transfer applicants offered admission: 30. Transfer applicants enrolled: 23. **International students:** Number of foreign undergraduates: 7 (4% of student body). Number of countries represented: 1. Minimum TOEFL score required: 525 (paper); 197 (computer).

Concordia University

- **Address:** 1530 Concordia W, Irvine, CA 92612-3299
- **Website:** http://www.cui.edu
- **Private; Religious affiliation:** Lutheran Church-Missouri Synod
- **Enrollment:** 1,365 full-time; 66 part-time

KEY STATS

✔ **U.S News College Ranking:** 44, Regional Universities (West)
✔ **SAT Score (25th/75th percentile):** 910-1130
✔ **Tuition:** 2010-2011: $26,000

Selectivity: Selective	**Room/board:** $8,380
Acceptance rate: 62%	**Average debt:** $23,113
Student/faculty ratio: 19/1	**Proportion who borrowed:** 68%

UNDERGRADUATE STUDENT BODY STATS

2009-2010 enrollment: 1,365 full-time; 66 part-time. Men: 39%; women: 61%. **Ethnic makeup:** African American: 2%; American-Indian: 1%; Asian American: 4%; Hispanic: 13%; White: 76%; International: 4%. **Religious preference:** Roman Catholic: 9%; Protestant: 26%; No preference: 1%; Unknown: 45%; Lutheran Church-Missouri Synod: 16%; Atheist/agnostic: 0%; Other: 3%.

ADMISSIONS FACTS AND FIGURES

Phone: (949) 854-8002. **Email:** admission@cui.edu. **Website:** http://www.cui.edu. **Application deadlines for fall 2011:** Regular decision: Rolling. Early decision: Not offered. Early action: Send application by: December 1; Decision sent by: December 15. Admission can be deferred. **Application fee:** $50. **To apply online, go to:** http://www.cui.edu/admissions/undergraduate/index.aspx?id=16444. **Admissions requirements/recommendations:** High school units required (recommended): English: 4; Mathematics: 3; Science: 3; Foreign language: (4); Social studies: (2); History: 2; Total units: 14 (6). Tests: The college uses SAT or ACT scores in admissions decisions. Either SAT or ACT required. For admission to the fall 2011 entering class, the school will accept: ACT with or without writing accepted. Campus visit: Recommended. Admissions interview: Neither required nor recommended. Off-campus interview: May be arranged. **Factors that count in admissions decisions:** *Academic:* Secondary school record: Important. Class rank: Considered. Letters of recommendation: Very Important. Standardized test scores: Very Important. Essay: Important. *Nonacademic:*

Interview: Considered. Extracurricular activities: Considered. Talent/ability: Considered. Character/personal qualities: Important. Alumni/ae relationship: Considered. Geographical residence: Not Considered. State residency: Not Considered. Religious affiliation/commitment: Considered. Minority status: Not Considered. Volunteer work: Considered. Work experience: Considered. **Other schools with the greatest overlap in applicants:** Azusa Pacific University; California Lutheran University; California State University–Fullerton; California State University–Long Beach; Westmont College. **Admissions statistics for the fall 2009 entering class:** Total applicants: 1,915. Total accepted: 1,192. Freshmen enrolled: 328; 20% were from out of state. Accepted through early-decision or early-action plans: 41%. Overall acceptance rate: 62%. Non-early acceptance rate: 73%. **Credentials of fall 2009 freshmen:** 18% ranked in the top 10 percent of their high school class; 55% were in the top 25 percent. **Average high school grade point average:** 3.5. **First-year students who submitted SAT scores:** 85%. Scores (25/75 percentile): Critical Reading: 460-560, Math: 450-570, Combined: 910-1130. **First-year students submitting ACT scores:** 42%. Scores (25/75 percentile): English: N/A, Math: N/A, Composite: 19-25.

ACADEMICS

Year founded: 1972. **Academic calendar:** Semester. **Degrees offered:** associate, bachelor's, master's. **Most popular majors:** 25% business administration and management, 17% liberal arts and sciences/liberal studies, 15% elementary education and teaching, 10% psychology, 7% communication, journalism, and related programs. **Major fields of study:** biological and biomedical sciences; business, management, marketing, and related support services; communication, journalism, and related programs; English language and literature/letters; history; liberal arts and sciences studies, and humanities; mathematics and statistics; multi/interdisciplinary studies; parks, recreation, leisure, and fitness studies; philosophy and religious studies; physical sciences; psychology; social sciences; theology and religious vocations; visual and performing arts. **Areas of required coursework:** arts/fine arts, humanities, mathematics, English (including composition), philosophy, foreign languages, sciences (biological or physical), history, social science, other. **Pre-professional programs:** pre-law, pre-medicine, pre-theology, other. **Special academic programs (% participation):** accelerated program (22%), distance learning (35%), double major (1%), exchange student program (domestic) (1%), honors program (20%), independent study (28%), internships (31%), study abroad (6%), teacher certificate program (14%). **Teacher certification offered in:** elementary, middle/junior high, secondary. **Reserve Officers Training Corps (ROTC):** Army ROTC: Offered at cooperating institution (California State University–Fullerton). **Faculty and instruction (2009-2010):** Total instructional faculty: 73 full-time, 206 part-time (68% men; 32% women; 13% minorities). Full-time faculty with Ph.D. or other terminal degree: 71%. Student/faculty ratio: 19/1. Classes of fewer than 20 students: 56%; of 20 to 49 students: 41%; of 50 or more students: 3%. **Advanced Placement and International Baccalaureate credit:** AP tests may be used for: Credit only. Scores accepted: 3, 4, 5. International Baccalaureate exams may be used for: Credit only. **Freshmen returning for sophomore year:** 75%. **Graduation rates:** Four-year: 57%; five-year: 63%; six-year: 61%. **Graduate study:** 33% of students pursue further study immediately upon graduation. Fields in which graduates pursue further study: Master of Business Administration (MBA), 12%; law, 6%; education, 35%.

COSTS AND FINANCIAL AID

Financial aid office: (949) 854-8002. **Expenses (2010-2011):** Tuition and fees 2010-2011: $26,000; room/board: $8,380. Estimated books and supplies: $1,600; transportation: $730; personal expenses: $2,200. **Financial aid:** Priority filing date for institution's financial aid form: March 2; deadline: February 1. In 2009-2010, 86% of undergraduates applied for financial aid. Of those, 67% were determined to have financial need; 19% had their need fully met. Average financial aid package (proportion receiving): $24,529 (67%). Average amount of gift aid, such as scholarships or grants (proportion receiving): $12,705 (57%). Average amount of self-help aid, such as work study or loans (proportion receiving): $4,519 (48%). Average need-based loan (excluding PLUS or other private loans): $4,382. Among students who received need-based aid, the average percentage of need met: 62%. Among students who received aid based on merit, the average award (and the proportion receiving): $7,043 (20%). The average athletic scholarship (and the proportion receiving): $14,837 (9%). Average amount of debt of borrowers graduating in 2009: $23,113. Proportion who borrowed: 68%.

CAMPUS LIFE AND EXTRACURRICULAR ACTIVITIES

Campus housing available (% using): coed dorms (99%), special housing for disabled students (1%). Students who live in college-owned, operated, or affiliated housing: 64%. **Student employment:** During the 2009-2010

academic year, 7% of undergraduates worked on campus. Average per-year earnings: $2,000. **Clubs and organizations:** Number of student organizations: 12. Activities include: campus ministries, choral groups, concert band, dance, drama/theater, international student organization, jazz band, literary magazine, music ensembles, musical theater, pep band, student government, student newspaper, yearbook. Number of fraternities: 0; sororities: 0. Average proportion of students who stay on campus on weekends: 60%. **Sports program (2009-2010):** Member of NAIA. *Men's intercollegiate varsity sports:* baseball, basketball, cross country, soccer, swimming, tennis, track and field (indoor), track and field (outdoor), water polo. *Women's intercollegiate varsity sports:* basketball, cross country, soccer, softball, swimming, tennis, track and field (indoor), track and field (outdoor), volleyball, water polo.

SERVICES AND FACILITIES

Basic services: nonremedial tutoring, health service, health insurance, other. **Remedial assistance:** reading, math, writing, study skills, other. **Counseling services:** minority student, career, personal, academic, psychological, religious. **For learning-disabled students:** School does not offer a structured program with separate admission and additional fees. Total undergraduates in learning-disabled program or receiving services: 49. **Library:** Number of titles: 77,783; number of current serial subscriptions: 24,480. **Information technology resources:** Students are not required to lease or own a computer. Number of campus computers available to all students: 93. School has a wireless network. Approximate number of users that can be accommodated: 3,000. Proportion of college-owned housing units wired for high-speed internet access: 100%. **Campus safety:** Security services offered: 24-hour foot-and-vehicle patrols, late-night transport/escort service, lighted pathways/sidewalks, student patrols, controlled dormitory access (key, security card, etc).

TRANSFER AND INTERNATIONAL STUDENTS

Transfer students: May apply for admission for the following academic terms: Fall, Spring. Applicants need a minimum number of credits to apply. For fall 2009: Transfer applications received: 483. Transfer applicants offered admission: 286. Transfer applicants enrolled: 204. **International students:** Number of foreign undergraduates: 50 (4% of student body). Number of countries represented: 11. Minimum TOEFL score required: 550 (paper); 79 (computer).

Dominican University of California

- **Address:** 50 Acacia Avenue, San Rafael, CA 94901-2298
- **Website:** http://www.dominican.edu
- **Private**
- **Enrollment:** 1,171 full-time; 278 part-time

KEY STATS

✔ **U.S News College Ranking:** 37, Regional Universities (West)
✔ **SAT Score (25th/75th percentile):** 920-1120
✔ **Tuition:** 2010-2011: $35,540

Selectivity: Selective	**Room/board:** $13,560
Acceptance rate: 56%	**Average debt:** $26,176
Student/faculty ratio: 11/1	**Proportion who borrowed:** 84%

UNDERGRADUATE STUDENT BODY STATS

2009-2010 enrollment: 1,171 full-time; 278 part-time. Men: 26%; women: 74%. **Ethnic makeup:** African American: 6%; American-Indian: 1%; Asian American: 24%; Hispanic: 17%; White: 51%; International: 2%. **Religious preference:** Roman Catholic: 36%; Protestant: 1%; Jewish: 1%; Buddhist: 1%; No preference: 9%; Unknown: 37%; Other Christian: 7%; Other: 8%.

ADMISSIONS FACTS AND FIGURES

Phone: (415) 485-3204. **Email:** enroll@dominican.edu. **Website:** http://www.dominican.edu. **Application deadlines for fall 2011:** Regular decision: Rolling. Early decision: Not offered. Early action: Not offered. Admission can be deferred. **Application fee:** $40. **To apply online, go to:** http://www.dominican.edu/admissions/online.html. **Admissions requirements/recommendations:** High school units required (recommended): English: 4; Mathematics: 2 (3); Science: 1 (2); Foreign language: 2; History: 1 (2); Total units: 11 (15). Tests: The college uses SAT or ACT scores in admissions decisions. Either SAT or ACT required. For admission to the fall 2011 entering class, the school will accept: ACT with writing required. Campus visit: Recommended. Admissions interview: Recommended. Off-campus interview: May be arranged. **Factors that count in admissions decisions:** *Academic:* Secondary school record: Very Important. Class rank: Important. Letters of recommendation: Very Important. Standardized test scores: Very Important. Essay: Very Important. *Nonacademic:* Interview: Important. Extracurricular activities: Important. Talent/ability: Important. Character/personal qualities: Very Important. Alumni/ae relationship: Considered. Geographical residence: Not Considered. State residency: Not Considered. Religious affiliation/commitment: Not Considered. Minority status: Not Considered. Volunteer work: Important. Work experience: Important. **Other schools with the greatest overlap in applicants:** San Francisco State University; Sonoma State University; St. Mary's College of California; University of California–Santa Cruz; University of San Francisco. **Admissions statistics for the fall 2009 entering class:** Total applicants: 2,425. Total accepted: 1,353. Freshmen enrolled: 289; 14% were from out of state. Overall acceptance rate: 56%. **Credentials of fall 2009 freshmen:** 28% ranked in the top 10 percent of their high school class; 62% were in the top 25 percent; 89% were in the top half. (Proportion submitting class standing: 46%.) **Average high school grade point average:** 3.4. **First-year students who submitted SAT scores:** 92%. Scores (25/75 percentile): Critical Reading: 460-560, Math: 460-560, Combined: 920-1120. **First-year students submitting ACT scores:** 43%. Scores (25/75 percentile): English: N/A, Math: N/A, Composite: 20-25.

ACADEMICS

Year founded: 1890. **Academic calendar:** Semester. **Degrees offered:** bachelor's, post-bachelor's certificate, master's. **Most popular majors:** 29% nursing/registered nurse training (R.N., A.S.N., B.S.N., M.S.N.), 22% business administration and management, 13% liberal arts and sciences, general studies, and humanities, 12% psychology, 7% biology/biological sciences. **Major fields of study:** area, ethnic, cultural, and gender studies; biological and biomedical sciences; business, management, marketing, and related support services; communication, journalism, and related programs; education; English language and literature/letters; health professions and related clinical sciences; history; liberal arts and sciences studies, and humanities; multi/interdisciplinary; philosophy and religious studies; psychology; social sciences; visual and performing arts. **Areas of required coursework:** arts/fine arts, humanities, computer literacy, mathematics, English (including composition), philosophy, sciences (biological or physical), history, social science. **Pre-professional programs:** pre-law, pre-dentistry, pre-medicine, pre-veterinary science, pre-optometry, pre-pharmacy. **Special academic programs:** accelerated program, cross-registration, distance learning, double major, dual enrollment, exchange student program (domestic), honors program, independent study, internships, student-designed major, study abroad, teacher certificate program, weekend college. **Teacher certification offered in:** special education, elementary, middle/junior high, secondary. **Faculty and instruction (2009-2010):** Total instructional faculty: 83 full-time, 272 part-time (34% men; 66% women; 15% minorities). Full-time faculty with Ph.D. or other terminal degree: 76%. Student/faculty ratio: 11/1. Classes of fewer than 20 students: 64%; of 20 to 49 students: 34%; of 50 or more students: 2%. **Advanced Placement and International Baccalaureate credit:** AP tests may be used for: Credit and/or placement. Scores accepted: 3, 4, 5. International Baccalaureate exams may be used for: Credit and/or placement. **Freshmen returning for sophomore year:** 76%. **Graduation rates:** Four-year: 38%; five-year: 44%; six-year: 50%.

COSTS AND FINANCIAL AID

Financial aid office: (415) 257-1321. **Expenses (2010-2011):** Tuition and fees 2010-2011: $35,540; room/board: $13,560. Estimated books and supplies: $1,620; transportation: $729; personal expenses: $2,250. **Financial aid:** Priority filing date for institution's financial aid form: March 2. In 2009-2010, 84% of undergraduates applied for financial aid. Of those, 77% were determined to have financial need; 8% had their need fully met. Average financial aid package (proportion receiving): $21,904 (77%). Average amount of gift aid, such as scholarships or grants (proportion receiving): $17,736 (75%). Average amount of self-help aid, such as work study or loans (proportion receiving): $4,745 (72%). Average need-based loan (excluding PLUS or other private loans): $4,667. Among students who received need-based aid, the average percentage of need met: 54%. Among students who received aid based on merit, the average award (and the proportion receiving): $10,746 (6%). The average athletic scholarship (and the proportion receiving): $6,630 (1%). Average amount of debt of borrowers graduating in 2009: $26,176. Proportion who borrowed: 84%.

CAMPUS LIFE AND EXTRACURRICULAR ACTIVITIES

Campus housing available (% using): coed dorms (100%). Students who live in college-owned, operated, or affiliated housing: 44%. **Student employment:** During the 2009-2010 academic year, 15% of undergraduates worked on campus. Average per-year earnings: $1,833. **Clubs and organizations:** Number of student organizations: 19. Activities include: campus ministries, choral groups, dance, drama/theater, jazz band, literary magazine, music ensembles, musical theater, radio station, student government, student newspaper, yearbook. Number of fraternities: 0; sororities: 0. Average proportion of students who stay on campus on weekends: 60%. **Sports program (2009-2010):** Member of NAIA. *Men's intercollegiate varsity sports:* basketball, golf, lacrosse, soccer. *Women's intercollegiate varsity sports:* basketball, golf, soccer, softball, tennis, volleyball.

SERVICES AND FACILITIES

Basic services: nonremedial tutoring, placement service, health service, health insurance. **Remedial assistance:** math, writing, study skills. **Counseling services:** career, personal, academic, older student, psychological, religious. **For learning-disabled students:** School does not offer a structured program with separate admission and additional fees. Total undergraduates in learning-disabled program or receiving services: 54. Services include: tape recorders, note-taking services, oral tests, learning center, readers, extended time for tests, tutors, substitution of courses, typist/scribe, exams on tape or computer, other testing accommodations. **Library:** Number of titles: 120,646; number of current serial subscriptions: 300. **Information technology resources:** Students are not required to lease or own a computer. Number of campus computers available to all students: 210. School has a wireless network. Approximate number of users that can be accommodated: 200. Proportion of college-owned housing units wired for high-speed internet access: 100%. **Campus safety:** Security services offered: 24-hour foot-and-vehicle patrols, late-night transport/escort service, 24-hour emergency telephones, lighted pathways/sidewalks, controlled dormitory access (key, security card, etc).

TRANSFER AND INTERNATIONAL STUDENTS

Transfer students: May apply for admission for the following academic terms: Fall, Spring. Applicants need a minimum number of credits to apply. For fall 2009: Transfer applications received: 392. Transfer applicants offered admission: 189. Transfer applicants enrolled: 78. **International students:** Number of foreign undergraduates: 27 (2% of student body). Number of countries represented: 13. Minimum TOEFL score required: 550 (paper); 213 (computer). Average TOEFL score: 550 (paper).

Fresno Pacific University

- **Address:** 1717 S. Chestnut Avenue, Fresno, CA 93702
- **Website:** http://www.fresno.edu
- **Private; Religious affiliation:** Mennonite Brethren
- **Enrollment:** 1,536 full-time; 274 part-time

KEY STATS

✔ **U.S News College Ranking:** 40, Regional Universities (West)
✔ **SAT Score (25th/75th percentile):** 840-1100
✔ **Tuition:** 2010-2011: $23,904

Selectivity: Selective	**Room/board:** $7,320
Acceptance rate: 71%	**Average debt:** $18,929
Student/faculty ratio: 16/1	**Proportion who borrowed:** 82%

UNDERGRADUATE STUDENT BODY STATS

2009-2010 enrollment: 1,536 full-time; 274 part-time. Men: 34%; women: 66%. **Ethnic makeup:** African American: 6%; American-Indian: 1%; Asian American: 3%; Hispanic: 34%; White: 53%; International: 3%. **Religious preference:** Roman Catholic: 19%; Protestant: 53%; No preference: 2%; Unknown: 19%; Mennonite Brethren: 6%; Other: 1%.

ADMISSIONS FACTS AND FIGURES

Phone: (559) 453-2039. **Email:** ugadmis@fresno.edu. **Website:** http://www.fresno.edu. **Application deadlines for fall 2011:** Regular decision: July 31. Early decision: Not offered. Early action: Not offered. Admission can be deferred. **Application fee:** $40. **To apply online, go to:** http://fresno.edu/apply. **Admissions requirements/recommendations:** High school units required (recommended): English: 4; Mathematics: 3; Science: 1; Foreign language: 2; Social studies: 2; Total units: 13. Tests: The college uses SAT or ACT scores in admissions decisions. Either SAT or ACT required. For admission to the fall 2011 entering class, the school will accept: ACT with or without writing accepted. Campus visit: Recommended. Admissions interview: Neither required nor recommended. Off-campus interview: May be arranged. **Factors that count in admissions decisions: *Academic:*** Secondary school record: Very Important. Class rank: Important. Letters of recommendation: Important. Standardized test scores: Important. Essay: Very Important. ***Nonacademic:*** Interview: Not Considered. Extracurricular activities: Not Considered. Talent/ability: Not Considered. Character/personal qualities: Considered. Alumni/ae relationship: Not Considered. Geographical residence: Not Considered. State residency: Not Considered. Religious affiliation/commitment: Important. Minority status: Not Considered. Volunteer work: Not Considered. Work experience: Not Considered. **Other schools with the greatest overlap in applicants:** Azusa Pacific University; Biola University; California State University–Fresno; Point Loma Nazarene University; University of California–Davis. **Admissions statistics for the fall 2009 entering class:** Total applicants: 792. Total accepted: 559. Freshmen enrolled: 174; Overall acceptance rate: 71%. **Credentials of fall 2009 freshmen:** 34% ranked in the top 10 percent of their high school class; 63% were in the top 25 percent; 91% were in the top half. (Proportion submitting class standing: 79%.) **Average high school grade point average:** 3.4. **First-year students who submitted SAT scores:** 87%. Scores (25/75 percentile): Critical Reading: 420-540, Math: 420-560, Combined: 840-1100. **First-year students submitting ACT scores:** 31%. Scores (25/75 percentile): English: 16-24, Math: 17-24, Composite: 18-24.

ACADEMICS

Year founded: 1944. **Academic calendar:** Semester. **Degrees offered:** associate, bachelor's, master's. **Most popular majors:** 39% education, 29% business, management, marketing, and related support services, 10% family and consumer sciences/human sciences, 6% health professions and related clinical sciences, 4% psychology. **Major fields of study:** area, ethnic, cultural, and gender studies; biological and biomedical sciences; business, management, marketing, and related support services; communication, journalism, and related programs; education; English language and literature/letters; foreign languages, literatures, and linguistics; health professions and related clinical sciences; history; liberal arts and sciences studies, and humanities; mathematics and statistics; natural resources and conservation; parks, recreation, leisure, and fitness studies; philosophy and religious studies; physical sciences; psychology; public administration and social service professions; social sciences; theology and religious vocations; visual and performing arts. **Areas of required coursework:** arts/fine arts, humanities, mathematics, English (including composition), sciences (biological or physical), history, social science, other. **Pre-professional programs:** pre-law, pre-dentistry, pre-medicine, pre-theology, pre-veterinary science, other. **Special academic programs (% participation):** accelerated program, distance learning, double major (8%), dual enrollment, English as a Second Language (ESL) (2%), exchange student program (domestic) (8%), independent study (12%), internships (14%), student-designed major (5%), study abroad (8%), teacher certificate program. **Teacher certification offered in:** special education, elementary, middle/junior high, secondary, bilingual/bicultural. **Cooperative education programs:** health professions. **Faculty and instruction (2009-2010):** Total instructional faculty: 79 full-time, 195 part-time (51% men; 49% women; 33% minorities). Full-time faculty with Ph.D. or other terminal degree: 62%. Student/faculty ratio: 16/1. Classes of fewer than 20 students: 72%; of 20 to 49 students: 27%; of 50 or more students: 1%. **Advanced Placement and International Baccalaureate credit:** AP tests may be used for: Credit only. International Baccalaureate exams may be used for: Credit only. **Freshmen returning for sophomore year:** 73%. **Graduation rates:** Six-year: 60%. **Graduate study:** 36% of students pursue further study immediately upon graduation; 56% within one year; 56% within five years.

COSTS AND FINANCIAL AID

Financial aid office: (559) 453-2027. **Expenses (2010-2011):** Tuition and fees 2010-2011: $23,904; room/board: $7,320. Estimated books and supplies: $1,620; transportation: $729; personal expenses: $2,250. **Financial aid:** Priority filing date for institution's financial aid form: March 2. In 2009-2010, 79% of undergraduates applied for financial aid. Of those, 73% were determined to have financial need; 8% had their need fully met. Average financial aid package (proportion receiving): $15,215 (72%). Average amount of gift aid, such as scholarships or grants (proportion receiving): $8,667 (55%). Average amount of self-help aid, such as work study or loans (proportion receiving): $5,111 (64%). Average need-based loan (excluding PLUS or other private loans): $4,616. Among students who received need-based aid, the average percentage of need met: 58%. Average amount of debt of borrowers graduating in 2009: $18,929. Proportion who borrowed: 82%.

CAMPUS LIFE AND EXTRACURRICULAR ACTIVITIES

Campus housing available (% using): women's dorms (39%), men's dorms (23%), apartment for single students (19%), special housing for disabled students (1%), other housing options (18%). **Student employment:** During the 2009-2010 academic year, 30% of undergraduates worked on campus. Average per-year earnings: $3,270. **Clubs and organizations:** Number of student organizations: 20. Activities include: choral groups, dance, drama/theater, jazz band, music ensembles, pep band, student government, student newspaper, yearbook. Number of fraternities: 0; sororities: 0. Average proportion of students who stay on campus on weekends: 50%. **Sports program (2009-2010):** Member of NAIA. *Men's intercollegiate varsity sports:* baseball, basketball, cross country, soccer, swimming, tennis, track and field (outdoor), water polo. *Women's intercollegiate varsity sports:* basketball, cross country, soccer, swimming, tennis, track and field (outdoor), volleyball, water polo.

SERVICES AND FACILITIES

Basic services: nonremedial tutoring, health service, health insurance, other. **Remedial assistance:** writing, study skills. **Counseling services:** career, personal, academic, psychological, religious, other. **For learning-disabled students:** School does not offer a structured program with separate admission and additional fees. Services include: tape recorders, untimed tests, note-taking services, oral tests, learning center, readers, extended time for tests, tutors, priority seating, texts on tape, other testing accommodations. **Library:** Number of titles: 197,532; number of current serial subscriptions: 3,200. **Information technology resources:** Students are not required to lease or own a computer. Number of campus computers available to all students: 90. School has a wireless network. Approximate number of users that can be accommodated: 768. Proportion of college-owned housing units wired for high-speed internet access: 100%. **Campus safety:** Security services offered: 24-hour foot-and-vehicle patrols, late-night transport/escort service, 24-hour emergency telephones, lighted pathways/sidewalks, controlled dormitory access (key, security card, etc).

TRANSFER AND INTERNATIONAL STUDENTS

Transfer students: May apply for admission for the following academic terms: Fall, Spring. Applicants need a minimum number of credits to apply. **International students:** Number of foreign undergraduates: 46 (3% of student body). Number of countries represented: 40. Minimum TOEFL score required: 500 (paper); 173 (computer).

Golden Gate University

- **Address:** 536 Mission Street, San Francisco, CA 94105
- **Website:** http://www.ggu.edu
- **Private**
- **Enrollment:** 78 full-time; 344 part-time

KEY STATS

- ✔ **U.S News College Ranking:** second tier, National Universities
- ✔ **SAT or ACT Score (25th/75th percentile):** N/A
- ✔ **Tuition:** 2010-2011: $20,520

Selectivity: Selective	**Room/board:** N/A
Acceptance rate: 88%	**Average debt:** N/A
Student/faculty ratio: 11/1	**Proportion who borrowed:** N/A

UNDERGRADUATE STUDENT BODY STATS

2009-2010 enrollment: 78 full-time; 344 part-time. Men: 43%; women: 57%. **Ethnic makeup:** African American: 10%; Asian American: 23%; Hispanic: 12%; White: 50%; International: 4%.

ADMISSIONS FACTS AND FIGURES

Phone: (415) 442-7800. **Email:** info@ggu.edu. **Website:** http://www.ggu.edu. **Application deadlines for fall 2011:** Regular decision: Rolling. Early decision: Not offered. Early action: Not offered. Admission can be deferred. **Application fee:** $60. **To apply online, go to:** http://www.ggu.edu/admissions_and_costs/admissions/apply. **Admissions requirements/recommendations:** High school units required (recommended): English: (4); Mathematics: (3); Science: (2); Foreign language: (2); Social studies: (1); History: (1); Total units: (14). Tests: The college uses SAT or ACT scores in admissions decisions. Neither SAT nor ACT required. Campus visit: Neither required nor recommended. Admissions interview: Recommended. Off-campus interview: Not available. **Factors that count in admissions**

decisions: *Academic:* Secondary school record: Very Important. Class rank: Considered. Letters of recommendation: Considered. Standardized test scores: Considered. Essay: Considered. *Nonacademic:* Interview: Not Considered. Extracurricular activities: Not Considered. Talent/ability: Not Considered. Character/personal qualities: Not Considered. Alumni/ae relationship: Not Considered. Geographical residence: Not Considered. State residency: Not Considered. Religious affiliation/commitment: Not Considered. Minority status: Considered. Volunteer work: Considered. Work experience: Considered. **Admissions statistics for the fall 2009 entering class:** Total applicants: 8. Total accepted: 7. Freshmen enrolled: 5; 20% were from out of state. Overall acceptance rate: 88%.

ACADEMICS

Year founded: 1901. **Academic calendar:** Trimester. **Degrees offered:** certificate, bachelor's, master's, doctorate. **Most popular majors:** 64% business administration and management, 13% information science/studies, 11% accounting, 5% computer and information sciences and support services. **Major fields of study:** business, management, marketing, and related support services; computer and information sciences and support services. **Areas of required coursework:** humanities, mathematics, English (including composition), philosophy, history, social science. **Special academic programs:** accelerated program, cooperative (work-study plan) program, distance learning, double major, dual enrollment, English as a Second Language (ESL), independent study, internships, weekend college. **Faculty and instruction (2009-2010):** Total instructional faculty: 71 full-time, 313 part-time (29% men; 71% women; 13% minorities). Student/faculty ratio: 11/1. Classes of fewer than 20 students: 83%; of 20 to 49 students: 17%. **Freshmen returning for sophomore year:** 50%. **Graduation rates:** Four-year: 0%; five-year: 0%; six-year: 30%.

COSTS AND FINANCIAL AID

Financial aid office: (415) 442-7270. **Expenses (2010-2011):** Tuition and fees 2010-2011: $20,520. Estimated books and supplies: $2,880; transportation: $1,800; personal expenses: $4,800. **Financial aid:** In 2009-2010, 83% of undergraduates applied for financial aid. Of those, 83% were determined to have financial need; 37% had their need fully met. Average financial aid package (proportion receiving): N/A (83%). Average amount of gift aid, such as scholarships or grants (proportion receiving): $1,850 (31%). Average amount of self-help aid, such as work study or loans (proportion receiving): $4,500 (31%). Average need-based loan (excluding PLUS or other private loans): $4,500. Among students who received aid based on merit, the average award (and the proportion receiving): $1,850 (40%). The average athletic scholarship (and the proportion receiving): $0 (0%).

CAMPUS LIFE AND EXTRACURRICULAR ACTIVITIES

Clubs and organizations: Number of student organizations: 12. Activities include: international student organization, student government, student newspaper. Number of fraternities: 0; sororities: 0.

SERVICES AND FACILITIES

Counseling services: minority student, career, personal, academic, older student. **For learning-disabled students:** School does not offer a structured program with separate admission and additional fees. Services include: tape recorders, note-taking services, extended time for tests, early syllabus, substitution of courses, typist/scribe, take home exams, other testing accommodations. **Library:** Number of titles: 85,193; number of current serial subscriptions: 592. **Information technology resources:** Students are not required to lease or own a computer. School has a wireless network. Approximate number of users that can be accommodated: 500. Proportion of college-owned housing units wired for high-speed internet access: 0%. **Campus safety:** Security services offered: 24-hour emergency telephones, lighted pathways/sidewalks.

TRANSFER AND INTERNATIONAL STUDENTS

Transfer students: May apply for admission for the following academic terms: Fall, Spring, Summer. Applicants need a minimum number of credits to apply. For fall 2009: Transfer applications received: 229. Transfer applicants offered admission: 131. Transfer applicants enrolled: 80. **International students:** Number of foreign undergraduates: 17 (4% of student body). Minimum TOEFL score required: 500 (paper); 61 (computer).

Harvey Mudd College

- **Address:** 301 Platt Boulevard, Claremont, CA 91711
- **Website:** http://www.hmc.edu
- **Private**
- **Enrollment:** 756 full-time; 1 part-time

KEY STATS

✔ **U.S News College Ranking:** 18, National Liberal Arts Colleges
✔ **SAT Score (25th/75th percentile):** 1420-1560
✔ **Tuition:** 2010-2011: $40,390

Selectivity: Most selective	**Room/board:** $13,198
Acceptance rate: 34%	**Average debt:** $16,384
Student/faculty ratio: 8/1	**Proportion who borrowed:** 59%

UNDERGRADUATE STUDENT BODY STATS

2009-2010 enrollment: 756 full-time; 1 part-time. Men: 64%; women: 36%. **Ethnic makeup:** African American: 1%; American-Indian: 1%; Asian American: 20%; Hispanic: 7%; White: 68%; International: 3%. **Religious preference:** Roman Catholic: 11%; Protestant: 22%; Jewish: 8%; Muslim: 1%; Hindu: 1%; Buddhist: 1%; No preference: 50%.

ADMISSIONS FACTS AND FIGURES

Phone: (909) 621-8011. **Email:** admission@hmc.edu. **Website:** http://www.hmc.edu. **Application deadlines for fall 2011:** Regular decision: January 2; decision sent by April 1. Early decision: Send application by: November 15; Decision sent by: December 15. Early action: Not offered. Admission can be deferred. **Application fee:** $60. **To apply online, go to:** http://www.hmc.edu/admission1/applyingforadmission.html. **Admissions requirements/recommendations:** High school units required (recommended): English: 4; Mathematics: 3 (4); Science: 3 (4); Foreign language: (2); Social studies: (2); History: 1 (2); Total units: 16 (3). Tests: The college uses SAT or ACT scores in admissions decisions. Either SAT or ACT required. For admission to the fall 2011 entering class, the school will accept: ACT with writing required. Campus visit: Recommended. Admissions interview: Recommended. Off-campus interview: May be arranged. **Factors that count in admissions decisions:** *Academic:* Secondary school record: Very Important. Class rank: Important. Letters of recommendation: Very Important. Standardized test scores: Important. Essay: Very Important. *Nonacademic:* Interview: Considered. Extracurricular activities: Important. Talent/ability: Very Important. Character/personal qualities: Very Important. Alumni/ae relationship: Considered. Geographical residence: Considered. State residency: Considered. Religious affiliation/commitment: Not Considered. Minority status: Considered. Volunteer work: Considered. Work experience: Considered. **Other schools with the greatest overlap in applicants:** California Institute of Technology; Cornell University; Massachusetts Institute of Technology; Stanford University; University of California–Berkeley. **Admissions statistics for the fall 2009 entering class:** Total applicants: 2,205. Total accepted: 751. Freshmen enrolled: 207; 62% were from out of state. Accepted through early-decision or early-action plans: 23%. Overall acceptance rate: 34%. Early-decision acceptance rate: 46%. Non-early acceptance rate: 33%. **Size of waiting list:** 522 applicants; enrolled from waiting list: 0. **Credentials of fall 2009 freshmen:** 94% ranked in the top 10 percent of their high school class; 100% were in the top 25 percent; 100% were in the top half. (Proportion submitting class standing: 73%.) **First-year students who submitted SAT scores:** 99%. Scores (25/75 percentile): Critical Reading: 680-770, Math: 740-790, Combined: 1420-1560. **First-year students submitting ACT scores:** 35%. Scores (25/75 percentile): English: 32-35, Math: 34-36, Composite: 32-35.

ACADEMICS

Year founded: 1955. **Academic calendar:** Semester. **Degrees offered:** bachelor's. **Most popular majors:** 34% engineering, 19% physical sciences, 14% computer and information sciences and support services, 11% biological and biomedical sciences, 11% mathematics and statistics. **Major fields of study:** biological and biomedical sciences; computer and information sciences and support services; engineering; mathematics and statistics; multi/interdisciplinary studies; physical sciences. **Areas of required coursework:** arts/fine arts, humanities, computer literacy, mathematics, English (including composition), sciences (biological or physical), social science, other. **Special academic programs (% participation):** cross-registration (100%), double major (7%), independent study, internships, liberal arts/career combination, student-designed major, study abroad (12%), other. **Reserve Officers Training Corps (ROTC):** Army ROTC: Offered at cooperating institution (Claremont

McKenna College); Air Force ROTC: Offered on campus. **Faculty and instruction (2009-2010):** Total instructional faculty: 81 full-time, 14 part-time (67% men; 33% women; 18% minorities). Full-time faculty with Ph.D. or other terminal degree: 100%. Student/faculty ratio: 8/1. Classes of fewer than 20 students: 59%; of 20 to 49 students: 34%; of 50 or more students: 7%. **Advanced Placement and International Baccalaureate credit:** AP tests may be used for: Credit and/or placement. Scores accepted: 5. International Baccalaureate exams may be used for: Placement only. **Freshmen returning for sophomore year:** 94%. **Graduation rates:** Four-year: 79%; five-year: 89%; six-year: 91%. **Graduate study:** 45% of students pursue further study immediately upon graduation. Fields in which graduates pursue further study: Master of Business Administration (MBA), 2%; law, 2%; engineering, 31%; education, 2%; arts and sciences, 30%.

COSTS AND FINANCIAL AID

Financial aid office: (909) 621-8055. **Expenses (2010-2011):** Tuition and fees 2010-2011: $40,390; room/board: $13,198. Estimated books and supplies: $800 personal expenses: $900. **Financial aid:** Priority filing date for institution's financial aid form: February 1; deadline: February 1. In 2009-2010, 61% of undergraduates applied for financial aid. Of those, 54% were determined to have financial need; 100% had their need fully met. Average financial aid package (proportion receiving): $32,547 (54%). Average amount of gift aid, such as scholarships or grants (proportion receiving): $29,269 (54%). Average amount of self-help aid, such as work study or loans (proportion receiving): $6,343 (39%). Average need-based loan (excluding PLUS or other private loans): $5,052. Among students who received need-based aid, the average percentage of need met: 100%. Among students who received aid based on merit, the average award (and the proportion receiving): $11,375 (23%). The average athletic scholarship (and the proportion receiving): $0 (0%). Average amount of debt of borrowers graduating in 2009: $16,384. Proportion who borrowed: 59%.

CAMPUS LIFE AND EXTRACURRICULAR ACTIVITIES

Campus housing available (% using): coed dorms (98%), apartments for married students (1%), apartment for single students (1%), special housing for disabled students (0%), other housing options (0%). Students who live in college-owned, operated, or affiliated housing: 99%. **Student employment:** During the 2009-2010 academic year, 48% of undergraduates worked on campus. Average per-year earnings: $805. **Clubs and organizations:** Number of student organizations: 90. Activities include: campus ministries, choral groups, concert band, dance, drama/theater, international student organization, jazz band, literary magazine, music ensembles, musical theater, pep band, radio station, student government, student newspaper, student film society, symphony orchestra, television station, yearbook. Number of fraternities: 0; sororities: 0. Average proportion of students who stay on campus on weekends: 85%. **Sports program (2009-2010):** Member of NCAA III. **Men's intercollegiate varsity sports:** baseball, basketball, cross country, football, golf, soccer, swimming, tennis, track and field (outdoor), water polo. **Women's intercollegiate varsity sports:** basketball, cross country, golf, lacrosse, soccer, softball, swimming, tennis, track and field (outdoor), volleyball, water polo.

SERVICES AND FACILITIES

Basic services: nonremedial tutoring, women's center, placement service, health service, health insurance. **Counseling services:** minority student, career, personal, academic, psychological, birth control, religious. **For learning-disabled students:** School does not offer a structured program with separate admission and additional fees. Total undergraduates in learning-disabled program or receiving services: 8. Services include: tape recorders, untimed tests, extended time for tests, tutors, other testing accommodations. **Library:** Number of titles: 2,618,747; number of current serial subscriptions: 47,450. **Information technology resources:** Students are not required to lease or own a computer. Number of campus computers available to all students: 120. School has a wireless network. Approximate number of users that can be accommodated: 1,280. Proportion of college-owned housing units wired for high-speed internet access: 100%. **Campus safety:** Security services offered: 24-hour foot-and-vehicle patrols, late-night transport/escort service, 24-hour emergency telephones, lighted pathways/sidewalks, controlled dormitory access (key, security card, etc).

TRANSFER AND INTERNATIONAL STUDENTS

Transfer students: May apply for admission for the following academic terms: Fall. Applicants do not need a minimum number of credits to apply. For fall 2009: Transfer applications received: 70. Transfer applicants offered admission: 1. Transfer applicants enrolled: 0. **International students:** Number of foreign undergraduates: 26 (3% of student body). Number of

countries represented: 20. Minimum TOEFL score required: 600 (paper); 250 (computer).

Holy Names University

- **Address:** 3500 Mountain Boulevard, Oakland, CA 94619
- **Website:** http://www.hnu.edu
- **Private; Religious affiliation:** Roman Catholic
- **Enrollment:** 536 full-time; 157 part-time

KEY STATS
✔ **U.S News College Ranking:** second tier, Regional Universities (West)
✔ **SAT Score (25th/75th percentile):** 788-971
✔ **Tuition:** 2010-2011: $28,690

Selectivity: Less selective	**Room/board:** $9,780
Acceptance rate: 77%	**Average debt:** $21,478
Student/faculty ratio: 16/1	**Proportion who borrowed:** 84%

UNDERGRADUATE STUDENT BODY STATS

2009-2010 enrollment: 536 full-time; 157 part-time. Men: 26%; women: 74%. **Ethnic makeup:** African American: 24%; Asian American: 9%; Hispanic: 18%; White: 45%; International: 4%.

ADMISSIONS FACTS AND FIGURES

Phone: (510) 436-1351. **Email:** admissions@hnu.edu. **Website:** http://www.hnu.edu. **Application deadlines for fall 2011:** Regular decision: August 15. Early decision: Not offered. Early action: Not offered. Admission can be deferred. **Application fee:** None. **To apply online, go to:** http://www.hnu.edu/admissions/applyOnline.html. **Admissions requirements/recommendations:** High school units required (recommended): English: 4; Mathematics: 3; Science: 1; Foreign language: 2 (3); History: 1; Academic electives: 3 (1); Total units: 15. Tests: The college uses SAT or ACT scores in admissions decisions. Either SAT or ACT required. For admission to the fall 2011 entering class, the school will accept: ACT with or without writing accepted. Campus visit: Recommended. Admissions interview: Recommended. Off-campus interview: May be arranged. **Factors that count in admissions decisions:** *Academic:* Secondary school record: Considered. Class rank: Not Considered. Letters of recommendation: Important. Standardized test scores: Important. Essay: Important. *Nonacademic:* Interview: Considered. Extracurricular activities: Considered. Talent/ability: Considered. Character/personal qualities: Considered. Alumni/ae relationship: Considered. Geographical residence: Not Considered. State residency: Not Considered. Religious affiliation/commitment: Not Considered. Minority status: Not Considered. Volunteer work: Considered. Work experience: Considered. **Other schools with the greatest overlap in applicants:** California State University–East Bay; Dominican University of California; Menlo College; Notre Dame de Namur University; St. Mary's College of California. **Admissions statistics for the fall 2009 entering class:** Total applicants: 452. Total accepted: 346. Freshmen enrolled: 127; Overall acceptance rate: 77%. **Credentials of fall 2009 freshmen:** 11% ranked in the top 10 percent of their high school class; 34% were in the top 25 percent. **Average high school grade point average:** 3.0. **First-year students who submitted SAT scores:** 84%. Scores (25/75 percentile): Critical Reading: 390-478, Math: 398-493, Combined: 788-971. **First-year students submitting ACT scores:** 40%. Scores (25/75 percentile): English: N/A, Math: N/A, Composite: 16-20.

ACADEMICS

Year founded: 1868. **Academic calendar:** Semester. **Degrees offered:** bachelor's, post-bachelor's certificate, master's, post-master's certificate. **Most popular majors:** 48% business administration and management, 17% nursing/registered nurse training (R.N., A.S.N., B.S.N., M.S.N.). **Major fields of study:** biological and biomedical sciences; business, management, marketing, and related support services; communication, journalism, and related programs; computer and information sciences and support services; English language and literature/letters; foreign languages, literatures, and linguistics; health professions and related clinical sciences; history; liberal arts and sciences studies, and humanities; philosophy and religious studies; psychology; public administration and social service professions; social sciences; visual and performing arts. **Areas of required coursework:** arts/fine arts, computer literacy, mathematics, English (including composition), philosophy, foreign languages, sciences (biological or physical), social science, other. **Pre-professional programs:** pre-law, pre-dentistry, pre-medicine, pre-veterinary science, pre-optometry, pre-pharmacy. **Special academic programs**

(% participation): accelerated program (1%), cross-registration, distance learning (5%), double major (17%), English as a Second Language (ESL), exchange student program (domestic), independent study, internships, liberal arts/career combination, student-designed major, study abroad, weekend college. **Reserve Officers Training Corps (ROTC):** Army ROTC: Offered at cooperating institution (University of California–Berkeley); Air Force ROTC: Offered at cooperating institution (University of California–Berkeley). **Faculty and instruction (2009-2010):** Total instructional faculty: 37 full-time, 126 part-time (34% men; 66% women; 10% minorities). Full-time faculty with Ph.D. or other terminal degree: 84%. Student/faculty ratio: 16/1. Classes of fewer than 20 students: 66%; of 20 to 49 students: 34%; of 50 or more students: 0%. **Advanced Placement and International Baccalaureate credit:** AP tests may be used for: Credit only. Scores accepted: 3, 4, 5. International Baccalaureate exams may be used for: Credit only. **Freshmen returning for sophomore year:** 70%. **Graduation rates:** Four-year: 26%; five-year: 31%; six-year: 33%.

COSTS AND FINANCIAL AID

Financial aid office: (510) 436-1327. **Expenses (2010-2011):** Tuition and fees 2010-2011: $28,690; room/board: $9,780. Estimated books and supplies: $1,620; transportation: $729. **Financial aid:** Priority filing date for institution's financial aid form: March 2; deadline: June 30. In 2009-2010, 100% of undergraduates applied for financial aid. Of those, 93% were determined to have financial need; 1% had their need fully met. Average financial aid package (proportion receiving): $20,413 (92%). Average amount of gift aid, such as scholarships or grants (proportion receiving): $17,912 (87%). Average amount of self-help aid, such as work study or loans (proportion receiving): $5,381 (83%). Average need-based loan (excluding PLUS or other private loans): $4,822. Among students who received need-based aid, the average percentage of need met: 53%. Among students who received aid based on merit, the average award (and the proportion receiving): $800 (4%). The average athletic scholarship (and the proportion receiving): $8,000 (1%). Average amount of debt of borrowers graduating in 2009: $21,478. Proportion who borrowed: 84%.

CAMPUS LIFE AND EXTRACURRICULAR ACTIVITIES

Campus housing available (% using): coed dorms (80%), women's dorms (16%), men's dorms (4%). **Student employment:** During the 2009-2010 academic year, 3% of undergraduates worked on campus. Average per-year earnings: $1,502. **Clubs and organizations:** Number of student organizations: 11. Activities include: campus ministries, choral groups, drama/theater, music ensembles, student government, symphony orchestra. Number of fraternities: 0; sororities: 0. Average proportion of students who stay on campus on weekends: 65%. **Sports program (2009-2010):** Member of NAIA. *Men's intercollegiate varsity sports:* basketball, cross country, golf, soccer. *Women's intercollegiate varsity sports:* basketball, cross country, soccer, softball, volleyball.

SERVICES AND FACILITIES

Basic services: nonremedial tutoring, health insurance, other. **Remedial assistance:** math, writing, study skills, other. **Counseling services:** career, personal, academic, psychological, religious. **For learning-disabled students:** School does not offer a structured program with separate admission and additional fees. Services include: remedial math, remedial English, reading machines, tape recorders, videotaped classes, note-taking services, oral tests, learning center, readers, extended time for tests, tutors, texts on tape, other testing accommodations. **Library:** Number of titles: 84,770; number of current serial subscriptions: 175. **Information technology resources:** Students are not required to lease or own a computer. Number of campus computers available to all students: 86. School has a wireless network. Approximate number of users that can be accommodated: 100. Proportion of college-owned housing units wired for high-speed internet access: 100%. **Campus safety:** Security services offered: late-night transport/escort service, 24-hour emergency telephones, lighted pathways/sidewalks, controlled dormitory access (key, security card, etc).

TRANSFER AND INTERNATIONAL STUDENTS

Transfer students: May apply for admission for the following academic terms: Fall, Spring. Applicants need a minimum number of credits to apply. For fall 2009: Transfer applications received: 175. Transfer applicants offered admission: 120. Transfer applicants enrolled: 80. **International students:** Number of foreign undergraduates: 26 (5% of student body). Number of countries represented: 21. Minimum TOEFL score required: 490 (paper); 163 (computer).

Hope International University

- **Address:** 2500 E. Nutwood Avenue, Fullerton, CA 92831
- **Website:** http://www.hiu.edu
- **Private; Religious affiliation:** Christian Churches/Churches of Christ
- **Enrollment:** 526 full-time; 187 part-time

KEY STATS
- ✔ **U.S News College Ranking:** second tier, Regional Universities (West)
- ✔ **SAT Score (25th/75th percentile):** 856-1058
- ✔ **Tuition:** 2010-2011: $23,190

Selectivity: Selective	**Room/board:** $7,400
Acceptance rate: 38%	**Average debt:** $27,000
Student/faculty ratio: 14/1	**Proportion who borrowed:** 97%

UNDERGRADUATE STUDENT BODY STATS

2009-2010 enrollment: 526 full-time; 187 part-time. Men: 43%; women: 57%. **Ethnic makeup:** African American: 6%; American-Indian: 1%; Asian American: 5%; Hispanic: 13%; White: 72%; International: 2%. **Religious preference:** Protestant: 30%; Christian Churches/Churches of Christ: 70%.

ADMISSIONS FACTS AND FIGURES

Phone: (714) 879-3901. **Email:** ug-admissions@hiu.edu. **Website:** http://www.hiu.edu. **Application deadlines for fall 2011:** Regular decision: Rolling. Early decision: Not offered. Early action: Not offered. Admission can be deferred. **Application fee:** $40. **To apply online, go to:** https://my.hiu.edu/Applicant/ApplyOnline_Login.aspx. **Admissions requirements/recommendations:** High school units required (recommended): English: (4); Mathematics: (2); Science: (1); Foreign language: (1); Social studies: (0); History: (1); Academic electives: (3); Total units: (13). Tests: The college uses SAT or ACT scores in admissions decisions. Either SAT or ACT required. For admission to the fall 2011 entering class, the school will accept: ACT with or without writing accepted. Campus visit: Recommended. Admissions interview: Recommended. Off-campus interview: May be arranged. **Factors that count in admissions decisions:** *Academic:* Secondary school record: Not Considered. Class rank: Very Important. Letters of recommendation: Very Important. Standardized test scores: Very Important. Essay: Very Important. *Nonacademic:* Interview: Very Important. Extracurricular activities: Considered. Talent/ability: Not Considered. Character/personal qualities: Very Important. Alumni/ae relationship: Not Considered. Geographical residence: Not Considered. State residency: Not Considered. Religious affiliation/commitment: Very Important. Minority status: Not Considered. Volunteer work: Not Considered. Work experience: Not Considered. **Other schools with the greatest overlap in applicants:** Azusa Pacific University; Biola University; California Baptist University; Concordia University; Vanguard University of Southern California. **Admissions statistics for the fall 2009 entering class:** Total applicants: 489. Total accepted: 188. Freshmen enrolled: 113; 18% were from out of state. Overall acceptance rate: 38%. **Credentials of fall 2009 freshmen:** 17% ranked in the top 10 percent of their high school class; 36% were in the top 25 percent; 75% were in the top half. (Proportion submitting class standing: 43%.) **Average high school grade point average:** 3.2. **First-year students who submitted SAT scores:** 70%. Scores (25/75 percentile): Critical Reading: 423-520, Math: 433-538, Combined: 856-1058. **First-year students submitting ACT scores:** 18%. Scores (25/75 percentile): English: 17-25, Math: 19-23, Composite: 19-26.

ACADEMICS

Year founded: 1928. **Academic calendar:** Semester. **Degrees offered:** certificate, diploma, associate, transfer-associate, terminal-associate, bachelor's, post-bachelor's certificate, master's. **Most popular majors:** 33% business, management, marketing, and related support services, 28% family and consumer sciences/human sciences, 18% theology and religious vocations, 8% psychology, 6% social sciences. **Major fields of study:** business, management, marketing, and related support services; education; family and consumer sciences/human sciences; psychology; social sciences; theology and religious vocations. **Areas of required coursework:** humanities, computer literacy, mathematics, English (including composition), philosophy, sciences (biological or physical), history, social science, other. **Pre-professional programs:** pre-theology. **Special academic programs (% participation):** accelerated program (25%), distance learning (25%), double major (0%), English as a Second Language (ESL) (0%), exchange student program (domestic) (0%), external degree program (0%), honors program, independent study, internships (43%), liberal arts/career combination, student-designed major, teacher certificate program (0%). **Teacher certification offered in:** elemen-

tary. **Cooperative education programs:** social/behavioral science, other.
Reserve Officers Training Corps (ROTC): Air Force ROTC: Offered at cooperating institution (University of Southern California). **Faculty and instruction (2009-2010):** Total instructional faculty: 31 full-time, 107 part-time (57% men; 43% women; 10% minorities). Full-time faculty with Ph.D. or other terminal degree: 77%. Student/faculty ratio: 14/1. Classes of fewer than 20 students: 77%; of 20 to 49 students: 23%; of 50 or more students: 0%. **Advanced Placement and International Baccalaureate credit:** AP tests may be used for: Credit only. Scores accepted: 3, 4, 5. International Baccalaureate exams may be used for: Credit only. **Freshmen returning for sophomore year:** 69%. **Graduation rates:** Four-year: 20%; five-year: 25%; six-year: 38%. **Graduate study:** 30% of students pursue further study immediately upon graduation. Fields in which graduates pursue further study: theology (or the seminary), 7%; education, 17%; arts and sciences, 7%.

COSTS AND FINANCIAL AID

Financial aid office: (714) 879-3901. **Expenses (2010-2011):** Tuition and fees 2010-2011: $23,190; room/board: $7,400. Estimated books and supplies: $1,620; transportation: $729; personal expenses: $2,250. **Financial aid:** Priority filing date for institution's financial aid form: March 2. In 2009-2010, 83% of undergraduates applied for financial aid. Of those, 38% were determined to have financial need; 2% had their need fully met. Average financial aid package (proportion receiving): $14,609 (38%). Average amount of gift aid, such as scholarships or grants (proportion receiving): $9,344 (38%). Average amount of self-help aid, such as work study or loans (proportion receiving): $5,866 (38%). Average need-based loan (excluding PLUS or other private loans): $5,005. Among students who received need-based aid, the average percentage of need met: 39%. Among students who received aid based on merit, the average award (and the proportion receiving): $7,477 (1%). The average athletic scholarship (and the proportion receiving): $13,320 (23%). Average amount of debt of borrowers graduating in 2009: $27,000. Proportion who borrowed: 97%.

CAMPUS LIFE AND EXTRACURRICULAR ACTIVITIES

Campus housing available (% using): women's dorms (59%), men's dorms (41%). Students who live in college-owned, operated, or affiliated housing: 43%. **Student employment:** During the 2009-2010 academic year, 40% of undergraduates worked on campus. Average per-year earnings: $1,904. **Clubs and organizations:** Number of student organizations: 3. Activities include: campus ministries, choral groups, drama/theater, international student organization, jazz band, music ensembles, musical theater, student government, student newspaper, yearbook. Number of fraternities: 0; sororities: 0. Average proportion of students who stay on campus on weekends: 70%. **Sports program (2009-2010):** Member of NAIA. *Men's intercollegiate varsity sports:* basketball, soccer, tennis, volleyball. *Women's intercollegiate varsity sports:* basketball, soccer, softball, tennis, volleyball.

SERVICES AND FACILITIES

Basic services: nonremedial tutoring, health insurance. **Remedial assistance:** reading, math, writing, study skills. **Counseling services:** minority student, career, veteran student, academic, psychological, religious. **For learning-disabled students:** School does not offer a structured program with separate admission and additional fees. Total undergraduates in learning-disabled program or receiving services: 0. Services include: remedial math, remedial English, tape recorders, oral tests, extended time for tests, tutors, early syllabus, priority seating, other testing accommodations. **Library:** Number of titles: 89,519; number of current serial subscriptions: 483. **Information technology resources:** Students are not required to lease or own a computer. Number of campus computers available to all students: 56. School has a wireless network. Approximate number of users that can be accommodated: 250. Proportion of college-owned housing units wired for high-speed internet access: 100%. **Campus safety:** Security services offered: 24-hour foot-and-vehicle patrols, late-night transport/escort service, 24-hour emergency telephones, lighted pathways/sidewalks, student patrols, controlled dormitory access (key, security card, etc).

TRANSFER AND INTERNATIONAL STUDENTS

Transfer students: May apply for admission for the following academic terms: Fall, Winter, Spring, Summer. Applicants do not need a minimum number of credits to apply. For fall 2009: Transfer applications received: 824. Transfer applicants offered admission: 557. Transfer applicants enrolled: 264. **International students:** Number of foreign undergraduates: 14 (2% of student body). Number of countries represented: 31. Minimum TOEFL score required: 500 (paper); 83 (computer). Average TOEFL score: 500 (paper).

Humboldt State University

- **Address:** 1 Harpst Street, Arcata, CA 95521-8299
- **Website:** http://www.humboldt.edu
- **Public**
- **Enrollment:** 6,536 full-time; 633 part-time

KEY STATS

✔ **U.S News College Ranking:** 37, Regional Universities (West)
✔ **SAT Score (25th/75th percentile):** 930-1160
✔ **Tuition:** 2009-2010: $5,166 in state, $14,094 out of state
  Selectivity: Selective   **Room/board:** $9,986
  Acceptance rate: 84%   **Average debt:** $17,668
  Student/faculty ratio: 22/1   **Proportion who borrowed:** 66%

UNDERGRADUATE STUDENT BODY STATS

2009-2010 enrollment: 6,536 full-time; 633 part-time. Men: 46%; women: 54%. **Ethnic makeup:** African American: 3%; American-Indian: 2%; Asian American: 4%; Hispanic: 13%; White: 77%; International: 1%.

ADMISSIONS FACTS AND FIGURES

Phone: (707) 826-4402. **Email:** hsuinfo@humboldt.edu. **Website:** http://www.humboldt.edu. **Application deadlines for fall 2011:** Regular decision: November 30. Early decision: Not offered. Early action: Not offered. Admission cannot be deferred. **Application fee:** $55. **To apply online, go to:** http://www.csumentor.edu/AdmissionApp/. **Admissions requirements/recommendations:** High school units required (recommended): English: 4; Mathematics: 3; Science: 2; Foreign language: 2; Social studies: 1; History: 1; Academic electives: 1; Total units: 15. Tests: The college uses SAT or ACT scores in admissions decisions. Neither SAT nor ACT required. For admission to the fall 2011 entering class, the school will accept: ACT with or without writing accepted. Campus visit: Recommended. Admissions interview: Neither required nor recommended. Off-campus interview: Not available. **Factors that count in admissions decisions: Academic:** Secondary school record: Important. Class rank: Not Considered. Letters of recommendation: Not Considered. Standardized test scores: Very Important. Essay: Not Considered. *Nonacademic:* Interview: Not Considered. Extracurricular activities: Not Considered. Talent/ability: Not Considered. Character/personal qualities: Not Considered. Alumni/ae relationship: Not Considered. Geographical residence: Not Considered. State residency: Considered. Religious affiliation/commitment: Not Considered. Minority status: Not Considered. Volunteer work: Not Considered. Work experience: Not Considered. **Other schools with the greatest overlap in applicants:** California State University–Long Beach; San Diego State University; San Francisco State University; University of California–Davis; University of California–Santa Cruz. **Admissions statistics for the fall 2009 entering class:** Total applicants: 9,379. Total accepted: 7,900. Freshmen enrolled: 1,385; 17% were from out of state. Overall acceptance rate: 84%. **Credentials of fall 2009 freshmen:** 15% ranked in the top 10 percent of their high school class; 38% were in the top 25 percent; 82% were in the top half. (Proportion submitting class standing: 58%.) **Average high school grade point average:** 3.2. **First-year students who submitted SAT scores:** 91%. Scores (25/75 percentile): Critical Reading: 470-590, Math: 460-570, Combined: 930-1160. **First-year students submitting ACT scores:** 36%. Scores (25/75 percentile): English: 18-25, Math: 18-25, Composite: 19-25.

ACADEMICS

Year founded: 1913. **Academic calendar:** Semester. **Degrees offered:** bachelor's, post-bachelor's certificate, master's. **Most popular majors:** 11% natural resources and conservation, 11% social sciences, 10% liberal arts and sciences studies, and humanities, 10% visual and performing arts, 9% biological and biomedical sciences. **Major fields of study:** agriculture, agriculture operations, and related sciences; area, ethnic, cultural, and gender studies; biological and biomedical sciences; business, management, marketing, and related support services; communication, journalism, and related programs; computer and information sciences and support services; education; engineering; engineering technologies/technicians; English language and literature/letters; foreign languages, literatures, and linguistics; health professions and related clinical sciences; history; liberal arts and sciences studies, and humanities; mathematics and statistics; multi/interdisciplinary studies; natural resources and conservation; philosophy and religious studies; physical sciences; psychology; public administration and social service professions; science technologies/technicians; social sciences; transportation and materials moving; visual and performing arts. **Areas of required**

coursework: humanities, mathematics, English (including composition), sciences (biological or physical), history, social science. **Pre-professional programs:** pre-law, pre-dentistry, pre-medicine, pre-veterinary science, pre-optometry, pre-pharmacy. **Special academic programs:** cooperative (work-study plan) program, cross-registration, distance learning, double major, dual enrollment, English as a Second Language (ESL), exchange student program (domestic), honors program, independent study, internships, student-designed major, study abroad, teacher certificate program. **Teacher certification offered in:** early childhood, special education, elementary, middle/junior high, secondary, bilingual/bicultural. **Faculty and instruction (2009-2010):** Total instructional faculty: 254 full-time, 254 part-time (52% men; 48% women; 12% minorities). Full-time faculty with Ph.D. or other terminal degree: 99%. Student/faculty ratio: 22/1. Classes of fewer than 20 students: 37%; of 20 to 49 students: 51%; of 50 or more students: 11%. **Advanced Placement and International Baccalaureate credit:** AP tests may be used for: Credit and/or placement. Scores accepted: 3, 4, 5. International Baccalaureate exams may be used for: Credit only. **Freshmen returning for sophomore year:** 75%. **Graduation rates:** Four-year: 11%; five-year: 31%; six-year: 43%.

COSTS AND FINANCIAL AID
Financial aid office: (707) 826-4321. **Expenses (2009-2010):** Tuition and fees 2009-2010: $5,166 in state, $14,094 out of state; room/board: $9,986. Estimated books and supplies: $1,528; transportation: $1,010; personal expenses: $2,224. **Financial aid:** Priority filing date for institution's financial aid form: March 2. In 2009-2010, 74% of undergraduates applied for financial aid. Of those, 61% were determined to have financial need; 2% had their need fully met. Average financial aid package (proportion receiving): $10,984 (59%). Average amount of gift aid, such as scholarships or grants (proportion receiving): $8,560 (48%). Average amount of self-help aid, such as work study or loans (proportion receiving): $4,468 (46%). Average need-based loan (excluding PLUS or other private loans): $4,248. Among students who received need-based aid, the average percentage of need met: 71%. Among students who received aid based on merit, the average award (and the proportion receiving): $2,011 (3%). The average athletic scholarship (and the proportion receiving): $2,931 (3%). Average amount of debt of borrowers graduating in 2009: $17,668. Proportion who borrowed: 66%.

CAMPUS LIFE AND EXTRACURRICULAR ACTIVITIES
Campus housing available (% using): coed dorms (80%), apartment for single students (3%). Students who live in college-owned, operated, or affiliated housing: 23%. **Clubs and organizations:** Number of student organizations: 180. Activities include: choral groups, concert band, dance, drama/theater, international student organization, jazz band, literary magazine, marching band, model UN, music ensembles, musical theater, pep band, radio station, student government, student newspaper, student film society, symphony orchestra. Number of fraternities: 2; sororities: 2. Average proportion of students who stay on campus on weekends: 20%. **Sports program (2009-2010):** Member of NCAA II. *Men's intercollegiate varsity sports:* basketball, cross country, football, soccer, track and field (outdoor). *Women's intercollegiate varsity sports:* basketball, cross country, crew (lightweight), soccer, softball, track and field (outdoor), volleyball.

SERVICES AND FACILITIES
Basic services: nonremedial tutoring, women's center, day care, health service, health insurance. **Remedial assistance:** reading, math, writing, study skills. **Counseling services:** career, personal, veteran student, academic, psychological, birth control. **For learning-disabled students:** School does not offer a structured program with separate admission and additional fees. Total undergraduates in learning-disabled program or receiving services: 150. Services include: remedial math, remedial English, reading machines, remedial reading, tape recorders, untimed tests, note-taking services, learning center, readers, extended time for tests, tutors, priority registration, other. **Library:** Number of titles: 1,000,000; number of current serial subscriptions: 429. **Information technology resources:** Students are not required to lease or own a computer. Number of campus computers available to all students: 1,098. School has a wireless network. Proportion of college-owned housing units wired for high-speed internet access: 100%. **Campus safety:** Security services offered: 24-hour foot-and-vehicle patrols, late-night transport/escort service, 24-hour emergency telephones, lighted pathways/sidewalks, controlled dormitory access (key, security card, etc).

TRANSFER AND INTERNATIONAL STUDENTS
Transfer students: May apply for admission for the following academic terms: Fall. Applicants do not need a minimum number of credits to apply. For fall 2009: Transfer applications received: 3,014. Transfer applicants

offered admission: 1,376. Transfer applicants enrolled: 804. **International students:** Number of foreign undergraduates: 61 (1% of student body). Number of countries represented: 19. Minimum TOEFL score required: 500 (paper); 173 (computer).

Humphreys College

- **Address:** 6650 Inglewood Avenue, Stockton, CA 95207
- **Website:** http://www.humphreys.edu
- **Private**
- **Enrollment:** N/A

KEY STATS
✔ **U.S News College Ranking:** Unranked, Regional Colleges (West)
✔ **SAT or ACT Score (25th/75th percentile):** N/A
✔ **Tuition:** 2009-2010: $12,864

Selectivity: N/A	Room/board: $7,524
Acceptance rate: N/A	Average debt: N/A
Student/faculty ratio: N/A	Proportion who borrowed: N/A

John F. Kennedy University

- **Address:** 100 Ellinwood Way, Pleasant Hill, CA 94523
- **Website:** http://www.jfku.edu
- **Private**
- **Enrollment:** N/A

KEY STATS
✔ **U.S News College Ranking:** Unranked, Regional Universities (West)
✔ **SAT or ACT Score (25th/75th percentile):** N/A
✔ **Tuition:** 2009-2010: $16,680

Selectivity: N/A	Room/board: N/A
Acceptance rate: N/A	Average debt: N/A
Student/faculty ratio: N/A	Proportion who borrowed: N/A

Laguna College of Art and Design

- **Address:** 2222 Laguna Canyon Road, Laguna Beach, CA 92651
- **Website:** http://www.lagunacollege.edu
- **Private**
- **Enrollment:** N/A

KEY STATS
✔ **U.S News College Ranking:** Unranked Specialty School–Fine Arts
✔ **SAT or ACT Score (25th/75th percentile):** N/A
✔ **Tuition:** 2009-2010: $21,600

Selectivity: N/A	Room/board: N/A
Acceptance rate: N/A	Average debt: N/A
Student/faculty ratio: N/A	Proportion who borrowed: N/A

La Sierra University

- **Address:** 4500 Riverwalk Parkway, Riverside, CA 92515
- **Website:** http://www.lasierra.edu
- **Private; Religious affiliation:** Seventh-day Adventist
- **Enrollment:** 1,304 full-time; 201 part-time

KEY STATS
✔ **U.S News College Ranking:** second tier, Regional Universities (West)
✔ **SAT Score (25th/75th percentile):** 830-1120
✔ **Tuition:** 2009-2010: $24,573

Selectivity: Selective	Room/board: $6,990
Acceptance rate: 53%	Average debt: N/A
Student/faculty ratio: 15/1	Proportion who borrowed: N/A

UNDERGRADUATE STUDENT BODY STATS

2009-2010 enrollment: 1,304 full-time; 201 part-time. Men: 44%; women: 56%. **Ethnic makeup:** African American: 9%; American-Indian: 1%; Asian American: 25%; Hispanic: 29%; White: 25%; International: 12%. **Religious preference:** Roman Catholic: 9%; Protestant: 14%; Hindu: 1%; Buddhist: 1%; Seventh-day Adventist: 66%; Other: 9%.

ADMISSIONS FACTS AND FIGURES

Phone: (951) 785-2176. **Email:** admissions@lasierra.edu. **Website:** http://www.lasierra.edu. **Application deadlines for fall 2011:** Regular decision: Rolling. Early decision: Not offered. Early action: Not offered. Admission can be deferred. **Application fee:** $30. **To apply online, go to:** http://www.lasierra.edu/admission-application/. **Admissions requirements/recommendations:** High school units required (recommended): English: 4; Mathematics: 3 (4); Science: 2 (3); Foreign language: 2 (3); Social studies: 2; Academic electives: 1; Total units: 15. Tests: The college uses SAT or ACT scores in admissions decisions. Either SAT or ACT required. For admission to the fall 2011 entering class, the school will accept: ACT with or without writing accepted. Campus visit: Recommended. Admissions interview: Recommended. Off-campus interview: May be arranged. **Factors that count in admissions decisions: Academic:** Secondary school record: Very Important. Class rank: Not Considered. Letters of recommendation: Important. Standardized test scores: Very Important. Essay: Important. *Nonacademic:* Interview: Considered. Extracurricular activities: Not Considered. Talent/ability: Not Considered. Character/personal qualities: Important. Alumni/ae relationship: Not Considered. Geographical residence: Not Considered. State residency: Not Considered. Religious affiliation/commitment: Important. Minority status: Not Considered. Volunteer work: Not Considered. Work experience: Not Considered. **Admissions statistics for the fall 2009 entering class:** Total applicants: 1,444. Total accepted: 759. Freshmen enrolled: 348; 12% were from out of state. Overall acceptance rate: 53%. **Credentials of fall 2009 freshmen:** 13% ranked in the top 10 percent of their high school class; 39% were in the top 25 percent; 72% were in the top half. (Proportion submitting class standing: 70%.) **Average high school grade point average:** 3.3. **First-year students who submitted SAT scores:** 81%. Scores (25/75 percentile): Critical Reading: 420-560, Math: 410-560, Combined: 830-1120. **First-year students submitting ACT scores:** 26%. Scores (25/75 percentile): English: 16-23, Math: 16-23, Composite: 17-22.

ACADEMICS

Year founded: 1922. **Academic calendar:** Quarter. **Degrees offered:** certificate, transfer-associate, bachelor's, master's, post-master's certificate, doctorate. **Most popular majors:** 29% business administration and management, 18% biology/biological sciences, 10% liberal arts and sciences/liberal studies, 8% psychology, 4% graphic design. **Major fields of study:** biological and biomedical sciences; business, management, marketing, and related support services; communication, journalism, and related programs; computer and information sciences and support services; education; English language and literature/letters; foreign languages, literatures, and linguistics; history; liberal arts and sciences studies, and humanities; mathematics and statistics; parks, recreation, leisure, and fitness studies; philosophy and religious studies; physical sciences; psychology; public administration and social service professions; social sciences; visual and performing arts. **Areas of required coursework:** arts/fine arts, humanities, computer literacy, mathematics, English (including composition), foreign languages, sciences (biological or physical), history, social science. **Pre-professional programs:** pre-law, pre-dentistry, pre-medicine, pre-theology, pre-veterinary science, pre-optometry, pre-pharmacy. **Special academic programs:** accelerated program, cross-registration, distance learning, double major, dual enrollment, English as a Second Language (ESL), honors program, independent study, internships, student-designed major, study abroad, teacher certificate program. **Teacher certification offered in:** elementary, middle/junior high, secondary. **Faculty and instruction (2009-2010):** Total instructional faculty: 93 full-time, 87 part-time (56% men; 44% women; 36% minorities). Full-time faculty with Ph.D. or other terminal degree: 84%. Student/faculty ratio: 15/1. Classes of fewer than 20 students: 66%; of 20 to 49 students: 30%; of 50 or more students: 4%. **Advanced Placement and International Baccalaureate credit:** AP tests may be used for: Credit only. Scores accepted: 3, 4, 5. **Freshmen returning for sophomore year:** 66%. **Graduation rates:** Four-year: 14%; five-year: 25%; six-year: 31%.

COSTS AND FINANCIAL AID

Financial aid office: (909) 785-2175. **Expenses (2009-2010):** Tuition and fees 2009-2010: $24,573; room/board: $6,990. Estimated books and supplies: $1,605; transportation: $763; personal expenses: $2,322. **Financial aid:** Priority filing date for institution's financial aid form: March 2.

CAMPUS LIFE AND EXTRACURRICULAR ACTIVITIES

Campus housing available (% using): coed dorms (9%), women's dorms (45%), men's dorms (28%), apartments for married students (8%), apartment for single students (8%), special housing for disabled students (0%). Students who live in college-owned, operated, or affiliated housing: 36%. **Student employment:** During the 2009-2010 academic year, 24% of undergraduates worked on campus. **Clubs and organizations:** Number of student organizations: 45. Activities include: campus ministries, choral groups, concert band, drama/theater, international student organization, jazz band, literary magazine, music ensembles, student government, student newspaper, symphony orchestra, yearbook. Number of fraternities: 0; sororities: 0. Average proportion of students who stay on campus on weekends: 35%. **Sports program (2009-2010):** Member of NCAA III. *Men's intercollegiate varsity sports:* baseball, basketball, golf, soccer, tennis. *Women's intercollegiate varsity sports:* basketball, soccer, softball, tennis, volleyball.

SERVICES AND FACILITIES

Basic services: nonremedial tutoring, women's center, placement service, health service, health insurance. **Remedial assistance:** reading, math, writing, study skills. **Counseling services:** minority student, career, personal, academic, psychological, religious. **For learning-disabled students:** School does not offer a structured program with separate admission and additional fees. Total undergraduates in learning-disabled program or receiving services: 22. Services include: remedial math, remedial English, remedial reading, tape recorders, note-taking services, oral tests, learning center, readers, extended time for tests, tutors, early syllabus, priority registration, priority seating, proofreading services, texts on tape, typist/scribe, exams on tape or computer, take home exams, other testing accommodations. **Library:** Number of titles: 255,050; number of current serial subscriptions: 1,011. **Information technology resources:** Students are not required to lease or own a computer. Number of campus computers available to all students: 262. School has a wireless network. Approximate number of users that can be accommodated: 800. Proportion of college-owned housing units wired for high-speed internet access: 100%. **Campus safety:** Security services offered: 24-hour foot-and-vehicle patrols, late-night transport/escort service, 24-hour emergency telephones, lighted pathways/sidewalks, controlled dormitory access (key, security card, etc).

TRANSFER AND INTERNATIONAL STUDENTS

Transfer students: May apply for admission for the following academic terms: Fall, Winter, Spring, Summer. Applicants need a minimum number of credits to apply. For fall 2009: Transfer applications received: 1,444. Transfer applicants offered admission: 759. Transfer applicants enrolled: 348. **International students:** Number of foreign undergraduates: 176 (12% of student body). Number of countries represented: 42. Minimum TOEFL score required: 550 (paper).

Loyola Marymount University

- **Address:** 1 LMU Drive, Los Angeles, CA 90045-2659
- **Website:** http://www.lmu.edu
- **Private; Religious affiliation:** Roman Catholic
- **Enrollment:** 5,522 full-time; 311 part-time

KEY STATS

✔ **U.S News College Ranking:** 3, Regional Universities (West)
✔ **SAT Score (25th/75th percentile):** 1080-1280
✔ **Tuition:** 2010-2011: $36,404

Selectivity: More selective	**Room/board:** $13,930
Acceptance rate: 59%	**Average debt:** $28,596
Student/faculty ratio: 11/1	**Proportion who borrowed:** 61%

UNDERGRADUATE STUDENT BODY STATS

2009-2010 enrollment: 5,522 full-time; 311 part-time. Men: 43%; women: 57%. **Ethnic makeup:** African American: 8%; American-Indian: 1%; Asian American: 13%; Hispanic: 19%; White: 56%; International: 3%. **Religious preference:** Protestant: 10%; Jewish: 3%; Muslim: 1%; Buddhist: 1%; Unknown: 31%; Roman Catholic: 46%; Other Christian: 8%.

ADMISSIONS FACTS AND FIGURES

Phone: (310) 338-2750. **Email:** admissions@lmu.edu. **Website:** http://www.lmu.edu. **Application deadlines for fall 2011:** Regular decision: January 15. Early decision: Not offered. Early action: Send application by: November 1; Decision sent by: December 21. Admission can be deferred. **Application fee:** $60. **To apply online, go to:** http://www.lmu.edu/admissions. **Admissions requirements/recommendations:** High school units required (recommended): English: (4); Mathematics: (3); Science: (2); Foreign language: (3); Social studies: (3); Academic electives: (1); Total units: (18). Tests: The college uses SAT or ACT scores in admissions decisions. Either SAT or ACT required. For admission to the fall 2011 entering class, the school will accept: ACT with writing recommended. Campus visit: Recommended. Admissions interview: Neither required nor recommended. Off-campus interview: Not available. **Factors that count in admissions decisions:** *Academic:* Secondary school record: Important. Class rank: Considered. Letters of recommendation: Considered. Standardized test scores: Important. Essay: Important. *Nonacademic:* Interview: Not Considered. Extracurricular activities: Considered. Talent/ability: Important. Character/personal qualities: Important. Alumni/ae relationship: Considered. Geographical residence: Not Considered. State residency: Not Considered. Religious affiliation/commitment: Not Considered. Minority status: Not Considered. Volunteer work: Not Considered. Work experience: Not Considered. **Other schools with the greatest overlap in applicants:** University of California–Irvine; University of California–Los Angeles; University of California–Santa Barbara; University of San Diego; University of Southern California. **Admissions statistics for the fall 2009 entering class:** Total applicants: 9,456. Total accepted: 5,594. Freshmen enrolled: 1,385; 30% were from out of state. Accepted through early-decision or early-action plans: 29%. Overall acceptance rate: 59%. Non-early acceptance rate: 56%. **Size of waiting list:** 1165 applicants; enrolled from waiting list: 232. **Credentials of fall 2009 freshmen:** 29% ranked in the top 10 percent of their high school class; 65% were in the top 25 percent; 96% were in the top half. (Proportion submitting class standing: 39%.) **Average high school grade point average:** 3.7. **First-year students who submitted SAT scores:** 88%. Scores (25/75 percentile): Critical Reading: 530-630, Math: 550-650, Combined: 1080-1280. **First-year students submitting ACT scores:** 46%. Scores (25/75 percentile): English: 24-29, Math: 23-29, Composite: 24-28.

ACADEMICS

Year founded: 1911. **Academic calendar:** Semester. **Degrees offered:** certificate, bachelor's, post-bachelor's certificate, master's, post-master's certificate, doctorate. **Most popular majors:** 26% business/commerce, 8% communication studies/speech communication and rhetoric, 6% social sciences, 5% English language and literature, 5% psychology. **Major fields of study:** area, ethnic, cultural, and gender studies; biological and biomedical sciences; business, management, marketing, and related support services; communications technologies/technicians and support services; computer and information sciences and support services; engineering; English language and literature/letters; foreign languages, literatures, and linguistics; health professions and related clinical sciences; history; liberal arts and sciences studies, and humanities; mathematics and statistics; multi/interdisciplinary studies; philosophy and religious studies; physical sciences; psychology; social sciences; theology and religious vocations; visual and performing arts. **Areas of required coursework:** arts/fine arts, humanities, mathematics, English (including composition), philosophy, sciences (biological or physical), history, social science, other. **Pre-professional programs:** pre-law, pre-dentistry, pre-medicine, pre-theology, pre-veterinary science, pre-optometry, pre-pharmacy, other. **Special academic programs:** accelerated program, cross-registration, distance learning, double major, dual enrollment, English as a Second Language (ESL), exchange student program (domestic), honors program, independent study, internships, liberal arts/career combination, student-designed major, study abroad, teacher certificate program, other. **Teacher certification offered in:** special education, elementary, middle/junior high, secondary, bilingual/bicultural. **Reserve Officers Training Corps (ROTC):** Army ROTC: Offered at cooperating institution (University of California–Los Angeles); Navy ROTC: Offered at cooperating institution (University of California–Los Angeles); Air Force ROTC: Offered on campus. **Faculty and instruction (2009-2010):** Total instructional faculty: 507 full-time, 502 part-time (56% men; 44% women; 24% minorities). Full-time faculty with Ph.D. or other terminal degree: 99%. Student/faculty ratio: 11/1. Classes of fewer than 20 students: 48%; of 20 to 49 students: 51%; of 50 or more students: 1%. **Advanced Placement and International Baccalaureate credit:** AP tests may be used for: Credit only. Scores accepted: 4, 5. International Baccalaureate exams may be used for: Credit only. **Freshmen returning for sophomore year:** 88%. **Graduation rates:** Four-year: 71%; five-year: 78%; six-year: 77%. **Graduate study:** 16% of students pursue further study within one year. Fields in which graduates pursue further study: Master of Business Administration (MBA), 15%; law, 13%; medicine, 18%; dentistry, 3%; engineering, 8%; theology (or the seminary), 7%; education, 22%; arts and sciences, 12%; veterinary medicine, 2%.

COSTS AND FINANCIAL AID

Financial aid office: (310) 338-2753. **Expenses (2010-2011):** Tuition and fees 2010-2011: $36,404; room/board: $13,930. Estimated books and supplies: $1,620; transportation: $729; personal expenses: $2,250. **Financial aid:** Priority filing date for institution's financial aid form: February 1; deadline: July 30. In 2009-2010, 72% of undergraduates applied for financial aid. Of those, 57% were determined to have financial need; 27% had their need fully met. Average financial aid package (proportion receiving): $29,477 (57%). Average amount of gift aid, such as scholarships or grants (proportion receiving): $19,354 (51%). Average amount of self-help aid, such as work study or loans (proportion receiving): $8,760 (52%). Average need-based loan (excluding PLUS or other private loans): $5,517. Among students who received need-based aid, the average percentage of need met: 75%. Among students who received aid based on merit, the average award (and the proportion receiving): $10,954 (12%). The average athletic scholarship (and the proportion receiving): $24,363 (3%). Average amount of debt of borrowers graduating in 2009: $28,596. Proportion who borrowed: 61%.

CAMPUS LIFE AND EXTRACURRICULAR ACTIVITIES

Campus housing available: coed dorms, women's dorms, men's dorms, apartment for single students, special housing for disabled students, special housing for international students, other housing options. Students who live in college-owned, operated, or affiliated housing: 57%. **Student employment:** During the 2009-2010 academic year, 51% of undergraduates worked on campus. Average per-year earnings: $2,800. **Clubs and organizations:** Number of student organizations: 150. Activities include: campus ministries, choral groups, dance, drama/theater, international student organization, literary magazine, music ensembles, pep band, radio station, student government, student newspaper, student film society, television station, yearbook. Number of fraternities: 6; sororities: 9. Proportion of men in fraternities: 11%; of women in sororities: 20%. Average proportion of students who stay on campus on weekends: 75%. **Sports program (2009-2010):** Member of NCAA I. *Men's intercollegiate varsity sports:* baseball, basketball, cross country, golf, soccer, tennis, track and field (outdoor), water polo. *Women's intercollegiate varsity sports:* basketball, crew (heavyweight), cross country, soccer, softball, swimming, tennis, track and field (outdoor), volleyball, water polo.

SERVICES AND FACILITIES

Basic services: nonremedial tutoring, placement service, day care, health service, health insurance, other. **Remedial assistance:** reading, math, writing, study skills, other. **Counseling services:** minority student, career, military, personal, academic, older student, psychological, religious. **For learning-disabled students:** School does not offer a structured program with separate admission and additional fees. Total undergraduates in learning-disabled program or receiving services: 200. Services include: reading machines, tape recorders, note-taking services, oral tests, learning center, readers, extended time for tests, tutors, priority registration, priority seating, texts on tape, exams on tape or computer, other testing accommodations, other. **Library:** Number of titles: 524,565; number of current serial subscriptions: 19,366. **Information technology resources:** Students are not required to lease or own a computer. School has a wireless network. Approximate number of users that can be accommodated: 3,000. Proportion of college-owned housing units wired for high-speed internet access: 100%. **Campus safety:** Security services offered: 24-hour foot-and-vehicle patrols, late-night transport/escort service, 24-hour emergency telephones, lighted pathways/sidewalks, controlled dormitory access (key, security card, etc).

TRANSFER AND INTERNATIONAL STUDENTS

Transfer students: May apply for admission for the following academic terms: Fall, Spring. Applicants do not need a minimum number of credits to apply. For fall 2009: Transfer applications received: 1,298. Transfer applicants offered admission: 711. Transfer applicants enrolled: 358. **International students:** Number of foreign undergraduates: 178 (3% of student body). Number of countries represented: 58. Minimum TOEFL score required: 550 (paper); 80 (computer). Average TOEFL score: 598 (paper).

Master's College and Seminary

- **Address:** 21726 Placerita Canyon Road, Santa Clarita, CA 91321-1200
- **Website:** http://www.masters.edu
- **Private; Religious affiliation:** Evangelical
- **Enrollment:** 876 full-time; 110 part-time

KEY STATS
✔ **U.S News College Ranking:** 2, Regional Colleges (West)
✔ **SAT Score (25th/75th percentile):** 960-1240
✔ **Tuition:** 2010-2011: $25,640

Selectivity: Selective	**Room/board:** $8,320
Acceptance rate: 49%	**Average debt:** $30,003
Student/faculty ratio: 10/1	**Proportion who borrowed:** 68%

UNDERGRADUATE STUDENT BODY STATS
2009-2010 enrollment: 876 full-time; 110 part-time. Men: 52%; women: 48%. **Ethnic makeup:** African American: 3%; American-Indian: 1%; Asian American: 5%; Hispanic: 8%; White: 78%; International: 5%.

ADMISSIONS FACTS AND FIGURES
Phone: (800) 568-6248. **Email:** admissions@masters.edu. **Website:** http://www.masters.edu. **Application deadlines for fall 2011:** Regular decision: Rolling. Early decision: Send application by: November 15; Decision sent by: December 22. Early action: Send application by: November 15; Decision sent by: December 22. Admission can be deferred. **Application fee:** $40. **Admissions requirements/recommendations:** High school units required (recommended): English: 4; Mathematics: 3; Science: 2; History: 2; Academic electives: (3). Tests: The college uses SAT or ACT scores in admissions decisions. Either SAT or ACT required. For admission to the fall 2011 entering class, the school will accept: ACT with writing required. Campus visit: Recommended. Admissions interview: Recommended. Off-campus interview: May be arranged. **Factors that count in admissions decisions:** *Academic:* Secondary school record: Very Important. Class rank: Not Considered. Letters of recommendation: Very Important. Standardized test scores: Very Important. Essay: Very Important. *Nonacademic:* Interview: Very Important. Extracurricular activities: Considered. Talent/ability: Considered. Character/personal qualities: Very Important. Alumni/ae relationship: Considered. Geographical residence: Not Considered. State residency: Not Considered. Religious affiliation/commitment: Very Important. Minority status: Not Considered. Volunteer work: Not Considered. Work experience: Not Considered. **Other schools with the greatest overlap in applicants:** Azusa Pacific University; Biola University; Point Loma Nazarene University; Westmont College. **Admissions statistics for the fall 2009 entering class:** Total applicants: 360. Total accepted: 177. Freshmen enrolled: 177; 39% were from out of state. Overall acceptance rate: 49%. Non-early acceptance rate: 49%. **Credentials of fall 2009 freshmen:** 23% ranked in the top 10 percent of their high school class; 43% were in the top 25 percent; 69% were in the top half. (Proportion submitting class standing: 34%.) **Average high school grade point average:** 3.6. **First-year students who submitted SAT scores:** 77%. Scores (25/75 percentile): Critical Reading: 480-630, Math: 480-610, Combined: 960-1240. **First-year students submitting ACT scores:** 26%. Scores (25/75 percentile): English: N/A, Math: N/A, Composite: 22-27.

ACADEMICS
Year founded: 1927. **Academic calendar:** Semester. **Degrees offered:** certificate, bachelor's, master's, doctorate. **Most popular majors:** 26% Bible/biblical studies, 20% business, management, marketing, and related support services, 15% liberal arts and sciences studies, and humanities, 8% history, 8% music. **Major fields of study:** biological and biomedical sciences; business, management, marketing, and related support services; communication, journalism, and related programs; computer and information sciences and support services; education; English language and literature/letters; family and consumer sciences/human sciences; foreign languages, literatures, and linguistics; health professions and related clinical sciences; history; legal professions and studies; liberal arts and sciences studies, and humanities; mathematics and statistics; parks, recreation, leisure, and fitness studies; social sciences; theology and religious vocations; visual and performing arts. **Areas of required coursework:** arts/fine arts, humanities, computer literacy, mathematics, English (including composition), philosophy, sciences (biological or physical), history, social science, other. **Pre-professional programs:** pre-law, pre-dentistry, pre-medicine, pre-theology. **Special academic programs (% participation):** accelerated program, coopera-

tive (work-study plan) program (18%), distance learning (2%), double major (8%), English as a Second Language (ESL) (0%), independent study (34%), internships (5%), study abroad (20%), teacher certificate program (9%). **Teacher certification offered in:** elementary, secondary. **Cooperative education programs:** education, home economics. **Faculty and instruction (2009-2010):** Total instructional faculty: 66 full-time, 133 part-time (74% men; 26% women; 7% minorities). Full-time faculty with Ph.D. or other terminal degree: 71%. Student/faculty ratio: 10/1. Classes of fewer than 20 students: 75%; of 20 to 49 students: 19%; of 50 or more students: 6%. **Advanced Placement and International Baccalaureate credit:** AP tests may be used for: Placement only. Scores accepted: 3, 4, 5. International Baccalaureate exams may be used for: Placement only. **Freshmen returning for sophomore year:** 81%. **Graduation rates:** Four-year: 50%; five-year: 59%; six-year: 58%. **Graduate study:** 25% of students pursue further study immediately upon graduation; 35% within five years. Fields in which graduates pursue further study: Master of Business Administration (MBA), 10%; medicine, 4%; theology (or the seminary), 10%; education, 9%; arts and sciences, 8%.

COSTS AND FINANCIAL AID
Financial aid office: (661) 259-3540. **Expenses (2010-2011):** Tuition and fees 2010-2011: $25,640; room/board: $8,320. Estimated books and supplies: $1,620; transportation: $729; personal expenses: $2,250. **Financial aid:** Priority filing date for institution's financial aid form: March 2; deadline: March 2. In 2009-2010, 100% of undergraduates applied for financial aid. Of those, 89% were determined to have financial need; 17% had their need fully met. Average financial aid package (proportion receiving): $18,028 (88%). Average amount of gift aid, such as scholarships or grants (proportion receiving): $13,630 (81%). Average amount of self-help aid, such as work study or loans (proportion receiving): $6,153 (77%). Average need-based loan (excluding PLUS or other private loans): $5,232. Among students who received need-based aid, the average percentage of need met: 70%. Among students who received aid based on merit, the average award (and the proportion receiving): $6,381 (7%). The average athletic scholarship (and the proportion receiving): $9,241 (4%). Average amount of debt of borrowers graduating in 2009: $30,003. Proportion who borrowed: 68%.

CAMPUS LIFE AND EXTRACURRICULAR ACTIVITIES
Campus housing available (% using): women's dorms (51%), men's dorms (49%). Students who live in college-owned, operated, or affiliated housing: 73%. **Student employment:** During the 2009-2010 academic year, 40% of undergraduates worked on campus. Average per-year earnings: $2,775. **Clubs and organizations:** Number of student organizations: 7. Activities include: choral groups, concert band, drama/theater, international student organization, jazz band, music ensembles, opera, pep band, student government, symphony orchestra. Number of fraternities: 0; sororities: 0. Average proportion of students who stay on campus on weekends: 50%. **Sports program (2009-2010):** Member of NAIA. *Men's intercollegiate varsity sports:* baseball, basketball, cross country, golf, soccer, track and field (outdoor). *Women's intercollegiate varsity sports:* basketball, cross country, soccer, tennis, track and field (outdoor), volleyball.

SERVICES AND FACILITIES
Basic services: placement service, health service, other. **Remedial assistance:** math. **Counseling services:** career, personal, veteran student, academic, older student, religious, other. **For learning-disabled students:** School does not offer a structured program with separate admission and additional fees. Services include: remedial math, note-taking services, readers, extended time for tests, tutors, other. **Library:** Number of titles: 170,136; number of current serial subscriptions: 230. **Information technology resources:** Students are required to lease or own a computer. Number of campus computers available to all students: 60. School has a wireless network. Approximate number of users that can be accommodated: 800. Proportion of college-owned housing units wired for high-speed internet access: 100%. **Campus safety:** Security services offered: 24-hour foot-and-vehicle patrols, late-night transport/escort service, 24-hour emergency telephones, lighted pathways/sidewalks, student patrols, controlled dormitory access (key, security card, etc.).

TRANSFER AND INTERNATIONAL STUDENTS
Transfer students: May apply for admission for the following academic terms: Fall, Spring. Applicants need a minimum number of credits to apply. For fall 2009: Transfer applications received: 239. Transfer applicants offered admission: 198. Transfer applicants enrolled: 112. **International students:** Number of foreign undergraduates: 54 (5% of student body). Number of countries represented: 38. Minimum TOEFL score required: 530 (paper); 78 (computer).

Menlo College

- **Address:** 1000 El Camino Real, Atherton, CA 94027
- **Website:** http://www.menlo.edu
- **Private**
- **Enrollment:** 569 full-time; 25 part-time

....

KEY STATS

✔ **U.S News College Ranking:** Unranked Specialty School–Business
✔ **SAT Score (25th/75th percentile):** 850-1100
✔ **Tuition:** 2010-2011: $33,550

Selectivity: Selective	**Room/board:** $11,330
Acceptance rate: 52%	**Average debt:** $25,696
Student/faculty ratio: 14/1	**Proportion who borrowed:** 76%

UNDERGRADUATE STUDENT BODY STATS

2009-2010 enrollment: 569 full-time; 25 part-time. Men: 64%; women: 36%. **Ethnic makeup:** African American: 4%; Asian American: 12%; Hispanic: 14%; White: 58%; International: 12%.

ADMISSIONS FACTS AND FIGURES

Phone: (800) 556-3656. **Email:** admissions@menlo.edu. **Website:** http://www.menlo.edu. **Application deadlines for fall 2011:** Regular decision: Rolling. Early decision: Not offered. Early action: Send application by: December 1; Decision sent by: December 15. Admission can be deferred. **Application fee:** $40. **To apply online, go to:** https://www.menlo.edu/undergrad_application.php. **Admissions requirements/recommendations:** High school units required (recommended): English: 4 (4); Mathematics: 3 (3); Science: 2 (3); Foreign language: 2 (3); Social studies: 3 (2); History: 0 (0); Academic electives: 0 (0); Total units: 16 (17). Tests: The college uses SAT or ACT scores in admissions decisions. Either SAT or ACT required. For admission to the fall 2011 entering class, the school will accept: ACT with writing recommended. Campus visit: Recommended. Admissions interview: Recommended. Off-campus interview: May be arranged. **Factors that count in admissions decisions:** *Academic:* Secondary school record: Very Important. Class rank: Important. Letters of recommendation: Important. Standardized test scores: Important. Essay: Important. *Nonacademic:* Interview: Considered. Extracurricular activities: Important. Talent/ability: Considered. Character/personal qualities: Very Important. Alumni/ae relationship: Important. Geographical residence: Not Considered. State residency: Not Considered. Religious affiliation/commitment: Not Considered. Minority status: Not Considered. Volunteer work: Important. Work experience: Considered. **Admissions statistics for the fall 2009 entering class:** Total applicants: 1,492. Total accepted: 772. Freshmen enrolled: 133; 33% were from out of state. Overall acceptance rate: 52%. Non-early acceptance rate: 52%. **Credentials of fall 2009 freshmen:** 11% ranked in the top 10 percent of their high school class; 40% were in the top 25 percent; 80% were in the top half. (Proportion submitting class standing: 26%.) **Average high school grade point average:** 3.1. **First-year students who submitted SAT scores:** 79%. Scores (25/75 percentile): Critical Reading: 420-540; Math: 430-560; Combined: 850-1100. **First-year students submitting ACT scores:** 45%. Scores (25/75 percentile): English: 16-22, Math: 17-25, Composite: 17-23.

ACADEMICS

Year founded: 1927. **Academic calendar:** Semester. **Degrees offered:** bachelor's. **Most popular majors:** 68% business administration and management, 18% liberal arts and sciences, general studies, and humanities, 14% mass communication/media studies. **Major fields of study:** business, management, marketing, and related support services; communication, journalism, and related programs; liberal arts and sciences studies, and humanities. **Areas of required coursework:** humanities, computer literacy, mathematics, English (including composition), foreign languages, sciences (biological or physical), history, social science, other. **Special academic programs (% participation):** accelerated program (8%), double major (0%), internships (20%), student-designed major (10%), study abroad. **Reserve Officers Training Corps (ROTC):** Army ROTC: Offered at cooperating institution (San Jose State University). **Faculty and instruction (2009-2010):** Total instructional faculty: 25 full-time, 49 part-time (54% men; 46% women; 23% minorities). Full-time faculty with Ph.D. or other terminal degree: 92%. Student/faculty ratio: 14/1. Classes of fewer than 20 students: 49%; of 20 to 49 students: 51%. **Advanced Placement and International Baccalaureate credit:** AP tests may be used for: Credit and/or placement. Scores accepted: 3, 4, 5. International Baccalaureate exams may be used for: Credit and/or

placement. **Freshmen returning for sophomore year:** 60%. **Graduation rates:** Four-year: 30%; five-year: 36%; six-year: 35%.

COSTS AND FINANCIAL AID

Financial aid office: (650) 543-3880. **Expenses (2010-2011):** Tuition and fees 2010-2011: $33,550; room/board: $11,330. Estimated books and supplies: $1,620; transportation: $728; personal expenses: $2,250. **Financial aid:** Priority filing date for institution's financial aid form: March 2. In 2009-2010, 64% of undergraduates applied for financial aid. Of those, 59% were determined to have financial need; 8% had their need fully met. Average financial aid package (proportion receiving): $26,274 (59%). Average amount of gift aid, such as scholarships or grants (proportion receiving): $22,421 (58%). Average amount of self-help aid, such as work study or loans (proportion receiving): $4,610 (54%). Average need-based loan (excluding PLUS or other private loans): $3,780. Among students who received need-based aid, the average percentage of need met: 70%. Among students who received aid based on merit, the average award (and the proportion receiving): $9,818 (33%). The average athletic scholarship (and the proportion receiving): $0 (0%). Average amount of debt of borrowers graduating in 2009: $25,696. Proportion who borrowed: 76%.

CAMPUS LIFE AND EXTRACURRICULAR ACTIVITIES

Campus housing available (% using): coed dorms (87%), men's dorms (13%). Students who live in college-owned, operated, or affiliated housing: 61%. **Student employment:** During the 2009-2010 academic year, 6% of undergraduates worked on campus. Average per-year earnings: $3,000. **Clubs and organizations:** Number of student organizations: 28. Activities include: dance, international student organization, radio station, student government, student newspaper, student film society, television station, yearbook. Number of fraternities: 0; sororities: 0. Average proportion of students who stay on campus on weekends: 65%. **Sports program (2009-2010):** Member of NCAA III. *Men's intercollegiate varsity sports:* baseball, basketball, cross country, football, golf, soccer, wrestling. *Women's intercollegiate varsity sports:* basketball, cross country, golf, soccer, softball, volleyball.

SERVICES AND FACILITIES

Basic services: nonremedial tutoring, placement service, health insurance. **Remedial assistance:** math, writing, study skills. **Counseling services:** career, academic, psychological. **For learning-disabled students:** School does not offer a structured program with separate admission and additional fees. Total undergraduates in learning-disabled program or receiving services: 84. Services include: remedial math, remedial English, tape recorders, other special classes, note-taking services, learning center, extended time for tests, tutors, exams on tape or computer, other testing accommodations, other. **Library:** Number of titles: 81,600; number of current serial subscriptions: 13,700. **Information technology resources:** Students are not required to lease or own a computer. Number of campus computers available to all students: 135. School has a wireless network. Approximate number of users that can be accommodated: 100. Proportion of college-owned housing units wired for high-speed internet access: 100%. **Campus safety:** Security services offered: 24-hour foot-and-vehicle patrols, late-night transport/escort service, 24-hour emergency telephones, lighted pathways/sidewalks, controlled dormitory access (key, security card, etc).

TRANSFER AND INTERNATIONAL STUDENTS

Transfer students: May apply for admission for the following academic terms: Fall, Spring. Applicants need a minimum number of credits to apply. For fall 2009: Transfer applications received: 393. Transfer applicants offered admission: 288. Transfer applicants enrolled: 70. **International students:** Number of foreign undergraduates: 70 (12% of student body). Number of countries represented: 23. Minimum TOEFL score required: 500 (paper); 173 (computer). Average TOEFL score: 520 (paper).

Mills College

- **Address:** 5000 MacArthur Boulevard, Oakland, CA 94613
- **Website:** http://www.mills.edu
- **Private**
- **Enrollment:** 870 full-time; 51 part-time

KEY STATS

✔ **U.S News College Ranking:** 4, Regional Universities (West)
✔ **SAT Score (25th/75th percentile):** 1030-1250
✔ **Tuition:** 2010-2011: $37,605

Selectivity: More selective	**Room/board:** $11,644
Acceptance rate: 57%	**Average debt:** N/A
Student/faculty ratio: 12/1	**Proportion who borrowed:** N/A

UNDERGRADUATE STUDENT BODY STATS

2009-2010 enrollment: 870 full-time; 51 part-time. Men: 0%; women: 100%. **Ethnic makeup:** African American: 9%; American-Indian: 1%; Asian American: 7%; Hispanic: 14%; White: 66%; International: 3%. **Religious preference:** Roman Catholic: 16%; Protestant: 25%; Jewish: 6%; Muslim: 2%; Buddhist: 5%; No preference: 36%.

ADMISSIONS FACTS AND FIGURES

Phone: (510) 430-2135. **Email:** admission@mills.edu. **Website:** http://www.mills.edu. **Application deadlines for fall 2011:** Regular decision: March 1; decision sent by April 1. Early decision: Not offered. Early action: Send application by: November 15; Decision sent by: December 15. Admission can be deferred. **Application fee:** $50. **To apply online, go to:** http://www.applyweb.com/apply/millsug/menu.html. **Admissions requirements/recommendations:** High school units required (recommended): English: 4 (4); Mathematics: 3 (4); Science: 2 (4); Foreign language: 2 (4); Social studies: 2 (4); History: 2 (4); Academic electives: (2); Total units: 15 (28). Tests: The college uses SAT or ACT scores in admissions decisions. Either SAT or ACT required. For admission to the fall 2011 entering class, the school will accept: ACT with or without writing accepted. Off-campus visit: Recommended. Admissions interview: Recommended. Off-campus interview: May be arranged. **Factors that count in admissions decisions:** *Academic:* Secondary school record: Very Important. Class rank: Important. Letters of recommendation: Important. Standardized test scores: Important. Essay: Very Important. *Nonacademic:* Interview: Considered. Extracurricular activities: Important. Talent/ability: Considered. Character/personal qualities: Important. Alumni/ae relationship: Considered. Geographical residence: Not Considered. State residency: Not Considered. Religious affiliation/commitment: Not Considered. Minority status: Not Considered. Volunteer work: Considered. Work experience: Considered. **Other schools with the greatest overlap in applicants:** University of California–Berkeley; University of California–Davis; University of California–Santa Barbara; University of California–Santa Cruz; University of San Francisco. **Admissions statistics for the fall 2009 entering class:** Total applicants: 1,519. Total accepted: 862. Freshmen enrolled: 162; 27% were from out of state. Accepted through early-decision or early-action plans: 31%. Overall acceptance rate: 57%. Non-early acceptance rate: 54%. **Credentials of fall 2009 freshmen:** 44% ranked in the top 10 percent of their high school class; 76% were in the top 25 percent; 96% were in the top half. (Proportion submitting class standing: 65%.) **Average high school grade point average:** 3.7. **First-year students who submitted SAT scores:** 86%. Scores (25/75 percentile): Critical Reading: 530-650, Math: 500-600, Combined: 1030-1250. **First-year students submitting ACT scores:** 38%. Scores (25/75 percentile): English: N/A, Math: N/A, Composite: 22-27.

ACADEMICS

Year founded: 1852. **Academic calendar:** Semester. **Degrees offered:** certificate, bachelor's, post-bachelor's certificate, master's, doctorate. **Most popular majors:** 15% social sciences, 14% English language and literature/letters, 13% visual and performing arts, 11% multi/interdisciplinary studies, 10% psychology. **Major fields of study:** area, ethnic, cultural, and gender studies; biological and biomedical sciences; business, management, marketing, and related support services; communication, journalism, and related programs; computer and information sciences and support services; engineering; English language and literature/letters; family and consumer sciences/human sciences; foreign languages, literatures, and linguistics; history; liberal arts and sciences studies, and humanities; mathematics and statistics; multi/interdisciplinary studies; natural resources and conservation; philosophy and religious studies; physical sciences; psychology; public administra-

tion and social service professions; social sciences; visual and performing arts. **Areas of required coursework:** arts/fine arts, humanities, computer literacy, mathematics, English (including composition), sciences (biological or physical), history, social science, other. **Pre-professional programs:** pre-law, pre-medicine. **Special academic programs (% participation):** cross-registration (3%), double major (6%), exchange student program (domestic) (1%), independent study (10%), internships (1%), student-designed major (1%), study abroad (30%), teacher certificate program. **Teacher certification offered in:** early childhood, special education, elementary, middle/junior high, secondary. **Cooperative education programs:** engineering, health professions. **Reserve Officers Training Corps (ROTC):** Army ROTC: Offered at cooperating institution (University of California–Berkeley); Navy ROTC: Offered at cooperating institution (University of California–Berkeley); Air Force ROTC: Offered on campus. **Faculty and instruction (2009-2010):** Total instructional faculty: 93 full-time, 88 part-time (34% men; 66% women; 25% minorities). Full-time faculty with Ph.D. or other terminal degree: 88%. Student/faculty ratio: 12/1. Classes of fewer than 20 students: 74%; of 20 to 49 students: 24%; of 50 or more students: 2%. **Advanced Placement and International Baccalaureate credit:** AP tests may be used for: Credit and/or placement. Scores accepted: 4, 5. International Baccalaureate exams may be used for: Credit only. **Freshmen returning for sophomore year:** 74%. **Graduation rates:** Four-year: 53%; five-year: 53%; six-year: 63%. **Graduate study:** 40% of students pursue further study immediately upon graduation; 40% within one year; 60% within five years. Fields in which graduates pursue further study: Master of Business Administration (MBA), 15%; law, 10%; medicine, 5%; dentistry, 3%; engineering, 1%; theology (or the seminary), 1%; education, 15%; arts and sciences, 45%; veterinary medicine, 5%.

COSTS AND FINANCIAL AID

Financial aid office: (510) 430-2000. **Expenses (2010-2011):** Tuition and fees 2010-2011: $37,605; room/board: $11,644. Estimated books and supplies: $1,400; transportation: $0; personal expenses: $2,000. **Financial aid:** Priority filing date for institution's financial aid form: February 15. In 2009-2010, 87% of undergraduates applied for financial aid. Of those, 84% were determined to have financial need; 47% had their need fully met. Average financial aid package (proportion receiving): $30,185 (84%). Average amount of gift aid, such as scholarships or grants (proportion receiving): $23,193 (84%). Average amount of self-help aid, such as work study or loans (proportion receiving): $7,102 (84%). Average need-based loan (excluding PLUS or other private loans): $6,515. Among students who received need-based aid, the average percentage of need met: 85%. Among students who received aid based on merit, the average award (and the proportion receiving): $14,955 (8%). The average athletic scholarship (and the proportion receiving): $0 (0%).

CAMPUS LIFE AND EXTRACURRICULAR ACTIVITIES

Campus housing available (% using): coed dorms (10%), women's dorms (74%), apartments for married students (2%), apartment for single students (6%), special housing for disabled students (1%), cooperative housing (1%), other housing options (6%). Students who live in college-owned, operated, or affiliated housing: 56%. **Student employment:** During the 2009-2010 academic year, 25% of undergraduates worked on campus. Average per-year earnings: $1,884. **Clubs and organizations:** Number of student organizations: 53. Activities include: campus ministries, choral groups, dance, drama/theater, literary magazine, model UN, music ensembles, musical theater, student government, student newspaper, student film society, yearbook. Number of fraternities: 0; sororities: 0. Average proportion of students who stay on campus on weekends: 50%. **Sports program (2009-2010):** Member of NCAA III. *Women's intercollegiate varsity sports:* cross country, crew (lightweight), soccer, swimming, tennis, track and field (outdoor), volleyball.

SERVICES AND FACILITIES

Basic services: nonremedial tutoring, women's center, placement service, health service, health insurance. **Remedial assistance:** reading, math, writing, study skills. **Counseling services:** minority student, career, personal, academic, older student, psychological, birth control, religious. **For learning-disabled students:** School does not offer a structured program with separate admission and additional fees. Total undergraduates in learning-disabled program or receiving services: 72. Services include: reading machines, tape recorders, note-taking services, oral tests, readers, extended time for tests, tutors, early syllabus, priority seating, texts on tape, typist/scribe, exams on tape or computer, take home exams. **Library:** Number of titles: 331,940; number of current serial subscriptions: 42,009. **Information technology resources:** Students are not required to lease or own a computer. Number of campus computers available to all students: 341. School has a wireless network. Approximate number of users that can be accommodated: 2,048. Proportion of college-owned housing units wired for high-speed internet access: 100%. **Campus safety:** Security services offered: 24-hour foot-and-vehicle patrols, late-night transport/escort service, 24-hour emergency telephones, lighted pathways/sidewalks, controlled dormitory access (key, security card, etc).

TRANSFER AND INTERNATIONAL STUDENTS
Transfer students: May apply for admission for the following academic terms: Fall, Spring. Applicants do not need a minimum number of credits to apply. For fall 2009: Transfer applications received: 344. Transfer applicants offered admission: 240. Transfer applicants enrolled: 129. **International students:** Number of foreign undergraduates: 23 (3% of student body). Number of countries represented: 11. Minimum TOEFL score required: 550 (paper); 213 (computer). Average TOEFL score: 587 (paper).

Mount St. Mary's College

- **Address:** 12001 Chalon Road, Los Angeles, CA 90049
- **Website:** http://www.msmc.la.edu
- **Private; Religious affiliation:** Roman Catholic
- **Enrollment:** 1,489 full-time; 491 part-time

KEY STATS
✔ **U.S News College Ranking:** 25, Regional Universities (West)
✔ **SAT Score (25th/75th percentile):** 920-1110
✔ **Tuition:** 2010-2011: $30,132

Selectivity: Less selective	**Room/board:** $9,830
Acceptance rate: 79%	**Average debt:** $33,030
Student/faculty ratio: 11/1	**Proportion who borrowed:** 90%

UNDERGRADUATE STUDENT BODY STATS
2009-2010 enrollment: 1,489 full-time; 491 part-time. Men: 8%; women: 92%. **Ethnic makeup:** African American: 9%; Asian American: 20%; Hispanic: 48%; White: 22%. **Religious preference:** Roman Catholic: 62%; Protestant: 13%; Jewish: 1%; No preference: 1%; Unknown: 23%.

ADMISSIONS FACTS AND FIGURES
Phone: (310) 954-4250. **Email:** admissions@msmc.la.edu. **Website:** http://www.msmc.la.edu. **Application deadlines for fall 2011:** Regular decision: Rolling. Early decision: Not offered. Early action: Send application by: December 1; Decision sent by: January 1. Admission can be deferred. **Application fee:** $40. **To apply online, go to:** http://www.msmc.la.edu/admissions/applyingtoMSMC/apply_online.htm. **Admissions requirements/recommendations:** High school units required (recommended): English: 4 (4); Mathematics: 2 (3); Science: 2 (3); Foreign language: 0 (0); Social studies: 1 (0); History: 0 (2); Academic electives: 0 (0). Tests: The college uses SAT or ACT scores in admissions decisions. Either SAT or ACT required. For admission to the fall 2011 entering class, the school will accept: ACT with or without writing accepted. Campus visit: Recommended. Admissions interview: Recommended. Off-campus interview: May be arranged. **Factors that count in admissions decisions:** *Academic:* Secondary school record: Important. Class rank: Not Considered. Letters of recommendation: Important. Standardized test scores: Very Important. Essay: Very Important. *Nonacademic:* Interview: Considered. Extracurricular activities: Considered. Talent/ability: Considered. Character/personal qualities: Considered. Alumni/ae relationship: Important. Geographical residence: Considered. State residency: Considered. Religious affiliation/commitment: Not Considered. Minority status: Considered. Volunteer work: Considered. Work experience: Considered. **Other schools with the greatest overlap in applicants:** California State University–Long Beach; California State University–Los Angeles; California State University–Northridge; Loyola Marymount University; University of California–Los Angeles. **Admissions statistics for the fall 2009 entering class:** Total applicants: 1,131. Total accepted: 892. Freshmen enrolled: 371; 1% were from out of state. Overall acceptance rate: 79%. Non-early acceptance rate: 79%. **Credentials of fall 2009 freshmen:** 12% ranked in the top 10 percent of their high school class; 56% were in the top 25 percent. **Average high school grade point average:** 3.1. **First-year students who submitted SAT scores:** 71%. Scores (25/75 percentile): Critical Reading: 470-560, Math: 450-550, Combined: 920-1110. **First-year students submitting ACT scores:** 28%. Scores (25/75 percentile): English: N/A, Math: N/A, Composite: 19-23.

ACADEMICS
Year founded: 1925. **Academic calendar:** Semester. **Degrees offered:** associate, transfer-associate, bachelor's, master's, post-master's certificate. **Most popular majors:** 35% nursing/registered nurse training (R.N., A.S.N., B.S.N., M.S.N.), 14% sociology, 6% business administration and management, 6% business/commerce, 6% psychology. **Major fields of study:** area, ethnic, cultural, and gender studies; biological and biomedical sciences; business, management, marketing, and related support services; education; English language and literature/letters; foreign languages, literatures, and linguistics; health professions and related clinical sciences; history; liberal arts and sciences studies, and humanities; mathematics and statistics; philosophy and religious studies; physical sciences; psychology; public administration and social service professions; social sciences; visual and performing arts. **Areas of required coursework:** arts/fine arts, humanities, mathematics, English (including composition), philosophy, foreign languages, sciences (biological or physical), history, social science, other. **Pre-professional programs:** pre-law, pre-medicine. **Special academic programs:** accelerated program, cross-registration, double major, exchange student program (domestic), honors program, independent study, internships, student-designed major, study abroad, teacher certificate program, weekend college. **Faculty and instruction (2009-2010):** Total instructional faculty: 89 full-time, 263 part-time (28% men; 72% women; 35% minorities). Full-time faculty with Ph.D. or other terminal degree: 61%. Student/faculty ratio: 11/1. Classes of fewer than 20 students: 69%; of 20 to 49 students: 31%; of 50 or more students: 0%. **Advanced Placement and International Baccalaureate credit:** AP tests may be used for: Placement only. Scores accepted: 3, 4, 5. **Freshmen returning for sophomore year:** 77%. **Graduation rates:** Four-year: 50%; five-year: 61%; six-year: 61%.

COSTS AND FINANCIAL AID
Financial aid office: (310) 954-4191. **Expenses (2010-2011):** Tuition and fees 2010-2011: $30,132; room/board: $9,830. Estimated books and supplies: $1,640; transportation: $1,550; personal expenses: $2,600. **Financial aid:** Priority filing date for institution's financial aid form: March 5; deadline: May 15. In 2009-2010, 93% of undergraduates applied for financial aid. Of those, 83% were determined to have financial need; 10% had their need fully met. Average financial aid package (proportion receiving): $30,185 (90%). Average amount of gift aid, such as scholarships or grants (proportion receiving): N/A (80%). Average amount of self-help aid, such as work study or loans (proportion receiving): N/A (83%). Among students who received need-based aid, the average percentage of need met: 93%. Among students who received aid based on merit, the average award (and the proportion receiving): $9,821 (3%). Average amount of debt of borrowers graduating in 2009: $33,030. Proportion who borrowed: 90%.

CAMPUS LIFE AND EXTRACURRICULAR ACTIVITIES
Campus housing available: women's dorms, men's dorms. Students who live in college-owned, operated, or affiliated housing: 69%. **Clubs and organizations:** Number of student organizations: 31. Activities include: campus ministries, choral groups, dance, literary magazine, student government, student newspaper, yearbook. Number of fraternities: 0; sororities: 1. of women in sororities: 1%. Average proportion of students who stay on campus on weekends: 50%. **Sports program (2009-2010):** Member of NCAA I.

SERVICES AND FACILITIES
Basic services: placement service, health service, health insurance. **Remedial assistance:** reading, math, writing, study skills. **Counseling services:** career, academic, psychological, religious. **For learning-disabled students:** School does not offer a structured program with separate admission and additional fees. Total undergraduates in learning-disabled program or receiving services: 25. Services include: remedial math, remedial English, reading machines, remedial reading, tape recorders, note-taking services, oral tests, learning center, extended time for tests, tutors, priority registration, priority seating, substitution of courses, texts on tape, exams on tape or computer, other testing accommodations, waiver of foreign language degree requirement, waiver of math degree requirement. **Library:** Number of titles: 140,000; number of current serial subscriptions: 26,000. **Information technology resources:** Students are not required to lease or own a computer. Number of campus computers available to all students: 350. School has a wireless network. Approximate number of users that can be accommodated: 600. Proportion of college-owned housing units wired for high-speed internet access: 100%. **Campus safety:** Security services offered: 24-hour foot-and-vehicle patrols, late-night transport/escort service, 24-hour emergency telephones, controlled dormitory access (key, security card, etc).

TRANSFER AND INTERNATIONAL STUDENTS

Transfer students: May apply for admission for the following academic terms: Fall, Spring. Applicants need a minimum number of credits to apply. For fall 2009: Transfer applications received: 316. Transfer applicants offered admission: 135. Transfer applicants enrolled: 77. **International students:** Number of foreign undergraduates: 4. Minimum TOEFL score required: 550 (paper); 213 (computer).

National Hispanic University

- **Address:** 14271 Story Road, San Jose, CA 95127-3823
- **Website:** http://www.nhu.edu
- **Private**
- **Enrollment:** N/A

KEY STATS

✔ **U.S News College Ranking:** Unranked, Regional Colleges (West)
✔ **SAT or ACT Score (25th/75th percentile):** N/A
✔ **Tuition:** 2009-2010: $6,640

Selectivity: N/A	Room/board: N/A
Acceptance rate: N/A	Average debt: N/A
Student/faculty ratio: N/A	Proportion who borrowed: N/A

National University

- **Address:** 11255 N. Torrey Pines Road, La Jolla, CA 92037
- **Website:** http://www.nu.edu
- **Private**
- **Enrollment:** N/A

KEY STATS

✔ **U.S News College Ranking:** Unranked, Regional Universities (West)
✔ **SAT or ACT Score (25th/75th percentile):** N/A
✔ **Tuition:** 2009-2010: $10,728

Selectivity: N/A	Room/board: N/A
Acceptance rate: N/A	Average debt: N/A
Student/faculty ratio: N/A	Proportion who borrowed: N/A

Notre Dame de Namur University

- **Address:** 1500 Ralston Avenue, Belmont, CA 94002-1908
- **Website:** http://www.ndnu.edu
- **Private; Religious affiliation:** Catholic
- **Enrollment:** 522 full-time; 353 part-time

KEY STATS

✔ **U.S News College Ranking:** 59, Regional Universities (West)
✔ **SAT Score (25th/75th percentile):** 840-1060
✔ **Tuition:** 2010-2011: $28,590

Selectivity: Less selective	Room/board: $11,600
Acceptance rate: 79%	Average debt: $21,758
Student/faculty ratio: 11/1	Proportion who borrowed: 82%

UNDERGRADUATE STUDENT BODY STATS

2009-2010 enrollment: 522 full-time; 353 part-time. Men: 34%; women: 66%. **Ethnic makeup:** African American: 8%; American-Indian: 1%; Asian American: 15%; Hispanic: 25%; White: 49%; International: 2%. **Religious preference:** Protestant: 8%; Jewish: 1%; Muslim: 1%; Hindu: 1%; Buddhist: 1%; Unknown: 59%; Catholic: 23%; Other: 6%.

ADMISSIONS FACTS AND FIGURES

Phone: (650) 508-3600. **Email:** admissions@ndnu.edu. **Website:** http://www.ndnu.edu. **Application deadlines for fall 2011:** Regular decision: Rolling. Early decision: Not offered. Early action: Send application by: December 1; Decision sent by: December 15. Admission can be deferred. **Application fee:** $50. **To apply online, go to:** http://app.commonapp.org/. **Admissions requirements/recommendations:** High school units required

(recommended): English: 4 (4); Mathematics: 2 (3); Science: 1 (2); Foreign language: 2 (3); Social studies: 2 (2); History: 1 (1); Academic electives: 3 (3); Total units: 15 (18). **Tests:** The college uses SAT or ACT scores in admissions decisions. Either SAT or ACT required. For admission to the fall 2011 entering class, the school will accept: ACT with writing required. Campus visit: Recommended. Admissions interview: Recommended. Off-campus interview: May be arranged. **Factors that count in admissions decisions:** *Academic:* Secondary school record: Important. Class rank: Important. Letters of recommendation: Important. Standardized test scores: Important. Essay: Important. *Nonacademic:* Interview: Considered. Extracurricular activities: Important. Talent/ability: Important. Character/personal qualities: Very Important. Alumni/ae relationship: Considered. Geographical residence: Not Considered. State residency: Not Considered. Religious affiliation/commitment: Not Considered. Minority status: Not Considered. Volunteer work: Considered. Work experience: Considered. **Other schools with the greatest overlap in applicants:** California State University–East Bay; Dominican University of California; Holy Names University; Menlo College; San Francisco State University. **Admissions statistics for the fall 2009 entering class:** Total applicants: 998. Total accepted: 791. Freshmen enrolled: 116; 25% were from out of state. Overall acceptance rate: 79%. Non-early acceptance rate: 79%. **Size of waiting list:** 0 applicants; enrolled from waiting list: 0. **Credentials of fall 2009 freshmen:** 10% ranked in the top 10 percent of their high school class; 25% were in the top 25 percent; 50% were in the top half. (Proportion submitting class standing: 40%.) **Average high school grade point average:** 2.9. **First-year students who submitted SAT scores:** 75%. Scores (25/75 percentile): Critical Reading: 420-540, Math: 420-520, Combined: 840-1060. **First-year students submitting ACT scores:** 30%. Scores (25/75 percentile): English: 14-22, Math: 16-21, Composite: 17-21.

ACADEMICS

Year founded: 1851. **Academic calendar:** Semester. **Degrees offered:** certificate, bachelor's, post-bachelor's certificate, master's. **Most popular majors:** 26% business administration and management, 14% liberal arts and sciences/liberal studies, 13% human services, 8% biology/biological sciences, 8% psychology. **Major fields of study:** biological and biomedical sciences; business, management, marketing, and related support services; communication, journalism, and related programs; computer and information sciences and support services; English language and literature/letters; health professions and related clinical sciences; history; liberal arts and sciences studies, and humanities; parks, recreation, leisure, and fitness studies; philosophy and religious studies; psychology; public administration and social service professions; social sciences; visual and performing arts. **Areas of required coursework:** arts/fine arts, humanities, computer literacy, mathematics, English (including composition), philosophy, foreign languages, sciences (biological or physical), history, social science, other. **Pre-professional programs:** pre-law, pre-dentistry, pre-medicine, pre-veterinary science, pre-pharmacy, other. **Special academic programs:** accelerated program, double major, English as a Second Language (ESL), exchange student program (domestic), independent study, internships, liberal arts/career combination, student-designed major, study abroad, teacher certificate program. **Teacher certification offered in:** special education, elementary, middle/junior high, secondary. **Faculty and instruction (2009-2010):** Total instructional faculty: 55 full-time, 113 part-time (39% men; 61% women; 19% minorities). Full-time faculty with Ph.D. or other terminal degree: 91%. Student/faculty ratio: 11/1. Classes of fewer than 20 students: 73%; of 20 to 49 students: 27%; of 50 or more students: 0%. **Advanced Placement and International Baccalaureate credit:** AP tests may be used for: Credit and/or placement. Scores accepted: 3, 4, 5. International Baccalaureate exams may be used for: Credit and/or placement. **Freshmen returning for sophomore year:** 72%. **Graduation rates:** Four-year: 48%; five-year: 56%; six-year: 55%.

COSTS AND FINANCIAL AID

Financial aid office: (650) 508-3600. **Expenses (2010-2011):** Tuition and fees 2010-2011: $28,590; room/board: $11,600. Estimated books and supplies: $1,560; transportation: $846; personal expenses: $3,150. **Financial aid:** Priority filing date for institution's financial aid form: March 2. In 2009-2010, 79% of undergraduates applied for financial aid. Of those, 75% were determined to have financial need; 10% had their need fully met. Average financial aid package (proportion receiving): $24,693 (75%). Average amount of gift aid, such as scholarships or grants (proportion receiving): $19,236 (74%). Average amount of self-help aid, such as work study or loans (proportion receiving): $6,050 (72%). Average need-based loan (excluding PLUS or other private loans): $4,980. Among students who received need-based aid, the average percentage of need met: 70%. Average amount of debt of borrowers graduating in 2009: $21,758. Proportion who borrowed: 82%.

CAMPUS LIFE AND EXTRACURRICULAR ACTIVITIES
Campus housing available (% using): coed dorms (75%), apartment for single students (25%). Students who live in college-owned, operated, or affiliated housing: 39%. **Student employment:** During the 2009-2010 academic year, 10% of undergraduates worked on campus. Average per-year earnings: $2,000. **Clubs and organizations:** Number of student organizations: 22. Activities include: choral groups, dance, drama/theater, international student organization, literary magazine, musical theater, opera, student government, student newspaper. Number of fraternities: 0; sororities: 0. Average proportion of students who stay on campus on weekends: 75%. **Sports program (2009-2010):** Member of NCAA II. *Men's intercollegiate varsity sports:* basketball, cross country, golf, lacrosse, soccer. *Women's intercollegiate varsity sports:* basketball, cross country, soccer, softball, tennis, volleyball.

SERVICES AND FACILITIES
Basic services: nonremedial tutoring, placement service, health service, health insurance. **Remedial assistance:** reading, math, writing, study skills. **Counseling services:** minority student, career, personal, academic, older student, psychological, religious. **For learning-disabled students:** School does not offer a structured program with separate admission and additional fees. Services include: remedial math, remedial English, remedial reading, tape recorders, diagnostic testing service, untimed tests, note-taking services, oral tests, learning center, readers, extended time for tests, tutors, priority seating, substitution of courses, texts on tape, other testing accommodations, waiver of foreign language degree requirement, waiver of math degree requirement. **Library:** Number of titles: 91,389; number of current serial subscriptions: 12,500. **Information technology resources:** Students are not required to lease or own a computer. Number of campus computers available to all students: 85. School has a wireless network. Approximate number of users that can be accommodated: 50. Proportion of college-owned housing units wired for high-speed internet access: 100%. **Campus safety:** Security services offered: 24-hour foot-and-vehicle patrols, late-night transport/escort service, 24-hour emergency telephones, lighted pathways/sidewalks, controlled dormitory access (key, security card, etc).

TRANSFER AND INTERNATIONAL STUDENTS
Transfer students: May apply for admission for the following academic terms: Fall, Spring, Summer. Applicants need a minimum number of credits to apply. For fall 2009: Transfer applications received: 326. Transfer applicants offered admission: 250. Transfer applicants enrolled: 153. **International students:** Number of foreign undergraduates: 20 (2% of student body). Number of countries represented: 12. Minimum TOEFL score required: 500 (paper); 173 (computer). Average TOEFL score: 525 (paper).

Occidental College

■ **Address:** 1600 Campus Road, Los Angeles, CA 90041-3314
■ **Website:** http://www.oxy.edu
■ **Private**
■ **Enrollment:** 1,957 full-time; 15 part-time

KEY STATS
✔ **U.S News College Ranking:** 36, National Liberal Arts Colleges
✔ **SAT Score (25th/75th percentile):** 1200-1380
✔ **Tuition:** 2010-2011: $40,903

Selectivity: More selective	**Room/board:** $11,360
Acceptance rate: 43%	**Average debt:** $17,561
Student/faculty ratio: 9/1	**Proportion who borrowed:** 67%

UNDERGRADUATE STUDENT BODY STATS
2009-2010 enrollment: 1,957 full-time; 15 part-time. Men: 44%; women: 56%. **Ethnic makeup:** African American: 6%; American-Indian: 1%; Asian American: 16%; Hispanic: 13%; White: 62%; International: 1%. **Religious preference:** Roman Catholic: 19%; Protestant: 35%; Jewish: 11%; Muslim: 1%; Buddhist: 2%; No preference: 1%; Other: 26%.

ADMISSIONS FACTS AND FIGURES
Phone: (800) 825-5262. **Email:** admission@oxy.edu. **Website:** http://www.oxy.edu. **Application deadlines for fall 2011:** Regular decision: January 10;

decision sent by April 1. Early decision: Send application by: November 15; Decision sent by: December 15. Early action: Not offered. Admission can be deferred. **Application fee:** $50. **To apply online, go to:** http://www.oxy.edu/Apply.xml. **Admissions requirements/recommendations:** High school units required (recommended): English: (4); Mathematics: (4); Science: (3); Foreign language: (3); Social studies: (2); History: (2); Academic electives: (2); Total units: (20). Tests: The college uses SAT or ACT scores in admissions decisions. Either SAT or ACT required. For admission to the fall 2011 entering class, the school will accept: ACT with writing required. Campus visit: Recommended. Admissions interview: Recommended. Off-campus interview: May be arranged. **Factors that count in admissions decisions:** *Academic:* Secondary school record: Very Important. Class rank: Important. Letters of recommendation: Important. Standardized test scores: Important. Essay: Important. *Nonacademic:* Interview: Considered. Extracurricular activities: Very Important. Talent/ability: Considered. Character/personal qualities: Important. Alumni/ae relationship: Considered. Geographical residence: Considered. State residency: Not Considered. Religious affiliation/commitment: Not Considered. Minority status: Considered. Volunteer work: Very Important. Work experience: Very Important. **Other schools with the greatest overlap in applicants:** Claremont McKenna College; Pomona College; University of California–Berkeley; University of California–Los Angeles; University of Southern California. **Admissions statistics for the fall 2009 entering class:** Total applicants: 6,013. Total accepted: 2,583. Freshmen enrolled: 576; 55% were from out of state. Accepted through early-decision or early-action plans: 8%. Overall acceptance rate: 43%. Early-decision acceptance rate: 65%. Non-early acceptance rate: 43%. **Size of waiting list:** 0 applicants; enrolled from waiting list: 0. **Credentials of fall 2009 freshmen:** 63% ranked in the top 10 percent of their high school class; 94% were in the top 25 percent; 99% were in the top half. (Proportion submitting class standing: 43%.) **Average high school grade point average:** 3.6. **First-year students who submitted SAT scores:** 72%. Scores (25/75 percentile): Critical Reading: 600-700, Math: 600-680, Combined: 1200-1380. **First-year students submitting ACT scores:** 28%. Scores (25/75 percentile): English: N/A, Math: N/A, Composite: 28-32.

ACADEMICS
Year founded: 1887. **Academic calendar:** Semester. **Degrees offered:** bachelor's, master's. **Most popular majors:** 12% economics, 8% art/art studies, 8% international relations and affairs, 7% English language and literature/letters, 7% biology/biological sciences. **Major fields of study:** area, ethnic, cultural, and gender studies; biological and biomedical sciences; English language and literature/letters; foreign languages, literatures, and linguistics; history; mathematics and statistics; natural resources and conservation; parks, recreation, leisure, and fitness studies; philosophy and religious studies; physical sciences; psychology; social sciences; visual and performing arts. **Areas of required coursework:** arts/fine arts, humanities, English (including composition), foreign languages, sciences (biological or physical), history, social science, other. **Pre-professional programs:** pre-law, pre-dentistry, pre-medicine, pre-veterinary science, pre-optometry, pre-pharmacy, other. **Special academic programs (% participation):** cross-registration (3%), double major (5%), exchange student program (domestic) (3%), honors program (20%), independent study (53%), internships (23%), student-designed major (.2%), study abroad (34%). **Teacher certification offered in:** elementary, secondary. **Reserve Officers Training Corps (ROTC):** Army ROTC: Offered at cooperating institution (University of Southern California); Air Force ROTC: Offered at cooperating institution (University of California–Los Angeles). **Faculty and instruction (2009-2010):** Total instructional faculty: 170 full-time, 90 part-time (54% men; 46% women; 26% minorities). Full-time faculty with Ph.D. or other terminal degree: 92%. Student/faculty ratio: 9/1. Classes of fewer than 20 students: 66%; of 20 to 49 students: 33%; of 50 or more students: 1%. **Advanced Placement and International Baccalaureate credit:** AP tests may be used for: Placement only. Scores accepted: 4, 5. International Baccalaureate exams may be used for: Placement only. **Freshmen returning for sophomore year:** 92%. **Graduation rates:** Four-year: 78%; five-year: 84%; six-year: 85%. **Graduate study:** 23% of students pursue further study immediately upon graduation; 5% within one year; 45% within five years. Fields in which graduates pursue further study: Master of Business Administration (MBA), 13%; law, 13%; medicine, 7%; dentistry, 1%; theology (or the seminary), 1%; education, 18%; arts and sciences, 47%; veterinary medicine, 1%.

COSTS AND FINANCIAL AID
Financial aid office: (323) 259-2548. **Expenses (2010-2011):** Tuition and fees 2010-2011: $40,903; room/board: $11,360. Estimated books and supplies: $1,116; transportation: $849; personal expenses: $1,427. **Financial aid:** Priority filing date for institution's financial aid form: February 1; deadline:

February 1. In 2009-2010, 64% of undergraduates applied for financial aid. Of those, 55% were determined to have financial need; 99% had their need fully met. Average financial aid package (proportion receiving): $36,048 (55%). Average amount of gift aid, such as scholarships or grants (proportion receiving): $28,994 (54%). Average amount of self-help aid, such as work study or loans (proportion receiving): $8,385 (50%). Average need-based loan (excluding PLUS or other private loans): $6,346. Among students who received need-based aid, the average percentage of need met: 100%. Among students who received aid based on merit, the average award (and the proportion receiving): $9,316 (20%). The average athletic scholarship (and the proportion receiving): $0 (0%). Average amount of debt of borrowers graduating in 2009: $17,561. Proportion who borrowed: 67%.

CAMPUS LIFE AND EXTRACURRICULAR ACTIVITIES

Campus housing available (% using): coed dorms (96%), women's dorms (3%), fraternity housing (1%). Students who live in college-owned, operated, or affiliated housing: 77%. **Student employment:** During the 2009-2010 academic year, 43% of undergraduates worked on campus. **Clubs and organizations:** Number of student organizations: 82. Activities include: campus ministries, choral groups, concert band, dance, drama/theater, international student organization, jazz band, literary magazine, music ensembles, musical theater, radio station, student government, student newspaper, student film society, symphony orchestra, yearbook. Number of fraternities: 4; sororities: 4. Proportion of men in fraternities: 10%; of women in sororities: 15%. Average proportion of students who stay on campus on weekends: 60%. **Sports program (2009-2010):** Member of NCAA III. *Men's intercollegiate varsity sports:* baseball, basketball, cross country, football, golf, soccer, swimming, tennis, track and field (outdoor), water polo. *Women's intercollegiate varsity sports:* basketball, cross country, golf, lacrosse, soccer, softball, swimming, tennis, track and field (outdoor), volleyball, water polo.

SERVICES AND FACILITIES

Basic services: nonremedial tutoring, women's center, health service, health insurance, other. **Counseling services:** minority student, career, personal, academic, psychological, birth control, religious. **For learning-disabled students:** School does not offer a structured program with separate admission and additional fees. Total undergraduates in learning-disabled program or receiving services: 120. Services include: tape recorders, note-taking services, learning center, extended time for tests, texts on tape, other testing accommodations, other. **Library:** Number of titles: 450,828; number of current serial subscriptions: 37,275. **Information technology resources:** Students are not required to lease or own a computer. Number of campus computers available to all students: 300. School has a wireless network. Approximate number of users that can be accommodated: 1,800. Proportion of college-owned housing units wired for high-speed internet access: 100%. **Campus safety:** Security services offered: 24-hour foot-and-vehicle patrols, late-night transport/escort service, 24-hour emergency telephones, lighted pathways/sidewalks, controlled dormitory access (key, security card, etc).

TRANSFER AND INTERNATIONAL STUDENTS

Transfer students: May apply for admission for the following academic terms: Fall, Spring. Applicants need a minimum number of credits to apply. For fall 2009: Transfer applications received: 455. Transfer applicants offered admission: 102. Transfer applicants enrolled: 41. **International students:** Number of foreign undergraduates: 27 (1% of student body). Number of countries represented: 23. Minimum TOEFL score required: 600 (paper); 250 (computer).

Otis College of Art and Design

- **Address:** 9045 Lincoln Boulevard, Los Angeles, CA 90045
- **Website:** http://www.otis.edu
- **Private**
- **Enrollment:** 1,141 full-time; 12 part-time

KEY STATS
- ✔ **U.S News College Ranking:** Unranked Specialty School–Fine Arts
- ✔ **SAT Score (25th/75th percentile):** 900-1150
- ✔ **Tuition:** 2010-2011: $32,900

Selectivity: N/A	Room/board: $11,800
Acceptance rate: 44%	Average debt: $27,903
Student/faculty ratio: 9/1	Proportion who borrowed: 65%

UNDERGRADUATE STUDENT BODY STATS

2009-2010 enrollment: 1,141 full-time; 12 part-time. Men: 32%; women: 68%.

ADMISSIONS FACTS AND FIGURES

Phone: (310) 665-6820. **Email:** admissions@otis.edu. **Website:** http://www.otis.edu. **Application deadlines for fall 2011:** Regular decision: Rolling. Early decision: Not offered. Early action: Not offered. Admission cannot be deferred. **Application fee:** $50. **To apply online, go to:** http://www.otis.edu/admissions/undergraduate_admissions/how_to_apply_overview.html. **Admissions requirements/recommendations:** High school units required (recommended): English: 4 (4); Mathematics: 3 (4); Science: 2 (4); Foreign language: (2); Social studies: 1 (2); History: 2 (3); Total units: 13 (23). Tests: The college uses SAT or ACT scores in admissions decisions. Either SAT or ACT required. For admission to the fall 2011 entering class, the school will accept: ACT with or without writing accepted. Campus visit: Recommended. Admissions interview: Neither required nor recommended. Off-campus interview: Not available. **Factors that count in admissions decisions:** *Academic:* Secondary school record: Very Important. Class rank: Not Considered. Letters of recommendation: Considered. Standardized test scores: Important. Essay: Very Important. *Nonacademic:* Interview: Considered. Extracurricular activities: Considered. Talent/ability: Very Important. Character/personal qualities: Considered. Alumni/ae relationship: Considered. Geographical residence: Not Considered. State residency: Not Considered. Religious affiliation/commitment: Not Considered. Minority status: Not Considered. Volunteer work: Considered. Work experience: Considered. **Admissions statistics for the fall 2009 entering class:** Total applicants: 1,634. Total-accepted: 714. Freshmen enrolled: 171; Overall acceptance rate: 44%. **Average high school grade point average:** 3.1. **First-year students who submitted SAT scores:** 78%. Scores (25/75 percentile): Critical Reading: 450-560, Math: 450-590, Combined: 900-1150. **First-year students submitting ACT scores:** 12%. Scores (25/75 percentile): English: 19-25, Math: 17-26, Composite: 19-24.

ACADEMICS

Year founded: 1918. **Academic calendar:** Semester. **Degrees offered:** bachelor's, master's. **Major fields of study:** architecture and related services; communication, journalism, and related programs; communications technologies/technicians and support services; visual and performing arts. **Areas of required coursework:** arts/fine arts, humanities, computer literacy, mathematics, English (including composition), sciences (biological or physical), history, social science. **Special academic programs:** cooperative (work-study plan) program, exchange student program (domestic), honors program, internships, study abroad, teacher certificate program. **Faculty and instruction (2009-2010):** Total instructional faculty: 56 full-time, 222 part-time (51% men; 49% women; 16% minorities). Full-time faculty with Ph.D. or other terminal degree: 9%. Student/faculty ratio: 9/1. Classes of fewer than 20 students: 78%; of 20 to 49 students: 21%; of 50 or more students: 1%. **Freshmen returning for sophomore year:** 80%. **Graduation rates:** Four-year: 47%; five-year: 53%; six-year: 51%.

COSTS AND FINANCIAL AID

Financial aid office: (310) 665-6880. **Expenses (2010-2011):** Tuition and fees 2010-2011: $32,900; room/board: $11,800. Estimated books and supplies: $1,400. **Financial aid:** Priority filing date for institution's financial aid form: February 15. In 2009-2010, 81% of undergraduates applied for financial aid. Of those, 67% were determined to have financial need; 4% had their need fully met. Average financial aid package (proportion receiving): $21,146 (67%). Average amount of gift aid, such as scholarships or grants (proportion receiving): $15,903 (66%). Average amount of self-help aid, such as work study or loans (proportion receiving): $5,848 (62%). Average need-based loan (excluding PLUS or other private loans): $4,715. Among students who received need-based aid, the average percentage of need met: 52%. Among students who received aid based on merit, the average award (and the proportion receiving): $6,432 (14%). Average amount of debt of borrowers graduating in 2009: $27,903. Proportion who borrowed: 65%.

CAMPUS LIFE AND EXTRACURRICULAR ACTIVITIES

Campus housing available (% using): apartment for single students (33%). Activities include: international student organization, literary magazine, student government. Number of fraternities: 0; sororities: 0.

SERVICES AND FACILITIES

Basic services: health insurance. **Remedial assistance:** reading, writing, study skills. **Counseling services:** personal, veteran student, psychological. **For learning-disabled students:** School does not offer a structured program with separate admission and additional fees. **Information technology resources:** Students are not required to lease or own a computer. Number of campus computers available to all students: 380. School has a wireless network. **Campus safety:** Security services offered: 24-hour foot-and-vehicle patrols, 24-hour emergency telephones, lighted pathways/sidewalks.

TRANSFER AND INTERNATIONAL STUDENTS

Transfer students: May apply for admission for the following academic terms: Fall, Spring. Applicants need a minimum number of credits to apply. For fall 2009: Transfer applications received: 720. Transfer applicants offered admission: 313. Transfer applicants enrolled: 152. **International students:** Minimum TOEFL score required: 550 (paper); 213 (computer).

Pacific Union College

- **Address:** 1 Angwin Avenue, Angwin, CA 94508
- **Website:** http://www.puc.edu
- **Private; Religious affiliation:** Seventh-day Adventist
- **Enrollment:** 1,309 full-time; 217 part-time

KEY STATS

✔ **U.S News College Ranking:** 10, Regional Colleges (West)
✔ **SAT Score (25th/75th percentile):** 880-1160
✔ **Tuition:** 2010-2011: $25,221

- **Selectivity:** Selective   **Room/board:** $7,059
- **Acceptance rate:** 48%   **Average debt:** $19,000
- **Student/faculty ratio:** 13/1   **Proportion who borrowed:** 70%

UNDERGRADUATE STUDENT BODY STATS

2009-2010 enrollment: 1,309 full-time; 217 part-time. Men: 44%; women: 56%. **Ethnic makeup:** African American 5%; Asian American: 24%; Hispanic: 20%; White: 46%; International: 6%.

ADMISSIONS FACTS AND FIGURES

Phone: (707) 965-6336. **Email:** enroll@puc.edu. **Website:** http://www.puc.edu. **Application deadlines for fall 2011:** Regular decision: Rolling. Early decision: Not offered. Early action: Not offered. Admission can be deferred. **Application fee:** $30. **To apply online, go to:** http://www.puc.edu/enrollment/apply. **Admissions requirements/recommendations:** High school units required (recommended): English: 4; Mathematics: 2 (3); Science: 1 (3); Foreign language: (2); History: 1 (2); Total units: 8. Tests: The college uses SAT or ACT scores in admissions decisions. Either SAT or ACT required. For admission to the fall 2011 entering class, the school will accept: ACT with or without writing accepted. Campus visit: Recommended. Admissions interview: Neither required nor recommended. Off-campus interview: May be arranged. **Factors that count in admissions decisions:** *Academic:* Secondary school record: Very Important. Class rank: Not Considered. Letters of recommendation: Very Important. Standardized test scores: Considered. Essay: Not Considered. *Nonacademic:* Interview: Considered. Extracurricular activities: Considered. Talent/ability: Not Considered. Character/personal qualities: Important. Alumni/ae relationship: Not Considered. Geographical residence: Not Considered. State residency: Not Considered. Religious affiliation/commitment: Considered. Minority status: Not Considered. Volunteer work: Not Considered. Work experience: Not Considered. **Other schools with the greatest overlap in applicants:** La Sierra University; Walla Walla University. **Admissions statistics for the fall 2009 entering class:** Total applicants: 1,700. Total accepted: 810. Freshmen enrolled: 324; 21% were from out of state. Overall acceptance rate: 48%. **Average high school grade point average:** 3.3. **First-year students who submitted SAT scores:** 52%. Scores (25/75 percentile): Critical Reading: 440-580, Math: 440-580, Combined: 880-1160. **First-year students submitting ACT scores:** 32%. Scores (25/75 percentile): English: 17-25, Math: 17-24, Composite: 18-25.

ACADEMICS

Year founded: 1882. **Academic calendar:** Quarter. **Degrees offered:** associate, bachelor's, master's. **Most popular majors:** 37% health professions and related clinical sciences, 15% business, management, marketing, and related support services, 11% biological and biomedical sciences, 6% education, 5% foreign languages, literatures, and linguistics. **Major fields of study:** biological and biomedical sciences; business, management, marketing, and related support services; communication, journalism, and related programs; computer and information sciences and support services; education;

English language and literature/letters; foreign languages, literatures, and linguistics; health professions and related clinical sciences; history; liberal arts and sciences studies, and humanities; mathematics and statistics; parks, recreation, leisure, and fitness studies; philosophy and religious studies; physical sciences; psychology; public administration and social service professions; social sciences; theology and religious vocations; transportation and materials moving; visual and performing arts. **Areas of required coursework:** arts/fine arts, humanities, computer literacy, mathematics, English (including composition), philosophy, sciences (biological or physical), history, social science, other. **Pre-professional programs:** pre-law, pre-dentistry, pre-medicine, pre-theology, pre-veterinary science, pre-optometry, pre-pharmacy, other. **Special academic programs (% participation):** cooperative (work-study plan) program, double major (2%), dual enrollment (5%), English as a Second Language (ESL) (1%), external degree program, honors program (4%), independent study (9%), internships (27%), study abroad (13%), teacher certificate program (1%). **Teacher certification offered in:** early childhood, elementary, middle/junior high, secondary. **Cooperative education programs:** education, social/behavioral science. **Faculty and instruction (2009-2010):** Total instructional faculty: 89 full-time, 13 part-time (52% men; 48% women; 23% minorities). Full-time faculty with Ph.D. or other terminal degree: 54%. Student/faculty ratio: 13/1. Classes of fewer than 20 students: 65%; of 20 to 49 students: 30%; of 50 or more students: 4%. **Advanced Placement and International Baccalaureate credit:** AP tests may be used for: Credit only. Scores accepted: 3. **Freshmen returning for sophomore year:** 75%. **Graduation rates:** Four-year: 38%; five-year: 57%; six-year: 47%.

COSTS AND FINANCIAL AID

Financial aid office: (707) 965-7200. **Expenses (2010-2011):** Tuition and fees 2010-2011: $25,221; room/board: $7,059. Estimated books and supplies: $1,620; transportation: $729; personal expenses: $2,250. **Financial aid:** Priority filing date for institution's financial aid form: March 2. In 2009-2010, 97% of undergraduates applied for financial aid. Of those, 97% were determined to have financial need; 22% had their need fully met. Average financial aid package (proportion receiving): $17,290 (97%). Average amount of gift aid, such as scholarships or grants (proportion receiving): $14,400 (97%). Average amount of self-help aid, such as work study or loans (proportion receiving): $4,080 (74%). Average need-based loan (excluding PLUS or other private loans): $3,488. Among students who received need-based aid, the average percentage of need met: 44%. Among students who received aid based on merit, the average award (and the proportion receiving): $3,444 (32%). The average athletic scholarship (and the proportion receiving): $0 (0%). Average amount of debt of borrowers graduating in 2009: $19,000. Proportion who borrowed: 70%.

CAMPUS LIFE AND EXTRACURRICULAR ACTIVITIES

Campus housing available (% using): women's dorms (40%), men's dorms (38%), apartments for married students. Students who live in college-owned, operated, or affiliated housing: 73%. **Student employment:** During the 2009-2010 academic year, 52% of undergraduates worked on campus. Average per-year earnings: $2,000. **Clubs and organizations:** Number of student organizations: 37. Activities include: campus ministries, choral groups, concert band, drama/theater, jazz band, literary magazine, music ensembles, musical theater, radio station, student government, student newspaper, student film society, symphony orchestra, yearbook. Number of fraternities: 0; sororities: 0. Average proportion of students who stay on campus on weekends: 45%. **Sports program (2009-2010):** Member of NAIA.

SERVICES AND FACILITIES

Basic services: nonremedial tutoring, day care, health service. **Remedial assistance:** reading, math, writing, study skills. **Counseling services:** minority student, career, personal, academic, older student, psychological, birth control, religious. **For learning-disabled students:** School does not offer a structured program with separate admission and additional fees. Total undergraduates in learning-disabled program or receiving services: 106. Services include: remedial math, remedial English, reading machines, tape recorders, diagnostic testing service, note-taking services, oral tests, learning center, readers, extended time for tests, tutors, priority seating, texts on tape, other testing accommodations, other. **Library:** Number of titles: 178,314; number of current serial subscriptions: 806. **Information technology resources:** Students are not required to lease or own a computer. Number of campus computers available to all students: 195. School has a wireless network. Approximate number of users that can be accommodated: 1,000. Proportion of college-owned housing units wired for high-speed internet access: 95%. **Campus safety:** Security services offered: 24-hour foot-and-vehicle patrols, late-night transport/escort service, 24-hour emergency telephones, lighted pathways/sidewalks.

TRANSFER AND INTERNATIONAL STUDENTS

Transfer students: May apply for admission for the following academic terms: Fall, Winter, Spring, Summer. Applicants need a minimum number of credits to apply. For fall 2009: Transfer applications received: 217. Transfer applicants offered admission: 189. Transfer applicants enrolled: 142. **International students:** Number of foreign undergraduates: 54 (6% of student body). Number of countries represented: 26. Minimum TOEFL score required: 525 (paper); 195 (computer). Average TOEFL score: 560 (paper).

Patten University

- **Address:** 2433 Coolidge Avenue, Oakland, CA 94601
- **Website:** http://www.patten.edu/
- **Private; Religious affiliation:** interdenominational
- **Enrollment:** N/A

....

KEY STATS

✔ **U.S News College Ranking:** second tier, Regional Colleges (West)
✔ **ACT Score:** 23
✔ **Tuition:** 2010-2011: $13,440

Selectivity: Selective	**Room/board:** $7,090
Acceptance rate: 65%	**Average debt:** $9,500
Student/faculty ratio: N/A	**Proportion who borrowed:** 75%

Pepperdine University

- **Address:** 24255 Pacific Coast Highway, Malibu, CA 90263
- **Website:** http://www.pepperdine.edu
- **Private; Religious affiliation:** Church of Christ
- **Enrollment:** 3,052 full-time; 387 part-time

....

KEY STATS

✔ **U.S News College Ranking:** 53, National Universities
✔ **SAT Score (25th/75th percentile):** 1110-1340
✔ **Tuition:** 2010-2011: $39,080

Selectivity: More selective	**Room/board:** $11,390
Acceptance rate: 41%	**Average debt:** $28,299
Student/faculty ratio: 14/1	**Proportion who borrowed:** 58%

UNDERGRADUATE STUDENT BODY STATS

2009-2010 enrollment: 3,052 full-time; 387 part-time. Men: 45%; women: 55%. **Ethnic makeup:** African American: 7%; American-Indian: 1%; Asian American: 10%; Hispanic: 12%; White: 65%; International: 6%. **Religious preference:** Roman Catholic: 15%; Protestant: 3%; Jewish: 1%; Muslim: 1%; Hindu: 1%; Buddhist: 1%; No preference: 2%; Unknown: 33%; Church of Christ: 16%; Other: 26%.

ADMISSIONS FACTS AND FIGURES

Phone: (310) 506-4392. **Email:** admission-seaver@pepperdine.edu. **Website:** http://www.pepperdine.edu. **Application deadlines for fall 2011:** Regular decision: January 15; decision sent by April 1. Early decision: Not offered. Early action: Not offered. Admission cannot be deferred. **Application fee:** $65. **To apply online, go to:** http://www.pepperdine.edu/admission/. **Admissions requirements/recommendations:** High school units required (recommended): English: (4); Mathematics: (4); Science: (4); Foreign language: (3); Social studies: (3); History: (3); Academic electives: (3); Total units: (28). Tests: The college uses SAT or ACT scores in admissions decisions. Either SAT or ACT required. For admission to the fall 2011 entering class, the school will accept: ACT with writing required. Campus visit: Recommended. Admissions interview: Neither required nor recommended. Off-campus interview: Not available. **Factors that count in admissions decisions:** *Academic:* Secondary school record: Very Important. Class rank: Not Considered. Letters of recommendation: Very Important. Standardized test scores: Very Important. Essay: Very Important. *Nonacademic:* Interview: Not Considered. Extracurricular activities: Very Important. Talent/ability: Very Important. Character/personal qualities: Very Important. Alumni/ae relationship: Considered. Geographical residence: Not Considered. State residency: Not Considered. Religious affiliation/commitment: Important. Minority status: Considered. Volunteer work: Important. Work experi-

ence: Considered. **Other schools with the greatest overlap in applicants:** Loyola Marymount University; University of California–Los Angeles; University of California–San Diego; University of San Diego; University of Southern California. **Admissions statistics for the fall 2009 entering class:** Total applicants: 6,426. Total accepted: 2,656. Freshmen enrolled: 766; 44% were from out of state. Overall acceptance rate: 41%. **Credentials of fall 2009 freshmen:** 45% ranked in the top 10 percent of their high school class; 77% were in the top 25 percent; 95% were in the top half. (Proportion submitting class standing: 45%.) **Average high school grade point average:** 3.7. **First-year students who submitted SAT scores:** 84%. Scores (25/75 percentile): Critical Reading: 550-660, Math: 560-680, Combined: 1110-1340. **First-year students submitting ACT scores:** 43%. Scores (25/75 percentile): English: N/A, Math: N/A, Composite: 26-30.

ACADEMICS

Year founded: 1937. **Academic calendar:** Semester. **Degrees offered:** bachelor's, master's, doctorate. **Most popular majors:** 30% business, management, marketing, and related support services, 25% communication, journalism, and related programs, 9% social sciences, 6% multi/interdisciplinary studies, 5% psychology. **Major fields of study:** area, ethnic, cultural, and gender studies; biological and biomedical sciences; business, management, marketing, and related support services; communication, journalism, and related programs; computer and information sciences and support services; education; English language and literature/letters; family and consumer sciences/human sciences; foreign languages, literatures, and linguistics; health professions and related clinical sciences; history; liberal arts and sciences studies, and humanities; mathematics and statistics; multi/interdisciplinary studies; parks, recreation, leisure, and fitness studies; philosophy and religious studies; physical sciences; psychology; security and protective services; social sciences; visual and performing arts. **Areas of required coursework:** arts/fine arts, humanities, mathematics, English (including composition), foreign languages, sciences (biological or physical), history, social science, other. **Pre-professional programs:** pre-law, pre-dentistry, pre-medicine, pre-theology, pre-veterinary science. **Special academic programs:** double major, honors program, independent study, internships, student-designed major, study abroad, teacher certificate program, other. **Teacher certification offered in:** elementary, middle/junior high, secondary. **Reserve Officers Training Corps (ROTC):** Army ROTC: Offered at cooperating institution (University of California–Los Angeles); Air Force ROTC: Offered at cooperating institution (University of Southern California). **Faculty and instruction (2009-2010):** Total instructional faculty: 365 full-time, 271 part-time (59% men; 41% women; 12% minorities). Full-time faculty with Ph.D. or other terminal degree: 90%. Student/faculty ratio: 14/1. Classes of fewer than 20 students: 65%; of 20 to 49 students: 32%; of 50 or more students: 3%. **Advanced Placement and International Baccalaureate credit:** AP tests may be used for: Credit and/or placement. Scores accepted: 3, 4, 5. International Baccalaureate exams may be used for: Placement only. **Freshmen returning for sophomore year:** 89%. **Graduation rates:** Four-year: 73%; five-year: 80%; six-year: 80%.

COSTS AND FINANCIAL AID

Financial aid office: (310) 506-4301. **Expenses (2010-2011):** Tuition and fees 2010-2011: $39,080; room/board: $11,390. Estimated books and supplies: $1,200; transportation: $600; personal expenses: $900. **Financial aid:** Priority filing date for institution's financial aid form: February 15; deadline: February 15. In 2009-2010, 62% of undergraduates applied for financial aid. Of those, 53% were determined to have financial need; 33% had their need fully met. Average financial aid package (proportion receiving): $34,721 (53%). Average amount of gift aid, such as scholarships or grants (proportion receiving): $27,829 (48%). Average amount of self-help aid, such as work study or loans (proportion receiving): $6,134 (49%). Average need-based loan (excluding PLUS or other private loans): $4,823. Among students who received need-based aid, the average percentage of need met: 85%. Among students who received aid based on merit, the average award (and the proportion receiving): $16,964 (18%). The average athletic scholarship (and the proportion receiving): $32,988 (3%). Average amount of debt of borrowers graduating in 2009: $28,299. Proportion who borrowed: 58%.

CAMPUS LIFE AND EXTRACURRICULAR ACTIVITIES

Campus housing available (% using): women's dorms (37%), men's dorms (28%), apartments for married students (1%), apartment for single students (34%), special housing for disabled students (0%). Students who live in college-owned, operated, or affiliated housing: 58%. **Student employment:** During the 2009-2010 academic year, 15% of undergraduates worked on campus. Average per-year earnings: $2,500. **Clubs and organizations:** Number of student organizations: 73. Activities include: campus ministries, choral groups, concert band, dance, drama/theater, international student organization, jazz band, literary magazine, model UN, music ensembles, musical theater, opera, pep band, radio station, student government, student newspaper, student film society, symphony orchestra, television station, yearbook. Number of fraternities: 5; sororities: 7. Proportion of men in fraternities: 18%; of women in sororities: 31%. Average proportion of students who stay on campus on weekends: 50%. **Sports program (2009-2010):** Member of NCAA I. *Men's intercollegiate varsity sports:* baseball, basketball, cross country, golf, tennis, volleyball, water polo. *Women's intercollegiate varsity sports:* basketball, cross country, golf, soccer, swimming, tennis, track and field (outdoor), volleyball.

SERVICES AND FACILITIES

Basic services: health service, health insurance. **Remedial assistance:** writing. **Counseling services:** career, personal, academic, psychological, religious. **For learning-disabled students:** School does not offer a structured program with separate admission and additional fees. Total undergraduates in learning-disabled program or receiving services: 538. Services include: reading machines, tape recorders, note-taking services, oral tests, readers, extended time for tests, priority registration, priority seating, texts on tape, other testing accommodations. **Library:** Number of titles: 373,872; number of current serial subscriptions: 37,651. **Information technology resources:** Students are not required to lease or own a computer. Number of campus computers available to all students: 500. School has a wireless network. Approximate number of users that can be accommodated: 4,000. Proportion of college-owned housing units wired for high-speed internet access: 100%. **Campus safety:** Security services offered: 24-hour foot-and-vehicle patrols, late-night transport/escort service, 24-hour emergency telephones, lighted pathways/sidewalks, student patrols, controlled dormitory access (key, security card, etc).

TRANSFER AND INTERNATIONAL STUDENTS

Transfer students: May apply for admission for the following academic terms: Fall, Spring. Applicants need a minimum number of credits to apply. For fall 2009: Transfer applications received: 537. Transfer applicants offered admission: 161. Transfer applicants enrolled: 74. **International students:** Number of foreign undergraduates: 198 (6% of student body). Number of countries represented: 66. Minimum TOEFL score required: 550 (paper); 80 (computer).

Pitzer College

- **Address:** 1050 N. Mills Avenue, Claremont, CA 91711-6101
- **Website:** http://www.pitzer.edu
- **Private**
- **Enrollment:** 986 full-time; 57 part-time

KEY STATS
✔ **U.S News College Ranking:** 46, National Liberal Arts Colleges
✔ **SAT Score (25th/75th percentile):** 1196-1373
✔ **Tuition:** 2010-2011: $41,174
  Selectivity: More selective   **Room/board:** $12,008
  Acceptance rate: 20%   **Average debt:** $20,448
  Student/faculty ratio: 11/1   **Proportion who borrowed:** 45%

UNDERGRADUATE STUDENT BODY STATS

2009-2010 enrollment: 986 full-time; 57 part-time. Men: 41%; women: 59%. **Ethnic makeup:** African American: 6%; American-Indian: 1%; Asian American: 8%; Hispanic: 15%; White: 67%; International: 3%.

ADMISSIONS FACTS AND FIGURES

Phone: (909) 621-8129. **Email:** admission@pitzer.edu. **Website:** http://www.pitzer.edu. **Application deadlines for fall 2011:** Regular decision: January 1; decision sent by April 1. Early decision: Send application by: November 15; Decision sent by: December 22. Early action: Not offered. Admission can be deferred. **Application fee:** $60. **To apply online, go to:** http://www.pitzer.edu/admission/apply_to_pitzer.asp. **Admissions requirements/recommendations:** High school units required (recommended): English: 4; Mathematics: 3; Science: 3; Foreign language: 3; Social studies: 3; History: 1; Total units: 21. Tests: The college uses SAT or ACT scores in admissions decisions. Neither SAT nor ACT required. For admission to the fall 2011 entering class, the school will accept: ACT with writing recommended. Campus visit: Recommended. Admissions interview: Recommended.

Off-campus interview: May be arranged. **Factors that count in admissions decisions:** *Academic:* Secondary school record: Very Important. Class rank: Very Important. Letters of recommendation: Very Important. Standardized test scores: Considered. Essay: Very Important. *Nonacademic:* Interview: Important. Extracurricular activities: Very Important. Talent/ability: Important. Character/personal qualities: Very Important. Alumni/ae relationship: Considered. Geographical residence: Important. State residency: Not Considered. Religious affiliation/commitment: Not Considered. Minority status: Very Important. Volunteer work: Important. Work experience: Considered. **Other schools with the greatest overlap in applicants:** Lewis & Clark College; Occidental College; Pomona College; Reed College; University of California–Los Angeles. **Admissions statistics for the fall 2009 entering class:** Total applicants: 4,081. Total accepted: 828. Freshmen enrolled: 256; 48% were from out of state. Accepted through early-decision or early-action plans: 28%. Overall acceptance rate: 20%. Early-decision acceptance rate: 55%. Non-early acceptance rate: 19%. **Size of waiting list:** 0 applicants; enrolled from waiting list: 0. **Credentials of fall 2009 freshmen:** 47% ranked in the top 10 percent of their high school class; 89% were in the top 25 percent; 100% were in the top half. (Proportion submitting class standing: 29%.) **Average high school grade point average:** 3.8. **First-year students who submitted SAT scores:** 38%. Scores (25/75 percentile): Critical Reading: 608-693, Math: 588-680, Combined: 1196-1373. **First-year students submitting ACT scores:** 18%. Scores (25/75 percentile): English: N/A, Math: N/A, Composite: 26-30.

ACADEMICS

Year founded: 1963. **Academic calendar:** Semester. **Degrees offered:** bachelor's. **Most popular majors:** 17% psychology, 9% political science and government, 9% sociology, 9% visual and performing arts, 6% environmental studies. **Major fields of study:** area, ethnic, cultural, and gender studies; biological and biomedical sciences; business, management, marketing, and related support services; English language and literature/letters; foreign languages, literatures, and linguistics; history; mathematics and statistics; multi/interdisciplinary studies; natural resources and conservation; philosophy and religious studies; physical sciences; psychology; social sciences; visual and performing arts. **Areas of required coursework:** humanities, mathematics, English (including composition), sciences (biological or physical), social science, other. **Pre-professional programs:** pre-medicine. **Special academic programs (% participation):** cooperative (work-study plan) program (34%), cross-registration (99%), double major (21%), English as a Second Language (ESL) (0%), exchange student program (domestic) (0%), honors program (20%), independent study (57%), internships, liberal arts/career combination, student-designed major (11%), study abroad (74%). **Cooperative education programs:** computer science, health professions, social/behavioral science. **Reserve Officers Training Corps (ROTC):** Army ROTC: Offered at cooperating institution (Claremont McKenna College); Air Force ROTC: Offered at cooperating institution (Harvey Mudd College). **Faculty and instruction (2009-2010):** Total instructional faculty: 73 full-time, 34 part-time (54% men; 46% women; 33% minorities). Full-time faculty with Ph.D. or other terminal degree: 100%. Student/faculty ratio: 11/1. Classes of fewer than 20 students: 67%; of 20 to 49 students: 32%; of 50 or more students: 1%. **Advanced Placement and International Baccalaureate credit:** International Baccalaureate exams may be used for: Credit only. **Freshmen returning for sophomore year:** 91%. **Graduation rates:** Four-year: 70%; five-year: 78%; six-year: 80%. **Graduate study:** 15% of students pursue further study immediately upon graduation. Fields in which graduates pursue further study: law, 1%; medicine, 1%; education, 1%; arts and sciences, 2%.

COSTS AND FINANCIAL AID

Financial aid office: (909) 621-8208. **Expenses (2010-2011):** Tuition and fees 2010-2011: $41,174; room/board: $12,008. Estimated books and supplies: $1,000; transportation: $300; personal expenses: $1,000. **Financial aid:** Priority filing date for institution's financial aid form: February 1; deadline: February 1. In 2009-2010, 44% of undergraduates applied for financial aid. Of those, 40% were determined to have financial need; 100% had their need fully met. Average financial aid package (proportion receiving): $35,835 (40%). Average amount of gift aid, such as scholarships or grants (proportion receiving): $30,356 (40%). Average amount of self-help aid, such as work study or loans (proportion receiving): $5,735 (39%). Average need-based loan (excluding PLUS or other private loans): $3,647. Among students who received need-based aid, the average percentage of need met: 100%. Among students who received aid based on merit, the average award (and the proportion receiving): $5,000 (5%). The average athletic scholarship (and the proportion receiving): $0 (0%). Average amount of debt of borrowers graduating in 2009: $20,448. Proportion who borrowed: 45%.

CAMPUS LIFE AND EXTRACURRICULAR ACTIVITIES

Campus housing available (% using): coed dorms (99%), apartment for single students (1%). Students who live in college-owned, operated, or affiliated housing: 74%. **Clubs and organizations:** Number of student organizations: 68. Activities include: campus ministries, choral groups, dance, drama/theater, international student organization, literary magazine, model UN, music ensembles, radio station, student government, student newspaper, symphony orchestra. Number of fraternities: 0; sororities: 0. Average proportion of students who stay on campus on weekends: 75%. **Sports program (2009-2010):** Member of NCAA III. *Men's intercollegiate varsity sports:* baseball, basketball, cross country, football, soccer, swimming, tennis, track and field (indoor), track and field (outdoor), water polo. *Women's intercollegiate varsity sports:* basketball, cross country, soccer, swimming, tennis, track and field (indoor), track and field (outdoor), water polo.

SERVICES AND FACILITIES

Basic services: nonremedial tutoring, women's center, placement service, health service, health insurance. **Remedial assistance:** writing, other. **Counseling services:** minority student, career, personal, academic, older student, psychological, birth control, religious. **For learning-disabled students:** School does not offer a structured program with separate admission and additional fees. Total undergraduates in learning-disabled program or receiving services: 101. Services include: reading machines, tape recorders, note-taking services, extended time for tests, tutors, early syllabus. **Library:** Number of titles: 2,576,646; number of current serial subscriptions: 51,226. **Information technology resources:** Students are not required to lease or own a computer. Number of campus computers available to all students: 90. School has a wireless network. Approximate number of users that can be accommodated: 1,600. Proportion of college-owned housing units wired for high-speed internet access: 100%. **Campus safety:** Security services offered: 24-hour foot-and-vehicle patrols, late-night transport/escort service, 24-hour emergency telephones, lighted pathways/sidewalks, controlled dormitory access (key, security card, etc).

TRANSFER AND INTERNATIONAL STUDENTS

Transfer students: May apply for admission for the following academic terms: Fall, Spring. Applicants need a minimum number of credits to apply. For fall 2009: Transfer applications received: 157. Transfer applicants offered admission: 33. Transfer applicants enrolled: 21. **International students:** Number of foreign undergraduates: 32 (3% of student body). Number of countries represented: 13. Minimum TOEFL score required: 520 (paper); 190 (computer). Average TOEFL score: 600 (paper).

Point Loma Nazarene University

- **Address:** 3900 Lomaland Drive, San Diego, CA 92106
- **Website:** http://www.pointloma.edu
- **Private; Religious affiliation:** Church of the Nazarene
- **Enrollment:** 2,306 full-time; 81 part-time

KEY STATS

✔ **U.S News College Ranking:** 16, Regional Universities (West)
✔ **SAT Score (25th/75th percentile):** 990-1230
✔ **Tuition:** 2010-2011: $27,100

Selectivity: Selective	**Room/board:** $9,000
Acceptance rate: 74%	**Average debt:** $29,491
Student/faculty ratio: 13/1	**Proportion who borrowed:** 87%

UNDERGRADUATE STUDENT BODY STATS

2009-2010 enrollment: 2,306 full-time; 81 part-time. Men: 38%; women: 62%. **Ethnic makeup:** African American: 3%; American-Indian: 1%; Asian American: 7%; Hispanic: 12%; White: 77%; International: 1%. **Religious preference:** Roman Catholic: 6%; No preference: 3%; Church of the Nazarene: 23%; Non-denominational: 24%; Other: 44%.

ADMISSIONS FACTS AND FIGURES

Phone: (619) 849-2273. **Email:** admissions@pointloma.edu. **Website:** http://www.pointloma.edu. **Application deadlines for fall 2011:** Regular decision: Rolling; decision sent by April 1. Early decision: Not offered. Early action: Send application by: December 1; Decision sent by: January 15. Admission cannot be deferred. **Application fee:** $50. **To apply online, go to:** http://www.pointloma.edu/Apply/. **Admissions requirements/recommendations:** High school units required (recommended): English: (4); Mathematics: (3);

Science: (2); Foreign language: (2); Social studies: (2); History: (1); Total units: (18). Tests: The college uses SAT or ACT scores in admissions decisions. Either SAT or ACT required. For admission to the fall 2011 entering class, the school will accept: ACT with or without writing accepted. Campus visit: Recommended. Admissions interview: Recommended. Off-campus interview: May be arranged. **Factors that count in admissions decisions:** *Academic:* Secondary school record: Very Important. Class rank: Important. Letters of recommendation: Important. Standardized test scores: Very Important. Essay: Important. *Nonacademic:* Interview: Important. Extracurricular activities: Considered. Talent/ability: Considered. Character/personal qualities: Very Important. Alumni/ae relationship: Considered. Geographical residence: Not Considered. State residency: Not Considered. Religious affiliation/commitment: Very Important. Minority status: Not Considered. Volunteer work: Not Considered. Work experience: Not Considered. **Admissions statistics for the fall 2009 entering class:** Total applicants: 2,490. Total accepted: 1,852. Freshmen enrolled: 535; 20% were from out of state. Overall acceptance rate: 74%. Non-early acceptance rate: 74%. **Size of waiting list:** 246 applicants; enrolled from waiting list: 109. **Credentials of fall 2009 freshmen:** 33% ranked in the top 10 percent of their high school class; 64% were in the top 25 percent; 89% were in the top half. (Proportion submitting class standing: 68%.) **Average high school grade point average:** 3.7. **First-year students who submitted SAT scores:** 91%. Scores (25/75 percentile): Critical Reading: 500-610, Math: 490-620, Combined: 990-1230. **First-year students submitting ACT scores:** 45%. Scores (25/75 percentile): English: N/A, Math: N/A, Composite: 21-27.

ACADEMICS

Year founded: 1902. **Academic calendar:** Semester. **Degrees offered:** bachelor's, master's. **Most popular majors:** 22% business, management, marketing, and related support services, 10% communication, journalism, and related programs, 10% health professions and related clinical sciences, 7% biological and biomedical sciences, 7% visual and performing arts. **Major fields of study:** biological and biomedical sciences; business, management, marketing, and related support services; communication, journalism, and related programs; communications technologies/technicians and support services; computer and information sciences and support services; education; engineering; English language and literature/letters; family and consumer sciences/human sciences; foreign languages, literatures, and linguistics; health professions and related clinical sciences; history; liberal arts and sciences studies, and humanities; mathematics and statistics; multi/interdisciplinary studies; parks, recreation, leisure, and fitness studies; philosophy and religious studies; physical sciences; psychology; public administration and social service professions; social sciences; theology and religious vocations; visual and performing arts. **Areas of required coursework:** arts/fine arts, mathematics, English (including composition), philosophy, foreign languages, sciences (biological or physical), history, social science, other. **Pre-professional programs:** pre-law, pre-dentistry, pre-medicine, pre-theology, other. **Special academic programs:** double major, honors program, independent study, internships, study abroad, teacher certificate program. **Teacher certification offered in:** special education, elementary, middle/junior high, secondary. **Cooperative education programs:** art, business, computer science, education, health professions, home economics, humanities, natural science, social/behavioral science. **Reserve Officers Training Corps (ROTC):** Army ROTC: Offered at cooperating institution (San Diego State University); Navy ROTC: Offered at cooperating institution (University of San Diego); Air Force ROTC: Offered at cooperating institution (San Diego State University). **Faculty and instruction (2009-2010):** Total instructional faculty: 149 full-time, 236 part-time (52% men; 48% women; 14% minorities). Full-time faculty with Ph.D. or other terminal degree: 79%. Student/faculty ratio: 13/1. **Advanced Placement and International Baccalaureate credit:** AP tests may be used for: Credit only. Scores accepted: 3, 4, 5. International Baccalaureate exams may be used for: Credit only. **Freshmen returning for sophomore year:** 85%. **Graduation rates:** Four-year: 62%; five-year: 71%; six-year: 70%.

COSTS AND FINANCIAL AID

Financial aid office: (619) 849-2538. **Expenses (2010-2011):** Tuition and fees 2010-2011: $27,100; room/board: $9,000. Estimated books and supplies: $1,620; transportation: $729; personal expenses: $2,250. **Financial aid:** Priority filing date for institution's financial aid form: March 2; deadline: March 2. In 2009-2010, 79% of undergraduates applied for financial aid. Of those, 64% were determined to have financial need; 19% had their need fully met. Average financial aid package (proportion receiving): $18,695 (64%). Average amount of gift aid, such as scholarships or grants (proportion receiving): $13,258 (56%). Average amount of self-help aid, such as work study or loans (proportion receiving): $7,749 (57%). Average need-based loan (excluding PLUS or other private loans): $5,785. Among students who received need-based aid, the average percentage of need met: 68%. Among students who received aid based on merit, the average award (and the proportion receiving): $6,256 (19%). The average athletic scholarship (and the proportion receiving): $11,606 (4%). Average amount of debt of borrowers graduating in 2009: $29,491. Proportion who borrowed: 87%.

CAMPUS LIFE AND EXTRACURRICULAR ACTIVITIES

Campus housing available: women's dorms, men's dorms, apartment for single students. Students who live in college-owned, operated, or affiliated housing: 68%. **Student employment:** During the 2009-2010 academic year, 26% of undergraduates worked on campus. Average per-year earnings: $3,960. **Clubs and organizations:** Number of student organizations: 31. Activities include: choral groups, concert band, drama/theater, jazz band, literary magazine, music ensembles, musical theater, radio station, student government, student newspaper, student film society, television station, yearbook. Number of fraternities: 2; sororities: 3. Average proportion of students who stay on campus on weekends: 50%. **Sports program (2009-2010):** Member of NAIA. *Men's intercollegiate varsity sports:* baseball, basketball, cross country, golf, soccer, tennis, track and field (outdoor). *Women's intercollegiate varsity sports:* basketball, cross country, soccer, softball, tennis, track and field (outdoor), volleyball.

SERVICES AND FACILITIES

Basic services: nonremedial tutoring, women's center, health service, health insurance. **Remedial assistance:** math, writing, study skills. **Counseling services:** career, personal, academic, psychological, religious, other. **For learning-disabled students:** School does not offer a structured program with separate admission and additional fees. Total undergraduates in learning-disabled program or receiving services: 145. Services include: reading machines, tape recorders, untimed tests, note-taking services, oral tests, learning center, readers, extended time for tests, tutors, priority registration, priority seating, substitution of courses, texts on tape, exams on tape or computer, waiver of foreign language degree requirement, other. **Library:** Number of titles: 170,958; number of current serial subscriptions: 1,084. **Information technology resources:** Students are not required to lease or own a computer. Number of campus computers available to all students: 485. School has a wireless network. Approximate number of users that can be accommodated: 5,000. Proportion of college-owned housing units wired for high-speed internet access: 100%. **Campus safety:** Security services offered: 24-hour foot-and-vehicle patrols, late-night transport/escort service, lighted pathways/sidewalks, controlled dormitory access (key, security card, etc).

TRANSFER AND INTERNATIONAL STUDENTS

Transfer students: May apply for admission for the following academic terms: Fall, Spring. Applicants do not need a minimum number of credits to apply. For fall 2009: Transfer applications received: 490. Transfer applicants offered admission: 319. Transfer applicants enrolled: 166. **International students:** Number of foreign undergraduates: 17 (1% of student body). Number of countries represented: 11. Minimum TOEFL score required: 550 (paper); 216 (computer). Average TOEFL score: 557 (paper).

Pomona College

- **Address:** 550 N. College Avenue, Claremont, CA 91711
- **Website:** http://www.pomona.edu
- **Private**
- **Enrollment:** 1,535 full-time; 15 part-time

KEY STATS

✔ **U.S News College Ranking:** 6, National Liberal Arts Colleges
✔ **SAT Score (25th/75th percentile):** 1400-1550
✔ **Tuition:** 2010-2011: $38,394

Selectivity: Most selective	**Room/board:** $12,936
Acceptance rate: 16%	**Average debt:** $11,700
Student/faculty ratio: 7/1	**Proportion who borrowed:** 55%

UNDERGRADUATE STUDENT BODY STATS

2009-2010 enrollment: 1,535 full-time; 15 part-time. Men: 50%; women: 50%. **Ethnic makeup:** African American: 9%; Asian American: 14%; Hispanic: 11%; White: 62%; International: 4%.

ADMISSIONS FACTS AND FIGURES

Phone: (909) 621-8134. **Email:** admissions@pomona.edu. **Website:** http://www.pomona.edu. **Application deadlines for fall 2011:** Regular decision: January 2; decision sent by April 5. Early decision: Send application by: November 15; Decision sent by: December 15. Early action: Not offered. Admission can be deferred. **Application fee:** $65. **To apply online, go to:** http://www.pomona.edu/admissions/applying/appinstructions.asp. **Admissions requirements/recommendations:** High school units required (recommended): English: 4; Mathematics: 3 (4); Science: 3 (4); Foreign language: 2 (3); Social studies: 2 (2); History: 3 (3). Tests: The college uses SAT or ACT scores in admissions decisions. Either SAT or ACT required. For admission to the fall 2011 entering class, the school will accept: ACT with writing required. Campus visit: Recommended. Admissions interview: Recommended. Off-campus interview: May be arranged. **Factors that count in admissions decisions:** *Academic:* Secondary school record: Very Important. Class rank: Very Important. Letters of recommendation: Very Important. Standardized test scores: Very Important. Essay: Very Important. *Nonacademic:* Interview: Important. Extracurricular activities: Very Important. Talent/ability: Very Important. Character/personal qualities: Very Important. Alumni/ae relationship: Considered. Geographical residence: Considered. State residency: Not Considered. Religious affiliation/commitment: Not Considered. Minority status: Considered. Volunteer work: Considered. Work experience: Considered. **Other schools with the greatest overlap in applicants:** Amherst College; Harvard University; Stanford University; University of California–Berkeley; Yale University. **Admissions statistics for the fall 2009 entering class:** Total applicants: 6,149. Total accepted: 992. Freshmen enrolled: 390; 73% were from out of state. Overall acceptance rate: 16%. Non-early acceptance rate: 16%. **Credentials of fall 2009 freshmen:** 92% ranked in the top 10 percent of their high school class; 99% were in the top 25 percent; 100% were in the top half. (Proportion submitting class standing: 55%.) **First-year students who submitted SAT scores:** 78%. Scores (25/75 percentile): Critical Reading: 710-780, Math: 690-770, Combined: 1400-1550. **First-year students submitting ACT scores:** 46%. Scores (25/75 percentile): English: 32-35, Math: 29-34, Composite: 31-34.

ACADEMICS

Year founded: 1887. **Academic calendar:** Semester. **Degrees offered:** bachelor's. **Most popular majors:** 13% economics, 7% mathematics, 6% English language and literature, 6% neuroscience, 5% environmental science. **Major fields of study:** area, ethnic, cultural, and gender studies; biological and biomedical sciences; communication, journalism, and related programs; computer and information sciences and support services; English language and literature/letters; foreign languages, literatures, and linguistics; history; mathematics and statistics; multi/interdisciplinary studies; natural resources and conservation; philosophy and religious studies; physical sciences; psychology; public administration and social service professions; social sciences; visual and performing arts. **Areas of required coursework:** arts/fine arts, humanities, computer literacy, mathematics, English (including composition), philosophy, foreign languages, sciences (biological or physical), history, social science, other. **Pre-professional programs:** pre-law, pre-medicine. **Special academic programs (% participation):** cross-registration (96%), double major (14%), exchange student program (domestic) (1%), independent study (30%), internships (40%), student-designed major (3%), study abroad (57%), other. **Cooperative education programs:** engineering. **Reserve Officers Training Corps (ROTC):** Army ROTC: Offered at cooperating institution (Claremont McKenna College); Air Force ROTC: Offered at cooperating institution (Harvey Mudd College). **Faculty and instruction (2009-2010):** Total instructional faculty: 188 full-time, 37 part-time (56% men; 44% women; 26% minorities). Full-time faculty with Ph.D. or other terminal degree: 98%. Student/faculty ratio: 7/1. Classes of fewer than 20 students: 66%; of 20 to 49 students: 32%; of 50 or more students: 2%. **Advanced Placement and International Baccalaureate credit:** AP tests may be used for: Credit only. Scores accepted: 4, 5. International Baccalaureate exams may be used for: Placement only. **Freshmen returning for sophomore year:** 98%. **Graduation rates:** Four-year: 89%; five-year: 94%; six-year: 95%. **Graduate study:** 23% of students pursue further study immediately upon graduation; 80% within five years.

COSTS AND FINANCIAL AID

Financial aid office: (909) 621-8205. **Expenses (2010-2011):** Tuition and fees 2010-2011: $38,394; room/board: $12,936. Estimated books and supplies: $900; transportation: $650; personal expenses: $1,100. **Financial aid:** Priority filing date for institution's financial aid form: February 1; deadline: February 1. In 2009-2010, 55% of undergraduates applied for financial aid. Of those, 54% were determined to have financial need; 100% had their need fully met. Average financial aid package (proportion receiving): $35,416 (54%). Average amount of gift aid, such as scholarships or grants (proportion receiving): $34,061 (54%). Average amount of self-help aid, such as work study or loans (proportion receiving): $1,355 (54%). Average need-based loan (excluding PLUS or other private loans): $0. Among students who received need-based aid, the average percentage of need met: 100%. Among students who received aid based on merit, the average award (and the proportion receiving): $0 (0%). The average athletic scholarship (and the proportion receiving): $0 (0%). Average amount of debt of borrowers graduating in 2009: $11,700. Proportion who borrowed: 55%.

CAMPUS LIFE AND EXTRACURRICULAR ACTIVITIES

Campus housing available (% using): coed dorms (97%), other housing options (3%). Students who live in college-owned, operated, or affiliated housing: 98%. **Student employment:** During the 2009-2010 academic year, 73% of undergraduates worked on campus. Average per-year earnings: $980. **Clubs and organizations:** Number of student organizations: 150. Activities include: campus ministries, choral groups, concert band, dance, drama/theater, international student organization, jazz band, literary magazine, model UN, music ensembles, musical theater, pep band, radio station, student government, student newspaper, student film society, symphony orchestra, television station, yearbook. Number of fraternities: 3; sororities: 0. Proportion of men in fraternities: 5%; Average proportion of students who stay on campus on weekends: 90%. **Sports program (2009-2010):** Member of NCAA III. *Men's intercollegiate varsity sports:* baseball, basketball, cross country, football, golf, soccer, swimming, tennis, track and field (outdoor), water polo. *Women's intercollegiate varsity sports:* basketball, cross country, lacrosse, soccer, softball, swimming, tennis, track and field (outdoor), volleyball, water polo.

SERVICES AND FACILITIES

Basic services: nonremedial tutoring, women's center, placement service, health service, health insurance. **Counseling services:** minority student, career, personal, academic, psychological, birth control, religious. **For learning-disabled students:** School does not offer a structured program with separate admission and additional fees. Total undergraduates in learning-disabled program or receiving services: 16. Services include: tape recorders, note-taking services, oral tests, readers, extended time for tests, tutors, priority registration, priority seating, substitution of courses, exams on tape or computer, other testing accommodations, waiver of foreign language degree requirement. **Library:** Number of titles: 2,618,747; number of current serial subscriptions: 47,450. **Information technology resources:** Students are not required to lease or own a computer. Number of campus computers available to all students: 500. School has a wireless network. Approximate number of users that can be accommodated: 10,000. Proportion of college-owned housing units wired for high-speed internet access: 100%. **Campus safety:** Security services offered: 24-hour foot-and-vehicle patrols, late-night transport/escort service, 24-hour emergency telephones, lighted pathways/sidewalks, student patrols, controlled dormitory access (key, security card, etc).

TRANSFER AND INTERNATIONAL STUDENTS

Transfer students: May apply for admission for the following academic terms: Fall. Applicants need a minimum number of credits to apply. For fall 2009: Transfer applications received: 265. Transfer applicants offered admission: 30. Transfer applicants enrolled: 13. **International students:** Number of foreign undergraduates: 64 (4% of student body). Number of countries represented: 10. Minimum TOEFL score required: 600 (paper); 250 (computer).

San Diego State University

- **Address:** 5500 Campanile Drive, San Diego, CA 92182-7455
- **Website:** http://www.sdsu.edu
- **Public**
- **Enrollment:** 23,264 full-time; 4,273 part-time

KEY STATS
✔ **U.S News College Ranking:** 183, National Universities
✔ **SAT Score (25th/75th percentile):** 910-1170
✔ **Tuition:** 2010-2011: $4,992 in state, $16,152 out of state

Selectivity: Selective	**Room/board:** $11,485
Acceptance rate: 36%	**Average debt:** $14,700
Student/faculty ratio: 22/1	**Proportion who borrowed:** 44%

UNDERGRADUATE STUDENT BODY STATS

2009-2010 enrollment: 23,264 full-time; 4,273 part-time. Men: 43%; women: 57%. **Ethnic makeup:** African American: 4%; American-Indian: 1%; Asian American: 15%; Hispanic: 26%; White: 51%; International: 3%.

ADMISSIONS FACTS AND FIGURES

Phone: (619) 594-6336. **Email:** admissions@sdsu.edu. **Website:** http://www.sdsu.edu. **Application deadlines for fall 2011:** Regular decision: November 30; decision sent by March 1. Early decision: Not offered. Early action: Not offered. Admission cannot be deferred. **Application fee:** $55. **To apply online, go to:** http://www.sdsu.edu/apply. **Admissions requirements/recommendations:** High school units required (recommended): English: 4; Mathematics: 3 (4); Science: 2; Foreign language: 2; Social studies: 1; History: 1; Academic electives: 1; Total units: 15. Tests: The college uses SAT or ACT scores in admissions decisions. Either SAT or ACT required. For admission to the fall 2011 entering class, the school will accept: ACT with or without writing accepted. Campus visit: Neither required nor recommended. Admissions interview: Neither required nor recommended. Off-campus interview: Not available. **Factors that count in admissions decisions:** *Academic:* Secondary school record: Very Important. Class rank: Not Considered. Letters of recommendation: Not Considered. Standardized test scores: Very Important. Essay: Not Considered. *Nonacademic:* Interview: Not Considered. Extracurricular activities: Not Considered. Talent/ability: Not Considered. Character/personal qualities: Not Considered. Alumni/ae relationship: Not Considered. Geographical residence: Important. State residency: Important. Religious affiliation/commitment: Not Considered. Minority status: Not Considered. Volunteer work: Not Considered. Work experience: Not Considered. **Admissions statistics for the fall 2009 entering class:** Total applicants: 41,986. Total accepted: 15,273. Freshmen enrolled: 4,273; 8% were from out of state. Overall acceptance rate: 36%. **Average high school grade point average:** 3.5. **First-year students who submitted SAT scores:** 95%. Scores (25/75 percentile): Critical Reading: 450-570, Math: 460-600, Combined: 910-1170. **First-year students submitting ACT scores:** 41%. Scores (25/75 percentile): English: 19-26, Math: 19-25, Composite: 19-25.

ACADEMICS

Year founded: 1897. **Academic calendar:** Semester. **Degrees offered:** bachelor's, post-bachelor's certificate, master's, doctorate. **Most popular majors:** 21% business, management, marketing, and related support services, 12% social sciences, 9% psychology, 7% English language and literature/letters, 6% parks, recreation, leisure, and fitness studies. **Major fields of study:** agriculture, agriculture operations, and related sciences; area, ethnic, cultural, and gender studies; biological and biomedical sciences; business, management, marketing, and related support services; communication, journalism, and related programs; communications technologies/technicians and support services; computer and information sciences and support services; education; engineering; English language and literature/letters; family and consumer sciences/human sciences; foreign languages, literatures, and linguistics; health professions and related clinical sciences; history; liberal arts and sciences studies, and humanities; mathematics and statistics; multi/interdisciplinary studies; natural resources and conservation; parks, recreation, leisure, and fitness studies; philosophy and religious studies; physical sciences; psychology; public administration and social service professions; security and protective services; social sciences; visual and performing arts. **Areas of required coursework:** arts/fine arts, humanities, mathematics, English (including composition), philosophy, foreign languages, sciences (biological or physical), history, social science. **Pre-professional programs:** pre-law, pre-dentistry, pre-medicine, pre-veterinary science. **Special academic programs:** distance learning, double major, English as a Second

Language (ESL), exchange student program (domestic), external degree program, honors program, independent study, internships, liberal arts/career combination, study abroad, teacher certificate program. **Teacher certification offered in:** early childhood, special education, elementary, vo-tech, middle/junior high, adult education, secondary, bilingual/bicultural. **Reserve Officers Training Corps (ROTC):** Army ROTC: Offered on campus; Navy ROTC: Offered on campus; Air Force ROTC: Offered on campus. **Faculty and instruction (2009-2010):** Total instructional faculty: 841 full-time, 689 part-time (53% men; 47% women; 23% minorities). Full-time faculty with Ph.D. or other terminal degree: 85%. Student/faculty ratio: 22/1. Classes of fewer than 20 students: 19%; of 20 to 49 students: 56%; of 50 or more students: 25%. **Advanced Placement and International Baccalaureate credit:** AP tests may be used for: Credit only. Scores accepted: 3, 4, 5. International Baccalaureate exams may be used for: Credit only. **Freshmen returning for sophomore year:** 82%. **Graduation rates:** Four-year: 29%; five-year: 58%; six-year: 66%.

COSTS AND FINANCIAL AID
Financial aid office: (619) 594-6323. **Expenses (2010-2011):** Tuition and fees 2010-2011: $4,992 in state, $16,152 out of state; room/board: $11,485. Estimated books and supplies: $1,638; transportation: $1,320; personal expenses: $2,657. **Financial aid:** Priority filing date for institution's financial aid form: March 2. In 2009-2010, 74% of undergraduates applied for financial aid. Of those, 53% were determined to have financial need; 19% had their need fully met. Average financial aid package (proportion receiving): $8,500 (52%). Average amount of gift aid, such as scholarships or grants (proportion receiving): $7,100 (39%). Average amount of self-help aid, such as work study or loans (proportion receiving): $4,100 (52%). Average need-based loan (excluding PLUS or other private loans): $4,100. Among students who received need-based aid, the average percentage of need met: 73%. Among students who received aid based on merit, the average award (and the proportion receiving): $1,800 (5%). The average athletic scholarship (and the proportion receiving): $13,500 (2%). Average amount of debt of borrowers graduating in 2009: $14,700. Proportion who borrowed: 44%.

CAMPUS LIFE AND EXTRACURRICULAR ACTIVITIES
Campus housing available: coed dorms, sorority housing, fraternity housing, apartment for single students, special housing for international students, other housing options. Students who live in college-owned, operated, or affiliated housing: 12%. **Student employment:** During the 2009-2010 academic year, 30% of undergraduates worked on campus. **Clubs and organizations:** Number of student organizations: 264. Activities include: campus ministries, choral groups, concert band, dance, drama/theater, international student organization, jazz band, literary magazine, marching band, model UN, music ensembles, musical theater, opera, pep band, radio station, student government, student newspaper, student film society, symphony orchestra, television station. Number of fraternities: 21; sororities: 23. Proportion of men in fraternities: 9%; of women in sororities: 9%. **Sports program (2009-2010):** Member of NCAA I. *Men's intercollegiate varsity sports:* baseball, basketball, football, golf, soccer, tennis. *Women's intercollegiate varsity sports:* basketball, crew (heavyweight), cross country, golf, soccer, softball, swimming, tennis, track and field (indoor), track and field (outdoor), volleyball, water polo.

SERVICES AND FACILITIES
Basic services: nonremedial tutoring, placement service, day care, health service, health insurance. **Remedial assistance:** reading, math. **Counseling services:** career, military, academic, psychological, birth control. **For learning-disabled students:** School does not offer a structured program with separate admission and additional fees. Services include: remedial math, remedial English, tape recorders, note-taking services, learning center, readers, extended time for tests, tutors, priority registration, texts on tape, other testing accommodations. **Information technology resources:** Students are not required to lease or own a computer. Number of campus computers available to all students: 400. School does not have a wireless network. Proportion of college-owned housing units wired for high-speed internet access: 100%. **Campus safety:** Security services offered: 24-hour foot-and-vehicle patrols, late-night transport/escort service, 24-hour emergency telephones, lighted pathways/sidewalks, student patrols.

TRANSFER AND INTERNATIONAL STUDENTS
Transfer students: May apply for admission for the following academic terms: Fall. Applicants need a minimum number of credits to apply. For fall 2009: Transfer applications received: 13,852. Transfer applicants offered admission: 3,671. Transfer applicants enrolled: 2,599. **International students:** Number of foreign undergraduates: 938 (3% of student body).

Number of countries represented: 60. Minimum TOEFL score required: 550 (paper); 213 (computer). Average TOEFL score: 589 (paper).

San Francisco Art Institute

■ **Address:** 800 Chestnut Street, San Francisco, CA 94133
■ **Website:** http://www.sfai.edu
■ **Private**
■ **Enrollment:** N/A

KEY STATS
✔ **U.S News College Ranking:** Unranked Specialty School–Fine Arts
✔ **SAT or ACT Score (25th/75th percentile):** N/A
✔ **Tuition:** 2009-2010: $31,350

Selectivity: N/A	Room/board: $12,524
Acceptance rate: N/A	Average debt: N/A
Student/faculty ratio: N/A	Proportion who borrowed: N/A

San Francisco Conservatory of Music

■ **Address:** 50 Oak Street, San Francisco, CA 94102
■ **Website:** http://www.sfcm.edu
■ **Private**
■ **Enrollment:** 201 full-time; 5 part-time

KEY STATS
✔ **U.S News College Ranking:** Unranked Specialty School–Fine Arts
✔ **SAT or ACT Score (25th/75th percentile):** N/A
✔ **Tuition:** 2010-2011: $35,180

Selectivity: N/A	Room/board: $10,950
Acceptance rate: 44%	Average debt: $34,000
Student/faculty ratio: 7/1	Proportion who borrowed: 93%

UNDERGRADUATE STUDENT BODY STATS
2009-2010 enrollment: 201 full-time; 5 part-time. Men: 55%; women: 45%. **Ethnic makeup:** African American: 4%; American-Indian: 1%; Asian American: 13%; Hispanic: 7%; White: 53%; International: 21%.

ADMISSIONS FACTS AND FIGURES
Phone: (800) 899-7326. **Email:** admit@sfcm.edu. **Website:** http://www.sfcm.edu. **Application deadlines for fall 2011:** Regular decision: December 1; decision sent by April 1. Early decision: Not offered. Early action: Not offered. Admission can be deferred. **Application fee:** $100. **To apply online, go to:** http://www.unifiedapps.org. **Admissions requirements/recommendations:** Tests: The college does not use SAT or ACT scores in admissions decisions. Neither SAT nor ACT required. Campus visit: Recommended. Admissions interview: Neither required nor recommended. Off-campus interview: Not available. **Factors that count in admissions decisions:** *Academic:* Secondary school record: Considered. Class rank: Considered. Letters of recommendation: Very Important. Standardized test scores: Considered. Essay: Considered. *Nonacademic:* Interview: Not Considered. Extracurricular activities: Very Important. Talent/ability: Very Important. Character/personal qualities: Important. Alumni/ae relationship: Considered. Geographical residence: Not Considered. State residency: Not Considered. Religious affiliation/commitment: Not Considered. Minority status: Not Considered. Volunteer work: Not Considered. Work experience: Not Considered. **Other schools with the greatest overlap in applicants:** Cleveland Institute of Music; Manhattan School of Music; New England Conservatory of Music; Oberlin College; University of Rochester. **Admissions statistics for the fall 2009 entering class:** Total applicants: 393. Total accepted: 173. Freshmen enrolled: 56; 43% were from out of state. Overall acceptance rate: 44%. **Size of waiting list:** 42 applicants; enrolled from waiting list: 27.

ACADEMICS
Year founded: 1917. **Academic calendar:** Semester. **Degrees offered:** certificate, diploma, bachelor's, master's, post-master's certificate. **Major fields of study:** visual and performing arts. **Areas of required coursework:** arts/fine arts, humanities, English (including composition), foreign languages, history, other. **Special academic programs (% participation):** English as a

Second Language (ESL) (8%), independent study (5%), internships (3%).
Faculty and instruction (2009-2010): Total instructional faculty: 31 full-time, 69 part-time (70% men; 30% women; 10% minorities). Full-time faculty with Ph.D. or other terminal degree: 23%. Student/faculty ratio: 7/1. Classes of fewer than 20 students: 66%; of 20 to 49 students: 31%; of 50 or more students: 3%. **Advanced Placement and International Baccalaureate credit:** AP tests may be used for: Credit and/or placement. Scores accepted: 3, 4, 5. **Freshmen returning for sophomore year:** 85%. **Graduation rates:** Six-year: 65%. **Graduate study:** 15% of students pursue further study immediately upon graduation; 20% within one year; 25% within five years. Fields in which graduates pursue further study: education, 10%; arts and sciences, 90%.

COSTS AND FINANCIAL AID

Financial aid office: (415) 759-3414. **Expenses (2010-2011):** Tuition and fees 2010-2011: $35,180; room/board: $10,950. Estimated books and supplies: $620; transportation: $200; personal expenses: $2,000. **Financial aid:** Priority filing date for institution's financial aid form: March 1; deadline: March 1. In 2009-2010, 68% of undergraduates applied for financial aid. Of those, 60% were determined to have financial need; 14% had their need fully met. Average financial aid package (proportion receiving): $22,952 (60%). Average amount of gift aid, such as scholarships or grants (proportion receiving): $17,133 (60%). Average amount of self-help aid, such as work study or loans (proportion receiving): $6,326 (55%). Average need-based loan (excluding PLUS or other private loans): $6,127. Among students who received need-based aid, the average percentage of need met: 66%. Among students who received aid based on merit, the average award (and the proportion receiving): $12,389 (37%). The average athletic scholarship (and the proportion receiving): $0 (0%). Average amount of debt of borrowers graduating in 2009: $34,000. Proportion who borrowed: 93%.

CAMPUS LIFE AND EXTRACURRICULAR ACTIVITIES

Campus housing available (% using): other housing options (100%). Students who live in college-owned, operated, or affiliated housing: 9%. **Student employment:** During the 2009-2010 academic year, 27% of undergraduates worked on campus. Average per-year earnings: $2,800. Activities include: choral groups, music ensembles, musical theater, opera, student government, symphony orchestra, yearbook. Number of fraternities: 0; sororities: 0. Average proportion of students who stay on campus on weekends: 95%.

SERVICES AND FACILITIES

Basic services: health insurance. **Counseling services:** psychological. **For learning-disabled students:** School does not offer a structured program with separate admission and additional fees. Services include: tutors. **Library:** Number of titles: 60,000; number of current serial subscriptions: 80. **Information technology resources:** Students are not required to lease or own a computer. Number of campus computers available to all students: 18. School has a wireless network. Approximate number of users that can be accommodated: 400. Proportion of college-owned housing units wired for high-speed internet access: 100%.

TRANSFER AND INTERNATIONAL STUDENTS

Transfer students: May apply for admission for the following academic terms: Fall, Spring. Applicants do not need a minimum number of credits to apply. For fall 2009: Transfer applications received: 91. Transfer applicants offered admission: 32. Transfer applicants enrolled: 19. **International students:** Number of foreign undergraduates: 43 (21% of student body). Number of countries represented: 31. Minimum TOEFL score required: 500 (paper); 173 (computer). Average TOEFL score: 513 (paper).

San Francisco State University

- **Address:** 1600 Holloway Avenue, San Francisco, CA 94132
- **Website:** http://www.sfsu.edu
- **Public**
- **Enrollment:** 19,877 full-time; 5,124 part-time

KEY STATS

✔ **U.S News College Ranking:** 51, Regional Universities (West)
✔ **SAT Score (25th/75th percentile):** 890-1130
✔ **Tuition:** 2009-2010: $4,740 in state, $15,900 out of state
   Selectivity: Selective   **Room/board:** $10,904
   Acceptance rate: 73%   **Average debt:** $15,684
   Student/faculty ratio: 25/1   **Proportion who borrowed:** 39%

UNDERGRADUATE STUDENT BODY STATS

2009-2010 enrollment: 19,877 full-time; 5,124 part-time. Men: 41%; women: 59%. **Ethnic makeup:** African American: 5%; Asian American: 28%; Hispanic: 18%; White: 41%; International: 7%.

ADMISSIONS FACTS AND FIGURES

Phone: (415) 338-6486. **Email:** ugadmit@sfsu.edu. **Website:** http://www.sfsu.edu. **Application deadlines for fall 2011:** Regular decision: November 30. Early decision: Not offered. Early action: Not offered. Admission cannot be deferred. **Application fee:** $55. **To apply online, go to:** http://www.sfsu.edu/future/appcentral/appcentral.html. **Admissions requirements/recommendations:** High school units required (recommended): English: 4; Mathematics: 3; Science: 2; Foreign language: 2; Social studies: 1; History: 1; Academic electives: (1); Total units: 14. Tests: The college uses SAT or ACT scores in admissions decisions. Neither SAT nor ACT required. For admission to the fall 2011 entering class, the school will accept: ACT with or without writing accepted. Campus visit: Neither required nor recommended. Admissions interview: Neither required nor recommended. Off-campus interview: Not available. **Factors that count in admissions decisions: *Academic:*** Secondary school record: Very Important. Class rank: Not Considered. Letters of recommendation: Considered. Standardized test scores: Very Important. Essay: Not Considered. ***Nonacademic:*** Interview: Not Considered. Extracurricular activities: Not Considered. Talent/ability: Considered. Character/personal qualities: Not Considered. Alumni/ae relationship: Not Considered. Geographical residence: Not Considered. State residency: Important. Religious affiliation/commitment: Not Considered. Minority status: Not Considered. Volunteer work: Not Considered. Work experience: Not Considered. **Other schools with the greatest overlap in applicants:** California State University–East Bay; San Jose State University. **Admissions statistics for the fall 2009 entering class:** Total applicants: 28,218. Total accepted: 20,465. Freshmen enrolled: 4,032; 1% were from out of state. Overall acceptance rate: 73%. **Average high school grade point average:** 3.1. **First-year students who submitted SAT scores:** 82%. Scores (25/75 percentile): Critical Reading: 440-560, Math: 450-570, Combined: 890-1130. **First-year students submitting ACT scores:** 23%. Scores (25/75 percentile): English: 18-24, Math: 18-25, Composite: 19-24.

ACADEMICS

Year founded: 1899. **Academic calendar:** Semester. **Degrees offered:** certificate, bachelor's, post-bachelor's certificate, master's, doctorate. **Most popular majors:** 20% business, management, marketing, and related support services, 10% social sciences, 9% psychology, 8% communication, journalism, and related programs, 8% visual and performing arts. **Major fields of study:** area, ethnic, cultural, and gender studies; biological and biomedical sciences; business, management, marketing, and related support services; communication, journalism, and related programs; communications technologies/technicians and support services; computer and information sciences and support services; education; engineering; English language and literature/letters; family and consumer sciences/human sciences; foreign languages, literatures, and linguistics; health professions and related clinical sciences; history; liberal arts and sciences studies, and humanities; mathematics and statistics; mechanic and repair technologies/technicians; multi/interdisciplinary studies; natural resources and conservation; parks, recreation, leisure, and fitness studies; philosophy and religious studies; physical sciences; psychology; public administration and social service professions; security and protective services; social sciences; visual and performing arts. **Areas of required coursework:** arts/fine arts, humanities, mathematics, English (including composition), philosophy, sciences (biological or physical), history, social science, other. **Pre-professional programs:** pre-law, pre-medicine, other. **Special academic programs:** cooperative (work-study plan) program, cross-registration, distance learning, double major, dual enrollment, English as a Second Language (ESL), honors program, independent study, internships, liberal arts/career combination, student-designed major, study abroad, teacher certificate program. **Teacher certification offered in:** early childhood, special education, elementary, vo-tech, middle/junior high, adult education, secondary, bilingual/bicultural. **Cooperative education programs:** other. **Reserve Officers Training Corps (ROTC):** Army ROTC: Offered at cooperating institution (University of San Francisco); Navy ROTC: Offered at cooperating institution (University of California–Berkeley); Air Force ROTC: Offered at cooperating institution (University of California–Berkeley). **Faculty and instruction (2009-2010):** Total instructional faculty: 818 full-time, 748 part-time (48% men; 52% women; 36% minorities). Full-time faculty with Ph.D. or other terminal degree: 74%. Student/faculty ratio: 25/1. Classes of fewer than 20 students: 16%; of 20 to 49 students: 58%; of 50 or more students: 26%. **Advanced Placement and International Baccalaureate credit:** AP tests may be used for: Credit only. **Freshmen returning for sophomore year:** 76%. **Graduation rates:** Four-year: 12%; five-year: 35%; six-year: 45%.

COSTS AND FINANCIAL AID

Financial aid office: (415) 338-7000. **Expenses (2009-2010):** Tuition and fees 2009-2010: $4,740 in state, $15,900 out of state; room/board: $10,904. Estimated books and supplies: $1,656; transportation: $1,254; personal expenses: $3,024. **Financial aid:** Priority filing date for institution's financial aid form: March 2. In 2009-2010, 66% of undergraduates applied for financial aid. Of those, 56% were determined to have financial need; 7% had their need fully met. Average financial aid package (proportion receiving): $10,668 (55%). Average amount of gift aid, such as scholarships or grants (proportion receiving): $8,635 (41%). Average amount of self-help aid, such as work study or loans (proportion receiving): $4,327 (54%). Average need-based loan (excluding PLUS or other private loans): $3,245. Among students who received need-based aid, the average percentage of need met: 64%. Among students who received aid based on merit, the average award (and the proportion receiving): $2,799 (1%). The average athletic scholarship (and the proportion receiving): $2,507 (0%). Average amount of debt of borrowers graduating in 2009: $15,684. Proportion who borrowed: 39%.

CAMPUS LIFE AND EXTRACURRICULAR ACTIVITIES

Campus housing available (% using): coed dorms (30%), apartments for married students (2%), apartment for single students (60%), special housing for disabled students (5%), special housing for international students (2%), other housing options (1%). Students who live in college-owned, operated, or affiliated housing: 11%. **Clubs and organizations:** Number of student organizations: 213. Activities include: choral groups, concert band, dance, drama/theater, international student organization, jazz band, literary magazine, music ensembles, musical theater, opera, pep band, radio station, student government, student newspaper, student film society, symphony orchestra, television station. Number of fraternities: 3; sororities: 4. Average proportion of students who stay on campus on weekends: 4%. **Sports program (2009-2010):** Member of NCAA II. **Men's intercollegiate varsity sports:** baseball, basketball, cross country, soccer, wrestling. **Women's intercollegiate varsity sports:** basketball, cross country, soccer, softball, track and field (indoor), track and field (outdoor), volleyball.

SERVICES AND FACILITIES

Basic services: nonremedial tutoring, women's center, placement service, day care, health service, health insurance. **Remedial assistance:** reading, math, writing, study skills. **Counseling services:** minority student, career, military, personal, veteran student, academic, older student, psychological, birth control. **For learning-disabled students:** School does not offer a structured program with separate admission and additional fees. **Library:** Number of titles: 1,143,765; number of current serial subscriptions: 40,184. **Information technology resources:** Students are not required to lease or own a computer. Number of campus computers available to all students: 2,800. School has a wireless network. Approximate number of users that can be accommodated: 2,000. Proportion of college-owned housing units wired for high-speed internet access: 100%. **Campus safety:** Security services offered: 24-hour foot-and-vehicle patrols, late-night transport/escort service, 24-hour emergency telephones, lighted pathways/sidewalks, student patrols, controlled dormitory access (key, security card, etc).

TRANSFER AND INTERNATIONAL STUDENTS

Transfer students: May apply for admission for the following academic terms: Fall, Spring. Applicants need a minimum number of credits to apply. For fall 2009: Transfer applications received: 11,220. Transfer applicants offered admission: 8,603. Transfer applicants enrolled: 3,228. **International students:** Number of foreign undergraduates: 1653 (7% of student body). Number of countries represented: 87. Minimum TOEFL score required: 500 (paper); 61 (computer). Average TOEFL score: 550 (paper).

San Jose State University

- **Address:** 1 Washington Square, San Jose, CA 95192
- **Website:** http://www.sjsu.edu
- **Public**
- **Enrollment:** 18,304 full-time; 5,969 part-time

KEY STATS

✔ **U.S News College Ranking:** 44, Regional Universities (West)
✔ **SAT Score (25th/75th percentile):** 900-1120
✔ **Tuition:** 2010-2011: $6,250 in state, $15,178 out of state

Selectivity: Selective	**Room/board:** $10,733
Acceptance rate: 74%	**Average debt:** $12,313
Student/faculty ratio: 25/1	**Proportion who borrowed:** 49%

UNDERGRADUATE STUDENT BODY STATS

2009-2010 enrollment: 18,304 full-time; 5,969 part-time. Men: 48%; women: 52%. **Ethnic makeup:** African American: 5%; Asian American: 34%; Hispanic: 19%; White: 38%; International: 4%.

ADMISSIONS FACTS AND FIGURES

Phone: (408) 283-7500. **Email:** admissions@sjsu.edu. **Website:** http://www.sjsu.edu. **Application deadlines for fall 2011:** Regular decision: November 30; decision sent by February 25. Early decision: Not offered. Early action: Not offered. Admission cannot be deferred. **Application fee:** $55. **To apply online, go to:** http://www.csumentor.edu. **Admissions requirements/recommendations:** High school units required (recommended): English: 4 (0); Mathematics: 3 (4); Science: 2 (3); Foreign language: 2 (0); Social studies: 1 (0); History: 1 (0); Academic electives: 1 (0); Total units: 15 (0). Tests: The college uses SAT or ACT scores in admissions decisions. Neither SAT nor ACT required. For admission to the fall 2011 entering class, the school will accept: ACT with writing required. Campus visit: Recommended. Admissions interview: Neither required nor recommended. Off-campus interview: Not available. **Factors that count in admissions decisions:** *Academic:* Secondary school record: Very Important. Class rank: Not Considered. Letters of recommendation: Not Considered. Standardized test scores: Very Important. Essay: Not Considered. *Nonacademic:* Interview: Not Considered. Extracurricular activities: Not Considered. Talent/ability: Not Considered. Character/personal qualities: Not Considered. Alumni/ae relationship: Not Considered. Geographical residence: Not Considered. State residency: Not Considered. Religious affiliation/commitment: Not Considered. Minority status: Not Considered. Volunteer work: Not Considered. Work experience: Not Considered. **Other schools with the greatest overlap in applicants:** California State University–Long Beach; San Diego State University; San Francisco State University; University of California–Davis. **Admissions statistics for the fall 2009 entering class:** Total applicants: 21,836. Total accepted: 16,251. Freshmen enrolled: 2,764; 1% were from out of state. Overall acceptance rate: 74%. **Average high school grade point average:** 3.2. **First-year students who submitted SAT scores:** 93%. Scores (25/75 percentile): Critical Reading: 440-540, Math: 460-580, Combined: 900-1120. **First-year students submitting ACT scores:** 23%. Scores (25/75 percentile): English: 17-23, Math: 18-25, Composite: 18-24.

ACADEMICS

Year founded: 1857. **Academic calendar:** Semester. **Degrees offered:** bachelor's, master's. **Most popular majors:** 30% business, management, marketing, and related support services, 9% engineering, 9% health professions and related clinical sciences, 8% visual and performing arts, 6% social sciences. **Major fields of study:** area, ethnic, cultural, and gender studies; biological and biomedical sciences; business, management, marketing, and related support services; communication, journalism, and related programs; education; engineering; English language and literature/letters; family and consumer sciences/human sciences; foreign languages, literatures, and linguistics; health professions and related clinical sciences; history; liberal arts and sciences studies, and humanities; mathematics and statistics; multi/interdisciplinary studies; natural resources and conservation; parks, recreation, leisure, and fitness studies; philosophy and religious studies; physical sciences; psychology; public administration and social service professions; security and protective services; social sciences; transportation and materials moving; visual and performing arts. **Areas of required coursework:** arts/fine arts, humanities, mathematics, English (including composition), sciences (biological or physical), history, social science, other. **Pre-professional programs:** pre-law, pre-medicine. **Special academic programs:** distance learning, double major, dual enrollment, honors program, independent study, internships, student-designed major, study abroad, teacher certificate program. **Teacher certification offered in:** early childhood, special education, elementary, middle/junior high, secondary, bilingual/bicultural. **Cooperative education programs:** engineering. **Reserve Officers Training Corps (ROTC):** Army ROTC: Offered at cooperating institution (Santa Clara University); Air Force ROTC: Offered on campus. **Faculty and instruction (2009-2010):** Total instructional faculty: 683 full-time, 1,002 part-time (51% men; 49% women; 26% minorities). Student/faculty ratio: 25/1. Classes of fewer than 20 students: 24%; of 20 to 49 students: 65%; of 50 or more students: 12%. **Advanced Placement and International Baccalaureate credit:** AP tests may be used for: Credit only. Scores accepted: 3, 4, 5. International Baccalaureate exams may be used for: Credit only. **Freshmen returning for sophomore year:** 80%. **Graduation rates:** Four-year: 9%; five-year: 32%; six-year: 43%.

COSTS AND FINANCIAL AID

Financial aid office: (408) 283-7500. **Expenses (2010-2011):** Tuition and fees 2010-2011: $6,250 in state, $15,178 out of state; room/board: $10,733. Estimated books and supplies: $1,704; transportation: $1,140; personal expenses: $2,934. **Financial aid:** Priority filing date for institution's financial aid form: March 2; deadline: June 12. In 2009-2010, 64% of undergraduates applied for financial aid. Of those, 55% were determined to have financial need; 35% had their need fully met. Average financial aid package (proportion receiving): $12,240 (53%). Average amount of gift aid, such as scholarships or grants (proportion receiving): $6,034 (39%). Average amount of self-help aid, such as work study or loans (proportion receiving): $5,783 (43%). Average need-based loan (excluding PLUS or other private loans): $5,280. Among students who received need-based aid, the average percentage of need met: 85%. Among students who received aid based on merit, the average award (and the proportion receiving): $3,405 (1%). The average athletic scholarship (and the proportion receiving): $8,485 (0%). Average amount of debt of borrowers graduating in 2009: $12,313. Proportion who borrowed: 49%.

CAMPUS LIFE AND EXTRACURRICULAR ACTIVITIES

Campus housing available (% using): coed dorms (65%), apartment for single students (34%), special housing for disabled students (1%). Students who live in college-owned, operated, or affiliated housing: 12%. **Student employment:** During the 2009-2010 academic year, 5% of undergraduates worked on campus. Average per-year earnings: $8,976. **Clubs and organizations:** Number of student organizations: 338. Activities include: choral groups, concert band, dance, drama/theater, international student organization, jazz band, literary magazine, marching band, music ensembles, pep band, radio station, student government, student newspaper, student film society, symphony orchestra. Number of fraternities: 22; sororities: 14. Average proportion of students who stay on campus on weekends: 60%. **Sports program (2009-2010):** Member of NCAA I. *Men's intercollegiate varsity sports:* baseball, basketball, cross country, football, golf, soccer. *Women's intercollegiate varsity sports:* basketball, cross country, golf, gymnastics, soccer, softball, swimming, tennis, volleyball, water polo.

SERVICES AND FACILITIES

Basic services: nonremedial tutoring, women's center, placement service, day care, health service, health insurance. **Remedial assistance:** reading, math, writing, study skills. **Counseling services:** minority student, career, military, personal, veteran, academic, older student, psychological, birth control, religious. **For learning-disabled students:** School does not offer a structured program with separate admission and additional fees. Total undergraduates in learning-disabled program or receiving services: 571. Services include: reading machines, diagnostic testing service, note-taking services, learning center, readers, extended time for tests, tutors, priority registration, texts on tape, other testing accommodations, other. **Library:** Number of titles: 1,331,942; number of current serial subscriptions: 720. **Information technology resources:** Students are not required to lease or own a computer. Number of campus computers available to all students: 1,355. School has a wireless network. Approximate number of users that can be accommodated: 32,000. Proportion of college-owned housing units wired for high-speed internet access: 100%. **Campus safety:** Security services offered: 24-hour foot-and-vehicle patrols, late-night transport/escort service,

24-hour emergency telephones, lighted pathways/sidewalks, student patrols, controlled dormitory access (key, security card, etc).

TRANSFER AND INTERNATIONAL STUDENTS

Transfer students: May apply for admission for the following academic terms: Fall, Spring. Applicants need a minimum number of credits to apply. For fall 2009: Transfer applications received: 7,971. Transfer applicants offered admission: 6,210. Transfer applicants enrolled: 2,088. **International students:** Number of foreign undergraduates: 1011 (4% of student body). Number of countries represented: 83. Minimum TOEFL score required: 500 (paper); 213 (computer). Average TOEFL score: 515 (paper).

Santa Clara University

- **Address:** 500 El Camino Real, Santa Clara, CA 95053
- **Website:** http://www.scu.edu
- **Private; Religious affiliation:** Catholic
- **Enrollment:** 5,087 full-time; 113 part-time

KEY STATS

✔ **U.S News College Ranking:** 2, Regional Universities (West)
✔ **SAT Score (25th/75th percentile):** 1120-1340
✔ **Tuition:** 2010-2011: $37,368

Selectivity: More selective	**Room/board:** $11,742
Acceptance rate: 59%	**Average debt:** $23,909
Student/faculty ratio: 13/1	**Proportion who borrowed:** 43%

UNDERGRADUATE STUDENT BODY STATS

2009-2010 enrollment: 5,087 full-time; 113 part-time. Men: 47%; women: 53%. **Ethnic makeup:** African American: 4%; American-Indian: 1%; Asian American: 17%; Hispanic: 15%; White: 60%; International: 3%. **Religious preference:** Protestant: 14%; Jewish: 1%; Muslim: 1%; Hindu: 1%; Buddhist: 2%; No preference: 20%; Catholic: 49%; Other Christian: 10%; Other: 2%.

ADMISSIONS FACTS AND FIGURES

Phone: (408) 554-4700. **Website:** http://www.scu.edu. **Application deadlines for fall 2011:** Regular decision: January 7; decision sent by April 1. Early decision: Not offered. Early action: Send application by: November 1; Decision sent by: December 23. Admission can be deferred. **Application fee:** $55. **To apply online, go to:** http://www.scu.edu/ugrad/apply/. **Admissions requirements/recommendations:** High school units required (recommended): English: 4 (4); Mathematics: 3 (4); Science: 2 (3); Foreign language: 2 (3); Social studies: 3 (3); Academic electives: 1 (1); Total units: 15 (19). Tests: The college uses SAT or ACT scores in admissions decisions. Either SAT or ACT required. For admission to the fall 2011 entering class, the school will accept: ACT with writing required. Campus visit: Recommended. Admissions interview: Neither required nor recommended. Off-campus interview: Not available. **Factors that count in admissions decisions:** *Academic:* Secondary school record: Very Important. Class rank: Considered. Letters of recommendation: Very Important. Standardized test scores: Important. Essay: Very Important. *Nonacademic:* Interview: Not Considered. Extracurricular activities: Important. Talent/ability: Important. Character/personal qualities: Important. Alumni/ae relationship: Considered. Geographical residence: Considered. State residency: Considered. Religious affiliation/commitment: Considered. Minority status: Important. Volunteer work: Important. Work experience: Considered. **Other schools with the greatest overlap in applicants:** University of California–Berkeley; University of California–Davis; University of California–Los Angeles; University of California–Santa Barbara; University of Southern California. **Admissions statistics for the fall 2009 entering class:** Total applicants: 10,226. Total accepted: 6,057. Freshmen enrolled: 1,085; 41% were from out of state. Accepted through early-decision or early-action plans: 33%. Overall acceptance rate: 59%. Non-early acceptance rate: 56%. **Size of waiting list:** 2262 applicants; enrolled from waiting list: 228. **Credentials of fall 2009 freshmen:** 37% ranked in the top 10 percent of their high school class; 76% were in the top 25 percent; 93% were in the top half. (Proportion submitting class standing: 30%.) **Average high school grade point average:** 3.5. **First-year students who submitted SAT scores:** 85%. Scores (25/75 percentile): Critical Reading: 550-660; Math: 570-680, Combined: 1120-1340. **First-year students submitting ACT scores:** 44%. Scores (25/75 percentile): English: 26-32, Math: 25-31, Composite: 26-30.

ACADEMICS

Year founded: 1851. **Academic calendar:** Quarter. **Degrees offered:** bachelor's, post-bachelor's certificate, master's, post-master's certificate, doctorate. **Most popular majors:** 35% business, management, marketing, and related support services, 13% social sciences, 9% communication, journalism, and related programs, 9% engineering, 7% psychology. **Major fields of study:** biological and biomedical sciences; business, management, marketing, and related support services; communication, journalism, and related programs; engineering; English language and literature/letters; foreign languages, literatures, and linguistics; history; liberal arts and sciences studies, and humanities; mathematics and statistics; multi/interdisciplinary studies; natural resources and conservation; philosophy and religious studies; physical sciences; psychology; social sciences; visual and performing arts. **Areas of required coursework:** arts/fine arts, humanities, mathematics, English (including composition), foreign languages, sciences (biological or physical), social science, other. **Pre-professional programs:** pre-law, pre-dentistry, pre-medicine, pre-veterinary science, pre-optometry, pre-pharmacy, other. **Special academic programs:** cooperative (work-study plan) program, double major, honors program, independent study, internships, student-designed major, study abroad, teacher certificate program. **Teacher certification offered in:** special education, elementary, middle/junior high, secondary. **Cooperative education programs:** engineering. **Reserve Officers Training Corps (ROTC):** Army ROTC: Offered on campus; Air Force ROTC: Offered at cooperating institution (San Jose State University). **Faculty and instruction (2009-2010):** Total instructional faculty: 436 full-time, 362 part-time (59% men; 41% women; 18% minorities). Full-time faculty with Ph.D. or other terminal degree: 94%. Student/faculty ratio: 13/1. Classes of fewer than 20 students: 35%; of 20 to 49 students: 63%; of 50 or more students: 2%. **Advanced Placement and International Baccalaureate credit:** AP tests may be used for: Credit and/or placement. Scores accepted: 4, 5. International Baccalaureate exams may be used for: Credit and/or placement. **Freshmen returning for sophomore year:** 93%. **Graduation rates:** Four-year: 78%; five-year: 84%; six-year: 85%. **Graduate study:** 14% of students pursue further study immediately upon graduation; 25% within one year; 82% within five years. Fields in which graduates pursue further study: Master of Business Administration (MBA), 22%; law, 19%; medicine, 5%; dentistry, 1%; engineering, 8%; education, 4%; arts and sciences, 41%; veterinary medicine, 1%.

COSTS AND FINANCIAL AID

Financial aid office: (408) 554-4505. **Expenses (2010-2011):** Tuition and fees 2010-2011: $37,368; room/board: $11,742. Estimated books and supplies: $1,620; transportation: $729; personal expenses: $2,250. **Financial aid:** Priority filing date for institution's financial aid form: February 1. In 2009-2010, 59% of undergraduates applied for financial aid. Of those, 45% were determined to have financial need; 33% had their need fully met. Average financial aid package (proportion receiving): $23,774 (38%). Average amount of gift aid, such as scholarships or grants (proportion receiving): $18,666 (30%). Average amount of self-help aid, such as work study or loans (proportion receiving): $5,425 (24%). Average need-based loan (excluding PLUS or other private loans): $4,461. Among students who received need-based aid, the average percentage of need met: 67%. Among students who received aid based on merit, the average award (and the proportion receiving): $11,557 (26%). The average athletic scholarship (and the proportion receiving): $25,180 (6%). Average amount of debt of borrowers graduating in 2009: $23,909. Proportion who borrowed: 43%.

CAMPUS LIFE AND EXTRACURRICULAR ACTIVITIES

Campus housing available (% using): coed dorms (77%), apartment for single students (22%), special housing for disabled students (1%). Students who live in college-owned, operated, or affiliated housing: 48%. **Student employment:** During the 2009-2010 academic year, 31% of undergraduates worked on campus. Average per-year earnings: $2,393. **Clubs and organizations:** Number of student organizations: 86. Activities include: campus ministries, choral groups, dance, drama/theater, international student organization, jazz band, literary magazine, model UN, music ensembles, musical theater, opera, pep band, radio station, student government, student newspaper, symphony orchestra, yearbook. Number of fraternities: 0; sororities: 0. Average proportion of students who stay on campus on weekends: 49%. **Sports program (2009-2010):** Member of NCAA I. *Men's intercollegiate varsity sports:* baseball, basketball, cross country, golf, soccer, tennis, track and field (outdoor), water polo. *Women's intercollegiate varsity sports:* basketball, crew (heavyweight), cross country, golf, soccer, softball, tennis, track and field (outdoor), volleyball, water polo.

SERVICES AND FACILITIES

Basic services: nonremedial tutoring, day care, health service, health insurance. **Counseling services:** minority student, career, military, personal, veteran student, academic, older student, psychological, birth control, religious. **For learning-disabled students:** School does not offer a structured program with separate admission and additional fees. Total undergraduates in learning-disabled program or receiving services: 136. Services include: reading machines, tape recorders, note-taking services, learning center, extended time for tests, tutors, early syllabus, priority registration, priority seating, substitution of courses, texts on tape, other testing accommodations, other. **Library:** Number of titles: 1,199,462; number of current serial subscriptions: 8,928. **Information technology resources:** Students are not required to lease or own a computer. Number of campus computers available to all students: 640. School has a wireless network. Approximate number of users that can be accommodated: 4,000. Proportion of college-owned housing units wired for high-speed internet access: 100%. **Campus safety:** Security services offered: 24-hour foot-and-vehicle patrols, late-night transport/escort service, 24-hour emergency telephones, lighted pathways/sidewalks, controlled dormitory access (key, security card, etc).

TRANSFER AND INTERNATIONAL STUDENTS

Transfer students: May apply for admission for the following academic terms: Fall. Applicants need a minimum number of credits to apply. For fall 2009: Transfer applications received: 689. Transfer applicants offered admission: 483. Transfer applicants enrolled: 242. **International students:** Number of foreign undergraduates: 162 (3% of student body). Number of countries represented: 23. Minimum TOEFL score required: 550 (paper); 79 (computer). Average TOEFL score: 593 (paper).

Scripps College

- **Address:** 1030 Columbia Avenue, Claremont, CA 91711
- **Website:** http://www.scrippscol.edu
- **Private**
- **Enrollment:** 902 full-time; 5 part-time

KEY STATS

✔ **U.S News College Ranking:** 23, National Liberal Arts Colleges
✔ **SAT Score (25th/75th percentile):** 1260-1430
✔ **Tuition:** 2010-2011: $40,450

Selectivity: Most selective	**Room/board:** $12,450
Acceptance rate: 33%	**Average debt:** $11,270
Student/faculty ratio: 10/1	**Proportion who borrowed:** 38%

UNDERGRADUATE STUDENT BODY STATS

2009-2010 enrollment: 902 full-time; 5 part-time. Men: 0%; women: 100%. **Ethnic makeup:** African American: 4%; American-Indian: 1%; Asian American: 13%; Hispanic: 9%; White: 71%; International: 2%.

ADMISSIONS FACTS AND FIGURES

Phone: (800) 770-1333. **Email:** admission@scrippscollege.edu. **Website:** http://www.scrippscol.edu. **Application deadlines for fall 2011:** Regular decision: January 1; decision sent by April 1. Early decision: Send application by: November 1; Decision sent by: December 15. Early action: Not offered. Admission can be deferred. **Application fee:** $60. **To apply online, go to:** http://www.scrippscollege.edu/admission/pdf/application-instructions.pdf. **Admissions requirements/recommendations:** High school units required (recommended): English: 4; Mathematics: 3; Science: 3; Foreign language: 3; Social studies: 3; Total units: 16. Tests: The college uses SAT or ACT scores in admissions decisions. Either SAT or ACT required. For admission to the fall 2011 entering class, the school will accept: ACT with or without writing accepted. Campus visit: Recommended. Admissions interview: Recommended. Off-campus interview: May be arranged. **Factors that count in admissions decisions:** *Academic:* Secondary school record: Very Important. Class rank: Very Important. Letters of recommendation: Very Important. Standardized test scores: Very Important. Essay: Very Important. *Nonacademic:* Interview: Very Important. Extracurricular activities: Very Important. Talent/ability: Very Important. Character/personal qualities: Very Important. Alumni/ae relationship: Very Important. Geographical residence: Important. State residency: Not Considered. Religious affiliation/commitment: Not Considered. Minority status: Very Important. Volunteer work: Very Important. Work experience: Very Important. **Other schools with the greatest overlap in applicants:** Pomona College; Stanford University;

University of California–Berkeley; University of Southern California; Wellesley College. **Admissions statistics for the fall 2009 entering class:** Total applicants: 2,061. Total accepted: 678. Freshmen enrolled: 203; 59% were from out of state. Overall acceptance rate: 33%. Early-decision acceptance rate: 54%. Non-early acceptance rate: 32%. **Size of waiting list:** 519 applicants; enrolled from waiting list: 26. **Credentials of fall 2009 freshmen:** 69% ranked in the top 10 percent of their high school class; 94% were in the top 25 percent; 99% were in the top half. (Proportion submitting class standing: 41%.) **Average high school grade point average:** 4.0. **First-year students who submitted SAT scores:** 82%. Scores (25/75 percentile): Critical Reading: 640-730, Math: 620-700, Combined: 1260-1430. **First-year students submitting ACT scores:** 48%. Scores (25/75 percentile): English: N/A, Math: N/A, Composite: 27-32.

ACADEMICS

Year founded: 1926. **Academic calendar:** Semester. **Degrees offered:** bachelor's, post-bachelor's certificate. **Most popular majors:** 12% psychology, 9% English language and literature, 8% political science and government, 5% history, 4% multi/interdisciplinary studies. **Major fields of study:** area, ethnic, cultural, and gender studies; biological and biomedical sciences; business, management, marketing, and related support services; communication, journalism, and related programs; computer and information sciences and support services; engineering; English language and literature/letters; foreign languages, literatures, and linguistics; history; mathematics and statistics; multi/interdisciplinary studies; natural resources and conservation; philosophy and religious studies; physical sciences; psychology; social sciences; visual and performing arts. **Areas of required coursework:** arts/fine arts, humanities, mathematics, English (including composition), foreign languages, sciences (biological or physical), social science, other. **Pre-professional programs:** pre-medicine. **Special academic programs (% participation):** accelerated program (3%), cross-registration (100%), double major (18%), exchange student program (domestic) (3%), independent study (30%), internships (10%), student-designed major (4%), study abroad (60%). **Reserve Officers Training Corps (ROTC):** Army ROTC: Offered at cooperating institution (Claremont McKenna College); Air Force ROTC: Offered at cooperating institution (Harvey Mudd College). **Faculty and instruction (2009-2010):** Total instructional faculty: 81 full-time, 23 part-time (44% men; 56% women; 16% minorities). Full-time faculty with Ph.D. or other terminal degree: 100%. Student/faculty ratio: 10/1. Classes of fewer than 20 students: 81%; of 20 to 49 students: 19%; of 50 or more students: 1%. **Advanced Placement and International Baccalaureate credit:** AP tests may be used for: Credit only. Scores accepted: 4, 5. International Baccalaureate exams may be used for: Credit only. **Freshmen returning for sophomore year:** 92%. **Graduation rates:** Four-year: 85%; five-year: 87%; six-year: 87%.

COSTS AND FINANCIAL AID

Financial aid office: (909) 621-8275. **Expenses (2010-2011):** Tuition and fees 2010-2011: $40,450; room/board: $12,450. Estimated books and supplies: $800; transportation: $0; personal expenses: $1,000. **Financial aid:** Priority filing date for institution's financial aid form: February 1; deadline: February 1. In 2009-2010, 53% of undergraduates applied for financial aid. Of those, 42% were determined to have financial need; 99% had their need fully met. Average financial aid package (proportion receiving): $34,330 (41%). Average amount of gift aid, such as scholarships or grants (proportion receiving): $31,456 (39%). Average amount of self-help aid, such as work study or loans (proportion receiving): $4,066 (36%). Average need-based loan (excluding PLUS or other private loans): $2,614. Among students who received need-based aid, the average percentage of need met: 100%. Among students who received aid based on merit, the average award (and the proportion receiving): $18,671 (8%). The average athletic scholarship (and the proportion receiving): $0 (0%). Average amount of debt of borrowers graduating in 2009: $11,270. Proportion who borrowed: 38%.

CAMPUS LIFE AND EXTRACURRICULAR ACTIVITIES

Campus housing available (% using): women's dorms (98%), apartment for single students (2%), special housing for disabled students, other housing options. Students who live in college-owned, operated, or affiliated housing: 96%. **Student employment:** During the 2009-2010 academic year, 20% of undergraduates worked on campus. Average per-year earnings: $5,000. **Clubs and organizations:** Number of student organizations: 61. Activities include: campus ministries, choral groups, dance, drama/theater, international student organization, literary magazine, model UN, music ensembles, radio station, student government, student newspaper, symphony orchestra, yearbook. Number of fraternities: 0; sororities: 0. Average proportion of students who stay on campus on weekends: 90%. **Sports**

program (2009-2010): Member of NCAA III. ***Women's intercollegiate varsity sports:*** basketball, cross country, golf, lacrosse, soccer, softball, swimming, tennis, track and field (outdoor), volleyball, water polo.

SERVICES AND FACILITIES

Basic services: nonremedial tutoring, women's center, placement service, health service, health insurance. **Counseling services:** minority student, career, military, personal, academic, older student, psychological, birth control, religious. **For learning-disabled students:** School does not offer a structured program with separate admission and additional fees. Services include: tape recorders, untimed tests, note-taking services, readers, extended time for tests, tutors, priority seating, other testing accommodations, other. **Library:** Number of titles: 2,604,795; number of current serial subscriptions: 46,862. **Information technology resources:** Students are not required to lease or own a computer. Number of campus computers available to all students: 85. School has a wireless network. Approximate number of users that can be accommodated: 350. Proportion of college-owned housing units wired for high-speed internet access: 100%. **Campus safety:** Security services offered: 24-hour foot-and-vehicle patrols, late-night transport/escort service, 24-hour emergency telephones, lighted pathways/sidewalks, controlled dormitory access (key, security card, etc).

TRANSFER AND INTERNATIONAL STUDENTS

Transfer students: May apply for admission for the following academic terms: Fall, Spring. Applicants need a minimum number of credits to apply. For fall 2009: Transfer applications received: 120. Transfer applicants offered admission: 34. Transfer applicants enrolled: 14. **International students:** Number of foreign undergraduates: 21 (2% of student body). Number of countries represented: 6. Minimum TOEFL score required: 600 (paper); 100 (computer).

Simpson University

- **Address:** 2211 College View Drive, Redding, CA 96003-8606
- **Website:** http://www.simpsonu.edu
- **Private; Religious affiliation:** Christian and Missionary Alliance
- **Enrollment:** 951 full-time; 5 part-time

KEY STATS

✔ **U.S News College Ranking:** second tier, National Liberal Arts Colleges
✔ **SAT Score (25th/75th percentile):** 860-1080
✔ **Tuition:** 2010-2011: $21,000

Selectivity: Selective	**Room/board:** $7,000
Acceptance rate: 59%	**Average debt:** $20,855
Student/faculty ratio: 16/1	**Proportion who borrowed:** 83%

UNDERGRADUATE STUDENT BODY STATS

2009-2010 enrollment: 951 full-time; 5 part-time. Men: 37%; women: 63%. **Ethnic makeup:** African American: 4%; American-Indian: 2%; Asian American: 10%; Hispanic: 8%; White: 77%. **Religious preference:** Protestant: 74%; No preference: 3%; Unknown: 1%; Christian and Missionary Alliance: 22%.

ADMISSIONS FACTS AND FIGURES

Phone: (530) 226-4606. **Email:** admissions@simpsonu.edu. **Website:** http://www.simpsonu.edu. **Application deadlines for fall 2011:** Regular decision: Rolling. Early decision: Not offered. Early action: Not offered. Admission can be deferred. **Application fee:** $25. **To apply online, go to:** https://app.applyyourself.com//?id=simpson. **Admissions requirements/recommendations:** High school units required (recommended): English: (4); Mathematics: (3); Science: (2); Foreign language: (2); Social studies: (3); History: (1); Academic electives: (1). Tests: The college uses SAT or ACT scores in admissions decisions. Either SAT or ACT required. For admission to the fall 2011 entering class, the school will accept: ACT with or without writing accepted. Campus visit: Recommended. Admissions interview: Neither required nor recommended. Off-campus interview: Not available. **Factors that count in admissions decisions:** *Academic:* Secondary school record: Very Important. Class rank: Important. Letters of recommendation: Very Important. Standardized test scores: Very Important. Essay: Very Important. *Nonacademic:* Interview: Considered. Extracurricular activities: Considered. Talent/ability: Considered. Character/personal qualities: Very Important. Alumni/ae relationship: Considered. Geographical residence: Not Considered. State residency: Not Considered. Religious affiliation/commitment: Very Important. Minority status: Not Considered. Volunteer work: Considered. Work experience: Considered. **Other schools with the greatest overlap in applicants:** Azusa Pacific University; Biola University; Fresno Pacific University; San Jose State University; University of California–Davis. **Admissions statistics for the fall 2009 entering class:** Total applicants: 662. Total accepted: 392. Freshmen enrolled: 145; 19% were from out of state. Overall acceptance rate: 59%. **Credentials of fall 2009 freshmen:** 17% ranked in the top 10 percent of their high school class; 43% were in the top 25 percent; 79% were in the top half. (Proportion submitting class standing: 69%.) **Average high school grade point average:** 3.4. **First-year students who submitted SAT scores:** 83%. Scores (25/75 percentile): Critical Reading: 440-550, Math: 420-530, Combined: 860-1080. **First-year students submitting ACT scores:** 29%. Scores (25/75 percentile): English: 19-27, Math: 18-23, Composite: 18-24.

ACADEMICS
Year founded: 1921. **Academic calendar:** Semester. **Degrees offered:** certificate, associate, bachelor's, master's. **Most popular majors:** 19% liberal arts and sciences/liberal studies, 18% psychology, 9% business administration and management, 9% human resources management and services, 7% organizational behavior studies. **Major fields of study:** business, management, marketing, and related support services; communication, journalism, and related programs; education; English language and literature/letters; history; liberal arts and sciences studies, and humanities; mathematics and statistics; philosophy and religious studies; psychology; social sciences; theology and religious vocations; visual and performing arts. **Areas of required coursework:** arts/fine arts, humanities, mathematics, English (including composition), philosophy, sciences (biological or physical), history, social science. **Special academic programs:** accelerated program, cooperative (work-study plan) program, distance learning, double major, honors program, independent study, internships, student-designed major, study abroad, teacher certificate program, weekend college. **Teacher certification offered in:** elementary, middle/junior high, secondary. **Reserve Officers Training Corps (ROTC):** Army ROTC: Offered on campus. **Faculty and instruction (2009-2010):** Total instructional faculty: 39 full-time, 82 part-time (65% men; 35% women; 5% minorities). Full-time faculty with Ph.D. or other terminal degree: 72%. Student/faculty ratio: 16/1. Classes of fewer than 20 students: 71%; of 20 to 49 students: 25%; of 50 or more students: 3%. **Advanced Placement and International Baccalaureate credit:** AP tests may be used for: Credit and/or placement. Scores accepted: 3, 4, 5. **Freshmen returning for sophomore year:** 68%. **Graduation rates:** Four-year: 36%; five-year: 43%; six-year: 45%. **Graduate study:** 23% of students pursue further study within one year.

COSTS AND FINANCIAL AID
Financial aid office: (530) 226-4111. **Expenses (2010-2011):** Tuition and fees 2010-2011: $21,000; room/board: $7,000. Estimated books and supplies: $1,440; transportation: $648; personal expenses: $2,000. **Financial aid:** Priority filing date for institution's financial aid form: March 2. In 2009-2010, 94% of undergraduates applied for financial aid. Of those, 87% were determined to have financial need; 14% had their need fully met. Average financial aid package (proportion receiving): $19,486 (87%). Average amount of gift aid, such as scholarships or grants (proportion receiving): $14,586 (86%). Average amount of self-help aid, such as work study or loans (proportion receiving): $5,399 (79%). Average need-based loan (excluding PLUS or other private loans): $4,655. Among students who received need-based aid, the average percentage of need met: 75%. Among students who received aid based on merit, the average award (and the proportion receiving): $6,785 (13%). The average athletic scholarship (and the proportion receiving): $3,941 (22%). Average amount of debt of borrowers graduating in 2009: $20,855. Proportion who borrowed: 83%.

CAMPUS LIFE AND EXTRACURRICULAR ACTIVITIES
Campus housing available (% using): women's dorms (56%), men's dorms (37%), apartments for married students (2%), apartment for single students (2%), special housing for disabled students (1%), special housing for international students (2%). Students who live in college-owned, operated, or affiliated housing: 51%. **Student employment:** During the 2009-2010 academic year, 34% of undergraduates worked on campus. Average per-year earnings: $2,616. **Clubs and organizations:** Number of student organizations: 19. Activities include: campus ministries, choral groups, dance, drama/theater, international student organization, jazz band, music ensembles, student government, student newspaper, student film society, symphony orchestra, yearbook. Number of fraternities: 0; sororities: 0. Average proportion of students who stay on campus on weekends: 85%. **Sports program (2009-2010):** Member of NAIA. *Men's intercollegiate varsity sports:*

baseball, basketball, cross country, golf, soccer. *Women's intercollegiate varsity sports:* basketball, cross country, golf, soccer, softball, volleyball.

SERVICES AND FACILITIES
Basic services: nonremedial tutoring, health service, other. **Remedial assistance:** math, writing. **Counseling services:** minority student, career, military, personal, veteran student, academic, older student, psychological, birth control, religious. **For learning-disabled students:** School does not offer a structured program with separate admission and additional fees. Total undergraduates in learning-disabled program or receiving services: 28. Services include: tape recorders, diagnostic testing service, note-taking services, oral tests, readers, extended time for tests, tutors, early syllabus, priority registration, priority seating, texts on tape, exams on tape or computer, other testing accommodations. **Library:** Number of titles: 138,642; number of current serial subscriptions: 23,697. **Information technology resources:** Students are not required to lease or own a computer. Number of campus computers available to all students: 25. School has a wireless network. Approximate number of users that can be accommodated: 960. Proportion of college-owned housing units wired for high-speed internet access: 100%. **Campus safety:** Security services offered: 24-hour foot-and-vehicle patrols, late-night transport/escort service, 24-hour emergency telephones, lighted pathways/sidewalks, student patrols, controlled dormitory access (key, security card, etc).

TRANSFER AND INTERNATIONAL STUDENTS
Transfer students: May apply for admission for the following academic terms: Fall, Spring, Summer. Applicants need a minimum number of credits to apply. For fall 2009: Transfer applications received: 302. Transfer applicants offered admission: 172. Transfer applicants enrolled: 91. **International students:** Number of foreign undergraduates: 1. Minimum TOEFL score required: 500 (paper); 180 (computer).

Sonoma State University

- **Address:** 1801 E. Cotati Avenue, Rohnert Park, CA 94928
- **Website:** http://www.sonoma.edu
- **Public**
- **Enrollment:** 6,618 full-time; 865 part-time

KEY STATS
✔ **U.S News College Ranking:** 35, Regional Universities (West)
✔ **SAT Score (25th/75th percentile):** 910-1130
✔ **Tuition:** 2010-2011: $5,302 in state, $14,230 out of state

Selectivity: Selective	**Room/board:** $10,522
Acceptance rate: 77%	**Average debt:** $15,954
Student/faculty ratio: 23/1	**Proportion who borrowed:** 44%

UNDERGRADUATE STUDENT BODY STATS
2009-2010 enrollment: 6,618 full-time; 865 part-time. Men: 38%; women: 62%. **Ethnic makeup:** African American: 1%; American-Indian: 1%; Asian American: 4%; Hispanic: 12%; White: 81%; International: 1%.

ADMISSIONS FACTS AND FIGURES
Phone: (707) 664-2778. **Email:** student.outreach@sonoma.edu. **Website:** http://www.sonoma.edu. **Application deadlines for fall 2011:** Regular decision: December 31. Early decision: Not offered. Early action: Not offered. Admission cannot be deferred. **Application fee:** $55. **To apply online, go to:** http://www.csumentor.edu. **Admissions requirements/recommendations:** High school units required (recommended): English: 4 (4); Mathematics: 3 (3); Science: 2 (2); Foreign language: 2 (2); History: 2 (2); Academic electives: 1 (1); Total units: 15 (15). Tests: The college uses SAT or ACT scores in admissions decisions. Either SAT or ACT required. For admission to the fall 2011 entering class, the school will accept: ACT with or without writing accepted. Campus visit: Recommended. Admissions interview: Neither required nor recommended. Off-campus interview: Not available. **Factors that count in admissions decisions:** *Academic:* Secondary school record: Very Important. Class rank: Not Considered. Letters of recommendation: Not Considered. Standardized test scores: Very Important. Essay: Not Considered. *Nonacademic:* Interview: Not Considered. Extracurricular activities: Not Considered. Talent/ability: Not Considered. Character/personal qualities: Not Considered. Alumni/ae relationship: Not Considered. Geographical residence: Important. State residency: Important. Religious affiliation/commitment: Not Considered. Minority status: Not Considered.

Volunteer work: Not Considered. Work experience: Not Considered. **Other schools with the greatest overlap in applicants:** San Francisco State University; University of California–Berkeley; University of California–Davis; University of California–Santa Cruz. **Admissions statistics for the fall 2009 entering class:** Total applicants: 11,244. Total accepted: 8,690. Freshmen enrolled: 2,215; 1% were from out of state. Overall acceptance rate: 77%. **Average high school grade point average:** 3.2. **First-year students who submitted SAT scores:** 54%. Scores (25/75 percentile): Critical Reading: 450-560, Math: 460-570, Combined: 910-1130. **First-year students submitting ACT scores:** 2%. Scores (25/75 percentile): English: N/A, Math: N/A, Composite: 19-24.

ACADEMICS

Year founded: 1960. **Academic calendar:** Semester. **Degrees offered:** bachelor's, master's. **Most popular majors:** 22% business administration and management, 12% psychology, 12% sociology, 9% liberal arts and sciences/liberal studies, 6% communication and media studies. **Major fields of study:** area, ethnic, cultural, and gender studies; biological and biomedical sciences; business, management, marketing, and related support services; communication, journalism, and related programs; computer and information sciences and support services; education; English language and literature/letters; foreign languages, literatures, and linguistics; health professions and related clinical sciences; history; liberal arts and sciences studies, and humanities; mathematics and statistics; multi/interdisciplinary studies; natural resources and conservation; parks, recreation, leisure, and fitness studies; philosophy and religious studies; physical sciences; psychology; security and protective services; social sciences; visual and performing arts. **Areas of required coursework:** arts/fine arts, humanities, computer literacy, mathematics, English (including composition), philosophy, sciences (biological or physical), history, social science. **Pre-professional programs:** pre-law, pre-dentistry, pre-medicine, pre-veterinary science, pre-optometry, pre-pharmacy. **Special academic programs:** accelerated program, cooperative (work-study plan) program, cross-registration, distance learning, double major, dual enrollment, English as a Second Language (ESL), exchange student program (domestic), external degree program, honors program, independent study, liberal arts/career combination, student-designed major, study abroad, teacher certificate program. **Teacher certification offered in:** early childhood, special education, elementary, middle/junior high, secondary, bilingual/bicultural. **Cooperative education programs:** natural science, social/behavioral science. **Reserve Officers Training Corps (ROTC):** Army ROTC: Offered at cooperating institution; Navy ROTC: Offered at cooperating institution; Air Force ROTC: Offered at cooperating institution. **Faculty and instruction (2009-2010):** Total instructional faculty: 278 full-time, 263 part-time (49% men; 51% women; 14% minorities). Full-time faculty with Ph.D. or other terminal degree: 91%. Student/faculty ratio: 23/1. Classes of fewer than 20 students: 39%; of 20 to 49 students: 54%; of 50 or more students: 7%. **Advanced Placement and International Baccalaureate credit:** AP tests may be used for: Credit only. Scores accepted: 3, 4. International Baccalaureate exams may be used for: Placement only. **Freshmen returning for sophomore year:** 75%. **Graduation rates:** Four-year: 24%; five-year: 45%; six-year: 54%. **Graduate study:** 24% of students pursue further study within one year; 25% within five years.

COSTS AND FINANCIAL AID

Financial aid office: (707) 664-2287. **Expenses (2010-2011):** Tuition and fees 2010-2011: $5,302 in state, $14,230 out of state; room/board: $10,522. Estimated books and supplies: $1,704. **Financial aid:** Priority filing date for institution's financial aid form: January 31. In 2009-2010, 57% of undergraduates applied for financial aid. Of those, 42% were determined to have financial need; 13% had their need fully met. Average financial aid package (proportion receiving): $9,782 (41%). Average amount of gift aid, such as scholarships or grants (proportion receiving): $8,889 (24%). Average amount of self-help aid, such as work study or loans (proportion receiving): $4,412 (35%). Average need-based loan (excluding PLUS or other private loans): $4,251. Among students who received need-based aid, the average percentage of need met: 70%. Among students who received aid based on merit, the average award (and the proportion receiving): $1,610 (2%). The average athletic scholarship (and the proportion receiving): $2,292 (1%). Average amount sent of debt of borrowers graduating in 2009: $15,954. Proportion who borrowed: 44%.

CAMPUS LIFE AND EXTRACURRICULAR ACTIVITIES

Campus housing available (% using): apartment for single students (78%), special housing for disabled students (2%), other housing options (20%). Students who live in college-owned, operated, or affiliated housing: 24%. **Student employment:** During the 2009-2010 academic year, 12% of under-

graduates worked on campus. Average per-year earnings: $5,406. **Clubs and organizations:** Number of student organizations: 110. Activities include: choral groups, dance, drama/theater, jazz band, literary magazine, music ensembles, musical theater, opera, pep band, radio station, student government, student newspaper, symphony orchestra. Number of fraternities: 5; sororities: 7. Proportion of men in fraternities: 4%; of women in sororities: 6%. Average proportion of students who stay on campus on weekends: 80%. **Sports program (2009-2010):** Member of NCAA II. **Men's intercollegiate varsity sports:** baseball, basketball, golf, soccer, tennis. **Women's intercollegiate varsity sports:** basketball, cross country, golf, soccer, softball, tennis, volleyball, water polo.

SERVICES AND FACILITIES

Basic services: nonremedial tutoring, women's center, placement service, day care, health service, other. **Remedial assistance:** reading, math, writing, study skills. **Counseling services:** minority student, career, military, personal, veteran student, academic, older student, psychological, birth control. **For learning-disabled students:** School does not offer a structured program with separate admission and additional fees. Total undergraduates in learning-disabled program or receiving services: 73. Services include: remedial math, remedial English, reading machines, remedial reading, tape recorders, other special classes, note-taking services, learning center, readers, extended time for tests, priority registration, texts on tape, other testing accommodations. **Library:** Number of titles: 619,514; number of current serial subscriptions: 33,156. **Information technology resources:** Students are required to lease or own a computer. Number of campus computers available to all students: 200. School has a wireless network. Approximate number of users that can be accommodated: 2,400. Proportion of college-owned housing units wired for high-speed internet access: 90%. **Campus safety:** Security services offered: 24-hour foot-and-vehicle patrols, late-night transport/escort service, 24-hour emergency telephones, lighted pathways/sidewalks, controlled dormitory access (key, security card, etc).

TRANSFER AND INTERNATIONAL STUDENTS

Transfer students: May apply for admission for the following academic terms: Fall, Spring. Applicants need a minimum number of credits to apply. For fall 2009: Transfer applications received: 2,544. Transfer applicants offered admission: 1,208. Transfer applicants enrolled: 613. **International students:** Number of foreign undergraduates: 82 (1% of student body). Number of countries represented: 26. Minimum TOEFL score required: 500 (paper); 173 (computer). Average TOEFL score: 533 (paper).

Southern California Inst. of Architecture

- **Address:** 960 E. Third Street, Los Angeles, CA 90013
- **Website:** http://www.sciarc.edu
- **Private**
- **Enrollment:** 265 full-time

KEY STATS

✔ **U.S News College Ranking:** Unranked Specialty School–Fine Arts
✔ **SAT or ACT Score (25th/75th percentile):** N/A
✔ **Tuition:** 2009-2010: $25,350

Selectivity: N/A	**Room/board:** N/A
Acceptance rate: 61%	**Average debt:** N/A
Student/faculty ratio: 15/1	**Proportion who borrowed:** N/A

UNDERGRADUATE STUDENT BODY STATS

2009-2010 enrollment: 265 full-time. Men: 69%; women: 31%. **Ethnic makeup:** African American: 3%; Asian American: 24%; Hispanic: 13%; White: 38%; International: 22%.

ADMISSIONS FACTS AND FIGURES

Phone: (800) 774-7242. **Email:** admissions@sciarc.edu. **Website:** http://www.sciarc.edu. **Application deadlines for fall 2011:** Regular decision: May 1; decision sent by April 1. Early decision: Not offered. Early action: Not offered. Admission can be deferred. **Application fee:** $75. **To apply online, go to:** http://www.sciarc.edu/portal/admissions/apply/index.html. **Admissions requirements/recommendations:** High school units required (recommended): English: 4; Mathematics: 3; Science: 2; Foreign language: 2; Social studies: 1; History: 2; Academic electives: 2; Total units: 17. Tests: The college uses SAT or ACT scores in admissions decisions. Either SAT or ACT required. For admission to the fall 2011 entering class, the school will accept: ACT with or without writing accepted. Campus visit: Recommended. Admissions interview: Neither required nor recommended. Off-campus interview: Not available. **Factors that count in admissions decisions:** *Academic:* Secondary school record: Important. Class rank: Considered. Letters of recommendation: Important. Standardized test scores: Important. Essay: Important. *Nonacademic:* Interview: Considered. Extracurricular activities: Considered. Talent/ability: Very Important. Character/personal qualities: Important. Alumni/ae relationship: Not Considered. Geographical residence: Not Considered. State residency: Not Considered. Religious affiliation/commitment: Not Considered. Minority status: Considered. Volunteer work: Considered. Work experience: Considered. **Other schools with the greatest overlap in applicants:** Columbia University; Otis College of Art and Design; Pratt Institute; University of Southern California; Woodbury University. **Admissions statistics for the fall 2009 entering class:** Total applicants: 77. Total accepted: 47. Freshmen enrolled: 47; Overall acceptance rate: 61%. **Size of waiting list:** 16 applicants; enrolled from waiting list: 7.

ACADEMICS
Year founded: 1972. **Academic calendar:** Semester. **Degrees offered:** bachelor's, master's. **Major fields of study:** architecture and related services. **Special academic programs (% participation):** cooperative (work-study plan) program (10%), internships (75%), study abroad (8%). **Faculty and instruction (2009-2010):** Total instructional faculty: 36 full-time, 90 part-time (63% men; 37% women; 25% minorities). Student/faculty ratio: 15/1. **Graduation rates:** Six-year: 75%.

COSTS AND FINANCIAL AID
Financial aid office: (213) 613-2200. **Expenses (2009-2010):** Tuition and fees 2009-2010: $25,350. Estimated books and supplies: $2,800.

CAMPUS LIFE AND EXTRACURRICULAR ACTIVITIES
Student employment: During the 2009-2010 academic year, 8% of undergraduates worked on campus. Average per-year earnings: $3,000. **Clubs and organizations:** Number of student organizations: 1. Activities include: student government. Number of fraternities: 0; sororities: 0.

SERVICES AND FACILITIES
Remedial assistance: writing, study skills. **Counseling services:** personal, academic, psychological. **Library:** Number of titles: 24,000; number of current serial subscriptions: 110. **Information technology resources:** Students are not required to lease or own a computer. Number of campus computers available to all students: 80. School has a wireless network. **Campus safety:** Security services offered: 24-hour foot-and-vehicle patrols, late-night transport/escort service, lighted pathways/sidewalks.

TRANSFER AND INTERNATIONAL STUDENTS
Transfer students: May apply for admission for the following academic terms: Fall, Spring. Applicants do not need a minimum number of credits to apply. For fall 2009: Transfer applications received: 66. Transfer applicants offered admission: 60. Transfer applicants enrolled: 49. **International students:** Number of foreign undergraduates: 57 (22% of student body). Number of countries represented: 33. Minimum TOEFL score required: 560 (paper); 220 (computer).

Stanford University

- **Address:** Stanford, CA 94305
- **Website:** http://www.stanford.edu
- **Private**
- **Enrollment:** 6,565 full-time; 37 part-time

KEY STATS
- ✔ **U.S News College Ranking:** 5, National Universities
- ✔ **SAT Score (25th/75th percentile):** 1340-1540
- ✔ **Tuition:** 2010-2011: $39,201

Selectivity: Most selective	**Room/board:** $11,876
Acceptance rate: 8%	**Average debt:** $16,219
Student/faculty ratio: 6/1	**Proportion who borrowed:** 36%

UNDERGRADUATE STUDENT BODY STATS
2009-2010 enrollment: 6,565 full-time; 37 part-time. Men: 51%; women: 49%. **Ethnic makeup:** African American: 10%; American-Indian: 3%; Asian American: 23%; Hispanic: 13%; White: 44%; International: 7%. **Religious**

preference: Roman Catholic: 19%; Protestant: 22%; Jewish: 7%; Muslim: 2%; Hindu: 3%; Buddhist: 2%; No preference: 38%; Other: 7%.

ADMISSIONS FACTS AND FIGURES
Phone: (650) 723-2091. **Email:** admission@stanford.edu. **Website:** http://www.stanford.edu. **Application deadlines for fall 2011:** Regular decision: January 1; decision sent by April 1. Early decision: Not offered. Early action: Send application by: November 1; Decision sent by: December 15. Admission can be deferred. **Application fee:** $90. **To apply online, go to:** http://www.stanford.edu/dept/uga/application/freshman/index.html. **Admissions requirements/recommendations:** High school units required (recommended): English: (4); Mathematics: (4); Science: (3); Foreign language: (3); Social studies: (2); History: (1); Total units: (20). Tests: The college uses SAT or ACT scores in admissions decisions. Either SAT or ACT required. For admission to the fall 2011 entering class, the school will accept: ACT with writing required. Campus visit: Neither required nor recommended. Admissions interview: Neither required nor recommended. Off-campus interview: Not available. **Factors that count in admissions decisions:** *Academic:* Secondary school record: Very Important. Class rank: Very Important. Letters of recommendation: Very Important. Standardized test scores: Very Important. Essay: Very Important. *Nonacademic:* Interview: Not Considered. Extracurricular activities: Very Important. Talent/ability: Very Important. Character/personal qualities: Very Important. Alumni/ae relationship: Considered. Geographical residence: Considered. State residency: Not Considered. Religious affiliation/commitment: Not Considered. Minority status: Considered. Volunteer work: Considered. Work experience: Considered. **Other schools with the greatest overlap in applicants:** Harvard University; Princeton University; University of California–Berkeley; University of California–Los Angeles; Yale University. **Admissions statistics for the fall 2009 entering class:** Total applicants: 30,429. Total accepted: 2,426. Freshmen enrolled: 1,694; 57% were from out of state. Accepted through early-decision or early-action plans: 32%. Overall acceptance rate: 8%. Non-early acceptance rate: 7%. **Size of waiting list:** 1354 applicants; enrolled from waiting list: 127. **Credentials of fall 2009 freshmen:** 91% ranked in the top 10 percent of their high school class; 99% were in the top 25 percent; 100% were in the top half. (Proportion submitting class standing: 50%.) **First-year students who submitted SAT scores:** 92%. Scores (25/75 percentile): Critical Reading: 660-760, Math: 680-780, Combined: 1340-1540. **First-year students submitting ACT scores:** 5%. Scores (25/75 percentile): English: 30-35, Math: 29-34, Composite: 30-34.

ACADEMICS
Year founded: 1885. **Academic calendar:** Quarter. **Degrees offered:** bachelor's, master's, doctorate. **Most popular majors:** 23% social sciences, 17% multi/interdisciplinary studies, 14% engineering, 7% biological and biomedical sciences, 5% physical sciences. **Major fields of study:** architecture and related services; area, ethnic, cultural, and gender studies; biological and biomedical sciences; communication, journalism, and related programs; computer and information sciences and support services; engineering; engineering technologies/technicians; English language and literature/letters; foreign languages, literatures, and linguistics; history; mathematics and statistics; multi/interdisciplinary studies; natural resources and conservation; philosophy and religious studies; physical sciences; psychology; public administration and social service professions; social sciences; visual and performing arts. **Areas of required coursework:** humanities, mathematics, English (including composition), foreign languages, sciences (biological or physical), social science, other. **Special academic programs (% participation):** accelerated program (.4%), double major (6%), dual enrollment (15%), exchange student program (domestic) (.2%), honors program (20%), independent study (75%), internships, student-designed major (.4%), study abroad (36%), other (4%). **Reserve Officers Training Corps (ROTC):** Army ROTC: Offered at cooperating institution (Santa Clara University); Navy ROTC: Offered at cooperating institution (University of California–Berkeley); Air Force ROTC: Offered at cooperating institution (San Jose State University). **Faculty and instruction (2009-2010):** Total instructional faculty: 1,008 full-time, 15 part-time (75% men; 25% women; 18% minorities). Full-time faculty with Ph.D. or other terminal degree: 99%. Student/faculty ratio: 6/1. Classes of fewer than 20 students: 68%; of 20 to 49 students: 20%; of 50 or more students: 12%. **Advanced Placement and International Baccalaureate credit:** AP tests may be used for: Credit and/or placement. Scores accepted: 4, 5. International Baccalaureate exams may be used for: Placement only. **Freshmen returning for sophomore year:** 98%. **Graduation rates:** Four-year: 79%; five-year: 92%; six-year: 95%. **Graduate study:** 30% of students pursue further study immediately upon graduation. Fields in which graduates pursue further study: Master of Business

Administration (MBA), 1%; law, 4%; medicine, 15%; arts and sciences, 80%.

COSTS AND FINANCIAL AID

Financial aid office: (650) 723-3058. **Expenses (2010-2011):** Tuition and fees 2010-2011: $39,201; room/board: $11,876. Estimated books and supplies: $1,485; transportation: $665; personal expenses: $2,385. **Financial aid:** Priority filing date for institution's financial aid form: February 15. In 2009-2010, 57% of undergraduates applied for financial aid. Of those, 50% were determined to have financial need; 85% had their need fully met. Average financial aid package (proportion receiving): $39,900 (50%). Average amount of gift aid, such as scholarships or grants (proportion receiving): $37,400 (49%). Average amount of self-help aid, such as work study or loans (proportion receiving): $2,200 (36%). Average need-based loan (excluding PLUS or other private loans): $2,700. Among students who received need-based aid, the average percentage of need met: 100%. Among students who received aid based on merit, the average award (and the proportion receiving): $3,600 (12%). The average athletic scholarship (and the proportion receiving): $23,500 (8%). Average amount of debt of borrowers graduating in 2009: $16,219. Proportion who borrowed: 36%.

CAMPUS LIFE AND EXTRACURRICULAR ACTIVITIES

Campus housing available (% using): coed dorms (66%), women's dorms (1%), sorority housing (3%), fraternity housing (5%), apartments for married students (1%), apartment for single students (6%), special housing for disabled students (2%), cooperative housing (5%), other housing options (11%). Students who live in college-owned, operated, or affiliated housing: 91%. Average per-year earnings: $12. **Clubs and organizations:** Number of student organizations: 630. Activities include: campus ministries, choral groups, concert band, dance, drama/theater, international student organization, jazz band, literary magazine, marching band, model UN, music ensembles, musical theater, opera, pep band, radio station, student government, student newspaper, student film society, symphony orchestra, television station, yearbook. Number of fraternities: 17; sororities: 11. Proportion of men in fraternities: 13%; of women in sororities: 13%. Average proportion of students who stay on campus on weekends: 95%. **Sports program (2009-2010):** Member of NCAA I. *Men's intercollegiate varsity sports:* baseball, basketball, cross country, fencing, football, golf, gymnastics, soccer, swimming, tennis, track and field (indoor), track and field (outdoor), volleyball, water polo, wrestling. *Women's intercollegiate varsity sports:* basketball, crew (heavyweight), cross country, fencing, field hockey, golf, gymnastics, lacrosse, crew (lightweight), soccer, softball, squash, swimming, sync swimming, tennis, track and field (indoor), track and field (outdoor), volleyball, water polo.

SERVICES AND FACILITIES

Basic services: nonremedial tutoring, women's center, placement service, day care, health service, health insurance, other. **Counseling services:** career, personal, academic, psychological, birth control, religious. **For learning-disabled students:** School does not offer a structured program with separate admission and additional fees. Services include: reading machines, tape recorders, diagnostic testing service, note-taking services, oral tests, learning center, readers, extended time for tests, tutors, texts on tape, other testing accommodations, other. **Library:** Number of titles: 8,500,000; number of current serial subscriptions: 75,000. **Information technology resources:** Students are not required to lease or own a computer. Number of campus computers available to all students: 1,000. School has a wireless network. Approximate number of users that can be accommodated: 100,000. Proportion of college-owned housing units wired for high-speed internet access: 100%. **Campus safety:** Security services offered: 24-hour foot-and-vehicle patrols, late-night transport/escort service, 24-hour emergency telephones, lighted pathways/sidewalks, controlled dormitory access (key, security card, etc).

TRANSFER AND INTERNATIONAL STUDENTS

Transfer students: May apply for admission for the following academic terms: Fall. Applicants need a minimum number of credits to apply. For fall 2009: Transfer applications received: 1,302. Transfer applicants offered admission: 25. Transfer applicants enrolled: 23. **International students:** Number of foreign undergraduates: 469 (7% of student body). Number of countries represented: 88.

St. Mary's College of California

- **Address:** 1928 St. Mary's Road, Moraga, CA 94556
- **Website:** http://www.stmarys-ca.edu
- **Private; Religious affiliation:** Roman Catholic
- **Enrollment:** 2,294 full-time; 245 part-time

KEY STATS

✔ **U.S News College Ranking:** 12, Regional Universities (West)
✔ **SAT Score (25th/75th percentile):** 980-1190
✔ **Tuition:** 2010-2011: $35,430

Selectivity: Selective	**Room/board:** $12,350
Acceptance rate: 79%	**Average debt:** $31,330
Student/faculty ratio: 12/1	**Proportion who borrowed:** 80%

UNDERGRADUATE STUDENT BODY STATS

2009-2010 enrollment: 2,294 full-time; 245 part-time. Men: 37%; women: 63%. **Ethnic makeup:** African American: 7%; American-Indian: 1%; Asian American: 11%; Hispanic: 20%; White: 58%; International: 2%. **Religious preference:** Jewish: 4%; Hindu: 1%; Buddhist: 1%; No preference: 23%; Roman Catholic: 51%; Christian: 8%; Other: 12%.

ADMISSIONS FACTS AND FIGURES

Phone: (925) 631-4224. **Email:** smcadmit@stmarys-ca.edu. **Website:** http://www.stmarys-ca.edu. **Application deadlines for fall 2011:** Regular decision: February 1. Early decision: Not offered. Early action: Send application by: November 15; Decision sent by: January 15. Admission can be deferred. **Application fee:** $55. To apply online, go to: http://www.stmarys-ca.edu/prospective/undergraduate_admissions/first_year_students/application.html. **Admissions requirements/recommendations:** High school units required (recommended): English: 4 (4); Mathematics: 3 (4); Science: 2 (3); Foreign language: 2 (3); Social studies: 1 (1); History: 1 (1); Academic electives: 2 (2); Total units: 16 (19). Tests: The college uses SAT or ACT scores in admissions decisions. Either SAT or ACT required. For admission to the fall 2011 entering class, the school will accept: ACT with or without writing accepted. Campus visit: Recommended. Admissions interview: Neither required nor recommended. Off-campus interview: May be arranged. **Factors that count in admissions decisions:** *Academic:* Secondary school record: Very Important. Class rank: Considered. Letters of recommendation: Important. Standardized test scores: Very Important. Essay: Important. *Nonacademic:* Interview: Considered. Extracurricular activities: Considered. Talent/ability: Considered. Character/personal qualities: Considered. Alumni/ae relationship: Considered. Geographical residence: Considered. State residency: Not Considered. Religious affiliation/commitment: Considered. Minority status: Considered. Volunteer work: Considered. Work experience: Considered. **Other schools with the greatest overlap in applicants:** Loyola Marymount University; Santa Clara University; University of California–Davis; University of California–Santa Barbara; University of San Diego. **Admissions statistics for the fall 2009 entering class:** Total applicants: 3,241. Total accepted: 2,555. Freshmen enrolled: 572; 7% were from out of state. Accepted through early-decision or early-action plans: 22%. Overall acceptance rate: 79%. Non-early acceptance rate: 85%. **Size of waiting list:** 279 applicants; enrolled from waiting list: 48. **Credentials of fall 2009 freshmen:** 38% ranked in the top 10 percent of their high school class; 74% were in the top 25 percent; 92% were in the top half. (Proportion submitting class standing: 42%.) **Average high school grade point average:** 3.4. **First-year students who submitted SAT scores:** 88%. Scores (25/75 percentile): Critical Reading: 490-590, Math: 490-600, Combined: 980-1190. **First-year students submitting ACT scores:** 12%. Scores (25/75 percentile): English: N/A, Math: N/A, Composite: 20-26.

ACADEMICS

Year founded: 1863. **Academic calendar:** 4-1-4. **Degrees offered:** associate, bachelor's, master's, doctorate. **Most popular majors:** 32% business/commerce, 12% liberal arts and sciences/liberal studies, 9% social sciences, 8% communication studies/speech communication and rhetoric, 8% psychology. **Major fields of study:** area, ethnic, cultural, and gender studies; biological and biomedical sciences; business, management, marketing, and related support services; communication, journalism, and related programs; computer and information sciences and support services; English language and literature/letters; foreign languages, literatures, and linguistics; health professions and related clinical sciences; history; liberal arts and sciences studies, and humanities; mathematics and statistics; multi/interdisciplinary studies; natural resources and conservation; parks, recreation, leisure, and fitness studies; philosophy and religious studies; physical sciences; psychology; social sciences; visual and performing arts. **Areas of required coursework:** arts/fine arts, humanities, mathematics, English (including composition), philosophy, foreign languages, sciences (biological or physical), history, social science, other. **Pre-professional programs:** pre-law, pre-dentistry, pre-medicine, pre-veterinary science, pre-optometry, pre-pharmacy, other. **Special academic programs (% participation):** cross-registration (1%), double major (2%), exchange student program (domestic) (2%), independent study (9%), internships (40%), student-designed major (0%), study abroad (39%). **Teacher certification offered in:** early childhood, special education, elementary, secondary. **Reserve Officers Training Corps (ROTC):** Army ROTC: Offered at cooperating institution (University of California–Berkeley); Air Force ROTC: Offered at cooperating institution (University of California–Berkeley). **Faculty and instruction (2009-2010):** Total instructional faculty: 202 full-time, 201 part-time (44% men; 56% women; 15% minorities). Full-time faculty with Ph.D. or other terminal degree: 95%. Student/faculty ratio: 12/1. Classes of fewer than 20 students: 53%; of 20 to 49 students: 47%; of 50 or more students: 0%. **Advanced Placement and International Baccalaureate credit:** AP tests may be used for: Credit only. International Baccalaureate exams may be used for: Placement only. **Freshmen returning for sophomore year:** 81%. **Graduation rates:** Four-year: 50%; five-year: 56%; six-year: 64%. **Graduate study:** 42% of students pursue further study immediately upon graduation; 45% within one year; 51% within five years. Fields in which graduates pursue further study: Master of Business Administration (MBA), 34%; law, 4%; medicine, 5%; education, 15%; arts and sciences, 31%.

COSTS AND FINANCIAL AID

Financial aid office: (925) 631-4370. **Expenses (2010-2011):** Tuition and fees 2010-2011: $35,430; room/board: $12,350. Estimated books and supplies: $1,620; transportation: $729; personal expenses: $2,250. **Financial aid:** Priority filing date for institution's financial aid form: February 15. In 2009-2010, 81% of undergraduates applied for financial aid. Of those, 78% were determined to have financial need; 6% had their need fully met. Average financial aid package (proportion receiving): $25,104 (76%). Average amount of gift aid, such as scholarships or grants (proportion receiving): $21,692 (59%). Average amount of self-help aid, such as work study or loans (proportion receiving): $5,641 (61%). Average need-based loan (excluding PLUS or other private loans): $4,789. Among students who received need-based aid, the average percentage of need met: 75%. Among students who received aid based on merit, the average award (and the proportion receiving): $12,574 (4%). The average athletic scholarship (and the proportion receiving): $31,120 (4%). Average amount of debt of borrowers graduating in 2009: $31,330. Proportion who borrowed: 80%.

CAMPUS LIFE AND EXTRACURRICULAR ACTIVITIES

Campus housing available (% using): coed dorms (96%), special housing for disabled students (4%). Students who live in college-owned, operated, or affiliated housing: 67%. **Student employment:** During the 2009-2010 academic year, 4% of undergraduates worked on campus. Average per-year earnings: $2,000. **Clubs and organizations:** Number of student organizations: 40. Activities include: campus ministries, choral groups, dance, drama/theater, jazz band, literary magazine, music ensembles, musical theater, pep band, radio station, student government, student newspaper, television station. Number of fraternities: 0; sororities: 0. Average proportion of students who stay on campus on weekends: 50%. **Sports program (2009-2010):** Member of NCAA I. **Men's intercollegiate varsity sports:** baseball, basketball, cross country, golf, soccer, tennis. **Women's intercollegiate varsity sports:** basketball, crew (heavyweight), cross country, lacrosse, soccer, softball, tennis, volleyball.

SERVICES AND FACILITIES

Basic services: nonremedial tutoring, women's center, health service. **Remedial assistance:** writing. **Counseling services:** minority student, career, personal, academic, psychological, birth control, religious. **For learning-disabled students:** School does not offer a structured program with separate admission and additional fees. Services include: remedial English, reading machines, tape recorders, untimed tests, note-taking services, oral tests, learning center, readers, extended time for tests, tutors, priority registration, texts on tape, other testing accommodations, other. **Library:** Number of titles: 230,133; number of current serial subscriptions: 40,355. **Information technology resources:** Students are not required to lease or own a computer. Number of campus computers available to all students: 244. School has a wireless network. Approximate number of users that can be accommodated: 1,000. Proportion of college-owned housing units wired for high-speed internet access: 100%. **Campus safety:** Security services offered: 24-hour foot-and-vehicle patrols, late-night transport/escort service, 24-hour emergency telephones, lighted pathways/sidewalks, controlled dormitory access (key, security card, etc).

TRANSFER AND INTERNATIONAL STUDENTS

Transfer students: May apply for admission for the following academic terms: Fall, Winter, Spring. Applicants need a minimum number of credits to apply. For fall 2009: Transfer applications received: 375. Transfer applicants offered admission: 247. Transfer applicants enrolled: 123. **International students:** Number of foreign undergraduates: 63 (2% of student body). Number of countries represented: 33. Minimum TOEFL score required: 527 (paper); 197 (computer). Average TOEFL score: 583 (paper).

Thomas Aquinas College

- **Address:** 10000 N. Ojai Road, Santa Paula, CA 93060-9621
- **Website:** http://www.thomasaquinas.edu
- **Private; Religious affiliation:** Catholic
- **Enrollment:** 345 full-time

KEY STATS

✔ **U.S News College Ranking:** 71, National Liberal Arts Colleges
✔ **SAT Score (25th/75th percentile):** 1160-1370
✔ **Tuition:** 2010-2011: $22,400

Selectivity: More selective **Room/board:** $7,400
Acceptance rate: 78% **Average debt:** $15,000
Student/faculty ratio: 11/1 **Proportion who borrowed:** 71%

UNDERGRADUATE STUDENT BODY STATS

2009-2010 enrollment: 345 full-time. Men: 46%; women: 54%. **Ethnic makeup:** American-Indian: 1%; Asian American: 2%; Hispanic: 8%; White: 83%; International: 6%. **Religious preference:** Protestant: 4%; No preference: 1%; Catholic: 95%.

ADMISSIONS FACTS AND FIGURES

Phone: (800) 634-9797. **Email:** admissions@thomasaquinas.edu. **Website:** http://www.thomasaquinas.edu. **Application deadlines for fall 2011:** Regular decision: Rolling. Early decision: Not offered. Early action: Not offered. Admission can be deferred. **To apply online, go to:** http://www.thomasaquinas.edu/admission/application.htm. **Admissions requirements/recommendations:** High school units required (recommended): English: 4 (4); Mathematics: 3 (4); Science: 2 (3); Foreign language: 2; History: 2 (2); Academic electives: (3); Total units: 13 (18). Tests: The college uses SAT or ACT scores in admissions decisions. Either SAT or ACT required. For admission to the fall 2011 entering class, the school will accept: ACT with writing recommended. Campus visit: Recommended. Admissions interview: Neither required nor recommended. Off-campus interview: May be arranged. **Factors that count in admissions decisions: Academic:** Secondary school record: Very Important. Class rank: Considered. Letters of recommendation: Very Important. Standardized test scores: Very Important. Essay: Very Important. **Nonacademic:** Interview: Considered. Extracurricular activities: Considered. Talent/ability: Considered. Character/personal qualities: Very Important. Alumni/ae relationship: Not Considered. Geographical residence: Not Considered. State residency: Not Considered. Religious affiliation/commitment: Considered. Minority status: Not Considered. Volunteer work: Considered. Work experience: Considered. **Other schools with the greatest overlap in applicants:** Catholic University of America; Christendom College; Franciscan University of Steubenville; University of Dallas; University of Notre Dame. **Admissions statistics for the fall 2009 entering class:** Total applicants: 184. Total accepted: 144. Freshmen enrolled: 102; 60% were from out of state. Overall acceptance rate: 78%. **Size of waiting list:** 2 applicants; enrolled from waiting list: 1. **Credentials of fall 2009 freshmen:** 50% ranked in the top 10 percent of their high school class; 80% were in the top 25 percent; 100% were in the top half. (Proportion submitting class standing: 10%.) **Average high school grade point average:** 3.7. **First-year students who submitted SAT scores:** 76%. Scores (25/75 percentile): Critical Reading: 610-730, Math: 550-640, Combined: 1160-1370. **First-year students submitting ACT scores:** 33%. Scores (25/75 percentile): English: 26-34, Math: 23-29, Composite: 25-30.

ACADEMICS

Year founded: 1971. **Academic calendar:** Semester. **Degrees offered:** bachelor's. **Major fields of study:** liberal arts and sciences studies, and humanities.

Areas of required coursework: humanities, mathematics, English (including composition), philosophy, foreign languages, sciences (biological or physical), history, social science, other. **Faculty and instruction (2009-2010):** Total instructional faculty: 28 full-time, 7 part-time (94% men; 6% women). Full-time faculty with Ph.D. or other terminal degree: 64%. Student/faculty ratio: 11/1. **Freshmen returning for sophomore year:** 85%. **Graduation rates:** Four-year: 71%; five-year: 78%; six-year: 78%. **Graduate study:** 18% of students pursue further study immediately upon graduation; 23% within one year; 33% within five years. Fields in which graduates pursue further study: Master of Business Administration (MBA), 1%; law, 11%; medicine, 4%; dentistry, 1%; engineering, 1%; theology (or the seminary), 12%; education, 5%; arts and sciences, 55%; veterinary medicine, 1%.

COSTS AND FINANCIAL AID

Financial aid office: (805) 525-4417. **Expenses (2010-2011):** Tuition and fees 2010-2011: $22,400; room/board: $7,400. Estimated books and supplies: $450; transportation: $728; personal expenses: $2,250. **Financial aid:** In 2009-2010, 77% of undergraduates applied for financial aid. Of those, 76% were determined to have financial need; 100% had their need fully met. Average financial aid package (proportion receiving): $19,294 (76%). Average amount of gift aid, such as scholarships or grants (proportion receiving): $14,076 (68%). Average amount of self-help aid, such as work study or loans (proportion receiving): $6,775 (75%). Average need-based loan (excluding PLUS or other private loans): $3,729. Among students who received need-based aid, the average percentage of need met: 100%. Among students who received aid based on merit, the average award (and the proportion receiving): $0 (0%). The average athletic scholarship (and the proportion receiving): $0 (0%). Average amount of debt of borrowers graduating in 2009: $15,000. Proportion who borrowed: 71%.

CAMPUS LIFE AND EXTRACURRICULAR ACTIVITIES

Campus housing available (% using): women's dorms (50%), men's dorms (49%), other housing options (1%). Students who live in college-owned, operated, or affiliated housing: 99%. **Clubs and organizations:** Number of student organizations: 2. Activities include: choral groups, dance, drama/theater, music ensembles, musical theater. Number of fraternities: 0; sororities: 0. Average proportion of students who stay on campus on weekends: 95%.

SERVICES AND FACILITIES

Basic services: health service. **Remedial assistance:** writing. **Counseling services:** career, personal, academic, psychological, religious. **For learning-disabled students:** School does not offer a structured program with separate admission and additional fees. **Library:** Number of titles: 63,000; number of current serial subscriptions: 72. **Information technology resources:** Students are not required to lease or own a computer. Number of campus computers available to all students: 16. School does not have a wireless network. Proportion of college-owned housing units wired for high-speed internet access: 0%. **Campus safety:** Security services offered: lighted pathways/sidewalks, controlled dormitory access (key, security card, etc).

TRANSFER AND INTERNATIONAL STUDENTS

International students: Number of foreign undergraduates: 21 (6% of student body). Number of countries represented: 7. Minimum TOEFL score required: 570 (paper); 230 (computer). Average TOEFL score: 597 (paper).

University of California–Berkeley

- **Address:** 110 Sproul Hall, Berkeley, CA 94720-5800
- **Website:** http://www.berkeley.edu
- **Public**
- **Enrollment:** 24,797 full-time; 733 part-time

KEY STATS

✔ **U.S News College Ranking:** 22, National Universities
✔ **SAT Score (25th/75th percentile):** 1230-1470
✔ **Tuition:** 2010-2011: $10,868 in state, $33,747 out of state

Selectivity: Most selective	**Room/board:** $15,308
Acceptance rate: 22%	**Average debt:** $14,493
Student/faculty ratio: 16/1	**Proportion who borrowed:** 41%

UNDERGRADUATE STUDENT BODY STATS

2009-2010 enrollment: 24,797 full-time; 733 part-time. Men: 47%; women: 53%. **Ethnic makeup:** African American: 4%; American-Indian: 1%; Asian American: 40%; Hispanic: 12%; White: 38%; International: 5%.

ADMISSIONS FACTS AND FIGURES

Phone: (510) 642-3175. **Email:** ouars@uclink4.berkeley.edu. **Website:** http://www.berkeley.edu. **Application deadlines for fall 2011:** Regular decision: November 30. Early decision: Not offered. Early action: Not offered. Admission cannot be deferred. **Application fee:** $60. **To apply online, go to:** http://www.universityofcalifornia.edu/admissions/. **Admissions requirements/recommendations:** High school units required (recommended): English: 4 (4); Mathematics: 3 (4); Science: 2 (3); Foreign language: 2 (3); History: 2 (2); Academic electives: 1 (1); Total units: 15 (18). Tests: The college uses SAT or ACT scores in admissions decisions. Either SAT or ACT required. For admission to the fall 2011 entering class, the school will accept: ACT with writing required. Campus visit: Neither required nor recommended. Admissions interview: Neither required nor recommended. Off-campus interview: Not available. **Factors that count in admissions decisions:** *Academic:* Secondary school record: Very Important. Class rank: Not Considered. Letters of recommendation: Not Considered. Standardized test scores: Important. Essay: Very Important. *Nonacademic:* Interview: Not Considered. Extracurricular activities: Important. Talent/ability: Important. Character/personal qualities: Important. Alumni/ae relationship: Not Considered. Geographical residence: Considered. State residency: Very Important. Religious affiliation/commitment: Not Considered. Minority status: Not Considered. Volunteer work: Important. Work experience: Important. **Admissions statistics for the fall 2009 entering class:** Total applicants: 48,650. Total accepted: 10,528. Freshmen enrolled: 4,356; 8% were from out of state. Overall acceptance rate: 22%. **Credentials of fall 2009 freshmen:** 98% ranked in the top 10 percent of their high school class; 100% were in the top 25 percent; 100% were in the top half. (Proportion submitting class standing: 100%.) **First-year students who submitted SAT scores:** 97%. Scores (25/75 percentile): Critical Reading: 590-710, Math: 640-760, Combined: 1230-1470. **First-year students submitting ACT scores:** 36%. Scores (25/75 percentile): English: 26-33, Math: 27-34, Composite: 27-32.

ACADEMICS

Year founded: 1868. **Academic calendar:** Semester. **Degrees offered:** certificate, bachelor's, master's, doctorate. **Major fields of study:** architecture and related services; area, ethnic, cultural, and gender studies; biological and biomedical sciences; business, management, marketing, and related support services; communication, journalism, and related programs; computer and information sciences and support services; engineering; English language and literature/letters; foreign languages, literatures, and linguistics; health professions and related clinical sciences; history; legal professions and studies; mathematics and statistics; multi/interdisciplinary studies; natural resources and conservation; philosophy and religious studies; physical sciences; psychology; public administration and social service professions; social sciences; visual and performing arts. **Areas of required coursework:** arts/fine arts, English (including composition), philosophy, sciences (biological or physical), history, social science, other. **Special academic programs:** accelerated program, cross-registration, double major, dual enrollment, English as a Second Language (ESL), exchange student program (domestic), honors program, independent study, internships, student-designed major, study abroad, teacher certificate program. **Reserve Officers Training Corps (ROTC):** Army ROTC: Offered on campus; Navy ROTC: Offered on campus; Air Force ROTC: Offered on campus. **Faculty and instruction (2009-2010):** Total instructional faculty: 1,582 full-time, 500 part-time (65% men; 35% women; 20% minorities). Full-time faculty with Ph.D. or other terminal degree: 99%. Student/faculty ratio: 16/1. Classes of fewer than 20 students: 60%; of 20 to 49 students: 25%; of 50 or more students: 15%. **Advanced Placement and International Baccalaureate credit:** AP tests may be used for: Credit and/or placement. **Freshmen returning for sophomore year:** 97%. **Graduation rates:** Four-year: 66%; five-year: 87%; six-year: 90%.

COSTS AND FINANCIAL AID

Financial aid office: (510) 642-6442. **Expenses (2010-2011):** Tuition and fees 2010-2011: $10,868 in state, $33,747 out of state; room/board: $15,308. Estimated books and supplies: $1,314; transportation: $618; personal expenses: $2,866. **Financial aid:** Priority filing date for institution's financial aid form: March 2; deadline: March 2. In 2009-2010, 64% of undergraduates applied for financial aid. Of those, 52% were determined to have financial need; 47% had their need fully met. Average financial aid package (proportion receiving): $18,322 (51%). Average amount of gift aid, such as scholarships or grants (proportion receiving): $13,976 (48%). Average amount of self-help aid, such as work study or loans (proportion receiving): $6,254 (40%). Average need-based loan (excluding PLUS or other private loans): $5,215. Among students who received need-based aid, the average percentage of need met: 87%. Among students who received aid based on merit, the average award (and the proportion receiving): $5,984 (5%). The average athletic scholarship (and the proportion receiving): $18,773 (1%). Average amount of debt of borrowers graduating in 2009: $14,493. Proportion who borrowed: 41%.

CAMPUS LIFE AND EXTRACURRICULAR ACTIVITIES

Campus housing available: coed dorms, women's dorms, men's dorms, sorority housing, fraternity housing, apartments for married students, apartment for single students, special housing for disabled students, special housing for international students, cooperative housing, other housing options. Students who live in college-owned, operated, or affiliated housing: 35%. Activities include: campus ministries, choral groups, concert band, dance, drama/theater, international student organization, jazz band, literary magazine, marching band, model UN, music ensembles, musical theater, pep band, radio station, student government, student newspaper, student film society, symphony orchestra, television station, yearbook. Proportion of men in fraternities: 10%; of women in sororities: 10%. **Sports program (2009-2010):** Member of NCAA I.

SERVICES AND FACILITIES

Campus safety: Security services offered: 24-hour foot-and-vehicle patrols, late-night transport/escort service, 24-hour emergency telephones, lighted pathways/sidewalks, student patrols, controlled dormitory access (key, security card, etc).

TRANSFER AND INTERNATIONAL STUDENTS

Transfer students: May apply for admission for the following academic terms: Fall. Applicants need a minimum number of credits to apply. For fall 2009: Transfer applications received: 13,266. Transfer applicants offered admission: 3,392. Transfer applicants enrolled: 2,213. **International students:** Number of foreign undergraduates: 1401 (5% of student body). Minimum TOEFL score required: 550 (paper); 220 (computer).

University of California–Davis

- **Address:** 1 Shields Avenue, Davis, CA 95616
- **Website:** http://www.ucdavis.edu
- **Public**
- **Enrollment:** 24,351 full-time; 304 part-time

KEY STATS

✔ **U.S News College Ranking:** 39, National Universities
✔ **SAT Score (25th/75th percentile):** 1080-1320
✔ **Tuition:** 2010-2011: $11,984 in state, $34,863 out of state
  Selectivity: Most selective   **Room/board:** $12,498
  Acceptance rate: 46%   **Average debt:** $16,222
  Student/faculty ratio: 16/1   **Proportion who borrowed:** 51%

UNDERGRADUATE STUDENT BODY STATS

2009-2010 enrollment: 24,351 full-time; 304 part-time. Men: 44%; women: 56%. **Ethnic makeup:** African American: 3%; American-Indian: 1%; Asian American: 40%; Hispanic: 14%; White: 41%; International: 2%.

ADMISSIONS FACTS AND FIGURES

Phone: (530) 752-2971. **Email:** undergraduateadmissions@ucdavis.edu. **Website:** http://www.ucdavis.edu. **Application deadlines for fall 2011:** Regular decision: November 30; decision sent by March 31. Early decision: Not offered. Early action: Not offered. Admission cannot be deferred. **Application fee:** $60. **To apply online, go to:** http://www.universityof-california.edu/apply. **Admissions requirements/recommendations:** High school units required (recommended): English: 4 (4); Mathematics: 3 (4); Science: 2 (3); Foreign language: 2 (3); Social studies: 1 (1); History: 1 (1); Academic electives: 1 (1); Total units: 15 (18). Tests: The college uses SAT or ACT scores in admissions decisions. Either SAT or ACT required. For admission to the fall 2011 entering class, the school will accept: ACT with writing required. Campus visit: Recommended. Admissions interview: Neither required nor recommended. Off-campus interview: Not available. **Factors that count in admissions decisions:** *Academic:* Secondary school

record: Very Important. Class rank: Important. Letters of recommendation: Not Considered. Standardized test scores: Very Important. Essay: Very Important. *Nonacademic:* Interview: Not Considered. Extracurricular activities: Important. Talent/ability: Important. Character/personal qualities: Important. Alumni/ae relationship: Not Considered. Geographical residence: Not Considered. State residency: Considered. Religious affiliation/commitment: Not Considered. Minority status: Not Considered. Volunteer work: Important. Work experience: Considered. **Admissions statistics for the fall 2009 entering class:** Total applicants: 42,374. Total accepted: 19,581. Freshmen enrolled: 4,412; 3% were from out of state. Overall acceptance rate: 46%. **Credentials of fall 2009 freshmen:** 100% ranked in the top 10 percent of their high school class; 100% were in the top 25 percent; 100% were in the top half. (Proportion submitting class standing: 100%.) **Average high school grade point average:** 3.9. **First-year students who submitted SAT scores:** 75%. Scores (25/75 percentile): Critical Reading: 520-640, Math: 560-680, Combined: 1080-1320. **First-year students submitting ACT scores:** 25%. Scores (25/75 percentile): English: 22-30, Math: 24-31, Composite: 24-30.

ACADEMICS

Year founded: 1905. **Academic calendar:** Quarter. **Degrees offered:** bachelor's, post-bachelor's certificate, master's, post-master's certificate, doctorate. **Most popular majors:** 10% psychology, 6% biology/biological sciences, 6% economics, 4% agricultural business and management, 4% communication studies/speech communication and rhetoric. **Major fields of study:** agriculture, agriculture operations, and related sciences; architecture and related services; area, ethnic, cultural, and gender studies; biological and biomedical sciences; computer and information sciences and support services; engineering; English language and literature/letters; family and consumer sciences/human sciences; foreign languages, literatures, and linguistics; history; mathematics and statistics; multi/interdisciplinary studies; natural resources and conservation; philosophy and religious studies; physical sciences; psychology; social sciences; visual and performing arts. **Areas of required coursework:** arts/fine arts, humanities, English (including composition), sciences (biological or physical), social science, other. **Special academic programs:** accelerated program, cross-registration, double major, dual enrollment, English as a Second Language (ESL), honors program, independent study, internships, student-designed major, study abroad, teacher certificate program, other. **Teacher certification offered in:** elementary, middle/junior high, secondary, bilingual/bicultural. **Cooperative education programs:** education, health professions. **Reserve Officers Training Corps (ROTC):** Army ROTC: Offered on campus; Navy ROTC: Offered at cooperating institution; Air Force ROTC: Offered at cooperating institution. **Faculty and instruction (2009-2010):** Total instructional faculty: 1,673 full-time, 205 part-time (65% men; 35% women; 20% minorities). Full-time faculty with Ph.D. or other terminal degree: 98%. Student/faculty ratio: 16/1. Classes of fewer than 20 students: 35%; of 20 to 49 students: 41%; of 50 or more students: 24%. **Advanced Placement and International Baccalaureate credit:** AP tests may be used for: Credit only. Scores accepted: 3, 4, 5. **Freshmen returning for sophomore year:** 91%. **Graduation rates:** Four-year: 51%; five-year: 76%; six-year: 81%. **Graduate study:** 38% of students pursue further study within one year. Fields in which graduates pursue further study: Master of Business Administration (MBA), 10%; law, 9%; medicine, 10%; dentistry, 2%; engineering, 6%; theology (or the seminary), 1%; education, 20%; arts and sciences, 50%; veterinary medicine, 3%.

COSTS AND FINANCIAL AID

Financial aid office: (530) 752-2396. **Expenses (2010-2011):** Tuition and fees 2010-2011: $11,984 in state, $34,863 out of state; room/board: $12,498. Estimated books and supplies: $1,601; transportation: $722; personal expenses: $2,454. **Financial aid:** Priority filing date for institution's financial aid form: March 2. In 2009-2010, 70% of undergraduates applied for financial aid. Of those, 58% were determined to have financial need; 21% had their need fully met. Average financial aid package (proportion receiving): $16,066 (57%). Average amount of gift aid, such as scholarships or grants (proportion receiving): $12,800 (54%). Average amount of self-help aid, such as work study or loans (proportion receiving): $5,304 (42%). Average need-based loan (excluding PLUS or other private loans): $5,140. Among students who received need-based aid, the average percentage of need met: 82%. Among students who received aid based on merit, the average award (and the proportion receiving): $5,879 (4%). The average athletic scholarship (and the proportion receiving): $12,121 (1%). Average amount of debt of borrowers graduating in 2009: $16,222. Proportion who borrowed: 51%.

CAMPUS LIFE AND EXTRACURRICULAR ACTIVITIES

Campus housing available (% using): coed dorms (77%), women's dorms (8%), men's dorms (1%), sorority housing (1%), fraternity housing (2%), apartments for married students (5%), apartment for single students (4%), special housing for disabled students (0%), special housing for international students (1%), cooperative housing (1%), other housing options. Students who live in college-owned, operated, or affiliated housing: 19%. **Student employment:** During the 2009-2010 academic year, 12% of undergraduates worked on campus. Average per-year earnings: $2,745. **Clubs and organizations:** Number of student organizations: 452. Activities include: campus ministries, choral groups, concert band, dance, drama/theater, international student organization, jazz band, literary magazine, marching band, model UN, music ensembles, musical theater, pep band, radio station, student government, student newspaper, student film society, symphony orchestra, television station, yearbook. Number of fraternities: 37; sororities: 28. **Sports program (2009-2010):** Member of NCAA I. *Men's intercollegiate varsity sports:* baseball, basketball, cross country, football, golf, soccer, swimming, tennis, track and field (indoor), track and field (outdoor), water polo, wrestling. *Women's intercollegiate varsity sports:* basketball, crew (heavyweight), cross country, field hockey, golf, gymnastics, lacrosse, crew (lightweight), soccer, softball, swimming, tennis, track and field (indoor), track and field (outdoor), volleyball, water polo.

SERVICES AND FACILITIES

Basic services: nonremedial tutoring, women's center, placement service, day care, health service, health insurance. **Remedial assistance:** reading, math, writing, study skills. **Counseling services:** minority student, career, military, personal, veteran student, academic, older student, psychological, birth control. **For learning-disabled students:** School does not offer a structured program with separate admission and additional fees. **Library:** Number of titles: 4,156,110; number of current serial subscriptions: 67,604. **Information technology resources:** Students are not required to lease or own a computer. Number of campus computers available to all students: 1,500. School has a wireless network. Approximate number of users that can be accommodated: 8,000. Proportion of college-owned housing units wired for high-speed internet access: 100%. **Campus safety:** Security services offered: 24-hour foot-and-vehicle patrols, late-night transport/escort service, 24-hour emergency telephones, lighted pathways/sidewalks, student patrols, controlled dormitory access (key, security card, etc).

TRANSFER AND INTERNATIONAL STUDENTS

Transfer students: May apply for admission for the following academic terms: Fall. Applicants need a minimum number of credits to apply. For fall 2009: Transfer applications received: 8,991. Transfer applicants offered admission: 6,288. Transfer applicants enrolled: 2,219. **International students:** Number of foreign undergraduates: 556 (2% of student body). Number of countries represented: 31. Minimum TOEFL score required: 500 (paper); 213 (computer).

University of California–Irvine

- **Address:** Irvine, CA 92697
- **Website:** http://www.uci.edu
- **Public**
- **Enrollment:** 21,705 full-time; 521 part-time

KEY STATS

✔ **U.S News College Ranking:** 41, National Universities
✔ **SAT Score (25th/75th percentile):** 1090-1320
✔ **Tuition:** 2010-2011: $11,913 in state, $34,792 out of state

Selectivity: Most selective	**Room/board:** $11,400
Acceptance rate: 44%	**Average debt:** $15,529
Student/faculty ratio: 19/1	**Proportion who borrowed:** 48%

UNDERGRADUATE STUDENT BODY STATS

2009-2010 enrollment: 21,705 full-time; 521 part-time. Men: 47%; women: 53%. **Ethnic makeup:** African American: 2%; Asian American: 53%; Hispanic: 14%; White: 28%; International: 3%.

ADMISSIONS FACTS AND FIGURES

Phone: (949) 824-6703. **Email:** admissions@uci.edu. **Website:** http://www.uci.edu. **Application deadlines for fall 2011:** Regular decision: November 30; decision sent by March 31. Early decision: Not offered. Early action:

Not offered. Admission cannot be deferred. **Application fee:** $60. **To apply online, go to:** http://www.universityofcalifornia.edu/admissions/. **Admissions requirements/recommendations:** High school units required (recommended): English: 4 (4); Mathematics: 3 (4); Science: 2 (3); Foreign language: 2 (3); Social studies: 0 (0); History: 2 (2); Academic electives: 1 (1); Total units: 15 (18). Tests: The college uses SAT or ACT scores in admissions decisions. Either SAT or ACT required. For admission to the fall 2011 entering class, the school will accept: ACT with writing required. Campus visit: Neither required nor recommended. Admissions interview: Neither required nor recommended. Off-campus interview: Not available. **Factors that count in admissions decisions:** *Academic:* Secondary school record: Very Important. Class rank: Not Considered. Letters of recommendation: Not Considered. Standardized test scores: Very Important. Essay: Very Important. *Nonacademic:* Interview: Not Considered. Extracurricular activities: Very Important. Talent/ability: Very Important. Character/personal qualities: Very Important. Alumni/ae relationship: Not Considered. Geographical residence: Not Considered. State residency: Considered. Religious affiliation/commitment: Not Considered. Minority status: Not Considered. Volunteer work: Very Important. Work experience: Very Important. **Admissions statistics for the fall 2009 entering class:** Total applicants: 44,123. Total accepted: 19,484. Freshmen enrolled: 4,030; 2% were from out of state. Overall acceptance rate: 44%. **Size of waiting list:** 742 applicants; enrolled from waiting list: 333. **Credentials of fall 2009 freshmen:** 96% ranked in the top 10 percent of their high school class; 100% were in the top 25 percent; 100% were in the top half. (Proportion submitting class standing: 86%.) **Average high school grade point average:** 3.9. **First-year students who submitted SAT scores:** 100%. Scores (25/75 percentile): Critical Reading: 520-640, Math: 570-680, Combined: 1090-1320.

ACADEMICS

Year founded: 1965. **Academic calendar:** Quarter. **Degrees offered:** bachelor's, post-bachelor's certificate, master's, doctorate. **Most popular majors:** 13% biology/biological sciences, 7% social psychology, 6% criminology, 6% psychology, 6% sociology. **Major fields of study:** architecture and related services; area, ethnic, cultural, and gender studies; biological and biomedical sciences; communication, journalism, and related programs; computer and information sciences and support services; engineering; English language and literature/letters; foreign languages, literatures, and linguistics; history; liberal arts and sciences studies, and humanities; mathematics and statistics; multi/interdisciplinary studies; philosophy and religious studies; physical sciences; psychology; social sciences; visual and performing arts. **Areas of required coursework:** arts/fine arts, humanities, computer literacy, mathematics, English (including composition), foreign languages, sciences (biological or physical), social science, other. **Special academic programs:** accelerated program, distance learning, double major, dual enrollment, English as a Second Language (ESL), honors program, independent study, internships, liberal arts/career combination, study abroad, teacher certificate program. **Teacher certification offered in:** elementary, middle/junior high, secondary. **Reserve Officers Training Corps (ROTC):** Army ROTC: Offered at cooperating institution (California State University–Long Beach); Air Force ROTC: Offered at cooperating institution (University of California–Los Angeles). **Faculty and instruction (2009-2010):** Total instructional faculty: 1,113 full-time, 261 part-time (65% men; 35% women; 25% minorities). Full-time faculty with Ph.D. or other terminal degree: 98%. Student/faculty ratio: 19/1. Classes of fewer than 20 students: 45%; of 20 to 49 students: 35%; of 50 or more students: 20%. **Advanced Placement and International Baccalaureate credit:** AP tests may be used for: Credit and/or placement. Scores accepted: 3, 4, 5. International Baccalaureate exams may be used for: Credit and/or placement. **Freshmen returning for sophomore year:** 94%. **Graduation rates:** Four-year: 58%; five-year: 79%; six-year: 82%. **Graduate study:** 29% of students pursue further study immediately upon graduation; 32% within one year; 39% within five years. Fields in which graduates pursue further study: Master of Business Administration (MBA), 17%; law, 10%; medicine, 13%; dentistry, 2%; engineering, 4%; theology (or the seminary), 1%; education, 12%; arts and sciences, 41%.

COSTS AND FINANCIAL AID

Financial aid office: (949) 824-5337. **Expenses (2010-2011):** Tuition and fees 2010-2011: $11,913 in state, $34,792 out of state; room/board: $11,400. Estimated books and supplies: $1,661; transportation: $1,445; personal expenses: $1,646. **Financial aid:** Priority filing date for institution's financial aid form: March 2; deadline: May 1. In 2009-2010, 68% of undergraduates applied for financial aid. Of those, 55% were determined to have financial need; 38% had their need fully met. Average financial aid package (proportion receiving): $16,286 (53%). Average amount of gift aid, such as scholarships or grants (proportion receiving): $13,035 (49%). Average amount of self-help aid, such as work study or loans (proportion receiving): $6,102 (37%). Average need-based loan (excluding PLUS or other private loans): $6,093. Among students who received need-based aid, the average percentage of need met: 84%. Among students who received aid based on merit, the average award (and the proportion receiving): $8,121 (3%). The average athletic scholarship (and the proportion receiving): $11,046 (1%). Average amount of debt of borrowers graduating in 2009: $15,529. Proportion who borrowed: 48%.

CAMPUS LIFE AND EXTRACURRICULAR ACTIVITIES

Campus housing available: coed dorms, women's dorms, men's dorms, sorority housing, fraternity housing, apartments for married students, apartment for single students, special housing for disabled students, special housing for international students, cooperative housing. Students who live in college-owned, operated, or affiliated housing: 35%. **Clubs and organizations:** Number of student organizations: 484. Activities include: choral groups, concert band, dance, drama/theater, international student organization, jazz band, literary magazine, model UN, music ensembles, musical theater, opera, pep band, radio station, student government, student newspaper, student film society, symphony orchestra, yearbook. Number of fraternities: 20; sororities: 23. Proportion of men in fraternities: 8%; of women in sororities: 12%. **Sports program (2009-2010):** Member of NCAA I. *Men's intercollegiate varsity sports:* baseball, basketball, cross country, golf, soccer, tennis, track and field (outdoor), volleyball, water polo. *Women's intercollegiate varsity sports:* basketball, cross country, golf, soccer, tennis, track and field (indoor), track and field (outdoor), volleyball, water polo.

SERVICES AND FACILITIES

Basic services: nonremedial tutoring, day care, health service, health insurance. **Counseling services:** minority student, career, personal, veteran student, academic, psychological, birth control. **For learning-disabled students:** School does not offer a structured program with separate admission and additional fees. Services include: reading machines, tape recorders, note-taking services, oral tests, learning center, readers, extended time for tests, tutors, early syllabus, priority registration, priority seating, substitution of courses, texts on tape, typist/scribe, exams on tape or computer, other testing accommodations. **Library:** Number of titles: 3,145,926; number of current serial subscriptions: 53,981. **Information technology resources:** Students are not required to lease or own a computer. School has a wireless network. Proportion of college-owned housing units wired for high-speed internet access: 100%. **Campus safety:** Security services offered: 24-hour foot-and-vehicle patrols, late-night transport/escort service, 24-hour emergency telephones, lighted pathways/sidewalks, student patrols, controlled dormitory access (key, security card, etc).

TRANSFER AND INTERNATIONAL STUDENTS

Transfer students: May apply for admission for the following academic terms: Fall. Applicants need a minimum number of credits to apply. For fall 2009: Transfer applications received: 10,554. Transfer applicants offered admission: 6,409. Transfer applicants enrolled: 1,733. **International students:** Number of foreign undergraduates: 577 (3% of student body). Number of countries represented: 126. Minimum TOEFL score required: 550 (paper); 80 (computer). Average TOEFL score: 620 (paper).

University of California—Los Angeles

- **Address:** 405 Hilgard Avenue, Los Angeles, CA 90095
- **Website:** http://www.ucla.edu/
- **Public**
- **Enrollment:** 25,756 full-time; 931 part-time

KEY STATS

✔ **U.S News College Ranking:** 25, National Universities
✔ **SAT Score (25th/75th percentile):** 1170-1410
✔ **Tuition:** 2010-2011: $10,781 in state, $33,660 out of state

Selectivity: Most selective	**Room/board:** $13,733
Acceptance rate: 22%	**Average debt:** $16,824
Student/faculty ratio: 17/1	**Proportion who borrowed:** 46%

UNDERGRADUATE STUDENT BODY STATS

2009-2010 enrollment: 25,756 full-time; 931 part-time. Men: 44%; women: 56%. **Ethnic makeup:** African American: 4%; Asian American: 38%; Hispanic: 15%; White: 38%; International: 5%.

ADMISSIONS FACTS AND FIGURES

Phone: (310) 825-3101. **Email:** ugadm@saonet.ucla.edu. **Website:** http://www.ucla.edu/. **Application deadlines for fall 2011:** Regular decision: November 30; decision sent by March 31. Early decision: Not offered. Early action: Not offered. Admission cannot be deferred. **Application fee:** $60. **To apply online, go to:** http://www.universityofcalifornia.edu/admissions/undergrad_adm/apply_to_uc.html. **Admissions requirements/recommendations:** High school units required (recommended): English: 4 (4); Mathematics: 3 (4); Science: 2 (3); Foreign language: 2 (3); History: 2 (2); Academic electives: (1); Total units: 15 (18). Tests: The college uses SAT or ACT scores in admissions decisions. Either SAT or ACT required. For admission to the fall 2011 entering class, the school will accept: ACT with writing required. Campus visit: Recommended. Admissions interview: Neither required nor recommended. Off-campus interview: Not available. **Factors that count in admissions decisions:** *Academic:* Secondary school record: Very Important. Class rank: Not Considered. Letters of recommendation: Not Considered. Standardized test scores: Very Important. Essay: Very Important. *Nonacademic:* Interview: Not Considered. Extracurricular activities: Important. Talent/ability: Important. Character/personal qualities: Important. Alumni/ae relationship: Not Considered. Geographical residence: Considered. State residency: Not Considered. Religious affiliation/commitment: Not Considered. Minority status: Not Considered. Volunteer work: Important. Work experience: Important. **Admissions statistics for the fall 2009 entering class:** Total applicants: 55,708. Total accepted: 12,179. Freshmen enrolled: 4,472; 10% were from out of state. Overall acceptance rate: 22%. **Credentials of fall 2009 freshmen:** 97% ranked in the top 10 percent of their high school class; 100% were in the top 25 percent; 100% were in the top half. (Proportion submitting class standing: 100%.) **Average high school grade point average:** 4.0. **First-year students who submitted SAT scores:** 98%. Scores (25/75 percentile): Critical Reading: 570-680, Math: 600-730, Combined: 1170-1410. **First-year students submitting ACT scores:** 47%. Scores (25/75 percentile): English: 24-32, Math: 26-33, Composite: 24-31.

ACADEMICS

Year founded: 1919. **Academic calendar:** Quarter. **Degrees offered:** bachelor's, master's, doctorate. **Most popular majors:** 9% political science and government, 8% history, 8% psychology, 7% sociology, 5% economics. **Major fields of study:** architecture and related services; area, ethnic, cultural, and gender studies; biological and biomedical sciences; business, management, marketing, and related support services; communication, journalism, and related programs; engineering; engineering technologies/technicians; English language and literature/letters; foreign languages, literatures, and linguistics; health professions and related clinical sciences; history; mathematics and statistics; multi/interdisciplinary studies; philosophy and religious studies; physical sciences; psychology; social sciences; visual and performing arts. **Areas of required coursework:** humanities, English (including composition), foreign languages, sciences (biological or physical), history, social science. **Special academic programs:** accelerated program, double major, honors program, independent study, internships, student-designed major, study abroad. **Reserve Officers Training Corps (ROTC):** Army ROTC: Offered on campus; Navy ROTC: Offered on campus; Air Force ROTC: Offered on campus. **Faculty and instruction (2009-2010):** Total instructional faculty: 1,998 full-time, 597 part-time (66% men; 34% women; 26% minorities). Full-time faculty with Ph.D. or other terminal degree: 98%. Student/faculty ratio: 17/1. Classes of fewer than 20 students: 52%; of 20 to 49 students: 26%; of 50 or more students: 22%. **Advanced Placement and International Baccalaureate credit:** AP tests may be used for: Placement only. Scores accepted: 3, 4, 5. International Baccalaureate exams may be used for: Placement only. **Freshmen returning for sophomore year:** 97%. **Graduation rates:** Four-year: 67%; five-year: 88%; six-year: 89%.

COSTS AND FINANCIAL AID

Financial aid office: (310) 206-0400. **Expenses (2010-2011):** Tuition and fees 2010-2011: $10,781 in state, $33,660 out of state; room/board: $13,733. Estimated books and supplies: $1,608; transportation: $911; personal expenses: $2,577. **Financial aid:** In 2009-2010, 59% of undergraduates applied for financial aid. Of those, 53% were determined to have financial need; 25% had their need fully met. Average financial aid package (proportion receiving): $17,008 (53%). Average amount of gift aid, such as scholarships or grants (proportion receiving): $13,302 (50%). Average amount of self-help aid, such as work study or loans (proportion receiving): $6,203 (38%). Average need-based loan (excluding PLUS or other private loans): $6,387. Among students who received need-based aid, the average percentage of need met: 81%. Among students who received aid based on merit, the average award (and the proportion receiving): $4,169 (4%). The average athletic scholarship (and the proportion receiving): $15,697 (1%). Average amount of debt of borrowers graduating in 2009: $16,824. Proportion who borrowed: 46%.

CAMPUS LIFE AND EXTRACURRICULAR ACTIVITIES

Campus housing available (% using): coed dorms (62%), sorority housing (4%), fraternity housing (4%), apartments for married students (8%), apartment for single students (21%), special housing for disabled students, cooperative housing (1%). Students who live in college-owned, operated, or affiliated housing: 36%. **Clubs and organizations:** Number of student organizations: 908. Activities include: campus ministries, choral groups, concert band, dance, drama/theater, international student organization, jazz band, literary magazine, marching band, model UN, music ensembles, musical theater, opera, pep band, radio station, student government, student newspaper, student film society, symphony orchestra, television station, yearbook. Number of fraternities: 31; sororities: 28. Proportion of men in fraternities: 13%; of women in sororities: 13%. Average proportion of students who stay on campus on weekends: 50%. **Sports program (2009-2010):** Member of NCAA I. *Men's intercollegiate varsity sports:* baseball, basketball, cross country, football, golf, soccer, tennis, track and field (indoor), track and field (outdoor), volleyball, water polo. *Women's intercollegiate varsity sports:* basketball, crew (heavyweight), cross country, golf, gymnastics, crew (lightweight), soccer, softball, swimming, tennis, track and field (indoor), track and field (outdoor), volleyball, water polo.

SERVICES AND FACILITIES

Basic services: nonremedial tutoring, women's center, placement service, day care, health service, health insurance, other. **Counseling services:** minority student, career, military, personal, veteran student, academic, older student, psychological, birth control, religious, other. **For learning-disabled students:** School does not offer a structured program with separate admission and additional fees. Services include: reading machines, tape recorders, note-taking services, readers, extended time for tests, tutors, priority registration, texts on tape, typist/scribe, exams on tape or computer, other testing accommodations, other. **Library:** Number of titles: 8,466,626; number of current serial subscriptions: 175,207. **Information technology resources:** Students are not required to lease or own a computer. Number of campus computers available to all students: 3,930. School has a wireless network. Approximate number of users that can be accommodated: 11,193. Proportion of college-owned housing units wired for high-speed internet access: 100%. **Campus safety:** Security services offered: 24-hour foot-and-vehicle patrols, late-night transport/escort service, 24-hour emergency telephones, lighted pathways/sidewalks, student patrols, controlled dormitory access (key, security card, etc).

TRANSFER AND INTERNATIONAL STUDENTS

Transfer students: May apply for admission for the following academic terms: Fall. Applicants need a minimum number of credits to apply. For fall 2009: Transfer applications received: 16,587. Transfer applicants offered admission: 5,261. Transfer applicants enrolled: 3,235. **International students:** Number of foreign undergraduates: 1280 (5% of student body). Number of countries represented: 59. Minimum TOEFL score required: 550 (paper); 220 (computer).

University of California–Riverside

- **Address:** 900 University Avenue, Riverside, CA 92521
- **Website:** http://www.ucr.edu
- **Public**
- **Enrollment:** 16,515 full-time; 481 part-time

KEY STATS

✔ **U.S News College Ranking:** 94, National Universities
✔ **SAT Score (25th/75th percentile):** 930-1190
✔ **Tuition:** 2010-2011: $11,022 in state, $33,901 out of state

Selectivity: More selective	**Room/board:** $11,600
Acceptance rate: 78%	**Average debt:** $16,398
Student/faculty ratio: 18/1	**Proportion who borrowed:** 62%

UNDERGRADUATE STUDENT BODY STATS

2009-2010 enrollment: 16,515 full-time; 481 part-time. Men: 48%; women: 52%. **Ethnic makeup:** African American: 8%; Asian American: 40%; Hispanic: 29%; White: 21%; International: 2%.

ADMISSIONS FACTS AND FIGURES

Phone: (951) 827-3411. **Email:** admit@ucr.edu. **Website:** http://www.ucr.edu. **Application deadlines for fall 2011:** Regular decision: November 30. Early decision: Not offered. Early action: Not offered. Admission cannot be deferred. **Application fee:** $60. **To apply online, go to:** http://www.ucop.edu/pathways. **Admissions requirements/recommendations:** High school units required (recommended): English: 4; Mathematics: 3 (4); Science: 2 (3); Foreign language: 2 (3); History: 2; Academic electives: 1; Total units: 15 (18). Tests: The college uses SAT or ACT scores in admissions decisions. Either SAT or ACT required. For admission to the fall 2011 entering class, the school will accept: ACT with writing required. Campus visit: Recommended. Admissions interview: Neither required nor recommended. Off-campus interview: Not available. **Factors that count in admissions decisions:** *Academic:* Secondary school record: Very Important. Class rank: Not Considered. Letters of recommendation: Not Considered. Standardized test scores: Very Important. Essay: Considered. *Nonacademic:* Interview: Not Considered. Extracurricular activities: Not Considered. Talent/ability: Not Considered. Character/personal qualities: Not Considered. Alumni/ae relationship: Not Considered. Geographical residence: Not Considered. State residency: Considered. Religious affiliation/commitment: Not Considered. Minority status: Not Considered. Volunteer work: Not Considered. Work experience: Not Considered. **Other schools with the greatest overlap in applicants:** University of California–Davis; University of California–Irvine; University of California–Los Angeles; University of California–San Diego; University of California–Santa Barbara. **Admissions statistics for the fall 2009 entering class:** Total applicants: 22,744. Total accepted: 17,762. Freshmen enrolled: 4,299; Overall acceptance rate: 78%. **Credentials of fall 2009 freshmen:** 94% ranked in the top 10 percent of their high school class; 100% were in the top 25 percent; 100% were in the top half. (Proportion submitting class standing: 100%.) **Average high school grade point average:** 3.5. **First-year students who submitted SAT scores:** 99%. Scores (25/75 percentile): Critical Reading: 450-570, Math: 480-620, Combined: 930-1190. **First-year students submitting ACT scores:** 40%. Scores (25/75 percentile): English: 19-24, Math: 19-26, Composite: 19-25.

ACADEMICS

Year founded: 1954. **Academic calendar:** Quarter. **Degrees offered:** bachelor's, post-bachelor's certificate, master's, doctorate. **Most popular majors:** 21% business, management, marketing, and related support services, 19% social sciences, 13% biological and biomedical sciences, 10% psychology, 5% history. **Major fields of study:** area, ethnic, cultural, and gender studies; biological and biomedical sciences; business, management, marketing, and related support services; computer and information sciences and support services; education; engineering; English language and literature/letters; foreign languages, literatures, and linguistics; health professions and related clinical sciences; history; legal professions and studies; liberal arts and sciences studies, and humanities; mathematics and statistics; multi/interdisciplinary studies; natural resources and conservation; philosophy and religious studies; physical sciences; psychology; public administration and social service professions; social sciences; visual and performing arts. **Areas of required coursework:** arts/fine arts, humanities, mathematics, English (including composition), foreign languages, sciences (biological or physical), history, social science, other. **Special academic programs:** accelerated program, cooperative (work-study plan) program, cross-registration, double major, English as a Second Language (ESL), honors program, independent study, internships, liberal arts/career combination, student-designed major, study abroad, teacher certificate program. **Teacher certification offered in:** special education, elementary, secondary, bilingual/bicultural. **Cooperative education programs:** art, business, engineering, humanities, social/behavioral science. **Reserve Officers Training Corps (ROTC):** Army ROTC: Offered at cooperating institution (California State University–San Bernardino); Air Force ROTC: Offered at cooperating institution (California State University–San Bernardino). **Faculty and instruction (2009-2010):** Total instructional faculty: 741 full-time, 149 part-time (64% men; 36% women; 28% minorities). Full-time faculty with Ph.D. or other terminal degree: 98%. Student/faculty ratio: 18/1. Classes of fewer than 20 students: 39%; of 20 to 49 students: 40%; of 50 or more students: 20%. **Advanced Placement and International Baccalaureate credit:** AP tests may be used for: Credit and/or placement. Scores accepted: 3, 4, 5. International Baccalaureate exams may be used for: Credit and/or placement. **Freshmen returning for sophomore year:** 86%. **Graduation rates:** Four-year: 41%; five-year: 65%; six-year: 68%. **Graduate study:** 16% of students pursue further study immediately upon graduation; 32% within one year. Fields in which graduates pursue further study: Master of Business Administration (MBA), 15%; law, 11%; medicine, 9%; dentistry, 2%; engineering, 5%; education, 13%; arts and sciences, 29%.

COSTS AND FINANCIAL AID

Financial aid office: (951) 827-3878. **Expenses (2010-2011):** Tuition and fees 2010-2011: $11,022 in state, $33,901 out of state; room/board: $11,600. Estimated books and supplies: $1,800; transportation: $1,350; personal expenses: $1,750. **Financial aid:** Priority filing date for institution's financial aid form: March 2; deadline: March 2. In 2009-2010, 80% of undergraduates applied for financial aid. Of those, 70% were determined to have financial need; 34% had their need fully met. Average financial aid package (proportion receiving): $16,903 (69%). Average amount of gift aid, such as scholarships or grants (proportion receiving): $12,935 (64%). Average amount of self-help aid, such as work study or loans (proportion receiving): $6,146 (53%). Average need-based loan (excluding PLUS or other private loans): $5,991. Among students who received need-based aid, the average percentage of need met: 84%. Among students who received aid based on merit, the average award (and the proportion receiving): $7,687 (1%). The average athletic scholarship (and the proportion receiving): $12,734 (1%). Average amount of debt of borrowers graduating in 2009: $16,398. Proportion who borrowed: 62%.

CAMPUS LIFE AND EXTRACURRICULAR ACTIVITIES

Campus housing available (% using): coed dorms (64%), apartments for married students (1%), apartment for single students (35%), special housing for disabled students, special housing for international students. Students who live in college-owned, operated, or affiliated housing: 33%. **Clubs and organizations:** Number of student organizations: 203. Activities include: choral groups, concert band, dance, drama/theater, international student organization, jazz band, literary magazine, marching band, model UN, music ensembles, musical theater, pep band, radio station, student government, student newspaper, student film society. Number of fraternities: 20; sororities: 20. Proportion of men in fraternities: 7%; of women in sororities: 7%. Average proportion of students who stay on campus on weekends: 55%. **Sports program (2009-2010):** Member of NCAA I. *Men's intercollegiate varsity sports:* baseball, basketball, cross country, golf, soccer, tennis, track and field (indoor), track and field (outdoor). *Women's intercollegiate varsity sports:* badminton, basketball, cross country, golf, soccer, softball, tennis, track and field (indoor), track and field (outdoor), volleyball.

SERVICES AND FACILITIES

Basic services: nonremedial tutoring, women's center, placement service, day care, health service, health insurance. **Remedial assistance:** reading, math, writing, study skills. **Counseling services:** minority student, career, military, personal, veteran student, academic, older student, psychological, birth control, religious. **For learning-disabled students:** School does not offer a structured program with separate admission and additional fees. Total undergraduates in learning-disabled program or receiving services: 51. **Library:** Number of titles: 2,955,171; number of current serial subscriptions: 90,153. **Information technology resources:** Students are not required to lease or own a computer. Number of campus computers available to all students: 1,072. School has a wireless network. Approximate number of users that can be accommodated: 25,000. Proportion of college-owned housing units wired for high-speed internet access: 100%. **Campus safety:** Security services offered: 24-hour foot-and-vehicle patrols, late-night transport/escort service, 24-hour emergency telephones, lighted pathways/sidewalks, student patrols, controlled dormitory access (key, security card, etc).

TRANSFER AND INTERNATIONAL STUDENTS

Transfer students: May apply for admission for the following academic terms: Fall. Applicants do not need a minimum number of credits to apply. For fall 2009: Transfer applications received: 5,418. Transfer applicants offered admission: 3,991. Transfer applicants enrolled: 960. **International students:** Number of foreign undergraduates: 261 (2% of student body). Number of countries represented: 13. Minimum TOEFL score required: 550 (paper); 79 (computer). Average TOEFL score: 550 (paper).

University of California–San Diego

- **Address:** 9500 Gilman Drive, La Jolla, CA 92093
- **Website:** http://www.ucsd.edu/
- **Public**
- **Enrollment:** 22,797 full-time; 346 part-time

KEY STATS
- ✔ **U.S News College Ranking:** 35, National Universities
- ✔ **SAT Score (25th/75th percentile):** 1150-1380
- ✔ **Tuition:** 2010-2011: $11,306 in state, $34,185 out of state
  - **Selectivity:** Most selective   **Room/board:** $11,719
  - **Acceptance rate:** 38%   **Average debt:** $17,679
  - **Student/faculty ratio:** 19/1   **Proportion who borrowed:** 51%

UNDERGRADUATE STUDENT BODY STATS

2009-2010 enrollment: 22,797 full-time; 346 part-time. Men: 48%; women: 52%. **Ethnic makeup:** African American: 2%; Asian American: 44%; Hispanic: 13%; White: 35%; International: 7%. **Religious preference:** Roman Catholic: 17%; Protestant: 10%; Jewish: 2%; Muslim: 2%; Hindu: 3%; Buddhist: 7%; No preference: 38%; Christian: 21%.

ADMISSIONS FACTS AND FIGURES

Phone: (858) 534-4831. **Email:** admissionsinfo@ucsd.edu. **Website:** http://www.ucsd.edu/. **Application deadlines for fall 2011:** Regular decision: November 30; decision sent by March 31. Early decision: Not offered. Early action: Not offered. Admission cannot be deferred. **Application fee:** $60. **To apply online, go to:** http://www.universityofcalifornia.edu/admissions/. **Admissions requirements/recommendations:** High school units required (recommended): English: 4 (4); Mathematics: 3 (4); Science: 2 (3); Foreign language: 2 (3); History: 2 (2); Academic electives: (1); Total units: 16 (21). Tests: The college uses SAT or ACT scores in admissions decisions. Either SAT or ACT required. For admission to the fall 2011 entering class, the school will accept: ACT with writing required. Campus visit: Recommended. Admissions interview: Neither required nor recommended. Off-campus interview: Not available. **Factors that count in admissions decisions:** *Academic:* Secondary school record: Very Important. Class rank: Not Considered. Letters of recommendation: Not Considered. Standardized test scores: Very Important. Essay: Very Important. *Nonacademic:* Interview: Not Considered. Extracurricular activities: Important. Talent/ability: Important. Character/personal qualities: Important. Alumni/ae relationship: Not Considered. Geographical residence: Considered. State residency: Important. Religious affiliation/commitment: Not Considered. Minority status: Not Considered. Volunteer work: Important. Work experience: Considered. **Other schools with the greatest overlap in applicants:** Harvard University; Stanford University; University of California–Berkeley; University of California–Los Angeles; University of Southern California. **Admissions statistics for the fall 2009 entering class:** Total applicants: 47,046. Total accepted: 17,679. Freshmen enrolled: 3,749; 5% were from out of state. Overall acceptance rate: 38%. **Credentials of fall 2009 freshmen:** 100% ranked in the top 10 percent of their high school class; 100% were in the top 25 percent; 100% were in the top half. (Proportion submitting class standing: 100%.) **Average high school grade point average:** 4.0. **First-year students who submitted SAT scores:** 99%. Scores (25/75 percentile): Critical Reading: 540-660, Math: 610-720, Combined: 1150-1380. **First-year students submitting ACT scores:** 38%. Scores (25/75 percentile): English: N/A, Math: N/A, Composite: 24-30.

ACADEMICS

Year founded: 1960. **Academic calendar:** Quarter. **Degrees offered:** bachelor's, master's, doctorate. **Most popular majors:** 22% biology, 13% economics, 8% psychology, 7% political science and government, 5% communication and media studies. **Major fields of study:** area, ethnic, cultural, and gender studies; biological and biomedical sciences; communication, journalism, and related programs; computer and information sciences and support services; engineering; English language and literature/letters; family and consumer sciences/human sciences; foreign languages, literatures, and linguistics; history; mathematics and statistics; multi/interdisciplinary studies; philosophy and religious studies; physical sciences; psychology; social sciences; theology and religious vocations; visual and performing arts. **Areas of required coursework:** arts/fine arts, humanities, mathematics, English (including composition), philosophy, foreign languages, sciences (biological or physical), history, social science. **Pre-professional programs:** pre-law, pre-medicine, pre-pharmacy, other. **Special academic programs:**

accelerated program, cross-registration, double major, dual enrollment, English as a Second Language (ESL), exchange student program (domestic), honors program, independent study, internships, liberal arts/career combination, student-designed major, study abroad, teacher certificate program. **Teacher certification offered in:** special education, elementary, middle/junior high, secondary, bilingual/bicultural. **Cooperative education programs:** art, computer science, engineering, humanities, natural science, social/behavioral science. **Faculty and instruction (2009-2010):** Total instructional faculty: 979 full-time, 211 part-time (71% men; 29% women; 24% minorities). Full-time faculty with Ph.D. or other terminal degree: 98%. Student/faculty ratio: 19/1. Classes of fewer than 20 students: 40%; of 20 to 49 students: 27%; of 50 or more students: 32%. **Advanced Placement and International Baccalaureate credit:** AP tests may be used for: Placement only. Scores accepted: 3, 4, 5. International Baccalaureate exams may be used for: Placement only. **Freshmen returning for sophomore year:** 94%. **Graduation rates:** Four-year: 56%; five-year: 80%; six-year: 84%. **Graduate study:** 35% of students pursue further study immediately upon graduation; 47% within one year; 58% within five years. Fields in which graduates pursue further study: Master of Business Administration (MBA), 8%; law, 15%; medicine, 16%; dentistry, 4%; engineering, 8%; education, 19%; arts and sciences, 37%; veterinary medicine, 1%.

COSTS AND FINANCIAL AID
Financial aid office: (858) 534-4480. **Expenses (2010-2011):** Tuition and fees 2010-2011: $11,306 in state, $34,185 out of state; room/board: $11,719. Estimated books and supplies: $1,573; transportation: $1,095; personal expenses: $2,451. **Financial aid:** Priority filing date for institution's financial aid form: March 2. In 2009-2010, 70% of undergraduates applied for financial aid. Of those, 61% were determined to have financial need; 36% had their need fully met. Average financial aid package (proportion receiving): $18,560 (60%). Average amount of gift aid, such as scholarships or grants (proportion receiving): $13,983 (57%). Average amount of self-help aid, such as work study or loans (proportion receiving): $6,298 (49%). Average need-based loan (excluding PLUS or other private loans): $5,833. Among students who received need-based aid, the average percentage of need met: 86%. Among students who received aid based on merit, the average award (and the proportion receiving): $9,419 (3%). The average athletic scholarship (and the proportion receiving): $538 (1%). Average amount of debt of borrowers graduating in 2009: $17,679. Proportion who borrowed: 51%.

CAMPUS LIFE AND EXTRACURRICULAR ACTIVITIES
Campus housing available (% using): coed dorms (74%), apartments for married students (5%), apartment for single students (16%), special housing for disabled students (1%), special housing for international students (3%), other housing options (1%). Students who live in college-owned, operated, or affiliated housing: 34%. **Student employment:** During the 2009-2010 academic year, 26% of undergraduates worked on campus. Average per-year earnings: $3,500. **Clubs and organizations:** Number of student organizations: 405. Activities include: campus ministries, choral groups, concert band, dance, drama/theater, international student organization, jazz band, literary magazine, marching band, model UN, music ensembles, musical theater, opera, pep band, radio station, student government, student newspaper, student film society, symphony orchestra, television station, yearbook. Number of fraternities: 19; sororities: 14. Proportion of men in fraternities: 14%; of women in sororities: 14%. Average proportion of students who stay on campus on weekends: 35%. **Sports program (2009-2010):** Member of NCAA II. *Men's intercollegiate varsity sports:* baseball, basketball, cross country, fencing, golf, soccer, swimming, tennis, track and field (outdoor), volleyball, water polo. *Women's intercollegiate varsity sports:* basketball, crew (heavyweight), cross country, fencing, crew (lightweight), soccer, softball, swimming, tennis, track and field (outdoor), volleyball, water polo.

SERVICES AND FACILITIES
Basic services: nonremedial tutoring, women's center, placement service, day care, health service, health insurance, other. **Remedial assistance:** study skills. **Counseling services:** minority student, career, military, personal, veteran student, academic, older student, psychological, birth control, religious. **For learning-disabled students:** School does not offer a structured program with separate admission and additional fees. Services include: reading machines, tape recorders, diagnostic testing service, untimed tests, note-taking services, special bookstore section, oral tests, learning center, readers, extended time for tests, tutors, priority registration, priority seating, texts on tape, other testing accommodations. **Library:** Number of titles: 3,328,368; number of current serial subscriptions: 72,314. **Information technology resources:** Students are not required to lease or own a computer.

Number of campus computers available to all students: 2,500. School has a wireless network. Approximate number of users that can be accommodated: 15,000. Proportion of college-owned housing units wired for high-speed internet access: 100%. **Campus safety:** Security services offered: 24-hour foot-and-vehicle patrols, late-night transport/escort service, 24-hour emergency telephones, lighted pathways/sidewalks, student patrols, controlled dormitory access (key, security card, etc).

TRANSFER AND INTERNATIONAL STUDENTS
Transfer students: May apply for admission for the following academic terms: Fall. Applicants need a minimum number of credits to apply. For fall 2009: Transfer applications received: 11,572. Transfer applicants offered admission: 7,160. Transfer applicants enrolled: 1,942. **International students:** Number of foreign undergraduates: 1532 (7% of student body). Number of countries represented: 108. Minimum TOEFL score required: 550 (paper); 220 (computer).

University of California–Santa Barbara

- **Address:** Santa Barbara, CA 93106
- **Website:** http://www.ucsb.edu
- **Public**
- **Enrollment:** 19,307 full-time; 489 part-time

KEY STATS
✔ **U.S News College Ranking:** 39, National Universities
✔ **SAT Score (25th/75th percentile):** 1090-1330
✔ **Tuition:** 2010-2011: $11,630 in state, $34,509 out of state
  Selectivity: Most selective   **Room/board:** $13,113
  Acceptance rate: 48%   **Average debt:** $17,768
  Student/faculty ratio: 17/1   **Proportion who borrowed:** 47%

UNDERGRADUATE STUDENT BODY STATS
2009-2010 enrollment: 19,307 full-time; 489 part-time. Men: 46%; women: 54%. **Ethnic makeup:** African American: 3%; American-Indian: 1%; Asian American: 16%; Hispanic: 21%; White: 57%; International: 1%.

ADMISSIONS FACTS AND FIGURES
Phone: (805) 893-2485. **Email:** admissions@sa.ucsb.edu. **Website:** http://www.ucsb.edu. **Application deadlines for fall 2011:** Regular decision: November 30; decision sent by March 15. Early decision: Not offered. Early action: Not offered. Admission cannot be deferred. **Application fee:** $60. **To apply online, go to:** http://www.universityofcalifornia.edu/admissions/. **Admissions requirements/recommendations:** High school units required (recommended): English: 4 (4); Mathematics: 3 (4); Science: 2 (3); Foreign language: 2 (3); Social studies: 0 (0); History: 2 (2); Academic electives: 1 (1); Total units: 15 (18). Tests: The college uses SAT or ACT scores in admissions decisions. Either SAT or ACT required. For admission to the fall 2011 entering class, the school will accept: ACT with writing required. Campus visit: Recommended. Admissions interview: Neither required nor recommended. Off-campus interview: Not available. **Factors that count in admissions decisions:** *Academic:* Secondary school record: Very Important. Class rank: Considered. Letters of recommendation: Not Considered. Standardized test scores: Very Important. Essay: Very Important. *Nonacademic:* Interview: Not Considered. Extracurricular activities: Considered. Talent/ability: Considered. Character/personal qualities: Considered. Alumni/ae relationship: Not Considered. Geographical residence: Not Considered. State residency: Considered. Religious affiliation/commitment: Not Considered. Minority status: Not Considered. Volunteer work: Considered. Work experience: Considered. **Other schools with the greatest overlap in applicants:** University of California–Berkeley; University of California–Davis; University of California–Irvine; University of California–Los Angeles; University of California–San Diego. **Admissions statistics for the fall 2009 entering class:** Total applicants: 44,707. Total accepted: 21,540. Freshmen enrolled: 4,583; 3% were from out of state. Overall acceptance rate: 48%. **Credentials of fall 2009 freshmen:** 96% ranked in the top 10 percent of their high school class; 98% were in the top 25 percent; 100% were in the top half. (Proportion submitting class standing: 100%.) **Average high school grade point average:** 3.9. **First-year students who submitted SAT scores:** 98%. Scores (25/75 percentile): Critical Reading: 540-660, Math: 550-670, Combined: 1090-1330. **First-year students submitting ACT scores:** 48%. Scores (25/75 percentile): English: 24-31, Math: 24-31, Composite: 24-30.

ACADEMICS

Year founded: 1909. **Academic calendar:** Quarter. **Degrees offered:** bachelor's, post-bachelor's certificate, master's, post-master's certificate, doctorate. **Most popular majors:** 12% business, management, marketing, and related support services, 10% sociology, 7% psychology, 6% communication and media studies, 6% international/global studies. **Major fields of study:** architecture and related services; area, ethnic, cultural, and gender studies; biological and biomedical sciences; business, management, marketing, and related support services; communication, journalism, and related programs; computer and information sciences and support services; engineering; English language and literature/letters; foreign languages, literatures, and linguistics; history; legal professions and studies; mathematics and statistics; multi/interdisciplinary studies; natural resources and conservation; philosophy and religious studies; physical sciences; psychology; social sciences; visual and performing arts. **Areas of required coursework:** arts/fine arts, humanities, mathematics, English (including composition), philosophy, foreign languages, sciences (biological or physical), history, social science, other. **Special academic programs:** accelerated program, cross-registration, distance learning, double major, dual enrollment, English as a Second Language (ESL), exchange student program (domestic), honors program, independent study, internships, student-designed major, study abroad, teacher certificate program. **Teacher certification offered in:** special education, elementary, middle/junior high, secondary. **Reserve Officers Training Corps (ROTC):** Army ROTC: Offered on campus. **Faculty and instruction (2009-2010):** Total instructional faculty: 906 full-time, 151 part-time (64% men; 36% women; 18% minorities). Full-time faculty with Ph.D. or other terminal degree: 98%. Student/faculty ratio: 17/1. Classes of fewer than 20 students: 47%; of 20 to 49 students: 35%; of 50 or more students: 18%. **Advanced Placement and International Baccalaureate credit:** AP tests may be used for: Credit and/or placement. Scores accepted: 3, 4, 5. International Baccalaureate exams may be used for: Credit only. **Freshmen returning for sophomore year:** 91%. **Graduation rates:** Four-year: 66%; five-year: 82%; six-year: 86%.

COSTS AND FINANCIAL AID

Financial aid office: (805) 893-2432. **Expenses (2010-2011):** Tuition and fees 2010-2011: $11,630 in state, $34,509 out of state; room/board: $13,113. Estimated books and supplies: $1,606; transportation: $1,224; personal expenses: $2,712. **Financial aid:** Priority filing date for institution's financial aid form: March 2; deadline: May 31. In 2009-2010, 66% of undergraduates applied for financial aid. Of those, 53% were determined to have financial need; 28% had their need fully met. Average financial aid package (proportion receiving): $17,380 (50%). Average amount of gift aid, such as scholarships or grants (proportion receiving): $13,876 (45%). Average amount of self-help aid, such as work study or loans (proportion receiving): N/A (38%). Average need-based loan (excluding PLUS or other private loans): $6,264. Among students who received need-based aid, the average percentage of need met: 82%. Among students who received aid based on merit, the average award (and the proportion receiving): $6,021 (2%). The average athletic scholarship (and the proportion receiving): $11,940 (1%). Average amount of debt of borrowers graduating in 2009: $17,768. Proportion who borrowed: 47%.

CAMPUS LIFE AND EXTRACURRICULAR ACTIVITIES

Campus housing available (% using): coed dorms (63%), sorority housing (4%), fraternity housing (3%), apartments for married students (7%), apartment for single students (22%), cooperative housing (1%). Students who live in college-owned, operated, or affiliated housing: 31%. **Student employment:** During the 2009-2010 academic year, 17% of undergraduates worked on campus. **Clubs and organizations:** Number of student organizations: 421. Activities include: campus ministries, choral groups, concert band, dance, drama/theater, international student organization, jazz band, literary magazine, model UN, music ensembles, musical theater, opera, pep band, radio station, student government, student newspaper, student film society, symphony orchestra, television station, yearbook. Number of fraternities: 15; sororities: 19. Proportion of men in fraternities: 7%; of women in sororities: 11%. **Sports program (2009-2010):** Member of NCAA I. *Men's intercollegiate varsity sports:* baseball, basketball, cross country, golf, soccer, swimming, tennis, track and field (outdoor), volleyball, water polo. *Women's intercollegiate varsity sports:* basketball, cross country, soccer, softball, swimming, tennis, track and field (indoor), track and field (outdoor), volleyball, water polo.

SERVICES AND FACILITIES

Basic services: nonremedial tutoring, women's center, day care, health service. **Remedial assistance:** reading, math, writing, study skills. **Counseling**

services: minority student, career, military, personal, academic, psychological, birth control. **For learning-disabled students:** School does not offer a structured program with separate admission and additional fees. Services include: reading machines, note-taking services, learning center, extended time for tests, tutors, substitution of courses, texts on tape, other testing accommodations. **Library:** Number of titles: 3,444,662; number of current serial subscriptions: 69,327. **Information technology resources:** Students are not required to lease or own a computer. Number of campus computers available to all students: 777. School has a wireless network. Approximate number of users that can be accommodated: 10,000. Proportion of college-owned housing units wired for high-speed internet access: 100%. **Campus safety:** Security services offered: 24-hour foot-and-vehicle patrols, late-night transport/escort service, 24-hour emergency telephones, lighted pathways/sidewalks, student patrols, controlled dormitory access (key, security card, etc).

TRANSFER AND INTERNATIONAL STUDENTS

Transfer students: May apply for admission for the following academic terms: Fall, Winter. Applicants need a minimum number of credits to apply. For fall 2009: Transfer applications received: 10,069. Transfer applicants offered admission: 6,685. Transfer applicants enrolled: 1,871. **International students:** Number of foreign undergraduates: 219 (1% of student body). Number of countries represented: 70. Minimum TOEFL score required: 550 (paper); 213 (computer).

University of California—Santa Cruz

- **Address:** 1156 High Street, Santa Cruz, CA 95064
- **Website:** http://www.ucsc.edu
- **Public**
- **Enrollment:** 15,076 full-time; 183 part-time

KEY STATS

✔ **U.S News College Ranking:** 72, National Universities
✔ **SAT Score (25th/75th percentile):** 1030-1270
✔ **Tuition:** 2010-2011: $10,626 in state, $33,505 out of state
  Selectivity: More selective   **Room/board:** $14,205
  Acceptance rate: 64%   **Average debt:** $16,024
  Student/faculty ratio: 18/1   **Proportion who borrowed:** 53%

UNDERGRADUATE STUDENT BODY STATS

2009-2010 enrollment: 15,076 full-time; 183 part-time. Men: 47%; women: 53%. **Ethnic makeup:** African American: 3%; American-Indian: 1%; Asian American: 22%; Hispanic: 18%; White: 56%.

ADMISSIONS FACTS AND FIGURES

Phone: (831) 459-4008. **Email:** admissions@cats.ucsc.edu. **Website:** http://www.ucsc.edu. **Application deadlines for fall 2011:** Regular decision: November 30; decision sent by March 31. Early decision: Not offered. Early action: Not offered. Admission cannot be deferred. **Application fee:** $60. **To apply online, go to:** http://www.ucop.edu/pathways. **Admissions requirements/recommendations:** High school units required (recommended): English: 4 (4); Mathematics: 3 (4); Science: 2 (3); Foreign language: 2 (3); Social studies: 1 (1); History: 1 (1); Academic electives: 1 (1); Total units: 15 (18). Tests: The college uses SAT or ACT scores in admissions decisions. Either SAT or ACT required. For admission to the fall 2011 entering class, the school will accept: ACT with writing required. Campus visit: Recommended. Admissions interview: Neither required nor recommended. Off-campus interview: Not available. **Factors that count in admissions decisions:** *Academic:* Secondary school record: Very Important. Class rank: Important. Letters of recommendation: Not Considered. Standardized test scores: Very Important. Essay: Important. *Nonacademic:* Interview: Not Considered. Extracurricular activities: Important. Talent/ability: Important. Character/personal qualities: Important. Alumni/ae relationship: Not Considered. Geographical residence: Considered. State residency: Very Important. Religious affiliation/commitment: Not Considered. Minority status: Not Considered. Volunteer work: Considered. Work experience: Considered. **Other schools with the greatest overlap in applicants:** University of California–Berkeley; University of California–Davis; University of California–Los Angeles; University of California–San Diego; University of California–Santa Barbara. **Admissions statistics for the fall 2009 entering class:** Total applicants: 27,249. Total accepted: 17,490. Freshmen enrolled: 3,214; 3% were from out of state. Overall acceptance rate: 64%.

Credentials of fall 2009 freshmen: 96% ranked in the top 10 percent of their high school class; 100% were in the top 25 percent; 100% were in the top half. (Proportion submitting class standing: 92%.) **Average high school grade point average:** 3.6. **First-year students who submitted SAT scores:** 98%. Scores (25/75 percentile): Critical Reading: 510-630, Math: 520-640, Combined: 1030-1270. **First-year students submitting ACT scores:** 37%. Scores (25/75 percentile): English: 22-28, Math: 22-28, Composite: 22-28.

ACADEMICS

Year founded: 1965. **Academic calendar:** Quarter. **Degrees offered:** bachelor's, post-bachelor's certificate, master's, doctorate. **Most popular majors:** 10% psychology, 8% business/managerial economics, 7% English language and literature/letters, 5% environmental studies, 5% history. **Major fields of study:** area, ethnic, cultural, and gender studies; biological and biomedical sciences; business, management, marketing, and related support services; computer and information sciences and support services; engineering; foreign languages, literatures, and linguistics; health professions and related clinical sciences; history; legal professions and studies; mathematics and statistics; multi/interdisciplinary studies; natural resources and conservation; philosophy and religious studies; physical sciences; psychology; social sciences; visual and performing arts. **Areas of required coursework:** arts/fine arts, humanities, mathematics, English (including composition), sciences (biological or physical), social science, other. **Pre-professional programs:** pre-law, pre-dentistry, pre-medicine, pre-veterinary science. **Special academic programs:** cooperative (work-study plan) program, double major, exchange student program (domestic), independent study, internships, student-designed major, study abroad, teacher certificate program. **Teacher certification offered in:** elementary, middle/junior high, secondary, bilingual/bicultural. **Reserve Officers Training Corps (ROTC):** Army ROTC: Offered at cooperating institution (Santa Clara University); Navy ROTC: Offered at cooperating institution (University of California–Berkeley); Air Force ROTC: Offered at cooperating institution (University of California–Berkeley). **Faculty and instruction (2009-2010):** Total instructional faculty: 563 full-time, 236 part-time (58% men; 42% women; 21% minorities). Full-time faculty with Ph.D. or other terminal degree: 98%. Student/faculty ratio: 18/1. Classes of fewer than 20 students: 46%; of 20 to 49 students: 31%; of 50 or more students: 23%. **Advanced Placement and International Baccalaureate credit:** AP tests may be used for: Credit and/or placement. Scores accepted: 3, 4, 5. International Baccalaureate exams may be used for: Credit and/or placement. **Freshmen returning for sophomore year:** 89%. **Graduation rates:** Four-year: 51%; five-year: 72%; six-year: 76%.

COSTS AND FINANCIAL AID

Financial aid office: (831) 459-2963. **Expenses (2010-2011):** Tuition and fees 2010-2011: $10,626 in state, $33,505 out of state; room/board: $14,205. Estimated books and supplies: $1,405; transportation: $871; personal expenses: $2,906. **Financial aid:** Priority filing date for institution's financial aid form: March 17; deadline: June 1. In 2009-2010, 69% of undergraduates applied for financial aid. Of those, 55% were determined to have financial need; 47% had their need fully met. Average financial aid package (proportion receiving): $18,545 (53%). Average amount of gift aid, such as scholarships or grants (proportion receiving): $13,735 (49%). Average amount of self-help aid, such as work study or loans (proportion receiving): $6,529 (48%). Average need-based loan (excluding PLUS or other private loans): $5,617. Among students who received need-based aid, the average percentage of need met: 89%. Among students who received aid based on merit, the average award (and the proportion receiving): $8,010 (2%). The average athletic scholarship (and the proportion receiving): $0 (0%). Average amount of debt of borrowers graduating in 2009: $16,024. Proportion who borrowed: 53%.

CAMPUS LIFE AND EXTRACURRICULAR ACTIVITIES

Campus housing available: coed dorms, women's dorms, men's dorms, apartments for married students, apartment for single students, special housing for disabled students, special housing for international students, other housing options. Students who live in college-owned, operated, or affiliated housing: 48%. **Student employment:** During the 2009-2010 academic year, 25% of undergraduates worked on campus. Average per-year earnings: $2,359. **Clubs and organizations:** Number of student organizations: 185. Activities include: campus ministries, choral groups, dance, drama/theater, jazz band, literary magazine, model UN, music ensembles, musical theater, opera, radio station, student government, student newspaper, student film society, symphony orchestra, television station. Number of fraternities: 7; sororities: 14. Proportion of men in fraternities: 1%; of women in sororities: 1%. **Sports program (2009-2010):** Member of NCAA III. **Men's intercollegiate varsity sports:** basketball, soccer, swimming, tennis, volleyball. **Women's intercollegiate varsity sports:** basketball, cross country, golf, soccer, swimming, tennis, volleyball.

SERVICES AND FACILITIES

Basic services: nonremedial tutoring, women's center, placement service, day care, health service, health insurance. **Counseling services:** minority student, career, personal, academic, psychological, birth control. **For learning-disabled students:** School does not offer a structured program with separate admission and additional fees. Services include: tape recorders, note-taking services, learning center, extended time for tests, tutors, priority registration, texts on tape, typist/scribe, other testing accommodations. **Library:** Number of titles: 1,638,857; number of current serial subscriptions: 37,299. **Information technology resources:** Students are not required to lease or own a computer. School has a wireless network. Approximate number of users that can be accommodated: 16,000. Proportion of college-owned housing units wired for high-speed internet access: 100%. **Campus safety:** Security services offered: 24-hour foot-and-vehicle patrols, late-night transport/escort service, 24-hour emergency telephones, lighted pathways/sidewalks, controlled dormitory access (key, security card, etc).

TRANSFER AND INTERNATIONAL STUDENTS

Transfer students: May apply for admission for the following academic terms: Fall, Winter. Applicants need a minimum number of credits to apply. For fall 2009: Transfer applications received: 5,625. Transfer applicants offered admission: 3,864. Transfer applicants enrolled: 870. **International students:** Number of foreign undergraduates: 55. Number of countries represented: 99. Minimum TOEFL score required: 550 (paper); 220 (computer). Average TOEFL score: 580 (paper).

University of La Verne

- **Address:** 1950 Third Street, La Verne, CA 91750
- **Website:** http://www.laverne.edu
- **Private**
- **Enrollment:** 1,435 full-time; 105 part-time

KEY STATS

✔ **U.S News College Ranking:** 136, National Universities
✔ **SAT Score (25th/75th percentile):** 880-1110
✔ **Tuition:** 2010-2011: $29,800

Selectivity: Selective	**Room/board:** $10,440
Acceptance rate: 68%	**Average debt:** $25,491
Student/faculty ratio: 12/1	**Proportion who borrowed:** 83%

UNDERGRADUATE STUDENT BODY STATS

2009-2010 enrollment: 1,435 full-time; 105 part-time. Men: 41%; women: 59%. **Ethnic makeup:** African American: 7%; American-Indian: 1%; Asian American: 4%; Hispanic: 39%; White: 48%; International: 1%. **Religious preference:** Roman Catholic: 14%; Protestant: 12%; Unknown: 68%; None: 3%; Other: 3%.

ADMISSIONS FACTS AND FIGURES

Phone: (800) 876-4858. **Email:** admissions@laverne.edu. **Website:** http://www.laverne.edu. **Application deadlines for fall 2011:** Regular decision: Rolling. Early decision: Not offered. Early action: Not offered. Admission can be deferred. **Application fee:** $50. **To apply online, go to:** http://www.laverne.edu/admission/undergraduate/. **Admissions requirements/recommendations:** High school units required (recommended): English: 4 (4); Mathematics: 3 (4); Science: 2 (2); Foreign language: 0 (2); Social studies: 2 (2); History: 3 (3); Academic electives: 0 (2); Total units: 14 (19). Tests: The college uses SAT or ACT scores in admissions decisions. Either SAT or ACT required. For admission to the fall 2011 entering class, the school will accept: ACT with writing required. Campus visit: Recommended. Admissions interview: Recommended. Off-campus interview: May be arranged. **Factors that count in admissions decisions:** *Academic:* Secondary school record: Very Important. Class rank: Important. Letters of recommendation: Very Important. Standardized test scores: Very Important. Essay: Very Important. *Nonacademic:* Interview: Considered. Extracurricular activities: Very Important. Talent/ability: Considered. Character/personal qualities: Very Important. Alumni/ae relationship: Considered. Geographical residence: Not Considered. State residency: Not Considered. Religious affiliation/commitment: Not Considered. Minority status: Considered. Volunteer work: Considered. Work experience: Considered. **Other schools**

with the greatest overlap in applicants: California State Polytechnic University–Pomona; California State University–Fullerton; Chapman University; University of Redlands; Whittier College. **Admissions statistics for the fall 2009 entering class:** Total applicants: 1,452. Total accepted: 989. Freshmen enrolled: 333; 4% were from out of state. Overall acceptance rate: 68%. **Credentials of fall 2009 freshmen:** 24% ranked in the top 10 percent of their high school class; 55% were in the top 25 percent; 85% were in the top half. (Proportion submitting class standing: 69%.) **Average high school grade point average:** 3.3. **First-year students who submitted SAT scores:** 90%. Scores (25/75 percentile): Critical Reading: 440-550, Math: 440-560, Combined: 880-1110. **First-year students submitting ACT scores:** 27%. Scores (25/75 percentile): English: 17-23, Math: 17-23, Composite: 17-23.

ACADEMICS

Year founded: 1891. **Academic calendar:** 4-1-4. **Degrees offered:** certificate, associate, bachelor's, post-bachelor's certificate, master's, doctorate. **Most popular majors:** 16% business administration and management, 11% psychology, 10% liberal arts and sciences/liberal studies, 8% communication studies/speech communication and rhetoric, 5% physical education teaching and coaching. **Major fields of study:** biological and biomedical sciences; business, management, marketing, and related support services; communication, journalism, and related programs; computer and information sciences and support services; education; English language and literature/letters; family and consumer sciences/human sciences; foreign languages, literatures, and linguistics; health professions and related clinical sciences; history; legal professions and studies; liberal arts and sciences studies, and humanities; mathematics and statistics; multi/interdisciplinary studies; natural resources and conservation; philosophy and religious studies; physical sciences; psychology; public administration and social service professions; social sciences; visual and performing arts. **Areas of required coursework:** arts/fine arts, humanities, mathematics, English (including composition), philosophy, foreign languages, sciences (biological or physical), history, social science, other. **Pre-professional programs:** pre-law, pre-dentistry, pre-medicine, other. **Special academic programs:** accelerated program, distance learning, double major, English as a Second Language (ESL), exchange student program (domestic), honors program, independent study, internships, liberal arts/career combination, student-designed major, study abroad, teacher certificate program, weekend college. **Teacher certification offered in:** early childhood, special education, elementary, middle/junior high, secondary, bilingual/bicultural. **Reserve Officers Training Corps (ROTC):** Army ROTC: Offered at cooperating institution (Pomona College). **Faculty and instruction (2009-2010):** Total instructional faculty: 190 full-time, 204 part-time (54% men; 46% women; 16% minorities). Full-time faculty with Ph.D. or other terminal degree: 86%. Student/faculty ratio: 12/1. Classes of fewer than 20 students: 76%; of 20 to 49 students: 23%; of 50 or more students: 0%. **Advanced Placement and International Baccalaureate credit:** AP tests may be used for: Placement only. Scores accepted: 3, 4, 5. International Baccalaureate exams may be used for: Placement only. **Freshmen returning for sophomore year:** 81%. **Graduation rates:** Four-year: 44%; five-year: 61%; six-year: 68%.

COSTS AND FINANCIAL AID

Financial aid office: (800) 649-0160. **Expenses (2010-2011):** Tuition and fees 2010-2011: $29,800; room/board: $10,440. Estimated books and supplies: $1,638; transportation: $792; personal expenses: $2,350. **Financial aid:** Priority filing date for institution's financial aid form: March 2. In 2009-2010, 88% of undergraduates applied for financial aid. Of those, 83% were determined to have financial need; 12% had their need fully met. Average financial aid package (proportion receiving): $24,932 (83%). Average amount of gift aid, such as scholarships or grants (proportion receiving): $11,941 (71%). Average amount of self-help aid, such as work study or loans (proportion receiving): $5,372 (78%). Average need-based loan (excluding PLUS or other private loans): $4,884. Among students who received need-based aid, the average percentage of need met: 60%. Among students who received aid based on merit, the average award (and the proportion receiving): $15,146 (11%). The average athletic scholarship (and the proportion receiving): $0 (0%). Average amount of debt of borrowers graduating in 2009: $25,491. Proportion who borrowed: 83%.

CAMPUS LIFE AND EXTRACURRICULAR ACTIVITIES

Campus housing available: coed dorms, women's dorms, special housing for disabled students, special housing for international students. Students who live in college-owned, operated, or affiliated housing: 29%. **Clubs and organizations:** Number of student organizations: 43. Activities include: campus ministries, choral groups, dance, drama/theater, international student organization, literary magazine, model UN, music ensembles, musical theater, radio station, student government, student newspaper, television station. Number of fraternities: 3; sororities: 6. Proportion of men in fraternities: 4%; of women in sororities: 13%. Average proportion of students who stay on campus on weekends: 25%. **Sports program (2009-2010):** Member of NCAA III. **Men's intercollegiate varsity sports:** baseball, basketball, cross country, football, golf, soccer, swimming, tennis, track and field (outdoor), water polo. **Women's intercollegiate varsity sports:** basketball, cross country, soccer, softball, swimming, tennis, track and field (outdoor), volleyball, water polo.

SERVICES AND FACILITIES

Basic services: nonremedial tutoring, placement service, health service, health insurance. **Remedial assistance:** math, writing, study skills, other. **Counseling services:** minority student, career, military, personal, veteran student, academic, older student, psychological, birth control, religious. **For learning-disabled students:** School does not offer a structured program with separate admission and additional fees. Services include: remedial math, remedial English, reading machines, tape recorders, untimed tests, note-taking services, oral tests, learning center, readers, extended time for tests, tutors, priority registration, priority seating, texts on tape, other testing accommodations, other. **Library:** Number of titles: 196,842; number of current serial subscriptions: 38,178. **Information technology resources:** Students are not required to lease or own a computer. Number of campus computers available to all students: 393. School has a wireless network. Proportion of college-owned housing units wired for high-speed internet access: 80%. **Campus safety:** Security services offered: 24-hour foot-and-vehicle patrols, late-night transport/escort service, 24-hour emergency telephones, lighted pathways/sidewalks, controlled dormitory access (key, security card, etc).

TRANSFER AND INTERNATIONAL STUDENTS

Transfer students: May apply for admission for the following academic terms: Fall, Spring. Applicants need a minimum number of credits to apply. For fall 2009: Transfer applications received: 303. Transfer applicants offered admission: 198. Transfer applicants enrolled: 114. **International students:** Number of foreign undergraduates: 21 (1% of student body). Number of countries represented: 6. Minimum TOEFL score required: 500 (paper); 213 (computer). Average TOEFL score: 583 (paper).

University of Redlands

- **Address:** PO Box 3080, Redlands, CA 92373
- **Website:** http://www.redlands.edu
- **Private**
- **Enrollment:** 2,269 full-time; 681 part-time

KEY STATS

✔ **U.S News College Ranking:** 9, Regional Universities (West)
✔ **SAT Score (25th/75th percentile):** 1060-1250
✔ **Tuition:** 2010-2011: $35,540

Selectivity: Selective	**Room/board:** $10,832
Acceptance rate: 70%	**Average debt:** $24,218
Student/faculty ratio: 11/1	**Proportion who borrowed:** 70%

UNDERGRADUATE STUDENT BODY STATS

2009-2010 enrollment: 2,269 full-time; 681 part-time. Men: 45%; women: 55%. **Ethnic makeup:** African American: 4%; American-Indian: 1%; Asian American: 5%; Hispanic: 15%; White: 73%; International: 2%.

ADMISSIONS FACTS AND FIGURES

Phone: (800) 455-5064. **Email:** admissions@redlands.edu. **Website:** http://www.redlands.edu. **Application deadlines for fall 2011:** Regular decision: June 1. Early decision: Not offered. Early action: Not offered. Admission can be deferred. **Application fee:** $35. **To apply online, go to:** http://www.redlands.edu/x7134.xml. **Admissions requirements/recommendations:** High school units required (recommended): English: 4 (4); Mathematics: 3 (3); Science: 2 (3); Foreign language: 2 (3); Social studies: 2 (3); Total units: 13 (16). Tests: The college uses SAT or ACT scores in admissions decisions. Either SAT or ACT required. For admission to the fall 2011 entering class, the school will accept: ACT with or without writing accepted. Campus visit: Recommended. Admissions interview: Recommended. Off-campus interview: May be arranged. **Factors that count in admissions decisions:** *Academic:* Secondary school record: Very Important. Class rank: Not Considered. Letters of recommendation: Very Important. Standardized test scores: Important. Essay: Important. *Nonacademic:* Interview: Considered. Extracurricular activities: Considered. Talent/ability: Very Important. Character/personal qualities: Very Important. Alumni/ae relationship: Considered. Geographical residence: Considered. State residency: Not Considered. Religious affiliation/commitment: Not Considered. Minority status: Considered. Volunteer work: Considered. Work experience: Considered. **Other schools with the greatest overlap in applicants:** Chapman University; Loyola Marymount University; Occidental College; University of San Diego; University of Southern California. **Admissions statistics for the fall 2009 entering class:** Total applicants: 3,267. Total accepted: 2,299. Freshmen enrolled: 561; 39% were from out of state. Overall acceptance rate: 70%. **Size of waiting list:** 0 applicants; enrolled from waiting list: 0. **Credentials of fall 2009 freshmen:** 31% ranked in the top 10 percent of their high school class; 67% were in the top 25 percent; 92% were in the top half. (Proportion submitting class standing: 58%.) **Average high school grade point average:** 3.5. **First-year students who submitted SAT scores:** 73%. Scores (25/75 percentile): Critical Reading: 520-620, Math: 540-630, Combined: 1060-1250. **First-year students submitting ACT scores:** 43%. Scores (25/75 percentile): English: N/A, Math: N/A, Composite: 22-27.

ACADEMICS

Year founded: 1907. **Academic calendar:** 4-1-4. **Degrees offered:** bachelor's, post-bachelor's certificate, master's, post-master's certificate, doctorate. **Most popular majors:** 42% business, management, marketing, and related support services, 9% social sciences, 7% health professions and related clinical sciences, 6% psychology, 5% English language and literature/letters. **Major fields of study:** area, ethnic, cultural, and gender studies; biological and biomedical sciences; business, management, marketing, and related support services; computer and information sciences and support services; education; English language and literature/letters; foreign languages, literatures, and linguistics; health professions and related clinical sciences; history; liberal arts and sciences studies, and humanities; mathematics and statistics; multi/interdisciplinary studies; natural resources and conservation; philosophy and religious studies; physical sciences; psychology; social sciences; visual and performing arts. **Areas of required coursework:** arts/fine arts, humanities, computer literacy, mathematics, English (including composition), philosophy, foreign languages, sciences (biological or physical), history, social science. **Pre-professional programs:** pre-law, pre-medicine. **Special academic programs:** cross-registration, double major, exchange student program (domestic), honors program, independent study, internships, liberal arts/career combination, student-designed major, study abroad, teacher certificate program. **Teacher certification offered in:** elementary, middle/junior high, secondary. **Reserve Officers Training Corps (ROTC):** Army ROTC: Offered at cooperating institution (California State University–San Bernardino); Navy ROTC: Offered at cooperating institution (California State University–San Bernardino); Air Force ROTC: Offered at cooperating institution (California State University–San Bernardino). **Faculty and instruction (2009-2010):** Total instructional faculty: 221 full-time, 239 part-time (58% men; 42% women; 11% minorities). Full-time faculty with Ph.D. or other terminal degree: 87%. Student/faculty ratio: 11/1. Classes of fewer than 20 students: 70%; of 20 to 49 students: 30%; of 50 or more students: 0%. **Advanced Placement and International Baccalaureate credit:** AP tests may be used for: Placement only. Scores accepted: 3, 4, 5. International Baccalaureate exams may be used for: Credit only. **Freshmen returning for sophomore year:** 84%. **Graduation rates:** Four-year: 61%; five-year: 66%; six-year: 69%. **Graduate study:** 32% of students pursue further study immediately upon graduation; 15% within one year; 17% within five years. Fields in which graduates pursue further study: Master of Business Administration (MBA), 9%; law, 7%; medicine, 9%; dentistry, 1%; engineering, 1%; theology (or the seminary), 1%; education, 22%; arts and sciences, 10%.

COSTS AND FINANCIAL AID

Financial aid office: (909) 335-4047. **Expenses (2010-2011):** Tuition and fees 2010-2011: $35,540; room/board: $10,832. Estimated books and supplies: $1,650; transportation: $1,170; personal expenses: $2,350. **Financial aid:** Priority filing date for institution's financial aid form: February 15. In 2009-2010, 82% of undergraduates applied for financial aid. Of those, 79% were determined to have financial need; 16% had their need fully met. Average financial aid package (proportion receiving): $28,324 (76%). Average amount of gift aid, such as scholarships or grants (proportion receiving): $23,039 (75%). Average amount of self-help aid, such as work study or loans (proportion receiving): $2,445 (49%). Average need-based loan (excluding PLUS or other private loans): $6,122. Among students who received need-based aid, the average percentage of need met: 66%. Among students who received aid based on merit, the average award (and the pro-

portion receiving): $12,888 (12%). Average amount of debt of borrowers graduating in 2009: $24,218. Proportion who borrowed: 70%.

CAMPUS LIFE AND EXTRACURRICULAR ACTIVITIES

Campus housing available (% using): coed dorms (53%), women's dorms (13%), men's dorms (5%), sorority housing (1%), fraternity housing (1%), apartment for single students (14%), special housing for disabled students (1%), other housing options (2%). Students who live in college-owned, operated, or affiliated housing: 51%. **Student employment:** During the 2009-2010 academic year, 39% of undergraduates worked on campus. Average per-year earnings: $1,250. **Clubs and organizations:** Number of student organizations: 102. Activities include: choral groups, concert band, dance, drama/theater, jazz band, literary magazine, music ensembles, musical theater, opera, student government, student newspaper, symphony orchestra, yearbook. Number of fraternities: 7; sororities: 5. Proportion of men in fraternities: 1%; of women in sororities: 1%. Average proportion of students who stay on campus on weekends: 75%. **Sports program (2009-2010):** Member of NCAA III.

SERVICES AND FACILITIES

Basic services: nonremedial tutoring, women's center, health service. **Counseling services:** career, personal, academic, psychological, religious. **For learning-disabled students:** School does not offer a structured program with separate admission and additional fees. Total undergraduates in learning-disabled program or receiving services: 150. Services include: reading machines, tape recorders, untimed tests, note-taking services, oral tests, extended time for tests, tutors, substitution of courses, texts on tape, exams on tape or computer, other testing accommodations. **Library:** Number of titles: 282,056; number of current serial subscriptions: 21,502. **Information technology resources:** Students are not required to lease or own a computer. Number of campus computers available to all students: 742. School has a wireless network. Approximate number of users that can be accommodated: 5,000. Proportion of college-owned housing units wired for high-speed internet access: 100%. **Campus safety:** Security services offered: 24-hour foot-and-vehicle patrols, late-night transport/escort service, 24-hour emergency telephones, lighted pathways/sidewalks, controlled dormitory access (key, security card, etc).

TRANSFER AND INTERNATIONAL STUDENTS

Transfer students: May apply for admission for the following academic terms: Fall, Spring. Applicants need a minimum number of credits to apply. For fall 2009: Transfer applications received: 182. Transfer applicants offered admission: 150. Transfer applicants enrolled: 87. **International students:** Number of foreign undergraduates: 55 (2% of student body). Number of countries represented: 11. Minimum TOEFL score required: 550 (paper); 213 (computer).

University of San Diego

- **Address:** 5998 Alcala Park, San Diego, CA 92110-2492
- **Website:** http://www.SanDiego.edu
- **Private; Religious affiliation:** Roman Catholic
- **Enrollment:** 4,896 full-time; 215 part-time

KEY STATS

✔ **U.S News College Ranking:** 94, National Universities
✔ **SAT Score (25th/75th percentile):** 1115-1300
✔ **Tuition:** 2010-2011: $37,378

Selectivity: More selective	**Room/board:** $11,602
Acceptance rate: 49%	**Average debt:** $27,999
Student/faculty ratio: 15/1	**Proportion who borrowed:** 57%

UNDERGRADUATE STUDENT BODY STATS

2009-2010 enrollment: 4,896 full-time; 215 part-time. Men: 43%; women: 57%. **Ethnic makeup:** African American: 3%; American-Indian: 2%; Asian American: 11%; Hispanic: 15%; White: 66%; International: 4%. **Religious preference:** Protestant: 25%; Jewish: 1%; Muslim: 2%; Buddhist: 1%; No preference: 9%; Unknown: 9%; Roman Catholic: 52%; Other: 1%.

ADMISSIONS FACTS AND FIGURES

Phone: (619) 260-4506. **Email:** admissions@SanDiego.edu. **Website:** http://www.SanDiego.edu. **Application deadlines for fall 2011:** Regular decision: March 1; decision sent by April 15. Early decision: Not offered.

Early action: Send application by: November 15; Decision sent by: January 31. Admission can be deferred. **Application fee:** $55. **To apply online, go to:** http://www.sandiego.edu/admissions/undergraduate/apply/application.php. **Admissions requirements/recommendations:** High school units required (recommended): English: 4 (4); Mathematics: 3 (4); Science: 3 (4); Foreign language: 2 (3); Social studies: 3 (4); Total units: 15 (19). Tests: The college uses SAT or ACT scores in admissions decisions. Either SAT or ACT required. For admission to the fall 2011 entering class, the school will accept: ACT with writing required. Campus visit: Recommended. Admissions interview: Neither required nor recommended. Off-campus interview: Not available. **Factors that count in admissions decisions:** *Academic:* Secondary school record: Very Important. Class rank: Important. Letters of recommendation: Important. Standardized test scores: Very Important. Essay: Important. *Nonacademic:* Interview: Not Considered. Extracurricular activities: Important. Talent/ability: Important. Character/personal qualities: Important. Alumni/ae relationship: Considered. Geographical residence: Considered. State residency: Not Considered. Religious affiliation/commitment: Very Important. Minority status: Considered. Volunteer work: Important. Work experience: Considered. **Other schools with the greatest overlap in applicants:** Loyola Marymount University; Santa Clara University; University of California–Los Angeles; University of California–Santa Barbara; University of Southern California. **Admissions statistics for the fall 2009 entering class:** Total applicants: 11,000. Total accepted: 5,434. Freshmen enrolled: 1,082; 47% were from out of state. Accepted through early-decision or early-action plans: 39%. Overall acceptance rate: 49%. Non-early acceptance rate: 45%. **Size of waiting list:** 1600 applicants; enrolled from waiting list: 387. **Credentials of fall 2009 freshmen:** 45% ranked in the top 10 percent of their high school class; 80% were in the top 25 percent; 98% were in the top half. (Proportion submitting class standing: 67%.) **Average high school grade point average:** 3.8. **First-year students who submitted SAT scores:** 82%. Scores (25/75 percentile): Critical Reading: 550-640, Math: 565-660, Combined: 1115-1300. **First-year students submitting ACT scores:** 50%. Scores (25/75 percentile): English: 24-30, Math: 25-29, Composite: 25-29.

ACADEMICS

Year founded: 1949. **Academic calendar:** 4-1-4. **Degrees offered:** bachelor's, post-bachelor's certificate, master's, post-master's certificate, doctorate. **Most popular majors:** 41% business, management, marketing, and related support services, 14% social sciences, 10% communication, journalism, and related programs, 7% psychology, 6% biological and biomedical sciences. **Major fields of study:** biological and biomedical sciences; business, management, marketing, and related support services; communication, journalism, and related programs; computer and information sciences and support services; engineering; English language and literature/letters; foreign languages, literatures, and linguistics; health professions and related clinical sciences; history; liberal arts and sciences studies, and humanities; mathematics and statistics; multi/interdisciplinary studies; philosophy and religious studies; physical sciences; psychology; social sciences; visual and performing arts. **Areas of required coursework:** arts/fine arts, humanities, mathematics, English (including composition), philosophy, foreign languages, sciences (biological or physical), history, social science, other. **Preprofessional programs:** pre-law, pre-dentistry, pre-medicine, pre-theology, pre-veterinary science, pre-optometry, pre-pharmacy. **Special academic programs:** double major, English as a Second Language (ESL), honors program, independent study, internships, liberal arts/career combination, study abroad, teacher certificate program. **Teacher certification offered in:** early childhood, special education, elementary, middle/junior high, secondary. **Reserve Officers Training Corps (ROTC):** Army ROTC: Offered at cooperating institution (San Diego State University); Navy ROTC: Offered on campus; Air Force ROTC: Offered at cooperating institution (San Diego State University). **Faculty and instruction (2009-2010):** Total instructional faculty: 381 full-time, 427 part-time (51% men; 49% women; 17% minorities). Full-time faculty with Ph.D. or other terminal degree: 94%. Student/faculty ratio: 15/1. Classes of fewer than 20 students: 42%; of 20 to 49 students: 58%; of 50 or more students: 0%. **Advanced Placement and International Baccalaureate credit:** AP tests may be used for: Placement only. Scores accepted: 3, 4, 5. International Baccalaureate exams may be used for: Placement only. **Freshmen returning for sophomore year:** 86%. **Graduation rates:** Four-year: 66%; five-year: 73%; six-year: 74%. **Graduate study:** 18% of students pursue further study within one year. Fields in which graduates pursue further study: Master of Business Administration (MBA), 16%; law, 20%; medicine, 8%; engineering, 4%; education, 14%; arts and sciences, 37%.

COSTS AND FINANCIAL AID

Financial aid office: (619) 260-4514. **Expenses (2010-2011):** Tuition and fees 2010-2011: $37,378; room/board: $11,602. Estimated books and supplies: $1,620; transportation: $729; personal expenses: $2,250. **Financial aid:** Priority filing date for institution's financial aid form: March 2. In 2009-2010, 54% of undergraduates applied for financial aid. Of those, 48% were determined to have financial need; 20% had their need fully met. Average financial aid package (proportion receiving): $28,993 (48%). Average amount of gift aid, such as scholarships or grants (proportion receiving): $21,139 (45%). Average amount of self-help aid, such as work study or loans (proportion receiving): $8,741 (41%). Average need-based loan (excluding PLUS or other private loans): $8,037. Among students who received need-based aid, the average percentage of need met: 74%. Among students who received aid based on merit, the average award (and the proportion receiving): $13,385 (16%). The average athletic scholarship (and the proportion receiving): $31,338 (3%). Average amount of debt of borrowers graduating in 2009: $27,999. Proportion who borrowed: 57%.

CAMPUS LIFE AND EXTRACURRICULAR ACTIVITIES

Campus housing available (% using): coed dorms (88%), women's dorms (7%), men's dorms (5%), apartments for married students, apartment for single students, special housing for disabled students. Students who live in college-owned, operated, or affiliated housing: 48%. **Student employment:** During the 2009-2010 academic year, 27% of undergraduates worked on campus. Average per-year earnings: $2,870. **Clubs and organizations:** Number of student organizations: 134. Activities include: campus ministries, choral groups, dance, drama/theater, international student organization, jazz band, literary magazine, model UN, music ensembles, musical theater, pep band, radio station, student government, student newspaper, symphony orchestra, television station, yearbook. Number of fraternities: 5; sororities: 6. Proportion of men in fraternities: 19%; of women in sororities: 26%. Average proportion of students who stay on campus on weekends: 75%. **Sports program (2009-2010):** Member of NCAA I. *Men's intercollegiate varsity sports:* baseball, basketball, cross country, football, golf, soccer, tennis. *Women's intercollegiate varsity sports:* basketball, cross country, crew (lightweight), soccer, softball, swimming, tennis, track and field (outdoor), volleyball.

SERVICES AND FACILITIES

Basic services: nonremedial tutoring, women's center, placement service, day care, health service, health insurance. **Counseling services:** minority student, career, military, personal, veteran student, academic, psychological, religious. **For learning-disabled students:** School does not offer a structured program with separate admission and additional fees. Total undergraduates in learning-disabled program or receiving services: 268. Services include: texts on tape, other. **Library:** Number of titles: 704,887; number of current serial subscriptions: 38,488. **Information technology resources:** Students are not required to lease or own a computer. Number of campus computers available to all students: 1,283. School has a wireless network. Approximate number of users that can be accommodated: 25,500. Proportion of college-owned housing units wired for high-speed internet access: 100%. **Campus safety:** Security services offered: 24-hour foot-and-vehicle patrols, late-night transport/escort service, 24-hour emergency telephones, lighted pathways/sidewalks, controlled dormitory access (key, security card, etc).

TRANSFER AND INTERNATIONAL STUDENTS

Transfer students: May apply for admission for the following academic terms: Fall, Spring. Applicants need a minimum number of credits to apply. For fall 2009: Transfer applications received: 1,303. Transfer applicants offered admission: 886. Transfer applicants enrolled: 401. **International students:** Number of foreign undergraduates: 184 (4% of student body). Number of countries represented: 61. Minimum TOEFL score required: 550 (paper); 80 (computer).

University of San Francisco

- **Address:** Ignatian Heights, San Francisco, CA 94117-1080
- **Website:** http://www.usfca.edu
- **Private; Religious affiliation:** Roman Catholic
- **Enrollment:** 5,314 full-time; 211 part-time

KEY STATS
- ✔ **U.S News College Ranking:** 117, National Universities
- ✔ **SAT Score (25th/75th percentile):** 1010-1220
- ✔ **Tuition:** 2010-2011: $36,380

Selectivity: Selective	**Room/board:** $11,990
Acceptance rate: 71%	**Average debt:** $26,886
Student/faculty ratio: 15/1	**Proportion who borrowed:** 64%

UNDERGRADUATE STUDENT BODY STATS
2009-2010 enrollment: 5,314 full-time; 211 part-time. Men: 37%; women: 63%. **Ethnic makeup:** African American: 5%; American-Indian: 1%; Asian American: 21%; Hispanic: 14%; White: 50%; International: 9%. **Religious preference:** Roman Catholic: 44%; Protestant: 7%; Jewish: 2%; Muslim: 1%; Hindu: 1%; Buddhist: 2%; No preference: 6%; Unknown: 32%.

ADMISSIONS FACTS AND FIGURES
Phone: (415) 422-6563. **Email:** admission@usfca.edu. **Website:** http://www.usfca.edu. **Application deadlines for fall 2011:** Regular decision: Rolling. Early decision: Not offered. Early action: Send application by: November 15; Decision sent by: January 16. Admission can be deferred. **Application fee:** $55. **To apply online, go to:** http://www.usfca.edu/applyusf/. **Admissions requirements/recommendations:** High school units required (recommended): English: 4; Mathematics: 3; Science: 2; Foreign language: 2; Social studies: 3; Academic electives: 6; Total units: 20. Tests: The college uses SAT or ACT scores in admissions decisions. Either SAT or ACT required. For admission to the fall 2011 entering class, the school will accept: ACT with writing required. Campus visit: Recommended. Admissions interview: Recommended. Off-campus interview: May be arranged. **Factors that count in admissions decisions:** *Academic:* Secondary school record: Very Important. Class rank: Important. Letters of recommendation: Important. Standardized test scores: Very Important. Essay: Very Important. *Nonacademic:* Interview: Not Considered. Extracurricular activities: Considered. Talent/ability: Considered. Character/personal qualities: Considered. Alumni/ae relationship: Considered. Geographical residence: Not Considered. State residency: Not Considered. Religious affiliation/commitment: Not Considered. Minority status: Not Considered. Volunteer work: Considered. Work experience: Not Considered. **Other schools with the greatest overlap in applicants:** San Francisco State University; Santa Clara University; Stanford University; University of California–Berkeley; University of California–Santa Cruz. **Admissions statistics for the fall 2009 entering class:** Total applicants: 8,281. Total accepted: 5,906. Freshmen enrolled: 1,073; 33% were from out of state. Accepted through early-decision or early-action plans: 28%. Overall acceptance rate: 71%. Non-early acceptance rate: 69%. **Credentials of fall 2009 freshmen:** 24% ranked in the top 10 percent of their high school class; 61% were in the top 25 percent; 91% were in the top half. (Proportion submitting class standing: 31%.) **Average high school grade point average:** 3.5. **First-year students who submitted SAT scores:** 84%. Scores (25/75 percentile): Critical Reading: 500-610, Math: 510-610, Combined: 1010-1220. **First-year students submitting ACT scores:** 43%. Scores (25/75 percentile): English: N/A, Math: N/A, Composite: 22-27.

ACADEMICS
Year founded: 1855. **Academic calendar:** 4-1-4. **Degrees offered:** bachelor's, master's, post-master's certificate, doctorate. **Most popular majors:** 12% nursing/registered nurse training (R.N., A.S.N., B.S.N., M.S.N.), 7% finance, 7% psychology, 6% business administration and management, 6% communication and media studies. **Major fields of study:** architecture and related services; area, ethnic, cultural, and gender studies; biological and biomedical sciences; business, management, marketing, and related support services; communication, journalism, and related programs; computer and information sciences and support services; English language and literature/letters; foreign languages, literatures, and linguistics; health professions and related clinical sciences; history; liberal arts and sciences studies, and humanities; mathematics and statistics; multi/interdisciplinary studies; natural resources and conservation; parks, recreation, leisure, and fitness studies; philosophy and religious studies; physical sciences; psychology; public administration and social service professions; social sciences; theol-

ogy and religious vocations; visual and performing arts. **Areas of required coursework:** arts/fine arts, humanities, computer literacy, mathematics, English (including composition), philosophy, foreign languages, sciences (biological or physical), history, social science, other. **Pre-professional programs:** pre-law, pre-dentistry, pre-medicine, pre-veterinary science, pre-optometry, pre-pharmacy. **Special academic programs:** cooperative (work-study plan) program, cross-registration, double major, English as a Second Language (ESL), exchange student program (domestic), external degree program, honors program, independent study, internships, liberal arts/career combination, study abroad, teacher certificate program. **Teacher certification offered in:** early childhood, special education, elementary, middle/junior high, secondary, bilingual/bicultural. **Reserve Officers Training Corps (ROTC):** Army ROTC: Offered on campus; Air Force ROTC: Offered at cooperating institution (University of California–Berkeley). **Faculty and instruction (2009-2010):** Total instructional faculty: 386 full-time, 185 part-time (50% men; 50% women; 22% minorities). Student/faculty ratio: 15/1. Classes of fewer than 20 students: 49%; of 20 to 49 students: 48%; of 50 or more students: 2%. **Advanced Placement and International Baccalaureate credit:** AP tests may be used for: Credit only. Scores accepted: 3. International Baccalaureate exams may be used for: Placement only. **Freshmen returning for sophomore year:** 83%. **Graduation rates:** Four-year: 49%; five-year: 66%; six-year: 70%. **Graduate study:** 30% of students pursue further study immediately upon graduation. Fields in which graduates pursue further study: Master of Business Administration (MBA), 15%; law, 3%; medicine, 2%; dentistry, 2%; education, 1%.

COSTS AND FINANCIAL AID
Financial aid office: (415) 422-2620. **Expenses (2010-2011):** Tuition and fees 2010-2011: $36,380; room/board: $11,990. Estimated books and supplies: $1,500; transportation: $1,100; personal expenses: $2,500. **Financial aid:** Priority filing date for institution's financial aid form: February 1. In 2009-2010, 66% of undergraduates applied for financial aid. Of those, 60% were determined to have financial need; 6% had their need fully met. Average financial aid package (proportion receiving): $26,830 (59%). Average amount of gift aid, such as scholarships or grants (proportion receiving): $21,762 (52%). Average amount of self-help aid, such as work study or loans (proportion receiving): $6,697 (53%). Average need-based loan (excluding PLUS or other private loans): $4,795. Among students who received need-based aid, the average percentage of need met: 65%. Among students who received aid based on merit, the average award (and the proportion receiving): $18,254 (2%). The average athletic scholarship (and the proportion receiving): $28,695 (3%). Average amount of debt of borrowers graduating in 2009: $26,886. Proportion who borrowed: 64%.

CAMPUS LIFE AND EXTRACURRICULAR ACTIVITIES
Campus housing available (% using): coed dorms (71%), women's dorms (8%), apartment for single students (20%), special housing for disabled students, other housing options (1%). Students who live in college-owned, operated, or affiliated housing: 38%. **Student employment:** During the 2009-2010 academic year, 18% of undergraduates worked on campus. Average per-year earnings: $3,736. **Clubs and organizations:** Number of student organizations: 95. Activities include: choral groups, dance, drama/theater, international student organization, literary magazine, music ensembles, musical theater, pep band, radio station, student government, student newspaper, television station, yearbook. Number of fraternities: 1; sororities: 1. Proportion of men in fraternities: 1%; of women in sororities: 1%. Average proportion of students who stay on campus on weekends: 35%. **Sports program (2009-2010):** Member of NCAA I. *Men's intercollegiate varsity sports:* baseball, basketball, cross country, golf, soccer, tennis, track and field (outdoor). *Women's intercollegiate varsity sports:* basketball, cross country, golf, soccer, tennis, track and field (outdoor), volleyball.

SERVICES AND FACILITIES
Basic services: nonremedial tutoring, placement service, health service, health insurance. **Remedial assistance:** study skills. **Counseling services:** minority student, career, personal, academic, older student, psychological, religious, other. **For learning-disabled students:** School does not offer a structured program with separate admission and additional fees. Services include: reading machines, tape recorders, videotaped classes, diagnostic testing service, untimed tests, note-taking services, oral tests, learning center, readers, extended time for tests, tutors, texts on tape, other testing accommodations, other. **Library:** Number of titles: 1,026,387; number of current serial subscriptions: 4,500. **Information technology resources:** Students are not required to lease or own a computer. Number of campus computers available to all students: 200. School has a wireless network. Proportion of college-owned housing units wired for high-speed internet

access: 100%. **Campus safety:** Security services offered: 24-hour foot-and-vehicle patrols, late-night transport/escort service, 24-hour emergency telephones, lighted pathways/sidewalks, controlled dormitory access (key, security card, etc).

TRANSFER AND INTERNATIONAL STUDENTS
Transfer students: May apply for admission for the following academic terms: Fall, Spring. Applicants need a minimum number of credits to apply. For fall 2009: Transfer applications received: 1,511. Transfer applicants offered admission: 892. Transfer applicants enrolled: 377. **International students:** Number of foreign undergraduates: 477 (9% of student body). Number of countries represented: 70. Minimum TOEFL score required: 550 (paper); 213 (computer). Average TOEFL score: 545 (paper).

University of Southern California

■ **Address:** University Park, Los Angeles, CA 90089
■ **Website:** http://www.usc.edu/
■ **Private**
■ **Enrollment:** 16,096 full-time; 655 part-time

KEY STATS
✔ **U.S News College Ranking:** 23, National Universities
✔ **SAT Score (25th/75th percentile):** 1270-1450
✔ **Tuition:** 2010-2011: $41,022

Selectivity: Most selective	**Room/board:** $11,580
Acceptance rate: 24%	**Average debt:** $30,097
Student/faculty ratio: 9/1	**Proportion who borrowed:** 45%

2009-2010 enrollment: 16,096 full-time; 655 part-time. Men: 50%; women: 50%. **Ethnic makeup:** African American: 6%; American-Indian: 1%; Asian American: 24%; Hispanic: 13%; White: 46%; International: 10%. **Religious preference:** Roman Catholic: 18%; Protestant: 29%; Jewish: 7%; Muslim: 2%; Hindu: 2%; Buddhist: 3%; No preference: 35%; Eastern Orthodox: 1%; Other: 3%.

ADMISSIONS FACTS AND FIGURES
Phone: (213) 740-1111. **Email:** admitusc@usc.edu. **Website:** http://www.usc.edu/. **Application deadlines for fall 2011:** Regular decision: January 10; decision sent by April 1. Early decision: Not offered. Early action: Not offered. Admission cannot be deferred. **Application fee:** $65. **To apply online, go to:** http://www.usc.edu/admission/undergraduate/apply/. **Admissions requirements/recommendations:** High school units required (recommended): English: 4 (4); Mathematics: 3 (4); Science: 2 (3); Foreign language: 2 (3); Social studies: 2 (3); Academic electives: 3 (3); Total units: 16 (20). Tests: The college uses SAT or ACT scores in admissions decisions. Either SAT or ACT required. For admission to the fall 2011 entering class, the school will accept: ACT with writing required. Campus visit: Recommended. Admissions interview: Neither required nor recommended. Off-campus interview: May be arranged. **Factors that count in admissions decisions:** *Academic:* Secondary school record: Very Important. Class rank: Considered. Letters of recommendation: Very Important. Standardized test scores: Very Important. Essay: Very Important. *Nonacademic:* Interview: Considered. Extracurricular activities: Important. Talent/ability: Important. Character/personal qualities: Considered. Alumni/ae relationship: Considered. Geographical residence: Not Considered. State residency: Not Considered. Religious affiliation/commitment: Not Considered. Minority status: Considered. Volunteer work: Considered. Work experience: Considered. **Other schools with the greatest overlap in applicants:** New York University; Northwestern University; Stanford University; University of California–Berkeley; University of California–Los Angeles. **Admissions statistics for the fall 2009 entering class:** Total applicants: 35,753. Total accepted: 8,724. Freshmen enrolled: 2,869; 41% were from out of state. Overall acceptance rate: 24%. **Credentials of fall 2009 freshmen:** 86% ranked in the top 10 percent of their high school class; 97% were in the top 25 percent; 100% were in the top half. (Proportion submitting class standing: 50%.) **Average high school grade point average:** 3.7. **First-year students who submitted SAT scores:** 82%. Scores (25/75 percentile): Critical Reading: 620-710, Math: 650-740, Combined: 1270-1450. **First-year students submitting ACT scores:** 39%. Scores (25/75 percentile): English: 28-34, Math: 28-33, Composite: 29-32.

ACADEMICS
Year founded: 1880. **Academic calendar:** Semester. **Degrees offered:** bachelor's, post-bachelor's certificate, master's, post-master's certificate, doctorate. **Most popular majors:** 27% business, management, marketing, and related support services, 14% social sciences, 14% visual and performing arts, 9% communication, journalism, and related programs, 9% engineering. **Major fields of study:** architecture and related services; area, ethnic, cultural, and gender studies; biological and biomedical sciences; business, management, marketing, and related support services; communication, journalism, and related programs; computer and information sciences and support services; education; engineering; English language and literature/letters; foreign languages, literatures, and linguistics; health professions and related clinical sciences; history; liberal arts and sciences studies, and humanities; mathematics and statistics; multi/interdisciplinary studies; natural resources and conservation; parks, recreation, leisure, and fitness studies; philosophy and religious studies; physical sciences; psychology; public administration and social service professions; social sciences; visual and performing arts. **Areas of required coursework:** humanities, English (including composition), foreign languages, sciences (biological or physical), history, social science, other. **Pre-professional programs:** pre-law, pre-dentistry, pre-medicine, pre-pharmacy, other. **Special academic programs:** cooperative (work-study plan) program, distance learning, double major, English as a Second Language (ESL), exchange student program (domestic), honors program, independent study, internships, liberal arts/career combination, student-designed major, study abroad, other. **Cooperative education programs:** engineering. **Reserve Officers Training Corps (ROTC):** Army ROTC: Offered on campus; Navy ROTC: Offered on campus; Air Force ROTC: Offered on campus. **Faculty and instruction (2009-2010):** Total instructional faculty: 1,638 full-time, 1,133 part-time (64% men; 36% women; 29% minorities). Full-time faculty with Ph.D. or other terminal degree: 90%. Student/faculty ratio: 9/1. Classes of fewer than 20 students: 63%; of 20 to 49 students: 27%; of 50 or more students: 11%. **Advanced Placement and International Baccalaureate credit:** AP tests may be used for: Credit and/or placement. Scores accepted: 4, 5. International Baccalaureate exams may be used for: Credit and/or placement. **Freshmen returning for sophomore year:** 96%. **Graduation rates:** Four-year: 72%; five-year: 86%; six-year: 88%. **Graduate study:** 24% of students pursue further study within one year. Fields in which graduates pursue further study: law, 4%; medicine, 2%.

COSTS AND FINANCIAL AID
Financial aid office: (213) 740-1111. **Expenses (2010-2011):** Tuition and fees 2010-2011: $41,022; room/board: $11,580. Estimated books and supplies: $1,500; transportation: $580; personal expenses: $896. **Financial aid:** Priority filing date for institution's financial aid form: February 2. In 2009-2010, 54% of undergraduates applied for financial aid. Of those, 40% were determined to have financial need; 96% had their need fully met. Average financial aid package (proportion receiving): $35,593 (40%). Average amount of gift aid, such as scholarships or grants (proportion receiving): $24,801 (36%). Average amount of self-help aid, such as work study or loans (proportion receiving): $7,556 (39%). Average need-based loan (excluding PLUS or other private loans): $5,617. Among students who received need-based aid, the average percentage of need met: 100%. Among students who received aid based on merit, the average award (and the proportion receiving): $18,179 (18%). The average athletic scholarship (and the proportion receiving): $42,030 (2%). Average amount of debt of borrowers graduating in 2009: $30,097. Proportion who borrowed: 45%.

CAMPUS LIFE AND EXTRACURRICULAR ACTIVITIES
Campus housing available (% using): coed dorms (17%), fraternity housing (4%), apartments for married students (1%), apartment for single students (52%), special housing for disabled students (1%), other housing options (21%). Students who live in college-owned, operated, or affiliated housing: 43%. **Clubs and organizations:** Number of student organizations: 676. Activities include: campus ministries, choral groups, concert band, dance, drama/theater, international student organization, jazz band, literary magazine, marching band, model UN, music ensembles, musical theater, opera, pep band, radio station, student government, student newspaper, student film society, symphony orchestra, television station, yearbook. Number of fraternities: 35; sororities: 25. Proportion of men in fraternities: 21%; of women in sororities: 21%. **Sports program (2009-2010):** Member of NCAA I. *Men's intercollegiate varsity sports:* baseball, basketball, football, golf, swimming, tennis, track and field (indoor), track and field (outdoor), volleyball, water polo. *Women's intercollegiate varsity sports:* basketball, crew (heavyweight), cross country, golf, crew (lightweight), soccer, swimming, tennis, track and field (indoor), track and field (outdoor), volleyball, water polo.

SERVICES AND FACILITIES

Basic services: nonremedial tutoring, placement service, health service, health insurance, other. **Counseling services:** minority student, career, military, personal, veteran student, academic, psychological, birth control, religious. **For learning-disabled students:** School does not offer a structured program with separate admission and additional fees. Total undergraduates in learning-disabled program or receiving services: 241. Services include: reading machines, tape recorders, videotaped classes, note-taking services, oral tests, learning center, readers, extended time for tests, tutors, texts on tape, typist/scribe, other testing accommodations, other. **Library:** Number of titles: 4,124,253; number of current serial subscriptions: 98,728. **Information technology resources:** Students are not required to lease or own a computer. Number of campus computers available to all students: 2,700. School has a wireless network. Approximate number of users that can be accommodated: 22,840. Proportion of college-owned housing units wired for high-speed internet access: 100%. **Campus safety:** Security services offered: 24-hour foot-and-vehicle patrols, late-night transport/escort service, 24-hour emergency telephones, lighted pathways/sidewalks, student patrols, controlled dormitory access (key, security card, etc).

TRANSFER AND INTERNATIONAL STUDENTS

Transfer students: May apply for admission for the following academic terms: Fall, Spring. Applicants do not need a minimum number of credits to apply. For fall 2009: Transfer applications received: 9,524. Transfer applicants offered admission: 2,465. Transfer applicants enrolled: 1,370. **International students:** Number of foreign undergraduates: 1672 (10% of student body). Number of countries represented: 87.

University of the Pacific

- **Address:** 3601 Pacific Avenue, Stockton, CA 95211
- **Website:** http://www.pacific.edu
- **Private**
- **Enrollment:** 3,384 full-time; 117 part-time

KEY STATS

✔ **U.S News College Ranking:** 99, National Universities
✔ **SAT Score (25th/75th percentile):** 1050-1320
✔ **Tuition:** 2010-2011: $34,100

Selectivity: More selective	**Room/board:** $11,142
Acceptance rate: 42%	**Average debt:** N/A
Student/faculty ratio: 12/1	**Proportion who borrowed:** N/A

UNDERGRADUATE STUDENT BODY STATS

2009-2010 enrollment: 3,384 full-time; 117 part-time. Men: 45%; women: 55%. **Ethnic makeup:** African American: 4%; American-Indian: 1%; Asian American: 35%; Hispanic: 12%; White: 45%; International: 4%.

ADMISSIONS FACTS AND FIGURES

Phone: (800) 959-2867. **Email:** admissions@pacific.edu. **Website:** http://www.pacific.edu. **Application deadlines for fall 2011:** Regular decision: January 15. Early decision: Not offered. Early action: Send application by: November 15; Decision sent by: January 15. Admission can be deferred. **Application fee:** $60. **To apply online, go to:** http://web.pacific.edu/x16059.xml. **Admissions requirements/recommendations:** High school units required (recommended): English: 4 (4); Mathematics: 3 (4); Science: 2 (3); Foreign language: 2 (2); Social studies: 2 (2); History: 1 (1); Academic electives: 1 (1); Total units: 16 (18). Tests: The college uses SAT or ACT scores in admissions decisions. Either SAT or ACT required. For admission to the fall 2011 entering class, the school will accept: ACT with or without writing accepted. Campus visit: Neither required nor recommended. Admissions interview: Neither required nor recommended. Off-campus interview: May be arranged. **Factors that count in admissions decisions:** *Academic:* Secondary school record: Very Important. Class rank: Considered. Letters of recommendation: Important. Standardized test scores: Important. Essay: Important. *Nonacademic:* Interview: Not Considered. Extracurricular activities: Important. Talent/ability: Considered. Character/personal qualities: Considered. Alumni/ae relationship: Considered. Geographical residence: Considered. State residency: Not Considered. Religious affiliation/commitment: Not Considered. Minority status: Not Considered. Volunteer work: Considered. Work experience: Considered. **Other schools with the greatest overlap in applicants:** California Polytechnic State University–San Luis Obispo; University of California–Berkeley; University of California–

Davis; University of California–Irvine; University of California–San Diego. **Admissions statistics for the fall 2009 entering class:** Total applicants: 14,970. Total accepted: 6,218. Freshmen enrolled: 894; 12% were from out of state. Overall acceptance rate: 42%. Non-early acceptance rate: 42%. **Size of waiting list:** 50 applicants; enrolled from waiting list: 30. **Credentials of fall 2009 freshmen:** 42% ranked in the top 10 percent of their high school class; 76% were in the top 25 percent; 95% were in the top half. (Proportion submitting class standing: 44%.) **Average high school grade point average:** 3.5. **First-year students who submitted SAT scores:** 93%. Scores (25/75 percentile): Critical Reading: 510-640, Math: 540-680, Combined: 1050-1320. **First-year students submitting ACT scores:** 37%. Scores (25/75 percentile): English: N/A, Math: N/A, Composite: 23-30.

ACADEMICS

Year founded: 1851. **Academic calendar:** Semester. **Degrees offered:** bachelor's, master's, doctorate. **Most popular majors:** 19% business administration and management, 15% biology/biological sciences, 11% engineering, 5% social sciences, 4% education. **Major fields of study:** biological and biomedical sciences; business, management, marketing, and related support services; communication, journalism, and related programs; computer and information sciences and support services; education; engineering; engineering technologies/technicians; English language and literature/letters; foreign languages, literatures, and linguistics; health professions and related clinical sciences; history; liberal arts and sciences studies, and humanities; mathematics and statistics; multi/interdisciplinary studies; natural resources and conservation; parks, recreation, leisure, and fitness studies; philosophy and religious studies; physical sciences; psychology; social sciences; visual and performing arts. **Areas of required coursework:** arts/fine arts, humanities, computer literacy, mathematics, English (including composition), philosophy, foreign languages, sciences (biological or physical), history, social science, other. **Pre-professional programs:** pre-dentistry, pre-pharmacy. **Special academic programs (% participation):** accelerated program (9%), cooperative (work-study plan) program (59%), double major (5%), English as a Second Language (ESL) (2%), exchange student program (domestic), honors program (16%), independent study (39%), internships (48%), liberal arts/career combination (6%), student-designed major (1%), study abroad (9%), teacher certificate program. **Teacher certification offered in:** special education, elementary, middle/junior high, secondary. **Cooperative education programs:** business, education, engineering, health professions. **Faculty and instruction (2009-2010):** Total instructional faculty: 440 full-time, 342 part-time (59% men; 41% women; 23% minorities). Full-time faculty with Ph.D. or other terminal degree: 92%. Student/faculty ratio: 12/1. Classes of fewer than 20 students: 63%; of 20 to 49 students: 33%; of 50 or more students: 4%. **Advanced Placement and International Baccalaureate credit:** AP tests may be used for: Credit only. Scores accepted: 3, 4, 5. International Baccalaureate exams may be used for: Credit only. **Freshmen returning for sophomore year:** 83%. **Graduation rates:** Four-year: 41%; five-year: 59%; six-year: 64%.

COSTS AND FINANCIAL AID

Financial aid office: (209) 946-2421. **Expenses (2010-2011):** Tuition and fees 2010-2011: $34,100; room/board: $11,142. Estimated books and supplies: $1,620; transportation: $729; personal expenses: $2,250. **Financial aid:** Priority filing date for institution's financial aid form: February 15. In 2009-2010, 78% of undergraduates applied for financial aid. Of those, 69% were determined to have financial need; 28% had their need fully met. Average financial aid package (proportion receiving): $29,320 (69%). Average amount of gift aid, such as scholarships or grants (proportion receiving): $22,044 (66%). Average amount of self-help aid, such as work study or loans (proportion receiving): $6,563 (65%). Average need-based loan (excluding PLUS or other private loans): $5,013. Among students who received aid based on merit, the average award (and the proportion receiving): $9,534 (14%). The average athletic scholarship (and the proportion receiving): $25,964 (3%).

CAMPUS LIFE AND EXTRACURRICULAR ACTIVITIES

Campus housing available (% using): coed dorms (58%), sorority housing (3%), fraternity housing (5%), apartments for married students (1%), apartment for single students (32%), special housing for disabled students (1%). Students who live in college-owned, operated, or affiliated housing: 56%. **Student employment:** During the 2009-2010 academic year, 21% of undergraduates worked on campus. Average per-year earnings: $1,242. **Clubs and organizations:** Number of student organizations: 100. Activities include: campus ministries, choral groups, concert band, dance, drama/theater, international student organization, jazz band, literary magazine, model UN, music ensembles, musical theater, opera, pep band, radio station, student government, student newspaper, student film society, symphony orchestra, yearbook. Number of fraternities: 8; sororities: 7. Proportion of men in fraternities: 17%; of women in sororities: 16%. Average proportion of students who stay on campus on weekends: 75%. **Sports program (2009-2010):** Member of NCAA I. *Men's intercollegiate varsity sports:* baseball, basketball, golf, swimming, tennis, volleyball, water polo. *Women's intercollegiate varsity sports:* basketball, cross country, field hockey, soccer, softball, swimming, tennis, volleyball, water polo.

SERVICES AND FACILITIES

Basic services: nonremedial tutoring, placement service, health service, health insurance. **Remedial assistance:** reading, math, writing. **Counseling services:** career, personal, veteran student, academic, psychological. **For learning-disabled students:** School does not offer a structured program with separate admission and additional fees. Total undergraduates in learning-disabled program or receiving services: 250. Services include: remedial math, remedial English, reading machines, remedial reading, note-taking services, learning center, extended time for tests, tutors, priority registration, texts on tape, typist/scribe, other testing accommodations, other. **Library:** Number of titles: 376,012; number of current serial subscriptions: 1,781. **Information technology resources:** Students are not required to lease or own a computer. Number of campus computers available to all students: 750. School has a wireless network. Approximate number of users that can be accommodated: 2,000. Proportion of college-owned housing units wired for high-speed internet access: 100%. **Campus safety:** Security services offered: 24-hour foot-and-vehicle patrols, late-night transport/escort service, 24-hour emergency telephones, lighted pathways/sidewalks, student patrols, controlled dormitory access (key, security card, etc).

TRANSFER AND INTERNATIONAL STUDENTS

Transfer students: May apply for admission for the following academic terms: Fall, Spring. Applicants need a minimum number of credits to apply. For fall 2009: Transfer applications received: 883. Transfer applicants offered admission: 422. Transfer applicants enrolled: 232. **International students:** Number of foreign undergraduates: 137 (4% of student body). Number of countries represented: 60. Minimum TOEFL score required: 475 (paper); 52 (computer). Average TOEFL score: 550 (paper).

Vanguard University of Southern California

- **Address:** 55 Fair Drive, Costa Mesa, CA 92626
- **Website:** http://www.vanguard.edu
- **Private; Religious affiliation:** Assemblies of God
- **Enrollment:** 1,293 full-time; 359 part-time

KEY STATS

✔ **U.S News College Ranking:** 9, Regional Colleges (West)
✔ **SAT Score (25th/75th percentile):** 860-1080
✔ **Tuition:** 2010-2011: $26,342

Selectivity: Selective	**Room/board:** $8,274
Acceptance rate: 79%	**Average debt:** $26,435
Student/faculty ratio: 15/1	**Proportion who borrowed:** 77%

UNDERGRADUATE STUDENT BODY STATS

2009-2010 enrollment: 1,293 full-time; 359 part-time. Men: 38%; women: 62%. **Ethnic makeup:** African American: 4%; American-Indian: 2%; Asian American: 4%; Hispanic: 17%; White: 71%; International: 1%. **Religious preference:** Roman Catholic: 4%; Protestant: 73%; No preference: 2%; Unknown: 1%; Assemblies of God: 20%.

ADMISSIONS FACTS AND FIGURES

Phone: (800) 722-6279. **Email:** admissions@vanguard.edu. **Website:** http://www.vanguard.edu. **Application deadlines for fall 2011:** Regular decision: Rolling; decision sent by March 1. Early decision: Not offered. Early action: Send application by: December 1; Decision sent by: January 15. Admission cannot be deferred. **Application fee:** $45. **To apply online, go to:** http://www.vanguard.edu/index.aspx?id=5737. **Admissions requirements/recommendations:** High school units required (recommended): English: (4); Mathematics: (2); Science: (2); Social studies: (3). Tests: The college uses SAT or ACT scores in admissions decisions. Either SAT or ACT required. For admission to the fall 2011 entering class, the school will accept: ACT with writing recommended. Campus visit: Recommended. Admissions interview: Recommended. Off-campus interview: Not available. **Factors that**

count in admissions decisions: *Academic:* Secondary school record: Very Important. Class rank: Not Considered. Letters of recommendation: Very Important. Standardized test scores: Important. Essay: Very Important. *Nonacademic:* Interview: Considered. Extracurricular activities: Considered. Talent/ability: Considered. Character/personal qualities: Very Important. Alumni/ae relationship: Not Considered. Geographical residence: Not Considered. State residency: Not Considered. Religious affiliation/commitment: Very Important. Minority status: Not Considered. Volunteer work: Considered. Work experience: Considered. **Other schools with the greatest overlap in applicants:** Azusa Pacific University; Biola University; Point Loma Nazarene University. **Admissions statistics for the fall 2009 entering class:** Total applicants: 787. Total accepted: 625. Freshmen enrolled: 268; 24% were from out of state. Overall acceptance rate: 79%. Non-early acceptance rate: 79%. **Credentials of fall 2009 freshmen:** 20% ranked in the top 10 percent of their high school class; 42% were in the top 25 percent; 79% were in the top half. (Proportion submitting class standing: 60%.) **Average high school grade point average:** 3.4. **First-year students who submitted SAT scores:** 83%. Scores (25/75 percentile): Critical Reading: 440-550, Math: 420-530, Combined: 860-1080. **First-year students submitting ACT scores:** 22%. Scores (25/75 percentile): English: N/A, Math: N/A, Composite: 18-23.

ACADEMICS

Year founded: 1920. **Academic calendar:** Semester. **Degrees offered:** certificate, bachelor's, master's. **Most popular majors:** 24% business, management, marketing, and related support services, 16% psychology, 11% communication, journalism, and related programs, 9% health professions and related clinical sciences, 9% social sciences. **Major fields of study:** biological and biomedical sciences; business, management, marketing, and related support services; communication, journalism, and related programs; computer and information sciences and support services; education; English language and literature/letters; foreign languages, literatures, and linguistics; health professions and related clinical sciences; history; legal professions and studies; liberal arts and sciences studies, and humanities; mathematics and statistics; multi/interdisciplinary studies; parks, recreation, leisure, and fitness studies; philosophy and religious studies; physical sciences; psychology; social sciences; theology and religious vocations; visual and performing arts. **Areas of required coursework:** arts/fine arts, humanities, computer literacy, mathematics, English (including composition), sciences (biological or physical), history, social science, other. **Pre-professional programs:** pre-law, pre-dentistry, pre-medicine, pre-theology, pre-veterinary science, pre-optometry, pre-pharmacy. **Special academic programs (% participation):** accelerated program (28%), cross-registration, distance learning, double major, independent study, internships, liberal arts/career combination, study abroad, teacher certificate program. **Teacher certification offered in:** early childhood, elementary, middle/junior high, secondary. **Reserve Officers Training Corps (ROTC):** Army ROTC: Offered at cooperating institution (California State University–Fullerton); Air Force ROTC: Offered at cooperating institution (Loyola Marymount University). **Faculty and instruction (2009-2010):** Total instructional faculty: 62 full-time, 113 part-time (49% men; 51% women; 17% minorities). Full-time faculty with Ph.D. or other terminal degree: 82%. Student/faculty ratio: 15/1. Classes of fewer than 20 students: 57%; of 20 to 49 students: 38%; of 50 or more students: 5%. **Advanced Placement and International Baccalaureate credit:** AP tests may be used for: Credit and/or placement. Scores accepted: 3. International Baccalaureate exams may be used for: Credit and/or placement. **Freshmen returning for sophomore year:** 72%. **Graduation rates:** Four-year: 45%; five-year: 53%; six-year: 52%.

COSTS AND FINANCIAL AID

Financial aid office: (714) 556-3610. **Expenses (2010-2011):** Tuition and fees 2010-2011: $26,342; room/board: $8,274. Estimated books and supplies: $1,620; transportation: $729; personal expenses: $2,250. **Financial aid:** Priority filing date for institution's financial aid form: March 2; deadline: March 2. In 2009-2010, 89% of undergraduates applied for financial aid. Of those, 79% were determined to have financial need; 15% had their need fully met. Average financial aid package (proportion receiving): $18,766 (79%). Average amount of gift aid, such as scholarships or grants (proportion receiving): $9,347 (64%). Average amount of self-help aid, such as work study or loans (proportion receiving): $5,208 (65%). Average need-based loan (excluding PLUS or other private loans): $4,681. Among students who received need-based aid, the average percentage of need met: 68%. Among students who received aid based on merit, the average award (and the proportion receiving): $8,187 (16%). The average athletic scholarship (and the proportion receiving): $12,558 (12%). Average amount of debt of borrowers graduating in 2009: $26,435. Proportion who borrowed: 77%.

CAMPUS LIFE AND EXTRACURRICULAR ACTIVITIES

Campus housing available (% using): coed dorms (10%), women's dorms (60%), men's dorms (30%), apartments for married students (0%), special housing for disabled students (0%). Students who live in college-owned, operated, or affiliated housing: 68%. **Student employment:** During the 2009-2010 academic year, 25% of undergraduates worked on campus. Average per-year earnings: $2,000. **Clubs and organizations:** Number of student organizations: 13. Activities include: campus ministries, choral groups, concert band, dance, drama/theater, international student organization, jazz band, literary magazine, music ensembles, musical theater, student government, student newspaper, yearbook. Number of fraternities: 0; sororities: 0. Average proportion of students who stay on campus on weekends: 60%. **Sports program (2009-2010):** Member of NAIA. *Men's intercollegiate varsity sports:* baseball, basketball, cross country, soccer, swimming, tennis, track and field (indoor), track and field (outdoor). *Women's intercollegiate varsity sports:* basketball, cross country, soccer, softball, swimming, tennis, track and field (indoor), track and field (outdoor), volleyball.

SERVICES AND FACILITIES

Basic services: nonremedial tutoring, placement service, health insurance, other. **Remedial assistance:** writing, study skills. **Counseling services:** minority student, career, personal, veteran student, academic, older student, psychological, religious. **For learning-disabled students:** School does not offer a structured program with separate admission and additional fees. Total undergraduates in learning-disabled program or receiving services: 36. Services include: untimed tests, note-taking services, oral tests, learning center, extended time for tests, tutors, priority seating, proofreading services, other testing accommodations, other. **Library:** Number of titles: 128,048; number of current serial subscriptions: 17,342. **Information technology resources:** Students are not required to lease or own a computer. Number of campus computers available to all students: 100. School has a wireless network. Approximate number of users that can be accommodated: 2,500. Proportion of college-owned housing units wired for high-speed internet access: 100%. **Campus safety:** Security services offered: 24-hour foot-and-vehicle patrols, late-night transport/escort service, lighted pathways/sidewalks, student patrols, controlled dormitory access (key, security card, etc).

TRANSFER AND INTERNATIONAL STUDENTS

Transfer students: May apply for admission for the following academic terms: Fall, Spring. Applicants do not need a minimum number of credits to apply. For fall 2009: Transfer applications received: 272. Transfer applicants offered admission: 198. Transfer applicants enrolled: 118. **International students:** Number of foreign undergraduates: 18 (1% of student body). Number of countries represented: 16. Minimum TOEFL score required: 550 (paper); 213 (computer).

Westmont College

- **Address:** 955 La Paz Road, Santa Barbara, CA 93108
- **Website:** http://www.westmont.edu
- **Private; Religious affiliation:** Christian nondenominational
- **Enrollment:** 1,293 full-time; 11 part-time

KEY STATS

✔ **U.S News College Ranking:** 99, National Liberal Arts Colleges
✔ **SAT Score (25th/75th percentile):** 1050-1300
✔ **Tuition:** 2010-2011: $34,460

Selectivity: More selective	**Room/board:** $10,960
Acceptance rate: 80%	**Average debt:** $25,565
Student/faculty ratio: 12/1	**Proportion who borrowed:** 54%

UNDERGRADUATE STUDENT BODY STATS

2009-2010 enrollment: 1,293 full-time; 11 part-time. Men: 38%; women: 63%. **Ethnic makeup:** African American: 3%; American-Indian: 2%; Asian American: 9%; Hispanic: 11%; White: 74%; International: 1%. **Religious preference:** Roman Catholic: 5%; Protestant: 90%; Unknown: 5%.

ADMISSIONS FACTS AND FIGURES

Phone: (800) 777-9011. **Email:** admissions@westmont.edu. **Website:** http://www.westmont.edu. **Application deadlines for fall 2011:** Regular decision: Rolling; decision sent by April 1. Early decision: Not offered. Early action: Send application by: November 1; Decision sent by: December 20.

Admission cannot be deferred. **Application fee:** $35. **To apply online, go to:** http://www.westmont.edu/admissions/apply.html. **Admissions requirements/recommendations:** High school units required (recommended): English: 4; Mathematics: 3; Science: 3; Foreign language: 2 (3); Social studies: 1; History: 1; Academic electives: (4); Total units: 16. Tests: The college uses SAT or ACT scores in admissions decisions. Either SAT or ACT required. For admission to the fall 2011 entering class, the school will accept: ACT with writing required. Campus visit: Recommended. Admissions interview: Recommended. Off-campus interview: May be arranged. **Factors that count in admissions decisions:** *Academic:* Secondary school record: Important. Class rank: Considered. Letters of recommendation: Important. Standardized test scores: Very Important. Essay: Important. *Nonacademic:* Interview: Important. Extracurricular activities: Important. Talent/ability: Important. Character/personal qualities: Very Important. Alumni/ae relationship: Considered. Geographical residence: Considered. State residency: Not Considered. Religious affiliation/commitment: Important. Minority status: Considered. Volunteer work: Considered. Work experience: Considered. **Other schools with the greatest overlap in applicants:** Azusa Pacific University; Biola University; Pepperdine University; Point Loma Nazarene University; University of California–Santa Barbara. **Admissions statistics for the fall 2009 entering class:** Total applicants: 1,817. Total accepted: 1,455. Freshmen enrolled: 320; 33% were from out of state. Accepted through early-decision or early-action plans: 62%. Overall acceptance rate: 80%. Non-early acceptance rate: 70%. **Size of waiting list:** 83 applicants; enrolled from waiting list: 57. **Credentials of fall 2009 freshmen:** 38% ranked in the top 10 percent of their high school class; 66% were in the top 25 percent; 90% were in the top half. (Proportion submitting class standing: 56%.) **Average high school grade point average:** 3.8. **First-year students who submitted SAT scores:** 87%. Scores (25/75 percentile): Critical Reading: 520-650, Math: 530-650, Combined: 1050-1300. **First-year students submitting ACT scores:** 51%. Scores (25/75 percentile): English: 21-28, Math: 23-30, Composite: 23-29.

ACADEMICS

Year founded: 1937. **Academic calendar:** Semester. **Degrees offered:** bachelor's, post-bachelor's certificate. **Most popular majors:** 16% business/managerial economics, 13% English language and literature, 10% biology/biological sciences, 10% communication studies/speech communication and rhetoric, 10% kinesiology and exercise science. **Major fields of study:** area, ethnic, cultural, and gender studies; biological and biomedical sciences; communication, journalism, and related programs; computer and information sciences and support services; engineering; English language and literature/letters; foreign languages, literatures, and linguistics; history; liberal arts and sciences studies, and humanities; mathematics and statistics; parks, recreation, leisure, and fitness studies; philosophy and religious studies; physical sciences; psychology; social sciences; visual and performing arts. **Areas of required coursework:** arts/fine arts, humanities, mathematics, English (including composition), philosophy, foreign languages, sciences (biological or physical), history, social science, other. **Preprofessional programs:** pre-law, pre-dentistry, pre-medicine, pre-theology, pre-veterinary science. **Special academic programs (% participation):** accelerated program (5%), cross-registration (1%), double major (10%), exchange student program (domestic) (25%), honors program (30%), independent study (60%), internships (65%), liberal arts/career combination (1%), student-designed major (1%), study abroad (50%), teacher certificate program (5%). **Teacher certification offered in:** elementary, secondary, bilingual/bicultural. **Reserve Officers Training Corps (ROTC):** Army ROTC: Offered at cooperating institution (University of California–Santa Barbara); Air Force ROTC: Offered at cooperating institution (Loyola Marymount University). **Faculty and instruction (2009-2010):** Total instructional faculty: 93 full-time, 40 part-time (60% men; 40% women; 14% minorities). Full-time faculty with Ph.D. or other terminal degree: 91%. Student/faculty ratio: 12/1. Classes of fewer than 20 students: 61%; of 20 to 49 students: 35%; of 50 or more students: 4%. **Advanced Placement and International Baccalaureate credit:** AP tests may be used for: Credit and/or placement. Scores accepted: 4, 5. International Baccalaureate exams may be used for: Credit and/or placement. **Freshmen returning for sophomore year:** 87%. **Graduation rates:** Four-year: 75%; five-year: 79%; six-year: 80%. **Graduate study:** 30% of students pursue further study immediately upon graduation; 60% within five years. Fields in which graduates pursue further study: Master of Business Administration (MBA), 10%; law, 3%; medicine, 5%; dentistry, 1%; engineering, 2%; theology (or the seminary), 10%; education, 25%; arts and sciences, 40%; veterinary medicine, 1%.

COSTS AND FINANCIAL AID

Financial aid office: (805) 565-6063. **Expenses (2010-2011):** Tuition and fees 2010-2011: $34,460; room/board: $10,960. Estimated books and supplies: $1,610; transportation: $730; personal expenses: $2,230. **Financial aid:** Priority filing date for institution's financial aid form: March 1. In 2009-2010, 70% of undergraduates applied for financial aid. Of those, 62% were determined to have financial need; 10% had their need fully met. Average financial aid package (proportion receiving): $24,129 (62%). Average amount of gift aid, such as scholarships or grants (proportion receiving): $19,229 (62%). Average amount of self-help aid, such as work study or loans (proportion receiving): $6,037 (51%). Average need-based loan (excluding PLUS or other private loans): $5,483. Among students who received need-based aid, the average percentage of need met: 70%. Among students who received aid based on merit, the average award (and the proportion receiving): $10,128 (27%). The average athletic scholarship (and the proportion receiving): $11,512 (4%). Average amount of debt of borrowers graduating in 2009: $25,565. Proportion who borrowed: 54%.

CAMPUS LIFE AND EXTRACURRICULAR ACTIVITIES

Campus housing available (% using): coed dorms (93%), apartments for married students (1%), apartment for single students (5%), special housing for disabled students (1%). Students who live in college-owned, operated, or affiliated housing: 83%. **Student employment:** During the 2009-2010 academic year, 35% of undergraduates worked on campus. Average per-year earnings: $2,000. **Clubs and organizations:** Number of student organizations: 0. Activities include: campus ministries, choral groups, dance, drama/theater, international student organization, jazz band, literary magazine, model UN, music ensembles, musical theater, pep band, radio station, student government, student newspaper, student film society, symphony orchestra, yearbook. Number of fraternities: 0; sororities: 0. Average proportion of students who stay on campus on weekends: 50%. **Sports program (2009-2010):** Member of NAIA. *Men's intercollegiate varsity sports:* baseball, basketball, cross country, soccer, tennis, track and field (outdoor). *Women's intercollegiate varsity sports:* basketball, cross country, soccer, tennis, track and field (outdoor), volleyball.

SERVICES AND FACILITIES

Basic services: nonremedial tutoring, placement service, health service, health insurance. **Remedial assistance:** math, writing, study skills. **Counseling services:** minority student, career, personal, academic, psychological, birth control, religious. **For learning-disabled students:** School does not offer a structured program with separate admission and additional fees. Total undergraduates in learning-disabled program or receiving services: 57. Services include: tape recorders, untimed tests, note-taking services, oral tests, readers, extended time for tests, tutors, priority registration, substitution of courses, texts on tape, typist/scribe, exams on tape or computer, other testing accommodations, other. **Library:** Number of titles: 150,385; number of current serial subscriptions: 3,100. **Information technology resources:** Students are not required to lease or own a computer. Number of campus computers available to all students: 90. School has a wireless network. Approximate number of users that can be accommodated: 2,500. Proportion of college-owned housing units wired for high-speed internet access: 100%. **Campus safety:** Security services offered: 24-hour foot-and-vehicle patrols, late-night transport/escort service, 24-hour emergency telephones, lighted pathways/sidewalks, controlled dormitory access (key, security card, etc).

TRANSFER AND INTERNATIONAL STUDENTS

Transfer students: May apply for admission for the following academic terms: Fall, Spring. Applicants need a minimum number of credits to apply. For fall 2009: Transfer applications received: 243. Transfer applicants offered admission: 158. Transfer applicants enrolled: 56. **International students:** Number of foreign undergraduates: 10 (1% of student body). Number of countries represented: 8. Minimum TOEFL score required: 560 (paper); 220 (computer). Average TOEFL score: 600 (paper).

Whittier College

- **Address:** 13406 Philadelphia Street, PO Box 634, Whittier, CA 90608
- **Website:** http://www.whittier.edu
- **Private**
- **Enrollment:** 1,354 full-time; 17 part-time

KEY STATS

✔ **U.S News College Ranking:** 137, National Liberal Arts Colleges
✔ **SAT Score (25th/75th percentile):** 940-1170
✔ **Tuition:** 2010-2011: $35,442

Selectivity: Selective	**Room/board:** $10,026
Acceptance rate: 72%	**Average debt:** $40,220
Student/faculty ratio: 13/1	**Proportion who borrowed:** 78%

UNDERGRADUATE STUDENT BODY STATS

2009-2010 enrollment: 1,354 full-time; 17 part-time. Men: 47%; women: 53%. **Ethnic makeup:** African American: 6%; American-Indian: 1%; Asian American: 9%; Hispanic: 30%; White: 54%; International: 2%.

ADMISSIONS FACTS AND FIGURES

Phone: (562) 907-4238. **Email:** admission@whittier.edu. **Website:** http://www.whittier.edu. **Application deadlines for fall 2011:** Regular decision: Rolling. Early decision: Not offered. Early action: Send application by: December 1; Decision sent by: December 30. Admission can be deferred. **Application fee:** $50. **To apply online, go to:** http://www.whittier.edu/AdmissionAndAid/Applying/default.aspx. **Admissions requirements/recommendations:** High school units required (recommended): English: 3 (4); Mathematics: 2 (3); Science: 1 (2); Foreign language: 2 (3); Social studies: 1 (2); Total units: 10 (14). Tests: The college uses SAT or ACT scores in admissions decisions. Either SAT or ACT required. For admission to the fall 2011 entering class, the school will accept: ACT with writing required. Campus visit: Recommended. Admissions interview: Recommended. Off-campus interview: May be arranged. **Factors that count in admissions decisions:** *Academic:* Secondary school record: Very Important. Class rank: Considered. Letters of recommendation: Important. Standardized test scores: Important. Essay: Very Important. *Nonacademic:* Interview: Important. Extracurricular activities: Important. Talent/ability: Important. Character/personal qualities: Important. Alumni/ae relationship: Considered. Geographical residence: Considered. State residency: Considered. Religious affiliation/commitment: Not Considered. Minority status: Considered. Volunteer work: Important. Work experience: Considered. **Other schools with the greatest overlap in applicants:** Chapman University; Loyola Marymount University; Occidental College; Pitzer College; University of Redlands. **Admissions statistics for the fall 2009 entering class:** Total applicants: 2,263. Total accepted: 1,626. Freshmen enrolled: 358; 26% were from out of state. Overall acceptance rate: 72%. Non-early acceptance rate: 72%. **Credentials of fall 2009 freshmen:** 30% ranked in the top 10 percent of their high school class; 42% were in the top 25 percent; 82% were in the top half. (Proportion submitting class standing: 54%.) **Average high school grade point average:** 3.4. **First-year students who submitted SAT scores:** 89%. Scores (25/75 percentile): Critical Reading: 470-580, Math: 470-590, Combined: 940-1170. **First-year students submitting ACT scores:** 34%. Scores (25/75 percentile): English: N/A, Math: N/A, Composite: 19-25.

ACADEMICS

Year founded: 1887. **Academic calendar:** 4-1-4. **Degrees offered:** bachelor's, master's. **Most popular majors:** 25% social sciences, 17% business, management, marketing, and related support services, 9% parks, recreation, leisure, and fitness studies, 8% English language and literature/letters, 7% biological and biomedical sciences. **Major fields of study:** area, ethnic, cultural, and gender studies; biological and biomedical sciences; business, management, marketing, and related support services; education; English language and literature/letters; foreign languages, literatures, and linguistics; history; liberal arts and sciences studies, and humanities; mathematics and statistics; natural resources and conservation; philosophy and religious studies; physical sciences; psychology; public administration and social service professions; social sciences; visual and performing arts. **Areas of required coursework:** arts/fine arts, humanities, mathematics, English (including composition), sciences (biological or physical), history, social science. **Pre-professional programs:** pre-law, pre-dentistry, pre-medicine, pre-veterinary science, pre-optometry, pre-pharmacy. **Special academic programs (% participation):** double major (7.7%), independent study (20%), internships (30%), liberal arts/career combination (50%), student-designed major (10%), study abroad (20%), teacher certificate program (15%). **Teacher certification offered in:** elementary, middle/junior high, secondary. **Reserve Officers Training Corps (ROTC):** Army ROTC: Offered at cooperating institution (California State University–Fullerton). **Faculty and instruction (2009-2010):** Total instructional faculty: 96 full-time, 34 part-time (51% men; 49% women; 28% minorities). Full-time faculty with Ph.D. or other terminal degree: 99%. Student/faculty ratio: 13/1. Classes of fewer than 20 students: 59%; of 20 to 49 students: 40%; of 50 or more students: 1%. **Advanced Placement and International Baccalaureate credit:** AP tests may be used for: Credit and/or placement. Scores accepted: 4, 5. International Baccalaureate exams may be used for: Credit and/or placement. **Freshmen returning for sophomore year:** 78%. **Graduation rates:** Four-year: 55%; five-year: 61%; six-year: 61%. **Graduate study:** 39% of students pursue further study immediately upon graduation; 52% within one year; 4% within five years. Fields in which graduates pursue further study: Master of Business Administration (MBA), 3%; law, 5%; medicine, 5%; education, 19%; arts and sciences, 38%.

COSTS AND FINANCIAL AID

Financial aid office: (562) 907-4285. **Expenses (2010-2011):** Tuition and fees 2010-2011: $35,442; room/board: $10,026. Estimated books and supplies: $1,638; transportation: $792; personal expenses: $2,696. **Financial aid:** Priority filing date for institution's financial aid form: February 1; deadline: June 30. In 2009-2010, 99% of undergraduates applied for financial aid. Of those, 72% were determined to have financial need; 26% had their need fully met. Average financial aid package (proportion receiving): $33,257 (72%). Average amount of gift aid, such as scholarships or grants (proportion receiving): $12,980 (58%). Average amount of self-help aid, such as work study or loans (proportion receiving): $12,033 (70%). Average need-based loan (excluding PLUS or other private loans): $10,564. Among students who received need-based aid, the average percentage of need met: 87%. Among students who received aid based on merit, the average award (and the proportion receiving): $14,448 (21%). Average amount of debt of borrowers graduating in 2009: $40,220. Proportion who borrowed: 78%.

CAMPUS LIFE AND EXTRACURRICULAR ACTIVITIES

Campus housing available (% using): coed dorms (100%), special housing for international students. Students who live in college-owned, operated, or affiliated housing: 60%. **Student employment:** During the 2009-2010 academic year, 9% of undergraduates worked on campus. Average per-year earnings: $1,389. **Clubs and organizations:** Number of student organizations: 70. Activities include: campus ministries, choral groups, dance, drama/theater, international student organization, jazz band, literary magazine, model UN, music ensembles, musical theater, radio station, student government, student newspaper, student film society, symphony orchestra, yearbook. Number of fraternities: 4; sororities: 5. Proportion of men in fraternities: 14%; of women in sororities: 20%. Average proportion of students who stay on campus on weekends: 85%. **Sports program (2009-2010):** Member of NCAA III. *Men's intercollegiate varsity sports:* baseball, basketball, cross country, football, golf, lacrosse, soccer, swimming, tennis, track and field (outdoor), water polo. *Women's intercollegiate varsity sports:* basketball, cross country, lacrosse, soccer, softball, swimming, tennis, track and field (outdoor), volleyball, water polo.

SERVICES AND FACILITIES

Basic services: nonremedial tutoring, health service, health insurance. **Remedial assistance:** writing, study skills, other. **Counseling services:** minority student, career, personal, academic, psychological, birth control. **For learning-disabled students:** School does not offer a structured program with separate admission and additional fees. Services include: reading machines, tape recorders, note-taking services, learning center, extended time for tests, tutors, priority registration, texts on tape, exams on tape or computer, other testing accommodations, waiver of foreign language degree requirement. **Library:** Number of titles: 305,746; number of current serial subscriptions: 12,586. **Information technology resources:** Students are not required to lease or own a computer. Number of campus computers available to all students: 325. School has a wireless network. Approximate number of users that can be accommodated: 2,750. Proportion of college-owned housing units wired for high-speed internet access: 100%. **Campus safety:** Security services offered: 24-hour foot-and-vehicle patrols, late-night transport/escort service, 24-hour emergency telephones, lighted pathways/sidewalks, student patrols, controlled dormitory access (key, security card, etc).

TRANSFER AND INTERNATIONAL STUDENTS

Transfer students: May apply for admission for the following academic terms: Fall, Spring. Applicants do not need a minimum number of credits to apply. For fall 2009: Transfer applications received: 268. Transfer applicants offered admission: 170. Transfer applicants enrolled: 95. **International students:** Number of foreign undergraduates: 24 (2% of student body). Number of countries represented: 23. Minimum TOEFL score required: 550 (paper); 213 (computer). Average TOEFL score: 635 (paper).

Woodbury University

- **Address:** 7500 Glenoaks Boulevard, Burbank, CA 91510
- **Website:** http://www.woodbury.edu
- **Private**
- **Enrollment:** 1,079 full-time; 222 part-time

KEY STATS

✔ **U.S News College Ranking:** 68, Regional Universities (West)
✔ **SAT Score (25th/75th percentile):** 709-1050
✔ **Tuition:** 2010-2011: $28,025

Selectivity: Less selective	Room/board: $8,978
Acceptance rate: 41%	Average debt: $47,059
Student/faculty ratio: 11/1	Proportion who borrowed: 91%

UNDERGRADUATE STUDENT BODY STATS

2009-2010 enrollment: 1,079 full-time; 222 part-time. Men: 48%; women: 52%. **Ethnic makeup:** African American: 5%; Asian American: 10%; Hispanic: 33%; White: 42%; International: 10%.

ADMISSIONS FACTS AND FIGURES

Phone: (818) 767-0888. **Email:** info@woodbury.edu. **Website:** http://www.woodbury.edu. **Application deadlines for fall 2011:** Regular decision: Rolling. Early decision: Not offered. Early action: Not offered. Admission can be deferred. **Application fee:** $50. **To apply online, go to:** https://woodbury.myuniversityapp.net/apply/authentication.do?cmd=login-check. **Admissions requirements/recommendations:** High school units required (recommended): English: (4); Mathematics: (3); Science: (2); Foreign language: (2); Social studies: (1); History: (2); Total units: (16). Tests: The college uses SAT or ACT scores in admissions decisions. Either SAT or ACT required. For admission to the fall 2011 entering class, the school will accept: ACT with or without writing accepted. Campus visit: Recommended. Admissions interview: Recommended. Off-campus interview: May be arranged. **Factors that count in admissions decisions:** *Academic:* Secondary school record: Very Important. Class rank: Considered. Letters of recommendation: Considered. Standardized test scores: Very Important. Essay: Considered. *Nonacademic:* Interview: Considered. Extracurricular activities: Considered. Talent/ability: Not Considered. Character/personal qualities: Not Considered. Alumni/ae relationship: Considered. Geographical residence: Not Considered. State residency: Not Considered. Religious affiliation/commitment: Not Considered. Minority status: Not Considered. Volunteer work: Considered. Work experience: Considered. **Other schools with the greatest overlap in applicants:** Mount St. Mary's College; Pacific Lutheran University; Pepperdine University; University of California–Los Angeles. **Admissions statistics for the fall 2009 entering class:** Total applicants: 514. Total accepted: 211. Freshmen enrolled: 128; Overall acceptance rate: 41%. **Size of waiting list:** 0 applicants; enrolled from waiting list: 0. **First-year students who submitted SAT scores:** 62%. Scores (25/75 percentile): Critical Reading: 309-520, Math: 400-530, Combined: 709-1050. **First-year students submitting ACT scores:** 10%. Scores (25/75 percentile): English: 17-24, Math: 15-23, Composite: 16-23.

ACADEMICS

Year founded: 1884. **Academic calendar:** Semester. **Degrees offered:** bachelor's, master's. **Most popular majors:** 32% business administration and management, 26% architecture (B.Arch., B.A./B.S., M.Arch., M.A./M.S., Ph.D.), 18% organizational behavior studies, 6% fashion/apparel design, 4% commercial and advertising art. **Major fields of study:** architecture and related services; business, management, marketing, and related support services; communication, journalism, and related programs; computer and information sciences and support services; history; psychology; visual and performing arts. **Areas of required coursework:** arts/fine arts, humanities, computer literacy, mathematics, English (including composition), sciences (biological or physical), social science. **Special academic programs:** accelerated program, double major, dual enrollment, English as a Second Language (ESL), exchange student program (domestic), independent study, internships, liberal arts/career combination, student-designed major, study abroad, weekend college. **Faculty and instruction (2009-2010):** Total instructional faculty: 59 full-time, 221 part-time (59% men; 41% women). Full-time faculty with Ph.D. or other terminal degree: 83%. Student/faculty ratio: 11/1. Classes of fewer than 20 students: 80%; of 20 to 49 students: 20%; of 50 or more students: 0%. **Advanced Placement and International Baccalaureate credit:** AP tests may be used for: Credit and/or placement. Scores accepted: 3. International Baccalaureate exams may be used for: Credit and/or placement. **Freshmen returning for sophomore year:** 78%. **Graduation rates:** Four-year: 26%; five-year: 40%; six-year: 50%. **Graduate study:** Fields in which graduates pursue further study: Master of Business Administration (MBA), 71%; engineering, 22%; arts and sciences, 7%.

COSTS AND FINANCIAL AID
Financial aid office: (818) 767-0888. **Expenses (2010-2011):** Tuition and fees 2010-2011: $28,025; room/board: $8,978. Estimated books and supplies: $1,638; transportation: $795; personal expenses: $2,250. **Financial aid:** Priority filing date for institution's financial aid form: March 2. In 2009-2010, 92% of undergraduates applied for financial aid. Of those, 88% were determined to have financial need; 3% had their need fully met. Average financial aid package (proportion receiving): $19,622 (88%). Average amount of gift aid, such as scholarships or grants (proportion receiving): $15,051 (86%). Average amount of self-help aid, such as work study or loans (proportion receiving): $5,234 (83%). Average need-based loan (excluding PLUS or other private loans): $4,988. Among students who received need-based aid, the average percentage of need met: 55%. Among students who received aid based on merit, the average award (and the proportion receiving): $6,549 (9%). The average athletic scholarship (and the proportion receiving): $0 (0%). Average amount of debt of borrowers graduating in 2009: $47,059. Proportion who borrowed: 91%.

CAMPUS LIFE AND EXTRACURRICULAR ACTIVITIES
Campus housing available (% using): coed dorms (94%), apartment for single students (6%). Students who live in college-owned, operated, or affili-

ated housing: 16%. **Clubs and organizations:** Number of student organizations: 22. Activities include: student government. Number of fraternities: 2; sororities: 3. Proportion of men in fraternities: 3%; of women in sororities: 2%.

SERVICES AND FACILITIES
Basic services: nonremedial tutoring, placement service, health service, health insurance. **Remedial assistance:** reading, math, writing, study skills. **Counseling services:** career, academic, psychological. **For learning-disabled students:** School does not offer a structured program with separate admission and additional fees. Total undergraduates in learning-disabled program or receiving services: 15. Services include: untimed tests, note-taking services, learning center, extended time for tests, tutors, priority seating, other testing accommodations. **Library:** Number of titles: 68,515; number of current serial subscriptions: 278. **Information technology resources:** Students are required to lease or own a computer. Number of campus computers available to all students: 310. School has a wireless network. Approximate number of users that can be accommodated: 500. Proportion of college-owned housing units wired for high-speed internet access: 100%. **Campus safety:** Security services offered: 24-hour foot-and-vehicle patrols, late-night transport/escort service, 24-hour emergency telephones, lighted pathways/sidewalks, controlled dormitory access (key, security card, etc).

TRANSFER AND INTERNATIONAL STUDENTS
Transfer students: May apply for admission for the following academic terms: Fall, Spring, Summer. Applicants do not need a minimum number of credits to apply. For fall 2009: Transfer applications received: 251. Transfer applicants offered admission: 202. Transfer applicants enrolled: 188. **International students:** Number of foreign undergraduates: 131 (10% of student body). Number of countries represented: 18. Minimum TOEFL score required: 500 (paper); 61 (computer).

Colorado

Adams State College

- **Address:** 208 Edgemont Boulevard, Alamosa, CO 81102
- **Website:** http://www.adams.edu
- **Public**
- **Enrollment:** N/A

....

KEY STATS
✔ **U.S News College Ranking:** second tier, Regional Universities (West)
✔ **SAT or ACT Score (25th/75th percentile):** N/A
✔ **Tuition:** 2009-2010: $4,454 in state, $13,598 out of state

Selectivity: Less selective	**Room/board:** $7,220
Acceptance rate: N/A	**Average debt:** N/A
Student/faculty ratio: N/A	**Proportion who borrowed:** N/A

Colorado Christian University

- **Address:** 180 S. Garrison Street, Lakewood, CO 80226
- **Website:** http://www.ccu.edu
- **Private; Religious affiliation:** Christian nondenominational
- **Enrollment:** N/A

....

KEY STATS
✔ **U.S News College Ranking:** 80, Regional Universities (West)
✔ **SAT Score (25th/75th percentile):** 930-1150
✔ **Tuition:** 2010-2011: $22,040

Selectivity: Selective	**Room/board:** $9,120
Acceptance rate: 42%	**Average debt:** N/A
Student/faculty ratio: N/A	**Proportion who borrowed:** N/A

Colorado College

- **Address:** 14 E. Cache La Poudre Street, Colorado Springs, CO 80903
- **Website:** http://www.ColoradoCollege.edu
- **Private**
- **Enrollment:** 1,966 full-time; 34 part-time

....

KEY STATS
✔ **U.S News College Ranking:** 26, National Liberal Arts Colleges
✔ **SAT Score (25th/75th percentile):** 1240-1420
✔ **Tuition:** 2010-2011: $38,748

Selectivity: More selective	**Room/board:** $9,416
Acceptance rate: 32%	**Average debt:** $16,172
Student/faculty ratio: 10/1	**Proportion who borrowed:** 35%

UNDERGRADUATE STUDENT BODY STATS
2009-2010 enrollment: 1,966 full-time; 34 part-time. Men: 47%; women: 53%. **Ethnic makeup:** African American: 2%; American-Indian: 1%; Asian American: 6%; Hispanic: 7%; White: 81%; International: 4%.

ADMISSIONS FACTS AND FIGURES
Phone: (719) 389-6344. **Email:** admission@ColoradoCollege.edu. **Website:** http://www.ColoradoCollege.edu. **Application deadlines for fall 2011:** Regular decision: January 15; decision sent by April 1. Early decision: Send application by: November 15; Decision sent by: December 20. Early action: Send application by: November 15; Decision sent by: January 15. Admission can be deferred. **Application fee:** $50. **To apply online, go to:** http://www.colora-docollege.edu/admission/firstyear/index.asp. **Admissions requirements/recommendations:** High school units required (recommended): English: 4 (4); Total units: 16 (20). Tests: The college uses SAT or ACT scores in admis-

sions decisions. Either SAT or ACT required. For admission to the fall 2011 entering class, the school will accept: ACT with or without writing accepted. Campus visit: Recommended. Admissions interview: Neither required nor recommended. Off-campus interview: May be arranged. **Factors that count in admissions decisions:** *Academic:* Secondary school record: Very Important. Class rank: Important. Letters of recommendation: Important. Standardized test scores: Important. Essay: Important. *Nonacademic:* Interview: Important. Extracurricular activities: Important. Talent/ability: Considered. Character/personal qualities: Considered. Alumni/ae relationship: Considered. Geographical residence: Not Considered. State residency: Not Considered. Religious affiliation/commitment: Considered. Minority status: Considered. Volunteer work: Considered. Work experience: Considered. **Admissions statistics for the fall 2009 entering class:** Total applicants: 4,941. Total accepted: 1,600. Freshmen enrolled: 526; 81% were from out of state. Accepted through early-decision or early-action plans: 63%. Overall acceptance rate: 32%. Early-decision acceptance rate: 43%. Non-early acceptance rate: 26%. **Size of waiting list:** 775 applicants; enrolled from waiting list: 24. **Credentials of fall 2009 freshmen:** 63% ranked in the top 10 percent of their high school class; 87% were in the top 25 percent; 99% were in the top half. (Proportion submitting class standing: 37%.) **First-year students who submitted SAT scores:** 56%. Scores (25/75 percentile): Critical Reading: 620-710, Math: 620-710, Combined: 1240-1420. **First-year students submitting ACT scores:** 44%. Scores (25/75 percentile): English: 28-33, Math: 26-31, Composite: 28-31.

ACADEMICS
Year founded: 1874. **Academic calendar:** Other. **Degrees offered:** bachelor's, master's. **Most popular majors:** 11% biology/biological sciences, 8% political science and government, 6% economics, 6% sociology, 5% history. **Major fields of study:** area, ethnic, cultural, and gender studies; biological and biomedical sciences; computer and information sciences and support services; English language and literature/letters; foreign languages, literatures, and linguistics; history; liberal arts and sciences studies, and humanities; mathematics and statistics; multi/interdisciplinary studies; natural resources and conservation; parks, recreation, leisure, and fitness studies; philosophy and religious studies; physical sciences; psychology; social sciences; visual and performing arts. **Areas of required coursework:** humanities, foreign languages, sciences (biological or physical), social science. **Pre-professional programs:** pre-law, pre-dentistry, pre-medicine, pre-veterinary science, other. **Special academic programs:** double major, English as a Second Language (ESL), independent study, internships, liberal arts/career combination, student-designed major, study abroad. **Cooperative education programs:** engineering, other. **Reserve Officers Training Corps (ROTC):** Army ROTC: Offered at cooperating institution (University of Colorado–Colorado Springs). **Faculty and instruction (2009-2010):** Total instructional faculty: 164 full-time, 33 part-time (; 17% minorities). Full-time faculty with Ph.D. or other terminal degree: 98%. Student/faculty ratio: 10/1. Classes of fewer than 20 students: 60%; of 20 to 49 students: 40%; of 50 or more students: 0%. **Advanced Placement and International Baccalaureate credit:** AP tests may be used for: Placement only. Scores accepted: 3, 4, 5. International Baccalaureate exams may be used for: Credit and/or placement. **Freshmen returning for sophomore year:** 95%. **Graduation rates:** Four-year: 78%; five-year: 83%; six-year: 85%.

COSTS AND FINANCIAL AID
Financial aid office: (719) 389-6651. **Expenses (2010-2011):** Tuition and fees 2010-2011: $38,748; room/board: $9,416. Estimated books and supplies: $1,116 personal expenses: $920. **Financial aid:** Priority filing date for institution's financial aid form: February 15; deadline: February 15. In 2009-2010, 44% of undergraduates applied for financial aid. Of those, 37% were determined to have financial need; 48% had their need fully met. Average financial aid package (proportion receiving): $30,203 (37%). Average amount of gift aid, such as scholarships or grants (proportion receiving): $28,207 (36%). Average amount of self-help aid, such as work study or loans (proportion receiving): $4,439 (24%). Average need-based loan (excluding PLUS or other private loans): $3,284. Among students who received need-based aid, the average percentage of need met: 92%. Among students who received aid based on merit, the average award (and the proportion receiv-

ing): $17,773 (10%). The average athletic scholarship (and the proportion receiving): $31,471 (2%). Average amount of debt of borrowers graduating in 2009: $16,172. Proportion who borrowed: 35%.

CAMPUS LIFE AND EXTRACURRICULAR ACTIVITIES

Campus housing available: coed dorms, women's dorms, men's dorms, fraternity housing, apartment for single students, special housing for disabled students, other housing options. Students who live in college-owned, operated, or affiliated housing: 76%. **Clubs and organizations:** Number of student organizations: 133. Activities include: campus ministries, choral groups, concert band, dance, drama/theater, international student organization, jazz band, literary magazine, music ensembles, musical theater, radio station, student government, student newspaper, student film society, yearbook. Number of fraternities: 1; sororities: 3. Proportion of men in fraternities: 3%; of women in sororities: 10%. **Sports program (2009-2010):** Member of NCAA III. *Men's intercollegiate varsity sports:* basketball, cross country, football, ice hockey, lacrosse, soccer, swimming, tennis, track and field (outdoor). *Women's intercollegiate varsity sports:* basketball, cross country, lacrosse, soccer, softball, swimming, tennis, track and field (indoor), track and field (outdoor), volleyball, water polo.

SERVICES AND FACILITIES

Basic services: nonremedial tutoring, day care, health service, health insurance. **Remedial assistance:** math, writing, study skills. **Counseling services:** career, personal, academic, psychological, birth control, religious. **For learning-disabled students:** School does not offer a structured program with separate admission and additional fees. Total undergraduates in learning-disabled program or receiving services: 118. Services include: tape recorders, note-taking services, extended time for tests, early syllabus, priority seating, substitution of courses, texts on tape, exams on tape or computer, other testing accommodations. **Library:** Number of titles: 819,028; number of current serial subscriptions: 26,233. **Information technology resources:** Students are not required to lease or own a computer. Number of campus computers available to all students: 200. School has a wireless network. Approximate number of users that can be accommodated: 5,500. Proportion of college-owned housing units wired for high-speed internet access: 100%. **Campus safety:** Security services offered: 24-hour foot-and-vehicle patrols, late-night transport/escort service, 24-hour emergency telephones, lighted pathways/sidewalks, controlled dormitory access (key, security card, etc).

TRANSFER AND INTERNATIONAL STUDENTS

Transfer students: May apply for admission for the following academic terms: Fall, Spring. Applicants need a minimum number of credits to apply. For fall 2009: Transfer applications received: 427. Transfer applicants offered admission: 70. Transfer applicants enrolled: 36. **International students:** Number of foreign undergraduates: 69 (4% of student body). Number of countries represented: 34. Minimum TOEFL score required: 550 (paper); 213 (computer). Average TOEFL score: 620 (paper).

Colorado School of Mines

- **Address:** 1500 Illinois Street, Golden, CO 80401
- **Website:** http://www.mines.edu
- **Public**
- **Enrollment:** 3,488 full-time; 187 part-time

KEY STATS

✔ **U.S News College Ranking:** 72, National Universities
✔ **ACT Score (25th/75th percentile):** 26-30
✔ **Tuition:** 2009-2010: $12,244 in state, $26,404 out of state

Selectivity: More selective	Room/board: $8,120
Acceptance rate: 63%	Average debt: $22,500
Student/faculty ratio: 15/1	Proportion who borrowed: 62%

UNDERGRADUATE STUDENT BODY STATS

2009-2010 enrollment: 3,488 full-time; 187 part-time. Men: 75%; women: 25%. **Ethnic makeup:** African American: 2%; American-Indian: 1%; Asian American: 6%; Hispanic: 7%; White: 80%; International: 6%.

ADMISSIONS FACTS AND FIGURES

Phone: (303) 273-3220. **Email:** admit@mines.edu. **Website:** http://www.mines.edu. **Application deadlines for fall 2011:** Regular decision: May 1. Early decision: Not offered. Early action: Not offered. Admission can be deferred. **Application fee:** $45. **To apply online, go to:** http://www.mines.edu/applynow. **Admissions requirements/recommendations:** High school units required (recommended): English: 4; Mathematics: 4; Science: 3; Foreign language: 1 (2); Social studies: 3; Academic electives: 2; Total units: 17. Tests: The college uses SAT or ACT scores in admissions decisions. Either SAT or ACT required. For admission to the fall 2011 entering class, the school will accept: ACT with writing recommended. Campus visit: Recommended. Admissions interview: Recommended. Off-campus interview: Not available. **Factors that count in admissions decisions:** *Academic:* Secondary school record: Very Important. Class rank: Very Important. Letters of recommendation: Considered. Standardized test scores: Very Important. Essay: Considered. *Nonacademic:* Interview: Considered. Extracurricular activities: Considered. Talent/ability: Considered. Character/personal qualities: Considered. Alumni/ae relationship: Considered. Geographical residence: Considered. State residency: Considered. Religious affiliation/commitment: Not Considered. Minority status: Not Considered. Volunteer work: Not Considered. Work experience: Not Considered. **Other schools with the greatest overlap in applicants:** Colorado State University; Massachusetts Institute of Technology; Purdue University–West Lafayette; Texas A&M University–College Station; University of Colorado–Boulder. **Admissions statistics for the fall 2009 entering class:** Total applicants: 7,190. Total accepted: 4,515. Freshmen enrolled: 880; 29% were from out of state. Overall acceptance rate: 63%. **Credentials of fall 2009 freshmen:** 52% ranked in the top 10 percent of their high school class; 85% were in the top 25 percent; 99% were in the top half. (Proportion submitting class standing: 65%.) **Average high school grade point average:** 3.7. **First-year students who submitted SAT scores:** 50%. Scores (25/75 percentile): Critical Reading: 550-650, Math: 620-700, Combined: 1170-1350. **First-year students submitting ACT scores:** 85%. Scores (25/75 percentile): English: 24-30, Math: 27-32, Composite: 26-30.

ACADEMICS

Year founded: 1874. **Academic calendar:** Semester. **Degrees offered:** bachelor's, master's, post-master's certificate, doctorate. **Most popular majors:** 86% engineering, 8% mathematics and statistics, 3% physical sciences, 3% social sciences. **Major fields of study:** computer and information sciences and support services; engineering; mathematics and statistics; physical sciences; social sciences. **Areas of required coursework:** humanities, computer literacy, mathematics, English (including composition), sciences (biological or physical), social science. **Special academic programs (% participation):** accelerated program (2%), cooperative (work-study plan) program (3%), double major (3%), dual enrollment, English as a Second Language (ESL), exchange student program (domestic), honors program (4%), independent study (4%), internships (84%), study abroad (4%). **Cooperative education programs:** business, computer science, engineering, humanities, social/behavioral science. **Reserve Officers Training Corps (ROTC):** Army ROTC: Offered on campus; Air Force ROTC: Offered on campus. **Faculty and instruction (2009-2010):** Total instructional faculty: 235 full-time, 96 part-time (77% men; 23% women; 15% minorities). Full-time faculty with Ph.D. or other terminal degree: 88%. Student/faculty ratio: 15/1. Classes of fewer than 20 students: 46%; of 20 to 49 students: 41%; of 50 or more students: 13%. **Advanced Placement and International Baccalaureate credit:** AP tests may be used for: Credit and/or placement. Scores accepted: 4, 5. International Baccalaureate exams may be used for: Credit and/or placement. **Freshmen returning for sophomore year:** 86%. **Graduation rates:** Four-year: 41%; five-year: 64%; six-year: 69%. **Graduate study:** 31% of students pursue further study immediately upon graduation; 1% within one year. Fields in which graduates pursue further study: Master of Business Administration (MBA), 20%; law, 8%; medicine, 5%; dentistry, 1%; engineering, 67%.

COSTS AND FINANCIAL AID

Financial aid office: (303) 273-3220. **Expenses (2009-2010):** Tuition and fees 2009-2010: $12,244 in state, $26,404 out of state; room/board: $8,120. Estimated books and supplies: $1,300; transportation: $0; personal expenses: $1,800. **Financial aid:** Priority filing date for institution's financial aid form: February 15. In 2009-2010, 63% of undergraduates applied for financial aid. Of those, 45% were determined to have financial need; 22% had their need fully met. Average financial aid package (proportion receiving): $11,927 (43%). Average amount of gift aid, such as scholarships or grants (proportion receiving): $6,586 (30%). Average amount of self-help aid, such as work study or loans (proportion receiving): $5,742 (42%). Average need-based loan (excluding PLUS or other private loans): $5,041. Among students who received need-based aid, the average percentage of need met: 68%. Among students who received aid based on merit, the average award (and the proportion receiving): $4,633 (21%). The average athletic scholarship (and the proportion receiving): $6,304 (9%). Average amount of debt of borrowers graduating in 2009: $22,500. Proportion who borrowed: 62%.

CAMPUS LIFE AND EXTRACURRICULAR ACTIVITIES

Campus housing available (% using): coed dorms (50%), sorority housing (4%), fraternity housing (16%), apartments for married students (2%), apartment for single students (28%), special housing for disabled students (0%). Students who live in college-owned, operated, or affiliated housing: 43%. **Student employment:** During the 2009-2010 academic year, 30% of undergraduates worked on campus. Average per-year earnings: $1,500.
Clubs and organizations: Number of student organizations: 162. Activities include: campus ministries, choral groups, concert band, dance, drama/theater, international student organization, jazz band, literary magazine, marching band, model UN, music ensembles, musical theater, pep band, radio station, student government, student newspaper, symphony orchestra, yearbook. Number of fraternities: 7; sororities: 3. Proportion of men in fraternities: 12%; of women in sororities: 15%. Average proportion of students who stay on campus on weekends: 40%. **Sports program (2009-2010):** Member of NCAA II. *Men's intercollegiate varsity sports:* baseball, basketball, cross country, football, golf, soccer, swimming, track and field (indoor), track and field (outdoor), wrestling. *Women's intercollegiate varsity sports:* basketball, cross country, soccer, softball, swimming, track and field (indoor), track and field (outdoor), volleyball.

SERVICES AND FACILITIES

Basic services: nonremedial tutoring, women's center, placement service, health service, health insurance, other. **Remedial assistance:** writing, study skills. **Counseling services:** minority student, career, military, personal, veteran student, academic, older student, psychological, birth control. **For learning-disabled students:** School does not offer a structured program with separate admission and additional fees. Total undergraduates in learning-disabled program or receiving services: 26. Services include: note-taking services, extended time for tests, tutors, priority seating, other testing accommodations. **Library:** Number of titles: 428,676; number of current serial subscriptions: 28,802. **Information technology resources:** Students are not required to lease or own a computer. Number of campus computers available to all students: 400. School has a wireless network. Approximate number of users that can be accommodated: 5,000. Proportion of college-owned housing units wired for high-speed internet access: 99%. **Campus safety:** Security services offered: 24-hour foot-and-vehicle patrols, late-night transport/escort service, 24-hour emergency telephones, lighted pathways/sidewalks, controlled dormitory access (key, security card, etc).

TRANSFER AND INTERNATIONAL STUDENTS

Transfer students: May apply for admission for the following academic terms: Fall, Spring, Summer. Applicants need a minimum number of credits to apply. For fall 2009: Transfer applications received: 520. Transfer applicants offered admission: 189. Transfer applicants enrolled: 94.
International students: Number of foreign undergraduates: 206 (6% of student body). Number of countries represented: 39. Minimum TOEFL score required: 550 (paper); 213 (computer).

Colorado State University

- **Address:** 1062 Campus Delivery, Fort Collins, CO 80523
- **Website:** http://www.colostate.edu
- **Public**
- **Enrollment:** 19,936 full-time; 2,222 part-time

KEY STATS

✔ **U.S News College Ranking:** 124, National Universities
✔ **ACT Score (25th/75th percentile):** 22-27
✔ **Tuition:** 2009-2010: $6,318 in state, $22,240 out of state
Selectivity: More selective   **Room/board:** $8,346
Acceptance rate: 72%   **Average debt:** $20,432
Student/faculty ratio: 17/1   **Proportion who borrowed:** 57%

UNDERGRADUATE STUDENT BODY STATS

2009-2010 enrollment: 19,936 full-time; 2,222 part-time. Men: 48%; women: 52%. **Ethnic makeup:** African American: 3%; American-Indian: 2%; Asian American: 3%; Hispanic: 7%; White: 85%; International: 2%.

ADMISSIONS FACTS AND FIGURES

Phone: (970) 491-6909. **Email:** admissions@colostate.edu. **Website:** http://www.colostate.edu. **Application deadlines for fall 2011:** Regular decision: February 1. Early decision: Not offered. Early action: Not offered. Admission can be deferred. **Application fee:** $50. **To apply online, go to:** http://admissions.colostate.edu/apply/. **Admissions requirements/recommendations:** High school units required (recommended): English: 4 (4); Mathematics: 4 (4); Science: 3 (3); Foreign language: 1 (2); Social studies: 2 (2); History: 1 (1); Academic electives: 2 (2); Total units: 17 (18). Tests: The college uses SAT or ACT scores in admissions decisions. Either SAT or ACT required. For admission to the fall 2011 entering class, the school will accept: ACT with or without writing accepted. Campus visit: Recommended. Admissions interview: Neither required nor recommended. Off-campus interview: Not available. **Factors that count in admissions decisions:** *Academic:* Secondary school record: Very Important. Class rank: Very Important. Letters of recommendation: Important. Standardized test scores: Important. Essay: Important. *Nonacademic:* Interview: Considered. Extracurricular activities: Important. Talent/ability: Important. Character/personal qualities: Important. Alumni/ae relationship: Considered. Geographical residence: Considered. State residency: Considered. Religious affiliation/commitment: Not Considered. Minority status: Not Considered. Volunteer work: Important. Work experience: Considered. **Other schools with the greatest overlap in applicants:** Arizona State University; Colorado School of Mines; Cornell University; University of Colorado–Boulder; University of Denver. **Admissions statistics for the fall 2009 entering class:** Total applicants: 15,253. Total accepted: 11,013. Freshmen enrolled: 4,322; 21% were from out of state. Overall acceptance rate: 72%. **Credentials of fall 2009 freshmen:** 22% ranked in the top 10 percent of their high school class; 50% were in the top 25 percent; 87% were in the top half. (Proportion submitting class standing: 84%.) **Average high school grade point average:** 3.6. **First-year students who submitted SAT scores:** 34%. Scores (25/75 percentile): Critical Reading: 500-610, Math: 510-640, Combined: 1010-1250. **First-year students submitting ACT scores:** 92%. Scores (25/75 percentile): English: 21-27, Math: 21-27, Composite: 22-27.

ACADEMICS

Year founded: 1870. **Academic calendar:** Semester. **Degrees offered:** bachelor's, master's, doctorate. **Most popular majors:** 15% business, management, marketing, and related support services, 9% biological and biomedical sciences, 8% family and consumer sciences/human sciences, 8% social sciences, 7% parks, recreation, leisure, and fitness studies. **Major fields of study:** agriculture, agriculture operations, and related sciences; architecture and related services; biological and biomedical sciences; business, management, marketing, and related support services; communication, journalism, and related programs; computer and information sciences and support services; education; engineering; English language and literature/letters; family and consumer sciences/human sciences; foreign languages, literatures, and linguistics; health professions and related clinical sciences; history; liberal arts and sciences studies, and humanities; mathematics and statistics; multi/interdisciplinary studies; natural resources and conservation; parks, recreation, leisure, and fitness studies; philosophy and religious studies; physical sciences; psychology; public administration and social service professions; security and protective services; social sciences; visual and performing arts. **Areas of required coursework:** arts/fine arts, humanities, mathematics, English (including composition), sciences (biological or physical), history, social science, other. **Pre-professional programs:** pre-law, pre-dentistry, pre-medicine, pre-veterinary science, pre-optometry, pre-pharmacy, other. **Special academic programs:** accelerated program, cooperative (work-study plan) program, cross-registration, distance learning, double major, dual enrollment, English as a Second Language (ESL), exchange student program (domestic), honors program, independent study, internships, liberal arts/career combination, study abroad, teacher certificate program. **Teacher certification offered in:** early childhood, vo-tech, middle/junior high, adult education, secondary, bilingual/bicultural. **Cooperative education programs:** computer science, engineering. **Reserve Officers Training Corps (ROTC):** Army ROTC: Offered on campus; Air Force ROTC: Offered on campus. **Faculty and instruction (2009-2010):** Total instructional faculty: 944 full-time, 45 part-time (68% men; 32% women; 13% minorities). Full-time faculty with Ph.D. or other terminal degree: 99%. Student/faculty ratio: 17/1. Classes of fewer than 20 students: 35%; of 20 to 49 students: 46%; of 50 or more students: 18%. **Advanced Placement and International Baccalaureate credit:** AP tests may be used for: Credit and/or placement. Scores accepted: 3, 4, 5. International Baccalaureate exams may be used for: Credit and/or placement. **Freshmen returning for sophomore year:** 82%. **Graduation rates:** Four-year: 35%; five-year: 59%; six-year: 64%.

COSTS AND FINANCIAL AID

Financial aid office: (970) 491-6321. **Expenses (2009-2010):** Tuition and fees 2009-2010: $6,318 in state, $22,240 out of state; room/board: $8,346. Estimated books and supplies: $1,126 personal expenses: $1,692. **Financial aid:** Priority filing date for institution's financial aid form: March 1. In 2009-2010, 63% of undergraduates applied for financial aid. Of those, 42% were determined to have financial need; 42% had their need fully met. Average financial aid package (proportion receiving): $10,051 (42%). Average amount of gift aid, such as scholarships or grants (proportion receiving): $5,170 (37%). Average amount of self-help aid, such as work study or loans (proportion receiving): $6,542 (32%). Average need-based loan (excluding PLUS or other private loans): $6,525. Among students who received need-based aid, the average percentage of need met: 74%. Among students who received aid based on merit, the average award (and the proportion receiving): $3,371 (9%). The average athletic scholarship (and the proportion receiving): $20,000 (1%). Average amount of debt of borrowers graduating in 2009: $20,432. Proportion who borrowed: 57%.

CAMPUS LIFE AND EXTRACURRICULAR ACTIVITIES

Campus housing available (% using): coed dorms (57%), apartments for married students (2%), apartment for single students (5%), special housing for disabled students (1%), special housing for international students. Students who live in college-owned, operated, or affiliated housing: 26%. **Student employment:** During the 2009-2010 academic year, 27% of undergraduates worked on campus. Average per-year earnings: $3,188. **Clubs and organizations:** Number of student organizations: 350. Activities include: campus ministries, choral groups, concert band, dance, drama/theater, international student organization, jazz band, literary magazine, marching band, music ensembles, musical theater, opera, pep band, radio station, student government, student newspaper, symphony orchestra, television station. Number of fraternities: 21; sororities: 14. Proportion of men in fraternities: 5%; of women in sororities: 7%. Average proportion of students who stay on campus on weekends: 45%. **Sports program (2009-2010):** Member of NCAA I. *Men's intercollegiate varsity sports:* basketball, cross country, football, golf, track and field (indoor), track and field (outdoor). *Women's intercollegiate varsity sports:* basketball, cross country, golf, softball, swimming, tennis, track and field (indoor), track and field (outdoor), volleyball, water polo.

SERVICES AND FACILITIES

Basic services: nonremedial tutoring, women's center, placement service, day care, health service, health insurance. **Counseling services:** minority student, career, military, personal, veteran student, academic, older student, psychological, birth control, religious. **For learning-disabled students:** School does not offer a structured program with separate admission and additional fees. Services include: reading machines, tape recorders, diagnostic testing service, note-taking services, readers, extended time for tests, tutors, priority registration, substitution of courses, texts on tape, exams on tape or computer, other testing accommodations, other. **Library:** Number of titles: 2,366,608; number of current serial subscriptions: 52,433. **Information technology resources:** Students are not required to lease or own a computer. Number of campus computers available to all students: 2,700. School has a wireless network. Approximate number of users that can be accommodated: 12,000. Proportion of college-owned housing units wired for high-speed internet access: 100%. **Campus safety:** Security services offered: 24-hour foot-and-vehicle patrols, late-night transport/escort service, 24-hour emergency telephones, lighted pathways/sidewalks, controlled dormitory access (key, security card, etc).

TRANSFER AND INTERNATIONAL STUDENTS

Transfer students: May apply for admission for the following academic terms: Fall, Spring, Summer. Applicants need a minimum number of credits to apply. For fall 2009: Transfer applications received: 3,083. Transfer applicants offered admission: 1,926. Transfer applicants enrolled: 1,353. **International students:** Number of foreign undergraduates: 361 (2% of student body). Number of countries represented: 85. Minimum TOEFL score required: 450 (paper); 45 (computer). Average TOEFL score: 501 (paper).

Colorado State University—Pueblo

■ **Address:** 2200 Bonforte Boulevard, Pueblo, CO 81001
■ **Website:** http://www.colostate-pueblo.edu
■ **Public**
■ **Enrollment:** 3,894 full-time; 1,685 part-time

KEY STATS

✔ **U.S News College Ranking:** second tier, National Liberal Arts Colleges
✔ **ACT Score (25th/75th percentile):** 18-23
✔ **Tuition:** 2009-2010: $5,210 in state, $15,602 out of state
   Selectivity: Less selective   **Room/board:** $7,244
   Acceptance rate: 95%   **Average debt:** N/A
   Student/faculty ratio: 16/1   **Proportion who borrowed:** N/A

UNDERGRADUATE STUDENT BODY STATS

2009-2010 enrollment: 3,894 full-time; 1,685 part-time. Men: 44%; women: 56%. **Ethnic makeup:** African American: 9%; American-Indian: 2%; Asian American: 3%; Hispanic: 25%; White: 60%; International: 1%.

ADMISSIONS FACTS AND FIGURES

Phone: (719) 549-2461. **Email:** info@colostate-pueblo.edu. **Website:** http://www.colostate-pueblo.edu. **Application deadlines for fall 2011:** Regular decision: August 1. Early decision: Not offered. Early action: Not offered. Admission can be deferred. **Application fee:** $25. **To apply online, go to:** http://www.gocsupueblo.com/Admissions/Pages/Apply-Now.aspx. **Admissions requirements/recommendations:** High school units required (recommended): English: 4; Mathematics: 4; Science: 3; Foreign language: 1 (2); Social studies: 2; History: 1; Academic electives: 2; Total units: 17. Tests: The college uses SAT or ACT scores in admissions decisions. Either SAT or ACT required. For admission to the fall 2011 entering class, the school will accept: ACT with or without writing accepted. Campus visit: Recommended. Admissions interview: Neither required nor recommended. Off-campus interview: Not available. **Factors that count in admissions decisions:** *Academic:* Secondary school record: Very Important. Class rank: Important. Letters of recommendation: Considered. Standardized test scores: Very Important. Essay: Considered. *Nonacademic:* Interview: Considered. Extracurricular activities: Not Considered. Talent/ability: Considered. Character/personal qualities: Considered. Alumni/ae relationship: Not Considered. Geographical residence: Not Considered. State residency: Not Considered. Religious affiliation/commitment: Not Considered. Minority status: Not Considered. Volunteer work: Considered. Work experience: Considered. **Admissions statistics for the fall 2009 entering class:** Total applicants: 2,758. Total accepted: 2,614. Freshmen enrolled: 1,054; 8% were from out of state. Overall acceptance rate: 95%. **Credentials of fall 2009 freshmen:** 2% ranked in the top 10 percent of their high school class; 7% were in the top 25 percent; 30% were in the top half. (Proportion submitting class standing: 88%.) **Average high school grade point average:** 3.1. **First-year students who submitted SAT scores:** 12%. Scores (25/75 percentile): Critical Reading: 420-550, Math: 430-570, Combined: 850-1120. **First-year students submitting ACT scores:** 90%. Scores (25/75 percentile): English: N/A, Math: N/A, Composite: 18-23.

ACADEMICS

Year founded: 1933. **Academic calendar:** Semester. **Degrees offered:** bachelor's, master's. **Most popular majors:** 16% sociology, 12% business/commerce, 10% nursing/registered nurse training (R.N., A.S.N., B.S.N., M.S.N.), 7% mass communication/media studies, 6% kinesiology and exercise science. **Major fields of study:** biological and biomedical sciences; business, management, marketing, and related support services; communication, journalism, and related programs; computer and information sciences and support services; engineering; engineering technologies/technicians; English language and literature/letters; foreign languages, literatures, and linguistics; health professions and related clinical sciences; history; liberal arts and sciences studies, and humanities; mathematics and statistics; parks, recreation, leisure, and fitness studies; physical sciences; psychology; public administration and social service professions; social sciences; visual and performing arts. **Areas of required coursework:** humanities, mathematics, English (including composition), sciences (biological or physical), history, social science. **Pre-professional programs:** pre-law, pre-dentistry, pre-medicine, pre-veterinary science, pre-optometry, pre-pharmacy, other. **Special academic programs:** accelerated program, cooperative (work-study plan) program, distance learning, double major, dual enrollment, English as a Second Language (ESL), external degree program, independent study, internships, liberal arts/career combination, study abroad, teacher certificate program, weekend college. **Teacher certification offered in:** elementary, secondary, bilingual/bicultural. **Cooperative education programs:** art, business, computer science, engineering, humanities, technologies. **Reserve Officers Training Corps (ROTC):** Army ROTC: Offered on campus. **Faculty and instruction (2009-2010):** Total instructional faculty: 180 full-time, 183 part-time. Student/faculty ratio: 16/1. Classes of fewer than 20 students: 42%; of 20 to 49 students: 50%; of 50 or more students: 8%. **Advanced Placement and International Baccalaureate credit:** AP tests may be used for: Credit only. Scores accepted: 3, 4, 5. International Baccalaureate exams may be used for: Credit only. **Freshmen returning for sophomore year:** 64%. **Graduation rates:** Four-year: 14%; five-year: 25%; six-year: 27%. **Graduate study:** 24% of students pursue further study within five years.

COSTS AND FINANCIAL AID

Financial aid office: (719) 549-2753. **Expenses (2009-2010):** Tuition and fees 2009-2010: $5,210 in state, $15,602 out of state; room/board: $7,244. Estimated books and supplies: $1,200; transportation: $1,296; personal expenses: $2,080. **Financial aid:** Priority filing date for institution's financial aid form: March 1. In 2009-2010, 87% of undergraduates applied for financial aid. Of those, 73% were determined to have financial need; 5% had their need fully met. Average financial aid package (proportion receiving): $8,512 (72%). Average amount of gift aid, such as scholarships or grants (proportion receiving): $5,936 (63%). Average amount of self-help aid, such as work study or loans (proportion receiving): $3,895 (61%). Average need-based loan (excluding PLUS or other private loans): $3,235. Among students who received need-based aid, the average percentage of need met: 58%. Among students who received aid based on merit, the average award (and the proportion receiving): $2,556 (6%). The average athletic scholarship (and the proportion receiving): $3,456 (4%).

CAMPUS LIFE AND EXTRACURRICULAR ACTIVITIES

Campus housing available (% using): coed dorms (62%), apartment for single students (38%), special housing for disabled students. Students who live in college-owned, operated, or affiliated housing: 19%. **Student employment:** During the 2009-2010 academic year, 11% of undergraduates worked on campus. Average per-year earnings: $1,384. **Clubs and organizations:** Number of student organizations: 54. Activities include: campus ministries, choral groups, concert band, dance, international student organization, jazz band, literary magazine, marching band, music ensembles, pep band, radio station, student government, student newspaper, symphony orchestra, television station. Number of fraternities: 3; sororities: 1. Proportion of men in fraternities: 1%; of women in sororities: 1%. Average proportion of students who stay on campus on weekends: 14%. **Sports program (2009-2010):** Member of NCAA II. *Men's intercollegiate varsity sports:* baseball, basketball, football, golf, soccer, tennis, wrestling. *Women's intercollegiate varsity sports:* basketball, cross country, golf, soccer, softball, tennis, track and field (indoor), track and field (outdoor), volleyball.

SERVICES AND FACILITIES

Basic services: nonremedial tutoring, women's center, day care, health service. **Remedial assistance:** reading, math, writing. **Counseling services:** minority student, career, personal, veteran student, academic, older student, psychological, birth control, other. **For learning-disabled students:** School does not offer a structured program with separate admission and additional fees. Services include: tape recorders, note-taking services, readers, extended time for tests, other. **Library:** Number of titles: 274,890; number of current serial subscriptions: 7,658. **Information technology resources:** Students are not required to lease or own a computer. Number of campus computers available to all students: 800. School has a wireless network. Approximate number of users that can be accommodated: 1,000. Proportion of college-owned housing units wired for high-speed internet access: 100%. **Campus safety:** Security services offered: 24-hour foot-and-vehicle patrols, late-night transport/escort service, 24-hour emergency telephones, lighted pathways/sidewalks, student patrols, controlled dormitory access (key, security card, etc).

TRANSFER AND INTERNATIONAL STUDENTS

Transfer students: May apply for admission for the following academic terms: Fall, Spring, Summer. Applicants need a minimum number of credits to apply. For fall 2009: Transfer applications received: 2,758. Transfer applicants offered admission: 2,614. Transfer applicants enrolled: 1,050. **International students:** Number of foreign undergraduates: 46 (1% of student body). Number of countries represented: 20. Minimum TOEFL score required: 500 (paper); 173 (computer). Average TOEFL score: 533 (paper).

Fort Lewis College

■ **Address:** 1000 Rim Drive, Durango, CO 81301
■ **Website:** http://www.fortlewis.edu
■ **Public**
■ **Enrollment:** 3,380 full-time; 305 part-time

KEY STATS

✔ **U.S News College Ranking:** second tier, National Liberal Arts Colleges
✔ **ACT Score (25th/75th percentile):** 20-24
✔ **Tuition:** 2010-2011: $4,820 in state, $18,952 out of state

Selectivity: Selective	**Room/board:** $9,134
Acceptance rate: 68%	**Average debt:** $15,962
Student/faculty ratio: 17/1	**Proportion who borrowed:** 54%

UNDERGRADUATE STUDENT BODY STATS

2009-2010 enrollment: 3,380 full-time; 305 part-time. Men: 51%; women: 49%. **Ethnic makeup:** African American: 1%; American-Indian: 21%; Asian American: 1%; Hispanic: 5%; White: 71%; International: 1%.

ADMISSIONS FACTS AND FIGURES

Phone: (970) 247-7184. **Email:** admission@fortlewis.edu. **Website:** http://www.fortlewis.edu. **Application deadlines for fall 2011:** Regular decision: August 1. Early decision: Not offered. Early action: Not offered. Admission can be deferred. **Application fee:** $40. **To apply online, go to:** https://webopus.fortlewis.edu/pls/banner/bwskalog.P_DispLoginNon. **Admissions requirements/recommendations:** High school units required (recommended): English: 4; Mathematics: 4; Science: 3; Foreign language: 1; Social studies: 2; History: 1; Academic electives: 2; Total units: 17. Tests: The college uses SAT or ACT scores in admissions decisions. Either SAT or ACT required. For admission to the fall 2011 entering class, the school will accept: ACT with or without writing accepted. Campus visit: Recommended. Admissions interview: Recommended. Off-campus interview: May be arranged. **Factors that count in admissions decisions:** *Academic:* Secondary school record: Very Important. Class rank: Very Important. Letters of recommendation: Considered. Standardized test scores: Very Important. Essay: Considered. *Nonacademic:* Interview: Considered. Extracurricular activities: Considered. Talent/ability: Considered. Character/personal qualities: Considered. Alumni/ae relationship: Considered. Geographical residence: Not Considered. State residency: Not Considered. Religious affiliation/commitment: Not Considered. Minority status: Not Considered. Volunteer work: Considered. Work experience: Considered. **Other schools with the greatest overlap in applicants:** Colorado State University; Mesa State College; University of Colorado–Boulder; University of Northern Colorado; Western State College of Colorado. **Admissions statistics for the fall 2009 entering class:** Total applicants: 2,722. Total accepted: 1,845. Freshmen enrolled: 802; 36% were from out of state. Overall acceptance rate: 68%. **Credentials of fall 2009 freshmen:** 11% ranked in the top 10 percent of their high school class; 30% were in the top 25 percent; 64% were in the top half. (Proportion submitting class standing: 65%.) **Average high school grade point average:** 3.1. **First-year students who submitted SAT scores:** 28%. Scores (25/75 percentile): Critical Reading: 470-575, Math: 460-570, Combined: 930-1145. **First-year students submitting ACT scores:** 87%. Scores (25/75 percentile): English: 18-24, Math: 19-25, Composite: 20-24.

ACADEMICS

Year founded: 1911. **Academic calendar:** Semester. **Degrees offered:** bachelor's. **Most popular majors:** 27% business, management, marketing, and related support services, 12% social sciences, 11% liberal arts and sciences studies, and humanities, 8% psychology, 8% visual and performing arts. **Major fields of study:** agriculture, agriculture operations, and related sciences; area, ethnic, cultural, and gender studies; biological and biomedical sciences; business, management, marketing, and related support services; communication, journalism, and related programs; computer and information sciences and support services; education; engineering; English language and literature/letters; foreign languages, literatures, and linguistics; health professions and related clinical sciences; history; liberal arts and sciences studies, and humanities; mathematics and statistics; multi/interdisciplinary studies; parks, recreation, leisure, and fitness studies; philosophy and religious studies; physical sciences; psychology; social sciences; visual and performing arts. **Areas of required coursework:** computer literacy, mathematics, English (including composition), sciences (biological or physical), social science, other. **Pre-professional programs:** pre-law, pre-medicine. **Special academic programs:** accelerated program, cooperative (work-study plan) program, distance learning, double major, dual enrollment, English as a Second Language (ESL), exchange student program (domestic), honors program, independent study, internships, liberal arts/career combination, student-designed major, study abroad, teacher certificate program. **Teacher certification offered in:** early childhood, elementary, secondary. **Cooperative education programs:** agriculture, art, business, computer science, education, engineering, health professions, humanities, natural science, social/behavioral science, technologies. **Faculty and instruction (2009-2010):** Total instructional faculty: 171 full-time, 90 part-time (51% men; 49% women; 10% minorities). Full-time faculty with Ph.D. or other terminal degree: 83%. Student/faculty ratio: 17/1. Classes of fewer than 20 students: 57%; of 20 to 49 students: 41%; of 50 or more students: 1%. **Advanced Placement and International Baccalaureate credit:** AP tests may be used for: Placement only. Scores accepted: 3, 4, 5. International Baccalaureate exams may be used for: Credit only. **Freshmen returning for sophomore year:** 58%. **Graduation rates:** Four-year: 15%; five-year: 29%; six-year: 34%. **Graduate study:** 14% of students pursue further study within one year; 21% within five years.

COSTS AND FINANCIAL AID

Financial aid office: (970) 247-7142. **Expenses (2010-2011):** Tuition and fees 2010-2011: $4,820 in state, $18,952 out of state; room/board: $9,134. Estimated books and supplies: $1,680; transportation: $1,590; personal expenses: $2,094. **Financial aid:** Priority filing date for institution's financial aid form: February 15. In 2009-2010, 66% of undergraduates applied for financial aid. Of those, 52% were determined to have financial need; 24% had their need fully met. Average financial aid package (proportion receiving): $8,042 (51%). Average amount of gift aid, such as scholarships or grants (proportion receiving): $3,660 (41%). Average amount of self-help aid, such as work study or loans (proportion receiving): $4,075 (42%). Average need-based loan (excluding PLUS or other private loans): $3,835. Among students who received need-based aid, the average percentage of need met: 71%. Among students who received aid based on merit, the average award (and the proportion receiving): $1,241 (12%). The average athletic scholarship (and the proportion receiving): $6,322 (6%). Average amount of debt of borrowers graduating in 2009: $15,962. Proportion who borrowed: 54%.

CAMPUS LIFE AND EXTRACURRICULAR ACTIVITIES

Campus housing available (% using): coed dorms (72%), apartments for married students (2%), apartment for single students (26%), special housing for disabled students. Students who live in college-owned, operated, or affiliated housing: 37%. **Student employment:** During the 2009-2010 academic year, 9% of undergraduates worked on campus. Average per-year earnings: $3,980. **Clubs and organizations:** Number of student organizations: 65. Activities include: campus ministries, choral groups, concert band, drama/theater, jazz band, literary magazine, pep band, radio station, student government, student newspaper. Number of fraternities: 0; sororities: 0. Average proportion of students who stay on campus on weekends: 30%. **Sports program (2009-2010):** Member of NCAA II. ***Men's intercollegiate varsity sports:*** basketball, cross country, football, golf, soccer. ***Women's intercollegiate varsity sports:*** basketball, cross country, lacrosse, soccer, softball, volleyball.

SERVICES AND FACILITIES

Basic services: nonremedial tutoring, placement service, day care, health service, health insurance. **Remedial assistance:** reading, math, writing. **Counseling services:** minority student, career, personal, veteran student, academic, older student, psychological, birth control, religious. **For learning-disabled students:** School does not offer a structured program with separate admission and additional fees. Services include: remedial math, remedial English, reading machines, remedial reading, tape recorders, untimed tests, note-taking services, oral tests, readers, extended time for tests, tutors, priority registration, priority seating, texts on tape, exams on tape or computer, other testing accommodations. **Library:** Number of titles: 167,287; number of current serial subscriptions: 1,790. **Information technology resources:** Students are not required to lease or own a computer. Number of campus computers available to all students: 740. School has a wireless network. Approximate number of users that can be accommodated: 1,000. Proportion of college-owned housing units wired for high-speed internet access: 100%. **Campus safety:** Security services offered: 24-hour foot-and-vehicle patrols, late-night transport/escort service, 24-hour emergency telephones, lighted pathways/sidewalks, controlled dormitory access (key, security card, etc).

TRANSFER AND INTERNATIONAL STUDENTS

Transfer students: May apply for admission for the following academic terms: Fall, Winter, Summer. Applicants do not need a minimum number of credits to apply. For fall 2009: Transfer applications received: 777. Transfer applicants offered admission: 508. Transfer applicants enrolled: 323. **International students:** Number of foreign undergraduates: 27 (1% of student body). Number of countries represented: 15. Minimum TOEFL score required: 500 (paper); 173 (computer).

Mesa State College

■ **Address:** 1100 North Avenue, Grand Junction, CO 81501-3122
■ **Website:** http://www.mesastate.edu
■ **Public**
■ **Enrollment:** 5,118 full-time; 1,821 part-time

KEY STATS
✔ **U.S News College Ranking:** second tier, National Liberal Arts Colleges
✔ **ACT Score (25th/75th percentile):** 18-23
✔ **Tuition:** 2009-2010: $5,374 in state, $14,340 out of state
Selectivity: Selective   **Room/board:** $7,507
Acceptance rate: 81%   **Average debt:** $18,834
Student/faculty ratio: 20/1   **Proportion who borrowed:** 43%

UNDERGRADUATE STUDENT BODY STATS

2009-2010 enrollment: 5,118 full-time; 1,821 part-time. Men: 43%; women: 57%. **Ethnic makeup:** African American: 2%; American-Indian: 2%; Asian American: 3%; Hispanic: 9%; White: 84%.

ADMISSIONS FACTS AND FIGURES

Phone: (800) 982-6372. **Email:** admissions@mesastate.edu. **Website:** http://www.mesastate.edu. **Application deadlines for fall 2011:** Regular decision: Rolling. Early decision: Not offered. Early action: Not offered. Admission can be deferred. **Application fee:** $30. **To apply online, go to:** https://mesaweb.mesastate.edu/BannerPROD/bwskalog.P_DispLoginNon. **Admissions requirements/recommendations:** High school units required (recommended): English: (4); Mathematics: (3); Science: (3); Social studies: (3); History: (1); Academic electives: (2); Total units: (18). Tests: The college uses SAT or ACT scores in admissions decisions. Either SAT or ACT required. For admission to the fall 2011 entering class, the school will accept: ACT with or without writing accepted. Campus visit: Recommended. Admissions interview: Neither required nor recommended. Off-campus interview: May be arranged. **Factors that count in admissions decisions:** *Academic:* Secondary school record: Important. Class rank: Important. Letters of recommendation: Considered. Standardized test scores: Important. Essay: Considered. *Nonacademic:* Interview: Considered. Extracurricular activities: Considered. Talent/ability: Considered. Character/personal qualities: Considered. Alumni/ae relationship: Considered. Geographical residence: Considered. State residency: Considered. Religious affiliation/commitment: Not Considered. Minority status: Considered. Volunteer work: Considered. Work experience: Considered. **Other schools with the greatest overlap in applicants:** Colorado State University; Fort Lewis College; University of Colorado–Boulder; University of Northern Colorado; Western State College of Colorado. **Admissions statistics for the fall 2009 entering class:** Total applicants: 4,225. Total accepted: 3,426. Freshmen enrolled: 1,602; 12% were from out of state. Overall acceptance rate: 81%. **Credentials of fall 2009 freshmen:** 7% ranked in the top 10 percent of their high school class; 22% were in the top 25 percent; 51% were in the top half. (Proportion submitting class standing: 78%.) **Average high school grade point average:** 2.9. **First-year students who submitted SAT scores:** 10%. Scores (25/75 percentile): Critical Reading: 430-550, Math: 430-560, Combined: 860-1110. **First-year students submitting ACT scores:** 81%. Scores (25/75 percentile): English: 17-23, Math: 17-23, Composite: 18-23.

ACADEMICS

Year founded: 1925. **Academic calendar:** Semester. **Degrees offered:** certificate, associate, transfer-associate, terminal-associate, bachelor's, master's. **Most popular majors:** 17% business/commerce, 10% nursing/registered nurse training (R.N., A.S.N., B.S.N., M.S.N.), 9% kinesiology and exercise science, 6% liberal arts and sciences/liberal studies, 6% psychology. **Major fields of study:** biological and biomedical sciences; business, management, marketing, and related support services; communication, journalism, and related programs; computer and information sciences and support services;

engineering technologies/technicians; English language and literature/ letters; foreign languages, literatures, and linguistics; health professions and related clinical sciences; history; liberal arts and sciences studies, and humanities; mathematics and statistics; natural resources and conservation; parks, recreation, leisure, and fitness studies; physical sciences; psychology; social sciences; visual and performing arts. **Areas of required coursework:** arts/fine arts, humanities, mathematics, English (including composition), sciences (biological or physical), social science. **Special academic programs:** accelerated program, distance learning, double major, exchange student program (domestic), honors program, independent study, internships, study abroad, teacher certificate program. **Teacher certification offered in:** early childhood, elementary, middle/junior high, secondary. **Faculty and instruction (2009-2010):** Total instructional faculty: 230 full-time, 188 part-time. Student/faculty ratio: 20/1. Classes of fewer than 20 students: 49%; of 20 to 49 students: 43%; of 50 or more students: 8%. **Advanced Placement and International Baccalaureate credit:** AP tests may be used for: Placement only. Scores accepted: 3, 4, 5. International Baccalaureate exams may be used for: Placement only. **Freshmen returning for sophomore year:** 58%. **Graduation rates:** Four-year: 10%; five-year: 21%; six-year: 26%.

COSTS AND FINANCIAL AID

Financial aid office: (970) 248-1396. **Expenses (2009-2010):** Tuition and fees 2009-2010: $5,374 in state, $14,340 out of state; room/board: $7,507. **Financial aid:** In 2009-2010, 75% of undergraduates applied for financial aid. Of those, 59% were determined to have financial need; 6% had their need fully met. Average financial aid package (proportion receiving): $6,913 (56%). Average amount of gift aid, such as scholarships or grants (proportion receiving): $4,749 (44%). Average amount of self-help aid, such as work study or loans (proportion receiving): $3,905 (47%). Average need-based loan (excluding PLUS or other private loans): $3,721. Among students who received need-based aid, the average percentage of need met: 59%. Among students who received aid based on merit, the average award (and the proportion receiving): $1,938 (8%). The average athletic scholarship (and the proportion receiving): $2,999 (4%). Average amount of debt of borrowers graduating in 2009: $18,834. Proportion who borrowed: 43%.

CAMPUS LIFE AND EXTRACURRICULAR ACTIVITIES

Campus housing available (% using): coed dorms (74%), women's dorms (10%), apartment for single students (13%), special housing for disabled students (1%). Students who live in college-owned, operated, or affiliated housing: 22%. **Student employment:** During the 2009-2010 academic year, 9% of undergraduates worked on campus. Average per-year earnings: $2,250. Activities include: choral groups, concert band, dance, drama/theater, international student organization, jazz band, literary magazine, music ensembles, musical theater, pep band, radio station, student government, student newspaper, student film society, symphony orchestra. Number of fraternities: 0; sororities: 0. Average proportion of students who stay on campus on weekends: 20%. **Sports program (2009-2010):** Member of NCAA II. *Men's intercollegiate varsity sports:* baseball, basketball, football, golf, lacrosse, soccer, swimming, tennis, wrestling. *Women's intercollegiate varsity sports:* basketball, cross country, golf, lacrosse, soccer, softball, swimming, tennis, track and field (indoor), track and field (outdoor), volleyball.

SERVICES AND FACILITIES

Basic services: nonremedial tutoring, placement service, day care, health service, health insurance, other. **Remedial assistance:** reading, math, writing, study skills. **Counseling services:** minority student, career, personal, academic, older student. **For learning-disabled students:** School does not offer a structured program with separate admission and additional fees. Total undergraduates in learning-disabled program or receiving services: 186. Services include: remedial math, remedial English, reading machines, remedial reading, tape recorders, note-taking services, oral tests, learning center, readers, extended time for tests, tutors, priority registration, priority seating, substitution of courses, texts on tape, typist/scribe. **Library:** Number of titles: 394,063; number of current serial subscriptions: 24,591. **Information technology resources:** Students are not required to lease or own a computer. Number of campus computers available to all students: 950. School has a wireless network. Approximate number of users that can be accommodated: 6,000. Proportion of college-owned housing units wired for high-speed internet access: 100%. **Campus safety:** Security services offered: 24-hour foot-and-vehicle patrols, late-night transport/escort service, 24-hour emergency telephones, lighted pathways/sidewalks, student patrols, controlled dormitory access (key, security card, etc).

TRANSFER AND INTERNATIONAL STUDENTS

Transfer students: May apply for admission for the following academic terms: Fall, Spring, Summer. Applicants need a minimum number of credits to apply. For fall 2009: Transfer applications received: 1,166. Transfer applicants offered admission: 887. Transfer applicants enrolled: 632. **International students:** Number of foreign undergraduates: 15. Number of countries represented: 12. Minimum TOEFL score required: 525 (paper); 190 (computer). Average TOEFL score: 550 (paper).

Metropolitan State College of Denver

■ **Address:** 1201 Fifth Street, Denver, CO 80217-3362
■ **Website:** http://www.mscd.edu
■ **Public**
■ **Enrollment:** 14,321 full-time; 8,516 part-time

KEY STATS

✔ **U.S News College Ranking:** second tier, National Liberal Arts Colleges
✔ **ACT Score (25th/75th percentile):** 18-23
✔ **Tuition:** 2010-2011: $4,093 in state, $14,440 out of state
   Selectivity: Selective   **Room/board:** N/A
   Acceptance rate: 72%   **Average debt:** $26,635
   Student/faculty ratio: 22/1   **Proportion who borrowed:** 61%

UNDERGRADUATE STUDENT BODY STATS

2009-2010 enrollment: 14,321 full-time; 8,516 part-time. Men: 45%; women: 55%. **Ethnic makeup:** African American: 6%; American-Indian: 1%; Asian American: 4%; Hispanic: 14%; White: 74%; International: 1%.

ADMISSIONS FACTS AND FIGURES

Phone: (303) 556-3058. **Email:** askmetro@mscd.edu. **Website:** http://www. mscd.edu. **Application deadlines for fall 2011:** Regular decision: August 1. Early decision: Not offered. Early action: Not offered. Admission can be deferred. **Application fee:** $25. **To apply online, go to:** http://www.mscd. edu/admissions/application/. **Admissions requirements/recommendations:** High school units required (recommended): English: 4 (4); Mathematics: 3 (3); Science: 3 (3); Foreign language: 2 (2); Social studies: 2 (2); History: 1 (1); Total units: 15 (15). Tests: The college uses SAT or ACT scores in admissions decisions. Either SAT or ACT required. For admission to the fall 2011 entering class, the school will accept: ACT with or without writing accepted. Campus visit: Recommended. Admissions interview: Neither required nor recommended. Off-campus interview: May be arranged. **Factors that count in admissions decisions:** *Academic:* Secondary school record: Important. Class rank: Important. Letters of recommendation: Considered. Standardized test scores: Important. Essay: Not Considered. *Nonacademic:* Interview: Not Considered. Extracurricular activities: Not Considered. Talent/ability: Not Considered. Character/personal qualities: Not Considered. Alumni/ae relationship: Not Considered. Geographical residence: Not Considered. State residency: Not Considered. Religious affiliation/commitment: Not Considered. Minority status: Not Considered. Volunteer work: Not Considered. Work experience: Not Considered. **Admissions statistics for the fall 2009 entering class:** Total applicants: 6,387. Total accepted: 4,576. Freshmen enrolled: 2,205; Overall acceptance rate: 72%. **Credentials of fall 2009 freshmen:** 7% ranked in the top 10 percent of their high school class; 20% were in the top 25 percent; 53% were in the top half. (Proportion submitting class standing: 74%.) **Average high school grade point average:** 2.9. **First-year students who submitted SAT scores:** 5%. Scores (25/75 percentile): Critical Reading: 450-570, Math: 430-590, Combined: 880-1160. **First-year students submitting ACT scores:** 84%. Scores (25/75 percentile): English: 17-23, Math: 17-23, Composite: 18-23.

ACADEMICS

Year founded: 1963. **Academic calendar:** Semester. **Degrees offered:** certificate, bachelor's, post-bachelor's certificate. **Major fields of study:** architecture and related services; area, ethnic, cultural, and gender studies; biological and biomedical sciences; business, management, marketing, and related support services; communication, journalism, and related programs; computer and information sciences and support services; education; engineering; engineering technologies/technicians; English language and literature/ letters; foreign languages, literatures, and linguistics; health professions and related clinical sciences; history; mathematics and statistics; multi/ interdisciplinary studies; parks, recreation, leisure, and fitness studies; philosophy and religious studies; physical sciences; psychology; public administration and social service professions; security and protective services; social sciences; transportation and materials moving; visual and performing arts. **Areas of required coursework:** mathematics, English (including composition), foreign languages, sciences (biological or physical), history, social science, other. **Special academic programs:** cooperative (work-study plan) program, distance learning, double major, dual enrollment, honors program, independent study, internships, liberal arts/career combination, student-designed major, study abroad, teacher certificate program. **Teacher certification offered in:** early childhood, special education, elementary, middle/junior high, secondary. **Cooperative education programs:** business, computer science, education. **Reserve Officers Training Corps (ROTC):** Army ROTC: Offered at cooperating institution (University of Colorado–Boulder); Air Force ROTC: Offered at cooperating institution (University of Colorado–Boulder). **Faculty and instruction (2009-2010):** Total instructional faculty: 509 full-time, 808 part-time (51% men; 49% women; 16% minorities). Full-time faculty with Ph.D. or other terminal degree: 70%. Student/faculty ratio: 22/1. Classes of fewer than 20 students: 31%; of 20 to 49 students: 66%; of 50 or more students: 3%. **Advanced Placement and International Baccalaureate credit:** AP tests may be used for: Credit only. Scores accepted: 3, 4, 5. **Freshmen returning for sophomore year:** 66%. **Graduation rates:** Four-year: 5%; five-year: 14%; six-year: 21%.

COSTS AND FINANCIAL AID
Financial aid office: (303) 556-4741. **Expenses (2010-2011):** Tuition and fees 2010-2011: $4,093 in state, $14,440 out of state. Estimated books and supplies: $1,600. **Financial aid:** In 2009-2010, 65% of undergraduates applied for financial aid. Of those, 51% were determined to have financial need; 2% had their need fully met. Average financial aid package (proportion receiving): $7,774 (49%). Average amount of gift aid, such as scholarships or grants (proportion receiving): $3,943 (35%). Average amount of self-help aid, such as work study or loans (proportion receiving): $4,448 (52%). Average need-based loan (excluding PLUS or other private loans): $4,174. Among students who received need-based aid, the average percentage of need met: 59%. Among students who received aid based on merit, the average award (and the proportion receiving): $991 (17%). The average athletic scholarship (and the proportion receiving): $5,558 (1%). Average amount of debt of borrowers graduating in 2009: $26,635. Proportion who borrowed: 61%.

CAMPUS LIFE AND EXTRACURRICULAR ACTIVITIES
Student employment: During the 2009-2010 academic year, 20% of undergraduates worked on campus. Average per-year earnings: $7,000. Activities include: choral groups, dance, drama/theater, jazz band, literary magazine, music ensembles, musical theater, pep band, radio station, student government, student newspaper, television station. Number of fraternities: 5; sororities: 7. **Sports program (2009-2010):** Member of NCAA II. *Men's intercollegiate varsity sports:* baseball, basketball, cross country, soccer, swimming, tennis, track and field (indoor), track and field (outdoor). *Women's intercollegiate varsity sports:* basketball, cross country, soccer, softball, swimming, tennis, track and field (indoor), track and field (outdoor).

SERVICES AND FACILITIES
Basic services: nonremedial tutoring, women's center, placement service, day care, health service, health insurance. **Remedial assistance:** reading, math, writing, study skills. **Counseling services:** career, military, personal, veteran student, academic, older student, psychological. **For learning-disabled students:** School does not offer a structured program with separate admission and additional fees. Services include: oral tests, learning center, readers, extended time for tests, tutors. **Information technology resources:** Students are not required to lease or own a computer. Number of campus computers available to all students: 800. School has a wireless network. **Campus safety:** Security services offered: 24-hour foot-and-vehicle patrols, late-night transport/escort service, 24-hour emergency telephones, lighted pathways/sidewalks.

TRANSFER AND INTERNATIONAL STUDENTS
Transfer students: May apply for admission for the following academic terms: Fall, Spring, Summer. Applicants need a minimum number of credits to apply. For fall 2009: Transfer applications received: 3,658. Transfer applicants offered admission: 3,412. Transfer applicants enrolled: 1,926. **International students:** Number of foreign undergraduates: 124 (1% of student body). Number of countries represented: 40. Minimum TOEFL score required: 533 (paper); 72 (computer).

Naropa University

■ **Address:** 2130 Arapahoe Avenue, Boulder, CO 80302
■ **Website:** http://www.naropa.edu
■ **Private**
■ **Enrollment:** 432 full-time; 48 part-time

KEY STATS
✔ **U.S News College Ranking:** Unranked, Regional Universities (West)
✔ **SAT or ACT Score (25th/75th percentile):** N/A
✔ **Tuition:** 2010-2011: $25,100

Selectivity: N/A	Room/board: $5,076
Acceptance rate: 75%	Average debt: $23,717
Student/faculty ratio: 9/1	Proportion who borrowed: 71%

UNDERGRADUATE STUDENT BODY STATS
2009-2010 enrollment: 432 full-time; 48 part-time. Men: 39%; women: 61%. **Ethnic makeup:** African American: 2%; American-Indian: 3%; Asian American: 3%; Hispanic: 4%; White: 86%; International: 3%.

ADMISSIONS FACTS AND FIGURES
Phone: (303) 546-3572. **Email:** admissions@naropa.edu. **Website:** http://www.naropa.edu. **Application deadlines for fall 2011:** Regular decision: Rolling. Early decision: Not offered. Early action: Not offered. Admission can be deferred. **Application fee:** $50. **To apply online, go to:** http://www.naropa.edu/admissions/undergrad.cfm. **Admissions requirements/recommendations:** High school units required (recommended): English: (4); Mathematics: (3); Science: (3); Foreign language: (3); Social studies: (3); History: (3); Total units: (23). Tests: The college does not use SAT or ACT scores in admissions decisions. Neither SAT nor ACT required. For admission to the fall 2011 entering class, the school will accept: ACT with or without writing accepted. Campus visit: Recommended. Admissions interview: Required. Off-campus interview: May be arranged. **Factors that count in admissions decisions:** *Academic:* Secondary school record: Very Important. Class rank: Not Considered. Letters of recommendation: Very Important. Standardized test scores: Considered. Essay: Very Important. *Nonacademic:* Interview: Very Important. Extracurricular activities: Important. Talent/ability: Important. Character/personal qualities: Important. Alumni/ae relationship: Considered. Geographical residence: Not Considered. State residency: Not Considered. Religious affiliation/commitment: Considered. Minority status: Considered. Volunteer work: Important. Work experience: Considered. **Other schools with the greatest overlap in applicants:** Evergreen State College; Hampshire College; Kalamazoo College; New School; St. Lawrence University. **Admissions statistics for the fall 2009 entering class:** Total applicants: 152. Total accepted: 114. Freshmen enrolled: 45; 71% were from out of state. Overall acceptance rate: 75%. **Average high school grade point average:** 3.2.

ACADEMICS
Year founded: 1974. **Academic calendar:** Semester. **Degrees offered:** certificate, bachelor's, master's. **Areas of required coursework:** arts/fine arts, humanities, English (including composition), social science, other. **Special academic programs:** double major, dual enrollment, independent study, internships, student-designed major. **Faculty and instruction (2009-2010):** Total instructional faculty: 51 full-time, 148 part-time (35% men; 65% women; 13% minorities). Full-time faculty with Ph.D. or other terminal degree: 57%. Student/faculty ratio: 9/1. Classes of fewer than 20 students: 90%; of 20 to 49 students: 10%; of 50 or more students: 1%. **Advanced Placement and International Baccalaureate credit:** AP tests may be used for: Credit only. Scores accepted: 3. International Baccalaureate exams may be used for: Credit only. **Freshmen returning for sophomore year:** 60%. **Graduation rates:** Four-year: 19%; five-year: 42%; six-year: 41%.

COSTS AND FINANCIAL AID
Financial aid office: (303) 546-3565. **Expenses (2010-2011):** Tuition and fees 2010-2011: $25,100; room/board: $5,076. Estimated books and supplies: $1,200; transportation: $1,300; personal expenses: $3,402. **Financial aid:** Priority filing date for institution's financial aid form: March 1. In 2009-2010, 72% of undergraduates applied for financial aid. Of those, 66% were determined to have financial need; 2% had their need fully met. Average financial aid package (proportion receiving): $25,123 (66%). Average amount of gift aid, such as scholarships or grants (proportion receiving): $15,279 (66%). Average amount of self-help aid, such as work study or loans (proportion receiving): $11,470 (66%). Average need-based

loan (excluding PLUS or other private loans): $9,226. Among students who received need-based aid, the average percentage of need met: 88%. Among students who received aid based on merit, the average award (and the proportion receiving): $0 (0%). The average athletic scholarship (and the proportion receiving): $0 (0%). Average amount of debt of borrowers graduating in 2009: $23,717. Proportion who borrowed: 71%.

CAMPUS LIFE AND EXTRACURRICULAR ACTIVITIES

Campus housing available: apartments for married students, apartment for single students. Students who live in college-owned, operated, or affiliated housing: 15%. **Clubs and organizations:** Number of student organizations: 38. Activities include: campus ministries, choral groups, dance, drama/theater, international student organization, jazz band, literary magazine, music ensembles, musical theater, student government. Number of fraternities: 0; sororities: 0.

SERVICES AND FACILITIES

Basic services: nonremedial tutoring, health insurance. **Remedial assistance:** writing, study skills, other. **Counseling services:** minority student, career, personal, veteran student, academic, older student, psychological, religious. **For learning-disabled students:** School does not offer a structured program with separate admission and additional fees. Total undergraduates in learning-disabled program or receiving services: 27. Services include: tape recorders, other special classes, untimed tests, note-taking services, oral tests, readers, extended time for tests, tutors, early syllabus, priority registration, priority seating, texts on tape, exams on tape or computer, other testing accommodations. **Library:** Number of titles: 29,175; number of current serial subscriptions: 81. **Information technology resources:** Students are not required to lease or own a computer. Number of campus computers available to all students: 75. School has a wireless network. Approximate number of users that can be accommodated: 240. Proportion of college-owned housing units wired for high-speed internet access: 100%. **Campus safety:** Security services offered: late-night transport/escort service, lighted pathways/sidewalks, controlled dormitory access (key, security card, etc).

TRANSFER AND INTERNATIONAL STUDENTS

Transfer students: May apply for admission for the following academic terms: Fall, Spring. Applicants do not need a minimum number of credits to apply. For fall 2009: Transfer applications received: 197. Transfer applicants offered admission: 171. Transfer applicants enrolled: 105. **International students:** Number of foreign undergraduates: 12 (3% of student body). Number of countries represented: 8. Minimum TOEFL score required: 550 (paper); 213 (computer).

Regis University

- **Address:** 3333 Regis Boulevard, B-20, Denver, CO 80221
- **Website:** http://www.regis.edu
- **Private; Religious affiliation:** Roman Catholic (Jesuit)
- **Enrollment:** 2,364 full-time; 3,222 part-time

KEY STATS

✔ **U.S News College Ranking:** 28, Regional Universities (West)
✔ **ACT Score (25th/75th percentile):** 21-27
✔ **Tuition:** 2010-2011: $30,588

Selectivity: More selective	**Room/board:** $9,100
Acceptance rate: 80%	**Average debt:** $25,558
Student/faculty ratio: 11/1	**Proportion who borrowed:** 66%

UNDERGRADUATE STUDENT BODY STATS

2009-2010 enrollment: 2,364 full-time; 3,222 part-time. Men: 35%; women: 65%. **Ethnic makeup:** African American: 6%; American-Indian: 1%; Asian American: 4%; Hispanic: 11%; White: 77%; International: 1%. **Religious preference:** Roman Catholic: 31%; Protestant: 8%; Jewish: 1%; Buddhist: 1%; No preference: 1%; Unknown: 33%; Other: 14%.

ADMISSIONS FACTS AND FIGURES

Phone: (303) 458-4900. **Email:** regisadm@regis.edu. **Website:** http://www.regis.edu. **Application deadlines for fall 2011:** Regular decision: August 1. Early decision: Not offered. Early action: Not offered. Admission can be deferred. **Application fee:** $40. **To apply online, go to:** http://www.regis.edu/rc.asp?page=applications.downloadapp. **Admissions requirements/recommendations:** High school units required (recommended): English:

(4); Mathematics: (3); Science: (3); Foreign language: (2); History: (2); Total units: 15. Tests: The college uses SAT or ACT scores in admissions decisions. Either SAT or ACT required. For admission to the fall 2011 entering class, the school will accept: ACT with writing recommended. Campus visit: Recommended. Admissions interview: Recommended. Off-campus interview: May be arranged. **Factors that count in admissions decisions:** *Academic:* Secondary school record: Very Important. Class rank: Not Considered. Letters of recommendation: Very Important. Standardized test scores: Important. Essay: Very Important. *Nonacademic:* Interview: Considered. Extracurricular activities: Important. Talent/ability: Considered. Character/personal qualities: Important. Alumni/ae relationship: Considered. Geographical residence: Considered. State residency: Not Considered. Religious affiliation/commitment: Considered. Minority status: Considered. Volunteer work: Important. Work experience: Not Considered. **Other schools with the greatest overlap in applicants:** Creighton University; Gonzaga University; St. Louis University; University of Colorado–Boulder; University of Denver. **Admissions statistics for the fall 2009 entering class:** Total applicants: 1,942. Total accepted: 1,544. Freshmen enrolled: 375; 42% were from out of state. Overall acceptance rate: 80%. **Size of waiting list:** N/A applicants; enrolled from waiting list: 0. **Credentials of fall 2009 freshmen:** 30% ranked in the top 10 percent of their high school class; 60% were in the top 25 percent; 86% were in the top half. (Proportion submitting class standing: 56%.) **Average high school grade point average:** 3.5. **First-year students who submitted SAT scores:** 43%. Scores (25/75 percentile): Critical Reading: 470-590, Math: 470-590, Combined: 940-1180. **First-year students submitting ACT scores:** 87%. Scores (25/75 percentile): English: 21-27, Math: 19-26, Composite: 21-27.

ACADEMICS

Year founded: 1877. **Academic calendar:** Semester. **Degrees offered:** bachelor's, master's. **Most popular majors:** 35% business, management, marketing, and related support services, 27% health professions and related clinical sciences, 7% computer and information sciences and support services, 6% liberal arts and sciences studies, and humanities, 4% psychology. **Major fields of study:** agriculture, agriculture operations, and related sciences; area, ethnic, cultural, and gender studies; biological and biomedical sciences; business, management, marketing, and related support services; communication, journalism, and related programs; computer and information sciences and support services; education; engineering; engineering technologies/technicians; English language and literature/letters; foreign languages, literatures, and linguistics; health professions and related clinical sciences; legal professions and studies; liberal arts and sciences studies, and humanities; mathematics and statistics; multi/interdisciplinary studies; philosophy and religious studies; physical sciences; psychology; public administration and social service professions; science technologies/technicians; security and protective services; social sciences; theology and religious vocations; visual and performing arts. **Areas of required coursework:** arts/fine arts, humanities, mathematics, English (including composition), philosophy, foreign languages, sciences (biological or physical), history, social science, other. **Pre-professional programs:** pre-law, pre-dentistry, pre-medicine, pre-theology, pre-veterinary science, pre-optometry, pre-pharmacy, other. **Special academic programs (% participation):** accelerated program (65%), distance learning (30%), double major (10%), dual enrollment, honors program (1%), independent study, internships (45%), student-designed major (4%), study abroad, teacher certificate program (8%). **Teacher certification offered in:** early childhood, special education, elementary, middle/junior high, secondary, bilingual/bicultural. **Reserve Officers Training Corps (ROTC):** Army ROTC: Offered at cooperating institution (Metropolitan State College of Denver); Navy ROTC: Offered at cooperating institution (University of Colorado–Boulder); Air Force ROTC: Offered at cooperating institution (University of Colorado–Boulder). **Faculty and instruction (2009-2010):** Total instructional faculty: 204 full-time, 790 part-time (46% men; 54% women; 9% minorities). Full-time faculty with Ph.D. or other terminal degree: 67%. Student/faculty ratio: 11/1. Classes of fewer than 20 students: 80%; of 20 to 49 students: 19%; of 50 or more students: 1%. **Advanced Placement and International Baccalaureate credit:** AP tests may be used for: Placement only. Scores accepted: 3, 4, 5. International Baccalaureate exams may be used for: Placement only. **Freshmen returning for sophomore year:** 83%. **Graduation rates:** Four-year: 44%; five-year: 64%; six-year: 61%. **Graduate study:** 30% of students pursue further study immediately upon graduation; 29% within one year.

COSTS AND FINANCIAL AID

Financial aid office: (303) 458-4066. **Expenses (2010-2011):** Tuition and fees 2010-2011: $30,588; room/board: $9,100. Estimated books and supplies: $1,749; transportation: $1,296; personal expenses: $1,269. **Financial aid:**

Priority filing date for institution's financial aid form: March 1. In 2009-2010, 96% of undergraduates applied for financial aid. Of those, 61% were determined to have financial need; 56% had their need fully met. Average financial aid package (proportion receiving): $15,333 (60%). Average amount of gift aid, such as scholarships or grants (proportion receiving): $10,756 (40%). Average amount of self-help aid, such as work study or loans (proportion receiving): $4,578 (40%). Average need-based loan (excluding PLUS or other private loans): $2,226. Among students who received need-based aid, the average percentage of need met: 54%. Among students who received aid based on merit, the average award (and the proportion receiving): $10,411 (24%). The average athletic scholarship (and the proportion receiving): $6,723 (5%). Average amount of debt of borrowers graduating in 2009: $25,558. Proportion who borrowed: 66%.

CAMPUS LIFE AND EXTRACURRICULAR ACTIVITIES
Campus housing available (% using): coed dorms (68%), apartment for single students (21%), special housing for disabled students (1%). Students who live in college-owned, operated, or affiliated housing: 21%. **Clubs and organizations:** Number of student organizations: 30. Activities include: campus ministries, choral groups, dance, drama/theater, jazz band, literary magazine, music ensembles, musical theater, radio station, student government, student newspaper, yearbook. Number of fraternities: 0; sororities: 0. Average proportion of students who stay on campus on weekends: 70%. **Sports program (2009-2010):** Member of NCAA II. *Men's intercollegiate varsity sports:* baseball, basketball, cross country, golf, soccer. *Women's intercollegiate varsity sports:* basketball, cross country, golf, lacrosse, soccer, softball, volleyball.

SERVICES AND FACILITIES
Basic services: nonremedial tutoring, placement service, health service, health insurance, other. **Remedial assistance:** reading, math, writing, study skills. **Counseling services:** career, personal, academic, older student, psychological, religious, other. **For learning-disabled students:** School does not offer a structured program with separate admission and additional fees. Total undergraduates in learning-disabled program or receiving services: 167. Services include: reading machines, tape recorders, note-taking services, oral tests, learning center, readers, extended time for tests, texts on tape, exams on tape or computer, other. **Library:** Number of titles: 350,000; number of current serial subscriptions: 17,000. **Information technology resources:** Students are not required to lease or own a computer. Number of campus computers available to all students: 480. School has a wireless network. Approximate number of users that can be accommodated: 2,500. Proportion of college-owned housing units wired for high-speed internet access: 100%. **Campus safety:** Security services offered: 24-hour foot-and-vehicle patrols, late-night transport/escort service, 24-hour emergency telephones, lighted pathways/sidewalks, controlled dormitory access (key, security card, etc).

TRANSFER AND INTERNATIONAL STUDENTS
Transfer students: May apply for admission for the following academic terms: Fall, Spring, Summer. Applicants need a minimum number of credits to apply. For fall 2009: Transfer applications received: 233. Transfer applicants offered admission: 126. Transfer applicants enrolled: 64. **International students:** Number of foreign undergraduates: 27 (1% of student body). Number of countries represented: 33. Minimum TOEFL score required: 550 (paper); 213 (computer). Average TOEFL score: 600 (paper).

United States Air Force Academy

- **Address:** HQ USAFA/RRS, 2304 Cadet Drive, Suite 2300, USAF Academy, CO 80840
- **Website:** http://www.usafa.edu
- **Public**
- **Enrollment:** 4,620 full-time

KEY STATS
✔ **U.S News College Ranking:** 1, Regional Colleges (West)
✔ **ACT Score (25th/75th percentile):** 28-32
✔ **Tuition:** N/A

Selectivity: Most selective	**Room/board:** N/A
Acceptance rate: 17%	**Average debt:** N/A
Student/faculty ratio: 9/1	**Proportion who borrowed:** N/A

UNDERGRADUATE STUDENT BODY STATS
2009-2010 enrollment: 4,620 full-time. Men: 80%; women: 20%. **Ethnic makeup:** African American: 5%; American-Indian: 1%; Asian American: 8%; Hispanic: 8%; White: 76%; International: 1%. **Religious preference:** Roman Catholic: 29%; Protestant: 55%; Jewish: 1%; No preference: 12%; Unknown: 1%; Other: 2%.

ADMISSIONS FACTS AND FIGURES
Phone: (800) 443-9266. **Email:** rr_webmail@usafa.edu. **Website:** http://www.usafa.edu. **Application deadlines for fall 2011:** Regular decision: February 15. Early decision: Not offered. Early action: Not offered. Admission cannot be deferred. **Application fee:** None. **To apply online, go to:** https://admissions.usafa.edu/secure/Online/Eligibility.htm. **Admissions requirements/recommendations:** High school units required (recommended): English: (4); Mathematics: (4); Science: (4); Foreign language: (2); Social studies: (3); History: (3); Total units: (22). Tests: The college uses SAT or ACT scores in admissions decisions. Either SAT or ACT required. For admission to the fall 2011 entering class, the school will accept: ACT with writing recommended. Campus visit: Recommended. Admissions interview: Required. Off-campus interview: May be arranged. **Factors that count in admissions decisions:** *Academic:* Secondary school record: Very Important. Class rank: Very Important. Letters of recommendation: Very Important. Standardized test scores: Very Important. Essay: Very Important. *Nonacademic:* Interview: Very Important. Extracurricular activities: Important. Talent/ability: Important. Character/personal qualities: Very Important. Alumni/ae relationship: Considered. Geographical residence: Considered. State residency: Considered. Religious affiliation/commitment: Not Considered. Minority status: Considered. Volunteer work: Important. Work experience: Important. **Other schools with the greatest overlap in applicants:** United States Coast Guard Academy; United States Merchant Marine Academy; United States Military Academy; United States Naval Academy. **Admissions statistics for the fall 2009 entering class:** Total applicants: 9,897. Total accepted: 1,667. Freshmen enrolled: 1,362; 92% were from out of state. Overall acceptance rate: 17%. **Size of waiting list:** 0 applicants; enrolled from waiting list: 0. **Credentials of fall 2009 freshmen:** 52% ranked in the top 10 percent of their high school class; 81% were in the top 25 percent; 97% were in the top half. (Proportion submitting class standing: 100%.) **Average high school grade point average:** 3.9. **First-year students who submitted SAT scores:** 49%. Scores (25/75 percentile): Critical Reading: 600-680, Math: 630-700, Combined: 1230-1380. **First-year students submitting ACT scores:** 51%. Scores (25/75 percentile): English: 25-31, Math: 26-32, Composite: 28-32.

ACADEMICS
Year founded: 1954. **Academic calendar:** Semester. **Degrees offered:** bachelor's. **Most popular majors:** 36% engineering, 12% social sciences, 11% business, management, marketing, and related support services, 11% multi/interdisciplinary studies, 10% physical sciences. **Major fields of study:** biological and biomedical sciences; business, management, marketing, and related support services; computer and information sciences and support services; engineering; English language and literature/letters; history; legal professions and studies; liberal arts and sciences studies, and humanities; multi/interdisciplinary studies; physical sciences; social sciences. **Areas of required coursework:** humanities, computer literacy, mathematics, English (including composition), philosophy, foreign languages, sciences (biological or physical), history, social science, other. **Special academic programs (% participation):** double major (2%), English as a Second Language (ESL) (1%), exchange student program (domestic) (6%), honors program (5%), independent study, internships, student-designed major, study abroad (7%). **Faculty and instruction (2009-2010):** Total instructional faculty: 506 full-time, 21 part-time (77% men; 23% women; 8% minorities). Full-time faculty with Ph.D. or other terminal degree: 53%. Student/faculty ratio: 9/1. Classes of fewer than 20 students: 64%; of 20 to 49 students: 35%; of 50 or more students: 0%. **Advanced Placement and International Baccalaureate credit:** AP tests may be used for: Credit and/or placement. **Freshmen returning for sophomore year:** 87%. **Graduation rates:** Four-year: 77%; five-year: 78%; six-year: 79%. **Graduate study:** 8% of students pursue further study immediately upon graduation. Fields in which graduates pursue further study: Master of Business Administration (MBA), 1%; law, 1%; medicine, 1%; engineering, 3%; arts and sciences, 1%.

COSTS AND FINANCIAL AID
Financial aid office: (719) 333-3160. **Financial aid:** Average financial aid package (proportion receiving): $0 (N/A). Average amount of gift aid, such as scholarships or grants (proportion receiving): $0 (N/A). Average amount of self-help aid, such as work study or loans (proportion receiving): $0 (N/A).

Average need-based loan (excluding PLUS or other private loans): $0. Among students who received aid based on merit, the average award (and the proportion receiving): $0 (N/A). The average athletic scholarship (and the proportion receiving): $0 (N/A).

CAMPUS LIFE AND EXTRACURRICULAR ACTIVITIES

Campus housing available (% using): coed dorms (100%). Students who live in college-owned, operated, or affiliated housing: 100%. **Clubs and organizations:** Number of student organizations: 77. Activities include: campus ministries, choral groups, dance, drama/theater, marching band, model UN, musical theater, pep band, radio station, student government, television station, yearbook. Number of fraternities: 0; sororities: 0. Average proportion of students who stay on campus on weekends: 100%. **Sports program (2009-2010):** Member of NCAA I. **Men's intercollegiate varsity sports:** baseball, basketball, cross country, fencing, football, golf, gymnastics, ice hockey, lacrosse, rifle, soccer, swimming, tennis, track and field (indoor), track and field (outdoor), water polo, wrestling. **Women's intercollegiate varsity sports:** basketball, cross country, fencing, gymnastics, rifle, soccer, swimming, tennis, track and field (indoor), track and field (outdoor), volleyball.

SERVICES AND FACILITIES

Basic services: nonremedial tutoring, women's center, health service, health insurance. **Remedial assistance:** reading, math, writing, study skills. **Counseling services:** military, personal, academic, psychological, birth control, religious, other. **Library:** Number of titles: 970,952; number of current serial subscriptions: 1,156. **Information technology resources:** Students are required to lease or own a computer. Number of campus computers available to all students: 500. School has a wireless network. Approximate number of users that can be accommodated: 4,500. Proportion of college-owned housing units wired for high-speed internet access: 100%. **Campus safety:** Security services offered: 24-hour foot-and-vehicle patrols, late-night transport/escort service, 24-hour emergency telephones, lighted pathways/sidewalks, controlled dormitory access (key, security card, etc).

TRANSFER AND INTERNATIONAL STUDENTS

Transfer students: May apply for admission for the following academic terms: Fall. Applicants do not need a minimum number of credits to apply. **International students:** Number of foreign undergraduates: 59 (1% of student body). Number of countries represented: 39.

University of Colorado—Boulder

- **Address:** Regent Administration Center, Room 125, 552 UCB, Boulder, CO 80309-0552
- **Website:** http://www.colorado.edu
- **Public**
- **Enrollment:** 24,847 full-time; 2,222 part-time

KEY STATS

✔ **U.S News College Ranking:** 86, National Universities
✔ **ACT Score (25th/75th percentile):** 24-29
✔ **Tuition:** 2010-2011: $8,511 in state, $28,193 out of state

Selectivity: More selective	**Room/board:** $10,792
Acceptance rate: 84%	**Average debt:** $19,211
Student/faculty ratio: 18/1	**Proportion who borrowed:** 42%

UNDERGRADUATE STUDENT BODY STATS

2009-2010 enrollment: 24,847 full-time; 2,222 part-time. Men: 53%; women: 47%. **Ethnic makeup:** African American: 2%; American-Indian: 1%; Asian American: 6%; Hispanic: 6%; White: 83%; International: 2%.

ADMISSIONS FACTS AND FIGURES

Phone: (303) 492-6301. **Email:** apply@colorado.edu. **Website:** http://www.colorado.edu. **Application deadlines for fall 2011:** Regular decision: January 15; decision sent by April 1. Early decision: Not offered. Early action: Send application by: December 1; Decision sent by: January 15. Admission can be deferred. **Application fee:** $50. **To apply online, go to:** http://www.colorado.edu/prospective/freshman/apply/. **Admissions requirements/recommendations:** High school units required (recommended): English: 4; Mathematics: 4; Science: 3; Foreign language: 3; Social studies: 3; History: 1; Total units: 17. Tests: The college uses SAT or ACT scores in admissions decisions. Either SAT or ACT required. For admission to the fall 2011 entering class, the school will accept: ACT with or without writing accepted. Campus visit:

Recommended. Admissions interview: Neither required nor recommended. Off-campus interview: Not available. **Factors that count in admissions decisions: Academic:** Secondary school record: Very Important. Class rank: Very Important. Letters of recommendation: Important. Standardized test scores: Very Important. Essay: Very Important. **Nonacademic:** Interview: Not Considered. Extracurricular activities: Considered. Talent/ability: Considered. Character/personal qualities: Important. Alumni/ae relationship: Considered. Geographical residence: Considered. State residency: Important. Religious affiliation/commitment: Not Considered. Minority status: Not Considered. Volunteer work: Considered. Work experience: Considered. **Other schools with the greatest overlap in applicants:** Arizona State University; Colorado State University; University of California–Los Angeles; University of Denver; University of Washington. **Admissions statistics for the fall 2009 entering class:** Total applicants: 19,649. Total accepted: 16,514. Freshmen enrolled: 5,555; 41% were from out of state. Accepted through early-decision or early-action plans: 60%. Overall acceptance rate: 84%. Non-early acceptance rate: 80%. **Size of waiting list:** 926 applicants; enrolled from waiting list: 81. **Credentials of fall 2009 freshmen:** 25% ranked in the top 10 percent of their high school class; 58% were in the top 25 percent; 92% were in the top half. (Proportion submitting class standing: 68%.) **Average high school grade point average:** 3.6. **First-year students who submitted SAT scores:** 58%. Scores (25/75 percentile): Critical Reading: 530-630, Math: 550-650, Combined: 1080-1280. **First-year students submitting ACT scores:** 80%. Scores (25/75 percentile): English: 23-29, Math: 23-29, Composite: 24-29.

ACADEMICS

Year founded: 1876. **Academic calendar:** Semester. **Degrees offered:** bachelor's, master's, post-master's certificate, doctorate. **Most popular majors:** 16% social sciences, 14% business, management, marketing, and related support services, 10% biological and biomedical sciences, 9% communication, journalism, and related programs, 9% psychology. **Major fields of study:** architecture and related services; area, ethnic, cultural, and gender studies; biological and biomedical sciences; business, management, marketing, and related support services; communication, journalism, and related programs; computer and information sciences and support services; education; engineering; English language and literature/letters; foreign languages, literatures, and linguistics; health professions and related clinical sciences; history; liberal arts and sciences studies, and humanities; mathematics and statistics; multi/interdisciplinary studies; natural resources and conservation; philosophy and religious studies; physical sciences; psychology; social sciences; visual and performing arts. **Areas of required coursework:** humanities, mathematics, English (including composition), foreign languages, sciences (biological or physical), history, social science, other. **Pre-professional programs:** pre-law, pre-dentistry, pre-medicine, pre-veterinary science, pre-optometry, pre-pharmacy, other. **Special academic programs (% participation):** accelerated program (5%), cooperative (work-study plan) program, cross-registration, distance learning (25%), double major (14%), dual enrollment (3%), English as a Second Language (ESL), honors program (17%), independent study (11%), internships (14%), liberal arts/career combination (2%), student-designed major, study abroad (18%), teacher certificate program (5%), other. **Teacher certification offered in:** elementary, secondary. **Cooperative education programs:** computer science, engineering. **Reserve Officers Training Corps (ROTC):** Army ROTC: Offered on campus; Navy ROTC: Offered on campus; Air Force ROTC: Offered on campus. **Faculty and instruction (2009-2010):** Total instructional faculty: 1,392 full-time, 699 part-time (59% men; 41% women; 14% minorities). Full-time faculty with Ph.D. or other terminal degree: 90%. Student/faculty ratio: 18/1. Classes of fewer than 20 students: 47%; of 20 to 49 students: 39%; of 50 or more students: 13%. **Advanced Placement and International Baccalaureate credit:** AP tests may be used for: Credit and/or placement. Scores accepted: 3, 4, 5. International Baccalaureate exams may be used for: Credit and/or placement. **Freshmen returning for sophomore year:** 84%. **Graduation rates:** Four-year: 41%; five-year: 63%; six-year: 67%. **Graduate study:** 21% of students pursue further study within one year; 41% within five years. Fields in which graduates pursue further study: Master of Business Administration (MBA), 5%; law, 5%; medicine, 2%; engineering, 2%; education, 3%; arts and sciences, 9%.

COSTS AND FINANCIAL AID

Financial aid office: (303) 492-5091. **Expenses (2010-2011):** Tuition and fees 2010-2011: $8,511 in state, $28,193 out of state; room/board: $10,792. Estimated books and supplies: $1,748; transportation: $1,296; personal expenses: $3,400. **Financial aid:** Priority filing date for institution's financial aid form: April 1. In 2009-2010, 69% of undergraduates applied for financial aid. Of those, 35% were determined to have financial need; 69% had their need fully met. Average financial aid package (proportion receiving): $14,790 (34%). Average amount of gift aid, such as scholarships or grants (proportion receiving): $8,125 (29%). Average amount of self-help aid, such as work study or loans (proportion receiving): $7,113 (32%). Average need-based loan (excluding PLUS or other private loans): $6,796. Among students who received need-based aid, the average percentage of need met: 92%. Among students who received aid based on merit, the average award (and the proportion receiving): $6,707 (26%). The average athletic scholarship (and the proportion receiving): $16,962 (1%). Average amount of debt of borrowers graduating in 2009: $19,211. Proportion who borrowed: 42%.

CAMPUS LIFE AND EXTRACURRICULAR ACTIVITIES

Campus housing available: coed dorms, sorority housing, apartments for married students, apartment for single students, special housing for disabled students, other housing options. Students who live in college-owned, operated, or affiliated housing: 24%. **Student employment:** During the 2009-2010 academic year, 12% of undergraduates worked on campus. Average per-year earnings: $1,485. **Clubs and organizations:** Number of student organizations: 400. Activities include: campus ministries, choral groups, concert band, dance, drama/theater, international student organization, jazz band, literary magazine, marching band, model UN, music ensembles, musical theater, opera, pep band, radio station, student government, student newspaper, student film society, symphony orchestra, television station. Number of fraternities: 20; sororities: 19. Proportion of men in fraternities: 9%; of women in sororities: 16%. Average proportion of students who stay on campus on weekends: 75%. **Sports program (2009-2010):** Member of NCAA I. *Men's intercollegiate varsity sports:* basketball, cross country, football, golf, skiing (nordic), skiing (alpine), track and field (indoor), track and field (outdoor). *Women's intercollegiate varsity sports:* basketball, cross country, golf, skiing (nordic), skiing (alpine), soccer, tennis, track and field (indoor), track and field (outdoor), volleyball.

SERVICES AND FACILITIES

Basic services: nonremedial tutoring, women's center, placement service, day care, health service, health insurance, other. **Counseling services:** minority student, career, personal, veteran student, academic, older student, psychological, birth control, other. **For learning-disabled students:** School does not offer a structured program with separate admission and additional fees. Total undergraduates in learning-disabled program or receiving services: 473. Services include: learning center, other. **Library:** Number of titles: 4,348,639; number of current serial subscriptions: 60,805. **Information technology resources:** Students are not required to lease or own a computer. Number of campus computers available to all students: 1,600. School has a wireless network. Approximate number of users that can be accommodated: 200,000. Proportion of college-owned housing units wired for high-speed internet access: 100%. **Campus safety:** Security services offered: 24-hour foot-and-vehicle patrols, late-night transport/escort service, 24-hour emergency telephones, lighted pathways/sidewalks, student patrols, controlled dormitory access (key, security card, etc).

TRANSFER AND INTERNATIONAL STUDENTS

Transfer students: May apply for admission for the following academic terms: Fall, Spring, Summer. Applicants do not need a minimum number of credits to apply. For fall 2009: Transfer applications received: 3,284. Transfer applicants offered admission: 2,050. Transfer applicants enrolled: 1,284. **International students:** Number of foreign undergraduates: 442 (2% of student body). Number of countries represented: 95. Minimum TOEFL score required: 500 (paper); 173 (computer). Average TOEFL score: 582 (paper).

University of Colorado–Colorado Springs

■ **Address:** 1420 Austin Bluffs Parkway, Colorado Springs, CO 80918
■ **Website:** http://www.uccs.edu
■ **Public**
■ **Enrollment:** 5,459 full-time; 1,461 part-time

KEY STATS

✔ **U.S News College Ranking:** 32, Regional Universities (West)
✔ **ACT Score (25th/75th percentile):** 21-26
✔ **Tuition:** 2010-2011: $7,486 in state, $17,482 out of state
   Selectivity: Selective   **Room/board:** $8,758
   Acceptance rate: 65%   **Average debt:** $20,923
   Student/faculty ratio: 16/1   **Proportion who borrowed:** 61%

UNDERGRADUATE STUDENT BODY STATS

2009-2010 enrollment: 5,459 full-time; 1,461 part-time. Men: 45%; women: 55%. **Ethnic makeup:** African American: 4%; American-Indian: 1%; Asian American: 5%; Hispanic: 10%; White: 80%.

ADMISSIONS FACTS AND FIGURES

Phone: (719) 262-3383. **Email:** admrecor@uccs.edu. **Website:** http://www.uccs.edu. **Application deadlines for fall 2011:** Regular decision: July 1. Early decision: Not offered. Early action: Not offered. Admission can be deferred. **Application fee:** $50. **To apply online, go to:** http://www.uccs.edu/appintro.htm. **Admissions requirements/recommendations:** High school units required (recommended): English: 4 (4); Mathematics: 4 (4); Science: 3 (3); Foreign language: 2 (2); Social studies: 2 (2); History: 0 (0); Academic electives: 1 (1); Total units: 16 (16). Tests: The college uses SAT or ACT scores in admissions decisions. Either SAT or ACT required. For admission to the fall 2011 entering class, the school will accept: ACT with or without writing accepted. Campus visit: Recommended. Admissions interview: Neither required nor recommended. Off-campus interview: May be arranged. **Factors that count in admissions decisions:** *Academic:* Secondary school record: Very Important. Class rank: Very Important. Letters of recommendation: Considered. Standardized test scores: Very Important. Essay: Considered. *Nonacademic:* Interview: Not Considered. Extracurricular activities: Considered. Talent/ability: Considered. Character/personal qualities: Not Considered. Alumni/ae relationship: Considered. Geographical residence: Considered. State residency: Not Considered. Religious affiliation/commitment: Not Considered. Minority status: Not Considered. Volunteer work: Not Considered. Work experience: Not Considered. **Other schools with the greatest overlap in applicants:** Colorado State University; Colorado State University–Pueblo; University of Colorado–Boulder; University of Colorado–Denver; University of Northern Colorado. **Admissions statistics for the fall 2009 entering class:** Total applicants: 4,757. Total accepted: 3,072. Freshmen enrolled: 1,097; 14% were from out of state. Overall acceptance rate: 65%. **Credentials of fall 2009 freshmen:** 14% ranked in the top 10 percent of their high school class; 40% were in the top 25 percent; 72% were in the top half. (Proportion submitting class standing: 84%.) **Average high school grade point average:** 3.3. **First-year students who submitted SAT scores:** 28%. Scores (25/75 percentile): Critical Reading: 480-590, Math: 490-600, Combined: 970-1190. **First-year students submitting ACT scores:** 92%. Scores (25/75 percentile): English: 20-26, Math: 20-26, Composite: 21-26.

ACADEMICS

Year founded: 1965. **Academic calendar:** Semester. **Degrees offered:** certificate, bachelor's, master's, doctorate. **Most popular majors:** 20% business administration and management, 15% social sciences, 13% health services/allied health/health sciences, 9% communication studies/speech communication and rhetoric, 9% psychology. **Major fields of study:** biological and biomedical sciences; business, management, marketing, and related support services; communication, journalism, and related programs; computer and information sciences and support services; engineering; English language and literature/letters; foreign languages, literatures, and linguistics; health professions and related clinical sciences; history; mathematics and statistics; multi/interdisciplinary studies; philosophy and religious studies; physical sciences; psychology; security and protective services; social sciences; visual and performing arts. **Areas of required coursework:** humanities, mathematics, English (including composition), sciences (biological or physical), history, social science. **Pre-professional programs:** pre-law, pre-dentistry, pre-medicine, pre-veterinary science, pre-pharmacy, other. **Special academic programs:** accelerated program, cooperative (work-study plan) program, distance learning, double major, English as a Second Language (ESL), honors program, independent study, internships, liberal arts/career combination, student-designed major, study abroad, teacher certificate program, other. **Teacher certification offered in:** special education, elementary, middle/junior high, secondary. **Cooperative education programs:** art, business, computer science, education, engineering, health professions, natural science, social/behavioral science. **Reserve Officers Training Corps (ROTC):** Army ROTC: Offered on campus. **Faculty and instruction (2009-2010):** Total instructional faculty: 227 full-time, 139 part-time (48% men; 52% women; 11% minorities). Full-time faculty with Ph.D. or other terminal degree: 100%. Student/faculty ratio: 16/1. Classes of fewer than 20 students: 39%; of 20 to 49 students: 49%; of 50 or more students: 11%. **Advanced Placement and International Baccalaureate credit:** AP tests may be used for: Credit only. Scores accepted: 4. **Freshmen returning for sophomore year:** 69%. **Graduation rates:** Four-year: 22%; five-year: 40%; six-year: 44%. **Graduate study:** 15% of students pursue further study immediately upon graduation; 21% within one year; 13% within five years. Fields in which graduates pursue further study: Master of Business Administration (MBA), 21%; law, 3%; medicine, 6%; dentistry, 1%; engineering, 6%; education, 32%; arts and sciences, 12%.

COSTS AND FINANCIAL AID

Financial aid office: (719) 262-3460. **Expenses (2010-2011):** Tuition and fees 2010-2011: $7,486 in state, $17,482 out of state; room/board: $8,758. Estimated books and supplies: $1,728; transportation: $1,696; personal expenses: $1,268. **Financial aid:** Priority filing date for institution's financial aid form: April 1. In 2009-2010, 85% of undergraduates applied for financial aid. Of those, 58% were determined to have financial need; 8% had their need fully met. Average financial aid package (proportion receiving): $8,396 (55%). Average amount of gift aid, such as scholarships or grants (proportion receiving): $6,282 (43%). Average amount of self-help aid, such as work study or loans (proportion receiving): $4,412 (43%). Average need-based loan (excluding PLUS or other private loans): $4,160. Among students who received need-based aid, the average percentage of need met: 53%. Among students who received aid based on merit, the average award (and the proportion receiving): $1,506 (4%). The average athletic scholarship (and the proportion receiving): $3,523 (1%). Average amount of debt of borrowers graduating in 2009: $20,923. Proportion who borrowed: 61%.

CAMPUS LIFE AND EXTRACURRICULAR ACTIVITIES

Campus housing available (% using): coed dorms (47%), women's dorms (8%), men's dorms, apartment for single students (35%), special housing for disabled students. Students who live in college-owned, operated, or affiliated housing: 13%. **Student employment:** During the 2009-2010 academic year, 12% of undergraduates worked on campus. Average per-year earnings: $5,000. **Clubs and organizations:** Number of student organizations: 11. Activities include: choral groups, dance, drama/theater, jazz band, literary magazine, music ensembles, musical theater, radio station, student government, student newspaper, student film society. Number of fraternities: 1; sororities: 1. **Sports program (2009-2010):** Member of NCAA II. *Men's intercollegiate varsity sports:* basketball, cross country, golf, soccer, track and field (indoor), track and field (outdoor). *Women's intercollegiate varsity sports:* basketball, cross country, soccer, softball, track and field (indoor), track and field (outdoor), volleyball.

SERVICES AND FACILITIES

Basic services: nonremedial tutoring, placement service, day care, health service, health insurance. **Remedial assistance:** reading, math, writing. **Counseling services:** minority student, career, military, personal, veteran student, academic, older student, psychological. **For learning-disabled students:** School does not offer a structured program with separate admission and additional fees. Services include: remedial math, remedial English, reading machines, tape recorders, note-taking services, learning center, extended time for tests, early syllabus, priority seating, texts on tape, typist/scribe, exams on tape or computer, other testing accommodations, other. **Library:** Number of titles: 470,672; number of current serial subscriptions: 10,875. **Information technology resources:** Students are not required to lease or own a computer. School has a wireless network. Proportion of college-owned housing units wired for high-speed internet access: 100%. **Campus safety:** Security services offered: 24-hour foot-and-vehicle patrols, late-night transport/escort service, 24-hour emergency telephones, lighted pathways/sidewalks, student patrols, controlled dormitory access (key, security card, etc).

TRANSFER AND INTERNATIONAL STUDENTS

Transfer students: May apply for admission for the following academic terms: Fall, Spring, Summer. Applicants need a minimum number of credits to apply. For fall 2009: Transfer applications received: 2,042. Transfer applicants offered admission: 1,375. Transfer applicants enrolled: 825. **International students:** Number of foreign undergraduates: 30. Number of countries represented: 25. Minimum TOEFL score required: 550 (paper); 79 (computer).

University of Colorado—Denver

- **Address:** Campus Box 167 PO Box 173364, Denver, CO 80217-3364
- **Website:** http://www.cudenver.edu
- **Public**
- **Enrollment:** 7,247 full-time; 5,999 part-time

KEY STATS

✔ **U.S News College Ranking:** 191, National Universities
✔ **ACT Score (25th/75th percentile):** 20-25
✔ **Tuition:** 2010-2011: $6,657 in state, $19,689 out of state

Selectivity: Selective	**Room/board:** $11,374
Acceptance rate: 61%	**Average debt:** $21,264
Student/faculty ratio: 15/1	**Proportion who borrowed:** 66%

UNDERGRADUATE STUDENT BODY STATS

2009-2010 enrollment: 7,247 full-time; 5,999 part-time. Men: 44%; women: 56%. **Ethnic makeup:** African American: 5%; American-Indian: 1%; Asian American: 11%; Hispanic: 12%; White: 66%; International: 5%.

ADMISSIONS FACTS AND FIGURES

Phone: (303) 556-2704. **Email:** admissions@carbon.cudenver.edu. **Website:** http://www.cudenver.edu. **Application deadlines for fall 2011:** Regular decision: Rolling. Early decision: Not offered. Early action: Not offered. Admission can be deferred. **Application fee:** $50. **To apply online, go to:** http://www.cudenver.edu/Admissions/UndergradFresh/Pages/FreshApply.aspx. **Admissions requirements/recommendations:** High school units required (recommended): English: 4 (4); Mathematics: 3 (3); Science: 3 (3); Foreign language: (2); Social studies: 2 (2); History: 1 (1); Academic electives: 2 (1); Total units: 15 (15). Tests: The college uses SAT or ACT scores in admissions decisions. Either SAT or ACT required. For admission to the fall 2011 entering class, the school will accept: ACT with or without writing accepted. Campus visit: Recommended. Admissions interview: Neither required nor recommended. Off-campus interview: May be arranged. **Factors that count in admissions decisions:** *Academic:* Secondary school record: Very Important. Class rank: Very Important. Letters of recommendation: Important. Standardized test scores: Very Important. Essay: Important. *Nonacademic:* Interview: Not Considered. Extracurricular activities: Considered. Talent/ability: Considered. Character/personal qualities: Considered. Alumni/ae relationship: Not Considered. Geographical residence: Not Considered. State residency: Not Considered. Religious affiliation/commitment: Not Considered. Minority status: Not Considered. Volunteer work: Not Considered. Work experience: Not Considered. **Admissions statistics for the fall 2009 entering class:** Total applicants: 4,850. Total accepted: 2,941. Freshmen enrolled: 1,053; 5% were from out of state. Overall acceptance rate: 61%. **Credentials of fall 2009 freshmen:** 16% ranked in the top 10 percent of their high school class; 40% were in the top 25 percent; 79% were in the top half. (Proportion submitting class standing: 88%.) **Average high school grade point average:** 3.3. **First-year students who submitted SAT scores:** 23%. Scores (25/75 percentile): Critical Reading: 480-600, Math: 485-610, Combined: 965-1210. **First-year students submitting ACT scores:** 93%. Scores (25/75 percentile): English: N/A, Math: N/A, Composite: 20-25.

ACADEMICS

Year founded: 1912. **Academic calendar:** Semester. **Degrees offered:** bachelor's, master's, post-master's certificate, doctorate. **Major fields of study:** biological and biomedical sciences; business, management, marketing, and related support services; communication, journalism, and related programs; computer and information sciences and support services; engineering; English language and literature/letters; foreign languages, literatures, and linguistics; health professions and related clinical sciences; history; mathematics and statistics; multi/interdisciplinary studies; philosophy and religious studies; physical sciences; psychology; social sciences; visual and performing arts. **Areas of required coursework:** arts/fine arts, humanities, mathematics, English (including composition), sciences (biological or physical), social science, other. **Pre-professional programs:** pre-dentistry, pre-medicine, pre-veterinary science, pre-pharmacy, other. **Special academic programs:** accelerated program, cooperative (work-study plan) program, cross-registration, distance learning, double major, English as a Second Language (ESL), honors program, independent study, internships, student-designed major, study abroad, teacher certificate program, weekend college. **Teacher certification offered in:** early childhood, special education, elementary, secondary. **Cooperative education programs:** art, business, computer science, education, engineering, humanities, natural science, social/behavioral science. **Reserve Officers Training Corps (ROTC):** Army ROTC: Offered at cooperating institution; Air Force ROTC: Offered at cooperating institution. **Faculty and instruction (2009-2010):** Total instructional faculty: 2,420 full-time, 516 part-time (49% men; 51% women; 11% minorities). Full-time faculty with Ph.D. or other terminal degree: 69%. Student/faculty ratio: 15/1. Classes of fewer than 20 students: 29%; of 20 to 49 students: 60%; of 50 or more students: 11%. **Advanced Placement and International Baccalaureate credit:** AP tests may be used for: Credit only. Scores accepted: 4, 5. **Freshmen returning for sophomore year:** 71%. **Graduation rates:** Four-year: 17%; five-year: 37%; six-year: 43%. **Graduate study:** 9% of students pursue further study within one year.

COSTS AND FINANCIAL AID

Financial aid office: (303) 556-2886. **Expenses (2010-2011):** Tuition and fees 2010-2011: $6,657 in state, $19,689 out of state; room/board: $11,374. Estimated books and supplies: $1,801; transportation: $1,335; personal expenses: $2,230. **Financial aid:** Priority filing date for institution's financial aid form: April 1. In 2009-2010, 68% of undergraduates applied for financial aid. Of those, 57% were determined to have financial need; 8% had their need fully met. Average financial aid package (proportion receiving): $8,804 (54%). Average amount of gift aid, such as scholarships or grants (proportion receiving): $2,189 (41%). Average amount of self-help aid, such as work study or loans (proportion receiving): $3,638 (44%). Average need-based loan (excluding PLUS or other private loans): $3,611. Among students who received need-based aid, the average percentage of need met: 55%. Among students who received aid based on merit, the average award (and the proportion receiving): $2,138 (5%). The average athletic scholarship (and the proportion receiving): $0 (0%). Average amount of debt of borrowers graduating in 2009: $21,264. Proportion who borrowed: 66%.

CAMPUS LIFE AND EXTRACURRICULAR ACTIVITIES

Campus housing available: apartment for single students. Students who live in college-owned, operated, or affiliated housing: 4%. **Clubs and organizations:** Number of student organizations: 77. Activities include: choral groups, dance, drama/theater, jazz band, music ensembles, musical theater, student government, student newspaper. Number of fraternities: 0; sororities: 0. Average proportion of students who stay on campus on weekends: 5%.

SERVICES AND FACILITIES

Basic services: nonremedial tutoring, placement service, day care, health service, health insurance. **Counseling services:** minority student, career, personal, veteran student, academic. **For learning-disabled students:** School does not offer a structured program with separate admission and additional fees. Services include: reading machines, diagnostic testing service, note-taking services, oral tests, readers, extended time for tests, tutors. **Information technology resources:** Students are not required to lease or own a computer. Number of campus computers available to all students: 150. School has a wireless network. Approximate number of users that can be accommodated: 2,000. Proportion of college-owned housing units wired for high-speed internet access: 100%. **Campus safety:** Security services offered: 24-hour foot-and-vehicle patrols, late-night transport/escort service, 24-hour emergency telephones, lighted pathways/sidewalks.

TRANSFER AND INTERNATIONAL STUDENTS

Transfer students: May apply for admission for the following academic terms: Fall, Spring, Summer. Applicants need a minimum number of credits to apply. For fall 2009: Transfer applications received: 2,549. Transfer applicants offered admission: 1,973. Transfer applicants enrolled: 1,089. **International students:** Number of foreign undergraduates: 494 (5% of student body). Number of countries represented: 60. Minimum TOEFL score required: 525 (paper); 197 (computer). Average TOEFL score: 589 (paper).

University of Denver

■ **Address:** 2199 S. University Boulevard, Denver, CO 80208
■ **Website:** http://www.du.edu
■ **Private**
■ **Enrollment:** 4,825 full-time; 518 part-time

KEY STATS

✔ **U.S News College Ranking:** 86, National Universities
✔ **ACT Score (25th/75th percentile):** 24-29
✔ **Tuition:** 2010-2011: $36,501

Selectivity: More selective	**Room/board:** $10,224
Acceptance rate: 70%	**Average debt:** $26,986
Student/faculty ratio: 9/1	**Proportion who borrowed:** 45%

UNDERGRADUATE STUDENT BODY STATS

2009-2010 enrollment: 4,825 full-time; 518 part-time. Men: 44%; women: 56%. **Ethnic makeup:** African American: 4%; American-Indian: 1%; Asian American: 5%; Hispanic: 8%; White: 76%; International: 6%.

ADMISSIONS FACTS AND FIGURES

Phone: (303) 871-2036. **Email:** admission@du.edu. **Website:** http://www.du.edu. **Application deadlines for fall 2011:** Regular decision: January 15; decision sent by March 15. Early decision: Not offered. Early action: Send application by: November 1; Decision sent by: January 15. Admission can be deferred. **Application fee:** $50. **To apply online, go to:** http://www.du.edu/admission/app.html. **Admissions requirements/recommendations:** High school units required (recommended): English: 4 (4); Mathematics: 4 (4); Science: 4 (4); Foreign language: 4 (4); Social studies: 2 (2); History: 2 (2); Total units: 21 (21). Tests: The college uses SAT or ACT scores in admissions decisions. Either SAT or ACT required. For admission to the fall 2011 entering class, the school will accept: ACT with or without writing accepted. Campus visit: Recommended. Admissions interview: Recommended. Off-campus interview: May be arranged. **Factors that count in admissions decisions:** *Academic:* Secondary school record: Very Important. Class rank: Not Considered. Letters of recommendation: Important. Standardized test scores: Very Important. Essay: Important. *Nonacademic:* Interview: Important. Extracurricular activities: Important. Talent/ability: Important. Character/personal qualities: Very Important. Alumni/ae relationship: Not Considered. Geographical residence: Not Considered. State residency: Not Considered. Religious affiliation/commitment: Not Considered. Minority status: Not Considered. Volunteer work: Important. Work experience: Important. **Other schools with the greatest overlap in applicants:** Boston University; Colorado College; Colorado State University; Santa Clara University; University of Colorado–Boulder. **Admissions statistics for the fall 2009 entering class:** Total applicants: 8,411. Total accepted: 5,926. Freshmen enrolled: 1,207; 53% were from out of state. Accepted through early-decision or early-action plans: 48%. Overall acceptance rate: 70%. Non-early acceptance rate: 63%. **Size of waiting list:** 1304 applicants; enrolled from waiting list: 47. **Credentials of fall 2009 freshmen:** 45% ranked in the top 10 percent of their high school class; 75% were in the top 25 percent; 96% were in the top half. (Proportion submitting class standing: 54%.) **Average high school grade point average:** 3.7. **First-year students who submitted SAT scores:** 58%. Scores (25/75 percentile): Critical Reading: 540-640; Math: 550-650, Combined: 1090-1290. **First-year students submitting ACT scores:** 74%. Scores (25/75 percentile): English: 24-31, Math: 24-29, Composite: 24-29.

ACADEMICS

Year founded: 1864. **Academic calendar:** Quarter. **Degrees offered:** certificate, bachelor's, post-bachelor's certificate, master's, post-master's certificate, doctorate. **Most popular majors:** 46% business, management, marketing, and related support services, 13% social sciences, 8% communication, journalism, and related programs, 7% biological and biomedical sciences, 6% psychology. **Major fields of study:** agriculture, agriculture operations, and related sciences; area, ethnic, cultural, and gender studies; biological and biomedical sciences; business, management, marketing, and related support services; communication, journalism, and related programs; computer and information sciences and support services; education; engineering; English language and literature/letters; foreign languages, literatures, and linguistics; history; legal professions and studies; mathematics and statistics; multi/interdisciplinary studies; natural resources and conservation; philosophy and religious studies; physical sciences; psychology; public administration and social service professions; social sciences; visual and performing arts. **Areas of required coursework:** humanities, mathematics, English (including composition), foreign languages, sciences (biological or physical), social science. **Pre-professional programs:** pre-law, pre-dentistry, pre-medicine, pre-veterinary science, pre-pharmacy. **Special academic programs (% participation):** accelerated program, cooperative (work-study plan) program, distance learning, double major (13%), dual enrollment (14%), English as a Second Language (ESL), honors program, independent study, internships, student-designed major, study abroad (74%), teacher certificate program, weekend college, other. **Teacher certification offered in:** early childhood, elementary, middle/junior high, secondary. **Cooperative education programs:** engineering. **Reserve Officers Training Corps (ROTC):** Army ROTC: Offered at cooperating institution (University of Colorado–Boulder); Air Force ROTC: Offered at cooperating institution (University of Colorado–Boulder). **Faculty and instruction (2009-2010):** Total instructional faculty: 612 full-time, 644 part-time (55% men; 45% women; 11% minorities). Full-time faculty with Ph.D. or other terminal degree: 90%. Student/faculty ratio: 9/1. Classes of fewer than 20 students: 62%; of 20 to 49 students: 33%; of 50 or more students: 5%. **Advanced Placement and International Baccalaureate credit:** AP tests may be used for: Credit and/or placement. Scores accepted: 3, 4, 5. International Baccalaureate exams may be used for: Credit and/or placement. **Freshmen returning for sophomore year:** 87%. **Graduation rates:** Four-year: 58%; five-year: 71%; six-year: 74%. **Graduate study:** 12% of students pursue further study immediately upon graduation; 24% within one year.

COSTS AND FINANCIAL AID
Financial aid office: (303) 871-4020. **Expenses (2010-2011):** Tuition and fees 2010-2011: $36,501; room/board: $10,224. Estimated books and supplies: $1,749; transportation: $1,191; personal expenses: $1,269. **Financial aid:** In 2009-2010, 53% of undergraduates applied for financial aid. Of those, 43% were determined to have financial need; 27% had their need fully met. Average financial aid package (proportion receiving): $28,632 (43%). Average amount of gift aid, such as scholarships or grants (proportion receiving): $23,435 (42%). Average amount of self-help aid, such as work study or loans (proportion receiving): $5,234 (34%). Average need-based loan (excluding PLUS or other private loans): $4,310. Among students who received need-based aid, the average percentage of need met: 81%. Among students who received aid based on merit, the average award (and the proportion receiving): $11,172 (37%). The average athletic scholarship (and the proportion receiving): $28,880 (4%). Average amount of debt of borrowers graduating in 2009: $26,986. Proportion who borrowed: 45%.

CAMPUS LIFE AND EXTRACURRICULAR ACTIVITIES
Campus housing available (% using): coed dorms (79%), sorority housing (7%), fraternity housing (5%), apartments for married students (1%), apartment for single students (7%), special housing for disabled students (1%). Students who live in college-owned, operated, or affiliated housing: 43%. **Clubs and organizations:** Number of student organizations: 120. Activities include: campus ministries, choral groups, concert band, dance, drama/theater, international student organization, jazz band, literary magazine, model UN, music ensembles, musical theater, opera, pep band, radio station, student government, student newspaper, student film society, symphony orchestra. Number of fraternities: 9; sororities: 5. Proportion of men in fraternities: 24%; of women in sororities: 16%. Average proportion of students who stay on campus on weekends: 60%. **Sports program (2009-2010):** Member of NCAA I. **Men's intercollegiate varsity sports:** basketball, golf, ice hockey, lacrosse, skiing (nordic), skiing (alpine), soccer, swimming, tennis. **Women's intercollegiate varsity sports:** basketball, golf, gymnastics, lacrosse, skiing (nordic), skiing (alpine), soccer, swimming, tennis, volleyball.

SERVICES AND FACILITIES
Basic services: nonremedial tutoring, women's center, placement service, health service, health insurance. **Counseling services:** minority student, career, military, personal, veteran student, academic, older student, psychological, birth control, religious. **For learning-disabled students:** School does not offer a structured program with separate admission and additional fees. Services include: reading machines, tape recorders, videotaped classes, diagnostic testing service, note-taking services, oral tests, learning center, readers, extended time for tests, tutors, priority registration, texts on tape, other. **Library:** Number of titles: 1,376,337; number of current serial subscriptions: 31,300. **Information technology resources:** Students are required to lease or own a computer. Number of campus computers available to all students: 170. School has a wireless network. Approximate number of users that can be accommodated: 28,000. Proportion of college-owned housing units wired for high-speed internet access: 95%. **Campus safety:** Security services offered: 24-hour foot-and-vehicle patrols, late-night transport/escort service, 24-hour emergency telephones, lighted pathways/sidewalks, controlled dormitory access (key, security card, etc).

TRANSFER AND INTERNATIONAL STUDENTS
Transfer students: May apply for admission for the following academic terms: Fall, Winter, Spring, Summer. Applicants do not need a minimum number of credits to apply. For fall 2009: Transfer applications received: 511. Transfer applicants offered admission: 402. Transfer applicants enrolled: 191. **International students:** Number of foreign undergraduates: 311 (6% of student body). Number of countries represented: 44. Minimum TOEFL score required: 525 (paper); 70 (computer). Average TOEFL score: 547 (paper).

University of Northern Colorado

- **Address:** Greeley, CO 80639
- **Website:** http://www.unco.edu
- **Public**
- **Enrollment:** 8,996 full-time; 977 part-time

KEY STATS
- ✔ **U.S News College Ranking:** second tier, National Universities
- ✔ **ACT Score (25th/75th percentile):** 20-25
- ✔ **Tuition:** 2009-2010: $5,451 in state, $14,499 out of state

Selectivity: Selective	**Room/board:** $8,370
Acceptance rate: 92%	**Average debt:** N/A
Student/faculty ratio: 19/1	**Proportion who borrowed:** N/A

UNDERGRADUATE STUDENT BODY STATS
2009-2010 enrollment: 8,996 full-time; 977 part-time. Men: 39%; women: 61%. **Ethnic makeup:** African American: 5%; American-Indian: 1%; Asian American: 3%; Hispanic: 14%; White: 76%; International: 1%.

ADMISSIONS FACTS AND FIGURES
Phone: (970) 351-2881. **Email:** admissions.help@unco.edu. **Website:** http://www.unco.edu. **Application deadlines for fall 2011:** Regular decision: Rolling. Early decision: Not offered. Early action: Not offered. Admission can be deferred. **Application fee:** $45. **To apply online, go to:** http://www.unco.edu/decide.shtml. **Admissions requirements/recommendations:** High school units required (recommended): English: 4; Mathematics: 3 (4); Science: 3; Foreign language: (1); Social studies: 3; Academic electives: 2; Total units: 15. Tests: The college uses SAT or ACT scores in admissions decisions. Either SAT or ACT required. For admission to the fall 2011 entering class, the school will accept: ACT with or without writing accepted. Campus visit: Recommended. Admissions interview: Neither required nor recommended. Off-campus interview: May be arranged. **Factors that count in admissions decisions:** *Academic:* Secondary school record: Considered. Class rank: Very Important. Letters of recommendation: Important. Standardized test scores: Very Important. Essay: Not Considered. *Nonacademic:* Interview: Considered. Extracurricular activities: Considered. Talent/ability: Considered. Character/personal qualities: Considered. Alumni/ae relationship: Not Considered. Geographical residence: Not Considered. State residency: Considered. Religious affiliation/commitment: Not Considered. Minority status: Considered. Volunteer work: Not Considered. Work experience: Considered. **Other schools with the greatest overlap in applicants:** Colorado State University; Mesa State College; Metropolitan State College of Denver; University of Denver. **Admissions statistics for the fall 2009 entering class:** Total applicants: 6,136. Total accepted: 5,661. Freshmen enrolled: 2,351; 10% were from out of state. Overall acceptance rate: 92%. **Credentials of fall 2009 freshmen:** 11% ranked in the top 10 percent of their high school class; 33% were in the top 25 percent; 69% were in the top half. (Proportion submitting class standing: 89%.) **Average high school grade point average:** 3.2. **First-year students who submitted SAT scores:** 19%. Scores (25/75 percentile): Critical Reading: 470-590, Math: 470-590, Combined: 940-1180. **First-year students submitting ACT scores:** 94%. Scores (25/75 percentile): English: 20-25, Math: 19-25, Composite: 20-25.

ACADEMICS
Year founded: 1890. **Academic calendar:** Semester. **Degrees offered:** bachelor's, master's, post-master's certificate, doctorate. **Most popular majors:** 14% business administration and management, 14% multi/interdisciplinary studies, 11% health professions and related clinical sciences, 10% communication, journalism, and related programs, 7% visual and performing arts.

Major fields of study: area, ethnic, cultural, and gender studies; biological and biomedical sciences; business, management, marketing, and related support services; communication, journalism, and related programs; education; English language and literature/letters; family and consumer sciences/human sciences; foreign languages, literatures, and linguistics; health professions and related clinical sciences; history; mathematics and statistics; multi/interdisciplinary studies; parks, recreation, leisure, and fitness studies; philosophy and religious studies; physical sciences; psychology; public administration and social service professions; security and protective services; social sciences; visual and performing arts. **Areas of required coursework:** arts/fine arts, mathematics, English (including composition), sciences (biological or physical), history, social science. **Pre-professional programs:** pre-law, pre-dentistry, pre-medicine, pre-veterinary science, pre-optometry, pre-pharmacy, other. **Special academic programs:** cooperative (work-study plan) program, cross-registration, distance learning, double major, English as a Second Language (ESL), exchange student program (domestic), external degree program, honors program, independent study, internships, student-designed major, study abroad, teacher certificate program. **Teacher certification offered in:** early childhood, special education, elementary, middle/junior high, secondary, bilingual/bicultural. **Reserve Officers Training Corps (ROTC):** Army ROTC: Offered on campus; Air Force ROTC: Offered on campus. **Faculty and instruction (2009-2010):** Total instructional faculty: 491 full-time, 214 part-time (45% men; 55% women; 10% minorities). Student/faculty ratio: 19/1. Classes of fewer than 20 students: 26%; of 20 to 49 students: 60%; of 50 or more students: 15%. **Advanced Placement and International Baccalaureate credit:** AP tests may be used for: Credit only. Scores accepted: 3, 4, 5. International Baccalaureate exams may be used for: Credit only. **Freshmen returning for sophomore year:** 68%. **Graduation rates:** Four-year: 28%; five-year: 46%; six-year: 49%. **Graduate study:** 13% of students pursue further study within one year. Fields in which graduates pursue further study: Master of Business Administration (MBA), 1%; law, 1%; medicine, 4%; education, 3%; arts and sciences, 4%.

COSTS AND FINANCIAL AID

Financial aid office: (970) 351-2502. **Expenses (2009-2010):** Tuition and fees 2009-2010: $5,451 in state, $14,499 out of state; room/board: $8,370. Estimated books and supplies: $1,300 personal expenses: $2,854. **Financial aid:** Priority filing date for institution's financial aid form: March 1. In 2009-2010, 80% of undergraduates applied for financial aid. Of those, 51% were determined to have financial need; 60% had their need fully met. Average financial aid package (proportion receiving): $14,872 (51%). Average amount of gift aid, such as scholarships or grants (proportion receiving): $6,877 (35%). Average amount of self-help aid, such as work study or loans (proportion receiving): $4,663 (40%). Average need-based loan (excluding PLUS or other private loans): $4,496. Among students who received need-based aid, the average percentage of need met: 100%. Among students who received aid based on merit, the average award (and the proportion receiving): $2,743 (16%). The average athletic scholarship (and the proportion receiving): $8,609 (1%).

CAMPUS LIFE AND EXTRACURRICULAR ACTIVITIES

Campus housing available (% using): coed dorms (87%), sorority housing (2%), fraternity housing (2%), apartments for married students (2%), apartment for single students (4%), special housing for disabled students (3%). Students who live in college-owned, operated, or affiliated housing: 32%. **Student employment:** During the 2009-2010 academic year, 15% of undergraduates worked on campus. Average per-year earnings: $2,775. **Clubs and organizations:** Number of student organizations: 137. Activities include: campus ministries, choral groups, concert band, dance, drama/theater, international student organization, jazz band, literary magazine, marching band, music ensembles, musical theater, opera, pep band, radio station, student government, student newspaper, student film society, symphony orchestra, television station. Number of fraternities: 9; sororities: 8. Proportion of men in fraternities: 2%; of women in sororities: 3%. Average proportion of students who stay on campus on weekends: 64%. **Sports program (2009-2010):** Member of NCAA I. *Men's intercollegiate varsity sports:* baseball, basketball, cross country, football, golf, tennis, track and field (outdoor), wrestling. *Women's intercollegiate varsity sports:* basketball, cross country, golf, soccer, softball, swimming, tennis, track and field (outdoor), volleyball.

SERVICES AND FACILITIES

Basic services: nonremedial tutoring, women's center, placement service, health service, health insurance. **Remedial assistance:** study skills. **Counseling services:** career, personal, psychological, birth control. **For learning-disabled students:** School does not offer a structured program

with separate admission and additional fees. Total undergraduates in learning-disabled program or receiving services: 111. Services include: tape recorders, note-taking services, readers, extended time for tests, texts on tape, other testing accommodations. **Library:** Number of titles: 1,081,133; number of current serial subscriptions: 29,985. **Information technology resources:** Students are not required to lease or own a computer. Number of campus computers available to all students: 1,644. School has a wireless network. Approximate number of users that can be accommodated: 11,500. Proportion of college-owned housing units wired for high-speed internet access: 100%. **Campus safety:** Security services offered: 24-hour foot-and-vehicle patrols, late-night transport/escort service, 24-hour emergency telephones, lighted pathways/sidewalks, student patrols, controlled dormitory access (key, security card, etc).

TRANSFER AND INTERNATIONAL STUDENTS

Transfer students: May apply for admission for the following academic terms: Fall, Spring, Summer. Applicants need a minimum number of credits to apply. For fall 2009: Transfer applications received: 1,136. Transfer applicants offered admission: 1,092. Transfer applicants enrolled: 699. **International students:** Number of foreign undergraduates: 41 (1% of student body). Number of countries represented: 35. Minimum TOEFL score required: 520 (paper); 197 (computer). Average TOEFL score: 528 (paper).

Western State College of Colorado

- **Address:** 600 N. Adams Street, Gunnison, CO 81231
- **Website:** http://www.western.edu
- **Public**
- **Enrollment:** 1,873 full-time; 320 part-time

KEY STATS
- ✔ **U.S News College Ranking:** Unranked, National Liberal Arts Colleges
- ✔ **ACT Score (25th/75th percentile):** 19-24
- ✔ **Tuition:** 2010-2011: $4,358 in state, $13,824 out of state

Selectivity: N/A	**Room/board:** $7,710
Acceptance rate: 72%	**Average debt:** $17,750
Student/faculty ratio: 17/1	**Proportion who borrowed:** 75%

UNDERGRADUATE STUDENT BODY STATS

2009-2010 enrollment: 1,873 full-time; 320 part-time. Men: 61%; women: 39%. **Ethnic makeup:** African American: 2%; American-Indian: 1%; Asian American: 1%; Hispanic: 5%; White: 91%.

ADMISSIONS FACTS AND FIGURES

Phone: (800) 876-5309. **Email:** discover@western.edu. **Website:** http://www.western.edu. **Application deadlines for fall 2011:** Regular decision: June 1. Early decision: Not offered. Early action: Not offered. Admission can be deferred. **Application fee:** $30. **To apply online, go to:** http://www.western.edu/admissions/apply.html. **Admissions requirements/recommendations:** High school units required (recommended): English: 4; Mathematics: 4; Science: 3; Foreign language: (1); Social studies: 3; History: (2); Academic electives: (2). Tests: The college does not use SAT or ACT scores in admissions decisions. Neither SAT nor ACT required. For admission to the fall 2011 entering class, the school will accept: ACT with or without writing accepted. Campus visit: Recommended. Admissions interview: Neither required nor recommended. Off-campus interview: May be arranged. **Factors that count in admissions decisions:** *Academic:* Secondary school record: Very Important. Class rank: Very Important. Letters of recommendation: Considered. Standardized test scores: Very Important. Essay: Considered. *Nonacademic:* Interview: Considered. Extracurricular activities: Important. Talent/ability: Important. Character/personal qualities: Important. Alumni/ae relationship: Not Considered. Geographical residence: Not Considered. State residency: Not Considered. Religious affiliation/commitment: Not Considered. Minority status: Not Considered. Volunteer work: Considered. Work experience: Considered. **Other schools with the greatest overlap in applicants:** Colorado State University; University of Colorado–Boulder; University of Colorado–Colorado Springs. **Admissions statistics for the fall 2009 entering class:** Total applicants: 2,311. Total accepted: 1,664. Freshmen enrolled: 499; 21% were from out of state. Overall acceptance rate: 72%. **Credentials of fall 2009 freshmen:** 6% ranked in the top 10 percent of their high school class; 22% were in the top 25 percent; 49% were in the top half. (Proportion submitting class standing: 99%.) **Average high school grade point average:** 2.9. **First-year students**

who submitted SAT scores: 21%. Scores (25/75 percentile): Critical Reading: 445-565, Math: 465-565, Combined: 910-1130. **First-year students submitting ACT scores:** 88%. Scores (25/75 percentile): English: 18-24, Math: 17-23, Composite: 19-24.

ACADEMICS

Year founded: 1901. **Academic calendar:** Semester. **Degrees offered:** bachelor's, master's. **Most popular majors:** 28% business, management, marketing, and related support services, 19% parks, recreation, leisure, and fitness studies, 10% social sciences, 7% psychology, 6% visual and performing arts. **Major fields of study:** biological and biomedical sciences; business, management, marketing, and related support services; communication, journalism, and related programs; computer and information sciences and support services; education; English language and literature/letters; foreign languages, literatures, and linguistics; history; mathematics and statistics; multi/interdisciplinary studies; natural resources and conservation; parks, recreation, leisure, and fitness studies; philosophy and religious studies; physical sciences; psychology; social sciences; visual and performing arts. **Areas of required coursework:** arts/fine arts, humanities, mathematics, English (including composition), sciences (biological or physical), social science. **Pre-professional programs:** pre-law, pre-dentistry, pre-medicine, pre-optometry. **Special academic programs (% participation):** distance learning (5%), double major (25%), dual enrollment (5%), honors program (5%), independent study, internships, liberal arts/career combination, study abroad, teacher certificate program (8%). **Teacher certification offered in:** special education, elementary, middle/junior high, secondary. **Cooperative education programs:** art, business, computer science, education, humanities, natural science, social/behavioral science. **Faculty and instruction (2009-2010):** Total instructional faculty: 107 full-time, 43 part-time (52% men; 48% women; 2% minorities). Full-time faculty with Ph.D. or other terminal degree: 83%. Student/faculty ratio: 17/1. Classes of fewer than 20 students: 50%; of 20 to 49 students: 50%; of 50 or more students: 0%. **Advanced Placement and International Baccalaureate credit:** AP tests may be used for: Credit only. Scores accepted: 4, 5. International Baccalaureate exams may be used for: Credit only. **Freshmen returning for sophomore year:** 61%. **Graduation rates:** Four-year: 20%; five-year: 35%; six-year: 36%.

COSTS AND FINANCIAL AID

Financial aid office: (970) 943-3085. **Expenses (2010-2011):** Tuition and fees 2010-2011: $4,358 in state, $13,824 out of state; room/board: $7,710. Estimated books and supplies: $1,500; transportation: $1,296; personal expenses: $1,269. **Financial aid:** Priority filing date for institution's financial aid form: April 1. In 2009-2010, 67% of undergraduates applied for financial aid. Of those, 45% were determined to have financial need; 8% had their need fully met. Average financial aid package (proportion receiving): $9,500 (38%). Average amount of gift aid, such as scholarships or grants (proportion receiving): $2,500 (19%). Average amount of self-help aid, such as work study or loans (proportion receiving): $2,300 (34%). Average need-based loan (excluding PLUS or other private loans): $5,300. Among students who received need-based aid, the average percentage of need met:

40%. Among students who received aid based on merit, the average award (and the proportion receiving): $1,700 (22%). The average athletic scholarship (and the proportion receiving): $2,400 (7%). Average amount of debt of borrowers graduating in 2009: $17,750. Proportion who borrowed: 75%.

CAMPUS LIFE AND EXTRACURRICULAR ACTIVITIES

Campus housing available (% using): coed dorms (97%), apartments for married students (3%). Students who live in college-owned, operated, or affiliated housing: 19%. **Student employment:** During the 2009-2010 academic year, 30% of undergraduates worked on campus. Average per-year earnings: $1,500. **Clubs and organizations:** Number of student organizations: 60. Activities include: choral groups, concert band, dance, drama/theater, international student organization, jazz band, literary magazine, music ensembles, pep band, radio station, student government, student newspaper, student film society, symphony orchestra, television station. Number of fraternities: 0; sororities: 0. Average proportion of students who stay on campus on weekends: 90%. **Sports program (2009-2010):** Member of NCAA II. *Men's intercollegiate varsity sports:* basketball, cross country, football, track and field (indoor), track and field (outdoor), wrestling. *Women's intercollegiate varsity sports:* basketball, cross country, track and field (indoor), track and field (outdoor), volleyball.

SERVICES AND FACILITIES

Basic services: nonremedial tutoring, placement service, day care, health service, health insurance. **Remedial assistance:** reading, math, writing, study skills. **Counseling services:** minority student, career, personal, veteran student, academic, older student, psychological, birth control. **For learning-disabled students:** School does not offer a structured program with separate admission and additional fees. Services include: remedial math, remedial English, reading machines, remedial reading, tape recorders, note-taking services, oral tests, learning center, readers, extended time for tests, priority registration, priority seating, substitution of courses, texts on tape, typist/scribe, exams on tape or computer, other testing accommodations. **Library:** Number of titles: 467,079; number of current serial subscriptions: 169. **Information technology resources:** Students are not required to lease or own a computer. Number of campus computers available to all students: 425. School has a wireless network. Approximate number of users that can be accommodated: 10,000. Proportion of college-owned housing units wired for high-speed internet access: 100%. **Campus safety:** Security services offered: 24-hour foot-and-vehicle patrols, late-night transport/escort service, lighted pathways/sidewalks, controlled dormitory access (key, security card, etc).

TRANSFER AND INTERNATIONAL STUDENTS

Transfer students: May apply for admission for the following academic terms: Fall, Spring. Applicants do not need a minimum number of credits to apply. For fall 2009: Transfer applications received: 567. Transfer applicants offered admission: 356. Transfer applicants enrolled: 134. **International students:** Number of foreign undergraduates: 0. Number of countries represented: 9. Minimum TOEFL score required: 550 (paper); 96 (computer).

Connecticut

Albertus Magnus College

- **Address:** 700 Prospect Street, New Haven, CT 06511
- **Website:** http://www.albertus.edu
- **Private; Religious affiliation:** Roman Catholic
- **Enrollment:** 1,505 full-time; 108 part-time

KEY STATS

✔ **U.S News College Ranking:** second tier, National Liberal Arts Colleges

✔ **SAT Score (25th/75th percentile):** 740-1020

✔ **Tuition:** 2010-2011: $24,374

Selectivity: Less selective	**Room/board:** $10,460
Acceptance rate: 84%	**Average debt:** $28,009
Student/faculty ratio: 16/1	**Proportion who borrowed:** N/A

UNDERGRADUATE STUDENT BODY STATS

2009-2010 enrollment: 1,505 full-time; 108 part-time. Men: 32%; women: 68%. **Ethnic makeup:** African American: 31%; Asian American: 1%; Hispanic: 12%; White: 55%. **Religious preference:** Roman Catholic: 47%; Protestant: 37%; Buddhist: 2%; No preference: 11%.

ADMISSIONS FACTS AND FIGURES

Phone: (800) 578-9160. **Email:** admissions@albertus.edu. **Website:** http://www.albertus.edu. **Application deadlines for fall 2011:** Regular decision: August 15. Early decision: Not offered. Early action: Not offered. Admission can be deferred. **Application fee:** $35. **To apply online, go to:** https://www.applyweb.com/apply/alma/indexa.html. **Admissions requirements/recommendations:** High school units required (recommended): English: 4 (4); Mathematics: 2 (3); Science: 2 (3); Foreign language: 2 (3); Social studies: 2 (3); History: 2 (1); Academic electives: 2 (3); Total units: 16 (16). Tests: The college uses SAT or ACT scores in admissions decisions. Either SAT or ACT required. For admission to the fall 2011 entering class, the school will accept: ACT with or without writing accepted. Campus visit: Recommended. Admissions interview: Recommended. Off-campus interview: May be arranged. **Factors that count in admissions decisions:** *Academic:* Secondary school record: Very Important. Class rank: Considered. Letters of recommendation: Important. Standardized test scores: Important. Essay: Considered. *Nonacademic:* Interview: Considered. Extracurricular activities: Considered. Talent/ability: Considered. Character/personal qualities: Considered. Alumni/ae relationship: Considered. Geographical residence: Not Considered. State residency: Not Considered. Religious affiliation/commitment: Not Considered. Minority status: Not Considered. Volunteer work: Considered. Work experience: Considered. **Admissions statistics for the fall 2009 entering class:** Total applicants: 595. Total accepted: 497. Freshmen enrolled: 168; 15% were from out of state. Overall acceptance rate: 84%. **Credentials of fall 2009 freshmen:** 12% ranked in the top 10 percent of their high school class; 23% were in the top 25 percent; 85% were in the top half. (Proportion submitting class standing: 94%.) **Average high school grade point average:** 2.6. **First-year students who submitted SAT scores:** 95%. Scores (25/75 percentile): Critical Reading: 380-500, Math: 360-520, Combined: 740-1020.

ACADEMICS

Year founded: 1925. **Academic calendar:** Semester. **Degrees offered:** associate, bachelor's, master's. **Most popular majors:** 32% business, management, marketing, and related support services, 25% sociology, 10% psychology, 7% English language and literature, 6% communications technologies/technicians and support services. **Major fields of study:** biological and biomedical sciences; business, management, marketing, and related support services; communication, journalism, and related programs; computer and information sciences and support services; education; English language and literature/letters; foreign languages, literatures, and linguistics; health professions and related clinical sciences; history; liberal arts and sciences studies, and humanities; mathematics and statistics; multi/interdisciplinary studies; physical sciences; psychology; public administration and social service professions; security and protective services; social sciences; visual and performing arts. **Areas of required coursework:** arts/fine arts, humanities, computer literacy, mathematics, English (including composition), philosophy, sciences (biological or physical), history, social science, other. **Pre-professional programs:** pre-law, pre-dentistry, pre-medicine, pre-veterinary science, pre-optometry, pre-pharmacy. **Special academic programs (% participation):** accelerated program (75%), distance learning (35%), double major (1%), honors program (3%), internships (30%), teacher certificate program (30%). **Teacher certification offered in:** middle/junior high, secondary. **Faculty and instruction (2009-2010):** Total instructional faculty: 41 full-time, 55 part-time (56% men; 44% women; 8% minorities). Full-time faculty with Ph.D. or other terminal degree: 88%. Student/faculty ratio: 16/1. Classes of fewer than 20 students: 75%; of 20 to 49 students: 25%. **Advanced Placement and International Baccalaureate credit:** AP tests may be used for: Placement only. **Freshmen returning for sophomore year:** 75%. **Graduation rates:** Four-year: 39%; five-year: 48%; six-year: 48%. **Graduate study:** 20% of students pursue further study immediately upon graduation; 30% within one year; 5% within five years. Fields in which graduates pursue further study: Master of Business Administration (MBA), 35%; law, 9%; medicine, 5%; dentistry, 2%; education, 15%; arts and sciences, 4%; veterinary medicine, 1%.

COSTS AND FINANCIAL AID

Financial aid office: (203) 773-8508. **Expenses (2010-2011):** Tuition and fees 2010-2011: $24,374; room/board: $10,460. Estimated books and supplies: $984; transportation: $2,142; personal expenses: $3,140. **Financial aid:** Priority filing date for institution's financial aid form: February 28. 8% had their need fully met. Average financial aid package (proportion receiving): $10,828 (N/A). Average amount of gift aid, such as scholarships or grants (proportion receiving): $7,146 (N/A). Average amount of self-help aid, such as work study or loans (proportion receiving): $4,381 (N/A). Average need-based loan (excluding PLUS or other private loans): $4,271. Among students who received need-based aid, the average percentage of need met: 49%. Among students who received aid based on merit, the average award (and the proportion receiving): $7,414 (N/A). The average athletic scholarship (and the proportion receiving): $0 (N/A). Average amount of debt of borrowers graduating in 2009: $28,009.

CAMPUS LIFE AND EXTRACURRICULAR ACTIVITIES

Campus housing available (% using): coed dorms (85%), women's dorms (15%), other housing options. Students who live in college-owned, operated, or affiliated housing: 45%. **Student employment:** During the 2009-2010 academic year, 24% of undergraduates worked on campus. **Clubs and organizations:** Number of student organizations: 10. Activities include: campus ministries, choral groups, dance, drama/theater, literary magazine, musical theater, student government, yearbook. Number of fraternities: 0; sororities: 0. Average proportion of students who stay on campus on weekends: 60%. **Sports program (2009-2010):** Member of NCAA III. *Men's intercollegiate varsity sports:* baseball, basketball, cross country, soccer, tennis, volleyball. *Women's intercollegiate varsity sports:* basketball, cross country, soccer, softball, tennis, volleyball.

SERVICES AND FACILITIES

Basic services: placement service, health service, health insurance. **Remedial assistance:** reading, math, writing, study skills. **Counseling services:** career, personal, academic, religious. **For learning-disabled students:** School does not offer a structured program with separate admission and additional fees. Services include: remedial math, remedial English, remedial reading, tape recorders, untimed tests, learning center, extended time for tests. **Library:** Number of titles: 86,846; number of current serial subscriptions: 19,172. **Information technology resources:** Students are not required to lease or own a computer. Number of campus computers available to all students: 135. School has a wireless network. Approximate number of users that can be accommodated: 12,500. Proportion of college-owned housing units wired for high-speed internet access: 100%. **Campus safety:** Security services offered: 24-hour foot-and-vehicle patrols, late-night transport/escort service, 24-hour emergency telephones, lighted pathways/sidewalks, controlled dormitory access (key, security card, etc).

TRANSFER AND INTERNATIONAL STUDENTS

Transfer students: May apply for admission for the following academic terms: Fall, Spring, Summer. Applicants do not need a minimum number of credits to apply. For fall 2009: Transfer applications received: 243. Transfer applicants offered admission: 195. Transfer applicants enrolled: 108. **International students:** Number of foreign undergraduates: 4. Minimum TOEFL score required: 550 (paper).

Central Connecticut State University

- **Address:** 1615 Stanley Street, New Britain, CT 06050
- **Website:** http://www.ccsu.edu
- **Public**
- **Enrollment:** 7,859 full-time; 2,130 part-time

KEY STATS

✔ **U.S News College Ranking:** 99, Regional Universities (North)
✔ **SAT Score (25th/75th percentile):** 930-1110
✔ **Tuition:** 2010-2011: $7,861 in state, $16,858 out of state

Selectivity: Selective	**Room/board:** $9,576
Acceptance rate: 54%	**Average debt:** $19,200
Student/faculty ratio: 16/1	**Proportion who borrowed:** 48%

UNDERGRADUATE STUDENT BODY STATS

2009-2010 enrollment: 7,859 full-time; 2,130 part-time. Men: 51%; women: 49%. **Ethnic makeup:** African American: 8%; Asian American: 3%; Hispanic: 7%; White: 81%; International: 1%.

ADMISSIONS FACTS AND FIGURES

Phone: (860) 832-2278. **Email:** admissions@ccsu.edu. **Website:** http://www.ccsu.edu. **Application deadlines for fall 2011:** Regular decision: June 1. Early decision: Not offered. Early action: Not offered. Admission cannot be deferred. **Application fee:** $50. **To apply online, go to:** http://www.ccsu.edu/page.cfm?p=2434. **Admissions requirements/recommendations:** High school units required (recommended): English: 4; Mathematics: 3 (1); Science: 2; Foreign language: (3); Social studies: 2; History: 1; Total units: 13 (4). Tests: The college uses SAT or ACT scores in admissions decisions. Either SAT or ACT required. For admission to the fall 2011 entering class, the school will accept: ACT with or without writing accepted. Campus visit: Neither required nor recommended. Admissions interview: Recommended. Off-campus interview: May be arranged. **Factors that count in admissions decisions:** *Academic:* Secondary school record: Very Important. Class rank: Important. Letters of recommendation: Considered. Standardized test scores: Important. Essay: Considered. *Nonacademic:* Interview: Considered. Extracurricular activities: Considered. Talent/ability: Considered. Character/personal qualities: Not Considered. Alumni/ae relationship: Not Considered. Geographical residence: Not Considered. State residency: Considered. Religious affiliation/commitment: Not Considered. Minority status: Considered. Volunteer work: Not Considered. Work experience: Not Considered. **Admissions statistics for the fall 2009 entering class:** Total applicants: 6,791. Total accepted: 3,697. Freshmen enrolled: 1,288; 4% were from out of state. Overall acceptance rate: 54%. **Credentials of fall 2009 freshmen:** 8% ranked in the top 10 percent of their high school class; 30% were in the top 25 percent; 72% were in the top half. (Proportion submitting class standing: 3%.) **Average high school grade point average:** 3.0. **First-year students who submitted SAT scores:** 99%. Scores (25/75 percentile): Critical Reading: 460-550, Math: 470-560, Combined: 930-1110.

ACADEMICS

Year founded: 1849. **Academic calendar:** Semester. **Degrees offered:** certificate, bachelor's, post-bachelor's certificate, master's, post-master's certificate, doctorate. **Most popular majors:** 28% business, management, marketing, and related support services, 13% social sciences, 11% education, 9% psychology, 7% engineering technologies/technicians. **Major fields of study:** biological and biomedical sciences; business, management, marketing, and related support services; computer and information sciences and support services; construction trades; education; engineering; engineering technologies/technicians; English language and literature/letters; foreign languages, literatures, and linguistics; health professions and related clinical sciences; history; mathematics and statistics; multi/interdisciplinary studies; philosophy and religious studies; physical sciences; psychology; public administration and social service professions; social sciences; visual and performing arts. **Areas of required coursework:** arts/fine arts, humanities,

computer literacy, mathematics, English (including composition), philosophy, foreign languages, sciences (biological or physical), history, social science. **Special academic programs:** cooperative (work-study plan) program, cross-registration, distance learning, double major, dual enrollment, English as a Second Language (ESL), exchange student program (domestic), honors program, independent study, internships, student-designed major, study abroad, teacher certificate program. **Teacher certification offered in:** early childhood, elementary, middle/junior high. **Cooperative education programs:** business, computer science, technologies, other. **Reserve Officers Training Corps (ROTC):** Army ROTC: Offered at cooperating institution; Air Force ROTC: Offered at cooperating institution. **Faculty and instruction (2009-2010):** Total instructional faculty: 433 full-time, 491 part-time (58% men; 42% women; 12% minorities). Full-time faculty with Ph.D. or other terminal degree: 82%. Student/faculty ratio: 16/1. Classes of fewer than 20 students: 40%; of 20 to 49 students: 58%; of 50 or more students: 2%. **Advanced Placement and International Baccalaureate credit:** AP tests may be used for: Credit only. Scores accepted: 3, 4, 5. **Freshmen returning for sophomore year:** 78%. **Graduation rates:** Four-year: 14%; five-year: 41%; six-year: 45%.

COSTS AND FINANCIAL AID

Financial aid office: (860) 832-2200. **Expenses (2010-2011):** Tuition and fees 2010-2011: $7,861 in state, $16,858 out of state; room/board: $9,576. Estimated books and supplies: $1,156; transportation: $782; personal expenses: $2,016. **Financial aid:** Priority filing date for institution's financial aid form: February 15; deadline: September 15. In 2009-2010, 74% of undergraduates applied for financial aid. Of those, 57% were determined to have financial need; 11% had their need fully met. Average financial aid package (proportion receiving): $6,601 (56%). Average amount of gift aid, such as scholarships or grants (proportion receiving): $3,501 (47%). Average amount of self-help aid, such as work study or loans (proportion receiving): $4,071 (49%). Average need-based loan (excluding PLUS or other private loans): $3,988. Among students who received need-based aid, the average percentage of need met: 63%. Among students who received aid based on merit, the average award (and the proportion receiving): $2,781 (1%). The average athletic scholarship (and the proportion receiving): $9,269 (2%). Average amount of debt of borrowers graduating in 2009: $19,200. Proportion who borrowed: 48%.

CAMPUS LIFE AND EXTRACURRICULAR ACTIVITIES

Campus housing available: coed dorms, women's dorms, men's dorms. Students who live in college-owned, operated, or affiliated housing: 22%. **Student employment:** During the 2009-2010 academic year, 15% of undergraduates worked on campus. **Clubs and organizations:** Number of student organizations: 100. Activities include: campus ministries, choral groups, concert band, dance, drama/theater, jazz band, literary magazine, music ensembles, pep band, radio station, student government, student newspaper, television station, yearbook. Number of fraternities: 3; sororities: 2. Proportion of men in fraternities: 1%; of women in sororities: 1%. **Sports program (2009-2010):** Member of NCAA I. *Men's intercollegiate varsity sports:* baseball, basketball, cross country, football, golf, soccer, track and field (indoor), track and field (outdoor). *Women's intercollegiate varsity sports:* basketball, cross country, golf, lacrosse, soccer, softball, swimming, track and field (indoor), track and field (outdoor), volleyball.

SERVICES AND FACILITIES

Basic services: nonremedial tutoring, women's center, placement service, day care, health service, health insurance. **Remedial assistance:** reading, math. **Counseling services:** minority student, career, personal, veteran student, academic, psychological, religious. **For learning-disabled students:** School does not offer a structured program with separate admission and additional fees. Services include: remedial math, remedial English, remedial reading, tape recorders, note-taking services, oral tests, learning center, readers, extended time for tests, tutors, priority registration, texts on tape, typist/scribe, exams on tape or computer, take home exams, other testing accommodations, other. **Library:** Number of titles: 725,978; number of current serial subscriptions: 40,128. **Information technology resources:** Students are not required to lease or own a computer. Number of campus computers available to all students: 750. School has a wireless network. Approximate number of users that can be accommodated: 1,000. Proportion of college-owned housing units wired for high-speed internet access: 100%. **Campus safety:** Security services offered: 24-hour foot-and-vehicle patrols, late-night transport/escort service, 24-hour emergency telephones, lighted pathways/sidewalks, student patrols, controlled dormitory access (key, security card, etc).

Transfer students: May apply for admission for the following academic terms: Fall, Spring. Applicants need a minimum number of credits to apply. For fall 2009: Transfer applications received: 2,106. Transfer applicants offered admission: 1,491. Transfer applicants enrolled: 974. **International students:** Number of foreign undergraduates: 98 (1% of student body). Number of countries represented: 45. Minimum TOEFL score required: 500 (paper); 177 (computer). Average TOEFL score: 500 (paper).

Connecticut College

- **Address:** 270 Mohegan Avenue, New London, CT 06320-4196
- **Website:** http://www.conncoll.edu
- **Private**
- **Enrollment:** 1,839 full-time; 67 part-time

KEY STATS

✔ **U.S News College Ranking:** 41, National Liberal Arts Colleges
✔ **ACT Score (25th/75th percentile):** 25-30
✔ **Tuition:** 2010-2011: $43,990

Selectivity: More selective	**Room/board:** $9,120
Acceptance rate: 37%	**Average debt:** $22,038
Student/faculty ratio: 9/1	**Proportion who borrowed:** 34%

UNDERGRADUATE STUDENT BODY STATS

2009-2010 enrollment: 1,839 full-time; 67 part-time. Men: 39%; women: 61%. **Ethnic makeup:** African American: 4%; Asian American: 5%; Hispanic: 6%; White: 81%; International: 4%. **Religious preference:** Roman Catholic: 21%; Protestant: 22%; Jewish: 13%; Muslim: 1%; Hindu: 1%; Buddhist: 1%; No preference: 35%; Other: 6%.

ADMISSIONS FACTS AND FIGURES

Phone: (860) 439-2200. **Email:** admission@conncoll.edu. **Website:** http://www.conncoll.edu. **Application deadlines for fall 2011:** Regular decision: January 1. Early decision: Send application by: November 15; Decision sent by: December 15. Early action: Not offered. Admission can be deferred. **Application fee:** $60. **To apply online, go to:** http://www.conncoll.edu/admission/adm_applying_to_conn.htm. **Admissions requirements/recommendations:** Tests: The college uses SAT or ACT scores in admissions decisions. Neither SAT nor ACT required. For admission to the fall 2011 entering class, the school will accept: ACT with or without writing accepted. Campus visit: Recommended. Admissions interview: Recommended. Off-campus interview: May be arranged. **Factors that count in admissions decisions:** *Academic:* Secondary school record: Very Important. Class rank: Very Important. Letters of recommendation: Important. Standardized test scores: Considered. Essay: Important. *Nonacademic:* Interview: Important. Extracurricular activities: Important. Talent/ability: Important. Character/personal qualities: Very Important. Alumni/ae relationship: Considered. Geographical residence: Considered. State residency: Considered. Religious affiliation/commitment: Considered. Minority status: Important. Volunteer work: Important. Work experience: Important. **Other schools with the greatest overlap in applicants:** Bates College; Bowdoin College; Brown University; Middlebury College; Vassar College. **Admissions statistics for the fall 2009 entering class:** Total applicants: 4,733. Total accepted: 1,738. Freshmen enrolled: 502; 88% were from out of state. Accepted through early-decision or early-action plans: 42%. Overall acceptance rate: 37%. Early-decision acceptance rate: 71%. Non-early acceptance rate: 34%. **Size of waiting list:** 1274 applicants; enrolled from waiting list: 49. **Credentials of fall 2009 freshmen:** 56% ranked in the top 10 percent of their high school class; 93% were in the top 25 percent; 100% were in the top half. (Proportion submitting class standing: 35%.) **First-year students who submitted SAT scores:** 37%. Scores (25/75 percentile): Critical Reading: 610-700, Math: 610-690, Combined: 1220-1390. **First-year students submitting ACT scores:** 46%. Scores (25/75 percentile): English: N/A, Math: N/A, Composite: 25-30.

ACADEMICS

Year founded: 1911. **Academic calendar:** Semester. **Degrees offered:** bachelor's, master's. **Most popular majors:** 15% economics, 9% political science and government, 8% English language and literature, 6% history, 6% international relations and affairs. **Major fields of study:** architecture and related services; area, ethnic, cultural, and gender studies; biological and biomedical sciences; computer and information sciences and support services; education; engineering; English language and literature/letters; family and consumer sciences/human sciences; foreign languages, literatures, and linguistics; history; mathematics and statistics; multi/interdisciplinary studies; philosophy and religious studies; physical sciences; psychology; social sciences; visual and performing arts. **Areas of required coursework:** arts/fine arts, humanities, mathematics, foreign languages, sciences (biological or physical), history, social science, other. **Pre-professional programs:** other. **Special academic programs (% participation):** cross-registration, double major (30%), independent study, internships (75%), student-designed major (2%), study abroad (53%), teacher certificate program (4%). **Teacher certification offered in:** elementary, secondary. **Faculty and instruction (2009-2010):** Total instructional faculty: 177 full-time, 65 part-time (52% men; 48% women; 19% minorities). Full-time faculty with Ph.D. or other terminal degree: 91%. Student/faculty ratio: 9/1. Classes of fewer than 20 students: 63%; of 20 to 49 students: 35%; of 50 or more students: 2%. **Advanced Placement and International Baccalaureate credit:** AP tests may be used for: Credit and/or placement. Scores accepted: 4, 5. International Baccalaureate exams may be used for: Placement only. **Freshmen returning for sophomore year:** 90%. **Graduation rates:** Four-year: 83%; five-year: 85%; six-year: 85%. **Graduate study:** 25% of students pursue further study immediately upon graduation.

COSTS AND FINANCIAL AID

Financial aid office: (860) 439-2058. **Expenses (2010-2011):** Tuition and fees 2010-2011: $43,990; room/board: $9,120. Estimated books and supplies: $1,000; transportation: $400; personal expenses: $500. **Financial aid:** In 2009-2010, 53% of undergraduates applied for financial aid. Of those, 45% were determined to have financial need; 100% had their need fully met. Average financial aid package (proportion receiving): $31,101 (45%). Average amount of gift aid, such as scholarships or grants (proportion receiving): $29,616 (41%). Average amount of self-help aid, such as work study or loans (proportion receiving): $5,397 (40%). Average need-based loan (excluding PLUS or other private loans): $4,389. Among students who received need-based aid, the average percentage of need met: 100%. Among students who received aid based on merit, the average award (and the proportion receiving): $0 (0%). The average athletic scholarship (and the proportion receiving): $0 (0%). Average amount of debt of borrowers graduating in 2009: $22,038. Proportion who borrowed: 34%.

CAMPUS LIFE AND EXTRACURRICULAR ACTIVITIES

Campus housing available (% using): coed dorms (96%), apartment for single students (4%). Students who live in college-owned, operated, or affiliated housing: 99%. **Clubs and organizations:** Number of student organizations: 60. Activities include: campus ministries, choral groups, concert band, dance, drama/theater, international student organization, jazz band, literary magazine, music ensembles, musical theater, radio station, student government, student newspaper, student film society, symphony orchestra, yearbook. Number of fraternities: 0; sororities: 0. **Sports program (2009-2010):** Member of NCAA III. *Men's intercollegiate varsity sports:* basketball, cross country, ice hockey, lacrosse, soccer, swimming, tennis, track and field (indoor), track and field (outdoor), water polo. *Women's intercollegiate varsity sports:* basketball, cross country, field hockey, ice hockey, lacrosse, soccer, squash, swimming, tennis, track and field (indoor), track and field (outdoor), volleyball, water polo.

SERVICES AND FACILITIES

Basic services: nonremedial tutoring, women's center, placement service, health service, health insurance, other. **Counseling services:** minority student, career, personal, academic, older student, psychological, birth control, religious, other. **For learning-disabled students:** School does not offer a structured program with separate admission and additional fees. Services include: note-taking services, extended time for tests, other testing accommodations, other. **Library:** Number of titles: 604,615; number of current serial subscriptions: 6,197. **Information technology resources:** Students are not required to lease or own a computer. Number of campus computers available to all students: 300. School has a wireless network. Approximate number of users that can be accommodated: 3,100. Proportion of college-owned housing units wired for high-speed internet access: 100%. **Campus safety:** Security services offered: 24-hour foot-and-vehicle patrols, late-night transport/escort service, 24-hour emergency telephones, lighted pathways/sidewalks, student patrols, controlled dormitory access (key, security card, etc).

TRANSFER AND INTERNATIONAL STUDENTS

Transfer students: May apply for admission for the following academic terms: Fall, Spring. Applicants need a minimum number of credits to apply. For fall 2009: Transfer applications received: 233. Transfer applicants offered admission: 76. Transfer applicants enrolled: 31. **International students:** Number of foreign undergraduates: 69 (4% of student body). Number of countries represented: 71. Minimum TOEFL score required: 600 (paper); 100 (computer). Average TOEFL score: 623 (paper).

Eastern Connecticut State University

- **Address:** 83 Windham Street, Willimantic, CT 06226
- **Website:** http://www.easternct.edu
- **Public**
- **Enrollment:** 4,326 full-time; 916 part-time

KEY STATS

✔ **U.S News College Ranking:** 91, Regional Universities (North)
✔ **SAT Score (25th/75th percentile):** 950-1110
✔ **Tuition:** 2010-2011: $8,350 in state, $17,347 out of state

Selectivity: Selective	**Room/board:** $10,088
Acceptance rate: 57%	**Average debt:** $22,659
Student/faculty ratio: 16/1	**Proportion who borrowed:** 73%

UNDERGRADUATE STUDENT BODY STATS

2009-2010 enrollment: 4,326 full-time; 916 part-time. Men: 46%; women: 54%. **Ethnic makeup:** African American: 7%; American-Indian: 1%; Asian American: 2%; Hispanic: 6%; White: 83%; International: 1%.

ADMISSIONS FACTS AND FIGURES

Phone: (860) 465-5286. **Email:** admissions@easternct.edu. **Website:** http://www.easternct.edu. **Application deadlines for fall 2011:** Regular decision: Rolling. Early decision: Not offered. Early action: Not offered. Admission can be deferred. **Application fee:** $50. **To apply online, go to:** http://www.easternct.edu/admissions/apply.htm. **Admissions requirements/recommendations:** High school units required (recommended): English: 4; Mathematics: 3 (4); Science: 2; Foreign language: (3); Social studies: 1; History: 1. Tests: The college uses SAT or ACT scores in admissions decisions. Either SAT or ACT required. For admission to the fall 2011 entering class, the school will accept: ACT with or without writing accepted. Campus visit: Recommended. Admissions interview: Neither required nor recommended. Off-campus interview: May be arranged. **Factors that count in admissions decisions:** *Academic:* Secondary school record: Important. Class rank: Very Important. Letters of recommendation: Important. Standardized test scores: Very Important. Essay: Considered. *Nonacademic:* Interview: Considered. Extracurricular activities: Considered. Talent/ability: Very Important. Character/personal qualities: Considered. Alumni/ae relationship: Not Considered. Geographical residence: Not Considered. State residency: Not Considered. Religious affiliation/commitment: Not Considered. Minority status: Not Considered. Volunteer work: Considered. Work experience: Considered. **Other schools with the greatest overlap in applicants:** Central Connecticut State University; Southern Connecticut State University; University of Connecticut; Western Connecticut State University. **Admissions statistics for the fall 2009 entering class:** Total applicants: 3,785. Total accepted: 2,155. Freshmen enrolled: 981; 10% were from out of state. Overall acceptance rate: 57%. **Size of waiting list:** 150 applicants; enrolled from waiting list: 25. **Credentials of fall 2009 freshmen:** 6% ranked in the top 10 percent of their high school class; 32% were in the top 25 percent; 73% were in the top half. (Proportion submitting class standing: 76%.) **Average high school grade point average:** 0.0. **First-year students who submitted SAT scores:** 99%. Scores (25/75 percentile): Critical Reading: 470-550, Math: 480-560, Combined: 950-1110. **First-year students submitting ACT scores:** 1%. Scores (25/75 percentile): English: N/A, Math: N/A, Composite: N/A.

ACADEMICS

Year founded: 1889. **Academic calendar:** Semester. **Degrees offered:** associate, bachelor's, master's. **Most popular majors:** 15% business, management, marketing, and related support services, 11% psychology, 9% liberal arts and sciences studies, and humanities, 7% English language and literature/letters, 7% communication, journalism, and related programs. **Major fields of study:** biological and biomedical sciences; business, management, marketing, and related support services; communication, journalism, and related programs; computer and information sciences and support services; education; English language and literature/letters; foreign languages, literatures, and linguistics; history; liberal arts and sciences studies, and humanities; mathematics and statistics; multi/interdisciplinary studies;

parks, recreation, leisure, and fitness studies; physical sciences; psychology; public administration and social service professions; social sciences; visual and performing arts. **Areas of required coursework:** arts/fine arts, humanities, computer literacy, mathematics, English (including composition), foreign languages, sciences (biological or physical), social science, other. **Pre-professional programs:** other. **Special academic programs (% participation):** accelerated program (3%), cooperative (work-study plan) program (1%), cross-registration (0%), distance learning (6%), double major (8%), dual enrollment (1%), exchange student program (domestic) (1%), honors program (5%), independent study (30%), internships (65%), student-designed major (5%), study abroad (3%), teacher certificate program (10%), weekend college (15%), other (10%). **Teacher certification offered in:** early childhood, elementary, secondary. **Cooperative education programs:** business, computer science, education, engineering, natural science, technologies, other. **Reserve Officers Training Corps (ROTC):** Army ROTC: Offered at cooperating institution (University of Connecticut); Air Force ROTC: Offered at cooperating institution (University of Connecticut). **Faculty and instruction (2009-2010):** Total instructional faculty: 198 full-time, 253 part-time (54% men; 46% women; 15% minorities). Full-time faculty with Ph.D. or other terminal degree: 97%. Student/faculty ratio: 16/1. Classes of fewer than 20 students: 40%; of 20 to 49 students: 59%; of 50 or more students: 0%. **Advanced Placement and International Baccalaureate credit:** AP tests may be used for: Credit only. Freshmen returning for sophomore year: 75%. **Graduation rates:** Four-year: 32%; five-year: 47%; six-year: 48%. **Graduate study:** 35% of students pursue further study immediately upon graduation. Fields in which graduates pursue further study: Master of Business Administration (MBA), 15%; medicine, 5%; education, 45%; arts and sciences, 35%.

COSTS AND FINANCIAL AID

Financial aid office: (860) 465-5205. **Expenses (2010-2011):** Tuition and fees 2010-2011: $8,350 in state, $17,347 out of state; room/board: $10,088. Estimated books and supplies: $1,554; transportation: $1,580; personal expenses: $3,124. **Financial aid:** Priority filing date for institution's financial aid form: March 15. In 2009-2010, 75% of undergraduates applied for financial aid. Of those, 52% were determined to have financial need; 9% had their need fully met. Average financial aid package (proportion receiving): $8,000 (50%). Average amount of gift aid, such as scholarships or grants (proportion receiving): $6,000 (35%). Average amount of self-help aid, such as work study or loans (proportion receiving): $4,192 (46%). Average need-based loan (excluding PLUS or other private loans): $4,273. Among students who received need-based aid, the average percentage of need met: 56%. Among students who received aid based on merit, the average award (and the proportion receiving): $3,470 (0%). The average athletic scholarship (and the proportion receiving): $0 (0%). Average amount of debt of borrowers graduating in 2009: $22,659. Proportion who borrowed: 73%.

CAMPUS LIFE AND EXTRACURRICULAR ACTIVITIES

Campus housing available (% using): coed dorms (12%), apartment for single students (60%), other housing options (28%). Students who live in college-owned, operated, or affiliated housing: 53%. **Student employment:** During the 2009-2010 academic year, 17% of undergraduates worked on campus. Average per-year earnings: $2,652. **Clubs and organizations:** Number of student organizations: 75. Activities include: campus ministries, choral groups, concert band, dance, drama/theater, international student organization, jazz band, literary magazine, music ensembles, musical theater, radio station, student government, student newspaper, television station, yearbook. Number of fraternities: 0; sororities: 0. Average proportion of students who stay on campus on weekends: 50%. **Sports program (2009-2010):** Member of NCAA III. *Men's intercollegiate varsity sports:* baseball, basketball, cross country, lacrosse, soccer, track and field (indoor), track and field (outdoor). *Women's intercollegiate varsity sports:* basketball, cross country, field hockey, lacrosse, soccer, softball, swimming, track and field (indoor), track and field (outdoor), volleyball.

SERVICES AND FACILITIES

Basic services: nonremedial tutoring, women's center, placement service, day care, health service, health insurance, other. **Remedial assistance:** math, writing, study skills. **Counseling services:** career, personal, veteran student, academic, psychological, birth control, religious, other. **For learning-disabled students:** School does not offer a structured program with separate admission and additional fees. Services include: remedial math, reading machines, tape recorders, note-taking services, oral tests, learning center, readers, extended time for tests, tutors, priority registration, priority seating, texts on tape, other testing accommodations. **Library:** Number of titles: 359,755; number of current serial subscriptions: 3,845. **Information technology resources:** Students are not required to lease or own a computer. Number of campus computers available to all students: 360. School has a wireless network. Proportion of college-owned housing units wired for high-speed internet access: 100%. **Campus safety:** Security services offered: 24-hour foot-and-vehicle patrols, late-night transport/escort service, 24-hour emergency telephones, lighted pathways/sidewalks, controlled dormitory access (key, security card, etc).

TRANSFER AND INTERNATIONAL STUDENTS

Transfer students: May apply for admission for the following academic terms: Fall, Spring. Applicants do not need a minimum number of credits to apply. For fall 2009: Transfer applications received: 862. Transfer applicants offered admission: 679. Transfer applicants enrolled: 441. **International students:** Number of foreign undergraduates: 62 (1% of student body). Number of countries represented: 18. Minimum TOEFL score required: 550 (paper); 213 (computer). Average TOEFL score: 557 (paper).

Fairfield University

- **Address:** 1073 N. Benson Road, Fairfield, CT 06824-5195
- **Website:** http://www.fairfield.edu
- **Private; Religious affiliation:** Roman Catholic (Jesuit)
- **Enrollment:** 3,320 full-time; 566 part-time

KEY STATS

- ✔ **U.S News College Ranking:** 4, Regional Universities (North)
- ✔ **SAT Score (25th/75th percentile):** 1050-1240
- ✔ **Tuition:** 2010-2011: $39,040

Selectivity: More selective	**Room/board:** $11,740
Acceptance rate: 65%	**Average debt:** $35,161
Student/faculty ratio: 13/1	**Proportion who borrowed:** 60%

UNDERGRADUATE STUDENT BODY STATS

2009-2010 enrollment: 3,320 full-time; 566 part-time. Men: 42%; women: 58%. **Ethnic makeup:** African American: 4%; American-Indian: 1%; Asian American: 3%; Hispanic: 8%; White: 83%; International: 1%. **Religious preference:** Roman Catholic: 73%; Protestant: 9%; Jewish: 1%; Muslim: 1%; No preference: 9%; Unknown: 1%; Other Christian: 5%; Other: 1%.

ADMISSIONS FACTS AND FIGURES

Phone: (203) 254-4100. **Email:** admis@fairfield.edu. **Website:** http://www.fairfield.edu. **Application deadlines for fall 2011:** Regular decision: January 15; decision sent by April 1. Early decision: Not offered. Early action: Send application by: November 1; Decision sent by: January 1. Admission can be deferred. **Application fee:** $60. **To apply online, go to:** http://www.fairfield.edu/admission/uga_index.html. **Admissions requirements/recommendations:** High school units required (recommended): English: 4 (4); Mathematics: 3 (4); Science: 2 (3); Foreign language: 2 (4); Social studies: 2 (2); History: 2 (2); Academic electives: 1 (1); Total units: 16 (20). Tests: The college uses SAT or ACT scores in admissions decisions. Neither SAT nor ACT required. For admission to the fall 2011 entering class, the school will accept: ACT with or without writing accepted. Campus visit: Recommended. Admissions interview: Recommended. Off-campus interview: May be arranged. **Factors that count in admissions decisions:** *Academic:* Secondary school record: Very Important. Class rank: Considered. Letters of recommendation: Very Important. Standardized test scores: Considered. Essay: Very Important. *Nonacademic:* Interview: Important. Extracurricular activities: Important. Talent/ability: Important. Character/personal qualities: Important. Alumni/ae relationship: Considered. Geographical residence: Considered. State residency: Not Considered. Religious affiliation/commitment: Not Considered. Minority status: Considered. Volunteer work: Important. Work experience: Important. **Other schools with the greatest overlap in applicants:** Boston College; College of the Holy Cross; Loyola University Maryland; Providence College; Villanova University. **Admissions statistics for the fall 2009 entering class:** Total applicants: 8,316. Total accepted: 5,376. Freshmen enrolled: 849; 76% were from out of state. Accepted through early-decision or early-action plans: 41%. Overall acceptance rate: 65%. Non-early acceptance rate: 70%. **Size of waiting list:** 2151 applicants; enrolled from waiting list: 143. **Credentials of fall 2009 freshmen:** 41% ranked in the top 10 percent of their high school class; 78% were in the top 25 percent; 95% were in the top half. (Proportion submitting class standing: 28%.) **Average high school grade point average:** 3.4. **First-year**

students who submitted SAT scores: 96%. Scores (25/75 percentile): Critical Reading: 520-610, Math: 530-630, Combined: 1050-1240.

ACADEMICS

Year founded: 1942. **Academic calendar:** Semester. **Degrees offered:** associate, bachelor's, master's, post-master's certificate. **Most popular majors:** 32% business, management, marketing, and related support services; 14% social sciences, 9% health professions and related clinical sciences, 9% psychology, 8% communication, journalism, and related programs. **Major fields of study:** area, ethnic, cultural, and gender studies; biological and biomedical sciences; business, management, marketing, and related support services; communication, journalism, and related programs; computer and information sciences and support services; engineering; engineering technologies/technicians; English language and literature/letters; foreign languages, literatures, and linguistics; health professions and related clinical sciences; history; liberal arts and sciences studies, and humanities; mathematics and statistics; multi/interdisciplinary studies; philosophy and religious studies; physical sciences; psychology; social sciences; visual and performing arts. **Areas of required coursework:** arts/fine arts, humanities, mathematics, English (including composition), philosophy, foreign languages, sciences (biological or physical), history, social science, other. **Pre-professional programs:** pre-law, pre-dentistry, pre-medicine, pre-veterinary science. **Special academic programs (% participation):** cross-registration, double major (14%), exchange student program (domestic), honors program (4%), independent study (26%), internships (72%), liberal arts/career combination (0%), student-designed major (.5%), study abroad (46%), teacher certificate program (2%). **Teacher certification offered in:** middle/junior high, secondary. **Reserve Officers Training Corps (ROTC):** Army ROTC: Offered at cooperating institution (Sacred Heart University); Air Force ROTC: Offered at cooperating institution (Manhattan College). **Faculty and instruction (2009-2010):** Total instructional faculty: 253 full-time, 229 part-time (53% men; 47% women; 9% minorities). Full-time faculty with Ph.D. or other terminal degree: 92%. Student/faculty ratio: 13/1. Classes of fewer than 20 students: 43%; of 20 to 49 students: 56%; of 50 or more students: 1%. **Advanced Placement and International Baccalaureate credit:** AP tests may be used for: Credit and/or placement. Scores accepted: 4, 5. International Baccalaureate exams may be used for: Placement only. **Freshmen returning for sophomore year:** 89%. **Graduation rates:** Four-year: 83%; five-year: 84%; six-year: 82%. **Graduate study:** 22% of students pursue further study immediately upon graduation. Fields in which graduates pursue further study: Master of Business Administration (MBA), 23%; law, 13%; medicine, 16%; education, 17%; arts and sciences, 24%.

COSTS AND FINANCIAL AID

Financial aid office: (203) 254-4125. **Expenses (2010-2011):** Tuition and fees 2010-2011: $39,040; room/board: $11,740. Estimated books and supplies: $900; transportation: $1,000; personal expenses: $1,465. **Financial aid:** Priority filing date for institution's financial aid form: February 15; deadline: February 15. In 2009-2010, 66% of undergraduates applied for financial aid. Of those, 55% were determined to have financial need; 21% had their need fully met. Average financial aid package (proportion receiving): $27,082 (55%). Average amount of gift aid, such as scholarships or grants (proportion receiving): $20,623 (49%). Average amount of self-help aid, such as work study or loans (proportion receiving): $5,379 (46%). Average need-based loan (excluding PLUS or other private loans): $4,671. Among students who received need-based aid, the average percentage of need met: 85%. Among students who received aid based on merit, the average award (and the proportion receiving): $13,813 (6%). The average athletic scholarship (and the proportion receiving): $20,919 (7%). Average amount of debt of borrowers graduating in 2009: $35,161. Proportion who borrowed: 60%.

CAMPUS LIFE AND EXTRACURRICULAR ACTIVITIES

Campus housing available (% using): coed dorms (65%), apartment for single students (21%), special housing for disabled students (1%), other housing options. Students who live in college-owned, operated, or affiliated housing: 79%. **Student employment:** During the 2009-2010 academic year, 18% of undergraduates worked on campus. Average per-year earnings: $1,500. **Clubs and organizations:** Number of student organizations: 106. Activities include: campus ministries, choral groups, concert band, dance, drama/theater, international student organization, jazz band, literary magazine, model UN, music ensembles, pep band, radio station, student government, student newspaper, student film society, television station, yearbook. Number of fraternities: 0; sororities: 0. Average proportion of students who stay on campus on weekends: 90%. **Sports program (2009-2010):** Member of NCAA I. *Men's intercollegiate varsity sports:* baseball, basketball, cross country, golf, lacrosse, soccer, swimming, tennis. *Women's intercollegiate*

varsity sports: basketball, crew (heavyweight), cross country, field hockey, golf, lacrosse, soccer, softball, swimming, tennis, volleyball.

SERVICES AND FACILITIES

Basic services: nonremedial tutoring, placement service, day care, health service, health insurance. **Counseling services:** minority student, career, personal, academic, psychological, religious. **For learning-disabled students:** School does not offer a structured program with separate admission and additional fees. Total undergraduates in learning-disabled program or receiving services: 190. Services include: reading machines, tape recorders, note-taking services, readers, extended time for tests, tutors, priority seating, other. **Library:** Number of titles: 394,588; number of current serial subscriptions: 34,405. **Information technology resources:** Students are not required to lease or own a computer. School has a wireless network. Approximate number of users that can be accommodated: 3,000. Proportion of college-owned housing units wired for high-speed internet access: 100%. **Campus safety:** Security services offered: 24-hour foot-and-vehicle patrols, late-night transport/escort service, 24-hour emergency telephones, lighted pathways/sidewalks, controlled dormitory access (key, security card, etc).

TRANSFER AND INTERNATIONAL STUDENTS

Transfer students: May apply for admission for the following academic terms: Fall, Spring. Applicants need a minimum number of credits to apply. For fall 2009: Transfer applications received: 273. Transfer applicants offered admission: 101. Transfer applicants enrolled: 37. **International students:** Number of foreign undergraduates: 33 (1% of student body). Number of countries represented: 37. Minimum TOEFL score required: 550 (paper); 213 (computer). Average TOEFL score: 590 (paper).

Mitchell College

- **Address:** 437 Pequot Avenue, New London, CT 06320
- **Website:** http://www.mitchell.edu
- **Private**
- **Enrollment:** 818 full-time; 143 part-time

KEY STATS

✔ **U.S News College Ranking:** Unranked, Regional Colleges (North)
✔ **SAT or ACT Score (25th/75th percentile):** N/A
✔ **Tuition:** 2009-2010: $25,627

Selectivity: N/A	**Room/board:** $11,548
Acceptance rate: 83%	**Average debt:** N/A
Student/faculty ratio: 15/1	**Proportion who borrowed:** N/A

UNDERGRADUATE STUDENT BODY STATS

2009-2010 enrollment: 818 full-time; 143 part-time. Men: 51%; women: 49%. **Ethnic makeup:** African American: 13%; American-Indian: 2%; Asian American: 1%; Hispanic: 8%; White: 76%; International: 1%.

ADMISSIONS FACTS AND FIGURES

Phone: (800) 443-2811. **Email:** admissions@mitchell.edu. **Website:** http://www.mitchell.edu. **Application deadlines for fall 2011:** Regular decision: Rolling. Early decision: Send application by: November 15; Decision sent by: December 15. Early action: Not offered. Admission can be deferred. **Application fee:** $30. **To apply online, go to:** https://applications.mitchell.edu/applyonline/Default.aspx?S=A. **Admissions requirements/recommendations:** High school units required (recommended): English: 4 (4); Mathematics: 3 (3); Science: 3 (3); Social studies: 3 (3); Academic electives: 2 (2); Total units: 16 (16). Tests: The college does not use SAT or ACT scores in admissions decisions. Neither SAT nor ACT required. Campus visit: Recommended. Admissions interview: Required. Off-campus interview: May be arranged. **Factors that count in admissions decisions:** *Academic:* Secondary school record: Important. Class rank: Not Considered. Letters of recommendation: Important. Standardized test scores: Not Considered. Essay: Important. *Nonacademic:* Interview: Very Important. Extracurricular activities: Important. Talent/ability: Considered. Character/personal qualities: Important. Alumni/ae relationship: Considered. Geographical residence: Not Considered. State residency: Not Considered. Religious affiliation/commitment: Not Considered. Minority status: Not Considered. Volunteer work: Important. Work experience: Considered. **Other schools with the greatest overlap in applicants:** Curry College; Eastern Connecticut State University; Mount Ida College; New England College; Quinnipiac University. **Admissions statistics for the fall 2009 entering class:** Total appli-

cants: 802. Total accepted: 663. Freshmen enrolled: 260; 51% were from out of state. Overall acceptance rate: 83%. Non-early acceptance rate: 83%. Size of waiting list: 0 applicants; enrolled from waiting list: 0. **Average high school grade point average:** 2.7.

ACADEMICS

Year founded: 1938. **Academic calendar:** Semester. **Degrees offered:** certificate, associate, bachelor's. **Most popular majors:** 29% liberal arts and sciences studies, and humanities, 27% business, management, marketing, and related support services, 13% security and protective services, 10% psychology, 9% education. **Major fields of study:** business, management, marketing, and related support services; communication, journalism, and related programs; education; family and consumer sciences/human sciences; legal professions and studies; liberal arts and sciences studies, and humanities; natural resources and conservation; parks, recreation, leisure, and fitness studies; psychology; security and protective services. **Areas of required coursework:** arts/fine arts, humanities, computer literacy, mathematics, English (including composition), sciences (biological or physical), history, social science. **Pre-professional programs:** pre-law. **Special academic programs:** independent study, internships, student-designed major, study abroad, teacher certificate program. **Teacher certification offered in:** early childhood. **Faculty and instruction (2009-2010):** Total instructional faculty: 35 full-time, 72 part-time (53% men; 47% women; 5% minorities). Full-time faculty with Ph.D. or other terminal degree: 77%. Student/faculty ratio: 15/1. Classes of fewer than 20 students: 77%; of 20 to 49 students: 23%. **Advanced Placement and International Baccalaureate credit:** AP tests may be used for: Credit only. International Baccalaureate exams may be used for: Credit only. **Freshmen returning for sophomore year:** 65%. **Graduation rates:** Four-year: 25%; five-year: 34%; six-year: 37%.

COSTS AND FINANCIAL AID

Expenses (2009-2010): Tuition and fees 2009-2010: $25,627; room/board: $11,548. Estimated books and supplies: $1,500. **Financial aid:** Priority filing date for institution's financial aid form: February 1.

CAMPUS LIFE AND EXTRACURRICULAR ACTIVITIES

Campus housing available (% using): coed dorms (70%), women's dorms (10%), men's dorms (10%), other housing options (10%). Students who live in college-owned, operated, or affiliated housing: 59%. **Student employment:** During the 2009-2010 academic year, 2% of undergraduates worked on campus. **Clubs and organizations:** Number of student organizations: 29. Activities include: campus ministries, choral groups, dance, drama/theater, literary magazine, music ensembles, musical theater, radio station, student government, student newspaper, yearbook. Number of fraternities: 0; sororities: 0. Average proportion of students who stay on campus on weekends: 65%. **Sports program (2009-2010):** Member of NCAA III. *Men's intercollegiate varsity sports:* baseball, basketball, cross country, golf, lacrosse, soccer, tennis. *Women's intercollegiate varsity sports:* basketball, cross country, soccer, softball, tennis, volleyball.

SERVICES AND FACILITIES

Basic services: day care, health service, health insurance. **Counseling services:** minority student, career, personal, veteran student, academic, birth control. **For learning-disabled students:** School does not offer a structured program with separate admission and additional fees. Services include: reading machines, tape recorders, diagnostic testing service, note-taking services, oral tests, learning center, readers, extended time for tests, tutors, priority seating, texts on tape, other testing accommodations. **Library:** Number of titles: 88,500; number of current serial subscriptions: 106. **Information technology resources:** Students are not required to lease or own a computer. Number of campus computers available to all students: 155. School has a wireless network. Approximate number of users that can be accommodated: 200. Proportion of college-owned housing units wired for high-speed internet access: 100%. **Campus safety:** Security services offered: 24-hour foot-and-vehicle patrols, late-night transport/escort service, 24-hour emergency telephones, lighted pathways/sidewalks, controlled dormitory access (key, security card, etc).

TRANSFER AND INTERNATIONAL STUDENTS

Transfer students: May apply for admission for the following academic terms: Fall, Spring. Applicants do not need a minimum number of credits to apply. For fall 2009: Transfer applications received: 90. Transfer applicants offered admission: 74. Transfer applicants enrolled: 53. **International students:** Number of foreign undergraduates: 5 (1% of student body). Number of countries represented: 6. Minimum TOEFL score required: 500 (paper); 173 (computer).

Post University

■ **Address:** 800 Country Club Road, PO Box 2540, Waterbury, CT 06723
■ **Website:** http://www.post.edu
■ **Enrollment:** 1,228 full-time; 969 part-time

KEY STATS

✔ **U.S News College Ranking:** second tier, Regional Colleges (North)
✔ **SAT Score (25th/75th percentile):** 780-1020
✔ **Tuition:** 2009-2010: $0 in state, $0 out of state

Selectivity: Less selective	**Room/board:** $9,400
Acceptance rate: 59%	**Average debt:** N/A
Student/faculty ratio: 19/1	**Proportion who borrowed:** 79%

UNDERGRADUATE STUDENT BODY STATS

2009-2010 enrollment: 1,228 full-time; 969 part-time. Men: 41%; women: 59%. **Ethnic makeup:** African American: 18%; Asian American: 1%; Hispanic: 7%; White: 73%; International: 1%.

ADMISSIONS FACTS AND FIGURES

Phone: (203) 596-4520. **Email:** admissions@post.edu. **Website:** http://www.post.edu. **Application deadlines for fall 2011:** Regular decision: Rolling. Early decision: Not offered. Early action: Not offered. Admission can be deferred. **Application fee:** $40. **To apply online, go to:** http://www.post.edu/applications.shtml. **Admissions requirements/recommendations:** High school units required (recommended): English: 4 (4); Mathematics: 3 (3); Science: 2 (2); Foreign language: 2 (2); Social studies: 1 (1); History: 2 (2); Academic electives: 2 (2); Total units: 16 (16). Tests: The college uses SAT or ACT scores in admissions decisions. Either SAT or ACT required. For admission to the fall 2011 entering class, the school will accept: ACT with or without writing accepted. Campus visit: Recommended. Admissions interview: Recommended. Off-campus interview: May be arranged. **Factors that count in admissions decisions:** *Academic:* Secondary school record: Important. Class rank: Considered. Letters of recommendation: Considered. Standardized test scores: Important. Essay: Considered. *Nonacademic:* Interview: Important. Extracurricular activities: Considered. Talent/ability: Considered. Character/personal qualities: Important. Alumni/ae relationship: Considered. Geographical residence: Considered. State residency: Not Considered. Religious affiliation/commitment: Not Considered. Minority status: Not Considered. Volunteer work: Considered. Work experience: Considered. **Other schools with the greatest overlap in applicants:** Central Connecticut State University; Quinnipiac University; Southern Connecticut State University; University of Bridgeport; University of New Haven. **Admissions statistics for the fall 2009 entering class:** Total applicants: 1,965. Total accepted: 1,152. Freshmen enrolled: 246; 66% were from out of state. Overall acceptance rate: 59%. **Credentials of fall 2009 freshmen:** 5% ranked in the top 10 percent of their high school class; 20% were in the top 25 percent; 50% were in the top half. (Proportion submitting class standing: 50%.) **Average high school grade point average:** 2.4. **First-year students who submitted SAT scores:** 92%. Scores (25/75 percentile): Critical Reading: 390-500, Math: 390-520, Combined: 780-1020. **First-year students submitting ACT scores:** 4%. Scores (25/75 percentile): English: 17-22, Math: 18-23, Composite: 17-22.

ACADEMICS

Year founded: 1890. **Academic calendar:** Semester. **Degrees offered:** certificate, associate, transfer-associate, terminal-associate, bachelor's, post-bachelor's certificate, master's, post-master's certificate. **Most popular majors:** 60% business administration and management, 15% accounting, 11% criminal justice/safety studies, 8% legal assistant/paralegal, 5% social work. **Major fields of study:** agriculture, agriculture operations, and related sciences; biological and biomedical sciences; business, management, marketing, and related support services; computer and information sciences and support services; English language and literature/letters; history; legal professions and studies; liberal arts and sciences studies, and humanities; natural resources and conservation; psychology; public administration and social service professions; security and protective services; social sciences. **Areas of required coursework:** humanities, computer literacy, mathematics, English (including composition), sciences (biological or physical), history, social science. **Special academic programs (% participation):** accelerated program (61%), cooperative (work-study plan) program (5%), cross-registration (0%), distance learning (46%), double major (2%), English as a Second Language (ESL) (0%), honors program (1%), independent study (30%), internships (1%), study abroad (3%), weekend college (5%). **Cooperative education pro-**

grams: business, computer science, social/behavioral science. **Faculty and instruction (2009-2010):** Total instructional faculty: 30 full-time, 188 part-time (49% men; 51% women; 15% minorities). Full-time faculty with Ph.D. or other terminal degree: 57%. Student/faculty ratio: 19/1. Classes of fewer than 20 students: 69%; of 20 to 49 students: 31%. **Advanced Placement and International Baccalaureate credit:** AP tests may be used for: Credit and/or placement. Scores accepted: 3, 4, 5. International Baccalaureate exams may be used for: Placement only. **Freshmen returning for sophomore year:** 57%. **Graduation rates:** Four-year: 21%; five-year: 26%; six-year: 30%. **Graduate study:** 12% of students pursue further study immediately upon graduation. Fields in which graduates pursue further study: Master of Business Administration (MBA), 10%; law, 5%; education, 13%; arts and sciences, 40%; veterinary medicine, 1%.

COSTS AND FINANCIAL AID

Financial aid office: (203) 596-4526. **Expenses (2009-2010):** Tuition and fees 2009-2010: $0 in state, $0 out of state; room/board: $9,400. Estimated books and supplies: $1,500; transportation: $2,250; personal expenses: $2,000. **Financial aid:** Priority filing date for institution's financial aid form: March 15. In 2009-2010, 98% of undergraduates applied for financial aid. Of those, 98% were determined to have financial need; Average financial aid package (proportion receiving): $11,812 (98%). Average amount of gift aid, such as scholarships or grants (proportion receiving): $4,247 (55%). Average amount of self-help aid, such as work study or loans (proportion receiving): $3,255 (82%). Average need-based loan (excluding PLUS or other private loans): $4,075. Among students who received need-based aid, the average percentage of need met: 69%. Among students who received aid based on merit, the average award (and the proportion receiving): $0 (0%). The average athletic scholarship (and the proportion receiving): $0 (0%). Proportion who borrowed: 79%.

CAMPUS LIFE AND EXTRACURRICULAR ACTIVITIES

Campus housing available (% using): coed dorms (100%), other housing options. Students who live in college-owned, operated, or affiliated housing: 61%. **Student employment:** During the 2009-2010 academic year, 65% of undergraduates worked on campus. Average per-year earnings: $2,896. **Clubs and organizations:** Number of student organizations: 15. Activities include: dance, drama/theater, international student organization, literary magazine, musical theater, student government, yearbook. Number of fraternities: 0; sororities: 0. Average proportion of students who stay on campus on weekends: 60%. **Sports program (2009-2010):** Member of NCAA II. *Men's intercollegiate varsity sports:* baseball, basketball, cross country, golf, soccer, swimming, tennis. *Women's intercollegiate varsity sports:* basketball, cross country, lacrosse, soccer, softball, swimming, tennis, volleyball.

SERVICES AND FACILITIES

Basic services: nonremedial tutoring, placement service, health service, health insurance. **Remedial assistance:** reading, math, writing, study skills. **Counseling services:** minority student, career, military, personal, veteran student, academic, psychological, birth control. **For learning-disabled students:** School does not offer a structured program with separate admission and additional fees. Total undergraduates in learning-disabled program or receiving services: 36. Services include: remedial math, remedial English, remedial reading, tape recorders, untimed tests, note-taking services, oral tests, learning center, extended time for tests, tutors, priority seating, substitution of courses, other testing accommodations. **Library:** Number of titles: 64,889; number of current serial subscriptions: 315. **Information technology resources:** Students are not required to lease or own a computer. Number of campus computers available to all students: 105. School has a wireless network. Approximate number of users that can be accommodated: 500. Proportion of college-owned housing units wired for high-speed internet access: 100%. **Campus safety:** Security services offered: 24-hour foot-and-vehicle patrols, late-night transport/escort service, 24-hour emergency telephones, lighted pathways/sidewalks, controlled dormitory access (key, security card, etc).

TRANSFER AND INTERNATIONAL STUDENTS

Transfer students: May apply for admission for the following academic terms: Fall, Spring. Applicants need a minimum number of credits to apply. For fall 2009: Transfer applications received: 210. Transfer applicants offered admission: 128. Transfer applicants enrolled: 64. **International students:** Number of foreign undergraduates: 19 (1% of student body). Number of countries represented: 8. Minimum TOEFL score required: 500 (paper); 177 (computer). Average TOEFL score: 520 (paper).

Quinnipiac University

- **Address:** 275 Mount Carmel Avenue, Hamden, CT 06518
- **Website:** http://www.quinnipiac.edu
- **Private**
- **Enrollment:** 5,686 full-time; 285 part-time

KEY STATS

✔ **U.S News College Ranking:** 9, Regional Universities (North)
✔ **SAT Score (25th/75th percentile):** 1120-1230
✔ **Tuition:** 2010-2011: $34,250

Selectivity: More selective	**Room/board:** $12,730
Acceptance rate: 60%	**Average debt:** $34,621
Student/faculty ratio: 12/1	**Proportion who borrowed:** 69%

UNDERGRADUATE STUDENT BODY STATS

2009-2010 enrollment: 5,686 full-time; 285 part-time. Men: 38%; women: 62%. **Ethnic makeup:** African American: 3%; Asian American: 3%; Hispanic: 5%; White: 87%; International: 1%. **Religious preference:** Roman Catholic: 60%; Protestant: 15%; Jewish: 11%; Muslim: 1%; Unknown: 13%.

ADMISSIONS FACTS AND FIGURES

Phone: (800) 462-1944. **Email:** admissions@quinnipiac.edu. **Website:** http://www.quinnipiac.edu. **Application deadlines for fall 2011:** Regular decision: February 1. Early decision: Not offered. Early action: Not offered. Admission can be deferred. **Application fee:** $45. **To apply online, go to:** http://www.quinnipiac.edu/x76.xml. **Admissions requirements/recommendations:** High school units required (recommended): English: 4 (4); Mathematics: 3 (3); Science: 2 (3); Foreign language: 2 (2); Social studies: 3 (3); Academic electives: 2 (2); Total units: 16 (16). Tests: The college uses SAT or ACT scores in admissions decisions. Either SAT or ACT required. For admission to the fall 2011 entering class, the school will accept: ACT with writing required. Campus visit: Recommended. Admissions interview: Recommended. Off-campus interview: May be arranged. **Factors that count in admissions decisions:** *Academic:* Secondary school record: Very Important. Class rank: Very Important. Letters of recommendation: Important. Standardized test scores: Very Important. Essay: Important. *Nonacademic:* Interview: Important. Extracurricular activities: Important. Talent/ability: Considered. Character/personal qualities: Important. Alumni/ae relationship: Considered. Geographical residence: Not Considered. State residency: Not Considered. Religious affiliation/commitment: Not Considered. Minority status: Considered. Volunteer work: Considered. Work experience: Considered. **Other schools with the greatest overlap in applicants:** Boston University; Fairfield University; Ithaca College; Northeastern University; University of Connecticut. **Admissions statistics for the fall 2009 entering class:** Total applicants: 13,847. Total accepted: 8,330. Freshmen enrolled: 1,587; 78% were from out of state. Overall acceptance rate: 60%. **Size of waiting list:** 1658 applicants; enrolled from waiting list: 180. **Credentials of fall 2009 freshmen:** 28% ranked in the top 10 percent of their high school class; 68% were in the top 25 percent; 98% were in the top half. (Proportion submitting class standing: 64%.) **Average high school grade point average:** 3.4. **First-year students who submitted SAT scores:** 94%. Scores (25/75 percentile): Critical Reading: 550-610, Math: 570-620, Combined: 1120-1230. **First-year students submitting ACT scores:** 30%. Scores (25/75 percentile): English: N/A, Math: N/A, Composite: 24-29.

ACADEMICS

Year founded: 1929. **Academic calendar:** Semester. **Degrees offered:** certificate, bachelor's, post-bachelor's certificate, master's. **Most popular majors:** 26% health services/allied health/health sciences, 20% accounting, 15% public relations, advertising, and applied communication , 7% physiological psychology/psychobiology, 6% economics. **Major fields of study:** biological and biomedical sciences; business, management, marketing, and related support services; communication, journalism, and related programs; computer and information sciences and support services; English language and literature/letters; family and consumer sciences/human sciences; foreign languages, literatures, and linguistics; health professions and related clinical sciences; history; legal professions and studies; liberal arts and sciences studies, and humanities; mathematics and statistics; multi/interdisciplinary studies; physical sciences; psychology; security and protective services; social sciences; visual and performing arts. **Areas of required coursework:** arts/fine arts, humanities, mathematics, English (including composition), foreign languages, sciences (biological or physical), history, social science.

Pre-professional programs: pre-law, pre-dentistry, pre-medicine, pre-veterinary science. **Special academic programs (% participation):** distance learning (4%), double major (2%), honors program (3%), internships (40%), liberal arts/career combination (28%), student-designed major (1%), study abroad (5%), teacher certificate program (12%). **Teacher certification offered in:** elementary, secondary. **Reserve Officers Training Corps (ROTC):** Army ROTC: Offered at cooperating institution; Air Force ROTC: Offered at cooperating institution. **Faculty and instruction (2009-2010):** Total instructional faculty: 286 full-time, 543 part-time (47% men; 53% women; 7% minorities). Full-time faculty with Ph.D. or other terminal degree: 87%. Student/faculty ratio: 12/1. Classes of fewer than 20 students: 46%; of 20 to 49 students: 54%. **Advanced Placement and International Baccalaureate credit:** AP tests may be used for: Credit and/or placement. Scores accepted: 3, 4, 5. International Baccalaureate exams may be used for: Credit and/or placement. **Freshmen returning for sophomore year:** 88%. **Graduation rates:** Four-year: 69%; five-year: 73%; six-year: 73%. **Graduate study:** 32% of students pursue further study immediately upon graduation; 6% within one year; 8% within five years. Fields in which graduates pursue further study: Master of Business Administration (MBA), 7%; law, 2%; medicine, 2%; dentistry, 1%; education, 6%; arts and sciences, 3%; veterinary medicine, 1%.

COSTS AND FINANCIAL AID

Financial aid office: (203) 582-8750. **Expenses (2010-2011):** Tuition and fees 2010-2011: $34,250; room/board: $12,730. Estimated books and supplies: $800; transportation: $500; personal expenses: $900. **Financial aid:** Priority filing date for institution's financial aid form: March 1; deadline: April 15. In 2009-2010, 72% of undergraduates applied for financial aid. Of those, 59% were determined to have financial need; 13% had their need fully met. Average financial aid package (proportion receiving): $19,785 (59%). Average amount of gift aid, such as scholarships or grants (proportion receiving): $14,200 (57%). Average amount of self-help aid, such as work study or loans (proportion receiving): $5,586 (50%). Average need-based loan (excluding PLUS or other private loans): $4,476. Among students who received need-based aid, the average percentage of need met: 65%. Among students who received aid based on merit, the average award (and the proportion receiving): $9,748 (14%). The average athletic scholarship (and the proportion receiving): $26,450 (5%). Average amount of debt of borrowers graduating in 2009: $34,621. Proportion who borrowed: 69%.

CAMPUS LIFE AND EXTRACURRICULAR ACTIVITIES

Campus housing available (% using): coed dorms (71%), apartment for single students (26%), other housing options (3%). Students who live in college-owned, operated, or affiliated housing: 78%. **Student employment:** During the 2009-2010 academic year, 20% of undergraduates worked on campus. Average per-year earnings: $2,100. **Clubs and organizations:** Number of student organizations: 80. Activities include: campus ministries, choral groups, dance, drama/theater, literary magazine, pep band, radio station, student government, student newspaper, television station, yearbook. Number of fraternities: 4; sororities: 5. Proportion of men in fraternities: 7%; of women in sororities: 6%. Average proportion of students who stay on campus on weekends: 75%. **Sports program (2009-2010):** Member of NCAA I.

SERVICES AND FACILITIES

Basic services: nonremedial tutoring, placement service, health service, health insurance. **Counseling services:** minority student, career, personal, veteran student, academic, older student, psychological, religious. **For learning-disabled students:** School does not offer a structured program with separate admission and additional fees. Services include: learning center, tutors. **Library:** Number of titles: 285,000; number of current serial subscriptions: 21,000. **Information technology resources:** Students are required to lease or own a computer. Number of campus computers available to all students: 450. School has a wireless network. Approximate number of users that can be accommodated: 8,000. Proportion of college-owned housing units wired for high-speed internet access: 100%. **Campus safety:** Security services offered: 24-hour foot-and-vehicle patrols, late-night transport/escort service, 24-hour emergency telephones, lighted pathways/sidewalks, controlled dormitory access (key, security card, etc).

TRANSFER AND INTERNATIONAL STUDENTS

Transfer students: May apply for admission for the following academic terms: Fall, Spring. Applicants need a minimum number of credits to apply. For fall 2009: Transfer applications received: 612. Transfer applicants offered admission: 468. Transfer applicants enrolled: 168. **International students:** Number of foreign undergraduates: 79 (1% of stu-

dent body). Number of countries represented: 18. Minimum TOEFL score required: 550 (paper); 213 (computer). Average TOEFL score: 555 (paper).

Sacred Heart University

- **Address:** 5151 Park Avenue, Fairfield, CT 06825
- **Website:** http://www.sacredheart.edu
- **Private; Religious affiliation:** Roman Catholic
- **Enrollment:** 3,534 full-time; 658 part-time

KEY STATS

✔ **U.S News College Ranking:** 33, Regional Universities (North)
✔ **SAT Score (25th/75th percentile):** 960-1150
✔ **Tuition:** 2009-2010: $30,298

Selectivity: Selective	**Room/board:** $11,684
Acceptance rate: 66%	**Average debt:** $27,500
Student/faculty ratio: 13/1	**Proportion who borrowed:** 96%

UNDERGRADUATE STUDENT BODY STATS

2009-2010 enrollment: 3,534 full-time; 658 part-time. Men: 39%; women: 61%. **Ethnic makeup:** African American: 3%; Asian American: 2%; Hispanic: 6%; White: 88%; International: 1%. **Religious preference:** Protestant: 9%; Jewish: 1%; Muslim: 1%; Buddhist: 1%; No preference: 12%; Roman Catholic: 66%; Other: 5%.

ADMISSIONS FACTS AND FIGURES

Phone: (203) 371-7880. **Email:** enroll@sacredheart.edu. **Website:** http://www.sacredheart.edu. **Application deadlines for fall 2011:** Regular decision: Rolling. Early decision: Send application by: December 1; Decision sent by: December 15. Early action: Not offered. Admission can be deferred. **Application fee:** $50. **To apply online, go to:** http://www.sacredheart.edu/apply.cfm. **Admissions requirements/recommendations:** High school units required (recommended): English: 4 (4); Mathematics: 3 (4); Science: 3 (4); Foreign language: 2 (4); Social studies: 3 (4); History: 3 (4); Academic electives: 3 (4); Total units: 22 (30). Tests: The college uses SAT or ACT scores in admissions decisions. Neither SAT nor ACT required. For admission to the fall 2011 entering class, the school will accept: ACT with or without writing accepted. Campus visit: Recommended. Admissions interview: Recommended. Off-campus interview: May be arranged. **Factors that count in admissions decisions:** *Academic:* Secondary school record: Very Important. Class rank: Important. Letters of recommendation: Important. Standardized test scores: Considered. Essay: Considered. *Nonacademic:* Interview: Very Important. Extracurricular activities: Very Important. Talent/ability: Important. Character/personal qualities: Important. Alumni/ae relationship: Considered. Geographical residence: Considered. State residency: Considered. Religious affiliation/commitment: Considered. Minority status: Considered. Volunteer work: Very Important. Work experience: Important. **Other schools with the greatest overlap in applicants:** Fairfield University; Marist College; Providence College; Quinnipiac University; University of Connecticut. **Admissions statistics for the fall 2009 entering class:** Total applicants: 7,343. Total accepted: 4,864. Freshmen enrolled: 909; 71% were from out of state. Overall acceptance rate: 66%. Non-early acceptance rate: 66%. **Credentials of fall 2009 freshmen:** 18% ranked in the top 10 percent of their high school class; 54% were in the top 25 percent; 83% were in the top half. (Proportion submitting class standing: 42%.) **Average high school grade point average:** 3.3. **First-year students who submitted SAT scores:** 95%. Scores (25/75 percentile): Critical Reading: 470-570, Math: 490-580, Combined: 960-1150. **First-year students submitting ACT scores:** 31%. Scores (25/75 percentile): English: N/A; Math: N/A, Composite: 20-24.

ACADEMICS

Year founded: 1963. **Academic calendar:** Semester. **Degrees offered:** certificate, associate, terminal-associate, bachelor's, post-bachelor's certificate, master's, post-master's certificate. **Most popular majors:** 19% business administration and management, 17% psychology, 8% nursing, 6% accounting, 6% kinesiology and exercise science. **Major fields of study:** biological and biomedical sciences; business, management, marketing, and related support services; communication, journalism, and related programs; computer and information sciences and support services; English language and literature/letters; foreign languages, literatures, and linguistics; health professions and related clinical sciences; history; legal professions and studies; liberal arts and sciences studies, and humanities; mathematics

and statistics; parks, recreation, leisure, and fitness studies; philosophy and religious studies; physical sciences; psychology; public administration and social service professions; security and protective services; social sciences; visual and performing arts. **Areas of required coursework:** arts/fine arts, humanities, computer literacy, mathematics, English (including composition), philosophy, sciences (biological or physical), history, social science. **Pre-professional programs:** pre-law, pre-dentistry, pre-medicine, pre-theology, pre-veterinary science, pre-optometry, pre-pharmacy, other. **Special academic programs (% participation):** distance learning (35%), double major (20%), English as a Second Language (ESL) (2%), honors program (6%), independent study (25%), internships (75%), study abroad (5%), teacher certificate program (10%). **Teacher certification offered in:** elementary, middle/junior high, secondary. **Reserve Officers Training Corps (ROTC):** Army ROTC: Offered on campus. **Faculty and instruction (2009-2010):** Total instructional faculty: 204 full-time, 363 part-time (52% men; 48% women; 11% minorities). Full-time faculty with Ph.D. or other terminal degree: 76%. Student/faculty ratio: 13/1. Classes of fewer than 20 students: 41%; of 20 to 49 students: 59%. **Advanced Placement and International Baccalaureate credit:** AP tests may be used for: Credit and/or placement. Scores accepted: 4, 5. International Baccalaureate exams may be used for: Placement only. **Freshmen returning for sophomore year:** 80%. **Graduation rates:** Four-year: 56%; five-year: 64%; six-year: 65%. **Graduate study:** 49% of students pursue further study within one year. Fields in which graduates pursue further study: Master of Business Administration (MBA), 11%; law, 3%; medicine, 2%; dentistry, 1%; education, 44%; arts and sciences, 24%; veterinary medicine, 1%.

COSTS AND FINANCIAL AID

Financial aid office: (203) 371-7980. **Expenses (2009-2010):** Tuition and fees 2009-2010: $30,298; room/board: $11,684. Estimated books and supplies: $1,000; transportation: $1,000; personal expenses: $1,000. **Financial aid:** Priority filing date for institution's financial aid form: February 15. In 2009-2010, 84% of undergraduates applied for financial aid. Of those, 69% were determined to have financial need; 14% had their need fully met. Average financial aid package (proportion receiving): $18,782 (69%). Average amount of gift aid, such as scholarships or grants (proportion receiving): $14,508 (68%). Average amount of self-help aid, such as work study or loans (proportion receiving): $5,172 (59%). Average need-based loan (excluding PLUS or other private loans): $4,527. Among students who received need-based aid, the average percentage of need met: 65%. Among students who received aid based on merit, the average award (and the proportion receiving): $5,541 (16%). The average athletic scholarship (and the proportion receiving): $19,301 (6%). Average amount of debt of borrowers graduating in 2009: $27,500. Proportion who borrowed: 96%.

CAMPUS LIFE AND EXTRACURRICULAR ACTIVITIES

Campus housing available (% using): coed dorms (66%), apartment for single students (33%), special housing for disabled students (1%). Students who live in college-owned, operated, or affiliated housing: 60%. **Student employment:** During the 2009-2010 academic year, 25% of undergraduates worked on campus. Average per-year earnings: $1,376. **Clubs and organizations:** Number of student organizations: 85. Activities include: campus ministries, choral groups, concert band, dance, drama/theater, international student organization, jazz band, literary magazine, marching band, music ensembles, musical theater, pep band, radio station, student government, student newspaper, student film society, television station, yearbook. Number of fraternities: 4; sororities: 5. Proportion of men in fraternities: 11%; of women in sororities: 10%. Average proportion of students who stay on campus on weekends: 75%. **Sports program (2009-2010):** Member of NCAA I. *Men's intercollegiate varsity sports:* baseball, basketball, cross country, fencing, football, golf, ice hockey, lacrosse, soccer, tennis, track and field (indoor), track and field (outdoor), volleyball, wrestling. *Women's intercollegiate varsity sports:* basketball, bowling, crew (heavyweight), cross country, equestrian, fencing, field hockey, golf, ice hockey, lacrosse, soccer, softball, swimming, team handball, tennis, track and field (indoor), track and field (outdoor), volleyball.

SERVICES AND FACILITIES

Basic services: nonremedial tutoring, health service, health insurance. **Remedial assistance:** reading, math, writing, study skills, other. **Counseling services:** minority student, career, personal, academic, older student, psychological, religious. **For learning-disabled students:** School does not offer a structured program with separate admission and additional fees. Services include: remedial math, reading machines, remedial reading, tape recorders, untimed tests, note-taking services, oral tests, learning center, readers, extended time for tests, tutors, other testing accommodations. **Library:**

Number of titles: 148,803; number of current serial subscriptions: 1,770. **Information technology resources:** Students are required to lease or own a computer. Number of campus computers available to all students: 78. School has a wireless network. Approximate number of users that can be accommodated: 7,000. Proportion of college-owned housing units wired for high-speed internet access: 100%. **Campus safety:** Security services offered: 24-hour foot-and-vehicle patrols, late-night transport/escort service, 24-hour emergency telephones, lighted pathways/sidewalks, controlled dormitory access (key, security card, etc).

TRANSFER AND INTERNATIONAL STUDENTS
Transfer students: May apply for admission for the following academic terms: Fall, Spring. Applicants do not need a minimum number of credits to apply. For fall 2009: Transfer applications received: 403. Transfer applicants offered admission: 328. Transfer applicants enrolled: 159. **International students:** Number of foreign undergraduates: 45 (1% of student body). Number of countries represented: 41. Minimum TOEFL score required: 550 (paper); 70 (computer).

Southern Connecticut State University

- **Address:** 501 Crescent Street, New Haven, CT 06515-1355
- **Website:** http://www.southernct.edu/
- **Public**
- **Enrollment:** 7,366 full-time; 1,228 part-time

KEY STATS
✔ **U.S News College Ranking:** 126, Regional Universities (North)
✔ **SAT Score (25th/75th percentile):** 870-1050
✔ **Tuition:** 2010-2011: $8,050 in state, $17,047 out of state
Selectivity: Less selective   **Room/board:** $9,938
Acceptance rate: 71%   **Average debt:** $17,374
Student/faculty ratio: 16/1   **Proportion who borrowed:** 66%

UNDERGRADUATE STUDENT BODY STATS
2009-2010 enrollment: 7,366 full-time; 1,228 part-time. Men: 37%; women: 63%. **Ethnic makeup:** African American: 13%; Asian American: 2%; Hispanic: 6%; White: 78%; International: 1%. **Religious preference:** Roman Catholic: 51%; Protestant: 11%; Jewish: 2%; Muslim: 1%; Buddhist: 1%; None: 1%; Other: 19%.

ADMISSIONS FACTS AND FIGURES
Phone: (203) 392-5656. **Website:** http://www.southernct.edu/. **Application deadlines for fall 2011:** Regular decision: April 1. Early decision: Not offered. Early action: Not offered. Admission can be deferred. **Application fee:** $50. **To apply online, go to:** http://www.southernct.edu/admissions/applications/. **Admissions requirements/recommendations:** High school units required (recommended): English: 4; Mathematics: 3 (4); Science: 2; Foreign language: 2 (3); Social studies: 2; History: 2; Total units: 16. Tests: The college uses SAT or ACT scores in admissions decisions. Either SAT or ACT required. For admission to the fall 2011 entering class, the school will accept: ACT with writing required. Campus visit: Recommended. Admissions interview: Neither required nor recommended. Off-campus interview: Not available. **Factors that count in admissions decisions:** *Academic:* Secondary school record: Very Important. Class rank: Important. Letters of recommendation: Important. Standardized test scores: Important. Essay: Important. *Nonacademic:* Interview: Not Considered. Extracurricular activities: Considered. Talent/ability: Considered. Character/personal qualities: Considered. Alumni/ae relationship: Considered. Geographical residence: Considered. State residency: Not Considered. Religious affiliation/commitment: Not Considered. Minority status: Considered. Volunteer work: Considered. Work experience: Considered. **Other schools with the greatest overlap in applicants:** Central Connecticut State University; Eastern Connecticut State University; University of Connecticut; University of New Haven; Western Connecticut State University. **Admissions statistics for the fall 2009 entering class:** Total applicants: 5,596. Total accepted: 3,993. Freshmen enrolled: 1,244; 11% were from out of state. Overall acceptance rate: 71%. **Credentials of fall 2009 freshmen:** 5% ranked in the top 10 percent of their high school class; 24% were in the top 25 percent; 67% were in the top half. (Proportion submitting class standing: 70%.) **Average high school grade point average:** 2.9. **First-year students who submitted SAT scores:** 98%. Scores (25/75 percentile): Critical Reading: 440-520, Math:

430-530, Combined: 870-1050. **First-year students submitting ACT scores:** 10%. Scores (25/75 percentile): English: N/A, Math: N/A, Composite: 18-23.

ACADEMICS
Year founded: 1893. **Academic calendar:** Semester. **Degrees offered:** bachelor's, master's, post-master's certificate, doctorate. **Most popular majors:** 14% business/commerce, 12% liberal arts and sciences/liberal studies, 12% psychology, 7% communication studies/speech communication and rhetoric, 7% nursing science (M.S., Ph.D.). **Major fields of study:** agriculture, agriculture operations, and related sciences; biological and biomedical sciences; business, management, marketing, and related support services; communication, journalism, and related programs; computer and information sciences and support services; education; English language and literature/letters; foreign languages, literatures, and linguistics; health professions and related clinical sciences; history; liberal arts and sciences studies, and humanities; library science; mathematics and statistics; parks, recreation, leisure, and fitness studies; philosophy and religious studies; physical sciences; psychology; public administration and social service professions; visual and performing arts. **Areas of required coursework:** arts/fine arts, humanities, mathematics, English (including composition), philosophy, foreign languages, sciences (biological or physical), history, social science. **Pre-professional programs:** pre-law, pre-dentistry, pre-medicine, pre-veterinary science, other. **Special academic programs:** accelerated program, cooperative (work-study plan) program, cross-registration, distance learning, double major, dual enrollment, exchange student program (domestic), external degree program, honors program, independent study, internships, liberal arts/career combination, student-designed major, study abroad, teacher certificate program. **Teacher certification offered in:** early childhood, special education, elementary, middle/junior high, secondary, bilingual/bicultural. **Cooperative education programs:** art, business, computer science, education, health professions, humanities, natural science, social/behavioral science. **Reserve Officers Training Corps (ROTC):** Army ROTC: Offered at cooperating institution (University of Connecticut); Air Force ROTC: Offered at cooperating institution (University of Connecticut). **Faculty and instruction (2009-2010):** Total instructional faculty: 407 full-time, 678 part-time (47% men; 53% women; 14% minorities). Full-time faculty with Ph.D. or other terminal degree: 86%. Student/faculty ratio: 16/1. Classes of fewer than 20 students: 40%; of 20 to 49 students: 58%; of 50 or more students: 2%. **Advanced Placement and International Baccalaureate credit:** AP tests may be used for: Credit only. Scores accepted: 3, 4, 5. **Freshmen returning for sophomore year:** 77%. **Graduation rates:** Four-year: 12%; five-year: 36%; six-year: 38%. **Graduate study:** 70% of students pursue further study within one year.

COSTS AND FINANCIAL AID
Financial aid office: (203) 392-5222. **Expenses (2010-2011):** Tuition and fees 2010-2011: $8,050 in state, $17,047 out of state; room/board: $9,938. Estimated books and supplies: $1,400; transportation: $800; personal expenses: $512. **Financial aid:** Priority filing date for institution's financial aid form: March 5; deadline: March 9. In 2009-2010, 86% of undergraduates applied for financial aid. Of those, 57% were determined to have financial need; 32% had their need fully met. Average financial aid package (proportion receiving): $8,355 (55%). Average amount of gift aid, such as scholarships or grants (proportion receiving): $5,784 (45%). Average amount of self-help aid, such as work study or loans (proportion receiving): $4,332 (46%). Average need-based loan (excluding PLUS or other private loans): $3,731. Among students who received need-based aid, the average percentage of need met: 79%. Among students who received aid based on merit, the average award (and the proportion receiving): $3,677 (4%). The average athletic scholarship (and the proportion receiving): $7,762 (2%). Average amount of debt of borrowers graduating in 2009: $17,374. Proportion who borrowed: 66%.

CAMPUS LIFE AND EXTRACURRICULAR ACTIVITIES
Campus housing available: coed dorms, apartment for single students, special housing for disabled students. Students who live in college-owned, operated, or affiliated housing: 32%. **Student employment:** During the 2009-2010 academic year, 2% of undergraduates worked on campus. Average per-year earnings: $3,500. **Clubs and organizations:** Number of student organizations: 113. Activities include: choral groups, concert band, dance, drama/theater, jazz band, literary magazine, music ensembles, musical theater, pep band, radio station, student government, student newspaper, television station. Number of fraternities: 4; sororities: 5. Proportion of men in fraternities: 1%; of women in sororities: 1%. Average proportion of students who stay on campus on weekends: 25%. **Sports program (2009-2010):** Member of NCAA II. *Men's intercollegiate varsity sports:* baseball, basketball, cross country, football, soccer, swimming, track and field

(indoor). *Women's intercollegiate varsity sports:* basketball, cross country, field hockey, lacrosse, soccer, softball, swimming, track and field (indoor), volleyball.

SERVICES AND FACILITIES

Basic services: nonremedial tutoring, women's center, placement service, health service, health insurance. **Remedial assistance:** reading, math, writing, study skills. **Counseling services:** career, personal, academic, psychological. **For learning-disabled students:** School does not offer a structured program with separate admission and additional fees. Services include: remedial math, remedial English, reading machines, tape recorders, other special classes, note-taking services, special bookstore section, oral tests, learning center, readers, extended time for tests, tutors, priority registration, priority seating, texts on tape, other. **Library:** Number of titles: 445,021; number of current serial subscriptions: 43,960. **Information technology resources:** Students are not required to lease or own a computer. Number of campus computers available to all students: 700. School has a wireless network. Approximate number of users that can be accommodated: 600. Proportion of college-owned housing units wired for high-speed internet access: 100%. **Campus safety:** Security services offered: 24-hour foot-and-vehicle patrols, late-night transport/escort service, 24-hour emergency telephones, lighted pathways/sidewalks, controlled dormitory access (key, security card, etc).

TRANSFER AND INTERNATIONAL STUDENTS

Transfer students: May apply for admission for the following academic terms: Fall, Spring. Applicants need a minimum number of credits to apply. For fall 2009: Transfer applications received: 1,984. Transfer applicants offered admission: 1,540. Transfer applicants enrolled: 973. **International students:** Number of foreign undergraduates: 53 (1% of student body). Number of countries represented: 36. Minimum TOEFL score required: 525 (paper); 197 (computer). Average TOEFL score: 550 (paper).

St. Joseph College

- **Address:** 1678 Asylum Avenue, West Hartford, CT 06117
- **Website:** http://www.sjc.edu
- **Private; Religious affiliation:** Roman Catholic
- **Enrollment:** 768 full-time; 195 part-time

KEY STATS

✔ **U.S News College Ranking:** 61, Regional Universities (North)
✔ **SAT Score (25th/75th percentile):** 880-1040
✔ **Tuition:** 2010-2011: $28,530

Selectivity: Selective	**Room/board:** $12,940
Acceptance rate: 84%	**Average debt:** $39,743
Student/faculty ratio: 10/1	**Proportion who borrowed:** 82%

UNDERGRADUATE STUDENT BODY STATS

2009-2010 enrollment: 768 full-time; 195 part-time. Men: 1%; women: 99%. **Ethnic makeup:** African American: 11%; Asian American: 2%; Hispanic: 10%; White: 76%.

ADMISSIONS FACTS AND FIGURES

Phone: (860) 231-5216. **Email:** admissions@sjc.edu. **Website:** http://www.sjc.edu. **Application deadlines for fall 2011:** Regular decision: Rolling. Early decision: Not offered. Early action: Not offered. Admission can be deferred. **Application fee:** $50. **To apply online, go to:** http://sjc.edu/admissions/undergraduate_admissions/. **Admissions requirements/recommendations:** High school units required (recommended): English: 4; Mathematics: 3; Science: 3; Foreign language: 3; Social studies: 3; Total units: 16. Tests: The college uses SAT or ACT scores in admissions decisions. Either SAT or ACT required. For admission to the fall 2011 entering class, the school will accept: ACT with or without writing accepted. Campus visit: Recommended. Admissions interview: Recommended. Off-campus interview: May be arranged. **Factors that count in admissions decisions:** *Academic:* Secondary school record: Very Important. Class rank: Considered. Letters of recommendation: Considered. Standardized test scores: Very Important. Essay: Considered. *Nonacademic:* Interview: Considered. Extracurricular activities: Considered. Talent/ability: Considered. Character/personal qualities: Considered. Alumni/ae relationship: Considered. Geographical residence: Considered. State residency: Considered. Religious affiliation/commitment: Considered. Minority status: Considered. Volunteer work: Considered.

Work experience: Considered. **Admissions statistics for the fall 2009 entering class:** Total applicants: 1,150. Total accepted: 961. Freshmen enrolled: 184; 15% were from out of state. Overall acceptance rate: 84%. **Credentials of fall 2009 freshmen:** 19% ranked in the top 10 percent of their high school class; 47% were in the top 25 percent; 85% were in the top half. (Proportion submitting class standing: 74%.) **Average high school grade point average:** 3.2. **First-year students who submitted SAT scores:** 99%. Scores (25/75 percentile): Critical Reading: 440-520, Math: 440-520, Combined: 880-1040.

ACADEMICS

Year founded: 1932. **Academic calendar:** Semester. **Degrees offered:** certificate, bachelor's, post-bachelor's certificate, master's. **Most popular majors:** 21% nursing/registered nurse training (R.N., A.S.N., B.S.N., M.S.N.), 12% psychology, 10% social work, 9% child development, 7% biology/biological sciences. **Major fields of study:** biological and biomedical sciences; business, management, marketing, and related support services; education; English language and literature/letters; family and consumer sciences/human sciences; foreign languages, literatures, and linguistics; health professions and related clinical sciences; liberal arts and sciences studies, and humanities; mathematics and statistics; philosophy and religious studies; physical sciences; psychology; public administration and social service professions; social sciences; visual and performing arts. **Areas of required coursework:** humanities, computer literacy, mathematics, English (including composition), philosophy, foreign languages, sciences (biological or physical), social science, other. **Pre-professional programs:** pre-pharmacy. **Special academic programs:** accelerated program, distance learning, double major, honors program, independent study, internships, liberal arts/career combination, student-designed major, study abroad, teacher certificate program, weekend college. **Teacher certification offered in:** early childhood, special education, elementary, secondary. **Faculty and instruction (2009-2010):** Total instructional faculty: 78 full-time, 140 part-time. Student/faculty ratio: 10/1. Classes of fewer than 20 students: 72%; of 20 to 49 students: 27%; of 50 or more students: 1%. **Freshmen returning for sophomore year:** 75%. **Graduation rates:** Four-year: 31%; five-year: 43%; six-year: 53%.

COSTS AND FINANCIAL AID

Financial aid office: (860) 231-5223. **Expenses (2010-2011):** Tuition and fees 2010-2011: $28,530; room/board: $12,940. Estimated books and supplies: $1,000; transportation: $500; personal expenses: $900. **Financial aid:** In 2009-2010, 92% of undergraduates applied for financial aid. Of those, 85% were determined to have financial need; 8% had their need fully met. Average financial aid package (proportion receiving): $20,293 (85%). Average amount of gift aid, such as scholarships or grants (proportion receiving): $15,867 (82%). Average amount of self-help aid, such as work study or loans (proportion receiving): $566 (77%). Average need-based loan (excluding PLUS or other private loans): $4,536. Among students who received need-based aid, the average percentage of need met: 71%. Among students who received aid based on merit, the average award (and the proportion receiving): $8,651 (11%). The average athletic scholarship (and the proportion receiving): $0 (0%). Average amount of debt of borrowers graduating in 2009: $39,743. Proportion who borrowed: 82%.

CAMPUS LIFE AND EXTRACURRICULAR ACTIVITIES

Campus housing available: women's dorms, special housing for disabled students, other housing options. Students who live in college-owned, operated, or affiliated housing: 40%. Activities include: campus ministries, choral groups, dance, drama/theater, literary magazine, music ensembles, student government, yearbook. Number of fraternities: 0; sororities: 0. **Sports program (2009-2010):** Member of NCAA III.

SERVICES AND FACILITIES

Basic services: nonremedial tutoring, placement service, health service, health insurance. **Counseling services:** career, personal, academic, psychological. **For learning-disabled students:** School does not offer a structured program with separate admission and additional fees. Services include: reading machines, tape recorders, videotaped classes, untimed tests, note-taking services, oral tests, learning center, readers, extended time for tests, tutors, early syllabus, priority registration, priority seating, proofreading services, substitution of courses, texts on tape, exams on tape or computer, take home exams, other testing accommodations, waiver of foreign language degree requirement. **Information technology resources:** Students are not required to lease or own a computer. School has a wireless network. Proportion of college-owned housing units wired for high-speed internet access: 100%. **Campus safety:** Security services offered: 24-hour foot-and-vehicle patrols, late-night transport/escort service, 24-hour emergency telephones, lighted pathways/sidewalks, controlled dormitory access (key, security card, etc).

TRANSFER AND INTERNATIONAL STUDENTS

Transfer students: May apply for admission for the following academic terms: Fall, Spring. Applicants need a minimum number of credits to apply. For fall 2009: Transfer applications received: 255. Transfer applicants offered admission: 184. Transfer applicants enrolled: 99. **International students:** Number of foreign undergraduates: 3.

Trinity College

- **Address:** 300 Summit Street, Hartford, CT 06106
- **Website:** http://www.trincoll.edu
- **Private**
- **Enrollment:** 2,207 full-time; 134 part-time

KEY STATS

✔ **U.S News College Ranking:** 36, National Liberal Arts Colleges
✔ **SAT Score (25th/75th percentile):** 1200-1370
✔ **Tuition:** 2010-2011: $42,420

Selectivity: More selective	**Room/board:** $10,960
Acceptance rate: 41%	**Average debt:** $20,174
Student/faculty ratio: 9/1	**Proportion who borrowed:** 42%

UNDERGRADUATE STUDENT BODY STATS

2009-2010 enrollment: 2,207 full-time; 134 part-time. Men: 50%; women: 50%. **Ethnic makeup:** African American: 6%; Asian American: 6%; Hispanic: 6%; White: 77%; International: 5%. **Religious preference:** Roman Catholic: 26%; Protestant: 29%; Jewish: 8%; Muslim: 1%; Hindu: 1%; Buddhist: 2%; No preference: 30%; Eastern Orthodox: 1%; Other: 2%.

ADMISSIONS FACTS AND FIGURES

Phone: (860) 297-2180. **Email:** admissions.office@trincoll.edu. **Website:** http://www.trincoll.edu. **Application deadlines for fall 2011:** Regular decision: January 1; decision sent by April 1. Early decision: Send application by: November 15; Decision sent by: December 15. Early action: Not offered. Admission can be deferred. **Application fee:** $60. **To apply online, go to:** http://www.trincoll.edu/depts/admissio/commonapp/. **Admissions requirements/recommendations:** High school units required (recommended): English: 4; Mathematics: 3; Science: 2; Foreign language: 3; History: 2; Total units: 16. Tests: The college uses SAT or ACT scores in admissions decisions. Either SAT or ACT required. For admission to the fall 2011 entering class, the school will accept: ACT with writing recommended. Campus visit: Recommended. Admissions interview: Recommended. Off-campus interview: May be arranged. **Factors that count in admissions decisions:** *Academic:* Secondary school record: Very Important. Class rank: Important. Letters of recommendation: Important. Standardized test scores: Important. Essay: Important. *Nonacademic:* Interview: Important. Extracurricular activities: Important. Talent/ability: Important. Character/personal qualities: Important. Alumni/ae relationship: Considered. Geographical residence: Considered. State residency: Not Considered. Religious affiliation/commitment: Not Considered. Minority status: Important. Volunteer work: Considered. Work experience: Considered. **Other schools with the greatest overlap in applicants:** Boston College; Brown University; Colby College; Georgetown University; Tufts University. **Admissions statistics for the fall 2009 entering class:** Total applicants: 4,532. Total accepted: 1,874. Freshmen enrolled: 573; 83% were from out of state. Overall acceptance rate: 41%. Non-early acceptance rate: 41%. **Size of waiting list:** 1432 applicants; enrolled from waiting list: 104. **Credentials of fall 2009 freshmen:** 68% ranked in the top 10 percent of their high school class; 93% were in the top 25 percent; 99% were in the top half. (Proportion submitting class standing: 17%.) **First-year students who submitted SAT scores:** 49%. Scores (25/75 percentile): Critical Reading: 590-680, Math: 610-690, Combined: 1200-1370. **First-year students submitting ACT scores:** 26%. Scores (25/75 percentile): English: 26-31, Math: 25-29, Composite: 26-30.

ACADEMICS

Year founded: 1823. **Academic calendar:** Semester. **Degrees offered:** bachelor's, master's. **Most popular majors:** 16% economics, 8% history, 8% psychology, 7% political science and government, 6% English language and literature. **Major fields of study:** area, ethnic, cultural, and gender studies; biological and biomedical sciences; computer and information sciences and support services; education; engineering; English language and literature/letters; foreign languages, literatures, and linguistics; history; mathematics and statistics; natural resources and conservation; philosophy and religious studies; physical sciences; psychology; public administration and social service professions; social sciences; visual and performing arts. **Areas of required coursework:** arts/fine arts, humanities, foreign languages, sciences (biological or physical), social science, other. **Pre-professional programs:** pre-law, pre-medicine. **Special academic programs (% participation):** accelerated program (.4%), cross-registration (2%), double major (15%), exchange student program (domestic) (0%), honors program (14%), independent study (63%), internships (35%), student-designed major (2%), study abroad (58%), teacher certificate program (0%), other (0%). **Reserve Officers Training Corps (ROTC):** Army ROTC: Offered at cooperating institution (University of Connecticut). **Faculty and instruction (2009-2010):** Total instructional faculty: 193 full-time, 81 part-time (60% men; 40% women; 19% minorities). Full-time faculty with Ph.D. or other terminal degree: 92%. Student/faculty ratio: 9/1. Classes of fewer than 20 students: 66%; of 20 to 49 students: 30%; of 50 or more students: 3%. **Advanced Placement and International Baccalaureate credit:** AP tests may be used for: Credit and/or placement. Scores accepted: 4, 5. International Baccalaureate exams may be used for: Placement only. **Freshmen returning for sophomore year:** 91%. **Graduation rates:** Four-year: 76%; five-year: 85%; six-year: 86%. **Graduate study:** 19% of students pursue further study immediately upon graduation; 26% within one year; 85% within five years. Fields in which graduates pursue further study: Master of Business Administration (MBA), 12%; law, 7%; medicine, 2%; dentistry, 1%; engineering, 3%; theology (or the seminary), 1%; education, 6%; arts and sciences, 37%.

COSTS AND FINANCIAL AID

Financial aid office: (860) 297-2046. **Expenses (2010-2011):** Tuition and fees 2010-2011: $42,420; room/board: $10,960. Estimated books and supplies: $1,000; transportation: $229; personal expenses: $900. **Financial aid:** Priority filing date for institution's financial aid form: February 1; deadline: March 1. In 2009-2010, 46% of undergraduates applied for financial aid. Of those, 42% were determined to have financial need; 100% had their need fully met. Average financial aid package (proportion receiving): N/A (42%). Average amount of gift aid, such as scholarships or grants (proportion receiving): $35,047 (39%). Average amount of self-help aid, such as work study or loans (proportion receiving): $5,167 (32%). Average need-based loan (excluding PLUS or other private loans): $4,341. Among students who received need-based aid, the average percentage of need met: 100%. Among students who received aid based on merit, the average award (and the proportion receiving): $29,375 (2%). The average athletic scholarship (and the proportion receiving): $0 (0%). Average amount of debt of borrowers graduating in 2009: $20,174. Proportion who borrowed: 42%.

CAMPUS LIFE AND EXTRACURRICULAR ACTIVITIES

Campus housing available (% using): coed dorms (97%), fraternity housing (2%). Students who live in college-owned, operated, or affiliated housing: 95%. **Student employment:** During the 2009-2010 academic year, 44% of undergraduates worked on campus. Average per-year earnings: $2,508. **Clubs and organizations:** Number of student organizations: 104. Activities include: choral groups, dance, drama/theater, international student organization, jazz band, literary magazine, model UN, music ensembles, musical theater, radio station, student government, student newspaper, student film society, yearbook. Number of fraternities: 7; sororities: 7. Proportion of men in fraternities: 20%; of women in sororities: 16%. Average proportion of students who stay on campus on weekends: 99%. **Sports program (2009-2010):** Member of NCAA III. *Men's intercollegiate varsity sports:* baseball, basketball, cross country, football, golf, ice hockey, lacrosse, soccer, swimming, tennis, track and field (indoor), track and field (outdoor), wrestling. *Women's intercollegiate varsity sports:* basketball, crew (heavyweight), cross country, field hockey, ice hockey, lacrosse, soccer, softball, squash, swimming, tennis, track and field (indoor), track and field (outdoor), volleyball.

SERVICES AND FACILITIES

Basic services: nonremedial tutoring, women's center, placement service, health service, health insurance. **Remedial assistance:** math, writing, study skills, other. **Counseling services:** minority student, career, personal, academic, older student, psychological, birth control, religious. **For learning-disabled students:** School does not offer a structured program with separate admission and additional fees. Total undergraduates in learning-disabled program or receiving services: 184. Services include: tape recorders, note-taking services, oral tests, readers, extended time for tests, tutors, priority seating, texts on tape, other testing accommodations. **Library:** Number of titles: 904,988; number of current serial subscriptions: 18,445. **Information**

technology resources: Students are not required to lease or own a computer. Number of campus computers available to all students: 356. School has a wireless network. Approximate number of users that can be accommodated: 4,000. Proportion of college-owned housing units wired for high-speed internet access: 100%. **Campus safety:** Security services offered: 24-hour foot-and-vehicle patrols, late-night transport/escort service, 24-hour emergency telephones, lighted pathways/sidewalks, controlled dormitory access (key, security card, etc).

TRANSFER AND INTERNATIONAL STUDENTS

Transfer students: May apply for admission for the following academic terms: Fall, Spring. Applicants do not need a minimum number of credits to apply. For fall 2009: Transfer applications received: 143. Transfer applicants offered admission: 45. Transfer applicants enrolled: 22. **International students:** Number of foreign undergraduates: 108 (5% of student body). Number of countries represented: 41. Average TOEFL score: 623 (paper).

United States Coast Guard Academy

- **Address:** 15 Mohegan Avenue, New London, CT 06320
- **Website:** http://www.uscga.edu
- **Public**
- **Enrollment:** 973 full-time

....

KEY STATS
✔ **U.S News College Ranking:** 1, Regional Colleges (North)
✔ **SAT Score (25th/75th percentile):** 1160-1340
✔ **Tuition:** N/A

Selectivity: More selective	**Room/board:** N/A
Acceptance rate: 25%	**Average debt:** $0
Student/faculty ratio: 8/1	**Proportion who borrowed:** 0%

UNDERGRADUATE STUDENT BODY STATS

2009-2010 enrollment: 973 full-time. Men: 73%; women: 27%. **Ethnic makeup:** African American: 3%; American-Indian: 1%; Asian American: 4%; Hispanic: 7%; White: 84%; International: 2%. **Religious preference:** Roman Catholic: 36%; Protestant: 48%; Jewish: 2%; No preference: 11%; Other: 3%.

ADMISSIONS FACTS AND FIGURES

Phone: (800) 883-8724. **Email:** admissions@uscga.edu. **Website:** http://www.uscga.edu. **Application deadlines for fall 2011:** Regular decision: February 1. Early decision: Not offered. Early action: Send application by: November 1; Decision sent by: December 24. Admission cannot be deferred. **Application fee:** None. **To apply online, go to:** http://www.admissions.uscga.edu/i2e/app/. **Admissions requirements/recommendations:** High school units required (recommended): English: 4; Mathematics: 4; Science: 3. Tests: The college uses SAT or ACT scores in admissions decisions. Either SAT or ACT required. For admission to the fall 2011 entering class, the school will accept: ACT with writing required. Campus visit: Recommended. Admissions interview: Recommended. Off-campus interview: May be arranged. **Factors that count in admissions decisions:** *Academic:* Secondary school record: Very Important. Class rank: Very Important. Letters of recommendation: Important. Standardized test scores: Very Important. Essay: Important. *Nonacademic:* Interview: Considered. Extracurricular activities: Very Important. Talent/ability: Important. Character/personal qualities: Very Important. Alumni/ae relationship: Considered. Geographical residence: Not Considered. State residency: Not Considered. Religious affiliation/commitment: Not Considered. Minority status: Not Considered. Volunteer work: Considered. Work experience: Considered. **Other schools with the greatest overlap in applicants:** United States Air Force Academy; United States Merchant Marine Academy; United States Military Academy; United States Naval Academy. **Admissions statistics for the fall 2009 entering class:** Total applicants: 1,672. Total accepted: 411. Freshmen enrolled: 288; 96% were from out of state. Accepted through early-decision or early-action plans: 50%. Overall acceptance rate: 25%. Non-early acceptance rate: 22%. **Credentials of fall 2009 freshmen:** 49% ranked in the top 10 percent of their high school class; 83% were in the top 25 percent; 99% were in the top half. (Proportion submitting class standing: 96%.) **Average high school grade point average:** 3.7. **First-year students who submitted SAT scores:** 87%. Scores (25/75 percentile): Critical Reading: 560-660, Math: 600-680, Combined: 1160-1340.

First-year students submitting ACT scores: 43%. Scores (25/75 percentile): English: 24-30, Math: 25-30, Composite: 24-30.

ACADEMICS

Year founded: 1931. **Academic calendar:** Semester. **Degrees offered:** bachelor's. **Most popular majors:** 41% engineering, 22% political science and government, 13% marine biology and biological oceanography, 12% business administration and management, 12% mathematics and statistics. **Major fields of study:** biological and biomedical sciences; business, management, marketing, and related support services; engineering; mathematics and statistics; social sciences. **Areas of required coursework:** humanities, computer literacy, mathematics, English (including composition), philosophy, foreign languages, sciences (biological or physical), history, social science, other. **Special academic programs (% participation):** double major (1%), exchange student program (domestic) (2%), honors program, independent study, internships. **Faculty and instruction (2009-2010):** Total instructional faculty: 116 full-time, 14 part-time (72% men; 28% women; 13% minorities). Full-time faculty with Ph.D. or other terminal degree: 43%. Student/faculty ratio: 8/1. Classes of fewer than 20 students: 71%; of 20 to 49 students: 29%. **Freshmen returning for sophomore year:** 89%. **Graduation rates:** Four-year: 73%; five-year: 76%; six-year: 76%.

COSTS AND FINANCIAL AID

Financial aid: Average financial aid package (proportion receiving): $0 (N/A). Average amount of gift aid, such as scholarships or grants (proportion receiving): $0 (N/A). Average amount of self-help aid, such as work study or loans (proportion receiving): $0 (N/A). Average need-based loan (excluding PLUS or other private loans): $0. Among students who received need-based aid, the average percentage of need met: 100%. Among students who received aid based on merit, the average award (and the proportion receiving): $0 (N/A). The average athletic scholarship (and the proportion receiving): $0 (N/A). Average amount of debt of borrowers graduating in 2009: $0.

CAMPUS LIFE AND EXTRACURRICULAR ACTIVITIES

Campus housing available (% using): coed dorms (100%). Students who live in college-owned, operated, or affiliated housing: 100%. **Student employment:** During the 2009-2010 academic year, 0% of undergraduates worked on campus. Average per-year earnings: $0. **Clubs and organizations:** Number of student organizations: 66. Activities include: campus ministries, choral groups, concert band, dance, drama/theater, jazz band, marching band, model UN, music ensembles, musical theater, pep band, student government, yearbook. Number of fraternities: 0; sororities: 0. Average proportion of students who stay on campus on weekends: 100%. **Sports program (2009-2010):** Member of NCAA III. *Men's intercollegiate varsity sports:* baseball, basketball, cross country, football, rifle, soccer, swimming, tennis, track and field (indoor), track and field (outdoor), wrestling. *Women's intercollegiate varsity sports:* basketball, crew (heavyweight), cross country, crew (lightweight), rifle, soccer, softball, swimming, track and field (indoor), track and field (outdoor), volleyball.

SERVICES AND FACILITIES

Basic services: nonremedial tutoring, health service, health insurance. **Remedial assistance:** reading, math, writing, study skills. **Counseling services:** minority student, career, military, personal, veteran student, academic, psychological, birth control, religious. **Library:** Number of titles: 169,275; number of current serial subscriptions: 16,224. **Information technology resources:** Students are required to lease or own a computer. Number of campus computers available to all students: 323. School has a wireless network. Approximate number of users that can be accommodated: 315. Proportion of college-owned housing units wired for high-speed internet access: 100%. **Campus safety:** Security services offered: 24-hour foot-and-vehicle patrols, lighted pathways/sidewalks.

TRANSFER AND INTERNATIONAL STUDENTS

Transfer students: May apply for admission for the following academic terms: Fall. Applicants do not need a minimum number of credits to apply. **International students:** Number of foreign undergraduates: 15 (2% of student body). Number of countries represented: 8. Minimum TOEFL score required: 560 (paper); 220 (computer). Average TOEFL score: 585 (paper).

University of Bridgeport

- **Address:** 126 Park Avenue, Bridgeport, CT 06604
- **Website:** http://www.bridgeport.edu
- **Private**
- **Enrollment:** 1,504 full-time; 744 part-time

KEY STATS

✔ **U.S News College Ranking:** second tier, National Universities
✔ **SAT Score (25th/75th percentile):** 810-990
✔ **Tuition:** 2010-2011: $26,495

Selectivity: Less selective	**Room/board:** $11,400
Acceptance rate: 55%	**Average debt:** N/A
Student/faculty ratio: 12/1	**Proportion who borrowed:** N/A

UNDERGRADUATE STUDENT BODY STATS

2009-2010 enrollment: 1,504 full-time; 744 part-time. Men: 32%; women: 68%. **Ethnic makeup:** African American: 37%; Asian American: 3%; Hispanic: 15%; White: 33%; International: 11%.

ADMISSIONS FACTS AND FIGURES

Phone: (203) 576-4552. **Email:** admit@bridgeport.edu. **Website:** http://www.bridgeport.edu. **Application deadlines for fall 2011:** Regular decision: Rolling. Early decision: Not offered. Early action: Not offered. Admission can be deferred. **Application fee:** $25. **To apply online, go to:** http://www.bridgeport.edu/pages/2588.asp. **Admissions requirements/recommendations:** High school units required (recommended): English: 4 (4); Mathematics: 3 (3); Science: 2 (2); Social studies: 2 (2); Academic electives: 5 (5); Total units: 16 (16). Tests: The college uses SAT or ACT scores in admissions decisions. Either SAT or ACT required. For admission to the fall 2011 entering class, the school will accept: ACT with or without writing accepted. Campus visit: Recommended. Admissions interview: Recommended. Off-campus interview: May be arranged. **Factors that count in admissions decisions:** *Academic:* Secondary school record: Very Important. Class rank: Important. Letters of recommendation: Important. Standardized test scores: Very Important. Essay: Important. *Nonacademic:* Interview: Considered. Extracurricular activities: Considered. Talent/ability: Important. Character/personal qualities: Important. Alumni/ae relationship: Not Considered. Geographical residence: Not Considered. State residency: Not Considered. Religious affiliation/commitment: Not Considered. Minority status: Not Considered. Volunteer work: Considered. Work experience: Considered. **Admissions statistics for the fall 2009 entering class:** Total applicants: 8,165. Total accepted: 4,510. Freshmen enrolled: 440; 65% were from out of state. Overall acceptance rate: 55%. **Credentials of fall 2009 freshmen:** 7% ranked in the top 10 percent of their high school class; 29% were in the top 25 percent; 64% were in the top half. (Proportion submitting class standing: 50%.) **Average high school grade point average:** 2.8. **First-year students who submitted SAT scores:** 94%. Scores (25/75 percentile): Critical Reading: 400-490, Math: 410-500, Combined: 810-990. **First-year students submitting ACT scores:** 8%. Scores (25/75 percentile): English: 15-21, Math: 16-19, Composite: 15-20.

ACADEMICS

Year founded: 1927. **Academic calendar:** Semester. **Degrees offered:** certificate, associate, bachelor's, master's, post-master's certificate, doctorate. **Most popular majors:** 20% general studies, 13% dental hygiene/hygienist, 11% clinical psychology, 9% human services, 6% business/commerce. **Major fields of study:** business, management, marketing, and related support services; health professions and related clinical sciences; liberal arts and sciences studies, and humanities; psychology; public administration and social service professions. **Areas of required coursework:** arts/fine arts, humanities, computer literacy, mathematics, English (including composition), philosophy, foreign languages, sciences (biological or physical), history, social science. **Pre-professional programs:** pre-law, pre-dentistry, pre-medicine, pre-veterinary science. **Special academic programs (% participation):** accelerated program (15%), cooperative (work-study plan) program (10%), cross-registration (1%), distance learning (5%), double major (10%), English as a Second Language (ESL) (5%), honors program (2%), independent study (5%), internships (5%), liberal arts/career combination (20%), student-designed major (5%), study abroad (5%), teacher certificate program (5%), weekend college (5%). **Teacher certification offered in:** elementary, middle/junior high, secondary. **Cooperative education programs:** art, business, computer science, education, engineering, health professions, humanities, natural science, social/behavioral science, technologies. **Reserve**

Officers Training Corps (ROTC): Army ROTC: Offered at cooperating institution. **Faculty and instruction (2009-2010):** Total instructional faculty: 125 full-time, 368 part-time (58% men; 42% women; 14% minorities). Full-time faculty with Ph.D. or other terminal degree: 82%. Student/faculty ratio: 12/1. Classes of fewer than 20 students: 65%; of 20 to 49 students: 34%; of 50 or more students: 1%. **Advanced Placement and International Baccalaureate credit:** AP tests may be used for: Credit and/or placement. Scores accepted: 3, 4, 5. International Baccalaureate exams may be used for: Placement only. **Freshmen returning for sophomore year:** 52%. **Graduation rates:** Four-year: 21%; five-year: 28%; six-year: 30%. **Graduate study:** 15% of students pursue further study immediately upon graduation; 25% within one year; 40% within five years. Fields in which graduates pursue further study: Master of Business Administration (MBA), 20%; law, 10%; medicine, 25%; engineering, 20%; education, 25%.

COSTS AND FINANCIAL AID

Financial aid office: (203) 576-4568. **Expenses (2010-2011):** Tuition and fees 2010-2011: $26,495; room/board: $11,400. Estimated books and supplies: $1,500; transportation: $2,850; personal expenses: $2,270. **Financial aid:** Priority filing date for institution's financial aid form: March 1. In 2009-2010, 96% of undergraduates applied for financial aid. Of those, 79% were determined to have financial need; 12% had their need fully met. Average financial aid package (proportion receiving): $22,618 (79%). Average amount of gift aid, such as scholarships or grants (proportion receiving): $8,420 (72%). Average amount of self-help aid, such as work study or loans (proportion receiving): $7,212 (76%). Average need-based loan (excluding PLUS or other private loans): $5,539. Among students who received need-based aid, the average percentage of need met: 56%. Among students who received aid based on merit, the average award (and the proportion receiving): $15,194 (21%). The average athletic scholarship (and the proportion receiving): $20,164 (9%).

CAMPUS LIFE AND EXTRACURRICULAR ACTIVITIES

Campus housing available (% using): coed dorms (100%). Students who live in college-owned, operated, or affiliated housing: 47%. **Student employment:** During the 2009-2010 academic year, 50% of undergraduates worked on campus. Average per-year earnings: $2,000. **Clubs and organizations:** Number of student organizations: 30. Activities include: choral groups, dance, international student organization, literary magazine, model UN, music ensembles, student government, student newspaper, yearbook. Number of fraternities: 1; sororities: 3. Proportion of men in fraternities: 2%; of women in sororities: 2%. Average proportion of students who stay on campus on weekends: 75%. **Sports program (2009-2010):** Member of NCAA II. *Men's intercollegiate varsity sports:* baseball, basketball, cross country, soccer, swimming. *Women's intercollegiate varsity sports:* basketball, cross country, gymnastics, lacrosse, soccer, softball, swimming, volleyball.

SERVICES AND FACILITIES

Basic services: nonremedial tutoring, placement service, health service, health insurance. **Remedial assistance:** reading, math, writing, study skills. **Counseling services:** minority student, career, personal, veteran student, academic, older student, psychological, birth control, religious. **For learning-disabled students:** School does not offer a structured program with separate admission and additional fees. Total undergraduates in learning-disabled program or receiving services: 22. Services include: remedial math, remedial English, remedial reading, untimed tests, oral tests, learning center, extended time for tests, tutors, early syllabus, exams on tape or computer, other testing accommodations. **Library:** Number of titles: 293,440; number of current serial subscriptions: 57,006. **Information technology resources:** Students are not required to lease or own a computer. Number of campus computers available to all students: 600. School has a wireless network. Proportion of college-owned housing units wired for high-speed internet access: 100%. **Campus safety:** Security services offered: 24-hour foot-and-vehicle patrols, late-night transport/escort service, 24-hour emergency telephones, lighted pathways/sidewalks, student patrols, controlled dormitory access (key, security card, etc.).

TRANSFER AND INTERNATIONAL STUDENTS

Transfer students: May apply for admission for the following academic terms: Fall, Spring, Summer. Applicants need a minimum number of credits to apply. For fall 2009: Transfer applications received: 843. Transfer applicants offered admission: 438. Transfer applicants enrolled: 170. **International students:** Number of foreign undergraduates: 253 (11% of student body). Number of countries represented: 50. Minimum TOEFL score required: 500 (paper). Average TOEFL score: 592 (paper).

University of Connecticut

- **Address:** 2131 Hillside Road, Unit 3088, Storrs, CT 06269-3088
- **Website:** http://www.uconn.edu
- **Public**
- **Enrollment:** 16,336 full-time; 672 part-time

KEY STATS

- ✔ **U.S News College Ranking:** 69, National Universities
- ✔ **SAT Score (25th/75th percentile):** 1120-1310
- ✔ **Tuition:** 2010-2011: $10,416 in state, $26,880 out of state

  Selectivity: More selective **Room/board:** $10,782
  Acceptance rate: 50% **Average debt:** $21,257
  Student/faculty ratio: 18/1 **Proportion who borrowed:** 61%

UNDERGRADUATE STUDENT BODY STATS

2009-2010 enrollment: 16,336 full-time; 672 part-time. Men: 50%; women: 50%. **Ethnic makeup:** African American: 5%; Asian American: 8%; Hispanic: 5%; White: 80%; International: 1%.

ADMISSIONS FACTS AND FIGURES

Phone: (860) 486-3137. **Email:** beahusky@uconn.edu. **Website:** http://www.uconn.edu. **Application deadlines for fall 2011:** Regular decision: February 1. Early decision: Not offered. Early action: Send application by: December 1; Decision sent by: February 1. Admission can be deferred. **Application fee:** $70. **To apply online, go to:** http://www.admissions.uconn.edu/apply/survey.php. **Admissions requirements/recommendations:** High school units required (recommended): English: 4; Mathematics: 3; Science: 2; Foreign language: 2 (3); Social studies: 2; Academic electives: 3; Total units: 16. Tests: The college uses SAT or ACT scores in admissions decisions. Either SAT or ACT required. For admission to the fall 2011 entering class, the school will accept: ACT with writing required. Campus visit: Recommended. Admissions interview: Neither required nor recommended. Off-campus interview: Not available. **Factors that count in admissions decisions:** *Academic:* Secondary school record: Very Important. Class rank: Very Important. Letters of recommendation: Important. Standardized test scores: Very Important. Essay: Important. *Nonacademic:* Interview: Not Considered. Extracurricular activities: Important. Talent/ability: Important. Character/personal qualities: Important. Alumni/ae relationship: Considered. Geographical residence: Considered. State residency: Considered. Religious affiliation/commitment: Not Considered. Minority status: Important. Volunteer work: Important. Work experience: Considered. **Other schools with the greatest overlap in applicants:** Boston University; Northeastern University; Pennsylvania State University–University Park; University of Massachusetts–Amherst; University of Vermont. **Admissions statistics for the fall 2009 entering class:** Total applicants: 21,999. Total accepted: 10,931. Freshmen enrolled: 3,221; 32% were from out of state. Accepted through early-decision or early-action plans: 81%. Overall acceptance rate: 50%. Non-early acceptance rate: 32%. **Size of waiting list:** 4186 applicants; enrolled from waiting list: 434. **Credentials of fall 2009 freshmen:** 44% ranked in the top 10 percent of their high school class; 83% were in the top 25 percent; 99% were in the top half. (Proportion submitting class standing: 60%.) **First-year students who submitted SAT scores:** 96%. Scores (25/75 percentile): Critical Reading: 550-640, Math: 570-670, Combined: 1120-1310. **First-year students submitting ACT scores:** 24%. Scores (25/75 percentile): English: N/A, Math: N/A, Composite: 24-29.

ACADEMICS

Year founded: 1881. **Academic calendar:** Semester. **Degrees offered:** associate, transfer-associate, terminal-associate, bachelor's, post-bachelor's certificate, master's, post-master's certificate, doctorate. **Most popular majors:** 15% social sciences, 14% business, management, marketing, and related support services, 9% health professions and related clinical sciences, 7% engineering, 7% psychology. **Major fields of study:** agriculture, agriculture operations, and related sciences; architecture and related services; area, ethnic, cultural, and gender studies; biological and biomedical sciences; business, management, marketing, and related support services; communication, journalism, and related programs; computer and information sciences and support services; education; engineering; English language and literature/letters; family and consumer sciences/human sciences; foreign languages, literatures, and linguistics; health professions and related clinical sciences; history; liberal arts and sciences studies, and humanities; mathematics and statistics; multi/interdisciplinary studies; natural resources and conserva-

tion; parks, recreation, leisure, and fitness studies; philosophy and religious studies; physical sciences; psychology; social sciences; visual and performing arts. **Areas of required coursework:** arts/fine arts, humanities, computer literacy, mathematics, English (including composition), philosophy, foreign languages, sciences (biological or physical), history, social science. **Pre-professional programs:** pre-law, pre-dentistry, pre-medicine, pre-veterinary science, pre-pharmacy, other. **Special academic programs (% participation):** accelerated program (3%), cooperative (work-study plan) program (3%), distance learning (20%), double major (6%), dual enrollment, English as a Second Language (ESL) (0%), exchange student program (domestic) (1%), honors program (9%), independent study (29%), internships (20%), liberal arts/career combination (25%), student-designed major (1%), study abroad (15%), teacher certificate program (3%), other. **Teacher certification offered in:** special education, elementary, adult education, secondary. **Cooperative education programs:** art, computer science, social/behavioral science, other. **Reserve Officers Training Corps (ROTC):** Army ROTC: Offered on campus; Air Force ROTC: Offered on campus. **Faculty and instruction (2009-2010):** Total instructional faculty: 1,003 full-time, 330 part-time (61% men; 39% women; 17% minorities). Full-time faculty with Ph.D. or other terminal degree: 94%. Student/faculty ratio: 18/1. Classes of fewer than 20 students: 43%; of 20 to 49 students: 39%; of 50 or more students: 18%. **Advanced Placement and International Baccalaureate credit:** AP tests may be used for: Credit and/or placement. Scores accepted: 4, 5. International Baccalaureate exams may be used for: Credit and/or placement. **Freshmen returning for sophomore year:** 93%. **Graduation rates:** Four-year: 61%; five-year: 76%; six-year: 78%. **Graduate study:** 34% of students pursue further study within one year.

COSTS AND FINANCIAL AID

Financial aid office: (860) 486-2819. **Expenses (2010-2011):** Tuition and fees 2010-2011: $10,416 in state, $26,880 out of state; room/board: $10,782. Estimated books and supplies: $800; transportation: $1,100; personal expenses: $1,640. **Financial aid:** Priority filing date for institution's financial aid form: March 1. In 2009-2010, 71% of undergraduates applied for financial aid. Of those, 53% were determined to have financial need; 18% had their need fully met. Average financial aid package (proportion receiving): $12,238 (52%). Average amount of gift aid, such as scholarships or grants (proportion receiving): $7,796 (39%). Average amount of self-help aid, such as work study or loans (proportion receiving): $4,836 (41%). Average need-based loan (excluding PLUS or other private loans): $4,204. Among students who received need-based aid, the average percentage of need met: 68%. Among students who received aid based on merit, the average award (and the proportion receiving): $6,280 (8%). The average athletic scholarship (and the proportion receiving): $22,683 (2%). Average amount of debt of borrowers graduating in 2009: $21,257. Proportion who borrowed: 61%.

CAMPUS LIFE AND EXTRACURRICULAR ACTIVITIES

Campus housing available (% using): coed dorms (63%), women's dorms (1%), men's dorms (1%), sorority housing (1%), fraternity housing (1%), apartments for married students (1%), apartment for single students (16%), special housing for disabled students (2%), special housing for international students (1%), other housing options (13%). Students who live in college-owned, operated, or affiliated housing: 73%. **Student employment:** During the 2009-2010 academic year, 51% of undergraduates worked on campus. Average per-year earnings: $2,000. **Clubs and organizations:** Number of student organizations: 463. Activities include: campus ministries, choral groups, concert band, dance, drama/theater, international student organization, jazz band, literary magazine, marching band, model UN, music ensembles, musical theater, opera, pep band, radio station, student government, student newspaper, student film society, symphony orchestra, television station, yearbook. Number of fraternities: 19; sororities: 14. Proportion of men in fraternities: 8%; of women in sororities: 10%. Average proportion of students who stay on campus on weekends: 74%. **Sports program (2009-2010):** Member of NCAA I. *Men's intercollegiate varsity sports:* baseball, basketball, cross country, football, golf, ice hockey, soccer, swimming, tennis, track and field (indoor), track and field (outdoor). *Women's intercollegiate varsity sports:* basketball, crew (heavyweight), cross country, field hockey, ice hockey, lacrosse, crew (lightweight), soccer, softball, swimming, tennis, track and field (indoor), track and field (outdoor), volleyball.

SERVICES AND FACILITIES

Basic services: nonremedial tutoring, women's center, placement service, day care, health service, other. **Remedial assistance:** other. **Counseling services:** minority student, career, military, personal, veteran student, academic, older student, psychological, birth control, religious. **For learning-disabled students:** School does not offer a structured program with separate admission and additional fees. Total undergraduates in learning-disabled program or receiving services: 150. Services include: remedial math, remedial English, reading machines, remedial reading, tape recorders, videotaped classes, diagnostic testing service, note-taking services, oral tests, learning center, readers, extended time for tests, tutors, early syllabus, priority registration, priority seating, substitution of courses, texts on tape, typist/scribe, exams on tape or computer, take home exams, other testing accommodations, other. **Library:** Number of titles: 3,435,579; number of current serial subscriptions: 72,795. **Information technology resources:** Students are not required to lease or own a computer. Number of campus computers available to all students: 100. School has a wireless network. Approximate number of users that can be accommodated: 1,500. Proportion of college-owned housing units wired for high-speed internet access: 100%. **Campus safety:** Security services offered: 24-hour foot-and-vehicle patrols, late-night transport/escort service, 24-hour emergency telephones, lighted pathways/sidewalks, student patrols, controlled dormitory access (key, security card, etc).

TRANSFER AND INTERNATIONAL STUDENTS

Transfer students: May apply for admission for the following academic terms: Fall, Spring. Applicants need a minimum number of credits to apply. For fall 2009: Transfer applications received: 2,107. Transfer applicants offered admission: 1,248. Transfer applicants enrolled: 780. **International students:** Number of foreign undergraduates: 215 (1% of student body). Number of countries represented: 72. Minimum TOEFL score required: 550 (paper); 79 (computer). Average TOEFL score: 570 (paper).

University of Hartford

- ■ **Address:** 200 Bloomfield Avenue, West Hartford, CT 06117-1599
- ■ **Website:** http://www.hartford.edu
- ■ **Private**
- ■ **Enrollment:** 4,697 full-time; 819 part-time

KEY STATS

✔ **U.S News College Ranking:** 183, National Universities
✔ **SAT Score (25th/75th percentile):** 900-1120
✔ **Tuition:** 2010-2011: $29,852

Selectivity: Selective	**Room/board:** $11,572
Acceptance rate: 68%	**Average debt:** $29,869
Student/faculty ratio: 12/1	**Proportion who borrowed:** 75%

UNDERGRADUATE STUDENT BODY STATS

2009-2010 enrollment: 4,697 full-time; 819 part-time. Men: 47%; women: 53%. **Ethnic makeup:** African American: 13%; Asian American: 3%; Hispanic: 7%; White: 74%; International: 3%.

ADMISSIONS FACTS AND FIGURES

Phone: (860) 768-4296. **Email:** admission@hartford.edu. **Website:** http://www.hartford.edu. **Application deadlines for fall 2011:** Regular decision: Rolling. Early decision: Not offered. Early action: Send application by: November 15; Decision sent by: December 1. Admission can be deferred. **Application fee:** $40. **To apply online, go to:** http://admission.hartford.edu/applying/applyOnline.php. **Admissions requirements/recommendations:** High school units required (recommended): English: 4; Mathematics: 2 (3); Science: 2 (3); Foreign language: (2); Social studies: 2 (3); History: 2; Academic electives: 4; Total units: 16. Tests: The college uses SAT or ACT scores in admissions decisions. Either SAT or ACT required. For admission to the fall 2011 entering class, the school will accept: ACT with writing recommended. Campus visit: Recommended. Admissions interview: Recommended. Off-campus interview: May be arranged. **Factors that count in admissions decisions:** *Academic:* Secondary school record: Very Important. Class rank: Important. Letters of recommendation: Considered. Standardized test scores: Important. Essay: Considered. *Nonacademic:* Interview: Considered. Extracurricular activities: Considered. Talent/ability: Considered. Character/personal qualities: Considered. Alumni/ae relationship: Not Considered. Geographical residence: Not Considered. State residency: Not Considered. Religious affiliation/commitment: Not Considered. Minority status: Not Considered. Volunteer work: Not Considered. Work experience: Not Considered. **Other schools with the greatest overlap in applicants:** Hofstra University; Ithaca College; Northeastern University; Quinnipiac University; University of New Haven. **Admissions statistics for the fall 2009 entering class:** Total applicants: 12,869. Total accepted:

8,802. Freshmen enrolled: 1,394; 67% were from out of state. Overall acceptance rate: 68%. Non-early acceptance rate: 68%. **First-year students who submitted SAT scores:** 94%. Scores (25/75 percentile): Critical Reading: 450-550, Math: 450-570, Combined: 900-1120. **First-year students submitting ACT scores:** 17%. Scores (25/75 percentile): English: N/A, Math: N/A, Composite: 19-24.

ACADEMICS

Year founded: 1877. **Academic calendar:** Semester. **Degrees offered:** certificate, diploma, associate, bachelor's, post-bachelor's certificate, master's, post-master's certificate, doctorate. **Most popular majors:** 20% visual and performing arts, 16% business, management, marketing, and related support services, 12% health professions and related clinical sciences, 8% education, 7% engineering technologies/technicians. **Major fields of study:** area, ethnic, cultural, and gender studies; biological and biomedical sciences; business, management, marketing, and related support services; communication, journalism, and related programs; computer and information sciences and support services; education; engineering; engineering technologies/technicians; English language and literature/letters; foreign languages, literatures, and linguistics; health professions and related clinical sciences; history; legal professions and studies; liberal arts and sciences studies, and humanities; mathematics and statistics; multi/interdisciplinary studies; philosophy and religious studies; physical sciences; psychology; security and protective services; social sciences; visual and performing arts. **Areas of required coursework:** arts/fine arts, humanities, computer literacy, mathematics, English (including composition), philosophy, foreign languages, sciences (biological or physical), history, social science, other. **Preprofessional programs:** pre-law, pre-dentistry, pre-medicine, pre-veterinary science, pre-optometry, other. **Special academic programs:** cooperative (work-study plan) program, cross-registration, distance learning, double major, dual enrollment, English as a Second Language (ESL), exchange student program (domestic), honors program, independent study, internships, liberal arts/career combination, student-designed major, study abroad, teacher certificate program, weekend college. **Teacher certification offered in:** early childhood, special education, elementary. **Cooperative education programs:** engineering. **Reserve Officers Training Corps (ROTC):** Army ROTC: Offered at cooperating institution; Air Force ROTC: Offered at cooperating institution. **Faculty and instruction (2009-2010):** Total instructional faculty: 345 full-time, 542 part-time (56% men; 44% women; 8% minorities). Full-time faculty with Ph.D. or other terminal degree: 85%. Student/faculty ratio: 12/1. Classes of fewer than 20 students: 69%; of 20 to 49 students: 30%; of 50 or more students: 1%. **Advanced Placement and International Baccalaureate credit:** AP tests may be used for: Placement only. Scores accepted: 3, 4, 5. International Baccalaureate exams may be used for: Credit only. Freshmen returning for sophomore year: 73%. **Graduation rates:** Four-year: 40%; five-year: 51%; six-year: 53%. **Graduate study:** 41% of students pursue further study immediately upon graduation; 79% within five years.

COSTS AND FINANCIAL AID

Financial aid office: (860) 768-4296. **Expenses (2010-2011):** Tuition and fees 2010-2011: $29,852; room/board: $11,572. Estimated books and supplies: $1,000; transportation: $1,620; personal expenses: $1,320. **Financial aid:** Priority filing date for institution's financial aid form: February 1; deadline: May 1. In 2009-2010, 94% of undergraduates applied for financial aid. Of those, 78% were determined to have financial need; 26% had their need fully met. Average financial aid package (proportion receiving): $22,400 (78%). Average amount of gift aid, such as scholarships or grants (proportion receiving): $8,365 (68%). Average amount of self-help aid, such as work study or loans (proportion receiving): $1,437 (15%). Average need-based loan (excluding PLUS or other private loans): $3,979. Among students who received need-based aid, the average percentage of need met: 90%. Among students who received aid based on merit, the average award (and the proportion receiving): $6,484 (0%). The average athletic scholarship (and the proportion receiving): $11,731 (4%). Average amount of debt of borrowers graduating in 2009: $29,869. Proportion who borrowed: 75%.

CAMPUS LIFE AND EXTRACURRICULAR ACTIVITIES

Campus housing available: coed dorms, women's dorms, men's dorms, apartment for single students, special housing for disabled students, other housing options. Students who live in college-owned, operated, or affiliated housing: 60%. **Clubs and organizations:** Number of student organizations: 46. Activities include: choral groups, concert band, dance, drama/theater, jazz band, literary magazine, music ensembles, musical theater, opera, pep band, radio station, student government, student newspaper, symphony orchestra, television station, yearbook. Number of fraternities: 7; sororities: 7. Average proportion of students who stay on campus on weekends: 85%.

Sports program (2009-2010): Member of NCAA I. *Men's intercollegiate varsity sports:* baseball, basketball, cross country, golf, lacrosse, soccer, tennis, track and field (indoor), track and field (outdoor). *Women's intercollegiate varsity sports:* basketball, cross country, golf, soccer, softball, tennis, track and field (indoor), track and field (outdoor), volleyball.

SERVICES AND FACILITIES
Basic services: nonremedial tutoring, women's center, placement service, health service, health insurance. **Remedial assistance:** reading, math, writing, study skills. **Counseling services:** minority student, career, personal, veteran student, academic, psychological, birth control, religious, other. **For learning-disabled students:** School does not offer a structured program with separate admission and additional fees. Total undergraduates in learning-disabled program or receiving services: 400. Services include: reading machines, tape recorders, note-taking services, learning center, readers, extended time for tests, tutors, priority registration, priority seating, substitution of courses, texts on tape, typist/scribe, other testing accommodations, waiver of foreign language degree requirement, other. **Library:** Number of titles: 481,685; number of current serial subscriptions: 3,903. **Information technology resources:** Students are not required to lease or own a computer. Number of campus computers available to all students: 500. School has a wireless network. Approximate number of users that can be accommodated: 600. Proportion of college-owned housing units wired for high-speed internet access: 100%. **Campus safety:** Security services offered: 24-hour foot-and-vehicle patrols, late-night transport/escort service, 24-hour emergency telephones, controlled dormitory access (key, security card, etc).

TRANSFER AND INTERNATIONAL STUDENTS
Transfer students: May apply for admission for the following academic terms: Fall, Spring. Applicants need a minimum number of credits to apply. For fall 2009: Transfer applications received: 941. Transfer applicants offered admission: 501. Transfer applicants enrolled: 247. **International students:** Number of foreign undergraduates: 170 (3% of student body). Number of countries represented: 49. Minimum TOEFL score required: 550 (paper); 213 (computer).

University of New Haven

- **Address:** 300 Boston Post Road, West Haven, CT 06516
- **Website:** http://www.newhaven.edu
- **Private**
- **Enrollment:** 3,540 full-time; 473 part-time

KEY STATS
✔ **U.S News College Ranking:** 99, Regional Universities (North)
✔ **SAT Score (25th/75th percentile):** 900-1120
✔ **Tuition:** 2009-2010: $29,470

Selectivity: Selective	**Room/board:** $12,372
Acceptance rate: 47%	**Average debt:** $36,272
Student/faculty ratio: 15/1	**Proportion who borrowed:** 86%

UNDERGRADUATE STUDENT BODY STATS
2009-2010 enrollment: 3,540 full-time; 473 part-time. Men: 50%; women: 50%. **Ethnic makeup:** African American: 9%; Asian American: 2%; Hispanic: 8%; White: 78%; International: 2%.

ADMISSIONS FACTS AND FIGURES
Phone: (203) 932-7319. **Email:** adminfo@newhaven.edu. **Website:** http://www.newhaven.edu. **Application deadlines for fall 2011:** Regular decision: Rolling. Early decision: Not offered. Early action: Send application by: November 15; Decision sent by: December 17. Admission cannot be deferred. **Application fee:** $75. **To apply online, go to:** http://www.newhaven.edu/admissions/ugrad/process/. **Admissions requirements/recommendations:** High school units required (recommended): English: 4; Mathematics: 3; Science: 2; Foreign language: 2; Social studies: 2; History: 0; Academic electives: 0; Total units: 13. Tests: The college uses SAT or ACT scores in admissions decisions. Either SAT or ACT required. For admission to the fall 2011 entering class, the school will accept: ACT with or without writing accepted. Campus visit: Recommended. Admissions interview: Recommended. Off-campus interview: May be arranged. **Factors that count in admissions decisions:** *Academic:* Secondary school record: Considered. Class rank: Not Considered. Letters of recommendation: Important. Standardized test scores: Very Important. Essay: Important. *Nonacademic:*

Interview: Considered. Extracurricular activities: Considered. Talent/ability: Not Considered. Character/personal qualities: Considered. Alumni/ae relationship: Not Considered. Geographical residence: Not Considered. State residency: Not Considered. Religious affiliation/commitment: Not Considered. Minority status: Not Considered. Volunteer work: Considered. Work experience: Considered. **Other schools with the greatest overlap in applicants:** Quinnipiac University; Southern Connecticut State University; University of Connecticut; University of Hartford; Western New England College. **Admissions statistics for the fall 2009 entering class:** Total applicants: 8,013. Total accepted: 3,753. Freshmen enrolled: 1,271; 59% were from out of state. Overall acceptance rate: 47%. Non-early acceptance rate: 47%. **Size of waiting list:** 59 applicants; enrolled from waiting list: 0. **Credentials of fall 2009 freshmen:** 14% ranked in the top 10 percent of their high school class; 39% were in the top 25 percent; 72% were in the top half. (Proportion submitting class standing: 59%.) **Average high school grade point average:** 3.2. **First-year students who submitted SAT scores:** 95%. Scores (25/75 percentile): Critical Reading: 450-550, Math: 450-570, Combined: 900-1120. **First-year students submitting ACT scores:** 18%. Scores (25/75 percentile): English: 19-24, Math: 18-25, Composite: 19-25.

ACADEMICS
Year founded: 1920. **Academic calendar:** 4-1-4. **Degrees offered:** certificate, associate, bachelor's, post-bachelor's certificate, master's, post-master's certificate. **Most popular majors:** 17% criminal justice/law enforcement administration, 8% fire protection and safety technology/technician, 7% forensic science and technology, 7% music management and merchandising, 3% business administration and management. **Major fields of study:** architecture and related services; biological and biomedical sciences; business, management, marketing, and related support services; communication, journalism, and related programs; computer and information sciences and support services; engineering; engineering technologies/technicians; English language and literature/letters; health professions and related clinical sciences; history; legal professions and studies; liberal arts and sciences studies, and humanities; mathematics and statistics; physical sciences; psychology; public administration and social service professions; science technologies/technicians; security and protective services; social sciences; visual and performing arts. **Areas of required coursework:** arts/fine arts, humanities, computer literacy, mathematics, English (including composition), philosophy, sciences (biological or physical), history, social science, other. **Pre-professional programs:** pre-law, pre-dentistry, pre-medicine, pre-veterinary science, other. **Special academic programs (% participation):** accelerated program, cooperative (work-study plan) program, distance learning, double major, English as a Second Language (ESL), honors program, independent study, internships (14%), study abroad (20%), teacher certificate program, other (31%). **Teacher certification offered in:** elementary, secondary. **Cooperative education programs:** business, computer science, engineering, natural science, social/behavioral science, technologies. **Reserve Officers Training Corps (ROTC):** Army ROTC: Offered on campus; Air Force ROTC: Offered at cooperating institution (University of Connecticut). **Faculty and instruction (2009-2010):** Total instructional faculty: 200 full-time, 362 part-time. Full-time faculty with Ph.D. or other terminal degree: 83%. Student/faculty ratio: 15/1. Classes of fewer than 20 students: 51%; of 20 to 49 students: 46%; of 50 or more students: 2%. **Advanced Placement and International Baccalaureate credit:** AP tests may be used for: Placement only. Scores accepted: 3, 4, 5. International Baccalaureate exams may be used for: Placement only. **Freshmen returning for sophomore year:** 75%. **Graduation rates:** Four-year: 39%; five-year: 49%; six-year: 44%. **Graduate study:** 36% of students pursue further study immediately upon graduation. Fields in which graduates pursue further study: Master of Business Administration (MBA), 9%; law, 6%.

COSTS AND FINANCIAL AID
Financial aid office: (203) 932-7315. **Expenses (2009-2010):** Tuition and fees 2009-2010: $29,470; room/board: $12,372. Estimated books and supplies: $1,000; transportation: $340; personal expenses: $1,000. **Financial aid:** In 2009-2010, 88% of undergraduates applied for financial aid. Of those, 79% were determined to have financial need; 16% had their need fully met. Average financial aid package (proportion receiving): $19,495 (79%). Average amount of gift aid, such as scholarships or grants (proportion receiving): $15,882 (79%). Average amount of self-help aid, such as work study or loans (proportion receiving): $4,195 (69%). Average need-based loan (excluding PLUS or other private loans): $4,129. Among students who received need-based aid, the average percentage of need met: 65%. Among students who received aid based on merit, the average award (and the proportion receiving): $9,607 (12%). The average athletic scholarship (and the

proportion receiving): $14,433 (1%). Average amount of debt of borrowers graduating in 2009: $36,272. Proportion who borrowed: 86%.

CAMPUS LIFE AND EXTRACURRICULAR ACTIVITIES

Campus housing available (% using): coed dorms (44%), apartment for single students (56%). Students who live in college-owned, operated, or affiliated housing: 38%. **Student employment:** During the 2009-2010 academic year, 12% of undergraduates worked on campus. Average per-year earnings: $1,215. **Clubs and organizations:** Number of student organizations: 54. Activities include: campus ministries, choral groups, dance, drama/theater, international student organization, jazz band, literary magazine, marching band, model UN, pep band, radio station, student government, student newspaper, symphony orchestra, yearbook. Number of fraternities: 6; sororities: 6. Proportion of men in fraternities: 5%; of women in sororities: 8%. Average proportion of students who stay on campus on weekends: 60%. **Sports program (2009-2010):** Member of NCAA II. *Men's intercollegiate varsity sports:* baseball, basketball, cross country, football, golf, soccer, track and field (indoor), track and field (outdoor), volleyball. *Women's intercollegiate varsity sports:* basketball, cross country, lacrosse, soccer, softball, tennis, track and field (indoor), track and field (outdoor), volleyball.

SERVICES AND FACILITIES

Basic services: nonremedial tutoring, placement service, health service, health insurance. **Remedial assistance:** reading, math, writing, study skills. **Counseling services:** minority student, career, personal, academic, psychological. **For learning-disabled students:** School does not offer a structured program with separate admission and additional fees. Total undergraduates in learning-disabled program or receiving services: 290. Services include: remedial math, remedial English, reading machines, remedial reading, tape recorders, diagnostic testing service, note-taking services, learning center, readers, extended time for tests, tutors, priority seating, texts on tape, other testing accommodations, other. **Library:** Number of titles: 411,328; number of current serial subscriptions: 1,895. **Information technology resources:** Students are not required to lease or own a computer. Number of campus computers available to all students: 450. School has a wireless network. Approximate number of users that can be accommodated: 1,000. Proportion of college-owned housing units wired for high-speed internet access: 100%. **Campus safety:** Security services offered: 24-hour foot-and-vehicle patrols, late-night transport/escort service, 24-hour emergency telephones, lighted pathways/sidewalks, student patrols, controlled dormitory access (key, security card, etc).

TRANSFER AND INTERNATIONAL STUDENTS

Transfer students: May apply for admission for the following academic terms: Fall, Spring, Summer. Applicants do not need a minimum number of credits to apply. For fall 2009: Transfer applications received: 661. Transfer applicants offered admission: 327. Transfer applicants enrolled: 229. **International students:** Number of foreign undergraduates: 96 (2% of student body). Number of countries represented: 26. Minimum TOEFL score required: 520 (paper); 190 (computer).

Wesleyan University

- **Address:** 237 High Street, Middletown, CT 06459
- **Website:** http://www.wesleyan.edu
- **Private**
- **Enrollment:** 2,774 full-time; 13 part-time

KEY STATS

✔ **U.S News College Ranking:** 12, National Liberal Arts Colleges
✔ **SAT Score (25th/75th percentile):** 1290-1500
✔ **Tuition:** 2010-2011: $42,084

Selectivity: Most selective	**Room/board:** $11,592
Acceptance rate: 22%	**Average debt:** $29,174
Student/faculty ratio: 9/1	**Proportion who borrowed:** 44%

UNDERGRADUATE STUDENT BODY STATS

2009-2010 enrollment: 2,774 full-time; 13 part-time. Men: 49%; women: 51%. **Ethnic makeup:** African American: 7%; American-Indian: 1%; Asian American: 10%; Hispanic: 9%; White: 67%; International: 7%. **Religious preference:** Roman Catholic: 12%; Protestant: 14%; Jewish: 18%; Muslim: 1%; Buddhist: 2%; No preference: 46%; Other: 7%.

ADMISSIONS FACTS AND FIGURES

Phone: (860) 685-3000. **Email:** admissions@wesleyan.edu. **Website:** http://www.wesleyan.edu. **Application deadlines for fall 2011:** Regular decision: January 1; decision sent by April 1. Early decision: Send application by: November 15; Decision sent by: December 15. Early action: Not offered. Admission can be deferred. **Application fee:** $55. **To apply online, go to:** http://www.admiss.wesleyan.edu. **Admissions requirements/recommendations:** High school units required (recommended): English: (4); Mathematics: (4); Science: (4); Foreign language: (4); Social studies: (4); History: (4); Total units: (24). Tests: The college uses SAT or ACT scores in admissions decisions. Either SAT or ACT required. For admission to the fall 2011 entering class, the school will accept: ACT with writing recommended. Campus visit: Recommended. Admissions interview: Recommended. Off-campus interview: May be arranged. **Factors that count in admissions decisions:** *Academic:* Secondary school record: Very Important. Class rank: Important. Letters of recommendation: Important. Standardized test scores: Important. Essay: Important. *Nonacademic:* Interview: Considered. Extracurricular activities: Considered. Talent/ability: Important. Character/personal qualities: Important. Alumni/ae relationship: Considered. Geographical residence: Considered. State residency: Not Considered. Religious affiliation/commitment: Not Considered. Minority status: Important. Volunteer work: Considered. Work experience: Considered. **Other schools with the greatest overlap in applicants:** Amherst College; Brown University; Harvard University; Tufts University; Yale University. **Admissions statistics for the fall 2009 entering class:** Total applicants: 10,068. Total accepted: 2,218. Freshmen enrolled: 745; 93% were from out of state. Accepted through early-decision or early-action plans: 47%. Overall acceptance rate: 22%. Early-decision acceptance rate: 41%. Non-early acceptance rate: 20%. Size of waiting list: 1838 applicants; enrolled from waiting list: 40. **Credentials of fall 2009 freshmen:** 70% ranked in the top 10 percent of their high school class; 90% were in the top 25 percent; 100% were in the top half. (Proportion submitting class standing: 47%.) **Average high school grade point average:** 3.8. **First-year students who submitted SAT scores:** 74%. Scores (25/75 percentile): Critical Reading: 640-750, Math: 650-750, Combined: 1290-1500. **First-year students submitting ACT scores:** 26%. Scores (25/75 percentile): English: 30-34, Math: 27-33, Composite: 29-33.

ACADEMICS

Year founded: 1831. **Academic calendar:** Semester. **Degrees offered:** bachelor's, master's, post-master's certificate, doctorate. **Most popular majors:** 8% psychology, 7% English language and literature, 7% economics, 7% political science and government, 5% American/United States studies/civilization. **Major fields of study:** agriculture, agriculture operations, and related sciences; area, ethnic, cultural, and gender studies; biological and biomedical sciences; computer and information sciences and support services; foreign languages, literatures, and linguistics; history; mathematics and statistics; multi/interdisciplinary studies; natural resources and conservation; philosophy and religious studies; physical sciences; psychology; social sciences; visual and performing arts. **Pre-professional programs:** pre-law, pre-dentistry, pre-medicine, pre-veterinary science. **Special academic programs (% participation):** cross-registration (0%), double major (28%), dual enrollment (.1%), exchange student program (domestic) (1.5%), honors program (27%), independent study (35%), internships (43%), student-designed major (.4%), study abroad (36%). **Reserve Officers Training Corps (ROTC):** Air Force ROTC: Offered at cooperating institution (University of Connecticut). **Faculty and instruction (2009-2010):** Total instructional faculty: 330 full-time, 31 part-time (58% men; 42% women; 19% minorities). Full-time faculty with Ph.D. or other terminal degree: 94%. Student/faculty ratio: 9/1. Classes of fewer than 20 students: 67%; of 20 to 49 students: 28%; of 50 or more students: 5%. **Advanced Placement and International Baccalaureate credit:** AP tests may be used for: Placement only. Scores accepted: 4, 5. International Baccalaureate exams may be used for: Placement only. **Freshmen returning for sophomore year:** 95%. **Graduation rates:** Four-year: 88%; five-year: 91%; six-year: 93%. **Graduate study:** 17% of students pursue further study immediately upon graduation. Fields in which graduates pursue further study: Master of Business Administration (MBA), 6%; law, 12%; medicine, 19%; theology (or the seminary), 3%; education, 7%; arts and sciences, 29%; veterinary medicine, 1%.

COSTS AND FINANCIAL AID

Financial aid office: (860) 685-2800. **Expenses (2010-2011):** Tuition and fees 2010-2011: $42,084; room/board: $11,592. Estimated books and supplies: $2,665; transportation: $285; personal expenses: $140. **Financial aid:** In 2009-2010, 51% of undergraduates applied for financial aid. Of those, 48% were determined to have financial need; 100% had their need fully

met. Average financial aid package (proportion receiving): $37,187 (48%). Average amount of gift aid, such as scholarships or grants (proportion receiving): $33,168 (43%). Average amount of self-help aid, such as work study or loans (proportion receiving): $6,076 (48%). Average need-based loan (excluding PLUS or other private loans): $4,069. Among students who received need-based aid, the average percentage of need met: 100%. Among students who received aid based on merit, the average award (and the proportion receiving): $46,085 (2%). The average athletic scholarship (and the proportion receiving): $0 (0%). Average amount of debt of borrowers graduating in 2009: $29,174. Proportion who borrowed: 44%.

CAMPUS LIFE AND EXTRACURRICULAR ACTIVITIES

Campus housing available (% using): coed dorms (45%), women's dorms (1%), men's dorms (1%), fraternity housing (3%), apartments for married students (0%), apartment for single students (17%), special housing for disabled students (1%), special housing for international students (0%), other housing options (19%). Students who live in college-owned, operated, or affiliated housing: 98%. **Student employment:** During the 2009-2010 academic year, 28% of undergraduates worked on campus. Average per-year earnings: $939. **Clubs and organizations:** Number of student organizations: 270. Activities include: campus ministries, choral groups, concert band, dance, drama/theater, jazz band, literary magazine, music ensembles, musical theater, pep band, radio station, student government, student newspaper, student film society, symphony orchestra, yearbook. Number of fraternities: 6; sororities: 0. Proportion of men in fraternities: 4%; of women in sororities: 1%. Average proportion of students who stay on campus on weekends: 98%. **Sports program (2009-2010):** Member of NCAA III. *Men's intercollegiate varsity sports:* baseball, basketball, cross country, football, golf, ice hockey, lacrosse, soccer, swimming, tennis, track and field (indoor), track and field (outdoor), wrestling. *Women's intercollegiate varsity sports:* basketball, crew (heavyweight), cross country, field hockey, golf, ice hockey, lacrosse, soccer, softball, squash, swimming, tennis, track and field (indoor), track and field (outdoor), volleyball.

SERVICES AND FACILITIES

Basic services: nonremedial tutoring, women's center, placement service, health service, health insurance, other. **Counseling services:** minority student, career, personal, veteran student, academic, older student, psychological, birth control, religious. **For learning-disabled students:** School does not offer a structured program with separate admission and additional fees. Total undergraduates in learning-disabled program or receiving services: 122. Services include: reading machines, tape recorders, videotaped classes, note-taking services, oral tests, readers, extended time for tests, tutors, early syllabus, priority registration, priority seating, texts on tape, typist/scribe, exams on tape or computer, other testing accommodations, other. **Library:** Number of titles: 1,663,183; number of current serial subscriptions: 10,489. **Information technology resources:** Students are not required to lease or own a computer. Number of campus computers available to all students: 205. School has a wireless network. Approximate number of users that can be accommodated: 3,000. Proportion of college-owned housing units wired for high-speed internet access: 100%. **Campus safety:** Security services offered: 24-hour foot-and-vehicle patrols, late-night transport/escort service, 24-hour emergency telephones, lighted pathways/sidewalks, controlled dormitory access (key, security card, etc).

TRANSFER AND INTERNATIONAL STUDENTS

Transfer students: May apply for admission for the following academic terms: Fall. Applicants need a minimum number of credits to apply. For fall 2009: Transfer applications received: 604. Transfer applicants offered admission: 131. Transfer applicants enrolled: 60. **International students:** Number of foreign undergraduates: 189 (7% of student body). Number of countries represented: 53. Minimum TOEFL score required: 100 (computer). Average TOEFL score: 640 (paper).

Western Connecticut State University

- **Address:** 181 White Street, Danbury, CT 06810
- **Website:** http://www.wcsu.edu
- **Public**
- **Enrollment:** 4,756 full-time; 1,113 part-time

KEY STATS
✔ **U.S News College Ranking:** second tier, Regional Universities (North)
✔ **SAT Score (25th/75th percentile):** 880-1090
✔ **Tuition:** 2010-2011: $7,909 in state, $16,906 out of state
   Selectivity: Less selective   **Room/board:** $9,970
   Acceptance rate: 62%   **Average debt:** $26,024
   Student/faculty ratio: 15/1   **Proportion who borrowed:** 36%

UNDERGRADUATE STUDENT BODY STATS
2009-2010 enrollment: 4,756 full-time; 1,113 part-time. Men: 46%; women: 54%. **Ethnic makeup:** African American: 7%; Asian American: 3%; Hispanic: 8%; White: 81%.

ADMISSIONS FACTS AND FIGURES
Phone: (203) 837-9000. **Email:** admissions@wcsu.edu. **Website:** http://www.wcsu.edu. **Application deadlines for fall 2011:** Regular decision: Rolling. Early decision: Not offered. Early action: Not offered. Admission can be deferred. **Application fee:** $50. **To apply online, go to:** http://www.wcsu.edu/admissions/application/. **Admissions requirements/recommendations:** High school units required (recommended): English: 4; Mathematics: 3; Science: 2; Foreign language: 2; Social studies: 1; History: 1; Total units: 13. Tests: The college uses SAT or ACT scores in admissions decisions. Either SAT or ACT required. For admission to the fall 2011 entering class, the school will accept: ACT with writing required. Campus visit: Neither required nor recommended. Admissions interview: Neither required nor recommended. Off-campus interview: May not be arranged. **Factors that count in admissions decisions:** *Academic:* Secondary school record: Very Important. Class rank: Important. Letters of recommendation: Considered. Standardized test scores: Very Important. Essay: Considered. *Nonacademic:* Interview: Considered. Extracurricular activities: Important. Talent/ability: Very Important. Character/personal qualities: Considered. Alumni/ae relationship: Considered. Geographical residence: Not Considered. State residency: Considered. Religious affiliation/commitment: Not Considered. Minority status: Considered. Volunteer work: Considered. Work experience: Considered. **Other schools with the greatest overlap in applicants:** Central Connecticut State University; Eastern Connecticut State University; Southern Connecticut State University; University of Connecticut; University of Hartford. **Admissions statistics for the fall 2009 entering class:** Total applicants: 4,175. Total accepted: 2,596. Freshmen enrolled: 1,019; 9% were from out of state. Overall acceptance rate: 62%. **Credentials of fall 2009 freshmen:** 4% ranked in the top 10 percent of their high school class; 21% were in the top 25 percent; 63% were in the top half. (Proportion submitting class standing: 20%.) **First-year students who submitted SAT scores:** 95%. Scores (25/75 percentile): Critical Reading: 440-540, Math: 440-550, Combined: 880-1090.

ACADEMICS
Year founded: 1903. **Academic calendar:** Semester. **Degrees offered:** associate, bachelor's, master's. **Most popular majors:** 25% business, management, marketing, and related support services, 10% education, 9% health professions and related clinical sciences, 9% security and protective services, 8% psychology. **Major fields of study:** area, ethnic, cultural, and gender studies; biological and biomedical sciences; business, management, marketing, and related support services; communication, journalism, and related programs; computer and information sciences and support services; education; English language and literature/letters; foreign languages, literatures, and linguistics; health professions and related clinical sciences; history; liberal arts and sciences studies, and humanities; mathematics and statistics; physical sciences; psychology; public administration and social service professions; security and protective services; social sciences; visual and performing arts. **Areas of required coursework:** humanities, mathematics, English (including composition), sciences (biological or physical), social science. **Special academic programs:** cooperative (work-study plan) program, cross-registration, distance learning, dual enrollment, honors program, independent study, internships, student-designed major, study abroad, teacher certificate program, other. **Teacher certification offered in:** elementary, secondary. **Cooperative education programs:** art, business, computer science, education,

humanities, natural science, social/behavioral science, technologies, other. **Reserve Officers Training Corps (ROTC):** Army ROTC: Offered at cooperating institution (University of Connecticut); Air Force ROTC: Offered at cooperating institution (University of Connecticut). **Faculty and instruction (2009-2010):** Total instructional faculty: 218 full-time, 364 part-time (55% men; 45% women; 9% minorities). Full-time faculty with Ph.D. or other terminal degree: 86%. Student/faculty ratio: 15/1. Classes of fewer than 20 students: 30%; of 20 to 49 students: 69%; of 50 or more students: 1%. **Advanced Placement and International Baccalaureate credit:** AP tests may be used for: Placement only. International Baccalaureate exams may be used for: Credit and/or placement. **Freshmen returning for sophomore year:** 71%. **Graduation rates:** Four-year: 13%; five-year: 33%; six-year: 39%. **Graduate study:** 2% of students pursue further study immediately upon graduation; 5% within one year; 20% within five years.

COSTS AND FINANCIAL AID

Financial aid office: (203) 837-8580. **Expenses (2010-2011):** Tuition and fees 2010-2011: $7,909 in state, $16,906 out of state; room/board: $9,970. Estimated books and supplies: $1,300; transportation: $1,458; personal expenses: $2,325. **Financial aid:** In 2009-2010, 76% of undergraduates applied for financial aid. Of those, 70% were determined to have financial need; 57% had their need fully met. Average financial aid package (proportion receiving): $8,090 (68%). Average amount of gift aid, such as scholarships or grants (proportion receiving): N/A (47%). Average amount of self-help aid, such as work study or loans (proportion receiving): N/A (61%). Among students who received need-based aid, the average percentage of need met: 54%. Among students who received aid based on merit, the average award (and the proportion receiving): $2,740 (1%). The average athletic scholarship (and the proportion receiving): $0 (0%). Average amount of debt of borrowers graduating in 2009: $26,024. Proportion who borrowed: 36%.

CAMPUS LIFE AND EXTRACURRICULAR ACTIVITIES

Campus housing available (% using): coed dorms (33%), women's dorms, apartment for single students (67%). Students who live in college-owned, operated, or affiliated housing: 29%. **Student employment:** During the 2009-2010 academic year, 13% of undergraduates worked on campus. Average per-year earnings: $1,500. **Clubs and organizations:** Number of student organizations: 89. Activities include: campus ministries, choral groups, concert band, dance, drama/theater, international student organization, jazz band, literary magazine, music ensembles, musical theater, opera, pep band, radio station, student government, student newspaper, symphony orchestra, yearbook. Number of fraternities: 3; sororities: 4. Proportion of men in fraternities: 3%; of women in sororities: 3%. **Sports program (2009-2010):** Member of NCAA III. **Men's intercollegiate varsity sports:** baseball, basketball, football, lacrosse, soccer, tennis. **Women's intercollegiate varsity sports:** basketball, field hockey, lacrosse, soccer, softball, swimming, tennis, volleyball.

SERVICES AND FACILITIES

Basic services: nonremedial tutoring, women's center, placement service, day care, health service, other. **Remedial assistance:** reading, math, writing, study skills, other. **Counseling services:** minority student, career, personal, veteran student, academic, older student, psychological, birth control, religious, other. **For learning-disabled students:** School does not offer a structured program with separate admission and additional fees. Services include: remedial math, remedial English, reading machines, tape recorders, untimed tests, note-taking services, oral tests, learning center, extended time for tests, tutors, priority registration, priority seating, texts on tape, other testing accommodations. **Library:** Number of titles: 215,096; number of current serial subscriptions: 31,337. **Information technology resources:** Students are not required to lease or own a computer. Number of campus computers available to all students: 1,021. School has a wireless network. Approximate number of users that can be accommodated: 5,000. Proportion of college-owned housing units wired for high-speed internet access: 100%. **Campus safety:** Security services offered: 24-hour foot-and-vehicle patrols, late-night transport/escort service, 24-hour emergency telephones, lighted pathways/sidewalks, student patrols, controlled dormitory access (key, security card, etc.).

TRANSFER AND INTERNATIONAL STUDENTS

Transfer students: May apply for admission for the following academic terms: Fall, Spring. Applicants need a minimum number of credits to apply. For fall 2009: Transfer applications received: 1,104. Transfer applicants offered admission: 795. Transfer applicants enrolled: 454. **International students:** Number of foreign undergraduates: 25. Number of

countries represented: 6. Minimum TOEFL score required: 550 (paper); 213 (computer). Average TOEFL score: 143 (paper).

Yale University

- **Address:** PO Box 208234, New Haven, CT 06520
- **Website:** http://www.yale.edu/
- **Private**
- **Enrollment:** 5,260 full-time; 15 part-time

KEY STATS

✔ **U.S News College Ranking:** 3, National Universities
✔ **SAT Score (25th/75th percentile):** 1400-1580
✔ **Tuition:** 2010-2011: $38,300

Selectivity: Most selective	**Room/board:** $11,500
Acceptance rate: 8%	**Average debt:** $10,717
Student/faculty ratio: 6/1	**Proportion who borrowed:** 31%

UNDERGRADUATE STUDENT BODY STATS

2009-2010 enrollment: 5,260 full-time; 15 part-time. Men: 50%; women: 50%. **Ethnic makeup:** African American: 9%; American-Indian: 1%; Asian American: 14%; Hispanic: 9%; White: 58%; International: 9%.

ADMISSIONS FACTS AND FIGURES

Phone: (203) 432-9316. **Email:** student.questions@yale.edu. **Website:** http://www.yale.edu/. **Application deadlines for fall 2011:** Regular decision: December 31; decision sent by April 1. Early decision: Not offered. Early action: Send application by: November 1; Decision sent by: December 15. Admission can be deferred. **Application fee:** $75. **To apply online, go to:** http://www.yale.edu/admit/freshmen/application/index.html. **Admissions requirements/recommendations:** Tests: The college uses SAT or ACT scores in admissions decisions. Either SAT or ACT required. For admission to the fall 2011 entering class, the school will accept: ACT with writing required. Campus visit: Recommended. Admissions interview: Recommended. Off-campus interview: May be arranged. **Factors that count in admissions decisions:** *Academic:* Secondary school record: Very Important. Class rank: Very Important. Letters of recommendation: Very Important. Standardized test scores: Very Important. Essay: Very Important. *Nonacademic:* Interview: Considered. Extracurricular activities: Very Important. Talent/ability: Very Important. Character/personal qualities: Very Important. Alumni/ae relationship: Considered. Geographical residence: Considered. State residency: Considered. Religious affiliation/commitment: Not Considered. Minority status: Considered. Volunteer work: Considered. Work experience: Considered. **Other schools with the greatest overlap in applicants:** Brown University; Columbia University; Harvard University; Princeton University; Stanford University. **Admissions statistics for the fall 2009 entering class:** Total applicants: 26,003. Total accepted: 1,958. Freshmen enrolled: 1,307; 93% were from out of state. Accepted through early-decision or early-action plans: 46%. Overall acceptance rate: 8%. Non-early acceptance rate: 6%. **Size of waiting list:** 769 applicants; enrolled from waiting list: 7. **Credentials of fall 2009 freshmen:** 96% ranked in the top 10 percent of their high school class; 100% were in the top 25 percent; 100% were in the top half. (Proportion submitting class standing: 35%.) **First-year students who submitted SAT scores:** 91%. Scores (25/75 percentile): Critical Reading: 700-800, Math: 700-780, Combined: 1400-1580. **First-year students submitting ACT scores:** 32%. Scores (25/75 percentile): English: N/A, Math: N/A, Composite: 30-34.

ACADEMICS

Year founded: 1701. **Academic calendar:** Semester. **Degrees offered:** bachelor's, master's, post-master's certificate, doctorate. **Most popular majors:** 13% political science and government, 12% history, 10% economics, 7% psychology, 6% biology/biological sciences. **Major fields of study:** architecture and related services; area, ethnic, cultural, and gender studies; biological and biomedical sciences; computer and information sciences and support services; engineering; English language and literature/letters; foreign languages, literatures, and linguistics; history; liberal arts and sciences studies, and humanities; mathematics and statistics; multi/interdisciplinary studies; natural resources and conservation; philosophy and religious studies; physical sciences; psychology; social sciences; visual and performing arts. **Areas of required coursework:** humanities, English (including composition), foreign languages, sciences (biological or physical), social science, other. **Pre-professional programs:** pre-medicine. **Special academic programs:**

accelerated program, double major, English as a Second Language (ESL), independent study, internships, liberal arts/career combination, student-designed major, study abroad, teacher certificate program. **Teacher certification offered in:** early childhood, elementary, middle/junior high, secondary. **Reserve Officers Training Corps (ROTC):** Army ROTC: Offered at cooperating institution (University of Connecticut); Air Force ROTC: Offered at cooperating institution (University of Connecticut). **Faculty and instruction (2009-2010):** Total instructional faculty: 1,198 full-time, 474 part-time (64% men; 36% women; 16% minorities). Full-time faculty with Ph.D. or other terminal degree: 91%. Student/faculty ratio: 6/1. Classes of fewer than 20 students: 79%; of 20 to 49 students: 14%; of 50 or more students: 7%. **Advanced Placement and International Baccalaureate credit:** AP tests may be used for: Credit and/or placement. Scores accepted: 4, 5. International Baccalaureate exams may be used for: Placement only. **Freshmen returning for sophomore year:** 99%. **Graduation rates:** Four-year: 90%; five-year: 97%; six-year: 98%. **Graduate study:** 23% of students pursue further study within one year. Fields in which graduates pursue further study: Master of Business Administration (MBA), 1%; law, 4%; medicine, 7%; engineering, 1%; theology (or the seminary), 1%; education, 1%; arts and sciences, 7%.

COSTS AND FINANCIAL AID

Financial aid office: (203) 432-2700. **Expenses (2010-2011):** Tuition and fees 2010-2011: $38,300; room/board: $11,500. Estimated books and supplies: $1,000; transportation: $720; personal expenses: $2,100. **Financial aid:** Priority filing date for institution's financial aid form: March 1; deadline: March 1. In 2009-2010, 56% of undergraduates applied for financial aid. Of those, 54% were determined to have financial need; 100% had their need fully met. Average financial aid package (proportion receiving): $39,270 (54%). Average amount of gift aid, such as scholarships or grants (proportion receiving): $37,639 (54%). Average amount of self-help aid, such as work study or loans (proportion receiving): $2,108 (45%). Average need-based loan (excluding PLUS or other private loans): $2,136. Among students who received need-based aid, the average percentage of need met: 100%. Average amount of debt of borrowers graduating in 2009: $10,717. Proportion who borrowed: 31%.

CAMPUS LIFE AND EXTRACURRICULAR ACTIVITIES

Campus housing available: coed dorms, special housing for disabled students. Students who live in college-owned, operated, or affiliated housing: 88%. **Student employment:** During the 2009-2010 academic year, 58% of undergraduates worked on campus. Average per-year earnings: $2,588. **Clubs and organizations:** Number of student organizations: 500. Activities include: campus ministries, choral groups, concert band, dance, drama/theater, international student organization, jazz band, literary magazine, marching band, model UN, music ensembles, musical theater, opera, pep band, radio station, student government, student newspaper, student film society, symphony orchestra, television station, yearbook. Average proportion of students who stay on campus on weekends: 93%. **Sports program (2009-2010):** Member of NCAA I. **Men's intercollegiate varsity sports:** baseball, basketball, cross country, fencing, football, golf, gymnastics, ice hockey, lacrosse, soccer, swimming, tennis, track and field (indoor), track and field (outdoor). **Women's intercollegiate varsity sports:** basketball, crew (heavyweight), cross country, fencing, field hockey, golf, gymnastics, ice hockey, lacrosse, crew (lightweight), soccer, squash, swimming, tennis, track and field (indoor), track and field (outdoor), volleyball.

SERVICES AND FACILITIES

Basic services: nonremedial tutoring, women's center, placement service, health service, health insurance. **Remedial assistance:** writing. **Counseling services:** minority student, career, military, personal, academic, older student, psychological, birth control, religious. **For learning-disabled students:** School does not offer a structured program with separate admission and additional fees. Total undergraduates in learning-disabled program or receiving services: 14. Services include: reading machines, tape recorders, diagnostic testing service, note-taking services, readers, extended time for tests, tutors, texts on tape, waiver of foreign language degree requirement, other. **Library:** Number of titles: 12,600,000; number of current serial subscriptions: 86,846. **Information technology resources:** Students are not required to lease or own a computer. Number of campus computers available to all students: 450. School has a wireless network. Approximate number of users that can be accommodated: 15,000. Proportion of college-owned housing units wired for high-speed internet access: 100%. **Campus safety:** Security services offered: 24-hour foot-and-vehicle patrols, late-night transport/escort service, 24-hour emergency telephones, lighted pathways/sidewalks, controlled dormitory access (key, security card, etc.).

TRANSFER AND INTERNATIONAL STUDENTS

Transfer students: May apply for admission for the following academic terms: Fall. Applicants need a minimum number of credits to apply. For fall 2009: Transfer applications received: 811. Transfer applicants offered admission: 19. Transfer applicants enrolled: 18. **International students:** Number of foreign undergraduates: 467 (9% of student body). Number of countries represented: 102. Minimum TOEFL score required: 600 (paper); 100 (computer).

Delaware

Delaware State University

- **Address:** 1200 N. Dupont Highway, Dover, DE 19901
- **Website:** http://www.desu.edu
- **Public**
- **Enrollment:** 2,818 full-time; 404 part-time

KEY STATS

✔ **U.S News College Ranking:** second tier, Regional Universities (North)
✔ **SAT Score (25th/75th percentile):** 790-960
✔ **Tuition:** 2009-2010: $6,481 in state, $13,742 out of state

Selectivity: Less selective	**Room/board:** $9,386
Acceptance rate: 37%	**Average debt:** N/A
Student/faculty ratio: 15/1	**Proportion who borrowed:** N/A

UNDERGRADUATE STUDENT BODY STATS

2009-2010 enrollment: 2,818 full-time; 404 part-time. Men: 40%; women: 60%. **Ethnic makeup:** African American: 70%; Asian American: 1%; Hispanic: 2%; White: 25%; International: 1%.

ADMISSIONS FACTS AND FIGURES

Phone: (302) 857-6353. **Email:** admissions@desu.edu. **Website:** http://www.desu.edu. **Application deadlines for fall 2011:** Regular decision: Rolling. Early decision: Send application by: N/A; Decision sent by: N/A. Early action: Not offered. Admission can be deferred. **Application fee:** $25. **To apply online, go to:** https://bnrweb.desu.edu/SSBDADPROD/bwskalog.P_DispLoginNon. **Admissions requirements/recommendations:** High school units required (recommended): English: 4; Mathematics: 3; Science: 3 (4); Foreign language: 4 (4); Social studies: 2; History: 2; Academic electives: 4 (4); Total units: 16. Tests: The college uses SAT or ACT scores in admissions decisions. Either SAT or ACT required. For admission to the fall 2011 entering class, the school will accept: ACT with or without writing accepted. Campus visit: Recommended. Admissions interview: Neither required nor recommended. Off-campus interview: May be arranged. **Factors that count in admissions decisions: Academic:** Secondary school record: Considered. Class rank: Not Considered. Letters of recommendation: Not Considered. Standardized test scores: Very Important. Essay: Not Considered. **Nonacademic:** Interview: Considered. Extracurricular activities: Considered. Talent/ability: Considered. Character/personal qualities: Considered. Alumni/ae relationship: Not Considered. Geographical residence: Not Considered. State residency: Not Considered. Religious affiliation/commitment: Not Considered. Minority status: Not Considered. Volunteer work: Not Considered. Work experience: Not Considered. **Other schools with the greatest overlap in applicants:** Hampton University; Morgan State University; Temple University; University of Maryland–Eastern Shore; Virginia State University. **Admissions statistics for the fall 2009 entering class:** Total applicants: 8,075. Total accepted: 2,999. Freshmen enrolled: 757; 67% were from out of state. Overall acceptance rate: 37%. Non-early acceptance rate: 37%. **Credentials of fall 2009 freshmen:** 6% ranked in the top 10 percent of their high school class; 22% were in the top 25 percent; 56% were in the top half. (Proportion submitting class standing: 72%.) **Average high school grade point average:** 2.8. **First-year students who submitted SAT scores:** 92%. Scores (25/75 percentile): Critical Reading: 400-480, Math: 390-480. Combined: 790-960. **First-year students submitting ACT scores:** 14%. Scores (25/75 percentile): English: 13-19, Math: 15-18, Composite: 15-19.

ACADEMICS

Year founded: 1891. **Academic calendar:** Semester. **Degrees offered:** bachelor's, master's, doctorate. **Most popular majors:** 18% business, management, marketing, and related support services, 13% communication, journalism, and related programs, 13% social sciences, 11% psychology, 9% public administration and social service professions. **Major fields of study:** agriculture, agriculture operations, and related sciences; biological and biomedical sciences; business, management, marketing, and related support services; communication, journalism, and related programs; computer and information sciences and support services; education; English language and literature/letters; family and consumer sciences/human sciences; health professions and related clinical sciences; mathematics and statistics; multi/interdisciplinary studies; natural resources and conservation; parks, recreation, leisure, and fitness studies; physical sciences; psychology; public administration and social service professions; social sciences; transportation and materials moving; visual and performing arts. **Areas of required coursework:** English (including composition), other. **Pre-professional programs:** pre-law, pre-veterinary science. **Special academic programs:** accelerated program, cooperative (work-study plan) program, distance learning, double major, English as a Second Language (ESL), exchange student program (domestic), honors program, independent study, internships, study abroad, teacher certificate program, weekend college. **Teacher certification offered in:** early childhood, special education, elementary, middle/junior high, secondary. **Cooperative education programs:** agriculture. **Reserve Officers Training Corps (ROTC):** Army ROTC: Offered on campus; Air Force ROTC: Offered at cooperating institution (University of Delaware). **Faculty and instruction (2009-2010):** Total instructional faculty: 190 full-time, 149 part-time (56% men; 44% women; 53% minorities). Full-time faculty with Ph.D. or other terminal degree: 92%. Student/faculty ratio: 15/1. Classes of fewer than 20 students: 50%; of 20 to 49 students: 47%; of 50 or more students: 3%. **Advanced Placement and International Baccalaureate credit:** International Baccalaureate exams may be used for: Placement only. **Freshmen returning for sophomore year:** 63%. **Graduation rates:** Four-year: 15%; five-year: 29%; six-year: 36%.

COSTS AND FINANCIAL AID

Financial aid office: (302) 857-6250. **Expenses (2009-2010):** Tuition and fees 2009-2010: $6,481 in state, $13,742 out of state; room/board: $9,386. Estimated books and supplies: $1,500 personal expenses: $1,600. **Financial aid:** Priority filing date for institution's financial aid form: March 15. In 2009-2010, 93% of undergraduates applied for financial aid. Of those, 85% were determined to have financial need; 30% had their need fully met. Average financial aid package (proportion receiving): $11,526 (84%). Average amount of gift aid, such as scholarships or grants (proportion receiving): $3,642 (61%). Average amount of self-help aid, such as work study or loans (proportion receiving): $3,578 (71%). Average need-based loan (excluding PLUS or other private loans): $3,494. Among students who received need-based aid, the average percentage of need met: 70%. Among students who received aid based on merit, the average award (and the proportion receiving): $9,784 (12%). The average athletic scholarship (and the proportion receiving): $18,574 (3%).

CAMPUS LIFE AND EXTRACURRICULAR ACTIVITIES

Campus housing available (% using): coed dorms (39%), women's dorms (9%), men's dorms (5%), apartment for single students (47%), special housing for disabled students, other housing options. Students who live in college-owned, operated, or affiliated housing: 64%. **Student employment:** During the 2009-2010 academic year, 10% of undergraduates worked on campus. Average per-year earnings: $2,000. **Clubs and organizations:** Number of student organizations: 67. Activities include: choral groups, concert band, dance, drama/theater, jazz band, marching band, music ensembles, musical theater, opera, pep band, radio station, student government, student newspaper, television station, yearbook. Number of fraternities: 5; sororities: 4. Proportion of men in fraternities: 1%; Average proportion of students who stay on campus on weekends: 55%. **Sports program (2009-2010):** Member of NCAA I. *Men's intercollegiate varsity sports:* baseball, basketball, cross country, football, swimming, tennis, track and field (indoor), track and field (outdoor). *Women's intercollegiate varsity sports:* basketball, bowling, cross country, soccer, softball, swimming, tennis, track and field (indoor), track and field (outdoor), volleyball.

SERVICES AND FACILITIES

Basic services: nonremedial tutoring, placement service, health service. **Remedial assistance:** reading, math, writing, study skills. **Counseling services:** minority student, career, military, personal, veteran student, academic, older student, psychological, birth control, religious. **For learning-disabled students:** School does not offer a structured program with separate admission and additional fees. Total undergraduates in learning-disabled program or receiving services: 55. Services include: remedial math, remedial English, remedial reading, tape recorders, diagnostic testing service, untimed tests, note-taking services, oral tests, learning center, readers, extended time for tests, tutors, early syllabus, priority registration, priority seating, proofreading services, substitution of courses, texts on tape, typist/scribe, exams on tape or computer, other testing accommodations, waiver of foreign language degree requirement, waiver of math degree requirement, other. **Library:** Number of titles: 415,622; number of current serial subscriptions: 30,732. **Information technology resources:** Students are not required to lease or own a computer. Number of campus computers available to all students: 1,200. School has a wireless network. Approximate number of users that can be accommodated: 500. Proportion of college-owned housing units wired for high-speed internet access: 100%. **Campus safety:** Security services offered: 24-hour foot-and-vehicle patrols, late-night transport/escort service, 24-hour emergency telephones, lighted pathways/sidewalks, controlled dormitory access (key, security card, etc.).

TRANSFER AND INTERNATIONAL STUDENTS

Transfer students: May apply for admission for the following academic terms: Fall, Spring. Applicants need a minimum number of credits to apply. For fall 2009: Transfer applications received: 940. Transfer applicants offered admission: 372. Transfer applicants enrolled: 219. **International students:** Number of foreign undergraduates: 39 (1% of student body). Number of countries represented: 29. Minimum TOEFL score required: 550 (paper); 213 (computer). Average TOEFL score: 570 (paper).

Goldey Beacom College

■ **Address:** 4701 Limestone Road, Wilmington, DE 19808
■ **Website:** http://gbc.edu
■ **Private**
■ **Enrollment:** N/A

KEY STATS
✔ **U.S News College Ranking:** Unranked Specialty School–Business
✔ **SAT or ACT Score (25th/75th percentile):** N/A
✔ **Tuition:** 2009-2010: $17,880

Selectivity: Less selective	**Room/board:** $4,782
Acceptance rate: N/A	**Average debt:** N/A
Student/faculty ratio: N/A	**Proportion who borrowed:** N/A

University of Delaware

■ **Address:** Newark, DE 19716
■ **Website:** http://www.udel.edu/
■ **Public**
■ **Enrollment:** 15,054 full-time; 1,686 part-time

KEY STATS
✔ **U.S News College Ranking:** 75, National Universities
✔ **SAT Score (25th/75th percentile):** 1060-1280
✔ **Tuition:** 2010-2011: $9,486 in state, $23,186 out of state

Selectivity: More selective	**Room/board:** $4,654
Acceptance rate: 57%	**Average debt:** $21,370
Student/faculty ratio: 12/1	**Proportion who borrowed:** 49%

UNDERGRADUATE STUDENT BODY STATS
2009-2010 enrollment: 15,054 full-time; 1,686 part-time. Men: 42%; women: 58%. **Ethnic makeup:** African American: 5%; Asian American: 5%; Hispanic: 6%; White: 82%; International: 2%.

ADMISSIONS FACTS AND FIGURES
Phone: (302) 831-8123. **Email:** admissions@udel.edu. **Website:** http://www.udel.edu/. **Application deadlines for fall 2011:** Regular decision: January 15; decision sent by March 15. Early decision: Not offered. Early action: Not offered. Admission can be deferred. **Application fee:** $75. **To apply online, go to:** http://admissions.udel.edu/apply. **Admissions requirements/recommendations:** High school units required (recommended): English: 4 (4); Mathematics: 3 (4); Science: 3 (4); Foreign language: 2 (4);

Social studies: 2 (2); History: 2 (2); Academic electives: 2 (2); Total units: 18 (22). Tests: The college uses SAT or ACT scores in admissions decisions. Either SAT or ACT required. For admission to the fall 2011 entering class, the school will accept: ACT with writing required. Campus visit: Recommended. Admissions interview: Neither required nor recommended. Off-campus interview: Not available. **Factors that count in admissions decisions: Academic:** Secondary school record: Very Important. Class rank: Considered. Letters of recommendation: Important. Standardized test scores: Important. Essay: Important. **Nonacademic:** Interview: Considered. Extracurricular activities: Important. Talent/ability: Important. Character/personal qualities: Important. Alumni/ae relationship: Considered. Geographical residence: Considered. State residency: Very Important. Religious affiliation/commitment: Not Considered. Minority status: Considered. Volunteer work: Important. Work experience: Important. **Other schools with the greatest overlap in applicants:** Pennsylvania State University–University Park; Rutgers, the State University of New Jersey–New Brunswick; University of Connecticut; University of Maryland–College Park; Villanova University. **Admissions statistics for the fall 2009 entering class:** Total applicants: 24,744. Total accepted: 14,109. Freshmen enrolled: 4,223; 69% were from out of state. Overall acceptance rate: 57%. **Size of waiting list:** 1603 applicants; enrolled from waiting list: 196. **Credentials of fall 2009 freshmen:** 37% ranked in the top 10 percent of their high school class; 74% were in the top 25 percent; 96% were in the top half. (Proportion submitting class standing: 52%.) **Average high school grade point average:** 3.5. **First-year students who submitted SAT scores:** 98%. Scores (25/75 percentile): Critical Reading: 520-630, Math: 540-650, Combined: 1060-1280. **First-year students submitting ACT scores:** 23%. Scores (25/75 percentile): English: 23-29, Math: 23-29, Composite: 24-28.

ACADEMICS
Year founded: 1743. **Academic calendar:** 4-1-4. **Degrees offered:** associate, bachelor's, master's, doctorate. **Most popular majors:** 20% business, management, marketing, and related support services, 13% social sciences, 10% education, 7% engineering, 7% health professions and related clinical sciences. **Major fields of study:** agriculture, agriculture operations, and related sciences; area, ethnic, cultural, and gender studies; biological and biomedical sciences; business, management, marketing, and related support services; computer and information sciences and support services; education; engineering technologies/technicians; English language and literature/letters; family and consumer sciences/human sciences; foreign languages, literatures, and linguistics; health professions and related clinical sciences; history; liberal arts and sciences studies, and humanities; mathematics and statistics; multi/interdisciplinary studies; natural resources and conservation; parks, recreation, leisure, and fitness studies; philosophy and religious studies; physical sciences; social sciences; visual and performing arts. **Areas of required coursework:** humanities, mathematics, English (including composition), foreign languages, sciences (biological or physical), social science, other. **Pre-professional programs:** pre-law, pre-dentistry, pre-medicine, pre-veterinary science, pre-optometry, pre-pharmacy, other. **Special academic programs (% participation):** accelerated program, cooperative (work-study plan) program, distance learning, double major (7%), dual enrollment (1%), English as a Second Language (ESL) (1%), honors program (12%), independent study, internships, liberal arts/career combination, student-designed major (2%), study abroad (38.4%), teacher certificate program (10%). **Teacher certification offered in:** early childhood, special education, elementary, middle/junior high, secondary. **Reserve Officers Training Corps (ROTC):** Army ROTC: Offered on campus; Air Force ROTC: Offered on campus. **Faculty and instruction (2009-2010):** Total instructional faculty: 1,159 full-time, 281 part-time (58% men; 42% women; 16% minorities). Full-time faculty with Ph.D. or other terminal degree: 85%. Student/faculty ratio: 12/1. Classes of fewer than 20 students: 40%; of 20 to 49 students: 48%; of 50 or more students: 12%. **Advanced Placement and International Baccalaureate credit:** AP tests may be used for: Placement only. Scores accepted: 2. International Baccalaureate exams may be used for: Credit only. **Freshmen returning for sophomore year:** 91%. **Graduation rates:** Four-year: 61%; five-year: 74%; six-year: 75%. **Graduate study:** 15% of students pursue further study immediately upon graduation. Fields in which graduates pursue further study: Master of Business Administration (MBA), 4%; law, 14%; medicine, 10%; dentistry, 3%; engineering, 11%; education, 6%; arts and sciences, 22%; veterinary medicine, 3%.

COSTS AND FINANCIAL AID
Financial aid office: (302) 831-8761. **Expenses (2010-2011):** Tuition and fees 2010-2011: $9,486 in state, $23,186 out of state; room/board: $4,654. Estimated books and supplies: $800 personal expenses: $1,500. **Financial aid:** Priority filing date for institution's financial aid form: February 1; dead-

line: March 15. In 2009-2010, 91% of undergraduates applied for financial aid. Of those, 58% were determined to have financial need; 49% had their need fully met. Average financial aid package (proportion receiving): $12,675 (57%). Average amount of gift aid, such as scholarships or grants (proportion receiving): $6,398 (39%). Average amount of self-help aid, such as work study or loans (proportion receiving): $7,697 (48%). Average need-based loan (excluding PLUS or other private loans): $7,543. Among students who received need-based aid, the average percentage of need met: 76%. Among students who received aid based on merit, the average award (and the proportion receiving): $5,965 (20%). The average athletic scholarship (and the proportion receiving): $12,823 (4%). Average amount of debt of borrowers graduating in 2009: $21,370. Proportion who borrowed: 49%.

CAMPUS LIFE AND EXTRACURRICULAR ACTIVITIES

Campus housing available (% using): coed dorms (76%), women's dorms (1%), sorority housing (2%), fraternity housing (0%), apartments for married students (1%), apartment for single students (16%), special housing for disabled students (1%), other housing options (2%). Students who live in college-owned, operated, or affiliated housing: 46%. **Student employment:** During the 2009-2010 academic year, 26% of undergraduates worked on campus. Average per-year earnings: $3,369. **Clubs and organizations:** Number of student organizations: 260. Activities include: campus ministries, choral groups, concert band, dance, drama/theater, international student organization, jazz band, literary magazine, marching band, model UN, music ensembles, musical theater, opera, pep band, radio station, student government, student newspaper, student film society, symphony orchestra, television station. Number of fraternities: 25; sororities: 19. Proportion of men in fraternities: 6%; of women in sororities: 7%. Average proportion of students who stay on campus on weekends: 67%. **Sports program (2009-2010):** Member of NCAA I. *Men's intercollegiate varsity sports:* baseball, basketball, cross country, football, golf, lacrosse, soccer, swimming, tennis, track and field (indoor), track and field (outdoor). *Women's intercollegiate varsity sports:* basketball, crew (heavyweight), cross country, lacrosse, soccer, softball, swimming, tennis, track and field (indoor), track and field (outdoor), volleyball.

SERVICES AND FACILITIES

Basic services: nonremedial tutoring, placement service, day care, health service, health insurance. **Remedial assistance:** reading, math, writing, study skills, other. **Counseling services:** minority student, career, personal, academic, older student, psychological, birth control, religious. **For learning-disabled students:** School does not offer a structured program with separate admission and additional fees. **Library:** Number of titles: 2,807,445; number of current serial subscriptions: 31,706. **Information technology resources:** Students are not required to lease or own a computer. Number of campus computers available to all students: 1,310. School has a wireless network. Approximate number of users that can be accommodated: 16,000. Proportion of college-owned housing units wired for high-speed internet access: 100%. **Campus safety:** Security services offered: 24-hour foot-and-vehicle patrols, late-night transport/escort service, 24-hour emergency telephones, lighted pathways/sidewalks, student patrols, controlled dormitory access (key, security card, etc).

TRANSFER AND INTERNATIONAL STUDENTS

Transfer students: May apply for admission for the following academic terms: Fall, Spring. Applicants do not need a minimum number of credits to apply. For fall 2009: Transfer applications received: 1,999. Transfer applicants offered admission: 817. Transfer applicants enrolled: 467. **International students:** Number of foreign undergraduates: 305 (2% of student body). Number of countries represented: 39. Minimum TOEFL score required: 575 (paper); 90 (computer).

Wesley College

■ **Address:** 120 N. State Street, Dover, DE 19901-3875
■ **Website:** http://www.wesley.edu
■ **Private; Religious affiliation:** United Methodist
■ **Enrollment:** 1,907 full-time; 394 part-time

KEY STATS

✔ **U.S News College Ranking:** 42, Regional Colleges (North)
✔ **SAT Score (25th/75th percentile):** 760-950
✔ **Tuition:** 2010-2011: $20,580

Selectivity: Less selective	**Room/board:** $9,550
Acceptance rate: 63%	**Average debt:** $25,900
Student/faculty ratio: 17/1	**Proportion who borrowed:** 65%

UNDERGRADUATE STUDENT BODY STATS

2009-2010 enrollment: 1,907 full-time; 394 part-time. Men: 45%; women: 55%. **Ethnic makeup:** African American: 35%; American-Indian: 1%; Asian American: 1%; Hispanic: 5%; White: 58%. **Religious preference:** Roman Catholic: 32%; Protestant: 43%; Jewish: 1%; United Methodist: 13%; Other: 11%.

ADMISSIONS FACTS AND FIGURES

Phone: (302) 736-2400. **Email:** admissions@wesley.edu. **Website:** http://www.wesley.edu. **Application deadlines for fall 2011:** Regular decision: April 30. Early decision: Send application by: November 1; Decision sent by: November 15. Early action: Not offered. Admission can be deferred. **Application fee:** $25. **To apply online, go to:** http://www.wesley.edu/index.cfm?fuseaction=home.apply. **Admissions requirements/recommendations:** High school units required (recommended): English: 0 (4); Mathematics: 0 (3); Science: 0 (2); Foreign language: (2); Social studies: 0 (2); History: 0 (2); Academic electives: 0 (2); Total units: 16. Tests: The college uses SAT or ACT scores in admissions decisions. SAT required. Campus visit: Recommended. Admissions interview: Recommended. Off-campus interview: May be arranged. **Factors that count in admissions decisions:** *Academic:* Secondary school record: Very Important. Class rank: Important. Letters of recommendation: Important. Standardized test scores: Important. Essay: Considered. *Nonacademic:* Interview: Important. Extracurricular activities: Important. Talent/ability: Important. Character/personal qualities: Important. Alumni/ae relationship: Considered. Geographical residence: Not Considered. State residency: Not Considered. Religious affiliation/commitment: Not Considered. Minority status: Not Considered. Volunteer work: Considered. Work experience: Considered. **Other schools with the greatest overlap in applicants:** Alvernia University; Gwynedd-Mercy College; Misericordia University; Stevenson University; University of Delaware. **Admissions statistics for the fall 2009 entering class:** Total applicants: 3,306. Total accepted: 2,078. Freshmen enrolled: 591; 73% were from out of state. Overall acceptance rate: 63%. Non-early acceptance rate: 63%. Size of waiting list: 0 applicants; enrolled from waiting list: 0. **Credentials of fall 2009 freshmen:** 25% ranked in the top 10 percent of their high school class; 57% were in the top 25 percent; 82% were in the top half. (Proportion submitting class standing: 100%.) **Average high school grade point average:** 2.7. **First-year students who submitted SAT scores:** 94%. Scores (25/75 percentile): Critical Reading: 380-470, Math: 380-480, Combined: 760-950.

ACADEMICS

Year founded: 1873. **Academic calendar:** Semester. **Degrees offered:** certificate, bachelor's, post-bachelor's certificate, master's. **Most popular majors:** 31% nursing, 18% business/commerce, 18% social sciences, 9% education, 8% liberal arts and sciences studies, and humanities. **Major fields of study:** area, ethnic, cultural, and gender studies; biological and biomedical sciences; business, management, marketing, and related support services; communication, journalism, and related programs; education; English language and literature/letters; health professions and related clinical sciences; history; legal professions and studies; liberal arts and sciences studies, and humanities; parks, recreation, leisure, and fitness studies; psychology; social sciences. **Areas of required coursework:** arts/fine arts, humanities, mathematics, English (including composition), philosophy, sciences (biological or physical), history, social science. **Pre-professional programs:** pre-law, pre-dentistry, pre-medicine, pre-theology. **Special academic programs (% participation):** double major (3%), English as a Second Language (ESL) (.1%), honors program (5%), independent study (8%), internships (4%), liberal arts/career combination (3%), study abroad (3%), teacher certificate program (16%). **Teacher certification offered in:** elementary. **Cooperative educa-**

tion programs: other. **Reserve Officers Training Corps (ROTC):** Army ROTC: Offered at cooperating institution (Delaware State University); Air Force ROTC: Offered at cooperating institution. **Faculty and instruction (2009-2010):** Total instructional faculty: 72 full-time, 85 part-time (50% men; 50% women; 13% minorities). Full-time faculty with Ph.D. or other terminal degree: 81%. Student/faculty ratio: 17/1. Classes of fewer than 20 students: 67%; of 20 to 49 students: 33%. **Advanced Placement and International Baccalaureate credit:** AP tests may be used for: Credit and/or placement. Scores accepted: 3, 4, 5. **Freshmen returning for sophomore year:** 50%. **Graduation rates:** Four-year: 19%; five-year: 33%; six-year: 37%. **Graduate study:** 30% of students pursue further study immediately upon graduation; 45% within one year; 50% within five years. Fields in which graduates pursue further study: Master of Business Administration (MBA), 25%; law, 2%; theology (or the seminary), 1%; education, 17%; arts and sciences, 5%.

COSTS AND FINANCIAL AID

Financial aid office: (302) 736-2321. **Expenses (2010-2011):** Tuition and fees 2010-2011: $20,580; room/board: $9,550. Estimated books and supplies: $1,100; transportation: $1,000; personal expenses: $1,000. **Financial aid:** Priority filing date for institution's financial aid form: April 15. In 2009-2010, 95% of undergraduates applied for financial aid. Of those, 91% were determined to have financial need; Average financial aid package (proportion receiving): $16,500 (91%). Average amount of gift aid, such as scholarships or grants (proportion receiving): $7,755 (78%). Average amount of self-help aid, such as work study or loans (proportion receiving): $4,110 (0%). Average need-based loan (excluding PLUS or other private loans): $5,660. Among students who received need-based aid, the average percentage of need met: 80%. Among students who received aid based on merit, the average award (and the proportion receiving): $3,100 (5%). The average athletic scholarship (and the proportion receiving): $0 (0%). Average amount of debt of borrowers graduating in 2009: $25,900. Proportion who borrowed: 65%.

CAMPUS LIFE AND EXTRACURRICULAR ACTIVITIES

Campus housing available (% using): coed dorms (63%), apartment for single students (36%), other housing options (1%). Students who live in college-owned, operated, or affiliated housing: 70%. **Student employment:** During the 2009-2010 academic year, 15% of undergraduates worked on campus. Average per-year earnings: $2,250. **Clubs and organizations:** Number of student organizations: 30. Activities include: choral groups, drama/theater, literary magazine, music ensembles, radio station, student government, student newspaper, television station, yearbook. Number of fraternities: 1; sororities: 3. Proportion of men in fraternities: 1%; of women in sororities: 5%. Average proportion of students who stay on campus on weekends: 25%. **Sports program (2009-2010):** Member of NCAA III. *Men's intercollegiate varsity sports:* baseball, basketball, cross country, football, golf, lacrosse, soccer, track and field (outdoor). *Women's intercollegiate varsity sports:* basketball, cross country, field hockey, lacrosse, soccer, softball, track and field (outdoor), volleyball.

SERVICES AND FACILITIES

Basic services: nonremedial tutoring, placement service, health service, health insurance. **Remedial assistance:** reading, math, writing, study skills, other. **Counseling services:** career, personal, veteran student, academic, psychological, birth control, religious. **For learning-disabled students:** School does not offer a structured program with separate admission and additional fees. Total undergraduates in learning-disabled program or receiving services: 100. Services include: remedial math, remedial English, tape recorders, untimed tests, note-taking services, extended time for tests, tutors, priority registration, priority seating. **Library:** Number of titles: 112,000; number of current serial subscriptions: 275. **Information technology resources:** Students are not required to lease or own a computer. Number of campus computers available to all students: 242. School has a wireless network. Approximate number of users that can be accommodated: 500. Proportion of college-owned housing units wired for high-speed internet access: 100%. **Campus safety:** Security services offered: 24-hour foot-and-vehicle patrols, 24-hour emergency telephones, lighted pathways/sidewalks, student patrols, controlled dormitory access (key, security card, etc).

TRANSFER AND INTERNATIONAL STUDENTS

Transfer students: May apply for admission for the following academic terms: Fall, Spring, Summer. Applicants need a minimum number of credits to apply. For fall 2009: Transfer applications received: 87. Transfer applicants offered admission: 78. Transfer applicants enrolled: 73. **International students:** Number of foreign undergraduates: 0. Minimum TOEFL score required: 500 (paper); 200 (computer). Average TOEFL score: 525 (paper).

Wilmington University

- ■ **Address:** 320 Dupont Highway, New Castle, DE 19720
- ■ **Website:** http://www.wilmu.edu
- ■ **Private**
- ■ **Enrollment:** 3,201 full-time; 2,692 part-time

KEY STATS
- ✔ **U.S News College Ranking:** Unranked, National Universities
- ✔ **SAT or ACT Score (25th/75th percentile):** N/A
- ✔ **Tuition:** 2009-2010: $9,080

Selectivity: N/A	**Room/board:** N/A
Acceptance rate: 99%	**Average debt:** N/A
Student/faculty ratio: N/A	**Proportion who borrowed:** N/A

UNDERGRADUATE STUDENT BODY STATS

2009-2010 enrollment: 3,201 full-time; 2,692 part-time. Men: 36%; women: 64%. **Ethnic makeup:** African American: 19%; Asian American: 1%; Hispanic: 3%; White: 76%.

ADMISSIONS FACTS AND FIGURES

Phone: (302) 328-9407. **Email:** undergradadmissions@wilmu.edu. **Website:** http://www.wilmu.edu. **Application deadlines for fall 2011:** Regular decision: Rolling. Early decision: Not offered. Early action: Not offered. Admission can be deferred. **Application fee:** $25. **To apply online, go to:** http://www.wilmu.edu/admission/applyonline.aspx. **Admissions requirements/recommendations:** Tests: The college does not use SAT or ACT scores in admissions decisions. Neither SAT nor ACT required. Campus visit: Neither required nor recommended. Admissions interview: Recommended. **Factors that count in admissions decisions:** *Academic:* Secondary school record: Not Considered. Class rank: Not Considered. Letters of recommendation: Not Considered. Standardized test scores: Not Considered. Essay: Not Considered. *Nonacademic:* Interview: Not Considered. Extracurricular activities: Not Considered. Talent/ability: Not Considered. Character/personal qualities: Not Considered. Alumni/ae relationship: Not Considered. Geographical residence: Not Considered. State residency: Not Considered. Religious affiliation/commitment: Not Considered. Minority status: Not Considered. Volunteer work: Not Considered. Work experience: Not Considered. **Other schools with the greatest overlap in applicants:** Delaware State University; University of Delaware; Wesley College. **Admissions statistics for the fall 2009 entering class:** Total applicants: 1,307. Total accepted: 1,292. Freshmen enrolled: 695; Overall acceptance rate: 99%.

ACADEMICS

Year founded: 1967. **Academic calendar:** Trimester. **Degrees offered:** certificate, associate, bachelor's, master's, doctorate. **Major fields of study:** business, management, marketing, and related support services; computer and information sciences and support services; education; health professions and related clinical sciences; legal professions and studies; liberal arts and sciences studies, and humanities; multi/interdisciplinary studies; parks, recreation, leisure, and fitness studies; psychology; security and protective services; transportation and materials moving; visual and performing arts. **Areas of required coursework:** arts/fine arts, humanities, computer literacy, mathematics, English (including composition), sciences (biological or physical), social science. **Special academic programs:** accelerated program, cross-registration, distance learning, double major, dual enrollment, English as a Second Language (ESL), independent study, internships, study abroad. **Teacher certification offered in:** early childhood, special education, elementary, middle/junior high, secondary. **Reserve Officers Training Corps (ROTC):** Army ROTC: Offered at cooperating institution. **Freshmen returning for sophomore year:** 69%. **Graduation rates:** Four-year: 17%; five-year: 30%; six-year: 41%.

COSTS AND FINANCIAL AID

Financial aid office: (302) 328-9437. **Expenses (2009-2010):** Tuition and fees 2009-2010: $9,080. Estimated books and supplies: $750.

CAMPUS LIFE AND EXTRACURRICULAR ACTIVITIES

Activities include: student government, yearbook. Number of fraternities: 0; sororities: 0. **Sports program (2009-2010):** Member of NCAA II. *Men's intercollegiate varsity sports:* baseball, basketball, cross country, golf, soccer. *Women's intercollegiate varsity sports:* basketball, cross country, lacrosse, soccer, softball, volleyball.

SERVICES AND FACILITIES

Basic services: nonremedial tutoring. **Remedial assistance:** reading, math, writing, study skills. **Counseling services:** academic. **For learning-disabled students:** School does not offer a structured program with separate admission and additional fees. **Information technology resources:** Students are not required to lease or own a computer. School has a wireless network. **Campus safety:** Security services offered: 24-hour foot-and-vehicle patrols, 24-hour emergency telephones, lighted pathways/sidewalks.

TRANSFER AND INTERNATIONAL STUDENTS

Transfer students: May apply for admission for the following academic terms: Fall, Winter, Spring, Summer. Applicants need a minimum number of credits to apply. For fall 2009: Transfer applications received: 1,444. Transfer applicants enrolled: 1,183. **International students:** Number of foreign undergraduates: 0. Minimum TOEFL score required: 550 (paper).

District of Columbia

American University

- **Address:** 4400 Massachusetts Avenue NW, Washington, DC 20016
- **Website:** http://www.american.edu
- **Private; Religious affiliation:** United Methodist
- **Enrollment:** 6,404 full-time; 244 part-time

KEY STATS

✔ **U.S News College Ranking:** 79, National Universities
✔ **SAT Score (25th/75th percentile):** 1170-1370
✔ **Tuition:** 2010-2011: $36,697
  Selectivity: More selective   **Room/board:** $13,468
  Acceptance rate: 53%   **Average debt:** $40,966
  Student/faculty ratio: 14/1   **Proportion who borrowed:** 54%

UNDERGRADUATE STUDENT BODY STATS

2009-2010 enrollment: 6,404 full-time; 244 part-time. Men: 40%; women: 60%. **Ethnic makeup:** African American: 4%; Asian American: 6%; Hispanic: 5%; White: 79%; International: 6%.

ADMISSIONS FACTS AND FIGURES

Phone: (202) 885-6000. **Email:** admissions@american.edu. **Website:** http://www.american.edu. **Application deadlines for fall 2011:** Regular decision: January 15; decision sent by April 1. Early decision: Send application by: November 15; Decision sent by: December 31. Early action: Not offered. Admission can be deferred. **Application fee:** $60. **To apply online, go to:** http://american.edu/admissions/apply.cfm. **Admissions requirements/recommendations:** High school units required (recommended): English: 4; Mathematics: 3 (4); Science: 3 (4); Foreign language: 2 (3); Social studies: 2 (4); Academic electives: 3 (4); Total units: 16 (18). Tests: The college uses SAT or ACT scores in admissions decisions. Either SAT or ACT required. For admission to the fall 2011 entering class, the school will accept: ACT with writing required. Campus visit: Recommended. Admissions interview: Neither required nor recommended. Off-campus interview: May be arranged. **Factors that count in admissions decisions:** *Academic:* Secondary school record: Very Important. Class rank: Not Considered. Letters of recommendation: Important. Standardized test scores: Important. Essay: Important. *Nonacademic:* Interview: Not Considered. Extracurricular activities: Important. Talent/ability: Considered. Character/personal qualities: Important. Alumni/ae relationship: Considered. Geographical residence: Considered. State residency: Not Considered. Religious affiliation/commitment: Not Considered. Minority status: Considered. Volunteer work: Important. Work experience: Considered. **Other schools with the greatest overlap in applicants:** Boston College; Cornell University; George Washington University; Georgetown University; Princeton University. **Admissions statistics for the fall 2009 entering class:** Total applicants: 14,935. Total accepted: 7,950. Freshmen enrolled: 1,533; 85% were from out of state. Accepted through early-decision or early-action plans: 19%. Overall acceptance rate: 53%. Early-decision acceptance rate: 73%. Non-early acceptance rate: 53%. **Size of waiting list:** 1225 applicants; enrolled from waiting list: 0. **Credentials of fall 2009 freshmen:** 50% ranked in the top 10 percent of their high school class; 83% were in the top 25 percent; 98% were in the top half. (Proportion submitting class standing: 38%.) **Average high school grade point average:** 3.7. **First-year students who submitted SAT scores:** 88%. Scores (25/75 percentile): Critical Reading: 590-700, Math: 580-670, Combined: 1170-1370. **First-year students submitting ACT scores:** 50%. Scores (25/75 percentile): English: 26-32, Math: 24-29, Composite: 26-30.

ACADEMICS

Year founded: 1893. **Academic calendar:** Semester. **Degrees offered:** certificate, associate, bachelor's, post-bachelor's certificate, master's, doctorate. **Most popular majors:** 25% international relations and affairs, 16% business administration and management, 10% political science and government, 6% communication studies/speech communication and rhetoric, 4% journalism. **Major fields of study:** area, ethnic, cultural, and gender studies; biological and biomedical sciences; business, management, marketing, and related support services; communication, journalism, and related programs; communications technologies/technicians and support services; computer and information sciences and support services; education; English language and literature/letters; foreign languages, literatures, and linguistics; history; liberal arts and sciences studies, and humanities; mathematics and statistics; multi/interdisciplinary studies; natural resources and conservation; parks, recreation, leisure, and fitness studies; philosophy and religious studies; physical sciences; psychology; security and protective services; social sciences; visual and performing arts. **Areas of required coursework:** arts/fine arts, humanities, mathematics, English (including composition), sciences (biological or physical), social science, other. **Pre-professional programs:** prelaw, pre-dentistry, pre-medicine, pre-veterinary science, pre-optometry, pre-pharmacy, other. **Special academic programs (% participation):** accelerated program, cooperative (work-study plan) program, cross-registration, double major (11.9%), exchange student program (domestic), honors program (22.4%), independent study, internships (80.6%), student-designed major, study abroad (58.5%), teacher certificate program, weekend college. **Teacher certification offered in:** early childhood, special education, elementary, secondary. **Cooperative education programs:** other. **Reserve Officers Training Corps (ROTC):** Army ROTC: Offered at cooperating institution (Georgetown University); Air Force ROTC: Offered at cooperating institution (Howard University). **Faculty and instruction (2009-2010):** Total instructional faculty: 626 full-time, 549 part-time (54% men; 46% women; 13% minorities). Full-time faculty with Ph.D. or other terminal degree: 95%. Student/faculty ratio: 14/1. Classes of fewer than 20 students: 45%; of 20 to 49 students: 52%; of 50 or more students: 3%. **Advanced Placement and International Baccalaureate credit:** AP tests may be used for: Credit and/or placement. Scores accepted: 4, 5. International Baccalaureate exams may be used for: Placement only. Freshmen returning for sophomore year: 88%. **Graduation rates:** Four-year: 71%; five-year: 76%; six-year: 77%. **Graduate study:** Fields in which graduates pursue further study: law, 25%.

COSTS AND FINANCIAL AID

Financial aid office: (202) 885-6100. **Expenses (2010-2011):** Tuition and fees 2010-2011: $36,697; room/board: $13,468. Estimated books and supplies: $600; transportation: $700; personal expenses: $600. **Financial aid:** In 2009-2010, 62% of undergraduates applied for financial aid. Of those, 51% were determined to have financial need; 77% had their need fully met. Average financial aid package (proportion receiving): $31,258 (50%). Average amount of gift aid, such as scholarships or grants (proportion receiving): $13,290 (24%). Average amount of self-help aid, such as work study or loans (proportion receiving): $7,747 (44%). Average need-based loan (excluding PLUS or other private loans): $4,838. Among students who received need-based aid, the average percentage of need met: 87%. Among students who received aid based on merit, the average award (and the proportion receiving): $18,412 (17%). The average athletic scholarship (and the proportion receiving): $23,013 (2%). Average amount of debt of borrowers graduating in 2009: $40,966. Proportion who borrowed: 54%.

CAMPUS LIFE AND EXTRACURRICULAR ACTIVITIES

Campus housing available: coed dorms, special housing for disabled students, special housing for international students, other housing options. Students who live in college-owned, operated, or affiliated housing: 64%. **Student employment:** During the 2009-2010 academic year, 8% of undergraduates worked on campus. **Clubs and organizations:** Number of student organizations: 220. Activities include: choral groups, dance, drama/theater, jazz band, literary magazine, music ensembles, musical theater, opera, pep band, radio station, student government, student newspaper, student film society, symphony orchestra, television station, yearbook. Number of fraternities: 11; sororities: 12. Proportion of men in fraternities: 14%; of women in sororities: 16%. **Sports program (2009-2010):** Member of NCAA I. *Men's intercollegiate varsity sports:* basketball, cross country, soccer, swimming, track and field (outdoor), wrestling. *Women's intercollegiate varsity sports:* basketball, cross country, field hockey, lacrosse, soccer, swimming, track and field (outdoor), volleyball.

SERVICES AND FACILITIES

Basic services: nonremedial tutoring, day care, health service, health insurance. **Remedial assistance:** other. **Counseling services:** minority student, career, personal, academic, psychological, religious. **For learning-disabled students:** School does not offer a structured program with separate admission and additional fees. Total undergraduates in learning-disabled program or receiving services: 300. Services include: tape recorders, other special classes, note-taking services, learning center, readers, extended time for tests, tutors, priority registration, texts on tape, other testing accommodations, other. **Library:** Number of titles: 942,486; number of current serial subscriptions: 46,306. **Information technology resources:** Students are not required to lease or own a computer. Number of campus computers available to all students: 600. School has a wireless network. Proportion of college-owned housing units wired for high-speed internet access: 100%. **Campus safety:** Security services offered: 24-hour foot-and-vehicle patrols, late-night transport/escort service, 24-hour emergency telephones, lighted pathways/sidewalks, controlled dormitory access (key, security card, etc).

TRANSFER AND INTERNATIONAL STUDENTS

Transfer students: May apply for admission for the following academic terms: Fall, Spring, Summer. Applicants do not need a minimum number of credits to apply. For fall 2009: Transfer applications received: 1,335. Transfer applicants offered admission: 882. Transfer applicants enrolled: 335. **International students:** Number of foreign undergraduates: 407 (6% of student body). Number of countries represented: 81. Minimum TOEFL score required: 550 (paper); 80 (computer). Average TOEFL score: 615 (paper).

Catholic University of America

- **Address:** 620 Michigan Avenue NE, Washington, DC 20064
- **Website:** http://www.cua.edu
- **Private; Religious affiliation:** Roman Catholic
- **Enrollment:** 3,234 full-time; 232 part-time

KEY STATS

✔ **U.S News College Ranking:** 120, National Universities
✔ **SAT Score (25th/75th percentile):** 1010-1210
✔ **Tuition:** 2010-2011: $33,780

Selectivity: Selective	**Room/board:** $12,742
Acceptance rate: 86%	**Average debt:** N/A
Student/faculty ratio: 10/1	**Proportion who borrowed:** N/A

UNDERGRADUATE STUDENT BODY STATS

2009-2010 enrollment: 3,234 full-time; 232 part-time. Men: 46%; women: 54%. **Ethnic makeup:** African American: 5%; Asian American: 3%; Hispanic: 7%; White: 81%; International: 3%. **Religious preference:** Protestant: 2%; Unknown: 38%; Roman Catholic: 55%.

ADMISSIONS FACTS AND FIGURES

Phone: (800) 673-2772. **Email:** cua-admissions@cua.edu. **Website:** http://www.cua.edu. **Application deadlines for fall 2011:** Regular decision: February 15; decision sent by March 15. Early decision: Not offered. Early action: Send application by: November 15; Decision sent by: December 15. Admission can be deferred. **Application fee:** $55. **To apply online, go to:** http://apply-online.cua.edu. **Admissions requirements/recommendations:** High school units required (recommended): English: (4); Mathematics: (3); Science: (3); Foreign language: (2); Social studies: (4); Total units: (17). Tests: The college uses SAT or ACT scores in admissions decisions. Either SAT or ACT required. For admission to the fall 2011 entering class, the school will accept: ACT with writing required. Campus visit: Recommended. Admissions interview: Recommended. Off-campus interview: May be arranged. **Factors that count in admissions decisions:** *Academic:* Secondary school record: Very Important. Class rank: Considered. Letters of recommendation: Very Important. Standardized test scores: Very Important. Essay: Important. *Nonacademic:* Interview: Important. Extracurricular activities: Important. Talent/ability: Important. Character/personal qualities: Very Important. Alumni/ae relationship: Considered. Geographical residence: Not Considered. State residency: Not Considered. Religious affiliation/commitment: Not Considered. Minority status: Considered. Volunteer work: Very Important. Work experience: Considered. **Other schools with the greatest overlap in applicants:** American University; Boston College; George Washington University; Georgetown University; Loyola University

Maryland. **Admissions statistics for the fall 2009 entering class:** Total applicants: 5,044. Total accepted: 4,336. Freshmen enrolled: 814; 99% were from out of state. Overall acceptance rate: 86%. Non-early acceptance rate: 86%. **Credentials of fall 2009 freshmen:** 24% ranked in the top 10 percent of their high school class; 50% were in the top 25 percent. **Average high school grade point average:** 3.3. **First-year students who submitted SAT scores:** 94%. Scores (25/75 percentile): Critical Reading: 510-610, Math: 500-600, Combined: 1010-1210. **First-year students submitting ACT scores:** 27%. Scores (25/75 percentile): English: N/A, Math: N/A, Composite: 21-26.

ACADEMICS

Year founded: 1887. **Academic calendar:** Semester. **Degrees offered:** associate, bachelor's, post-bachelor's certificate, master's, post-master's certificate, doctorate. **Most popular majors:** 13% architecture (B.Arch., B.A./B.S., M.Arch., M.A./M.S., Ph.D.), 13% political science and government, 8% nursing/registered nurse training (R.N., A.S.N., B.S.N., M.S.N.), 7% psychology, 4% music. **Major fields of study:** architecture and related services; biological and biomedical sciences; business, management, marketing, and related support services; communication, journalism, and related programs; computer and information sciences and support services; education; engineering; English language and literature/letters; foreign languages, literatures, and linguistics; health professions and related clinical sciences; history; liberal arts and sciences studies, and humanities; mathematics and statistics; multi/interdisciplinary studies; philosophy and religious studies; physical sciences; psychology; public administration and social service professions; social sciences; visual and performing arts. **Areas of required coursework:** humanities, mathematics, English (including composition), philosophy, foreign languages, social science, other. **Pre-professional programs:** pre-law, pre-dentistry, pre-medicine, pre-theology, pre-veterinary science. **Special academic programs:** accelerated program, cross-registration, distance learning, double major, dual enrollment, English as a Second Language (ESL), honors program, independent study, internships, study abroad, teacher certificate program. **Teacher certification offered in:** early childhood, special education, elementary, secondary. **Reserve Officers Training Corps (ROTC):** Army ROTC: Offered at cooperating institution (Georgetown University); Navy ROTC: Offered at cooperating institution (George Washington University); Air Force ROTC: Offered at cooperating institution (Howard University). **Faculty and instruction (2009-2010):** Total instructional faculty: 354 full-time, 349 part-time (58% men; 42% women; 11% minorities). Full-time faculty with Ph.D. or other terminal degree: 97%. Student/faculty ratio: 10/1. Classes of fewer than 20 students: 57%; of 20 to 49 students: 36%; of 50 or more students: 7%. **Advanced Placement and International Baccalaureate credit:** AP tests may be used for: Credit only. Scores accepted: 4, 5. International Baccalaureate exams may be used for: Credit only. **Freshmen returning for sophomore year:** 81%. **Graduation rates:** Four-year: 65%; five-year: 71%; six-year: 72%. **Graduate study:** 38% of students pursue further study within one year. Fields in which graduates pursue further study: Master of Business Administration (MBA), 4%; law, 13%; medicine, 4%; engineering, 1%; education, 12%; arts and sciences, 31%; veterinary medicine, 1%.

COSTS AND FINANCIAL AID

Financial aid office: (202) 319-5307. **Expenses (2010-2011):** Tuition and fees 2010-2011: $33,780; room/board: $12,742. Estimated books and supplies: $1,250; transportation: $800; personal expenses: $1,500. **Financial aid:** Priority filing date for institution's financial aid form: February 15; deadline: April 10. In 2009-2010, 69% of undergraduates applied for financial aid. Of those, 58% were determined to have financial need; 46% had their need fully met. Average financial aid package (proportion receiving): $20,209 (58%). Average amount of gift aid, such as scholarships or grants (proportion receiving): $15,576 (56%). Average amount of self-help aid, such as work study or loans (proportion receiving): $5,158 (54%). Average need-based loan (excluding PLUS or other private loans): $4,377. Among students who received need-based aid, the average percentage of need met: 81%. Among students who received aid based on merit, the average award (and the proportion receiving): $10,449 (31%).

CAMPUS LIFE AND EXTRACURRICULAR ACTIVITIES

Campus housing available: coed dorms, women's dorms, men's dorms, apartment for single students, special housing for disabled students, other housing options. Students who live in college-owned, operated, or affiliated housing: 70%. **Clubs and organizations:** Number of student organizations: 87. Activities include: campus ministries, choral groups, dance, drama/theater, international student organization, jazz band, literary magazine, music ensembles, musical theater, opera, radio station, student government, student newspaper, student film society, symphony orchestra, yearbook.

Number of fraternities: 1; sororities: 1. Proportion of men in fraternities: 1%; of women in sororities: 1%. **Sports program (2009-2010):** Member of NCAA III. **Men's intercollegiate varsity sports:** baseball, basketball, cross country, football, lacrosse, soccer, swimming, tennis, track and field (indoor), track and field (outdoor). **Women's intercollegiate varsity sports:** basketball, cross country, field hockey, lacrosse, soccer, softball, swimming, tennis, track and field (indoor), track and field (outdoor), volleyball.

SERVICES AND FACILITIES
Basic services: nonremedial tutoring, placement service, health service, health insurance. **Counseling services:** minority student, career, military, personal, veteran student, academic, older student, psychological, religious. **For learning-disabled students:** School does not offer a structured program with separate admission and additional fees. Total undergraduates in learning-disabled program or receiving services: 180. Services include: reading machines, tape recorders, note-taking services, readers, extended time for tests, priority registration, priority seating, other testing accommodations, other. **Library:** Number of titles: 1,642,234; number of current serial subscriptions: 10,047. **Information technology resources:** Students are not required to lease or own a computer. Number of campus computers available to all students: 500. School has a wireless network. Approximate number of users that can be accommodated: 2,500. Proportion of college-owned housing units wired for high-speed internet access: 100%. **Campus safety:** Security services offered: 24-hour foot-and-vehicle patrols, late-night transport/escort service, 24-hour emergency telephones, lighted pathways/sidewalks, student patrols, controlled dormitory access (key, security card, etc).

TRANSFER AND INTERNATIONAL STUDENTS
Transfer students: May apply for admission for the following academic terms: Fall, Spring. Applicants need a minimum number of credits to apply. For fall 2009: Transfer applications received: 594. Transfer applicants offered admission: 232. Transfer applicants enrolled: 109. **International students:** Number of foreign undergraduates: 94 (3% of student body). Number of countries represented: 42. Minimum TOEFL score required: 550 (paper); 213 (computer). Average TOEFL score: 563 (paper).

Corcoran College of Art and Design

- **Address:** 500 17th Street NW, Washington, DC 20006-4804
- **Website:** http://www.corcoran.edu
- **Private**
- **Enrollment:** 309 full-time; 382 part-time

KEY STATS
- ✔ **U.S News College Ranking:** Unranked Specialty School–Fine Arts
- ✔ **SAT Score (25th/75th percentile):** 910-1150
- ✔ **Tuition:** 2010-2011: $29,180

Selectivity: N/A	Room/board: N/A
Acceptance rate: 53%	Average debt: N/A
Student/faculty ratio: 23/1	Proportion who borrowed: N/A

UNDERGRADUATE STUDENT BODY STATS
2009-2010 enrollment: 309 full-time; 382 part-time. Men: 29%; women: 71%. **Ethnic makeup:** African American: 8%; American-Indian: 1%; Asian American: 7%; Hispanic: 10%; White: 70%; International: 4%.

ADMISSIONS FACTS AND FIGURES
Phone: (202) 639-1814. **Email:** admissions@corcoran.org. **Website:** http://www.corcoran.edu. **Application deadlines for fall 2011:** Regular decision: Rolling. Early decision: Not offered. Early action: Not offered. Admission can be deferred. **Application fee:** $45. **To apply online, go to:** https://www.corcoran.org/college/corcoran/apply_step1.asp. **Admissions requirements/recommendations:** High school units required (recommended): English: (4). Tests: The college uses SAT or ACT scores in admissions decisions. Either SAT or ACT required. For admission to the fall 2011 entering class, the school will accept: ACT with or without writing accepted. Campus visit: Recommended. Admissions interview: Recommended. Off-campus interview: May be arranged. **Factors that count in admissions decisions: *Academic:*** Secondary school record: Important. Class rank: Important. Letters of recommendation: Considered. Standardized test scores: Important. Essay: Considered. ***Nonacademic:*** Interview: Considered. Extracurricular activities: Considered. Talent/ability: Very Important. Character/personal qualities: Considered. Alumni/ae relation-

ship: Considered. Geographical residence: Not Considered. State residency: Not Considered. Religious affiliation/commitment: Not Considered. Minority status: Not Considered. Volunteer work: Considered. Work experience: Considered. **Other schools with the greatest overlap in applicants:** Maryland Institute College of Art; Pratt Institute; Savannah College of Art and Design; Virginia Commonwealth University. **Admissions statistics for the fall 2009 entering class:** Total applicants: 435. Total accepted: 229. Freshmen enrolled: 77; 93% were from out of state. Overall acceptance rate: 53%. **Credentials of fall 2009 freshmen:** 14% ranked in the top 10 percent of their high school class; 52% were in the top 25 percent; 86% were in the top half. (Proportion submitting class standing: 30%.) **Average high school grade point average:** 2.9. **First-year students who submitted SAT scores:** 85%. Scores (25/75 percentile): Critical Reading: 460-610, Math: 450-540, Combined: 910-1150. **First-year students submitting ACT scores:** 26%. Scores (25/75 percentile): English: 19-25, Math: 17-23, Composite: 20-26.

ACADEMICS
Year founded: 1890. **Academic calendar:** Semester. **Degrees offered:** certificate, associate, bachelor's, master's. **Most popular majors:** 33% photography, 31% fine/studio arts, 16% graphic design, 15% photojournalism, 5% digital communication and media/multimedia. **Major fields of study:** communication, journalism, and related programs; education; visual and performing arts. **Areas of required coursework:** arts/fine arts, humanities, computer literacy, English (including composition), other. **Special academic programs (% participation):** cross-registration (3%), exchange student program (domestic) (2%), independent study (16%), internships (45%), study abroad (6%). **Faculty and instruction (2009-2010):** Total instructional faculty: 24 full-time, 143 part-time. Full-time faculty with Ph.D. or other terminal degree: 21%. Student/faculty ratio: 23/1. **Advanced Placement and International Baccalaureate credit:** AP tests may be used for: Credit only. Scores accepted: 4, 5. International Baccalaureate exams may be used for: Credit only. **Freshmen returning for sophomore year:** 69%. **Graduation rates:** Four-year: 60%; five-year: 60%; six-year: 59%. **Graduate study:** 15% of students pursue further study immediately upon graduation; 20% within one year; 25% within five years. Fields in which graduates pursue further study: education, 10%; arts and sciences, 90%.

COSTS AND FINANCIAL AID
Financial aid office: (202) 639-1818. **Expenses (2010-2011):** Tuition and fees 2010-2011: $29,180. Estimated books and supplies: $2,600; transportation: $1,400; personal expenses: $1,200. **Financial aid:** Priority filing date for institution's financial aid form: March 15. In 2009-2010, 82% of undergraduates applied for financial aid. Of those, 64% were determined to have financial need; Average financial aid package (proportion receiving): N/A (64%). Average amount of gift aid, such as scholarships or grants (proportion receiving): N/A (64%). Average amount of self-help aid, such as work study or loans (proportion receiving): N/A (64%). The average athletic scholarship (and the proportion receiving): $0 (N/A).

CAMPUS LIFE AND EXTRACURRICULAR ACTIVITIES
Campus housing available (% using): coed dorms (100%), apartment for single students. Students who live in college-owned, operated, or affiliated housing: 28%. **Student employment:** During the 2009-2010 academic year, 24% of undergraduates worked on campus. Average per-year earnings: $1,000. Activities include: student government. Number of fraternities: 0; sororities: 0. Average proportion of students who stay on campus on weekends: 76%.

SERVICES AND FACILITIES
Basic services: nonremedial tutoring, health insurance. **Remedial assistance:** writing. **Counseling services:** personal, academic, psychological. **For learning-disabled students:** School does not offer a structured program with separate admission and additional fees. Services include: learning center, extended time for tests, tutors. **Library:** Number of titles: 47,052; number of current serial subscriptions: 217. **Information technology resources:** Students are not required to lease or own a computer. Number of campus computers available to all students: 117. School has a wireless network. Approximate number of users that can be accommodated: 300. Proportion of college-owned housing units wired for high-speed internet access: 100%. **Campus safety:** Security services offered: 24-hour foot-and-vehicle patrols, lighted pathways/sidewalks, controlled dormitory access (key, security card, etc).

TRANSFER AND INTERNATIONAL STUDENTS
Transfer students: May apply for admission for the following academic terms: Fall, Spring. Applicants need a minimum number of credits to apply. For fall 2009: Transfer applications received: 159. Transfer applicants

offered admission: 84. Transfer applicants enrolled: 54. **International students:** Number of foreign undergraduates: 15 (4% of student body). Number of countries represented: 12. Minimum TOEFL score required: 550 (paper); 213 (computer). Average TOEFL score: 523 (paper).

Gallaudet University

- ■ **Address:** 800 Florida Avenue NE, Washington, DC 20002
- ■ **Website:** http://www.gallaudet.edu
- ■ **Private**
- ■ **Enrollment:** N/A

KEY STATS

✔ **U.S News College Ranking:** second tier, Regional Universities (North)
✔ **SAT or ACT Score (25th/75th percentile):** N/A
✔ **Tuition:** 2009-2010: $11,226

Selectivity: Less selective	**Room/board:** $9,660
Acceptance rate: N/A	**Average debt:** N/A
Student/faculty ratio: N/A	**Proportion who borrowed:** N/A

Georgetown University

- ■ **Address:** 37th and O Streets NW, Washington, DC 20057
- ■ **Website:** http://www.georgetown.edu
- ■ **Private; Religious affiliation:** Roman Catholic (Jesuit)
- ■ **Enrollment:** 7,115 full-time; 318 part-time

KEY STATS

✔ **U.S News College Ranking:** 21, National Universities
✔ **SAT Score (25th/75th percentile):** 1300-1500
✔ **Tuition:** 2010-2011: $40,203

Selectivity: Most selective	**Room/board:** $12,240
Acceptance rate: 20%	**Average debt:** $25,085
Student/faculty ratio: 10/1	**Proportion who borrowed:** 45%

UNDERGRADUATE STUDENT BODY STATS

2009-2010 enrollment: 7,115 full-time; 318 part-time. Men: 45%; women: 55%. **Ethnic makeup:** African American: 7%; Asian American: 9%; Hispanic: 6%; White: 71%; International: 7%. **Religious preference:** Roman Catholic: 49%; Protestant: 25%; Jewish: 6%; Muslim: 2%; Hindu: 1%; Buddhist: 1%; No preference: 13%; Other: 3%.

ADMISSIONS FACTS AND FIGURES

Phone: (202) 687-3600. **Email:** guadmiss@georgetown.edu. **Website:** http://www.georgetown.edu. **Application deadlines for fall 2011:** Regular decision: January 10; decision sent by April 1. Early decision: Not offered. Early action: Send application by: November 1; Decision sent by: December 15. Admission can be deferred. **Application fee:** $65. **To apply online, go to:** http://uadmissions.georgetown.edu/applying_firstyear_forms.cfm. **Admissions requirements/recommendations:** High school units required (recommended): English: 4 (4); Mathematics: 2 (4); Science: 1 (4); Foreign language: 2 (4); Social studies: 2 (4); History: 2 (2). Tests: The college uses SAT or ACT scores in admissions decisions. Either SAT or ACT required. For admission to the fall 2011 entering class, the school will accept: ACT with or without writing accepted. Campus visit: Recommended. Admissions interview: Required. Off-campus interview: May be arranged. **Factors that count in admissions decisions:** *Academic:* Secondary school record: Very Important. Class rank: Very Important. Letters of recommendation: Very Important. Standardized test scores: Very Important. Essay: Very Important. *Nonacademic:* Interview: Important. Extracurricular activities: Important. Talent/ability: Very Important. Character/personal qualities: Very Important. Alumni/ae relationship: Considered. Geographical residence: Considered. State residency: Considered. Religious affiliation/commitment: Not Considered. Minority status: Considered. Volunteer work: Important. Work experience: Considered. **Other schools with the greatest overlap in applicants:** Boston College; Duke University; New York University; University of Pennsylvania; University of Virginia. **Admissions statistics for the fall 2009 entering class:** Total applicants: 18,616. Total accepted: 3,682. Freshmen enrolled: 1,555; 99% were from out of state. Overall acceptance rate: 20%. Non-early acceptance rate: 20%. **Size of waiting list:** 2425 appli-

cants; enrolled from waiting list: 158. **Credentials of fall 2009 freshmen:** 94% ranked in the top 10 percent of their high school class; 99% were in the top 25 percent; 100% were in the top half. (Proportion submitting class standing: 50%.) **First-year students who submitted SAT scores:** 94%. Scores (25/75 percentile): Critical Reading: 650-750, Math: 650-750, Combined: 1300-1500. **First-year students submitting ACT scores:** 5%. Scores (25/75 percentile): English: N/A, Math: N/A, Composite: 27-33.

ACADEMICS

Year founded: 1789. **Academic calendar:** Semester. **Degrees offered:** certificate, bachelor's, master's, doctorate. **Most popular majors:** 21% international relations and affairs, 11% finance, 9% political science and government. **Major fields of study:** area, ethnic, cultural, and gender studies; biological and biomedical sciences; business, management, marketing, and related support services; computer and information sciences and support services; English language and literature/letters; foreign languages, literatures, and linguistics; health professions and related clinical sciences; history; liberal arts and sciences studies, and humanities; mathematics and statistics; multi/interdisciplinary studies; philosophy and religious studies; physical sciences; psychology; social sciences; visual and performing arts. **Areas of required coursework:** English (including composition), philosophy, other. **Pre-professional programs:** pre-law, pre-medicine. **Special academic programs:** cross-registration, double major, English as a Second Language (ESL), honors program, independent study, internships, student-designed major, study abroad. **Reserve Officers Training Corps (ROTC):** Army ROTC: Offered on campus; Navy ROTC: Offered at cooperating institution (George Washington University); Air Force ROTC: Offered at cooperating institution (Howard University). **Faculty and instruction (2009-2010):** Total instructional faculty: 873 full-time, 904 part-time (62% men; 38% women; 13% minorities). Full-time faculty with Ph.D. or other terminal degree: 88%. Student/faculty ratio: 10/1. Classes of fewer than 20 students: 61%; of 20 to 49 students: 35%; of 50 or more students: 4%. **Advanced Placement and International Baccalaureate credit:** AP tests may be used for: Placement only. Scores accepted: 4, 5. International Baccalaureate exams may be used for: Placement only. **Freshmen returning for sophomore year:** 96%. **Graduation rates:** Four-year: 85%; five-year: 92%; six-year: 93%. **Graduate study:** 24% of students pursue further study immediately upon graduation.

COSTS AND FINANCIAL AID

Financial aid office: (202) 687-4547. **Expenses (2010-2011):** Tuition and fees 2010-2011: $40,203; room/board: $12,240. Estimated books and supplies: $1,184; transportation: $550; personal expenses: $1,790. **Financial aid:** Priority filing date for institution's financial aid form: February 1. In 2009-2010, 52% of undergraduates applied for financial aid. Of those, 43% were determined to have financial need; 100% had their need fully met. Average financial aid package (proportion receiving): $31,181 (43%). Average amount of gift aid, such as scholarships or grants (proportion receiving): $30,140 (37%). Average amount of self-help aid, such as work study or loans (proportion receiving): $5,675 (39%). Average need-based loan (excluding PLUS or other private loans): $4,492. Among students who received need-based aid, the average percentage of need met: 100%. Among students who received aid based on merit, the average award (and the proportion receiving): $0 (0%). The average athletic scholarship (and the proportion receiving): $15,870 (4%). Average amount of debt of borrowers graduating in 2009: $25,085. Proportion who borrowed: 45%.

CAMPUS LIFE AND EXTRACURRICULAR ACTIVITIES

Campus housing available (% using): coed dorms (80%), apartment for single students (14%), other housing options (6%). Students who live in college-owned, operated, or affiliated housing: 70%. **Clubs and organizations:** Number of student organizations: 144. Activities include: choral groups, concert band, dance, drama/theater, jazz band, literary magazine, music ensembles, musical theater, pep band, radio station, student government, student newspaper, student film society, symphony orchestra, television station, yearbook. Number of fraternities: 0; sororities: 0. Average proportion of students who stay on campus on weekends: 95%. **Sports program (2009-2010):** Member of NCAA I. *Men's intercollegiate varsity sports:* baseball, basketball, cross country, football, golf, lacrosse, soccer, swimming, tennis, track and field (indoor), track and field (outdoor). *Women's intercollegiate varsity sports:* basketball, crew (heavyweight), cross country, field hockey, golf, lacrosse, crew (lightweight), soccer, softball, tennis, track and field (indoor), track and field (outdoor), volleyball.

SERVICES AND FACILITIES

Basic services: nonremedial tutoring, women's center, placement service, health service. **Counseling services:** minority student, career, personal, academic, psychological, religious. **For learning-disabled students:** School does not offer a structured program with separate admission and additional fees. Services include: reading machines, tape recorders, note-taking services, extended time for tests, other. **Library:** Number of titles: 2,660,742; number of current serial subscriptions: 70,518. **Information technology resources:** Students are not required to lease or own a computer. School has a wireless network. Approximate number of users that can be accommodated: 11,910. Proportion of college-owned housing units wired for high-speed internet access: 99%. **Campus safety:** Security services offered: 24-hour foot-and-vehicle patrols, late-night transport/escort service, 24-hour emergency telephones, lighted pathways/sidewalks, student patrols, controlled dormitory access (key, security card, etc).

TRANSFER AND INTERNATIONAL STUDENTS

Transfer students: May apply for admission for the following academic terms: Fall. Applicants need a minimum number of credits to apply. For fall 2009: Transfer applications received: 2,028. Transfer applicants offered admission: 284. Transfer applicants enrolled: 174. **International students:** Number of foreign undergraduates: 477 (7% of student body). Number of countries represented: 88. Minimum TOEFL score required: 550 (paper); 213 (computer).

George Washington University

- **Address:** 2121 I Street NW, Washington, DC 20052
- **Website:** http://www.gwu.edu
- **Private**
- **Enrollment:** 9,640 full-time; 918 part-time

KEY STATS

✔ **U.S News College Ranking:** 51, National Universities
✔ **SAT Score (25th/75th percentile):** 1200-1380
✔ **Tuition:** 2010-2011: $41,242

Selectivity: More selective	**Room/board:** $12,680
Acceptance rate: 37%	**Average debt:** $32,547
Student/faculty ratio: 13/1	**Proportion who borrowed:** 47%

UNDERGRADUATE STUDENT BODY STATS

2009-2010 enrollment: 9,640 full-time; 918 part-time. Men: 45%; women: 55%. **Ethnic makeup:** African American: 7%; American-Indian: 1%; Asian American: 11%; Hispanic: 7%; White: 68%; International: 6%.

ADMISSIONS FACTS AND FIGURES

Phone: (202) 994-6040. **Email:** gwadm@gwu.edu. **Website:** http://www.gwu.edu. **Application deadlines for fall 2011:** Regular decision: January 10; decision sent by April 1. Early decision: Send application by: November 10; Decision sent by: December 15. Early action: Not offered. Admission can be deferred. **Application fee:** $65. **To apply online, go to:** http://gwired.gwu.edu/adm/apply/. **Admissions requirements/recommendations:** High school units required (recommended): English: 4 (4); Mathematics: 2 (4); Science: 2 (4); Foreign language: 2 (4); Social studies: 2 (4); Total units: 13 (20). Tests: The college uses SAT or ACT scores in admissions decisions. Either SAT or ACT required. For admission to the fall 2011 entering class, the school will accept: ACT with or without writing accepted. Campus visit: Recommended. Admissions interview: Recommended. Off-campus interview: May be arranged. **Factors that count in admissions decisions:** *Academic:* Secondary school record: Very Important. Class rank: Important. Letters of recommendation: Important. Standardized test scores: Important. Essay: Important. *Nonacademic:* Interview: Important. Extracurricular activities: Important. Talent/ability: Important. Character/personal qualities: Considered. Alumni/ae relationship: Considered. Geographical residence: Considered. State residency: Not Considered. Religious affiliation/commitment: Not Considered. Minority status: Considered. Volunteer work: Important. Work experience: Considered. **Other schools with the greatest overlap in applicants:** Boston University; Emory University; Georgetown University; New York University. **Admissions statistics for the fall 2009 entering class:** Total applicants: 19,842. Total accepted: 7,292. Freshmen enrolled: 2,592; 99% were from out of state. Accepted through early-decision or early-action plans: 34%. Overall acceptance rate: 37%. Early-decision acceptance rate: 47%. Non-early acceptance rate: 36%. **Size of waiting list:** 2100 applicants; enrolled from waiting list: 74. **Credentials of fall 2009 freshmen:** 67% ranked in the top 10 percent of their high school class; 93% were in the top 25 percent; 100% were in the top half. (Proportion submit-

ting class standing: 52%.) **First-year students who submitted SAT scores:** 80%. Scores (25/75 percentile): Critical Reading: 600-690, Math: 600-690, Combined: 1200-1380. **First-year students submitting ACT scores:** 27%. Scores (25/75 percentile): English: N/A, Math: N/A, Composite: 27-30.

ACADEMICS

Year founded: 1821. **Academic calendar:** Semester. **Degrees offered:** certificate, associate, bachelor's, post-bachelor's certificate, master's, post-master's certificate, doctorate. **Most popular majors:** 37% social sciences, 19% business, management, marketing, and related support services, 7% psychology, 4% English language and literature/letters, 4% health professions and related clinical sciences. **Major fields of study:** area, ethnic, cultural, and gender studies; biological and biomedical sciences; business, management, marketing, and related support services; communication, journalism, and related programs; computer and information sciences and support services; education; engineering; English language and literature/letters; foreign languages, literatures, and linguistics; health professions and related clinical sciences; history; liberal arts and sciences studies, and humanities; mathematics and statistics; multi/interdisciplinary studies; philosophy and religious studies; physical sciences; psychology; security and protective services; social sciences; visual and performing arts. **Areas of required coursework:** humanities, mathematics, English (including composition), sciences (biological or physical), social science. **Pre-professional programs:** pre-law, pre-medicine. **Special academic programs (% participation):** accelerated program, cooperative (work-study plan) program (1%), cross-registration (1%), distance learning (16%), double major (17%), dual enrollment, honors program (4%), independent study, internships (68%), liberal arts/career combination, student-designed major, study abroad (43%). **Cooperative education programs:** art, business, computer science, engineering, humanities, natural science, social/behavioral science, technologies. **Reserve Officers Training Corps (ROTC):** Army ROTC: Offered at cooperating institution (Georgetown University); Navy ROTC: Offered on campus; Air Force ROTC: Offered at cooperating institution (University of Maryland–College Park). **Faculty and instruction (2009-2010):** Total instructional faculty: 903 full-time, 1,416 part-time (59% men; 41% women; 17% minorities). Full-time faculty with Ph.D. or other terminal degree: 92%. Student/faculty ratio: 13/1. Classes of fewer than 20 students: 56%; of 20 to 49 students: 34%; of 50 or more students: 10%. **Advanced Placement and International Baccalaureate credit:** AP tests may be used for: Credit and/or placement. Scores accepted: 4, 5. International Baccalaureate exams may be used for: Placement only. **Freshmen returning for sophomore year:** 91%. **Graduation rates:** Four-year: 76%; five-year: 81%; six-year: 81%. **Graduate study:** 17% of students pursue further study immediately upon graduation; 22% within one year. Fields in which graduates pursue further study: law, 35%; medicine, 12%; education, 2%; arts and sciences, 46%.

COSTS AND FINANCIAL AID

Financial aid office: (202) 994-6620. **Expenses (2010-2011):** Tuition and fees 2010-2011: $41,242; room/board: $12,680. Estimated books and supplies: $1,200; transportation: $1,000; personal expenses: $1,400. **Financial aid:** Priority filing date for institution's financial aid form: February 1; deadline: February 1. In 2009-2010, 53% of undergraduates applied for financial aid. Of those, 45% were determined to have financial need; 84% had their need fully met. Average financial aid package (proportion receiving): $39,572 (43%). Average amount of gift aid, such as scholarships or grants (proportion receiving): $27,633 (42%). Average amount of self-help aid, such as work study or loans (proportion receiving): $6,644 (36%). Average need-based loan (excluding PLUS or other private loans): $5,229. Among students who received need-based aid, the average percentage of need met: 93%. Among students who received aid based on merit, the average award (and the proportion receiving): $13,050 (12%). The average athletic scholarship (and the proportion receiving): $25,477 (2%). Average amount of debt of borrowers graduating in 2009: $32,547. Proportion who borrowed: 47%.

CAMPUS LIFE AND EXTRACURRICULAR ACTIVITIES

Campus housing available (% using): coed dorms (95%), women's dorms (2%), sorority housing (2%), fraternity housing (1%), apartment for single students. Students who live in college-owned, operated, or affiliated housing: 67%. **Clubs and organizations:** Number of student organizations: 378. Activities include: choral groups, concert band, dance, drama/theater, international student organization, jazz band, literary magazine, marching band, model UN, music ensembles, musical theater, pep band, radio station, student government, student newspaper, student film society, television station, yearbook. Number of fraternities: 17; sororities: 14. Proportion of men in fraternities: 23%; of women in sororities: 23%. Average proportion of students who stay on campus on weekends: 95%. **Sports program (2009-2010):**

Member of NCAA I. *Men's intercollegiate varsity sports:* baseball, basketball, cross country, golf, soccer, swimming, tennis, water polo. *Women's intercollegiate varsity sports:* basketball, crew (heavyweight), cross country, gymnastics, lacrosse, crew (lightweight), soccer, softball, squash, swimming, tennis, volleyball, water polo.

SERVICES AND FACILITIES

Basic services: nonremedial tutoring, placement service, health service, health insurance. **Counseling services:** minority student, career, personal, veteran student, academic, older student, psychological, birth control, religious, other. **For learning-disabled students:** School does not offer a structured program with separate admission and additional fees. Total undergraduates in learning-disabled program or receiving services: 241. Services include: reading machines, tape recorders, untimed tests, note-taking services, readers, extended time for tests, tutors, priority registration, priority seating, texts on tape, other testing accommodations. **Library:** Number of titles: 2,300,013; number of current serial subscriptions: 65,556. **Information technology resources:** Students are not required to lease or own a computer. School has a wireless network. Approximate number of users that can be accommodated: 4,000. Proportion of college-owned housing units wired for high-speed internet access: 100%. **Campus safety:** Security services offered: 24-hour foot-and-vehicle patrols, late-night transport/escort service, 24-hour emergency telephones, lighted pathways/sidewalks, controlled dormitory access (key, security card, etc).

TRANSFER AND INTERNATIONAL STUDENTS

Transfer students: May apply for admission for the following academic terms: Fall, Spring, Summer. Applicants do not need a minimum number of credits to apply. For fall 2009: Transfer applications received: 2,436. Transfer applicants offered admission: 540. Transfer applicants enrolled: 310. **International students:** Number of foreign undergraduates: 624 (6% of student body). Number of countries represented: 89. Minimum TOEFL score required: 550 (paper); 213 (computer).

Howard University

- **Address:** 2400 Sixth Street NW, Washington, DC 20059
- **Website:** http://www.howard.edu
- **Private**
- **Enrollment:** 6,791 full-time; 385 part-time

KEY STATS

✔ **U.S News College Ranking:** 104, National Universities
✔ **SAT Score (25th/75th percentile):** 900-1320
✔ **Tuition:** 2010-2011: $17,905

Selectivity: Selective	**Room/board:** $7,966
Acceptance rate: 54%	**Average debt:** $12,000
Student/faculty ratio: 11/1	**Proportion who borrowed:** 81%

UNDERGRADUATE STUDENT BODY STATS

2009-2010 enrollment: 6,791 full-time; 385 part-time. Men: 32%; women: 68%. **Ethnic makeup:** African American: 47%; White: 49%; International: 3%.

ADMISSIONS FACTS AND FIGURES

Phone: (202) 806-2700. **Email:** admission@howard.edu. **Website:** http://www.howard.edu. **Application deadlines for fall 2011:** Regular decision: February 15. Early decision: Send application by: November 1; Decision sent by: December 24. Early action: Send application by: November 1; Decision sent by: N/A. Admission can be deferred. **Application fee:** $45. **To apply online, go to:** http://www.howard.edu/enrollment/apply/default.htm. **Admissions requirements/recommendations:** High school units required (recommended): English: 4 (4); Mathematics: 2 (3); Science: 2 (4); Foreign language: 2 (2); Social studies: 2 (2); History: 2 (2); Total units: 14 (21). Tests: The college uses SAT or ACT scores in admissions decisions. Either SAT or ACT required. For admission to the fall 2011 entering class, the school will accept: ACT with writing required. Campus visit: Recommended. Admissions interview: Neither required nor recommended. Off-campus interview: Not available. **Factors that count in admissions decisions:** *Academic:* Secondary school record: Very Important. Class rank: Very Important. Letters of recommendation: Important. Standardized test scores: Very Important. Essay: Considered. *Nonacademic:* Interview: Not Considered. Extracurricular activities: Considered. Talent/ability:

Considered. Character/personal qualities: Important. Alumni/ae relationship: Considered. Geographical residence: Not Considered. State residency: Not Considered. Religious affiliation/commitment: Not Considered. Minority status: Not Considered. Volunteer work: Considered. Work experience: Considered. **Other schools with the greatest overlap in applicants:** Hampton University; Morehouse College; Spelman College; University of Maryland–College Park. **Admissions statistics for the fall 2009 entering class:** Total applicants: 9,209. Total accepted: 4,976. Freshmen enrolled: 1,598; Accepted through early-decision or early-action plans: 34%. Overall acceptance rate: 54%. Early-decision acceptance rate: 72%. Non-early acceptance rate: 49%. **Credentials of fall 2009 freshmen:** 24% ranked in the top 10 percent of their high school class; 52% were in the top 25 percent; 84% were in the top half. (Proportion submitting class standing: 49%.) **Average high school grade point average:** 3.2. **First-year students who submitted SAT scores:** 82%. Scores (25/75 percentile): Critical Reading: 460-660, Math: 440-660, Combined: 900-1320. **First-year students submitting ACT scores:** 40%. Scores (25/75 percentile): English: 17-30, Math: 18-29, Composite: 19-29.

ACADEMICS

Year founded: 1867. **Academic calendar:** Semester. **Degrees offered:** certificate, bachelor's, master's, post-master's certificate, doctorate. **Most popular majors:** 8% biology, 7% journalism, 6% political science and government, 6% psychology, 5% radio, television, and digital communication. **Major fields of study:** architecture and related services; area, ethnic, cultural, and gender studies; biological and biomedical sciences; business, management, marketing, and related support services; communication, journalism, and related programs; education; engineering; English language and literature/letters; family and consumer sciences/human sciences; foreign languages, literatures, and linguistics; health professions and related clinical sciences; history; mathematics and statistics; multi/interdisciplinary studies; parks, recreation, leisure, and fitness studies; philosophy and religious studies; physical sciences; psychology; security and protective services; social sciences; visual and performing arts. **Areas of required coursework:** arts/fine arts, humanities, computer literacy, mathematics, English (including composition), philosophy, foreign languages, sciences (biological or physical), history, social science, other. **Pre-professional programs:** pre-law, pre-dentistry, pre-medicine, pre-veterinary science, pre-optometry, pre-pharmacy, other. **Special academic programs (% participation):** accelerated program (3%), cooperative (work-study plan) program (10%), cross-registration (2%), distance learning (2%), double major (4%), dual enrollment (.1%), exchange student program (domestic) (19%), honors program (10%), independent study (10%), internships (23%), liberal arts/career combination (15%), student-designed major (3%), study abroad (12%), teacher certificate program (5%), other (1%). **Teacher certification offered in:** early childhood, special education, elementary, middle/junior high, secondary. **Cooperative education programs:** business, computer science, engineering, other. **Reserve Officers Training Corps (ROTC):** Army ROTC: Offered on campus; Air Force ROTC: Offered on campus. **Faculty and instruction (2009-2010):** Total instructional faculty: 960 full-time, 316 part-time (57% men; 43% women; 84% minorities). Full-time faculty with Ph.D. or other terminal degree: 91%. Student/faculty ratio: 11/1. Classes of fewer than 20 students: 63%; of 20 to 49 students: 33%; of 50 or more students: 4%. **Advanced Placement and International Baccalaureate credit:** AP tests may be used for: Placement only. Scores accepted: 3, 4, 5. International Baccalaureate exams may be used for: Placement only. **Freshmen returning for sophomore year:** 86%. **Graduation rates:** Four-year: 47%; five-year: 62%; six-year: 62%. **Graduate study:** 21% of students pursue further study immediately upon graduation; 60% within one year; 70% within five years. Fields in which graduates pursue further study: Master of Business Administration (MBA), 1%; law, 1%; medicine, 10%; dentistry, 6%; engineering, 17%; theology (or the seminary), 1%; education, 10%; arts and sciences, 12%.

COSTS AND FINANCIAL AID

Financial aid office: (202) 806-2762. **Expenses (2010-2011):** Tuition and fees 2010-2011: $17,905; room/board: $7,966. Estimated books and supplies: $2,240; transportation: $1,994; personal expenses: $1,085. **Financial aid:** Priority filing date for institution's financial aid form: February 15; deadline: August 15. In 2009-2010, 94% of undergraduates applied for financial aid. Of those, 95% were determined to have financial need; 17% had their need fully met. Average financial aid package (proportion receiving): $11,133 (81%). Average amount of gift aid, such as scholarships or grants (proportion receiving): $3,356 (43%). Average amount of self-help aid, such as work study or loans (proportion receiving): $2,249 (67%). Average need-based loan (excluding PLUS or other private loans): $2,249. Among students who received need-based aid, the average percentage of need met: 81%. Among students who received aid based on merit, the average award (and the proportion receiving): $4,927 (4%). The average athletic scholarship (and the proportion receiving): $4,955 (5%). Average amount of debt of borrowers graduating in 2009: $12,000. Proportion who borrowed: 81%.

CAMPUS LIFE AND EXTRACURRICULAR ACTIVITIES
Campus housing available (% using): coed dorms (10%), women's dorms (16%), men's dorms (14%), apartments for married students (3%), apartment for single students (15%), other housing options (42%). **Student employment:** During the 2009-2010 academic year, 13% of undergraduates worked on campus. Average per-year earnings: $10,000. **Clubs and organizations:** Number of student organizations: 225. Activities include: campus ministries, choral groups, concert band, dance, drama/theater, international student organization, jazz band, literary magazine, marching band, music ensembles, musical theater, opera, pep band, radio station, student government, student newspaper, student film society, television station, yearbook. Number of fraternities: 10; sororities: 8. Average proportion of students who stay on campus on weekends: 40%. **Sports program (2009-2010):** Member of NCAA I. *Men's intercollegiate varsity sports:* basketball, cross country, football, soccer, swimming, tennis, track and field (indoor), track and field (outdoor). *Women's intercollegiate varsity sports:* basketball, crew (heavyweight), cross country, lacrosse, soccer, softball, swimming, tennis, track and field (indoor), track and field (outdoor), volleyball.

SERVICES AND FACILITIES
Basic services: nonremedial tutoring, women's center, placement service, health service, health insurance. **Remedial assistance:** reading, math, writing, study skills. **Counseling services:** minority student, career, personal, veteran student, academic, older student, psychological, birth control, religious. **For learning-disabled students:** School does not offer a structured program with separate admission and additional fees. Total undergraduates in learning-disabled program or receiving services: 7. Services include: remedial math, reading machines, remedial reading, tape recorders, diagnostic testing service, oral tests, learning center, extended time for tests, tutors, priority seating, substitution of courses, texts on tape, exams on tape or computer, other testing accommodations. **Library:** Number of titles: 2,455,985; number of current serial subscriptions: 26,382. **Information technology resources:** Students are not required to lease or own a computer. Number of campus computers available to all students: 4,010. School has a wireless network. Approximate number of users that can be accommodated: 5,000. Proportion of college-owned housing units wired for high-speed internet access: 100%. **Campus safety:** Security services offered: 24-hour foot-and-vehicle patrols, late-night transport/escort service, 24-hour emergency telephones, lighted pathways/sidewalks, student patrols, controlled dormitory access (key, security card, etc).

TRANSFER AND INTERNATIONAL STUDENTS
Transfer students: May apply for admission for the following academic terms: Fall, Spring, Summer. Applicants need a minimum number of credits to apply. For fall 2009: Transfer applications received: 1,430. Transfer applicants offered admission: 748. Transfer applicants enrolled: 399. **International students:** Number of foreign undergraduates: 229 (3% of student body). Number of countries represented: 86. Minimum TOEFL score required: 550 (paper); 213 (computer). Average TOEFL score: 550 (paper).

Trinity University

■ **Address:** 125 Michigan Avenue NE, Washington, DC 20017
■ **Website:** http://www.trinitydc.edu
■ **Private; Religious affiliation:** Roman Catholic
■ **Enrollment:** N/A

KEY STATS
✔ **U.S News College Ranking:** second tier, Regional Universities (North)
✔ **SAT or ACT Score (25th/75th percentile):** N/A
✔ **Tuition:** 2009-2010: $20,159

Selectivity: Less selective	**Room/board:** $8,850
Acceptance rate: N/A	**Average debt:** N/A
Student/faculty ratio: N/A	**Proportion who borrowed:** N/A

University of the District of Columbia

■ **Address:** 4200 Connecticut Avenue NW, Washington, DC 20008
■ **Website:** http://www.udc.edu/
■ **Public**
■ **Enrollment:** 2,182 full-time; 2,588 part-time

KEY STATS
✔ **U.S News College Ranking:** Unranked, Regional Universities (North)
✔ **SAT or ACT Score (25th/75th percentile):** N/A
✔ **Tuition:** 2010-2011: $7,000 in state, $14,000 out of state

Selectivity: N/A	**Room/board:** $0
Acceptance rate: 68%	**Average debt:** N/A
Student/faculty ratio: N/A	**Proportion who borrowed:** N/A

UNDERGRADUATE STUDENT BODY STATS
2009-2010 enrollment: 2,182 full-time; 2,588 part-time. Men: 38%; women: 62%. **Ethnic makeup:** African American: 74%; Asian American: 3%; Hispanic: 6%; White: 17%.

ADMISSIONS FACTS AND FIGURES
Phone: (202) 274-5010. **Website:** http://www.udc.edu/. **Application deadlines for fall 2011:** Regular decision: June 15. Early decision: Send application by: N/A; Decision sent by: N/A. Early action: Not offered. Admission can be deferred. **Application fee:** $75. **To apply online, go to:** http://www.udc.edu/admission/93069_UndergradApp.pdf. **Admissions requirements/recommendations:** High school units required (recommended): English: 4 (0); Mathematics: 2 (0); Science: 2 (0); Foreign language: 2 (0); Social studies: 0 (0); History: 0 (0); Academic electives: 0 (0); Total units: 14 (0). Tests: The college does not use SAT or ACT scores in admissions decisions. Neither SAT nor ACT required. Campus visit: Recommended. Admissions interview: Neither required nor recommended. Off-campus interview: Not available. **Factors that count in admissions decisions:** *Academic:* Secondary school record: Very Important. Class rank: Not Considered. Letters of recommendation: Not Considered. Standardized test scores: Considered. Essay: Not Considered. *Nonacademic:* Interview: Not Considered. Extracurricular activities: Not Considered. Talent/ability: Considered. Character/personal qualities: Not Considered. Geographical residence: Not Considered. State residency: Not Considered. Religious affiliation/commitment: Not Considered. Minority status: Not Considered. Volunteer work: Not Considered. Work experience: Not Considered. **Admissions statistics for the fall 2009 entering class:** Total applicants: 4,279. Total accepted: 2,913. Freshmen enrolled: 940; 6% were from out of state. Overall acceptance rate: 68%. Non-early acceptance rate: 68%. **Size of waiting list:** 1348 applicants; enrolled from waiting list: 1340.

ACADEMICS
Year founded: 1976. **Academic calendar:** Semester. **Degrees offered:** certificate, associate, bachelor's, master's. **Major fields of study:** architecture and related services; biological and biomedical sciences; business, management, marketing, and related support services; computer and information sciences and support services; construction trades; education; engineering; engineering technologies/technicians; English language and literature/letters; family and consumer sciences/human sciences; foreign languages, literatures, and linguistics; health professions and related clinical sciences; history; mathematics and statistics; natural resources and conservation; parks, recreation, leisure, and fitness studies; physical sciences; psychology; public administration and social service professions; security and protective services; social sciences; transportation and materials moving; visual and performing arts. **Areas of required coursework:** computer literacy, mathematics, English (including composition), foreign languages, sciences (biological or physical), social science. **Special academic programs (% participation):** cooperative (work-study plan) program (29%), English as a Second Language (ESL) (28%), honors program (16%), independent study (26%), internships (27%), teacher certificate program (15%). **Teacher certification offered in:** early childhood, special education, elementary, middle/junior high, adult education, secondary. **Cooperative education programs:** computer science, health professions, vocational arts, other. **Reserve Officers Training Corps (ROTC):** Army ROTC: Offered at cooperating institution (Howard University); Navy ROTC: Offered at cooperating institution (Howard University); Air Force ROTC: Offered at cooperating institution (Howard University). **Freshmen returning for sophomore year:** 55%. **Graduation rates:** Six-year: 15%.

COSTS AND FINANCIAL AID

Financial aid office: (202) 274-5060. **Expenses (2010-2011):** Tuition and fees 2010-2011: $7,000 in state, $14,000 out of state; room/board: $0. Estimated books and supplies: $1,400; transportation: $1,500; personal expenses: $1,900. **Financial aid:** Priority filing date for institution's financial aid form: April 15; deadline: June 30.

CAMPUS LIFE AND EXTRACURRICULAR ACTIVITIES

Students who live in college-owned, operated, or affiliated housing: 0%. **Student employment:** During the 2009-2010 academic year, 3% of undergraduates worked on campus. Average per-year earnings: $4,000. **Clubs and organizations:** Number of student organizations: 54. Activities include: choral groups, concert band, dance, drama/theater, jazz band, music ensembles, musical theater, opera, pep band, student government, student newspaper, symphony orchestra, television station, yearbook. Number of fraternities: 4; sororities: 3. Proportion of men in fraternities: 3%; of women in sororities: 7%. Average proportion of students who stay on campus on weekends: 15%. **Sports program (2009-2010):** Member of NCAA II. *Men's intercollegiate varsity sports:* basketball, cross country, soccer, track and field (outdoor). *Women's intercollegiate varsity sports:* basketball, cross country, soccer, track and field (outdoor).

SERVICES AND FACILITIES

Basic services: nonremedial tutoring, placement service, day care, health service, health insurance. **Remedial assistance:** reading, math, writing, study skills, other. **Counseling services:** minority student, career, military, personal, veteran student, academic, older student, psychological. **For learning-disabled students:** School does not offer a structured program with separate admission and additional fees. Services include: remedial math, remedial English, reading machines, remedial reading, tape recorders, other special classes, diagnostic testing service, untimed tests, note-taking services, oral tests, learning center, readers, extended time for tests, tutors, other. **Information technology resources:** Students are not required to lease or own a computer. Number of campus computers available to all students: 265. School does not have a wireless network. **Campus safety:** Security services offered: 24-hour foot-and-vehicle patrols, late-night transport/escort service, 24-hour emergency telephones, lighted pathways/sidewalks.

TRANSFER AND INTERNATIONAL STUDENTS

Transfer students: May apply for admission for the following academic terms: Fall, Spring, Summer. Applicants need a minimum number of credits to apply. **International students:** Number of foreign undergraduates: 0. Minimum TOEFL score required: 500 (paper); 213 (computer).

Florida

- **Address:** 11300 N.E. Second Avenue, Miami Shores, FL 33161-6695
- **Website:** http://www.barry.edu
- **Private; Religious affiliation:** Roman Catholic
- **Enrollment:** 4,156 full-time; 942 part-time

KEY STATS

✔ **U.S News College Ranking:** second tier, National Universities
✔ **SAT Score (25th/75th percentile):** 830-990
✔ **Tuition:** 2010-2011: $27,200

Selectivity: Less selective	**Room/board:** $9,426
Acceptance rate: 62%	**Average debt:** $35,880
Student/faculty ratio: 18/1	**Proportion who borrowed:** 66%

UNDERGRADUATE STUDENT BODY STATS

2009-2010 enrollment: 4,156 full-time; 942 part-time. Men: 31%; women: 69%. **Ethnic makeup:** African American: 20%; Asian American: 1%; Hispanic: 25%; White: 48%; International: 5%.

ADMISSIONS FACTS AND FIGURES

Phone: (305) 899-3100. **Email:** admissions@mail.barry.edu. **Website:** http://www.barry.edu. **Application deadlines for fall 2011:** Regular decision: Rolling. Early decision: Not offered. Early action: Not offered. Admission can be deferred. **Application fee:** $30. **To apply online, go to:** http://www.barry.edu/undergrad-apply. **Admissions requirements/recommendations:** High school units required (recommended): English: (4); Mathematics: (3); Science: (3); Social studies: (3); Total units: (12). Tests: The college uses SAT or ACT scores in admissions decisions. Either SAT or ACT required. For admission to the fall 2011 entering class, the school will accept: ACT with or without writing accepted. Campus visit: Recommended. Admissions interview: Recommended. **Factors that count in admissions decisions:** *Academic:* Secondary school record: Considered. Class rank: Considered. Letters of recommendation: Considered. Standardized test scores: Very Important. Essay: Considered. *Nonacademic:* Interview: Important. Extracurricular activities: Considered. Talent/ability: Important. Character/personal qualities: Important. Alumni/ae relationship: Not Considered. Geographical residence: Not Considered. State residency: Not Considered. Religious affiliation/commitment: Not Considered. Minority status: Not Considered. Volunteer work: Considered. Work experience: Considered. **Other schools with the greatest overlap in applicants:** Florida International University; Florida State University; University of Central Florida; University of Florida; University of Miami. **Admissions statistics for the fall 2009 entering class:** Total applicants: 4,327. Total accepted: 2,695. Freshmen enrolled: 648; Overall acceptance rate: 62%. **First-year students who submitted SAT scores:** 75%. Scores (25/75 percentile): Critical Reading: 420-500, Math: 410-490, Combined: 830-990. **First-year students submitting ACT scores:** 46%. Scores (25/75 percentile): English: 16-21, Math: 16-20, Composite: 18-21.

ACADEMICS

Year founded: 1940. **Academic calendar:** Semester. **Degrees offered:** certificate, bachelor's, post-bachelor's certificate, master's, post-master's certificate, doctorate. **Major fields of study:** biological and biomedical sciences; business, management, marketing, and related support services; communication, journalism, and related programs; computer and information sciences and support services; education; English language and literature/letters; foreign languages, literatures, and linguistics; health professions and related clinical sciences; history; legal professions and studies; liberal arts and sciences studies, and humanities; mathematics and statistics; natural resources and conservation; parks, recreation, leisure, and fitness studies; philosophy and religious studies; physical sciences; psychology; public administration and social service professions; security and protective services; social sciences; theology and religious vocations; visual and performing arts. **Areas of required coursework:** arts/fine arts, humanities, computer literacy, mathematics, English (including composition), philosophy, sciences (biological or physical), social science, other. **Pre-professional

programs: pre-law, pre-dentistry, pre-medicine, pre-veterinary science, pre-pharmacy. **Special academic programs:** accelerated program, double major, English as a Second Language (ESL), honors program, internships, study abroad, teacher certificate program. **Teacher certification offered in:** early childhood, elementary, middle/junior high, secondary. **Reserve Officers Training Corps (ROTC):** Army ROTC: Offered at cooperating institution (Acadia University); Air Force ROTC: Offered at cooperating institution. **Faculty and instruction (2009-2010):** Total instructional faculty: 341 full-time, 539 part-time (50% men; 50% women; 29% minorities). Student/faculty ratio: 18/1. **Freshmen returning for sophomore year:** 63%. **Graduation rates:** Six-year: 38%.

COSTS AND FINANCIAL AID

Financial aid office: (800) 899-3673. **Expenses (2010-2011):** Tuition and fees 2010-2011: $27,200; room/board: $9,426. **Financial aid:** Priority filing date for institution's financial aid form: March 15. In 2009-2010, 85% of undergraduates applied for financial aid. Of those, 82% were determined to have financial need; 4% had their need fully met. Average financial aid package (proportion receiving): $18,528 (81%). Average amount of gift aid, such as scholarships or grants (proportion receiving): $6,975 (58%). Average amount of self-help aid, such as work study or loans (proportion receiving): $7,537 (76%). Average need-based loan (excluding PLUS or other private loans): $5,332. Among students who received need-based aid, the average percentage of need met: 52%. Among students who received aid based on merit, the average award (and the proportion receiving): $6,871 (10%). The average athletic scholarship (and the proportion receiving): $16,328 (4%). Average amount of debt of borrowers graduating in 2009: $35,880. Proportion who borrowed: 66%.

CAMPUS LIFE AND EXTRACURRICULAR ACTIVITIES

Campus housing available: coed dorms, women's dorms, men's dorms, special housing for disabled students. **Clubs and organizations:** Number of student organizations: 45. Activities include: choral groups, dance, drama/theater, literary magazine, music ensembles, musical theater, radio station, student government, student newspaper, television station. Number of fraternities: 4; sororities: 4. Average proportion of students who stay on campus on weekends: 75%. **Sports program (2009-2010):** Member of NCAA II. *Men's intercollegiate varsity sports:* baseball, golf, soccer, tennis. *Women's intercollegiate varsity sports:* basketball, golf, soccer, softball, tennis, volleyball.

SERVICES AND FACILITIES

Basic services: health service, health insurance. **Remedial assistance:** reading, math, writing, study skills. **Counseling services:** career, personal, academic. **For learning-disabled students:** School does not offer a structured program with separate admission and additional fees. Services include: remedial math, remedial English, reading machines, remedial reading, tape recorders, other special classes, untimed tests, note-taking services, oral tests, learning center, readers, extended time for tests, tutors, texts on tape, other. **Library:** Number of titles: 316,517; number of current serial subscriptions: 28,119. **Information technology resources:** Students are not required to lease or own a computer. Number of campus computers available to all students: 368. School has a wireless network. Proportion of college-owned housing units wired for high-speed internet access: 100%. **Campus safety:** Security services offered: 24-hour foot-and-vehicle patrols, late-night transport/escort service, 24-hour emergency telephones, lighted pathways/sidewalks, controlled dormitory access (key, security card, etc).

TRANSFER AND INTERNATIONAL STUDENTS

Transfer students: May apply for admission for the following academic terms: Fall, Winter, Spring, Summer. Applicants need a minimum number of credits to apply. **International students:** Number of foreign undergraduates: 274 (5% of student body). Minimum TOEFL score required: 550 (paper); 213 (computer).

Beacon College

- **Address:** 105 E. Main Street, Leesburg, FL 34748
- **Website:** http://www.beaconcollege.edu/
- **Private**
- **Enrollment:** 128 full-time

KEY STATS

✔ **U.S News College Ranking:** Unranked, National Liberal Arts Colleges
✔ **SAT or ACT Score (25th/75th percentile):** N/A
✔ **Tuition:** 2010-2011: $28,410

Selectivity: N/A	**Room/board:** $8,150
Acceptance rate: 92%	**Average debt:** $35,000
Student/faculty ratio: N/A	**Proportion who borrowed:** 12%

UNDERGRADUATE STUDENT BODY STATS

2009-2010 enrollment: 128 full-time. Men: 63%; women: 38%. **Ethnic makeup:** African American: 9%; Asian American: 2%; Hispanic: 3%; White: 86%.

ADMISSIONS FACTS AND FIGURES

Phone: (706) 323-5364. **Email:** admissions@beaconcollege.edu. **Website:** http://www.beaconcollege.edu/. **Application deadlines for fall 2011:** Regular decision: Rolling. Early decision: Not offered. Early action: Not offered. Admission can be deferred. **Application fee:** $50. **Admissions requirements/recommendations:** High school units required (recommended): English: 4; Mathematics: 3; Science: 3; Foreign language: 0; Social studies: 1; History: 3; Academic electives: 9; Total units: 25 (2). Tests: The college does not use SAT or ACT scores in admissions decisions. Neither SAT nor ACT required. Campus visit: Recommended. Admissions interview: Required. Off-campus interview: Not available. **Factors that count in admissions decisions:** *Academic:* Secondary school record: Important. Class rank: Considered. Letters of recommendation: Very Important. Standardized test scores: Important. Essay: Important. *Nonacademic:* Interview: Very Important. Extracurricular activities: Important. Talent/ability: Important. Character/personal qualities: Very Important. Alumni/ae relationship: Considered. Geographical residence: Not Considered. State residency: Not Considered. Religious affiliation/commitment: Not Considered. Minority status: Not Considered. Volunteer work: Important. Work experience: Important. **Admissions statistics for the fall 2009 entering class:** Total applicants: 53. Total accepted: 49. Freshmen enrolled: 28; Overall acceptance rate: 92%. **Size of waiting list:** 0 applicants; enrolled from waiting list: 0.

ACADEMICS

Year founded: 1989. **Academic calendar:** Semester. **Degrees offered:** associate, bachelor's. **Most popular majors:** 41% liberal arts and sciences/liberal studies, 38% human services, 21% computer and information sciences. **Major fields of study:** computer and information sciences and support services; liberal arts and sciences studies, and humanities; public administration and social service professions. **Areas of required coursework:** arts/fine arts, humanities, computer literacy, mathematics, English (including composition), sciences (biological or physical), history, social science, other. **Special academic programs:** independent study. **Faculty and instruction (2009-2010):** Total instructional faculty: N/A. **Freshmen returning for sophomore year:** 85%. **Graduation rates:** Four-year: 50%; five-year: 50%; six-year: 64%. **Graduate study:** 20% of students pursue further study within one year; 20% within five years. Fields in which graduates pursue further study: Master of Business Administration (MBA), 10%; education, 35%.

COSTS AND FINANCIAL AID

Financial aid office: (352) 787-7660. **Expenses (2010-2011):** Tuition and fees 2010-2011: $28,410; room/board: $8,150. Estimated books and supplies: $600; transportation: $400; personal expenses: $500. **Financial aid:** In 2009-2010, 67% of undergraduates applied for financial aid. Of those, 67% were determined to have financial need; Average financial aid package (proportion receiving): $30,000 (67%). Average amount of gift aid, such as scholarships or grants (proportion receiving): $20,000 (67%). Average amount of self-help aid, such as work study or loans (proportion receiving): $5,500 (67%). Average need-based loan (excluding PLUS or other private loans): $5,500. Among students who received need-based aid, the average percentage of need met: 80%. Among students who received aid based on merit, the average award (and the proportion receiving): $0 (0%). The average athletic scholarship (and the proportion receiving): $0 (0%). Average

amount of debt of borrowers graduating in 2009: $35,000. Proportion who borrowed: 12%.

CAMPUS LIFE AND EXTRACURRICULAR ACTIVITIES

Campus housing available (% using): apartment for single students (94%), special housing for disabled students (1%), other housing options (5%). Activities include: dance, literary magazine, music ensembles, student government, student newspaper, student film society, yearbook. Number of fraternities: 2; sororities: 2.

SERVICES AND FACILITIES

Basic services: nonremedial tutoring, placement service. **Remedial assistance:** reading, math, writing, study skills. **Counseling services:** career, personal, academic, psychological, birth control. **For learning-disabled students:** School does not offer a structured program with separate admission and additional fees. Services include: remedial math, remedial English, reading machines, remedial reading, other special classes, diagnostic testing service, untimed tests, note-taking services, oral tests, learning center, readers, extended time for tests, tutors, early syllabus, priority seating, texts on tape, typist/scribe, exams on tape or computer, other testing accommodations. **Library:** Number of titles: 22,670; number of current serial subscriptions: 120. **Information technology resources:** Students are not required to lease or own a computer. Number of campus computers available to all students: 46. School has a wireless network. Proportion of college-owned housing units wired for high-speed internet access: 100%. **Campus safety:** Security services offered: late-night transport/escort service, lighted pathways/sidewalks, student patrols, controlled dormitory access (key, security card, etc).

TRANSFER AND INTERNATIONAL STUDENTS

Transfer students: May apply for admission for the following academic terms: Fall, Spring. Applicants do not need a minimum number of credits to apply. **International students:** Number of foreign undergraduates: 0.

Bethune-Cookman University

- **Address:** 640 Dr. Mary McLeod Bethune Boulevard, Daytona Beach, FL 32114
- **Website:** http://www.bethune.cookman.edu
- **Private; Religious affiliation:** Methodist
- **Enrollment:** 3,450 full-time; 144 part-time

KEY STATS

✔ **U.S News College Ranking:** 55, Regional Colleges (South)
✔ **SAT Score (25th/75th percentile):** 770-930
✔ **Tuition:** 2010-2011: $13,452

Selectivity: Less selective	**Room/board:** $7,980
Acceptance rate: 69%	**Average debt:** $27,103
Student/faculty ratio: 17/1	**Proportion who borrowed:** 96%

UNDERGRADUATE STUDENT BODY STATS

2009-2010 enrollment: 3,450 full-time; 144 part-time. Men: 40%; women: 60%. **Ethnic makeup:** African American: 93%; Hispanic: 2%; White: 2%; International: 3%. **Religious preference:** Roman Catholic: 4%; Protestant: 60%; No preference: 19%; Unknown: 7%; Methodist: 8%; Other: 2%.

ADMISSIONS FACTS AND FIGURES

Phone: (800) 448-0228. **Email:** admissions@cookman.edu. **Website:** http://www.bethune.cookman.edu. **Application deadlines for fall 2011:** Regular decision: Rolling. Early decision: Not offered. Early action: Not offered. Admission can be deferred. **Application fee:** $25. **To apply online, go to:** http://www.bethune.cookman.edu/admissions/apply.html. **Admissions requirements/recommendations:** High school units required (recommended): English: 4; Mathematics: 3; Science: 3; Foreign language: (2); Social studies: 1; History: 2; Academic electives: 6; Total units: 19 (3). Tests: The college uses SAT or ACT scores in admissions decisions. Either SAT or ACT required. For admission to the fall 2011 entering class, the school will accept: ACT with or without writing accepted. Campus visit: Neither required nor recommended. Admissions interview: Neither required nor recommended. Off-campus interview: May be arranged. **Factors that count in admissions decisions:** *Academic:* Secondary school record: Very Important. Class rank: Considered. Letters of recommendation: Important. Standardized test scores: Very Important. Essay: Considered. *Nonacademic:* Interview: Considered. Extracurricular activities: Considered. Talent/ability:

Considered. Character/personal qualities: Important. Alumni/ae relationship: Considered. Geographical residence: Not Considered. State residency: Not Considered. Religious affiliation/commitment: Not Considered. Minority status: Not Considered. Volunteer work: Considered. Work experience: Considered. **Other schools with the greatest overlap in applicants:** Florida A&M University; Savannah State University; South Carolina State University; University of Central Florida; University of Florida. **Admissions statistics for the fall 2009 entering class:** Total applicants: 5,188. Total accepted: 3,587. Freshmen enrolled: 2,047; 0% were from out of state. Overall acceptance rate: 69%. **Credentials of fall 2009 freshmen:** 5% ranked in the top 10 percent of their high school class; 15% were in the top 25 percent; 52% were in the top half. (Proportion submitting class standing: 93%.) **Average high school grade point average:** 2.9. **First-year students who submitted SAT scores:** 92%. Scores (25/75 percentile): Critical Reading: 390-470, Math: 380-460, Combined: 770-930. **First-year students submitting ACT scores:** 85%. Scores (25/75 percentile): English: 16-19, Math: 16-19, Composite: 16-19.

ACADEMICS

Year founded: 1904. **Academic calendar:** Semester. **Degrees offered:** bachelor's, master's. **Most popular majors:** 14% business administration and management, 13% corrections and criminal justice, 8% psychology, 6% sociology, 5% elementary education and teaching. **Major fields of study:** biological and biomedical sciences; business, management, marketing, and related support services; communication, journalism, and related programs; computer and information sciences and support services; education; engineering; English language and literature/letters; health professions and related clinical sciences; history; liberal arts and sciences studies, and humanities; mathematics and statistics; multi/interdisciplinary studies; philosophy and religious studies; physical sciences; psychology; security and protective services; social sciences; visual and performing arts. **Areas of required coursework:** arts/fine arts, humanities, computer literacy, mathematics, English (including composition), philosophy, foreign languages, sciences (biological or physical), history, social science, other. **Pre-professional programs:** pre-medicine. **Special academic programs (% participation):** cooperative (work-study plan) program (15%), distance learning (1%), double major (0%), honors program (1%), internships (5%), study abroad (1%), weekend college (2%). **Teacher certification offered in:** special education, elementary, middle/junior high, secondary. **Cooperative education programs:** business, computer science, education, engineering, health professions, humanities, natural science, social/behavioral science. **Reserve Officers Training Corps (ROTC):** Army ROTC: Offered at cooperating institution (Embry-Riddle Aeronautical University); Air Force ROTC: Offered at cooperating institution (Embry-Riddle Aeronautical University). **Faculty and instruction (2009-2010):** Total instructional faculty: 210 full-time, 28 part-time (49% men; 51% women; 58% minorities). Full-time faculty with Ph.D. or other terminal degree: 48%. Student/faculty ratio: 17/1. Classes of fewer than 20 students: 47%; of 20 to 49 students: 52%; of 50 or more students: 1%. **Advanced Placement and International Baccalaureate credit:** AP tests may be used for: Credit only. Scores accepted: 3. International Baccalaureate exams may be used for: Credit only. **Freshmen returning for sophomore year:** 69%. **Graduation rates:** Four-year: 16%; five-year: 30%; six-year: 37%. **Graduate study:** 12% of students pursue further study immediately upon graduation; 30% within one year; 35% within five years. Fields in which graduates pursue further study: Master of Business Administration (MBA), 12%; law, 1%; medicine, 1%; dentistry, 1%; engineering, 2%; theology (or the seminary), 1%; education, 9%; arts and sciences, 4%.

COSTS AND FINANCIAL AID

Financial aid office: (386) 481-2620. **Expenses (2010-2011):** Tuition and fees 2010-2011: $13,452; room/board: $7,980. Estimated books and supplies: $900; transportation: $900; personal expenses: $3,000. **Financial aid:** Priority filing date for institution's financial aid form: April 1; deadline: June 30. In 2009-2010, 98% of undergraduates applied for financial aid. Of those, 94% were determined to have financial need; 6% had their need fully met. Average financial aid package (proportion receiving): $13,046 (94%). Average amount of gift aid, such as scholarships or grants (proportion receiving): $9,245 (90%). Average amount of self-help aid, such as work study or loans (proportion receiving): $4,660 (85%). Average need-based loan (excluding PLUS or other private loans): $4,659. Among students who received need-based aid, the average percentage of need met: 52%. Among students who received aid based on merit, the average award (and the proportion receiving): $8,636 (3%). The average athletic scholarship (and the proportion receiving): $11,244 (2%). Average amount of debt of borrowers graduating in 2009: $27,103. Proportion who borrowed: 96%.

CAMPUS LIFE AND EXTRACURRICULAR ACTIVITIES

Campus housing available (% using): women's dorms (56%), men's dorms (42%), other housing options (2%). Students who live in college-owned, operated, or affiliated housing: 25%. **Student employment:** During the 2009-2010 academic year, 10% of undergraduates worked on campus. Average per-year earnings: $2,300. **Clubs and organizations:** Number of student organizations: 60. Activities include: choral groups, concert band, drama/theater, jazz band, marching band, model UN, music ensembles, radio station, student government, student newspaper, television station, yearbook. Number of fraternities: 5; sororities: 4. Proportion of men in fraternities: 8%; of women in sororities: 4%. Average proportion of students who stay on campus on weekends: 80%. **Sports program (2009-2010):** Member of NCAA I. *Men's intercollegiate varsity sports:* baseball, basketball, cross country, football, golf, tennis, track and field (indoor), track and field (outdoor). *Women's intercollegiate varsity sports:* basketball, bowling, cross country, golf, softball, tennis, track and field (indoor), track and field (outdoor), volleyball.

SERVICES AND FACILITIES

Basic services: nonremedial tutoring, placement service, health service, health insurance. **Remedial assistance:** reading, math, writing, study skills. **Counseling services:** minority student, career, military, personal, veteran student, academic, older student, psychological, birth control, religious. **For learning-disabled students:** School does not offer a structured program with separate admission and additional fees. Total undergraduates in learning-disabled program or receiving services: 49. Services include: remedial math, remedial English, remedial reading, tape recorders, untimed tests, note-taking services, oral tests, learning center, readers, extended time for tests, tutors, priority registration, priority seating, texts on tape, other testing accommodations. **Library:** Number of titles: 126,631; number of current serial subscriptions: 138. **Information technology resources:** Students are not required to lease or own a computer. Number of campus computers available to all students: 512. School has a wireless network. Approximate number of users that can be accommodated: 900. Proportion of college-owned housing units wired for high-speed internet access: 100%. **Campus safety:** Security services offered: 24-hour foot-and-vehicle patrols, late-night transport/escort service, 24-hour emergency telephones, lighted pathways/sidewalks, controlled dormitory access (key, security card, etc).

TRANSFER AND INTERNATIONAL STUDENTS

Transfer students: May apply for admission for the following academic terms: Fall, Spring, Summer. Applicants need a minimum number of credits to apply. For fall 2009: Transfer applicants enrolled: 99. **International students:** Number of foreign undergraduates: 64 (3% of student body). Minimum TOEFL score required: 550 (paper); 213 (computer). Average TOEFL score: 600 (paper).

Clearwater Christian College

- **Address:** 3400 Gulf-to-Bay Boulevard, Clearwater, FL 33759-4595
- **Website:** http://www.clearwater.edu
- **Private; Religious affiliation:** Christian nondenominational
- **Enrollment:** 555 full-time; 15 part-time

KEY STATS

✔ **U.S News College Ranking:** 42, Regional Colleges (South)
✔ **ACT Score (25th/75th percentile):** 19-25
✔ **Tuition:** 2009-2010: $14,710

Selectivity: Selective	Room/board: $6,740
Acceptance rate: 89%	Average debt: N/A
Student/faculty ratio: N/A	Proportion who borrowed: N/A

UNDERGRADUATE STUDENT BODY STATS

2009-2010 enrollment: 555 full-time; 15 part-time. Men: 51%; women: 49%. **Ethnic makeup:** African American: 4%; Asian American: 1%; Hispanic: 3%; White: 91%. **Religious preference:** Protestant: 90%; Christian nondenominational: 10%.

ADMISSIONS FACTS AND FIGURES

Phone: (800) 348-4463. **Email:** admissions@clearwater.edu. **Website:** http://www.clearwater.edu. **Application deadlines for fall 2011:** Regular decision: Rolling. Early decision: Not offered. Early action: Not offered. Admission can be deferred. **Application fee:** $35. **To apply online, go to:** https://www.

clearwater.edu/admissions/undergrad/application/signup.asp. **Admissions requirements/recommendations:** High school units required (recommended): English: (4); Mathematics: (3); Science: (3); Foreign language: (2); Social studies: (2); History: (1); Total units: (15). Tests: The college uses SAT or ACT scores in admissions decisions. Either SAT or ACT required. For admission to the fall 2011 entering class, the school will accept: ACT with or without writing accepted. Campus visit: Recommended. Admissions interview: Recommended. Off-campus interview: May be arranged. **Factors that count in admissions decisions:** *Academic:* Secondary school record: Important. Class rank: Considered. Letters of recommendation: Very Important. Standardized test scores: Very Important. Essay: Very Important. *Nonacademic:* Interview: Important. Extracurricular activities: Considered. Talent/ability: Considered. Character/personal qualities: Very Important. Alumni/ae relationship: Considered. Geographical residence: Not Considered. State residency: Not Considered. Religious affiliation/commitment: Very Important. Minority status: Not Considered. Volunteer work: Considered. Work experience: Not Considered. **Other schools with the greatest overlap in applicants:** Cedarville University; Liberty University; University of Central Florida; University of South Florida. **Admissions statistics for the fall 2009 entering class:** Total applicants: 278. Total accepted: 247. Freshmen enrolled: 157; 55% were from out of state. Overall acceptance rate: 89%. **Size of waiting list:** 0 applicants; enrolled from waiting list: 0. **Credentials of fall 2009 freshmen:** 10% ranked in the top 10 percent of their high school class; 33% were in the top 25 percent; 67% were in the top half. (Proportion submitting class standing: 25%.) **Average high school grade point average:** 3.3.

ACADEMICS

Year founded: 1966. **Academic calendar:** Semester. **Degrees offered:** certificate, associate, bachelor's, master's. **Major fields of study:** biological and biomedical sciences; business, management, marketing, and related support services; communication, journalism, and related programs; computer and information sciences and support services; education; English language and literature/letters; health professions and related clinical sciences; history; legal professions and studies; liberal arts and sciences studies, and humanities; mathematics and statistics; multi/interdisciplinary studies; parks, recreation, leisure, and fitness studies; psychology; theology and religious vocations; visual and performing arts. **Areas of required coursework:** arts/fine arts, humanities, computer literacy, mathematics, English (including composition), sciences (biological or physical), history, social science. **Preprofessional programs:** pre-law, pre-medicine. **Special academic programs (% participation):** distance learning (10%), double major (1%), dual enrollment (1%), honors program (4%), independent study (1%), internships (5%), student-designed major (4%), study abroad (5%), teacher certificate program (16%). **Teacher certification offered in:** special education, elementary, secondary. **Reserve Officers Training Corps (ROTC):** Army ROTC: Offered at cooperating institution (University of South Florida); Navy ROTC: Offered at cooperating institution (University of South Florida); Air Force ROTC: Offered at cooperating institution (University of South Florida). **Faculty and instruction (2009-2010):** Total instructional faculty: N/A. Classes of fewer than 20 students: 69%; of 20 to 49 students: 29%; of 50 or more students: 3%. **Advanced Placement and International Baccalaureate credit:** AP tests may be used for: Placement only. Scores accepted: 3, 4, 5. International Baccalaureate exams may be used for: Placement only. **Freshmen returning for sophomore year:** 66%. **Graduation rates:** Four-year: 40%; five-year: 42%; six-year: 43%. **Graduate study:** 25% of students pursue further study immediately upon graduation. Fields in which graduates pursue further study: Master of Business Administration (MBA), 25%; law, 5%; medicine, 5%; theology (or the seminary), 25%; education, 25%; arts and sciences, 15%.

COSTS AND FINANCIAL AID

Financial aid office: (727) 726-1153. **Expenses (2009-2010):** Tuition and fees 2009-2010: $14,710; room/board: $6,740. Estimated books and supplies: $1,000; transportation: $1,500; personal expenses: $2,200. **Financial aid:** Priority filing date for institution's financial aid form: March 15.

CAMPUS LIFE AND EXTRACURRICULAR ACTIVITIES

Campus housing available (% using): women's dorms (50%), men's dorms (50%). Students who live in college-owned, operated, or affiliated housing: 80%. **Student employment:** During the 2009-2010 academic year, 40% of undergraduates worked on campus. Average per-year earnings: $1,600. **Clubs and organizations:** Number of student organizations: 10. Activities include: campus ministries, choral groups, concert band, drama/theater, music ensembles, pep band, student government, student newspaper, student film society, symphony orchestra, yearbook. Number of fraternities: 6; sororities: 6. Proportion of men in fraternities: 100%; of women in

sororities: 100%. Average proportion of students who stay on campus on weekends: 30%.

SERVICES AND FACILITIES

Basic services: nonremedial tutoring, placement service, health insurance. **Remedial assistance:** reading, math, writing, study skills, other. **Counseling services:** career, personal, academic, psychological, religious. **For learning-disabled students:** School does not offer a structured program with separate admission and additional fees. Services include: remedial math, remedial English, tape recorders, videotaped classes, untimed tests, note-taking services, oral tests, readers, extended time for tests, tutors, priority registration, priority seating, substitution of courses, texts on tape, other testing accommodations, other. **Library:** Number of titles: 105,013; number of current serial subscriptions: 3,409. **Information technology resources:** Students are not required to lease or own a computer. Number of campus computers available to all students: 46. School has a wireless network. Approximate number of users that can be accommodated: 500. Proportion of college-owned housing units wired for high-speed internet access: 100%. **Campus safety:** Security services offered: 24-hour foot-and-vehicle patrols, lighted pathways/sidewalks, student patrols, controlled dormitory access (key, security card, etc).

TRANSFER AND INTERNATIONAL STUDENTS

Transfer students: May apply for admission for the following academic terms: Fall, Spring, Summer. Applicants do not need a minimum number of credits to apply. For fall 2009: Transfer applications received: 70. Transfer applicants offered admission: 68. Transfer applicants enrolled: 51. **International students:** Number of foreign undergraduates: 2. Number of countries represented: 5. Minimum TOEFL score required: 500 (paper); 173 (computer).

Eckerd College

- **Address:** 4200 54th Avenue S, St. Petersburg, FL 33711
- **Website:** http://www.eckerd.edu
- **Private; Religious affiliation:** Presbyterian
- **Enrollment:** 1,845 full-time; 18 part-time

KEY STATS

✔ **U.S News College Ranking:** 137, National Liberal Arts Colleges
✔ **SAT Score (25th/75th percentile):** 1020-1240
✔ **Tuition:** 2010-2011: $33,228

Selectivity: Selective	**Room/board:** $9,326
Acceptance rate: 72%	**Average debt:** $30,494
Student/faculty ratio: 14/1	**Proportion who borrowed:** 63%

UNDERGRADUATE STUDENT BODY STATS

2009-2010 enrollment: 1,845 full-time; 18 part-time. Men: 42%; women: 58%. **Ethnic makeup:** African American: 4%; Asian American: 2%; Hispanic: 4%; White: 87%; International: 3%. **Religious preference:** Roman Catholic: 17%; Protestant: 17%; Jewish: 7%; Hindu: 1%; Buddhist: 2%; No preference: 40%; Presbyterian: 4%; Other Christian: 8%; Other: 4%.

ADMISSIONS FACTS AND FIGURES

Phone: (727) 864-8331. **Email:** admissions@eckerd.edu. **Website:** http://www.eckerd.edu. **Application deadlines for fall 2011:** Regular decision: Rolling. Early decision: Not offered. Early action: Not offered. Admission can be deferred. **Application fee:** $35. **To apply online, go to:** http://www.eckerd.edu/admissions/index.php?f=apply. **Admissions requirements/recommendations:** High school units required (recommended): English: (4); Mathematics: (3); Science: (3); Foreign language: (2); Social studies: (2); History: (1); Academic electives: (3); Total units: (18). Tests: The college uses SAT or ACT scores in admissions decisions. Either SAT or ACT required. For admission to the fall 2011 entering class, the school will accept: ACT with or without writing accepted. Campus visit: Recommended. Admissions interview: Recommended. Off-campus interview: May be arranged. **Factors that count in admissions decisions:** *Academic:* Secondary school record: Very Important. Class rank: Considered. Letters of recommendation: Important. Standardized test scores: Important. Essay: Important. *Nonacademic:* Interview: Important. Extracurricular activities: Important. Talent/ability: Important. Character/personal qualities: Important. Alumni/ae relationship: Considered. Geographical residence: Not Considered. State residency: Not Considered. Religious affiliation/commitment: Not Considered.

Minority status: Not Considered. Volunteer work: Considered. Work experience: Considered. **Other schools with the greatest overlap in applicants:** Rollins College; Stetson University; University of Florida; University of Miami; University of Tampa. **Admissions statistics for the fall 2009 entering class:** Total applicants: 3,200. Total accepted: 2,293. Freshmen enrolled: 505; 80% were from out of state. Overall acceptance rate: 72%. **Size of waiting list:** 79 applicants; enrolled from waiting list: 33. **Credentials of fall 2009 freshmen:** 15% ranked in the top 10 percent of their high school class; 45% were in the top 25 percent; 85% were in the top half. (Proportion submitting class standing: 46%.) **Average high school grade point average:** 3.3. **First-year students who submitted SAT scores:** 77%. Scores (25/75 percentile): Critical Reading: 520-630, Math: 500-610, Combined: 1020-1240. **First-year students submitting ACT scores:** 48%. Scores (25/75 percentile): English: 22-28, Math: 20-27, Composite: 22-28.

ACADEMICS

Year founded: 1958. **Academic calendar:** 4-1-4. **Degrees offered:** bachelor's. **Most popular majors:** 9% biology/biological sciences, 9% environmental studies, 9% marine biology and biological oceanography, 7% business administration and management, 6% developmental and child psychology. **Major fields of study:** area, ethnic, cultural, and gender studies; biological and biomedical sciences; business, management, marketing, and related support services; communication, journalism, and related programs; computer and information sciences and support services; English language and literature/letters; foreign languages, literatures, and linguistics; history; liberal arts and sciences studies, and humanities; mathematics and statistics; multi/interdisciplinary studies; natural resources and conservation; philosophy and religious studies; physical sciences; psychology; social sciences; visual and performing arts. **Areas of required coursework:** arts/fine arts, humanities, mathematics, foreign languages, sciences (biological or physical), social science, other. **Pre-professional programs:** pre-law, pre-dentistry, pre-medicine, pre-veterinary science, pre-pharmacy. **Special academic programs (% participation):** accelerated program (3%), double major (13%), honors program (5%), independent study (22%), internships (64%), liberal arts/career combination (0%), student-designed major (13%), study abroad (62%). **Reserve Officers Training Corps (ROTC):** Army ROTC: Offered at cooperating institution (University of South Florida); Air Force ROTC: Offered at cooperating institution (University of South Florida). **Faculty and instruction (2009-2010):** Total instructional faculty: 110 full-time, 52 part-time (56% men; 44% women; 13% minorities). Full-time faculty with Ph.D. or other terminal degree: 95%. Student/faculty ratio: 14/1. Classes of fewer than 20 students: 35%; of 20 to 49 students: 63%; of 50 or more students: 1%. **Advanced Placement and International Baccalaureate credit:** AP tests may be used for: Credit and/or placement. Scores accepted: 4, 5. International Baccalaureate exams may be used for: Placement only. **Freshmen returning for sophomore year:** 78%. **Graduation rates:** Four-year: 58%; five-year: 64%; six-year: 65%. **Graduate study:** 35% of students pursue further study within one year; 57% within five years. Fields in which graduates pursue further study: Master of Business Administration (MBA), 10%; law, 10%; medicine, 2%; education, 7%; arts and sciences, 71%.

COSTS AND FINANCIAL AID

Financial aid office: (727) 864-8334. **Expenses (2010-2011):** Tuition and fees 2010-2011: $33,228; room/board: $9,326. Estimated books and supplies: $1,200; transportation: $1,750; personal expenses: $1,400. **Financial aid:** Priority filing date for institution's financial aid form: March 1. In 2009-2010, 68% of undergraduates applied for financial aid. Of those, 57% were determined to have financial need; 23% had their need fully met. Average financial aid package (proportion receiving): $27,743 (57%). Average amount of gift aid, such as scholarships or grants (proportion receiving): $18,255 (57%). Average amount of self-help aid, such as work study or loans (proportion receiving): $6,479 (49%). Average need-based loan (excluding PLUS or other private loans): $4,807. Among students who received need-based aid, the average percentage of need met: 87%. Among students who received aid based on merit, the average award (and the proportion receiving): $10,777 (32%). The average athletic scholarship (and the proportion receiving): $28,896 (2%). Average amount of debt of borrowers graduating in 2009: $30,494. Proportion who borrowed: 63%.

CAMPUS LIFE AND EXTRACURRICULAR ACTIVITIES

Campus housing available (% using): coed dorms (84%), women's dorms (16%), men's dorms (0%), special housing for disabled students (0%). Students who live in college-owned, operated, or affiliated housing: 78%. **Student employment:** During the 2009-2010 academic year, 17% of undergraduates worked on campus. Average per-year earnings: $1,600. **Clubs and organizations:** Number of student organizations: 62. Activities include: campus ministries, choral groups, concert band, dance, drama/theater, international student organization, literary magazine, model UN, music ensembles, radio station, student government, student newspaper, television station. Number of fraternities: 0; sororities: 0. Average proportion of students who stay on campus on weekends: 80%. **Sports program (2009-2010):** Member of NCAA II. **Men's intercollegiate varsity sports:** baseball, basketball, golf, soccer, tennis. **Women's intercollegiate varsity sports:** basketball, golf, soccer, softball, tennis, volleyball.

SERVICES AND FACILITIES

Basic services: nonremedial tutoring, women's center, placement service, health service, health insurance. **Counseling services:** minority student, career, personal, academic, psychological, birth control, religious. **For learning-disabled students:** School does not offer a structured program with separate admission and additional fees. **Library:** Number of titles: 169,029; number of current serial subscriptions: 6,069. **Information technology resources:** Students are not required to lease or own a computer. Number of campus computers available to all students: 320. School has a wireless network. Approximate number of users that can be accommodated: 2,000. Proportion of college-owned housing units wired for high-speed internet access: 100%. **Campus safety:** Security services offered: 24-hour foot-and-vehicle patrols, late-night transport/escort service, 24-hour emergency telephones, lighted pathways/sidewalks, student patrols, controlled dormitory access (key, security card, etc).

TRANSFER AND INTERNATIONAL STUDENTS

Transfer students: May apply for admission for the following academic terms: Fall, Winter, Spring, Summer. Applicants do not need a minimum number of credits to apply. For fall 2009: Transfer applications received: 336. Transfer applicants offered admission: 161. Transfer applicants enrolled: 71. **International students:** Number of foreign undergraduates: 63 (3% of student body). Number of countries represented: 39. Minimum TOEFL score required: 550 (paper); 213 (computer). Average TOEFL score: 590 (paper).

Edward Waters College

- **Address:** 1658 Kings Road, Jacksonville, FL 32209
- **Website:** http://www.ewc.edu
- **Private; Religious affiliation:** African Methodist Episcopal
- **Enrollment:** N/A

KEY STATS

✔ **U.S News College Ranking:** Unranked, Regional Colleges (South)
✔ **SAT or ACT Score (25th/75th percentile):** N/A
✔ **Tuition:** 2009-2010: $9,990

Selectivity: N/A	**Room/board:** $6,474
Acceptance rate: N/A	**Average debt:** N/A
Student/faculty ratio: N/A	**Proportion who borrowed:** N/A

Embry-Riddle Aeronautical University

- **Address:** 600 S. Clyde Morris Boulevard, Daytona Beach, FL 32114
- **Website:** http://www.embryriddle.edu
- **Private**
- **Enrollment:** 4,158 full-time; 272 part-time

KEY STATS

✔ **U.S News College Ranking:** 10, Regional Universities (South)
✔ **SAT Score (25th/75th percentile):** 950-1210
✔ **Tuition:** 2010-2011: $29,248

Selectivity: Selective	**Room/board:** $8,790
Acceptance rate: 81%	**Average debt:** N/A
Student/faculty ratio: 16/1	**Proportion who borrowed:** 66%

UNDERGRADUATE STUDENT BODY STATS

2009-2010 enrollment: 4,158 full-time; 272 part-time. Men: 83%; women: 17%. **Ethnic makeup:** African American: 6%; Asian American: 6%; Hispanic: 8%; White: 67%; International: 13%.

ADMISSIONS FACTS AND FIGURES

Phone: (800) 862-2416. **Email:** dbadmit@erau.edu. **Website:** http://www.embryriddle.edu. **Application deadlines for fall 2011:** Regular decision: Rolling. Early decision: Not offered. Early action: Not offered. Admission can be deferred. **Application fee:** $50. **To apply online, go to:** https://app.applyyourself.com/?id=erau. **Admissions requirements/recommendations:** High school units required (recommended): English: 4 (4); Mathematics: 4 (4); Science: 2 (3); Foreign language: 0 (1); Social studies: 3 (3); History: 1 (2); Academic electives: 3 (3); Total units: 15 (19). Tests: The college uses SAT or ACT scores in admissions decisions. Either SAT or ACT required. For admission to the fall 2011 entering class, the school will accept: ACT with or without writing accepted. Campus visit: Recommended. Admissions interview: Neither required nor recommended. Off-campus interview: Not available. **Factors that count in admissions decisions:** *Academic:* Secondary school record: Considered. Class rank: Very Important. Letters of recommendation: Very Important. Standardized test scores: Very Important. Essay: Considered. *Nonacademic:* Interview: Considered. Extracurricular activities: Considered. Talent/ability: Not Considered. Character/personal qualities: Considered. Alumni/ae relationship: Considered. Geographical residence: Not Considered. State residency: Not Considered. Religious affiliation/commitment: Not Considered. Minority status: Not Considered. Volunteer work: Considered. Work experience: Considered. **Admissions statistics for the fall 2009 entering class:** Total applicants: 3,536. Total accepted: 2,851. Freshmen enrolled: 862; 69% were from out of state. Overall acceptance rate: 81%. **Credentials of fall 2009 freshmen:** 20% ranked in the top 10 percent of their high school class; 44% were in the top 25 percent; 75% were in the top half. (Proportion submitting class standing: 61%.) **Average high school grade point average:** 3.2. **First-year students who submitted SAT scores:** 80%. Scores (25/75 percentile): Critical Reading: 460-580, Math: 490-630, Combined: 950-1210. **First-year students submitting ACT scores:** 47%. Scores (25/75 percentile): English: 19-26, Math: 21-28, Composite: 21-27.

ACADEMICS

Year founded: 1926. **Academic calendar:** Semester. **Degrees offered:** associate, bachelor's, master's. **Most popular majors:** 24% aerospace, aeronautical, and astronautical engineering, 17% airline/commercial/professional pilot and flight crew, 11% aeronautics/aviation/aerospace science and technology, 9% air traffic controller, 7% business administration, management, and operations. **Major fields of study:** business, management, marketing, and related support services; communication, journalism, and related programs; computer and information sciences and support services; engineering; engineering technologies/technicians; mechanic and repair technologies/technicians; physical sciences; psychology; security and protective services; transportation and materials moving. **Areas of required coursework:** humanities, computer literacy, mathematics, English (including composition), sciences (biological or physical), social science. **Special academic programs:** accelerated program, cooperative (work-study plan) program, distance learning, double major, dual enrollment, English as a Second Language (ESL), honors program, independent study, internships, student-designed major, study abroad. **Cooperative education programs:** business, computer science, engineering, other. **Reserve Officers Training Corps (ROTC):** Army ROTC: Offered on campus; Navy ROTC: Offered on campus; Air Force ROTC: Offered on campus. **Faculty and instruction (2009-2010):** Total instructional faculty: 242 full-time, 82 part-time (75% men; 25% women; 9% minorities). Full-time faculty with Ph.D. or other terminal degree: 66%. Student/faculty ratio: 16/1. Classes of fewer than 20 students: 29%; of 20 to 49 students: 69%; of 50 or more students: 2%. **Advanced Placement and International Baccalaureate credit:** AP tests may be used for: Placement only. Scores accepted: 3, 4, 5. International Baccalaureate exams may be used for: Credit only. **Freshmen returning for sophomore year:** 75%. **Graduation rates:** Four-year: 29%; five-year: 52%; six-year: 60%. **Graduate study:** 20% of students pursue further study immediately upon graduation; 31% within one year; 49% within five years. Fields in which graduates pursue further study: Master of Business Administration (MBA), 12%; engineering, 47%; arts and sciences, 10%.

COSTS AND FINANCIAL AID

Financial aid office: (800) 943-6279. **Expenses (2010-2011):** Tuition and fees 2010-2011: $29,248; room/board: $8,790. Estimated books and supplies: $1,400; transportation: $2,518; personal expenses: $1,488. **Financial aid:** Priority filing date for institution's financial aid form: March 1. In 2009-2010, 70% of undergraduates applied for financial aid. Of those, 61% were determined to have financial need; Average financial aid package (proportion receiving): $15,246 (61%). Average amount of gift aid, such as scholarships or grants (proportion receiving): $9,085 (59%). Average amount of

self-help aid, such as work study or loans (proportion receiving): $5,628 (52%). Average need-based loan (excluding PLUS or other private loans): $4,672. Among students who received aid based on merit, the average award (and the proportion receiving): $0 (0%). The average athletic scholarship (and the proportion receiving): $6,435 (4%). Proportion who borrowed: 66%.

CAMPUS LIFE AND EXTRACURRICULAR ACTIVITIES

Campus housing available (% using): coed dorms (61%), apartment for single students (37%), other housing options (2%). Students who live in college-owned, operated, or affiliated housing: 37%. **Student employment:** During the 2009-2010 academic year, 22% of undergraduates worked on campus. Average per-year earnings: $1,960. **Clubs and organizations:** Number of student organizations: 140. Activities include: choral groups, dance, drama/theater, international student organization, music ensembles, pep band, radio station, student government, student newspaper, yearbook. Number of fraternities: 12; sororities: 4. Proportion of men in fraternities: 12%; of women in sororities: 19%. **Sports program (2009-2010):** Member of NAIA. *Men's intercollegiate varsity sports:* baseball, basketball, cross country, golf, soccer, tennis, track and field (outdoor). *Women's intercollegiate varsity sports:* cross country, golf, soccer, tennis, track and field (outdoor), volleyball.

SERVICES AND FACILITIES

Basic services: nonremedial tutoring, women's center, placement service, health service, health insurance. **Remedial assistance:** math, other. **Counseling services:** minority student, career, personal, veteran student, academic. **For learning-disabled students:** School does not offer a structured program with separate admission and additional fees. Services include: reading machines, tape recorders, untimed tests, note-taking services, tutors. **Library:** Number of titles: 137,472; number of current serial subscriptions: 906. **Information technology resources:** Students are not required to lease or own a computer. Number of campus computers available to all students: 1,041. School has a wireless network. Approximate number of users that can be accommodated: 1,500. Proportion of college-owned housing units wired for high-speed internet access: 100%. **Campus safety:** Security services offered: 24-hour foot-and-vehicle patrols, late-night transport/escort service, 24-hour emergency telephones, lighted pathways/sidewalks, controlled dormitory access (key, security card, etc).

TRANSFER AND INTERNATIONAL STUDENTS

Transfer students: May apply for admission for the following academic terms: Fall, Spring, Summer. Applicants do not need a minimum number of credits to apply. For fall 2009: Transfer applications received: 931. Transfer applicants offered admission: 550. Transfer applicants enrolled: 248. **International students:** Number of foreign undergraduates: 567 (13% of student body). Number of countries represented: 96. Minimum TOEFL score required: 550 (paper); 79 (computer). Average TOEFL score: 585 (paper).

Flagler College

- **Address:** 74 King Street, St. Augustine, FL 32084
- **Website:** http://www.flagler.edu
- **Private**
- **Enrollment:** 2,640 full-time; 76 part-time

KEY STATS

✔ **U.S News College Ranking:** 9, Regional Colleges (South)
✔ **SAT Score (25th/75th percentile):** 1030-1180
✔ **Tuition:** 2010-2011: $13,860

Selectivity: Selective	**Room/board:** $7,590
Acceptance rate: 44%	**Average debt:** $18,190
Student/faculty ratio: 20/1	**Proportion who borrowed:** 55%

UNDERGRADUATE STUDENT BODY STATS

2009-2010 enrollment: 2,640 full-time; 76 part-time. Men: 40%; women: 60%. **Ethnic makeup:** African American: 2%; Hispanic: 4%; White: 91%; International: 2%.

ADMISSIONS FACTS AND FIGURES

Phone: (800) 304-4208. **Email:** admiss@flagler.edu. **Website:** http://www.flagler.edu. **Application deadlines for fall 2011:** Regular decision: March 1;

decision sent by March 30. Early decision: Send application by: December 1; Decision sent by: December 15. Early action: Not offered. Admission can be deferred. **Application fee:** $40. **To apply online, go to:** https://www.applyweb.com/aw?flagler. **Admissions requirements/recommendations:** High school units required (recommended): English: 4 (4); Mathematics: 3 (4); Science: 2 (3); Foreign language: 0 (2); Social studies: 3 (3); History: 1 (2); Academic electives: 2 (2); Total units: 16 (24). Tests: The college uses SAT or ACT scores in admissions decisions. Either SAT or ACT required. For admission to the fall 2011 entering class, the school will accept: ACT with or without writing accepted. Campus visit: Recommended. Admissions interview: Recommended. Off-campus interview: Not available. **Factors that count in admissions decisions: *Academic:*** Secondary school record: Very Important. Class rank: Considered. Letters of recommendation: Considered. Standardized test scores: Important. Essay: Important. ***Nonacademic:*** Interview: Considered. Extracurricular activities: Important. Talent/ability: Considered. Character/personal qualities: Considered. Alumni/ae relationship: Important. Geographical residence: Not Considered. State residency: Not Considered. Religious affiliation/commitment: Not Considered. Minority status: Not Considered. Volunteer work: Considered. Work experience: Not Considered. **Other schools with the greatest overlap in applicants:** Florida State University; University of Central Florida; University of Florida; University of North Florida; University of South Florida. **Admissions statistics for the fall 2009 entering class:** Total applicants: 2,585. Total accepted: 1,149. Freshmen enrolled: 564; 38% were from out of state. Overall acceptance rate: 44%. Early-decision acceptance rate: 60%. Non-early acceptance rate: 39%. **Size of waiting list:** 519 applicants; enrolled from waiting list: 4. **Credentials of fall 2009 freshmen:** 18% ranked in the top 10 percent of their high school class; 56% were in the top 25 percent; 95% were in the top half. (Proportion submitting class standing: 66%.) **Average high school grade point average:** 3.3. **First-year students who submitted SAT scores:** 71%. Scores (25/75 percentile): Critical Reading: 520-590, Math: 510-590, Combined: 1030-1180. **First-year students submitting ACT scores:** 56%. Scores (25/75 percentile): English: 21-26, Math: 20-24, Composite: 21-24.

ACADEMICS

Year founded: 1968. **Academic calendar:** Semester. **Degrees offered:** bachelor's. **Most popular majors:** 24% business, management, marketing, and related support services, 12% communication, journalism, and related programs, 12% visual and performing arts, 11% education, 9% psychology. **Major fields of study:** area, ethnic, cultural, and gender studies; business, management, marketing, and related support services; communication, journalism, and related programs; education; English language and literature/letters; foreign languages, literatures, and linguistics; history; liberal arts and sciences studies, and humanities; parks, recreation, leisure, and fitness studies; philosophy and religious studies; psychology; social sciences; visual and performing arts. **Areas of required coursework:** humanities, computer literacy, mathematics, English (including composition), social science. **Pre-professional programs:** pre-law. **Special academic programs (% participation):** double major (8%), independent study (15%), internships (46%), study abroad (2%), teacher certificate program (12%). **Teacher certification offered in:** special education, elementary, middle/junior high, secondary. **Faculty and instruction (2009-2010):** Total instructional faculty: 95 full-time, 102 part-time (52% men; 48% women; 4% minorities). Full-time faculty with Ph.D. or other terminal degree: 57%. Student/faculty ratio: 20/1. Classes of fewer than 20 students: 40%; of 20 to 49 students: 60%; of 50 or more students: 0%. **Advanced Placement and International Baccalaureate credit:** AP tests may be used for: Credit only. Scores accepted: 4, 5. International Baccalaureate exams may be used for: Credit only. **Freshmen returning for sophomore year:** 77%. **Graduation rates:** Four-year: 49%; five-year: 62%; six-year: 61%. **Graduate study:** Fields in which graduates pursue further study: Master of Business Administration (MBA), 25%; law, 16%; theology (or the seminary), 2%; education, 28%; arts and sciences, 3%.

COSTS AND FINANCIAL AID

Financial aid office: (904) 819-6225. **Expenses (2010-2011):** Tuition and fees 2010-2011: $13,860; room/board: $7,590. Estimated books and supplies: $1,000; transportation: $1,600; personal expenses: $2,300. **Financial aid:** Priority filing date for institution's financial aid form: April 1. In 2009-2010, 68% of undergraduates applied for financial aid. Of those, 52% were determined to have financial need; 12% had their need fully met. Average financial aid package (proportion receiving): $17,705 (52%). Average amount of gift aid, such as scholarships or grants (proportion receiving): $4,664 (39%). Average amount of self-help aid, such as work study or loans (proportion receiving): $4,376 (40%). Average need-based loan (excluding PLUS or other private loans): $4,151. Among students who received need-based aid, the average percentage of need met: 61%. Among students

who received aid based on merit, the average award (and the proportion receiving): $1,731 (7%). The average athletic scholarship (and the proportion receiving): $6,002 (6%). Average amount of debt of borrowers graduating in 2009: $18,190. Proportion who borrowed: 55%.

CAMPUS LIFE AND EXTRACURRICULAR ACTIVITIES

Campus housing available (% using): women's dorms (62%), men's dorms (38%). Students who live in college-owned, operated, or affiliated housing: 40%. **Student employment:** During the 2009-2010 academic year, 10% of undergraduates worked on campus. Average per-year earnings: $900. **Clubs and organizations:** Number of student organizations: 32. Activities include: campus ministries, choral groups, dance, drama/theater, literary magazine, musical theater, radio station, student government, student newspaper. Number of fraternities: 0; sororities: 0. Average proportion of students who stay on campus on weekends: 35%. **Sports program (2009-2010):** Member of NCAA II. ***Men's intercollegiate varsity sports:*** baseball, basketball, cross country, golf, soccer, tennis. ***Women's intercollegiate varsity sports:*** basketball, cross country, golf, soccer, softball, tennis, volleyball.

SERVICES AND FACILITIES

Basic services: health service, health insurance. **Remedial assistance:** reading, math, writing, study skills. **Counseling services:** career, personal, academic, psychological. **For learning-disabled students:** School does not offer a structured program with separate admission and additional fees. Total undergraduates in learning-disabled program or receiving services: 79. Services include: remedial math, remedial English, reading machines, remedial reading, tape recorders, untimed tests, note-taking services, oral tests, learning center, readers, extended time for tests, tutors, priority registration, texts on tape, other testing accommodations. **Library:** Number of titles: 187,945; number of current serial subscriptions: 533. **Information technology resources:** Students are not required to lease or own a computer. Number of campus computers available to all students: 260. School has a wireless network. Approximate number of users that can be accommodated: 1,500. Proportion of college-owned housing units wired for high-speed internet access: 100%. **Campus safety:** Security services offered: 24-hour foot-and-vehicle patrols, late-night transport/escort service, 24-hour emergency telephones, controlled dormitory access (key, security card, etc).

TRANSFER AND INTERNATIONAL STUDENTS

Transfer students: May apply for admission for the following academic terms: Fall, Spring. Applicants need a minimum number of credits to apply. For fall 2009: Transfer applications received: 607. Transfer applicants offered admission: 334. Transfer applicants enrolled: 222. **International students:** Number of foreign undergraduates: 48 (2% of student body). Number of countries represented: 20. Minimum TOEFL score required: 550 (paper); 213 (computer). Average TOEFL score: 605 (paper).

Florida A&M University

■ **Address:** Tallahassee, FL 32307
■ **Website:** http://www.famu.edu
■ **Public**
■ **Enrollment:** 9,268 full-time; 976 part-time

KEY STATS

✔ **U.S News College Ranking:** second tier, National Universities
✔ **ACT Score (25th/75th percentile):** 17-21
✔ **Tuition:** 2010-2011: $4,589 in state, $16,530 out of state

Selectivity: Selective	**Room/board:** $7,814
Acceptance rate: 61%	**Average debt:** $27,662
Student/faculty ratio: 18/1	**Proportion who borrowed:** 81%

UNDERGRADUATE STUDENT BODY STATS

2009-2010 enrollment: 9,268 full-time; 976 part-time. Men: 41%; women: 59%. **Ethnic makeup:** African American: 94%; Asian American: 1%; Hispanic: 1%; White: 2%; International: 1%.

ADMISSIONS FACTS AND FIGURES

Phone: (850) 599-3796. **Email:** ugradmissions@famu.edu. **Website:** http://www.famu.edu. **Application deadlines for fall 2011:** Regular decision: May 15. Early decision: Not offered. Early action: Not offered. Admission can be deferred. **Application fee:** $30. **To apply online, go to:** http://www.famu.edu/index.cfm?a=admissions&amp;amp;amp;amp;p=App

lyOnline. **Admissions requirements/recommendations:** High school units required (recommended): English: 4 (4); Mathematics: 3 (3); Science: 3 (3); Foreign language: 2 (2); Social studies: 3 (3); History: (3); Academic electives: 3 (3); Total units: 18 (18). Tests: The college uses SAT or ACT scores in admissions decisions. Either SAT or ACT required. For admission to the fall 2011 entering class, the school will accept: ACT with or without writing accepted. Campus visit: Neither required nor recommended. Admissions interview: Neither required nor recommended. Off-campus interview: Not available. **Factors that count in admissions decisions:** *Academic:* Secondary school record: Very Important. Class rank: Not Considered. Letters of recommendation: Very Important. Standardized test scores: Very Important. Essay: Considered. *Nonacademic:* Interview: Not Considered. Extracurricular activities: Considered. Talent/ability: Considered. Character/personal qualities: Considered. Alumni/ae relationship: Considered. Geographical residence: Not Considered. State residency: Considered. Religious affiliation/commitment: Not Considered. Minority status: Not Considered. Volunteer work: Considered. Work experience: Considered. **Other schools with the greatest overlap in applicants:** College of William and Mary; Howard University; North Carolina A&T State University; Tennessee State University; University of Northern Colorado. **Admissions statistics for the fall 2009 entering class:** Total applicants: 7,952. Total accepted: 4,824. Freshmen enrolled: 2,444; 19% were from out of state. Overall acceptance rate: 61%. **Average high school grade point average:** 2.9. **First-year students who submitted SAT scores:** 63%. Scores (25/75 percentile): Critical Reading: 410-500, Math: 410-500, Combined: 820-1000. **First-year students submitting ACT scores:** 74%. Scores (25/75 percentile): English: N/A, Math: N/A, Composite: 17-21.

ACADEMICS

Year founded: 1887. **Academic calendar:** Semester. **Degrees offered:** associate, bachelor's, master's, post-master's certificate, doctorate. **Most popular majors:** 21% business, management, marketing, and related support services, 17% health professions and related clinical sciences, 10% security and protective services, 8% social sciences, 6% education. **Major fields of study:** agriculture, agriculture operations, and related sciences; architecture and related services; area, ethnic, cultural, and gender studies; communication, journalism, and related programs; computer and information sciences and support services; education; engineering; engineering technologies/technicians; natural resources and conservation; visual and performing arts. **Areas of required coursework:** humanities, computer literacy, mathematics, English (including composition), sciences (biological or physical), history, social science. **Pre-professional programs:** pre-law, pre-medicine, pre-pharmacy. **Special academic programs:** accelerated program, cooperative (work-study plan) program, cross-registration, distance learning, double major, dual enrollment, honors program, independent study, internships, study abroad, teacher certificate program, weekend college, other. **Teacher certification offered in:** early childhood, elementary, middle/junior high, secondary. **Cooperative education programs:** agriculture, business, education, health professions, social/behavioral science. **Reserve Officers Training Corps (ROTC):** Army ROTC: Offered on campus; Navy ROTC: Offered on campus; Air Force ROTC: Offered at cooperating institution (Florida State University). **Faculty and instruction (2009-2010):** Total instructional faculty: 590 full-time, 140 part-time (55% men; 45% women; 78% minorities). Full-time faculty with Ph.D. or other terminal degree: 74%. Student/faculty ratio: 18/1. Classes of fewer than 20 students: 30%; of 20 to 49 students: 52%; of 50 or more students: 18%. **Advanced Placement and International Baccalaureate credit:** AP tests may be used for: Credit only. Scores accepted: 3, 4, 5. International Baccalaureate exams may be used for: Credit and/or placement. **Freshmen returning for sophomore year:** 82%. **Graduation rates:** Four-year: 12%; five-year: 28%; six-year: 39%. **Graduate study:** 40% of students pursue further study immediately upon graduation; 18% within one year. Fields in which graduates pursue further study: Master of Business Administration (MBA), 5%; law, 3%; medicine, 5%; dentistry, 1%; engineering, 3%; theology (or the seminary), 1%; education, 4%; arts and sciences, 3%; veterinary medicine, 1%.

COSTS AND FINANCIAL AID

Financial aid office: (850) 412-7927. **Expenses (2010-2011):** Tuition and fees 2010-2011: $4,589 in state, $16,530 out of state; room/board: $7,814. Estimated books and supplies: $1,078; transportation: $1,010; personal expenses: $1,872. **Financial aid:** Priority filing date for institution's financial aid form: March 1; deadline: May 15. In 2009-2010, 78% of undergraduates applied for financial aid. Of those, 76% were determined to have financial need; 30% had their need fully met. Average financial aid package (proportion receiving): $12,216 (75%). Average amount of gift aid, such as scholarships or grants (proportion receiving): $5,077 (58%). Average amount of

self-help aid, such as work study or loans (proportion receiving): $4,058 (61%). Average need-based loan (excluding PLUS or other private loans): $3,982. Among students who received need-based aid, the average percentage of need met: 80%. Among students who received aid based on merit, the average award (and the proportion receiving): $5,285 (4%). The average athletic scholarship (and the proportion receiving): $7,882 (2%). Average amount of debt of borrowers graduating in 2009: $27,662. Proportion who borrowed: 81%.

CAMPUS LIFE AND EXTRACURRICULAR ACTIVITIES

Campus housing available (% using): coed dorms (14%), women's dorms (32%), men's dorms (12%), apartments for married students (1%), apartment for single students (36%), special housing for disabled students (0%), other housing options (0%). Students who live in college-owned, operated, or affiliated housing: 70%. Average per-year earnings: $5,600. **Clubs and organizations:** Number of student organizations: 145. Activities include: campus ministries, choral groups, concert band, dance, drama/theater, international student organization, jazz band, literary magazine, marching band, music ensembles, musical theater, pep band, radio station, student government, student newspaper, symphony orchestra, television station, yearbook. Number of fraternities: 4; sororities: 4. Proportion of men in fraternities: 2%; of women in sororities: 3%. Average proportion of students who stay on campus on weekends: 95%. **Sports program (2009-2010):** Member of NCAA I. *Men's intercollegiate varsity sports:* baseball, basketball, cross country, football, golf, swimming, tennis, track and field (indoor). *Women's intercollegiate varsity sports:* basketball, bowling, cross country, golf, softball, swimming, tennis, track and field (outdoor), volleyball.

SERVICES AND FACILITIES

Basic services: nonremedial tutoring, placement service, day care, health service, health insurance. **Remedial assistance:** reading, math, writing, study skills. **Counseling services:** minority student, career, military, personal, veteran student, academic, older student, psychological, birth control. **For learning-disabled students:** School does not offer a structured program with separate admission and additional fees. Total undergraduates in learning-disabled program or receiving services: 431. Services include: remedial math, remedial English, remedial reading, tape recorders, diagnostic testing service, note-taking services, oral tests, readers, extended time for tests, tutors, early syllabus, priority seating, proofreading services, substitution of courses, texts on tape, typist/scribe, exams on tape or computer, take home exams, waiver of foreign language degree requirement, waiver of math degree requirement. **Library:** Number of titles: 965,125; number of current serial subscriptions: 64,703. **Information technology resources:** Students are not required to lease or own a computer. Number of campus computers available to all students: 3,000. School has a wireless network. Approximate number of users that can be accommodated: 15,000. Proportion of college-owned housing units wired for high-speed internet access: 100%. **Campus safety:** Security services offered: 24-hour foot-and-vehicle patrols, late-night transport/escort service, 24-hour emergency telephones, lighted pathways/sidewalks.

TRANSFER AND INTERNATIONAL STUDENTS

Transfer students: May apply for admission for the following academic terms: Fall, Spring, Summer. Applicants need a minimum number of credits to apply. For fall 2009: Transfer applications received: 2,088. Transfer applicants offered admission: 820. Transfer applicants enrolled: 513. **International students:** Number of foreign undergraduates: 69 (1% of student body). Number of countries represented: 23. Minimum TOEFL score required: 500 (paper); 80 (computer). Average TOEFL score: 550 (paper).

Florida Atlantic University

- **Address:** 777 Glades Road, PO Box 3091, Boca Raton, FL 33431
- **Website:** http://www.fau.edu
- **Public**
- **Enrollment:** 13,096 full-time; 9,212 part-time

KEY STATS

✔ **U.S News College Ranking:** second tier, National Universities

✔ **SAT Score (25th/75th percentile):** 970-1150

✔ **Tuition:** 2009-2010: $4,187 in state, $4,187 out of state

Selectivity: Selective	**Room/board:** $9,582
Acceptance rate: 46%	**Average debt:** $17,338
Student/faculty ratio: 20/1	**Proportion who borrowed:** 47%

UNDERGRADUATE STUDENT BODY STATS

2009-2010 enrollment: 13,096 full-time; 9,212 part-time. Men: 42%; women: 58%. **Ethnic makeup:** African American: 18%; Asian American: 5%; Hispanic: 20%; White: 54%; International: 3%.

ADMISSIONS FACTS AND FIGURES

Phone: (561) 297-3040. **Email:** admisweb@fau.edu. **Website:** http://www.fau.edu. **Application deadlines for fall 2011:** Regular decision: May 1. Early decision: Not offered. Early action: Not offered. Admission can be deferred. **Application fee:** $30. **To apply online, go to:** http://fauapps.fau.edu/uapp/. **Admissions requirements/recommendations:** High school units required (recommended): English: 4 (4); Mathematics: 3 (4); Science: 3 (3); Foreign language: 2 (2); Social studies: 3 (3); History: 0 (0); Academic electives: 3 (3); Total units: 18 (19). Tests: The college uses SAT or ACT scores in admissions decisions. Either SAT or ACT required. For admission to the fall 2011 entering class, the school will accept: ACT with or without writing accepted. Campus visit: Required. Admissions interview: Neither required nor recommended. Off-campus interview: Not available. **Factors that count in admissions decisions:** *Academic:* Secondary school record: Important. Class rank: Important. Letters of recommendation: Considered. Standardized test scores: Very Important. Essay: Considered. *Nonacademic:* Interview: Not Considered. Extracurricular activities: Considered. Talent/ability: Considered. Character/personal qualities: Considered. Alumni/ae relationship: Considered. Geographical residence: Not Considered. State residency: Not Considered. Religious affiliation/commitment: Not Considered. Minority status: Not Considered. Volunteer work: Considered. Work experience: Not Considered. **Other schools with the greatest overlap in applicants:** Florida International University; Florida State University; University of Central Florida; University of Florida; University of South Florida. **Admissions statistics for the fall 2009 entering class:** Total applicants: 14,532. Total accepted: 6,745. Freshmen enrolled: 2,569; 6% were from out of state. Overall acceptance rate: 46%. **Credentials of fall 2009 freshmen:** 12% ranked in the top 10 percent of their high school class; 39% were in the top 25 percent; 77% were in the top half. (Proportion submitting class standing: 82%.) **Average high school grade point average:** 3.4. **First-year students who submitted SAT scores:** 68%. Scores (25/75 percentile): Critical Reading: 480-570, Math: 490-580, Combined: 970-1150. **First-year students submitting ACT scores:** 38%. Scores (25/75 percentile): English: N/A, Math: N/A, Composite: 21-25.

ACADEMICS

Year founded: 1961. **Academic calendar:** Semester. **Degrees offered:** certificate, associate, bachelor's, master's, post-master's certificate, doctorate. **Most popular majors:** 9% elementary education and teaching, 8% business administration and management, 7% marketing/marketing management, 6% criminal justice/safety studies, 5% biology/biological sciences. **Major fields of study:** architecture and related services; biological and biomedical sciences; business, management, marketing, and related support services; communication, journalism, and related programs; computer and information sciences and support services; education; engineering; engineering technologies/technicians; English language and literature/letters; foreign languages, literatures, and linguistics; health professions and related clinical sciences; history; liberal arts and sciences studies, and humanities; mathematics and statistics; parks, recreation, leisure, and fitness studies; philosophy and religious studies; physical sciences; psychology; public administration and social service professions; security and protective services; social sciences; visual and performing arts. **Areas of required coursework:** arts/fine arts, humanities, mathematics, English (including composition), foreign languages, sciences (biological or physical), history,

social science. **Pre-professional programs:** pre-law, pre-dentistry, pre-medicine, pre-veterinary science, pre-optometry, pre-pharmacy. **Special academic programs (% participation):** accelerated program, cooperative (work-study plan) program, distance learning (14%), double major, dual enrollment (1%), English as a Second Language (ESL), honors program (2%), independent study, internships, liberal arts/career combination, study abroad (2%), teacher certificate program, weekend college. **Teacher certification offered in:** early childhood, special education, elementary, adult education, secondary, bilingual/bicultural. **Cooperative education programs:** art, business, computer science, education, engineering, health professions, humanities, natural science, social/behavioral science. **Reserve Officers Training Corps (ROTC):** Army ROTC: Offered on campus; Air Force ROTC: Offered at cooperating institution (University of Miami). **Faculty and instruction (2009-2010):** Total instructional faculty: 785 full-time, 498 part-time (54% men; 46% women; 18% minorities). Full-time faculty with Ph.D. or other terminal degree: 86%. Student/faculty ratio: 20/1. Classes of fewer than 20 students: 29%; of 20 to 49 students: 57%; of 50 or more students: 13%. **Advanced Placement and International Baccalaureate credit:** International Baccalaureate exams may be used for: Credit only. **Freshmen returning for sophomore year:** 75%. **Graduation rates:** Four-year: 16%; five-year: 32%; six-year: 38%. **Graduate study:** 61% of students pursue further study immediately upon graduation; 11% within one year.

COSTS AND FINANCIAL AID

Financial aid office: (561) 297-3530. **Expenses (2009-2010):** Tuition and fees 2009-2010: $4,187 in state, $4,187 out of state; room/board: $9,582. Estimated books and supplies: $900; transportation: $1,906; personal expenses: $1,608. **Financial aid:** Priority filing date for institution's financial aid form: March 1. In 2009-2010, 65% of undergraduates applied for financial aid. Of those, 53% were determined to have financial need; 11% had their need fully met. Average financial aid package (proportion receiving): $8,271 (51%). Average amount of gift aid, such as scholarships or grants (proportion receiving): $6,358 (44%). Average amount of self-help aid, such as work study or loans (proportion receiving): $4,103 (32%). Average need-based loan (excluding PLUS or other private loans): $3,972. Among students who received need-based aid, the average percentage of need met: 69%. Among students who received aid based on merit, the average award (and the proportion receiving): $0 (0%). The average athletic scholarship (and the proportion receiving): $0 (0%). Average amount of debt of borrowers graduating in 2009: $17,338. Proportion who borrowed: 47%.

CAMPUS LIFE AND EXTRACURRICULAR ACTIVITIES

Campus housing available (% using): coed dorms (75%), women's dorms (1%), apartment for single students (24%). Students who live in college-owned, operated, or affiliated housing: 4%. **Student employment:** During the 2009-2010 academic year, 14% of undergraduates worked on campus. Average per-year earnings: $2,250. **Clubs and organizations:** Number of student organizations: 215. Activities include: campus ministries, choral groups, concert band, dance, drama/theater, international student organization, jazz band, literary magazine, marching band, model UN, music ensembles, musical theater, opera, pep band, radio station, student government, student newspaper, student film society, symphony orchestra, television station. Number of fraternities: 11; sororities: 9. Proportion of men in fraternities: 1%; of women in sororities: 1%. Average proportion of students who stay on campus on weekends: 80%. **Sports program (2009-2010):** Member of NCAA I. *Men's intercollegiate varsity sports:* baseball, basketball, cross country, football, golf, soccer, swimming, tennis. *Women's intercollegiate varsity sports:* basketball, cross country, golf, soccer, softball, swimming, tennis, track and field (indoor), track and field (outdoor), volleyball.

SERVICES AND FACILITIES

Basic services: nonremedial tutoring, women's center, placement service, health service, health insurance. **Counseling services:** minority student, career, military, personal, veteran student, academic, older student, psychological, birth control, religious. **For learning-disabled students:** School does not offer a structured program with separate admission and additional fees. Services include: reading machines, tape recorders, other. **Library:** Number of titles: 1,330,817; number of current serial subscriptions: 12,811. **Information technology resources:** Students are not required to lease or own a computer. Number of campus computers available to all students: 2,100. School has a wireless network. Proportion of college-owned housing units wired for high-speed internet access: 98%. **Campus safety:** Security services offered: 24-hour foot-and-vehicle patrols, late-night transport/escort service, 24-hour emergency telephones, lighted pathways/sidewalks, student patrols, controlled dormitory access (key, security card, etc).

Transfer students: May apply for admission for the following academic terms: Fall, Spring, Summer. Applicants need a minimum number of credits to apply. For fall 2009: Transfer applications received: 9,071. Transfer applicants offered admission: 5,698. Transfer applicants enrolled: 2,984. **International students:** Number of foreign undergraduates: 561 (3% of student body). Number of countries represented: 143. Minimum TOEFL score required: 550 (paper); 80 (computer). Average TOEFL score: 600 (paper).

Florida Gulf Coast University

- **Address:** 10501 FGCU Boulevard S, Fort Myers, FL 33965-6565
- **Website:** http://www.fgcu.edu
- **Public**
- **Enrollment:** 7,854 full-time; 1,859 part-time

KEY STATS

✔ **U.S News College Ranking:** 83, Regional Universities (South)
✔ **SAT Score (25th/75th percentile):** 950-1110
✔ **Tuition:** 2009-2010: $4,337 in state, $18,869 out of state

Selectivity: Selective	**Room/board:** $8,659
Acceptance rate: 66%	**Average debt:** $21,247
Student/faculty ratio: 22/1	**Proportion who borrowed:** 35%

UNDERGRADUATE STUDENT BODY STATS

2009-2010 enrollment: 7,854 full-time; 1,859 part-time. Men: 44%; women: 56%. **Ethnic makeup:** African American: 5%; American-Indian: 1%; Asian American: 2%; Hispanic: 14%; White: 76%; International: 2%.

ADMISSIONS FACTS AND FIGURES

Phone: (239) 590-7878. **Email:** admissions@fgcu.edu. **Website:** http://www.fgcu.edu. **Application deadlines for fall 2011:** Regular decision: June 2. Early decision: Send application by: N/A; Decision sent by: N/A. Early action: Not offered. Admission can be deferred. **Application fee:** $30. **To apply online, go to:** https://gulfline.fgcu.edu/pls/fgpo/bwskalog.P_DispLoginNon. **Admissions requirements/recommendations:** High school units required (recommended): English: 4; Mathematics: 3; Science: 3; Foreign language: 2; Social studies: 3; Academic electives: 3; Total units: 18. Tests: The college uses SAT or ACT scores in admissions decisions. Either SAT or ACT required. For admission to the fall 2011 entering class, the school will accept: ACT with writing required. Campus visit: Recommended. Admissions interview: Neither required nor recommended. Off-campus interview: May be arranged. **Factors that count in admissions decisions:** *Academic:* Secondary school record: Important. Class rank: Considered. Letters of recommendation: Considered. Standardized test scores: Very Important. Essay: Not Considered. *Nonacademic:* Interview: Not Considered. Extracurricular activities: Not Considered. Talent/ability: Not Considered. Character/personal qualities: Not Considered. Alumni/ae relationship: Not Considered. Geographical residence: Not Considered. State residency: Not Considered. Religious affiliation/commitment: Not Considered. Minority status: Not Considered. Volunteer work: Not Considered. Work experience: Not Considered. **Other schools with the greatest overlap in applicants:** Florida Atlantic University; Florida International University; University of Central Florida; University of South Florida. **Admissions statistics for the fall 2009 entering class:** Total applicants: 8,298. Total accepted: 5,441. Freshmen enrolled: 1,991; 9% were from out of state. Overall acceptance rate: 66%. Non-early acceptance rate: 66%. **Credentials of fall 2009 freshmen:** 13% ranked in the top 10 percent of their high school class; 39% were in the top 25 percent; 81% were in the top half. (Proportion submitting class standing: 3%.) **Average high school grade point average:** 3.3. **First-year students who submitted SAT scores:** 91%. Scores (25/75 percentile): Critical Reading: 480-560, Math: 470-550, Combined: 950-1110. **First-year students submitting ACT scores:** 68%. Scores (25/75 percentile): English: 19-23, Math: 19-24, Composite: 20-23.

ACADEMICS

Year founded: 1991. **Academic calendar:** Semester. **Degrees offered:** certificate, associate, transfer-associate, bachelor's, master's. **Most popular majors:** 29% business, management, marketing, and related support services; 13% education; 11% health professions and related clinical sciences. **Major fields of study:** biological and biomedical sciences; business, management, marketing, and related support services; computer and information sciences and support services; education; health professions and related clinical sci-

ences; legal professions and studies; liberal arts and sciences studies, and humanities; parks, recreation, leisure, and fitness studies; public administration and social service professions; security and protective services; social sciences. **Areas of required coursework:** arts/fine arts, humanities, mathematics, English (including composition), foreign languages, sciences (biological or physical), social science, other. **Special academic programs:** accelerated program, cross-registration, distance learning, double major, dual enrollment, honors program, independent study, internships, student-designed major, study abroad, teacher certificate program. **Teacher certification offered in:** early childhood, special education, elementary, secondary. **Faculty and instruction (2009-2010):** Total instructional faculty: 348 full-time, 208 part-time (51% men; 49% women; 15% minorities). Full-time faculty with Ph.D. or other terminal degree: 76%. Student/faculty ratio: 22/1. Classes of fewer than 20 students: 22%; of 20 to 49 students: 66%; of 50 or more students: 12%. **Advanced Placement and International Baccalaureate credit:** AP tests may be used for: Credit only. Scores accepted: 3, 4, 5. International Baccalaureate exams may be used for: Credit only. **Freshmen returning for sophomore year:** 75%. **Graduation rates:** Six-year: 37%.

COSTS AND FINANCIAL AID

Financial aid office: (239) 590-7920. **Expenses (2009-2010):** Tuition and fees 2009-2010: $4,337 in state, $18,869 out of state; room/board: $8,659. **Financial aid:** Priority filing date for institution's financial aid form: March 1; deadline: June 30. In 2009-2010, 75% of undergraduates applied for financial aid. Of those, 33% were determined to have financial need; 9% had their need fully met. Average financial aid package (proportion receiving): $7,231 (33%). Average amount of gift aid, such as scholarships or grants (proportion receiving): $4,430 (19%). Average amount of self-help aid, such as work study or loans (proportion receiving): $5,153 (21%). Average need-based loan (excluding PLUS or other private loans): $5,272. Among students who received need-based aid, the average percentage of need met: 62%. Among students who received aid based on merit, the average award (and the proportion receiving): $3,869 (4%). The average athletic scholarship (and the proportion receiving): $10,589 (2%). Average amount of debt of borrowers graduating in 2009: $21,247. Proportion who borrowed: 35%.

CAMPUS LIFE AND EXTRACURRICULAR ACTIVITIES

Campus housing available: coed dorms, apartment for single students, special housing for disabled students. Students who live in college-owned, operated, or affiliated housing: 29%. Average per-year earnings: $6,000. Activities include: dance, drama/theater, literary magazine, student government, student newspaper, student film society. Number of fraternities: 2; sororities: 3. Proportion of men in fraternities: 7%; of women in sororities: 8%. Average proportion of students who stay on campus on weekends: 50%. **Sports program (2009-2010):** Member of NCAA II.

SERVICES AND FACILITIES

Basic services: nonremedial tutoring, day care, health service. **Remedial assistance:** reading, math, writing, study skills. **Counseling services:** career, personal, academic, psychological. **For learning-disabled students:** School does not offer a structured program with separate admission and additional fees. Total undergraduates in learning-disabled program or receiving services: 328. Services include: reading machines, tape recorders, diagnostic testing service, untimed tests, note-taking services, learning center, readers, extended time for tests, tutors, priority registration, priority seating, texts on tape, other testing accommodations. **Library:** Number of titles: 387,860; number of current serial subscriptions: 8,007. **Information technology resources:** Students are not required to lease or own a computer. Number of campus computers available to all students: 315. School has a wireless network. Approximate number of users that can be accommodated: 1,400. Proportion of college-owned housing units wired for high-speed internet access: 100%. **Campus safety:** Security services offered: 24-hour foot-and-vehicle patrols, late-night transport/escort service, 24-hour emergency telephones, lighted pathways/sidewalks.

TRANSFER AND INTERNATIONAL STUDENTS

Transfer students: May apply for admission for the following academic terms: Fall, Spring, Summer. Applicants need a minimum number of credits to apply. For fall 2009: Transfer applications received: 2,416. Transfer applicants offered admission: 1,550. Transfer applicants enrolled: 1,022. **International students:** Number of foreign undergraduates: 155 (2% of student body). Number of countries represented: 80. Minimum TOEFL score required: 550 (paper); 213 (computer). Average TOEFL score: 550 (paper).

Florida Institute of Technology

- **Address:** 150 W. University Boulevard, Melbourne, FL 32901-6975
- **Website:** http://www.fit.edu
- **Private**
- **Enrollment:** 3,929 full-time; 1,093 part-time

KEY STATS

✔ **U.S News College Ranking:** 159, National Universities
✔ **SAT Score (25th/75th percentile):** 1040-1270
✔ **Tuition:** 2010-2011: $32,294

Selectivity: Selective	**Room/board:** $11,210
Acceptance rate: 74%	**Average debt:** $40,630
Student/faculty ratio: 14/1	**Proportion who borrowed:** 69%

UNDERGRADUATE STUDENT BODY STATS

2009-2010 enrollment: 3,929 full-time; 1,093 part-time. Men: 54%; women: 46%. **Ethnic makeup:** African American: 14%; American-Indian: 1%; Asian American: 2%; Hispanic: 7%; White: 62%; International: 14%.

ADMISSIONS FACTS AND FIGURES

Phone: (800) 888-4348. **Email:** admission@fit.edu. **Website:** http://www. fit.edu. **Application deadlines for fall 2011:** Regular decision: Rolling. Early decision: Not offered. Early action: Not offered. Admission can be deferred. **Application fee:** $50. **To apply online, go to:** http://www.fit.edu/ugrad/ apply.htm. **Admissions requirements/recommendations:** High school units required (recommended): English: 4 (4); Mathematics: 3 (4); Science: 3 (4); Foreign language: (2); Social studies: 1 (3); History: 2 (2); Academic electives: 7 (5); Total units: 20 (26). Tests: The college uses SAT or ACT scores in admissions decisions. Either SAT or ACT required. For admission to the fall 2011 entering class, the school will accept: ACT with or without writing accepted. Campus visit: Recommended. Admissions interview: Recommended. Off-campus interview: May be arranged. **Factors that count in admissions decisions:** *Academic:* Secondary school record: Very Important. Class rank: Considered. Letters of recommendation: Considered. Standardized test scores: Important. Essay: Considered. *Nonacademic:* Interview: Considered. Extracurricular activities: Considered. Talent/ability: Not Considered. Character/personal qualities: Considered. Alumni/ae relationship: Considered. Geographical residence: Not Considered. State residency: Not Considered. Religious affiliation/commitment: Not Considered. Minority status: Not Considered. Volunteer work: Not Considered. Work experience: Considered. **Other schools with the greatest overlap in applicants:** Embry-Riddle Aeronautical University; Florida State University; University of Central Florida; University of Florida; University of South Florida. **Admissions statistics for the fall 2009 entering class:** Total applicants: 3,340. Total accepted: 2,477. Freshmen enrolled: 539; 60% were from out of state. Overall acceptance rate: 74%. **Credentials of fall 2009 freshmen:** 27% ranked in the top 10 percent of their high school class; 52% were in the top 25 percent; 88% were in the top half. (Proportion submitting class standing: 63%.) **Average high school grade point average:** 3.5. **First-year students who submitted SAT scores:** 71%. Scores (25/75 percentile): Critical Reading: 500-610, Math: 540-660, Combined: 1040-1270. **First-year students submitting ACT scores:** 39%. Scores (25/75 percentile): English: 21-28, Math: 23-29, Composite: 23-28.

ACADEMICS

Year founded: 1958. **Academic calendar:** Semester. **Degrees offered:** associate, bachelor's, master's, post-master's certificate, doctorate. **Most popular majors:** 13% aerospace, aeronautical, and astronautical engineering, 10% aviation/airway management and operations, 7% marine biology and biological oceanography, 7% mechanical engineering, 5% electrical, electronics, and communications engineering. **Major fields of study:** biological and biomedical sciences; business, management, marketing, and related support services; communication, journalism, and related programs; computer and information sciences and support services; education; engineering; liberal arts and sciences studies, and humanities; mathematics and statistics; multi/interdisciplinary studies; natural resources and conservation; physical sciences; psychology; transportation and materials moving. **Areas of required coursework:** humanities, computer literacy, mathematics, English (including composition), sciences (biological or physical), social science. **Pre-professional programs:** pre-medicine, pre-veterinary science, pre-optometry, pre-pharmacy, other. **Special academic programs (% participation):** accelerated program (0%), cooperative (work-study plan) program (11%), cross-registration (3%), distance learning (2%), double major (5%),

dual enrollment (7%), English as a Second Language (ESL) (1%), independent study (5%), internships (65%), study abroad (4%), teacher certificate program (1%), other (1%). **Teacher certification offered in:** elementary, middle/junior high, secondary. **Cooperative education programs:** business, computer science, education, engineering, humanities, natural science, social/behavioral science, technologies, other. **Reserve Officers Training Corps (ROTC):** Army ROTC: Offered on campus. **Faculty and instruction (2009-2010):** Total instructional faculty: 226 full-time, 66 part-time (78% men; 22% women; 12% minorities). Full-time faculty with Ph.D. or other terminal degree: 88%. Student/faculty ratio: 14/1. Classes of fewer than 20 students: 55%; of 20 to 49 students: 42%; of 50 or more students: 3%. **Advanced Placement and International Baccalaureate credit:** AP tests may be used for: Credit only. Scores accepted: 4, 5. International Baccalaureate exams may be used for: Credit only. **Freshmen returning for sophomore year:** 75%. **Graduation rates:** Four-year: 39%; five-year: 54%; six-year: 58%. **Graduate study:** 28% of students pursue further study immediately upon graduation. Fields in which graduates pursue further study: Master of Business Administration (MBA), 8%; law, 4%; medicine, 8%; engineering, 55%; arts and sciences, 25%.

COSTS AND FINANCIAL AID

Financial aid office: (321) 674-8070. **Expenses (2010-2011):** Tuition and fees 2010-2011: $32,294; room/board: $11,210. Estimated books and supplies: $1,200; transportation: $1,500; personal expenses: $1,500. **Financial aid:** Priority filing date for institution's financial aid form: March 1. In 2009-2010, 68% of undergraduates applied for financial aid. Of those, 61% were determined to have financial need; 25% had their need fully met. Average financial aid package (proportion receiving): $27,868 (61%). Average amount of gift aid, such as scholarships or grants (proportion receiving): $19,004 (60%). Average amount of self-help aid, such as work study or loans (proportion receiving): $5,525 (48%). Average need-based loan (excluding PLUS or other private loans): $4,704. Among students who received need-based aid, the average percentage of need met: 81%. Among students who received aid based on merit, the average award (and the proportion receiving): $10,155 (26%). The average athletic scholarship (and the proportion receiving): $22,165 (3%). Average amount of debt of borrowers graduating in 2009: $40,630. Proportion who borrowed: 69%.

CAMPUS LIFE AND EXTRACURRICULAR ACTIVITIES

Campus housing available (% using): coed dorms (90%), apartment for single students (10%). Students who live in college-owned, operated, or affiliated housing: 54%. **Student employment:** During the 2009-2010 academic year, 5% of undergraduates worked on campus. Average per-year earnings: $6,775. **Clubs and organizations:** Number of student organizations: 106. Activities include: campus ministries, choral groups, dance, drama/theater, international student organization, jazz band, literary magazine, musical theater, pep band, radio station, student government, student newspaper, television station. Number of fraternities: 7; sororities: 3. Proportion of men in fraternities: 11%; of women in sororities: 5%. Average proportion of students who stay on campus on weekends: 80%. **Sports program (2009-2010):** Member of NCAA II. *Men's intercollegiate varsity sports:* baseball, basketball, cross country, golf, soccer, tennis. *Women's intercollegiate varsity sports:* basketball, crew (heavyweight), cross country, golf, crew (lightweight), soccer, softball, tennis, volleyball.

SERVICES AND FACILITIES

Basic services: nonremedial tutoring, placement service, health service, health insurance. **Remedial assistance:** reading, math, writing, study skills. **Counseling services:** career, military, personal, veteran student, academic, psychological, birth control, religious. **For learning-disabled students:** School does not offer a structured program with separate admission and additional fees. Total undergraduates in learning-disabled program or receiving services: 76. Services include: remedial math, remedial English, diagnostic testing service, untimed tests, note-taking services, learning center, extended time for tests, tutors, priority seating, other. **Library:** Number of titles: 342,791; number of current serial subscriptions: 38,452. **Information technology resources:** Students are not required to lease or own a computer. Number of campus computers available to all students: 400. School has a wireless network. Approximate number of users that can be accommodated: 3,000. Proportion of college-owned housing units wired for high-speed internet access: 100%. **Campus safety:** Security services offered: 24-hour foot-and-vehicle patrols, late-night transport/escort service, 24-hour emergency telephones, lighted pathways/sidewalks, controlled dormitory access (key, security card, etc).

TRANSFER AND INTERNATIONAL STUDENTS

Transfer students: May apply for admission for the following academic terms: Fall, Spring. Applicants need a minimum number of credits to apply. For fall 2009: Transfer applications received: 621. Transfer applicants offered admission: 361. Transfer applicants enrolled: 132. **International students:** Number of foreign undergraduates: 674 (14% of student body). Number of countries represented: 90. Minimum TOEFL score required: 550 (paper); 79 (computer). Average TOEFL score: 570 (paper).

Florida International University

- **Address:** University Park, Miami, FL 33199
- **Website:** http://www.fiu.edu
- **Public**
- **Enrollment:** 19,513 full-time; 12,277 part-time

KEY STATS

✔ **U.S News College Ranking:** second tier, National Universities
✔ **SAT Score (25th/75th percentile):** 1070-1230
✔ **Tuition:** 2009-2010: $4,168 in state, $16,567 out of state

Selectivity: Selective	**Room/board:** $11,946
Acceptance rate: 35%	**Average debt:** $14,901
Student/faculty ratio: 28/1	**Proportion who borrowed:** 39%

UNDERGRADUATE STUDENT BODY STATS

2009-2010 enrollment: 19,513 full-time; 12,277 part-time. Men: 44%; women: 56%. **Ethnic makeup:** African American: 12%; Asian American: 3%; Hispanic: 65%; White: 15%; International: 5%.

ADMISSIONS FACTS AND FIGURES

Phone: (305) 348-2363. **Email:** admiss@fiu.edu. **Website:** http://www.fiu.edu. **Application deadlines for fall 2011:** Regular decision: May 1. Early decision: Not offered. Early action: Not offered. Admission cannot be deferred. **Application fee:** $30. **To apply online, go to:** https://app.applyyourself.com/?ID=fiu-u. **Admissions requirements/recommendations:** High school units required (recommended): English: 4; Mathematics: 3; Science: 3; Foreign language: 2; Social studies: 3; History: 0; Academic electives: 3; Total units: 18. Tests: The college uses SAT or ACT scores in admissions decisions. Either SAT or ACT required. For admission to the fall 2011 entering class, the school will accept: ACT with or without writing accepted. Campus visit: Recommended. Admissions interview: Neither required nor recommended. Off-campus interview: May be arranged. **Factors that count in admissions decisions:** *Academic:* Secondary school record: Very Important. Class rank: Very Important. Letters of recommendation: Considered. Standardized test scores: Very Important. Essay: Considered. *Nonacademic:* Interview: Considered. Extracurricular activities: Considered. Talent/ability: Considered. Character/personal qualities: Considered. Alumni/ae relationship: Considered. Geographical residence: Considered. State residency: Considered. Religious affiliation/commitment: Not Considered. Minority status: Not Considered. Volunteer work: Considered. Work experience: Considered. **Admissions statistics for the fall 2009 entering class:** Total applicants: 15,979. Total accepted: 5,591. Freshmen enrolled: 2,013; 4% were from out of state. Overall acceptance rate: 35%. **Average high school grade point average:** 3.7. **First-year students who submitted SAT scores:** 75%. Scores (25/75 percentile): Critical Reading: 540-620, Math: 530-610, Combined: 1070-1230. **First-year students submitting ACT scores:** 25%. Scores (25/75 percentile): English: 23-28, Math: 23-27, Composite: 24-27.

ACADEMICS

Year founded: 1965. **Academic calendar:** Semester. **Degrees offered:** certificate, associate, bachelor's, post-bachelor's certificate, master's, doctorate. **Most popular majors:** 33% business, management, marketing, and related support services, 10% health professions and related clinical sciences, 8% psychology, 8% social sciences, 6% education. **Major fields of study:** architecture and related services; area, ethnic, cultural, and gender studies; biological and biomedical sciences; business, management, marketing, and related support services; communication, journalism, and related programs; computer and information sciences and support services; education; engineering; engineering technologies/technicians; English language and literature/letters; foreign languages, literatures, and linguistics; health professions and related clinical sciences; history; liberal arts and sciences studies, and humanities; mathematics and statistics; natural resources and

conservation; parks, recreation, leisure, and fitness studies; philosophy and religious studies; physical sciences; psychology; public administration and social service professions; security and protective services; social sciences; visual and performing arts. **Areas of required coursework:** arts/fine arts, humanities, computer literacy, mathematics, English (including composition), foreign languages, sciences (biological or physical), social science. **Pre-professional programs:** pre-law, pre-medicine. **Special academic programs:** accelerated program, cooperative (work-study plan) program, distance learning, double major, dual enrollment, English as a Second Language (ESL), exchange student program (domestic), honors program, independent study, internships, study abroad, teacher certificate program, weekend college. **Teacher certification offered in:** early childhood, special education, elementary, secondary. **Cooperative education programs:** computer science, education, engineering, natural science, social/behavioral science. **Reserve Officers Training Corps (ROTC):** Army ROTC: Offered on campus; Air Force ROTC: Offered on campus. **Faculty and instruction (2009-2010):** Total instructional faculty: 871 full-time, 683 part-time (56% men; 44% women; 39% minorities). Full-time faculty with Ph.D. or other terminal degree: 87%. Student/faculty ratio: 28/1. Classes of fewer than 20 students: 24%; of 20 to 49 students: 55%; of 50 or more students: 21%. **Advanced Placement and International Baccalaureate credit:** AP tests may be used for: Placement only. Scores accepted: 3. International Baccalaureate exams may be used for: Credit only. **Freshmen returning for sophomore year:** 80%. **Graduation rates:** Four-year: 20%; five-year: 38%; six-year: 46%.

COSTS AND FINANCIAL AID

Financial aid office: (305) 348-2431. **Expenses (2009-2010):** Tuition and fees 2009-2010: $4,168 in state, $16,567 out of state; room/board: $11,946. Estimated books and supplies: $1,048; transportation: $2,616; personal expenses: $2,216. **Financial aid:** Priority filing date for institution's financial aid form: March 1; deadline: May 15. Average amount of debt of borrowers graduating in 2009: $14,901. Proportion who borrowed: 39%.

CAMPUS LIFE AND EXTRACURRICULAR ACTIVITIES

Campus housing available: coed dorms, fraternity housing, apartments for married students, apartment for single students, special housing for disabled students. Students who live in college-owned, operated, or affiliated housing: 8%. **Clubs and organizations:** Number of student organizations: 250. Activities include: campus ministries, choral groups, drama/theater, international student organization, jazz band, model UN, music ensembles, opera, radio station, student government, student newspaper, symphony orchestra, yearbook. Number of fraternities: 21; sororities: 16. Average proportion of students who stay on campus on weekends: 75%. **Sports program (2009-2010):** Member of NCAA I. *Men's intercollegiate varsity sports:* baseball, basketball, cross country, football, soccer, track and field (indoor), track and field (outdoor). *Women's intercollegiate varsity sports:* basketball, cross country, golf, soccer, softball, swimming, tennis, track and field (indoor), track and field (outdoor), volleyball.

SERVICES AND FACILITIES

Basic services: nonremedial tutoring, women's center, placement service, day care, health service. **Remedial assistance:** other. **Counseling services:** career, academic, psychological. **For learning-disabled students:** School does not offer a structured program with separate admission and additional fees. Services include: reading machines, tape recorders, diagnostic testing service, note-taking services, oral tests, learning center, extended time for tests, priority registration, priority seating, proofreading services, substitution of courses, texts on tape, typist/scribe, other testing accommodations, waiver of foreign language degree requirement, other. **Library:** Number of titles: 2,042,919; number of current serial subscriptions: 48,143. **Information technology resources:** Students are not required to lease or own a computer. Number of campus computers available to all students: 4,000. School has a wireless network. Approximate number of users that can be accommodated: 40,000. Proportion of college-owned housing units wired for high-speed internet access: 100%. **Campus safety:** Security services offered: 24-hour foot-and-vehicle patrols, late-night transport/escort service, 24-hour emergency telephones, lighted pathways/sidewalks, student patrols, controlled dormitory access (key, security card, etc).

TRANSFER AND INTERNATIONAL STUDENTS

Transfer students: May apply for admission for the following academic terms: Fall, Spring, Summer. Applicants need a minimum number of credits to apply. For fall 2009: Transfer applications received: 9,572. Transfer applicants offered admission: 6,815. Transfer applicants enrolled: 4,336. **International students:** Number of foreign undergraduates: 1603 (5% of stu-

dent body). Number of countries represented: 76. Minimum TOEFL score required: 500 (paper); 173 (computer). Average TOEFL score: 596 (paper).

Florida Memorial University

- **Address:** 15800 N.W. 42nd Avenue, Miami, FL 33054
- **Website:** http://www.fmuniv.edu/
- **Private; Religious affiliation:** Baptist
- **Enrollment:** N/A

KEY STATS
✔ **U.S News College Ranking:** second tier, Regional Colleges (South)
✔ **SAT or ACT Score (25th/75th percentile):** N/A
✔ **Tuition:** 2009-2010: $13,356

Selectivity: Less selective	**Room/board:** $5,820
Acceptance rate: N/A	**Average debt:** N/A
Student/faculty ratio: N/A	**Proportion who borrowed:** N/A

Florida Southern College

- **Address:** 111 Lake Hollingsworth Drive, Lakeland, FL 33801-5698
- **Website:** http://www.flsouthern.edu
- **Private; Religious affiliation:** United Methodist
- **Enrollment:** 1,832 full-time; 79 part-time

KEY STATS
✔ **U.S News College Ranking:** 8, Regional Colleges (South)
✔ **SAT Score (25th/75th percentile):** 970-1170
✔ **Tuition:** 2010-2011: $24,162

Selectivity: Selective	**Room/board:** $8,310
Acceptance rate: 69%	**Average debt:** $22,910
Student/faculty ratio: 13/1	**Proportion who borrowed:** 63%

UNDERGRADUATE STUDENT BODY STATS
2009-2010 enrollment: 1,832 full-time; 79 part-time. Men: 43%; women: 57%. **Ethnic makeup:** African American: 6%; American-Indian: 1%; Asian American: 2%; Hispanic: 8%; White: 80%; International: 3%. **Religious preference:** Roman Catholic: 20%; Protestant: 21%; Jewish: 1%; No preference: 25%; United Methodist: 14%; Other: 19%.

ADMISSIONS FACTS AND FIGURES
Phone: (863) 680-4131. **Email:** fscadm@flsouthern.edu. **Website:** http://www.flsouthern.edu. **Application deadlines for fall 2011:** Regular decision: March 1. Early decision: Send application by: December 1; Decision sent by: December 15. Early action: Not offered. Admission can be deferred. **Application fee:** $30. **To apply online, go to:** http://www.applyweb.com/aw?fsc. **Admissions requirements/recommendations:** High school units required (recommended): English: 4; Mathematics: 3; Science: 2; Foreign language: (2); Social studies: 3; History: 3; Academic electives: 1; Total units: 18. Tests: The college uses SAT or ACT scores in admissions decisions. Either SAT or ACT required. For admission to the fall 2011 entering class, the school will accept: ACT with or without writing accepted. Campus visit: Recommended. Admissions interview: Recommended. Off-campus interview: May be arranged. **Factors that count in admissions decisions:** *Academic:* Secondary school record: Very Important. Class rank: Considered. Letters of recommendation: Important. Standardized test scores: Very Important. Essay: Important. *Nonacademic:* Interview: Considered. Extracurricular activities: Important. Talent/ability: Important. Character/personal qualities: Important. Alumni/ae relationship: Considered. Geographical residence: Important. State residency: Considered. Religious affiliation/commitment: Not Considered. Minority status: Not Considered. Volunteer work: Considered. Work experience: Considered. **Other schools with the greatest overlap in applicants:** Stetson University; University of Central Florida; University of Florida; University of South Florida; University of Tampa. **Admissions statistics for the fall 2009 entering class:** Total applicants: 2,437. Total accepted: 1,692. Freshmen enrolled: 553; 31% were from out of state. Accepted through early-decision or early-action plans: 11%. Overall acceptance rate: 69%. Early-decision acceptance rate: 86%. Non-early acceptance rate: 69%. **Size of waiting list:** 0 applicants; enrolled from waiting list: 0. **Credentials of fall 2009 freshmen:**

23% ranked in the top 10 percent of their high school class; 49% were in the top 25 percent; 80% were in the top half. (Proportion submitting class standing: 71%.) **Average high school grade point average:** 3.4. **First-year students who submitted SAT scores:** 83%. Scores (25/75 percentile): Critical Reading: 490-590, Math: 480-580, Combined: 970-1170. **First-year students submitting ACT scores:** 63%. Scores (25/75 percentile): English: 19-25, Math: 20-26, Composite: 21-25.

ACADEMICS
Year founded: 1885. **Academic calendar:** Semester. **Degrees offered:** bachelor's, master's. **Most popular majors:** 29% business, management, marketing, and related support services, 17% education, 10% social sciences, 8% health professions and related clinical sciences, 7% communication, journalism, and related programs. **Major fields of study:** agriculture, agriculture operations, and related sciences; biological and biomedical sciences; business, management, marketing, and related support services; communication, journalism, and related programs; education; English language and literature/letters; foreign languages, literatures, and linguistics; health professions and related clinical sciences; history; mathematics and statistics; parks, recreation, leisure, and fitness studies; philosophy and religious studies; physical sciences; psychology; social sciences; visual and performing arts. **Areas of required coursework:** arts/fine arts, humanities, computer literacy, mathematics, English (including composition), philosophy, sciences (biological or physical), history, social science, other. **Pre-professional programs:** pre-law, pre-dentistry, pre-medicine, pre-theology, pre-veterinary science, pre-pharmacy, other. **Special academic programs (% participation):** double major (10%), dual enrollment (1%), exchange student program (domestic) (0%), honors program (2%), independent study (2%), internships (55%), liberal arts/career combination (0%), student-designed major (0%), study abroad (29%), teacher certificate program (14%). **Teacher certification offered in:** elementary, middle/junior high, secondary. **Cooperative education programs:** health professions, natural science. **Reserve Officers Training Corps (ROTC):** Army ROTC: Offered on campus; Air Force ROTC: Offered at cooperating institution (University of South Florida). **Faculty and instruction (2009-2010):** Total instructional faculty: 109 full-time, 86 part-time (55% men; 45% women; 7% minorities). Full-time faculty with Ph.D. or other terminal degree: 87%. Student/faculty ratio: 13/1. Classes of fewer than 20 students: 47%; of 20 to 49 students: 53%; of 50 or more students: 0%. **Advanced Placement and International Baccalaureate credit:** AP tests may be used for: Credit only. Scores accepted: 3, 4, 5. International Baccalaureate exams may be used for: Placement only. **Freshmen returning for sophomore year:** 74%. **Graduation rates:** Four-year: 38%; five-year: 54%; six-year: 54%. **Graduate study:** 27% of students pursue further study immediately upon graduation.

COSTS AND FINANCIAL AID
Financial aid office: (863) 680-4140. **Expenses (2010-2011):** Tuition and fees 2010-2011: $24,162; room/board: $8,310. Estimated books and supplies: $1,150 personal expenses: $1,180. **Financial aid:** Priority filing date for institution's financial aid form: March 1; deadline: July 1. In 2009-2010, 77% of undergraduates applied for financial aid. Of those, 67% were determined to have financial need; 28% had their need fully met. Average financial aid package (proportion receiving): $19,093 (67%). Average amount of gift aid, such as scholarships or grants (proportion receiving): $6,615 (47%). Average amount of self-help aid, such as work study or loans (proportion receiving): $4,800 (48%). Average need-based loan (excluding PLUS or other private loans): $4,228. Among students who received need-based aid, the average percentage of need met: 71%. Among students who received aid based on merit, the average award (and the proportion receiving): $9,903 (11%). The average athletic scholarship (and the proportion receiving): $9,379 (12%). Average amount of debt of borrowers graduating in 2009: $22,910. Proportion who borrowed: 63%.

CAMPUS LIFE AND EXTRACURRICULAR ACTIVITIES
Campus housing available (% using): coed dorms (28%), women's dorms (20%), men's dorms (18%), sorority housing (14%), fraternity housing (10%), apartments for married students (1%), apartment for single students (1%), special housing for disabled students (1%). Students who live in college-owned, operated, or affiliated housing: 70%. **Student employment:** During the 2009-2010 academic year, 25% of undergraduates worked on campus. Average per-year earnings: $1,500. **Clubs and organizations:** Number of student organizations: 70. Activities include: campus ministries, choral groups, concert band, dance, drama/theater, international student organization, jazz band, literary magazine, music ensembles, musical theater, opera, pep band, student government, student newspaper, symphony orchestra, television station, yearbook. Number of fraternities: 7; sororities:

7. Proportion of men in fraternities: 28%; of women in sororities: 23%. Average proportion of students who stay on campus on weekends: 85%. **Sports program (2009-2010):** Member of NCAA II. *Men's intercollegiate varsity sports:* baseball, basketball, cross country, golf, lacrosse, soccer, swimming, tennis, track and field (outdoor). *Women's intercollegiate varsity sports:* basketball, cross country, golf, soccer, softball, swimming, tennis, track and field (outdoor), volleyball.

SERVICES AND FACILITIES

Basic services: nonremedial tutoring, placement service, health service, health insurance. **Remedial assistance:** math, writing, study skills. **Counseling services:** minority student, career, military, personal, academic, psychological, religious, other. **For learning-disabled students:** School does not offer a structured program with separate admission and additional fees. Total undergraduates in learning-disabled program or receiving services: 85. Services include: extended time for tests, other. **Library:** Number of titles: 175,213; number of current serial subscriptions: 641. **Information technology resources:** Students are not required to lease or own a computer. Number of campus computers available to all students: 394. School has a wireless network. Approximate number of users that can be accommodated: 300. Proportion of college-owned housing units wired for high-speed internet access: 100%. **Campus safety:** Security services offered: 24-hour foot-and-vehicle patrols, late-night transport/escort service, 24-hour emergency telephones, lighted pathways/sidewalks, student patrols, controlled dormitory access (key, security card, etc).

TRANSFER AND INTERNATIONAL STUDENTS

Transfer students: May apply for admission for the following academic terms: Fall, Spring, Summer. Applicants need a minimum number of credits to apply. For fall 2009: Transfer applications received: 300. Transfer applicants offered admission: 194. Transfer applicants enrolled: 107. **International students:** Number of foreign undergraduates: 61 (3% of student body). Number of countries represented: 31. Minimum TOEFL score required: 550 (paper); 213 (computer). Average TOEFL score: 546 (paper).

Florida State University

- **Address:** Tallahassee, FL 32306
- **Website:** http://www.fsu.edu
- **Public**
- **Enrollment:** 27,705 full-time; 3,098 part-time

KEY STATS

✔ **U.S News College Ranking:** 104, National Universities
✔ **SAT Score (25th/75th percentile):** 1110-1290
✔ **Tuition:** 2009-2010: $4,566 in state, $18,804 out of state
  Selectivity: More selective   **Room/board:** $8,000
  Acceptance rate: 61%   **Average debt:** $19,364
  Student/faculty ratio: 22/1   **Proportion who borrowed:** 48%

UNDERGRADUATE STUDENT BODY STATS

2009-2010 enrollment: 27,705 full-time; 3,098 part-time. Men: 45%; women: 55%. **Ethnic makeup:** African American: 10%; American-Indian: 1%; Asian American: 4%; Hispanic: 13%; White: 72%.

ADMISSIONS FACTS AND FIGURES

Phone: (850) 644-6200. **Email:** admissions@admin.fsu.edu. **Website:** http://www.fsu.edu. **Application deadlines for fall 2011:** Regular decision: January 19. Early decision: Not offered. Early action: Not offered. Admission cannot be deferred. **Application fee:** $30. **To apply online, go to:** https://admissions.fsu.edu/undergradapp/. **Admissions requirements/recommendations:** High school units required (recommended): English: 4 (4); Mathematics: 4 (4); Science: 3 (4); Foreign language: 2 (4); Social studies: 1 (2); History: 2 (2); Academic electives: 3 (3); Total units: 19 (23). Tests: The college uses SAT or ACT scores in admissions decisions. Either SAT or ACT required. For admission to the fall 2011 entering class, the school will accept: ACT with writing required. Campus visit: Recommended. Admissions interview: Neither required nor recommended. Off-campus interview: Not available. **Factors that count in admissions decisions:** *Academic:* Secondary school record: Very Important. Class rank: Considered. Letters of recommendation: Considered. Standardized test scores: Important. Essay: Considered. *Nonacademic:* Interview: Not Considered. Extracurricular activities: Considered. Talent/ability:

Important. Character/personal qualities: Considered. Alumni/ae relationship: Considered. Geographical residence: Considered. State residency: Important. Religious affiliation/commitment: Not Considered. Minority status: Not Considered. Volunteer work: Considered. Work experience: Considered. **Other schools with the greatest overlap in applicants:** Florida International University; University of Central Florida; University of Florida; University of Miami; University of South Florida. **Admissions statistics for the fall 2009 entering class:** Total applicants: 23,439. Total accepted: 14,308. Freshmen enrolled: 5,967; 11% were from out of state. Overall acceptance rate: 61%. **Size of waiting list:** 1052 applicants; enrolled from waiting list: 86. **Credentials of fall 2009 freshmen:** 34% ranked in the top 10 percent of their high school class; 61% were in the top 25 percent; 93% were in the top half. (Proportion submitting class standing: 76%.) **Average high school grade point average:** 3.7. **First-year students who submitted SAT scores:** 52%. Scores (25/75 percentile): Critical Reading: 550-640, Math: 560-650, Combined: 1110-1290. **First-year students submitting ACT scores:** 48%. Scores (25/75 percentile): English: 23-29, Math: 24-28, Composite: 24-28.

ACADEMICS

Year founded: 1851. **Academic calendar:** Semester. **Degrees offered:** certificate, associate, transfer-associate, bachelor's, post-bachelor's certificate, master's, post-master's certificate, doctorate. **Most popular majors:** 6% English language and literature, 5% criminal justice/safety studies, 5% finance, 5% political science and government, 5% psychology. **Major fields of study:** area, ethnic, cultural, and gender studies; biological and biomedical sciences; business, management, marketing, and related support services; communication, journalism, and related programs; computer and information sciences and support services; education; engineering; English language and literature/letters; family and consumer sciences/human sciences; foreign languages, literatures, and linguistics; health professions and related clinical sciences; history; liberal arts and sciences studies, and humanities; mathematics and statistics; parks, recreation, leisure, and fitness studies; philosophy and religious studies; physical sciences; psychology; public administration and social service professions; security and protective services; social sciences; visual and performing arts. **Areas of required coursework:** arts/fine arts, humanities, computer literacy, mathematics, English (including composition), sciences (biological or physical), history, social science, other. **Pre-professional programs:** pre-law, pre-dentistry, pre-medicine, pre-theology, pre-veterinary science, pre-optometry, pre-pharmacy, other. **Special academic programs:** accelerated program, cooperative (work-study plan) program, cross-registration, distance learning, double major, dual enrollment, English as a Second Language (ESL), honors program, independent study, internships, study abroad, teacher certificate program. **Teacher certification offered in:** early childhood, special education, elementary, middle/junior high, secondary. **Cooperative education programs:** business, computer science, education, engineering, natural science, social/behavioral science, other. **Reserve Officers Training Corps (ROTC):** Army ROTC: Offered on campus; Navy ROTC: Offered at cooperating institution (Florida A&M University); Air Force ROTC: Offered on campus. **Faculty and instruction (2009-2010):** Total instructional faculty: 1,293 full-time, 329 part-time (60% men; 40% women; 14% minorities). Full-time faculty with Ph.D. or other terminal degree: 92%. Student/faculty ratio: 22/1. Classes of fewer than 20 students: 36%; of 20 to 49 students: 48%; of 50 or more students: 16%. **Advanced Placement and International Baccalaureate credit:** AP tests may be used for: Credit and/or placement. Scores accepted: 3, 4, 5. International Baccalaureate exams may be used for: Credit and/or placement. **Freshmen returning for sophomore year:** 89%. **Graduation rates:** Four-year: 47%; five-year: 68%; six-year: 71%. **Graduate study:** 29% of students pursue further study immediately upon graduation.

COSTS AND FINANCIAL AID

Financial aid office: (850) 644-1993. **Expenses (2009-2010):** Tuition and fees 2009-2010: $4,566 in state, $18,804 out of state; room/board: $8,000. Estimated books and supplies: $1,000; transportation: $1,434; personal expenses: $2,880. **Financial aid:** In 2009-2010, 69% of undergraduates applied for financial aid. Of those, 34% were determined to have financial need; 77% had their need fully met. Average financial aid package (proportion receiving): $10,419 (34%). Average amount of gift aid, such as scholarships or grants (proportion receiving): $4,071 (20%). Average amount of self-help aid, such as work study or loans (proportion receiving): $3,767 (25%). Average need-based loan (excluding PLUS or other private loans): $3,648. Among students who received need-based aid, the average percentage of need met: 76%. Among students who received aid based on merit, the average award (and the proportion receiving): $2,254 (6%). The average athletic scholarship (and the proportion receiving): $14,368 (1%). Average amount of debt of borrowers graduating in 2009: $19,364. Proportion who borrowed: 48%.

CAMPUS LIFE AND EXTRACURRICULAR ACTIVITIES

Campus housing available: coed dorms, women's dorms, sorority housing, fraternity housing, apartments for married students, apartment for single students, special housing for disabled students, other housing options. Students who live in college-owned, operated, or affiliated housing: 20%. **Student employment:** During the 2009-2010 academic year, 9% of undergraduates worked on campus. Average per-year earnings: $4,300. **Clubs and organizations:** Number of student organizations: 530. Activities include: campus ministries, choral groups, concert band, dance, drama/theater, international student organization, jazz band, literary magazine, marching band, model UN, music ensembles, musical theater, opera, pep band, radio station, student government, student newspaper, student film society, symphony orchestra, television station, yearbook. Number of fraternities: 32; sororities: 28. Proportion of men in fraternities: 7%; of women in sororities: 8%. **Sports program (2009-2010):** Member of NCAA I. *Men's intercollegiate varsity sports:* baseball, basketball, cross country, football, golf, swimming, tennis, track and field (indoor), track and field (outdoor). *Women's intercollegiate varsity sports:* basketball, cross country, golf, soccer, softball, swimming, tennis, track and field (indoor), track and field (outdoor), volleyball.

SERVICES AND FACILITIES

Basic services: nonremedial tutoring, women's center, placement service, day care, health service, health insurance. **Remedial assistance:** reading, math, writing, study skills. **Counseling services:** minority student, career, military, personal, veteran student, academic, older student, psychological, birth control, religious. **For learning-disabled students:** School does not offer a structured program with separate admission and additional fees. Services include: reading machines, tape recorders, diagnostic testing service, note-taking services, oral tests, readers, extended time for tests, priority registration, priority seating, texts on tape, other testing accommodations, other. **Library:** Number of titles: 3,034,491; number of current serial subscriptions: 78,300. **Information technology resources:** Students are required to lease or own a computer. Number of campus computers available to all students: 2,958. School has a wireless network. Approximate number of users that can be accommodated: 9,240. Proportion of college-owned housing units wired for high-speed internet access: 100%. **Campus safety:** Security services offered: 24-hour foot-and-vehicle patrols, late-night transport/escort service, 24-hour emergency telephones, lighted pathways/sidewalks, controlled dormitory access (key, security card, etc).

TRANSFER AND INTERNATIONAL STUDENTS

Transfer students: May apply for admission for the following academic terms: Fall, Spring, Summer. Applicants need a minimum number of credits to apply. For fall 2009: Transfer applications received: 7,654. Transfer applicants offered admission: 3,665. Transfer applicants enrolled: 2,079. **International students:** Number of foreign undergraduates: 124. Number of countries represented: 54. Minimum TOEFL score required: 550 (paper); 213 (computer). Average TOEFL score: 601 (paper).

Hodges University

- **Address:** 2655 Northbrooke Drive, Naples, FL 34119
- **Website:** http://www.hodges.edu
- **Private**
- **Enrollment:** 1,587 full-time; 451 part-time

KEY STATS

✔ **U.S News College Ranking:** Unranked, Regional Universities (South)
✔ **SAT or ACT Score (25th/75th percentile):** N/A
✔ **Tuition:** 2010-2011: $14,330

Selectivity: N/A	Room/board: N/A
Acceptance rate: 91%	Average debt: $17,600
Student/faculty ratio: 23/1	Proportion who borrowed: 78%

UNDERGRADUATE STUDENT BODY STATS

2009-2010 enrollment: 1,587 full-time; 451 part-time. Men: 31%; women: 69%. **Ethnic makeup:** African American: 17%; Asian American: 2%; Hispanic: 27%; White: 54%.

ADMISSIONS FACTS AND FIGURES

Phone: (239) 513-1122. **Email:** admit@hodges.edu. **Website:** http://www.hodges.edu. **Application deadlines for fall 2011:** Regular decision: Rolling. Early decision: Not offered. Early action: Not offered. Admission cannot be deferred. **Application fee:** $20. **To apply online, go to:** http://www.hodges.edu/admissions/apply/. **Admissions requirements/recommendations:** Tests: The college does not use SAT or ACT scores in admissions decisions. Neither SAT nor ACT required. For admission to the fall 2011 entering class, the school will accept: ACT with or without writing accepted. Campus visit: Recommended. Admissions interview: Recommended. Off-campus interview: Not available. **Factors that count in admissions decisions:** *Academic:* Secondary school record: Not Considered. Class rank: Not Considered. Letters of recommendation: Not Considered. Standardized test scores: Not Considered. Essay: Not Considered. *Nonacademic:* Interview: Important. Extracurricular activities: Not Considered. Talent/ability: Not Considered. Character/personal qualities: Not Considered. Alumni/ae relationship: Not Considered. Geographical residence: Not Considered. State residency: Not Considered. Religious affiliation/commitment: Not Considered. Minority status: Not Considered. Volunteer work: Not Considered. Work experience: Not Considered. **Admissions statistics for the fall 2009 entering class:** Total applicants: 331. Total accepted: 300. Freshmen enrolled: 287; 5% were from out of state. Overall acceptance rate: 91%.

ACADEMICS

Year founded: 1990. **Academic calendar:** Trimester. **Degrees offered:** certificate, associate, bachelor's, master's. **Most popular majors:** 46% business administration, management, and operations, 23% multi/interdisciplinary studies, 12% health/health care administration/management, 7% information technology, 5% criminal justice/safety studies. **Major fields of study:** business, management, marketing, and related support services; computer and information sciences and support services; health professions and related clinical sciences; legal professions and studies; multi/interdisciplinary studies; psychology; security and protective services. **Areas of required coursework:** humanities, computer literacy, mathematics, English (including composition), social science. **Special academic programs:** accelerated program, distance learning, double major, English as a Second Language (ESL). **Faculty and instruction (2009-2010):** Total instructional faculty: 58 full-time, 57 part-time (51% men; 49% women; 10% minorities). Full-time faculty with Ph.D. or other terminal degree: 59%. Student/faculty ratio: 23/1. Classes of fewer than 20 students: 68%; of 20 to 49 students: 30%; of 50 or more students: 2%. **Advanced Placement and International Baccalaureate credit:** AP tests may be used for: Credit only. Scores accepted: 3, 4, 5. International Baccalaureate exams may be used for: Credit only. **Freshmen returning for sophomore year:** 39%. **Graduation rates:** Six-year: 32%.

COSTS AND FINANCIAL AID

Financial aid office: (239) 513-1122. **Expenses (2010-2011):** Tuition and fees 2010-2011: $14,330. **Financial aid:** Priority filing date for institution's financial aid form: September 10; deadline: September 10. In 2009-2010, 89% of undergraduates applied for financial aid. Of those, 74% were determined to have financial need; 20% had their need fully met. Average financial aid package (proportion receiving): $9,200 (74%). Average amount of gift aid, such as scholarships or grants (proportion receiving): $4,600 (67%). Average amount of self-help aid, such as work study or loans (proportion receiving): $4,300 (57%). Average need-based loan (excluding PLUS or other private loans): $4,300. Among students who received need-based aid, the average percentage of need met: 74%. Among students who received aid based on merit, the average award (and the proportion receiving): $260 (4%). The average athletic scholarship (and the proportion receiving): $0 (0%). Average amount of debt of borrowers graduating in 2009: $17,600. Proportion who borrowed: 78%.

CAMPUS LIFE AND EXTRACURRICULAR ACTIVITIES

Activities include: literary magazine. Number of fraternities: 0; sororities: 0.

SERVICES AND FACILITIES

Basic services: nonremedial tutoring, placement service. **Remedial assistance:** math, writing. **Counseling services:** career, academic. **For learning-disabled students:** School does not offer a structured program with separate admission and additional fees. **Library:** Number of titles: 38,008; number of current serial subscriptions: 230. **Information technology resources:** Students are not required to lease or own a computer. Number of campus computers available to all students: 800. School has a wireless network. Proportion of college-owned housing units wired for high-speed internet access: 100%.

TRANSFER AND INTERNATIONAL STUDENTS

Transfer students: May apply for admission for the following academic terms: Fall, Winter, Summer. Applicants need a minimum number of credits to apply. For fall 2009: Transfer applications received: 382. Transfer applicants offered admission: 358. Transfer applicants enrolled: 382. **International students:** Number of foreign undergraduates: 2. Minimum TOEFL score required: 500 (paper); 273 (computer).

Jacksonville University

- **Address:** 2800 University Boulevard N, Jacksonville, FL 32211
- **Website:** http://www.jacksonville.edu
- **Private**
- **Enrollment:** 2,316 full-time; 857 part-time

KEY STATS

✔ **U.S News College Ranking:** 44, Regional Universities (South)
✔ **SAT Score (25th/75th percentile):** 940-1120
✔ **Tuition:** 2010-2011: $26,300

Selectivity: Selective	**Room/board:** $9,320
Acceptance rate: 54%	**Average debt:** N/A
Student/faculty ratio: 14/1	**Proportion who borrowed:** N/A

UNDERGRADUATE STUDENT BODY STATS

2009-2010 enrollment: 2,316 full-time; 857 part-time. Men: 40%; women: 60%. **Ethnic makeup:** African American: 19%; American-Indian: 1%; Asian American: 3%; Hispanic: 6%; White: 70%; International: 2%.

ADMISSIONS FACTS AND FIGURES

Phone: (800) 225-2027. **Email:** admissions@ju.edu. **Website:** http://www.jacksonville.edu. **Application deadlines for fall 2011:** Regular decision: Rolling. Early decision: Not offered. Early action: Not offered. Admission can be deferred. **Application fee:** $30. **To apply online, go to:** http://www.ju.edu/apply.aspx. **Admissions requirements/recommendations:** High school units required (recommended): English: 4 (4); Mathematics: 3 (4); Science: 3 (3); Foreign language: 0 (2); Social studies: 3 (3); Total units: 13 (16). Tests: The college uses SAT or ACT scores in admissions decisions. Either SAT or ACT required. For admission to the fall 2011 entering class, the school will accept: ACT with or without writing accepted. Campus visit: Recommended. Admissions interview: Recommended. Off-campus interview: May be arranged. **Factors that count in admissions decisions:** *Academic:* Secondary school record: Important. Class rank: Not Considered. Letters of recommendation: Considered. Standardized test scores: Very Important. Essay: Considered. *Nonacademic:* Interview: Considered. Extracurricular activities: Considered. Talent/ability: Important. Character/personal qualities: Considered. Alumni/ae relationship: Not Considered. Geographical residence: Not Considered. State residency: Not Considered. Religious affiliation/commitment: Not Considered. Minority status: Not Considered. Volunteer work: Considered. Work experience: Considered. **Other schools with the greatest overlap in applicants:** Florida State University; University of Central Florida; University of Florida; University of North Florida; University of Tampa. **Admissions statistics for the fall 2009 entering class:** Total applicants: 6,854. Total accepted: 3,668. Freshmen enrolled: 669; 36% were from out of state. Overall acceptance rate: 54%. **Average high school grade point average:** 3.4. **First-year students who submitted SAT scores:** 66%. Scores (25/75 percentile): Critical Reading: 470-560, Math: 470-560, Combined: 940-1120. **First-year students submitting ACT scores:** 34%. Scores (25/75 percentile): English: N/A, Math: N/A, Composite: 19-25.

ACADEMICS

Year founded: 1934. **Academic calendar:** Semester. **Degrees offered:** bachelor's, master's. **Most popular majors:** 43% health professions and related clinical sciences, 19% business, management, marketing, and related support services, 10% social sciences, 6% visual and performing arts, 5% transportation and materials moving. **Major fields of study:** biological and biomedical sciences; business, management, marketing, and related support services; communication, journalism, and related programs; computer and information sciences and support services; education; English language and literature/letters; foreign languages, literatures, and linguistics; health professions and related clinical sciences; history; liberal arts and sciences studies, and humanities; mathematics and statistics; parks, recreation, leisure, and fitness studies; philosophy and religious studies; physical sciences; psychology; social sciences; theology and religious vocations; transportation and materials moving; visual and performing arts. **Areas of required coursework:** arts/fine arts, humanities, computer literacy, mathematics, English (including composition), philosophy, sciences (biological or physical), history, social science, other. **Pre-professional programs:** pre-law, pre-dentistry, pre-medicine, pre-veterinary science, pre-pharmacy. **Special academic programs (% participation):** accelerated program (11%), cooperative (work-study plan) program, distance learning (24%), double major (7%), dual enrollment, honors program, independent study, internships, liberal arts/career combination, student-designed major, study abroad, teacher certificate program. **Teacher certification offered in:** early childhood, elementary, secondary. **Reserve Officers Training Corps (ROTC):** Navy ROTC: Offered on campus. **Faculty and instruction (2009-2010):** Total instructional faculty: 166 full-time, 105 part-time (52% men; 48% women; 13% minorities). Full-time faculty with Ph.D. or other terminal degree: 81%. Student/faculty ratio: 14/1. Classes of fewer than 20 students: 58%; of 20 to 49 students: 42%; of 50 or more students: 0%. **Advanced Placement and International Baccalaureate credit:** AP tests may be used for: Credit only. Scores accepted: 3, 4. International Baccalaureate exams may be used for: Credit only. **Freshmen returning for sophomore year:** 64%. **Graduation rates:** Four-year: 29%; five-year: 40%; six-year: 52%. **Graduate study:** 13% of students pursue further study immediately upon graduation.

COSTS AND FINANCIAL AID

Financial aid office: (904) 256-7060. **Expenses (2010-2011):** Tuition and fees 2010-2011: $26,300; room/board: $9,320. Estimated books and supplies: $800; transportation: $1,732; personal expenses: $1,178. **Financial aid:** Priority filing date for institution's financial aid form: March 1. In 2009-2010, 80% of undergraduates applied for financial aid. Of those, 71% were determined to have financial need; 17% had their need fully met. Average financial aid package (proportion receiving): $19,580 (71%). Average amount of gift aid, such as scholarships or grants (proportion receiving): $15,432 (61%). Average amount of self-help aid, such as work study or loans (proportion receiving): $4,700 (51%). Average need-based loan (excluding PLUS or other private loans): $4,433. Among students who received need-based aid, the average percentage of need met: 61%. Among students who received aid based on merit, the average award (and the proportion receiving): $8,925 (25%). The average athletic scholarship (and the proportion receiving): $13,642 (12%).

CAMPUS LIFE AND EXTRACURRICULAR ACTIVITIES

Campus housing available: coed dorms, women's dorms, men's dorms, sorority housing, fraternity housing, apartment for single students. Students who live in college-owned, operated, or affiliated housing: 43%. **Clubs and organizations:** Number of student organizations: 60. Activities include: choral groups, concert band, dance, drama/theater, jazz band, literary magazine, music ensembles, musical theater, pep band, radio station, student government, student newspaper, symphony orchestra, television station, yearbook. Number of fraternities: 6; sororities: 7. Proportion of men in fraternities: 10%; of women in sororities: 14%. Average proportion of students who stay on campus on weekends: 60%. **Sports program (2009-2010):** Member of NCAA I. *Men's intercollegiate varsity sports:* baseball, basketball, football, golf, lacrosse, soccer, tennis. *Women's intercollegiate varsity sports:* basketball, cross country, golf, lacrosse, crew (lightweight), soccer, softball, tennis, track and field (indoor), track and field (outdoor), volleyball.

SERVICES AND FACILITIES

Basic services: nonremedial tutoring, placement service, health service, health insurance. **Remedial assistance:** reading, math, writing, study skills. **Counseling services:** career, personal, academic, psychological. **For learning-disabled students:** School does not offer a structured program with separate admission and additional fees. Total undergraduates in learning-disabled program or receiving services: 51. Services include: learning center, extended time for tests, tutors, priority seating, substitution of courses, other testing accommodations. **Library:** Number of titles: 250,552; number of current serial subscriptions: 49,554. **Information technology resources:** Students are not required to lease or own a computer. Number of campus computers available to all students: 596. School has a wireless network. Approximate number of users that can be accommodated: 2,250. Proportion of college-owned housing units wired for high-speed internet access: 100%. **Campus safety:** Security services offered: 24-hour foot-and-vehicle patrols, late-night transport/escort service, 24-hour emergency telephones, lighted pathways/sidewalks, controlled dormitory access (key, security card, etc).

TRANSFER AND INTERNATIONAL STUDENTS

Transfer students: May apply for admission for the following academic terms: Fall, Spring, Summer. Applicants need a minimum number of credits to apply. For fall 2009: Transfer applications received: 1,814. Transfer applicants offered admission: 964. Transfer applicants enrolled: 302. **International students:** Number of foreign undergraduates: 51 (2% of student body). Number of countries represented: 50. Minimum TOEFL score required: 540 (paper); 207 (computer). Average TOEFL score: 540 (paper).

Lynn University

- **Address:** 3601 N. Military Trail, Boca Raton, FL 33431
- **Website:** http://www.lynn.edu
- **Private**
- **Enrollment:** 1,576 full-time; 210 part-time

KEY STATS

✔ **U.S News College Ranking:** 78, Regional Universities (South)
✔ **SAT Score (25th/75th percentile):** 840-1050
✔ **Tuition:** 2010-2011: $30,900

Selectivity: Less selective	**Room/board:** $10,900
Acceptance rate: 72%	**Average debt:** $34,075
Student/faculty ratio: 16/1	**Proportion who borrowed:** 43%

UNDERGRADUATE STUDENT BODY STATS

2009-2010 enrollment: 1,576 full-time; 210 part-time. Men: 51%; women: 49%. **Ethnic makeup:** African American: 3%; Hispanic: 7%; White: 74%; International: 15%.

ADMISSIONS FACTS AND FIGURES

Phone: (800) 888-5966. **Email:** admission@lynn.edu. **Website:** http://www.lynn.edu. **Application deadlines for fall 2011:** Regular decision: Rolling. Early decision: Not offered. Early action: Not offered. Admission can be deferred. **Application fee:** $35. **To apply online, go to:** http://www.lynn.edu/getting-started/applying-to-lynn. **Admissions requirements/recommendations:** High school units required (recommended): English: 4; Mathematics: 4; Science: 4; Foreign language: 0; Social studies: 2; History: 2; Total units: 16. Tests: The college uses SAT or ACT scores in admissions decisions. Either SAT or ACT required. For admission to the fall 2011 entering class, the school will accept: ACT with or without writing accepted. Campus visit: Recommended. Admissions interview: Recommended. **Factors that count in admissions decisions:** *Academic:* Secondary school record: Very Important. Class rank: Important. Letters of recommendation: Important. Standardized test scores: Very Important. Essay: Important. *Nonacademic:* Interview: Considered. Extracurricular activities: Considered. Talent/ability: Considered. Character/personal qualities: Important. Alumni/ae relationship: Considered. Geographical residence: Not Considered. State residency: Considered. Religious affiliation/commitment: Not Considered. Minority status: Not Considered. Volunteer work: Considered. Work experience: Important. **Other schools with the greatest overlap in applicants:** Barry University; Florida Southern College; Rollins College; University of Tampa. **Admissions statistics for the fall 2009 entering class:** Total applicants: 2,454. Total accepted: 1,773. Freshmen enrolled: 477; 73% were from out of state. Overall acceptance rate: 72%. **Credentials of fall 2009 freshmen:** 7% ranked in the top 10 percent of their high school class; 23% were in the top 25 percent; 51% were in the top half. (Proportion submitting class standing: 27%.) **First-year students who submitted SAT scores:** 82%. Scores (25/75 percentile): Critical Reading: 420-520, Math: 420-530, Combined: 840-1050. **First-year students submitting ACT scores:** 33%. Scores (25/75 percentile): English: 16-21, Math: 16-22, Composite: 17-22.

ACADEMICS

Year founded: 1962. **Academic calendar:** Semester. **Degrees offered:** certificate, bachelor's, post-bachelor's certificate, master's, post-master's certificate. **Most popular majors:** 43% business, management, marketing, and related support services, 16% communication, journalism, and related programs, 13% psychology, 9% security and protective services, 8% visual and performing arts. **Major fields of study:** biological and biomedical sciences; business, management, marketing, and related support services; communication, journalism, and related programs; education; health professions and related clinical sciences; liberal arts and sciences studies, and humanities; parks, recreation, leisure, and fitness studies; psychology; public administration and social service professions; security and protective services; social sciences; visual and performing arts. **Areas of required coursework:** arts/fine arts, humanities, computer literacy, mathematics, English (including composition), sciences (biological or physical), history, social science, other. **Special academic programs (% participation):** accelerated program, cooperative (work-study plan) program, distance learning (49%), double major (0%), dual enrollment, English as a Second Language (ESL) (8%), honors program (2%), independent study (15%), internships (30%), liberal arts/career combination, study abroad (18%), teacher certificate program. **Teacher certification offered in:** elementary, secondary. **Reserve Officers Training Corps (ROTC):** Air Force ROTC: Offered at cooperating institution (University of Miami). **Faculty and instruction (2009-2010):** Total instructional faculty: 103 full-time, 57 part-time (61% men; 39% women; 28% minorities). Full-time faculty with Ph.D. or other terminal degree: 69%. Student/faculty ratio: 16/1. Classes of fewer than 20 students: 61%; of 20 to 49 students: 39%; of 50 or more students: 0%. **Advanced Placement and International Baccalaureate credit:** AP tests may be used for: Credit and/or placement. International Baccalaureate exams may be used for: Placement only. **Freshmen returning for sophomore year:** 61%. **Graduation rates:** Four-year: 23%; five-year: 33%; six-year: 35%.

COSTS AND FINANCIAL AID

Financial aid office: (561) 237-7186. **Expenses (2010-2011):** Tuition and fees 2010-2011: $30,900; room/board: $10,900. Estimated books and supplies: $1,200; transportation: $650. **Financial aid:** Priority filing date for institution's financial aid form: March 1. In 2009-2010, 68% of undergraduates applied for financial aid. Of those, 42% were determined to have financial need; 98% had their need fully met. Average financial aid package (proportion receiving): $20,853 (42%). Average amount of gift aid, such as scholarships or grants (proportion receiving): $13,761 (36%). Average amount of self-help aid, such as work study or loans (proportion receiving): $7,098 (30%). Average need-based loan (excluding PLUS or other private loans): $5,643. Among students who received need-based aid, the average percentage of need met: 60%. Among students who received aid based on merit, the average award (and the proportion receiving): $11,381 (22%). The average athletic scholarship (and the proportion receiving): $9,212 (12%). Average amount of debt of borrowers graduating in 2009: $34,075. Proportion who borrowed: 43%.

CAMPUS LIFE AND EXTRACURRICULAR ACTIVITIES

Campus housing available (% using): coed dorms (99%), women's dorms, special housing for disabled students (1%), special housing for international students. Students who live in college-owned, operated, or affiliated housing: 42%. **Student employment:** During the 2009-2010 academic year, 2% of undergraduates worked on campus. Average per-year earnings: $3,400. **Clubs and organizations:** Number of student organizations: 31. Activities include: campus ministries, choral groups, dance, drama/theater, international student organization, literary magazine, music ensembles, radio station, student government, student newspaper, student film society, symphony orchestra, television station, yearbook. Number of fraternities: 1; sororities: 1. Average proportion of students who stay on campus on weekends: 95%. **Sports program (2009-2010):** Member of NCAA II.

SERVICES AND FACILITIES

Basic services: nonremedial tutoring, health service, health insurance. **Remedial assistance:** math, writing, study skills. **Counseling services:** career, personal, academic. **For learning-disabled students:** School does not offer a structured program with separate admission and additional fees. Services include: remedial math, remedial English, reading machines, tape recorders, other special classes, untimed tests, oral tests, learning center, readers, extended time for tests, tutors. **Library:** Number of titles: 110,000; number of current serial subscriptions: 400. **Information technology resources:** Students are not required to lease or own a computer. Number of campus computers available to all students: 235. School has a wireless network. Approximate number of users that can be accommodated: 50. Proportion of college-owned housing units wired for high-speed internet access: 100%. **Campus safety:** Security services offered: late-night transport/escort service, lighted pathways/sidewalks.

TRANSFER AND INTERNATIONAL STUDENTS

Transfer students: May apply for admission for the following academic terms: Fall, Spring. Applicants need a minimum number of credits to apply. For fall 2009: Transfer applications received: 178. Transfer applicants offered admission: 174. Transfer applicants enrolled: 99. **International students:** Number of foreign undergraduates: 266 (15% of student body). Minimum TOEFL score required: 500 (paper); 173 (computer). Average TOEFL score: 580 (paper).

New College of Florida

- **Address:** 5800 Bay Shore Road, Sarasota, FL 34243-2109
- **Website:** http://www.ncf.edu
- **Public**
- **Enrollment:** 825 full-time

KEY STATS

✔ **U.S News College Ranking:** 99, National Liberal Arts Colleges
✔ **SAT Score (25th/75th percentile):** 1220-1410
✔ **Tuition:** 2009-2010: $4,784 in state, $26,386 out of state
  Selectivity: More selective   **Room/board:** $7,783
  Acceptance rate: 53%   **Average debt:** $14,794
  Student/faculty ratio: 10/1   **Proportion who borrowed:** 41%

UNDERGRADUATE STUDENT BODY STATS

2009-2010 enrollment: 825 full-time. Men: 38%; women: 62%. **Ethnic makeup:** African American: 2%; American-Indian: 1%; Asian American: 3%; Hispanic: 11%; White: 83%.

ADMISSIONS FACTS AND FIGURES

Phone: (941) 487-5000. **Email:** admissions@ncf.edu. **Website:** http://www.ncf.edu. **Application deadlines for fall 2011:** Regular decision: April 15. Early decision: Not offered. Early action: Not offered. Admission can be deferred. **Application fee:** $30. **To apply online, go to:** http://www.ncf.edu/admissions/apply. **Admissions requirements/recommendations:** High school units required (recommended): English: 4 (4); Mathematics: 4 (4); Science: 3 (4); Foreign language: 2 (4); Social studies: 3 (4); History: 0 (0); Academic electives: 2 (5); Total units: 18 (20). Tests: The college uses SAT or ACT scores in admissions decisions. Either SAT or ACT required. For admission to the fall 2011 entering class, the school will accept: ACT with writing required. Campus visit: Recommended. Admissions interview: Neither required nor recommended. Off-campus interview: May be arranged. **Factors that count in admissions decisions:** *Academic:* Secondary school record: Very Important. Class rank: Considered. Letters of recommendation: Important. Standardized test scores: Important. Essay: Very Important. *Nonacademic:* Interview: Considered. Extracurricular activities: Considered. Talent/ability: Considered. Character/personal qualities: Important. Alumni/ae relationship: Considered. Geographical residence: Considered. State residency: Considered. Religious affiliation/commitment: Not Considered. Minority status: Not Considered. Volunteer work: Considered. Work experience: Considered. **Other schools with the greatest overlap in applicants:** Eckerd College; Florida State University; Hampshire College; New York University; University of Florida. **Admissions statistics for the fall 2009 entering class:** Total applicants: 1,403. Total accepted: 739. Freshmen enrolled: 218; 21% were from out of state. Overall acceptance rate: 53%. **Size of waiting list:** 203 applicants; enrolled from waiting list: 1. **Credentials of fall 2009 freshmen:** 49% ranked in the top 10 percent of their high school class; 84% were in the top 25 percent; 96% were in the top half. (Proportion submitting class standing: 63%.) **Average high school grade point average:** 4.0. **First-year students who submitted SAT scores:** 95%. Scores (25/75 percentile): Critical Reading: 630-730, Math: 590-680, Combined: 1220-1410. **First-year students submitting ACT scores:** 52%. Scores (25/75 percentile): English: 28-34, Math: 24-29, Composite: 27-30.

ACADEMICS

Year founded: 2001. **Academic calendar:** 4-1-4. **Degrees offered:** bachelor's. **Most popular majors:** 100% liberal arts and sciences, general studies, and humanities. **Major fields of study:** liberal arts and sciences studies, and humanities. **Areas of required coursework:** humanities, sciences (biological or physical), social science. **Special academic programs (% participation):** cross-registration (16%), double major (9%), exchange student program (domestic) (20%), honors program (100%), independent study (100%), internships (54%), student-designed major (100%), study abroad (30%). **Faculty and instruction (2009-2010):** Total instructional faculty: 71 full-time, 23 part-time (48% men; 52% women; 14% minorities). Full-time faculty with Ph.D. or other terminal degree: 99%. Student/faculty ratio: 10/1. Classes of fewer than 20 students: 64%; of 20 to 49 students: 33%; of 50 or more students: 3%. **Freshmen returning for sophomore year:** 84%. **Graduation rates:** Four-year: 46%; five-year: 59%; six-year: 60%. **Graduate study:** 29% of students pursue further study immediately upon graduation; 55% within one year; 73% within five years. Fields in which graduates pursue further study: Master of Business Administration (MBA), 10%; law, 11%; medicine, 2%; theology (or the seminary), 2%; education, 9%; arts and sciences, 66%; veterinary medicine, 1%.

COSTS AND FINANCIAL AID

Financial aid office: (941) 359-4255. **Expenses (2009-2010):** Tuition and fees 2009-2010: $4,784 in state, $26,386 out of state; room/board: $7,783. Estimated books and supplies: $800; transportation: $1,100; personal expenses: $2,600. **Financial aid:** Priority filing date for institution's financial aid form: February 15. In 2009-2010, 63% of undergraduates applied for financial aid. Of those, 45% were determined to have financial need; 56% had their need fully met. Average financial aid package (proportion receiving): $13,282 (45%). Average amount of gift aid, such as scholarships or grants (proportion receiving): $9,844 (44%). Average amount of self-help aid, such as work study or loans (proportion receiving): $4,393 (36%). Average need-based loan (excluding PLUS or other private loans): $3,857. Among students who received need-based aid, the average percentage of need met: 92%. Among students who received aid based on merit, the average award (and the proportion receiving): $2,778 (49%). The average athletic scholarship (and the proportion receiving): $0 (0%). Average amount of debt of borrowers graduating in 2009: $14,794. Proportion who borrowed: 41%.

CAMPUS LIFE AND EXTRACURRICULAR ACTIVITIES

Campus housing available (% using): coed dorms (99%), special housing for disabled students (1%). Students who live in college-owned, operated, or affiliated housing: 79%. **Student employment:** During the 2009-2010 academic year, 24% of undergraduates worked on campus. Average per-year earnings: $2,309. **Clubs and organizations:** Number of student organizations: 60. Activities include: campus ministries, choral groups, dance, drama/theater, literary magazine, music ensembles, musical theater, radio station, student government, student newspaper, student film society. Number of fraternities: 0; sororities: 0. Average proportion of students who stay on campus on weekends: 79%.

SERVICES AND FACILITIES

Basic services: nonremedial tutoring, women's center, placement service, day care, health service, health insurance. **Remedial assistance:** study skills. **Counseling services:** minority student, career, military, personal, veteran student, academic, older student, psychological, birth control, religious. **For learning-disabled students:** School does not offer a structured program with separate admission and additional fees. Total undergraduates in learning-disabled program or receiving services: 4. Services include: tape recorders, note-taking services, oral tests, readers, extended time for tests, priority seating, typist/scribe, other testing accommodations. **Library:** Number of titles: 285,897; number of current serial subscriptions: 953. **Information technology resources:** Students are not required to lease or own a computer. Number of campus computers available to all students: 120. School has a wireless network. Approximate number of users that can be accommodated: 1,000. Proportion of college-owned housing units wired for high-speed internet access: 100%. **Campus safety:** Security services offered: 24-hour foot-and-vehicle patrols, late-night transport/escort service, 24-hour emergency telephones, lighted pathways/sidewalks, student patrols, controlled dormitory access (key, security card, etc).

TRANSFER AND INTERNATIONAL STUDENTS

Transfer students: May apply for admission for the following academic terms: Fall, Spring. Applicants do not need a minimum number of credits to apply. For fall 2009: Transfer applications received: 250. Transfer applicants offered admission: 55. Transfer applicants enrolled: 35. **International students:** Number of foreign undergraduates: 2. Number of countries represented: 21. Minimum TOEFL score required: 560 (paper); 220 (computer).

Nova Southeastern University

- **Address:** 3301 College Avenue, Ft. Lauderdale, FL 33314
- **Website:** http://www.nova.edu
- **Private**
- **Enrollment:** 3,879 full-time; 1,989 part-time

KEY STATS

✔ **U.S News College Ranking:** second tier, National Universities
✔ **SAT Score (25th/75th percentile):** 910-1110
✔ **Tuition:** 2009-2010: $21,100

Selectivity: Selective	**Room/board:** $8,634
Acceptance rate: 45%	**Average debt:** $36,908
Student/faculty ratio: 22/1	**Proportion who borrowed:** 71%

UNDERGRADUATE STUDENT BODY STATS

2009-2010 enrollment: 3,879 full-time; 1,989 part-time. Men: 28%; women: 72%. **Ethnic makeup:** African American: 27%; Asian American: 5%; Hispanic: 28%; White: 35%; International: 4%.

ADMISSIONS FACTS AND FIGURES

Phone: (954) 262-8000. **Email:** admissions@nova.edu. **Website:** http://www.nova.edu. **Application deadlines for fall 2011:** Regular decision: Rolling. Early decision: Not offered. Early action: Not offered. Admission can be deferred. **Application fee:** $50. **To apply online, go to:** http://www.undergrad.nova.edu/admissions/. **Admissions requirements/recommendations:** High school units required (recommended): English: (4); Mathematics: (3); Science: (3); Social studies: (3); Total units: (13). Tests: The college uses SAT or ACT scores in admissions decisions. Either SAT or ACT required. For admission to the fall 2011 entering class, the school will accept: ACT with or without writing accepted. Campus visit: Recommended. Admissions interview: Recommended. Off-campus interview: May be arranged. **Factors that count in admissions decisions:** *Academic:* Secondary school record: Important. Class rank: Not Considered. Letters of recommendation: Considered. Standardized test scores: Very Important. Essay: Considered. *Nonacademic:* Interview: Considered. Extracurricular activities: Considered. Talent/ability: Considered. Character/personal qualities: Considered. Alumni/ae relationship: Not Considered. Geographical residence: Not Considered. State residency: Not Considered. Religious affiliation/commitment: Not Considered. Minority status: Not Considered. Volunteer work: Considered. Work experience: Not Considered. **Admissions statistics for the fall 2009 entering class:** Total applicants: 4,124. Total accepted: 1,849. Freshmen enrolled: 579; Overall acceptance rate: 45%. **Credentials of fall 2009 freshmen:** 13% ranked in the top 10 percent of their high school class; 38% were in the top 25 percent; 91% were in the top half. **First-year students who submitted SAT scores:** 69%. Scores (25/75 percentile): Critical Reading: 460-550, Math: 450-560, Combined: 910-1110. **First-year students submitting ACT scores:** 42%. Scores (25/75 percentile): English: 18-23, Math: 18-23, Composite: 19-23.

ACADEMICS

Year founded: 1964. **Academic calendar:** Trimester. **Degrees offered:** certificate, associate, bachelor's, post-bachelor's certificate, master's, post-master's certificate, doctorate. **Most popular majors:** 31% business, management, marketing, and related support services, 20% health professions and related clinical sciences, 18% biological and biomedical sciences, 10% psychology, 9% education. **Major fields of study:** area, ethnic, cultural, and gender studies; biological and biomedical sciences; business, management, marketing, and related support services; communication, journalism, and related programs; computer and information sciences and support services; education; English language and literature/letters; health professions and related clinical sciences; history; legal professions and studies; liberal arts and sciences studies, and humanities; multi/interdisciplinary studies; natural resources and conservation; parks, recreation, leisure, and fitness studies; psychology; security and protective services; social sciences. **Areas of required coursework:** arts/fine arts, humanities, mathematics, English (including composition), sciences (biological or physical), social science. **Pre-professional programs:** pre-law, pre-dentistry, pre-medicine, pre-optometry, pre-pharmacy. **Special academic programs:** distance learning, double major, honors program, independent study, internships, study abroad, teacher certificate program. **Teacher certification offered in:** early childhood, special education, elementary, secondary. **Cooperative education programs:** business, computer science, education, health professions, humanities, natural science, social/behavioral science, other. **Faculty and instruction (2009-2010):**

Total instructional faculty: 712 full-time, 1,001 part-time (51% men; 49% women; 27% minorities). Full-time faculty with Ph.D. or other terminal degree: 82%. Student/faculty ratio: 22/1. Classes of fewer than 20 students: 79%; of 20 to 49 students: 20%; of 50 or more students: 0%. **Advanced Placement and International Baccalaureate credit:** AP tests may be used for: Credit and/or placement. International Baccalaureate exams may be used for: Credit and/or placement. **Freshmen returning for sophomore year:** 64%. **Graduation rates:** Four-year: 22%; five-year: 31%; six-year: 36%.

COSTS AND FINANCIAL AID

Financial aid office: (954) 262-3380. **Expenses (2009-2010):** Tuition and fees 2009-2010: $21,100; room/board: $8,634. Estimated books and supplies: $1,500; transportation: $440; personal expenses: $2,898. **Financial aid:** Priority filing date for institution's financial aid form: April 15. In 2009-2010, 85% of undergraduates applied for financial aid. Of those, 76% were determined to have financial need; 99% had their need fully met. Average financial aid package (proportion receiving): $16,863 (76%). Average amount of gift aid, such as scholarships or grants (proportion receiving): $6,287 (75%). Average amount of self-help aid, such as work study or loans (proportion receiving): $6,672 (46%). Average need-based loan (excluding PLUS or other private loans): $5,568. Among students who received need-based aid, the average percentage of need met: 67%. Among students who received aid based on merit, the average award (and the proportion receiving): $5,631 (6%). The average athletic scholarship (and the proportion receiving): $12,328 (6%). Average amount of debt of borrowers graduating in 2009: $36,908. Proportion who borrowed: 71%.

CAMPUS LIFE AND EXTRACURRICULAR ACTIVITIES

Campus housing available (% using): coed dorms (100%), apartments for married students, apartment for single students, special housing for disabled students, special housing for international students. Students who live in college-owned, operated, or affiliated housing: 38%. **Student employment:** During the 2009-2010 academic year, 10% of undergraduates worked on campus. Average per-year earnings: $2,154. **Clubs and organizations:** Number of student organizations: 38. Activities include: choral groups, concert band, dance, drama/theater, international student organization, jazz band, literary magazine, music ensembles, musical theater, pep band, radio station, student government, student newspaper, student film society. Number of fraternities: 4; sororities: 6. Proportion of men in fraternities: 5%; of women in sororities: 3%. Average proportion of students who stay on campus on weekends: 67%. **Sports program (2009-2010):** Member of NCAA II. *Men's intercollegiate varsity sports:* baseball, basketball, cross country, golf, soccer, track and field (outdoor). *Women's intercollegiate varsity sports:* basketball, crew (heavyweight), cross country, golf, soccer, softball, tennis, track and field (outdoor), volleyball.

SERVICES AND FACILITIES

Basic services: nonremedial tutoring, women's center, placement service, health service, health insurance. **Remedial assistance:** reading, math, writing, study skills. **Counseling services:** career, military, personal, veteran student, academic, older student, psychological, birth control. **For learning-disabled students:** School does not offer a structured program with separate admission and additional fees. Services include: reading machines, tape recorders, note-taking services, oral tests, learning center, readers, extended time for tests, tutors, priority seating, texts on tape, other testing accommodations, other. **Library:** Number of titles: 700,217; number of current serial subscriptions: 44,573. **Information technology resources:** Students are not required to lease or own a computer. Number of campus computers available to all students: 2,500. School has a wireless network. Approximate number of users that can be accommodated: 4,000. Proportion of college-owned housing units wired for high-speed internet access: 100%. **Campus safety:** Security services offered: 24-hour foot-and-vehicle patrols, late-night transport/escort service, 24-hour emergency telephones, lighted pathways/sidewalks, controlled dormitory access (key, security card, etc).

TRANSFER AND INTERNATIONAL STUDENTS

Transfer students: May apply for admission for the following academic terms: Fall, Winter, Spring, Summer. Applicants need a minimum number of credits to apply. For fall 2009: Transfer applications received: 4,474. Transfer applicants offered admission: 2,207. Transfer applicants enrolled: 1,560. **International students:** Number of foreign undergraduates: 228 (4% of student body). Number of countries represented: 106. Minimum TOEFL score required: 515 (paper); 213 (computer).

Palm Beach Atlantic University

- **Address:** 901 S. Flagler Drive, West Palm Beach, FL 33416-4708
- **Website:** http://www.pba.edu
- **Private; Religious affiliation:** Christian nondenominational
- **Enrollment:** 2,244 full-time; 190 part-time

KEY STATS

✔ **U.S News College Ranking:** 54, Regional Universities (South)
✔ **SAT Score (25th/75th percentile):** 920-1130
✔ **Tuition:** 2010-2011: $23,400

Selectivity: Selective	**Room/board:** $8,400
Acceptance rate: 69%	**Average debt:** $22,443
Student/faculty ratio: 14/1	**Proportion who borrowed:** 68%

UNDERGRADUATE STUDENT BODY STATS

2009-2010 enrollment: 2,244 full-time; 190 part-time. Men: 36%; women: 64%. **Ethnic makeup:** African American: 17%; Asian American: 1%; Hispanic: 14%; White: 65%; International: 2%. **Religious preference:** Roman Catholic: 12%; Protestant: 52%; No preference: 1%; Unknown: 4%; Christian nondenominational: 28%; Other: 3%.

ADMISSIONS FACTS AND FIGURES

Phone: (888) 468-6722. **Email:** admit@pba.edu. **Website:** http://www.pba.edu. **Application deadlines for fall 2011:** Regular decision: Rolling. Early decision: Not offered. Early action: Not offered. Admission can be deferred. **Application fee:** $35. **To apply online, go to:** http://www.pba.edu/admissions/applyonline.cfm. **Admissions requirements/recommendations:** High school units required (recommended): English: 4; Mathematics: 3; Science: 4. Tests: The college uses SAT or ACT scores in admissions decisions. Either SAT or ACT required. For admission to the fall 2011 entering class, the school will accept: ACT with or without writing accepted. Campus visit: Recommended. Admissions interview: Recommended. Off-campus interview: May be arranged. **Factors that count in admissions decisions:** *Academic:* Secondary school record: Important. Class rank: Considered. Letters of recommendation: Important. Standardized test scores: Very Important. Essay: Important. *Nonacademic:* Interview: Important. Extracurricular activities: Considered. Talent/ability: Considered. Character/personal qualities: Very Important. Alumni/ae relationship: Considered. Geographical residence: Not Considered. State residency: Not Considered. Religious affiliation/commitment: Considered. Minority status: Not Considered. Volunteer work: Considered. Work experience: Not Considered. **Other schools with the greatest overlap in applicants:** Florida Atlantic University; Florida State University; University of Central Florida; University of Florida; University of South Florida. **Admissions statistics for the fall 2009 entering class:** Total applicants: 1,401. Total accepted: 965. Freshmen enrolled: 422; 40% were from out of state. Overall acceptance rate: 69%. **Credentials of fall 2009 freshmen:** 25% ranked in the top 10 percent of their high school class; 54% were in the top 25 percent. **Average high school grade point average:** 3.5. **First-year students who submitted SAT scores:** 79%. Scores (25/75 percentile): Critical Reading: 470-580, Math: 450-550, Combined: 920-1130. **First-year students submitting ACT scores:** 59%. Scores (25/75 percentile): English: 19-26, Math: 18-25, Composite: 20-26.

ACADEMICS

Year founded: 1968. **Academic calendar:** Semester. **Degrees offered:** associate, bachelor's, master's. **Most popular majors:** 47% business, management, marketing, and related support services, 9% communication, journalism, and related programs, 7% health professions and related clinical sciences, 7% psychology, 7% theology and religious vocations. **Major fields of study:** biological and biomedical sciences; business, management, marketing, and related support services; communication, journalism, and related programs; computer and information sciences and support services; education; English language and literature/letters; health professions and related clinical sciences; history; legal professions and studies; liberal arts and sciences studies, and humanities; mathematics and statistics; multi/interdisciplinary studies; parks, recreation, leisure, and fitness studies; philosophy and religious studies; psychology; social sciences; theology and religious vocations; visual and performing arts. **Areas of required coursework:** arts/fine arts, humanities, mathematics, English (including composition), sciences (biological or physical), social science, other. **Pre-professional programs:** pre-law, pre-pharmacy, other. **Special academic programs:** accelerated program, distance learning, double major, dual enrollment, honors program, independent study, internships, student-designed major, study abroad, teacher certificate program. **Teacher certification offered in:** early childhood, special education, elementary, middle/junior high, secondary. **Reserve Officers Training Corps (ROTC):** Army ROTC: Offered at cooperating institution (Florida Atlantic University). **Faculty and instruction (2009-2010):** Total instructional faculty: 157 full-time, 173 part-time (54% men; 46% women; 13% minorities). Full-time faculty with Ph.D. or other terminal degree: 77%. Student/faculty ratio: 14/1. Classes of fewer than 20 students: 60%; of 20 to 49 students: 39%; of 50 or more students: 1%. **Advanced Placement and International Baccalaureate credit:** AP tests may be used for: Credit only. Scores accepted: 3, 4, 5. International Baccalaureate exams may be used for: Credit only. **Freshmen returning for sophomore year:** 71%. **Graduation rates:** Four-year: 41%; five-year: 48%; six-year: 51%.

COSTS AND FINANCIAL AID

Financial aid office: (561) 803-2000. **Expenses (2010-2011):** Tuition and fees 2010-2011: $23,400; room/board: $8,400. Estimated books and supplies: $1,300; transportation: $1,000; personal expenses: $1,650. **Financial aid:** Priority filing date for institution's financial aid form: February 1; deadline: August 1. In 2009-2010, 86% of undergraduates applied for financial aid. Of those, 75% were determined to have financial need; 30% had their need fully met. Average financial aid package (proportion receiving): $20,405 (75%). Average amount of gift aid, such as scholarships or grants (proportion receiving): $5,521 (50%). Average amount of self-help aid, such as work study or loans (proportion receiving): $4,532 (60%). Average need-based loan (excluding PLUS or other private loans): $4,242. Among students who received need-based aid, the average percentage of need met: 63%. Among students who received aid based on merit, the average award (and the proportion receiving): $5,946 (9%). The average athletic scholarship (and the proportion receiving): $8,344 (6%). Average amount of debt of borrowers graduating in 2009: $22,443. Proportion who borrowed: 68%.

CAMPUS LIFE AND EXTRACURRICULAR ACTIVITIES

Campus housing available: coed dorms, women's dorms, men's dorms, apartments for married students, apartment for single students. Students who live in college-owned, operated, or affiliated housing: 55%. **Student employment:** During the 2009-2010 academic year, 28% of undergraduates worked on campus. **Clubs and organizations:** Number of student organizations: 67. Activities include: campus ministries, choral groups, dance, drama/theater, international student organization, jazz band, literary magazine, music ensembles, musical theater, pep band, radio station, student government, student newspaper, symphony orchestra, television station, yearbook. Number of fraternities: 0; sororities: 0. Average proportion of students who stay on campus on weekends: 60%. **Sports program (2009-2010):** Member of NCAA II. *Men's intercollegiate varsity sports:* baseball, basketball, cross country, soccer, tennis. *Women's intercollegiate varsity sports:* basketball, cross country, soccer, softball, tennis, volleyball.

SERVICES AND FACILITIES

Basic services: health service, health insurance. **Remedial assistance:** reading, math, writing, study skills. **Counseling services:** minority student, career, personal, veteran student, academic, older student, psychological, religious. **For learning-disabled students:** School does not offer a structured program with separate admission and additional fees. Total undergraduates in learning-disabled program or receiving services: 110. Services include: remedial math, remedial English, tape recorders, note-taking services, learning center, readers, extended time for tests, tutors, priority registration, substitution of courses, texts on tape, typist/scribe, exams on tape or computer, other testing accommodations, waiver of math degree requirement. **Library:** Number of titles: 160,714; number of current serial subscriptions: 317. **Information technology resources:** Students are not required to lease or own a computer. Number of campus computers available to all students: 460. School has a wireless network. Approximate number of users that can be accommodated: 5,000. Proportion of college-owned housing units wired for high-speed internet access: 100%. **Campus safety:** Security services offered: 24-hour foot-and-vehicle patrols, late-night transport/escort service, 24-hour emergency telephones, lighted pathways/sidewalks, controlled dormitory access (key, security card, etc).

TRANSFER AND INTERNATIONAL STUDENTS

Transfer students: May apply for admission for the following academic terms: Fall, Spring, Summer. Applicants need a minimum number of credits to apply. For fall 2009: Transfer applications received: 859. Transfer applicants offered admission: 669. Transfer applicants enrolled: 422. **International students:** Number of foreign undergraduates: 59 (2% of stu-

dent body). Number of countries represented: 26. Minimum TOEFL score required: 550 (paper); 213 (computer).

Ringling College of Art and Design

- ■ **Address:** 2700 N. Tamiami Trail, Sarasota, FL 34234-5895
- ■ **Website:** http://www.ringling.edu
- ■ **Private**
- ■ **Enrollment:** 1,268 full-time; 50 part-time

....

KEY STATS

✔ **U.S News College Ranking:** Unranked Specialty School–Fine Arts

✔ **SAT or ACT Score (25th/75th percentile):** N/A

✔ **Tuition:** 2010-2011: $30,128

Selectivity: N/A **Room/board:** $14,840

Acceptance rate: 73% **Average debt:** $53,702

Student/faculty ratio: 12/1 **Proportion who borrowed:** 86%

UNDERGRADUATE STUDENT BODY STATS

2009-2010 enrollment: 1,268 full-time; 50 part-time. Men: 43%; women: 57%. **Ethnic makeup:** African American: 4%; American-Indian: 1%; Asian American: 7%; Hispanic: 12%; White: 69%; International: 6%.

ADMISSIONS FACTS AND FIGURES

Phone: (800) 255-7695. **Email:** admissions@ringling.edu. **Website:** http://www.ringling.edu. **Application deadlines for fall 2011:** Regular decision: Rolling. Early decision: Not offered. Early action: Not offered. Admission can be deferred. **Application fee:** $70. **To apply online, go to:** https://saffron.ringling.edu/OAPP/. **Admissions requirements/recommendations:** Tests: The college does not use SAT or ACT scores in admissions decisions. Neither SAT nor ACT required. Campus visit: Recommended. Admissions interview: Recommended. Off-campus interview: May be arranged. **Factors that count in admissions decisions:** *Academic:* Secondary school record: Very Important. Class rank: Not Considered. Letters of recommendation: Important. Standardized test scores: Not Considered. Essay: Important. *Nonacademic:* Interview: Considered. Extracurricular activities: Considered. Talent/ability: Very Important. Character/personal qualities: Not Considered. Alumni/ae relationship: Considered. Geographical residence: Considered. State residency: Not Considered. Religious affiliation/commitment: Not Considered. Minority status: Not Considered. Volunteer work: Considered. Work experience: Considered. **Other schools with the greatest overlap in applicants:** Maryland Institute College of Art; Pratt Institute; Rhode Island School of Design; Savannah College of Art and Design; School of Visual Arts. **Admissions statistics for the fall 2009 entering class:** Total applicants: 1,147. Total accepted: 842. Freshmen enrolled: 319; 47% were from out of state. Overall acceptance rate: 73%. **Average high school grade point average:** 3.2.

ACADEMICS

Year founded: 1931. **Academic calendar:** Semester. **Degrees offered:** certificate, bachelor's. **Major fields of study:** communications technologies/technicians and support services; visual and performing arts. **Areas of required coursework:** arts/fine arts, humanities, computer literacy, mathematics, English (including composition), philosophy, history, social science, other. **Special academic programs (% participation):** dual enrollment (0%), exchange student program (domestic) (1%), independent study (22%), internships (12%), study abroad (1%). **Faculty and instruction (2009-2010):** Total instructional faculty: 83 full-time, 65 part-time (64% men; 36% women; 4% minorities). Full-time faculty with Ph.D. or other terminal degree: 66%. Student/faculty ratio: 12/1. Classes of fewer than 20 students: 64%; of 20 to 49 students: 35%; of 50 or more students: 1%. **Advanced Placement and International Baccalaureate credit:** International Baccalaureate exams may be used for: Credit only. **Freshmen returning for sophomore year:** 81%. **Graduation rates:** Four-year: 52%; five-year: 63%; six-year: 63%. **Graduate study:** 8% of students pursue further study within one year.

COSTS AND FINANCIAL AID

Financial aid office: (941) 351-5100. **Expenses (2010-2011):** Tuition and fees 2010-2011: $30,128; room/board: $14,840. Estimated books and supplies: $2,625; transportation: $810; personal expenses: $2,935. **Financial aid:** Priority filing date for institution's financial aid form: March 1; deadline: May 1. In 2009-2010, 100% of undergraduates applied for financial aid. Of

those, 89% were determined to have financial need; 4% had their need fully met. Average financial aid package (proportion receiving): $17,057 (88%). Average amount of gift aid, such as scholarships or grants (proportion receiving): $8,646 (76%). Average amount of self-help aid, such as work study or loans (proportion receiving): $10,225 (82%). Average need-based loan (excluding PLUS or other private loans): $9,929. Among students who received need-based aid, the average percentage of need met: 46%. Among students who received aid based on merit, the average award (and the proportion receiving): $3,310 (5%). The average athletic scholarship (and the proportion receiving): $0 (0%). Average amount of debt of borrowers graduating in 2009: $53,702. Proportion who borrowed: 86%.

CAMPUS LIFE AND EXTRACURRICULAR ACTIVITIES

Campus housing available (% using): coed dorms (42%), women's dorms (11%), men's dorms (7%), apartments for married students (1%), apartment for single students (38%), other housing options (1%). Students who live in college-owned, operated, or affiliated housing: 53%. **Student employment:** During the 2009-2010 academic year, 13% of undergraduates worked on campus. Average per-year earnings: $4,476. **Clubs and organizations:** Number of student organizations: 29. Activities include: campus ministries, dance, drama/theater, international student organization, student government. Number of fraternities: 0; sororities: 0. Average proportion of students who stay on campus on weekends: 90%.

SERVICES AND FACILITIES

Basic services: nonremedial tutoring, placement service, health service, health insurance. **Remedial assistance:** reading, math, writing, study skills. **Counseling services:** minority student, career, personal, veteran student, academic, older student, psychological, religious, other. **For learning-disabled students:** School does not offer a structured program with separate admission and additional fees. Total undergraduates in learning-disabled program or receiving services: 52. Services include: remedial math, remedial English, reading machines, tape recorders, other special classes, note-taking services, learning center, extended time for tests, tutors, priority seating, texts on tape, other testing accommodations. **Library:** Number of titles: 54,151; number of current serial subscriptions: 419. **Information technology resources:** Students are not required to lease or own a computer. Number of campus computers available to all students: 2,500. School has a wireless network. Approximate number of users that can be accommodated: 10,000. Proportion of college-owned housing units wired for high-speed internet access: 100%. **Campus safety:** Security services offered: 24-hour foot-and-vehicle patrols, late-night transport/escort service, 24-hour emergency telephones, lighted pathways/sidewalks, controlled dormitory access (key, security card, etc).

TRANSFER AND INTERNATIONAL STUDENTS

Transfer students: May apply for admission for the following academic terms: Fall, Spring. Applicants need a minimum number of credits to apply. For fall 2009: Transfer applications received: 384. Transfer applicants offered admission: 249. Transfer applicants enrolled: 136. **International students:** Number of foreign undergraduates: 85 (6% of student body). Number of countries represented: 30. Minimum TOEFL score required: 500 (paper); 173 (computer).

Rollins College

- ■ **Address:** 1000 Holt Avenue, Winter Park, FL 32789-4499
- ■ **Website:** http://www.rollins.edu
- ■ **Private**
- ■ **Enrollment:** 1,773 full-time

....

KEY STATS

✔ **U.S News College Ranking:** 1, Regional Universities (South)

✔ **SAT Score (25th/75th percentile):** 1130-1305

✔ **Tuition:** 2010-2011: $37,640

Selectivity: More selective **Room/board:** $11,760

Acceptance rate: 62% **Average debt:** $22,255

Student/faculty ratio: 10/1 **Proportion who borrowed:** 51%

UNDERGRADUATE STUDENT BODY STATS

2009-2010 enrollment: 1,773 full-time. Men: 42%; women: 58%. **Ethnic makeup:** African American: 4%; American-Indian: 1%; Asian American: 4%; Hispanic: 10%; White: 78%; International: 4%.

ADMISSIONS FACTS AND FIGURES

Phone: (407) 646-2161. **Email:** admission@rollins.edu. **Website:** http://www.rollins.edu. **Application deadlines for fall 2011:** Regular decision: February 15; decision sent by April 1. Early decision: Send application by November 15; Decision sent by: December 15. Early action: Not offered. Admission can be deferred. **Application fee:** $40. **To apply online, go to:** http://www.rollins.edu/admission/application.shtml. **Admissions requirements/recommendations:** High school units required (recommended): English: 4 (4); Mathematics: 3 (4); Science: 2 (4); Foreign language: 2 (3); Social studies: 2 (3); History: 2 (3); Academic electives: 2 (3); Total units: 17 (24). Tests: The college uses SAT or ACT scores in admissions decisions. Neither SAT nor ACT required. For admission to the fall 2011 entering class, the school will accept: ACT with writing recommended. Campus visit: Recommended. Admissions interview: Recommended. Off-campus interview: Not available. **Factors that count in admissions decisions:** *Academic:* Secondary school record: Very Important. Class rank: Considered. Letters of recommendation: Important. Standardized test scores: Important. Essay: Important. *Nonacademic:* Interview: Considered. Extracurricular activities: Important. Talent/ability: Important. Character/personal qualities: Considered. Alumni/ae relationship: Considered. Geographical residence: Not Considered. State residency: Not Considered. Religious affiliation/commitment: Not Considered. Minority status: Not Considered. Volunteer work: Considered. Work experience: Considered. **Other schools with the greatest overlap in applicants:** Boston College; Florida State University; University of Central Florida; University of Florida; University of Miami. **Admissions statistics for the fall 2009 entering class:** Total applicants: 2,999. Total accepted: 1,847. Freshmen enrolled: 464; 52% were from out of state. Overall acceptance rate: 62%. Early-decision acceptance rate: 76%. Non-early acceptance rate: 60%. **Size of waiting list:** 345 applicants; enrolled from waiting list: 63. **Credentials of fall 2009 freshmen:** 39% ranked in the top 10 percent of their high school class; 65% were in the top 25 percent; 91% were in the top half. (Proportion submitting class standing: 47%.) **Average high school grade point average:** 3.3. **First-year students who submitted SAT scores:** 76%. Scores (25/75 percentile): Critical Reading: 565-652, Math: 565-653, Combined: 1130-1305. **First-year students submitting ACT scores:** 49%. Scores (25/75 percentile): English: N/A, Math: N/A, Composite: 24-29.

ACADEMICS

Year founded: 1885. **Academic calendar:** Semester. **Degrees offered:** bachelor's, master's. **Most popular majors:** 32% social sciences, 15% psychology, 12% business, management, marketing, and related support services, 10% visual and performing arts, 6% biological and biomedical sciences. **Major fields of study:** area, ethnic, cultural, and gender studies; biological and biomedical sciences; business, management, marketing, and related support services; communication, journalism, and related programs; computer and information sciences and support services; education; English language and literature/letters; foreign languages, literatures, and linguistics; history; mathematics and statistics; multi/interdisciplinary studies; philosophy and religious studies; physical sciences; psychology; social sciences; visual and performing arts. **Areas of required coursework:** arts/fine arts, humanities, computer literacy, mathematics, English (including composition), philosophy, foreign languages, sciences (biological or physical), history, social science. **Pre-professional programs:** pre-law, pre-dentistry, pre-medicine, pre-veterinary science, pre-optometry, pre-pharmacy. **Special academic programs:** accelerated program, cross-registration, double major, dual enrollment, exchange student program (domestic), honors program, independent study, internships, student-designed major, study abroad, teacher certificate program. **Teacher certification offered in:** elementary, secondary. **Faculty and instruction (2009-2010):** Total instructional faculty: 196 full-time, 40 part-time (57% men; 43% women; 12% minorities). Full-time faculty with Ph.D. or other terminal degree: 93%. Student/faculty ratio: 10/1. Classes of fewer than 20 students: 69%; of 20 to 49 students: 31%. **Advanced Placement and International Baccalaureate credit:** AP tests may be used for: Placement only. Scores accepted: 4, 5. International Baccalaureate exams may be used for: Credit and/or placement. **Freshmen returning for sophomore year:** 85%. **Graduation rates:** Four-year: 59%; five-year: 64%; six-year: 68%. **Graduate study:** 24% of students pursue further study immediately upon graduation; 33% within one year. Fields in which graduates pursue further study: Master of Business Administration (MBA), 6%; law, 7%; medicine, 2%; education, 7%; arts and sciences, 3%.

COSTS AND FINANCIAL AID

Financial aid office: (407) 646-2395. **Expenses (2010-2011):** Tuition and fees 2010-2011: $37,640; room/board: $11,760. Estimated books and supplies: $770; transportation: $760; personal expenses: $3,060. **Financial aid:** Priority filing date for institution's financial aid form: March 1; deadline:

March 1. In 2009-2010, 53% of undergraduates applied for financial aid. Of those, 47% were determined to have financial need; 21% had their need fully met. Average financial aid package (proportion receiving): $33,763 (47%). Average amount of gift aid, such as scholarships or grants (proportion receiving): $28,226 (46%). Average amount of self-help aid, such as work study or loans (proportion receiving): $5,349 (37%). Average need-based loan (excluding PLUS or other private loans): $4,380. Among students who received need-based aid, the average percentage of need met: 86%. Among students who received aid based on merit, the average award (and the proportion receiving): $15,291 (16%). The average athletic scholarship (and the proportion receiving): $24,935 (4%). Average amount of debt of borrowers graduating in 2009: $22,255. Proportion who borrowed: 51%.

CAMPUS LIFE AND EXTRACURRICULAR ACTIVITIES

Campus housing available (% using): coed dorms (61%), sorority housing (9%), fraternity housing (8%), apartment for single students (22%), special housing for disabled students. Students who live in college-owned, operated, or affiliated housing: 67%. **Student employment:** During the 2009-2010 academic year, 16% of undergraduates worked on campus. Average per-year earnings: $1,527. **Clubs and organizations:** Number of student organizations: 82. Activities include: campus ministries, choral groups, dance, drama/theater, international student organization, literary magazine, model UN, music ensembles, musical theater, pep band, radio station, student government, student newspaper, student film society, television station. Number of fraternities: 5; sororities: 6. Proportion of men in fraternities: 19%; of women in sororities: 25%. Average proportion of students who stay on campus on weekends: 60%. **Sports program (2009-2010):** Member of NCAA II. **Men's intercollegiate varsity sports:** baseball, basketball, cross country, golf, lacrosse, soccer, swimming, tennis. **Women's intercollegiate varsity sports:** basketball, crew (lightweight), cross country, golf, lacrosse, soccer, softball, swimming, tennis, volleyball.

SERVICES AND FACILITIES

Basic services: nonremedial tutoring, women's center, placement service, health service, health insurance. **Remedial assistance:** reading, math, writing. **Counseling services:** minority student, career, military, personal, veteran student, academic, older student, psychological, birth control, religious. **For learning-disabled students:** School does not offer a structured program with separate admission and additional fees. Services include: reading machines, tape recorders, untimed tests, note-taking services, learning center, readers, extended time for tests, tutors, priority seating, texts on tape, other. **Library:** Number of titles: 309,274; number of current serial subscriptions: 36,989. **Information technology resources:** Students are not required to lease or own a computer. Number of campus computers available to all students: 240. School has a wireless network. Approximate number of users that can be accommodated: 2,001. Proportion of college-owned housing units wired for high-speed internet access: 100%. **Campus safety:** Security services offered: 24-hour foot-and-vehicle patrols, late-night transport/escort service, 24-hour emergency telephones, lighted pathways/sidewalks, controlled dormitory access (key, security card, etc).

TRANSFER AND INTERNATIONAL STUDENTS

Transfer students: May apply for admission for the following academic terms: Fall, Spring. Applicants need a minimum number of credits to apply. For fall 2009: Transfer applications received: 310. Transfer applicants offered admission: 143. Transfer applicants enrolled: 72. **International students:** Number of foreign undergraduates: 77 (4% of student body). Number of countries represented: 52. Minimum TOEFL score required: 550 (paper); 80 (computer). Average TOEFL score: 605 (paper).

Southeastern University

- **Address:** 1000 Longfellow Boulevard, Lakeland, FL 33801
- **Website:** http://www.seuniversity.edu
- **Private; Religious affiliation:** Assemblies of God
- **Enrollment:** 2,348 full-time; 317 part-time

KEY STATS

✔ **U.S News College Ranking:** 53, Regional Colleges (South)

✔ **SAT Score (25th/75th percentile):** 861-1100

✔ **Tuition:** 2010-2011: $16,430

Selectivity: Less selective	**Room/board:** $7,900
Acceptance rate: 76%	**Average debt:** $17,044
Student/faculty ratio: 25/1	**Proportion who borrowed:** 100%

UNDERGRADUATE STUDENT BODY STATS

2009-2010 enrollment: 2,348 full-time; 317 part-time. Men: 42%; women: 58%. **Ethnic makeup:** African American: 9%; Asian American: 1%; Hispanic: 12%; White: 77%. **Religious preference:** Roman Catholic: 1%; Protestant: 42%; Unknown: 25%; Assemblies of God: 32%.

ADMISSIONS FACTS AND FIGURES

Phone: (863) 667-5018. **Email:** admission@seuniversity.edu. **Website:** http://www.seuniversity.edu. **Application deadlines for fall 2011:** Regular decision: July 1. Early decision: Not offered. Early action: Not offered. Admission can be deferred. **Application fee:** $40. **To apply online, go to:** https://www.seuniversity.edu/forms/app.html. **Admissions requirements/recommendations:** High school units required (recommended): English: (4); Mathematics: (4); Science: (4); Foreign language: (2); Social studies: (4); Total units: (18). Tests: The college uses SAT or ACT scores in admissions decisions. Either SAT or ACT required. For admission to the fall 2011 entering class, the school will accept: ACT with or without writing accepted. Campus visit: Recommended. Admissions interview: Recommended. Off-campus interview: May be arranged. **Factors that count in admissions decisions:** *Academic:* Secondary school record: Considered. Class rank: Considered. Letters of recommendation: Important. Standardized test scores: Important. Essay: Important. *Nonacademic:* Interview: Considered. Extracurricular activities: Considered. Talent/ability: Considered. Character/personal qualities: Very Important. Alumni/ae relationship: Considered. Geographical residence: Not Considered. State residency: Not Considered. Religious affiliation/commitment: Very Important. Minority status: Not Considered. Volunteer work: Considered. Work experience: Considered. **Other schools with the greatest overlap in applicants:** Evangel University; Florida State University; Palm Beach Atlantic University; University of Florida; University of South Florida. **Admissions statistics for the fall 2009 entering class:** Total applicants: 1,163. Total accepted: 882. Freshmen enrolled: 569; 42% were from out of state. Overall acceptance rate: 76%. **First-year students who submitted SAT scores:** 68%. Scores (25/75 percentile): Critical Reading: 441-560, Math: 420-540, Combined: 861-1100. **First-year students submitting ACT scores:** 50%. Scores (25/75 percentile): English: N/A, Math: N/A, Composite: 17-23.

ACADEMICS

Year founded: 1935. **Academic calendar:** Semester. **Degrees offered:** bachelor's, master's. **Most popular majors:** 22% theology and religious vocations, 13% business/commerce, 10% human services, 7% psychology, 5% English language and literature. **Major fields of study:** biological and biomedical sciences; business, management, marketing, and related support services; communication, journalism, and related programs; education; English language and literature/letters; health professions and related clinical sciences; history; mathematics and statistics; psychology; public administration and social service professions; security and protective services; theology and religious vocations; visual and performing arts. **Areas of required coursework:** arts/fine arts, humanities, mathematics, English (including composition), sciences (biological or physical), history, social science, other. **Pre-professional programs:** pre-law, pre-medicine, pre-theology. **Special academic programs:** distance learning, double major, dual enrollment, honors program, independent study, internships, study abroad, teacher certificate program, weekend college. **Teacher certification offered in:** elementary, middle/junior high, secondary. **Reserve Officers Training Corps (ROTC):** Army ROTC: Offered at cooperating institution (Florida Southern College). **Faculty and instruction (2009-2010):** Total instructional faculty: 83 full-time, 71 part-time (67% men; 33% women; 15% minorities). Full-time faculty with Ph.D. or other terminal degree: 65%. Student/faculty ratio: 25/1. Classes of

fewer than 20 students: 53%; of 20 to 49 students: 41%; of 50 or more students: 6%. **Advanced Placement and International Baccalaureate credit:** AP tests may be used for: Placement only. International Baccalaureate exams may be used for: Credit only. **Freshmen returning for sophomore year:** 66%. **Graduation rates:** Four-year: 33%; five-year: 45%; six-year: 43%.

COSTS AND FINANCIAL AID

Financial aid office: (863) 667-5026. **Expenses (2010-2011):** Tuition and fees 2010-2011: $16,430; room/board: $7,900. Estimated books and supplies: $1,200; transportation: $1,200; personal expenses: $1,200. **Financial aid:** Priority filing date for institution's financial aid form: April 15. In 2009-2010, 84% of undergraduates applied for financial aid. Of those, 72% were determined to have financial need; 14% had their need fully met. Average financial aid package (proportion receiving): $10,890 (72%). Average amount of gift aid, such as scholarships or grants (proportion receiving): $7,917 (69%). Average amount of self-help aid, such as work study or loans (proportion receiving): $4,181 (57%). Average need-based loan (excluding PLUS or other private loans): $4,048. Among students who received need-based aid, the average percentage of need met: 55%. Among students who received aid based on merit, the average award (and the proportion receiving): $3,224 (11%). The average athletic scholarship (and the proportion receiving): $3,864 (1%). Average amount of debt of borrowers graduating in 2009: $17,044. Proportion who borrowed: 100%.

CAMPUS LIFE AND EXTRACURRICULAR ACTIVITIES

Campus housing available (% using): women's dorms (61%), men's dorms (39%), other housing options (0%). Students who live in college-owned, operated, or affiliated housing: 80%. **Clubs and organizations:** Number of student organizations: 55. Activities include: campus ministries, choral groups, concert band, drama/theater, international student organization, jazz band, music ensembles, musical theater, opera, radio station, student government, student newspaper, television station, yearbook. Number of fraternities: 0; sororities: 0. Average proportion of students who stay on campus on weekends: 60%. **Sports program (2009-2010):** *Men's intercollegiate varsity sports:* baseball, basketball, golf, soccer. *Women's intercollegiate varsity sports:* basketball, soccer, tennis, volleyball.

SERVICES AND FACILITIES

Basic services: nonremedial tutoring, placement service, health service, health insurance. **Remedial assistance:** reading, math, writing. **Counseling services:** career, personal, veteran student, academic, religious. **For learning-disabled students:** School does not offer a structured program with separate admission and additional fees. Total undergraduates in learning-disabled program or receiving services: 35. Services include: remedial math, remedial English, reading machines, remedial reading, tape recorders, diagnostic testing service, untimed tests, note-taking services, special bookstore section, oral tests, learning center, readers, extended time for tests, tutors, early syllabus, priority registration, priority seating, proofreading services, texts on tape, exams on tape or computer, other testing accommodations. **Library:** Number of titles: 108,966; number of current serial subscriptions: 21,543. **Information technology resources:** Students are not required to lease or own a computer. Number of campus computers available to all students: 90. School has a wireless network. Approximate number of users that can be accommodated: 550. Proportion of college-owned housing units wired for high-speed internet access: 100%. **Campus safety:** Security services offered: 24-hour foot-and-vehicle patrols, lighted pathways/sidewalks, controlled dormitory access (key, security card, etc).

TRANSFER AND INTERNATIONAL STUDENTS

Transfer students: May apply for admission for the following academic terms: Fall, Spring, Summer. Applicants do not need a minimum number of credits to apply. For fall 2009: Transfer applications received: 525. Transfer applicants offered admission: 521. Transfer applicants enrolled: 268. **International students:** Number of foreign undergraduates: 1. Number of countries represented: 39. Minimum TOEFL score required: 500 (paper); 173 (computer).

Stetson University

- **Address:** 421 N. Woodland Boulevard, DeLand, FL 32723
- **Website:** http://www.stetson.edu
- **Private**
- **Enrollment:** 2,079 full-time; 83 part-time

KEY STATS

✔ **U.S News College Ranking:** 3, Regional Universities (South)
✔ **SAT Score (25th/75th percentile):** 990-1200
✔ **Tuition:** 2010-2011: $33,424

Selectivity: Selective	Room/board: $9,805
Acceptance rate: 53%	Average debt: $30,914
Student/faculty ratio: 11/1	Proportion who borrowed: 83%

UNDERGRADUATE STUDENT BODY STATS

2009-2010 enrollment: 2,079 full-time; 83 part-time. Men: 43%; women: 57%. **Ethnic makeup:** African American: 6%; Asian American: 2%; Hispanic: 11%; White: 78%; International: 3%. **Religious preference:** Roman Catholic: 20%; Protestant: 27%; Jewish: 2%; No preference: 10%; Unknown: 29%; Muslim/Hindu/Buddhist: 1%; Other: 11%.

ADMISSIONS FACTS AND FIGURES

Phone: (800) 688-0101. **Email:** admissions@stetson.edu. **Website:** http://www.stetson.edu. **Application deadlines for fall 2011:** Regular decision: Rolling. Early decision: Send application by: November 1; Decision sent by: November 15. Early action: Not offered. Admission can be deferred. **Application fee:** $40. **To apply online, go to:** http://www.stetson.edu/apply. **Admissions requirements/recommendations:** High school units required (recommended): English: 4; Mathematics: 3; Science: 3; Foreign language: 2; Social studies: 2; Total units: 14. Tests: The college uses SAT or ACT scores in admissions decisions. Neither SAT nor ACT required. For admission to the fall 2011 entering class, the school will accept: ACT with or without writing accepted. Campus visit: Recommended. Admissions interview: Recommended. Off-campus interview: May be arranged. **Factors that count in admissions decisions:** *Academic:* Secondary school record: Very Important. Class rank: Important. Letters of recommendation: Important. Standardized test scores: Important. Essay: Important. *Nonacademic:* Interview: Important. Extracurricular activities: Important. Talent/ability: Important. Character/personal qualities: Important. Alumni/ae relationship: Considered. Geographical residence: Considered. State residency: Considered. Religious affiliation/commitment: Not Considered. Minority status: Considered. Volunteer work: Important. Work experience: Important. **Other schools with the greatest overlap in applicants:** Florida State University; Rollins College; University of Central Florida; University of Florida; University of South Florida. **Admissions statistics for the fall 2009 entering class:** Total applicants: 4,640. Total accepted: 2,479. Freshmen enrolled: 502; 15% were from out of state. Accepted through early-decision or early-action plans: 4%. Overall acceptance rate: 53%. Early-decision acceptance rate: 87%. Non-early acceptance rate: 53%. **Credentials of fall 2009 freshmen:** 28% ranked in the top 10 percent of their high school class; 63% were in the top 25 percent; 91% were in the top half. (Proportion submitting class standing: 76%.) **Average high school grade point average:** 3.8. **First-year students who submitted SAT scores:** 90%. Scores (25/75 percentile): Critical Reading: 500-600, Math: 490-600, Combined: 990-1200. **First-year students submitting ACT scores:** 62%. Scores (25/75 percentile): English: 20-26, Math: 19-26, Composite: 21-26.

ACADEMICS

Year founded: 1883. **Academic calendar:** Semester. **Degrees offered:** bachelor's, master's. **Most popular majors:** 38% business, management, marketing, and related support services, 17% social sciences, 7% education, 6% biological and biomedical sciences, 6% visual and performing arts. **Major fields of study:** area, ethnic, cultural, and gender studies; biological and biomedical sciences; business, management, marketing, and related support services; communication, journalism, and related programs; computer and information sciences and support services; education; English language and literature/letters; foreign languages, literatures, and linguistics; health professions and related clinical sciences; history; liberal arts and sciences studies, and humanities; mathematics and statistics; natural resources and conservation; parks, recreation, leisure, and fitness studies; philosophy and religious studies; physical sciences; psychology; social sciences; visual and performing arts. **Areas of required coursework:** arts/fine arts, humanities, computer literacy, mathematics, English (including composition), foreign languages, sciences (biological or physical), history, social science, other. **Pre-professional programs:** pre-law, pre-dentistry, pre-medicine, pre-veterinary science. **Special academic programs:** accelerated program, distance learning, double major, honors program, independent study, internships, liberal arts/career combination, student-designed major, study abroad, teacher certificate program, weekend college. **Teacher certification offered in:** elementary, middle/junior high, secondary. **Cooperative education programs:** engineering, health professions, other. **Reserve Officers Training Corps (ROTC):** Army ROTC: Offered at cooperating institution. **Faculty and instruction (2009-2010):** Total instructional faculty: 229 full-time, 124 part-time (59% men; 41% women; 9% minorities). Full-time faculty with Ph.D. or other terminal degree: 95%. Student/faculty ratio: 11/1. Classes of fewer than 20 students: 61%; of 20 to 49 students: 39%; of 50 or more students: 0%. **Advanced Placement and International Baccalaureate credit:** AP tests may be used for: Placement only. Scores accepted: 4, 5. International Baccalaureate exams may be used for: Credit only. **Freshmen returning for sophomore year:** 79%. **Graduation rates:** Four-year: 50%; five-year: 60%; six-year: 65%. **Graduate study:** Fields in which graduates pursue further study: Master of Business Administration (MBA), 26%; law, 15%; medicine, 7%; dentistry, 3%; theology (or the seminary), 2%; education, 10%; arts and sciences, 36%; veterinary medicine, 1%.

COSTS AND FINANCIAL AID

Financial aid office: (386) 822-7120. **Expenses (2010-2011):** Tuition and fees 2010-2011: $33,424; room/board: $9,805. Estimated books and supplies: $1,200; transportation: $950; personal expenses: $1,000. **Financial aid:** Priority filing date for institution's financial aid form: March 15. In 2009-2010, 72% of undergraduates applied for financial aid. Of those, 64% were determined to have financial need; 26% had their need fully met. Average financial aid package (proportion receiving): $27,435 (64%). Average amount of gift aid, such as scholarships or grants (proportion receiving): $20,704 (63%). Average amount of self-help aid, such as work study or loans (proportion receiving): $6,259 (50%). Average need-based loan (excluding PLUS or other private loans): $4,877. Among students who received need-based aid, the average percentage of need met: 81%. Among students who received aid based on merit, the average award (and the proportion receiving): $12,241 (28%). The average athletic scholarship (and the proportion receiving): $23,884 (4%). Average amount of debt of borrowers graduating in 2009: $30,914. Proportion who borrowed: 83%.

CAMPUS LIFE AND EXTRACURRICULAR ACTIVITIES

Campus housing available (% using): coed dorms (45%), women's dorms (20%), men's dorms (8%), sorority housing (6%), fraternity housing (6%), apartment for single students (14%), other housing options (1%). Students who live in college-owned, operated, or affiliated housing: 69%. **Student employment:** During the 2009-2010 academic year, 13% of undergraduates worked on campus. Average per-year earnings: $2,500. **Clubs and organizations:** Number of student organizations: 124. Activities include: campus ministries, choral groups, concert band, dance, drama/theater, jazz band, literary magazine, model UN, music ensembles, musical theater, opera, pep band, radio station, student government, student newspaper, student film society, symphony orchestra. Number of fraternities: 6; sororities: 5. Proportion of men in fraternities: 26%; of women in sororities: 22%. Average proportion of students who stay on campus on weekends: 60%. **Sports program (2009-2010):** Member of NCAA I. *Men's intercollegiate varsity sports:* baseball, basketball, cross country, golf, soccer, tennis. *Women's intercollegiate varsity sports:* basketball, crew (heavyweight), crew (lightweight), cross country, golf, soccer, softball, tennis, volleyball.

SERVICES AND FACILITIES

Basic services: nonremedial tutoring, women's center, placement service, health service, health insurance, other. **Remedial assistance:** math, writing, study skills, other. **Counseling services:** minority student, career, personal, academic, psychological, birth control, religious. **For learning-disabled students:** School does not offer a structured program with separate admission and additional fees. Total undergraduates in learning-disabled program or receiving services: 61. Services include: tape recorders, note-taking services, oral tests, learning center, readers, extended time for tests, tutors, priority registration, priority seating, substitution of courses, texts on tape, typist/scribe, exams on tape or computer, waiver of foreign language degree requirement. **Library:** Number of titles: 404,061; number of current serial subscriptions: 36,000. **Information technology resources:** Students are not required to lease or own a computer. Number of campus computers available to all students: 473. School has a wireless network. Approximate number of users that can be accommodated: 900. Proportion of college-owned housing units wired for high-speed internet access: 100%. **Campus**

safety: Security services offered: 24-hour foot-and-vehicle patrols, late-night transport/escort service, 24-hour emergency telephones, lighted pathways/sidewalks, controlled dormitory access (key, security card, etc).

TRANSFER AND INTERNATIONAL STUDENTS

Transfer students: May apply for admission for the following academic terms: Fall, Spring, Summer. Applicants do not need a minimum number of credits to apply. For fall 2009: Transfer applications received: 280. Transfer applicants offered admission: 176. Transfer applicants enrolled: 84. **International students:** Number of foreign undergraduates: 72 (3% of student body). Number of countries represented: 29. Minimum TOEFL score required: 550 (paper); 213 (computer).

St. Leo University

- **Address:** PO Box 6665, Saint Leo, FL 33574-6665
- **Website:** http://www.saintleo.edu
- **Private; Religious affiliation:** Roman Catholic
- **Enrollment:** 1,640 full-time; 104 part-time

KEY STATS

✔ **U.S News College Ranking:** 59, Regional Universities (South)
✔ **SAT Score (25th/75th percentile):** 890-1080
✔ **Tuition:** 2010-2011: $17,850

Selectivity: Selective	**Room/board:** $8,848
Acceptance rate: 76%	**Average debt:** $23,787
Student/faculty ratio: 15/1	**Proportion who borrowed:** 63%

UNDERGRADUATE STUDENT BODY STATS

2009-2010 enrollment: 1,640 full-time; 104 part-time. Men: 49%; women: 51%. **Ethnic makeup:** African American: 10%; Asian American: 1%; Hispanic: 11%; White: 70%; International: 8%. **Religious preference:** Protestant: 18%; Jewish: 1%; No preference: 45%; Roman Catholic: 33%; Other: 3%.

ADMISSIONS FACTS AND FIGURES

Phone: (800) 334-5532. **Email:** admission@saintleo.edu. **Website:** http://www.saintleo.edu. **Application deadlines for fall 2011:** Regular decision: August 15. Early decision: Not offered. Early action: Not offered. Admission can be deferred. **Application fee:** $35. **To apply online, go to:** https://go2.saintleo.edu/i2e/app/login.asp?. **Admissions requirements/recommendations:** High school units required (recommended): English: (4); Mathematics: (3); Science: (2); Foreign language: (2); Social studies: (3); Academic electives: (2); Total units: (16). Tests: The college uses SAT or ACT scores in admissions decisions. Either SAT or ACT required. For admission to the fall 2011 entering class, the school will accept: ACT with or without writing accepted. Campus visit: Recommended. Admissions interview: Recommended. Off-campus interview: May be arranged. **Factors that count in admissions decisions:** *Academic:* Secondary school record: Very Important. Class rank: Considered. Letters of recommendation: Very Important. Standardized test scores: Very Important. Essay: Considered. *Nonacademic:* Interview: Important. Extracurricular activities: Important. Talent/ability: Important. Character/personal qualities: Very Important. Alumni/ae relationship: Important. Geographical residence: Not Considered. State residency: Not Considered. Religious affiliation/commitment: Not Considered. Minority status: Considered. Volunteer work: Important. Work experience: Considered. **Other schools with the greatest overlap in applicants:** Florida Southern College; University of Central Florida; University of Florida; University of South Florida; University of Tampa. **Admissions statistics for the fall 2009 entering class:** Total applicants: 2,074. Total accepted: 1,586. Freshmen enrolled: 489; 39% were from out of state. Overall acceptance rate: 76%. **Credentials of fall 2009 freshmen:** 11% ranked in the top 10 percent of their high school class; 34% were in the top 25 percent; 64% were in the top half. (Proportion submitting class standing: 69%.) **Average high school grade point average:** 3.3. **First-year students who submitted SAT scores:** 57%. Scores (25/75 percentile): Critical Reading: 440-530, Math: 450-550, Combined: 890-1080. **First-year students submitting ACT scores:** 40%. Scores (25/75 percentile): English: 18-23, Math: 18-23, Composite: 20-24.

ACADEMICS

Year founded: 1889. **Academic calendar:** Semester. **Degrees offered:** associate, bachelor's, post-bachelor's certificate, master's. **Most popular majors:**

36% business, management, marketing, and related support services, 10% psychology, 10% security and protective services, 9% biological and biomedical sciences, 7% education. **Major fields of study:** biological and biomedical sciences; business, management, marketing, and related support services; communication, journalism, and related programs; education; English language and literature/letters; health professions and related clinical sciences; history; mathematics and statistics; natural resources and conservation; parks, recreation, leisure, and fitness studies; psychology; public administration and social service professions; security and protective services; social sciences; theology and religious vocations. **Areas of required coursework:** arts/fine arts, humanities, computer literacy, mathematics, English (including composition), philosophy, sciences (biological or physical), history, social science, other. **Pre-professional programs:** pre-law, pre-dentistry, pre-medicine, pre-veterinary science, pre-optometry, pre-pharmacy, other. **Special academic programs (% participation):** distance learning (85%), double major (6%), honors program (17%), independent study (20%), internships (48%), liberal arts/career combination (1%), study abroad (5%), teacher certificate program (7%), weekend college (42%). **Teacher certification offered in:** elementary, middle/junior high. **Reserve Officers Training Corps (ROTC):** Army ROTC: Offered on campus; Air Force ROTC: Offered at cooperating institution (University of South Florida). **Faculty and instruction (2009-2010):** Total instructional faculty: 106 full-time, 51 part-time (64% men; 36% women; 10% minorities). Full-time faculty with Ph.D. or other terminal degree: 87%. Student/faculty ratio: 15/1. Classes of fewer than 20 students: 49%; of 20 to 49 students: 51%; of 50 or more students: 0%. **Advanced Placement and International Baccalaureate credit:** AP tests may be used for: Credit and/or placement. Scores accepted: 3. International Baccalaureate exams may be used for: Credit and/or placement. **Freshmen returning for sophomore year:** 71%. **Graduation rates:** Four-year: 24%; five-year: 40%; six-year: 42%. **Graduate study:** 36% of students pursue further study within one year.

COSTS AND FINANCIAL AID

Financial aid office: (352) 588-8270. **Expenses (2010-2011):** Tuition and fees 2010-2011: $17,850; room/board: $8,848. Estimated books and supplies: $1,200; transportation: $1,100; personal expenses: $1,330. **Financial aid:** Priority filing date for institution's financial aid form: March 1. In 2009-2010, 87% of undergraduates applied for financial aid. Of those, 72% were determined to have financial need; 28% had their need fully met. Average financial aid package (proportion receiving): $16,532 (72%). Average amount of gift aid, such as scholarships or grants (proportion receiving): $11,571 (72%). Average amount of self-help aid, such as work study or loans (proportion receiving): $5,294 (61%). Average need-based loan (excluding PLUS or other private loans): $4,111. Among students who received need-based aid, the average percentage of need met: 76%. Among students who received aid based on merit, the average award (and the proportion receiving): $7,217 (2%). The average athletic scholarship (and the proportion receiving): $9,182 (4%). Average amount of debt of borrowers graduating in 2009: $23,787. Proportion who borrowed: 63%.

CAMPUS LIFE AND EXTRACURRICULAR ACTIVITIES

Campus housing available: coed dorms, women's dorms, men's dorms, apartment for single students, special housing for disabled students, other housing options. Students who live in college-owned, operated, or affiliated housing: 72%. **Student employment:** During the 2009-2010 academic year, 40% of undergraduates worked on campus. Average per-year earnings: $3,500. **Clubs and organizations:** Number of student organizations: 58. Activities include: campus ministries, choral groups, concert band, dance, drama/theater, international student organization, literary magazine, music ensembles, musical theater, student government, student newspaper, television station, yearbook. Number of fraternities: 6; sororities: 4. Proportion of men in fraternities: 18%; of women in sororities: 13%. Average proportion of students who stay on campus on weekends: 85%. **Sports program (2009-2010):** Member of NCAA II. *Men's intercollegiate varsity sports:* baseball, basketball, cross country, golf, lacrosse, soccer, swimming, tennis. *Women's intercollegiate varsity sports:* basketball, cross country, golf, soccer, softball, swimming, tennis, volleyball.

SERVICES AND FACILITIES

Basic services: nonremedial tutoring, health service, health insurance. **Remedial assistance:** math, writing, study skills. **Counseling services:** minority student, career, personal, veteran student, academic, older student, psychological, religious. **For learning-disabled students:** School does not offer a structured program with separate admission and additional fees. Services include: remedial math, remedial English, reading machines, tape recorders, note-taking services, oral tests, learning center, readers, extended time for tests, tutors, other. **Library:** Number of titles: 115,463; number of current serial subscriptions: 42,388. **Information technology resources:** Students are not required to lease or own a computer. Number of campus computers available to all students: 1,371. School has a wireless network. Approximate number of users that can be accommodated: 1,300. Proportion of college-owned housing units wired for high-speed internet access: 100%. **Campus safety:** Security services offered: 24-hour foot-and-vehicle patrols, late-night transport/escort service, 24-hour emergency telephones, lighted pathways/sidewalks, student patrols, controlled dormitory access (key, security card, etc).

TRANSFER AND INTERNATIONAL STUDENTS

Transfer students: May apply for admission for the following academic terms: Fall, Spring. Applicants need a minimum number of credits to apply. For fall 2009: Transfer applications received: 307. Transfer applicants offered admission: 296. Transfer applicants enrolled: 144. **International students:** Number of foreign undergraduates: 131 (8% of student body). Number of countries represented: 45. Minimum TOEFL score required: 550 (paper); 79 (computer). Average TOEFL score: 610 (paper).

St. Thomas University

- ■ **Address:** 16401 N.W. 37th Avenue, Miami Gardens, FL 33054
- ■ **Website:** http://www.stu.edu
- ■ **Private; Religious affiliation:** Roman Catholic
- ■ **Enrollment:** 1,109 full-time; 67 part-time

KEY STATS
✔ **U.S News College Ranking:** 63, Regional Universities (South)
✔ **SAT Score (25th/75th percentile):** 773-960
✔ **Tuition:** 2009-2010: $21,690

Selectivity: Less selective	**Room/board:** $6,516
Acceptance rate: 59%	**Average debt:** N/A
Student/faculty ratio: 13/1	**Proportion who borrowed:** N/A

UNDERGRADUATE STUDENT BODY STATS

2009-2010 enrollment: 1,109 full-time; 67 part-time. Men: 44%; women: 56%. **Ethnic makeup:** African American: 25%; Asian American: 1%; Hispanic: 48%; White: 17%; International: 9%.

ADMISSIONS FACTS AND FIGURES

Phone: (305) 628-6546. **Email:** signup@stu.edu. **Website:** http://www.stu.edu. **Application deadlines for fall 2011:** Regular decision: Rolling. Early decision: Not offered. Early action: Not offered. Admission can be deferred. **Application fee:** $40. **To apply online, go to:** http://www.stu.edu/ProspectiveStudents/tabid/449/Default.aspx. **Admissions requirements/recommendations:** High school units required (recommended): English: 4; Mathematics: 3; Science: 2; Social studies: 3; Academic electives: 6; Total units: 18. Tests: The college uses SAT or ACT scores in admissions decisions. Either SAT or ACT required. For admission to the fall 2011 entering class, the school will accept: ACT with or without writing accepted. Campus visit: Recommended. Admissions interview: Recommended. Off-campus interview: May be arranged. **Factors that count in admissions decisions:** *Academic:* Secondary school record: Important. Class rank: Very Important. Letters of recommendation: Important. Standardized test scores: Very Important. Essay: Important. *Nonacademic:* Interview: Not Considered. Extracurricular activities: Considered. Talent/ability: Considered. Character/personal qualities: Considered. Alumni/ae relationship: Important. Geographical residence: Not Considered. State residency: Not Considered. Religious affiliation/commitment: Not Considered. Minority status: Not Considered. Volunteer work: Considered. Work experience: Considered. **Other schools with the greatest overlap in applicants:** Barry University; Florida International University; Florida Memorial University; Miami-Dade College; University of Miami. **Admissions statistics for the fall 2009 entering class:** Total applicants: 674. Total accepted: 400. Freshmen enrolled: 238; 16% were from out of state. Overall acceptance rate: 59%. **Credentials of fall 2009 freshmen:** 5% ranked in the top 10 percent of their high school class; 20% were in the top 25 percent. **First-year students who submitted SAT scores:** 61%. Scores (25/75 percentile): Critical Reading: 390-480, Math: 383-480, Combined: 773-960. **First-year students submitting ACT scores:** 38%. Scores (25/75 percentile): English: N/A, Math: N/A, Composite: 16-19.

ACADEMICS

Year founded: 1961. **Academic calendar:** Semester. **Degrees offered:** certificate, bachelor's, post-bachelor's certificate, master's, post-master's certificate, doctorate. **Most popular majors:** 51% business, management, marketing, and related support services, 9% education, 9% security and protective services, 8% psychology, 5% social sciences. **Major fields of study:** biological and biomedical sciences; business, management, marketing, and related support services; communication, journalism, and related programs; computer and information sciences and support services; education; English language and literature/letters; health professions and related clinical sciences; history; liberal arts and sciences studies, and humanities; parks, recreation, leisure, and fitness studies; philosophy and religious studies; psychology; public administration and social service professions; security and protective services; social sciences. **Areas of required coursework:** computer literacy, mathematics, English (including composition), philosophy, sciences (biological or physical), history, social science, other. **Pre-professional programs:** pre-law, pre-dentistry, pre-medicine. **Special academic programs:** distance learning, double major, dual enrollment, honors program, independent study, internships, liberal arts/career combination, teacher certificate program. **Teacher certification offered in:** elementary, secondary. **Faculty and instruction (2009-2010):** Total instructional faculty: N/A. Student/faculty ratio: 13/1. Classes of fewer than 20 students: 65%; of 20 to 49 students: 35%; of 50 or more students: 0%. **Advanced Placement and International Baccalaureate credit:** AP tests may be used for: Credit only. Scores accepted: 3, 4, 5. International Baccalaureate exams may be used for: Credit only. **Freshmen returning for sophomore year:** 68%. **Graduation rates:** Four-year: 28%; five-year: 34%; six-year: 36%.

COSTS AND FINANCIAL AID

Financial aid office: (305) 474-6960. **Expenses (2009-2010):** Tuition and fees 2009-2010: $21,690; room/board: $6,516. **Financial aid:** Priority filing date for institution's financial aid form: April 1.

CAMPUS LIFE AND EXTRACURRICULAR ACTIVITIES

Campus housing available: women's dorms, men's dorms. Students who live in college-owned, operated, or affiliated housing: 19%. Average per-year earnings: $3,200. **Clubs and organizations:** Number of student organizations: 17. Activities include: campus ministries, choral groups, international student organization, literary magazine, music ensembles, student government, television station, yearbook. Number of fraternities: 0; sororities: 0. **Sports program (2009-2010):** Member of NAIA.

SERVICES AND FACILITIES

Basic services: nonremedial tutoring, health service, health insurance. **Remedial assistance:** reading, math, writing, study skills. **Counseling services:** career, personal, academic, psychological, religious. **For learning-disabled students:** School does not offer a structured program with separate admission and additional fees. Services include: remedial math, remedial English, remedial reading, tape recorders, untimed tests, learning center, extended time for tests, tutors. **Library:** Number of titles: 228,795; number of current serial subscriptions: 3,894. **Information technology resources:** Students are not required to lease or own a computer. Number of campus computers available to all students: 250. School has a wireless network. Approximate number of users that can be accommodated: 100. **Campus safety:** Security services offered: 24-hour foot-and-vehicle patrols, late-night transport/escort service, 24-hour emergency telephones, lighted pathways/sidewalks, controlled dormitory access (key, security card, etc).

TRANSFER AND INTERNATIONAL STUDENTS

Transfer students: May apply for admission for the following academic terms: Fall, Spring, Summer. Applicants need a minimum number of credits to apply. For fall 2009: Transfer applications received: 293. Transfer applicants offered admission: 240. Transfer applicants enrolled: 0. **International students:** Number of foreign undergraduates: 108 (9% of student body). Number of countries represented: 49. Minimum TOEFL score required: 193 (computer).

University of Central Florida

- **Address:** 4000 Central Florida Boulevard, Orlando, FL 32816
- **Website:** http://www.ucf.edu
- **Public**
- **Enrollment:** 34,095 full-time; 11,206 part-time

KEY STATS

✔ **U.S News College Ranking:** 179, National Universities
✔ **SAT Score (25th/75th percentile):** 1090-1270
✔ **Tuition:** 2009-2010: $4,526 in state, $20,005 out of state

Selectivity: More selective   **Room/board:** $8,540
Acceptance rate: 47%   **Average debt:** $17,044
Student/faculty ratio: 31/1   **Proportion who borrowed:** 41%

UNDERGRADUATE STUDENT BODY STATS

2009-2010 enrollment: 34,095 full-time; 11,206 part-time. Men: 45%; women: 55%. **Ethnic makeup:** African American: 9%; Asian American: 6%; Hispanic: 15%; White: 68%; International: 1%.

ADMISSIONS FACTS AND FIGURES

Phone: (407) 823-3000. **Email:** admission@mail.ucf.edu. **Website:** http://www.ucf.edu. **Application deadlines for fall 2011:** Regular decision: May 1. Early decision: Not offered. Early action: Not offered. Admission cannot be deferred. **Application fee:** $30. **To apply online, go to:** https://www.admissions.mca.ucf.edu/. **Admissions requirements/recommendations:** High school units required (recommended): English: 4; Mathematics: 4; Science: 3; Foreign language: 2; Social studies: 3; Academic electives: 2; Total units: 18. Tests: The college uses SAT or ACT scores in admissions decisions. Either SAT or ACT required. For admission to the fall 2011 entering class, the school will accept: ACT with writing required. Campus visit: Recommended. Admissions interview: Recommended. Off-campus interview: Not available. **Factors that count in admissions decisions:** *Academic:* Secondary school record: Very Important. Class rank: Considered. Letters of recommendation: Important. Standardized test scores: Very Important. Essay: Important. *Nonacademic:* Interview: Considered. Extracurricular activities: Considered. Talent/ability: Considered. Character/personal qualities: Considered. Alumni/ae relationship: Considered. Geographical residence: Considered. State residency: Considered. Religious affiliation/commitment: Not Considered. Minority status: Not Considered. Volunteer work: Considered. Work experience: Considered. **Other schools with the greatest overlap in applicants:** Florida International University; Florida State University; University of Florida; University of Miami; University of South Florida. **Admissions statistics for the fall 2009 entering class:** Total applicants: 32,335. Total accepted: 15,125. Freshmen enrolled: 6,397; 7% were from out of state. Overall acceptance rate: 47%. **Size of waiting list:** 578 applicants; enrolled from waiting list: 31. **Credentials of fall 2009 freshmen:** 35% ranked in the top 10 percent of their high school class; 77% were in the top 25 percent; 95% were in the top half. (Proportion submitting class standing: 80%.) **Average high school grade point average:** 3.7. **First-year students who submitted SAT scores:** 56%. Scores (25/75 percentile): Critical Reading: 530-620, Math: 560-650, Combined: 1090-1270. **First-year students submitting ACT scores:** 44%. Scores (25/75 percentile): English: N/A, Math: N/A, Composite: 23-28.

ACADEMICS

Year founded: 1963. **Academic calendar:** Semester. **Degrees offered:** certificate, associate, bachelor's, post-bachelor's certificate, master's, doctorate. **Most popular majors:** 26% business, management, marketing, and related support services, 11% education, 10% health professions and related clinical sciences, 8% psychology, 6% liberal arts and sciences studies, and humanities. **Major fields of study:** biological and biomedical sciences; business, management, marketing, and related support services; communication, journalism, and related programs; computer and information sciences and support services; education; engineering; engineering technologies/technicians; English language and literature/letters; foreign languages, literatures, and linguistics; health professions and related clinical sciences; history; legal professions and studies; liberal arts and sciences studies, and humanities; mathematics and statistics; philosophy and religious studies; physical sciences; psychology; public administration and social service professions; security and protective services; social sciences; visual and performing arts. **Areas of required coursework:** humanities, mathematics, English (including composition), sciences (biological or physical), history, social science. **Pre-professional programs:** pre-law, pre-medicine. **Special academic programs**

(% participation): cooperative (work-study plan) program (11%), distance learning (72%), double major (3%), dual enrollment (.1%), honors program (5%), independent study (11%), internships (32%), study abroad (.9%), teacher certificate program (11%). **Teacher certification offered in:** early childhood, special education, elementary, secondary. **Cooperative education programs:** art, business, computer science, education, engineering, health professions, humanities, natural science, social/behavioral science, technologies. **Reserve Officers Training Corps (ROTC):** Army ROTC: Offered on campus; Air Force ROTC: Offered on campus. **Faculty and instruction (2009-2010):** Total instructional faculty: 1,240 full-time, 467 part-time (58% men; 42% women; 20% minorities). Full-time faculty with Ph.D. or other terminal degree: 78%. Student/faculty ratio: 31/1. Classes of fewer than 20 students: 27%; of 20 to 49 students: 48%; of 50 or more students: 25%. **Advanced Placement and International Baccalaureate credit:** AP tests may be used for: Credit only. Scores accepted: 3, 4, 5. International Baccalaureate exams may be used for: Credit only. **Freshmen returning for sophomore year:** 85%. **Graduation rates:** Four-year: 34%; five-year: 57%; six-year: 63%. **Graduate study:** 25% of students pursue further study immediately upon graduation; 34% within one year; 47% within five years. Fields in which graduates pursue further study: Master of Business Administration (MBA), 28%; law, 8%; medicine, 10%; dentistry, 1%; engineering, 6%; education, 23%; arts and sciences, 24%.

COSTS AND FINANCIAL AID

Financial aid office: (407) 823-2827. **Expenses (2009-2010):** Tuition and fees 2009-2010: $4,526 in state, $20,005 out of state; room/board: $8,540. Estimated books and supplies: $924; transportation: $1,800; personal expenses: $2,276. **Financial aid:** Priority filing date for institution's financial aid form: March 1; deadline: June 30. In 2009-2010, 62% of undergraduates applied for financial aid. Of those, 44% were determined to have financial need; 16% had their need fully met. Average financial aid package (proportion receiving): $7,951 (42%). Average amount of gift aid, such as scholarships or grants (proportion receiving): $4,640 (28%). Average amount of self-help aid, such as work study or loans (proportion receiving): $4,790 (24%). Average need-based loan (excluding PLUS or other private loans): $4,681. Among students who received need-based aid, the average percentage of need met: 67%. Among students who received aid based on merit, the average award (and the proportion receiving): $2,327 (6%). The average athletic scholarship (and the proportion receiving): $8,186 (1%). Average amount of debt of borrowers graduating in 2009: $17,044. Proportion who borrowed: 41%.

CAMPUS LIFE AND EXTRACURRICULAR ACTIVITIES

Campus housing available (% using): coed dorms (21%), sorority housing (3%), fraternity housing (1%), apartment for single students (72%). Students who live in college-owned, operated, or affiliated housing: 21%. Average per-year earnings: $5,180. **Clubs and organizations:** Number of student organizations: 302. Activities include: campus ministries, choral groups, concert band, drama/theater, international student organization, jazz band, literary magazine, marching band, model UN, music ensembles, musical theater, pep band, radio station, student government, student newspaper, student film society, symphony orchestra. Number of fraternities: 24; sororities: 19. Proportion of men in fraternities: 11%; of women in sororities: 9%. Average proportion of students who stay on campus on weekends: 50%. **Sports program (2009-2010):** Member of NCAA I. *Men's intercollegiate varsity sports:* baseball, basketball, cross country, football, golf, soccer, tennis. *Women's intercollegiate varsity sports:* basketball, crew (heavyweight), crew (lightweight), cross country, golf, soccer, softball, tennis, track and field (indoor), track and field (outdoor), volleyball.

SERVICES AND FACILITIES

Basic services: nonremedial tutoring, women's center, day care, health service, health insurance. **Counseling services:** minority student, career, personal, veteran student, academic, psychological, birth control. **For learning-disabled students:** School does not offer a structured program with separate admission and additional fees. Services include: reading machines, tape recorders, videotaped classes, note-taking services, readers, extended time for tests, tutors, priority registration, other. **Library:** Number of titles: 1,936,014; number of current serial subscriptions: 32,009. **Information technology resources:** Students are not required to lease or own a computer. Number of campus computers available to all students: 2,937. School has a wireless network. Approximate number of users that can be accommodated: 10,000. Proportion of college-owned housing units wired for high-speed internet access: 100%. **Campus safety:** Security services offered: 24-hour foot-and-vehicle patrols, late-night transport/escort service, 24-hour emergency telephones, lighted pathways/sidewalks, controlled dormitory access (key, security card, etc.).

TRANSFER AND INTERNATIONAL STUDENTS

Transfer students: May apply for admission for the following academic terms: Fall, Spring, Summer. Applicants need a minimum number of credits to apply. For fall 2009: Transfer applications received: 12,280. Transfer applicants offered admission: 7,525. Transfer applicants enrolled: 5,336. **International students:** Number of foreign undergraduates: 559 (1% of student body). Number of countries represented: 131. Minimum TOEFL score required: 550 (paper); 213 (computer). Average TOEFL score: 563 (paper).

University of Florida

- **Address:** 201 Criser Hall, Gainesville, FL 32611
- **Website:** http://www.ufl.edu
- **Public**
- **Enrollment:** 31,304 full-time; 2,324 part-time

KEY STATS

✔ **U.S News College Ranking:** 53, National Universities
✔ **SAT Score (25th/75th percentile):** 1140-1360
✔ **Tuition:** 2009-2010: $4,373 in state, $23,744 out of state
   Selectivity: More selective   **Room/board:** $7,500
   Acceptance rate: 42%   **Average debt:** $15,932
   Student/faculty ratio: 20/1   **Proportion who borrowed:** 41%

UNDERGRADUATE STUDENT BODY STATS

2009-2010 enrollment: 31,304 full-time; 2,324 part-time. Men: 45%; women: 55%. **Ethnic makeup:** African American: 10%; American-Indian: 1%; Asian American: 9%; Hispanic: 16%; White: 64%; International: 1%.

ADMISSIONS FACTS AND FIGURES

Phone: (352) 392-1365. **Website:** http://www.ufl.edu. **Application deadlines for fall 2011:** Regular decision: November 1. Early decision: Not offered. Early action: Not offered. Admission cannot be deferred. **Application fee:** $30. **To apply online, go to:** http://admissions.ufl.edu. **Admissions requirements/recommendations:** High school units required (recommended): English: 4; Mathematics: 3; Science: 3; Foreign language: 2; Social studies: 3; History: 0; Academic electives: 3; Total units: 18. Tests: The college uses SAT or ACT scores in admissions decisions. Either SAT or ACT required. For admission to the fall 2011 entering class, the school will accept: ACT with writing required. Campus visit: Recommended. Admissions interview: Neither required nor recommended. Off-campus interview: Not available. **Factors that count in admissions decisions:** *Academic:* Secondary school record: Very Important. Class rank: Considered. Letters of recommendation: Not Considered. Standardized test scores: Important. Essay: Very Important. *Nonacademic:* Interview: Not Considered. Extracurricular activities: Important. Talent/ability: Important. Character/personal qualities: Important. Alumni/ae relationship: Considered. Geographical residence: Considered. State residency: Considered. Religious affiliation/commitment: Not Considered. Minority status: Not Considered. Volunteer work: Important. Work experience: Important. **Other schools with the greatest overlap in applicants:** Florida International University; Florida State University; University of Central Florida; University of Miami; University of South Florida. **Admissions statistics for the fall 2009 entering class:** Total applicants: 25,798. Total accepted: 10,821. Freshmen enrolled: 6,253; 3% were from out of state. Overall acceptance rate: 42%. **Credentials of fall 2009 freshmen:** 77% ranked in the top 10 percent of their high school class; 93% were in the top 25 percent; 99% were in the top half. (Proportion submitting class standing: 72%.) **Average high school grade point average:** 4.0. **First-year students who submitted SAT scores:** 76%. Scores (25/75 percentile): Critical Reading: 560-670, Math: 580-690, Combined: 1140-1360. **First-year students submitting ACT scores:** 25%. Scores (25/75 percentile): English: N/A, Math: N/A, Composite: 26-31.

ACADEMICS

Year founded: 1853. **Academic calendar:** Semester. **Degrees offered:** bachelor's, master's, doctorate. **Most popular majors:** 15% business, management, marketing, and related support services, 13% social sciences, 11% engineering, 8% communication, journalism, and related programs, 8% health professions and related clinical sciences. **Major fields of study:** agriculture, agriculture operations, and related sciences; architecture and

related services; area, ethnic, cultural, and gender studies; biological and biomedical sciences; business, management, marketing, and related support services; communication, journalism, and related programs; computer and information sciences and support services; education; engineering; engineering technologies/technicians; English language and literature/letters; family and consumer sciences/human sciences; foreign languages, literatures, and linguistics; health professions and related clinical sciences; history; legal professions and studies; mathematics and statistics; multi/interdisciplinary studies; natural resources and conservation; parks, recreation, leisure, and fitness studies; philosophy and religious studies; physical sciences; psychology; security and protective services; social sciences; visual and performing arts. **Areas of required coursework:** humanities, mathematics, English (including composition), sciences (biological or physical), social science. **Pre-professional programs:** pre-law, pre-dentistry, pre-medicine, pre-veterinary science, pre-pharmacy. **Special academic programs:** accelerated program, cooperative (work-study plan) program, cross-registration, distance learning, double major, dual enrollment, English as a Second Language (ESL), exchange student program (domestic), external degree program, honors program, independent study, internships, liberal arts/career combination, student-designed major, study abroad, teacher certificate program, weekend college, other. **Teacher certification offered in:** early childhood, elementary, secondary. **Cooperative education programs:** business, computer science, engineering. **Reserve Officers Training Corps (ROTC):** Army ROTC: Offered on campus; Navy ROTC: Offered on campus; Air Force ROTC: Offered on campus. **Faculty and instruction (2009-2010):** Total instructional faculty: 3,372 full-time, 224 part-time (67% men; 33% women; 24% minorities). Full-time faculty with Ph.D. or other terminal degree: 75%. Student/faculty ratio: 20/1. Classes of fewer than 20 students: 39%; of 20 to 49 students: 39%; of 50 or more students: 22%. **Advanced Placement and International Baccalaureate credit:** AP tests may be used for: Credit and/or placement. Scores accepted: 3, 4, 5. International Baccalaureate exams may be used for: Credit and/or placement. **Freshmen returning for sophomore year:** 95%. **Graduation rates:** Four-year: 58%; five-year: 79%; six-year: 82%.

COSTS AND FINANCIAL AID

Financial aid office: (352) 392-1271. **Expenses (2009-2010):** Tuition and fees 2009-2010: $4,373 in state, $23,744 out of state; room/board: $7,500. Estimated books and supplies: $990; transportation: $540; personal expenses: $3,320. **Financial aid:** Priority filing date for institution's financial aid form: March 15. In 2009-2010, 55% of undergraduates applied for financial aid. Of those, 44% were determined to have financial need; 36% had their need fully met. Average financial aid package (proportion receiving): $13,448 (43%). Average amount of gift aid, such as scholarships or grants (proportion receiving): $6,942 (30%). Average amount of self-help aid, such as work study or loans (proportion receiving): $4,240 (24%). Average need-based loan (excluding PLUS or other private loans): $4,196. Among students who received need-based aid, the average percentage of need met: 85%. Among students who received aid based on merit, the average award (and the proportion receiving): $4,700 (47%). The average athletic scholarship (and the proportion receiving): $14,301 (1%). Average amount of debt of borrowers graduating in 2009: $15,932. Proportion who borrowed: 41%.

CAMPUS LIFE AND EXTRACURRICULAR ACTIVITIES

Campus housing available (% using): coed dorms (31%), sorority housing (7%), fraternity housing (8%), apartments for married students (10%), apartment for single students (16%), special housing for disabled students (1%), special housing for international students (2%). Students who live in college-owned, operated, or affiliated housing: 23%. **Student employment:** During the 2009-2010 academic year, 10% of undergraduates worked on campus. Average per-year earnings: $1,579. **Clubs and organizations:** Number of student organizations: 907. Activities include: choral groups, concert band, dance, drama/theater, jazz band, literary magazine, marching band, music ensembles, musical theater, pep band, radio station, student government, student newspaper, student film society, symphony orchestra, television station, yearbook. Number of fraternities: 37; sororities: 26. Average proportion of students who stay on campus on weekends: 70%. **Sports program (2009-2010):** Member of NCAA I. *Men's intercollegiate varsity sports:* baseball, basketball, cross country, football, golf, swimming, tennis, track and field (indoor), track and field (outdoor). *Women's intercollegiate varsity sports:* basketball, cross country, golf, gymnastics, lacrosse, soccer, softball, swimming, tennis, track and field (indoor), track and field (outdoor), volleyball.

SERVICES AND FACILITIES

Basic services: nonremedial tutoring, placement service, day care, health service, health insurance. **Remedial assistance:** reading, math, writing, study skills, other. **Counseling services:** minority student, career, military, personal, veteran student, academic, older student, psychological, birth control, religious, other. **For learning-disabled students:** School does not offer a structured program with separate admission and additional fees. Total undergraduates in learning-disabled program or receiving services: 700. Services include: tape recorders, note-taking services, readers, extended time for tests, early syllabus, priority registration, priority seating, substitution of courses, texts on tape, typist/scribe, exams on tape or computer. **Library:** Number of titles: 5,618,880; number of current serial subscriptions: 89,741. **Information technology resources:** Students are required to lease or own a computer. Number of campus computers available to all students: 1,120. School has a wireless network. Approximate number of users that can be accommodated: 14,150. Proportion of college-owned housing units wired for high-speed internet access: 98%. **Campus safety:** Security services offered: 24-hour foot-and-vehicle patrols, late-night transport/escort service, 24-hour emergency telephones, lighted pathways/sidewalks, student patrols, controlled dormitory access (key, security card, etc).

TRANSFER AND INTERNATIONAL STUDENTS

Transfer students: May apply for admission for the following academic terms: Fall, Spring, Summer. Applicants need a minimum number of credits to apply. For fall 2009: Transfer applications received: 5,026. Transfer applicants offered admission: 1,668. Transfer applicants enrolled: 1,326. **International students:** Number of foreign undergraduates: 262 (1% of student body). Number of countries represented: 31. Minimum TOEFL score required: 550 (paper); 213 (computer). Average TOEFL score: 550 (paper).

University of Miami

- **Address:** PO Box 248025, Coral Gables, FL 33124
- **Website:** http://www.miami.edu
- **Private**
- **Enrollment:** 9,451 full-time; 919 part-time

KEY STATS

- ✔ **U.S News College Ranking:** 47, National Universities
- ✔ **SAT Score (25th/75th percentile):** 1170-1380
- ✔ **Tuition:** 2010-2011: $37,836

Selectivity: More selective	**Room/board:** $11,062
Acceptance rate: 44%	**Average debt:** $24,396
Student/faculty ratio: 11/1	**Proportion who borrowed:** 55%

UNDERGRADUATE STUDENT BODY STATS

2009-2010 enrollment: 9,451 full-time; 919 part-time. Men: 48%; women: 52%. **Ethnic makeup:** African American: 8%; Asian American: 5%; Hispanic: 24%; White: 54%; International: 9%. **Religious preference:** Roman Catholic: 14%; Protestant: 18%; Jewish: 4%; Muslim: 1%; Hindu: 1%; Unknown: 59%; Other: 3%.

ADMISSIONS FACTS AND FIGURES

Phone: (305) 284-4323. **Email:** admission@miami.edu. **Website:** http://www.miami.edu. **Application deadlines for fall 2011:** Regular decision: January 15; decision sent by April 15. Early decision: Send application by: November 1; Decision sent by: December 15. Early action: Send application by: November 1; Decision sent by: February 1. Admission can be deferred. **Application fee:** $65. **To apply online, go to:** http://www.miami.edu/apply/. **Admissions requirements/recommendations:** High school units required (recommended): English: (4); Mathematics: (4); Science: (3); Foreign language: (2); Social studies: (3); History: (2); Total units: (20). Tests: The college uses SAT or ACT scores in admissions decisions. Either SAT or ACT required. For admission to the fall 2011 entering class, the school will accept: ACT with or without writing accepted. Campus visit: Recommended. Admissions interview: Neither required nor recommended. Off-campus interview: May be arranged. **Factors that count in admissions decisions:** *Academic:* Secondary school record: Very Important. Class rank: Very Important. Letters of recommendation: Very Important. Standardized test scores: Very Important. Essay: Very Important. *Nonacademic:* Interview: Not Considered. Extracurricular activities: Very Important. Talent/ability: Considered. Character/personal qualities: Considered. Alumni/ae relationship: Considered. Geographical residence: Considered. State residency:

Not Considered. Religious affiliation/commitment: Not Considered. Minority status: Considered. Volunteer work: Important. Work experience: Considered. **Other schools with the greatest overlap in applicants:** Boston University; New York University; Pennsylvania State University–University Park; Tulane University; University of Southern California. **Admissions statistics for the fall 2009 entering class:** Total applicants: 21,844. Total accepted: 9,700. Freshmen enrolled: 2,006; 56% were from out of state. Accepted through early-decision or early-action plans: 57%. Overall acceptance rate: 44%. Early-decision acceptance rate: 26%. Non-early acceptance rate: 41%. **Credentials of fall 2009 freshmen:** 63% ranked in the top 10 percent of their high school class; 87% were in the top 25 percent; 97% were in the top half. (Proportion submitting class standing: 34%.) **Average high school grade point average:** 4.0. **First-year students who submitted SAT scores:** 58%. Scores (25/75 percentile): Critical Reading: 570-680, Math: 600-700, Combined: 1170-1380. **First-year students submitting ACT scores:** 33%. Scores (25/75 percentile): English: 27-33, Math: 26-32, Composite: 27-31.

ACADEMICS

Year founded: 1925. **Academic calendar:** Semester. **Degrees offered:** certificate, bachelor's, post-bachelor's certificate, master's, post-master's certificate, doctorate. **Most popular majors:** 21% business, management, marketing, and related support services, 13% social sciences, 9% biological and biomedical sciences, 9% visual and performing arts, 8% communication, journalism, and related programs. **Major fields of study:** architecture and related services; area, ethnic, cultural, and gender studies; biological and biomedical sciences; business, management, marketing, and related support services; communication, journalism, and related programs; communications technologies/technicians and support services; computer and information sciences and support services; education; engineering; English language and literature/letters; foreign languages, literatures, and linguistics; health professions and related clinical sciences; history; legal professions and studies; liberal arts and sciences studies, and humanities; mathematics and statistics; multi/interdisciplinary studies; parks, recreation, leisure, and fitness studies; philosophy and religious studies; physical sciences; psychology; social sciences; visual and performing arts. **Areas of required coursework:** arts/fine arts, humanities, mathematics, English (including composition), philosophy, sciences (biological or physical), history, social science. **Pre-professional programs:** pre-law, pre-dentistry, pre-medicine, pre-veterinary science, pre-pharmacy, other. **Special academic programs:** accelerated program, distance learning, double major, dual enrollment, English as a Second Language (ESL), honors program, independent study, internships, liberal arts/career combination, student-designed major, study abroad, teacher certificate program, weekend college. **Teacher certification offered in:** elementary, secondary. **Reserve Officers Training Corps (ROTC):** Army ROTC: Offered on campus; Air Force ROTC: Offered on campus. **Faculty and instruction (2009-2010):** Total instructional faculty: 961 full-time, 335 part-time (63% men; 37% women; 28% minorities). Full-time faculty with Ph.D. or other terminal degree: 87%. Student/faculty ratio: 11/1. Classes of fewer than 20 students: 52%; of 20 to 49 students: 41%; of 50 or more students: 7%. **Advanced Placement and International Baccalaureate credit:** AP tests may be used for: Credit and/or placement. Scores accepted: 3, 4, 5. International Baccalaureate exams may be used for: Credit only. **Freshmen returning for sophomore year:** 90%. **Graduation rates:** Four-year: 67%; five-year: 78%; six-year: 80%. **Graduate study:** 26% of students pursue further study immediately upon graduation. Fields in which graduates pursue further study: Master of Business Administration (MBA), 6%; law, 16%; medicine, 16%; arts and sciences, 21%.

COSTS AND FINANCIAL AID

Financial aid office: (305) 284-5212. **Expenses (2010-2011):** Tuition and fees 2010-2011: $37,836; room/board: $11,062. Estimated books and supplies: $1,250; transportation: $1,350; personal expenses: $2,456. **Financial aid:** Priority filing date for institution's financial aid form: February 1. In 2009-2010, 57% of undergraduates applied for financial aid. Of those, 48% were determined to have financial need; 35% had their need fully met. Average financial aid package (proportion receiving): $30,640 (48%). Average amount of gift aid, such as scholarships or grants (proportion receiving): $22,869 (47%). Average amount of self-help aid, such as work study or loans (proportion receiving): $6,705 (42%). Average need-based loan (excluding PLUS or other private loans): $5,078. Among students who received need-based aid, the average percentage of need met: 82%. Among students who received aid based on merit, the average award (and the proportion receiving): $18,529 (20%). The average athletic scholarship (and the proportion receiving): $27,667 (2%). Average amount of debt of borrowers graduating in 2009: $24,396. Proportion who borrowed: 55%.

CAMPUS LIFE AND EXTRACURRICULAR ACTIVITIES

Campus housing available (% using): coed dorms (70%), apartment for single students (23%), special housing for disabled students (1%). Students who live in college-owned, operated, or affiliated housing: 43%. **Student employment:** During the 2009-2010 academic year, 25% of undergraduates worked on campus. Average per-year earnings: $3,000. **Clubs and organizations:** Number of student organizations: 293. Activities include: campus ministries, choral groups, concert band, dance, drama/theater, international student organization, jazz band, literary magazine, marching band, model UN, music ensembles, musical theater, opera, pep band, radio station, student government, student newspaper, student film society, symphony orchestra, television station, yearbook. Number of fraternities: 19; sororities: 13. Proportion of men in fraternities: 15%; of women in sororities: 14%. **Sports program (2009-2010):** Member of NCAA I. *Men's intercollegiate varsity sports:* baseball, basketball, cross country, football, swimming, tennis, track and field (indoor), track and field (outdoor). *Women's intercollegiate varsity sports:* basketball, crew (heavyweight), cross country, golf, soccer, swimming, tennis, track and field (indoor), track and field (outdoor), volleyball.

SERVICES AND FACILITIES

Basic services: nonremedial tutoring, placement service, health service, health insurance. **Remedial assistance:** reading, math, writing, study skills. **Counseling services:** minority student, career, personal, academic, older student, psychological, other. **For learning-disabled students:** School does not offer a structured program with separate admission and additional fees. Total undergraduates in learning-disabled program or receiving services: 238. Services include: note-taking services, learning center, readers, extended time for tests, tutors. **Library:** Number of titles: 3,300,370; number of current serial subscriptions: 76,869. **Information technology resources:** Students are not required to lease or own a computer. School has a wireless network. Proportion of college-owned housing units wired for high-speed internet access: 100%. **Campus safety:** Security services offered: 24-hour foot-and-vehicle patrols, late-night transport/escort service, 24-hour emergency telephones, lighted pathways/sidewalks, controlled dormitory access (key, security card, etc).

TRANSFER AND INTERNATIONAL STUDENTS

Transfer students: May apply for admission for the following academic terms: Fall, Spring, Summer. Applicants do not need a minimum number of credits to apply. For fall 2009: Transfer applications received: 3,698. Transfer applicants offered admission: 1,449. Transfer applicants enrolled: 619. **International students:** Number of foreign undergraduates: 838 (9% of student body). Number of countries represented: 73. Minimum TOEFL score required: 550 (paper); 80 (computer). Average TOEFL score: 499 (paper).

University of North Florida

- **Address:** 4567 St. Johns Bluff Road S, Jacksonville, FL 32224-2645
- **Website:** http://www.unf.edu
- **Public**
- **Enrollment:** 10,453 full-time; 4,042 part-time

KEY STATS

✔ **U.S News College Ranking:** 51, Regional Universities (South)
✔ **SAT Score (25th/75th percentile):** 1020-1210
✔ **Tuition:** 2009-2010: $4,193 in state, $17,582 out of state
   Selectivity: Selective   **Room/board:** $9,982
   Acceptance rate: 64%   **Average debt:** $15,619
   Student/faculty ratio: 23/1   **Proportion who borrowed:** 41%

UNDERGRADUATE STUDENT BODY STATS

2009-2010 enrollment: 10,453 full-time; 4,042 part-time. Men: 44%; women: 56%. **Ethnic makeup:** African American: 11%; Asian American: 6%; Hispanic: 7%; White: 75%; International: 1%. **Religious preference:** Roman Catholic: 1%; Unknown: 96%; Baptist: 1%; Other: 2%.

ADMISSIONS FACTS AND FIGURES

Phone: (904) 620-2624. **Email:** admissions@unf.edu. **Website:** http://www.unf.edu. **Application deadlines for fall 2011:** Regular decision: June 11. Early decision: Not offered. Early action: Not offered. Admission can be deferred. **Application fee:** $30. **To apply online, go to:** http://www.unf.edu/admis-sions/applying/applyonline.html. **Admissions requirements/recommendations:** High school units required (recommended): English: 4; Mathematics: 3; Science: 3; Foreign language: 2; Social studies: 3; Academic electives: 4; Total units: 19. Tests: The college uses SAT or ACT scores in admissions decisions. Either SAT or ACT required. For admission to the fall 2011 entering class, the school will accept: ACT with writing required. Campus visit: Recommended. Admissions interview: Recommended. Off-campus interview: Not available. **Factors that count in admissions decisions:** *Academic:* Secondary school record: Very Important. Class rank: Considered. Letters of recommendation: Considered. Standardized test scores: Very Important. Essay: Considered. *Nonacademic:* Interview: Not Considered. Extracurricular activities: Considered. Talent/ability: Considered. Character/personal qualities: Not Considered. Alumni/ae relationship: Not Considered. Geographical residence: Not Considered. State residency: Not Considered. Religious affiliation/commitment: Not Considered. Minority status: Not Considered. Volunteer work: Considered. Work experience: Considered. **Other schools with the greatest overlap in applicants:** Florida Atlantic University; Florida State University; University of Central Florida; University of Florida; University of South Florida. **Admissions statistics for the fall 2009 entering class:** Total applicants: 10,159. Total accepted: 6,459. Freshmen enrolled: 2,227; 3% were from out of state. Overall acceptance rate: 64%. **Credentials of fall 2009 freshmen:** 22% ranked in the top 10 percent of their high school class; 53% were in the top 25 percent; 86% were in the top half. (Proportion submitting class standing: 59%.) **Average high school grade point average:** 3.5. **First-year students who submitted SAT scores:** 51%. Scores (25/75 percentile): Critical Reading: 510-610, Math: 510-600, Combined: 1020-1210. **First-year students submitting ACT scores:** 49%. Scores (25/75 percentile): English: 19-24, Math: 20-24, Composite: 21-24.

ACADEMICS

Year founded: 1965. **Academic calendar:** Semester. **Degrees offered:** associate, transfer-associate, terminal-associate, bachelor's, post-bachelor's certificate, master's, post-master's certificate. **Most popular majors:** 23% business, management, marketing, and related support services, 14% health professions and related clinical sciences, 11% education, 9% communication, journalism, and related programs, 7% psychology. **Major fields of study:** biological and biomedical sciences; business, management, marketing, and related support services; communication, journalism, and related programs; computer and information sciences and support services; education; engineering; engineering technologies/technicians; English language and literature/letters; foreign languages, literatures, and linguistics; health professions and related clinical sciences; history; liberal arts and sciences studies, and humanities; mathematics and statistics; multi/interdisciplinary studies; philosophy and religious studies; physical sciences; psychology; security and protective services; social sciences; visual and performing arts. **Areas of required coursework:** arts/fine arts, humanities, computer literacy, mathematics, English (including composition), philosophy, foreign languages, sciences (biological or physical), history, social science, other. **Pre-professional programs:** pre-law, pre-dentistry, pre-medicine. **Special academic programs (% participation):** accelerated program (35%), cooperative (work-study plan) program (1%), distance learning (10%), double major (0%), dual enrollment (.002%), English as a Second Language (ESL), honors program (2.7%), independent study (11%), internships (41%), student-designed major (.07%), study abroad (2%), teacher certificate program, weekend college (.5%). **Teacher certification offered in:** special education, elementary, middle/junior high, secondary. **Cooperative education programs:** business, computer science, engineering, health professions, natural science, social/behavioral science. **Reserve Officers Training Corps (ROTC):** Army ROTC: Offered on campus; Navy ROTC: Offered at cooperating institution (Jacksonville University). **Faculty and instruction (2009-2010):** Total instructional faculty: 495 full-time, 246 part-time (50% men; 50% women; 13% minorities). Full-time faculty with Ph.D. or other terminal degree: 79%. Student/faculty ratio: 23/1. Classes of fewer than 20 students: 20%; of 20 to 49 students: 68%; of 50 or more students: 13%. **Advanced Placement and International Baccalaureate credit:** AP tests may be used for: Credit and/or placement. Scores accepted: 3, 4, 5. International Baccalaureate exams may be used for: Credit and/or placement. **Freshmen returning for sophomore year:** 79%. **Graduation rates:** Four-year: 23%; five-year: 43%; six-year: 46%.

COSTS AND FINANCIAL AID

Financial aid office: (904) 620-2604. **Expenses (2009-2010):** Tuition and fees 2009-2010: $4,193 in state, $17,582 out of state; room/board: $9,982. Estimated books and supplies: $900; transportation: $3,123; personal expenses: $1,030. **Financial aid:** Priority filing date for institution's financial aid form: April 1. In 2009-2010, 60% of undergraduates applied for financial aid. Of those, 47% were determined to have financial need; 9% had their need fully met. Average financial aid package (proportion receiving): $1,822 (45%). Average amount of gift aid, such as scholarships or grants (proportion receiving): $1,500 (29%). Average amount of self-help aid, such as work study or loans (proportion receiving): $1,867 (26%). Average need-based loan (excluding PLUS or other private loans): $1,793. Among students who received need-based aid, the average percentage of need met: 90%. Among students who received aid based on merit, the average award (and the proportion receiving): $1,210 (13%). The average athletic scholarship (and the proportion receiving): $2,327 (2%). Average amount of debt of borrowers graduating in 2009: $15,619. Proportion who borrowed: 41%.

CAMPUS LIFE AND EXTRACURRICULAR ACTIVITIES

Campus housing available: coed dorms, apartment for single students, special housing for disabled students, other housing options. Students who live in college-owned, operated, or affiliated housing: 27%. **Student employment:** During the 2009-2010 academic year, 4% of undergraduates worked on campus. Average per-year earnings: $7,693. **Clubs and organizations:** Number of student organizations: 140. Activities include: campus ministries, choral groups, concert band, dance, drama/theater, jazz band, literary magazine, music ensembles, pep band, radio station, student government, student newspaper, television station. Number of fraternities: 9; sororities: 8. Average proportion of students who stay on campus on weekends: 60%. **Sports program (2009-2010):** Member of NCAA I. *Men's intercollegiate varsity sports:* baseball, basketball, cross country, golf, soccer, tennis, track and field (outdoor). *Women's intercollegiate varsity sports:* basketball, cross country, soccer, softball, tennis, track and field (outdoor), volleyball.

SERVICES AND FACILITIES

Basic services: nonremedial tutoring, women's center, day care, health service, health insurance. **Remedial assistance:** reading, math, writing, study skills, other. **Counseling services:** minority student, career, personal, academic, psychological, birth control, religious. **For learning-disabled students:** School does not offer a structured program with separate admission and additional fees. Total undergraduates in learning-disabled program or receiving services: 454. Services include: reading machines, tape recorders, untimed tests, note-taking services, oral tests, learning center, readers, extended time for tests, tutors, priority registration, priority seating, texts on tape, other testing accommodations, other. **Library:** Number of titles: 844,402; number of current serial subscriptions: 3,979. **Information technology resources:** Students are not required to lease or own a computer. Number of campus computers available to all students: 904. School has a wireless network. Approximate number of users that can be accommodated: 1,500. Proportion of college-owned housing units wired for high-speed internet access: 100%. **Campus safety:** Security services offered: 24-hour foot-and-vehicle patrols, late-night transport/escort service, 24-hour emergency telephones, lighted pathways/sidewalks, controlled dormitory access (key, security card, etc).

TRANSFER AND INTERNATIONAL STUDENTS

Transfer students: May apply for admission for the following academic terms: Fall, Spring, Summer. Applicants need a minimum number of credits to apply. For fall 2009: Transfer applications received: 3,576. Transfer applicants offered admission: 2,191. Transfer applicants enrolled: 1,476. **International students:** Number of foreign undergraduates: 83 (1% of student body). Number of countries represented: 71. Minimum TOEFL score required: 500 (paper); 61 (computer). Average TOEFL score: 585 (paper).

University of South Florida

- **Address:** 4202 E. Fowler Avenue, Tampa, FL 33620-9951
- **Website:** http://www.usf.edu
- **Public**
- **Enrollment:** 22,706 full-time; 7,830 part-time

KEY STATS

✔ **U.S News College Ranking:** 183, National Universities
✔ **SAT Score (25th/75th percentile):** 1050-1260
✔ **Tuition:** 2009-2010: $4,577 in state, $15,386 out of state

Selectivity: More selective	Room/board: $8,750
Acceptance rate: 48%	Average debt: $20,266
Student/faculty ratio: 27/1	Proportion who borrowed: 52%

UNDERGRADUATE STUDENT BODY STATS

2009-2010 enrollment: 22,706 full-time; 7,830 part-time. Men: 44%; women: 56%. **Ethnic makeup:** African American: 13%; Asian American: 7%; Hispanic: 15%; White: 64%; International: 1%.

ADMISSIONS FACTS AND FIGURES

Phone: (813) 974-3350. **Email:** admission@admin.usf.edu. **Website:** http://www.usf.edu. **Application deadlines for fall 2011:** Regular decision: March 1; decision sent by April 15. Early decision: Not offered. Early action: Not offered. Admission cannot be deferred. **Application fee:** $30. **To apply online, go to:** http://www.usf.edu/Prospective-Students/. **Admissions requirements/recommendations:** High school units required (recommended): English: 4 (4); Mathematics: 3 (4); Science: 3 (4); Foreign language: 2 (4); Social studies: 3 (3); History: 0 (0); Academic electives: 3 (3); Total units: 18 (21). Tests: The college uses SAT or ACT scores in admissions decisions. Either SAT or ACT required. For admission to the fall 2011 entering class, the school will accept: ACT with writing required. Campus visit: Recommended. Admissions interview: Neither required nor recommended. Off-campus interview: Not available. **Factors that count in admissions decisions:** *Academic:* Secondary school record: Very Important. Class rank: Considered. Letters of recommendation: Considered. Standardized test scores: Important. Essay: Considered. *Nonacademic:* Interview: Not Considered. Extracurricular activities: Considered. Talent/ability: Considered. Character/personal qualities: Considered. Alumni/ae relationship: Not Considered. Geographical residence: Considered. State residency: Considered. Religious affiliation/commitment: Not Considered. Minority status: Not Considered. Volunteer work: Considered. Work experience: Considered. **Other schools with the greatest overlap in applicants:** Florida State University; University of Central Florida; University of Florida. **Admissions statistics for the fall 2009 entering class:** Total applicants: 24,932. Total accepted: 11,855. Freshmen enrolled: 3,857; 5% were from out of state. Overall acceptance rate: 48%. **Credentials of fall 2009 freshmen:** 35% ranked in the top 10 percent of their high school class; 67% were in the top 25 percent; 83% were in the top half. (Proportion submitting class standing: 100%.) **Average high school grade point average:** 3.7. **First-year students who submitted SAT scores:** 57%. Scores (25/75 percentile): Critical Reading: 520-620, Math: 530-640, Combined: 1050-1260. **First-year students submitting ACT scores:** 43%. Scores (25/75 percentile): English: N/A, Math: N/A, Composite: 22-28.

ACADEMICS

Year founded: 1956. **Academic calendar:** Semester. **Degrees offered:** associate, bachelor's, post-bachelor's certificate, master's, doctorate. **Most popular majors:** 8% psychology, 6% biomedical sciences, 6% criminology, 6% elementary education and teaching, 6% finance. **Major fields of study:** area, ethnic, cultural, and gender studies; biological and biomedical sciences; business, management, marketing, and related support services; communication, journalism, and related programs; computer and information sciences and support services; education; engineering; English language and literature/letters; foreign languages, literatures, and linguistics; health professions and related clinical sciences; history; liberal arts and sciences studies, and humanities; mathematics and statistics; multi/interdisciplinary studies; natural resources and conservation; philosophy and religious studies; physical sciences; psychology; public administration and social service professions; social sciences; visual and performing arts. **Areas of required coursework:** arts/fine arts, humanities, mathematics, English (including composition), sciences (biological or physical), history, social science, other. **Pre-professional programs:** pre-medicine. **Special academic programs:** accelerated program, cooperative (work-study plan) program, cross-registration, distance learning, double major, dual enrollment, English as a Second Language (ESL), exchange student program (domestic), honors program, internships, study abroad, teacher certificate program, weekend college. **Teacher certification offered in:** early childhood, special education, elementary, vo-tech, middle/junior high, adult education, secondary. **Cooperative education programs:** art, business, computer science, health professions, technologies. **Reserve Officers Training Corps (ROTC):** Army ROTC: Offered on campus; Navy ROTC: Offered on campus; Air Force ROTC: Offered on campus. **Faculty and instruction (2009-2010):** Total instructional faculty: 1,098 full-time, 114 part-time (58% men; 42% women; 24% minorities). Full-time faculty with Ph.D. or other terminal degree: 82%. Student/faculty ratio: 27/1. Classes of fewer than 20 students: 24%; of 20 to 49 students: 60%; of 50 or more students: 15%. **Advanced Placement and International Baccalaureate credit:** AP tests may be used for: Credit only. Scores accepted: 3, 4, 5. International Baccalaureate exams may be used for: Placement only. **Freshmen returning for sophomore year:** 84%. **Graduation rates:** Four-year:

21%; five-year: 40%; six-year: 48%. **Graduate study:** 20% of students pursue further study immediately upon graduation.

COSTS AND FINANCIAL AID

Financial aid office: (813) 974-4700. **Expenses (2009-2010):** Tuition and fees 2009-2010: $4,577 in state, $15,386 out of state; room/board: $8,750. Estimated books and supplies: $1,500 personal expenses: $4,100. **Financial aid:** Priority filing date for institution's financial aid form: March 1. In 2009-2010, 66% of undergraduates applied for financial aid. Of those, 55% were determined to have financial need; Average financial aid package (proportion receiving): $8,470 (53%). Average amount of gift aid, such as scholarships or grants (proportion receiving): $4,999 (6%). Average amount of self-help aid, such as work study or loans (proportion receiving): $4,825 (34%). Average need-based loan (excluding PLUS or other private loans): $4,505. Among students who received need-based aid, the average percentage of need met: 48%. Among students who received aid based on merit, the average award (and the proportion receiving): $1,951 (16%). The average athletic scholarship (and the proportion receiving): $5,610 (2%). Average amount of debt of borrowers graduating in 2009: $20,266. Proportion who borrowed: 52%.

CAMPUS LIFE AND EXTRACURRICULAR ACTIVITIES

Campus housing available (% using): coed dorms (43%), women's dorms (8%), sorority housing (4%), fraternity housing (4%), apartments for married students (1%), apartment for single students (40%), special housing for disabled students. Students who live in college-owned, operated, or affiliated housing: 16%. **Student employment:** During the 2009-2010 academic year, 15% of undergraduates worked on campus. **Clubs and organizations:** Number of student organizations: 450. Activities include: campus ministries, choral groups, concert band, dance, drama/theater, international student organization, jazz band, literary magazine, marching band, music ensembles, musical theater, opera, pep band, radio station, student government, student newspaper, student film society, symphony orchestra, television station. Number of fraternities: 21; sororities: 16. Proportion of men in fraternities: 8%; of women in sororities: 6%. Average proportion of students who stay on campus on weekends: 15%. **Sports program (2009-2010):** Member of NCAA I. *Men's intercollegiate varsity sports:* baseball, basketball, cross country, football, golf, soccer, tennis, track and field (outdoor). *Women's intercollegiate varsity sports:* basketball, cross country, golf, soccer, softball, tennis, track and field (outdoor), volleyball.

SERVICES AND FACILITIES

Basic services: nonremedial tutoring, placement service, day care, health service, health insurance. **Remedial assistance:** reading, math, writing, study skills. **Counseling services:** minority student, career, military, personal, veteran student, academic, older student, psychological. **For learning-disabled students:** School does not offer a structured program with separate admission and additional fees. Services include: reading machines, tape recorders, note-taking services, oral tests, readers, extended time for tests, priority registration, other. **Library:** Number of titles: 1,777,504; number of current serial subscriptions: 79,412. **Information technology resources:** Students are not required to lease or own a computer. Number of campus computers available to all students: 550. School has a wireless network. Approximate number of users that can be accommodated: 1,500. Proportion of college-owned housing units wired for high-speed internet access: 100%. **Campus safety:** Security services offered: 24-hour foot-and-vehicle patrols, late-night transport/escort service, 24-hour emergency telephones, lighted pathways/sidewalks, student patrols, controlled dormitory access (key, security card, etc).

TRANSFER AND INTERNATIONAL STUDENTS

Transfer students: May apply for admission for the following academic terms: Fall, Spring, Summer. Applicants need a minimum number of credits to apply. For fall 2009: Transfer applications received: 8,352. Transfer applicants offered admission: 5,677. Transfer applicants enrolled: 3,696. **International students:** Number of foreign undergraduates: 382 (1% of student body). Number of countries represented: 131. Minimum TOEFL score required: 550 (paper); 213 (computer).

University of Tampa

- **Address:** 401 W. Kennedy Boulevard, Tampa, FL 33606-1490
- **Website:** http://www.ut.edu
- **Private**
- **Enrollment:** 5,196 full-time; 363 part-time

KEY STATS

✔ **U.S News College Ranking:** 26, Regional Universities (South)
✔ **SAT Score (25th/75th percentile):** 970-1150
✔ **Tuition:** 2010-2011: $23,218

Selectivity: Selective	**Room/board:** $8,590
Acceptance rate: 62%	**Average debt:** $28,129
Student/faculty ratio: 17/1	**Proportion who borrowed:** 62%

UNDERGRADUATE STUDENT BODY STATS

2009-2010 enrollment: 5,196 full-time; 363 part-time. Men: 43%; women: 57%. **Ethnic makeup:** African American: 5%; Asian American: 2%; Hispanic: 10%; White: 73%; International: 9%.

ADMISSIONS FACTS AND FIGURES

Phone: (888) 646-2738. **Email:** admissions@ut.edu. **Website:** http://www.ut.edu. **Application deadlines for fall 2011:** Regular decision: Rolling. Early decision: Not offered. Early action: Send application by November 15; Decision sent by: December 15. Admission can be deferred. **Application fee:** $40. **To apply online, go to:** https://spartanweb.ut.edu/utadmapp/. **Admissions requirements/recommendations:** High school units required (recommended): English: 4; Mathematics: 3; Science: 3; Foreign language: 2; Social studies: 3; Academic electives: 3; Total units: 18. Tests: The college uses SAT or ACT scores in admissions decisions. Either SAT or ACT required. For admission to the fall 2011 entering class, the school will accept ACT with or without writing accepted. Campus visit: Recommended. Admissions interview: Recommended. Off-campus interview: May be arranged. **Factors that count in admissions decisions:** *Academic:* Secondary school record: Very Important. Class rank: Considered. Letters of recommendation: Important. Standardized test scores: Very Important. Essay: Important. *Nonacademic:* Interview: Considered. Extracurricular activities: Considered. Talent/ability: Important. Character/personal qualities: Considered. Alumni/ae relationship: Considered. Geographical residence: Not Considered. State residency: Not Considered. Religious affiliation/commitment: Not Considered. Minority status: Not Considered. Volunteer work: Considered. Work experience: Considered. **Admissions statistics for the fall 2009 entering class:** Total applicants: 9,929. Total accepted: 6,109. Freshmen enrolled: 1,419; 69% were from out of state. Overall acceptance rate: 62%. Non-early acceptance rate: 62%. **Size of waiting list:** 193 applicants; enrolled from waiting list: 7. **Credentials of fall 2009 freshmen:** 15% ranked in the top 10 percent of their high school class; 43% were in the top 25 percent; 83% were in the top half. (Proportion submitting class standing: 54%.) **Average high school grade point average:** 3.2. **First-year students who submitted SAT scores:** 83%. Scores (25/75 percentile): Critical Reading: 480-570, Math: 490-580, Combined: 970-1150. **First-year students submitting ACT scores:** 44%. Scores (25/75 percentile): English: 20-25, Math: 19-25, Composite: 21-25.

ACADEMICS

Year founded: 1931. **Academic calendar:** Semester. **Degrees offered:** certificate, associate, bachelor's, post-bachelor's certificate, master's, post-master's certificate. **Most popular majors:** 7% business administration and management, 7% communication studies/speech communication and rhetoric, 7% nursing/registered nurse training (R.N., A.S.N., B.S.N., M.S.N.), 6% marketing/marketing management, 6% psychology. **Major fields of study:** biological and biomedical sciences; business, management, marketing, and related support services; communication, journalism, and related programs; computer and information sciences and support services; education; English language and literature/letters; foreign languages, literatures, and linguistics; health professions and related clinical sciences; history; liberal arts and sciences studies, and humanities; mathematics and statistics; natural resources and conservation; physical sciences; psychology; security and protective services; social sciences; visual and performing arts. **Areas of required coursework:** arts/fine arts, humanities, computer literacy, mathematics, English (including composition), sciences (biological or physical), social science, other. **Pre-professional programs:** pre-law, pre-dentistry, pre-medicine, pre-veterinary science. **Special academic programs (% participation):** double major (4%), dual enrollment (0%), exchange student program (domestic), honors program (23%), independent study (33%), internships (30%), liberal arts/career combination, study abroad (7%), teacher certificate program (6%), other (1%). **Teacher certification offered in:** early childhood, elementary, middle/junior high, secondary. **Reserve Officers Training Corps (ROTC):** Army ROTC: Offered on campus; Navy ROTC: Offered at cooperating institution (University of South Florida); Air Force ROTC: Offered at cooperating institution (University of South Florida). **Faculty and instruction (2009-2010):** Total instructional faculty: 238 full-time, 293 part-time (49% men; 51% women; 13% minorities). Full-time faculty with Ph.D. or other terminal degree: 91%. Student/faculty ratio: 17/1. Classes of fewer than 20 students: 35%; of 20 to 49 students: 65%; of 50 or more students: 0%. **Advanced Placement and International Baccalaureate credit:** AP tests may be used for: Credit only. Scores accepted: 3, 4, 5. International Baccalaureate exams may be used for: Credit only. **Freshmen returning for sophomore year:** 74%. **Graduation rates:** Four-year: 44%; five-year: 55%; six-year: 56%. **Graduate study:** 84% of students pursue further study immediately upon graduation; 15% within one year. Fields in which graduates pursue further study: Master of Business Administration (MBA), 25%; law, 7%; medicine, 16%; engineering, 1%; education, 11%; arts and sciences, 8%; veterinary medicine, 1%.

COSTS AND FINANCIAL AID

Financial aid office: (813) 253-6219. **Expenses (2010-2011):** Tuition and fees 2010-2011: $23,218; room/board: $8,590. Estimated books and supplies: $1,086; transportation: $832; personal expenses: $1,440. **Financial aid:** Priority filing date for institution's financial aid form: February 1. In 2009-2010, 67% of undergraduates applied for financial aid. Of those, 55% were determined to have financial need; 19% had their need fully met. Average financial aid package (proportion receiving): $16,003 (55%). Average amount of gift aid, such as scholarships or grants (proportion receiving): $5,644 (39%). Average amount of self-help aid, such as work study or loans (proportion receiving): $4,502 (48%). Average need-based loan (excluding PLUS or other private loans): $4,315. Among students who received need-based aid, the average percentage of need met: 83%. Among students who received aid based on merit, the average award (and the proportion receiving): $5,443 (33%). The average athletic scholarship (and the proportion receiving): $8,854 (3%). Average amount of debt of borrowers graduating in 2009: $28,129. Proportion who borrowed: 62%.

CAMPUS LIFE AND EXTRACURRICULAR ACTIVITIES

Campus housing available (% using): coed dorms (91%), apartment for single students (5%), other housing options (4%). Students who live in college-owned, operated, or affiliated housing: 59%. **Student employment:** During the 2009-2010 academic year, 12% of undergraduates worked on campus. Average per-year earnings: $2,000. **Clubs and organizations:** Number of student organizations: 145. Activities include: campus ministries, choral groups, concert band, dance, drama/theater, international student organization, jazz band, literary magazine, model UN, music ensembles, musical theater, pep band, radio station, student government, student newspaper, student film society, symphony orchestra, television station, yearbook. Number of fraternities: 9; sororities: 10. Proportion of men in fraternities: 10%; of women in sororities: 12%. Average proportion of students who stay on campus on weekends: 75%. **Sports program (2009-2010):** Member of NCAA II. *Men's intercollegiate varsity sports:* baseball, basketball, cross country, golf, soccer, swimming. *Women's intercollegiate varsity sports:* basketball, crew (heavyweight), cross country, soccer, softball, swimming, tennis, volleyball.

SERVICES AND FACILITIES

Basic services: nonremedial tutoring, placement service, health service, health insurance. **Remedial assistance:** reading, math, writing, study skills. **Counseling services:** minority student, career, military, personal, academic, older student. **For learning-disabled students:** School does not offer a structured program with separate admission and additional fees. Services include: remedial math, remedial English, reading machines, tape recorders, note-taking services, oral tests, learning center, readers, extended time for tests, tutors, priority seating, proofreading services, texts on tape, typist/scribe, other testing accommodations. **Library:** Number of titles: 292,202; number of current serial subscriptions: 42,916. **Information technology resources:** Students are not required to lease or own a computer. Number of campus computers available to all students: 795. School has a wireless network. Approximate number of users that can be accommodated: 3,750. Proportion of college-owned housing units wired for high-speed internet access: 100%. **Campus safety:** Security services offered: 24-hour foot-and-vehicle patrols, late-night transport/escort service, 24-hour emergency tele-phones, lighted pathways/sidewalks, student patrols, controlled dormitory access (key, security card, etc).

TRANSFER AND INTERNATIONAL STUDENTS

Transfer students: May apply for admission for the following academic terms: Fall, Spring, Summer. Applicants need a minimum number of credits to apply. For fall 2009: Transfer applications received: 1,949. Transfer applicants offered admission: 1,096. Transfer applicants enrolled: 462. **International students:** Number of foreign undergraduates: 505 (9% of student body). Number of countries represented: 100. Minimum TOEFL score required: 550 (paper); 80 (computer). Average TOEFL score: 571 (paper).

University of West Florida

- **Address:** 11000 University Parkway, Pensacola, FL 32514-5750
- **Website:** http://uwf.edu
- **Public**
- **Enrollment:** 6,533 full-time; 2,592 part-time

KEY STATS

✔ **U.S News College Ranking:** second tier, National Universities
✔ **ACT Score (25th/75th percentile):** 21-25
✔ **Tuition:** 2009-2010: $4,210 in state, $17,092 out of state

Selectivity: Selective	**Room/board:** $6,900
Acceptance rate: 70%	**Average debt:** N/A
Student/faculty ratio: 22/1	**Proportion who borrowed:** N/A

UNDERGRADUATE STUDENT BODY STATS

2009-2010 enrollment: 6,533 full-time; 2,592 part-time. Men: 41%; women: 59%. **Ethnic makeup:** African American: 10%; American-Indian: 1%; Asian American: 5%; Hispanic: 6%; White: 76%; International: 1%.

ADMISSIONS FACTS AND FIGURES

Phone: (850) 474-2230. **Email:** admissions@uwf.edu. **Website:** http://uwf.edu. **Application deadlines for fall 2011:** Regular decision: June 30. Early decision: Not offered. Early action: Not offered. Admission can be deferred. **Application fee:** $30. **To apply online, go to:** http://uwf.edu/admissions/apply.cfm. **Admissions requirements/recommendations:** High school units required (recommended): English: 4; Mathematics: 3; Science: 3; Foreign language: 2; Social studies: 3; Academic electives: 4; Total units: 19. Tests: The college uses SAT or ACT scores in admissions decisions. Either SAT or ACT required. For admission to the fall 2011 entering class, the school will accept: ACT with or without writing accepted. Campus visit: Recommended. Admissions interview: Neither required nor recommended. Off-campus interview: Not available. **Factors that count in admissions decisions: *Academic:*** Secondary school record: Very Important. Class rank: Not Considered. Letters of recommendation: Considered. Standardized test scores: Very Important. Essay: Considered. ***Nonacademic:*** Interview: Not Considered. Extracurricular activities: Considered. Talent/ability: Considered. Character/personal qualities: Considered. Alumni/ae relationship: Considered. Geographical residence: Considered. State residency: Considered. Religious affiliation/commitment: Not Considered. Minority status: Not Considered. Volunteer work: Considered. Work experience: Considered. **Other schools with the greatest overlap in applicants:** Faulkner University; Florida State University; Troy State University–Dothan; Troy State University–Montgomery; University of South Alabama. **Admissions statistics for the fall 2009 entering class:** Total applicants: 4,513. Total accepted: 3,154. Freshmen enrolled: 1,110; 10% were from out of state. Overall acceptance rate: 70%. **Credentials of fall 2009 freshmen:** 18% ranked in the top 10 percent of their high school class; 43% were in the top 25 percent; 79% were in the top half. (Proportion submitting class standing: 85%.) **Average high school grade point average:** 3.5. **First-year students who submitted SAT scores:** 33%. Scores (25/75 percentile): Critical Reading: 490-590, Math: 470-570, Combined: 960-1160. **First-year students submitting ACT scores:** 80%. Scores (25/75 percentile): English: N/A, Math: N/A, Composite: 21-25.

ACADEMICS

Year founded: 1963. **Academic calendar:** Semester. **Degrees offered:** diploma, associate, bachelor's, master's, doctorate. **Most popular majors:** 10% elementary education and teaching, 8% mass communication/media studies, 7% special education and teaching, 6% psychology, 5% criminal justice/safety studies. **Major fields of study:** biological and biomedical sciences; business, management, marketing, and related support services; communication, journalism, and related programs; computer and information sciences and support services; education; engineering; engineering technologies/technicians; English language and literature/letters; health professions and related clinical sciences; history; legal professions and studies; liberal arts and sciences studies, and humanities; mathematics and statistics; multi/interdisciplinary studies; natural resources and conservation; parks, recreation, leisure, and fitness studies; philosophy and religious studies; physical sciences; psychology; public administration and social service professions; security and protective services; social sciences; visual and performing arts. **Areas of required coursework:** mathematics, English (including composition). **Pre-professional programs:** pre-law, pre-dentistry, other. **Special academic programs:** cooperative (work-study plan) program, distance learning, double major, dual enrollment, exchange student program (domestic), honors program, independent study, internships, study abroad, teacher certificate program, other. **Teacher certification offered in:** early childhood, special education, elementary, middle/junior high, secondary. **Cooperative education programs:** art, business, computer science, education, engineering, health professions, humanities, natural science, social/behavioral science, other. **Reserve Officers Training Corps (ROTC):** Army ROTC: Offered on campus; Air Force ROTC: Offered on campus. **Faculty and instruction (2009-2010):** Total instructional faculty: 312 full-time, 197 part-time (56% men; 44% women; 14% minorities). Full-time faculty with Ph.D. or other terminal degree: 81%. Student/faculty ratio: 22/1. Classes of fewer than 20 students: 31%; of 20 to 49 students: 60%; of 50 or more students: 8%. **Advanced Placement and International Baccalaureate credit:** AP tests may be used for: Credit only. International Baccalaureate exams may be used for: Credit only. **Freshmen returning for sophomore year:** 75%. **Graduation rates:** Four-year: 21%; five-year: 39%; six-year: 45%.

COSTS AND FINANCIAL AID
Financial aid office: (850) 474-3127. **Expenses (2009-2010):** Tuition and fees 2009-2010: $4,210 in state, $17,092 out of state; room/board: $6,900. Estimated books and supplies: $1,200; transportation: $900; personal expenses: $2,300. **Financial aid:** Priority filing date for institution's financial aid form: February 1.

CAMPUS LIFE AND EXTRACURRICULAR ACTIVITIES
Campus housing available: coed dorms, sorority housing, fraternity housing, special housing for disabled students, other housing options. Students who live in college-owned, operated, or affiliated housing: 12%. **Clubs and organizations:** Number of student organizations: 157. Activities include: choral groups, concert band, dance, drama/theater, jazz band, music ensembles, musical theater, radio station, student government, student newspaper, symphony orchestra, television station. Number of fraternities: 10; sororities: 7. Proportion of men in fraternities: 5%; of women in sororities: 5%. Average proportion of students who stay on campus on weekends: 15%. **Sports program (2009-2010):** Member of NCAA II. *Men's intercollegiate varsity sports:* baseball, basketball, cross country, golf, soccer, tennis. *Women's intercollegiate varsity sports:* basketball, cross country, golf, soccer, softball, tennis, volleyball.

SERVICES AND FACILITIES
Basic services: nonremedial tutoring, placement service, day care, health service, health insurance. **Counseling services:** minority student, career, military, personal, veteran student, academic, religious. **For learning-disabled students:** School does not offer a structured program with separate admission and additional fees. Services include: reading machines, tape recorders, note-taking services, oral tests, learning center, readers, extended time for tests, tutors, priority registration, priority seating, substitution of courses, texts on tape, typist/scribe, exams on tape or computer, other testing accommodations, other. **Library:** Number of titles: 1,000,558; number of current serial subscriptions: 4,619. **Information technology resources:** Students are not required to lease or own a computer. Number of campus computers available to all students: 200. School has a wireless network. Approximate number of users that can be accommodated: 2,100. Proportion of college-owned housing units wired for high-speed internet access: 100%. **Campus safety:** Security services offered: 24-hour foot-and-vehicle patrols, late-night transport/escort service, 24-hour emergency telephones, lighted pathways/sidewalks, student patrols, controlled dormitory access (key, security card, etc).

TRANSFER AND INTERNATIONAL STUDENTS
Transfer students: May apply for admission for the following academic terms: Fall, Spring, Summer. Applicants do not need a minimum number of credits to apply. For fall 2009: Transfer applications received: 2,431.

Transfer applicants offered admission: 1,850. Transfer applicants enrolled: 1,223. **International students:** Number of foreign undergraduates: 124 (1% of student body). Number of countries represented: 35. Minimum TOEFL score required: 525 (paper); 193 (computer). Average TOEFL score: 556 (paper).

Warner University

- **Address:** 13895 US 27, Lake Wales, FL 33859
- **Website:** http://www.warner.edu
- **Private; Religious affiliation:** Church of God
- **Enrollment:** 845 full-time; 119 part-time

KEY STATS
✔ **U.S News College Ranking:** 63, Regional Colleges (South)
✔ **SAT Score (25th/75th percentile):** 727-1125
✔ **Tuition:** 2009-2010: $15,320

Selectivity: Less selective	**Room/board:** $6,815
Acceptance rate: 44%	**Average debt:** N/A
Student/faculty ratio: 16/1	**Proportion who borrowed:** N/A

UNDERGRADUATE STUDENT BODY STATS
2009-2010 enrollment: 845 full-time; 119 part-time. Men: 43%; women: 57%. **Ethnic makeup:** African American: 23%; Asian American: 1%; Hispanic: 11%; White: 63%; International: 2%. **Religious preference:** Roman Catholic: 7%; Protestant: 34%; Jewish: 1%; No preference: 16%; Unknown: 24%; Church of God: 11%; Other: 7%.

ADMISSIONS FACTS AND FIGURES
Phone: (800) 309-9563. **Email:** admissions@warner.edu. **Website:** http://www.warner.edu. **Application deadlines for fall 2011:** Regular decision: Rolling. Early decision: Not offered. Early action: Not offered. Admission can be deferred. **Application fee:** $20. **To apply online, go to:** http://www.warner.edu/apply/. **Admissions requirements/recommendations:** High school units required (recommended): English: 0 (4); Mathematics: 0 (3); Science: 0 (2); Foreign language: 0 (1); Social studies: 0 (1); History: 0 (1); Academic electives: 0 (2); Total units: 0 (14). Tests: The college uses SAT or ACT scores in admissions decisions. Either SAT or ACT required. For admission to the fall 2011 entering class, the school will accept: ACT with or without writing accepted. Campus visit: Recommended. Admissions interview: Recommended. Off-campus interview: May be arranged. **Factors that count in admissions decisions:** *Academic:* Secondary school record: Considered. Class rank: Important. Letters of recommendation: Important. Standardized test scores: Important. Essay: Considered. *Nonacademic:* Interview: Considered. Extracurricular activities: Considered. Talent/ability: Considered. Character/personal qualities: Considered. Alumni/ae relationship: Considered. Geographical residence: Not Considered. State residency: Not Considered. Religious affiliation/commitment: Not Considered. Minority status: Not Considered. Volunteer work: Considered. Work experience: Not Considered. **Other schools with the greatest overlap in applicants:** Anderson University; Florida Southern College; University of Central Florida; University of South Florida; Webber International University. **Admissions statistics for the fall 2009 entering class:** Total applicants: 579. Total accepted: 254. Freshmen enrolled: 131; 6% were from out of state. Overall acceptance rate: 44%. **Size of waiting list:** 0 applicants; enrolled from waiting list: 0. **Credentials of fall 2009 freshmen:** 6% ranked in the top 10 percent of their high school class; 27% were in the top 25 percent; 62% were in the top half. (Proportion submitting class standing: 74%.) **Average high school grade point average:** 3.3. **First-year students who submitted SAT scores:** 55%. Scores (25/75 percentile): Critical Reading: 373-551, Math: 354-574, Combined: 727-1125. **First-year students submitting ACT scores:** 47%. Scores (25/75 percentile): English: N/A, Math: N/A, Composite: 16-23.

ACADEMICS
Year founded: 1968. **Academic calendar:** Semester. **Degrees offered:** certificate, associate, bachelor's, master's. **Most popular majors:** 56% business, management, marketing, and related support services, 25% education, 9% theology and religious vocations, 4% parks, recreation, leisure, and fitness studies, 3% communication, journalism, and related programs. **Major fields of study:** biological and biomedical sciences; business, management, marketing, and related support services; communication, journalism, and related programs; education; English language and literature/letters; history; parks, recreation, and fitness studies; psychology; public

administration and social service professions; social sciences; theology and religious vocations. **Areas of required coursework:** arts/fine arts, humanities, computer literacy, mathematics, English (including composition), foreign languages, sciences (biological or physical), history, social science, other. **Pre-professional programs:** pre-law, pre-theology, other. **Special academic programs (% participation):** accelerated program (70%), distance learning (60%), double major (1%), dual enrollment (1%), English as a Second Language (ESL) (1%), honors program (1%), independent study (10%), internships (20%), study abroad (1%), teacher certificate program (13%). **Teacher certification offered in:** special education, elementary, middle/junior high, secondary. **Faculty and instruction (2009-2010):** Total instructional faculty: 32 full-time, 78 part-time (51% men; 49% women; 10% minorities). Full-time faculty with Ph.D. or other terminal degree: 63%. Student/faculty ratio: 16/1. Classes of fewer than 20 students: 70%; of 20 to 49 students: 29%; of 50 or more students: 1%. **Advanced Placement and International Baccalaureate credit:** AP tests may be used for: Placement only. Scores accepted: 3, 4, 5. International Baccalaureate exams may be used for: Placement only. **Freshmen returning for sophomore year:** 72%. **Graduation rates:** Four-year: 21%; five-year: 37%; six-year: 35%. **Graduate study:** 28% of students pursue further study immediately upon graduation. Fields in which graduates pursue further study: Master of Business Administration (MBA), 45%; law, 1%; medicine, 1%; theology (or the seminary), 10%; education, 20%; arts and sciences, 23%.

COSTS AND FINANCIAL AID

Financial aid office: (863) 638-7202. **Expenses (2009-2010):** Tuition and fees 2009-2010: $15,320; room/board: $6,815. Estimated books and supplies: $1,000. **Financial aid:** Priority filing date for institution's financial aid form: May 1; deadline: January 15.

CAMPUS LIFE AND EXTRACURRICULAR ACTIVITIES

Campus housing available (% using): women's dorms (51%), men's dorms (49%). Students who live in college-owned, operated, or affiliated housing: 26%. **Student employment:** During the 2009-2010 academic year, 29% of undergraduates worked on campus. Average per-year earnings: $2,400. **Clubs and organizations:** Number of student organizations: 6. Activities include: campus ministries, choral groups, drama/theater, music ensembles, pep band, student government, student newspaper. Number of fraternities: 2; sororities: 2. Average proportion of students who stay on campus on weekends: 65%. **Sports program (2009-2010):** Member of NAIA. *Men's intercollegiate varsity sports:* baseball, basketball, cross country, golf, soccer, tennis, track and field (indoor), track and field (outdoor), volleyball. *Women's intercollegiate varsity sports:* cross country, golf, soccer, softball, tennis, track and field (indoor), track and field (outdoor), volleyball.

SERVICES AND FACILITIES

Basic services: nonremedial tutoring. **Remedial assistance:** reading, math, writing, study skills. **Counseling services:** career, academic, religious. **For learning-disabled students:** School does not offer a structured program with separate admission and additional fees. Services include: remedial math, remedial English, remedial reading, oral tests, learning center, readers, extended time for tests, tutors. **Library:** Number of titles: 89,548; number of current serial subscriptions: 204. **Information technology resources:** Students are not required to lease or own a computer. Number of campus computers available to all students: 80. School has a wireless network. Approximate number of users that can be accommodated: 1,000. Proportion of college-owned housing units wired for high-speed internet access: 0%. **Campus safety:** Security services offered: 24-hour foot-and-vehicle patrols, late-night transport/escort service, lighted pathways/sidewalks, controlled dormitory access (key, security card, etc).

TRANSFER AND INTERNATIONAL STUDENTS

Transfer students: May apply for admission for the following academic terms: Fall, Spring, Summer. Applicants need a minimum number of credits to apply. **International students:** Number of foreign undergraduates: 17 (2% of student body). Number of countries represented: 10. Minimum TOEFL score required: 500 (paper); 173 (computer).

Webber International University

- ■ **Address:** PO Box 96, Babson Park, FL 33827
- ■ **Website:** http://www.webber.edu
- ■ **Private**
- ■ **Enrollment:** 553 full-time; 52 part-time

KEY STATS

✔ **U.S News College Ranking:** Unranked Specialty School–Business
✔ **ACT Score (25th/75th percentile):** 18-21
✔ **Tuition:** 2010-2011: $18,742

Selectivity: Selective	**Room/board:** $7,322
Acceptance rate: 74%	**Average debt:** $25,963
Student/faculty ratio: 22/1	**Proportion who borrowed:** 54%

UNDERGRADUATE STUDENT BODY STATS

2009-2010 enrollment: 553 full-time; 52 part-time. Men: 65%; women: 35%. **Ethnic makeup:** African American: 23%; Asian American: 1%; Hispanic: 9%; White: 53%; International: 15%.

ADMISSIONS FACTS AND FIGURES

Phone: (800) 741-1844. **Email:** admissions@webber.edu. **Website:** http://www.webber.edu. **Application deadlines for fall 2011:** Regular decision: August 1. Early decision: Not offered. Early action: Send application by: N/A; Decision sent by: N/A. Admission can be deferred. **Application fee:** $35. **To apply online, go to:** http://www.webber.edu/ADMISSIONS/apply.aspx. **Admissions requirements/recommendations:** High school units required (recommended): English: 4; Mathematics: 2 (3); Science: 1 (3); Foreign language: (1); Social studies: 2; History: (2); Academic electives: (4); Total units: (15). Tests: The college uses SAT or ACT scores in admissions decisions. Either SAT or ACT required. For admission to the fall 2011 entering class, the school will accept: ACT with writing recommended. Campus visit: Required. Admissions interview: Required. Off-campus interview: Not available. **Factors that count in admissions decisions:** *Academic:* Secondary school record: Important. Class rank: Considered. Letters of recommendation: Considered. Standardized test scores: Very Important. Essay: Considered. *Nonacademic:* Interview: Considered. Extracurricular activities: Not Considered. Talent/ability: Not Considered. Character/personal qualities: Considered. Alumni/ae relationship: Considered. Geographical residence: Not Considered. State residency: Not Considered. Religious affiliation/commitment: Not Considered. Minority status: Not Considered. Volunteer work: Not Considered. Work experience: Not Considered. **Other schools with the greatest overlap in applicants:** Flagler College; Florida Southern College; Jacksonville University; Lynn University. **Admissions statistics for the fall 2009 entering class:** Total applicants: 411. Total accepted: 305. Freshmen enrolled: 173; 5% were from out of state. Overall acceptance rate: 74%. Non-early acceptance rate: 74%. **Credentials of fall 2009 freshmen:** 8% ranked in the top 10 percent of their high school class; 27% were in the top 25 percent; 57% were in the top half. (Proportion submitting class standing: 65%.) **Average high school grade point average:** 3.1. **First-year students who submitted SAT scores:** 51%. Scores (25/75 percentile): Critical Reading: 420-510, Math: 430-530, Combined: 850-1040. **First-year students submitting ACT scores:** 63%. Scores (25/75 percentile): English: 16-21, Math: 17-23, Composite: 18-21.

ACADEMICS

Year founded: 1927. **Academic calendar:** Semester. **Degrees offered:** associate, bachelor's, master's. **Most popular majors:** 74% business, management, marketing, and related support services, 21% parks, recreation, leisure, and fitness studies, 4% computer and information sciences and support services, 1% legal professions and studies. **Major fields of study:** business, management, marketing, and related support services; computer and information sciences and support services; legal professions and studies; parks, recreation, leisure, and fitness studies. **Areas of required coursework:** humanities, computer literacy, mathematics, English (including composition), sciences (biological or physical), social science, other. **Pre-professional programs:** pre-law. **Special academic programs (% participation):** internships (75%). **Faculty and instruction (2009-2010):** Total instructional faculty: 19 full-time, 22 part-time (51% men; 49% women; 2% minorities). Full-time faculty with Ph.D. or other terminal degree: 74%. Student/faculty ratio: 22/1. Classes of fewer than 20 students: 49%; of 20 to 49 students: 50%; of 50 or more students: 1%. **Advanced Placement and International Baccalaureate credit:** International Baccalaureate exams may be used for: Credit only. **Freshmen returning for sophomore year:** 50%. **Graduation rates:**

Four-year: 24%; five-year: 31%; six-year: 39%. **Graduate study:** 30% of students pursue further study immediately upon graduation; 30% within one year. Fields in which graduates pursue further study: Master of Business Administration (MBA), 70%; law, 5%; education, 10%.

COSTS AND FINANCIAL AID

Financial aid office: (863) 638-2930. **Expenses (2010-2011):** Tuition and fees 2010-2011: $18,742; room/board: $7,322. Estimated books and supplies: $900; transportation: $1,178; personal expenses: $3,263. **Financial aid:** Priority filing date for institution's financial aid form: May 1; deadline: August 1. In 2009-2010, 79% of undergraduates applied for financial aid. Of those, 63% were determined to have financial need; 11% had their need fully met. Average financial aid package (proportion receiving): $17,601 (63%). Average amount of gift aid, such as scholarships or grants (proportion receiving): $13,616 (63%). Average amount of self-help aid, such as work study or loans (proportion receiving): $4,405 (61%). Average need-based loan (excluding PLUS or other private loans): $5,001. Among students who received need-based aid, the average percentage of need met: 50%. Among students who received aid based on merit, the average award (and the proportion receiving): $7,491 (27%). The average athletic scholarship (and the proportion receiving): $6,589 (24%). Average amount of debt of borrowers graduating in 2009: $25,963. Proportion who borrowed: 54%.

CAMPUS LIFE AND EXTRACURRICULAR ACTIVITIES

Campus housing available (% using): women's dorms (31%), men's dorms (69%). Students who live in college-owned, operated, or affiliated housing: 53%. **Student employment:** During the 2009-2010 academic year, 16% of undergraduates worked on campus. Average per-year earnings: $3,000. **Clubs and organizations:** Number of student organizations: 11. Activities include: international student organization, marching band, student govern-

ment, student newspaper. Number of fraternities: 0; sororities: 0. Average proportion of students who stay on campus on weekends: 65%. **Sports program (2009-2010):** Member of NAIA. *Men's intercollegiate varsity sports:* baseball, basketball, cross country, football, golf, soccer, track and field (outdoor). *Women's intercollegiate varsity sports:* cross country, golf, soccer, softball, track and field (outdoor), volleyball.

SERVICES AND FACILITIES

Basic services: nonremedial tutoring, placement service, health service, health insurance. **Remedial assistance:** reading, math, writing, study skills, other. **Counseling services:** career, personal, academic. **For learning-disabled students:** School does not offer a structured program with separate admission and additional fees. **Library:** Number of titles: 15,000; number of current serial subscriptions: 55. **Information technology resources:** Students are not required to lease or own a computer. Number of campus computers available to all students: 100. School does not have a wireless network. Proportion of college-owned housing units wired for high-speed internet access: 100%. **Campus safety:** Security services offered: 24-hour foot-and-vehicle patrols, lighted pathways/sidewalks, controlled dormitory access (key, security card, etc.).

TRANSFER AND INTERNATIONAL STUDENTS

Transfer students: May apply for admission for the following academic terms: Fall, Spring, Summer. Applicants need a minimum number of credits to apply. For fall 2009: Transfer applications received: 176. Transfer applicants offered admission: 105. Transfer applicants enrolled: 75. **International students:** Number of foreign undergraduates: 79 (15% of student body). Number of countries represented: 37. Minimum TOEFL score required: 500 (paper); 173 (computer). Average TOEFL score: 428 (paper).

Georgia

Agnes Scott College

- **Address:** 141 E. College Avenue, Decatur, GA 30030
- **Website:** http://www.agnesscott.edu
- **Private; Religious affiliation:** Presbyterian Church (USA)
- **Enrollment:** 810 full-time; 32 part-time

KEY STATS
✔ **U.S News College Ranking:** 67, National Liberal Arts Colleges
✔ **SAT Score (25th/75th percentile):** 1010-1270
✔ **Tuition:** 2010-2011: $31,283

Selectivity: More selective	**Room/board:** $9,850
Acceptance rate: 46%	**Average debt:** $23,176
Student/faculty ratio: 9/1	**Proportion who borrowed:** 69%

UNDERGRADUATE STUDENT BODY STATS
2009-2010 enrollment: 810 full-time; 32 part-time. Men: 1%; women: 99%. **Ethnic makeup:** African American: 25%; Asian American: 4%; Hispanic: 5%; White: 59%; International: 7%. **Religious preference:** Roman Catholic: 6%; Protestant: 31%; Jewish: 2%; Muslim: 3%; Hindu: 1%; No preference: 4%; Unknown: 44%; Presbyterian Church (USA): 4%; Other: 3%.

ADMISSIONS FACTS AND FIGURES
Phone: (800) 868-8602. **Email:** admission@agnesscott.edu. **Website:** http://www.agnesscott.edu. **Application deadlines for fall 2011:** Regular decision: May 1. Early decision: Not offered. Early action: Send application by: November 15; Decision sent by: December 15. Admission can be deferred. **Application fee:** $35. **To apply online, go to:** http://www.agnesscott.edu/admission/undergraduate/apply. **Admissions requirements/recommendations:** High school units required (recommended): English: (4); Mathematics: (3); Science: (2); Foreign language: (2); Social studies: (2); History: (2); Total units: (16). Tests: The college uses SAT or ACT scores in admissions decisions. Neither SAT nor ACT required. For admission to the fall 2011 entering class, the school will accept: ACT with writing required. Campus visit: Recommended. Admissions interview: Recommended. Off-campus interview: May be arranged. **Factors that count in admissions decisions:** *Academic:* Secondary school record: Very Important. Class rank: Very Important. Letters of recommendation: Very Important. Standardized test scores: Considered. Essay: Very Important. *Nonacademic:* Interview: Considered. Extracurricular activities: Important. Talent/ability: Very Important. Character/personal qualities: Very Important. Alumni/ae relationship: Considered. Geographical residence: Considered. State residency: Considered. Religious affiliation/commitment: Not Considered. Minority status: Considered. Volunteer work: Important. Work experience: Important. **Other schools with the greatest overlap in applicants:** Emory University; Georgia Institute of Technology; Georgia State University; Spelman College; University of Georgia. **Admissions statistics for the fall 2009 entering class:** Total applicants: 1,984. Total accepted: 918. Freshmen enrolled: 237; 41% were from out of state. Accepted through early-decision or early-action plans: 22%. Overall acceptance rate: 46%. Non-early acceptance rate: 44%. **Size of waiting list:** 44 applicants; enrolled from waiting list: 4. **Credentials of fall 2009 freshmen:** 33% ranked in the top 10 percent of their high school class; 66% were in the top 25 percent; 93% were in the top half. (Proportion submitting class standing: 56%.) **Average high school grade point average:** 3.6. **First-year students who submitted SAT scores:** 83%. Scores (25/75 percentile): Critical Reading: 520-650, Math: 490-620, Combined: 1010-1270. **First-year students submitting ACT scores:** 45%. Scores (25/75 percentile): English: N/A, Math: N/A, Composite: 22-28.

ACADEMICS
Year founded: 1889. **Academic calendar:** Semester. **Degrees offered:** bachelor's, post-bachelor's certificate. **Most popular majors:** 22% social sciences, 13% psychology, 11% history, 10% English language and literature/letters, 8% biological and biomedical sciences. **Major fields of study:** area, ethnic, cultural, and gender studies; biological and biomedical sciences; English language and literature/letters; foreign languages, literatures, and linguistics; history; mathematics and statistics; multi/interdisciplinary studies; philosophy and religious studies; physical sciences; psychology; social sciences; visual and performing arts. **Areas of required coursework:** arts/fine arts, humanities, mathematics, English (including composition), philosophy, foreign languages, sciences (biological or physical), history, social science, other. **Pre-professional programs:** pre-law, pre-dentistry, pre-medicine, pre-veterinary science, other. **Special academic programs (% participation):** accelerated program (1.6%), cross-registration (14.1%), double major (17.8%), dual enrollment (2.7%), exchange student program (domestic) (0%), independent study (13.5%), internships (78%), student-designed major (1.1%), study abroad (52%), teacher certificate program (.5%). **Reserve Officers Training Corps (ROTC):** Army ROTC: Offered at cooperating institution (Georgia Institute of Technology); Air Force ROTC: Offered at cooperating institution (Georgia Institute of Technology). **Faculty and instruction (2009-2010):** Total instructional faculty: 82 full-time, 26 part-time (39% men; 61% women; 18% minorities). Full-time faculty with Ph.D. or other terminal degree: 98%. Student/faculty ratio: 9/1. Classes of fewer than 20 students: 75%; of 20 to 49 students: 25%; of 50 or more students: 0%. **Advanced Placement and International Baccalaureate credit:** AP tests may be used for: Credit and/or placement. Scores accepted: 4, 5. International Baccalaureate exams may be used for: Credit and/or placement. **Freshmen returning for sophomore year:** 82%. **Graduation rates:** Four-year: 60%; five-year: 65%; six-year: 67%. **Graduate study:** 33% of students pursue further study immediately upon graduation; 45% within five years. Fields in which graduates pursue further study: Master of Business Administration (MBA), 4%; law, 12%; medicine, 5%; dentistry, 1%; engineering, 1%; theology (or the seminary), 4%; education, 12%; arts and sciences, 60%; veterinary medicine, 1%.

COSTS AND FINANCIAL AID
Financial aid office: (404) 471-6395. **Expenses (2010-2011):** Tuition and fees 2010-2011: $31,283; room/board: $9,850. Estimated books and supplies: $1,000 personal expenses: $1,000. **Financial aid:** Priority filing date for institution's financial aid form: February 15; deadline: May 1. In 2009-2010, 80% of undergraduates applied for financial aid. Of those, 74% were determined to have financial need; 34% had their need fully met. Average financial aid package (proportion receiving): $28,845 (74%). Average amount of gift aid, such as scholarships or grants (proportion receiving): $23,525 (73%). Average amount of self-help aid, such as work study or loans (proportion receiving): $5,285 (65%). Average need-based loan (excluding PLUS or other private loans): $3,767. Among students who received need-based aid, the average percentage of need met: 91%. Among students who received aid based on merit, the average award (and the proportion receiving): $15,195 (24%). Average amount of debt of borrowers graduating in 2009: $23,176. Proportion who borrowed: 69%.

CAMPUS LIFE AND EXTRACURRICULAR ACTIVITIES
Campus housing available (% using): women's dorms (79%), apartment for single students (18%). Students who live in college-owned, operated, or affiliated housing: 86%. **Student employment:** During the 2009-2010 academic year, 62% of undergraduates worked on campus. Average per-year earnings: $2,000. **Clubs and organizations:** Number of student organizations: 99. Activities include: campus ministries, choral groups, dance, drama/theater, international student organization, jazz band, literary magazine, marching band, model UN, music ensembles, musical theater, pep band, student government, student newspaper, symphony orchestra, television station, yearbook. Number of fraternities: 0; sororities: 0. Average proportion of students who stay on campus on weekends: 70%. **Sports program (2009-2010):** Member of NCAA III. *Women's intercollegiate varsity sports:* basketball, lacrosse, soccer, softball, tennis, volleyball.

SERVICES AND FACILITIES
Basic services: nonremedial tutoring, placement service, health service, health insurance. **Counseling services:** minority student, career, personal, academic, older student, psychological, birth control, religious. **For learning-disabled students:** School does not offer a structured program with separate admission and additional fees. Total undergraduates in learning-disabled program or receiving services: 16. Services include: reading machines, tape

recorders, note-taking services, special bookstore section, oral tests, readers, extended time for tests, tutors, early syllabus, priority registration, priority seating, substitution of courses, texts on tape, typist/scribe, exams on tape or computer, other testing accommodations, other. **Library:** Number of titles: 231,399; number of current serial subscriptions: 26,956. **Information technology resources:** Students are not required to lease or own a computer. Number of campus computers available to all students: 429. School has a wireless network. Approximate number of users that can be accommodated: 500. Proportion of college-owned housing units wired for high-speed internet access: 100%. **Campus safety:** Security services offered: 24-hour foot-and-vehicle patrols, late-night transport/escort service, 24-hour emergency telephones, lighted pathways/sidewalks, controlled dormitory access (key, security card, etc).

TRANSFER AND INTERNATIONAL STUDENTS

Transfer students: May apply for admission for the following academic terms: Fall, Spring. Applicants do not need a minimum number of credits to apply. For fall 2009: Transfer applications received: 77. Transfer applicants offered admission: 35. Transfer applicants enrolled: 18. **International students:** Number of foreign undergraduates: 52 (7% of student body). Number of countries represented: 27. Minimum TOEFL score required: 577 (paper); 233 (computer). Average TOEFL score: 622 (paper).

Albany State University

- **Address:** 504 College Drive, Albany, GA 31705
- **Website:** http://www.asurams.edu/
- **Public**
- **Enrollment:** 3,149 full-time; 604 part-time

KEY STATS

✔ **U.S News College Ranking:** 86, Regional Universities (South)
✔ **SAT Score (25th/75th percentile):** 830-960
✔ **Tuition:** 2009-2010: $962 in state, $13,352 out of state

Selectivity: Less selective	**Room/board:** $5,240
Acceptance rate: 42%	**Average debt:** N/A
Student/faculty ratio: 21/1	**Proportion who borrowed:** N/A

UNDERGRADUATE STUDENT BODY STATS

2009-2010 enrollment: 3,149 full-time; 604 part-time. Men: 33%; women: 67%. **Ethnic makeup:** African American: 92%; White: 7%; International: 1%.

ADMISSIONS FACTS AND FIGURES

Phone: (229) 430-4646. **Email:** admissions@asurams.edu. **Website:** http://www.asurams.edu/. **Application deadlines for fall 2011:** Regular decision: July 1. Early decision: Not offered. Early action: Send application by: N/A; Decision sent by: N/A. Admission can be deferred. **Application fee:** $20. **To apply online, go to:** http://www.gacollege411.org/Applications/USG_Common_App_Short/apply.html?application_id=2871. **Admissions requirements/recommendations:** High school units required (recommended): English: 4; Mathematics: 4; Science: 3; Foreign language: 2; Social studies: 3; Total units: 16. Tests: The college uses SAT or ACT scores in admissions decisions. Either SAT or ACT required. For admission to the fall 2011 entering class, the school will accept: ACT with or without writing accepted. Campus visit: Recommended. Admissions interview: Neither required nor recommended. Off-campus interview: Not available. **Factors that count in admissions decisions:** *Academic:* Secondary school record: Not Considered. Class rank: Not Considered. Letters of recommendation: Not Considered. Standardized test scores: Very Important. Essay: Not Considered. *Nonacademic:* Interview: Considered. Extracurricular activities: Not Considered. Talent/ability: Not Considered. Character/personal qualities: Not Considered. Alumni/ae relationship: Not Considered. Geographical residence: Not Considered. State residency: Not Considered. Religious affiliation/commitment: Not Considered. Minority status: Not Considered. Volunteer work: Not Considered. Work experience: Not Considered. **Admissions statistics for the fall 2009 entering class:** Total applicants: 4,773. Total accepted: 1,993. Freshmen enrolled: 732; 4% were from out of state. Overall acceptance rate: 42%. Non-early acceptance rate: 42%. **Average high school grade point average:** 2.8. **First-year students who submitted SAT scores:** 75%. Scores (25/75 percentile): Critical Reading: 420-480, Math: 410-480, Combined: 830-960. **First-year students submitting ACT scores:** 51%. Scores (25/75 percentile): English: N/A, Math: N/A, Composite: 17-19.

ACADEMICS

Year founded: 1903. **Academic calendar:** Semester. **Degrees offered:** bachelor's, master's, post-master's certificate. **Major fields of study:** biological and biomedical sciences; business, management, marketing, and related support services; communication, journalism, and related programs; computer and information sciences and support services; education; English language and literature/letters; foreign languages, literatures, and linguistics; health professions and related clinical sciences; history; mathematics and statistics; parks, recreation, leisure, and fitness studies; physical sciences; psychology; public administration and social service professions; security and protective services; social sciences; visual and performing arts. **Areas of required coursework:** arts/fine arts, humanities, computer literacy, mathematics, English (including composition), sciences (biological or physical), social science, other. **Pre-professional programs:** pre-law, pre-dentistry, pre-medicine, pre-pharmacy. **Teacher certification offered in:** early childhood, special education, middle/junior high, secondary. **Cooperative education programs:** art, business, computer science, education, engineering, health professions, humanities, social/behavioral science, technologies. **Reserve Officers Training Corps (ROTC):** Army ROTC: Offered on campus. **Faculty and instruction (2009-2010):** Total instructional faculty: 152 full-time, 132 part-time (51% men; 49% women). Student/faculty ratio: 21/1. Classes of fewer than 20 students: 44%; of 20 to 49 students: 53%; of 50 or more students: 3%. **Freshmen returning for sophomore year:** 77%. **Graduation rates:** Six-year: 44%.

COSTS AND FINANCIAL AID

Financial aid office: (229) 430-4650. **Expenses (2009-2010):** Tuition and fees 2009-2010: $962 in state, $13,352 out of state; room/board: $5,240. Estimated books and supplies: $1,700; transportation: $1,652; personal expenses: $3,736. **Financial aid:** Priority filing date for institution's financial aid form: April 15; deadline: April 30.

CAMPUS LIFE AND EXTRACURRICULAR ACTIVITIES

Campus housing available: coed dorms, women's dorms, men's dorms, apartment for single students, special housing for disabled students. Activities include: campus ministries, choral groups, concert band, dance, drama/theater, international student organization, jazz band, marching band, model UN, music ensembles, opera, pep band, radio station, student government, student newspaper, television station. Number of fraternities: 6; sororities: 4. **Sports program (2009-2010):** Member of NCAA II. *Men's intercollegiate varsity sports:* baseball, basketball, cross country, football. *Women's intercollegiate varsity sports:* basketball, cross country, softball, tennis, volleyball.

SERVICES AND FACILITIES

Basic services: nonremedial tutoring, placement service, health service, health insurance. **Remedial assistance:** reading, math, writing, other. **Counseling services:** career, military, personal, veteran student, academic, psychological, birth control, other. **For learning-disabled students:** School does not offer a structured program with separate admission and additional fees. Services include: remedial math, remedial English, reading machines, remedial reading, tape recorders, untimed tests, note-taking services, oral tests, readers, extended time for tests, tutors, priority registration, priority seating, texts on tape. **Library:** Number of titles: 196,411; number of current serial subscriptions: 791,635. **Information technology resources:** Students are not required to lease or own a computer. Number of campus computers available to all students: 2,412. School has a wireless network. Proportion of college-owned housing units wired for high-speed internet access: 100%. **Campus safety:** Security services offered: 24-hour foot-and-vehicle patrols, 24-hour emergency telephones, lighted pathways/sidewalks, controlled dormitory access (key, security card, etc).

TRANSFER AND INTERNATIONAL STUDENTS

Transfer students: May apply for admission for the following academic terms: Fall, Spring, Summer. Applicants need a minimum number of credits to apply. For fall 2009: Transfer applications received: 609. Transfer applicants offered admission: 383. Transfer applicants enrolled: 259. **International students:** Number of foreign undergraduates: 41 (1% of student body). Number of countries represented: 18. Minimum TOEFL score required: 523 (paper); 193 (computer).

Armstrong Atlantic State University

- **Address:** 11935 Abercorn Street, Savannah, GA 31419
- **Website:** http://www.armstrong.edu
- **Public**
- **Enrollment:** 4,623 full-time; 1,964 part-time

KEY STATS

✔ **U.S News College Ranking:** second tier, Regional Universities (South)
✔ **SAT Score (25th/75th percentile):** 890-1100
✔ **Tuition:** 2010-2011: $4,198 in state, $13,486 out of state
  Selectivity: Less selective   **Room/board:** $7,840
  Acceptance rate: 82%   **Average debt:** $19,000
  Student/faculty ratio: 21/1   **Proportion who borrowed:** 49%

UNDERGRADUATE STUDENT BODY STATS

2009-2010 enrollment: 4,623 full-time; 1,964 part-time. Men: 35%; women: 65%. **Ethnic makeup:** African American: 21%; American-Indian: 1%; Asian American: 2%; Hispanic: 4%; White: 68%; International: 4%.

ADMISSIONS FACTS AND FIGURES

Phone: (912) 344-2503. **Email:** adm-info@mail.armstrong.edu. **Website:** http://www.armstrong.edu. **Application deadlines for fall 2011:** Regular decision: June 29. Early decision: Not offered. Early action: Not offered. Admission can be deferred. **Application fee:** $25. **To apply online, go to:** https://www.applyweb.com/apply/aasu/. **Admissions requirements/recommendations:** High school units required (recommended): English: 4; Mathematics: 4; Science: 3; Foreign language: 2; Social studies: 3. Tests: The college uses SAT or ACT scores in admissions decisions. Either SAT or ACT required. For admission to the fall 2011 entering class, the school will accept: ACT with or without writing accepted. Campus visit: Recommended. Admissions interview: Neither required nor recommended. Off-campus interview: Not available. **Factors that count in admissions decisions:** *Academic:* Secondary school record: Not Considered. Class rank: Not Considered. Letters of recommendation: Not Considered. Standardized test scores: Very Important. Essay: Not Considered. *Nonacademic:* Interview: Not Considered. Extracurricular activities: Not Considered. Talent/ability: Not Considered. Character/personal qualities: Not Considered. Alumni/ae relationship: Not Considered. Geographical residence: Not Considered. State residency: Not Considered. Religious affiliation/commitment: Not Considered. Minority status: Not Considered. Volunteer work: Not Considered. Work experience: Not Considered. **Other schools with the greatest overlap in applicants:** Georgia Southern University; Savannah College of Art and Design; Savannah State University; University of Georgia; Valdosta State University. **Admissions statistics for the fall 2009 entering class:** Total applicants: 2,167. Total accepted: 1,775. Freshmen enrolled: 1,091; 11% were from out of state. Overall acceptance rate: 82%. **Average high school grade point average:** 3.1. **First-year students who submitted SAT scores:** 74%. Scores (25/75 percentile): Critical Reading: 450-550, Math: 440-550, Combined: 890-1100. **First-year students submitting ACT scores:** 29%. Scores (25/75 percentile): English: 19-22, Math: 17-22, Composite: 18-23.

ACADEMICS

Year founded: 1935. **Academic calendar:** Semester. **Degrees offered:** certificate, associate, bachelor's, post-bachelor's certificate, master's, post-master's certificate. **Most popular majors:** 36% health professions and related clinical sciences, 19% education, 10% liberal arts and sciences studies, and humanities, 8% social sciences, 5% biological and biomedical sciences. **Major fields of study:** biological and biomedical sciences; computer and information sciences and support services; education; English language and literature/letters; foreign languages, literatures, and linguistics; health professions and related clinical sciences; history; legal professions and studies; liberal arts and sciences studies, and humanities; mathematics and statistics; physical sciences; psychology; security and protective services; social sciences; visual and performing arts. **Areas of required coursework:** arts/fine arts, humanities, computer literacy, mathematics, English (including composition), philosophy, foreign languages, sciences (biological or physical), history, social science. **Pre-professional programs:** pre-law, pre-dentistry, pre-medicine, pre-veterinary science, pre-pharmacy, other. **Special academic programs:** cooperative (work-study plan) program, distance learning, double major, dual enrollment, honors program, independent study, internships, study abroad, teacher certificate program, weekend college. **Teacher certification offered in:** early childhood, special education, elementary, middle/junior high, secondary. **Cooperative education programs:** computer science,

engineering, other. **Reserve Officers Training Corps (ROTC):** Army ROTC: Offered on campus; Navy ROTC: Offered at cooperating institution. **Faculty and instruction (2009-2010):** Total instructional faculty: 206 full-time, 192 part-time (40% men; 60% women; 11% minorities). Student/faculty ratio: 21/1. Classes of fewer than 20 students: 46%; of 20 to 49 students: 51%; of 50 or more students: 3%. **Advanced Placement and International Baccalaureate credit:** AP tests may be used for: Credit and/or placement. Scores accepted: 3, 4, 5. International Baccalaureate exams may be used for: Placement only. **Freshmen returning for sophomore year:** 70%. **Graduation rates:** Four-year: 7%; five-year: 22%; six-year: 26%.

COSTS AND FINANCIAL AID

Financial aid office: (912) 921-5990. **Expenses (2010-2011):** Tuition and fees 2010-2011: $4,198 in state, $13,486 out of state; room/board: $7,840. Estimated books and supplies: $1,000; transportation: $3,816; personal expenses: $2,366. **Financial aid:** Priority filing date for institution's financial aid form: March 15. In 2009-2010, 81% of undergraduates applied for financial aid. Of those, 53% were determined to have financial need; 53% had their need fully met. Average financial aid package (proportion receiving): $7,750 (34%). Average amount of gift aid, such as scholarships or grants (proportion receiving): $4,000 (27%). Average amount of self-help aid, such as work study or loans (proportion receiving): $7,750 (27%). Average need-based loan (excluding PLUS or other private loans): $4,500. Among students who received need-based aid, the average percentage of need met: 82%. Among students who received aid based on merit, the average award (and the proportion receiving): $3,000 (19%). The average athletic scholarship (and the proportion receiving): $6,800 (2%). Average amount of debt of borrowers graduating in 2009: $19,000. Proportion who borrowed: 49%.

CAMPUS LIFE AND EXTRACURRICULAR ACTIVITIES

Campus housing available (% using): coed dorms, apartment for single students (100%). Students who live in college-owned, operated, or affiliated housing: 13%. **Student employment:** During the 2009-2010 academic year, 2% of undergraduates worked on campus. Average per-year earnings: $4,500. **Clubs and organizations:** Number of student organizations: 63. Activities include: campus ministries, choral groups, concert band, dance, drama/theater, international student organization, jazz band, literary magazine, music ensembles, musical theater, pep band, student government, student newspaper, symphony orchestra. Number of fraternities: 4; sororities: 5. Proportion of men in fraternities: 3%; of women in sororities: 2%. Average proportion of students who stay on campus on weekends: 9%. **Sports program (2009-2010):** Member of NCAA II. *Men's intercollegiate varsity sports:* baseball, basketball, golf, tennis. *Women's intercollegiate varsity sports:* basketball, golf, softball, tennis, volleyball.

SERVICES AND FACILITIES

Basic services: nonremedial tutoring, health service. **Remedial assistance:** reading, math, writing. **Counseling services:** minority student, career, personal, veteran student, academic, older student, psychological, birth control. **For learning-disabled students:** School does not offer a structured program with separate admission and additional fees. Services include: remedial math, remedial English, reading machines, remedial reading, tape recorders, other special classes, videotaped classes, diagnostic testing service, note-taking services, oral tests, learning center, readers, extended time for tests, tutors. **Library:** Number of titles: 231,500; number of current serial subscriptions: 925. **Information technology resources:** Students are not required to lease or own a computer. Number of campus computers available to all students: 300. School has a wireless network. Proportion of college-owned housing units wired for high-speed internet access: 100%. **Campus safety:** Security services offered: 24-hour foot-and-vehicle patrols, late-night transport/escort service, 24-hour emergency telephones, lighted pathways/sidewalks, controlled dormitory access (key, security card, etc).

TRANSFER AND INTERNATIONAL STUDENTS

Transfer students: May apply for admission for the following academic terms: Fall, Spring, Summer. Applicants need a minimum number of credits to apply. For fall 2009: Transfer applications received: 1,155. Transfer applicants offered admission: 1,053. Transfer applicants enrolled: 787. **International students:** Number of foreign undergraduates: 263 (4% of student body). Number of countries represented: 71. Minimum TOEFL score required: 523 (paper); 193 (computer). Average TOEFL score: 556 (paper).

Atlanta Christian College

- **Address:** 2605 Ben Hill Road, East Point, GA 30344
- **Website:** http://www.acc.edu
- **Private; Religious affiliation:** Christian Churches/Churches of Christ
- **Enrollment:** 664 full-time; 26 part-time

KEY STATS

✔ **U.S News College Ranking:** second tier, Regional Colleges (South)
✔ **SAT Score (25th/75th percentile):** 820-1040
✔ **Tuition:** 2010-2011: $15,902

Selectivity: Less selective	**Room/board:** $5,670
Acceptance rate: 66%	**Average debt:** N/A
Student/faculty ratio: 22/1	**Proportion who borrowed:** N/A

UNDERGRADUATE STUDENT BODY STATS

2009-2010 enrollment: 664 full-time; 26 part-time. Men: 44%; women: 56%. **Ethnic makeup:** African American: 55%; Hispanic: 4%; White: 40%; International: 1%. **Religious preference:** Roman Catholic: 2%; Protestant: 98%.

ADMISSIONS FACTS AND FIGURES

Phone: (404) 669-3202. **Email:** admissions@acc.edu. **Website:** http://www.acc.edu. **Application deadlines for fall 2011:** Regular decision: August 1. Early decision: Not offered. Early action: Not offered. Admission can be deferred. **Application fee:** $25. **To apply online, go to:** http://choose.acc.edu. **Admissions requirements/recommendations:** High school units required (recommended): English: (4); Mathematics: (3); Science: (3); Foreign language: (2); Social studies: (3); History: (3); Academic electives: (4); Total units: (24). Tests: The college uses SAT or ACT scores in admissions decisions. Either SAT or ACT required. For admission to the fall 2011 entering class, the school will accept: ACT with writing recommended. Campus visit: Recommended. Admissions interview: Neither required nor recommended. Off-campus interview: Not available. **Factors that count in admissions decisions:** *Academic:* Secondary school record: Very Important. Class rank: Considered. Letters of recommendation: Very Important. Standardized test scores: Very Important. Essay: Considered. *Nonacademic:* Interview: Not Considered. Extracurricular activities: Considered. Talent/ability: Important. Character/personal qualities: Important. Alumni/ae relationship: Considered. Geographical residence: Not Considered. State residency: Not Considered. Religious affiliation/commitment: Considered. Minority status: Not Considered. Volunteer work: Considered. Work experience: Not Considered. **Other schools with the greatest overlap in applicants:** Georgia State University; Gordon College; Kennesaw State University; Toccoa Falls College; University of West Georgia. **Admissions statistics for the fall 2009 entering class:** Total applicants: 335. Total accepted: 222. Freshmen enrolled: 111; Overall acceptance rate: 66%. **First-year students who submitted SAT scores:** 71%. Scores (25/75 percentile): Critical Reading: 410-540, Math: 410-500, Combined: 820-1040. **First-year students submitting ACT scores:** 48%. Scores (25/75 percentile): English: N/A, Math: N/A, Composite: 18-23.

ACADEMICS

Year founded: 1937. **Academic calendar:** Semester. **Degrees offered:** associate, bachelor's. **Major fields of study:** business, management, marketing, and related support services; education; English language and literature/letters; liberal arts and sciences studies, and humanities; psychology; theology and religious vocations; visual and performing arts. **Areas of required coursework:** arts/fine arts, humanities, mathematics, English (including composition), philosophy, sciences (biological or physical), history, social science, other. **Special academic programs:** distance learning, double major, dual enrollment, independent study, internships. **Teacher certification offered in:** early childhood. **Faculty and instruction (2009-2010):** Total instructional faculty: 16 full-time, 49 part-time. Student/faculty ratio: 22/1. **Advanced Placement and International Baccalaureate credit:** AP tests may be used for: Credit only. Scores accepted: 3, 4. **Freshmen returning for sophomore year:** 63%. **Graduation rates:** Six-year: 30%.

COSTS AND FINANCIAL AID

Financial aid office: (800) 766-1222. **Expenses (2010-2011):** Tuition and fees 2010-2011: $15,902; room/board: $5,670.

CAMPUS LIFE AND EXTRACURRICULAR ACTIVITIES

Campus housing available: women's dorms, men's dorms, apartments for married students, apartment for single students. Students who live in college-owned, operated, or affiliated housing: 59%. **Clubs and organizations:** Number of student organizations: 12. Activities include: campus ministries, choral groups, dance, drama/theater, literary magazine, music ensembles, student government, student newspaper. Number of fraternities: 0; sororities: 1.

SERVICES AND FACILITIES

Basic services: nonremedial tutoring, health service, health insurance. **Remedial assistance:** reading, math, writing, study skills. **Counseling services:** minority student, career, personal, academic, older student, psychological, religious. **For learning-disabled students:** School does not offer a structured program with separate admission and additional fees. Total undergraduates in learning-disabled program or receiving services: 17. Services include: note-taking services, oral tests, learning center, readers, extended time for tests, tutors, priority seating, proofreading services, typist/scribe, other testing accommodations, other. **Information technology resources:** Students are not required to lease or own a computer. Number of campus computers available to all students: 36. School has a wireless network. Proportion of college-owned housing units wired for high-speed internet access: 100%. **Campus safety:** Security services offered: 24-hour foot-and-vehicle patrols, lighted pathways/sidewalks, controlled dormitory access (key, security card, etc).

TRANSFER AND INTERNATIONAL STUDENTS

Transfer students: May apply for admission for the following academic terms: Fall, Spring, Summer. Applicants do not need a minimum number of credits to apply. For fall 2009: Transfer applications received: 522. Transfer applicants offered admission: 450. Transfer applicants enrolled: 202. **International students:** Number of foreign undergraduates: 3 (1% of student body). Number of countries represented: 3. Minimum TOEFL score required: 550 (paper); 80 (computer).

Augusta State University

- **Address:** 2500 Walton Way, Augusta, GA 30904-2200
- **Website:** http://www.aug.edu
- **Public**
- **Enrollment:** N/A

KEY STATS

✔ **U.S News College Ranking:** second tier, Regional Universities (South)
✔ **SAT or ACT Score (25th/75th percentile):** N/A
✔ **Tuition:** 2009-2010: $3,730 in state, $13,018 out of state

Selectivity: Less selective	**Room/board:** $9,600
Acceptance rate: N/A	**Average debt:** N/A
Student/faculty ratio: N/A	**Proportion who borrowed:** N/A

Berry College

- **Address:** PO Box 490279, Mount Berry, GA 30149
- **Website:** http://www.berry.edu
- **Private**
- **Enrollment:** 1,737 full-time; 40 part-time

KEY STATS

✔ **U.S News College Ranking:** 122, National Liberal Arts Colleges
✔ **SAT Score (25th/75th percentile):** 1030-1250
✔ **Tuition:** 2010-2011: $24,620

Selectivity: More selective	**Room/board:** $8,724
Acceptance rate: 67%	**Average debt:** $17,502
Student/faculty ratio: 12/1	**Proportion who borrowed:** 82%

UNDERGRADUATE STUDENT BODY STATS

2009-2010 enrollment: 1,737 full-time; 40 part-time. Men: 31%; women: 69%. **Ethnic makeup:** African American: 5%; Asian American: 2%; Hispanic: 3%; White: 88%; International: 2%. **Religious preference:** Roman Catholic: 10%; Protestant: 75%; No preference: 9%; Jewish, Muslim, Hindu, Buddist, Orthodox Christian, indigenous religion : 6%.

ADMISSIONS FACTS AND FIGURES

Phone: (706) 236-2215. **Email:** admissions@berry.edu. **Website:** http://www.berry.edu. **Application deadlines for fall 2011:** Regular decision: July 23. Early decision: Not offered. Early action: Not offered. Admission can be deferred. **Application fee:** $50. **To apply online, go to:** http://www.berry.edu/admissions/stn_applications.asp. **Admissions requirements/recommendations:** High school units required (recommended): English: 4; Mathematics: 4; Science: 3; Foreign language: 2; Social studies: 3; Total units: 20. Tests: The college uses SAT or ACT scores in admissions decisions. Either SAT or ACT required. For admission to the fall 2011 entering class, the school will accept: ACT with or without writing accepted. Campus visit: Recommended. Admissions interview: Recommended. Off-campus interview: Not available. **Factors that count in admissions decisions:** *Academic:* Secondary school record: Very Important. Class rank: Considered. Letters of recommendation: Considered. Standardized test scores: Very Important. Essay: Considered. *Nonacademic:* Interview: Considered. Extracurricular activities: Important. Talent/ability: Not Considered. Character/personal qualities: Not Considered. Alumni/ae relationship: Not Considered. Geographical residence: Not Considered. State residency: Not Considered. Religious affiliation/commitment: Not Considered. Minority status: Not Considered. Volunteer work: Considered. Work experience: Considered. **Other schools with the greatest overlap in applicants:** Auburn University; Georgia Institute of Technology; Georgia Southern University; Mercer University. **Admissions statistics for the fall 2009 entering class:** Total applicants: 2,412. Total accepted: 1,616. Freshmen enrolled: 569; 21% were from out of state. Overall acceptance rate: 67%. **Credentials of fall 2009 freshmen:** 32% ranked in the top 10 percent of their high school class; 66% were in the top 25 percent; 92% were in the top half. (Proportion submitting class standing: 75%.) **Average high school grade point average:** 3.6. **First-year students who submitted SAT scores:** 60%. Scores (25/75 percentile): Critical Reading: 520-640, Math: 510-610, Combined: 1030-1250. **First-year students submitting ACT scores:** 40%. Scores (25/75 percentile): English: 23-30, Math: 21-27, Composite: 22-28.

ACADEMICS

Year founded: 1902. **Academic calendar:** Semester. **Degrees offered:** bachelor's, master's, post-master's certificate. **Most popular majors:** 18% business, management, marketing, and related support services, 11% communication, journalism, and related programs, 11% education, 10% biological and biomedical sciences, 7% agriculture, agriculture operations, and related sciences. **Major fields of study:** agriculture, agriculture operations, and related sciences; biological and biomedical sciences; business, management, marketing, and related support services; communication, journalism, and related programs; computer and information sciences and support services; education; engineering technologies/technicians; English language and literature/letters; foreign languages, literatures, and linguistics; health professions and related clinical sciences; history; mathematics and statistics; multi/interdisciplinary studies; natural resources and conservation; philosophy and religious studies; physical sciences; psychology; social sciences; visual and performing arts. **Areas of required coursework:** arts/fine arts, humanities, computer literacy, mathematics, English (including composition), sciences (biological or physical), history, social science, other. **Preprofessional programs:** pre-law, pre-dentistry, pre-medicine, pre-veterinary science, pre-pharmacy. **Special academic programs:** cooperative (work-study plan) program, cross-registration, double major, dual enrollment, honors program, independent study, internships, student-designed major, study abroad, teacher certificate program, other. **Teacher certification offered in:** early childhood, elementary, middle/junior high, secondary, bilingual/bicultural. **Cooperative education programs:** business, computer science, humanities, natural science, social/behavioral science. **Faculty and instruction (2009-2010):** Total instructional faculty: 145 full-time, 59 part-time (61% men; 39% women; 4% minorities). Full-time faculty with Ph.D. or other terminal degree: 90%. Student/faculty ratio: 12/1. Classes of fewer than 20 students: 65%; of 20 to 49 students: 34%; of 50 or more students: 0%. **Advanced Placement and International Baccalaureate credit:** AP tests may be used for: Credit and/or placement. Scores accepted: 3, 4, 5. International Baccalaureate exams may be used for: Placement only. **Freshmen returning for sophomore year:** 76%. **Graduation rates:** Four-year: 48%; five-year: 58%; six-year: 60%. **Graduate study:** 26% of students pursue further study within one year; 37% within five years. Fields in which graduates pursue further study: Master of Business Administration (MBA), 7%; law, 4%; medicine, 7%; dentistry, 4%; engineering, 4%; theology (or the seminary), 6%; education, 11%; arts and sciences, 42%; veterinary medicine, 16%.

COSTS AND FINANCIAL AID

Financial aid office: (706) 236-1714. **Expenses (2010-2011):** Tuition and fees 2010-2011: $24,620; room/board: $8,724. Estimated books and supplies: $1,200; transportation: $1,380; personal expenses: $1,840. **Financial aid:** Priority filing date for institution's financial aid form: April 1. In 2009-2010, 83% of undergraduates applied for financial aid. Of those, 68% were determined to have financial need; 21% had their need fully met. Average financial aid package (proportion receiving): $20,606 (68%). Average amount of gift aid, such as scholarships or grants (proportion receiving): $15,281 (68%). Average amount of self-help aid, such as work study or loans (proportion receiving): $6,497 (56%). Average need-based loan (excluding PLUS or other private loans): $3,833. Among students who received need-based aid, the average percentage of need met: 83%. Among students who received aid based on merit, the average award (and the proportion receiving): $9,206 (28%). The average athletic scholarship (and the proportion receiving): $12,977 (5%). Average amount of debt of borrowers graduating in 2009: $17,502. Proportion who borrowed: 82%.

CAMPUS LIFE AND EXTRACURRICULAR ACTIVITIES

Campus housing available (% using): coed dorms (55%), women's dorms (30%), men's dorms (3%), apartment for single students (7%), special housing for disabled students (5%), cooperative housing (0%). Students who live in college-owned, operated, or affiliated housing: 84%. **Student employment:** During the 2009-2010 academic year, 85% of undergraduates worked on campus. Average per-year earnings: $4,736. **Clubs and organizations:** Number of student organizations: 75. Activities include: campus ministries, choral groups, concert band, dance, drama/theater, international student organization, jazz band, literary magazine, model UN, music ensembles, musical theater, student government, student newspaper, symphony orchestra, television station, yearbook. Number of fraternities: 0; sororities: 0. Average proportion of students who stay on campus on weekends: 60%. **Sports program (2009-2010):** Member of NCAA III. *Men's intercollegiate varsity sports:* baseball, basketball, cross country, golf, lacrosse, soccer, swimming, tennis. *Women's intercollegiate varsity sports:* basketball, cross country, equestrian, golf, lacrosse, soccer, softball, swimming, tennis, volleyball.

SERVICES AND FACILITIES

Basic services: nonremedial tutoring, placement service, health service. **Remedial assistance:** study skills. **Counseling services:** minority student, career, personal, veteran student, academic, older student, psychological, religious. **For learning-disabled students:** School does not offer a structured program with separate admission and additional fees. Total undergraduates in learning-disabled program or receiving services: 38. Services include: remedial English, tape recorders, note-taking services, oral tests, readers, extended time for tests, tutors, priority registration, priority seating, texts on tape, typist/scribe, exams on tape or computer, other testing accommodations, other. **Library:** Number of titles: 347,056; number of current serial subscriptions: 2,082. **Information technology resources:** Students are not required to lease or own a computer. Number of campus computers available to all students: 140. School has a wireless network. Approximate number of users that can be accommodated: 2,500. Proportion of college-owned housing units wired for high-speed internet access: 100%. **Campus safety:** Security services offered: 24-hour foot-and-vehicle patrols, 24-hour emergency telephones, lighted pathways/sidewalks, controlled dormitory access (key, security card, etc).

TRANSFER AND INTERNATIONAL STUDENTS

Transfer students: May apply for admission for the following academic terms: Fall, Spring, Summer. Applicants do not need a minimum number of credits to apply. For fall 2009: Transfer applications received: 219. Transfer applicants offered admission: 109. Transfer applicants enrolled: 53. **International students:** Number of foreign undergraduates: 29 (2% of student body). Number of countries represented: 20. Minimum TOEFL score required: 550 (paper); 213 (computer). Average TOEFL score: 552 (paper).

Brenau University

- **Address:** 500 Washington Street SE, Gainesville, GA 30501
- **Website:** http://www.brenau.edu
- **Private**
- **Enrollment:** 766 full-time; 67 part-time

KEY STATS

✔ **U.S News College Ranking:** 29, Regional Universities (South)
✔ **SAT Score (25th/75th percentile):** 870-1050
✔ **Tuition:** 2010-2011: $20,130

Selectivity: Selective	**Room/board:** $10,065
Acceptance rate: 38%	**Average debt:** $17,999
Student/faculty ratio: 8/1	**Proportion who borrowed:** 64%

UNDERGRADUATE STUDENT BODY STATS

2009-2010 enrollment: 766 full-time; 67 part-time. Men: 0%; women: 100%. **Ethnic makeup:** African American: 21%; Asian American: 3%; Hispanic: 5%; White: 64%; International: 6%.

ADMISSIONS FACTS AND FIGURES

Phone: (770) 534-6100. **Email:** admissions@brenau.edu. **Website:** http://www.brenau.edu. **Application deadlines for fall 2011:** Regular decision: Rolling. Early decision: Not offered. Early action: Not offered. Admission can be deferred. **Application fee:** $35. **To apply online, go to:** https://secure.brenau.edu/WCApp.htm. **Admissions requirements/recommendations:** Tests: The college uses SAT or ACT scores in admissions decisions. Either SAT or ACT required. For admission to the fall 2011 entering class, the school will accept: ACT with or without writing accepted. Campus visit: Recommended. Admissions interview: Recommended. Off-campus interview: May be arranged. **Factors that count in admissions decisions:** *Academic:* Secondary school record: Important. Class rank: Considered. Letters of recommendation: Not Considered. Standardized test scores: Important. Essay: Not Considered. *Nonacademic:* Interview: Considered. Extracurricular activities: Considered. Talent/ability: Considered. Character/personal qualities: Considered. Alumni/ae relationship: Not Considered. Geographical residence: Not Considered. State residency: Not Considered. Religious affiliation/commitment: Not Considered. Minority status: Not Considered. Volunteer work: Considered. Work experience: Considered. **Other schools with the greatest overlap in applicants:** Agnes Scott College; Berry College; Georgia Southern University; North Georgia College and State University; University of Georgia. **Admissions statistics for the fall 2009 entering class:** Total applicants: 3,493. Total accepted: 1,329. Freshmen enrolled: 159; 12% were from out of state. Overall acceptance rate: 38%. **Size of waiting list:** 0 applicants; enrolled from waiting list: 0. **First-year students who submitted SAT scores:** 85%. Scores (25/75 percentile): Critical Reading: 450-540, Math: 420-510, Combined: 870-1050.

ACADEMICS

Year founded: 1878. **Academic calendar:** Semester. **Degrees offered:** bachelor's, master's. **Most popular majors:** 39% health professions and related clinical sciences, 17% education, 14% visual and performing arts, 10% business, management, marketing, and related support services, 6% communication, journalism, and related programs. **Major fields of study:** biological and biomedical sciences; business, management, marketing, and related support services; communication, journalism, and related programs; education; English language and literature/letters; health professions and related clinical sciences; history; legal professions and studies; liberal arts and sciences studies, and humanities; psychology; social sciences; visual and performing arts. **Areas of required coursework:** humanities, mathematics, English (including composition), foreign languages, sciences (biological or physical), history, social science, other. **Pre-professional programs:** pre-law, other. **Special academic programs:** cross-registration, distance learning, double major, dual enrollment, English as a Second Language (ESL), honors program, independent study, internships, student-designed major, study abroad, teacher certificate program, weekend college. **Teacher certification offered in:** early childhood, special education, middle/junior high. **Faculty and instruction (2009-2010):** Total instructional faculty: 73 full-time, 89 part-time (36% men; 64% women; 11% minorities). Full-time faculty with Ph.D. or other terminal degree: 82%. Student/faculty ratio: 8/1. Classes of fewer than 20 students: 74%; of 20 to 49 students: 24%; of 50 or more students: 2%. **Advanced Placement and International Baccalaureate credit:** AP tests may be used for: Credit and/or placement. Scores accepted: 3, 4, 5. International Baccalaureate exams may be used for: Credit and/or

placement. **Freshmen returning for sophomore year:** 67%. **Graduation rates:** Four-year: 32%; five-year: 44%; six-year: 49%. **Graduate study:** 7% of students pursue further study immediately upon graduation; 22% within one year; 35% within five years. Fields in which graduates pursue further study: Master of Business Administration (MBA), 14%; law, 4%; medicine, 2%; dentistry, 1%; education, 13%.

COSTS AND FINANCIAL AID

Financial aid office: (770) 534-6176. **Expenses (2010-2011):** Tuition and fees 2010-2011: $20,130; room/board: $10,065. Estimated books and supplies: $1,100; transportation: $850; personal expenses: $1,400. **Financial aid:** Priority filing date for institution's financial aid form: March 15. In 2009-2010, 83% of undergraduates applied for financial aid. Of those, 73% were determined to have financial need; 14% had their need fully met. Average financial aid package (proportion receiving): $18,874 (73%). Average amount of gift aid, such as scholarships or grants (proportion receiving): $14,244 (73%). Average amount of self-help aid, such as work study or loans (proportion receiving): $4,904 (55%). Average need-based loan (excluding PLUS or other private loans): $4,319. Among students who received need-based aid, the average percentage of need met: 73%. Among students who received aid based on merit, the average award (and the proportion receiving): $10,492 (18%). The average athletic scholarship (and the proportion receiving): $15,125 (6%). Average amount of debt of borrowers graduating in 2009: $17,999. Proportion who borrowed: 64%.

CAMPUS LIFE AND EXTRACURRICULAR ACTIVITIES

Campus housing available: women's dorms, sorority housing, apartment for single students, special housing for disabled students, special housing for international students, cooperative housing. Students who live in college-owned, operated, or affiliated housing: 55%. Average per-year earnings: $2,175. **Clubs and organizations:** Number of student organizations: 52. Activities include: campus ministries, choral groups, dance, drama/theater, international student organization, literary magazine, music ensembles, musical theater, radio station, student government, student newspaper, television station, yearbook. Number of fraternities: 0; sororities: 8. of women in sororities: 22%. Average proportion of students who stay on campus on weekends: 50%. **Sports program (2009-2010):** Member of NAIA. *Women's intercollegiate varsity sports:* basketball, cross country, soccer, softball, swimming, tennis, volleyball.

SERVICES AND FACILITIES

Basic services: nonremedial tutoring, women's center, placement service, health service. **Remedial assistance:** reading, math, writing, study skills. **Counseling services:** minority student, career, personal, academic, older student, psychological, birth control, religious. **For learning-disabled students:** School does not offer a structured program with separate admission and additional fees. Total undergraduates in learning-disabled program or receiving services: 19. Services include: remedial math, remedial English, reading machines, remedial reading, tape recorders, other special classes, note-taking services, oral tests, learning center, readers, extended time for tests, tutors, priority registration, priority seating, texts on tape, exams on tape or computer. **Library:** Number of titles: 86,787; number of current serial subscriptions: 15,541. **Information technology resources:** Students are not required to lease or own a computer. Number of campus computers available to all students: 130. School has a wireless network. Approximate number of users that can be accommodated: 1,584. Proportion of college-owned housing units wired for high-speed internet access: 100%. **Campus safety:** Security services offered: 24-hour foot-and-vehicle patrols, late-night transport/escort service, 24-hour emergency telephones, lighted pathways/sidewalks, controlled dormitory access (key, security card, etc).

TRANSFER AND INTERNATIONAL STUDENTS

Transfer students: May apply for admission for the following academic terms: Fall, Spring, Summer. Applicants need a minimum number of credits to apply. For fall 2009: Transfer applications received: 553. Transfer applicants offered admission: 375. Transfer applicants enrolled: 133. **International students:** Number of foreign undergraduates: 47 (6% of student body). Number of countries represented: 20. Minimum TOEFL score required: 550 (paper); 173 (computer).

Brewton-Parker College

- **Address:** 201 David-Eliza Fountain Circle, Mount Vernon, GA 30445
- **Website:** http://www.bpc.edu
- **Private; Religious affiliation:** Baptist
- **Enrollment:** N/A

KEY STATS

✔ **U.S News College Ranking:** second tier, Regional Colleges (South)
✔ **SAT or ACT Score (25th/75th percentile):** N/A
✔ **Tuition:** 2009-2010: $15,390

Selectivity: Less selective	**Room/board:** $6,323
Acceptance rate: N/A	**Average debt:** N/A
Student/faculty ratio: N/A	**Proportion who borrowed:** N/A

Clark Atlanta University

- **Address:** 223 James P. Brawley Drive SW, Atlanta, GA 30314
- **Website:** http://www.cau.edu
- **Private; Religious affiliation:** Methodist
- **Enrollment:** 3,067 full-time; 135 part-time

KEY STATS

✔ **U.S News College Ranking:** second tier, National Universities
✔ **SAT Score (25th/75th percentile):** 810-950
✔ **Tuition:** 2010-2011: $17,954

Selectivity: Less selective	**Room/board:** $8,124
Acceptance rate: 59%	**Average debt:** $41,979
Student/faculty ratio: 17/1	**Proportion who borrowed:** 94%

UNDERGRADUATE STUDENT BODY STATS

2009-2010 enrollment: 3,067 full-time; 135 part-time. Men: 27%; women: 73%. **Ethnic makeup:** African American: 90%; White: 9%; International: 1%. **Religious preference:** Roman Catholic: 3%; Muslim: 1%; No preference: 16%; Unknown: 16%; Methodist: 3%; Christian Non-Denominational: 24%; Other: 37%.

ADMISSIONS FACTS AND FIGURES

Phone: (800) 688-3228. **Email:** cauadmissions@cau.edu. **Website:** http://www.cau.edu. **Application deadlines for fall 2011:** Regular decision: June 1. Early decision: Not offered. Early action: Not offered. Admission can be deferred. **Application fee:** $35. **To apply online, go to:** http://admissions.cau.edu/. **Admissions requirements/recommendations:** High school units required (recommended): English: 4; Mathematics: 3; Science: 3; Foreign language: 2; Social studies: 3; Academic electives: 3; Total units: 18. Tests: The college uses SAT or ACT scores in admissions decisions. Either SAT or ACT required. For admission to the fall 2011 entering class, the school will accept: ACT with or without writing accepted. Campus visit: Recommended. Admissions interview: Neither required nor recommended. Off-campus interview: Not available. **Factors that count in admissions decisions:** *Academic:* Secondary school record: Very Important. Class rank: Not Considered. Letters of recommendation: Important. Standardized test scores: Very Important. Essay: Important. *Nonacademic:* Interview: Not Considered. Extracurricular activities: Not Considered. Talent/ability: Important. Character/personal qualities: Very Important. Alumni/ae relationship: Considered. Geographical residence: Not Considered. State residency: Not Considered. Religious affiliation/commitment: Not Considered. Minority status: Not Considered. Volunteer work: Not Considered. Work experience: Considered. **Admissions statistics for the fall 2009 entering class:** Total applicants: 6,681. Total accepted: 3,954. Freshmen enrolled: 703; 74% were from out of state. Overall acceptance rate: 59%. **Credentials of fall 2009 freshmen:** 8% ranked in the top 10 percent of their high school class; 23% were in the top 25 percent; 46% were in the top half. (Proportion submitting class standing: 6%.) **Average high school grade point average:** 3.0. **First-year students who submitted SAT scores:** 70%. Scores (25/75 percentile): Critical Reading: 410-480, Math: 400-470, Combined: 810-950. **First-year students submitting ACT scores:** 30%. Scores (25/75 percentile): English: N/A, Math: N/A, Composite: 18-20.

ACADEMICS

Year founded: 1988. **Academic calendar:** Semester. **Degrees offered:** bachelor's, post-bachelor's certificate, master's, post-master's certificate, doctorate. **Most popular majors:** 26% communication, journalism, and related programs, 22% business, management, marketing, and related support services, 8% psychology, 7% biological and biomedical sciences, 7% visual and performing arts. **Major fields of study:** biological and biomedical sciences; business, management, marketing, and related support services; communication, journalism, and related programs; computer and information sciences and support services; education; engineering; English language and literature/letters; foreign languages, literatures, and linguistics; health professions and related clinical sciences; history; liberal arts and sciences studies, and humanities; mathematics and statistics; philosophy and religious studies; physical sciences; psychology; public administration and social service professions; security and protective services; social sciences; visual and performing arts. **Areas of required coursework:** humanities, computer literacy, mathematics, English (including composition), philosophy, foreign languages, sciences (biological or physical), history, social science, other. **Special academic programs:** accelerated program, cooperative (work-study plan) program, cross-registration, double major, dual enrollment, exchange student program (domestic), honors program, independent study, internships, study abroad, teacher certificate program, weekend college. **Teacher certification offered in:** early childhood, special education. **Cooperative education programs:** other. **Reserve Officers Training Corps (ROTC):** Army ROTC: Offered at cooperating institution (Morehouse College); Navy ROTC: Offered at cooperating institution (Morehouse College). **Faculty and instruction (2009-2010):** Total instructional faculty: 178 full-time, 98 part-time (58% men; 42% women; 89% minorities). Full-time faculty with Ph.D. or other terminal degree: 77%. Student/faculty ratio: 17/1. Classes of fewer than 20 students: 30%; of 20 to 49 students: 63%; of 50 or more students: 7%. **Advanced Placement and International Baccalaureate credit:** AP tests may be used for: Credit only. Scores accepted: 3. International Baccalaureate exams may be used for: Credit only. **Freshmen returning for sophomore year:** 70%. **Graduation rates:** Four-year: 30%; five-year: 41%; six-year: 43%. **Graduate study:** 20% of students pursue further study immediately upon graduation; 22% within one year; 24% within five years. Fields in which graduates pursue further study: Master of Business Administration (MBA), 3%; law, 1%; medicine, 1%; engineering, 1%; education, 1%; arts and sciences, 13%.

COSTS AND FINANCIAL AID

Financial aid office: (404) 880-8111. **Expenses (2010-2011):** Tuition and fees 2010-2011: $17,954; room/board: $8,124. Estimated books and supplies: $2,200; transportation: $1,412; personal expenses: $1,540. **Financial aid:** Priority filing date for institution's financial aid form: March 1; deadline: March 1. In 2009-2010, 98% of undergraduates applied for financial aid. Of those, 91% were determined to have financial need; 20% had their need fully met. Average financial aid package (proportion receiving): $5,876 (91%). Average amount of gift aid, such as scholarships or grants (proportion receiving): $4,209 (76%). Average amount of self-help aid, such as work study or loans (proportion receiving): $2,526 (87%). Average need-based loan (excluding PLUS or other private loans): $2,429. Among students who received need-based aid, the average percentage of need met: 20%. Among students who received aid based on merit, the average award (and the proportion receiving): $9,577 (0%). The average athletic scholarship (and the proportion receiving): $6,601 (0%). Average amount of debt of borrowers graduating in 2009: $41,979. Proportion who borrowed: 94%.

CAMPUS LIFE AND EXTRACURRICULAR ACTIVITIES

Campus housing available (% using): coed dorms (28%), women's dorms (39%), men's dorms (18%), apartment for single students (15%). Students who live in college-owned, operated, or affiliated housing: 34%. **Student employment:** During the 2009-2010 academic year, 10% of undergraduates worked on campus. Average per-year earnings: $8,500. **Clubs and organizations:** Number of student organizations: 80. Activities include: campus ministries, choral groups, concert band, dance, drama/theater, international student organization, literary magazine, marching band, music ensembles, musical theater, opera, pep band, radio station, student government, student newspaper, student film society, symphony orchestra, television station, yearbook. Number of fraternities: 5; sororities: 4. Proportion of men in fraternities: 2%; of women in sororities: 3%. Average proportion of students who stay on campus on weekends: 80%. **Sports program (2009-2010):** Member of NCAA II. **Men's intercollegiate varsity sports:** baseball, basketball, cross country, football, track and field (outdoor). **Women's intercollegiate varsity sports:** basketball, cross country, softball, tennis, track and field (outdoor), volleyball.

SERVICES AND FACILITIES

Basic services: nonremedial tutoring, placement service, health service, health insurance. **Remedial assistance:** reading, math, writing, study skills, other. **Counseling services:** minority student, career, personal, veteran student, academic, older student, psychological, religious, other. **For learning-disabled students:** School does not offer a structured program with separate admission and additional fees. Total undergraduates in learning-disabled program or receiving services: 12. Services include: tape recorders, untimed tests, note-taking services, oral tests, learning center, readers, extended time for tests, tutors, priority registration, priority seating, texts on tape, other testing accommodations. **Library:** Number of titles: 375,956; number of current serial subscriptions: 31,840. **Information technology resources:** Students are not required to lease or own a computer. Number of campus computers available to all students: 700. School has a wireless network. Approximate number of users that can be accommodated: 2,825. Proportion of college-owned housing units wired for high-speed internet access: 100%. **Campus safety:** Security services offered: 24-hour foot-and-vehicle patrols, late-night transport/escort service, 24-hour emergency telephones, lighted pathways/sidewalks, controlled dormitory access (key, security card, etc).

TRANSFER AND INTERNATIONAL STUDENTS

Transfer students: May apply for admission for the following academic terms: Fall, Spring, Summer. Applicants need a minimum number of credits to apply. For fall 2009: Transfer applications received: 729. Transfer applicants offered admission: 465. Transfer applicants enrolled: 173. **International students:** Number of foreign undergraduates: 19 (1% of student body). Number of countries represented: 9. Minimum TOEFL score required: 500 (paper); 173 (computer). Average TOEFL score: 550 (paper).

Clayton State University

- **Address:** 2000 Clayton State Boulevard, Morrow, GA 30260
- **Website:** http://www.clayton.edu
- **Public**
- **Enrollment:** 3,674 full-time; 2,738 part-time

KEY STATS

✔ **U.S News College Ranking:** 57, Regional Colleges (South)
✔ **SAT Score (25th/75th percentile):** 880-1070
✔ **Tuition:** 2009-2010: $4,858 in state, $16,472 out of state

Selectivity: Selective	**Room/board:** $8,078
Acceptance rate: 38%	**Average debt:** N/A
Student/faculty ratio: 19/1	**Proportion who borrowed:** N/A

UNDERGRADUATE STUDENT BODY STATS

2009-2010 enrollment: 3,674 full-time; 2,738 part-time. Men: 30%; women: 70%. **Ethnic makeup:** African American: 63%; Asian American: 4%; Hispanic: 3%; White: 28%; International: 1%.

ADMISSIONS FACTS AND FIGURES

Phone: (678) 466-4115. **Email:** ccsu-info@mail.clayton.edu. **Website:** http://www.clayton.edu. **Application deadlines for fall 2011:** Regular decision: July 1. Early decision: Not offered. Early action: Not offered. Admission can be deferred. **Application fee:** $40. **To apply online, go to:** http://www.clayton.edu/futurestudents.htm. **Admissions requirements/recommendations:** High school units required (recommended): English: 4 (4); Mathematics: 4 (4); Science: 3 (4); Foreign language: 2 (3); Social studies: 3 (3); History: (2); Academic electives: (2); Total units: 16 (22). Tests: The college uses SAT or ACT scores in admissions decisions. Either SAT or ACT required. For admission to the fall 2011 entering class, the school will accept: ACT with or without writing accepted. Campus visit: Recommended. Admissions interview: Neither required nor recommended. Off-campus interview: Not available. **Factors that count in admissions decisions:** *Academic:* Secondary school record: Very Important. Class rank: Considered. Letters of recommendation: Considered. Standardized test scores: Very Important. Essay: Important. *Nonacademic:* Interview: Not Considered. Extracurricular activities: Considered. Talent/ability: Considered. Character/personal qualities: Not Considered. Alumni/ae relationship: Not Considered. Geographical residence: Not Considered. State residency: Not Considered. Religious affiliation/commitment: Not Considered. Minority status: Not Considered. Volunteer work: Not Considered. Work experience: Not Considered. **Other schools with the greatest overlap in applicants:** Georgia College & State University; Georgia State University; Kennesaw State University; Southern

Polytechnic State University; University of West Georgia. **Admissions statistics for the fall 2009 entering class:** Total applicants: 2,137. Total accepted: 821. Freshmen enrolled: 535; 1% were from out of state. Overall acceptance rate: 38%. **Credentials of fall 2009 freshmen:** 18% ranked in the top 10 percent of their high school class; 44% were in the top 25 percent; 82% were in the top half. (Proportion submitting class standing: 44%.) **Average high school grade point average:** 3.0. **First-year students who submitted SAT scores:** 69%. Scores (25/75 percentile): Critical Reading: 450-540, Math: 430-530, Combined: 880-1070. **First-year students submitting ACT scores:** 36%. Scores (25/75 percentile): English: 17-21, Math: 18-21, Composite: 18-22.

ACADEMICS

Year founded: 1969. **Academic calendar:** Semester. **Degrees offered:** certificate, associate, transfer-associate, terminal-associate, bachelor's, master's. **Most popular majors:** 13% community psychology, 12% liberal arts and sciences/liberal studies, 11% nursing/registered nurse training (R.N., A.S.N., B.S.N., M.S.N.), 10% hospital and health care facilities administration/management, 6% junior high/intermediate/middle school education and teaching. **Major fields of study:** biological and biomedical sciences; business, management, marketing, and related support services; communication, journalism, and related programs; computer and information sciences and support services; education; health professions and related clinical sciences; history; liberal arts and sciences studies, and humanities; mathematics and statistics; psychology; security and protective services; social sciences; visual and performing arts. **Areas of required coursework:** arts/fine arts, humanities, computer literacy, mathematics, English (including composition), philosophy, foreign languages, sciences (biological or physical), history, social science, other. **Pre-professional programs:** pre-law, pre-dentistry, pre-medicine, pre-veterinary science, pre-pharmacy, other. **Special academic programs (% participation):** cross-registration (1%), distance learning (12%), double major (9%), dual enrollment (3%), honors program (2%), independent study (31%), internships (70%), student-designed major (3%), study abroad (14%), teacher certificate program (2%). **Teacher certification offered in:** middle/junior high. **Reserve Officers Training Corps (ROTC):** Army ROTC: Offered on campus; Navy ROTC: Offered at cooperating institution; Air Force ROTC: Offered at cooperating institution. **Faculty and instruction (2009-2010):** Total instructional faculty: 196 full-time, 162 part-time (49% men; 51% women; 36% minorities). Full-time faculty with Ph.D. or other terminal degree: 86%. Student/faculty ratio: 19/1. Classes of fewer than 20 students: 37%; of 20 to 49 students: 58%; of 50 or more students: 5%. **Advanced Placement and International Baccalaureate credit:** AP tests may be used for: Credit only. Scores accepted: 3, 4, 5. International Baccalaureate exams may be used for: Credit only. **Freshmen returning for sophomore year:** 61%. **Graduation rates:** Four-year: 12%; five-year: 24%; six-year: 25%. **Graduate study:** 17% of students pursue further study immediately upon graduation; 24% within one year; 40% within five years. Fields in which graduates pursue further study: Master of Business Administration (MBA), 6%; law, 3%; medicine, 2%; dentistry, 1%; engineering, 3%; education, 9%; arts and sciences, 32%.

COSTS AND FINANCIAL AID

Financial aid office: (678) 466-4185. **Expenses (2009-2010):** Tuition and fees 2009-2010: $4,858 in state, $16,472 out of state; room/board: $8,078. Estimated books and supplies: $2,000; transportation: $1,002; personal expenses: $2,500. **Financial aid:** Priority filing date for institution's financial aid form: July 1. In 2009-2010, 85% of undergraduates applied for financial aid. Of those, 80% were determined to have financial need; 10% had their need fully met. Average financial aid package (proportion receiving): $4,163 (79%). Average amount of gift aid, such as scholarships or grants (proportion receiving): $2,442 (58%). Average amount of self-help aid, such as work study or loans (proportion receiving): $2,190 (66%). Average need-based loan (excluding PLUS or other private loans): $1,901. Among students who received need-based aid, the average percentage of need met: 35%. Among students who received aid based on merit, the average award (and the proportion receiving): $745 (3%). The average athletic scholarship (and the proportion receiving): $2,359 (2%).

CAMPUS LIFE AND EXTRACURRICULAR ACTIVITIES

Campus housing available (% using): coed dorms (100%). Students who live in college-owned, operated, or affiliated housing: 8%. **Student employment:** During the 2009-2010 academic year, 4% of undergraduates worked on campus. Average per-year earnings: $5,000. **Clubs and organizations:** Number of student organizations: 42. Activities include: choral groups, concert band, drama/theater, jazz band, literary magazine, music ensembles, musical theater, opera, pep band, student government, student newspaper, student film society. Number of fraternities: 5; sororities: 5. Average proportion of students who stay on campus on weekends: 10%. **Sports program (2009-2010):** Member of NCAA II. *Men's intercollegiate varsity sports:* basketball, cross country, golf, soccer, track and field (indoor). *Women's intercollegiate varsity sports:* basketball, cross country, soccer, track and field (indoor).

SERVICES AND FACILITIES
Basic services: nonremedial tutoring, placement service, health service. **Remedial assistance:** reading, math, writing, study skills. **Counseling services:** minority student, career, military, personal, veteran student, academic, older student. **For learning-disabled students:** School does not offer a structured program with separate admission and additional fees. Services include: reading machines, tape recorders, note-taking services, readers, extended time for tests, priority registration, priority seating, texts on tape, other testing accommodations. **Library:** Number of titles: 113,004; number of current serial subscriptions: 507. **Information technology resources:** Students are required to lease or own a computer. Number of campus computers available to all students: 64. School has a wireless network. Approximate number of users that can be accommodated: 1,500. Proportion of college-owned housing units wired for high-speed internet access: 100%. **Campus safety:** Security services offered: 24-hour foot-and-vehicle patrols, late-night transport/escort service, 24-hour emergency telephones, lighted pathways/sidewalks.

TRANSFER AND INTERNATIONAL STUDENTS
Transfer students: May apply for admission for the following academic terms: Fall, Spring, Summer. Applicants need a minimum number of credits to apply. For fall 2009: Transfer applications received: 1,838. Transfer applicants offered admission: 1,201. Transfer applicants enrolled: 819. **International students:** Number of foreign undergraduates: 92 (1% of student body). Number of countries represented: 82. Minimum TOEFL score required: 550 (paper); 210 (computer). Average TOEFL score: 573 (paper).

Columbus State University

- **Address:** 4225 University Avenue, Columbus, GA 31907
- **Website:** http://www.colstate.edu
- **Public**
- **Enrollment:** 4,908 full-time; 2,061 part-time

KEY STATS
✔ **U.S News College Ranking:** second tier, Regional Universities (South)
✔ **SAT Score (25th/75th percentile):** 850-1115
✔ **Tuition:** 2009-2010: $4,250 in state, $13,548 out of state

Selectivity: Less selective	**Room/board:** $7,800
Acceptance rate: 64%	**Average debt:** $21,538
Student/faculty ratio: 18/1	**Proportion who borrowed:** 64%

UNDERGRADUATE STUDENT BODY STATS
2009-2010 enrollment: 4,908 full-time; 2,061 part-time. Men: 40%; women: 60%. **Ethnic makeup:** African American: 34%; American-Indian: 1%; Asian American: 2%; Hispanic: 5%; White: 58%; International: 1%.

ADMISSIONS FACTS AND FIGURES
Phone: (706) 568-2035. **Email:** admissions@colstate.edu. **Website:** http://www.colstate.edu. **Application deadlines for fall 2011:** Regular decision: June 30. Early decision: Not offered. Early action: Not offered. Admission can be deferred. **Application fee:** $30. **To apply online, go to:** http://www.colstate.edu/future/apply/. **Admissions requirements/recommendations:** High school units required (recommended): English: 4; Mathematics: 4; Science: 3; Foreign language: 2; Social studies: 3; Total units: 16. Tests: The college uses SAT or ACT scores in admissions decisions. Either SAT or ACT required. For admission to the fall 2011 entering class, the school will accept: ACT with or without writing accepted. Campus visit: Recommended. Admissions interview: Neither required nor recommended. Off-campus interview: Not available. **Factors that count in admissions decisions:** *Academic:* Secondary school record: Very Important. Class rank: Not Considered. Letters of recommendation: Not Considered. Standardized test scores: Important. Essay: Not Considered. *Nonacademic:* Interview: Considered. Extracurricular activities: Considered. Talent/ability: Considered. Character/personal qualities: Not Considered. Alumni/ae relationship: Not Considered. Geographical residence: Considered. State resi-

dency: Not Considered. Religious affiliation/commitment: Not Considered. Minority status: Not Considered. Volunteer work: Not Considered. Work experience: Not Considered. **Admissions statistics for the fall 2009 entering class:** Total applicants: 3,445. Total accepted: 2,204. Freshmen enrolled: 1,319; 10% were from out of state. Overall acceptance rate: 64%. **Average high school grade point average:** 3.0. **First-year students who submitted SAT scores:** 78%. Scores (25/75 percentile): Critical Reading: 430-575, Math: 420-540, Combined: 850-1115. **First-year students submitting ACT scores:** 35%. Scores (25/75 percentile): English: 16-22, Math: 15-22, Composite: 17-22.

ACADEMICS
Year founded: 1958. **Academic calendar:** Semester. **Degrees offered:** certificate, associate, bachelor's, post-bachelor's certificate, master's, post-master's certificate, doctorate. **Most popular majors:** 27% business, management, marketing, and related support services, 17% education, 13% health professions and related clinical sciences, 9% security and protective services, 8% English language and literature/letters. **Major fields of study:** biological and biomedical sciences; business, management, marketing, and related support services; communication, journalism, and related programs; education; English language and literature/letters; foreign languages, literatures, and linguistics; health professions and related clinical sciences; history; mathematics and statistics; physical sciences; psychology; social sciences; visual and performing arts. **Areas of required coursework:** arts/fine arts, humanities, computer literacy, mathematics, English (including composition), sciences (biological or physical), history, social science. **Pre-professional programs:** pre-medicine, other. **Special academic programs:** accelerated program, cooperative (work-study plan) program, distance learning, double major, dual enrollment, English as a Second Language (ESL), honors program, independent study, internships, liberal arts/career combination, study abroad, teacher certificate program. **Teacher certification offered in:** early childhood, special education, middle/junior high, secondary. **Reserve Officers Training Corps (ROTC):** Army ROTC: Offered on campus. **Faculty and instruction (2009-2010):** Total instructional faculty: 261 full-time, 192 part-time (54% men; 46% women; 20% minorities). Full-time faculty with Ph.D. or other terminal degree: 79%. Student/faculty ratio: 18/1. Classes of fewer than 20 students: 38%; of 20 to 49 students: 58%; of 50 or more students: 5%. **Advanced Placement and International Baccalaureate credit:** AP tests may be used for: Credit only. **Freshmen returning for sophomore year:** 69%. **Graduation rates:** Four-year: 11%; five-year: 25%; six-year: 33%.

COSTS AND FINANCIAL AID
Financial aid office: (706) 568-2036. **Expenses (2009-2010):** Tuition and fees 2009-2010: $4,250 in state, $13,548 out of state; room/board: $7,800. Estimated books and supplies: $933; transportation: $1,387; personal expenses: $1,844. **Financial aid:** Priority filing date for institution's financial aid form: May 1. In 2009-2010, 78% of undergraduates applied for financial aid. Of those, 62% were determined to have financial need; 22% had their need fully met. Average financial aid package (proportion receiving): $8,161 (60%). Average amount of gift aid, such as scholarships or grants (proportion receiving): $4,804 (41%). Average amount of self-help aid, such as work study or loans (proportion receiving): $4,194 (46%). Average need-based loan (excluding PLUS or other private loans): $3,993. Among students who received need-based aid, the average percentage of need met: 72%. Among students who received aid based on merit, the average award (and the proportion receiving): $1,514 (3%). The average athletic scholarship (and the proportion receiving): $4,810 (4%). Average amount of debt of borrowers graduating in 2009: $21,538. Proportion who borrowed: 64%.

CAMPUS LIFE AND EXTRACURRICULAR ACTIVITIES
Campus housing available (% using): coed dorms (94%), apartment for single students (4%), special housing for disabled students (1%), special housing for international students (1%). Students who live in college-owned, operated, or affiliated housing: 18%. **Student employment:** During the 2009-2010 academic year, 4% of undergraduates worked on campus. Average per-year earnings: $6. **Clubs and organizations:** Number of student organizations: 62. Activities include: campus ministries, choral groups, concert band, dance, drama/theater, international student organization, jazz band, literary magazine, model UN, music ensembles, musical theater, opera, pep band, student government, student newspaper, symphony orchestra. Number of fraternities: 8; sororities: 8. Proportion of men in fraternities: 2%; of women in sororities: 2%. **Sports program (2009-2010):** Member of NCAA II. *Men's intercollegiate varsity sports:* baseball, basketball, cross country, golf, rifle, tennis, track and field (indoor). *Women's intercollegiate varsity sports:* basketball, cross country, golf, rifle, soccer, softball, tennis, track and field (indoor).

SERVICES AND FACILITIES

Basic services: nonremedial tutoring, placement service, health service, other. **Remedial assistance:** reading, math, writing, study skills. **Counseling services:** minority student, career, military, personal, veteran student, academic, older student, psychological. **For learning-disabled students:** School does not offer a structured program with separate admission and additional fees. Total undergraduates in learning-disabled program or receiving services: 46. Services include: remedial math, remedial English, reading machines, remedial reading, tape recorders, videotaped classes, diagnostic testing service, untimed tests, note-taking services, oral tests, learning center, readers, extended time for tests, tutors, early syllabus, priority registration, priority seating, substitution of courses, texts on tape, typist/scribe, exams on tape or computer, waiver of foreign language degree requirement. **Library:** Number of titles: 384,219; number of current serial subscriptions: 1,879. **Information technology resources:** Students are not required to lease or own a computer. School has a wireless network. Approximate number of users that can be accommodated: 9,000. Proportion of college-owned housing units wired for high-speed internet access: 100%. **Campus safety:** Security services offered: 24-hour foot-and-vehicle patrols, late-night transport/escort service, 24-hour emergency telephones, lighted pathways/sidewalks, controlled dormitory access (key, security card, etc).

TRANSFER AND INTERNATIONAL STUDENTS

Transfer students: May apply for admission for the following academic terms: Fall, Spring, Summer. Applicants need a minimum number of credits to apply. For fall 2009: Transfer applications received: 1,547. Transfer applicants offered admission: 1,095. Transfer applicants enrolled: 631. **International students:** Number of foreign undergraduates: 74 (1% of student body). Minimum TOEFL score required: 550 (paper); 213 (computer). Average TOEFL score: 564 (paper).

Covenant College

- **Address:** 14049 Scenic Highway, Lookout Mountain, GA 30750
- **Website:** http://www.covenant.edu
- **Private; Religious affiliation:** Presbyterian Church in America
- **Enrollment:** 965 full-time; 33 part-time

KEY STATS
- ✔ **U.S News College Ranking:** 6, Regional Colleges (South)
- ✔ **SAT Score (25th/75th percentile):** 1050-1280
- ✔ **Tuition:** 2010-2011: $26,226

Selectivity: More selective	**Room/board:** $7,450
Acceptance rate: 60%	**Average debt:** $15,478
Student/faculty ratio: 14/1	**Proportion who borrowed:** 70%

UNDERGRADUATE STUDENT BODY STATS

2009-2010 enrollment: 965 full-time; 33 part-time. Men: 44%; women: 56%. **Ethnic makeup:** African American: 2%; Asian American: 2%; Hispanic: 2%; White: 93%; International: 1%. **Religious preference:** Roman Catholic: 1%; Protestant: 41%; Presbyterian Church in America: 52%; Other: 6%.

ADMISSIONS FACTS AND FIGURES

Phone: (706) 820-2398. **Email:** admissions@covenant.edu. **Website:** http://www.covenant.edu. **Application deadlines for fall 2011:** Regular decision: Rolling. Early decision: Not offered. Early action: Not offered. Admission can be deferred. **Application fee:** $35. **To apply online, go to:** http://www.covenant.edu/admissions/trad/application.php. **Admissions requirements/recommendations:** High school units required (recommended): English: 4 (4); Mathematics: 3 (3); Science: 2 (2); Foreign language: (2); Social studies: 2 (2); Academic electives: 3 (3); Total units: 16 (16). Tests: The college uses SAT or ACT scores in admissions decisions. Either SAT or ACT required. For admission to the fall 2011 entering class, the school will accept: ACT with or without writing accepted. Campus visit: Recommended. Admissions interview: Neither required nor recommended. Off-campus interview: Not available. **Factors that count in admissions decisions:** *Academic:* Secondary school record: Very Important. Class rank: Considered. Letters of recommendation: Very Important. Standardized test scores: Very Important. Essay: Very Important. *Nonacademic:* Interview: Important. Extracurricular activities: Considered. Talent/ability: Not Considered. Character/personal qualities: Very Important. Alumni/ae relationship: Considered. Geographical residence: Not Considered. State residency: Not Considered. Religious affiliation/commitment: Considered. Minority status: Considered.

Volunteer work: Considered. Work experience: Not Considered. **Other schools with the greatest overlap in applicants:** Berry College; Gordon College; Samford University; University of Georgia; Wheaton College. **Admissions statistics for the fall 2009 entering class:** Total applicants: 1,078. Total accepted: 649. Freshmen enrolled: 277; 75% were from out of state. Overall acceptance rate: 60%. **Credentials of fall 2009 freshmen:** 31% ranked in the top 10 percent of their high school class; 56% were in the top 25 percent; 76% were in the top half. (Proportion submitting class standing: 35%.) **Average high school grade point average:** 3.7. **First-year students who submitted SAT scores:** 72%. Scores (25/75 percentile): Critical Reading: 540-660, Math: 510-620, Combined: 1050-1280. **First-year students submitting ACT scores:** 61%. Scores (25/75 percentile): English: 22-30, Math: 21-27, Composite: 22-28.

ACADEMICS

Year founded: 1955. **Academic calendar:** Semester. **Degrees offered:** associate, bachelor's, master's. **Most popular majors:** 21% social sciences, 12% visual and performing arts, 9% education, 8% theology and religious vocations, 7% English language and literature/letters. **Major fields of study:** biological and biomedical sciences; business, management, marketing, and related support services; computer and information sciences and support services; education; English language and literature/letters; health professions and related clinical sciences; history; mathematics and statistics; multi/interdisciplinary studies; philosophy and religious studies; physical sciences; psychology; social sciences; theology and religious vocations; visual and performing arts. **Areas of required coursework:** arts/fine arts, humanities, mathematics, English (including composition), philosophy, foreign languages, sciences (biological or physical), history, social science, other. **Pre-professional programs:** pre-law, pre-medicine, other. **Special academic programs (% participation):** double major (4%), dual enrollment (0%), exchange student program (domestic) (1%), independent study (100%), internships (10%), student-designed major (8%), study abroad (10%), teacher certificate program (9%). **Teacher certification offered in:** early childhood, elementary, middle/junior high, secondary. **Reserve Officers Training Corps (ROTC):** Army ROTC: Offered at cooperating institution (University of Tennessee–Chattanooga). **Faculty and instruction (2009-2010):** Total instructional faculty: 58 full-time, 29 part-time (78% men; 22% women; 8% minorities). Full-time faculty with Ph.D. or other terminal degree: 88%. Student/faculty ratio: 14/1. Classes of fewer than 20 students: 59%; of 20 to 49 students: 41%; of 50 or more students: 0%. **Advanced Placement and International Baccalaureate credit:** AP tests may be used for: Placement only. Scores accepted: 3. International Baccalaureate exams may be used for: Credit and/or placement. **Freshmen returning for sophomore year:** 75%. **Graduation rates:** Four-year: 47%; five-year: 56%; six-year: 61%. **Graduate study:** 16% of students pursue further study immediately upon graduation. Fields in which graduates pursue further study: Master of Business Administration (MBA), 5%; medicine, 5%; dentistry, 5%; theology (or the seminary), 15%; education, 5%; arts and sciences, 65%.

COSTS AND FINANCIAL AID

Financial aid office: (706) 419-1126. **Expenses (2010-2011):** Tuition and fees 2010-2011: $26,226; room/board: $7,450. Estimated books and supplies: $1,000; transportation: $650; personal expenses: $650. **Financial aid:** Priority filing date for institution's financial aid form: March 1. In 2009-2010, 71% of undergraduates applied for financial aid. Of those, 61% were determined to have financial need; 28% had their need fully met. Average financial aid package (proportion receiving): $18,697 (61%). Average amount of gift aid, such as scholarships or grants (proportion receiving): $14,104 (59%). Average amount of self-help aid, such as work study or loans (proportion receiving): $7,014 (53%). Average need-based loan (excluding PLUS or other private loans): $4,336. Among students who received need-based aid, the average percentage of need met: 77%. Among students who received aid based on merit, the average award (and the proportion receiving): $8,403 (22%). The average athletic scholarship (and the proportion receiving): $5,125 (6%). Average amount of debt of borrowers graduating in 2009: $15,478. Proportion who borrowed: 70%.

CAMPUS LIFE AND EXTRACURRICULAR ACTIVITIES

Campus housing available (% using): women's dorms (52%), men's dorms (41%), apartment for single students (7%). Students who live in college-owned, operated, or affiliated housing: 84%. **Clubs and organizations:** Number of student organizations: 43. Activities include: campus ministries, choral groups, concert band, dance, drama/theater, international student organization, jazz band, literary magazine, music ensembles, musical theater, radio station, student government, student newspaper, student film society, yearbook. Number of fraternities: 0; sororities: 0. Average proportion of students who stay on campus on weekends: 90%. **Sports program (2009-2010):** Member of NAIA. *Men's intercollegiate varsity sports:* baseball, basketball, cross country, golf, soccer, tennis. *Women's intercollegiate varsity sports:* basketball, cross country, golf, soccer, softball, tennis, volleyball.

SERVICES AND FACILITIES

Basic services: placement service, health service, health insurance. **Remedial assistance:** math, writing, study skills, other. **Counseling services:** career, personal, psychological, religious, other. **For learning-disabled students:** School does not offer a structured program with separate admission and additional fees. Total undergraduates in learning-disabled program or receiving services: 11. Services include: remedial math, remedial English, reading machines, tape recorders, other special classes, extended time for tests, tutors, proofreading services, texts on tape. **Library:** Number of titles: 83,720; number of current serial subscriptions: 525. **Information technology resources:** Students are not required to lease or own a computer. Number of campus computers available to all students: 130. School has a wireless network. Approximate number of users that can be accommodated: 900. Proportion of college-owned housing units wired for high-speed internet access: 100%. **Campus safety:** Security services offered: late-night transport/escort service, lighted pathways/sidewalks, controlled dormitory access (key, security card, etc).

TRANSFER AND INTERNATIONAL STUDENTS

Transfer students: May apply for admission for the following academic terms: Fall, Spring. Applicants need a minimum number of credits to apply. For fall 2009: Transfer applications received: 193. Transfer applicants offered admission: 77. Transfer applicants enrolled: 31. **International students:** Number of foreign undergraduates: 14 (1% of student body). Number of countries represented: 9. Minimum TOEFL score required: 540 (paper); 76 (computer). Average TOEFL score: 590 (paper).

Dalton State College

- **Address:** 650 College Drive, Dalton, GA 30720
- **Website:** http://www.daltonstate.edu/
- **Public**
- **Enrollment:** N/A

KEY STATS

- ✔ **U.S News College Ranking:** Unranked, Regional Colleges (South)
- ✔ **SAT or ACT Score (25th/75th percentile):** N/A
- ✔ **Tuition:** 2009-2010: $2,900 in state, $10,382 out of state

Selectivity: N/A	Room/board: $4,440
Acceptance rate: N/A	Average debt: N/A
Student/faculty ratio: N/A	Proportion who borrowed: N/A

Emmanuel College

- **Address:** PO Box 129, Franklin Springs, GA 30639
- **Website:** http://www.ec.edu
- **Private; Religious affiliation:** International Pentecostal Holiness
- **Enrollment:** 660 full-time; 72 part-time

KEY STATS

- ✔ **U.S News College Ranking:** 64, Regional Colleges (South)
- ✔ **SAT Score (25th/75th percentile):** 840-1080
- ✔ **Tuition:** 2009-2010: $12,880

Selectivity: Less selective	Room/board: $5,520
Acceptance rate: 32%	Average debt: N/A
Student/faculty ratio: 15/1	Proportion who borrowed: N/A

UNDERGRADUATE STUDENT BODY STATS

2009-2010 enrollment: 660 full-time; 72 part-time. Men: 46%; women: 54%. **Ethnic makeup:** African American: 21%; Asian American: 1%; Hispanic: 6%; White: 71%; International: 1%. **Religious preference:** Protestant: 79%; International Pentecostal Holiness: 21%.

ADMISSIONS FACTS AND FIGURES

Phone: (800) 860-8800. **Email:** admissions@ec.edu. **Website:** http://www.ec.edu. **Application deadlines for fall 2011:** Regular decision: August 1. Early decision: Not offered. Early action: Not offered. Admission can be deferred. **Application fee:** $25. **To apply online, go to:** http://www.gacollege411.org/Applications/Emmanuel_College_GA/apply.html. **Admissions requirements/recommendations:** Tests: The college uses SAT or ACT scores in admissions decisions. Either SAT or ACT required. For admission to the fall 2011 entering class, the school will accept: ACT with or without writing accepted. Campus visit: Recommended. Admissions interview: Neither required nor recommended. Off-campus interview: May be arranged. **Factors that count in admissions decisions:** *Academic:* Secondary school record: Very Important. Class rank: Not Considered. Letters of recommendation: Considered. Standardized test scores: Very Important. Essay: Not Considered. *Nonacademic:* Interview: Considered. Extracurricular activities: Not Considered. Talent/ability: Not Considered. Character/personal qualities: Not Considered. Alumni/ae relationship: Not Considered. Geographical residence: Not Considered. State residency: Not Considered. Religious affiliation/commitment: Considered. Minority status: Not Considered. Volunteer work: Not Considered. Work experience: Not Considered. **Other schools with the greatest overlap in applicants:** Piedmont College; University of Georgia. **Admissions statistics for the fall 2009 entering class:** Total applicants: 912. Total accepted: 295. Freshmen enrolled: 164; 23% were from out of state. Overall acceptance rate: 32%. **Average high school grade point average:** 3.1. **First-year students who submitted SAT scores:** 67%. Scores (25/75 percentile): Critical Reading: 420-540, Math: 420-540, Combined: 840-1080. **First-year students submitting ACT scores:** 1%. Scores (25/75 percentile): English: N/A, Math: N/A, Composite: N/A.

ACADEMICS

Year founded: 1919. **Academic calendar:** Semester. **Degrees offered:** associate, bachelor's. **Most popular majors:** 27% teacher education and professional development, 16% business administration, management, and operations, 12% theological and ministerial studies. **Major fields of study:** biological and biomedical sciences; business, management, marketing, and related support services; communication, journalism, and related programs; computer and information sciences and support services; education; English language and literature/letters; health professions and related clinical sciences; history; legal professions and studies; mathematics and statistics; parks, recreation, leisure, and fitness studies; psychology; theology and religious vocations; visual and performing arts. **Areas of required coursework:** humanities, mathematics, English (including composition), philosophy, sciences (biological or physical), history, social science. **Pre-professional programs:** pre-law, pre-medicine, pre-pharmacy. **Special academic programs (% participation):** distance learning (5%), dual enrollment (3%), independent study (5%), internships (15%), teacher certificate program (15%). **Teacher certification offered in:** early childhood, middle/junior high, secondary. **Faculty and instruction (2009-2010):** Total instructional faculty: 36 full-time, 33 part-time (58% men; 42% women; 1% minorities). Full-time faculty with Ph.D. or other terminal degree: 69%. Student/faculty ratio: 15/1. Classes of fewer than 20 students: 59%; of 20 to 49 students: 41%; of 50 or more students: 0%. **Advanced Placement and International Baccalaureate credit:** AP tests may be used for: Credit only. Scores accepted: 3, 4, 5. **Freshmen returning for sophomore year:** 65%. **Graduation rates:** Four-year: 29%; five-year: 36%; six-year: 36%. **Graduate study:** 50% of students pursue further study immediately upon graduation.

COSTS AND FINANCIAL AID

Financial aid office: (706) 245-2843. **Expenses (2009-2010):** Tuition and fees 2009-2010: $12,880; room/board: $5,520. Estimated books and supplies: $800. **Financial aid:** Priority filing date for institution's financial aid form: March 15; deadline: May 1.

CAMPUS LIFE AND EXTRACURRICULAR ACTIVITIES

Campus housing available (% using): women's dorms (40%), men's dorms (40%), apartments for married students (20%). Students who live in college-owned, operated, or affiliated housing: 46%. **Clubs and organizations:** Number of student organizations: 20. Activities include: campus ministries, choral groups, drama/theater, international student organization, literary magazine, music ensembles, musical theater, student government, student newspaper, yearbook. Number of fraternities: 0; sororities: 0. Average proportion of students who stay on campus on weekends: 30%. **Sports program (2009-2010):** Member of NAIA. *Men's intercollegiate varsity sports:* baseball, basketball, soccer, tennis. *Women's intercollegiate varsity sports:* basketball, soccer, softball, tennis.

SERVICES AND FACILITIES

Basic services: nonremedial tutoring, health insurance. **Remedial assistance:** reading, math, writing. **Counseling services:** minority student, career, personal, veteran student, academic, religious. **For learning-disabled students:** School does not offer a structured program with separate admission and additional fees. Services include: remedial math, remedial English, remedial reading. **Library:** Number of titles: 83,700; number of current serial subscriptions: 74. **Information technology resources:** Students are not required to lease or own a computer. Number of campus computers available to all students: 60. School has a wireless network. Approximate number of users that can be accommodated: 200. Proportion of college-owned housing units wired for high-speed internet access: 100%. **Campus safety:** Security services offered: 24-hour foot-and-vehicle patrols, lighted pathways/sidewalks, student patrols, controlled dormitory access (key, security card, etc).

TRANSFER AND INTERNATIONAL STUDENTS

Transfer students: May apply for admission for the following academic terms: Fall, Spring, Summer. Applicants do not need a minimum number of credits to apply. For fall 2009: Transfer applications received: 204. Transfer applicants offered admission: 119. Transfer applicants enrolled: 75. **International students:** Number of foreign undergraduates: 9 (1% of student body). Number of countries represented: 5. Minimum TOEFL score required: 550 (paper); 213 (computer).

Emory University

- **Address:** 201 Dowman Drive, Atlanta, GA 30322
- **Website:** http://www.emory.edu
- **Private; Religious affiliation:** Methodist
- **Enrollment:** 6,884 full-time; 96 part-time

KEY STATS

✔ **U.S News College Ranking:** 20, National Universities
✔ **SAT Score (25th/75th percentile):** 1300-1480
✔ **Tuition:** 2010-2011: $39,158

Selectivity: Most selective	**Room/board:** $11,198
Acceptance rate: 30%	**Average debt:** $25,865
Student/faculty ratio: 7/1	**Proportion who borrowed:** 42%

UNDERGRADUATE STUDENT BODY STATS

2009-2010 enrollment: 6,884 full-time; 96 part-time. Men: 45%; women: 55%. **Ethnic makeup:** African American: 10%; Asian American: 22%; Hispanic: 4%; White: 55%; International: 8%. **Religious preference:** Roman Catholic: 13%; Protestant: 23%; Jewish: 25%; Muslim: 2%; Hindu: 6%; Buddhist: 1%; No preference: 22%; Methodist: 6%; Other: 2%.

ADMISSIONS FACTS AND FIGURES

Phone: (404) 727-6036. **Email:** admiss@emory.edu. **Website:** http://www.emory.edu. **Application deadlines for fall 2011:** Regular decision: January 15; decision sent by April 1. Early decision: Send application by: November 1; Decision sent by: December 15. Early action: Not offered. Admission can be deferred. **Application fee:** $50. **To apply online, go to:** http://www.emory.edu/ADMISSIONS/admission-aid/application.htm. **Admissions requirements/recommendations:** High school units required (recommended): English: 4; Mathematics: 3 (4); Science: 2 (3); Foreign language: 2 (3); Social studies: 2; History: 2; Academic electives: 2; Total units: 16. Tests: The college uses SAT or ACT scores in admissions decisions. Either SAT or ACT required. For admission to the fall 2011 entering class, the school will accept: ACT with writing required. Campus visit: Neither required nor recommended. Admissions interview: Neither required nor recommended. **Factors that count in admissions decisions:** *Academic:* Secondary school record: Very Important. Class rank: Considered. Letters of recommendation: Very Important. Standardized test scores: Very Important. Essay: Very Important. *Nonacademic:* Interview: Considered. Extracurricular activities: Very Important. Talent/ability: Very Important. Character/personal qualities: Very Important. Alumni/ae relationship: Important. Geographical residence: Important. State residency: Not Considered. Religious affiliation/commitment: Not Considered. Minority status: Important. Volunteer work: Important. Work experience: Important. **Other schools with the greatest overlap in applicants:** Duke University; Georgetown University; University of Pennsylvania; Vanderbilt University; Washington University in St. Louis. **Admissions statistics for the fall 2009 entering class:** Total applicants: 15,599. Total accepted: 4,627. Freshmen enrolled: 1,315; 73% were from

out of state. Overall acceptance rate: 30%. Early-decision acceptance rate: 35%. Non-early acceptance rate: 29%. **Size of waiting list:** 4585 applicants; enrolled from waiting list: 140. **Credentials of fall 2009 freshmen:** 85% ranked in the top 10 percent of their high school class; 98% were in the top 25 percent; 100% were in the top half. (Proportion submitting class standing: 39%.) **First-year students who submitted SAT scores:** 84%. Scores (25/75 percentile): Critical Reading: 640-730; Math: 660-750; Combined: 1300-1480. **First-year students submitting ACT scores:** 46%. Scores (25/75 percentile): English: N/A, Math: N/A, Composite: 29-33.

ACADEMICS

Year founded: 1836. **Academic calendar:** Semester. **Degrees offered:** associate, bachelor's, master's, doctorate. **Most popular majors:** 25% social sciences, 17% business administration and management, 9% psychology, 8% biology/biological sciences. **Major fields of study:** area, ethnic, cultural, and gender studies; biological and biomedical sciences; business, management, marketing, and related support services; computer and information sciences and support services; education; English language and literature/letters; foreign languages, literatures, and linguistics; health professions and related clinical sciences; history; mathematics and statistics; natural resources and conservation; philosophy and religious studies; physical sciences; psychology; social sciences; visual and performing arts. **Areas of required coursework:** arts/fine arts, humanities, mathematics, English (including composition), foreign languages, sciences (biological or physical), history, social science, other. **Special academic programs (% participation):** cooperative (work-study plan) program (29%), cross-registration, double major, dual enrollment, English as a Second Language (ESL), honors program, independent study (29%), internships (49%), liberal arts/career combination, study abroad (40%), teacher certificate program, other. **Teacher certification offered in:** middle/junior high, secondary. **Cooperative education programs:** business, education. **Reserve Officers Training Corps (ROTC):** Army ROTC: Offered at cooperating institution (Georgia Institute of Technology); Navy ROTC: Offered at cooperating institution (Georgia Institute of Technology); Air Force ROTC: Offered at cooperating institution (Georgia Institute of Technology). **Faculty and instruction (2009-2010):** Total instructional faculty: 1,279 full-time, 200 part-time (59% men; 41% women; 16% minorities). Full-time faculty with Ph.D. or other terminal degree: 99%. Student/faculty ratio: 7/1. Classes of fewer than 20 students: 64%; of 20 to 49 students: 27%; of 50 or more students: 9%. **Advanced Placement and International Baccalaureate credit:** AP tests may be used for: Credit and/or placement. Scores accepted: 4, 5. International Baccalaureate exams may be used for: Credit and/or placement. **Freshmen returning for sophomore year:** 95%. **Graduation rates:** Four-year: 84%; five-year: 88%; six-year: 90%. **Graduate study:** 37% of students pursue further study immediately upon graduation. Fields in which graduates pursue further study: Master of Business Administration (MBA), 6%; law, 21%; medicine, 30%; arts and sciences, 32%.

COSTS AND FINANCIAL AID

Financial aid office: (404) 727-6039. **Expenses (2010-2011):** Tuition and fees 2010-2011: $39,158; room/board: $11,198. Estimated books and supplies: $1,100; transportation: $900; personal expenses: $1,200. **Financial aid:** Priority filing date for institution's financial aid form: February 15; deadline: March 1. In 2009-2010, 51% of undergraduates applied for financial aid. Of those, 45% were determined to have financial need; 95% had their need fully met. Average financial aid package (proportion receiving): $32,415 (45%). Average amount of gift aid, such as scholarships or grants (proportion receiving): $28,053 (43%). Average amount of self-help aid, such as work study or loans (proportion receiving): $4,848 (39%). Average need-based loan (excluding PLUS or other private loans): $4,333. Among students who received need-based aid, the average percentage of need met: 100%. Among students who received aid based on merit, the average award (and the proportion receiving): $21,345 (6%). Average amount of debt of borrowers graduating in 2009: $25,865. Proportion who borrowed: 42%.

CAMPUS LIFE AND EXTRACURRICULAR ACTIVITIES

Campus housing available: coed dorms, women's dorms, men's dorms, sorority housing, fraternity housing, apartments for married students, apartment for single students, special housing for disabled students, special housing for international students. Students who live in college-owned, operated, or affiliated housing: 67%. **Student employment:** During the 2009-2010 academic year, 28% of undergraduates worked on campus. Average per-year earnings: $1,505. **Clubs and organizations:** Number of student organizations: 252. Activities include: campus ministries, choral groups, concert band, dance, drama/theater, international student organization, jazz band, literary magazine, marching band, music ensembles, musical theater, opera, pep band, radio station, student government, student newspaper, student film society, symphony orchestra, television station. Number of fraternities: 14; sororities: 11. Proportion of men in fraternities: 25%; of women in sororities: 31%. **Sports program (2009-2010):** Member of NCAA III. *Men's intercollegiate varsity sports:* baseball, basketball, cross country, golf, soccer, swimming, tennis, track and field (outdoor). *Women's intercollegiate varsity sports:* basketball, cross country, soccer, softball, swimming, tennis, track and field (outdoor), volleyball.

SERVICES AND FACILITIES

Basic services: nonremedial tutoring, women's center, placement service, day care, health service, health insurance. **Counseling services:** career, personal, academic, psychological. **For learning-disabled students:** School does not offer a structured program with separate admission and additional fees. Services include: other special classes, note-taking services, oral tests, readers, extended time for tests, tutors. **Library:** Number of titles: 3,226,137; number of current serial subscriptions: 55,411. **Information technology resources:** Students are not required to lease or own a computer. Number of campus computers available to all students: 650. School has a wireless network. Proportion of college-owned housing units wired for high-speed internet access: 100%. **Campus safety:** Security services offered: 24-hour foot-and-vehicle patrols, late-night transport/escort service, 24-hour emergency telephones, lighted pathways/sidewalks, student patrols, controlled dormitory access (key, security card, etc).

TRANSFER AND INTERNATIONAL STUDENTS

Transfer students: May apply for admission for the following academic terms: Fall, Spring, Summer. Applicants need a minimum number of credits to apply. For fall 2009: Transfer applications received: 522. Transfer applicants offered admission: 206. Transfer applicants enrolled: 124. **International students:** Number of foreign undergraduates: 558 (8% of student body). Number of countries represented: 73.

Fort Valley State University

- **Address:** 1005 State University Drive, Fort Valley, GA 31030
- **Website:** http://www.fvsu.edu
- **Public**
- **Enrollment:** 3,001 full-time; 420 part-time

KEY STATS

✔ **U.S News College Ranking:** second tier, Regional Universities (South)
✔ **SAT Score (25th/75th percentile):** 822-1021
✔ **Tuition:** 2009-2010: $5,012 in state, $16,626 out of state

Selectivity: Less selective	**Room/board:** $6,188
Acceptance rate: 40%	**Average debt:** $34,190
Student/faculty ratio: 19/1	**Proportion who borrowed:** 98%

UNDERGRADUATE STUDENT BODY STATS

2009-2010 enrollment: 3,001 full-time; 420 part-time. Men: 43%; women: 57%. **Ethnic makeup:** African American: 97%; White: 2%; International: 1%.

ADMISSIONS FACTS AND FIGURES

Phone: (478) 825-6307. **Email:** admissap@mail.fvsu.edu. **Website:** http://www.fvsu.edu. **Application deadlines for fall 2011:** Regular decision: July 19. Early decision: Not offered. Early action: Not offered. Admission can be deferred. **Application fee:** $30. **Admissions requirements/recommendations:** High school units required (recommended): English: 4 (4); Mathematics: 4 (4); Science: 3 (3); Foreign language: 2 (2); Social studies: 1 (1); History: 2 (2); Total units: 16 (16). Tests: The college uses SAT or ACT scores in admissions decisions. Either SAT or ACT required. For admission to the fall 2011 entering class, the school will accept: ACT with or without writing accepted. Campus visit: Recommended. Admissions interview: Neither required nor recommended. Off-campus interview: Not available. **Factors that count in admissions decisions:** *Academic:* Secondary school record: Very Important. Class rank: Important. Letters of recommendation: Considered. Standardized test scores: Very Important. Essay: Important. *Nonacademic:* Interview: Considered. Extracurricular activities: Considered. Talent/ability: Considered. Character/personal qualities: Considered. Alumni/ae relationship: Important. Geographical residence: Considered. State residency: Considered. Religious affiliation/commitment: Not Considered. Minority status: Not Considered. Volunteer work: Considered. Work experience: Considered. **Other schools with the greatest**

overlap in applicants: Albany State University; Clark Atlanta University; Morehouse College; Morris Brown College; Savannah State University. **Admissions statistics for the fall 2009 entering class:** Total applicants: 5,343. Total accepted: 2,161. Freshmen enrolled: 998; 3% were from out of state. Overall acceptance rate: 40%. **Size of waiting list:** 807 applicants; enrolled from waiting list: 0. **Credentials of fall 2009 freshmen:** 5% ranked in the top 10 percent of their high school class; 27% were in the top 25 percent; 60% were in the top half. (Proportion submitting class standing: 39%.) **Average high school grade point average:** 2.8. **First-year students who submitted SAT scores:** 65%. Scores (25/75 percentile): Critical Reading: 412-513, Math: 410-508, Combined: 822-1021. **First-year students submitting ACT scores:** 32%. Scores (25/75 percentile): English: 16-21, Math: 17-22, Composite: 17-21.

ACADEMICS

Year founded: 1895. **Academic calendar:** Semester. **Degrees offered:** associate, bachelor's, master's. **Most popular majors:** 19% history, 17% visual and performing arts, 10% biology, 10% criminal justice and corrections, 10% psychology. **Major fields of study:** agriculture, agriculture operations, and related sciences; biological and biomedical sciences; business, management, marketing, and related support services; communication, journalism, and related programs; computer and information sciences and support services; education; engineering technologies/technicians; English language and literature/letters; family and consumer sciences/human sciences; health professions and related clinical sciences; history; mathematics and statistics; physical sciences; psychology; public administration and social service professions; security and protective services; social sciences; visual and performing arts. **Areas of required coursework:** arts/fine arts, humanities, computer literacy, mathematics, English (including composition), philosophy, foreign languages, sciences (biological or physical), history, social science. **Pre-professional programs:** pre-law, pre-dentistry, pre-medicine, pre-veterinary science, pre-pharmacy. **Special academic programs (% participation):** cross-registration (2%), distance learning (5%), double major (2%), honors program (3%), internships (30%), teacher certificate program (1%). **Teacher certification offered in:** early childhood, vo-tech, middle/junior high, secondary. **Cooperative education programs:** agriculture, computer science, health professions, home economics, natural science, technologies. **Reserve Officers Training Corps (ROTC):** Army ROTC: Offered on campus. **Faculty and instruction (2009-2010):** Total instructional faculty: 153 full-time, 49 part-time (50% men; 50% women; 71% minorities). Full-time faculty with Ph.D. or other terminal degree: 75%. Student/faculty ratio: 19/1. Classes of fewer than 20 students: 48%; of 20 to 49 students: 43%; of 50 or more students: 9%. **Advanced Placement and International Baccalaureate credit:** AP tests may be used for: Placement only. **Freshmen returning for sophomore year:** 80%. **Graduation rates:** Four-year: 13%; five-year: 34%; six-year: 35%. **Graduate study:** 27% of students pursue further study immediately upon graduation; 30% within one year; 32% within five years. Fields in which graduates pursue further study: Master of Business Administration (MBA), 5%; law, 6%; medicine, 5%; dentistry, 4%; engineering, 4%; education, 9%; arts and sciences, 13%; veterinary medicine, 3%.

COSTS AND FINANCIAL AID

Financial aid office: (478) 825-6351. **Expenses (2009-2010):** Tuition and fees 2009-2010: $5,012 in state, $16,626 out of state; room/board: $6,188. Estimated books and supplies: $1,200; transportation: $1,200; personal expenses: $400. **Financial aid:** Priority filing date for institution's financial aid form: April 15; deadline: June 30. In 2009-2010, 96% of undergraduates applied for financial aid. Of those, 96% were determined to have financial need; Average financial aid package (proportion receiving): $4,400 (84%). Average amount of gift aid, such as scholarships or grants (proportion receiving): N/A (72%). Average amount of self-help aid, such as work study or loans (proportion receiving): N/A (7%). Among students who received need-based aid, the average percentage of need met: 82%. Among students who received aid based on merit, the average award (and the proportion receiving): $1,776 (0%). The average athletic scholarship (and the proportion receiving): $2,174 (5%). Average amount of debt of borrowers graduating in 2009: $34,190. Proportion who borrowed: 98%.

CAMPUS LIFE AND EXTRACURRICULAR ACTIVITIES

Campus housing available (% using): women's dorms (53%), men's dorms (44%), special housing for international students (3%). Students who live in college-owned, operated, or affiliated housing: 62%. **Student employment:** During the 2009-2010 academic year, 2% of undergraduates worked on campus. Average per-year earnings: $4,000. **Clubs and organizations:** Number of student organizations: 75. Activities include: choral groups, concert band, drama/theater, international student organization, jazz band, marching band, music ensembles, pep band, radio station, student government, student newspaper, student film society, television station, yearbook. Number of fraternities: 5; sororities: 4. Proportion of men in fraternities: 5%; of women in sororities: 2%. Average proportion of students who stay on campus on weekends: 42%. **Sports program (2009-2010):** Member of NCAA II. **Men's intercollegiate varsity sports:** basketball, cross country, football, tennis, track and field (outdoor). **Women's intercollegiate varsity sports:** basketball, cross country, softball, tennis, track and field (outdoor), volleyball.

SERVICES AND FACILITIES
Basic services: nonremedial tutoring, placement service, health service, health insurance. **Remedial assistance:** reading, math, writing, study skills. **Counseling services:** minority student, career, personal, veteran student, academic, older student, religious. **For learning-disabled students:** School does not offer a structured program with separate admission and additional fees. Services include: remedial math, remedial English, remedial reading, tape recorders, diagnostic testing service, oral tests, readers, extended time for tests, tutors, priority registration, priority seating, substitution of courses, exams on tape or computer. **Library:** Number of titles: 192,397; number of current serial subscriptions: 835. **Information technology resources:** Students are not required to lease or own a computer. Number of campus computers available to all students: 255. School has a wireless network. Approximate number of users that can be accommodated: 1,500. Proportion of college-owned housing units wired for high-speed internet access: 54%. **Campus safety:** Security services offered: 24-hour foot-and-vehicle patrols, late-night transport/escort service, 24-hour emergency telephones, lighted pathways/sidewalks, controlled dormitory access (key, security card, etc).

TRANSFER AND INTERNATIONAL STUDENTS
Transfer students: May apply for admission for the following academic terms: Fall, Spring, Summer. Applicants need a minimum number of credits to apply. For fall 2009: Transfer applications received: 471. Transfer applicants offered admission: 218. Transfer applicants enrolled: 135. **International students:** Number of foreign undergraduates: 23 (1% of student body). Number of countries represented: 21. Minimum TOEFL score required: 523 (paper); 69 (computer).

Georgia College & State University

- **Address:** 231 W. Hancock Street, Milledgeville, GA 31061
- **Website:** http://www.gcsu.edu
- **Public**
- **Enrollment:** 5,089 full-time; 555 part-time

KEY STATS
✔ **U.S News College Ranking:** 32, Regional Universities (South)
✔ **SAT Score (25th/75th percentile):** 1040-1200
✔ **Tuition:** 2010-2011: $7,852 in state, $24,890 out of state

Selectivity: Selective	**Room/board:** $8,688
Acceptance rate: 62%	**Average debt:** $15,800
Student/faculty ratio: 17/1	**Proportion who borrowed:** 52%

UNDERGRADUATE STUDENT BODY STATS
2009-2010 enrollment: 5,089 full-time; 555 part-time. Men: 40%; women: 60%. **Ethnic makeup:** African American: 6%; Asian American: 1%; Hispanic: 3%; White: 88%; International: 1%. **Religious preference:** Roman Catholic: 9%; Protestant: 21%; Jewish: 1%; No preference: 22%; baptist: 14%; Other: 33%.

ADMISSIONS FACTS AND FIGURES
Phone: (478) 445-1283. **Email:** info@gcsu.edu. **Website:** http://www.gcsu.edu. **Application deadlines for fall 2011:** Regular decision: April 1. Early decision: Not offered. Early action: Send application by: November 1; Decision sent by: December 15. Admission can be deferred. **Application fee:** $40. **To apply online, go to:** http://www.applyweb.com/aw?gcsu. **Admissions requirements/recommendations:** High school units required (recommended): English: 4; Mathematics: 4; Science: 3; Foreign language: 2; Social studies: 3; Total units: 16. Tests: The college uses SAT or ACT scores in admissions decisions. Either SAT or ACT required. For admission to the fall 2011 entering class, the school will accept: ACT with writing required. Campus visit: Recommended. Admissions interview: Neither required nor recommended. Off-campus interview: Not available. **Factors that count in admissions decisions:** *Academic:* Secondary school record: Very Important. Class rank: Important. Letters of recommendation: Important.

Standardized test scores: Very Important. Essay: Important. *Nonacademic:* Interview: Not Considered. Extracurricular activities: Important. Talent/ability: Important. Character/personal qualities: Considered. Alumni/ae relationship: Considered. Geographical residence: Considered. State residency: Considered. Religious affiliation/commitment: Not Considered. Minority status: Considered. Volunteer work: Considered. Work experience: Considered. **Other schools with the greatest overlap in applicants:** Georgia Southern University; Georgia State University; Kennesaw State University; University of Georgia; Valdosta State University. **Admissions statistics for the fall 2009 entering class:** Total applicants: 4,080. Total accepted: 2,520. Freshmen enrolled: 1,204; 2% were from out of state. Accepted through early-decision or early-action plans: 15%. Overall acceptance rate: 62%. Non-early acceptance rate: 72%. **Size of waiting list:** 196 applicants; enrolled from waiting list: 49. **Credentials of fall 2009 freshmen:** 20% ranked in the top 10 percent of their high school class; 59% were in the top 25 percent. **Average high school grade point average:** 3.3. **First-year students who submitted SAT scores:** 85%. Scores (25/75 percentile): Critical Reading: 520-600, Math: 520-600, Combined: 1040-1200. **First-year students submitting ACT scores:** 46%. Scores (25/75 percentile): English: 22-26, Math: 21-26, Composite: 22-25.

ACADEMICS
Year founded: 1889. **Academic calendar:** Semester. **Degrees offered:** bachelor's, master's, post-master's certificate. **Most popular majors:** 9% psychology, 8% business administration and management, 8% marketing/marketing management, 8% nursing/registered nurse training (R.N., A.S.N., B.S.N., M.S.N.), 7% health teacher education. **Major fields of study:** biological and biomedical sciences; business, management, marketing, and related support services; communication, journalism, and related programs; computer and information sciences and support services; education; English language and literature/letters; foreign languages, literatures, and linguistics; health professions and related clinical sciences; history; liberal arts and sciences studies, and humanities; mathematics and statistics; natural resources and conservation; parks, recreation, leisure, and fitness studies; philosophy and religious studies; physical sciences; psychology; security and protective services; social sciences; visual and performing arts. **Areas of required coursework:** arts/fine arts, humanities, mathematics, English (including composition), foreign languages, sciences (biological or physical), history, social science. **Pre-professional programs:** pre-law, pre-dentistry, pre-medicine, pre-veterinary science, pre-optometry, pre-pharmacy, other. **Special academic programs (% participation):** accelerated program, distance learning (14.8%), double major, dual enrollment (1.22%), English as a Second Language (ESL) (.31%), honors program (4.07%), independent study (16.7%), internships (47.1%), student-designed major (.92%), study abroad (21.5%), teacher certificate program (7.32%). **Teacher certification offered in:** early childhood, special education, elementary, middle/junior high, secondary. **Reserve Officers Training Corps (ROTC):** Army ROTC: Offered at cooperating institution. **Faculty and instruction (2009-2010):** Total instructional faculty: 301 full-time, 112 part-time (47% men; 53% women; 14% minorities). Full-time faculty with Ph.D. or other terminal degree: 79%. Student/faculty ratio: 17/1. Classes of fewer than 20 students: 33%; of 20 to 49 students: 59%; of 50 or more students: 7%. **Advanced Placement and International Baccalaureate credit:** AP tests may be used for: Credit and/or placement. Scores accepted: 3, 4, 5. International Baccalaureate exams may be used for: Credit only. **Freshmen returning for sophomore year:** 84%. **Graduation rates:** Four-year: 25%; five-year: 45%; six-year: 45%.

COSTS AND FINANCIAL AID
Financial aid office: (478) 445-5149. **Expenses (2010-2011):** Tuition and fees 2010-2011: $7,852 in state, $24,890 out of state; room/board: $8,688. Estimated books and supplies: $1,200; transportation: $1,220; personal expenses: $2,489. **Financial aid:** Priority filing date for institution's financial aid form: March 1. In 2009-2010, 92% of undergraduates applied for financial aid. Of those, 45% were determined to have financial need; Average financial aid package (proportion receiving): $7,514 (43%). Average amount of gift aid, such as scholarships or grants (proportion receiving): $4,104 (20%). Average amount of self-help aid, such as work study or loans (proportion receiving): $4,122 (27%). Average need-based loan (excluding PLUS or other private loans): $4,057. Among students who received need-based aid, the average percentage of need met: 34%. Among students who received aid based on merit, the average award (and the proportion receiving): $1,197 (1%). The average athletic scholarship (and the proportion receiving): $4,708 (3%). Average amount of debt of borrowers graduating in 2009: $15,800. Proportion who borrowed: 52%.

CAMPUS LIFE AND EXTRACURRICULAR ACTIVITIES
Campus housing available (% using): coed dorms (61%), apartment for single students (37%), special housing for disabled students (1%), special housing for international students (1%). Students who live in college-owned, operated, or affiliated housing: 38%. **Student employment:** During the 2009-2010 academic year, 6% of undergraduates worked on campus. Average per-year earnings: $7,540. **Clubs and organizations:** Number of student organizations: 238. Activities include: campus ministries, choral groups, concert band, dance, drama/theater, international student organization, jazz band, literary magazine, music ensembles, musical theater, pep band, radio station, student government, student newspaper, television station. Number of fraternities: 7; sororities: 7. Proportion of men in fraternities: 2%; of women in sororities: 8%. Average proportion of students who stay on campus on weekends: 70%. **Sports program (2009-2010):** Member of NCAA II. *Men's intercollegiate varsity sports:* baseball, basketball, cross country, golf, tennis. *Women's intercollegiate varsity sports:* basketball, cross country, soccer, softball, tennis.

SERVICES AND FACILITIES
Basic services: nonremedial tutoring, women's center, health service, health insurance. **Counseling services:** minority student, career, personal, veteran student, academic, psychological. **For learning-disabled students:** School does not offer a structured program with separate admission and additional fees. Total undergraduates in learning-disabled program or receiving services: 80. Services include: reading machines, tape recorders, diagnostic testing service, untimed tests, note-taking services, oral tests, learning center, readers, extended time for tests, tutors, early syllabus, priority registration, priority seating, proofreading services, substitution of courses, texts on tape, typist/scribe, exams on tape or computer, other testing accommodations, waiver of foreign language degree requirement, other. **Library:** Number of titles: 202,254; number of current serial subscriptions: 6,381. **Information technology resources:** Students are not required to lease or own a computer. Number of campus computers available to all students: 203. School has a wireless network. Approximate number of users that can be accommodated: 3,500. Proportion of college-owned housing units wired for high-speed internet access: 100%. **Campus safety:** Security services offered: 24-hour foot-and-vehicle patrols, late-night transport/escort service, 24-hour emergency telephones, lighted pathways/sidewalks, student patrols, controlled dormitory access (key, security card, etc).

TRANSFER AND INTERNATIONAL STUDENTS
Transfer students: May apply for admission for the following academic terms: Fall, Spring, Summer. Applicants need a minimum number of credits to apply. For fall 2009: Transfer applications received: 1,123. Transfer applicants offered admission: 719. Transfer applicants enrolled: 409. **International students:** Number of foreign undergraduates: 72 (1% of student body). Number of countries represented: 39. Minimum TOEFL score required: 500 (paper); 61 (computer). Average TOEFL score: 568 (paper).

Georgia Institute of Technology

- **Address:** 225 North Avenue NW, Atlanta, GA 30332
- **Website:** http://www.gatech.edu/welcome
- **Public**
- **Enrollment:** 12,422 full-time; 1,093 part-time

KEY STATS
✔ **U.S News College Ranking:** 35, National Universities
✔ **SAT Score (25th/75th percentile):** 1230-1430
✔ **Tuition:** 2009-2010: $7,606 in state, $25,816 out of state
  Selectivity: Most selective **Room/board:** $8,204
  Acceptance rate: 59% **Average debt:** $23,352
  Student/faculty ratio: 20/1 **Proportion who borrowed:** 62%

UNDERGRADUATE STUDENT BODY STATS
2009-2010 enrollment: 12,422 full-time; 1,093 part-time. Men: 70%; women: 30%. **Ethnic makeup:** African American: 6%; Asian American: 17%; Hispanic: 4%; White: 66%; International: 6%.

ADMISSIONS FACTS AND FIGURES
Phone: (404) 894-4154. **Email:** admission@gatech.edu. **Website:** http://www.gatech.edu/welcome. **Application deadlines for fall 2011:** Regular decision: January 15; decision sent by March 15. Early decision: Not offered.

Early action: Send application by: November 1; Decision sent by: December 15. Admission cannot be deferred. **Application fee:** $65. **To apply online, go to:** http://www.admissions.gatech.edu/apply/. **Admissions requirements/recommendations:** High school units required (recommended): English: 4; Mathematics: 4; Science: 3; Foreign language: 2; Social studies: 3; History: 0; Academic electives: 0; Total units: 16. Tests: The college uses SAT or ACT scores in admissions decisions. Either SAT or ACT required. For admission to the fall 2011 entering class, the school will accept: ACT with writing required. Campus visit: Recommended. Admissions interview: Neither required nor recommended. Off-campus interview: Not available. **Factors that count in admissions decisions:** *Academic:* Secondary school record: Very Important. Class rank: Not Considered. Letters of recommendation: Not Considered. Standardized test scores: Important. Essay: Important. *Nonacademic:* Interview: Not Considered. Extracurricular activities: Very Important. Talent/ability: Important. Character/personal qualities: Important. Alumni/ae relationship: Considered. Geographical residence: Important. State residency: Important. Religious affiliation/commitment: Not Considered. Minority status: Considered. Volunteer work: Important. Work experience: Important. **Other schools with the greatest overlap in applicants:** Duke University; Emory University; University of Georgia; University of Michigan–Ann Arbor; Virginia Tech. **Admissions statistics for the fall 2009 entering class:** Total applicants: 11,432. Total accepted: 6,721. Freshmen enrolled: 2,660; 32% were from out of state. Overall acceptance rate: 59%. Non-early acceptance rate: 59%. **Size of waiting list:** 450 applicants; enrolled from waiting list: 123. **Credentials of fall 2009 freshmen:** 81% ranked in the top 10 percent of their high school class; 95% were in the top 25 percent; 100% were in the top half. (Proportion submitting class standing: 53%.) **Average high school grade point average:** 3.8. **First-year students who submitted SAT scores:** 93%. Scores (25/75 percentile): Critical Reading: 580-680, Math: 650-750, Combined: 1230-1430. **First-year students submitting ACT scores:** 49%. Scores (25/75 percentile): English: 26-32, Math: 28-33, Composite: 27-31.

ACADEMICS
Year founded: 1885. **Academic calendar:** Semester. **Degrees offered:** bachelor's, master's, doctorate. **Most popular majors:** 57% engineering, 14% business, management, marketing, and related support services, 6% computer and information sciences and support services, 5% architecture and related services, 4% biological and biomedical sciences. **Major fields of study:** architecture and related services; biological and biomedical sciences; business, management, marketing, and related support services; communication, journalism, and related programs; computer and information sciences and support services; engineering; history; mathematics and statistics; multi/interdisciplinary studies; physical sciences; psychology; public administration and social service professions; social sciences; visual and performing arts. **Areas of required coursework:** humanities, computer literacy, mathematics, English (including composition), sciences (biological or physical), history, social science, other. **Pre-professional programs:** pre-law, pre-dentistry, pre-medicine, pre-veterinary science, pre-optometry, pre-pharmacy. **Special academic programs (% participation):** accelerated program, cooperative (work-study plan) program (21%), cross-registration (2%), distance learning, double major (5%), dual enrollment (.2%), English as a Second Language (ESL), honors program, independent study, internships (13%), student-designed major, study abroad (26%), other. **Cooperative education programs:** business, computer science, engineering, other. **Reserve Officers Training Corps (ROTC):** Army ROTC: Offered on campus; Navy ROTC: Offered on campus; Air Force ROTC: Offered on campus. **Faculty and instruction (2009-2010):** Total instructional faculty: 939 full-time, 125 part-time (78% men; 22% women; 27% minorities). Full-time faculty with Ph.D. or other terminal degree: 97%. Student/faculty ratio: 20/1. Classes of fewer than 20 students: 38%; of 20 to 49 students: 38%; of 50 or more students: 24%. **Advanced Placement and International Baccalaureate credit:** AP tests may be used for: Credit and/or placement. Scores accepted: 4, 5. International Baccalaureate exams may be used for: Credit only. **Freshmen returning for sophomore year:** 93%. **Graduation rates:** Four-year: 31%; five-year: 71%; six-year: 79%. **Graduate study:** 28% of students pursue further study immediately upon graduation; 42% within five years. Fields in which graduates pursue further study: Master of Business Administration (MBA), 2%; law, 8%; medicine, 20%; dentistry, 1%; engineering, 46%; theology (or the seminary), 1%; education, 2%; arts and sciences, 16%.

COSTS AND FINANCIAL AID
Financial aid office: (404) 894-4582. **Expenses (2009-2010):** Tuition and fees 2009-2010: $7,606 in state, $25,816 out of state; room/board: $8,204. **Financial aid:** Priority filing date for institution's financial aid form: March 1; deadline: March 1. In 2009-2010, 58% of undergraduates applied for

financial aid. Of those, 34% were determined to have financial need; 26% had their need fully met. Average financial aid package (proportion receiving): $10,933 (33%). Average amount of gift aid, such as scholarships or grants (proportion receiving): $9,265 (29%). Average amount of self-help aid, such as work study or loans (proportion receiving): $4,772 (22%). Average need-based loan (excluding PLUS or other private loans): $4,532. Among students who received need-based aid, the average percentage of need met: 72%. Among students who received aid based on merit, the average award (and the proportion receiving): $4,368 (5%). The average athletic scholarship (and the proportion receiving): $14,917 (2%). Average amount of debt of borrowers graduating in 2009: $23,352. Proportion who borrowed: 62%.

CAMPUS LIFE AND EXTRACURRICULAR ACTIVITIES

Campus housing available (% using): coed dorms (22%), women's dorms (5%), men's dorms (11%), sorority housing (2%), fraternity housing (14%), apartments for married students (4%), apartment for single students (38%), special housing for disabled students (1%), special housing for international students (0%). Students who live in college-owned, operated, or affiliated housing: 60%. **Clubs and organizations:** Number of student organizations: 429. Activities include: campus ministries, choral groups, concert band, dance, drama/theater, international student organization, jazz band, literary magazine, marching band, model UN, music ensembles, musical theater, pep band, radio station, student government, student newspaper, student film society, symphony orchestra, television station, yearbook. Number of fraternities: 38; sororities: 14. Proportion of men in fraternities: 23%; of women in sororities: 33%. Average proportion of students who stay on campus on weekends: 65%. **Sports program (2009-2010):** Member of NCAA I. *Men's intercollegiate varsity sports:* baseball, basketball, cross country, football, golf, swimming, tennis, track and field (indoor), track and field (outdoor). *Women's intercollegiate varsity sports:* basketball, cross country, softball, swimming, tennis, track and field (indoor), track and field (outdoor), volleyball.

SERVICES AND FACILITIES

Basic services: nonremedial tutoring, women's center, placement service, day care, health service, health insurance. **Remedial assistance:** reading, math, writing. **Counseling services:** minority student, career, personal, academic, older student, psychological, birth control, other. **For learning-disabled students:** School does not offer a structured program with separate admission and additional fees. Services include: tape recorders, videotaped classes, diagnostic testing service, note-taking services, oral tests, learning center, readers, extended time for tests, tutors, priority registration, priority seating, substitution of courses, texts on tape, typist/scribe, exams on tape or computer, other testing accommodations, other. **Library:** Number of titles: 2,541,880; number of current serial subscriptions: 41,412. **Information technology resources:** Students are required to lease or own a computer. Number of campus computers available to all students: 800. School has a wireless network. Approximate number of users that can be accommodated: 17,000. Proportion of college-owned housing units wired for high-speed internet access: 100%. **Campus safety:** Security services offered: 24-hour foot-and-vehicle patrols, late-night transport/escort service, 24-hour emergency telephones, lighted pathways/sidewalks, controlled dormitory access (key, security card, etc).

TRANSFER AND INTERNATIONAL STUDENTS

Transfer students: May apply for admission for the following academic terms: Fall, Spring, Summer. Applicants need a minimum number of credits to apply. For fall 2009: Transfer applications received: 1,741. Transfer applicants offered admission: 617. Transfer applicants enrolled: 524. **International students:** Number of foreign undergraduates: 813 (6% of student body). Number of countries represented: 68.

Georgia Southern University

■ **Address:** PO Box 8033, Statesboro, GA 30460
■ **Website:** http://www.georgiasouthern.edu/
■ **Public**
■ **Enrollment:** 14,799 full-time; 1,687 part-time

KEY STATS

✔ **U.S News College Ranking:** second tier, National Universities
✔ **SAT Score (25th/75th percentile):** 1020-1170
✔ **Tuition:** 2010-2011: $6,240 in state, $18,216 out of state
  Selectivity: Selective   **Room/board:** $8,414
  Acceptance rate: 56%   **Average debt:** $18,618
  Student/faculty ratio: 22/1   **Proportion who borrowed:** 65%

UNDERGRADUATE STUDENT BODY STATS

2009-2010 enrollment: 14,799 full-time; 1,687 part-time. Men: 52%; women: 48%. **Ethnic makeup:** African American: 22%; Asian American: 1%; Hispanic: 3%; White: 72%; International: 1%.

ADMISSIONS FACTS AND FIGURES

Phone: (912) 478-5391. **Email:** admissions@georgiasouthern.edu. **Website:** http://www.georgiasouthern.edu/. **Application deadlines for fall 2011:** Regular decision: May 1. Early decision: Not offered. Early action: Not offered. Admission can be deferred. **Application fee:** $30. **To apply online, go to:** https://www.applyweb.com/apply/gasou/menu.html. **Admissions requirements/recommendations:** High school units required (recommended): English: 4; Mathematics: 4; Science: 3; Foreign language: 2; Social studies: 3; Total units: 16. Tests: The college uses SAT or ACT scores in admissions decisions. Either SAT or ACT required. For admission to the fall 2011 entering class, the school will accept: ACT with writing required. Campus visit: Recommended. Admissions interview: Required. Off-campus interview: May be arranged. **Factors that count in admissions decisions:** *Academic:* Secondary school record: Very Important. Class rank: Considered. Letters of recommendation: Not Considered. Standardized test scores: Very Important. Essay: Not Considered. *Nonacademic:* Interview: Not Considered. Extracurricular activities: Not Considered. Talent/ability: Not Considered. Character/personal qualities: Not Considered. Alumni/ae relationship: Not Considered. Geographical residence: Not Considered. State residency: Not Considered. Religious affiliation/commitment: Not Considered. Minority status: Not Considered. Volunteer work: Not Considered. Work experience: Not Considered. **Other schools with the greatest overlap in applicants:** Georgia Institute of Technology; Georgia State University; Kennesaw State University; University of Georgia; University of West Georgia. **Admissions statistics for the fall 2009 entering class:** Total applicants: 9,214. Total accepted: 5,154. Freshmen enrolled: 3,539; 4% were from out of state. Overall acceptance rate: 56%. **Credentials of fall 2009 freshmen:** 14% ranked in the top 10 percent of their high school class; 42% were in the top 25 percent; 74% were in the top half. (Proportion submitting class standing: 61%.) **Average high school grade point average:** 3.2. **First-year students who submitted SAT scores:** 81%. Scores (25/75 percentile): Critical Reading: 510-580, Math: 510-590, Combined: 1020-1170. **First-year students submitting ACT scores:** 44%. Scores (25/75 percentile): English: 21-25, Math: 20-25, Composite: 21-25.

ACADEMICS

Year founded: 1906. **Academic calendar:** Semester. **Degrees offered:** certificate, bachelor's, post-bachelor's certificate, master's, post-master's certificate, doctorate. **Most popular majors:** 25% business, management, marketing, and related support services, 13% education, 7% engineering technologies/technicians, 7% parks, recreation, leisure, and fitness studies, 6% health professions and related clinical sciences. **Major fields of study:** area, ethnic, cultural, and gender studies; biological and biomedical sciences; business, management, marketing, and related support services; communication, journalism, and related programs; communications technologies/technicians and support services; computer and information sciences and support services; education; engineering technologies/technicians; English language and literature/letters; family and consumer sciences/human sciences; foreign languages, literatures, and linguistics; health professions and related clinical sciences; history; liberal arts and sciences studies, and humanities; mathematics and statistics; parks, recreation, leisure, and fitness studies; philosophy and religious studies; physical sciences; psychology; public administration and social service professions; security and protective services; social sciences; visual and performing arts. **Areas of required coursework:** arts/fine arts, humanities, computer literacy, mathematics, English (including composition), sciences (biological or physical), history, social science, other. **Pre-professional programs:** pre-law, pre-dentistry, pre-medicine, pre-veterinary science, pre-optometry, pre-pharmacy. **Special academic programs (% participation):** accelerated program (34%), cooperative (work-study plan) program (.4%), distance learning (52%), double major (2.1%), English as a Second Language (ESL) (.1%), honors program (5.5%), independent study (10.9%), internships (46.7%), student-designed major (5.5%), study abroad (10.7%), teacher certificate program (10.9%). **Teacher certification offered in:** early childhood, special education, middle/junior high, secondary. **Cooperative education programs:** business, computer science, engineering, health professions, natural science, technologies, other. **Reserve Officers Training Corps (ROTC):** Army ROTC: Offered on campus. **Faculty and instruction (2009-2010):** Total instructional faculty: 728 full-time, 109 part-time (50% men; 50% women; 16% minorities). Full-time faculty with Ph.D. or other terminal degree: 80%. Student/faculty ratio: 22/1. Classes of fewer than 20 students: 23%; of 20 to 49 students: 64%; of 50 or more students: 13%. **Advanced Placement and International Baccalaureate credit:** AP tests may be used for: Placement only. Scores accepted: 3, 4, 5. International Baccalaureate exams may be used for: Placement only. **Freshmen returning for sophomore year:** 79%. **Graduation rates:** Four-year: 17%; five-year: 41%; six-year: 48%. **Graduate study:** 29% of students pursue further study immediately upon graduation. Fields in which graduates pursue further study: Master of Business Administration (MBA), 12%; law, 2%; medicine, 2%.

COSTS AND FINANCIAL AID
Financial aid office: (912) 681-5413. **Expenses (2010-2011):** Tuition and fees 2010-2011: $6,240 in state, $18,216 out of state; room/board: $8,414. Estimated books and supplies: $1,200; transportation: $2,550; personal expenses: $3,100. **Financial aid:** Priority filing date for institution's financial aid form: April 20. In 2009-2010, 87% of undergraduates applied for financial aid. Of those, 59% were determined to have financial need; 13% had their need fully met. Average financial aid package (proportion receiving): $8,704 (57%). Average amount of gift aid, such as scholarships or grants (proportion receiving): $6,494 (46%). Average amount of self-help aid, such as work study or loans (proportion receiving): $4,224 (46%). Average need-based loan (excluding PLUS or other private loans): $4,158. Among students who received need-based aid, the average percentage of need met: 58%. Among students who received aid based on merit, the average award (and the proportion receiving): $1,846 (3%). The average athletic scholarship (and the proportion receiving): $6,108 (1%). Average amount of debt of borrowers graduating in 2009: $18,618. Proportion who borrowed: 65%.

CAMPUS LIFE AND EXTRACURRICULAR ACTIVITIES
Campus housing available (% using): coed dorms (13%), apartment for single students (85%), special housing for disabled students (2%), special housing for international students (0%). Students who live in college-owned, operated, or affiliated housing: 27%. **Student employment:** During the 2009-2010 academic year, 12% of undergraduates worked on campus. Average per-year earnings: $2,142. **Clubs and organizations:** Number of student organizations: 235. Activities include: campus ministries, choral groups, concert band, dance, drama/theater, international student organization, jazz band, literary magazine, marching band, music ensembles, musical theater, pep band, radio station, student government, student newspaper, student film society, symphony orchestra, television station. Number of fraternities: 20; sororities: 9. Proportion of men in fraternities: 10%; of women in sororities: 11%. Average proportion of students who stay on campus on weekends: 64%. **Sports program (2009-2010):** Member of NCAA I. *Men's intercollegiate varsity sports:* baseball, basketball, football, golf, soccer, tennis. *Women's intercollegiate varsity sports:* basketball, bowling, cross country, soccer, softball, swimming, tennis, track and field (outdoor), volleyball.

SERVICES AND FACILITIES
Basic services: nonremedial tutoring, women's center, placement service, day care, health service, health insurance, other. **Remedial assistance:** reading, math, writing, study skills, other. **Counseling services:** minority student, career, military, personal, veteran student, academic, older student, psychological, birth control. **For learning-disabled students:** School does not offer a structured program with separate admission and additional fees. Total undergraduates in learning-disabled program or receiving services: 429. Services include: remedial math, remedial English, reading machines, remedial reading, tape recorders, other special classes, diagnostic testing service, note-taking services, oral tests, learning center, readers, extended time for tests, tutors, priority registration, priority seating, texts on tape,

other testing accommodations. **Library:** Number of titles: 607,542; number of current serial subscriptions: 2,389. **Information technology resources:** Students are not required to lease or own a computer. Number of campus computers available to all students: 3,260. School has a wireless network. Approximate number of users that can be accommodated: 11,940. Proportion of college-owned housing units wired for high-speed internet access: 100%. **Campus safety:** Security services offered: 24-hour foot-and-vehicle patrols, late-night transport/escort service, 24-hour emergency telephones, lighted pathways/sidewalks, student patrols, controlled dormitory access (key, security card, etc).

TRANSFER AND INTERNATIONAL STUDENTS
Transfer students: May apply for admission for the following academic terms: Fall, Spring, Summer. Applicants need a minimum number of credits to apply. For fall 2009: Transfer applications received: 1,619. Transfer applicants offered admission: 1,320. Transfer applicants enrolled: 1,080. **International students:** Number of foreign undergraduates: 196 (1% of student body). Number of countries represented: 57. Minimum TOEFL score required: 523 (paper); 193 (computer). Average TOEFL score: 523 (paper).

Georgia Southwestern State University

- **Address:** 800 Wheatley Street, Americus, GA 31709
- **Website:** http://www.gsw.edu
- **Public**
- **Enrollment:** 1,934 full-time; 725 part-time

KEY STATS
✔ **U.S News College Ranking:** 87, Regional Universities (South)
✔ **SAT Score (25th/75th percentile):** 880-1060
✔ **Tuition:** 2009-2010: $4,762 in state, $16,376 out of state

Selectivity: Selective	**Room/board:** $7,115
Acceptance rate: 70%	**Average debt:** $20,505
Student/faculty ratio: 21/1	**Proportion who borrowed:** 62%

UNDERGRADUATE STUDENT BODY STATS
2009-2010 enrollment: 1,934 full-time; 725 part-time. Men: 35%; women: 65%. **Ethnic makeup:** African American: 30%; Asian American: 1%; Hispanic: 2%; White: 63%; International: 3%.

ADMISSIONS FACTS AND FIGURES
Phone: (229) 928-1273. **Email:** gswapps@canes.gsw.edu. **Website:** http://www.gsw.edu. **Application deadlines for fall 2011:** Regular decision: July 21. Early decision: Send application by: N/A; Decision sent by: N/A. Early action: Not offered. Admission can be deferred. **Application fee:** $25. **To apply online, go to:** https://www.ganet.org/gsw. **Admissions requirements/ recommendations:** High school units required (recommended): English: 4; Mathematics: 4; Science: 3; Foreign language: 2; Social studies: 1; History: 2; Academic electives: (2); Total units: 16. Tests: The college uses SAT or ACT scores in admissions decisions. Either SAT or ACT required. For admission to the fall 2011 entering class, the school will accept: ACT with or without writing accepted. Campus visit: Recommended. Admissions interview: Recommended. **Factors that count in admissions decisions:** *Academic:* Secondary school record: Very Important. Class rank: Important. Letters of recommendation: Considered. Standardized test scores: Very Important. Essay: Considered. *Nonacademic:* Interview: Considered. Extracurricular activities: Considered. Talent/ability: Considered. **Admissions statistics for the fall 2009 entering class:** Total applicants: 1,347. Total accepted: 944. Freshmen enrolled: 490; 4% were from out of state. Overall acceptance rate: 70%. Non-early acceptance rate: 70%. **Credentials of fall 2009 freshmen:** 13% ranked in the top 10 percent of their high school class; 39% were in the top 25 percent; 69% were in the top half. (Proportion submitting class standing: 54%.) **Average high school grade point average:** 3.1. **First-year students who submitted SAT scores:** 62%. Scores (25/75 percentile): Critical Reading: 440-530, Math: 440-530, Combined: 880-1060. **First-year students submitting ACT scores:** 24%. Scores (25/75 percentile): English: 17-21, Math: 17-21, Composite: 18-21.

ACADEMICS
Year founded: 1906. **Academic calendar:** Semester. **Degrees offered:** bachelor's, post-bachelor's certificate, master's, post-master's certificate. **Most popular majors:** 17% business administration and management, 11% elementary education and teaching, 10% accounting, 10% psychology, 8%

nursing/registered nurse training (R.N., A.S.N., B.S.N., M.S.N.). **Major fields of study:** biological and biomedical sciences; business, management, marketing, and related support services; computer and information sciences and support services; education; engineering technologies/technicians; English language and literature/letters; health professions and related clinical sciences; history; mathematics and statistics; physical sciences; psychology; social sciences; visual and performing arts. **Areas of required coursework:** arts/fine arts, humanities, mathematics, English (including composition), sciences (biological or physical), history, social science. **Preprofessional programs:** pre-dentistry, pre-medicine, pre-veterinary science, pre-pharmacy. **Special academic programs:** accelerated program, distance learning, double major, dual enrollment, English as a Second Language (ESL), honors program, independent study, internships, study abroad, teacher certification program. **Teacher certification offered in:** early childhood, special education, middle/junior high. **Faculty and instruction (2009-2010):** Total instructional faculty: 96 full-time, 47 part-time (43% men; 57% women; 16% minorities). Full-time faculty with Ph.D. or other terminal degree: 78%. Student/faculty ratio: 21/1. Classes of fewer than 20 students: 45%; of 20 to 49 students: 52%; of 50 or more students: 3%. **Advanced Placement and International Baccalaureate credit:** AP tests may be used for: Credit and/or placement. Scores accepted: 3, 4, 5. **Freshmen returning for sophomore year:** 69%. **Graduation rates:** Four-year: 15%; five-year: 30%; six-year: 35%.

COSTS AND FINANCIAL AID

Financial aid office: (229) 928-1378. **Expenses (2009-2010):** Tuition and fees 2009-2010: $4,762 in state, $16,376 out of state; room/board: $7,115. **Financial aid:** Priority filing date for institution's financial aid form: April 1. In 2009-2010, 81% of undergraduates applied for financial aid. Of those, 68% were determined to have financial need; 21% had their need fully met. Average financial aid package (proportion receiving): $7,655 (66%). Average amount of gift aid, such as scholarships or grants (proportion receiving): $4,323 (45%). Average amount of self-help aid, such as work study or loans (proportion receiving): $3,937 (46%). Average need-based loan (excluding PLUS or other private loans): $3,914. Among students who received need-based aid, the average percentage of need met: 56%. Among students who received aid based on merit, the average award (and the proportion receiving): $1,886 (6%). The average athletic scholarship (and the proportion receiving): $2,949 (2%). Average amount of debt of borrowers graduating in 2009: $20,505. Proportion who borrowed: 62%.

CAMPUS LIFE AND EXTRACURRICULAR ACTIVITIES

Campus housing available: coed dorms, apartment for single students. Students who live in college-owned, operated, or affiliated housing: 31%. **Clubs and organizations:** Number of student organizations: 65. Activities include: campus ministries, choral groups, concert band, dance, drama/theater, international student organization, jazz band, literary magazine, student government, student newspaper, television station. Number of fraternities: 7; sororities: 6. Proportion of men in fraternities: 17%; of women in sororities: 10%. **Sports program (2009-2010):** Member of NCAA II. **Men's intercollegiate varsity sports:** baseball, basketball, golf, soccer, tennis. **Women's intercollegiate varsity sports:** basketball, cross country, soccer, softball, tennis.

SERVICES AND FACILITIES

Basic services: nonremedial tutoring, health service, health insurance. **Remedial assistance:** reading, math, writing, study skills. **Counseling services:** minority student, career, personal, academic. **For learning-disabled students:** School does not offer a structured program with separate admission and additional fees. Services include: remedial math, remedial English, reading machines, tape recorders, note-taking services, special bookstore section, readers, extended time for tests, tutors, priority seating, other testing accommodations. **Library:** Number of titles: 583,239; number of current serial subscriptions: 362. **Information technology resources:** Students are not required to lease or own a computer. Number of campus computers available to all students: 562. School has a wireless network. Proportion of college-owned housing units wired for high-speed internet access: 100%. **Campus safety:** Security services offered: 24-hour foot-and-vehicle patrols, late-night transport/escort service, 24-hour emergency telephones, lighted pathways/sidewalks, controlled dormitory access (key, security card, etc.).

TRANSFER AND INTERNATIONAL STUDENTS

Transfer students: May apply for admission for the following academic terms: Fall, Spring, Summer. Applicants need a minimum number of credits to apply. For fall 2009: Transfer applications received: 747. Transfer applicants offered admission: 590. Transfer applicants enrolled: 362.

International students: Number of foreign undergraduates: 71 (3% of student body). Number of countries represented: 16. Minimum TOEFL score required: 523 (paper); 193 (computer).

Georgia State University

- **Address:** University Plaza, Atlanta, GA 30303-3083
- **Website:** http://www.gsu.edu
- **Public**
- **Enrollment:** 16,973 full-time; 5,411 part-time

KEY STATS

✔ **U.S News College Ranking:** second tier, National Universities
✔ **SAT Score (25th/75th percentile):** 980-1180
✔ **Tuition:** 2010-2011: $7,293 in state, $21,861 out of state

Selectivity: Selective	**Room/board:** $11,370
Acceptance rate: 51%	**Average debt:** $13,166
Student/faculty ratio: 19/1	**Proportion who borrowed:** 58%

UNDERGRADUATE STUDENT BODY STATS

2009-2010 enrollment: 16,973 full-time; 5,411 part-time. Men: 40%; women: 60%. **Ethnic makeup:** African American: 34%; Asian American: 12%; Hispanic: 7%; White: 45%; International: 2%.

ADMISSIONS FACTS AND FIGURES

Phone: (404) 413-2500. **Email:** admissions@gsu.edu. **Website:** http://www.gsu.edu. **Application deadlines for fall 2011:** Regular decision: March 1; decision sent by April 1. Early decision: Not offered. Early action: Not offered. Admission can be deferred. **Application fee:** $60. **To apply online, go to:** http://www.gsu.edu/~wwwadm/adm30.html. **Admissions requirements/recommendations:** High school units required (recommended): English: 4; Mathematics: 4; Science: 3; Foreign language: 2; Social studies: 2; History: 1; Total units: 16. Tests: The college uses SAT or ACT scores in admissions decisions. Either SAT or ACT required. For admission to the fall 2011 entering class, the school will accept: ACT with writing required. Campus visit: Neither required nor recommended. Admissions interview: Neither required nor recommended. Off-campus interview: Not available. **Factors that count in admissions decisions:** *Academic:* Secondary school record: Very Important. Class rank: Not Considered. Letters of recommendation: Considered. Standardized test scores: Very Important. Essay: Not Considered. *Nonacademic:* Interview: Not Considered. Extracurricular activities: Not Considered. Talent/ability: Considered. Character/personal qualities: Not Considered. Alumni/ae relationship: Not Considered. Geographical residence: Considered. State residency: Not Considered. Religious affiliation/commitment: Not Considered. Minority status: Not Considered. Volunteer work: Not Considered. Work experience: Not Considered. **Other schools with the greatest overlap in applicants:** Georgia Institute of Technology; Georgia Southern University; Kennesaw State University; Mercer University; University of Georgia. **Admissions statistics for the fall 2009 entering class:** Total applicants: 11,913. Total accepted: 6,049. Freshmen enrolled: 2,934; 3% were from out of state. Overall acceptance rate: 51%. **Size of waiting list:** 392 applicants; enrolled from waiting list: 120. **Average high school grade point average:** 3.3. **First-year students who submitted SAT scores:** 89%. Scores (25/75 percentile): Critical Reading: 490-590, Math: 490-590, Combined: 980-1180. **First-year students submitting ACT scores:** 39%. Scores (25/75 percentile): English: 20-25, Math: 21-26, Composite: 21-25.

ACADEMICS

Year founded: 1913. **Academic calendar:** Semester. **Degrees offered:** certificate, bachelor's, post-bachelor's certificate, master's, post-master's certificate, doctorate. **Most popular majors:** 33% business, management, marketing, and related support services, 13% social sciences, 8% psychology, 7% visual and performing arts, 6% biological and biomedical sciences. **Major fields of study:** area, ethnic, cultural, and gender studies; biological and biomedical sciences; business, management, marketing, and related support services; communication, journalism, and related programs; computer and information sciences and support services; education; English language and literature/letters; family and consumer sciences/human sciences; foreign languages, literatures, and linguistics; health professions and related clinical sciences; history; legal professions and studies; mathematics and statistics; multi/interdisciplinary studies; natural resources and conservation; parks, recreation, leisure, and fitness studies; philosophy and religious studies; physical sciences; psychology; public administration and social service professions; security and protective services; social sciences; visual and performing arts. **Areas of required coursework:** humanities, mathematics, English (including composition), philosophy, foreign languages, sciences (biological or physical), history, social science, other. **Pre-professional programs:** pre-law, pre-medicine. **Special academic programs (% participation):** accelerated program (2%), cooperative (work-study plan) program (3.4%), cross-registration, distance learning (1%), double major (4%), dual enrollment, English as a Second Language (ESL) (1%), honors program (2%), independent study, internships, student-designed major, study abroad (3%), teacher certificate program, weekend college. **Teacher certification offered in:** early childhood, special education, elementary, middle/junior high, secondary, bilingual/bicultural. **Cooperative education programs:** education. **Reserve Officers Training Corps (ROTC):** Army ROTC: Offered on campus; Navy ROTC: Offered at cooperating institution (Georgia Institute of Technology); Air Force ROTC: Offered at cooperating institution (Georgia Institute of Technology). **Faculty and instruction (2009-2010):** Total instructional faculty: 1,103 full-time, 399 part-time (50% men; 50% women; 22% minorities). Full-time faculty with Ph.D. or other terminal degree: 87%. Student/faculty ratio: 19/1. Classes of fewer than 20 students: 17%; of 20 to 49 students: 68%; of 50 or more students: 15%. **Advanced Placement and International Baccalaureate credit:** AP tests may be used for: Credit only. Scores accepted: 3, 4, 5. International Baccalaureate exams may be used for: Credit only. **Freshmen returning for sophomore year:** 82%. **Graduation rates:** Four-year: 18%; five-year: 41%; six-year: 50%.

COSTS AND FINANCIAL AID

Financial aid office: (404) 651-2227. **Expenses (2010-2011):** Tuition and fees 2010-2011: $7,293 in state, $21,861 out of state; room/board: $11,370. Estimated books and supplies: $1,000; transportation: $2,070; personal expenses: $1,970. **Financial aid:** Priority filing date for institution's financial aid form: April 1; deadline: November 1. In 2009-2010, 79% of undergraduates applied for financial aid. Of those, 65% were determined to have financial need; 8% had their need fully met. Average financial aid package (proportion receiving): $8,393 (63%). Average amount of gift aid, such as scholarships or grants (proportion receiving): $4,443 (42%). Average amount of self-help aid, such as work study or loans (proportion receiving): $5,341 (42%). Average need-based loan (excluding PLUS or other private loans): $5,341. Among students who received need-based aid, the average percentage of need met: 12%. Among students who received aid based on merit, the average award (and the proportion receiving): $3,503 (1%). The average athletic scholarship (and the proportion receiving): $4,651 (1%). Average amount of debt of borrowers graduating in 2009: $13,166. Proportion who borrowed: 58%.

CAMPUS LIFE AND EXTRACURRICULAR ACTIVITIES

Campus housing available (% using): coed dorms, apartments for married students (1%), apartment for single students (96%), special housing for disabled students (1%), special housing for international students (2%), other housing options. Students who live in college-owned, operated, or affiliated housing: 13%. **Student employment:** During the 2009-2010 academic year, 10% of undergraduates worked on campus. Average per-year earnings: $5,086. **Clubs and organizations:** Number of student organizations: 326. Activities include: campus ministries, choral groups, concert band, dance, drama/theater, international student organization, jazz band, literary magazine, marching band, model UN, music ensembles, musical theater, opera, pep band, radio station, student government, student newspaper, student film society, symphony orchestra, television station. Number of fraternities: 9; sororities: 12. Proportion of men in fraternities: 1%; of women in sororities: 1%. **Sports program (2009-2010):** Member of NCAA I. *Men's intercollegiate varsity sports:* baseball, basketball, cross country, golf, soccer, tennis, track and field (indoor), track and field (outdoor). *Women's intercollegiate varsity sports:* basketball, cross country, golf, soccer, softball, tennis, track and field (indoor), track and field (outdoor), volleyball.

SERVICES AND FACILITIES

Basic services: nonremedial tutoring, placement service, day care, health service, health insurance, other. **Remedial assistance:** reading, math, writing, study skills. **Counseling services:** minority student, career, personal, veteran student, academic, psychological, other. **For learning-disabled students:** School does not offer a structured program with separate admission and additional fees. Total undergraduates in learning-disabled program or receiving services: 250. Services include: tape recorders, diagnostic testing service, note-taking services, readers, extended time for tests, priority registration, priority seating, texts on tape, other testing accommodations, waiver of foreign language degree requirement. **Library:** Number of titles:

1,640,392; number of current serial subscriptions: 15,498. **Information technology resources:** Students are not required to lease or own a computer. Number of campus computers available to all students: 1,200. School has a wireless network. Approximate number of users that can be accommodated: 4,000. Proportion of college-owned housing units wired for high-speed internet access: 100%. **Campus safety:** Security services offered: 24-hour foot-and-vehicle patrols, late-night transport/escort service, 24-hour emergency telephones, lighted pathways/sidewalks, controlled dormitory access (key, security card, etc.).

TRANSFER AND INTERNATIONAL STUDENTS

Transfer students: May apply for admission for the following academic terms: Fall, Spring, Summer. Applicants need a minimum number of credits to apply. For fall 2009: Transfer applications received: 6,764. Transfer applicants offered admission: 4,005. Transfer applicants enrolled: 2,286. **International students:** Number of foreign undergraduates: 505 (2% of student body). Number of countries represented: 74. Minimum TOEFL score required: 550 (paper); 213 (computer). Average TOEFL score: 613 (paper).

Kennesaw State University

- **Address:** 1000 Chastain Road, Kennesaw, GA 30144-5591
- **Website:** http://www.kennesaw.edu
- **Public**
- **Enrollment:** 15,508 full-time; 4,796 part-time

KEY STATS

✔ **U.S News College Ranking:** 69, Regional Universities (South)
✔ **SAT Score (25th/75th percentile):** 990-1160
✔ **Tuition:** 2010-2011: $5,942 in state, $17,918 out of state

Selectivity: Selective	**Room/board:** $5,852
Acceptance rate: 64%	**Average debt:** $17,262
Student/faculty ratio: 21/1	**Proportion who borrowed:** 43%

UNDERGRADUATE STUDENT BODY STATS

2009-2010 enrollment: 15,508 full-time; 4,796 part-time. Men: 41%; women: 59%. **Ethnic makeup:** African American: 13%; Asian American: 3%; Hispanic: 5%; White: 76%; International: 2%.

ADMISSIONS FACTS AND FIGURES

Phone: (770) 423-6300. **Email:** ksuadmit@kennesaw.edu. **Website:** http://www.kennesaw.edu. **Application deadlines for fall 2011:** Regular decision: May 14. Early decision: Not offered. Early action: Not offered. Admission can be deferred. **Application fee:** $40. **To apply online, go to:** http://www.kennesaw.edu/admissions/. **Admissions requirements/recommendations:** High school units required (recommended): English: 4; Mathematics: 4; Science: 3; Foreign language: 2; Social studies: 3; Total units: 16. Tests: The college uses SAT or ACT scores in admissions decisions. Either SAT or ACT required. For admission to the fall 2011 entering class, the school will accept: ACT with or without writing accepted. Campus visit: Recommended. Admissions interview: Neither required nor recommended. Off-campus interview: Not available. **Factors that count in admissions decisions:** *Academic:* Secondary school record: Not Considered. Class rank: Not Considered. Letters of recommendation: Not Considered. Standardized test scores: Very Important. Essay: Not Considered. *Nonacademic:* Interview: Not Considered. Extracurricular activities: Not Considered. Talent/ability: Not Considered. Character/personal qualities: Not Considered. Alumni/ae relationship: Not Considered. Geographical residence: Not Considered. State residency: Not Considered. Religious affiliation/commitment: Not Considered. Minority status: Not Considered. Volunteer work: Not Considered. Work experience: Not Considered. **Other schools with the greatest overlap in applicants:** Georgia Southern University; Georgia State University; University of Georgia; University of West Georgia; Valdosta State University. **Admissions statistics for the fall 2009 entering class:** Total applicants: 7,877. Total accepted: 5,010. Freshmen enrolled: 2,749; 3% were from out of state. Overall acceptance rate: 64%. **Credentials of fall 2009 freshmen:** 21% ranked in the top 10 percent of their high school class; 53% were in the top 25 percent; 81% were in the top half. (Proportion submitting class standing: 50%.) **Average high school grade point average:** 3.2. **First-year students who submitted SAT scores:** 78%. Scores (25/75 percentile): Critical Reading: 500-580, Math: 490-580, Combined: 990-1160. **First-year students submitting ACT scores:** 38%. Scores (25/75 percentile): English: 19-24, Math: 20-24, Composite: 20-24.

ACADEMICS

Year founded: 1963. **Academic calendar:** Semester. **Degrees offered:** certificate, bachelor's, post-bachelor's certificate, master's, doctorate. **Most popular majors:** 27% business, management, marketing, and related support services; 17% education, 7% communication, journalism, and related programs, 7% health professions and related clinical sciences, 7% social sciences. **Major fields of study:** area, ethnic, cultural, and gender studies; biological and biomedical sciences; business, management, marketing, and related support services; communication, journalism, and related programs; computer and information sciences and support services; education; English language and literature/letters; foreign languages, literatures, and linguistics; health professions and related clinical sciences; history; mathematics and statistics; multi/interdisciplinary studies; parks, recreation, leisure, and fitness studies; physical sciences; psychology; public administration and social service professions; security and protective services; social sciences; visual and performing arts. **Areas of required coursework:** arts/fine arts, humanities, mathematics, English (including composition), foreign languages, sciences (biological or physical), history, social science, other. **Pre-professional programs:** pre-law, pre-dentistry, pre-medicine, pre-veterinary science, pre-optometry, pre-pharmacy, other. **Special academic programs (% participation):** cooperative (work-study plan) program (5%), cross-registration (1%), distance learning (6%), double major (1%), dual enrollment (1%), English as a Second Language (ESL) (2%), honors program (2%), independent study (7%), internships (21%), study abroad (8%), teacher certificate program (18%). **Teacher certification offered in:** early childhood, elementary, middle/junior high, secondary. **Cooperative education programs:** art, business, computer science, health professions, humanities, natural science, social/behavioral science. **Reserve Officers Training Corps (ROTC):** Army ROTC: Offered at cooperating institution (Georgia Institute of Technology); Air Force ROTC: Offered at cooperating institution (Georgia Institute of Technology). **Faculty and instruction (2009-2010):** Total instructional faculty: 701 full-time, 533 part-time (46% men; 54% women; 20% minorities). Full-time faculty with Ph.D. or other terminal degree: 75%. Student/faculty ratio: 21/1. Classes of fewer than 20 students: 20%; of 20 to 49 students: 66%; of 50 or more students: 14%. **Advanced Placement and International Baccalaureate credit:** AP tests may be used for: Credit only. Scores accepted: 3, 4, 5. International Baccalaureate exams may be used for: Credit only. **Freshmen returning for sophomore year:** 75%. **Graduation rates:** Four-year: 10%; five-year: 30%; six-year: 34%.

COSTS AND FINANCIAL AID

Financial aid office: (770) 423-6074. **Expenses (2010-2011):** Tuition and fees 2010-2011: $5,942 in state, $17,918 out of state; room/board: $5,852. Estimated books and supplies: $1,500; transportation: $2,421; personal expenses: $1,739. **Financial aid:** Priority filing date for institution's financial aid form: April 1. In 2009-2010, 73% of undergraduates applied for financial aid. Of those, 56% were determined to have financial need; 13% had their need fully met. Average financial aid package (proportion receiving): $3,970 (54%). Average amount of gift aid, such as scholarships or grants (proportion receiving): $2,321 (29%). Average amount of self-help aid, such as work study or loans (proportion receiving): $2,115 (45%). Average need-based loan (excluding PLUS or other private loans): $2,115. Among students who received need-based aid, the average percentage of need met: 24%. Among students who received aid based on merit, the average award (and the proportion receiving): $1,087 (19%). The average athletic scholarship (and the proportion receiving): $1,628 (4%). Average amount of debt of borrowers graduating in 2009: $17,262. Proportion who borrowed: 43%.

CAMPUS LIFE AND EXTRACURRICULAR ACTIVITIES

Campus housing available (% using): apartment for single students (100%). Students who live in college-owned, operated, or affiliated housing: 15%. **Student employment:** During the 2009-2010 academic year, 7% of undergraduates worked on campus. Average per-year earnings: $3,096. **Clubs and organizations:** Number of student organizations: 151. Activities include: campus ministries, choral groups, concert band, dance, drama/theater, international student organization, jazz band, model UN, music ensembles, musical theater, radio station, student government, student newspaper, symphony orchestra. Number of fraternities: 10; sororities: 8. Proportion of men in fraternities: 3%; of women in sororities: 4%. Average proportion of students who stay on campus on weekends: 30%. **Sports program (2009-2010):** Member of NCAA I. *Men's intercollegiate varsity sports:* baseball, basketball, cross country, golf, tennis, track and field (indoor), track and field (outdoor). *Women's intercollegiate varsity sports:* basketball, cross country, golf, soccer, softball, tennis, track and field (indoor), track and field (outdoor), volleyball.

SERVICES AND FACILITIES

Basic services: nonremedial tutoring, women's center, placement service, health service, health insurance. **Remedial assistance:** reading, math, writing, study skills. **Counseling services:** minority student, career, military, personal, veteran student, academic, older student, psychological, birth control. **For learning-disabled students:** School does not offer a structured program with separate admission and additional fees. Services include: remedial math, remedial English, reading machines, remedial reading, tape recorders, diagnostic testing service, oral tests, extended time for tests, priority registration, priority seating, texts on tape, exams on tape or computer, other. **Library:** Number of titles: 645,788; number of current serial subscriptions: 200. **Information technology resources:** Students are not required to lease or own a computer. Number of campus computers available to all students: 1,087. School has a wireless network. Approximate number of users that can be accommodated: 7,500. Proportion of college-owned housing units wired for high-speed internet access: 100%. **Campus safety:** Security services offered: 24-hour foot-and-vehicle patrols, late-night transport/escort service, 24-hour emergency telephones, lighted pathways/sidewalks, student patrols, controlled dormitory access (key, security card, etc).

TRANSFER AND INTERNATIONAL STUDENTS

Transfer students: May apply for admission for the following academic terms: Fall, Spring, Summer. Applicants need a minimum number of credits to apply. For fall 2009: Transfer applications received: 3,992. Transfer applicants offered admission: 2,929. Transfer applicants enrolled: 1,944. **International students:** Number of foreign undergraduates: 449 (2% of student body). Number of countries represented: 133. Minimum TOEFL score required: 527 (paper); 75 (computer). Average TOEFL score: 560 (paper).

LaGrange College

- **Address:** 601 Broad Street, LaGrange, GA 30240
- **Website:** http://www.lagrange.edu
- **Private; Religious affiliation:** United Methodist
- **Enrollment:** 776 full-time; 89 part-time

KEY STATS
- ✔ **U.S News College Ranking:** 7, Regional Colleges (South)
- ✔ **SAT Score (25th/75th percentile):** 920-1140
- ✔ **Tuition:** 2010-2011: $22,148

Selectivity: Selective	Room/board: $9,230
Acceptance rate: 65%	Average debt: $24,561
Student/faculty ratio: 10/1	Proportion who borrowed: 75%

UNDERGRADUATE STUDENT BODY STATS

2009-2010 enrollment: 776 full-time; 89 part-time. Men: 45%; women: 55%. **Ethnic makeup:** African American: 22%; Asian American: 1%; Hispanic: 2%; White: 73%; International: 2%. **Religious preference:** Roman Catholic: 5%; No preference: 19%; United Methodist: 18%; Other: 58%.

ADMISSIONS FACTS AND FIGURES

Phone: (706) 880-8005. **Email:** admission@lagrange.edu. **Website:** http://www.lagrange.edu. **Application deadlines for fall 2011:** Regular decision: Rolling. Early decision: Not offered. Early action: Send application by: N/A; Decision sent by: N/A. Admission can be deferred. **Application fee:** $30. **To apply online, go to:** https://www.applyweb.com/apply/lgc/index.html. **Admissions requirements/recommendations:** High school units required (recommended): English: 4 (4); Mathematics: 4 (4); Science: 3 (3); Foreign language: (2); Social studies: 3 (3); Total units: 14 (16). Tests: The college uses SAT or ACT scores in admissions decisions. Either SAT or ACT required. For admission to the fall 2011 entering class, the school will accept: ACT with or without writing accepted. Campus visit: Recommended. Admissions interview: Recommended. Off-campus interview: May be arranged. **Factors that count in admissions decisions:** *Academic:* Secondary school record: Considered. Class rank: Important. Letters of recommendation: Important. Standardized test scores: Very Important. Essay: Considered. *Nonacademic:* Interview: Considered. Extracurricular activities: Important. Talent/ability: Considered. Character/personal qualities: Very Important. Alumni/ae relationship: Considered. Geographical residence: Considered. State residency: Not Considered. Religious affiliation/commitment: Not Considered. Minority status: Not Considered. Volunteer work: Considered. Work experience: Not Considered. **Other schools with the greatest overlap in applicants:** Berry College; Elon University; Georgia

College & State University; Mercer University; University of Georgia. **Admissions statistics for the fall 2009 entering class:** Total applicants: 1,342. Total accepted: 869. Freshmen enrolled: 231; 13% were from out of state. Overall acceptance rate: 65%. Non-early acceptance rate: 65%. **Credentials of fall 2009 freshmen:** 25% ranked in the top 10 percent of their high school class; 54% were in the top 25 percent; 92% were in the top half. (Proportion submitting class standing: 57%.) **Average high school grade point average:** 3.5. **First-year students who submitted SAT scores:** 79%. Scores (25/75 percentile): Critical Reading: 460-570, Math: 460-570, Combined: 920-1140. **First-year students submitting ACT scores:** 16%. Scores (25/75 percentile): English: 19-25, Math: 19-25, Composite: 20-25.

ACADEMICS

Year founded: 1831. **Academic calendar:** 4-1-4. **Degrees offered:** associate, bachelor's, master's, post-master's certificate. **Most popular majors:** 21% business administration and management, 16% nursing/registered nurse training (R.N., A.S.N., B.S.N., M.S.N.), 11% biology/biological sciences, 11% social work, 10% visual and performing arts. **Major fields of study:** biological and biomedical sciences; business, management, marketing, and related support services; computer and information sciences and support services; education; English language and literature/letters; foreign languages, literatures, and linguistics; health professions and related clinical sciences; history; liberal arts and sciences studies, and humanities; mathematics and statistics; philosophy and religious studies; physical sciences; psychology; social sciences; theology and religious vocations; visual and performing arts. **Areas of required coursework:** arts/fine arts, humanities, computer literacy, mathematics, English (including composition), foreign languages, sciences (biological or physical), other. **Pre-professional programs:** pre-dentistry, pre-medicine, pre-theology, pre-veterinary science, pre-optometry, pre-pharmacy, other. **Special academic programs:** double major, dual enrollment, independent study, internships, liberal arts/career combination, study abroad, teacher certificate program. **Teacher certification offered in:** early childhood, elementary, middle/junior high, secondary. **Faculty and instruction (2009-2010):** Total instructional faculty: 64 full-time, 83 part-time (52% men; 48% women; 7% minorities). Full-time faculty with Ph.D. or other terminal degree: 84%. Student/faculty ratio: 10/1. Classes of fewer than 20 students: 86%; of 20 to 49 students: 14%; of 50 or more students: 0%. **Advanced Placement and International Baccalaureate credit:** AP tests may be used for: Credit only. Scores accepted: 4, 5. International Baccalaureate exams may be used for: Placement only. **Freshmen returning for sophomore year:** 64%. **Graduation rates:** Four-year: 37%; five-year: 49%; six-year: 52%. **Graduate study:** 20% of students pursue further study immediately upon graduation. Fields in which graduates pursue further study: Master of Business Administration (MBA), 45%; theology (or the seminary), 5%; education, 14%; arts and sciences, 58%.

COSTS AND FINANCIAL AID

Financial aid office: (706) 880-8229. **Expenses (2010-2011):** Tuition and fees 2010-2011: $22,148; room/board: $9,230. Estimated books and supplies: $1,000; transportation: $1,200; personal expenses: $1,300. **Financial aid:** Priority filing date for institution's financial aid form: March 1. In 2009-2010, 91% of undergraduates applied for financial aid. Of those, 81% were determined to have financial need; 22% had their need fully met. Average financial aid package (proportion receiving): $17,664 (81%). Average amount of gift aid, such as scholarships or grants (proportion receiving): $12,967 (80%). Average amount of self-help aid, such as work study or loans (proportion receiving): $4,667 (64%). Average need-based loan (excluding PLUS or other private loans): $4,268. Among students who received need-based aid, the average percentage of need met: 75%. Among students who received aid based on merit, the average award (and the proportion receiving): $10,356 (13%). The average athletic scholarship (and the proportion receiving): $0 (0%). Average amount of debt of borrowers graduating in 2009: $24,561. Proportion who borrowed: 75%.

CAMPUS LIFE AND EXTRACURRICULAR ACTIVITIES

Campus housing available (% using): coed dorms (19%), women's dorms (19%), men's dorms (17%), sorority housing (2%), fraternity housing (0%), apartment for single students (41%). Students who live in college-owned, operated, or affiliated housing: 62%. **Student employment:** During the 2009-2010 academic year, 0% of undergraduates worked on campus. **Clubs and organizations:** Number of student organizations: 52. Activities include: campus ministries, choral groups, drama/theater, international student organization, literary magazine, music ensembles, musical theater, pep band, student government, student newspaper, symphony orchestra, yearbook. Number of fraternities: 3; sororities: 6. Proportion of men in fraternities: 3%; of women in sororities: 4%. Average proportion of students who stay on campus on weekends: 70%. **Sports program (2009-2010):** Member of NCAA III. *Men's intercollegiate varsity sports:* baseball, basketball, cross country, football, golf, soccer, swimming, tennis. *Women's intercollegiate varsity sports:* basketball, cross country, lacrosse, soccer, softball, swimming, tennis, volleyball.

SERVICES AND FACILITIES

Basic services: nonremedial tutoring, placement service, health service, health insurance. **Remedial assistance:** writing, study skills. **Counseling services:** minority student, career, personal, veteran student, academic, older student, psychological, birth control, religious. **For learning-disabled students:** School does not offer a structured program with separate admission and additional fees. Services include: tape recorders, untimed tests, note-taking services, oral tests, readers, extended time for tests, tutors, priority registration, priority seating. **Library:** Number of titles: 118,598; number of current serial subscriptions: 402. **Information technology resources:** Students are not required to lease or own a computer. Number of campus computers available to all students: 186. School has a wireless network. Approximate number of users that can be accommodated: 820. Proportion of college-owned housing units wired for high-speed internet access: 100%. **Campus safety:** Security services offered: 24-hour foot-and-vehicle patrols, late-night transport/escort service, 24-hour emergency telephones, lighted pathways/sidewalks, controlled dormitory access (key, security card, etc).

TRANSFER AND INTERNATIONAL STUDENTS

Transfer students: May apply for admission for the following academic terms: Fall, Winter, Spring, Summer. Applicants need a minimum number of credits to apply. For fall 2009: Transfer applications received: 219. Transfer applicants offered admission: 127. Transfer applicants enrolled: 62. **International students:** Number of foreign undergraduates: 13 (2% of student body). Number of countries represented: 12. Minimum TOEFL score required: 500 (paper); 173 (computer). Average TOEFL score: 677 (paper).

Life University

- **Address:** 1269 Barclay Circle, Marietta, GA 30060
- **Website:** http://www.life.edu
- **Private**
- **Enrollment:** 528 full-time; 199 part-time

KEY STATS

✔ **U.S News College Ranking:** second tier, Regional Universities (South)
✔ **SAT Score (25th/75th percentile):** 805-995
✔ **Tuition:** 2009-2010: $8,352

Selectivity: Less selective	**Room/board:** $12,480
Acceptance rate: 82%	**Average debt:** $17,600
Student/faculty ratio: 14/1	**Proportion who borrowed:** 60%

UNDERGRADUATE STUDENT BODY STATS

2009-2010 enrollment: 528 full-time; 199 part-time. Men: 52%; women: 48%. **Ethnic makeup:** African American: 30%; American-Indian: 1%; Asian American: 4%; Hispanic: 6%; White: 60%.

ADMISSIONS FACTS AND FIGURES

Phone: (770) 426-2884. **Email:** admissions@life.edu. **Website:** http://www.life.edu. **Application deadlines for fall 2011:** Regular decision: September 1. Early decision: Not offered. Early action: Send application by: N/A; Decision sent by: N/A. Admission can be deferred. **Application fee:** $50. **To apply online, go to:** http://apply.life.edu. **Admissions requirements/recommendations:** Tests: The college uses SAT or ACT scores in admissions decisions. Either SAT or ACT required. For admission to the fall 2011 entering class, the school will accept: ACT with writing required. Campus visit: Recommended. Admissions interview: Recommended. **Factors that count in admissions decisions:** *Academic:* Secondary school record: Considered. Class rank: Considered. Letters of recommendation: Not Considered. Standardized test scores: Important. Essay: Not Considered. *Nonacademic:* Interview: Not Considered. Extracurricular activities: Considered. Talent/ability: Considered. Character/personal qualities: Not Considered. Alumni/ae relationship: Considered. Geographical residence: Not Considered. State residency: Not Considered. Religious affiliation/commitment: Not Considered. Minority status: Not Considered. Volunteer work: Not Considered. Work experience: Not Considered. **Admissions statistics for the fall 2009 entering class:** Total applicants: 322. Total accepted: 263. Freshmen enrolled: 208; Overall acceptance rate: 82%. Non-early acceptance rate: 82%. **First-year students who submitted SAT scores:** 19%. Scores (25/75 percentile): Critical Reading: 405-485, Math: 400-510, Combined: 805-995. **First-year students submitting ACT scores:** 6%. Scores (25/75 percentile): English: 16-23, Math: 17-21, Composite: 18-23.

ACADEMICS
Year founded: 1974. **Academic calendar:** Quarter. **Degrees offered:** certificate, associate, bachelor's, post-bachelor's certificate, master's. **Major fields of study:** biological and biomedical sciences; business, management, marketing, and related support services; computer and information sciences and support services; health professions and related clinical sciences; multi/interdisciplinary studies; psychology. **Areas of required coursework:** humanities, computer literacy, mathematics, English (including composition), sciences (biological or physical), history, social science. **Pre-professional programs:** other. **Special academic programs:** accelerated program, double major, English as a Second Language (ESL), independent study, internships. **Faculty and instruction (2009-2010):** Total instructional faculty: 119 full-time, 47 part-time (61% men; 39% women; 20% minorities). Full-time faculty with Ph.D. or other terminal degree: 85%. Student/faculty ratio: 14/1. Classes of fewer than 20 students: 67%; of 20 to 49 students: 31%; of 50 or more students: 1%. **Freshmen returning for sophomore year:** 65%. **Graduation rates:** Four-year: 3%; five-year: 13%; six-year: 14%.

COSTS AND FINANCIAL AID
Financial aid office: (770) 426-2901. **Expenses (2009-2010):** Tuition and fees 2009-2010: $8,352; room/board: $12,480. **Financial aid:** Priority filing date for institution's financial aid form: March 1. In 2009-2010, 84% of undergraduates applied for financial aid. Of those, 78% were determined to have financial need; 1% had their need fully met. Average financial aid package (proportion receiving): $9,750 (75%). Average amount of gift aid, such as scholarships or grants (proportion receiving): $4,825 (50%). Average amount of self-help aid, such as work study or loans (proportion receiving): $5,500 (75%). Average need-based loan (excluding PLUS or other private loans): $500. Among students who received need-based aid, the average percentage of need met: 1%. Among students who received aid based on merit, the average award (and the proportion receiving): $1,000 (0%). The average athletic scholarship (and the proportion receiving): $10,600 (9%). Average amount of debt of borrowers graduating in 2009: $17,600. Proportion who borrowed: 60%.

CAMPUS LIFE AND EXTRACURRICULAR ACTIVITIES
Campus housing available: apartments for married students, apartment for single students. Activities include: student government. Number of fraternities: 0; sororities: 0.

SERVICES AND FACILITIES
Basic services: day care. **Remedial assistance:** reading, math, writing, study skills. **Information technology resources:** Students are not required to lease or own a computer. School has a wireless network. **Campus safety:** Security services offered: 24-hour foot-and-vehicle patrols, 24-hour emergency telephones.

TRANSFER AND INTERNATIONAL STUDENTS
Transfer students: May apply for admission for the following academic terms: Fall, Winter, Spring, Summer. Applicants need a minimum number of credits to apply. For fall 2009: Transfer applications received: 141. Transfer applicants offered admission: 84. Transfer applicants enrolled: 58.

Macon State College

- **Address:** 100 College Station Drive, Macon, GA 31206
- **Website:** http://www.maconstate.edu/
- **Public**
- **Enrollment:** N/A

KEY STATS
✔ **U.S News College Ranking:** second tier, Regional Colleges (South)
✔ **SAT or ACT Score (25th/75th percentile):** N/A
✔ **Tuition:** 2009-2010: $2,304 in state, $8,280 out of state
  Selectivity: Less selective **Room/board:** N/A
  Acceptance rate: N/A **Average debt:** N/A
  Student/faculty ratio: N/A **Proportion who borrowed:** N/A

Mercer University

- **Address:** 1400 Coleman Avenue, Macon, GA 31207-0003
- **Website:** http://www.mercer.edu
- **Private; Religious affiliation:** Baptist
- **Enrollment:** 3,837 full-time; 694 part-time

KEY STATS
✔ **U.S News College Ranking:** 8, Regional Universities (South)
✔ **SAT Score (25th/75th percentile):** 1090-1270
✔ **Tuition:** 2010-2011: $30,560
  Selectivity: More selective **Room/board:** $10,088
  Acceptance rate: 62% **Average debt:** $29,065
  Student/faculty ratio: 14/1 **Proportion who borrowed:** 58%

UNDERGRADUATE STUDENT BODY STATS
2009-2010 enrollment: 3,837 full-time; 694 part-time. Men: 31%; women: 69%. **Ethnic makeup:** African American: 26%; Asian American: 4%; Hispanic: 2%; White: 64%; International: 3%. **Religious preference:** Roman Catholic: 8%; Protestant: 18%; Muslim: 1%; Hindu: 2%; No preference: 29%; Unknown: 10%; Baptist: 32%.

ADMISSIONS FACTS AND FIGURES
Phone: (478) 301-2650. **Email:** admissions@mercer.edu. **Website:** http://www.mercer.edu. **Application deadlines for fall 2011:** Regular decision: July 1. Early decision: Not offered. Early action: Send application by: November 1; Decision sent by: November 15. Admission can be deferred. **Application fee:** $50. **To apply online, go to:** https://sis.mercer.edu/mhomepg.htm. **Admissions requirements/recommendations:** High school units required (recommended): English: 4 (4); Mathematics: 4 (4); Science: 3 (3); Foreign language: 2 (2); Social studies: 1 (1); History: 2 (2); Total units: 16 (16). Tests: The college uses SAT or ACT scores in admissions decisions. Either SAT or ACT required. For admission to the fall 2011 entering class, the school will accept: ACT with or without writing accepted. Campus visit: Recommended. Admissions interview: Recommended. Off-campus interview: May be arranged. **Factors that count in admissions decisions:** *Academic:* Secondary school record: Very Important. Class rank: Considered. Letters of recommendation: Considered. Standardized test scores: Very Important. Essay: Not Considered. *Nonacademic:* Interview: Considered. Extracurricular activities: Important. Talent/ability: Important. Character/personal qualities: Important. Alumni/ae relationship: Considered. Geographical residence: Not Considered. State residency: Not Considered. Religious affiliation/commitment: Not Considered. Minority status: Not Considered. Volunteer work: Important. Work experience: Considered. **Other schools with the greatest overlap in applicants:** Emory University; Furman University; Georgia Institute of Technology; Samford University; University of Georgia. **Admissions statistics for the fall 2009 entering class:** Total applicants: 4,877. Total accepted: 3,034. Freshmen enrolled: 616; 18% were from out of state. Overall acceptance rate: 62%. Non-early acceptance rate: 62%. **Credentials of fall 2009 freshmen:** 43% ranked in the top 10 percent of their high school class; 73% were in the top 25 percent; 94% were in the top half. (Proportion submitting class standing: 63%.) **Average high school grade point average:** 3.7. **First-year students who submitted SAT scores:** 73%. Scores (25/75 percentile): Critical Reading: 540-630, Math: 550-640, Combined: 1090-1270. **First-year students submitting ACT scores:** 27%. Scores (25/75 percentile): English: 24-31, Math: 23-28, Composite: 24-29.

ACADEMICS
Year founded: 1833. **Academic calendar:** Semester. **Degrees offered:** bachelor's, master's, post-master's certificate, doctorate. **Most popular majors:** 24% business, management, marketing, and related support services, 11% social sciences, 10% biological and biomedical sciences, 10% communication, journalism, and related programs, 9% engineering. **Major fields of study:** area, ethnic, cultural, and gender studies; biological and biomedical sciences; business, management, marketing, and related support services; communication, journalism, and related programs; computer and information sciences and support services; education; engineering; English language and literature/letters; foreign languages, literatures, and linguistics; history; liberal arts and sciences studies, and humanities; mathematics and statistics; natural resources and conservation; philosophy and religious studies; physical sciences; psychology; social sciences; visual and performing arts. **Areas of required coursework:** arts/fine arts, humanities, computer literacy, mathematics, English (including composition),

philosophy, foreign languages, sciences (biological or physical), history, social science, other. **Pre-professional programs:** pre-law, pre-dentistry, pre-medicine, pre-theology, pre-veterinary science, pre-pharmacy, other. **Special academic programs:** accelerated program, cooperative (work-study plan) program, cross-registration, double major, dual enrollment, honors program, independent study, internships, liberal arts/career combination, student-designed major, study abroad, teacher certificate program. **Teacher certification offered in:** elementary, middle/junior high, secondary. **Cooperative education programs:** art, business, computer science, engineering, humanities, natural science, social/behavioral science, other. **Reserve Officers Training Corps (ROTC):** Army ROTC: Offered on campus. **Faculty and instruction (2009-2010):** Total instructional faculty: 370 full-time, 264 part-time (53% men; 47% women; 20% minorities). Full-time faculty with Ph.D. or other terminal degree: 88%. Student/faculty ratio: 14/1. Classes of fewer than 20 students: 57%; of 20 to 49 students: 41%; of 50 or more students: 2%. **Advanced Placement and International Baccalaureate credit:** AP tests may be used for: Credit and/or placement. Scores accepted: 3, 4, 5. International Baccalaureate exams may be used for: Credit only. **Freshmen returning for sophomore year:** 80%. **Graduation rates:** Four-year: 44%; five-year: 59%; six-year: 56%. **Graduate study:** 23% of students pursue further study immediately upon graduation.

COSTS AND FINANCIAL AID

Financial aid office: (478) 301-2670. **Expenses (2010-2011):** Tuition and fees 2010-2011: $30,560; room/board: $10,088. Estimated books and supplies: $1,200; transportation: $800; personal expenses: $1,201. **Financial aid:** Priority filing date for institution's financial aid form: April 1. In 2009-2010, 80% of undergraduates applied for financial aid. Of those, 71% were determined to have financial need; 47% had their need fully met. Average financial aid package (proportion receiving): $30,024 (71%). Average amount of gift aid, such as scholarships or grants (proportion receiving): $19,558 (71%). Average amount of self-help aid, such as work study or loans (proportion receiving): $8,881 (47%). Average need-based loan (excluding PLUS or other private loans): $8,304. Among students who received need-based aid, the average percentage of need met: 88%. Among students who received aid based on merit, the average award (and the proportion receiving): $19,395 (28%). The average athletic scholarship (and the proportion receiving): $15,572 (6%). Average amount of debt of borrowers graduating in 2009: $29,065. Proportion who borrowed: 58%.

CAMPUS LIFE AND EXTRACURRICULAR ACTIVITIES

Campus housing available: coed dorms, women's dorms, men's dorms, sorority housing, fraternity housing, apartments for married students, apartment for single students, special housing for disabled students, special housing for international students. Students who live in college-owned, operated, or affiliated housing: 70%. **Clubs and organizations:** Number of student organizations: 96. Activities include: campus ministries, choral groups, concert band, dance, drama/theater, international student organization, jazz band, literary magazine, model UN, music ensembles, musical theater, opera, pep band, radio station, student government, student newspaper, student film society, television station. Number of fraternities: 10; sororities: 6. Proportion of men in fraternities: 22%; of women in sororities: 26%. Average proportion of students who stay on campus on weekends: 65%. **Sports program (2009-2010):** Member of NCAA I. *Men's intercollegiate varsity sports:* baseball, basketball, cross country, golf, rifle, soccer, tennis. *Women's intercollegiate varsity sports:* basketball, cross country, golf, soccer, softball, tennis, volleyball.

SERVICES AND FACILITIES

Basic services: nonremedial tutoring, placement service, health service, health insurance. **Counseling services:** minority student, career, military, personal, veteran student, academic, older student, psychological, religious. **For learning-disabled students:** School does not offer a structured program with separate admission and additional fees. Services include: remedial math, tape recorders, learning center, extended time for tests, tutors, priority registration, priority seating, texts on tape, other testing accommodations, other. **Library:** Number of titles: 796,693; number of current serial subscriptions: 25,037. **Information technology resources:** Students are not required to lease or own a computer. Number of campus computers available to all students: 500. School has a wireless network. Proportion of college-owned housing units wired for high-speed internet access: 100%. **Campus safety:** Security services offered: 24-hour foot-and-vehicle patrols, late-night transport/escort service, 24-hour emergency telephones, lighted pathways/sidewalks, student patrols, controlled dormitory access (key, security card, etc).

TRANSFER AND INTERNATIONAL STUDENTS

Transfer students: May apply for admission for the following academic terms: Fall, Spring, Summer. Applicants need a minimum number of credits to apply. For fall 2009: Transfer applications received: 255. Transfer applicants offered admission: 227. Transfer applicants enrolled: 80. **International students:** Number of foreign undergraduates: 117 (3% of student body). Number of countries represented: 35. Minimum TOEFL score required: 80 (computer).

Morehouse College

- **Address:** 830 Westview Drive SW, Atlanta, GA 30314
- **Website:** http://www.morehouse.edu
- **Private**
- **Enrollment:** 2,512 full-time; 177 part-time

KEY STATS

✔ **U.S News College Ranking:** 127, National Liberal Arts Colleges
✔ **SAT Score (25th/75th percentile):** 930-1150
✔ **Tuition:** 2010-2011: $22,444

Selectivity: Selective	**Room/board:** $11,494
Acceptance rate: 67%	**Average debt:** $32,125
Student/faculty ratio: 15/1	**Proportion who borrowed:** 90%

UNDERGRADUATE STUDENT BODY STATS

2009-2010 enrollment: 2,512 full-time; 177 part-time. Men: 100%; women: 0%. **Ethnic makeup:** African American: 95%; White: 2%; International: 3%.

ADMISSIONS FACTS AND FIGURES

Phone: (404) 215-2632. **Email:** admissions@morehouse.edu. **Website:** http://www.morehouse.edu. **Application deadlines for fall 2011:** Regular decision: February 15; decision sent by April 1. Early decision: Send application by: November 1; Decision sent by: December 15. Early action: Send application by: November 1; Decision sent by: December 15. Admission cannot be deferred. **Application fee:** $45. **To apply online, go to:** http://www.morehouse.edu/admissions/. **Admissions requirements/recommendations:** High school units required (recommended): English: 4 (4); Mathematics: 3 (3); Science: 2 (2); Foreign language: 2 (2); Social studies: 2 (2); Academic electives: (3); Total units: 13 (16). Tests: The college uses SAT or ACT scores in admissions decisions. Either SAT or ACT required. For admission to the fall 2011 entering class, the school will accept: ACT with writing recommended. Campus visit: Recommended. Admissions interview: Recommended. Off-campus interview: May be arranged. **Factors that count in admissions decisions:** *Academic:* Secondary school record: Important. Class rank: Important. Letters of recommendation: Important. Standardized test scores: Very Important. Essay: Important. *Nonacademic:* Interview: Considered. Extracurricular activities: Considered. Talent/ability: Considered. Character/personal qualities: Considered. Alumni/ae relationship: Considered. Geographical residence: Considered. State residency: Not Considered. Religious affiliation/commitment: Not Considered. Minority status: Considered. Volunteer work: Considered. Work experience: Not Considered. **Other schools with the greatest overlap in applicants:** Duke University; Harvard University; Howard University; University of North Carolina–Chapel Hill; Washington State University. **Admissions statistics for the fall 2009 entering class:** Total applicants: 2,352. Total accepted: 1,584. Freshmen enrolled: 655; Overall acceptance rate: 67%. Early-decision acceptance rate: 100%. Non-early acceptance rate: 66%. **Size of waiting list:** 0 applicants; enrolled from waiting list: 0. **Credentials of fall 2009 freshmen:** 17% ranked in the top 10 percent of their high school class; 43% were in the top 25 percent; 81% were in the top half. (Proportion submitting class standing: 48%.) **Average high school grade point average:** 3.2. **First-year students who submitted SAT scores:** 65%. Scores (25/75 percentile): Critical Reading: 460-570, Math: 470-580, Combined: 930-1150. **First-year students submitting ACT scores:** 35%. Scores (25/75 percentile): English: 19-25, Math: 19-24, Composite: 19-25.

ACADEMICS

Year founded: 1867. **Academic calendar:** Semester. **Degrees offered:** bachelor's. **Most popular majors:** 36% business administration and management, 10% political science and government, 8% psychology, 7% English language and literature, 5% biology/biological sciences. **Major fields of study:** area, ethnic, cultural, and gender studies; biological and biomedical sciences; business, management, marketing, and related support services;

communication, journalism, and related programs; computer and information sciences and support services; education; engineering; English language and literature/letters; foreign languages, literatures, and linguistics; history; mathematics and statistics; parks, recreation, leisure, and fitness studies; philosophy and religious studies; physical sciences; psychology; social sciences; visual and performing arts. **Areas of required coursework:** arts/fine arts, humanities, computer literacy, mathematics, English (including composition), philosophy, foreign languages, sciences (biological or physical), history, social science, other. **Pre-professional programs:** pre-law, pre-medicine, other. **Special academic programs (% participation):** cross-registration (69%), double major (2%), dual enrollment (1%), exchange student program (domestic), honors program (9%), independent study (4%), internships (89%), study abroad (7.5%), teacher certificate program (1%). **Teacher certification offered in:** early childhood. **Cooperative education programs:** business, computer science, education, engineering, social/behavioral science. **Reserve Officers Training Corps (ROTC):** Army ROTC: Offered on campus; Navy ROTC: Offered on campus; Air Force ROTC: Offered at cooperating institution (Georgia Institute of Technology). **Faculty and instruction (2009-2010):** Total instructional faculty: 158 full-time, 55 part-time (64% men; 36% women; 82% minorities). Full-time faculty with Ph.D. or other terminal degree: 90%. Student/faculty ratio: 15/1. Classes of fewer than 20 students: 45%; of 20 to 49 students: 53%; of 50 or more students: 2%. **Advanced Placement and International Baccalaureate credit:** AP tests may be used for: Placement only. Scores accepted: 3, 4, 5. International Baccalaureate exams may be used for: Placement only. **Freshmen returning for sophomore year:** 85%. **Graduation rates:** Four-year: 39%; five-year: 55%; six-year: 60%. **Graduate study:** 23% of students pursue further study immediately upon graduation. Fields in which graduates pursue further study: law, 21%; medicine, 14%; engineering, 7%; theology (or the seminary), 12%; arts and sciences, 37%.

COSTS AND FINANCIAL AID

Financial aid office: (404) 681-2800. **Expenses (2010-2011):** Tuition and fees 2010-2011: $22,444; room/board: $11,494. Estimated books and supplies: $2,000; transportation: $2,750; personal expenses: $2,500. **Financial aid:** Priority filing date for institution's financial aid form: February 15; deadline: April 1. In 2009-2010, 97% of undergraduates applied for financial aid. Of those, 97% were determined to have financial need; 8% had their need fully met. Average financial aid package (proportion receiving): $12,425 (97%). Average amount of gift aid, such as scholarships or grants (proportion receiving): $10,850 (45%). Average amount of self-help aid, such as work study or loans (proportion receiving): $7,500 (69%). Average need-based loan (excluding PLUS or other private loans): $5,500. Among students who received need-based aid, the average percentage of need met: 64%. Average amount of debt of borrowers graduating in 2009: $32,125. Proportion who borrowed: 90%.

CAMPUS LIFE AND EXTRACURRICULAR ACTIVITIES

Campus housing available (% using): men's dorms (100%), special housing for disabled students. **Student employment:** During the 2009-2010 academic year, 1% of undergraduates worked on campus. Average per-year earnings: $8,680. **Clubs and organizations:** Number of student organizations: 78. Activities include: choral groups, concert band, dance, drama/theater, international student organization, jazz band, literary magazine, marching band, model UN, music ensembles, pep band, student government, student newspaper, student film society, symphony orchestra, yearbook. Number of fraternities: 8; sororities: 0. Average proportion of students who stay on campus on weekends: 50%. **Sports program (2009-2010):** Member of NCAA II. *Men's intercollegiate varsity sports:* baseball, basketball, cross country, football, golf, tennis, track and field (outdoor).

SERVICES AND FACILITIES

Basic services: nonremedial tutoring, placement service, health service, health insurance. **Remedial assistance:** reading, math, writing, study skills. **Counseling services:** minority student, career, personal, academic, older student, psychological, birth control, religious. **For learning-disabled students:** School does not offer a structured program with separate admission and additional fees. Total undergraduates in learning-disabled program or receiving services: 82. Services include: remedial math, remedial English, reading machines, remedial reading, tape recorders, note-taking services, oral tests, learning center, readers, extended time for tests, tutors, early syllabus, priority registration, priority seating, proofreading services, substitution of courses, texts on tape, typist/scribe, exams on tape or computer, take home exams, other testing accommodations, other. **Library:** Number of titles: 585,338; number of current serial subscriptions: 1,522. **Information technology resources:** Students are not required to lease or own a computer.

School has a wireless network. Approximate number of users that can be accommodated: 99. Proportion of college-owned housing units wired for high-speed internet access: 0%. **Campus safety:** Security services offered: 24-hour foot-and-vehicle patrols, late-night transport/escort service, 24-hour emergency telephones, lighted pathways/sidewalks, controlled dormitory access (key, security card, etc).

TRANSFER AND INTERNATIONAL STUDENTS

Transfer students: May apply for admission for the following academic terms: Fall, Spring, Summer. Applicants need a minimum number of credits to apply. For fall 2009: Transfer applications received: 170. Transfer applicants offered admission: 143. Transfer applicants enrolled: 99. **International students:** Number of foreign undergraduates: 70 (3% of student body). Number of countries represented: 26. Minimum TOEFL score required: 500 (paper). Average TOEFL score: 550 (paper).

North Georgia College and State University

- **Address:** 82 College Circle, Dahlonega, GA 30597
- **Website:** http://www.ngcsu.edu
- **Public**
- **Enrollment:** 4,111 full-time; 903 part-time

KEY STATS

✔ **U.S News College Ranking:** 59, Regional Universities (South)
✔ **SAT Score (25th/75th percentile):** 1010-1180
✔ **Tuition:** 2009-2010: $5,036 in state, $16,650 out of state

Selectivity: Selective	**Room/board:** $5,248
Acceptance rate: 54%	**Average debt:** $9,885
Student/faculty ratio: 20/1	**Proportion who borrowed:** 65%

UNDERGRADUATE STUDENT BODY STATS

2009-2010 enrollment: 4,111 full-time; 903 part-time. Men: 43%; women: 57%. **Ethnic makeup:** African American: 2%; Asian American: 1%; Hispanic: 4%; White: 91%; International: 1%.

ADMISSIONS FACTS AND FIGURES

Phone: (800) 498-9581. **Email:** admissions@ngcsu.edu. **Website:** http://www.ngcsu.edu. **Application deadlines for fall 2011:** Regular decision: July 1. Early decision: Not offered. Early action: Not offered. Admission cannot be deferred. **Application fee:** $30. **To apply online, go to:** http://www.applyweb.com/aw?ngcsu. **Admissions requirements/recommendations:** High school units required (recommended): English: 4; Mathematics: 4; Science: 3; Foreign language: 2; Social studies: 3; Academic electives: 0; Total units: 17. Tests: The college uses SAT or ACT scores in admissions decisions. Either SAT or ACT required. For admission to the fall 2011 entering class, the school will accept: ACT with or without writing accepted. Campus visit: Recommended. Admissions interview: Neither required nor recommended. Off-campus interview: Not available. **Factors that count in admissions decisions:** *Academic:* Secondary school record: Considered. Class rank: Considered. Letters of recommendation: Considered. Standardized test scores: Very Important. Essay: Not Considered. *Nonacademic:* Interview: Not Considered. Extracurricular activities: Considered. Talent/ability: Considered. Character/personal qualities: Considered. Alumni/ae relationship: Considered. Geographical residence: Not Considered. State residency: Not Considered. Religious affiliation/commitment: Not Considered. Minority status: Not Considered. Volunteer work: Considered. Work experience: Considered. **Other schools with the greatest overlap in applicants:** Berry College; Georgia Southern University; Georgia State University; University of Georgia; University of West Georgia. **Admissions statistics for the fall 2009 entering class:** Total applicants: 2,993. Total accepted: 1,620. Freshmen enrolled: 822; 5% were from out of state. Overall acceptance rate: 54%. **Average high school grade point average:** 3.4. **First-year students who submitted SAT scores:** 83%. Scores (25/75 percentile): Critical Reading: 510-590, Math: 500-590, Combined: 1010-1180. **First-year students submitting ACT scores:** 38%. Scores (25/75 percentile): English: N/A, Math: N/A, Composite: 21-25.

ACADEMICS

Year founded: 1873. **Academic calendar:** Semester. **Degrees offered:** certificate, associate, bachelor's, post-bachelor's certificate, master's, post-master's certificate. **Most popular majors:** 26% business, management, marketing, and related support services, 22% education, 10% social sciences, 7% security and protective services, 6% biological and biomedical sciences. **Major fields of study:** biological and biomedical sciences; business, management, marketing, and related support services; computer and information sciences and support services; education; English language and literature/letters; foreign languages, literatures, and linguistics; health professions and related clinical sciences; history; mathematics and statistics; physical sciences; psychology; public administration and social service professions; security and protective services; social sciences; visual and performing arts. **Areas of required coursework:** arts/fine arts, humanities, computer literacy, mathematics, English (including composition), philosophy, foreign languages, sciences (biological or physical), history, social science. **Pre-professional programs:** pre-law, pre-dentistry, pre-medicine, pre-veterinary science, pre-pharmacy, other. **Special academic programs:** cooperative (work-study plan) program, distance learning, double major, dual enrollment, external degree program, honors program, independent study, internships, liberal arts/career combination, study abroad, teacher certificate program, other. **Teacher certification offered in:** early childhood, special education, elementary, middle/junior high, secondary. **Reserve Officers Training Corps (ROTC):** Army ROTC: Offered on campus. **Faculty and instruction (2009-2010):** Total instructional faculty: 220 full-time, 124 part-time (42% men; 58% women; 7% minorities). Student/faculty ratio: 20/1. Classes of fewer than 20 students: 35%; of 20 to 49 students: 61%; of 50 or more students: 4%. **Advanced Placement and International Baccalaureate credit:** AP tests may be used for: Credit only. International Baccalaureate exams may be used for: Credit only. **Freshmen returning for sophomore year:** 77%. **Graduation rates:** Four-year: 24%; five-year: 40%; six-year: 49%.

COSTS AND FINANCIAL AID

Financial aid office: (706) 864-1412. **Expenses (2009-2010):** Tuition and fees 2009-2010: $5,036 in state, $16,650 out of state; room/board: $5,248. Estimated books and supplies: $1,000; transportation: $1,000; personal expenses: $1,646. **Financial aid:** Priority filing date for institution's financial aid form: March 17. In 2009-2010, 92% of undergraduates applied for financial aid. Of those, 39% were determined to have financial need; 66% had their need fully met. Average financial aid package (proportion receiving): $8,400 (38%). Average amount of gift aid, such as scholarships or grants (proportion receiving): $2,000 (34%). Average amount of self-help aid, such as work study or loans (proportion receiving): $2,000 (37%). Average need-based loan (excluding PLUS or other private loans): $5,500. Among students who received need-based aid, the average percentage of need met: 79%. Among students who received aid based on merit, the average award (and the proportion receiving): $1,500 (4%). The average athletic scholarship (and the proportion receiving): $2,000 (2%). Average amount of debt of borrowers graduating in 2009: $9,885. Proportion who borrowed: 65%.

CAMPUS LIFE AND EXTRACURRICULAR ACTIVITIES

Campus housing available: coed dorms, women's dorms, men's dorms, apartment for single students, other housing options. Students who live in college-owned, operated, or affiliated housing: 31%. **Clubs and organizations:** Number of student organizations: 140. Activities include: campus ministries, choral groups, concert band, dance, drama/theater, international student organization, jazz band, literary magazine, music ensembles, student government, student newspaper, yearbook. Number of fraternities: 9; sororities: 5. Proportion of men in fraternities: 11%; of women in sororities: 12%. **Sports program (2009-2010):** Member of NCAA II. *Men's intercollegiate varsity sports:* baseball, basketball, cross country, golf, soccer, tennis, track and field (outdoor). *Women's intercollegiate varsity sports:* basketball, cross country, golf, soccer, softball, tennis, track and field (outdoor).

SERVICES AND FACILITIES

Basic services: nonremedial tutoring, placement service, health service, health insurance. **Remedial assistance:** reading, math, writing, study skills. **Counseling services:** minority student, career, military, personal, veteran student, academic, older student, psychological, birth control. **For learning-disabled students:** School does not offer a structured program with separate admission and additional fees. Services include: remedial math, remedial English, reading machines, remedial reading, tape recorders, diagnostic testing service, untimed tests, note-taking services, readers, extended time for tests, tutors, priority registration, priority seating. **Library:** Number of titles: 173,074; number of current serial subscriptions: 4,633. **Information technology resources:** Students are not required to lease or own a computer. Number of campus computers available to all students: 850. School has a wireless network. Proportion of college-owned housing units wired for high-speed internet access: 100%. **Campus safety:** Security services offered:

24-hour foot-and-vehicle patrols, 24-hour emergency telephones, lighted pathways/sidewalks, controlled dormitory access (key, security card, etc).

TRANSFER AND INTERNATIONAL STUDENTS

Transfer students: May apply for admission for the following academic terms: Fall, Spring, Summer. Applicants need a minimum number of credits to apply. For fall 2009: Transfer applications received: 1,048. Transfer applicants offered admission: 785. Transfer applicants enrolled: 448. **International students:** Number of foreign undergraduates: 60 (1% of student body). Number of countries represented: 53. Minimum TOEFL score required: 550 (paper); 213 (computer).

Oglethorpe University

■ **Address:** 4484 Peachtree Road NE, Atlanta, GA 30319-2797
■ **Website:** http://www.oglethorpe.edu
■ **Private**
■ **Enrollment:** 923 full-time; 107 part-time

KEY STATS
✔ **U.S News College Ranking:** 166, National Liberal Arts Colleges
✔ **SAT Score (25th/75th percentile):** 1060-1280
✔ **Tuition:** 2010-2011: $27,950
  Selectivity: More selective   **Room/board:** $9,990
  Acceptance rate: 42%   **Average debt:** $18,650
  Student/faculty ratio: 16/1   **Proportion who borrowed:** 42%

UNDERGRADUATE STUDENT BODY STATS

2009-2010 enrollment: 923 full-time; 107 part-time. Men: 40%; women: 60%. **Ethnic makeup:** African American: 23%; Asian American: 4%; Hispanic: 5%; White: 64%; International: 3%.

ADMISSIONS FACTS AND FIGURES

Phone: (404) 364-8307. **Email:** admission@oglethorpe.edu. **Website:** http://www.oglethorpe.edu. **Application deadlines for fall 2011:** Regular decision: Rolling. Early decision: Not offered. Early action: Send application by: December 5; Decision sent by: December 20. Admission can be deferred. **Application fee:** $40. **To apply online, go to:** http://www.oglethorpe.edu/Admission/undergraduate/applications/. **Admissions requirements/recommendations:** High school units required (recommended): English: 4; Mathematics: 3; Science: 2; Foreign language: (2); Social studies: 3. Tests: The college uses SAT or ACT scores in admissions decisions. Either SAT or ACT required. For admission to the fall 2011 entering class, the school will accept: ACT with writing recommended. Campus visit: Recommended. Admissions interview: Recommended. **Factors that count in admissions decisions:** *Academic:* Secondary school record: Very Important. Class rank: Important. Letters of recommendation: Important. Standardized test scores: Very Important. Essay: Important. *Nonacademic:* Interview: Important. Extracurricular activities: Important. Talent/ability: Considered. Character/personal qualities: Considered. Alumni/ae relationship: Considered. Geographical residence: Not Considered. State residency: Not Considered. Religious affiliation/commitment: Not Considered. Minority status: Not Considered. Volunteer work: Important. Work experience: Considered. **Admissions statistics for the fall 2009 entering class:** Total applicants: 4,891. Total accepted: 2,040. Freshmen enrolled: 232; Overall acceptance rate: 42%. Non-early acceptance rate: 42%. **Credentials of fall 2009 freshmen:** 24% ranked in the top 10 percent of their high school class; 63% were in the top 25 percent; 87% were in the top half. (Proportion submitting class standing: 57%.) **Average high school grade point average:** 3.6. **First-year students who submitted SAT scores:** 76%. Scores (25/75 percentile): Critical Reading: 550-650, Math: 510-630, Combined: 1060-1280. **First-year students submitting ACT scores:** 40%. Scores (25/75 percentile): English: N/A, Math: N/A, Composite: 23-27.

ACADEMICS

Year founded: 1835. **Academic calendar:** Semester. **Degrees offered:** diploma, bachelor's, master's. **Most popular majors:** 23% business, management, marketing, and related support services; 18% psychology; 16% English language and literature/letters; 11% social sciences; 6% history. **Major fields of study:** area, ethnic, cultural, and gender studies; biological and biomedical sciences; business, management, marketing, and related support services; communication, journalism, and related programs; English language and literature/letters; history; liberal arts and sciences studies, and humanities; mathematics and statistics; multi/interdisciplinary studies; philosophy and religious studies; physical sciences; psychology; public administration and social service professions; social sciences; visual and performing arts. **Areas of required coursework:** arts/fine arts, humanities, computer literacy, mathematics, English (including composition), philosophy, foreign languages, sciences (biological or physical), history, social science, other. **Pre-professional programs:** pre-law, pre-dentistry, pre-medicine, pre-theology, pre-veterinary science, pre-optometry, pre-pharmacy. **Special academic programs:** accelerated program, cooperative (work-study plan) program, cross-registration, double major, dual enrollment, honors program, independent study, internships, liberal arts/career combination, student-designed major, study abroad. **Reserve Officers Training Corps (ROTC):** Air Force ROTC: Offered at cooperating institution (Georgia Institute of Technology). **Faculty and instruction (2009-2010):** Total instructional faculty: 46 full-time, 53 part-time (57% men; 43% women; 11% minorities). Full-time faculty with Ph.D. or other terminal degree: 93%. Student/faculty ratio: 16/1. Classes of fewer than 20 students: 73%; of 20 to 49 students: 27%. **Advanced Placement and International Baccalaureate credit:** AP tests may be used for: Credit and/or placement. Scores accepted: 4, 5. International Baccalaureate exams may be used for: Credit only. **Freshmen returning for sophomore year:** 78%. **Graduation rates:** Four-year: 43%; five-year: 53%; six-year: 56%.

COSTS AND FINANCIAL AID

Financial aid office: (404) 364-8356. **Expenses (2010-2011):** Tuition and fees 2010-2011: $27,950; room/board: $9,990. Estimated books and supplies: $900; transportation: $750; personal expenses: $2,000. **Financial aid:** Priority filing date for institution's financial aid form: February 1. In 2009-2010, 64% of undergraduates applied for financial aid. Of those, 56% were determined to have financial need; 38% had their need fully met. Average financial aid package (proportion receiving): $26,500 (56%). Average amount of gift aid, such as scholarships or grants (proportion receiving): $19,876 (56%). Average amount of self-help aid, such as work study or loans (proportion receiving): $6,618 (30%). Average need-based loan (excluding PLUS or other private loans): $6,326. Among students who received need-based aid, the average percentage of need met: 86%. Among students who received aid based on merit, the average award (and the proportion receiving): $12,291 (27%). Average amount of debt of borrowers graduating in 2009: $18,650. Proportion who borrowed: 42%.

CAMPUS LIFE AND EXTRACURRICULAR ACTIVITIES

Campus housing available (% using): coed dorms (92%), women's dorms, men's dorms, sorority housing (4%), fraternity housing (4%). Activities include: campus ministries, choral groups, dance, drama/theater, international student organization, literary magazine, musical theater, radio station, student government, student newspaper, student film society, yearbook. Number of fraternities: 4; sororities: 3. **Sports program (2009-2010):** Member of NCAA III. *Men's intercollegiate varsity sports:* baseball, basketball, cross country, golf, lacrosse, soccer, tennis, track and field (outdoor). *Women's intercollegiate varsity sports:* basketball, cross country, golf, soccer, tennis, track and field (outdoor), volleyball.

SERVICES AND FACILITIES

Basic services: nonremedial tutoring, placement service, health service, health insurance. **Counseling services:** career, academic, psychological. **Information technology resources:** Students are not required to lease or own a computer. School has a wireless network. Proportion of college-owned housing units wired for high-speed internet access: 100%. **Campus safety:** Security services offered: 24-hour foot-and-vehicle patrols, 24-hour emergency telephones, lighted pathways/sidewalks, controlled dormitory access (key, security card, etc).

TRANSFER AND INTERNATIONAL STUDENTS

Transfer students: May apply for admission for the following academic terms: Fall, Spring, Summer. Applicants need a minimum number of credits to apply. For fall 2009: Transfer applications received: 118. Transfer applicants offered admission: 56. Transfer applicants enrolled: 38. **International students:** Number of foreign undergraduates: 27 (3% of student body). Number of countries represented: 32. Minimum TOEFL score required: 500 (paper).

Paine College

- **Address:** 1235 15th Street, Augusta, GA 30901-3182
- **Website:** http://www.paine.edu
- **Private; Religious affiliation:** Christian Methodist Episcopal and United Methodist Churches
- **Enrollment:** 855 full-time; 53 part-time

KEY STATS

✔ **U.S News College Ranking:** second tier, National Liberal Arts Colleges
✔ **SAT Score (25th/75th percentile):** 670-850
✔ **Tuition:** 2009-2010: $11,794

Selectivity: Less selective	**Room/board:** $5,748
Acceptance rate: 39%	**Average debt:** N/A
Student/faculty ratio: 13/1	**Proportion who borrowed:** N/A

UNDERGRADUATE STUDENT BODY STATS

2009-2010 enrollment: 855 full-time; 53 part-time. Men: 35%; women: 65%. **Ethnic makeup:** African American: 96%; Hispanic: 1%; White: 4%. **Religious preference:** Roman Catholic: 1%; Protestant: 27%; No preference: 49%; Unknown: 7%; Christian Methodist Episcopal and United Methodist Churches: 5%; CHGC, EPIS, HOLI, JEHW, NDM, PENT, PRES, SDA: 11%.

ADMISSIONS FACTS AND FIGURES

Phone: (706) 821-8320. **Email:** tinsleyj@mail.paine.edu. **Website:** http://www.paine.edu. **Application deadlines for fall 2011:** Regular decision: August 1. Early decision: Not offered. Early action: Not offered. Admission can be deferred. **Application fee:** $25. **To apply online, go to:** http://www.paine.edu/admissions/apply.aspx. **Admissions requirements/recommendations:** High school units required (recommended): English: 4 (4); Mathematics: 3 (3); Science: 3 (3); Foreign language: (1); Social studies: 2 (2); History: 1 (1); Academic electives: 3; Total units: 16 (16). Tests: The college uses SAT or ACT scores in admissions decisions. Either SAT or ACT required. For admission to the fall 2011 entering class, the school will accept: ACT with or without writing accepted. Campus visit: Neither required nor recommended. Admissions interview: Neither required nor recommended. Off-campus interview: May be arranged. **Factors that count in admissions decisions:** *Academic:* Secondary school record: Very Important. Class rank: Not Considered. Letters of recommendation: Very Important. Standardized test scores: Very Important. Essay: Considered. *Nonacademic:* Interview: Not Considered. Extracurricular activities: Considered. Talent/ability: Important. Character/personal qualities: Very Important. Alumni/ae relationship: Considered. Geographical residence: Not Considered. State residency: Not Considered. Religious affiliation/commitment: Not Considered. Minority status: Not Considered. Volunteer work: Not Considered. Work experience: Not Considered. **Admissions statistics for the fall 2009 entering class:** Total applicants: 3,424. Total accepted: 1,331. Freshmen enrolled: 274; 28% were from out of state. Overall acceptance rate: 39%. **Credentials of fall 2009 freshmen:** 7% ranked in the top 10 percent of their high school class; 14% were in the top 25 percent; 49% were in the top half. (Proportion submitting class standing: 51%.) **Average high school grade point average:** 2.7. **First-year students who submitted SAT scores:** 76%. Scores (25/75 percentile): Critical Reading: 340-430, Math: 330-420, Combined: 670-850. **First-year students submitting ACT scores:** 48%. Scores (25/75 percentile): English: 11-17, Math: 15-17, Composite: 14-17.

ACADEMICS

Year founded: 1882. **Academic calendar:** Semester. **Degrees offered:** bachelor's. **Most popular majors:** 29% counseling psychology, 12% sociology, 9% business administration and management, 8% English language and literature, 7% biology/biological sciences. **Major fields of study:** biological and biomedical sciences; business, management, marketing, and related support services; communication, journalism, and related programs; education; English language and literature/letters; history; mathematics and statistics; multi/interdisciplinary studies; natural resources and conservation; philosophy and religious studies; physical sciences; psychology; social sciences; visual and performing arts. **Areas of required coursework:** arts/fine arts, humanities, computer literacy, mathematics, English (including composition), philosophy, foreign languages, sciences (biological or physical), history, social science, other. **Pre-professional programs:** other. **Special academic programs (% participation):** cross-registration (1%), distance learning (15%), dual enrollment (0%), honors program (1%), independent study (0%), internships (2%), liberal arts/career combination (35%), study abroad (2%), teacher certificate program (16%). **Teacher certification offered**

in: early childhood, elementary, middle/junior high, secondary. **Reserve Officers Training Corps (ROTC):** Army ROTC: Offered at cooperating institution (Augusta State University). **Faculty and instruction (2009-2010):** Total instructional faculty: 59 full-time, 19 part-time (54% men; 46% women; 79% minorities). Full-time faculty with Ph.D. or other terminal degree: 61%. Student/faculty ratio: 13/1. Classes of fewer than 20 students: 62%; of 20 to 49 students: 38%; of 50 or more students: 0%. **Advanced Placement and International Baccalaureate credit:** AP tests may be used for: Credit only. Scores accepted: 3. **Freshmen returning for sophomore year:** 58%. **Graduation rates:** Four-year: 9%; five-year: 24%; six-year: 28%. **Graduate study:** 15% of students pursue further study immediately upon graduation; 20% within one year; 30% within five years. Fields in which graduates pursue further study: Master of Business Administration (MBA), 10%; law, 5%; medicine, 5%; dentistry, 5%; engineering, 5%; theology (or the seminary), 5%; education, 15%; arts and sciences, 50%.

COSTS AND FINANCIAL AID
Financial aid office: (706) 821-8262. **Expenses (2009-2010):** Tuition and fees 2009-2010: $11,794; room/board: $5,748. **Financial aid:** Priority filing date for institution's financial aid form: March 1.

CAMPUS LIFE AND EXTRACURRICULAR ACTIVITIES
Campus housing available (% using): women's dorms (66%), men's dorms (34%). Students who live in college-owned, operated, or affiliated housing: 58%. **Student employment:** During the 2009-2010 academic year, 0% of undergraduates worked on campus. Average per-year earnings: $0. **Clubs and organizations:** Number of student organizations: 18. Activities include: choral groups, dance, drama/theater, international student organization, literary magazine, music ensembles, student government, student newspaper, yearbook. Number of fraternities: 4; sororities: 4. Proportion of men in fraternities: 10%; of women in sororities: 10%. **Sports program (2009-2010):** Member of NCAA II. **Men's intercollegiate varsity sports:** baseball, basketball, cross country, golf, track and field (outdoor). **Women's intercollegiate varsity sports:** basketball, cross country, softball, track and field (outdoor), volleyball.

SERVICES AND FACILITIES
Basic services: nonremedial tutoring, placement service, health service, health insurance. **Remedial assistance:** reading, math, writing, study skills. **Counseling services:** career, military, personal, veteran student, academic, religious, other. **For learning-disabled students:** School does not offer a structured program with separate admission and additional fees. Services include: remedial math, remedial English, remedial reading, diagnostic testing service, learning center, extended time for tests, tutors. **Library:** Number of titles: 76,157; number of current serial subscriptions: 23,194. **Information technology resources:** Students are not required to lease or own a computer. Number of campus computers available to all students: 225. School has a wireless network. Proportion of college-owned housing units wired for high-speed internet access: 100%. **Campus safety:** Security services offered: 24-hour foot-and-vehicle patrols, late-night transport/escort service, 24-hour emergency telephones, lighted pathways/sidewalks, controlled dormitory access (key, security card, etc).

TRANSFER AND INTERNATIONAL STUDENTS
Transfer students: May apply for admission for the following academic terms: Fall, Spring, Summer. Applicants need a minimum number of credits to apply. For fall 2009: Transfer applications received: 146. Transfer applicants offered admission: 72. Transfer applicants enrolled: 48. **International students:** Number of foreign undergraduates: 1. Number of countries represented: 1. Minimum TOEFL score required: 500 (paper).

Piedmont College

- **Address:** PO Box 10, Demorest, GA 30535
- **Website:** http://www.piedmont.edu
- **Private; Religious affiliation:** United Church of Christ
- **Enrollment:** 1,116 full-time; 152 part-time

KEY STATS
✔ U.S News College Ranking: 69, Regional Universities (South)
✔ SAT Score (25th/75th percentile): 878-1090
✔ Tuition: 2010-2011: $18,000

Selectivity: Selective	**Room/board:** $7,500
Acceptance rate: 60%	**Average debt:** $16,986
Student/faculty ratio: 15/1	**Proportion who borrowed:** 71%

UNDERGRADUATE STUDENT BODY STATS
2009-2010 enrollment: 1,116 full-time; 152 part-time. Men: 30%; women: 70%. **Ethnic makeup:** African American: 11%; Asian American: 1%; Hispanic: 2%; White: 85%.

ADMISSIONS FACTS AND FIGURES
Phone: (800) 277-7020. **Email:** ugrad@piedmont.edu. **Website:** http://www.piedmont.edu. **Application deadlines for fall 2011:** Regular decision: July 1. Early decision: Not offered. Early action: Not offered. Admission can be deferred. **To apply online, go to:** http://www.piedmont.edu/it/forms/undergrad.html. **Admissions requirements/recommendations:** High school units required (recommended): English: 4 (4); Mathematics: 3 (3); Science: 3 (3); Foreign language: 2 (2); Social studies: 1 (1); History: 2 (2); Total units: 21 (21). Tests: The college uses SAT or ACT scores in admissions decisions. Either SAT or ACT required. For admission to the fall 2011 entering class, the school will accept: ACT with writing recommended. Campus visit: Recommended. Admissions interview: Recommended. Off-campus interview: May be arranged. **Factors that count in admissions decisions:** *Academic:* Secondary school record: Very Important. Class rank: Important. Letters of recommendation: Important. Standardized test scores: Very Important. Essay: Important. *Nonacademic:* Interview: Important. Extracurricular activities: Important. Talent/ability: Important. Character/personal qualities: Important. Alumni/ae relationship: Considered. Geographical residence: Considered. State residency: Considered. Religious affiliation/commitment: Not Considered. Minority status: Not Considered. Volunteer work: Considered. Work experience: Considered. **Other schools with the greatest overlap in applicants:** Berry College; LaGrange College; North Georgia College and State University; Shorter College. **Admissions statistics for the fall 2009 entering class:** Total applicants: 1,321. Total accepted: 788. Freshmen enrolled: 239; 1% were from out of state. Overall acceptance rate: 60%. **Size of waiting list:** 0 applicants; enrolled from waiting list: 0. **Credentials of fall 2009 freshmen:** 14% ranked in the top 10 percent of their high school class; 41% were in the top 25 percent; 81% were in the top half. (Proportion submitting class standing: 65%.) **Average high school grade point average:** 3.4. **First-year students who submitted SAT scores:** 78%. Scores (25/75 percentile): Critical Reading: 448-540, Math: 430-550, Combined: 878-1090. **First-year students submitting ACT scores:** 37%. Scores (25/75 percentile): English: N/A, Math: N/A, Composite: 18-23.

ACADEMICS
Year founded: 1897. **Academic calendar:** Semester. **Degrees offered:** bachelor's, master's, doctorate. **Most popular majors:** 33% education, 27% business, management, marketing, and related support services, 13% social sciences, 6% visual and performing arts, 5% health professions and related clinical sciences. **Major fields of study:** biological and biomedical sciences; business, management, marketing, and related support services; communication, journalism, and related programs; education; English language and literature/letters; foreign languages, literatures, and linguistics; history; multi/interdisciplinary studies; philosophy and religious studies; physical sciences; psychology; security and protective services; social sciences; visual and performing arts. **Areas of required coursework:** arts/fine arts, humanities, computer literacy, mathematics, English (including composition), philosophy, foreign languages, sciences (biological or physical), history, social science. **Special academic programs:** accelerated program, distance learning, double major, dual enrollment, student-designed major, study abroad, teacher certificate program. **Teacher certification offered in:** early childhood, special education, middle/junior high, secondary. **Faculty and instruction (2009-2010):** Total instructional faculty: 113 full-time, 134 part-time (54% men; 46% women). Student/faculty ratio: 15/1. Classes of fewer than 20

students: 74%; of 20 to 49 students: 26%; of 50 or more students: 0%. **Freshmen returning for sophomore year:** 69%. **Graduation rates:** Four-year: 34%; five-year: 40%; six-year: 48%.

COSTS AND FINANCIAL AID
Financial aid office: (706) 776-0114. **Expenses (2010-2011):** Tuition and fees 2010-2011: $18,000; room/board: $7,500. Estimated books and supplies: $1,500; transportation: $1,400; personal expenses: $2,350. **Financial aid:** Priority filing date for institution's financial aid form: May 1. In 2009-2010, 86% of undergraduates applied for financial aid. Of those, 68% were determined to have financial need; 21% had their need fully met. Average financial aid package (proportion receiving): $16,890 (65%). Average amount of gift aid, such as scholarships or grants (proportion receiving): $2,696 (23%). Average amount of self-help aid, such as work study or loans (proportion receiving): $4,510 (17%). Average need-based loan (excluding PLUS or other private loans): $4,465. Among students who received need-based aid, the average percentage of need met: 59%. Among students who received aid based on merit, the average award (and the proportion receiving): $9,166 (9%). The average athletic scholarship (and the proportion receiving): $0 (0%). Average amount of debt of borrowers graduating in 2009: $16,986. Proportion who borrowed: 71%.

CAMPUS LIFE AND EXTRACURRICULAR ACTIVITIES
Campus housing available: coed dorms, women's dorms, men's dorms, apartments for married students, special housing for international students. Students who live in college-owned, operated, or affiliated housing: 41%. **Clubs and organizations:** Number of student organizations: 27. Activities include: choral groups, dance, drama/theater, music ensembles, radio station, student government, student newspaper, television station, yearbook. Number of fraternities: 0; sororities: 0. Average proportion of students who stay on campus on weekends: 30%. **Sports program (2009-2010):** Member of NCAA III. *Men's intercollegiate varsity sports:* baseball, basketball, cross country, golf, soccer, tennis. *Women's intercollegiate varsity sports:* basketball, cross country, golf, soccer, softball, tennis.

SERVICES AND FACILITIES
Counseling services: career, academic, psychological, religious. **For learning-disabled students:** School does not offer a structured program with separate admission and additional fees. Services include: tape recorders, untimed tests, oral tests, tutors. **Library:** Number of titles: 115,400; number of current serial subscriptions: 365. **Information technology resources:** Students are not required to lease or own a computer. Number of campus computers available to all students: 250. School has a wireless network. Proportion of college-owned housing units wired for high-speed internet access: 100%. **Campus safety:** Security services offered: 24-hour foot-and-vehicle patrols, late-night transport/escort service, lighted pathways/sidewalks.

TRANSFER AND INTERNATIONAL STUDENTS
Transfer students: May apply for admission for the following academic terms: Fall, Spring, Summer. Applicants do not need a minimum number of credits to apply. **International students:** Number of foreign undergraduates: 5. Number of countries represented: 23. Minimum TOEFL score required: 550 (paper); 213 (computer).

Reinhardt University

- **Address:** 7300 Reinhardt University, Waleska, GA 30183-0128
- **Website:** http://www.reinhardt.edu/
- **Private; Religious affiliation:** United Methodist
- **Enrollment:** 978 full-time; 78 part-time

KEY STATS
✔ **U.S News College Ranking:** 55, Regional Colleges (South)
✔ **SAT Score (25th/75th percentile):** 840-1070
✔ **Tuition:** 2010-2011: $17,166

Selectivity: Less selective	**Room/board:** $6,386
Acceptance rate: 68%	**Average debt:** N/A
Student/faculty ratio: 12/1	**Proportion who borrowed:** N/A

UNDERGRADUATE STUDENT BODY STATS
2009-2010 enrollment: 978 full-time; 78 part-time. Men: 39%; women: 61%. **Ethnic makeup:** African American: 9%; Asian American: 1%; Hispanic: 5%;

White: 85%. **Religious preference:** Roman Catholic: 8%; No preference: 12%; Unknown: 35%; United Methodist: 19%; Baptist: 24%; Other: 2%.

ADMISSIONS FACTS AND FIGURES
Phone: (770) 720-5526. **Email:** admissions@reinhardt.edu. **Website:** http://www.reinhardt.edu/. **Application deadlines for fall 2011:** Regular decision: Rolling. Early decision: Not offered. Early action: Not offered. Admission can be deferred. **Application fee:** $25. **To apply online, go to:** http://www.reinhardt.edu/Admissions/application.htm. **Admissions requirements/recommendations:** High school units required (recommended): English: 4; Mathematics: 4; Science: 3; Foreign language: (2); Social studies: 3; Total units: 14 (2). Tests: The college uses SAT or ACT scores in admissions decisions. Either SAT or ACT required. For admission to the fall 2011 entering class, the school will accept: ACT with or without writing accepted. Campus visit: Recommended. Admissions interview: Neither required nor recommended. Off-campus interview: May be arranged. **Factors that count in admissions decisions:** *Academic:* Secondary school record: Important. Class rank: Considered. Letters of recommendation: Considered. Standardized test scores: Very Important. Essay: Not Considered. *Nonacademic:* Interview: Not Considered. Extracurricular activities: Considered. Talent/ability: Considered. Character/personal qualities: Considered. Alumni/ae relationship: Considered. Geographical residence: Considered. State residency: Not Considered. Religious affiliation/commitment: Considered. Minority status: Considered. Volunteer work: Considered. Work experience: Considered. **Other schools with the greatest overlap in applicants:** Berry College; Georgia State University; Kennesaw State University; Shorter College; University of Georgia. **Admissions statistics for the fall 2009 entering class:** Total applicants: 1,191. Total accepted: 810. Freshmen enrolled: 239; Overall acceptance rate: 68%. **Credentials of fall 2009 freshmen:** 10% ranked in the top 10 percent of their high school class; 20% were in the top 25 percent; 53% were in the top half. (Proportion submitting class standing: 60%.) **Average high school grade point average:** 3.0. **First-year students who submitted SAT scores:** 72%. Scores (25/75 percentile): Critical Reading: 430-540, Math: 410-530, Combined: 840-1070. **First-year students submitting ACT scores:** 23%. Scores (25/75 percentile): English: N/A, Math: N/A, Composite: 17-23.

ACADEMICS
Year founded: 1883. **Academic calendar:** Semester. **Degrees offered:** associate, transfer-associate, bachelor's, master's. **Most popular majors:** 32% business, management, marketing, and related support services, 26% education, 9% visual and performing arts, 8% biological and biomedical sciences, 6% liberal arts and sciences studies, and humanities. **Major fields of study:** biological and biomedical sciences; business, management, marketing, and related support services; communication, journalism, and related programs; education; English language and literature/letters; history; liberal arts and sciences studies, and humanities; mathematics and statistics; philosophy and religious studies; psychology; security and protective services; social sciences; visual and performing arts. **Areas of required coursework:** arts/fine arts, humanities, mathematics, English (including composition), foreign languages, sciences (biological or physical), history, social science. **Pre-professional programs:** pre-law, pre-dentistry, pre-medicine, pre-pharmacy. **Special academic programs:** accelerated program, distance learning, double major, dual enrollment, external degree program, honors program, independent study, internships, study abroad, teacher certificate program, weekend college. **Teacher certification offered in:** early childhood, middle/junior high, secondary. **Faculty and instruction (2009-2010):** Total instructional faculty: 60 full-time, 100 part-time (51% men; 49% women; 7% minorities). Full-time faculty with Ph.D. or other terminal degree: 78%. Student/faculty ratio: 12/1. Classes of fewer than 20 students: 77%; of 20 to 49 students: 23%; of 50 or more students: 0%. **Advanced Placement and International Baccalaureate credit:** AP tests may be used for: Credit and/or placement. Scores accepted: 3. International Baccalaureate exams may be used for: Credit and/or placement. **Freshmen returning for sophomore year:** 60%. **Graduation rates:** Four-year: 31%; five-year: 40%; six-year: 36%. **Graduate study:** 10% of students pursue further study immediately upon graduation; 15% within one year; 0% within five years. Fields in which graduates pursue further study: Master of Business Administration (MBA), 30%; law, 5%; dentistry, 2%; theology (or the seminary), 10%; education, 30%; arts and sciences, 23%.

COSTS AND FINANCIAL AID
Financial aid office: (770) 720-5667. **Expenses (2010-2011):** Tuition and fees 2010-2011: $17,166; room/board: $6,386. Estimated books and supplies: $1,200; transportation: $4,000; personal expenses: $1,100. **Financial aid:** Priority filing date for institution's financial aid form: May 1. In 2009-2010,

100% of undergraduates applied for financial aid. Of those, 83% were determined to have financial need; 12% had their need fully met. Average financial aid package (proportion receiving): $11,498 (83%). Average amount of gift aid, such as scholarships or grants (proportion receiving): $8,852 (83%). Average amount of self-help aid, such as work study or loans (proportion receiving): $3,670 (61%). Average need-based loan (excluding PLUS or other private loans): $3,547. Among students who received need-based aid, the average percentage of need met: 53%. Among students who received aid based on merit, the average award (and the proportion receiving): $4,835 (14%). The average athletic scholarship (and the proportion receiving): $3,685 (7%).

CAMPUS LIFE AND EXTRACURRICULAR ACTIVITIES

Campus housing available (% using): coed dorms (20%), women's dorms (34%), men's dorms (16%), apartment for single students (30%), special housing for disabled students, other housing options. Students who live in college-owned, operated, or affiliated housing: 44%. **Student employment:** During the 2009-2010 academic year, 6% of undergraduates worked on campus. Average per-year earnings: $500. **Clubs and organizations:** Number of student organizations: 38. Activities include: campus ministries, choral groups, concert band, drama/theater, international student organization, jazz band, music ensembles, radio station, student government, student newspaper, student film society, television station, yearbook. Number of fraternities: 0; sororities: 0. Average proportion of students who stay on campus on weekends: 20%. **Sports program (2009-2010):** Member of NAIA. *Men's intercollegiate varsity sports:* baseball, basketball, cross country, golf, lacrosse, soccer, tennis. *Women's intercollegiate varsity sports:* basketball, cross country, golf, lacrosse, soccer, softball, tennis, volleyball.

SERVICES AND FACILITIES

Basic services: nonremedial tutoring, placement service, health service, health insurance. **Remedial assistance:** reading, math, writing, study skills. **Counseling services:** career, veteran student, academic, psychological, religious. **For learning-disabled students:** School does not offer a structured program with separate admission and additional fees. Total undergraduates in learning-disabled program or receiving services: 122. Services include: remedial math, remedial English, remedial reading, tape recorders, note-taking services, oral tests, learning center, readers, extended time for tests, tutors, priority registration, priority seating, proofreading services, texts on tape, other testing accommodations. **Library:** Number of titles: 60,278; number of current serial subscriptions: 371. **Information technology resources:** Students are not required to lease or own a computer. Number of campus computers available to all students: 164. School has a wireless network. Approximate number of users that can be accommodated: 150. Proportion of college-owned housing units wired for high-speed internet access: 100%. **Campus safety:** Security services offered: 24-hour foot-and-vehicle patrols, late-night transport/escort service, 24-hour emergency telephones, lighted pathways/sidewalks, controlled dormitory access (key, security card, etc).

TRANSFER AND INTERNATIONAL STUDENTS

Transfer students: May apply for admission for the following academic terms: Fall, Spring. Applicants need a minimum number of credits to apply. For fall 2009: Transfer applications received: 195. Transfer applicants offered admission: 126. Transfer applicants enrolled: 80. **International students:** Number of foreign undergraduates: 1. Number of countries represented: 23. Minimum TOEFL score required: 500 (paper); 173 (computer). Average TOEFL score: 500 (paper).

Savannah College of Art and Design

- **Address:** 342 Bull Street, PO Box 3146, Savannah, GA 31402-3146
- **Website:** http://www.scad.edu
- **Private**
- **Enrollment:** 7,194 full-time; 994 part-time

....

KEY STATS

✔ **U.S News College Ranking:** Unranked Specialty School–Fine Arts
✔ **SAT Score (25th/75th percentile):** 960-1190
✔ **Tuition:** 2010-2011: $29,070

Selectivity: N/A	Room/board: $11,750
Acceptance rate: 68%	Average debt: N/A
Student/faculty ratio: 17/1	Proportion who borrowed: N/A

UNDERGRADUATE STUDENT BODY STATS

2009-2010 enrollment: 7,194 full-time; 994 part-time. Men: 40%; women: 60%. **Ethnic makeup:** African American: 4%; Asian American: 1%; Hispanic: 3%; White: 83%; International: 9%.

ADMISSIONS FACTS AND FIGURES

Phone: (912) 525-5100. **Email:** admission@scad.edu. **Website:** http://www.scad.edu. **Application deadlines for fall 2011:** Regular decision: August 1. Early decision: Not offered. Early action: Not offered. Admission can be deferred. **Application fee:** $50. **To apply online, go to:** http://www.scad.edu/admission/apply/continue.cfm. **Admissions requirements/recommendations:** Tests: The college uses SAT or ACT scores in admissions decisions. Either SAT or ACT required. For admission to the fall 2011 entering class, the school will accept: ACT with writing required. Campus visit: Recommended. Admissions interview: Recommended. Off-campus interview: May be arranged. **Factors that count in admissions decisions:** *Academic:* Secondary school record: Important. Class rank: Considered. Letters of recommendation: Considered. Standardized test scores: Very Important. Essay: Considered. *Nonacademic:* Interview: Considered. Extracurricular activities: Important. Talent/ability: Important. Character/personal qualities: Considered. Alumni/ae relationship: Not Considered. Geographical residence: Not Considered. State residency: Not Considered. Religious affiliation/commitment: Not Considered. Minority status: Not Considered. Volunteer work: Considered. Work experience: Considered. **Admissions statistics for the fall 2009 entering class:** Total applicants: 8,108. Total accepted: 5,503. Freshmen enrolled: 1,682; 79% were from out of state. Overall acceptance rate: 68%. **Average high school grade point average:** 3.4. **First-year students who submitted SAT scores:** 71%. Scores (25/75 percentile): Critical Reading: 490-600, Math: 470-590, Combined: 960-1190. **First-year students submitting ACT scores:** 33%. Scores (25/75 percentile): English: 21-27, Math: 18-25, Composite: 20-26.

ACADEMICS

Year founded: 1978. **Academic calendar:** Quarter. **Degrees offered:** certificate, bachelor's, post-bachelor's certificate, master's. **Major fields of study:** architecture and related services; communication, journalism, and related programs; communications technologies/technicians and support services; computer and information sciences and support services; English language and literature/letters; multi/interdisciplinary studies; visual and performing arts. **Areas of required coursework:** arts/fine arts, humanities, computer literacy, mathematics, English (including composition), sciences (biological or physical), social science. **Special academic programs:** distance learning, double major, dual enrollment, English as a Second Language (ESL), independent study, internships, study abroad, teacher certificate program. **Reserve Officers Training Corps (ROTC):** Army ROTC: Offered at cooperating institution (Armstrong Atlantic State University). **Faculty and instruction (2009-2010):** Total instructional faculty: 491 full-time, 167 part-time (58% men; 42% women; 11% minorities). Full-time faculty with Ph.D. or other terminal degree: 73%. Student/faculty ratio: 17/1. Classes of fewer than 20 students: 84%; of 20 to 49 students: 16%; of 50 or more students: 0%. **Advanced Placement and International Baccalaureate credit:** AP tests may be used for: Placement only. Scores accepted: 3, 4, 5. International Baccalaureate exams may be used for: Placement only. **Freshmen returning for sophomore year:** 81%. **Graduation rates:** Four-year: 51%; five-year: 64%; six-year: 65%. **Graduate study:** 10% of students pursue further study immediately upon graduation. Fields in which graduates pursue further study: education, 20%; arts and sciences, 80%.

COSTS AND FINANCIAL AID

Financial aid office: (912) 525-6104. **Expenses (2010-2011):** Tuition and fees 2010-2011: $29,070; room/board: $11,750. Estimated books and supplies: $2,400; transportation: $1,248; personal expenses: $1,560. **Financial aid:** Priority filing date for institution's financial aid form: February 15. In 2009-2010, 65% of undergraduates applied for financial aid. Of those, 56% were determined to have financial need; 7% had their need fully met. Average financial aid package (proportion receiving): $14,040 (56%). Average amount of gift aid, such as scholarships or grants (proportion receiving): $5,145 (28%). Average amount of self-help aid, such as work study or loans (proportion receiving): $4,416 (55%). Average need-based loan (excluding PLUS or other private loans): $4,413. Among students who received need-based aid, the average percentage of need met: 20%. Among students who received aid based on merit, the average award (and the proportion receiving): $9,576 (29%). The average athletic scholarship (and the proportion receiving): $19,751 (2%).

CAMPUS LIFE AND EXTRACURRICULAR ACTIVITIES

Campus housing available (% using): coed dorms (93%), women's dorms (2%), apartment for single students (5%), other housing options. Students who live in college-owned, operated, or affiliated housing: 35%. **Student employment:** During the 2009-2010 academic year, 20% of undergraduates worked on campus. Average per-year earnings: $3,200. **Clubs and organizations:** Number of student organizations: 63. Activities include: choral groups, dance, drama/theater, international student organization, literary magazine, music ensembles, musical theater, radio station, student government, student newspaper, television station. Number of fraternities: 0; sororities: 0. Average proportion of students who stay on campus on weekends: 35%. **Sports program (2009-2010):** Member of NAIA. *Men's intercollegiate varsity sports:* baseball, basketball, cross country, golf, soccer, swimming, tennis. *Women's intercollegiate varsity sports:* basketball, cross country, equestrian, golf, soccer, softball, swimming, tennis, volleyball.

SERVICES AND FACILITIES

Basic services: nonremedial tutoring, health service, health insurance, other. **Remedial assistance:** other. **Counseling services:** career, personal, academic, other. **For learning-disabled students:** School does not offer a structured program with separate admission and additional fees. Services include: reading machines, tape recorders, note-taking services, oral tests, learning center, readers, extended time for tests, tutors, priority registration, priority seating, texts on tape, other testing accommodations, other. **Library:** Number of titles: 203,002; number of current serial subscriptions: 1,219. **Information technology resources:** Students are not required to lease or own a computer. Number of campus computers available to all students: 3,400. School has a wireless network. Approximate number of users that can be accommodated: 5,000. Proportion of college-owned housing units wired for high-speed internet access: 100%. **Campus safety:** Security services offered: 24-hour foot-and-vehicle patrols, late-night transport/escort service, 24-hour emergency telephones, lighted pathways/sidewalks, student patrols, controlled dormitory access (key, security card, etc).

TRANSFER AND INTERNATIONAL STUDENTS

Transfer students: May apply for admission for the following academic terms: Fall, Winter, Spring, Summer. Applicants do not need a minimum number of credits to apply. For fall 2009: Transfer applications received: 2,954. Transfer applicants offered admission: 1,584. Transfer applicants enrolled: 662. **International students:** Number of foreign undergraduates: 702 (9% of student body). Number of countries represented: 97. Minimum TOEFL score required: 550 (paper); 85 (computer). Average TOEFL score: 400 (paper).

Savannah State University

- **Address:** PO Box 20482, Savannah, GA 31404
- **Website:** http://www.savannahstate.edu
- **Public**
- **Enrollment:** 3,171 full-time; 515 part-time

KEY STATS

✔ **U.S News College Ranking:** second tier, Regional Universities (South)
✔ **SAT Score (25th/75th percentile):** 810-950
✔ **Tuition:** 2009-2010: $4,774 in state, $16,388 out of state

Selectivity: Less selective	Room/board: $5,958
Acceptance rate: 40%	Average debt: N/A
Student/faculty ratio: 21/1	Proportion who borrowed: N/A

UNDERGRADUATE STUDENT BODY STATS

2009-2010 enrollment: 3,171 full-time; 515 part-time. Men: 44%; women: 56%. **Ethnic makeup:** African American: 95%; White: 3%; International: 1%.

ADMISSIONS FACTS AND FIGURES

Phone: (912) 356-2181. **Email:** admissions@savannahstate.edu. **Website:** http://www.savannahstate.edu. **Application deadlines for fall 2011:** Regular decision: July 1. Early decision: Send application by: N/A; Decision sent by: N/A. Early action: Not offered. Admission can be deferred. **Application fee:** $20. **To apply online, go to:** https://www.applyweb.com/aw?ssu. **Admissions requirements/recommendations:** High school units required (recommended): English: 4; Mathematics: 4; Science: 3; Foreign language: 2; Social studies: 3; Total units: 16. Tests: The college uses SAT or ACT scores in admissions decisions. Either SAT or ACT required. For admission to the fall 2011 entering class, the school will accept: ACT with or without writing accepted. Campus visit: Recommended. **Factors that count in admissions decisions:** *Academic:* Secondary school record: Not Considered. Class rank: Not Considered. Letters of recommendation: Not Considered. Standardized test scores: Important. Essay: Not Considered. *Nonacademic:* Interview: Not Considered. Extracurricular activities: Not Considered. Talent/ability: Not Considered. Character/personal qualities: Not Considered. Alumni/ae relationship: Not Considered. Geographical residence: Not Considered. State residency: Not Considered. Religious affiliation/commitment: Not Considered. Minority status: Not Considered. Volunteer work: Not Considered. Work experience: Not Considered. **Admissions statistics for the fall 2009 entering class:** Total applicants: 4,450. Total accepted: 1,783. Freshmen enrolled: 916; 9% were from out of state. Overall acceptance rate: 40%. Non-early acceptance rate: 40%. **Average high school grade point average:** 2.7. **First-year students who submitted SAT scores:** 78%. Scores (25/75 percentile): Critical Reading: 410-480, Math: 400-470, Combined: 810-950. **First-year students submitting ACT scores:** 42%. Scores (25/75 percentile): English: N/A, Math: N/A, Composite: 17-19.

ACADEMICS

Year founded: 1890. **Academic calendar:** Semester. **Degrees offered:** bachelor's, master's. **Most popular majors:** 13% biology/biological sciences; 11% journalism, 10% business administration and management, 8% developmental and child psychology, 7% accounting. **Major fields of study:** area, ethnic, cultural, and gender studies; biological and biomedical sciences; business, management, marketing, and related support services; communication, journalism, and related programs; computer and information sciences and support services; engineering; engineering technologies/technicians; English language and literature/letters; history; mathematics and statistics; parks, recreation, leisure, and fitness studies; physical sciences; public administration and social service professions; security and protective services; social sciences; visual and performing arts. **Special academic programs:** accelerated program, cooperative (work-study plan) program, double major, honors program, independent study, internships, study abroad. **Reserve Officers Training Corps (ROTC):** Army ROTC: Offered on campus; Navy ROTC: Offered on campus. **Faculty and instruction (2009-2010):** Total instructional faculty: 151 full-time, 29 part-time (50% men; 50% women). Student/faculty ratio: 21/1. **Freshmen returning for sophomore year:** 73%. **Graduation rates:** Four-year: 13%; five-year: 23%; six-year: 34%.

COSTS AND FINANCIAL AID

Financial aid office: (912) 356-2253. **Expenses (2009-2010):** Tuition and fees 2009-2010: $4,774 in state, $16,388 out of state; room/board: $5,958. Estimated books and supplies: $1,500.

CAMPUS LIFE AND EXTRACURRICULAR ACTIVITIES

Campus housing available: coed dorms, women's dorms, men's dorms, apartment for single students, special housing for disabled students. Activities include: choral groups, drama/theater, international student organization, marching band, radio station, student government, student newspaper, television station. **Sports program (2009-2010):** Member of NCAA I. *Men's intercollegiate varsity sports:* baseball, basketball, cross country, football, golf, track and field (indoor), track and field (outdoor). *Women's intercollegiate varsity sports:* basketball, cross country, golf, softball, tennis, track and field (indoor), track and field (outdoor), water polo.

SERVICES AND FACILITIES

Basic services: placement service, health service, health insurance. **Remedial assistance:** reading, math, writing, study skills. **Counseling services:** minority student, career, military, personal, academic. **For learning-disabled students:** Services include: reading machines, tape recorders, note-taking services, readers, extended time for tests, priority seating, exams on tape or computer, other testing accommodations, waiver of foreign language degree requirement, other. **Library:** Number of titles: 187,916; number of current serial subscriptions: 812. **Information technology resources:** Students are not required to lease or own a computer. School has a wireless network. **Campus safety:** Security services offered: 24-hour foot-and-vehicle patrols, late-night transport/escort service, 24-hour emergency telephones, lighted pathways/sidewalks, controlled dormitory access (key, security card, etc).

TRANSFER AND INTERNATIONAL STUDENTS

Transfer students: May apply for admission for the following academic terms: Fall, Spring, Summer. Applicants need a minimum number of credits to apply. For fall 2009: Transfer applications received: 365. Transfer applicants offered admission: 220. Transfer applicants enrolled: 147.

International students: Number of foreign undergraduates: 29 (1% of student body). Minimum TOEFL score required: 523 (paper); 70 (computer).

Shorter College

- **Address:** 315 Shorter Avenue, Rome, GA 30165-4298
- **Website:** http://www.shorter.edu
- **Private; Religious affiliation:** Baptist
- **Enrollment:** 1,167 full-time; 38 part-time

KEY STATS

- ✔ **U.S News College Ranking:** 17, Regional Colleges (South)
- ✔ **SAT Score (25th/75th percentile):** 860-1120
- ✔ **Tuition:** 2010-2011: $17,070

Selectivity: Selective	**Room/board:** $8,200
Acceptance rate: 65%	**Average debt:** $22,967
Student/faculty ratio: 11/1	**Proportion who borrowed:** 75%

UNDERGRADUATE STUDENT BODY STATS

2009-2010 enrollment: 1,167 full-time; 38 part-time. Men: 50%; women: 50%. **Ethnic makeup:** African American: 14%; Asian American: 1%; Hispanic: 2%; White: 78%; International: 5%. **Religious preference:** Roman Catholic: 6%; Protestant: 31%; No preference: 10%; Baptist: 52%; Other: 1%.

ADMISSIONS FACTS AND FIGURES

Phone: (800) 868-6980. **Email:** admissions@shorter.edu. **Website:** http://www.shorter.edu. **Application deadlines for fall 2011:** Regular decision: Rolling. Early decision: Not offered. Early action: Not offered. Admission can be deferred. **Application fee:** $25. **To apply online, go to:** https://scholar.shorter.edu/ics/Admissions/Admissions_Homepage.jnz?portlet=Apply_For_Admissions. **Admissions requirements/recommendations:** High school units required (recommended): English: 4; Mathematics: 4; Science: 3; Foreign language: 2; Social studies: 0; History: 3; Academic electives: 0; Total units: 16. Tests: The college uses SAT or ACT scores in admissions decisions. Either SAT or ACT required. For admission to the fall 2011 entering class, the school will accept: ACT with writing required. Campus visit: Recommended. Admissions interview: Recommended. Off-campus interview: May be arranged. **Factors that count in admissions decisions:** *Academic:* Secondary school record: Important. Class rank: Important. Letters of recommendation: Considered. Standardized test scores: Very Important. Essay: Important. *Nonacademic:* Interview: Considered. Extracurricular activities: Considered. Talent/ability: Important. Character/personal qualities: Considered. Alumni/ae relationship: Considered. Geographical residence: Not Considered. State residency: Not Considered. Religious affiliation/commitment: Not Considered. Minority status: Not Considered. Volunteer work: Considered. Work experience: Considered. **Other schools with the greatest overlap in applicants:** Berry College; Kennesaw State University; University of Georgia. **Admissions statistics for the fall 2009 entering class:** Total applicants: 1,672. Total accepted: 1,089. Freshmen enrolled: 333; 9% were from out of state. Overall acceptance rate: 65%. **Credentials of fall 2009 freshmen:** 23% ranked in the top 10 percent of their high school class; 50% were in the top 25 percent; 72% were in the top half. (Proportion submitting class standing: 77%.) **Average high school grade point average:** 3.3. **First-year students who submitted SAT scores:** 76%. Scores (25/75 percentile): Critical Reading: 430-570, Math: 430-550, Combined: 860-1120. **First-year students submitting ACT scores:** 56%. Scores (25/75 percentile): English: 17-24, Math: 17-24, Composite: 18-23.

ACADEMICS

Year founded: 1873. **Academic calendar:** Semester. **Degrees offered:** bachelor's. **Most popular majors:** 26% business, management, marketing, and related support services, 14% education, 12% visual and performing arts, 8% biological and biomedical sciences, 6% history. **Major fields of study:** biological and biomedical sciences; business, management, marketing, and related support services; communication, journalism, and related programs; computer and information sciences and support services; education; English language and literature/letters; foreign languages, literatures, and linguistics; history; liberal arts and sciences studies, and humanities; mathematics and statistics; multi/interdisciplinary studies; natural resources and conservation; parks, recreation, leisure, and fitness studies; philosophy and religious studies; physical sciences; psychology; social sciences; theology and religious vocations; visual and performing arts. **Areas of required coursework:** arts/fine arts, computer literacy, mathematics, English (including composition), sciences (biological or physical), history, social science, other. **Special academic programs (% participation):** cross-registration (1%), distance learning (10%), double major (2%), dual enrollment (1%), honors program (4%), independent study (15%), internships (65%), student-designed major (6%), study abroad (11%), teacher certificate program (23%). **Teacher certification offered in:** early childhood, elementary, middle/junior high, secondary. **Faculty and instruction (2009-2010):** Total instructional faculty: 83 full-time, 66 part-time (48% men; 52% women; 7% minorities). Full-time faculty with Ph.D. or other terminal degree: 73%. Student/faculty ratio: 11/1. Classes of fewer than 20 students: 62%; of 20 to 49 students: 38%; of 50 or more students: 1%. **Advanced Placement and International Baccalaureate credit:** AP tests may be used for: Placement only. Scores accepted: 3. International Baccalaureate exams may be used for: Credit and/or placement. **Freshmen returning for sophomore year:** 68%. **Graduation rates:** Four-year: 43%; five-year: 51%; six-year: 49%. **Graduate study:** 40% of students pursue further study within one year; 47% within five years. Fields in which graduates pursue further study: Master of Business Administration (MBA), 13%; medicine, 14%; theology (or the seminary), 12%; education, 25%; arts and sciences, 25%.

COSTS AND FINANCIAL AID

Financial aid office: (706) 233-7227. **Expenses (2010-2011):** Tuition and fees 2010-2011: $17,070; room/board: $8,200. Estimated books and supplies: $1,200; transportation: $1,160; personal expenses: $1,770. **Financial aid:** Priority filing date for institution's financial aid form: April 1. In 2009-2010, 86% of undergraduates applied for financial aid. Of those, 73% were determined to have financial need; 28% had their need fully met. Average financial aid package (proportion receiving): $15,152 (73%). Average amount of gift aid, such as scholarships or grants (proportion receiving): $12,411 (73%). Average amount of self-help aid, such as work study or loans (proportion receiving): $3,939 (51%). Average need-based loan (excluding PLUS or other private loans): $3,588. Among students who received need-based aid, the average percentage of need met: 71%. Among students who received aid based on merit, the average award (and the proportion receiving): $4,845 (16%). The average athletic scholarship (and the proportion receiving): $10,770 (15%). Average amount of debt of borrowers graduating in 2009: $22,967. Proportion who borrowed: 75%.

CAMPUS LIFE AND EXTRACURRICULAR ACTIVITIES

Campus housing available (% using): women's dorms (43%), men's dorms (32%), apartment for single students (25%). Students who live in college-owned, operated, or affiliated housing: 54%. **Student employment:** During the 2009-2010 academic year, 19% of undergraduates worked on campus. Average per-year earnings: $2,500. **Clubs and organizations:** Number of student organizations: 50. Activities include: campus ministries, choral groups, concert band, dance, drama/theater, international student organization, literary magazine, marching band, model UN, music ensembles, musical theater, opera, pep band, radio station, student government, student newspaper, student film society, television station, yearbook. Number of fraternities: 3; sororities: 3. Proportion of men in fraternities: 13%; of women in sororities: 24%. Average proportion of students who stay on campus on weekends: 25%. **Sports program (2009-2010):** Member of NAIA. *Men's intercollegiate varsity sports:* baseball, basketball, cross country, football, golf, soccer, track and field (outdoor). *Women's intercollegiate varsity sports:* basketball, cross country, golf, soccer, softball, track and field (outdoor), volleyball.

SERVICES AND FACILITIES

Basic services: nonremedial tutoring, placement service, health service, health insurance. **Remedial assistance:** math, writing. **Counseling services:** career, personal, academic, religious. **For learning-disabled students:** School does not offer a structured program with separate admission and additional fees. **Library:** Number of titles: 144,475; number of current serial subscriptions: 8,511. **Information technology resources:** Students are not required to lease or own a computer. Number of campus computers available to all students: 159. School has a wireless network. Approximate number of users that can be accommodated: 1,200. Proportion of college-owned housing units wired for high-speed internet access: 100%. **Campus safety:** Security services offered: 24-hour foot-and-vehicle patrols, lighted pathways/sidewalks, controlled dormitory access (key, security card, etc).

TRANSFER AND INTERNATIONAL STUDENTS

Transfer students: May apply for admission for the following academic terms: Fall, Spring, Summer. Applicants need a minimum number of credits to apply. For fall 2009: Transfer applications received: 364. Transfer applicants offered admission: 197. Transfer applicants enrolled: 110.

International students: Number of foreign undergraduates: 63 (5% of student body). Number of countries represented: 25. Minimum TOEFL score required: 500 (paper); 173 (computer).

Southern Polytechnic State University

- **Address:** 1100 S. Marietta Parkway, Marietta, GA 30060-2896
- **Website:** http://www.spsu.edu
- **Public**
- **Enrollment:** 3,331 full-time; 1,212 part-time

KEY STATS

✔ **U.S News College Ranking:** 81, Regional Universities (South)
✔ **SAT Score (25th/75th percentile):** 1030-1220
✔ **Tuition:** 2010-2011: $6,174 in state, $19,294 out of state

Selectivity: Selective	**Room/board:** $6,604
Acceptance rate: 75%	**Average debt:** $16,280
Student/faculty ratio: 19/1	**Proportion who borrowed:** 50%

UNDERGRADUATE STUDENT BODY STATS

2009-2010 enrollment: 3,331 full-time; 1,212 part-time. Men: 81%; women: 19%. **Ethnic makeup:** African American: 20%; Asian American: 5%; Hispanic: 5%; White: 63%; International: 6%.

ADMISSIONS FACTS AND FIGURES

Phone: (678) 915-4188. **Email:** admiss@spsu.edu. **Website:** http://www.spsu.edu. **Application deadlines for fall 2011:** Regular decision: July 1. Early decision: Not offered. Early action: Not offered. Admission can be deferred. **Application fee:** $20. **To apply online, go to:** http://www.gacollege411.org/Applications/USG_Common_App_Short/apply.html?application_id=3425. **Admissions requirements/recommendations:** High school units required (recommended): English: 4; Mathematics: 4; Science: 3; Foreign language: 2; Academic electives: 2; Total units: 18. Tests: The college uses SAT or ACT scores in admissions decisions. Either SAT or ACT required. For admission to the fall 2011 entering class, the school will accept: ACT with writing required. Campus visit: Recommended. Admissions interview: Recommended. Off-campus interview: Not available. **Factors that count in admissions decisions:** *Academic:* Secondary school record: Very Important. Class rank: Not Considered. Letters of recommendation: Not Considered. Standardized test scores: Very Important. Essay: Not Considered. *Nonacademic:* Interview: Not Considered. Extracurricular activities: Not Considered. Talent/ability: Not Considered. Character/personal qualities: Not Considered. Alumni/ae relationship: Not Considered. Geographical residence: Not Considered. State residency: Not Considered. Religious affiliation/commitment: Not Considered. Minority status: Not Considered. Volunteer work: Not Considered. Work experience: Not Considered. **Other schools with the greatest overlap in applicants:** Georgia Institute of Technology; Georgia Southern University; Georgia State University; Kennesaw State University; University of Georgia. **Admissions statistics for the fall 2009 entering class:** Total applicants: 1,289. Total accepted: 961. Freshmen enrolled: 539; 1% were from out of state. Overall acceptance rate: 75%. **Size of waiting list:** 0 applicants; enrolled from waiting list: 0. **Average high school grade point average:** 3.2. **First-year students who submitted SAT scores:** 80%. Scores (25/75 percentile): Critical Reading: 500-590, Math: 530-630, Combined: 1030-1220. **First-year students submitting ACT scores:** 22%. Scores (25/75 percentile): English: 20-24, Math: 21-25, Composite: 21-25.

ACADEMICS

Year founded: 1948. **Academic calendar:** Semester. **Degrees offered:** certificate, associate, transfer-associate, bachelor's, post-bachelor's certificate, master's. **Most popular majors:** 43% engineering technologies/technicians, 22% business, management, marketing, and related support services, 13% computer and information sciences and support services, 9% architecture and related services, 3% communication, journalism, and related programs. **Major fields of study:** architecture and related services; biological and biomedical sciences; business, management, marketing, and related support services; communication, journalism, and related programs; computer and information sciences and support services; engineering; engineering technologies/technicians; mathematics and statistics; physical sciences; social sciences. **Areas of required coursework:** arts/fine arts, humanities, mathematics, English (including composition), sciences (biological or physical), history, social science. **Pre-professional programs:** pre-law, pre-dentistry,

pre-medicine, pre-veterinary science, pre-optometry, pre-pharmacy. **Special academic programs:** cooperative (work-study plan) program, cross-registration, distance learning, double major, dual enrollment, honors program, independent study, internships, study abroad. **Cooperative education programs:** business, computer science, engineering, technologies. **Reserve Officers Training Corps (ROTC):** Army ROTC: Offered on campus; Navy ROTC: Offered at cooperating institution (Georgia Institute of Technology); Air Force ROTC: Offered at cooperating institution (Georgia Institute of Technology). **Faculty and instruction (2009-2010):** Total instructional faculty: 178 full-time, 98 part-time (69% men; 31% women; 36% minorities). Full-time faculty with Ph.D. or other terminal degree: 76%. Student/faculty ratio: 19/1. Classes of fewer than 20 students: 43%; of 20 to 49 students: 57%; of 50 or more students: 1%. **Advanced Placement and International Baccalaureate credit:** AP tests may be used for: Credit only. Scores accepted: 3, 4, 5. International Baccalaureate exams may be used for: Credit only. **Freshmen returning for sophomore year:** 76%. **Graduation rates:** Four-year: 7%; five-year: 20%; six-year: 27%. **Graduate study:** 10% of students pursue further study immediately upon graduation; 10% within one year.

COSTS AND FINANCIAL AID

Financial aid office: (678) 915-7290. **Expenses (2010-2011):** Tuition and fees 2010-2011: $6,174 in state, $19,294 out of state; room/board: $6,604. **Financial aid:** Priority filing date for institution's financial aid form: March 1. In 2009-2010, 65% of undergraduates applied for financial aid. Of those, 52% were determined to have financial need; 14% had their need fully met. Average financial aid package (proportion receiving): $3,678 (50%). Average amount of gift aid, such as scholarships or grants (proportion receiving): $3,739 (46%). Average amount of self-help aid, such as work study or loans (proportion receiving): $5,075 (42%). Average need-based loan (excluding PLUS or other private loans): $4,824. Among students who received need-based aid, the average percentage of need met: 78%. Among students who received aid based on merit, the average award (and the proportion receiving): $8,269 (0%). The average athletic scholarship (and the proportion receiving): $3,524 (2%). Average amount of debt of borrowers graduating in 2009: $16,280. Proportion who borrowed: 50%.

CAMPUS LIFE AND EXTRACURRICULAR ACTIVITIES

Campus housing available (% using): coed dorms (35%), apartment for single students (65%). Students who live in college-owned, operated, or affiliated housing: 17%. **Student employment:** During the 2009-2010 academic year, 18% of undergraduates worked on campus. Average per-year earnings: $3,000. **Clubs and organizations:** Number of student organizations: 92. Activities include: choral groups, dance, international student organization, jazz band, pep band, radio station, student government, student newspaper. Number of fraternities: 8; sororities: 3. Proportion of men in fraternities: 7%; of women in sororities: 7%. Average proportion of students who stay on campus on weekends: 70%. **Sports program (2009-2010):** Member of NAIA. *Men's intercollegiate varsity sports:* baseball, basketball, soccer. *Women's intercollegiate varsity sports:* basketball.

SERVICES AND FACILITIES

Basic services: nonremedial tutoring, placement service, health service, health insurance. **Remedial assistance:** study skills. **Counseling services:** minority student, career, personal, veteran student, academic, older student, psychological. **For learning-disabled students:** School does not offer a structured program with separate admission and additional fees. Total undergraduates in learning-disabled program or receiving services: 27. Services include: reading machines, note-taking services, oral tests, learning center, readers, extended time for tests, tutors, priority registration, priority seating, texts on tape, typist/scribe, other. **Library:** Number of titles: 125,636; number of current serial subscriptions: 1,016. **Information technology resources:** Students are not required to lease or own a computer. Number of campus computers available to all students: 1,300. School has a wireless network. Approximate number of users that can be accommodated: 10,000. Proportion of college-owned housing units wired for high-speed internet access: 100%. **Campus safety:** Security services offered: 24-hour foot-and-vehicle patrols, late-night transport/escort service, 24-hour emergency telephones, lighted pathways/sidewalks, controlled dormitory access (key, security card, etc).

TRANSFER AND INTERNATIONAL STUDENTS

Transfer students: May apply for admission for the following academic terms: Fall, Spring, Summer. Applicants need a minimum number of credits to apply. For fall 2009: Transfer applications received: 817. Transfer applicants offered admission: 728. Transfer applicants enrolled: 582. **International students:** Number of foreign undergraduates: 267 (6% of stu-

dent body). Number of countries represented: 53. Minimum TOEFL score required: 550 (paper); 79 (computer). Average TOEFL score: 588 (paper).

Spelman College

- **Address:** 350 Spelman Lane SW, Atlanta, GA 30314-4399
- **Website:** http://www.spelman.edu
- **Private**
- **Enrollment:** 2,121 full-time; 108 part-time

KEY STATS

✔ **U.S News College Ranking:** 59, National Liberal Arts Colleges
✔ **SAT Score (25th/75th percentile):** 950-1128
✔ **Tuition:** 2010-2011: $22,010

Selectivity: Selective	**Room/board:** $10,464
Acceptance rate: 40%	**Average debt:** $14,070
Student/faculty ratio: 11/1	**Proportion who borrowed:** 70%

UNDERGRADUATE STUDENT BODY STATS

2009-2010 enrollment: 2,121 full-time; 108 part-time. Men: 0%; women: 100%. **Ethnic makeup:** African American: 91%; White: 1%; International: 7%. **Religious preference:** Roman Catholic: 7%; Protestant: 68%; Muslim: 2%; No preference: 6%; Other: 17%.

ADMISSIONS FACTS AND FIGURES

Phone: (800) 982-2411. **Email:** admiss@spelman.edu. **Website:** http://www.spelman.edu. **Application deadlines for fall 2011:** Regular decision: February 1; decision sent by April 1. Early decision: Send application by: November 1; Decision sent by: December 15. Early action: Send application by: November 15; Decision sent by: December 31. Admission can be deferred. **Application fee:** $35. **To apply online, go to:** http://www.spelman.edu/applyonline. **Admissions requirements/recommendations:** High school units required (recommended): English: 4 (4); Mathematics: 3 (4); Science: 3 (4); Foreign language: 3 (4); Social studies: 3 (4); History: 2 (3); Academic electives: 2 (2); Total units: 16 (19). Tests: The college uses SAT or ACT scores in admissions decisions. Either SAT or ACT required. For admission to the fall 2011 entering class, the school will accept: ACT with or without writing accepted. Campus visit: Recommended. Admissions interview: Neither required nor recommended. Off-campus interview: May be arranged. **Factors that count in admissions decisions:** *Academic:* Secondary school record: Very Important. Class rank: Considered. Letters of recommendation: Important. Standardized test scores: Very Important. Essay: Very Important. *Nonacademic:* Interview: Not Considered. Extracurricular activities: Important. Talent/ability: Considered. Character/personal qualities: Very Important. Alumni/ae relationship: Considered. Geographical residence: Not Considered. State residency: Not Considered. Religious affiliation/commitment: Not Considered. Minority status: Not Considered. Volunteer work: Important. Work experience: Important. **Other schools with the greatest overlap in applicants:** Duke University; Florida A&M University; Hampton University; Howard University; Smith College. **Admissions statistics for the fall 2009 entering class:** Total applicants: 5,436. Total accepted: 2,181. Freshmen enrolled: 553; 74% were from out of state. Accepted through early-decision or early-action plans: 58%. Overall acceptance rate: 40%. Early-decision acceptance rate: 39%. Non-early acceptance rate: 33%. **Size of waiting list:** 324 applicants; enrolled from waiting list: 19. **Credentials of fall 2009 freshmen:** 33% ranked in the top 10 percent of their high school class; 66% were in the top 25 percent; 92% were in the top half. (Proportion submitting class standing: 62%.) **Average high school grade point average:** 3.5. **First-year students who submitted SAT scores:** 76%. Scores (25/75 percentile): Critical Reading: 480-568, Math: 470-560, Combined: 950-1128. **First-year students submitting ACT scores:** 56%. Scores (25/75 percentile): English: N/A, Math: N/A, Composite: 20-24.

ACADEMICS

Year founded: 1881. **Academic calendar:** Semester. **Degrees offered:** bachelor's. **Most popular majors:** 29% social sciences, 17% psychology, 14% English language and literature/letters, 14% biological and biomedical sciences, 5% physical sciences. **Major fields of study:** area, ethnic, cultural, and gender studies; biological and biomedical sciences; computer and information sciences and support services; education; engineering; English language and literature/letters; foreign languages, literatures, and linguistics; legal professions and studies; mathematics and statistics; multi/interdisciplinary studies; natural resources and conservation; philosophy

and religious studies; physical sciences; psychology; public administration and social service professions; social sciences; visual and performing arts. **Areas of required coursework:** arts/fine arts, humanities, computer literacy, mathematics, English (including composition), philosophy, foreign languages, sciences (biological or physical), history, social science, other. **Preprofessional programs:** pre-law, pre-dentistry, pre-medicine, other. **Special academic programs (% participation):** cross-registration (35%), double major (8%), dual enrollment (1%), exchange student program (domestic) (2%), honors program (15%), independent study (2%), internships (20%), liberal arts/career combination (100%), student-designed major (5%), study abroad (5%), teacher certificate program (7%). **Teacher certification offered in:** early childhood, elementary, secondary. **Reserve Officers Training Corps (ROTC):** Army ROTC: Offered at cooperating institution (Georgia Institute of Technology); Navy ROTC: Offered on campus; Air Force ROTC: Offered at cooperating institution (Clark Atlanta University). **Faculty and instruction (2009-2010):** Total instructional faculty: 172 full-time, 76 part-time (35% men; 65% women). Full-time faculty with Ph.D. or other terminal degree: 85%. Student/faculty ratio: 11/1. Classes of fewer than 20 students: 63%; of 20 to 49 students: 33%; of 50 or more students: 4%. **Advanced Placement and International Baccalaureate credit:** AP tests may be used for: Credit only. Scores accepted: 3, 4, 5. International Baccalaureate exams may be used for: Credit only. **Freshmen returning for sophomore year:** 89%. **Graduation rates:** Four-year: 65%; five-year: 73%; six-year: 83%. **Graduate study:** 41% of students pursue further study immediately upon graduation. Fields in which graduates pursue further study: Master of Business Administration (MBA), 2%; law, 15%; medicine, 12%; dentistry, 1%; engineering, 15%; theology (or the seminary), 3%; education, 23%; arts and sciences, 27%; veterinary medicine, 2%.

COSTS AND FINANCIAL AID

Financial aid office: (404) 270-5212. **Expenses (2010-2011):** Tuition and fees 2010-2011: $22,010; room/board: $10,464. Estimated books and supplies: $1,800; transportation: $1,500; personal expenses: $2,200. **Financial aid:** Priority filing date for institution's financial aid form: February 1. In 2009-2010, 94% of undergraduates applied for financial aid. Of those, 79% were determined to have financial need; 34% had their need fully met. Average financial aid package (proportion receiving): $15,439 (79%). Average amount of gift aid, such as scholarships or grants (proportion receiving): $12,829 (67%). Average amount of self-help aid, such as work study or loans (proportion receiving): $4,560 (67%). Average need-based loan (excluding PLUS or other private loans): $4,307. Among students who received need-based aid, the average percentage of need met: 47%. Among students who received aid based on merit, the average award (and the proportion receiving): $0 (0%). The average athletic scholarship (and the proportion receiving): $0 (0%). Average amount of debt of borrowers graduating in 2009: $14,070. Proportion who borrowed: 70%.

CAMPUS LIFE AND EXTRACURRICULAR ACTIVITIES

Campus housing available (% using): women's dorms (100%). Students who live in college-owned, operated, or affiliated housing: 50%. **Student employment:** During the 2009-2010 academic year, 24% of undergraduates worked on campus. Average per-year earnings: $2,500. **Clubs and organizations:** Number of student organizations: 82. Activities include: campus ministries, choral groups, concert band, dance, drama/theater, jazz band, literary magazine, marching band, model UN, music ensembles, student government, student newspaper, student film society, symphony orchestra, yearbook. ; sororities: 4. Average proportion of students who stay on campus on weekends: 70%. **Sports program (2009-2010):** Member of NCAA III. **Women's intercollegiate varsity sports:** basketball, cross country, golf, soccer, softball, tennis, volleyball.

SERVICES AND FACILITIES

Basic services: nonremedial tutoring, women's center, placement service, health service, health insurance. **Counseling services:** career, personal, academic, birth control, religious. **For learning-disabled students:** School does not offer a structured program with separate admission and additional fees. Total undergraduates in learning-disabled program or receiving services: 52. Services include: tape recorders, diagnostic testing service, note-taking services, oral tests, learning center, readers, extended time for tests, tutors, early syllabus, priority registration, priority seating, substitution of courses, texts on tape, other testing accommodations, other. **Library:** Number of titles: 585,338; number of current serial subscriptions: 1,522. **Information technology resources:** Students are not required to lease or own a computer. Number of campus computers available to all students: 550. School has a wireless network. Approximate number of users that can be accommodated: 3,000. Proportion of college-owned housing units wired for high-speed internet access: 85%. **Campus safety:** Security services offered: 24-hour foot-and-vehicle patrols, late-night transport/escort service, 24-hour emergency telephones, lighted pathways/sidewalks, controlled dormitory access (key, security card, etc).

TRANSFER AND INTERNATIONAL STUDENTS

Transfer students: May apply for admission for the following academic terms: Fall, Spring. Applicants need a minimum number of credits to apply. For fall 2009: Transfer applications received: 552. Transfer applicants offered admission: 78. Transfer applicants enrolled: 51. **International students:** Number of foreign undergraduates: 119 (7% of student body). Number of countries represented: 21. Minimum TOEFL score required: 500 (paper); 250 (computer).

Thomas University

- **Address:** 1501 Millpond Road, Thomasville, GA 31792
- **Website:** http://www.thomasu.edu
- **Private**
- **Enrollment:** 379 full-time; 197 part-time

KEY STATS

✔ **U.S News College Ranking:** Unranked, Regional Colleges (South)
✔ **SAT or ACT Score (25th/75th percentile):** N/A
✔ **Tuition:** 2009-2010: $11,894

Selectivity: N/A	Room/board: $5,698
Acceptance rate: N/A	Average debt: N/A
Student/faculty ratio: 8/1	Proportion who borrowed: N/A

UNDERGRADUATE STUDENT BODY STATS

2009-2010 enrollment: 379 full-time; 197 part-time. Men: 29%; women: 71%. **Ethnic makeup:** African American: 24%; American-Indian: 1%; Asian American: 2%; Hispanic: 4%; White: 65%; International: 4%.

ADMISSIONS FACTS AND FIGURES

Phone: (229) 227-6934. **Email:** dglass@thomasu.edu. **Website:** http://www.thomasu.edu. **Application deadlines for fall 2011:** Regular decision: Rolling. Early decision: Not offered. Early action: Not offered. Admission cannot be deferred. **Application fee:** $25. **Admissions requirements/recommendations:** Tests: The college does not use SAT or ACT scores in admissions decisions. Neither SAT nor ACT required. Campus visit: Recommended. Admissions interview: Neither required nor recommended. Off-campus interview: Not available. **Factors that count in admissions decisions:** *Academic:* Secondary school record: Very Important. Class rank: Not Considered. Letters of recommendation: Not Considered. Standardized test scores: Considered. Essay: Not Considered. *Nonacademic:* Interview: Not Considered. Extracurricular activities: Not Considered. Talent/ability: Not Considered. Character/personal qualities: Not Considered. Alumni/ae relationship: Not Considered. Geographical residence: Not Considered. State residency: Not Considered. Religious affiliation/commitment: Not Considered. Minority status: Not Considered. Volunteer work: Not Considered. Work experience: Not Considered.

ACADEMICS

Year founded: 1950. **Academic calendar:** Semester. **Degrees offered:** associate, bachelor's, post-bachelor's certificate, master's. **Major fields of study:** biological and biomedical sciences; business, management, marketing, and related support services; education; health professions and related clinical sciences; liberal arts and sciences studies, and humanities; natural resources and conservation; public administration and social service professions; security and protective services. **Areas of required coursework:** arts/fine arts, humanities, computer literacy, mathematics, English (including composition), sciences (biological or physical), history, social science, other. **Special academic programs (% participation):** distance learning (7%), double major (1%), internships (3%), study abroad (0%), teacher certificate program (1%). **Teacher certification offered in:** early childhood, middle/junior high, secondary. **Faculty and instruction (2009-2010):** Total instructional faculty: 44 full-time, 2 part-time (28% men; 72% women; 4% minorities). Full-time faculty with Ph.D. or other terminal degree: 50%. Student/faculty ratio: 8/1. **Advanced Placement and International Baccalaureate credit:** AP tests may be used for: Placement only. Scores accepted: 4, 5. International Baccalaureate exams may be used for: Placement only. **Graduation rates:** Four-year: 13%; five-year: 76%; six-year: 66%.

COSTS AND FINANCIAL AID

Financial aid office: (229) 227-6925. **Expenses (2009-2010):** Tuition and fees 2009-2010: $11,894; room/board: $5,698. Estimated books and supplies: $1,500.

CAMPUS LIFE AND EXTRACURRICULAR ACTIVITIES

Campus housing available: coed dorms, apartments for married students. Activities include: choral groups, jazz band, student government, student newspaper. Number of fraternities: 0; sororities: 0. Average proportion of students who stay on campus on weekends: 10%. **Sports program (2009-2010):** Member of NAIA.

SERVICES AND FACILITIES

Basic services: nonremedial tutoring, placement service, health insurance. **Remedial assistance:** reading, math, writing, study skills. **Counseling services:** personal, academic. **Information technology resources:** Students are not required to lease or own a computer. Number of campus computers available to all students: 50. School has a wireless network. Proportion of college-owned housing units wired for high-speed internet access: 100%. **Campus safety:** Security services offered: controlled dormitory access (key, security card, etc).

TRANSFER AND INTERNATIONAL STUDENTS

Transfer students: May apply for admission for the following academic terms: Fall, Spring, Summer. Applicants need a minimum number of credits to apply. **International students:** Number of foreign undergraduates: 5 (4% of student body). Minimum TOEFL score required: 550 (paper); 213 (computer). Average TOEFL score: 560 (paper).

Toccoa Falls College

- **Address:** 325 Chapel Drive, Toccoa Falls, GA 30598
- **Website:** http://www.tfc.edu
- **Private; Religious affiliation:** Christian and Missionary Alliance
- **Enrollment:** 762 full-time; 54 part-time

KEY STATS

✔ **U.S News College Ranking:** 46, Regional Colleges (South)
✔ **SAT Score (25th/75th percentile):** 910-1120
✔ **Tuition:** 2010-2011: $15,885

Selectivity: Less selective	Room/board: $5,950
Acceptance rate: 56%	Average debt: N/A
Student/faculty ratio: 13/1	Proportion who borrowed: N/A

UNDERGRADUATE STUDENT BODY STATS

2009-2010 enrollment: 762 full-time; 54 part-time. Men: 45%; women: 55%. **Ethnic makeup:** African American: 4%; Asian American: 7%; Hispanic: 1%; White: 81%; International: 6%. **Religious preference:** Protestant: 65%; Christian and Missionary Alliance: 35%.

ADMISSIONS FACTS AND FIGURES

Phone: (706) 886-6831. **Email:** admissions@tfc.edu. **Website:** http://www.tfc.edu. **Application deadlines for fall 2011:** Regular decision: Rolling. Early decision: Not offered. Early action: Not offered. Admission can be deferred. **Application fee:** $25. **To apply online, go to:** http://www.tfc.edu/adm/application/undergrad_application.htm. **Admissions requirements/recommendations:** High school units required (recommended): English: 4 (4); Mathematics: 3 (3); Science: 3 (3); Foreign language: 0 (0); Social studies: 3 (3); History: 0 (0); Academic electives: 6 (6); Total units: 19 (19). Tests: The college uses SAT or ACT scores in admissions decisions. Either SAT or ACT required. For admission to the fall 2011 entering class, the school will accept: ACT with writing recommended. Campus visit: Recommended. Admissions interview: Neither required nor recommended. Off-campus interview: May be arranged. **Factors that count in admissions decisions:** *Academic:* Secondary school record: Very Important. Class rank: Not Considered. Letters of recommendation: Considered. Standardized test scores: Very Important. Essay: Very Important. *Nonacademic:* Interview: Considered. Extracurricular activities: Considered. Talent/ability: Considered. Character/personal qualities: Very Important. Alumni/ae relationship: Not Considered. Geographical residence: Not Considered. State residency: Not Considered. Religious affiliation/commitment: Very Important. Minority status: Not Considered. Volunteer work: Considered. Work experience: Considered. **Other schools with the greatest overlap**

in applicants: Columbia International University; Crown College; Nyack College; Simpson University. **Admissions statistics for the fall 2009 entering class:** Total applicants: 679. Total accepted: 378. Freshmen enrolled: 171; Overall acceptance rate: 56%. **First-year students who submitted SAT scores:** 71%. Scores (25/75 percentile): Critical Reading: 470-570, Math: 440-550, Combined: 910-1120. **First-year students submitting ACT scores:** 46%. Scores (25/75 percentile): English: 16-25, Math: 16-23, Composite: 17-22.

ACADEMICS

Year founded: 1907. **Academic calendar:** 4-1-4. **Degrees offered:** certificate, associate, bachelor's. **Most popular majors:** 38% theology and religious vocations, 23% education, 15% psychology, 6% communication, journalism, and related programs, 4% biological and biomedical sciences. **Major fields of study:** biological and biomedical sciences; business, management, marketing, and related support services; communication, journalism, and related programs; education; English language and literature/letters; legal professions and studies; philosophy and religious studies; psychology; theology and religious vocations; visual and performing arts. **Areas of required coursework:** humanities, computer literacy, mathematics, English (including composition), history, social science, other. **Pre-professional programs:** pre-medicine. **Special academic programs (% participation):** distance learning, double major, dual enrollment, independent study (35%), internships (46%), study abroad (1%), teacher certificate program (18%). **Teacher certification offered in:** early childhood, elementary, middle/junior high, secondary. **Faculty and instruction (2009-2010):** Total instructional faculty: 49 full-time, 29 part-time (73% men; 27% women; 6% minorities). Full-time faculty with Ph.D. or other terminal degree: 55%. Student/faculty ratio: 13/1. Classes of fewer than 20 students: 81%; of 20 to 49 students: 19%; of 50 or more students: 0%. **Advanced Placement and International Baccalaureate credit:** International Baccalaureate exams may be used for: Placement only. **Freshmen returning for sophomore year:** 67%. **Graduation rates:** Four-year: 56%; five-year: 59%; six-year: 51%. **Graduate study:** 30% of students pursue further study within one year; 60% within five years.

COSTS AND FINANCIAL AID

Financial aid office: (706) 886-6831. **Expenses (2010-2011):** Tuition and fees 2010-2011: $15,885; room/board: $5,950. Estimated books and supplies: $1,000. **Financial aid:** Priority filing date for institution's financial aid form: May 1.

CAMPUS LIFE AND EXTRACURRICULAR ACTIVITIES

Campus housing available (% using): women's dorms (55%), men's dorms (36%), apartments for married students (5%), special housing for international students (2%), other housing options (2%). **Student employment:** During the 2009-2010 academic year, 34% of undergraduates worked on campus. Average per-year earnings: $1,875. Activities include: campus ministries, choral groups, concert band, drama/theater, international student organization, jazz band, music ensembles, radio station, student government, student newspaper, symphony orchestra, yearbook. Number of fraternities: 0; sororities: 0. Average proportion of students who stay on campus on weekends: 60%.

SERVICES AND FACILITIES

Basic services: nonremedial tutoring, placement service, health service, health insurance. **Counseling services:** career, personal, academic, older student, psychological, religious. **For learning-disabled students:** School does not offer a structured program with separate admission and additional fees. Services include: untimed tests, note-taking services, oral tests, learning center, readers, extended time for tests, tutors, priority seating, other testing accommodations, other. **Library:** Number of titles: 142,674; number of current serial subscriptions: 25,305. **Information technology resources:** Students are not required to lease or own a computer. Number of campus computers available to all students: 60. School has a wireless network. Approximate number of users that can be accommodated: 600. Proportion of college-owned housing units wired for high-speed internet access: 90%. **Campus safety:** Security services offered: 24-hour foot-and-vehicle patrols, late-night transport/escort service, 24-hour emergency telephones, lighted pathways/sidewalks, controlled dormitory access (key, security card, etc).

TRANSFER AND INTERNATIONAL STUDENTS

Transfer students: May apply for admission for the following academic terms: Fall, Winter, Spring, Summer. Applicants need a minimum number of credits to apply. For fall 2009: Transfer applications received: 161. Transfer applicants offered admission: 104. Transfer applicants enrolled: 62. **International students:** Number of foreign undergraduates: 46 (6% of student body). Number of countries represented: 11. Minimum TOEFL score required: 550 (paper); 213 (computer). Average TOEFL score: 566 (paper).

University of Georgia

- **Address:** Terrell Hall, Athens, GA 30602
- **Website:** http://www.uga.edu
- **Public**
- **Enrollment:** 24,670 full-time; 1,472 part-time

KEY STATS

✔ **U.S News College Ranking:** 56, National Universities
✔ **SAT Score (25th/75th percentile):** 1130-1330
✔ **Tuition:** 2010-2011: $7,530 in state, $25,740 out of state
Selectivity: More selective   **Room/board:** $8,460
Acceptance rate: 54%   **Average debt:** $14,766
Student/faculty ratio: 18/1   **Proportion who borrowed:** 44%

UNDERGRADUATE STUDENT BODY STATS

2009-2010 enrollment: 24,670 full-time; 1,472 part-time. Men: 42%; women: 58%. **Ethnic makeup:** African American: 7%; Asian American: 7%; Hispanic: 3%; White: 82%; International: 1%. **Religious preference:** Roman Catholic: 13%; Protestant: 49%; Jewish: 3%; Hindu: 1%; Buddhist: 1%; No preference: 21%; Other: 12%.

ADMISSIONS FACTS AND FIGURES

Phone: (706) 542-8776. **Email:** adm-info@uga.edu. **Website:** http://www.uga.edu. **Application deadlines for fall 2011:** Regular decision: January 15. Early decision: Not offered. Early action: Send application by: October 15; Decision sent by: December 15. Admission can be deferred. **Application fee:** $60. **To apply online, go to:** http://www.admissions.uga.edu/article/apply_now.html. **Admissions requirements/recommendations:** High school units required (recommended): English: 4 (4); Mathematics: 4 (4); Science: 3 (3); Foreign language: 2 (3); Social studies: 3 (1); History: (2); Total units: 16 (18). Tests: The college uses SAT or ACT scores in admissions decisions. Either SAT or ACT required. For admission to the fall 2011 entering class, the school will accept: ACT with writing required. Campus visit: Recommended. Admissions interview: Neither required nor recommended. Off-campus interview: Not available. **Factors that count in admissions decisions:** *Academic:* Secondary school record: Very Important. Class rank: Not Considered. Letters of recommendation: Considered. Standardized test scores: Important. Essay: Considered. *Nonacademic:* Interview: Not Considered. Extracurricular activities: Considered. Talent/ability: Considered. Character/personal qualities: Considered. Alumni/ae relationship: Not Considered. Geographical residence: Not Considered. State residency: Not Considered. Religious affiliation/commitment: Not Considered. Minority status: Not Considered. Volunteer work: Not Considered. Work experience: Considered. **Other schools with the greatest overlap in applicants:** Clemson University; Emory University; Georgia Institute of Technology; University of North Carolina–Chapel Hill; University of South Carolina. **Admissions statistics for the fall 2009 entering class:** Total applicants: 17,776. Total accepted: 9,557. Freshmen enrolled: 4,684; 11% were from out of state. Accepted through early-decision or early-action plans: 78%. Overall acceptance rate: 54%. Non-early acceptance rate: 36%. **Size of waiting list:** 1141 applicants; enrolled from waiting list: 724. **Credentials of fall 2009 freshmen:** 54% ranked in the top 10 percent of their high school class; 89% were in the top 25 percent; 98% were in the top half. (Proportion submitting class standing: 77%.) **Average high school grade point average:** 3.8. **First-year students who submitted SAT scores:** 93%. Scores (25/75 percentile): Critical Reading: 560-660, Math: 570-670, Combined: 1130-1330. **First-year students submitting ACT scores:** 54%. Scores (25/75 percentile): English: 25-31, Math: 24-29, Composite: 25-29.

ACADEMICS

Year founded: 1785. **Academic calendar:** Semester. **Degrees offered:** certificate, bachelor's, post-bachelor's certificate, master's, post-master's certificate, doctorate. **Most popular majors:** 6% biology/biological sciences, 6% finance, 6% psychology, 4% marketing/marketing management, 4% political science and government. **Major fields of study:** agriculture, agriculture operations, and related sciences; architecture and related services; area, ethnic, cultural, and gender studies; biological and biomedical sciences; business, management, marketing, and related support services; communication, journalism, and related programs; communications technologies/

technicians and support services; computer and information sciences and support services; education; engineering; English language and literature/letters; family and consumer sciences/human sciences; foreign languages, literatures, and linguistics; health professions and related clinical sciences; history; liberal arts and sciences studies, and humanities; mathematics and statistics; multi/interdisciplinary studies; natural resources and conservation; parks, recreation, leisure, and fitness studies; philosophy and religious studies; physical sciences; psychology; public administration and social service professions; security and protective services; social sciences; visual and performing arts. **Areas of required coursework:** arts/fine arts, humanities, computer literacy, mathematics, English (including composition), sciences (biological or physical), history, social science, other. **Pre-professional programs:** pre-law, pre-dentistry, pre-medicine, pre-theology, pre-veterinary science, pre-optometry, pre-pharmacy. **Special academic programs (% participation):** accelerated program, cooperative (work-study plan) program, cross-registration, distance learning, double major (14%), dual enrollment, exchange student program (domestic) (1%), external degree program, honors program (3%), independent study (4%), internships (28%), liberal arts/career combination, student-designed major, study abroad (26%), teacher certificate program (7%). **Teacher certification offered in:** early childhood, special education, elementary, vo-tech, middle/junior high, secondary, bilingual/bicultural. **Cooperative education programs:** agriculture, business, engineering, natural science, other. **Reserve Officers Training Corps (ROTC):** Army ROTC: Offered on campus; Air Force ROTC: Offered on campus. **Faculty and instruction (2009-2010):** Total instructional faculty: 1,775 full-time, 438 part-time (63% men; 37% women; 15% minorities). Full-time faculty with Ph.D. or other terminal degree: 94%. Student/faculty ratio: 18/1. Classes of fewer than 20 students: 36%; of 20 to 49 students: 52%; of 50 or more students: 13%. **Advanced Placement and International Baccalaureate credit:** AP tests may be used for: Credit and/or placement. Scores accepted: 3, 4, 5. International Baccalaureate exams may be used for: Credit and/or placement. **Freshmen returning for sophomore year:** 94%. **Graduation rates:** Four-year: 51%; five-year: 77%; six-year: 81%. **Graduate study:** 28% of students pursue further study immediately upon graduation. Fields in which graduates pursue further study: Master of Business Administration (MBA), 13%; law, 13%; medicine, 17%; dentistry, 1%; engineering, 1%; theology (or the seminary), 1%; education, 13%; arts and sciences, 31%; veterinary medicine, 10%.

COSTS AND FINANCIAL AID

Financial aid office: (706) 542-6147. **Expenses (2010-2011):** Tuition and fees 2010-2011: $7,530 in state, $25,740 out of state; room/board: $8,460. Estimated books and supplies: $960; transportation: $270; personal expenses: $1,194. **Financial aid:** Priority filing date for institution's financial aid form: March 1. In 2009-2010, 54% of undergraduates applied for financial aid. Of those, 33% were determined to have financial need; 18% had their need fully met. Average financial aid package (proportion receiving): $9,509 (32%). Average amount of gift aid, such as scholarships or grants (proportion receiving): $7,953 (29%). Average amount of self-help aid, such as work study or loans (proportion receiving): $3,915 (21%). Average need-based loan (excluding PLUS or other private loans): $3,809. Among students who received need-based aid, the average percentage of need met: 76%. Among students who received aid based on merit, the average award (and the proportion receiving): $1,872 (5%). The average athletic scholarship (and the proportion receiving): $13,520 (2%). Average amount of debt of borrowers graduating in 2009: $14,766. Proportion who borrowed: 44%.

CAMPUS LIFE AND EXTRACURRICULAR ACTIVITIES

Campus housing available (% using): coed dorms (42%), women's dorms (15%), sorority housing (2%), fraternity housing (3%), apartments for married students (8%), apartment for single students (16%), special housing for disabled students, special housing for international students, other housing options. Students who live in college-owned, operated, or affiliated housing: 27%. **Student employment:** During the 2009-2010 academic year, 8% of undergraduates worked on campus. Average per-year earnings: $4,640. **Clubs and organizations:** Number of student organizations: 623. Activities include: campus ministries, choral groups, concert band, dance, drama/theater, international student organization, jazz band, literary magazine, marching band, model UN, music ensembles, musical theater, opera, pep band, radio station, student government, student newspaper, student film society, symphony orchestra, television station, yearbook. Number of fraternities: 34; sororities: 25. Proportion of men in fraternities: 21%; of women in sororities: 24%. Average proportion of students who stay on campus on weekends: 75%. **Sports program (2009-2010):** Member of NCAA I. *Men's intercollegiate varsity sports:* baseball, basketball, cross country, football, golf, swimming, tennis, track and field (indoor), track and field (outdoor).

Women's intercollegiate varsity sports: basketball, cross country, equestrian, golf, gymnastics, soccer, softball, swimming, tennis, track and field (indoor), track and field (outdoor), volleyball.

SERVICES AND FACILITIES

Basic services: nonremedial tutoring, women's center, placement service, day care, health service, health insurance. **Remedial assistance:** reading, math, writing, study skills. **Counseling services:** minority student, career, military, personal, veteran student, academic, older student, psychological, birth control, religious. **For learning-disabled students:** School does not offer a structured program with separate admission and additional fees. Total undergraduates in learning-disabled program or receiving services: 258. Services include: remedial math, remedial English, reading machines, remedial reading, tape recorders, videotaped classes, diagnostic testing service, note-taking services, oral tests, learning center, readers, extended time for tests, tutors, early syllabus, priority registration, priority seating, substitution of courses, texts on tape, typist/scribe, exams on tape or computer, other testing accommodations, waiver of foreign language degree requirement, waiver of math degree requirement, other. **Library:** Number of titles: 4,637,291; number of current serial subscriptions: 84,495. **Information technology resources:** Students are not required to lease or own a computer. Number of campus computers available to all students: 3,440. School has a wireless network. Approximate number of users that can be accommodated: 25,000. Proportion of college-owned housing units wired for high-speed internet access: 100%. **Campus safety:** Security services offered: 24-hour foot-and-vehicle patrols, late-night transport/escort service, 24-hour emergency telephones, lighted pathways/sidewalks, controlled dormitory access (key, security card, etc).

TRANSFER AND INTERNATIONAL STUDENTS

Transfer students: May apply for admission for the following academic terms: Fall, Spring, Summer. Applicants need a minimum number of credits to apply. For fall 2009: Transfer applications received: 2,989. Transfer applicants offered admission: 1,749. Transfer applicants enrolled: 1,355. **International students:** Number of foreign undergraduates: 194 (1% of student body). Number of countries represented: 106. Minimum TOEFL score required: 550 (paper); 80 (computer).

University of West Georgia

- **Address:** 1601 Maple Street, Carrollton, GA 30118
- **Website:** http://www.westga.edu
- **Public**
- **Enrollment:** 8,126 full-time; 1,496 part-time

KEY STATS

✔ **U.S News College Ranking:** second tier, Regional Universities (South)
✔ **ACT Score (25th/75th percentile):** 18-22
✔ **Tuition:** 2009-2010: $5,382 in state, $17,358 out of state

Selectivity: Selective	**Room/board:** $6,254
Acceptance rate: 58%	**Average debt:** N/A
Student/faculty ratio: 20/1	**Proportion who borrowed:** N/A

UNDERGRADUATE STUDENT BODY STATS

2009-2010 enrollment: 8,126 full-time; 1,496 part-time. Men: 40%; women: 60%. **Ethnic makeup:** African American: 27%; Asian American: 1%; Hispanic: 2%; White: 68%; International: 1%.

ADMISSIONS FACTS AND FIGURES

Phone: (678) 839-4000. **Email:** admiss@westga.edu. **Website:** http://www.westga.edu. **Application deadlines for fall 2011:** Regular decision: June 1. Early decision: Not offered. Early action: Not offered. Admission can be deferred. **Application fee:** $30. **To apply online, go to:** http://www.westga.edu/~admiss/. **Admissions requirements/recommendations:** High school units required (recommended): English: 4; Mathematics: 4; Science: 3 (4); Foreign language: 2; Social studies: 1; History: 2; Total units: 16. Tests: The college uses SAT or ACT scores in admissions decisions. Either SAT or ACT required. For admission to the fall 2011 entering class, the school will accept: ACT with or without writing accepted. Campus visit: Recommended. Admissions interview: Recommended. **Factors that count in admissions decisions:** *Academic:* Secondary school record: Very Important. Class rank: Not Considered. Letters of recommendation: Not Considered. Standardized test scores: Very Important. Essay: Not

Considered. **Nonacademic:** Interview: Not Considered. Extracurricular activities: Not Considered. Talent/ability: Not Considered. Character/personal qualities: Not Considered. Alumni/ae relationship: Not Considered. Geographical residence: Not Considered. State residency: Not Considered. Religious affiliation/commitment: Not Considered. Minority status: Not Considered. Volunteer work: Not Considered. Work experience: Not Considered. **Other schools with the greatest overlap in applicants:** Georgia Southern University; Georgia State University; Kennesaw State University; University of Georgia; Valdosta State University. **Admissions statistics for the fall 2009 entering class:** Total applicants: 5,981. Total accepted: 3,444. Freshmen enrolled: 2,033; 3% were from out of state. Overall acceptance rate: 58%. **Average high school grade point average:** 2.9. **First-year students who submitted SAT scores:** 70%. Scores (25/75 percentile): Critical Reading: 450-540, Math: 450-530, Combined: 900-1070. **First-year students submitting ACT scores:** 70%. Scores (25/75 percentile): English: 17-22, Math: 18-23, Composite: 18-22.

ACADEMICS

Year founded: 1906. **Academic calendar:** Semester. **Degrees offered:** bachelor's, post-bachelor's certificate, master's, post-master's certificate, doctorate. **Most popular majors:** 25% business, management, marketing, and related support services, 20% education, 12% social sciences, 9% health professions and related clinical sciences, 7% psychology. **Major fields of study:** biological and biomedical sciences; business, management, marketing, and related support services; communication, journalism, and related programs; computer and information sciences and support services; education; English language and literature/letters; foreign languages, literatures, and linguistics; health professions and related clinical sciences; history; mathematics and statistics; natural resources and conservation; parks, recreation, leisure, and fitness studies; philosophy and religious studies; physical sciences; psychology; social sciences; visual and performing arts. **Areas of required coursework:** arts/fine arts, humanities, computer literacy, mathematics, English (including composition), foreign languages, sciences (biological or physical), history, social science. **Pre-professional programs:** pre-law, pre-dentistry, pre-medicine, pre-veterinary science, pre-pharmacy, other. **Special academic programs:** accelerated program, cooperative (work-study plan) program, distance learning, double major, dual enrollment, external degree program, honors program, independent study, internships, study abroad, teacher certificate program. **Teacher certification offered in:** early childhood, special education, elementary, middle/junior high, secondary. **Cooperative education programs:** other. **Reserve Officers Training Corps (ROTC):** Army ROTC: Offered on campus. **Faculty and instruction (2009-2010):** Total instructional faculty: 431 full-time, 134 part-time (45% men; 55% women; 14% minorities). Full-time faculty with Ph.D. or other terminal degree: 78%. Student/faculty ratio: 20/1. Classes of fewer than 20 students: 35%; of 20 to 49 students: 55%; of 50 or more students: 10%. **Advanced Placement and International Baccalaureate credit:** AP tests may be used for: Credit only. Scores accepted: 3, 4, 5. International Baccalaureate exams may be used for: Credit only. **Freshmen returning for sophomore year:** 73%. **Graduation rates:** Four-year: 12%; five-year: 29%; six-year: 35%.

COSTS AND FINANCIAL AID

Financial aid office: (678) 839-6421. **Expenses (2009-2010):** Tuition and fees 2009-2010: $5,382 in state, $17,358 out of state; room/board: $6,254. Estimated books and supplies: $1,000; transportation: $952; personal expenses: $3,060. **Financial aid:** Priority filing date for institution's financial aid form: April 1; deadline: July 1. In 2009-2010, 80% of undergraduates applied for financial aid. Of those, 61% were determined to have financial need; 17% had their need fully met. Average financial aid package (proportion receiving): $8,224 (60%). Average amount of gift aid, such as scholarships or grants (proportion receiving): $5,804 (50%). Average amount of self-help aid, such as work study or loans (proportion receiving): $4,304 (46%). Average need-based loan (excluding PLUS or other private loans): $3,980. Among students who received need-based aid, the average percentage of need met: 60%. Among students who received aid based on merit, the average award (and the proportion receiving): $1,532 (3%). The average athletic scholarship (and the proportion receiving): $5,453 (2%).

CAMPUS LIFE AND EXTRACURRICULAR ACTIVITIES

Campus housing available: coed dorms, women's dorms, sorority housing, fraternity housing, special housing for disabled students. Students who live in college-owned, operated, or affiliated housing: 28%. **Student employment:** During the 2009-2010 academic year, 5% of undergraduates worked on campus. Average per-year earnings: $4,716. **Clubs and organizations:** Number of student organizations: 147. Activities include: campus ministries, choral groups, concert band, dance, drama/theater, international

student organization, jazz band, literary magazine, marching band, music ensembles, musical theater, opera, pep band, radio station, student government, student newspaper, television station. Number of fraternities: 14; sororities: 9. Proportion of men in fraternities: 3%; of women in sororities: 3%. Average proportion of students who stay on campus on weekends: 25%. **Sports program (2009-2010):** Member of NCAA II. *Men's intercollegiate varsity sports:* baseball, basketball, cross country, football, golf. *Women's intercollegiate varsity sports:* basketball, cross country, golf, soccer, softball, volleyball.

SERVICES AND FACILITIES

Basic services: nonremedial tutoring, placement service, health service. **Remedial assistance:** reading, math, writing, study skills. **Counseling services:** minority student, career, military, personal, veteran student, academic, older student, psychological. **For learning-disabled students:** School does not offer a structured program with separate admission and additional fees. Total undergraduates in learning-disabled program or receiving services: 300. Services include: remedial math, remedial English, reading machines, remedial reading, tape recorders, untimed tests, note-taking services, oral tests, learning center, readers, extended time for tests, tutors, priority registration, priority seating, substitution of courses, texts on tape, typist/scribe, other testing accommodations, waiver of foreign language degree requirement, other. **Library:** Number of titles: 541,488; number of current serial subscriptions: 17,000. **Information technology resources:** Students are not required to lease or own a computer. Number of campus computers available to all students: 1,144. School has a wireless network. Approximate number of users that can be accommodated: 2,048. Proportion of college-owned housing units wired for high-speed internet access: 100%. **Campus safety:** Security services offered: 24-hour foot-and-vehicle patrols, 24-hour emergency telephones, lighted pathways/sidewalks, controlled dormitory access (key, security card, etc).

TRANSFER AND INTERNATIONAL STUDENTS

Transfer students: May apply for admission for the following academic terms: Fall, Spring, Summer. Applicants need a minimum number of credits to apply. For fall 2009: Transfer applications received: 1,547. Transfer applicants offered admission: 985. Transfer applicants enrolled: 611. **International students:** Number of foreign undergraduates: 115 (1% of student body). Number of countries represented: 36. Minimum TOEFL score required: 523 (paper); 193 (computer).

Valdosta State University

■ **Address:** 1500 N. Patterson Street, Valdosta, GA 31698
■ **Website:** http://www.valdosta.edu
■ **Public**
■ **Enrollment:** 9,019 full-time; 1,309 part-time

KEY STATS

✔ **U.S News College Ranking:** 69, Regional Universities (South)
✔ **SAT Score (25th/75th percentile):** 930-1090
✔ **Tuition:** 2009-2010: $5,706 in state, $13,617 out of state

Selectivity: Selective	**Room/board:** $7,062
Acceptance rate: 71%	**Average debt:** $17,840
Student/faculty ratio: 22/1	**Proportion who borrowed:** 65%

UNDERGRADUATE STUDENT BODY STATS

2009-2010 enrollment: 9,019 full-time; 1,309 part-time. Men: 42%; women: 58%. **Ethnic makeup:** African American: 31%; Asian American: 1%; Hispanic: 1%; White: 65%; International: 2%.

ADMISSIONS FACTS AND FIGURES

Phone: (229) 333-5791. **Email:** admissions@valdosta.edu. **Website:** http://www.valdosta.edu. **Application deadlines for fall 2011:** Regular decision: June 15. Early decision: Not offered. Early action: Not offered. Admission can be deferred. **Application fee:** $40. **To apply online, go to:** https://www.gacollege411.com. **Admissions requirements/recommendations:** High school units required (recommended): English: 4 (4); Mathematics: 4 (4); Science: 3 (3); Foreign language: 2 (2); Social studies: 3 (3); Total units: 16 (16). Tests: The college uses SAT or ACT scores in admissions decisions. Either SAT or ACT required. For admission to the fall 2011 entering class, the school will accept: ACT with or without writing accepted. Campus visit: Neither required nor recommended. Admissions interview: Neither required nor recommended. Off-campus interview: Not available. **Factors that count in admissions decisions:** *Academic:* Secondary school record: Not Considered. Class rank: Not Considered. Letters of recommendation: Not Considered. Standardized test scores: Very Important. Essay: Not Considered. *Nonacademic:* Interview: Not Considered. Extracurricular activities: Not Considered. Talent/ability: Not Considered. Character/personal qualities: Not Considered. Alumni/ae relationship: Not Considered. Geographical residence: Not Considered. State residency: Not Considered. Religious affiliation/commitment: Not Considered. Minority status: Not Considered. Volunteer work: Not Considered. Work experience: Not Considered. **Other schools with the greatest overlap in applicants:** Georgia College & State University; Georgia Southern University; Georgia State University; University of Georgia; University of West Georgia. **Admissions statistics for the fall 2009 entering class:** Total applicants: 6,703. Total accepted: 4,744. Freshmen enrolled: 2,467; 3% were from out of state. Overall acceptance rate: 71%. **Average high school grade point average:** 3.0. **First-year students who submitted SAT scores:** 77%. Scores (25/75 percentile): Critical Reading: 470-550, Math: 460-540, Combined: 930-1090. **First-year students submitting ACT scores:** 20%. Scores (25/75 percentile): English: 20-24, Math: 19-23, Composite: 20-23.

ACADEMICS

Year founded: 1906. **Academic calendar:** Semester. **Degrees offered:** associate, bachelor's, master's, post-master's certificate, doctorate. **Most popular majors:** 22% education, 19% business, management, marketing, and related support services, 9% English language and literature/letters, 9% health professions and related clinical sciences, 7% social sciences. **Major fields of study:** biological and biomedical sciences; business, management, marketing, and related support services; communication, journalism, and related programs; computer and information sciences and support services; education; engineering technologies/technicians; English language and literature/letters; foreign languages, literatures, and linguistics; health professions and related clinical sciences; history; legal professions and studies; liberal arts and sciences studies, and humanities; mathematics and statistics; natural resources and conservation; parks, recreation, leisure, and fitness studies; philosophy and religious studies; physical sciences; psychology; security and protective services; social sciences; visual and performing arts. **Areas of required coursework:** humanities, mathematics, English (including composition), sciences (biological or physical), history, social science, other. **Special academic programs:** cooperative (work-study plan) program, distance learning, double major, dual enrollment, English as a Second Language (ESL), external degree program, honors program, independent study, internships, study abroad, teacher certificate program, weekend college. **Teacher certification offered in:** early childhood, special education, middle/junior high, adult education, secondary. **Cooperative education programs:** agriculture, art, business, computer science, education, engineering, health professions, humanities, natural science, social/behavioral science, technologies, vocational arts, other. **Reserve Officers Training Corps (ROTC):** Air Force ROTC: Offered on campus. **Faculty and instruction (2009-2010):** Total instructional faculty: 472 full-time, 120 part-time (48% men; 52% women; 9% minorities). Full-time faculty with Ph.D. or other terminal degree: 72%. Student/faculty ratio: 22/1. Classes of fewer than 20 students: 34%; of 20 to 49 students: 63%; of 50 or more students: 3%. **Advanced Placement and International Baccalaureate credit:** International Baccalaureate exams may be used for: Credit only. **Freshmen returning for sophomore year:** 72%. **Graduation rates:** Four-year: 16%; five-year: 37%; six-year: 42%.

COSTS AND FINANCIAL AID

Financial aid office: (229) 333-5935. **Expenses (2009-2010):** Tuition and fees 2009-2010: $5,706 in state, $13,617 out of state; room/board: $7,062. Estimated books and supplies: $1,200; transportation: $3,316; personal expenses: $2,760. **Financial aid:** Priority filing date for institution's financial aid form: May 1. In 2009-2010, 78% of undergraduates applied for financial aid. Of those, 63% were determined to have financial need; 14% had their need fully met. Average financial aid package (proportion receiving): $8,550 (63%). Average amount of gift aid, such as scholarships or grants (proportion receiving): $6,092 (50%). Average amount of self-help aid, such as work study or loans (proportion receiving): $4,032 (58%). Average need-based loan (excluding PLUS or other private loans): $3,948. Among students who received need-based aid, the average percentage of need met: 58%. Among students who received aid based on merit, the average award (and the proportion receiving): $1,653 (1%). The average athletic scholarship (and the proportion receiving): $3,356 (0%). Average amount of debt of borrowers graduating in 2009: $17,840. Proportion who borrowed: 65%.

CAMPUS LIFE AND EXTRACURRICULAR ACTIVITIES

Campus housing available (% using): coed dorms (64%), apartment for single students (21%), special housing for disabled students (3%), special housing for international students (1%). Students who live in college-owned, operated, or affiliated housing: 28%. **Student employment:** During the 2009-2010 academic year, 12% of undergraduates worked on campus. Average per-year earnings: $6,000. **Clubs and organizations:** Number of student organizations: 158. Activities include: campus ministries, choral groups, concert band, dance, drama/theater, international student organization, jazz band, literary magazine, marching band, model UN, music ensembles, pep band, radio station, student government, student newspaper, symphony orchestra, television station. Number of fraternities: 13; sororities: 10. Proportion of men in fraternities: 5%; of women in sororities: 7%. Average proportion of students who stay on campus on weekends: 65%. **Sports program (2009-2010):** Member of NCAA II. *Men's intercollegiate varsity sports:* baseball, basketball, cross country, football, golf, tennis. *Women's intercollegiate varsity sports:* basketball, cross country, softball, tennis, volleyball.

SERVICES AND FACILITIES

Basic services: nonremedial tutoring, placement service, health service, health insurance. **Remedial assistance:** other. **Counseling services:** minority student, career, personal, veteran student, academic, older student, psychological, birth control, other. **For learning-disabled students:** School does not offer a structured program with separate admission and additional fees. Total undergraduates in learning-disabled program or receiving services: 50. Services include: remedial math, remedial English, reading machines, remedial reading, tape recorders, note-taking services, oral tests, learning center, readers, extended time for tests, tutors, priority registration, priority seating, substitution of courses, texts on tape, exams on tape or computer, other testing accommodations. **Library:** Number of titles: 633,876; number of current serial subscriptions: 2,732. **Information technology resources:** Students are not required to lease or own a computer. Number of campus computers available to all students: 1,225. School has a wireless network. Approximate number of users that can be accommodated: 2,500. Proportion of college-owned housing units wired for high-speed internet access: 100%. **Campus safety:** Security services offered: 24-hour foot-and-vehicle patrols, late-night transport/escort service, 24-hour emergency telephones, lighted pathways/sidewalks, controlled dormitory access (key, security card, etc).

TRANSFER AND INTERNATIONAL STUDENTS

Transfer students: May apply for admission for the following academic terms: Fall, Spring, Summer. Applicants need a minimum number of credits to apply. For fall 2009: Transfer applications received: 1,247. Transfer applicants offered admission: 738. Transfer applicants enrolled: 684. **International students:** Number of foreign undergraduates: 204 (2% of student body). Number of countries represented: 67. Minimum TOEFL score required: 523 (paper); 193 (computer). Average TOEFL score: 574 (paper).

Wesleyan College

- **Address:** 4760 Forsyth Road, Macon, GA 31210-4462
- **Website:** http://www.wesleyancollege.edu
- **Private; Religious affiliation:** United Methodist
- **Enrollment:** 387 full-time; 237 part-time

KEY STATS

✔ **U.S News College Ranking:** 158, National Liberal Arts Colleges
✔ **SAT Score (25th/75th percentile):** 960-1210
✔ **Tuition:** 2010-2011: $18,000

Selectivity: Selective		**Room/board:** $8,100
Acceptance rate: 53%		**Average debt:** $20,983
Student/faculty ratio: 10/1		**Proportion who borrowed:** 63%

UNDERGRADUATE STUDENT BODY STATS

2009-2010 enrollment: 387 full-time; 237 part-time. Men: 2%; women: 98%. **Ethnic makeup:** African American: 24%; Asian American: 3%; Hispanic: 2%; White: 49%; International: 20%. **Religious preference:** Roman Catholic: 7%; Protestant: 39%; Jewish: 1%; Muslim: 1%; Hindu: 2%; Buddhist: 1%; No preference: 33%; United Methodist: 13%.

ADMISSIONS FACTS AND FIGURES

Phone: (800) 447-6610. **Email:** admissions@wesleyancollege.edu. **Website:** http://www.wesleyancollege.edu. **Application deadlines for fall 2011:** Regular decision: June 1. Early decision: Send application by: November 15; Decision sent by: December 15. Early action: Send application by: February 15; Decision sent by: March 15. Admission can be deferred. **Application fee:** $30. **To apply online, go to:** http://www.wesleyancollege.edu/Admission/Apply/tabid/1226/Default.aspx. **Admissions requirements/recommendations:** High school units required (recommended): English: 4 (4); Mathematics: 3 (4); Science: 3 (4); Foreign language: 2 (4); Social studies: 3 (4); History: 0 (0); Academic electives: 0 (2); Total units: 15 (22). Tests: The college uses SAT or ACT scores in admissions decisions. Either SAT or ACT required. For admission to the fall 2011 entering class, the school will accept: ACT with or without writing accepted. Campus visit: Recommended. Admissions interview: Recommended. Off-campus interview: May be arranged. **Factors that count in admissions decisions:** *Academic:* Secondary school record: Very Important. Class rank: Important. Letters of recommendation: Important. Standardized test scores: Important. Essay: Considered. *Nonacademic:* Interview: Important. Extracurricular activities: Important. Talent/ability: Important. Character/personal qualities: Not Considered. Alumni/ae relationship: Considered. Geographical residence: Not Considered. State residency: Not Considered. Religious affiliation/commitment: Not Considered. Minority status: Not Considered. Volunteer work: Considered. Work experience: Considered. **Other schools with the greatest overlap in applicants:** Agnes Scott College; Berry College; Georgia College & State University; Mercer University; University of Georgia. **Admissions statistics for the fall 2009 entering class:** Total applicants: 536. Total accepted: 286. Freshmen enrolled: 99; 23% were from out of state. Overall acceptance rate: 53%. Non-early acceptance rate: 53%. **Size of waiting list:** 0 applicants; enrolled from waiting list: 0. **Credentials of fall 2009 freshmen:** 34% ranked in the top 10 percent of their high school class; 61% were in the top 25 percent; 78% were in the top half. (Proportion submitting class standing: 68%.) **First-year students who submitted SAT scores:** 74%. Scores (25/75 percentile): Critical Reading: 500-610, Math: 460-600, Combined: 960-1210. **First-year students submitting ACT scores:** 39%. Scores (25/75 percentile): English: N/A, Math: N/A, Composite: 20-28.

ACADEMICS

Year founded: 1836. **Academic calendar:** Semester. **Degrees offered:** bachelor's, master's. **Most popular majors:** 24% visual and performing arts, 17% psychology, 13% communication, journalism, and related programs, 8% business administration, management, and operations, 7% liberal arts and sciences/liberal studies. **Major fields of study:** area, ethnic, cultural, and gender studies; biological and biomedical sciences; business, management, marketing, and related support services; communication, journalism, and related programs; computer and information sciences and support services; education; engineering; English language and literature/letters; foreign languages, literatures, and linguistics; history; liberal arts and sciences studies, and humanities; mathematics and statistics; multi/interdisciplinary studies; natural resources and conservation; philosophy and religious studies; physical sciences; psychology; social sciences; visual and performing arts. **Areas of required coursework:** arts/fine arts, humanities, mathematics, English (including composition), foreign languages, sciences (biological or physical), social science. **Pre-professional programs:** pre-law, pre-dentistry, pre-medicine, pre-veterinary science, pre-pharmacy, other. **Special academic programs (% participation):** cross-registration (2%), double major (14%), exchange student program (domestic) (0%), honors program (9%), independent study (40%), internships (60%), student-designed major (1%), study abroad (3%), teacher certificate program (2%). **Teacher certification offered in:** early childhood. **Cooperative education programs:** education, engineering. **Faculty and instruction (2009-2010):** Total instructional faculty: 47 full-time, 33 part-time (39% men; 61% women; 5% minorities). Full-time faculty with Ph.D. or other terminal degree: 100%. Student/faculty ratio: 10/1. Classes of fewer than 20 students: 91%; of 20 to 49 students: 9%. **Advanced Placement and International Baccalaureate credit:** AP tests may be used for: Credit only. Scores accepted: 3, 4, 5. International Baccalaureate exams may be used for: Credit only. **Freshmen returning for sophomore year:** 72%. **Graduation rates:** Four-year: 41%; five-year: 41%; six-year: 41%. **Graduate study:** 32% of students pursue further study immediately upon graduation; 30% within one year; 25% within five years. Fields in which graduates pursue further study: Master of Business Administration (MBA), 4%; law, 2%; medicine, 2%; arts and sciences, 25%.

COSTS AND FINANCIAL AID

Financial aid office: (888) 665-5723. **Expenses (2010-2011):** Tuition and fees 2010-2011: $18,000; room/board: $8,100. Estimated books and supplies: $1,200; transportation: $800; personal expenses: $1,200. **Financial aid:** Priority filing date for institution's financial aid form: February 15. In 2009-2010, 77% of undergraduates applied for financial aid. Of those, 67% were determined to have financial need; 23% had their need fully met. Average financial aid package (proportion receiving): $16,980 (67%). Average amount of gift aid, such as scholarships or grants (proportion receiving): $13,510 (67%). Average amount of self-help aid, such as work study or loans (proportion receiving): $4,587 (52%). Average need-based loan (excluding PLUS or other private loans): $4,359. Among students who received need-based aid, the average percentage of need met: 81%. Among students who received aid based on merit, the average award (and the proportion receiving): $15,208 (32%). The average athletic scholarship (and the proportion receiving): $0 (0%). Average amount of debt of borrowers graduating in 2009: $20,983. Proportion who borrowed: 63%.

CAMPUS LIFE AND EXTRACURRICULAR ACTIVITIES

Campus housing available (% using): women's dorms (72%), apartment for single students (28%). Students who live in college-owned, operated, or affiliated housing: 82%. **Student employment:** During the 2009-2010 academic year, 45% of undergraduates worked on campus. Average per-year earnings: $1,000. **Clubs and organizations:** Number of student organizations: 44. Activities include: campus ministries, choral groups, dance, drama/theater, international student organization, literary magazine, model UN, music ensembles, student government, student newspaper, yearbook. Number of fraternities: 0; sororities: 0. Average proportion of students who stay on campus on weekends: 70%. **Sports program (2009-2010):** Member of NCAA III. *Women's intercollegiate varsity sports:* basketball, cross country, equestrian, soccer, softball, tennis.

SERVICES AND FACILITIES

Basic services: nonremedial tutoring, placement service, health service, health insurance. **Remedial assistance:** reading, math, writing, study skills. **Counseling services:** career, personal, academic, psychological, birth control, religious. **For learning-disabled students:** School does not offer a structured program with separate admission and additional fees. Services include: note-taking services, oral tests, learning center, readers, extended time for tests, tutors, priority seating. **Library:** Number of titles: 143,071; number of current serial subscriptions: 615. **Information technology resources:** Students are not required to lease or own a computer. Number of campus computers available to all students: 30. School has a wireless network. Proportion of college-owned housing units wired for high-speed internet access: 100%. **Campus safety:** Security services offered: 24-hour foot-and-vehicle patrols, late-night transport/escort service, 24-hour emergency telephones, lighted pathways/sidewalks, controlled dormitory access (key, security card, etc).

TRANSFER AND INTERNATIONAL STUDENTS

Transfer students: May apply for admission for the following academic terms: Fall, Spring. Applicants need a minimum number of credits to apply. For fall 2009: Transfer applications received: 56. Transfer applicants offered admission: 23. Transfer applicants enrolled: 9. **International students:** Number of foreign undergraduates: 94 (20% of student body). Number of countries represented: 24. Minimum TOEFL score required: 550 (paper); 213 (computer). Average TOEFL score: 597 (paper).

Hawaii

Brigham Young University–Hawaii

- **Address:** 55-220 Kulanui Street, Laie Oahu, HI 96762-1294
- **Website:** http://www.byuh.edu
- **Private; Religious affiliation:** Church of Jesus Christ of Latter-day Saints
- **Enrollment:** N/A

KEY STATS

- ✔ **U.S News College Ranking:** second tier, National Liberal Arts Colleges
- ✔ **SAT or ACT Score (25th/75th percentile):** N/A
- ✔ **Tuition:** 2009-2010: $3,800

Selectivity: Selective	**Room/board:** $4,580
Acceptance rate: N/A	**Average debt:** N/A
Student/faculty ratio: N/A	**Proportion who borrowed:** N/A

Chaminade University of Honolulu

- **Address:** 3140 Waialae Avenue, Honolulu, HI 96816-1578
- **Website:** http://www.chaminade.edu
- **Private; Religious affiliation:** Roman Catholic
- **Enrollment:** 989 full-time; 39 part-time

KEY STATS

- ✔ **U.S News College Ranking:** 80, Regional Universities (West)
- ✔ **SAT Score (25th/75th percentile):** 840-1040
- ✔ **Tuition:** 2010-2011: $17,740

Selectivity: Less selective	**Room/board:** $10,700
Acceptance rate: 95%	**Average debt:** N/A
Student/faculty ratio: 12/1	**Proportion who borrowed:** N/A

UNDERGRADUATE STUDENT BODY STATS

2009-2010 enrollment: 989 full-time; 39 part-time. Men: 34%; women: 66%. **Ethnic makeup:** African American: 3%; American-Indian: 1%; Asian American: 68%; Hispanic: 7%; White: 19%; International: 3%.

ADMISSIONS FACTS AND FIGURES

Phone: (808) 735-4735. **Email:** admissions@chaminade.edu. **Website:** http://www.chaminade.edu. **Application deadlines for fall 2011:** Regular decision: Rolling. Early decision: Not offered. Early action: Not offered. Admission can be deferred. **Application fee:** $50. **To apply online, go to:** https://www.chaminade.edu/forms/apps/ug/. **Admissions requirements/ recommendations:** High school units required (recommended): English: 4 (4); Mathematics: 3 (3); Science: 2 (2); Social studies: 3 (3). Tests: The college uses SAT or ACT scores in admissions decisions. Either SAT or ACT required. For admission to the fall 2011 entering class, the school will accept: ACT with or without writing accepted. Campus visit: Recommended. Admissions interview: Recommended. Off-campus interview: May be arranged. **Factors that count in admissions decisions:** *Academic:* Secondary school record: Very Important. Class rank: Not Considered. Letters of recommendation: Considered. Standardized test scores: Very Important. Essay: Important. *Nonacademic:* Interview: Considered. Extracurricular activities: Important. Talent/ability: Important. Character/personal quali- ties: Important. Alumni/ae relationship: Not Considered. Geographical residence: Not Considered. State residency: Not Considered. Religious affiliation/commitment: Not Considered. Minority status: Not Considered. Volunteer work: Important. Work experience: Considered. **Admissions sta- tistics for the fall 2009 entering class:** Total applicants: 1,037. Total accepted: 989. Freshmen enrolled: 264; Overall acceptance rate: 95%. **Credentials of fall 2009 freshmen:** 9% ranked in the top 10 percent of their high school class; 34% were in the top 25 percent; 75% were in the top half. (Proportion submitting class standing: 65%.) **Average high school grade point average:** 3.2. **First-year students who submitted SAT scores:** 88%. Scores (25/75 per- centile): Critical Reading: 420-520, Math: 420-520, Combined: 840-1040.

First-year students submitting ACT scores: 35%. Scores (25/75 percentile): English: 16-23, Math: 16-22, Composite: 18-22.

ACADEMICS

Year founded: 1955. **Academic calendar:** Semester. **Degrees offered:** associ- ate, bachelor's, post-bachelor's certificate, master's. **Most popular majors:** 17% criminal justice/safety studies, 17% education, 15% psychology, 7% forensic science and technology, 7% interior design. **Major fields of study:** biological and biomedical sciences; business, management, marketing, and related support services; communication, journalism, and related pro- grams; computer and information sciences and support services; education; English language and literature/letters; history; multi/interdisciplinary studies; philosophy and religious studies; psychology; security and protec- tive services; social sciences; visual and performing arts. **Areas of required coursework:** arts/fine arts, humanities, computer literacy, mathematics, English (including composition), philosophy, foreign languages, sciences (biological or physical), history, social science, other. **Pre-professional programs:** pre-law, pre-medicine. **Special academic programs:** accelerated program, distance learning, double major, exchange student program (domestic), internships, student-designed major, study abroad, teacher certificate program. **Teacher certification offered in:** early childhood, spe- cial education, elementary, middle/junior high, secondary. **Cooperative education programs:** education, social/behavioral science. **Reserve Officers Training Corps (ROTC):** Army ROTC: Offered at cooperating institution (University of Hawaii–Manoa); Air Force ROTC: Offered at cooperating institution (University of Hawaii–West Oahu). **Faculty and instruction (2009-2010):** Total instructional faculty: 70 full-time, 50 part-time (58% men; 43% women; 37% minorities). Full-time faculty with Ph.D. or other terminal degree: 71%. Student/faculty ratio: 12/1. Classes of fewer than 20 students: 59%; of 20 to 49 students: 41%. **Advanced Placement and International Baccalaureate credit:** AP tests may be used for: Credit only. Scores accepted: 3, 4, 5. International Baccalaureate exams may be used for: Credit only. **Freshmen returning for sophomore year:** 67%. **Graduation rates:** Four-year: 21%; five-year: 38%; six-year: 37%.

COSTS AND FINANCIAL AID

Financial aid office: (808) 735-4780. **Expenses (2010-2011):** Tuition and fees 2010-2011: $17,740; room/board: $10,700. Estimated books and supplies: $1,200; transportation: $864; personal expenses: $1,254. **Financial aid:** Priority filing date for institution's financial aid form: March 1.

CAMPUS LIFE AND EXTRACURRICULAR ACTIVITIES

Campus housing available: coed dorms, women's dorms. **Student employ- ment:** During the 2009-2010 academic year, 15% of undergraduates worked on campus. **Clubs and organizations:** Number of student organizations: 38. Activities include: campus ministries, choral groups, drama/theater, literary magazine, musical theater, student government, student newspaper, year- book. Number of fraternities: 0; sororities: 0. **Sports program (2009-2010):** Member of NCAA II. *Men's intercollegiate varsity sports:* basketball, cross country, golf, soccer. *Women's intercollegiate varsity sports:* basketball, cross country, soccer, softball, tennis, volleyball.

SERVICES AND FACILITIES

Basic services: nonremedial tutoring, placement service, health insurance. **Remedial assistance:** reading, math, writing, study skills. **Counseling ser- vices:** career, personal, veteran student, academic, psychological, religious, other. **For learning-disabled students:** School does not offer a structured pro- gram with separate admission and additional fees. **Library:** Number of titles: 68,256; number of current serial subscriptions: 273. **Information technology resources:** Students are not required to lease or own a computer. Number of campus computers available to all students: 150. School has a wireless network. Approximate number of users that can be accommodated: 3,000. Proportion of college-owned housing units wired for high-speed internet access: 100%. **Campus safety:** Security services offered: 24-hour foot-and- vehicle patrols, late-night transport/escort service, 24-hour emergency telephones, lighted pathways/sidewalks, controlled dormitory access (key, security card, etc).

TRANSFER AND INTERNATIONAL STUDENTS

Transfer students: May apply for admission for the following academic terms: Fall, Spring. Applicants need a minimum number of credits to apply. For fall 2009: Transfer applications received: 209. Transfer applicants offered admission: 207. Transfer applicants enrolled: 83. **International students:** Number of foreign undergraduates: 28 (3% of student body). Number of countries represented: 9. Minimum TOEFL score required: 550 (paper); 213 (computer).

Hawaii Pacific University

- **Address:** 1164 Bishop Street, Honolulu, HI 96813
- **Website:** http://www.hpu.edu
- **Private**
- **Enrollment:** 3,849 full-time; 3,057 part-time

KEY STATS

✔ **U.S News College Ranking:** 68, Regional Universities (West)
✔ **SAT Score (25th/75th percentile):** 880-1130
✔ **Tuition:** 2010-2011: $15,820

Selectivity: Selective	**Room/board:** $11,648
Acceptance rate: 73%	**Average debt:** $22,802
Student/faculty ratio: 15/1	**Proportion who borrowed:** N/A

UNDERGRADUATE STUDENT BODY STATS

2009-2010 enrollment: 3,849 full-time; 3,057 part-time. Men: 42%; women: 58%. **Ethnic makeup:** African American: 7%; American-Indian: 2%; Asian American: 37%; Hispanic: 9%; White: 39%; International: 7%.

ADMISSIONS FACTS AND FIGURES

Phone: (808) 544-0238. **Email:** admissions@hpu.edu. **Website:** http://www.hpu.edu. **Application deadlines for fall 2011:** Regular decision: August 15. Early decision: Not offered. Early action: Not offered. Admission can be deferred. **Application fee:** $50. **To apply online, go to:** http://web1.hpu.edu/index.cfm?section=admissions. **Admissions requirements/recommendations:** High school units required (recommended): English: 4 (4); Mathematics: 4 (4); Science: 2 (2); Foreign language: 2 (2); Social studies: 3 (3); History: 2 (2); Total units: 14 (14). Tests: The college uses SAT or ACT scores in admissions decisions. Either SAT or ACT required. For admission to the fall 2011 entering class, the school will accept: ACT with or without writing accepted. Campus visit: Recommended. Admissions interview: Recommended. Off-campus interview: May be arranged. **Factors that count in admissions decisions:** *Academic:* Secondary school record: Very Important. Class rank: Considered. Letters of recommendation: Considered. Standardized test scores: Important. Essay: Considered. *Nonacademic:* Interview: Important. Extracurricular activities: Important. Talent/ability: Considered. Character/personal qualities: Considered. Alumni/ae relationship: Not Considered. Geographical residence: Not Considered. State residency: Not Considered. Religious affiliation/commitment: Not Considered. Minority status: Not Considered. Volunteer work: Considered. Work experience: Considered. **Other schools with the greatest overlap in applicants:** Boston University; New York University; University of Hawaii–Manoa; University of Southern California; University of Washington. **Admissions statistics for the fall 2009 entering class:** Total applicants: 3,645. Total accepted: 2,668. Freshmen enrolled: 637; 53% were from out of state. Overall acceptance rate: 73%. **Credentials of fall 2009 freshmen:** 24% ranked in the top 10 percent of their high school class; 49% were in the top 25 percent; 82% were in the top half. (Proportion submitting class standing: 62%.) **Average high school grade point average:** 3.3. **First-year students who submitted SAT scores:** 84%. Scores (25/75 percentile): Critical Reading: 430-560, Math: 450-570, Combined: 880-1130. **First-year students submitting ACT scores:** 35%. Scores (25/75 percentile): English: 17-24, Math: 18-24, Composite: 18-24.

ACADEMICS

Year founded: 1965. **Academic calendar:** Semester. **Degrees offered:** certificate, associate, bachelor's, post-bachelor's certificate, master's, post-master's certificate. **Most popular majors:** 35% business, management, marketing, and related support services, 24% health professions and related clinical sciences, 9% communication, journalism, and related programs, 5% psychology, 5% social sciences. **Major fields of study:** area, ethnic, cultural, and gender studies; biological and biomedical sciences; business, management, marketing, and related support services; communication, journalism, and

related programs; computer and information sciences and support services; education; English language and literature/letters; health professions and related clinical sciences; liberal arts and sciences studies, and humanities; mathematics and statistics; multi/interdisciplinary studies; natural resources and conservation; physical sciences; psychology; public administration and social service professions; security and protective services; social sciences. **Areas of required coursework:** humanities, computer literacy, mathematics, English (including composition), foreign languages, sciences (biological or physical), history, social science, other. **Pre-professional programs:** pre-law, pre-medicine, pre-pharmacy. **Special academic programs (% participation):** accelerated program (30%), cooperative (work-study plan) program (6%), distance learning (26%), double major (2%), English as a Second Language (ESL) (3%), honors program (8%), internships (25%), student-designed major (.1%), study abroad (1%). **Teacher certification offered in:** secondary. **Cooperative education programs:** business, computer science, education, health professions, humanities, natural science, social/behavioral science. **Reserve Officers Training Corps (ROTC):** Army ROTC: Offered at cooperating institution (University of Hawaii–Manoa); Air Force ROTC: Offered at cooperating institution (University of Hawaii–Manoa). **Faculty and instruction (2009-2010):** Total instructional faculty: 253 full-time, 346 part-time (54% men; 46% women; 30% minorities). Full-time faculty with Ph.D. or other terminal degree: 64%. Student/faculty ratio: 15/1. Classes of fewer than 20 students: 63%; of 20 to 49 students: 37%. **Advanced Placement and International Baccalaureate credit:** AP tests may be used for: Placement only. Scores accepted: 2, 3, 4. International Baccalaureate exams may be used for: Placement only. **Freshmen returning for sophomore year:** 67%. **Graduation rates:** Four-year: 23%; five-year: 36%; six-year: 41%. **Graduate study:** 46% of students pursue further study immediately upon graduation; 75% within one year; 88% within five years. Fields in which graduates pursue further study: Master of Business Administration (MBA), 40%; law, 5%; medicine, 2%; education, 12%; arts and sciences, 25%.

COSTS AND FINANCIAL AID

Financial aid office: (808) 544-0253. **Expenses (2010-2011):** Tuition and fees 2010-2011: $15,820; room/board: $11,648. Estimated books and supplies: $1,200; transportation: $500; personal expenses: $1,192. **Financial aid:** Priority filing date for institution's financial aid form: March 1. In 2009-2010, 76% of undergraduates applied for financial aid. Of those, 47% were determined to have financial need; 11% had their need fully met. Average financial aid package (proportion receiving): $14,529 (46%). Average amount of gift aid, such as scholarships or grants (proportion receiving): $2,016 (27%). Average amount of self-help aid, such as work study or loans (proportion receiving): $6,983 (43%). Average need-based loan (excluding PLUS or other private loans): $6,501. Among students who received need-based aid, the average percentage of need met: 77%. Among students who received aid based on merit, the average award (and the proportion receiving): $4,402 (52%). Average amount of debt of borrowers graduating in 2009: $22,802.

CAMPUS LIFE AND EXTRACURRICULAR ACTIVITIES

Campus housing available (% using): coed dorms (3%), apartment for single students (10%). **Student employment:** During the 2009-2010 academic year, 5% of undergraduates worked on campus. Average per-year earnings: $6,409. **Clubs and organizations:** Number of student organizations: 66. Activities include: campus ministries, choral groups, dance, drama/theater, international student organization, jazz band, literary magazine, model UN, music ensembles, musical theater, pep band, student government, student newspaper, student film society, symphony orchestra. Number of fraternities: 0; sororities: 0. Average proportion of students who stay on campus on weekends: 25%. **Sports program (2009-2010):** Member of NCAA II. *Men's intercollegiate varsity sports:* baseball, basketball, cross country, golf, soccer, tennis. *Women's intercollegiate varsity sports:* basketball, cross country, soccer, softball, tennis, volleyball.

SERVICES AND FACILITIES

Basic services: nonremedial tutoring, placement service, health insurance. **Remedial assistance:** reading, math, writing, study skills, other. **Counseling services:** career, military, personal, veteran student, academic, older student, psychological, religious. **For learning-disabled students:** School does not offer a structured program with separate admission and additional fees. Services include: remedial math, remedial English, remedial reading, tape recorders, untimed tests, oral tests, learning center, readers, extended time for tests, tutors, priority registration, priority seating, texts on tape, other testing accommodations. **Library:** Number of titles: 108,500; number of current serial subscriptions: 30,000. **Information technology resources:** Students are not required to lease or own a computer. Number of campus computers available to all students: 650. School has a wireless network. Approximate number of users that can be accommodated: 400. Proportion of college-owned housing units wired for high-speed internet access: 100%. **Campus safety:** Security services offered: 24-hour foot-and-vehicle patrols, lighted pathways/sidewalks, controlled dormitory access (key, security card, etc).

TRANSFER AND INTERNATIONAL STUDENTS

Transfer students: May apply for admission for the following academic terms: Fall, Winter, Spring, Summer. Applicants need a minimum number of credits to apply. For fall 2009: Transfer applications received: 1,449. Transfer applicants offered admission: 1,042. Transfer applicants enrolled: 430. **International students:** Number of foreign undergraduates: 436 (7% of student body). Number of countries represented: 105. Minimum TOEFL score required: 550 (paper); 213 (computer). Average TOEFL score: 569 (paper).

University of Hawaii–Hilo

- **Address:** 200 W. Kawili Street, Hilo, HI 96720-4091
- **Website:** http://www.uhh.hawaii.edu
- **Public**
- **Enrollment:** N/A

KEY STATS

✔ **U.S News College Ranking:** second tier, National Liberal Arts Colleges
✔ **SAT or ACT Score (25th/75th percentile):** N/A
✔ **Tuition:** 2009-2010: $4,888 in state, $14,392 out of state

Selectivity: Selective	**Room/board:** $6,914
Acceptance rate: N/A	**Average debt:** N/A
Student/faculty ratio: N/A	**Proportion who borrowed:** N/A

University of Hawaii–Manoa

- **Address:** 2500 Campus Road, Honolulu, HI 96822
- **Website:** http://www.manoa.hawaii.edu/
- **Public**
- **Enrollment:** 11,361 full-time; 2,591 part-time

KEY STATS

✔ **U.S News College Ranking:** 159, National Universities
✔ **SAT Score (25th/75th percentile):** 990-1200
✔ **Tuition:** 2010-2011: $8,095 in state, $21,535 out of state

Selectivity: Selective	**Room/board:** $9,410
Acceptance rate: 67%	**Average debt:** $16,528
Student/faculty ratio: 14/1	**Proportion who borrowed:** 35%

UNDERGRADUATE STUDENT BODY STATS

2009-2010 enrollment: 11,361 full-time; 2,591 part-time. Men: 46%; women: 54%. **Ethnic makeup:** African American: 1%; American-Indian: 1%; Asian American: 67%; Hispanic: 3%; White: 24%; International: 4%.

ADMISSIONS FACTS AND FIGURES

Phone: (808) 956-8975. **Email:** ar-info@hawaii.edu. **Website:** http://www.manoa.hawaii.edu/. **Application deadlines for fall 2011:** Regular decision: May 1. Early decision: Not offered. Early action: Not offered. Admission cannot be deferred. **Application fee:** $50. **To apply online, go to:** http://www.hawaii.edu/admrec/. **Admissions requirements/recommendations:** High school units required (recommended): English: 4; Mathematics: 3; Science: 3; Social studies: 3; Academic electives: 5; Total units: 22. Tests: The college uses SAT or ACT scores in admissions decisions. Either SAT or ACT required. For admission to the fall 2011 entering class, the school will accept: ACT with writing required. Campus visit: Neither required nor recommended. Admissions interview: Neither required nor recommended. Off-campus interview: Not available. **Factors that count in admissions decisions:** *Academic:* Secondary school record: Very Important. Class rank: Important. Letters of recommendation: Considered. Standardized test scores: Very Important. Essay: Considered. ***Nonacademic:*** Interview: Considered. Extracurricular activities: Considered. Talent/ability: Considered. Character/personal qualities: Not Considered. Alumni/ae

relationship: Not Considered. Geographical residence: Considered. State residency: Important. Religious affiliation/commitment: Not Considered. Minority status: Not Considered. Volunteer work: Not Considered. Work experience: Not Considered. **Other schools with the greatest overlap in applicants:** Colorado State University; Hawaii Pacific University; University of Colorado–Boulder; University of Hawaii–Hilo; University of Washington. **Admissions statistics for the fall 2009 entering class:** Total applicants: 7,196. Total accepted: 4,837. Freshmen enrolled: 1,922; 28% were from out of state. Overall acceptance rate: 67%. **Size of waiting list:** 0 applicants; enrolled from waiting list: 0. **Credentials of fall 2009 freshmen:** 28% ranked in the top 10 percent of their high school class; 60% were in the top 25 percent; 91% were in the top half. (Proportion submitting class standing: 65%.) **Average high school grade point average:** 3.4. **First-year students who submitted SAT scores:** 87%. Scores (25/75 percentile): Critical Reading: 480-580, Math: 510-620, Combined: 990-1200. **First-year students submitting ACT scores:** 25%. Scores (25/75 percentile): English: 20-25, Math: 20-26, Composite: 21-25.

ACADEMICS

Year founded: 1907. **Academic calendar:** Semester. **Degrees offered:** certificate, bachelor's, post-bachelor's certificate, master's, doctorate. **Most popular majors:** 21% business, management, marketing, and related support services, 11% social sciences, 6% education, 6% engineering, 6% psychology. **Major fields of study:** agriculture, agriculture operations, and related sciences; area, ethnic, cultural, and gender studies; biological and biomedical sciences; business, management, marketing, and related support services; communication, journalism, and related programs; computer and information sciences and support services; education; engineering; English language and literature/letters; family and consumer sciences/human sciences; foreign languages, literatures, and linguistics; health professions and related clinical sciences; history; liberal arts and sciences studies, and humanities; mathematics and statistics; multi/interdisciplinary studies; natural resources and conservation; parks, recreation, leisure, and fitness studies; philosophy and religious studies; physical sciences; psychology; public administration and social service professions; social sciences; visual and performing arts. **Areas of required coursework:** arts/fine arts, humanities, English (including composition), foreign languages, sciences (biological or physical), social science, other. **Pre-professional programs:** pre-law, pre-dentistry, pre-medicine, pre-veterinary science, pre-optometry, pre-pharmacy. **Special academic programs (% participation):** cooperative (work-study plan) program, distance learning (10%), double major (8%), English as a Second Language (ESL), exchange student program (domestic), honors program (5%), independent study, internships, student-designed major (6%), study abroad, teacher certificate program (8%). **Teacher certification offered in:** early childhood, special education, elementary, vo-tech, secondary. **Cooperative education programs:** agriculture, art, business, computer science, education, engineering, health professions, humanities, natural science, social/behavioral science, technologies, other. **Reserve Officers Training Corps (ROTC):** Army ROTC: Offered on campus; Air Force ROTC: Offered on campus. **Faculty and instruction (2009-2010):** Total instructional faculty: 1,200 full-time, 70 part-time (58% men; 42% women; 35% minorities). Full-time faculty with Ph.D. or other terminal degree: 87%. Student/faculty ratio: 14/1. Classes of fewer than 20 students: 45%; of 20 to 49 students: 44%; of 50 or more students: 10%. **Advanced Placement and International Baccalaureate credit:** AP tests may be used for: Placement only. Scores accepted: 4, 5. International Baccalaureate exams may be used for: Placement only. **Freshmen returning for sophomore year:** 78%. **Graduation rates:** Four-year: 16%; five-year: 38%; six-year: 48%. **Graduate study:** 10% of students pursue further study immediately upon graduation; 11% within one year; 20% within five years. Fields in which graduates pursue further study: Master of Business Administration (MBA), 9%; law, 4%; medicine, 6%; engineering, 3%; education, 27%; arts and sciences, 22%.

COSTS AND FINANCIAL AID

Financial aid office: (808) 956-7251. **Expenses (2010-2011):** Tuition and fees 2010-2011: $8,095 in state, $21,535 out of state; room/board: $9,410. Estimated books and supplies: $1,146. **Financial aid:** Priority filing date for institution's financial aid form: March 1. In 2009-2010, 67% of undergraduates applied for financial aid. Of those, 45% were determined to have financial need; 16% had their need fully met. Average financial aid package (proportion receiving): $8,703 (42%). Average amount of gift aid, such as scholarships or grants (proportion receiving): $6,561 (33%). Average amount of self-help aid, such as work study or loans (proportion receiving): $4,109 (29%). Average need-based loan (excluding PLUS or other private loans): $3,796. Among students who received need-based aid, the average percentage of need met: 60%. Among students who received aid based on merit, the average award (and the proportion receiving): $7,427 (12%). The average athletic scholarship (and the proportion receiving): $10,187 (2%). Average amount of debt of borrowers graduating in 2009: $16,528. Proportion who borrowed: 35%.

CAMPUS LIFE AND EXTRACURRICULAR ACTIVITIES
Campus housing available (% using): coed dorms (67%), apartments for married students (1%), apartment for single students (32%), special housing for disabled students. Students who live in college-owned, operated, or affiliated housing: 23%. **Student employment:** During the 2009-2010 academic year, 32% of undergraduates worked on campus. Average per-year earnings: $5,035. **Clubs and organizations:** Number of student organizations: 150. Activities include: campus ministries, choral groups, concert band, dance, drama/theater, international student organization, jazz band, literary magazine, marching band, music ensembles, musical theater, pep band, radio station, student government, student newspaper, student film society, symphony orchestra. Number of fraternities: 4; sororities: 2. Proportion of men in fraternities: 1%; of women in sororities: 1%. Average proportion of students who stay on campus on weekends: 25%. **Sports program (2009-2010):** Member of NCAA I. **Men's intercollegiate varsity sports:** baseball, basketball, football, golf, swimming, tennis, volleyball. **Women's intercollegiate varsity sports:** basketball, cross country, golf, soccer, softball, swimming, tennis, track and field (indoor), track and field (outdoor), volleyball, water polo.

SERVICES AND FACILITIES
Basic services: nonremedial tutoring, women's center, placement service, day care, health service, health insurance, other. **Remedial assistance:** study skills. **Counseling services:** career, military, personal, academic, psychological, birth control. **For learning-disabled students:** School does not offer a structured program with separate admission and additional fees. Services include: reading machines, tape recorders, note-taking services, readers, extended time for tests, tutors, priority registration, texts on tape. **Library:** Number of titles: 3,418,840; number of current serial subscriptions: 58,434. **Information technology resources:** Students are not required to lease or own a computer. Number of campus computers available to all students: 300. School has a wireless network. Approximate number of users that can be accommodated: 2,000. Proportion of college-owned housing units wired for high-speed internet access: 100%. **Campus safety:** Security services offered: 24-hour foot-and-vehicle patrols, late-night transport/escort service, 24-hour emergency telephones, lighted pathways/sidewalks, student patrols, controlled dormitory access (key, security card, etc).

TRANSFER AND INTERNATIONAL STUDENTS
Transfer students: May apply for admission for the following academic terms: Fall, Spring. Applicants need a minimum number of credits to apply. For fall 2009: Transfer applications received: 4,262. Transfer applicants offered admission: 3,110. Transfer applicants enrolled: 1,834. **International students:** Number of foreign undergraduates: 540 (4% of student body). Number of countries represented: 49. Minimum TOEFL score required: 500 (paper); 173 (computer).

University of Hawaii–West Oahu

- **Address:** 96-129 Ala Ike Street, Pearl City, HI 96782
- **Website:** http://www.uhwo.hawaii.edu
- **Public**
- **Enrollment:** 408 full-time; 885 part-time

KEY STATS
✔ **U.S News College Ranking:** second tier, National Liberal Arts Colleges
✔ **SAT or ACT Score (25th/75th percentile):** N/A
✔ **Tuition:** 2010-2011: $4,666 in state, $14,362 out of state

Selectivity: Selective	**Room/board:** N/A
Acceptance rate: 81%	**Average debt:** N/A
Student/faculty ratio: 13/1	**Proportion who borrowed:** N/A

UNDERGRADUATE STUDENT BODY STATS
2009-2010 enrollment: 408 full-time; 885 part-time. Men: 29%; women: 71%. **Ethnic makeup:** African American: 2%; Asian American: 64%; Hispanic: 2%; White: 29%; International: 3%.

ADMISSIONS FACTS AND FIGURES
Phone: (808) 454-4700. **Email:** info@uhwo.hawaii.edu. **Website:** http://www.uhwo.hawaii.edu. **Application deadlines for fall 2011:** Regular decision: August 1. Early decision: Not offered. Early action: Not offered. Admission can be deferred. **Application fee:** $50. **To apply online, go to:** http://www.hawaii.edu/admissions. **Admissions requirements/recommendations:** High school units required (recommended): English: 4; Mathematics: 3; Science: 3; Social studies: 3; Academic electives: 5; Total units: 22. Tests: The college uses SAT or ACT scores in admissions decisions. Neither SAT nor ACT required. For admission to the fall 2011 entering class, the school will accept: ACT with writing recommended. **Factors that count in admissions decisions:** *Academic:* Secondary school record: Important. Class rank: Not Considered. Letters of recommendation: Considered. Standardized test scores: Considered. Essay: Considered. *Nonacademic:* Interview: Not Considered. Extracurricular activities: Considered. Talent/ability: Not Considered. Character/personal qualities: Not Considered. Alumni/ae relationship: Not Considered. Geographical residence: Considered. State residency: Considered. Religious affiliation/commitment: Not Considered. Minority status: Not Considered. Volunteer work: Not Considered. Work experience: Not Considered. **Other schools with the greatest overlap in applicants:** University of Hawaii–Manoa. **Admissions statistics for the fall 2009 entering class:** Total applicants: 241. Total accepted: 196. Freshmen enrolled: 77; 1% were from out of state. Overall acceptance rate: 81%. **Average high school grade point average:** 3.2.

ACADEMICS
Academic calendar: Semester. **Degrees offered:** certificate, bachelor's. **Most popular majors:** 37% business, management, marketing, and related support services, 20% public administration and social service professions, 18% psychology, 14% social sciences, 3% English language and literature/letters. **Major fields of study:** business, management, marketing, and related support services; education; liberal arts and sciences studies, and humanities; public administration and social service professions; social sciences. **Areas of required coursework:** humanities, mathematics, English (including composition), philosophy, sciences (biological or physical), history, social science. **Special academic programs:** distance learning, double major, teacher certificate program. **Reserve Officers Training Corps (ROTC):** Army ROTC: Offered at cooperating institution (University of Hawaii–Manoa); Air Force ROTC: Offered at cooperating institution (University of Hawaii–Manoa). **Faculty and instruction (2009-2010):** Total instructional faculty: 46 full-time, 28 part-time (54% men; 46% women; 43% minorities). Full-time faculty with Ph.D. or other terminal degree: 96%. Student/faculty ratio: 13/1. Classes of fewer than 20 students: 60%; of 20 to 49 students: 40%. **Freshmen returning for sophomore year:** 60%. **Graduation rates:** Four-year: 20%; five-year: 46%; six-year: 56%.

COSTS AND FINANCIAL AID
Expenses (2010-2011): Tuition and fees 2010-2011: $4,666 in state, $14,362 out of state. Estimated books and supplies: $1,123; transportation: $200; personal expenses: $1,474. **Financial aid:** Priority filing date for institution's financial aid form: April 1.

CAMPUS LIFE AND EXTRACURRICULAR ACTIVITIES
Student employment: During the 2009-2010 academic year, 1% of undergraduates worked on campus. Activities include: student government. Number of fraternities: 0; sororities: 0.

SERVICES AND FACILITIES
Remedial assistance: reading, math, writing, study skills. **Library:** Number of titles: 81,365; number of current serial subscriptions: 28,300. **Information technology resources:** Students are not required to lease or own a computer. School has a wireless network. Proportion of college-owned housing units wired for high-speed internet access: 0%.

TRANSFER AND INTERNATIONAL STUDENTS
Transfer students: May apply for admission for the following academic terms: Fall. Applicants need a minimum number of credits to apply. For fall 2009: Transfer applications received: 573. Transfer applicants offered admission: 502. Transfer applicants enrolled: 340. **International students:** Number of foreign undergraduates: 37 (3% of student body).

Idaho

Boise State University

- **Address:** 1910 University Drive, Boise, ID 83725
- **Website:** http://www.BoiseState.edu
- **Public**
- **Enrollment:** 12,142 full-time; 4,551 part-time

KEY STATS

✔ **U.S News College Ranking:** 51, Regional Universities (West)
✔ **ACT Score (25th/75th percentile):** 19-25
✔ **Tuition:** 2010-2011: $5,300 in state, $14,756 out of state

Selectivity: Selective	**Room/board:** $5,610
Acceptance rate: 87%	**Average debt:** $23,256
Student/faculty ratio: 21/1	**Proportion who borrowed:** 64%

UNDERGRADUATE STUDENT BODY STATS

2009-2010 enrollment: 12,142 full-time; 4,551 part-time. Men: 46%; women: 54%. **Ethnic makeup:** African American: 2%; American-Indian: 1%; Asian American: 3%; Hispanic: 7%; White: 85%; International: 2%.

ADMISSIONS FACTS AND FIGURES

Phone: (208) 426-1156. **Email:** bsuinfo@boisestate.edu. **Website:** http://www.BoiseState.edu. **Application deadlines for fall 2011:** Regular decision: June 30. Early decision: Not offered. Early action: Not offered. Admission cannot be deferred. **Application fee:** $50. **To apply online, go to:** http://admissions.boisestate.edu/applynow/. **Admissions requirements/recommendations:** High school units required (recommended): English: 8 (8); Mathematics: 6 (6); Science: 6 (6); Foreign language: 0 (0); Social studies: 5 (5); History: 2 (2); Academic electives: 3 (2); Total units: 30 (30). Tests: The college uses SAT or ACT scores in admissions decisions. Either SAT or ACT required. For admission to the fall 2011 entering class, the school will accept: ACT with or without writing accepted. Campus visit: Recommended. Admissions interview: Neither required nor recommended. Off-campus interview: Not available. **Factors that count in admissions decisions:** *Academic:* Secondary school record: Very Important. Class rank: Important. Letters of recommendation: Not Considered. Standardized test scores: Very Important. Essay: Not Considered. *Nonacademic:* Interview: Not Considered. Extracurricular activities: Considered. Talent/ability: Considered. Character/personal qualities: Not Considered. Alumni/ae relationship: Not Considered. Geographical residence: Not Considered. State residency: Not Considered. Religious affiliation/commitment: Not Considered. Minority status: Considered. Volunteer work: Not Considered. Work experience: Not Considered. **Other schools with the greatest overlap in applicants:** Brigham Young University–Provo; College of Idaho; Idaho State University; Lewis-Clark State College; University of Idaho. **Admissions statistics for the fall 2009 entering class:** Total applicants: 4,127. Total accepted: 3,606. Freshmen enrolled: 2,194; 12% were from out of state. Overall acceptance rate: 87%. **Credentials of fall 2009 freshmen:** 13% ranked in the top 10 percent of their high school class; 36% were in the top 25 percent; 71% were in the top half. (Proportion submitting class standing: 77%.) **Average high school grade point average:** 3.3. **First-year students who submitted SAT scores:** 39%. Scores (25/75 percentile): Critical Reading: 460-570, Math: 470-590, Combined: 930-1160. **First-year students submitting ACT scores:** 69%. Scores (25/75 percentile): English: 18-24, Math: 18-25, Composite: 19-25.

ACADEMICS

Year founded: 1932. **Academic calendar:** Semester. **Degrees offered:** associate, bachelor's, post-bachelor's certificate, master's, doctorate. **Most popular majors:** 6% communication studies/speech communication and rhetoric, 6% elementary education and teaching, 6% psychology, 5% accounting, 5% business/commerce. **Major fields of study:** agriculture, agriculture operations, and related sciences; area, ethnic, cultural, and gender studies; biological and biomedical sciences; business, management, marketing, and related support services; computer and information sciences and support services; construction trades; education; engineering; engineering technologies/technicians; English language and literature/letters; family and consumer sciences/human sciences; foreign languages, literatures, and linguistics; health professions and related clinical sciences; history; mathematics and statistics; mechanic and repair technologies/technicians; multi/interdisciplinary studies; parks, recreation, leisure, and fitness studies; philosophy and religious studies; physical sciences; precision production; psychology; public administration and social service professions; security and protective services; social sciences; visual and performing arts. **Areas of required coursework:** arts/fine arts, humanities, computer literacy, mathematics, English (including composition), sciences (biological or physical), history, social science. **Pre-professional programs:** pre-law, pre-dentistry, pre-medicine, pre-veterinary science, pre-optometry, pre-pharmacy. **Special academic programs:** accelerated program, cooperative (work-study plan) program, distance learning, double major, dual enrollment, English as a Second Language (ESL), honors program, internships, liberal arts/career combination, study abroad, teacher certificate program, weekend college. **Teacher certification offered in:** early childhood, special education, elementary, middle/junior high, secondary, bilingual/bicultural. **Reserve Officers Training Corps (ROTC):** Army ROTC: Offered on campus. **Faculty and instruction (2009-2010):** Total instructional faculty: 542 full-time, 461 part-time (52% men; 48% women; 8% minorities). Full-time faculty with Ph.D. or other terminal degree: 78%. Student/faculty ratio: 21/1. Classes of fewer than 20 students: 40%; of 20 to 49 students: 51%; of 50 or more students: 9%. **Advanced Placement and International Baccalaureate credit:** AP tests may be used for: Credit only. International Baccalaureate exams may be used for: Credit only. **Freshmen returning for sophomore year:** 66%. **Graduation rates:** Four-year: 6%; five-year: 19%; six-year: 27%. **Graduate study:** 5% of students pursue further study immediately upon graduation; 10% within one year; 15% within five years. Fields in which graduates pursue further study: Master of Business Administration (MBA), 3%; law, 1%; engineering, 1%; education, 10%.

COSTS AND FINANCIAL AID

Financial aid office: (208) 426-1540. **Expenses (2010-2011):** Tuition and fees 2010-2011: $5,300 in state, $14,756 out of state; room/board: $5,610. Estimated books and supplies: $1,188; transportation: $1,832; personal expenses: $2,296. **Financial aid:** Priority filing date for institution's financial aid form: April 1. In 2009-2010, 68% of undergraduates applied for financial aid. Of those, 67% were determined to have financial need; 13% had their need fully met. Average financial aid package (proportion receiving): $8,282 (67%). Average amount of gift aid, such as scholarships or grants (proportion receiving): $4,453 (50%). Average amount of self-help aid, such as work study or loans (proportion receiving): $7,205 (50%). Average need-based loan (excluding PLUS or other private loans): $6,599. Among students who received need-based aid, the average percentage of need met: 23%. Among students who received aid based on merit, the average award (and the proportion receiving): $1,071 (5%). The average athletic scholarship (and the proportion receiving): $10,380 (0%). Average amount of debt of borrowers graduating in 2009: $23,256. Proportion who borrowed: 64%.

CAMPUS LIFE AND EXTRACURRICULAR ACTIVITIES

Campus housing available (% using): coed dorms (50%), women's dorms (15%), men's dorms (10%), apartments for married students (10%), apartment for single students (15%), special housing for disabled students. Students who live in college-owned, operated, or affiliated housing: 11%. **Student employment:** During the 2009-2010 academic year, 8% of undergraduates worked on campus. Average per-year earnings: $2,000. **Clubs and organizations:** Number of student organizations: 210. Activities include: choral groups, dance, drama/theater, marching band, music ensembles, musical theater, pep band, radio station, student government, student newspaper. Number of fraternities: 2; sororities: 2. Proportion of men in fraternities: 1%; of women in sororities: 1%. Average proportion of students who stay on campus on weekends: 9%. **Sports program (2009-2010):** Member of NCAA I. *Men's intercollegiate varsity sports:* basketball, cross country, football, golf, tennis, track and field (indoor), track and field (outdoor), wrestling. *Women's intercollegiate varsity sports:* basketball, cross country, golf, gymnastics, soccer, softball, swimming, tennis, track and field (indoor), track and field (outdoor), volleyball.

SERVICES AND FACILITIES

Basic services: nonremedial tutoring, women's center, placement service, day care, health service, health insurance. **Remedial assistance:** reading, math, writing. **Counseling services:** minority student, career, personal, veteran student, academic. **For learning-disabled students:** School does not offer a structured program with separate admission and additional fees. Services include: remedial math, remedial English, remedial reading, tape recorders, diagnostic testing service, oral tests, learning center, tutors. **Library:** Number of titles: 838,932; number of current serial subscriptions: 5,575. **Information technology resources:** Students are not required to lease or own a computer. Number of campus computers available to all students: 900. School has a wireless network. Proportion of college-owned housing units wired for high-speed internet access: 100%. **Campus safety:** Security services offered: 24-hour foot-and-vehicle patrols, late-night transport/escort service, 24-hour emergency telephones, lighted pathways/sidewalks, controlled dormitory access (key, security card, etc).

TRANSFER AND INTERNATIONAL STUDENTS

Transfer students: May apply for admission for the following academic terms: Fall, Spring, Summer. Applicants do not need a minimum number of credits to apply. For fall 2009: Transfer applications received: 2,182. Transfer applicants offered admission: 2,127. Transfer applicants enrolled: 995. **International students:** Number of foreign undergraduates: 250 (2% of student body). Number of countries represented: 65. Minimum TOEFL score required: 500 (paper); 173 (computer). Average TOEFL score: 583 (paper).

Brigham Young University–Idaho

- **Address:** 525 S. Center Street, Rexburg, ID 83460
- **Website:** http://www.byui.edu
- **Private**
- **Enrollment** N/A

KEY STATS

✔ **U.S News College Ranking:** 21, Regional Colleges (West)
✔ **SAT or ACT Score (25th/75th percentile):** N/A
✔ **Tuition:** 2009-2010: $3,580

Selectivity: Less selective	**Room/board:** $4,486
Acceptance rate: N/A	**Average debt:** N/A
Student/faculty ratio: N/A	**Proportion who borrowed:** N/A

College of Idaho

- **Address:** 2112 Cleveland Boulevard, Caldwell, ID 83605
- **Website:** http://www.collegeofidaho.edu
- **Private; Religious affiliation:** Association of Presbyterian Colleges and Universities
- **Enrollment:** 945 full-time; 57 part-time

KEY STATS

✔ **U.S News College Ranking:** 174, National Liberal Arts Colleges
✔ **ACT Score (25th/75th percentile):** 22-27
✔ **Tuition:** 2010-2011: $21,050

Selectivity: More selective	**Room/board:** $7,777
Acceptance rate: 62%	**Average debt:** $24,237
Student/faculty ratio: 12/1	**Proportion who borrowed:** 67%

UNDERGRADUATE STUDENT BODY STATS

2009-2010 enrollment: 945 full-time; 57 part-time. Men: 42%; women: 58%. **Ethnic makeup:** African American: 1%; Asian American: 2%; Hispanic: 8%; White: 82%; International: 6%.

ADMISSIONS FACTS AND FIGURES

Phone: (800) 224-3246. **Email:** admission@collegeofidaho.edu. **Website:** http://www.collegeofidaho.edu. **Application deadlines for fall 2011:** Regular decision: August 1. Early decision: Not offered. Early action: Send application by: December 15; Decision sent by: November 15. Admission can be deferred. **Application fee:** None. **To apply online, go to:** http://www.collegeofidaho.edu/admission/default.asp?ID=admission. **Admissions requirements/**

recommendations: High school units required (recommended): English: (4); Mathematics: (4); Science: (3); Foreign language: (3); Social studies: (4); Total units: (18). Tests: The college uses SAT or ACT scores in admissions decisions. Either SAT or ACT required. For admission to the fall 2011 entering class, the school will accept: ACT with writing required. Campus visit: Recommended. Admissions interview: Recommended. Off-campus interview: May be arranged. **Factors that count in admissions decisions:** *Academic:* Secondary school record: Very Important. Class rank: Important. Letters of recommendation: Very Important. Standardized test scores: Very Important. Essay: Important. *Nonacademic:* Interview: Important. Extracurricular activities: Important. Talent/ability: Considered. Character/personal qualities: Very Important. Alumni/ae relationship: Considered. Geographical residence: Not Considered. State residency: Not Considered. Religious affiliation/commitment: Not Considered. Minority status: Not Considered. Volunteer work: Considered. Work experience: Not Considered. **Other schools with the greatest overlap in applicants:** Boise State University; Brigham Young University–Idaho; Idaho State University; Northwest Nazarene University; University of Idaho. **Admissions statistics for the fall 2009 entering class:** Total applicants: 1,214. Total accepted: 758. Freshmen enrolled: 306; 21% were from out of state. Accepted through early-decision or early-action plans: 25%. Overall acceptance rate: 62%. Non-early acceptance rate: 57%. **Credentials of fall 2009 freshmen:** 30% ranked in the top 10 percent of their high school class; 64% were in the top 25 percent; 88% were in the top half. (Proportion submitting class standing: 71%.) **Average high school grade point average:** 3.6. **First-year students who submitted SAT scores:** 32%. Scores (25/75 percentile): Critical Reading: 440-575, Math: 460-595, Combined: 900-1170. **First-year students submitting ACT scores:** 65%. Scores (25/75 percentile): English: 21-28, Math: 21-27, Composite: 22-27.

ACADEMICS

Year founded: 1891. **Academic calendar:** Other. **Degrees offered:** bachelor's, master's. **Most popular majors:** 22% business, management, marketing, and related support services; 12% psychology, 12% social sciences, 9% biological and biomedical sciences, 9% history. **Major fields of study:** biological and biomedical sciences; business, management, marketing, and related support services; education; engineering; English language and literature/letters; foreign languages, literatures, and linguistics; health professions and related clinical sciences; history; liberal arts and sciences studies, and humanities; mathematics and statistics; multi/interdisciplinary studies; natural resources and conservation; parks, recreation, leisure, and fitness studies; philosophy and religious studies; physical sciences; psychology; social sciences; visual and performing arts. **Areas of required coursework:** arts/fine arts, humanities, mathematics, English (including composition), sciences (biological or physical), history, social science, other. **Pre-professional programs:** pre-law, pre-dentistry, pre-medicine, pre-veterinary science, pre-optometry, pre-pharmacy, other. **Special academic programs (% participation):** cross-registration, double major (13.5%), dual enrollment, English as a Second Language (ESL), exchange student program (domestic), honors program, independent study (63.2%), internships (36.8%), liberal arts/career combination, student-designed major, study abroad, teacher certificate program. **Teacher certification offered in:** elementary, middle/junior high, secondary. **Cooperative education programs:** business, engineering, health professions, natural science, other. **Reserve Officers Training Corps (ROTC):** Army ROTC: Offered on campus. **Faculty and instruction (2009-2010):** Total instructional faculty: 74 full-time, 27 part-time (56% men; 44% women; 3% minorities). Full-time faculty with Ph.D. or other terminal degree: 81%. Student/faculty ratio: 12/1. Classes of fewer than 20 students: 61%; of 20 to 49 students: 36%; of 50 or more students: 3%. **Advanced Placement and International Baccalaureate credit:** AP tests may be used for: Placement only. Scores accepted: 3, 4, 5. International Baccalaureate exams may be used for: Credit and/or placement. **Freshmen returning for sophomore year:** 79%. **Graduation rates:** Four-year: 55%; five-year: 60%; six-year: 61%.

COSTS AND FINANCIAL AID

Financial aid office: (208) 459-5307. **Expenses (2010-2011):** Tuition and fees 2010-2011: $21,050; room/board: $7,777. Estimated books and supplies: $1,200; transportation: $1,000; personal expenses: $700. **Financial aid:** Priority filing date for institution's financial aid form: February 15. In 2009-2010, 59% of undergraduates applied for financial aid. Of those, 59% were determined to have financial need; 21% had their need fully met. Average financial aid package (proportion receiving): $16,324 (58%). Average amount of gift aid, such as scholarships or grants (proportion receiving): $5,178 (38%). Average amount of self-help aid, such as work study or loans (proportion receiving): $4,548 (42%). Average need-based loan (excluding PLUS or other private loans): $4,415. Among students who received need-based aid, the average percentage of need met: 88%. Among students who received aid based on merit, the average award (and the proportion receiving): $11,583 (35%). The average athletic scholarship (and the proportion receiving): $5,536 (25%). Average amount of debt of borrowers graduating in 2009: $24,237. Proportion who borrowed: 67%.

CAMPUS LIFE AND EXTRACURRICULAR ACTIVITIES

Campus housing available (% using): coed dorms (84%), fraternity housing, apartment for single students (8%), special housing for disabled students, special housing for international students, other housing options (8%). Students who live in college-owned, operated, or affiliated housing: 58%. **Student employment:** During the 2009-2010 academic year, 5% of undergraduates worked on campus. Average per-year earnings: $1,638. **Clubs and organizations:** Number of student organizations: 55. Activities include: campus ministries, choral groups, concert band, dance, drama/theater, international student organization, jazz band, literary magazine, model UN, music ensembles, musical theater, opera, pep band, radio station, student government, student newspaper, student film society, symphony orchestra, yearbook. Number of fraternities: 3; sororities: 4. Proportion of men in fraternities: 16%; of women in sororities: 13%. Average proportion of students who stay on campus on weekends: 70%. **Sports program (2009-2010):** Member of NAIA. **Men's intercollegiate varsity sports:** baseball, basketball, cross country, golf, skiing (alpine), soccer, swimming, tennis, track and field (outdoor). **Women's intercollegiate varsity sports:** basketball, cross country, golf, skiing (alpine), soccer, softball, swimming, tennis, track and field (outdoor), volleyball.

SERVICES AND FACILITIES

Basic services: nonremedial tutoring, placement service, health service, health insurance, other. **Remedial assistance:** reading, math, writing, study skills. **Counseling services:** minority student, career, military, personal, academic, older student, psychological, birth control, religious, other. **For learning-disabled students:** School does not offer a structured program with separate admission and additional fees. Total undergraduates in learning-disabled program or receiving services: 33. Services include: remedial math, reading machines, tape recorders, diagnostic testing service, untimed tests, note-taking services, oral tests, learning center, readers, extended time for tests, tutors, priority seating, texts on tape, other testing accommodations, other. **Library:** Number of titles: 155,000; number of current serial subscriptions: 1,975. **Information technology resources:** Students are not required to lease or own a computer. Number of campus computers available to all students: 250. School has a wireless network. Approximate number of users that can be accommodated: 40,000. Proportion of college-owned housing units wired for high-speed internet access: 100%. **Campus safety:** Security services offered: 24-hour foot-and-vehicle patrols, late-night transport/escort service, 24-hour emergency telephones, lighted pathways/sidewalks, student patrols, controlled dormitory access (key, security card, etc).

TRANSFER AND INTERNATIONAL STUDENTS

Transfer students: May apply for admission for the following academic terms: Fall, Winter, Spring. Applicants need a minimum number of credits to apply. For fall 2009: Transfer applications received: 164. Transfer applicants offered admission: 76. Transfer applicants enrolled: 52. **International students:** Number of foreign undergraduates: 40 (6% of student body). Number of countries represented: 40. Minimum TOEFL score required: 550 (paper); 79 (computer). Average TOEFL score: 510 (paper).

Idaho State University

- ■ **Address:** 921 S. Eigth Avenue, Pocatello, ID 83209
- ■ **Website:** http://www.isu.edu
- ■ **Public**
- ■ **Enrollment:** 7,638 full-time; 3,620 part-time

KEY STATS

✔ **U.S News College Ranking:** second tier, National Universities
✔ **ACT Score (25th/75th percentile):** 18-24
✔ **Tuition:** 2009-2010: $4,968 in state, $14,770 out of state

Selectivity: Selective	**Room/board:** $5,050
Acceptance rate: 73%	**Average debt:** N/A
Student/faculty ratio: 16/1	**Proportion who borrowed:** N/A

UNDERGRADUATE STUDENT BODY STATS

2009-2010 enrollment: 7,638 full-time; 3,620 part-time. Men: 45%; women: 55%. **Ethnic makeup:** African American: 1%; American-Indian: 2%; Asian American: 2%; Hispanic: 6%; White: 87%; International: 1%. **Religious preference:** Roman Catholic: 6%; Protestant: 4%; Unknown: 47%; Church of Jesus Christ of Latter-day Saints: 31%; Other: 12%.

ADMISSIONS FACTS AND FIGURES

Phone: (208) 282-2475. **Email:** info@isu.edu. **Website:** http://www.isu.edu. **Application deadlines for fall 2011:** Regular decision: Rolling. Early decision: Not offered. Early action: Not offered. Admission can be deferred. **Application fee:** $40. **To apply online, go to:** http://apply.isu.edu/. **Admissions requirements/recommendations:** High school units required (recommended): English: 4; Mathematics: 3 (4); Science: 3; Foreign language: 1; Social studies: 3; History: 0; Academic electives: 0; Total units: 16 (4). Tests: The college uses SAT or ACT scores in admissions decisions. Either SAT or ACT required. For admission to the fall 2011 entering class, the school will accept: ACT with or without writing accepted. Campus visit: Recommended. Admissions interview: Neither required nor recommended. Off-campus interview: Not available. **Factors that count in admissions decisions:** *Academic:* Secondary school record: Not Considered. Class rank: Not Considered. Letters of recommendation: Not Considered. Standardized test scores: Considered. Essay: Not Considered. *Nonacademic:* Interview: Not Considered. Extracurricular activities: Not Considered. Talent/ability: Not Considered. Character/personal qualities: Not Considered. Alumni/ae relationship: Not Considered. Geographical residence: Not Considered. State residency: Not Considered. Religious affiliation/commitment: Not Considered. Minority status: Not Considered. Volunteer work: Not Considered. Work experience: Not Considered. **Other schools with the greatest overlap in applicants:** Boise State University; Brigham Young University–Idaho; University of Idaho; Utah State University. **Admissions statistics for the fall 2009 entering class:** Total applicants: 3,889. Total accepted: 2,856. Freshmen enrolled: 1,906; 7% were from out of state. Overall acceptance rate: 73%. **Credentials of fall 2009 freshmen:** 13% ranked in the top 10 percent of their high school class; 31% were in the top 25 percent; 61% were in the top half. (Proportion submitting class standing: 13%.) **Average high school grade point average:** 3.2. **First-year students who submitted SAT scores:** 8%. **First-year students submitting ACT scores:** 61%. Scores (25/75 percentile): English: 17-24, Math: 17-24, Composite: 18-24.

ACADEMICS

Year founded: 1901. **Academic calendar:** Semester. **Degrees offered:** certificate, associate, bachelor's, post-bachelor's certificate, master's, post-master's certificate, doctorate. **Most popular majors:** 10% nursing/registered nurse training (R.N., A.S.N., B.S.N., M.S.N.), 6% human resources management/personnel administration, 5% elementary education and teaching, 4% physical education teaching and coaching, 4% social work. **Major fields of study:** area, ethnic, cultural, and gender studies; biological and biomedical sciences; business, management, marketing, and related support services; communication, journalism, and related programs; computer and information sciences and support services; education; engineering; engineering technologies/technicians; English language and literature/letters; family and consumer sciences/human sciences; foreign languages, literatures, and linguistics; health professions and related clinical sciences; history; liberal arts and sciences studies, and humanities; mathematics and statistics; multi/interdisciplinary studies; philosophy and religious studies; physical sciences; psychology; public administration and social service professions; social sciences; visual and performing arts. **Areas of required coursework:** arts/fine arts, humanities, mathematics, English (including composition), philosophy, foreign languages, sciences (biological or physical), history, social science, other. **Pre-professional programs:** pre-law, pre-dentistry, pre-medicine, pre-veterinary science, pre-optometry, pre-pharmacy, other. **Special academic programs:** accelerated program, cooperative (work-study plan) program, cross-registration, distance learning, double major, dual enrollment, English as a Second Language (ESL), exchange student program (domestic), honors program, independent study, internships, liberal arts/career combination, student-designed major, study abroad, teacher certificate program, weekend college. **Teacher certification offered in:** early childhood, special education, elementary, vo-tech, secondary. **Cooperative education programs:** health professions, natural science, other. **Reserve Officers Training Corps (ROTC):** Army ROTC: Offered on campus. **Faculty and instruction (2009-2010):** Total instructional faculty: 602 full-time, 236 part-time (56% men; 44% women; 7% minorities). Full-time faculty with Ph.D. or other terminal degree: 76%. Student/faculty ratio: 16/1. Classes of fewer than 20 students: 59%; of 20 to 49 students: 36%; of 50 or more students: 5%. **Advanced Placement and International Baccalaureate credit:**

AP tests may be used for: Credit only. Scores accepted: 3, 4, 5. **Freshmen returning for sophomore year:** 57%. **Graduation rates:** Four-year: 7%; five-year: 21%; six-year: 30%. **Graduate study:** Fields in which graduates pursue further study: Master of Business Administration (MBA), 5%; medicine, 15%; veterinary medicine, 1%.

COSTS AND FINANCIAL AID
Financial aid office: (208) 282-2756. **Expenses (2009-2010):** Tuition and fees 2009-2010: $4,968 in state, $14,770 out of state; room/board: $5,050. Estimated books and supplies: $900; transportation: $1,344; personal expenses: $2,869. **Financial aid:** Priority filing date for institution's financial aid form: March 1.

CAMPUS LIFE AND EXTRACURRICULAR ACTIVITIES
Campus housing available: coed dorms, women's dorms, men's dorms, sorority housing, fraternity housing, apartments for married students, apartment for single students, special housing for disabled students, other housing options. Students who live in college-owned, operated, or affiliated housing: 7%. **Student employment:** During the 2009-2010 academic year, 16% of undergraduates worked on campus. Average per-year earnings: $4,480. **Clubs and organizations:** Number of student organizations: 138. Activities include: campus ministries, choral groups, concert band, dance, drama/theater, international student organization, jazz band, literary magazine, marching band, music ensembles, musical theater, opera, pep band, radio station, student government, student newspaper, symphony orchestra, television station, yearbook. Number of fraternities: 3; sororities: 2. Proportion of men in fraternities: 1%; of women in sororities: 1%. **Sports program (2009-2010):** Member of NCAA I. *Men's intercollegiate varsity sports:* basketball, cross country, football, tennis, track and field (indoor), track and field (outdoor). *Women's intercollegiate varsity sports:* basketball, cross country, golf, soccer, softball, tennis, track and field (indoor), track and field (outdoor), volleyball.

SERVICES AND FACILITIES
Basic services: nonremedial tutoring, placement service, day care, health service, health insurance, other. **Remedial assistance:** reading, math, writing, study skills. **Counseling services:** minority student, career, personal, academic, other. **For learning-disabled students:** School does not offer a structured program with separate admission and additional fees. Services include: remedial math, remedial English, reading machines, remedial reading, tape recorders, diagnostic testing service, untimed tests, note-taking services, oral tests, learning center, readers, extended time for tests, tutors, priority registration, other testing accommodations. **Library:** Number of titles: 2,164,443; number of current serial subscriptions: 5,124. **Information technology resources:** Students are not required to lease or own a computer. Number of campus computers available to all students: 786. School has a wireless network. Approximate number of users that can be accommodated: 500. Proportion of college-owned housing units wired for high-speed internet access: 42%. **Campus safety:** Security services offered: 24-hour foot-and-vehicle patrols, late-night transport/escort service, 24-hour emergency telephones, lighted pathways/sidewalks, controlled dormitory access (key, security card, etc).

TRANSFER AND INTERNATIONAL STUDENTS
Transfer students: May apply for admission for the following academic terms: Fall, Spring, Summer. Applicants need a minimum number of credits to apply. For fall 2009: Transfer applications received: 1,595. Transfer applicants offered admission: 1,203. Transfer applicants enrolled: 903. **International students:** Number of foreign undergraduates: 104 (1% of student body). Number of countries represented: 65. Minimum TOEFL score required: 500 (paper); 173 (computer). Average TOEFL score: 550 (paper).

Lewis-Clark State College

- **Address:** 500 Eighth Avenue, Lewiston, ID 83501
- **Website:** http://www.lcsc.edu
- **Public**
- **Enrollment:** 2,534 full-time; 1,666 part-time

KEY STATS
✔ **U.S News College Ranking:** 26, Regional Colleges (West)
✔ **ACT Score (25th/75th percentile):** 17-22
✔ **Tuition:** 2010-2011: $5,000 in state, $13,908 out of state
  Selectivity: Less selective   **Room/board:** $7,530
  Acceptance rate: 98%   **Average debt:** N/A
  Student/faculty ratio: 15/1   **Proportion who borrowed:** 61%

UNDERGRADUATE STUDENT BODY STATS
2009-2010 enrollment: 2,534 full-time; 1,666 part-time. Men: 40%; women: 60%. **Ethnic makeup:** African American: 1%; American-Indian: 4%; Asian American: 2%; Hispanic: 4%; White: 87%; International: 3%.

ADMISSIONS FACTS AND FIGURES
Phone: (208) 792-2210. **Email:** admissions@lcsc.edu. **Website:** http://www.lcsc.edu. **Application deadlines for fall 2011:** Regular decision: Rolling. Early decision: Not offered. Early action: Not offered. Admission can be deferred. **Application fee:** $35. **To apply online, go to:** http://www.lcsc.edu/Admissions/forms.htm. **Admissions requirements/recommendations:** High school units required (recommended): English: 4; Mathematics: 3; Science: 3; Foreign language: (1); Total units: 15. Tests: The college uses SAT or ACT scores in admissions decisions. Neither SAT nor ACT required. For admission to the fall 2011 entering class, the school will accept: ACT with or without writing accepted. Campus visit: Recommended. Admissions interview: Neither required nor recommended. Off-campus interview: Not available. **Factors that count in admissions decisions:** *Academic:* Secondary school record: Very Important. Class rank: Not Considered. Letters of recommendation: Not Considered. Standardized test scores: Very Important. Essay: Not Considered. *Nonacademic:* Interview: Not Considered. Extracurricular activities: Not Considered. Talent/ability: Not Considered. Character/personal qualities: Not Considered. Alumni/ae relationship: Not Considered. Geographical residence: Not Considered. State residency: Not Considered. Religious affiliation/commitment: Not Considered. Minority status: Not Considered. Volunteer work: Not Considered. Work experience: Not Considered. **Other schools with the greatest overlap in applicants:** Boise State University; University of Idaho. **Admissions statistics for the fall 2009 entering class:** Total applicants: 1,273. Total accepted: 1,252. Freshmen enrolled: 635; 16% were from out of state. Overall acceptance rate: 98%. **Credentials of fall 2009 freshmen:** 5% ranked in the top 10 percent of their high school class; 18% were in the top 25 percent; 47% were in the top half. (Proportion submitting class standing: 72%.) **First-year students who submitted SAT scores:** 17%. Scores (25/75 percentile): Critical Reading: 450-540, Math: 438-540, Combined: 888-1080. **First-year students submitting ACT scores:** 63%. Scores (25/75 percentile): English: 17-22, Math: 15-21, Composite: 17-22.

ACADEMICS
Year founded: 1893. **Academic calendar:** Semester. **Degrees offered:** certificate, diploma, associate, transfer-associate, terminal-associate, bachelor's. **Most popular majors:** 26% business, management, marketing, and related support services, 14% education, 14% health professions and related clinical sciences, 8% public administration and social service professions, 7% security and protective services. **Major fields of study:** biological and biomedical sciences; business, management, marketing, and related support services; communication, journalism, and related programs; communications technologies/technicians and support services; computer and information sciences and support services; education; engineering technologies/technicians; English language and literature/letters; family and consumer sciences/human sciences; health professions and related clinical sciences; legal professions and studies; mathematics and statistics; mechanic and repair technologies/technicians; multi/interdisciplinary studies; parks, recreation, leisure, and fitness studies; physical sciences; precision production; psychology; public administration and social service professions; security and protective services; social sciences. **Areas of required coursework:** arts/fine arts, humanities, mathematics, English (including composition), sciences (biological or physical), social science. **Pre-professional programs:** pre-dentistry, pre-medicine, pre-veterinary science, pre-pharmacy, other.

Special academic programs: accelerated program, cooperative (work-study plan) program, distance learning, dual enrollment, English as a Second Language (ESL), independent study, internships, study abroad, teacher certificate program. Teacher certification offered in: special education, elementary, secondary. Cooperative education programs: business, computer science, education, health professions, humanities, natural science, social/behavioral science, technologies. Reserve Officers Training Corps (ROTC): Army ROTC: Offered at cooperating institution (University of Idaho); Navy ROTC: Offered at cooperating institution (University of Idaho); Air Force ROTC: Offered at cooperating institution (University of Idaho). Faculty and instruction (2009-2010): Total instructional faculty: N/A. Student/faculty ratio: 15/1. Classes of fewer than 20 students: 25%; of 20 to 49 students: 2%; of 50 or more students: 73%. Advanced Placement and International Baccalaureate credit: AP tests may be used for: Credit only. Scores accepted: 3, 4, 5. International Baccalaureate exams may be used for: Credit only. Freshmen returning for sophomore year: 54%. Graduation rates: Six-year: 23%. Graduate study: 6% of students pursue further study immediately upon graduation.

COSTS AND FINANCIAL AID

Financial aid office: (208) 792-2224. Expenses (2010-2011): Tuition and fees 2010-2011: $5,000 in state, $13,908 out of state; room/board: $7,530. Estimated books and supplies: $1,520; transportation: $2,280; personal expenses: $2,232. Financial aid: Priority filing date for institution's financial aid form: March 1. In 2009-2010, 77% of undergraduates applied for financial aid. Of those, 66% were determined to have financial need; 10% had their need fully met. Average financial aid package (proportion receiving): $8,048 (65%). Average amount of gift aid, such as scholarships or grants (proportion receiving): $3,796 (43%). Average amount of self-help aid, such as work study or loans (proportion receiving): $3,708 (53%). Average need-based loan (excluding PLUS or other private loans): $3,918. Among students who received need-based aid, the average percentage of need met: 10%. Among students who received aid based on merit, the average award (and the proportion receiving): $2,758 (11%). The average athletic scholarship (and the proportion receiving): $8,382 (8%). Proportion who borrowed: 61%.

CAMPUS LIFE AND EXTRACURRICULAR ACTIVITIES

Campus housing available (% using): coed dorms (12%), apartments for married students, apartment for single students. Student employment: During the 2009-2010 academic year, 5% of undergraduates worked on campus. Average per-year earnings: $2,000. Clubs and organizations: Number of student organizations: 50. Activities include: campus ministries, drama/theater, international student organization, jazz band, literary magazine, radio station, student government, student newspaper. Number of fraternities: 0; sororities: 0. Average proportion of students who stay on campus on weekends: 25%. Sports program (2009-2010): Member of NAIA. Men's intercollegiate varsity sports: baseball, basketball, cross country, golf, tennis, track and field (indoor). Women's intercollegiate varsity sports: basketball, cross country, golf, tennis, track and field (indoor), volleyball.

SERVICES AND FACILITIES

Basic services: nonremedial tutoring, placement service, day care, health service, health insurance. Remedial assistance: reading, math, writing, study skills. Counseling services: minority student, career, military, personal, veteran student, academic, older student, psychological, birth control. For learning-disabled students: School does not offer a structured program with separate admission and additional fees. Services include: remedial math, remedial English, reading machines, remedial reading, tape recorders, note-taking services, oral tests, learning center, readers, extended time for tests, tutors, texts on tape, typist/scribe, other testing accommodations. Library: Number of titles: 185,487; number of current serial subscriptions: 674. Information technology resources: Students are not required to lease or own a computer. Number of campus computers available to all students: 492. School has a wireless network. Approximate number of users that can be accommodated: 1,500. Proportion of college-owned housing units wired for high-speed internet access: 95%. Campus safety: Security services offered: 24-hour foot-and-vehicle patrols, late-night transport/escort service, 24-hour emergency telephones, lighted pathways/sidewalks, controlled dormitory access (key, security card, etc).

TRANSFER AND INTERNATIONAL STUDENTS

Transfer students: May apply for admission for the following academic terms: Fall, Spring, Summer. Applicants need a minimum number of credits to apply. For fall 2009: Transfer applications received: 540. Transfer applicants offered admission: 530. Transfer applicants enrolled: 313.

International students: Number of foreign undergraduates: 85 (3% of student body). Number of countries represented: 29. Minimum TOEFL score required: 500 (paper); 173 (computer). Average TOEFL score: 535 (paper).

Northwest Nazarene University

- **Address:** 623 Holly Street, Nampa, ID 83686
- **Website:** http://www.nnu.edu
- **Private; Religious affiliation:** Church of the Nazarene
- **Enrollment:** 1,184 full-time; 152 part-time

KEY STATS

✔ U.S News College Ranking: 40, Regional Universities (West)
✔ ACT Score (25th/75th percentile): 20-26
✔ Tuition: 2010-2011: $23,090

Selectivity: Selective	Room/board: $6,070
Acceptance rate: 58%	Average debt: $35,808
Student/faculty ratio: 13/1	Proportion who borrowed: 85%

UNDERGRADUATE STUDENT BODY STATS

2009-2010 enrollment: 1,184 full-time; 152 part-time. Men: 43%; women: 57%. Ethnic makeup: African American: 1%; American-Indian: 1%; Asian American: 2%; Hispanic: 5%; White: 89%; International: 2%. Religious preference: Roman Catholic: 3%; Protestant: 42%; No preference: 3%; Unknown: 3%; Church of the Nazarene: 49%.

ADMISSIONS FACTS AND FIGURES

Phone: (208) 467-8000. Email: Admissions@nnu.edu. Website: http://www.nnu.edu. Application deadlines for fall 2011: Regular decision: August 15. Early decision: Not offered. Early action: Send application by: December 15; Decision sent by: January 15. Admission can be deferred. Application fee: $25. To apply online, go to: http://www.nnu.edu/apply/. Admissions requirements/recommendations: High school units required (recommended): English: 4 (4); Mathematics: 3 (3); Science: 3 (3); Foreign language: 2 (2); Social studies: 0 (3); History: 3 (3); Total units: 15 (21). Tests: The college uses SAT or ACT scores in admissions decisions. Either SAT or ACT required. For admission to the fall 2011 entering class, the school will accept: ACT with or without writing accepted. Campus visit: Recommended. Admissions interview: Recommended. Off-campus interview: May be arranged. Factors that count in admissions decisions: Academic: Secondary school record: Considered. Class rank: Very Important. Letters of recommendation: Considered. Standardized test scores: Very Important. Essay: Not Considered. Nonacademic: Interview: Not Considered. Extracurricular activities: Considered. Talent/ability: Considered. Character/personal qualities: Very Important. Alumni/ae relationship: Considered. Geographical residence: Not Considered. State residency: Not Considered. Religious affiliation/commitment: Considered. Minority status: Not Considered. Volunteer work: Considered. Work experience: Not Considered. Other schools with the greatest overlap in applicants: Boise State University; College of Idaho; Idaho State University; Point Loma Nazarene University; University of Idaho. Admissions statistics for the fall 2009 entering class: Total applicants: 2,001. Total accepted: 1,166. Freshmen enrolled: 277; 44% were from out of state. Overall acceptance rate: 58%. Non-early acceptance rate: 58%. Credentials of fall 2009 freshmen: 24% ranked in the top 10 percent of their high school class; 47% were in the top 25 percent; 76% were in the top half. (Proportion submitting class standing: 71%.) Average high school grade point average: 3.4. First-year students who submitted SAT scores: 48%. Scores (25/75 percentile): Critical Reading: 480-600, Math: 490-590, Combined: 970-1190. First-year students submitting ACT scores: 76%. Scores (25/75 percentile): English: 18-25, Math: 18-25, Composite: 20-26.

ACADEMICS

Year founded: 1913. Academic calendar: Semester. Degrees offered: bachelor's, master's. Most popular majors: 24% business/commerce, 20% pre-medicine/pre-medical studies, 11% education, 8% philosophy, 7% general studies. Major fields of study: biological and biomedical sciences; business, management, marketing, and related support services; communication, journalism, and related programs; computer and information sciences and support services; education; engineering; English language and literature/letters; foreign languages, literatures, and linguistics; health professions and related clinical sciences; history; liberal arts and sciences studies, and humanities; parks, recreation, leisure, and fitness studies; philosophy and religious studies; physical sciences; psychology; public administration and social service professions; social sciences; theology and religious vocations; visual and performing arts. **Areas of required coursework:** arts/fine arts, humanities, computer literacy, mathematics, English (including composition), philosophy, sciences (biological or physical), history, social science, other. **Pre-professional programs:** pre-law, pre-dentistry, pre-medicine, pre-theology, pre-veterinary science, pre-optometry, pre-pharmacy, other. **Special academic programs (% participation):** accelerated program (12%), cross-registration (0%), distance learning (0%), double major (2%), exchange student program (domestic) (0%), honors program (4%), independent study (0%), internships (30%), liberal arts/career combination (100%), student-designed major (0%), study abroad (5%), teacher certificate program (9%). **Teacher certification offered in:** special education, elementary, middle/junior high, secondary. **Cooperative education programs:** education, engineering, health professions. **Reserve Officers Training Corps (ROTC):** Army ROTC: Offered on campus. **Faculty and instruction (2009-2010):** Total instructional faculty: 102 full-time, 4 part-time (; 7% minorities). Full-time faculty with Ph.D. or other terminal degree: 69%. Student/faculty ratio: 13/1. Classes of fewer than 20 students: 57%; of 20 to 49 students: 37%; of 50 or more students: 6%. **Advanced Placement and International Baccalaureate credit:** AP tests may be used for: Placement only. Scores accepted: 3, 4, 5. International Baccalaureate exams may be used for: Credit only. **Freshmen returning for sophomore year:** 69%. **Graduation rates:** Four-year: 37%; five-year: 51%; six-year: 51%.

COSTS AND FINANCIAL AID

Financial aid office: (208) 467-8347. **Expenses (2010-2011):** Tuition and fees 2010-2011: $23,090; room/board: $6,070. Estimated books and supplies: $1,100; transportation: $990; personal expenses: $990. **Financial aid:** Priority filing date for institution's financial aid form: March 1. In 2009-2010, 85% of undergraduates applied for financial aid. Of those, 75% were determined to have financial need; 23% had their need fully met. Average financial aid package (proportion receiving): $16,918 (75%). Average amount of gift aid, such as scholarships or grants (proportion receiving): $8,356 (61%). Average amount of self-help aid, such as work study or loans (proportion receiving): $3,541 (56%). Average need-based loan (excluding PLUS or other private loans): $3,436. Among students who received need-based aid, the average percentage of need met: 84%. Among students who received aid based on merit, the average award (and the proportion receiving): $5,566 (24%). The average athletic scholarship (and the proportion receiving): $7,311 (20%). Average amount of debt of borrowers graduating in 2009: $35,808. Proportion who borrowed: 85%.

CAMPUS LIFE AND EXTRACURRICULAR ACTIVITIES

Campus housing available (% using): coed dorms (26%), women's dorms (27%), men's dorms (19%), apartments for married students (5%), apartment for single students, other housing options (23%). Students who live in college-owned, operated, or affiliated housing: 57%. **Student employment:** During the 2009-2010 academic year, 28% of undergraduates worked on campus. Average per-year earnings: $3,000. **Clubs and organizations:** Number of student organizations: 31. Activities include: campus ministries, choral groups, concert band, drama/theater, international student organization, jazz band, literary magazine, music ensembles, musical theater, opera, pep band, student government, student newspaper, symphony orchestra, yearbook. Number of fraternities: 0; sororities: 0. Average proportion of students who stay on campus on weekends: 60%. **Sports program (2009-2010):** Member of NCAA II. *Men's intercollegiate varsity sports:* baseball, basketball, cross country, golf, soccer, track and field (indoor), track and field (outdoor). *Women's intercollegiate varsity sports:* basketball, cross country, soccer, softball, track and field (indoor), track and field (outdoor), volleyball.

SERVICES AND FACILITIES

Basic services: nonremedial tutoring, health service, health insurance. **Remedial assistance:** reading, math, writing, study skills, other. **Counseling services:** minority student, career, military, personal, veteran student, academic, older student, psychological, birth control, religious. **For learning-disabled students:** School does not offer a structured program with separate admission and additional fees. Total undergraduates in learning-disabled program or receiving services: 14. Services include: remedial math, remedial English, remedial reading, tape recorders, other special classes, untimed tests, note-taking services, oral tests, learning center, readers, extended time for tests, tutors, priority registration, priority seating, texts on tape, other testing accommodations. **Library:** Number of titles: 176,802; number of current serial subscriptions: 648. **Information technology resources:** Students are not required to lease or own a computer. Number of campus computers available to all students: 275. School has a wireless network. Approximate number of users that can be accommodated: 255. Proportion of college-

owned housing units wired for high-speed internet access: 100%. **Campus safety:** Security services offered: 24-hour foot-and-vehicle patrols, late-night transport/escort service, 24-hour emergency telephones, lighted pathways/sidewalks, student patrols, controlled dormitory access (key, security card, etc).

TRANSFER AND INTERNATIONAL STUDENTS

Transfer students: May apply for admission for the following academic terms: Fall, Spring, Summer. Applicants do not need a minimum number of credits to apply. For fall 2009: Transfer applications received: 200. Transfer applicants offered admission: 147. Transfer applicants enrolled: 70. **International students:** Number of foreign undergraduates: 24 (2% of student body). Number of countries represented: 6. Minimum TOEFL score required: 500 (paper); 173 (computer).

University of Idaho

- **Address:** 875 Perimeter Drive, PO Box 442282, Moscow, ID 83844-2282
- **Website:** http://www.its.uidaho.edu/uihome/
- **Public**
- **Enrollment:** 8,288 full-time; 1,055 part-time

KEY STATS

✔ **U.S News College Ranking:** 153, National Universities
✔ **ACT Score (25th/75th percentile):** 20-26
✔ **Tuition:** 2010-2011: $5,402 in state, $16,994 out of state

Selectivity: Selective	**Room/board:** $7,194
Acceptance rate: 80%	**Average debt:** $22,527
Student/faculty ratio: 17/1	**Proportion who borrowed:** 68%

UNDERGRADUATE STUDENT BODY STATS

2009-2010 enrollment: 8,288 full-time; 1,055 part-time. Men: 53%; women: 47%. **Ethnic makeup:** African American: 1%; American-Indian: 1%; Asian American: 2%; Hispanic: 6%; White: 87%; International: 2%.

ADMISSIONS FACTS AND FIGURES

Phone: (888) 884-3246. **Email:** admissions@uidaho.edu. **Website:** http://www.its.uidaho.edu/uihome/. **Application deadlines for fall 2011:** Regular decision: August 1. Early decision: Not offered. Early action: Not offered. Admission can be deferred. **Application fee:** $40. **To apply online, go to:** http://www.students.uidaho.edu/default.aspx?pid=15568. **Admissions requirements/recommendations:** High school units required (recommended): English: 4 (4); Mathematics: 3 (3); Science: 3 (3); Foreign language: 1 (1); Social studies: 3 (3); Academic electives: 2 (2); Total units: 15 (15). Tests: The college uses SAT or ACT scores in admissions decisions. Either SAT or ACT required. For admission to the fall 2011 entering class, the school will accept: ACT with or without writing accepted. Campus visit: Recommended. Admissions interview: Neither required nor recommended. Off-campus interview: May be arranged. **Factors that count in admissions decisions:** *Academic:* Secondary school record: Not Considered. Class rank: Not Considered. Letters of recommendation: Not Considered. Standardized test scores: Very Important. Essay: Not Considered. *Nonacademic:* Interview: Not Considered. Extracurricular activities: Not Considered. Talent/ability: Not Considered. Character/personal qualities: Not Considered. Alumni/ae relationship: Not Considered. Geographical residence: Not Considered. State residency: Not Considered. Religious affiliation/commitment: Not Considered. Minority status: Not Considered. Volunteer work: Not Considered. Work experience: Not Considered. **Other schools with the greatest overlap in applicants:** Boise State University; Eastern Washington University; University of Montana; University of Washington; Washington State University. **Admissions statistics for the fall 2009 entering class:** Total applicants: 5,110. Total accepted: 4,068. Freshmen enrolled: 1,780; 40% were from out of state. Overall acceptance rate: 80%. **Credentials of fall 2009 freshmen:** 19% ranked in the top 10 percent of their high school class; 46% were in the top 25 percent; 79% were in the top half. (Proportion submitting class standing: 70%.) **Average high school grade point average:** 3.4. **First-year students who submitted SAT scores:** 59%. Scores (25/75 percentile): Critical Reading: 490-600, Math: 490-610, Combined: 980-1210. **First-year students submitting ACT scores:** 67%. Scores (25/75 percentile): English: 19-26, Math: 19-26, Composite: 20-26.

ACADEMICS

Year founded: 1889. **Academic calendar:** Semester. **Degrees offered:** certificate, bachelor's, post-bachelor's certificate, master's, post-master's certificate, doctorate. **Major fields of study:** agriculture, agriculture operations, and related sciences; architecture and related services; area, ethnic, cultural, and gender studies; biological and biomedical sciences; business, management, marketing, and related support services; communication, journalism, and related programs; communications technologies/technicians and support services; computer and information sciences and support services; education; engineering; English language and literature/letters; family and consumer sciences/human sciences; foreign languages, literatures, and linguistics; health professions and related clinical sciences; history; legal professions and studies; liberal arts and sciences studies, and humanities; mathematics and statistics; military technologies; multi/interdisciplinary studies; natural resources and conservation; parks, recreation, leisure, and fitness studies; philosophy and religious studies; physical sciences; psychology; security and protective services; social sciences; visual and performing arts. **Areas of required coursework:** arts/fine arts, humanities, mathematics, English (including composition), sciences (biological or physical), history, social science, other. **Pre-professional programs:** pre-law, pre-medicine, pre-veterinary science. **Special academic programs:** accelerated program, cooperative (work-study plan) program, cross-registration, distance learning, double major, dual enrollment, English as a Second Language (ESL), exchange student program (domestic), honors program, independent study, internships, student-designed major, study abroad, teacher certificate program. **Teacher certification offered in:** early childhood, special education, elementary, vo-tech, middle/junior high, adult education, secondary. **Cooperative education programs:** agriculture, art, business, computer science, education, engineering, health professions, home economics, humanities, natural science, social/behavioral science, technologies, vocational arts. **Reserve Officers Training Corps (ROTC):** Army ROTC: Offered on campus; Navy ROTC: Offered on campus; Air Force ROTC: Offered at cooperating institution (Washington State University). **Faculty and instruction (2009-2010):** Total instructional faculty: 545 full-time, 122 part-time (66% men; 34% women; 8% minorities). Full-time faculty with Ph.D. or other terminal degree: 77%. Student/faculty ratio: 17/1. Classes of fewer than 20 students: 52%; of 20 to 49 students: 39%; of 50 or more students: 9%. **Advanced Placement and International Baccalaureate credit:** AP tests may be used for: Credit and/or placement. Scores accepted: 3, 4, 5. International Baccalaureate exams may be used for: Placement only. **Freshmen returning for sophomore year:** 76%. **Graduation rates:** Four-year: 25%; five-year: 50%; six-year: 56%.

COSTS AND FINANCIAL AID

Financial aid office: (208) 885-6312. **Expenses (2010-2011):** Tuition and fees 2010-2011: $5,402 in state, $16,994 out of state; room/board: $7,194. Estimated books and supplies: $1,474; transportation: $1,460; personal expenses: $3,170. **Financial aid:** Priority filing date for institution's financial aid form: February 15. In 2009-2010, 77% of undergraduates applied for financial aid. Of those, 64% were determined to have financial need; 26% had their need fully met. Average financial aid package (proportion receiving): $12,076 (62%). Average amount of gift aid, such as scholarships or grants (proportion receiving): $4,365 (41%). Average amount of self-help aid, such as work study or loans (proportion receiving): $7,319 (51%). Average need-based loan (excluding PLUS or other private loans): $7,208.

Among students who received need-based aid, the average percentage of need met: 76%. Among students who received aid based on merit, the average award (and the proportion receiving): $4,810 (14%). The average athletic scholarship (and the proportion receiving): $16,057 (3%). Average amount of debt of borrowers graduating in 2009: $22,527. Proportion who borrowed: 68%.

CAMPUS LIFE AND EXTRACURRICULAR ACTIVITIES

Campus housing available: coed dorms, women's dorms, men's dorms, sorority housing, fraternity housing, apartments for married students, apartment for single students, special housing for disabled students, special housing for international students, cooperative housing. Students who live in college-owned, operated, or affiliated housing: 9%. **Student employment:** During the 2009-2010 academic year, 35% of undergraduates worked on campus. Average per-year earnings: $1,500. **Clubs and organizations:** Number of student organizations: 200. Activities include: campus ministries, choral groups, concert band, dance, drama/theater, international student organization, jazz band, literary magazine, marching band, music ensembles, musical theater, opera, pep band, radio station, student government, student newspaper, student film society, symphony orchestra, television station. Number of fraternities: 19; sororities: 12. Proportion of men in fraternities: 7%; of women in sororities: 7%. **Sports program (2009-2010):** Member of NCAA I. *Men's intercollegiate varsity sports:* basketball, cross country, football, golf, tennis, track and field (indoor), track and field (outdoor). *Women's intercollegiate varsity sports:* basketball, cross country, golf, soccer, tennis, track and field (indoor), track and field (outdoor), volleyball.

SERVICES AND FACILITIES

Basic services: nonremedial tutoring, women's center, placement service, day care, health service, health insurance. **Remedial assistance:** reading, math, writing, study skills. **Counseling services:** minority student, career, military, personal, veteran student, academic, older student, psychological, birth control. **For learning-disabled students:** School does not offer a structured program with separate admission and additional fees. Services include: reading machines, tape recorders, videotaped classes, note-taking services, oral tests, learning center, readers, extended time for tests, tutors, priority registration, other testing accommodations, other. **Library:** Number of titles: 2,840,000; number of current serial subscriptions: 8,609. **Information technology resources:** Students are not required to lease or own a computer. Number of campus computers available to all students: 604. School has a wireless network. Proportion of college-owned housing units wired for high-speed internet access: 100%. **Campus safety:** Security services offered: 24-hour foot-and-vehicle patrols, late-night transport/escort service, 24-hour emergency telephones, lighted pathways/sidewalks, controlled dormitory access (key, security card, etc).

TRANSFER AND INTERNATIONAL STUDENTS

Transfer students: May apply for admission for the following academic terms: Fall, Spring, Summer. Applicants need a minimum number of credits to apply. For fall 2009: Transfer applications received: 1,738. Transfer applicants offered admission: 1,006. Transfer applicants enrolled: 736. **International students:** Number of foreign undergraduates: 174 (2% of student body). Number of countries represented: 35. Minimum TOEFL score required: 525 (paper); 193 (computer). Average TOEFL score: 573 (paper).

Illinois

Augustana College

- **Address:** 639 38th Street, Rock Island, IL 61201-2296
- **Website:** http://www.augustana.edu
- **Private; Religious affiliation:** Evangelical Lutheran Church in America
- **Enrollment:** 2,446 full-time; 26 part-time

KEY STATS

✔ **U.S News College Ranking:** 88, National Liberal Arts Colleges
✔ **ACT Score (25th/75th percentile):** 23-29
✔ **Tuition:** 2010-2011: $30,012

Selectivity: More selective	**Room/board:** $8,181
Acceptance rate: 73%	**Average debt:** N/A
Student/faculty ratio: 11/1	**Proportion who borrowed:** N/A

UNDERGRADUATE STUDENT BODY STATS

2009-2010 enrollment: 2,446 full-time; 26 part-time. Men: 43%; women: 57%. **Ethnic makeup:** African American: 2%; Asian American: 2%; Hispanic: 3%; White: 92%; International: 1%. **Religious preference:** Roman Catholic: 34%; Protestant: 18%; Jewish: 1%; Muslim: 1%; No preference: 1%; Unknown: 18%; Evangelical Lutheran Church in America: 19%; Other: 8%.

ADMISSIONS FACTS AND FIGURES

Phone: (800) 798-8100. **Email:** admissions@augustana.edu. **Website:** http://www.augustana.edu. **Application deadlines for fall 2011:** Regular decision: Rolling. Early decision: Not offered. Early action: Not offered. Admission can be deferred. **Application fee:** $35. **To apply online, go to:** http://www.augustana.edu/admissions/apply/. **Admissions requirements/ recommendations:** High school units required (recommended): English: 3 (4); Mathematics: 3 (4); Science: 3 (4); Foreign language: 1 (2); Social studies: 1 (2); History: 1 (1); Academic electives: (4); Total units: (16). Tests: The college uses SAT or ACT scores in admissions decisions. Neither SAT nor ACT required. For admission to the fall 2011 entering class, the school will accept: ACT with or without writing accepted. Campus visit: Recommended. Admissions interview: Recommended. Off-campus interview: Not available. **Factors that count in admissions decisions: Academic:** Secondary school record: Very Important. Class rank: Very Important. Letters of recommendation: Important. Standardized test scores: Important. Essay: Important. **Nonacademic:** Interview: Important. Extracurricular activities: Important. Talent/ability: Important. Character/personal qualities: Important. Alumni/ ae relationship: Considered. Geographical residence: Considered. State residency: Not Considered. Religious affiliation/commitment: Considered. Minority status: Considered. Volunteer work: Considered. Work experience: Considered. **Admissions statistics for the fall 2009 entering class:** Total applicants: 3,633. Total accepted: 2,638. Freshmen enrolled: 616; 13% were from out of state. Overall acceptance rate: 73%. **Credentials of fall 2009 freshmen:** 35% ranked in the top 10 percent of their high school class; 64% were in the top 25 percent; 90% were in the top half. (Proportion submitting class standing: 82%.) **First-year students submitting ACT scores:** 95%. Scores (25/75 percentile): English: N/A, Math: N/A, Composite: 23-29.

ACADEMICS

Year founded: 1860. **Academic calendar:** Quarter. **Degrees offered:** bachelor's. **Most popular majors:** 22% business, management, marketing, and related support services, 16% biological and biomedical sciences, 10% social sciences, 8% health professions and related clinical sciences, 7% psychology. **Major fields of study:** area, ethnic, cultural, and gender studies; biological and biomedical sciences; business, management, marketing, and related support services; computer and information sciences and support services; education; engineering; English language and literature/letters; foreign languages, literatures, and linguistics; health professions and related clinical sciences; history; mathematics and statistics; multi/interdisciplinary studies; natural resources and conservation; philosophy and religious studies; physical sciences; psychology; public administration and social service professions; social sciences; visual and performing arts. **Areas of required coursework:** arts/fine arts, humanities, mathematics, English (including

composition), foreign languages, sciences (biological or physical), history, social science, other. **Pre-professional programs:** pre-law, pre-dentistry, pre-medicine, pre-veterinary science, pre-optometry, pre-pharmacy, other. **Special academic programs (% participation):** accelerated program, double major (30%), honors program (8%), independent study, internships (34%), liberal arts/career combination, student-designed major (1%), study abroad (30%), teacher certificate program. **Teacher certification offered in:** elementary, middle/junior high, secondary. **Faculty and instruction (2009-2010):** Total instructional faculty: 174 full-time, 89 part-time (56% men; 44% women; 14% minorities). Full-time faculty with Ph.D. or other terminal degree: 94%. Student/faculty ratio: 11/1. Classes of fewer than 20 students: 61%; of 20 to 49 students: 38%; of 50 or more students: 1%. **Advanced Placement and International Baccalaureate credit:** AP tests may be used for: Credit and/or placement. Scores accepted: 3, 4, 5. International Baccalaureate exams may be used for: Placement only. **Freshmen returning for sophomore year:** 85%. **Graduation rates:** Four-year: 72%; five-year: 78%; six-year: 78%. **Graduate study:** 47% of students pursue further study immediately upon graduation. Fields in which graduates pursue further study: Master of Business Administration (MBA), 3%; law, 1%; medicine, 4%; dentistry, 1%; engineering, 1%; education, 4%; arts and sciences, 19%; veterinary medicine, 4%.

COSTS AND FINANCIAL AID

Financial aid office: (309) 794-7207. **Expenses (2010-2011):** Tuition and fees 2010-2011: $30,012; room/board: $8,181. Estimated books and supplies: $1,000; transportation: $400; personal expenses: $800. **Financial aid:** Priority filing date for institution's financial aid form: April 1. In 2009-2010, 84% of undergraduates applied for financial aid. Of those, 70% were determined to have financial need; 42% had their need fully met. Average financial aid package (proportion receiving): $25,819 (69%). Average amount of gift aid, such as scholarships or grants (proportion receiving): $15,738 (69%). Average amount of self-help aid, such as work study or loans (proportion receiving): $7,836 (57%). Average need-based loan (excluding PLUS or other private loans): $7,306. Among students who received need-based aid, the average percentage of need met: 85%. Among students who received aid based on merit, the average award (and the proportion receiving): $11,868 (29%). The average athletic scholarship (and the proportion receiving): $0 (0%).

CAMPUS LIFE AND EXTRACURRICULAR ACTIVITIES

Campus housing available: coed dorms, apartment for single students. Students who live in college-owned, operated, or affiliated housing: 70%. **Student employment:** During the 2009-2010 academic year, 43% of undergraduates worked on campus. Average per-year earnings: $2,000. **Clubs and organizations:** Number of student organizations: 166. Activities include: campus ministries, choral groups, concert band, dance, drama/theater, international student organization, jazz band, literary magazine, model UN, music ensembles, musical theater, opera, pep band, radio station, student government, student newspaper, symphony orchestra, yearbook. Number of fraternities: 6; sororities: 6. Proportion of men in fraternities: 20%; of women in sororities: 26%. Average proportion of students who stay on campus on weekends: 80%. **Sports program (2009-2010):** Member of NCAA III. **Men's intercollegiate varsity sports:** baseball, basketball, cross country, football, golf, soccer, swimming, tennis, track and field (outdoor), wrestling. **Women's intercollegiate varsity sports:** basketball, cross country, golf, soccer, softball, swimming, tennis, track and field (outdoor), volleyball.

SERVICES AND FACILITIES

Basic services: nonremedial tutoring, women's center, placement service, health service, health insurance, other. **Counseling services:** minority student, career, personal, academic, psychological, religious. **For learning-disabled students:** School does not offer a structured program with separate admission and additional fees. Services include: tape recorders, untimed tests, note-taking services, oral tests, learning center, extended time for tests, tutors, priority registration, priority seating, texts on tape, other testing accommodations, other. **Library:** Number of titles: 209,688; number of current serial subscriptions: 20,662. **Information technology resources:** Students are not required to lease or own a computer. Number of campus computers available to all students: 600. School has a wireless network. Approximate number of users that can be accommodated: 1,000. Proportion of college-owned housing units wired for high-speed internet access: 100%. **Campus safety:** Security services offered: 24-hour foot-and-vehicle patrols, late-night transport/escort service, 24-hour emergency telephones, lighted pathways/sidewalks, controlled dormitory access (key, security card, etc).

TRANSFER AND INTERNATIONAL STUDENTS
Transfer students: May apply for admission for the following academic terms: Fall, Winter, Spring, Summer. Applicants need a minimum number of credits to apply. For fall 2009: Transfer applications received: 97. Transfer applicants offered admission: 69. Transfer applicants enrolled: 31. **International students:** Number of foreign undergraduates: 14 (1% of student body). Number of countries represented: 20. Minimum TOEFL score required: 550 (paper); 203 (computer).

Aurora University

■ **Address:** 347 S. Gladstone Avenue, Aurora, IL 60506-4892
■ **Website:** http://www.aurora.edu
■ **Private**
■ **Enrollment:** N/A

KEY STATS
✔ **U.S News College Ranking:** second tier, Regional Universities (Midwest)
✔ **SAT or ACT Score (25th/75th percentile):** N/A
✔ **Tuition:** 2009-2010: $18,200

Selectivity: Selective	**Room/board:** $7,618
Acceptance rate: N/A	**Average debt:** N/A
Student/faculty ratio: N/A	**Proportion who borrowed:** N/A

Benedictine University

■ **Address:** 5700 College Road, Lisle, IL 60532
■ **Website:** http://www.ben.edu
■ **Private; Religious affiliation:** Roman Catholic
■ **Enrollment:** 2,262 full-time; 1,093 part-time

KEY STATS
✔ **U.S News College Ranking:** 52, Regional Universities (Midwest)
✔ **ACT Score (25th/75th percentile):** 20-26
✔ **Tuition:** 2010-2011: $23,200

Selectivity: Selective	**Room/board:** $7,280
Acceptance rate: 79%	**Average debt:** $25,781
Student/faculty ratio: N/A	**Proportion who borrowed:** 65%

UNDERGRADUATE STUDENT BODY STATS
2009-2010 enrollment: 2,262 full-time; 1,093 part-time. Men: 43%; women: 57%. **Ethnic makeup:** African American: 10%; Asian American: 14%; Hispanic: 7%; White: 68%; International: 1%.

ADMISSIONS FACTS AND FIGURES
Phone: (630) 829-6300. **Email:** admissions@ben.edu. **Website:** http://www.ben.edu. **Application deadlines for fall 2011:** Regular decision: Rolling. Early decision: Not offered. Early action: Not offered. Admission can be deferred. **Application fee:** $40. **To apply online, go to:** http://www.ben.edu/admissions/applynow.asp. **Admissions requirements/recommendations:** High school units required (recommended): English: 4; Mathematics: 3 (4); Science: 2 (3); Foreign language: 2; Social studies: 3; History: 1; Total units: 16. Tests: The college uses SAT or ACT scores in admissions decisions. Either SAT or ACT required. For admission to the fall 2011 entering class, the school will accept: ACT with or without writing accepted. Campus visit: Recommended. Admissions interview: Neither required nor recommended. Off-campus interview: May be arranged. **Factors that count in admissions decisions:** *Academic:* Secondary school record: Very Important. Class rank: Very Important. Letters of recommendation: Considered. Standardized test scores: Very Important. Essay: Considered. *Nonacademic:* Interview: Considered. Extracurricular activities: Considered. Talent/ability: Not Considered. Character/personal qualities: Not Considered. Alumni/ae relationship: Not Considered. Geographical residence: Not Considered. State residency: Not Considered. Religious affiliation/commitment: Not Considered. Minority status: Not Considered. Volunteer work: Not Considered. Work experience: Not Considered. **Admissions statistics for the fall 2009 entering class:** Total applicants: 1,667. Total accepted: 1,317. Freshmen enrolled: 445; 8% were from out of state. Overall acceptance rate: 79%. **Credentials of fall 2009 freshmen:** 15% ranked in the top 10 percent of their high school class; 39% were in the top 25 percent; 70% were in the top half. (Proportion submitting class standing: 99%.) **Average high school grade point average:** 3.3. **First-year students submitting ACT scores:** 99%. Scores (25/75 percentile): English: 20-26, Math: 19-26, Composite: 20-26.

ACADEMICS
Year founded: 1887. **Academic calendar:** Semester. **Degrees offered:** certificate, associate, bachelor's, post-bachelor's certificate, master's, doctorate. **Major fields of study:** biological and biomedical sciences; business, management, marketing, and related support services; communication, journalism, and related programs; computer and information sciences and support services; education; engineering; English language and literature/letters; family and consumer sciences/human sciences; foreign languages, literatures, and linguistics; health professions and related clinical sciences; history; legal professions and studies; liberal arts and sciences studies, and humanities; mathematics and statistics; multi/interdisciplinary studies; natural resources and conservation; philosophy and religious studies; physical sciences; psychology; social sciences; visual and performing arts. **Areas of required coursework:** arts/fine arts, humanities, mathematics, English (including composition), philosophy, sciences (biological or physical), social science. **Pre-professional programs:** pre-law, pre-dentistry, pre-medicine, pre-veterinary science, pre-optometry, pre-pharmacy. **Special academic programs:** accelerated program, cooperative (work-study plan) program, cross-registration, distance learning, double major, exchange student program (domestic), honors program, independent study, internships, study abroad, teacher certificate program, weekend college. **Teacher certification offered in:** special education, elementary, middle/junior high, secondary. **Reserve Officers Training Corps (ROTC):** Army ROTC: Offered at cooperating institution. **Faculty and instruction (2009-2010):** Total instructional faculty: 103 full-time, 467 part-time (48% men; 52% women; 16% minorities). Full-time faculty with Ph.D. or other terminal degree: 88%. Classes of fewer than 20 students: 60%; of 20 to 49 students: 40%; of 50 or more students: 0%. **Advanced Placement and International Baccalaureate credit:** International Baccalaureate exams may be used for: Credit only. **Freshmen returning for sophomore year:** 76%. **Graduation rates:** Four-year: 38%; five-year: 50%; six-year: 58%.

COSTS AND FINANCIAL AID
Financial aid office: (630) 829-6108. **Expenses (2010-2011):** Tuition and fees 2010-2011: $23,200; room/board: $7,280. Estimated books and supplies: $1,340; transportation: $0; personal expenses: $2,290. **Financial aid:** Priority filing date for institution's financial aid form: April 15. In 2009-2010, 78% of undergraduates applied for financial aid. Of those, 70% were determined to have financial need; Average financial aid package (proportion receiving): $16,602 (68%). Average amount of gift aid, such as scholarships or grants (proportion receiving): $7,641 (44%). Average amount of self-help aid, such as work study or loans (proportion receiving): $5,499 (57%). Average need-based loan (excluding PLUS or other private loans): $4,394. Among students who received aid based on merit, the average award (and the proportion receiving): $8,536 (44%). The average athletic scholarship (and the proportion receiving): $0 (0%). Average amount of debt of borrowers graduating in 2009: $25,781. Proportion who borrowed: 65%.

CAMPUS LIFE AND EXTRACURRICULAR ACTIVITIES
Campus housing available: coed dorms, women's dorms, men's dorms, apartments for married students, apartment for single students. Students who live in college-owned, operated, or affiliated housing: 31%. **Student employment:** During the 2009-2010 academic year, 26% of undergraduates worked on campus. **Clubs and organizations:** Number of student organizations: 30. Activities include: campus ministries, choral groups, concert band, dance, drama/theater, international student organization, jazz band, literary magazine, model UN, music ensembles, pep band, student government, student newspaper, student film society, symphony orchestra, television station. Number of fraternities: 0; sororities: 0. Average proportion of students who stay on campus on weekends: 40%. **Sports program (2009-2010):** Member of NCAA III. *Men's intercollegiate varsity sports:* baseball, basketball, cross country, football, golf, soccer, track and field (indoor). *Women's intercollegiate varsity sports:* basketball, cross country, golf, soccer, softball, tennis, track and field (indoor), volleyball.

SERVICES AND FACILITIES

Basic services: nonremedial tutoring, placement service, health service. **Counseling services:** career, military, personal, academic, psychological, religious. **For learning-disabled students:** School does not offer a structured program with separate admission and additional fees. Services include: reading machines, tape recorders, videotaped classes, untimed tests, note-taking services, oral tests, learning center, readers, extended time for tests, tutors, priority seating, texts on tape, other testing accommodations. **Library:** Number of titles: 100,507; number of current serial subscriptions: 25,851. **Information technology resources:** Students are not required to lease or own a computer. Number of campus computers available to all students: 200. School has a wireless network. Proportion of college-owned housing units wired for high-speed internet access: 100%. **Campus safety:** Security services offered: 24-hour foot-and-vehicle patrols, late-night transport/escort service, 24-hour emergency telephones, lighted pathways/sidewalks, controlled dormitory access (key, security card, etc.).

TRANSFER AND INTERNATIONAL STUDENTS

Transfer students: May apply for admission for the following academic terms: Fall, Spring, Summer. Applicants do not need a minimum number of credits to apply. For fall 2009: Transfer applications received: 526. Transfer applicants offered admission: 414. Transfer applicants enrolled: 253. **International students:** Number of foreign undergraduates: 36 (1% of student body). Number of countries represented: 9. Minimum TOEFL score required: 550 (paper); 213 (computer).

Blackburn College

- **Address:** 700 College Avenue, Carlinville, IL 62626
- **Website:** http://www.blackburn.edu
- **Private; Religious affiliation:** Presbyterian
- **Enrollment:** 585 full-time; 22 part-time

KEY STATS

✔ **U.S News College Ranking:** 50, Regional Colleges (Midwest)
✔ **ACT Score (25th/75th percentile):** 19-25
✔ **Tuition:** 2010-2011: $14,996

Selectivity: Selective	**Room/board:** $4,790
Acceptance rate: 54%	**Average debt:** $20,077
Student/faculty ratio: 13/1	**Proportion who borrowed:** 85%

UNDERGRADUATE STUDENT BODY STATS

2009-2010 enrollment: 585 full-time; 22 part-time. Men: 41%; women: 59%. **Ethnic makeup:** African American: 7%; Asian American: 1%; Hispanic: 2%; White: 90%. **Religious preference:** Roman Catholic: 15%; Protestant: 1%; Unknown: 55%; Presbyterian: 2%; Other: 27%.

ADMISSIONS FACTS AND FIGURES

Phone: (800) 233-3550. **Email:** admit@mail.blackburn.edu. **Website:** http://www.blackburn.edu. **Application deadlines for fall 2011:** Regular decision: Rolling. Early decision: Not offered. Early action: Not offered. Admission can be deferred. **Application fee:** None. **To apply online, go to:** http://www.blackburn.edu/futurestudents/apply.asp. **Admissions requirements/recommendations:** High school units required (recommended): English: 4 (4); Mathematics: 3 (3); Science: 2 (3); Foreign language: 0 (2); Social studies: 2 (2); History: 2 (2); Academic electives: 2 (2); Total units: 17 (20). Tests: The college uses SAT or ACT scores in admissions decisions. Either SAT or ACT required. For admission to the fall 2011 entering class, the school will accept: ACT with or without writing accepted. Campus visit: Recommended. Admissions interview: Recommended. Off-campus interview: May be arranged. **Factors that count in admissions decisions:** *Academic:* Secondary school record: Very Important. Class rank: Very Important. Letters of recommendation: Considered. Standardized test scores: Very Important. Essay: Considered. *Nonacademic:* Interview: Important. Extracurricular activities: Considered. Talent/ability: Important. Character/personal qualities: Very Important. Alumni/ae relationship: Considered. Geographical residence: Not Considered. State residency: Not Considered. Religious affiliation/commitment: Not Considered. Minority status: Not Considered. Volunteer work: Considered. Work experience: Important. **Other schools with the greatest overlap in applicants:** Illinois College; Millikin University; Southern Illinois University–Edwardsville; University of Illinois–Springfield; University of Illinois–Urbana-Champaign. **Admissions statistics for the fall 2009 entering class:** Total applicants: 912. Total accepted: 491. Freshmen enrolled: 146;

Overall acceptance rate: 54%. **Size of waiting list:** 0 applicants; enrolled from waiting list: 0. **Credentials of fall 2009 freshmen:** 19% ranked in the top 10 percent of their high school class; 42% were in the top 25 percent; 84% were in the top half. (Proportion submitting class standing: 95%.) **Average high school grade point average:** 3.5. **First-year students who submitted SAT scores:** 1%. **First-year students submitting ACT scores:** 99%. Scores (25/75 percentile): English: 20-25, Math: 20-24, Composite: 19-25.

ACADEMICS

Year founded: 1837. **Academic calendar:** Semester. **Degrees offered:** bachelor's. **Most popular majors:** 17% criminal justice/safety studies, 10% biology/biological sciences, 10% elementary education and teaching, 10% marketing/marketing management, 8% accounting. **Major fields of study:** biological and biomedical sciences; communication, journalism, and related programs; computer and information sciences and support services; education; English language and literature/letters; mathematics and statistics; multi/interdisciplinary studies. **Areas of required coursework:** arts/fine arts, humanities, mathematics, English (including composition), philosophy, sciences (biological or physical), social science. **Pre-professional programs:** pre-law, pre-dentistry, pre-medicine, pre-theology, pre-veterinary science, other. **Special academic programs (% participation):** cooperative (work-study plan) program (0%), double major (15%), independent study (9%), internships (29%), study abroad (2%), teacher certificate program (19%). **Teacher certification offered in:** elementary, middle/junior high, secondary. **Faculty and instruction (2009-2010):** Total instructional faculty: 36 full-time, 33 part-time (57% men; 43% women; 10% minorities). Full-time faculty with Ph.D. or other terminal degree: 86%. Student/faculty ratio: 13/1. Classes of fewer than 20 students: 76%; of 20 to 49 students: 23%; of 50 or more students: 0%. **Advanced Placement and International Baccalaureate credit:** AP tests may be used for: Credit only. Scores accepted: 3, 4, 5. **Freshmen returning for sophomore year:** 61%. **Graduation rates:** Four-year: 27%; five-year: 35%; six-year: 42%. **Graduate study:** 18% of students pursue further study immediately upon graduation; 20% within one year; 22% within five years. Fields in which graduates pursue further study: Master of Business Administration (MBA), 2%; law, 1%; medicine, 33%; arts and sciences, 33%; veterinary medicine, 1%.

COSTS AND FINANCIAL AID

Financial aid office: (800) 233-3550. **Expenses (2010-2011):** Tuition and fees 2010-2011: $14,996; room/board: $4,790. Estimated books and supplies: $700; transportation: $150; personal expenses: $800. **Financial aid:** Priority filing date for institution's financial aid form: April 1. In 2009-2010, 96% of undergraduates applied for financial aid. Of those, 83% were determined to have financial need; 39% had their need fully met. Average financial aid package (proportion receiving): $13,873 (83%). Average amount of gift aid, such as scholarships or grants (proportion receiving): $11,209 (81%). Average amount of self-help aid, such as work study or loans (proportion receiving): $5,297 (77%). Average need-based loan (excluding PLUS or other private loans): $4,107. Among students who received need-based aid, the average percentage of need met: 80%. Among students who received aid based on merit, the average award (and the proportion receiving): $5,163 (10%). The average athletic scholarship (and the proportion receiving): $0 (0%). Average amount of debt of borrowers graduating in 2009: $20,077. Proportion who borrowed: 85%.

CAMPUS LIFE AND EXTRACURRICULAR ACTIVITIES

Campus housing available (% using): coed dorms (70%), women's dorms (19%), men's dorms (11%). **Student employment:** During the 2009-2010 academic year, 82% of undergraduates worked on campus. Average per-year earnings: $4,030. **Clubs and organizations:** Number of student organizations: 32. Activities include: campus ministries, choral groups, concert band, dance, drama/theater, literary magazine, model UN, musical theater, student government, student newspaper, yearbook. Number of fraternities: 0; sororities: 0. Average proportion of students who stay on campus on weekends: 65%. **Sports program (2009-2010):** Member of NCAA III. *Men's intercollegiate varsity sports:* baseball, basketball, cross country, football, golf, soccer. *Women's intercollegiate varsity sports:* basketball, cross country, soccer, softball, tennis, volleyball.

SERVICES AND FACILITIES

Basic services: nonremedial tutoring, placement service, health insurance. **Remedial assistance:** math, writing, study skills. **Counseling services:** minority student, career, personal, academic, psychological, religious. **For learning-disabled students:** School does not offer a structured program with separate admission and additional fees. Services include: remedial math, remedial English, tape recorders, videotaped classes, untimed tests, note-taking services, oral tests, learning center, readers, extended time for tests, tutors, priority seating, texts on tape, other. **Library:** Number of titles: 61,586; number of current serial subscriptions: 79. **Information technology resources:** Students are not required to lease or own a computer. Number of campus computers available to all students: 58. School has a wireless network. Proportion of college-owned housing units wired for high-speed internet access: 100%. **Campus safety:** Security services offered: late-night transport/escort service, 24-hour emergency telephones, lighted pathways/sidewalks, student patrols, controlled dormitory access (key, security card, etc).

TRANSFER AND INTERNATIONAL STUDENTS

Transfer students: May apply for admission for the following academic terms: Fall, Spring, Summer. Applicants do not need a minimum number of credits to apply. For fall 2009: Transfer applications received: 157. Transfer applicants offered admission: 87. Transfer applicants enrolled: 56. **International students:** Number of foreign undergraduates: 0. Minimum TOEFL score required: 525 (paper); 197 (computer).

Bradley University

- **Address:** 1501 W. Bradley Avenue, Peoria, IL 61625
- **Website:** http://www.bradley.edu
- **Private**
- **Enrollment:** 4,801 full-time; 260 part-time

KEY STATS

✔ **U.S News College Ranking:** 6, Regional Universities (Midwest)
✔ **ACT Score (25th/75th percentile):** 22-27
✔ **Tuition:** 2010-2011: $25,424

Selectivity: More selective	**Room/board:** $7,950
Acceptance rate: 74%	**Average debt:** N/A
Student/faculty ratio: 13/1	**Proportion who borrowed:** N/A

UNDERGRADUATE STUDENT BODY STATS

2009-2010 enrollment: 4,801 full-time; 260 part-time. Men: 46%; women: 54%. **Ethnic makeup:** African American: 8%; Asian American: 4%; Hispanic: 4%; White: 83%; International: 1%. **Religious preference:** Roman Catholic: 32%; Protestant: 21%; Jewish: 4%; No preference: 14%; Other: 29%.

ADMISSIONS FACTS AND FIGURES

Phone: (800) 447-6460. **Email:** admissions@bradley.edu. **Website:** http://www.bradley.edu. **Application deadlines for fall 2011:** Regular decision: Rolling. Early decision: Not offered. Early action: Not offered. Admission can be deferred. **Application fee:** $35. **To apply online, go to:** http://admissions.bradley.edu/freshman/application/. **Admissions requirements/recommendations:** High school units required (recommended): English: 4 (5); Mathematics: 3 (4); Science: 2 (3); Foreign language: (2); Social studies: 2 (3); Total units: 11 (17). **Tests:** The college uses SAT or ACT scores in admissions decisions. Either SAT or ACT required. For admission to the fall 2011 entering class, the school will accept: ACT with or without writing accepted. Campus visit: Recommended. Admissions interview: Recommended. Off-campus interview: May be arranged. **Factors that count in admissions decisions:** *Academic:* Secondary school record: Very Important. Class rank: Important. Letters of recommendation: Considered. Standardized test scores: Important. Essay: Considered. *Nonacademic:* Interview: Considered. Extracurricular activities: Important. Talent/ability: Considered. Character/personal qualities: Considered. Alumni/ae relationship: Considered. Geographical residence: Considered. State residency: Not Considered. Religious affiliation/commitment: Not Considered. Minority status: Considered. Volunteer work: Considered. Work experience: Considered. **Other schools with the greatest overlap in applicants:** Illinois State University; Marquette University; Northern Illinois University; University of Illinois–Chicago; University of Illinois–Urbana-Champaign. **Admissions statistics for the fall 2009 entering class:** Total applicants: 6,221. Total accepted: 4,573. Freshmen enrolled: 1,106; 13% were from out of state. Overall acceptance rate: 74%. **Size of waiting list:** 0 applicants; enrolled from waiting list: 0. **Credentials of fall 2009 freshmen:** 26% ranked in the top 10 percent of their high school class; 60% were in the top 25 percent; 91% were in the top half. (Proportion submitting class standing: 77%.) **Average high school grade point average:** 3.6. **First-year students who submitted SAT scores:** 7%. Scores (25/75 percentile): Critical Reading: 480-600, Math: 510-

640, Combined: 990-1240. **First-year students submitting ACT scores:** 97%. Scores (25/75 percentile): English: 22-28, Math: 22-28, Composite: 22-27.

ACADEMICS

Year founded: 1897. **Academic calendar:** Semester. **Degrees offered:** bachelor's, master's. **Most popular majors:** 6% nursing/registered nurse training (R.N., A.S.N., B.S.N., M.S.N.), 5% elementary education and teaching, 5% health professions and related clinical sciences, 5% psychology, 4% business administration and management. **Major fields of study:** agriculture, agriculture operations, and related sciences; biological and biomedical sciences; business, management, marketing, and related support services; communication, journalism, and related programs; communications technologies/technicians and support services; computer and information sciences and support services; education; engineering; engineering technologies/technicians; English language and literature/letters; family and consumer sciences/human sciences; foreign languages, literatures, and linguistics; health professions and related clinical sciences; history; liberal arts and sciences studies, and humanities; mathematics and statistics; natural resources and conservation; philosophy and religious studies; physical sciences; psychology; public administration and social service professions; security and protective services; social sciences; visual and performing arts. **Areas of required coursework:** arts/fine arts, humanities, computer literacy, mathematics, English (including composition), sciences (biological or physical), social science, other. **Pre-professional programs:** pre-law, other. **Special academic programs (% participation):** cooperative (work-study plan) program (10%), double major (8%), honors program (10%), independent study, internships (26%), student-designed major, study abroad (20%), teacher certificate program (13%). **Teacher certification offered in:** early childhood, special education, elementary, secondary. **Cooperative education programs:** art, business, computer science, education, engineering, health professions, home economics, humanities, natural science, social/behavioral science, technologies. **Reserve Officers Training Corps (ROTC):** Army ROTC: Offered on campus. **Faculty and instruction (2009-2010):** Total instructional faculty: 345 full-time, 204 part-time (58% men; 42% women; 11% minorities). Full-time faculty with Ph.D. or other terminal degree: 83%. Student/faculty ratio: 13/1. Classes of fewer than 20 students: 47%; of 20 to 49 students: 49%; of 50 or more students: 4%. **Advanced Placement and International Baccalaureate credit:** AP tests may be used for: Credit only. Scores accepted: 4, 5. International Baccalaureate exams may be used for: Credit only. **Freshmen returning for sophomore year:** 88%. **Graduation rates:** Four-year: 52%; five-year: 73%; six-year: 76%. **Graduate study:** 19% of students pursue further study immediately upon graduation. Fields in which graduates pursue further study: Master of Business Administration (MBA), 2%; law, 6%; medicine, 1%; dentistry, 1%; engineering, 61%; education, 6%; arts and sciences, 16%.

COSTS AND FINANCIAL AID

Financial aid office: (309) 677-3089. **Expenses (2010-2011):** Tuition and fees 2010-2011: $25,424; room/board: $7,950. Estimated books and supplies: $1,200; transportation: $250; personal expenses: $1,876. **Financial aid:** Priority filing date for institution's financial aid form: March 1. In 2009-2010, 84% of undergraduates applied for financial aid. Of those, 72% were determined to have financial need; 18% had their need fully met. Average financial aid package (proportion receiving): $16,201 (71%). Average amount of gift aid, such as scholarships or grants (proportion receiving): $12,618 (68%). Average amount of self-help aid, such as work study or loans (proportion receiving): $4,810 (60%). Average need-based loan (excluding PLUS or other private loans): $4,608. Among students who received need-based aid, the average percentage of need met: 69%. Among students who received aid based on merit, the average award (and the proportion receiving): $7,764 (28%). The average athletic scholarship (and the proportion receiving): $15,581 (2%).

CAMPUS LIFE AND EXTRACURRICULAR ACTIVITIES

Campus housing available (% using): coed dorms (60%), sorority housing (7%), fraternity housing (11%), apartments for married students, apartment for single students (3%), other housing options (19%). Students who live in college-owned, operated, or affiliated housing: 68%. **Student employment:** During the 2009-2010 academic year, 20% of undergraduates worked on campus. Average per-year earnings: $1,100. **Clubs and organizations:** Number of student organizations: 250. Activities include: campus ministries, choral groups, concert band, dance, drama/theater, international student organization, jazz band, literary magazine, music ensembles, pep band, radio station, student government, student newspaper, student film society, symphony orchestra. Number of fraternities: 17; sororities: 12. Proportion of men in fraternities: 35%; of women in sororities: 27%.

Average proportion of students who stay on campus on weekends: 75%.
Sports program (2009-2010): Member of NCAA I. *Men's intercollegiate varsity sports:* baseball, basketball, cross country, golf, soccer, tennis. *Women's intercollegiate varsity sports:* basketball, cross country, golf, softball, tennis, track and field (indoor), track and field (outdoor), volleyball.

SERVICES AND FACILITIES
Basic services: nonremedial tutoring, placement service, health service, health insurance. **Remedial assistance:** study skills, other. **Counseling services:** minority student, career, academic, psychological. **For learning-disabled students:** School does not offer a structured program with separate admission and additional fees. Total undergraduates in learning-disabled program or receiving services: 188. Services include: tape recorders, video-taped classes, untimed tests, learning center, extended time for tests, tutors. **Library:** Number of titles: 511,000; number of current serial subscriptions: 41,689. **Information technology resources:** Students are not required to lease or own a computer. Number of campus computers available to all students: 2,500. School has a wireless network. Approximate number of users that can be accommodated: 1,600. Proportion of college-owned housing units wired for high-speed internet access: 100%. **Campus safety:** Security services offered: 24-hour foot-and-vehicle patrols, late-night transport/escort service, 24-hour emergency telephones, lighted pathways/sidewalks, controlled dormitory access (key, security card, etc).

TRANSFER AND INTERNATIONAL STUDENTS
Transfer students: May apply for admission for the following academic terms: Fall, Winter, Spring, Summer. Applicants need a minimum number of credits to apply. For fall 2009: Transfer applications received: 1,057. Transfer applicants offered admission: 664. Transfer applicants enrolled: 303. **International students:** Number of foreign undergraduates: 30 (1% of student body). Number of countries represented: 21. Minimum TOEFL score required: 530 (paper); 79 (computer).

Chicago State University

- **Address:** 9501 S. King Drive, Chicago, IL 60628
- **Website:** http://www.csu.edu
- **Public**
- **Enrollment:** N/A

KEY STATS
✔ **U.S News College Ranking:** second tier, Regional Universities (Midwest)
✔ **SAT or ACT Score (25th/75th percentile):** N/A
✔ **Tuition:** 2009-2010: $8,006 in state, $13,922 out of state

Selectivity: Selective	**Room/board:** $7,540
Acceptance rate: N/A	**Average debt:** N/A
Student/faculty ratio: N/A	**Proportion who borrowed:** N/A

Columbia College

- **Address:** 600 S. Michigan Avenue, Chicago, IL 60605-1996
- **Website:** http://www.colum.edu
- **Private**
- **Enrollment:** N/A

KEY STATS
✔ **U.S News College Ranking:** Unranked, Regional Universities (Midwest)
✔ **SAT or ACT Score (25th/75th percentile):** N/A
✔ **Tuition:** 2009-2010: $18,960

Selectivity: N/A	**Room/board:** $12,360
Acceptance rate: N/A	**Average debt:** N/A
Student/faculty ratio: N/A	**Proportion who borrowed:** N/A

Concordia University Chicago

- **Address:** 7400 Augusta Street, River Forest, IL 60305-1499
- **Website:** http://www.cuchicago.edu/index.asp
- **Private; Religious affiliation:** Lutheran
- **Enrollment:** 1,180 full-time; 90 part-time

KEY STATS
✔ **U.S News College Ranking:** 92, Regional Universities (Midwest)
✔ **ACT Score (25th/75th percentile):** 19-24
✔ **Tuition:** 2010-2011: $24,406

Selectivity: Selective	**Room/board:** $8,000
Acceptance rate: 83%	**Average debt:** $26,577
Student/faculty ratio: 17/1	**Proportion who borrowed:** 82%

UNDERGRADUATE STUDENT BODY STATS
2009-2010 enrollment: 1,180 full-time; 90 part-time. Men: 43%; women: 57%. **Ethnic makeup:** African American: 12%; Asian American: 2%; Hispanic: 13%; White: 73%; International: 1%.

ADMISSIONS FACTS AND FIGURES
Phone: (708) 209-3100. **Email:** admission@cuchicago.edu. **Website:** http://www.cuchicago.edu/index.asp. **Application deadlines for fall 2011:** Regular decision: Rolling. Early decision: Not offered. Early action: Not offered. Admission can be deferred. **To apply online, go to:** https://www.cuchicago.edu/admission/undergrad/freshman/online_app.asp. **Admissions requirements/recommendations:** High school units required (recommended): English: 4 (4); Mathematics: 3 (3); Science: 2 (4); Foreign language: (2); Social studies: 2 (2); History: (1); Total units: 15. Tests: The college uses SAT or ACT scores in admissions decisions. ACT required. For admission to the fall 2011 entering class, the school will accept: ACT with or without writing accepted. Campus visit: Recommended. Admissions interview: Recommended. Off-campus interview: May be arranged. **Factors that count in admissions decisions:** *Academic:* Secondary school record: Important. Class rank: Important. Letters of recommendation: Considered. Standardized test scores: Important. Essay: Considered. *Nonacademic:* Interview: Considered. Extracurricular activities: Considered. Talent/ability: Not Considered. Character/personal qualities: Considered. Alumni/ae relationship: Not Considered. Geographical residence: Not Considered. State residency: Not Considered. Religious affiliation/commitment: Not Considered. Minority status: Not Considered. Volunteer work: Not Considered. Work experience: Not Considered. **Admissions statistics for the fall 2009 entering class:** Total applicants: 1,742. Total accepted: 1,452. Freshmen enrolled: 363; 38% were from out of state. Overall acceptance rate: 83%. **Average high school grade point average:** 3.1. **First-year students who submitted SAT scores:** 12%. Scores (25/75 percentile): Critical Reading: 460-580, Math: 460-570, Combined: 920-1150. **First-year students submitting ACT scores:** 93%. Scores (25/75 percentile): English: N/A, Math: N/A, Composite: 19-24.

ACADEMICS
Year founded: 1864. **Academic calendar:** Semester. **Degrees offered:** bachelor's, post-bachelor's certificate, master's, post-master's certificate, doctorate. **Most popular majors:** 36% teacher education, 18% business, management, marketing, and related support services, 8% psychology, 7% communication, journalism, and related programs, 7% visual and performing arts. **Major fields of study:** biological and biomedical sciences; business, management, marketing, and related support services; computer and information sciences and support services; education; English language and literature/letters; health professions and related clinical sciences; history; liberal arts and sciences studies, and humanities; mathematics and statistics; multi/interdisciplinary studies; physical sciences; psychology; public administration and social service professions; social sciences; theology and religious vocations; visual and performing arts. **Areas of required coursework:** arts/fine arts, humanities, computer literacy, mathematics, English (including composition), foreign languages, sciences (biological or physical), history, social science. **Pre-professional programs:** pre-law, pre-dentistry, pre-medicine, pre-theology. **Special academic programs:** distance learning, double major, exchange student program (domestic), honors program, independent study, internships, study abroad, teacher certificate program. **Teacher certification offered in:** early childhood, special education, elementary, middle/junior high, secondary. **Faculty and instruction (2009-2010):** Total instructional faculty: 122 full-time, 200 part-time. Full-time faculty with Ph.D. or other terminal degree: 76%. Student/faculty ratio: 17/1. Classes of fewer than 20 students: 58%; of 20 to 49 students: 41%; of 50 or more students:

1%. **Advanced Placement and International Baccalaureate credit:** AP tests may be used for: Credit only. **Freshmen returning for sophomore year:** 73%. **Graduation rates:** Four-year: 39%; five-year: 45%; six-year: 50%. **Graduate study:** 24% of students pursue further study immediately upon graduation.

COSTS AND FINANCIAL AID

Financial aid office: (708) 209-3113. **Expenses (2010-2011):** Tuition and fees 2010-2011: $24,406; room/board: $8,000. Estimated books and supplies: $1,200; transportation: $600; personal expenses: $800. **Financial aid:** Priority filing date for institution's financial aid form: April 1; deadline: June 1. In 2009-2010, 94% of undergraduates applied for financial aid. Of those, 84% were determined to have financial need; 20% had their need fully met. Average financial aid package (proportion receiving): $17,219 (84%). Average amount of gift aid, such as scholarships or grants (proportion receiving): $13,364 (83%). Average amount of self-help aid, such as work study or loans (proportion receiving): $4,057 (67%). Average need-based loan (excluding PLUS or other private loans): $4,077. Among students who received need-based aid, the average percentage of need met: 76%. Among students who received aid based on merit, the average award (and the proportion receiving): $10,057 (15%). The average athletic scholarship (and the proportion receiving): $0 (0%). Average amount of debt of borrowers graduating in 2009: $26,577. Proportion who borrowed: 82%.

CAMPUS LIFE AND EXTRACURRICULAR ACTIVITIES

Campus housing available: coed dorms, women's dorms, men's dorms, special housing for disabled students. Students who live in college-owned, operated, or affiliated housing: 70%. **Clubs and organizations:** Number of student organizations: 30. Activities include: campus ministries, choral groups, concert band, dance, drama/theater, jazz band, literary magazine, music ensembles, musical theater, pep band, radio station, student government, student newspaper, yearbook. Number of fraternities: 0; sororities: 0. **Sports program (2009-2010):** Member of NCAA III. *Men's intercollegiate varsity sports:* baseball, basketball, cross country, football, soccer, tennis, track and field (outdoor). *Women's intercollegiate varsity sports:* basketball, cross country, soccer, softball, tennis, track and field (outdoor), volleyball.

SERVICES AND FACILITIES

Basic services: nonremedial tutoring, placement service, day care, health insurance. **Remedial assistance:** writing. **Counseling services:** career, personal, academic, psychological, religious. **Library:** Number of titles: 159,716; number of current serial subscriptions: 160. **Information technology resources:** Students are not required to lease or own a computer. Number of campus computers available to all students: 95. School has a wireless network. Proportion of college-owned housing units wired for high-speed internet access: 100%. **Campus safety:** Security services offered: 24-hour foot-and-vehicle patrols, late-night transport/escort service, 24-hour emergency telephones, lighted pathways/sidewalks, student patrols, controlled dormitory access (key, security card, etc).

TRANSFER AND INTERNATIONAL STUDENTS

Transfer students: May apply for admission for the following academic terms: Fall, Spring, Summer. Applicants need a minimum number of credits to apply. For fall 2009: Transfer applications received: 248. Transfer applicants offered admission: 234. Transfer applicants enrolled: 101. **International students:** Number of foreign undergraduates: 8 (1% of student body). Number of countries represented: 1. Minimum TOEFL score required: 525 (paper); 72 (computer).

DePaul University

- **Address:** 1 E. Jackson Boulevard, Chicago, IL 60604-2287
- **Website:** http://www.depaul.edu
- **Private; Religious affiliation:** Roman Catholic
- **Enrollment:** 13,213 full-time; 2,986 part-time

KEY STATS

✔ **U.S News College Ranking:** 136, National Universities
✔ **ACT Score (25th/75th percentile):** 22-27
✔ **Tuition:** 2010-2011: $28,858

Selectivity: More selective	**Room/board:** $10,955
Acceptance rate: 74%	**Average debt:** $19,072
Student/faculty ratio: 17/1	**Proportion who borrowed:** 64%

UNDERGRADUATE STUDENT BODY STATS

2009-2010 enrollment: 13,213 full-time; 2,986 part-time. Men: 45%; women: 55%. **Ethnic makeup:** African American: 9%; Asian American: 8%; Hispanic: 13%; White: 68%; International: 1%. **Religious preference:** Protestant: 2%; Jewish: 2%; Muslim: 3%; Hindu: 1%; Buddhist: 1%; No preference: 6%; Unknown: 23%; Roman Catholic: 37%; Christian Orthodox: 3%; Other: 22%.

ADMISSIONS FACTS AND FIGURES

Phone: (312) 362-8300. **Email:** admission@depaul.edu. **Website:** http://www.depaul.edu. **Application deadlines for fall 2011:** Regular decision: February 1; decision sent by March 15. Early decision: Not offered. Early action: Send application by: November 15; Decision sent by: January 15. Admission can be deferred. **Application fee:** $40. **To apply online, go to:** https://wa.is.depaul.edu/AdmissionApp/login.aspx. **Admissions requirements/recommendations:** High school units required (recommended): English: 4; Mathematics: 3; Science: 3; Foreign language: (2); Total units: 12 (2). Tests: The college uses SAT or ACT scores in admissions decisions. Either SAT or ACT required. For admission to the fall 2011 entering class, the school will accept: ACT with or without writing accepted. Campus visit: Recommended. Admissions interview: Neither required nor recommended. Off-campus interview: May be arranged. **Factors that count in admissions decisions:** *Academic:* Secondary school record: Very Important. Class rank: Important. Letters of recommendation: Important. Standardized test scores: Very Important. Essay: Very Important. *Nonacademic:* Interview: Considered. Extracurricular activities: Important. Talent/ability: Important. Character/personal qualities: Important. Alumni/ae relationship: Considered. Geographical residence: Considered. State residency: Considered. Religious affiliation/commitment: Considered. Minority status: Considered. Volunteer work: Important. Work experience: Important. **Other schools with the greatest overlap in applicants:** Loyola University Chicago; Northern Illinois University; Northwestern University; University of Illinois–Chicago; University of Illinois–Urbana-Champaign. **Admissions statistics for the fall 2009 entering class:** Total applicants: 11,564. Total accepted: 8,584. Freshmen enrolled: 2,531; 31% were from out of state. Overall acceptance rate: 74%. Non-early acceptance rate: 74%. **Credentials of fall 2009 freshmen:** 22% ranked in the top 10 percent of their high school class; 51% were in the top 25 percent; 85% were in the top half. (Proportion submitting class standing: 43%.) **Average high school grade point average:** 3.5. **First-year students who submitted SAT scores:** 21%. Scores (25/75 percentile): Critical Reading: 520-640, Math: 520-620, Combined: 1040-1260. **First-year students submitting ACT scores:** 88%. Scores (25/75 percentile): English: 22-28, Math: 21-27, Composite: 22-27.

ACADEMICS

Year founded: 1898. **Academic calendar:** Quarter. **Degrees offered:** certificate, bachelor's, post-bachelor's certificate, master's, post-master's certificate, doctorate. **Most popular majors:** 33% business, management, marketing, and related support services, 10% communication, journalism, and related programs, 10% social sciences, 9% liberal arts and sciences studies, and humanities, 8% psychology. **Major fields of study:** area, ethnic, cultural, and gender studies; biological and biomedical sciences; business, management, marketing, and related support services; communication, journalism, and related programs; computer and information sciences and support services; education; English language and literature/letters; foreign languages, literatures, and linguistics; health professions and related clinical sciences; liberal arts and sciences studies, and humanities; mathematics and statistics; natural resources and conservation; philosophy and religious studies; physical sciences; psychology; public administration and social service professions; social sciences; visual and performing arts. **Areas of required coursework:** arts/fine arts, humanities, computer literacy, mathematics, English (including composition), philosophy, foreign languages, sciences (biological or physical), history, social science, other. **Pre-professional programs:** pre-law, pre-dentistry, pre-medicine, pre-veterinary science, other. **Special academic programs (% participation):** accelerated program, cooperative (work-study plan) program, distance learning (10.2%), double major (9.7%), dual enrollment, English as a Second Language (ESL) (.2%), honors program (6.4%), independent study (14.4%), internships (38%), student-designed major (9.1%), study abroad (7.53%), teacher certificate program (5.71%), weekend college. **Teacher certification offered in:** early childhood, special education, elementary, middle/junior high, secondary, bilingual/bicultural. **Cooperative education programs:** art, business, computer science, education, engineering, health professions, home economics, humanities, natural science, social/behavioral science, technologies, vocational arts, other. **Reserve Officers Training Corps (ROTC):** Army ROTC: Offered at cooperating institution (University of Illinois–Chicago). **Faculty**

and instruction (2009-2010): Total instructional faculty: 919 full-time, 906 part-time (57% men; 43% women; 18% minorities). Full-time faculty with Ph.D. or other terminal degree: 88%. Student/faculty ratio: 17/1. Classes of fewer than 20 students: 35%; of 20 to 49 students: 64%; of 50 or more students: 1%. **Advanced Placement and International Baccalaureate credit:** AP tests may be used for: Credit and/or placement. Scores accepted: 4, 5. International Baccalaureate exams may be used for: Credit and/or placement. **Freshmen returning for sophomore year:** 84%. **Graduation rates:** Four-year: 43%; five-year: 60%; six-year: 63%. **Graduate study:** 21% of students pursue further study immediately upon graduation. Fields in which graduates pursue further study: Master of Business Administration (MBA), 14%; law, 22%; medicine, 1%; dentistry, 1%; theology (or the seminary), 1%; education, 11%; arts and sciences, 53%.

COSTS AND FINANCIAL AID

Financial aid office: (312) 362-8091. **Expenses (2010-2011):** Tuition and fees 2010-2011: $28,858; room/board: $10,955. Estimated books and supplies: $1,134; transportation: $744; personal expenses: $1,750. **Financial aid:** Priority filing date for institution's financial aid form: March 1. In 2009-2010, 81% of undergraduates applied for financial aid. Of those, 66% were determined to have financial need; 10% had their need fully met. Average financial aid package (proportion receiving): $20,459 (63%). Average amount of gift aid, such as scholarships or grants (proportion receiving): $14,428 (51%). Average amount of self-help aid, such as work study or loans (proportion receiving): $6,228 (54%). Average need-based loan (excluding PLUS or other private loans): $4,732. Among students who received need-based aid, the average percentage of need met: 67%. Among students who received aid based on merit, the average award (and the proportion receiving): $9,128 (4%). The average athletic scholarship (and the proportion receiving): $20,056 (2%). Average amount of debt of borrowers graduating in 2009: $19,072. Proportion who borrowed: 64%.

CAMPUS LIFE AND EXTRACURRICULAR ACTIVITIES

Campus housing available (% using): coed dorms (100%), apartment for single students, special housing for disabled students, special housing for international students, other housing options. Students who live in college-owned, operated, or affiliated housing: 17%. **Student employment:** During the 2009-2010 academic year, 18% of undergraduates worked on campus. Average per-year earnings: $5,000. **Clubs and organizations:** Number of student organizations: 311. Activities include: campus ministries, choral groups, concert band, dance, drama/theater, international student organization, jazz band, literary magazine, marching band, model UN, music ensembles, musical theater, opera, pep band, radio station, student government, student newspaper, student film society, symphony orchestra, yearbook. Number of fraternities: 9; sororities: 13. Average proportion of students who stay on campus on weekends: 75%. **Sports program (2009-2010):** Member of NCAA I. **Men's intercollegiate varsity sports:** basketball, cross country, golf, soccer, tennis, track and field (indoor), track and field (outdoor). **Women's intercollegiate varsity sports:** basketball, cross country, soccer, softball, tennis, track and field (indoor), track and field (outdoor), volleyball.

SERVICES AND FACILITIES

Basic services: nonremedial tutoring, women's center, placement service, health service, health insurance. **Remedial assistance:** reading, math, writing, study skills. **Counseling services:** minority student, career, military, personal, veteran student, academic, older student, psychological, birth control, religious. **For learning-disabled students:** School does not offer a structured program with separate admission and additional fees. Total undergraduates in learning-disabled program or receiving services: 420. Services include: remedial math, remedial English, untimed tests, oral tests, readers, extended time for tests, tutors, priority registration, texts on tape, exams on tape or computer, other testing accommodations, other. **Library:** Number of titles: 925,495; number of current serial subscriptions: 54,841. **Information technology resources:** Students are not required to lease or own a computer. Number of campus computers available to all students: 1,800. School has a wireless network. Approximate number of users that can be accommodated: 3,575. Proportion of college-owned housing units wired for high-speed internet access: 100%. **Campus safety:** Security services offered: 24-hour foot-and-vehicle patrols, late-night transport/escort service, 24-hour emergency telephones, lighted pathways/sidewalks, controlled dormitory access (key, security card, etc).

TRANSFER AND INTERNATIONAL STUDENTS

Transfer students: May apply for admission for the following academic terms: Fall, Winter, Spring, Summer. Applicants do not need a minimum

number of credits to apply. For fall 2009: Transfer applications received: 4,674. Transfer applicants offered admission: 2,979. Transfer applicants enrolled: 1,655. **International students:** Number of foreign undergraduates: 198 (1% of student body). Number of countries represented: 61. Minimum TOEFL score required: 550 (paper); 80 (computer).

Dominican University

■ **Address:** 7900 W. Division, River Forest, IL 60305
■ **Website:** http://www.dom.edu
■ **Private; Religious affiliation:** Roman Catholic
■ **Enrollment:** 1,707 full-time; 197 part-time

KEY STATS

✔ **U.S News College Ranking:** 19, Regional Universities (Midwest)
✔ **ACT Score (25th/75th percentile):** 20-25
✔ **Tuition:** 2010-2011: $25,710

Selectivity: Selective	**Room/board:** $8,000
Acceptance rate: 72%	**Average debt:** $21,392
Student/faculty ratio: 12/1	**Proportion who borrowed:** 89%

UNDERGRADUATE STUDENT BODY STATS

2009-2010 enrollment: 1,707 full-time; 197 part-time. Men: 31%; women: 69%. **Ethnic makeup:** African American: 6%; Asian American: 2%; Hispanic: 26%; White: 63%; International: 2%. **Religious preference:** Protestant: 1%; Jewish: 1%; Muslim: 1%; Buddhist: 1%; No preference: 5%; Unknown: 15%; Roman Catholic: 60%; Christian: 8%; Other: 8%.

ADMISSIONS FACTS AND FIGURES

Phone: (708) 524-6800. **Email:** domadmis@dom.edu. **Website:** http://www.dom.edu. **Application deadlines for fall 2011:** Regular decision: Rolling. Early decision: Not offered. Early action: Not offered. Admission can be deferred. **Application fee:** $25. **To apply online, go to:** http://www.illinoismentor.org/Applications/Dominican_University/apply.html. **Admissions requirements/recommendations:** High school units required (recommended): English: (4); Mathematics: (3); Science: (3); Foreign language: (2); Social studies: (1); History: (2); Total units: 16. Tests: The college uses SAT or ACT scores in admissions decisions. Either SAT or ACT required. For admission to the fall 2011 entering class, the school will accept: ACT with or without writing accepted. Campus visit: Recommended. Admissions interview: Recommended. Off-campus interview: May be arranged. **Factors that count in admissions decisions:** *Academic:* Secondary school record: Very Important. Class rank: Important. Letters of recommendation: Considered. Standardized test scores: Important. Essay: Important. *Nonacademic:* Interview: Considered. Extracurricular activities: Considered. Talent/ability: Considered. Character/personal qualities: Important. Alumni/ae relationship: Considered. Geographical residence: Not Considered. State residency: Not Considered. Religious affiliation/commitment: Not Considered. Minority status: Not Considered. Volunteer work: Considered. Work experience: Considered. **Other schools with the greatest overlap in applicants:** DePaul University; Elmhurst College; Loyola University Chicago; Northeastern Illinois University; University of Illinois–Chicago. **Admissions statistics for the fall 2009 entering class:** Total applicants: 1,768. Total accepted: 1,277. Freshmen enrolled: 405; 9% were from out of state. Overall acceptance rate: 72%. **Credentials of fall 2009 freshmen:** 19% ranked in the top 10 percent of their high school class; 50% were in the top 25 percent; 85% were in the top half. (Proportion submitting class standing: 75%.) **Average high school grade point average:** 3.5. **First-year students who submitted SAT scores:** 7%. Scores (25/75 percentile): Critical Reading: 460-580, Math: 430-580, Combined: 890-1160. **First-year students submitting ACT scores:** 99%. Scores (25/75 percentile): English: 20-26, Math: 18-25, Composite: 20-25.

ACADEMICS

Year founded: 1901. **Academic calendar:** Semester. **Degrees offered:** certificate, bachelor's, post-bachelor's certificate, master's, post-master's certificate, doctorate. **Most popular majors:** 13% business administration and management, 8% psychology, 7% dietetics/dietitian (R.D.), 6% natural sciences, 5% English language and literature. **Major fields of study:** area, ethnic, cultural, and gender studies; biological and biomedical sciences; business, management, marketing, and related support services; communication, journalism, and related programs; computer and information sciences and support services; English language and literature/letters; family and consumer sciences/human sciences; foreign languages, literatures, and linguistics; health professions and related clinical sciences; history; liberal arts and sciences studies, and humanities; mathematics and statistics; multi/interdisciplinary studies; natural resources and conservation; philosophy and religious studies; physical sciences; psychology; social sciences; theology and religious vocations; visual and performing arts. **Areas of required coursework:** arts/fine arts, humanities, computer literacy, mathematics, English (including composition), philosophy, foreign languages, sciences (biological or physical), history, social science, other. **Pre-professional programs:** pre-law, pre-dentistry, pre-medicine, pre-veterinary science, pre-optometry, pre-pharmacy, other. **Special academic programs (% participation):** accelerated program (3%), cross-registration, distance learning (1%), double major (10%), dual enrollment, exchange student program (domestic) (1%), honors program (8%), independent study (5%), internships (10%), liberal arts/career combination, student-designed major (1%), study abroad (8%), teacher certificate program (5%). **Teacher certification offered in:** early childhood, special education, elementary, middle/junior high, secondary, bilingual/bicultural. **Faculty and instruction (2009-2010):** Total instructional faculty: 142 full-time, 224 part-time (41% men; 59% women; 14% minorities). Full-time faculty with Ph.D. or other terminal degree: 84%. Student/faculty ratio: 12/1. Classes of fewer than 20 students: 63%; of 20 to 49 students: 37%; of 50 or more students: 0%. **Advanced Placement and International Baccalaureate credit:** AP tests may be used for: Credit and/or placement. Scores accepted: 3, 4, 5. International Baccalaureate exams may be used for: Credit and/or placement. **Freshmen returning for sophomore year:** 80%. **Graduation rates:** Four-year: 60%; five-year: 71%; six-year: 68%. **Graduate study:** 25% of students pursue further study immediately upon graduation; 35% within one year; 50% within five years. Fields in which graduates pursue further study: Master of Business Administration (MBA), 30%; law, 5%; medicine, 5%; dentistry, 1%; engineering, 1%; theology (or the seminary), 1%; education, 30%; arts and sciences, 15%.

COSTS AND FINANCIAL AID
Financial aid office: (708) 524-6809. **Expenses (2010-2011):** Tuition and fees 2010-2011: $25,710; room/board: $8,000. Estimated books and supplies: $1,200; transportation: $90; personal expenses: $1,000. **Financial aid:** Priority filing date for institution's financial aid form: April 15. In 2009-2010, 90% of undergraduates applied for financial aid. Of those, 83% were determined to have financial need; 14% had their need fully met. Average financial aid package (proportion receiving): $18,277 (83%). Average amount of gift aid, such as scholarships or grants (proportion receiving): $14,403 (81%). Average amount of self-help aid, such as work study or loans (proportion receiving): $4,922 (71%). Average need-based loan (excluding PLUS or other private loans): $4,132. Among students who received need-based aid, the average percentage of need met: 74%. Among students who received aid based on merit, the average award (and the proportion receiving): $7,912 (12%). The average athletic scholarship (and the proportion receiving): $0 (0%). Average amount of debt of borrowers graduating in 2009: $21,392. Proportion who borrowed: 89%.

CAMPUS LIFE AND EXTRACURRICULAR ACTIVITIES
Campus housing available (% using): coed dorms (94%), special housing for disabled students (1%), other housing options (5%). Students who live in college-owned, operated, or affiliated housing: 35%. **Student employment:** During the 2009-2010 academic year, 30% of undergraduates worked on campus. Average per-year earnings: $2,500. **Clubs and organizations:** Number of student organizations: 52. Activities include: choral groups, dance, drama/theater, literary magazine, musical theater, student government, student newspaper. Number of fraternities: 0; sororities: 0. Average proportion of students who stay on campus on weekends: 60%. **Sports program (2009-2010):** Member of NCAA III. *Men's intercollegiate varsity sports:* baseball, basketball, cross country, golf, soccer, tennis. *Women's intercollegiate varsity sports:* basketball, cross country, soccer, softball, tennis, volleyball.

SERVICES AND FACILITIES
Basic services: nonremedial tutoring, placement service, day care, health service, health insurance. **Remedial assistance:** math, writing, study skills, other. **Counseling services:** minority student, career, personal, veteran student, academic, psychological, religious. **For learning-disabled students:** School does not offer a structured program with separate admission and additional fees. Total undergraduates in learning-disabled program or receiving services: 53. Services include: reading machines, tape recorders, note-taking services, learning center, readers, extended time for tests, tutors, priority seating, proofreading services, texts on tape, typist/scribe, exams on tape or computer, other testing accommodations. **Library:** Number of

titles: 347,164; number of current serial subscriptions: 656. **Information technology resources:** Students are not required to lease or own a computer. Number of campus computers available to all students: 625. School has a wireless network. Approximate number of users that can be accommodated: 500. Proportion of college-owned housing units wired for high-speed internet access: 100%. **Campus safety:** Security services offered: 24-hour foot-and-vehicle patrols, late-night transport/escort service, 24-hour emergency telephones, lighted pathways/sidewalks, controlled dormitory access (key, security card, etc).

TRANSFER AND INTERNATIONAL STUDENTS
Transfer students: May apply for admission for the following academic terms: Fall, Spring, Summer. Applicants need a minimum number of credits to apply. For fall 2009: Transfer applications received: 327. Transfer applicants offered admission: 230. Transfer applicants enrolled: 128. **International students:** Number of foreign undergraduates: 42 (2% of student body). Minimum TOEFL score required: 550 (paper); 213 (computer).

Eastern Illinois University

- **Address:** 600 Lincoln Avenue, Charleston, IL 61920-3099
- **Website:** http://www.eiu.edu
- **Public**
- **Enrollment:** 9,205 full-time; 1,020 part-time

KEY STATS
✔ **U.S News College Ranking:** 52, Regional Universities (Midwest)
✔ **ACT Score (25th/75th percentile):** 19-24
✔ **Tuition:** 2009-2010: $9,429 in state, $23,769 out of state

Selectivity: Selective	**Room/board:** $8,078
Acceptance rate: 68%	**Average debt:** $11,547
Student/faculty ratio: 16/1	**Proportion who borrowed:** 53%

UNDERGRADUATE STUDENT BODY STATS
2009-2010 enrollment: 9,205 full-time; 1,020 part-time. Men: 42%; women: 58%. **Ethnic makeup:** African American: 12%; American-Indian: 1%; Asian American: 1%; Hispanic: 3%; White: 84%.

ADMISSIONS FACTS AND FIGURES
Phone: (877) 581-2348. **Email:** admissions@eiu.edu. **Website:** http://www.eiu.edu. **Application deadlines for fall 2011:** Regular decision: Rolling. Early decision: Not offered. Early action: Not offered. Admission can be deferred. **Application fee:** $30. **To apply online, go to:** http://www.applyweb.com/apply/eiu/menu.html. **Admissions requirements/recommendations:** High school units required (recommended): English: 4; Mathematics: 3; Science: 3; Foreign language: (2); Social studies: 3; Academic electives: 2; Total units: 15 (2). Tests: The college uses SAT or ACT scores in admissions decisions. Either SAT or ACT required. For admission to the fall 2011 entering class, the school will accept: ACT with or without writing accepted. Campus visit: Recommended. Admissions interview: Neither required nor recommended. Off-campus interview: May be arranged. **Factors that count in admissions decisions:** *Academic:* Secondary school record: Very Important. Class rank: Important. Letters of recommendation: Considered. Standardized test scores: Very Important. Essay: Considered. *Nonacademic:* Extracurricular activities: Important. Character/personal qualities: Very Important. **Other schools with the greatest overlap in applicants:** Illinois State University; Millikin University; Northern Illinois University; Southern Illinois University–Edwardsville; University of Illinois–Urbana-Champaign. **Admissions statistics for the fall 2009 entering class:** Total applicants: 7,563. Total accepted: 5,173. Freshmen enrolled: 1,654; 2% were from out of state. Overall acceptance rate: 68%. **Credentials of fall 2009 freshmen:** 3% ranked in the top 10 percent of their high school class; 12% were in the top 25 percent; 43% were in the top half. (Proportion submitting class standing: 83%.) **Average high school grade point average:** 3.2. **First-year students submitting ACT scores:** 100%. Scores (25/75 percentile): English: 19-24, Math: 17-24, Composite: 19-24.

ACADEMICS
Year founded: 1895. **Academic calendar:** Semester. **Degrees offered:** bachelor's, post-bachelor's certificate, master's, post-master's certificate. **Most popular majors:** 29% education, 13% business, management, marketing, and related support services, 9% English language and literature/letters, 8% liberal arts and sciences studies, and humanities, 7% family and consumer

sciences/human sciences. **Major fields of study:** area, ethnic, cultural, and gender studies; biological and biomedical sciences; business, management, marketing, and related support services; communication, journalism, and related programs; computer and information sciences and support services; education; engineering; engineering technologies/technicians; English language and literature/letters; family and consumer sciences/human sciences; foreign languages, literatures, and linguistics; health professions and related clinical sciences; history; liberal arts and sciences studies, and humanities; mathematics and statistics; multi/interdisciplinary studies; parks, recreation, leisure, and fitness studies; philosophy and religious studies; physical sciences; psychology; social sciences; visual and performing arts. **Areas of required coursework:** arts/fine arts, humanities, computer literacy, mathematics, English (including composition), foreign languages, sciences (biological or physical), social science, other. **Pre-professional programs:** pre-law, pre-dentistry, pre-medicine, pre-veterinary science, pre-optometry, pre-pharmacy, other. **Special academic programs (% participation):** distance learning (5%), double major (5%), dual enrollment (0%), exchange student program (domestic) (0%), external degree program (8%), honors program (10%), independent study (15%), internships (15%), study abroad (10%), teacher certificate program (28%). **Teacher certification offered in:** early childhood, special education, elementary, vo-tech, middle/junior high, secondary. **Cooperative education programs:** engineering, health professions, other. **Reserve Officers Training Corps (ROTC):** Army ROTC: Offered on campus. **Faculty and instruction (2009-2010):** Total instructional faculty: 629 full-time, 163 part-time (51% men; 49% women; 9% minorities). Full-time faculty with Ph.D. or other terminal degree: 70%. Student/faculty ratio: 16/1. Classes of fewer than 20 students: 32%; of 20 to 49 students: 63%; of 50 or more students: 4%. **Advanced Placement and International Baccalaureate credit:** AP tests may be used for: Credit and/or placement. Scores accepted: 3, 4, 5. **Freshmen returning for sophomore year:** 80%. **Graduation rates:** Four-year: 30%; five-year: 53%; six-year: 59%. **Graduate study:** 23% of students pursue further study within one year; 48% within five years.

COSTS AND FINANCIAL AID

Financial aid office: (217) 581-3713. **Expenses (2009-2010):** Tuition and fees 2009-2010: $9,429 in state, $23,769 out of state; room/board: $8,078. Estimated books and supplies: $120; transportation: $650; personal expenses: $1,600. **Financial aid:** Priority filing date for institution's financial aid form: March 1. In 2009-2010, 96% of undergraduates applied for financial aid. Of those, 53% were determined to have financial need; 9% had their need fully met. Average financial aid package (proportion receiving): $8,912 (50%). Average amount of gift aid, such as scholarships or grants (proportion receiving): $3,632 (28%). Average amount of self-help aid, such as work study or loans (proportion receiving): $3,839 (41%). Average need-based loan (excluding PLUS or other private loans): $4,136. Among students who received need-based aid, the average percentage of need met: 67%. Among students who received aid based on merit, the average award (and the proportion receiving): $3,934 (4%). The average athletic scholarship (and the proportion receiving): $9,282 (2%). Average amount of debt of borrowers graduating in 2009: $11,547. Proportion who borrowed: 53%.

CAMPUS LIFE AND EXTRACURRICULAR ACTIVITIES

Campus housing available (% using): coed dorms (17%), women's dorms (39%), men's dorms (24%), sorority housing (7%), fraternity housing (4%), apartments for married students (3%), apartment for single students (6%), special housing for disabled students (0%). Students who live in college-owned, operated, or affiliated housing: 41%. **Clubs and organizations:** Number of student organizations: 237. Activities include: campus ministries, choral groups, concert band, dance, drama/theater, international student organization, jazz band, literary magazine, marching band, music ensembles, musical theater, opera, pep band, radio station, student government, student newspaper, symphony orchestra, television station, yearbook. Number of fraternities: 16; sororities: 13. Proportion of men in fraternities: 20%; of women in sororities: 13%. Average proportion of students who stay on campus on weekends: 64%. **Sports program (2009-2010):** Member of NCAA I. **Men's intercollegiate varsity sports:** baseball, basketball, cross country, football, golf, soccer, swimming, tennis, track and field (indoor), track and field (outdoor). **Women's intercollegiate varsity sports:** basketball, cross country, golf, rugby, soccer, softball, swimming, tennis, track and field (indoor), track and field (outdoor), volleyball.

SERVICES AND FACILITIES

Basic services: nonremedial tutoring, women's center, placement service, health service, health insurance, other. **Remedial assistance:** reading, math, writing, study skills, other. **Counseling services:** minority student, career, personal, veteran student, academic, psychological, birth control, other.

For learning-disabled students: School does not offer a structured program with separate admission and additional fees. Total undergraduates in learning-disabled program or receiving services: 109. Services include: remedial math, remedial English, reading machines, remedial reading, tape recorders, other special classes, note-taking services, oral tests, learning center, readers, extended time for tests, tutors, priority registration, priority seating, texts on tape, other testing accommodations. **Library:** Number of titles: 992,487; number of current serial subscriptions: 34,190. **Information technology resources:** Students are not required to lease or own a computer. Number of campus computers available to all students: 750. School has a wireless network. Approximate number of users that can be accommodated: 10,000. Proportion of college-owned housing units wired for high-speed internet access: 100%. **Campus safety:** Security services offered: 24-hour foot-and-vehicle patrols, late-night transport/escort service, 24-hour emergency telephones, lighted pathways/sidewalks, student patrols, controlled dormitory access (key, security card, etc).

TRANSFER AND INTERNATIONAL STUDENTS

Transfer students: May apply for admission for the following academic terms: Fall, Spring, Summer. Applicants need a minimum number of credits to apply. For fall 2009: Transfer applications received: 2,151. Transfer applicants offered admission: 1,646. Transfer applicants enrolled: 1,113. **International students:** Number of foreign undergraduates: 49. Number of countries represented: 26. Minimum TOEFL score required: 500 (paper); 173 (computer).

East-West University

- ■ **Address:** 816 S. Michigan Avenue, Chicago, IL 60605
- ■ **Website:** http://www.eastwest.edu
- ■ **Private**
- ■ **Enrollment:** 1,039 full-time; 14 part-time

KEY STATS

✔ **U.S News College Ranking:** second tier, Regional Colleges (Midwest)
✔ **ACT Score:** 18
✔ **Tuition:** 2009-2010: $15,795

Selectivity: Less selective	**Room/board:** N/A
Acceptance rate: 77%	**Average debt:** N/A
Student/faculty ratio: N/A	**Proportion who borrowed:** N/A

UNDERGRADUATE STUDENT BODY STATS

2009-2010 enrollment: 1,039 full-time; 14 part-time. Men: 40%; women: 60%. **Ethnic makeup:** African American: 60%; Asian American: 3%; Hispanic: 13%; White: 7%; International: 16%.

ADMISSIONS FACTS AND FIGURES

Phone: (312) 939-0111. **Email:** seeyou@eastwest.edu. **Website:** http://www.eastwest.edu. **Application deadlines for fall 2011:** Regular decision: Rolling. Early decision: Not offered. Early action: Not offered. Admission can be deferred. **Application fee:** $40. **Admissions requirements/recommendations:** Tests: The college uses SAT or ACT scores in admissions decisions. Either SAT or ACT required. For admission to the fall 2011 entering class, the school will accept: ACT with or without writing accepted. Campus visit: Recommended. Admissions interview: Required. Off-campus interview: May be arranged. **Factors that count in admissions decisions:** *Academic:* Secondary school record: Considered. Class rank: Considered. Letters of recommendation: Considered. Standardized test scores: Very Important. Essay: Considered. *Nonacademic:* Interview: Important. Extracurricular activities: Considered. Talent/ability: Not Considered. Character/personal qualities: Considered. Alumni/ae relationship: Considered. Geographical residence: Considered. State residency: Considered. Religious affiliation/commitment: Not Considered. Minority status: Not Considered. Volunteer work: Not Considered. Work experience: Not Considered. **Admissions statistics for the fall 2009 entering class:** Overall acceptance rate: 77%. First-year students who submitted SAT scores: 1%. First-year students submitting ACT scores: 82%. Scores (25/75 percentile): English: N/A, Math: N/A, Composite: N/A.

ACADEMICS

Year founded: 1980. **Academic calendar:** Quarter. **Degrees offered:** certificate, associate, bachelor's. **Most popular majors:** 42% business administration and management, 27% liberal arts and sciences/liberal studies, 13% English language and literature, 12% computer and information sciences,

4% engineering technology. **Major fields of study:** business, management, marketing, and related support services; computer and information sciences and support services; engineering technologies/technicians; English language and literature/letters; liberal arts and sciences studies, and humanities; mathematics and statistics; multi/interdisciplinary studies. **Areas of required coursework:** arts/fine arts, humanities, computer literacy, mathematics, English (including composition), philosophy, foreign languages, sciences (biological or physical), history, social science. **Special academic programs (% participation):** cooperative (work-study plan) program (50%), double major (5%), dual enrollment (5%), English as a Second Language (ESL) (2%), honors program (0%), independent study (5%), internships (5%). **Cooperative education programs:** business, computer science, humanities, social/behavioral science, technologies. **Faculty and instruction (2009-2010):** Total instructional faculty: N/A. Classes of fewer than 20 students: 45%; of 20 to 49 students: 54%; of 50 or more students: 1%. **Graduation rates:** Four-year: 8%; five-year: 10%; six-year: 11%.

COSTS AND FINANCIAL AID

Financial aid office: (312) 939-0111. **Expenses (2009-2010):** Tuition and fees 2009-2010: $15,795. Estimated books and supplies: $1,500. **Financial aid:** Priority filing date for institution's financial aid form: June 30.

CAMPUS LIFE AND EXTRACURRICULAR ACTIVITIES

Student employment: During the 2009-2010 academic year, 5% of undergraduates worked on campus. Activities include: choral groups, dance, drama/theater, international student organization, student government, student newspaper. **Sports program (2009-2010):** Member of NAIA.

SERVICES AND FACILITIES

Basic services: other. **Remedial assistance:** reading, math, writing, study skills. **Counseling services:** academic, psychological. **Library:** Number of titles: 18,500; number of current serial subscriptions: 136. **Information technology resources:** Students are not required to lease or own a computer. Number of campus computers available to all students: 300. School has a wireless network. Approximate number of users that can be accommodated: 128.

TRANSFER AND INTERNATIONAL STUDENTS

Transfer students: May apply for admission for the following academic terms: Fall, Winter, Spring. Applicants need a minimum number of credits to apply. **International students:** Number of foreign undergraduates: 169 (16% of student body). Minimum TOEFL score required: 65 (computer).

Elmhurst College

- **Address:** 190 Prospect Avenue, Elmhurst, IL 60126
- **Website:** http://www.elmhurst.edu
- **Private; Religious affiliation:** United Church of Christ
- **Enrollment:** 2,851 full-time; 242 part-time

KEY STATS

✔ **U.S News College Ranking:** 12, Regional Universities (Midwest)
✔ **ACT Score (25th/75th percentile):** 21-27
✔ **Tuition:** 2010-2011: $28,660

Selectivity: Selective	**Room/board:** $8,216
Acceptance rate: 70%	**Average debt:** $18,329
Student/faculty ratio: 14/1	**Proportion who borrowed:** 90%

UNDERGRADUATE STUDENT BODY STATS

2009-2010 enrollment: 2,851 full-time; 242 part-time. Men: 38%; women: 62%. **Ethnic makeup:** African American: 4%; Asian American: 4%; Hispanic: 8%; White: 83%; International: 1%. **Religious preference:** Roman Catholic: 38%; Protestant: 20%; Jewish: 1%; Muslim: 3%; Hindu: 1%; No preference: 18%; Unknown: 5%; United Church of Christ: 6%; Other: 8%.

ADMISSIONS FACTS AND FIGURES

Phone: (630) 617-3400. **Email:** admit@elmhurst.edu. **Website:** http://www.elmhurst.edu. **Application deadlines for fall 2011:** Regular decision: July 15. Early decision: Not offered. Early action: Not offered. Admission can be deferred. **Application fee:** None. **To apply online, go to:** http://www.illinoismentor.org/Applications/Elmhurst_College/apply.html?application_id=169. **Admissions requirements/recommendations:** High school units required (recommended): English: 4 (4); Mathematics: 2 (3); Science: 2 (3); Foreign

language: 0 (1); Social studies: 2 (3); History: 1 (2); Academic electives: 4 (4); Total units: 16 (21). Tests: The college uses SAT or ACT scores in admissions decisions. Either SAT or ACT required. For admission to the fall 2011 entering class, the school will accept: ACT with or without writing accepted. Campus visit: Recommended. Admissions interview: Recommended. Off-campus interview: Not available. **Factors that count in admissions decisions:** *Academic:* Secondary school record: Very Important. Class rank: Very Important. Letters of recommendation: Important. Standardized test scores: Very Important. Essay: Important. *Nonacademic:* Interview: Important. Extracurricular activities: Considered. Talent/ability: Considered. Character/personal qualities: Considered. Alumni/ae relationship: Considered. Geographical residence: Not Considered. State residency: Not Considered. Religious affiliation/commitment: Not Considered. Minority status: Not Considered. Volunteer work: Not Considered. Work experience: Not Considered. **Other schools with the greatest overlap in applicants:** Augustana College; DePaul University; Loyola University Chicago; North Central College; Northern Illinois University. **Admissions statistics for the fall 2009 entering class:** Total applicants: 2,762. Total accepted: 1,935. Freshmen enrolled: 587; 15% were from out of state. Overall acceptance rate: 70%. **Credentials of fall 2009 freshmen:** 21% ranked in the top 10 percent of their high school class; 51% were in the top 25 percent; 82% were in the top half. (Proportion submitting class standing: 85%.) **Average high school grade point average:** 3.4. **First-year students who submitted SAT scores:** 7%. Scores (25/75 percentile): Critical Reading: 460-560, Math: 480-610, Combined: 940-1170. **First-year students submitting ACT scores:** 97%. Scores (25/75 percentile): English: 21-27, Math: 20-27, Composite: 21-27.

ACADEMICS

Year founded: 1871. **Academic calendar:** 4-1-4. **Degrees offered:** bachelor's, master's. **Most popular majors:** 25% business, management, marketing, and related support services, 14% health professions and related clinical sciences, 13% education, 7% communication, journalism, and related programs, 7% psychology. **Major fields of study:** agriculture, agriculture operations, and related sciences; area, ethnic, cultural, and gender studies; biological and biomedical sciences; business, management, marketing, and related support services; communication, journalism, and related programs; computer and information sciences and support services; education; English language and literature/letters; foreign languages, literatures, and linguistics; health professions and related clinical sciences; history; liberal arts and sciences studies, and humanities; mathematics and statistics; multi/interdisciplinary studies; natural resources and conservation; parks, recreation, leisure, and fitness studies; philosophy and religious studies; physical sciences; psychology; public administration and social service professions; social sciences; theology and religious vocations; visual and performing arts. **Areas of required coursework:** arts/fine arts, humanities, mathematics, English (including composition), philosophy, foreign languages, sciences (biological or physical), history, social science. **Preprofessional programs:** pre-law, pre-dentistry, pre-medicine, pre-theology, pre-veterinary science, pre-optometry, pre-pharmacy. **Special academic programs (% participation):** accelerated program (6%), double major (10%), dual enrollment (1%), honors program (12%), independent study (15%), internships (25%), liberal arts/career combination (75%), student-designed major (1%), study abroad (20%), teacher certificate program (25%). **Teacher certification offered in:** early childhood, special education, elementary, middle/junior high, secondary. **Reserve Officers Training Corps (ROTC):** Army ROTC: Offered at cooperating institution (Wheaton College); Air Force ROTC: Offered at cooperating institution (Illinois Institute of Technology). **Faculty and instruction (2009-2010):** Total instructional faculty: 134 full-time, 228 part-time (49% men; 51% women; 10% minorities). Full-time faculty with Ph.D. or other terminal degree: 86%. Student/faculty ratio: 14/1. Classes of fewer than 20 students: 63%; of 20 to 49 students: 37%; of 50 or more students: 0%. **Advanced Placement and International Baccalaureate credit:** AP tests may be used for: Credit and/or placement. Scores accepted: 3, 4, 5. International Baccalaureate exams may be used for: Placement only. **Freshmen returning for sophomore year:** 84%. **Graduation rates:** Four-year: 53%; five-year: 67%; six-year: 70%. **Graduate study:** 28% of students pursue further study immediately upon graduation; 30% within one year; 50% within five years. Fields in which graduates pursue further study: Master of Business Administration (MBA), 30%; law, 2%; medicine, 5%; dentistry, 2%; theology (or the seminary), 5%; education, 50%; arts and sciences, 6%.

COSTS AND FINANCIAL AID

Financial aid office: (630) 617-3075. **Expenses (2010-2011):** Tuition and fees 2010-2011: $28,660; room/board: $8,216. Estimated books and supplies: $1,000; transportation: $524; personal expenses: $1,100. **Financial aid:** Priority filing date for institution's financial aid form: April 15. In

2009-2010, 75% of undergraduates applied for financial aid. Of those, 69% were determined to have financial need; 31% had their need fully met. Average financial aid package (proportion receiving): $21,073 (69%). Average amount of gift aid, such as scholarships or grants (proportion receiving): $17,050 (67%). Average amount of self-help aid, such as work study or loans (proportion receiving): $5,052 (54%). Average need-based loan (excluding PLUS or other private loans): $4,575. Among students who received need-based aid, the average percentage of need met: 78%. Among students who received aid based on merit, the average award (and the proportion receiving): $10,816 (6%). The average athletic scholarship (and the proportion receiving): $0 (0%). Average amount of debt of borrowers graduating in 2009: $18,329. Proportion who borrowed: 90%.

CAMPUS LIFE AND EXTRACURRICULAR ACTIVITIES

Campus housing available (% using): coed dorms (77%), apartment for single students (23%). Students who live in college-owned, operated, or affiliated housing: 42%. **Student employment:** During the 2009-2010 academic year, 25% of undergraduates worked on campus. Average per-year earnings: $1,250. **Clubs and organizations:** Number of student organizations: 89. Activities include: campus ministries, choral groups, concert band, dance, drama/theater, international student organization, jazz band, literary magazine, model UN, music ensembles, musical theater, radio station, student government, student newspaper, symphony orchestra, yearbook. Number of fraternities: 3; sororities: 3. Proportion of men in fraternities: 7%; of women in sororities: 11%. Average proportion of students who stay on campus on weekends: 25%. **Sports program (2009-2010):** Member of NCAA III. *Men's intercollegiate varsity sports:* baseball, basketball, cross country, football, golf, soccer, tennis, track and field (indoor), track and field (outdoor), wrestling. *Women's intercollegiate varsity sports:* basketball, bowling, cross country, golf, soccer, softball, tennis, track and field (indoor), track and field (outdoor), volleyball.

SERVICES AND FACILITIES

Basic services: nonremedial tutoring, women's center, placement service, day care, health service, health insurance. **Remedial assistance:** reading, math, writing, study skills. **Counseling services:** minority student, career, personal, academic, older student, psychological, birth control, religious. **For learning-disabled students:** School does not offer a structured program with separate admission and additional fees. **Library:** Number of titles: 230,055; number of current serial subscriptions: 1,859. **Information technology resources:** Students are not required to lease or own a computer. Number of campus computers available to all students: 800. School has a wireless network. Approximate number of users that can be accommodated: 1,000. Proportion of college-owned housing units wired for high-speed internet access: 100%. **Campus safety:** Security services offered: 24-hour foot-and-vehicle patrols, late-night transport/escort service, 24-hour emergency telephones, lighted pathways/sidewalks, controlled dormitory access (key, security card, etc).

TRANSFER AND INTERNATIONAL STUDENTS

Transfer students: May apply for admission for the following academic terms: Fall, Winter, Spring. Applicants do not need a minimum number of credits to apply. For fall 2009: Transfer applications received: 890. Transfer applicants offered admission: 525. Transfer applicants enrolled: 267. **International students:** Number of foreign undergraduates: 33 (1% of student body). Number of countries represented: 32. Minimum TOEFL score required: 550 (paper); 213 (computer). Average TOEFL score: 600 (paper).

Eureka College

- **Address:** 300 E. College Avenue, Eureka, IL 61530-1500
- **Website:** http://www.eureka.edu
- **Private; Religious affiliation:** Christian Church (Disciples of Christ)
- **Enrollment:** 698 full-time; 68 part-time

KEY STATS

✔ **U.S News College Ranking:** 29, Regional Colleges (Midwest)
✔ **ACT Score (25th/75th percentile):** 19-24
✔ **Tuition:** 2010-2011: $18,045

Selectivity: Selective	**Room/board:** $7,760
Acceptance rate: 71%	**Average debt:** $15,390
Student/faculty ratio: N/A	**Proportion who borrowed:** 79%

UNDERGRADUATE STUDENT BODY STATS

2009-2010 enrollment: 698 full-time; 68 part-time. Men: 44%; women: 56%. **Religious preference:** Roman Catholic: 14%; Protestant: 45%; Unknown: 36%; Christian Church (Disciples of Christ): 5%.

ADMISSIONS FACTS AND FIGURES

Phone: (309) 467-6345. **Email:** admissions@eureka.edu. **Website:** http://www.eureka.edu. **Application deadlines for fall 2011:** Regular decision: August 1. Early decision: Not offered. Early action: Not offered. Admission can be deferred. **Application fee:** None. **To apply online, go to:** http://www.eureka.edu/admissions/apply.htm. **Admissions requirements/recommendations:** High school units required (recommended): English: 0 (4); Mathematics: 0 (3); Science: 0 (2); Foreign language: 0 (2); Social studies: 0 (1); History: 0 (1); Academic electives: 0 (0); Total units: 0 (13). Tests: The college uses SAT or ACT scores in admissions decisions. Either SAT or ACT required. For admission to the fall 2011 entering class, the school will accept: ACT with or without writing accepted. Campus visit: Recommended. Admissions interview: Recommended. Off-campus interview: Not available. **Factors that count in admissions decisions:** *Academic:* Secondary school record: Very Important. Class rank: Important. Letters of recommendation: Important. Standardized test scores: Very Important. Essay: Not Considered. *Nonacademic:* Interview: Considered. Extracurricular activities: Important. Talent/ability: Important. Character/personal qualities: Very Important. Alumni/ae relationship: Not Considered. Geographical residence: Not Considered. State residency: Not Considered. Religious affiliation/commitment: Not Considered. Minority status: Not Considered. Volunteer work: Not Considered. Work experience: Not Considered. **Other schools with the greatest overlap in applicants:** Bradley University; Illinois College; Illinois State University; Millikin University; Monmouth College. **Admissions statistics for the fall 2009 entering class:** Total applicants: 1,052. Total accepted: 748. Freshmen enrolled: 143; 5% were from out of state. Overall acceptance rate: 71%. **Size of waiting list:** 0 applicants; enrolled from waiting list: 0. **Credentials of fall 2009 freshmen:** 13% ranked in the top 10 percent of their high school class; 35% were in the top 25 percent; 74% were in the top half. (Proportion submitting class standing: 95%.) **Average high school grade point average:** 3.2. **First-year students submitting ACT scores:** 100%. Scores (25/75 percentile): English: 19-25, Math: 17-24, Composite: 19-24.

ACADEMICS

Year founded: 1855. **Academic calendar:** Semester. **Degrees offered:** bachelor's. **Most popular majors:** 18% elementary education and teaching, 14% business administration and management, 8% organizational behavior studies, 6% communication studies/speech communication and rhetoric, 6% psychology. **Major fields of study:** biological and biomedical sciences; business, management, marketing, and related support services; communication, journalism, and related programs; computer and information sciences and support services; education; English language and literature/letters; health professions and related clinical sciences; history; liberal arts and sciences studies, and humanities; mathematics and statistics; multi/interdisciplinary studies; natural resources and conservation; parks, recreation, leisure, and fitness studies; philosophy and religious studies; physical sciences; psychology; security and protective services; social sciences; visual and performing arts. **Areas of required coursework:** arts/fine arts, humanities, mathematics, English (including composition), philosophy, sciences (biological or physical), history, social science, other. **Pre-professional programs:** pre-law, pre-dentistry, pre-medicine, pre-theology, pre-veterinary science. **Special academic programs (% participation):** double major (7.7%), dual enrollment (0%), honors program (2.2%), independent study (8.8%), internships (24.8%), student-designed major (2.7%), study abroad (2.7%), teacher certificate program (23.2%). **Teacher certification offered in:** special education, elementary, middle/junior high, secondary. **Reserve Officers Training Corps (ROTC):** Army ROTC: Offered at cooperating institution (Illinois State University). **Faculty and instruction (2009-2010):** Total instructional faculty: N/A. Classes of fewer than 20 students: 63%; of 20 to 49 students: 37%; of 50 or more students: 0%. **Advanced Placement and International Baccalaureate credit:** Scores accepted: 3, 4, 5. International Baccalaureate exams may be used for: Credit only. **Freshmen returning for sophomore year:** 77%. **Graduation rates:** Six-year: 52%. **Graduate study:** 12% of students pursue further study immediately upon graduation.

COSTS AND FINANCIAL AID

Financial aid office: (309) 467-6311. **Expenses (2010-2011):** Tuition and fees 2010-2011: $18,045; room/board: $7,760. Estimated books and supplies: $1,000; transportation: $500; personal expenses: $500. **Financial aid:** Priority filing date for institution's financial aid form: April 1; deadline:

April 1. In 2009-2010, 87% of undergraduates applied for financial aid. Of those, 72% were determined to have financial need; 13% had their need fully met. Average financial aid package (proportion receiving): $11,105 (72%). Average amount of gift aid, such as scholarships or grants (proportion receiving): $7,062 (72%). Average amount of self-help aid, such as work study or loans (proportion receiving): $4,042 (61%). Average need-based loan (excluding PLUS or other private loans): $3,846. Among students who received need-based aid, the average percentage of need met: 61%. Among students who received aid based on merit, the average award (and the proportion receiving): $3,232 (15%). The average athletic scholarship (and the proportion receiving): $0 (0%). Average amount of debt of borrowers graduating in 2009: $15,390. Proportion who borrowed: 79%.

CAMPUS LIFE AND EXTRACURRICULAR ACTIVITIES

Campus housing available (% using): coed dorms (21%), women's dorms (30%), men's dorms (29%), sorority housing (16%), fraternity housing (4%), special housing for disabled students (0%). Students who live in college-owned, operated, or affiliated housing: 52%. **Student employment:** During the 2009-2010 academic year, 14% of undergraduates worked on campus. Average per-year earnings: $1,734. **Clubs and organizations:** Number of student organizations: 45. Activities include: campus ministries, choral groups, dance, drama/theater, international student organization, literary magazine, marching band, music ensembles, pep band, student government, student newspaper, yearbook. Number of fraternities: 3; sororities: 3. Proportion of men in fraternities: 24%; of women in sororities: 24%. Average proportion of students who stay on campus on weekends: 70%. **Sports program (2009-2010):** Member of NCAA III. *Men's intercollegiate varsity sports:* baseball, basketball, cross country, football, golf, soccer, swimming, tennis, track and field (outdoor). *Women's intercollegiate varsity sports:* basketball, cross country, golf, soccer, softball, swimming, tennis, track and field (outdoor), volleyball.

SERVICES AND FACILITIES

Basic services: nonremedial tutoring, placement service, health service, health insurance. **Remedial assistance:** reading, math, writing, study skills. **Counseling services:** career, academic, religious. **For learning-disabled students:** School does not offer a structured program with separate admission and additional fees. Total undergraduates in learning-disabled program or receiving services: 33. Services include: note-taking services, learning center, readers, extended time for tests, tutors, typist/scribe, exams on tape or computer. **Library:** Number of titles: 91,400; number of current serial subscriptions: 265. **Information technology resources:** Students are not required to lease or own a computer. Number of campus computers available to all students: 90. School has a wireless network. Approximate number of users that can be accommodated: 30. Proportion of college-owned housing units wired for high-speed internet access: 100%. **Campus safety:** Security services offered: lighted pathways/sidewalks, controlled dormitory access (key, security card, etc).

TRANSFER AND INTERNATIONAL STUDENTS

Transfer students: May apply for admission for the following academic terms: Fall, Spring, Summer. Applicants need a minimum number of credits to apply. For fall 2009: Transfer applications received: 317. Transfer applicants offered admission: 206. Transfer applicants enrolled: 117. **International students:** Minimum TOEFL score required: 550 (paper); 79 (computer).

Greenville College

- **Address:** 315 E. College Avenue, Greenville, IL 62246-0159
- **Website:** http://www.greenville.edu
- **Private; Religious affiliation:** Free Methodist
- **Enrollment:** 1,330 full-time; 52 part-time

....

KEY STATS

✔ **U.S News College Ranking:** 31, Regional Colleges (Midwest)
✔ **ACT Score (25th/75th percentile):** 20-27
✔ **Tuition:** 2010-2011: $20,924

Selectivity: Selective	**Room/board:** $7,227
Acceptance rate: 78%	**Average debt:** $24,070
Student/faculty ratio: 17/1	**Proportion who borrowed:** 94%

UNDERGRADUATE STUDENT BODY STATS

2009-2010 enrollment: 1,330 full-time; 52 part-time. Men: 45%; women: 55%. **Ethnic makeup:** African American: 8%; American-Indian: 1%; Asian American: 1%; Hispanic: 3%; White: 87%; International: 2%. **Religious preference:** Roman Catholic: 8%; Protestant: 68%; Unknown: 15%; Free Methodist: 7%.

ADMISSIONS FACTS AND FIGURES

Phone: (618) 664-7100. **Email:** admissions@greenville.edu. **Website:** http://www.greenville.edu. **Application deadlines for fall 2011:** Regular decision: August 1; decision sent by September 1. Early decision: Not offered. Early action: Not offered. Admission can be deferred. **Application fee:** $25. **To apply online, go to:** http://www.greenville.edu/apply. **Admissions requirements/recommendations:** High school units required (recommended): English: (4); Mathematics: (2); Science: (1); Foreign language: (2); History: (1); Total units: (11). Tests: The college uses SAT or ACT scores in admissions decisions. Either SAT or ACT required. For admission to the fall 2011 entering class, the school will accept: ACT with or without writing accepted. Campus visit: Recommended. Admissions interview: Recommended. Off-campus interview: Not available. **Factors that count in admissions decisions:** *Academic:* Secondary school record: Considered. Class rank: Considered. Letters of recommendation: Considered. Standardized test scores: Important. Essay: Very Important. *Nonacademic:* Interview: Considered. Extracurricular activities: Considered. Talent/ability: Considered. Character/personal qualities: Important. Alumni/ae relationship: Considered. Geographical residence: Not Considered. State residency: Not Considered. Religious affiliation/commitment: Important. Minority status: Considered. Volunteer work: Considered. Work experience: Considered. **Other schools with the greatest overlap in applicants:** Eastern Illinois University; McKendree University; Olivet Nazarene University; Southern Illinois University–Carbondale; Southern Illinois University–Edwardsville. **Admissions statistics for the fall 2009 entering class:** Total applicants: 932. Total accepted: 727. Freshmen enrolled: 253; 40% were from out of state. Overall acceptance rate: 78%. **Credentials of fall 2009 freshmen:** 16% ranked in the top 10 percent of their high school class; 39% were in the top 25 percent; 73% were in the top half. (Proportion submitting class standing: 88%.) **Average high school grade point average:** 3.3. **First-year students who submitted SAT scores:** 19%. Scores (25/75 percentile): Critical Reading: 435-585, Math: 410-560, Combined: 845-1145. **First-year students submitting ACT scores:** 87%. Scores (25/75 percentile): English: 20-28, Math: 19-26, Composite: 20-27.

ACADEMICS

Year founded: 1892. **Academic calendar:** 4-1-4. **Degrees offered:** bachelor's, master's. **Most popular majors:** 39% business, management, marketing, and related support services, 26% education, 5% biological and biomedical sciences, 5% visual and performing arts, 4% communications technologies/technicians and support services. **Major fields of study:** biological and biomedical sciences; business, management, marketing, and related support services; communication, journalism, and related programs; communications technologies/technicians and support services; education; English language and literature/letters; foreign languages, literatures, and linguistics; history; liberal arts and sciences studies, and humanities; mathematics and statistics; multi/interdisciplinary studies; parks, recreation, leisure, and fitness studies; philosophy and religious studies; physical sciences; psychology; public administration and social service professions; security and protective services; social sciences; theology and religious vocations; visual and performing arts. **Areas of required coursework:** humanities, mathematics, English (including composition), philosophy, foreign languages, sciences (biological and physical), history, social science, other. **Pre-professional programs:** pre-law, pre-dentistry, pre-medicine, pre-theology, pre-veterinary science, pre-optometry, pre-pharmacy, other. **Special academic programs (% participation):** cooperative (work-study plan) program (4%), double major (9%), honors program (1%), independent study (15%), internships (75%), student-designed major (5%), study abroad (1%), teacher certificate program (27%). **Teacher certification offered in:** early childhood, special education, elementary, secondary. **Cooperative education programs:** art, business, computer science, education, humanities, natural science, social/behavioral science, technologies. **Faculty and instruction (2009-2010):** Total instructional faculty: 67 full-time, 111 part-time (53% men; 47% women; 3% minorities). Full-time faculty with Ph.D. or other terminal degree: 69%. Student/faculty ratio: 17/1. Classes of fewer than 20 students: 54%; of 20 to 49 students: 41%; of 50 or more students: 5%. **Advanced Placement and International Baccalaureate credit:** AP tests may be used for: Credit and/or placement. Scores accepted: 3, 4, 5. International Baccalaureate exams may be used for:

Credit and/or placement. **Freshmen returning for sophomore year:** 69%.
Graduation rates: Four-year: 38%; five-year: 44%; six-year: 50%.

COSTS AND FINANCIAL AID
Financial aid office: (618) 664-7110. **Expenses (2010-2011):** Tuition and fees 2010-2011: $20,924; room/board: $7,227. Estimated books and supplies: $900; transportation: $1,324; personal expenses: $1,500. **Financial aid:** Priority filing date for institution's financial aid form: April 15; deadline: July 1. In 2009-2010, 93% of undergraduates applied for financial aid. Of those, 87% were determined to have financial need; 11% had their need fully met. Average financial aid package (proportion receiving): $15,347 (87%). Average amount of gift aid, such as scholarships or grants (proportion receiving): $11,629 (82%). Average amount of self-help aid, such as work study or loans (proportion receiving): $4,774 (79%). Average need-based loan (excluding PLUS or other private loans): $4,158. Among students who received need-based aid, the average percentage of need met: 68%. Among students who received aid based on merit, the average award (and the proportion receiving): $6,763 (11%). The average athletic scholarship (and the proportion receiving): $0 (0%). Average amount of debt of borrowers graduating in 2009: $24,070. Proportion who borrowed: 94%.

CAMPUS LIFE AND EXTRACURRICULAR ACTIVITIES
Campus housing available (% using): women's dorms (32%), men's dorms (36%), apartment for single students (19%), other housing options (13%). Students who live in college-owned, operated, or affiliated housing: 56%. **Student employment:** During the 2009-2010 academic year, 25% of undergraduates worked on campus. Average per-year earnings: $1,200. **Clubs and organizations:** Number of student organizations: 25. Activities include: choral groups, concert band, drama/theater, jazz band, music ensembles, musical theater, pep band, radio station, student government, student newspaper, yearbook. Number of fraternities: 0; sororities: 0. Average proportion of students who stay on campus on weekends: 70%. **Sports program (2009-2010):** Member of NCAA III. *Men's intercollegiate varsity sports:* baseball, basketball, cross country, football, soccer, tennis, track and field (outdoor). *Women's intercollegiate varsity sports:* basketball, cross country, soccer, softball, tennis, track and field (outdoor), volleyball.

SERVICES AND FACILITIES
Basic services: nonremedial tutoring, health insurance. **Remedial assistance:** math, study skills, other. **Counseling services:** career, personal, academic, older student, psychological, religious. **For learning-disabled students:** School does not offer a structured program with separate admission and additional fees. Services include: remedial math, remedial English, extended time for tests, tutors, priority seating. **Library:** Number of titles: 135,210; number of current serial subscriptions: 8,543. **Information technology resources:** Students are not required to lease or own a computer. Number of campus computers available to all students: 65. School has a wireless network. Approximate number of users that can be accommodated: 2,000. Proportion of college-owned housing units wired for high-speed internet access: 100%. **Campus safety:** Security services offered: late-night transport/escort service, 24-hour emergency telephones, lighted pathways/sidewalks, student patrols, controlled dormitory access (key, security card, etc).

TRANSFER AND INTERNATIONAL STUDENTS
Transfer students: May apply for admission for the following academic terms: Fall, Winter, Spring, Summer. Applicants do not need a minimum number of credits to apply. For fall 2009: Transfer applications received: 255. Transfer applicants offered admission: 123. Transfer applicants enrolled: 74. **International students:** Number of foreign undergraduates: 22 (2% of student body). Number of countries represented: 10. Minimum TOEFL score required: 500 (paper); 173 (computer). Average TOEFL score: 530 (paper).

Illinois College

- **Address:** 1101 W. College Avenue, Jacksonville, IL 62650-2299
- **Website:** http://www.ic.edu
- **Private; Religious affiliation:** Presbyterian Church (USA) and United Church of Christ
- **Enrollment:** 864 full-time; 30 part-time

KEY STATS
✔ **U.S News College Ranking:** 158, National Liberal Arts Colleges
✔ **ACT Score (25th/75th percentile):** 21-27
✔ **Tuition:** 2010-2011: $21,300

Selectivity: Selective	**Room/board:** $7,600
Acceptance rate: 55%	**Average debt:** $21,258
Student/faculty ratio: 11/1	**Proportion who borrowed:** 76%

UNDERGRADUATE STUDENT BODY STATS
2009-2010 enrollment: 864 full-time; 30 part-time. Men: 49%; women: 51%. **Ethnic makeup:** African American: 5%; American-Indian: 1%; Asian American: 1%; Hispanic: 2%; White: 90%; International: 3%. **Religious preference:** Roman Catholic: 23%; Protestant: 44%; No preference: 12%; Unknown: 3%; Presbyterian Church (USA) and United Church of Christ: 6%; Methodist: 12%.

ADMISSIONS FACTS AND FIGURES
Phone: (217) 245-3030. **Email:** admissions@ic.edu. **Website:** http://www.ic.edu. **Application deadlines for fall 2011:** Regular decision: Rolling. Early decision: Not offered. Early action: Not offered. Admission can be deferred. **To apply online, go to:** http://www.commonapp.org. **Admissions requirements/recommendations:** High school units required (recommended): English: 4 (4); Mathematics: 3 (3); Science: 2 (3); Foreign language: 0 (2); Social studies: 1 (1); History: 1 (1); Academic electives: 3 (3); Total units: 16 (20). Tests: The college uses SAT or ACT scores in admissions decisions. Neither SAT nor ACT required. For admission to the fall 2011 entering class, the school will accept: ACT with or without writing accepted. Campus visit: Recommended. Admissions interview: Recommended. Off-campus interview: May be arranged. **Factors that count in admissions decisions:** *Academic:* Secondary school record: Very Important. Class rank: Important. Letters of recommendation: Considered. Standardized test scores: Important. Essay: Important. *Nonacademic:* Interview: Important. Extracurricular activities: Important. Talent/ability: Important. Character/personal qualities: Very Important. Alumni/ae relationship: Considered. Geographical residence: Considered. State residency: Important. Religious affiliation/commitment: Not Considered. Minority status: Considered. Volunteer work: Considered. Work experience: Considered. **Other schools with the greatest overlap in applicants:** Illinois State University; Millikin University; Southern Illinois University–Carbondale; Southern Illinois University–Edwardsville; University of Illinois–Urbana-Champaign. **Admissions statistics for the fall 2009 entering class:** Total applicants: 1,313. Total accepted: 719. Freshmen enrolled: 225; 12% were from out of state. Overall acceptance rate: 55%. **Size of waiting list:** 13 applicants; enrolled from waiting list: 4. **Credentials of fall 2009 freshmen:** 26% ranked in the top 10 percent of their high school class; 56% were in the top 25 percent; 85% were in the top half. (Proportion submitting class standing: 95%.) **Average high school grade point average:** 3.4. **First-year students who submitted SAT scores:** 2%. **First-year students submitting ACT scores:** 98%. Scores (25/75 percentile): English: 20-27, Math: 20-27, Composite: 21-27.

ACADEMICS
Year founded: 1829. **Academic calendar:** Semester. **Degrees offered:** bachelor's. **Most popular majors:** 16% biological and biomedical sciences, 16% social sciences, 14% multi/interdisciplinary studies, 12% education, 10% English language and literature/letters. **Major fields of study:** biological and biomedical sciences; business, management, marketing, and related support services; computer and information sciences and support services; education; engineering; English language and literature/letters; foreign languages, literatures, and linguistics; health professions and related clinical sciences; history; mathematics and statistics; multi/interdisciplinary studies; parks, recreation, leisure, and fitness studies; philosophy and religious studies; physical sciences; psychology; social sciences; visual and performing arts. **Areas of required coursework:** arts/fine arts, humanities, mathematics, English (including composition), philosophy, foreign languages, sciences (biological or physical), history, social science. **Special academic programs (% participation):** cross-registration (1%), double major

(13%), dual enrollment (0%), independent study (38%), internships (60%), liberal arts/career combination (45%), student-designed major (0%), study abroad (15%), teacher certificate program (16%). **Teacher certification offered in:** early childhood, elementary, middle/junior high, secondary. **Cooperative education programs:** engineering. **Faculty and instruction (2009-2010):** Total instructional faculty: 74 full-time, 17 part-time (52% men; 48% women; 10% minorities). Full-time faculty with Ph.D. or other terminal degree: 84%. Student/faculty ratio: 11/1. Classes of fewer than 20 students: 68%; of 20 to 49 students: 31%; of 50 or more students: 1%. **Advanced Placement and International Baccalaureate credit:** AP tests may be used for: Credit only. Scores accepted: 3, 4, 5. International Baccalaureate exams may be used for: Credit only. **Freshmen returning for sophomore year:** 77%. **Graduation rates:** Four-year: 50%; five-year: 57%; six-year: 60%. **Graduate study:** 25% of students pursue further study immediately upon graduation; 33% within one year; 43% within five years. Fields in which graduates pursue further study: Master of Business Administration (MBA), 20%; law, 10%; medicine, 10%; dentistry, 3%; engineering, 5%; theology (or the seminary), 5%; education, 25%; arts and sciences, 20%; veterinary medicine, 2%.

COSTS AND FINANCIAL AID
Financial aid office: (217) 245-3035. **Expenses (2010-2011):** Tuition and fees 2010-2011: $21,300; room/board: $7,600. Estimated books and supplies: $900; transportation: $500; personal expenses: $900. **Financial aid:** Priority filing date for institution's financial aid form: March 1. In 2009-2010, 92% of undergraduates applied for financial aid. Of those, 82% were determined to have financial need; 29% had their need fully met. Average financial aid package (proportion receiving): $18,014 (82%). Average amount of gift aid, such as scholarships or grants (proportion receiving): $13,434 (81%). Average amount of self-help aid, such as work study or loans (proportion receiving): $5,572 (68%). Average need-based loan (excluding PLUS or other private loans): $4,660. Among students who received need-based aid, the average percentage of need met: 89%. Among students who received aid based on merit, the average award (and the proportion receiving): $8,805 (17%). The average athletic scholarship (and the proportion receiving): $0 (0%). Average amount of debt of borrowers graduating in 2009: $21,258. Proportion who borrowed: 76%.

CAMPUS LIFE AND EXTRACURRICULAR ACTIVITIES
Campus housing available (% using): coed dorms (66%), women's dorms (12%), men's dorms (12%), apartment for single students (8%), special housing for disabled students (1%). Students who live in college-owned, operated, or affiliated housing: 78%. **Student employment:** During the 2009-2010 academic year, 48% of undergraduates worked on campus. Average per-year earnings: $1,920. **Clubs and organizations:** Number of student organizations: 81. Activities include: campus ministries, choral groups, concert band, drama/theater, international student organization, literary magazine, model UN, music ensembles, student government, student newspaper, yearbook. Number of fraternities: 0; sororities: 0. Average proportion of students who stay on campus on weekends: 65%. **Sports program (2009-2010):** Member of NCAA III.

SERVICES AND FACILITIES
Basic services: nonremedial tutoring, placement service, health service. **Remedial assistance:** writing, study skills. **Counseling services:** career, personal, academic, psychological, birth control, religious. **For learning-disabled students:** School does not offer a structured program with separate admission and additional fees. Services include: reading machines, tape recorders, diagnostic testing service, untimed tests, note-taking services, oral tests, readers, extended time for tests, tutors, priority registration, priority seating, texts on tape, other testing accommodations, other. **Library:** Number of titles: 183,172; number of current serial subscriptions: 648. **Information technology resources:** Students are not required to lease or own a computer. Number of campus computers available to all students: 158. School has a wireless network. Approximate number of users that can be accommodated: 1,000. Proportion of college-owned housing units wired for high-speed internet access: 99%. **Campus safety:** Security services offered: 24-hour foot-and-vehicle patrols, late-night transport/escort service, 24-hour emergency telephones, lighted pathways/sidewalks, student patrols, controlled dormitory access (key, security card, etc.).

TRANSFER AND INTERNATIONAL STUDENTS
Transfer students: May apply for admission for the following academic terms: Fall, Spring. Applicants need a minimum number of credits to apply. For fall 2009: Transfer applications received: 123. Transfer applicants offered admission: 69. Transfer applicants enrolled: 42. **International students:** Number of foreign undergraduates: 22 (3% of student body).

Number of countries represented: 15. Minimum TOEFL score required: 550 (paper); 213 (computer). Average TOEFL score: 580 (paper).

Illinois Institute of Technology

- **Address:** 3300 S. Federal Street, Chicago, IL 60616-3793
- **Website:** http://www.iit.edu
- **Private**
- **Enrollment:** 2,480 full-time; 185 part-time

KEY STATS
✔ **U.S News College Ranking:** 111, National Universities
✔ **ACT Score (25th/75th percentile):** 25-31
✔ **Tuition:** 2010-2011: $31,253
  Selectivity: More selective **Room/board:** $10,338
  Acceptance rate: 60% **Average debt:** N/A
  Student/faculty ratio: 10/1 **Proportion who borrowed:** N/A

UNDERGRADUATE STUDENT BODY STATS
2009-2010 enrollment: 2,480 full-time; 185 part-time. Men: 71%; women: 29%. **Ethnic makeup:** African American: 4%; American-Indian: 1%; Asian American: 13%; Hispanic: 8%; White: 57%; International: 17%.

ADMISSIONS FACTS AND FIGURES
Phone: (800) 448-2329. **Email:** admission@iit.edu. **Website:** http://www.iit.edu. **Application deadlines for fall 2011:** Regular decision: Rolling. Early decision: Send application by: November 1; Decision sent by: December 1. Early action: Send application by: December 1; Decision sent by: January 1. Admission can be deferred. **Application fee:** None. **To apply online, go to:** http://www.iit.edu/admission/undergrad. **Admissions requirements/recommendations:** High school units required (recommended): English: 4 (4); Mathematics: 4 (4); Science: 3 (3); Foreign language: 2 (2); Social studies: 2 (2); History: (2); Total units: 15 (19). Tests: The college uses SAT or ACT scores in admissions decisions. Neither SAT nor ACT required. For admission to the fall 2011 entering class, the school will accept: ACT with writing recommended. Campus visit: Recommended. Admissions interview: Recommended. Off-campus interview: May be arranged. **Factors that count in admissions decisions:** *Academic:* Secondary school record: Very Important. Class rank: Important. Letters of recommendation: Important. Standardized test scores: Important. Essay: Important. *Nonacademic:* Interview: Considered. Extracurricular activities: Considered. Talent/ability: Considered. Character/personal qualities: Considered. Alumni/ae relationship: Considered. Geographical residence: Not Considered. State residency: Not Considered. Religious affiliation/commitment: Not Considered. Minority status: Not Considered. Volunteer work: Considered. Work experience: Considered. **Other schools with the greatest overlap in applicants:** Loyola University Chicago; Northwestern University; Purdue University–West Lafayette; University of Illinois–Chicago; University of Illinois–Urbana-Champaign. **Admissions statistics for the fall 2009 entering class:** Total applicants: 2,918. Total accepted: 1,759. Freshmen enrolled: 459; 41% were from out of state. Overall acceptance rate: 60%. Non-early acceptance rate: 51%. **Credentials of fall 2009 freshmen:** 41% ranked in the top 10 percent of their high school class; 72% were in the top 25 percent; 96% were in the top half. (Proportion submitting class standing: 60%.) **First-year students who submitted SAT scores:** 40%. Scores (25/75 percentile): Critical Reading: 540-670, Math: 630-723, Combined: 1170-1393. **First-year students submitting ACT scores:** 74%. Scores (25/75 percentile): English: 24-31, Math: 26-32, Composite: 25-31.

ACADEMICS
Year founded: 1890. **Academic calendar:** Semester. **Degrees offered:** bachelor's, master's, doctorate. **Most popular majors:** 21% architecture (B.Arch., B.A./B.S., M.Arch., M.A./M.S., Ph.D.), 11% electrical, electronics, and communications engineering, 9% mechanical engineering, 6% aerospace, aeronautical, and astronautical engineering, 6% computer science. **Major fields of study:** architecture and related services; biological and biomedical sciences; business, management, marketing, and related support services; communication, journalism, and related programs; computer and information sciences and support services; engineering; engineering technologies/technicians; mathematics and statistics; multi/interdisciplinary studies; physical sciences; psychology; social sciences. **Areas of required coursework:** humanities, computer literacy, mathematics, sciences (biological or physical), social science, other. **Pre-professional programs:** pre-law, pre-medicine,

pre-optometry, pre-pharmacy. **Special academic programs (% participation):** cooperative (work-study plan) program (3%), cross-registration, distance learning (15%), double major (8%), English as a Second Language (ESL) (1%), independent study (43%), liberal arts/career combination, study abroad (6%), teacher certificate program, other. **Teacher certification offered in:** secondary. **Cooperative education programs:** business, computer science, education, engineering, health professions, humanities, natural science, social/behavioral science, technologies, other. **Reserve Officers Training Corps (ROTC):** Army ROTC: Offered on campus; Navy ROTC: Offered on campus; Air Force ROTC: Offered on campus. **Faculty and instruction (2009-2010):** Total instructional faculty: 385 full-time, 270 part-time (78% men; 22% women; 4% minorities). Full-time faculty with Ph.D. or other terminal degree: 89%. Student/faculty ratio: 10/1. Classes of fewer than 20 students: 55%; of 20 to 49 students: 39%; of 50 or more students: 6%. **Advanced Placement and International Baccalaureate credit:** AP tests may be used for: Credit and/or placement. Scores accepted: 3, 4, 5. International Baccalaureate exams may be used for: Credit only. **Freshmen returning for sophomore year:** 87%. **Graduation rates:** Four-year: 35%; five-year: 61%; six-year: 66%. **Graduate study:** 34% of students pursue further study immediately upon graduation.

COSTS AND FINANCIAL AID
Financial aid office: (312) 567-7219. **Expenses (2010-2011):** Tuition and fees 2010-2011: $31,253; room/board: $10,338. Estimated books and supplies: $1,000; transportation: $1,200; personal expenses: $2,100. **Financial aid:** Priority filing date for institution's financial aid form: April 15. In 2009-2010, 68% of undergraduates applied for financial aid. Of those, 63% were determined to have financial need; 18% had their need fully met. Average financial aid package (proportion receiving): $24,602 (63%). Average amount of gift aid, such as scholarships or grants (proportion receiving): $18,411 (62%). Average amount of self-help aid, such as work study or loans (proportion receiving): $6,183 (49%). Average need-based loan (excluding PLUS or other private loans): $4,555. Among students who received need-based aid, the average percentage of need met: 75%. Among students who received aid based on merit, the average award (and the proportion receiving): $12,584 (36%). The average athletic scholarship (and the proportion receiving): $9,687 (2%).

CAMPUS LIFE AND EXTRACURRICULAR ACTIVITIES
Campus housing available (% using): coed dorms (79%), sorority housing (6%), fraternity housing (15%), other housing options (0%). Students who live in college-owned, operated, or affiliated housing: 34%. **Student employment:** During the 2009-2010 academic year, 18% of undergraduates worked on campus. Average per-year earnings: $3,282. **Clubs and organizations:** Number of student organizations: 105. Activities include: campus ministries, choral groups, concert band, dance, drama/theater, international student organization, literary magazine, music ensembles, musical theater, radio station, student government, student newspaper, student film society, television station. Number of fraternities: 7; sororities: 3. Proportion of men in fraternities: 12%; of women in sororities: 12%. **Sports program (2009-2010):** Member of NAIA. *Men's intercollegiate varsity sports:* baseball, cross country, soccer, swimming. *Women's intercollegiate varsity sports:* cross country, soccer, swimming, volleyball.

SERVICES AND FACILITIES
Basic services: health service. **Counseling services:** minority student, career, personal, psychological, religious, other. **For learning-disabled students:** School does not offer a structured program with separate admission and additional fees. Services include: tape recorders, other special classes, videotaped classes, note-taking services, oral tests, learning center, readers, extended time for tests, tutors, priority registration, texts on tape, typist/scribe, exams on tape or computer, other testing accommodations, other. **Library:** Number of titles: 1,765,169; number of current serial subscriptions: 34,652. **Information technology resources:** Students are not required to lease or own a computer. Number of campus computers available to all students: 624. School has a wireless network. Proportion of college-owned housing units wired for high-speed internet access: 100%. **Campus safety:** Security services offered: 24-hour foot-and-vehicle patrols, late-night transport/escort service, 24-hour emergency telephones, lighted pathways/sidewalks, controlled dormitory access (key, security card, etc).

TRANSFER AND INTERNATIONAL STUDENTS
Transfer students: May apply for admission for the following academic terms: Fall, Spring. Applicants need a minimum number of credits to apply. For fall 2009: Transfer applications received: 845. Transfer applicants offered admission: 309. Transfer applicants enrolled: 176.

International students: Number of foreign undergraduates: 442 (17% of student body). Number of countries represented: 72. Minimum TOEFL score required: 550 (paper); 213 (computer). Average TOEFL score: 597 (paper).

Illinois State University

- **Address:** Campus Box 2200, Normal, IL 61790-2200
- **Website:** http://www.ilstu.edu
- **Public**
- **Enrollment:** 17,290 full-time; 1,099 part-time

KEY STATS
✔ **U.S News College Ranking:** 156, National Universities
✔ **ACT Score (25th/75th percentile):** 22-26
✔ **Tuition:** 2009-2010: $10,531 in state, $16,561 out of state

Selectivity: Selective	**Room/board:** $7,882
Acceptance rate: 62%	**Average debt:** $20,105
Student/faculty ratio: 19/1	**Proportion who borrowed:** 61%

UNDERGRADUATE STUDENT BODY STATS
2009-2010 enrollment: 17,290 full-time; 1,099 part-time. Men: 44%; women: 56%. **Ethnic makeup:** African American: 6%; Asian American: 2%; Hispanic: 5%; White: 87%.

ADMISSIONS FACTS AND FIGURES
Phone: (309) 438-2181. **Email:** admissions@ilstu.edu. **Website:** http://www.ilstu.edu. **Application deadlines for fall 2011:** Regular decision: March 1. Early decision: Not offered. Early action: Not offered. Admission cannot be deferred. **Application fee:** $40. **To apply online, go to:** http://www.admissions.ilstu.edu/apply/. **Admissions requirements/recommendations:** High school units required (recommended): English: 4; Mathematics: 3; Science: 2; Foreign language: 2; Social studies: 2; Academic electives: 2; Total units: 15. Tests: The college uses SAT or ACT scores in admissions decisions. Either SAT or ACT required. For admission to the fall 2011 entering class, the school will accept: ACT with or without writing accepted. Campus visit: Required. Admissions interview: Neither required nor recommended. **Factors that count in admissions decisions:** *Academic:* Secondary school record: Very Important. Class rank: Not Considered. Letters of recommendation: Not Considered. Standardized test scores: Very Important. Essay: Important. *Nonacademic:* Interview: Not Considered. Extracurricular activities: Not Considered. Talent/ability: Considered. Character/personal qualities: Considered. Alumni/ae relationship: Not Considered. Geographical residence: Not Considered. State residency: Not Considered. Religious affiliation/commitment: Not Considered. Minority status: Not Considered. Volunteer work: Not Considered. Work experience: Not Considered. **Other schools with the greatest overlap in applicants:** Eastern Illinois University; Northern Illinois University; Southern Illinois University–Carbondale; University of Illinois–Urbana-Champaign; Western Illinois University. **Admissions statistics for the fall 2009 entering class:** Total applicants: 14,114. Total accepted: 8,711. Freshmen enrolled: 3,033; 1% were from out of state. Overall acceptance rate: 62%. **Size of waiting list:** 254 applicants; enrolled from waiting list: 240. **Average high school grade point average:** 3.4. **First-year students submitting ACT scores:** 99%. Scores (25/75 percentile): English: 21-27, Math: 22-27, Composite: 22-26.

ACADEMICS
Year founded: 1857. **Academic calendar:** Semester. **Degrees offered:** bachelor's, post-bachelor's certificate, master's, post-master's certificate, doctorate. **Most popular majors:** 19% education, 18% business, management, marketing, and related support services, 7% health professions and related clinical sciences, 6% communication, journalism, and related programs, 6% security and protective services. **Major fields of study:** agriculture, agriculture operations, and related sciences; biological and biomedical sciences; business, management, marketing, and related support services; communication, journalism, and related programs; computer and information sciences and support services; education; engineering technologies/technicians; English language and literature/letters; family and consumer sciences/human sciences; foreign languages, literatures, and linguistics; health professions and related clinical sciences; history; liberal arts and sciences studies, and humanities; mathematics and statistics; parks, recreation, leisure, and fitness studies; philosophy and religious studies; physical sciences; psychology; public administration and social service professions; security and protective services; social sciences; visual and performing

arts. **Areas of required coursework:** arts/fine arts, humanities, computer literacy, mathematics, English (including composition), philosophy, sciences (biological or physical), history, social science. **Pre-professional programs:** pre-law, pre-medicine, pre-veterinary science. **Special academic programs (% participation):** distance learning (50%), double major (5%), dual enrollment (.05%), exchange student program (domestic) (.3%), honors program (9%), independent study (30%), internships (40%), student-designed major (2.8%), study abroad (4.7%), teacher certificate program (25%). **Cooperative education programs:** agriculture, health professions, home economics, natural science, social/behavioral science, technologies. **Reserve Officers Training Corps (ROTC):** Army ROTC: Offered on campus. **Faculty and instruction (2009-2010):** Total instructional faculty: 876 full-time, 304 part-time (51% men; 49% women; 12% minorities). Full-time faculty with Ph.D. or other terminal degree: 83%. Student/faculty ratio: 19/1. Classes of fewer than 20 students: 31%; of 20 to 49 students: 58%; of 50 or more students: 11%. **Advanced Placement and International Baccalaureate credit:** AP tests may be used for: Credit only. **Freshmen returning for sophomore year:** 84%. **Graduation rates:** Four-year: 42%; five-year: 65%; six-year: 69%. **Graduate study:** 45% of students pursue further study within one year; 21% within five years. Fields in which graduates pursue further study: Master of Business Administration (MBA), 8%; law, 6%; medicine, 12%; engineering, 4%; education, 24%; arts and sciences, 39%.

COSTS AND FINANCIAL AID

Financial aid office: (309) 438-2231. **Expenses (2009-2010):** Tuition and fees 2009-2010: $10,531 in state, $16,561 out of state; room/board: $7,882. Estimated books and supplies: $1,084; transportation: $917; personal expenses: $2,337. **Financial aid:** Priority filing date for institution's financial aid form: March 1. In 2009-2010, 72% of undergraduates applied for financial aid. Of those, 55% were determined to have financial need; 38% had their need fully met. Average financial aid package (proportion receiving): $11,678 (52%). Average amount of gift aid, such as scholarships or grants (proportion receiving): $8,857 (31%). Average amount of self-help aid, such as work study or loans (proportion receiving): $7,189 (46%). Average need-based loan (excluding PLUS or other private loans): $7,103. Among students who received need-based aid, the average percentage of need met: 79%. Among students who received aid based on merit, the average award (and the proportion receiving): $3,231 (2%). The average athletic scholarship (and the proportion receiving): $12,175 (1%). Average amount of debt of borrowers graduating in 2009: $20,105. Proportion who borrowed: 61%.

CAMPUS LIFE AND EXTRACURRICULAR ACTIVITIES

Campus housing available: coed dorms, sorority housing, fraternity housing, apartments for married students, apartment for single students, special housing for disabled students, special housing for international students. Students who live in college-owned, operated, or affiliated housing: 33%. **Student employment:** During the 2009-2010 academic year, 15% of undergraduates worked on campus. Average per-year earnings: $2,948. **Clubs and organizations:** Number of student organizations: 250. Activities include: campus ministries, choral groups, concert band, dance, drama/theater, international student organization, jazz band, literary magazine, marching band, music ensembles, musical theater, pep band, radio station, student government, student newspaper, student film society, symphony orchestra, television station. Number of fraternities: 14; sororities: 16. Proportion of men in fraternities: 8%; of women in sororities: 8%. **Sports program (2009-2010):** Member of NCAA I. **Men's intercollegiate varsity sports:** baseball, basketball, cross country, football, golf, gymnastics, swimming, tennis, track and field (indoor). **Women's intercollegiate varsity sports:** basketball, cross country, golf, gymnastics, soccer, softball, swimming, tennis, track and field (indoor), volleyball.

SERVICES AND FACILITIES

Basic services: placement service, day care, health service, health insurance, other. **Remedial assistance:** reading, math, study skills. **Counseling services:** minority student, career, military, personal, veteran student, academic, older student, psychological, birth control, religious. **For learning-disabled students:** School does not offer a structured program with separate admission and additional fees. Total undergraduates in learning-disabled program or receiving services: 184. Services include: reading machines, diagnostic testing service, note-taking services, learning center, readers, extended time for tests, tutors, other testing accommodations. **Library:** Number of titles: 1,519,687; number of current serial subscriptions: 8,878. **Information technology resources:** Students are not required to lease or own a computer. Number of campus computers available to all students: 2,292. School has a wireless network. Approximate number of users that can be accommodated: 1,100. Proportion of college-owned housing units wired for high-speed

internet access: 90%. **Campus safety:** Security services offered: 24-hour foot-and-vehicle patrols, late-night transport/escort service, 24-hour emergency telephones, lighted pathways/sidewalks, student patrols, controlled dormitory access (key, security card, etc).

TRANSFER AND INTERNATIONAL STUDENTS

Transfer students: May apply for admission for the following academic terms: Fall, Spring, Summer. Applicants need a minimum number of credits to apply. For fall 2009: Transfer applications received: 3,993. Transfer applicants offered admission: 3,381. Transfer applicants enrolled: 1,926. **International students:** Number of foreign undergraduates: 90. Number of countries represented: 39. Minimum TOEFL score required: 550 (paper); 213 (computer). Average TOEFL score: 594 (paper).

Illinois Wesleyan University

- **Address:** Box 2900, Bloomington, IL 61702-2900
- **Website:** http://www.iwu.edu
- **Private**
- **Enrollment:** 2,057 full-time; 9 part-time

KEY STATS

✔ **U.S News College Ranking:** 62, National Liberal Arts Colleges
✔ **ACT Score (25th/75th percentile):** 26-30
✔ **Tuition:** 2010-2011: $35,256

Selectivity: More selective	**Room/board:** $8,106
Acceptance rate: 54%	**Average debt:** $26,458
Student/faculty ratio: 11/1	**Proportion who borrowed:** 56%

UNDERGRADUATE STUDENT BODY STATS

2009-2010 enrollment: 2,057 full-time; 9 part-time. Men: 41%; women: 59%. **Ethnic makeup:** African American: 5%; Asian American: 5%; Hispanic: 3%; White: 83%; International: 4%.

ADMISSIONS FACTS AND FIGURES

Phone: (800) 332-2498. **Email:** iwuadmit@iwu.edu. **Website:** http://www.iwu.edu. **Application deadlines for fall 2011:** Regular decision: Rolling. Early decision: Not offered. Early action: Send application by: November 15; Decision sent by: January 15. Admission can be deferred. **To apply online, go to:** http://www2.iwu.edu/admissions/applications/. **Admissions requirements/recommendations:** High school units required (recommended): English: (4); Mathematics: (3); Science: (3); Foreign language: (3); Social studies: (2); Total units: (15). Tests: The college uses SAT or ACT scores in admissions decisions. Either SAT or ACT required. For admission to the fall 2011 entering class, the school will accept: ACT with or without writing accepted. Campus visit: Recommended. Admissions interview: Recommended. Off-campus interview: Not available. **Factors that count in admissions decisions:** *Academic:* Secondary school record: Very Important. Class rank: Important. Letters of recommendation: Considered. Standardized test scores: Important. Essay: Important. *Nonacademic:* Interview: Very Important. Extracurricular activities: Important. Talent/ability: Important. Character/personal qualities: Important. Alumni/ae relationship: Considered. Geographical residence: Considered. State residency: Considered. Religious affiliation/commitment: Not Considered. Minority status: Considered. Volunteer work: Considered. Work experience: Considered. **Other schools with the greatest overlap in applicants:** Augustana College; Northwestern University; University of Illinois–Urbana-Champaign; University of Notre Dame; Washington University in St. Louis. **Admissions statistics for the fall 2009 entering class:** Total applicants: 3,321. Total accepted: 1,785. Freshmen enrolled: 518; 13% were from out of state. Overall acceptance rate: 54%. Non-early acceptance rate: 54%. **Size of waiting list:** 411 applicants; enrolled from waiting list: 26. **Credentials of fall 2009 freshmen:** 45% ranked in the top 10 percent of their high school class; 81% were in the top 25 percent; 99% were in the top half. (Proportion submitting class standing: 67%.) **Average high school grade point average:** 3.9. **First-year students who submitted SAT scores:** 23%. Scores (25/75 percentile): Critical Reading: 570-680, Math: 600-720, Combined: 1170-1400. **First-year students submitting ACT scores:** 94%. Scores (25/75 percentile): English: 25-30, Math: 26-32, Composite: 26-30.

ACADEMICS

Year founded: 1850. **Academic calendar:** Other. **Degrees offered:** bachelor's. **Most popular majors:** 14% business/commerce, 9% English language and literature, 8% accounting, 7% psychology, 6% political science and government. **Major fields of study:** area, ethnic, cultural, and gender studies; biological and biomedical sciences; business, management, marketing, and related support services; computer and information sciences and support services; education; English language and literature/letters; foreign languages, literatures, and linguistics; health professions and related clinical sciences; history; mathematics and statistics; multi/interdisciplinary studies; natural resources and conservation; philosophy and religious studies; physical sciences; psychology; social sciences; visual and performing arts. **Areas of required coursework:** arts/fine arts, humanities, mathematics, English (including composition), foreign languages, sciences (biological or physical), history, social science, other. **Pre-professional programs:** pre-law, pre-dentistry, pre-medicine, pre-theology, pre-veterinary science, pre-optometry, pre-pharmacy. **Special academic programs (% participation):** double major (20%), honors program (10%), independent study (75%), internships (60%), student-designed major (1%), study abroad (50%), teacher certificate program (5%). **Teacher certification offered in:** elementary, middle/junior high, secondary. **Reserve Officers Training Corps (ROTC):** Army ROTC: Offered at cooperating institution (Illinois State University). **Faculty and instruction (2009-2010):** Total instructional faculty: 162 full-time, 67 part-time (54% men; 46% women; 10% minorities). Full-time faculty with Ph.D. or other terminal degree: 92%. Student/faculty ratio: 11/1. Classes of fewer than 20 students: 63%; of 20 to 49 students: 36%; of 50 or more students: 1%. **Advanced Placement and International Baccalaureate credit:** AP tests may be used for: Credit only. Scores accepted: 4, 5. International Baccalaureate exams may be used for: Credit only. **Freshmen returning for sophomore year:** 92%. **Graduation rates:** Four-year: 81%; five-year: 86%; six-year: 86%. **Graduate study:** 40% of students pursue further study within one year. Fields in which graduates pursue further study: Master of Business Administration (MBA), 5%; law, 13%; medicine, 21%; dentistry, 2%; engineering, 2%; theology (or the seminary), 2%; education, 6%; arts and sciences, 34%; veterinary medicine, 1%.

COSTS AND FINANCIAL AID

Financial aid office: (309) 556-3096. **Expenses (2010-2011):** Tuition and fees 2010-2011: $35,256; room/board: $8,106. Estimated books and supplies: $780 personal expenses: $660. **Financial aid:** Priority filing date for institution's financial aid form: March 1; deadline: March 1. In 2009-2010, 66% of undergraduates applied for financial aid. Of those, 59% were determined to have financial need; 67% had their need fully met. Average financial aid package (proportion receiving): $25,753 (59%). Average amount of gift aid, such as scholarships or grants (proportion receiving): $18,340 (59%). Average amount of self-help aid, such as work study or loans (proportion receiving): $7,289 (55%). Average need-based loan (excluding PLUS or other private loans): $5,313. Among students who received need-based aid, the average percentage of need met: 97%. Among students who received aid based on merit, the average award (and the proportion receiving): $11,861 (30%). The average athletic scholarship (and the proportion receiving): $0 (0%). Average amount of debt of borrowers graduating in 2009: $26,458. Proportion who borrowed: 56%.

CAMPUS LIFE AND EXTRACURRICULAR ACTIVITIES

Campus housing available (% using): coed dorms (77%), sorority housing (13%), fraternity housing (9%), apartment for single students (1%). Students who live in college-owned, operated, or affiliated housing: 75%. **Student employment:** During the 2009-2010 academic year, 19% of undergraduates worked on campus. Average per-year earnings: $2,400. **Clubs and organizations:** Number of student organizations: 165. Activities include: campus ministries, choral groups, concert band, dance, drama/theater, international student organization, jazz band, literary magazine, music ensembles, musical theater, opera, pep band, radio station, student government, student newspaper, student film society, symphony orchestra, television station, yearbook. Number of fraternities: 6; sororities: 5. Proportion of men in fraternities: 32%; of women in sororities: 31%. Average proportion of students who stay on campus on weekends: 80%. **Sports program (2009-2010):** Member of NCAA III.

SERVICES AND FACILITIES

Basic services: nonremedial tutoring, placement service, health service, health insurance. **Counseling services:** minority student, career, personal, academic, psychological, birth control, religious, other. **For learning-disabled students:** School does not offer a structured program with separate admission and additional fees. Services include: tape recorders, oral tests, extended time for tests, tutors, other testing accommodations, other. **Library:** Number of titles: 328,368; number of current serial subscriptions: 33,435. **Information technology resources:** Students are not required to lease or own

a computer. Number of campus computers available to all students: 400. School has a wireless network. Approximate number of users that can be accommodated: 1,340. Proportion of college-owned housing units wired for high-speed internet access: 100%. **Campus safety:** Security services offered: 24-hour foot-and-vehicle patrols, late-night transport/escort service, 24-hour emergency telephones, lighted pathways/sidewalks, controlled dormitory access (key, security card, etc).

TRANSFER AND INTERNATIONAL STUDENTS

Transfer students: May apply for admission for the following academic terms: Fall, Spring. Applicants do not need a minimum number of credits to apply. For fall 2009: Transfer applications received: 170. Transfer applicants offered admission: 54. Transfer applicants enrolled: 30. **International students:** Number of foreign undergraduates: 84 (4% of student body). Number of countries represented: 22. Minimum TOEFL score required: 550 (paper); 80 (computer). Average TOEFL score: 606 (paper).

Judson University

- **Address:** 1151 N. State Street, Elgin, IL 60123-1498
- **Website:** http://www.judsonu.edu
- **Private; Religious affiliation:** American Baptist
- **Enrollment:** 860 full-time; 253 part-time

KEY STATS
✔ **U.S News College Ranking:** 20, Regional Colleges (Midwest)
✔ **ACT Score (25th/75th percentile):** 20-26
✔ **Tuition:** 2010-2011: $24,780

Selectivity: Selective	**Room/board:** $8,500
Acceptance rate: 71%	**Average debt:** $26,493
Student/faculty ratio: 12/1	**Proportion who borrowed:** 88%

UNDERGRADUATE STUDENT BODY STATS

2009-2010 enrollment: 860 full-time; 253 part-time. Men: 43%; women: 57%. **Ethnic makeup:** African American: 4%; Asian American: 2%; Hispanic: 7%; White: 83%; International: 5%. **Religious preference:** Roman Catholic: 6%; Protestant: 36%; No preference: 1%; Unknown: 42%; American Baptist: 3%; Non-Denominational: 11%; Other: 1%.

ADMISSIONS FACTS AND FIGURES

Phone: (800) 879-5376. **Email:** admissions@judsonu.edu. **Website:** http://www.judsonu.edu. **Application deadlines for fall 2011:** Regular decision: Rolling. Early decision: Not offered. Early action: Not offered. Admission can be deferred. **Application fee:** $50. **To apply online, go to:** http://www.illinoismentor.org/Applications/Judson_University/apply.html. **Admissions requirements/recommendations:** High school units required (recommended): English: 4 (4); Mathematics: 3 (3); Science: 2 (2); Social studies: 2 (2); Total units: 11 (11). Tests: The college uses SAT or ACT scores in admissions decisions. Either SAT or ACT required. For admission to the fall 2011 entering class, the school will accept: ACT with or without writing accepted. Campus visit: Recommended. Admissions interview: Recommended. Off-campus interview: May be arranged. **Factors that count in admissions decisions:** *Academic:* Secondary school record: Very Important. Class rank: Considered. Letters of recommendation: Important. Standardized test scores: Very Important. Essay: Considered. *Nonacademic:* Interview: Not Considered. Extracurricular activities: Not Considered. Talent/ability: Considered. Character/personal qualities: Considered. Alumni/ae relationship: Not Considered. Geographical residence: Not Considered. State residency: Not Considered. Religious affiliation/commitment: Not Considered. Minority status: Not Considered. Volunteer work: Not Considered. Work experience: Not Considered. **Other schools with the greatest overlap in applicants:** Aurora University; Northern Illinois University; Trinity Christian College; Trinity International University. **Admissions statistics for the fall 2009 entering class:** Total applicants: 532. Total accepted: 377. Freshmen enrolled: 174; 29% were from out of state. Overall acceptance rate: 71%. **Credentials of fall 2009 freshmen:** 14% ranked in the top 10 percent of their high school class; 43% were in the top 25 percent; 73% were in the top half. (Proportion submitting class standing: 61%.) **Average high school grade point average:** 3.3. **First-year students who submitted SAT scores:** 10%. Scores (25/75 percentile): Critical Reading: 490-600, Math: 540-600, Combined: 1030-1200. **First-year students submitting ACT scores:** 75%. Scores (25/75 percentile): English: 20-26, Math: 19-26, Composite: 20-26.

ACADEMICS

Year founded: 1963. **Academic calendar:** Semester. **Degrees offered:** certificate, bachelor's, master's. **Most popular majors:** 41% business, management, marketing, and related support services, 18% public administration and social service professions, 10% architecture and related services, 8% education, 8% theology and religious vocations. **Major fields of study:** architecture and related services; biological and biomedical sciences; business, management, marketing, and related support services; communication, journalism, and related programs; education; English language and literature/letters; history; mathematics and statistics; multi/interdisciplinary studies; parks, recreation, leisure, and fitness studies; physical sciences; psychology; public administration and social service professions; security and protective services; social sciences; theology and religious vocations; visual and performing arts. **Areas of required coursework:** arts/fine arts, humanities, mathematics, English (including composition), sciences (biological or physical), history, social science, other. **Pre-professional programs:** pre-law, pre-dentistry, pre-medicine, pre-theology. **Special academic programs (% participation):** accelerated program (44%), distance learning (1%), double major (6%), honors program (3%), independent study (2%), internships (77%), student-designed major (1%), study abroad (5%), teacher certificate program (0%). **Teacher certification offered in:** early childhood, elementary, secondary, bilingual/bicultural. **Reserve Officers Training Corps (ROTC):** Army ROTC: Offered at cooperating institution (Wheaton College). **Faculty and instruction (2009-2010):** Total instructional faculty: 64 full-time, 82 part-time (60% men; 40% women; 25% minorities). Full-time faculty with Ph.D. or other terminal degree: 73%. Student/faculty ratio: 12/1. Classes of fewer than 20 students: 81%; of 20 to 49 students: 19%; of 50 or more students: 0%. **Advanced Placement and International Baccalaureate credit:** AP tests may be used for: Placement only. Scores accepted: 3, 4, 5. International Baccalaureate exams may be used for: Credit only. **Freshmen returning for sophomore year:** 70%. **Graduation rates:** Four-year: 34%; five-year: 52%; six-year: 53%. **Graduate study:** 51% of students pursue further study immediately upon graduation. Fields in which graduates pursue further study: Master of Business Administration (MBA), 33%; theology (or the seminary), 7%; education, 8%; arts and sciences, 43%.

COSTS AND FINANCIAL AID

Financial aid office: (847) 628-2532. **Expenses (2010-2011):** Tuition and fees 2010-2011: $24,780; room/board: $8,500. Estimated books and supplies: $1,500; transportation: $750; personal expenses: $2,000. **Financial aid:** Priority filing date for institution's financial aid form: March 1; deadline: May 1. In 2009-2010, 87% of undergraduates applied for financial aid. Of those, 79% were determined to have financial need; Average financial aid package (proportion receiving): N/A (79%). Average amount of gift aid, such as scholarships or grants (proportion receiving): $7,949 (55%). Average amount of self-help aid, such as work study or loans (proportion receiving): N/A (73%). Among students who received aid based on merit, the average award (and the proportion receiving): $9,388 (11%). The average athletic scholarship (and the proportion receiving): $14,309 (15%). Average amount of debt of borrowers graduating in 2009: $26,493. Proportion who borrowed: 88%.

CAMPUS LIFE AND EXTRACURRICULAR ACTIVITIES

Campus housing available (% using): coed dorms (45%), women's dorms (20%), men's dorms (30%), apartments for married students (5%), special housing for disabled students (0%). Students who live in college-owned, operated, or affiliated housing: 40%. **Student employment:** During the 2009-2010 academic year, 38% of undergraduates worked on campus. Average per-year earnings: $1,500. **Clubs and organizations:** Number of student organizations: 23. Activities include: campus ministries, choral groups, concert band, dance, drama/theater, international student organization, jazz band, music ensembles, musical theater, student government, student film society, symphony orchestra. Number of fraternities: 0; sororities: 0. Average proportion of students who stay on campus on weekends: 40%. **Sports program (2009-2010):** Member of NAIA. *Men's intercollegiate varsity sports:* baseball, basketball, cross country, golf, soccer, tennis, track and field (indoor), track and field (outdoor). *Women's intercollegiate varsity sports:* basketball, cross country, golf, soccer, softball, tennis, track and field (indoor), track and field (outdoor), volleyball.

SERVICES AND FACILITIES

Basic services: nonremedial tutoring, placement service, health service, health insurance. **Remedial assistance:** reading, math, writing, study skills. **Counseling services:** minority student, career, personal, academic, older student, psychological, religious. **For learning-disabled students:** School does not offer a structured program with separate admission and additional fees. Services include: remedial math, remedial English, remedial reading, tape recorders, videotaped classes, untimed tests, note-taking services, oral tests, learning center, readers, extended time for tests, tutors, priority seating, texts on tape, other testing accommodations, other. **Library:** Number of titles: 114,024; number of current serial subscriptions: 532. **Information technology resources:** Students are not required to lease or own a computer. Number of campus computers available to all students: 260. School has a wireless network. Approximate number of users that can be accommodated: 600. Proportion of college-owned housing units wired for high-speed internet access: 100%. **Campus safety:** Security services offered: 24-hour foot-and-vehicle patrols, late-night transport/escort service, 24-hour emergency telephones, lighted pathways/sidewalks, controlled dormitory access (key, security card, etc).

TRANSFER AND INTERNATIONAL STUDENTS

Transfer students: May apply for admission for the following academic terms: Fall, Spring. Applicants need a minimum number of credits to apply. For fall 2009: Transfer applications received: 180. Transfer applicants offered admission: 133. Transfer applicants enrolled: 93. **International students:** Number of foreign undergraduates: 47 (5% of student body). Number of countries represented: 25. Minimum TOEFL score required: 550 (paper); 213 (computer). Average TOEFL score: 533 (paper).

Kendall College

- **Address:** 900 N. North Branch Street, Chicago, IL 60642
- **Website:** http://www.kendall.edu
- **Enrollment:** 1,421 full-time; 968 part-time

KEY STATS

✔ **U.S News College Ranking:** second tier, Regional Colleges (Midwest)
✔ **SAT or ACT Score (25th/75th percentile):** N/A
✔ **Tuition:** 2009-2010: $0 in state, $0 out of state

Selectivity: Less selective	**Room/board:** $10,485
Acceptance rate: 99%	**Average debt:** N/A
Student/faculty ratio: 19/1	**Proportion who borrowed:** N/A

UNDERGRADUATE STUDENT BODY STATS

2009-2010 enrollment: 1,421 full-time; 968 part-time. Men: 30%; women: 70%. **Ethnic makeup:** African American: 18%; Asian American: 4%; Hispanic: 13%; White: 60%; International: 5%.

ADMISSIONS FACTS AND FIGURES

Phone: (877) 588-8860. **Email:** admissions@kendall.edu. **Website:** http://www.kendall.edu. **Application deadlines for fall 2011:** Regular decision: Rolling. Early decision: Not offered. Early action: Not offered. Admission cannot be deferred. **Application fee:** $50. **To apply online, go to:** http://www.kendall.edu/admissions/apply-for-admission/. **Admissions requirements/recommendations:** High school units required (recommended): Total units: 12 (12). Tests: The college uses SAT or ACT scores in admissions decisions. Neither SAT nor ACT required. For admission to the fall 2011 entering class, the school will accept: ACT with or without writing accepted. Campus visit: Recommended. Admissions interview: Required. Off-campus interview: Not available. **Factors that count in admissions decisions:** *Academic:* Secondary school record: Very Important. Class rank: Considered. Letters of recommendation: Very Important. Standardized test scores: Very Important. Essay: Very Important. *Nonacademic:* Interview: Considered. Extracurricular activities: Considered. Talent/ability: Considered. Character/personal qualities: Important. Alumni/ae relationship: Not Considered. Geographical residence: Considered. State residency: Not Considered. Religious affiliation/commitment: Not Considered. Minority status: Not Considered. Volunteer work: Not Considered. Work experience: Considered. **Other schools with the greatest overlap in applicants:** Johnson and Wales University; National-Louis University; Robert Morris University; Roosevelt University; School of the Art Institute of Chicago. **Admissions statistics for the fall 2009 entering class:** Total applicants: 447. Total accepted: 443. Freshmen enrolled: 154; 18% were from out of state. Overall acceptance rate: 99%.

ACADEMICS

Year founded: 1934. **Academic calendar:** Quarter. **Degrees offered:** certificate, associate, transfer-associate, bachelor's. **Most popular majors:** 46% early childhood education and teaching, 46% hospitality administration/management, 8% culinary arts/chef training. **Major fields of study:** business, management, marketing, and related support services; education; personal and culinary services. **Areas of required coursework:** arts/fine arts, humanities, computer literacy, mathematics, English (including composition), foreign languages, sciences (biological or physical), social science. **Special academic programs:** accelerated program, cooperative (work-study plan) program, distance learning, double major, honors program, internships, study abroad, teacher certificate program. **Teacher certification offered in:** early childhood. **Faculty and instruction (2009-2010):** Total instructional faculty: 43 full-time, 154 part-time (42% men; 58% women). Student/faculty ratio: 19/1. Classes of fewer than 20 students: 56%; of 20 to 49 students: 44%; of 50 or more students: 0%. **Advanced Placement and International Baccalaureate credit:** International Baccalaureate exams may be used for: Placement only. **Graduation rates:** Six-year: 38%.

COSTS AND FINANCIAL AID
Financial aid office: (312) 752-2028. **Expenses (2009-2010):** Tuition and fees 2009-2010: $0 in state, $0 out of state; room/board: $10,485. Estimated books and supplies: $1,800.

CAMPUS LIFE AND EXTRACURRICULAR ACTIVITIES
Campus housing available (% using): other housing options (100%). Students who live in college-owned, operated, or affiliated housing: 14%. **Student employment:** During the 2009-2010 academic year, 9% of undergraduates worked on campus. Average per-year earnings: $6,800. **Clubs and organizations:** Number of student organizations: 15. Activities include: dance, international student organization, student government. Number of fraternities: 0; sororities: 0. Average proportion of students who stay on campus on weekends: 13%.

SERVICES AND FACILITIES
Basic services: nonremedial tutoring, health insurance, other. **Remedial assistance:** reading, math, writing, study skills. **Counseling services:** career, academic, psychological. **For learning-disabled students:** School does not offer a structured program with separate admission and additional fees. Total undergraduates in learning-disabled program or receiving services: 52. Services include: remedial math, remedial English, remedial reading, tape recorders, videotaped classes, untimed tests, note-taking services, oral tests, learning center, readers, extended time for tests, tutors, priority registration, priority seating, proofreading services, substitution of courses, texts on tape, exams on tape or computer, take home exams, other testing accommodations, waiver of foreign language degree requirement, other. **Library:** Number of titles: 33,000; number of current serial subscriptions: 300. **Information technology resources:** Students are not required to lease or own a computer. Number of campus computers available to all students: 156. School has a wireless network. **Campus safety:** Security services offered: 24-hour emergency telephones, lighted pathways/sidewalks, controlled dormitory access (key, security card, etc).

TRANSFER AND INTERNATIONAL STUDENTS
Transfer students: May apply for admission for the following academic terms: Fall, Winter, Spring, Summer. Applicants need a minimum number of credits to apply. For fall 2009: Transfer applications received: 836. Transfer applicants offered admission: 834. Transfer applicants enrolled: 457. **International students:** Number of foreign undergraduates: 111 (5% of student body). Number of countries represented: 37. Minimum TOEFL score required: 525 (paper); 71 (computer).

Knox College

- **Address:** 2 E. South Street, Galesburg, IL 61401
- **Website:** http://www.knox.edu
- **Private**
- **Enrollment:** 1,384 full-time; 23 part-time

....

KEY STATS
✔ **U.S News College Ranking:** 75, National Liberal Arts Colleges
✔ **ACT Score (25th/75th percentile):** 26-31
✔ **Tuition:** 2010-2011: $33,024

Selectivity: More selective	**Room/board:** $7,341
Acceptance rate: 74%	**Average debt:** $24,018
Student/faculty ratio: 12/1	**Proportion who borrowed:** 73%

UNDERGRADUATE STUDENT BODY STATS
2009-2010 enrollment: 1,384 full-time; 23 part-time. Men: 40%; women: 60%. **Ethnic makeup:** African American: 5%; American-Indian: 1%; Asian American: 7%; Hispanic: 5%; White: 75%; International: 7%.

ADMISSIONS FACTS AND FIGURES
Phone: (800) 678-5669. **Email:** admission@knox.edu. **Website:** http://www.knox.edu. **Application deadlines for fall 2011:** Regular decision: February 1; decision sent by March 31. Early decision: Not offered. Early action: Send application by: December 1; Decision sent by: December 31. Admission can be deferred. **Application fee:** $40. **To apply online, go to:** http://www.knox.edu/apply. **Admissions requirements/recommendations:** High school units required (recommended): English: (4); Mathematics: (4); Science: (4); Foreign language: (3); Social studies: (2); History: (2); Total units: (19). Tests: The college uses SAT or ACT scores in admissions decisions. Neither SAT nor ACT required. For admission to the fall 2011 entering class, the school will accept: ACT with or without writing accepted. Campus visit: Recommended. Admissions interview: Recommended. Off-campus interview: May be arranged. **Factors that count in admissions decisions:** *Academic:* Secondary school record: Very Important. Class rank: Very Important. Letters of recommendation: Important. Standardized test scores: Considered. Essay: Important. *Nonacademic:* Interview: Considered. Extracurricular activities: Considered. Talent/ability: Considered. Character/personal qualities: Important. Alumni/ae relationship: Considered. Geographical residence: Considered. State residency: Considered. Religious affiliation/commitment: Not Considered. Minority status: Considered. Volunteer work: Considered. Work experience: Not Considered. **Other schools with the greatest overlap in applicants:** Beloit College; Grinnell College; Illinois Wesleyan University; Northwestern University; University of Illinois-Urbana-Champaign. **Admissions statistics for the fall 2009 entering class:** Total applicants: 2,427. Total accepted: 1,788. Freshmen enrolled: 359; 53% were from out of state. Accepted through early-decision or early-action plans: 47%. Overall acceptance rate: 74%. Non-early acceptance rate: 65%. **Size of waiting list:** 67 applicants; enrolled from waiting list: 11. **Credentials of fall 2009 freshmen:** 37% ranked in the top 10 percent of their high school class; 67% were in the top 25 percent; 97% were in the top half. (Proportion submitting class standing: 100%.) **Average high school grade point average:** 3.3. **First-year students who submitted SAT scores:** 23%. Scores (25/75 percentile): Critical Reading: 600-730, Math: 560-690, Combined: 1160-1420. **First-year students submitting ACT scores:** 60%. Scores (25/75 percentile): English: 26-33, Math: 24-30, Composite: 26-31.

ACADEMICS
Year founded: 1837. **Academic calendar:** Trimester. **Degrees offered:** bachelor's. **Most popular majors:** 8% political science and government, 7% economics, 7% education, 7% psychology, 6% biology/biological sciences. **Major fields of study:** area, ethnic, cultural, and gender studies; biological and biomedical sciences; computer and information sciences and support services; education; English language and literature/letters; foreign languages, literatures, and linguistics; history; liberal arts and sciences studies, and humanities; mathematics and statistics; multi/interdisciplinary studies; natural resources and conservation; philosophy and religious studies; physical sciences; psychology; social sciences; visual and performing arts. **Areas of required coursework:** arts/fine arts, humanities, computer literacy, mathematics, foreign languages, sciences (biological or physical), social science, other. **Pre-professional programs:** pre-law, pre-medicine, pre-optometry. **Special academic programs (% participation):** double major (22%), dual enrollment (0%), honors program (12%), independent study (76%), internships (70%), student-designed major (4%), study abroad (42%), teacher certificate program (5%). **Teacher certification offered in:** elementary, middle/junior high, secondary. **Faculty and instruction (2009-2010):** Total instructional faculty: 108 full-time, 29 part-time (58% men; 42% women; 15% minorities). Full-time faculty with Ph.D. or other terminal degree: 94%. Student/faculty ratio: 12/1. Classes of fewer than 20 students: 66%; of 20 to 49 students: 34%; of 50 or more students: 0%. **Advanced Placement and International Baccalaureate credit:** AP tests may be used for: Credit and/or placement. Scores accepted: 4, 5. International Baccalaureate exams may be used for: Credit and/or placement. **Freshmen returning for sophomore year:** 90%. **Graduation rates:** Four-year: 66%; five-year: 72%; six-year: 73%. **Graduate study:** 30% of students pursue further study within one year. Fields in which graduates pursue further study: Master of Business Administration (MBA), 3%; law, 13%; medicine, 7%; arts and sciences, 77%.

COSTS AND FINANCIAL AID
Financial aid office: (309) 341-7130. **Expenses (2010-2011):** Tuition and fees 2010-2011: $33,024; room/board: $7,341. Estimated books and sup-

plies: $900; transportation: $450; personal expenses: $1,000. **Financial aid:** Priority filing date for institution's financial aid form: February 15. In 2009-2010, 77% of undergraduates applied for financial aid. Of those, 70% were determined to have financial need; 27% had their need fully met. Average financial aid package (proportion receiving): $25,642 (70%). Average amount of gift aid, such as scholarships or grants (proportion receiving): $19,765 (69%). Average amount of self-help aid, such as work study or loans (proportion receiving): $6,481 (63%). Average need-based loan (excluding PLUS or other private loans): $5,062. Among students who received need-based aid, the average percentage of need met: 90%. Among students who received aid based on merit, the average award (and the proportion receiving): $10,845 (20%). The average athletic scholarship (and the proportion receiving): $0 (0%). Average amount of debt of borrowers graduating in 2009: $24,018. Proportion who borrowed: 73%.

CAMPUS LIFE AND EXTRACURRICULAR ACTIVITIES

Campus housing available (% using): coed dorms (58%), women's dorms (1%), men's dorms (1%), fraternity housing (13%), apartments for married students (1%), apartment for single students (1%), special housing for disabled students (1%), special housing for international students (1%). Students who live in college-owned, operated, or affiliated housing: 87%. **Student employment:** During the 2009-2010 academic year, 42% of undergraduates worked on campus. **Clubs and organizations:** Number of student organizations: 99. Activities include: campus ministries, choral groups, dance, drama/theater, international student organization, jazz band, literary magazine, model UN, music ensembles, radio station, student government, student newspaper, symphony orchestra. Number of fraternities: 6; sororities: 5. Proportion of men in fraternities: 32%; of women in sororities: 18%. Average proportion of students who stay on campus on weekends: 95%. **Sports program (2009-2010):** Member of NCAA III. *Men's intercollegiate varsity sports:* baseball, basketball, cross country, football, golf, soccer, swimming, tennis, track and field (indoor), track and field (outdoor), wrestling. *Women's intercollegiate varsity sports:* basketball, cross country, golf, soccer, softball, swimming, tennis, track and field (indoor), track and field (outdoor), volleyball.

SERVICES AND FACILITIES

Basic services: nonremedial tutoring, health service, health insurance. **Counseling services:** minority student, career, personal, academic, psychological, birth control. **For learning-disabled students:** School does not offer a structured program with separate admission and additional fees. Total undergraduates in learning-disabled program or receiving services: 65. Services include: learning center, tutors. **Library:** Number of titles: 327,910; number of current serial subscriptions: 7,446. **Information technology resources:** Students are not required to lease or own a computer. Number of campus computers available to all students: 250. School has a wireless network. Approximate number of users that can be accommodated: 4,000. Proportion of college-owned housing units wired for high-speed internet access: 100%. **Campus safety:** Security services offered: 24-hour foot-and-vehicle patrols, late-night transport/escort service, 24-hour emergency telephones, lighted pathways/sidewalks, controlled dormitory access (key, security card, etc).

TRANSFER AND INTERNATIONAL STUDENTS

Transfer students: May apply for admission for the following academic terms: Fall, Winter, Spring. Applicants need a minimum number of credits to apply. For fall 2009: Transfer applications received: 126. Transfer applicants offered admission: 70. Transfer applicants enrolled: 35. **International students:** Number of foreign undergraduates: 95 (7% of student body). Number of countries represented: 36. Minimum TOEFL score required: 550 (paper); 80 (computer).

Lake Forest College

- **Address:** 555 N. Sheridan Road, Lake Forest, IL 60045
- **Website:** http://www.lakeforest.edu
- **Private**
- **Enrollment:** 1,384 full-time; 14 part-time

KEY STATS

✔ **U.S News College Ranking:** 105, National Liberal Arts Colleges
✔ **ACT Score (25th/75th percentile):** 23-28
✔ **Tuition:** 2009-2010: $34,206

Selectivity: More selective	**Room/board:** $8,006
Acceptance rate: 69%	**Average debt:** $29,279
Student/faculty ratio: 12/1	**Proportion who borrowed:** 74%

UNDERGRADUATE STUDENT BODY STATS

2009-2010 enrollment: 1,384 full-time; 14 part-time. Men: 41%; women: 59%. **Ethnic makeup:** African American: 5%; Asian American: 4%; Hispanic: 7%; White: 73%; International: 11%.

ADMISSIONS FACTS AND FIGURES

Phone: (847) 735-5000. **Email:** admissions@lakeforest.edu. **Website:** http://www.lakeforest.edu. **Application deadlines for fall 2011:** Regular decision: Rolling; decision sent by March 20. Early decision: Send application by: December 1; Decision sent by: December 20. Early action: Send application by: December 1; Decision sent by: January 20. Admission can be deferred. **To apply online, go to:** http://www.lakeforest.edu/admissions/application/default.asp. **Admissions requirements/recommendations:** High school units required (recommended): English: 4 (4); Mathematics: 3 (4); Science: 3 (4); Foreign language: 2 (4); Social studies: 2 (2); History: 2 (2); Academic electives: 3 (3); Total units: 19 (23). Tests: The college uses SAT or ACT scores in admissions decisions. Neither SAT nor ACT required. For admission to the fall 2011 entering class, the school will accept: ACT with or without writing accepted. Campus visit: Recommended. Admissions interview: Recommended. Off-campus interview: May be arranged. **Factors that count in admissions decisions:** *Academic:* Secondary school record: Very Important. Class rank: Considered. Letters of recommendation: Very Important. Standardized test scores: Considered. Essay: Important. *Nonacademic:* Interview: Very Important. Extracurricular activities: Important. Talent/ability: Important. Character/personal qualities: Important. Alumni/ae relationship: Considered. Geographical residence: Considered. State residency: Not Considered. Religious affiliation/commitment: Not Considered. Minority status: Not Considered. Volunteer work: Considered. Work experience: Considered. **Other schools with the greatest overlap in applicants:** DePaul University; Illinois Wesleyan University; Knox College; Loyola University Chicago; University of Illinois–Urbana-Champaign. **Admissions statistics for the fall 2009 entering class:** Total applicants: 2,026. Total accepted: 1,398. Freshmen enrolled: 355; 53% were from out of state. Overall acceptance rate: 69%. Non-early acceptance rate: 69%. **Size of waiting list:** 47 applicants; enrolled from waiting list: 18. **Credentials of fall 2009 freshmen:** 38% ranked in the top 10 percent of their high school class; 62% were in the top 25 percent; 92% were in the top half. (Proportion submitting class standing: 51%.) **Average high school grade point average:** 3.5. First-year students who submitted SAT scores: 33%. **First-year students submitting ACT scores:** 62%. Scores (25/75 percentile): English: 23-29, Math: 23-28, Composite: 23-28.

ACADEMICS

Year founded: 1857. **Academic calendar:** Semester. **Degrees offered:** bachelor's, master's. **Most popular majors:** 11% communication studies/speech communication and rhetoric, 9% economics, 8% business/commerce, 7% English language and literature, 7% history. **Major fields of study:** area, ethnic, cultural, and gender studies; biological and biomedical sciences; business, management, marketing, and related support services; communication, journalism, and related programs; computer and information sciences and support services; education; English language and literature/letters; foreign languages, literatures, and linguistics; history; liberal arts and sciences studies, and humanities; mathematics and statistics; natural resources and conservation; philosophy and religious studies; physical sciences; psychology; social sciences; visual and performing arts. **Areas of required coursework:** humanities, mathematics, English (including composition), sciences (biological or physical), social science. **Pre-professional programs:** pre-law, pre-medicine. **Special academic programs (% participation):** accelerated program (0%), double major (35%), independent study (58%), internships (39%), liberal arts/career combination, student-designed major (1%), study abroad (31%), teacher certificate program (4%). **Teacher certification offered in:** elementary, middle/junior high, secondary, bilingual/bicultural. **Cooperative education programs:** engineering. **Faculty and instruction (2009-2010):** Total instructional faculty: 95 full-time, 76 part-time (50% men; 50% women; 11% minorities). Full-time faculty with Ph.D. or other terminal degree: 98%. Student/faculty ratio: 12/1. Classes of fewer than 20 students: 63%; of 20 to 49 students: 37%; of 50 or more students: 0%. **Advanced Placement and International Baccalaureate credit:** AP tests may be used for: Credit and/or placement. Scores accepted: 3, 4, 5. International Baccalaureate exams may be used for: Credit and/or placement. **Freshmen returning for sophomore year:** 80%. **Graduation rates:** Four-year: 59%; five-year: 66%; six-year: 67%. **Graduate study:** 25% of students pursue further study immediately upon graduation; 27% within one year; 40% within five years. Fields in which graduates pursue further study: Master of Business Administration (MBA), 6%; law, 22%; medicine, 28%; engineering, 6%; education, 8%; arts and sciences, 29%; veterinary medicine, 2%.

COSTS AND FINANCIAL AID

Financial aid office: (847) 735-5104. **Expenses (2009-2010):** Tuition and fees 2009-2010: $34,206; room/board: $8,006. Estimated books and supplies: $1,000; transportation: $500; personal expenses: $3,088. **Financial aid:** Priority filing date for institution's financial aid form: February 15; deadline: May 1. In 2009-2010, 76% of undergraduates applied for financial aid. Of those, 76% were determined to have financial need; 100% had their need fully met. Average financial aid package (proportion receiving): $26,500 (76%). Average amount of gift aid, such as scholarships or grants (proportion receiving): $23,300 (76%). Average amount of self-help aid, such as work study or loans (proportion receiving): $5,750 (44%). Average need-based loan (excluding PLUS or other private loans): $4,900. Among students who received aid based on merit, the average award (and the proportion receiving): $12,400 (17%). The average athletic scholarship (and the proportion receiving): $0 (0%). Average amount of debt of borrowers graduating in 2009: $29,279. Proportion who borrowed: 74%.

CAMPUS LIFE AND EXTRACURRICULAR ACTIVITIES

Campus housing available (% using): coed dorms (89%), women's dorms (9%), apartment for single students (2%), special housing for disabled students, special housing for international students. Students who live in college-owned, operated, or affiliated housing: 77%. **Student employment:** During the 2009-2010 academic year, 47% of undergraduates worked on campus. Average per-year earnings: $2,000. **Clubs and organizations:** Number of student organizations: 80. Activities include: campus ministries, choral groups, concert band, dance, drama/theater, international student organization, jazz band, literary magazine, model UN, music ensembles, musical theater, radio station, student government, student newspaper, student film society. Number of fraternities: 1; sororities: 5. Proportion of men in fraternities: 9%; of women in sororities: 15%. Average proportion of students who stay on campus on weekends: 80%. **Sports program (2009-2010):** Member of NCAA III. **Men's intercollegiate varsity sports:** basketball, cross country, football, ice hockey, soccer, swimming, tennis. **Women's intercollegiate varsity sports:** basketball, cross country, ice hockey, soccer, softball, swimming, tennis, volleyball.

SERVICES AND FACILITIES

Basic services: nonremedial tutoring, placement service, health service, health insurance, other. **Counseling services:** minority student, career, personal, veteran student, academic, older student, psychological, birth control, religious. **For learning-disabled students:** School does not offer a structured program with separate admission and additional fees. Total undergraduates in learning-disabled program or receiving services: 28. Services include: reading machines, tape recorders, untimed tests, note-taking services, oral tests, learning center, readers, extended time for tests, tutors, early syllabus, priority registration, priority seating, texts on tape, typist/scribe, exams on tape or computer, other testing accommodations. **Library:** Number of titles: 402,367; number of current serial subscriptions: 2,540. **Information technology resources:** Students are not required to lease or own a computer. Number of campus computers available to all students: 190. School has a wireless network. Approximate number of users that can be accommodated: 1,100. Proportion of college-owned housing units wired for high-speed internet access: 100%. **Campus safety:** Security services offered: 24-hour foot-and-vehicle patrols, late-night transport/escort service, 24-hour emergency telephones, lighted pathways/sidewalks, student patrols, controlled dormitory access (key, security card, etc.).

TRANSFER AND INTERNATIONAL STUDENTS

Transfer students: May apply for admission for the following academic terms: Fall, Spring. Applicants do not need a minimum number of credits to apply. For fall 2009: Transfer applications received: 148. Transfer applicants offered admission: 93. Transfer applicants enrolled: 65. **International students:** Number of foreign undergraduates: 150 (11% of student body). Number of countries represented: 31. Minimum TOEFL score required: 550 (paper); 220 (computer). Average TOEFL score: 601 (paper).

Lewis University

- **Address:** 1 University Parkway, Romeoville, IL 60446-2200
- **Website:** http://www.lewisu.edu
- **Private; Religious affiliation:** Roman Catholic
- **Enrollment:** 3,252 full-time; 827 part-time

KEY STATS

✔ **U.S News College Ranking:** 43, Regional Universities (Midwest)
✔ **ACT Score (25th/75th percentile):** 20-25
✔ **Tuition:** 2010-2011: $23,780

Selectivity: Selective	**Room/board:** $8,600
Acceptance rate: 74%	**Average debt:** $20,413
Student/faculty ratio: 14/1	**Proportion who borrowed:** 70%

UNDERGRADUATE STUDENT BODY STATS

2009-2010 enrollment: 3,252 full-time; 827 part-time. Men: 42%; women: 58%. **Ethnic makeup:** African American: 9%; Asian American: 4%; Hispanic: 11%; White: 72%; International: 3%. **Religious preference:** Unknown: 9%; Roman Catholic: 61%; Other: 30%.

ADMISSIONS FACTS AND FIGURES

Phone: (800) 897-9000. **Email:** admissions@lewisu.edu. **Website:** http://www.lewisu.edu. **Application deadlines for fall 2011:** Regular decision: Rolling. Early decision: Not offered. Early action: Not offered. Admission can be deferred. **Application fee:** $40. **To apply online, go to:** http://www.illinoismentor.org/applications/lewis_university/apply.html. **Admissions requirements/recommendations:** High school units required (recommended): English: 3 (4); Mathematics: 0 (3); Science: 0 (2); Foreign language: 0 (2); Social studies: 0 (2); History: 0 (1); Academic electives: 0 (4); Total units: 18 (18). Tests: The college uses SAT or ACT scores in admissions decisions. Either SAT or ACT required. For admission to the fall 2011 entering class, the school will accept: ACT with or without writing accepted. Campus visit: Recommended. Admissions interview: Recommended. Off-campus interview: Not available. **Factors that count in admissions decisions:** *Academic:* Secondary school record: Very Important. Class rank: Considered. Letters of recommendation: Considered. Standardized test scores: Very Important. Essay: Important. *Nonacademic:* Interview: Considered. Extracurricular activities: Considered. Talent/ability: Considered. Character/personal qualities: Considered. Alumni/ae relationship: Considered. Geographical residence: Considered. State residency: Not Considered. Religious affiliation/commitment: Not Considered. Minority status: Considered. Volunteer work: Considered. Work experience: Considered. **Other schools with the greatest overlap in applicants:** Benedictine University; DePaul University; Loyola University Chicago; Northern Illinois University; St. Xavier University. **Admissions statistics for the fall 2009 entering class:** Total applicants: 2,674. Total accepted: 1,991. Freshmen enrolled: 658; 7% were from out of state. Overall acceptance rate: 74%. **Credentials of fall 2009 freshmen:** 15% ranked in the top 10 percent of their high school class; 39% were in the top 25 percent; 71% were in the top half. (Proportion submitting class standing: 77%.) **Average high school grade point average:** 3.2. **First-year students who submitted SAT scores:** 3%. Scores (25/75 percentile): Critical Reading: 420-530, Math: 470-580, Combined: 890-1110. **First-year students submitting ACT scores:** 95%. Scores (25/75 percentile): English: 19-25, Math: 18-25, Composite: 20-25.

ACADEMICS

Year founded: 1932. **Academic calendar:** Semester. **Degrees offered:** certificate, associate, bachelor's, master's, post-master's certificate, doctorate. **Most popular majors:** 26% business/commerce, 19% nursing/registered nurse training (R.N., A.S.N., B.S.N., M.S.N.), 12% criminal justice/safety studies, 8% psychology, 7% education. **Major fields of study:** agriculture, agriculture operations, and related sciences; area, ethnic, cultural, and gender studies; biological and biomedical sciences; business, management, marketing, and related support services; communication, journalism, and related programs; communications technologies/technicians and support services; computer and information sciences and support services; education; English language and literature/letters; health professions and related clinical sciences; liberal arts and sciences studies, and humanities; mathematics and statistics; natural resources and conservation; parks, recreation, leisure, and fitness studies; philosophy and religious studies; physical sciences; psychology; public administration and social service professions; security and protective services; social sciences; transportation and materials moving; visual and performing arts. **Areas of required coursework:** arts/fine arts, humanities, mathematics, English (including composition), philosophy, sciences (biological or physical), history, social science. **Pre-professional programs:** pre-law, pre-dentistry, pre-medicine, pre-theology, pre-veterinary science, pre-optometry, pre-pharmacy, other. **Special academic programs (% participation):** accelerated program (17%), distance learning, double major (10%), dual enrollment, English as a Second Language (ESL) (1%), exchange student program (domestic), honors program (5%), independent study (9%), internships (20%), liberal arts/career combination (75%), student-designed major, study abroad (5%), teacher certificate program (10%). **Teacher certification offered in:** special education, elementary, middle/junior high, secondary. **Reserve Officers Training Corps (ROTC):** Army ROTC: Offered at cooperating institution (Olivet Nazarene University); Air Force ROTC: Offered at cooperating institution (Illinois Institute of Technology). **Faculty and instruction (2009-2010):** Total instructional faculty: 189 full-time, 352 part-time (55% men; 45% women; 8% minorities). Full-time faculty with Ph.D. or other terminal degree: 68%. Student/faculty ratio: 14/1. Classes of fewer than 20 students: 65%; of 20 to 49 students: 35%; of 50 or more students: 0%. **Advanced Placement and International Baccalaureate credit:** AP tests may be used for: Placement only. Scores accepted: 3, 4, 5. International Baccalaureate exams may be used for: Placement only. **Freshmen returning for sophomore year:** 79%. **Graduation rates:** Four-year: 39%; five-year: 58%; six-year: 55%. **Graduate study:** 10% of students pursue further study immediately upon graduation; 25% within one year; 40% within five years. Fields in which graduates pursue further study: Master of Business Administration (MBA), 23%; law, 5%; medicine, 21%; theology (or the seminary), 1%; education, 31%; arts and sciences, 20%.

COSTS AND FINANCIAL AID

Financial aid office: (815) 836-5263. **Expenses (2010-2011):** Tuition and fees 2010-2011: $23,780; room/board: $8,600. Estimated books and supplies: $1,000; transportation: $500; personal expenses: $1,600. **Financial aid:** Priority filing date for institution's financial aid form: May 1; deadline: May 1. In 2009-2010, 85% of undergraduates applied for financial aid. Of those, 73% were determined to have financial need; 68% had their need fully met. Average financial aid package (proportion receiving): $18,419 (72%). Average amount of gift aid, such as scholarships or grants (proportion receiving): $8,954 (36%). Average amount of self-help aid, such as work study or loans (proportion receiving): $5,670 (56%). Average need-based loan (excluding PLUS or other private loans): $4,322. Among students who received need-based aid, the average percentage of need met: 84%. Among students who received aid based on merit, the average award (and the proportion receiving): $7,538 (9%). The average athletic scholarship (and the proportion receiving): $6,255 (6%). Average amount of debt of borrowers graduating in 2009: $20,413. Proportion who borrowed: 70%.

CAMPUS LIFE AND EXTRACURRICULAR ACTIVITIES

Campus housing available (% using): coed dorms (100%), special housing for disabled students. Students who live in college-owned, operated, or affiliated housing: 30%. **Student employment:** During the 2009-2010 academic year, 25% of undergraduates worked on campus. Average per-year earnings: $3,600. **Clubs and organizations:** Number of student organizations: 97. Activities include: campus ministries, choral groups, dance, drama/theater, international student organization, jazz band, literary magazine, music ensembles, musical theater, radio station, student government, student newspaper, television station. Number of fraternities: 5; sororities: 7. Proportion of men in fraternities: 1%; of women in sororities: 1%. Average proportion of students who stay on campus on weekends: 60%. **Sports program (2009-2010):** Member of NCAA II. *Men's intercollegiate varsity sports:* baseball, basketball, cross country, golf, soccer, swimming, tennis, track and field (indoor), track and field (outdoor), volleyball. *Women's intercollegiate varsity sports:* basketball, cross country, golf, soccer, softball, swimming, tennis, track and field (indoor), track and field (outdoor), volleyball.

SERVICES AND FACILITIES

Basic services: nonremedial tutoring, health service, health insurance. **Remedial assistance:** reading, math, writing, study skills. **Counseling ser-**

vices: minority student, career, military, personal, academic, older student, psychological, religious. **For learning-disabled students:** School does not offer a structured program with separate admission and additional fees. Services include: diagnostic testing service, untimed tests, note-taking services, oral tests, learning center, readers, extended time for tests, tutors, priority registration, priority seating, other testing accommodations. **Library:** Number of titles: 172,059; number of current serial subscriptions: 1,238. **Information technology resources:** Students are not required to lease or own a computer. Number of campus computers available to all students: 540. School has a wireless network. Approximate number of users that can be accommodated: 3,000. Proportion of college-owned housing units wired for high-speed internet access: 100%. **Campus safety:** Security services offered: 24-hour foot-and-vehicle patrols, late-night transport/escort service, 24-hour emergency telephones, lighted pathways/sidewalks, student patrols, controlled dormitory access (key, security card, etc).

TRANSFER AND INTERNATIONAL STUDENTS

Transfer students: May apply for admission for the following academic terms: Fall, Spring, Summer. Applicants need a minimum number of credits to apply. For fall 2009: Transfer applications received: 1,085. Transfer applicants offered admission: 603. Transfer applicants enrolled: 372. **International students:** Number of foreign undergraduates: 122 (3% of student body). Number of countries represented: 31. Minimum TOEFL score required: 500 (paper); 173 (computer). Average TOEFL score: 515 (paper).

Lincoln College

- ■ **Address:** 715 W. Raab Road, Normal, IL 61761
- ■ **Website:** http://www.lincolncollege.edu
- ■ **Private**
- ■ **Enrollment:** N/A

KEY STATS

✔ **U.S News College Ranking:** second tier, Regional Colleges (Midwest)
✔ **SAT or ACT Score (25th/75th percentile):** N/A
✔ **Tuition:** 2009-2010: $21,000

Selectivity: Less selective	**Room/board:** $6,500
Acceptance rate: N/A	**Average debt:** N/A
Student/faculty ratio: N/A	**Proportion who borrowed:** N/A

Loyola University Chicago

- ■ **Address:** 1032 W. Sheridan Road, Chicago, IL 60660
- ■ **Website:** http://www.luc.edu
- ■ **Private; Religious affiliation:** Roman Catholic
- ■ **Enrollment:** 9,348 full-time; 729 part-time

KEY STATS

✔ **U.S News College Ranking:** 117, National Universities
✔ **ACT Score (25th/75th percentile):** 24-29
✔ **Tuition:** 2010-2011: $32,114

Selectivity: More selective	**Room/board:** $11,220
Acceptance rate: 78%	**Average debt:** $35,526
Student/faculty ratio: 15/1	**Proportion who borrowed:** 77%

UNDERGRADUATE STUDENT BODY STATS

2009-2010 enrollment: 9,348 full-time; 729 part-time. Men: 35%; women: 65%. **Ethnic makeup:** African American: 5%; Asian American: 12%; Hispanic: 10%; White: 73%; International: 1%. **Religious preference:** Roman Catholic: 67%; Protestant: 3%; Jewish: 2%; Muslim: 5%; Hindu: 3%; No preference: 6%; Orthodox: 4%; Other: 10%.

ADMISSIONS FACTS AND FIGURES

Phone: (312) 915-6500. **Email:** admission@luc.edu. **Website:** http://www.luc.edu. **Application deadlines for fall 2011:** Regular decision: Rolling. Early decision: Not offered. Early action: Not offered. Admission cannot be deferred. **Application fee:** None. **To apply online, go to:** http://www.luc.edu/undergrad/admission.shtml. **Admissions requirements/recommendations:** High school units required (recommended): English: 4 (4); Mathematics: 3 (4); Science: 3 (3); Foreign language: 2 (2); Social studies: 2 (2); History: 1 (2);

Academic electives: 0 (3); Total units: 15 (20). Tests: The college uses SAT or ACT scores in admissions decisions. Either SAT or ACT required. For admission to the fall 2011 entering class, the school will accept: ACT with or without writing accepted. Campus visit: Recommended. Admissions interview: Recommended. Off-campus interview: May be arranged. **Factors that count in admissions decisions:** *Academic:* Secondary school record: Very Important. Class rank: Considered. Letters of recommendation: Important. Standardized test scores: Very Important. Essay: Important. *Nonacademic:* Interview: Considered. Extracurricular activities: Important. Talent/ability: Considered. Character/personal qualities: Important. Alumni/ae relationship: Considered. Geographical residence: Considered. State residency: Considered. Religious affiliation/commitment: Not Considered. Minority status: Not Considered. Volunteer work: Important. Work experience: Considered. **Other schools with the greatest overlap in applicants:** DePaul University; Marquette University; Northwestern University; University of Illinois–Chicago; University of Illinois–Urbana-Champaign. **Admissions statistics for the fall 2009 entering class:** Total applicants: 17,383. Total accepted: 13,583. Freshmen enrolled: 2,076; 42% were from out of state. Overall acceptance rate: 78%. **Size of waiting list:** 0 applicants; enrolled from waiting list: 0. **Credentials of fall 2009 freshmen:** 32% ranked in the top 10 percent of their high school class; 67% were in the top 25 percent; 96% were in the top half. (Proportion submitting class standing: 62%.) **Average high school grade point average:** 3.7. **First-year students who submitted SAT scores:** 29%. Scores (25/75 percentile): Critical Reading: 540-650, Math: 530-650, Combined: 1070-1300. **First-year students submitting ACT scores:** 90%. Scores (25/75 percentile): English: 24-30, Math: 23-29, Composite: 24-29.

ACADEMICS

Year founded: 1870. **Academic calendar:** Semester. **Degrees offered:** certificate, bachelor's, post-bachelor's certificate, master's, post-master's certificate, doctorate. **Most popular majors:** 24% business, management, marketing, and related support services, 12% social sciences, 11% biological and biomedical sciences, 11% psychology, 8% health professions and related clinical sciences. **Major fields of study:** biological and biomedical sciences; business, management, marketing, and related support services; communication, journalism, and related programs; computer and information sciences and support services; education; English language and literature/letters; foreign languages, literatures, and linguistics; health professions and related clinical sciences; history; liberal arts and sciences studies, and humanities; mathematics and statistics; multi/interdisciplinary studies; natural resources and conservation; philosophy and religious studies; physical sciences; psychology; public administration and social service professions; security and protective services; social sciences; theology and religious vocations; visual and performing arts. **Areas of required coursework:** arts/fine arts, humanities, computer literacy, mathematics, philosophy, foreign languages, sciences (biological or physical), history, social science, other. **Preprofessional programs:** pre-law, pre-dentistry, pre-medicine, pre-veterinary science, pre-optometry, pre-pharmacy, other. **Special academic programs (% participation):** accelerated program (.9%), distance learning (4%), double major (22%), dual enrollment (0%), exchange student program (domestic), honors program (4%), independent study, internships, study abroad (27.7%), teacher certificate program (4%). **Teacher certification offered in:** early childhood, special education, elementary, secondary, bilingual/bicultural. **Reserve Officers Training Corps (ROTC):** Army ROTC: Offered at cooperating institution (University of Illinois–Chicago); Navy ROTC: Offered at cooperating institution (Northwestern University); Air Force ROTC: Offered at cooperating institution (Illinois Institute of Technology). **Faculty and instruction (2009-2010):** Total instructional faculty: 629 full-time, 723 part-time (51% men; 49% women; 10% minorities). Full-time faculty with Ph.D. or other terminal degree: 93%. Student/faculty ratio: 15/1. Classes of fewer than 20 students: 32%; of 20 to 49 students: 59%; of 50 or more students: 9%. **Advanced Placement and International Baccalaureate credit:** AP tests may be used for: Credit and/or placement. Scores accepted: 3, 4, 5. International Baccalaureate exams may be used for: Credit and/or placement. **Freshmen returning for sophomore year:** 84%. **Graduation rates:** Four-year: 48%; five-year: 65%; six-year: 68%.

COSTS AND FINANCIAL AID

Financial aid office: (773) 508-3155. **Expenses (2010-2011):** Tuition and fees 2010-2011: $32,114; room/board: $11,220. Estimated books and supplies: $1,200; transportation: $450; personal expenses: $1,600. **Financial aid:** Priority filing date for institution's financial aid form: March 1. In 2009-2010, 82% of undergraduates applied for financial aid. Of those, 73% were determined to have financial need; 8% had their need fully met. Average financial aid package (proportion receiving): $27,092 (73%).

Average amount of gift aid, such as scholarships or grants (proportion receiving): $16,380 (70%). Average amount of self-help aid, such as work study or loans (proportion receiving): $6,514 (65%). Average need-based loan (excluding PLUS or other private loans): $4,891. Among students who received need-based aid, the average percentage of need met: 82%. Among students who received aid based on merit, the average award (and the proportion receiving): $7,524 (17%). The average athletic scholarship (and the proportion receiving): $22,146 (1%). Average amount of debt of borrowers graduating in 2009: $35,526. Proportion who borrowed: 77%.

CAMPUS LIFE AND EXTRACURRICULAR ACTIVITIES

Campus housing available (% using): coed dorms (63%), sorority housing, fraternity housing, apartment for single students (35%), special housing for disabled students (1%), special housing for international students (1%). Students who live in college-owned, operated, or affiliated housing: 40%. **Student employment:** During the 2009-2010 academic year, 8% of undergraduates worked on campus. Average per-year earnings: $1,500. **Clubs and organizations:** Number of student organizations: 185. Activities include: campus ministries, choral groups, concert band, dance, drama/theater, international student organization, jazz band, literary magazine, model UN, music ensembles, musical theater, pep band, radio station, student government, student newspaper, student film society, television station, yearbook. Number of fraternities: 7; sororities: 9. Proportion of men in fraternities: 5%; of women in sororities: 8%. Average proportion of students who stay on campus on weekends: 65%. **Sports program (2009-2010):** Member of NCAA I. *Men's intercollegiate varsity sports:* basketball, cross country, golf, soccer, track and field (indoor), track and field (outdoor), volleyball. *Women's intercollegiate varsity sports:* basketball, cross country, golf, soccer, softball, track and field (indoor), track and field (outdoor), volleyball.

SERVICES AND FACILITIES

Basic services: nonremedial tutoring, women's center, placement service, health service, health insurance. **Remedial assistance:** reading, math, writing, study skills, other. **Counseling services:** minority student, career, personal, academic, older student, psychological, religious. **For learning-disabled students:** School does not offer a structured program with separate admission and additional fees. Services include: reading machines, tape recorders, note-taking services, oral tests, readers, extended time for tests, tutors, early syllabus, priority seating, texts on tape, typist/scribe, exams on tape or computer. **Library:** Number of titles: 1,731,343; number of current serial subscriptions: 54,309. **Information technology resources:** Students are not required to lease or own a computer. Number of campus computers available to all students: 1,314. School has a wireless network. Approximate number of users that can be accommodated: 3,000. Proportion of college-owned housing units wired for high-speed internet access: 100%. **Campus safety:** Security services offered: 24-hour foot-and-vehicle patrols, late-night transport/escort service, 24-hour emergency telephones, lighted pathways/sidewalks, controlled dormitory access (key, security card, etc).

TRANSFER AND INTERNATIONAL STUDENTS

Transfer students: May apply for admission for the following academic terms: Fall, Spring, Summer. Applicants need a minimum number of credits to apply. For fall 2009: Transfer applications received: 2,257. Transfer applicants offered admission: 1,600. Transfer applicants enrolled: 590. **International students:** Number of foreign undergraduates: 99 (1% of student body). Number of countries represented: 72. Minimum TOEFL score required: 550 (paper); 213 (computer).

MacMurray College

- **Address:** 447 E. College, Jacksonville, IL 62650
- **Website:** http://www.mac.edu
- **Private; Religious affiliation:** United Methodist
- **Enrollment:** 473 full-time; 45 part-time

KEY STATS

✔ **U.S News College Ranking:** 52, Regional Colleges (Midwest)
✔ **ACT Score (25th/75th percentile):** 17-22
✔ **Tuition:** 2010-2011: $18,810

Selectivity: Less selective	**Room/board:** $6,710
Acceptance rate: 59%	**Average debt:** $27,524
Student/faculty ratio: 12/1	**Proportion who borrowed:** 94%

UNDERGRADUATE STUDENT BODY STATS

2009-2010 enrollment: 473 full-time; 45 part-time. Men: 37%; women: 63%. **Ethnic makeup:** African American: 16%; Asian American: 1%; Hispanic: 4%; White: 78%. **Religious preference:** Roman Catholic: 16%; Protestant: 34%; Jewish: 1%; No preference: 3%; Unknown: 31%; United Methodist: 15%.

ADMISSIONS FACTS AND FIGURES

Phone: (217) 479-7056. **Email:** admissions@mac.edu. **Website:** http://www.mac.edu. **Application deadlines for fall 2011:** Regular decision: Rolling. Early decision: Not offered. Early action: Not offered. Admission can be deferred. **To apply online, go to:** https://www.mac.edu/admission/apply_online.asp. **Admissions requirements/recommendations:** High school units required (recommended): English: (4); Mathematics: (3); Science: (3); Foreign language: (2); Social studies: (2); History: (3); Total units: (17). Tests: The college uses SAT or ACT scores in admissions decisions. Either SAT or ACT required. For admission to the fall 2011 entering class, the school will accept: ACT with or without writing accepted. Campus visit: Recommended. Admissions interview: Neither required nor recommended. Off-campus interview: May be arranged. **Factors that count in admissions decisions: Academic:** Secondary school record: Important. Class rank: Important. Letters of recommendation: Considered. Standardized test scores: Very Important. Essay: Considered. **Nonacademic:** Interview: Considered. Extracurricular activities: Important. Talent/ability: Important. Character/personal qualities: Considered. Alumni/ae relationship: Not Considered. Geographical residence: Not Considered. State residency: Not Considered. Religious affiliation/commitment: Not Considered. Minority status: Not Considered. Volunteer work: Considered. Work experience: Considered. **Other schools with the greatest overlap in applicants:** Illinois College; Southern Illinois University–Carbondale; Southern Illinois University–Edwardsville; Western Illinois University. **Admissions statistics for the fall 2009 entering class:** Total applicants: 492. Total accepted: 291. Freshmen enrolled: 96; 29% were from out of state. Overall acceptance rate: 59%. **Size of waiting list:** 0 applicants; enrolled from waiting list: 0. **First-year students who submitted SAT scores:** 2%. **First-year students submitting ACT scores:** 97%. Scores (25/75 percentile): English: 15-21, Math: 16-22, Composite: 17-22.

ACADEMICS

Year founded: 1846. **Academic calendar:** Semester. **Degrees offered:** associate, bachelor's. **Most popular majors:** 19% nursing/registered nurse training (R.N., A.S.N., B.S.N., M.S.N.), 12% criminal justice/law enforcement administration, 10% social work, 9% education/teaching of individuals with hearing impairments, including deafness, 8% English language and literature. **Major fields of study:** area, ethnic, cultural, and gender studies; biological and biomedical sciences; business, management, marketing, and related support services; education; English language and literature/letters; foreign languages, literatures, and linguistics; health professions and related clinical sciences; history; legal professions and studies; liberal arts and sciences studies, and humanities; parks, recreation, leisure, and fitness studies; philosophy and religious studies; psychology; public administration and social service professions; security and protective services; social sciences; theology and religious vocations; visual and performing arts. **Areas of required coursework:** arts/fine arts, humanities, mathematics, English (including composition), sciences (biological or physical), social science. **Pre-professional programs:** pre-law, pre-dentistry, pre-medicine, pre-theology, pre-veterinary science, other. **Special academic programs (% participation):** cross-registration (2%), distance learning (4%), double major (15%), dual enrollment (4%), independent study (5%), internships (50%), liberal arts/career combination (100%), student-designed major (1%), study abroad (5%), teacher certificate program (30%), weekend college (1%). **Teacher certification offered in:** special education, elementary, middle/junior high, secondary. **Faculty and instruction (2009-2010):** Total instructional faculty: 33 full-time, 24 part-time (35% men; 65% women; 4% minorities). Full-time faculty with Ph.D. or other terminal degree: 58%. Student/faculty ratio: 12/1. Classes of fewer than 20 students: 61%; of 20 to 49 students: 38%; of 50 or more students: 1%. **Advanced Placement and International Baccalaureate credit:** AP tests may be used for: Credit and/or placement. Scores accepted: 3, 4, 5. International Baccalaureate exams may be used for: Credit only. **Freshmen returning for sophomore year:** 60%. **Graduation rates:** Four-year: 30%; five-year: 35%; six-year: 48%. **Graduate study:** 11% of students pursue further study within one year.

COSTS AND FINANCIAL AID

Financial aid office: (217) 479-7041. **Expenses (2010-2011):** Tuition and fees 2010-2011: $18,810; room/board: $6,710. Estimated books and supplies:

$800; transportation: $700; personal expenses: $982. **Financial aid:** Priority filing date for institution's financial aid form: April 1. In 2009-2010, 98% of undergraduates applied for financial aid. Of those, 95% were determined to have financial need; 47% had their need fully met. Average financial aid package (proportion receiving): $24,166 (95%). Average amount of gift aid, such as scholarships or grants (proportion receiving): $14,107 (93%). Average amount of self-help aid, such as work study or loans (proportion receiving): $10,195 (95%). Average need-based loan (excluding PLUS or other private loans): $10,059. Among students who received need-based aid, the average percentage of need met: 93%. Among students who received aid based on merit, the average award (and the proportion receiving): $9,212 (3%). The average athletic scholarship (and the proportion receiving): $0 (0%). Average amount of debt of borrowers graduating in 2009: $27,524. Proportion who borrowed: 94%.

CAMPUS LIFE AND EXTRACURRICULAR ACTIVITIES

Campus housing available (% using): coed dorms (100%). Students who live in college-owned, operated, or affiliated housing: 44%. **Student employment:** During the 2009-2010 academic year, 4% of undergraduates worked on campus. Average per-year earnings: $396. **Clubs and organizations:** Number of student organizations: 32. Activities include: campus ministries, choral groups, dance, drama/theater, literary magazine, music ensembles, student government. Number of fraternities: 2; sororities: 2. Average proportion of students who stay on campus on weekends: 45%. **Sports program (2009-2010):** Member of NCAA III. **Men's intercollegiate varsity sports:** baseball, basketball, football, golf, soccer. **Women's intercollegiate varsity sports:** basketball, golf, soccer, softball, volleyball.

SERVICES AND FACILITIES

Basic services: nonremedial tutoring, placement service, health service, health insurance. **Remedial assistance:** study skills. **Counseling services:** career, personal, veteran student, academic, older student, psychological, religious. **For learning-disabled students:** School does not offer a structured program with separate admission and additional fees. Services include: untimed tests, note-taking services, oral tests, learning center, readers, tutors, texts on tape. **Library:** Number of titles: 1,795,627; number of current serial subscriptions: 115. **Information technology resources:** Students are not required to lease or own a computer. Number of campus computers available to all students: 61. School has a wireless network. Proportion of college-owned housing units wired for high-speed internet access: 100%. **Campus safety:** Security services offered: 24-hour foot-and-vehicle patrols, late-night transport/escort service, 24-hour emergency telephones, lighted pathways/sidewalks, controlled dormitory access (key, security card, etc).

TRANSFER AND INTERNATIONAL STUDENTS

Transfer students: May apply for admission for the following academic terms: Fall, Spring, Summer. Applicants need a minimum number of credits to apply. **International students:** Number of foreign undergraduates: 1. Number of countries represented: 1. Minimum TOEFL score required: 550 (paper); 79 (computer). Average TOEFL score: 565 (paper).

McKendree University

- **Address:** 701 College Road, Lebanon, IL 62254-1299
- **Website:** http://www.mckendree.edu
- **Private; Religious affiliation:** Methodist
- **Enrollment:** 1,714 full-time; 598 part-time

KEY STATS

✔ **U.S News College Ranking:** 20, Regional Colleges (Midwest)
✔ **ACT Score (25th/75th percentile):** 19-25
✔ **Tuition:** 2010-2011: $23,130

Selectivity: Selective	Room/board: $8,240
Acceptance rate: 71%	Average debt: $19,445
Student/faculty ratio: 15/1	Proportion who borrowed: 73%

UNDERGRADUATE STUDENT BODY STATS

2009-2010 enrollment: 1,714 full-time; 598 part-time. Men: 45%; women: 55%. **Ethnic makeup:** African American: 13%; Asian American: 1%; Hispanic: 24%; White: 60%; International: 2%. **Religious preference:** Roman Catholic: 23%; Protestant: 24%; No preference: 2%; Unknown: 29%; Methodist: 20%; Other: 2%.

ADMISSIONS FACTS AND FIGURES

Phone: (618) 537-6831. **Email:** inquiry@mckendree.edu. **Website:** http://www.mckendree.edu. **Application deadlines for fall 2011:** Regular decision: Rolling; decision sent by March 1. Early decision: Not offered. Early action: Not offered. Admission can be deferred. **Application fee:** $40. **To apply online, go to:** http://www.mckendree.edu/prospective/Apply_Online.aspx. **Admissions requirements/recommendations:** High school units required (recommended): English: 4 (4); Mathematics: 3 (3); Science: 3 (3); Foreign language: 2 (2); Social studies: 2 (2); History: 2 (2); Total units: 14 (14). Tests: The college uses SAT or ACT scores in admissions decisions. Either SAT or ACT required. For admission to the fall 2011 entering class, the school will accept: ACT with or without writing accepted. Campus visit: Recommended. Admissions interview: Recommended. Off-campus interview: Not available. **Factors that count in admissions decisions:** *Academic:* Secondary school record: Very Important. Class rank: Very Important. Letters of recommendation: Important. Standardized test scores: Important. Essay: Important. *Nonacademic:* Interview: Important. Extracurricular activities: Important. Talent/ability: Very Important. Character/personal qualities: Very Important. Alumni/ae relationship: Considered. Geographical residence: Not Considered. State residency: Not Considered. Religious affiliation/commitment: Not Considered. Minority status: Not Considered. Volunteer work: Important. Work experience: Important. **Other schools with the greatest overlap in applicants:** Illinois College; Millikin University; Southern Illinois University–Edwardsville; University of Illinois–Urbana-Champaign. **Admissions statistics for the fall 2009 entering class:** Total applicants: 1,291. Total accepted: 914. Freshmen enrolled: 307; 11% were from out of state. Overall acceptance rate: 71%. **Credentials of fall 2009 freshmen:** 19% ranked in the top 10 percent of their high school class; 43% were in the top 25 percent; 82% were in the top half. (Proportion submitting class standing: 100%.) **Average high school grade point average:** 3.4. **First-year students who submitted SAT scores:** 3%. Scores (25/75 percentile): Critical Reading: 410-590, Math: 470-560, Combined: 880-1150. **First-year students submitting ACT scores:** 97%. Scores (25/75 percentile): English: 19-24, Math: 18-25, Composite: 19-25.

ACADEMICS

Year founded: 1828. **Academic calendar:** Semester. **Degrees offered:** associate, bachelor's, master's. **Most popular majors:** 30% elementary education and teaching, 17% nursing, 16% business administration and management, 7% management science, 4% accounting. **Major fields of study:** biological and biomedical sciences; business, management, marketing, and related support services; communication, journalism, and related programs; computer and information sciences and support services; education; English language and literature/letters; health professions and related clinical sciences; history; liberal arts and sciences studies, and humanities; mathematics and statistics; philosophy and religious studies; physical sciences; psychology; social sciences; visual and performing arts. **Areas of required coursework:** arts/fine arts, humanities, computer literacy, mathematics, English (including composition), philosophy, foreign languages, sciences (biological or physical), history, social science, other. **Pre-professional programs:** pre-law, pre-dentistry, pre-medicine, pre-theology, pre-veterinary science, pre-optometry, pre-pharmacy. **Special academic programs (% participation):** accelerated program (1%), cross-registration (4%), distance learning (2%), double major (.5%), external degree program (1%), honors program (1%), independent study (12%), internships (24%), liberal arts/career combination (100%), student-designed major (0%), study abroad (1%), teacher certificate program (21%). **Teacher certification offered in:** special education, elementary, secondary. **Cooperative education programs:** business, engineering, health professions. **Reserve Officers Training Corps (ROTC):** Army ROTC: Offered at cooperating institution; Air Force ROTC: Offered at cooperating institution. **Faculty and instruction (2009-2010):** Total instructional faculty: 94 full-time, 210 part-time (57% men; 43% women; 6% minorities). Full-time faculty with Ph.D. or other terminal degree: 83%. Student/faculty ratio: 15/1. Classes of fewer than 20 students: 69%; of 20 to 49 students: 31%. **Advanced Placement and International Baccalaureate credit:** AP tests may be used for: Placement only. Scores accepted: 3, 4, 5. International Baccalaureate exams may be used for: Credit only. **Freshmen returning for sophomore year:** 77%. **Graduation rates:** Four-year: 39%; five-year: 57%; six-year: 60%. **Graduate study:** 20% of students pursue further study immediately upon graduation; 24% within one year; 30% within five years. Fields in which graduates pursue further study: Master of Business Administration (MBA), 23%; law, 15%; medicine, 5%; theology (or the seminary), 5%; education, 22%; arts and sciences, 25%; veterinary medicine, 5%.

COSTS AND FINANCIAL AID

Financial aid office: (618) 537-6828. **Expenses (2010-2011):** Tuition and fees 2010-2011: $23,130; room/board: $8,240. Estimated books and supplies: $1,200; transportation: $1,100; personal expenses: $1,100. **Financial aid:** Priority filing date for institution's financial aid form: May 31. In 2009-2010, 90% of undergraduates applied for financial aid. Of those, 78% were determined to have financial need; 28% had their need fully met. Average financial aid package (proportion receiving): $17,718 (77%). Average amount of gift aid, such as scholarships or grants (proportion receiving): $14,101 (74%). Average amount of self-help aid, such as work study or loans (proportion receiving): $4,866 (59%). Average need-based loan (excluding PLUS or other private loans): $3,996. Among students who received need-based aid, the average percentage of need met: 79%. Among students who received aid based on merit, the average award (and the proportion receiving): $8,591 (17%). The average athletic scholarship (and the proportion receiving): $8,042 (12%). Average amount of debt of borrowers graduating in 2009: $19,445. Proportion who borrowed: 73%.

CAMPUS LIFE AND EXTRACURRICULAR ACTIVITIES

Campus housing available (% using): coed dorms (42%), apartment for single students (58%). Students who live in college-owned, operated, or affiliated housing: 55%. **Student employment:** During the 2009-2010 academic year, 25% of undergraduates worked on campus. Average per-year earnings: $2,000. **Clubs and organizations:** Number of student organizations: 62. Activities include: campus ministries, choral groups, concert band, dance, drama/theater, jazz band, literary magazine, marching band, model UN, music ensembles, musical theater, pep band, radio station, student government, student newspaper, student film society, yearbook. Number of fraternities: 4; sororities: 3. Proportion of men in fraternities: 6%; of women in sororities: 6%. Average proportion of students who stay on campus on weekends: 60%. **Sports program (2009-2010):** Member of NAIA. *Men's intercollegiate varsity sports:* baseball, basketball, cross country, football, golf, soccer, tennis, track and field (indoor), track and field (outdoor), wrestling. *Women's intercollegiate varsity sports:* basketball, bowling, cross country, golf, soccer, softball, tennis, track and field (indoor), track and field (outdoor), volleyball.

SERVICES AND FACILITIES

Basic services: nonremedial tutoring, placement service, health service, health insurance. **Remedial assistance:** reading, math, writing, study skills. **Counseling services:** minority student, career, military, personal, veteran student, academic, psychological, religious. **For learning-disabled students:** School does not offer a structured program with separate admission and additional fees. Services include: remedial math, remedial English, reading machines, tape recorders, untimed tests, oral tests, learning center, extended time for tests, tutors, priority seating, texts on tape. **Library:** Number of titles: 94,000; number of current serial subscriptions: 155. **Information technology resources:** Students are not required to lease or own a computer. Number of campus computers available to all students: 355. School has a wireless network. Approximate number of users that can be accommodated: 1,010. Proportion of college-owned housing units wired for high-speed internet access: 100%. **Campus safety:** Security services offered: 24-hour foot-and-vehicle patrols, late-night transport/escort service, lighted pathways/sidewalks, controlled dormitory access (key, security card, etc).

TRANSFER AND INTERNATIONAL STUDENTS

Transfer students: May apply for admission for the following academic terms: Fall, Spring, Summer. Applicants do not need a minimum number of credits to apply. For fall 2009: Transfer applications received: 430. Transfer applicants offered admission: 286. Transfer applicants enrolled: 182. **International students:** Number of foreign undergraduates: 37 (2% of student body). Number of countries represented: 15. Minimum TOEFL score required: 520 (paper); 190 (computer). Average TOEFL score: 525 (paper).

Millikin University

- **Address:** 1184 W. Main Street, Decatur, IL 62522-2084
- **Website:** http://www.millikin.edu
- **Private; Religious affiliation:** Presbyterian
- **Enrollment:** 2,157 full-time; 119 part-time

KEY STATS

✔ **U.S News College Ranking:** 144, National Liberal Arts Colleges
✔ **ACT Score (25th/75th percentile):** 20-25
✔ **Tuition:** 2010-2011: $27,425

Selectivity: Selective	Room/board: $8,291
Acceptance rate: 60%	Average debt: $28,449
Student/faculty ratio: 11/1	Proportion who borrowed: 82%

UNDERGRADUATE STUDENT BODY STATS

2009-2010 enrollment: 2,157 full-time; 119 part-time. Men: 40%; women: 60%. **Ethnic makeup:** African American: 10%; Asian American: 1%; Hispanic: 3%; White: 84%; International: 1%.

ADMISSIONS FACTS AND FIGURES

Phone: (217) 424-6210. **Email:** admis@millikin.edu. **Website:** http://www.millikin.edu. **Application deadlines for fall 2011:** Regular decision: Rolling. Early decision: Not offered. Early action: Not offered. Admission can be deferred. **To apply online, go to:** http://www.millikin.edu/admission/howapply/. **Admissions requirements/recommendations:** High school units required (recommended): English: (4); Mathematics: (3); Science: (3); Foreign language: (2); Social studies: (2); History: (2); Total units: 15 (16). Tests: The college uses SAT or ACT scores in admissions decisions. Either SAT or ACT required. For admission to the fall 2011 entering class, the school will accept: ACT with or without writing accepted. Campus visit: Recommended. Admissions interview: Recommended. Off-campus interview: May be arranged. **Factors that count in admissions decisions:** *Academic:* Secondary school record: Very Important. Class rank: Important. Letters of recommendation: Important. Standardized test scores: Important. Essay: Not Considered. *Nonacademic:* Interview: Important. Extracurricular activities: Considered. Talent/ability: Considered. Character/personal qualities: Considered. Alumni/ae relationship: Considered. Geographical residence: Not Considered. State residency: Not Considered. Religious affiliation/commitment: Not Considered. Minority status: Not Considered. Volunteer work: Considered. Work experience: Considered. **Admissions statistics for the fall 2009 entering class:** Total applicants: 3,167. Total accepted: 1,905. Freshmen enrolled: 542; 18% were from out of state. Overall acceptance rate: 60%. **Credentials of fall 2009 freshmen:** 17% ranked in the top 10 percent of their high school class; 40% were in the top 25 percent; 76% were in the top half. (Proportion submitting class standing: 91%.) **Average high school grade point average:** 3.3. **First-year students who submitted SAT scores:** 8%. Scores (25/75 percentile): Critical Reading: 480-590, Math: 480-560, Combined: 960-1150. **First-year students submitting ACT scores:** 95%. Scores (25/75 percentile): English: 21-26, Math: 18-25, Composite: 20-25.

ACADEMICS

Year founded: 1901. **Academic calendar:** Semester. **Degrees offered:** bachelor's, master's. **Most popular majors:** 21% business, management, marketing, and related support services, 18% visual and performing arts, 15% education, 11% health professions and related clinical sciences, 6% biological and biomedical sciences. **Major fields of study:** area, ethnic, cultural, and gender studies; biological and biomedical sciences; business, management, marketing, and related support services; communication, journalism, and related programs; computer and information sciences and support services; education; English language and literature/letters; foreign languages, literatures, and linguistics; health professions and related clinical sciences; history; legal professions and studies; mathematics and statistics; multi/interdisciplinary studies; parks, recreation, leisure, and fitness studies; philosophy and religious studies; physical sciences; psychology; public administration and social service professions; security and protective services; social sciences; visual and performing arts. **Areas of required coursework:** arts/fine arts, mathematics, English (including composition), sciences (biological or physical), other. **Pre-professional programs:** pre-law, pre-dentistry, pre-medicine, pre-veterinary science, pre-optometry, pre-pharmacy, other. **Special academic programs (% participation):** accelerated program (18%), double major (8%), exchange student program (domestic) (.2%), honors program (3%), independent study (18%), internships (54%), student-designed major (1%), study abroad (27%), teacher certificate program (18%).

Teacher certification offered in: early childhood, elementary, middle/junior high, secondary. **Faculty and instruction (2009-2010):** Total instructional faculty: 154 full-time, 123 part-time (44% men; 56% women; 10% minorities). Full-time faculty with Ph.D. or other terminal degree: 81%. Student/faculty ratio: 11/1. Classes of fewer than 20 students: 55%; of 20 to 49 students: 43%; of 50 or more students: 2%. **Advanced Placement and International Baccalaureate credit:** AP tests may be used for: Credit only. Scores accepted: 3, 4, 5. International Baccalaureate exams may be used for: Credit only. **Freshmen returning for sophomore year:** 78%. **Graduation rates:** Four-year: 54%; five-year: 63%; six-year: 63%. **Graduate study:** 25% of students pursue further study immediately upon graduation. Fields in which graduates pursue further study: Master of Business Administration (MBA), 5%; law, 5%; medicine, 12%; dentistry, 2%; engineering, 2%; education, 3%; arts and sciences, 70%; veterinary medicine, 1%.

COSTS AND FINANCIAL AID

Financial aid office: (217) 424-6343. **Expenses (2010-2011):** Tuition and fees 2010-2011: $27,425; room/board: $8,291. Estimated books and supplies: $1,000 personal expenses: $2,100. **Financial aid:** Priority filing date for institution's financial aid form: March 15. In 2009-2010, 91% of undergraduates applied for financial aid. Of those, 79% were determined to have financial need; 54% had their need fully met. Average financial aid package (proportion receiving): $19,958 (79%). Average amount of gift aid, such as scholarships or grants (proportion receiving): $8,811 (74%). Average amount of self-help aid, such as work study or loans (proportion receiving): $4,204 (63%). Average need-based loan (excluding PLUS or other private loans): $4,204. Among students who received need-based aid, the average percentage of need met: 92%. Among students who received aid based on merit, the average award (and the proportion receiving): $9,108 (10%). The average athletic scholarship (and the proportion receiving): $0 (0%). Average amount of debt of borrowers graduating in 2009: $28,449. Proportion who borrowed: 82%.

CAMPUS LIFE AND EXTRACURRICULAR ACTIVITIES

Campus housing available (% using): coed dorms (33%), women's dorms (8%), sorority housing (5%), fraternity housing (3%), apartments for married students (2%), apartment for single students (25%), special housing for disabled students (1%), special housing for international students (1%), other housing options (17%). Students who live in college-owned, operated, or affiliated housing: 69%. **Student employment:** During the 2009-2010 academic year, 10% of undergraduates worked on campus. Average per-year earnings: $750. **Clubs and organizations:** Number of student organizations: 94. Activities include: choral groups, concert band, dance, drama/theater, international student organization, jazz band, literary magazine, model UN, music ensembles, musical theater, opera, pep band, radio station, student government, student newspaper, student film society, symphony orchestra. Number of fraternities: 5; sororities: 5. Proportion of men in fraternities: 22%; of women in sororities: 19%. Average proportion of students who stay on campus on weekends: 75%. **Sports program (2009-2010):** Member of NCAA III. **Men's intercollegiate varsity sports:** baseball, basketball, cross country, football, golf, soccer, swimming, track and field (indoor), track and field (outdoor). **Women's intercollegiate varsity sports:** basketball, cross country, golf, soccer, softball, swimming, tennis, track and field (indoor), track and field (outdoor), volleyball.

SERVICES AND FACILITIES

Basic services: nonremedial tutoring, placement service, health service. **Remedial assistance:** writing, study skills. **Counseling services:** minority student, career, personal, academic, older student, psychological, birth control, religious. **For learning-disabled students:** School does not offer a structured program with separate admission and additional fees. Services include: remedial math, remedial English, tape recorders, other special classes, untimed tests, note-taking services, oral tests, learning center, readers, extended time for tests, tutors, texts on tape, other. **Library:** Number of titles: 218,110; number of current serial subscriptions: 365. **Information technology resources:** Students are not required to lease or own a computer. Number of campus computers available to all students: 280. School has a wireless network. Approximate number of users that can be accommodated: 1,000. Proportion of college-owned housing units wired for high-speed internet access: 100%. **Campus safety:** Security services offered: 24-hour foot-and-vehicle patrols, late-night transport/escort service, 24-hour emergency telephones, lighted pathways/sidewalks, controlled dormitory access (key, security card, etc).

TRANSFER AND INTERNATIONAL STUDENTS

Transfer students: May apply for admission for the following academic terms: Fall, Spring, Summer. Applicants need a minimum number of credits to apply. For fall 2009: Transfer applications received: 543. Transfer applicants offered admission: 298. Transfer applicants enrolled: 138. **International students:** Number of foreign undergraduates: 30 (1% of student body). Number of countries represented: 9. Minimum TOEFL score required: 550 (paper); 213 (computer).

Monmouth College

- **Address:** 700 E. Broadway, Monmouth, IL 61462
- **Website:** http://www.monm.edu
- **Private; Religious affiliation:** Presbyterian
- **Enrollment:** 1,366 full-time; 13 part-time

KEY STATS

✔ **U.S News College Ranking:** 174, National Liberal Arts Colleges
✔ **ACT Score (25th/75th percentile):** 20-25
✔ **Tuition:** 2010-2011: $26,900

Selectivity: Selective	**Room/board:** $7,300
Acceptance rate: 70%	**Average debt:** $24,476
Student/faculty ratio: 14/1	**Proportion who borrowed:** 81%

UNDERGRADUATE STUDENT BODY STATS

2009-2010 enrollment: 1,366 full-time; 13 part-time. Men: 48%; women: 52%. **Ethnic makeup:** African American: 6%; American-Indian: 1%; Asian American: 1%; Hispanic: 5%; White: 86%; International: 1%. **Religious preference:** Roman Catholic: 25%; Protestant: 23%; Jewish: 1%; Hindu: 5%; Buddhist: 1%; No preference: 15%; Other: 15%.

ADMISSIONS FACTS AND FIGURES

Phone: (800) 747-2687. **Email:** admit@monm.edu. **Website:** http://www.monm.edu. **Application deadlines for fall 2011:** Regular decision: Rolling. Early decision: Not offered. Early action: Not offered. Admission can be deferred. **To apply online, go to:** https://www.monm.edu/admission/app.htm. **Admissions requirements/recommendations:** High school units required (recommended): English: 4 (4); Mathematics: 3 (3); Science: 2 (3); Foreign language: 2 (3); Social studies: 2 (3); History: 1 (2); Total units: 14 (22). **Tests:** The college uses SAT or ACT scores in admissions decisions. Either SAT or ACT required. For admission to the fall 2011 entering class, the school will accept: ACT with or without writing accepted. Campus visit: Recommended. Admissions interview: Recommended. Off-campus interview: May be arranged. **Factors that count in admissions decisions:** *Academic:* Secondary school record: Very Important. Class rank: Important. Letters of recommendation: Considered. Standardized test scores: Important. Essay: Considered. *Nonacademic:* Interview: Important. Extracurricular activities: Important. Talent/ability: Important. Character/personal qualities: Important. Alumni/ae relationship: Considered. Geographical residence: Considered. State residency: Not Considered. Religious affiliation/commitment: Not Considered. Minority status: Not Considered. Volunteer work: Considered. Work experience: Considered. **Other schools with the greatest overlap in applicants:** Augustana College; Illinois Wesleyan University; Knox College; Lake Forest College; University of Illinois–Urbana-Champaign. **Admissions statistics for the fall 2009 entering class:** Total applicants: 2,070. Total accepted: 1,450. Freshmen enrolled: 440; 2% were from out of state. Overall acceptance rate: 70%. **Credentials of fall 2009 freshmen:** 9% ranked in the top 10 percent of their high school class; 32% were in the top 25 percent; 66% were in the top half. (Proportion submitting class standing: 98%.) **Average high school grade point average:** 3.2. **First-year students who submitted SAT scores:** 2%. Scores (25/75 percentile): Critical Reading: 510-590, Math: 430-570, Combined: 940-1160. **First-year students submitting ACT scores:** 98%. Scores (25/75 percentile): English: 19-25, Math: 19-25, Composite: 20-25.

ACADEMICS

Year founded: 1853. **Academic calendar:** Semester. **Degrees offered:** bachelor's. **Most popular majors:** 26% business, management, marketing, and related support services, 17% education, 9% English language and literature/letters, 9% social sciences, 7% psychology. **Major fields of study:** biological and biomedical sciences; business, management, marketing, and related support services; computer and information sciences and support services; education; engineering; English language and literature/

letters; foreign languages, literatures, and linguistics; health professions and related clinical sciences; history; legal professions and studies; mathematics and statistics; philosophy and religious studies; physical sciences; psychology; social sciences; visual and performing arts. **Areas of required coursework:** arts/fine arts, humanities, mathematics, English (including composition), foreign languages, sciences (biological or physical), social science, other. **Pre-professional programs:** pre-law, pre-dentistry, pre-medicine, pre-theology, pre-veterinary science, pre-optometry. **Special academic programs (% participation):** double major (21%), English as a Second Language (ESL) (.5%), honors program (1%), independent study (49%), internships (42%), student-designed major (1%), study abroad (24%), teacher certificate program (7%). **Teacher certification offered in:** elementary, middle/junior high, secondary. **Cooperative education programs:** art, engineering, health professions. **Reserve Officers Training Corps (ROTC):** Army ROTC: Offered on campus. **Faculty and instruction (2009-2010):** Total instructional faculty: 83 full-time, 43 part-time (54% men; 46% women; 8% minorities). Full-time faculty with Ph.D. or other terminal degree: 83%. Student/faculty ratio: 14/1. Classes of fewer than 20 students: 45%; of 20 to 49 students: 55%; of 50 or more students: 0%. **Advanced Placement and International Baccalaureate credit:** AP tests may be used for: Placement only. Scores accepted: 3, 4, 5. International Baccalaureate exams may be used for: Credit only. **Freshmen returning for sophomore year:** 73%. **Graduation rates:** Four-year: 51%; five-year: 63%; six-year: 64%. **Graduate study:** 24% of students pursue further study immediately upon graduation; 1% within one year; 5% within five years. Fields in which graduates pursue further study: Master of Business Administration (MBA), 15%; law, 21%; medicine, 8%; engineering, 2%; theology (or the seminary), 3%; education, 10%; arts and sciences, 44%; veterinary medicine, 1%.

COSTS AND FINANCIAL AID

Financial aid office: (309) 457-2129. **Expenses (2010-2011):** Tuition and fees 2010-2011: $26,900; room/board: $7,300. Estimated books and supplies: $1,000; transportation: $600; personal expenses: $1,050. **Financial aid:** Priority filing date for institution's financial aid form: March 1. In 2009-2010, 94% of undergraduates applied for financial aid. Of those, 84% were determined to have financial need; 20% had their need fully met. Average financial aid package (proportion receiving): $20,775 (84%). Average amount of gift aid, such as scholarships or grants (proportion receiving): $16,052 (84%). Average amount of self-help aid, such as work study or loans (proportion receiving): $5,027 (67%). Average need-based loan (excluding PLUS or other private loans): $4,085. Among students who received need-based aid, the average percentage of need met: 84%. Among students who received aid based on merit, the average award (and the proportion receiving): $10,425 (16%). The average athletic scholarship (and the proportion receiving): $0 (0%). Average amount of debt of borrowers graduating in 2009: $24,476. Proportion who borrowed: 81%.

CAMPUS LIFE AND EXTRACURRICULAR ACTIVITIES

Campus housing available (% using): coed dorms (15%), women's dorms (33%), men's dorms (24%), fraternity housing (6%), apartment for single students (17%), special housing for disabled students (1%), special housing for international students (1%). Students who live in college-owned, operated, or affiliated housing: 94%. **Student employment:** During the 2009-2010 academic year, 40% of undergraduates worked on campus. Average per-year earnings: $1,600. **Clubs and organizations:** Number of student organizations: 80. Activities include: campus ministries, choral groups, concert band, dance, drama/theater, international student organization, jazz band, literary magazine, marching band, music ensembles, musical theater, pep band, radio station, student government, student newspaper, student film society, television station. Number of fraternities: 4; sororities: 3. Proportion of men in fraternities: 8%; of women in sororities: 10%. Average proportion of students who stay on campus on weekends: 70%. **Sports program (2009-2010):** Member of NCAA III. *Men's intercollegiate varsity sports:* baseball, basketball, cross country, football, golf, soccer, swimming, tennis, track and field (indoor), track and field (outdoor). *Women's intercollegiate varsity sports:* basketball, cross country, golf, soccer, softball, swimming, tennis, track and field (indoor), track and field (outdoor), volleyball.

SERVICES AND FACILITIES

Basic services: nonremedial tutoring, placement service, health service, health insurance, other. **Counseling services:** minority student, career, personal, veteran student, academic, psychological, religious. **For learning-disabled students:** School does not offer a structured program with separate admission and additional fees. Services include: tape recorders, untimed tests, note-taking services, oral tests, learning center, readers, extended time for tests, tutors, priority seating, texts on tape, typist/scribe, take home exams, other testing accommodations. **Library:** Number of titles: 191,866; number of current serial subscriptions: 2,408. **Information technology resources:** Students are not required to lease or own a computer. Number of campus computers available to all students: 140. School has a wireless network. Approximate number of users that can be accommodated: 5,000. Proportion of college-owned housing units wired for high-speed internet access: 100%. **Campus safety:** Security services offered: 24-hour foot-and-vehicle patrols, late-night transport/escort service, 24-hour emergency telephones, lighted pathways/sidewalks, controlled dormitory access (key, security card, etc).

TRANSFER AND INTERNATIONAL STUDENTS

Transfer students: May apply for admission for the following academic terms: Fall, Spring. Applicants need a minimum number of credits to apply. For fall 2009: Transfer applications received: 225. Transfer applicants offered admission: 127. Transfer applicants enrolled: 61. **International students:** Number of foreign undergraduates: 20 (1% of student body). Number of countries represented: 12. Minimum TOEFL score required: 550 (paper); 173 (computer). Average TOEFL score: 565 (paper).

National-Louis University

- **Address:** 122 S. Michigan Avenue, Chicago, IL 60603
- **Website:** http://www.nl.edu
- **Private**
- **Enrollment:** 1,023 full-time; 449 part-time

KEY STATS

✔ **U.S News College Ranking:** second tier, Regional Universities (Midwest)
✔ **SAT or ACT Score (25th/75th percentile):** N/A
✔ **Tuition:** 2009-2010: $18,435

Selectivity: Selective	**Room/board:** N/A
Acceptance rate: 33%	**Average debt:** N/A
Student/faculty ratio: 9/1	**Proportion who borrowed:** N/A

UNDERGRADUATE STUDENT BODY STATS

2009-2010 enrollment: 1,023 full-time; 449 part-time. Men: 21%; women: 79%. **Ethnic makeup:** African American: 35%; Asian American: 2%; Hispanic: 14%; White: 49%.

ADMISSIONS FACTS AND FIGURES

Phone: (888) 658-8632. **Email:** nluinfo@nl.edu. **Website:** http://www.nl.edu. **Application deadlines for fall 2011:** Regular decision: Rolling. Early decision: Not offered. Early action: Send application by: N/A; Decision sent by: N/A. Admission can be deferred. **Application fee:** $40. **To apply online, go to:** http://www.nl.edu/applyonline/. **Admissions requirements/recommendations:** High school units required (recommended): English: 0 (4); Mathematics: 0 (3); Science: 0 (2); Foreign language: 0 (2); Social studies: 0 (3); History: 0 (0); Academic electives: 0 (0); Total units: 0 (0). Tests: The college uses SAT or ACT scores in admissions decisions. Either SAT or ACT required. Campus visit: Recommended. Admissions interview: Recommended. Off-campus interview: May be arranged. **Factors that count in admissions decisions:** *Academic:* Secondary school record: Very Important. Class rank: Not Considered. Letters of recommendation: Considered. Standardized test scores: Important. Essay: Considered. *Nonacademic:* Interview: Considered. Extracurricular activities: Not Considered. Talent/ability: Not Considered. Character/personal qualities: Not Considered. Alumni/ae relationship: Not Considered. Geographical residence: Not Considered. State residency: Not Considered. Religious affiliation/commitment: Not Considered. Minority status: Not Considered. Volunteer work: Not Considered. Work experience: Not Considered. **Other schools with the greatest overlap in applicants:** Columbia College; Roosevelt University. **Admissions statistics for the fall 2009 entering class:** Total applicants: 27. Total accepted: 9. Freshmen enrolled: 1; 0% were from out of state. Overall acceptance rate: 33%. Non-early acceptance rate: 33%. **Size of waiting list:** 0 applicants; enrolled from waiting list: 0.

ACADEMICS

Year founded: 1886. **Academic calendar:** Quarter. **Degrees offered:** certificate, bachelor's, post-bachelor's certificate, master's, post-master's certificate, doctorate. **Major fields of study:** biological and biomedical sciences; business, management, marketing, and related support services; computer and information sciences and support services; education; English lan-

guage and literature/letters; health professions and related clinical sciences; mathematics and statistics; multi/interdisciplinary studies; psychology; public administration and social service professions; social sciences; visual and performing arts. **Areas of required coursework:** arts/fine arts, humanities, computer literacy, mathematics, English (including composition), philosophy, sciences (biological or physical), history, social science. **Special academic programs:** accelerated program, cross-registration, distance learning, double major, dual enrollment, English as a Second Language (ESL), independent study, internships, study abroad, teacher certificate program, weekend college. **Teacher certification offered in:** early childhood, special education, elementary, middle/junior high, adult education, secondary, bilingual/bicultural. **Cooperative education programs:** art, business, computer science, education, health professions, humanities, natural science, social/behavioral science, technologies. **Faculty and instruction (2009-2010):** Total instructional faculty: 254 full-time, 448 part-time. Student/faculty ratio: 9/1. **Advanced Placement and International Baccalaureate credit:** AP tests may be used for: Credit only. International Baccalaureate exams may be used for: Credit only. **Freshmen returning for sophomore year:** 49%. **Graduation rates:** Six-year: 11%.

COSTS AND FINANCIAL AID

Financial aid office: (847) 465-5350. **Expenses (2009-2010):** Tuition and fees 2009-2010: $18,435.

CAMPUS LIFE AND EXTRACURRICULAR ACTIVITIES

Student employment: During the 2009-2010 academic year, 2% of undergraduates worked on campus. Average per-year earnings: $2,600. Activities include: drama/theater, musical theater, student government, student newspaper. Number of fraternities: 0; sororities: 0.

SERVICES AND FACILITIES

Basic services: nonremedial tutoring, health service. **Remedial assistance:** reading, math, writing, study skills. **Counseling services:** minority student, career, military, personal, veteran student, academic, older student, psychological, birth control. **For learning-disabled students:** Services include: remedial math, remedial English, reading machines, remedial reading, tape recorders, other special classes, videotaped classes, diagnostic testing service, oral tests, learning center, readers, tutors. **Information technology resources:** Students are not required to lease or own a computer. Number of campus computers available to all students: 165. **Campus safety:** Security services offered: late-night transport/escort service, 24-hour emergency telephones, lighted pathways/sidewalks, student patrols, controlled dormitory access (key, security card, etc).

TRANSFER AND INTERNATIONAL STUDENTS

Transfer students: May apply for admission for the following academic terms: Fall, Winter, Spring, Summer. Applicants need a minimum number of credits to apply. **International students:** Number of foreign undergraduates: 0. Minimum TOEFL score required: 550 (paper).

North Central College

- **Address:** 30 N. Brainard Street, PO Box 3063, Naperville, IL 60540
- **Website:** http://www.noctrl.edu
- **Private; Religious affiliation:** United Methodist
- **Enrollment:** 2,333 full-time; 189 part-time

KEY STATS

✔ **U.S News College Ranking:** 19, Regional Universities (Midwest)
✔ **ACT Score (25th/75th percentile):** 22-27
✔ **Tuition:** 2010-2011: $28,224

Selectivity: Selective	**Room/board:** $8,463
Acceptance rate: 67%	**Average debt:** $27,285
Student/faculty ratio: 16/1	**Proportion who borrowed:** 72%

UNDERGRADUATE STUDENT BODY STATS

2009-2010 enrollment: 2,333 full-time; 189 part-time. Men: 43%; women: 57%. **Ethnic makeup:** African American: 4%; Asian American: 3%; Hispanic: 6%; White: 87%; International: 1%. **Religious preference:** Roman Catholic: 25%; Protestant: 26%; Jewish: 1%; Muslim: 1%; No preference: 2%; Unknown: 36%; United Methodist: 6%; Greek Orthodox: 1%; Other: 2%.

ADMISSIONS FACTS AND FIGURES

Phone: (630) 637-5800. **Email:** ncadm@noctrl.edu. **Website:** http://www.noctrl.edu. **Application deadlines for fall 2011:** Regular decision: Rolling. Early decision: Not offered. Early action: Not offered. Admission can be deferred. **Application fee:** $25. **To apply online, go to:** https://www2.noctrl.edu/cgi-bin/applogin.pl. **Admissions requirements/recommendations:** High school units required (recommended): English: 4 (4); Mathematics: 3 (3); Science: 3 (3); Foreign language: 0 (3); Social studies: 2 (2); History: 1 (1); Academic electives: 3 (3); Total units: 16 (19). Tests: The college uses SAT or ACT scores in admissions decisions. Either SAT or ACT required. For admission to the fall 2011 entering class, the school will accept: ACT with or without writing accepted. Campus visit: Recommended. Admissions interview: Recommended. Off-campus interview: May be arranged. **Factors that count in admissions decisions:** *Academic:* Secondary school record: Very Important. Class rank: Not Considered. Letters of recommendation: Considered. Standardized test scores: Very Important. Essay: Considered. *Nonacademic:* Interview: Considered. Extracurricular activities: Important. Talent/ability: Important. Character/personal qualities: Very Important. Alumni/ae relationship: Considered. Geographical residence: Not Considered. State residency: Not Considered. Religious affiliation/commitment: Not Considered. Minority status: Not Considered. Volunteer work: Important. Work experience: Considered. **Other schools with the greatest overlap in applicants:** Augustana College; Elmhurst College; Illinois State University; Loyola University Chicago; University of Illinois–Urbana-Champaign. **Admissions statistics for the fall 2009 entering class:** Total applicants: 2,762. Total accepted: 1,854. Freshmen enrolled: 543; 12% were from out of state. Overall acceptance rate: 67%. **Average high school grade point average:** 3.5. **First-year students who submitted SAT scores:** 10%. **First-year students submitting ACT scores:** 98%. Scores (25/75 percentile): English: 21-27, Math: 21-27, Composite: 22-27.

ACADEMICS

Year founded: 1861. **Academic calendar:** Quarter. **Degrees offered:** bachelor's, post-bachelor's certificate, master's. **Most popular majors:** 8% business administration, management, and operations, 7% elementary education and teaching, 6% finance, 6% marketing/marketing management, 6% psychology. **Major fields of study:** area, ethnic, cultural, and gender studies; biological and biomedical sciences; business, management, marketing, and related support services; communication, journalism, and related programs; communications technologies/technicians and support services; computer and information sciences and support services; education; English language and literature/letters; foreign languages, literatures, and linguistics; health professions and related clinical sciences; history; liberal arts and sciences studies, and humanities; mathematics and statistics; multi/interdisciplinary studies; parks, recreation, leisure, and fitness studies; philosophy and religious studies; physical sciences; psychology; social sciences; visual and performing arts. **Areas of required coursework:** humanities, mathematics, English (including composition), foreign languages, sciences (biological or physical), social science, other. **Pre-professional programs:** pre-law, pre-dentistry, pre-medicine, pre-theology, pre-veterinary science, pre-pharmacy. **Special academic programs (% participation):** accelerated program (1%), cross-registration (1%), double major (23%), English as a Second Language (ESL), exchange student program (domestic), honors program (24%), independent study (17%), internships (26%), student-designed major (.1%), study abroad (21%), teacher certificate program (19%). **Teacher certification offered in:** elementary, middle/junior high, secondary. **Cooperative education programs:** other. **Reserve Officers Training Corps (ROTC):** Army ROTC: Offered at cooperating institution (Wheaton College); Air Force ROTC: Offered at cooperating institution (Illinois Institute of Technology). **Faculty and instruction (2009-2010):** Total instructional faculty: 118 full-time, 134 part-time (50% men; 50% women; 10% minorities). Full-time faculty with Ph.D. or other terminal degree: 84%. Student/faculty ratio: 16/1. Classes of fewer than 20 students: 39%; of 20 to 49 students: 60%; of 50 or more students: 1%. **Advanced Placement and International Baccalaureate credit:** AP tests may be used for: Credit and/or placement. Scores accepted: 3, 4, 5. International Baccalaureate exams may be used for: Credit and/or placement. **Freshmen returning for sophomore year:** 78%. **Graduation rates:** Four-year: 53%; five-year: 63%; six-year: 63%. **Graduate study:** 13% of students pursue further study within one year. Fields in which graduates pursue further study: Master of Business Administration (MBA), 18%; law, 1%; medicine, 1%; education, 1%; arts and sciences, 78%; veterinary medicine, 1%.

COSTS AND FINANCIAL AID

Financial aid office: (630) 637-5600. **Expenses (2010-2011):** Tuition and fees 2010-2011: $28,224; room/board: $8,463. Estimated books and supplies: $1,200; transportation: $447; personal expenses: $1,182. **Financial aid:** In 2009-2010, 85% of undergraduates applied for financial aid. Of those, 76% were determined to have financial need; 25% had their need fully met. Average financial aid package (proportion receiving): $19,870 (76%). Average amount of gift aid, such as scholarships or grants (proportion receiving): $15,023 (75%). Average amount of self-help aid, such as work study or loans (proportion receiving): $4,661 (62%). Average need-based loan (excluding PLUS or other private loans): $4,531. Among students who received need-based aid, the average percentage of need met: 76%. Among students who received aid based on merit, the average award (and the proportion receiving): $10,390 (20%). The average athletic scholarship (and the proportion receiving): $0 (0%). Average amount of debt of borrowers graduating in 2009: $27,285. Proportion who borrowed: 72%.

CAMPUS LIFE AND EXTRACURRICULAR ACTIVITIES

Campus housing available (% using): coed dorms (77%), women's dorms (16%), men's dorms (6%), special housing for disabled students (1%), other housing options. Students who live in college-owned, operated, or affiliated housing: 53%. **Student employment:** During the 2009-2010 academic year, 30% of undergraduates worked on campus. Average per-year earnings: $1,300. **Clubs and organizations:** Number of student organizations: 54. Activities include: campus ministries, choral groups, concert band, dance, drama/theater, international student organization, jazz band, literary magazine, music ensembles, musical theater, opera, pep band, radio station, student government, student newspaper. Number of fraternities: 0; sororities: 0. Average proportion of students who stay on campus on weekends: 85%. **Sports program (2009-2010):** Member of NCAA III. *Men's intercollegiate varsity sports:* baseball, basketball, cross country, football, golf, soccer, swimming, tennis, track and field (indoor), track and field (outdoor), wrestling. *Women's intercollegiate varsity sports:* basketball, cross country, golf, lacrosse, soccer, softball, swimming, tennis, track and field (indoor), track and field (outdoor), volleyball.

SERVICES AND FACILITIES

Basic services: nonremedial tutoring, placement service, health service, health insurance. **Remedial assistance:** math, writing, study skills, other. **Counseling services:** minority student, career, personal, academic, psychological, birth control, religious. **For learning-disabled students:** School does not offer a structured program with separate admission and additional fees. Services include: remedial math, reading machines, tape recorders, diagnostic testing service, untimed tests, note-taking services, oral tests, learning center, readers, extended time for tests, tutors, priority seating, substitution of courses, texts on tape, exams on tape or computer, other testing accommodations, other. **Library:** Number of titles: 151,296; number of current serial subscriptions: 3,190. **Information technology resources:** Students are not required to lease or own a computer. Number of campus computers available to all students: 325. School has a wireless network. Approximate number of users that can be accommodated: 300. Proportion of college-owned housing units wired for high-speed internet access: 100%. **Campus safety:** Security services offered: 24-hour foot-and-vehicle patrols, late-night transport/escort service, 24-hour emergency telephones, lighted pathways/sidewalks, controlled dormitory access (key, security card, etc).

TRANSFER AND INTERNATIONAL STUDENTS

Transfer students: May apply for admission for the following academic terms: Fall, Winter, Spring, Summer. Applicants need a minimum number of credits to apply. For fall 2009: Transfer applications received: 882. Transfer applicants offered admission: 517. Transfer applicants enrolled: 266. **International students:** Number of foreign undergraduates: 21 (1% of student body). Number of countries represented: 20. Minimum TOEFL score required: 520 (paper); 68 (computer).

Northeastern Illinois University

- **Address:** 5500 N. St. Louis Avenue, Chicago, IL 60625
- **Website:** http://www.neiu.edu
- **Public**
- **Enrollment:** 5,350 full-time; 3,841 part-time

KEY STATS

✔ **U.S News College Ranking:** second tier, Regional Universities (Midwest)
✔ **ACT Score (25th/75th percentile):** 16-21
✔ **Tuition:** 2010-2011: $7,492 in state, $13,732 out of state

Selectivity: Less selective	**Room/board:** $0
Acceptance rate: 74%	**Average debt:** $10,903
Student/faculty ratio: 17/1	**Proportion who borrowed:** 16%

UNDERGRADUATE STUDENT BODY STATS

2009-2010 enrollment: 5,350 full-time; 3,841 part-time. Men: 42%; women: 58%. **Ethnic makeup:** African American: 10%; Asian American: 10%; Hispanic: 30%; White: 46%; International: 4%.

ADMISSIONS FACTS AND FIGURES

Phone: (773) 442-4000. **Email:** admrec@neiu.edu. **Website:** http://www.neiu.edu. **Application deadlines for fall 2011:** Regular decision: July 1. Early decision: Not offered. Early action: Not offered. Admission can be deferred. **Application fee:** $25. **To apply online, go to:** http://applyweb.com/apply/neiu/. **Admissions requirements/recommendations:** High school units required (recommended): English: 4; Mathematics: 3; Science: 3; Social studies: 3; Total units: 15. Tests: The college uses SAT or ACT scores in admissions decisions. Either SAT or ACT required. For admission to the fall 2011 entering class, the school will accept: ACT with or without writing accepted. Campus visit: Recommended. Admissions interview: Neither required nor recommended. Off-campus interview: Not available. **Factors that count in admissions decisions:** *Academic:* Secondary school record: Not Considered. Class rank: Very Important. Letters of recommendation: Not Considered. Standardized test scores: Very Important. Essay: Not Considered. *Nonacademic:* Interview: Not Considered. Extracurricular activities: Not Considered. Talent/ability: Not Considered. Character/personal qualities: Not Considered. Alumni/ae relationship: Not Considered. Geographical residence: Not Considered. State residency: Not Considered. Religious affiliation/commitment: Not Considered. Minority status: Not Considered. Volunteer work: Not Considered. Work experience: Not Considered. **Admissions statistics for the fall 2009 entering class:** Total applicants: 4,035. Total accepted: 2,997. Freshmen enrolled: 1,070; 0% were from out of state. Overall acceptance rate: 74%. **Credentials of fall 2009 freshmen:** 11% ranked in the top 10 percent of their high school class; 24% were in the top 25 percent. **Average high school grade point average:** 2.9. **First-year students submitting ACT scores:** 95%. Scores (25/75 percentile): English: 16-21, Math: 15-22, Composite: 16-21.

ACADEMICS

Year founded: 1867. **Academic calendar:** Semester. **Degrees offered:** bachelor's, master's. **Most popular majors:** 18% business, management, marketing, and related support services, 15% education, 12% liberal arts and sciences studies, and humanities, 10% security and protective services, 9% English language and literature/letters. **Major fields of study:** area, ethnic, cultural, and gender studies; biological and biomedical sciences; business, management, marketing, and related support services; communication, journalism, and related programs; computer and information sciences and support services; education; English language and literature/letters; foreign languages, literatures, and linguistics; history; mathematics and statistics; natural resources and conservation; parks, recreation, leisure, and fitness studies; philosophy and religious studies; physical sciences; psychology; public administration and social service professions; social sciences; visual and performing arts. **Areas of required coursework:** arts/fine arts, humanities, mathematics, English (including composition), sciences (biological or physical), social science. **Pre-professional programs:** pre-law, pre-dentistry, pre-medicine, pre-veterinary science, pre-pharmacy. **Special academic programs:** accelerated program, cooperative (work-study plan) program, distance learning, double major, dual enrollment, English as a Second Language (ESL), exchange student program (domestic), honors program, independent study, internships, student-designed major, study abroad, teacher certificate program. **Teacher certification offered in:** early childhood, special education, elementary, secondary, bilingual/bicultural. **Reserve Officers Training Corps (ROTC):** Army ROTC: Offered at cooperating institu-

tion (University of Illinois–Chicago); Air Force ROTC: Offered at cooperating institution (Illinois Institute of Technology). **Faculty and instruction (2009-2010):** Total instructional faculty: 404 full-time, 295 part-time (50% men; 50% women; 27% minorities). Full-time faculty with Ph.D. or other terminal degree: 73%. Student/faculty ratio: 17/1. Classes of fewer than 20 students: 39%; of 20 to 49 students: 59%; of 50 or more students: 2%. **Advanced Placement and International Baccalaureate credit:** AP tests may be used for: Credit only. Scores accepted: 4, 5. International Baccalaureate exams may be used for: Credit only. **Freshmen returning for sophomore year:** 66%. **Graduation rates:** Four-year: 3%; five-year: 13%; six-year: 19%. **Graduate study:** 26% of students pursue further study within one year. Fields in which graduates pursue further study: Master of Business Administration (MBA), 28%; law, 3%; medicine, 2%.

COSTS AND FINANCIAL AID

Financial aid office: (773) 442-5000. **Expenses (2010-2011):** Tuition and fees 2010-2011: $7,492 in state, $13,732 out of state; room/board: $0. **Financial aid:** Priority filing date for institution's financial aid form: February 15. In 2009-2010, 73% of undergraduates applied for financial aid. Of those, 63% were determined to have financial need; 3% had their need fully met. Average financial aid package (proportion receiving): $8,362 (58%). Average amount of gift aid, such as scholarships or grants (proportion receiving): $7,038 (51%). Average amount of self-help aid, such as work study or loans (proportion receiving): $4,608 (25%). Average need-based loan (excluding PLUS or other private loans): $4,477. Among students who received need-based aid, the average percentage of need met: 48%. Among students who received aid based on merit, the average award (and the proportion receiving): $3,063 (3%). Average amount of debt of borrowers graduating in 2009: $10,903. Proportion who borrowed: 16%.

CAMPUS LIFE AND EXTRACURRICULAR ACTIVITIES

Clubs and organizations: Number of student organizations: 67. Activities include: choral groups, concert band, dance, drama/theater, jazz band, literary magazine, music ensembles, musical theater, radio station, student government, student newspaper. Number of fraternities: 2; sororities: 4.

SERVICES AND FACILITIES

Basic services: nonremedial tutoring, women's center, placement service, day care, health service, health insurance. **Remedial assistance:** reading, math, writing, study skills. **Counseling services:** minority student, career, military, personal, veteran student, academic, older student, psychological, birth control, religious. **For learning-disabled students:** School does not offer a structured program with separate admission and additional fees. Services include: remedial math, remedial English, reading machines, remedial reading, tape recorders, other special classes, untimed tests, note-taking services, oral tests, learning center, readers, extended time for tests, tutors, priority registration, priority seating, texts on tape. **Library:** Number of titles: 711,087; number of current serial subscriptions: 22,233. **Information technology resources:** Students are not required to lease or own a computer. Number of campus computers available to all students: 430. School has a wireless network. Approximate number of users that can be accommodated: 100. **Campus safety:** Security services offered: 24-hour foot-and-vehicle patrols, late-night transport/escort service, 24-hour emergency telephones, lighted pathways/sidewalks.

TRANSFER AND INTERNATIONAL STUDENTS

Transfer students: May apply for admission for the following academic terms: Fall, Spring, Summer. Applicants need a minimum number of credits to apply. For fall 2009: Transfer applications received: 2,217. Transfer applicants offered admission: 1,796. Transfer applicants enrolled: 1,398. **International students:** Number of foreign undergraduates: 342 (4% of student body). Number of countries represented: 16. Minimum TOEFL score required: 500 (paper); 173 (computer).

Northern Illinois University

- **Address:** PO Box 3001, DeKalb, IL 60115
- **Website:** http://www.niu.edu/
- **Public**
- **Enrollment:** 16,352 full-time; 1,925 part-time

KEY STATS

✔ **U.S News College Ranking:** second tier, National Universities

✔ **ACT Score:** 22

✔ **Tuition:** 2010-2011: $12,126 in state, $20,646 out of state

Selectivity: Selective	**Room/board:** $8,790
Acceptance rate: 59%	**Average debt:** $24,154
Student/faculty ratio: 17/1	**Proportion who borrowed:** 63%

UNDERGRADUATE STUDENT BODY STATS

2009-2010 enrollment: 16,352 full-time; 1,925 part-time. Men: 49%; women: 51%. **Ethnic makeup:** African American: 14%; American-Indian: 1%; Asian American: 6%; Hispanic: 8%; White: 71%; International: 1%.

ADMISSIONS FACTS AND FIGURES

Phone: (815) 753-0446. **Email:** admission-info@niu.edu. **Website:** http://www.niu.edu/. **Application deadlines for fall 2011:** Regular decision: August 1. Early decision: Not offered. Early action: Not offered. Admission can be deferred. **Application fee:** $30. **To apply online, go to:** http://www.niu.edu/Admissions/freshman/application.shtml. **Admissions requirements/recommendations:** High school units required (recommended): English: 4; Mathematics: 2 (4); Science: 2 (4); Foreign language: 1 (2); Social studies: 2 (3); History: 1; Total units: 15. Tests: The college uses SAT or ACT scores in admissions decisions. Either SAT or ACT required. For admission to the fall 2011 entering class, the school will accept: ACT with or without writing accepted. Campus visit: Recommended. Admissions interview: Neither required nor recommended. Off-campus interview: Not available. **Factors that count in admissions decisions:** *Academic:* Secondary school record: Very Important. Class rank: Very Important. Letters of recommendation: Considered. Standardized test scores: Very Important. Essay: Considered. *Nonacademic:* Interview: Considered. Extracurricular activities: Considered. Talent/ability: Considered. Character/personal qualities: Not Considered. Alumni/ae relationship: Not Considered. Geographical residence: Not Considered. State residency: Not Considered. Religious affiliation/commitment: Not Considered. Minority status: Considered. Volunteer work: Not Considered. Work experience: Not Considered. **Admissions statistics for the fall 2009 entering class:** Total applicants: 17,787. Total accepted: 10,409. Freshmen enrolled: 3,033; Overall acceptance rate: 59%. **Size of waiting list:** 0 applicants; enrolled from waiting list: 0. **Credentials of fall 2009 freshmen:** 9% ranked in the top 10 percent of their high school class; 33% were in the top 25 percent; 75% were in the top half. (Proportion submitting class standing: 93%.)

ACADEMICS

Year founded: 1895. **Academic calendar:** Semester. **Degrees offered:** bachelor's, master's, doctorate. **Most popular majors:** 7% communication studies/speech communication and rhetoric, 5% accounting, 5% marketing/marketing management, 5% nursing/registered nurse training (R.N., A.S.N., B.S.N., M.S.N.), 5% psychology. **Major fields of study:** biological and biomedical sciences; business, management, marketing, and related support services; communication, journalism, and related programs; computer and information sciences and support services; education; engineering; engineering technologies/technicians; English language and literature/letters; family and consumer sciences/human sciences; foreign languages, literatures, and linguistics; health professions and related clinical sciences; history; liberal arts and sciences studies, and humanities; mathematics and statistics; philosophy and religious studies; physical sciences; psychology; social sciences; visual and performing arts. **Areas of required coursework:** humanities, mathematics, English (including composition), philosophy, foreign languages, history, social science. **Pre-professional programs:** pre-law, pre-dentistry, pre-medicine. **Special academic programs:** accelerated program, cooperative (work-study plan) program, cross-registration, distance learning, double major, external degree program, honors program, independent study, internships, liberal arts/career combination, student-designed major, study abroad, teacher certificate program. **Teacher certification offered in:** early childhood, special education, elementary, middle/junior high, adult education, secondary. **Reserve Officers Training Corps (ROTC):** Army ROTC: Offered on campus. **Faculty and instruction (2009-2010):** Total

instructional faculty: 922 full-time, 251 part-time (54% men; 46% women; 12% minorities). Full-time faculty with Ph.D. or other terminal degree: 83%. Student/faculty ratio: 17/1. Classes of fewer than 20 students: 41%; of 20 to 49 students: 47%; of 50 or more students: 12%. **Advanced Placement and International Baccalaureate credit:** AP tests may be used for: Placement only. **Freshmen returning for sophomore year:** 76%. **Graduation rates:** Four-year: 23%; five-year: 42%; six-year: 48%. **Graduate study:** 10% of students pursue further study immediately upon graduation.

COSTS AND FINANCIAL AID

Financial aid office: (815) 753-1300. **Expenses (2010-2011):** Tuition and fees 2010-2011: $12,126 in state, $20,646 out of state; room/board: $8,790. Estimated books and supplies: $1,400; transportation: $700; personal expenses: $2,524. **Financial aid:** Priority filing date for institution's financial aid form: March 1. In 2009-2010, 78% of undergraduates applied for financial aid. Of those, 65% were determined to have financial need; 11% had their need fully met. Average financial aid package (proportion receiving): $11,087 (64%). Average amount of gift aid, such as scholarships or grants (proportion receiving): $7,582 (42%). Average amount of self-help aid, such as work study or loans (proportion receiving): $6,031 (61%). Average need-based loan (excluding PLUS or other private loans): $4,278. Among students who received need-based aid, the average percentage of need met: 65%. Among students who received aid based on merit, the average award (and the proportion receiving): $912 (0%). The average athletic scholarship (and the proportion receiving): $15,650 (2%). Average amount of debt of borrowers graduating in 2009: $24,154. Proportion who borrowed: 63%.

CAMPUS LIFE AND EXTRACURRICULAR ACTIVITIES

Campus housing available: coed dorms, sorority housing, fraternity housing, apartments for married students, special housing for disabled students, special housing for international students. **Student employment:** During the 2009-2010 academic year, 24% of undergraduates worked on campus. Average per-year earnings: $1,700. **Clubs and organizations:** Number of student organizations: 400. Activities include: choral groups, concert band, dance, drama/theater, jazz band, marching band, music ensembles, musical theater, radio station, student government, student newspaper, student film society, symphony orchestra, television station. Number of fraternities: 26; sororities: 17. Proportion of men in fraternities: 5%; of women in sororities: 4%. Average proportion of students who stay on campus on weekends: 60%. **Sports program (2009-2010):** Member of NCAA I. *Men's intercollegiate varsity sports:* baseball, basketball, football, golf, soccer, tennis, volleyball. *Women's intercollegiate varsity sports:* basketball, cross country, golf, gymnastics, soccer, tennis, volleyball.

SERVICES AND FACILITIES

Basic services: nonremedial tutoring, women's center, placement service, day care, health service, health insurance. **Remedial assistance:** reading, math, writing, study skills. **Counseling services:** minority student, career, personal, veteran student, academic, older student, psychological, birth control, religious. **For learning-disabled students:** School does not offer a structured program with separate admission and additional fees. Total undergraduates in learning-disabled program or receiving services: 158. Services include: reading machines, tape recorders, note-taking services, extended time for tests, early syllabus, priority registration, priority seating, texts on tape, exams on tape or computer, other testing accommodations, other. **Library:** Number of titles: 3,578,601; number of current serial subscriptions: 34,844. **Information technology resources:** Students are not required to lease or own a computer. School has a wireless network. Approximate number of users that can be accommodated: 1,000. Proportion of college-owned housing units wired for high-speed internet access: 100%. **Campus safety:** Security services offered: 24-hour foot-and-vehicle patrols, late-night transport/escort service, 24-hour emergency telephones, lighted pathways/sidewalks, controlled dormitory access (key, security card, etc).

TRANSFER AND INTERNATIONAL STUDENTS

Transfer students: May apply for admission for the following academic terms: Fall, Spring, Summer. Applicants need a minimum number of credits to apply. For fall 2009: Transfer applications received: 5,072. Transfer applicants offered admission: 3,663. Transfer applicants enrolled: 2,100. **International students:** Number of foreign undergraduates: 186 (1% of student body). Number of countries represented: 100. Minimum TOEFL score required: 550 (paper); 197 (computer). Average TOEFL score: 560 (paper).

North Park University

- **Address:** 3225 W. Foster Avenue, Chicago, IL 60625-4895
- **Website:** http://www.northpark.edu
- **Private; Religious affiliation:** Evangelical Covenant Church
- **Enrollment:** 1,773 full-time; 425 part-time

KEY STATS

✔ **U.S News College Ranking:** 43, Regional Universities (Midwest)
✔ **ACT Score (25th/75th percentile):** 19-25
✔ **Tuition:** 2010-2011: $19,900

Selectivity: Selective	Room/board: $8,350
Acceptance rate: 71%	Average debt: $23,343
Student/faculty ratio: 12/1	Proportion who borrowed: 72%

UNDERGRADUATE STUDENT BODY STATS

2009-2010 enrollment: 1,773 full-time; 425 part-time. Men: 39%; women: 61%. **Ethnic makeup:** African American: 8%; Asian American: 6%; Hispanic: 10%; White: 72%; International: 3%. **Religious preference:** Roman Catholic: 19%; Protestant: 38%; Jewish: 1%; No preference: 9%; Unknown: 5%; Evangelical Covenant Church: 20%.

ADMISSIONS FACTS AND FIGURES

Phone: (773) 244-5500. **Email:** admissions@northpark.edu. **Website:** http://www.northpark.edu. **Application deadlines for fall 2011:** Regular decision: July 1. Early decision: Not offered. Early action: Not offered. Admission can be deferred. **Application fee:** $40. **To apply online, go to:** https://www.applyweb.com/apply/northp/menu.html. **Admissions requirements/recommendations:** High school units required (recommended): English: 3 (4); Mathematics: 3 (4); Science: 2 (3); Foreign language: 1 (1); Social studies: 1 (1); History: (1). Tests: The college uses SAT or ACT scores in admissions decisions. Either SAT or ACT required. For admission to the fall 2011 entering class, the school will accept: ACT with writing recommended. Campus visit: Recommended. Admissions interview: Recommended. Off-campus interview: May be arranged. **Factors that count in admissions decisions:** *Academic:* Secondary school record: Very Important. Class rank: Very Important. Letters of recommendation: Very Important. Standardized test scores: Very Important. Essay: Very Important. *Nonacademic:* Interview: Very Important. Extracurricular activities: Important. Talent/ability: Important. Character/personal qualities: Very Important. Alumni/ae relationship: Important. Geographical residence: Considered. State residency: Not Considered. Religious affiliation/commitment: Not Considered. Minority status: Considered. Volunteer work: Important. Work experience: Considered. **Other schools with the greatest overlap in applicants:** DePaul University; Elmhurst College; North Central College; University of Illinois–Chicago; Wheaton College. **Admissions statistics for the fall 2009 entering class:** Total applicants: 1,473. Total accepted: 1,039. Freshmen enrolled: 364; 44% were from out of state. Overall acceptance rate: 71%. **Credentials of fall 2009 freshmen:** 10% ranked in the top 10 percent of their high school class; 34% were in the top 25 percent; 68% were in the top half. (Proportion submitting class standing: 94%.) **Average high school grade point average:** 3.1. **First-year students who submitted SAT scores:** 22%. Scores (25/75 percentile): Critical Reading: 490-600, Math: 460-550, Combined: 950-1150. **First-year students submitting ACT scores:** 81%. Scores (25/75 percentile): English: 19-26, Math: 17-25, Composite: 19-25.

ACADEMICS

Year founded: 1891. **Academic calendar:** Semester. **Degrees offered:** certificate, bachelor's, post-bachelor's certificate, master's. **Most popular majors:** 16% business administration and management, 16% nursing/registered nurse training (R.N., A.S.N., B.S.N., M.S.N.), 8% biology/biological sciences, 6% elementary education and teaching, 6% psychology. **Major fields of study:** area, ethnic, cultural, and gender studies; biological and biomedical sciences; business, management, marketing, and related support services; communication, journalism, and related programs; education; English language and literature/letters; foreign languages, literatures, and linguistics; health professions and related clinical sciences; history; mathematics and statistics; multi/interdisciplinary studies; parks, recreation, leisure, and fitness studies; philosophy and religious studies; physical sciences; psychology; social sciences; theology and religious vocations; visual and performing arts. **Areas of required coursework:** arts/fine arts, humanities, mathematics, English (including composition), foreign languages, sciences (biological or physical). **Pre-professional programs:** pre-law, pre-dentistry, pre-medicine, pre-theology, pre-veterinary science, pre-optometry,

pre-pharmacy. **Special academic programs (% participation):** double major (7%), English as a Second Language (ESL) (1%), honors program (3%), independent study (10%), internships (25%), student-designed major, study abroad (5%), teacher certificate program (10%). **Teacher certification offered in:** early childhood, special education, elementary, middle/junior high, secondary, bilingual/bicultural. **Cooperative education programs:** engineering. **Reserve Officers Training Corps (ROTC):** Army ROTC: Offered at cooperating institution (University of Illinois–Chicago); Air Force ROTC: Offered at cooperating institution (Illinois Institute of Technology). **Faculty and instruction (2009-2010):** Total instructional faculty: 125 full-time, 162 part-time (48% men; 52% women; 16% minorities). Full-time faculty with Ph.D. or other terminal degree: 90%. Student/faculty ratio: 12/1. Classes of fewer than 20 students: 56%; of 20 to 49 students: 43%; of 50 or more students: 1%. **Advanced Placement and International Baccalaureate credit:** AP tests may be used for: Credit and/or placement. Scores accepted: 3, 4, 5. International Baccalaureate exams may be used for: Credit and/or placement. **Freshmen returning for sophomore year:** 74%. **Graduation rates:** Four-year: 34%; five-year: 46%; six-year: 53%. **Graduate study:** 15% of students pursue further study immediately upon graduation; 40% within five years.

COSTS AND FINANCIAL AID

Financial aid office: (773) 244-5526. **Expenses (2010-2011):** Tuition and fees 2010-2011: $19,900; room/board: $8,350. Estimated books and supplies: $1,000; transportation: $400; personal expenses: $1,600. **Financial aid:** Priority filing date for institution's financial aid form: April 1; deadline: June 1. Average amount of debt of borrowers graduating in 2009: $23,343. Proportion who borrowed: 72%.

CAMPUS LIFE AND EXTRACURRICULAR ACTIVITIES

Campus housing available (% using): coed dorms (20%), women's dorms (25%), men's dorms (9%), apartment for single students (46%). Students who live in college-owned, operated, or affiliated housing: 50%. **Student employment:** During the 2009-2010 academic year, 20% of undergraduates worked on campus. Average per-year earnings: $2,000. **Clubs and organizations:** Number of student organizations: 25. Activities include: campus ministries, choral groups, concert band, drama/theater, international student organization, jazz band, literary magazine, music ensembles, musical theater, opera, student government, student newspaper, symphony orchestra, yearbook. Number of fraternities: 0; sororities: 0. Average proportion of students who stay on campus on weekends: 80%. **Sports program (2009-2010):** Member of NCAA III. *Men's intercollegiate varsity sports:* baseball, basketball, cross country, football, golf, soccer, track and field (indoor). *Women's intercollegiate varsity sports:* basketball, crew (heavyweight), cross country, golf, soccer, softball, track and field (indoor), volleyball.

SERVICES AND FACILITIES

Basic services: nonremedial tutoring, placement service, health service, health insurance. **Remedial assistance:** reading, math, writing, study skills. **Counseling services:** career, personal, academic, psychological, religious. **For learning-disabled students:** School does not offer a structured program with separate admission and additional fees. Total undergraduates in learning-disabled program or receiving services: 75. Services include: remedial math, remedial English, remedial reading, tape recorders, untimed tests, note-taking services, oral tests, learning center, readers, extended time for tests, tutors, priority seating, substitution of courses, texts on tape, exams on tape or computer, other testing accommodations. **Library:** Number of titles: 225,000; number of current serial subscriptions: 995. **Information technology resources:** Students are not required to lease or own a computer. Number of campus computers available to all students: 100. School has a wireless network. Proportion of college-owned housing units wired for high-speed internet access: 100%. **Campus safety:** Security services offered: 24-hour foot-and-vehicle patrols, late-night transport/escort service, 24-hour emergency telephones, lighted pathways/sidewalks, controlled dormitory access (key, security card, etc.).

TRANSFER AND INTERNATIONAL STUDENTS

Transfer students: May apply for admission for the following academic terms: Fall, Spring. Applicants need a minimum number of credits to apply. For fall 2009: Transfer applications received: 495. Transfer applicants offered admission: 316. Transfer applicants enrolled: 205. **International students:** Number of foreign undergraduates: 72 (3% of student body). Number of countries represented: 28. Minimum TOEFL score required: 550 (paper); 213 (computer).

Northwestern University

- **Address:** 633 Clark Street, Evanston, IL 60208
- **Website:** http://www.northwestern.edu
- **Private**
- **Enrollment:** 8,437 full-time; 99 part-time

KEY STATS

✔ **U.S News College Ranking:** 12, National Universities
✔ **SAT Score (25th/75th percentile):** 1360-1530
✔ **Tuition: 2010-2011:** $40,247

Selectivity: Most selective	**Room/board:** $12,240
Acceptance rate: 27%	**Average debt:** $20,802
Student/faculty ratio: 7/1	**Proportion who borrowed:** 48%

UNDERGRADUATE STUDENT BODY STATS

2009-2010 enrollment: 8,437 full-time; 99 part-time. Men: 48%; women: 52%. **Ethnic makeup:** African American: 6%; Asian American: 19%; Hispanic: 7%; White: 62%; International: 6%. **Religious preference:** Roman Catholic: 21%; Protestant: 27%; Jewish: 14%; Muslim: 3%; Hindu: 4%; Buddhist: 1%; No preference: 27%; Other: 3%.

ADMISSIONS FACTS AND FIGURES

Phone: (847) 491-7271. **Email:** ug-admission@northwestern.edu. **Website:** http://www.northwestern.edu. **Application deadlines for fall 2011:** Regular decision: January 1; decision sent by April 15. Early decision: Send application by: November 1; Decision sent by: December 15. Early action: Not offered. Admission can be deferred. **Application fee:** $65. **To apply online, go to:** http://www.ugadm.northwestern.edu. **Admissions requirements/recommendations:** High school units required (recommended): English: (4); Mathematics: (3); Science: (2); Foreign language: (2); Social studies: (2); Academic electives: (1); Total units: (16). Tests: The college uses SAT or ACT scores in admissions decisions. Either SAT or ACT required. For admission to the fall 2011 entering class, the school will accept: ACT with writing required. Campus visit: Recommended. Admissions interview: Neither required nor recommended. Off-campus interview: May be arranged. **Factors that count in admissions decisions:** *Academic:* Secondary school record: Very Important. Class rank: Very Important. Letters of recommendation: Important. Standardized test scores: Very Important. Essay: Very Important. *Nonacademic:* Interview: Considered. Extracurricular activities: Important. Talent/ability: Important. Character/personal qualities: Important. Alumni/ae relationship: Considered. Geographical residence: Not Considered. State residency: Not Considered. Religious affiliation/commitment: Not Considered. Minority status: Considered. Volunteer work: Considered. Work experience: Considered. **Other schools with the greatest overlap in applicants:** Cornell University; Duke University; University of Chicago; University of Pennsylvania; Washington University in St. Louis. **Admissions statistics for the fall 2009 entering class:** Total applicants: 25,369. Total accepted: 6,887. Freshmen enrolled: 2,128; Accepted through early-decision or early-action plans: 27%. Overall acceptance rate: 27%. Early-decision acceptance rate: 39%. Non-early acceptance rate: 26%. **Size of waiting list:** 2850 applicants; enrolled from waiting list: 45. **Credentials of fall 2009 freshmen:** 90% ranked in the top 10 percent of their high school class; 99% were in the top 25 percent; 100% were in the top half. (Proportion submitting class standing: 43%.) **First-year students who submitted SAT scores:** 75%. Scores (25/75 percentile): Critical Reading: 670-750, Math: 690-780, Combined: 1360-1530. **First-year students submitting ACT scores:** 62%. Scores (25/75 percentile): English: N/A, Math: N/A, Composite: 31-33.

ACADEMICS

Year founded: 1851. **Academic calendar:** Quarter. **Degrees offered:** certificate, bachelor's, master's, post-master's certificate, doctorate. **Most popular majors:** 16% communication, journalism, and related programs, 15% engineering, 11% economics, 10% visual and performing arts, 9% psychology. **Major fields of study:** area, ethnic, cultural, and gender studies; biological and biomedical sciences; business, management, marketing, and related support services; communication, journalism, and related programs; computer and information sciences and support services; education; engineering; English language and literature/letters; foreign languages, literatures, and linguistics; health professions and related clinical sciences; history; legal professions and studies; liberal arts and sciences studies, and humanities; mathematics and statistics; multi/interdisciplinary studies; natural resources and conservation; philosophy and religious studies; physical

sciences; psychology; public administration and social service professions; social sciences; visual and performing arts. **Areas of required coursework:** arts/fine arts, humanities, mathematics, English (including composition), foreign languages, sciences (biological or physical), social science. **Pre-professional programs:** pre-law, pre-medicine. **Special academic programs:** accelerated program, cooperative (work-study plan) program, double major, honors program, independent study, internships, liberal arts/career combination, student-designed major, study abroad, teacher certificate program. **Teacher certification offered in:** secondary. **Cooperative education programs:** engineering. **Reserve Officers Training Corps (ROTC):** Army ROTC: Offered at cooperating institution (University of Illinois–Chicago); Navy ROTC: Offered on campus; Air Force ROTC: Offered at cooperating institution (Illinois Institute of Technology). **Faculty and instruction (2009-2010):** Total instructional faculty: 1,092 full-time, 126 part-time (63% men; 37% women; 16% minorities). Full-time faculty with Ph.D. or other terminal degree: 100%. Student/faculty ratio: 7/1. Classes of fewer than 20 students: 73%; of 20 to 49 students: 20%; of 50 or more students: 6%. **Advanced Placement and International Baccalaureate credit:** AP tests may be used for: Credit and/or placement. Scores accepted: 3, 4, 5. International Baccalaureate exams may be used for: Credit and/or placement. **Freshmen returning for sophomore year:** 97%. **Graduation rates:** Four-year: 87%; five-year: 94%; six-year: 95%. **Graduate study:** Fields in which graduates pursue further study: Master of Business Administration (MBA), 37%; law, 1%; medicine, 6%; engineering, 15%; education, 14%; arts and sciences, 1%; veterinary medicine, 6%.

COSTS AND FINANCIAL AID

Financial aid office: (847) 491-7400. **Expenses (2010-2011):** Tuition and fees 2010-2011: $40,247; room/board: $12,240. Estimated books and supplies: $1,737; transportation: $400; personal expenses: $1,782. **Financial aid:** Priority filing date for institution's financial aid form: February 15; deadline: February 15. In 2009-2010, 50% of undergraduates applied for financial aid. Of those, 43% were determined to have financial need; 100% had their need fully met. Average financial aid package (proportion receiving): $30,080 (43%). Average amount of gift aid, such as scholarships or grants (proportion receiving): $26,817 (41%). Average amount of self-help aid, such as work study or loans (proportion receiving): $5,430 (38%). Average need-based loan (excluding PLUS or other private loans): $4,625. Among students who received need-based aid, the average percentage of need met: 100%. Among students who received aid based on merit, the average award (and the proportion receiving): $2,521 (5%). The average athletic scholarship (and the proportion receiving): $32,403 (5%). Average amount of debt of borrowers graduating in 2009: $20,802. Proportion who borrowed: 48%.

CAMPUS LIFE AND EXTRACURRICULAR ACTIVITIES

Campus housing available: coed dorms, women's dorms, men's dorms, sorority housing, fraternity housing, other housing options. **Student employment:** During the 2009-2010 academic year, 45% of undergraduates worked on campus. Average per-year earnings: $2,216. **Clubs and organizations:** Number of student organizations: 415. Activities include: campus ministries, choral groups, concert band, dance, drama/theater, international student organization, jazz band, literary magazine, marching band, model UN, music ensembles, musical theater, opera, pep band, radio station, student government, student newspaper, student film society, symphony orchestra, television station, yearbook. Number of fraternities: 21; sororities: 18. **Sports program (2009-2010):** Member of NCAA I. *Men's intercollegiate varsity sports:* baseball, basketball, football, golf, soccer, swimming, tennis, wrestling. *Women's intercollegiate varsity sports:* basketball, cross country, fencing, field hockey, golf, lacrosse, soccer, softball, swimming, tennis, volleyball.

SERVICES AND FACILITIES

Basic services: nonremedial tutoring, women's center, placement service, health service, health insurance. **Counseling services:** minority student, career, personal, academic, psychological, birth control, religious. **For learning-disabled students:** School does not offer a structured program with separate admission and additional fees. Services include: reading machines, tape recorders, diagnostic testing service, note-taking services, oral tests, readers, extended time for tests, priority registration, priority seating, texts on tape, other testing accommodations, other. **Library:** Number of titles: 4,842,949; number of current serial subscriptions: 77,933. **Information technology resources:** Students are not required to lease or own a computer. Number of campus computers available to all students: 725. School has a wireless network. Proportion of college-owned housing units wired for high-speed internet access: 100%. **Campus safety:** Security services offered: 24-hour foot-and-vehicle patrols, late-night transport/escort service, 24-hour emergency telephones, lighted pathways/sidewalks, student patrols, controlled dormitory access (key, security card, etc).

TRANSFER AND INTERNATIONAL STUDENTS

Transfer students: May apply for admission for the following academic terms: Fall, Winter, Spring, Summer. Applicants need a minimum number of credits to apply. For fall 2009: Transfer applications received: 1,225. Transfer applicants offered admission: 195. Transfer applicants enrolled: 99. **International students:** Number of foreign undergraduates: 480 (6% of student body). Number of countries represented: 42. Minimum TOEFL score required: 600 (paper); 250 (computer). Average TOEFL score: 637 (paper).

Olivet Nazarene University

- **Address:** 1 University Avenue, Bourbonnais, IL 60914
- **Website:** http://www.olivet.edu
- **Private; Religious affiliation:** Church of the Nazarene
- **Enrollment:** 2,618 full-time; 553 part-time

KEY STATS

- ✔ **U.S News College Ranking:** 66, Regional Universities (Midwest)
- ✔ **ACT Score (25th/75th percentile):** 20-27
- ✔ **Tuition:** 2010-2011: $25,590

Selectivity: Selective	**Room/board:** $6,400
Acceptance rate: 81%	**Average debt:** $28,473
Student/faculty ratio: 19/1	**Proportion who borrowed:** 77%

UNDERGRADUATE STUDENT BODY STATS

2009-2010 enrollment: 2,618 full-time; 553 part-time. Men: 38%; women: 62%. **Ethnic makeup:** African American: 11%; Asian American: 1%; Hispanic: 4%; White: 83%. **Religious preference:** Roman Catholic: 6%; Protestant: 50%; No preference: 9%; Church of the Nazarene: 35%.

ADMISSIONS FACTS AND FIGURES

Phone: (815) 939-5011. **Email:** admissions@olivet.edu. **Website:** http://www.olivet.edu. **Application deadlines for fall 2011:** Regular decision: Rolling. Early decision: Not offered. Early action: Not offered. Admission can be deferred. **Application fee:** $25. **To apply online, go to:** http://www.olivet.edu/admissions/adm_apply.asp. **Admissions requirements/recommendations:** High school units required (recommended): English: 4 (4); Mathematics: 3 (3); Science: 3 (3); Foreign language: 0 (2); Social studies: 3 (3); History: 2 (2); Academic electives: 0 (0); Total units: 15 (17). Tests: The college uses SAT or ACT scores in admissions decisions. ACT required. For admission to the fall 2011 entering class, the school will accept: ACT with or without writing accepted. Campus visit: Recommended. Admissions interview: Recommended. Off-campus interview: May be arranged. **Factors that count in admissions decisions:** *Academic:* Secondary school record: Very Important. Class rank: Considered. Letters of recommendation: Considered. Standardized test scores: Very Important. Essay: Considered. *Nonacademic:* Interview: Very Important. Extracurricular activities: Important. Talent/ability: Important. Character/personal qualities: Very Important. Alumni/ae relationship: Considered. Geographical residence: Not Considered. State residency: Not Considered. Religious affiliation/commitment: Important. Minority status: Not Considered. Volunteer work: Considered. Work experience: Considered. **Other schools with the greatest overlap in applicants:** Calvin College; Indiana Wesleyan University; Loyola University Chicago; Northern Illinois University; Taylor University. **Admissions statistics for the fall 2009 entering class:** Total applicants: 2,892. Total accepted: 2,341. Freshmen enrolled: 778; 58% were from out of state. Overall acceptance rate: 81%. **Credentials of fall 2009 freshmen:** 24% ranked in the top 10 percent of their high school class; 50% were in the top 25 percent; 79% were in the top half. (Proportion submitting class standing: 84%.) **Average high school grade point average:** 3.5. **First-year students who submitted SAT scores:** 17%. **First-year students submitting ACT scores:** 99%. Scores (25/75 percentile): English: N/A, Math: N/A, Composite: 20-27.

ACADEMICS

Year founded: 1907. **Academic calendar:** Semester. **Degrees offered:** associate, bachelor's, master's, doctorate. **Most popular majors:** 20% health professions and related clinical sciences, 19% business, management, marketing, and related support services, 11% education, 5% biological and biomedical sciences, 5% communication, journalism, and related programs.

Major fields of study: architecture and related services; biological and biomedical sciences; business, management, marketing, and related support services; communication, journalism, and related programs; computer and information sciences and support services; education; English language and literature/letters; foreign languages, literatures, and linguistics; health professions and related clinical sciences; history; liberal arts and sciences studies, and humanities; mathematics and statistics; parks, recreation, leisure, and fitness studies; philosophy and religious studies; physical sciences; psychology; public administration and social service professions; security and protective services; social sciences; theology and religious vocations; visual and performing arts. **Areas of required coursework:** arts/fine arts, humanities, mathematics, English (including composition), foreign languages, sciences (biological or physical), history, social science, other. **Pre-professional programs:** pre-law, pre-dentistry, pre-medicine, pre-veterinary science, pre-optometry, pre-pharmacy, other. **Special academic programs:** accelerated program, distance learning, double major, dual enrollment, English as a Second Language (ESL), honors program, independent study, internships, student-designed major, study abroad, teacher certificate program. **Teacher certification offered in:** early childhood, elementary, middle/junior high, secondary. **Reserve Officers Training Corps (ROTC):** Army ROTC: Offered on campus. **Faculty and instruction (2009-2010):** Total instructional faculty: 115 full-time, 52 part-time (60% men; 40% women; 6% minorities). Full-time faculty with Ph.D. or other terminal degree: 71%. Student/faculty ratio: 19/1. Classes of fewer than 20 students: 35%; of 20 to 49 students: 56%; of 50 or more students: 9%. **Advanced Placement and International Baccalaureate credit:** AP tests may be used for: Credit and/or placement. Scores accepted: 3, 4, 5. International Baccalaureate exams may be used for: Credit only. **Freshmen returning for sophomore year:** 73%. **Graduation rates:** Four-year: 44%; five-year: 53%; six-year: 56%. **Graduate study:** 27% of students pursue further study immediately upon graduation.

COSTS AND FINANCIAL AID

Financial aid office: (815) 939-5249. **Expenses (2010-2011):** Tuition and fees 2010-2011: $25,590; room/board: $6,400. Estimated books and supplies: $1,000; transportation: $400; personal expenses: $1,300. **Financial aid:** Priority filing date for institution's financial aid form: March 1. In 2009-2010, 85% of undergraduates applied for financial aid. Of those, 76% were determined to have financial need; 32% had their need fully met. Average financial aid package (proportion receiving): $17,812 (76%). Average amount of gift aid, such as scholarships or grants (proportion receiving): $13,112 (76%). Average amount of self-help aid, such as work study or loans (proportion receiving): $4,566 (59%). Average need-based loan (excluding PLUS or other private loans): $4,419. Among students who received need-based aid, the average percentage of need met: 82%. Among students who received aid based on merit, the average award (and the proportion receiving): $10,134 (24%). The average athletic scholarship (and the proportion receiving): $6,270 (15%). Average amount of debt of borrowers graduating in 2009: $28,473. Proportion who borrowed: 77%.

CAMPUS LIFE AND EXTRACURRICULAR ACTIVITIES

Campus housing available (% using): women's dorms (26%), men's dorms (24%), apartments for married students (1%), apartment for single students (49%), special housing for disabled students (0%). Students who live in college-owned, operated, or affiliated housing: 67%. **Student employment:** During the 2009-2010 academic year, 32% of undergraduates worked on campus. Average per-year earnings: $1,100. **Clubs and organizations:** Number of student organizations: 80. Activities include: campus ministries, choral groups, concert band, dance, drama/theater, international student organization, jazz band, literary magazine, marching band, music ensembles, musical theater, opera, pep band, radio station, student government, student newspaper, student film society, symphony orchestra, television station, yearbook. Number of fraternities: 0; sororities: 0. Average proportion of students who stay on campus on weekends: 75%. **Sports program (2009-2010):** Member of NAIA. *Men's intercollegiate varsity sports:* baseball, basketball, cross country, football, golf, soccer, tennis, track and field (indoor), track and field (outdoor). *Women's intercollegiate varsity sports:* basketball, cross country, soccer, softball, tennis, track and field (indoor), track and field (outdoor), volleyball.

SERVICES AND FACILITIES

Basic services: nonremedial tutoring, placement service, health service, health insurance. **Remedial assistance:** math, writing, study skills. **Counseling services:** minority student, career, military, personal, veteran student, academic, older student, psychological, religious. **For learning-disabled students:** School does not offer a structured program with separate admission and additional fees. Services include: remedial math, remedial English, remedial reading, tape recorders, diagnostic testing service, untimed tests, note-taking services, oral tests, learning center, readers, extended time for tests, tutors, priority registration, priority seating, other testing accommodations. **Library:** Number of titles: 209,618; number of current serial subscriptions: 40,395. **Information technology resources:** Students are not required to lease or own a computer. Number of campus computers available to all students: 600. School has a wireless network. Approximate number of users that can be accommodated: 11,000. Proportion of college-owned housing units wired for high-speed internet access: 100%. **Campus safety:** Security services offered: 24-hour foot-and-vehicle patrols, late-night transport/escort service, 24-hour emergency telephones, lighted pathways/sidewalks, student patrols, controlled dormitory access (key, security card, etc).

TRANSFER AND INTERNATIONAL STUDENTS
Transfer students: May apply for admission for the following academic terms: Fall, Spring, Summer. Applicants need a minimum number of credits to apply. For fall 2009: Transfer applications received: 623. Transfer applicants offered admission: 331. Transfer applicants enrolled: 144. **International students:** Number of foreign undergraduates: 14. Number of countries represented: 17. Minimum TOEFL score required: 500 (paper); 173 (computer).

Principia College

- **Address:** 1 Maybeck Place, Elsah, IL 62028
- **Website:** http://www.prin.edu/college
- **Private; Religious affiliation:** Christian Science
- **Enrollment:** 520 full-time; 7 part-time

KEY STATS
✔ **U.S News College Ranking:** 127, National Liberal Arts Colleges
✔ **SAT Score (25th/75th percentile):** 1010-1270
✔ **Tuition:** 2010-2011: $24,015

Selectivity: Selective	**Room/board:** $9,000
Acceptance rate: 81%	**Average debt:** $14,963
Student/faculty ratio: 8/1	**Proportion who borrowed:** 64%

UNDERGRADUATE STUDENT BODY STATS
2009-2010 enrollment: 520 full-time; 7 part-time. Men: 48%; women: 52%. **Ethnic makeup:** African American: 1%; Hispanic: 2%; White: 80%; International: 17%.

ADMISSIONS FACTS AND FIGURES
Phone: (618) 374-5181. **Email:** collegeadmissions@prin.edu. **Website:** http://www.prin.edu/college. **Application deadlines for fall 2011:** Regular decision: Rolling. Early decision: Not offered. Early action: Send application by: November 15; Decision sent by: December 1. Admission can be deferred. **Application fee:** None. **Admissions requirements/recommendations:** High school units required (recommended): English: 4 (4); Mathematics: 4 (4); Science: 3 (3); Foreign language: 2 (3); Social studies: 2 (2); History: 1 (2); Academic electives: 2 (2); Total units: 16 (20). Tests: The college uses SAT or ACT scores in admissions decisions. Either SAT or ACT required. For admission to the fall 2011 entering class, the school will accept: ACT with writing required. Campus visit: Recommended. Admissions interview: Recommended. Off-campus interview: May be arranged. **Factors that count in admissions decisions:** *Academic:* Secondary school record: Important. Class rank: Important. Letters of recommendation: Very Important. Standardized test scores: Very Important. Essay: Very Important. *Nonacademic:* Interview: Important. Extracurricular activities: Important. Talent/ability: Important. Character/personal qualities: Very Important. Alumni/ae relationship: Considered. Geographical residence: Not Considered. State residency: Not Considered. Religious affiliation/commitment: Very Important. Minority status: Considered. Volunteer work: Considered. Work experience: Considered. **Other schools with the greatest overlap in applicants:** Ball State University; Indiana University–Bloomington; University of California–Santa Barbara; University of Chicago; University of Puget Sound. **Admissions statistics for the fall 2009 entering class:** Total applicants: 191. Total accepted: 155. Freshmen enrolled: 111; 15% were from out of state. Overall acceptance rate: 81%. Non-early acceptance rate: 81%. **Size of waiting list:** 0 applicants; enrolled from waiting list: 0. **Credentials of fall 2009 freshmen:** 36% ranked in the top 10 percent of their high school class; 64% were in the top 25 percent; 79% were in the

top half. (Proportion submitting class standing: 56%.) **Average high school grade point average:** 3.4. **First-year students who submitted SAT scores:** 86%. Scores (25/75 percentile): Critical Reading: 520-650, Math: 490-620, Combined: 1010-1270. **First-year students submitting ACT scores:** 37%. Scores (25/75 percentile): English: 24-32, Math: 19-28, Composite: 22-29.

ACADEMICS
Year founded: 1910. **Academic calendar:** Quarter. **Degrees offered:** bachelor's. **Most popular majors:** 16% mass communication/media studies, 14% business administration and management, 12% fine/studio arts, 8% political science and government, 7% elementary education and teaching. **Major fields of study:** biological and biomedical sciences; business, management, marketing, and related support services; communication, journalism, and related programs; computer and information sciences and support services; education; engineering; English language and literature/letters; foreign languages, literatures, and linguistics; history; mathematics and statistics; natural resources and conservation; parks, recreation, leisure, and fitness studies; philosophy and religious studies; physical sciences; social sciences; visual and performing arts. **Areas of required coursework:** arts/fine arts, humanities, mathematics, English (including composition), philosophy, foreign languages, sciences (biological or physical), history, social science, other. **Special academic programs (% participation):** double major (21%), independent study (2%), internships (7%), student-designed major (1%), study abroad (65%). **Teacher certification offered in:** elementary, middle/junior high, secondary. **Faculty and instruction (2009-2010):** Total instructional faculty: N/A. Student/faculty ratio: 8/1. **Advanced Placement and International Baccalaureate credit:** AP tests may be used for: Placement only. Scores accepted: 3, 4, 5. International Baccalaureate exams may be used for: Placement only. **Freshmen returning for sophomore year:** 93%. **Graduation rates:** Six-year: 74%. **Graduate study:** 12% of students pursue further study immediately upon graduation; 0% within one year; 0% within five years. Fields in which graduates pursue further study: Master of Business Administration (MBA), 17%; law, 8%; engineering, 2%; theology (or the seminary), 1%; education, 12%; arts and sciences, 60%.

COSTS AND FINANCIAL AID
Financial aid office: (618) 374-5186. **Expenses (2010-2011):** Tuition and fees 2010-2011: $24,015; room/board: $9,000. Estimated books and supplies: $900; transportation: $1,000; personal expenses: $750. **Financial aid:** Priority filing date for institution's financial aid form: March 1. In 2009-2010, 100% of undergraduates applied for financial aid. Of those, 72% were determined to have financial need; 82% had their need fully met. Average financial aid package (proportion receiving): $24,175 (70%). Average amount of gift aid, such as scholarships or grants (proportion receiving): $20,119 (70%). Average amount of self-help aid, such as work study or loans (proportion receiving): $5,342 (53%). Average need-based loan (excluding PLUS or other private loans): $5,342. Among students who received need-based aid, the average percentage of need met: 85%. Among students who received aid based on merit, the average award (and the proportion receiving): $16,727 (17%). The average athletic scholarship (and the proportion receiving): $0 (0%). Average amount of debt of borrowers graduating in 2009: $14,963. Proportion who borrowed: 64%.

CAMPUS LIFE AND EXTRACURRICULAR ACTIVITIES
Campus housing available (% using): coed dorms, women's dorms (49%), men's dorms (49%), apartments for married students (2%). Students who live in college-owned, operated, or affiliated housing: 99%. **Student employment:** During the 2009-2010 academic year, 50% of undergraduates worked on campus. Average per-year earnings: $3,000. **Clubs and organizations:** Number of student organizations: 28. Activities include: choral groups, dance, drama/theater, international student organization, model UN, music ensembles, musical theater, pep band, radio station, student government, student newspaper, symphony orchestra, television station, yearbook. Number of fraternities: 0; sororities: 0. Average proportion of students who stay on campus on weekends: 100%. **Sports program (2009-2010):** Member of NCAA III. **Men's intercollegiate varsity sports:** baseball, basketball, cross country, soccer. **Women's intercollegiate varsity sports:** basketball, cross country, soccer, softball.

SERVICES AND FACILITIES
Basic services: health service. **Remedial assistance:** reading, writing, study skills. **Counseling services:** career, personal, academic, other. **Library:** Number of titles: 210,000; number of current serial subscriptions: 12,000. **Information technology resources:** Students are not required to lease or own a computer. Number of campus computers available to all students: 250. School has a wireless network. Approximate number of users that can be

accommodated: 500. Proportion of college-owned housing units wired for high-speed internet access: 100%. **Campus safety:** Security services offered: 24-hour foot-and-vehicle patrols, 24-hour emergency telephones, lighted pathways/sidewalks, controlled dormitory access (key, security card, etc.).

TRANSFER AND INTERNATIONAL STUDENTS

Transfer students: May apply for admission for the following academic terms: Fall, Winter, Spring. Applicants do not need a minimum number of credits to apply. For fall 2009: Transfer applications received: 26. Transfer applicants offered admission: 26. Transfer applicants enrolled: 26. **International students:** Number of foreign undergraduates: 89 (17% of student body). Minimum TOEFL score required: 550 (paper); 213 (computer). Average TOEFL score: 563 (paper).

Quincy University

- **Address:** 1800 College Avenue, Quincy, IL 62301
- **Website:** http://www.quincy.edu
- **Private; Religious affiliation:** Catholic
- **Enrollment:** 1,094 full-time; 147 part-time

KEY STATS

✔ **U.S News College Ranking:** 35, Regional Colleges (Midwest)
✔ **ACT Score (25th/75th percentile):** 19-24
✔ **Tuition:** 2010-2011: $23,000

Selectivity: Selective	**Room/board:** $8,960
Acceptance rate: 90%	**Average debt:** $21,785
Student/faculty ratio: 14/1	**Proportion who borrowed:** 77%

UNDERGRADUATE STUDENT BODY STATS

2009-2010 enrollment: 1,094 full-time; 147 part-time. Men: 44%; women: 56%. **Ethnic makeup:** African American: 10%; Asian American: 1%; Hispanic: 4%; White: 84%; International: 1%. **Religious preference:** Protestant: 23%; Muslim: 1%; No preference: 32%; Catholic: 43%.

ADMISSIONS FACTS AND FIGURES

Phone: (217) 228-5210. **Email:** admissions@quincy.edu. **Website:** http://www.quincy.edu. **Application deadlines for fall 2011:** Regular decision: Rolling. Early decision: Not offered. Early action: Not offered. Admission can be deferred. **Application fee:** $25. **To apply online, go to:** http://www.quincy.edu/Admissions/ApplyOnline.php. **Admissions requirements/recommendations:** High school units required (recommended): English: (4); Mathematics: (3); Science: (3); Foreign language: (2); Social studies: (3); Total units: (16). Tests: The college uses SAT or ACT scores in admissions decisions. Either SAT or ACT required. For admission to the fall 2011 entering class, the school will accept: ACT with or without writing accepted. Campus visit: Recommended. Admissions interview: Recommended. Off-campus interview: May be arranged. **Factors that count in admissions decisions:** *Academic:* Secondary school record: Very Important. Class rank: Important. Letters of recommendation: Important. Standardized test scores: Important. Essay: Important. *Nonacademic:* Interview: Considered. Extracurricular activities: Important. Talent/ability: Considered. Character/personal qualities: Important. Alumni/ae relationship: Not Considered. Geographical residence: Not Considered. State residency: Not Considered. Religious affiliation/commitment: Not Considered. Minority status: Not Considered. Volunteer work: Important. Work experience: Important. **Other schools with the greatest overlap in applicants:** Augustana College; Bradley University; Illinois Wesleyan University; St. Louis University; Truman State University. **Admissions statistics for the fall 2009 entering class:** Total applicants: 986. Total accepted: 892. Freshmen enrolled: 249; 34% were from out of state. Overall acceptance rate: 90%. **Credentials of fall 2009 freshmen:** 12% ranked in the top 10 percent of their high school class; 35% were in the top 25 percent; 65% were in the top half. (Proportion submitting class standing: 87%.) **Average high school grade point average:** 3.2. **First-year students who submitted SAT scores:** 8%. Scores (25/75 percentile): Critical Reading: 420-480, Math: 430-540, Combined: 850-1020. **First-year students submitting ACT scores:** 92%. Scores (25/75 percentile): English: 18-24, Math: 17-24, Composite: 19-24.

ACADEMICS

Year founded: 1860. **Academic calendar:** Semester. **Degrees offered:** associate, bachelor's, master's. **Most popular majors:** 26% business, management, marketing, and related support services, 13% education, 12% health profes-

sions and related clinical sciences, 7% public administration and social service professions, 6% communication, journalism, and related programs. **Major fields of study:** biological and biomedical sciences; business, management, marketing, and related support services; communication, journalism, and related programs; computer and information sciences and support services; education; English language and literature/letters; foreign languages, literatures, and linguistics; health professions and related clinical sciences; history; liberal arts and sciences studies, and humanities; mathematics and statistics; parks, recreation, leisure, and fitness studies; philosophy and religious studies; physical sciences; psychology; public administration and social service professions; security and protective services; social sciences; transportation and materials moving; visual and performing arts. **Areas of required coursework:** arts/fine arts, humanities, computer literacy, mathematics, English (including composition), philosophy, sciences (biological or physical), history, social science, other. **Pre-professional programs:** pre-law, pre-dentistry, pre-medicine, pre-veterinary science, pre-pharmacy, other. **Special academic programs:** accelerated program, distance learning, double major, dual enrollment, honors program, independent study, internships, student-designed major, study abroad, teacher certificate program. **Teacher certification offered in:** special education, elementary, secondary, bilingual/bicultural. **Cooperative education programs:** engineering. **Faculty and instruction (2009-2010):** Total instructional faculty: 53 full-time, 116 part-time (45% men; 55% women; 6% minorities). Full-time faculty with Ph.D. or other terminal degree: 75%. Student/faculty ratio: 14/1. Classes of fewer than 20 students: 70%; of 20 to 49 students: 30%. **Advanced Placement and International Baccalaureate credit:** AP tests may be used for: Credit and/or placement. Scores accepted: 4, 5. International Baccalaureate exams may be used for: Credit and/or placement. **Freshmen returning for sophomore year:** 70%. **Graduation rates:** Four-year: 31%; five-year: 41%; six-year: 47%. **Graduate study:** 23% of students pursue further study within one year. Fields in which graduates pursue further study: Master of Business Administration (MBA), 5%; law, 4%; education, 8%; arts and sciences, 6%.

COSTS AND FINANCIAL AID

Financial aid office: (217) 228-5260. **Expenses (2010-2011):** Tuition and fees 2010-2011: $23,000; room/board: $8,960. Estimated books and supplies: $1,250; transportation: $1,060; personal expenses: $1,090. **Financial aid:** Priority filing date for institution's financial aid form: March 1. In 2009-2010, 91% of undergraduates applied for financial aid. Of those, 83% were determined to have financial need; 21% had their need fully met. Average financial aid package (proportion receiving): $20,172 (80%). Average amount of gift aid, such as scholarships or grants (proportion receiving): $15,730 (79%). Average amount of self-help aid, such as work study or loans (proportion receiving): $4,831 (62%). Average need-based loan (excluding PLUS or other private loans): $4,704. Among students who received need-based aid, the average percentage of need met: 79%. Among students who received aid based on merit, the average award (and the proportion receiving): $9,884 (3%). The average athletic scholarship (and the proportion receiving): $11,314 (9%). Average amount of debt of borrowers graduating in 2009: $21,785. Proportion who borrowed: 77%.

CAMPUS LIFE AND EXTRACURRICULAR ACTIVITIES

Campus housing available (% using): coed dorms (57%), women's dorms (7%), men's dorms (12%), sorority housing (2%), fraternity housing (1%), apartments for married students, apartment for single students (4%), special housing for disabled students, other housing options (7%). Students who live in college-owned, operated, or affiliated housing: 54%. **Student employment:** During the 2009-2010 academic year, 17% of undergraduates worked on campus. Average per-year earnings: $1,000. **Clubs and organizations:** Number of student organizations: 40. Activities include: campus ministries, choral groups, concert band, dance, drama/theater, jazz band, literary magazine, marching band, music ensembles, musical theater, pep band, radio station, student government, student newspaper, symphony orchestra. Number of fraternities: 1; sororities: 2. Proportion of men in fraternities: 3%; of women in sororities: 12%. Average proportion of students who stay on campus on weekends: 75%. **Sports program (2009-2010):** Member of NCAA II. *Men's intercollegiate varsity sports:* baseball, basketball, cross country, football, golf, soccer, tennis, volleyball. *Women's intercollegiate varsity sports:* basketball, cross country, golf, soccer, softball, tennis, volleyball.

SERVICES AND FACILITIES

Basic services: nonremedial tutoring, placement service, health service, health insurance. **Remedial assistance:** math, writing, study skills. **Counseling services:** minority student, career, personal, academic, older student, psychological, religious. **For learning-disabled students:** School does not offer a structured program with separate admission and additional fees. Total undergraduates in learning-disabled program or receiving services: 24. Services include: remedial math, remedial English, reading machines, tape recorders, untimed tests, note-taking services, oral tests, learning center, readers, extended time for tests, tutors, priority registration, priority seating, texts on tape, typist/scribe, exams on tape or computer, other testing accommodations. **Library:** Number of titles: 210,318; number of current serial subscriptions: 324. **Information technology resources:** Students are not required to lease or own a computer. Number of campus computers available to all students: 160. School has a wireless network. Approximate number of users that can be accommodated: 2,700. Proportion of college-owned housing units wired for high-speed internet access: 100%. **Campus safety:** Security services offered: 24-hour foot-and-vehicle patrols, late-night transport/escort service, 24-hour emergency telephones, lighted pathways/sidewalks, controlled dormitory access (key, security card, etc).

TRANSFER AND INTERNATIONAL STUDENTS

Transfer students: May apply for admission for the following academic terms: Fall, Spring, Summer. Applicants need a minimum number of credits to apply. For fall 2009: Transfer applications received: 229. Transfer applicants offered admission: 212. Transfer applicants enrolled: 122. **International students:** Number of foreign undergraduates: 7 (1% of student body). Number of countries represented: 6. Minimum TOEFL score required: 500 (paper); 173 (computer). Average TOEFL score: 550 (paper).

Robert Morris University

- **Address:** 401 S. State Street, Chicago, IL 60605
- **Website:** http://www.robertmorris.edu/
- **Private**
- **Enrollment:** 3,949 full-time; 201 part-time

KEY STATS
✔ **U.S News College Ranking:** 61, Regional Colleges (Midwest)
✔ **ACT Score:** 18
✔ **Tuition:** 2010-2011: $20,100

Selectivity: Less selective	**Room/board:** $10,422
Acceptance rate: 81%	**Average debt:** $26,752
Student/faculty ratio: 23/1	**Proportion who borrowed:** 94%

UNDERGRADUATE STUDENT BODY STATS

2009-2010 enrollment: 3,949 full-time; 201 part-time. Men: 38%; women: 62%. **Ethnic makeup:** African American: 35%; Asian American: 2%; Hispanic: 23%; White: 39%; International: 1%.

ADMISSIONS FACTS AND FIGURES

Phone: (312) 935-4400. **Email:** enroll@robertmorris.edu. **Website:** http://www.robertmorris.edu/. **Application deadlines for fall 2011:** Regular decision: Rolling. Early decision: Not offered. Early action: Not offered. Admission can be deferred. **Application fee:** $30. **To apply online, go to:** http://www.robertmorris.edu/apply/. **Admissions requirements/recommendations:** High school units required (recommended): English: 4; Mathematics: 3; Science: 3; Foreign language: (1); Social studies: (2). Tests: The college uses SAT or ACT scores in admissions decisions. Neither SAT nor ACT required. For admission to the fall 2011 entering class, the school will accept: ACT with or without writing accepted. Campus visit: Recommended. Admissions interview: Recommended. Off-campus interview: May be arranged. **Factors that count in admissions decisions:** *Academic:* Secondary school record: Very Important. Class rank: Very Important. Letters of recommendation: Not Considered. Standardized test scores: Not Considered. Essay: Not Considered. *Nonacademic:* Interview: Very Important. Extracurricular activities: Considered. Talent/ability: Not Considered. Character/personal qualities: Not Considered. Alumni/ae relationship: Not Considered. Geographical residence: Not Considered. State residency: Not Considered. Religious affiliation/commitment: Not Considered. Minority status: Not Considered. Volunteer work: Not Considered. Work experience: Considered. **Other schools with the greatest overlap in applicants:** Columbia College; DePaul University; DeVry University–Addison; Roosevelt University; University of Illinois–Chicago. **Admissions statistics for the fall 2009 entering class:** Total applicants: 2,982. Total accepted: 2,404. Freshmen enrolled: 959; 8% were from out of state. Overall acceptance rate: 81%. **Size of waiting list:** 10 applicants; enrolled from waiting list: 0. **Credentials of fall 2009 freshmen:** 5% ranked in the top 10 percent of their high school class; 20%

were in the top 25 percent; 52% were in the top half. (Proportion submitting class standing: 80%.) **Average high school grade point average:** 2.7. **First-year students submitting ACT scores:** 63%. Scores (25/75 percentile): English: N/A, Math: N/A, Composite: N/A.

ACADEMICS

Year founded: 1913. **Academic calendar:** Other. **Degrees offered:** diploma, associate, bachelor's, master's. **Most popular majors:** 80% business, management, marketing, and related support services, 10% computer and information sciences and support services, 8% visual and performing arts, 2% multi/interdisciplinary studies. **Major fields of study:** business, management, marketing, and related support services; computer and information sciences and support services; visual and performing arts. **Areas of required coursework:** arts/fine arts, humanities, computer literacy, mathematics, English (including composition), philosophy, sciences (biological or physical), history, social science, other. **Special academic programs:** accelerated program, distance learning, dual enrollment, honors program, independent study, internships, study abroad, other. **Reserve Officers Training Corps (ROTC):** Army ROTC: Offered at cooperating institution (University of Illinois–Chicago). **Faculty and instruction (2009-2010):** Total instructional faculty: 113 full-time, 179 part-time (55% men; 45% women; 20% minorities). Full-time faculty with Ph.D. or other terminal degree: 35%. Student/faculty ratio: 23/1. Classes of fewer than 20 students: 44%; of 20 to 49 students: 54%; of 50 or more students: 1%. **Advanced Placement and International Baccalaureate credit:** AP tests may be used for: Credit only. **Freshmen returning for sophomore year:** 55%. **Graduation rates:** Six-year: 49%. **Graduate study:** 6% of students pursue further study immediately upon graduation; 7% within one year. Fields in which graduates pursue further study: Master of Business Administration (MBA), 92%; law, 3%; medicine, 1%; education, 2%; arts and sciences, 2%.

COSTS AND FINANCIAL AID

Financial aid office: (312) 935-4408. **Expenses (2010-2011):** Tuition and fees 2010-2011: $20,100; room/board: $10,422. Estimated books and supplies: $1,500; transportation: $510; personal expenses: $2,190. **Financial aid:** In 2009-2010, 97% of undergraduates applied for financial aid. Of those, 92% were determined to have financial need; 3% had their need fully met. Average financial aid package (proportion receiving): $12,121 (91%). Average amount of gift aid, such as scholarships or grants (proportion receiving): $8,739 (65%). Average amount of self-help aid, such as work study or loans (proportion receiving): $4,543 (69%). Average need-based loan (excluding PLUS or other private loans): $4,482. Among students who received need-based aid, the average percentage of need met: 45%. Among students who received aid based on merit, the average award (and the proportion receiving): $6,819 (3%). The average athletic scholarship (and the proportion receiving): $10,111 (2%). Average amount of debt of borrowers graduating in 2009: $26,752. Proportion who borrowed: 94%.

CAMPUS LIFE AND EXTRACURRICULAR ACTIVITIES

Campus housing available (% using): coed dorms (100%). Students who live in college-owned, operated, or affiliated housing: 5%. **Student employment:** During the 2009-2010 academic year, 7% of undergraduates worked on campus. Average per-year earnings: $2,047. **Clubs and organizations:** Number of student organizations: 37. Activities include: choral groups, dance, jazz band, literary magazine, pep band, student newspaper. Number of fraternities: 0; sororities: 0. Average proportion of students who stay on campus on weekends: 10%. **Sports program (2009-2010):** Member of NAIA. *Men's intercollegiate varsity sports:* baseball, basketball, cross country, golf, soccer, volleyball. *Women's intercollegiate varsity sports:* basketball, cross country, golf, crew (lightweight), soccer, softball, swimming, tennis, track and field (outdoor), volleyball.

SERVICES AND FACILITIES

Basic services: placement service. **Counseling services:** minority student, career, personal, academic, older student, psychological. **For learning-disabled students:** School does not offer a structured program with separate admission and additional fees. Total undergraduates in learning-disabled program or receiving services: 45. Services include: tape recorders, note-taking services, oral tests, learning center, readers, extended time for tests, tutors, early syllabus, priority seating, texts on tape, other testing accommodations, other. **Library:** Number of titles: 149,673; number of current serial subscriptions: 42. **Information technology resources:** Students are not required to lease or own a computer. Number of campus computers available to all students: 1,538. School has a wireless network. Approximate number of users that can be accommodated: 1,000. Proportion of college-owned housing units wired for high-speed internet access: 100%. **Campus**

safety: Security services offered: 24-hour emergency telephones, lighted pathways/sidewalks.

TRANSFER AND INTERNATIONAL STUDENTS

Transfer students: May apply for admission for the following academic terms: Fall, Winter, Spring, Summer. Applicants need a minimum number of credits to apply. For fall 2009: Transfer applications received: 1,088. Transfer applicants offered admission: 869. Transfer applicants enrolled: 618. **International students:** Number of foreign undergraduates: 26 (1% of student body). Number of countries represented: 26. Minimum TOEFL score required: 500 (paper); 173 (computer).

Rockford College

- **Address:** 5050 E. State Street, Rockford, IL 61108-2393
- **Website:** http://www.rockford.edu
- **Private**
- **Enrollment:** 753 full-time; 116 part-time

KEY STATS

✔ **U.S News College Ranking:** 95, Regional Universities (Midwest)
✔ **ACT Score (25th/75th percentile):** 19-24
✔ **Tuition:** 2010-2011: $24,750

Selectivity: Selective	**Room/board:** $6,950
Acceptance rate: 41%	**Average debt:** $25,844
Student/faculty ratio: 10/1	**Proportion who borrowed:** 100%

UNDERGRADUATE STUDENT BODY STATS

2009-2010 enrollment: 753 full-time; 116 part-time. Men: 40%; women: 60%. **Ethnic makeup:** African American: 8%; Asian American: 2%; Hispanic: 6%; White: 83%.

ADMISSIONS FACTS AND FIGURES

Phone: (815) 226-4050. **Email:** rcadmissions@rockford.edu. **Website:** http://www.rockford.edu. **Application deadlines for fall 2011:** Regular decision: Rolling. Early decision: Not offered. Early action: Not offered. Admission can be deferred. **Application fee:** $35. **To apply online, go to:** http://www.rockford.edu/?page=ApplyNowAll. **Admissions requirements/recommendations:** High school units required (recommended): English: 4; Mathematics: 3; Science: 3; Foreign language: 0; Social studies: 3; History: 0; Academic electives: 2; Total units: 15. Tests: The college uses SAT or ACT scores in admissions decisions. Either SAT or ACT required. For admission to the fall 2011 entering class, the school will accept: ACT with or without writing accepted. Campus visit: Recommended. Admissions interview: Neither required nor recommended. Off-campus interview: Not available. **Factors that count in admissions decisions:** *Academic:* Secondary school record: Important. Class rank: Considered. Letters of recommendation: Considered. Standardized test scores: Important. Essay: Important. *Nonacademic:* Interview: Not Considered. Extracurricular activities: Not Considered. Talent/ability: Not Considered. Character/personal qualities: Not Considered. Alumni/ae relationship: Not Considered. Geographical residence: Not Considered. State residency: Not Considered. Religious affiliation/commitment: Not Considered. Minority status: Not Considered. Volunteer work: Not Considered. Work experience: Not Considered. **Other schools with the greatest overlap in applicants:** Elmhurst College; Monmouth College; North Central College; Northern Illinois University; Southern Illinois University–Carbondale. **Admissions statistics for the fall 2009 entering class:** Total applicants: 967. Total accepted: 398. Freshmen enrolled: 92; 22% were from out of state. Overall acceptance rate: 41%. **Credentials of fall 2009 freshmen:** 18% ranked in the top 10 percent of their high school class; 33% were in the top 25 percent; 65% were in the top half. (Proportion submitting class standing: 85%.) **Average high school grade point average:** 3.1. **First-year students who submitted SAT scores:** 9%. **First-year students submitting ACT scores:** 97%. Scores (25/75 percentile): English: 18-25, Math: 17-24, Composite: 19-24.

ACADEMICS

Year founded: 1847. **Academic calendar:** Semester. **Degrees offered:** bachelor's, post-bachelor's certificate, master's. **Most popular majors:** 30% education, 22% business, management, marketing, and related support services, 11% health professions and related clinical sciences, 8% psychology, 5% visual and performing arts. **Major fields of study:** biological and biomedical sciences; business, management, marketing, and related support services; computer and information sciences and support services; education; English language and literature/letters; foreign languages, literatures, and linguistics; health professions and related clinical sciences; history; mathematics and statistics; multi/interdisciplinary studies; philosophy and religious studies; physical sciences; psychology; social sciences; visual and performing arts. **Areas of required coursework:** arts/fine arts, humanities, mathematics, English (including composition), sciences (biological or physical), social science, other. **Pre-professional programs:** pre-law, pre-dentistry, pre-medicine, pre-veterinary science, pre-pharmacy, other. **Special academic programs:** accelerated program, distance learning, double major, English as a Second Language (ESL), exchange student program (domestic), honors program, independent study, internships, study abroad, teacher certificate program, other. **Teacher certification offered in:** special education, elementary, middle/junior high, secondary, bilingual/bicultural. **Faculty and instruction (2009-2010):** Total instructional faculty: 67 full-time, 82 part-time (51% men; 49% women; 4% minorities). Full-time faculty with Ph.D. or other terminal degree: 70%. Student/faculty ratio: 10/1. Classes of fewer than 20 students: 80%; of 20 to 49 students: 20%; of 50 or more students: 0%. **Advanced Placement and International Baccalaureate credit:** AP tests may be used for: Credit and/or placement. Scores accepted: 3, 4, 5. **Freshmen returning for sophomore year:** 62%. **Graduation rates:** Four-year: 29%; five-year: 42%; six-year: 40%. **Graduate study:** Fields in which graduates pursue further study: Master of Business Administration (MBA), 23%; law, 1%; medicine, 2%; engineering, 1%; education, 37%; arts and sciences, 16%.

COSTS AND FINANCIAL AID

Financial aid office: (815) 226-3396. **Expenses (2010-2011):** Tuition and fees 2010-2011: $24,750; room/board: $6,950. Estimated books and supplies: $1,200; transportation: $1,000; personal expenses: $2,460. **Financial aid:** Priority filing date for institution's financial aid form: March 1. In 2009-2010, 96% of undergraduates applied for financial aid. Of those, 91% were determined to have financial need; 13% had their need fully met. Average financial aid package (proportion receiving): $17,247 (90%). Average amount of gift aid, such as scholarships or grants (proportion receiving): $12,354 (87%). Average amount of self-help aid, such as work study or loans (proportion receiving): $5,471 (87%). Average need-based loan (excluding PLUS or other private loans): $4,706. Among students who received need-based aid, the average percentage of need met: 68%. Among students who received aid based on merit, the average award (and the proportion receiving): $8,620 (9%). The average athletic scholarship (and the proportion receiving): $0 (0%). Average amount of debt of borrowers graduating in 2009: $25,844. Proportion who borrowed: 100%.

CAMPUS LIFE AND EXTRACURRICULAR ACTIVITIES

Campus housing available: coed dorms, special housing for disabled students, other housing options. Students who live in college-owned, operated, or affiliated housing: 35%. **Clubs and organizations:** Number of student organizations: 26. Activities include: campus ministries, choral groups, dance, drama/theater, international student organization, literary magazine, music ensembles, musical theater, pep band, student government. Number of fraternities: 0; sororities: 0. **Sports program (2009-2010):** Member of NCAA III. *Men's intercollegiate varsity sports:* baseball, basketball, cross country, football, golf, soccer, tennis, track and field (indoor), track and field (outdoor). *Women's intercollegiate varsity sports:* basketball, cross country, soccer, softball, tennis, track and field (indoor), track and field (outdoor), volleyball.

SERVICES AND FACILITIES

Basic services: nonremedial tutoring, placement service, health service, health insurance. **Remedial assistance:** reading, math, study skills. **Counseling services:** career, personal, veteran student, academic, psychological, religious, other. **For learning-disabled students:** School does not offer a structured program with separate admission and additional fees. Services include: remedial math, remedial English, reading machines, remedial reading, tape recorders, diagnostic testing service, untimed tests, note-taking services, oral tests, learning center, readers, extended time for tests, tutors, priority seating, texts on tape, typist/scribe, exams on tape or computer, other testing accommodations, other. **Library:** Number of titles: 139,976; number of current serial subscriptions: 400. **Information technology resources:** Students are not required to lease or own a computer. Number of campus computers available to all students: 160. School has a wireless network. Approximate number of users that can be accommodated: 1,000. Proportion of college-owned housing units wired for high-speed internet access: 100%. **Campus safety:** Security services offered: 24-hour foot-and-vehicle patrols, late-night transport/escort service, 24-hour emergency telephones, lighted pathways/sidewalks, student patrols, controlled dormitory access (key, security card, etc).

TRANSFER AND INTERNATIONAL STUDENTS

Transfer students: May apply for admission for the following academic terms: Fall, Spring, Summer. Applicants need a minimum number of credits to apply. For fall 2009: Transfer applications received: 611. Transfer applicants offered admission: 364. Transfer applicants enrolled: 177. **International students:** Number of foreign undergraduates: 2. Number of countries represented: 6. Minimum TOEFL score required: 550 (paper); 213 (computer).

Roosevelt University

- **Address:** 430 S. Michigan Avenue, Chicago, IL 60605
- **Website:** http://www.roosevelt.edu
- **Private**
- **Enrollment:** 2,834 full-time; 1,348 part-time

KEY STATS

✔ **U.S News College Ranking:** 88, Regional Universities (Midwest)
✔ **ACT Score (25th/75th percentile):** 19-25
✔ **Tuition:** 2010-2011: $23,000

Selectivity: Selective	**Room/board:** $11,174
Acceptance rate: 79%	**Average debt:** N/A
Student/faculty ratio: 13/1	**Proportion who borrowed:** N/A

UNDERGRADUATE STUDENT BODY STATS

2009-2010 enrollment: 2,834 full-time; 1,348 part-time. Men: 34%; women: 66%. **Ethnic makeup:** African American: 20%; Asian American: 5%; Hispanic: 15%; White: 58%; International: 2%.

ADMISSIONS FACTS AND FIGURES

Phone: (312) 341-3515. **Email:** applyRU@roosevelt.edu. **Website:** http://www.roosevelt.edu. **Application deadlines for fall 2011:** Regular decision: Rolling. Early decision: Not offered. Early action: Not offered. Admission can be deferred. **Application fee:** $25. **To apply online, go to:** http://www.roosevelt.edu/admission/apps.htm. **Admissions requirements/recommendations:** High school units required (recommended): English: 4 (4); Mathematics: 3 (4); Science: 2 (3); Foreign language: 0 (2); Social studies: 2 (3); History: 0 (2); Academic electives: 0 (2); Total units: 11 (23). Tests: The college uses SAT or ACT scores in admissions decisions. Either SAT or ACT required. For admission to the fall 2011 entering class, the school will accept: ACT with or without writing accepted. Campus visit: Recommended. Admissions interview: Recommended. Off-campus interview: May be arranged. **Factors that count in admissions decisions:** *Academic:* Secondary school record: Very Important. Class rank: Considered. Letters of recommendation: Considered. Standardized test scores: Important. Essay: Considered. *Nonacademic:* Interview: Considered. Extracurricular activities: Considered. Talent/ability: Considered. Character/personal qualities: Important. Alumni/ae relationship: Considered. Geographical residence: Not Considered. State residency: Not Considered. Religious affiliation/commitment: Not Considered. Minority status: Not Considered. Volunteer work: Not Considered. Work experience: Not Considered. **Other schools with the greatest overlap in applicants:** DePaul University; Loyola University Chicago; Northern Illinois University; University of Illinois–Chicago. **Admissions statistics for the fall 2009 entering class:** Total applicants: 2,589. Total accepted: 2,048. Freshmen enrolled: 597; 34% were from out of state. Overall acceptance rate: 79%. **Size of waiting list:** 0 applicants; enrolled from waiting list: 0. **Credentials of fall 2009 freshmen:** 2% ranked in the top 10 percent of their high school class; 6% were in the top 25 percent; 26% were in the top half. (Proportion submitting class standing: 31%.) **First-year students who submitted SAT scores:** 8%. Scores (25/75 percentile): Critical Reading: 513-628, Math: 470-580, Combined: 983-1208. **First-year students submitting ACT scores:** 80%. Scores (25/75 percentile): English: 20-26, Math: 17-24, Composite: 19-25.

ACADEMICS

Year founded: 1945. **Academic calendar:** Semester. **Degrees offered:** certificate, bachelor's, post-bachelor's certificate, master's, post-master's certificate, doctorate. **Most popular majors:** 34% business, management, marketing, and related support services, 14% psychology, 8% visual and performing arts, 7% education, 6% social sciences. **Major fields of study:** area, ethnic, cultural, and gender studies; biological and biomedical sciences; business, management, marketing, and related support services; communication, journalism, and related programs; computer and information sciences and support services; education; engineering; engineering technologies/technicians; English language and literature/letters; foreign languages, literatures, and linguistics; health professions and related clinical sciences; legal professions and studies; liberal arts and sciences studies, and humanities; mathematics and statistics; multi/interdisciplinary studies; natural resources and conservation; philosophy and religious studies; physical sciences; psychology; public administration and social service professions; security and protective services; social sciences; visual and performing arts. **Areas of required coursework:** humanities, mathematics, English (including composition), sciences (biological or physical). **Pre-professional programs:** pre-law, pre-medicine, pre-pharmacy. **Special academic programs:** accelerated program, distance learning, double major, dual enrollment, English as a Second Language (ESL), exchange student program (domestic), honors program, independent study, internships, student-designed major, study abroad, teacher certification program. **Teacher certification offered in:** early childhood, special education, elementary, secondary. **Faculty and instruction (2009-2010):** Total instructional faculty: 235 full-time, 456 part-time (55% men; 45% women; 16% minorities). Full-time faculty with Ph.D. or other terminal degree: 88%. Student/faculty ratio: 13/1. Classes of fewer than 20 students: 57%; of 20 to 49 students: 42%; of 50 or more students: 1%. **Advanced Placement and International Baccalaureate credit:** AP tests may be used for: Credit and/or placement. International Baccalaureate exams may be used for: Placement only. **Freshmen returning for sophomore year:** 63%. **Graduation rates:** Four-year: 28%; five-year: 42%; six-year: 39%. **Graduate study:** 23% of students pursue further study immediately upon graduation; 25% within one year; 22% within five years.

COSTS AND FINANCIAL AID

Financial aid office: (312) 341-3565. **Expenses (2010-2011):** Tuition and fees 2010-2011: $23,000; room/board: $11,174. Estimated books and supplies: $1,000; transportation: $1,100; personal expenses: $2,900. **Financial aid:** Priority filing date for institution's financial aid form: April 1. In 2009-2010, 95% of undergraduates applied for financial aid. Of those, 79% were determined to have financial need; 11% had their need fully met. Average financial aid package (proportion receiving): $18,843 (78%). Average amount of gift aid, such as scholarships or grants (proportion receiving): $8,305 (65%). Average amount of self-help aid, such as work study or loans (proportion receiving): $7,960 (72%). Average need-based loan (excluding PLUS or other private loans): $7,600. Among students who received need-based aid, the average percentage of need met: 75%. Among students who received aid based on merit, the average award (and the proportion receiving): $5,330 (15%). The average athletic scholarship (and the proportion receiving): $0 (0%).

CAMPUS LIFE AND EXTRACURRICULAR ACTIVITIES

Campus housing available (% using): coed dorms (90%), apartments for married students (1%), apartment for single students (9%), other housing options. Students who live in college-owned, operated, or affiliated housing: 19%. **Student employment:** During the 2009-2010 academic year, 25% of undergraduates worked on campus. Average per-year earnings: $2,200. **Clubs and organizations:** Number of student organizations: 50. Activities include: choral groups, concert band, dance, drama/theater, jazz band, literary magazine, music ensembles, musical theater, opera, radio station, student government, student newspaper, symphony orchestra. Number of fraternities: 2; sororities: 4. Average proportion of students who stay on campus on weekends: 75%. **Sports program (2009-2010):** Member of NAIA. *Men's intercollegiate varsity sports:* baseball, basketball, cross country, tennis. *Women's intercollegiate varsity sports:* basketball, cross country, tennis.

SERVICES AND FACILITIES

Basic services: nonremedial tutoring, placement service, day care, health insurance. **Remedial assistance:** reading, math, writing, study skills. **Counseling services:** minority student, career, personal, veteran student, academic, older student, psychological. **For learning-disabled students:** Services include: remedial math, remedial English, reading machines, remedial reading, tape recorders, diagnostic testing service, untimed tests, note-taking services, oral tests, learning center, readers, extended time for tests, tutors, priority seating, texts on tape, other testing accommodations. **Library:** Number of titles: 207,947; number of current serial subscriptions: 2,479. **Information technology resources:** Students are not required to lease or own a computer. Number of campus computers available to all students: 925. School has a wireless network. Proportion of college-owned housing units wired for high-speed internet access: 50%. **Campus safety:** Security services offered: 24-hour foot-and-vehicle patrols, late-night transport/escort service, 24-hour emergency telephones, lighted pathways/sidewalks, controlled dormitory access (key, security card, etc.).

TRANSFER AND INTERNATIONAL STUDENTS

Transfer students: May apply for admission for the following academic terms: Fall, Spring, Summer. Applicants need a minimum number of credits to apply. For fall 2009: Transfer applications received: 2,698. Transfer applicants offered admission: 1,621. Transfer applicants enrolled: 735. **International students:** Number of foreign undergraduates: 102 (2% of student body). Number of countries represented: 42. Minimum TOEFL score required: 213 (computer). Average TOEFL score: 550 (paper).

School of the Art Institute of Chicago

- **Address:** 37 S. Wabash Avenue, Chicago, IL 60603
- **Website:** http://www.saic.edu
- **Private**
- **Enrollment:** 2,219 full-time; 226 part-time

KEY STATS

✔ **U.S News College Ranking:** Unranked Specialty School–Fine Arts
✔ **SAT or ACT Score (25th/75th percentile):** N/A
✔ **Tuition:** 2010-2011: $36,120

Selectivity: N/A	Room/board: $9,800
Acceptance rate: 81%	Average debt: N/A
Student/faculty ratio: 8/1	Proportion who borrowed: N/A

UNDERGRADUATE STUDENT BODY STATS

2009-2010 enrollment: 2,219 full-time; 226 part-time. Men: 34%; women: 66%. **Ethnic makeup:** African American: 4%; American-Indian: 1%; Asian American: 12%; Hispanic: 9%; White: 58%; International: 17%.

ADMISSIONS FACTS AND FIGURES

Phone: (312) 629-6100. **Email:** admiss@saic.edu. **Website:** http://www.saic.edu. **Application deadlines for fall 2011:** Regular decision: June 1. Early decision: Not offered. Early action: Send application by: January 2; Decision sent by: February 1. Admission can be deferred. **Application fee:** $65. **To apply online, go to:** http://www.saic.edu/ugapp. **Admissions requirements/recommendations:** Tests: The college uses SAT or ACT scores in admissions decisions. Either SAT or ACT required. For admission to the fall 2011 entering class, the school will accept: ACT with or without writing accepted. Campus visit: Recommended. Admissions interview: Recommended. Off-campus interview: May be arranged. **Factors that count in admissions decisions:** *Academic:* Secondary school record: Very Important. Class rank: Important. Letters of recommendation: Very Important. Standardized test scores: Very Important. Essay: Very Important. *Nonacademic:* Interview: Important. Extracurricular activities: Important. Talent/ability: Very Important. Character/personal qualities: Very Important. Alumni/ae relationship: Considered. Geographical residence: Considered. State residency: Considered. Religious affiliation/commitment: Not Considered. Minority status: Important. Volunteer work: Important. Work experience: Considered. **Other schools with the greatest overlap in applicants:** Kansas City Art Institute; Maryland Institute College of Art; Pratt Institute; Rhode Island School of Design; University of Illinois–Chicago. **Admissions statistics for the fall 2009 entering class:** Total applicants: 3,114. Total accepted: 2,533. Freshmen enrolled: 462; 81% were from out of state. Overall acceptance rate: 81%. Non-early acceptance rate: 81%.

ACADEMICS

Year founded: 1866. **Academic calendar:** Semester. **Degrees offered:** bachelor's, post-bachelor's certificate, master's. **Major fields of study:** architecture and related services; education; English language and literature/letters; visual and performing arts. **Areas of required coursework:** arts/fine arts, humanities, English (including composition), sciences (biological or physical), social science, other. **Special academic programs:** cooperative (work-study plan) program, cross-registration, double major, English as a Second Language (ESL), exchange student program (domestic), independent study, internships, student-designed major, study abroad, teacher certificate program. **Teacher certification offered in:** elementary, middle/junior high, secondary. **Cooperative education programs:** art. **Faculty and instruction (2009-2010):** Total instructional faculty: 135 full-time, 450 part-time (53% men; 47% women; 15% minorities). Student/faculty ratio: 8/1. Classes of

fewer than 20 students: 82%; of 20 to 49 students: 17%; of 50 or more students: 1%. **Advanced Placement and International Baccalaureate credit:** AP tests may be used for: Credit only. Scores accepted: 3, 4, 5. International Baccalaureate exams may be used for: Credit only. **Freshmen returning for sophomore year:** 76%. **Graduation rates:** Four-year: 50%; five-year: 61%; six-year: 60%. **Graduate study:** 12% of students pursue further study immediately upon graduation.

COSTS AND FINANCIAL AID

Financial aid office: (312) 629-6600. **Expenses (2010-2011):** Tuition and fees 2010-2011: $36,120; room/board: $9,800. Estimated books and supplies: $2,740; transportation: $700; personal expenses: $2,100. **Financial aid:** Priority filing date for institution's financial aid form: March 15. In 2009-2010, 63% of undergraduates applied for financial aid. Of those, 58% were determined to have financial need; 4% had their need fully met. Average financial aid package (proportion receiving): $28,084 (58%). Average amount of gift aid, such as scholarships or grants (proportion receiving): $13,067 (57%). Average amount of self-help aid, such as work study or loans (proportion receiving): $7,411 (55%). Average need-based loan (excluding PLUS or other private loans): $4,572. Among students who received need-based aid, the average percentage of need met: 79%. Among students who received aid based on merit, the average award (and the proportion receiving): $5,630 (32%). The average athletic scholarship (and the proportion receiving): $0 (0%).

CAMPUS LIFE AND EXTRACURRICULAR ACTIVITIES

Campus housing available (% using): coed dorms (100%), special housing for disabled students. Students who live in college-owned, operated, or affiliated housing: 36%. **Student employment:** During the 2009-2010 academic year, 20% of undergraduates worked on campus. Average per-year earnings: $3,500. **Clubs and organizations:** Number of student organizations: 44. Activities include: campus ministries, dance, drama/theater, international student organization, literary magazine, radio station, student government, student newspaper, student film society, television station. Number of fraternities: 0; sororities: 0.

SERVICES AND FACILITIES

Basic services: nonremedial tutoring, placement service, health service, health insurance, other. **Remedial assistance:** reading, math, writing, study skills, other. **Counseling services:** minority student, career, personal, veteran student, academic, psychological, birth control. **For learning-disabled students:** School does not offer a structured program with separate admission and additional fees. Services include: remedial English, remedial reading, tape recorders, videotaped classes, untimed tests, note-taking services, oral tests, learning center, readers, extended time for tests, tutors, priority registration, priority seating, substitution of courses, texts on tape, typist/scribe, exams on tape or computer, other testing accommodations, other. **Library:** Number of titles: 102,511; number of current serial subscriptions: 409. **Information technology resources:** Students are required to lease or own a computer. Number of campus computers available to all students: 300. School has a wireless network. Approximate number of users that can be accommodated: 3,000. Proportion of college-owned housing units wired for high-speed internet access: 100%. **Campus safety:** Security services offered: 24-hour foot-and-vehicle patrols, late-night transport/escort service, 24-hour emergency telephones, lighted pathways/sidewalks, controlled dormitory access (key, security card, etc.).

TRANSFER AND INTERNATIONAL STUDENTS

Transfer students: May apply for admission for the following academic terms: Fall, Spring. Applicants do not need a minimum number of credits to apply. For fall 2009: Transfer applications received: 797. Transfer applicants offered admission: 675. Transfer applicants enrolled: 283. **International students:** Number of foreign undergraduates: 401 (17% of student body). Number of countries represented: 25. Minimum TOEFL score required: 550 (paper); 213 (computer).

Shimer College

■ **Address:** 3424 S. State Street, Chicago, IL 60616
■ **Website:** http://www.shimer.edu
■ **Private**
■ **Enrollment:** N/A

KEY STATS

✔ **U.S News College Ranking:** Unranked, National Liberal Arts Colleges
✔ **ACT Score:** 28
✔ **Tuition:** 2009-2010: $25,960

Selectivity: N/A	**Room/board:** $11,696
Acceptance rate: 90%	**Average debt:** N/A
Student/faculty ratio: N/A	**Proportion who borrowed:** N/A

Southern Illinois University—Carbondale

■ **Address:** Carbondale, IL 62901-6899
■ **Website:** http://www.siuc.edu
■ **Public**
■ **Enrollment:** 13,619 full-time; 1,932 part-time

KEY STATS

✔ **U.S News College Ranking:** 183, National Universities
✔ **ACT Score (25th/75th percentile):** 19-24
✔ **Tuition:** 2010-2011: $10,468 in state, $21,403 out of state

Selectivity: Selective	**Room/board:** $8,292
Acceptance rate: 69%	**Average debt:** $21,359
Student/faculty ratio: 16/1	**Proportion who borrowed:** 50%

UNDERGRADUATE STUDENT BODY STATS

2009-2010 enrollment: 13,619 full-time; 1,932 part-time. Men: 56%; women: 44%. **Ethnic makeup:** African American: 19%; Asian American: 2%; Hispanic: 5%; White: 72%; International: 2%.

ADMISSIONS FACTS AND FIGURES

Phone: (618) 536-4405. **Email:** joinsiuc@siu.edu. **Website:** http://www.siuc.edu. **Application deadlines for fall 2011:** Regular decision: Rolling. Early decision: Not offered. Early action: Not offered. Admission can be deferred. **Application fee:** $30. **To apply online, go to:** http://admissions.siu.edu/admpp.htm. **Admissions requirements/recommendations:** High school units required (recommended): English: 4; Mathematics: 3; Science: 3; Social studies: 3; Academic electives: 2; Total units: 15. Tests: The college uses SAT or ACT scores in admissions decisions. Either SAT or ACT required. For admission to the fall 2011 entering class, the school will accept: ACT with or without writing accepted. Campus visit: Recommended. Admissions interview: Neither required nor recommended. Off-campus interview: May be arranged. **Factors that count in admissions decisions:** *Academic:* Secondary school record: Considered. Class rank: Very Important. Letters of recommendation: Considered. Standardized test scores: Very Important. Essay: Not Considered. *Nonacademic:* Interview: Not Considered. Extracurricular activities: Considered. Talent/ability: Considered. Character/personal qualities: Not Considered. Alumni/ae relationship: Not Considered. Geographical residence: Not Considered. State residency: Not Considered. Religious affiliation/commitment: Not Considered. Minority status: Not Considered. Volunteer work: Considered. Work experience: Considered. **Admissions statistics for the fall 2009 entering class:** Total applicants: 11,509. Total accepted: 7,900. Freshmen enrolled: 2,450; 8% were from out of state. Overall acceptance rate: 69%. **Credentials of fall 2009 freshmen:** 10% ranked in the top 10 percent of their high school class; 28% were in the top 25 percent; 61% were in the top half. (Proportion submitting class standing: 86%.) **First-year students who submitted SAT scores:** 3%. **First-year students submitting ACT scores:** 94%. Scores (25/75 percentile): English: 18-24, Math: 17-25, Composite: 19-24.

ACADEMICS

Year founded: 1869. **Academic calendar:** Semester. **Degrees offered:** associate, bachelor's, post-bachelor's certificate, master's, doctorate. **Most popular majors:** 20% education, 10% business, management, marketing, and related support services, 8% engineering technologies/technicians, 8% health professions and related clinical sciences, 6% visual and performing arts. **Major fields of study:** agriculture, agriculture operations, and related sciences; architecture and related services; biological and biomedical sciences; business, management, marketing, and related support services; communication, journalism, and related programs; computer and information sciences and support services; education; engineering; engineering technologies/technicians; English language and literature/letters; family and consumer sciences/human sciences; foreign languages, literatures, and linguistics; health professions and related clinical sciences; history; legal professions and studies; liberal arts and sciences studies, and humanities; mathematics and statistics; mechanic and repair technologies/technicians; multi/interdisciplinary studies; natural resources and conservation; parks, recreation, leisure, and fitness studies; personal and culinary services; philosophy and religious studies; physical sciences; psychology; public administration and social service professions; security and protective services; social sciences; transportation and materials moving; visual and performing arts. **Areas of required coursework:** arts/fine arts, mathematics, English (including composition), sciences (biological or physical), social science, other. **Pre-professional programs:** pre-law, pre-dentistry, pre-medicine, pre-veterinary science, pre-optometry, pre-pharmacy, other. **Special academic programs:** cooperative (work-study plan) program, distance learning, double major, English as a Second Language (ESL), honors program, independent study, internships, student-designed major, study abroad, teacher certificate program. **Teacher certification offered in:** early childhood, special education, elementary, vo-tech, middle/junior high, secondary, bilingual/bicultural. **Cooperative education programs:** agriculture, art, business, computer science, education, engineering, health professions, home economics, humanities, natural science, social/behavioral science, technologies, vocational arts. **Reserve Officers Training Corps (ROTC):** Army ROTC: Offered on campus; Air Force ROTC: Offered on campus. **Faculty and instruction (2009-2010):** Total instructional faculty: 958 full-time, 136 part-time (63% men; 37% women; 17% minorities). Full-time faculty with Ph.D. or other terminal degree: 81%. Student/faculty ratio: 16/1. Classes of fewer than 20 students: 50%; of 20 to 49 students: 45%; of 50 or more students: 5%. **Advanced Placement and International Baccalaureate credit:** AP tests may be used for: Credit only. Scores accepted: 3, 4, 5. International Baccalaureate exams may be used for: Credit only. **Freshmen returning for sophomore year:** 68%. **Graduation rates:** Four-year: 24%; five-year: 40%; six-year: 44%. **Graduate study:** 55% of students pursue further study within one year. Fields in which graduates pursue further study: law, 2%; medicine, 2%.

COSTS AND FINANCIAL AID

Financial aid office: (618) 453-4334. **Expenses (2010-2011):** Tuition and fees 2010-2011: $10,468 in state, $21,403 out of state; room/board: $8,292. Estimated books and supplies: $1,100 personal expenses: $2,672. **Financial aid:** Priority filing date for institution's financial aid form: April 1. In 2009-2010, 77% of undergraduates applied for financial aid. Of those, 65% were determined to have financial need; 84% had their need fully met. Average financial aid package (proportion receiving): $11,809 (63%). Average amount of gift aid, such as scholarships or grants (proportion receiving): $6,934 (47%). Average amount of self-help aid, such as work study or loans (proportion receiving): $5,027 (55%). Average need-based loan (excluding PLUS or other private loans): $4,121. Among students who received need-based aid, the average percentage of need met: 95%. Among students who received aid based on merit, the average award (and the proportion receiving): $6,359 (9%). The average athletic scholarship (and the proportion receiving): $12,668 (1%). Average amount of debt of borrowers graduating in 2009: $21,359. Proportion who borrowed: 50%.

CAMPUS LIFE AND EXTRACURRICULAR ACTIVITIES

Campus housing available (% using): coed dorms (36%), women's dorms (7%), men's dorms, sorority housing, fraternity housing, apartments for married students (10%), apartment for single students (3%), special housing for disabled students (1%), special housing for international students (1%), other housing options. Students who live in college-owned, operated, or affiliated housing: 25%. **Student employment:** During the 2009-2010 academic year, 26% of undergraduates worked on campus. Average per-year earnings: $5,500. **Clubs and organizations:** Number of student organizations: 405. Activities include: campus ministries, choral groups, concert band, dance, drama/theater, international student organization, jazz band, literary magazine, marching band, music ensembles, musical theater, opera, pep band, radio station, student government, student newspaper, student film society, symphony orchestra, television station, yearbook. Number of fraternities: 18; sororities: 7. Proportion of men in fraternities: 5%; of women in sororities: 4%. Average proportion of students who stay on campus on weekends: 75%. **Sports program (2009-2010):** Member of NCAA I. *Men's intercollegiate varsity sports:* baseball, basketball, cross country, football, golf, swimming, tennis, track and field (indoor), track and field (outdoor). **Women's intercollegiate varsity sports:** basketball, cross country, golf, softball, swimming, tennis, track and field (indoor), track and field (outdoor), volleyball.

SERVICES AND FACILITIES

Basic services: nonremedial tutoring, women's center, placement service, day care, health service, health insurance. **Remedial assistance:** reading, math, writing, study skills. **Counseling services:** minority student, career, military, personal, veteran student, academic, older student, psychological, birth control, religious. **For learning-disabled students:** School does not offer a structured program with separate admission and additional fees. Total undergraduates in learning-disabled program or receiving services: 120. Services include: remedial math, remedial English, reading machines, remedial reading, tape recorders, other special classes, videotaped classes, diagnostic testing service, untimed tests, note-taking services, special bookstore section, oral tests, learning center, readers, extended time for tests, tutors, priority registration, priority seating, texts on tape, typist/scribe, exams on tape or computer, other testing accommodations, other. **Library:** Number of titles: 2,890,200; number of current serial subscriptions: 40,345. **Information technology resources:** Students are not required to lease or own a computer. Number of campus computers available to all students: 1,776. School has a wireless network. Approximate number of users that can be accommodated: 8,000. Proportion of college-owned housing units wired for high-speed internet access: 100%. **Campus safety:** Security services offered: 24-hour foot-and-vehicle patrols, late-night transport/escort service, 24-hour emergency telephones, lighted pathways/sidewalks, student patrols, controlled dormitory access (key, security card, etc).

TRANSFER AND INTERNATIONAL STUDENTS

Transfer students: May apply for admission for the following academic terms: Fall, Spring, Summer. Applicants need a minimum number of credits to apply. For fall 2009: Transfer applications received: 4,168. Transfer applicants offered admission: 3,032. Transfer applicants enrolled: 2,250. **International students:** Number of foreign undergraduates: 236 (2% of student body). Number of countries represented: 108. Minimum TOEFL score required: 520 (paper); 68 (computer). Average TOEFL score: 520 (paper).

Southern Illinois University—Edwardsville

- **Address:** Box 1600, Edwardsville, IL 62026
- **Website:** http://www.siue.edu
- **Public**
- **Enrollment:** 9,491 full-time; 1,653 part-time

KEY STATS

✔ **U.S News College Ranking:** 61, Regional Universities (Midwest)
✔ **ACT Score (25th/75th percentile):** 20-25
✔ **Tuition:** 2009-2010: $8,336 in state, $17,638 out of state

Selectivity: Selective	**Room/board:** $7,430
Acceptance rate: 87%	**Average debt:** $20,603
Student/faculty ratio: 17/1	**Proportion who borrowed:** 44%

UNDERGRADUATE STUDENT BODY STATS

2009-2010 enrollment: 9,491 full-time; 1,653 part-time. Men: 46%; women: 54%. **Ethnic makeup:** African American: 11%; Asian American: 2%; Hispanic: 2%; White: 83%; International: 1%.

ADMISSIONS FACTS AND FIGURES

Phone: (618) 650-3705. **Email:** admissions@siue.edu. **Website:** http://www.siue.edu. **Application deadlines for fall 2011:** Regular decision: May 1. Early decision: Not offered. Early action: Not offered. Admission can be deferred. **Application fee:** $30. **To apply online, go to:** http://www.siue.edu/apply. **Admissions requirements/recommendations:** High school units required (recommended): English: 4; Mathematics: 3; Science: 3; Foreign language: (2); Social studies: 3 (0); History: (2); Academic electives: 2; Total units: 15. Tests: The college uses SAT or ACT scores in admissions decisions. ACT required. For admission to the fall 2011 entering class, the school will accept: ACT with or without writing accepted. Campus visit: Recommended. Admissions interview: Neither required nor recommended. Off-campus interview: Not available. **Factors that count in admissions decisions:** *Academic:* Secondary school record: Important. Class rank: Very Important. Letters of recommendation: Not Considered. Standardized test

scores: Very Important. Essay: Not Considered. *Nonacademic:* Interview: Not Considered. Extracurricular activities: Not Considered. Talent/ability: Not Considered. Character/personal qualities: Not Considered. Alumni/ae relationship: Not Considered. Geographical residence: Not Considered. State residency: Not Considered. Religious affiliation/commitment: Not Considered. Minority status: Not Considered. Volunteer work: Not Considered. Work experience: Not Considered. **Other schools with the greatest overlap in applicants:** Illinois State University; Lewis & Clark College; McKendree University; University of Illinois–Urbana-Champaign. **Admissions statistics for the fall 2009 entering class:** Total applicants: 6,952. Total accepted: 6,077. Freshmen enrolled: 1,950; Overall acceptance rate: 87%. **Credentials of fall 2009 freshmen:** 18% ranked in the top 10 percent of their high school class; 42% were in the top 25 percent; 76% were in the top half. (Proportion submitting class standing: 91%.) **First-year students submitting ACT scores:** 99%. Scores (25/75 percentile): English: N/A, Math: N/A, Composite: 20-25.

ACADEMICS

Year founded: 1957. **Academic calendar:** Semester. **Degrees offered:** bachelor's, post-bachelor's certificate, master's, post-master's certificate. **Most popular majors:** 12% business administration and management, 9% nursing/registered nurse training (R.N., A.S.N., B.S.N., M.S.N.), 6% biology/biological sciences, 6% psychology, 5% elementary education and teaching. **Major fields of study:** biological and biomedical sciences; business, management, marketing, and related support services; communication, journalism, and related programs; computer and information sciences and support services; education; engineering; engineering technologies/technicians; English language and literature/letters; foreign languages, literatures, and linguistics; health professions and related clinical sciences; history; liberal arts and sciences studies, and humanities; mathematics and statistics; parks, recreation, leisure, and fitness studies; philosophy and religious studies; physical sciences; psychology; public administration and social service professions; security and protective services; social sciences; visual and performing arts. **Areas of required coursework:** arts/fine arts, humanities, computer literacy, mathematics, English (including composition), philosophy, sciences (biological or physical), history, social science, other. **Pre-professional programs:** pre-law, pre-dentistry, pre-medicine, pre-veterinary science, pre-pharmacy. **Special academic programs:** accelerated program, cooperative (work-study plan) program, cross-registration, distance learning, double major, dual enrollment, English as a Second Language (ESL), honors program, independent study, internships, student-designed major, study abroad, teacher certificate program, other. **Teacher certification offered in:** early childhood, special education, elementary, middle/junior high, secondary. **Cooperative education programs:** business, computer science, education, engineering, health professions, humanities, natural science, social/behavioral science. **Reserve Officers Training Corps (ROTC):** Army ROTC: Offered on campus; Air Force ROTC: Offered on campus. **Faculty and instruction (2009-2010):** Total instructional faculty: 622 full-time, 248 part-time (52% men; 48% women; 14% minorities). Full-time faculty with Ph.D. or other terminal degree: 80%. Student/faculty ratio: 17/1. Classes of fewer than 20 students: 41%; of 20 to 49 students: 49%; of 50 or more students: 10%. **Advanced Placement and International Baccalaureate credit:** AP tests may be used for: Credit and/or placement. Scores accepted: 3, 4, 5. International Baccalaureate exams may be used for: Placement only. **Freshmen returning for sophomore year:** 72%. **Graduation rates:** Four-year: 16%; five-year: 25%; six-year: 42%. **Graduate study:** 32% of students pursue further study within one year; 21% within five years.

COSTS AND FINANCIAL AID

Financial aid office: (618) 650-3839. **Expenses (2009-2010):** Tuition and fees 2009-2010: $8,336 in state, $17,638 out of state; room/board: $7,430. Estimated books and supplies: $715; transportation: $6,464; personal expenses: $1,555. **Financial aid:** Priority filing date for institution's financial aid form: March 1; deadline: June 1. In 2009-2010, 74% of undergraduates applied for financial aid. Of those, 67% were determined to have financial need; 17% had their need fully met. Average financial aid package (proportion receiving): $15,749 (63%). Average amount of gift aid, such as scholarships or grants (proportion receiving): $9,606 (34%). Average amount of self-help aid, such as work study or loans (proportion receiving): $8,849 (54%). Average need-based loan (excluding PLUS or other private loans): $10,045. Among students who received need-based aid, the average percentage of need met: 46%. Among students who received aid based on merit, the average award (and the proportion receiving): $7,261 (4%). The average athletic scholarship (and the proportion receiving): $12,279 (1%). Average amount of debt of borrowers graduating in 2009: $20,603. Proportion who borrowed: 44%.

CAMPUS LIFE AND EXTRACURRICULAR ACTIVITIES

Campus housing available (% using): coed dorms (56%), fraternity housing, apartments for married students (4%), apartment for single students (38%), other housing options. **Student employment:** During the 2009-2010 academic year, 14% of undergraduates worked on campus. Average per-year earnings: $2,900. **Clubs and organizations:** Number of student organizations: 200. Activities include: campus ministries, choral groups, concert band, dance, drama/theater, international student organization, jazz band, literary magazine, music ensembles, musical theater, opera, pep band, radio station, student government, student newspaper, symphony orchestra, television station. Number of fraternities: 9; sororities: 8. **Sports program (2009-2010):** Member of NCAA II. *Men's intercollegiate varsity sports:* baseball, basketball, cross country, golf, soccer, tennis, track and field (outdoor), wrestling. *Women's intercollegiate varsity sports:* basketball, cross country, golf, soccer, softball, tennis, track and field (outdoor), volleyball.

SERVICES AND FACILITIES

Basic services: nonremedial tutoring, day care, health service, health insurance. **Remedial assistance:** reading, math, writing, study skills. **Counseling services:** minority student, career, military, personal, veteran student, academic, older student, psychological, birth control, religious, other. **For learning-disabled students:** School does not offer a structured program with separate admission and additional fees. Services include: remedial math, remedial English, reading machines, remedial reading, tape recorders, other special classes, diagnostic testing service, untimed tests, note-taking services, oral tests, learning center, readers, extended time for tests, tutors, priority registration, priority seating, other. **Library:** Number of titles: 818,957; number of current serial subscriptions: 19,034. **Information technology resources:** Students are not required to lease or own a computer. Number of campus computers available to all students: 800. School has a wireless network. Approximate number of users that can be accommodated: 5,000. Proportion of college-owned housing units wired for high-speed internet access: 100%. **Campus safety:** Security services offered: 24-hour foot-and-vehicle patrols, late-night transport/escort service, 24-hour emergency telephones, lighted pathways/sidewalks, controlled dormitory access (key, security card, etc).

TRANSFER AND INTERNATIONAL STUDENTS

Transfer students: May apply for admission for the following academic terms: Fall, Spring, Summer. Applicants need a minimum number of credits to apply. For fall 2009: Transfer applications received: 2,348. Transfer applicants offered admission: 2,237. Transfer applicants enrolled: 1,222. **International students:** Number of foreign undergraduates: 73 (1% of student body). Number of countries represented: 48. Minimum TOEFL score required: 550 (paper); 213 (computer).

St. Xavier University

- **Address:** 3700 W. 103rd Street, Chicago, IL 60655
- **Website:** http://www.sxu.edu
- **Private; Religious affiliation:** Roman Catholic
- **Enrollment:** 2,495 full-time; 589 part-time

KEY STATS

✔ **U.S News College Ranking:** 34, Regional Universities (Midwest)
✔ **ACT Score (25th/75th percentile):** 20-25
✔ **Tuition:** 2010-2011: $25,520

Selectivity: Selective	**Room/board:** $8,692
Acceptance rate: 87%	**Average debt:** $26,939
Student/faculty ratio: 14/1	**Proportion who borrowed:** 78%

UNDERGRADUATE STUDENT BODY STATS

2009-2010 enrollment: 2,495 full-time; 589 part-time. Men: 30%; women: 70%. **Ethnic makeup:** African American: 17%; Asian American: 3%; Hispanic: 14%; White: 64%. **Religious preference:** Roman Catholic: 57%; Protestant: 5%; Muslim: 3%; No preference: 3%; Unknown: 12%; : N/A; Other: 20%.

ADMISSIONS FACTS AND FIGURES

Phone: (773) 298-3050. **Email:** admission@sxu.edu. **Website:** http://www.sxu.edu. **Application deadlines for fall 2011:** Regular decision: Rolling. Early decision: Not offered. Early action: Not offered. Admission can be deferred. **Application fee:** $25. **To apply online, go to:** http://www.sxu.edu/admission.

Admissions requirements/recommendations: High school units required (recommended): English: 4 (4); Mathematics: 3 (3); Foreign language: 2 (2); Academic electives: 3 (3); Total units: 16 (16). Tests: The college uses SAT or ACT scores in admissions decisions. Either SAT or ACT required. For admission to the fall 2011 entering class, the school will accept: ACT with or without writing accepted. Campus visit: Recommended. Admissions interview: Recommended. Off-campus interview: Not available. **Factors that count in admissions decisions:** *Academic:* Secondary school record: Important. Class rank: Not Considered. Letters of recommendation: Considered. Standardized test scores: Very Important. Essay: Very Important. *Nonacademic:* Interview: Considered. Extracurricular activities: Considered. Talent/ability: Considered. Character/personal qualities: Considered. Alumni/ae relationship: Not Considered. Geographical residence: Not Considered. State residency: Not Considered. Religious affiliation/commitment: Not Considered. Minority status: Not Considered. Volunteer work: Considered. Work experience: Considered. **Other schools with the greatest overlap in applicants:** DePaul University; Lewis University; Loyola University Chicago; Northern Illinois University; University of Illinois–Chicago. **Admissions statistics for the fall 2009 entering class:** Total applicants: 3,509. Total accepted: 3,039. Freshmen enrolled: 439; 9% were from out of state. Overall acceptance rate: 87%. **Credentials of fall 2009 freshmen:** 17% ranked in the top 10 percent of their high school class; 44% were in the top 25 percent; 74% were in the top half. (Proportion submitting class standing: 79%.) **Average high school grade point average:** 3.2. **First-year students who submitted SAT scores:** 5%. Scores (25/75 percentile): Critical Reading: 512-580, Math: 487-597, Combined: 999-1177. **First-year students submitting ACT scores:** 97%. Scores (25/75 percentile): English: 18-25, Math: 20-25, Composite: 20-25.

ACADEMICS

Year founded: 1846. **Academic calendar:** Semester. **Degrees offered:** bachelor's, post-bachelor's certificate, master's, post-master's certificate. **Most popular majors:** 24% business, management, marketing, and related support services, 19% health professions and related clinical sciences, 16% education, 8% liberal arts and sciences studies, and humanities, 8% social sciences. **Major fields of study:** biological and biomedical sciences; business, management, marketing, and related support services; communication, journalism, and related programs; computer and information sciences and support services; education; English language and literature/letters; foreign languages, literatures, and linguistics; health professions and related clinical sciences; history; liberal arts and sciences studies, and humanities; mathematics and statistics; multi/interdisciplinary studies; philosophy and religious studies; physical sciences; psychology; security and protective services; social sciences; theology and religious vocations; visual and performing arts. **Areas of required coursework:** humanities, mathematics, English (including composition), philosophy, sciences (biological or physical), history, social science, other. **Pre-professional programs:** pre-dentistry, pre-medicine, pre-pharmacy. **Special academic programs (% participation):** accelerated program (20%), cooperative (work-study plan) program (5%), distance learning (5%), double major (5%), English as a Second Language (ESL), exchange student program (domestic), honors program, independent study, internships, liberal arts/career combination, student-designed major, study abroad (1.7%), teacher certificate program (14.3%). **Teacher certification offered in:** early childhood, special education, elementary, middle/junior high, secondary, bilingual/bicultural. **Faculty and instruction (2009-2010):** Total instructional faculty: 180 full-time, 226 part-time (40% men; 60% women; 10% minorities). Full-time faculty with Ph.D. or other terminal degree: 100%. Student/faculty ratio: 14/1. Classes of fewer than 20 students: 46%; of 20 to 49 students: 53%; of 50 or more students: 1%. **Advanced Placement and International Baccalaureate credit:** AP tests may be used for: Credit only. Scores accepted: 3, 4, 5. International Baccalaureate exams may be used for: Credit only. **Freshmen returning for sophomore year:** 74%. **Graduation rates:** Four-year: 29%; five-year: 49%; six-year: 55%. **Graduate study:** 18% of students pursue further study within one year. Fields in which graduates pursue further study: Master of Business Administration (MBA), 20%; law, 6%; theology (or the seminary), 2%; education, 10%; arts and sciences, 62%.

COSTS AND FINANCIAL AID

Financial aid office: (773) 298-3070. **Expenses (2010-2011):** Tuition and fees 2010-2011: $25,520; room/board: $8,692. Estimated books and supplies: $1,200; transportation: $452; personal expenses: $1,054. **Financial aid:** Priority filing date for institution's financial aid form: March 1. In 2009-2010, 99% of undergraduates applied for financial aid. Of those, 84% were determined to have financial need; 19% had their need fully met. Average financial aid package (proportion receiving): $19,878 (84%). Average amount of gift aid, such as scholarships or grants (proportion receiving): $14,015 (83%). Average amount of self-help aid, such as work study or loans (proportion receiving): $6,772 (73%). Average need-based loan (excluding PLUS or other private loans): $4,626. Among students who received need-based aid, the average percentage of need met: 80%. Among students who received aid based on merit, the average award (and the proportion receiving): $9,765 (15%). The average athletic scholarship (and the proportion receiving): $10,310 (8%). Average amount of debt of borrowers graduating in 2009: $26,939. Proportion who borrowed: 78%.

CAMPUS LIFE AND EXTRACURRICULAR ACTIVITIES

Campus housing available (% using): coed dorms (81%), apartment for single students (19%). Students who live in college-owned, operated, or affiliated housing: 29%. **Student employment:** During the 2009-2010 academic year, 4% of undergraduates worked on campus. Average per-year earnings: $3,500. **Clubs and organizations:** Number of student organizations: 33. Activities include: campus ministries, choral groups, concert band, dance, drama/theater, jazz band, literary magazine, marching band, music ensembles, radio station, student government, student newspaper, student film society, symphony orchestra. Number of fraternities: 0; sororities: 0. Average proportion of students who stay on campus on weekends: 50%. **Sports program (2009-2010):** Member of NAIA. *Men's intercollegiate varsity sports:* baseball, basketball, cross country, football, soccer, track and field (indoor), track and field (outdoor), volleyball. *Women's intercollegiate varsity sports:* basketball, cross country, soccer, softball, track and field (indoor), track and field (outdoor), volleyball.

SERVICES AND FACILITIES

Basic services: nonremedial tutoring, placement service, health service, health insurance. **Remedial assistance:** reading, math, writing, study skills. **Counseling services:** career, personal, academic. **For learning-disabled students:** School does not offer a structured program with separate admission and additional fees. Services include: remedial math, reading machines, tape recorders, untimed tests, note-taking services, oral tests, learning center, readers, extended time for tests, tutors, priority registration, priority seating, texts on tape, other testing accommodations, other. **Library:** Number of titles: 179,000; number of current serial subscriptions: 35,000. **Information technology resources:** Students are not required to lease or own a computer. Number of campus computers available to all students: 500. School has a wireless network. Approximate number of users that can be accommodated: 1,500. Proportion of college-owned housing units wired for high-speed internet access: 100%. **Campus safety:** Security services offered: 24-hour foot-and-vehicle patrols, late-night transport/escort service, 24-hour emergency telephones, lighted pathways/sidewalks, student patrols, controlled dormitory access (key, security card, etc).

TRANSFER AND INTERNATIONAL STUDENTS

Transfer students: May apply for admission for the following academic terms: Fall, Spring, Summer. Applicants do not need a minimum number of credits to apply. For fall 2009: Transfer applications received: 1,844. Transfer applicants offered admission: 874. Transfer applicants enrolled: 407. **International students:** Number of foreign undergraduates: 4. Number of countries represented: 12. Minimum TOEFL score required: 550 (paper); 213 (computer). Average TOEFL score: 550 (paper).

Trinity Christian College

- ■ **Address:** 6601 W. College Drive, Palos Heights, IL 60463
- ■ **Website:** http://www.trnty.edu
- ■ **Private; Religious affiliation:** Reformed
- ■ **Enrollment:** 1,081 full-time; 369 part-time

KEY STATS

- ✔ **U.S News College Ranking:** 20, Regional Colleges (Midwest)
- ✔ **ACT Score (25th/75th percentile):** 17-29
- ✔ **Tuition:** 2010-2011: $21,518

Selectivity: Selective	**Room/board:** $7,964
Acceptance rate: 86%	**Average debt:** $33,133
Student/faculty ratio: 12/1	**Proportion who borrowed:** 77%

UNDERGRADUATE STUDENT BODY STATS

2009-2010 enrollment: 1,081 full-time; 369 part-time. Men: 33%; women: 67%. **Ethnic makeup:** African American: 8%; Asian American: 2%;

Hispanic: 7%; White: 80%; International: 2%. **Religious preference:** Roman Catholic: 16%; No preference: 1%; Reformed: 35%; Baptist: 7%; Other: 41%.

ADMISSIONS FACTS AND FIGURES

Phone: (800) 748-0085. **Email:** admissions@trnty.edu. **Website:** http://www.trnty.edu. **Application deadlines for fall 2011:** Regular decision: August 31. Early decision: Not offered. Early action: Not offered. Admission can be deferred. **Application fee:** $20. **To apply online, go to:** https://www.applyweb.com/apply/tcc/index.html. **Admissions requirements/recommendations:** High school units required (recommended): English: 3 (4); Mathematics: 3 (3); Science: 2; Foreign language: (2); Social studies: 2 (3); History: (2); Total units: 16 (18). Tests: The college uses SAT or ACT scores in admissions decisions. Either SAT or ACT required. For admission to the fall 2011 entering class, the school will accept: ACT with or without writing accepted. Campus visit: Recommended. Admissions interview: Recommended. Off-campus interview: May be arranged. **Factors that count in admissions decisions:** *Academic:* Secondary school record: Very Important. Class rank: Important. Letters of recommendation: Important. Standardized test scores: Very Important. Essay: Important. *Nonacademic:* Interview: Important. Extracurricular activities: Important. Talent/ability: Important. Character/personal qualities: Important. Alumni/ae relationship: Considered. Geographical residence: Considered. State residency: Considered. Religious affiliation/commitment: Important. Minority status: Considered. Volunteer work: Considered. Work experience: Considered. **Other schools with the greatest overlap in applicants:** Calvin College; Dordt College; Hope College; Northwestern College. **Admissions statistics for the fall 2009 entering class:** Total applicants: 625. Total accepted: 536. Freshmen enrolled: 201; 43% were from out of state. Overall acceptance rate: 86%. **Credentials of fall 2009 freshmen:** 22% ranked in the top 10 percent of their high school class; 40% were in the top 25 percent; 67% were in the top half. (Proportion submitting class standing: 78%.) **Average high school grade point average:** 3.4. **First-year students who submitted SAT scores:** 11%. Scores (25/75 percentile): Critical Reading: 443-642, Math: 430-674, Combined: 873-1316. **First-year students submitting ACT scores:** 89%. Scores (25/75 percentile): English: 16-30, Math: 16-29, Composite: 17-29.

ACADEMICS

Year founded: 1959. **Academic calendar:** Semester. **Degrees offered:** bachelor's. **Most popular majors:** 38% education, 17% business, management, marketing, and related support services, 13% health professions and related clinical sciences, 5% psychology, 4% theology and religious vocations. **Major fields of study:** biological and biomedical sciences; business, management, marketing, and related support services; communication, journalism, and related programs; computer and information sciences and support services; education; English language and literature/letters; foreign languages, literatures, and linguistics; health professions and related clinical sciences; history; mathematics and statistics; parks, recreation, leisure, and fitness studies; philosophy and religious studies; physical sciences; psychology; public administration and social service professions; social sciences; theology and religious vocations; visual and performing arts. **Areas of required coursework:** arts/fine arts, humanities, mathematics, English (including composition), philosophy, sciences (biological or physical), history, social science, other. **Pre-professional programs:** pre-law, pre-dentistry, pre-medicine, pre-theology, pre-veterinary science, pre-optometry, pre-pharmacy. **Special academic programs:** cooperative (work-study plan) program, double major, honors program, independent study, internships, liberal arts/career combination, study abroad, teacher certificate program. **Teacher certification offered in:** special education, elementary, middle/junior high, secondary, bilingual/bicultural. **Faculty and instruction (2009-2010):** Total instructional faculty: 79 full-time, 72 part-time (58% men; 42% women; 13% minorities). Full-time faculty with Ph.D. or other terminal degree: 67%. Student/faculty ratio: 12/1. Classes of fewer than 20 students: 58%; of 20 to 49 students: 42%. **Advanced Placement and International Baccalaureate credit:** AP tests may be used for: Placement only. Scores accepted: 3, 4, 5. **Freshmen returning for sophomore year:** 74%. **Graduation rates:** Four-year: 54%; five-year: 58%; six-year: 59%. **Graduate study:** 10% of students pursue further study immediately upon graduation. Fields in which graduates pursue further study: Master of Business Administration (MBA), 1%; law, 1%; medicine, 1%; engineering, 1%; theology (or the seminary), 4%; arts and sciences, 3%; veterinary medicine, 1%.

COSTS AND FINANCIAL AID

Financial aid office: (708) 239-4706. **Expenses (2010-2011):** Tuition and fees 2010-2011: $21,518; room/board: $7,964. Estimated books and supplies: $1,200; transportation: $1,550; personal expenses: $2,658. **Financial aid:** Priority filing date for institution's financial aid form: February 15; deadline:

March 1. In 2009-2010, 96% of undergraduates applied for financial aid. Of those, 86% were determined to have financial need; 5% had their need fully met. Average financial aid package (proportion receiving): $12,219 (86%). Average amount of gift aid, such as scholarships or grants (proportion receiving): $4,120 (65%). Average amount of self-help aid, such as work study or loans (proportion receiving): $3,900 (69%). Average need-based loan (excluding PLUS or other private loans): $4,447. Among students who received need-based aid, the average percentage of need met: 49%. Among students who received aid based on merit, the average award (and the proportion receiving): $7,024 (10%). The average athletic scholarship (and the proportion receiving): $6,027 (15%). Average amount of debt of borrowers graduating in 2009: $33,133. Proportion who borrowed: 77%.

CAMPUS LIFE AND EXTRACURRICULAR ACTIVITIES

Campus housing available (% using): coed dorms (94%), apartment for single students (6%). Students who live in college-owned, operated, or affiliated housing: 42%. **Student employment:** During the 2009-2010 academic year, 28% of undergraduates worked on campus. Average per-year earnings: $1,500. **Clubs and organizations:** Number of student organizations: 20. Activities include: campus ministries, choral groups, concert band, dance, drama/theater, jazz band, literary magazine, music ensembles, musical theater, student government, student newspaper, yearbook. Number of fraternities: 0; sororities: 0. Average proportion of students who stay on campus on weekends: 50%. **Sports program (2009-2010):** Member of NAIA. *Men's intercollegiate varsity sports:* baseball, basketball, cross country, soccer, track and field (indoor), track and field (outdoor). *Women's intercollegiate varsity sports:* basketball, cross country, soccer, softball, track and field (indoor), track and field (outdoor), volleyball.

SERVICES AND FACILITIES

Basic services: nonremedial tutoring, placement service, health service, health insurance. **Remedial assistance:** reading, math, writing, study skills. **Counseling services:** minority student, career, personal, academic, older student, psychological, religious. **For learning-disabled students:** School does not offer a structured program with separate admission and additional fees. Services include: remedial English, tape recorders, untimed tests, notetaking services, oral tests, learning center, readers, extended time for tests, tutors, priority registration, priority seating, texts on tape, other. **Library:** Number of titles: 66,232; number of current serial subscriptions: 221. **Information technology resources:** Students are not required to lease or own a computer. Number of campus computers available to all students: 150. School has a wireless network. Approximate number of users that can be accommodated: 1,300. Proportion of college-owned housing units wired for high-speed internet access: 100%. **Campus safety:** Security services offered: 24-hour foot-and-vehicle patrols, late-night transport/escort service, 24-hour emergency telephones, lighted pathways/sidewalks, student patrols, controlled dormitory access (key, security card, etc).

TRANSFER AND INTERNATIONAL STUDENTS

Transfer students: May apply for admission for the following academic terms: Fall, Spring. Applicants need a minimum number of credits to apply. For fall 2009: Transfer applications received: 245. Transfer applicants offered admission: 190. Transfer applicants enrolled: 114. **International students:** Number of foreign undergraduates: 32 (2% of student body). Number of countries represented: 12. Minimum TOEFL score required: 550 (paper); 213 (computer).

Trinity International University

- **Address:** 2065 Half Day Road, Deerfield, IL 60015
- **Website:** http://www.tiu.edu
- **Private; Religious affiliation:** Evangelical Free Church of America
- **Enrollment:** 981 full-time; 299 part-time

KEY STATS

✔ **U.S News College Ranking:** second tier, National Universities
✔ **ACT Score (25th/75th percentile):** 19-26
✔ **Tuition:** 2010-2011: $23,370

Selectivity: Selective	**Room/board:** $7,660
Acceptance rate: 97%	**Average debt:** $23,864
Student/faculty ratio: 13/1	**Proportion who borrowed:** 88%

UNDERGRADUATE STUDENT BODY STATS

2009-2010 enrollment: 981 full-time; 299 part-time. Men: 43%; women: 57%. **Ethnic makeup:** African American: 23%; Asian American: 4%; Hispanic: 11%; White: 61%; International: 1%. **Religious preference:** Protestant: 91%; Other: 9%.

ADMISSIONS FACTS AND FIGURES

Phone: (800) 822-3225. **Email:** tcadmissions@tiu.edu. **Website:** http://www.tiu.edu. **Application deadlines for fall 2011:** Regular decision: Rolling. Early decision: Not offered. Early action: Not offered. Admission can be deferred. **Application fee:** $25. **To apply online, go to:** https://www.tiu.edu/forms/undergradapplication1.php. **Admissions requirements/recommendations:** High school units required (recommended): English: 4; Mathematics: 2; Science: 2; Foreign language: 2; Social studies: 2; History: 2; Total units: 17. Tests: The college uses SAT or ACT scores in admissions decisions. Either SAT or ACT required. For admission to the fall 2011 entering class, the school will accept: ACT with or without writing accepted. Campus visit: Recommended. Admissions interview: Neither required nor recommended. Off-campus interview: Not available. **Factors that count in admissions decisions:** *Academic:* Secondary school record: Considered. Class rank: Very Important. Letters of recommendation: Very Important. Standardized test scores: Very Important. Essay: Very Important. *Nonacademic:* Interview: Not Considered. Extracurricular activities: Considered. Talent/ability: Considered. Character/personal qualities: Very Important. Alumni/ae relationship: Not Considered. Geographical residence: Not Considered. State residency: Not Considered. Religious affiliation/commitment: Very Important. Minority status: Not Considered. Volunteer work: Not Considered. Work experience: Not Considered. **Other schools with the greatest overlap in applicants:** Bethel College; Judson College; Taylor University; Trinity Christian College; Wheaton College. **Admissions statistics for the fall 2009 entering class:** Total applicants: 384. Total accepted: 372. Freshmen enrolled: 156; 42% were from out of state. Overall acceptance rate: 97%. **Credentials of fall 2009 freshmen:** 18% ranked in the top 10 percent of their high school class; 36% were in the top 25 percent; 63% were in the top half. (Proportion submitting class standing: 72%.) **Average high school grade point average:** 3.1. **First-year students who submitted SAT scores:** 15%. Scores (25/75 percentile): Critical Reading: 390-580, Math: 440-560, Combined: 830-1140. **First-year students submitting ACT scores:** 90%. Scores (25/75 percentile): English: 18-26, Math: 17-25, Composite: 19-26.

ACADEMICS

Year founded: 1897. **Academic calendar:** Semester. **Degrees offered:** certificate, bachelor's, post-bachelor's certificate, master's, doctorate. **Most popular majors:** 22% business, management, marketing, and related support services, 22% education, 19% theology and religious vocations, 10% psychology, 7% liberal arts and sciences studies, and humanities. **Major fields of study:** biological and biomedical sciences; business, management, marketing, and related support services; communication, journalism, and related programs; education; English language and literature/letters; health professions and related clinical sciences; history; legal professions and studies; liberal arts and sciences studies, and humanities; mathematics and statistics; philosophy and religious studies; physical sciences; psychology; social sciences; theology and religious vocations; visual and performing arts. **Areas of required coursework:** arts/fine arts, humanities, mathematics, English (including composition), philosophy, foreign languages, sciences (biological or physical), history, social science, other. **Pre-professional programs:** pre-law, pre-medicine, pre-theology, other. **Special academic programs:** cross-registration, double major, dual enrollment, honors program, independent study, internships, study abroad, teacher certificate program. **Teacher certification offered in:** elementary, middle/junior high, secondary. **Cooperative education programs:** health professions. **Faculty and instruction (2009-2010):** Total instructional faculty: 42 full-time, 36 part-time (53% men; 47% women; 10% minorities). Full-time faculty with Ph.D. or other terminal degree: 83%. Student/faculty ratio: 13/1. Classes of fewer than 20 students: 56%; of 20 to 49 students: 40%; of 50 or more students: 3%. **Advanced Placement and International Baccalaureate credit:** AP tests may be used for: Credit only. **Freshmen returning for sophomore year:** 72%. **Graduation rates:** Four-year: 38%; five-year: 49%; six-year: 51%. **Graduate study:** 32% of students pursue further study immediately upon graduation; 33% within one year.

COSTS AND FINANCIAL AID

Financial aid office: (847) 317-8060. **Expenses (2010-2011):** Tuition and fees 2010-2011: $23,370; room/board: $7,660. Estimated books and supplies: $1,120; transportation: $1,400; personal expenses: $1,460. **Financial aid:**

Priority filing date for institution's financial aid form: April 1. In 2009-2010, 87% of undergraduates applied for financial aid. Of those, 77% were determined to have financial need; 11% had their need fully met. Average financial aid package (proportion receiving): $20,273 (77%). Average amount of gift aid, such as scholarships or grants (proportion receiving): $9,420 (60%). Average amount of self-help aid, such as work study or loans (proportion receiving): $6,041 (67%). Average need-based loan (excluding PLUS or other private loans): $4,810. Among students who received need-based aid, the average percentage of need met: 96%. Among students who received aid based on merit, the average award (and the proportion receiving): $4,591 (7%). The average athletic scholarship (and the proportion receiving): $8,954 (4%). Average amount of debt of borrowers graduating in 2009: $23,864. Proportion who borrowed: 88%.

CAMPUS LIFE AND EXTRACURRICULAR ACTIVITIES
Campus housing available (% using): women's dorms (24%), men's dorms (26%), other housing options (50%). Average per-year earnings: $2,800. **Clubs and organizations:** Number of student organizations: 35. Activities include: campus ministries, choral groups, concert band, drama/theater, international student organization, jazz band, music ensembles, musical theater, pep band, student government, student newspaper, symphony orchestra, yearbook. Number of fraternities: 0; sororities: 0. Average proportion of students who stay on campus on weekends: 50%. **Sports program (2009-2010):** Member of NAIA. *Men's intercollegiate varsity sports:* baseball, basketball, cross country, football, golf, soccer. *Women's intercollegiate varsity sports:* basketball, cross country, golf, soccer, softball, volleyball.

SERVICES AND FACILITIES
Basic services: nonremedial tutoring, health service, health insurance. **Remedial assistance:** math, writing, study skills. **Counseling services:** minority student, career, personal, academic, older student, psychological, religious. **For learning-disabled students:** School does not offer a structured program with separate admission and additional fees. Total undergraduates in learning-disabled program or receiving services: 20. Services include: untimed tests, note-taking services, oral tests, learning center, extended time for tests, tutors, priority seating, substitution of courses, texts on tape, exams on tape or computer, other testing accommodations. **Library:** Number of titles: 266,586; number of current serial subscriptions: 979. **Information technology resources:** Students are not required to lease or own a computer. Number of campus computers available to all students: 100. School has a wireless network. Approximate number of users that can be accommodated: 1,500. Proportion of college-owned housing units wired for high-speed internet access: 100%. **Campus safety:** Security services offered: 24-hour foot-and-vehicle patrols, late-night transport/escort service, 24-hour emergency telephones, lighted pathways/sidewalks, student patrols, controlled dormitory access (key, security card, etc).

TRANSFER AND INTERNATIONAL STUDENTS
Transfer students: May apply for admission for the following academic terms: Fall, Winter, Spring, Summer. Applicants do not need a minimum number of credits to apply. For fall 2009: Transfer applications received: 117. Transfer applicants offered admission: 114. Transfer applicants enrolled: 87. **International students:** Number of foreign undergraduates: 16 (1% of student body). Number of countries represented: 10. Minimum TOEFL score required: 580 (paper); 237 (computer). Average TOEFL score: 586 (paper).

University of Chicago

- **Address:** 5801 S. Ellis Avenue, Chicago, IL 60637
- **Website:** http://www.uchicago.edu
- **Private**
- **Enrollment:** 5,017 full-time; 49 part-time

....

KEY STATS
✔ **U.S News College Ranking:** 9, National Universities
✔ **SAT Score (25th/75th percentile):** 1370-1560
✔ **Tuition:** 2010-2011: $41,091

Selectivity: Most selective	**Room/board:** $12,153
Acceptance rate: 27%	**Average debt:** $24,238
Student/faculty ratio: 6/1	**Proportion who borrowed:** 48%

UNDERGRADUATE STUDENT BODY STATS
2009-2010 enrollment: 5,017 full-time; 49 part-time. Men: 51%; women: 49%. **Ethnic makeup:** African American: 6%; Asian American: 15%; Hispanic: 9%; White: 61%; International: 9%.

ADMISSIONS FACTS AND FIGURES
Phone: (773) 702-8650. **Email:** collegeadmissions@uchicago.edu. **Website:** http://www.uchicago.edu. **Application deadlines for fall 2011:** Regular decision: January 2; decision sent by April 1. Early decision: Not offered. Early action: Send application by: November 1; Decision sent by: December 15. Admission can be deferred. **Application fee:** $65. **To apply online, go to:** http://www.commonapp.org. **Admissions requirements/recommendations:** High school units required (recommended): English: (4); Mathematics: (4); Science: (4); Foreign language: (3); Social studies: (2); History: (2); Total units: (19). Tests: The college uses SAT or ACT scores in admissions decisions. Either SAT or ACT required. For admission to the fall 2011 entering class, the school will accept: ACT with or without writing accepted. Campus visit: Recommended. Admissions interview: Recommended. Off-campus interview: May be arranged. **Factors that count in admissions decisions:** *Academic:* Secondary school record: Very Important. Class rank: Important. Letters of recommendation: Very Important. Standardized test scores: Considered. Essay: Very Important. *Nonacademic:* Interview: Considered. Extracurricular activities: Important. Talent/ability: Very Important. Character/personal qualities: Very Important. Alumni/ae relationship: Considered. Geographical residence: Not Considered. State residency: Not Considered. Religious affiliation/commitment: Not Considered. Minority status: Considered. Volunteer work: Important. Work experience: Considered. **Other schools with the greatest overlap in applicants:** Columbia University; Harvard University; Northwestern University; University of Pennsylvania; Yale University. **Admissions statistics for the fall 2009 entering class:** Total applicants: 13,564. Total accepted: 3,708. Freshmen enrolled: 1,336; 79% were from out of state. Overall acceptance rate: 27%. Non-early acceptance rate: 27%. **Size of waiting list:** 2153 applicants; enrolled from waiting list: 89. **Credentials of fall 2009 freshmen:** 87% ranked in the top 10 percent of their high school class; 97% were in the top 25 percent; 100% were in the top half. (Proportion submitting class standing: 61%.) **First-year students who submitted SAT scores:** 85%. Scores (25/75 percentile): Critical Reading: 690-780, Math: 680-780, Combined: 1370-1560. **First-year students submitting ACT scores:** 52%. Scores (25/75 percentile): English: 28-34, Math: 27-33, Composite: 28-32.

ACADEMICS
Year founded: 1892. **Academic calendar:** Quarter. **Degrees offered:** bachelor's, master's, doctorate. **Most popular majors:** 34% social sciences, 11% biological and biomedical sciences, 7% mathematics and statistics, 6% English language and literature/letters, 5% history. **Major fields of study:** area, ethnic, cultural, and gender studies; biological and biomedical sciences; computer and information sciences and support services; English language and literature/letters; foreign languages, literatures, and linguistics; history; liberal arts and sciences studies, and humanities; mathematics and statistics; multi/interdisciplinary studies; natural resources and conservation; philosophy and religious studies; physical sciences; psychology; public administration and social service professions; social sciences; theology and religious vocations; visual and performing arts. **Areas of required coursework:** arts/fine arts, humanities, mathematics, English (including composition), foreign languages, sciences (biological or physical), history, social science. **Pre-professional programs:** pre-law, pre-medicine. **Special academic programs (% participation):** accelerated program, cross-registration, double major (20%), dual enrollment, exchange student program (domestic), independent study, internships, student-designed major, study abroad (10%), teacher certificate program. **Teacher certification offered in:** elementary. **Reserve Officers Training Corps (ROTC):** Army ROTC: Offered at cooperating institution (Illinois Institute of Technology); Air Force ROTC: Offered at cooperating institution (Illinois Institute of Technology). **Faculty and instruction (2009-2010):** Total instructional faculty: 1,092 full-time, 570 part-time (70% men; 30% women; 17% minorities). Full-time faculty with Ph.D. or other terminal degree: 100%. Student/faculty ratio: 6/1. Classes of fewer than 20 students: 78%; of 20 to 49 students: 18%; of 50 or more students: 4%. **Advanced Placement and International Baccalaureate credit:** AP tests may be used for: Placement only. Scores accepted: 4, 5. International Baccalaureate exams may be used for: Placement only. **Freshmen returning for sophomore year:** 98%. **Graduation rates:** Four-year: 86%; five-year: 90%; six-year: 91%. **Graduate study:** 20% of students pursue further study immediately upon graduation; 24% within one year.

COSTS AND FINANCIAL AID

Financial aid office: (773) 702-8666. **Expenses (2010-2011):** Tuition and fees 2010-2011: $41,091; room/board: $12,153. Estimated books and supplies: $1,201 personal expenses: $2,195. **Financial aid:** In 2009-2010, 65% of undergraduates applied for financial aid. Of those, 49% were determined to have financial need; 80% had their need fully met. Average financial aid package (proportion receiving): $36,915 (49%). Average amount of gift aid, such as scholarships or grants (proportion receiving): $33,027 (39%). Average amount of self-help aid, such as work study or loans (proportion receiving): $5,434 (39%). Average need-based loan (excluding PLUS or other private loans): $5,074. Among students who received need-based aid, the average percentage of need met: 100%. Among students who received aid based on merit, the average award (and the proportion receiving): $13,208 (11%). The average athletic scholarship (and the proportion receiving): $0 (0%). Average amount of debt of borrowers graduating in 2009: $24,238. Proportion who borrowed: 48%.

CAMPUS LIFE AND EXTRACURRICULAR ACTIVITIES

Campus housing available: coed dorms, fraternity housing, apartments for married students. **Clubs and organizations:** Number of student organizations: 400. Activities include: campus ministries, choral groups, concert band, dance, drama/theater, international student organization, jazz band, literary magazine, model UN, music ensembles, musical theater, pep band, radio station, student government, student newspaper, student film society, symphony orchestra, yearbook. Number of fraternities: 10; sororities: 3. Average proportion of students who stay on campus on weekends: 95%. **Sports program (2009-2010):** Member of NCAA III. *Men's intercollegiate varsity sports:* baseball, basketball, cross country, football, soccer, swimming, tennis, track and field (indoor), track and field (outdoor), volleyball, wrestling. *Women's intercollegiate varsity sports:* basketball, cross country, soccer, softball, squash, swimming, tennis, track and field (indoor), track and field (outdoor), volleyball.

SERVICES AND FACILITIES

Basic services: nonremedial tutoring, health service, health insurance. **Counseling services:** minority student, career, personal, academic, psychological, birth control, religious. **Library:** Number of titles: 8,597,159; number of current serial subscriptions: 153,214. **Information technology resources:** Students are not required to lease or own a computer. School has a wireless network. Approximate number of users that can be accommodated: 6,000. Proportion of college-owned housing units wired for high-speed internet access: 100%. **Campus safety:** Security services offered: 24-hour foot-and-vehicle patrols, late-night transport/escort service, 24-hour emergency telephones, lighted pathways/sidewalks, controlled dormitory access (key, security card, etc).

TRANSFER AND INTERNATIONAL STUDENTS

Transfer students: May apply for admission for the following academic terms: Fall. Applicants need a minimum number of credits to apply. For fall 2009: Transfer applications received: 649. Transfer applicants offered admission: 115. Transfer applicants enrolled: 54. **International students:** Number of foreign undergraduates: 437 (9% of student body). Number of countries represented: 55. Minimum TOEFL score required: 600 (paper); 104 (computer).

University of Illinois–Chicago

- ■ **Address:** 601 S. Morgan M/C 102, Chicago, IL 60607
- ■ **Website:** http://www.uic.edu
- ■ **Public**
- ■ **Enrollment:** 14,898 full-time; 1,146 part-time

....

KEY STATS

✔ **U.S News College Ranking:** 143, National Universities
✔ **ACT Score (25th/75th percentile):** 21-26
✔ **Tuition:** 2010-2011: $13,074 in state, $25,464 out of state

Selectivity: More selective	**Room/board:** $10,882
Acceptance rate: 63%	**Average debt:** $18,440
Student/faculty ratio: 18/1	**Proportion who borrowed:** 61%

UNDERGRADUATE STUDENT BODY STATS

2009-2010 enrollment: 14,898 full-time; 1,146 part-time. Men: 48%; women: 52%. **Ethnic makeup:** African American: 8%; Asian American: 22%; Hispanic: 18%; White: 49%; International: 1%.

ADMISSIONS FACTS AND FIGURES

Phone: (312) 996-4350. **Email:** uicadmit@uic.edu. **Website:** http://www.uic.edu. **Application deadlines for fall 2011:** Regular decision: January 15. Early decision: Not offered. Early action: Not offered. Admission cannot be deferred. **Application fee:** $40. **To apply online, go to:** http://www.uic.edu/depts/oar/undergrad/apply_undergrad.html. **Admissions requirements/recommendations:** High school units required (recommended): English: 4; Mathematics: 3 (4); Science: 3; Foreign language: 2 (4); Social studies: 3; Academic electives: 1; Total units: 15. Tests: The college uses SAT or ACT scores in admissions decisions. Either SAT or ACT required. For admission to the fall 2011 entering class, the school will accept: ACT with or without writing accepted. Campus visit: Recommended. Admissions interview: Neither required nor recommended. Off-campus interview: Not available. **Factors that count in admissions decisions:** *Academic:* Secondary school record: Very Important. Class rank: Very Important. Letters of recommendation: Considered. Standardized test scores: Very Important. Essay: Very Important. *Nonacademic:* Interview: Not Considered. Extracurricular activities: Considered. Talent/ability: Not Considered. Character/personal qualities: Considered. Alumni/ae relationship: Not Considered. Geographical residence: Not Considered. State residency: Not Considered. Religious affiliation/commitment: Not Considered. Minority status: Not Considered. Volunteer work: Not Considered. Work experience: Not Considered. **Admissions statistics for the fall 2009 entering class:** Total applicants: 14,661. Total accepted: 9,244. Freshmen enrolled: 3,147; 2% were from out of state. Overall acceptance rate: 63%. **Size of waiting list:** 0 applicants; enrolled from waiting list: 0. **Credentials of fall 2009 freshmen:** 28% ranked in the top 10 percent of their high school class; 62% were in the top 25 percent; 93% were in the top half. (Proportion submitting class standing: 100%.) **First-year students who submitted SAT scores:** 6%. Scores (25/75 percentile): Critical Reading: 460-630, Math: 510-660, Combined: 970-1290. **First-year students submitting ACT scores:** 98%. Scores (25/75 percentile): English: 21-27, Math: 21-27, Composite: 21-26.

ACADEMICS

Year founded: 1965. **Academic calendar:** Semester. **Degrees offered:** certificate, bachelor's, master's, post-master's certificate, doctorate. **Most popular majors:** 20% business, management, marketing, and related support services, 12% psychology, 10% biological and biomedical sciences, 10% social sciences, 9% engineering. **Major fields of study:** architecture and related services; area, ethnic, cultural, and gender studies; biological and biomedical sciences; business, management, marketing, and related support services; communication, journalism, and related programs; computer and information sciences and support services; education; engineering; engineering technologies/technicians; English language and literature/letters; foreign languages, literatures, and linguistics; health professions and related clinical sciences; history; liberal arts and sciences studies, and humanities; mathematics and statistics; multi/interdisciplinary studies; parks, recreation, leisure, and fitness studies; philosophy and religious studies; physical sciences; psychology; public administration and social service professions; security and protective services; social sciences; visual and performing arts. **Areas of required coursework:** arts/fine arts, humanities, mathematics, English (including composition), sciences (biological or physical), history, social science, other. **Pre-professional programs:** pre-law, pre-dentistry, pre-medicine, pre-veterinary science, pre-pharmacy, other. **Special academic programs:** accelerated program, cooperative (work-study plan) program, distance learning, double major, dual enrollment, exchange student program (domestic), honors program, independent study, internships, student-designed major, study abroad, teacher certificate program. **Teacher certification offered in:** early childhood, special education, elementary, secondary, bilingual/bicultural. **Cooperative education programs:** business, engineering, other. **Reserve Officers Training Corps (ROTC):** Army ROTC: Offered on campus; Navy ROTC: Offered at cooperating institution (Illinois Institute of Technology); Air Force ROTC: Offered at cooperating institution (Illinois Institute of Technology). **Faculty and instruction (2009-2010):** Total instructional faculty: 1,160 full-time, 380 part-time (54% men; 46% women; 24% minorities). Full-time faculty with Ph.D. or other terminal degree: 73%. Student/faculty ratio: 18/1. Classes of fewer than 20 students: 33%; of 20 to 49 students: 49%; of 50 or more students: 19%. **Advanced Placement and International Baccalaureate credit:** AP tests may be used for: Credit only. Scores accepted: 3, 4, 5. International Baccalaureate exams may be used for: Credit only. **Freshmen returning for sophomore year:** 79%. **Graduation rates:**

Five-year: 0%; six-year: 54%. **Graduate study:** 31% of students pursue further study immediately upon graduation. Fields in which graduates pursue further study: law, 6%; medicine, 9%; arts and sciences, 5%.

COSTS AND FINANCIAL AID

Financial aid office: (312) 996-3126. **Expenses (2010-2011):** Tuition and fees 2010-2011: $13,074 in state, $25,464 out of state; room/board: $10,882. Estimated books and supplies: $1,200; transportation: $1,398; personal expenses: $2,176. **Financial aid:** Priority filing date for institution's financial aid form: March 1. In 2009-2010, 79% of undergraduates applied for financial aid. Of those, 68% were determined to have financial need; 14% had their need fully met. Average financial aid package (proportion receiving): $12,980 (65%). Average amount of gift aid, such as scholarships or grants (proportion receiving): $11,628 (52%). Average amount of self-help aid, such as work study or loans (proportion receiving): $4,893 (49%). Average need-based loan (excluding PLUS or other private loans): $4,149. Among students who received need-based aid, the average percentage of need met: 72%. Among students who received aid based on merit, the average award (and the proportion receiving): $3,650 (4%). The average athletic scholarship (and the proportion receiving): $16,741 (1%). Average amount of debt of borrowers graduating in 2009: $18,440. Proportion who borrowed: 61%.

CAMPUS LIFE AND EXTRACURRICULAR ACTIVITIES

Campus housing available (% using): coed dorms (64%), apartment for single students (36%). Students who live in college-owned, operated, or affiliated housing: 21%. **Clubs and organizations:** Number of student organizations: 370. Activities include: campus ministries, choral groups, concert band, dance, drama/theater, international student organization, jazz band, literary magazine, music ensembles, pep band, radio station, student government, student newspaper, yearbook. Number of fraternities: 13; sororities: 15. Proportion of men in fraternities: 3%; of women in sororities: 4%. Average proportion of students who stay on campus on weekends: 50%. **Sports program (2009-2010):** Member of NCAA I. *Men's intercollegiate varsity sports:* baseball, basketball, cross country, gymnastics, soccer, swimming, tennis, track and field (indoor), track and field (outdoor). *Women's intercollegiate varsity sports:* basketball, cross country, gymnastics, softball, swimming, tennis, track and field (indoor), track and field (outdoor), volleyball.

SERVICES AND FACILITIES

Basic services: nonremedial tutoring, women's center, placement service, day care, health service, health insurance. **Remedial assistance:** reading, math, writing, study skills, other. **Counseling services:** minority student, career, military, personal, veteran student, academic, psychological, birth control, religious, other. **For learning-disabled students:** School does not offer a structured program with separate admission and additional fees. Total undergraduates in learning-disabled program or receiving services: 64. Services include: remedial math, remedial English, reading machines, remedial reading, tape recorders, note-taking services, oral tests, learning center, readers, extended time for tests, priority registration, priority seating, substitution of courses, texts on tape, typist/scribe, exams on tape or computer, other testing accommodations. **Library:** Number of titles: 3,324,390; number of current serial subscriptions: 66,350. **Information technology resources:** Students are not required to lease or own a computer. Number of campus computers available to all students: 600. School has a wireless network. Approximate number of users that can be accommodated: 7,000. Proportion of college-owned housing units wired for high-speed internet access: 100%. **Campus safety:** Security services offered: 24-hour foot-and-vehicle patrols, late-night transport/escort service, 24-hour emergency telephones, lighted pathways/sidewalks, student patrols, controlled dormitory access (key, security card, etc).

TRANSFER AND INTERNATIONAL STUDENTS

Transfer students: May apply for admission for the following academic terms: Fall, Spring. Applicants need a minimum number of credits to apply. For fall 2009: Transfer applications received: 6,036. Transfer applicants offered admission: 2,335. Transfer applicants enrolled: 1,393. **International students:** Number of foreign undergraduates: 218 (1% of student body). Number of countries represented: 37. Minimum TOEFL score required: 520 (paper); 190 (computer).

University of Illinois–Springfield

- **Address:** 1 University Plaza, Springfield, IL 62703-5407
- **Website:** http://www.uis.edu
- **Public**
- **Enrollment:** 1,954 full-time; 1,073 part-time

KEY STATS
✔ **U.S News College Ranking:** 22, Regional Universities (Midwest)
✔ **ACT Score (25th/75th percentile):** 20-26
✔ **Tuition:** 2010-2011: $9,815 in state, $18,965 out of state
  Selectivity: Selective   **Room/board:** $8,660
  Acceptance rate: 58%   **Average debt:** $14,717
  Student/faculty ratio: 13/1   **Proportion who borrowed:** 64%

UNDERGRADUATE STUDENT BODY STATS
2009-2010 enrollment: 1,954 full-time; 1,073 part-time. Men: 45%; women: 55%. **Ethnic makeup:** African American: 13%; American-Indian: 1%; Asian American: 3%; Hispanic: 3%; White: 78%; International: 1%.

ADMISSIONS FACTS AND FIGURES
Phone: (217) 206-4847. **Email:** admissions@uis.edu. **Website:** http://www.uis.edu. **Application deadlines for fall 2011:** Regular decision: Rolling. Early decision: Not offered. Early action: Not offered. Admission can be deferred. **Application fee:** $40. **To apply online, go to:** http://www.uis.edu/admissions/apply.html. **Admissions requirements/recommendations:** High school units required (recommended): English: 4; Mathematics: 3 (4); Science: 3 (4); Foreign language: 2 (4); Social studies: 2 (4); History: 2; Total units: 16. Tests: The college uses SAT or ACT scores in admissions decisions. Either SAT or ACT required. For admission to the fall 2011 entering class, the school will accept: ACT with or without writing accepted. Campus visit: Recommended. Admissions interview: Neither required nor recommended. Off-campus interview: Not available. **Factors that count in admissions decisions:** *Academic:* Secondary school record: Very Important. Class rank: Considered. Letters of recommendation: Considered. Standardized test scores: Important. Essay: Very Important. *Nonacademic:* Interview: Not Considered. Extracurricular activities: Considered. Talent/ability: Not Considered. Character/personal qualities: Not Considered. Alumni/ae relationship: Not Considered. Geographical residence: Not Considered. State residency: Not Considered. Religious affiliation/commitment: Not Considered. Minority status: Not Considered. Volunteer work: Not Considered. Work experience: Considered. **Admissions statistics for the fall 2009 entering class:** Total applicants: 1,349. Total accepted: 777. Freshmen enrolled: 288; 2% were from out of state. Overall acceptance rate: 58%. **Size of waiting list:** 0 applicants; enrolled from waiting list: 0. **Credentials of fall 2009 freshmen:** 18% ranked in the top 10 percent of their high school class; 43% were in the top 25 percent; 78% were in the top half. (Proportion submitting class standing: 87%.) **Average high school grade point average:** 3.2. **First-year students submitting ACT scores:** 99%. Scores (25/75 percentile): English: 18-25, Math: 20-26, Composite: 20-26.

ACADEMICS
Year founded: 1969. **Academic calendar:** Semester. **Degrees offered:** bachelor's, post-bachelor's certificate, master's, post-master's certificate, doctorate. **Most popular majors:** 14% business administration and management, 11% psychology, 10% liberal arts and sciences/liberal studies, 9% computer science, 7% communication and media studies. **Major fields of study:** biological and biomedical sciences; business, management, marketing, and related support services; communication, journalism, and related programs; computer and information sciences and support services; English language and literature/letters; health professions and related clinical sciences; history; legal professions and studies; liberal arts and sciences studies, and humanities; mathematics and statistics; philosophy and religious studies; physical sciences; psychology; public administration and social service professions; security and protective services; social sciences; visual and performing arts. **Areas of required coursework:** arts/fine arts, humanities, mathematics, English (including composition), sciences (biological or physical), social science, other. **Pre-professional programs:** pre-law, pre-medicine, pre-veterinary science. **Special academic programs:** distance learning, double major, English as a Second Language (ESL), honors program, independent study, internships, study abroad, teacher certificate program. **Teacher certification offered in:** elementary, secondary. **Faculty and instruction (2009-2010):** Total instructional faculty: 211 full-time, 147 part-time (55% men; 45% women; 13% minorities). Full-time faculty with Ph.D. or other terminal degree:

90%. Student/faculty ratio: 13/1. Classes of fewer than 20 students: 46%; of 20 to 49 students: 52%; of 50 or more students: 2%. **Advanced Placement and International Baccalaureate credit:** AP tests may be used for: Credit and/ or placement. Scores accepted: 3, 4, 5. International Baccalaureate exams may be used for: Credit only. **Freshmen returning for sophomore year:** 73%. **Graduation rates:** Four-year: 47%; five-year: 64%; six-year: 60%.

COSTS AND FINANCIAL AID

Financial aid office: (217) 206-6724. **Expenses (2010-2011):** Tuition and fees 2010-2011: $9,815 in state, $18,965 out of state; room/board: $8,660. Estimated books and supplies: $1,200; transportation: $900; personal expenses: $1,800. **Financial aid:** Priority filing date for institution's financial aid form: April 1; deadline: November 15. In 2009-2010, 83% of undergraduates applied for financial aid. Of those, 68% were determined to have financial need; 8% had their need fully met. Average financial aid package (proportion receiving): $10,929 (66%). Average amount of gift aid, such as scholarships or grants (proportion receiving): $7,928 (55%). Average amount of self-help aid, such as work study or loans (proportion receiving): $5,052 (59%). Average need-based loan (excluding PLUS or other private loans): $4,204. Among students who received need-based aid, the average percentage of need met: 74%. Among students who received aid based on merit, the average award (and the proportion receiving): $3,903 (12%). The average athletic scholarship (and the proportion receiving): $5,825 (2%). Average amount of debt of borrowers graduating in 2009: $14,717. Proportion who borrowed: 64%.

CAMPUS LIFE AND EXTRACURRICULAR ACTIVITIES

Campus housing available: coed dorms, apartments for married students, apartment for single students, special housing for disabled students, special housing for international students. Students who live in college-owned, operated, or affiliated housing: 27%. **Clubs and organizations:** Number of student organizations: 83. Activities include: campus ministries, choral groups, concert band, dance, drama/theater, international student organization, jazz band, model UN, music ensembles, pep band, student government, student newspaper, student film society. Number of fraternities: 0; sororities: 0. Average proportion of students who stay on campus on weekends: 65%. **Sports program (2009-2010):** Member of NCAA II. *Men's intercollegiate varsity sports:* baseball, basketball, golf, soccer, tennis. *Women's intercollegiate varsity sports:* basketball, golf, soccer, softball, tennis, volleyball.

SERVICES AND FACILITIES

Basic services: women's center, day care, health service, health insurance. **Remedial assistance:** reading, math, writing, study skills. **Counseling services:** minority student, career, military, personal, veteran student, academic, older student, psychological, birth control, religious. **For learning-disabled students:** School does not offer a structured program with separate admission and additional fees. Total undergraduates in learning-disabled program or receiving services: 47. Services include: remedial math, tape recorders, videotaped classes, untimed tests, note-taking services, oral tests, learning center, readers, extended time for tests, tutors, early syllabus, priority registration, priority seating, substitution of courses, texts on tape, typist/ scribe, exams on tape or computer, other testing accommodations, other. **Library:** Number of titles: 568,154; number of current serial subscriptions: 42,777. **Information technology resources:** Students are not required to lease or own a computer. School has a wireless network. Approximate number of users that can be accommodated: 2,000. Proportion of college-owned housing units wired for high-speed internet access: 100%. **Campus safety:** Security services offered: 24-hour foot-and-vehicle patrols, 24-hour emergency telephones, lighted pathways/sidewalks, controlled dormitory access (key, security card, etc).

TRANSFER AND INTERNATIONAL STUDENTS

Transfer students: May apply for admission for the following academic terms: Fall, Spring, Summer. Applicants need a minimum number of credits to apply. For fall 2009: Transfer applications received: 1,449. Transfer applicants offered admission: 915. Transfer applicants enrolled: 635. **International students:** Number of foreign undergraduates: 22 (1% of student body). Number of countries represented: 11. Minimum TOEFL score required: 500 (paper); 69 (computer).

University of Illinois–Urbana-Champaign

- **Address:** 601 E. John Street, Champaign, IL 61820-5711
- **Website:** http://www.uiuc.edu
- **Public**
- **Enrollment:** 30,639 full-time; 838 part-time

KEY STATS
- ✔ **U.S News College Ranking:** 47, National Universities
- ✔ **ACT Score (25th/75th percentile):** 26-31
- ✔ **Tuition:** 2009-2010: $12,286 in state, $26,070 out of state

Selectivity: More selective   **Room/board:** $9,284
Acceptance rate: 65%   **Average debt:** $21,145
Student/faculty ratio: 16/1   **Proportion who borrowed:** 55%

UNDERGRADUATE STUDENT BODY STATS

2009-2010 enrollment: 30,639 full-time; 838 part-time. Men: 54%; women: 46%. **Ethnic makeup:** African American: 7%; Asian American: 13%; Hispanic: 7%; White: 65%; International: 8%.

ADMISSIONS FACTS AND FIGURES

Phone: (217) 333-0302. **Email:** ugradadmissions@uiuc.edu. **Website:** http://www.uiuc.edu. **Application deadlines for fall 2011:** Regular decision: January 2; decision sent by February 18. Early decision: Not offered. Early action: Not offered. Admission can be deferred. **Application fee:** $40. **To apply online, go to:** http://www.apply.uiuc.edu. **Admissions requirements/recommendations:** High school units required (recommended): English: 4 (4); Mathematics: 3 (4); Science: 2 (4); Foreign language: 2 (4); Social studies: 2 (4); Academic electives: 2 (4); Total units: 15 (24). Tests: The college uses SAT or ACT scores in admissions decisions. Either SAT or ACT required. For admission to the fall 2011 entering class, the school will accept: ACT with writing required. Campus visit: Recommended. Admissions interview: Neither required nor recommended. Off-campus interview: May be arranged. **Factors that count in admissions decisions:** *Academic:* Secondary school record: Very Important. Class rank: Important. Letters of recommendation: Not Considered. Standardized test scores: Important. Essay: Important. *Nonacademic:* Interview: Not Considered. Extracurricular activities: Important. Talent/ability: Important. Character/personal qualities: Considered. Alumni/ae relationship: Not Considered. Geographical residence: Considered. State residency: Considered. Religious affiliation/commitment: Not Considered. Minority status: Considered. Volunteer work: Considered. Work experience: Considered. **Other schools with the greatest overlap in applicants:** Northwestern University; Purdue University–West Lafayette; University of Michigan–Ann Arbor; University of Wisconsin–Madison; Washington University in St. Louis. **Admissions statistics for the fall 2009 entering class:** Total applicants: 26,057. Total accepted: 16,979. Freshmen enrolled: 6,991; 7% were from out of state. Overall acceptance rate: 65%. **Size of waiting list:** 1040 applicants; enrolled from waiting list: 691. **Credentials of fall 2009 freshmen:** 58% ranked in the top 10 percent of their high school class; 94% were in the top 25 percent; 100% were in the top half. (Proportion submitting class standing: 63%.) **First-year students who submitted SAT scores:** 23%. Scores (25/75 percentile): Critical Reading: 540-660, Math: 660-770, Combined: 1200-1430. **First-year students submitting ACT scores:** 86%. Scores (25/75 percentile): English: 26-32, Math: 26-32, Composite: 26-31.

ACADEMICS

Year founded: 1867. **Academic calendar:** Semester. **Degrees offered:** certificate, bachelor's, post-bachelor's certificate, master's, post-master's certificate, doctorate. **Most popular majors:** 13% engineering, 12% business, management, marketing, and related support services, 11% social sciences, 8% English language and literature/letters, 7% biological and biomedical sciences. **Major fields of study:** agriculture, agriculture operations, and related sciences; architecture and related services; area, ethnic, cultural, and gender studies; biological and biomedical sciences; business, management, marketing, and related support services; communication, journalism, and related programs; computer and information sciences and support services; education; engineering; English language and literature/letters; family and consumer sciences/human sciences; foreign languages, literatures, and linguistics; health professions and related clinical sciences; history; legal professions and studies; liberal arts and sciences studies, and humanities; mathematics and statistics; multi/interdisciplinary studies; natural resources and conservation; parks, recreation, leisure, and fitness studies; philosophy and religious studies; physical sciences; psychology; social sciences; transportation and materials moving; visual and performing arts. **Areas of required coursework:** humanities, mathematics, English (including composition), philosophy, foreign languages, sciences (biological or physical), history, social science, other. **Pre-professional programs:** pre-law, pre-dentistry, pre-medicine, pre-veterinary science, pre-optometry, pre-pharmacy. **Special academic programs (% participation):** accelerated program (13%), cooperative (work-study plan) program (2%), cross-registration (1%), distance learning (5%), double major (10%), dual enrollment (1%), English as a Second Language (ESL) (2%), exchange student program (domestic) (1%), honors program (25%), independent study (72%), internships (30%), liberal arts/career combination (20%), student-designed major (1%), study abroad (21%), teacher certificate program (6%), weekend college, other (100%). **Teacher certification offered in:** early childhood, special education, elementary, secondary. **Cooperative education programs:** computer science, engineering, other. **Reserve Officers Training Corps (ROTC):** Army ROTC: Offered on campus; Navy ROTC: Offered on campus; Air Force ROTC: Offered on campus. **Faculty and instruction (2009-2010):** Total instructional faculty: 1,880 full-time, 57 part-time (69% men; 31% women; 24% minorities). Full-time faculty with Ph.D. or other terminal degree: 92%. Student/faculty ratio: 16/1. Classes of fewer than 20 students: 38%; of 20 to 49 students: 42%; of 50 or more students: 20%. **Advanced Placement and International Baccalaureate credit:** AP tests may be used for: Credit and/or placement. Scores accepted: 3, 4, 5. International Baccalaureate exams may be used for: Credit and/or placement. **Freshmen returning for sophomore year:** 93%. **Graduation rates:** Four-year: 65%; five-year: 81%; six-year: 83%. **Graduate study:** 21% of students pursue further study immediately upon graduation; 34% within one year; 45% within five years. Fields in which graduates pursue further study: Master of Business Administration (MBA), 23%; law, 14%; medicine, 11%; dentistry, 3%; engineering, 27%; theology (or the seminary), 2%; education, 25%; arts and sciences, 57%; veterinary medicine, 3%.

COSTS AND FINANCIAL AID

Financial aid office: (217) 333-0100. **Expenses (2009-2010):** Tuition and fees 2009-2010: $12,286 in state, $26,070 out of state; room/board: $9,284. Estimated books and supplies: $1,200 personal expenses: $2,642. **Financial aid:** Priority filing date for institution's financial aid form: March 15. In 2009-2010, 59% of undergraduates applied for financial aid. Of those, 45% were determined to have financial need; 31% had their need fully met. Average financial aid package (proportion receiving): $12,614 (44%). Average amount of gift aid, such as scholarships or grants (proportion receiving): $10,570 (34%). Average amount of self-help aid, such as work study or loans (proportion receiving): $5,111 (38%). Average need-based loan (excluding PLUS or other private loans): $4,473. Among students who received need-based aid, the average percentage of need met: 70%. Among students who received aid based on merit, the average award (and the proportion receiving): $3,359 (11%). The average athletic scholarship (and the proportion receiving): $17,548 (1%). Average amount of debt of borrowers graduating in 2009: $21,145. Proportion who borrowed: 55%.

CAMPUS LIFE AND EXTRACURRICULAR ACTIVITIES

Campus housing available (% using): coed dorms (46%), women's dorms (6%), men's dorms (1%), sorority housing (8%), fraternity housing (17%), apartments for married students (6%), apartment for single students (0%), special housing for disabled students (1%), special housing for international students (0%), cooperative housing (1%), other housing options (14%). Students who live in college-owned, operated, or affiliated housing: 14%. **Student employment:** During the 2009-2010 academic year, 25% of undergraduates worked on campus. Average per-year earnings: $1,500. **Clubs and organizations:** Number of student organizations: 999. Activities include: choral groups, concert band, dance, drama/theater, jazz band, literary magazine, marching band, music ensembles, musical theater, opera, pep band, radio station, student government, student newspaper, student film society, symphony orchestra, television station, yearbook. Number of fraternities: 59; sororities: 36. Proportion of men in fraternities: 51%; of women in sororities: 49%. Average proportion of students who stay on campus on weekends: 75%. **Sports program (2009-2010):** Member of NCAA I.

SERVICES AND FACILITIES

Basic services: nonremedial tutoring, women's center, placement service, day care, health service, health insurance, other. **Remedial assistance:** reading, math, writing, study skills. **Counseling services:** minority student, career, military, personal, veteran student, academic, older student, psychological, birth control, other. **For learning-disabled students:** School does not offer a structured program with separate admission and additional fees. Services include: reading machines, tape recorders, other special classes,

note-taking services, special bookstore section, oral tests, learning center, readers, extended time for tests, priority registration, priority seating, texts on tape, other testing accommodations, other. **Library:** Number of titles: 11,000,000; number of current serial subscriptions: 127,666. **Information technology resources:** Students are not required to lease or own a computer. Number of campus computers available to all students: 3,500. School has a wireless network. Approximate number of users that can be accommodated: 10,500. Proportion of college-owned housing units wired for high-speed internet access: 100%. **Campus safety:** Security services offered: 24-hour foot-and-vehicle patrols, late-night transport/escort service, 24-hour emergency telephones, lighted pathways/sidewalks, student patrols, controlled dormitory access (key, security card, etc).

TRANSFER AND INTERNATIONAL STUDENTS

Transfer students: May apply for admission for the following academic terms: Fall, Spring, Summer. Applicants do not need a minimum number of credits to apply. For fall 2009: Transfer applications received: 3,379. Transfer applicants offered admission: 1,744. Transfer applicants enrolled: 1,195. **International students:** Number of foreign undergraduates: 2510 (8% of student body). Number of countries represented: 62. Minimum TOEFL score required: 550 (paper); 213 (computer).

University of St. Francis

- ■ **Address:** 500 Wilcox Street, Joliet, IL 60435
- ■ **Website:** http://www.stfrancis.edu
- ■ **Private; Religious affiliation:** Roman Catholic
- ■ **Enrollment:** 1,210 full-time; 66 part-time

KEY STATS

- ✔ **U.S News College Ranking:** 37, Regional Universities (Midwest)
- ✔ **ACT Score (25th/75th percentile):** 21-26
- ✔ **Tuition:** 2009-2010: $22,698

Selectivity: Selective	**Room/board:** $7,938
Acceptance rate: 50%	**Average debt:** $21,594
Student/faculty ratio: 12/1	**Proportion who borrowed:** 96%

UNDERGRADUATE STUDENT BODY STATS

2009-2010 enrollment: 1,210 full-time; 66 part-time. Men: 33%; women: 67%. **Ethnic makeup:** African American: 7%; Asian American: 4%; Hispanic: 12%; White: 76%; International: 1%. **Religious preference:** Protestant: 30%; Jewish: 1%; Muslim: 1%; Roman Catholic: 55%; Other: 13%.

ADMISSIONS FACTS AND FIGURES

Phone: (800) 735-7500. **Email:** admissions@stfrancis.edu. **Website:** http://www.stfrancis.edu. **Application deadlines for fall 2011:** Regular decision: August 1. Early decision: Not offered. Early action: Not offered. Admission can be deferred. **Application fee:** $30. **To apply online, go to:** http://www.stfrancis.edu/admissions/apply.htm. **Admissions requirements/recommendations:** High school units required (recommended): English: 4; Mathematics: 3; Science: 2; Foreign language: (1); Social studies: 2; Academic electives: 3; Total units: 17. Tests: The college uses SAT or ACT scores in admissions decisions. Either SAT or ACT required. For admission to the fall 2011 entering class, the school will accept: ACT with or without writing accepted. Campus visit: Recommended. Admissions interview: Recommended. Off-campus interview: May be arranged. **Factors that count in admissions decisions:** *Academic:* Secondary school record: Very Important. Class rank: Very Important. Letters of recommendation: Considered. Standardized test scores: Very Important. Essay: Considered. *Nonacademic:* Interview: Considered. Extracurricular activities: Not Considered. Talent/ability: Not Considered. Character/personal qualities: Not Considered. Alumni/ae relationship: Not Considered. Geographical residence: Not Considered. State residency: Not Considered. Religious affiliation/commitment: Not Considered. Minority status: Not Considered. Volunteer work: Not Considered. Work experience: Not Considered. **Other schools with the greatest overlap in applicants:** Illinois State University; Lewis University; North Central College; Northern Illinois University; St. Xavier University. **Admissions statistics for the fall 2009 entering class:** Total applicants: 1,274. Total accepted: 632. Freshmen enrolled: 223; 9% were from out of state. Overall acceptance rate: 50%. **Credentials of fall 2009 freshmen:** 20% ranked in the top 10 percent of their high school class; 50% were in the top 25 percent; 90% were in the top half. (Proportion submitting class standing: 87%.) **Average high school grade point average:** 3.3. **First-year students submitting ACT scores:** 100%. Scores (25/75 percentile): English: 21-27, Math: 19-26, Composite: 21-26.

ACADEMICS

Year founded: 1920. **Academic calendar:** Semester. **Degrees offered:** bachelor's, master's, post-master's certificate. **Most popular majors:** 32% nursing/registered nurse training (R.N., A.S.N., B.S.N., M.S.N.), 12% elementary education and teaching, 5% psychology, 4% biology/biological sciences, 4% marketing/marketing management. **Major fields of study:** biological and biomedical sciences; business, management, marketing, and related support services; communication, journalism, and related programs; computer and information sciences and support services; education; English language and literature/letters; health professions and related clinical sciences; history; liberal arts and sciences studies, and humanities; mathematics and statistics; multi/interdisciplinary studies; natural resources and conservation; parks, recreation, leisure, and fitness studies; psychology; public administration and social service professions; social sciences; theology and religious vocations; visual and performing arts. **Areas of required coursework:** arts/fine arts, computer literacy, mathematics, English (including composition), philosophy, sciences (biological or physical), history, social science, other. **Pre-professional programs:** pre-law, pre-dentistry, pre-medicine, pre-veterinary science, pre-optometry, pre-pharmacy, other. **Special academic programs (% participation):** accelerated program, distance learning (73%), double major (1%), honors program, independent study (7%), internships (73%), student-designed major, study abroad (1%), teacher certificate program (21%). **Teacher certification offered in:** special education, elementary, middle/junior high, secondary. **Faculty and instruction (2009-2010):** Total instructional faculty: 88 full-time, 147 part-time (42% men; 58% women; 10% minorities). Full-time faculty with Ph.D. or other terminal degree: 68%. Student/faculty ratio: 12/1. Classes of fewer than 20 students: 68%; of 20 to 49 students: 32%; of 50 or more students: 0%. **Advanced Placement and International Baccalaureate credit:** AP tests may be used for: Credit and/or placement. Scores accepted: 3, 4, 5. International Baccalaureate exams may be used for: Credit only. **Freshmen returning for sophomore year:** 76%. **Graduation rates:** Four-year: 33%; five-year: 56%; six-year: 59%. **Graduate study:** 27% of students pursue further study immediately upon graduation.

COSTS AND FINANCIAL AID

Financial aid office: (815) 740-3403. **Expenses (2009-2010):** Tuition and fees 2009-2010: $22,698; room/board: $7,938. Estimated books and supplies: $800; transportation: $500; personal expenses: $1,000. **Financial aid:** Priority filing date for institution's financial aid form: March 15. In 2009-2010, 99% of undergraduates applied for financial aid. Of those, 81% were determined to have financial need; 49% had their need fully met. Average financial aid package (proportion receiving): $18,171 (81%). Average amount of gift aid, such as scholarships or grants (proportion receiving): $7,816 (56%). Average amount of self-help aid, such as work study or loans (proportion receiving): $5,275 (62%). Average need-based loan (excluding PLUS or other private loans): $4,538. Among students who received need-based aid, the average percentage of need met: 72%. Among students who received aid based on merit, the average award (and the proportion receiving): $6,748 (17%). The average athletic scholarship (and the proportion receiving): $9,209 (7%). Average amount of debt of borrowers graduating in 2009: $21,594. Proportion who borrowed: 96%.

CAMPUS LIFE AND EXTRACURRICULAR ACTIVITIES

Campus housing available (% using): coed dorms (97%), apartment for single students (3%). Students who live in college-owned, operated, or affiliated housing: 30%. **Student employment:** During the 2009-2010 academic year, 18% of undergraduates worked on campus. Average per-year earnings: $2,166. **Clubs and organizations:** Number of student organizations: 28. Activities include: campus ministries, choral groups, dance, drama/theater, international student organization, literary magazine, music ensembles, musical theater, opera, radio station, student government, student newspaper, symphony orchestra, television station. Number of fraternities: 0; sororities: 0. Average proportion of students who stay on campus on weekends: 50%. **Sports program (2009-2010):** Member of NAIA. *Men's intercollegiate varsity sports:* baseball, basketball, cross country, football, golf, soccer, tennis, track and field (indoor), track and field (outdoor). *Women's intercollegiate varsity sports:* basketball, cross country, golf, soccer, softball, tennis, track and field (indoor), track and field (outdoor), volleyball.

SERVICES AND FACILITIES

Basic services: nonremedial tutoring, health insurance, other. **Remedial assistance:** math, writing, study skills, other. **Counseling services:** career,

personal, academic, older student, psychological, religious. **For learning-disabled students:** School does not offer a structured program with separate admission and additional fees. Total undergraduates in learning-disabled program or receiving services: 20. Services include: tape recorders, note-taking services, oral tests, learning center, readers, extended time for tests, tutors, priority seating, texts on tape, other testing accommodations, other. **Library:** Number of titles: 134,400; number of current serial subscriptions: 15,002. **Information technology resources:** Students are not required to lease or own a computer. Number of campus computers available to all students: 382. School has a wireless network. Approximate number of users that can be accommodated: 10,000. Proportion of college-owned housing units wired for high-speed internet access: 100%. **Campus safety:** Security services offered: 24-hour foot-and-vehicle patrols, late-night transport/escort service, 24-hour emergency telephones, lighted pathways/sidewalks, student patrols, controlled dormitory access (key, security card, etc).

TRANSFER AND INTERNATIONAL STUDENTS

Transfer students: May apply for admission for the following academic terms: Fall, Spring, Summer. Applicants need a minimum number of credits to apply. For fall 2009: Transfer applications received: 988. Transfer applicants offered admission: 365. Transfer applicants enrolled: 168. **International students:** Number of foreign undergraduates: 15 (1% of student body). Minimum TOEFL score required: 550 (paper); 213 (computer).

VanderCook College of Music

- **Address:** 3140 S. Federal Street, Chicago, IL 60616
- **Website:** http://www.vandercook.edu
- **Private**
- **Enrollment:** 135 full-time; 40 part-time

KEY STATS

✔ **U.S News College Ranking:** Unranked Specialty School–Fine Arts
✔ **ACT Score (25th/75th percentile):** 19-26
✔ **Tuition:** 2010-2011: $22,270

Selectivity: N/A	Room/board: $10,338
Acceptance rate: 98%	Average debt: N/A
Student/faculty ratio: 9/1	Proportion who borrowed: 95%

UNDERGRADUATE STUDENT BODY STATS

2009-2010 enrollment: 135 full-time; 40 part-time. Men: 58%; women: 42%. **Ethnic makeup:** African American: 14%; Asian American: 4%; Hispanic: 11%; White: 66%; International: 4%.

ADMISSIONS FACTS AND FIGURES

Phone: (800) 448-2655. **Email:** admissions@vandercook.edu. **Website:** http://www.vandercook.edu. **Application deadlines for fall 2011:** Regular decision: Rolling. Early decision: Not offered. Early action: Not offered. Admission can be deferred. **Application fee:** $35. **To apply online, go to:** http://www.vandercook.edu/PDF/UgApp.pdf. **Admissions requirements/recommendations:** High school units required (recommended): English: (3); Mathematics: (2); Science: (2); Foreign language: (2); Social studies: (3); History: (0); Total units: (15). Tests: The college uses SAT or ACT scores in admissions decisions. Neither SAT nor ACT required. For admission to the fall 2011 entering class, the school will accept: ACT with or without writing accepted. Campus visit: Recommended. Admissions interview: Required. Off-campus interview: May be arranged. **Factors that count in admissions decisions:** *Academic:* Secondary school record: Considered. Class rank: Important. Letters of recommendation: Important. Standardized test scores: Important. Essay: Very Important. *Nonacademic:* Interview: Important. Extracurricular activities: Considered. Talent/ability: Very Important. Character/personal qualities: Very Important. Alumni/ae relationship: Important. Geographical residence: Considered. State residency: Not Considered. Religious affiliation/commitment: Not Considered. Minority status: Not Considered. Volunteer work: Considered. Work experience: Considered. **Admissions statistics for the fall 2009 entering class:** Total applicants: 52. Total accepted: 51. Freshmen enrolled: 31; 28% were from out of state. Overall acceptance rate: 98%. **Size of waiting list:** 2 applicants; enrolled from waiting list: 0. **Credentials of fall 2009 freshmen:** 19% ranked in the top 10 percent of their high school class; 42% were in the top 25 percent; 85% were in the top half. (Proportion submitting class standing: 84%.) **Average high school grade point average:** 3.3. **First-year students who submitted SAT scores:** 19%. Scores (25/75 percentile): Critical Reading: 510-

700, Math: 540-620, Combined: 1050-1320. **First-year students submitting ACT scores:** 81%. Scores (25/75 percentile): English: 19-25, Math: 19-25, Composite: 19-26.

ACADEMICS

Year founded: 1909. **Academic calendar:** Semester. **Degrees offered:** bachelor's, master's. **Most popular majors:** 100% music teacher education. **Major fields of study:** education. **Areas of required coursework:** arts/fine arts, humanities, computer literacy, mathematics, English (including composition), sciences (biological or physical), history, social science, other. **Special academic programs (% participation):** teacher certificate program (100%). **Teacher certification offered in:** elementary, middle/junior high, secondary. **Cooperative education programs:** education. **Faculty and instruction (2009-2010):** Total instructional faculty: 11 full-time, 24 part-time (60% men; 40% women; 9% minorities). Full-time faculty with Ph.D. or other terminal degree: 45%. Student/faculty ratio: 9/1. Classes of fewer than 20 students: 65%; of 20 to 49 students: 30%; of 50 or more students: 5%. **Advanced Placement and International Baccalaureate credit:** AP tests may be used for: Placement only. Scores accepted: 3, 4, 5. **Freshmen returning for sophomore year:** 90%. **Graduation rates:** Four-year: 42%; five-year: 58%; six-year: 60%.

COSTS AND FINANCIAL AID

Financial aid office: (312) 225-6288. **Expenses (2010-2011):** Tuition and fees 2010-2011: $22,270; room/board: $10,338. Estimated books and supplies: $1,900. **Financial aid:** Priority filing date for institution's financial aid form: April 1. In 2009-2010, 98% of undergraduates applied for financial aid. Of those, 96% were determined to have financial need; Average financial aid package (proportion receiving): $12,947 (100%). Average amount of gift aid, such as scholarships or grants (proportion receiving): $12,172 (47%). Average amount of self-help aid, such as work study or loans (proportion receiving): $5,388 (73%). Average need-based loan (excluding PLUS or other private loans): $4,696. Among students who received aid based on merit, the average award (and the proportion receiving): $6,313 (4%). The average athletic scholarship (and the proportion receiving): $0 (0%). Proportion who borrowed: 95%.

CAMPUS LIFE AND EXTRACURRICULAR ACTIVITIES

Campus housing available: coed dorms, sorority housing, fraternity housing, apartments for married students, other housing options. Students who live in college-owned, operated, or affiliated housing: 9%. **Student employment:** During the 2009-2010 academic year, 5% of undergraduates worked on campus. Average per-year earnings: $1,000. Activities include: choral groups, concert band, jazz band, music ensembles, musical theater. Number of fraternities: 1; sororities: 1.

SERVICES AND FACILITIES

Basic services: placement service. **Remedial assistance:** other. **Library:** Number of titles: 13,885; number of current serial subscriptions: 181. **Information technology resources:** Students are not required to lease or own a computer. Number of campus computers available to all students: 18. School has a wireless network. Proportion of college-owned housing units wired for high-speed internet access: 100%. **Campus safety:** Security services offered: 24-hour foot-and-vehicle patrols, 24-hour emergency telephones, lighted pathways/sidewalks, controlled dormitory access (key, security card, etc).

TRANSFER AND INTERNATIONAL STUDENTS

Transfer students: May apply for admission for the following academic terms: Fall, Spring. Applicants do not need a minimum number of credits to apply. For fall 2009: Transfer applications received: 13. Transfer applicants offered admission: 10. Transfer applicants enrolled: 6. **International students:** Number of foreign undergraduates: 5 (4% of student body). Number of countries represented: 2. Minimum TOEFL score required: 500 (paper); 173 (computer).

Western Illinois University

- **Address:** 1 University Circle, Macomb, IL 61455
- **Website:** http://www.wiu.edu
- **Public**
- **Enrollment:** 9,556 full-time; 997 part-time

KEY STATS

✔ **U.S News College Ranking:** 49, Regional Universities (Midwest)
✔ **ACT Score (25th/75th percentile):** 19-23
✔ **Tuition:** 2010-2011: $9,466 in state, $12,855 out of state

Selectivity: Selective	**Room/board:** $7,642
Acceptance rate: 64%	**Average debt:** $20,550
Student/faculty ratio: 16/1	**Proportion who borrowed:** 68%

UNDERGRADUATE STUDENT BODY STATS

2009-2010 enrollment: 9,556 full-time; 997 part-time. Men: 53%; women: 47%. **Ethnic makeup:** African American: 9%; Asian American: 1%; Hispanic: 5%; White: 83%; International: 1%.

ADMISSIONS FACTS AND FIGURES

Phone: (309) 298-3157. **Email:** admissions@wiu.edu. **Website:** http://www.wiu.edu. **Application deadlines for fall 2011:** Regular decision: May 15. Early decision: Not offered. Early action: Not offered. Admission can be deferred. **Application fee:** $30. **To apply online, go to:** http://www.student.services.wiu.edu/admissions/application/. **Admissions requirements/recommendations:** High school units required (recommended): English: (4); Mathematics: (3); Science: (3); Social studies: (3); Academic electives: (2); Total units: (15). Tests: The college uses SAT or ACT scores in admissions decisions. Either SAT or ACT required. For admission to the fall 2011 entering class, the school will accept: ACT with or without writing accepted. Campus visit: Recommended. Admissions interview: Neither required nor recommended. Off-campus interview: May be arranged. **Factors that count in admissions decisions:** *Academic:* Secondary school record: Very Important. Class rank: Very Important. Letters of recommendation: Not Considered. Standardized test scores: Very Important. Essay: Not Considered. *Nonacademic:* Interview: Not Considered. Extracurricular activities: Not Considered. Talent/ability: Not Considered. Character/personal qualities: Not Considered. Alumni/ae relationship: Not Considered. Geographical residence: Not Considered. State residency: Not Considered. Religious affiliation/commitment: Not Considered. Minority status: Not Considered. Volunteer work: Not Considered. Work experience: Not Considered. **Other schools with the greatest overlap in applicants:** Eastern Illinois University; Illinois State University; Northern Illinois University. **Admissions statistics for the fall 2009 entering class:** Total applicants: 8,331. Total accepted: 5,301. Freshmen enrolled: 1,641; 6% were from out of state. Overall acceptance rate: 64%. **Credentials of fall 2009 freshmen:** 7% ranked in the top 10 percent of their high school class; 24% were in the top 25 percent; 58% were in the top half. (Proportion submitting class standing: 78%.) **Average high school grade point average:** 3.0. **First-year students submitting ACT scores:** 97%. Scores (25/75 percentile): English: N/A, Math: N/A, Composite: 19-23.

ACADEMICS

Year founded: 1899. **Academic calendar:** Semester. **Degrees offered:** bachelor's, post-bachelor's certificate, master's, post-master's certificate, doctorate. **Most popular majors:** 15% criminal justice/law enforcement administration, 10% liberal arts and sciences/liberal studies, 8% communication studies/speech communication and rhetoric, 8% elementary education and teaching, 7% parks, recreation, and leisure facilities management. **Major fields of study:** agriculture, agriculture operations, and related sciences; area, ethnic, cultural, and gender studies; biological and biomedical sciences; business, management, marketing, and related support services; communication, journalism, and related programs; communications technologies/technicians and support services; computer and information sciences and support services; education; engineering technologies/technicians; English language and literature/letters; family and consumer sciences/human sciences; foreign languages, literatures, and linguistics; health professions and related clinical sciences; history; liberal arts and sciences studies, and humanities; mathematics and statistics; parks, recreation, leisure, and fitness studies; philosophy and religious studies; physical sciences; psychology; public administration and social service professions; security and protective services; social sciences; visual and performing arts. **Areas of required coursework:** humanities, mathematics, English (including composition), sciences (biological or physical), history, social science, other. **Pre-**

professional programs: pre-law, pre-dentistry, pre-medicine, pre-veterinary science, pre-optometry, pre-pharmacy, other. **Special academic programs (% participation):** distance learning (42%), double major (3%), dual enrollment, English as a Second Language (ESL) (.8%), external degree program (9.3%), honors program (5%), independent study (24%), internships (10.7%), student-designed major (1.2%), study abroad (1%), teacher certificate program (11.4%), weekend college (4%). **Teacher certification offered in:** early childhood, special education, elementary, middle/junior high, secondary, bilingual/bicultural. **Reserve Officers Training Corps (ROTC):** Army ROTC: Offered on campus. **Faculty and instruction (2009-2010):** Total instructional faculty: 672 full-time, 82 part-time (56% men; 44% women; 14% minorities). Full-time faculty with Ph.D. or other terminal degree: 71%. Student/faculty ratio: 16/1. Classes of fewer than 20 students: 43%; of 20 to 49 students: 52%; of 50 or more students: 5%. **Advanced Placement and International Baccalaureate credit:** AP tests may be used for: Placement only. Scores accepted: 2, 3, 4, 5. International Baccalaureate exams may be used for: Credit only. **Freshmen returning for sophomore year:** 73%. **Graduation rates:** Four-year: 35%; five-year: 55%; six-year: 57%. **Graduate study:** 25% of students pursue further study within one year. Fields in which graduates pursue further study: law, 4%; medicine, 1%; dentistry, 1%; arts and sciences, 50%.

COSTS AND FINANCIAL AID

Financial aid office: (309) 298-2446. **Expenses (2010-2011):** Tuition and fees 2010-2011: $9,466 in state, $12,855 out of state; room/board: $7,642. Estimated books and supplies: $1,200; transportation: $1,225; personal expenses: $1,773. **Financial aid:** Priority filing date for institution's financial aid form: February 15. In 2009-2010, 82% of undergraduates applied for financial aid. Of those, 68% were determined to have financial need; 35% had their need fully met. Average financial aid package (proportion receiving): $9,261 (65%). Average amount of gift aid, such as scholarships or grants (proportion receiving): $7,479 (46%). Average amount of self-help aid, such as work study or loans (proportion receiving): $4,407 (59%). Average need-based loan (excluding PLUS or other private loans): $4,159. Among students who received need-based aid, the average percentage of need met: 61%. Among students who received aid based on merit, the average award (and the proportion receiving): $3,081 (5%). The average athletic scholarship (and the proportion receiving): $7,995 (4%). Average amount of debt of borrowers graduating in 2009: $20,550. Proportion who borrowed: 68%.

CAMPUS LIFE AND EXTRACURRICULAR ACTIVITIES

Campus housing available (% using): coed dorms (73%), women's dorms (6%), men's dorms (6%), sorority housing (3%), fraternity housing (3%), apartments for married students (2%), apartment for single students (5%), special housing for disabled students (1%), special housing for international students (1%). Students who live in college-owned, operated, or affiliated housing: 44%. **Student employment:** During the 2009-2010 academic year, 20% of undergraduates worked on campus. Average per-year earnings: $1,665. **Clubs and organizations:** Number of student organizations: 250. Activities include: choral groups, concert band, dance, drama/theater, jazz band, marching band, music ensembles, musical theater, pep band, radio station, student government, student newspaper, television station, yearbook. Number of fraternities: 18; sororities: 9. Proportion of men in fraternities: 9%; of women in sororities: 9%. **Sports program (2009-2010):** Member of NCAA I. *Men's intercollegiate varsity sports:* baseball, basketball, cross country, football, golf, swimming, tennis. *Women's intercollegiate varsity sports:* basketball, cross country, golf, soccer, softball, swimming, tennis, volleyball.

SERVICES AND FACILITIES

Basic services: nonremedial tutoring, women's center, placement service, day care, health service, health insurance. **Remedial assistance:** math, writing. **Counseling services:** personal, academic, psychological. **For learning-disabled students:** School does not offer a structured program with separate admission and additional fees. Services include: remedial math, remedial English, remedial reading, tape recorders, note-taking services, readers, extended time for tests, tutors, priority registration, texts on tape, other testing accommodations. **Library:** Number of titles: 718,241; number of current serial subscriptions: 3,445. **Information technology resources:** Students are not required to lease or own a computer. Number of campus computers available to all students: 1,000. School has a wireless network. Approximate number of users that can be accommodated: 15,000. Proportion of college-owned housing units wired for high-speed internet access: 100%. **Campus safety:** Security services offered: 24-hour foot-and-vehicle patrols, late-night transport/escort service, 24-hour emergency telephones, lighted pathways/ sidewalks, controlled dormitory access (key, security card, etc).

TRANSFER AND INTERNATIONAL STUDENTS

Transfer students: May apply for admission for the following academic terms: Fall, Spring, Summer. Applicants need a minimum number of credits to apply. For fall 2009: Transfer applications received: 2,737. Transfer applicants offered admission: 2,028. Transfer applicants enrolled: 1,332. **International students:** Number of foreign undergraduates: 157 (1% of student body). Number of countries represented: 55. Minimum TOEFL score required: 550 (paper); 213 (computer).

Wheaton College

- **Address:** 501 College Avenue, Wheaton, IL 60187
- **Website:** http://www.wheaton.edu
- **Private; Religious affiliation:** Christian nondenominational
- **Enrollment:** 2,332 full-time; 67 part-time

KEY STATS

✔ **U.S News College Ranking:** 55, National Liberal Arts Colleges
✔ **ACT Score (25th/75th percentile):** 27-31
✔ **Tuition:** 2010-2011: $27,580
  Selectivity: More selective   **Room/board:** $8,050
  Acceptance rate: 71%   **Average debt:** $20,455
  Student/faculty ratio: 11/1   **Proportion who borrowed:** 51%

UNDERGRADUATE STUDENT BODY STATS

2009-2010 enrollment: 2,332 full-time; 67 part-time. Men: 50%; women: 50%. **Ethnic makeup:** African American: 4%; Asian American: 8%; Hispanic: 4%; White: 83%; International: 1%.

ADMISSIONS FACTS AND FIGURES

Phone: (630) 752-5005. **Email:** admissions@wheaton.edu. **Website:** http://www.wheaton.edu. **Application deadlines for fall 2011:** Regular decision: January 10; decision sent by April 1. Early decision: Not offered. Early action: Send application by: November 1; Decision sent by: December 31. Admission can be deferred. **Application fee:** $50. **To apply online, go to:** http://www.wheaton.edu/admissions/UndGrad/applying/forms.php4. **Admissions requirements/recommendations:** High school units required (recommended): English: (4); Mathematics: (4); Science: (4); Foreign language: (3); Social studies: (4); Total units: 15 (19). Tests: The college uses SAT or ACT scores in admissions decisions. Either SAT or ACT required. For admission to the fall 2011 entering class, the school will accept: ACT with writing required. Campus visit: Recommended. Admissions interview: Recommended. Off-campus interview: May be arranged. **Factors that count in admissions decisions:** *Academic:* Secondary school record: Very Important. Class rank: Considered. Letters of recommendation: Very Important. Standardized test scores: Very Important. Essay: Very Important. *Nonacademic:* Interview: Very Important. Extracurricular activities: Important. Talent/ability: Important. Character/personal qualities: Very Important. Alumni/ae relationship: Considered. Geographical residence: Considered. State residency: Considered. Religious affiliation/commitment: Very Important. Minority status: Considered. Volunteer work: Important. Work experience: Important. **Other schools with the greatest overlap in applicants:** Baylor University; Calvin College; Gordon College; Grove City College; Taylor University. **Admissions statistics for the fall 2009 entering class:** Total applicants: 1,950. Total accepted: 1,390. Freshmen enrolled: 620; 77% were from out of state. Accepted through early-decision or early-action plans: 56%. Overall acceptance rate: 71%. Non-early acceptance rate: 74%. **Size of waiting list:** 351 applicants; enrolled from waiting list: 11. **Credentials of fall 2009 freshmen:** 59% ranked in the top 10 percent of their high school class; 83% were in the top 25 percent; 96% were in the top half. (Proportion submitting class standing: 53%.) **Average high school grade point average:** 3.7. **First-year students who submitted SAT scores:** 61%. Scores (25/75 percentile): Critical Reading: 600-710, Math: 600-700, Combined: 1200-1410. **First-year students submitting ACT scores:** 66%. Scores (25/75 percentile): English: 27-34, Math: 25-31, Composite: 27-31.

ACADEMICS

Year founded: 1860. **Academic calendar:** Semester. **Degrees offered:** bachelor's, post-bachelor's certificate, master's, doctorate. **Most popular majors:** 18% social sciences, 11% theology and religious vocations, 8% English language and literature/letters, 8% business, management, marketing, and related support services, 7% education. **Major fields of study:** biological and biomedical sciences; business, management, marketing, and related support services; communication, journalism, and related programs; computer and information sciences and support services; education; engineering; English language and literature/letters; foreign languages, literatures, and linguistics; health professions and related clinical sciences; history; mathematics and statistics; multi/interdisciplinary studies; natural resources and conservation; parks, recreation, leisure, and fitness studies; philosophy and religious studies; physical sciences; psychology; social sciences; theology and religious vocations; visual and performing arts. **Areas of required coursework:** arts/fine arts, humanities, mathematics, English (including composition), philosophy, foreign languages, sciences (biological or physical), history, social science, other. **Pre-professional programs:** pre-law, pre-dentistry, pre-medicine, pre-theology. **Special academic programs:** cross-registration, double major, exchange student program (domestic), independent study, internships, liberal arts/career combination, student-designed major, study abroad, teacher certificate program. **Teacher certification offered in:** elementary, middle/junior high, secondary. **Reserve Officers Training Corps (ROTC):** Army ROTC: Offered on campus; Air Force ROTC: Offered at cooperating institution (Illinois Institute of Technology). **Faculty and instruction (2009-2010):** Total instructional faculty: 202 full-time, 104 part-time (65% men; 35% women; 10% minorities). Full-time faculty with Ph.D. or other terminal degree: 95%. Student/faculty ratio: 11/1. Classes of fewer than 20 students: 57%; of 20 to 49 students: 39%; of 50 or more students: 4%. **Advanced Placement and International Baccalaureate credit:** AP tests may be used for: Credit and/or placement. Scores accepted: 3, 4, 5. International Baccalaureate exams may be used for: Credit and/or placement. **Freshmen returning for sophomore year:** 95%. **Graduation rates:** Four-year: 80%; five-year: 87%; six-year: 88%. **Graduate study:** 32% of students pursue further study within one year; 61% within five years. Fields in which graduates pursue further study: Master of Business Administration (MBA), 3%; law, 7%; medicine, 26%; engineering, 1%; theology (or the seminary), 14%; education, 9%; arts and sciences, 40%.

COSTS AND FINANCIAL AID

Financial aid office: (630) 752-5021. **Expenses (2010-2011):** Tuition and fees 2010-2011: $27,580; room/board: $8,050. Estimated books and supplies: $800 personal expenses: $2,000. **Financial aid:** Priority filing date for institution's financial aid form: February 15. In 2009-2010, 75% of undergraduates applied for financial aid. Of those, 54% were determined to have financial need; 28% had their need fully met. Average financial aid package (proportion receiving): $22,934 (54%). Average amount of gift aid, such as scholarships or grants (proportion receiving): $16,241 (50%). Average amount of self-help aid, such as work study or loans (proportion receiving): $5,202 (51%). Average need-based loan (excluding PLUS or other private loans): $4,803. Among students who received need-based aid, the average percentage of need met: 84%. Among students who received aid based on merit, the average award (and the proportion receiving): $5,397

(16%). The average athletic scholarship (and the proportion receiving): $0 (0%). Average amount of debt of borrowers graduating in 2009: $20,455. Proportion who borrowed: 51%.

CAMPUS LIFE AND EXTRACURRICULAR ACTIVITIES

Campus housing available: coed dorms, women's dorms, men's dorms, apartments for married students, apartment for single students, cooperative housing, other housing options. Students who live in college-owned, operated, or affiliated housing: 90%. **Student employment:** During the 2009-2010 academic year, 48% of undergraduates worked on campus. Average per-year earnings: $1,000. **Clubs and organizations:** Number of student organizations: 85. Activities include: campus ministries, choral groups, concert band, dance, drama/theater, international student organization, jazz band, literary magazine, model UN, music ensembles, musical theater, opera, pep band, radio station, student government, student newspaper, student film society, symphony orchestra, television station, yearbook. Number of fraternities: 0; sororities: 0. Average proportion of students who stay on campus on weekends: 90%. **Sports program (2009-2010):** Member of NCAA III. *Men's intercollegiate varsity sports:* baseball, basketball, cross country, football, golf, soccer, swimming, tennis, track and field (indoor), track and field (outdoor), wrestling. *Women's intercollegiate varsity sports:* basketball, cross country, golf, soccer, softball, swimming, tennis, track and field (indoor), track and field (outdoor), volleyball, water polo.

SERVICES AND FACILITIES

Basic services: health service, health insurance, other. **Remedial assistance:** writing, study skills. **Counseling services:** minority student, career, military, personal, veteran student, academic, psychological, birth control, religious. **For learning-disabled students:** School does not offer a structured program with separate admission and additional fees. Total undergraduates in learning-disabled program or receiving services: 45. **Library:** Number of titles: 473,968; number of current serial subscriptions: 7,864. **Information technology resources:** Students are not required to lease or own a computer. Number of campus computers available to all students: 125. School has a wireless network. Approximate number of users that can be accommodated: 3,700. Proportion of college-owned housing units wired for high-speed internet access: 100%. **Campus safety:** Security services offered: 24-hour foot-and-vehicle patrols, late-night transport/escort service, 24-hour emergency telephones, lighted pathways/sidewalks, student patrols, controlled dormitory access (key, security card, etc).

TRANSFER AND INTERNATIONAL STUDENTS

Transfer students: May apply for admission for the following academic terms: Fall, Spring, Summer. Applicants need a minimum number of credits to apply. For fall 2009: Transfer applications received: 162. Transfer applicants offered admission: 115. Transfer applicants enrolled: 79. **International students:** Number of foreign undergraduates: 35 (1% of student body). Number of countries represented: 16. Minimum TOEFL score required: 550 (paper); 213 (computer).

Indiana

Anderson University

- **Address:** 1100 E. Fifth Street, Anderson, IN 46012
- **Website:** http://www.anderson.edu
- **Private; Religious affiliation:** Church of God
- **Enrollment:** 1,927 full-time; 207 part-time

KEY STATS
✔ **U.S News College Ranking:** 37, Regional Universities (Midwest)
✔ **SAT Score (25th/75th percentile):** 920-1140
✔ **Tuition:** 2010-2011: $24,000

Selectivity: Selective	**Room/board:** $8,350
Acceptance rate: 60%	**Average debt:** $25,401
Student/faculty ratio: 13/1	**Proportion who borrowed:** 84%

UNDERGRADUATE STUDENT BODY STATS
2009-2010 enrollment: 1,927 full-time; 207 part-time. Men: 43%; women: 57%. **Ethnic makeup:** African American: 6%; Asian American: 1%; Hispanic: 1%; White: 89%; International: 2%. **Religious preference:** Roman Catholic: 4%; Protestant: 52%; No preference: 23%; Church of God: 21%.

ADMISSIONS FACTS AND FIGURES
Phone: (765) 641-4080. **Email:** info@anderson.edu. **Website:** http://www.anderson.edu. **Application deadlines for fall 2011:** Regular decision: July 1. Early decision: Not offered. Early action: Not offered. Admission can be deferred. **Application fee:** $25. **To apply online, go to:** https://accessau.anderson.edu/oa/. **Admissions requirements/recommendations:** High school units required (recommended): English: 4 (4); Mathematics: 3 (4); Science: 3 (4); Foreign language: 2 (3); Social studies: 1 (2); History: 1 (2); Academic electives: (5); Total units: 17 (30). Tests: The college uses SAT or ACT scores in admissions decisions. Either SAT or ACT required. For admission to the fall 2011 entering class, the school will accept: ACT with writing required. Campus visit: Recommended. Admissions interview: Recommended. Off-campus interview: May be arranged. **Factors that count in admissions decisions:** *Academic:* Secondary school record: Very Important. Class rank: Important. Letters of recommendation: Very Important. Standardized test scores: Important. Essay: Considered. *Nonacademic:* Interview: Important. Extracurricular activities: Important. Talent/ability: Considered. Character/personal qualities: Important. Alumni/ae relationship: Considered. Geographical residence: Not Considered. State residency: Not Considered. Religious affiliation/commitment: Very Important. Minority status: Considered. Volunteer work: Important. Work experience: Not Considered. **Other schools with the greatest overlap in applicants:** Ball State University; Butler University; Huntington University; Indiana Wesleyan University; Taylor University. **Admissions statistics for the fall 2009 entering class:** Total applicants: 2,115. Total accepted: 1,278. Freshmen enrolled: 552; 28% were from out of state. Overall acceptance rate: 60%. **Credentials of fall 2009 freshmen:** 23% ranked in the top 10 percent of their high school class; 47% were in the top 25 percent; 78% were in the top half. (Proportion submitting class standing: 79%.) **Average high school grade point average:** 3.3. **First-year students who submitted SAT scores:** 77%. Scores (25/75 percentile): Critical Reading: 460-570, Math: 460-570, Combined: 920-1140. **First-year students submitting ACT scores:** 54%. Scores (25/75 percentile): English: 20-26, Math: 20-26, Composite: 21-26.

ACADEMICS
Year founded: 1917. **Academic calendar:** Semester. **Degrees offered:** associate, bachelor's, master's, doctorate. **Most popular majors:** 26% business, management, marketing, and related support services, 14% education, 10% visual and performing arts, 9% health professions and related clinical sciences, 5% psychology. **Major fields of study:** biological and biomedical sciences; business, management, marketing, and related support services; communication, journalism, and related programs; computer and information sciences and support services; education; English language and literature/letters; family and consumer sciences/human sciences; foreign languages, literatures, and linguistics; health professions and related clinical sciences; history; liberal arts and sciences studies, and humanities; mathematics and statistics; multi/interdisciplinary studies; parks, recreation, leisure, and fitness studies; philosophy and religious studies; physical sciences; psychology; public administration and social service professions; security and protective services; social sciences; theology and religious vocations; visual and performing arts. **Areas of required coursework:** arts/fine arts, humanities, mathematics, English (including composition), philosophy, foreign languages, sciences (biological or physical), history, social science. **Pre-professional programs:** pre-law, pre-dentistry, pre-medicine, pre-theology, pre-veterinary science, pre-optometry, pre-pharmacy. **Special academic programs (% participation):** accelerated program (12%), cross-registration (69%), double major (10%), honors program (8%), independent study (46%), internships (26%), student-designed major (0%), study abroad (7%), teacher certificate program (15%). **Teacher certification offered in:** elementary, secondary. **Faculty and instruction (2009-2010):** Total instructional faculty: 146 full-time, 84 part-time (56% men; 44% women; 4% minorities). Full-time faculty with Ph.D. or other terminal degree: 65%. Student/faculty ratio: 13/1. Classes of fewer than 20 students: 61%; of 20 to 49 students: 36%; of 50 or more students: 3%. **Advanced Placement and International Baccalaureate credit:** AP tests may be used for: Placement only. Scores accepted: 3, 4, 5. International Baccalaureate exams may be used for: Placement only. **Freshmen returning for sophomore year:** 76%. **Graduation rates:** Four-year: 44%; five-year: 59%; six-year: 55%. **Graduate study:** 11% of students pursue further study immediately upon graduation; 25% within one year; 0% within five years. Fields in which graduates pursue further study: Master of Business Administration (MBA), 27%; law, 1%; medicine, 17%; theology (or the seminary), 14%; education, 22%; arts and sciences, 19%.

COSTS AND FINANCIAL AID
Financial aid office: (765) 641-4180. **Expenses (2010-2011):** Tuition and fees 2010-2011: $24,000; room/board: $8,350. Estimated books and supplies: $1,050; transportation: $1,000; personal expenses: $1,650. **Financial aid:** Priority filing date for institution's financial aid form: March 1. In 2009-2010, 90% of undergraduates applied for financial aid. Of those, 82% were determined to have financial need; 22% had their need fully met. Average financial aid package (proportion receiving): $20,553 (81%). Average amount of gift aid, such as scholarships or grants (proportion receiving): $13,414 (80%). Average amount of self-help aid, such as work study or loans (proportion receiving): $1,421 (77%). Average need-based loan (excluding PLUS or other private loans): $1,651. Among students who received need-based aid, the average percentage of need met: 93%. Among students who received aid based on merit, the average award (and the proportion receiving): $9,500 (18%). The average athletic scholarship (and the proportion receiving): $0 (0%). Average amount of debt of borrowers graduating in 2009: $25,401. Proportion who borrowed: 84%.

CAMPUS LIFE AND EXTRACURRICULAR ACTIVITIES
Campus housing available (% using): coed dorms (6%), women's dorms (40%), men's dorms (30%), apartment for single students (22%), special housing for disabled students (2%). Students who live in college-owned, operated, or affiliated housing: 76%. **Student employment:** During the 2009-2010 academic year, 49% of undergraduates worked on campus. Average per-year earnings: $3,000. **Clubs and organizations:** Number of student organizations: 41. Activities include: campus ministries, choral groups, concert band, dance, drama/theater, international student organization, jazz band, literary magazine, model UN, music ensembles, musical theater, opera, pep band, radio station, student government, student newspaper, symphony orchestra, yearbook. Number of fraternities: 0; sororities: 0. Average proportion of students who stay on campus on weekends: 65%. **Sports program (2009-2010):** Member of NCAA III. *Men's intercollegiate varsity sports:* baseball, basketball, cross country, football, golf, soccer, tennis, track and field (indoor), track and field (outdoor). *Women's intercollegiate varsity sports:* basketball, cross country, golf, soccer, softball, tennis, track and field (indoor), track and field (outdoor), volleyball.

SERVICES AND FACILITIES

Basic services: nonremedial tutoring, health service. **Remedial assistance:** reading, math, writing, study skills. **Counseling services:** minority student, career, personal, veteran student, academic, older student, psychological, religious, other. **For learning-disabled students:** School does not offer a structured program with separate admission and additional fees. Total undergraduates in learning-disabled program or receiving services: 55. Services include: reading machines, tape recorders, other special classes, note-taking services, oral tests, learning center, readers, extended time for tests, tutors, texts on tape, exams on tape or computer, other. **Library:** Number of titles: 307,239; number of current serial subscriptions: 656. **Information technology resources:** Students are not required to lease or own a computer. Number of campus computers available to all students: 250. School has a wireless network. Approximate number of users that can be accommodated: 500. Proportion of college-owned housing units wired for high-speed internet access: 100%. **Campus safety:** Security services offered: 24-hour foot-and-vehicle patrols, late-night transport/escort service, 24-hour emergency telephones, lighted pathways/sidewalks, student patrols, controlled dormitory access (key, security card, etc).

TRANSFER AND INTERNATIONAL STUDENTS

Transfer students: May apply for admission for the following academic terms: Fall, Spring, Summer. Applicants need a minimum number of credits to apply. For fall 2009: Transfer applications received: 266. Transfer applicants offered admission: 79. Transfer applicants enrolled: 62. **International students:** Number of foreign undergraduates: 41 (2% of student body). Number of countries represented: 35. Minimum TOEFL score required: 530 (paper); 71 (computer). Average TOEFL score: 560 (paper).

Ball State University

- **Address:** 2000 University Avenue, Muncie, IN 47306
- **Website:** http://www.bsu.edu
- **Public**
- **Enrollment:** 16,412 full-time; 1,325 part-time

KEY STATS

- ✔ **U.S News College Ranking:** 179, National Universities
- ✔ **SAT Score (25th/75th percentile):** 940-1150
- ✔ **Tuition:** 2010-2011: $8,214 in state, $21,666 out of state
  - **Selectivity:** Selective
  - **Acceptance rate:** 74%
  - **Student/faculty ratio:** 18/1
  - **Room/board:** $8,438
  - **Average debt:** $22,598
  - **Proportion who borrowed:** 67%

UNDERGRADUATE STUDENT BODY STATS

2009-2010 enrollment: 16,412 full-time; 1,325 part-time. Men: 48%; women: 52%. **Ethnic makeup:** African American: 7%; Asian American: 1%; Hispanic: 2%; White: 88%; International: 2%.

ADMISSIONS FACTS AND FIGURES

Phone: (765) 285-8300. **Email:** askus@bsu.edu. **Website:** http://www.bsu.edu. **Application deadlines for fall 2011:** Regular decision: August 15. Early decision: Not offered. Early action: Not offered. Admission can be deferred. **Application fee:** $25. **To apply online, go to:** http://www.bsu.edu/admissions. **Admissions requirements/recommendations:** High school units required (recommended): English: 4; Mathematics: 3; Science: 3; Foreign language: (3); Social studies: 3; Total units: 15 (3). Tests: The college uses SAT or ACT scores in admissions decisions. Neither SAT nor ACT required. For admission to the fall 2011 entering class, the school will accept: ACT with writing recommended. Campus visit: Recommended. Admissions interview: Neither required nor recommended. Off-campus interview: Not available. **Factors that count in admissions decisions:** *Academic:* Secondary school record: Very Important. Class rank: Considered. Letters of recommendation: Considered. Standardized test scores: Very Important. Essay: Considered. *Nonacademic:* Interview: Not Considered. Extracurricular activities: Considered. Talent/ability: Considered. Character/personal qualities: Considered. Alumni/ae relationship: Not Considered. Geographical residence: Not Considered. State residency: Not Considered. Religious affiliation/commitment: Not Considered. Minority status: Not Considered. Volunteer work: Considered. Work experience: Considered. **Other schools with the greatest overlap in applicants:** Indiana University–Bloomington; Purdue University–West Lafayette. **Admissions statistics for the fall 2009 entering class:** Total applicants: 13,022. Total accepted: 9,592. Freshmen

enrolled: 4,178; 10% were from out of state. Overall acceptance rate: 74%. **Credentials of fall 2009 freshmen:** 16% ranked in the top 10 percent of their high school class; 45% were in the top 25 percent; 87% were in the top half. (Proportion submitting class standing: 78%.) **Average high school grade point average:** 3.3. **First-year students who submitted SAT scores:** 78%. Scores (25/75 percentile): Critical Reading: 470-570, Math: 470-580, Combined: 940-1150. **First-year students submitting ACT scores:** 22%. Scores (25/75 percentile): English: 19-24, Math: 19-25, Composite: 19-24.

ACADEMICS

Year founded: 1918. **Academic calendar:** Semester. **Degrees offered:** associate, bachelor's, post-bachelor's certificate, master's, post-master's certificate, doctorate. **Most popular majors:** 16% business, management, marketing, and related support services, 14% education, 12% liberal arts and sciences studies, and humanities, 7% health professions and related clinical sciences, 6% visual and performing arts. **Major fields of study:** architecture and related services; area, ethnic, cultural, and gender studies; biological and biomedical sciences; business, management, marketing, and related support services; communication, journalism, and related programs; computer and information sciences and support services; education; engineering; engineering technologies/technicians; English language and literature/letters; family and consumer sciences/human sciences; foreign languages, literatures, and linguistics; health professions and related clinical sciences; history; legal professions and studies; liberal arts and sciences studies, and humanities; library science; mathematics and statistics; natural resources and conservation; parks, recreation, leisure, and fitness studies; philosophy and religious studies; physical sciences; psychology; public administration and social service professions; security and protective services; social sciences; visual and performing arts. **Areas of required coursework:** arts/fine arts, humanities, mathematics, English (including composition), sciences (biological or physical), history, social science, other. **Pre-professional programs:** pre-law, pre-dentistry, pre-medicine, pre-veterinary science, pre-optometry, pre-pharmacy, other. **Special academic programs:** accelerated program, distance learning, double major, dual enrollment, English as a Second Language (ESL), exchange student program (domestic), external degree program, honors program, independent study, internships, student-designed major, study abroad, teacher certificate program. **Teacher certification offered in:** early childhood, special education, elementary, vo-tech, middle/junior high, secondary. **Cooperative education programs:** computer science. **Reserve Officers Training Corps (ROTC):** Army ROTC: Offered on campus. **Faculty and instruction (2009-2010):** Total instructional faculty: 940 full-time, 240 part-time (54% men; 46% women; 12% minorities). Full-time faculty with Ph.D. or other terminal degree: 74%. Student/faculty ratio: 18/1. Classes of fewer than 20 students: 32%; of 20 to 49 students: 58%; of 50 or more students: 10%. **Advanced Placement and International Baccalaureate credit:** AP tests may be used for: Credit and/or placement. Scores accepted: 3, 4, 5. International Baccalaureate exams may be used for: Credit and/or placement. **Freshmen returning for sophomore year:** 77%. **Graduation rates:** Four-year: 35%; five-year: 55%; six-year: 58%. **Graduate study:** 16% of students pursue further study within one year. Fields in which graduates pursue further study: Master of Business Administration (MBA), 10%; law, 5%; medicine, 8%; dentistry, 1%; engineering, 1%; education, 21%; arts and sciences, 54%; veterinary medicine, 1%.

COSTS AND FINANCIAL AID

Financial aid office: (765) 285-5600. **Expenses (2010-2011):** Tuition and fees 2010-2011: $8,214 in state, $21,666 out of state; room/board: $8,438. Estimated books and supplies: $1,000; transportation: $1,038; personal expenses: $1,600. **Financial aid:** Priority filing date for institution's financial aid form: March 10. In 2009-2010, 82% of undergraduates applied for financial aid. Of those, 63% were determined to have financial need; 25% had their need fully met. Average financial aid package (proportion receiving): $9,450 (63%). Average amount of gift aid, such as scholarships or grants (proportion receiving): $6,145 (38%). Average amount of self-help aid, such as work study or loans (proportion receiving): $4,475 (52%). Average need-based loan (excluding PLUS or other private loans): $4,170. Among students who received need-based aid, the average percentage of need met: 60%. Among students who received aid based on merit, the average award (and the proportion receiving): $5,062 (6%). The average athletic scholarship (and the proportion receiving): $16,147 (2%). Average amount of debt of borrowers graduating in 2009: $22,598. Proportion who borrowed: 67%.

CAMPUS LIFE AND EXTRACURRICULAR ACTIVITIES

Campus housing available: coed dorms, women's dorms, men's dorms, sorority housing, fraternity housing, apartments for married students, apartment for single students, special housing for disabled students, special housing for international students, other housing options. Students who live in college-owned, operated, or affiliated housing: 44%. **Student employment:** During the 2009-2010 academic year, 27% of undergraduates worked on campus. Average per-year earnings: $1,586. **Clubs and organizations:** Number of student organizations: 355. Activities include: campus ministries, choral groups, concert band, dance, drama/theater, international student organization, jazz band, literary magazine, marching band, music ensembles, musical theater, opera, pep band, radio station, student government, student newspaper, student film society, symphony orchestra, television station. Number of fraternities: 15; sororities: 12. Proportion of men in fraternities: 9%; of women in sororities: 8%. **Sports program (2009-2010):** Member of NCAA I. *Men's intercollegiate varsity sports:* baseball, basketball, football, golf, swimming, tennis, volleyball. *Women's intercollegiate varsity sports:* basketball, cross country, field hockey, golf, gymnastics, soccer, softball, swimming, tennis, track and field (indoor), track and field (outdoor), volleyball.

SERVICES AND FACILITIES

Basic services: nonremedial tutoring, women's center, placement service, day care, health service, health insurance. **Remedial assistance:** study skills. **Counseling services:** minority student, career, military, personal, veteran student, academic, older student, psychological, birth control, religious, other. **For learning-disabled students:** School does not offer a structured program with separate admission and additional fees. Total undergraduates in learning-disabled program or receiving services: 300. Services include: reading machines, tape recorders, note-taking services, oral tests, learning center, readers, extended time for tests, tutors, priority registration, texts on tape. **Library:** Number of titles: 1,078,583; number of current serial subscriptions: 26,651. **Information technology resources:** Students are not required to lease or own a computer. Number of campus computers available to all students: 1,023. School has a wireless network. Approximate number of users that can be accommodated: 45,000. Proportion of college-owned housing units wired for high-speed internet access: 100%. **Campus safety:** Security services offered: 24-hour foot-and-vehicle patrols, late-night transport/escort service, 24-hour emergency telephones, lighted pathways/sidewalks, controlled dormitory access (key, security card, etc).

TRANSFER AND INTERNATIONAL STUDENTS

Transfer students: May apply for admission for the following academic terms: Fall, Spring, Summer. Applicants need a minimum number of credits to apply. For fall 2009: Transfer applications received: 1,581. Transfer applicants offered admission: 1,008. Transfer applicants enrolled: 672. **International students:** Number of foreign undergraduates: 265 (2% of student body). Number of countries represented: 74. Minimum TOEFL score required: 550 (paper); 213 (computer). Average TOEFL score: 575 (paper).

Bethel College

- **Address:** 1001 Bethel Circle, Mishawaka, IN 46545
- **Website:** http://www.bethelcollege.edu
- **Private; Religious affiliation:** Missionary Church
- **Enrollment:** 1,482 full-time; 446 part-time

KEY STATS

✔ **U.S News College Ranking:** 16, Regional Colleges (Midwest)
✔ **SAT Score (25th/75th percentile):** 910-1160
✔ **Tuition:** 2010-2011: $21,990

Selectivity: Selective	**Room/board:** $6,670
Acceptance rate: 78%	**Average debt:** $20,800
Student/faculty ratio: 14/1	**Proportion who borrowed:** 75%

UNDERGRADUATE STUDENT BODY STATS

2009-2010 enrollment: 1,482 full-time; 446 part-time. Men: 33%; women: 67%. **Ethnic makeup:** African American: 13%; American-Indian: 1%; Asian American: 1%; Hispanic: 3%; White: 80%; International: 2%. **Religious preference:** Roman Catholic: 7%; Protestant: 64%; Unknown: 13%; Missionary Church: 16%.

ADMISSIONS FACTS AND FIGURES

Phone: (800) 422-4101. **Email:** admissions@bethelcollege.edu. **Website:** http://www.bethelcollege.edu. **Application deadlines for fall 2011:** Regular decision: Rolling. Early decision: Not offered. Early action: Not offered.

Admission can be deferred. **Application fee:** $25. **To apply online, go to:** http://www.bethelcollege.edu/admission/apply.php. **Admissions requirements/recommendations:** High school units required (recommended): English: 4 (4); Mathematics: 3 (3); Science: 3 (3); Foreign language: 2 (2); Social studies: 1 (2); History: 2 (2); Academic electives: 2 (3); Total units: 17 (19). Tests: The college uses SAT or ACT scores in admissions decisions. Either SAT or ACT required. For admission to the fall 2011 entering class, the school will accept: ACT with or without writing accepted. Campus visit: Recommended. Admissions interview: Recommended. Off-campus interview: May be arranged. **Factors that count in admissions decisions:** *Academic:* Secondary school record: Very Important. Class rank: Important. Letters of recommendation: Important. Standardized test scores: Important. Essay: Important. *Nonacademic:* Interview: Considered. Extracurricular activities: Important. Talent/ability: Considered. Character/personal qualities: Important. Alumni/ae relationship: Considered. Geographical residence: Not Considered. State residency: Not Considered. Religious affiliation/commitment: Not Considered. Minority status: Considered. Volunteer work: Considered. Work experience: Considered. **Other schools with the greatest overlap in applicants:** Ball State University; Grace College and Seminary; Huntington University; Indiana Wesleyan University. **Admissions statistics for the fall 2009 entering class:** Total applicants: 847. Total accepted: 657. Freshmen enrolled: 309; 72% were from out of state. Overall acceptance rate: 78%. **Size of waiting list:** 0 applicants; enrolled from waiting list: 0. **Credentials of fall 2009 freshmen:** 24% ranked in the top 10 percent of their high school class; 51% were in the top 25 percent; 82% were in the top half. (Proportion submitting class standing: 72%.) **Average high school grade point average:** 3.4. **First-year students who submitted SAT scores:** 64%. Scores (25/75 percentile): Critical Reading: 450-580, Math: 460-580, Combined: 910-1160. **First-year students submitting ACT scores:** 53%. Scores (25/75 percentile): English: 20-26, Math: 19-26, Composite: 19-26.

ACADEMICS

Year founded: 1947. **Academic calendar:** Semester. **Degrees offered:** associate, bachelor's, master's. **Most popular majors:** 39% business, management, marketing, and related support services, 13% liberal arts and sciences studies, and humanities, 11% health professions and related clinical sciences, 8% theology and religious vocations, 6% education. **Major fields of study:** agriculture, agriculture operations, and related sciences; biological and biomedical sciences; business, management, marketing, and related support services; communication, journalism, and related programs; computer and information sciences and support services; education; engineering; English language and literature/letters; foreign languages, literatures, and linguistics; health professions and related clinical sciences; history; legal professions and studies; liberal arts and sciences studies, and humanities; mathematics and statistics; multi/interdisciplinary studies; parks, recreation, leisure, and fitness studies; philosophy and religious studies; physical sciences; psychology; security and protective services; social sciences; theology and religious vocations; visual and performing arts. **Areas of required coursework:** arts/fine arts, humanities, mathematics, English (including composition), philosophy, foreign languages, sciences (biological or physical), history, social science, other. **Pre-professional programs:** pre-law, pre-dentistry, pre-medicine, pre-theology, pre-veterinary science, pre-optometry, other. **Special academic programs:** accelerated program, cross-registration, double major, dual enrollment, English as a Second Language (ESL), exchange student program (domestic), independent study, internships, student-designed major, study abroad, teacher certificate program, other. **Teacher certification offered in:** early childhood, elementary, middle/junior high, secondary. **Reserve Officers Training Corps (ROTC):** Army ROTC: Offered at cooperating institution (University of Notre Dame); Air Force ROTC: Offered at cooperating institution (University of Notre Dame). **Faculty and instruction (2009-2010):** Total instructional faculty: 91 full-time, 114 part-time (47% men; 53% women; 6% minorities). Full-time faculty with Ph.D. or other terminal degree: 62%. Student/faculty ratio: 14/1. Classes of fewer than 20 students: 69%; of 20 to 49 students: 29%; of 50 or more students: 2%. **Advanced Placement and International Baccalaureate credit:** AP tests may be used for: Placement only. Scores accepted: 3, 4, 5. International Baccalaureate exams may be used for: Credit only. **Freshmen returning for sophomore year:** 79%. **Graduation rates:** Four-year: 44%; five-year: 59%; six-year: 61%.

COSTS AND FINANCIAL AID

Financial aid office: (574) 257-3316. **Expenses (2010-2011):** Tuition and fees 2010-2011: $21,990; room/board: $6,670. Estimated books and supplies: $1,600; transportation: $1,200; personal expenses: $1,400. **Financial aid:** Priority filing date for institution's financial aid form: March 1. In 2009-

2010, 91% of undergraduates applied for financial aid. Of those, 80% were determined to have financial need; 16% had their need fully met. Average financial aid package (proportion receiving): $18,230 (80%). Average amount of gift aid, such as scholarships or grants (proportion receiving): $8,140 (54%). Average amount of self-help aid, such as work study or loans (proportion receiving): $6,580 (78%). Average need-based loan (excluding PLUS or other private loans): $5,330. Among students who received need-based aid, the average percentage of need met: 69%. Among students who received aid based on merit, the average award (and the proportion receiving): $6,240 (12%). The average athletic scholarship (and the proportion receiving): $6,220 (18%). Average amount of debt of borrowers graduating in 2009: $20,800. Proportion who borrowed: 75%.

CAMPUS LIFE AND EXTRACURRICULAR ACTIVITIES

Campus housing available (% using): women's dorms (41%), men's dorms (21%), apartment for single students (20%), other housing options (18%). Students who live in college-owned, operated, or affiliated housing: 47%. **Student employment:** During the 2009-2010 academic year, 30% of undergraduates worked on campus. Average per-year earnings: $2,000. **Clubs and organizations:** Number of student organizations: 13. Activities include: campus ministries, choral groups, concert band, drama/theater, international student organization, jazz band, literary magazine, music ensembles, musical theater, opera, pep band, radio station, student government, student newspaper, student film society, symphony orchestra, yearbook. Number of fraternities: 0; sororities: 0. Average proportion of students who stay on campus on weekends: 40%. **Sports program (2009-2010):** Member of NAIA. **Men's intercollegiate varsity sports:** baseball, basketball, cross country, golf, soccer, tennis, track and field (indoor), track and field (outdoor). **Women's intercollegiate varsity sports:** basketball, cross country, golf, soccer, softball, tennis, track and field (indoor), track and field (outdoor), volleyball.

SERVICES AND FACILITIES

Basic services: nonremedial tutoring, placement service, health service, health insurance. **Remedial assistance:** reading, math, writing, study skills, other. **Counseling services:** minority student, career, personal, academic, older student, psychological, religious. **For learning-disabled students:** School does not offer a structured program with separate admission and additional fees. Total undergraduates in learning-disabled program or receiving services: 54. Services include: remedial math, remedial English, remedial reading, tape recorders, note-taking services, oral tests, learning center, readers, extended time for tests, tutors, priority seating, proofreading services, substitution of courses, texts on tape, typist/scribe, exams on tape or computer, other testing accommodations, other. **Library:** Number of titles: 144,670; number of current serial subscriptions: 1,380. **Information technology resources:** Students are not required to lease or own a computer. Number of campus computers available to all students: 188. School has a wireless network. Approximate number of users that can be accommodated: 2,000. Proportion of college-owned housing units wired for high-speed internet access: 100%. **Campus safety:** Security services offered: 24-hour foot-and-vehicle patrols, late-night transport/escort service, 24-hour emergency telephones, lighted pathways/sidewalks, controlled dormitory access (key, security card, etc).

TRANSFER AND INTERNATIONAL STUDENTS

Transfer students: May apply for admission for the following academic terms: Fall, Spring, Summer. Applicants need a minimum number of credits to apply. For fall 2009: Transfer applications received: 349. Transfer applicants offered admission: 288. Transfer applicants enrolled: 242. **International students:** Number of foreign undergraduates: 44 (2% of student body). Number of countries represented: 10. Minimum TOEFL score required: 540 (paper); 207 (computer).

Butler University

- **Address:** 4600 Sunset Avenue, Indianapolis, IN 46208
- **Website:** http://www.butler.edu
- **Private**
- **Enrollment:** 3,670 full-time; 56 part-time

KEY STATS

✔ **U.S News College Ranking:** 2, Regional Universities (Midwest)
✔ **ACT Score (25th/75th percentile):** 25-30
✔ **Tuition:** 2010-2011: $30,558

Selectivity: More selective	**Room/board:** $10,130
Acceptance rate: 79%	**Average debt:** $30,470
Student/faculty ratio: 11/1	**Proportion who borrowed:** 64%

UNDERGRADUATE STUDENT BODY STATS

2009-2010 enrollment: 3,670 full-time; 56 part-time. Men: 40%; women: 60%. **Ethnic makeup:** African American: 4%; Asian American: 2%; Hispanic: 2%; White: 90%; International: 2%. **Religious preference:** Roman Catholic: 33%; Protestant: 48%; Jewish: 1%; No preference: 15%; Other: 3%.

ADMISSIONS FACTS AND FIGURES

Phone: (888) 940-8100. **Email:** admission@butler.edu. **Website:** http://www.butler.edu. **Application deadlines for fall 2011:** Regular decision: August 1. Early decision: Not offered. Early action: Send application by: November 15; Decision sent by: December 17. Admission can be deferred. **Application fee:** $35. **To apply online, go to:** https://www.butler.edu/boa/. **Admissions requirements/recommendations:** High school units required (recommended): English: 4; Mathematics: 3; Science: 3; Foreign language: 2; Social studies: 2; History: 2; Total units: 16. Tests: The college uses SAT or ACT scores in admissions decisions. Either SAT or ACT required. For admission to the fall 2011 entering class, the school will accept: ACT with writing required. Campus visit: Recommended. Admissions interview: Neither required nor recommended. Off-campus interview: Not available. **Factors that count in admissions decisions: Academic:** Secondary school record: Very Important. Class rank: Important. Letters of recommendation: Considered. Standardized test scores: Very Important. Essay: Very Important. **Nonacademic:** Interview: Not Considered. Extracurricular activities: Important. Talent/ability: Important. Character/personal qualities: Considered. Alumni/ae relationship: Considered. Geographical residence: Not Considered. State residency: Not Considered. Religious affiliation/commitment: Not Considered. Minority status: Not Considered. Volunteer work: Considered. Work experience: Considered. **Other schools with the greatest overlap in applicants:** Ball State University; DePauw University; Indiana University–Bloomington; Miami University–Oxford; Purdue University–West Lafayette. **Admissions statistics for the fall 2009 entering class:** Total applicants: 6,246. Total accepted: 4,928. Freshmen enrolled: 946; 46% were from out of state. Accepted through early-decision or early-action plans: 79%. Overall acceptance rate: 79%. Non-early acceptance rate: 77%. **Size of waiting list:** 54 applicants; enrolled from waiting list: 10. **Credentials of fall 2009 freshmen:** 50% ranked in the top 10 percent of their high school class; 79% were in the top 25 percent; 98% were in the top half. (Proportion submitting class standing: 70%.) **Average high school grade point average:** 3.8. **First-year students who submitted SAT scores:** 42%. Scores (25/75 percentile): Critical Reading: 520-630, Math: 540-650, Combined: 1060-1280. **First-year students submitting ACT scores:** 58%. Scores (25/75 percentile): English: 25-31, Math: 24-30, Composite: 25-30.

ACADEMICS

Year founded: 1855. **Academic calendar:** Semester. **Degrees offered:** associate, bachelor's, master's. **Most popular majors:** 24% health professions and related clinical sciences, 17% business, management, marketing, and related support services, 9% education, 8% communication, journalism, and related programs, 7% visual and performing arts. **Major fields of study:** biological and biomedical sciences; business, management, marketing, and related support services; communication, journalism, and related programs; communications technologies/technicians and support services; computer and information sciences and support services; education; English language and literature/letters; foreign languages, literatures, and linguistics; health professions and related clinical sciences; history; liberal arts and sciences studies, and humanities; mathematics and statistics; multi/interdisciplinary studies; philosophy and religious studies; physical sciences; psychology; security and protective services; social sciences; visual and performing arts. **Areas of required coursework:** arts/fine arts, humanities, mathematics, English (including composition), sciences (biological or physical), social science, other. **Pre-professional programs:** pre-law, pre-dentistry, pre-medicine, pre-theology, pre-veterinary science, pre-pharmacy, other. **Special academic programs (% participation):** accelerated program (7%), cross-registration (4%), double major (14%), dual enrollment (.3%), honors program (15%), independent study (22%), internships (60%), liberal arts/career combination (2%), student-designed major (.5%), study abroad (21%), teacher certificate program (18.5%). **Teacher certification offered in:** early childhood, special education, elementary, middle/junior high, secondary. **Cooperative education programs:** business, other. **Reserve Officers Training Corps (ROTC):** Army ROTC: Offered on campus; Air Force ROTC: Offered at cooperating institution (Indiana University–Bloomington). **Faculty and instruction (2009-2010):** Total instructional faculty: 327 full-time, 139 part-time (56% men; 44% women; 12% minorities). Full-time faculty with Ph.D. or other terminal degree: 83%. Student/faculty ratio: 11/1. Classes of fewer than 20 students: 58%; of 20 to 49 students: 39%; of 50 or more students: 4%. **Advanced Placement and International Baccalaureate credit:** AP tests may be used for: Credit only. Scores accepted: 3, 4, 5. International Baccalaureate exams may be used for: Credit only. **Freshmen returning for sophomore year:** 88%. **Graduation rates:** Four-year: 57%; five-year: 63%; six-year: 73%. **Graduate study:** 33% of students pursue further study immediately upon graduation; 38% within one year; 40% within five years. Fields in which graduates pursue further study: Master of Business Administration (MBA), 7%; law, 8%; medicine, 10%; dentistry, 1%; education, 3%; arts and sciences, 71%.

COSTS AND FINANCIAL AID

Financial aid office: (317) 940-8200. **Expenses (2010-2011):** Tuition and fees 2010-2011: $30,558; room/board: $10,130. Estimated books and supplies: $1,000; transportation: $600; personal expenses: $1,550. **Financial aid:** Priority filing date for institution's financial aid form: March 1. In 2009-2010, 92% of undergraduates applied for financial aid. Of those, 66% were determined to have financial need; 19% had their need fully met. Average financial aid package (proportion receiving): $20,922 (66%). Average amount of gift aid, such as scholarships or grants (proportion receiving): $15,800 (63%). Average amount of self-help aid, such as work study or loans (proportion receiving): $6,092 (53%). Average need-based loan (excluding PLUS or other private loans): $5,387. Among students who received aid based on merit, the average award (and the proportion receiving): $11,674 (22%). The average athletic scholarship (and the proportion receiving): $20,353 (2%). Average amount of debt of borrowers graduating in 2009: $30,470. Proportion who borrowed: 64%.

CAMPUS LIFE AND EXTRACURRICULAR ACTIVITIES

Campus housing available (% using): coed dorms (37%), women's dorms (15%), sorority housing (17%), fraternity housing (10%), apartment for single students (21%). Students who live in college-owned, operated, or affiliated housing: 66%. **Student employment:** During the 2009-2010 academic year, 25% of undergraduates worked on campus. Average per-year earnings: $1,100. **Clubs and organizations:** Number of student organizations: 140. Activities include: campus ministries, choral groups, concert band, dance, drama/theater, international student organization, jazz band, literary magazine, marching band, model UN, music ensembles, musical theater, opera, pep band, student government, student newspaper, symphony orchestra, television station, yearbook. Number of fraternities: 8; sororities: 8. Proportion of men in fraternities: 27%; of women in sororities: 27%. Average proportion of students who stay on campus on weekends: 80%. **Sports program (2009-2010):** Member of NCAA I. *Men's intercollegiate varsity sports:* baseball, basketball, cross country, football, golf, soccer, tennis, track and field (indoor), track and field (outdoor). *Women's intercollegiate varsity sports:* basketball, cross country, golf, soccer, softball, swimming, tennis, track and field (indoor), track and field (outdoor), volleyball.

SERVICES AND FACILITIES

Basic services: placement service, health service. **Counseling services:** career, personal, academic, psychological. **For learning-disabled students:** School does not offer a structured program with separate admission and additional fees. Total undergraduates in learning-disabled program or receiving services: 45. Services include: tape recorders, learning center, extended time for tests, texts on tape, other testing accommodations. **Library:** Number of titles: 339,944; number of current serial subscriptions: 33,627. **Information technology resources:** Students are not required to lease or own a computer. Number of campus computers available to all students: 430. School has a wireless network. Approximate number of users that can be accommodated: 10,000. Proportion of college-owned housing units wired for high-speed internet access: 100%. **Campus safety:** Security services offered: 24-hour

foot-and-vehicle patrols, late-night transport/escort service, 24-hour emergency telephones, lighted pathways/sidewalks, controlled dormitory access (key, security card, etc).

TRANSFER AND INTERNATIONAL STUDENTS

Transfer students: May apply for admission for the following academic terms: Fall, Spring, Summer. Applicants need a minimum number of credits to apply. For fall 2009: Transfer applications received: 1,368. Transfer applicants offered admission: 250. Transfer applicants enrolled: 98. **International students:** Number of foreign undergraduates: 84 (2% of student body). Number of countries represented: 47. Minimum TOEFL score required: 550 (paper); 213 (computer). Average TOEFL score: 613 (paper).

Calumet College of St. Joseph

- **Address:** 2400 New York Avenue, Whiting, IN 46394
- **Website:** http://www.ccsj.edu
- **Private; Religious affiliation:** Roman Catholic
- **Enrollment:** 561 full-time; 554 part-time

KEY STATS
✔ **U.S News College Ranking:** second tier, Regional Universities (Midwest)
✔ **SAT Score:** 838
✔ **Tuition:** 2010-2011: $14,200

Selectivity: Less selective	**Room/board:** N/A
Acceptance rate: 53%	**Average debt:** $22,524
Student/faculty ratio: 12/1	**Proportion who borrowed:** 80%

UNDERGRADUATE STUDENT BODY STATS

2009-2010 enrollment: 561 full-time; 554 part-time. Men: 52%; women: 48%. **Ethnic makeup:** African American: 28%; Asian American: 1%; Hispanic: 25%; White: 45%. **Religious preference:** Roman Catholic: 44%; Other: 56%.

ADMISSIONS FACTS AND FIGURES

Phone: (219) 473-4215. **Email:** admissions@ccsj.edu. **Website:** http://www. ccsj.edu. **Application deadlines for fall 2011:** Regular decision: Rolling. Early decision: Not offered. Early action: Not offered. Admission can be deferred. **To apply online, go to:** http://sos.ccsj.edu/form_index.cfm. **Admissions requirements/recommendations:** High school units required (recommended): English: 4 (4); Mathematics: 3 (3); Science: 3 (3); Foreign language: 2 (2); Social studies: 3 (3); History: 1 (1). Tests: The college uses SAT or ACT scores in admissions decisions. Neither SAT nor ACT required. For admission to the fall 2011 entering class, the school will accept: ACT with or without writing accepted. Campus visit: Recommended. Admissions interview: Recommended. Off-campus interview: May be arranged. **Factors that count in admissions decisions:** *Academic:* Secondary school record: Important. Class rank: Important. Letters of recommendation: Considered. Standardized test scores: Important. Essay: Important. *Nonacademic:* Interview: Considered. Extracurricular activities: Considered. Talent/ability: Considered. Character/personal qualities: Considered. Alumni/ae relationship: Considered. Geographical residence: Not Considered. State residency: Not Considered. Religious affiliation/commitment: Considered. Minority status: Not Considered. Volunteer work: Important. Work experience: Considered. **Other schools with the greatest overlap in applicants:** Indiana University Northwest; Purdue University–Calumet. **Admissions statistics for the fall 2009 entering class:** Total applicants: 456. Total accepted: 240. Freshmen enrolled: 156; 24% were from out of state. Overall acceptance rate: 53%. **Credentials of fall 2009 freshmen:** 10% ranked in the top 10 percent of their high school class; 25% were in the top 25 percent; 50% were in the top half. (Proportion submitting class standing: 92%.) **Average high school grade point average:** 2.4. **First-year students who submitted SAT scores:** 47%. **First-year students submitting ACT scores:** 35%. Scores (25/75 percentile): English: N/A, Math: N/A, Composite: N/A.

ACADEMICS

Year founded: 1951. **Academic calendar:** Semester. **Degrees offered:** certificate, diploma, associate, bachelor's, post-bachelor's certificate, master's. **Most popular majors:** 42% criminal justice/police science, 15% business administration, management, and operations, 11% elementary education and teaching, 8% criminal justice/law enforcement administration, 6% business administration and management. **Major fields of study:** business, management, marketing, and related support services; communication, journalism, and related programs; computer and information sciences and support services; education; English language and literature/letters; health professions and related clinical sciences; legal professions and studies; liberal arts and sciences studies, and humanities; philosophy and religious studies; psychology; public administration and social service professions; security and protective services; social sciences; visual and performing arts. **Areas of required coursework:** arts/fine arts, humanities, computer literacy, mathematics, English (including composition), sciences (biological or physical), history. **Special academic programs (% participation):** accelerated program (30%), cooperative (work-study plan) program (5%), cross-registration (5%), distance learning (5%), double major (2%), independent study (5%), internships (5%), teacher certificate program (10%), weekend college (10%). **Teacher certification offered in:** elementary, middle/junior high, secondary. **Cooperative education programs:** art, business, computer science, education, humanities, natural science, social/behavioral science, technologies. **Faculty and instruction (2009-2010):** Total instructional faculty: 34 full-time, 92 part-time (60% men; 40% women; 16% minorities). Full-time faculty with Ph.D. or other terminal degree: 68%. Student/faculty ratio: 12/1. Classes of fewer than 20 students: 71%; of 20 to 49 students: 28%; of 50 or more students: 0%. **Freshmen returning for sophomore year:** 58%. **Graduation rates:** Four-year: 23%; five-year: 31%; six-year: 17%. **Graduate study:** 3% of students pursue further study immediately upon graduation; 5% within one year; 10% within five years. Fields in which graduates pursue further study: Master of Business Administration (MBA), 20%; law, 3%; education, 10%; arts and sciences, 4%.

COSTS AND FINANCIAL AID

Financial aid office: (219) 473-4213. **Expenses (2010-2011):** Tuition and fees 2010-2011: $14,200. Estimated books and supplies: $750; transportation: $1,210; personal expenses: $1,140. **Financial aid:** Priority filing date for institution's financial aid form: March 1. In 2009-2010, 94% of undergraduates applied for financial aid. Of those, 79% were determined to have financial need; 4% had their need fully met. Average financial aid package (proportion receiving): $11,510 (77%). Average amount of gift aid, such as scholarships or grants (proportion receiving): $7,300 (61%). Average amount of self-help aid, such as work study or loans (proportion receiving): $3,507 (61%). Average need-based loan (excluding PLUS or other private loans): $3,591. Among students who received need-based aid, the average percentage of need met: 72%. Among students who received aid based on merit, the average award (and the proportion receiving): $2,400 (0%). The average athletic scholarship (and the proportion receiving): $5,341 (39%). Average amount of debt of borrowers graduating in 2009: $22,524. Proportion who borrowed: 80%.

CAMPUS LIFE AND EXTRACURRICULAR ACTIVITIES

Student employment: During the 2009-2010 academic year, 0% of undergraduates worked on campus. Average per-year earnings: $4,000. **Clubs and organizations:** Number of student organizations: 13. Activities include: dance, drama/theater, literary magazine, musical theater, pep band, student government, student newspaper. Number of fraternities: 0; sororities: 1. **Sports program (2009-2010):** Member of NAIA. *Men's intercollegiate varsity sports:* baseball, basketball, cross country, golf, soccer, tennis, track and field (indoor), track and field (outdoor), wrestling. *Women's intercollegiate varsity sports:* basketball, bowling, cross country, golf, soccer, softball, tennis, track and field (indoor), track and field (outdoor), volleyball.

SERVICES AND FACILITIES

Basic services: nonremedial tutoring, placement service. **Remedial assistance:** reading, math, writing, study skills. **Counseling services:** career, personal, academic, religious. **For learning-disabled students:** School does not offer a structured program with separate admission and additional fees. Total undergraduates in learning-disabled program or receiving services: 5. Services include: remedial math, remedial English, tape recorders, untimed tests, note-taking services, oral tests, learning center, readers, extended time for tests, tutors, texts on tape. **Library:** Number of titles: 112,200; number of current serial subscriptions: 79. **Information technology resources:** Students are not required to lease or own a computer. Number of campus computers available to all students: 161. School has a wireless network. Approximate number of users that can be accommodated: 80. Proportion of college-owned housing units wired for high-speed internet access: 0%. **Campus safety:** Security services offered: 24-hour emergency telephones, lighted pathways/sidewalks.

TRANSFER AND INTERNATIONAL STUDENTS

Transfer students: May apply for admission for the following academic terms: Fall, Winter, Spring, Summer. Applicants need a minimum number of credits to apply. For fall 2009: Transfer applications received: 299. Transfer applicants offered admission: 160. Transfer applicants enrolled: 128. **International students:** Number of foreign undergraduates: 2. Minimum TOEFL score required: 515 (paper); 190 (computer).

DePauw University

- **Address:** 313 S. Locust Street, Greencastle, IN 46135
- **Website:** http://www.depauw.edu
- **Private; Religious affiliation:** United Methodist
- **Enrollment:** 2,368 full-time; 28 part-time

KEY STATS
✔ **U.S News College Ranking:** 51, National Liberal Arts Colleges
✔ **SAT Score (25th/75th percentile):** 1080-1320
✔ **Tuition:** 2010-2011: $34,905

Selectivity: More selective	**Room/board:** $9,180
Acceptance rate: 66%	**Average debt:** $24,210
Student/faculty ratio: 10/1	**Proportion who borrowed:** 48%

UNDERGRADUATE STUDENT BODY STATS

2009-2010 enrollment: 2,368 full-time; 28 part-time. Men: 43%; women: 57%. **Ethnic makeup:** African American: 6%; Asian American: 3%; Hispanic: 4%; White: 79%; International: 7%. **Religious preference:** Roman Catholic: 20%; Protestant: 28%; Jewish: 1%; No preference: 12%; Unknown: 29%; United Methodist: 8%; Orthodox (Eastern), Mennonite, Quaker, Unitarian, B'hai: 1%; Other: 1%.

ADMISSIONS FACTS AND FIGURES

Phone: (765) 658-4006. **Email:** admission@depauw.edu. **Website:** http://www.depauw.edu. **Application deadlines for fall 2011:** Regular decision: February 1; decision sent by April 1. Early decision: Send application by: November 1; Decision sent by: January 1. Early action: Send application by: December 1; Decision sent by: February 15. Admission can be deferred. **Application fee:** $40. **To apply online, go to:** http://www.depauw.edu/admission/applying/index.asp. **Admissions requirements/recommendations:** High school units required (recommended): English: (4); Mathematics: (4); Science: (3); Foreign language: (2); Social studies: (2). Tests: The college uses SAT or ACT scores in admissions decisions. Either SAT or ACT required. For admission to the fall 2011 entering class, the school will accept: ACT with or without writing accepted. Campus visit: Recommended. Admissions interview: Recommended. Off-campus interview: May be arranged. **Factors that count in admissions decisions:** *Academic:* Secondary school record: Very Important. Class rank: Important. Letters of recommendation: Important. Standardized test scores: Very Important. Essay: Important. *Nonacademic:* Interview: Considered. Extracurricular activities: Considered. Talent/ability: Considered. Character/personal qualities: Considered. Alumni/ae relationship: Considered. Geographical residence: Considered. State residency: Considered. Religious affiliation/commitment: Not Considered. Minority status: Not Considered. Volunteer work: Considered. Work experience: Considered. **Other schools with the greatest overlap in applicants:** Indiana University–Bloomington; Miami University–Oxford; University of Notre Dame; Vanderbilt University; Washington University in St. Louis. **Admissions statistics for the fall 2009 entering class:** Total applicants: 4,347. Total accepted: 2,877. Freshmen enrolled: 717; 59% were from out of state. Accepted through early-decision or early-action plans: 53%. Overall acceptance rate: 66%. Early-decision acceptance rate: 81%. **Size of waiting list:** 157 applicants; enrolled from waiting list: 107. **Credentials of fall 2009 freshmen:** 51% ranked in the top 10 percent of their high school class; 82% were in the top 25 percent; 100% were in the top half. (Proportion submitting class standing: 60%.) **Average high school grade point average:** 3.6. **First-year students who submitted SAT scores:** 68%. Scores (25/75 percentile): Critical Reading: 530-650, Math: 550-670, Combined: 1080-1320. **First-year students submitting ACT scores:** 67%. Scores (25/75 percentile): English: 24-29, Math: 24-31, Composite: 24-29.

ACADEMICS

Year founded: 1837. **Academic calendar:** 4-1-4. **Degrees offered:** bachelor's. **Most popular majors:** 19% social sciences, 12% English language and literature/letters, 12% communication, journalism, and related programs, 11% biological and biomedical sciences, 7% foreign languages, literatures, and linguistics. **Major fields of study:** area, ethnic, cultural, and gender studies; biological and biomedical sciences; communication, journalism, and related programs; computer and information sciences and support services; education; English language and literature/letters; foreign languages, literatures, and linguistics; health professions and related clinical sciences; history; mathematics and statistics; multi/interdisciplinary studies; natural resources and conservation; parks, recreation, leisure, and fitness studies; philosophy and religious studies; physical sciences; psychology; social sciences; visual and performing arts. **Areas of required coursework:** arts/fine arts, humanities, English (including composition), philosophy, foreign languages, sciences (biological or physical), history, social science. **Preprofessional programs:** pre-law, pre-dentistry, pre-medicine, pre-theology, pre-veterinary science, pre-optometry, pre-pharmacy. **Special academic programs (% participation):** double major (18%), dual enrollment (6%), exchange student program (domestic), honors program (26%), independent study (9%), internships (63%), student-designed major (0%), study abroad (60%), teacher certificate program (5.2%). **Teacher certification offered in:** elementary, middle/junior high, secondary. **Cooperative education programs:** other. **Reserve Officers Training Corps (ROTC):** Army ROTC: Offered at cooperating institution (Rose-Hulman Institute of Technology); Air Force ROTC: Offered at cooperating institution (Indiana University–Bloomington). **Faculty and instruction (2009-2010):** Total instructional faculty: 224 full-time, 55 part-time (55% men; 45% women; 19% minorities). Full-time faculty with Ph.D. or other terminal degree: 98%. Student/faculty ratio: 10/1. Classes of fewer than 20 students: 61%; of 20 to 49 students: 39%; of 50 or more students: 0%. **Advanced Placement and International Baccalaureate credit:** AP tests may be used for: Credit and/or placement. Scores accepted: 4, 5. International Baccalaureate exams may be used for: Credit and/or placement. **Freshmen returning for sophomore year:** 89%. **Graduation rates:** Four-year: 79%; five-year: 82%; six-year: 83%. **Graduate study:** 23% of students pursue further study immediately upon graduation; 50% within five years. Fields in which graduates pursue further study: Master of Business Administration (MBA), 6%; law, 26%; medicine, 6%; dentistry, 2%; education, 11%; arts and sciences, 45%.

COSTS AND FINANCIAL AID

Financial aid office: (765) 658-4030. **Expenses (2010-2011):** Tuition and fees 2010-2011: $34,905; room/board: $9,180. Estimated books and supplies: $800; transportation: $300; personal expenses: $1,800. **Financial aid:** Priority filing date for institution's financial aid form: February 15; deadline: March 10. In 2009-2010, 63% of undergraduates applied for financial aid. Of those, 53% were determined to have financial need; 33% had their need fully met. Average financial aid package (proportion receiving): $28,224 (53%). Average amount of gift aid, such as scholarships or grants (proportion receiving): $24,150 (53%). Average amount of self-help aid, such as work study or loans (proportion receiving): $5,306 (41%). Average need-based loan (excluding PLUS or other private loans): $3,870. Among students who received need-based aid, the average percentage of need met: 90%. Among students who received aid based on merit, the average award (and the proportion receiving): $15,637 (45%). Average amount of debt of borrowers graduating in 2009: $24,210. Proportion who borrowed: 48%.

CAMPUS LIFE AND EXTRACURRICULAR ACTIVITIES

Campus housing available (% using): coed dorms (45%), sorority housing (17%), fraternity housing (21%), apartment for single students (16%), special housing for disabled students, special housing for international students. Students who live in college-owned, operated, or affiliated housing: 95%. **Student employment:** During the 2009-2010 academic year, 17% of undergraduates worked on campus. Average per-year earnings: $900. **Clubs and organizations:** Number of student organizations: 111. Activities include: campus ministries, choral groups, concert band, dance, drama/theater, international student organization, jazz band, literary magazine, music ensembles, musical theater, opera, pep band, radio station, student government, student newspaper, student film society, symphony orchestra, television station. Number of fraternities: 13; sororities: 12. Proportion of men in fraternities: 63%; of women in sororities: 72%. **Sports program (2009-2010):** Member of NCAA III. **Men's intercollegiate varsity sports:** baseball, basketball, cross country, football, golf, soccer, swimming, tennis, track and field (indoor), track and field (outdoor), volleyball. **Women's intercollegiate varsity sports:** basketball, cross country, field hockey, golf, soccer, softball, swimming, tennis, track and field (indoor), track and field (outdoor), volleyball.

SERVICES AND FACILITIES

Basic services: nonremedial tutoring, women's center, placement service, health service. **Remedial assistance:** reading, math, writing, study skills. **Counseling services:** minority student, career, personal, academic, psychological, birth control, religious. **For learning-disabled students:** School does not offer a structured program with separate admission and additional

fees. Services include: remedial math, remedial English, reading machines, remedial reading, tape recorders, diagnostic testing service, untimed tests, note-taking services, oral tests, learning center, readers, extended time for tests, tutors, priority registration, priority seating, texts on tape, other testing accommodations. **Library:** Number of titles: 818,618; number of current serial subscriptions: 2,859. **Information technology resources:** Students are required to lease or own a computer. Number of campus computers available to all students: 424. School has a wireless network. Approximate number of users that can be accommodated: 1,000. Proportion of college-owned housing units wired for high-speed internet access: 100%. **Campus safety:** Security services offered: 24-hour foot-and-vehicle patrols, late-night transport/escort service, 24-hour emergency telephones, lighted pathways/sidewalks, student patrols, controlled dormitory access (key, security card, etc).

TRANSFER AND INTERNATIONAL STUDENTS

Transfer students: May apply for admission for the following academic terms: Fall, Spring. Applicants do not need a minimum number of credits to apply. For fall 2009: Transfer applications received: 64. Transfer applicants offered admission: 30. Transfer applicants enrolled: 15. **International students:** Number of foreign undergraduates: 175 (7% of student body). Number of countries represented: 32. Minimum TOEFL score required: 560 (paper); 220 (computer).

Earlham College

- **Address:** 801 National Road W, Richmond, IN 47374
- **Website:** http://www.earlham.edu
- **Private; Religious affiliation:** Quaker
- **Enrollment:** 1,105 full-time; 22 part-time

KEY STATS
✔ **U.S News College Ranking:** 75, National Liberal Arts Colleges
✔ **SAT Score (25th/75th percentile):** 1090-1330
✔ **Tuition:** 2010-2011: $36,694

Selectivity: More selective	**Room/board:** $7,400
Acceptance rate: 76%	**Average debt:** $23,752
Student/faculty ratio: 12/1	**Proportion who borrowed:** 55%

UNDERGRADUATE STUDENT BODY STATS

2009-2010 enrollment: 1,105 full-time; 22 part-time. Men: 45%; women: 55%. **Ethnic makeup:** African American: 6%; American-Indian: 1%; Asian American: 3%; Hispanic: 2%; White: 74%; International: 14%.

ADMISSIONS FACTS AND FIGURES

Phone: (765) 983-1600. **Email:** admission@earlham.edu. **Website:** http://www.earlham.edu. **Application deadlines for fall 2011:** Regular decision: February 15; decision sent by March 15. Early decision: Send application by: December 1; Decision sent by: December 15. Early action: Send application by: January 1; Decision sent by: February 1. Admission can be deferred. **Application fee:** None. **To apply online, go to:** https://www.applyweb.com/apply/earlham/. **Admissions requirements/recommendations:** High school units required (recommended): English: 4 (4); Mathematics: 3 (4); Science: 3 (4); Foreign language: 2 (4); Social studies: 4 (4); History: 2 (2); Total units: 19 (23). Tests: The college uses SAT or ACT scores in admissions decisions. Either SAT or ACT required. For admission to the fall 2011 entering class, the school will accept: ACT with writing required. Campus visit: Recommended. Admissions interview: Recommended. Off-campus interview: May be arranged. **Factors that count in admissions decisions:** *Academic:* Secondary school record: Very Important. Class rank: Very Important. Letters of recommendation: Important. Standardized test scores: Important. Essay: Important. *Nonacademic:* Interview: Considered. Extracurricular activities: Important. Talent/ability: Important. Character/personal qualities: Very Important. Alumni/ae relationship: Not Considered. Geographical residence: Not Considered. State residency: Not Considered. Religious affiliation/commitment: Not Considered. Minority status: Not Considered. Volunteer work: Important. Work experience: Not Considered. **Other schools with the greatest overlap in applicants:** Beloit College; College of Wooster; Kenyon College; Macalester College; Oberlin College. **Admissions statistics for the fall 2009 entering class:** Total applicants: 1,668. Total accepted: 1,272. Freshmen enrolled: 292; 74% were from out of state. Accepted through early-decision or early-action plans: 49%. Overall acceptance rate: 76%. Early-decision acceptance rate: 88%. Non-early acceptance rate: 72%. **Size of waiting list:** 29 applicants; enrolled from waiting list: 12. **Credentials of fall 2009 freshmen:** 31% ranked in the top 10 percent of their high school class; 59% were in the top 25 percent; 92% were in the top half. (Proportion submitting class standing: 36%.) **Average high school grade point average:** 3.5. **First-year students who submitted SAT scores:** 67%. Scores (25/75 percentile): Critical Reading: 560-690, Math: 530-640, Combined: 1090-1330. **First-year students submitting ACT scores:** 37%. Scores (25/75 percentile): English: N/A, Math: N/A, Composite: 24-29.

ACADEMICS

Year founded: 1847. **Academic calendar:** Semester. **Degrees offered:** bachelor's, master's. **Most popular majors:** 11% psychology, 9% biology, 8% English language and literature, 7% business/commerce, 7% fine and studio art. **Major fields of study:** area, ethnic, cultural, and gender studies; biological and biomedical sciences; business, management, marketing, and related support services; computer and information sciences and support services; English language and literature/letters; foreign languages, literatures, and linguistics; health professions and related clinical sciences; history; mathematics and statistics; multi/interdisciplinary studies; natural resources and conservation; philosophy and religious studies; physical sciences; psychology; social sciences; visual and performing arts. **Areas of required coursework:** arts/fine arts, humanities, mathematics, English (including composition), foreign languages, sciences (biological or physical), social science. **Pre-professional programs:** pre-law, pre-medicine, other. **Special academic programs (% participation):** accelerated program (0%), cross-registration (.5%), double major (23%), dual enrollment (0%), English as a Second Language (ESL) (3%), independent study (55%), internships (18%), student-designed major (1%), study abroad (78%). **Teacher certification offered in:** middle/junior high, secondary. **Cooperative education programs:** engineering. **Faculty and instruction (2009-2010):** Total instructional faculty: 89 full-time, 9 part-time (55% men; 45% women; 20% minorities). Full-time faculty with Ph.D. or other terminal degree: 87%. Student/faculty ratio: 12/1. Classes of fewer than 20 students: 61%; of 20 to 49 students: 34%; of 50 or more students: 5%. **Advanced Placement and International Baccalaureate credit:** AP tests may be used for: Credit only. Scores accepted: 4, 5. International Baccalaureate exams may be used for: Credit only. **Freshmen returning for sophomore year:** 83%. **Graduation rates:** Four-year: 60%; five-year: 71%; six-year: 72%. **Graduate study:** 60% of students pursue further study within five years. Fields in which graduates pursue further study: Master of Business Administration (MBA), 5%; law, 8%; medicine, 12%; theology (or the seminary), 1%; education, 16%; arts and sciences, 57%; veterinary medicine, 1%.

COSTS AND FINANCIAL AID

Financial aid office: (765) 983-1217. **Expenses (2010-2011):** Tuition and fees 2010-2011: $36,694; room/board: $7,400. Estimated books and supplies: $850; transportation: $500; personal expenses: $1,000. **Financial aid:** Priority filing date for institution's financial aid form: March 1. In 2009-2010, 64% of undergraduates applied for financial aid. Of those, 58% were determined to have financial need; 32% had their need fully met. Average financial aid package (proportion receiving): $27,660 (58%). Average amount of gift aid, such as scholarships or grants (proportion receiving): $19,870 (50%). Average amount of self-help aid, such as work study or loans (proportion receiving): $6,126 (49%). Average need-based loan (excluding PLUS or other private loans): $4,832. Among students who received need-based aid, the average percentage of need met: 90%. Among students who received aid based on merit, the average award (and the proportion receiving): $10,413 (26%). The average athletic scholarship (and the proportion receiving): $0 (0%). Average amount of debt of borrowers graduating in 2009: $23,752. Proportion who borrowed: 55%.

CAMPUS LIFE AND EXTRACURRICULAR ACTIVITIES

Campus housing available (% using): coed dorms (60%), special housing for disabled students (1%), special housing for international students (3%), cooperative housing (5%), other housing options (8%). Students who live in college-owned, operated, or affiliated housing: 88%. **Student employment:** During the 2009-2010 academic year, 14% of undergraduates worked on campus. Average per-year earnings: $800. **Clubs and organizations:** Number of student organizations: 70. Activities include: campus ministries, choral groups, concert band, dance, drama/theater, international student organization, jazz band, literary magazine, model UN, music ensembles, radio station, student government, student newspaper, student film society, symphony orchestra, yearbook. Number of fraternities: 0; sororities: 0. Average proportion of students who stay on campus on weekends: 95%. **Sports program (2009-2010):** Member of NCAA III. *Men's intercollegiate varsity sports:* baseball, basketball, cross country, football, soccer, tennis, track and field (indoor), track and field (outdoor). *Women's intercollegiate*

varsity sports: basketball, cross country, field hockey, soccer, tennis, track and field (indoor), track and field (outdoor), volleyball.

SERVICES AND FACILITIES

Basic services: nonremedial tutoring, women's center, placement service, day care, health service, health insurance. **Counseling services:** minority student, career, personal, academic, psychological, birth control, religious. **For learning-disabled students:** School does not offer a structured program with separate admission and additional fees. Services include: reading machines, tape recorders, note-taking services, extended time for tests, priority seating, texts on tape. **Library:** Number of titles: 406,423; number of current serial subscriptions: 20,673. **Information technology resources:** Students are not required to lease or own a computer. Number of campus computers available to all students: 170. School has a wireless network. Approximate number of users that can be accommodated: 400. Proportion of college-owned housing units wired for high-speed internet access: 100%. **Campus safety:** Security services offered: 24-hour foot-and-vehicle patrols, late-night transport/escort service, 24-hour emergency telephones, lighted pathways/sidewalks, controlled dormitory access (key, security card, etc).

TRANSFER AND INTERNATIONAL STUDENTS

Transfer students: May apply for admission for the following academic terms: Fall, Spring. Applicants need a minimum number of credits to apply. For fall 2009: Transfer applications received: 77. Transfer applicants offered admission: 43. Transfer applicants enrolled: 14. **International students:** Number of foreign undergraduates: 150 (14% of student body). Number of countries represented: 74. Minimum TOEFL score required: 550 (paper); 213 (computer). Average TOEFL score: 600 (paper).

Franklin College

- **Address:** 101 Branigin Boulevard, Franklin, IN 46131-2623
- **Website:** http://www.franklincollege.edu
- **Private; Religious affiliation:** American Baptist
- **Enrollment:** 1,018 full-time; 135 part-time

KEY STATS

✔ **U.S News College Ranking:** 10, Regional Colleges (Midwest)
✔ **SAT Score (25th/75th percentile):** 880-1090
✔ **Tuition:** 2010-2011: $24,655

Selectivity: Selective	**Room/board:** $7,295
Acceptance rate: 67%	**Average debt:** $26,903
Student/faculty ratio: 12/1	**Proportion who borrowed:** 85%

UNDERGRADUATE STUDENT BODY STATS

2009-2010 enrollment: 1,018 full-time; 135 part-time. Men: 50%; women: 50%. **Ethnic makeup:** African American: 3%; Asian American: 1%; Hispanic: 1%; White: 94%. **Religious preference:** Roman Catholic: 12%; Protestant: 45%; Unknown: 35%; American Baptist: 8%.

ADMISSIONS FACTS AND FIGURES

Phone: (317) 738-8062. **Email:** admissions@franklincollege.edu. **Website:** http://www.franklincollege.edu. **Application deadlines for fall 2011:** Regular decision: Rolling. Early decision: Not offered. Early action: Not offered. Admission can be deferred. **Application fee:** $30. **To apply online, go to:** https://www.applyweb.com/aw?fc. **Admissions requirements/recommendations:** High school units required (recommended): English: 4; Mathematics: 3; Science: 2; Foreign language: (2); Social studies: 3. Tests: The college uses SAT or ACT scores in admissions decisions. Either SAT or ACT required. For admission to the fall 2011 entering class, the school will accept: ACT with writing required. Campus visit: Recommended. Admissions interview: Recommended. Off-campus interview: May be arranged. **Factors that count in admissions decisions:** *Academic:* Secondary school record: Very Important. Class rank: Very Important. Letters of recommendation: Considered. Standardized test scores: Very Important. Essay: Important. *Nonacademic:* Interview: Considered. Extracurricular activities: Important. Talent/ability: Considered. Character/personal qualities: Important. Alumni/ae relationship: Important. Geographical residence: Considered. State residency: Considered. Religious affiliation/commitment: Considered. Minority status: Considered. Volunteer work: Considered. Work experience: Considered. **Other schools with the greatest overlap in applicants:** Ball State University; Hanover College; Indiana University–Bloomington; Manchester College; Purdue University–West Lafayette. **Admissions statistics for the fall**

2009 entering class: Total applicants: 1,734. Total accepted: 1,156. Freshmen enrolled: 325; Overall acceptance rate: 67%. **Size of waiting list:** 0 applicants; enrolled from waiting list: 0. **Credentials of fall 2009 freshmen:** 21% ranked in the top 10 percent of their high school class; 56% were in the top 25 percent; 92% were in the top half. (Proportion submitting class standing: 84%.) **Average high school grade point average:** 3.4. **First-year students who submitted SAT scores:** 90%. Scores (25/75 percentile): Critical Reading: 420-520, Math: 460-570, Combined: 880-1090. **First-year students submitting ACT scores:** 31%. Scores (25/75 percentile): English: 19-26, Math: 18-25, Composite: 19-24.

ACADEMICS

Year founded: 1834. **Academic calendar:** 4-1-4. **Degrees offered:** bachelor's. **Most popular majors:** 17% journalism, 13% business/commerce, 13% elementary education and teaching, 10% biology/biological sciences, 6% sociology. **Major fields of study:** area, ethnic, cultural, and gender studies; biological and biomedical sciences; business, management, marketing, and related support services; communication, journalism, and related programs; computer and information sciences and support services; education; English language and literature/letters; foreign languages, literatures, and linguistics; health professions and related clinical sciences; history; mathematics and statistics; parks, recreation, leisure, and fitness studies; philosophy and religious studies; physical sciences; psychology; social sciences; visual and performing arts. **Areas of required coursework:** arts/fine arts, humanities, mathematics, English (including composition), foreign languages, sciences (biological or physical), history, social science, other. **Pre-professional programs:** pre-law, pre-dentistry, pre-medicine, pre-veterinary science, pre-optometry, pre-pharmacy, other. **Special academic programs (% participation):** cooperative (work-study plan) program (84%), cross-registration (1%), double major (11%), dual enrollment, independent study (20%), internships (66%), student-designed major (0%), study abroad, teacher certificate program (27%). **Teacher certification offered in:** elementary, middle/junior high, secondary. **Cooperative education programs:** engineering, health professions, technologies, other. **Reserve Officers Training Corps (ROTC):** Army ROTC: Offered at cooperating institution. **Faculty and instruction (2009-2010):** Total instructional faculty: 67 full-time, 36 part-time (51% men; 49% women; 4% minorities). Full-time faculty with Ph.D. or other terminal degree: 90%. Student/faculty ratio: 12/1. Classes of fewer than 20 students: 67%; of 20 to 49 students: 33%. **Advanced Placement and International Baccalaureate credit:** AP tests may be used for: Credit only. **Freshmen returning for sophomore year:** 72%. **Graduation rates:** Four-year: 50%; five-year: 55%; six-year: 57%. **Graduate study:** 14% of students pursue further study immediately upon graduation. Fields in which graduates pursue further study: law, 1%; medicine, 4%; dentistry, 1%; theology (or the seminary), 4%; education, 18%; arts and sciences, 9%; veterinary medicine, 1%.

COSTS AND FINANCIAL AID

Financial aid office: (317) 738-8075. **Expenses (2010-2011):** Tuition and fees 2010-2011: $24,655; room/board: $7,295. Estimated books and supplies: $1,200 personal expenses: $185. **Financial aid:** Priority filing date for institution's financial aid form: March 1; deadline: March 1. In 2009-2010, 93% of undergraduates applied for financial aid. Of those, 81% were determined to have financial need; 26% had their need fully met. Average financial aid package (proportion receiving): $17,703 (80%). Average amount of gift aid, such as scholarships or grants (proportion receiving): $13,782 (80%). Average amount of self-help aid, such as work study or loans (proportion receiving): $4,910 (65%). Average need-based loan (excluding PLUS or other private loans): $4,665. Among students who received need-based aid, the average percentage of need met: 80%. Among students who received aid based on merit, the average award (and the proportion receiving): $8,013 (19%). The average athletic scholarship (and the proportion receiving): $0 (0%). Average amount of debt of borrowers graduating in 2009: $26,903. Proportion who borrowed: 85%.

CAMPUS LIFE AND EXTRACURRICULAR ACTIVITIES

Campus housing available (% using): coed dorms (65%), fraternity housing (35%), special housing for disabled students. Students who live in college-owned, operated, or affiliated housing: 69%. **Student employment:** During the 2009-2010 academic year, 52% of undergraduates worked on campus. Average per-year earnings: $1,293. **Clubs and organizations:** Number of student organizations: 62. Activities include: choral groups, dance, drama/theater, literary magazine, musical theater, pep band, radio station, student government, student newspaper, television station, yearbook. Number of fraternities: 5; sororities: 4. Proportion of men in fraternities: 34%; of women in sororities: 43%. **Sports program (2009-2010):** Member of NCAA

III. **Men's intercollegiate varsity sports:** basketball, cross country, football, golf, soccer, swimming, tennis, track and field (indoor), track and field (outdoor). **Women's intercollegiate varsity sports:** basketball, cross country, golf, soccer, softball, swimming, tennis, track and field (indoor), track and field (outdoor), volleyball.

SERVICES AND FACILITIES

Basic services: nonremedial tutoring, placement service, health service, health insurance. **Remedial assistance:** reading, math, writing, study skills. **Counseling services:** minority student, career, personal, veteran student, academic, older student, psychological, birth control, religious. **For learning-disabled students:** School does not offer a structured program with separate admission and additional fees. Services include: remedial math, remedial English, remedial reading, tape recorders, other special classes, videotaped classes, untimed tests, note-taking services, oral tests, learning center, readers, extended time for tests, tutors, priority registration, texts on tape. **Library:** Number of titles: 124,434; number of current serial subscriptions: 12,673. **Information technology resources:** Students are not required to lease or own a computer. Number of campus computers available to all students: 400. School has a wireless network. Approximate number of users that can be accommodated: 10,000. Proportion of college-owned housing units wired for high-speed internet access: 100%. **Campus safety:** Security services offered: 24-hour foot-and-vehicle patrols, late-night transport/escort service, 24-hour emergency telephones, lighted pathways/sidewalks, controlled dormitory access (key, security card, etc).

TRANSFER AND INTERNATIONAL STUDENTS

Transfer students: May apply for admission for the following academic terms: Fall, Winter, Spring, Summer. Applicants do not need a minimum number of credits to apply. For fall 2009: Transfer applications received: 77. Transfer applicants offered admission: 48. Transfer applicants enrolled: 26. **International students:** Number of foreign undergraduates: 0. Number of countries represented: 3. Minimum TOEFL score required: 550 (paper); 213 (computer). Average TOEFL score: 570 (paper).

Goshen College

- **Address:** 1700 S. Main Street, Goshen, IN 46526
- **Website:** http://www.goshen.edu
- **Private; Religious affiliation:** Mennonite Church USA
- **Enrollment:** 903 full-time; 71 part-time

KEY STATS

✔ **U.S News College Ranking:** 137, National Liberal Arts Colleges
✔ **SAT Score (25th/75th percentile):** 960-1270
✔ **Tuition:** 2010-2011: $24,500

Selectivity: Selective	**Room/board:** $8,300
Acceptance rate: 68%	**Average debt:** $16,564
Student/faculty ratio: 11/1	**Proportion who borrowed:** 75%

UNDERGRADUATE STUDENT BODY STATS

2009-2010 enrollment: 903 full-time; 71 part-time. Men: 39%; women: 61%. **Ethnic makeup:** African American: 4%; Asian American: 2%; Hispanic: 7%; White: 83%; International: 4%. **Religious preference:** Roman Catholic: 6%; Protestant: 28%; No preference: 2%; Unknown: 6%; Mennonite Church USA: 55%; Other: 3%.

ADMISSIONS FACTS AND FIGURES

Phone: (574) 535-7535. **Email:** admissions@goshen.edu. **Website:** http://www.goshen.edu. **Application deadlines for fall 2011:** Regular decision: August 1. Early decision: Not offered. Early action: Not offered. Admission can be deferred. **Application fee:** $25. **To apply online, go to:** http://www.goshen.edu/admission/ap_main.php. **Admissions requirements/recommendations:** High school units required (recommended): English: 4 (4); Mathematics: 2 (3); Science: 2 (3); Foreign language: 2 (2); Social studies: 2 (2); History: 2 (2); Total units: 12 (16). Tests: The college uses SAT or ACT scores in admissions decisions. Either SAT or ACT required. For admission to the fall 2011 entering class, the school will accept: ACT with or without writing accepted. Campus visit: Recommended. Admissions interview: Recommended. Off-campus interview: May be arranged. **Factors that count in admissions decisions:** *Academic:* Secondary school record: Very Important. Class rank: Important. Letters of recommendation: Important. Standardized test scores: Very Important. Essay: Considered. *Nonacademic:*

Interview: Important. Extracurricular activities: Considered. Talent/ability: Considered. Character/personal qualities: Considered. Alumni/ae relationship: Considered. Geographical residence: Not Considered. State residency: Not Considered. Religious affiliation/commitment: Not Considered. Minority status: Not Considered. Volunteer work: Considered. Work experience: Considered. **Other schools with the greatest overlap in applicants:** Bluffton University; Eastern Mennonite University; Indiana University–South Bend; Indiana University-Purdue University–Fort Wayne; Manchester College. **Admissions statistics for the fall 2009 entering class:** Total applicants: 788. Total accepted: 532. Freshmen enrolled: 238; 48% were from out of state. Overall acceptance rate: 68%. **Size of waiting list:** 0 applicants; enrolled from waiting list: 0. **Credentials of fall 2009 freshmen:** 30% ranked in the top 10 percent of their high school class; 58% were in the top 25 percent; 82% were in the top half. (Proportion submitting class standing: 87%.) **Average high school grade point average:** 3.6. **First-year students who submitted SAT scores:** 73%. Scores (25/75 percentile): Critical Reading: 470-640, Math: 490-630, Combined: 960-1270. **First-year students submitting ACT scores:** 41%. Scores (25/75 percentile): English: 20-30, Math: 21-28, Composite: 21-29.

ACADEMICS

Year founded: 1894. **Academic calendar:** Semester. **Degrees offered:** certificate, bachelor's, master's. **Most popular majors:** 16% business, management, marketing, and related support services, 14% health professions and related clinical sciences, 13% visual and performing arts, 9% education, 7% public administration and social service professions. **Major fields of study:** biological and biomedical sciences; business, management, marketing, and related support services; communication, journalism, and related programs; computer and information sciences and support services; education; English language and literature/letters; foreign languages, literatures, and linguistics; health professions and related clinical sciences; history; mathematics and statistics; multi/interdisciplinary studies; natural resources and conservation; philosophy and religious studies; physical sciences; psychology; public administration and social service professions; social sciences; visual and performing arts. **Areas of required coursework:** arts/fine arts, humanities, mathematics, English (including composition), philosophy, foreign languages, sciences (biological or physical), history, social science, other. **Pre-professional programs:** pre-dentistry, pre-medicine, pre-theology, pre-veterinary science. **Special academic programs (% participation):** cross-registration (1%), double major (6%), dual enrollment (1%), independent study (3%), internships (97%), liberal arts/career combination, student-designed major (3%), study abroad (85%), teacher certificate program (8%), other (20%). **Teacher certification offered in:** special education, elementary, middle/junior high, secondary. **Faculty and instruction (2009-2010):** Total instructional faculty: 68 full-time, 54 part-time (50% men; 50% women; 5% minorities). Full-time faculty with Ph.D. or other terminal degree: 68%. Student/faculty ratio: 11/1. Classes of fewer than 20 students: 56%; of 20 to 49 students: 40%; of 50 or more students: 4%. **Advanced Placement and International Baccalaureate credit:** AP tests may be used for: Placement only. Scores accepted: 3. International Baccalaureate exams may be used for: Placement only. **Freshmen returning for sophomore year:** 84%. **Graduation rates:** Four-year: 56%; five-year: 67%; six-year: 70%. **Graduate study:** 10% of students pursue further study within one year.

COSTS AND FINANCIAL AID

Financial aid office: (574) 535-7583. **Expenses (2010-2011):** Tuition and fees 2010-2011: $24,500; room/board: $8,300. Estimated books and supplies: $890; transportation: $700; personal expenses: $1,100. **Financial aid:** Priority filing date for institution's financial aid form: March 10. In 2009-2010, 83% of undergraduates applied for financial aid. Of those, 75% were determined to have financial need; 17% had their need fully met. Average financial aid package (proportion receiving): $17,727 (74%). Average amount of gift aid, such as scholarships or grants (proportion receiving): $14,462 (72%). Average amount of self-help aid, such as work study or loans (proportion receiving): $4,566 (59%). Average need-based loan (excluding PLUS or other private loans): $4,193. Among students who received need-based aid, the average percentage of need met: 81%. Among students who received aid based on merit, the average award (and the proportion receiving): $10,361 (20%). The average athletic scholarship (and the proportion receiving): $4,634 (7%). Average amount of debt of borrowers graduating in 2009: $16,564. Proportion who borrowed: 75%.

CAMPUS LIFE AND EXTRACURRICULAR ACTIVITIES

Campus housing available (% using): coed dorms (58%), apartment for single students (24%), other housing options (18%). Students who live in college-owned, operated, or affiliated housing: 75%. **Student employment:**

During the 2009-2010 academic year, 54% of undergraduates worked on campus. Average per-year earnings: $3,000. **Clubs and organizations:** Number of student organizations: 29. Activities include: campus ministries, choral groups, drama/theater, international student organization, jazz band, music ensembles, musical theater, opera, radio station, student government, student newspaper, student film society, symphony orchestra, television station, yearbook. Number of fraternities: 0; sororities: 0. Average proportion of students who stay on campus on weekends: 80%. **Sports program (2009-2010):** Member of NAIA. *Men's intercollegiate varsity sports:* baseball, basketball, cross country, golf, soccer, tennis, track and field (indoor), track and field (outdoor). *Women's intercollegiate varsity sports:* basketball, cross country, soccer, softball, tennis, track and field (indoor), track and field (outdoor), volleyball.

SERVICES AND FACILITIES

Basic services: placement service, day care, health service, health insurance. **Remedial assistance:** math, writing, study skills. **Counseling services:** minority student, career, personal, academic, older student, psychological, religious. **For learning-disabled students:** School does not offer a structured program with separate admission and additional fees. Total undergraduates in learning-disabled program or receiving services: 30. Services include: remedial math, remedial English, reading machines, tape recorders, videotaped classes, note-taking services, oral tests, learning center, readers, extended time for tests, tutors, priority registration, priority seating, other testing accommodations, other. **Library:** Number of titles: 134,453; number of current serial subscriptions: 1,083. **Information technology resources:** Students are not required to lease or own a computer. Number of campus computers available to all students: 125. School has a wireless network. Approximate number of users that can be accommodated: 2,500. Proportion of college-owned housing units wired for high-speed internet access: 100%. **Campus safety:** Security services offered: 24-hour emergency telephones, lighted pathways/sidewalks, controlled dormitory access (key, security card, etc).

TRANSFER AND INTERNATIONAL STUDENTS

Transfer students: May apply for admission for the following academic terms: Fall, Spring, Summer. Applicants need a minimum number of credits to apply. For fall 2009: Transfer applications received: 121. Transfer applicants offered admission: 81. Transfer applicants enrolled: 55. **International students:** Number of foreign undergraduates: 41 (4% of student body). Number of countries represented: 24. Minimum TOEFL score required: 550 (paper); 79 (computer). Average TOEFL score: 547 (paper).

Grace College and Seminary

- **Address:** 200 Seminary Drive, Winona Lake, IN 46590
- **Website:** http://www.grace.edu
- **Private; Religious affiliation:** Fellowship of Grace Brethren Churches
- **Enrollment:** 1,296 full-time; 170 part-time

KEY STATS

✔ **U.S News College Ranking:** 35, Regional Colleges (Midwest)
✔ **SAT Score (25th/75th percentile):** 930-1190
✔ **Tuition:** 2010-2011: $21,700

Selectivity: Selective	**Room/board:** $7,074
Acceptance rate: 97%	**Average debt:** N/A
Student/faculty ratio: 18/1	**Proportion who borrowed:** N/A

UNDERGRADUATE STUDENT BODY STATS

2009-2010 enrollment: 1,296 full-time; 170 part-time. Men: 52%; women: 48%. **Ethnic makeup:** African American: 11%; American-Indian: 1%; Asian American: 1%; Hispanic: 2%; White: 85%; International: 1%. **Religious preference:** Roman Catholic: 2%; Protestant: 82%; Fellowship of Grace Brethren Churches: 16%.

ADMISSIONS FACTS AND FIGURES

Phone: (574) 372-5100. **Email:** enroll@grace.edu. **Website:** http://www.grace.edu. **Application deadlines for fall 2011:** Regular decision: March 1. Early decision: Not offered. Early action: Send application by: December 1; Decision sent by: December 20. Admission can be deferred. **Application fee:** $30. **To apply online, go to:** http://www.grace.edu/admissions/apply/. **Admissions requirements/recommendations:** High school units required (recommended): English: 3 (4); Mathematics: 2 (4); Science: 2 (3); Foreign language: 2 (4); Social studies: 2 (3); History: 2 (3); Total units: 13 (21). Tests: The college uses SAT or ACT scores in admissions decisions. Either SAT or ACT required. For admission to the fall 2011 entering class, the school will accept: ACT with writing recommended. Campus visit: Recommended. Admissions interview: Neither required nor recommended. Off-campus interview: Not available. **Factors that count in admissions decisions: Academic:** Secondary school record: Important. Class rank: Important. Letters of recommendation: Important. Standardized test scores: Important. Essay: Considered. **Nonacademic:** Interview: Considered. Extracurricular activities: Considered. Talent/ability: Considered. Character/personal qualities: Considered. Alumni/ae relationship: Not Considered. Geographical residence: Considered. State residency: Not Considered. Religious affiliation/commitment: Very Important. Minority status: Not Considered. Volunteer work: Considered. Work experience: Considered. **Other schools with the greatest overlap in applicants:** Bethel College; Cedarville University; Huntington University; Indiana Wesleyan University; Taylor University. **Admissions statistics for the fall 2009 entering class:** Total applicants: 1,027. Total accepted: 994. Freshmen enrolled: 229; 45% were from out of state. Overall acceptance rate: 97%. Non-early acceptance rate: 97%. **Size of waiting list:** 12 applicants; enrolled from waiting list: 2. **Credentials of fall 2009 freshmen:** 28% ranked in the top 10 percent of their high school class; 57% were in the top 25 percent; 85% were in the top half. (Proportion submitting class standing: 82%.) **Average high school grade point average:** 3.5. **First-year students who submitted SAT scores:** 69%. Scores (25/75 percentile): Critical Reading: 460-600, Math: 470-590, Combined: 930-1190. **First-year students submitting ACT scores:** 52%. Scores (25/75 percentile): English: N/A, Math: N/A, Composite: 21-28.

ACADEMICS

Year founded: 1948. **Academic calendar:** Semester. **Degrees offered:** certificate, diploma, associate, bachelor's, post-bachelor's certificate, master's. **Most popular majors:** 39% business administration and management, 16% elementary education and teaching, 9% psychology, 6% music performance, 5% communication studies/speech communication and rhetoric. **Major fields of study:** biological and biomedical sciences; business, management, marketing, and related support services; communication, journalism, and related programs; computer and information sciences and support services; education; English language and literature/letters; foreign languages, literatures, and linguistics; mathematics and statistics; parks, recreation, leisure, and fitness studies; physical sciences; psychology; public administration and social service professions; security and protective services; social sciences; theology and religious vocations; visual and performing arts. **Areas of required coursework:** arts/fine arts, humanities, mathematics, English (including composition), philosophy, sciences (biological or physical), history. **Pre-professional programs:** pre-law, pre-dentistry, pre-medicine, pre-theology, pre-veterinary science, pre-pharmacy. **Special academic programs:** distance learning, double major, English as a Second Language (ESL), honors program, independent study, internships, study abroad, teacher certificate program. **Teacher certification offered in:** special education, elementary, middle/junior high, secondary. **Faculty and instruction (2009-2010):** Total instructional faculty: 57 full-time, 71 part-time (75% men; 25% women; 2% minorities). Full-time faculty with Ph.D. or other terminal degree: 67%. Student/faculty ratio: 18/1. Classes of fewer than 20 students: 54%; of 20 to 49 students: 42%; of 50 or more students: 4%. **Advanced Placement and International Baccalaureate credit:** AP tests may be used for: Credit and/or placement. International Baccalaureate exams may be used for: Placement only. **Freshmen returning for sophomore year:** 79%. **Graduation rates:** Four-year: 50%; five-year: 57%; six-year: 56%. **Graduate study:** 17% of students pursue further study immediately upon graduation. Fields in which graduates pursue further study: law, 1%; medicine, 4%; dentistry, 1%; theology (or the seminary), 6%; arts and sciences, 1%.

COSTS AND FINANCIAL AID

Financial aid office: (574) 372-5100. **Expenses (2010-2011):** Tuition and fees 2010-2011: $21,700; room/board: $7,074. Estimated books and supplies: $1,000; transportation: $800; personal expenses: $1,000. **Financial aid:** Priority filing date for institution's financial aid form: March 1.

CAMPUS LIFE AND EXTRACURRICULAR ACTIVITIES

Campus housing available (% using): women's dorms (58%), men's dorms (29%), apartment for single students (13%). Students who live in college-owned, operated, or affiliated housing: 67%. **Student employment:** During the 2009-2010 academic year, 31% of undergraduates worked on campus. Average per-year earnings: $2,000. **Clubs and organizations:** Number of student organizations: 9. Activities include: campus ministries, choral groups, concert band, drama/theater, international student organization, literary

magazine, music ensembles, musical theater, opera, pep band, student government, student newspaper, symphony orchestra, yearbook. Number of fraternities: 0; sororities: 0. Average proportion of students who stay on campus on weekends: 65%. **Sports program (2009-2010):** Member of NAIA. **Men's intercollegiate varsity sports:** baseball, basketball, cross country, golf, soccer, tennis, track and field (indoor), track and field (outdoor). **Women's intercollegiate varsity sports:** basketball, cross country, soccer, softball, tennis, track and field (indoor), track and field (outdoor), volleyball.

SERVICES AND FACILITIES

Basic services: nonremedial tutoring, placement service, health service, health insurance. **Remedial assistance:** reading, math, writing, study skills. **Counseling services:** career, personal, academic, psychological, religious. **For learning-disabled students:** School does not offer a structured program with separate admission and additional fees. Services include: remedial math, remedial English, reading machines, tape recorders, untimed tests, note-taking services, oral tests, learning center, readers, extended time for tests, tutors, other testing accommodations. **Library:** Number of titles: 154,687; number of current serial subscriptions: 402. **Information technology resources:** Students are not required to lease or own a computer. Number of campus computers available to all students: 150. School has a wireless network. Approximate number of users that can be accommodated: 500. Proportion of college-owned housing units wired for high-speed internet access: 100%. **Campus safety:** Security services offered: late-night transport/escort service, 24-hour emergency telephones, lighted pathways/sidewalks, controlled dormitory access (key, security card, etc).

TRANSFER AND INTERNATIONAL STUDENTS

Transfer students: May apply for admission for the following academic terms: Fall, Spring. Applicants need a minimum number of credits to apply. For fall 2009: Transfer applications received: 142. Transfer applicants offered admission: 91. Transfer applicants enrolled: 56. **International students:** Number of foreign undergraduates: 10 (1% of student body). Number of countries represented: 5. Minimum TOEFL score required: 500 (paper); 173 (computer).

Hanover College

- **Address:** Box 108, Hanover, IN 47243
- **Website:** http://www.hanover.edu
- **Private; Religious affiliation:** Presbyterian
- **Enrollment:** 932 full-time; 6 part-time

KEY STATS

✔ **U.S News College Ranking:** 114, National Liberal Arts Colleges
✔ **SAT Score (25th/75th percentile):** 990-1220
✔ **Tuition:** 2010-2011: $27,500

Selectivity: More selective	**Room/board:** $8,300
Acceptance rate: 61%	**Average debt:** $27,807
Student/faculty ratio: 10/1	**Proportion who borrowed:** 67%

UNDERGRADUATE STUDENT BODY STATS

2009-2010 enrollment: 932 full-time; 6 part-time. Men: 46%; women: 54%. **Ethnic makeup:** African American: 2%; Asian American: 1%; Hispanic: 2%; White: 92%; International: 3%. **Religious preference:** Roman Catholic: 12%; Protestant: 33%; No preference: 1%; Unknown: 49%; Presbyterian: 4%; Other: 1%.

ADMISSIONS FACTS AND FIGURES

Phone: (812) 866-7021. **Email:** admission@hanover.edu. **Website:** http://www.hanover.edu. **Application deadlines for fall 2011:** Regular decision: March 1. Early decision: Not offered. Early action: Send application by: December 1; Decision sent by: December 20. Admission can be deferred. **Application fee:** $40. **To apply online, go to:** https://www.applyweb.com/aw?hanover. **Admissions requirements/recommendations:** High school units required (recommended): English: 4 (4); Mathematics: 3 (4); Science: 3 (4); Foreign language: 2 (4); Social studies: 2 (3); History: 2 (3); Academic electives: 2 (3); Total units: 18 (25). Tests: The college uses SAT or ACT scores in admissions decisions. Either SAT or ACT required. For admission to the fall 2011 entering class, the school will accept: ACT with writing recommended. Campus visit: Recommended. Admissions interview: Recommended. Off-campus interview: May be arranged. **Factors that count in admissions decisions: Academic:** Secondary school record: Very Important. Class rank: Very Important. Letters of recommendation: Important. Standardized test scores: Important. Essay: Considered. *Nonacademic:* Interview: Considered. Extracurricular activities: Considered. Talent/ability: Important. Character/personal qualities: Considered. Alumni/ae relationship: Considered. Geographical residence: Considered. State residency: Considered. Religious affiliation/commitment: Not Considered. Minority status: Considered. Volunteer work: Considered. Work experience: Considered. **Other schools with the greatest overlap in applicants:** DePauw University; Earlham College; Franklin College; Indiana University–Bloomington; Taylor University. **Admissions statistics for the fall 2009 entering class:** Total applicants: 3,019. Total accepted: 1,830. Freshmen enrolled: 293; 31% were from out of state. Accepted through early-decision or early-action plans: 63%. Overall acceptance rate: 61%. Non-early acceptance rate: 52%. **Size of waiting list:** 0 applicants; enrolled from waiting list: 0. **Credentials of fall 2009 freshmen:** 32% ranked in the top 10 percent of their high school class; 71% were in the top 25 percent; 96% were in the top half. (Proportion submitting class standing: 80%.) **Average high school grade point average:** 3.6. **First-year students who submitted SAT scores:** 63%. Scores (25/75 percentile): Critical Reading: 490-600, Math: 500-620, Combined: 990-1220. **First-year students submitting ACT scores:** 36%. Scores (25/75 percentile): English: N/A, Math: N/A, Composite: 22-28.

ACADEMICS

Year founded: 1827. **Academic calendar:** Other. **Degrees offered:** bachelor's. **Most popular majors:** 9% psychology, 7% communication studies/speech communication and rhetoric, 7% history, 6% English language and literature, 5% economics. **Major fields of study:** area, ethnic, cultural, and gender studies; biological and biomedical sciences; business, management, marketing, and related support services; communication, journalism, and related programs; computer and information sciences and support services; English language and literature/letters; foreign languages, literatures, and linguistics; history; mathematics and statistics; multi/interdisciplinary studies; parks, recreation, leisure, and fitness studies; philosophy and religious studies; physical sciences; psychology; social sciences; theology and religious vocations; visual and performing arts. **Areas of required coursework:** arts/fine arts, humanities, mathematics, English (including composition), philosophy, foreign languages, sciences (biological or physical), history, social science, other. **Pre-professional programs:** other. **Special academic programs (% participation):** double major (15%), independent study (64%), internships (45%), student-designed major (1%), study abroad (52%), teacher certificate program (7%). **Teacher certification offered in:** early childhood, elementary, middle/junior high, secondary. **Faculty and instruction (2009-2010):** Total instructional faculty: 91 full-time, 4 part-time (61% men; 39% women; 7% minorities). Full-time faculty with Ph.D. or other terminal degree: 100%. Student/faculty ratio: 10/1. Classes of fewer than 20 students: 81%; of 20 to 49 students: 19%; of 50 or more students: 0%. **Advanced Placement and International Baccalaureate credit:** AP tests may be used for: Credit and/or placement. Scores accepted: 4, 5. International Baccalaureate exams may be used for: Credit and/or placement. **Freshmen returning for sophomore year:** 81%. **Graduation rates:** Four-year: 58%; five-year: 63%; six-year: 63%. **Graduate study:** 26% of students pursue further study immediately upon graduation. Fields in which graduates pursue further study: Master of Business Administration (MBA), 1%; law, 12%; medicine, 3%; dentistry, 1%; theology (or the seminary), 7%; education, 7%; arts and sciences, 37%; veterinary medicine, 1%.

COSTS AND FINANCIAL AID

Financial aid office: (800) 213-2178. **Expenses (2010-2011):** Tuition and fees 2010-2011: $27,500; room/board: $8,300. Estimated books and supplies: $900; transportation: $600; personal expenses: $900. **Financial aid:** Priority filing date for institution's financial aid form: March 10. In 2009-2010, 84% of undergraduates applied for financial aid. Of those, 76% were determined to have financial need; 31% had their need fully met. Average financial aid package (proportion receiving): $23,495 (76%). Average amount of gift aid, such as scholarships or grants (proportion receiving): $19,414 (76%). Average amount of self-help aid, such as work study or loans (proportion receiving): $4,792 (65%). Average need-based loan (excluding PLUS or other private loans): $3,530. Among students who received need-based aid, the average percentage of need met: 88%. Among students who received aid based on merit, the average award (and the proportion receiving): $12,193 (22%). The average athletic scholarship (and the proportion receiving): $0 (0%). Average amount of debt of borrowers graduating in 2009: $27,807. Proportion who borrowed: 67%.

CAMPUS LIFE AND EXTRACURRICULAR ACTIVITIES

Campus housing available (% using): coed dorms (41%), women's dorms (16%), men's dorms (6%), sorority housing (20%), fraternity housing (15%), apartments for married students (0%), apartment for single students (0%). Students who live in college-owned, operated, or affiliated housing: 95%. **Student employment:** During the 2009-2010 academic year, 31% of undergraduates worked on campus. Average per-year earnings: $1,540. **Clubs and organizations:** Number of student organizations: 56. Activities include: campus ministries, choral groups, concert band, dance, drama/theater, international student organization, jazz band, literary magazine, music ensembles, musical theater, pep band, radio station, student government, student newspaper, student film society, symphony orchestra, television station, yearbook. Number of fraternities: 4; sororities: 4. Proportion of men in fraternities: 31%; of women in sororities: 34%. **Sports program (2009-2010):** Member of NCAA III.

SERVICES AND FACILITIES

Basic services: nonremedial tutoring, placement service, health service. **Counseling services:** career, personal, academic, psychological, religious. **For learning-disabled students:** School does not offer a structured program with separate admission and additional fees. Services include: tape recorders, untimed tests, note-taking services, oral tests, learning center, readers, extended time for tests, tutors, priority seating, proofreading services, texts on tape, exams on tape or computer, other testing accommodations. **Library:** Number of titles: 340,662; number of current serial subscriptions: 2,212. **Information technology resources:** Students are not required to lease or own a computer. Number of campus computers available to all students: 158. School has a wireless network. Approximate number of users that can be accommodated: 1,500. Proportion of college-owned housing units wired for high-speed internet access: 100%. **Campus safety:** Security services offered: 24-hour foot-and-vehicle patrols, late-night transport/escort service, 24-hour emergency telephones, lighted pathways/sidewalks, controlled dormitory access (key, security card, etc).

TRANSFER AND INTERNATIONAL STUDENTS

Transfer students: May apply for admission for the following academic terms: Fall, Winter. Applicants do not need a minimum number of credits to apply. For fall 2009: Transfer applications received: 74. Transfer applicants offered admission: 34. Transfer applicants enrolled: 20. **International students:** Number of foreign undergraduates: 24 (3% of student body). Number of countries represented: 13. Minimum TOEFL score required: 550 (paper); 80 (computer). Average TOEFL score: 588 (paper).

Huntington University

- **Address:** 2303 College Avenue, Huntington, IN 46750
- **Website:** http://www.huntington.edu
- **Private; Religious affiliation:** United Brethren in Christ
- **Enrollment:** 1,050 full-time; 140 part-time

KEY STATS

✔ **U.S News College Ranking:** 8, Regional Colleges (Midwest)
✔ **ACT Score (25th/75th percentile):** 20-26
✔ **Tuition:** 2010-2011: $22,330

Selectivity: Selective	**Room/board:** $7,430
Acceptance rate: 89%	**Average debt:** $27,541
Student/faculty ratio: 13/1	**Proportion who borrowed:** 55%

UNDERGRADUATE STUDENT BODY STATS

2009-2010 enrollment: 1,050 full-time; 140 part-time. Men: 44%; women: 56%. **Ethnic makeup:** African American: 1%; Hispanic: 2%; White: 94%; International: 3%. **Religious preference:** Roman Catholic: 4%; Protestant: 76%; United Brethren in Christ: 10%; Other: 10%.

ADMISSIONS FACTS AND FIGURES

Phone: (800) 642-6493. **Email:** admissions@huntington.edu. **Website:** http://www.huntington.edu. **Application deadlines for fall 2011:** Regular decision: August 1. Early decision: Not offered. Early action: Not offered. Admission can be deferred. **Application fee:** $20. **To apply online, go to:** http://www.huntington.edu/admissions. **Admissions requirements/recommendations:** High school units required (recommended): English: 4 (0); Mathematics: 3 (0); Science: 2 (0); Foreign language: 0 (2); Social studies: 2 (0); History: 2 (0); Academic electives: 0 (2); Total units: 14 (8). Tests:

The college uses SAT or ACT scores in admissions decisions. Either SAT or ACT required. For admission to the fall 2011 entering class, the school will accept: ACT with writing required. Campus visit: Recommended. Admissions interview: Recommended. Off-campus interview: Not available. **Factors that count in admissions decisions:** *Academic:* Secondary school record: Very Important. Class rank: Important. Letters of recommendation: Considered. Standardized test scores: Very Important. Essay: Important. *Nonacademic:* Interview: Considered. Extracurricular activities: Important. Talent/ability: Considered. Character/personal qualities: Important. Alumni/ae relationship: Considered. Geographical residence: Not Considered. State residency: Not Considered. Religious affiliation/commitment: Very Important. Minority status: Considered. Volunteer work: Considered. Work experience: Considered. **Other schools with the greatest overlap in applicants:** Anderson University; Ball State University; Grace College and Seminary; Indiana Wesleyan University; Taylor University. **Admissions statistics for the fall 2009 entering class:** Total applicants: 897. Total accepted: 802. Freshmen enrolled: 260; 44% were from out of state. Overall acceptance rate: 89%. **Credentials of fall 2009 freshmen:** 28% ranked in the top 10 percent of their high school class; 58% were in the top 25 percent; 86% were in the top half. (Proportion submitting class standing: 83%.) **Average high school grade point average:** 3.3. **First-year students who submitted SAT scores:** 37%. Scores (25/75 percentile): Critical Reading: 480-580, Math: 480-560, Combined: 960-1140. **First-year students submitting ACT scores:** 62%. Scores (25/75 percentile): English: 19-26, Math: 19-26, Composite: 20-26.

ACADEMICS

Year founded: 1897. **Academic calendar:** 4-1-4. **Degrees offered:** associate, transfer-associate, bachelor's, post-bachelor's certificate, master's. **Most popular majors:** 21% business administration and management, 17% education, 15% theology and religious vocations, 10% communication, journalism, and related programs, 6% visual and performing arts. **Major fields of study:** biological and biomedical sciences; business, management, marketing, and related support services; communication, journalism, and related programs; computer and information sciences and support services; education; English language and literature/letters; foreign languages, literatures, and linguistics; health professions and related clinical sciences; history; legal professions and studies; mathematics and statistics; natural resources and conservation; parks, recreation, leisure, and fitness studies; philosophy and religious studies; physical sciences; psychology; public administration and social service professions; social sciences; theology and religious vocations; visual and performing arts. **Areas of required coursework:** arts/fine arts, humanities, mathematics, English (including composition), philosophy, sciences (biological or physical), history, social science, other. **Pre-professional programs:** pre-law, pre-medicine. **Special academic programs (% participation):** accelerated program (10%), distance learning (3%), double major (9%), independent study (5%), internships (12%), study abroad (2%), teacher certificate program (25%). **Teacher certification offered in:** special education, elementary, middle/junior high, secondary. **Faculty and instruction (2009-2010):** Total instructional faculty: 62 full-time, 41 part-time (61% men; 39% women; 6% minorities). Full-time faculty with Ph.D. or other terminal degree: 76%. Student/faculty ratio: 13/1. Classes of fewer than 20 students: 72%; of 20 to 49 students: 27%; of 50 or more students: 0%. **Advanced Placement and International Baccalaureate credit:** AP tests may be used for: Credit and/or placement. Scores accepted: 3, 4, 5. International Baccalaureate exams may be used for: Credit and/or placement. **Freshmen returning for sophomore year:** 74%. **Graduation rates:** Four-year: 54%; five-year: 61%; six-year: 61%. **Graduate study:** 11% of students pursue further study within one year. Fields in which graduates pursue further study: Master of Business Administration (MBA), 1%; medicine, 2%; theology (or the seminary), 1%; education, 1%; arts and sciences, 6%.

COSTS AND FINANCIAL AID

Financial aid office: (260) 359-4015. **Expenses (2010-2011):** Tuition and fees 2010-2011: $22,330; room/board: $7,430. Estimated books and supplies: $950; transportation: $900; personal expenses: $1,300. **Financial aid:** Priority filing date for institution's financial aid form: March 1. In 2009-2010, 87% of undergraduates applied for financial aid. Of those, 75% were determined to have financial need; 8% had their need fully met. Average financial aid package (proportion receiving): $16,098 (74%). Average amount of gift aid, such as scholarships or grants (proportion receiving): $12,852 (70%). Average amount of self-help aid, such as work study or loans (proportion receiving): $4,976 (68%). Average need-based loan (excluding PLUS or other private loans): $4,495. Among students who received need-based aid, the average percentage of need met: 72%. Among students who received aid based on merit, the average award (and the pro-

portion receiving): $7,555 (16%). The average athletic scholarship (and the proportion receiving): $8,177 (4%). Average amount of debt of borrowers graduating in 2009: $27,541. Proportion who borrowed: 55%.

CAMPUS LIFE AND EXTRACURRICULAR ACTIVITIES

Campus housing available (% using): women's dorms (48%), men's dorms (42%), apartments for married students (1%), apartment for single students (9%), special housing for disabled students (0%). Students who live in college-owned, operated, or affiliated housing: 80%. **Student employment:** During the 2009-2010 academic year, 62% of undergraduates worked on campus. Average per-year earnings: $997. **Clubs and organizations:** Number of student organizations: 12. Activities include: campus ministries, choral groups, drama/theater, international student organization, jazz band, literary magazine, music ensembles, musical theater, pep band, radio station, student government, student newspaper, student film society, symphony orchestra, television station, yearbook. Number of fraternities: 0; sororities: 1. of women in sororities: 8%. Average proportion of students who stay on campus on weekends: 50%. **Sports program (2009-2010):** Member of NAIA. *Men's intercollegiate varsity sports:* baseball, basketball, cross country, golf, soccer, tennis, track and field (indoor), track and field (outdoor). *Women's intercollegiate varsity sports:* basketball, cross country, soccer, softball, tennis, track and field (indoor), track and field (outdoor), volleyball.

SERVICES AND FACILITIES

Basic services: nonremedial tutoring, health service, health insurance. **Remedial assistance:** math, writing, study skills. **Counseling services:** career, personal, academic, psychological, religious. **For learning-disabled students:** School does not offer a structured program with separate admission and additional fees. Total undergraduates in learning-disabled program or receiving services: 15. Services include: remedial math, remedial English, note-taking services, oral tests, learning center, readers, extended time for tests, tutors, priority registration, priority seating, exams on tape or computer, other testing accommodations, other. **Library:** Number of titles: 178,144; number of current serial subscriptions: 1,005. **Information technology resources:** Students are not required to lease or own a computer. Number of campus computers available to all students: 270. School has a wireless network. Approximate number of users that can be accommodated: 2,880. Proportion of college-owned housing units wired for high-speed internet access: 100%. **Campus safety:** Security services offered: late-night transport/escort service, 24-hour emergency telephones, lighted pathways/sidewalks, controlled dormitory access (key, security card, etc).

TRANSFER AND INTERNATIONAL STUDENTS

Transfer students: May apply for admission for the following academic terms: Fall, Spring. Applicants need a minimum number of credits to apply. For fall 2009: Transfer applications received: 112. Transfer applicants offered admission: 83. Transfer applicants enrolled: 60. **International students:** Number of foreign undergraduates: 27 (3% of student body). Number of countries represented: 14. Minimum TOEFL score required: 525 (paper); 75 (computer). Average TOEFL score: 600 (paper).

Indiana Institute of Technology

- **Address:** 1600 E. Washington Boulevard, Fort Wayne, IN 46803
- **Website:** http://www.indianatech.edu
- **Private**
- **Enrollment:** 2,326 full-time; 1,308 part-time

KEY STATS

✔ **U.S News College Ranking:** Unranked Specialty School–Business
✔ **SAT Score (25th/75th percentile):** 830-1070
✔ **Tuition:** 2009-2010: $21,400

Selectivity: Less selective	**Room/board:** $8,050
Acceptance rate: 74%	**Average debt:** N/A
Student/faculty ratio: 31/1	**Proportion who borrowed:** N/A

UNDERGRADUATE STUDENT BODY STATS

2009-2010 enrollment: 2,326 full-time; 1,308 part-time. Men: 44%; women: 56%. **Ethnic makeup:** African American: 23%; American-Indian: 1%; Asian American: 1%; Hispanic: 3%; White: 71%; International: 1%.

ADMISSIONS FACTS AND FIGURES

Phone: (800) 937-2448. **Email:** admissions@indianatech.edu. **Website:** http://www.indianatech.edu. **Application deadlines for fall 2011:** Regular decision: September 1. Early decision: Not offered. Early action: Not offered. Admission can be deferred. **Application fee:** $25. **To apply online, go to:** https://secure.indianatech.edu/eForms/Apply/. **Admissions requirements/recommendations:** High school units required (recommended): English: 4 (4); Mathematics: 2 (3); Science: 2 (3); Social studies: 3 (4); Academic electives: 7 (4). Tests: The college uses SAT or ACT scores in admissions decisions. Either SAT or ACT required. For admission to the fall 2011 entering class, the school will accept: ACT with or without writing accepted. Campus visit: Recommended. Admissions interview: Recommended. Off-campus interview: May be arranged. **Factors that count in admissions decisions:** *Academic:* Secondary school record: Very Important. Class rank: Important. Letters of recommendation: Considered. Standardized test scores: Important. Essay: Considered. *Nonacademic:* Interview: Important. Extracurricular activities: Considered. Talent/ability: Considered. Character/personal qualities: Important. Alumni/ae relationship: Considered. Geographical residence: Not Considered. State residency: Not Considered. Religious affiliation/commitment: Not Considered. Minority status: Not Considered. Volunteer work: Considered. Work experience: Considered. **Admissions statistics for the fall 2009 entering class:** Total applicants: 1,823. Total accepted: 1,346. Freshmen enrolled: 0; 42% were from out of state. Overall acceptance rate: 74%. **Credentials of fall 2009 freshmen:** 5% ranked in the top 10 percent of their high school class; 20% were in the top 25 percent; 54% were in the top half. (Proportion submitting class standing: 60%.) **Average high school grade point average:** 2.8. **First-year students who submitted SAT scores:** 57%. Scores (25/75 percentile): Critical Reading: 400-510, Math: 430-560, Combined: 830-1070. **First-year students submitting ACT scores:** 54%. Scores (25/75 percentile): English: 16-22, Math: 17-24, Composite: 17-22.

ACADEMICS

Year founded: 1930. **Academic calendar:** Semester. **Degrees offered:** associate, bachelor's, master's. **Most popular majors:** 72% business administration and management, 8% accounting, 7% engineering, 4% criminal justice and corrections, 3% computer and information sciences and support services. **Major fields of study:** business, management, marketing, and related support services; communication, journalism, and related programs; computer and information sciences and support services; education; engineering; health professions and related clinical sciences; liberal arts and sciences studies, and humanities; parks, recreation, leisure, and fitness studies; psychology; security and protective services. **Areas of required coursework:** humanities, computer literacy, mathematics, English (including composition), social science. **Special academic programs (% participation):** accelerated program (93%), cross-registration, distance learning (49%), double major, dual enrollment, external degree program, independent study (14%), internships (6%). **Teacher certification offered in:** elementary. **Reserve Officers Training Corps (ROTC):** Army ROTC: Offered at cooperating institution (Indiana University-Purdue University–Fort Wayne). **Faculty and instruction (2009-2010):** Total instructional faculty: 38 full-time, 173 part-time (64% men; 36% women; 16% minorities). Full-time faculty with Ph.D. or other terminal degree: 32%. Student/faculty ratio: 31/1. Classes of fewer than 20 students: 87%; of 20 to 49 students: 13%; of 50 or more students: 0%. **Advanced Placement and International Baccalaureate credit:** AP tests may be used for: Placement only. International Baccalaureate exams may be used for: Credit only. **Freshmen returning for sophomore year:** 57%. **Graduation rates:** Four-year: 10%; five-year: 17%; six-year: 30%. **Graduate study:** 20% of students pursue further study immediately upon graduation; 11% within one year. Fields in which graduates pursue further study: Master of Business Administration (MBA), 80%; engineering, 20%.

COSTS AND FINANCIAL AID

Financial aid office: (260) 422-5561. **Expenses (2009-2010):** Tuition and fees 2009-2010: $21,400; room/board: $8,050. **Financial aid:** Priority filing date for institution's financial aid form: March 10; deadline: March 10.

CAMPUS LIFE AND EXTRACURRICULAR ACTIVITIES

Campus housing available (% using): coed dorms (80%), fraternity housing (9%), apartment for single students (11%). Students who live in college-owned, operated, or affiliated housing: 45%. **Student employment:** During the 2009-2010 academic year, 1% of undergraduates worked on campus. Average per-year earnings: $4,500. **Clubs and organizations:** Number of student organizations: 26. Activities include: campus ministries, choral groups, dance, pep band, radio station, student government, student newspaper. Number of fraternities: 2; sororities: 0. Proportion of men in fraternities: 1%; Average proportion of students who stay on campus on weekends: 50%. **Sports program (2009-2010):** Member of NAIA. *Men's intercollegiate varsity sports:* baseball, basketball, cross country, golf, soccer, tennis, track and field (indoor), track and field (outdoor). *Women's intercollegiate varsity sports:* basketball, cross country, golf, soccer, softball, tennis, track and field (indoor), track and field (outdoor), volleyball.

SERVICES AND FACILITIES

Basic services: placement service, health service. **Remedial assistance:** study skills. **Counseling services:** career, academic. **For learning-disabled students:** School does not offer a structured program with separate admission and additional fees. Services include: remedial math, remedial English, remedial reading, note-taking services, oral tests, extended time for tests, tutors, priority seating. **Library:** Number of titles: 40,000; number of current serial subscriptions: 53. **Information technology resources:** Students are required to lease or own a computer. Number of campus computers available to all students: 360. School has a wireless network. Approximate number of users that can be accommodated: 480. Proportion of college-owned housing units wired for high-speed internet access: 100%. **Campus safety:** Security services offered: 24-hour foot-and-vehicle patrols, 24-hour emergency telephones, lighted pathways/sidewalks, controlled dormitory access (key, security card, etc).

TRANSFER AND INTERNATIONAL STUDENTS

Transfer students: May apply for admission for the following academic terms: Fall, Spring, Summer. Applicants do not need a minimum number of credits to apply. For fall 2009: Transfer applications received: 285. Transfer applicants offered admission: 149. Transfer applicants enrolled: 76. **International students:** Number of foreign undergraduates: 30 (1% of student body). Number of countries represented: 9. Minimum TOEFL score required: 545 (paper); 185 (computer).

Indiana State University

- **Address:** 200 N. Seventh Street, Terre Haute, IN 47809-9989
- **Website:** http://web.indstate.edu/
- **Public**
- **Enrollment:** 7,301 full-time; 1,159 part-time

KEY STATS

✔ **U.S News College Ranking:** second tier, National Universities
✔ **SAT Score (25th/75th percentile):** 830-1030
✔ **Tuition:** 2010-2011: $7,714 in state, $16,626 out of state

Selectivity: Less selective	**Room/board:** $7,752
Acceptance rate: 68%	**Average debt:** $23,963
Student/faculty ratio: 18/1	**Proportion who borrowed:** 65%

UNDERGRADUATE STUDENT BODY STATS

2009-2010 enrollment: 7,301 full-time; 1,159 part-time. Men: 49%; women: 51%. **Ethnic makeup:** African American: 15%; Asian American: 1%; Hispanic: 2%; White: 80%; International: 3%.

ADMISSIONS FACTS AND FIGURES

Phone: (812) 237-2121. **Email:** admisu@isugw.indstate.edu. **Website:** http://web.indstate.edu/. **Application deadlines for fall 2011:** Regular decision: August 15. Early decision: Not offered. Early action: Not offered. Admission can be deferred. **Application fee:** $25. **To apply online, go to:** http://www.indstate.edu/admissions/apply.htm. **Admissions requirements/recommendations:** High school units required (recommended): English: 8 (8); Mathematics: 6 (6); Science: 6 (6); Foreign language: (2); Social studies: 4 (4); History: 2 (2); Academic electives: 4 (4); Total units: 40 (40). Tests: The college uses SAT or ACT scores in admissions decisions. Either SAT or ACT required. For admission to the fall 2011 entering class, the school will accept: ACT with writing required. Campus visit: Recommended. Admissions interview: Neither required nor recommended. Off-campus interview: Not available. **Factors that count in admissions decisions:** *Academic:* Secondary school record: Very Important. Class rank: Very Important. Letters of recommendation: Important. Standardized test scores: Important. Essay: Important. *Nonacademic:* Interview: Considered. Extracurricular activities: Considered. Talent/ability: Considered. Character/personal qualities: Considered. Alumni/ae relationship: Not Considered. Geographical residence: Not Considered. State residency: Not Considered. Religious affiliation/commitment: Not Considered. Minority status: Not

Considered. Volunteer work: Not Considered. Work experience: Not Considered. **Other schools with the greatest overlap in applicants:** Ball State University; Indiana University–Bloomington; Purdue University–West Lafayette. **Admissions statistics for the fall 2009 entering class:** Total applicants: 8,154. Total accepted: 5,582. Freshmen enrolled: 2,035; 9% were from out of state. Overall acceptance rate: 68%. **Credentials of fall 2009 freshmen:** 9% ranked in the top 10 percent of their high school class; 29% were in the top 25 percent; 64% were in the top half. (Proportion submitting class standing: 82%.) **Average high school grade point average:** 3.0. **First-year students who submitted SAT scores:** 72%. Scores (25/75 percentile): Critical Reading: 410-510, Math: 420-520, Combined: 830-1030. **First-year students submitting ACT scores:** 26%. Scores (25/75 percentile): English: 15-22, Math: 16-22, Composite: 17-22.

ACADEMICS

Year founded: 1865. **Academic calendar:** Semester. **Degrees offered:** certificate, associate, transfer-associate, terminal-associate, bachelor's, post-bachelor's certificate, master's, post-master's certificate, doctorate. **Most popular majors:** 18% business, management, marketing, and related support services, 16% education, 12% social sciences, 11% health professions and related clinical sciences, 7% engineering technologies/technicians. **Major fields of study:** architecture and related services; area, ethnic, cultural, and gender studies; biological and biomedical sciences; business, management, marketing, and related support services; communication, journalism, and related programs; computer and information sciences and support services; education; engineering technologies/technicians; English language and literature/letters; family and consumer sciences/human sciences; foreign languages, literatures, and linguistics; health professions and related clinical sciences; history; liberal arts and sciences studies, and humanities; mathematics and statistics; parks, recreation, leisure, and fitness studies; philosophy and religious studies; physical sciences; psychology; public administration and social service professions; social sciences; transportation and materials moving; visual and performing arts. **Areas of required coursework:** arts/fine arts, computer literacy, mathematics, English (including composition), foreign languages, sciences (biological or physical), history, social science, other. **Pre-professional programs:** pre-law, pre-dentistry, pre-medicine, pre-veterinary science, pre-optometry, pre-pharmacy, other. **Special academic programs:** accelerated program, cooperative (work-study plan) program, distance learning, double major, dual enrollment, English as a Second Language (ESL), honors program, independent study, internships, study abroad, teacher certificate program. **Teacher certification offered in:** early childhood, special education, elementary, middle/junior high, secondary. **Cooperative education programs:** business, computer science, education, health professions, home economics, technologies, other. **Reserve Officers Training Corps (ROTC):** Army ROTC: Offered on campus; Air Force ROTC: Offered on campus. **Faculty and instruction (2009-2010):** Total instructional faculty: 430 full-time, 213 part-time (55% men; 45% women; 10% minorities). Full-time faculty with Ph.D. or other terminal degree: 85%. Student/faculty ratio: 18/1. Classes of fewer than 20 students: 35%; of 20 to 49 students: 56%; of 50 or more students: 9%. **Advanced Placement and International Baccalaureate credit:** AP tests may be used for: Credit only. Scores accepted: 3, 4, 5. **Freshmen returning for sophomore year:** 67%. **Graduation rates:** Four-year: 19%; five-year: 36%; six-year: 40%. **Graduate study:** 10% of students pursue further study immediately upon graduation; 17% within one year.

COSTS AND FINANCIAL AID

Financial aid office: (812) 237-2215. **Expenses (2010-2011):** Tuition and fees 2010-2011: $7,714 in state, $16,626 out of state; room/board: $7,752. Estimated books and supplies: $1,170; transportation: $1,022; personal expenses: $1,670. **Financial aid:** Priority filing date for institution's financial aid form: March 1. In 2009-2010, 84% of undergraduates applied for financial aid. Of those, 69% were determined to have financial need; 16% had their need fully met. Average financial aid package (proportion receiving): $9,198 (67%). Average amount of gift aid, such as scholarships or grants (proportion receiving): $6,110 (44%). Average amount of self-help aid, such as work study or loans (proportion receiving): $4,242 (49%). Average need-based loan (excluding PLUS or other private loans): $3,755. Among students who received need-based aid, the average percentage of need met: 80%. Among students who received aid based on merit, the average award (and the proportion receiving): $4,820 (10%). The average athletic scholarship (and the proportion receiving): $10,775 (4%). Average amount of debt of borrowers graduating in 2009: $23,963. Proportion who borrowed: 65%.

CAMPUS LIFE AND EXTRACURRICULAR ACTIVITIES

Campus housing available: coed dorms, women's dorms, men's dorms, sorority housing, fraternity housing, apartments for married students, apartment for single students, special housing for disabled students. Students who live in college-owned, operated, or affiliated housing: 37%. **Student employment:** During the 2009-2010 academic year, 13% of undergraduates worked on campus. Average per-year earnings: $3,100. **Clubs and organizations:** Number of student organizations: 152. Activities include: campus ministries, choral groups, concert band, dance, drama/theater, international student organization, jazz band, literary magazine, marching band, music ensembles, musical theater, pep band, radio station, student government, student newspaper, student film society, symphony orchestra, yearbook. Number of fraternities: 11; sororities: 10. Proportion of men in fraternities: 10%; of women in sororities: 9%. **Sports program (2009-2010):** Member of NCAA I. *Men's intercollegiate varsity sports:* baseball, basketball, cross country, football, track and field (indoor), track and field (outdoor). *Women's intercollegiate varsity sports:* basketball, cross country, golf, soccer, softball, track and field (indoor), track and field (outdoor), volleyball.

SERVICES AND FACILITIES

Basic services: women's center, placement service, day care, health service, health insurance. **Remedial assistance:** reading, writing, study skills. **Counseling services:** minority student, career, personal, veteran student, academic, psychological. **For learning-disabled students:** School does not offer a structured program with separate admission and additional fees. Services include: tape recorders, note-taking services, oral tests, learning center, readers, extended time for tests, tutors, texts on tape, other testing accommodations, other. **Library:** Number of titles: 1,246,771; number of current serial subscriptions: 53,422. **Information technology resources:** Students are required to lease or own a computer. Number of campus computers available to all students: 393. School has a wireless network. Approximate number of users that can be accommodated: 10,375. Proportion of college-owned housing units wired for high-speed internet access: 100%. **Campus safety:** Security services offered: 24-hour foot-and-vehicle patrols, late-night transport/escort service, 24-hour emergency telephones, lighted pathways/sidewalks, controlled dormitory access (key, security card, etc).

TRANSFER AND INTERNATIONAL STUDENTS

Transfer students: May apply for admission for the following academic terms: Fall, Spring, Summer. Applicants do not need a minimum number of credits to apply. For fall 2009: Transfer applications received: 2,942. Transfer applicants offered admission: 1,739. Transfer applicants enrolled: 763. **International students:** Number of foreign undergraduates: 227 (3% of student body). Number of countries represented: 39. Minimum TOEFL score required: 500 (paper); 173 (computer).

Indiana University–Bloomington

- **Address:** 107 S. Indiana Avenue, Bloomington, IN 47405-7000
- **Website:** http://www.iub.edu
- **Public**
- **Enrollment:** 31,061 full-time; 1,429 part-time

KEY STATS

✔ **U.S News College Ranking:** 75, National Universities
✔ **SAT Score (25th/75th percentile):** 1060-1290
✔ **Tuition:** 2010-2011: $9,028 in state, $27,689 out of state

Selectivity: More selective   **Room/board:** $7,918
Acceptance rate: 73%   **Average debt:** $25,522
Student/faculty ratio: 19/1   **Proportion who borrowed:** 54%

UNDERGRADUATE STUDENT BODY STATS

2009-2010 enrollment: 31,061 full-time; 1,429 part-time. Men: 50%; women: 50%. **Ethnic makeup:** African American: 5%; Asian American: 4%; Hispanic: 3%; White: 82%; International: 6%.

ADMISSIONS FACTS AND FIGURES

Phone: (812) 855-0661. **Email:** iuadmit@indiana.edu. **Website:** http://www.iub.edu. **Application deadlines for fall 2011:** Regular decision: Rolling. Early decision: Not offered. Early action: Not offered. Admission can be deferred. **Application fee:** $55. **To apply online, go to:** http://admit.indiana.edu/application/. **Admissions requirements/recommendations:** High school units required (recommended): English: 4; Mathematics: 3 (4); Science: 1

(3); Foreign language: (3); Social studies: 2 (3); Academic electives: 4; Total units: 14 (19). Tests: The college uses SAT or ACT scores in admissions decisions. Either SAT or ACT required. For admission to the fall 2011 entering class, the school will accept: ACT with writing required. Campus visit: Recommended. Admissions interview: Neither required nor recommended. Off-campus interview: Not available. **Factors that count in admissions decisions:** *Academic:* Secondary school record: Very Important. Class rank: Very Important. Letters of recommendation: Considered. Standardized test scores: Important. Essay: Considered. *Nonacademic:* Interview: Considered. Extracurricular activities: Considered. Talent/ability: Considered. Character/personal qualities: Considered. Alumni/ae relationship: Considered. Geographical residence: Considered. State residency: Considered. Religious affiliation/commitment: Not Considered. Minority status: Considered. Volunteer work: Considered. Work experience: Considered. **Other schools with the greatest overlap in applicants:** Ball State University; Miami University–Oxford; Purdue University–West Lafayette; University of Illinois–Urbana-Champaign; University of Iowa. **Admissions statistics for the fall 2009 entering class:** Total applicants: 33,011. Total accepted: 23,975. Freshmen enrolled: 7,327; 32% were from out of state. Overall acceptance rate: 73%. **Credentials of fall 2009 freshmen:** 34% ranked in the top 10 percent of their high school class; 71% were in the top 25 percent; 96% were in the top half. (Proportion submitting class standing: 55%.) **Average high school grade point average:** 3.6. **First-year students who submitted SAT scores:** 78%. Scores (25/75 percentile): Critical Reading: 520-630, Math: 540-660, Combined: 1060-1290. **First-year students submitting ACT scores:** 53%. Scores (25/75 percentile): English: 24-30, Math: 24-29, Composite: 24-29.

ACADEMICS

Year founded: 1820. **Academic calendar:** Semester. **Degrees offered:** certificate, bachelor's, post-bachelor's certificate, master's, post-master's certificate, doctorate. **Most popular majors:** 20% business, management, marketing, and related support services, 16% education, 10% communication, journalism, and related programs, 7% social sciences, 6% public administration and social service professions. **Major fields of study:** biological and biomedical sciences; business, management, marketing, and related support services; communications technologies/technicians and support services; computer and information sciences and support services; education; English language and literature/letters; family and consumer sciences/human sciences; foreign languages, literatures, and linguistics; health professions and related clinical sciences; history; liberal arts and sciences studies, and humanities; mathematics and statistics; multi/interdisciplinary studies; parks, recreation, leisure, and fitness studies; philosophy and religious studies; physical sciences; psychology; public administration and social service professions; security and protective services; social sciences; visual and performing arts. **Areas of required coursework:** arts/fine arts, English (including composition), foreign languages, sciences (biological or physical), history. **Pre-professional programs:** pre-law, pre-dentistry, pre-medicine, pre-optometry. **Special academic programs:** accelerated program, cooperative (work-study plan) program, distance learning, double major, dual enrollment, English as a Second Language (ESL), external degree program, honors program, independent study, internships, liberal arts/career combination, student-designed major, study abroad, teacher certificate program. **Teacher certification offered in:** early childhood, special education, elementary, secondary. **Cooperative education programs:** business, computer science, education, health professions, humanities, natural science, social/behavioral science. **Reserve Officers Training Corps (ROTC):** Army ROTC: Offered on campus; Air Force ROTC: Offered on campus. **Faculty and instruction (2009-2010):** Total instructional faculty: 1,917 full-time, 368 part-time (61% men; 39% women; 16% minorities). Full-time faculty with Ph.D. or other terminal degree: 78%. Student/faculty ratio: 19/1. Classes of fewer than 20 students: 32%; of 20 to 49 students: 48%; of 50 or more students: 19%. **Advanced Placement and International Baccalaureate credit:** AP tests may be used for: Placement only. Scores accepted: 3, 4, 5. International Baccalaureate exams may be used for: Placement only. **Freshmen returning for sophomore year:** 89%. **Graduation rates:** Four-year: 53%; five-year: 70%; six-year: 74%.

COSTS AND FINANCIAL AID

Financial aid office: (812) 855-0321. **Expenses (2010-2011):** Tuition and fees 2010-2011: $9,028 in state, $27,689 out of state; room/board: $7,918. Estimated books and supplies: $812; transportation: $820; personal expenses: $2,412. **Financial aid:** Priority filing date for institution's financial aid form: March 1. In 2009-2010, 60% of undergraduates applied for financial aid. Of those, 43% were determined to have financial need; 14% had their need fully met. Average financial aid package (proportion receiving):

$10,440 (41%). Average amount of gift aid, such as scholarships or grants (proportion receiving): $8,677 (32%). Average amount of self-help aid, such as work study or loans (proportion receiving): $4,323 (30%). Average need-based loan (excluding PLUS or other private loans): $4,322. Among students who received need-based aid, the average percentage of need met: 89%. Among students who received aid based on merit, the average award (and the proportion receiving): $5,708 (22%). The average athletic scholarship (and the proportion receiving): $20,145 (1%). Average amount of debt of borrowers graduating in 2009: $25,522. Proportion who borrowed: 54%.

CAMPUS LIFE AND EXTRACURRICULAR ACTIVITIES

Campus housing available: coed dorms, women's dorms, men's dorms, sorority housing, fraternity housing, apartments for married students, apartment for single students, special housing for disabled students, special housing for international students, cooperative housing, other housing options. Students who live in college-owned, operated, or affiliated housing: 36%. Activities include: campus ministries, choral groups, concert band, dance, drama/theater, jazz band, literary magazine, marching band, music ensembles, musical theater, opera, radio station, student government, student newspaper, symphony orchestra, television station, yearbook. Number of fraternities: 44; sororities: 26. Proportion of men in fraternities: 16%; of women in sororities: 18%. **Sports program (2009-2010):** Member of NCAA I. *Men's intercollegiate varsity sports:* baseball, basketball, cross country, football, golf, soccer, swimming, tennis, track and field (outdoor), wrestling. *Women's intercollegiate varsity sports:* basketball, cross country, field hockey, golf, crew (lightweight), soccer, softball, swimming, tennis, track and field (outdoor), volleyball, water polo.

SERVICES AND FACILITIES

Basic services: nonremedial tutoring, women's center, placement service, day care, health service. **Remedial assistance:** reading, math, writing, study skills. **Counseling services:** minority student, career, military, personal, veteran student, academic, older student, psychological, birth control, religious. **For learning-disabled students:** School does not offer a structured program with separate admission and additional fees. Services include: reading machines, tape recorders, note-taking services, oral tests, readers, extended time for tests, priority registration, priority seating, texts on tape, other testing accommodations, other. **Library:** Number of titles: 7,617,989; number of current serial subscriptions: 103,228. **Information technology resources:** Students are not required to lease or own a computer. Number of campus computers available to all students: 2,262. School has a wireless network. **Campus safety:** Security services offered: 24-hour foot-and-vehicle patrols, late-night transport/escort service, 24-hour emergency telephones, lighted pathways/sidewalks, controlled dormitory access (key, security card, etc).

TRANSFER AND INTERNATIONAL STUDENTS

Transfer students: May apply for admission for the following academic terms: Fall, Spring, Summer. Applicants need a minimum number of credits to apply. For fall 2009: Transfer applications received: 3,505. Transfer applicants offered admission: 2,113. Transfer applicants enrolled: 1,020. **International students:** Number of foreign undergraduates: 1885 (6% of student body). Number of countries represented: 67.

Indiana University East

- **Address:** 2325 Chester Boulevard, Richmond, IN 47374-1289
- **Website:** http://www.iue.edu
- **Public**
- **Enrollment:** 1,514 full-time; 1,313 part-time

KEY STATS

✔ **U.S News College Ranking:** second tier, Regional Colleges (Midwest)
✔ **SAT Score (25th/75th percentile):** 820-1020
✔ **Tuition:** 2010-2011: $6,069 in state, $16,305 out of state

Selectivity: Less selective	Room/board: N/A
Acceptance rate: 74%	Average debt: $27,300
Student/faculty ratio: 16/1	Proportion who borrowed: 78%

UNDERGRADUATE STUDENT BODY STATS

2009-2010 enrollment: 1,514 full-time; 1,313 part-time. Men: 33%; women: 67%. **Ethnic makeup:** African American: 4%; Asian American: 1%; Hispanic: 1%; White: 93%.

ADMISSIONS FACTS AND FIGURES

Phone: (765) 973-8208. **Email:** eaadmit@indiana.edu. **Website:** http://www.iue.edu. **Application deadlines for fall 2011:** Regular decision: Rolling. Early decision: Not offered. Early action: Not offered. Admission can be deferred. **Application fee:** $35. **To apply online, go to:** http://www.iue.edu/admissions/now.php. **Admissions requirements/recommendations:** High school units required (recommended): English: 4; Mathematics: 3 (3); Science: 1; Social studies: 2; Academic electives: 4; Total units: 14 (16). Tests: The college uses SAT or ACT scores in admissions decisions. Either SAT or ACT required. For admission to the fall 2011 entering class, the school will accept: ACT with writing required. Campus visit: Recommended. Admissions interview: Neither required nor recommended. Off-campus interview: May be arranged. **Factors that count in admissions decisions:** *Academic:* Secondary school record: Very Important. Class rank: Important. Letters of recommendation: Not Considered. Standardized test scores: Very Important. Essay: Not Considered. *Nonacademic:* Interview: Not Considered. Extracurricular activities: Not Considered. Talent/ability: Not Considered. Character/personal qualities: Not Considered. Alumni/ae relationship: Not Considered. Geographical residence: Considered. State residency: Considered. Religious affiliation/commitment: Not Considered. Minority status: Not Considered. Volunteer work: Not Considered. Work experience: Not Considered. **Admissions statistics for the fall 2009 entering class:** Total applicants: 861. Total accepted: 633. Freshmen enrolled: 400; 15% were from out of state. Overall acceptance rate: 74%. **Credentials of fall 2009 freshmen:** 5% ranked in the top 10 percent of their high school class; 24% were in the top 25 percent; 62% were in the top half. (Proportion submitting class standing: 76%.) **Average high school grade point average:** 3.0. **First-year students who submitted SAT scores:** 56%. Scores (25/75 percentile): Critical Reading: 400-510, Math: 420-510, Combined: 820-1020. **First-year students submitting ACT scores:** 34%. Scores (25/75 percentile): English: 16-22, Math: 16-21, Composite: 17-22.

ACADEMICS

Year founded: 1971. **Academic calendar:** Semester. **Degrees offered:** bachelor's, post-bachelor's certificate, master's. **Most popular majors:** 34% business, management, marketing, and related support services, 14% liberal arts and sciences studies, and humanities, 12% health professions and related clinical sciences, 10% education, 8% public administration and social service professions. **Major fields of study:** biological and biomedical sciences; business, management, marketing, and related support services; communication, journalism, and related programs; computer and information sciences and support services; education; English language and literature/letters; health professions and related clinical sciences; history; liberal arts and sciences studies, and humanities; mathematics and statistics; multi/interdisciplinary studies; natural resources and conservation; psychology; public administration and social service professions; security and protective services; social sciences; visual and performing arts. **Areas of required coursework:** humanities, computer literacy, English (including composition), sciences (biological or physical), social science. **Special academic programs:** cooperative (work-study plan) program, cross-registration, distance learning, double major, dual enrollment, external degree program, independent study, internships, teacher certificate program, weekend college, other. **Teacher certification offered in:** elementary, secondary. **Faculty and instruction (2009-2010):** Total instructional faculty: 86 full-time, 119 part-time (43% men; 57% women; 8% minorities). Full-time faculty with Ph.D. or other terminal degree: 56%. Student/faculty ratio: 16/1. Classes of fewer than 20 students: 58%; of 20 to 49 students: 41%; of 50 or more students: 2%. **Advanced Placement and International Baccalaureate credit:** AP tests may be used for: Credit only. Scores accepted: 3, 4, 5. **Freshmen returning for sophomore year:** 60%. **Graduation rates:** Four-year: 9%; five-year: 15%; six-year: 20%.

COSTS AND FINANCIAL AID

Financial aid office: (765) 973-8206. **Expenses (2010-2011):** Tuition and fees 2010-2011: $6,069 in state, $16,305 out of state. Estimated books and supplies: $970; transportation: $2,244; personal expenses: $2,322. **Financial aid:** Priority filing date for institution's financial aid form: March 1. In 2009-2010, 91% of undergraduates applied for financial aid. Of those, 81% were determined to have financial need; 5% had their need fully met. Average financial aid package (proportion receiving): $7,943 (79%). Average amount of gift aid, such as scholarships or grants (proportion receiving): $5,769 (69%). Average amount of self-help aid, such as work study or loans (proportion receiving): $3,684 (62%). Average need-based loan (excluding PLUS or other private loans): $3,684. Among students who received need-based aid, the average percentage of need met: 95%. Among students who received aid based on merit, the average award (and the proportion receiving): $1,275 (4%). The average athletic scholarship (and the proportion receiving): $0 (0%). Average amount of debt of borrowers graduating in 2009: $27,300. Proportion who borrowed: 78%.

CAMPUS LIFE AND EXTRACURRICULAR ACTIVITIES

Activities include: drama/theater, literary magazine, student government, student newspaper, television station. **Sports program (2009-2010):** Member of NAIA. *Men's intercollegiate varsity sports:* basketball, cross country, golf, tennis, track and field (outdoor). *Women's intercollegiate varsity sports:* cross country, golf, tennis, track and field (outdoor), volleyball.

SERVICES AND FACILITIES

Basic services: nonremedial tutoring, placement service, health service, health insurance, other. **Remedial assistance:** reading, math, writing, study skills. **Counseling services:** minority student, career, personal, veteran student, academic, older student, psychological. **For learning-disabled students:** Services include: remedial math, remedial English, reading machines, remedial reading, tape recorders, diagnostic testing service, untimed tests, note-taking services, oral tests, learning center, readers, tutors. **Information technology resources:** Students are not required to lease or own a computer. **Campus safety:** Security services offered: 24-hour foot-and-vehicle patrols, lighted pathways/sidewalks.

TRANSFER AND INTERNATIONAL STUDENTS

Transfer students: May apply for admission for the following academic terms: Fall, Spring, Summer. Applicants need a minimum number of credits to apply. For fall 2009: Transfer applications received: 440. Transfer applicants offered admission: 356. Transfer applicants enrolled: 262. **International students:** Number of foreign undergraduates: 4. Number of countries represented: 2.

Indiana University—Kokomo

- **Address:** 2300 S. Washington Street, PO Box 9003, Kokomo, IN 46904-9003
- **Website:** http://www.iuk.edu
- **Public**
- **Enrollment:** 1,549 full-time; 1,299 part-time

KEY STATS

✔ **U.S News College Ranking:** 66, Regional Colleges (Midwest)
✔ **SAT Score (25th/75th percentile):** 850-1050
✔ **Tuition:** 2010-2011: $6,109 in state, $15,374 out of state

Selectivity: Less selective	**Room/board:** N/A
Acceptance rate: 81%	**Average debt:** $24,788
Student/faculty ratio: 17/1	**Proportion who borrowed:** 65%

UNDERGRADUATE STUDENT BODY STATS

2009-2010 enrollment: 1,549 full-time; 1,299 part-time. Men: 35%; women: 65%. **Ethnic makeup:** African American: 5%; Asian American: 1%; Hispanic: 2%; White: 91%.

ADMISSIONS FACTS AND FIGURES

Phone: (765) 455-9531. **Email:** Iuadmiss@iuk.edu. **Website:** http://www.iuk.edu. **Application deadlines for fall 2011:** Early decision: Not offered. Early action: Not offered. Admission can be deferred. **Application fee:** $45. **To apply online, go to:** http://www.iuk.edu/~koadms/apply.shtml. **Admissions requirements/recommendations:** High school units required (recommended): English: 4; Mathematics: 3; Science: 2; Foreign language: (2); Social studies: 2; Academic electives: 4; Total units: 15. Tests: The college uses SAT or ACT scores in admissions decisions. Either SAT or ACT required. For admission to the fall 2011 entering class, the school will accept: ACT with writing required. Campus visit: Recommended. Admissions interview: Recommended. Off-campus interview: May be arranged. **Factors that count in admissions decisions:** *Academic:* Secondary school record: Very Important. Class rank: Very Important. Letters of recommendation: Considered. Standardized test scores: Important. Essay: Not Considered. *Nonacademic:* Interview: Not Considered. Extracurricular activities: Not Considered. Talent/ability: Not Considered. Character/personal qualities: Not Considered. Alumni/ae relationship: Not Considered. Geographical residence: Not Considered. State residency: Not Considered. Religious affiliation/commitment: Not Considered. Minority status: Not Considered. Volunteer work: Not Considered. Work experience: Not

Considered. **Admissions statistics for the fall 2009 entering class:** Total applicants: 758. Total accepted: 615. Freshmen enrolled: 434; 1% were from out of state. Overall acceptance rate: 81%. **Credentials of fall 2009 freshmen:** 9% ranked in the top 10 percent of their high school class; 32% were in the top 25 percent; 66% were in the top half. (Proportion submitting class standing: 89%.) **Average high school grade point average:** 2.9. **First-year students who submitted SAT scores:** 78%. Scores (25/75 percentile): Critical Reading: 420-520, Math: 430-530, Combined: 850-1050. **First-year students submitting ACT scores:** 22%. Scores (25/75 percentile): English: 15-21, Math: 16-22, Composite: 17-22.

ACADEMICS

Year founded: 1945. **Academic calendar:** Semester. **Degrees offered:** certificate, associate, bachelor's, post-bachelor's certificate, master's. **Most popular majors:** 33% health professions and related clinical sciences, 24% liberal arts and sciences studies, and humanities, 14% business, management, marketing, and related support services, 12% education, 4% communication, journalism, and related programs. **Major fields of study:** biological and biomedical sciences; business, management, marketing, and related support services; communication, journalism, and related programs; computer and information sciences and support services; education; English language and literature/letters; health professions and related clinical sciences; liberal arts and sciences studies, and humanities; mathematics and statistics; multi/interdisciplinary studies; physical sciences; psychology; public administration and social service professions; security and protective services; social sciences. **Areas of required coursework:** computer literacy, mathematics, English (including composition). **Pre-professional programs:** pre-law, pre-dentistry, pre-medicine. **Special academic programs:** accelerated program, cross-registration, distance learning, double major, dual enrollment, external degree program, honors program, independent study, internships, liberal arts/career combination, study abroad, teacher certificate program. **Teacher certification offered in:** early childhood, elementary, middle/junior high, secondary. **Faculty and instruction (2009-2010):** Total instructional faculty: 89 full-time, 86 part-time (43% men; 57% women; 11% minorities). Full-time faculty with Ph.D. or other terminal degree: 63%. Student/faculty ratio: 17/1. Classes of fewer than 20 students: 46%; of 20 to 49 students: 50%; of 50 or more students: 4%. **Advanced Placement and International Baccalaureate credit:** AP tests may be used for: Placement only. Scores accepted: 4, 5. **Freshmen returning for sophomore year:** 56%. **Graduation rates:** Four-year: 9%; five-year: 19%; six-year: 27%.

COSTS AND FINANCIAL AID

Financial aid office: (765) 455-9216. **Expenses (2010-2011):** Tuition and fees 2010-2011: $6,109 in state, $15,374 out of state. Estimated books and supplies: $890; transportation: $2,244; personal expenses: $4,238. **Financial aid:** Priority filing date for institution's financial aid form: March 1. In 2009-2010, 87% of undergraduates applied for financial aid. Of those, 70% were determined to have financial need; 4% had their need fully met. Average financial aid package (proportion receiving): $7,733 (67%). Average amount of gift aid, such as scholarships or grants (proportion receiving): $6,231 (53%). Average amount of self-help aid, such as work study or loans (proportion receiving): $3,668 (49%). Average need-based loan (excluding PLUS or other private loans): $3,671. Among students who received need-based aid, the average percentage of need met: 92%. Among students who received aid based on merit, the average award (and the proportion receiving): $1,237 (4%). The average athletic scholarship (and the proportion receiving): $0 (0%). Average amount of debt of borrowers graduating in 2009: $24,788. Proportion who borrowed: 65%.

CAMPUS LIFE AND EXTRACURRICULAR ACTIVITIES

Clubs and organizations: Number of student organizations: 25. Activities include: choral groups, drama/theater, music ensembles, student government, student newspaper.

SERVICES AND FACILITIES

Basic services: nonremedial tutoring, placement service, day care, health insurance. **Remedial assistance:** math. **Counseling services:** minority student, career, personal, veteran student, academic, older student, psychological. **For learning-disabled students:** School does not offer a structured program with separate admission and additional fees. Services include: remedial math, remedial English, reading machines, diagnostic testing service, untimed tests, note-taking services, oral tests, learning center, readers, extended time for tests, tutors, priority registration, priority seating, texts on tape, other. **Library:** Number of titles: 689,237; number of current serial subscriptions: 29,085. **Information technology resources:** Students are not required to lease or own a computer. Number of campus computers

available to all students: 400. School has a wireless network. Approximate number of users that can be accommodated: 200. **Campus safety:** Security services offered: 24-hour foot-and-vehicle patrols, late-night transport/escort service, 24-hour emergency telephones, lighted pathways/sidewalks.

TRANSFER AND INTERNATIONAL STUDENTS

Transfer students: May apply for admission for the following academic terms: Fall, Spring, Summer. Applicants need a minimum number of credits to apply. For fall 2009: Transfer applications received: 426. Transfer applicants offered admission: 354. Transfer applicants enrolled: 226. **International students:** Number of foreign undergraduates: 4. Number of countries represented: 8. Minimum TOEFL score required: 550 (paper).

Indiana University Northwest

- **Address:** 3400 Broadway, Gary, IN 46408
- **Website:** http://www.iun.edu
- **Public**
- **Enrollment:** 3,098 full-time; 1,781 part-time

KEY STATS

✔ **U.S News College Ranking:** second tier, Regional Universities (Midwest)
✔ **SAT Score (25th/75th percentile):** 790-1000
✔ **Tuition:** 2010-2011: $6,193 in state, $16,381 out of state
  Selectivity: Less selective **Room/board:** N/A
  Acceptance rate: 79% **Average debt:** $28,403
  Student/faculty ratio: 16/1 **Proportion who borrowed:** 68%

UNDERGRADUATE STUDENT BODY STATS

2009-2010 enrollment: 3,098 full-time; 1,781 part-time. Men: 32%; women: 68%. **Ethnic makeup:** African American: 21%; Asian American: 2%; Hispanic: 13%; White: 63%.

ADMISSIONS FACTS AND FIGURES

Phone: (219) 980-6991. **Email:** admit@iun.edu. **Website:** http://www.iun.edu. **Application deadlines for fall 2011:** Regular decision: Rolling. Early decision: Not offered. Early action: Not offered. Admission can be deferred. **Application fee:** $25. **To apply online, go to:** http://www.iun.edu/~admit/apps.shtml. **Admissions requirements/recommendations:** High school units required (recommended): English: 4; Mathematics: 3; Science: 1; Foreign language: (2); Social studies: 2; Academic electives: 4; Total units: 14. Tests: The college uses SAT or ACT scores in admissions decisions. Either SAT or ACT required. For admission to the fall 2011 entering class, the school will accept: ACT with writing required. Campus visit: Recommended. Admissions interview: Neither required nor recommended. Off-campus interview: May be arranged. **Factors that count in admissions decisions:** *Academic:* Secondary school record: Very Important. Class rank: Very Important. Letters of recommendation: Considered. Standardized test scores: Very Important. Essay: Not Considered. *Nonacademic:* Interview: Not Considered. Extracurricular activities: Not Considered. Talent/ability: Not Considered. Character/personal qualities: Not Considered. Alumni/ae relationship: Not Considered. Geographical residence: Not Considered. State residency: Not Considered. Religious affiliation/commitment: Not Considered. Minority status: Not Considered. Volunteer work: Not Considered. Work experience: Not Considered. **Other schools with the greatest overlap in applicants:** Purdue University–Calumet; Purdue University–North Central. **Admissions statistics for the fall 2009 entering class:** Total applicants: 1,707. Total accepted: 1,351. Freshmen enrolled: 954; 1% were from out of state. Overall acceptance rate: 79%. **Credentials of fall 2009 freshmen:** 7% ranked in the top 10 percent of their high school class; 22% were in the top 25 percent; 53% were in the top half. (Proportion submitting class standing: 58%.) **Average high school grade point average:** 2.6. **First-year students who submitted SAT scores:** 69%. Scores (25/75 percentile): Critical Reading: 400-500, Math: 390-500, Combined: 790-1000. **First-year students submitting ACT scores:** 15%. Scores (25/75 percentile): English: 15-22, Math: 16-22, Composite: 16-22.

ACADEMICS

Year founded: 1948. **Academic calendar:** Semester. **Degrees offered:** certificate, associate, bachelor's, post-bachelor's certificate, master's. **Most popular majors:** 25% health professions and related clinical sciences, 19% liberal arts and sciences studies, and humanities, 14% business, management, marketing, and related support services, 11% security and protective services, 9% education. **Major fields of study:** area, ethnic, cultural, and gender studies; biological and biomedical sciences; business, management, marketing, and related support services; communication, journalism, and related programs; computer and information sciences and support services; education; English language and literature/letters; foreign languages, literatures, and linguistics; health professions and related clinical sciences; history; liberal arts and sciences studies, and humanities; mathematics and statistics; multi/interdisciplinary studies; parks, recreation, leisure, and fitness studies; philosophy and religious studies; physical sciences; psychology; public administration and social service professions; security and protective services; social sciences; visual and performing arts. **Areas of required coursework:** humanities, computer literacy, mathematics, English (including composition), sciences (biological or physical), history, social science. **Pre-professional programs:** pre-law, pre-dentistry, pre-medicine, pre-veterinary science, pre-optometry, pre-pharmacy. **Special academic programs:** accelerated program, cooperative (work-study plan) program, distance learning, double major, dual enrollment, external degree program, independent study, internships, liberal arts/career combination, student-designed major, study abroad, teacher certificate program, weekend college, other. **Teacher certification offered in:** special education, elementary, middle/junior high, secondary. **Cooperative education programs:** business, computer science, humanities. **Reserve Officers Training Corps (ROTC):** Army ROTC: Offered on campus. **Faculty and instruction (2009-2010):** Total instructional faculty: 177 full-time, 182 part-time (47% men; 53% women; 21% minorities). Full-time faculty with Ph.D. or other terminal degree: 72%. Student/faculty ratio: 16/1. Classes of fewer than 20 students: 33%; of 20 to 49 students: 60%; of 50 or more students: 7%. **Advanced Placement and International Baccalaureate credit:** AP tests may be used for: Credit only. **Freshmen returning for sophomore year:** 65%. **Graduation rates:** Four-year: 9%; five-year: 19%; six-year: 26%.

COSTS AND FINANCIAL AID
Financial aid office: (877) 280-4593. **Expenses (2010-2011):** Tuition and fees 2010-2011: $6,193 in state, $16,381 out of state. Estimated books and supplies: $1,320; transportation: $2,940; personal expenses: $3,918. **Financial aid:** Priority filing date for institution's financial aid form: March 1. In 2009-2010, 82% of undergraduates applied for financial aid. Of those, 70% were determined to have financial need; 3% had their need fully met. Average financial aid package (proportion receiving): $8,238 (67%). Average amount of gift aid, such as scholarships or grants (proportion receiving): $6,334 (53%). Average amount of self-help aid, such as work study or loans (proportion receiving): $3,727 (56%). Average need-based loan (excluding PLUS or other private loans): $3,727. Among students who received need-based aid, the average percentage of need met: 90%. Among students who received aid based on merit, the average award (and the proportion receiving): $3,260 (5%). The average athletic scholarship (and the proportion receiving): $1,286 (0%). Average amount of debt of borrowers graduating in 2009: $28,403. Proportion who borrowed: 68%.

CAMPUS LIFE AND EXTRACURRICULAR ACTIVITIES
Clubs and organizations: Number of student organizations: 80. Activities include: choral groups, dance, drama/theater, international student organization, literary magazine, musical theater, radio station, student government, student newspaper. Number of fraternities: 4; sororities: 3. **Sports program (2009-2010):** Member of NAIA. *Men's intercollegiate varsity sports:* baseball, basketball. *Women's intercollegiate varsity sports:* basketball, volleyball.

SERVICES AND FACILITIES
Basic services: nonremedial tutoring, placement service, day care, health insurance. **Remedial assistance:** reading, math, writing, study skills, other. **Counseling services:** minority student, career, military, veteran student, academic, older student, psychological. **For learning-disabled students:** School does not offer a structured program with separate admission and additional fees. Services include: remedial math, remedial English, remedial reading, tape recorders, note-taking services, oral tests, learning center, readers, extended time for tests, tutors, priority seating, texts on tape, other testing accommodations, other. **Library:** Number of titles: 509,251; number of current serial subscriptions: 1,527. **Information technology resources:** Students are not required to lease or own a computer. Number of campus computers available to all students: 170. School has a wireless network. Approximate number of users that can be accommodated: 400. **Campus safety:** Security services offered: 24-hour foot-and-vehicle patrols, late-night transport/escort service, 24-hour emergency telephones, lighted pathways/sidewalks.

TRANSFER AND INTERNATIONAL STUDENTS
Transfer students: May apply for admission for the following academic terms: Fall, Spring, Summer. Applicants do not need a minimum number of credits to apply. For fall 2009: Transfer applications received: 835. Transfer applicants offered admission: 644. Transfer applicants enrolled: 399. **International students:** Number of foreign undergraduates: 10. Number of countries represented: 8.

Indiana Univ.-Purdue Univ.—Fort Wayne

■ **Address:** 2101 E. Coliseum Boulevard, Fort Wayne, IN 46805-1499
■ **Website:** http://www.ipfw.edu
■ **Public**
■ **Enrollment:** 8,389 full-time; 4,487 part-time

KEY STATS
✔ **U.S News College Ranking:** second tier, Regional Universities (Midwest)
✔ **SAT Score (25th/75th percentile):** 850-1080
✔ **Tuition:** 2009-2010: $6,233 in state, $14,829 out of state

Selectivity: Less selective	**Room/board:** $8,877
Acceptance rate: 96%	**Average debt:** N/A
Student/faculty ratio: 18/1	**Proportion who borrowed:** N/A

UNDERGRADUATE STUDENT BODY STATS
2009-2010 enrollment: 8,389 full-time; 4,487 part-time. Men: 45%; women: 55%. **Ethnic makeup:** African American: 7%; Asian American: 2%; Hispanic: 3%; White: 86%; International: 1%.

ADMISSIONS FACTS AND FIGURES
Phone: (260) 481-6812. **Email:** ask@ipfw.edu. **Website:** http://www.ipfw.edu. **Application deadlines for fall 2011:** Regular decision: August 1. Early decision: Not offered. Early action: Not offered. Admission can be deferred. **Application fee:** $50. **To apply online, go to:** http://www.ipfw.edu/admiss/. **Admissions requirements/recommendations:** High school units required (recommended): English: 4; Mathematics: 3; Science: 3; Foreign language: 2; Social studies: 3; Academic electives: 5; Total units: 20. Tests: The college uses SAT or ACT scores in admissions decisions. Either SAT or ACT required. For admission to the fall 2011 entering class, the school will accept: ACT with or without writing accepted. Campus visit: Recommended. Admissions interview: Neither required nor recommended. Off-campus interview: Not available. **Factors that count in admissions decisions:** *Academic:* Secondary school record: Very Important. Class rank: Very Important. Letters of recommendation: Considered. Standardized test scores: Very Important. Essay: Not Considered. *Nonacademic:* Interview: Not Considered. Extracurricular activities: Not Considered. Talent/ability: Considered. Character/personal qualities: Not Considered. Alumni/ae relationship: Not Considered. Geographical residence: Not Considered. State residency: Considered. Religious affiliation/commitment: Not Considered. Minority status: Not Considered. Volunteer work: Not Considered. Work experience: Not Considered. **Other schools with the greatest overlap in applicants:** Ball State University; Indiana University–Bloomington; Indiana University-Purdue University–Indianapolis; Purdue University–West Lafayette; University of St. Francis. **Admissions statistics for the fall 2009 entering class:** Total applicants: 3,597. Total accepted: 3,463. Freshmen enrolled: 2,222; 2% were from out of state. Overall acceptance rate: 96%. **Credentials of fall 2009 freshmen:** 10% ranked in the top 10 percent of their high school class; 30% were in the top 25 percent; 67% were in the top half. (Proportion submitting class standing: 85%.) **Average high school grade point average:** 3.0. **First-year students who submitted SAT scores:** 90%. Scores (25/75 percentile): Critical Reading: 420-530, Math: 430-550, Combined: 850-1080. **First-year students submitting ACT scores:** 23%. Scores (25/75 percentile): English: 17-23, Math: 18-25, Composite: 18-24.

ACADEMICS
Year founded: 1964. **Academic calendar:** Semester. **Degrees offered:** certificate, associate, terminal-associate, bachelor's, post-bachelor's certificate, master's. **Most popular majors:** 19% business administration and management, 17% general studies, 14% education, 6% health services/allied health/health sciences, 5% visual and performing arts. **Major fields of study:** area, ethnic, cultural, and gender studies; biological and biomedical sciences; business, management, marketing, and related support services; communication, journalism, and related programs; computer and information sciences and support services; education; engineering; engineering

technologies/technicians; English language and literature/letters; foreign languages, literatures, and linguistics; health professions and related clinical sciences; history; liberal arts and sciences studies, and humanities; mathematics and statistics; multi/interdisciplinary studies; philosophy and religious studies; physical sciences; psychology; public administration and social service professions; security and protective services; social sciences; visual and performing arts. **Areas of required coursework:** arts/fine arts, humanities, mathematics, English (including composition), sciences (biological or physical), social science. **Pre-professional programs:** pre-dentistry, pre-medicine, pre-veterinary science, pre-pharmacy. **Special academic programs:** accelerated program, cooperative (work-study plan) program, distance learning, double major, English as a Second Language (ESL), exchange student program (domestic), honors program, independent study, internships, liberal arts/career combination, student-designed major, study abroad, teacher certificate program, weekend college. **Teacher certification offered in:** early childhood, special education, elementary, middle/junior high, secondary. **Cooperative education programs:** business, humanities, natural science. **Reserve Officers Training Corps (ROTC):** Army ROTC: Offered on campus. **Faculty and instruction (2009-2010):** Total instructional faculty: 407 full-time, 405 part-time (51% men; 49% women; 13% minorities). Full-time faculty with Ph.D. or other terminal degree: 85%. Student/faculty ratio: 18/1. Classes of fewer than 20 students: 41%; of 20 to 49 students: 56%; of 50 or more students: 3%. **Advanced Placement and International Baccalaureate credit:** AP tests may be used for: Credit only. Scores accepted: 3, 4, 5. International Baccalaureate exams may be used for: Credit only. **Freshmen returning for sophomore year:** 61%. **Graduation rates:** Four-year: 6%; five-year: 17%; six-year: 22%. **Graduate study:** 15% of students pursue further study immediately upon graduation.

COSTS AND FINANCIAL AID
Financial aid office: (260) 481-6820. **Expenses (2009-2010):** Tuition and fees 2009-2010: $6,233 in state, $14,829 out of state; room/board: $8,877. Estimated books and supplies: $1,300. **Financial aid:** Priority filing date for institution's financial aid form: March 10.

CAMPUS LIFE AND EXTRACURRICULAR ACTIVITIES
Campus housing available (% using): apartment for single students (100%). Students who live in college-owned, operated, or affiliated housing: 5%. Average per-year earnings: $5,000. **Clubs and organizations:** Number of student organizations: 121. Activities include: campus ministries, choral groups, concert band, dance, drama/theater, international student organization, jazz band, literary magazine, music ensembles, musical theater, opera, pep band, student government, student newspaper, student film society, symphony orchestra, television station. Number of fraternities: 0; sororities: 1. of women in sororities: 1%. Average proportion of students who stay on campus on weekends: 20%. **Sports program (2009-2010):** Member of NCAA I. *Men's intercollegiate varsity sports:* baseball, basketball, cross country, golf, soccer, tennis, volleyball. *Women's intercollegiate varsity sports:* basketball, cross country, golf, soccer, softball, tennis, track and field (indoor), track and field (outdoor), volleyball.

SERVICES AND FACILITIES
Basic services: nonremedial tutoring, women's center, placement service, day care, health service, health insurance. **Remedial assistance:** reading, math, writing, study skills. **Counseling services:** minority student, career, military, personal, veteran student, academic, older student, psychological, birth control, religious. **For learning-disabled students:** School does not offer a structured program with separate admission and additional fees. Total undergraduates in learning-disabled program or receiving services: 153. Services include: remedial math, reading machines, remedial reading, tape recorders, note-taking services, oral tests, learning center, readers, extended time for tests, tutors, early syllabus, priority registration, priority seating, texts on tape, typist/scribe, exams on tape or computer, other testing accommodations. **Library:** Number of titles: 441,647; number of current serial subscriptions: 19,822. **Information technology resources:** Students are not required to lease or own a computer. Number of campus computers available to all students: 642. School has a wireless network. Approximate number of users that can be accommodated: 5,000. Proportion of college-owned housing units wired for high-speed internet access: 100%. **Campus safety:** Security services offered: 24-hour foot-and-vehicle patrols, late-night transport/escort service, 24-hour emergency telephones, lighted pathways/sidewalks, controlled dormitory access (key, security card, etc).

TRANSFER AND INTERNATIONAL STUDENTS
Transfer students: May apply for admission for the following academic terms: Fall, Spring, Summer. Applicants do not need a minimum number

of credits to apply. For fall 2009: Transfer applications received: 1,405. Transfer applicants offered admission: 1,347. Transfer applicants enrolled: 921. **International students:** Number of foreign undergraduates: 133 (1% of student body). Number of countries represented: 42. Minimum TOEFL score required: 550 (paper); 79 (computer).

Indiana Univ.-Purdue Univ.—Indianapolis

- **Address:** 425 N. University Boulevard, Indianapolis, IN 46202-5143
- **Website:** http://www.iupui.edu
- **Public**
- **Enrollment:** 15,696 full-time; 6,423 part-time

KEY STATS
✔ **U.S News College Ranking:** second tier, National Universities
✔ **SAT Score (25th/75th percentile):** 890-1110
✔ **Tuition:** 2010-2011: $7,885 in state, $24,428 out of state

Selectivity: Selective	**Room/board:** $7,944
Acceptance rate: 67%	**Average debt:** $27,062
Student/faculty ratio: 16/1	**Proportion who borrowed:** 72%

UNDERGRADUATE STUDENT BODY STATS
2009-2010 enrollment: 15,696 full-time; 6,423 part-time. Men: 42%; women: 58%. **Ethnic makeup:** African American: 10%; Asian American: 3%; Hispanic: 3%; White: 81%; International: 3%.

ADMISSIONS FACTS AND FIGURES
Phone: (317) 274-4591. **Email:** apply@iupui.edu. **Website:** http://www.iupui.edu. **Application deadlines for fall 2011:** Regular decision: May 1. Early decision: Not offered. Early action: Not offered. Admission can be deferred. **Application fee:** $50. **To apply online, go to:** http://www.enroll.iupui.edu/. **Admissions requirements/recommendations:** High school units required (recommended): English: 4; Mathematics: 3 (4); Science: 3; Social studies: 3; Academic electives: 4; Total units: 17. Tests: The college uses SAT or ACT scores in admissions decisions. Either SAT or ACT required. For admission to the fall 2011 entering class, the school will accept: ACT with writing required. Campus visit: Recommended. Admissions interview: Recommended. Off-campus interview: Not available. **Factors that count in admissions decisions:** *Academic:* Secondary school record: Very Important. Class rank: Considered. Letters of recommendation: Considered. Standardized test scores: Considered. Essay: Considered. *Nonacademic:* Interview: Not Considered. Extracurricular activities: Not Considered. Talent/ability: Not Considered. Character/personal qualities: Considered. Alumni/ae relationship: Not Considered. Geographical residence: Not Considered. State residency: Not Considered. Religious affiliation/commitment: Not Considered. Minority status: Not Considered. Volunteer work: Considered. Work experience: Considered. **Other schools with the greatest overlap in applicants:** Ball State University; Indiana State University; Indiana University–Bloomington; Purdue University–West Lafayette; University of Indianapolis. **Admissions statistics for the fall 2009 entering class:** Total applicants: 9,641. Total accepted: 6,414. Freshmen enrolled: 3,019; 3% were from out of state. Overall acceptance rate: 67%. **Credentials of fall 2009 freshmen:** 15% ranked in the top 10 percent of their high school class; 44% were in the top 25 percent; 87% were in the top half. (Proportion submitting class standing: 75%.) **Average high school grade point average:** 3.3. **First-year students who submitted SAT scores:** 83%. Scores (25/75 percentile): Critical Reading: 440-550, Math: 450-560, Combined: 890-1110. **First-year students submitting ACT scores:** 29%. Scores (25/75 percentile): English: 17-24, Math: 18-25, Composite: 19-24.

ACADEMICS
Year founded: 1969. **Academic calendar:** Semester. **Degrees offered:** certificate, associate, bachelor's, post-bachelor's certificate, master's, doctorate. **Most popular majors:** 17% business, management, marketing, and related support services, 16% health professions and related clinical sciences, 14% liberal arts and sciences studies, and humanities, 10% education, 5% communication, journalism, and related programs. **Major fields of study:** biological and biomedical sciences; business, management, marketing, and related support services; communication, journalism, and related programs; computer and information sciences and support services; education; engineering; engineering technologies/technicians; English language and literature/letters; foreign languages, literatures, and linguistics; health professions and related clinical sciences; history; liberal arts and sciences

studies, and humanities; mathematics and statistics; multi/interdisciplinary studies; natural resources and conservation; philosophy and religious studies; physical sciences; psychology; public administration and social service professions; security and protective services; social sciences; visual and performing arts. **Areas of required coursework:** computer literacy, mathematics, English (including composition), sciences (biological or physical), social science, other. **Pre-professional programs:** pre-law, pre-dentistry, pre-medicine, pre-veterinary science, pre-optometry, pre-pharmacy, other. **Special academic programs:** accelerated program, cooperative (work-study plan) program, cross-registration, distance learning, double major, dual enrollment, English as a Second Language (ESL), exchange student program (domestic), external degree program, honors program, independent study, internships, student-designed major, study abroad, teacher certificate program, weekend college. **Teacher certification offered in:** early childhood, special education, elementary, middle/junior high, secondary. **Cooperative education programs:** engineering, technologies. **Reserve Officers Training Corps (ROTC):** Army ROTC: Offered on campus; Air Force ROTC: Offered at cooperating institution (Indiana University–Bloomington). **Faculty and instruction (2009-2010):** Total instructional faculty: 2,116 full-time, 980 part-time (58% men; 42% women; 18% minorities). Full-time faculty with Ph.D. or other terminal degree: 83%. Student/faculty ratio: 16/1. Classes of fewer than 20 students: 34%; of 20 to 49 students: 56%; of 50 or more students: 10%. **Advanced Placement and International Baccalaureate credit:** AP tests may be used for: Placement only. Scores accepted: 3, 4, 5. International Baccalaureate exams may be used for: Credit only. **Freshmen returning for sophomore year:** 68%. **Graduation rates:** Four-year: 10%; five-year: 26%; six-year: 34%.

COSTS AND FINANCIAL AID

Financial aid office: (317) 274-4162. **Expenses (2010-2011):** Tuition and fees 2010-2011: $7,885 in state, $24,428 out of state; room/board: $7,944. Estimated books and supplies: $672; transportation: $3,200; personal expenses: $3,520. **Financial aid:** Priority filing date for institution's financial aid form: March 1. In 2009-2010, 81% of undergraduates applied for financial aid. Of those, 67% were determined to have financial need; 5% had their need fully met. Average financial aid package (proportion receiving): $8,978 (65%). Average amount of gift aid, such as scholarships or grants (proportion receiving): $6,925 (52%). Average amount of self-help aid, such as work study or loans (proportion receiving): $4,129 (51%). Average need-based loan (excluding PLUS or other private loans): $4,127. Among students who received need-based aid, the average percentage of need met: 90%. Among students who received aid based on merit, the average award (and the proportion receiving): $3,407 (7%). The average athletic scholarship (and the proportion receiving): $7,226 (1%). Average amount of debt of borrowers graduating in 2009: $27,062. Proportion who borrowed: 72%.

CAMPUS LIFE AND EXTRACURRICULAR ACTIVITIES

Campus housing available: coed dorms, apartments for married students, apartment for single students, special housing for international students, other housing options. Students who live in college-owned, operated, or affiliated housing: 5%. Activities include: campus ministries, choral groups, concert band, dance, drama/theater, jazz band, literary magazine, music ensembles, pep band, student government, student newspaper. Number of fraternities: 3; sororities: 5. Proportion of men in fraternities: 1%; of women in sororities: 1%. **Sports program (2009-2010):** Member of NCAA I. *Men's intercollegiate varsity sports:* basketball, cross country, golf, soccer, swimming, tennis, track and field (outdoor). *Women's intercollegiate varsity sports:* basketball, cross country, golf, soccer, softball, swimming, tennis, track and field (outdoor), volleyball.

SERVICES AND FACILITIES

Basic services: nonremedial tutoring, women's center, placement service, day care, health service, health insurance, other. **Remedial assistance:** math, writing. **Counseling services:** minority student, career, military, personal, veteran student, academic, older student, psychological, birth control. **For learning-disabled students:** School does not offer a structured program with separate admission and additional fees. Services include: remedial math, remedial English, reading machines, remedial reading, tape recorders, videotaped classes, diagnostic testing service, note-taking services, oral tests, learning center, readers, extended time for tests, tutors, texts on tape, other testing accommodations. **Library:** Number of titles: 1,687,336; number of current serial subscriptions: 9,073. **Information technology resources:** Students are not required to lease or own a computer. Number of campus computers available to all students: 3,000. School has a wireless network. Approximate number of users that can be accommodated: 13,500. Proportion of college-owned housing units wired for high-speed internet

access: 100%. **Campus safety:** Security services offered: 24-hour foot-and-vehicle patrols, late-night transport/escort service, 24-hour emergency telephones, lighted pathways/sidewalks, controlled dormitory access (key, security card, etc).

TRANSFER AND INTERNATIONAL STUDENTS

Transfer students: May apply for admission for the following academic terms: Fall, Spring, Summer. Applicants need a minimum number of credits to apply. For fall 2009: Transfer applications received: 3,535. Transfer applicants offered admission: 2,345. Transfer applicants enrolled: 1,475. **International students:** Number of foreign undergraduates: 635 (3% of student body). Number of countries represented: 121.

Indiana University–South Bend

- **Address:** 1700 Mishawaka Avenue, PO Box 7111, South Bend, IN 46634-7111
- **Website:** http://www.iusb.edu
- **Public**
- **Enrollment:** 4,328 full-time; 3,168 part-time

KEY STATS

✔ **U.S News College Ranking:** second tier, Regional Universities (Midwest)
✔ **SAT Score (25th/75th percentile):** 840-1050
✔ **Tuition:** 2010-2011: $6,290 in state, $16,617 out of state

Selectivity: Less selective	**Room/board:** $6,796
Acceptance rate: 80%	**Average debt:** $25,384
Student/faculty ratio: 15/1	**Proportion who borrowed:** 71%

UNDERGRADUATE STUDENT BODY STATS

2009-2010 enrollment: 4,328 full-time; 3,168 part-time. Men: 39%; women: 61%. **Ethnic makeup:** African American: 8%; Asian American: 1%; Hispanic: 5%; White: 83%; International: 2%.

ADMISSIONS FACTS AND FIGURES

Phone: (574) 520-4839. **Email:** admissions@iusb.edu. **Website:** http://www.iusb.edu. **Application deadlines for fall 2011:** Regular decision: Rolling. Early decision: Not offered. Early action: Not offered. Admission can be deferred. **Application fee:** $45. **To apply online, go to:** http://www.iusb.edu/~admissio/. **Admissions requirements/recommendations:** High school units required (recommended): English: 4; Mathematics: 3; Science: 1; Foreign language: (2); Social studies: 2; Total units: 13. Tests: The college uses SAT or ACT scores in admissions decisions. Either SAT or ACT required. For admission to the fall 2011 entering class, the school will accept: ACT with writing required. Campus visit: Recommended. Admissions interview: Recommended. Off-campus interview: May be arranged. **Factors that count in admissions decisions:** *Academic:* Secondary school record: Very Important. Class rank: Important. Letters of recommendation: Considered. Standardized test scores: Considered. Essay: Not Considered. *Nonacademic:* Interview: Considered. Extracurricular activities: Considered. Talent/ability: Not Considered. Character/personal qualities: Not Considered. Alumni/ae relationship: Not Considered. Geographical residence: Not Considered. State residency: Considered. Religious affiliation/commitment: Not Considered. Minority status: Not Considered. Volunteer work: Not Considered. Work experience: Not Considered. **Other schools with the greatest overlap in applicants:** Ball State University; Bethel College; Indiana University–Bloomington; Purdue University–West Lafayette. **Admissions statistics for the fall 2009 entering class:** Total applicants: 2,272. Total accepted: 1,816. Freshmen enrolled: 1,206; 2% were from out of state. Overall acceptance rate: 80%. **Credentials of fall 2009 freshmen:** 7% ranked in the top 10 percent of their high school class; 22% were in the top 25 percent; 60% were in the top half. (Proportion submitting class standing: 49%.) **Average high school grade point average:** 2.8. **First-year students who submitted SAT scores:** 72%. Scores (25/75 percentile): Critical Reading: 420-520, Math: 420-530, Combined: 840-1050. **First-year students submitting ACT scores:** 12%. Scores (25/75 percentile): English: 15-22, Math: 16-23, Composite: 17-23.

ACADEMICS

Year founded: 1922. **Academic calendar:** Semester. **Degrees offered:** certificate, diploma, associate, bachelor's, post-bachelor's certificate, master's. **Most popular majors:** 17% education, 17% liberal arts and sciences studies, and humanities, 16% business, management, marketing, and related support services, 15% health professions and related clinical sciences, 7% psychology. **Major fields of study:** area, ethnic, cultural, and gender studies; biological and biomedical sciences; business, management, marketing, and related support services; communication, journalism, and related programs; computer and information sciences and support services; education; engineering technologies/technicians; English language and literature/letters; family and consumer sciences/human sciences; foreign languages, literatures, and linguistics; history; liberal arts and sciences studies, and humanities; mathematics and statistics; multi/interdisciplinary studies; natural resources and conservation; philosophy and religious studies; physical sciences; psychology; public administration and social service professions; social sciences; visual and performing arts. **Areas of required coursework:** arts/fine arts, humanities, computer literacy, mathematics, English (including composition), sciences (biological or physical), social science, other. **Pre-professional programs:** pre-law, pre-dentistry, pre-medicine, pre-optometry, pre-pharmacy. **Special academic programs:** accelerated program, cross-registration, distance learning, double major, dual enrollment, English as a Second Language (ESL), external degree program, honors program, independent study, internships, liberal arts/career combination, study abroad, teacher certificate program, weekend college, other. **Teacher certification offered in:** early childhood, special education, elementary, secondary. **Reserve Officers Training Corps (ROTC):** Army ROTC: Offered at cooperating institution; Navy ROTC: Offered at cooperating institution; Air Force ROTC: Offered at cooperating institution. **Faculty and instruction (2009-2010):** Total instructional faculty: 292 full-time, 254 part-time (45% men; 55% women; 14% minorities). Full-time faculty with Ph.D. or other terminal degree: 63%. Student/faculty ratio: 15/1. Classes of fewer than 20 students: 41%; of 20 to 49 students: 56%; of 50 or more students: 4%. **Advanced Placement and International Baccalaureate credit:** AP tests may be used for: Credit only. **Freshmen returning for sophomore year:** 63%. **Graduation rates:** Four-year: 7%; five-year: 20%; six-year: 26%.

COSTS AND FINANCIAL AID

Financial aid office: (574) 237-4357. **Expenses (2010-2011):** Tuition and fees 2010-2011: $6,290 in state, $16,617 out of state; room/board: $6,796. Estimated books and supplies: $1,290; transportation: $2,758; personal expenses: $2,322. **Financial aid:** Priority filing date for institution's financial aid form: March 1. In 2009-2010, 84% of undergraduates applied for financial aid. Of those, 71% were determined to have financial need; 3% had their need fully met. Average financial aid package (proportion receiving): $7,902 (68%). Average amount of gift aid, such as scholarships or grants (proportion receiving): $6,266 (56%). Average amount of self-help aid, such as work study or loans (proportion receiving): $3,638 (50%). Average need-based loan (excluding PLUS or other private loans): $3,634. Among students who received need-based aid, the average percentage of need met: 93%. Among students who received aid based on merit, the average award (and the proportion receiving): $3,361 (4%). The average athletic scholarship (and the proportion receiving): $6,410 (0%). Average amount of debt of borrowers graduating in 2009: $25,384. Proportion who borrowed: 71%.

CAMPUS LIFE AND EXTRACURRICULAR ACTIVITIES

Campus housing available: apartment for single students, special housing for international students. **Clubs and organizations:** Number of student organizations: 55. Activities include: choral groups, drama/theater, jazz band, literary magazine, music ensembles, musical theater, opera, pep band, student government, student newspaper, student film society, symphony orchestra. Number of fraternities: 1; sororities: 1. **Sports program (2009-2010):** Member of NAIA. **Men's intercollegiate varsity sports:** basketball. **Women's intercollegiate varsity sports:** basketball.

SERVICES AND FACILITIES

Basic services: nonremedial tutoring, women's center, placement service, day care, other. **Remedial assistance:** reading, math, writing, study skills. **Counseling services:** minority student, career, personal, veteran student, academic, older student, psychological. **For learning-disabled students:** School does not offer a structured program with separate admission and additional fees. Services include: remedial math, remedial English, remedial reading, learning center, tutors, other. **Library:** Number of titles: 311,673; number of current serial subscriptions: 22,221. **Information technology resources:** Students are not required to lease or own a computer. Number of campus computers available to all students: 550. School has a wireless network. Approximate number of users that can be accommodated: 800. **Campus safety:** Security services offered: 24-hour foot-and-vehicle patrols, late-night transport/escort service, lighted pathways/sidewalks.

TRANSFER AND INTERNATIONAL STUDENTS

Transfer students: May apply for admission for the following academic terms: Fall, Spring, Summer. Applicants do not need a minimum number of credits to apply. For fall 2009: Transfer applications received: 1,155. Transfer applicants offered admission: 912. Transfer applicants enrolled: 586. **International students:** Number of foreign undergraduates: 143 (2% of student body). Number of countries represented: 38. Minimum TOEFL score required: 530 (paper); 197 (computer).

Indiana University Southeast

- **Address:** 4201 Grant Line Road, New Albany, IN 47150-6405
- **Website:** http://www.ius.edu
- **Public**
- **Enrollment:** 3,899 full-time; 2,044 part-time

KEY STATS

✔ **U.S News College Ranking:** second tier, Regional Universities (Midwest)
✔ **SAT Score (25th/75th percentile):** 840-1040
✔ **Tuition:** 2010-2011: $6,163 in state, $15,428 out of state

Selectivity: Less selective	**Room/board:** $9,310
Acceptance rate: 85%	**Average debt:** $22,649
Student/faculty ratio: 17/1	**Proportion who borrowed:** 60%

UNDERGRADUATE STUDENT BODY STATS

2009-2010 enrollment: 3,899 full-time; 2,044 part-time. Men: 40%; women: 60%. **Ethnic makeup:** African American: 6%; Asian American: 2%; Hispanic: 2%; White: 89%.

ADMISSIONS FACTS AND FIGURES

Phone: (812) 941-2212. **Email:** admissions@ius.edu. **Website:** http://www.ius.edu. **Application deadlines for fall 2011:** Regular decision: Rolling. Early decision: Not offered. Early action: Not offered. Admission can be deferred. **Application fee:** $30. **To apply online, go to:** http://www.ius.edu/apply. **Admissions requirements/recommendations:** High school units required (recommended): English: 4; Mathematics: 3 (4); Science: 1 (2); Foreign language: (2); Social studies: 2; History: (1); Academic electives: 4; Total units: 14 (19). Tests: The college uses SAT or ACT scores in admissions decisions. Either SAT or ACT required. For admission to the fall 2011 entering class, the school will accept: ACT with writing required. Campus visit: Recommended. Admissions interview: Recommended. Off-campus interview: Not available. **Factors that count in admissions decisions: *Academic:*** Secondary school record: Very Important. Class rank: Very Important. Letters of recommendation: Considered. Standardized test scores: Important. Essay: Not Considered. ***Nonacademic:*** Interview: Considered. Extracurricular activities: Not Considered. Talent/ability: Not Considered. Character/personal qualities: Not Considered. Alumni/ae relationship: Not Considered. Geographical residence: Not Considered. State residency: Not Considered. Religious affiliation/commitment: Not Considered. Minority status: Not Considered. Volunteer work: Not Considered. Work experience: Not Considered. **Admissions statistics for the fall 2009 entering class:** Total applicants: 1,985. Total accepted: 1,688. Freshmen enrolled: 1,094; 23% were from out of state. Overall acceptance rate: 85%. **Credentials of fall 2009 freshmen:** 6% ranked in the top 10 percent of their high school class; 27% were in the top 25 percent; 64% were in the top half. (Proportion submitting class standing: 73%.) **Average high school grade point average:** 2.9. **First-year students who submitted SAT scores:** 64%. Scores (25/75 percentile): Critical Reading: 420-520, Math: 420-520, Combined: 840-1040. **First-year students submitting ACT scores:** 39%. Scores (25/75 percentile): English: 16-22, Math: 16-21, Composite: 17-22.

ACADEMICS

Year founded: 1941. **Academic calendar:** Semester. **Degrees offered:** certificate, associate, bachelor's, post-bachelor's certificate, master's. **Most popular majors:** 24% business, management, marketing, and related support services, 21% liberal arts and sciences studies, and humanities, 13% education, 8% health professions and related clinical sciences, 6% communication, journalism, and related programs. **Major fields of study:** area, ethnic, cultural, and gender studies; biological and biomedical sciences; business, management, marketing, and related support services; communication, journalism, and related programs; computer and information sciences and support services; education; English language and literature/letters; foreign languages, literatures, and linguistics; health professions and related clinical sciences; history; liberal arts and sciences studies, and humanities; mathematics and statistics; philosophy and religious studies; physical sciences; psychology; security and protective services; social sciences; visual and performing arts. **Areas of required coursework:** arts/fine arts, humanities, computer literacy, mathematics, English (including composition), philosophy, sciences (biological or physical), social science. **Pre-professional programs:** pre-law, pre-dentistry, pre-medicine, pre-optometry. **Special academic programs:** accelerated program, cross-registration, distance learning, double major, dual enrollment, external degree program, honors program, independent study, internships, student-designed major, study abroad, teacher certificate program, weekend college, other. **Teacher certification offered in:** special education, elementary, secondary. **Reserve Officers Training Corps (ROTC):** Army ROTC: Offered at cooperating institution (University of Louisville); Air Force ROTC: Offered at cooperating institution (University of Louisville). **Faculty and instruction (2009-2010):** Total instructional faculty: 200 full-time, 265 part-time (50% men; 50% women; 12% minorities). Full-time faculty with Ph.D. or other terminal degree: 72%. Student/faculty ratio: 17/1. Classes of fewer than 20 students: 31%; of 20 to 49 students: 68%; of 50 or more students: 1%. **Advanced Placement and International Baccalaureate credit:** AP tests may be used for: Credit only. Scores accepted: 3, 4, 5. **Freshmen returning for sophomore year:** 61%. **Graduation rates:** Four-year: 8%; five-year: 19%; six-year: 29%.

COSTS AND FINANCIAL AID

Financial aid office: (812) 941-2246. **Expenses (2010-2011):** Tuition and fees 2010-2011: $6,163 in state, $15,428 out of state; room/board: $9,310. Estimated books and supplies: $1,100; transportation: $700; personal expenses: $2,030. **Financial aid:** Priority filing date for institution's financial aid form: March 1. In 2009-2010, 81% of undergraduates applied for financial aid. Of those, 64% were determined to have financial need; 5% had their need fully met. Average financial aid package (proportion receiving): $7,611 (62%). Average amount of gift aid, such as scholarships or grants (proportion receiving): $6,010 (51%). Average amount of self-help aid, such as work study or loans (proportion receiving): $3,793 (42%). Average need-based loan (excluding PLUS or other private loans): $3,793. Among students who received need-based aid, the average percentage of need met: 92%. Among students who received aid based on merit, the average award (and the proportion receiving): $1,482 (5%). The average athletic scholarship (and the proportion receiving): $1,085 (1%). Average amount of debt of borrowers graduating in 2009: $22,649. Proportion who borrowed: 60%.

CAMPUS LIFE AND EXTRACURRICULAR ACTIVITIES

Campus housing available: coed dorms. Activities include: choral groups, concert band, drama/theater, literary magazine, music ensembles, student government, student newspaper, symphony orchestra. Number of fraternities: 2; sororities: 4. **Sports program (2009-2010):** Member of NAIA. *Men's intercollegiate varsity sports:* baseball, basketball, tennis. *Women's intercollegiate varsity sports:* basketball, softball, tennis, volleyball.

SERVICES AND FACILITIES

Basic services: placement service, day care. **Remedial assistance:** reading, math, writing, study skills, other. **Counseling services:** career, personal, academic, psychological. **For learning-disabled students:** School does not offer a structured program with separate admission and additional fees. Services include: remedial math, remedial English, reading machines, remedial reading, other special classes, untimed tests, note-taking services, special bookstore section, oral tests, readers, tutors, other. **Information technology resources:** Students are not required to lease or own a computer. Number of campus computers available to all students: 830. **Campus safety:** Security services offered: 24-hour foot-and-vehicle patrols, 24-hour emergency telephones, lighted pathways/sidewalks.

TRANSFER AND INTERNATIONAL STUDENTS

Transfer students: May apply for admission for the following academic terms: Fall, Spring, Summer. Applicants need a minimum number of credits to apply. For fall 2009: Transfer applications received: 1,013. Transfer applicants offered admission: 740. Transfer applicants enrolled: 533. **International students:** Number of foreign undergraduates: 25. Number of countries represented: 12. Minimum TOEFL score required: 530 (paper); 197 (computer).

Indiana Wesleyan University

- **Address:** 4201 S. Washington Street, Marion, IN 46953-4999
- **Website:** http://www.indwes.edu
- **Private; Religious affiliation:** Wesleyan Church
- **Enrollment:** 2,980 full-time; 265 part-time

KEY STATS

✔ **U.S News College Ranking:** 28, Regional Universities (Midwest)
✔ **SAT Score (25th/75th percentile):** 960-1180
✔ **Tuition:** 2010-2011: $21,214

Selectivity: Selective	**Room/board:** $7,008
Acceptance rate: 76%	**Average debt:** $26,847
Student/faculty ratio: 14/1	**Proportion who borrowed:** 75%

UNDERGRADUATE STUDENT BODY STATS

2009-2010 enrollment: 2,980 full-time; 265 part-time. Men: 37%; women: 63%. **Ethnic makeup:** African American: 1%; Asian American: 1%; Hispanic: 2%; White: 96%. **Religious preference:** Protestant: 75%; No preference: 2%; Unknown: 3%; Wesleyan Church: 20%.

ADMISSIONS FACTS AND FIGURES

Phone: (800) 332-6901. **Email:** admissions@indwes.edu. **Website:** http://www.indwes.edu. **Application deadlines for fall 2011:** Regular decision: Rolling. Early decision: Not offered. Early action: Not offered. Admission can be deferred. **Application fee:** $25. To apply online, go to: http://cas.indwes.edu/Admissions/Apply/. **Admissions requirements/recommendations:** High school units required (recommended): English: (8); Mathematics: (8); Science: (6); Foreign language: (4); Social studies: (6); History: (0); Academic electives: (6); Total units: 0 (40). Tests: The college uses SAT or ACT scores in admissions decisions. Either SAT or ACT required. For admission to the fall 2011 entering class, the school will accept: ACT with writing recommended. Campus visit: Recommended. Admissions interview: Neither required nor recommended. Off-campus interview: Not available. **Factors that count in admissions decisions:** *Academic:* Secondary school record: Important. Class rank: Important. Letters of recommendation: Very Important. Standardized test scores: Very Important. Essay: Considered. *Nonacademic:* Interview: Considered. Extracurricular activities: Considered. Talent/ability: Considered. Character/personal qualities: Very Important. Alumni/ae relationship: Considered. Geographical residence: Not Considered. State residency: Not Considered. Religious affiliation/commitment: Considered. Minority status: Not Considered. Volunteer work: Considered. Work experience: Considered. **Other schools with the greatest overlap in applicants:** Ball State University; Bethel College; Olivet Nazarene University; Purdue University–West Lafayette; Taylor University. **Admissions statistics for the fall 2009 entering class:** Total applicants: 2,676. Total accepted: 2,034. Freshmen enrolled: 762; 50% were from out of state. Overall acceptance rate: 76%. **Size of waiting list:** 0 applicants; enrolled from waiting list: 0. **Credentials of fall 2009 freshmen:** 29% ranked in the top 10 percent of their high school class; 56% were in the top 25 percent; 82% were in the top half. (Proportion submitting class standing: 81%.) **Average high school grade point average:** 3.5. **First-year students who submitted SAT scores:** 63%. Scores (25/75 percentile): Critical Reading: 480-590, Math: 480-590, Combined: 960-1180. **First-year students submitting ACT scores:** 63%. Scores (25/75 percentile): English: 21-28, Math: 20-26, Composite: 21-27.

ACADEMICS

Year founded: 1920. **Academic calendar:** Semester. **Degrees offered:** certificate, associate, bachelor's. **Most popular majors:** 18% nursing/registered nurse training (R.N., A.S.N., B.S.N., M.S.N.), 9% elementary education and teaching, 7% business administration and management, 3% marketing/marketing management, 3% psychology. **Major fields of study:** biological and biomedical sciences; business, management, marketing, and related support services; communication, journalism, and related programs; computer and information sciences and support services; education; English language and literature/letters; foreign languages, literatures, and linguistics; health professions and related clinical sciences; history; liberal arts and sciences studies, and humanities; mathematics and statistics; multi/interdisciplinary studies; parks, recreation, leisure, and fitness studies; philosophy and religious studies; physical sciences; psychology; public administration and social service professions; science technologies/technicians; security and protective services; social sciences; theology and religious vocations; visual and performing arts. **Areas of required coursework:** arts/

fine arts, humanities, computer literacy, mathematics, English (including composition), philosophy, foreign languages, sciences (biological or physical), history, social science, other. **Pre-professional programs:** pre-law, pre-dentistry, pre-medicine, pre-theology, pre-veterinary science, other. **Special academic programs (% participation):** cross-registration (1%), double major (23%), dual enrollment (5%), honors program (3%), independent study (1%), internships (20%), study abroad (1%). **Teacher certification offered in:** special education, elementary, middle/junior high, secondary, bilingual/bicultural. **Reserve Officers Training Corps (ROTC):** Army ROTC: Offered on campus. **Faculty and instruction (2009-2010):** Total instructional faculty: 170 full-time, 128 part-time (58% men; 42% women; 7% minorities). Full-time faculty with Ph.D. or other terminal degree: 61%. Student/faculty ratio: 14/1. Classes of fewer than 20 students: %; of 20 to 49 students: %; of 50 or more students: %. **Advanced Placement and International Baccalaureate credit:** AP tests may be used for: Credit only. **Freshmen returning for sophomore year:** 81%. **Graduation rates:** Four-year: 55%; five-year: 66%; six-year: 70%.

COSTS AND FINANCIAL AID

Financial aid office: (765) 677-2116. **Expenses (2010-2011):** Tuition and fees 2010-2011: $21,214; room/board: $7,008. Estimated books and supplies: $1,266; transportation: $450; personal expenses: $1,456. **Financial aid:** Priority filing date for institution's financial aid form: March 1. In 2009-2010, 96% of undergraduates applied for financial aid. Of those, 72% were determined to have financial need; 31% had their need fully met. Average financial aid package (proportion receiving): $15,739 (71%). Average amount of gift aid, such as scholarships or grants (proportion receiving): $12,529 (66%). Average amount of self-help aid, such as work study or loans (proportion receiving): $3,849 (58%). Average need-based loan (excluding PLUS or other private loans): $4,203. Among students who received need-based aid, the average percentage of need met: 74%. Among students who received aid based on merit, the average award (and the proportion receiving): $5,450 (20%). The average athletic scholarship (and the proportion receiving): $5,840 (4%). Average amount of debt of borrowers graduating in 2009: $26,847. Proportion who borrowed: 75%.

CAMPUS LIFE AND EXTRACURRICULAR ACTIVITIES

Campus housing available (% using): women's dorms (50%), men's dorms (31%), apartment for single students (19%), other housing options. Students who live in college-owned, operated, or affiliated housing: 78%. **Student employment:** During the 2009-2010 academic year, 22% of undergraduates worked on campus. Average per-year earnings: $3,800. **Clubs and organizations:** Number of student organizations: 36. Activities include: campus ministries, choral groups, concert band, drama/theater, international student organization, jazz band, literary magazine, model UN, music ensembles, musical theater, opera, pep band, radio station, student government, student newspaper, student film society, symphony orchestra, television station, yearbook. Number of fraternities: 0; sororities: 0. Average proportion of students who stay on campus on weekends: 60%. **Sports program (2009-2010):** Member of NAIA. **Men's intercollegiate varsity sports:** baseball, basketball, cross country, golf, soccer, tennis, track and field (indoor), track and field (outdoor). **Women's intercollegiate varsity sports:** basketball, cross country, soccer, softball, tennis, track and field (indoor), track and field (outdoor), volleyball.

SERVICES AND FACILITIES

Basic services: nonremedial tutoring, placement service, health service. **Remedial assistance:** reading, math, writing, study skills, other. **Counseling services:** minority student, career, personal, academic, older student, psychological, religious. **For learning-disabled students:** School does not offer a structured program with separate admission and additional fees. Total undergraduates in learning-disabled program or receiving services: 59. Services include: note-taking services, readers, extended time for tests, tutors, priority seating, exams on tape or computer. **Library:** Number of titles: 168,362; number of current serial subscriptions: 85,496. **Information technology resources:** Students are not required to lease or own a computer. Number of campus computers available to all students: 691. School has a wireless network. Approximate number of users that can be accommodated: 5,000. Proportion of college-owned housing units wired for high-speed internet access: 100%. **Campus safety:** Security services offered: 24-hour foot-and-vehicle patrols, late-night transport/escort service, 24-hour emergency telephones, lighted pathways/sidewalks, controlled dormitory access (key, security card, etc).

TRANSFER AND INTERNATIONAL STUDENTS

Transfer students: May apply for admission for the following academic terms: Fall, Spring, Summer. Applicants need a minimum number of credits to apply. For fall 2009: Transfer applications received: 528. Transfer applicants offered admission: 223. Transfer applicants enrolled: 143. **International students:** Number of foreign undergraduates: 6. Number of countries represented: 16. Minimum TOEFL score required: 550 (paper); 213 (computer). Average TOEFL score: 555 (paper).

Manchester College

- **Address:** 604 E. College Avenue, North Manchester, IN 46962
- **Website:** http://www.manchester.edu
- **Private; Religious affiliation:** Church of the Brethren
- **Enrollment:** 1,182 full-time; 41 part-time

KEY STATS

✔ **U.S News College Ranking:** 18, Regional Colleges (Midwest)
✔ **SAT Score (25th/75th percentile):** 880-1120
✔ **Tuition:** 2010-2011: $24,920

Selectivity: Selective	**Room/board:** $8,860
Acceptance rate: 77%	**Average debt:** $16,235
Student/faculty ratio: 16/1	**Proportion who borrowed:** 80%

UNDERGRADUATE STUDENT BODY STATS

2009-2010 enrollment: 1,182 full-time; 41 part-time. Men: 49%; women: 51%. **Ethnic makeup:** African American: 3%; American-Indian: 1%; Asian American: 1%; Hispanic: 2%; White: 90%; International: 3%. **Religious preference:** Roman Catholic: 12%; Protestant: 31%; No preference: 3%; Unknown: 33%; Church of the Brethren: 8%; Other: 1%.

ADMISSIONS FACTS AND FIGURES

Phone: (800) 852-3648. **Email:** admitinfo@manchester.edu. **Website:** http://www.manchester.edu. **Application deadlines for fall 2011:** Regular decision: Rolling. Early decision: Not offered. Early action: Not offered. Admission can be deferred. **Application fee:** $25. **To apply online, go to:** http://www.manchester.edu/admissions/admissions/index.htm. **Admissions requirements/recommendations:** High school units required (recommended): English: 4 (4); Mathematics: 3 (4); Science: 2 (3); Foreign language: 2 (2); Social studies: 1 (1); History: 1 (1); Total units: 13 (15). Tests: The college uses SAT or ACT scores in admissions decisions. Either SAT or ACT required. For admission to the fall 2011 entering class, the school will accept: ACT with writing recommended. Campus visit: Recommended. Admissions interview: Neither required nor recommended. Off-campus interview: May be arranged. **Factors that count in admissions decisions:** *Academic:* Secondary school record: Very Important. Class rank: Very Important. Letters of recommendation: Very Important. Standardized test scores: Very Important. Essay: Not Considered. *Nonacademic:* Extracurricular activities: Considered. Talent/ability: Not Considered. Character/personal qualities: Considered. Alumni/ae relationship: Not Considered. Geographical residence: Not Considered. State residency: Not Considered. Religious affiliation/commitment: Not Considered. Minority status: Not Considered. Volunteer work: Considered. Work experience: Considered. **Other schools with the greatest overlap in applicants:** Anderson University; Ball State University; Hanover College; Indiana University-Purdue University–Fort Wayne; University of Indianapolis. **Admissions statistics for the fall 2009 entering class:** Total applicants: 2,991. Total accepted: 2,292. Freshmen enrolled: 426; 11% were from out of state. Overall acceptance rate: 77%. **Credentials of fall 2009 freshmen:** 20% ranked in the top 10 percent of their high school class; 54% were in the top 25 percent; 85% were in the top half. (Proportion submitting class standing: 87%.) **Average high school grade point average:** 3.3. **First-year students who submitted SAT scores:** 87%. Scores (25/75 percentile): Critical Reading: 430-550, Math: 450-570, Combined: 880-1120. **First-year students submitting ACT scores:** 32%. Scores (25/75 percentile): English: 16-25, Math: 18-25, Composite: 18-25.

ACADEMICS

Year founded: 1889. **Academic calendar:** 4-1-4. **Degrees offered:** associate, bachelor's, master's. **Most popular majors:** 27% business, management, marketing, and related support services, 17% education, 12% health professions and related clinical sciences, 6% psychology, 6% social sciences. **Major fields of study:** biological and biomedical sciences; business, management, marketing, and related support services; communication, journalism, and related programs; computer and information sciences and support services; education; engineering; English language and literature/letters; foreign languages, literatures, and linguistics; health professions and related clinical sciences; history; mathematics and statistics; multi/interdisciplinary studies; natural resources and conservation; philosophy and religious studies; physical sciences; psychology; public administration and social service professions; social sciences; visual and performing arts. **Areas of required coursework:** arts/fine arts, humanities, mathematics, English (including composition), philosophy, sciences (biological or physical), history, social science, other. **Pre-professional programs:** pre-law, pre-dentistry, pre-medicine, pre-theology, pre-veterinary science, other. **Special academic programs:** accelerated program, distance learning, double major, dual enrollment, exchange student program (domestic), honors program, independent study, internships, liberal arts/career combination, student-designed major, study abroad, teacher certificate program. **Teacher certification offered in:** early childhood, special education, elementary, middle/junior high, secondary, bilingual/bicultural. **Faculty and instruction (2009-2010):** Total instructional faculty: 68 full-time, 26 part-time (54% men; 46% women; 6% minorities). Full-time faculty with Ph.D. or other terminal degree: 81%. Student/faculty ratio: 16/1. Classes of fewer than 20 students: 50%; of 20 to 49 students: 49%; of 50 or more students: 1%. **Advanced Placement and International Baccalaureate credit:** AP tests may be used for: Credit and/or placement. Scores accepted: 3, 4, 5. International Baccalaureate exams may be used for: Placement only. **Freshmen returning for sophomore year:** 69%. **Graduation rates:** Four-year: 38%; five-year: 48%; six-year: 53%. **Graduate study:** 18% of students pursue further study within one year. Fields in which graduates pursue further study: Master of Business Administration (MBA), 14%; law, 6%; medicine, 6%; dentistry, 9%; theology (or the seminary), 3%; education, 9%; arts and sciences, 54%.

COSTS AND FINANCIAL AID
Financial aid office: (260) 982-5066. **Expenses (2010-2011):** Tuition and fees 2010-2011: $24,920; room/board: $8,860. Estimated books and supplies: $1,000; transportation: $680; personal expenses: $805. **Financial aid:** Priority filing date for institution's financial aid form: March 1. In 2009-2010, 94% of undergraduates applied for financial aid. Of those, 84% were determined to have financial need; 32% had their need fully met. Average financial aid package (proportion receiving): $21,729 (84%). Average amount of gift aid, such as scholarships or grants (proportion receiving): $16,881 (78%). Average amount of self-help aid, such as work study or loans (proportion receiving): $4,218 (73%). Average need-based loan (excluding PLUS or other private loans): $6,024. Among students who received need-based aid, the average percentage of need met: 92%. Among students who received aid based on merit, the average award (and the proportion receiving): $10,470 (9%). Average amount of debt of borrowers graduating in 2009: $16,235. Proportion who borrowed: 80%.

CAMPUS LIFE AND EXTRACURRICULAR ACTIVITIES
Campus housing available: coed dorms, apartments for married students, apartment for single students, special housing for disabled students. Students who live in college-owned, operated, or affiliated housing: 75%. **Student employment:** During the 2009-2010 academic year, 38% of undergraduates worked on campus. Average per-year earnings: $1,679. **Clubs and organizations:** Number of student organizations: 60. Activities include: campus ministries, choral groups, concert band, dance, drama/theater, international student organization, jazz band, literary magazine, model UN, music ensembles, opera, pep band, radio station, student government, student newspaper, symphony orchestra, yearbook. Number of fraternities: 0; sororities: 0. Average proportion of students who stay on campus on weekends: 75%. **Sports program (2009-2010):** Member of NCAA III. *Men's intercollegiate varsity sports:* baseball, basketball, cross country, football, golf, soccer, tennis, track and field (outdoor), wrestling. *Women's intercollegiate varsity sports:* basketball, cross country, golf, soccer, softball, tennis, track and field (outdoor), volleyball.

SERVICES AND FACILITIES
Basic services: nonremedial tutoring, placement service, health service, health insurance. **Remedial assistance:** reading, math, writing, study skills. **Counseling services:** minority student, career, personal, academic, psychological, birth control, religious. **For learning-disabled students:** School does not offer a structured program with separate admission and additional fees. Total undergraduates in learning-disabled program or receiving services: 55. Services include: tape recorders, untimed tests, note-taking services, oral tests, learning center, readers, extended time for tests, tutors, priority seating, texts on tape, other testing accommodations. **Library:** Number of titles: 180,895; number of current serial subscriptions: 595. **Information**

technology resources: Students are not required to lease or own a computer. Number of campus computers available to all students: 222. School has a wireless network. Approximate number of users that can be accommodated: 1,400. Proportion of college-owned housing units wired for high-speed internet access: 100%. **Campus safety:** Security services offered: 24-hour foot-and-vehicle patrols, late-night transport/escort service, 24-hour emergency telephones, lighted pathways/sidewalks, controlled dormitory access (key, security card, etc).

TRANSFER AND INTERNATIONAL STUDENTS
Transfer students: May apply for admission for the following academic terms: Fall, Winter, Spring, Summer. Applicants do not need a minimum number of credits to apply. For fall 2009: Transfer applications received: 93. Transfer applicants offered admission: 39. Transfer applicants enrolled: 25. **International students:** Number of foreign undergraduates: 40 (3% of student body). Number of countries represented: 17. Minimum TOEFL score required: 550 (paper); 213 (computer). Average TOEFL score: 550 (paper).

Marian University

- **Address:** 3200 Cold Spring Road, Indianapolis, IN 46222
- **Website:** http://www.marian.edu
- **Private; Religious affiliation:** Roman Catholic
- **Enrollment:** 1,488 full-time; 550 part-time

KEY STATS
✔ **U.S News College Ranking:** 41, Regional Colleges (Midwest)
✔ **SAT Score (25th/75th percentile):** 900-1100
✔ **Tuition:** 2009-2010: $24,000

Selectivity: Selective	**Room/board:** $7,512
Acceptance rate: 54%	**Average debt:** N/A
Student/faculty ratio: 14/1	**Proportion who borrowed:** N/A

UNDERGRADUATE STUDENT BODY STATS
2009-2010 enrollment: 1,488 full-time; 550 part-time. Men: 36%; women: 64%. **Ethnic makeup:** African American: 18%; Asian American: 1%; Hispanic: 3%; White: 77%. **Religious preference:** Protestant: 32%; No preference: 1%; Unknown: 31%; Roman Catholic: 35%; Other: 1%.

ADMISSIONS FACTS AND FIGURES
Phone: (317) 955-6300. **Email:** admissions@marian.edu. **Website:** http://www.marian.edu. **Application deadlines for fall 2011:** Regular decision: August 1. Early decision: Not offered. Early action: Not offered. Admission can be deferred. **Application fee:** $35. **To apply online, go to:** http://www.marian.edu/Admission/Pages/ApplyOnline.aspx. **Admissions requirements/recommendations:** High school units required (recommended): English: 4 (4); Mathematics: 2 (3); Science: 2 (3); Foreign language: 1 (2); Social studies: 1 (1); History: 1 (1); Academic electives: 9 (8); Total units: 20 (20). Tests: The college uses SAT or ACT scores in admissions decisions. Either SAT or ACT required. For admission to the fall 2011 entering class, the school will accept: ACT with writing required. Campus visit: Recommended. Admissions interview: Recommended. Off-campus interview: May be arranged. **Factors that count in admissions decisions:** *Academic:* Secondary school record: Important. Class rank: Important. Letters of recommendation: Important. Standardized test scores: Very Important. Essay: Considered. *Nonacademic:* Interview: Considered. Extracurricular activities: Considered. Talent/ability: Considered. Character/personal qualities: Considered. Alumni/ae relationship: Considered. Geographical residence: Not Considered. State residency: Not Considered. Religious affiliation/commitment: Not Considered. Minority status: Not Considered. Volunteer work: Considered. Work experience: Not Considered. **Other schools with the greatest overlap in applicants:** Ball State University; Franklin College; Indiana University–Bloomington; Indiana University-Purdue University–Indianapolis; University of Indianapolis. **Admissions statistics for the fall 2009 entering class:** Total applicants: 1,858. Total accepted: 1,002. Freshmen enrolled: 330; 11% were from out of state. Overall acceptance rate: 54%. **Credentials of fall 2009 freshmen:** 10% ranked in the top 10 percent of their high school class; 28% were in the top 25 percent; 67% were in the top half. (Proportion submitting class standing: 78%.) **Average high school grade point average:** 3.2. **First-year students who submitted SAT scores:** 81%. Scores (25/75 percentile): Critical Reading: 450-540, Math: 450-560,

Combined: 900-1100. **First-year students submitting ACT scores:** 49%.
Scores (25/75 percentile): English: N/A, Math: N/A, Composite: 19-23.

ACADEMICS

Year founded: 1851. **Academic calendar:** Semester. **Degrees offered:** associate, bachelor's, master's. **Most popular majors:** 44% business, management, marketing, and related support services, 20% health professions and related clinical sciences, 7% education, 5% biological and biomedical sciences, 4% psychology. **Major fields of study:** biological and biomedical sciences; business, management, marketing, and related support services; communication, journalism, and related programs; education; English language and literature/letters; foreign languages, literatures, and linguistics; health professions and related clinical sciences; history; mathematics and statistics; parks, recreation, leisure, and fitness studies; philosophy and religious studies; physical sciences; psychology; science technologies/technicians; social sciences; theology and religious vocations; visual and performing arts. **Areas of required coursework:** humanities, mathematics, English (including composition), philosophy, foreign languages, sciences (biological or physical), history, social science, other. **Pre-professional programs:** pre-law, pre-dentistry, pre-medicine, pre-theology, pre-veterinary science, pre-optometry, pre-pharmacy. **Special academic programs (% participation):** accelerated program (5%), cooperative (work-study plan) program (10%), cross-registration (5%), double major (12%), dual enrollment (3%), honors program (8%), independent study (12%), internships (34%), study abroad (5%), teacher certificate program (20%). **Teacher certification offered in:** special education, elementary, middle/junior high, secondary, bilingual/bicultural. **Cooperative education programs:** art, business, computer science, education, health professions, humanities, natural science, social/behavioral science. **Reserve Officers Training Corps (ROTC):** Army ROTC: Offered on campus. **Faculty and instruction (2009-2010):** Total instructional faculty: 86 full-time, 116 part-time (41% men; 59% women; 12% minorities). Full-time faculty with Ph.D. or other terminal degree: 52%. Student/faculty ratio: 14/1. Classes of fewer than 20 students: 61%; of 20 to 49 students: 38%; of 50 or more students: 1%. **Advanced Placement and International Baccalaureate credit:** AP tests may be used for: Credit and/or placement. Scores accepted: 3, 4, 5. International Baccalaureate exams may be used for: Placement only. **Freshmen returning for sophomore year:** 74%. **Graduation rates:** Four-year: 32%; five-year: 47%; six-year: 49%. **Graduate study:** 10% of students pursue further study immediately upon graduation; 18% within one year. Fields in which graduates pursue further study: Master of Business Administration (MBA), 10%; law, 10%; medicine, 6%; dentistry, 2%; theology (or the seminary), 8%; education, 20%; arts and sciences, 42%; veterinary medicine, 2%.

COSTS AND FINANCIAL AID

Financial aid office: (317) 955-6040. **Expenses (2009-2010):** Tuition and fees 2009-2010: $24,000; room/board: $7,512. Estimated books and supplies: $800 personal expenses: $4,600. **Financial aid:** Priority filing date for institution's financial aid form: March 10.

CAMPUS LIFE AND EXTRACURRICULAR ACTIVITIES

Campus housing available (% using): coed dorms (90%), apartments for married students (0%), apartment for single students (4%), cooperative housing (2%), other housing options (4%). Students who live in college-owned, operated, or affiliated housing: 49%. **Student employment:** During the 2009-2010 academic year, 28% of undergraduates worked on campus. Average per-year earnings: $3,000. **Clubs and organizations:** Number of student organizations: 39. Activities include: campus ministries, choral groups, concert band, dance, drama/theater, international student organization, jazz band, literary magazine, marching band, music ensembles, musical theater, pep band, student government, student newspaper, yearbook. Number of fraternities: 0; sororities: 0. Average proportion of students who stay on campus on weekends: 70%. **Sports program (2009-2010):** Member of NAIA. *Men's intercollegiate varsity sports:* baseball, basketball, cross country, football, golf, soccer, tennis, track and field (indoor), track and field (outdoor). *Women's intercollegiate varsity sports:* basketball, cross country, golf, soccer, softball, tennis, track and field (indoor), track and field (outdoor), volleyball.

SERVICES AND FACILITIES

Basic services: nonremedial tutoring, placement service, health service, health insurance. **Remedial assistance:** reading, math, writing, study skills. **Counseling services:** minority student, career, personal, veteran student, academic, psychological, religious. **For learning-disabled students:** School does not offer a structured program with separate admission and additional fees. Services include: remedial math, remedial English, reading machines, remedial reading, tape recorders, other special classes, diagnostic test-

ing service, untimed tests, note-taking services, learning center, readers, extended time for tests, tutors, typist/scribe, other testing accommodations. **Library:** Number of titles: 102,500; number of current serial subscriptions: 950. **Information technology resources:** Students are not required to lease or own a computer. Number of campus computers available to all students: 300. School has a wireless network. Approximate number of users that can be accommodated: 800. Proportion of college-owned housing units wired for high-speed internet access: 100%. **Campus safety:** Security services offered: 24-hour foot-and-vehicle patrols, late-night transport/escort service, lighted pathways/sidewalks, controlled dormitory access (key, security card, etc).

TRANSFER AND INTERNATIONAL STUDENTS

Transfer students: May apply for admission for the following academic terms: Fall, Spring, Summer. Applicants need a minimum number of credits to apply. For fall 2009: Transfer applicants enrolled: 154. **International students:** Number of foreign undergraduates: 4. Number of countries represented: 5. Minimum TOEFL score required: 530 (paper); 213 (computer). Average TOEFL score: 550 (paper).

Martin University

■ **Address:** PO Box 18567, 2171 Avondale Place, Indianapolis, IN 46218
■ **Website:** http://www.martin.edu
■ **Private**
■ **Enrollment:** N/A

KEY STATS

✔ **U.S News College Ranking:** Unranked, National Liberal Arts Colleges
✔ **SAT or ACT Score (25th/75th percentile):** N/A
✔ **Tuition:** 2009-2010: $13,520

Selectivity: N/A	**Room/board:** N/A
Acceptance rate: N/A	**Average debt:** N/A
Student/faculty ratio: N/A	**Proportion who borrowed:** N/A

Oakland City University

■ **Address:** 138 N. Lucretia Street, Oakland City, IN 47660
■ **Website:** http://www.oak.edu
■ **Private; Religious affiliation:** General Association of General Baptist
■ **Enrollment:** 1,225 full-time; 1,154 part-time

KEY STATS

✔ **U.S News College Ranking:** second tier, Regional Universities (Midwest)
✔ **SAT Score (25th/75th percentile):** 820-1045
✔ **Tuition:** 2009-2010: $15,410

Selectivity: Less selective	**Room/board:** $6,228
Acceptance rate: 77%	**Average debt:** N/A
Student/faculty ratio: N/A	**Proportion who borrowed:** N/A

UNDERGRADUATE STUDENT BODY STATS

2009-2010 enrollment: 1,225 full-time; 1,154 part-time. Men: 45%; women: 55%. **Ethnic makeup:** African American: 12%; Hispanic: 2%; White: 85%. **Religious preference:** Roman Catholic: 10%; Protestant: 34%; Unknown: 24%; General Association of General Baptist: 18%.

ADMISSIONS FACTS AND FIGURES

Phone: (800) 737-5125. **Email:** ocuadmit@oak.edu. **Website:** http://www.oak.edu. **Application deadlines for fall 2011:** Regular decision: August 1. Early decision: Not offered. Early action: Not offered. Admission can be deferred. **Application fee:** $35. **To apply online, go to:** https://bookstore.oak.edu/application/index.asp?AppKey=S6TYYQADM6TI1. **Admissions requirements/recommendations:** High school units required (recommended): English: 4 (4); Mathematics: 3 (3); Science: 3 (3); Foreign language: 0 (0); Social studies: 2 (2); History: 0 (0); Academic electives: 0 (0); Total units: 12 (12). Tests: The college uses SAT or ACT scores in admissions decisions. Either SAT or ACT required. For admission to the fall 2011 entering class, the school will accept: ACT with or without writing accepted. Campus visit: Required. Admissions interview: Required. Off-campus interview: May be arranged. **Factors that count in admissions decisions:** *Academic:*

Secondary school record: Very Important. Class rank: Considered. Letters of recommendation: Not Considered. Standardized test scores: Very Important. Essay: Not Considered. **Nonacademic:** Interview: Considered. Extracurricular activities: Not Considered. Talent/ability: Not Considered. Character/personal qualities: Important. Alumni/ae relationship: Considered. Geographical residence: Not Considered. State residency: Not Considered. Religious affiliation/commitment: Not Considered. Minority status: Not Considered. Volunteer work: Not Considered. Work experience: Not Considered. **Admissions statistics for the fall 2009 entering class:** Total applicants: 562. Total accepted: 431. Freshmen enrolled: 320; Overall acceptance rate: 77%. **Size of waiting list:** 0 applicants; enrolled from waiting list: 0. **Credentials of fall 2009 freshmen:** 15% ranked in the top 10 percent of their high school class; 37% were in the top 25 percent; 65% were in the top half. (Proportion submitting class standing: 64%.) **First-year students who submitted SAT scores:** 70%. Scores (25/75 percentile): Critical Reading: 400-515, Math: 420-530, Combined: 820-1045. **First-year students submitting ACT scores:** 40%. Scores (25/75 percentile): English: 18-24, Math: 17-23, Composite: 17-24.

ACADEMICS

Year founded: 1885. **Academic calendar:** Semester. **Degrees offered:** certificate, associate, bachelor's, master's, doctorate. **Major fields of study:** biological and biomedical sciences; business, management, marketing, and related support services; computer and information sciences and support services; education; English language and literature/letters; liberal arts and sciences studies, and humanities; mathematics and statistics; philosophy and religious studies; security and protective services; social sciences; visual and performing arts. **Areas of required coursework:** arts/fine arts, humanities, computer literacy, mathematics, English (including composition), philosophy, sciences (biological or physical), history, social science. **Special academic programs:** accelerated program, cooperative (work-study plan) program, distance learning, double major, dual enrollment, external degree program, honors program, independent study, internships, liberal arts/career combination, teacher certificate program. **Teacher certification offered in:** early childhood, special education, elementary, secondary. **Advanced Placement and International Baccalaureate credit:** AP tests may be used for: Credit only. Scores accepted: 3. **Freshmen returning for sophomore year:** 71%. **Graduation rates:** Four-year: 42%; five-year: 49%; six-year: 51%. **Graduate study:** 30% of students pursue further study immediately upon graduation. Fields in which graduates pursue further study: Master of Business Administration (MBA), 10%; theology (or the seminary), 10%; education, 10%.

COSTS AND FINANCIAL AID

Financial aid office: (812) 749-1224. **Expenses (2009-2010):** Tuition and fees 2009-2010: $15,410; room/board: $6,228. Estimated books and supplies: $1,950.

CAMPUS LIFE AND EXTRACURRICULAR ACTIVITIES

Campus housing available: women's dorms, men's dorms, apartments for married students, apartment for single students. **Student employment:** During the 2009-2010 academic year, 5% of undergraduates worked on campus. Activities include: campus ministries, choral groups, drama/theater, music ensembles, musical theater, pep band, student government, student newspaper, yearbook. Number of fraternities: 0; sororities: 0. Average proportion of students who stay on campus on weekends: 10%. **Sports program (2009-2010):** Member of NAIA.

SERVICES AND FACILITIES

Remedial assistance: math, writing. **Counseling services:** career, academic, religious. **Library:** Number of titles: 85,430; number of current serial subscriptions: 265. **Information technology resources:** Students are not required to lease or own a computer. Number of campus computers available to all students: 150. School has a wireless network. Proportion of college-owned housing units wired for high-speed internet access: 100%. **Campus safety:** Security services offered: lighted pathways/sidewalks, controlled dormitory access (key, security card, etc).

TRANSFER AND INTERNATIONAL STUDENTS

Transfer students: May apply for admission for the following academic terms: Fall, Spring, Summer. Applicants need a minimum number of credits to apply. For fall 2009: Transfer applications received: 126. Transfer applicants offered admission: 117. Transfer applicants enrolled: 109. **International students:** Number of foreign undergraduates: 2. Minimum TOEFL score required: 500 (paper). Average TOEFL score: 510 (paper).

Purdue University–Calumet

- **Address:** 2200 169th Street, Hammond, IN 46323-2094
- **Website:** http://www.calumet.purdue.edu/
- **Public**
- **Enrollment:** 5,858 full-time; 3,147 part-time

KEY STATS

✔ **U.S News College Ranking:** second tier, Regional Universities (Midwest)
✔ **SAT Score (25th/75th percentile):** 820-1030
✔ **Tuition:** 2009-2010: $6,308 in state, $14,115 out of state
  Selectivity: Less selective   **Room/board:** $7,073
  Acceptance rate: 69%   **Average debt:** $19,926
  Student/faculty ratio: 21/1   **Proportion who borrowed:** 62%

UNDERGRADUATE STUDENT BODY STATS

2009-2010 enrollment: 5,858 full-time; 3,147 part-time. Men: 45%; women: 55%. **Ethnic makeup:** African American: 19%; Asian American: 1%; Hispanic: 15%; White: 61%; International: 3%.

ADMISSIONS FACTS AND FIGURES

Phone: (219) 989-2213. **Email:** adms@calumet.purdue.edu. **Website:** http://www.calumet.purdue.edu/. **Application deadlines for fall 2011:** Regular decision: Rolling. Early decision: Not offered. Early action: Not offered. Admission can be deferred. **To apply online, go to:** http://webs.calumet.purdue.edu/admissions/. **Admissions requirements/recommendations:** High school units required (recommended): English: 4 (4); Mathematics: 2 (2); Science: 1 (2); Foreign language: 2 (2); Social studies: 1 (1); History: 1 (1); Total units: 14 (14). Tests: The college uses SAT or ACT scores in admissions decisions. Either SAT or ACT required. For admission to the fall 2011 entering class, the school will accept: ACT with writing required. Campus visit: Recommended. Admissions interview: Neither required nor recommended. Off-campus interview: Not available. **Factors that count in admissions decisions: Academic:** Secondary school record: Important. Class rank: Important. Letters of recommendation: Not Considered. Standardized test scores: Important. Essay: Not Considered. **Nonacademic:** Interview: Not Considered. Extracurricular activities: Not Considered. Talent/ability: Not Considered. Character/personal qualities: Not Considered. Alumni/ae relationship: Not Considered. Geographical residence: Not Considered. State residency: Not Considered. Religious affiliation/commitment: Not Considered. Minority status: Not Considered. Volunteer work: Not Considered. Work experience: Not Considered. **Other schools with the greatest overlap in applicants:** Ball State University; Indiana University Northwest; Indiana University–Bloomington; Purdue University–West Lafayette; Valparaiso University. **Admissions statistics for the fall 2009 entering class:** Total applicants: 5,884. Total accepted: 4,081. Freshmen enrolled: 1,359; 13% were from out of state. Overall acceptance rate: 69%. **Credentials of fall 2009 freshmen:** 10% ranked in the top 10 percent of their high school class; 28% were in the top 25 percent; 58% were in the top half. (Proportion submitting class standing: 90%.) **First-year students who submitted SAT scores:** 70%. Scores (25/75 percentile): Critical Reading: 410-510, Math: 410-520, Combined: 820-1030. **First-year students submitting ACT scores:** 30%. Scores (25/75 percentile): English: 16-23, Math: 16-23, Composite: N/A.

ACADEMICS

Year founded: 1946. **Academic calendar:** Semester. **Degrees offered:** certificate, associate, transfer-associate, terminal-associate, bachelor's, post-bachelor's certificate, master's, post-master's certificate. **Most popular majors:** 19% business, management, marketing, and related support services, 10% health professions and related clinical sciences, 7% engineering technologies/technicians, 6% communication, journalism, and related programs, 6% social sciences. **Major fields of study:** area, ethnic, cultural, and gender studies; biological and biomedical sciences; business, management, marketing, and related support services; communication, journalism, and related programs; communications technologies/technicians and support services; computer and information sciences and support services; education; engineering; engineering technologies/technicians; English language and literature/letters; family and consumer sciences/human sciences; foreign languages, literatures, and linguistics; health professions and related clinical sciences; history; mathematics and statistics; parks, recreation, leisure, and fitness studies; philosophy and religious studies; physical sciences; psychology; security and protective services; social sciences. **Areas of required coursework:** arts/fine arts, humanities, computer literacy, mathematics,

English (including composition), philosophy, foreign languages, sciences (biological or physical), history, social science. **Pre-professional programs:** pre-law, pre-dentistry, pre-medicine, pre-veterinary science, pre-optometry, pre-pharmacy. **Special academic programs (% participation):** accelerated program, cooperative (work-study plan) program (0%), distance learning, double major, dual enrollment, English as a Second Language (ESL), honors program (0%), independent study, internships (7%), study abroad, teacher certificate program (7%), weekend college. **Teacher certification offered in:** special education, elementary, middle/junior high, secondary. **Cooperative education programs:** engineering, technologies. **Faculty and instruction (2009-2010):** Total instructional faculty: 268 full-time, 250 part-time (53% men; 47% women; 18% minorities). Full-time faculty with Ph.D. or other terminal degree: 69%. Student/faculty ratio: 21/1. Classes of fewer than 20 students: 28%; of 20 to 49 students: 67%; of 50 or more students: 6%. **Advanced Placement and International Baccalaureate credit:** AP tests may be used for: Credit only. Scores accepted: 3, 4, 5. International Baccalaureate exams may be used for: Placement only. **Freshmen returning for sophomore year:** 64%. **Graduation rates:** Four-year: 6%; five-year: 17%; six-year: 22%.

COSTS AND FINANCIAL AID

Financial aid office: (219) 989-2301. **Expenses (2009-2010):** Tuition and fees 2009-2010: $6,308 in state, $14,115 out of state; room/board: $7,073. **Financial aid:** Priority filing date for institution's financial aid form: March 10; deadline: June 30. In 2009-2010, 73% of undergraduates applied for financial aid. Of those, 60% were determined to have financial need; 11% had their need fully met. Average financial aid package (proportion receiving): $6,632 (56%). Average amount of gift aid, such as scholarships or grants (proportion receiving): $4,989 (39%). Average amount of self-help aid, such as work study or loans (proportion receiving): $3,379 (43%). Average need-based loan (excluding PLUS or other private loans): $3,355. Among students who received need-based aid, the average percentage of need met: 12%. Among students who received aid based on merit, the average award (and the proportion receiving): $2,370 (5%). The average athletic scholarship (and the proportion receiving): $2,967 (0%). Average amount of debt of borrowers graduating in 2009: $19,926. Proportion who borrowed: 62%.

CAMPUS LIFE AND EXTRACURRICULAR ACTIVITIES

Campus housing available (% using): apartment for single students (100%). Students who live in college-owned, operated, or affiliated housing: 6%. **Student employment:** During the 2009-2010 academic year, 10% of undergraduates worked on campus. Average per-year earnings: $3,300. **Clubs and organizations:** Number of student organizations: 62. Activities include: campus ministries, choral groups, dance, drama/theater, international student organization, student government, student newspaper. Number of fraternities: 2; sororities: 2. Average proportion of students who stay on campus on weekends: 4%. **Sports program (2009-2010):** Member of NAIA.

SERVICES AND FACILITIES

Basic services: nonremedial tutoring, placement service, day care, health service, health insurance. **Remedial assistance:** reading, math, writing, study skills, other. **Counseling services:** minority student, career, personal, veteran student, academic, older student, psychological, other. **For learning-disabled students:** School does not offer a structured program with separate admission and additional fees. Services include: reading machines, tape recorders, note-taking services, oral tests, readers, extended time for tests, tutors, priority seating, texts on tape, other testing accommodations, other. **Library:** Number of titles: 267,156; number of current serial subscriptions: 1,390. **Information technology resources:** Students are not required to lease or own a computer. Number of campus computers available to all students: 1,300. School has a wireless network. Approximate number of users that can be accommodated: 250. Proportion of college-owned housing units wired for high-speed internet access: 100%. **Campus safety:** Security services offered: 24-hour foot-and-vehicle patrols, 24-hour emergency telephones, lighted pathways/sidewalks, student patrols, controlled dormitory access (key, security card, etc).

TRANSFER AND INTERNATIONAL STUDENTS

Transfer students: May apply for admission for the following academic terms: Fall, Spring, Summer. Applicants need a minimum number of credits to apply. For fall 2009: Transfer applications received: 1,335. Transfer applicants offered admission: 739. Transfer applicants enrolled: 478. **International students:** Number of foreign undergraduates: 277 (3% of student body). Number of countries represented: 27. Minimum TOEFL score required: 550 (paper); 213 (computer). Average TOEFL score: 562 (paper).

Purdue University–North Central

- **Address:** 1401 S. US Highway 421, Westville, IN 46391
- **Website:** http://www.pnc.edu
- **Public**
- **Enrollment:** 2,761 full-time; 1,618 part-time

KEY STATS
✔ **U.S News College Ranking:** second tier, Regional Colleges (Midwest)
✔ **SAT Score (25th/75th percentile):** 840-1060
✔ **Tuition:** 2010-2011: $6,704 in state, $15,960 out of state
Selectivity: Less selective   **Room/board:** N/A
Acceptance rate: 86%   **Average debt:** $20,859
Student/faculty ratio: 18/1   **Proportion who borrowed:** 75%

UNDERGRADUATE STUDENT BODY STATS

2009-2010 enrollment: 2,761 full-time; 1,618 part-time. Men: 43%; women: 57%. **Ethnic makeup:** African American: 7%; American-Indian: 1%; Asian American: 1%; Hispanic: 5%; White: 86%.

ADMISSIONS FACTS AND FIGURES

Phone: (219) 785-5455. **Email:** admissions@pnc.edu. **Website:** http://www.pnc.edu. **Application deadlines for fall 2011:** Regular decision: Rolling. Early decision: Not offered. Early action: Not offered. Admission can be deferred. **Application fee:** None. **To apply online, go to:** http://www.pnc.edu/admissions/applying.html. **Admissions requirements/recommendations:** High school units required (recommended): English: 4 (4); Mathematics: 3 (3); Science: 3 (3); Foreign language: 0 (0); Social studies: 1 (1); History: 1 (1); Academic electives: 0 (0); Total units: 15 (15). Tests: The college uses SAT or ACT scores in admissions decisions. Neither SAT nor ACT required. For admission to the fall 2011 entering class, the school will accept: ACT with writing recommended. Campus visit: Recommended. Admissions interview: Recommended. Off-campus interview: May be arranged. **Factors that count in admissions decisions:** *Academic:* Secondary school record: Not Considered. Class rank: Very Important. Letters of recommendation: Not Considered. Standardized test scores: Very Important. Essay: Not Considered. *Nonacademic:* Interview: Not Considered. Extracurricular activities: Not Considered. Talent/ability: Not Considered. Character/personal qualities: Not Considered. Alumni/ae relationship: Not Considered. Geographical residence: Not Considered. State residency: Not Considered. Religious affiliation/commitment: Not Considered. Minority status: Not Considered. Volunteer work: Not Considered. Work experience: Not Considered. **Other schools with the greatest overlap in applicants:** Ball State University; Indiana University Northwest; Indiana University–South Bend; Purdue University–Calumet; Purdue University–West Lafayette. **Admissions statistics for the fall 2009 entering class:** Total applicants: 1,563. Total accepted: 1,341. Freshmen enrolled: 768; 2% were from out of state. Overall acceptance rate: 86%. **Credentials of fall 2009 freshmen:** 4% ranked in the top 10 percent of their high school class; 16% were in the top 25 percent; 51% were in the top half. (Proportion submitting class standing: 79%.) **Average high school grade point average:** 2.8. **First-year students who submitted SAT scores:** 58%. Scores (25/75 percentile): Critical Reading: 420-520, Math: 420-540, Combined: 840-1060. **First-year students submitting ACT scores:** 12%. Scores (25/75 percentile): English: 16-23, Math: 16-23, Composite: 18-22.

ACADEMICS

Year founded: 1946. **Academic calendar:** Semester. **Degrees offered:** certificate, associate, terminal-associate, bachelor's, post-bachelor's certificate, master's. **Most popular majors:** 29% business, management, marketing, and related support services, 26% liberal arts and sciences studies, and humanities, 12% education, 11% engineering technologies/technicians, 6% health professions and related clinical sciences. **Major fields of study:** biological and biomedical sciences; business, management, marketing, and related support services; communication, journalism, and related programs; computer and information sciences and support services; education; engineering technologies/technicians; English language and literature/letters; health professions and related clinical sciences; liberal arts and sciences studies, and humanities; social sciences. **Areas of required coursework:** humanities, computer literacy, mathematics, English (including composition), sciences (biological or physical), social science. **Pre-professional programs:** pre-dentistry, pre-medicine, pre-veterinary science, pre-pharmacy. **Special academic programs:** distance learning, double major, dual enrollment, independent study, internships, teacher certificate program, weekend college. **Teacher certification offered in:** early childhood, elementary, secondary. **Faculty and instruction (2009-2010):** Total instructional faculty: 121 full-time, 193 part-time (52% men; 48% women; 13% minorities). Full-time faculty with Ph.D. or other terminal degree: 63%. Student/faculty ratio: 18/1. Classes of fewer than 20 students: 51%; of 20 to 49 students: 47%; of 50 or more students: 2%. **Advanced Placement and International Baccalaureate credit:** AP tests may be used for: Placement only. Scores accepted: 3, 4, 5. International Baccalaureate exams may be used for: Credit only. **Freshmen returning for sophomore year:** 54%. **Graduation rates:** Four-year: 6%; five-year: 15%; six-year: 15%.

COSTS AND FINANCIAL AID

Financial aid office: (219) 785-5279. **Expenses (2010-2011):** Tuition and fees 2010-2011: $6,704 in state, $15,960 out of state. Estimated books and supplies: $1,815; transportation: $2,103; personal expenses: $1,616. **Financial aid:** Priority filing date for institution's financial aid form: March 10; deadline: June 30. In 2009-2010, 75% of undergraduates applied for financial aid. Of those, 61% were determined to have financial need; 4% had their need fully met. Average financial aid package (proportion receiving): $6,947 (58%). Average amount of gift aid, such as scholarships or grants (proportion receiving): $4,063 (31%). Average amount of self-help aid, such as work study or loans (proportion receiving): $3,917 (42%). Average need-based loan (excluding PLUS or other private loans): $3,872. Among students who received need-based aid, the average percentage of need met: 40%. Among students who received aid based on merit, the average award (and the proportion receiving): $1,362 (1%). The average athletic scholarship (and the proportion receiving): $776 (2%). Average amount of debt of borrowers graduating in 2009: $20,859. Proportion who borrowed: 75%.

CAMPUS LIFE AND EXTRACURRICULAR ACTIVITIES

Student employment: During the 2009-2010 academic year, 2% of undergraduates worked on campus. Average per-year earnings: $1,425. **Clubs and organizations:** Number of student organizations: 30. Activities include: campus ministries, drama/theater, literary magazine, student government, student newspaper. Number of fraternities: 0; sororities: 0. **Sports program (2009-2010):** Member of NAIA. *Men's intercollegiate varsity sports:* baseball, basketball. *Women's intercollegiate varsity sports:* softball, volleyball.

SERVICES AND FACILITIES

Basic services: nonremedial tutoring, placement service, day care, health insurance. **Remedial assistance:** math, writing, study skills. **Counseling services:** career, personal, veteran student, academic. **For learning-disabled students:** School does not offer a structured program with separate admission and additional fees. Total undergraduates in learning-disabled program or receiving services: 17. Services include: remedial math, remedial English, tape recorders, note-taking services, oral tests, learning center, readers, extended time for tests, tutors, texts on tape, other testing accommodations. **Library:** Number of titles: 88,379; number of current serial subscriptions: 26,045. **Information technology resources:** Students are not required to lease or own a computer. Number of campus computers available to all students: 450. School has a wireless network. Approximate number of users that can be accommodated: 1,000. **Campus safety:** Security services offered: 24-hour foot-and-vehicle patrols, late-night transport/escort service, 24-hour emergency telephones, lighted pathways/sidewalks.

TRANSFER AND INTERNATIONAL STUDENTS

Transfer students: May apply for admission for the following academic terms: Fall, Spring, Summer. Applicants need a minimum number of credits to apply. For fall 2009: Transfer applications received: 260. Transfer applicants offered admission: 255. Transfer applicants enrolled: 229. **International students:** Number of foreign undergraduates: 9. Number of countries represented: 5. Minimum TOEFL score required: 550 (paper); 213 (computer).

Purdue University—West Lafayette

- **Address:** Schleman Hall, 475 Stadium Mall Drive, West Lafayette, IN 47907-2050
- **Website:** http://www.purdue.edu
- **Public**
- **Enrollment:** 29,646 full-time; 1,499 part-time

KEY STATS
✔ **U.S News College Ranking:** 56, National Universities
✔ **SAT Score (25th/75th percentile):** 1040-1280
✔ **Tuition:** 2010-2011: $9,070 in state, $26,622 out of state
  Selectivity: More selective   **Room/board:** $8,822
  Acceptance rate: 73%   **Average debt:** $23,924
  Student/faculty ratio: 14/1   **Proportion who borrowed:** 54%

UNDERGRADUATE STUDENT BODY STATS
2009-2010 enrollment: 29,646 full-time; 1,499 part-time. Men: 58%; women: 42%. **Ethnic makeup:** African American: 3%; Asian American: 5%; Hispanic: 3%; White: 79%; International: 9%.

ADMISSIONS FACTS AND FIGURES
Phone: (765) 494-1776. **Email:** admissions@purdue.edu. **Website:** http://www.purdue.edu. **Application deadlines for fall 2011:** Regular decision: March 1. Early decision: Not offered. Early action: Not offered. Admission can be deferred. **Application fee:** $50. **To apply online, go to:** http://www.purdue.edu/Admissions/Undergrad/. **Admissions requirements/recommendations:** High school units required (recommended): English: 4 (4); Mathematics: 4 (4); Science: 3 (3); Foreign language: 2 (2); Social studies: 3 (3); Total units: 16 (17). Tests: The college uses SAT or ACT scores in admissions decisions. Either SAT or ACT required. For admission to the fall 2011 entering class, the school will accept: ACT with writing required. Campus visit: Recommended. Admissions interview: Neither required nor recommended. Off-campus interview: Not available. **Factors that count in admissions decisions:** *Academic:* Secondary school record: Very Important. Class rank: Considered. Letters of recommendation: Considered. Standardized test scores: Important. Essay: Important. *Nonacademic:* Interview: Not Considered. Extracurricular activities: Considered. Talent/ability: Considered. Character/personal qualities: Considered. Alumni/ae relationship: Considered. Geographical residence: Considered. State residency: Considered. Religious affiliation/commitment: Not Considered. Minority status: Considered. Volunteer work: Considered. Work experience: Considered. **Other schools with the greatest overlap in applicants:** Ball State University; Indiana University—Bloomington; Indiana University-Purdue University—Indianapolis; University of Illinois—Urbana-Champaign; University of Michigan—Ann Arbor. **Admissions statistics for the fall 2009 entering class:** Total applicants: 27,213. Total accepted: 19,905. Freshmen enrolled: 6,171; 38% were from out of state. Overall acceptance rate: 73%. **Credentials of fall 2009 freshmen:** 35% ranked in the top 10 percent of their high school class; 70% were in the top 25 percent; 95% were in the top half. (Proportion submitting class standing: 62%.) **Average high school grade point average:** 3.5. **First-year students who submitted SAT scores:** 80%. Scores (25/75 percentile): Critical Reading: 500-610, Math: 540-670, Combined: 1040-1280. **First-year students submitting ACT scores:** 46%. Scores (25/75 percentile): English: 24-31, Math: 22-29, Composite: 23-29.

ACADEMICS
Year founded: 1869. **Academic calendar:** Semester. **Degrees offered:** certificate, associate, terminal-associate, bachelor's, post-bachelor's certificate, master's, post-master's certificate, doctorate. **Most popular majors:** 22% liberal arts and sciences studies, and humanities, 20% engineering, 16% business, management, marketing, and related support services, 8% agriculture, agriculture operations, and related sciences, 8% engineering technologies/technicians. **Major fields of study:** agriculture, agriculture operations, and related sciences; area, ethnic, cultural, and gender studies; biological and biomedical sciences; business, management, marketing, and related support services; communication, journalism, and related programs; computer and information sciences and support services; education; engineering; engineering technologies/technicians; English language and literature/letters; family and consumer sciences/human sciences; foreign languages, literatures, and linguistics; health professions and related clinical sciences; liberal arts and sciences studies, and humanities; mathematics and statistics; multi/interdisciplinary studies; natural resources and conservation;

parks, recreation, leisure, and fitness studies; philosophy and religious studies; physical sciences; psychology; public administration and social service professions; security and protective services; social sciences; transportation and materials moving; visual and performing arts. **Areas of required coursework:** humanities, computer literacy, mathematics, English (including composition), foreign languages, sciences (biological or physical), social science. **Pre-professional programs:** pre-law, pre-dentistry, pre-medicine, pre-veterinary science, pre-pharmacy, other. **Special academic programs:** accelerated program, cooperative (work-study plan) program, cross-registration, distance learning, double major, dual enrollment, exchange student program (domestic), honors program, independent study, internships, liberal arts/career combination, study abroad, teacher certificate program, weekend college. **Teacher certification offered in:** early childhood, special education, elementary, vo-tech, middle/junior high, adult education, secondary, bilingual/bicultural. **Cooperative education programs:** agriculture, computer science, engineering, natural science, technologies, vocational arts. **Reserve Officers Training Corps (ROTC):** Army ROTC: Offered on campus; Navy ROTC: Offered on campus; Air Force ROTC: Offered on campus. **Faculty and instruction (2009-2010):** Total instructional faculty: 2,111 full-time, 276 part-time (68% men; 32% women; 18% minorities). Full-time faculty with Ph.D. or other terminal degree: 99%. Student/faculty ratio: 14/1. Classes of fewer than 20 students: 37%; of 20 to 49 students: 46%; of 50 or more students: 16%. **Advanced Placement and International Baccalaureate credit:** AP tests may be used for: Credit and/or placement. Scores accepted: 3, 4, 5. International Baccalaureate exams may be used for: Credit and/or placement. **Freshmen returning for sophomore year:** 86%. **Graduation rates:** Four-year: 38%; five-year: 64%; six-year: 70%. **Graduate study:** 22% of students pursue further study immediately upon graduation. Fields in which graduates pursue further study: Master of Business Administration (MBA), 5%; law, 7%; medicine, 8%; dentistry, 1%; engineering, 22%; theology (or the seminary), 1%; education, 8%; arts and sciences, 22%; veterinary medicine, 3%.

COSTS AND FINANCIAL AID

Financial aid office: (765) 494-5090. **Expenses (2010-2011):** Tuition and fees 2010-2011: $9,070 in state, $26,622 out of state; room/board: $8,822. Estimated books and supplies: $1,270; transportation: $180; personal expenses: $2,180. **Financial aid:** Priority filing date for institution's financial aid form: March 1. In 2009-2010, 63% of undergraduates applied for financial aid. Of those, 46% were determined to have financial need; 32% had their need fully met. Average financial aid package (proportion receiving): $10,555 (46%). Average amount of gift aid, such as scholarships or grants (proportion receiving): $8,738 (32%). Average amount of self-help aid, such as work study or loans (proportion receiving): $4,621 (42%). Average need-based loan (excluding PLUS or other private loans): $4,562. Among students who received need-based aid, the average percentage of need met: 95%. Among students who received aid based on merit, the average award (and the proportion receiving): $5,637 (7%). The average athletic scholarship (and the proportion receiving): $18,413 (1%). Average amount of debt of borrowers graduating in 2009: $23,924. Proportion who borrowed: 54%.

CAMPUS LIFE AND EXTRACURRICULAR ACTIVITIES

Campus housing available (% using): coed dorms (49%), women's dorms (4%), men's dorms (13%), sorority housing (6%), fraternity housing (8%), apartments for married students (5%), apartment for single students (10%), cooperative housing (2%), other housing options (3%). Students who live in college-owned, operated, or affiliated housing: 34%. **Student employment:** During the 2009-2010 academic year, 22% of undergraduates worked on campus. Average per-year earnings: $1,550. **Clubs and organizations:** Number of student organizations: 878. Activities include: campus ministries, choral groups, concert band, dance, drama/theater, international student organization, jazz band, literary magazine, marching band, model UN, music ensembles, musical theater, pep band, radio station, student government, student newspaper, student film society, symphony orchestra, television station, yearbook. Number of fraternities: 47; sororities: 30. Proportion of men in fraternities: 7%; of women in sororities: 5%. Average proportion of students who stay on campus on weekends: 60%. **Sports program (2009-2010):** Member of NCAA I. *Men's intercollegiate varsity sports:* baseball, basketball, cross country, football, golf, swimming, tennis, track and field (indoor), track and field (outdoor), wrestling. *Women's intercollegiate varsity sports:* basketball, cross country, golf, soccer, softball, swimming, tennis, track and field (indoor), track and field (outdoor), volleyball.

SERVICES AND FACILITIES

Basic services: nonremedial tutoring, women's center, placement service, day care, health service, health insurance. **Remedial assistance:** reading,

math, writing, study skills. **Counseling services:** minority student, career, military, personal, veteran student, academic, older student, psychological, birth control. **For learning-disabled students:** School does not offer a structured program with separate admission and additional fees. Services include: remedial math, reading machines, tape recorders, other special classes, diagnostic testing service, note-taking services, oral tests, learning center, readers, extended time for tests, priority registration, priority seating, substitution of courses, texts on tape, typist/scribe, exams on tape or computer, other testing accommodations, other. **Library:** Number of titles: 2,509,156; number of current serial subscriptions: 48,283. **Information technology resources:** Students are not required to lease or own a computer. Number of campus computers available to all students: 5,970. School has a wireless network. Approximate number of users that can be accommodated: 30,000. Proportion of college-owned housing units wired for high-speed internet access: 100%. **Campus safety:** Security services offered: 24-hour foot-and-vehicle patrols, late-night transport/escort service, 24-hour emergency telephones, lighted pathways/sidewalks, student patrols, controlled dormitory access (key, security card, etc).

TRANSFER AND INTERNATIONAL STUDENTS

Transfer students: May apply for admission for the following academic terms: Fall, Spring, Summer. Applicants need a minimum number of credits to apply. For fall 2009: Transfer applications received: 3,307. Transfer applicants offered admission: 1,715. Transfer applicants enrolled: 1,034. **International students:** Number of foreign undergraduates: 2809 (9% of student body). Number of countries represented: 127. Minimum TOEFL score required: 550 (paper); 79 (computer). Average TOEFL score: 560 (paper).

Rose-Hulman Institute of Technology

- **Address:** 5500 Wabash Avenue, Terre Haute, IN 47803
- **Website:** http://www.rose-hulman.edu
- **Private**
- **Enrollment:** 1,835 full-time; 9 part-time

KEY STATS

✔ **U.S News College Ranking:** Unranked Specialty School–Engineering
✔ **SAT Score (25th/75th percentile):** 1190-1390
✔ **Tuition:** 2010-2011: $36,270

Selectivity: More selective	**Room/board:** $9,957
Acceptance rate: 70%	**Average debt:** $35,261
Student/faculty ratio: 12/1	**Proportion who borrowed:** 73%

UNDERGRADUATE STUDENT BODY STATS

2009-2010 enrollment: 1,835 full-time; 9 part-time. Men: 80%; women: 20%. **Ethnic makeup:** African American: 3%; Asian American: 5%; Hispanic: 2%; White: 87%; International: 3%.

ADMISSIONS FACTS AND FIGURES

Phone: (812) 877-8213. **Email:** admissions@rose-hulman.edu. **Website:** http://www.rose-hulman.edu. **Application deadlines for fall 2011:** Regular decision: March 1. Early decision: Not offered. Early action: Not offered. Admission can be deferred. **Application fee:** $40. **To apply online, go to:** http://www.rose-hulman.edu/admissions. **Admissions requirements/recommendations:** High school units required (recommended): English: 4; Mathematics: 4 (5); Science: 2 (3); Social studies: 2; Academic electives: 4; Total units: 16. Tests: The college uses SAT or ACT scores in admissions decisions. Either SAT or ACT required. For admission to the fall 2011 entering class, the school will accept: ACT with or without writing accepted. Campus visit: Recommended. Admissions interview: Recommended. Off-campus interview: Not available. **Factors that count in admissions decisions:** *Academic:* Secondary school record: Very Important. Class rank: Very Important. Letters of recommendation: Important. Standardized test scores: Important. Essay: Considered. *Nonacademic:* Interview: Considered. Extracurricular activities: Considered. Talent/ability: Considered. Character/personal qualities: Important. Alumni/ae relationship: Considered. Geographical residence: Not Considered. State residency: Not Considered. Religious affiliation/commitment: Not Considered. Minority status: Not Considered. Volunteer work: Considered. Work experience: Considered. **Other schools with the greatest overlap in applicants:** Indiana University–Bloomington; Purdue University–West Lafayette; Rensselaer Polytechnic Institute; University of Evansville; University of Illinois–Urbana-

Champaign. **Admissions statistics for the fall 2009 entering class:** Total applicants: 3,554. Total accepted: 2,495. Freshmen enrolled: 465; 52% were from out of state. Overall acceptance rate: 70%. **Credentials of fall 2009 freshmen:** 61% ranked in the top 10 percent of their high school class; 89% were in the top 25 percent; 99% were in the top half. (Proportion submitting class standing: 77%.) **First-year students who submitted SAT scores:** 77%. Scores (25/75 percentile): Critical Reading: 560-670, Math: 630-720, Combined: 1190-1390. **First-year students submitting ACT scores:** 64%. Scores (25/75 percentile): English: 25-32, Math: 28-34, Composite: 26-32.

ACADEMICS

Year founded: 1874. **Academic calendar:** Quarter. **Degrees offered:** bachelor's, master's. **Most popular majors:** 31% mechanical engineering, 12% chemical engineering, 11% electrical, electronics, and communications engineering, 9% biomedical/medical engineering, 8% computer engineering. **Major fields of study:** biological and biomedical sciences; computer and information sciences and support services; engineering; mathematics and statistics; physical sciences; social sciences. **Areas of required coursework:** humanities, computer literacy, mathematics, English (including composition), sciences (biological or physical), social science. **Pre-professional programs:** pre-law, pre-medicine, other. **Special academic programs (% participation):** accelerated program (13%), cooperative (work-study plan) program (11%), cross-registration, double major (12%), independent study (11%), internships, study abroad (3%). **Cooperative education programs:** computer science, engineering, natural science. **Reserve Officers Training Corps (ROTC):** Army ROTC: Offered on campus; Air Force ROTC: Offered on campus. **Faculty and instruction (2009-2010):** Total instructional faculty: 160 full-time, 8 part-time (77% men; 23% women; 10% minorities). Full-time faculty with Ph.D. or other terminal degree: 100%. Student/faculty ratio: 12/1. Classes of fewer than 20 students: 38%; of 20 to 49 students: 62%; of 50 or more students: 0%. **Advanced Placement and International Baccalaureate credit:** AP tests may be used for: Placement only. Scores accepted: 4, 5. International Baccalaureate exams may be used for: Placement only. **Freshmen returning for sophomore year:** 91%. **Graduation rates:** Four-year: 69%; five-year: 79%; six-year: 81%. **Graduate study:** 22% of students pursue further study immediately upon graduation; 22% within one year; 35% within five years. Fields in which graduates pursue further study: Master of Business Administration (MBA), 50%; law, 3%; medicine, 2%; dentistry, 1%; engineering, 38%; education, 1%; arts and sciences, 5%.

COSTS AND FINANCIAL AID

Financial aid office: (812) 877-8259. **Expenses (2010-2011):** Tuition and fees 2010-2011: $36,270; room/board: $9,957. Estimated books and supplies: $1,500 personal expenses: $1,500. **Financial aid:** Priority filing date for institution's financial aid form: March 1. In 2009-2010, 81% of undergraduates applied for financial aid. Of those, 70% were determined to have financial need; 19% had their need fully met. Average financial aid package (proportion receiving): $23,743 (70%). Average amount of gift aid, such as scholarships or grants (proportion receiving): $18,278 (70%). Average amount of self-help aid, such as work study or loans (proportion receiving): $5,352 (68%). Average need-based loan (excluding PLUS or other private loans): $5,014. Among students who received need-based aid, the average percentage of need met: 82%. Among students who received aid based on merit, the average award (and the proportion receiving): $9,661 (27%). Average amount of debt of borrowers graduating in 2009: $35,261. Proportion who borrowed: 73%.

CAMPUS LIFE AND EXTRACURRICULAR ACTIVITIES

Campus housing available (% using): coed dorms (45%), men's dorms (18%), sorority housing (1%), fraternity housing (18%), apartment for single students (18%). Students who live in college-owned, operated, or affiliated housing: 60%. **Student employment:** During the 2009-2010 academic year, 32% of undergraduates worked on campus. Average per-year earnings: $1,500. **Clubs and organizations:** Number of student organizations: 105. Activities include: choral groups, concert band, dance, drama/theater, international student organization, jazz band, literary magazine, music ensembles, musical theater, pep band, radio station, student government, student newspaper. Number of fraternities: 8; sororities: 3. Proportion of men in fraternities: 28%; of women in sororities: 28%. Average proportion of students who stay on campus on weekends: 75%. **Sports program (2009-2010):** Member of NCAA III. **Men's intercollegiate varsity sports:** baseball, basketball, cross country, football, golf, rifle, soccer, swimming, tennis, track and field (indoor), track and field (outdoor). **Women's intercollegiate varsity sports:** basketball, cross country, golf, rifle, soccer, softball, swimming, tennis, track and field (indoor), track and field (outdoor), volleyball.

SERVICES AND FACILITIES

Basic services: nonremedial tutoring, placement service, health service, health insurance. **Remedial assistance:** study skills. **Counseling services:** career, personal, academic, psychological, birth control. **For learning-disabled students:** School does not offer a structured program with separate admission and additional fees. Total undergraduates in learning-disabled program or receiving services: 66. Services include: tape recorders, note-taking services, learning center, extended time for tests, tutors, priority seating, texts on tape. **Library:** Number of titles: 79,708; number of current serial subscriptions: 18,000. **Information technology resources:** Students are required to lease or own a computer. Number of campus computers available to all students: 200. School has a wireless network. Approximate number of users that can be accommodated: 1,000. Proportion of college-owned housing units wired for high-speed internet access: 100%. **Campus safety:** Security services offered: 24-hour foot-and-vehicle patrols, late-night transport/escort service, 24-hour emergency telephones, lighted pathways/sidewalks, controlled dormitory access (key, security card, etc).

TRANSFER AND INTERNATIONAL STUDENTS

Transfer students: May apply for admission for the following academic terms: Fall, Winter, Spring. Applicants do not need a minimum number of credits to apply. For fall 2009: Transfer applications received: 101. Transfer applicants offered admission: 46. Transfer applicants enrolled: 15. **International students:** Number of foreign undergraduates: 56 (3% of student body). Number of countries represented: 13. Minimum TOEFL score required: 580 (paper); 237 (computer).

St. Joseph's College

- **Address:** PO Box 890, Rensselaer, IN 47978
- **Website:** http://www.saintjoe.edu
- **Private; Religious affiliation:** Roman Catholic
- **Enrollment:** 946 full-time; 64 part-time

KEY STATS

✔ **U.S News College Ranking:** 25, Regional Colleges (Midwest)
✔ **SAT Score (25th/75th percentile):** 850-1070
✔ **Tuition:** 2010-2011: $25,260

Selectivity: Selective	**Room/board:** $7,640
Acceptance rate: 73%	**Average debt:** $28,135
Student/faculty ratio: 14/1	**Proportion who borrowed:** 77%

UNDERGRADUATE STUDENT BODY STATS

2009-2010 enrollment: 946 full-time; 64 part-time. Men: 43%; women: 57%. **Ethnic makeup:** African American: 10%; Asian American: 1%; Hispanic: 5%; White: 84%; International: 1%. **Religious preference:** Protestant: 37%; No preference: 15%; Roman Catholic: 44%; Other: 4%.

ADMISSIONS FACTS AND FIGURES

Phone: (219) 866-6170. **Email:** admissions@saintjoe.edu. **Website:** http://www.saintjoe.edu. **Application deadlines for fall 2011:** Regular decision: Rolling. Early decision: Not offered. Early action: Not offered. Admission can be deferred. **Application fee:** $25. **To apply online, go to:** http://www.saintjoe.edu/ad/apply/. **Admissions requirements/recommendations:** High school units required (recommended): English: (4); Mathematics: (3); Science: (3); Foreign language: (2); Social studies: (3); Total units: (15). Tests: The college uses SAT or ACT scores in admissions decisions. Either SAT or ACT required. For admission to the fall 2011 entering class, the school will accept: ACT with or without writing accepted. Campus visit: Recommended. Admissions interview: Neither required nor recommended. Off-campus interview: Not available. **Factors that count in admissions decisions:** *Academic:* Secondary school record: Very Important. Class rank: Important. Letters of recommendation: Considered. Standardized test scores: Very Important. Essay: Considered. *Nonacademic:* Interview: Important. Extracurricular activities: Important. Talent/ability: Considered. Character/personal qualities: Important. Alumni/ae relationship: Considered. Geographical residence: Not Considered. State residency: Not Considered. Religious affiliation/commitment: Not Considered. Minority status: Not Considered. Volunteer work: Important. Work experience: Considered. **Other schools with the greatest overlap in applicants:** Ball State University; Indiana University–Bloomington; Manchester College; Purdue University–West Lafayette. **Admissions statistics for the fall 2009 entering class:** Total applicants: 1,218. Total accepted: 886. Freshmen enrolled: 231;

29% were from out of state. Overall acceptance rate: 73%. **Credentials of fall 2009 freshmen:** 14% ranked in the top 10 percent of their high school class; 38% were in the top 25 percent; 69% were in the top half. (Proportion submitting class standing: 81%.) **Average high school grade point average:** 3.1. **First-year students who submitted SAT scores:** 57%. Scores (25/75 percentile): Critical Reading: 420-520, Math: 430-550, Combined: 850-1070. **First-year students submitting ACT scores:** 42%. Scores (25/75 percentile): English: 17-25, Math: 18-26, Composite: 18-26.

ACADEMICS

Year founded: 1889. **Academic calendar:** Semester. **Degrees offered:** certificate, diploma, associate, bachelor's, master's. **Most popular majors:** 24% health professions and related clinical sciences, 17% business, management, marketing, and related support services, 9% biological and biomedical sciences, 8% education, 7% visual and performing arts. **Major fields of study:** biological and biomedical sciences; business, management, marketing, and related support services; communication, journalism, and related programs; computer and information sciences and support services; education; English language and literature/letters; health professions and related clinical sciences; history; mathematics and statistics; philosophy and religious studies; physical sciences; psychology; public administration and social service professions; security and protective services; social sciences; theology and religious vocations; visual and performing arts. **Areas of required coursework:** arts/fine arts, humanities, computer literacy, English (including composition), philosophy, sciences (biological or physical), history, social science. **Pre-professional programs:** pre-law, pre-dentistry, pre-medicine, pre-veterinary science, pre-optometry, pre-pharmacy. **Special academic programs (% participation):** accelerated program (3%), cross-registration (24%), double major (5%), dual enrollment (1%), honors program (8%), independent study (16%), internships (9%), liberal arts/career combination (100%), student-designed major (1%), study abroad (2%), teacher certificate program (12%). **Teacher certification offered in:** early childhood, special education, elementary, middle/junior high, secondary. **Cooperative education programs:** education, health professions, social/behavioral science. **Faculty and instruction (2009-2010):** Total instructional faculty: 57 full-time, 43 part-time (48% men; 52% women; 3% minorities). Full-time faculty with Ph.D. or other terminal degree: 86%. Student/faculty ratio: 14/1. Classes of fewer than 20 students: 78%; of 20 to 49 students: 21%; of 50 or more students: 1%. **Advanced Placement and International Baccalaureate credit:** AP tests may be used for: Credit only. Scores accepted: 3. **Freshmen returning for sophomore year:** 65%. **Graduation rates:** Four-year: 52%; five-year: 58%; six-year: 55%. **Graduate study:** 22% of students pursue further study immediately upon graduation. Fields in which graduates pursue further study: Master of Business Administration (MBA), 9%; law, 19%; medicine, 3%; theology (or the seminary), 3%; education, 6%; arts and sciences, 59%.

COSTS AND FINANCIAL AID

Financial aid office: (219) 866-6163. **Expenses (2010-2011):** Tuition and fees 2010-2011: $25,260; room/board: $7,640. Estimated books and supplies: $800; transportation: $540; personal expenses: $680. **Financial aid:** Priority filing date for institution's financial aid form: March 1. In 2009-2010, 100% of undergraduates applied for financial aid. Of those, 87% were determined to have financial need; 29% had their need fully met. Average financial aid package (proportion receiving): $21,891 (87%). Average amount of gift aid, such as scholarships or grants (proportion receiving): $14,856 (86%). Average amount of self-help aid, such as work study or loans (proportion receiving): $4,450 (63%). Average need-based loan (excluding PLUS or other private loans): $4,382. Among students who received need-based aid, the average percentage of need met: 80%. Among students who received aid based on merit, the average award (and the proportion receiving): $12,711 (11%). The average athletic scholarship (and the proportion receiving): $11,159 (5%). Average amount of debt of borrowers graduating in 2009: $28,135. Proportion who borrowed: 77%.

CAMPUS LIFE AND EXTRACURRICULAR ACTIVITIES

Campus housing available (% using): coed dorms (34%), women's dorms (27%), men's dorms (26%), apartment for single students (13%). Students who live in college-owned, operated, or affiliated housing: 65%. **Student employment:** During the 2009-2010 academic year, 34% of undergraduates worked on campus. Average per-year earnings: $1,500. **Clubs and organizations:** Number of student organizations: 35. Activities include: choral groups, concert band, dance, drama/theater, jazz band, literary magazine, marching band, music ensembles, musical theater, pep band, radio station, student government, student newspaper, student film society, television station. Number of fraternities: 0; sororities: 0. Average proportion of students who stay on campus on weekends: 60%. **Sports program (2009-2010):**

Member of NCAA II. **Men's intercollegiate varsity sports:** basketball, cross country, football, golf, soccer, tennis, track and field (indoor), track and field (outdoor). **Women's intercollegiate varsity sports:** basketball, cross country, golf, soccer, softball, tennis, track and field (indoor), track and field (outdoor), volleyball.

SERVICES AND FACILITIES

Basic services: nonremedial tutoring. **Remedial assistance:** reading, writing, study skills. **Counseling services:** career, personal, academic, religious. **For learning-disabled students:** School does not offer a structured program with separate admission and additional fees. Services include: remedial English, tape recorders, other special classes, untimed tests, oral tests, extended time for tests, tutors. **Library:** Number of titles: 228,858; number of current serial subscriptions: 326. **Information technology resources:** Students are not required to lease or own a computer. Number of campus computers available to all students: 69. School has a wireless network. Approximate number of users that can be accommodated: 2,000. Proportion of college-owned housing units wired for high-speed internet access: 100%. **Campus safety:** Security services offered: 24-hour foot-and-vehicle patrols, late-night transport/escort service, 24-hour emergency telephones, student patrols, controlled dormitory access (key, security card, etc).

TRANSFER AND INTERNATIONAL STUDENTS

Transfer students: May apply for admission for the following academic terms: Fall, Winter. Applicants need a minimum number of credits to apply. For fall 2009: Transfer applications received: 124. Transfer applicants offered admission: 55. Transfer applicants enrolled: 25. **International students:** Number of foreign undergraduates: 7 (1% of student body). Number of countries represented: 6. Minimum TOEFL score required: 550 (paper); 213 (computer).

St. Mary-of-the-Woods College

- **Address:** St. Mary-of-the-Woods, IN 47876
- **Website:** http://www.smwc.edu
- **Private; Religious affiliation:** Roman Catholic
- **Enrollment:** 592 full-time; 873 part-time

KEY STATS

✔ **U.S News College Ranking:** 18, Regional Colleges (Midwest)
✔ **SAT Score (25th/75th percentile):** 830-1060
✔ **Tuition:** 2010-2011: $24,500

Selectivity: Selective	**Room/board:** $8,890
Acceptance rate: 67%	**Average debt:** $25,500
Student/faculty ratio: 12/1	**Proportion who borrowed:** 97%

UNDERGRADUATE STUDENT BODY STATS

2009-2010 enrollment: 592 full-time; 873 part-time. Men: 5%; women: 95%. **Ethnic makeup:** African American: 4%; American-Indian: 1%; Asian American: 1%; Hispanic: 2%; White: 92%; International: 1%.

ADMISSIONS FACTS AND FIGURES

Phone: (800) 926-7692. **Email:** smwcadms@smwc.edu. **Website:** http://www.smwc.edu. **Application deadlines for fall 2011:** Regular decision: Rolling. Early decision: Not offered. Early action: Not offered. Admission can be deferred. **Application fee:** $30. **To apply online, go to:** https://apply.smwc.edu/apply/authentication.do?cmd=login-check. **Admissions requirements/recommendations:** High school units required (recommended): English: 4 (4); Mathematics: 3 (3); Science: 3 (3); Foreign language: 2 (2); Social studies: 3 (3); History: 0 (0); Academic electives: 0 (0); Total units: 18 (18). Tests: The college uses SAT or ACT scores in admissions decisions. Either SAT or ACT required. For admission to the fall 2011 entering class, the school will accept: ACT with or without writing accepted. Campus visit: Recommended. Admissions interview: Recommended. Off-campus interview: May be arranged. **Factors that count in admissions decisions:** *Academic:* Secondary school record: Important. Class rank: Important. Letters of recommendation: Important. Standardized test scores: Very Important. Essay: Important. *Nonacademic:* Interview: Considered. Extracurricular activities: Considered. Talent/ability: Not Considered. Character/personal qualities: Considered. Alumni/ae relationship: Considered. Geographical residence: Not Considered. State residency: Not Considered. Religious affiliation/commitment: Not Considered. Minority status: Not Considered. Volunteer work: Considered. Work experience: Not

Considered. **Other schools with the greatest overlap in applicants:** Indiana State University; Indiana University–Bloomington; St. Joseph's College. **Admissions statistics for the fall 2009 entering class:** Total applicants: 353. Total accepted: 236. Freshmen enrolled: 90; 20% were from out of state. Overall acceptance rate: 67%. **Size of waiting list:** 0 applicants; enrolled from waiting list: 0. **Credentials of fall 2009 freshmen:** 24% ranked in the top 10 percent of their high school class; 51% were in the top 25 percent; 72% were in the top half. (Proportion submitting class standing: 84%.) **Average high school grade point average:** 3.2. **First-year students who submitted SAT scores:** 72%. Scores (25/75 percentile): Critical Reading: 420-560, Math: 410-500, Combined: 830-1060. **First-year students submitting ACT scores:** 40%. Scores (25/75 percentile): English: N/A, Math: N/A, Composite: 19-26.

ACADEMICS

Year founded: 1840. **Academic calendar:** Semester. **Degrees offered:** certificate, associate, bachelor's, post-bachelor's certificate, master's. **Most popular majors:** 39% education, 11% business, management, marketing, and related support services, 9% psychology, 6% agriculture, agriculture operations, and related sciences, 6% biological and biomedical sciences. **Major fields of study:** agriculture, agriculture operations, and related sciences; biological and biomedical sciences; business, management, marketing, and related support services; communication, journalism, and related programs; computer and information sciences and support services; education; English language and literature/letters; health professions and related clinical sciences; legal professions and studies; liberal arts and sciences studies, and humanities; mathematics and statistics; multi/interdisciplinary studies; psychology; public administration and social service professions; social sciences; theology and religious vocations; visual and performing arts. **Areas of required coursework:** arts/fine arts, humanities, computer literacy, mathematics, English (including composition), philosophy, foreign languages, sciences (biological or physical), history, social science, other. **Pre-professional programs:** pre-law, pre-dentistry, pre-medicine, pre-veterinary science, pre-optometry, pre-pharmacy. **Special academic programs (% participation):** accelerated program, cross-registration, distance learning (80%), double major, external degree program (77%), honors program (5%), independent study, internships, student-designed major, study abroad, teacher certificate program. **Teacher certification offered in:** early childhood, special education, elementary, middle/junior high, secondary. **Reserve Officers Training Corps (ROTC):** Army ROTC: Offered at cooperating institution (Indiana State University); Air Force ROTC: Offered at cooperating institution (Rose-Hulman Institute of Technology). **Faculty and instruction (2009-2010):** Total instructional faculty: 66 full-time, 108 part-time (28% men; 72% women; 5% minorities). Full-time faculty with Ph.D. or other terminal degree: 58%. Student/faculty ratio: 12/1. Classes of fewer than 20 students: 94%; of 20 to 49 students: 7%; of 50 or more students: 0%. **Advanced Placement and International Baccalaureate credit:** AP tests may be used for: Credit and/or placement. Scores accepted: 3. International Baccalaureate exams may be used for: Credit and/or placement. **Freshmen returning for sophomore year:** 76%. **Graduation rates:** Four-year: 54%; five-year: 60%; six-year: 51%. **Graduate study:** 7% of students pursue further study immediately upon graduation; 8% within one year. Fields in which graduates pursue further study: Master of Business Administration (MBA), 17%; arts and sciences, 75%; veterinary medicine, 8%.

COSTS AND FINANCIAL AID

Financial aid office: (812) 535-5109. **Expenses (2010-2011):** Tuition and fees 2010-2011: $24,500; room/board: $8,890. Estimated books and supplies: $2,000; transportation: $600; personal expenses: $850. **Financial aid:** Priority filing date for institution's financial aid form: March 10; deadline: March 10. In 2009-2010, 99% of undergraduates applied for financial aid. Of those, 90% were determined to have financial need; 12% had their need fully met. Average financial aid package (proportion receiving): $15,681 (90%). Average amount of gift aid, such as scholarships or grants (proportion receiving): $7,724 (63%). Average amount of self-help aid, such as work study or loans (proportion receiving): $4,281 (90%). Average need-based loan (excluding PLUS or other private loans): $4,131. Among students who received need-based aid, the average percentage of need met: 77%. Among students who received aid based on merit, the average award (and the proportion receiving): $6,236 (10%). The average athletic scholarship (and the proportion receiving): $6,338 (10%). Average amount of debt of borrowers graduating in 2009: $25,500. Proportion who borrowed: 97%.

CAMPUS LIFE AND EXTRACURRICULAR ACTIVITIES

Campus housing available (% using): women's dorms (100%). Students who live in college-owned, operated, or affiliated housing: 17%. **Student employment:** During the 2009-2010 academic year, 36% of undergraduates worked on campus. Average per-year earnings: $1,500. **Clubs and organizations:** Number of student organizations: 30. Activities include: campus ministries, choral groups, concert band, dance, drama/theater, international student organization, jazz band, literary magazine, music ensembles, musical theater, student government, student newspaper. Number of fraternities: 0; sororities: 0. Average proportion of students who stay on campus on weekends: 50%. **Sports program (2009-2010):** *Men's intercollegiate varsity sports:* cross country, golf. *Women's intercollegiate varsity sports:* basketball, equestrian, soccer, softball.

SERVICES AND FACILITIES

Basic services: nonremedial tutoring, placement service, day care, health service. **Remedial assistance:** math, writing, study skills. **Counseling services:** career, personal, academic, psychological, religious. **For learning-disabled students:** School does not offer a structured program with separate admission and additional fees. Total undergraduates in learning-disabled program or receiving services: 32. Services include: remedial math, remedial English, tape recorders, other special classes, untimed tests, note-taking services, oral tests, learning center, readers, extended time for tests, tutors, proofreading services, substitution of courses, other testing accommodations, waiver of foreign language degree requirement, other. **Library:** Number of titles: 98,972; number of current serial subscriptions: 45. **Information technology resources:** Students are not required to lease or own a computer. Number of campus computers available to all students: 200. School has a wireless network. Approximate number of users that can be accommodated: 5,000. Proportion of college-owned housing units wired for high-speed internet access: 100%. **Campus safety:** Security services offered: 24-hour foot-and-vehicle patrols, lighted pathways/sidewalks, controlled dormitory access (key, security card, etc).

TRANSFER AND INTERNATIONAL STUDENTS

Transfer students: May apply for admission for the following academic terms: Fall, Winter. Applicants need a minimum number of credits to apply. For fall 2009: Transfer applications received: 43. Transfer applicants offered admission: 26. Transfer applicants enrolled: 13. **International students:** Number of foreign undergraduates: 8 (1% of student body). Number of countries represented: 6. Minimum TOEFL score required: 500 (paper); 62 (computer). Average TOEFL score: 534 (paper).

St. Mary's College

- **Address:** Notre Dame, IN 46556
- **Website:** http://www.saintmarys.edu
- **Private; Religious affiliation:** Roman Catholic
- **Enrollment:** 1,647 full-time; 17 part-time

KEY STATS

- ✔ **U.S News College Ranking:** 93, National Liberal Arts Colleges
- ✔ **ACT Score (25th/75th percentile):** 23-28
- ✔ **Tuition:** 2010-2011: $31,020

Selectivity: More selective	**Room/board:** $9,480
Acceptance rate: 86%	**Average debt:** $25,531
Student/faculty ratio: 11/1	**Proportion who borrowed:** 72%

UNDERGRADUATE STUDENT BODY STATS

2009-2010 enrollment: 1,647 full-time; 17 part-time. Men: 0%; women: 100%. **Ethnic makeup:** African American: 1%; Asian American: 1%; Hispanic: 7%; White: 89%; International: 1%. **Religious preference:** Protestant: 9%; No preference: 1%; Unknown: 13%; Roman Catholic: 76%; Other: 1%.

ADMISSIONS FACTS AND FIGURES

Phone: (574) 284-4587. **Email:** admission@saintmarys.edu. **Website:** http://www.saintmarys.edu. **Application deadlines for fall 2011:** Regular decision: Rolling. Early decision: Send application by: November 15; Decision sent by: December 15. Early action: Not offered. Admission can be deferred. **Application fee:** $30. **To apply online, go to:** http://www.saintmarys.edu/apply. **Admissions requirements/recommendations:** High school units required (recommended): English: 4 (4); Mathematics: 3 (4); Science: 2 (4); Foreign language: 2 (4); Social studies: 0 (0); History: 2 (2); Academic electives: 3 (3); Total units: 16 (20). Tests: The college uses SAT or ACT scores in admissions decisions. Either SAT or ACT required. For admission to the fall 2011 entering class, the school will accept: ACT with writing required. **Campus visit:** Recommended. **Admissions interview:** Recommended. **Off-campus interview:** May be arranged. **Factors that count in admissions decisions: Academic:** Secondary school record: Important. Class rank: Considered. Letters of recommendation: Considered. Standardized test scores: Important. Essay: Considered. **Nonacademic:** Interview: Considered. Extracurricular activities: Considered. Talent/ability: Considered. Character/personal qualities: Considered. Alumni/ae relationship: Considered. Geographical residence: Considered. State residency: Considered. Religious affiliation/commitment: Not Considered. Minority status: Considered. Volunteer work: Considered. Work experience: Considered. **Other schools with the greatest overlap in applicants:** Indiana University–Bloomington; Loyola University Chicago; Marquette University; Miami University–Oxford; University of Dayton. **Admissions statistics for the fall 2009 entering class:** Total applicants: 1,357. Total accepted: 1,162. Freshmen enrolled: 435; 69% were from out of state. Accepted through early-decision or early-action plans: 18%. Overall acceptance rate: 86%. Early-decision acceptance rate: 87%. Non-early acceptance rate: 86%. **Size of waiting list:** 0 applicants; enrolled from waiting list: 0. **Credentials of fall 2009 freshmen:** 38% ranked in the top 10 percent of their high school class; 58% were in the top 25 percent; 93% were in the top half. (Proportion submitting class standing: 58%.) **Average high school grade point average:** 3.7. **First-year students who submitted SAT scores:** 61%. Scores (25/75 percentile): Critical Reading: 510-620, Math: 510-600, Combined: 1020-1220. **First-year students submitting ACT scores:** 72%. Scores (25/75 percentile): English: 23-30, Math: 21-27, Composite: 23-28.

ACADEMICS

Year founded: 1844. **Academic calendar:** Semester. **Degrees offered:** bachelor's. **Most popular majors:** 12% communication studies/speech communication and rhetoric, 12% elementary education and teaching, 10% nursing/registered nurse training (R.N., A.S.N., B.S.N., M.S.N.), 9% biology/biological sciences, 8% history. **Major fields of study:** biological and biomedical sciences; business, management, marketing, and related support services; communication, journalism, and related programs; education; English language and literature/letters; foreign languages, literatures, and linguistics; health professions and related clinical sciences; history; liberal arts and sciences studies, and humanities; mathematics and statistics; multi/interdisciplinary studies; philosophy and religious studies; physical sciences; psychology; public administration and social service professions; social sciences; visual and performing arts. **Areas of required coursework:** mathematics, English (including composition), philosophy, foreign languages, history, other. **Pre-professional programs:** pre-law, pre-dentistry, pre-medicine, other. **Special academic programs (% participation):** accelerated program (2%), cross-registration (33%), double major (14%), exchange student program (domestic) (1%), independent study (31%), internships (78%), liberal arts/career combination (2%), student-designed major (1%), study abroad (42%), teacher certificate program (12%). **Teacher certification offered in:** early childhood, elementary, middle/junior high, secondary, bilingual/bicultural. **Reserve Officers Training Corps (ROTC):** Army ROTC: Offered at cooperating institution (University of Notre Dame); Navy ROTC: Offered at cooperating institution (University of Notre Dame); Air Force ROTC: Offered at cooperating institution (University of Notre Dame). **Faculty and instruction (2009-2010):** Total instructional faculty: 129 full-time, 62 part-time (31% men; 69% women; 7% minorities). Full-time faculty with Ph.D. or other terminal degree: 88%. Student/faculty ratio: 11/1. Classes of fewer than 20 students: 57%; of 20 to 49 students: 41%; of 50 or more students: 2%. **Advanced Placement and International Baccalaureate credit:** AP tests may be used for: Credit and/or placement. Scores accepted: 3, 4, 5. International Baccalaureate exams may be used for: Credit and/or placement. **Freshmen returning for sophomore year:** 85%. **Graduation rates:** Four-year: 73%; five-year: 78%; six-year: 78%. **Graduate study:** 29% of students pursue further study immediately upon graduation; 29% within one year; 54% within five years. Fields in which graduates pursue further study: Master of Business Administration (MBA), 14%; law, 9%; medicine, 15%; theology (or the seminary), 1%; education, 24%; arts and sciences, 37%.

COSTS AND FINANCIAL AID

Financial aid office: (574) 284-4557. **Expenses (2010-2011):** Tuition and fees 2010-2011: $31,020; room/board: $9,480. Estimated books and supplies: $1,200; transportation: $500; personal expenses: $1,000. **Financial aid:** Priority filing date for institution's financial aid form: March 1; deadline: March 1. In 2009-2010, 81% of undergraduates applied for financial aid. Of those, 70% were determined to have financial need; 16% had their need fully met. Average financial aid package (proportion receiving): $22,125 (69%). Average amount of gift aid, such as scholarships or grants

(proportion receiving): $15,340 (64%). Average amount of self-help aid, such as work study or loans (proportion receiving): $5,468 (50%). Average need-based loan (excluding PLUS or other private loans): $4,491. Among students who received need-based aid, the average percentage of need met: 71%. Among students who received aid based on merit, the average award (and the proportion receiving): $10,227 (23%). The average athletic scholarship (and the proportion receiving): $0 (0%). Average amount of debt of borrowers graduating in 2009: $25,531. Proportion who borrowed: 72%.

CAMPUS LIFE AND EXTRACURRICULAR ACTIVITIES

Campus housing available (% using): women's dorms (94%), apartment for single students (6%), special housing for international students. Students who live in college-owned, operated, or affiliated housing: 85%. **Student employment:** During the 2009-2010 academic year, 39% of undergraduates worked on campus. Average per-year earnings: $1,600. **Clubs and organizations:** Number of student organizations: 75. Activities include: campus ministries, choral groups, dance, drama/theater, international student organization, jazz band, literary magazine, marching band, music ensembles, musical theater, opera, pep band, radio station, student government, student newspaper, television station, yearbook. Number of fraternities: 0; sororities: 0. Average proportion of students who stay on campus on weekends: 75%. **Sports program (2009-2010):** Member of NCAA III. **Women's intercollegiate varsity sports:** basketball, cross country, golf, soccer, softball, swimming, tennis, volleyball.

SERVICES AND FACILITIES

Basic services: women's center, day care, health service. **Remedial assistance:** other. **Counseling services:** minority student, career, military, personal, academic, psychological, religious. **For learning-disabled students:** School does not offer a structured program with separate admission and additional fees. Total undergraduates in learning-disabled program or receiving services: 63. Services include: reading machines, tape recorders, note-taking services, oral tests, learning center, extended time for tests, tutors, early syllabus, priority seating, substitution of courses, texts on tape, typist/scribe, exams on tape or computer, other testing accommodations, waiver of foreign language degree requirement. **Library:** Number of titles: 271,161; number of current serial subscriptions: 20,780. **Information technology resources:** Students are not required to lease or own a computer. Number of campus computers available to all students: 236. School has a wireless network. Approximate number of users that can be accommodated: 1,000. Proportion of college-owned housing units wired for high-speed internet access: 100%. **Campus safety:** Security services offered: 24-hour foot-and-vehicle patrols, late-night transport/escort service, 24-hour emergency telephones, lighted pathways/sidewalks, controlled dormitory access (key, security card, etc).

TRANSFER AND INTERNATIONAL STUDENTS

Transfer students: May apply for admission for the following academic terms: Fall, Spring. Applicants need a minimum number of credits to apply. For fall 2009: Transfer applications received: 91. Transfer applicants offered admission: 42. Transfer applicants enrolled: 31. **International students:** Number of foreign undergraduates: 10 (1% of student body). Number of countries represented: 5. Minimum TOEFL score required: 500 (paper); 173 (computer). Average TOEFL score: 550 (paper).

Taylor University

- **Address:** 236 W. Reade Avenue, Upland, IN 46989-1002
- **Website:** http://www.taylor.edu
- **Private; Religious affiliation:** Christian interdenominational
- **Enrollment:** 1,900 full-time; 536 part-time

KEY STATS

✔ **U.S News College Ranking:** 1, Regional Colleges (Midwest)
✔ **ACT Score (25th/75th percentile):** 24-31
✔ **Tuition:** 2010-2011: $26,383

Selectivity: More selective	**Room/board:** $6,972
Acceptance rate: 83%	**Average debt:** $22,971
Student/faculty ratio: 13/1	**Proportion who borrowed:** 53%

UNDERGRADUATE STUDENT BODY STATS

2009-2010 enrollment: 1,900 full-time; 536 part-time. Men: 45%; women: 55%. **Ethnic makeup:** African American: 2%; Asian American: 3%; Hispanic: 2%; White: 90%; International: 3%.

ADMISSIONS FACTS AND FIGURES

Phone: (765) 998-5134. **Email:** admissions_u@taylor.edu. **Website:** http://www.taylor.edu. **Application deadlines for fall 2011:** Regular decision: Rolling. Early decision: Not offered. Early action: Not offered. Admission can be deferred. **Application fee:** $25. **To apply online, go to:** https://www.applyweb.com/apply/tuu/menu.html. **Admissions requirements/recommendations:** High school units required (recommended): English: 4; Mathematics: 3 (4); Science: 3 (4); Foreign language: (2); Social studies: 2 (3); Academic electives: 3 (1); Total units: 15 (20). Tests: The college uses SAT or ACT scores in admissions decisions. Either SAT or ACT required. For admission to the fall 2011 entering class, the school will accept: ACT with writing recommended. Campus visit: Recommended. Admissions interview: Recommended. Off-campus interview: May be arranged. **Factors that count in admissions decisions:** *Academic:* Secondary school record: Very Important. Class rank: Important. Letters of recommendation: Very Important. Standardized test scores: Very Important. Essay: Very Important. *Nonacademic:* Interview: Important. Extracurricular activities: Important. Talent/ability: Considered. Character/personal qualities: Very Important. Alumni/ae relationship: Considered. Geographical residence: Not Considered. State residency: Considered. Religious affiliation/commitment: Very Important. Minority status: Considered. Volunteer work: Important. Work experience: Considered. **Other schools with the greatest overlap in applicants:** Anderson University; Calvin College; Cedarville University; Indiana Wesleyan University; Wheaton College. **Admissions statistics for the fall 2009 entering class:** Total applicants: 1,975. Total accepted: 1,643. Freshmen enrolled: 486; 65% were from out of state. Overall acceptance rate: 83%. **Credentials of fall 2009 freshmen:** 41% ranked in the top 10 percent of their high school class; 66% were in the top 25 percent; 90% were in the top half. (Proportion submitting class standing: 100%.) **Average high school grade point average:** 3.6. **First-year students who submitted SAT scores:** 42%. Scores (25/75 percentile): Critical Reading: 500-650, Math: 510-640, Combined: 1010-1290. **First-year students submitting ACT scores:** 57%. Scores (25/75 percentile): English: 23-31, Math: 22-29, Composite: 24-31.

ACADEMICS

Year founded: 1846. **Academic calendar:** 4-1-4. **Degrees offered:** associate, bachelor's, master's. **Most popular majors:** 16% education, 12% business, management, marketing, and related support services, 10% psychology, 10% theology and religious vocations, 9% visual and performing arts. **Major fields of study:** biological and biomedical sciences; business, management, marketing, and related support services; communication, journalism, and related programs; computer and information sciences and support services; education; engineering; English language and literature/letters; foreign languages, literatures, and linguistics; history; mathematics and statistics; multi/interdisciplinary studies; natural resources and conservation; parks, recreation, leisure, and fitness studies; philosophy and religious studies; physical sciences; psychology; public administration and social service professions; social sciences; theology and religious vocations; visual and performing arts. **Areas of required coursework:** arts/fine arts, humanities, computer literacy, mathematics, English (including composition), philosophy, sciences (biological or physical), history, social science, other. **Pre-professional programs:** pre-law, pre-medicine. **Special academic programs (% participation):** distance learning (24%), double major (4%), dual enrollment (3%), English as a Second Language (ESL) (0%), exchange student program (domestic) (0%), honors program (19%), independent study (47%), internships (97%), student-designed major (0%), study abroad (60%), teacher certificate program (17%). **Teacher certification offered in:** early childhood, special education, elementary, middle/junior high, secondary. **Faculty and instruction (2009-2010):** Total instructional faculty: 129 full-time, 117 part-time (65% men; 35% women; 5% minorities). Full-time faculty with Ph.D. or other terminal degree: 80%. Student/faculty ratio: 13/1. Classes of fewer than 20 students: 59%; of 20 to 49 students: 37%; of 50 or more students: 4%. **Advanced Placement and International Baccalaureate credit:** AP tests may be used for: Placement only. Scores accepted: 3, 4, 5. International Baccalaureate exams may be used for: Credit only. **Freshmen returning for sophomore year:** 86%. **Graduation rates:** Four-year: 71%; five-year: 76%; six-year: 78%. **Graduate study:** 14% of students pursue further study within one year. Fields in which graduates pursue further study: Master of Business Administration (MBA), 10%; law, 2%;

medicine, 20%; engineering, 4%; theology (or the seminary), 13%; education, 3%; arts and sciences, 48%.

COSTS AND FINANCIAL AID

Financial aid office: (765) 998-5358. **Expenses (2010-2011):** Tuition and fees 2010-2011: $26,383; room/board: $6,972. Estimated books and supplies: $1,000; transportation: $0; personal expenses: $1,800. **Financial aid:** In 2009-2010, 73% of undergraduates applied for financial aid. Of those, 62% were determined to have financial need; 23% had their need fully met. Average financial aid package (proportion receiving): $18,002 (62%). Average amount of gift aid, such as scholarships or grants (proportion receiving): $14,157 (59%). Average amount of self-help aid, such as work study or loans (proportion receiving): $5,174 (54%). Average need-based loan (excluding PLUS or other private loans): $4,542. Among students who received need-based aid, the average percentage of need met: 79%. Among students who received aid based on merit, the average award (and the proportion receiving): $6,520 (23%). The average athletic scholarship (and the proportion receiving): $7,614 (4%). Average amount of debt of borrowers graduating in 2009: $22,971. Proportion who borrowed: 53%.

CAMPUS LIFE AND EXTRACURRICULAR ACTIVITIES

Campus housing available (% using): coed dorms (24%), women's dorms (36%), men's dorms (37%), apartments for married students (0%), apartment for single students (3%). Students who live in college-owned, operated, or affiliated housing: 81%. **Student employment:** During the 2009-2010 academic year, 26% of undergraduates worked on campus. Average per-year earnings: $944. **Clubs and organizations:** Number of student organizations: 86. Activities include: choral groups, concert band, drama/theater, jazz band, literary magazine, music ensembles, musical theater, opera, pep band, radio station, student government, student newspaper, student film society, symphony orchestra, television station, yearbook. Number of fraternities: 0; sororities: 0. Average proportion of students who stay on campus on weekends: 80%. **Sports program (2009-2010):** Member of NAIA. *Men's intercollegiate varsity sports:* baseball, basketball, cross country, football, golf, soccer, tennis, track and field (indoor), track and field (outdoor). *Women's intercollegiate varsity sports:* basketball, cross country, soccer, softball, tennis, track and field (indoor), track and field (outdoor), volleyball.

SERVICES AND FACILITIES

Basic services: nonremedial tutoring, placement service, health service, health insurance. **Remedial assistance:** reading, math, writing, study skills. **Counseling services:** minority student, career, personal, academic, psychological, religious. **For learning-disabled students:** School does not offer a structured program with separate admission and additional fees. Services include: remedial math, remedial English, reading machines, remedial reading, tape recorders, note-taking services, oral tests, learning center, readers, extended time for tests, tutors, priority registration, texts on tape, other testing accommodations, other. **Library:** Number of titles: 184,995; number of current serial subscriptions: 628. **Information technology resources:** Students are not required to lease or own a computer. Number of campus computers available to all students: 375. School has a wireless network. Approximate number of users that can be accommodated: 768. Proportion of college-owned housing units wired for high-speed internet access: 100%. **Campus safety:** Security services offered: 24-hour foot-and-vehicle patrols, late-night transport/escort service, 24-hour emergency telephones, lighted pathways/sidewalks, controlled dormitory access (key, security card, etc).

TRANSFER AND INTERNATIONAL STUDENTS

Transfer students: May apply for admission for the following academic terms: Fall, Winter, Spring, Summer. Applicants do not need a minimum number of credits to apply. For fall 2009: Transfer applications received: 126. Transfer applicants offered admission: 77. Transfer applicants enrolled: 38. **International students:** Number of foreign undergraduates: 51 (3% of student body). Number of countries represented: 29. Minimum TOEFL score required: 550 (paper); 80 (computer). Average TOEFL score: 600 (paper).

Trine University

- **Address:** 1 University Avenue, Angola, IN 46703
- **Website:** http://www.trine.edu
- **Private**
- **Enrollment:** 1,479 full-time; 129 part-time

UNDERGRADUATE STUDENT BODY STATS

2009-2010 enrollment: 1,479 full-time; 129 part-time. Men: 65%; women: 35%. **Ethnic makeup:** African American: 4%; Asian American: 1%; Hispanic: 2%; White: 90%; International: 3%.

ADMISSIONS FACTS AND FIGURES

Phone: (260) 665-4100. **Email:** admit@trine.edu. **Website:** http://www.trine.edu. **Application deadlines for fall 2011:** Regular decision: August 1. Early decision: Not offered. Early action: Not offered. Admission can be deferred. **To apply online, go to:** http://www.trine.edu/admission/undergraduate/steps_to_apply. **Admissions requirements/recommendations:** High school units required (recommended): English: 4; Mathematics: 3; Science: 3; Foreign language: (2); Social studies: 3; History: 2; Academic electives: 3; Total units: 18. Tests: The college uses SAT or ACT scores in admissions decisions. Either SAT or ACT required. For admission to the fall 2011 entering class, the school will accept: ACT with or without writing accepted. Campus visit: Recommended. Admissions interview: Recommended. Off-campus interview: Not available. **Factors that count in admissions decisions:** *Academic:* Secondary school record: Very Important. Class rank: Very Important. Letters of recommendation: Important. Standardized test scores: Very Important. Essay: Considered. *Nonacademic:* Interview: Important. Extracurricular activities: Important. Talent/ability: Considered. Character/personal qualities: Considered. Alumni/ae relationship: Considered. Geographical residence: Not Considered. State residency: Not Considered. Religious affiliation/commitment: Not Considered. Minority status: Not Considered. Volunteer work: Considered. Work experience: Considered. **Other schools with the greatest overlap in applicants:** Adrian College; Ball State University; Manchester College; Purdue University–West Lafayette; Rose-Hulman Institute of Technology. **Admissions statistics for the fall 2009 entering class:** Total applicants: 2,340. Total accepted: 1,760. Freshmen enrolled: 458; 38% were from out of state. Overall acceptance rate: 75%. **Credentials of fall 2009 freshmen:** 22% ranked in the top 10 percent of their high school class; 51% were in the top 25 percent; 83% were in the top half. (Proportion submitting class standing: 92%.) **Average high school grade point average:** 3.4. **First-year students who submitted SAT scores:** 54%. Scores (25/75 percentile): Critical Reading: 460-560, Math: 490-620, Combined: 950-1180. **First-year students submitting ACT scores:** 46%. Scores (25/75 percentile): English: 19-25, Math: 20-27, Composite: 21-26.

ACADEMICS

Year founded: 1884. **Academic calendar:** Semester. **Degrees offered:** associate, bachelor's, master's. **Most popular majors:** 37% engineering, 30% business/commerce, 11% criminal justice/law enforcement administration, 7% education, 5% psychology. **Major fields of study:** biological and biomedical sciences; business, management, marketing, and related support services; communication, journalism, and related programs; computer and information sciences and support services; education; engineering; engineering technologies/technicians; English language and literature/letters; health professions and related clinical sciences; liberal arts and sciences studies, and humanities; mathematics and statistics; natural resources and conservation; parks, recreation, leisure, and fitness studies; physical sciences; psychology; security and protective services; social sciences. **Areas of required coursework:** humanities, computer literacy, mathematics, English (including composition), sciences (biological or physical), social science. **Pre-professional programs:** pre-medicine. **Special academic programs (% participation):** cooperative (work-study plan) program (10%), distance learning (10%), double major (5%), honors program (7%), independent study (1%), internships (10%), study abroad (2%), teacher certificate program

(10%). **Teacher certification offered in:** elementary, middle/junior high, secondary. **Cooperative education programs:** business, computer science, engineering, natural science, technologies. **Reserve Officers Training Corps (ROTC):** Air Force ROTC: Offered at cooperating institution (University of Notre Dame). **Faculty and instruction (2009-2010):** Total instructional faculty: 72 full-time, 60 part-time (67% men; 33% women; 8% minorities). Full-time faculty with Ph.D. or other terminal degree: 61%. Student/faculty ratio: 15/1. Classes of fewer than 20 students: 46%; of 20 to 49 students: 54%; of 50 or more students: 0%. **Advanced Placement and International Baccalaureate credit:** AP tests may be used for: Credit and/or placement. Scores accepted: 3, 4, 5. International Baccalaureate exams may be used for: Credit and/or placement. **Freshmen returning for sophomore year:** 67%. **Graduation rates:** Four-year: 29%; five-year: 48%; six-year: 49%. **Graduate study:** 30% of students pursue further study immediately upon graduation; 10% within one year; 20% within five years. Fields in which graduates pursue further study: Master of Business Administration (MBA), 25%; law, 20%; medicine, 3%; dentistry, 2%; engineering, 20%; education, 10%; arts and sciences, 20%.

COSTS AND FINANCIAL AID

Financial aid office: (260) 665-4175. **Expenses (2010-2011):** Tuition and fees 2010-2011: $25,400; room/board: $8,500. Estimated books and supplies: $1,600; transportation: $2,250; personal expenses: $3,000. **Financial aid:** Priority filing date for institution's financial aid form: March 10; deadline: March 10. In 2009-2010, 97% of undergraduates applied for financial aid. Of those, 71% were determined to have financial need; 43% had their need fully met. Average financial aid package (proportion receiving): $16,957 (71%). Average amount of gift aid, such as scholarships or grants (proportion receiving): $4,373 (31%). Average amount of self-help aid, such as work study or loans (proportion receiving): $6,650 (31%). Average need-based loan (excluding PLUS or other private loans): $3,573. Among students who received need-based aid, the average percentage of need met: 91%. Among students who received aid based on merit, the average award (and the proportion receiving): $8,604 (5%). The average athletic scholarship (and the proportion receiving): $0 (0%). Average amount of debt of borrowers graduating in 2009: $19,334. Proportion who borrowed: 81%.

CAMPUS LIFE AND EXTRACURRICULAR ACTIVITIES

Campus housing available (% using): coed dorms (44%), women's dorms (10%), men's dorms (28%), apartment for single students (18%). Students who live in college-owned, operated, or affiliated housing: 80%. **Student employment:** During the 2009-2010 academic year, 28% of undergraduates worked on campus. Average per-year earnings: $1,377. **Clubs and organizations:** Number of student organizations: 35. Activities include: campus ministries, choral groups, dance, drama/theater, jazz band, marching band, music ensembles, pep band, radio station, student government, student newspaper, yearbook. Number of fraternities: 8; sororities: 4. Proportion of men in fraternities: 21%; of women in sororities: 20%. Average proportion of students who stay on campus on weekends: 65%. **Sports program (2009-2010):** Member of NCAA III. *Men's intercollegiate varsity sports:* baseball, basketball, cross country, football, golf, lacrosse, soccer, tennis, track and field (indoor), track and field (outdoor), wrestling. *Women's intercollegiate varsity sports:* basketball, cross country, golf, lacrosse, soccer, softball, tennis, track and field (indoor), track and field (outdoor), volleyball.

SERVICES AND FACILITIES

Basic services: nonremedial tutoring, placement service. **Remedial assistance:** math, writing, study skills. **Counseling services:** career, personal, academic, older student, psychological. **For learning-disabled students:** School does not offer a structured program with separate admission and additional fees. Total undergraduates in learning-disabled program or receiving services: 33. Services include: tape recorders, untimed tests, notetaking services, learning center, readers, extended time for tests, tutors, priority seating, texts on tape. **Library:** Number of titles: 48,845; number of current serial subscriptions: 255. **Information technology resources:** Students are not required to lease or own a computer. Number of campus computers available to all students: 200. School has a wireless network. Approximate number of users that can be accommodated: 50. Proportion of college-owned housing units wired for high-speed internet access: 100%. **Campus safety:** Security services offered: 24-hour foot-and-vehicle patrols, late-night transport/escort service, 24-hour emergency telephones, lighted pathways/sidewalks, controlled dormitory access (key, security card, etc).

TRANSFER AND INTERNATIONAL STUDENTS

Transfer students: May apply for admission for the following academic terms: Fall, Spring, Summer. Applicants do not need a minimum number of credits to apply. For fall 2009: Transfer applications received: 209. Transfer applicants offered admission: 86. Transfer applicants enrolled: 49. **International students:** Number of foreign undergraduates: 39 (3% of student body). Number of countries represented: 10. Minimum TOEFL score required: 550 (paper); 213 (computer).

University of Evansville

- **Address:** 1800 Lincoln Avenue, Evansville, IN 47722
- **Website:** http://www.evansville.edu
- **Private; Religious affiliation:** Methodist
- **Enrollment:** 2,477 full-time; 239 part-time

KEY STATS

✔ **U.S News College Ranking:** 10, Regional Universities (Midwest)
✔ **SAT Score (25th/75th percentile):** 1020-1238
✔ **Tuition:** 2010-2011: $28,076

Selectivity: More selective	**Room/board:** $9,110
Acceptance rate: 86%	**Average debt:** $25,598
Student/faculty ratio: 14/1	**Proportion who borrowed:** 72%

UNDERGRADUATE STUDENT BODY STATS

2009-2010 enrollment: 2,477 full-time; 239 part-time. Men: 40%; women: 60%. **Ethnic makeup:** African American: 2%; Asian American: 1%; Hispanic: 2%; White: 89%; International: 6%. **Religious preference:** Roman Catholic: 17%; Protestant: 21%; Unknown: 52%; Methodist: 9%; Other: 1%.

ADMISSIONS FACTS AND FIGURES

Phone: (812) 488-2468. **Email:** admission@evansville.edu. **Website:** http://www.evansville.edu. **Application deadlines for fall 2011:** Regular decision: February 1; decision sent by February 15. Early decision: Not offered. Early action: Send application by: December 1; Decision sent by: December 15. Admission can be deferred. **Application fee:** $35. **To apply online, go to:** http://www.evansville.edu/apply/. **Admissions requirements/recommendations:** High school units required (recommended): English: 4 (4); Mathematics: 3 (4); Science: 2 (3); Foreign language: 0 (2); Social studies: 1 (1); History: 1 (1); Academic electives: 0 (0); Total units: 11 (15). Tests: The college uses SAT or ACT scores in admissions decisions. Either SAT or ACT required. For admission to the fall 2011 entering class, the school will accept: ACT with writing required. Campus visit: Recommended. Admissions interview: Recommended. Off-campus interview: May be arranged. **Factors that count in admissions decisions:** *Academic:* Secondary school record: Very Important. Class rank: Considered. Letters of recommendation: Considered. Standardized test scores: Important. Essay: Not Considered. *Nonacademic:* Interview: Not Considered. Extracurricular activities: Important. Talent/ability: Considered. Character/personal qualities: Considered. Alumni/ae relationship: Considered. Geographical residence: Not Considered. State residency: Not Considered. Religious affiliation/commitment: Not Considered. Minority status: Considered. Volunteer work: Considered. Work experience: Considered. **Other schools with the greatest overlap in applicants:** Ball State University; Butler University; Indiana University–Bloomington; Purdue University–West Lafayette; University of Southern Indiana. **Admissions statistics for the fall 2009 entering class:** Total applicants: 3,012. Total accepted: 2,593. Freshmen enrolled: 701; 42% were from out of state. Accepted through early-decision or early-action plans: 75%. Overall acceptance rate: 86%. Non-early acceptance rate: 69%. **Credentials of fall 2009 freshmen:** 38% ranked in the top 10 percent of their high school class; 70% were in the top 25 percent; 96% were in the top half. (Proportion submitting class standing: 83%.) **Average high school grade point average:** 3.7. **First-year students who submitted SAT scores:** 69%. Scores (25/75 percentile): Critical Reading: 510-610, Math: 510-628, Combined: 1020-1238. **First-year students submitting ACT scores:** 62%. Scores (25/75 percentile): English: 21-29, Math: 21-28, Composite: 22-28.

ACADEMICS

Year founded: 1854. **Academic calendar:** Semester. **Degrees offered:** associate, bachelor's, master's. **Most popular majors:** 15% business, management, marketing, and related support services, 11% visual and performing arts, 9% education, 9% social sciences, 8% health professions and related clinical sciences. **Major fields of study:** biological and biomedical sciences; business, management, marketing, and related support services; communication, journalism, and related programs; computer and information sciences and support services; education; engineering; English language

and literature/letters; foreign languages, literatures, and linguistics; health professions and related clinical sciences; history; legal professions and studies; liberal arts and sciences studies, and humanities; mathematics and statistics; multi/interdisciplinary studies; natural resources and conservation; parks, recreation, leisure, and fitness studies; philosophy and religious studies; physical sciences; psychology; public administration and social service professions; social sciences; theology and religious vocations; visual and performing arts. **Areas of required coursework:** arts/fine arts, humanities, mathematics, philosophy, foreign languages, sciences (biological or physical), history, social science, other. **Pre-professional programs:** pre-law, pre-dentistry, pre-medicine, pre-theology, pre-veterinary science, pre-optometry, pre-pharmacy, other. **Special academic programs (% participation):** accelerated program (3%), cooperative (work-study plan) program (5%), double major (10%), dual enrollment (2%), English as a Second Language (ESL) (1%), external degree program (2%), honors program (5%), independent study (38%), internships (65%), student-designed major (0%), study abroad (52%), teacher certificate program (10%). **Teacher certification offered in:** special education, elementary, middle/junior high, secondary. **Cooperative education programs:** business, computer science, engineering, natural science. **Reserve Officers Training Corps (ROTC):** Army ROTC: Offered on campus. **Faculty and instruction (2009-2010):** Total instructional faculty: 172 full-time, 49 part-time (63% men; 37% women; 6% minorities). Full-time faculty with Ph.D. or other terminal degree: 87%. Student/faculty ratio: 14/1. Classes of fewer than 20 students: 56%; of 20 to 49 students: 42%; of 50 or more students: 2%. **Advanced Placement and International Baccalaureate credit:** AP tests may be used for: Credit and/or placement. Scores accepted: 4, 5. International Baccalaureate exams may be used for: Credit only. **Freshmen returning for sophomore year:** 81%. **Graduation rates:** Four-year: 52%; five-year: 63%; six-year: 62%. **Graduate study:** 23% of students pursue further study within one year.

COSTS AND FINANCIAL AID

Financial aid office: (812) 488-2364. **Expenses (2010-2011):** Tuition and fees 2010-2011: $28,076; room/board: $9,110. Estimated books and supplies: $1,000; transportation: $1,300; personal expenses: $944. **Financial aid:** Priority filing date for institution's financial aid form: March 10; deadline: March 10. In 2009-2010, 86% of undergraduates applied for financial aid. Of those, 72% were determined to have financial need; 25% had their need fully met. Average financial aid package (proportion receiving): $22,537 (72%). Average amount of gift aid, such as scholarships or grants (proportion receiving): $19,392 (71%). Average amount of self-help aid, such as work study or loans (proportion receiving): $5,020 (49%). Average need-based loan (excluding PLUS or other private loans): $4,615. Among students who received need-based aid, the average percentage of need met: 83%. Among students who received aid based on merit, the average award (and the proportion receiving): $12,866 (21%). The average athletic scholarship (and the proportion receiving): $23,980 (4%). Average amount of debt of borrowers graduating in 2009: $25,598. Proportion who borrowed: 72%.

CAMPUS LIFE AND EXTRACURRICULAR ACTIVITIES

Campus housing available (% using): coed dorms (41%), women's dorms (20%), men's dorms (11%), fraternity housing (8%), apartment for single students (20%). Students who live in college-owned, operated, or affiliated housing: 69%. **Student employment:** During the 2009-2010 academic year, 16% of undergraduates worked on campus. Average per-year earnings: $1,700. **Clubs and organizations:** Number of student organizations: 157. Activities include: campus ministries, choral groups, concert band, dance, drama/theater, international student organization, jazz band, literary magazine, model UN, music ensembles, musical theater, opera, pep band, radio station, student government, student newspaper, student film society, symphony orchestra, yearbook. Number of fraternities: 6; sororities: 5. Proportion of men in fraternities: 28%; of women in sororities: 23%. Average proportion of students who stay on campus on weekends: 65%. **Sports program (2009-2010):** Member of NCAA I. *Men's intercollegiate varsity sports:* baseball, basketball, cross country, golf, soccer, swimming. *Women's intercollegiate varsity sports:* basketball, cross country, golf, soccer, softball, swimming, tennis, volleyball.

SERVICES AND FACILITIES

Basic services: nonremedial tutoring, placement service, health service, health insurance, other. **Counseling services:** minority student, career, personal, veteran student, academic, older student, psychological, religious. **For learning-disabled students:** School does not offer a structured program with separate admission and additional fees. Total undergraduates in learning-disabled program or receiving services: 23. Services include: tape recorders, note-taking services, extended time for tests, tutors, priority seating, texts on tape, other testing accommodations. **Library:** Number of titles: 277,330; number of current serial subscriptions: 768. **Information technology resources:** Students are not required to lease or own a computer. Number of campus computers available to all students: 385. School has a wireless network. Approximate number of users that can be accommodated: 2,000. Proportion of college-owned housing units wired for high-speed internet access: 100%. **Campus safety:** Security services offered: 24-hour foot-and-vehicle patrols, late-night transport/escort service, 24-hour emergency telephones, lighted pathways/sidewalks, controlled dormitory access (key, security card, etc).

TRANSFER AND INTERNATIONAL STUDENTS

Transfer students: May apply for admission for the following academic terms: Fall, Spring. Applicants do not need a minimum number of credits to apply. For fall 2009: Transfer applications received: 337. Transfer applicants offered admission: 193. Transfer applicants enrolled: 105. **International students:** Number of foreign undergraduates: 145 (6% of student body). Number of countries represented: 50. Minimum TOEFL score required: 500 (paper); 61 (computer). Average TOEFL score: 523 (paper).

University of Indianapolis

- **Address:** 1400 E. Hanna Avenue, Indianapolis, IN 46227-3697
- **Website:** http://www.uindy.edu
- **Private; Religious affiliation:** United Methodist
- **Enrollment:** 2,880 full-time; 912 part-time

KEY STATS

✔ **U.S News College Ranking:** 33, Regional Universities (Midwest)
✔ **SAT Score (25th/75th percentile):** 910-1130
✔ **Tuition:** 2010-2011: $22,230

Selectivity: Selective	**Room/board:** $8,440
Acceptance rate: 80%	**Average debt:** $27,070
Student/faculty ratio: 14/1	**Proportion who borrowed:** 79%

UNDERGRADUATE STUDENT BODY STATS

2009-2010 enrollment: 2,880 full-time; 912 part-time. Men: 33%; women: 67%. **Ethnic makeup:** African American: 11%; Asian American: 1%; Hispanic: 2%; White: 80%; International: 5%. **Religious preference:** Roman Catholic: 14%; Protestant: 34%; Unknown: 38%; United Methodist: 8%; Other: 6%.

ADMISSIONS FACTS AND FIGURES

Phone: (317) 788-3216. **Email:** admissions@uindy.edu. **Website:** http://www.uindy.edu. **Application deadlines for fall 2011:** Regular decision: Rolling. Early decision: Not offered. Early action: Not offered. Admission can be deferred. **Application fee:** $25. **To apply online, go to:** http://admissions.uindy.edu/apply/. **Admissions requirements/recommendations:** High school units required (recommended): English: 4 (4); Mathematics: 3 (4); Science: 3 (4); Foreign language: 2 (3); Social studies: 1 (2); History: 1 (1); Academic electives: 1 (3); Total units: 15 (18). Tests: The college uses SAT or ACT scores in admissions decisions. Either SAT or ACT required. For admission to the fall 2011 entering class, the school will accept: ACT with or without writing accepted. Campus visit: Recommended. Admissions interview: Recommended. Off-campus interview: May be arranged. **Factors that count in admissions decisions:** *Academic:* Secondary school record: Very Important. Class rank: Important. Letters of recommendation: Not Considered. Standardized test scores: Important. Essay: Not Considered. *Nonacademic:* Interview: Not Considered. Extracurricular activities: Not Considered. Talent/ability: Not Considered. Character/personal qualities: Not Considered. Alumni/ae relationship: Not Considered. Geographical residence: Not Considered. State residency: Not Considered. Religious affiliation/commitment: Not Considered. Minority status: Not Considered. Volunteer work: Not Considered. Work experience: Not Considered. **Other schools with the greatest overlap in applicants:** Ball State University; Butler University; Indiana University–Bloomington; Indiana University-Purdue University–Indianapolis; Purdue University–West Lafayette. **Admissions statistics for the fall 2009 entering class:** Total applicants: 3,944. Total accepted: 3,151. Freshmen enrolled: 743; 7% were from out of state. Overall acceptance rate: 80%. **Size of waiting list:** 0 applicants; enrolled from waiting list: 0. **Credentials of fall 2009 freshmen:** 26% ranked in the top 10 percent of their high school class; 59% were in the top 25 percent; 89% were in the top half. (Proportion submitting class standing: 89%.) **Average**

high school grade point average: 3.4. **First-year students who submitted SAT scores:** 87%. Scores (25/75 percentile): Critical Reading: 450-560, Math: 460-570, Combined: 910-1130. **First-year students submitting ACT scores:** 52%. Scores (25/75 percentile): English: 19-25, Math: 19-25, Composite: 19-25.

ACADEMICS

Year founded: 1902. **Academic calendar:** Semester. **Degrees offered:** associate, bachelor's, master's, doctorate. **Most popular majors:** 15% nursing/registered nurse training (R.N., A.S.N., B.S.N., M.S.N.), 14% business administration and management, 12% education, 7% liberal arts and sciences/liberal studies, 7% psychology. **Major fields of study:** biological and biomedical sciences; business, management, marketing, and related support services; communication, journalism, and related programs; computer and information sciences and support services; education; engineering; English language and literature/letters; foreign languages, literatures, and linguistics; health professions and related clinical sciences; history; liberal arts and sciences studies, and humanities; mathematics and statistics; multi/interdisciplinary studies; natural resources and conservation; parks, recreation, leisure, and fitness studies; philosophy and religious studies; physical sciences; psychology; public administration and social service professions; security and protective services; social sciences; visual and performing arts. **Areas of required coursework:** arts/fine arts, humanities, computer literacy, mathematics, English (including composition), philosophy, foreign languages, sciences (biological or physical), history, social science, other. **Pre-professional programs:** pre-law, pre-dentistry, pre-medicine, pre-theology, pre-veterinary science, pre-optometry, other. **Special academic programs:** accelerated program, cross-registration, double major, dual enrollment, English as a Second Language (ESL), honors program, independent study, internships, liberal arts/career combination, student-designed major, study abroad, teacher certificate program, weekend college, other. **Teacher certification offered in:** elementary, middle/junior high, secondary. **Reserve Officers Training Corps (ROTC):** Army ROTC: Offered at cooperating institution (Indiana University-Purdue University–Indianapolis). **Faculty and instruction (2009-2010):** Total instructional faculty: 205 full-time, 253 part-time (50% men; 50% women; 8% minorities). Full-time faculty with Ph.D. or other terminal degree: 75%. Student/faculty ratio: 14/1. Classes of fewer than 20 students: 58%; of 20 to 49 students: 42%; of 50 or more students: 0%. **Advanced Placement and International Baccalaureate credit:** AP tests may be used for: Placement only. Scores accepted: 3, 4, 5. International Baccalaureate exams may be used for: Credit only. **Freshmen returning for sophomore year:** 73%. **Graduation rates:** Four-year: 38%; five-year: 48%; six-year: 52%. **Graduate study:** 27% of students pursue further study immediately upon graduation. Fields in which graduates pursue further study: Master of Business Administration (MBA), 11%; medicine, 4%; dentistry, 2%; theology (or the seminary), 2%; education, 4%; arts and sciences, 78%.

COSTS AND FINANCIAL AID

Financial aid office: (317) 788-3217. **Expenses (2010-2011):** Tuition and fees 2010-2011: $22,230; room/board: $8,440. Estimated books and supplies: $1,030; transportation: $1,050; personal expenses: $1,560. **Financial aid:** Priority filing date for institution's financial aid form: March 10. In 2009-2010, 84% of undergraduates applied for financial aid. Of those, 73% were determined to have financial need; 14% had their need fully met. Average financial aid package (proportion receiving): $15,526 (72%). Average amount of gift aid, such as scholarships or grants (proportion receiving): $8,000 (53%). Average amount of self-help aid, such as work study or loans (proportion receiving): $4,869 (60%). Average need-based loan (excluding PLUS or other private loans): $4,174. Among students who received need-based aid, the average percentage of need met: 70%. Among students who received aid based on merit, the average award (and the proportion receiving): $7,138 (45%). The average athletic scholarship (and the proportion receiving): $10,698 (6%). Average amount of debt of borrowers graduating in 2009: $27,070. Proportion who borrowed: 79%.

CAMPUS LIFE AND EXTRACURRICULAR ACTIVITIES

Campus housing available (% using): coed dorms (74%), women's dorms (13%), apartments for married students (0%), apartment for single students (13%). Students who live in college-owned, operated, or affiliated housing: 38%. **Student employment:** During the 2009-2010 academic year, 50% of undergraduates worked on campus. Average per-year earnings: $1,000. **Clubs and organizations:** Number of student organizations: 62. Activities include: campus ministries, choral groups, concert band, dance, drama/theater, international student organization, jazz band, literary magazine, music ensembles, musical theater, opera, pep band, radio station, student government, student newspaper, television station, yearbook. Number of fraternities: 0; sororities: 0. Average proportion of students who stay on campus on weekends: 50%. **Sports program (2009-2010):** Member of NCAA II. *Men's intercollegiate varsity sports:* baseball, basketball, cross country, football, golf, soccer, swimming, tennis, track and field (indoor), track and field (outdoor), wrestling. *Women's intercollegiate varsity sports:* basketball, cross country, golf, soccer, softball, swimming, tennis, track and field (indoor), track and field (outdoor), volleyball.

SERVICES AND FACILITIES

Basic services: nonremedial tutoring, placement service, day care, health service, health insurance. **Remedial assistance:** math, writing, study skills. **Counseling services:** minority student, career, personal, academic, psychological, religious, other. **For learning-disabled students:** School does not offer a structured program with separate admission and additional fees. Services include: remedial math, remedial English, reading machines, tape recorders, other special classes, diagnostic testing service, untimed tests, oral tests, learning center, readers, extended time for tests, tutors, priority seating, texts on tape, other testing accommodations, other. **Library:** Number of titles: 184,025; number of current serial subscriptions: 624. **Information technology resources:** Students are not required to lease or own a computer. Number of campus computers available to all students: 221. School has a wireless network. Approximate number of users that can be accommodated: 2,500. Proportion of college-owned housing units wired for high-speed internet access: 100%. **Campus safety:** Security services offered: 24-hour foot-and-vehicle patrols, late-night transport/escort service, 24-hour emergency telephones, lighted pathways/sidewalks, student patrols, controlled dormitory access (key, security card, etc).

TRANSFER AND INTERNATIONAL STUDENTS

Transfer students: May apply for admission for the following academic terms: Fall, Winter, Spring, Summer. Applicants do not need a minimum number of credits to apply. For fall 2009: Transfer applications received: 741. Transfer applicants offered admission: 488. Transfer applicants enrolled: 222. **International students:** Number of foreign undergraduates: 199 (5% of student body). Number of countries represented: 60. Minimum TOEFL score required: 500 (paper); 173 (computer). Average TOEFL score: 540 (paper).

University of Notre Dame

- ■ **Address:** Notre Dame, IN 46556
- ■ **Website:** http://www.nd.edu
- ■ **Private; Religious affiliation:** Roman Catholic
- ■ **Enrollment:** 8,356 full-time; 16 part-time

KEY STATS

✔ **U.S News College Ranking:** 19, National Universities
✔ **ACT Score (25th/75th percentile):** 31-34
✔ **Tuition:** 2010-2011: $39,919

Selectivity: Most selective	**Room/board:** $10,866
Acceptance rate: 29%	**Average debt:** $28,371
Student/faculty ratio: 12/1	**Proportion who borrowed:** 57%

UNDERGRADUATE STUDENT BODY STATS

2009-2010 enrollment: 8,356 full-time; 16 part-time. Men: 54%; women: 46%. **Ethnic makeup:** African American: 4%; American-Indian: 1%; Asian American: 7%; Hispanic: 10%; White: 76%; International: 3%. **Religious preference:** Protestant: 11%; Roman Catholic: 84%; Other: 5%.

ADMISSIONS FACTS AND FIGURES

Phone: (574) 631-7505. **Email:** admissions@nd.edu. **Website:** http://www.nd.edu. **Application deadlines for fall 2011:** Regular decision: December 31; decision sent by April 10. Early decision: Not offered. Early action: Send application by: November 1; Decision sent by: December 19. Admission can be deferred. **Application fee:** $65. **To apply online, go to:** http://admissions.nd.edu/onlineapplication. **Admissions requirements/recommendations:** High school units required (recommended): English: 4 (4); Mathematics: 3 (4); Science: 2 (4); Foreign language: 2 (4); History: 2 (4); Academic electives: 3; Total units: 16 (20). Tests: The college uses SAT or ACT scores in admissions decisions. Either SAT or ACT required. For admission to the fall 2011 entering class, the school will accept: ACT with or without writing accepted. Campus visit: Recommended. Admissions interview: Neither required nor recommended. Off-campus interview:

Not available. **Factors that count in admissions decisions:** *Academic:* Secondary school record: Very Important. Class rank: Important. Letters of recommendation: Important. Standardized test scores: Important. Essay: Important. *Nonacademic:* Interview: Not Considered. Extracurricular activities: Important. Talent/ability: Important. Character/personal qualities: Important. Alumni/ae relationship: Important. Geographical residence: Not Considered. State residency: Not Considered. Religious affiliation/commitment: Considered. Minority status: Considered. Volunteer work: Important. Work experience: Considered. **Other schools with the greatest overlap in applicants:** Boston College; Georgetown University; Northwestern University; Stanford University; Washington University in St. Louis. **Admissions statistics for the fall 2009 entering class:** Total applicants: 14,357. Total accepted: 4,113. Freshmen enrolled: 2,064; 93% were from out of state. Accepted through early-decision or early-action plans: 48%. Overall acceptance rate: 29%. Non-early acceptance rate: 23%. **Size of waiting list:** 2016 applicants; enrolled from waiting list: 257. **Credentials of fall 2009 freshmen:** 89% ranked in the top 10 percent of their high school class; 97% were in the top 25 percent; 100% were in the top half. (Proportion submitting class standing: 47%.) **First-year students who submitted SAT scores:** 48%. Scores (25/75 percentile): Critical Reading: 650-750, Math: 680-760, Combined: 1330-1510. **First-year students submitting ACT scores:** 52%. Scores (25/75 percentile): English: N/A, Math: N/A, Composite: 31-34.

ACADEMICS

Year founded: 1842. **Academic calendar:** Semester. **Degrees offered:** bachelor's, master's, doctorate. **Most popular majors:** 24% business/commerce, 10% engineering, 7% political science and government, 6% biology/biological sciences, 6% psychology. **Major fields of study:** architecture and related services; area, ethnic, cultural, and gender studies; biological and biomedical sciences; business, management, marketing, and related support services; computer and information sciences and support services; education; engineering; English language and literature/letters; foreign languages, literatures, and linguistics; health professions and related clinical sciences; history; liberal arts and sciences studies, and humanities; mathematics and statistics; multi/interdisciplinary studies; natural resources and conservation; philosophy and religious studies; physical sciences; psychology; social sciences; theology and religious vocations; visual and performing arts. **Areas of required coursework:** arts/fine arts, humanities, mathematics, English (including composition), philosophy, foreign languages, sciences (biological or physical), history, social science. **Pre-professional programs:** pre-medicine, pre-theology. **Special academic programs (% participation):** cross-registration (3.22%), double major (33%), dual enrollment (5.64%), exchange student program (domestic) (1.9%), honors program (19.2%), independent study (73.5%), internships (19.2%), liberal arts/career combination (1.85%), student-designed major (0%), study abroad (46.2%). **Reserve Officers Training Corps (ROTC):** Army ROTC: Offered on campus; Navy ROTC: Offered on campus; Air Force ROTC: Offered on campus. **Faculty and instruction (2009-2010):** Total instructional faculty: 947 full-time, 108 part-time (71% men; 29% women; 14% minorities). Full-time faculty with Ph.D. or other terminal degree: 93%. Student/faculty ratio: 12/1. Classes of fewer than 20 students: 54%; of 20 to 49 students: 36%; of 50 or more students: 9%. **Advanced Placement and International Baccalaureate credit:** AP tests may be used for: Credit and/or placement. Scores accepted: 4, 5. International Baccalaureate exams may be used for: Credit and/or placement. **Freshmen returning for sophomore year:** 98%. **Graduation rates:** Four-year: 90%; five-year: 95%; six-year: 96%. **Graduate study:** 36% of students pursue further study immediately upon graduation. Fields in which graduates pursue further study: Master of Business Administration (MBA), 10%; law, 11%; medicine, 19%; dentistry, 2%; engineering, 6%; theology (or the seminary), 3%; education, 10%; arts and sciences, 39%.

COSTS AND FINANCIAL AID

Financial aid office: (574) 631-6436. **Expenses (2010-2011):** Tuition and fees 2010-2011: $39,919; room/board: $10,866. Estimated books and supplies: $950; transportation: $500; personal expenses: $1,000. **Financial aid:** Priority filing date for institution's financial aid form: February 15; deadline: February 15. In 2009-2010, 62% of undergraduates applied for financial aid. Of those, 49% were determined to have financial need; 97% had their need fully met. Average financial aid package (proportion receiving): $34,101 (49%). Average amount of gift aid, such as scholarships or grants (proportion receiving): $26,847 (47%). Average amount of self-help aid, such as work study or loans (proportion receiving): $6,914 (42%). Average need-based loan (excluding PLUS or other private loans): $4,782. Among students who received need-based aid, the average percentage of need met: 99%. Among students who received aid based on merit, the average award (and the proportion receiving): $7,465 (3%). The average athletic scholarship (and the proportion receiving): $29,640 (5%). Average amount of debt of borrowers graduating in 2009: $28,371. Proportion who borrowed: 57%.

CAMPUS LIFE AND EXTRACURRICULAR ACTIVITIES
Campus housing available (% using): women's dorms (47%), men's dorms (53%). Students who live in college-owned, operated, or affiliated housing: 81%. **Student employment:** During the 2009-2010 academic year, 49% of undergraduates worked on campus. Average per-year earnings: $2,600. **Clubs and organizations:** Number of student organizations: 305. Activities include: campus ministries, choral groups, concert band, dance, drama/theater, jazz band, literary magazine, marching band, model UN, music ensembles, musical theater, opera, pep band, radio station, student government, student newspaper, student film society, symphony orchestra, television station, yearbook. Number of fraternities: 0; sororities: 0. **Sports program (2009-2010):** Member of NCAA I. *Men's intercollegiate varsity sports:* baseball, basketball, cross country, fencing, football, golf, ice hockey, lacrosse, soccer, swimming, tennis, track and field (indoor), track and field (outdoor). *Women's intercollegiate varsity sports:* basketball, crew (heavyweight), cross country, fencing, golf, lacrosse, crew (lightweight), soccer, softball, swimming, tennis, track and field (indoor), track and field (outdoor), volleyball.

SERVICES AND FACILITIES
Basic services: women's center, placement service, health service, health insurance, other. **Remedial assistance:** reading, math, writing, study skills. **Counseling services:** minority student, career, personal, academic, psychological, religious, other. **For learning-disabled students:** School does not offer a structured program with separate admission and additional fees. Total undergraduates in learning-disabled program or receiving services: 200. Services include: reading machines, tape recorders, note-taking services, readers, extended time for tests, tutors, priority registration, priority seating, texts on tape, typist/scribe, exams on tape or computer, other testing accommodations, waiver of foreign language degree requirement. **Library:** Number of titles: 3,469,001; number of current serial subscriptions: 88,352. **Information technology resources:** Students are not required to lease or own a computer. Number of campus computers available to all students: 261. School has a wireless network. Approximate number of users that can be accommodated: 20,000. Proportion of college-owned housing units wired for high-speed internet access: 100%. **Campus safety:** Security services offered: 24-hour foot-and-vehicle patrols, late-night transport/escort service, 24-hour emergency telephones, lighted pathways/sidewalks, student patrols, controlled dormitory access (key, security card, etc).

TRANSFER AND INTERNATIONAL STUDENTS
Transfer students: May apply for admission for the following academic terms: Fall, Spring. Applicants need a minimum number of credits to apply. For fall 2009: Transfer applications received: 440. Transfer applicants offered admission: 152. Transfer applicants enrolled: 113. **International students:** Number of foreign undergraduates: 213 (3% of student body). Number of countries represented: 41. Minimum TOEFL score required: 560 (paper); 250 (computer). Average TOEFL score: 560 (paper).

University of Southern Indiana

- **Address:** 8600 University Boulevard, Evansville, IN 47712
- **Website:** http://www.usi.edu
- **Public**
- **Enrollment:** 8,033 full-time; 1,615 part-time

KEY STATS
✔ **U.S News College Ranking:** second tier, Regional Universities (Midwest)
✔ **SAT Score (25th/75th percentile):** 850-1070
✔ **Tuition:** 2010-2011: $5,740 in state, $13,386 out of state

Selectivity: Less selective	**Room/board:** $6,700
Acceptance rate: 88%	**Average debt:** N/A
Student/faculty ratio: 18/1	**Proportion who borrowed:** N/A

UNDERGRADUATE STUDENT BODY STATS
2009-2010 enrollment: 8,033 full-time; 1,615 part-time. Men: 41%; women: 59%. **Ethnic makeup:** African American: 5%; Asian American: 1%; Hispanic: 1%; White: 90%; International: 2%.

ADMISSIONS FACTS AND FIGURES
Phone: (812) 464-1765. **Email:** enroll@usi.edu. **Website:** http://www.usi.edu. **Application deadlines for fall 2011:** Regular decision: August 15. Early decision: Not offered. Early action: Not offered. Admission cannot be deferred. **Application fee:** $25. **To apply online, go to:** http://www.usi.edu/admissn/apply.asp. **Admissions requirements/recommendations:** High school units required (recommended): English: (4); Mathematics: (4); Science: (2); Foreign language: (2); Social studies: (2); History: (2); Academic electives: (2); Total units: (18). Tests: The college uses SAT or ACT scores in admissions decisions. Either SAT or ACT required. For admission to the fall 2011 entering class, the school will accept: ACT with writing recommended. Campus visit: Recommended. Admissions interview: Neither required nor recommended. Off-campus interview: May be arranged. **Factors that count in admissions decisions:** *Academic:* Secondary school record: Considered. Class rank: Important. Letters of recommendation: Considered. Standardized test scores: Important. Essay: Considered. *Nonacademic:* Interview: Considered. Extracurricular activities: Considered. Talent/ability: Considered. Character/personal qualities: Considered. Alumni/ae relationship: Considered. Geographical residence: Not Considered. State residency: Not Considered. Religious affiliation/commitment: Not Considered. Minority status: Not Considered. Volunteer work: Not Considered. Work experience: Considered. **Admissions statistics for the fall 2009 entering class:** Total applicants: 5,324. Total accepted: 4,694. Freshmen enrolled: 2,093; 8% were from out of state. Overall acceptance rate: 88%. **Credentials of fall 2009 freshmen:** 12% ranked in the top 10 percent of their high school class; 31% were in the top 25 percent; 64% were in the top half. (Proportion submitting class standing: 91%.) **Average high school grade point average:** 3.0. **First-year students who submitted SAT scores:** 75%. Scores (25/75 percentile): Critical Reading: 420-530, Math: 430-540, Combined: 850-1070. **First-year students submitting ACT scores:** 40%. Scores (25/75 percentile): English: 16-23, Math: 17-23, Composite: 18-23.

ACADEMICS
Year founded: 1965. **Academic calendar:** Semester. **Degrees offered:** certificate, associate, transfer-associate, terminal-associate, bachelor's, post-bachelor's certificate, master's. **Most popular majors:** 25% health professions and related clinical sciences, 21% business, management, marketing, and related support services, 11% education, 10% communication, journalism, and related programs, 7% social sciences. **Major fields of study:** biological and biomedical sciences; business, management, marketing, and related support services; communication, journalism, and related programs; computer and information sciences and support services; education; engineering; engineering technologies/technicians; English language and literature/letters; foreign languages, literatures, and linguistics; health professions and related clinical sciences; history; liberal arts and sciences studies, and humanities; mathematics and statistics; multi/interdisciplinary studies; parks, recreation, leisure, and fitness studies; philosophy and religious studies; physical sciences; psychology; public administration and social service professions; social sciences; visual and performing arts. **Areas of required coursework:** arts/fine arts, humanities, computer literacy, mathematics, English (including composition), sciences (biological or physical), history, social science. **Pre-professional programs:** pre-law, pre-dentistry, pre-medicine, pre-veterinary science, pre-optometry, pre-pharmacy, other. **Special academic programs (% participation):** cooperative (work-study plan) program (2%), cross-registration (5%), distance learning (64%), double major (3%), dual enrollment (7%), English as a Second Language (ESL) (0%), honors program (5%), independent study (6%), internships (19%), study abroad (0%), teacher certificate program (19%). **Teacher certification offered in:** early childhood, special education, elementary, middle/junior high, secondary. **Cooperative education programs:** business, computer science, engineering. **Reserve Officers Training Corps (ROTC):** Army ROTC: Offered on campus. **Faculty and instruction (2009-2010):** Total instructional faculty: 338 full-time, 330 part-time (44% men; 56% women; 5% minorities). Full-time faculty with Ph.D. or other terminal degree: 64%. Student/faculty ratio: 18/1. Classes of fewer than 20 students: 36%; of 20 to 49 students: 60%; of 50 or more students: 4%. **Advanced Placement and International Baccalaureate credit:** AP tests may be used for: Placement only. Scores accepted: 3, 4, 5. International Baccalaureate exams may be used for: Credit only. **Freshmen returning for sophomore year:** 65%. **Graduation rates:** Four-year: 17%; five-year: 32%; six-year: 34%. **Graduate study:** 16% of students pursue further study within one year.

COSTS AND FINANCIAL AID
Financial aid office: (812) 464-1767. **Expenses (2010-2011):** Tuition and fees 2010-2011: $5,740 in state, $13,386 out of state; room/board: $6,700. Estimated books and supplies: $1,100; transportation: $1,250; personal

expenses: $2,800. **Financial aid:** Priority filing date for institution's financial aid form: March 1. In 2009-2010, 84% of undergraduates applied for financial aid. Of those, 62% were determined to have financial need; 15% had their need fully met. Average financial aid package (proportion receiving): $8,198 (60%). Average amount of gift aid, such as scholarships or grants (proportion receiving): $4,433 (43%). Average amount of self-help aid, such as work study or loans (proportion receiving): $3,553 (55%). Average need-based loan (excluding PLUS or other private loans): $3,494. Among students who received need-based aid, the average percentage of need met: 78%. Among students who received aid based on merit, the average award (and the proportion receiving): $2,730 (10%). The average athletic scholarship (and the proportion receiving): $6,260 (1%).

CAMPUS LIFE AND EXTRACURRICULAR ACTIVITIES

Campus housing available (% using): coed dorms (30%), sorority housing (2%), fraternity housing (0%), apartments for married students (0%), apartment for single students (66%), special housing for disabled students (1%), special housing for international students (1%). Students who live in college-owned, operated, or affiliated housing: 28%. **Student employment:** During the 2009-2010 academic year, 11% of undergraduates worked on campus. Average per-year earnings: $1,370. **Clubs and organizations:** Number of student organizations: 102. Activities include: campus ministries, choral groups, dance, drama/theater, international student organization, jazz band, literary magazine, model UN, pep band, radio station, student government, student newspaper. Number of fraternities: 7; sororities: 4. Proportion of men in fraternities: 4%; of women in sororities: 3%. Average proportion of students who stay on campus on weekends: 15%. **Sports program (2009-2010):** Member of NCAA II. *Men's intercollegiate varsity sports:* baseball, basketball, cross country, golf, soccer, tennis, track and field (indoor), track and field (outdoor). *Women's intercollegiate varsity sports:* basketball, cross country, golf, soccer, softball, tennis, track and field (indoor), track and field (outdoor), volleyball.

SERVICES AND FACILITIES

Basic services: nonremedial tutoring, placement service, day care, health service, health insurance. **Remedial assistance:** reading, math, writing, study skills. **Counseling services:** minority student, career, personal, academic, psychological, birth control. **For learning-disabled students:** School does not offer a structured program with separate admission and additional fees. Total undergraduates in learning-disabled program or receiving services: 246. Services include: remedial math, remedial English, remedial reading, note-taking services, oral tests, learning center, readers, extended time for tests, tutors, priority registration, priority seating, texts on tape, other testing accommodations. **Library:** Number of titles: 328,129; number of current serial subscriptions: 21,855. **Information technology resources:** Students are not required to lease or own a computer. Number of campus computers available to all students: 1,165. School has a wireless network. Approximate number of users that can be accommodated: 6,160. Proportion of college-owned housing units wired for high-speed internet access: 100%. **Campus safety:** Security services offered: 24-hour foot-and-vehicle patrols, late-night transport/escort service, 24-hour emergency telephones, lighted pathways/sidewalks, student patrols, controlled dormitory access (key, security card, etc).

TRANSFER AND INTERNATIONAL STUDENTS

Transfer students: May apply for admission for the following academic terms: Fall, Spring, Summer. Applicants do not need a minimum number of credits to apply. For fall 2009: Transfer applications received: 1,212. Transfer applicants offered admission: 949. Transfer applicants enrolled: 703. **International students:** Number of foreign undergraduates: 189 (2% of student body). Number of countries represented: 40. Minimum TOEFL score required: 525 (paper); 71 (computer). Average TOEFL score: 507 (paper).

University of St. Francis

■ **Address:** 2701 Spring Street, Fort Wayne, IN 46808
■ **Website:** http://www.sf.edu
■ **Private; Religious affiliation:** Roman Catholic
■ **Enrollment:** N/A

KEY STATS
✔ **U.S News College Ranking:** 81, Regional Universities (Midwest)
✔ **ACT Score (25th/75th percentile):** 19-23
✔ **Tuition:** 2009-2010: $21,760

Selectivity: Selective	**Room/board:** $6,750
Acceptance rate: 47%	**Average debt:** N/A
Student/faculty ratio: N/A	**Proportion who borrowed:** N/A

Valparaiso University

■ **Address:** Kretzmann Hall, 1700 Chapel Drive, Valparaiso, IN 46383
■ **Website:** http://www.valpo.edu
■ **Private; Religious affiliation:** Lutheran
■ **Enrollment:** 2,733 full-time; 155 part-time

KEY STATS
✔ **U.S News College Ranking:** 5, Regional Universities (Midwest)
✔ **ACT Score (25th/75th percentile):** 22-29
✔ **Tuition:** 2010-2011: $29,582

Selectivity: More selective	**Room/board:** $8,330
Acceptance rate: 91%	**Average debt:** $31,783
Student/faculty ratio: 14/1	**Proportion who borrowed:** 73%

UNDERGRADUATE STUDENT BODY STATS

2009-2010 enrollment: 2,733 full-time; 155 part-time. Men: 48%; women: 52%. **Ethnic makeup:** African American: 6%; American-Indian: 1%; Asian American: 2%; Hispanic: 5%; White: 84%; International: 3%. **Religious preference:** Roman Catholic: 21%; Protestant: 22%; Muslim: 2%; No preference: 4%; Unknown: 11%; Lutheran: 31%; Other Christian, Orthodox, Mormon, Christian Science: 8%; Other: 1%.

ADMISSIONS FACTS AND FIGURES

Phone: (888) 468-2576. **Email:** undergrad.admissions@valpo.edu. **Website:** http://www.valpo.edu. **Application deadlines for fall 2011:** Regular decision: August 15. Early decision: Not offered. Early action: Send application by: November 1; Decision sent by: December 1. Admission can be deferred. **Application fee:** $30. **To apply online, go to:** http://www.valpo.edu/admissions/apply/. **Admissions requirements/recommendations:** High school units required (recommended): English: 4 (4); Mathematics: 3 (4); Science: 2 (3); Foreign language: 2 (2); Social studies: 0 (1); History: 2 (2); Academic electives: 3 (3); Total units: 16 (19). Tests: The college uses SAT or ACT scores in admissions decisions. Either SAT or ACT required. For admission to the fall 2011 entering class, the school will accept: ACT with writing recommended. Campus visit: Recommended. Admissions interview: Recommended. Off-campus interview: May be arranged. **Factors that count in admissions decisions:** *Academic:* Secondary school record: Very Important. Class rank: Important. Letters of recommendation: Important. Standardized test scores: Important. Essay: Considered. *Nonacademic:* Interview: Considered. Extracurricular activities: Important. Talent/ability: Important. Character/personal qualities: Important. Alumni/ae relationship: Important. Geographical residence: Not Considered. State residency: Not Considered. Religious affiliation/commitment: Considered. Minority status: Considered. Volunteer work: Considered. Work experience: Not Considered. **Other schools with the greatest overlap in applicants:** Bradley University; Butler University; Indiana University–Bloomington; Marquette University; Purdue University–West Lafayette. **Admissions statistics for the fall 2009 entering class:** Total applicants: 2,932. Total accepted: 2,674. Freshmen enrolled: 671; 62% were from out of state. Accepted through early-decision or early-action plans: 43%. Overall acceptance rate: 91%. Non-early acceptance rate: 88%. **Credentials of fall 2009 freshmen:** 26% ranked in the top 10 percent of their high school class; 58% were in the top 25 percent; 86% were in the top half. (Proportion submitting class standing: 77%.) **Average high school grade point average:** 3.3. **First-year students who submitted SAT scores:** 47%. Scores (25/75 percentile): Critical Reading: 480-

630, Math: 500-620, Combined: 980-1250. **First-year students submitting ACT scores:** 71%. Scores (25/75 percentile): English: 22-30, Math: 22-29, Composite: 22-29.

ACADEMICS

Year founded: 1859. **Academic calendar:** Semester. **Degrees offered:** certificate, associate, terminal-associate, bachelor's, post-bachelor's certificate, master's, post-master's certificate, doctorate. **Most popular majors:** 11% nursing/registered nurse training (R.N., A.S.N., B.S.N., M.S.N.), 5% psychology, 4% political science and government, 3% history, 3% mechanical engineering. **Major fields of study:** area, ethnic, cultural, and gender studies; biological and biomedical sciences; business, management, marketing, and related support services; communication, journalism, and related programs; computer and information sciences and support services; education; engineering; English language and literature/letters; family and consumer sciences/human sciences; foreign languages, literatures, and linguistics; health professions and related clinical sciences; history; mathematics and statistics; multi/interdisciplinary studies; natural resources and conservation; parks, recreation, leisure, and fitness studies; philosophy and religious studies; physical sciences; psychology; public administration and social service professions; social sciences; theology and religious vocations; visual and performing arts. **Areas of required coursework:** humanities, foreign languages, sciences (biological or physical), social science, other. **Pre-professional programs:** pre-law, pre-dentistry, pre-medicine, pre-theology, pre-veterinary science, pre-optometry. **Special academic programs (% participation):** accelerated program (4%), cooperative (work-study plan) program (1%), distance learning (28%), double major (21%), English as a Second Language (ESL) (.5%), exchange student program (domestic) (3%), honors program (11%), independent study (27%), internships (36%), liberal arts/career combination (1%), student-designed major (3%), study abroad (18%), teacher certificate program (9%). **Teacher certification offered in:** special education, elementary, middle/junior high, secondary. **Cooperative education programs:** business, computer science, engineering, health professions, humanities, natural science, social/behavioral science, other. **Reserve Officers Training Corps (ROTC):** Army ROTC: Offered at cooperating institution (University of Notre Dame); Air Force ROTC: Offered at cooperating institution (University of Notre Dame). **Faculty and instruction (2009-2010):** Total instructional faculty: 242 full-time, 114 part-time (58% men; 42% women; 8% minorities). Full-time faculty with Ph.D. or other terminal degree: 92%. Student/faculty ratio: 14/1. Classes of fewer than 20 students: 43%; of 20 to 49 students: 51%; of 50 or more students: 5%. **Advanced Placement and International Baccalaureate credit:** AP tests may be used for: Credit and/or placement. Scores accepted: 3, 4, 5. International Baccalaureate exams may be used for: Credit and/or placement. **Freshmen returning for sophomore year:** 84%. **Graduation rates:** Four-year: 63%; five-year: 75%; six-year: 76%. **Graduate study:** 24% of students pursue further study within one year. Fields in which graduates pursue further study: Master of Business Administration (MBA), 11%; law, 8%; medicine, 1%; engineering, 7%; theology (or the seminary), 4%; arts and sciences, 69%.

COSTS AND FINANCIAL AID

Financial aid office: (219) 464-5015. **Expenses (2010-2011):** Tuition and fees 2010-2011: $29,582; room/board: $8,330. Estimated books and supplies: $1,200; transportation: $750; personal expenses: $890. **Financial aid:** Priority filing date for institution's financial aid form: March 1. In 2009-2010, 82% of undergraduates applied for financial aid. Of those, 72% were determined to have financial need; 24% had their need fully met. Average financial aid package (proportion receiving): $21,000 (72%). Average amount of gift aid, such as scholarships or grants (proportion receiving): $15,700 (71%). Average amount of self-help aid, such as work study or loans (proportion receiving): $5,600 (57%). Average need-based loan (excluding PLUS or other private loans): $5,000. Among students who received need-based aid, the average percentage of need met: 80%. Among students who received aid based on merit, the average award (and the proportion receiving): $9,200 (22%). The average athletic scholarship (and the proportion receiving): $20,700 (3%). Average amount of debt of borrowers graduating in 2009: $31,783. Proportion who borrowed: 73%.

CAMPUS LIFE AND EXTRACURRICULAR ACTIVITIES

Campus housing available (% using): coed dorms (67%), women's dorms (18%), fraternity housing (7%), apartment for single students (7%). Students who live in college-owned, operated, or affiliated housing: 66%. **Student employment:** During the 2009-2010 academic year, 50% of undergraduates worked on campus. Average per-year earnings: $850. **Clubs and organizations:** Number of student organizations: 93. Activities include: campus ministries, choral groups, concert band, dance, drama/theater, international

student organization, jazz band, literary magazine, music ensembles, musical theater, pep band, radio station, student government, student newspaper, symphony orchestra, yearbook. Number of fraternities: 9; sororities: 7. Proportion of men in fraternities: 24%; of women in sororities: 20%. **Sports program (2009-2010):** Member of NCAA I. ***Men's intercollegiate varsity sports:*** baseball, basketball, cross country, football, golf, soccer, swimming, tennis, track and field (indoor), track and field (outdoor). ***Women's intercollegiate varsity sports:*** basketball, bowling, cross country, golf, soccer, softball, swimming, tennis, track and field (indoor), track and field (outdoor), volleyball.

SERVICES AND FACILITIES

Basic services: nonremedial tutoring, placement service, health service, health insurance. **Remedial assistance:** writing, study skills. **Counseling services:** minority student, career, military, personal, academic, older student, psychological, religious. **For learning-disabled students:** School does not offer a structured program with separate admission and additional fees. Total undergraduates in learning-disabled program or receiving services: 23. Services include: tape recorders, note-taking services, oral tests, readers, extended time for tests, tutors, early syllabus, priority registration, priority seating, texts on tape, typist/scribe, exams on tape or computer, other testing accommodations, waiver of foreign language degree requirement, other. **Library:** Number of titles: 537,234; number of current serial subscriptions: 47,914. **Information technology resources:** Students are not required to lease or own a computer. Number of campus computers available to all students: 946. School has a wireless network. Approximate number of users that can be accommodated: 3,000. Proportion of college-owned housing units wired for high-speed internet access: 100%. **Campus safety:** Security services offered: 24-hour foot-and-vehicle patrols, late-night transport/escort service, 24-hour emergency telephones, lighted pathways/sidewalks, controlled dormitory access (key, security card, etc).

TRANSFER AND INTERNATIONAL STUDENTS

Transfer students: May apply for admission for the following academic terms: Fall, Spring, Summer. Applicants do not need a minimum number of credits to apply. For fall 2009: Transfer applications received: 289. Transfer applicants offered admission: 263. Transfer applicants enrolled: 124. **International students:** Number of foreign undergraduates: 92 (3% of student body). Number of countries represented: 21. Minimum TOEFL score required: 550 (paper); 213 (computer).

Wabash College

- **Address:** PO Box 352, Crawfordsville, IN 47933
- **Website:** http://www.wabash.edu
- **Private**
- **Enrollment:** 874 full-time; 9 part-time

KEY STATS
- ✔ **U.S News College Ranking:** 58, National Liberal Arts Colleges
- ✔ **SAT Score (25th/75th percentile):** 1030-1260
- ✔ **Tuition:** 2010-2011: $31,050

Selectivity: More selective	**Room/board:** $8,300
Acceptance rate: 49%	**Average debt:** $28,383
Student/faculty ratio: 10/1	**Proportion who borrowed:** 70%

UNDERGRADUATE STUDENT BODY STATS

2009-2010 enrollment: 874 full-time; 9 part-time. Men: 100%; women: 0%. **Ethnic makeup:** African American: 6%; American-Indian: 1%; Asian American: 2%; Hispanic: 5%; White: 80%; International: 7%.

ADMISSIONS FACTS AND FIGURES

Phone: (800) 345-5385. **Email:** admissions@wabash.edu. **Website:** http://www.wabash.edu. **Application deadlines for fall 2011:** Regular decision: Rolling. Early decision: Send application by: November 15; Decision sent by: December 1. Early action: Send application by: December 1; Decision sent by: December 22. Admission can be deferred. **Application fee:** $40. **To apply online, go to:** http://www.wabash.edu/admissions/apply/. **Admissions requirements/recommendations:** High school units required (recommended): English: (4); Mathematics: (4); Science: (2); Foreign language: (2); Social studies: (2); History: (0); Academic electives: (3); Total units: (17). Tests: The college uses SAT or ACT scores in admissions decisions. Either SAT or ACT required. For admission to the fall 2011 entering class, the school will accept: ACT with writing required. Campus visit: Recommended. Admissions interview: Recommended. Off-campus interview: May be arranged. **Factors that count in admissions decisions:** *Academic:* Secondary school record: Very Important. Class rank: Very Important. Letters of recommendation: Important. Standardized test scores: Important. Essay: Considered. *Nonacademic:* Interview: Important. Extracurricular activities: Important. Talent/ability: Important. Character/personal qualities: Considered. Alumni/ae relationship: Considered. Geographical residence: Considered. State residency: Not Considered. Religious affiliation/commitment: Not Considered. Minority status: Considered. Volunteer work: Considered. Work experience: Considered. **Other schools with the greatest overlap in applicants:** Butler University; DePauw University; Hanover College; Indiana University–Bloomington; Purdue University–West Lafayette. **Admissions statistics for the fall 2009 entering class:** Total applicants: 1,588. Total accepted: 775. Freshmen enrolled: 247; 28% were from out of state. Accepted through early-decision or early-action plans: 61%. Overall acceptance rate: 49%. Early-decision acceptance rate: 92%. Non-early acceptance rate: 40%. **Size of waiting list:** 40 applicants; enrolled from waiting list: 4. **Credentials of fall 2009 freshmen:** 31% ranked in the top 10 percent of their high school class; 70% were in the top 25 percent; 91% were in the top half. (Proportion submitting class standing: 79%.) **Average high school grade point average:** 3.5. **First-year students who submitted SAT scores:** 83%. Scores (25/75 percentile): Critical Reading: 500-600, Math: 530-660, Combined: 1030-1260. **First-year students submitting ACT scores:** 49%. Scores (25/75 percentile): English: 21-26, Math: 22-28, Composite: 21-27.

ACADEMICS

Year founded: 1832. **Academic calendar:** Semester. **Degrees offered:** bachelor's. **Most popular majors:** 20% social sciences, 15% philosophy and religious studies, 13% English language and literature, 12% psychology, 9% biology/biological sciences. **Major fields of study:** biological and biomedical sciences; English language and literature/letters; foreign languages, literatures, and linguistics; history; mathematics and statistics; philosophy and religious studies; physical sciences; psychology; social sciences; visual and performing arts. **Areas of required coursework:** arts/fine arts, humanities, mathematics, English (including composition), philosophy, foreign languages, sciences (biological or physical), history, social science. **Preprofessional programs:** pre-law, pre-dentistry, pre-medicine, other. **Special academic programs (% participation):** double major (8%), independent study (38%), internships (73%), student-designed major (0%), study abroad (23%), teacher certificate program (3%). **Teacher certification offered in:** secondary. **Cooperative education programs:** engineering. **Faculty and instruction (2009-2010):** Total instructional faculty: 90 full-time, 2 part-time (64% men; 36% women; 8% minorities). Full-time faculty with Ph.D. or other terminal degree: 99%. Student/faculty ratio: 10/1. Classes of fewer than 20 students: 77%; of 20 to 49 students: 20%; of 50 or more students: 2%. **Advanced Placement and International Baccalaureate credit:** AP tests may be used for: Placement only. Scores accepted: 4, 5. International Baccalaureate exams may be used for: Placement only. **Freshmen returning for sophomore year:** 87%. **Graduation rates:** Four-year: 62%; five-year: 65%; six-year: 67%. **Graduate study:** 29% of students pursue further study immediately upon graduation; 40% within one year; 65% within five years. Fields in which graduates pursue further study: Master of Business Administration (MBA), 1%; law, 6%; medicine, 8%; dentistry, 1%; engineering, 1%; theology (or the seminary), 3%; education, 1%; arts and sciences, 10%; veterinary medicine, 1%.

COSTS AND FINANCIAL AID

Financial aid office: (765) 361-6370. **Expenses (2010-2011):** Tuition and fees 2010-2011: $31,050; room/board: $8,300. Estimated books and supplies: $900 personal expenses: $1,500. **Financial aid:** Priority filing date for institution's financial aid form: February 15; deadline: March 1. In 2009-2010, 88% of undergraduates applied for financial aid. Of those, 80% were determined to have financial need; 88% had their need fully met. Average financial aid package (proportion receiving): $27,083 (80%). Average amount of gift aid, such as scholarships or grants (proportion receiving): $18,638 (79%). Average amount of self-help aid, such as work study or loans (proportion receiving): $7,905 (69%). Average need-based loan (excluding PLUS or other private loans): $5,319. Among students who received need-based aid, the average percentage of need met: 96%. Among students who received aid based on merit, the average award (and the proportion receiving): $16,398 (17%). Average amount of debt of borrowers graduating in 2009: $28,383. Proportion who borrowed: 70%.

CAMPUS LIFE AND EXTRACURRICULAR ACTIVITIES

Campus housing available (% using): men's dorms (36%), fraternity housing (50%), other housing options (14%). Students who live in college-owned, operated, or affiliated housing: 86%. **Student employment:** During the 2009-2010 academic year, 85% of undergraduates worked on campus. Average per-year earnings: $3,000. **Clubs and organizations:** Number of student organizations: 66. Activities include: campus ministries, choral groups, concert band, drama/theater, international student organization, jazz band, literary magazine, music ensembles, musical theater, pep band, radio station, student government, student newspaper, student film society, symphony orchestra, yearbook. Number of fraternities: 9 Proportion of men in fraternities: 49%; Average proportion of students who stay on campus on weekends: 60%. **Sports program (2009-2010):** Member of NCAA III. *Men's intercollegiate varsity sports:* baseball, basketball, cross country, football, golf, soccer, swimming, tennis, track and field (indoor), track and field (outdoor), wrestling.

SERVICES AND FACILITIES

Basic services: nonremedial tutoring, placement service, health service, health insurance. **Remedial assistance:** math, writing, study skills. **Counseling services:** minority student, career, personal, academic, psychological, religious. **For learning-disabled students:** School does not offer a structured program with separate admission and additional fees. Services include: tape recorders, untimed tests, learning center, extended time for tests, tutors, other. **Library:** Number of titles: 359,446; number of current serial subscriptions: 23,884. **Information technology resources:** Students are not required to lease or own a computer. Number of campus computers available to all students: 400. School has a wireless network. Approximate number of users that can be accommodated: 3,000. Proportion of college-owned housing units wired for high-speed internet access: 100%. **Campus safety:** Security services offered: 24-hour foot-and-vehicle patrols, late-night transport/escort service, 24-hour emergency telephones, lighted pathways/sidewalks.

TRANSFER AND INTERNATIONAL STUDENTS

Transfer students: May apply for admission for the following academic terms: Fall, Spring. Applicants need a minimum number of credits to apply. For fall 2009: Transfer applications received: 22. Transfer applicants offered admission: 5. Transfer applicants enrolled: 3. **International students:** Number of foreign undergraduates: 58 (7% of student body). Number of countries represented: 21. Minimum TOEFL score required: 79 (computer).

Iowa

Briar Cliff University

- **Address:** 3303 Rebecca Street, Box 2100, Sioux City, IA 51104
- **Website:** http://www.briarcliff.edu
- **Private; Religious affiliation:** Roman Catholic
- **Enrollment:** 893 full-time; 186 part-time

KEY STATS

✔ **U.S News College Ranking:** 29, Regional Colleges (Midwest)
✔ **ACT Score (25th/75th percentile):** 19-25
✔ **Tuition:** 2010-2011: $23,418

Selectivity: Selective	**Room/board:** $7,032
Acceptance rate: 62%	**Average debt:** N/A
Student/faculty ratio: 12/1	**Proportion who borrowed:** N/A

UNDERGRADUATE STUDENT BODY STATS

2009-2010 enrollment: 893 full-time; 186 part-time. Men: 44%; women: 56%. **Ethnic makeup:** African American: 7%; American-Indian: 2%; Asian American: 3%; Hispanic: 6%; White: 82%. **Religious preference:** Protestant: 26%; Unknown: 19%; Roman Catholic: 55%.

ADMISSIONS FACTS AND FIGURES

Phone: (712) 279-5200. **Email:** admissions@briarcliff.edu. **Website:** http://www.briarcliff.edu. **Application deadlines for fall 2011:** Regular decision: Rolling. Early decision: Not offered. Early action: Not offered. Admission can be deferred. **Application fee:** $20. **To apply online, go to:** https://www.briarcliff.edu/prospective_students/online_forms/application.asp. **Admissions requirements/recommendations:** High school units required (recommended): English: 4 (4); Mathematics: 3 (3); Science: 3 (3); Foreign language: 2 (2); Social studies: 1 (1); History: 1 (2); Academic electives: 1 (1); Total units: 16 (16). Tests: The college uses SAT or ACT scores in admissions decisions. ACT required. For admission to the fall 2011 entering class, the school will accept: ACT with or without writing accepted. Campus visit: Recommended. Admissions interview: Recommended. Off-campus interview: May be arranged. **Factors that count in admissions decisions:** *Academic:* Secondary school record: Very Important. Class rank: Important. Letters of recommendation: Considered. Standardized test scores: Very Important. Essay: Considered. *Nonacademic:* Interview: Considered. Extracurricular activities: Considered. Talent/ability: Considered. Character/personal qualities: Considered. Alumni/ae relationship: Considered. Geographical residence: Not Considered. State residency: Not Considered. Religious affiliation/commitment: Not Considered. Minority status: Not Considered. Volunteer work: Not Considered. Work experience: Not Considered. **Other schools with the greatest overlap in applicants:** Buena Vista University; Iowa State University; Morningside College; University of Iowa. **Admissions statistics for the fall 2009 entering class:** Total applicants: 1,579. Total accepted: 976. Freshmen enrolled: 223; 54% were from out of state. Overall acceptance rate: 62%. **Size of waiting list:** 0 applicants; enrolled from waiting list: 0. **Credentials of fall 2009 freshmen:** 11% ranked in the top 10 percent of their high school class; 34% were in the top 25 percent; 64% were in the top half. (Proportion submitting class standing: 95%.) **Average high school grade point average:** 3.2. **First-year students who submitted SAT scores:** 9%. **First-year students submitting ACT scores:** 99%. Scores (25/75 percentile): English: 18-34, Math: 18-35, Composite: 19-25.

ACADEMICS

Year founded: 1930. **Academic calendar:** Trimester. **Degrees offered:** associate, bachelor's, post-bachelor's certificate, master's. **Most popular majors:** 26% business administration and management, 21% nursing/registered nurse training (R.N., A.S.N., B.S.N., M.S.N.), 11% education, 6% parks, recreation, leisure, and fitness studies. **Major fields of study:** biological and biomedical sciences; business, management, marketing, and related support services; communication, journalism, and related programs; computer and information sciences and support services; education; English language and literature/letters; foreign languages, literatures, and linguistics; health professions and related clinical sciences; mathematics and statistics; natural resources and conservation; parks, recreation, leisure, and fitness studies; physical sciences; psychology; public administration and social service professions; security and protective services; social sciences; theology and religious vocations; visual and performing arts. **Areas of required coursework:** arts/fine arts, humanities, computer literacy, mathematics, English (including composition), philosophy, foreign languages, sciences (biological or physical), history, social science, other. **Pre-professional programs:** pre-law, pre-dentistry, pre-medicine, pre-veterinary science, pre-optometry, pre-pharmacy, other. **Special academic programs (% participation):** accelerated program (11%), cross-registration (0%), distance learning (6%), double major (11%), dual enrollment (0%), honors program (10%), independent study (100%), internships (60%), liberal arts/career combination (99%), study abroad (0%), teacher certificate program (11%), weekend college (11%). **Teacher certification offered in:** elementary, middle/junior high, secondary. **Reserve Officers Training Corps (ROTC):** Army ROTC: Offered at cooperating institution (University of South Dakota). **Faculty and instruction (2009-2010):** Total instructional faculty: 60 full-time, 48 part-time (44% men; 56% women; 3% minorities). Full-time faculty with Ph.D. or other terminal degree: 68%. Student/faculty ratio: 12/1. Classes of fewer than 20 students: 75%; of 20 to 49 students: 25%; of 50 or more students: 0%. **Advanced Placement and International Baccalaureate credit:** AP tests may be used for: Credit only. Scores accepted: 3, 4, 5. International Baccalaureate exams may be used for: Credit only. **Freshmen returning for sophomore year:** 65%. **Graduation rates:** Four-year: 41%; five-year: 47%; six-year: 49%. **Graduate study:** 27% of students pursue further study immediately upon graduation; 0% within one year. Fields in which graduates pursue further study: Master of Business Administration (MBA), 18%; law, 2%; medicine, 34%; theology (or the seminary), 6%; education, 12%; arts and sciences, 28%.

COSTS AND FINANCIAL AID

Financial aid office: (712) 279-5239. **Expenses (2010-2011):** Tuition and fees 2010-2011: $23,418; room/board: $7,032. Estimated books and supplies: $1,050; transportation: $1,020; personal expenses: $1,980. **Financial aid:** Priority filing date for institution's financial aid form: March 15. In 2009-2010, 98% of undergraduates applied for financial aid. Of those, 70% were determined to have financial need; 68% had their need fully met. Average financial aid package (proportion receiving): $6,300 (70%). Average amount of gift aid, such as scholarships or grants (proportion receiving): $6,200 (70%). Average amount of self-help aid, such as work study or loans (proportion receiving): $7,851 (70%). Average need-based loan (excluding PLUS or other private loans): $4,775. Among students who received need-based aid, the average percentage of need met: 78%. Among students who received aid based on merit, the average award (and the proportion receiving): $11,550 (30%). The average athletic scholarship (and the proportion receiving): $5,440 (47%).

CAMPUS LIFE AND EXTRACURRICULAR ACTIVITIES

Campus housing available (% using): coed dorms (84%), other housing options (16%). Students who live in college-owned, operated, or affiliated housing: 52%. **Student employment:** During the 2009-2010 academic year, 21% of undergraduates worked on campus. Average per-year earnings: $760. **Clubs and organizations:** Number of student organizations: 36. Activities include: campus ministries, choral groups, drama/theater, jazz band, literary magazine, music ensembles, musical theater, opera, radio station, student government, student newspaper. Number of fraternities: 0; sororities: 0. Average proportion of students who stay on campus on weekends: 70%. **Sports program (2009-2010):** Member of NAIA. *Men's intercollegiate varsity sports:* baseball, basketball, cross country, football, golf, soccer, tennis, track and field (indoor), track and field (outdoor), wrestling. *Women's intercollegiate varsity sports:* basketball, cross country, golf, soccer, softball, tennis, track and field (indoor), track and field (outdoor), volleyball.

SERVICES AND FACILITIES

Basic services: nonremedial tutoring, placement service, health service, health insurance. **Remedial assistance:** reading, math, writing, study skills. **Counseling services:** minority student, career, military, personal, veteran student, academic, older student, psychological, religious. **For learning-disabled students:** School does not offer a structured program with separate admission and additional fees. Total undergraduates in learning-disabled program or receiving services: 2. Services include: remedial math, reading machines, remedial reading, tape recorders, note-taking services, oral tests, extended time for tests, priority registration, other testing accommodations. **Information technology resources:** Students are not required to lease or own a computer. Number of campus computers available to all students: 134. School has a wireless network. Approximate number of users that can be accommodated: 550. Proportion of college-owned housing units wired for high-speed internet access: 100%. **Campus safety:** Security services offered: 24-hour foot-and-vehicle patrols, late-night transport/escort service, 24-hour emergency telephones, lighted pathways/sidewalks, controlled dormitory access (key, security card, etc).

TRANSFER AND INTERNATIONAL STUDENTS

Transfer students: May apply for admission for the following academic terms: Fall, Winter, Spring, Summer. Applicants need a minimum number of credits to apply. For fall 2009: Transfer applications received: 130. Transfer applicants offered admission: 65. Transfer applicants enrolled: 47. **International students:** Number of foreign undergraduates: 2. Number of countries represented: 2. Minimum TOEFL score required: 525 (paper); 193 (computer). Average TOEFL score: 525 (paper).

Buena Vista University

- **Address:** 610 W. Fourth Street, Storm Lake, IA 50588
- **Website:** http://www.bvu.edu
- **Private; Religious affiliation:** Presbyterian
- **Enrollment:** 943 full-time; 14 part-time

KEY STATS

✔ **U.S News College Ranking:** 14, Regional Colleges (Midwest)
✔ **ACT Score (25th/75th percentile):** 18-25
✔ **Tuition:** 2010-2011: $26,306

Selectivity: Selective	**Room/board:** $7,582
Acceptance rate: 72%	**Average debt:** $40,569
Student/faculty ratio: 10/1	**Proportion who borrowed:** 91%

UNDERGRADUATE STUDENT BODY STATS

2009-2010 enrollment: 943 full-time; 14 part-time. Men: 49%; women: 51%. **Ethnic makeup:** African American: 6%; Asian American: 2%; Hispanic: 5%; White: 83%; International: 4%. **Religious preference:** Roman Catholic: 26%; Protestant: 50%; Unknown: 10%; Presbyterian: 4%; Other: 10%.

ADMISSIONS FACTS AND FIGURES

Phone: (800) 383-9600. **Email:** admissions@bvu.edu. **Website:** http://www.bvu.edu. **Application deadlines for fall 2011:** Regular decision: Rolling. Early decision: Not offered. Early action: Not offered. Admission can be deferred. **To apply online, go to:** http://www.bvu.edu/attending_bvu/apply.dot. **Admissions requirements/recommendations:** High school units required (recommended): English: 4; Mathematics: (4); Science: 2 (4); Foreign language: (2); Social studies: 2; History: (2); Total units: 15. Tests: The college uses SAT or ACT scores in admissions decisions. Either SAT or ACT required. For admission to the fall 2011 entering class, the school will accept: ACT with or without writing accepted. Campus visit: Recommended. Admissions interview: Recommended. Off-campus interview: May be arranged. **Factors that count in admissions decisions:** *Academic:* Secondary school record: Very Important. Class rank: Very Important. Letters of recommendation: Very Important. Standardized test scores: Very Important. Essay: Considered. *Nonacademic:* Interview: Considered. Extracurricular activities: Considered. Talent/ability: Considered. Character/personal qualities: Considered. Alumni/ae relationship: Considered. Geographical residence: Not Considered. State residency: Not Considered. Religious affiliation/commitment: Not Considered. Minority status: Not Considered. Volunteer work: Considered. Work experience: Considered. **Other schools with the greatest overlap in applicants:** Central College; Iowa State University; Morningside College; Simpson College; University of Northern Iowa. **Admissions statistics for the fall 2009 entering class:** Total applicants: 1,433. Total accepted: 1,027. Freshmen enrolled: 273; 26% were from out of state. Overall acceptance rate: 72%. **Credentials of fall 2009 freshmen:** 15% ranked in the top 10 percent of their high school class; 38% were in the top 25 percent; 71% were in the top half. (Proportion submitting class standing: 94%.) **Average high school grade point average:** 3.3. **First-year students who submitted SAT scores:** 4%. Scores (25/75 percentile): Critical Reading:

350-530, Math: 450-580, Combined: 800-1110. **First-year students submitting ACT scores:** 95%. Scores (25/75 percentile): English: 17-25, Math: 18-25, Composite: 18-25.

ACADEMICS

Year founded: 1891. **Academic calendar:** 4-1-4. **Degrees offered:** bachelor's, master's. **Most popular majors:** 23% business, management, marketing, and related support services, 11% parks, recreation, leisure, and fitness studies, 10% biological and biomedical sciences, 9% education, 8% security and protective services. **Major fields of study:** biological and biomedical sciences; business, management, marketing, and related support services; communication, journalism, and related programs; computer and information sciences and support services; education; English language and literature/letters; foreign languages, literatures, and linguistics; health professions and related clinical sciences; history; mathematics and statistics; multi/interdisciplinary studies; parks, recreation, leisure, and fitness studies; philosophy and religious studies; physical sciences; psychology; public administration and social service professions; security and protective services; social sciences; visual and performing arts. **Areas of required coursework:** arts/fine arts, humanities, computer literacy, mathematics, English (including composition), sciences (biological or physical), social science, other. **Preprofessional programs:** pre-law, pre-dentistry, pre-medicine, pre-theology, pre-veterinary science, pre-optometry, pre-pharmacy, other. **Special academic programs:** distance learning, double major, dual enrollment, English as a Second Language (ESL), exchange student program (domestic), external degree program, honors program, independent study, internships, student-designed major, study abroad, teacher certificate program. **Teacher certification offered in:** special education, elementary, middle/junior high, secondary. **Reserve Officers Training Corps (ROTC):** Army ROTC: Offered on campus. **Faculty and instruction (2009-2010):** Total instructional faculty: 83 full-time, 23 part-time (54% men; 46% women; 6% minorities). Full-time faculty with Ph.D. or other terminal degree: 69%. Student/faculty ratio: 10/1. Classes of fewer than 20 students: 65%; of 20 to 49 students: 35%; of 50 or more students: 0%. **Advanced Placement and International Baccalaureate credit:** AP tests may be used for: Placement only. Scores accepted: 3, 4, 5. International Baccalaureate exams may be used for: Placement only. **Freshmen returning for sophomore year:** 69%. **Graduation rates:** Four-year: 46%; five-year: 58%; six-year: 59%. **Graduate study:** 26% of students pursue further study immediately upon graduation. Fields in which graduates pursue further study: Master of Business Administration (MBA), 4%; law, 4%; medicine, 24%; theology (or the seminary), 6%; education, 4%; arts and sciences, 56%; veterinary medicine, 2%.

COSTS AND FINANCIAL AID

Financial aid office: (712) 749-2164. **Expenses (2010-2011):** Tuition and fees 2010-2011: $26,306; room/board: $7,582. Estimated books and supplies: $885; transportation: $750; personal expenses: $1,000. **Financial aid:** Priority filing date for institution's financial aid form: June 1. In 2009-2010, 94% of undergraduates applied for financial aid. Of those, 87% were determined to have financial need; 52% had their need fully met. Average financial aid package (proportion receiving): $24,136 (87%). Average amount of gift aid, such as scholarships or grants (proportion receiving): $9,415 (74%). Average amount of self-help aid, such as work study or loans (proportion receiving): $5,827 (76%). Average need-based loan (excluding PLUS or other private loans): $5,120. Among students who received need-based aid, the average percentage of need met: 50%. Among students who received aid based on merit, the average award (and the proportion receiving): $11,139 (7%). The average athletic scholarship (and the proportion receiving): $0 (0%). Average amount of debt of borrowers graduating in 2009: $40,569. Proportion who borrowed: 91%.

CAMPUS LIFE AND EXTRACURRICULAR ACTIVITIES

Campus housing available (% using): coed dorms (66%), women's dorms (13%), men's dorms (21%). Students who live in college-owned, operated, or affiliated housing: 85%. **Clubs and organizations:** Number of student organizations: 65. Activities include: campus ministries, choral groups, concert band, dance, drama/theater, international student organization, jazz band, music ensembles, musical theater, pep band, radio station, student government, student newspaper, television station. Number of fraternities: 0; sororities: 0. Average proportion of students who stay on campus on weekends: 60%. **Sports program (2009-2010):** Member of NCAA III. *Men's intercollegiate varsity sports:* baseball, basketball, cross country, football, golf, soccer, tennis, track and field (indoor), track and field (outdoor), wrestling. *Women's intercollegiate varsity sports:* basketball, cross country, golf, soccer, softball, tennis, track and field (indoor), track and field (outdoor), volleyball.

SERVICES AND FACILITIES

Basic services: nonremedial tutoring, placement service, health service. **Remedial assistance:** reading, math, writing, study skills. **Counseling services:** minority student, career, personal, veteran student, academic, psychological, birth control, religious. **For learning-disabled students:** School does not offer a structured program with separate admission and additional fees. Services include: remedial math, remedial English, reading machines, tape recorders, learning center, extended time for tests, tutors, priority registration, priority seating, texts on tape. **Library:** Number of titles: 145,000; number of current serial subscriptions: 639. **Information technology resources:** Students are not required to lease or own a computer. School has a wireless network. Approximate number of users that can be accommodated: 4,800. Proportion of college-owned housing units wired for high-speed internet access: 100%. **Campus safety:** Security services offered: late-night transport/escort service, 24-hour emergency telephones, lighted pathways/sidewalks, controlled dormitory access (key, security card, etc).

TRANSFER AND INTERNATIONAL STUDENTS

Transfer students: May apply for admission for the following academic terms: Fall, Winter, Spring. Applicants do not need a minimum number of credits to apply. For fall 2009: Transfer applications received: 186. Transfer applicants offered admission: 113. Transfer applicants enrolled: 75. **International students:** Number of foreign undergraduates: 37 (4% of student body). Number of countries represented: 4. Minimum TOEFL score required: 475 (paper); 53 (computer). Average TOEFL score: 543 (paper).

Central College

- **Address:** 812 University Street, Pella, IA 50219
- **Website:** http://www.central.edu
- **Private; Religious affiliation:** Reformed Church in America
- **Enrollment:** 1,597 full-time; 39 part-time

KEY STATS

✔ **U.S News College Ranking:** 144, National Liberal Arts Colleges
✔ **ACT Score (25th/75th percentile):** 21-27
✔ **Tuition:** 2010-2011: $26,242

Selectivity: More selective	**Room/board:** $8,702
Acceptance rate: 74%	**Average debt:** $36,068
Student/faculty ratio: 15/1	**Proportion who borrowed:** 86%

UNDERGRADUATE STUDENT BODY STATS

2009-2010 enrollment: 1,597 full-time; 39 part-time. Men: 47%; women: 53%. **Ethnic makeup:** African American: 2%; Asian American: 2%; Hispanic: 2%; White: 93%; International: 1%. **Religious preference:** Roman Catholic: 16%; Protestant: 55%; Unknown: 19%; Reformed Church in America: 9%; Other: 1%.

ADMISSIONS FACTS AND FIGURES

Phone: (641) 628-7600. **Email:** admissions@central.edu. **Website:** http://www.central.edu. **Application deadlines for fall 2011:** Regular decision: Rolling. Early decision: Not offered. Early action: Not offered. Admission can be deferred. **Application fee:** $25. **To apply online, go to:** https://www.central.edu/admission/forms/apply/index.cfm. **Admissions requirements/recommendations:** High school units required (recommended): English: (4); Mathematics: (3); Science: (3); Foreign language: (2); Social studies: (3); History: (2); Academic electives: (0); Total units: 0 (15). Tests: The college uses SAT or ACT scores in admissions decisions. Either SAT or ACT required. For admission to the fall 2011 entering class, the school will accept: ACT with or without writing accepted. Campus visit: Recommended. Admissions interview: Recommended. Off-campus interview: May be arranged. **Factors that count in admissions decisions:** *Academic:* Secondary school record: Very Important. Class rank: Important. Letters of recommendation: Considered. Standardized test scores: Very Important. Essay: Considered. *Nonacademic:* Interview: Considered. Extracurricular activities: Considered. Talent/ability: Considered. Character/personal qualities: Considered. Alumni/ae relationship: Considered. Geographical residence: Not Considered. State residency: Not Considered. Religious affiliation/commitment: Not Considered. Minority status: Not Considered. Volunteer work: Considered. Work experience: Considered. **Other schools with the greatest overlap in applicants:** Coe College; Loras College; Northwestern College; Simpson College; Wartburg College. **Admissions statistics for the fall 2009 entering class:** Total applicants: 2,451. Total accepted: 1,823. Freshmen

enrolled: 443; 17% were from out of state. Overall acceptance rate: 74%. **Credentials of fall 2009 freshmen:** 28% ranked in the top 10 percent of their high school class; 54% were in the top 25 percent; 84% were in the top half. (Proportion submitting class standing: 94%.) **Average high school grade point average:** 3.5. **First-year students who submitted SAT scores:** 3%. Scores (25/75 percentile): Critical Reading: 470-670, Math: 480-650, Combined: 950-1320. **First-year students submitting ACT scores:** 98%. Scores (25/75 percentile): English: 20-27, Math: 20-27, Composite: 21-27.

ACADEMICS

Year founded: 1853. **Academic calendar:** Semester. **Degrees offered:** bachelor's. **Most popular majors:** 15% business, management, marketing, and related support services, 13% kinesiology and exercise science, 12% foreign languages, literatures, and linguistics, 10% education, 8% social sciences. **Major fields of study:** biological and biomedical sciences; business, management, marketing, and related support services; communication, journalism, and related programs; computer and information sciences and support services; education; English language and literature/letters; foreign languages, literatures, and linguistics; history; liberal arts and sciences studies, and humanities; mathematics and statistics; multi/interdisciplinary studies; natural resources and conservation; parks, recreation, leisure, and fitness studies; philosophy and religious studies; physical sciences; psychology; social sciences; visual and performing arts. **Areas of required coursework:** arts/fine arts, humanities, mathematics, foreign languages, sciences (biological or physical), history, social science, other. **Pre-professional programs:** pre-law, pre-dentistry, pre-medicine, pre-veterinary science, pre-optometry, pre-pharmacy, other. **Special academic programs (% participation):** accelerated program (26%), cooperative (work-study plan) program, double major (15%), dual enrollment, honors program (21%), independent study (23%), internships (45%), student-designed major (2%), study abroad (50%), teacher certificate program (11%). **Teacher certification offered in:** early childhood, special education, elementary, middle/junior high, secondary. **Cooperative education programs:** computer science, engineering, health professions. **Faculty and instruction (2009-2010):** Total instructional faculty: 88 full-time, 42 part-time (54% men; 5% minorities). Full-time faculty with Ph.D. or other terminal degree: 88%. Student/faculty ratio: 15/1. Classes of fewer than 20 students: 51%; of 20 to 49 students: 49%; of 50 or more students: 0%. **Advanced Placement and International Baccalaureate credit:** AP tests may be used for: Credit and/or placement. Scores accepted: 3, 4, 5. International Baccalaureate exams may be used for: Credit and/or placement. **Freshmen returning for sophomore year:** 80%. **Graduation rates:** Four-year: 56%; five-year: 62%; six-year: 63%. **Graduate study:** 25% of students pursue further study immediately upon graduation; 23% within one year. Fields in which graduates pursue further study: Master of Business Administration (MBA), 5%; law, 8%; medicine, 18%; dentistry, 5%; engineering, 8%; theology (or the seminary), 3%; education, 9%; arts and sciences, 43%; veterinary medicine, 1%.

COSTS AND FINANCIAL AID

Financial aid office: (641) 628-5187. **Expenses (2010-2011):** Tuition and fees 2010-2011: $26,242; room/board: $8,702. Estimated books and supplies: $1,014; transportation: $1,270; personal expenses: $1,734. **Financial aid:** Priority filing date for institution's financial aid form: March 15. In 2009-2010, 100% of undergraduates applied for financial aid. Of those, 82% were determined to have financial need; 20% had their need fully met. Average financial aid package (proportion receiving): $22,115 (82%). Average amount of gift aid, such as scholarships or grants (proportion receiving): $16,141 (82%). Average amount of self-help aid, such as work study or loans (proportion receiving): $5,904 (69%). Average need-based loan (excluding PLUS or other private loans): $4,643. Among students who received need-based aid, the average percentage of need met: 84%. Among students who received aid based on merit, the average award (and the proportion receiving): $10,799 (18%). The average athletic scholarship (and the proportion receiving): $0 (0%). Average amount of debt of borrowers graduating in 2009: $36,068. Proportion who borrowed: 86%.

CAMPUS LIFE AND EXTRACURRICULAR ACTIVITIES

Campus housing available (% using): coed dorms (66%), women's dorms (10%), men's dorms (10%), sorority housing (1%), fraternity housing (1%), special housing for disabled students (1%), special housing for international students (1%), other housing options (0%). Students who live in college-owned, operated, or affiliated housing: 93%. **Student employment:** During the 2009-2010 academic year, 0% of undergraduates worked on campus. Average per-year earnings: $0. **Clubs and organizations:** Number of student organizations: 55. Activities include: campus ministries, choral groups, concert band, drama/theater, international student organization, jazz band, literary magazine, music ensembles, pep band, radio station, student government, student newspaper, student film society, symphony orchestra. Number of fraternities: 5; sororities: 3. Proportion of men in fraternities: 6%; of women in sororities: 6%. Average proportion of students who stay on campus on weekends: 70%. **Sports program (2009-2010):** Member of NCAA III. *Men's intercollegiate varsity sports:* baseball, basketball, cross country, football, golf, soccer, tennis, track and field (indoor), track and field (outdoor), wrestling. *Women's intercollegiate varsity sports:* basketball, cross country, golf, soccer, softball, tennis, track and field (indoor), track and field (outdoor), volleyball.

SERVICES AND FACILITIES

Basic services: nonremedial tutoring, placement service, health service, health insurance. **Remedial assistance:** study skills. **Counseling services:** minority student, career, personal, veteran student, academic, older student, psychological, birth control, religious. **For learning-disabled students:** School does not offer a structured program with separate admission and additional fees. Total undergraduates in learning-disabled program or receiving services: 50. Services include: reading machines, tape recorders, videotaped classes, diagnostic testing service, untimed tests, note-taking services, oral tests, learning center, readers, extended time for tests, tutors, priority seating, proofreading services, texts on tape, typist/scribe, exams on tape or computer, other testing accommodations. **Library:** Number of titles: 229,038; number of current serial subscriptions: 410. **Information technology resources:** Students are not required to lease or own a computer. Number of campus computers available to all students: 516. School has a wireless network. Approximate number of users that can be accommodated: 2,000. Proportion of college-owned housing units wired for high-speed internet access: 100%. **Campus safety:** Security services offered: 24-hour foot-and-vehicle patrols, late-night transport/escort service, 24-hour emergency telephones, lighted pathways/sidewalks, student patrols, controlled dormitory access (key, security card, etc).

TRANSFER AND INTERNATIONAL STUDENTS

Transfer students: May apply for admission for the following academic terms: Fall, Spring, Summer. Applicants do not need a minimum number of credits to apply. For fall 2009: Transfer applications received: 179. Transfer applicants offered admission: 91. Transfer applicants enrolled: 53. **International students:** Number of foreign undergraduates: 15 (1% of student body). Number of countries represented: 11. Minimum TOEFL score required: 530 (paper); 197 (computer).

Clarke University

■ **Address:** 1550 Clarke Drive, Dubuque, IA 52001
■ **Website:** http://www.clarke.edu
■ **Private; Religious affiliation:** Roman Catholic
■ **Enrollment:** 802 full-time; 180 part-time

KEY STATS

✔ **U.S News College Ranking:** 162, National Liberal Arts Colleges
✔ **ACT Score (25th/75th percentile):** 20-26
✔ **Tuition:** 2010-2011: $24,610

Selectivity: Selective	**Room/board:** $7,340
Acceptance rate: 77%	**Average debt:** $34,386
Student/faculty ratio: 11/1	**Proportion who borrowed:** 90%

UNDERGRADUATE STUDENT BODY STATS

2009-2010 enrollment: 802 full-time; 180 part-time. Men: 32%; women: 68%. **Ethnic makeup:** African American: 1%; Asian American: 1%; Hispanic: 2%; White: 94%; International: 1%. **Religious preference:** Roman Catholic: 36%; Protestant: 5%; Unknown: 59%.

ADMISSIONS FACTS AND FIGURES

Phone: (563) 588-6316. **Email:** admissions@clarke.edu. **Website:** http://www.clarke.edu. **Application deadlines for fall 2011:** Regular decision: Rolling. Early decision: Not offered. Early action: Not offered. Admission can be deferred. **Application fee:** $25. **To apply online, go to:** http://www.clarke.edu/page.aspx?id=1790. **Admissions requirements/recommendations:** High school units required (recommended): English: 4; Mathematics: 3 (4); Science: 3 (4); Foreign language: 2 (3); Social studies: 3; Academic electives: 4; Total units: 21. Tests: The college uses SAT or ACT scores in admissions decisions. Either SAT or ACT required. For admission to the fall 2011

entering class, the school will accept: ACT with or without writing accepted. Campus visit: Recommended. Admissions interview: Recommended. Off-campus interview: May be arranged. **Factors that count in admissions decisions:** *Academic:* Secondary school record: Very Important. Class rank: Important. Letters of recommendation: Not Considered. Standardized test scores: Very Important. Essay: Not Considered. *Nonacademic:* Interview: Considered. Extracurricular activities: Considered. Talent/ability: Considered. Character/personal qualities: Not Considered. Alumni/ae relationship: Not Considered. Geographical residence: Not Considered. State residency: Not Considered. Religious affiliation/commitment: Not Considered. Minority status: Considered. Volunteer work: Considered. Work experience: Not Considered. **Other schools with the greatest overlap in applicants:** Loras College; St. Ambrose University; University of Dubuque; University of Northern Iowa; University of Wisconsin–Platteville. **Admissions statistics for the fall 2009 entering class:** Total applicants: 823. Total accepted: 637. Freshmen enrolled: 148; 58% were from out of state. Overall acceptance rate: 77%. **Credentials of fall 2009 freshmen:** 23% ranked in the top 10 percent of their high school class; 47% were in the top 25 percent; 76% were in the top half. (Proportion submitting class standing: 89%.) **Average high school grade point average:** 3.3. **First-year students who submitted SAT scores:** 4%. Scores (25/75 percentile): Critical Reading: 468-580, Math: 460-538, Combined: 928-1118. **First-year students submitting ACT scores:** 95%. Scores (25/75 percentile): English: 20-26, Math: 20-26, Composite: 20-26.

ACADEMICS

Year founded: 1843. **Academic calendar:** Semester. **Degrees offered:** certificate, associate, bachelor's, master's, post-master's certificate, doctorate. **Most popular majors:** 20% nursing/registered nurse training (R.N., A.S.N., B.S.N., M.S.N.), 13% education, 12% business administration and management, 9% psychology, 7% communication, journalism, and related programs. **Major fields of study:** biological and biomedical sciences; communication, journalism, and related programs; computer and information sciences and support services; education; English language and literature/letters; foreign languages, literatures, and linguistics; liberal arts and sciences studies, and humanities; mathematics and statistics; multi/interdisciplinary studies; philosophy and religious studies; physical sciences; psychology; public administration and social service professions; social sciences. **Areas of required coursework:** arts/fine arts, humanities, English (including composition), philosophy, sciences (biological or physical), social science. **Pre-professional programs:** pre-law, pre-dentistry, pre-medicine, pre-veterinary science, pre-pharmacy, other. **Special academic programs (% participation):** accelerated program (15%), cross-registration (3%), distance learning (1%), double major (6%), honors program (2%), independent study (1%), internships (2%), student-designed major (0%), study abroad (1%), teacher certificate program (1%). **Teacher certification offered in:** special education, elementary, middle/junior high, secondary. **Reserve Officers Training Corps (ROTC):** Army ROTC: Offered at cooperating institution (University of Dubuque). **Faculty and instruction (2009-2010):** Total instructional faculty: 75 full-time, 60 part-time (40% men; 60% women; 1% minorities). Full-time faculty with Ph.D. or other terminal degree: 68%. Student/faculty ratio: 11/1. Classes of fewer than 20 students: 81%; of 20 to 49 students: 19%; of 50 or more students: 0%. **Advanced Placement and International Baccalaureate credit:** AP tests may be used for: Placement only. Scores accepted: 2, 3, 4, 5. International Baccalaureate exams may be used for: Placement only. **Freshmen returning for sophomore year:** 76%. **Graduation rates:** Four-year: 48%; five-year: 65%; six-year: 66%. **Graduate study:** 18% of students pursue further study immediately upon graduation.

COSTS AND FINANCIAL AID

Financial aid office: (563) 588-6327. **Expenses (2010-2011):** Tuition and fees 2010-2011: $24,610; room/board: $7,340. Estimated books and supplies: $1,040; transportation: $1,250; personal expenses: $1,250. **Financial aid:** Priority filing date for institution's financial aid form: April 15. In 2009-2010, 96% of undergraduates applied for financial aid. Of those, 87% were determined to have financial need; 24% had their need fully met. Average financial aid package (proportion receiving): $19,614 (87%). Average amount of gift aid, such as scholarships or grants (proportion receiving): $15,231 (86%). Average amount of self-help aid, such as work study or loans (proportion receiving): $5,064 (77%). Average need-based loan (excluding PLUS or other private loans): $4,670. Among students who received need-based aid, the average percentage of need met: 88%. Among students who received aid based on merit, the average award (and the proportion receiving): $15,566 (11%). The average athletic scholarship (and the proportion receiving): $7,519 (19%). Average amount of debt of borrowers graduating in 2009: $34,386. Proportion who borrowed: 90%.

CAMPUS LIFE AND EXTRACURRICULAR ACTIVITIES

Campus housing available (% using): coed dorms (42%), women's dorms (38%), apartment for single students (20%). Students who live in college-owned, operated, or affiliated housing: 57%. **Student employment:** During the 2009-2010 academic year, 40% of undergraduates worked on campus. Average per-year earnings: $1,300. **Clubs and organizations:** Number of student organizations: 25. Activities include: choral groups, drama/theater, jazz band, literary magazine, music ensembles, radio station, student government, student newspaper, yearbook. Number of fraternities: 0; sororities: 0. Average proportion of students who stay on campus on weekends: 60%. **Sports program (2009-2010):** Member of NAIA. *Men's intercollegiate varsity sports:* baseball, basketball, cross country, golf, soccer, track and field (indoor), track and field (outdoor), volleyball. *Women's intercollegiate varsity sports:* basketball, bowling, cross country, golf, soccer, softball, track and field (indoor), track and field (outdoor), volleyball.

SERVICES AND FACILITIES

Basic services: health service. **Remedial assistance:** reading, math, writing, study skills. **Counseling services:** career, personal, academic, older student, psychological, religious. **For learning-disabled students:** School does not offer a structured program with separate admission and additional fees. Services include: remedial math, remedial English, remedial reading, untimed tests, oral tests, learning center, readers, extended time for tests, tutors, other. **Library:** Number of titles: 100,500; number of current serial subscriptions: 35,000. **Information technology resources:** Students are not required to lease or own a computer. Number of campus computers available to all students: 273. School has a wireless network. Approximate number of users that can be accommodated: 1,664. Proportion of college-owned housing units wired for high-speed internet access: 100%. **Campus safety:** Security services offered: 24-hour foot-and-vehicle patrols, 24-hour emergency telephones, lighted pathways/sidewalks, controlled dormitory access (key, security card, etc.).

TRANSFER AND INTERNATIONAL STUDENTS

Transfer students: May apply for admission for the following academic terms: Fall, Spring, Summer. Applicants need a minimum number of credits to apply. For fall 2009: Transfer applications received: 370. Transfer applicants offered admission: 188. Transfer applicants enrolled: 92. **International students:** Number of foreign undergraduates: 14 (1% of student body). Number of countries represented: 5. Minimum TOEFL score required: 525 (paper); 203 (computer).

Coe College

- ■ **Address:** 1220 First Avenue NE, Cedar Rapids, IA 52402
- ■ **Website:** http://www.coe.edu
- ■ **Private; Religious affiliation:** Presbyterian
- ■ **Enrollment:** 1,225 full-time; 62 part-time

KEY STATS

- ✔ **U.S News College Ranking:** 101, National Liberal Arts Colleges
- ✔ **ACT Score (25th/75th percentile):** 23-28
- ✔ **Tuition:** 2010-2011: $30,860

Selectivity: More selective	**Room/board:** $7,290
Acceptance rate: 65%	**Average debt:** $30,665
Student/faculty ratio: 11/1	**Proportion who borrowed:** 83%

UNDERGRADUATE STUDENT BODY STATS

2009-2010 enrollment: 1,225 full-time; 62 part-time. Men: 47%; women: 53%. **Ethnic makeup:** African American: 2%; Asian American: 1%; Hispanic: 2%; White: 91%; International: 4%. **Religious preference:** Roman Catholic: 18%; Protestant: 3%; Jewish: 1%; No preference: 52%; Presbyterian: 2%; Lutheran: 8%; Other: 16%.

ADMISSIONS FACTS AND FIGURES

Phone: (319) 399-8500. **Email:** admission@coe.edu. **Website:** http://www.coe.edu. **Application deadlines for fall 2011:** Regular decision: March 1. Early decision: Not offered. Early action: Send application by: December 10; Decision sent by: January 20. Admission can be deferred. **Application fee:** $30. **To apply online, go to:** http://www.coe.edu/admission/apply/. **Admissions requirements/recommendations:** High school units required (recommended): English: (4); Mathematics: (3); Science: (3); Foreign language: (2); Social studies: (3); History: (0); Academic electives: (2); Total

units: (18). Tests: The college uses SAT or ACT scores in admissions decisions. Either SAT or ACT required. For admission to the fall 2011 entering class, the school will accept: ACT with or without writing accepted. Campus visit: Recommended. Admissions interview: Recommended. Off-campus interview: May be arranged. **Factors that count in admissions decisions: *Academic:*** Secondary school record: Important. Class rank: Important. Letters of recommendation: Important. Standardized test scores: Very Important. Essay: Important. *Nonacademic:* Interview: Considered. Extracurricular activities: Considered. Talent/ability: Considered. Character/personal qualities: Considered. Alumni/ae relationship: Considered. Geographical residence: Not Considered. State residency: Not Considered. Religious affiliation/commitment: Not Considered. Minority status: Considered. Volunteer work: Considered. Work experience: Not Considered. **Other schools with the greatest overlap in applicants:** Beloit College; Cornell College; Luther College; Macalester College; University of Iowa. **Admissions statistics for the fall 2009 entering class:** Total applicants: 2,063. Total accepted: 1,336. Freshmen enrolled: 325; 41% were from out of state. Accepted through early-decision or early-action plans: 59%. Overall acceptance rate: 65%. **Credentials of fall 2009 freshmen:** 27% ranked in the top 10 percent of their high school class; 61% were in the top 25 percent; 94% were in the top half. (Proportion submitting class standing: 88%.) **Average high school grade point average:** 3.7. First-year students who submitted SAT scores: 13%. Scores (25/75 percentile): Critical Reading: 540-640, Math: 530-630, Combined: 1070-1270. **First-year students submitting ACT scores:** 95%. Scores (25/75 percentile): English: 22-29, Math: 22-28, Composite: 23-28.

ACADEMICS

Year founded: 1851. **Academic calendar:** Semester. **Degrees offered:** bachelor's, master's. **Most popular majors:** 12% psychology, 11% business, management, marketing, and related support services, 8% health professions and related clinical sciences, 7% biological and biomedical sciences, 6% English language and literature/letters. **Major fields of study:** area, ethnic, cultural, and gender studies; biological and biomedical sciences; business, management, marketing, and related support services; communication, journalism, and related programs; computer and information sciences and support services; education; English language and literature/letters; foreign languages, literatures, and linguistics; health professions and related clinical sciences; history; mathematics and statistics; philosophy and religious studies; physical sciences; psychology; social sciences; visual and performing arts. **Areas of required coursework:** arts/fine arts, humanities, English (including composition), sciences (biological or physical), social science. **Pre-professional programs:** pre-law, pre-dentistry, pre-medicine, pre-veterinary science. **Special academic programs (% participation):** accelerated program (0%), cross-registration (2%), double major (34%), dual enrollment (0%), English as a Second Language (ESL) (0%), exchange student program (domestic) (0%), honors program (7%), independent study (11%), internships (19%), student-designed major (1%), study abroad, teacher certificate program (8%). **Teacher certification offered in:** elementary, middle/junior high, secondary. **Reserve Officers Training Corps (ROTC):** Army ROTC: Offered at cooperating institution (University of Iowa); Air Force ROTC: Offered at cooperating institution (University of Iowa). **Faculty and instruction (2009-2010):** Total instructional faculty: 90 full-time, 84 part-time (51% men; 49% women; 6% minorities). Full-time faculty with Ph.D. or other terminal degree: 84%. Student/faculty ratio: 11/1. Classes of fewer than 20 students: 75%; of 20 to 49 students: 24%; of 50 or more students: 1%. **Advanced Placement and International Baccalaureate credit:** AP tests may be used for: Credit and/or placement. Scores accepted: 4, 5. International Baccalaureate exams may be used for: Credit and/or placement. **Freshmen returning for sophomore year:** 81%. **Graduation rates:** Four-year: 60%; five-year: 69%; six-year: 70%. **Graduate study:** 20% of students pursue further study immediately upon graduation; 25% within one year; 45% within five years. Fields in which graduates pursue further study: Master of Business Administration (MBA), 17%; law, 6%; medicine, 29%; engineering, 6%; theology (or the seminary), 2%; education, 14%; arts and sciences, 52%.

COSTS AND FINANCIAL AID

Financial aid office: (319) 399-8540. **Expenses (2010-2011):** Tuition and fees 2010-2011: $30,860; room/board: $7,290. Estimated books and supplies: $1,000; transportation: $1,000; personal expenses: $1,600. **Financial aid:** Priority filing date for institution's financial aid form: March 1. In 2009-2010, 85% of undergraduates applied for financial aid. Of those, 77% were determined to have financial need; 23% had their need fully met. Average financial aid package (proportion receiving): $23,085 (77%). Average amount of gift aid, such as scholarships or grants (proportion receiving): $18,611 (77%). Average amount of self-help aid, such as work study or loans (proportion receiving): $5,694 (63%). Average need-based loan (excluding

PLUS or other private loans): $5,054. Among students who received need-based aid, the average percentage of need met: 82%. Among students who received aid based on merit, the average award (and the proportion receiving): $16,112 (21%). The average athletic scholarship (and the proportion receiving): $0 (0%). Average amount of debt of borrowers graduating in 2009: $30,665. Proportion who borrowed: 83%.

CAMPUS LIFE AND EXTRACURRICULAR ACTIVITIES

Campus housing available (% using): coed dorms (43%), women's dorms (10%), men's dorms (10%), sorority housing (7%), fraternity housing (10%), apartment for single students (18%), other housing options (2%). Students who live in college-owned, operated, or affiliated housing: 85%. **Student employment:** During the 2009-2010 academic year, 45% of undergraduates worked on campus. Average per-year earnings: $700. **Clubs and organizations:** Number of student organizations: 74. Activities include: campus ministries, choral groups, concert band, dance, drama/theater, jazz band, literary magazine, music ensembles, musical theater, pep band, radio station, student government, student newspaper, symphony orchestra, television station, yearbook. Number of fraternities: 5; sororities: 3. Proportion of men in fraternities: 23%; of women in sororities: 18%. Average proportion of students who stay on campus on weekends: 85%. **Sports program (2009-2010):** Member of NCAA III. *Men's intercollegiate varsity sports:* baseball, basketball, cross country, football, golf, soccer, swimming, tennis, track and field (indoor), track and field (outdoor), wrestling. *Women's intercollegiate varsity sports:* basketball, cross country, golf, soccer, softball, swimming, tennis, track and field (indoor), track and field (outdoor), volleyball.

SERVICES AND FACILITIES

Basic services: nonremedial tutoring, placement service, health service. **Remedial assistance:** reading, math, writing, study skills. **Counseling services:** career, personal, academic, psychological, birth control, religious. **For learning-disabled students:** School does not offer a structured program with separate admission and additional fees. Services include: remedial reading, tape recorders, untimed tests, note-taking services, oral tests, learning center, extended time for tests, tutors, texts on tape, exams on tape or computer, other testing accommodations. **Library:** Number of titles: 276,805; number of current serial subscriptions: 27,228. **Information technology resources:** Students are not required to lease or own a computer. Number of campus computers available to all students: 280. School has a wireless network. Approximate number of users that can be accommodated: 1,000. Proportion of college-owned housing units wired for high-speed internet access: 100%. **Campus safety:** Security services offered: 24-hour foot-and-vehicle patrols, late-night transport/escort service, 24-hour emergency telephones, lighted pathways/sidewalks, controlled dormitory access (key, security card, etc).

TRANSFER AND INTERNATIONAL STUDENTS

Transfer students: May apply for admission for the following academic terms: Fall, Spring. Applicants do not need a minimum number of credits to apply. For fall 2009: Transfer applications received: 170. Transfer applicants offered admission: 109. Transfer applicants enrolled: 43. **International students:** Number of foreign undergraduates: 47 (4% of student body). Number of countries represented: 18. Minimum TOEFL score required: 520 (paper); 190 (computer). Average TOEFL score: 593 (paper).

Cornell College

- **Address:** 600 First Street SW, Mount Vernon, IA 52314-1098
- **Website:** http://www.cornellcollege.edu
- **Private; Religious affiliation:** United Methodist
- **Enrollment:** 1,121 full-time; 12 part-time

KEY STATS

✔ **U.S News College Ranking:** 81, National Liberal Arts Colleges
✔ **ACT Score (25th/75th percentile):** 24-29
✔ **Tuition:** 2010-2011: $31,050

Selectivity: More selective	**Room/board:** $7,660
Acceptance rate: 44%	**Average debt:** $27,990
Student/faculty ratio: 12/1	**Proportion who borrowed:** 72%

UNDERGRADUATE STUDENT BODY STATS

2009-2010 enrollment: 1,121 full-time; 12 part-time. Men: 48%; women: 52%. **Ethnic makeup:** African American: 3%; American-Indian: 1%; Asian American: 3%; Hispanic: 4%; White: 85%; International: 4%.

ADMISSIONS FACTS AND FIGURES

Phone: (800) 747-1112. **Email:** admissions@cornellcollege.edu. **Website:** http://www.cornellcollege.edu. **Application deadlines for fall 2011:** Regular decision: February 1; decision sent by March 20. Early decision: Send application by: November 1; Decision sent by: January 15. Early action: Send application by: December 1; Decision sent by: February 1. Admission can be deferred. **Application fee:** $30. **To apply online, go to:** http://www.cornellcollege.edu/admissions/apply-to-cornell/index.shtml. **Admissions requirements/recommendations:** High school units required (recommended): English: (4); Mathematics: (3); Science: (3); Foreign language: (2); Social studies: (3); History: (0); Academic electives: (0); Total units: (15). Tests: The college uses SAT or ACT scores in admissions decisions. Either SAT or ACT required. For admission to the fall 2011 entering class, the school will accept: ACT with or without writing accepted. Campus visit: Recommended. Admissions interview: Recommended. Off-campus interview: May be arranged. **Factors that count in admissions decisions:** *Academic:* Secondary school record: Very Important. Class rank: Important. Letters of recommendation: Very Important. Standardized test scores: Important. Essay: Very Important. *Nonacademic:* Interview: Important. Extracurricular activities: Important. Talent/ability: Important. Character/personal qualities: Important. Alumni/ae relationship: Considered. Geographical residence: Considered. State residency: Considered. Religious affiliation/commitment: Not Considered. Minority status: Considered. Volunteer work: Important. Work experience: Important. **Other schools with the greatest overlap in applicants:** Beloit College; Colorado College; Grinnell College; Knox College; Lawrence University. **Admissions statistics for the fall 2009 entering class:** Total applicants: 3,208. Total accepted: 1,411. Freshmen enrolled: 335; 82% were from out of state. Accepted through early-decision or early-action plans: 82%. Overall acceptance rate: 44%. Early-decision acceptance rate: 52%. Non-early acceptance rate: 49%. **Size of waiting list:** 142 applicants; enrolled from waiting list: 50. **Credentials of fall 2009 freshmen:** 35% ranked in the top 10 percent of their high school class; 57% were in the top 25 percent; 87% were in the top half. (Proportion submitting class standing: 67%.) **Average high school grade point average:** 3.5. **First-year students who submitted SAT scores:** 41%. Scores (25/75 percentile): Critical Reading: 550-680, Math: 550-680, Combined: 1100-1360. **First-year students submitting ACT scores:** 76%. Scores (25/75 percentile): English: 23-30, Math: 23-30, Composite: 24-29.

ACADEMICS

Year founded: 1853. **Academic calendar:** Other. **Degrees offered:** bachelor's. **Most popular majors:** 11% psychology, 10% history, 7% English language and literature, 7% economics, 6% kinesiology and exercise science. **Major fields of study:** area, ethnic, cultural, and gender studies; biological and biomedical sciences; business, management, marketing, and related support services; computer and information sciences and support services; education; English language and literature/letters; foreign languages, literatures, and linguistics; history; liberal arts and sciences studies, and humanities; mathematics and statistics; multi/interdisciplinary studies; natural resources and conservation; parks, recreation, leisure, and fitness studies; philosophy and religious studies; physical sciences; psychology; social sciences; visual and performing arts. **Areas of required coursework:** arts/fine arts, humanities, mathematics, English (including composition), foreign languages, sciences (biological or physical), social science. **Pre-professional programs:** pre-law, pre-dentistry, pre-medicine, pre-theology, pre-veterinary science, pre-optometry, pre-pharmacy. **Special academic programs (% participation):** double major (37%), English as a Second Language (ESL) (1%), independent study (17%), internships (29%), student-designed major (1%), study abroad (20%), teacher certificate program (12%). **Teacher certification offered in:** elementary, middle/junior high, secondary. **Cooperative education programs:** health professions. **Faculty and instruction (2009-2010):** Total instructional faculty: 87 full-time, 5 part-time (50% men; 50% women; 9% minorities). Full-time faculty with Ph.D. or other terminal degree: 97%. Student/faculty ratio: 12/1. Classes of fewer than 20 students: 62%; of 20 to 49 students: 38%. **Advanced Placement and International Baccalaureate credit:** AP tests may be used for: Placement only. Scores accepted: 3, 4, 5. International Baccalaureate exams may be used for: Credit only. **Freshmen returning for sophomore year:** 83%. **Graduation rates:** Four-year: 65%; five-year: 70%; six-year: 71%. **Graduate study:** 25% of students pursue further study immediately upon graduation; 33% within one year; 40% within five years. Fields in which graduates pursue further study: Master of Business

Administration (MBA), 7%; law, 9%; medicine, 10%; dentistry, 1%; theology (or the seminary), 4%; education, 10%; arts and sciences, 57%.

COSTS AND FINANCIAL AID

Financial aid office: (319) 895-4216. **Expenses (2010-2011):** Tuition and fees 2010-2011: $31,050; room/board: $7,660. Estimated books and supplies: $810; transportation: $1,520; personal expenses: $675. **Financial aid:** Priority filing date for institution's financial aid form: March 1; deadline: March 1. In 2009-2010, 82% of undergraduates applied for financial aid. Of those, 74% were determined to have financial need; 38% had their need fully met. Average financial aid package (proportion receiving): $25,535 (74%). Average amount of gift aid, such as scholarships or grants (proportion receiving): $20,545 (74%). Average amount of self-help aid, such as work study or loans (proportion receiving): $5,935 (60%). Average need-based loan (excluding PLUS or other private loans): $4,755. Among students who received need-based aid, the average percentage of need met: 93%. Among students who received aid based on merit, the average award (and the proportion receiving): $13,250 (19%). The average athletic scholarship (and the proportion receiving): $0 (0%). Average amount of debt of borrowers graduating in 2009: $27,990. Proportion who borrowed: 72%.

CAMPUS LIFE AND EXTRACURRICULAR ACTIVITIES

Campus housing available (% using): coed dorms (75%), women's dorms (17%), men's dorms (8%). Students who live in college-owned, operated, or affiliated housing: 90%. **Student employment:** During the 2009-2010 academic year, 20% of undergraduates worked on campus. Average per-year earnings: $1,200. **Clubs and organizations:** Number of student organizations: 78. Activities include: campus ministries, choral groups, concert band, dance, drama/theater, international student organization, jazz band, literary magazine, music ensembles, musical theater, opera, radio station, student government, student newspaper, symphony orchestra, yearbook. Number of fraternities: 7; sororities: 7. Proportion of men in fraternities: 20%; of women in sororities: 21%. Average proportion of students who stay on campus on weekends: 75%. **Sports program (2009-2010):** Member of NCAA III. *Men's intercollegiate varsity sports:* baseball, basketball, cross country, football, golf, soccer, tennis, track and field (indoor), track and field (outdoor), wrestling. *Women's intercollegiate varsity sports:* basketball, cross country, golf, soccer, softball, tennis, track and field (indoor), track and field (outdoor), volleyball.

SERVICES AND FACILITIES

Basic services: nonremedial tutoring, women's center, health service, health insurance. **Counseling services:** minority student, career, personal, academic, older student, psychological, birth control, religious. **For learning-disabled students:** School does not offer a structured program with separate admission and additional fees. Total undergraduates in learning-disabled program or receiving services: 82. Services include: tape recorders, untimed tests, oral tests, learning center, extended time for tests, tutors, priority registration, priority seating, texts on tape, exams on tape or computer, other testing accommodations, other. **Library:** Number of titles: 214,247; number of current serial subscriptions: 464. **Information technology resources:** Students are not required to lease or own a computer. Number of campus computers available to all students: 203. School has a wireless network. Approximate number of users that can be accommodated: 1,500. Proportion of college-owned housing units wired for high-speed internet access: 100%. **Campus safety:** Security services offered: 24-hour foot-and-vehicle patrols, late-night transport/escort service, 24-hour emergency telephones, lighted pathways/sidewalks, controlled dormitory access (key, security card, etc).

TRANSFER AND INTERNATIONAL STUDENTS

Transfer students: May apply for admission for the following academic terms: Fall, Winter, Spring. Applicants do not need a minimum number of credits to apply. For fall 2009: Transfer applications received: 387. Transfer applicants offered admission: 90. Transfer applicants enrolled: 36. **International students:** Number of foreign undergraduates: 50 (4% of student body). Number of countries represented: 20. Minimum TOEFL score required: 550 (paper); 213 (computer). Average TOEFL score: 618 (paper).

Dordt College

- **Address:** 498 Fourth Avenue NE, Sioux Center, IA 51250
- **Website:** http://www.dordt.edu
- **Private; Religious affiliation:** Christian Reformed
- **Enrollment:** 1,285 full-time; 43 part-time

KEY STATS

✔ **U.S News College Ranking:** 3, Regional Colleges (Midwest)
✔ **ACT Score (25th/75th percentile):** 22-27
✔ **Tuition:** 2010-2011: $23,180

Selectivity: More selective **Room/board:** $6,320
Acceptance rate: 84% **Average debt:** $19,988
Student/faculty ratio: 14/1 **Proportion who borrowed:** 85%

UNDERGRADUATE STUDENT BODY STATS

2009-2010 enrollment: 1,285 full-time; 43 part-time. Men: 49%; women: 51%. **Ethnic makeup:** Asian American: 1%; Hispanic: 1%; White: 83%; International: 15%. **Religious preference:** Roman Catholic: 2%; Protestant: 43%; Unknown: 2%; Christian Reformed: 53%.

ADMISSIONS FACTS AND FIGURES

Phone: (800) 343-6738. **Email:** admissions@dordt.edu. **Website:** http://www.dordt.edu. **Application deadlines for fall 2011:** Regular decision: August 1. Early decision: Not offered. Early action: Not offered. Admission cannot be deferred. **Application fee:** $25. **To apply online, go to:** http://www.dordt.edu/offices/admissions/apply/. **Admissions requirements/recommendations:** High school units required (recommended): English: 3 (4); Mathematics: 2 (3); Science: 2 (4); Foreign language: 2 (3); Social studies: (1); History: 2; Academic electives: 6; Total units: 17 (25). Tests: The college uses SAT or ACT scores in admissions decisions. Either SAT or ACT required. For admission to the fall 2011 entering class, the school will accept: ACT with or without writing accepted. Campus visit: Recommended. Admissions interview: Neither required nor recommended. **Factors that count in admissions decisions:** *Academic:* Secondary school record: Very Important. Class rank: Considered. Letters of recommendation: Not Considered. Standardized test scores: Very Important. Essay: Not Considered. *Nonacademic:* Interview: Not Considered. Extracurricular activities: Considered. Talent/ability: Considered. Character/personal qualities: Considered. Alumni/ae relationship: Considered. Geographical residence: Not Considered. State residency: Not Considered. Religious affiliation/commitment: Very Important. Minority status: Not Considered. Volunteer work: Not Considered. Work experience: Not Considered. **Other schools with the greatest overlap in applicants:** Calvin College; Iowa State University; Northwestern College; Trinity Christian College; University of Sioux Falls. **Admissions statistics for the fall 2009 entering class:** Total applicants: 1,006. Total accepted: 842. Freshmen enrolled: 364; 62% were from out of state. Overall acceptance rate: 84%. **Size of waiting list:** 0 applicants; enrolled from waiting list: 0. **Credentials of fall 2009 freshmen:** 35% ranked in the top 10 percent of their high school class; 57% were in the top 25 percent; 78% were in the top half. (Proportion submitting class standing: 85%.) **Average high school grade point average:** 3.5. **First-year students who submitted SAT scores:** 21%. Scores (25/75 percentile): Critical Reading: 460-610, Math: 480-620, Combined: 940-1230. **First-year students submitting ACT scores:** 86%. Scores (25/75 percentile): English: 21-28, Math: 21-27, Composite: 22-27.

ACADEMICS

Year founded: 1955. **Academic calendar:** Semester. **Degrees offered:** associate, bachelor's, master's. **Most popular majors:** 19% business/commerce, 15% elementary education and teaching, 6% engineering, 6% kinesiology and exercise science, 5% theology/theological studies. **Major fields of study:** agriculture, agriculture operations, and related sciences; biological and biomedical sciences; business, management, marketing, and related support services; communication, journalism, and related programs; computer and information sciences and support services; education; engineering; English language and literature/letters; foreign languages, literatures, and linguistics; health professions and related clinical sciences; history; liberal arts and sciences studies, and humanities; mathematics and statistics; natural resources and conservation; parks, recreation, leisure, and fitness studies; philosophy and religious studies; physical sciences; psychology; public administration and social service professions; social sciences; theology and religious vocations; visual and performing arts. **Areas of required coursework:** arts/fine arts, humanities, mathematics, English (including composition), philosophy, sciences (biological or physical), history, social science, other. **Pre-professional programs:** pre-law, pre-dentistry, pre-medicine, pre-theology, pre-veterinary science, pre-optometry, pre-pharmacy, other. **Special academic programs (% participation):** double major (9%), English as a Second Language (ESL) (0%), independent study (8%), internships (15%), student-designed major (1%), study abroad (8%). **Teacher certification offered in:** elementary, middle/junior high, secondary. **Cooperative education programs:** health professions. **Faculty and instruction (2009-2010):** Total instructional faculty: 80 full-time, 44 part-time (68% men; 32% women; 3% minorities). Full-time faculty with Ph.D. or other terminal degree: 74%. Student/faculty ratio: 14/1. Classes of fewer than 20 students: 55%; of 20 to 49 students: 42%; of 50 or more students: 3%. **Advanced Placement and International Baccalaureate credit:** AP tests may be used for: Credit and/or placement. Scores accepted: 3, 4, 5. International Baccalaureate exams may be used for: Credit and/or placement. **Freshmen returning for sophomore year:** 81%. **Graduation rates:** Four-year: 58%; five-year: 61%; six-year: 63%. **Graduate study:** 14% of students pursue further study immediately upon graduation. Fields in which graduates pursue further study: Master of Business Administration (MBA), 3%; law, 5%; medicine, 25%; dentistry, 3%; engineering, 14%; theology (or the seminary), 11%; education, 3%; arts and sciences, 33%; veterinary medicine, 3%.

COSTS AND FINANCIAL AID
Financial aid office: (712) 722-6087. **Expenses (2010-2011):** Tuition and fees 2010-2011: $23,180; room/board: $6,320. Estimated books and supplies: $1,010; transportation: $1,300; personal expenses: $2,100. **Financial aid:** Priority filing date for institution's financial aid form: April 1. In 2009-2010, 86% of undergraduates applied for financial aid. Of those, 74% were determined to have financial need; 16% had their need fully met. Average financial aid package (proportion receiving): $20,705 (74%). Average amount of gift aid, such as scholarships or grants (proportion receiving): $11,515 (74%). Average amount of self-help aid, such as work study or loans (proportion receiving): $9,190 (73%). Average need-based loan (excluding PLUS or other private loans): $5,437. Among students who received need-based aid, the average percentage of need met: 88%. Among students who received aid based on merit, the average award (and the proportion receiving): $11,435 (20%). The average athletic scholarship (and the proportion receiving): $5,393 (5%). Average amount of debt of borrowers graduating in 2009: $19,988. Proportion who borrowed: 85%.

CAMPUS LIFE AND EXTRACURRICULAR ACTIVITIES
Campus housing available (% using): coed dorms (33%), women's dorms (16%), men's dorms (16%), apartment for single students (35%). Students who live in college-owned, operated, or affiliated housing: 90%. **Student employment:** During the 2009-2010 academic year, 64% of undergraduates worked on campus. Average per-year earnings: $1,500. **Clubs and organizations:** Number of student organizations: 37. Activities include: campus ministries, choral groups, concert band, dance, drama/theater, international student organization, jazz band, literary magazine, music ensembles, musical theater, radio station, student government, student newspaper, student film society, symphony orchestra, yearbook. Number of fraternities: 0; sororities: 0. Average proportion of students who stay on campus on weekends: 75%. **Sports program (2009-2010):** Member of NAIA. ***Men's intercollegiate varsity sports:*** baseball, basketball, cross country, football, golf, soccer, track and field (indoor), track and field (outdoor). ***Women's intercollegiate varsity sports:*** basketball, cross country, golf, soccer, softball, track and field (indoor), track and field (outdoor), volleyball.

SERVICES AND FACILITIES
Basic services: nonremedial tutoring, placement service, health service, health insurance. **Remedial assistance:** reading, math, writing, study skills. **Counseling services:** minority student, career, personal, academic, religious. **For learning-disabled students:** School does not offer a structured program with separate admission and additional fees. Total undergraduates in learning-disabled program or receiving services: 32. Services include: remedial math, remedial English, reading machines, tape recorders, untimed tests, note-taking services, oral tests, learning center, readers, extended time for tests, tutors, priority seating, texts on tape, other testing accommodations, other. **Library:** Number of titles: 128,776; number of current serial subscriptions: 27,237. **Information technology resources:** Students are not required to lease or own a computer. Number of campus computers available to all students: 185. School has a wireless network. Approximate number of users that can be accommodated: 2,000. Proportion of college-owned housing units wired for high-speed internet access: 100%. **Campus safety:** Security services offered: late-night transport/escort service, lighted pathways/sidewalks, student patrols, controlled dormitory access (key, security card, etc).

TRANSFER AND INTERNATIONAL STUDENTS
Transfer students: May apply for admission for the following academic terms: Fall, Spring. Applicants need a minimum number of credits to apply. For fall 2009: Transfer applications received: 96. Transfer applicants offered admission: 61. Transfer applicants enrolled: 41. **International students:** Number of foreign undergraduates: 201 (15% of student body). Number of countries represented: 13. Minimum TOEFL score required: 550 (paper); 213 (computer). Average TOEFL score: 585 (paper).

Drake University

- **Address:** 2507 University Avenue, Des Moines, IA 50311
- **Website:** http://www.drake.edu
- **Private**
- **Enrollment:** 3,326 full-time; 222 part-time

KEY STATS
✔ **U.S News College Ranking:** 3, Regional Universities (Midwest)
✔ **ACT Score (25th/75th percentile):** 24-29
✔ **Tuition:** 2010-2011: $26,960

Selectivity: More selective	**Room/board:** $8,130
Acceptance rate: 74%	**Average debt:** $34,919
Student/faculty ratio: 13/1	**Proportion who borrowed:** 71%

UNDERGRADUATE STUDENT BODY STATS
2009-2010 enrollment: 3,326 full-time; 222 part-time. Men: 42%; women: 58%. **Ethnic makeup:** African American: 3%; Asian American: 3%; Hispanic: 2%; White: 86%; International: 7%.

ADMISSIONS FACTS AND FIGURES
Phone: (515) 271-3181. **Email:** admission@drake.edu. **Website:** http://www.drake.edu. **Application deadlines for fall 2011:** Regular decision: Rolling. Early decision: Not offered. Early action: Not offered. Admission can be deferred. **Application fee:** $25. **To apply online, go to:** http://www.drake.edu/admission/ugrad/admission/process.php. **Admissions requirements/recommendations:** High school units required (recommended): English: 0 (4); Mathematics: 0 (3); Science: 0 (2); Foreign language: 0 (2); Social studies: 0 (4); History: 0 (0); Academic electives: 0 (0); Total units: 0 (16). Tests: The college uses SAT or ACT scores in admissions decisions. Either SAT or ACT required. For admission to the fall 2011 entering class, the school will accept: ACT with or without writing accepted. Campus visit: Recommended. Admissions interview: Recommended. Off-campus interview: May be arranged. **Factors that count in admissions decisions:** *Academic:* Secondary school record: Important. Class rank: Considered. Letters of recommendation: Important. Standardized test scores: Very Important. Essay: Very Important. *Nonacademic:* Interview: Important. Extracurricular activities: Considered. Talent/ability: Considered. Character/personal qualities: Considered. Alumni/ae relationship: Not Considered. Geographical residence: Not Considered. State residency: Not Considered. Religious affiliation/commitment: Not Considered. Minority status: Not Considered. Volunteer work: Considered. Work experience: Considered. **Other schools with the greatest overlap in applicants:** Butler University; Creighton University; Iowa State University; Marquette University; University of Iowa. **Admissions statistics for the fall 2009 entering class:** Total applicants: 4,829. Total accepted: 3,577. Freshmen enrolled: 863; 67% were from out of state. Overall acceptance rate: 74%. **Size of waiting list:** 0 applicants; enrolled from waiting list: 0. **Credentials of fall 2009 freshmen:** 38% ranked in the top 10 percent of their high school class; 70% were in the top 25 percent; 92% were in the top half. (Proportion submitting class standing: 75%.) **Average high school grade point average:** 3.6. **First-year students who submitted SAT scores:** 15%. Scores (25/75 percentile): Critical Reading: 510-640, Math: 530-660, Combined: 1040-1300. **First-year students submitting ACT scores:** 94%. Scores (25/75 percentile): English: 23-29, Math: 24-30, Composite: 24-29.

ACADEMICS
Year founded: 1881. **Academic calendar:** Semester. **Degrees offered:** certificate, bachelor's, post-bachelor's certificate, master's, post-master's certificate, doctorate. **Most popular majors:** 34% business, management, marketing, and related support services, 13% communication, journalism, and related programs, 8% biological and biomedical sciences, 8% education, 8% social sciences. **Major fields of study:** biological and biomedical sciences; business, management, marketing, and related support services;

communication, journalism, and related programs; computer and information sciences and support services; education; English language and literature/letters; health professions and related clinical sciences; history; legal professions and studies; liberal arts and sciences studies, and humanities; mathematics and statistics; multi/interdisciplinary studies; natural resources and conservation; philosophy and religious studies; physical sciences; psychology; social sciences; visual and performing arts. **Areas of required coursework:** arts/fine arts, humanities, computer literacy, mathematics, English (including composition), sciences (biological or physical), history, social science, other. **Pre-professional programs:** pre-pharmacy. **Special academic programs (% participation):** accelerated program (0%), cross-registration (1%), distance learning (35%), double major (16%), dual enrollment (0%), English as a Second Language (ESL) (0%), exchange student program (domestic) (0%), honors program (6%), independent study (36%), internships (60%), liberal arts/career combination (10%), student-designed major (1%), study abroad (21%), teacher certificate program (10%). **Teacher certification offered in:** early childhood, special education, elementary, middle/junior high, adult education, secondary, bilingual/bicultural. **Reserve Officers Training Corps (ROTC):** Army ROTC: Offered on campus; Air Force ROTC: Offered at cooperating institution (Iowa State University). **Faculty and instruction (2009-2010):** Total instructional faculty: 275 full-time, 142 part-time (52% men; 48% women; 10% minorities). Full-time faculty with Ph.D. or other terminal degree: 89%. Student/faculty ratio: 13/1. Classes of fewer than 20 students: 40%; of 20 to 49 students: 50%; of 50 or more students: 9%. **Advanced Placement and International Baccalaureate credit:** AP tests may be used for: Credit and/or placement. Scores accepted: 3, 4. International Baccalaureate exams may be used for: Placement only. **Freshmen returning for sophomore year:** 87%. **Graduation rates:** Four-year: 61%; five-year: 72%; six-year: 73%. **Graduate study:** 13% of students pursue further study immediately upon graduation. Fields in which graduates pursue further study: Master of Business Administration (MBA), 20%; law, 19%; medicine, 15%; dentistry, 2%; education, 7%; arts and sciences, 37%.

COSTS AND FINANCIAL AID

Financial aid office: (515) 271-2905. **Expenses (2010-2011):** Tuition and fees 2010-2011: $26,960; room/board: $8,130. Estimated books and supplies: $900; transportation: $1,610; personal expenses: $1,950. **Financial aid:** Priority filing date for institution's financial aid form: March 1. In 2009-2010, 72% of undergraduates applied for financial aid. Of those, 57% were determined to have financial need; 32% had their need fully met. Average financial aid package (proportion receiving): $20,813 (57%). Average amount of gift aid, such as scholarships or grants (proportion receiving): $13,960 (56%). Average amount of self-help aid, such as work study or loans (proportion receiving): $6,702 (49%). Average need-based loan (excluding PLUS or other private loans): $4,951. Among students who received need-based aid, the average percentage of need met: 82%. Among students who received aid based on merit, the average award (and the proportion receiving): $10,664 (36%). The average athletic scholarship (and the proportion receiving): $20,260 (3%). Average amount of debt of borrowers graduating in 2009: $34,919. Proportion who borrowed: 71%.

CAMPUS LIFE AND EXTRACURRICULAR ACTIVITIES

Campus housing available (% using): coed dorms (45%), sorority housing (4%), fraternity housing (5%), other housing options (46%). Students who live in college-owned, operated, or affiliated housing: 76%. **Student employment:** During the 2009-2010 academic year, 20% of undergraduates worked on campus. Average per-year earnings: $1,600. **Clubs and organizations:** Number of student organizations: 191. Activities include: campus ministries, choral groups, concert band, drama/theater, jazz band, literary magazine, marching band, model UN, music ensembles, musical theater, pep band, radio station, student government, student newspaper, symphony orchestra. Number of fraternities: 8; sororities: 7. Proportion of men in fraternities: 26%; of women in sororities: 28%. Average proportion of students who stay on campus on weekends: 80%. **Sports program (2009-2010):** Member of NCAA I. **Men's intercollegiate varsity sports:** basketball, cross country, football, golf, soccer, tennis, track and field (indoor), track and field (outdoor). **Women's intercollegiate varsity sports:** basketball, crew (heavyweight), crew (lightweight), cross country, golf, soccer, softball, tennis, track and field (indoor), track and field (outdoor), volleyball.

SERVICES AND FACILITIES

Basic services: nonremedial tutoring, women's center, placement service, health service, health insurance. **Remedial assistance:** study skills. **Counseling services:** minority student, career, military, personal, veteran student, academic, older student, psychological, birth control, other. **For learning-disabled students:** School does not offer a structured program with separate admission and additional fees. Total undergraduates in learning-disabled program or receiving services: 70. Services include: reading machines, tape recorders, note-taking services, readers, extended time for tests, priority seating, texts on tape, other testing accommodations, other. **Library:** Number of titles: 749,845; number of current serial subscriptions: 4,609. **Information technology resources:** Students are not required to lease or own a computer. Number of campus computers available to all students: 400. School has a wireless network. Approximate number of users that can be accommodated: 2,000. Proportion of college-owned housing units wired for high-speed internet access: 100%. **Campus safety:** Security services offered: 24-hour foot-and-vehicle patrols, late-night transport/escort service, 24-hour emergency telephones, lighted pathways/sidewalks, controlled dormitory access (key, security card, etc).

TRANSFER AND INTERNATIONAL STUDENTS

Transfer students: May apply for admission for the following academic terms: Fall, Spring, Summer. Applicants need a minimum number of credits to apply. For fall 2009: Transfer applications received: 602. Transfer applicants offered admission: 375. Transfer applicants enrolled: 192. **International students:** Number of foreign undergraduates: 229 (7% of student body). Number of countries represented: 56. Minimum TOEFL score required: 530 (paper); 71 (computer).

Graceland University

- **Address:** 1 University Place, Lamoni, IA 50140-1698
- **Website:** http://www.graceland.edu
- **Private; Religious affiliation:** Community of Christ
- **Enrollment:** 1,177 full-time; 345 part-time

KEY STATS

✔ **U.S News College Ranking:** 107, Regional Universities (Midwest)
✔ **ACT Score (25th/75th percentile):** 16-23
✔ **Tuition:** 2010-2011: $20,980

Selectivity: Selective	**Room/board:** $7,040
Acceptance rate: 88%	**Average debt:** $29,924
Student/faculty ratio: 16/1	**Proportion who borrowed:** 89%

UNDERGRADUATE STUDENT BODY STATS

2009-2010 enrollment: 1,177 full-time; 345 part-time. Men: 39%; women: 61%. **Ethnic makeup:** African American: 10%; American-Indian: 1%; Asian American: 2%; Hispanic: 3%; White: 75%; International: 9%.

ADMISSIONS FACTS AND FIGURES

Phone: (866) 472-2352. **Email:** admissions@graceland.edu. **Website:** http://www.graceland.edu. **Application deadlines for fall 2011:** Regular decision: Rolling. Early decision: Not offered. Early action: Not offered. Admission can be deferred. **To apply online, go to:** http://www.graceland.edu/apply-now/. **Admissions requirements/recommendations:** High school units required (recommended): English: (4); Mathematics: (4); Science: (4); Social studies: (4); Total units: (16). Tests: The college uses SAT or ACT scores in admissions decisions. Either SAT or ACT required. For admission to the fall 2011 entering class, the school will accept: ACT with or without writing accepted. Campus visit: Recommended. Admissions interview: Recommended. Off-campus interview: May be arranged. **Factors that count in admissions decisions: Academic:** Secondary school record: Very Important. Class rank: Very Important. Letters of recommendation: Considered. Standardized test scores: Very Important. Essay: Considered. **Nonacademic:** Interview: Considered. Extracurricular activities: Considered. Talent/ability: Important. Character/personal qualities: Important. Alumni/ae relationship: Considered. Geographical residence: Not Considered. State residency: Not Considered. Religious affiliation/commitment: Considered. Minority status: Not Considered. Volunteer work: Not Considered. Work experience: Not Considered. **Admissions statistics for the fall 2009 entering class:** Total applicants: 598. Total accepted: 526. Freshmen enrolled: 222; 30% were from out of state. Overall acceptance rate: 88%. **Credentials of fall 2009 freshmen:** 11% ranked in the top 10 percent of their high school class; 30% were in the top 25 percent; 60% were in the top half. (Proportion submitting class standing: 87%.) **Average high school grade point average:** 3.1. **First-year students who submitted SAT scores:** 26%. Scores (25/75 percentile): Critical Reading: 420-530, Math: 420-550, Combined: 840-1080. **First-year students submitting ACT scores:** 74%. Scores (25/75 percentile): English: 16-23, Math: 16-24, Composite: 16-23.

ACADEMICS

Year founded: 1895. **Academic calendar:** 4-1-4. **Degrees offered:** bachelor's, master's, post-master's certificate. **Most popular majors:** 30% personal and culinary services, 28% health professions and related clinical sciences, 13% business, management, marketing, and related support services, 6% visual and performing arts, 3% psychology. **Major fields of study:** biological and biomedical sciences; business, management, marketing, and related support services; communication, journalism, and related programs; computer and information sciences and support services; education; English language and literature/letters; foreign languages, literatures, and linguistics; health professions and related clinical sciences; history; liberal arts and sciences studies, and humanities; mathematics and statistics; parks, recreation, leisure, and fitness studies; philosophy and religious studies; physical sciences; psychology; public administration and social service professions; security and protective services; social sciences; visual and performing arts. **Areas of required coursework:** arts/fine arts, humanities, mathematics, English (including composition), sciences (biological or physical), history, social science, other. **Pre-professional programs:** pre-dentistry, pre-medicine, pre-veterinary science. **Special academic programs (% participation):** accelerated program (4%), distance learning (21%), double major (9%), dual enrollment (6%), English as a Second Language (ESL) (4%), honors program (2%), independent study (12%), internships (61%), liberal arts/career combination, student-designed major (3%), study abroad (.2%), teacher certificate program (31%). **Teacher certification offered in:** early childhood, special education, elementary, middle/junior high, secondary. **Faculty and instruction (2009-2010):** Total instructional faculty: 85 full-time, 34 part-time (45% men; 55% women; 13% minorities). Full-time faculty with Ph.D. or other terminal degree: 68%. Student/faculty ratio: 16/1. Classes of fewer than 20 students: 64%; of 20 to 49 students: 34%; of 50 or more students: 2%. **Advanced Placement and International Baccalaureate credit:** AP tests may be used for: Credit only. Scores accepted: 3, 4, 5. International Baccalaureate exams may be used for: Credit only. **Freshmen returning for sophomore year:** 68%. **Graduation rates:** Four-year: 34%; five-year: 47%; six-year: 51%. **Graduate study:** 33% of students pursue further study immediately upon graduation. Fields in which graduates pursue further study: Master of Business Administration (MBA), 1%; law, 1%; medicine, 2%; education, 2%; arts and sciences, 3%.

COSTS AND FINANCIAL AID

Financial aid office: (641) 784-5136. **Expenses (2010-2011):** Tuition and fees 2010-2011: $20,980; room/board: $7,040. Estimated books and supplies: $1,000; transportation: $1,210; personal expenses: $1,760. **Financial aid:** In 2009-2010, 80% of undergraduates applied for financial aid. Of those, 73% were determined to have financial need; 20% had their need fully met. Average financial aid package (proportion receiving): $19,566 (70%). Average amount of gift aid, such as scholarships or grants (proportion receiving): $14,710 (70%). Average amount of self-help aid, such as work study or loans (proportion receiving): $5,631 (59%). Average need-based loan (excluding PLUS or other private loans): $4,891. Among students who received need-based aid, the average percentage of need met: 80%. Among students who received aid based on merit, the average award (and the proportion receiving): $10,029 (23%). The average athletic scholarship (and the proportion receiving): $5,282 (19%). Average amount of debt of borrowers graduating in 2009: $29,924. Proportion who borrowed: 89%.

CAMPUS LIFE AND EXTRACURRICULAR ACTIVITIES

Campus housing available (% using): women's dorms (47%), men's dorms (52%), apartments for married students (1%). Students who live in college-owned, operated, or affiliated housing: 70%. **Student employment:** During the 2009-2010 academic year, 43% of undergraduates worked on campus. Average per-year earnings: $1,575. **Clubs and organizations:** Number of student organizations: 54. Activities include: campus ministries, choral groups, concert band, dance, drama/theater, international student organization, jazz band, music ensembles, musical theater, pep band, radio station, student government, student newspaper, symphony orchestra, yearbook. Number of fraternities: 0; sororities: 0. Average proportion of students who stay on campus on weekends: 58%. **Sports program (2009-2010):** Member of NAIA. **Men's intercollegiate varsity sports:** baseball, basketball, cross country, football, golf, soccer, tennis, track and field (indoor), track and field (outdoor), volleyball. **Women's intercollegiate varsity sports:** basketball, cross country, golf, soccer, softball, tennis, track and field (indoor), track and field (outdoor), volleyball.

SERVICES AND FACILITIES

Basic services: nonremedial tutoring, placement service, health service, health insurance. **Remedial assistance:** reading, math, writing, study skills.

Counseling services: minority student, career, personal, veteran student, academic, older student, birth control, religious. **For learning-disabled students:** School does not offer a structured program with separate admission and additional fees. Total undergraduates in learning-disabled program or receiving services: 62. Services include: remedial math, remedial English, remedial reading, tape recorders, diagnostic testing service, note-taking services, oral tests, learning center, readers, extended time for tests, tutors, priority seating, proofreading services, typist/scribe, exams on tape or computer. **Library:** Number of titles: 153,328; number of current serial subscriptions: 558. **Information technology resources:** Students are not required to lease or own a computer. Number of campus computers available to all students: 249. School has a wireless network. Approximate number of users that can be accommodated: 350. Proportion of college-owned housing units wired for high-speed internet access: 100%. **Campus safety:** Security services offered: 24-hour foot-and-vehicle patrols, late-night transport/escort service, 24-hour emergency telephones, lighted pathways/sidewalks, controlled dormitory access (key, security card, etc).

TRANSFER AND INTERNATIONAL STUDENTS

Transfer students: May apply for admission for the following academic terms: Fall, Winter, Spring, Summer. Applicants need a minimum number of credits to apply. For fall 2009: Transfer applications received: 218. Transfer applicants offered admission: 196. Transfer applicants enrolled: 98. **International students:** Number of foreign undergraduates: 119 (9% of student body). Number of countries represented: 38. Minimum TOEFL score required: 450 (paper); 133 (computer). Average TOEFL score: 482 (paper).

Grand View University

- **Address:** 1200 Grandview Avenue, Des Moines, IA 50316
- **Website:** http://www.gvc.edu
- **Private; Religious affiliation:** Evangelical Lutheran Church in America
- **Enrollment:** 1,601 full-time; 384 part-time

KEY STATS
- ✔ **U.S News College Ranking:** 52, Regional Colleges (Midwest)
- ✔ **ACT Score (25th/75th percentile):** 18-23
- ✔ **Tuition:** 2010-2011: $20,292

Selectivity: Selective	**Room/board:** $6,732
Acceptance rate: 95%	**Average debt:** $28,041
Student/faculty ratio: 14/1	**Proportion who borrowed:** 83%

UNDERGRADUATE STUDENT BODY STATS

2009-2010 enrollment: 1,601 full-time; 384 part-time. Men: 38%; women: 62%. **Ethnic makeup:** African American: 7%; Asian American: 3%; Hispanic: 3%; White: 86%; International: 1%.

ADMISSIONS FACTS AND FIGURES

Phone: (515) 263-2810. **Email:** admissions@gvc.edu. **Website:** http://www.gvc.edu. **Application deadlines for fall 2011:** Regular decision: August 15. Early decision: Not offered. Early action: Not offered. Admission can be deferred. **Application fee:** $35. **To apply online, go to:** http://www.admissions.gvc.edu/bullAdmissionsbull/ApplyNow/tabid/1061/Default.aspx. **Admissions requirements/recommendations:** High school units required (recommended): English: (4); Mathematics: (3); Science: (3); Foreign language: (2); Social studies: (3); Total units: (15). Tests: The college uses SAT or ACT scores in admissions decisions. Either SAT or ACT required. For admission to the fall 2011 entering class, the school will accept: ACT with writing recommended. Campus visit: Recommended. Admissions interview: Recommended. **Factors that count in admissions decisions:** *Academic:* Secondary school record: Very Important. Class rank: Very Important. Letters of recommendation: Not Considered. Standardized test scores: Important. Essay: Not Considered. *Nonacademic:* Interview: Not Considered. Extracurricular activities: Considered. Talent/ability: Considered. Character/personal qualities: Very Important. Alumni/ae relationship: Considered. Geographical residence: Not Considered. State residency: Not Considered. Religious affiliation/commitment: Not Considered. Minority status: Not Considered. Volunteer work: Not Considered. Work experience: Not Considered. **Other schools with the greatest overlap in applicants:** Central College; Drake University; Iowa State University; Simpson College. **Admissions statistics for the fall 2009 entering class:** Total applicants: 689. Total accepted: 653. Freshmen enrolled: 233; 19% were from out of state. Overall acceptance rate: 95%. **Credentials of fall 2009 freshmen:** 16% ranked in the top 10 percent of their high school class; 36% were in the top 25 percent; 78% were in the top half. (Proportion submitting class standing: 88%.) **Average high school grade point average:** 3.2. **First-year students who submitted SAT scores:** 10%. Scores (25/75 percentile): Critical Reading: 410-500, Math: 380-500, Combined: 790-1000. **First-year students submitting ACT scores:** 91%. Scores (25/75 percentile): English: 17-22, Math: 16-22, Composite: 18-23.

ACADEMICS

Year founded: 1896. **Academic calendar:** Semester. **Degrees offered:** certificate, associate, bachelor's, post-bachelor's certificate, master's. **Most popular majors:** 21% business/commerce, 19% nursing/registered nurse training (R.N., A.S.N., B.S.N., M.S.N.), 7% art/art studies. **Major fields of study:** biological and biomedical sciences; business, management, marketing, and related support services; communication, journalism, and related programs; communications technologies/technicians and support services; computer and information sciences and support services; education; English language and literature/letters; health professions and related clinical sciences; liberal arts and sciences studies, and humanities; mathematics and statistics; philosophy and religious studies; physical sciences; psychology; public administration and social service professions; security and protective services; social sciences; visual and performing arts. **Areas of required coursework:** arts/fine arts, humanities, computer literacy, mathematics, English (including composition), sciences (biological or physical), history, social science. **Preprofessional programs:** pre-law, pre-dentistry, pre-medicine, pre-theology, pre-optometry, pre-pharmacy. **Special academic programs:** accelerated program, cooperative (work-study plan) program, cross-registration, distance learning, double major, dual enrollment, honors program, independent study, internships, liberal arts/career combination, student-designed major, study abroad, teacher certificate program, weekend college. **Teacher certification offered in:** early childhood, special education, elementary, secondary. **Reserve Officers Training Corps (ROTC):** Army ROTC: Offered at cooperating institution; Air Force ROTC: Offered at cooperating institution. **Faculty and instruction (2009-2010):** Total instructional faculty: 87 full-time, 116 part-time (41% men; 59% women; 4% minorities). Full-time faculty with Ph.D. or other terminal degree: 57%. Student/faculty ratio: 14/1. Classes of fewer than 20 students: 75%; of 20 to 49 students: 25%; of 50 or more students: 0%. **Freshmen returning for sophomore year:** 69%. **Graduation rates:** Four-year: 27%; five-year: 46%; six-year: 44%.

COSTS AND FINANCIAL AID

Financial aid office: (515) 263-2820. **Expenses (2010-2011):** Tuition and fees 2010-2011: $20,292; room/board: $6,732. Estimated books and supplies: $900; transportation: $600; personal expenses: $2,152. **Financial aid:** Priority filing date for institution's financial aid form: March 1. In 2009-2010, 92% of undergraduates applied for financial aid. Of those, 82% were determined to have financial need; 20% had their need fully met. Average financial aid package (proportion receiving): $14,309 (82%). Average amount of gift aid, such as scholarships or grants (proportion receiving): $11,883 (74%). Average amount of self-help aid, such as work study or loans (proportion receiving): $4,593 (71%). Average need-based loan (excluding PLUS or other private loans): $4,029. Among students who received need-based aid, the average percentage of need met: 75%. Among students who received aid based on merit, the average award (and the proportion receiving): $5,861 (15%). The average athletic scholarship (and the proportion receiving): $5,943 (7%). Average amount of debt of borrowers graduating in 2009: $28,041. Proportion who borrowed: 83%.

CAMPUS LIFE AND EXTRACURRICULAR ACTIVITIES

Campus housing available (% using): coed dorms (67%), apartment for single students (26%), other housing options (7%). Students who live in college-owned, operated, or affiliated housing: 29%. **Student employment:** During the 2009-2010 academic year, 15% of undergraduates worked on campus. Average per-year earnings: $1,500. **Clubs and organizations:** Number of student organizations: 40. Activities include: campus ministries, choral groups, concert band, dance, drama/theater, literary magazine, music ensembles, radio station, student government, student newspaper, television station, yearbook. Number of fraternities: 0; sororities: 0. **Sports program (2009-2010):** Member of NAIA.

SERVICES AND FACILITIES

Basic services: nonremedial tutoring, placement service, health service, health insurance. **Remedial assistance:** reading, math, writing, study skills. **Counseling services:** minority student, career, personal, academic, birth control, religious. **For learning-disabled students:** School does not offer

a structured program with separate admission and additional fees. Total undergraduates in learning-disabled program or receiving services: 64. Services include: remedial math, remedial English, reading machines, remedial reading, tape recorders, diagnostic testing service, note-taking services, oral tests, readers, extended time for tests, tutors, early syllabus, texts on tape, typist/scribe, exams on tape or computer. **Library:** Number of titles: 137,138; number of current serial subscriptions: 21,536. **Information technology resources:** Students are not required to lease or own a computer. Number of campus computers available to all students: 234. School has a wireless network. Proportion of college-owned housing units wired for high-speed internet access: 98%. **Campus safety:** Security services offered: 24-hour foot-and-vehicle patrols, late-night transport/escort service, 24-hour emergency telephones, lighted pathways/sidewalks, controlled dormitory access (key, security card, etc).

TRANSFER AND INTERNATIONAL STUDENTS

Transfer students: May apply for admission for the following academic terms: Fall, Spring, Summer. Applicants need a minimum number of credits to apply. For fall 2009: Transfer applications received: 629. Transfer applicants offered admission: 587. Transfer applicants enrolled: 356. **International students:** Number of foreign undergraduates: 24 (1% of student body). Minimum TOEFL score required: 550 (paper); 210 (computer).

Grinnell College

- **Address:** Grinnell, IA 50112-1690
- **Website:** http://www.grinnell.edu
- **Private**
- **Enrollment:** 1,633 full-time; 55 part-time

KEY STATS

✔ **U.S News College Ranking:** 18, National Liberal Arts Colleges
✔ **SAT Score (25th/75th percentile):** 1220-1460
✔ **Tuition:** 2010-2011: $37,482

Selectivity: Most selective	**Room/board:** $8,880
Acceptance rate: 34%	**Average debt:** $19,540
Student/faculty ratio: 9/1	**Proportion who borrowed:** 54%

UNDERGRADUATE STUDENT BODY STATS

2009-2010 enrollment: 1,633 full-time; 55 part-time. Men: 47%; women: 53%. **Ethnic makeup:** African American: 6%; American-Indian: 1%; Asian American: 8%; Hispanic: 7%; White: 67%; International: 11%. **Religious preference:** Roman Catholic: 14%; Protestant: 23%; Jewish: 5%; Muslim: 2%; Hindu: 1%; Buddhist: 2%; No preference: 40%; Unknown: 8%; Other: 5%.

ADMISSIONS FACTS AND FIGURES

Phone: (800) 247-0113. **Email:** askgrin@grinnell.edu. **Website:** http://www.grinnell.edu. **Application deadlines for fall 2011:** Regular decision: January 2; decision sent by April 1. Early decision: Send application by: November 15; Decision sent by: December 15. Early action: Not offered. Admission can be deferred. **Application fee:** $30. **To apply online, go to:** http://www.grinnell.edu/admission/apply/. **Admissions requirements/recommendations:** High school units required (recommended): English: (4); Mathematics: (4); Science: (4); Foreign language: (3); Social studies: (4); Total units: (20). Tests: The college uses SAT or ACT scores in admissions decisions. Either SAT or ACT required. For admission to the fall 2011 entering class, the school will accept: ACT with or without writing accepted. Campus visit: Recommended. Admissions interview: Recommended. Off-campus interview: May be arranged. **Factors that count in admissions decisions:** *Academic:* Secondary school record: Very Important. Class rank: Very Important. Letters of recommendation: Very Important. Standardized test scores: Very Important. Essay: Important. *Nonacademic:* Interview: Important. Extracurricular activities: Very Important. Talent/ability: Very Important. Character/personal qualities: Considered. Alumni/ae relationship: Considered. Geographical residence: Considered. State residency: Considered. Religious affiliation/commitment: Not Considered. Minority status: Important. Volunteer work: Considered. Work experience: Considered. **Other schools with the greatest overlap in applicants:** Brown University; Carleton College; Macalester College; Oberlin College; Washington University in St. Louis. **Admissions statistics for the fall 2009 entering class:** Total applicants: 3,291. Total accepted: 1,108. Freshmen enrolled: 378; 85% were from out of state. Accepted through early-decision or early-action plans: 35%. Overall acceptance rate: 34%. Early-decision acceptance rate: 48%. Non-early acceptance rate: 32%. **Size of waiting list:** 1026 applicants; enrolled from waiting list: 71. **Credentials of fall 2009 freshmen:** 65% ranked in the top 10 percent of their high school class; 93% were in the top 25 percent; 98% were in the top half. (Proportion submitting class standing: 48%.) **First-year students who submitted SAT scores:** 56%. Scores (25/75 percentile): Critical Reading: 600-730, Math: 620-730, Combined: 1220-1460. **First-year students submitting ACT scores:** 44%. Scores (25/75 percentile): English: 29-34, Math: 26-32, Composite: 28-32.

ACADEMICS

Year founded: 1846. **Academic calendar:** Semester. **Degrees offered:** bachelor's. **Most popular majors:** 10% economics, 10% psychology, 9% political science and government, 8% English language and literature, 8% biology/biological sciences. **Major fields of study:** biological and biomedical sciences; computer and information sciences and support services; English language and literature/letters; foreign languages, literatures, and linguistics; history; mathematics and statistics; multi/interdisciplinary studies; philosophy and religious studies; physical sciences; psychology; social sciences; visual and performing arts. **Special academic programs (% participation):** double major (19%), independent study (53%), internships (34%), liberal arts/career combination, student-designed major (3%), study abroad (54%), teacher certificate program (1%). **Teacher certification offered in:** middle/junior high, secondary. **Cooperative education programs:** other. **Faculty and instruction (2009-2010):** Total instructional faculty: 157 full-time, 46 part-time (55% men; 45% women; 15% minorities). Full-time faculty with Ph.D. or other terminal degree: 97%. Student/faculty ratio: 9/1. Classes of fewer than 20 students: 64%; of 20 to 49 students: 36%; of 50 or more students: 0%. **Advanced Placement and International Baccalaureate credit:** AP tests may be used for: Credit and/or placement. Scores accepted: 3, 4, 5. International Baccalaureate exams may be used for: Credit and/or placement. **Freshmen returning for sophomore year:** 94%. **Graduation rates:** Four-year: 78%; five-year: 84%; six-year: 84%. **Graduate study:** 29% of students pursue further study immediately upon graduation; 32% within one year; 76% within five years. Fields in which graduates pursue further study: Master of Business Administration (MBA), 12%; law, 18%; medicine, 10%; dentistry, 1%; engineering, 1%; theology (or the seminary), 2%; education, 1%; arts and sciences, 55%; veterinary medicine, 1%.

COSTS AND FINANCIAL AID

Financial aid office: (641) 269-3250. **Expenses (2010-2011):** Tuition and fees 2010-2011: $37,482; room/board: $8,880. Estimated books and supplies: $900; transportation: $700; personal expenses: $1,100. **Financial aid:** Priority filing date for institution's financial aid form: February 1; deadline: February 1. In 2009-2010, 71% of undergraduates applied for financial aid. Of those, 64% were determined to have financial need; 100% had their need fully met. Average financial aid package (proportion receiving): $32,958 (64%). Average amount of gift aid, such as scholarships or grants (proportion receiving): $27,997 (63%). Average amount of self-help aid, such as work study or loans (proportion receiving): $4,056 (55%). Average need-based loan (excluding PLUS or other private loans): $3,133. Among students who received need-based aid, the average percentage of need met: 100%. Among students who received aid based on merit, the average award (and the proportion receiving): $10,181 (21%). The average athletic scholarship (and the proportion receiving): $0 (0%). Average amount of debt of borrowers graduating in 2009: $19,540. Proportion who borrowed: 54%.

CAMPUS LIFE AND EXTRACURRICULAR ACTIVITIES

Campus housing available (% using): coed dorms (95%), special housing for disabled students, cooperative housing (2%), other housing options. Students who live in college-owned, operated, or affiliated housing: 87%. **Student employment:** During the 2009-2010 academic year, 64% of undergraduates worked on campus. Average per-year earnings: $2,000. **Clubs and organizations:** Number of student organizations: 250. Activities include: campus ministries, choral groups, concert band, dance, drama/theater, international student organization, jazz band, literary magazine, model UN, music ensembles, musical theater, pep band, radio station, student government, student newspaper, student film society, symphony orchestra, yearbook. Number of fraternities: 0; sororities: 0. Average proportion of students who stay on campus on weekends: 95%. **Sports program (2009-2010):** Member of NCAA III. *Men's intercollegiate varsity sports:* baseball, basketball, cross country, football, golf, soccer, swimming, tennis, track and field (indoor), track and field (outdoor). *Women's intercollegiate varsity sports:* basketball, cross country, golf, soccer, softball, swimming, tennis, track and field (indoor), track and field (outdoor), volleyball.

SERVICES AND FACILITIES

Basic services: nonremedial tutoring, health service, health insurance. **Counseling services:** career, personal, academic, psychological, birth control, religious. **For learning-disabled students:** School does not offer a structured program with separate admission and additional fees. Total undergraduates in learning-disabled program or receiving services: 55. Services include: tape recorders, note-taking services, learning center, readers, extended time for tests, tutors, other. **Library:** Number of titles: 1,230,201; number of current serial subscriptions: 22,059. **Information technology resources:** Students are not required to lease or own a computer. Number of campus computers available to all students: 457. School has a wireless network. Approximate number of users that can be accommodated: 5,000. Proportion of college-owned housing units wired for high-speed internet access: 100%. **Campus safety:** Security services offered: 24-hour foot-and-vehicle patrols, late-night transport/escort service, 24-hour emergency telephones, lighted pathways/sidewalks, student patrols, controlled dormitory access (key, security card, etc).

TRANSFER AND INTERNATIONAL STUDENTS

Transfer students: May apply for admission for the following academic terms: Fall, Spring. Applicants need a minimum number of credits to apply. For fall 2009: Transfer applications received: 115. Transfer applicants offered admission: 50. Transfer applicants enrolled: 28. **International students:** Number of foreign undergraduates: 176 (11% of student body). Number of countries represented: 54. Minimum TOEFL score required: 550 (paper); 80 (computer).

Iowa State University

- **Address:** 100 Alumni Hall, Ames, IA 50011
- **Website:** http://www.iastate.edu
- **Public**
- **Enrollment:** 21,394 full-time; 1,127 part-time

KEY STATS

✔ **U.S News College Ranking:** 94, National Universities
✔ **ACT Score (25th/75th percentile):** 22-28
✔ **Tuition:** 2010-2011: $6,997 in state, $18,563 out of state
  Selectivity: More selective   **Room/board:** $7,472
  Acceptance rate: 85%   **Average debt:** $30,411
  Student/faculty ratio: 16/1   **Proportion who borrowed:** 71%

UNDERGRADUATE STUDENT BODY STATS

2009-2010 enrollment: 21,394 full-time; 1,127 part-time. Men: 57%; women: 43%. **Ethnic makeup:** African American: 3%; Asian American: 3%; Hispanic: 3%; White: 86%; International: 5%.

ADMISSIONS FACTS AND FIGURES

Phone: (800) 262-3810. **Email:** admissions@iastate.edu. **Website:** http://www.iastate.edu. **Application deadlines for fall 2011:** Regular decision: Rolling. Early decision: Not offered. Early action: Not offered. Admission can be deferred. **Application fee:** $40. **To apply online, go to:** http://www.admissions.iastate.edu. **Admissions requirements/recommendations:** High school units required (recommended): English: 4 (4); Mathematics: 3 (4); Science: 3 (4); Foreign language: 2 (3); Social studies: 2 (4); Total units: 14 (19). Tests: The college uses SAT or ACT scores in admissions decisions. Either SAT or ACT required. For admission to the fall 2011 entering class, the school will accept: ACT with or without writing accepted. Campus visit: Recommended. Admissions interview: Neither required nor recommended. Off-campus interview: Not available. **Factors that count in admissions decisions:** *Academic:* Secondary school record: Very Important. Class rank: Very Important. Letters of recommendation: Considered. Standardized test scores: Very Important. Essay: Considered. *Nonacademic:* Interview: Considered. Extracurricular activities: Considered. Talent/ability: Considered. Character/personal qualities: Considered. Alumni/ae relationship: Not Considered. Geographical residence: Considered. State residency: Considered. Religious affiliation/commitment: Not Considered. Minority status: Not Considered. Volunteer work: Considered. Work experience: Considered. **Other schools with the greatest overlap in applicants:** Purdue University–West Lafayette; University of Illinois–Urbana-Champaign; University of Iowa; University of Minnesota–Twin Cities; University of Wisconsin–Madison. **Admissions statistics for the fall 2009 entering class:** Total applicants: 12,536. Total accepted: 10,662. Freshmen enrolled: 4,356;

30% were from out of state. Overall acceptance rate: 85%. **Credentials of fall 2009 freshmen:** 28% ranked in the top 10 percent of their high school class; 62% were in the top 25 percent; 93% were in the top half. (Proportion submitting class standing: 77%.) **Average high school grade point average:** 3.5. **First-year students who submitted SAT scores:** 10%. Scores (25/75 percentile): Critical Reading: 490-640, Math: 540-690, Combined: 1030-1330. **First-year students submitting ACT scores:** 93%. Scores (25/75 percentile): English: 21-28, Math: 22-28, Composite: 22-28.

ACADEMICS

Year founded: 1858. **Academic calendar:** Semester. **Degrees offered:** bachelor's, master's, post-master's certificate, doctorate. **Most popular majors:** 21% business, management, marketing, and related support services, 16% engineering, 10% agriculture, agriculture operations, and related sciences, 7% visual and performing arts, 5% biological and biomedical sciences. **Major fields of study:** agriculture, agriculture operations, and related sciences; architecture and related services; area, ethnic, cultural, and gender studies; biological and biomedical sciences; business, management, marketing, and related support services; communication, journalism, and related programs; computer and information sciences and support services; education; engineering; English language and literature/letters; family and consumer sciences/human sciences; foreign languages, literatures, and linguistics; health professions and related clinical sciences; history; liberal arts and sciences studies, and humanities; mathematics and statistics; multi/interdisciplinary studies; natural resources and conservation; parks, recreation, leisure, and fitness studies; philosophy and religious studies; physical sciences; psychology; public administration and social service professions; social sciences; visual and performing arts. **Areas of required coursework:** humanities, mathematics, English (including composition), sciences (biological or physical), social science, other. **Pre-professional programs:** pre-law, pre-dentistry, pre-medicine, pre-theology, pre-veterinary science, pre-optometry, pre-pharmacy, other. **Special academic programs:** accelerated program, cooperative (work-study plan) program, cross-registration, distance learning, double major, dual enrollment, English as a Second Language (ESL), exchange student program (domestic), external degree program, honors program, independent study, internships, liberal arts/career combination, student-designed major, study abroad, teacher certificate program, weekend college. **Teacher certification offered in:** early childhood, special education, elementary, vo-tech, middle/junior high, adult education, secondary, bilingual/bicultural. **Cooperative education programs:** agriculture, business, computer science, education, engineering, home economics, humanities, natural science, social/behavioral science, technologies, other. **Reserve Officers Training Corps (ROTC):** Army ROTC: Offered on campus; Navy ROTC: Offered on campus; Air Force ROTC: Offered on campus. **Faculty and instruction (2009-2010):** Total instructional faculty: 1,435 full-time, 228 part-time (66% men; 34% women; 19% minorities). Full-time faculty with Ph.D. or other terminal degree: 92%. Student/faculty ratio: 16/1. Classes of fewer than 20 students: 33%; of 20 to 49 students: 48%; of 50 or more students: 19%. **Advanced Placement and International Baccalaureate credit:** AP tests may be used for: Placement only. Scores accepted: 3, 4, 5. International Baccalaureate exams may be used for: Credit and/or placement. **Freshmen returning for sophomore year:** 84%. **Graduation rates:** Four-year: 35%; five-year: 65%; six-year: 69%. **Graduate study:** 17% of students pursue further study within one year.

COSTS AND FINANCIAL AID

Financial aid office: (515) 294-2223. **Expenses (2010-2011):** Tuition and fees 2010-2011: $6,997 in state, $18,563 out of state; room/board: $7,472. Estimated books and supplies: $1,014; transportation: $624; personal expenses: $2,814. **Financial aid:** Priority filing date for institution's financial aid form: March 1. In 2009-2010, 75% of undergraduates applied for financial aid. Of those, 53% were determined to have financial need; 39% had their need fully met. Average financial aid package (proportion receiving): $10,771 (52%). Average amount of gift aid, such as scholarships or grants (proportion receiving): $5,560 (52%). Average amount of self-help aid, such as work study or loans (proportion receiving): $4,541 (43%). Average need-based loan (excluding PLUS or other private loans): $4,359. Among students who received need-based aid, the average percentage of need met: 82%. Among students who received aid based on merit, the average award (and the proportion receiving): $2,285 (31%). The average athletic scholarship (and the proportion receiving): $14,639 (2%). Average amount of debt of borrowers graduating in 2009: $30,411. Proportion who borrowed: 71%.

CAMPUS LIFE AND EXTRACURRICULAR ACTIVITIES

Campus housing available (% using): coed dorms (48%), women's dorms (4%), men's dorms (4%), sorority housing (3%), fraternity housing (6%),

apartments for married students (6%), apartment for single students (19%), special housing for disabled students, special housing for international students (1%), other housing options (9%). Students who live in college-owned, operated, or affiliated housing: 36%. **Student employment:** During the 2009-2010 academic year, 33% of undergraduates worked on campus. Average per-year earnings: $3,500. **Clubs and organizations:** Number of student organizations: 745. Activities include: choral groups, concert band, dance, drama/theater, jazz band, literary magazine, marching band, music ensembles, musical theater, opera, pep band, radio station, student government, student newspaper, student film society, symphony orchestra, television station. Number of fraternities: 34; sororities: 19. Proportion of men in fraternities: 16%; of women in sororities: 17%. Average proportion of students who stay on campus on weekends: 62%. **Sports program (2009-2010):** Member of NCAA I. *Men's intercollegiate varsity sports:* basketball, cross country, football, golf, swimming, track and field (indoor), track and field (outdoor), wrestling. *Women's intercollegiate varsity sports:* basketball, cross country, golf, gymnastics, soccer, softball, tennis, track and field (indoor), track and field (outdoor), volleyball.

SERVICES AND FACILITIES

Basic services: nonremedial tutoring, women's center, placement service, day care, health service, health insurance, other. **Remedial assistance:** study skills. **Counseling services:** minority student, career, military, personal, veteran student, academic, older student, psychological, birth control, religious. **For learning-disabled students:** School does not offer a structured program with separate admission and additional fees. Services include: reading machines, tape recorders, videotaped classes, note-taking services, learning center, readers, extended time for tests, priority registration, priority seating, texts on tape, other testing accommodations, other. **Library:** Number of titles: 2,578,144; number of current serial subscriptions: 97,352. **Information technology resources:** Students are not required to lease or own a computer. Number of campus computers available to all students: 3,500. School has a wireless network. Approximate number of users that can be accommodated: 12,000. Proportion of college-owned housing units wired for high-speed internet access: 100%. **Campus safety:** Security services offered: 24-hour foot-and-vehicle patrols, late-night transport/escort service, 24-hour emergency telephones, lighted pathways/sidewalks, controlled dormitory access (key, security card, etc).

TRANSFER AND INTERNATIONAL STUDENTS

Transfer students: May apply for admission for the following academic terms: Fall, Spring, Summer. Applicants need a minimum number of credits to apply. For fall 2009: Transfer applications received: 3,068. Transfer applicants offered admission: 2,369. Transfer applicants enrolled: 1,622. **International students:** Number of foreign undergraduates: 1179 (5% of student body). Number of countries represented: 106. Minimum TOEFL score required: 530 (paper).

Iowa Wesleyan College

- **Address:** 601 N. Main Street, Mount Pleasant, IA 52641
- **Website:** http://www.iwc.edu
- **Private; Religious affiliation:** United Methodist
- **Enrollment:** N/A

KEY STATS

✔ **U.S News College Ranking:** second tier, Regional Colleges (Midwest)
✔ **SAT or ACT Score (25th/75th percentile):** N/A
✔ **Tuition:** 2009-2010: $21,000

Selectivity: Less selective	**Room/board:** $6,842
Acceptance rate: N/A	**Average debt:** N/A
Student/faculty ratio: N/A	**Proportion who borrowed:** N/A

Loras College

- **Address:** 1450 Alta Vista, Dubuque, IA 52004-0178
- **Website:** http://www.loras.edu
- **Private; Religious affiliation:** Roman Catholic
- **Enrollment:** 1,458 full-time; 41 part-time

KEY STATS

✔ **U.S News College Ranking:** 11, Regional Colleges (Midwest)
✔ **ACT Score (25th/75th percentile):** 21-26
✔ **Tuition:** 2010-2011: $26,286

Selectivity: Selective	Room/board: $7,306
Acceptance rate: 61%	Average debt: $30,100
Student/faculty ratio: 12/1	Proportion who borrowed: 82%

UNDERGRADUATE STUDENT BODY STATS

2009-2010 enrollment: 1,458 full-time; 41 part-time. Men: 51%; women: 49%. **Ethnic makeup:** African American: 1%; Hispanic: 3%; White: 92%; International: 3%. **Religious preference:** Protestant: 2%; Unknown: 24%; Roman Catholic: 64%.

ADMISSIONS FACTS AND FIGURES

Phone: (800) 245-6727. **Email:** adms@loras.edu. **Website:** http://www.loras.edu. **Application deadlines for fall 2011:** Regular decision: Rolling. Early decision: Not offered. Early action: Not offered. Admission can be deferred. **Application fee:** $25. **To apply online, go to:** http://www.loras.edu/admissions/application/apply.asp. **Admissions requirements/recommendations:** High school units required (recommended): English: 4 (4); Mathematics: 3 (3); Science: 4 (4); Social studies: 3 (3); History: 3 (3); Total units: 16 (16). Tests: The college uses SAT or ACT scores in admissions decisions. Neither SAT nor ACT required. For admission to the fall 2011 entering class, the school will accept: ACT with or without writing accepted. Campus visit: Recommended. Admissions interview: Recommended. Off-campus interview: May be arranged. **Factors that count in admissions decisions:** *Academic:* Secondary school record: Very Important. Class rank: Important. Letters of recommendation: Considered. Standardized test scores: Very Important. Essay: Considered. *Nonacademic:* Interview: Not Considered. Extracurricular activities: Considered. Talent/ability: Not Considered. Character/personal qualities: Considered. Alumni/ae relationship: Not Considered. Geographical residence: Not Considered. State residency: Not Considered. Religious affiliation/commitment: Not Considered. Minority status: Considered. Volunteer work: Considered. Work experience: Considered. **Other schools with the greatest overlap in applicants:** Clarke University; St. Ambrose University; University of Iowa; University of Northern Iowa; Wartburg College. **Admissions statistics for the fall 2009 entering class:** Total applicants: 4,141. Total accepted: 2,544. Freshmen enrolled: 414; 56% were from out of state. Overall acceptance rate: 61%. **Credentials of fall 2009 freshmen:** 15% ranked in the top 10 percent of their high school class; 38% were in the top 25 percent; 71% were in the top half. (Proportion submitting class standing: 65%.) **Average high school grade point average:** 3.3. **First-year students submitting ACT scores:** 96%. Scores (25/75 percentile): English: 19-26, Math: 20-26, Composite: 21-26.

ACADEMICS

Year founded: 1839. **Academic calendar:** Semester. **Degrees offered:** associate, bachelor's, master's. **Most popular majors:** 23% business, management, marketing, and related support services, 17% education, 8% communication, journalism, and related programs, 7% English language and literature/letters, 6% public administration and social service professions. **Major fields of study:** biological and biomedical sciences; business, management, marketing, and related support services; communication, journalism, and related programs; computer and information sciences and support services; education; engineering; English language and literature/letters; foreign languages, literatures, and linguistics; history; liberal arts and sciences studies, and humanities; mathematics and statistics; parks, recreation, leisure, and fitness studies; philosophy and religious studies; physical sciences; psychology; public administration and social service professions; security and protective services; social sciences; visual and performing arts. **Areas of required coursework:** arts/fine arts, humanities, mathematics, English (including composition), sciences (biological or physical), social science. **Pre-professional programs:** pre-law, pre-dentistry, pre-medicine, pre-optometry, pre-pharmacy, other. **Special academic programs (% participation):** cooperative (work-study plan) program (10%), cross-registration (23%), double major (30%), dual enrollment (8%), English as a Second Language

(ESL) (0%), honors program (11%), independent study (9%), internships (46%), student-designed major (1%), study abroad (15%), teacher certificate program (6%). **Teacher certification offered in:** early childhood, special education, elementary, middle/junior high, secondary. **Reserve Officers Training Corps (ROTC):** Army ROTC: Offered at cooperating institution (University of Dubuque). **Faculty and instruction (2009-2010):** Total instructional faculty: 111 full-time, 48 part-time (53% men; 47% women; 4% minorities). Full-time faculty with Ph.D. or other terminal degree: 74%. Student/faculty ratio: 12/1. Classes of fewer than 20 students: 57%; of 20 to 49 students: 43%; of 50 or more students: 0%. **Advanced Placement and International Baccalaureate credit:** AP tests may be used for: Credit only. Scores accepted: 3, 4, 5. International Baccalaureate exams may be used for: Credit only. Freshmen returning for sophomore year: 74%. **Graduation rates:** Four-year: 54%; five-year: 67%; six-year: 64%. **Graduate study:** 17% of students pursue further study immediately upon graduation. Fields in which graduates pursue further study: Master of Business Administration (MBA), 17%; law, 5%; medicine, 20%; dentistry, 2%; engineering, 2%; theology (or the seminary), 2%; education, 2%; arts and sciences, 29%; veterinary medicine, 1%.

COSTS AND FINANCIAL AID

Financial aid office: (563) 588-7136. **Expenses (2010-2011):** Tuition and fees 2010-2011: $26,286; room/board: $7,306. Estimated books and supplies: $1,100; transportation: $1,378; personal expenses: $600. **Financial aid:** Priority filing date for institution's financial aid form: April 15. In 2009-2010, 85% of undergraduates applied for financial aid. Of those, 76% were determined to have financial need; 40% had their need fully met. Average financial aid package (proportion receiving): $16,558 (76%). Average amount of gift aid, such as scholarships or grants (proportion receiving): $8,276 (67%). Average amount of self-help aid, such as work study or loans (proportion receiving): $3,262 (67%). Average need-based loan (excluding PLUS or other private loans): $3,071. Among students who received need-based aid, the average percentage of need met: 89%. Among students who received aid based on merit, the average award (and the proportion receiving): $9,620 (24%). The average athletic scholarship (and the proportion receiving): $0 (0%). Average amount of debt of borrowers graduating in 2009: $30,100. Proportion who borrowed: 82%.

CAMPUS LIFE AND EXTRACURRICULAR ACTIVITIES

Campus housing available (% using): coed dorms (75%), apartment for single students (18%), other housing options (7%). Students who live in college-owned, operated, or affiliated housing: 66%. **Student employment:** During the 2009-2010 academic year, 40% of undergraduates worked on campus. Average per-year earnings: $1,500. **Clubs and organizations:** Number of student organizations: 65. Activities include: choral groups, concert band, dance, drama/theater, jazz band, music ensembles, musical theater, radio station, student government, student newspaper, television station, yearbook. Number of fraternities: 0; sororities: 1. Average proportion of students who stay on campus on weekends: 50%. **Sports program (2009-2010):** Member of NCAA III. *Men's intercollegiate varsity sports:* baseball, basketball, cross country, football, golf, gymnastics, soccer, swimming, tennis, track and field (indoor), track and field (outdoor), volleyball, wrestling. *Women's intercollegiate varsity sports:* basketball, cross country, golf, gymnastics, soccer, softball, swimming, tennis, track and field (indoor), track and field (outdoor), volleyball.

SERVICES AND FACILITIES

Basic services: nonremedial tutoring, health service, health insurance. **Remedial assistance:** reading, math, writing, study skills. **Counseling services:** minority student, career, military, personal, veteran student, academic, older student, psychological, religious. **For learning-disabled students:** School does not offer a structured program with separate admission and additional fees. Services include: reading machines, tape recorders, other special classes, untimed tests, note-taking services, learning center, extended time for tests, tutors, other. **Library:** Number of titles: 370,766; number of current serial subscriptions: 499. **Information technology resources:** Students are required to lease or own a computer. School has a wireless network. Approximate number of users that can be accommodated: 2,500. Proportion of college-owned housing units wired for high-speed internet access: 100%. **Campus safety:** Security services offered: 24-hour foot-and-vehicle patrols, late-night transport/escort service, 24-hour emergency telephones, lighted pathways/sidewalks, controlled dormitory access (key, security card, etc).

TRANSFER AND INTERNATIONAL STUDENTS

Transfer students: May apply for admission for the following academic terms: Fall, Spring, Summer. Applicants need a minimum number of credits to apply. For fall 2009: Transfer applications received: 160. Transfer applicants offered admission: 84. Transfer applicants enrolled: 41. **International students:** Number of foreign undergraduates: 50 (3% of student body). Number of countries represented: 9. Minimum TOEFL score required: 550 (paper); 213 (computer).

Luther College

- ■ **Address:** 700 College Drive, Decorah, IA 52101-1045
- ■ **Website:** http://www.luther.edu
- ■ **Private; Religious affiliation:** Lutheran
- ■ **Enrollment:** 2,470 full-time; 49 part-time

KEY STATS
✔ **U.S News College Ranking:** 81, National Liberal Arts Colleges
✔ **ACT Score (25th/75th percentile):** 23-29
✔ **Tuition:** 2010-2011: $33,480
  Selectivity: More selective   **Room/board:** $5,800
  Acceptance rate: 70%   **Average debt:** $34,101
  Student/faculty ratio: 12/1   **Proportion who borrowed:** 82%

UNDERGRADUATE STUDENT BODY STATS
2009-2010 enrollment: 2,470 full-time; 49 part-time. Men: 42%; women: 58%. **Ethnic makeup:** African American: 2%; Asian American: 2%; Hispanic: 2%; White: 89%; International: 5%. **Religious preference:** Roman Catholic: 15%; Protestant: 12%; No preference: 18%; Lutheran: 45%; Other: 10%.

ADMISSIONS FACTS AND FIGURES
Phone: (563) 387-1287. **Email:** admissions@luther.edu. **Website:** http://www.luther.edu. **Application deadlines for fall 2011:** Regular decision: Rolling. Early decision: Not offered. Early action: Not offered. Admission can be deferred. **Application fee:** $25. **To apply online, go to:** http://www.luther.edu/admis/apply.html. **Admissions requirements/recommendations:** High school units required (recommended): English: (4); Mathematics: (3); Science: (2); Foreign language: (2); Social studies: (3); Total units: (14). Tests: The college uses SAT or ACT scores in admissions decisions. Either SAT or ACT required. For admission to the fall 2011 entering class, the school will accept: ACT with or without writing accepted. Campus visit: Recommended. Admissions interview: Recommended. Off-campus interview: May be arranged. **Factors that count in admissions decisions:** *Academic:* Secondary school record: Very Important. Class rank: Very Important. Letters of recommendation: Very Important. Standardized test scores: Very Important. Essay: Considered. *Nonacademic:* Interview: Considered. Extracurricular activities: Important. Talent/ability: Important. Character/personal qualities: Important. Alumni/ae relationship: Considered. Geographical residence: Not Considered. State residency: Not Considered. Religious affiliation/commitment: Not Considered. Minority status: Considered. Volunteer work: Considered. Work experience: Not Considered. **Other schools with the greatest overlap in applicants:** Concordia College–Moorhead; Gustavus Adolphus College; St. Olaf College; University of Iowa; Wartburg College. **Admissions statistics for the fall 2009 entering class:** Total applicants: 3,445. Total accepted: 2,403. Freshmen enrolled: 657; 69% were from out of state. Overall acceptance rate: 70%. **Credentials of fall 2009 freshmen:** 35% ranked in the top 10 percent of their high school class; 64% were in the top 25 percent; 91% were in the top half. (Proportion submitting class standing: 81%.) **Average high school grade point average:** 3.6. **First-year students who submitted SAT scores:** 14%. Scores (25/75 percentile): Critical Reading: 500-640, Math: 530-670, Combined: 1030-1310. **First-year students submitting ACT scores:** 94%. Scores (25/75 percentile): English: 23-30, Math: 23-29, Composite: 23-29.

ACADEMICS
Year founded: 1861. **Academic calendar:** 4-1-4. **Degrees offered:** bachelor's. **Most popular majors:** 12% biology/biological sciences, 10% music, 9% business administration and management, 7% elementary education and teaching, 7% psychology. **Major fields of study:** area, ethnic, cultural, and gender studies; biological and biomedical sciences; business, management, marketing, and related support services; communication, journalism, and related programs; computer and information sciences and support services; education; English language and literature/letters; foreign languages, literatures, and linguistics; health professions and related clinical sciences; history; mathematics and statistics; multi/interdisciplinary studies; natural

resources and conservation; parks, recreation, leisure, and fitness studies; philosophy and religious studies; physical sciences; psychology; public administration and social service professions; social sciences; visual and performing arts. **Areas of required coursework:** arts/fine arts, humanities, mathematics, English (including composition), philosophy, foreign languages, sciences (biological or physical), history, social science, other. **Pre-professional programs:** pre-law, pre-dentistry, pre-medicine, pre-theology, pre-veterinary science, pre-optometry, pre-pharmacy, other. **Special academic programs:** double major, dual enrollment, honors program, independent study, internships, student-designed major, study abroad, teacher certificate program. **Teacher certification offered in:** early childhood, special education, elementary, middle/junior high, secondary, bilingual/bicultural. **Faculty and instruction (2009-2010):** Total instructional faculty: 177 full-time, 74 part-time (57% men; 43% women; 2% minorities). Full-time faculty with Ph.D. or other terminal degree: 92%. Student/faculty ratio: 12/1. Classes of fewer than 20 students: 53%; of 20 to 49 students: 45%; of 50 or more students: 2%. **Advanced Placement and International Baccalaureate credit:** AP tests may be used for: Credit and/or placement. Scores accepted: 4, 5. International Baccalaureate exams may be used for: Credit and/or placement. **Freshmen returning for sophomore year:** 86%. **Graduation rates:** Four-year: 65%; five-year: 74%; six-year: 75%. **Graduate study:** 21% of students pursue further study immediately upon graduation. Fields in which graduates pursue further study: law, 10%; medicine, 13%; dentistry, 3%; engineering, 2%; theology (or the seminary), 3%; education, 2%; arts and sciences, 66%; veterinary medicine, 1%.

COSTS AND FINANCIAL AID
Financial aid office: (563) 387-1018. **Expenses (2010-2011):** Tuition and fees 2010-2011: $33,480; room/board: $5,800. Estimated books and supplies: $910; transportation: $1,020; personal expenses: $1,510. **Financial aid:** Priority filing date for institution's financial aid form: March 1. In 2009-2010, 81% of undergraduates applied for financial aid. Of those, 69% were determined to have financial need; 31% had their need fully met. Average financial aid package (proportion receiving): $24,932 (69%). Average amount of gift aid, such as scholarships or grants (proportion receiving): $17,454 (68%). Average amount of self-help aid, such as work study or loans (proportion receiving): $6,273 (58%). Average need-based loan (excluding PLUS or other private loans): $6,406. Among students who received need-based aid, the average percentage of need met: 88%. Among students who received aid based on merit, the average award (and the proportion receiving): $9,617 (10%). Average amount of debt of borrowers graduating in 2009: $34,101. Proportion who borrowed: 82%.

CAMPUS LIFE AND EXTRACURRICULAR ACTIVITIES
Campus housing available (% using): coed dorms (90%), apartments for married students (1%), apartment for single students (2%), special housing for disabled students, other housing options (7%). Students who live in college-owned, operated, or affiliated housing: 88%. **Student employment:** During the 2009-2010 academic year, 51% of undergraduates worked on campus. Average per-year earnings: $2,200. **Clubs and organizations:** Number of student organizations: 80. Activities include: campus ministries, choral groups, concert band, dance, drama/theater, international student organization, jazz band, literary magazine, model UN, music ensembles, musical theater, pep band, radio station, student government, student newspaper, symphony orchestra, yearbook. Number of fraternities: 1; sororities: 3. Proportion of men in fraternities: 1%; of women in sororities: 2%. Average proportion of students who stay on campus on weekends: 90%. **Sports program (2009-2010):** Member of NCAA III. *Men's intercollegiate varsity sports:* baseball, basketball, cross country, football, golf, soccer, swimming, tennis, track and field (indoor), track and field (outdoor), wrestling. *Women's intercollegiate varsity sports:* basketball, cross country, golf, soccer, softball, swimming, tennis, track and field (indoor), track and field (outdoor), volleyball.

SERVICES AND FACILITIES
Basic services: nonremedial tutoring, placement service, health service, health insurance. **Remedial assistance:** reading, writing, study skills. **Counseling services:** minority student, career, personal, academic, older student, psychological, birth control, religious. **For learning-disabled students:** School does not offer a structured program with separate admission and additional fees. Total undergraduates in learning-disabled program or receiving services: 23. Services include: tape recorders, note-taking services, oral tests, learning center, extended time for tests, tutors, priority registration, texts on tape, other testing accommodations, other. **Library:** Number of titles: 333,314; number of current serial subscriptions: 823. **Information technology resources:** Students are not required to lease or own a computer.

Number of campus computers available to all students: 500. School has a wireless network. Approximate number of users that can be accommodated: 5,000. Proportion of college-owned housing units wired for high-speed internet access: 100%. **Campus safety:** Security services offered: 24-hour foot-and-vehicle patrols, late-night transport/escort service, 24-hour emergency telephones, lighted pathways/sidewalks, controlled dormitory access (key, security card, etc).

TRANSFER AND INTERNATIONAL STUDENTS

Transfer students: May apply for admission for the following academic terms: Fall, Winter, Spring, Summer. Applicants do not need a minimum number of credits to apply. For fall 2009: Transfer applications received: 111. Transfer applicants offered admission: 75. Transfer applicants enrolled: 45. **International students:** Number of foreign undergraduates: 127 (5% of student body). Number of countries represented: 44. Minimum TOEFL score required: 550 (paper); 80 (computer). Average TOEFL score: 588 (paper).

Maharishi University of Management

- **Address:** Fairfield, IA 52557
- **Website:** http://www.mum.edu
- **Private**
- **Enrollment:** N/A

KEY STATS

- ✔ **U.S News College Ranking:** second tier, Regional Universities (Midwest)
- ✔ **SAT or ACT Score (25th/75th percentile):** N/A
- ✔ **Tuition:** 2009-2010: $24,430
  - **Selectivity:** Selective **Room/board:** $6,000
  - **Acceptance rate:** N/A **Average debt:** N/A
  - **Student/faculty ratio:** N/A **Proportion who borrowed:** N/A

Morningside College

- **Address:** 1501 Morningside Avenue, Sioux City, IA 51106
- **Website:** http://www.morningside.edu
- **Private; Religious affiliation:** United Methodist
- **Enrollment:** 1,198 full-time; 41 part-time

KEY STATS

- ✔ **U.S News College Ranking:** 27, Regional Colleges (Midwest)
- ✔ **ACT Score (25th/75th percentile):** 20-25
- ✔ **Tuition:** 2010-2011: $22,980
  - **Selectivity:** Selective **Room/board:** $7,040
  - **Acceptance rate:** 71% **Average debt:** $37,479
  - **Student/faculty ratio:** 14/1 **Proportion who borrowed:** 89%

UNDERGRADUATE STUDENT BODY STATS

2009-2010 enrollment: 1,198 full-time; 41 part-time. Men: 46%; women: 54%. **Ethnic makeup:** African American: 1%; American-Indian: 1%; Asian American: 1%; Hispanic: 2%; White: 92%; International: 2%. **Religious preference:** Roman Catholic: 20%; Protestant: 34%; No preference: 27%; United Methodist: 19%; 0: 0%.

ADMISSIONS FACTS AND FIGURES

Phone: (712) 274-5111. **Email:** mscadm@morningside.edu. **Website:** http://www.morningside.edu. **Application deadlines for fall 2011:** Regular decision: Rolling. Early decision: Not offered. Early action: Not offered. Admission can be deferred. **Application fee:** None. **To apply online, go to:** https://campusweb.morningside.edu/cgi-bin/web.asp?web=ADM. LOGIN&SECTIONS=MORN.APPLICATION.SECTIONS. **Admissions requirements/recommendations:** High school units required (recommended): English: 3 (3); Mathematics: 2 (2); Science: 2 (2); Social studies: 3 (3); Total units: 10 (10). Tests: The college uses SAT or ACT scores in admissions decisions. Either SAT or ACT required. For admission to the fall 2011 entering class, the school will accept: ACT with or without writing accepted. Campus visit: Recommended. Admissions interview: Recommended. Off-campus interview: Not available. **Factors that count in admissions decisions:** *Academic:* Secondary school record: Very Important.

Class rank: Very Important. Letters of recommendation: Very Important. Standardized test scores: Very Important. Essay: Considered. ***Nonacademic:*** Interview: Important. Extracurricular activities: Important. Talent/ability: Important. Character/personal qualities: Not Considered. Alumni/ae relationship: Not Considered. Geographical residence: Not Considered. State residency: Not Considered. Religious affiliation/commitment: Not Considered. Minority status: Not Considered. Volunteer work: Not Considered. Work experience: Not Considered. **Other schools with the greatest overlap in applicants:** Briar Cliff University; Iowa State University; University of Iowa; University of Nebraska–Lincoln; University of Northern Iowa. **Admissions statistics for the fall 2009 entering class:** Total applicants: 1,552. Total accepted: 1,101. Freshmen enrolled: 325; 36% were from out of state. Overall acceptance rate: 71%. **Credentials of fall 2009 freshmen:** 16% ranked in the top 10 percent of their high school class; 41% were in the top 25 percent; 79% were in the top half. (Proportion submitting class standing: 95%.) **Average high school grade point average:** 3.4. **First-year students who submitted SAT scores:** 3%. **First-year students submitting ACT scores:** 98%. Scores (25/75 percentile): English: 19-25, Math: 19-25, Composite: 20-25.

ACADEMICS

Year founded: 1894. **Academic calendar:** Semester. **Degrees offered:** bachelor's, master's. **Most popular majors:** 27% business administration and management, 20% elementary education and teaching, 9% nursing/registered nurse training (R.N., A.S.N., B.S.N., M.S.N.), 8% biology/biological sciences, 8% psychology. **Major fields of study:** biological and biomedical sciences; business, management, marketing, and related support services; communication, journalism, and related programs; computer and information sciences and support services; education; engineering; English language and literature/letters; foreign languages, literatures, and linguistics; health professions and related clinical sciences; history; mathematics and statistics; multi/interdisciplinary studies; philosophy and religious studies; physical sciences; psychology; social sciences; visual and performing arts. **Areas of required coursework:** arts/fine arts, humanities, mathematics, English (including composition), sciences (biological or physical). **Preprofessional programs:** pre-law, pre-dentistry, pre-medicine, pre-theology, pre-veterinary science, pre-optometry, pre-pharmacy. **Special academic programs (% participation):** distance learning, double major (24%), dual enrollment, English as a Second Language (ESL) (0%), honors program (15%), independent study (18%), internships (35%), student-designed major (0%), study abroad (2%), teacher certificate program (22%). **Teacher certification offered in:** special education, elementary, secondary. **Cooperative education programs:** health professions. **Reserve Officers Training Corps (ROTC):** Army ROTC: Offered at cooperating institution (University of South Dakota). **Faculty and instruction (2009-2010):** Total instructional faculty: 70 full-time, 103 part-time (38% men; 62% women; 3% minorities). Full-time faculty with Ph.D. or other terminal degree: 71%. Student/faculty ratio: 14/1. Classes of fewer than 20 students: 46%; of 20 to 49 students: 53%; of 50 or more students: 1%. **Advanced Placement and International Baccalaureate credit:** AP tests may be used for: Credit and/or placement. Scores accepted: 3, 4, 5. International Baccalaureate exams may be used for: Credit and/or placement. **Freshmen returning for sophomore year:** 73%. **Graduation rates:** Four-year: 39%; five-year: 46%; six-year: 46%. **Graduate study:** 13% of students pursue further study immediately upon graduation. Fields in which graduates pursue further study: Master of Business Administration (MBA), 16%; law, 8%; medicine, 5%; dentistry, 3%; theology (or the seminary), 8%; education, 11%; arts and sciences, 46%; veterinary medicine, 3%.

COSTS AND FINANCIAL AID

Financial aid office: (712) 274-5159. **Expenses (2010-2011):** Tuition and fees 2010-2011: $22,980; room/board: $7,040. Estimated books and supplies: $1,014; transportation: $1,270; personal expenses: $1,734. **Financial aid:** Priority filing date for institution's financial aid form: March 1. In 2009-2010, 94% of undergraduates applied for financial aid. Of those, 86% were determined to have financial need; 28% had their need fully met. Average financial aid package (proportion receiving): $18,517 (86%). Average amount of gift aid, such as scholarships or grants (proportion receiving): $6,774 (65%). Average amount of self-help aid, such as work study or loans (proportion receiving): $5,405 (74%). Average need-based loan (excluding PLUS or other private loans): $4,665. Among students who received need-based aid, the average percentage of need met: 81%. Among students who received aid based on merit, the average award (and the proportion receiving): $166 (14%). The average athletic scholarship (and the proportion receiving): $2,995 (49%). Average amount of debt of borrowers graduating in 2009: $37,479. Proportion who borrowed: 89%.

CAMPUS LIFE AND EXTRACURRICULAR ACTIVITIES

Campus housing available (% using): coed dorms (37%), sorority housing (2%), fraternity housing (5%), apartments for married students (1%), apartment for single students (19%), special housing for disabled students. Students who live in college-owned, operated, or affiliated housing: 64%. **Student employment:** During the 2009-2010 academic year, 39% of undergraduates worked on campus. Average per-year earnings: $1,334. **Clubs and organizations:** Number of student organizations: 41. Activities include: campus ministries, choral groups, concert band, dance, drama/theater, international student organization, jazz band, literary magazine, marching band, music ensembles, musical theater, pep band, radio station, student government, student newspaper, student film society, television station, yearbook. Number of fraternities: 2; sororities: 1. Proportion of men in fraternities: 6%; of women in sororities: 3%. Average proportion of students who stay on campus on weekends: 65%. **Sports program (2009-2010):** Member of NAIA. *Men's intercollegiate varsity sports:* baseball, basketball, cross country, football, golf, soccer, swimming, tennis, track and field (indoor), track and field (outdoor), wrestling. *Women's intercollegiate varsity sports:* basketball, cross country, golf, soccer, softball, swimming, tennis, track and field (indoor), track and field (outdoor), volleyball.

SERVICES AND FACILITIES

Basic services: nonremedial tutoring, placement service, health service, health insurance. **Remedial assistance:** reading, math, writing, study skills. **Counseling services:** minority student, career, personal, academic, older student, psychological, birth control, religious. **For learning-disabled students:** School does not offer a structured program with separate admission and additional fees. Services include: remedial math, remedial English, reading machines, remedial reading, tape recorders, diagnostic testing service, untimed tests, note-taking services, oral tests, learning center, readers, extended time for tests, tutors, priority seating, texts on tape. **Library:** Number of titles: 92,188; number of current serial subscriptions: 300. **Information technology resources:** Students are required to lease or own a computer. Number of campus computers available to all students: 30. School has a wireless network. Approximate number of users that can be accommodated: 1,500. Proportion of college-owned housing units wired for high-speed internet access: 100%. **Campus safety:** Security services offered: late-night transport/escort service, 24-hour emergency telephones, lighted pathways/sidewalks, student patrols, controlled dormitory access (key, security card, etc).

TRANSFER AND INTERNATIONAL STUDENTS

Transfer students: May apply for admission for the following academic terms: Fall, Spring, Summer. Applicants need a minimum number of credits to apply. For fall 2009: Transfer applications received: 190. Transfer applicants offered admission: 90. Transfer applicants enrolled: 66. **International students:** Number of foreign undergraduates: 23 (2% of student body). Number of countries represented: 9. Minimum TOEFL score required: 500 (paper); 173 (computer).

Mount Mercy College

- **Address:** 1330 Elmhurst Drive NE, Cedar Rapids, IA 52402
- **Website:** http://www.mtmercy.edu
- **Private; Religious affiliation:** Roman Catholic
- **Enrollment:** 939 full-time; 559 part-time

KEY STATS
✔ **U.S News College Ranking:** 24, Regional Colleges (Midwest)
✔ **ACT Score (25th/75th percentile):** 20-24
✔ **Tuition:** 2010-2011: $23,260

Selectivity: Selective	**Room/board:** $7,260
Acceptance rate: 78%	**Average debt:** $30,233
Student/faculty ratio: 13/1	**Proportion who borrowed:** 94%

UNDERGRADUATE STUDENT BODY STATS
2009-2010 enrollment: 939 full-time; 559 part-time. Men: 30%; women: 70%. **Ethnic makeup:** African American: 2%; Asian American: 1%; Hispanic: 3%; White: 92%; International: 2%. **Religious preference:** No preference: 40%; Roman Catholic: 27%; Other: 33%.

ADMISSIONS FACTS AND FIGURES

Phone: (319) 368-6460. **Email:** admission@mtmercy.edu. **Website:** http://www.mtmercy.edu. **Application deadlines for fall 2011:** Regular decision: Rolling. Early decision: Not offered. Early action: Not offered. Admission can be deferred. **To apply online, go to:** http://www.mtmercy.edu/admission/applynow.html. **Admissions requirements/recommendations:** High school units required (recommended): English: (4); Mathematics: (3); Science: (3); Foreign language: (2); Social studies: (3); Total units: (15). Tests: The college uses SAT or ACT scores in admissions decisions. Either SAT or ACT required. For admission to the fall 2011 entering class, the school will accept: ACT with or without writing accepted. Campus visit: Recommended. Admissions interview: Recommended. Off-campus interview: May be arranged. **Factors that count in admissions decisions:** *Academic:* Secondary school record: Very Important. Class rank: Not Considered. Letters of recommendation: Considered. Standardized test scores: Very Important. Essay: Not Considered. *Nonacademic:* Interview: Considered. Extracurricular activities: Considered. Talent/ability: Considered. Character/personal qualities: Important. Alumni/ae relationship: Considered. Geographical residence: Not Considered. State residency: Not Considered. Religious affiliation/commitment: Not Considered. Minority status: Not Considered. Volunteer work: Important. Work experience: Considered. **Other schools with the greatest overlap in applicants:** Coe College; Iowa State University; St. Ambrose University; University of Iowa; University of Northern Iowa. **Admissions statistics for the fall 2009 entering class:** Total applicants: 366. Total accepted: 284. Freshmen enrolled: 150; 5% were from out of state. Overall acceptance rate: 78%. **Credentials of fall 2009 freshmen:** 15% ranked in the top 10 percent of their high school class; 53% were in the top 25 percent; 82% were in the top half. (Proportion submitting class standing: 89%.) **Average high school grade point average:** 3.4. **First-year students submitting ACT scores:** 98%. Scores (25/75 percentile): English: 21-22, Math: 21-23, Composite: 20-24.

ACADEMICS

Year founded: 1928. **Academic calendar:** 4-1-4. **Degrees offered:** bachelor's, master's. **Most popular majors:** 21% business administration, management, and operations, 16% nursing/registered nurse training (R.N., A.S.N., B.S.N., M.S.N.), 7% elementary education and teaching, 6% accounting, 6% criminal justice/law enforcement administration. **Major fields of study:** biological and biomedical sciences; business, management, marketing, and related support services; communication, journalism, and related programs; computer and information sciences and support services; education; English language and literature/letters; health professions and related clinical sciences; history; mathematics and statistics; multi/interdisciplinary studies; philosophy and religious studies; psychology; security and protective services; social sciences; visual and performing arts. **Areas of required coursework:** arts/fine arts, humanities, mathematics, English (including composition), philosophy, sciences (biological or physical), history, social science, other. **Pre-professional programs:** pre-law, pre-dentistry, pre-medicine, pre-veterinary science, other. **Special academic programs (% participation):** accelerated program (32%), cooperative (work-study plan) program (0%), cross-registration (1%), double major (10%), dual enrollment (1%), honors program (2%), independent study (5%), internships (65%), liberal arts/career combination (4%), teacher certificate program (10%). **Teacher certification offered in:** early childhood, special education, elementary, middle/junior high, secondary. **Faculty and instruction (2009-2010):** Total instructional faculty: 75 full-time, 81 part-time (38% men; 62% women; 5% minorities). Full-time faculty with Ph.D. or other terminal degree: 60%. Student/faculty ratio: 13/1. Classes of fewer than 20 students: 60%; of 20 to 49 students: 39%; of 50 or more students: 1%. **Advanced Placement and International Baccalaureate credit:** AP tests may be used for: Credit only. Scores accepted: 3, 4, 5. International Baccalaureate exams may be used for: Credit only. **Freshmen returning for sophomore year:** 78%. **Graduation rates:** Four-year: 51%; five-year: 63%; six-year: 61%. **Graduate study:** 8% of students pursue further study immediately upon graduation.

COSTS AND FINANCIAL AID

Financial aid office: (319) 368-6467. **Expenses (2010-2011):** Tuition and fees 2010-2011: $23,260; room/board: $7,260. Estimated books and supplies: $1,200. **Financial aid:** Priority filing date for institution's financial aid form: March 1. In 2009-2010, 93% of undergraduates applied for financial aid. Of those, 85% were determined to have financial need; 19% had their need fully met. Average financial aid package (proportion receiving): $16,094 (84%). Average amount of gift aid, such as scholarships or grants (proportion receiving): $11,589 (81%). Average amount of self-help aid, such as work study or loans (proportion receiving): $5,533 (75%). Average need-based loan (excluding PLUS or other private loans): $4,952. Among students who received need-based aid, the average percentage of need met: 72%. Among students who received aid based on merit, the average award (and the proportion receiving): $8,107 (14%). The average athletic scholarship (and the proportion receiving): $3,628 (6%). Average amount of debt of borrowers graduating in 2009: $30,233. Proportion who borrowed: 94%.

CAMPUS LIFE AND EXTRACURRICULAR ACTIVITIES

Campus housing available (% using): coed dorms (89%), apartment for single students (11%), other housing options (0%). Students who live in college-owned, operated, or affiliated housing: 37%. **Student employment:** During the 2009-2010 academic year, 54% of undergraduates worked on campus. Average per-year earnings: $2,000. **Clubs and organizations:** Number of student organizations: 36. Activities include: campus ministries, choral groups, dance, drama/theater, literary magazine, student government, student newspaper. Number of fraternities: 0; sororities: 0. Average proportion of students who stay on campus on weekends: 30%. **Sports program (2009-2010):** Member of NAIA. *Men's intercollegiate varsity sports:* baseball, basketball, cross country, golf, soccer, track and field (indoor), track and field (outdoor). *Women's intercollegiate varsity sports:* basketball, cross country, golf, soccer, softball, track and field (indoor), track and field (outdoor), volleyball.

SERVICES AND FACILITIES

Basic services: nonremedial tutoring, placement service, health service. **Remedial assistance:** reading, math, writing, study skills. **Counseling services:** minority student, career, personal, veteran student, academic, older student, psychological, religious. **For learning-disabled students:** School does not offer a structured program with separate admission and additional fees. Total undergraduates in learning-disabled program or receiving services: 68. Services include: remedial math, remedial English, reading machines, remedial reading, tape recorders, videotaped classes, note-taking services, oral tests, learning center, readers, extended time for tests, tutors, priority registration, priority seating, texts on tape, typist/scribe, exams on tape or computer, other testing accommodations. **Library:** Number of titles: 140,319; number of current serial subscriptions: 870. **Information technology resources:** Students are not required to lease or own a computer. Number of campus computers available to all students: 172. School has a wireless network. Approximate number of users that can be accommodated: 1,500. Proportion of college-owned housing units wired for high-speed internet access: 100%. **Campus safety:** Security services offered: 24-hour foot-and-vehicle patrols, late-night transport/escort service, 24-hour emergency telephones, lighted pathways/sidewalks, controlled dormitory access (key, security card, etc).

TRANSFER AND INTERNATIONAL STUDENTS

Transfer students: May apply for admission for the following academic terms: Fall, Winter, Spring, Summer. Applicants need a minimum number of credits to apply. For fall 2009: Transfer applications received: 448. Transfer applicants offered admission: 324. Transfer applicants enrolled: 194. **International students:** Number of foreign undergraduates: 28 (2% of student body). Number of countries represented: 6. Minimum TOEFL score required: 550 (paper); 213 (computer).

Northwestern College

- **Address:** 101 Seventh Street SW, Orange City, IA 51041
- **Website:** http://www.nwciowa.edu
- **Private; Religious affiliation:** Reformed Church in America
- **Enrollment:** 1,164 full-time; 42 part-time

KEY STATS

✔ **U.S News College Ranking:** 9, Regional Colleges (Midwest)
✔ **ACT Score (25th/75th percentile):** 21-28
✔ **Tuition:** 2010-2011: $22,642

Selectivity: Selective	Room/board: $6,657
Acceptance rate: 75%	Average debt: $31,062
Student/faculty ratio: 14/1	Proportion who borrowed: 87%

UNDERGRADUATE STUDENT BODY STATS

2009-2010 enrollment: 1,164 full-time; 42 part-time. Men: 41%; women: 59%. **Ethnic makeup:** Asian American: 1%; Hispanic: 2%; White: 93%; International: 3%. **Religious preference:** Roman Catholic: 3%; Protestant: 93%; Unknown: 2%.

ADMISSIONS FACTS AND FIGURES

Phone: (712) 707-7130. **Email:** admissions@nwciowa.edu. **Website:** http://www.nwciowa.edu. **Application deadlines for fall 2011:** Regular decision: August 15. Early decision: Not offered. Early action: Not offered. Admission can be deferred. **Application fee:** $25. **To apply online, go to:** http://www.nwciowa.edu/apply/default.aspx. **Admissions requirements/recommendations:** High school units required (recommended): English: (4); Mathematics: (3); Science: (2); Foreign language: (3); Social studies: (3); Total units: (16). Tests: The college uses SAT or ACT scores in admissions decisions. Either SAT or ACT required. For admission to the fall 2011 entering class, the school will accept: ACT with or without writing accepted. Campus visit: Recommended. Admissions interview: Neither required nor recommended. Off-campus interview: May be arranged. **Factors that count in admissions decisions:** *Academic:* Secondary school record: Very Important. Class rank: Very Important. Letters of recommendation: Important. Standardized test scores: Very Important. Essay: Considered. *Nonacademic:* Interview: Considered. Extracurricular activities: Not Considered. Talent/ability: Considered. Character/personal qualities: Important. Alumni/ae relationship: Not Considered. Geographical residence: Not Considered. State residency: Not Considered. Religious affiliation/commitment: Considered. Minority status: Not Considered. Volunteer work: Not Considered. Work experience: Not Considered. **Other schools with the greatest overlap in applicants:** Central College; Iowa State University; Northwestern College; University of Northern Iowa; University of Sioux Falls. **Admissions statistics for the fall 2009 entering class:** Total applicants: 1,356. Total accepted: 1,018. Freshmen enrolled: 331; 47% were from out of state. Overall acceptance rate: 75%. **Credentials of fall 2009 freshmen:** 29% ranked in the top 10 percent of their high school class; 54% were in the top 25 percent; 82% were in the top half. (Proportion submitting class standing: 93%.) **Average high school grade point average:** 3.5. **First-year students submitting ACT scores:** 93%. Scores (25/75 percentile): English: 21-29, Math: 20-27, Composite: 21-28.

ACADEMICS

Year founded: 1882. **Academic calendar:** Semester. **Degrees offered:** certificate, bachelor's. **Major fields of study:** biological and biomedical sciences; business, management, marketing, and related support services; communication, journalism, and related programs; computer and information sciences and support services; education; English language and literature/letters; foreign languages, literatures, and linguistics; health professions and related clinical sciences; history; liberal arts and sciences studies, and humanities; mathematics and statistics; parks, recreation, leisure, and fitness studies; philosophy and religious studies; physical sciences; psychology; public administration and social service professions; social sciences; theology and religious vocations; visual and performing arts. **Areas of required coursework:** arts/fine arts, mathematics, English (including composition), philosophy, foreign languages, sciences (biological or physical), history, social science, other. **Pre-professional programs:** pre-law, pre-dentistry, pre-medicine, pre-theology, pre-veterinary science, pre-optometry, pre-pharmacy, other. **Special academic programs (% participation):** double major (1%), honors program (1%), internships (5%), student-designed major (1%), study abroad (5%), teacher certificate program (25%). **Teacher certification offered in:** early childhood, special education, elementary, middle/junior high, secondary, bilingual/bicultural. **Faculty and instruction (2009-2010):** Total instructional faculty: 85 full-time, 41 part-time (52% men; 48% women; 2% minorities). Full-time faculty with Ph.D. or other terminal degree: 81%. Student/faculty ratio: 14/1. Classes of fewer than 20 students: 68%; of 20 to 49 students: 32%; of 50 or more students: 0%. **Advanced Placement and International Baccalaureate credit:** AP tests may be used for: Placement only. Scores accepted: 3, 4, 5. International Baccalaureate exams may be used for: Placement only. **Freshmen returning for sophomore year:** 78%. **Graduation rates:** Four-year: 53%; five-year: 59%; six-year: 61%. **Graduate study:** 20% of students pursue further study immediately upon graduation.

COSTS AND FINANCIAL AID

Financial aid office: (712) 707-7131. **Expenses (2010-2011):** Tuition and fees 2010-2011: $22,642; room/board: $6,657. Estimated books and supplies: $1,014; transportation: $1,270; personal expenses: $1,734. **Financial aid:** Priority filing date for institution's financial aid form: April 1. In 2009-2010, 77% of undergraduates applied for financial aid. Of those, 77% were determined to have financial need; 41% had their need fully met. Average financial aid package (proportion receiving): $18,093 (77%). Average amount of gift aid, such as scholarships or grants (proportion receiving): $7,043 (75%). Average amount of self-help aid, such as work study or loans (proportion receiving): $4,652 (66%). Average need-based loan (excluding

PLUS or other private loans): $4,185. Among students who received need-based aid, the average percentage of need met: 89%. Among students who received aid based on merit, the average award (and the proportion receiving): $6,323 (19%). The average athletic scholarship (and the proportion receiving): $4,728 (34%). Average amount of debt of borrowers graduating in 2009: $31,062. Proportion who borrowed: 87%.

CAMPUS LIFE AND EXTRACURRICULAR ACTIVITIES

Campus housing available: women's dorms, men's dorms, apartments for married students, apartment for single students. Students who live in college-owned, operated, or affiliated housing: 89%. **Student employment:** During the 2009-2010 academic year, 32% of undergraduates worked on campus. Average per-year earnings: $1,170. Activities include: campus ministries, choral groups, concert band, dance, drama/theater, jazz band, literary magazine, music ensembles, musical theater, student government, student newspaper, symphony orchestra, television station. Number of fraternities: 0; sororities: 0. Average proportion of students who stay on campus on weekends: 80%. **Sports program (2009-2010):** Member of NAIA. *Men's intercollegiate varsity sports:* baseball, basketball, cross country, football, golf, soccer, tennis, track and field (indoor), track and field (outdoor), wrestling. *Women's intercollegiate varsity sports:* basketball, cross country, golf, soccer, softball, tennis, track and field (indoor), track and field (outdoor), volleyball.

SERVICES AND FACILITIES

Basic services: nonremedial tutoring, placement service, health service, health insurance. **Remedial assistance:** reading, math, writing, study skills. **Counseling services:** career, personal, veteran student, academic, psychological, religious. **For learning-disabled students:** School does not offer a structured program with separate admission and additional fees. Total undergraduates in learning-disabled program or receiving services: 21. Services include: remedial math, remedial English, reading machines, remedial reading, tape recorders, videotaped classes, untimed tests, note-taking services, oral tests, learning center, readers, extended time for tests, tutors, priority registration, priority seating, texts on tape, typist/scribe, other testing accommodations. **Library:** Number of titles: 127,000; number of current serial subscriptions: 20,000. **Information technology resources:** Students are not required to lease or own a computer. Number of campus computers available to all students: 250. School has a wireless network. Approximate number of users that can be accommodated: 800. Proportion of college-owned housing units wired for high-speed internet access: 100%. **Campus safety:** Security services offered: 24-hour emergency telephones, lighted pathways/sidewalks, controlled dormitory access (key, security card, etc).

TRANSFER AND INTERNATIONAL STUDENTS

Transfer students: May apply for admission for the following academic terms: Fall, Spring. Applicants do not need a minimum number of credits to apply. **International students:** Number of foreign undergraduates: 26 (3% of student body). Number of countries represented: 20. Minimum TOEFL score required: 550 (paper); 213 (computer).

Simpson College

- **Address:** 701 N. C Street, Indianola, IA 50125
- **Website:** http://www.simpson.edu
- **Private; Religious affiliation:** United Methodist
- **Enrollment:** 1,481 full-time; 507 part-time

KEY STATS

✔ **U.S News College Ranking:** 144, National Liberal Arts Colleges
✔ **ACT Score (25th/75th percentile):** 21-27
✔ **Tuition:** 2010-2011: $26,837
Selectivity: More selective   **Room/board:** $7,639
Acceptance rate: 89%   **Average debt:** $34,354
Student/faculty ratio: 14/1   **Proportion who borrowed:** 92%

UNDERGRADUATE STUDENT BODY STATS

2009-2010 enrollment: 1,481 full-time; 507 part-time. Men: 43%; women: 57%. **Ethnic makeup:** African American: 2%; Asian American: 2%; Hispanic: 2%; White: 94%; International: 1%. **Religious preference:** Roman Catholic: 18%; Protestant: 39%; No preference: 13%; Unknown: 12%; United Methodist: 17%; Jewish, Muslim, Hindu, Buddhist, Unknown: 1%.

ADMISSIONS FACTS AND FIGURES

Phone: (515) 961-1624. **Email:** admiss@simpson.edu. **Website:** http://www.simpson.edu. **Application deadlines for fall 2011:** Regular decision: Rolling. Early decision: Not offered. Early action: Not offered. Admission can be deferred. **To apply online, go to:** http://www.simpson.edu/admissions/apply/process.html. **Admissions requirements/recommendations:** High school units required (recommended): English: (4); Mathematics: (3); Science: (3); Foreign language: (3); Social studies: (3); Total units: (16). Tests: The college uses SAT or ACT scores in admissions decisions. Either SAT or ACT required. For admission to the fall 2011 entering class, the school will accept: ACT with or without writing accepted. Campus visit: Recommended. Admissions interview: Recommended. Off-campus interview: May be arranged. **Factors that count in admissions decisions:** *Academic:* Secondary school record: Very Important. Class rank: Very Important. Letters of recommendation: Very Important. Standardized test scores: Very Important. Essay: Not Considered. *Nonacademic:* Interview: Considered. Extracurricular activities: Considered. Talent/ability: Not Considered. Character/personal qualities: Considered. Alumni/ae relationship: Not Considered. Geographical residence: Not Considered. State residency: Not Considered. Religious affiliation/commitment: Not Considered. Minority status: Not Considered. Volunteer work: Considered. Work experience: Not Considered. **Admissions statistics for the fall 2009 entering class:** Total applicants: 1,290. Total accepted: 1,142. Freshmen enrolled: 390; 18% were from out of state. Overall acceptance rate: 89%. **Credentials of fall 2009 freshmen:** 31% ranked in the top 10 percent of their high school class; 61% were in the top 25 percent; 89% were in the top half. (Proportion submitting class standing: 96%.) **First-year students who submitted SAT scores:** 7%. **First-year students submitting ACT scores:** 97%. Scores (25/75 percentile): English: N/A, Math: N/A, Composite: 21-27.

ACADEMICS

Year founded: 1860. **Academic calendar:** Other. **Degrees offered:** bachelor's, post-bachelor's certificate, master's. **Most popular majors:** 29% business, management, marketing, and related support services, 8% biological and biomedical sciences, 8% education, 8% social sciences, 7% communication, journalism, and related programs. **Major fields of study:** biological and biomedical sciences; business, management, marketing, and related support services; communication, journalism, and related programs; computer and information sciences and support services; education; English language and literature/letters; foreign languages, literatures, and linguistics; health professions and related clinical sciences; history; legal professions and studies; liberal arts and sciences studies, and humanities; mathematics and statistics; multi/interdisciplinary studies; natural resources and conservation; parks, recreation, leisure, and fitness studies; philosophy and religious studies; physical sciences; psychology; security and protective services; social sciences; visual and performing arts. **Areas of required coursework:** arts/fine arts, humanities, mathematics, English (including composition), foreign languages, sciences (biological or physical), history, social science. **Pre-professional programs:** pre-law, pre-dentistry, pre-medicine, pre-theology, pre-veterinary science, pre-optometry, pre-pharmacy, other. **Special academic programs (% participation):** accelerated program (30%), cooperative (work-study plan) program (40%), double major (27%), honors program (4%), independent study (30%), internships (51%), liberal arts/career combination, student-designed major, study abroad (43%), teacher certificate program (11%), weekend college (5%). **Teacher certification offered in:** early childhood, special education, elementary, middle/junior high, secondary. **Cooperative education programs:** art, business, computer science, education, engineering, health professions, humanities, natural science, social/behavioral science, technologies. **Faculty and instruction (2009-2010):** Total instructional faculty: 99 full-time, 111 part-time (59% men; 41% women; 6% minorities). Full-time faculty with Ph.D. or other terminal degree: 88%. Student/faculty ratio: 14/1. Classes of fewer than 20 students: 62%; of 20 to 49 students: 37%; of 50 or more students: 1%. **Advanced Placement and International Baccalaureate credit:** AP tests may be used for: Credit and/or placement. Scores accepted: 3, 4, 5. International Baccalaureate exams may be used for: Credit only. **Freshmen returning for sophomore year:** 82%. **Graduation rates:** Four-year: 57%; five-year: 64%; six-year: 65%. **Graduate study:** 21% of students pursue further study within one year. Fields in which graduates pursue further study: Master of Business Administration (MBA), 6%; law, 6%; medicine, 31%; dentistry, 4%; engineering, 3%; theology (or the seminary), 4%; education, 13%; arts and sciences, 33%.

COSTS AND FINANCIAL AID

Financial aid office: (515) 961-1630. **Expenses (2010-2011):** Tuition and fees 2010-2011: $26,837; room/board: $7,639. Estimated books and supplies: $900; transportation: $700; personal expenses: $1,300. **Financial**

aid: Priority filing date for institution's financial aid form: April 1. In 2009-2010, 100% of undergraduates applied for financial aid. Of those, 86% were determined to have financial need; 25% had their need fully met. Average financial aid package (proportion receiving): $25,103 (86%). Average amount of gift aid, such as scholarships or grants (proportion receiving): $16,915 (86%). Average amount of self-help aid, such as work study or loans (proportion receiving): $3,751 (71%). Average need-based loan (excluding PLUS or other private loans): $3,506. Among students who received need-based aid, the average percentage of need met: 89%. Among students who received aid based on merit, the average award (and the proportion receiving): $12,819 (14%). The average athletic scholarship (and the proportion receiving): $0 (0%). Average amount of debt of borrowers graduating in 2009: $34,354. Proportion who borrowed: 92%.

CAMPUS LIFE AND EXTRACURRICULAR ACTIVITIES

Campus housing available (% using): coed dorms (51%), sorority housing (7%), fraternity housing (7%), apartment for single students (30%). Students who live in college-owned, operated, or affiliated housing: 84%. **Student employment:** During the 2009-2010 academic year, 49% of undergraduates worked on campus. Average per-year earnings: $1,261. **Clubs and organizations:** Number of student organizations: 67. Activities include: campus ministries, choral groups, concert band, dance, drama/theater, international student organization, jazz band, literary magazine, model UN, music ensembles, opera, pep band, radio station, student government, student newspaper, yearbook. Number of fraternities: 4; sororities: 3. Proportion of men in fraternities: 18%; of women in sororities: 21%. Average proportion of students who stay on campus on weekends: 75%. **Sports program (2009-2010):** Member of NCAA III. *Men's intercollegiate varsity sports:* baseball, basketball, cross country, football, golf, soccer, swimming, tennis, track and field (indoor), track and field (outdoor), wrestling. *Women's intercollegiate varsity sports:* basketball, cross country, golf, soccer, softball, swimming, tennis, track and field (indoor), track and field (outdoor), volleyball.

SERVICES AND FACILITIES

Basic services: nonremedial tutoring, women's center, health service, health insurance. **Remedial assistance:** study skills. **Counseling services:** career, personal, academic, psychological, religious. **For learning-disabled students:** School does not offer a structured program with separate admission and additional fees. Total undergraduates in learning-disabled program or receiving services: 24. Services include: untimed tests, note-taking services, oral tests, learning center, readers, extended time for tests, tutors, priority seating, proofreading services, substitution of courses, texts on tape, typist/scribe, exams on tape or computer, other testing accommodations, other. **Library:** Number of titles: 155,574; number of current serial subscriptions: 28,663. **Information technology resources:** Students are not required to lease or own a computer. Number of campus computers available to all students: 336. School has a wireless network. Approximate number of users that can be accommodated: 3,000. Proportion of college-owned housing units wired for high-speed internet access: 100%. **Campus safety:** Security services offered: 24-hour foot-and-vehicle patrols, late-night transport/escort service, 24-hour emergency telephones, lighted pathways/sidewalks, student patrols, controlled dormitory access (key, security card, etc).

TRANSFER AND INTERNATIONAL STUDENTS

Transfer students: May apply for admission for the following academic terms: Fall, Spring, Summer. Applicants need a minimum number of credits to apply. For fall 2009: Transfer applications received: 164. Transfer applicants offered admission: 140. Transfer applicants enrolled: 73. **International students:** Number of foreign undergraduates: 19 (1% of student body). Number of countries represented: 8. Minimum TOEFL score required: 550 (paper); 213 (computer).

St. Ambrose University

- **Address:** 518 W. Locust Street, Davenport, IA 52803-2898
- **Website:** http://www.sau.edu
- **Private; Religious affiliation:** Roman Catholic
- **Enrollment:** 2,414 full-time; 473 part-time

KEY STATS

✔ **U.S News College Ranking:** 43, Regional Universities (Midwest)
✔ **ACT Score (25th/75th percentile):** 20-25
✔ **Tuition:** 2010-2011: $23,910

Selectivity: Selective	**Room/board:** $8,585
Acceptance rate: 82%	**Average debt:** $33,216
Student/faculty ratio: 11/1	**Proportion who borrowed:** 77%

UNDERGRADUATE STUDENT BODY STATS

2009-2010 enrollment: 2,414 full-time; 473 part-time. Men: 39%; women: 61%. **Ethnic makeup:** African American: 3%; Asian American: 1%; Hispanic: 4%; White: 91%. **Religious preference:** Roman Catholic: 64%; Protestant: 36%.

ADMISSIONS FACTS AND FIGURES

Phone: (563) 333-6300. **Email:** admit@sau.edu. **Website:** http://www.sau.edu. **Application deadlines for fall 2011:** Regular decision: Rolling. Early decision: Not offered. Early action: Not offered. Admission can be deferred. **Application fee:** $25. **To apply online, go to:** http://www.sau.edu/apply.htm. **Admissions requirements/recommendations:** High school units required (recommended): English: 4 (4); Mathematics: 3 (3); Science: 2 (2); Foreign language: 1 (1); Social studies: 1 (1); History: 1 (1); Academic electives: 4 (4); Total units: 18 (18). Tests: The college uses SAT or ACT scores in admissions decisions. Either SAT or ACT required. For admission to the fall 2011 entering class, the school will accept: ACT with or without writing accepted. Campus visit: Recommended. Admissions interview: Recommended. Off-campus interview: May be arranged. **Factors that count in admissions decisions:** *Academic:* Secondary school record: Very Important. Class rank: Very Important. Letters of recommendation: Considered. Standardized test scores: Very Important. Essay: Considered. *Nonacademic:* Interview: Considered. Extracurricular activities: Considered. Talent/ability: Considered. Character/personal qualities: Considered. Alumni/ae relationship: Considered. Geographical residence: Considered. State residency: Not Considered. Religious affiliation/commitment: Not Considered. Minority status: Considered. Volunteer work: Considered. Work experience: Not Considered. **Other schools with the greatest overlap in applicants:** Augustana College; Bradley University; Loras College; University of Iowa; University of Northern Iowa. **Admissions statistics for the fall 2009 entering class:** Total applicants: 2,075. Total accepted: 1,702. Freshmen enrolled: 577; 71% were from out of state. Overall acceptance rate: 82%. **Size of waiting list:** 0 applicants; enrolled from waiting list: 0. **Credentials of fall 2009 freshmen:** 14% ranked in the top 10 percent of their high school class; 34% were in the top 25 percent; 65% were in the top half. (Proportion submitting class standing: 76%.) **Average high school grade point average:** 3.1. **First-year students submitting ACT scores:** 97%. Scores (25/75 percentile): English: 20-25, Math: 18-25, Composite: 20-25.

ACADEMICS

Year founded: 1882. **Academic calendar:** Semester. **Degrees offered:** certificate, bachelor's, post-bachelor's certificate, master's, post-master's certificate, doctorate. **Most popular majors:** 31% business, management, marketing, and related support services, 10% education, 9% health professions and related clinical sciences, 8% biological and biomedical sciences, 8% psychology. **Major fields of study:** biological and biomedical sciences; business, management, marketing, and related support services; communication, journalism, and related programs; computer and information sciences and support services; education; engineering; English language and literature/letters; foreign languages, literatures, and linguistics; health professions and related clinical sciences; history; legal professions and studies; mathematics and statistics; multi/interdisciplinary studies; philosophy and religious studies; physical sciences; psychology; public administration and social service professions; security and protective services; social sciences; theology and religious vocations; visual and performing arts. **Areas of required coursework:** arts/fine arts, humanities, mathematics, English (including composition), philosophy, foreign languages, sciences (biological or physical), history, social science, other. **Pre-professional programs:** pre-law, pre-medicine. **Special academic programs (% participation):** accelerated program (12%), cooperative (work-study plan) program, distance learning (2%), double major (11%), independent study (26%), internships (45%), liberal arts/career combination (22%), student-designed major (2.8%), study abroad (6%), teacher certificate program (12.8%). **Teacher certification offered in:** early childhood, special education, elementary, middle/junior high, secondary. **Cooperative education programs:** art, business, computer science, engineering, health professions, humanities, natural science, social/behavioral science. **Faculty and instruction (2009-2010):** Total instructional faculty: 186 full-time, 220 part-time (52% men; 48% women; 6% minorities). Full-time faculty with Ph.D. or other terminal degree: 74%. Student/faculty ratio: 11/1. Classes of fewer than 20 students: 61%; of 20 to 49 students: 39%; of 50 or more students: 0%. **Advanced Placement and International Baccalaureate credit:** AP tests may be used for: Credit only. Scores accepted: 3, 4, 5. International Baccalaureate exams may be used for: Credit only. **Freshmen returning for sophomore year:** 76%. **Graduation rates:** Four-year: 53%; five-year: 64%; six-year: 61%. **Graduate study:** 16% of students pursue further study within one year. Fields in which graduates pursue further study: Master of Business Administration (MBA), 17%; law, 3%; medicine, 4%; dentistry, 2%; education, 2%; arts and sciences, 72%; veterinary medicine, 2%.

COSTS AND FINANCIAL AID
Financial aid office: (563) 333-6314. **Expenses (2010-2011):** Tuition and fees 2010-2011: $23,910; room/board: $8,585. Estimated books and supplies: $1,200; transportation: $1,050; personal expenses: $1,200. **Financial aid:** Priority filing date for institution's financial aid form: March 15. In 2009-2010, 99% of undergraduates applied for financial aid. Of those, 75% were determined to have financial need; 41% had their need fully met. Average financial aid package (proportion receiving): $16,770 (74%). Average amount of gift aid, such as scholarships or grants (proportion receiving): $10,732 (73%). Average amount of self-help aid, such as work study or loans (proportion receiving): $5,080 (58%). Average need-based loan (excluding PLUS or other private loans): $4,713. Among students who received need-based aid, the average percentage of need met: 26%. Among students who received aid based on merit, the average award (and the proportion receiving): $7,158 (23%). The average athletic scholarship (and the proportion receiving): $4,260 (7%). Average amount of debt of borrowers graduating in 2009: $33,216. Proportion who borrowed: 77%.

CAMPUS LIFE AND EXTRACURRICULAR ACTIVITIES
Campus housing available (% using): coed dorms (52%), women's dorms (8%), men's dorms (2%), apartment for single students (23%), special housing for disabled students (1%), special housing for international students (1%), other housing options (13%). Students who live in college-owned, operated, or affiliated housing: 52%. **Student employment:** During the 2009-2010 academic year, 21% of undergraduates worked on campus. Average per-year earnings: $1,850. **Clubs and organizations:** Number of student organizations: 26. Activities include: campus ministries, choral groups, concert band, dance, drama/theater, international student organization, jazz band, literary magazine, music ensembles, musical theater, opera, pep band, radio station, student government, student newspaper, symphony orchestra, television station. Number of fraternities: 0; sororities: 0. Average proportion of students who stay on campus on weekends: 60%. **Sports program (2009-2010):** Member of NAIA. ***Men's intercollegiate varsity sports:*** baseball, basketball, cross country, football, golf, soccer, tennis, track and field (indoor), track and field (outdoor), volleyball. ***Women's intercollegiate varsity sports:*** basketball, bowling, cross country, golf, soccer, softball, tennis, track and field (indoor), track and field (outdoor), volleyball.

SERVICES AND FACILITIES
Basic services: nonremedial tutoring, women's center, placement service, day care, health service. **Remedial assistance:** reading, math, writing, study skills. **Counseling services:** career, personal, veteran student, academic, psychological, religious. **For learning-disabled students:** School does not offer a structured program with separate admission and additional fees. Total undergraduates in learning-disabled program or receiving services: 160. Services include: remedial math, remedial English, reading machines, remedial reading, tape recorders, untimed tests, note-taking services, oral tests, learning center, readers, extended time for tests, tutors, early syllabus, priority seating, proofreading services, substitution of courses, texts on tape, typist/scribe, exams on tape or computer, other testing accommodations, other. **Library:** Number of titles: 153,997; number of current serial subscriptions: 728. **Information technology resources:** Students are not required to lease or own a computer. Number of campus computers available to all students: 276. School has a wireless network. Proportion of college-owned housing units wired for high-speed internet access: 90%. **Campus safety:**

Security services offered: 24-hour foot-and-vehicle patrols, late-night transport/escort service, 24-hour emergency telephones, lighted pathways/sidewalks, student patrols, controlled dormitory access (key, security card, etc).

TRANSFER AND INTERNATIONAL STUDENTS
Transfer students: May apply for admission for the following academic terms: Fall, Winter, Spring, Summer. Applicants need a minimum number of credits to apply. For fall 2009: Transfer applications received: 667. Transfer applicants offered admission: 457. Transfer applicants enrolled: 284. **International students:** Number of foreign undergraduates: 7. Number of countries represented: 12. Minimum TOEFL score required: 500 (paper); 213 (computer). Average TOEFL score: 535 (paper).

University of Dubuque

- ■ **Address:** 2000 University Avenue, Dubuque, IA 52001
- ■ **Website:** http://www.dbq.edu
- ■ **Private; Religious affiliation:** Presbyterian
- ■ **Enrollment:** 1,355 full-time; 85 part-time

KEY STATS
✔ **U.S News College Ranking:** 49, Regional Colleges (Midwest)
✔ **SAT Score (25th/75th percentile):** 810-1050
✔ **Tuition:** 2010-2011: $21,590

Selectivity: Less selective	**Room/board:** $7,370
Acceptance rate: 75%	**Average debt:** $37,936
Student/faculty ratio: 14/1	**Proportion who borrowed:** 97%

UNDERGRADUATE STUDENT BODY STATS
2009-2010 enrollment: 1,355 full-time; 85 part-time. Men: 55%; women: 45%. **Ethnic makeup:** African American: 12%; American-Indian: 1%; Asian American: 2%; Hispanic: 4%; White: 80%; International: 1%. **Religious preference:** Roman Catholic: 26%; Protestant: 21%; Unknown: 47%; Presbyterian: 4%; Other: 2%.

ADMISSIONS FACTS AND FIGURES
Phone: (800) 722-5583. **Email:** admssns@univ.dbq.edu. **Website:** http://www.dbq.edu. **Application deadlines for fall 2011:** Regular decision: August 15. Early decision: Not offered. Early action: Not offered. Admission can be deferred. **Application fee:** $25. **To apply online, go to:** https://www.dbq.edu/admission/admit9.cfm. **Admissions requirements/recommendations:** High school units required (recommended): English: 4 (4); Mathematics: 3 (3); Science: 3 (3); Foreign language: 0 (0); Social studies: 3 (3); History: 0 (0); Academic electives: 3 (3); Total units: 16 (16). Tests: The college uses SAT or ACT scores in admissions decisions. Either SAT or ACT required. For admission to the fall 2011 entering class, the school will accept: ACT with or without writing accepted. Campus visit: Recommended. Admissions interview: Recommended. Off-campus interview: May be arranged. **Factors that count in admissions decisions:** *Academic:* Secondary school record: Very Important. Class rank: Very Important. Letters of recommendation: Very Important. Standardized test scores: Very Important. Essay: Very Important. *Nonacademic:* Interview: Considered. Extracurricular activities: Considered. Talent/ability: Considered. Character/personal qualities: Very Important. Alumni/ae relationship: Considered. Geographical residence: Not Considered. State residency: Not Considered. Religious affiliation/commitment: Not Considered. Minority status: Not Considered. Volunteer work: Considered. Work experience: Considered. **Other schools with the greatest overlap in applicants:** Clarke University; Iowa State University; Loras College; University of Northern Iowa; Wartburg College. **Admissions statistics for the fall 2009 entering class:** Total applicants: 1,181. Total accepted: 882. Freshmen enrolled: 354; 72% were from out of state. Overall acceptance rate: 75%. **Credentials of fall 2009 freshmen:** 8% ranked in the top 10 percent of their high school class; 22% were in the top 25 percent; 55% were in the top half. (Proportion submitting class standing: 91%.) **Average high school grade point average:** 2.9.

ACADEMICS
Year founded: 1852. **Academic calendar:** 4-1-4. **Degrees offered:** certificate, associate, bachelor's, master's, doctorate. **Most popular majors:** 20% business, management, marketing, and related support services, 15% transportation and materials moving, 12% health professions and related clinical sciences, 11% education, 7% social sciences. **Major fields of study:** biological and biomedical sciences; business, management, marketing, and related

support services; computer and information sciences and support services; education; English language and literature/letters; health professions and related clinical sciences; natural resources and conservation; parks, recreation, leisure, and fitness studies; philosophy and religious studies; psychology; security and protective services; social sciences; transportation and materials moving. **Areas of required coursework:** arts/fine arts, humanities, computer literacy, mathematics, English (including composition), philosophy, foreign languages, sciences (biological or physical), history, social science. **Pre-professional programs:** pre-dentistry, pre-medicine, pre-theology, pre-veterinary science. **Special academic programs:** cooperative (work-study plan) program, cross-registration, distance learning, double major, dual enrollment, independent study, internships, liberal arts/career combination, student-designed major, study abroad, teacher certificate program, other. **Teacher certification offered in:** special education, elementary, middle/junior high, secondary. **Cooperative education programs:** business, computer science, education, natural science, social/behavioral science, technologies, vocational arts. **Reserve Officers Training Corps (ROTC):** Army ROTC: Offered on campus. **Faculty and instruction (2009-2010):** Total instructional faculty: 83 full-time, 81 part-time (57% men; 43% women; 4% minorities). Full-time faculty with Ph.D. or other terminal degree: 49%. Student/faculty ratio: 14/1. Classes of fewer than 20 students: 60%; of 20 to 49 students: 40%; of 50 or more students: 0%. **Advanced Placement and International Baccalaureate credit:** AP tests may be used for: Placement only. Scores accepted: 3. International Baccalaureate exams may be used for: Placement only. **Freshmen returning for sophomore year:** 65%. **Graduation rates:** Four-year: 21%; five-year: 35%; six-year: 42%. **Graduate study:** 10% of students pursue further study immediately upon graduation; 5% within one year; 10% within five years. Fields in which graduates pursue further study: Master of Business Administration (MBA), 50%; law, 2%; medicine, 1%; theology (or the seminary), 3%; education, 10%; arts and sciences, 2%.

COSTS AND FINANCIAL AID

Financial aid office: (563) 589-3396. **Expenses (2010-2011):** Tuition and fees 2010-2011: $21,590; room/board: $7,370. Estimated books and supplies: $950; transportation: $900; personal expenses: $1,500. **Financial aid:** Priority filing date for institution's financial aid form: April 1. In 2009-2010, 97% of undergraduates applied for financial aid. Of those, 89% were determined to have financial need; 29% had their need fully met. Average financial aid package (proportion receiving): $18,833 (89%). Average amount of gift aid, such as scholarships or grants (proportion receiving): $12,769 (89%). Average amount of self-help aid, such as work study or loans (proportion receiving): $7,291 (74%). Average need-based loan (excluding PLUS or other private loans): $6,780. Among students who received need-based aid, the average percentage of need met: 78%. Among students who received aid based on merit, the average award (and the proportion receiving): $6,984 (10%). Average amount of debt of borrowers graduating in 2009: $37,936. Proportion who borrowed: 97%.

CAMPUS LIFE AND EXTRACURRICULAR ACTIVITIES

Campus housing available (% using): coed dorms (70%), apartments for married students, apartment for single students (30%). Students who live in college-owned, operated, or affiliated housing: 48%. **Student employment:** During the 2009-2010 academic year, 50% of undergraduates worked on campus. Average per-year earnings: $1,500. **Clubs and organizations:** Number of student organizations: 50. Activities include: campus ministries, choral groups, dance, drama/theater, international student organization, jazz band, literary magazine, music ensembles, musical theater, pep band, student government, student newspaper, student film society, yearbook. Number of fraternities: 7; sororities: 4. Proportion of men in fraternities: 6%; of women in sororities: 4%. Average proportion of students who stay on campus on weekends: 75%. **Sports program (2009-2010):** Member of NCAA III. *Men's intercollegiate varsity sports:* baseball, basketball, cross country, football, golf, soccer, tennis, track and field (indoor), track and field (outdoor), wrestling. *Women's intercollegiate varsity sports:* basketball, cross country, golf, soccer, softball, tennis, track and field (indoor), track and field (outdoor), volleyball.

SERVICES AND FACILITIES

Basic services: nonremedial tutoring, placement service, health service, health insurance. **Remedial assistance:** reading, math, writing, study skills. **Counseling services:** minority student, career, military, personal, veteran student, academic, psychological, religious. **For learning-disabled students:** School does not offer a structured program with separate admission and additional fees. Services include: remedial math, remedial English, reading machines, remedial reading, tape recorders, other special classes, videotaped classes, diagnostic testing service, untimed tests, note-taking services,

special bookstore section, oral tests, learning center, readers, extended time for tests, tutors, texts on tape, typist/scribe, exams on tape or computer, other testing accommodations, other. **Library:** Number of titles: 184,728; number of current serial subscriptions: 37,169. **Information technology resources:** Students are not required to lease or own a computer. Number of campus computers available to all students: 150. School does not have a wireless network. Proportion of college-owned housing units wired for high-speed internet access: 100%. **Campus safety:** Security services offered: 24-hour foot-and-vehicle patrols, late-night transport/escort service, 24-hour emergency telephones, lighted pathways/sidewalks, controlled dormitory access (key, security card, etc.).

TRANSFER AND INTERNATIONAL STUDENTS

Transfer students: May apply for admission for the following academic terms: Fall, Spring. Applicants need a minimum number of credits to apply. For fall 2009: Transfer applications received: 304. Transfer applicants offered admission: 222. Transfer applicants enrolled: 148. **International students:** Number of foreign undergraduates: 11 (1% of student body). Minimum TOEFL score required: 500 (paper); 170 (computer). Average TOEFL score: 525 (paper).

University of Iowa

- **Address:** 107 Calvin Hall, Iowa City, IA 52242-1396
- **Website:** http://www.uiowa.edu
- **Public**
- **Enrollment:** 18,476 full-time; 2,098 part-time

KEY STATS
✔ **U.S News College Ranking:** 72, National Universities
✔ **ACT Score (25th/75th percentile):** 23-28
✔ **Tuition:** 2010-2011: $7,417 in state, $23,713 out of state
  Selectivity: More selective   **Room/board:** $8,331
  Acceptance rate: 83%   **Average debt:** $22,684
  Student/faculty ratio: 15/1   **Proportion who borrowed:** 61%

UNDERGRADUATE STUDENT BODY STATS

2009-2010 enrollment: 18,476 full-time; 2,098 part-time. Men: 48%; women: 52%. **Ethnic makeup:** African American: 2%; American-Indian: 1%; Asian American: 4%; Hispanic: 3%; White: 87%; International: 4%.

ADMISSIONS FACTS AND FIGURES

Phone: (800) 553-4692. **Email:** admissions@uiowa.edu. **Website:** http://www.uiowa.edu. **Application deadlines for fall 2011:** Regular decision: April 1. Early decision: Not offered. Early action: Not offered. Admission can be deferred. **Application fee:** $40. **To apply online, go to:** http://www.uiowa.edu/admissions/undergrad/apply/index.html. **Admissions requirements/recommendations:** High school units required (recommended): English: 4; Mathematics: 3 (4); Science: 3; Foreign language: 2 (4); Social studies: 3; Total units: 15. Tests: The college uses SAT or ACT scores in admissions decisions. Either SAT or ACT required. For admission to the fall 2011 entering class, the school will accept: ACT with writing recommended. Campus visit: Recommended. Admissions interview: Neither required nor recommended. Off-campus interview: Not available. **Factors that count in admissions decisions:** *Academic:* Secondary school record: Very Important. Class rank: Very Important. Letters of recommendation: Considered. Standardized test scores: Very Important. Essay: Not Considered. *Nonacademic:* Interview: Not Considered. Extracurricular activities: Not Considered. Talent/ability: Considered. Character/personal qualities: Considered. Alumni/ae relationship: Not Considered. Geographical residence: Not Considered. State residency: Considered. Religious affiliation/commitment: Not Considered. Minority status: Not Considered. Volunteer work: Not Considered. Work experience: Not Considered. **Other schools with the greatest overlap in applicants:** Indiana University–Bloomington; Iowa State University; Purdue University–West Lafayette; University of Illinois–Urbana-Champaign; University of Wisconsin–Madison. **Admissions statistics for the fall 2009 entering class:** Total applicants: 15,060. Total accepted: 12,503. Freshmen enrolled: 4,063; 46% were from out of state. Overall acceptance rate: 83%. **Size of waiting list:** 0 applicants; enrolled from waiting list: 0. **Credentials of fall 2009 freshmen:** 23% ranked in the top 10 percent of their high school class; 55% were in the top 25 percent; 91% were in the top half. (Proportion submitting class standing: 75%.) **Average high school grade point average:** 3.6. **First-year students who submitted SAT**

scores: 9%. Scores (25/75 percentile): Critical Reading: 500-640, Math: 560-690, Combined: 1060-1330. **First-year students submitting ACT scores:** 93%. Scores (25/75 percentile): English: 22-28, Math: 22-28, Composite: 23-28.

ACADEMICS

Year founded: 1847. **Academic calendar:** Semester. **Degrees offered:** certificate, bachelor's, post-bachelor's certificate, master's, post-master's certificate, doctorate. **Most popular majors:** 19% business, management, marketing, and related support services, 10% communication, journalism, and related programs, 9% social sciences, 8% psychology, 7% health professions and related clinical sciences. **Major fields of study:** architecture and related services; area, ethnic, cultural, and gender studies; biological and biomedical sciences; business, management, marketing, and related support services; communication, journalism, and related programs; computer and information sciences and support services; education; engineering; English language and literature/letters; foreign languages, literatures, and linguistics; health professions and related clinical sciences; history; legal professions and studies; liberal arts and sciences studies, and humanities; mathematics and statistics; multi/interdisciplinary studies; natural resources and conservation; parks, recreation, leisure, and fitness studies; philosophy and religious studies; physical sciences; psychology; public administration and social service professions; security and protective services; social sciences; visual and performing arts. **Areas of required coursework:** humanities, mathematics, English (including composition), foreign languages, sciences (biological or physical), history, social science. **Preprofessional programs:** pre-law, pre-dentistry, pre-medicine, pre-veterinary science, pre-optometry, pre-pharmacy, other. **Special academic programs:** accelerated program, cooperative (work-study plan) program, distance learning, double major, dual enrollment, English as a Second Language (ESL), exchange student program (domestic), external degree program, honors program, independent study, internships, liberal arts/career combination, student-designed major, study abroad, teacher certificate program. **Teacher certification offered in:** early childhood, special education, elementary, middle/junior high, secondary, bilingual/bicultural. **Cooperative education programs:** business, engineering. **Reserve Officers Training Corps (ROTC):** Army ROTC: Offered on campus; Air Force ROTC: Offered on campus. **Faculty and instruction (2009-2010):** Total instructional faculty: 1,586 full-time, 93 part-time (69% men; 31% women; 16% minorities). Full-time faculty with Ph.D. or other terminal degree: 97%. Student/faculty ratio: 15/1. Classes of fewer than 20 students: 50%; of 20 to 49 students: 40%; of 50 or more students: 10%. **Advanced Placement and International Baccalaureate credit:** AP tests may be used for: Credit and/or placement. Scores accepted: 3, 4, 5. International Baccalaureate exams may be used for: Credit and/or placement. **Freshmen returning for sophomore year:** 83%. **Graduation rates:** Four-year: 42%; five-year: 65%; six-year: 69%. **Graduate study:** 30% of students pursue further study within one year.

COSTS AND FINANCIAL AID

Financial aid office: (319) 335-1450. **Expenses (2010-2011):** Tuition and fees 2010-2011: $7,417 in state, $23,713 out of state; room/board: $8,331. Estimated books and supplies: $1,090; transportation: $890; personal expenses: $2,625. **Financial aid:** In 2009-2010, 68% of undergraduates applied for financial aid. Of those, 48% were determined to have financial need; 62% had their need fully met. Average financial aid package (proportion receiving): $7,781 (46%). Average amount of gift aid, such as scholarships or grants (proportion receiving): $5,298 (29%). Average amount of self-help aid, such as work study or loans (proportion receiving): $4,412 (37%). Average need-based loan (excluding PLUS or other private loans): $4,102. Among students who received need-based aid, the average percentage of need met: 65%. Among students who received aid based on merit, the average award (and the proportion receiving): $3,279 (15%). The average athletic scholarship (and the proportion receiving): $17,262 (2%). Average amount of debt of borrowers graduating in 2009: $22,684. Proportion who borrowed: 61%.

CAMPUS LIFE AND EXTRACURRICULAR ACTIVITIES

Campus housing available: coed dorms, sorority housing, fraternity housing, apartments for married students, apartment for single students, special housing for disabled students, other housing options. Students who live in college-owned, operated, or affiliated housing: 29%. **Student employment:** During the 2009-2010 academic year, 30% of undergraduates worked on campus. Average per-year earnings: $6,000. **Clubs and organizations:** Number of student organizations: 486. Activities include: campus ministries, choral groups, concert band, dance, drama/theater, international student organization, jazz band, literary magazine, marching band, music

ensembles, musical theater, opera, pep band, radio station, student government, student newspaper, student film society, symphony orchestra, television station. Number of fraternities: 19; sororities: 18. Proportion of men in fraternities: 8%; of women in sororities: 12%. Average proportion of students who stay on campus on weekends: 95%. **Sports program (2009-2010):** Member of NCAA I. *Men's intercollegiate varsity sports:* baseball, basketball, cross country, football, golf, gymnastics, swimming, tennis, track and field (indoor), track and field (outdoor), wrestling. *Women's intercollegiate varsity sports:* basketball, crew (heavyweight), cross country, field hockey, golf, gymnastics, crew (lightweight), soccer, softball, swimming, tennis, track and field (indoor), track and field (outdoor), volleyball.

SERVICES AND FACILITIES

Basic services: nonremedial tutoring, women's center, placement service, day care, health service, health insurance. **Remedial assistance:** reading, math, writing, study skills. **Counseling services:** minority student, career, military, personal, veteran student, academic, older student, psychological, birth control. **For learning-disabled students:** School does not offer a structured program with separate admission and additional fees. Total undergraduates in learning-disabled program or receiving services: 200. Services include: reading machines, tape recorders, diagnostic testing service, note-taking services, readers, extended time for tests, tutors, priority registration, priority seating, texts on tape, other testing accommodations. **Library:** Number of titles: 4,304,186; number of current serial subscriptions: 61,679. **Information technology resources:** Students are not required to lease or own a computer. Number of campus computers available to all students: 1,200. School has a wireless network. Approximate number of users that can be accommodated: 30,000. Proportion of college-owned housing units wired for high-speed internet access: 100%. **Campus safety:** Security services offered: 24-hour foot-and-vehicle patrols, late-night transport/escort service, 24-hour emergency telephones, lighted pathways/sidewalks, controlled dormitory access (key, security card, etc).

TRANSFER AND INTERNATIONAL STUDENTS

Transfer students: May apply for admission for the following academic terms: Fall, Winter, Spring, Summer. Applicants need a minimum number of credits to apply. For fall 2009: Transfer applications received: 2,823. Transfer applicants offered admission: 1,874. Transfer applicants enrolled: 1,144. **International students:** Number of foreign undergraduates: 733 (4% of student body). Number of countries represented: 57. Minimum TOEFL score required: 530 (paper); 197 (computer).

University of Northern Iowa

- **Address:** 1227 W. 27th Street, Cedar Falls, IA 50614
- **Website:** http://www.uni.edu/
- **Public**
- **Enrollment:** 10,227 full-time; 1,154 part-time

KEY STATS

✔ **U.S News College Ranking:** 15, Regional Universities (Midwest)
✔ **ACT Score (25th/75th percentile):** 21-26
✔ **Tuition:** 2010-2011: $7,008 in state, $15,348 out of state

Selectivity: Selective	Room/board: $7,120
Acceptance rate: 85%	Average debt: $24,123
Student/faculty ratio: 17/1	Proportion who borrowed: 80%

UNDERGRADUATE STUDENT BODY STATS

2009-2010 enrollment: 10,227 full-time; 1,154 part-time. Men: 43%; women: 57%. **Ethnic makeup:** African American: 3%; Asian American: 1%; Hispanic: 2%; White: 92%; International: 2%.

ADMISSIONS FACTS AND FIGURES

Phone: (800) 772-2037. **Email:** admissions@uni.edu. **Website:** http://www.uni.edu/. **Application deadlines for fall 2011:** Regular decision: August 15. Early decision: Not offered. Early action: Not offered. Admission can be deferred. **Application fee:** $40. **To apply online, go to:** http://www.uni.edu/resources/prospective/index.shtml. **Admissions requirements/recommendations:** High school units required (recommended): English: 4; Mathematics: 3; Science: 3; Foreign language: (2); Social studies: 3; Academic electives: 2; Total units: 15. Tests: The college uses SAT or ACT scores in admissions decisions. Either SAT or ACT required. For admission to the fall 2011 entering class, the school will accept: ACT with or without writing accepted.

Campus visit: Recommended. Admissions interview: Neither required nor recommended. Off-campus interview: Not available. **Factors that count in admissions decisions: *Academic:*** Secondary school record: Very Important. Class rank: Very Important. Letters of recommendation: Considered. Standardized test scores: Very Important. Essay: Considered. ***Nonacademic:*** Interview: Considered. Extracurricular activities: Not Considered. Talent/ability: Considered. Character/personal qualities: Not Considered. Alumni/ae relationship: Not Considered. Geographical residence: Not Considered. State residency: Not Considered. Religious affiliation/commitment: Not Considered. Minority status: Not Considered. Volunteer work: Not Considered. Work experience: Not Considered. **Other schools with the greatest overlap in applicants:** Iowa State University; University of Iowa; Wartburg College. **Admissions statistics for the fall 2009 entering class:** Total applicants: 4,133. Total accepted: 3,505. Freshmen enrolled: 1,946; 5% were from out of state. Overall acceptance rate: 85%. **Credentials of fall 2009 freshmen:** 19% ranked in the top 10 percent of their high school class; 49% were in the top 25 percent; 85% were in the top half. (Proportion submitting class standing: 90%.) **Average high school grade point average:** 3.4. **First-year students who submitted SAT scores:** 1%. Scores (25/75 percentile): Critical Reading: 450-650, Math: 470-680, Combined: 920-1330. **First-year students submitting ACT scores:** 99%. Scores (25/75 percentile): English: 20-26, Math: 20-26, Composite: 21-26.

ACADEMICS
Year founded: 1876. **Academic calendar:** Semester. **Degrees offered:** bachelor's, master's, doctorate. **Most popular majors:** 22% business administration, management, and operations, 15% teacher education and professional development, 6% public administration and social service professions, 6% public relations, advertising, and applied communication , 6% visual and performing arts. **Major fields of study:** area, ethnic, cultural, and gender studies; biological and biomedical sciences; business, management, marketing, and related support services; communication, journalism, and related programs; communications technologies/technicians and support services; computer and information sciences and support services; education; engineering; engineering technologies/technicians; English language and literature/letters; family and consumer sciences/human sciences; foreign languages, literatures, and linguistics; health professions and related clinical sciences; history; liberal arts and sciences studies, and humanities; mathematics and statistics; multi/interdisciplinary studies; natural resources and conservation; parks, recreation, leisure, and fitness studies; philosophy and religious studies; physical sciences; psychology; public administration and social service professions; social sciences; visual and performing arts. **Areas of required coursework:** arts/fine arts, humanities, mathematics, English (including composition), philosophy, foreign languages, sciences (biological or physical), history, social science, other. **Pre-professional programs:** pre-law, pre-dentistry, pre-medicine, pre-theology, pre-veterinary science, pre-optometry, pre-pharmacy, other. **Special academic programs (% participation):** accelerated program, cooperative (work-study plan) program (.5%), distance learning, double major (14%), dual enrollment (.1%), English as a Second Language (ESL) (.4%), exchange student program (domestic), external degree program, honors program, independent study (.5%), internships (.5%), liberal arts/career combination, student-designed major (.2%), study abroad (.3%), teacher certificate program (19%), weekend college, other. **Teacher certification offered in:** early childhood, special education, elementary, middle/junior high, secondary, bilingual/bicultural. **Cooperative education programs:** art, business, computer science, education, health professions, home economics, humanities, natural science, social/behavioral science, technologies, other. **Reserve Officers Training Corps (ROTC):** Army ROTC: Offered on campus. **Faculty and instruction (2009-2010):** Total instructional faculty: 632 full-time, 178 part-time (53% men; 47% women; 12% minorities). Full-time faculty with Ph.D. or other terminal degree: 72%. Student/faculty ratio: 17/1. Classes of fewer than 20 students: 36%; of 20 to 49 students: 56%; of 50 or more students: 9%. **Advanced Placement and International Baccalaureate credit:** AP tests may be used for: Credit only. Scores accepted: 3, 4, 5. International Baccalaureate exams may be used for: Placement only. **Freshmen returning for sophomore year:** 83%. **Graduation rates:** Four-year: 35%; five-year: 62%; six-year: 65%. **Graduate study:** 15% of students pursue further study immediately upon graduation; 15% within one year. Fields in which graduates pursue further study: Master of Business Administration (MBA), 38%; law, 13%; medicine, 11%; dentistry, 4%; engineering, 7%; theology (or the seminary), 2%; education, 10%; arts and sciences, 15%.

COSTS AND FINANCIAL AID
Financial aid office: (319) 273-2700. **Expenses (2010-2011):** Tuition and fees 2010-2011: $7,008 in state, $15,348 out of state; room/board: $7,120.

Estimated books and supplies: $1,055; transportation: $872; personal expenses: $2,528. **Financial aid:** In 2009-2010, 81% of undergraduates applied for financial aid. Of those, 60% were determined to have financial need; 19% had their need fully met. Average financial aid package (proportion receiving): $8,243 (57%). Average amount of gift aid, such as scholarships or grants (proportion receiving): $4,691 (32%). Average amount of self-help aid, such as work study or loans (proportion receiving): $4,458 (48%). Average need-based loan (excluding PLUS or other private loans): $4,261. Among students who received need-based aid, the average percentage of need met: 65%. Among students who received aid based on merit, the average award (and the proportion receiving): $2,959 (14%). The average athletic scholarship (and the proportion receiving): $11,435 (3%). Average amount of debt of borrowers graduating in 2009: $24,123. Proportion who borrowed: 80%.

CAMPUS LIFE AND EXTRACURRICULAR ACTIVITIES
Campus housing available (% using): coed dorms (74%), women's dorms (17%), apartments for married students (5%), apartment for single students (3%), special housing for disabled students (1%), other housing options. Students who live in college-owned, operated, or affiliated housing: 39%. **Student employment:** During the 2009-2010 academic year, 37% of undergraduates worked on campus. Average per-year earnings: $1,610. **Clubs and organizations:** Number of student organizations: 288. Activities include: campus ministries, choral groups, concert band, dance, drama/theater, international student organization, jazz band, literary magazine, marching band, model UN, music ensembles, musical theater, opera, pep band, radio station, student government, student newspaper, symphony orchestra, yearbook. Number of fraternities: 5; sororities: 5. Proportion of men in fraternities: 3%; of women in sororities: 3%. Average proportion of students who stay on campus on weekends: 50%. **Sports program (2009-2010):** Member of NCAA I. *Men's intercollegiate varsity sports:* basketball, cross country, football, golf, track and field (indoor), track and field (outdoor), wrestling. *Women's intercollegiate varsity sports:* basketball, cross country, golf, soccer, softball, swimming, tennis, track and field (indoor), track and field (outdoor), volleyball.

SERVICES AND FACILITIES
Basic services: nonremedial tutoring, placement service, day care, health service, health insurance. **Remedial assistance:** reading, math, writing, study skills. **Counseling services:** minority student, career, military, personal, veteran student, academic, older student, psychological, birth control. **For learning-disabled students:** School does not offer a structured program with separate admission and additional fees. Total undergraduates in learning-disabled program or receiving services: 114. Services include: reading machines, tape recorders, diagnostic testing service, note-taking services, readers, extended time for tests, tutors, priority registration, priority seating, substitution of courses, texts on tape, typist/scribe, other testing accommodations. **Library:** Number of titles: 1,251,947; number of current serial subscriptions: 3,577. **Information technology resources:** Students are not required to lease or own a computer. Number of campus computers available to all students: 3,000. School has a wireless network. Approximate number of users that can be accommodated: 6,000. Proportion of college-owned housing units wired for high-speed internet access: 100%. **Campus safety:** Security services offered: 24-hour foot-and-vehicle patrols, late-night transport/escort service, 24-hour emergency telephones, lighted pathways/sidewalks, student patrols, controlled dormitory access (key, security card, etc).

TRANSFER AND INTERNATIONAL STUDENTS
Transfer students: May apply for admission for the following academic terms: Fall, Spring, Summer. Applicants need a minimum number of credits to apply. For fall 2009: Transfer applications received: 1,822. Transfer applicants offered admission: 1,470. Transfer applicants enrolled: 1,088. **International students:** Number of foreign undergraduates: 219 (2% of student body). Number of countries represented: 68. Minimum TOEFL score required: 550 (paper); 79 (computer). Average TOEFL score: 577 (paper).

Upper Iowa University

- **Address:** Box 1857, Fayette, IA 52142
- **Website:** http://www.uiu.edu
- **Private**
- **Enrollment:** 3,119 full-time; 3,039 part-time

KEY STATS

✔ **U.S News College Ranking:** second tier, Regional Universities (Midwest)
✔ **ACT Score (25th/75th percentile):** 16-25
✔ **Tuition:** 2010-2011: $22,350

Selectivity: Selective	**Room/board:** $6,870
Acceptance rate: 42%	**Average debt:** $24,769
Student/faculty ratio: 24/1	**Proportion who borrowed:** 97%

UNDERGRADUATE STUDENT BODY STATS

2009-2010 enrollment: 3,119 full-time; 3,039 part-time. Men: 39%; women: 61%. **Ethnic makeup:** African American: 14%; Asian American: 1%; Hispanic: 2%; White: 68%; International: 14%.

ADMISSIONS FACTS AND FIGURES

Phone: (563) 425-5281. **Email:** admission@uiu.edu. **Website:** http://www.uiu.edu. **Application deadlines for fall 2011:** Regular decision: Rolling. Early decision: Not offered. Early action: Not offered. Admission can be deferred. **Application fee:** $15. **Admissions requirements/recommendations:** High school units required (recommended): English: 4 (4); Mathematics: 3 (3); Science: 3 (3); Social studies: 2 (2); History: 1 (1); Total units: 14 (14). **Tests:** The college uses SAT or ACT scores in admissions decisions. Neither SAT nor ACT required. For admission to the fall 2011 entering class, the school will accept: ACT with or without writing accepted. Campus visit: Recommended. Admissions interview: Recommended. Off-campus interview: May be arranged. **Factors that count in admissions decisions:** *Academic:* Secondary school record: Considered. Class rank: Considered. Letters of recommendation: Considered. Standardized test scores: Very Important. Essay: Not Considered. *Nonacademic:* Interview: Not Considered. Extracurricular activities: Not Considered. Talent/ability: Not Considered. Character/personal qualities: Not Considered. Alumni/ae relationship: Considered. Geographical residence: Not Considered. State residency: Not Considered. Religious affiliation/commitment: Not Considered. Minority status: Not Considered. Volunteer work: Not Considered. Work experience: Not Considered. **Other schools with the greatest overlap in applicants:** Coe College; University of Iowa; University of Northern Iowa; Wartburg College; Winona State University. **Admissions statistics for the fall 2009 entering class:** Total applicants: 1,293. Total accepted: 544. Freshmen enrolled: 176; Overall acceptance rate: 42%. **Average high school grade point average:** 2.9. **First-year students who submitted SAT scores:** 8%. Scores (25/75 percentile): Critical Reading: 390-555, Math: 358-570, Combined: 748-1125. **First-year students submitting ACT scores:** 92%. Scores (25/75 percentile): English: N/A, Math: N/A, Composite: 16-25.

ACADEMICS

Year founded: 1857. **Academic calendar:** Other. **Degrees offered:** associate, bachelor's, master's. **Most popular majors:** 41% business, management, marketing, and related support services, 19% public administration and social service professions, 13% psychology, 7% security and protective services, 5% education. **Major fields of study:** biological and biomedical sciences; business, management, marketing, and related support services; communication, journalism, and related programs; computer and information sciences and support services; education; English language and literature/letters; mathematics and statistics; natural resources and conservation; parks, recreation, leisure, and fitness studies; physical sciences; psychology; social sciences; visual and performing arts. **Areas of required coursework:** arts/fine arts, humanities, computer literacy, mathematics, English (including composition), sciences (biological or physical), history, social science, other. **Special academic programs:** accelerated program, distance learning, double major, dual enrollment, English as a Second Language (ESL), external degree program, independent study, internships, student-designed major, study abroad, teacher certificate program. **Teacher certification offered in:** early childhood, special education, elementary, middle/junior high, secondary, bilingual/bicultural. **Faculty and instruction (2009-2010):** Total instructional faculty: 60 full-time, 402 part-time (55% men; 45% women; 14% minorities). Full-time faculty with Ph.D. or other terminal degree: 82%. Student/faculty ratio: 24/1. **Advanced Placement and International Baccalaureate credit:** AP tests may be used for: Credit only.

Scores accepted: 3, 4, 5. International Baccalaureate exams may be used for: Credit only. **Freshmen returning for sophomore year:** 66%. **Graduation rates:** Four-year: 21%; five-year: 32%; six-year: 40%. **Graduate study:** 19% of students pursue further study immediately upon graduation.

COSTS AND FINANCIAL AID

Financial aid office: (563) 425-5274. **Expenses (2010-2011):** Tuition and fees 2010-2011: $22,350; room/board: $6,870. Estimated books and supplies: $1,400; transportation: $600; personal expenses: $1,600. **Financial aid:** Priority filing date for institution's financial aid form: March 31. In 2009-2010, 95% of undergraduates applied for financial aid. Of those, 82% were determined to have financial need; 16% had their need fully met. Average financial aid package (proportion receiving): $8,513 (77%). Average amount of gift aid, such as scholarships or grants (proportion receiving): $6,761 (61%). Average amount of self-help aid, such as work study or loans (proportion receiving): $4,042 (60%). Average need-based loan (excluding PLUS or other private loans): $3,991. Among students who received need-based aid, the average percentage of need met: 52%. Among students who received aid based on merit, the average award (and the proportion receiving): $9,184 (4%). Average amount of debt of borrowers graduating in 2009: $24,769. Proportion who borrowed: 97%.

CAMPUS LIFE AND EXTRACURRICULAR ACTIVITIES

Campus housing available: women's dorms, men's dorms, apartment for single students, other housing options. Students who live in college-owned, operated, or affiliated housing: 27%. Activities include: campus ministries, choral groups, international student organization, pep band, student government, student newspaper. Number of fraternities: 4; sororities: 5. Proportion of men in fraternities: 17%; of women in sororities: 32%. Average proportion of students who stay on campus on weekends: 60%. **Sports program (2009-2010):** Member of NCAA II. *Men's intercollegiate varsity sports:* baseball, basketball, football, golf, soccer, wrestling. *Women's intercollegiate varsity sports:* basketball, golf, soccer, softball, tennis, volleyball.

SERVICES AND FACILITIES

Basic services: nonremedial tutoring. **Remedial assistance:** reading, math, writing, study skills. **Counseling services:** career, personal. **For learning-disabled students:** School does not offer a structured program with separate admission and additional fees. Total undergraduates in learning-disabled program or receiving services: 45. Services include: remedial math, remedial English, reading machines, remedial reading, tape recorders, untimed tests, note-taking services, oral tests, learning center, readers, extended time for tests, tutors, proofreading services, substitution of courses, texts on tape, other testing accommodations. **Library:** Number of titles: 73,237; number of current serial subscriptions: 282. **Information technology resources:** Students are not required to lease or own a computer. Number of campus computers available to all students: 75. School has a wireless network. Approximate number of users that can be accommodated: 1,500. Proportion of college-owned housing units wired for high-speed internet access: 100%. **Campus safety:** Security services offered: 24-hour foot-and-vehicle patrols, late-night transport/escort service, 24-hour emergency telephones, lighted pathways/sidewalks, student patrols, controlled dormitory access (key, security card, etc).

TRANSFER AND INTERNATIONAL STUDENTS

Transfer students: May apply for admission for the following academic terms: Fall, Spring, Summer. Applicants do not need a minimum number of credits to apply. For fall 2009: Transfer applications received: 287. Transfer applicants offered admission: 172. Transfer applicants enrolled: 110. **International students:** Number of foreign undergraduates: 878 (14% of student body). Minimum TOEFL score required: 500 (paper); 61 (computer). Average TOEFL score: 597 (paper).

Waldorf College

- **Address:** 106 S. Sixth Street, Forest City, IA 50436
- **Website:** http://www.waldorf.edu
- **Private; Religious affiliation:** Lutheran
- **Enrollment:** N/A

KEY STATS

✔ **U.S News College Ranking:** second tier, Regional Colleges (Midwest)
✔ **SAT or ACT Score (25th/75th percentile):** N/A
✔ **Tuition:** 2009-2010: $20,554

Selectivity: Less selective	**Room/board:** $5,954
Acceptance rate: N/A	**Average debt:** N/A
Student/faculty ratio: N/A	**Proportion who borrowed:** N/A

Wartburg College

- **Address:** PO Box 1003, Waverly, IA 50677-0903
- **Website:** http://www.wartburg.edu
- **Private; Religious affiliation:** Lutheran
- **Enrollment:** 1,736 full-time; 64 part-time

KEY STATS

✔ **U.S News College Ranking:** 152, National Liberal Arts Colleges
✔ **ACT Score (25th/75th percentile):** 21-27
✔ **Tuition:** 2010-2011: $29,020

Selectivity: Selective	**Room/board:** $7,975
Acceptance rate: 73%	**Average debt:** $27,225
Student/faculty ratio: 12/1	**Proportion who borrowed:** 81%

UNDERGRADUATE STUDENT BODY STATS

2009-2010 enrollment: 1,736 full-time; 64 part-time. Men: 48%; women: 52%. **Ethnic makeup:** African American: 5%; Asian American: 2%; Hispanic: 1%; White: 87%; International: 5%. **Religious preference:** Roman Catholic: 22%; Protestant: 25%; Muslim: 1%; Hindu: 1%; No preference: 3%; Unknown: 10%; Lutheran: 34%.

ADMISSIONS FACTS AND FIGURES

Phone: (319) 352-8264. **Email:** admissions@wartburg.edu. **Website:** http://www.wartburg.edu. **Application deadlines for fall 2011:** Regular decision: Rolling. Early decision: Not offered. Early action: Send application by: December 1; Decision sent by: N/A. Admission can be deferred. **To apply online, go to:** http://www.wartburg.edu/admissions/online.html. **Admissions requirements/recommendations:** High school units required (recommended): English: (4); Mathematics: (3); Science: (3); Foreign language: (2); Social studies: (2); Total units: (15). Tests: The college uses SAT or ACT scores in admissions decisions. Either SAT or ACT required. For admission to the fall 2011 entering class, the school will accept: ACT with or without writing accepted. Campus visit: Recommended. Admissions interview: Neither required nor recommended. Off-campus interview: May be arranged. **Factors that count in admissions decisions:** *Academic:* Secondary school record: Very Important. Class rank: Very Important. Letters of recommendation: Very Important. Standardized test scores: Very Important. Essay: Considered. *Nonacademic:* Interview: Important. Extracurricular activities: Considered. Talent/ability: Considered. Character/personal qualities: Important. Alumni/ae relationship: Not Considered. Geographical residence: Not Considered. State residency: Not Considered. Religious affiliation/commitment: Not Considered. Minority status: Considered. Volunteer work: Considered. Work experience: Considered. **Other schools with the greatest overlap in applicants:** Central College; Iowa State University; Luther College; University of Iowa; University of Northern Iowa. **Admissions statistics for the fall 2009 entering class:** Total applicants: 2,278. Total accepted: 1,652. Freshmen enrolled: 480; 26% were from out of state. Overall acceptance rate: 73%. Non-early acceptance rate: 73%. **Size of waiting list:** 0 applicants; enrolled from waiting list: 0. **Credentials of fall 2009 freshmen:** 28% ranked in the top 10 percent of their high school class; 56% were in the top 25 percent; 84% were in the top half. (Proportion submitting class standing: 87%.) **Average high school grade point average:** 3.5. **First-year students who submitted SAT scores:** 7%. Scores (25/75 percentile): Critical Reading: 420-600, Math: 470-610, Combined: 890-1210. **First-year students submitting**

ACT scores: 95%. Scores (25/75 percentile): English: 20-27, Math: 20-27, Composite: 21-27.

ACADEMICS

Year founded: 1852. **Academic calendar:** Other. **Degrees offered:** bachelor's. **Most popular majors:** 23% business/commerce, 13% biology/biological sciences, 13% elementary education and teaching, 10% communication studies/speech communication and rhetoric, 4% sport and fitness administration/management. **Major fields of study:** biological and biomedical sciences; business, management, marketing, and related support services; communication, journalism, and related programs; computer and information sciences and support services; education; engineering; English language and literature/letters; foreign languages, literatures, and linguistics; health professions and related clinical sciences; history; mathematics and statistics; parks, recreation, leisure, and fitness studies; philosophy and religious studies; physical sciences; psychology; public administration and social service professions; social sciences; theology and religious vocations; visual and performing arts. **Areas of required coursework:** humanities, mathematics, English (including composition), philosophy, foreign languages, sciences (biological or physical), social science, other. **Pre-professional programs:** pre-law, pre-dentistry, pre-medicine, pre-veterinary science, pre-optometry, pre-pharmacy. **Special academic programs:** accelerated program, double major, dual enrollment, honors program, independent study, internships, student-designed major, study abroad, teacher certificate program. **Teacher certification offered in:** early childhood, special education, elementary, middle/junior high, secondary. **Faculty and instruction (2009-2010):** Total instructional faculty: 109 full-time, 72 part-time (51% men; 49% women; 6% minorities). Full-time faculty with Ph.D. or other terminal degree: 84%. Student/faculty ratio: 12/1. Classes of fewer than 20 students: 41%; of 20 to 49 students: 56%; of 50 or more students: 3%. **Advanced Placement and International Baccalaureate credit:** AP tests may be used for: Placement only. Scores accepted: 3, 4. **Freshmen returning for sophomore year:** 78%. **Graduation rates:** Four-year: 61%; five-year: 63%; six-year: 64%. **Graduate study:** 23% of students pursue further study within one year. Fields in which graduates pursue further study: Master of Business Administration (MBA), 2%; law, 1%; medicine, 6%; education, 1%; arts and sciences, 11%.

COSTS AND FINANCIAL AID

Financial aid office: (319) 352-8262. **Expenses (2010-2011):** Tuition and fees 2010-2011: $29,020; room/board: $7,975. Estimated books and supplies: $1,100; transportation: $600; personal expenses: $700. **Financial aid:** Priority filing date for institution's financial aid form: March 1. In 2009-2010, 90% of undergraduates applied for financial aid. Of those, 79% were determined to have financial need; 40% had their need fully met. Average financial aid package (proportion receiving): $21,639 (79%). Average amount of gift aid, such as scholarships or grants (proportion receiving): $17,076 (79%). Average amount of self-help aid, such as work study or loans (proportion receiving): $5,495 (66%). Average need-based loan (excluding PLUS or other private loans): $4,637. Among students who received need-based aid, the average percentage of need met: 83%. Among students who received aid based on merit, the average award (and the proportion receiving): $13,202 (20%). The average athletic scholarship (and the proportion receiving): $0 (0%). Average amount of debt of borrowers graduating in 2009: $27,225. Proportion who borrowed: 81%.

CAMPUS LIFE AND EXTRACURRICULAR ACTIVITIES

Campus housing available (% using): coed dorms (81%), women's dorms (9%), men's dorms (10%). Students who live in college-owned, operated, or affiliated housing: 81%. **Student employment:** During the 2009-2010 academic year, 45% of undergraduates worked on campus. Average per-year earnings: $2,500. **Clubs and organizations:** Number of student organizations: 90. Activities include: campus ministries, choral groups, concert band, dance, drama/theater, international student organization, jazz band, literary magazine, music ensembles, musical theater, opera, pep band, radio station, student government, student newspaper, student film society, symphony orchestra, television station, yearbook. Number of fraternities: 0; sororities: 0. Average proportion of students who stay on campus on weekends: 70%. **Sports program (2009-2010):** Member of NCAA III. *Men's intercollegiate varsity sports:* baseball, basketball, cross country, football, golf, soccer, tennis, track and field (indoor), track and field (outdoor), wrestling. *Women's intercollegiate varsity sports:* basketball, cross country, golf, soccer, softball, tennis, track and field (indoor), track and field (outdoor), volleyball.

SERVICES AND FACILITIES

Basic services: health service. **Remedial assistance:** reading, math, writing, study skills. **Counseling services:** career, personal, academic, religious. **For learning-disabled students:** School does not offer a structured program with separate admission and additional fees. Total undergraduates in learning-disabled program or receiving services: 11. Services include: remedial math, remedial English, reading machines, tape recorders, note-taking services, oral tests, learning center, readers, extended time for tests, priority seating, texts on tape, other. **Library:** Number of titles: 194,178; number of current serial subscriptions: 50,445. **Information technology resources:** Students are not required to lease or own a computer. Number of campus computers available to all students: 275. School has a wireless network. Approximate number of users that can be accommodated: 250. Proportion of college-owned housing units wired for high-speed internet access: 100%. **Campus safety:** Security services offered: 24-hour foot-and-vehicle patrols, late-night transport/escort service, 24-hour emergency telephones, lighted pathways/sidewalks, student patrols, controlled dormitory access (key, security card, etc).

TRANSFER AND INTERNATIONAL STUDENTS

Transfer students: May apply for admission for the following academic terms: Fall, Winter, Spring, Summer. Applicants need a minimum number of credits to apply. For fall 2009: Transfer applications received: 173.

Transfer applicants offered admission: 80. Transfer applicants enrolled: 42. **International students:** Number of foreign undergraduates: 89 (5% of student body). Number of countries represented: 38. Minimum TOEFL score required: 480 (paper); 157 (computer).

William Penn University

- **Address:** 201 Trueblood Avenue, Oskaloosa, IA 52577
- **Website:** http://www.wmpenn.edu
- **Private; Religious affiliation:** Quaker
- **Enrollment:** N/A

KEY STATS

✔ **U.S News College Ranking:** second tier, Regional Colleges (Midwest)
✔ **ACT Score (25th/75th percentile):** 16-22
✔ **Tuition:** 2009-2010: $18,934

Selectivity: Less selective	**Room/board:** $5,292
Acceptance rate: 34%	**Average debt:** N/A
Student/faculty ratio: N/A	**Proportion who borrowed:** N/A

Kansas

Baker University

- **Address:** PO Box 65, Baldwin City, KS 66006
- **Website:** http://www.bakeru.edu
- **Private; Religious affiliation:** United Methodist
- **Enrollment:** 899 full-time; 93 part-time

KEY STATS

✔ **U.S News College Ranking:** 144, National Liberal Arts Colleges
✔ **ACT Score (25th/75th percentile):** 21-26
✔ **Tuition:** 2010-2011: $22,280

Selectivity: Selective	**Room/board:** $7,030
Acceptance rate: 56%	**Average debt:** N/A
Student/faculty ratio: 12/1	**Proportion who borrowed:** N/A

UNDERGRADUATE STUDENT BODY STATS

2009-2010 enrollment: 899 full-time; 93 part-time. Men: 47%; women: 53%. **Ethnic makeup:** African American: 8%; American-Indian: 1%; Asian American: 1%; Hispanic: 1%; White: 87%; International: 1%.

ADMISSIONS FACTS AND FIGURES

Phone: (800) 873-4282. **Email:** admission@bakeru.edu. **Website:** http://www.bakeru.edu. **Application deadlines for fall 2011:** Regular decision: Rolling. Early decision: Not offered. Early action: Not offered. Admission can be deferred. **To apply online, go to:** http://www.bakeru.edu/admissions/app/. **Admissions requirements/recommendations:** High school units required (recommended): English: (4); Mathematics: (3); Science: (3); Foreign language: (2); Social studies: (3); Total units: (17). Tests: The college uses SAT or ACT scores in admissions decisions. Either SAT or ACT required. For admission to the fall 2011 entering class, the school will accept: ACT with or without writing accepted. Campus visit: Recommended. Admissions interview: Recommended. Off-campus interview: May be arranged. **Factors that count in admissions decisions: Academic:** Secondary school record: Very Important. Class rank: Important. Letters of recommendation: Very Important. Standardized test scores: Very Important. Essay: Considered. **Nonacademic:** Interview: Considered. Extracurricular activities: Considered. Talent/ability: Considered. Character/personal qualities: Considered. Alumni/ae relationship: Considered. Geographical residence: Considered. State residency: Not Considered. Religious affiliation/commitment: Not Considered. Minority status: Not Considered. Volunteer work: Considered. Work experience: Considered. **Other schools with the greatest overlap in applicants:** Kansas State University; Pittsburg State University; Rockhurst University; University of Kansas; William Jewell College. **Admissions statistics for the fall 2009 entering class:** Total applicants: 1,266. Total accepted: 706. Freshmen enrolled: 257; 27% were from out of state. Overall acceptance rate: 56%. **Size of waiting list:** 0 applicants; enrolled from waiting list: 0. **Credentials of fall 2009 freshmen:** 24% ranked in the top 10 percent of their high school class; 54% were in the top 25 percent; 84% were in the top half. (Proportion submitting class standing: 97%.) **Average high school grade point average:** 3.5. **First-year students who submitted SAT scores:** 7%. Scores (25/75 percentile): Critical Reading: 453-575, Math: 433-563, Combined: 886-1138. **First-year students submitting ACT scores:** 96%. Scores (25/75 percentile): English: 20-26, Math: 19-26, Composite: 21-26.

ACADEMICS

Year founded: 1858. **Academic calendar:** 4-1-4. **Degrees offered:** bachelor's. **Most popular majors:** 25% business, management, marketing, and related support services, 13% education, 10% parks, recreation, leisure, and fitness studies, 6% biological and biomedical sciences, 6% communication, journalism, and related programs. **Major fields of study:** biological and biomedical sciences; business, management, marketing, and related support services; communication, journalism, and related programs; computer and information sciences and support services; education; English language and literature/letters; foreign languages, literatures, and linguistics; health professions and related clinical sciences; history; mathematics and statistics; multi/interdisciplinary studies; parks, recreation, leisure, and fitness stud-

ies; philosophy and religious studies; physical sciences; psychology; social sciences; visual and performing arts. **Areas of required coursework:** arts/fine arts, humanities, mathematics, English (including composition), sciences (biological or physical), history, social science, other. **Pre-professional programs:** pre-law, pre-dentistry, pre-medicine, pre-theology, pre-veterinary science, pre-optometry, pre-pharmacy, other. **Special academic programs (% participation):** distance learning (5%), double major (17%), honors program (13%), independent study (5%), internships (35%), student-designed major (1%), study abroad (10%), teacher certificate program (13%). **Teacher certification offered in:** special education, elementary, middle/junior high, secondary. **Reserve Officers Training Corps (ROTC):** Army ROTC: Offered at cooperating institution (University of Kansas); Air Force ROTC: Offered at cooperating institution (University of Kansas). **Faculty and instruction (2009-2010):** Total instructional faculty: 65 full-time, 36 part-time (53% men; 47% women; 4% minorities). Full-time faculty with Ph.D. or other terminal degree: 86%. Student/faculty ratio: 12/1. Classes of fewer than 20 students: 74%; of 20 to 49 students: 25%; of 50 or more students: 1%. **Advanced Placement and International Baccalaureate credit:** AP tests may be used for: Credit only. Scores accepted: 3, 4, 5. International Baccalaureate exams may be used for: Credit only. **Freshmen returning for sophomore year:** 76%. **Graduation rates:** Four-year: 36%; five-year: 53%; six-year: 54%. **Graduate study:** 28% of students pursue further study immediately upon graduation. Fields in which graduates pursue further study: Master of Business Administration (MBA), 1%; law, 5%; medicine, 3%; education, 3%; arts and sciences, 16%.

COSTS AND FINANCIAL AID

Financial aid office: (785) 594-4595. **Expenses (2010-2011):** Tuition and fees 2010-2011: $22,280; room/board: $7,030. Estimated books and supplies: $1,200; transportation: $2,930; personal expenses: $1,550. **Financial aid:** Priority filing date for institution's financial aid form: March 1. In 2009-2010, 97% of undergraduates applied for financial aid. Of those, 67% were determined to have financial need; 46% had their need fully met. Average financial aid package (proportion receiving): $9,417 (67%). Average amount of gift aid, such as scholarships or grants (proportion receiving): $5,710 (38%). Average amount of self-help aid, such as work study or loans (proportion receiving): $5,822 (67%). Average need-based loan (excluding PLUS or other private loans): $4,278. Among students who received need-based aid, the average percentage of need met: 85%. Among students who received aid based on merit, the average award (and the proportion receiving): $11,488 (13%). The average athletic scholarship (and the proportion receiving): $3,885 (7%).

CAMPUS LIFE AND EXTRACURRICULAR ACTIVITIES

Campus housing available (% using): coed dorms (42%), women's dorms (0%), men's dorms (19%), sorority housing (17%), fraternity housing (9%), apartment for single students (13%), special housing for disabled students. Students who live in college-owned, operated, or affiliated housing: 84%. **Clubs and organizations:** Number of student organizations: 45. Activities include: choral groups, concert band, dance, drama/theater, international student organization, jazz band, literary magazine, music ensembles, pep band, radio station, student government, student newspaper, television station, yearbook. Number of fraternities: 5; sororities: 5. Proportion of men in fraternities: 35%; of women in sororities: 40%. Average proportion of students who stay on campus on weekends: 50%. **Sports program (2009-2010):** Member of NAIA. *Men's intercollegiate varsity sports:* baseball, basketball, cross country, football, golf, soccer, tennis, track and field (indoor), track and field (outdoor), wrestling. *Women's intercollegiate varsity sports:* basketball, bowling, cross country, golf, soccer, softball, tennis, track and field (indoor), track and field (outdoor), volleyball.

SERVICES AND FACILITIES

Basic services: nonremedial tutoring, women's center, placement service, health service. **Remedial assistance:** reading, math, writing, study skills. **Counseling services:** minority student, career, personal, veteran student, academic, older student, psychological, birth control, religious. **For learning-disabled students:** School does not offer a structured program with separate admission and additional fees. Total undergraduates in learning-disabled program or receiving services: 14. Services include: tape recorders, note-taking services, oral tests, learning center, readers, extended time for tests, tutors, priority seating, typist/scribe, exams on tape or computer, other testing accommodations. **Library:** Number of titles: 103,243; number of current serial subscriptions: 567. **Information technology resources:** Students are not required to lease or own a computer. Number of campus computers available to all students: 237. School has a wireless network. Approximate number of users that can be accommodated: 1,025. Proportion of college-owned housing units wired for high-speed internet access: 100%. **Campus safety:** Security services offered: 24-hour foot-and-vehicle patrols, lighted pathways/sidewalks, controlled dormitory access (key, security card, etc).

TRANSFER AND INTERNATIONAL STUDENTS

Transfer students: May apply for admission for the following academic terms: Fall, Winter, Spring, Summer. Applicants need a minimum number of credits to apply. For fall 2009: Transfer applications received: 435. Transfer applicants offered admission: 80. Transfer applicants enrolled: 51. **International students:** Number of foreign undergraduates: 6 (1% of student body). Number of countries represented: 12. Minimum TOEFL score required: 525 (paper); 195 (computer).

Benedictine College

- **Address:** 1020 N. Second Street, Atchison, KS 66002
- **Website:** http://www.benedictine.edu
- **Private; Religious affiliation:** Roman Catholic
- **Enrollment:** 1,470 full-time; 345 part-time

KEY STATS

✔ **U.S News College Ranking:** 52, Regional Universities (Midwest)
✔ **ACT Score (25th/75th percentile):** 21-27
✔ **Tuition:** 2010-2011: $20,700

Selectivity: Selective	**Room/board:** $7,375
Acceptance rate: 61%	**Average debt:** $20,078
Student/faculty ratio: 15/1	**Proportion who borrowed:** 75%

UNDERGRADUATE STUDENT BODY STATS

2009-2010 enrollment: 1,470 full-time; 345 part-time. Men: 47%; women: 53%. **Ethnic makeup:** African American: 3%; Asian American: 1%; Hispanic: 5%; White: 88%; International: 2%. **Religious preference:** Protestant: 8%; Unknown: 7%; Roman Catholic: 81%.

ADMISSIONS FACTS AND FIGURES

Phone: (800) 467-5340. **Email:** bcadmiss@benedictine.edu. **Website:** http://www.benedictine.edu. **Application deadlines for fall 2011:** Regular decision: Rolling. Early decision: Not offered. Early action: Not offered. Admission can be deferred. **Application fee:** $25. **To apply online, go to:** http://www.benedictine.edu. **Admissions requirements/recommendations:** High school units required (recommended): English: 4; Mathematics: 3 (4); Science: 2 (4); Foreign language: 2 (4); Social studies: 2; History: 1; Total units: 14 (12). Tests: The college uses SAT or ACT scores in admissions decisions. Either SAT or ACT required. For admission to the fall 2011 entering class, the school will accept: ACT with or without writing accepted. Campus visit: Recommended. Admissions interview: Recommended. Off-campus interview: May be arranged. **Factors that count in admissions decisions:** *Academic:* Secondary school record: Very Important. Class rank: Very Important. Letters of recommendation: Considered. Standardized test scores: Very Important. Essay: Considered. *Nonacademic:* Interview: Considered. Extracurricular activities: Considered. Talent/ability: Considered. Character/personal qualities: Considered. Alumni/ae relationship: Considered. Geographical residence: Not Considered. State residency: Not Considered. Religious affiliation/commitment: Not Considered. Minority status: Considered. Volunteer work: Considered. Work experience: Considered. **Other schools with the greatest overlap in applicants:** Creighton University; Kansas State University; Rockhurst University; St. Louis University; University of Kansas. **Admissions statistics for the fall 2009 entering class:** Total applicants: 2,412. Total accepted: 1,478. Freshmen enrolled: 428; 69% were from out of state. Overall acceptance rate: 61%. **Size of waiting list:** 24 applicants; enrolled from waiting list: 5. **Credentials of fall 2009 freshmen:** 28% ranked in the top 10 percent of their high school class; 57% were in the top 25 percent; 74% were in the top half. (Proportion submitting class standing: 51%.) **Average high school grade point average:** 3.4. **First-year students who submitted SAT scores:** 14%. First-year students

submitting ACT scores: 86%. Scores (25/75 percentile): English: 21-27, Math: 19-26, Composite: 21-27.

ACADEMICS

Year founded: 1859. **Academic calendar:** Semester. **Degrees offered:** associate, bachelor's, master's. **Most popular majors:** 21% business, management, marketing, and related support services, 14% education, 8% theology and religious vocations, 6% biological and biomedical sciences, 6% communication, journalism, and related programs. **Major fields of study:** biological and biomedical sciences; business, management, marketing, and related support services; communication, journalism, and related programs; computer and information sciences and support services; education; English language and literature/letters; foreign languages, literatures, and linguistics; health professions and related clinical sciences; history; liberal arts and sciences studies, and humanities; mathematics and statistics; multi/interdisciplinary studies; philosophy and religious studies; physical sciences; psychology; social sciences; visual and performing arts. **Areas of required coursework:** arts/fine arts, humanities, mathematics, English (including composition), philosophy, foreign languages, sciences (biological or physical), history, social science, other. **Pre-professional programs:** pre-law. **Special academic programs (% participation):** cooperative (work-study plan) program (25%), double major (24%), dual enrollment (10%), English as a Second Language (ESL) (1%), independent study (11%), internships (44%), liberal arts/career combination (3%), student-designed major (2%), study abroad (7%), teacher certificate program (11%). **Teacher certification offered in:** special education, elementary, middle/junior high, secondary. **Cooperative education programs:** engineering, other. **Reserve Officers Training Corps (ROTC):** Army ROTC: Offered on campus. **Faculty and instruction (2009-2010):** Total instructional faculty: 75 full-time, 53 part-time (64% men; 36% women; 3% minorities). Full-time faculty with Ph.D. or other terminal degree: 83%. Student/faculty ratio: 15/1. Classes of fewer than 20 students: 61%; of 20 to 49 students: 38%; of 50 or more students: 1%. **Advanced Placement and International Baccalaureate credit:** AP tests may be used for: Placement only. Scores accepted: 3, 4, 5. International Baccalaureate exams may be used for: Credit and/or placement. **Freshmen returning for sophomore year:** 74%. **Graduation rates:** Four-year: 41%; five-year: 47%; six-year: 54%. **Graduate study:** 15% of students pursue further study immediately upon graduation; 25% within one year. Fields in which graduates pursue further study: Master of Business Administration (MBA), 27%; law, 5%; medicine, 10%; dentistry, 2%; engineering, 2%; theology (or the seminary), 5%; arts and sciences, 25%; veterinary medicine, 2%.

COSTS AND FINANCIAL AID

Financial aid office: (913) 360-7484. **Expenses (2010-2011):** Tuition and fees 2010-2011: $20,700; room/board: $7,375. Estimated books and supplies: $2,000; transportation: $2,000; personal expenses: $3,500. **Financial aid:** Priority filing date for institution's financial aid form: March 15; deadline: June 1. In 2009-2010, 85% of undergraduates applied for financial aid. Of those, 73% were determined to have financial need; 21% had their need fully met. Average financial aid package (proportion receiving): $22,755 (73%). Average amount of gift aid, such as scholarships or grants (proportion receiving): $12,418 (73%). Average amount of self-help aid, such as work study or loans (proportion receiving): $1,019 (46%). Average need-based loan (excluding PLUS or other private loans): $3,335. Among students who received need-based aid, the average percentage of need met: 75%. Among students who received aid based on merit, the average award (and the proportion receiving): $7,981 (12%). The average athletic scholarship (and the proportion receiving): $5,071 (8%). Average amount of debt of borrowers graduating in 2009: $20,078. Proportion who borrowed: 75%.

CAMPUS LIFE AND EXTRACURRICULAR ACTIVITIES

Campus housing available (% using): coed dorms (20%), women's dorms (35%), men's dorms (40%), other housing options (5%). Students who live in college-owned, operated, or affiliated housing: 75%. **Student employment:** During the 2009-2010 academic year, 22% of undergraduates worked on campus. Average per-year earnings: $800. **Clubs and organizations:** Number of student organizations: 52. Activities include: campus ministries, choral groups, concert band, dance, drama/theater, international student organization, jazz band, literary magazine, music ensembles, musical theater, pep band, radio station, student government, student newspaper, symphony orchestra, television station, yearbook. Number of fraternities: 0; sororities: 0. Average proportion of students who stay on campus on weekends: 75%. **Sports program (2009-2010):** Member of NAIA. *Men's intercollegiate varsity sports:* baseball, basketball, cross country, football, golf, soccer, swimming, track and field (indoor), track and field (outdoor). *Women's* *intercollegiate varsity sports:* basketball, cross country, golf, soccer, softball, swimming, track and field (indoor), track and field (outdoor), volleyball.

SERVICES AND FACILITIES

Basic services: nonremedial tutoring, placement service, health service. **Remedial assistance:** reading, study skills. **Counseling services:** minority student, career, military, personal, academic, psychological, religious. **For learning-disabled students:** School does not offer a structured program with separate admission and additional fees. Total undergraduates in learning-disabled program or receiving services: 70. Services include: tape recorders, untimed tests, note-taking services, oral tests, learning center, readers, extended time for tests, tutors. **Library:** Number of titles: 254,101; number of current serial subscriptions: 458. **Information technology resources:** Students are not required to lease or own a computer. Number of campus computers available to all students: 83. School has a wireless network. Proportion of college-owned housing units wired for high-speed internet access: 100%. **Campus safety:** Security services offered: 24-hour foot-and-vehicle patrols, late-night transport/escort service, 24-hour emergency telephones, lighted pathways/sidewalks, controlled dormitory access (key, security card, etc).

TRANSFER AND INTERNATIONAL STUDENTS

Transfer students: May apply for admission for the following academic terms: Fall, Spring, Summer. Applicants do not need a minimum number of credits to apply. For fall 2009: Transfer applications received: 221. Transfer applicants offered admission: 76. Transfer applicants enrolled: 65. **International students:** Number of foreign undergraduates: 16 (2% of student body). Number of countries represented: 23. Minimum TOEFL score required: 535 (paper); 200 (computer).

Bethany College

- **Address:** 421 N. First Street, Lindsborg, KS 67456-1897
- **Website:** http://www.bethanylb.edu
- **Private; Religious affiliation:** Evangelical Lutheran Church in America
- **Enrollment:** 574 full-time; 18 part-time

KEY STATS

✔ **U.S News College Ranking:** 44, Regional Colleges (Midwest)
✔ **ACT Score (25th/75th percentile):** 20-25
✔ **Tuition:** 2010-2011: $20,026

Selectivity: Selective	**Room/board:** $6,174
Acceptance rate: 58%	**Average debt:** $22,699
Student/faculty ratio: 10/1	**Proportion who borrowed:** 84%

UNDERGRADUATE STUDENT BODY STATS

2009-2010 enrollment: 574 full-time; 18 part-time. Men: 50%; women: 50%. **Ethnic makeup:** African American: 10%; American-Indian: 1%; Asian American: 1%; Hispanic: 6%; White: 77%; International: 5%. **Religious preference:** Roman Catholic: 15%; Protestant: 33%; Jewish: 1%; Muslim: 1%; No preference: 33%; Evangelical Lutheran Church in America: 17%; Christian: N/A.

ADMISSIONS FACTS AND FIGURES

Phone: (800) 826-2281. **Email:** admissions@bethanylb.edu. **Website:** http://www.bethanylb.edu. **Application deadlines for fall 2011:** Regular decision: Rolling. Early decision: Not offered. Early action: Not offered. Admission can be deferred. **To apply online, go to:** http://www.bethanylb.edu/contentm/gen/bethany_college_generated_pages/Apply_m18.html. **Admissions requirements/recommendations:** High school units required (recommended): English: (4); Mathematics: (3); Science: (3); Foreign language: (2); Social studies: (3). Tests: The college uses SAT or ACT scores in admissions decisions. Either SAT or ACT required. For admission to the fall 2011 entering class, the school will accept: ACT with or without writing accepted. Campus visit: Recommended. Admissions interview: Recommended. Off-campus interview: May be arranged. **Factors that count in admissions decisions:** *Academic:* Secondary school record: Important. Class rank: Very Important. Letters of recommendation: Considered. Standardized test scores: Very Important. Essay: Considered. *Nonacademic:* Interview: Considered. Extracurricular activities: Considered. Talent/ability: Considered. Character/personal qualities: Considered. Alumni/ae relationship: Considered. Geographical residence: Not Considered. State residency: Not Considered. Religious affiliation/commitment: Not Considered.

Minority status: Not Considered. Volunteer work: Not Considered. Work experience: Not Considered. **Other schools with the greatest overlap in applicants:** Fort Hays State University; Kansas State University; University of Kansas. **Admissions statistics for the fall 2009 entering class:** Total applicants: 840. Total accepted: 491. Freshmen enrolled: 182; 47% were from out of state. Overall acceptance rate: 58%. **Credentials of fall 2009 freshmen:** 14% ranked in the top 10 percent of their high school class; 36% were in the top 25 percent; 66% were in the top half. (Proportion submitting class standing: 89%.) **Average high school grade point average:** 3.3. **First-year students who submitted SAT scores:** 18%. Scores (25/75 percentile): Critical Reading: 390-490, Math: 430-520, Combined: 820-1010. **First-year students submitting ACT scores:** 81%. Scores (25/75 percentile): English: 19-24, Math: 18-25, Composite: 20-25.

ACADEMICS

Year founded: 1881. **Academic calendar:** 4-1-4. **Degrees offered:** bachelor's. **Most popular majors:** 16% elementary education and teaching, 11% biology/biological sciences, 11% criminology, 9% business, management, marketing, and related support services, 7% sport and fitness administration/management. **Major fields of study:** biological and biomedical sciences; business, management, marketing, and related support services; communication, journalism, and related programs; education; English language and literature/letters; history; mathematics and statistics; physical sciences; psychology; public administration and social service professions; security and protective services; theology and religious vocations; visual and performing arts. **Areas of required coursework:** arts/fine arts, humanities, mathematics, English (including composition), philosophy, sciences (biological or physical), history, social science. **Pre-professional programs:** pre-law, pre-medicine, pre-theology, pre-veterinary science, pre-pharmacy. **Special academic programs (% participation):** accelerated program (3%), cooperative (work-study plan) program (20%), cross-registration (5%), double major (4%), dual enrollment (0%), exchange student program (domestic) (1%), honors program (2%), independent study (5%), internships (35%), student-designed major (1%), study abroad (2%), teacher certificate program (16%). **Teacher certification offered in:** special education, elementary, middle/junior high, secondary. **Cooperative education programs:** education, engineering. **Faculty and instruction (2009-2010):** Total instructional faculty: 43 full-time, 41 part-time (60% men; 40% women; 4% minorities). Full-time faculty with Ph.D. or other terminal degree: 72%. Student/faculty ratio: 10/1. Classes of fewer than 20 students: 79%; of 20 to 49 students: 20%; of 50 or more students: 1%. **Freshmen returning for sophomore year:** 56%. **Graduation rates:** Four-year: 24%; five-year: 31%; six-year: 42%. **Graduate study:** 20% of students pursue further study immediately upon graduation. Fields in which graduates pursue further study: Master of Business Administration (MBA), 13%; law, 13%; medicine, 13%; engineering, 6%; theology (or the seminary), 13%; veterinary medicine, 6%.

COSTS AND FINANCIAL AID

Financial aid office: (785) 227-3311. **Expenses (2010-2011):** Tuition and fees 2010-2011: $20,026; room/board: $6,174. Estimated books and supplies: $1,000; transportation: $1,000; personal expenses: $2,600. **Financial aid:** Priority filing date for institution's financial aid form: March 15. In 2009-2010, 99% of undergraduates applied for financial aid. Of those, 81% were determined to have financial need; 42% had their need fully met. Average financial aid package (proportion receiving): $20,598 (81%). Average amount of gift aid, such as scholarships or grants (proportion receiving): $7,399 (69%). Average amount of self-help aid, such as work study or loans (proportion receiving): $5,686 (64%). Average need-based loan (excluding PLUS or other private loans): $4,783. Among students who received need-based aid, the average percentage of need met: 94%. Among students who received aid based on merit, the average award (and the proportion receiving): $6,948 (7%). The average athletic scholarship (and the proportion receiving): $3,637 (6%). Average amount of debt of borrowers graduating in 2009: $22,699. Proportion who borrowed: 84%.

CAMPUS LIFE AND EXTRACURRICULAR ACTIVITIES

Campus housing available (% using): coed dorms (75%), women's dorms (16%), apartment for single students (5%), other housing options (4%). Students who live in college-owned, operated, or affiliated housing: 59%. **Student employment:** During the 2009-2010 academic year, 58% of undergraduates worked on campus. Average per-year earnings: $1,500. **Clubs and organizations:** Number of student organizations: 53. Activities include: campus ministries, choral groups, concert band, dance, drama/theater, international student organization, jazz band, music ensembles, musical theater, pep band, student government, student newspaper, symphony orchestra, yearbook. Number of fraternities: 3; sororities: 3. Proportion of men in fraternities: 15%; of women in sororities: 18%. Average proportion of students who stay on campus on weekends: 60%. **Sports program (2009-2010):** Member of NAIA. **Men's intercollegiate varsity sports:** baseball, basketball, cross country, football, golf, soccer, tennis, track and field (indoor), track and field (outdoor). **Women's intercollegiate varsity sports:** basketball, cross country, soccer, softball, tennis, track and field (indoor), track and field (outdoor), volleyball.

SERVICES AND FACILITIES
Basic services: nonremedial tutoring, health service, health insurance. **Remedial assistance:** reading, math, writing, study skills. **Counseling services:** minority student, career, personal, academic, psychological, religious. **For learning-disabled students:** School does not offer a structured program with separate admission and additional fees. Total undergraduates in learning-disabled program or receiving services: 7. Services include: remedial math, remedial English, reading machines, remedial reading, tape recorders, other special classes, diagnostic testing service, untimed tests, note-taking services, oral tests, learning center, readers, extended time for tests, tutors, proofreading services, texts on tape. **Library:** Number of titles: 135,871; number of current serial subscriptions: 84. **Information technology resources:** Students are not required to lease or own a computer. Number of campus computers available to all students: 75. School has a wireless network. Approximate number of users that can be accommodated: 150. Proportion of college-owned housing units wired for high-speed internet access: 90%. **Campus safety:** Security services offered: late-night transport/escort service, 24-hour emergency telephones, lighted pathways/sidewalks, controlled dormitory access (key, security card, etc).

TRANSFER AND INTERNATIONAL STUDENTS
Transfer students: May apply for admission for the following academic terms: Fall, Winter, Spring, Summer. Applicants do not need a minimum number of credits to apply. For fall 2009: Transfer applications received: 227. Transfer applicants offered admission: 136. Transfer applicants enrolled: 67. **International students:** Number of foreign undergraduates: 27 (5% of student body). Number of countries represented: 22. Minimum TOEFL score required: 525 (paper); 71 (computer).

Bethel College

- **Address:** 300 E. 27th Street, North Newton, KS 67117-8061
- **Website:** http://www.bethelks.edu
- **Private; Religious affiliation:** Mennonite Church USA
- **Enrollment:** 416 full-time; 21 part-time

KEY STATS
- ✔ **U.S News College Ranking:** 137, National Liberal Arts Colleges
- ✔ **ACT Score (25th/75th percentile):** 21-29
- ✔ **Tuition:** 2010-2011: $20,700

Selectivity: More selective	**Room/board:** $6,980
Acceptance rate: 75%	**Average debt:** $24,858
Student/faculty ratio: 9/1	**Proportion who borrowed:** 79%

UNDERGRADUATE STUDENT BODY STATS
2009-2010 enrollment: 416 full-time; 21 part-time. Men: 51%; women: 49%. **Ethnic makeup:** African American: 5%; American-Indian: 1%; Asian American: 2%; Hispanic: 7%; White: 81%; International: 3%. **Religious preference:** Roman Catholic: 8%; Protestant: 27%; No preference: 1%; Unknown: 21%; Mennonite Church USA: 43%.

ADMISSIONS FACTS AND FIGURES
Phone: (800) 522-1887. **Email:** admissions@bethelks.edu. **Website:** http://www.bethelks.edu. **Application deadlines for fall 2011:** Regular decision: Rolling. Early decision: Not offered. Early action: Not offered. Admission can be deferred. **Application fee:** $20. **To apply online, go to:** http://www.bethelks.edu/future_students/apply_now/index.php. **Admissions requirements/recommendations:** High school units required (recommended): English: 4 (4); Mathematics: 4 (4); Science: 3 (3); Foreign language: 2 (2); Social studies: 3 (3); History: 1 (1); Total units: 18 (18). Tests: The college uses SAT or ACT scores in admissions decisions. Either SAT or ACT required. For admission to the fall 2011 entering class, the school will accept: ACT with or without writing accepted. Campus visit: Recommended. Admissions interview: Required. Off-campus interview: May be arranged. **Factors that count in admissions decisions: Academic:**

Secondary school record: Considered. Class rank: Important. Letters of recommendation: Considered. Standardized test scores: Very Important. Essay: Not Considered. **Nonacademic:** Interview: Not Considered. Extracurricular activities: Important. Talent/ability: Not Considered. Character/personal qualities: Important. Alumni/ae relationship: Important. Geographical residence: Not Considered. State residency: Not Considered. Religious affiliation/commitment: Not Considered. Minority status: Not Considered. Volunteer work: Not Considered. Work experience: Not Considered. **Other schools with the greatest overlap in applicants:** Kansas State University; University of Kansas; Wichita State University. **Admissions statistics for the fall 2009 entering class:** Total applicants: 386. Total accepted: 288. Freshmen enrolled: 92; 31% were from out of state. Overall acceptance rate: 75%. **Credentials of fall 2009 freshmen:** 36% ranked in the top 10 percent of their high school class; 58% were in the top 25 percent; 86% were in the top half. (Proportion submitting class standing: 92%.) **Average high school grade point average:** 3.6. **First-year students who submitted SAT scores:** 11%. Scores (25/75 percentile): Critical Reading: 420-700, Math: 460-730, Combined: 880-1430. **First-year students submitting ACT scores:** 89%. Scores (25/75 percentile): English: 21-29, Math: 20-29, Composite: 21-29.

ACADEMICS
Year founded: 1887. **Academic calendar:** 4-1-4. **Degrees offered:** certificate, bachelor's. **Most popular majors:** 37% nursing/registered nurse training (R.N., A.S.N., B.S.N., M.S.N.), 12% business/commerce, 7% biology/biological sciences, 7% social work, 6% history. **Major fields of study:** biological and biomedical sciences; business, management, marketing, and related support services; communication, journalism, and related programs; computer and information sciences and support services; education; English language and literature/letters; foreign languages, literatures, and linguistics; health professions and related clinical sciences; history; mathematics and statistics; multi/interdisciplinary studies; parks, recreation, leisure, and fitness studies; philosophy and religious studies; physical sciences; psychology; public administration and social service professions; visual and performing arts. **Areas of required coursework:** arts/fine arts, humanities, mathematics, English (including composition), philosophy, foreign languages, sciences (biological or physical), history, social science. **Preprofessional programs:** pre-law, pre-dentistry, pre-medicine, pre-veterinary science, pre-optometry, pre-pharmacy. **Special academic programs (% participation):** cross-registration (2%), double major (8%), dual enrollment (1%), exchange student program (domestic) (0%), independent study (33%), internships (20%), liberal arts/career combination (0%), study abroad (5%), teacher certificate program (9%). **Teacher certification offered in:** special education, elementary, middle/junior high, secondary. **Faculty and instruction (2009-2010):** Total instructional faculty: 40 full-time, 20 part-time (48% men; 52% women; 7% minorities). Full-time faculty with Ph.D. or other terminal degree: 63%. Student/faculty ratio: 9/1. Classes of fewer than 20 students: 75%; of 20 to 49 students: 23%; of 50 or more students: 1%. **Advanced Placement and International Baccalaureate credit:** AP tests may be used for: Credit and/or placement. Scores accepted: 4, 5. International Baccalaureate exams may be used for: Credit and/or placement. **Freshmen returning for sophomore year:** 73%. **Graduation rates:** Four-year: 51%; five-year: 66%; six-year: 69%.

COSTS AND FINANCIAL AID
Financial aid office: (316) 284-5232. **Expenses (2010-2011):** Tuition and fees 2010-2011: $20,700; room/board: $6,980. Estimated books and supplies: $800; transportation: $850; personal expenses: $2,550. **Financial aid:** Priority filing date for institution's financial aid form: August 15. In 2009-2010, 85% of undergraduates applied for financial aid. Of those, 81% were determined to have financial need; 48% had their need fully met. Average financial aid package (proportion receiving): $21,569 (81%). Average amount of gift aid, such as scholarships or grants (proportion receiving): $5,291 (57%). Average amount of self-help aid, such as work study or loans (proportion receiving): $7,625 (60%). Average need-based loan (excluding PLUS or other private loans): $6,787. Among students who received need-based aid, the average percentage of need met: 94%. Among students who received aid based on merit, the average award (and the proportion receiving): $9,003 (19%). The average athletic scholarship (and the proportion receiving): $3,246 (43%). Average amount of debt of borrowers graduating in 2009: $24,858. Proportion who borrowed: 79%.

CAMPUS LIFE AND EXTRACURRICULAR ACTIVITIES
Campus housing available (% using): coed dorms (99%), apartments for married students, apartment for single students (1%), special housing for disabled students. Students who live in college-owned, operated, or affiliated housing: 72%. **Student employment:** During the 2009-2010 academic

year, 39% of undergraduates worked on campus. Average per-year earnings: $1,200. **Clubs and organizations:** Number of student organizations: 50. Activities include: campus ministries, choral groups, concert band, drama/theater, international student organization, jazz band, literary magazine, music ensembles, musical theater, opera, radio station, student government, student newspaper, symphony orchestra, television station, yearbook. Number of fraternities: 0; sororities: 0. Average proportion of students who stay on campus on weekends: 80%. **Sports program (2009-2010):** Member of NAIA. *Men's intercollegiate varsity sports:* basketball, cross country, football, golf, soccer, tennis, track and field (indoor), track and field (outdoor). *Women's intercollegiate varsity sports:* basketball, cross country, golf, soccer, tennis, track and field (indoor), track and field (outdoor), volleyball.

SERVICES AND FACILITIES

Basic services: nonremedial tutoring, health service, health insurance. **Remedial assistance:** reading, math, writing, study skills. **Counseling services:** minority student, career, personal, academic, psychological, religious. **For learning-disabled students:** School does not offer a structured program with separate admission and additional fees. Total undergraduates in learning-disabled program or receiving services: 6. Services include: remedial math, remedial English, remedial reading, tape recorders, untimed tests, note-taking services, oral tests, learning center, readers, extended time for tests, tutors, other. **Library:** Number of titles: 147,965; number of current serial subscriptions: 32,765. **Information technology resources:** Students are not required to lease or own a computer. Number of campus computers available to all students: 41. School has a wireless network. Approximate number of users that can be accommodated: 200. Proportion of college-owned housing units wired for high-speed internet access: 100%. **Campus safety:** Security services offered: 24-hour emergency telephones, lighted pathways/sidewalks, controlled dormitory access (key, security card, etc).

TRANSFER AND INTERNATIONAL STUDENTS

Transfer students: May apply for admission for the following academic terms: Fall, Winter, Spring, Summer. Applicants do not need a minimum number of credits to apply. For fall 2009: Transfer applications received: 94. Transfer applicants offered admission: 56. Transfer applicants enrolled: 49. **International students:** Number of foreign undergraduates: 15 (3% of student body). Number of countries represented: 13. Minimum TOEFL score required: 540 (paper); 207 (computer). Average TOEFL score: 620 (paper).

Central Christian College

- **Address:** 1200 S. Main, PO Box 1403, McPherson, KS 67460-5799
- **Website:** http://www.centralchristian.edu/
- **Private; Religious affiliation:** Free Methodist
- **Enrollment:** 328 full-time; 138 part-time

KEY STATS

✔ **U.S News College Ranking:** second tier, Regional Colleges (Midwest)
✔ **ACT Score (25th/75th percentile):** 18-24
✔ **Tuition:** 2010-2011: $18,000

Selectivity: Selective	**Room/board:** $5,900
Acceptance rate: 59%	**Average debt:** $21,500
Student/faculty ratio: 14/1	**Proportion who borrowed:** 73%

UNDERGRADUATE STUDENT BODY STATS

2009-2010 enrollment: 328 full-time; 138 part-time. Men: 51%; women: 49%. **Ethnic makeup:** African American: 14%; American-Indian: 2%; Hispanic: 4%; White: 77%; International: 2%. **Religious preference:** Roman Catholic: 4%; Protestant: 60%; No preference: 5%; Free Methodist: 11%; Other: 20%.

ADMISSIONS FACTS AND FIGURES

Phone: (800) 835-0078. **Email:** rick.wyatt@centralchristian.edu. **Website:** http://www.centralchristian.edu/. **Application deadlines for fall 2011:** Regular decision: August 1. Early decision: Not offered. Early action: Not offered. Admission can be deferred. **Application fee:** $20. **To apply online, go to:** http://www.centralchristian.edu/admapp.html. **Admissions requirements/recommendations:** High school units required (recommended): English: (4); Mathematics: (2); Science: (2); Foreign language: (0); Social studies: (2); History: (1); Academic electives: (10); Total units: (22). Tests: The college uses SAT or ACT scores in admissions decisions. Either

SAT or ACT required. For admission to the fall 2011 entering class, the school will accept: ACT with or without writing accepted. Campus visit: Recommended. Admissions interview: Neither required nor recommended. Off-campus interview: Not available. **Factors that count in admissions decisions:** *Academic:* Secondary school record: Very Important. Class rank: Considered. Letters of recommendation: Very Important. Standardized test scores: Important. Essay: Considered. *Nonacademic:* Interview: Not Considered. Extracurricular activities: Not Considered. Talent/ability: Not Considered. Character/personal qualities: Important. Alumni/ae relationship: Not Considered. Geographical residence: Not Considered. State residency: Not Considered. Religious affiliation/commitment: Considered. Minority status: Not Considered. Volunteer work: Not Considered. Work experience: Not Considered. **Other schools with the greatest overlap in applicants:** Azusa Pacific University; Greenville College; Indiana Wesleyan University; Oklahoma Wesleyan University; Spring Arbor University. **Admissions statistics for the fall 2009 entering class:** Total applicants: 694. Total accepted: 410. Freshmen enrolled: 111; 67% were from out of state. Overall acceptance rate: 59%. **Credentials of fall 2009 freshmen:** 8% ranked in the top 10 percent of their high school class; 30% were in the top 25 percent; 67% were in the top half. (Proportion submitting class standing: 87%.) **Average high school grade point average:** 3.3. **First-year students who submitted SAT scores:** 13%. Scores (25/75 percentile): Critical Reading: 370-540, Math: 390-570, Combined: 760-1110. **First-year students submitting ACT scores:** 70%. Scores (25/75 percentile): English: 17-23, Math: 17-24, Composite: 18-24.

ACADEMICS

Year founded: 1884. **Academic calendar:** 4-1-4. **Degrees offered:** associate, bachelor's. **Most popular majors:** 25% business, management, marketing, and related support services, 17% theology and religious vocations, 14% liberal arts and sciences studies, and humanities, 10% natural resources and conservation, 7% psychology. **Major fields of study:** biological and biomedical sciences; business, management, marketing, and related support services; communication, journalism, and related programs; English language and literature/letters; health professions and related clinical sciences; history; legal professions and studies; liberal arts and sciences studies, and humanities; mathematics and statistics; multi/interdisciplinary studies; parks, recreation, leisure, and fitness studies; philosophy and religious studies; physical sciences; psychology; security and protective services; social sciences; theology and religious vocations; visual and performing arts. **Areas of required coursework:** arts/fine arts, humanities, mathematics, English (including composition), philosophy, sciences (biological or physical), history, social science, other. **Pre-professional programs:** pre-law, pre-medicine, pre-theology, pre-veterinary science, other. **Special academic programs (% participation):** cooperative (work-study plan) program (39%), cross-registration (2%), double major (.01%), dual enrollment (.04%), independent study (7%), internships (8%), student-designed major (14%). **Teacher certification offered in:** elementary, middle/junior high, secondary. **Cooperative education programs:** art, business, health professions, social/behavioral science, other. **Faculty and instruction (2009-2010):** Total instructional faculty: 18 full-time, 30 part-time (58% men; 42% women; 2% minorities). Full-time faculty with Ph.D. or other terminal degree: 11%. Student/faculty ratio: 14/1. Classes of fewer than 20 students: 76%; of 20 to 49 students: 21%; of 50 or more students: 3%. **Advanced Placement and International Baccalaureate credit:** AP tests may be used for: Credit and/or placement. Scores accepted: 3, 4, 5. International Baccalaureate exams may be used for: Credit and/or placement. **Freshmen returning for sophomore year:** 62%. **Graduation rates:** Four-year: 35%; five-year: 36%; six-year: 34%. **Graduate study:** 6% of students pursue further study immediately upon graduation; 6% within one year; 6% within five years. Fields in which graduates pursue further study: Master of Business Administration (MBA), 35%; law, 5%; medicine, 5%; theology (or the seminary), 10%; education, 5%; arts and sciences, 35%; veterinary medicine, 5%.

COSTS AND FINANCIAL AID

Financial aid office: (620) 241-0723. **Expenses (2010-2011):** Tuition and fees 2010-2011: $18,000; room/board: $5,900. Estimated books and supplies: $1,200; transportation: $1,000; personal expenses: $1,000. **Financial aid:** Priority filing date for institution's financial aid form: March 1. In 2009-2010, 88% of undergraduates applied for financial aid. Of those, 81% were determined to have financial need; Average financial aid package (proportion receiving): $14,480 (81%). Average amount of gift aid, such as scholarships or grants (proportion receiving): $5,081 (54%). Average amount of self-help aid, such as work study or loans (proportion receiving): $5,102 (66%). Average need-based loan (excluding PLUS or other private loans): $5,083. Among students who received need-based aid, the average percentage of need met: 70%. Among students who received aid based on merit, the average award (and the proportion receiving): $6,110 (21%). The average athletic scholarship (and the proportion receiving): $1,788 (14%). Average amount of debt of borrowers graduating in 2009: $21,500. Proportion who borrowed: 73%.

CAMPUS LIFE AND EXTRACURRICULAR ACTIVITIES
Campus housing available (% using): coed dorms (26%), women's dorms (31%), men's dorms (37%), apartments for married students (2%), apartment for single students (4%). Students who live in college-owned, operated, or affiliated housing: 91%. **Student employment:** During the 2009-2010 academic year, 62% of undergraduates worked on campus. Average per-year earnings: $1,400. **Clubs and organizations:** Number of student organizations: 2. Activities include: campus ministries, choral groups, drama/theater, jazz band, literary magazine, music ensembles, musical theater, pep band, student government, student newspaper, yearbook. Number of fraternities: 0; sororities: 0. Average proportion of students who stay on campus on weekends: 75%. **Sports program (2009-2010):** Member of NAIA. *Men's intercollegiate varsity sports:* baseball, basketball, golf, soccer, tennis. *Women's intercollegiate varsity sports:* basketball, golf, soccer, softball, tennis, volleyball.

SERVICES AND FACILITIES
Basic services: nonremedial tutoring, health service, health insurance. **Remedial assistance:** math, writing, study skills, other. **Counseling services:** minority student, career, personal, academic, older student, psychological, religious. **For learning-disabled students:** School does not offer a structured program with separate admission and additional fees. Services include: remedial math, remedial English, other special classes, untimed tests, note-taking services, oral tests, readers, extended time for tests, tutors, priority seating. **Library:** Number of titles: 27,829; number of current serial subscriptions: 142. **Information technology resources:** Students are not required to lease or own a computer. Number of campus computers available to all students: 38. School has a wireless network. Approximate number of users that can be accommodated: 250. Proportion of college-owned housing units wired for high-speed internet access: 96%. **Campus safety:** Security services offered: 24-hour emergency telephones, lighted pathways/sidewalks, controlled dormitory access (key, security card, etc).

TRANSFER AND INTERNATIONAL STUDENTS
Transfer students: May apply for admission for the following academic terms: Fall, Winter, Spring. Applicants need a minimum number of credits to apply. For fall 2009: Transfer applications received: 97. Transfer applicants offered admission: 32. Transfer applicants enrolled: 26. **International students:** Number of foreign undergraduates: 5 (2% of student body). Number of countries represented: 4. Minimum TOEFL score required: 500 (paper); 175 (computer). Average TOEFL score: 525 (paper).

Emporia State University

- **Address:** 1200 Commercial, Emporia, KS 66801-5087
- **Website:** http://www.emporia.edu
- **Public**
- **Enrollment:** 3,734 full-time; 474 part-time

KEY STATS
- ✔ **U.S News College Ranking:** 84, Regional Universities (Midwest)
- ✔ **ACT Score (25th/75th percentile):** 19-25
- ✔ **Tuition:** 2009-2010: $4,374 in state, $13,578 out of state

Selectivity: Selective	**Room/board:** $6,146
Acceptance rate: 88%	**Average debt:** $21,158
Student/faculty ratio: 18/1	**Proportion who borrowed:** 68%

UNDERGRADUATE STUDENT BODY STATS
2009-2010 enrollment: 3,734 full-time; 474 part-time. Men: 40%; women: 60%. **Ethnic makeup:** African American: 6%; American-Indian: 1%; Asian American: 1%; Hispanic: 5%; White: 80%; International: 7%.

ADMISSIONS FACTS AND FIGURES
Phone: (620) 341-5465. **Email:** go2esu@emporia.edu. **Website:** http://www.emporia.edu. **Application deadlines for fall 2011:** Regular decision: Rolling. Early decision: Not offered. Early action: Not offered. Admission can be deferred. **Application fee:** $30. **To apply online, go to:** http://www.

applyweb.com/apply/emporia/index2.html. **Admissions requirements/recommendations:** High school units required (recommended): English: 4 (4); Mathematics: 3 (3); Science: 3 (3); Social studies: 3 (3). Tests: The college uses SAT or ACT scores in admissions decisions. Either SAT or ACT required. For admission to the fall 2011 entering class, the school will accept: ACT with or without writing accepted. Campus visit: Recommended. Admissions interview: Neither required nor recommended. Off-campus interview: Not available. **Factors that count in admissions decisions:** *Academic:* Secondary school record: Not Considered. Class rank: Very Important. Letters of recommendation: Not Considered. Standardized test scores: Very Important. Essay: Considered. *Nonacademic:* Interview: Not Considered. Extracurricular activities: Considered. Talent/ability: Important. Character/personal qualities: Not Considered. Alumni/ae relationship: Not Considered. Geographical residence: Not Considered. State residency: Not Considered. Religious affiliation/commitment: Not Considered. Minority status: Not Considered. Volunteer work: Not Considered. Work experience: Not Considered. **Other schools with the greatest overlap in applicants:** Kansas State University; Pittsburg State University; University of Kansas; Washburn University; Wichita State University. **Admissions statistics for the fall 2009 entering class:** Total applicants: 1,420. Total accepted: 1,249. Freshmen enrolled: 677; 9% were from out of state. Overall acceptance rate: 88%. **Credentials of fall 2009 freshmen:** 14% ranked in the top 10 percent of their high school class; 33% were in the top 25 percent; 66% were in the top half. (Proportion submitting class standing: 68%.) **Average high school grade point average:** 3.2. **First-year students who submitted SAT scores:** 1%. **First-year students submitting ACT scores:** 89%. Scores (25/75 percentile): English: 17-24, Math: 18-25, Composite: 19-25.

ACADEMICS
Year founded: 1863. **Academic calendar:** Semester. **Degrees offered:** bachelor's, post-bachelor's certificate, master's, post-master's certificate, doctorate. **Most popular majors:** 26% education, 18% business, management, marketing, and related support services, 10% social sciences, 8% health professions and related clinical sciences, 6% visual and performing arts. **Major fields of study:** biological and biomedical sciences; business, management, marketing, and related support services; communication, journalism, and related programs; computer and information sciences and support services; education; English language and literature/letters; foreign languages, literatures, and linguistics; health professions and related clinical sciences; history; liberal arts and sciences studies, and humanities; mathematics and statistics; multi/interdisciplinary studies; parks, recreation, leisure, and fitness studies; physical sciences; psychology; security and protective services; social sciences; visual and performing arts. **Areas of required coursework:** arts/fine arts, humanities, computer literacy, mathematics, English (including composition), sciences (biological or physical), history, social science, other. **Pre-professional programs:** pre-law, pre-dentistry, pre-medicine, pre-veterinary science, pre-optometry, pre-pharmacy, other. **Special academic programs:** distance learning, double major, dual enrollment, honors program, independent study, internships, student-designed major, study abroad, teacher certificate program. **Teacher certification offered in:** early childhood, special education, elementary, middle/junior high, secondary, bilingual/bicultural. **Faculty and instruction (2009-2010):** Total instructional faculty: 253 full-time, 25 part-time (52% men; 48% women; 9% minorities). Full-time faculty with Ph.D. or other terminal degree: 81%. Student/faculty ratio: 18/1. Classes of fewer than 20 students: 38%; of 20 to 49 students: 56%; of 50 or more students: 6%. **Advanced Placement and International Baccalaureate credit:** AP tests may be used for: Placement only. Scores accepted: 3, 4, 5. International Baccalaureate exams may be used for: Placement only. **Freshmen returning for sophomore year:** 71%. **Graduation rates:** Four-year: 22%; five-year: 36%; six-year: 44%. **Graduate study:** 52% of students pursue further study within one year.

COSTS AND FINANCIAL AID
Financial aid office: (620) 341-5457. **Expenses (2009-2010):** Tuition and fees 2009-2010: $4,374 in state, $13,578 out of state; room/board: $6,146. Estimated books and supplies: $900; transportation: $1,106; personal expenses: $2,846. **Financial aid:** Priority filing date for institution's financial aid form: March 15. In 2009-2010, 77% of undergraduates applied for financial aid. Of those, 60% were determined to have financial need; 17% had their need fully met. Average financial aid package (proportion receiving): $7,960 (60%). Average amount of gift aid, such as scholarships or grants (proportion receiving): $5,258 (50%). Average amount of self-help aid, such as work study or loans (proportion receiving): $1,938 (50%). Average need-based loan (excluding PLUS or other private loans): $5,765. Among students who received need-based aid, the average percentage of need met: 88%. Among students who received aid based on merit, the aver-

age award (and the proportion receiving): $1,335 (14%). The average athletic scholarship (and the proportion receiving): $3,393 (5%). Average amount of debt of borrowers graduating in 2009: $21,158. Proportion who borrowed: 68%.

CAMPUS LIFE AND EXTRACURRICULAR ACTIVITIES

Campus housing available (% using): coed dorms (77%), sorority housing (9%), fraternity housing (8%), apartments for married students (6%), special housing for disabled students, special housing for international students. Students who live in college-owned, operated, or affiliated housing: 21%. **Student employment:** During the 2009-2010 academic year, 23% of undergraduates worked on campus. Average per-year earnings: $2,300. **Clubs and organizations:** Number of student organizations: 129. Activities include: campus ministries, choral groups, concert band, dance, drama/theater, international student organization, jazz band, literary magazine, marching band, music ensembles, musical theater, opera, pep band, student government, student newspaper, student film society, symphony orchestra, yearbook. Number of fraternities: 6; sororities: 5. Proportion of men in fraternities: 5%; of women in sororities: 5%. **Sports program (2009-2010):** Member of NCAA II. *Men's intercollegiate varsity sports:* baseball, basketball, cross country, football, tennis, track and field (indoor), track and field (outdoor). *Women's intercollegiate varsity sports:* basketball, cross country, soccer, softball, tennis, track and field (indoor), track and field (outdoor), volleyball.

SERVICES AND FACILITIES

Basic services: nonremedial tutoring, women's center, placement service, day care, health service, health insurance. **Remedial assistance:** reading, math, writing. **Counseling services:** minority student, career, military, personal, veteran student, academic, older student, psychological, birth control, religious, other. **For learning-disabled students:** School does not offer a structured program with separate admission and additional fees. Services include: remedial math, remedial English, reading machines, remedial reading, tape recorders, diagnostic testing service, note-taking services, oral tests, readers, extended time for tests, tutors, priority registration, priority seating, texts on tape, other testing accommodations, other. **Library:** Number of titles: 2,457,985; number of current serial subscriptions: 41,417. **Information technology resources:** Students are not required to lease or own a computer. Number of campus computers available to all students: 410. School has a wireless network. Approximate number of users that can be accommodated: 130. Proportion of college-owned housing units wired for high-speed internet access: 100%. **Campus safety:** Security services offered: 24-hour foot-and-vehicle patrols, late-night transport/escort service, 24-hour emergency telephones, lighted pathways/sidewalks, student patrols, controlled dormitory access (key, security card, etc).

TRANSFER AND INTERNATIONAL STUDENTS

Transfer students: May apply for admission for the following academic terms: Fall, Spring, Summer. Applicants need a minimum number of credits to apply. For fall 2009: Transfer applications received: 737. Transfer applicants offered admission: 567. Transfer applicants enrolled: 479. **International students:** Number of foreign undergraduates: 277 (7% of student body). Number of countries represented: 40. Minimum TOEFL score required: 520 (paper); 68 (computer). Average TOEFL score: 542 (paper).

Fort Hays State University

- **Address:** 600 Park Street, Hays, KS 67601-4099
- **Website:** http://www.fhsu.edu
- **Public**
- **Enrollment:** N/A

KEY STATS

✔ **U.S News College Ranking:** second tier, Regional Universities (Midwest)
✔ **ACT Score (25th/75th percentile):** 18-24
✔ **Tuition:** 2009-2010: $2,946 in state, $11,099 out of state
  Selectivity: Less selective   **Room/board:** $6,560
  Acceptance rate: 93%   **Average debt:** N/A
  Student/faculty ratio: N/A   **Proportion who borrowed:** N/A

Friends University

- **Address:** 2100 W. University Street, Wichita, KS 67213
- **Website:** http://www.friends.edu
- **Private**
- **Enrollment:** N/A

KEY STATS

✔ **U.S News College Ranking:** second tier, Regional Universities (Midwest)
✔ **SAT or ACT Score (25th/75th percentile):** N/A
✔ **Tuition:** 2009-2010: $19,230
  Selectivity: Selective   **Room/board:** $5,670
  Acceptance rate: N/A   **Average debt:** N/A
  Student/faculty ratio: N/A   **Proportion who borrowed:** N/A

Kansas State University

- **Address:** Anderson Hall, Manhattan, KS 66506
- **Website:** http://www.k-state.edu
- **Public**
- **Enrollment:** 16,510 full-time; 2,268 part-time

KEY STATS

✔ **U.S News College Ranking:** 132, National Universities
✔ **ACT Score:** 24
✔ **Tuition:** 2010-2011: $7,376 in state, $18,404 out of state
  Selectivity: More selective   **Room/board:** $6,954
  Acceptance rate: 55%   **Average debt:** $20,700
  Student/faculty ratio: 20/1   **Proportion who borrowed:** 62%

UNDERGRADUATE STUDENT BODY STATS

2009-2010 enrollment: 16,510 full-time; 2,268 part-time. Men: 52%; women: 48%. **Ethnic makeup:** African American: 4%; American-Indian: 1%; Asian American: 1%; Hispanic: 4%; White: 86%; International: 5%.

ADMISSIONS FACTS AND FIGURES

Phone: (785) 532-6250. **Email:** k-state@k-state.edu. **Website:** http://www.k-state.edu. **Application deadlines for fall 2011:** Regular decision: Rolling. Early decision: Not offered. Early action: Not offered. Admission cannot be deferred. **Application fee:** $30. **To apply online, go to:** http://www.k-state.edu/admit/apply/apply.html. **Admissions requirements/recommendations:** High school units required (recommended): English: 4 (4); Mathematics: 3 (3); Science: 3 (3); Social studies: 3 (2); History: 2 (2); Total units: 14 (14). Tests: The college uses SAT or ACT scores in admissions decisions. Neither SAT nor ACT required. For admission to the fall 2011 entering class, the school will accept: ACT with or without writing accepted. Campus visit: Recommended. Admissions interview: Neither required nor recommended. Off-campus interview: Not available. **Factors that count in admissions decisions:** *Academic:* Secondary school record: Very Important. Class rank: Very Important. Letters of recommendation: Considered. Standardized test scores: Very Important. Essay: Not Considered. *Nonacademic:* Interview: Not Considered. Extracurricular activities: Not Considered. Talent/ability: Not Considered. Character/personal qualities: Not Considered. Alumni/ae relationship: Not Considered. Geographical residence: Not Considered. State residency: Not Considered. Religious affiliation/commitment: Not Considered. Minority status: Not Considered. Volunteer work: Not Considered. Work experience: Not Considered. **Admissions statistics for the fall 2009 entering class:** Total applicants: 10,003. Total accepted: 5,550. Freshmen enrolled: 3,522; 18% were from out of state. Overall acceptance rate: 55%. **Credentials of fall 2009 freshmen:** 22% ranked in the top 10 percent of their high school class; 49% were in the top 25 percent; 79% were in the top half. (Proportion submitting class standing: 39%.) **Average high school grade point average:** 3.4. **First-year students submitting ACT scores:** 85%. Scores (25/75 percentile): English: N/A, Math: N/A, Composite: N/A.

ACADEMICS

Year founded: 1863. **Academic calendar:** Semester. **Degrees offered:** certificate, associate, bachelor's, post-bachelor's certificate, master's, doctorate. **Most popular majors:** 17% business, management, marketing, and related support services, 12% social sciences, 11% agriculture, agriculture operations, and related sciences, 10% education, 9% engineering. **Major fields of**

study: agriculture, agriculture operations, and related sciences; architecture and related services; area, ethnic, cultural, and gender studies; biological and biomedical sciences; business, management, marketing, and related support services; communication, journalism, and related programs; computer and information sciences and support services; education; engineering; engineering technologies/technicians; English language and literature/letters; family and consumer sciences/human sciences; foreign languages, literatures, and linguistics; health professions and related clinical sciences; history; liberal arts and sciences studies, and humanities; mathematics and statistics; mechanic and repair technologies/technicians; multi/interdisciplinary studies; parks, recreation, leisure, and fitness studies; philosophy and religious studies; physical sciences; psychology; public administration and social service professions; social sciences; transportation and materials moving; visual and performing arts. **Areas of required coursework:** humanities, computer literacy, mathematics, English (including composition), sciences (biological or physical), history, social science. **Pre-professional programs:** pre-law, pre-dentistry, pre-medicine, pre-veterinary science, pre-optometry, pre-pharmacy, other. **Special academic programs:** accelerated program, cooperative (work-study plan) program, distance learning, double major, English as a Second Language (ESL), exchange student program (domestic), honors program, independent study, internships, study abroad, teacher certificate program, other. **Teacher certification offered in:** early childhood, special education, elementary, middle/junior high, secondary. **Cooperative education programs:** engineering. **Reserve Officers Training Corps (ROTC):** Army ROTC: Offered on campus; Air Force ROTC: Offered on campus. **Faculty and instruction (2009-2010):** Total instructional faculty: 973 full-time, 138 part-time (61% men; 39% women; 16% minorities). Full-time faculty with Ph.D. or other terminal degree: 81%. Student/faculty ratio: 20/1. Classes of fewer than 20 students: 52%; of 20 to 49 students: 38%; of 50 or more students: 10%. **Advanced Placement and International Baccalaureate credit:** AP tests may be used for: Credit only. Scores accepted: 3, 4, 5. International Baccalaureate exams may be used for: Credit only. **Freshmen returning for sophomore year:** 79%. **Graduation rates:** Four-year: 26%; five-year: 53%; six-year: 59%. **Graduate study:** 21% of students pursue further study within one year.

COSTS AND FINANCIAL AID
Financial aid office: (785) 532-6420. **Expenses (2010-2011):** Tuition and fees 2010-2011: $7,376 in state, $18,404 out of state; room/board: $6,954. Estimated books and supplies: $1,100; transportation: $500; personal expenses: $2,900. **Financial aid:** Priority filing date for institution's financial aid form: March 1. In 2009-2010, 69% of undergraduates applied for financial aid. Of those, 51% were determined to have financial need; 18% had their need fully met. Average financial aid package (proportion receiving): $10,655 (50%). Average amount of gift aid, such as scholarships or grants (proportion receiving): $4,188 (31%). Average amount of self-help aid, such as work study or loans (proportion receiving): $4,506 (44%). Average need-based loan (excluding PLUS or other private loans): $4,264. Among students who received need-based aid, the average percentage of need met: 84%. Among students who received aid based on merit, the average award (and the proportion receiving): $3,024 (16%). The average athletic scholarship (and the proportion receiving): $11,404 (1%). Average amount of debt of borrowers graduating in 2009: $20,700. Proportion who borrowed: 62%.

CAMPUS LIFE AND EXTRACURRICULAR ACTIVITIES
Campus housing available (% using): coed dorms (34%), women's dorms (17%), men's dorms (10%), sorority housing (12%), fraternity housing (18%), apartments for married students (7%), apartment for single students (1%), cooperative housing (1%). Students who live in college-owned, operated, or affiliated housing: 31%. **Student employment:** During the 2009-2010 academic year, 31% of undergraduates worked on campus. Average per-year earnings: $4,467. **Clubs and organizations:** Number of student organizations: 418. Activities include: choral groups, concert band, dance, drama/theater, international student organization, jazz band, marching band, music ensembles, musical theater, pep band, radio station, student government, student newspaper, symphony orchestra, television station, yearbook. Number of fraternities: 28; sororities: 13. Proportion of men in fraternities: 14%; of women in sororities: 14%. Average proportion of students who stay on campus on weekends: 65%. **Sports program (2009-2010):** Member of NCAA I. *Men's intercollegiate varsity sports:* baseball, basketball, cross country, football, golf, track and field (indoor), track and field (outdoor). *Women's intercollegiate varsity sports:* basketball, crew (heavyweight), cross country, equestrian, golf, crew (lightweight), tennis, track and field (indoor), track and field (outdoor), volleyball.

SERVICES AND FACILITIES
Basic services: nonremedial tutoring, women's center, placement service, day care, health service, health insurance. **Remedial assistance:** reading, math, study skills, other. **Counseling services:** minority student, career, personal, veteran student, academic, psychological. **For learning-disabled students:** School does not offer a structured program with separate admission and additional fees. Services include: remedial math, reading machines, note-taking services, oral tests, readers, extended time for tests, tutors, priority registration, texts on tape, other testing accommodations. **Library:** Number of titles: 2,352,744; number of current serial subscriptions: 19,202. **Information technology resources:** Students are not required to lease or own a computer. Number of campus computers available to all students: 489. School has a wireless network. Approximate number of users that can be accommodated: 3,750. Proportion of college-owned housing units wired for high-speed internet access: 100%. **Campus safety:** Security services offered: 24-hour foot-and-vehicle patrols, late-night transport/escort service, 24-hour emergency telephones, lighted pathways/sidewalks, controlled dormitory access (key, security card, etc).

TRANSFER AND INTERNATIONAL STUDENTS
Transfer students: May apply for admission for the following academic terms: Fall, Spring, Summer. Applicants do not need a minimum number of credits to apply. For fall 2009: Transfer applications received: 2,466. Transfer applicants offered admission: 1,834. Transfer applicants enrolled: 1,312. **International students:** Number of foreign undergraduates: 827 (5% of student body). Number of countries represented: 59.

Kansas Wesleyan University

- **Address:** 100 E. Claflin, Salina, KS 67401
- **Website:** http://www.kwu.edu
- **Private; Religious affiliation:** United Methodist
- **Enrollment:** N/A

KEY STATS
✔ **U.S News College Ranking:** 58, Regional Colleges (Midwest)
✔ **ACT Score:** 22
✔ **Tuition:** 2009-2010: $19,200

Selectivity: Selective	**Room/board:** $6,600
Acceptance rate: 63%	**Average debt:** N/A
Student/faculty ratio: N/A	**Proportion who borrowed:** N/A

McPherson College

- **Address:** PO Box 1402, McPherson, KS 67460
- **Website:** http://www.mcpherson.edu
- **Private; Religious affiliation:** Church of the Brethren
- **Enrollment:** 542 full-time; 87 part-time

KEY STATS
✔ **U.S News College Ranking:** second tier, National Liberal Arts Colleges
✔ **ACT Score (25th/75th percentile):** 19-24
✔ **Tuition:** 2010-2011: $19,625

Selectivity: Selective	**Room/board:** $7,325
Acceptance rate: 87%	**Average debt:** $25,865
Student/faculty ratio: 15/1	**Proportion who borrowed:** 85%

UNDERGRADUATE STUDENT BODY STATS
2009-2010 enrollment: 542 full-time; 87 part-time. Men: 56%; women: 44%. **Ethnic makeup:** African American: 10%; American-Indian: 3%; Asian American: 2%; Hispanic: 7%; White: 77%; International: 1%. **Religious preference:** Roman Catholic: 13%; Protestant: 1%; No preference: 33%; Unknown: 6%; Church of the Brethren: 8%; Baptist: 7%; Other: 32%.

ADMISSIONS FACTS AND FIGURES
Phone: (800) 365-7402. **Email:** admiss@mcpherson.edu. **Website:** http://www.mcpherson.edu. **Application deadlines for fall 2011:** Regular decision: Rolling. Early decision: Not offered. Early action: Not offered. Admission can be deferred. **Application fee:** $25. **To apply online, go to:** http://www.mcpherson.edu/directory/forms.asp. **Admissions requirements/recom-**

mendations: Tests: The college uses SAT or ACT scores in admissions decisions. Either SAT or ACT required. For admission to the fall 2011 entering class, the school will accept: ACT with or without writing accepted. Campus visit: Recommended. Admissions interview: Neither required nor recommended. Off-campus interview: Not available. **Factors that count in admissions decisions:** *Academic:* Secondary school record: Very Important. Class rank: Considered. Letters of recommendation: Considered. Standardized test scores: Very Important. Essay: Not Considered. *Nonacademic:* Interview: Considered. Extracurricular activities: Considered. Talent/ability: Considered. Character/personal qualities: Considered. Alumni/ae relationship: Not Considered. Geographical residence: Not Considered. State residency: Not Considered. Religious affiliation/commitment: Not Considered. Minority status: Not Considered. Volunteer work: Considered. Work experience: Considered. **Other schools with the greatest overlap in applicants:** Bethany College; Bethel College; Kansas Wesleyan University; Sterling College; Tabor College. **Admissions statistics for the fall 2009 entering class:** Total applicants: 474. Total accepted: 411. Freshmen enrolled: 137; 10% were from out of state. Overall acceptance rate: 87%. **Credentials of fall 2009 freshmen:** 9% ranked in the top 10 percent of their high school class; 25% were in the top 25 percent; 60% were in the top half. (Proportion submitting class standing: 63%.) **Average high school grade point average:** 3.2. **First-year students who submitted SAT scores:** 15%. Scores (25/75 percentile): Critical Reading: 448-560, Math: 450-563, Combined: 898-1123. **First-year students submitting ACT scores:** 85%. Scores (25/75 percentile): English: 18-24, Math: 18-23, Composite: 19-24.

ACADEMICS

Year founded: 1887. **Academic calendar:** 4-1-4. **Degrees offered:** bachelor's. **Most popular majors:** 27% business, management, marketing, and related support services, 21% engineering technologies/technicians, 9% visual and performing arts, 8% parks, recreation, leisure, and fitness studies, 7% biological and biomedical sciences. **Major fields of study:** agriculture, agriculture operations, and related sciences; biological and biomedical sciences; business, management, marketing, and related support services; communication, journalism, and related programs; computer and information sciences and support services; education; engineering technologies/technicians; English language and literature/letters; foreign languages, literatures, and linguistics; history; mathematics and statistics; multi/interdisciplinary studies; parks, recreation, leisure, and fitness studies; philosophy and religious studies; physical sciences; psychology; social sciences; visual and performing arts. **Areas of required coursework:** arts/fine arts, humanities, computer literacy, mathematics, English (including composition), philosophy, sciences (biological or physical), history, social science, other. **Preprofessional programs:** pre-law, pre-dentistry, pre-medicine, pre-veterinary science, pre-optometry, pre-pharmacy, other. **Special academic programs (% participation):** cross-registration (16%), double major (10%), dual enrollment (0%), exchange student program (domestic) (3%), independent study (7%), internships (47%), student-designed major (0%), study abroad (7%), teacher certificate program (14%). **Teacher certification offered in:** special education, elementary, middle/junior high, secondary. **Cooperative education programs:** art, business, education, health professions, humanities, natural science, social/behavioral science, technologies, other. **Faculty and instruction (2009-2010):** Total instructional faculty: 34 full-time, 20 part-time (63% men; 37% women; 11% minorities). Full-time faculty with Ph.D. or other terminal degree: 82%. Student/faculty ratio: 15/1. Classes of fewer than 20 students: 69%; of 20 to 49 students: 30%; of 50 or more students: 1%. **Advanced Placement and International Baccalaureate credit:** AP tests may be used for: Credit only. Scores accepted: 3, 4, 5. International Baccalaureate exams may be used for: Placement only. **Freshmen returning for sophomore year:** 67%. **Graduation rates:** Four-year: 36%; five-year: 47%; six-year: 48%. **Graduate study:** 10% of students pursue further study immediately upon graduation.

COSTS AND FINANCIAL AID

Financial aid office: (620) 241-0731. **Expenses (2010-2011):** Tuition and fees 2010-2011: $19,625; room/board: $7,325. Estimated books and supplies: $1,290; transportation: $1,090; personal expenses: $1,900. **Financial aid:** Priority filing date for institution's financial aid form: March 1. In 2009-2010, 92% of undergraduates applied for financial aid. Of those, 85% were determined to have financial need; 33% had their need fully met. Average financial aid package (proportion receiving): $20,033 (85%). Average amount of gift aid, such as scholarships or grants (proportion receiving): $6,422 (73%). Average amount of self-help aid, such as work study or loans (proportion receiving): $5,501 (74%). Average need-based loan (excluding PLUS or other private loans): $5,184. Among students who received need-based aid, the average percentage of need met: 88%. Among students who received aid based on merit, the average award (and the proportion receiving): $9,344 (14%). The average athletic scholarship (and the proportion receiving): $2,915 (39%). Average amount of debt of borrowers graduating in 2009: $25,865. Proportion who borrowed: 85%.

CAMPUS LIFE AND EXTRACURRICULAR ACTIVITIES

Campus housing available (% using): coed dorms (42%), women's dorms (12%), men's dorms (46%), special housing for disabled students (0%). Students who live in college-owned, operated, or affiliated housing: 74%. **Student employment:** During the 2009-2010 academic year, 25% of undergraduates worked on campus. Average per-year earnings: $1,000. **Clubs and organizations:** Number of student organizations: 19. Activities include: choral groups, dance, drama/theater, jazz band, music ensembles, musical theater, student government, student newspaper, yearbook. Number of fraternities: 0; sororities: 0. Average proportion of students who stay on campus on weekends: 60%. **Sports program (2009-2010):** Member of NAIA. *Men's intercollegiate varsity sports:* basketball, cross country, football, soccer, tennis, track and field (indoor), track and field (outdoor). *Women's intercollegiate varsity sports:* basketball, cross country, soccer, softball, tennis, track and field (indoor), track and field (outdoor), volleyball.

SERVICES AND FACILITIES

Basic services: nonremedial tutoring, other. **Remedial assistance:** reading, math, writing, study skills. **Counseling services:** minority student, career, personal, academic, religious. **For learning-disabled students:** School does not offer a structured program with separate admission and additional fees. Services include: remedial math, reading machines, remedial reading, tape recorders, other special classes, untimed tests, note-taking services, oral tests, learning center, readers, extended time for tests, tutors, priority registration, priority seating, texts on tape, other testing accommodations. **Library:** Number of titles: 96,886; number of current serial subscriptions: 319. **Information technology resources:** Students are not required to lease or own a computer. Number of campus computers available to all students: 115. School has a wireless network. Proportion of college-owned housing units wired for high-speed internet access: 100%. **Campus safety:** Security services offered: lighted pathways/sidewalks, controlled dormitory access (key, security card, etc).

TRANSFER AND INTERNATIONAL STUDENTS

Transfer students: May apply for admission for the following academic terms: Fall, Winter, Spring. Applicants need a minimum number of credits to apply. For fall 2009: Transfer applications received: 100. Transfer applicants offered admission: 92. Transfer applicants enrolled: 53. **International students:** Number of foreign undergraduates: 7 (1% of student body). Number of countries represented: 1. Minimum TOEFL score required: 550 (paper); 213 (computer).

MidAmerica Nazarene University

- **Address:** 2030 E. College Way, Olathe, KS 66062
- **Website:** http://www.mnu.edu
- **Private; Religious affiliation:** Nazarene
- **Enrollment:** 1,045 full-time; 290 part-time

KEY STATS
✔ **U.S News College Ranking:** second tier, Regional Universities (Midwest)
✔ **ACT Score (25th/75th percentile):** 20-25
✔ **Tuition:** 2009-2010: $19,146

Selectivity: Selective	**Room/board:** $6,452
Acceptance rate: 74%	**Average debt:** N/A
Student/faculty ratio: 12/1	**Proportion who borrowed:** N/A

UNDERGRADUATE STUDENT BODY STATS
2009-2010 enrollment: 1,045 full-time; 290 part-time. Men: 42%; women: 58%. **Ethnic makeup:** African American: 11%; Asian American: 1%; Hispanic: 4%; White: 83%. **Religious preference:** Roman Catholic: 6%; Protestant: 38%; No preference: 7%; Nazarene: 49%.

ADMISSIONS FACTS AND FIGURES
Phone: (913) 971-3380. **Email:** admissions@mnu.edu. **Website:** http://www.mnu.edu. **Application deadlines for fall 2011:** Regular decision: August 1. Early decision: Not offered. Early action: Not offered. Admission can be deferred. **Application fee:** $25. **To apply online, go to:** http://www.mnu.edu/

admissions/online_app.pl. **Admissions requirements/recommendations:** High school units required (recommended): English: (4); Mathematics: (3); Science: (3); Foreign language: (1); Social studies: (3); Total units: (15). Tests: The college uses SAT or ACT scores in admissions decisions. Either SAT or ACT required. For admission to the fall 2011 entering class, the school will accept: ACT with or without writing accepted. Campus visit: Recommended. Admissions interview: Neither required nor recommended. Off-campus interview: May be arranged. **Factors that count in admissions decisions:** *Academic:* Secondary school record: Considered. Class rank: Important. Letters of recommendation: Important. Standardized test scores: Very Important. Essay: Not Considered. *Nonacademic:* Interview: Not Considered. Extracurricular activities: Considered. Talent/ability: Considered. Character/personal qualities: Important. Alumni/ae relationship: Considered. Geographical residence: Not Considered. State residency: Not Considered. Religious affiliation/commitment: Important. Minority status: Not Considered. Volunteer work: Considered. Work experience: Not Considered. **Other schools with the greatest overlap in applicants:** Kansas State University; Olivet Nazarene University; Southern Nazarene University; University of Kansas. **Admissions statistics for the fall 2009 entering class:** Total applicants: 476. Total accepted: 354. Freshmen enrolled: 196; 57% were from out of state. Overall acceptance rate: 74%. **Credentials of fall 2009 freshmen:** 23% ranked in the top 10 percent of their high school class; 41% were in the top 25 percent; 75% were in the top half. (Proportion submitting class standing: 84%.) **Average high school grade point average:** 3.4. **First-year students who submitted SAT scores:** 12%. Scores (25/75 percentile): Critical Reading: 440-590, Math: 470-580, Combined: 910-1170. **First-year students submitting ACT scores:** 95%. Scores (25/75 percentile): English: 19-27, Math: 19-26, Composite: 20-25.

ACADEMICS

Year founded: 1966. **Academic calendar:** Semester. **Degrees offered:** associate, bachelor's, master's, post-master's certificate. **Most popular majors:** 53% business, management, marketing, and related support services, 17% health professions and related clinical sciences, 8% education, 5% psychology, 4% security and protective services. **Major fields of study:** biological and biomedical sciences; business, management, marketing, and related support services; communication, journalism, and related programs; computer and information sciences and support services; education; English language and literature/letters; health professions and related clinical sciences; history; mathematics and statistics; philosophy and religious studies; physical sciences; psychology; social sciences; theology and religious vocations; visual and performing arts. **Areas of required coursework:** arts/fine arts, humanities, computer literacy, mathematics, English (including composition), philosophy, foreign languages, sciences (biological or physical), history, social science, other. **Pre-professional programs:** pre-law, pre-dentistry, pre-medicine, pre-theology, pre-veterinary science, pre-pharmacy. **Special academic programs:** accelerated program, cross-registration, distance learning, double major, dual enrollment, exchange student program (domestic), independent study, internships, student-designed major, study abroad, teacher certificate program, weekend college. **Teacher certification offered in:** elementary, middle/junior high, secondary. **Reserve Officers Training Corps (ROTC):** Army ROTC: Offered on campus; Air Force ROTC: Offered at cooperating institution (University of Kansas). **Faculty and instruction (2009-2010):** Total instructional faculty: 75 full-time, 123 part-time (54% men; 46% women; 1% minorities). Full-time faculty with Ph.D. or other terminal degree: 45%. Student/faculty ratio: 12/1. Classes of fewer than 20 students: 68%; of 20 to 49 students: 28%; of 50 or more students: 4%. **Advanced Placement and International Baccalaureate credit:** AP tests may be used for: Credit only. Scores accepted: 3, 4, 5. International Baccalaureate exams may be used for: Credit only. **Freshmen returning for sophomore year:** 71%. **Graduation rates:** Four-year: 40%; five-year: 57%; six-year: 54%. **Graduate study:** 11% of students pursue further study immediately upon graduation.

COSTS AND FINANCIAL AID

Financial aid office: (913) 791-3298. **Expenses (2009-2010):** Tuition and fees 2009-2010: $19,146; room/board: $6,452. Estimated books and supplies: $1,180; transportation: $1,212; personal expenses: $1,176. **Financial aid:** Priority filing date for institution's financial aid form: March 1.

CAMPUS LIFE AND EXTRACURRICULAR ACTIVITIES

Campus housing available: women's dorms, men's dorms. Students who live in college-owned, operated, or affiliated housing: 55%. **Student employment:** During the 2009-2010 academic year, 34% of undergraduates worked on campus. Average per-year earnings: $1,086. **Clubs and organizations:** Number of student organizations: 26. Activities include: campus ministries, choral groups, concert band, drama/theater, international student organiza-

tion, jazz band, literary magazine, music ensembles, musical theater, pep band, radio station, student government, student newspaper, television station, yearbook. Number of fraternities: 0; sororities: 0. Average proportion of students who stay on campus on weekends: 40%. **Sports program (2009-2010):** Member of NAIA. *Men's intercollegiate varsity sports:* baseball, basketball, football, soccer. *Women's intercollegiate varsity sports:* basketball, soccer, softball, volleyball.

SERVICES AND FACILITIES

Basic services: nonremedial tutoring. **Remedial assistance:** reading, math, writing, study skills. **Counseling services:** personal, psychological. **For learning-disabled students:** School does not offer a structured program with separate admission and additional fees. Services include: remedial math, remedial English, remedial reading, tape recorders, videotaped classes, diagnostic testing service, untimed tests, note-taking services, oral tests, learning center, readers, extended time for tests, tutors, priority seating, texts on tape, other testing accommodations. **Library:** Number of titles: 133,140; number of current serial subscriptions: 1,260. **Information technology resources:** Students are not required to lease or own a computer. Number of campus computers available to all students: 115. School has a wireless network. Approximate number of users that can be accommodated: 4,500. Proportion of college-owned housing units wired for high-speed internet access: 100%. **Campus safety:** Security services offered: 24-hour foot-and-vehicle patrols, late-night transport/escort service, 24-hour emergency telephones, lighted pathways/sidewalks, student patrols, controlled dormitory access (key, security card, etc).

TRANSFER AND INTERNATIONAL STUDENTS

Transfer students: May apply for admission for the following academic terms: Fall, Winter, Spring, Summer. Applicants need a minimum number of credits to apply. For fall 2009: Transfer applications received: 298. Transfer applicants offered admission: 181. Transfer applicants enrolled: 141. **International students:** Number of foreign undergraduates: 6. Minimum TOEFL score required: 550 (paper); 214 (computer).

Newman University

- **Address:** 3100 McCormick Avenue, Wichita, KS 67213
- **Website:** http://www.newmanu.edu
- **Private; Religious affiliation:** Roman Catholic
- **Enrollment:** 997 full-time; 871 part-time

KEY STATS

✔ **U.S News College Ranking:** second tier, Regional Universities (Midwest)
✔ **ACT Score (25th/75th percentile):** 19-27
✔ **Tuition:** 2010-2011: $19,872

Selectivity: More selective	**Room/board:** $6,938
Acceptance rate: 42%	**Average debt:** $23,996
Student/faculty ratio: 14/1	**Proportion who borrowed:** 77%

UNDERGRADUATE STUDENT BODY STATS

2009-2010 enrollment: 997 full-time; 871 part-time. Men: 34%; women: 66%. **Ethnic makeup:** African American: 6%; American-Indian: 2%; Asian American: 4%; Hispanic: 10%; White: 73%; International: 5%.

ADMISSIONS FACTS AND FIGURES

Phone: (877) 639-6268. **Email:** admissions@newmanu.edu. **Website:** http://www.newmanu.edu. **Application deadlines for fall 2011:** Regular decision: Rolling. Early decision: Not offered. Early action: Not offered. Admission can be deferred. **Application fee:** $20. **To apply online, go to:** https://www.discovernewman.org/secure/9509/preview_app.asp?wcc=nu1. **Admissions requirements/recommendations:** High school units required (recommended): English: (4); Mathematics: (3); Science: (3); Social studies: (3). Tests: The college uses SAT or ACT scores in admissions decisions. Either SAT or ACT required. For admission to the fall 2011 entering class, the school will accept: ACT with or without writing accepted. Campus visit: Recommended. Admissions interview: Neither required nor recommended. Off-campus interview: May be arranged. **Factors that count in admissions decisions:** *Academic:* Secondary school record: Very Important. Class rank: Not Considered. Letters of recommendation: Considered. Standardized test scores: Very Important. Essay: Not Considered. *Nonacademic:* Interview: Not Considered. Extracurricular activities: Not Considered. Talent/ability: Not Considered. Character/personal qualities: Considered. Alumni/

ae relationship: Not Considered. Geographical residence: Not Considered. State residency: Not Considered. Religious affiliation/commitment: Not Considered. Minority status: Not Considered. Volunteer work: Not Considered. Work experience: Not Considered. **Other schools with the greatest overlap in applicants:** Friends University; Kansas State University; University of Kansas; Wichita State University. **Admissions statistics for the fall 2009 entering class:** Total applicants: 2,193. Total accepted: 913. Freshmen enrolled: 176; 25% were from out of state. Overall acceptance rate: 42%. **Credentials of fall 2009 freshmen:** 27% ranked in the top 10 percent of their high school class; 52% were in the top 25 percent; 78% were in the top half. (Proportion submitting class standing: 78%.) **Average high school grade point average:** 3.4. **First-year students who submitted SAT scores:** 20%. Scores (25/75 percentile): Critical Reading: 430-530, Math: 420-570, Combined: 850-1100. **First-year students submitting ACT scores:** 89%. Scores (25/75 percentile): English: N/A, Math: N/A, Composite: 19-27.

ACADEMICS

Year founded: 1933. **Academic calendar:** Semester. **Degrees offered:** associate, bachelor's, master's. **Most popular majors:** 24% elementary education and teaching, 23% nursing/registered nurse training (R.N., A.S.N., B.S.N., M.S.N.), 14% business administration and management, 10% biology/biological sciences, 6% psychology. **Major fields of study:** biological and biomedical sciences; business, management, marketing, and related support services; communication, journalism, and related programs; education; health professions and related clinical sciences; history; liberal arts and sciences studies, and humanities; mathematics and statistics; philosophy and religious studies; psychology; social sciences; theology and religious vocations; visual and performing arts. **Areas of required coursework:** humanities, mathematics, English (including composition), philosophy, foreign languages, sciences (biological or physical), history, social science. **Pre-professional programs:** pre-law, pre-dentistry, pre-medicine, pre-theology, pre-veterinary science, pre-optometry, pre-pharmacy, other. **Special academic programs:** accelerated program, cooperative (work-study plan) program, cross-registration, distance learning, double major, dual enrollment, honors program, independent study, internships, student-designed major, study abroad, teacher certificate program. **Teacher certification offered in:** elementary, middle/junior high, secondary, bilingual/bicultural. **Cooperative education programs:** art, business, computer science, education, social/behavioral science. **Faculty and instruction (2009-2010):** Total instructional faculty: 77 full-time, 106 part-time (37% men; 63% women; 5% minorities). Full-time faculty with Ph.D. or other terminal degree: 52%. Student/faculty ratio: 14/1. Classes of fewer than 20 students: 65%; of 20 to 49 students: 34%; of 50 or more students: 1%. **Advanced Placement and International Baccalaureate credit:** AP tests may be used for: Credit and/or placement. Scores accepted: 3, 4, 5. International Baccalaureate exams may be used for: Credit and/or placement. **Freshmen returning for sophomore year:** 64%. **Graduation rates:** Four-year: 29%; five-year: 42%; six-year: 43%. **Graduate study:** Fields in which graduates pursue further study: Master of Business Administration (MBA), 4%; medicine, 2%; theology (or the seminary), 1%; education, 1%; arts and sciences, 1%.

COSTS AND FINANCIAL AID

Financial aid office: (316) 942-4291. **Expenses (2010-2011):** Tuition and fees 2010-2011: $19,872; room/board: $6,938. Estimated books and supplies: $1,017. **Financial aid:** Priority filing date for institution's financial aid form: March 1. In 2009-2010, 99% of undergraduates applied for financial aid. Of those, 81% were determined to have financial need; 17% had their need fully met. Average financial aid package (proportion receiving): $14,402 (81%). Average amount of gift aid, such as scholarships or grants (proportion receiving): $4,872 (67%). Average amount of self-help aid, such as work study or loans (proportion receiving): $4,007 (65%). Average need-based loan (excluding PLUS or other private loans): $4,056. Among students who received need-based aid, the average percentage of need met: 62%. Among students who received aid based on merit, the average award (and the proportion receiving): $5,673 (4%). The average athletic scholarship (and the proportion receiving): $5,279 (22%). Average amount of debt of borrowers graduating in 2009: $23,996. Proportion who borrowed: 77%.

CAMPUS LIFE AND EXTRACURRICULAR ACTIVITIES

Campus housing available (% using): apartments for married students (3%), apartment for single students (90%). Students who live in college-owned, operated, or affiliated housing: 24%. **Student employment:** During the 2009-2010 academic year, 9% of undergraduates worked on campus. Average per-year earnings: $4,720. **Clubs and organizations:** Number of student organizations: 29. Activities include: campus ministries, choral groups, dance, drama/theater, international student organization, literary magazine, pep band, student government, student newspaper. Number of fraternities: 0; sororities: 0. Average proportion of students who stay on campus on weekends: 35%. **Sports program (2009-2010):** Member of NCAA II. **Men's intercollegiate varsity sports:** baseball, basketball, cross country, golf, soccer, tennis, wrestling. **Women's intercollegiate varsity sports:** basketball, bowling, cross country, golf, soccer, softball, tennis, volleyball.

SERVICES AND FACILITIES

Basic services: nonremedial tutoring, placement service, day care, health insurance. **Remedial assistance:** reading; math, writing, study skills. **Counseling services:** career, personal, academic, older student, psychological, religious. **For learning-disabled students:** School does not offer a structured program with separate admission and additional fees. Services include: remedial math, remedial English, reading machines, remedial reading, tape recorders, untimed tests, note-taking services, oral tests, learning center, readers, extended time for tests, tutors, priority seating, texts on tape, other. **Library:** Number of titles: 107,057; number of current serial subscriptions: 327. **Information technology resources:** Students are not required to lease or own a computer. Number of campus computers available to all students: 130. School has a wireless network. Approximate number of users that can be accommodated: 300. Proportion of college-owned housing units wired for high-speed internet access: 100%. **Campus safety:** Security services offered: 24-hour foot-and-vehicle patrols, late-night transport/escort service, 24-hour emergency telephones, lighted pathways/sidewalks, student patrols, controlled dormitory access (key, security card, etc).

TRANSFER AND INTERNATIONAL STUDENTS

Transfer students: May apply for admission for the following academic terms: Fall, Spring, Summer. Applicants need a minimum number of credits to apply. For fall 2009: Transfer applications received: 814. Transfer applicants offered admission: 399. Transfer applicants enrolled: 209. **International students:** Number of foreign undergraduates: 53 (5% of student body). Minimum TOEFL score required: 530 (paper); 197 (computer).

Ottawa University

■ **Address:** 1001 S. Cedar Street, Ottawa, KS 66067-3399
■ **Website:** http://www.ottawa.edu
■ **Private; Religious affiliation:** American Baptist
■ **Enrollment:** N/A

KEY STATS
✔ **U.S News College Ranking:** second tier, Regional Colleges (Midwest)
✔ **SAT or ACT Score (25th/75th percentile):** N/A
✔ **Tuition:** 2009-2010: $19,450

Selectivity: Less selective	**Room/board:** $7,496
Acceptance rate: N/A	**Average debt:** N/A
Student/faculty ratio: N/A	**Proportion who borrowed:** N/A

Pittsburg State University

■ **Address:** 1701 S. Broadway, Pittsburg, KS 66762
■ **Website:** http://www.pittstate.edu
■ **Public**
■ **Enrollment:** 5,615 full-time; 319 part-time

KEY STATS
✔ **U.S News College Ranking:** 72, Regional Universities (Midwest)
✔ **ACT Score (25th/75th percentile):** 19-24
✔ **Tuition:** 2010-2011: $4,848 in state, $13,588 out of state

Selectivity: Selective	**Room/board:** $6,016
Acceptance rate: 86%	**Average debt:** $18,516
Student/faculty ratio: 19/1	**Proportion who borrowed:** 67%

UNDERGRADUATE STUDENT BODY STATS
2009-2010 enrollment: 5,615 full-time; 319 part-time. Men: 54%; women: 46%. **Ethnic makeup:** African American: 3%; American-Indian: 2%; Asian American: 1%; Hispanic: 3%; White: 87%; International: 4%.

ADMISSIONS FACTS AND FIGURES

Phone: (800) 854-7488. **Email:** psuadmit@pittstate.edu. **Website:** http://www.pittstate.edu. **Application deadlines for fall 2011:** Regular decision: Rolling. Early decision: Not offered. Early action: Not offered. Admission can be deferred. **Application fee:** $30. **To apply online, go to:** http://www.pittstate.edu/admit/applyingforms.html. **Admissions requirements/recommendations:** High school units required (recommended): English: 4 (4); Mathematics: 3 (3); Science: 3 (3); Foreign language: 0 (0); Social studies: 3 (3); History: 0 (0); Academic electives: 0 (0); Total units: 13 (13). Tests: The college uses SAT or ACT scores in admissions decisions. ACT required. For admission to the fall 2011 entering class, the school will accept: ACT with or without writing accepted. Campus visit: Recommended. Admissions interview: Neither required nor recommended. Off-campus interview: Not available. **Factors that count in admissions decisions:** *Academic:* Secondary school record: Very Important. Class rank: Very Important. Standardized test scores: Very Important. *Nonacademic:* Interview: Not Considered. Extracurricular activities: Not Considered. Talent/ability: Not Considered. Character/personal qualities: Not Considered. Alumni/ae relationship: Not Considered. Geographical residence: Not Considered. State residency: Not Considered. Religious affiliation/commitment: Not Considered. Minority status: Not Considered. Volunteer work: Not Considered. Work experience: Not Considered. **Other schools with the greatest overlap in applicants:** Kansas State University; Missouri Southern State University; University of Kansas; Washburn University; Wichita State University. **Admissions statistics for the fall 2009 entering class:** Total applicants: 1,816. Total accepted: 1,567. Freshmen enrolled: 864; Overall acceptance rate: 86%. **Credentials of fall 2009 freshmen:** 18% ranked in the top 10 percent of their high school class; 43% were in the top 25 percent; 72% were in the top half. (Proportion submitting class standing: 95%.) **Average high school grade point average:** 3.3. **First-year students submitting ACT scores:** 93%. Scores (25/75 percentile): English: 17-24, Math: 17-24, Composite: 19-24.

ACADEMICS

Year founded: 1903. **Academic calendar:** Semester. **Degrees offered:** certificate, associate, bachelor's, master's, post-master's certificate. **Major fields of study:** biological and biomedical sciences; business, management, marketing, and related support services; communication, journalism, and related programs; communications technologies/technicians and support services; computer and information sciences and support services; education; engineering technologies/technicians; English language and literature/letters; family and consumer sciences/human sciences; foreign languages, literatures, and linguistics; health professions and related clinical sciences; history; liberal arts and sciences studies, and humanities; mathematics and statistics; multi/interdisciplinary studies; parks, recreation, leisure, and fitness studies; physical sciences; psychology; public administration and social service professions; security and protective services; social sciences; visual and performing arts. **Areas of required coursework:** arts/fine arts, humanities, mathematics, English (including composition), foreign languages, sciences (biological or physical), history, social science, other. **Pre-professional programs:** pre-dentistry, pre-medicine, pre-pharmacy. **Special academic programs:** accelerated program, distance learning, double major, dual enrollment, English as a Second Language (ESL), honors program, independent study, internships, student-designed major, study abroad, teacher certificate program. **Teacher certification offered in:** early childhood, special education, elementary, middle/junior high, secondary, bilingual/bicultural. **Cooperative education programs:** business, education, engineering, health professions, social/behavioral science, technologies, vocational arts. **Reserve Officers Training Corps (ROTC):** Army ROTC: Offered on campus. **Faculty and instruction (2009-2010):** Total instructional faculty: 308 full-time, 96 part-time (59% men; 41% women; 8% minorities). Full-time faculty with Ph.D. or other terminal degree: 75%. Student/faculty ratio: 19/1. Classes of fewer than 20 students: 46%; of 20 to 49 students: 46%; of 50 or more students: 8%. **Advanced Placement and International Baccalaureate credit:** AP tests may be used for: Credit and/or placement. Scores accepted: 3, 4, 5. International Baccalaureate exams may be used for: Credit only. **Freshmen returning for sophomore year:** 74%. **Graduation rates:** Four-year: 43%; five-year: 48%; six-year: 51%. **Graduate study:** 20% of students pursue further study within one year.

COSTS AND FINANCIAL AID

Financial aid office: (620) 235-4240. **Expenses (2010-2011):** Tuition and fees 2010-2011: $4,848 in state, $13,588 out of state; room/board: $6,016. Estimated books and supplies: $1,000; transportation: $1,360; personal expenses: $2,170. **Financial aid:** Priority filing date for institution's financial aid form: March 1. In 2009-2010, 75% of undergraduates applied for financial aid. Of those, 59% were determined to have financial need; 8% had

their need fully met. Average financial aid package (proportion receiving): $9,900 (58%). Average amount of gift aid, such as scholarships or grants (proportion receiving): $4,525 (40%). Average amount of self-help aid, such as work study or loans (proportion receiving): $2,746 (15%). Average need-based loan (excluding PLUS or other private loans): $3,889. Among students who received need-based aid, the average percentage of need met: 75%. Among students who received aid based on merit, the average award (and the proportion receiving): $2,450 (8%). The average athletic scholarship (and the proportion receiving): $4,517 (2%). Average amount of debt of borrowers graduating in 2009: $18,516. Proportion who borrowed: 67%.

CAMPUS LIFE AND EXTRACURRICULAR ACTIVITIES

Campus housing available (% using): coed dorms (96%), apartments for married students (4%). **Student employment:** During the 2009-2010 academic year, 10% of undergraduates worked on campus. Average per-year earnings: $3,500. **Clubs and organizations:** Number of student organizations: 130. Activities include: campus ministries, choral groups, concert band, dance, drama/theater, international student organization, jazz band, literary magazine, marching band, music ensembles, pep band, radio station, student government, student newspaper, television station, yearbook. Number of fraternities: 8; sororities: 3. Average proportion of students who stay on campus on weekends: 55%. **Sports program (2009-2010):** Member of NCAA II. *Men's intercollegiate varsity sports:* baseball, basketball, cross country, football, golf, track and field (indoor), track and field (outdoor). *Women's intercollegiate varsity sports:* basketball, cross country, softball, track and field (indoor), track and field (outdoor), volleyball.

SERVICES AND FACILITIES

Basic services: placement service, health service. **Counseling services:** minority student, career, military, personal, veteran student, academic, older student, psychological, birth control. **For learning-disabled students:** School does not offer a structured program with separate admission and additional fees. Services include: tape recorders, diagnostic testing service, untimed tests, note-taking services, oral tests, learning center, readers, extended time for tests, tutors, priority seating, texts on tape, other testing accommodations. **Library:** Number of titles: 879,907; number of current serial subscriptions: 13,389. **Information technology resources:** Students are not required to lease or own a computer. Number of campus computers available to all students: 500. School has a wireless network. Approximate number of users that can be accommodated: 5,000. Proportion of college-owned housing units wired for high-speed internet access: 100%. **Campus safety:** Security services offered: 24-hour foot-and-vehicle patrols, 24-hour emergency telephones, lighted pathways/sidewalks, controlled dormitory access (key, security card, etc).

TRANSFER AND INTERNATIONAL STUDENTS

Transfer students: May apply for admission for the following academic terms: Fall, Spring, Summer. Applicants need a minimum number of credits to apply. For fall 2009: Transfer applications received: 1,026. Transfer applicants offered admission: 827. Transfer applicants enrolled: 588. **International students:** Number of foreign undergraduates: 239 (4% of student body). Number of countries represented: 29. Minimum TOEFL score required: 520 (paper); 190 (computer). Average TOEFL score: 520 (paper).

Southwestern College

- **Address:** 100 College Street, Winfield, KS 67156-2499
- **Website:** http://www.sckans.edu
- **Private; Religious affiliation:** United Methodist
- **Enrollment:** 575 full-time; 950 part-time

KEY STATS

✔ **U.S News College Ranking:** 92, Regional Universities (Midwest)
✔ **ACT Score (25th/75th percentile):** 19-24
✔ **Tuition:** 2010-2011: $20,656

Selectivity: Selective	**Room/board:** $6,056
Acceptance rate: 90%	**Average debt:** $27,973
Student/faculty ratio: 12/1	**Proportion who borrowed:** 86%

UNDERGRADUATE STUDENT BODY STATS

2009-2010 enrollment: 575 full-time; 950 part-time. Men: 52%; women: 48%. **Ethnic makeup:** African American: 8%; American-Indian: 2%; Asian American: 2%; Hispanic: 6%; White: 82%; International: 1%. **Religious**

preference: Roman Catholic: 3%; Unknown: 74%; United Methodist: 8%; Other: 15%.

ADMISSIONS FACTS AND FIGURES

Phone: (620) 229-6236. **Email:** scadmit@sckans.edu. **Website:** http://www.sckans.edu. **Application deadlines for fall 2011:** Regular decision: August 25. Early decision: Not offered. Early action: Not offered. Admission cannot be deferred. **Application fee:** $25. **To apply online, go to:** http://www.sckans.edu/admissions/apply/index.html. **Admissions requirements/recommendations:** High school units required (recommended): English: 4; Mathematics: 3; Science: 2; Social studies: 3; History: 1; Total units: 14. Tests: The college uses SAT or ACT scores in admissions decisions. Either SAT or ACT required. For admission to the fall 2011 entering class, the school will accept: ACT with or without writing accepted. Campus visit: Recommended. Admissions interview: Required. Off-campus interview: May be arranged. **Factors that count in admissions decisions:** *Academic:* Secondary school record: Very Important. Class rank: Considered. Letters of recommendation: Considered. Standardized test scores: Very Important. Essay: Important. *Nonacademic:* Interview: Considered. Extracurricular activities: Considered. Talent/ability: Considered. Character/personal qualities: Considered. Alumni/ae relationship: Considered. Geographical residence: Not Considered. State residency: Not Considered. Religious affiliation/commitment: Not Considered. Minority status: Not Considered. Volunteer work: Not Considered. Work experience: Not Considered. **Other schools with the greatest overlap in applicants:** Emporia State University; Kansas State University; University of Kansas; Wichita State University. **Admissions statistics for the fall 2009 entering class:** Total applicants: 293. Total accepted: 264. Freshmen enrolled: 119; 50% were from out of state. Overall acceptance rate: 90%. **Credentials of fall 2009 freshmen:** 16% ranked in the top 10 percent of their high school class; 44% were in the top 25 percent; 73% were in the top half. (Proportion submitting class standing: 81%.) **Average high school grade point average:** 3.3. **First-year students who submitted SAT scores:** 21%. Scores (25/75 percentile): Critical Reading: 380-540, Math: 430-550, Combined: 810-1090. **First-year students submitting ACT scores:** 87%. Scores (25/75 percentile): English: 17-25, Math: 17-24, Composite: 19-24.

ACADEMICS

Year founded: 1885. **Academic calendar:** Semester. **Degrees offered:** bachelor's, post-bachelor's certificate, master's, post-master's certificate. **Most popular majors:** 13% biology/biological sciences, 10% business administration and management, 10% elementary education and teaching, 9% journalism, 7% nursing/registered nurse training (R.N., A.S.N., B.S.N., M.S.N.). **Major fields of study:** biological and biomedical sciences; business, management, marketing, and related support services; communication, journalism, and related programs; computer and information sciences and support services; education; engineering; English language and literature/letters; health professions and related clinical sciences; history; liberal arts and sciences studies, and humanities; mathematics and statistics; parks, recreation, leisure, and fitness studies; philosophy and religious studies; physical sciences; psychology; social sciences; visual and performing arts. **Areas of required coursework:** arts/fine arts, humanities, mathematics, English (including composition), sciences (biological or physical), social science, other. **Special academic programs (% participation):** double major (6%), honors program (7%), independent study (31%), internships (17%), student-designed major (0%), teacher certificate program (2%). **Teacher certification offered in:** early childhood, elementary, middle/junior high, secondary. **Cooperative education programs:** other. **Faculty and instruction (2009-2010):** Total instructional faculty: 47 full-time, 122 part-time (56% men; 44% women; 4% minorities). Full-time faculty with Ph.D. or other terminal degree: 60%. Student/faculty ratio: 12/1. Classes of fewer than 20 students: 83%; of 20 to 49 students: 16%; of 50 or more students: 1%. **Advanced Placement and International Baccalaureate credit:** International Baccalaureate exams may be used for: Credit only. **Freshmen returning for sophomore year:** 68%. **Graduation rates:** Four-year: 29%; five-year: 44%; six-year: 47%. **Graduate study:** 53% of students pursue further study immediately upon graduation. Fields in which graduates pursue further study: Master of Business Administration (MBA), 35%; law, 5%.

COSTS AND FINANCIAL AID

Financial aid office: (620) 229-6215. **Expenses (2010-2011):** Tuition and fees 2010-2011: $20,656; room/board: $6,056. Estimated books and supplies: $600; transportation: $2,226; personal expenses: $3,748. **Financial aid:** Priority filing date for institution's financial aid form: April 1; deadline: August 15. In 2009-2010, 87% of undergraduates applied for financial aid. Of those, 80% were determined to have financial need; 24% had

their need fully met. Average financial aid package (proportion receiving): $18,500 (80%). Average amount of gift aid, such as scholarships or grants (proportion receiving): $10,894 (78%). Average amount of self-help aid, such as work study or loans (proportion receiving): $5,630 (68%). Average need-based loan (excluding PLUS or other private loans): $5,630. Among students who received need-based aid, the average percentage of need met: 88%. Among students who received aid based on merit, the average award (and the proportion receiving): $7,914 (18%). The average athletic scholarship (and the proportion receiving): $7,659 (25%). Average amount of debt of borrowers graduating in 2009: $27,973. Proportion who borrowed: 86%.

CAMPUS LIFE AND EXTRACURRICULAR ACTIVITIES

Campus housing available (% using): coed dorms (13%), women's dorms (19%), men's dorms (22%), apartments for married students (0%), apartment for single students (46%). Students who live in college-owned, operated, or affiliated housing: 72%. **Student employment:** During the 2009-2010 academic year, 20% of undergraduates worked on campus. Average per-year earnings: $2,100. **Clubs and organizations:** Number of student organizations: 25. Activities include: campus ministries, choral groups, concert band, dance, drama/theater, international student organization, jazz band, music ensembles, musical theater, pep band, radio station, student government, student newspaper, symphony orchestra, television station, yearbook. Number of fraternities: 1; sororities: 0. Average proportion of students who stay on campus on weekends: 60%. **Sports program (2009-2010):** Member of NAIA. *Men's intercollegiate varsity sports:* basketball, cross country, football, golf, soccer, tennis, track and field (indoor), track and field (outdoor). *Women's intercollegiate varsity sports:* basketball, cross country, golf, soccer, softball, tennis, track and field (indoor), track and field (outdoor), volleyball.

SERVICES AND FACILITIES

Basic services: nonremedial tutoring, placement service, health service. **Remedial assistance:** reading, math, writing, study skills, other. **Counseling services:** career, personal, academic, psychological, birth control, religious. **For learning-disabled students:** School does not offer a structured program with separate admission and additional fees. Total undergraduates in learning-disabled program or receiving services: 7. Services include: remedial math, remedial reading, note-taking services, tutors. **Library:** Number of titles: 56,237; number of current serial subscriptions: 40,660. **Information technology resources:** Students are required to lease or own a computer. Number of campus computers available to all students: 600. School has a wireless network. Approximate number of users that can be accommodated: 500. Proportion of college-owned housing units wired for high-speed internet access: 100%. **Campus safety:** Security services offered: 24-hour foot-and-vehicle patrols, late-night transport/escort service, 24-hour emergency telephones, lighted pathways/sidewalks, controlled dormitory access (key, security card, etc).

TRANSFER AND INTERNATIONAL STUDENTS

Transfer students: May apply for admission for the following academic terms: Fall, Spring. Applicants need a minimum number of credits to apply. For fall 2009: Transfer applications received: 90. Transfer applicants offered admission: 86. Transfer applicants enrolled: 57. **International students:** Number of foreign undergraduates: 20 (1% of student body). Number of countries represented: 13. Minimum TOEFL score required: 550 (paper); 213 (computer). Average TOEFL score: 570 (paper).

Sterling College

- **Address:** 125 W. Cooper, Sterling, KS 67579
- **Website:** http://www.sterling.edu
- **Private; Religious affiliation:** Presbyterian
- **Enrollment:** 602 full-time; 120 part-time

KEY STATS

✔ **U.S News College Ranking:** second tier, National Liberal Arts Colleges
✔ **ACT Score (25th/75th percentile):** 19-24
✔ **Tuition:** 2009-2010: $18,000

Selectivity: Selective	**Room/board:** $6,290
Acceptance rate: 55%	**Average debt:** N/A
Student/faculty ratio: 13/1	**Proportion who borrowed:** N/A

UNDERGRADUATE STUDENT BODY STATS

2009-2010 enrollment: 602 full-time; 120 part-time. Men: 51%; women: 49%. **Ethnic makeup:** African American: 7%; American-Indian: 2%; Asian American: 1%; Hispanic: 7%; White: 82%; International: 1%. **Religious preference:** Roman Catholic: 9%; Protestant: 49%; No preference: 35%; Presbyterian: 7%.

ADMISSIONS FACTS AND FIGURES

Phone: (800) 346-1017. **Email:** admissions@sterling.edu. **Website:** http://www.sterling.edu. **Application deadlines for fall 2011:** Regular decision: Rolling. Early decision: Not offered. Early action: Send application by: November 15; Decision sent by: December 1. Admission cannot be deferred. **Application fee:** $25. **To apply online, go to:** https://sterling.yourcollegeapplication.com/. **Admissions requirements/recommendations:** High school units required (recommended): English: (4); Mathematics: (3); Science: (3); Foreign language: (2); Social studies: (1); History: (2); Academic electives: (1); Total units: (18). Tests: The college uses SAT or ACT scores in admissions decisions. Either SAT or ACT required. For admission to the fall 2011 entering class, the school will accept: ACT with or without writing accepted. Campus visit: Recommended. Admissions interview: Recommended. Off-campus interview: May be arranged. **Factors that count in admissions decisions:** *Academic:* Secondary school record: Very Important. Class rank: Considered. Letters of recommendation: Important. Standardized test scores: Very Important. Essay: Important. *Nonacademic:* Interview: Important. Extracurricular activities: Important. Talent/ability: Considered. Character/personal qualities: Very Important. Alumni/ae relationship: Considered. Geographical residence: Not Considered. State residency: Not Considered. Religious affiliation/commitment: Important. Minority status: Not Considered. Volunteer work: Important. Work experience: Considered. **Other schools with the greatest overlap in applicants:** Bethany College; Kansas State University; Kansas Wesleyan University; McPherson College; Tabor College. **Admissions statistics for the fall 2009 entering class:** Total applicants: 953. Total accepted: 525. Freshmen enrolled: 187; 53% were from out of state. Overall acceptance rate: 55%. Non-early acceptance rate: 55%. **Credentials of fall 2009 freshmen:** 8% ranked in the top 10 percent of their high school class; 25% were in the top 25 percent; 55% were in the top half. (Proportion submitting class standing: 84%.) **Average high school grade point average:** 3.2. **First-year students who submitted SAT scores:** 15%. Scores (25/75 percentile): Critical Reading: 410-530, Math: 450-540, Combined: 860-1070. **First-year students submitting ACT scores:** 85%. Scores (25/75 percentile): English: 18-24, Math: 17-24, Composite: 19-24.

ACADEMICS

Year founded: 1887. **Academic calendar:** 4-1-4. **Degrees offered:** bachelor's. **Most popular majors:** 28% business, management, marketing, and related support services, 21% parks, recreation, leisure, and fitness studies, 9% theology and religious vocations, 6% biological and biomedical sciences, 6% visual and performing arts. **Major fields of study:** biological and biomedical sciences; business, management, marketing, and related support services; communication, journalism, and related programs; computer and information sciences and support services; education; English language and literature/letters; health professions and related clinical sciences; history; mathematics and statistics; multi/interdisciplinary studies; parks, recreation, leisure, and fitness studies; philosophy and religious studies; physical sciences; theology and religious vocations; visual and performing arts. **Areas of required coursework:** arts/fine arts, humanities, mathematics, English (including composition), philosophy, sciences (biological or physical), history, social science, other. **Pre-professional programs:** pre-dentistry, pre-medicine, pre-theology, pre-veterinary science. **Special academic programs (% participation):** cross-registration (1%), distance learning (1%), double major (6%), dual enrollment (3%), honors program (2%), independent study (15%), internships (80%), student-designed major (0%), study abroad (1%), teacher certificate program (21%). **Teacher certification offered in:** special education, elementary, middle/junior high, secondary. **Faculty and instruction (2009-2010):** Total instructional faculty: 41 full-time, 18 part-time (68% men; 32% women; 7% minorities). Full-time faculty with Ph.D. or other terminal degree: 46%. Student/faculty ratio: 13/1. Classes of fewer than 20 students: 69%; of 20 to 49 students: 27%; of 50 or more students: 4%. **Advanced Placement and International Baccalaureate credit:** AP tests may be used for: Credit and/or placement. Scores accepted: 3, 4, 5. International Baccalaureate exams may be used for: Placement only. **Freshmen returning for sophomore year:** 64%. **Graduation rates:** Four-year: 35%; five-year: 40%; six-year: 41%.

COSTS AND FINANCIAL AID

Financial aid office: (620) 278-4207. **Expenses (2009-2010):** Tuition and fees 2009-2010: $18,000; room/board: $6,290. Estimated books and supplies: $750; transportation: $1,500; personal expenses: $750. **Financial aid:** Priority filing date for institution's financial aid form: April 1.

CAMPUS LIFE AND EXTRACURRICULAR ACTIVITIES

Campus housing available (% using): women's dorms (45%), men's dorms (55%). Students who live in college-owned, operated, or affiliated housing: 72%. **Student employment:** During the 2009-2010 academic year, 20% of undergraduates worked on campus. Average per-year earnings: $1,100. **Clubs and organizations:** Number of student organizations: 15. Activities include: campus ministries, choral groups, concert band, dance, drama/theater, jazz band, literary magazine, music ensembles, musical theater, radio station, student government, student newspaper, television station, yearbook. Number of fraternities: 0; sororities: 0. Average proportion of students who stay on campus on weekends: 65%. **Sports program (2009-2010):** Member of NAIA. *Men's intercollegiate varsity sports:* baseball, basketball, cross country, football, golf, soccer, track and field (indoor), track and field (outdoor). *Women's intercollegiate varsity sports:* basketball, cross country, golf, soccer, softball, track and field (indoor), track and field (outdoor), volleyball.

SERVICES AND FACILITIES

Basic services: nonremedial tutoring, placement service, health service, health insurance. **Remedial assistance:** writing, study skills. **Counseling services:** career, personal, academic, psychological, religious. **For learning-disabled students:** School does not offer a structured program with separate admission and additional fees. Total undergraduates in learning-disabled program or receiving services: 15. Services include: remedial English, diagnostic testing service, untimed tests, note-taking services, oral tests, learning center, readers, extended time for tests, tutors, priority seating, typist/scribe. **Library:** Number of titles: 77,536; number of current serial subscriptions: 270. **Information technology resources:** Students are not required to lease or own a computer. Number of campus computers available to all students: 140. School has a wireless network. Approximate number of users that can be accommodated: 400. Proportion of college-owned housing units wired for high-speed internet access: 100%. **Campus safety:** Security services offered: lighted pathways/sidewalks, controlled dormitory access (key, security card, etc).

TRANSFER AND INTERNATIONAL STUDENTS

Transfer students: May apply for admission for the following academic terms: Fall, Spring. Applicants do not need a minimum number of credits to apply. For fall 2009: Transfer applications received: 239. Transfer applicants offered admission: 139. Transfer applicants enrolled: 63. **International students:** Number of foreign undergraduates: 7 (1% of student body). Number of countries represented: 6. Minimum TOEFL score required: 520 (paper); 190 (computer).

Tabor College

- **Address:** 400 S. Jefferson, Hillsboro, KS 67063
- **Website:** http://www.tabor.edu
- **Private; Religious affiliation:** Mennonite Brethren
- **Enrollment:** 515 full-time; 103 part-time

KEY STATS

✔ **U.S News College Ranking:** 40, Regional Colleges (Midwest)
✔ **ACT Score (25th/75th percentile):** 19-25
✔ **Tuition:** 2009-2010: $19,660

Selectivity: Selective	**Room/board:** $6,880
Acceptance rate: 94%	**Average debt:** N/A
Student/faculty ratio: 12/1	**Proportion who borrowed:** N/A

UNDERGRADUATE STUDENT BODY STATS

2009-2010 enrollment: 515 full-time; 103 part-time. Men: 50%; women: 50%. **Ethnic makeup:** African American: 7%; American-Indian: 1%; Asian American: 1%; Hispanic: 7%; White: 83%; International: 1%. **Religious preference:** Roman Catholic: 4%; Protestant: 66%; Mennonite Brethren: 30%.

ADMISSIONS FACTS AND FIGURES

Phone: (620) 947-3121. **Email:** admissions@tabor.edu. **Website:** http://www.tabor.edu. **Application deadlines for fall 2011:** Regular decision: Rolling. Early decision: Send application by: December 31; Decision sent by: N/A. Early action: Not offered. Admission cannot be deferred. **Application fee:** $30. **To apply online, go to:** http://www.tabor.edu/apply-now. **Admissions requirements/recommendations:** High school units required (recommended): English: (4); Mathematics: (3); Science: (3); Foreign language: (1); Social studies: (2); History: (2); Total units: (17). Tests: The college uses SAT or ACT scores in admissions decisions. Either SAT or ACT required. For admission to the fall 2011 entering class, the school will accept: ACT with or without writing accepted. Campus visit: Recommended. Admissions interview: Recommended. Off-campus interview: May be arranged. **Factors that count in admissions decisions: Academic:** Secondary school record: Important. Class rank: Not Considered. Letters of recommendation: Considered. Standardized test scores: Very Important. Essay: Important. *Nonacademic:* Interview: Important. Extracurricular activities: Considered. Talent/ability: Considered. Character/personal qualities: Very Important. Alumni/ae relationship: Considered. Geographical residence: Not Considered. State residency: Considered. Religious affiliation/commitment: Important. Minority status: Not Considered. Volunteer work: Considered. Work experience: Not Considered. **Other schools with the greatest overlap in applicants:** Bethel College; Friends University; Kansas State University; Sterling College; Wichita State University. **Admissions statistics for the fall 2009 entering class:** Total applicants: 343. Total accepted: 321. Freshmen enrolled: 140; 46% were from out of state. Overall acceptance rate: 94%. Non-early acceptance rate: 94%. **Credentials of fall 2009 freshmen:** 14% ranked in the top 10 percent of their high school class; 19% were in the top 25 percent; 70% were in the top half. (Proportion submitting class standing: 81%.) **First-year students who submitted SAT scores:** 12%. Scores (25/75 percentile): Critical Reading: 400-480, Math: 450-520, Combined: 850-1000. **First-year students submitting ACT scores:** 88%. Scores (25/75 percentile): English: 18-25, Math: 18-26, Composite: 19-25.

ACADEMICS

Year founded: 1908. **Academic calendar:** 4-1-4. **Degrees offered:** certificate, associate, bachelor's, master's. **Most popular majors:** 17% health professions and related clinical sciences, 16% business, management, marketing, and related support services, 12% education, 10% philosophy and religious studies, 8% visual and performing arts. **Major fields of study:** biological and biomedical sciences; business, management, marketing, and related support services; communication, journalism, and related programs; computer and information sciences and support services; education; English language and literature/letters; health professions and related clinical sciences; history; liberal arts and sciences studies, and humanities; mathematics and statistics; multi/interdisciplinary studies; parks, recreation, leisure, and fitness studies; philosophy and religious studies; physical sciences; psychology; social sciences; theology and religious vocations; visual and performing arts. **Areas of required coursework:** arts/fine arts, humanities, computer literacy, mathematics, English (including composition), philosophy, sciences (biological or physical), history, social science, other. **Pre-professional programs:** pre-law, pre-dentistry, pre-medicine, pre-theology, pre-veterinary science, pre-optometry, pre-pharmacy. **Special academic programs (% participation):** accelerated program (24%), cross-registration, distance learning (41%), double major (21%), dual enrollment (23%), exchange student program (domestic) (0%), independent study (54%), internships (48%), liberal arts/career combination, student-designed major (0%), study abroad (1%), teacher certificate program (15%). **Teacher certification offered in:** special education, elementary, middle/junior high, secondary. **Faculty and instruction (2009-2010):** Total instructional faculty: 30 full-time, 51 part-time (49% men; 51% women; 5% minorities). Full-time faculty with Ph.D. or other terminal degree: 67%. Student/faculty ratio: 12/1. Classes of fewer than 20 students: 63%; of 20 to 49 students: 34%; of 50 or more students: 2%. **Advanced Placement and International Baccalaureate credit:** AP tests may be used for: Credit and/or placement. Scores accepted: 3, 4, 5. International Baccalaureate exams may be used for: Credit and/or placement. **Freshmen returning for sophomore year:** 67%. **Graduation rates:** Four-year: 55%; five-year: 60%; six-year: 55%.

COSTS AND FINANCIAL AID

Financial aid office: (620) 947-3121. **Expenses (2009-2010):** Tuition and fees 2009-2010: $19,660; room/board: $6,880. Estimated books and supplies: $700; transportation: $1,000; personal expenses: $3,130. **Financial aid:** Priority filing date for institution's financial aid form: March 1.

CAMPUS LIFE AND EXTRACURRICULAR ACTIVITIES

Campus housing available (% using): women's dorms (41%), men's dorms (50%). Students who live in college-owned, operated, or affiliated housing: 87%. **Student employment:** During the 2009-2010 academic year, 52% of undergraduates worked on campus. Average per-year earnings: $925. **Clubs and organizations:** Number of student organizations: 9. Activities include: campus ministries, choral groups, concert band, drama/theater, music ensembles, musical theater, pep band, student government, student newspaper, yearbook. Number of fraternities: 0; sororities: 0. Average proportion of students who stay on campus on weekends: 80%. **Sports program (2009-2010):** Member of NAIA. *Men's intercollegiate varsity sports:* baseball, basketball, cross country, football, soccer, tennis, track and field (indoor), track and field (outdoor). *Women's intercollegiate varsity sports:* basketball, cross country, soccer, softball, tennis, track and field (indoor), track and field (outdoor), volleyball.

SERVICES AND FACILITIES

Basic services: nonremedial tutoring, placement service, health insurance, other. **Remedial assistance:** reading, math, writing, study skills. **Counseling services:** career, academic, psychological. **For learning-disabled students:** School does not offer a structured program with separate admission and additional fees. Services include: remedial math, remedial English, other special classes, untimed tests, note-taking services, oral tests, readers, extended time for tests, tutors, priority seating, texts on tape, other testing accommodations. **Library:** Number of titles: 73,997; number of current serial subscriptions: 149. **Information technology resources:** Students are not required to lease or own a computer. Number of campus computers available to all students: 65. School has a wireless network. Approximate number of users that can be accommodated: 450. Proportion of college-owned housing units wired for high-speed internet access: 100%. **Campus safety:** Security services offered: lighted pathways/sidewalks, controlled dormitory access (key, security card, etc).

TRANSFER AND INTERNATIONAL STUDENTS

Transfer students: May apply for admission for the following academic terms: Fall, Winter, Spring, Summer. Applicants need a minimum number of credits to apply. For fall 2009: Transfer applications received: 90. Transfer applicants offered admission: 86. Transfer applicants enrolled: 44. **International students:** Number of foreign undergraduates: 6 (1% of student body). Number of countries represented: 4. Minimum TOEFL score required: 525 (paper); 195 (computer). Average TOEFL score: 570 (paper).

University of Kansas

- **Address:** 1502 Iowa Street, Lawrence, KS 66045-7576
- **Website:** http://www.ku.edu
- **Public**
- **Enrollment:** 18,930 full-time; 2,136 part-time

KEY STATS

- ✔ **U.S News College Ranking:** 104, National Universities
- ✔ **ACT Score (25th/75th percentile):** 22-27
- ✔ **Tuition:** 2009-2010: $7,414 in state, $18,097 out of state

Selectivity: More selective	**Room/board:** $6,802
Acceptance rate: 91%	**Average debt:** $22,478
Student/faculty ratio: 20/1	**Proportion who borrowed:** 45%

UNDERGRADUATE STUDENT BODY STATS

2009-2010 enrollment: 18,930 full-time; 2,136 part-time. Men: 50%; women: 50%. **Ethnic makeup:** African American: 4%; American-Indian: 1%; Asian American: 4%; Hispanic: 4%; White: 82%; International: 4%.

ADMISSIONS FACTS AND FIGURES

Phone: (785) 864-3911. **Email:** adm@ku.edu. **Website:** http://www.ku.edu. **Application deadlines for fall 2011:** Regular decision: April 1. Early decision: Not offered. Early action: Not offered. Admission cannot be deferred. **Application fee:** $30. **To apply online, go to:** http://www.admissions.ku.edu. **Admissions requirements/recommendations:** High school units required (recommended): English: 4 (4); Mathematics: 3 (4); Science: 3 (3); Foreign language: (2); Social studies: 3 (3); Total units: 13 (16). Tests: The college uses SAT or ACT scores in admissions decisions. Either SAT or ACT required. For admission to the fall 2011 entering class, the school will accept: ACT with or without writing accepted. Campus visit:

Recommended. Admissions interview: Neither required nor recommended. Off-campus interview: Not available. **Factors that count in admissions decisions: *Academic:*** Secondary school record: Not Considered. Class rank: Very Important. Letters of recommendation: Not Considered. Standardized test scores: Very Important. Essay: Not Considered. ***Nonacademic:*** Interview: Not Considered. Extracurricular activities: Not Considered. Talent/ability: Not Considered. Character/personal qualities: Not Considered. Alumni/ae relationship: Not Considered. Geographical residence: Not Considered. State residency: Not Considered. Religious affiliation/commitment: Not Considered. Minority status: Not Considered. Volunteer work: Not Considered. Work experience: Not Considered. **Other schools with the greatest overlap in applicants:** Kansas State University; Texas A&M University–College Station; Texas Tech University; University of Oklahoma; University of Texas–Austin. **Admissions statistics for the fall 2009 entering class:** Total applicants: 10,653. Total accepted: 9,740. Freshmen enrolled: 3,942; 27% were from out of state. Overall acceptance rate: 91%. **Credentials of fall 2009 freshmen:** 27% ranked in the top 10 percent of their high school class; 55% were in the top 25 percent; 89% were in the top half. (Proportion submitting class standing: 68%.) **Average high school grade point average:** 3.4. **First-year students submitting ACT scores:** 97%. Scores (25/75 percentile): English: 21-28, Math: 21-27, Composite: 22-27.

ACADEMICS

Year founded: 1866. **Academic calendar:** Semester. **Degrees offered:** bachelor's, master's, post-master's certificate, doctorate. **Most popular majors:** 13% business, management, marketing, and related support services, 11% health professions and related clinical sciences, 11% social sciences, 7% communication, journalism, and related programs, 7% psychology. **Major fields of study:** architecture and related services; area, ethnic, cultural, and gender studies; biological and biomedical sciences; business, management, marketing, and related support services; communication, journalism, and related programs; computer and information sciences and support services; education; engineering; English language and literature/letters; foreign languages, literatures, and linguistics; health professions and related clinical sciences; history; liberal arts and sciences studies, and humanities; mathematics and statistics; multi/interdisciplinary studies; natural resources and conservation; parks, recreation, leisure, and fitness studies; philosophy and religious studies; physical sciences; psychology; public administration and social service professions; social sciences; visual and performing arts. **Areas of required coursework:** humanities, mathematics, English (including composition), foreign languages, sciences (biological or physical), social science, other. **Pre-professional programs:** pre-law, pre-dentistry, pre-medicine, pre-veterinary science, pre-optometry. **Special academic programs (% participation):** accelerated program, cooperative (work-study plan) program, distance learning (4%), double major (10%), dual enrollment, English as a Second Language (ESL) (2%), honors program (14%), independent study, internships, liberal arts/career combination (2%), student-designed major, study abroad (22%), teacher certificate program (4%). **Teacher certification offered in:** early childhood, special education, elementary, middle/junior high, secondary. **Cooperative education programs:** engineering. **Reserve Officers Training Corps (ROTC):** Army ROTC: Offered on campus; Navy ROTC: Offered on campus; Air Force ROTC: Offered on campus. **Faculty and instruction (2009-2010):** Total instructional faculty: 1,298 full-time, 401 part-time (59% men; 41% women; 16% minorities). Full-time faculty with Ph.D. or other terminal degree: 94%. Student/faculty ratio: 20/1. Classes of fewer than 20 students: 39%; of 20 to 49 students: 49%; of 50 or more students: 12%. **Advanced Placement and International Baccalaureate credit:** AP tests may be used for: Credit and/or placement. Scores accepted: 3, 4, 5. International Baccalaureate exams may be used for: Credit and/or placement. **Freshmen returning for sophomore year:** 80%. **Graduation rates:** Four-year: 32%; five-year: 55%; six-year: 61%. **Graduate study:** 38% of students pursue further study within one year.

COSTS AND FINANCIAL AID

Financial aid office: (785) 864-4700. **Expenses (2009-2010):** Tuition and fees 2009-2010: $7,414 in state, $18,097 out of state; room/board: $6,802. Estimated books and supplies: $800; transportation: $1,840; personal expenses: $2,386. **Financial aid:** Priority filing date for institution's financial aid form: March 1; deadline: June 30. In 2009-2010, 78% of undergraduates applied for financial aid. Of those, 44% were determined to have financial need; 22% had their need fully met. Average financial aid package (proportion receiving): $10,014 (42%). Average amount of gift aid, such as scholarships or grants (proportion receiving): $5,775 (29%). Average amount of self-help aid, such as work study or loans (proportion receiving): $4,862 (34%). Average need-based loan (excluding PLUS or other private loans): $3,664. Among students who received need-based aid, the aver-

age percentage of need met: 53%. Among students who received aid based on merit, the average award (and the proportion receiving): $3,234 (10%). The average athletic scholarship (and the proportion receiving): $16,687 (2%). Average amount of debt of borrowers graduating in 2009: $22,478. Proportion who borrowed: 45%.

CAMPUS LIFE AND EXTRACURRICULAR ACTIVITIES

Campus housing available (% using): coed dorms (63%), women's dorms (13%), apartments for married students (1%), apartment for single students (10%), cooperative housing (13%). Students who live in college-owned, operated, or affiliated housing: 22%. **Student employment:** During the 2009-2010 academic year, 14% of undergraduates worked on campus. Average per-year earnings: $4,800. **Clubs and organizations:** Number of student organizations: 580. Activities include: choral groups, concert band, dance, drama/theater, international student organization, jazz band, literary magazine, marching band, music ensembles, musical theater, opera, pep band, radio station, student government, student newspaper, symphony orchestra, television station. Number of fraternities: 27; sororities: 16. Proportion of men in fraternities: 13%; of women in sororities: 18%. Average proportion of students who stay on campus on weekends: 70%. **Sports program (2009-2010):** Member of NCAA I. ***Men's intercollegiate varsity sports:*** baseball, basketball, cross country, football, golf, track and field (indoor), track and field (outdoor). ***Women's intercollegiate varsity sports:*** basketball, crew (heavyweight), cross country, golf, crew (lightweight), soccer, softball, swimming, tennis, track and field (indoor), track and field (outdoor), volleyball.

SERVICES AND FACILITIES

Basic services: nonremedial tutoring, women's center, placement service, day care, health service, health insurance, other. **Remedial assistance:** math. **Counseling services:** minority student, career, military, personal, veteran student, academic, older student, psychological, birth control. **For learning-disabled students:** School does not offer a structured program with separate admission and additional fees. Total undergraduates in learning-disabled program or receiving services: 209. Services include: remedial math, reading machines, tape recorders, diagnostic testing service, note-taking services, learning center, readers, extended time for tests, priority registration, priority seating, texts on tape, exams on tape or computer, other testing accommodations, other. **Library:** Number of titles: 5,012,773; number of current serial subscriptions: 73,613. **Information technology resources:** Students are not required to lease or own a computer. Number of campus computers available to all students: 1,680. School has a wireless network. Approximate number of users that can be accommodated: 20,000. Proportion of college-owned housing units wired for high-speed internet access: 100%. **Campus safety:** Security services offered: 24-hour foot-and-vehicle patrols, late-night transport/escort service, 24-hour emergency telephones, lighted pathways/sidewalks, controlled dormitory access (key, security card, etc).

TRANSFER AND INTERNATIONAL STUDENTS

Transfer students: May apply for admission for the following academic terms: Fall, Spring, Summer. Applicants do not need a minimum number of credits to apply. For fall 2009: Transfer applications received: 2,555. Transfer applicants offered admission: 2,234. Transfer applicants enrolled: 1,434. **International students:** Number of foreign undergraduates: 899 (4% of student body). Number of countries represented: 82.

University of St. Mary

- **Address:** 4100 S. Fourth Street Trafficway, Leavenworth, KS 66048
- **Website:** http://www.stmary.edu
- **Private; Religious affiliation:** Roman Catholic
- **Enrollment:** 513 full-time; 266 part-time

KEY STATS

✔ **U.S News College Ranking:** second tier, Regional Universities (Midwest)
✔ **ACT Score (25th/75th percentile):** 18-24
✔ **Tuition:** 2009-2010: $18,950

Selectivity: Selective	**Room/board:** $6,600
Acceptance rate: 70%	**Average debt:** N/A
Student/faculty ratio: 11/1	**Proportion who borrowed:** N/A

UNDERGRADUATE STUDENT BODY STATS

2009-2010 enrollment: 513 full-time; 266 part-time. Men: 36%; women: 64%. **Ethnic makeup:** African American: 12%; American-Indian: 1%; Asian

American: 1%; Hispanic: 8%; White: 78%. **Religious preference:** Protestant: 27%; Jewish: 1%; No preference: 5%; Unknown: 33%; Roman Catholic: 34%.

ADMISSIONS FACTS AND FIGURES

Phone: (913) 758-6118. **Email:** admiss@stmary.edu. **Website:** http://www.stmary.edu. **Application deadlines for fall 2011:** Regular decision: Rolling. Early decision: Not offered. Early action: Not offered. Admission can be deferred. **Application fee:** $25. **To apply online, go to:** http://espire.stmary.edu/ics/Admissions/Admission_Application.jnz?portlet=Apply_Online_2.0&formid=7. **Admissions requirements/recommendations:** High school units required (recommended): English: 4 (4); Mathematics: 2 (4); Science: 2 (4); Foreign language: (2); Social studies: (2); History: 2 (4); Academic electives: 2 (2); Total units: 12 (24). Tests: The college uses SAT or ACT scores in admissions decisions. Either SAT or ACT required. For admission to the fall 2011 entering class, the school will accept: ACT with or without writing accepted. Campus visit: Recommended. Admissions interview: Recommended. Off-campus interview: May be arranged. **Factors that count in admissions decisions: *Academic:*** Secondary school record: Very Important. Class rank: Not Considered. Letters of recommendation: Considered. Standardized test scores: Important. Essay: Considered. ***Nonacademic:*** Interview: Important. Extracurricular activities: Important. Talent/ability: Important. Character/personal qualities: Very Important. Alumni/ae relationship: Considered. Geographical residence: Not Considered. State residency: Not Considered. Religious affiliation/commitment: Not Considered. Minority status: Not Considered. Volunteer work: Important. Work experience: Considered. **Other schools with the greatest overlap in applicants:** Baker University; Kansas State University; MidAmerica Nazarene University; Ottawa University; University of Kansas. **Admissions statistics for the fall 2009 entering class:** Total applicants: 581. Total accepted: 407. Freshmen enrolled: 129; 34% were from out of state. Overall acceptance rate: 70%. **Credentials of fall 2009 freshmen:** 10% ranked in the top 10 percent of their high school class; 31% were in the top 25 percent; 71% were in the top half. (Proportion submitting class standing: 98%.) **First-year students who submitted SAT scores:** 12%. Scores (25/75 percentile): Critical Reading: 410-550, Math: 430-580, Combined: 840-1130. **First-year students submitting ACT scores:** 88%. Scores (25/75 percentile): English: N/A, Math: N/A, Composite: 18-24.

ACADEMICS

Year founded: 1923. **Academic calendar:** Semester. **Degrees offered:** certificate, associate, bachelor's, master's. **Most popular majors:** 24% nursing/registered nurse training (R.N., A.S.N., B.S.N., M.S.N.), 18% business administration and management, 10% psychology, 8% elementary education and teaching, 8% sport and fitness administration/management. **Major fields of study:** biological and biomedical sciences; business, management, marketing, and related support services; communication, journalism, and related programs; computer and information sciences and support services; education; English language and literature/letters; family and consumer sciences/human sciences; health professions and related clinical sciences; history; liberal arts and sciences studies, and humanities; mathematics and statistics; parks, recreation, leisure, and fitness studies; physical sciences; psychology; social sciences; theology and religious vocations; visual and performing arts. **Areas of required coursework:** arts/fine arts, computer literacy, mathematics, English (including composition), philosophy, sciences (biological or physical), history, social science, other. **Pre-professional programs:** pre-law, pre-dentistry, pre-medicine, pre-pharmacy. **Special academic programs (% participation):** accelerated program (1%), distance learning (2%), double major (6%), dual enrollment (16%), exchange student program (domestic) (0%), honors program (12%), independent study (30%), internships (7%), student-designed major (6%), study abroad (0%), teacher certificate program (12%). **Teacher certification offered in:** elementary, secondary. **Reserve Officers Training Corps (ROTC):** Army ROTC: Offered at cooperating institution (University of Kansas); Air Force ROTC: Offered at cooperating institution (University of Kansas). **Faculty and instruction (2009-2010):** Total instructional faculty: 43 full-time, 67 part-time (45% men; 55% women; 5% minorities). Full-time faculty with Ph.D. or other terminal degree: 60%. Student/faculty ratio: 11/1. Classes of fewer than 20 students: 75%; of 20 to 49 students: 24%; of 50 or more students: 1%. **Advanced Placement and International Baccalaureate credit:** International Baccalaureate exams may be used for: Credit only. **Freshmen returning for sophomore year:** 63%. **Graduation rates:** Four-year: 29%; five-year: 37%; six-year: 41%. **Graduate study:** 23% of students pursue further study immediately upon graduation. Fields in which graduates pursue further study: Master of Business Administration (MBA), 4%; law, 1%; education, 4%; arts and sciences, 5%.

COSTS AND FINANCIAL AID

Financial aid office: (800) 752-7043. **Expenses (2009-2010):** Tuition and fees 2009-2010: $18,950; room/board: $6,600. Estimated books and supplies: $1,200. **Financial aid:** Priority filing date for institution's financial aid form: April 1.

CAMPUS LIFE AND EXTRACURRICULAR ACTIVITIES

Campus housing available (% using): coed dorms (100%). Students who live in college-owned, operated, or affiliated housing: 33%. **Clubs and organizations:** Number of student organizations: 17. Activities include: campus ministries, choral groups, concert band, drama/theater, literary magazine, music ensembles, musical theater, opera, student government. Number of fraternities: 0; sororities: 0. Average proportion of students who stay on campus on weekends: 45%. **Sports program (2009-2010):** Member of NAIA. *Men's intercollegiate varsity sports:* baseball, basketball, football, soccer. *Women's intercollegiate varsity sports:* basketball, soccer, softball, volleyball.

SERVICES AND FACILITIES

Basic services: nonremedial tutoring, placement service, day care, health service, health insurance. **Remedial assistance:** reading, math, writing, study skills. **Counseling services:** career, veteran student, academic, psychological, religious. **For learning-disabled students:** School does not offer a structured program with separate admission and additional fees. Services include: remedial math, tape recorders, untimed tests, learning center, extended time for tests, tutors, priority seating, other testing accommodations. **Library:** Number of titles: 120,753; number of current serial subscriptions: 157. **Information technology resources:** Students are not required to lease or own a computer. Number of campus computers available to all students: 380. School has a wireless network. Approximate number of users that can be accommodated: 1,200. Proportion of college-owned housing units wired for high-speed internet access: 100%. **Campus safety:** Security services offered: 24-hour emergency telephones, lighted pathways/sidewalks, controlled dormitory access (key, security card, etc).

TRANSFER AND INTERNATIONAL STUDENTS

Transfer students: May apply for admission for the following academic terms: Fall, Spring, Summer. Applicants need a minimum number of credits to apply. For fall 2009: Transfer applications received: 402. Transfer applicants offered admission: 257. Transfer applicants enrolled: 127. **International students:** Number of foreign undergraduates: 2. Number of countries represented: 1. Minimum TOEFL score required: 500 (paper); 173 (computer).

Washburn University

- **Address:** 1700 S.W. College, Topeka, KS 66621
- **Website:** http://www.washburn.edu
- **Public**
- **Enrollment:** 3,906 full-time; 1,860 part-time

KEY STATS

✔ **U.S News College Ranking:** 58, Regional Universities (Midwest)
✔ **ACT Score (25th/75th percentile):** 19-24
✔ **Tuition:** 2009-2010: $6,116 in state, $13,766 out of state

Selectivity: Selective	**Room/board:** $5,792
Acceptance rate: 100%	**Average debt:** $17,031
Student/faculty ratio: 16/1	**Proportion who borrowed:** 66%

UNDERGRADUATE STUDENT BODY STATS

2009-2010 enrollment: 3,906 full-time; 1,860 part-time. Men: 39%; women: 61%.

ADMISSIONS FACTS AND FIGURES

Phone: (785) 670-1030. **Email:** admissions@washburn.edu. **Website:** http://www.washburn.edu. **Application deadlines for fall 2011:** Regular decision: August 1. Early decision: Not offered. Early action: Not offered. Admission cannot be deferred. **Application fee:** $20. **To apply online, go to:** http://www.washburn.edu/admissions. **Admissions requirements/recommendations:** High school units required (recommended): English: (4); Mathematics: (3); Science: (3); Foreign language: (2); Social studies: (3); History: (1). Tests: The college uses SAT or ACT scores in admissions decisions. ACT required. For admission to the fall 2011 entering class, the school will accept: ACT with or without writing accepted. Campus visit: Recommended. Admissions interview: Neither required nor recommended. Off-campus interview: May be arranged. **Factors that count in admissions decisions: *Academic:*** Secondary school record: Very Important. Class rank: Not Considered. Letters of recommendation: Not Considered. Standardized test scores: Very Important. Essay: Not Considered. ***Nonacademic:*** Interview: Not Considered. Extracurricular activities: Not Considered. Talent/ability: Not Considered. Character/personal qualities: Not Considered. Alumni/ae relationship: Not Considered. Geographical residence: Not Considered. State residency: Not Considered. Religious affiliation/commitment: Not Considered. Minority status: Not Considered. Volunteer work: Not Considered. Work experience: Not Considered. **Admissions statistics for the fall 2009 entering class:** Total applicants: 1,587. Total accepted: 1,587. Freshmen enrolled: 820; 10% were from out of state. Overall acceptance rate: 100%. **Credentials of fall 2009 freshmen:** 12% ranked in the top 10 percent of their high school class; 30% were in the top 25 percent; 61% were in the top half. (Proportion submitting class standing: 82%.) **Average high school grade point average:** 3.2. **First-year students submitting ACT scores:** 76%. Scores (25/75 percentile): English: 17-24, Math: 17-25, Composite: 19-24.

ACADEMICS

Year founded: 1865. **Academic calendar:** Semester. **Degrees offered:** certificate, associate, bachelor's, post-bachelor's certificate, master's. **Most popular majors:** 25% business, management, marketing, and related support services, 23% health professions and related clinical sciences, 8% education, 7% security and protective services, 6% communication, journalism, and related programs. **Major fields of study:** biological and biomedical sciences; business, management, marketing, and related support services; communication, journalism, and related programs; computer and information sciences and support services; education; English language and literature/letters; foreign languages, literatures, and linguistics; health professions and related clinical sciences; history; legal professions and studies; liberal arts and sciences studies, and humanities; mathematics and statistics; multi/interdisciplinary studies; parks, recreation, leisure, and fitness studies; philosophy and religious studies; physical sciences; psychology; public administration and social service professions; security and protective services; social sciences; visual and performing arts. **Areas of required coursework:** arts/fine arts, humanities, mathematics, English (including composition), foreign languages, sciences (biological or physical), social science, other. **Pre-professional programs:** pre-law, pre-dentistry, pre-medicine, pre-theology, pre-veterinary science, pre-optometry, pre-pharmacy, other. **Special academic programs (% participation):** cooperative (work-study plan) program (6%), cross-registration (2%), distance learning (9%), double major (6%), dual enrollment (2%), English as a Second Language (ESL) (2%), honors program (8%), independent study (26%), internships (10%), liberal arts/career combination (5%), student-designed major (1%), study abroad (5%), teacher certificate program (7%). **Teacher certification offered in:** early childhood, special education, elementary, middle/junior high, secondary. **Cooperative education programs:** computer science, education, engineering, health professions, social/behavioral science. **Reserve Officers Training Corps (ROTC):** Army ROTC: Offered on campus; Navy ROTC: Offered at cooperating institution (University of Kansas); Air Force ROTC: Offered on campus. **Faculty and instruction (2009-2010):** Total instructional faculty: 256 full-time, 243 part-time (47% men; 53% women; 12% minorities). Full-time faculty with Ph.D. or other terminal degree: 86%. Student/faculty ratio: 16/1. Classes of fewer than 20 students: 41%; of 20 to 49 students: 56%; of 50 or more students: 3%. **Advanced Placement and International Baccalaureate credit:** AP tests may be used for: Credit and/or placement. Scores accepted: 3, 4, 5. **Freshmen returning for sophomore year:** 64%. **Graduation rates:** Four-year: 21%; five-year: 36%; six-year: 46%. **Graduate study:** 45% of students pursue further study immediately upon graduation; 53% within five years. Fields in which graduates pursue further study: Master of Business Administration (MBA), 23%; law, 10%; medicine, 28%; education, 8%; arts and sciences, 28%.

COSTS AND FINANCIAL AID

Financial aid office: (785) 670-1151. **Expenses (2009-2010):** Tuition and fees 2009-2010: $6,116 in state, $13,766 out of state; room/board: $5,792. Estimated books and supplies: $1,400; transportation: $2,559; personal expenses: $2,486. **Financial aid:** Priority filing date for institution's financial aid form: February 15. In 2009-2010, 89% of undergraduates applied for financial aid. Of those, 63% were determined to have financial need; 13% had their need fully met. Average financial aid package (proportion receiving): $8,748 (62%). Average amount of gift aid, such as scholarships or grants (proportion receiving): $4,778 (35%). Average amount of self-help aid, such as work study or loans (proportion receiving): $4,532 (55%). Average need-based loan (excluding PLUS or other private loans): $4,295.

Among students who received need-based aid, the average percentage of need met: 39%. Among students who received aid based on merit, the average award (and the proportion receiving): $1,888 (15%). The average athletic scholarship (and the proportion receiving): $4,500 (4%). Average amount of debt of borrowers graduating in 2009: $17,031. Proportion who borrowed: 66%.

CAMPUS LIFE AND EXTRACURRICULAR ACTIVITIES

Campus housing available (% using): coed dorms (61%), sorority housing (7%), fraternity housing (5%), apartment for single students (26%), other housing options (1%). Students who live in college-owned, operated, or affiliated housing: 13%. **Student employment:** During the 2009-2010 academic year, 15% of undergraduates worked on campus. Average per-year earnings: $1,600. **Clubs and organizations:** Number of student organizations: 116. Activities include: campus ministries, choral groups, concert band, dance, drama/theater, international student organization, jazz band, literary magazine, marching band, model UN, music ensembles, musical theater, pep band, student government, student newspaper, student film society, symphony orchestra, television station, yearbook. Number of fraternities: 4; sororities: 4. Proportion of men in fraternities: 6%; of women in sororities: 4%. Average proportion of students who stay on campus on weekends: 35%. **Sports program (2009-2010):** Member of NCAA II. ***Men's intercollegiate varsity sports:*** baseball, basketball, football, golf, tennis. ***Women's intercollegiate varsity sports:*** basketball, soccer, softball, tennis, volleyball.

SERVICES AND FACILITIES

Basic services: nonremedial tutoring, placement service, day care, health service, health insurance. **Remedial assistance:** math, writing, study skills. **Counseling services:** minority student, career, military, personal, veteran student, academic, older student, psychological, birth control. **For learning-disabled students:** School does not offer a structured program with separate admission and additional fees. Services include: reading machines, tape recorders, note-taking services, oral tests, learning center, readers, extended time for tests, tutors, other testing accommodations. **Library:** Number of titles: 356,990; number of current serial subscriptions: 31,870. **Information technology resources:** Students are not required to lease or own a computer. Number of campus computers available to all students: 1,200. School has a wireless network. Approximate number of users that can be accommodated: 1,800. Proportion of college-owned housing units wired for high-speed internet access: 100%. **Campus safety:** Security services offered: 24-hour foot-and-vehicle patrols, late-night transport/escort service, 24-hour emergency telephones, lighted pathways/sidewalks, student patrols, controlled dormitory access (key, security card, etc).

TRANSFER AND INTERNATIONAL STUDENTS

Transfer students: May apply for admission for the following academic terms: Fall, Spring, Summer. Applicants need a minimum number of credits to apply. For fall 2009: Transfer applications received: 1,100. Transfer applicants offered admission: 1,045. Transfer applicants enrolled: 591. **International students:** Number of countries represented: 43. Minimum TOEFL score required: 520 (paper); 193 (computer).

Wichita State University

- **Address:** 1845 Fairmount, Wichita, KS 67260
- **Website:** http://www.wichita.edu
- **Public**
- **Enrollment:** 8,138 full-time; 3,566 part-time

KEY STATS

✔ **U.S News College Ranking:** second tier, National Universities
✔ **ACT Score (25th/75th percentile):** 21-26
✔ **Tuition:** 2009-2010: $5,467 in state, $13,501 out of state

Selectivity: Selective	**Room/board:** $6,060
Acceptance rate: 89%	**Average debt:** $15,769
Student/faculty ratio: 20/1	**Proportion who borrowed:** 57%

UNDERGRADUATE STUDENT BODY STATS

2009-2010 enrollment: 8,138 full-time; 3,566 part-time. Men: 46%; women: 54%. **Ethnic makeup:** African American: 6%; American-Indian: 1%; Asian American: 6%; Hispanic: 5%; White: 77%; International: 6%.

ADMISSIONS FACTS AND FIGURES

Phone: (316) 978-3085. **Email:** admissions@wichita.edu. **Website:** http://www.wichita.edu. **Application deadlines for fall 2011:** Regular decision: Rolling. Early decision: Not offered. Early action: Not offered. Admission can be deferred. **Application fee:** $30. **To apply online, go to:** http://webs.wichita.edu/?u=ugrad&p=/apply. **Admissions requirements/recommendations:** High school units required (recommended): English: 4; Mathematics: 3; Science: 3; Social studies: 3; Total units: 14. Tests: The college uses SAT or ACT scores in admissions decisions. Neither SAT nor ACT required. For admission to the fall 2011 entering class, the school will accept: ACT with or without writing accepted. Campus visit: Recommended. Admissions interview: Neither required nor recommended. Off-campus interview: Not available. **Factors that count in admissions decisions:** *Academic:* Secondary school record: Very Important. Class rank: Very Important. Letters of recommendation: Not Considered. Standardized test scores: Very Important. Essay: Not Considered. *Nonacademic:* Interview: Not Considered. Extracurricular activities: Not Considered. Talent/ability: Not Considered. Character/personal qualities: Not Considered. Alumni/ae relationship: Not Considered. Geographical residence: Not Considered. State residency: Not Considered. Religious affiliation/commitment: Not Considered. Minority status: Not Considered. Volunteer work: Not Considered. Work experience: Not Considered. **Other schools with the greatest overlap in applicants:** Kansas State University; University of Kansas. **Admissions statistics for the fall 2009 entering class:** Total applicants: 2,963. Total accepted: 2,625. Freshmen enrolled: 1,390; 6% were from out of state. Overall acceptance rate: 89%. **Credentials of fall 2009 freshmen:** 18% ranked in the top 10 percent of their high school class; 45% were in the top 25 percent; 77% were in the top half. (Proportion submitting class standing: 87%.) **Average high school grade point average:** 3.3. **First-year students who submitted SAT scores:** 8%. Scores (25/75 percentile): Critical Reading: 470-600, Math: 500-623, Combined: 970-1223. **First-year students submitting ACT scores:** 89%. Scores (25/75 percentile): English: 19-26, Math: 20-26, Composite: 21-26.

ACADEMICS

Year founded: 1895. **Academic calendar:** Semester. **Degrees offered:** certificate, associate, bachelor's, post-bachelor's certificate, master's, post-master's certificate, doctorate. **Most popular majors:** 24% business, management, marketing, and related support services, 10% education, 10% health professions and related clinical sciences, 9% engineering, 6% psychology. **Major fields of study:** area, ethnic, cultural, and gender studies; biological and biomedical sciences; business, management, marketing, and related support services; communication, journalism, and related programs; computer and information sciences and support services; education; engineering; engineering technologies/technicians; English language and literature/letters; foreign languages, literatures, and linguistics; health professions and related clinical sciences; history; liberal arts and sciences studies, and humanities; mathematics and statistics; multi/interdisciplinary studies; parks, recreation, leisure, and fitness studies; philosophy and religious studies; physical sciences; psychology; public administration and social service professions; security and protective services; social sciences; visual and performing arts. **Areas of required coursework:** arts/fine arts, humanities, computer literacy, mathematics, English (including composition), sciences (biological or physical), social science, other. **Pre-professional programs:** pre-law, pre-medicine, pre-veterinary science, pre-optometry, pre-pharmacy, other. **Special academic programs:** accelerated program, cooperative (work-study plan) program, cross-registration, distance learning, double major, dual enrollment, English as a Second Language (ESL), exchange student program (domestic), honors program, independent study, internships, liberal arts/career combination, study abroad, teacher certificate program. **Teacher certification offered in:** early childhood, special education, elementary, middle/junior high, secondary, bilingual/bicultural. **Cooperative education programs:** art, business, computer science, education, engineering, health professions, humanities, natural science, social/behavioral science. **Faculty and instruction (2009-2010):** Total instructional faculty: 448 full-time, 40 part-time (57% men; 43% women; 16% minorities). Full-time faculty with Ph.D. or other terminal degree: 79%. Student/faculty ratio: 20/1. Classes of fewer than 20 students: 41%; of 20 to 49 students: 47%; of 50 or more students: 12%. **Advanced Placement and International Baccalaureate credit:** AP tests may be used for: Credit and/or placement. Scores accepted: 3, 4, 5. International Baccalaureate exams may be used for: Credit and/or

placement. **Freshmen returning for sophomore year:** 70%. **Graduation rates:** Four-year: 15%; five-year: 33%; six-year: 41%.

COSTS AND FINANCIAL AID

Financial aid office: (316) 978-3430. **Expenses (2009-2010):** Tuition and fees 2009-2010: $5,467 in state, $13,501 out of state; room/board: $6,060. Estimated books and supplies: $945; transportation: $1,620; personal expenses: $2,299. **Financial aid:** Priority filing date for institution's financial aid form: March 1. In 2009-2010, 82% of undergraduates applied for financial aid. Of those, 38% were determined to have financial need; 66% had their need fully met. Average financial aid package (proportion receiving): $7,278 (37%). Average amount of gift aid, such as scholarships or grants (proportion receiving): $3,604 (20%). Average amount of self-help aid, such as work study or loans (proportion receiving): $4,750 (31%). Average need-based loan (excluding PLUS or other private loans): $4,729. Among students who received need-based aid, the average percentage of need met: 50%. Among students who received aid based on merit, the average award (and the proportion receiving): $1,704 (21%). The average athletic scholarship (and the proportion receiving): $6,837 (3%). Average amount of debt of borrowers graduating in 2009: $15,769. Proportion who borrowed: 57%.

CAMPUS LIFE AND EXTRACURRICULAR ACTIVITIES

Campus housing available: coed dorms, fraternity housing, apartments for married students, apartment for single students, special housing for disabled students. Students who live in college-owned, operated, or affiliated housing: 8%. **Student employment:** During the 2009-2010 academic year, 9% of undergraduates worked on campus. Average per-year earnings: $7,900. **Clubs and organizations:** Number of student organizations: 141. Activities include: campus ministries, choral groups, concert band, dance, drama/theater, international student organization, jazz band, literary magazine, music ensembles, musical theater, opera, pep band, radio station, student government, student newspaper, student film society, symphony orchestra, television station. Number of fraternities: 10; sororities: 8. Proportion of men in fraternities: 5%; of women in sororities: 2%. **Sports program (2009-2010):** Member of NCAA I. *Men's intercollegiate varsity sports:* baseball, basketball, cross country, golf, tennis, track and field (outdoor). *Women's intercollegiate varsity sports:* basketball, bowling, cross country, golf, crew (lightweight), softball, tennis, track and field (outdoor), volleyball.

SERVICES AND FACILITIES

Basic services: nonremedial tutoring, placement service, day care, health service, health insurance. **Remedial assistance:** reading, math, writing, study skills. **Counseling services:** minority student, career, military, personal, veteran student, academic, older student, psychological, birth control, religious. **For learning-disabled students:** School does not offer a structured program with separate admission and additional fees. Total undergraduates in learning-disabled program or receiving services: 295. Services include: remedial math, remedial English, reading machines, tape recorders, videotaped classes, diagnostic testing service, untimed tests, note-taking services, oral tests, readers, extended time for tests, tutors, texts on tape, typist/scribe, exams on tape or computer, other testing accommodations. **Library:** Number of titles: 1,772,590; number of current serial subscriptions: 54,615. **Information technology resources:** Students are not required to lease or own a computer. Number of campus computers available to all students: 1,500. School has a wireless network. Proportion of college-owned housing units wired for high-speed internet access: 100%. **Campus safety:** Security services offered: 24-hour foot-and-vehicle patrols, late-night transport/escort service, 24-hour emergency telephones, lighted pathways/sidewalks, student patrols, controlled dormitory access (key, security card, etc).

TRANSFER AND INTERNATIONAL STUDENTS

Transfer students: May apply for admission for the following academic terms: Fall, Spring, Summer. Applicants do not need a minimum number of credits to apply. For fall 2009: Transfer applications received: 1,884. Transfer applicants offered admission: 1,697. Transfer applicants enrolled: 1,379. **International students:** Number of foreign undergraduates: 607 (6% of student body). Number of countries represented: 92. Minimum TOEFL score required: 530 (paper); 197 (computer). Average TOEFL score: 538 (paper).

Kentucky

Alice Lloyd College

- **Address:** 100 Purpose Road, Pippa Passes, KY 41844
- **Website:** http://www.alc.edu
- **Private**
- **Enrollment:** 567 full-time; 28 part-time

KEY STATS
- ✔ **U.S News College Ranking:** 35, Regional Colleges (South)
- ✔ **ACT Score (25th/75th percentile):** 18-23
- ✔ **Tuition:** 2010-2011: $9,500

Selectivity: Selective	**Room/board:** $4,650
Acceptance rate: 9%	**Average debt:** $6,500
Student/faculty ratio: 18/1	**Proportion who borrowed:** 42%

UNDERGRADUATE STUDENT BODY STATS
2009-2010 enrollment: 567 full-time; 28 part-time. Men: 44%; women: 56%. **Ethnic makeup:** African American: 1%; Hispanic: 1%; White: 98%.

ADMISSIONS FACTS AND FIGURES
Phone: (888) 280-4252. **Email:** admissions@alc.edu. **Website:** http://www.alc.edu. **Application deadlines for fall 2011:** Regular decision: July 1. Early decision: Not offered. Early action: Not offered. Admission can be deferred. **Application fee:** None. **To apply online, go to:** http://www.alc.edu/future_students/admission_application.php. **Admissions requirements/recommendations:** High school units required (recommended): English: 4; Mathematics: 3; Science: 3; History: 2; Total units: 12. Tests: The college uses SAT or ACT scores in admissions decisions. Either SAT or ACT required. For admission to the fall 2011 entering class, the school will accept: ACT with or without writing accepted. Campus visit: Recommended. Admissions interview: Recommended. Off-campus interview: May be arranged. **Factors that count in admissions decisions:** *Academic:* Secondary school record: Very Important. Class rank: Important. Letters of recommendation: Considered. Standardized test scores: Very Important. Essay: Considered. *Nonacademic:* Interview: Considered. Extracurricular activities: Considered. Talent/ability: Considered. Character/personal qualities: Important. Alumni/ae relationship: Considered. Geographical residence: Very Important. State residency: Not Considered. Religious affiliation/commitment: Not Considered. Minority status: Considered. Volunteer work: Considered. Work experience: Considered. **Other schools with the greatest overlap in applicants:** Eastern Kentucky University; Georgetown College; Morehead State University; Pikeville College. **Admissions statistics for the fall 2009 entering class:** Total applicants: 1,972. Total accepted: 172. Freshmen enrolled: 172; Overall acceptance rate: 9%. **Size of waiting list:** 20 applicants; enrolled from waiting list: 10. **Credentials of fall 2009 freshmen:** 13% ranked in the top 10 percent of their high school class; 41% were in the top 25 percent; 80% were in the top half. (Proportion submitting class standing: 65%.) **Average high school grade point average:** 3.3. **First-year students who submitted SAT scores:** 2%. Scores (25/75 percentile): Critical Reading: 410-540, Math: 420-530, Combined: 830-1070. **First-year students submitting ACT scores:** 98%. Scores (25/75 percentile): English: 17-23, Math: 16-21, Composite: 18-23.

ACADEMICS
Year founded: 1923. **Academic calendar:** Semester. **Degrees offered:** bachelor's. **Most popular majors:** 30% biological and biomedical sciences, 20% education, 18% business, management, marketing, and related support services, 11% history, 8% English language and literature/letters. **Major fields of study:** biological and biomedical sciences; business, management, marketing, and related support services; education; English language and literature/letters; multi/interdisciplinary studies; parks, recreation, leisure, and fitness studies; social sciences. **Areas of required coursework:** humanities, computer literacy, mathematics, English (including composition), sciences (biological or physical), history, social science, other. **Pre-professional programs:** pre-law, pre-dentistry, pre-medicine, pre-veterinary science, pre-optometry, pre-pharmacy. **Special academic programs (% participation):** cooperative (work-study plan) program (100%), double major, internships,

liberal arts/career combination, student-designed major, study abroad, teacher certificate program (20%), other. **Teacher certification offered in:** elementary, middle/junior high, secondary. **Faculty and instruction (2009-2010):** Total instructional faculty: 28 full-time, 16 part-time (55% men; 45% women; 5% minorities). Full-time faculty with Ph.D. or other terminal degree: 61%. Student/faculty ratio: 18/1. Classes of fewer than 20 students: 60%; of 20 to 49 students: 40%; of 50 or more students: 0%. **Freshmen returning for sophomore year:** 63%. **Graduation rates:** Four-year: 23%; five-year: 34%; six-year: 37%. **Graduate study:** 35% of students pursue further study immediately upon graduation; 15% within one year; 10% within five years. Fields in which graduates pursue further study: Master of Business Administration (MBA), 12%; law, 14%; medicine, 43%; dentistry, 6%; engineering, 1%; education, 18%; arts and sciences, 5%; veterinary medicine, 1%.

COSTS AND FINANCIAL AID
Financial aid office: (606) 368-6059. **Expenses (2010-2011):** Tuition and fees 2010-2011: $9,500; room/board: $4,650. Estimated books and supplies: $950; transportation: $1,950; personal expenses: $1,950. **Financial aid:** Priority filing date for institution's financial aid form: March 15; deadline: August 15. In 2009-2010, 99% of undergraduates applied for financial aid. Of those, 82% were determined to have financial need; 23% had their need fully met. Average financial aid package (proportion receiving): $10,395 (82%). Average amount of gift aid, such as scholarships or grants (proportion receiving): $7,833 (81%). Average amount of self-help aid, such as work study or loans (proportion receiving): $3,120 (70%). Average need-based loan (excluding PLUS or other private loans): $903. Among students who received need-based aid, the average percentage of need met: 78%. Among students who received aid based on merit, the average award (and the proportion receiving): $4,344 (16%). The average athletic scholarship (and the proportion receiving): $7,869 (4%). Average amount of debt of borrowers graduating in 2009: $6,500. Proportion who borrowed: 42%.

CAMPUS LIFE AND EXTRACURRICULAR ACTIVITIES
Campus housing available (% using): women's dorms (49%), men's dorms (51%), special housing for disabled students. **Clubs and organizations:** Number of student organizations: 21. Activities include: campus ministries, choral groups, drama/theater, literary magazine, pep band, radio station, student government, student newspaper, television station, yearbook. Number of fraternities: 0; sororities: 0. Average proportion of students who stay on campus on weekends: 10%. **Sports program (2009-2010):** Member of NAIA. *Men's intercollegiate varsity sports:* baseball, basketball, cross country. *Women's intercollegiate varsity sports:* basketball, cross country, softball.

SERVICES AND FACILITIES
Basic services: placement service, day care, health service. **Remedial assistance:** math, writing, other. **Counseling services:** career, personal, academic. **For learning-disabled students:** School does not offer a structured program with separate admission and additional fees. **Library:** Number of titles: 72,781; number of current serial subscriptions: 211. **Information technology resources:** Students are not required to lease or own a computer. Number of campus computers available to all students: 106. School has a wireless network. Approximate number of users that can be accommodated: 1,000. Proportion of college-owned housing units wired for high-speed internet access: 100%. **Campus safety:** Security services offered: 24-hour foot-and-vehicle patrols, late-night transport/escort service, lighted pathways/sidewalks, controlled dormitory access (key, security card, etc).

TRANSFER AND INTERNATIONAL STUDENTS
Transfer students: May apply for admission for the following academic terms: Fall, Spring. Applicants need a minimum number of credits to apply. For fall 2009: Transfer applications received: 50. Transfer applicants offered admission: 37. Transfer applicants enrolled: 32. **International students:** Number of foreign undergraduates: 0. Number of countries represented: 1. Minimum TOEFL score required: 550 (paper); 213 (computer). Average TOEFL score: 570 (paper).

Asbury University

- **Address:** 1 Macklem Drive, Wilmore, KY 40390
- **Website:** http://www.asbury.edu
- **Private; Religious affiliation:** non-denominational
- **Enrollment:** 1,377 full-time; 93 part-time

KEY STATS
- ✔ **U.S News College Ranking:** 162, National Liberal Arts Colleges
- ✔ **ACT Score (25th/75th percentile):** 21-27
- ✔ **Tuition:** 2010-2011: $23,303
  - **Selectivity:** More selective   **Room/board:** $5,566
  - **Acceptance rate:** 53%   **Average debt:** $26,150
  - **Student/faculty ratio:** 14/1   **Proportion who borrowed:** 85%

UNDERGRADUATE STUDENT BODY STATS

2009-2010 enrollment: 1,377 full-time; 93 part-time. Men: 37%; women: 63%. **Ethnic makeup:** African American: 2%; American-Indian: 1%; Asian American: 1%; Hispanic: 2%; White: 93%; International: 1%.

ADMISSIONS FACTS AND FIGURES

Phone: (800) 888-1818. **Email:** admissions@asbury.edu. **Website:** http://www.asbury.edu. **Application deadlines for fall 2011:** Regular decision: Rolling. Early decision: Not offered. Early action: Not offered. Admission can be deferred. **To apply online, go to:** http://www.asbury.edu/application/. **Admissions requirements/recommendations:** High school units required (recommended): English: (4); Mathematics: (4); Science: (3); Foreign language: (2); Social studies: (1); History: (1); Total units: (15). Tests: The college uses SAT or ACT scores in admissions decisions. Either SAT or ACT required. For admission to the fall 2011 entering class, the school will accept: ACT with or without writing accepted. Campus visit: Recommended. Admissions interview: Neither required nor recommended. Off-campus interview: Not available. **Factors that count in admissions decisions:** *Academic:* Secondary school record: Important. Class rank: Considered. Letters of recommendation: Important. Standardized test scores: Very Important. Essay: Not Considered. *Nonacademic:* Interview: Not Considered. Extracurricular activities: Considered. Talent/ability: Considered. Character/personal qualities: Important. Alumni/ae relationship: Not Considered. Geographical residence: Not Considered. State residency: Not Considered. Religious affiliation/commitment: Not Considered. Minority status: Not Considered. Volunteer work: Not Considered. Work experience: Not Considered. **Other schools with the greatest overlap in applicants:** Georgetown College; Greenville College; Indiana Wesleyan University; Southern Wesleyan University; Taylor University. **Admissions statistics for the fall 2009 entering class:** Total applicants: 1,734. Total accepted: 924. Freshmen enrolled: 315; 52% were from out of state. Overall acceptance rate: 53%. **Size of waiting list:** 0 applicants; enrolled from waiting list: 0. **Credentials of fall 2009 freshmen:** 32% ranked in the top 10 percent of their high school class; 63% were in the top 25 percent; 91% were in the top half. (Proportion submitting class standing: 63%.) **Average high school grade point average:** 3.6. **First-year students who submitted SAT scores:** 34%. Scores (25/75 percentile): Critical Reading: 510-650, Math: 490-630, Combined: 1000-1280. **First-year students submitting ACT scores:** 69%. Scores (25/75 percentile): English: 19-26, Math: 22-29, Composite: 21-27.

ACADEMICS

Year founded: 1890. **Academic calendar:** Semester. **Degrees offered:** associate, bachelor's, master's. **Most popular majors:** 17% radio and television broadcasting technology/technician, 6% business/commerce, 6% history, 5% psychology, 5% speech and rhetorical studies. **Major fields of study:** biological and biomedical sciences; business, management, marketing, and related support services; communication, journalism, and related programs; communications technologies/technicians and support services; education; English language and literature/letters; foreign languages, literatures, and linguistics; health professions and related clinical sciences; history; mathematics and statistics; parks, recreation, leisure, and fitness studies; philosophy and religious studies; physical sciences; psychology; public administration and social service professions; social sciences; theology and religious vocations; visual and performing arts. **Areas of required coursework:** arts/fine arts, humanities, computer literacy, mathematics, English (including composition), philosophy, foreign languages, sciences (biological or physical), history, social science, other. **Pre-professional programs:** pre-law, pre-dentistry, pre-medicine, pre-theology, pre-veterinary science. **Special academic programs:** double major, English as a Second Language

(ESL), internships, study abroad, teacher certificate program. **Teacher certification offered in:** special education, elementary, middle/junior high, secondary. **Reserve Officers Training Corps (ROTC):** Army ROTC: Offered at cooperating institution (University of Kentucky); Air Force ROTC: Offered at cooperating institution (University of Kentucky). **Faculty and instruction (2009-2010):** Total instructional faculty: 83 full-time, 84 part-time (60% men; 40% women; 5% minorities). Full-time faculty with Ph.D. or other terminal degree: 71%. Student/faculty ratio: 14/1. Classes of fewer than 20 students: 59%; of 20 to 49 students: 39%; of 50 or more students: 1%. **Advanced Placement and International Baccalaureate credit:** International Baccalaureate exams may be used for: Credit only. **Freshmen returning for sophomore year:** 82%. **Graduation rates:** Four-year: 57%; five-year: 64%; six-year: 65%.

COSTS AND FINANCIAL AID

Financial aid office: (800) 888-1818. **Expenses (2010-2011):** Tuition and fees 2010-2011: $23,303; room/board: $5,566. Estimated books and supplies: $815; transportation: $1,225; personal expenses: $1,240. **Financial aid:** Priority filing date for institution's financial aid form: March 1. In 2009-2010, 85% of undergraduates applied for financial aid. Of those, 74% were determined to have financial need; 25% had their need fully met. Average financial aid package (proportion receiving): $17,794 (74%). Average amount of gift aid, such as scholarships or grants (proportion receiving): $11,682 (73%). Average amount of self-help aid, such as work study or loans (proportion receiving): $4,941 (65%). Average need-based loan (excluding PLUS or other private loans): $3,907. Among students who received need-based aid, the average percentage of need met: 81%. Among students who received aid based on merit, the average award (and the proportion receiving): $9,343 (10%). The average athletic scholarship (and the proportion receiving): $4,160 (3%). Average amount of debt of borrowers graduating in 2009: $26,150. Proportion who borrowed: 85%.

CAMPUS LIFE AND EXTRACURRICULAR ACTIVITIES

Campus housing available (% using): women's dorms (48%), men's dorms (36%), apartments for married students (1%), apartment for single students (15%). Students who live in college-owned, operated, or affiliated housing: 87%. **Student employment:** During the 2009-2010 academic year, 54% of undergraduates worked on campus. Average per-year earnings: $991. **Clubs and organizations:** Number of student organizations: 37. Activities include: campus ministries, choral groups, concert band, drama/theater, jazz band, literary magazine, music ensembles, musical theater, opera, radio station, student government, student newspaper, symphony orchestra, television station, yearbook. Number of fraternities: 0; sororities: 0. Average proportion of students who stay on campus on weekends: 70%. **Sports program (2009-2010):** Member of NAIA. *Men's intercollegiate varsity sports:* baseball, basketball, cross country, soccer, swimming, tennis. *Women's intercollegiate varsity sports:* basketball, cross country, soccer, softball, swimming, tennis, volleyball.

SERVICES AND FACILITIES

Basic services: nonremedial tutoring, placement service, health service, health insurance. **Remedial assistance:** math, writing, study skills. **Counseling services:** minority student, career, military, personal, veteran student, academic, older student, psychological, birth control, religious. **For learning-disabled students:** School does not offer a structured program with separate admission and additional fees. **Library:** Number of titles: 150,965; number of current serial subscriptions: 545. **Information technology resources:** Students are not required to lease or own a computer. Number of campus computers available to all students: 200. School has a wireless network. Approximate number of users that can be accommodated: 360. Proportion of college-owned housing units wired for high-speed internet access: 100%. **Campus safety:** Security services offered: 24-hour foot-and-vehicle patrols, late-night transport/escort service, lighted pathways/sidewalks, controlled dormitory access (key, security card, etc).

TRANSFER AND INTERNATIONAL STUDENTS

Transfer students: May apply for admission for the following academic terms: Fall, Spring, Summer. Applicants need a minimum number of credits to apply. For fall 2009: Transfer applications received: 212. Transfer applicants offered admission: 112. Transfer applicants enrolled: 58. **International students:** Number of foreign undergraduates: 16 (1% of student body). Number of countries represented: 9. Minimum TOEFL score required: 550 (paper); 213 (computer).

Bellarmine University

- **Address:** 2001 Newburg Road, Louisville, KY 40205
- **Website:** http://www.bellarmine.edu
- **Private; Religious affiliation:** Roman Catholic
- **Enrollment:** 2,047 full-time; 370 part-time

KEY STATS

✔ **U.S News College Ranking:** 12, Regional Universities (South)
✔ **ACT Score (25th/75th percentile):** 22-27
✔ **Tuition:** 2010-2011: $30,310

Selectivity: More selective	**Room/board:** $8,820
Acceptance rate: 53%	**Average debt:** $21,639
Student/faculty ratio: 12/1	**Proportion who borrowed:** 69%

UNDERGRADUATE STUDENT BODY STATS

2009-2010 enrollment: 2,047 full-time; 370 part-time. Men: 35%; women: 65%. **Ethnic makeup:** African American: 4%; Asian American: 3%; Hispanic: 2%; White: 90%; International: 1%. **Religious preference:** Protestant: 27%; No preference: 2%; Unknown: 18%; Roman Catholic: 50%; Other: 3%.

ADMISSIONS FACTS AND FIGURES

Phone: (502) 452-8131. **Email:** admissions@bellarmine.edu. **Website:** http://www.bellarmine.edu. **Application deadlines for fall 2011:** Regular decision: August 15. Early decision: Not offered. Early action: Send application by: November 1; Decision sent by: November 15. Admission can be deferred. **Application fee:** $25. **To apply online, go to:** http://www.bellarmine.edu/admissions/applyNow.asp. **Admissions requirements/recommendations:** High school units required (recommended): English: 4 (4); Mathematics: 3 (4); Science: 3 (4); Foreign language: 2 (2); Social studies: 2 (3); History: 1 (2); Academic electives: 5 (7); Total units: 20 (26). Tests: The college uses SAT or ACT scores in admissions decisions. Either SAT or ACT required. For admission to the fall 2011 entering class, the school will accept: ACT with or without writing accepted. Campus visit: Recommended. Admissions interview: Recommended. Off-campus interview: May be arranged. **Factors that count in admissions decisions: Academic:** Secondary school record: Very Important. Class rank: Important. Letters of recommendation: Very Important. Standardized test scores: Very Important. Essay: Considered. **Nonacademic:** Interview: Considered. Extracurricular activities: Important. Talent/ability: Considered. Character/personal qualities: Very Important. Alumni/ae relationship: Considered. Geographical residence: Considered. State residency: Considered. Religious affiliation/commitment: Not Considered. Minority status: Considered. Volunteer work: Considered. Work experience: Considered. **Other schools with the greatest overlap in applicants:** Centre College; Transylvania University; University of Kentucky; University of Louisville; Xavier University. **Admissions statistics for the fall 2009 entering class:** Total applicants: 6,021. Total accepted: 3,214. Freshmen enrolled: 603; 36% were from out of state. Overall acceptance rate: 53%. Non-early acceptance rate: 53%. **Credentials of fall 2009 freshmen:** 23% ranked in the top 10 percent of their high school class; 51% were in the top 25 percent; 84% were in the top half. (Proportion submitting class standing: 57%.) **Average high school grade point average:** 3.5. **First-year students who submitted SAT scores:** 23%. Scores (25/75 percentile): Critical Reading: 480-600, Math: 510-600, Combined: 990-1200. **First-year students submitting ACT scores:** 77%. Scores (25/75 percentile): English: 21-26, Math: 22-29, Composite: 22-27.

ACADEMICS

Year founded: 1950. **Academic calendar:** Semester. **Degrees offered:** bachelor's, post-bachelor's certificate, master's. **Most popular majors:** 32% health professions and related clinical sciences, 17% business, management, marketing, and related support services, 10% psychology, 8% communication, journalism, and related programs, 5% social sciences. **Major fields of study:** agriculture, agriculture operations, and related sciences; biological and biomedical sciences; business, management, marketing, and related support services; communication, journalism, and related programs; computer and information sciences and support services; education; engineering; English language and literature/letters; health professions and related clinical sciences; history; liberal arts and sciences studies, and humanities; mathematics and statistics; multi/interdisciplinary studies; philosophy and religious studies; physical sciences; psychology; security and protective services; social sciences; theology and religious vocations; visual and performing arts. **Areas of required coursework:** arts/fine arts, humanities, mathematics, English (including composition), philosophy, sciences (biological or physical), history, social science, other. **Pre-professional programs:** pre-law, pre-dentistry, pre-medicine, pre-veterinary science, pre-pharmacy, other. **Special academic programs (% participation):** accelerated program (14%), cross-registration (1%), double major (10%), dual enrollment (5%), honors program (4%), independent study (3%), internships (56%), liberal arts/career combination (2%), student-designed major (0%), study abroad (28%), teacher certificate program (5%). **Teacher certification offered in:** special education, elementary, middle/junior high, secondary. **Reserve Officers Training Corps (ROTC):** Army ROTC: Offered at cooperating institution (University of Louisville); Air Force ROTC: Offered at cooperating institution (University of Louisville). **Faculty and instruction (2009-2010):** Total instructional faculty: 138 full-time, 162 part-time (52% men; 48% women; 8% minorities). Full-time faculty with Ph.D. or other terminal degree: 80%. Student/faculty ratio: 12/1. Classes of fewer than 20 students: 63%; of 20 to 49 students: 35%; of 50 or more students: 2%. **Advanced Placement and International Baccalaureate credit:** AP tests may be used for: Placement only. Scores accepted: 3, 4, 5. International Baccalaureate exams may be used for: Placement only. **Freshmen returning for sophomore year:** 80%. **Graduation rates:** Four-year: 52%; five-year: 65%; six-year: 63%. **Graduate study:** 23% of students pursue further study immediately upon graduation. Fields in which graduates pursue further study: Master of Business Administration (MBA), 15%; law, 5%; medicine, 54%; education, 5%; arts and sciences, 20%; veterinary medicine, 1%.

COSTS AND FINANCIAL AID

Financial aid office: (502) 452-8124. **Expenses (2010-2011):** Tuition and fees 2010-2011: $30,310; room/board: $8,820. Estimated books and supplies: $876; transportation: $2,178; personal expenses: $4,114. **Financial aid:** Priority filing date for institution's financial aid form: March 1. In 2009-2010, 83% of undergraduates applied for financial aid. Of those, 75% were determined to have financial need; 24% had their need fully met. Average financial aid package (proportion receiving): $23,927 (74%). Average amount of gift aid, such as scholarships or grants (proportion receiving): $15,752 (74%). Average amount of self-help aid, such as work study or loans (proportion receiving): $5,705 (49%). Average need-based loan (excluding PLUS or other private loans): $4,112. Among students who received need-based aid, the average percentage of need met: 77%. Among students who received aid based on merit, the average award (and the proportion receiving): $16,198 (24%). The average athletic scholarship (and the proportion receiving): $7,981 (8%). Average amount of debt of borrowers graduating in 2009: $21,639. Proportion who borrowed: 69%.

CAMPUS LIFE AND EXTRACURRICULAR ACTIVITIES

Campus housing available (% using): coed dorms (43%), women's dorms (30%), men's dorms (27%), special housing for disabled students, other housing options. Students who live in college-owned, operated, or affiliated housing: 47%. **Student employment:** During the 2009-2010 academic year, 10% of undergraduates worked on campus. Average per-year earnings: $2,000. **Clubs and organizations:** Number of student organizations: 70. Activities include: campus ministries, choral groups, concert band, dance, drama/theater, international student organization, jazz band, music ensembles, musical theater, pep band, radio station, student government, student newspaper, yearbook. Number of fraternities: 1; sororities: 1. Proportion of men in fraternities: 1%; of women in sororities: 1%. Average proportion of students who stay on campus on weekends: 45%. **Sports program (2009-2010):** Member of NCAA II. **Men's intercollegiate varsity sports:** baseball, basketball, cross country, golf, lacrosse, soccer, tennis, track and field (indoor), track and field (outdoor). **Women's intercollegiate varsity sports:** basketball, cross country, field hockey, golf, soccer, softball, tennis, track and field (indoor), track and field (outdoor), volleyball.

SERVICES AND FACILITIES

Basic services: nonremedial tutoring, placement service. **Counseling services:** career, personal, academic, psychological, religious. **For learning-disabled students:** School does not offer a structured program with separate admission and additional fees. Total undergraduates in learning-disabled program or receiving services: 20. Services include: reading machines, tape recorders, videotaped classes, untimed tests, note-taking services, oral tests, learning center, readers, extended time for tests, tutors, priority registration, priority seating, proofreading services, substitution of courses, texts on tape. **Library:** Number of titles: 132,323; number of current serial subscriptions: 420. **Information technology resources:** Students are not required to lease or own a computer. Number of campus computers available to all students: 356. School has a wireless network. Approximate number of users that can be accommodated: 1,500. Proportion of college-owned housing units wired for high-speed internet access: 100%. **Campus safety:** Security services offered: 24-hour foot-and-vehicle patrols, late-night transport/escort service, 24-hour emergency telephones, lighted pathways/sidewalks, controlled dormitory access (key, security card, etc).

TRANSFER AND INTERNATIONAL STUDENTS
Transfer students: May apply for admission for the following academic terms: Fall, Spring, Summer. Applicants do not need a minimum number of credits to apply. For fall 2009: Transfer applications received: 87. Transfer applicants offered admission: 77. Transfer applicants enrolled: 67. **International students:** Number of foreign undergraduates: 28 (1% of student body). Number of countries represented: 19. Minimum TOEFL score required: 550 (paper); 213 (computer).

Berea College

- Address: CPO Box 2142, Berea, KY 40404
- Website: http://www.berea.edu
- Private
- Enrollment: 1,501 full-time; 47 part-time

KEY STATS
✔ **U.S News College Ranking:** 67, National Liberal Arts Colleges
✔ **ACT Score (25th/75th percentile):** 21-26
✔ **Tuition:** 2010-2011: $910

Selectivity: More selective	**Room/board:** $5,574
Acceptance rate: 19%	**Average debt:** $8,133
Student/faculty ratio: 10/1	**Proportion who borrowed:** 79%

UNDERGRADUATE STUDENT BODY STATS
2009-2010 enrollment: 1,501 full-time; 47 part-time. Men: 41%; women: 59%. **Ethnic makeup:** African American: 18%; American-Indian: 1%; Asian American: 1%; Hispanic: 3%; White: 70%; International: 7%.

ADMISSIONS FACTS AND FIGURES
Phone: (859) 985-3500. **Email:** admissions@berea.edu. **Website:** http://www.berea.edu. **Application deadlines for fall 2011:** Regular decision: April 30. Early decision: Not offered. Early action: Not offered. Admission cannot be deferred. **Application fee:** None. **To apply online, go to:** http://www.berea.edu/prospectivestudents/. **Admissions requirements/recommendations:** High school units required (recommended): English: (4); Mathematics: (3); Science: (2); Foreign language: (2); Social studies: (1); History: (1); Total units: (13). Tests: The college uses SAT or ACT scores in admissions decisions. Either SAT or ACT required. For admission to the fall 2011 entering class, the school will accept: ACT with or without writing accepted. Campus visit: Recommended. Admissions interview: Required. Off-campus interview: May be arranged. **Factors that count in admissions decisions:** *Academic:* Secondary school record: Important. Class rank: Important. Letters of recommendation: Considered. Standardized test scores: Important. Essay: Important. *Nonacademic:* Interview: Very Important. Extracurricular activities: Considered. Talent/ability: Considered. Character/personal qualities: Important. Alumni/ae relationship: Not Considered. Geographical residence: Considered. State residency: Considered. Religious affiliation/commitment: Not Considered. Minority status: Considered. Volunteer work: Considered. Work experience: Considered. **Other schools with the greatest overlap in applicants:** Eastern Kentucky University; Morehead State University; University of Kentucky; University of Louisville; University of Tennessee. **Admissions statistics for the fall 2009 entering class:** Total applicants: 2,745. Total accepted: 516. Freshmen enrolled: 392; 54% were from out of state. Overall acceptance rate: 19%. **Credentials of fall 2009 freshmen:** 26% ranked in the top 10 percent of their high school class; 69% were in the top 25 percent; 91% were in the top half. (Proportion submitting class standing: 86%.) **Average high school grade point average:** 3.4. **First-year students who submitted SAT scores:** 16%. Scores (25/75 percentile): Critical Reading: 500-620, Math: 465-585, Combined: 965-1205. **First-year students submitting ACT scores:** 78%. Scores (25/75 percentile): English: 20-27, Math: 19-24, Composite: 21-26.

ACADEMICS
Year founded: 1855. **Academic calendar:** 4-1-4. **Degrees offered:** bachelor's. **Most popular majors:** 11% visual and performing arts, 9% business, management, marketing, and related support services, 8% engineering technologies/technicians, 7% biological and biomedical sciences, 7% family

and consumer sciences/human sciences. **Major fields of study:** agriculture, agriculture operations, and related sciences; area, ethnic, cultural, and gender studies; biological and biomedical sciences; business, management, marketing, and related support services; communication, journalism, and related programs; education; engineering technologies/technicians; English language and literature/letters; family and consumer sciences/human sciences; foreign languages, literatures, and linguistics; health professions and related clinical sciences; history; mathematics and statistics; multi/interdisciplinary studies; philosophy and religious studies; physical sciences; psychology; social sciences; visual and performing arts. **Areas of required coursework:** arts/fine arts, humanities, mathematics, English (including composition), sciences (biological or physical), history, social science, other. **Pre-professional programs:** pre-law, pre-medicine, pre-veterinary science. **Special academic programs:** double major, English as a Second Language (ESL), exchange student program (domestic), honors program, independent study, internships, student-designed major, study abroad, teacher certificate program, other. **Teacher certification offered in:** early childhood, elementary, middle/junior high, secondary. **Faculty and instruction (2009-2010):** Total instructional faculty: 130 full-time, 46 part-time (55% men; 45% women; 13% minorities). Full-time faculty with Ph.D. or other terminal degree: 91%. Student/faculty ratio: 10/1. Classes of fewer than 20 students: 62%; of 20 to 49 students: 38%; of 50 or more students: 0%. **Advanced Placement and International Baccalaureate credit:** AP tests may be used for: Credit and/or placement. Scores accepted: 3, 4, 5. International Baccalaureate exams may be used for: Credit only. **Freshmen returning for sophomore year:** 81%. **Graduation rates:** Four-year: 51%; five-year: 64%; six-year: 65%.

COSTS AND FINANCIAL AID
Financial aid office: (859) 985-3310. **Expenses (2010-2011):** Tuition and fees 2010-2011: $910; room/board: $5,574. Estimated books and supplies: $700; transportation: $426; personal expenses: $1,376. **Financial aid:** Priority filing date for institution's financial aid form: March 15. In 2009-2010, 100% of undergraduates applied for financial aid. Of those, 100% were determined to have financial need; Average financial aid package (proportion receiving): $32,141 (100%). Average amount of gift aid, such as scholarships or grants (proportion receiving): $29,964 (100%). Average amount of self-help aid, such as work study or loans (proportion receiving): $2,198 (100%). Average need-based loan (excluding PLUS or other private loans): $213. Among students who received need-based aid, the average percentage of need met: 93%. Among students who received aid based on merit, the average award (and the proportion receiving): $0 (0%). The average athletic scholarship (and the proportion receiving): $0 (0%). Average amount of debt of borrowers graduating in 2009: $8,133. Proportion who borrowed: 79%.

CAMPUS LIFE AND EXTRACURRICULAR ACTIVITIES
Campus housing available: women's dorms, men's dorms, apartments for married students, other housing options. Students who live in college-owned, operated, or affiliated housing: 87%. **Student employment:** During the 2009-2010 academic year, 100% of undergraduates worked on campus. Average per-year earnings: $2,700. **Clubs and organizations:** Number of student organizations: 86. Activities include: campus ministries, choral groups, dance, drama/theater, international student organization, jazz band, literary magazine, music ensembles, pep band, student government, student newspaper, yearbook. Number of fraternities: 0; sororities: 0. **Sports program (2009-2010):** Member of NAIA. *Men's intercollegiate varsity sports:* baseball, basketball, cross country, golf, soccer, swimming, tennis, track and field (outdoor). *Women's intercollegiate varsity sports:* basketball, cross country, soccer, softball, swimming, tennis, track and field (outdoor), volleyball.

SERVICES AND FACILITIES
Basic services: nonremedial tutoring, placement service, day care, health service, health insurance. **Remedial assistance:** reading, math, writing, study skills, other. **Counseling services:** minority student, career, personal, academic, older student, psychological, birth control, religious. **For learning-disabled students:** School does not offer a structured program with separate admission and additional fees. Total undergraduates in learning-disabled program or receiving services: 68. Services include: remedial math, tape recorders, diagnostic testing service, note-taking services, oral tests, learning center, readers, extended time for tests, tutors, priority seating, texts on tape, other testing accommodations. **Library:** Number of titles: 381,418; number of current serial subscriptions: 840. **Information technology resources:** Students are not required to lease or own a computer. Number of campus computers available to all students: 1,600. School has a wireless network. Approximate number of users that can be accommodated: 575. Proportion of college-owned housing units wired for high-speed internet access: 100%. **Campus safety:** Security services offered: 24-hour foot-and-

vehicle patrols, 24-hour emergency telephones, lighted pathways/sidewalks, controlled dormitory access (key, security card, etc).

TRANSFER AND INTERNATIONAL STUDENTS

Transfer students: May apply for admission for the following academic terms: Fall, Spring. Applicants do not need a minimum number of credits to apply. For fall 2009: Transfer applications received: 364. Transfer applicants offered admission: 38. Transfer applicants enrolled: 28. **International students:** Number of foreign undergraduates: 112 (7% of student body). Number of countries represented: 121. Minimum TOEFL score required: 500 (paper); 173 (computer). Average TOEFL score: 600 (paper).

Brescia University

- **Address:** 717 Frederica Street, Owensboro, KY 42301
- **Website:** http://www.brescia.edu
- **Private; Religious affiliation:** Roman Catholic
- **Enrollment:** 489 full-time; 181 part-time

KEY STATS

✔ **U.S News College Ranking:** 31, Regional Colleges (South)
✔ **ACT Score (25th/75th percentile):** 18-24
✔ **Tuition:** 2010-2011: $17,390

Selectivity: Selective	**Room/board:** $9,250
Acceptance rate: 67%	**Average debt:** N/A
Student/faculty ratio: 11/1	**Proportion who borrowed:** N/A

UNDERGRADUATE STUDENT BODY STATS

2009-2010 enrollment: 489 full-time; 181 part-time. Men: 40%; women: 60%. **Ethnic makeup:** African American: 6%; Asian American: 1%; Hispanic: 2%; White: 87%; International: 4%.

ADMISSIONS FACTS AND FIGURES

Phone: (270) 686-4241. **Email:** admissions@brescia.edu. **Website:** http://www.brescia.edu. **Application deadlines for fall 2011:** Regular decision: Rolling. Early decision: Not offered. Early action: Not offered. Admission can be deferred. **Application fee:** $25. **To apply online, go to:** http://www.brescia.edu/admissions/apply_now.php. **Admissions requirements/recommendations:** High school units required (recommended): English: (4); Mathematics: (3); Science: (2); Foreign language: (2); Social studies: (2); History: (2); Academic electives: (2); Total units: (17). Tests: The college uses SAT or ACT scores in admissions decisions. Either SAT or ACT required. For admission to the fall 2011 entering class, the school will accept: ACT with or without writing accepted. Campus visit: Recommended. Admissions interview: Recommended. Off-campus interview: May be arranged. **Factors that count in admissions decisions:** *Academic:* Secondary school record: Not Considered. Class rank: Not Considered. Letters of recommendation: Not Considered. Standardized test scores: Very Important. Essay: Not Considered. *Nonacademic:* Interview: Not Considered. Extracurricular activities: Not Considered. Talent/ability: Not Considered. Character/personal qualities: Not Considered. Alumni/ae relationship: Not Considered. Geographical residence: Not Considered. State residency: Not Considered. Religious affiliation/commitment: Not Considered. Minority status: Not Considered. Volunteer work: Not Considered. Work experience: Not Considered. **Other schools with the greatest overlap in applicants:** Bellarmine University; University of Louisville; Western Kentucky University. **Admissions statistics for the fall 2009 entering class:** Total applicants: 677. Total accepted: 453. Freshmen enrolled: 122; 11% were from out of state. Overall acceptance rate: 67%. **Average high school grade point average:** 3.3. **First-year students who submitted SAT scores:** 10%. **First-year students submitting ACT scores:** 89%. Scores (25/75 percentile): English: 18-24, Math: 16-23, Composite: 18-24.

ACADEMICS

Year founded: 1950. **Academic calendar:** Semester. **Degrees offered:** associate, bachelor's, post-bachelor's certificate, master's. **Most popular majors:** 17% accounting, 13% social work, 11% special education and teaching, 7% elementary education and teaching, 7% liberal arts and sciences/liberal studies. **Major fields of study:** biological and biomedical sciences; business, management, marketing, and related support services; education; English language and literature/letters; foreign languages, literatures, and linguistics; health professions and related clinical sciences; history; liberal arts and sciences studies, and humanities; mathematics and statistics; multi/

interdisciplinary studies; physical sciences; psychology; public administration and social service professions; social sciences; theology and religious vocations; visual and performing arts. **Areas of required coursework:** arts/fine arts, humanities, computer literacy, mathematics, English (including composition), philosophy, foreign languages, sciences (biological or physical), history, social science, other. **Pre-professional programs:** pre-law, pre-dentistry, pre-medicine, pre-veterinary science, pre-optometry, pre-pharmacy, other. **Special academic programs (% participation):** cross-registration, distance learning, double major (8%), English as a Second Language (ESL) (5%), exchange student program (domestic), honors program (5%), independent study (12%), internships (45%), liberal arts/career combination, student-designed major (9%), teacher certificate program (14%), weekend college (10%). **Teacher certification offered in:** early childhood, special education, elementary, middle/junior high, secondary. **Faculty and instruction (2009-2010):** Total instructional faculty: 41 full-time, 38 part-time (53% men; 47% women; 9% minorities). Full-time faculty with Ph.D. or other terminal degree: 66%. Student/faculty ratio: 11/1. Classes of fewer than 20 students: 78%; of 20 to 49 students: 22%; of 50 or more students: 0%. **Advanced Placement and International Baccalaureate credit:** AP tests may be used for: Credit and/or placement. Scores accepted: 3, 4, 5. International Baccalaureate exams may be used for: Credit and/or placement. **Freshmen returning for sophomore year:** 62%. **Graduation rates:** Four-year: 26%; five-year: 40%; six-year: 41%.

COSTS AND FINANCIAL AID

Financial aid office: (270) 686-4253. **Expenses (2010-2011):** Tuition and fees 2010-2011: $17,390; room/board: $9,250. Estimated books and supplies: $1,200; transportation: $1,120; personal expenses: $1,225. **Financial aid:** Priority filing date for institution's financial aid form: March 15. In 2009-2010, 97% of undergraduates applied for financial aid. Of those, 97% were determined to have financial need; Average financial aid package (proportion receiving): $14,241 (97%). Average amount of gift aid, such as scholarships or grants (proportion receiving): $5,772 (89%). Average amount of self-help aid, such as work study or loans (proportion receiving): $3,876 (59%). Average need-based loan (excluding PLUS or other private loans): $3,645. The average athletic scholarship (and the proportion receiving): $5,897 (38%).

CAMPUS LIFE AND EXTRACURRICULAR ACTIVITIES

Campus housing available (% using): coed dorms (60%), women's dorms, men's dorms, apartment for single students (35%), special housing for disabled students, other housing options. Students who live in college-owned, operated, or affiliated housing: 41%. **Student employment:** During the 2009-2010 academic year, 20% of undergraduates worked on campus. Average per-year earnings: $1,700. **Clubs and organizations:** Number of student organizations: 36. Activities include: campus ministries, choral groups, dance, drama/theater, international student organization, literary magazine, music ensembles, pep band, student government, student newspaper. Number of fraternities: 0; sororities: 0. Average proportion of students who stay on campus on weekends: 60%. **Sports program (2009-2010):** Member of NAIA. **Men's intercollegiate varsity sports:** baseball, basketball, cross country, golf, soccer, tennis. **Women's intercollegiate varsity sports:** basketball, cross country, golf, soccer, softball, tennis, volleyball.

SERVICES AND FACILITIES

Basic services: nonremedial tutoring, women's center, placement service, health insurance. **Remedial assistance:** reading, math, writing, study skills. **Counseling services:** minority student, career, personal, academic, psychological, religious, other. **For learning-disabled students:** School does not offer a structured program with separate admission and additional fees. Total undergraduates in learning-disabled program or receiving services: 21. Services include: remedial math, remedial English, remedial reading, tape recorders, untimed tests, note-taking services, oral tests, learning center, readers, extended time for tests, tutors, priority seating, substitution of courses, texts on tape, typist/scribe. **Library:** Number of titles: 161,814; number of current serial subscriptions: 26,045. **Information technology resources:** Students are not required to lease or own a computer. Number of campus computers available to all students: 115. School has a wireless network. Approximate number of users that can be accommodated: 500. Proportion of college-owned housing units wired for high-speed internet access: 100%. **Campus safety:** Security services offered: late-night transport/escort service, lighted pathways/sidewalks, controlled dormitory access (key, security card, etc).

TRANSFER AND INTERNATIONAL STUDENTS

Transfer students: May apply for admission for the following academic terms: Fall, Spring. Applicants do not need a minimum number of credits to apply. For fall 2009: Transfer applications received: 194. Transfer applicants offered admission: 107. Transfer applicants enrolled: 81. **International students:** Number of foreign undergraduates: 18 (4% of student body). Number of countries represented: 22. Minimum TOEFL score required: 550 (paper); 79 (computer).

Campbellsville University

- ■ **Address:** 1 University Drive, Campbellsville, KY 42718
- ■ **Website:** http://www.campbellsville.edu
- ■ **Private; Religious affiliation:** Baptist
- ■ **Enrollment:** 1,710 full-time; 1,023 part-time

KEY STATS

✔ **U.S News College Ranking:** 25, Regional Colleges (South)
✔ **ACT Score (25th/75th percentile):** 18-23
✔ **Tuition:** 2010-2011: $19,310

Selectivity: Selective	**Room/board:** N/A
Acceptance rate: 67%	**Average debt:** $21,500
Student/faculty ratio: 13/1	**Proportion who borrowed:** 90%

UNDERGRADUATE STUDENT BODY STATS

2009-2010 enrollment: 1,710 full-time; 1,023 part-time. Men: 43%; women: 57%. **Ethnic makeup:** African American: 10%; Hispanic: 1%; White: 84%; International: 4%. **Religious preference:** Roman Catholic: 6%; Protestant: 25%; No preference: 13%; Unknown: 10%; Baptist: 46%.

ADMISSIONS FACTS AND FIGURES

Phone: (270) 789-5220. **Email:** admissions@campbellsville.edu. **Website:** http://www.campbellsville.edu. **Application deadlines for fall 2011:** Regular decision: August 1. Early decision: Not offered. Early action: Not offered. Admission can be deferred. **Application fee:** $20. **To apply online, go to:** http://exweb.campbellsville.edu/exweb/login.asp. **Admissions requirements/recommendations:** High school units required (recommended): English: 4 (4); Mathematics: 3 (3); Science: 3 (3); Social studies: 2 (2); History: 1 (1); Academic electives: 6 (6); Total units: 21 (21). Tests: The college uses SAT or ACT scores in admissions decisions. Either SAT or ACT required. For admission to the fall 2011 entering class, the school will accept: ACT with or without writing accepted. Campus visit: Recommended. Admissions interview: Recommended. Off-campus interview: May be arranged. **Factors that count in admissions decisions:** *Academic:* Secondary school record: Very Important. Class rank: Important. Letters of recommendation: Important. Standardized test scores: Important. Essay: Considered. *Nonacademic:* Interview: Important. Extracurricular activities: Considered. Talent/ability: Considered. Character/personal qualities: Important. Alumni/ae relationship: Considered. Geographical residence: Not Considered. State residency: Not Considered. Religious affiliation/commitment: Considered. Minority status: Not Considered. Volunteer work: Considered. Work experience: Considered. **Other schools with the greatest overlap in applicants:** Eastern Kentucky University; Georgetown College; Lindsey Wilson College; University of the Cumberlands; Western Kentucky University. **Admissions statistics for the fall 2009 entering class:** Total applicants: 2,109. Total accepted: 1,421. Freshmen enrolled: 518; 17% were from out of state. Overall acceptance rate: 67%. **Credentials of fall 2009 freshmen:** 17% ranked in the top 10 percent of their high school class; 38% were in the top 25 percent; 69% were in the top half. (Proportion submitting class standing: 78%.) **Average high school grade point average:** 3.1. **First-year students who submitted SAT scores:** 1%. Scores (25/75 percentile): Critical Reading: 420-560, Math: 430-600, Combined: 850-1160. **First-year students submitting ACT scores:** 75%. Scores (25/75 percentile): English: N/A, Math: N/A, Composite: 18-23.

ACADEMICS

Year founded: 1906. **Academic calendar:** Semester. **Degrees offered:** certificate, associate, bachelor's, master's. **Most popular majors:** 28% business, management, marketing, and related support services, 27% education, 9% theology and religious vocations, 5% public administration and social service professions, 5% security and protective services. **Major fields of study:** biological and biomedical sciences; business, management, marketing, and related support services; communication, journalism, and related pro-grams; computer and information sciences and support services; education; English language and literature/letters; history; liberal arts and sciences studies, and humanities; mathematics and statistics; parks, recreation, leisure, and fitness studies; physical sciences; psychology; public administration and social service professions; security and protective services; social sciences; theology and religious vocations; visual and performing arts. **Areas of required coursework:** arts/fine arts, humanities, computer literacy, mathematics, English (including composition), philosophy, sciences (biological or physical), history, social science, other. **Pre-professional programs:** prelaw, pre-dentistry, pre-medicine, pre-theology, pre-veterinary science, pre-optometry, pre-pharmacy. **Special academic programs:** accelerated program, distance learning, double major, dual enrollment, English as a Second Language (ESL), honors program, independent study, internships, study abroad, teacher certificate program, weekend college. **Teacher certification offered in:** early childhood, special education, elementary, middle/junior high, secondary. **Reserve Officers Training Corps (ROTC):** Army ROTC: Offered at cooperating institution. **Faculty and instruction (2009-2010):** Total instructional faculty: 115 full-time, 179 part-time (44% men; 56% women; 8% minorities). Full-time faculty with Ph.D. or other terminal degree: 58%. Student/faculty ratio: 13/1. Classes of fewer than 20 students: 67%; of 20 to 49 students: 33%; of 50 or more students: 0%. **Advanced Placement and International Baccalaureate credit:** AP tests may be used for: Credit only. Scores accepted: 3. **Freshmen returning for sophomore year:** 67%. **Graduation rates:** Four-year: 26%; five-year: 37%; six-year: 38%.

COSTS AND FINANCIAL AID

Financial aid office: (270) 789-5013. **Expenses (2010-2011):** Tuition and fees 2010-2011: $19,310. Estimated books and supplies: $1,000; transportation: $1,400; personal expenses: $2,700. **Financial aid:** Priority filing date for institution's financial aid form: April 1. In 2009-2010, 98% of undergraduates applied for financial aid. Of those, 94% were determined to have financial need; 17% had their need fully met. Average financial aid package (proportion receiving): $14,521 (93%). Average amount of gift aid, such as scholarships or grants (proportion receiving): $11,351 (91%). Average amount of self-help aid, such as work study or loans (proportion receiving): $4,342 (73%). Average need-based loan (excluding PLUS or other private loans): $3,785. Among students who received need-based aid, the average percentage of need met: 74%. Among students who received aid based on merit, the average award (and the proportion receiving): $5,340 (6%). The average athletic scholarship (and the proportion receiving): $9,261 (6%). Average amount of debt of borrowers graduating in 2009: $21,500. Proportion who borrowed: 90%.

CAMPUS LIFE AND EXTRACURRICULAR ACTIVITIES

Campus housing available (% using): women's dorms (56%), men's dorms (43%), apartments for married students (1%). Students who live in college-owned, operated, or affiliated housing: 48%. **Student employment:** During the 2009-2010 academic year, 5% of undergraduates worked on campus. Average per-year earnings: $1,700. **Clubs and organizations:** Number of student organizations: 40. Activities include: campus ministries, choral groups, concert band, dance, drama/theater, jazz band, literary magazine, marching band, music ensembles, musical theater, pep band, radio station, student government, student newspaper, television station. Average proportion of students who stay on campus on weekends: 35%. **Sports program (2009-2010):** Member of NAIA.

SERVICES AND FACILITIES

Basic services: nonremedial tutoring, placement service, health service, health insurance. **Remedial assistance:** reading, math, writing, study skills. **Counseling services:** career, military, personal, academic, psychological, religious. **Library:** Number of titles: 117,456; number of current serial subscriptions: 348. **Information technology resources:** Students are not required to lease or own a computer. Number of campus computers available to all students: 180. School does not have a wireless network. **Campus safety:** Security services offered: 24-hour foot-and-vehicle patrols, late-night transport/escort service, 24-hour emergency telephones, lighted pathways/sidewalks, controlled dormitory access (key, security card, etc).

TRANSFER AND INTERNATIONAL STUDENTS

Transfer students: May apply for admission for the following academic terms: Fall, Spring, Summer. Applicants do not need a minimum number of credits to apply. For fall 2009: Transfer applications received: 485. Transfer applicants offered admission: 271. Transfer applicants enrolled: 190. **International students:** Number of foreign undergraduates: 118 (4% of student body). Minimum TOEFL score required: 500 (paper); 177 (computer).

Centre College

- **Address:** 600 W. Walnut Street, Danville, KY 40422
- **Website:** http://www.centre.edu
- **Private; Religious affiliation:** Presbyterian Church (USA)
- **Enrollment:** 1,216 full-time

KEY STATS

- ✔ **U.S News College Ranking:** 47, National Liberal Arts Colleges
- ✔ **ACT Score (25th/75th percentile):** 26-30
- ✔ **Tuition:** 2009-2010: $31,200

Selectivity: More selective	**Room/board:** $7,800
Acceptance rate: 69%	**Average debt:** $17,190
Student/faculty ratio: 11/1	**Proportion who borrowed:** 53%

UNDERGRADUATE STUDENT BODY STATS

2009-2010 enrollment: 1,216 full-time. Men: 45%; women: 55%. **Ethnic makeup:** African American: 4%; Asian American: 3%; Hispanic: 2%; White: 89%; International: 2%. **Religious preference:** Roman Catholic: 21%; Protestant: 47%; Jewish: 1%; Muslim: 1%; Buddhist: 1%; No preference: 18%; Unknown: 1%; Presbyterian Church (USA): 9%.

ADMISSIONS FACTS AND FIGURES

Phone: (859) 238-5350. **Email:** admission@centre.edu. **Website:** http://www.centre.edu. **Application deadlines for fall 2011:** Regular decision: February 1; decision sent by March 15. Early decision: Not offered. Early action: Send application by: December 1; Decision sent by: January 15. Admission can be deferred. **Application fee:** $40. **To apply online, go to:** http://www.centre.edu/web/admission/howtoapply.html. **Admissions requirements/recommendations:** High school units required (recommended): English: 4 (4); Mathematics: 3 (4); Science: 2 (4); Foreign language: 2 (4); Social studies: 1 (2); History: 1 (2); Academic electives: 0 (0); Total units: 13 (21). Tests: The college uses SAT or ACT scores in admissions decisions. Either SAT or ACT required. For admission to the fall 2011 entering class, the school will accept: ACT with writing recommended. Campus visit: Recommended. Admissions interview: Recommended. Off-campus interview: May be arranged. **Factors that count in admissions decisions:** *Academic:* Secondary school record: Very Important. Class rank: Important. Letters of recommendation: Important. Standardized test scores: Important. Essay: Important. *Nonacademic:* Interview: Considered. Extracurricular activities: Considered. Talent/ability: Considered. Character/personal qualities: Considered. Alumni/ae relationship: Considered. Geographical residence: Considered. State residency: Not Considered. Religious affiliation/commitment: Not Considered. Minority status: Considered. Volunteer work: Considered. Work experience: Considered. **Other schools with the greatest overlap in applicants:** Rhodes College; Sewanee–University of the South; Transylvania University; University of Kentucky; University of Louisville. **Admissions statistics for the fall 2009 entering class:** Total applicants: 2,056. Total accepted: 1,422. Freshmen enrolled: 333; 38% were from out of state. Overall acceptance rate: 69%. Non-early acceptance rate: 69%. **Size of waiting list:** 249 applicants; enrolled from waiting list: 28. **Credentials of fall 2009 freshmen:** 59% ranked in the top 10 percent of their high school class; 84% were in the top 25 percent; 98% were in the top half. (Proportion submitting class standing: 62%.) **Average high school grade point average:** 3.6. **First-year students who submitted SAT scores:** 26%. Scores (25/75 percentile): Critical Reading: 550-670, Math: 570-670, Combined: 1120-1340. **First-year students submitting ACT scores:** 74%. Scores (25/75 percentile): English: 25-33, Math: 25-30, Composite: 26-30.

ACADEMICS

Year founded: 1819. **Academic calendar:** 4-1-4. **Degrees offered:** bachelor's. **Most popular majors:** 15% history, 9% economics, 9% political science and government, 9% social sciences, 7% psychology. **Major fields of study:** biological and biomedical sciences; computer and information sciences and support services; education; English language and literature/letters; foreign languages, literatures, and linguistics; history; mathematics and statistics; multi/interdisciplinary studies; philosophy and religious studies; physical sciences; psychology; social sciences; visual and performing arts. **Areas of required coursework:** humanities, mathematics, philosophy, foreign languages, sciences (biological or physical), history, social science, other. **Special academic programs (% participation):** cross-registration (1%), double major (27%), honors program (3%), independent study (32%), internships (24%), student-designed major (1%), study abroad (85%), teacher certificate program (4%). **Teacher certification offered in:** elementary, secondary.

Reserve Officers Training Corps (ROTC): Army ROTC: Offered at cooperating institution (University of Kentucky); Air Force ROTC: Offered at cooperating institution (University of Kentucky). **Faculty and instruction (2009-2010):** Total instructional faculty: 103 full-time, 17 part-time (58% men; 42% women; 10% minorities). Full-time faculty with Ph.D. or other terminal degree: 89%. Student/faculty ratio: 11/1. Classes of fewer than 20 students: 58%; of 20 to 49 students: 42%; of 50 or more students: 0%. **Advanced Placement and International Baccalaureate credit:** AP tests may be used for: Credit and/or placement. Scores accepted: 4, 5. International Baccalaureate exams may be used for: Credit and/or placement. **Freshmen returning for sophomore year:** 91%. **Graduation rates:** Four-year: 79%; five-year: 81%; six-year: 81%. **Graduate study:** 40% of students pursue further study immediately upon graduation. Fields in which graduates pursue further study: Master of Business Administration (MBA), 1%; law, 10%; medicine, 12%; dentistry, 4%; theology (or the seminary), 3%; education, 4%; arts and sciences, 66%.

COSTS AND FINANCIAL AID

Financial aid office: (859) 238-5365. **Expenses (2009-2010):** Tuition and fees 2009-2010: $31,200; room/board: $7,800. Estimated books and supplies: $1,200; transportation: $400; personal expenses: $800. **Financial aid:** Priority filing date for institution's financial aid form: March 1; deadline: March 1. In 2009-2010, 71% of undergraduates applied for financial aid. Of those, 59% were determined to have financial need; 30% had their need fully met. Average financial aid package (proportion receiving): $25,091 (59%). Average amount of gift aid, such as scholarships or grants (proportion receiving): $21,641 (59%). Average amount of self-help aid, such as work study or loans (proportion receiving): $5,527 (42%). Average need-based loan (excluding PLUS or other private loans): $4,803. Among students who received need-based aid, the average percentage of need met: 85%. Among students who received aid based on merit, the average award (and the proportion receiving): $14,106 (36%). The average athletic scholarship (and the proportion receiving): $0 (0%). Average amount of debt of borrowers graduating in 2009: $17,190. Proportion who borrowed: 53%.

CAMPUS LIFE AND EXTRACURRICULAR ACTIVITIES

Campus housing available (% using): coed dorms (57%), women's dorms (24%), men's dorms (14%), sorority housing (1%), fraternity housing (1%), apartment for single students (1%), special housing for disabled students (0%), special housing for international students (0%), other housing options (0%). Students who live in college-owned, operated, or affiliated housing: 99%. **Student employment:** During the 2009-2010 academic year, 35% of undergraduates worked on campus. Average per-year earnings: $1,100. Activities include: campus ministries, choral groups, dance, drama/theater, international student organization, jazz band, literary magazine, music ensembles, musical theater, opera, pep band, radio station, student government, student newspaper, symphony orchestra, television station. Number of fraternities: 4; sororities: 4. Proportion of men in fraternities: 34%; of women in sororities: 37%. Average proportion of students who stay on campus on weekends: 70%. **Sports program (2009-2010):** Member of NCAA III. **Men's intercollegiate varsity sports:** baseball, basketball, cross country, football, golf, lacrosse, soccer, swimming, tennis, track and field (indoor), track and field (outdoor). **Women's intercollegiate varsity sports:** basketball, cross country, field hockey, golf, lacrosse, soccer, softball, swimming, tennis, track and field (indoor), track and field (outdoor), volleyball.

SERVICES AND FACILITIES

Basic services: nonremedial tutoring, placement service, health service. **Remedial assistance:** reading, math, writing, study skills. **Counseling services:** minority student, career, personal, academic, psychological, birth control, religious. **For learning-disabled students:** School does not offer a structured program with separate admission and additional fees. Total undergraduates in learning-disabled program or receiving services: 44. Services include: tape recorders, other special classes, videotaped classes, note-taking services, oral tests, learning center, extended time for tests, tutors, priority registration, priority seating, texts on tape, exams on tape or computer, other testing accommodations. **Library:** Number of titles: 223,652; number of current serial subscriptions: 28,221. **Information technology resources:** Students are not required to lease or own a computer. Number of campus computers available to all students: 260. School has a wireless network. Approximate number of users that can be accommodated: 1,800. Proportion of college-owned housing units wired for high-speed internet access: 100%. **Campus safety:** Security services offered: 24-hour foot-and-vehicle patrols, late-night transport/escort service, 24-hour emergency telephones, lighted pathways/sidewalks, controlled dormitory access (key, security card, etc).

TRANSFER AND INTERNATIONAL STUDENTS

Transfer students: May apply for admission for the following academic terms: Fall, Winter. Applicants do not need a minimum number of credits to apply. For fall 2009: Transfer applications received: 45. Transfer applicants offered admission: 20. Transfer applicants enrolled: 8. **International students:** Number of foreign undergraduates: 23 (2% of student body). Minimum TOEFL score required: 580 (paper); 237 (computer). Average TOEFL score: 604 (paper).

Eastern Kentucky University

- **Address:** 521 Lancaster Avenue, Richmond, KY 40475
- **Website:** http://www.eku.edu
- **Public**
- **Enrollment:** 11,698 full-time; 2,293 part-time

KEY STATS

- ✔ **U.S News College Ranking:** 59, Regional Universities (South)
- ✔ **ACT Score (25th/75th percentile):** 19-23
- ✔ **Tuition:** 2009-2010: $6,772 in state, $17,740 out of state

Selectivity: Selective	**Room/board:** $6,500
Acceptance rate: 69%	**Average debt:** $12,588
Student/faculty ratio: 17/1	**Proportion who borrowed:** 66%

UNDERGRADUATE STUDENT BODY STATS

2009-2010 enrollment: 11,698 full-time; 2,293 part-time. Men: 43%; women: 57%. **Ethnic makeup:** African American: 5%; Asian American: 1%; Hispanic: 1%; White: 92%; International: 1%.

ADMISSIONS FACTS AND FIGURES

Phone: (800) 465-9191. **Email:** admissions@eku.edu. **Website:** http://www.eku.edu. **Application deadlines for fall 2011:** Regular decision: August 1. Early decision: Not offered. Early action: Not offered. Admission can be deferred. **Application fee:** $30. **To apply online, go to:** http://www.admissions.eku.edu/. **Admissions requirements/recommendations:** High school units required (recommended): English: 4; Mathematics: 3; Science: 3; Foreign language: 2; Social studies: 3; History: 0; Academic electives: 7; Total units: 25. Tests: The college uses SAT or ACT scores in admissions decisions. Either SAT or ACT required. For admission to the fall 2011 entering class, the school will accept: ACT with or without writing accepted. Campus visit: Neither required nor recommended. Admissions interview: Neither required nor recommended. Off-campus interview: Not available. **Factors that count in admissions decisions:** *Academic:* Secondary school record: Very Important. Class rank: Not Considered. Letters of recommendation: Not Considered. Standardized test scores: Very Important. Essay: Not Considered. *Nonacademic:* Interview: Not Considered. Extracurricular activities: Not Considered. Talent/ability: Not Considered. Character/personal qualities: Not Considered. Alumni/ae relationship: Not Considered. Geographical residence: Not Considered. State residency: Not Considered. Religious affiliation/commitment: Not Considered. Minority status: Not Considered. Volunteer work: Not Considered. Work experience: Not Considered. **Other schools with the greatest overlap in applicants:** Morehead State University; Northern Kentucky University; University of Kentucky; Western Kentucky University. **Admissions statistics for the fall 2009 entering class:** Total applicants: 8,339. Total accepted: 5,742. Freshmen enrolled: 2,564; 14% were from out of state. Overall acceptance rate: 69%. **First-year students submitting ACT scores:** 98%. Scores (25/75 percentile): English: 18-24, Math: 17-23, Composite: 19-23.

ACADEMICS

Year founded: 1906. **Academic calendar:** Semester. **Degrees offered:** certificate, associate, bachelor's, post-bachelor's certificate, master's, post-master's certificate. **Most popular majors:** 13% elementary and middle school administration/principalship, 9% occupational therapy/therapist, 6% counselor education/school counseling and guidance services, 6% security and protective services, 5% secondary education and teaching. **Major fields of study:** agriculture, agriculture operations, and related sciences; biological and biomedical sciences; business, management, marketing, and related support services; communication, journalism, and related programs; communications technologies/technicians and support services; computer and information sciences and support services; education; engineering technologies/technicians; English language and literature/letters; family and consumer sciences/human sciences; foreign languages, literatures, and

linguistics; health professions and related clinical sciences; history; legal professions and studies; liberal arts and sciences studies, and humanities; mathematics and statistics; natural resources and conservation; parks, recreation, leisure, and fitness studies; philosophy and religious studies; physical sciences; psychology; public administration and social service professions; security and protective services; social sciences; transportation and materials moving; visual and performing arts. **Areas of required coursework:** arts/fine arts, humanities, computer literacy, mathematics, English (including composition), foreign languages, sciences (biological or physical), history, social science, other. **Pre-professional programs:** pre-law, pre-dentistry, pre-medicine, pre-veterinary science, pre-optometry, pre-pharmacy. **Special academic programs:** cooperative (work-study plan) program, distance learning, double major, dual enrollment, English as a Second Language (ESL), honors program, independent study, internships, student-designed major, study abroad, teacher certificate program. **Teacher certification offered in:** early childhood, special education, elementary, vo-tech, middle/junior high, secondary. **Cooperative education programs:** agriculture, business, computer science, education, health professions, home economics, humanities, natural science, social/behavioral science, technologies, vocational arts, other. **Reserve Officers Training Corps (ROTC):** Army ROTC: Offered on campus; Air Force ROTC: Offered at cooperating institution. **Faculty and instruction (2009-2010):** Total instructional faculty: 615 full-time, 451 part-time (47% men; 53% women; 55% minorities). Full-time faculty with Ph.D. or other terminal degree: 75%. Student/faculty ratio: 17/1. Classes of fewer than 20 students: 48%; of 20 to 49 students: 48%; of 50 or more students: 4%. **Advanced Placement and International Baccalaureate credit:** AP tests may be used for: Credit only. Scores accepted: 3, 4, 5. International Baccalaureate exams may be used for: Credit only. **Freshmen returning for sophomore year:** 65%. **Graduation rates:** Four-year: 14%; five-year: 31%; six-year: 37%. **Graduate study:** 46% of students pursue further study within one year.

COSTS AND FINANCIAL AID

Financial aid office: (859) 622-2361. **Expenses (2009-2010):** Tuition and fees 2009-2010: $6,772 in state, $17,740 out of state; room/board: $6,500. Estimated books and supplies: $1,000. **Financial aid:** Priority filing date for institution's financial aid form: March 15. In 2009-2010, 79% of undergraduates applied for financial aid. Of those, 64% were determined to have financial need; 9% had their need fully met. Average financial aid package (proportion receiving): $10,183 (63%). Average amount of gift aid, such as scholarships or grants (proportion receiving): $5,949 (41%). Average amount of self-help aid, such as work study or loans (proportion receiving): $4,139 (52%). Average need-based loan (excluding PLUS or other private loans): $3,652. Among students who received need-based aid, the average percentage of need met: 83%. Among students who received aid based on merit, the average award (and the proportion receiving): $5,126 (12%). The average athletic scholarship (and the proportion receiving): $13,429 (1%). Average amount of debt of borrowers graduating in 2009: $12,588. Proportion who borrowed: 66%.

CAMPUS LIFE AND EXTRACURRICULAR ACTIVITIES

Campus housing available (% using): coed dorms (47%), women's dorms (33%), men's dorms (17%), apartments for married students, apartment for single students (3%), special housing for disabled students (0%). Students who live in college-owned, operated, or affiliated housing: 30%. **Student employment:** During the 2009-2010 academic year, 12% of undergraduates worked on campus. Average per-year earnings: $4,590. **Clubs and organizations:** Number of student organizations: 192. Activities include: choral groups, concert band, dance, drama/theater, jazz band, literary magazine, marching band, music ensembles, musical theater, pep band, radio station, student government, student newspaper, student film society, symphony orchestra, yearbook. Number of fraternities: 16; sororities: 14. Average proportion of students who stay on campus on weekends: 40%. **Sports program (2009-2010):** Member of NCAA I. *Men's intercollegiate varsity sports:* baseball, basketball, cross country, football, golf, tennis, track and field (indoor), track and field (outdoor). *Women's intercollegiate varsity sports:* basketball, cross country, golf, soccer, softball, tennis, track and field (indoor), track and field (outdoor), volleyball.

SERVICES AND FACILITIES

Basic services: nonremedial tutoring, health service. **Remedial assistance:** reading, math, writing, study skills. **Counseling services:** minority student, career, personal, academic, psychological, religious. **For learning-disabled students:** School does not offer a structured program with separate admission and additional fees. Services include: remedial math, remedial English, reading machines, remedial reading, tape recorders, other special classes, diagnostic testing service, note-taking services, oral tests, learning center, readers, extended time for tests, tutors, other. **Library:** Number of titles: 661,952; number of current serial subscriptions: 18,394. **Information technology resources:** Students are not required to lease or own a computer. Number of campus computers available to all students: 532. School has a wireless network. Approximate number of users that can be accommodated: 5,000. Proportion of college-owned housing units wired for high-speed internet access: 99%. **Campus safety:** Security services offered: 24-hour foot-and-vehicle patrols, late-night transport/escort service, 24-hour emergency telephones, lighted pathways/sidewalks, controlled dormitory access (key, security card, etc).

TRANSFER AND INTERNATIONAL STUDENTS

Transfer students: May apply for admission for the following academic terms: Fall, Spring, Summer. Applicants do not need a minimum number of credits to apply. For fall 2009: Transfer applications received: 2,953. Transfer applicants offered admission: 1,745. Transfer applicants enrolled: 1,160. **International students:** Number of foreign undergraduates: 68 (1% of student body). Number of countries represented: 28. Minimum TOEFL score required: 500 (paper); 173 (computer). Average TOEFL score: 525 (paper).

Georgetown College

- ■ **Address:** 400 E. College Street, Georgetown, KY 40324
- ■ **Website:** http://www.georgetowncollege.edu
- ■ **Private; Religious affiliation:** Baptist
- ■ **Enrollment:** 1,281 full-time; 54 part-time

KEY STATS

- ✔ **U.S News College Ranking:** 162, National Liberal Arts Colleges
- ✔ **ACT Score (25th/75th percentile):** 21-26
- ✔ **Tuition:** 2010-2011: $27,640

Selectivity: More selective	**Room/board:** $7,320
Acceptance rate: 79%	**Average debt:** $24,462
Student/faculty ratio: 11/1	**Proportion who borrowed:** 76%

UNDERGRADUATE STUDENT BODY STATS

2009-2010 enrollment: 1,281 full-time; 54 part-time. Men: 44%; women: 56%. **Ethnic makeup:** African American: 7%; Hispanic: 1%; White: 90%; International: 1%. **Religious preference:** Roman Catholic: 11%; Protestant: 35%; No preference: 10%; Baptist: 38%; Other: 6%.

ADMISSIONS FACTS AND FIGURES

Phone: (502) 863-8009. **Email:** admissions@georgetowncollege.edu. **Website:** http://www.georgetowncollege.edu. **Application deadlines for fall 2011:** Regular decision: August 1. Early decision: Not offered. Early action: Not offered. Admission can be deferred. **Application fee:** $30. **To apply online, go to:** http://www.georgetowncollege.edu/Admissions/application-process.htm. **Admissions requirements/recommendations:** High school units required (recommended): English: 4 (4); Mathematics: 3 (3); Science: 3 (3); Foreign language: 2 (2); Social studies: 2 (2); Total units: 20 (20). Tests: The college uses SAT or ACT scores in admissions decisions. Either SAT or ACT required. For admission to the fall 2011 entering class, the school will accept: ACT with or without writing accepted. Campus visit: Recommended. Admissions interview: Recommended. Off-campus interview: May be arranged. **Factors that count in admissions decisions: Academic:** Secondary school record: Very Important. Class rank: Important. Letters of recommendation: Important. Standardized test scores: Important. Essay: Considered. *Nonacademic:* Interview: Considered. Extracurricular activities: Important. Talent/ability: Important. Character/personal qualities: Important. Alumni/ae relationship: Considered. Geographical residence: Considered. State residency: Considered. Religious affiliation/commitment: Considered. Minority status: Not Considered. Volunteer work: Considered. Work experience: Not Considered. **Other schools with the greatest overlap in applicants:** Centre College; Eastern Kentucky University; Transylvania University; University of Kentucky; Western Kentucky University. **Admissions statistics for the fall 2009 entering class:** Total applicants: 1,720. Total accepted: 1,363. Freshmen enrolled: 378; 14% were from out of state. Overall acceptance rate: 79%. **Size of waiting list:** 0 applicants; enrolled from waiting list: 0. **Credentials of fall 2009 freshmen:** 31% ranked in the top 10 percent of their high school class; 60% were in the top 25 percent; 93% were in the top half. (Proportion submitting class standing: 77%.) **Average high school grade point average:** 3.4. **First-year students who submitted SAT scores:** 8%. Scores (25/75 percentile):

Critical Reading: 430-570, Math: 480-560, Combined: 910-1130. **First-year students submitting ACT scores:** 95%. Scores (25/75 percentile): English: 19-26, Math: 20-27, Composite: 21-26.

ACADEMICS

Year founded: 1787. **Academic calendar:** Semester. **Degrees offered:** bachelor's, master's. **Most popular majors:** 15% business, management, marketing, and related support services, 11% psychology, 10% communication, journalism, and related programs, 9% parks, recreation, leisure, and fitness studies, 8% education. **Major fields of study:** area, ethnic, cultural, and gender studies; biological and biomedical sciences; business, management, marketing, and related support services; communication, journalism, and related programs; computer and information sciences and support services; education; English language and literature/letters; foreign languages, literatures, and linguistics; health professions and related clinical sciences; history; liberal arts and sciences studies, and humanities; mathematics and statistics; multi/interdisciplinary studies; parks, recreation, leisure, and fitness studies; philosophy and religious studies; physical sciences; psychology; social sciences; visual and performing arts. **Areas of required coursework:** arts/fine arts, humanities, computer literacy, mathematics, English (including composition), philosophy, foreign languages, sciences (biological or physical), history, social science. **Special academic programs:** accelerated program, cooperative (work-study plan) program, double major, dual enrollment, honors program, independent study, internships, liberal arts/career combination, student-designed major, study abroad, teacher certificate program. **Teacher certification offered in:** early childhood, special education, elementary, middle/junior high, secondary. **Reserve Officers Training Corps (ROTC):** Army ROTC: Offered at cooperating institution (University of Kentucky); Air Force ROTC: Offered at cooperating institution (University of Kentucky). **Faculty and instruction (2009-2010):** Total instructional faculty: 110 full-time, 53 part-time (56% men; 44% women; 6% minorities). Full-time faculty with Ph.D. or other terminal degree: 95%. Student/faculty ratio: 11/1. Classes of fewer than 20 students: 63%; of 20 to 49 students: 37%; of 50 or more students: 0%. **Advanced Placement and International Baccalaureate credit:** AP tests may be used for: Credit only. Scores accepted: 3. International Baccalaureate exams may be used for: Credit only. **Freshmen returning for sophomore year:** 79%. **Graduation rates:** Four-year: 49%; five-year: 60%; six-year: 60%. **Graduate study:** 48% of students pursue further study immediately upon graduation; 65% within one year. Fields in which graduates pursue further study: law, 15%; medicine, 18%; dentistry, 9%; theology (or the seminary), 6%; arts and sciences, 52%.

COSTS AND FINANCIAL AID

Financial aid office: (502) 863-8027. **Expenses (2010-2011):** Tuition and fees 2010-2011: $27,640; room/board: $7,320. Estimated books and supplies: $1,250; transportation: $700; personal expenses: $1,650. **Financial aid:** Priority filing date for institution's financial aid form: February 15; deadline: March 15. In 2009-2010, 84% of undergraduates applied for financial aid. Of those, 77% were determined to have financial need; 31% had their need fully met. Average financial aid package (proportion receiving): $22,830 (77%). Average amount of gift aid, such as scholarships or grants (proportion receiving): $19,189 (77%). Average amount of self-help aid, such as work study or loans (proportion receiving): $5,020 (56%). Average need-based loan (excluding PLUS or other private loans): $4,622. Among students who received need-based aid, the average percentage of need met: 83%. Among students who received aid based on merit, the average award (and the proportion receiving): $13,990 (22%). The average athletic scholarship (and the proportion receiving): $9,585 (7%). Average amount of debt of borrowers graduating in 2009: $24,462. Proportion who borrowed: 76%.

CAMPUS LIFE AND EXTRACURRICULAR ACTIVITIES

Campus housing available (% using): women's dorms (37%), men's dorms (22%), sorority housing (13%), fraternity housing (16%), apartment for single students (12%). Students who live in college-owned, operated, or affiliated housing: 87%. **Student employment:** During the 2009-2010 academic year, 50% of undergraduates worked on campus. Average per-year earnings: $1,400. **Clubs and organizations:** Number of student organizations: 100. Activities include: choral groups, concert band, dance, drama/theater, literary magazine, music ensembles, musical theater, pep band, radio station, student government, student newspaper, yearbook. Number of fraternities: 5; sororities: 4. Proportion of men in fraternities: 30%; of women in sororities: 42%. Average proportion of students who stay on campus on weekends: 70%. **Sports program (2009-2010):** Member of NAIA. *Men's intercollegiate varsity sports:* baseball, basketball, cross country, football, golf, soccer, tennis, track and field (indoor), track and field (outdoor).

Women's intercollegiate varsity sports: basketball, cross country, golf, soccer, softball, tennis, track and field (indoor), track and field (outdoor), volleyball.

SERVICES AND FACILITIES

Basic services: nonremedial tutoring, placement service, health service, health insurance. **Remedial assistance:** study skills. **Counseling services:** minority student, career, personal, academic, psychological, religious. **For learning-disabled students:** School does not offer a structured program with separate admission and additional fees. Services include: reading machines, tape recorders, untimed tests, note-taking services, readers, extended time for tests, tutors, texts on tape, other testing accommodations. **Library:** Number of titles: 180,711; number of current serial subscriptions: 478. **Information technology resources:** Students are not required to lease or own a computer. Number of campus computers available to all students: 250. School has a wireless network. Proportion of college-owned housing units wired for high-speed internet access: 100%. **Campus safety:** Security services offered: 24-hour foot-and-vehicle patrols, late-night transport/escort service, 24-hour emergency telephones, lighted pathways/sidewalks, controlled dormitory access (key, security card, etc).

TRANSFER AND INTERNATIONAL STUDENTS

Transfer students: May apply for admission for the following academic terms: Fall, Spring, Summer. Applicants do not need a minimum number of credits to apply. For fall 2009: Transfer applications received: 81. Transfer applicants offered admission: 72. Transfer applicants enrolled: 38. **International students:** Number of foreign undergraduates: 13 (1% of student body). Number of countries represented: 8. Minimum TOEFL score required: 520 (paper); 190 (computer).

Kentucky State University

- ■ **Address:** 400 E. Main Street, Frankfort, KY 40601
- ■ **Website:** http://www.kysu.edu
- ■ **Public**
- ■ **Enrollment:** 2,106 full-time; 532 part-time

KEY STATS

✔ **U.S News College Ranking:** 49, Regional Colleges (South)
✔ **ACT Score (25th/75th percentile):** 15-19
✔ **Tuition:** 2009-2010: $5,686 in state, $14,058 out of state

Selectivity: Less selective	**Room/board:** $6,480
Acceptance rate: 24%	**Average debt:** $35,552
Student/faculty ratio: 15/1	**Proportion who borrowed:** 76%

UNDERGRADUATE STUDENT BODY STATS

2009-2010 enrollment: 2,106 full-time; 532 part-time. Men: 42%; women: 58%. **Ethnic makeup:** African American: 64%; Hispanic: 1%; White: 34%; International: 1%.

ADMISSIONS FACTS AND FIGURES

Phone: (800) 325-1716. **Email:** james.burrell@kysu.edu. **Website:** http://www.kysu.edu. **Application deadlines for fall 2011:** Regular decision: Rolling. Early decision: Not offered. Early action: Not offered. Admission can be deferred. **Application fee:** $30. **To apply online, go to:** http://www.kysu.edu/admissions/. **Admissions requirements/recommendations:** High school units required (recommended): English: 4; Mathematics: 3; Science: 3; Foreign language: (2); Social studies: 3; History: 1; Academic electives: 7; Total units: 22 (2). Tests: The college uses SAT or ACT scores in admissions decisions. Either SAT or ACT required. For admission to the fall 2011 entering class, the school will accept: ACT with or without writing accepted. Campus visit: Neither required nor recommended. Admissions interview: Neither required nor recommended. Off-campus interview: Not available. **Factors that count in admissions decisions:** *Academic:* Secondary school record: Important. Class rank: Not Considered. Letters of recommendation: Considered. Standardized test scores: Very Important. Essay: Considered. *Nonacademic:* Interview: Considered. Extracurricular activities: Considered. Talent/ability: Not Considered. Character/personal qualities: Considered. Alumni/ae relationship: Considered. Geographical residence: Considered. State residency: Important. Religious affiliation/commitment: Not Considered. Minority status: Not Considered. Volunteer work: Not Considered. Work experience: Not Considered. **Admissions statistics for the fall 2009 entering class:** Total applicants: 10,765. Total accepted: 2,610. Freshmen enrolled: 540; 58% were from out of state. Overall acceptance

rate: 24%. **Size of waiting list:** 0 applicants; enrolled from waiting list: 0. **Average high school grade point average:** 2.6. **First-year students who submitted SAT scores:** 16%. Scores (25/75 percentile): Critical Reading: 360-460, Math: 340-460, Combined: 700-920. **First-year students submitting ACT scores:** 92%. Scores (25/75 percentile): English: 13-19, Math: 15-18, Composite: 15-19.

ACADEMICS

Year founded: 1886. **Academic calendar:** Semester. **Degrees offered:** associate, bachelor's, master's. **Most popular majors:** 17% liberal arts and sciences/liberal studies, 15% business/commerce, 10% biology/biological sciences, 8% criminal justice/safety studies, 5% social work. **Major fields of study:** biological and biomedical sciences; business, management, marketing, and related support services; computer and information sciences and support services; education; engineering; English language and literature/letters; family and consumer sciences/human sciences; health professions and related clinical sciences; history; liberal arts and sciences studies, and humanities; mathematics and statistics; physical sciences; psychology; public administration and social service professions; security and protective services; social sciences; visual and performing arts. **Areas of required coursework:** arts/fine arts, humanities, computer literacy, mathematics, English (including composition), foreign languages, sciences (biological or physical), history, social science. **Pre-professional programs:** pre-law, pre-dentistry, pre-medicine, pre-veterinary science, pre-optometry, pre-pharmacy, other. **Special academic programs:** cooperative (work-study plan) program, distance learning, double major, English as a Second Language (ESL), honors program, independent study, internships, liberal arts/career combination, student-designed major, study abroad, teacher certificate program. **Teacher certification offered in:** early childhood, special education, elementary, secondary. **Cooperative education programs:** agriculture, home economics, other. **Reserve Officers Training Corps (ROTC):** Army ROTC: Offered at cooperating institution (University of Kentucky); Air Force ROTC: Offered at cooperating institution (University of Kentucky). **Faculty and instruction (2009-2010):** Total instructional faculty: 128 full-time, 52 part-time (50% men; 50% women; 34% minorities). Full-time faculty with Ph.D. or other terminal degree: 68%. Student/faculty ratio: 15/1. Classes of fewer than 20 students: 58%; of 20 to 49 students: 41%; of 50 or more students: 0%. **Advanced Placement and International Baccalaureate credit:** Scores accepted: 3. International Baccalaureate exams may be used for: Credit only. **Freshmen returning for sophomore year:** 51%. **Graduation rates:** Four-year: 8%; five-year: 20%; six-year: 26%. **Graduate study:** 50% of students pursue further study immediately upon graduation. Fields in which graduates pursue further study: Master of Business Administration (MBA), 2%; law, 2%; medicine, 2%; dentistry, 2%; engineering, 2%; theology (or the seminary), 1%; education, 28%; arts and sciences, 50%; veterinary medicine, 1%.

COSTS AND FINANCIAL AID

Financial aid office: (502) 597-5960. **Expenses (2009-2010):** Tuition and fees 2009-2010: $5,686 in state, $14,058 out of state; room/board: $6,480. Estimated books and supplies: $1,300; transportation: $800; personal expenses: $3,000. **Financial aid:** In 2009-2010, 82% of undergraduates applied for financial aid. Of those, 81% were determined to have financial need; 17% had their need fully met. Average financial aid package (proportion receiving): $8,529 (76%). Average amount of gift aid, such as scholarships or grants (proportion receiving): $5,405 (62%). Average amount of self-help aid, such as work study or loans (proportion receiving): $4,401 (72%). Average need-based loan (excluding PLUS or other private loans): $3,972. Among students who received need-based aid, the average percentage of need met: 20%. Among students who received aid based on merit, the average award (and the proportion receiving): $4,918 (4%). The average athletic scholarship (and the proportion receiving): $6,044 (7%). Average amount of debt of borrowers graduating in 2009: $35,552. Proportion who borrowed: 76%.

CAMPUS LIFE AND EXTRACURRICULAR ACTIVITIES

Campus housing available (% using): coed dorms (75%), women's dorms (25%). Students who live in college-owned, operated, or affiliated housing: 39%. **Student employment:** During the 2009-2010 academic year, 5% of undergraduates worked on campus. Average per-year earnings: $895. **Clubs and organizations:** Number of student organizations: 33. Activities include: choral groups, concert band, dance, drama/theater, international student organization, jazz band, marching band, music ensembles, musical theater, opera, pep band, student government, student newspaper, yearbook. Number of fraternities: 1; sororities: 1. Proportion of men in fraternities: 2%; of women in sororities: 2%. **Sports program (2009-2010):** Member of

NCAA II. **Men's intercollegiate varsity sports:** baseball, basketball, cross country, football, golf, track and field (outdoor). **Women's intercollegiate varsity sports:** basketball, cross country, softball, track and field (outdoor), volleyball.

SERVICES AND FACILITIES

Basic services: nonremedial tutoring, placement service, health service, health insurance. **Remedial assistance:** reading, math, writing, study skills. **Counseling services:** career, academic, older student. **For learning-disabled students:** School does not offer a structured program with separate admission and additional fees. Services include: remedial math, remedial English, reading machines, remedial reading, tape recorders, untimed tests, note-taking services, oral tests, learning center, readers, extended time for tests, tutors, priority registration, priority seating, texts on tape, other testing accommodations. **Library:** Number of titles: 452,246; number of current serial subscriptions: 27,919. **Information technology resources:** Students are not required to lease or own a computer. Number of campus computers available to all students: 339. School has a wireless network. Approximate number of users that can be accommodated: 9,396. Proportion of college-owned housing units wired for high-speed internet access: 100%. **Campus safety:** Security services offered: 24-hour emergency telephones, lighted pathways/sidewalks, controlled dormitory access (key, security card, etc).

TRANSFER AND INTERNATIONAL STUDENTS

Transfer students: May apply for admission for the following academic terms: Fall, Spring, Summer. Applicants need a minimum number of credits to apply. For fall 2009: Transfer applications received: 597. Transfer applicants offered admission: 215. Transfer applicants enrolled: 116. **International students:** Number of foreign undergraduates: 19 (1% of student body). Number of countries represented: 10. Minimum TOEFL score required: 525 (paper); 173 (computer). Average TOEFL score: 560 (paper).

Kentucky Wesleyan College

- **Address:** 3000 Frederica Street, Owensboro, KY 42301
- **Website:** http://www.kwc.edu
- **Private; Religious affiliation:** United Methodist
- **Enrollment:** 834 full-time; 42 part-time

KEY STATS

✔ **U.S News College Ranking:** second tier, National Liberal Arts Colleges
✔ **ACT Score (25th/75th percentile):** 19-24
✔ **Tuition:** 2010-2011: $18,180

Selectivity: Selective	**Room/board:** $6,730
Acceptance rate: 67%	**Average debt:** $20,906
Student/faculty ratio: 15/1	**Proportion who borrowed:** 89%

UNDERGRADUATE STUDENT BODY STATS

2009-2010 enrollment: 834 full-time; 42 part-time. Men: 53%; women: 47%. **Ethnic makeup:** African American: 9%; Hispanic: 1%; White: 88%; International: 1%. **Religious preference:** Roman Catholic: 20%; Protestant: 54%; No preference: 2%; Unknown: 10%; United Methodist: 13%.

ADMISSIONS FACTS AND FIGURES

Phone: (800) 999-0592. **Email:** admitme@kwc.edu. **Website:** http://www.kwc.edu. **Application deadlines for fall 2011:** Regular decision: Rolling. Early decision: Not offered. Early action: Not offered. Admission can be deferred. **Application fee:** None. **Admissions requirements/recommendations:** High school units required (recommended): English: 4; Mathematics: 3; Science: 3; Foreign language: (2); Social studies: 3; Total units: 13 (2). Tests: The college uses SAT or ACT scores in admissions decisions. Either SAT or ACT required. For admission to the fall 2011 entering class, the school will accept: ACT with or without writing accepted. Campus visit: Recommended. Admissions interview: Recommended. Off-campus interview: May be arranged. **Factors that count in admissions decisions: Academic:** Secondary school record: Very Important. Class rank: Considered. Letters of recommendation: Considered. Standardized test scores: Very Important. Essay: Not Considered. **Nonacademic:** Interview: Important. Extracurricular activities: Important. Talent/ability: Considered. Character/personal qualities: Considered. Alumni/ae relationship: Considered. Geographical residence: Not Considered. State residency: Not Considered. Religious affiliation/commitment: Not Considered. Minority status: Not Considered. Volunteer work: Considered. Work experience: Considered. **Other schools with the**

greatest overlap in applicants: Brescia University; Murray State University; University of Kentucky; University of Louisville; Western Kentucky University. **Admissions statistics for the fall 2009 entering class:** Total applicants: 1,240. Total accepted: 828. Freshmen enrolled: 227; 25% were from out of state. Overall acceptance rate: 67%. **Credentials of fall 2009 freshmen:** 18% ranked in the top 10 percent of their high school class; 36% were in the top 25 percent; 68% were in the top half. (Proportion submitting class standing: 80%.) **Average high school grade point average:** 3.2. **First-year students who submitted SAT scores:** 9%. Scores (25/75 percentile): Critical Reading: 450-550, Math: 430-520, Combined: 880-1070. **First-year students submitting ACT scores:** 93%. Scores (25/75 percentile): English: 18-25, Math: 17-24, Composite: 19-24.

ACADEMICS

Year founded: 1858. **Academic calendar:** Semester. **Degrees offered:** bachelor's. **Most popular majors:** 20% business, management, marketing, and related support services, 13% education, 10% biological and biomedical sciences, 10% parks, recreation, leisure, and fitness studies, 9% security and protective services. **Major fields of study:** biological and biomedical sciences; business, management, marketing, and related support services; communication, journalism, and related programs; computer and information sciences and support services; education; English language and literature/letters; foreign languages, literatures, and linguistics; history; mathematics and statistics; multi/interdisciplinary studies; parks, recreation, leisure, and fitness studies; philosophy and religious studies; physical sciences; psychology; public administration and social service professions; security and protective services; social sciences; visual and performing arts. **Areas of required coursework:** arts/fine arts, humanities, computer literacy, mathematics, English (including composition), foreign languages, sciences (biological or physical), history, social science. **Pre-professional programs:** pre-law, pre-dentistry, pre-medicine, pre-veterinary science, pre-optometry, pre-pharmacy, other. **Special academic programs (% participation):** cooperative (work-study plan) program (20%), double major (10%), independent study (50%), internships (31%), liberal arts/career combination (100%), student-designed major (0%), study abroad (2%), teacher certificate program (10%). **Teacher certification offered in:** early childhood, special education, elementary, middle/junior high, secondary, bilingual/bicultural. **Cooperative education programs:** business, computer science, natural science, social/behavioral science. **Reserve Officers Training Corps (ROTC):** Army ROTC: Offered at cooperating institution (Western Kentucky University). **Faculty and instruction (2009-2010):** Total instructional faculty: 43 full-time, 44 part-time (53% men; 47% women; 6% minorities). Full-time faculty with Ph.D. or other terminal degree: 84%. **Student/faculty ratio:** 15/1. Classes of fewer than 20 students: 70%; of 20 to 49 students: 30%; of 50 or more students: 0%. **Advanced Placement and International Baccalaureate credit:** AP tests may be used for: Credit only. Scores accepted: 3, 4, 5. International Baccalaureate exams may be used for: Placement only. **Freshmen returning for sophomore year:** 61%. **Graduation rates:** Four-year: 35%; five-year: 50%; six-year: 52%. **Graduate study:** 25% of students pursue further study immediately upon graduation; 33% within one year; 49% within five years. Fields in which graduates pursue further study: Master of Business Administration (MBA), 8%; law, 1%; medicine, 1%; education, 10%; arts and sciences, 10%.

COSTS AND FINANCIAL AID

Financial aid office: (270) 926-3111. **Expenses (2010-2011):** Tuition and fees 2010-2011: $18,180; room/board: $6,730. Estimated books and supplies: $1,400; transportation: $2,000; personal expenses: $1,000. **Financial aid:** Priority filing date for institution's financial aid form: March 15. In 2009-2010, 92% of undergraduates applied for financial aid. Of those, 83% were determined to have financial need; 29% had their need fully met. Average financial aid package (proportion receiving): $16,017 (83%). Average amount of gift aid, such as scholarships or grants (proportion receiving): $12,886 (82%). Average amount of self-help aid, such as work study or loans (proportion receiving): $4,078 (60%). Average need-based loan (excluding PLUS or other private loans): $4,078. Among students who received need-based aid, the average percentage of need met: 78%. Among students who received aid based on merit, the average award (and the proportion receiving): $8,955 (16%). The average athletic scholarship (and the proportion receiving): $0 (0%). Average amount of debt of borrowers graduating in 2009: $20,906. Proportion who borrowed: 89%.

CAMPUS LIFE AND EXTRACURRICULAR ACTIVITIES

Campus housing available (% using): coed dorms (40%), women's dorms (30%), men's dorms (30%), sorority housing, fraternity housing, other housing options. Students who live in college-owned, operated, or affiliated housing: 45%. **Student employment:** During the 2009-2010 academic year, 10% of undergraduates worked on campus. Average per-year earnings: $1,000. **Clubs and organizations:** Number of student organizations: 42. Activities include: campus ministries, choral groups, concert band, dance, drama/theater, literary magazine, music ensembles, pep band, radio station, student government, student newspaper, yearbook. Number of fraternities: 3; sororities: 2. Proportion of men in fraternities: 9%; of women in sororities: 11%. Average proportion of students who stay on campus on weekends: 50%. **Sports program (2009-2010):** Member of NCAA II. *Men's intercollegiate varsity sports:* baseball, basketball, cross country, football, golf, soccer. *Women's intercollegiate varsity sports:* basketball, cross country, golf, soccer, softball, tennis, volleyball.

SERVICES AND FACILITIES

Basic services: nonremedial tutoring, women's center, placement service, health service, health insurance. **Remedial assistance:** reading, math, writing, study skills. **Counseling services:** career, personal, veteran student, academic, psychological, religious. **For learning-disabled students:** School does not offer a structured program with separate admission and additional fees. Total undergraduates in learning-disabled program or receiving services: 62. Services include: remedial math, remedial English, remedial reading, untimed tests, note-taking services, learning center, extended time for tests, tutors, priority seating, typist/scribe, other testing accommodations, other. **Library:** Number of titles: 100,919; number of current serial subscriptions: 149. **Information technology resources:** Students are not required to lease or own a computer. Number of campus computers available to all students: 125. School has a wireless network. Approximate number of users that can be accommodated: 1,000. Proportion of college-owned housing units wired for high-speed internet access: 100%. **Campus safety:** Security services offered: late-night transport/escort service, 24-hour emergency telephones, lighted pathways/sidewalks, controlled dormitory access (key, security card, etc).

TRANSFER AND INTERNATIONAL STUDENTS

Transfer students: May apply for admission for the following academic terms: Fall, Spring, Summer. Applicants need a minimum number of credits to apply. For fall 2009: Transfer applications received: 267. Transfer applicants offered admission: 135. Transfer applicants enrolled: 68. **International students:** Number of foreign undergraduates: 10 (1% of student body). Number of countries represented: 5. Minimum TOEFL score required: 500 (paper); 70 (computer).

Lindsey Wilson College

- **Address:** 210 Lindsey Wilson Street, Columbia, KY 42728
- **Website:** http://www.lindsey.edu
- **Private; Religious affiliation:** United Methodist
- **Enrollment:** 1,900 full-time; 92 part-time

KEY STATS

✔ **U.S News College Ranking:** second tier, National Liberal Arts Colleges
✔ **ACT Score (25th/75th percentile):** 16-22
✔ **Tuition:** 2010-2011: $18,950

Selectivity: Less selective	**Room/board:** $7,645
Acceptance rate: 80%	**Average debt:** N/A
Student/faculty ratio: 16/1	**Proportion who borrowed:** N/A

UNDERGRADUATE STUDENT BODY STATS

2009-2010 enrollment: 1,900 full-time; 92 part-time. Men: 39%; women: 61%. **Ethnic makeup:** African American: 8%; American-Indian: 1%; Hispanic: 1%; White: 85%; International: 5%. **Religious preference:** Roman Catholic: 5%; Protestant: 53%; Jewish: 1%; Buddhist: 1%; No preference: 2%; Unknown: 24%; United Methodist: 9%; Other: 5%.

ADMISSIONS FACTS AND FIGURES

Phone: (270) 384-8100. **Email:** admissions@lindsey.edu. **Website:** http://www.lindsey.edu. **Application deadlines for fall 2011:** Regular decision: Rolling. Early decision: Not offered. Early action: Not offered. Admission cannot be deferred. **To apply online, go to:** http://campus.lindsey.edu/admissions/ugapp.cfm. **Admissions requirements/recommendations:** Tests: The college uses SAT or ACT scores in admissions decisions. Neither SAT nor ACT required. For admission to the fall 2011 entering class, the school will accept: ACT with or without writing accepted. Campus

visit: Recommended. Admissions interview: Recommended. Off-campus interview: May be arranged. **Factors that count in admissions decisions:** *Academic:* Secondary school record: Considered. Class rank: Considered. Letters of recommendation: Considered. Standardized test scores: Considered. Essay: Considered. *Nonacademic:* Interview: Considered. Extracurricular activities: Considered. Talent/ability: Considered. Character/personal qualities: Important. Alumni/ae relationship: Considered. Geographical residence: Considered. State residency: Considered. Religious affiliation/commitment: Considered. Minority status: Considered. Volunteer work: Considered. Work experience: Considered. **Other schools with the greatest overlap in applicants:** Campbellsville University; University of Kentucky; Western Kentucky University. **Admissions statistics for the fall 2009 entering class:** Total applicants: 2,090. Total accepted: 1,669. Freshmen enrolled: 562; 8% were from out of state. Overall acceptance rate: 80%. **Credentials of fall 2009 freshmen:** 8% ranked in the top 10 percent of their high school class; 26% were in the top 25 percent; 58% were in the top half. (Proportion submitting class standing: 71%.) **Average high school grade point average:** 3.0. **First-year students submitting ACT scores:** 84%. Scores (25/75 percentile): English: 15-22, Math: 16-21, Composite: 16-22.

ACADEMICS

Year founded: 1903. **Academic calendar:** Semester. **Degrees offered:** associate, bachelor's, master's. **Most popular majors:** 56% multi/interdisciplinary studies, 8% business, management, marketing, and related support services, 8% communication, journalism, and related programs, 4% theology and religious vocations, 3% biological and biomedical sciences. **Major fields of study:** area, ethnic, cultural, and gender studies; biological and biomedical sciences; business, management, marketing, and related support services; communication, journalism, and related programs; education; English language and literature/letters; history; liberal arts and sciences studies, and humanities; mathematics and statistics; philosophy and religious studies; psychology; public administration and social service professions; security and protective services; social sciences; visual and performing arts. **Areas of required coursework:** humanities, mathematics, English (including composition), sciences (biological or physical), history, social science. **Pre-professional programs:** pre-law, pre-dentistry, pre-medicine, pre-veterinary science, pre-optometry, pre-pharmacy. **Special academic programs (% participation):** double major (4%), student-designed major (1%), study abroad (1%), teacher certificate program (7%), weekend college (52%). **Teacher certification offered in:** elementary, middle/junior high, secondary. **Faculty and instruction (2009-2010):** Total instructional faculty: 90 full-time, 88 part-time (49% men; 51% women; 5% minorities). Full-time faculty with Ph.D. or other terminal degree: 73%. Student/faculty ratio: 16/1. Classes of fewer than 20 students: 62%; of 20 to 49 students: 38%; of 50 or more students: 0%. **Advanced Placement and International Baccalaureate credit:** International Baccalaureate exams may be used for: Placement only. **Freshmen returning for sophomore year:** 53%. **Graduation rates:** Four-year: 15%; five-year: 24%; six-year: 28%.

COSTS AND FINANCIAL AID

Financial aid office: (270) 384-8022. **Expenses (2010-2011):** Tuition and fees 2010-2011: $18,950; room/board: $7,645. Estimated books and supplies: $900; transportation: $2,213; personal expenses: $2,877. **Financial aid:** Priority filing date for institution's financial aid form: March 15. In 2009-2010, 99% of undergraduates applied for financial aid. Of those, 94% were determined to have financial need; Average financial aid package (proportion receiving): $15,075 (91%). Average amount of gift aid, such as scholarships or grants (proportion receiving): $11,898 (91%). Average amount of self-help aid, such as work study or loans (proportion receiving): $4,096 (83%). Average need-based loan (excluding PLUS or other private loans): $4,234. Among students who received aid based on merit, the average award (and the proportion receiving): $0 (0%). The average athletic scholarship (and the proportion receiving): $0 (0%).

CAMPUS LIFE AND EXTRACURRICULAR ACTIVITIES

Campus housing available (% using): women's dorms (37%), men's dorms (44%), apartment for single students (19%). Students who live in college-owned, operated, or affiliated housing: 44%. **Student employment:** During the 2009-2010 academic year, 1% of undergraduates worked on campus. Average per-year earnings: $1,000. **Clubs and organizations:** Number of student organizations: 29. Activities include: campus ministries, choral groups, dance, drama/theater, international student organization, literary magazine, marching band, pep band, student government, student newspaper. Number of fraternities: 0; sororities: 0. Average proportion of students who stay on campus on weekends: 40%. **Sports program (2009-2010):** Member of NAIA. *Men's intercollegiate varsity sports:* baseball, basketball, cross country, football, golf, soccer, swimming, tennis, track and field (indoor), track and field (outdoor). *Women's intercollegiate varsity sports:* basketball, cross country, golf, soccer, softball, swimming, tennis, track and field (indoor), track and field (outdoor), volleyball.

SERVICES AND FACILITIES

Basic services: placement service, health service, health insurance, other. **Remedial assistance:** reading, math, writing, study skills. **Counseling services:** career, personal, academic, religious. **For learning-disabled students:** School does not offer a structured program with separate admission and additional fees. Services include: remedial math, remedial English, reading machines, remedial reading, tape recorders, untimed tests, note-taking services, oral tests, learning center, readers, extended time for tests, tutors, priority seating. **Library:** Number of titles: 50,261; number of current serial subscriptions: 13,000. **Information technology resources:** Students are not required to lease or own a computer. Number of campus computers available to all students: 200. School has a wireless network. Approximate number of users that can be accommodated: 2,000. Proportion of college-owned housing units wired for high-speed internet access: 100%. **Campus safety:** Security services offered: 24-hour foot-and-vehicle patrols, late-night transport/escort service, 24-hour emergency telephones, lighted pathways/sidewalks, controlled dormitory access (key, security card, etc).

TRANSFER AND INTERNATIONAL STUDENTS

Transfer students: May apply for admission for the following academic terms: Fall, Spring, Summer. Applicants do not need a minimum number of credits to apply. For fall 2009: Transfer applications received: 729. Transfer applicants offered admission: 70. Transfer applicants enrolled: 54. **International students:** Number of foreign undergraduates: 90 (5% of student body). Number of countries represented: 34. Minimum TOEFL score required: 450 (paper); 133 (computer). Average TOEFL score: 468 (paper).

Mid-Continent University

- **Address:** 99 Powell Road E, Mayfield, KY 42066
- **Website:** http://www.midcontinent.edu
- **Private; Religious affiliation:** Southern Baptist Convention
- **Enrollment:** 1,576 full-time; 247 part-time

KEY STATS

✔ **U.S News College Ranking:** Unranked Specialty School–Business
✔ **ACT Score (25th/75th percentile):** 17-20
✔ **Tuition:** 2010-2011: $7,300

Selectivity: Less selective	**Room/board:** $6,600
Acceptance rate: 57%	**Average debt:** $10,782
Student/faculty ratio: 14/1	**Proportion who borrowed:** 78%

UNDERGRADUATE STUDENT BODY STATS

2009-2010 enrollment: 1,576 full-time; 247 part-time. **Men:** 36%; **women:** 64%. **Ethnic makeup:** African American: 13%; Hispanic: 1%; White: 84%; International: 2%. **Religious preference:** Southern Baptist Convention: 90%; Other: 10%.

ADMISSIONS FACTS AND FIGURES

Phone: (270) 247-8521. **Email:** admissions@midcontinent.edu. **Website:** http://www.midcontinent.edu. **Application deadlines for fall 2011:** Regular decision: Rolling; decision sent by August 1. Early decision: Not offered. Early action: Not offered. Admission can be deferred. **Application fee:** $20. **To apply online, go to:** http://www.midcontinent.info/OnlineApplication.html. **Admissions requirements/recommendations:** High school units required (recommended): English: 4 (4); Mathematics: 2 (2); Science: 2 (2); Foreign language: 1 (1); Social studies: 2 (2); History: 0 (0); Total units: 12 (12). Tests: The college uses SAT or ACT scores in admissions decisions. Either SAT or ACT required. For admission to the fall 2011 entering class, the school will accept: ACT with or without writing accepted. Campus visit: Recommended. Admissions interview: Neither required nor recommended. Off-campus interview: May be arranged. **Factors that count in admissions decisions:** *Academic:* Secondary school record: Important. Class rank: Important. Letters of recommendation: Important. Standardized test scores: Very Important. Essay: Important. *Nonacademic:* Interview: Considered. Extracurricular activities: Considered. Talent/ability: Considered. Character/personal qualities: Very Important. Alumni/ae relationship: Not Considered. Geographic residence: Not Considered. State

residency: Not Considered. Religious affiliation/commitment: Important. Minority status: Important. Volunteer work: Considered. Work experience: Considered. **Other schools with the greatest overlap in applicants:** Murray State University. **Admissions statistics for the fall 2009 entering class:** Total applicants: 508. Total accepted: 289. Freshmen enrolled: 189; 11% were from out of state. Overall acceptance rate: 57%. **Size of waiting list:** 0 applicants; enrolled from waiting list: 0. **Credentials of fall 2009 freshmen:** 2% ranked in the top 10 percent of their high school class; 15% were in the top 25 percent; 56% were in the top half. (Proportion submitting class standing: 92%.) **Average high school grade point average:** 2.9. **First-year students who submitted SAT scores:** 1%. **First-year students submitting ACT scores:** 99%. Scores (25/75 percentile): English: N/A, Math: N/A, Composite: 17-20.

ACADEMICS

Year founded: 1949. **Academic calendar:** Semester. **Degrees offered:** associate, bachelor's, master's. **Most popular majors:** 90% business administration and management, 3% Bible/biblical studies, 3% counseling psychology, 2% elementary education and teaching, 1% social sciences. **Major fields of study:** business, management, marketing, and related support services; education; foreign languages, literatures, and linguistics; psychology; social sciences; theology and religious vocations. **Areas of required coursework:** arts/fine arts, humanities, computer literacy, mathematics, English (including composition), sciences (biological or physical), history, social science. **Special academic programs (% participation):** accelerated program (93%), distance learning (5%), double major (1%), independent study (8%), teacher certificate program (2%). **Teacher certification offered in:** elementary. **Faculty and instruction (2009-2010):** Total instructional faculty: 31 full-time, 110 part-time (70% men; 30% women; 8% minorities). Full-time faculty with Ph.D. or other terminal degree: 45%. Student/faculty ratio: 14/1. Classes of fewer than 20 students: 82%; of 20 to 49 students: 18%; of 50 or more students: 1%. **Advanced Placement and International Baccalaureate credit:** AP tests may be used for: Credit only. **Freshmen returning for sophomore year:** 62%. **Graduation rates:** Four-year: 15%; five-year: 24%; six-year: 25%.

COSTS AND FINANCIAL AID

Financial aid office: (270) 247-8521. **Expenses (2010-2011):** Tuition and fees 2010-2011: $7,300; room/board: $6,600. Estimated books and supplies: $1,500; transportation: $2,500; personal expenses: $1,750. **Financial aid:** Priority filing date for institution's financial aid form: March 15. In 2009-2010, 97% of undergraduates applied for financial aid. Of those, 95% were determined to have financial need; 3% had their need fully met. Average financial aid package (proportion receiving): $8,244 (95%). Average amount of gift aid, such as scholarships or grants (proportion receiving): $6,021 (84%). Average amount of self-help aid, such as work study or loans (proportion receiving): $3,797 (75%). Average need-based loan (excluding PLUS or other private loans): $3,587. Among students who received need-based aid, the average percentage of need met: 35%. Among students who received aid based on merit, the average award (and the proportion receiving): $8,359 (2%). The average athletic scholarship (and the proportion receiving): $0 (0%). Average amount of debt of borrowers graduating in 2009: $10,782. Proportion who borrowed: 78%.

CAMPUS LIFE AND EXTRACURRICULAR ACTIVITIES

Campus housing available (% using): women's dorms (42%), men's dorms (58%). Students who live in college-owned, operated, or affiliated housing: 5%. **Student employment:** During the 2009-2010 academic year, 2% of undergraduates worked on campus. Average per-year earnings: $2,534. **Clubs and organizations:** Number of student organizations: 5. Activities include: campus ministries, international student organization, music ensembles, student government. Number of fraternities: 0; sororities: 0. Average proportion of students who stay on campus on weekends: 20%. **Sports program (2009-2010):** Member of NAIA. *Men's intercollegiate varsity sports:* baseball, basketball, soccer. *Women's intercollegiate varsity sports:* basketball, softball, volleyball.

SERVICES AND FACILITIES

Basic services: nonremedial tutoring. **Remedial assistance:** reading, math, writing, study skills. **Counseling services:** career, personal, psychological, religious. **For learning-disabled students:** School does not offer a structured program with separate admission and additional fees. Total undergraduates in learning-disabled program or receiving services: 2. Services include: remedial math, remedial English, remedial reading, tape recorders, videotaped classes, untimed tests, note-taking services, oral tests, readers, extended time for tests, tutors. **Library:** Number of titles: 36,046; number of current serial subscriptions: 47. **Information technology resources:** Students are not required to lease or own a computer. Number of campus computers available to all students: 40. School does not have a wireless network. Proportion of college-owned housing units wired for high-speed internet access: 100%. **Campus safety:** Security services offered: 24-hour emergency telephones, lighted pathways/sidewalks, controlled dormitory access (key, security card, etc).

TRANSFER AND INTERNATIONAL STUDENTS

Transfer students: May apply for admission for the following academic terms: Fall, Spring, Summer. Applicants do not need a minimum number of credits to apply. For fall 2009: Transfer applicants offered admission: 38. Transfer applicants enrolled: 38. **International students:** Number of foreign undergraduates: 39 (2% of student body). Number of countries represented: 13. Minimum TOEFL score required: 500 (paper); 61 (computer).

Midway College

■ **Address:** 512 E. Stephens Street, Midway, KY 40347
■ **Website:** http://www.midway.edu
■ **Private; Religious affiliation:** Christian Church (Disciples of Christ)
■ **Enrollment:** N/A

KEY STATS

✔ **U.S News College Ranking:** second tier, Regional Colleges (South)
✔ **ACT Score (25th/75th percentile):** 19-22
✔ **Tuition:** 2009-2010: $18,000
  Selectivity: Selective   **Room/board:** $6,800
  Acceptance rate: 79%   **Average debt:** N/A
  Student/faculty ratio: N/A   **Proportion who borrowed:** N/A

Morehead State University

■ **Address:** 150 University Boulevard, Morehead, KY 40351
■ **Website:** http://www.moreheadstate.edu
■ **Public**
■ **Enrollment:** 5,586 full-time; 1,964 part-time

KEY STATS

✔ **U.S News College Ranking:** 52, Regional Universities (South)
✔ **ACT Score (25th/75th percentile):** 19-24
✔ **Tuition:** 2009-2010: $6,036 in state, $15,096 out of state
  Selectivity: Selective   **Room/board:** $6,192
  Acceptance rate: 80%   **Average debt:** $24,045
  Student/faculty ratio: 17/1   **Proportion who borrowed:** 69%

UNDERGRADUATE STUDENT BODY STATS

2009-2010 enrollment: 5,586 full-time; 1,964 part-time. Men: 39%; women: 61%. **Ethnic makeup:** African American: 3%; Hispanic: 1%; White: 95%.

ADMISSIONS FACTS AND FIGURES

Phone: (606) 783-2000. **Email:** admissions@moreheadstate.edu. **Website:** http://www.moreheadstate.edu. **Application deadlines for fall 2011:** Regular decision: Rolling. Early decision: Not offered. Early action: Not offered. Admission can be deferred. **Application fee:** $30. **To apply online, go to:** http://acampus21.moreheadstate.edu/prospective/undergrad/apply. **Admissions requirements/recommendations:** High school units required (recommended): English: 4; Mathematics: 3; Science: 3; Foreign language: 2; Social studies: 3; History: 1; Academic electives: 7; Total units: 22. Tests: The college uses SAT or ACT scores in admissions decisions. Either SAT or ACT required. For admission to the fall 2011 entering class, the school will accept: ACT with or without writing accepted. Campus visit: Recommended. Admissions interview: Neither required nor recommended. Off-campus interview: May not be arranged. **Factors that count in admissions decisions:** *Academic:* Secondary school record: Very Important. Class rank: Not Considered. Letters of recommendation: Considered. Standardized test scores: Very Important. Essay: Not Considered. *Nonacademic:* Interview: Not Considered. Extracurricular activities: Not Considered. Talent/ability: Not Considered. Character/personal qualities: Not Considered. Alumni/ae relationship: Not Considered. Geographical residence: Not Considered. State residency: Not Considered. Religious affiliation/commitment: Not Considered. Minority status: Not Considered. Volunteer work: Not

Considered. Work experience: Not Considered. **Admissions statistics for the fall 2009 entering class:** Total applicants: 2,772. Total accepted: 2,217. Freshmen enrolled: 1,260; 15% were from out of state. Overall acceptance rate: 80%. **Credentials of fall 2009 freshmen:** 21% ranked in the top 10 percent of their high school class; 46% were in the top 25 percent; 77% were in the top half. (Proportion submitting class standing: 73%.) **Average high school grade point average:** 3.3. **First-year students who submitted SAT scores:** 4%. Scores (25/75 percentile): Critical Reading: 440-560, Math: 460-570, Combined: 900-1130. **First-year students submitting ACT scores:** 99%. Scores (25/75 percentile): English: 18-24, Math: 17-23, Composite: 19-24.

ACADEMICS

Year founded: 1922. **Academic calendar:** Semester. **Degrees offered:** associate, bachelor's, post-bachelor's certificate, master's, post-master's certificate. **Most popular majors:** 12% general studies, 7% education, 7% elementary education and teaching, 5% social work, 4% communication studies/speech communication and rhetoric. **Major fields of study:** agriculture, agriculture operations, and related sciences; biological and biomedical sciences; business, management, marketing, and related support services; communication, journalism, and related programs; computer and information sciences and support services; education; engineering technologies/technicians; English language and literature/letters; family and consumer sciences/human sciences; foreign languages, literatures, and linguistics; health professions and related clinical sciences; history; legal professions and studies; liberal arts and sciences studies, and humanities; mathematics and statistics; parks, recreation, leisure, and fitness studies; philosophy and religious studies; physical sciences; psychology; public administration and social service professions; social sciences; visual and performing arts. **Areas of required coursework:** humanities, computer literacy, mathematics, English (including composition), sciences (biological or physical), social science, other. **Pre-professional programs:** pre-law, pre-dentistry, pre-medicine, pre-veterinary science, pre-optometry, pre-pharmacy, other. **Special academic programs:** accelerated program, cooperative (work-study plan) program, cross-registration, distance learning, double major, dual enrollment, exchange student program (domestic), honors program, independent study, internships, student-designed major, study abroad, teacher certificate program, weekend college. **Teacher certification offered in:** early childhood, special education, elementary, vo-tech, middle/junior high, secondary. **Cooperative education programs:** agriculture, art, business, computer science, education, engineering, health professions, humanities, natural science, social/behavioral science, technologies, other. **Reserve Officers Training Corps (ROTC):** Army ROTC: Offered on campus. **Faculty and instruction (2009-2010):** Total instructional faculty: 370 full-time, 99 part-time (50% men; 50% women; 11% minorities). Full-time faculty with Ph.D. or other terminal degree: 68%. Student/faculty ratio: 17/1. Classes of fewer than 20 students: 52%; of 20 to 49 students: 44%; of 50 or more students: 3%. **Advanced Placement and International Baccalaureate credit:** AP tests may be used for: Credit and/or placement. Scores accepted: 3, 4, 5. International Baccalaureate exams may be used for: Credit and/or placement. **Freshmen returning for sophomore year:** 69%. **Graduation rates:** Four-year: 16%; five-year: 34%; six-year: 41%.

COSTS AND FINANCIAL AID

Financial aid office: (606) 783-2011. **Expenses (2009-2010):** Tuition and fees 2009-2010: $6,036 in state, $15,096 out of state; room/board; $6,192. Estimated books and supplies: $912; transportation: $600; personal expenses: $1,200. **Financial aid:** Priority filing date for institution's financial aid form: March 15. In 2009-2010, 84% of undergraduates applied for financial aid. Of those, 71% were determined to have financial need; 37% had their need fully met. Average financial aid package (proportion receiving): $9,447 (70%). Average amount of gift aid, such as scholarships or grants (proportion receiving): $5,224 (48%). Average amount of self-help aid, such as work study or loans (proportion receiving): $3,887 (50%). Average need-based loan (excluding PLUS or other private loans): $3,657. Among students who received need-based aid, the average percentage of need met: 74%. Among students who received aid based on merit, the average award (and the proportion receiving): $6,526 (13%). The average athletic scholarship (and the proportion receiving): $6,510 (5%). Average amount of debt of borrowers graduating in 2009: $24,045. Proportion who borrowed: 69%.

CAMPUS LIFE AND EXTRACURRICULAR ACTIVITIES

Campus housing available (% using): coed dorms (89%), sorority housing (1%), fraternity housing (1%), apartments for married students (1%), apartment for single students (5%), special housing for disabled students (1%), special housing for international students (1%), other housing options (1%).

Students who live in college-owned, operated, or affiliated housing: 33%. **Student employment:** During the 2009-2010 academic year, 12% of undergraduates worked on campus. Average per-year earnings: $1,931. **Clubs and organizations:** Number of student organizations: 103. Activities include: campus ministries, choral groups, concert band, dance, drama/theater, international student organization, jazz band, literary magazine, marching band, music ensembles, musical theater, opera, pep band, radio station, student government, student newspaper, symphony orchestra, television station, yearbook. Number of fraternities: 10; sororities: 9. Proportion of men in fraternities: 11%; of women in sororities: 8%. **Sports program (2009-2010):** Member of NCAA I. *Men's intercollegiate varsity sports:* baseball, basketball, cross country, football, golf, rifle, tennis, track and field (outdoor). *Women's intercollegiate varsity sports:* basketball, cross country, golf, rifle, soccer, softball, tennis, track and field (outdoor), volleyball.

SERVICES AND FACILITIES

Basic services: nonremedial tutoring, health service, health insurance. **Remedial assistance:** reading, math, writing, study skills. **Counseling services:** minority student, career, personal, veteran student, academic, older student, psychological, birth control. **For learning-disabled students:** School does not offer a structured program with separate admission and additional fees. Total undergraduates in learning-disabled program or receiving services: 49. Services include: remedial math, remedial English, reading machines, remedial reading, tape recorders, videotaped classes, note-taking services, oral tests, readers, extended time for tests, tutors, priority seating, texts on tape, other testing accommodations, other. **Library:** Number of titles: 537,675; number of current serial subscriptions: 41,041. **Information technology resources:** Students are not required to lease or own a computer. Number of campus computers available to all students: 1,000. School has a wireless network. Approximate number of users that can be accommodated: 20,100. Proportion of college-owned housing units wired for high-speed internet access: 100%. **Campus safety:** Security services offered: 24-hour foot-and-vehicle patrols, late-night transport/escort service, 24-hour emergency telephones, lighted pathways/sidewalks, controlled dormitory access (key, security card, etc).

TRANSFER AND INTERNATIONAL STUDENTS

Transfer students: May apply for admission for the following academic terms: Fall, Spring, Summer. Applicants need a minimum number of credits to apply. For fall 2009: Transfer applications received: 911. Transfer applicants offered admission: 670. Transfer applicants enrolled: 431. **International students:** Number of foreign undergraduates: 28. Number of countries represented: 19. Minimum TOEFL score required: 500 (paper); 173 (computer).

Murray State University

- **Address:** 113 Sparks Hall, Murray, KY 42071
- **Website:** http://www.murraystate.edu
- **Public**
- **Enrollment:** 6,816 full-time; 1,426 part-time

KEY STATS

✔ **U.S News College Ranking:** 22, Regional Universities (South)
✔ **ACT Score (25th/75th percentile):** 19-25
✔ **Tuition:** 2009-2010: $5,976 in state, $16,236 out of state

Selectivity: Selective	Room/board: $6,562
Acceptance rate: 73%	Average debt: $18,000
Student/faculty ratio: 16/1	Proportion who borrowed: 65%

UNDERGRADUATE STUDENT BODY STATS

2009-2010 enrollment: 6,816 full-time; 1,426 part-time. Men: 41%; women: 59%. **Ethnic makeup:** African American: 6%; Asian American: 1%; Hispanic: 1%; White: 90%; International: 2%.

ADMISSIONS FACTS AND FIGURES

Phone: (270) 809-3741. **Email:** admissions@murraystate.edu. **Website:** http://www.murraystate.edu. **Application deadlines for fall 2011:** Regular decision: August 1. Early decision: Not offered. Early action: Not offered. Admission can be deferred. **Application fee:** $30. **To apply online, go to:** https://www.applyweb.com/apply/murray/menu.html. **Admissions requirements/recommendations:** High school units required (recommended): English: 4; Mathematics: 3 (4); Science: 3 (4); Foreign language: 2; Social

studies: 3; Academic electives: 6; Total units: 22. Tests: The college uses SAT or ACT scores in admissions decisions. ACT required. For admission to the fall 2011 entering class, the school will accept: ACT with writing recommended. Campus visit: Recommended. Admissions interview: Recommended. Off-campus interview: May be arranged. **Factors that count in admissions decisions:** *Academic:* Secondary school record: Very Important. Class rank: Very Important. Letters of recommendation: Considered. Standardized test scores: Very Important. Essay: Not Considered. *Nonacademic:* Interview: Considered. Extracurricular activities: Considered. Talent/ability: Considered. Character/personal qualities: Considered. Alumni/ae relationship: Considered. Geographical residence: Considered. State residency: Considered. Religious affiliation/commitment: Not Considered. Minority status: Not Considered. Volunteer work: Not Considered. Work experience: Not Considered. **Other schools with the greatest overlap in applicants:** Austin Peay State University; University of Kentucky; University of Louisville; University of Tennessee–Martin; Western Kentucky University. **Admissions statistics for the fall 2009 entering class:** Total applicants: 4,233. Total accepted: 3,108. Freshmen enrolled: 1,391; 31% were from out of state. Overall acceptance rate: 73%. **Credentials of fall 2009 freshmen:** 16% ranked in the top 10 percent of their high school class; 43% were in the top 25 percent; 75% were in the top half. (Proportion submitting class standing: 84%.) **Average high school grade point average:** 3.3. **First-year students submitting ACT scores:** 100%. Scores (25/75 percentile): English: 19-25, Math: 17-24, Composite: 19-25.

ACADEMICS

Year founded: 1922. **Academic calendar:** Semester. **Degrees offered:** associate, bachelor's, master's. **Most popular majors:** 15% education, 13% business, management, marketing, and related support services, 11% health professions and related clinical sciences, 9% liberal arts and sciences studies, and humanities, 8% communication, journalism, and related programs. **Major fields of study:** agriculture, agriculture operations, and related sciences; biological and biomedical sciences; business, management, marketing, and related support services; communication, journalism, and related programs; communications technologies/technicians and support services; computer and information sciences and support services; education; engineering; engineering technologies/technicians; English language and literature/letters; family and consumer sciences/human sciences; foreign languages, literatures, and linguistics; health professions and related clinical sciences; history; liberal arts and sciences studies, and humanities; mathematics and statistics; natural resources and conservation; parks, recreation, leisure, and fitness studies; philosophy and religious studies; physical sciences; psychology; public administration and social service professions; security and protective services; social sciences; visual and performing arts. **Areas of required coursework:** arts/fine arts, humanities, computer literacy, mathematics, English (including composition), sciences (biological or physical), history, social science, other. **Pre-professional programs:** pre-law, pre-dentistry, pre-medicine, pre-theology, pre-veterinary science, pre-optometry, pre-pharmacy. **Special academic programs:** cooperative (work-study plan) program, cross-registration, distance learning, double major, dual enrollment, English as a Second Language (ESL), exchange student program (domestic), external degree program, honors program, independent study, internships, liberal arts/career combination, study abroad, teacher certificate program, weekend college, other. **Teacher certification offered in:** early childhood, special education, elementary, vo-tech, middle/junior high, secondary, bilingual/bicultural. **Cooperative education programs:** agriculture, art, business, computer science, education, engineering, health professions, home economics, humanities, natural science, social/behavioral science, technologies, other. **Reserve Officers Training Corps (ROTC):** Army ROTC: Offered on campus. **Faculty and instruction (2009-2010):** Total instructional faculty: 406 full-time, 161 part-time (54% men; 46% women; 11% minorities). Full-time faculty with Ph.D. or other terminal degree: 77%. Student/faculty ratio: 16/1. Classes of fewer than 20 students: 54%; of 20 to 49 students: 42%; of 50 or more students: 4%. **Advanced Placement and International Baccalaureate credit:** AP tests may be used for: Credit only. Scores accepted: 3, 4, 5. International Baccalaureate exams may be used for: Credit only. **Freshmen returning for sophomore year:** 73%. **Graduation rates:** Four-year: 32%; five-year: 47%; six-year: 52%.

COSTS AND FINANCIAL AID

Financial aid office: (270) 809-2546. **Expenses (2009-2010):** Tuition and fees 2009-2010: $5,976 in state, $16,236 out of state; room/board: $6,562. Estimated books and supplies: $900; transportation: $1,000; personal expenses: $1,500. **Financial aid:** Priority filing date for institution's financial aid form: April 1. In 2009-2010, 79% of undergraduates applied for financial aid. Of those, 64% were determined to have financial need; 87% had their need fully met. Average financial aid package (proportion receiving): $5,825 (56%). Average amount of gift aid, such as scholarships or grants (proportion receiving): $2,738 (38%). Average amount of self-help aid, such as work study or loans (proportion receiving): $3,087 (54%). Average need-based loan (excluding PLUS or other private loans): $2,446. Among students who received aid based on merit, the average award (and the proportion receiving): $2,306 (35%). The average athletic scholarship (and the proportion receiving): $8,884 (4%). Average amount of debt of borrowers graduating in 2009: $18,000. Proportion who borrowed: 65%.

CAMPUS LIFE AND EXTRACURRICULAR ACTIVITIES

Campus housing available (% using): coed dorms (77%), women's dorms (13%), apartments for married students (2%), apartment for single students (6%), special housing for disabled students (2%). Students who live in college-owned, operated, or affiliated housing: 36%. **Student employment:** During the 2009-2010 academic year, 21% of undergraduates worked on campus. Average per-year earnings: $2,710. **Clubs and organizations:** Number of student organizations: 225. Activities include: campus ministries, choral groups, concert band, dance, drama/theater, international student organization, jazz band, literary magazine, marching band, music ensembles, musical theater, pep band, radio station, student government, student newspaper, student film society, symphony orchestra, television station, yearbook. Number of fraternities: 15; sororities: 7. Average proportion of students who stay on campus on weekends: 40%. **Sports program (2009-2010):** Member of NCAA I. *Men's intercollegiate varsity sports:* baseball, basketball, football, golf, rifle, tennis. *Women's intercollegiate varsity sports:* basketball, crew (heavyweight), cross country, equestrian, golf, rifle, soccer, softball, tennis, track and field (indoor), track and field (outdoor), volleyball.

SERVICES AND FACILITIES

Basic services: nonremedial tutoring, women's center, placement service, health service, health insurance, other. **Remedial assistance:** reading, math, writing, study skills, other. **Counseling services:** minority student, career, military, personal, veteran student, academic, older student, psychological, birth control, religious. **For learning-disabled students:** School does not offer a structured program with separate admission and additional fees. Total undergraduates in learning-disabled program or receiving services: 400. Services include: remedial math, remedial English, reading machines, remedial reading, tape recorders, other special classes, diagnostic testing service, note-taking services, special bookstore section, oral tests, learning center, readers, extended time for tests, tutors, texts on tape. **Library:** Number of titles: 933,635; number of current serial subscriptions: 1,418. **Information technology resources:** Students are not required to lease or own a computer. Number of campus computers available to all students: 1,800. School has a wireless network. Approximate number of users that can be accommodated: 5,000. Proportion of college-owned housing units wired for high-speed internet access: 100%. **Campus safety:** Security services offered: 24-hour foot-and-vehicle patrols, late-night transport/escort service, 24-hour emergency telephones, lighted pathways/sidewalks, student patrols, controlled dormitory access (key, security card, etc).

TRANSFER AND INTERNATIONAL STUDENTS

Transfer students: May apply for admission for the following academic terms: Fall, Spring, Summer. Applicants need a minimum number of credits to apply. For fall 2009: Transfer applications received: 1,306. Transfer applicants offered admission: 947. Transfer applicants enrolled: 579. **International students:** Number of foreign undergraduates: 157 (2% of student body). Number of countries represented: 46. Minimum TOEFL score required: 500 (paper); 173 (computer).

Northern Kentucky University

- **Address:** Nunn Drive, Highland Heights, KY 41099
- **Website:** http://www.nku.edu
- **Public**
- **Enrollment:** 9,969 full-time; 3,210 part-time

KEY STATS

✔ **U.S News College Ranking:** 66, Regional Universities (South)
✔ **ACT Score (25th/75th percentile):** 19-24
✔ **Tuition:** 2009-2010: $6,792 in state, $12,792 out of state

Selectivity: Selective	**Room/board:** $5,698
Acceptance rate: 69%	**Average debt:** N/A
Student/faculty ratio: 17/1	**Proportion who borrowed:** N/A

UNDERGRADUATE STUDENT BODY STATS

2009-2010 enrollment: 9,969 full-time; 3,210 part-time. Men: 44%; women: 56%. **Ethnic makeup:** African American: 6%; Asian American: 1%; Hispanic: 1%; White: 90%; International: 1%. **Religious preference:** Other: 100%.

ADMISSIONS FACTS AND FIGURES

Phone: (800) 637-9948. **Email:** admitnku@nku.edu. **Website:** http://www.nku.edu. **Application deadlines for fall 2011:** Regular decision: August 1. Early decision: Not offered. Early action: Not offered. Admission can be deferred. **Application fee:** $40. **To apply online, go to:** http://www.nku.edu/apply/index.php. **Admissions requirements/recommendations:** High school units required (recommended): English: 4; Mathematics: 3; Science: 3; Foreign language: 2; Social studies: 3; History: 1; Academic electives: 5; Total units: 22. Tests: The college uses SAT or ACT scores in admissions decisions. Either SAT or ACT required. For admission to the fall 2011 entering class, the school will accept: ACT with or without writing accepted. Campus visit: Recommended. Admissions interview: Neither required nor recommended. Off-campus interview: Not available. **Factors that count in admissions decisions:** *Academic:* Secondary school record: Important. Class rank: Important. Letters of recommendation: Not Considered. Standardized test scores: Considered. Essay: Considered. *Nonacademic:* Interview: Not Considered. Extracurricular activities: Not Considered. Talent/ability: Not Considered. Character/personal qualities: Not Considered. Alumni/ae relationship: Not Considered. Geographical residence: Not Considered. State residency: Not Considered. Religious affiliation/commitment: Not Considered. Minority status: Not Considered. Volunteer work: Not Considered. Work experience: Not Considered. **Other schools with the greatest overlap in applicants:** Eastern Kentucky University; University of Cincinnati; University of Kentucky; University of Louisville; Western Kentucky University. **Admissions statistics for the fall 2009 entering class:** Total applicants: 6,887. Total accepted: 4,767. Freshmen enrolled: 2,243; 30% were from out of state. Overall acceptance rate: 69%. **Credentials of fall 2009 freshmen:** 9% ranked in the top 10 percent of their high school class; 29% were in the top 25 percent. **Average high school grade point average:** 3.1. **First-year students who submitted SAT scores:** 15%. Scores (25/75 percentile): Critical Reading: 420-540, Math: 430-540, Combined: 850-1080. **First-year students submitting ACT scores:** 85%. Scores (25/75 percentile): English: 18-24, Math: 17-24, Composite: 19-24.

ACADEMICS

Year founded: 1968. **Academic calendar:** Semester. **Degrees offered:** certificate, associate, bachelor's, post-bachelor's certificate, master's, post-master's certificate, doctorate. **Most popular majors:** 24% business, management, marketing, and related support services, 12% health professions and related clinical sciences, 11% education, 8% visual and performing arts, 7% social sciences. **Major fields of study:** biological and biomedical sciences; business, management, marketing, and related support services; communication, journalism, and related programs; computer and information sciences and support services; education; engineering technologies/technicians; English language and literature/letters; foreign languages, literatures, and linguistics; health professions and related clinical sciences; history; liberal arts and sciences studies, and humanities; mathematics and statistics; natural resources and conservation; parks, recreation, leisure, and fitness studies; philosophy and religious studies; physical sciences; psychology; public administration and social service professions; security and protective services; social sciences; visual and performing arts. **Areas of required coursework:** arts/fine arts, humanities, mathematics, English (including composition), sciences (biological or physical), social science, other. **Pre-**

professional programs: pre-law, pre-dentistry, pre-medicine, pre-veterinary science, pre-optometry, pre-pharmacy, other. **Special academic programs:** accelerated program, cooperative (work-study plan) program, cross-registration, distance learning, double major, dual enrollment, English as a Second Language (ESL), honors program, independent study, internships, liberal arts/career combination, student-designed major, study abroad, teacher certificate program, weekend college. **Teacher certification offered in:** early childhood, special education, elementary, vo-tech, middle/junior high, secondary. **Cooperative education programs:** art, business, computer science, education, engineering, health professions, humanities, natural science, social/behavioral science, technologies, other. **Reserve Officers Training Corps (ROTC):** Army ROTC: Offered at cooperating institution (Xavier University); Air Force ROTC: Offered at cooperating institution (University of Cincinnati). **Faculty and instruction (2009-2010):** Total instructional faculty: 536 full-time, 617 part-time (47% men; 53% women; 10% minorities). Student/faculty ratio: 17/1. **Advanced Placement and International Baccalaureate credit:** AP tests may be used for: Credit only. Scores accepted: 3, 4, 5. International Baccalaureate exams may be used for: Credit only. **Freshmen returning for sophomore year:** 69%. **Graduation rates:** Four-year: 8%; five-year: 22%; six-year: 34%.

COSTS AND FINANCIAL AID
Financial aid office: (859) 572-5143. **Expenses (2009-2010):** Tuition and fees 2009-2010: $6,792 in state, $12,792 out of state; room/board: $5,698. Estimated books and supplies: $800. **Financial aid:** Priority filing date for institution's financial aid form: March 1.

CAMPUS LIFE AND EXTRACURRICULAR ACTIVITIES
Campus housing available: coed dorms, women's dorms, men's dorms, sorority housing, fraternity housing, apartment for single students, special housing for disabled students, other housing options. Students who live in college-owned, operated, or affiliated housing: 14%. **Clubs and organizations:** Number of student organizations: 170. Activities include: campus ministries, choral groups, concert band, dance, drama/theater, international student organization, jazz band, literary magazine, model UN, music ensembles, musical theater, pep band, radio station, student government, student newspaper, student film society, symphony orchestra, television station. Number of fraternities: 5; sororities: 5. Proportion of men in fraternities: 5%; of women in sororities: 5%. Average proportion of students who stay on campus on weekends: 30%. **Sports program (2009-2010):** Member of NCAA II. *Men's intercollegiate varsity sports:* baseball, basketball, cross country, golf, soccer, tennis. *Women's intercollegiate varsity sports:* basketball, cross country, golf, soccer, softball, tennis, volleyball.

SERVICES AND FACILITIES
Basic services: nonremedial tutoring, placement service, day care, health service, health insurance. **Remedial assistance:** reading, math, writing, study skills, other. **Counseling services:** minority student, career, personal, veteran student, academic, older student, psychological, birth control, religious. **For learning-disabled students:** School does not offer a structured program with separate admission and additional fees. Total undergraduates in learning-disabled program or receiving services: 184. Services include: remedial math, remedial English, reading machines, remedial reading, tape recorders, untimed tests, note-taking services, oral tests, learning center, readers, extended time for tests, tutors, priority registration, priority seating, proofreading services, texts on tape, typist/scribe, exams on tape or computer, take home exams, other testing accommodations. **Library:** Number of titles: 871,092; number of current serial subscriptions: 1,002. **Information technology resources:** Students are not required to lease or own a computer. Number of campus computers available to all students: 1,890. School has a wireless network. Approximate number of users that can be accommodated: 5,000. Proportion of college-owned housing units wired for high-speed internet access: 100%. **Campus safety:** Security services offered: 24-hour foot-and-vehicle patrols, late-night transport/escort service, 24-hour emergency telephones, lighted pathways/sidewalks, controlled dormitory access (key, security card, etc).

TRANSFER AND INTERNATIONAL STUDENTS
Transfer students: May apply for admission for the following academic terms: Fall, Winter, Spring, Summer. Applicants need a minimum number of credits to apply. For fall 2009: Transfer applications received: 1,701. Transfer applicants offered admission: 1,015. Transfer applicants enrolled: 715. **International students:** Number of foreign undergraduates: 139 (1% of student body). Number of countries represented: 62. Minimum TOEFL score required: 500 (paper); 173 (computer). Average TOEFL score: 570 (paper).

■ **Address:** 147 Sycamore Street, Pikeville, KY 41501-1194
■ **Website:** http://www.pc.edu/
■ **Private; Religious affiliation:** Presbyterian Church (USA)
■ **Enrollment:** 624 full-time; 81 part-time

KEY STATS
✔ **U.S News College Ranking:** Unranked, National Liberal Arts Colleges
✔ **ACT Score (25th/75th percentile):** 17-23
✔ **Tuition:** 2010-2011: $15,250

Selectivity: N/A	**Room/board:** $6,300
Acceptance rate: 100%	**Average debt:** $18,103
Student/faculty ratio: 11/1	**Proportion who borrowed:** 76%

UNDERGRADUATE STUDENT BODY STATS
2009-2010 enrollment: 624 full-time; 81 part-time. Men: 50%; women: 50%. **Ethnic makeup:** African American: 10%; Asian American: 1%; Hispanic: 1%; White: 88%. **Religious preference:** Roman Catholic: 4%; Protestant: 71%; No preference: 5%; Unknown: 19%; Presbyterian Church (USA): 1%.

ADMISSIONS FACTS AND FIGURES
Phone: (606) 218-5251. **Email:** wewantyou@pc.edu. **Website:** http://www.pc.edu/. **Application deadlines for fall 2011:** Regular decision: August 16. Early decision: Not offered. Early action: Not offered. Admission can be deferred. **Admissions requirements/recommendations:** High school units required (recommended): English: (4); Mathematics: (3); Science: (3); Social studies: (2); History: (1); Total units: (13). Tests: The college does not use SAT or ACT scores in admissions decisions. Neither SAT nor ACT required. For admission to the fall 2011 entering class, the school will accept: ACT with or without writing accepted. Campus visit: Recommended. Admissions interview: Neither required nor recommended. Off-campus interview: May be arranged. **Factors that count in admissions decisions:** *Academic:* Secondary school record: Not Considered. Class rank: Not Considered. Letters of recommendation: Not Considered. Standardized test scores: Not Considered. Essay: Not Considered. *Nonacademic:* Interview: Not Considered. Extracurricular activities: Not Considered. Talent/ability: Not Considered. Character/personal qualities: Not Considered. Alumni/ae relationship: Not Considered. Geographical residence: Not Considered. State residency: Not Considered. Religious affiliation/commitment: Not Considered. Minority status: Not Considered. Volunteer work: Not Considered. Work experience: Not Considered. **Other schools with the greatest overlap in applicants:** Alice Lloyd College; Eastern Kentucky University; Morehead State University; University of Kentucky; University of Louisville. **Admissions statistics for the fall 2009 entering class:** Total applicants: 770. Total accepted: 770. Freshmen enrolled: 186; 37% were from out of state. Overall acceptance rate: 100%. **Credentials of fall 2009 freshmen:** 52% ranked in the top 25 percent of their high school class; 87% were in the top half. (Proportion submitting class standing: 73%.) **Average high school grade point average:** 3.2. **First-year students submitting ACT scores:** 100%. Scores (25/75 percentile): English: 17-22, Math: 16-23, Composite: 17-23.

ACADEMICS
Year founded: 1889. **Academic calendar:** Semester. **Degrees offered:** associate, transfer-associate, terminal-associate, bachelor's, post-bachelor's certificate. **Most popular majors:** 30% business, management, marketing, and related support services, 11% biological and biomedical sciences, 11% psychology, 10% history, 7% communication, journalism, and related programs. **Major fields of study:** biological and biomedical sciences; business, management, marketing, and related support services; communication, journalism, and related programs; computer and information sciences and support services; education; English language and literature/letters; history; mathematics and statistics; multi/interdisciplinary studies; philosophy and religious studies; physical sciences; psychology; security and protective services; social sciences; visual and performing arts. **Areas of required coursework:** humanities, computer literacy, mathematics, English (including composition), sciences (biological or physical), history, social science, other. **Pre-professional programs:** pre-law, pre-dentistry, pre-medicine, pre-theology, pre-pharmacy. **Special academic programs (% participation):** double major (13%), independent study (47%), internships (13%), liberal arts/career combination, study abroad (1%), teacher certificate program. **Teacher certification offered in:** elementary, middle/junior high, secondary. **Reserve Officers Training Corps (ROTC):** Army ROTC: Offered at cooperat-

ing institution (Morehead State University). **Faculty and instruction (2009-2010):** Total instructional faculty: 53 full-time, 17 part-time (44% men; 56% women; 0% minorities). Full-time faculty with Ph.D. or other terminal degree: 53%. Student/faculty ratio: 11/1. Classes of fewer than 20 students: 69%; of 20 to 49 students: 31%; of 50 or more students: 0%. **Advanced Placement and International Baccalaureate credit:** AP tests may be used for: Credit only. Scores accepted: 3. **Freshmen returning for sophomore year:** 50%. **Graduation rates:** Four-year: 18%; five-year: 31%; six-year: 32%. **Graduate study:** 22% of students pursue further study within one year; 40% within five years. Fields in which graduates pursue further study: Master of Business Administration (MBA), 21%; law, 3%; medicine, 6%; dentistry, 5%; theology (or the seminary), 1%; arts and sciences, 50%.

COSTS AND FINANCIAL AID

Financial aid office: (606) 218-5253. **Expenses (2010-2011):** Tuition and fees 2010-2011: $15,250; room/board: $6,300. Estimated books and supplies: $2,500; transportation: $2,500; personal expenses: $2,500. **Financial aid:** Priority filing date for institution's financial aid form: March 15. In 2009-2010, 96% of undergraduates applied for financial aid. Of those, 93% were determined to have financial need; 85% had their need fully met. Average financial aid package (proportion receiving): $14,677 (93%). Average amount of gift aid, such as scholarships or grants (proportion receiving): $11,834 (92%). Average amount of self-help aid, such as work study or loans (proportion receiving): $4,458 (63%). Average need-based loan (excluding PLUS or other private loans): $4,202. Among students who received need-based aid, the average percentage of need met: 92%. Average amount of debt of borrowers graduating in 2009: $18,103. Proportion who borrowed: 76%.

CAMPUS LIFE AND EXTRACURRICULAR ACTIVITIES

Campus housing available (% using): coed dorms (15%), women's dorms (34%), men's dorms (51%). Students who live in college-owned, operated, or affiliated housing: 44%. **Student employment:** During the 2009-2010 academic year, 1% of undergraduates worked on campus. Average per-year earnings: $1,500. **Clubs and organizations:** Number of student organizations: 30. Activities include: campus ministries, choral groups, dance, pep band, student government, student newspaper, yearbook. Number of fraternities: 0; sororities: 0. Average proportion of students who stay on campus on weekends: 30%. **Sports program (2009-2010):** Member of NAIA.

SERVICES AND FACILITIES

Basic services: nonremedial tutoring, health insurance. **Remedial assistance:** reading, math, writing. **Counseling services:** personal, veteran student, academic. **For learning-disabled students:** School does not offer a structured program with separate admission and additional fees. Total undergraduates in learning-disabled program or receiving services: 28. Services include: remedial math, remedial English, remedial reading, oral tests, readers, extended time for tests, tutors. **Library:** Number of titles: 72,673; number of current serial subscriptions: 219. **Information technology resources:** Students are not required to lease or own a computer. Number of campus computers available to all students: 162. School has a wireless network. Approximate number of users that can be accommodated: 500. Proportion of college-owned housing units wired for high-speed internet access: 0%. **Campus safety:** Security services offered: 24-hour foot-and-vehicle patrols, late-night transport/escort service, 24-hour emergency telephones, lighted pathways/sidewalks, controlled dormitory access (key, security card, etc).

TRANSFER AND INTERNATIONAL STUDENTS

Transfer students: May apply for admission for the following academic terms: Fall, Spring, Summer. Applicants need a minimum number of credits to apply. For fall 2009: Transfer applications received: 96. Transfer applicants offered admission: 96. Transfer applicants enrolled: 59. **International students:** Number of foreign undergraduates: 3. Number of countries represented: 4. Minimum TOEFL score required: 500 (paper); 175 (computer).

Spalding University

- **Address:** 845 S. Third Street, Louisville, KY 40203-2188
- **Website:** http://www.spalding.edu
- **Private; Religious affiliation:** Roman Catholic
- **Enrollment:** N/A

KEY STATS

✔ **U.S News College Ranking:** second tier, National Universities
✔ **SAT Score (25th/75th percentile):** 912-1090
✔ **Tuition:** 2009-2010: $17,700

Selectivity: Selective	**Room/board:** $3,000
Acceptance rate: 43%	**Average debt:** N/A
Student/faculty ratio: N/A	**Proportion who borrowed:** N/A

Thomas More College

- **Address:** 333 Thomas More Parkway, Crestview Hills, KY 41017-3495
- **Website:** http://www.thomasmore.edu
- **Private; Religious affiliation:** Roman Catholic
- **Enrollment:** 1,327 full-time; 384 part-time

KEY STATS

✔ **U.S News College Ranking:** 44, Regional Universities (South)
✔ **ACT Score (25th/75th percentile):** 20-25
✔ **Tuition:** 2010-2011: $23,517

Selectivity: Selective	**Room/board:** $6,790
Acceptance rate: 93%	**Average debt:** $26,862
Student/faculty ratio: 16/1	**Proportion who borrowed:** 74%

UNDERGRADUATE STUDENT BODY STATS

2009-2010 enrollment: 1,327 full-time; 384 part-time. Men: 47%; women: 53%. **Ethnic makeup:** African American: 5%; American-Indian: 1%; Asian American: 1%; Hispanic: 1%; White: 92%. **Religious preference:** Roman Catholic: 36%; Protestant: 14%; No preference: 2%; Unknown: 48%.

ADMISSIONS FACTS AND FIGURES

Phone: (800) 825-4557. **Email:** admissions@thomasmore.edu. **Website:** http://www.thomasmore.edu. **Application deadlines for fall 2011:** Regular decision: August 1. Early decision: Not offered. Early action: Not offered. Admission can be deferred. **Application fee:** $25. **To apply online, go to:** http://gohigherky.org/Applications/Thomas_More_College/apply.html?application_id=466. **Admissions requirements/recommendations:** High school units required (recommended): English: 4; Mathematics: 3; Science: 3; Foreign language: 2; Social studies: 3; Total units: 17. Tests: The college uses SAT or ACT scores in admissions decisions. Either SAT or ACT required. For admission to the fall 2011 entering class, the school will accept: ACT with or without writing accepted. Campus visit: Recommended. Admissions interview: Neither required nor recommended. Off-campus interview: May be arranged. **Factors that count in admissions decisions:** *Academic:* Secondary school record: Very Important. Class rank: Considered. Letters of recommendation: Considered. Standardized test scores: Very Important. Essay: Considered. *Nonacademic:* Interview: Considered. Extracurricular activities: Considered. Talent/ability: Considered. Character/personal qualities: Important. Alumni/ae relationship: Considered. Geographical residence: Not Considered. State residency: Not Considered. Religious affiliation/commitment: Not Considered. Minority status: Not Considered. Volunteer work: Considered. Work experience: Not Considered. **Other schools with the greatest overlap in applicants:** College of Mount St. Joseph; Georgetown College; Northern Kentucky University; University of Kentucky; University of Louisville. **Admissions statistics for the fall 2009 entering class:** Total applicants: 1,047. Total accepted: 974. Freshmen enrolled: 312; 49% were from out of state. Overall acceptance rate: 93%. **Credentials of fall 2009 freshmen:** 13% ranked in the top 10 percent of their high school class; 36% were in the top 25 percent; 64% were in the top half. (Proportion submitting class standing: 70%.) **Average high school grade point average:** 3.3. **First-year students who submitted SAT scores:** 29%. Scores (25/75 percentile): Critical Reading: 440-560, Math: 430-550, Combined: 870-1110. **First-year students submitting ACT scores:** 91%. Scores (25/75 percentile): English: 20-25, Math: 19-25, Composite: 20-25.

ACADEMICS

Year founded: 1921. **Academic calendar:** Semester. **Degrees offered:** certificate, associate, bachelor's, master's. **Most popular majors:** 51% business, management, marketing, and related support services, 8% health professions and related clinical sciences, 7% liberal arts and sciences studies, and humanities, 6% biological and biomedical sciences, 4% education. **Major fields of study:** area, ethnic, cultural, and gender studies; biological and biomedical sciences; business, management, marketing, and related support services; communication, journalism, and related programs; computer and information sciences and support services; education; English language and literature/letters; foreign languages, literatures, and linguistics; health professions and related clinical sciences; history; legal professions and studies; liberal arts and sciences studies, and humanities; mathematics and statistics; natural resources and conservation; parks, recreation, leisure, and fitness studies; philosophy and religious studies; physical sciences; psychology; security and protective services; social sciences; visual and performing arts. **Areas of required coursework:** arts/fine arts, humanities, computer literacy, mathematics, English (including composition), philosophy, foreign languages, sciences (biological or physical), history, social science, other. **Pre-professional programs:** pre-law, pre-dentistry, pre-medicine, pre-veterinary science, pre-pharmacy. **Special academic programs:** accelerated program, cooperative (work-study plan) program, cross-registration, double major, dual enrollment, honors program, independent study, internships, student-designed major, study abroad. **Teacher certification offered in:** elementary, middle/junior high, secondary. **Cooperative education programs:** art, business, computer science, education, humanities, natural science, social/behavioral science, technologies. **Reserve Officers Training Corps (ROTC):** Army ROTC: Offered at cooperating institution (Xavier University); Air Force ROTC: Offered at cooperating institution (University of Cincinnati). **Faculty and instruction (2009-2010):** Total instructional faculty: 75 full-time, 58 part-time (51% men; 49% women; 5% minorities). Full-time faculty with Ph.D. or other terminal degree: 68%. Student/faculty ratio: 16/1. Classes of fewer than 20 students: 73%; of 20 to 49 students: 27%; of 50 or more students: 0%. **Advanced Placement and International Baccalaureate credit:** AP tests may be used for: Credit and/or placement. Scores accepted: 3, 4, 5. International Baccalaureate exams may be used for: Credit only. **Freshmen returning for sophomore year:** 70%. **Graduation rates:** Four-year: 28%; five-year: 46%; six-year: 45%. **Graduate study:** 15% of students pursue further study immediately upon graduation; 41% within one year; 65% within five years. Fields in which graduates pursue further study: Master of Business Administration (MBA), 37%; law, 5%; medicine, 7%; engineering, 1%; theology (or the seminary), 3%; education, 8%; arts and sciences, 17%.

COSTS AND FINANCIAL AID

Financial aid office: (859) 344-3319. **Expenses (2010-2011):** Tuition and fees 2010-2011: $23,517; room/board: $6,790. Estimated books and supplies: $1,000; transportation: $2,000; personal expenses: $2,300. **Financial aid:** Priority filing date for institution's financial aid form: March 15; deadline: March 15. In 2009-2010, 82% of undergraduates applied for financial aid. Of those, 70% were determined to have financial need; 23% had their need fully met. Average financial aid package (proportion receiving): $14,988 (70%). Average amount of gift aid, such as scholarships or grants (proportion receiving): $12,017 (61%). Average amount of self-help aid, such as work study or loans (proportion receiving): $4,209 (54%). Average need-based loan (excluding PLUS or other private loans): $4,073. Among students who received need-based aid, the average percentage of need met: 70%. Among students who received aid based on merit, the average award (and the proportion receiving): $12,022 (15%). The average athletic scholarship (and the proportion receiving): $0 (0%). Average amount of debt of borrowers graduating in 2009: $26,862. Proportion who borrowed: 74%.

CAMPUS LIFE AND EXTRACURRICULAR ACTIVITIES

Campus housing available (% using): coed dorms (36%), women's dorms (31%), men's dorms (33%). Students who live in college-owned, operated, or affiliated housing: 21%. **Student employment:** During the 2009-2010 academic year, 15% of undergraduates worked on campus. Average per-year earnings: $1,960. **Clubs and organizations:** Number of student organizations: 45. Activities include: campus ministries, choral groups, drama/theater, international student organization, literary magazine, student government, yearbook. Number of fraternities: 1; sororities: 1. Proportion of men in fraternities: 1%; of women in sororities: 3%. Average proportion of students who stay on campus on weekends: 60%. **Sports program (2009-2010):** Member of NCAA III. *Men's intercollegiate varsity sports:* baseball, basketball, cross country, football, golf, soccer, tennis. *Women's intercol-*

legiate varsity sports: basketball, cross country, golf, soccer, softball, tennis, volleyball.

SERVICES AND FACILITIES

Basic services: nonremedial tutoring, placement service. **Remedial assistance:** math, writing, study skills. **Counseling services:** minority student, career, personal, veteran student, academic, older student, psychological, religious. **For learning-disabled students:** School does not offer a structured program with separate admission and additional fees. Total undergraduates in learning-disabled program or receiving services: 26. Services include: remedial math, remedial English, remedial reading, tape recorders, other special classes, untimed tests, note-taking services, oral tests, learning center, readers, extended time for tests, tutors, priority seating, texts on tape, other. **Library:** Number of titles: 110,565; number of current serial subscriptions: 506. **Information technology resources:** Students are not required to lease or own a computer. Number of campus computers available to all students: 95. School has a wireless network. Proportion of college-owned housing units wired for high-speed internet access: 100%. **Campus safety:** Security services offered: 24-hour foot-and-vehicle patrols, late-night transport/escort service, lighted pathways/sidewalks, student patrols, controlled dormitory access (key, security card, etc.).

TRANSFER AND INTERNATIONAL STUDENTS

Transfer students: May apply for admission for the following academic terms: Fall, Spring, Summer. Applicants need a minimum number of credits to apply. For fall 2009: Transfer applicants enrolled: 67. **International students:** Number of foreign undergraduates: 3. Number of countries represented: 4. Minimum TOEFL score required: 515 (paper); 187 (computer).

Transylvania University

- **Address:** 300 N. Broadway, Lexington, KY 40508-1797
- **Website:** http://www.transy.edu
- **Private; Religious affiliation:** Christian Church (Disciples of Christ)
- **Enrollment:** 1,086 full-time; 6 part-time

KEY STATS

✔ **U.S News College Ranking:** 88, National Liberal Arts Colleges
✔ **ACT Score (25th/75th percentile):** 23-29
✔ **Tuition:** 2010-2011: $26,740

Selectivity: More selective	**Room/board:** $8,090
Acceptance rate: 81%	**Average debt:** $19,893
Student/faculty ratio: 12/1	**Proportion who borrowed:** 65%

UNDERGRADUATE STUDENT BODY STATS

2009-2010 enrollment: 1,086 full-time; 6 part-time. Men: 41%; women: 59%. **Ethnic makeup:** African American: 4%; Asian American: 1%; Hispanic: 1%; White: 92%; International: 1%. **Religious preference:** Roman Catholic: 15%; Protestant: 49%; No preference: 27%; Christian Church (Disciples of Christ): 8%; Other: 1%.

ADMISSIONS FACTS AND FIGURES

Phone: (859) 233-8242. **Email:** admissions@transy.edu. **Website:** http://www.transy.edu. **Application deadlines for fall 2011:** Regular decision: February 1; decision sent by March 1. Early decision: Not offered. Early action: Send application by: December 1; Decision sent by: January 15. Admission can be deferred. **Application fee:** $30. **To apply online, go to:** https://www.transy.edu/admissions/admissionform.htm. **Admissions requirements/recommendations:** High school units required (recommended): English: 4 (4); Mathematics: 3 (4); Science: 3 (4); Foreign language: 2 (4); Social studies: 2 (2); History: 1 (1); Academic electives: 2 (2); Total units: 16 (18). Tests: The college uses SAT or ACT scores in admissions decisions. Either SAT or ACT required. For admission to the fall 2011 entering class, the school will accept: ACT with or without writing accepted. Campus visit: Recommended. Admissions interview: Recommended. Off-campus interview: May be arranged. **Factors that count in admissions decisions:** *Academic:* Secondary school record: Very Important. Class rank: Considered. Letters of recommendation: Important. Standardized test scores: Very Important. Essay: Important. *Nonacademic:* Interview: Considered. Extracurricular activities: Important. Talent/ability: Considered. Character/personal qualities: Considered. Alumni/ae relationship: Considered. Geographical residence: Considered. State residency: Not Considered. Religious affiliation/commitment: Not Considered.

Minority status: Considered. Volunteer work: Important. Work experience: Considered. **Other schools with the greatest overlap in applicants:** Centre College; Denison University; Hanover College; University of Kentucky; Vanderbilt University. **Admissions statistics for the fall 2009 entering class:** Total applicants: 1,374. Total accepted: 1,118. Freshmen enrolled: 283; 14% were from out of state. Accepted through early-decision or early-action plans: 65%. Overall acceptance rate: 81%. Non-early acceptance rate: 88%. **Credentials of fall 2009 freshmen:** 42% ranked in the top 10 percent of their high school class; 69% were in the top 25 percent; 94% were in the top half. (Proportion submitting class standing: 76%.) **Average high school grade point average:** 3.7. **First-year students who submitted SAT scores:** 25%. Scores (25/75 percentile): Critical Reading: 530-650, Math: 510-630, Combined: 1040-1280. **First-year students submitting ACT scores:** 97%. Scores (25/75 percentile): English: 23-30, Math: 22-27, Composite: 23-29.

ACADEMICS

Year founded: 1780. **Academic calendar:** Other. **Degrees offered:** bachelor's. **Most popular majors:** 12% business/commerce, 10% biology/biological sciences, 10% psychology, 9% accounting, 7% Spanish language and literature. **Major fields of study:** biological and biomedical sciences; business, management, marketing, and related support services; computer and information sciences and support services; education; engineering; English language and literature/letters; foreign languages, literatures, and linguistics; history; liberal arts and sciences studies, and humanities; mathematics and statistics; parks, recreation, leisure, and fitness studies; philosophy and religious studies; physical sciences; psychology; social sciences; visual and performing arts. **Areas of required coursework:** arts/fine arts, humanities, mathematics, English (including composition), foreign languages, sciences (biological or physical), social science, other. **Special academic programs (% participation):** double major (14%), independent study (1%), internships (30%), liberal arts/career combination (0%), student-designed major (3%), study abroad (65%), teacher certificate program (5%). **Teacher certification offered in:** elementary, middle/junior high, secondary. **Reserve Officers Training Corps (ROTC):** Army ROTC: Offered at cooperating institution; Air Force ROTC: Offered at cooperating institution. **Faculty and instruction (2009-2010):** Total instructional faculty: 87 full-time, 10 part-time (61% men; 39% women; 7% minorities). Full-time faculty with Ph.D. or other terminal degree: 97%. Student/faculty ratio: 12/1. Classes of fewer than 20 students: 57%; of 20 to 49 students: 43%; of 50 or more students: 0%. **Advanced Placement and International Baccalaureate credit:** AP tests may be used for: Credit only. Scores accepted: 4, 5. International Baccalaureate exams may be used for: Credit only. **Freshmen returning for sophomore year:** 82%. **Graduation rates:** Four-year: 67%; five-year: 74%; six-year: 75%. **Graduate study:** 41% of students pursue further study immediately upon graduation; 20% within one year. Fields in which graduates pursue further study: Master of Business Administration (MBA), 5%; law, 26%; medicine, 6%; dentistry, 1%; theology (or the seminary), 5%; education, 5%; arts and sciences, 21%; veterinary medicine, 1%.

COSTS AND FINANCIAL AID

Financial aid office: (859) 233-8239. **Expenses (2010-2011):** Tuition and fees 2010-2011: $26,740; room/board: $8,090. Estimated books and supplies: $1,000; transportation: $750; personal expenses: $1,350. **Financial aid:** Priority filing date for institution's financial aid form: March 1. In 2009-2010, 75% of undergraduates applied for financial aid. Of those, 65% were determined to have financial need; 21% had their need fully met. Average financial aid package (proportion receiving): $21,670 (65%). Average amount of gift aid, such as scholarships or grants (proportion receiving): $17,805 (65%). Average amount of self-help aid, such as work study or loans (proportion receiving): $5,565 (54%). Average need-based loan (excluding PLUS or other private loans): $4,457. Among students who received need-based aid, the average percentage of need met: 83%. Among students who received aid based on merit, the average award (and the proportion receiving): $10,461 (33%). The average athletic scholarship (and the proportion receiving): $0 (0%). Average amount of debt of borrowers graduating in 2009: $19,893. Proportion who borrowed: 65%.

CAMPUS LIFE AND EXTRACURRICULAR ACTIVITIES

Campus housing available (% using): coed dorms (27%), women's dorms (40%), men's dorms (30%), apartment for single students (0%), special housing for disabled students (1%). Students who live in college-owned, operated, or affiliated housing: 75%. **Student employment:** During the 2009-2010 academic year, 34% of undergraduates worked on campus. Average per-year earnings: $1,500. **Clubs and organizations:** Number of student organizations: 55. Activities include: campus ministries, choral groups, concert band, dance, drama/theater, jazz band, literary magazine, music ensembles, musical theater, opera, pep band, radio station, student government, student newspaper, symphony orchestra, yearbook. Number of fraternities: 4; sororities: 4. Proportion of men in fraternities: 50%; of women in sororities: 55%. Average proportion of students who stay on campus on weekends: 70%. **Sports program (2009-2010):** Member of NCAA III. *Men's intercollegiate varsity sports:* baseball, basketball, cross country, golf, soccer, swimming, tennis, track and field (outdoor). *Women's intercollegiate varsity sports:* basketball, cross country, field hockey, golf, soccer, softball, swimming, tennis, track and field (outdoor), volleyball.

SERVICES AND FACILITIES

Basic services: placement service, health service, health insurance. **Remedial assistance:** writing. **Counseling services:** minority student, career, personal, academic, psychological, birth control, religious. **For learning-disabled students:** School does not offer a structured program with separate admission and additional fees. Services include: untimed tests, note-taking services, extended time for tests, tutors, priority registration, priority seating. **Library:** Number of titles: 136,360; number of current serial subscriptions: 500. **Information technology resources:** Students are not required to lease or own a computer. Number of campus computers available to all students: 220. School has a wireless network. Approximate number of users that can be accommodated: 250. Proportion of college-owned housing units wired for high-speed internet access: 100%. **Campus safety:** Security services offered: 24-hour foot-and-vehicle patrols, late-night transport/escort service, 24-hour emergency telephones, lighted pathways/sidewalks, controlled dormitory access (key, security card, etc).

TRANSFER AND INTERNATIONAL STUDENTS

Transfer students: May apply for admission for the following academic terms: Fall, Winter. Applicants do not need a minimum number of credits to apply. For fall 2009: Transfer applications received: 49. Transfer applicants offered admission: 27. Transfer applicants enrolled: 14. **International students:** Number of foreign undergraduates: 6 (1% of student body). Number of countries represented: 0. Minimum TOEFL score required: 550 (paper); 220 (computer). Average TOEFL score: 525 (paper).

Union College

- **Address:** 310 College Street, Barbourville, KY 40906
- **Website:** http://www.unionky.edu
- **Private; Religious affiliation:** Methodist
- **Enrollment:** 765 full-time; 60 part-time

KEY STATS
✔ **U.S News College Ranking:** second tier, Regional Universities (South)
✔ **ACT Score (25th/75th percentile):** 17-21
✔ **Tuition:** 2010-2011: $18,900

Selectivity: Less selective	**Room/board:** $5,950
Acceptance rate: 61%	**Average debt:** $24,083
Student/faculty ratio: 12/1	**Proportion who borrowed:** 79%

UNDERGRADUATE STUDENT BODY STATS

2009-2010 enrollment: 765 full-time; 60 part-time. Men: 53%; women: 47%. **Ethnic makeup:** African American: 12%; Hispanic: 1%; White: 83%; International: 3%. **Religious preference:** Roman Catholic: 2%; Protestant: 16%; No preference: 1%; Unknown: 79%; Methodist: 2%.

ADMISSIONS FACTS AND FIGURES

Phone: (800) 489-8646. **Email:** enroll@unionky.edu. **Website:** http://www.unionky.edu. **Application deadlines for fall 2011:** Regular decision: Rolling. Early decision: Not offered. Early action: Not offered. Admission can be deferred. **Application fee:** $10. **To apply online, go to:** https://www.unionky.edu/apply/applic.asp. **Admissions requirements/recommendations:** High school units required (recommended): English: (4); Mathematics: (3); Science: (2); Foreign language: (2); Social studies: (2). Tests: The college uses SAT or ACT scores in admissions decisions. Either SAT or ACT required. For admission to the fall 2011 entering class, the school will accept: ACT with or without writing accepted. Campus visit: Recommended. Admissions interview: Recommended. Off-campus interview: May be arranged. **Factors that count in admissions decisions:** *Academic:* Secondary school record: Important. Class rank: Important. Letters of recommendation: Considered. Standardized test scores: Important. Essay: Not Considered. *Nonacademic:* Interview: Not Considered. Extracurricular activities: Considered. Talent/ability: Considered. Character/personal qualities: Considered. Alumni/ae relationship: Considered. Geographical residence: Considered. State residency: Not Considered. Religious affiliation/commitment: Not Considered. Minority status: Not Considered. Volunteer work: Considered. Work experience: Not Considered. **Other schools with the greatest overlap in applicants:** Berea College; Eastern Kentucky University; Georgetown College; Lindsey Wilson College; University of the Cumberlands. **Admissions statistics for the fall 2009 entering class:** Total applicants: 1,226. Total accepted: 750. Freshmen enrolled: 191; 31% were from out of state. Overall acceptance rate: 61%. **Average high school grade point average:** 2.9. **First-year students who submitted SAT scores:** 6%. Scores (25/75 percentile): Critical Reading: 415-455, Math: 438-508, Combined: 853-963. **First-year students submitting ACT scores:** 94%. Scores (25/75 percentile): English: 16-21, Math: 15-22, Composite: 17-21.

ACADEMICS

Year founded: 1879. **Academic calendar:** Semester. **Degrees offered:** bachelor's, post-bachelor's certificate, master's, post-master's certificate. **Most popular majors:** 38% business administration and management, 22% education, 9% psychology, 8% parks, recreation, and leisure facilities management. **Major fields of study:** biological and biomedical sciences; business, management, marketing, and related support services; computer and information sciences and support services; education; English language and literature/letters; history; mathematics and statistics; parks, recreation, leisure, and fitness studies; philosophy and religious studies; physical sciences; psychology; public administration and social service professions; social sciences; visual and performing arts. **Areas of required coursework:** humanities, mathematics, English (including composition), sciences (biological or physical), history, social science. **Pre-professional programs:** pre-law, pre-dentistry, pre-medicine, pre-veterinary science, pre-optometry, pre-pharmacy, other. **Special academic programs:** distance learning, double major, honors program, independent study, liberal arts/career combination, student-designed major, study abroad, teacher certificate program. **Teacher certification offered in:** special education, elementary, middle/junior high, secondary. **Reserve Officers Training Corps (ROTC):** Army ROTC: Offered on campus. **Faculty and instruction (2009-2010):** Total instructional faculty: 61 full-time, 43 part-time (53% men; 47% women; 6% minorities). Full-time faculty with Ph.D. or other terminal degree: 72%. Student/faculty ratio: 12/1. Classes of fewer than 20 students: 78%; of 20 to 49 students: 22%; of 50 or more students: 0%. **Advanced Placement and International Baccalaureate credit:** AP tests may be used for: Credit only. Scores accepted: 3, 4, 5. **Freshmen returning for sophomore year:** 58%. **Graduation rates:** Four-year: 14%; five-year: 17%; six-year: 31%. **Graduate study:** 36% of students pursue further study immediately upon graduation; 14% within one year; 18% within five years. Fields in which graduates pursue further study: Master of Business Administration (MBA), 24%; education, 42%; arts and sciences, 36%.

COSTS AND FINANCIAL AID

Financial aid office: (606) 546-1229. **Expenses (2010-2011):** Tuition and fees 2010-2011: $18,900; room/board: $5,950. Estimated books and supplies: $1,470; transportation: $1,890; personal expenses: $1,680. **Financial aid:** Priority filing date for institution's financial aid form: March 15. In 2009-2010, 96% of undergraduates applied for financial aid. Of those, 89% were determined to have financial need; 25% had their need fully met. Average financial aid package (proportion receiving): $19,623 (86%). Average amount of gift aid, such as scholarships or grants (proportion receiving): $12,442 (85%). Average amount of self-help aid, such as work study or loans (proportion receiving): $8,029 (77%). Average need-based loan (excluding PLUS or other private loans): $7,501. Among students who received need-based aid, the average percentage of need met: 80%. Among students who received aid based on merit, the average award (and the proportion receiving): $10,421 (8%). The average athletic scholarship (and the proportion receiving): $0 (0%). Average amount of debt of borrowers graduating in 2009: $24,083. Proportion who borrowed: 79%.

CAMPUS LIFE AND EXTRACURRICULAR ACTIVITIES

Campus housing available (% using): women's dorms (34%), men's dorms (30%), apartments for married students (0%), apartment for single students (36%). **Student employment:** During the 2009-2010 academic year, 17% of undergraduates worked on campus. Average per-year earnings: $2,200. **Clubs and organizations:** Number of student organizations: 24. Activities include: campus ministries, choral groups, drama/theater, literary magazine, pep band, student government, yearbook. Number of fraternities: 0; sororities: 0. Average proportion of students who stay on campus on weekends: 50%. **Sports program (2009-2010):** Member of NAIA. *Men's intercolle-*

giate varsity sports: baseball, basketball, cross country, football, golf, soccer, swimming, tennis, track and field (outdoor). *Women's intercollegiate varsity sports:* basketball, bowling, cross country, golf, soccer, softball, swimming, tennis, track and field (outdoor), volleyball.

SERVICES AND FACILITIES

Basic services: nonremedial tutoring, placement service, health service, health insurance. **Remedial assistance:** reading, math, writing. **Counseling services:** career, personal, academic, older student, psychological, birth control, religious. **For learning-disabled students:** School does not offer a structured program with separate admission and additional fees. Services include: remedial math, remedial English, remedial reading, tape recorders, note-taking services, oral tests, readers, extended time for tests, tutors, priority seating. **Library:** Number of titles: 113,995; number of current serial subscriptions: 313. **Information technology resources:** Students are not required to lease or own a computer. Number of campus computers available to all students: 200. School has a wireless network. Approximate number of users that can be accommodated: 1,500. Proportion of college-owned housing units wired for high-speed internet access: 100%. **Campus safety:** Security services offered: 24-hour foot-and-vehicle patrols, late-night transport/escort service, 24-hour emergency telephones, lighted pathways/sidewalks, controlled dormitory access (key, security card, etc).

TRANSFER AND INTERNATIONAL STUDENTS

Transfer students: May apply for admission for the following academic terms: Fall, Spring, Summer. Applicants need a minimum number of credits to apply. For fall 2009: Transfer applications received: 267. Transfer applicants offered admission: 137. Transfer applicants enrolled: 64. **International students:** Number of foreign undergraduates: 25 (3% of student body). Number of countries represented: 9. Minimum TOEFL score required: 520 (paper); 212 (computer). Average TOEFL score: 530 (paper).

University of Kentucky

- **Address:** 101 Main Building, Lexington, KY 40506
- **Website:** http://www.uky.edu
- **Public**
- **Enrollment:** 17,619 full-time; 1,564 part-time

KEY STATS

✔ **U.S News College Ranking:** 129, National Universities
✔ **ACT Score (25th/75th percentile):** 22-28
✔ **Tuition:** 2010-2011: $8,610 in state, $17,678 out of state

Selectivity: More selective	**Room/board:** $9,439
Acceptance rate: 74%	**Average debt:** $22,943
Student/faculty ratio: 18/1	**Proportion who borrowed:** 33%

UNDERGRADUATE STUDENT BODY STATS

2009-2010 enrollment: 17,619 full-time; 1,564 part-time. Men: 50%; women: 50%. **Ethnic makeup:** African American: 7%; Asian American: 2%; Hispanic: 2%; White: 87%; International: 1%.

ADMISSIONS FACTS AND FIGURES

Phone: (859) 257-2000. **Email:** admissions@uky.edu. **Website:** http://www.uky.edu. **Application deadlines for fall 2011:** Regular decision: February 15. Early decision: Not offered. Early action: Not offered. Admission can be deferred. **Application fee:** $50. **To apply online, go to:** http://www.uky.edu/Admissions/application.html. **Admissions requirements/recommendations:** High school units required (recommended): English: 4 (4); Mathematics: 3 (4); Science: 3 (4); Foreign language: 2 (2); Social studies: 3 (3); Academic electives: 5 (3); Total units: 22 (22). Tests: The college uses SAT or ACT scores in admissions decisions. Either SAT or ACT required. For admission to the fall 2011 entering class, the school will accept: ACT with or without writing accepted. Campus visit: Recommended. Admissions interview: Neither required nor recommended. Off-campus interview: Not available. **Factors that count in admissions decisions:** *Academic:* Secondary school record: Very Important. Class rank: Considered. Letters of recommendation: Considered. Standardized test scores: Very Important. Essay: Considered. *Nonacademic:* Interview: Considered. Extracurricular activities: Considered. Talent/ability: Considered. Character/personal qualities: Considered. Alumni/ae relationship: Considered. Geographical residence: Considered. State residency: Not Considered. Religious affiliation/commitment: Not Considered. Minority status: Considered. Volunteer work: Considered.

Work experience: Not Considered. **Admissions statistics for the fall 2009 entering class:** Total applicants: 12,195. Total accepted: 8,966. Freshmen enrolled: 4,153; 21% were from out of state. Overall acceptance rate: 74%. **Credentials of fall 2009 freshmen:** 27% ranked in the top 10 percent of their high school class; 56% were in the top 25 percent; 84% were in the top half. (Proportion submitting class standing: 59%.) **Average high school grade point average:** 3.4. **First-year students who submitted SAT scores:** 22%. Scores (25/75 percentile): Critical Reading: 490-610, Math: 490-640, Combined: 980-1250. **First-year students submitting ACT scores:** 94%. Scores (25/75 percentile): English: 21-28, Math: 20-27, Composite: 22-28.

ACADEMICS

Year founded: 1865. **Academic calendar:** Semester. **Degrees offered:** bachelor's, master's, doctorate. **Most popular majors:** 6% psychology, 5% biology/biological sciences, 4% accounting, 4% finance, 4% marketing/marketing management. **Major fields of study:** agriculture, agriculture operations, and related sciences; architecture and related services; area, ethnic, cultural, and gender studies; biological and biomedical sciences; business, management, marketing, and related support services; communication, journalism, and related programs; computer and information sciences and support services; education; engineering; English language and literature/letters; family and consumer sciences/human sciences; foreign languages, literatures, and linguistics; health professions and related clinical sciences; history; legal professions and studies; liberal arts and sciences studies, and humanities; library science; mathematics and statistics; multi/interdisciplinary studies; natural resources and conservation; parks, recreation, leisure, and fitness studies; philosophy and religious studies; physical sciences; psychology; public administration and social service professions; social sciences; visual and performing arts. **Areas of required coursework:** humanities, mathematics, English (including composition), foreign languages, sciences (biological or physical), social science. **Pre-professional programs:** pre-dentistry, pre-medicine, pre-veterinary science, pre-optometry, pre-pharmacy. **Special academic programs (% participation):** accelerated program, cooperative (work-study plan) program, distance learning, double major, English as a Second Language (ESL), exchange student program (domestic), honors program, independent study, internships, student-designed major, study abroad (15%), teacher certificate program, weekend college. **Teacher certification offered in:** early childhood, special education, elementary, middle/junior high, secondary. **Cooperative education programs:** engineering. **Reserve Officers Training Corps (ROTC):** Army ROTC: Offered on campus; Air Force ROTC: Offered on campus. **Faculty and instruction (2009-2010):** Total instructional faculty: 1,301 full-time, 382 part-time (63% men; 37% women; 14% minorities). Full-time faculty with Ph.D. or other terminal degree: 91%. Student/faculty ratio: 18/1. Classes of fewer than 20 students: 29%; of 20 to 49 students: 54%; of 50 or more students: 17%. **Advanced Placement and International Baccalaureate credit:** AP tests may be used for: Credit and/or placement. International Baccalaureate exams may be used for: Credit only. **Freshmen returning for sophomore year:** 79%. **Graduation rates:** Four-year: 32%; five-year: 55%; six-year: 60%. **Graduate study:** 40% of students pursue further study immediately upon graduation.

COSTS AND FINANCIAL AID

Financial aid office: (859) 257-3172. **Expenses (2010-2011):** Tuition and fees 2010-2011: $8,610 in state, $17,678 out of state; room/board: $9,439. Estimated books and supplies: $800; transportation: $700; personal expenses: $1,526. **Financial aid:** Priority filing date for institution's financial aid form: February 15. In 2009-2010, 60% of undergraduates applied for financial aid. Of those, 46% were determined to have financial need; 47% had their need fully met. Average financial aid package (proportion receiving): $8,831 (45%). Average amount of gift aid, such as scholarships or grants (proportion receiving): $5,137 (20%). Average amount of self-help aid, such as work study or loans (proportion receiving): $4,202 (31%). Average need-based loan (excluding PLUS or other private loans): $4,011. Among students who received need-based aid, the average percentage of need met: 83%. Among students who received aid based on merit, the average award (and the proportion receiving): $5,451 (19%). The average athletic scholarship (and the proportion receiving): $13,990 (3%). Average amount of debt of borrowers graduating in 2009: $22,943. Proportion who borrowed: 33%.

CAMPUS LIFE AND EXTRACURRICULAR ACTIVITIES

Campus housing available (% using): coed dorms (73%), women's dorms (10%), men's dorms (13%), sorority housing (1%), fraternity housing (2%), apartments for married students, apartment for single students (1%), special housing for disabled students, special housing for international students. Students who live in college-owned, operated, or affiliated hous-

ing: 28%. **Clubs and organizations:** Number of student organizations: 420. Activities include: campus ministries, choral groups, concert band, dance, drama/theater, international student organization, jazz band, literary magazine, marching band, music ensembles, musical theater, opera, pep band, radio station, student government, student newspaper, symphony orchestra, yearbook. Number of fraternities: 24; sororities: 18. Proportion of men in fraternities: 16%; of women in sororities: 23%. Average proportion of students who stay on campus on weekends: 28%. **Sports program (2009-2010):** Member of NCAA I. *Men's intercollegiate varsity sports:* baseball, basketball, cross country, football, golf, rifle, soccer, swimming, tennis, track and field (indoor), track and field (outdoor). *Women's intercollegiate varsity sports:* basketball, cross country, golf, gymnastics, rifle, soccer, squash, swimming, tennis, track and field (indoor), track and field (outdoor), volleyball.

SERVICES AND FACILITIES

Basic services: nonremedial tutoring, women's center, placement service, health service, health insurance. **Remedial assistance:** math, study skills. **Counseling services:** minority student, career, military, academic, psychological. **For learning-disabled students:** School does not offer a structured program with separate admission and additional fees. Total undergraduates in learning-disabled program or receiving services: 376. Services include: remedial math, remedial English, reading machines, remedial reading, diagnostic testing service, oral tests, readers, extended time for tests, priority registration, substitution of courses, texts on tape, typist/scribe, exams on tape or computer, other testing accommodations. **Library:** Number of titles: 3,784,382; number of current serial subscriptions: 78,194. **Information technology resources:** Students are not required to lease or own a computer. Number of campus computers available to all students: 980. School has a wireless network. Approximate number of users that can be accommodated: 70,125. Proportion of college-owned housing units wired for high-speed internet access: 100%. **Campus safety:** Security services offered: 24-hour foot-and-vehicle patrols, late-night transport/escort service, 24-hour emergency telephones, lighted pathways/sidewalks, controlled dormitory access (key, security card, etc).

TRANSFER AND INTERNATIONAL STUDENTS

Transfer students: May apply for admission for the following academic terms: Fall, Spring, Summer. Applicants need a minimum number of credits to apply. For fall 2009: Transfer applications received: 2,200. Transfer applicants offered admission: 1,476. Transfer applicants enrolled: 1,039. **International students:** Number of foreign undergraduates: 236 (1% of student body). Number of countries represented: 50. Minimum TOEFL score required: 527 (paper); 71 (computer).

University of Louisville

- **Address:** 2301 S. Third Street, Louisville, KY 40292
- **Website:** http://www.louisville.edu
- **Public**
- **Enrollment:** 11,981 full-time; 3,496 part-time

KEY STATS

- ✔ **U.S News College Ranking:** 176, National Universities
- ✔ **ACT Score (25th/75th percentile):** 21-28
- ✔ **Tuition:** 2009-2010: $8,348 in state, $19,676 out of state

Selectivity: Selective	**Room/board:** $7,126
Acceptance rate: 73%	**Average debt:** $17,651
Student/faculty ratio: 18/1	**Proportion who borrowed:** 47%

UNDERGRADUATE STUDENT BODY STATS

2009-2010 enrollment: 11,981 full-time; 3,496 part-time. Men: 49%; women: 51%. **Ethnic makeup:** African American: 13%; Asian American: 3%; Hispanic: 2%; White: 81%; International: 1%.

ADMISSIONS FACTS AND FIGURES

Phone: (502) 852-6531. **Email:** admitme@louisville.edu. **Website:** http://www.louisville.edu. **Application deadlines for fall 2011:** Regular decision: August 25. Early decision: Not offered. Early action: Not offered. Admission can be deferred. **Application fee:** $40. **To apply online, go to:** http://louisville.edu/admissions. **Admissions requirements/recommendations:** High school units required (recommended): English: 4; Mathematics: 3 (4); Science: 3 (4); Foreign language: 2 (3); Social studies: 3; Academic electives: 5; Total units: 22 (11). Tests: The college uses SAT or ACT scores in admissions decisions. Either SAT or ACT required. For admission to the fall 2011 entering class, the school will accept: ACT with or without writing accepted. Campus visit: Recommended. Admissions interview: Neither required nor recommended. Off-campus interview: Not available. **Factors that count in admissions decisions:** *Academic:* Secondary school record: Very Important. Class rank: Considered. Letters of recommendation: Considered. Standardized test scores: Very Important. Essay: Not Considered. *Nonacademic:* Interview: Not Considered. Extracurricular activities: Considered. Talent/ability: Considered. Character/personal qualities: Not Considered. Alumni/ae relationship: Not Considered. Geographical residence: Not Considered. State residency: Considered. Religious affiliation/commitment: Not Considered. Minority status: Considered. Volunteer work: Considered. Work experience: Considered. **Other schools with the greatest overlap in applicants:** Bellarmine University; Eastern Kentucky University; Murray State University; University of Kentucky; Western Kentucky University. **Admissions statistics for the fall 2009 entering class:** Total applicants: 7,755. Total accepted: 5,625. Freshmen enrolled: 2,478; 18% were from out of state. Overall acceptance rate: 73%. **Credentials of fall 2009 freshmen:** 25% ranked in the top 10 percent of their high school class; 53% were in the top 25 percent; 84% were in the top half. (Proportion submitting class standing: 50%.) **Average high school grade point average:** 3.5. **First-year students who submitted SAT scores:** 11%. Scores (25/75 percentile): Critical Reading: 500-628, Math: 510-640, Combined: 1010-1268. **First-year students submitting ACT scores:** 89%. Scores (25/75 percentile): English: 20-27, Math: 21-28, Composite: 21-28.

ACADEMICS

Year founded: 1798. **Academic calendar:** Semester. **Degrees offered:** certificate, associate, terminal-associate, bachelor's, post-bachelor's certificate, master's, post-master's certificate, doctorate. **Most popular majors:** 22% business, management, marketing, and related support services, 10% engineering, 8% communication, journalism, and related programs, 8% parks, recreation, leisure, and fitness studies, 7% social sciences. **Major fields of study:** area, ethnic, cultural, and gender studies; biological and biomedical sciences; business, management, marketing, and related support services; communication, journalism, and related programs; education; engineering; English language and literature/letters; foreign languages, literatures, and linguistics; health professions and related clinical sciences; history; liberal arts and sciences studies, and humanities; mathematics and statistics; parks, recreation, leisure, and fitness studies; philosophy and religious studies; physical sciences; psychology; security and protective services; social sciences; visual and performing arts. **Areas of required coursework:** arts/fine arts, humanities, mathematics, English (including composition), sciences (biological or physical), history, social science, other. **Pre-professional programs:** pre-law, pre-dentistry, pre-medicine, pre-optometry, pre-pharmacy. **Special academic programs:** accelerated program, cooperative (work-study plan) program, cross-registration, distance learning, double major, dual enrollment, English as a Second Language (ESL), honors program, independent study, internships, student-designed major, study abroad, teacher certificate program. **Teacher certification offered in:** early childhood, special education, elementary, vo-tech, middle/junior high, secondary, bilingual/bicultural. **Cooperative education programs:** business, computer science, education, engineering. **Reserve Officers Training Corps (ROTC):** Army ROTC: Offered on campus; Air Force ROTC: Offered on campus. **Faculty and instruction (2009-2010):** Total instructional faculty: 867 full-time, 489 part-time (56% men; 44% women; 16% minorities). Full-time faculty with Ph.D. or other terminal degree: 89%. Student/faculty ratio: 18/1. Classes of fewer than 20 students: 24%; of 20 to 49 students: 63%; of 50 or more students: 13%. **Advanced Placement and International Baccalaureate credit:** AP tests may be used for: Credit only. International Baccalaureate exams may be used for: Placement only. **Freshmen returning for sophomore year:** 78%. **Graduation rates:** Four-year: 21%; five-year: 41%; six-year: 48%.

COSTS AND FINANCIAL AID

Financial aid office: (502) 852-5511. **Expenses (2009-2010):** Tuition and fees 2009-2010: $8,348 in state, $19,676 out of state; room/board: $7,126. Estimated books and supplies: $1,000; transportation: $2,194; personal expenses: $1,946. **Financial aid:** Priority filing date for institution's financial aid form: March 15. In 2009-2010, 70% of undergraduates applied for financial aid. Of those, 57% were determined to have financial need; 22% had their need fully met. Average financial aid package (proportion receiving): $10,170 (55%). Average amount of gift aid, such as scholarships or grants (proportion receiving): $7,641 (49%). Average amount of self-help aid, such as work study or loans (proportion receiving): $3,141 (37%). Average need-based loan (excluding PLUS or other private loans): $4,024. Among students who received need-based aid, the average percentage of

need met: 65%. Among students who received aid based on merit, the average award (and the proportion receiving): $6,948 (14%). The average athletic scholarship (and the proportion receiving): $17,793 (3%). Average amount of debt of borrowers graduating in 2009: $17,651. Proportion who borrowed: 47%.

CAMPUS LIFE AND EXTRACURRICULAR ACTIVITIES

Campus housing available: coed dorms, sorority housing, fraternity housing, apartments for married students, apartment for single students, special housing for disabled students, cooperative housing, other housing options. Students who live in college-owned, operated, or affiliated housing: 17%. **Clubs and organizations:** Number of student organizations: 256. Activities include: campus ministries, choral groups, concert band, dance, drama/theater, international student organization, jazz band, literary magazine, marching band, music ensembles, musical theater, opera, pep band, radio station, student government, student newspaper, symphony orchestra. Number of fraternities: 16; sororities: 10. Proportion of men in fraternities: 15%; of women in sororities: 10%. Average proportion of students who stay on campus on weekends: 33%. **Sports program (2009-2010):** Member of NCAA I. *Men's intercollegiate varsity sports:* baseball, basketball, cross country, football, golf, soccer, swimming, tennis, track and field (indoor), track and field (outdoor). *Women's intercollegiate varsity sports:* basketball, crew (heavyweight), cross country, field hockey, golf, lacrosse, soccer, softball, swimming, tennis, track and field (indoor), track and field (outdoor), volleyball.

SERVICES AND FACILITIES

Basic services: nonremedial tutoring, women's center, placement service, day care, health service, health insurance. **Remedial assistance:** other. **Counseling services:** minority student, career, military, personal, veteran student, academic, older student, psychological, birth control, religious, other. **For learning-disabled students:** School does not offer a structured program with separate admission and additional fees. Total undergraduates in learning-disabled program or receiving services: 70. Services include: remedial math, reading machines, tape recorders, diagnostic testing service, note-taking services, learning center, extended time for tests, tutors, priority seating, texts on tape, exams on tape or computer, other testing accommodations, other. **Library:** Number of titles: 2,244,103; number of current serial subscriptions: 74,116. **Information technology resources:** Students are not required to lease or own a computer. Number of campus computers available to all students: 400. School has a wireless network. Approximate number of users that can be accommodated: 3,500. Proportion of college-owned housing units wired for high-speed internet access: 100%. **Campus safety:** Security services offered: 24-hour foot-and-vehicle patrols, late-night transport/escort service, 24-hour emergency telephones, lighted pathways/sidewalks, controlled dormitory access (key, security card, etc).

TRANSFER AND INTERNATIONAL STUDENTS

Transfer students: May apply for admission for the following academic terms: Fall, Spring, Summer. Applicants need a minimum number of credits to apply. For fall 2009: Transfer applications received: 2,494. Transfer applicants offered admission: 1,851. Transfer applicants enrolled: 1,080. **International students:** Number of foreign undergraduates: 153 (1% of student body). Number of countries represented: 69. Minimum TOEFL score required: 550 (paper); 79 (computer).

University of the Cumberlands

- **Address:** 6178 College Station Drive, Williamsburg, KY 40769
- **Website:** http://www.ucumberlands.edu
- **Private; Religious affiliation:** Baptist
- **Enrollment:** N/A

KEY STATS

✔ **U.S News College Ranking:** 60, Regional Colleges (South)
✔ **SAT or ACT Score (25th/75th percentile):** N/A
✔ **Tuition:** 2009-2010: $15,658

Selectivity: Less selective	**Room/board:** $6,826
Acceptance rate: N/A	**Average debt:** N/A
Student/faculty ratio: N/A	**Proportion who borrowed:** N/A

Western Kentucky University

- **Address:** 1906 College Heights Boulevard, Bowling Green, KY 42101-3576
- **Website:** http://www.wku.edu
- **Public**
- **Enrollment:** 14,024 full-time; 3,621 part-time

KEY STATS

✔ **U.S News College Ranking:** 35, Regional Universities (South)
✔ **ACT Score (25th/75th percentile):** 18-24
✔ **Tuition:** 2009-2010: $7,200 in state, $17,784 out of state

Selectivity: Selective	**Room/board:** $6,351
Acceptance rate: 95%	**Average debt:** $15,168
Student/faculty ratio: 19/1	**Proportion who borrowed:** 55%

UNDERGRADUATE STUDENT BODY STATS

2009-2010 enrollment: 14,024 full-time; 3,621 part-time. Men: 43%; women: 57%. **Ethnic makeup:** African American: 11%; Asian American: 1%; Hispanic: 1%; White: 84%; International: 2%.

ADMISSIONS FACTS AND FIGURES

Phone: (270) 745-2551. **Email:** admission@wku.edu. **Website:** http://www.wku.edu. **Application deadlines for fall 2011:** Regular decision: August 1. Early decision: Not offered. Early action: Not offered. Admission can be deferred. **Application fee:** $40. **To apply online, go to:** http://www.wku.edu/Info/Admissions/. **Admissions requirements/recommendations:** High school units required (recommended): English: 4; Mathematics: 3; Science: 3; Foreign language: 2; Social studies: 3; Total units: 15. Tests: The college uses SAT or ACT scores in admissions decisions. Either SAT or ACT required. For admission to the fall 2011 entering class, the school will accept: ACT with or without writing accepted. Campus visit: Neither required nor recommended. Admissions interview: Neither required nor recommended. Off-campus interview: Not available. **Factors that count in admissions decisions:** *Academic:* Secondary school record: Not Considered. Class rank: Not Considered. Letters of recommendation: Not Considered. Standardized test scores: Very Important. Essay: Not Considered. *Nonacademic:* Interview: Not Considered. Extracurricular activities: Not Considered. Talent/ability: Not Considered. Character/personal qualities: Not Considered. Alumni/ae relationship: Not Considered. Geographical residence: Not Considered. State residency: Not Considered. Religious affiliation/commitment: Not Considered. Minority status: Not Considered. Volunteer work: Not Considered. Work experience: Not Considered. **Admissions statistics for the fall 2009 entering class:** Total applicants: 7,757. Total accepted: 7,331. Freshmen enrolled: 3,387; 17% were from out of state. Overall acceptance rate: 95%. **Credentials of fall 2009 freshmen:** 17% ranked in the top 10 percent of their high school class; 38% were in the top 25 percent; 67% were in the top half. (Proportion submitting class standing: 59%.) **Average high school grade point average:** 3.2. **First-year students who submitted SAT scores:** 3%. Scores (25/75 percentile): Critical Reading: 430-540, Math: 430-550, Combined: 860-1090. **First-year students submitting ACT scores:** 91%. Scores (25/75 percentile): English: 17-24, Math: 17-25, Composite: 18-24.

ACADEMICS

Year founded: 1906. **Academic calendar:** Semester. **Degrees offered:** certificate, associate, bachelor's, post-bachelor's certificate, master's, post-master's certificate, doctorate. **Most popular majors:** 16% business, management, marketing, and related support services, 14% education, 10% communication, journalism, and related programs, 9% health professions and related clinical sciences, 9% social sciences. **Major fields of study:** agriculture, agriculture operations, and related sciences; biological and biomedical sciences; business, management, marketing, and related support services; communication, journalism, and related programs; computer and information sciences and support services; education; engineering; engineering technologies/technicians; English language and literature/letters; family and consumer sciences/human sciences; foreign languages, literatures, and linguistics; health professions and related clinical sciences; history; liberal arts and sciences studies, and humanities; mathematics and statistics; multi/interdisciplinary studies; parks, recreation, leisure, and fitness studies; philosophy and religious studies; physical sciences; psychology; public administration and social service professions; social sciences; visual and performing arts. **Areas of required coursework:** arts/fine arts, humanities, mathematics,

English (including composition), foreign languages, sciences (biological or physical), history, social science, other. **Pre-professional programs:** pre-law, pre-dentistry, pre-medicine, pre-theology, pre-veterinary science, pre-optometry, pre-pharmacy, other. **Special academic programs:** cooperative (work-study plan) program, distance learning, double major, dual enrollment, English as a Second Language (ESL), exchange student program (domestic), external degree program, honors program, independent study, internships, student-designed major, study abroad, teacher certificate program, other. **Teacher certification offered in:** early childhood, special education, elementary, vo-tech, middle/junior high, secondary. **Cooperative education programs:** agriculture, art, business, computer science, education, engineering, health professions, home economics, humanities, natural science, social/behavioral science, technologies, other. **Reserve Officers Training Corps (ROTC):** Army ROTC: Offered on campus; Air Force ROTC: Offered at cooperating institution (Tennessee State University). **Faculty and instruction (2009-2010):** Total instructional faculty: 735 full-time, 415 part-time (51% men; 49% women; 10% minorities). Full-time faculty with Ph.D. or other terminal degree: 72%. Student/faculty ratio: 19/1. Classes of fewer than 20 students: 41%; of 20 to 49 students: 53%; of 50 or more students: 6%. **Advanced Placement and International Baccalaureate credit:** AP tests may be used for: Credit and/or placement. Scores accepted: 3, 4, 5. International Baccalaureate exams may be used for: Credit and/or placement. **Freshmen returning for sophomore year:** 73%. **Graduation rates:** Four-year: 22%; five-year: 44%; six-year: 49%.

COSTS AND FINANCIAL AID

Financial aid office: (270) 745-2755. **Expenses (2009-2010):** Tuition and fees 2009-2010: $7,200 in state, $17,784 out of state; room/board: $6,351. Estimated books and supplies: $1,000; transportation: $800; personal expenses: $1,679. **Financial aid:** Priority filing date for institution's financial aid form: March 15. In 2009-2010, 80% of undergraduates applied for financial aid. Of those, 64% were determined to have financial need; 30% had their need fully met. Average financial aid package (proportion receiving): $12,057 (63%). Average amount of gift aid, such as scholarships or grants (proportion receiving): $5,349 (44%). Average amount of self-help aid, such as work study or loans (proportion receiving): $3,916 (48%). Average need-based loan (excluding PLUS or other private loans): $3,826. Among students who received need-based aid, the average percentage of need met: 31%. Among students who received aid based on merit, the average award (and the proportion receiving): $5,052 (8%). The average athletic scholarship (and the proportion receiving): $11,056 (3%). Average amount of debt of borrowers graduating in 2009: $15,168. Proportion who borrowed: 55%.

CAMPUS LIFE AND EXTRACURRICULAR ACTIVITIES

Campus housing available (% using): coed dorms (50%), women's dorms (29%), men's dorms (21%), sorority housing, fraternity housing, special housing for international students, other housing options. Students who live in college-owned, operated, or affiliated housing: 28%. **Student employment:** During the 2009-2010 academic year, 6% of undergraduates worked on campus. Average per-year earnings: $1,365. **Clubs and organizations:** Number of student organizations: 251. Activities include: campus ministries, choral groups, concert band, dance, drama/theater, international student organization, jazz band, literary magazine, marching band, music ensembles, musical theater, opera, pep band, radio station, student government, student newspaper, student film society, symphony orchestra, television station, yearbook. Number of fraternities: 18; sororities: 13. Proportion of men in fraternities: 9%; of women in sororities: 9%. Average proportion of students who stay on campus on weekends: 60%. **Sports program (2009-2010):** Member of NCAA I. *Men's intercollegiate varsity sports:* baseball, basketball, cross country, football, golf, rifle, swimming, tennis, track and field (indoor), track and field (outdoor). *Women's intercollegiate varsity sports:* basketball, cross country, golf, rifle, soccer, softball, swimming, tennis, track and field (indoor), track and field (outdoor), volleyball.

SERVICES AND FACILITIES

Basic services: nonremedial tutoring, women's center, placement service, day care, health service, health insurance. **Remedial assistance:** reading, math, writing, study skills, other. **Counseling services:** minority student, career, military, personal, veteran student, academic, older student, psychological, birth control. **For learning-disabled students:** School does not offer a structured program with separate admission and additional fees. Total undergraduates in learning-disabled program or receiving services: 154. Services include: remedial math, remedial English, reading machines, remedial reading, tape recorders, other special classes, videotaped classes, diagnostic testing service, note-taking services, oral tests, learning center, readers, extended time for tests, tutors, priority registration, priority seating, substitution of courses, texts on tape, typist/scribe, other. **Library:** Number of titles: 1,804,147; number of current serial subscriptions: 3,600. **Information technology resources:** Students are not required to lease or own a computer. Number of campus computers available to all students: 1,410. School has a wireless network. Approximate number of users that can be accommodated: 4,700. Proportion of college-owned housing units wired for high-speed internet access: 100%. **Campus safety:** Security services offered: 24-hour foot-and-vehicle patrols, late-night transport/escort service, 24-hour emergency telephones, lighted pathways/sidewalks, controlled dormitory access (key, security card, etc).

TRANSFER AND INTERNATIONAL STUDENTS

Transfer students: May apply for admission for the following academic terms: Fall, Winter, Spring, Summer. Applicants need a minimum number of credits to apply. For fall 2009: Transfer applications received: 2,154. Transfer applicants offered admission: 1,846. Transfer applicants enrolled: 982. **International students:** Number of foreign undergraduates: 259 (2% of student body). Number of countries represented: 48. Minimum TOEFL score required: 525 (paper); 197 (computer). Average TOEFL score: 556 (paper).

Louisiana

Centenary College of Louisiana

- **Address:** PO Box 41188, Shreveport, LA 71134-1188
- **Website:** http://www.centenary.edu
- **Private; Religious affiliation:** United Methodist
- **Enrollment:** N/A

KEY STATS

✔ **U.S News College Ranking:** second tier, National Liberal Arts Colleges
✔ **ACT Score (25th/75th percentile):** 22-27
✔ **Tuition:** 2010-2011: $24,080

Selectivity: More selective	**Room/board:** $8,420
Acceptance rate: 93%	**Average debt:** $18,100
Student/faculty ratio: N/A	**Proportion who borrowed:** 58%

Dillard University

- **Address:** 2601 Gentilly Boulevard, New Orleans, LA 70122
- **Website:** http://www.dillard.edu
- **Private; Religious affiliation:** United Methodist
- **Enrollment:** 949 full-time; 62 part-time

KEY STATS

✔ **U.S News College Ranking:** second tier, National Liberal Arts Colleges
✔ **ACT Score (25th/75th percentile):** 16-20
✔ **Tuition:** 2009-2010: $13,880

Selectivity: Less selective	**Room/board:** $8,210
Acceptance rate: 48%	**Average debt:** N/A
Student/faculty ratio: 10/1	**Proportion who borrowed:** N/A

UNDERGRADUATE STUDENT BODY STATS

2009-2010 enrollment: 949 full-time; 62 part-time. Men: 27%; women: 73%. **Ethnic makeup:** African American: 95%; Hispanic: 1%; White: 3%; International: 1%. **Religious preference:** Roman Catholic: 12%; Protestant: 57%; Unknown: 18%; United Methodist: 1%.

ADMISSIONS FACTS AND FIGURES

Phone: (800) 216-6637. **Email:** admissions@dillard.edu. **Website:** http://www.dillard.edu. **Application deadlines for fall 2011:** Regular decision: August 1. Early decision: Not offered. Early action: Not offered. Admission can be deferred. **Application fee:** $30. **To apply online, go to:** https://campus-web.dillard.edu/cgi-bin/appinput.mbr/appinputform. **Admissions requirements/recommendations:** High school units required (recommended): English: 4; Mathematics: 3; Science: 3; Foreign language: (2); Social studies: 3; Academic electives: 6; Total units: 19. Tests: The college uses SAT or ACT scores in admissions decisions. Either SAT or ACT required. For admission to the fall 2011 entering class, the school will accept: ACT with or without writing accepted. Campus visit: Recommended. Admissions interview: Recommended. Off-campus interview: May be arranged. **Factors that count in admissions decisions:** *Academic:* Secondary school record: Very Important. Class rank: Considered. Letters of recommendation: Important. Standardized test scores: Very Important. Essay: Important. *Nonacademic:* Interview: Considered. Extracurricular activities: Considered. Talent/ability: Considered. Character/personal qualities: Not Considered. Alumni/ae relationship: Not Considered. Geographical residence: Not Considered. State residency: Not Considered. Religious affiliation/commitment: Not Considered. Minority status: Not Considered. Volunteer work: Considered. Work experience: Not Considered. **Other schools with the greatest overlap in applicants:** Morehouse College; Spelman College; University of New Orleans; Xavier University of Louisiana. **Admissions statistics for the fall 2009 entering class:** Total applicants: 3,993. Total accepted: 1,900. Freshmen enrolled: 326; 35% were from out of state. Overall acceptance rate: 48%. **Credentials of fall 2009 freshmen:** 16% ranked in the top 10

percent of their high school class; 30% were in the top 25 percent; 75% were in the top half. (Proportion submitting class standing: 72%.) **Average high school grade point average:** 2.9. **First-year students who submitted SAT scores:** 19%. Scores (25/75 percentile): Critical Reading: 370-470, Math: 340-440, Combined: 710-910. **First-year students submitting ACT scores:** 85%. Scores (25/75 percentile): English: 15-21, Math: 15-19, Composite: 16-20.

ACADEMICS

Year founded: 1869. **Academic calendar:** Semester. **Degrees offered:** bachelor's. **Most popular majors:** 15% public health education and promotion, 12% mass communication/media studies, 11% sociology, 9% biology/biological sciences, 8% psychology. **Major fields of study:** agriculture, agriculture operations, and related sciences; biological and biomedical sciences; business, management, marketing, and related support services; communication, journalism, and related programs; English language and literature/letters; history; legal professions and studies; mathematics and statistics; philosophy and religious studies; physical sciences; psychology; public administration and social service professions; security and protective services; social sciences; visual and performing arts. **Areas of required coursework:** humanities, computer literacy, mathematics, English (including composition), foreign languages, sciences (biological or physical), history, social science, other. **Pre-professional programs:** pre-medicine, other. **Special academic programs (% participation):** double major (.5%), dual enrollment (1%), exchange student program (domestic) (6%), honors program (7%), independent study (.5%), internships (75%), liberal arts/career combination (1%), study abroad (5%), teacher certificate program (1%). **Teacher certification offered in:** early childhood, special education, elementary, secondary. **Reserve Officers Training Corps (ROTC):** Army ROTC: Offered at cooperating institution; Air Force ROTC: Offered at cooperating institution. **Faculty and instruction (2009-2010):** Total instructional faculty: 92 full-time, 23 part-time (45% men; 55% women; 82% minorities). Full-time faculty with Ph.D. or other terminal degree: 63%. Student/faculty ratio: 10/1. Classes of fewer than 20 students: 73%; of 20 to 49 students: 25%; of 50 or more students: 1%. **Advanced Placement and International Baccalaureate credit:** AP tests may be used for: Placement only. Scores accepted: 3, 4, 5. International Baccalaureate exams may be used for: Placement only. **Freshmen returning for sophomore year:** 62%. **Graduation rates:** Four-year: 17%; five-year: 24%; six-year: 29%. **Graduate study:** 14% of students pursue further study immediately upon graduation; 28% within one year; 40% within five years. Fields in which graduates pursue further study: Master of Business Administration (MBA), 6%; law, 5%; medicine, 2%; engineering, 2%; education, 5%; arts and sciences, 35%.

COSTS AND FINANCIAL AID

Financial aid office: (504) 816-4677. **Expenses (2009-2010):** Tuition and fees 2009-2010: $13,880; room/board: $8,210. Estimated books and supplies: $1,200; transportation: $1,049; personal expenses: $1,819. **Financial aid:** Priority filing date for institution's financial aid form: March 3; deadline: May 1.

CAMPUS LIFE AND EXTRACURRICULAR ACTIVITIES

Campus housing available (% using): coed dorms (73%), apartments for married students (0%), apartment for single students (27%), special housing for disabled students (0%), special housing for international students (0%). Students who live in college-owned, operated, or affiliated housing: 41%. **Student employment:** During the 2009-2010 academic year, 25% of undergraduates worked on campus. Average per-year earnings: $2,100. **Clubs and organizations:** Number of student organizations: 40. Activities include: choral groups, dance, drama/theater, jazz band, music ensembles, musical theater, radio station, student government, student newspaper, yearbook. Number of fraternities: 2; sororities: 3. Proportion of men in fraternities: 4%; of women in sororities: 11%. Average proportion of students who stay on campus on weekends: 45%. **Sports program (2009-2010):** Member of NAIA. *Men's intercollegiate varsity sports:* basketball, cross country. *Women's intercollegiate varsity sports:* basketball, cross country, softball, volleyball.

SERVICES AND FACILITIES

Basic services: nonremedial tutoring, health service, health insurance. **Remedial assistance:** reading, math, writing, study skills. **Counseling services:** career, personal, academic, psychological, religious. **For learning-disabled students:** School does not offer a structured program with separate admission and additional fees. Services include: remedial math, remedial English, remedial reading, tape recorders, untimed tests, note-taking services, oral tests, learning center, readers, extended time for tests, tutors, priority registration, priority seating, other testing accommodations. **Library:** Number of titles: 103,795; number of current serial subscriptions: 0. **Information technology resources:** Students are not required to lease or own a computer. Number of campus computers available to all students: 440. School has a wireless network. Approximate number of users that can be accommodated: 200. Proportion of college-owned housing units wired for high-speed internet access: 100%. **Campus safety:** Security services offered: 24-hour foot-and-vehicle patrols, late-night transport/escort service, 24-hour emergency telephones, lighted pathways/sidewalks, controlled dormitory access (key, security card, etc).

TRANSFER AND INTERNATIONAL STUDENTS

Transfer students: May apply for admission for the following academic terms: Fall, Spring, Summer. Applicants need a minimum number of credits to apply. For fall 2009: Transfer applications received: 510. Transfer applicants offered admission: 136. Transfer applicants enrolled: 94. **International students:** Number of foreign undergraduates: 9 (1% of student body). Number of countries represented: 13. Minimum TOEFL score required: 550 (paper); 213 (computer).

Grambling State University

- **Address:** Box 607, Grambling, LA 71245
- **Website:** http://www.gram.edu/
- **Public**
- **Enrollment:** 4,222 full-time; 316 part-time

KEY STATS

✔ **U.S News College Ranking:** second tier, Regional Universities (South)
✔ **ACT Score (25th/75th percentile):** 16-19
✔ **Tuition:** 2009-2010: $4,016 in state, $9,902 out of state

Selectivity: Less selective	**Room/board:** $7,168
Acceptance rate: 33%	**Average debt:** $30,112
Student/faculty ratio: 19/1	**Proportion who borrowed:** 57%

UNDERGRADUATE STUDENT BODY STATS

2009-2010 enrollment: 4,222 full-time; 316 part-time. Men: 39%; women: 61%. **Ethnic makeup:** African American: 88%; White: 2%; International: 10%. **Religious preference:** Roman Catholic: 3%; Protestant: 54%; No preference: 22%; Unknown: 7%.

ADMISSIONS FACTS AND FIGURES

Phone: (318) 274-6183. **Email:** admissions@gram.edu. **Website:** http://www.gram.edu/. **Application deadlines for fall 2011:** Regular decision: June 1. Early decision: Not offered. Early action: Not offered. Admission cannot be deferred. **Application fee:** $20. **To apply online, go to:** http://www.gram.edu/admissions/default.asp. **Admissions requirements/recommendations:** High school units required (recommended): English: 4 (4); Mathematics: 3 (3); Science: 3 (3); Foreign language: 2 (2); Social studies: 1 (1); History: 2 (2); Academic electives: 2 (2); Total units: 18 (18). Tests: The college uses SAT or ACT scores in admissions decisions. Either SAT or ACT required. For admission to the fall 2011 entering class, the school will accept: ACT with or without writing accepted. Campus visit: Neither required nor recommended. Admissions interview: Neither required nor recommended. Off-campus interview: May be arranged. **Factors that count in admissions decisions:** *Academic:* Secondary school record: Very Important. Class rank: Very Important. Letters of recommendation: Not Considered. Standardized test scores: Very Important. Essay: Not Considered. *Nonacademic:* Interview: Not Considered. Extracurricular activities: Not Considered. Talent/ability: Not Considered. Character/personal qualities: Not Considered. Alumni/ae relationship: Considered. Geographical residence: Not Considered. State residency: Not Considered. Religious affiliation/commitment: Not Considered. Minority status: Not Considered. Volunteer work: Not Considered. Work experience: Not Considered. **Other schools with the greatest overlap in applicants:** Louisiana Tech University;

McNeese State University; Northwestern State University of Louisiana; Southern University and A&M College; University of Louisiana–Monroe. **Admissions statistics for the fall 2009 entering class:** Total applicants: 4,399. Total accepted: 1,463. Freshmen enrolled: 931; 52% were from out of state. Overall acceptance rate: 33%. **Credentials of fall 2009 freshmen:** 4% ranked in the top 10 percent of their high school class; 33% were in the top 25 percent; 47% were in the top half. (Proportion submitting class standing: 80%.) **Average high school grade point average:** 2.8. **First-year students who submitted SAT scores:** 28%. Scores (25/75 percentile): Critical Reading: 370-470, Math: 380-480, Combined: 750-950. **First-year students submitting ACT scores:** 80%. Scores (25/75 percentile): English: 15-20, Math: 16-19, Composite: 16-19.

ACADEMICS

Year founded: 1901. **Academic calendar:** Semester. **Degrees offered:** associate, bachelor's, master's, post-master's certificate. **Most popular majors:** 18% nursing/registered nurse training (R.N., A.S.N., B.S.N., M.S.N.), 13% criminal justice/safety studies, 7% business administration and management, 6% information science/studies, 5% mass communication/media studies. **Major fields of study:** biological and biomedical sciences; business, management, marketing, and related support services; communication, journalism, and related programs; computer and information sciences and support services; education; engineering technologies/technicians; English language and literature/letters; family and consumer sciences/human sciences; foreign languages, literatures, and linguistics; health professions and related clinical sciences; history; legal professions and studies; mathematics and statistics; parks, recreation, leisure, and fitness studies; physical sciences; psychology; public administration and social service professions; security and protective services; social sciences; visual and performing arts. **Areas of required coursework:** arts/fine arts, humanities, computer literacy, mathematics, English (including composition), foreign languages, sciences (biological or physical), history, social science. **Pre-professional programs:** pre-law. **Special academic programs:** cooperative (work-study plan) program, cross-registration, distance learning, double major, dual enrollment, honors program, independent study, internships, study abroad. **Cooperative education programs:** business, computer science, engineering, natural science. **Reserve Officers Training Corps (ROTC):** Army ROTC: Offered on campus; Air Force ROTC: Offered at cooperating institution (Louisiana Tech University). **Faculty and instruction (2009-2010):** Total instructional faculty: 242 full-time, 17 part-time (53% men; 47% women; 76% minorities). Full-time faculty with Ph.D. or other terminal degree: 60%. Student/faculty ratio: 19/1. Classes of fewer than 20 students: 44%; of 20 to 49 students: 51%; of 50 or more students: 4%. **Advanced Placement and International Baccalaureate credit:** AP tests may be used for: Credit only. Scores accepted: 4, 5. **Freshmen returning for sophomore year:** 59%. **Graduation rates:** Four-year: 12%; five-year: 25%; six-year: 33%.

COSTS AND FINANCIAL AID

Financial aid office: (318) 274-6056. **Expenses (2009-2010):** Tuition and fees 2009-2010: $4,016 in state, $9,902 out of state; room/board: $7,168. Estimated books and supplies: $1,200; transportation: $1,049; personal expenses: $3,638. **Financial aid:** Priority filing date for institution's financial aid form: April 1; deadline: June 1. In 2009-2010, 80% of undergraduates applied for financial aid. Of those, 80% were determined to have financial need; 11% had their need fully met. Average financial aid package (proportion receiving): $16,539 (80%). Average amount of gift aid, such as scholarships or grants (proportion receiving): $5,151 (69%). Average amount of self-help aid, such as work study or loans (proportion receiving): $4,352 (76%). Average need-based loan (excluding PLUS or other private loans): $3,397. Among students who received need-based aid, the average percentage of need met: 73%. Among students who received aid based on merit, the average award (and the proportion receiving): $2,501 (3%). The average athletic scholarship (and the proportion receiving): $5,453 (6%). Average amount of debt of borrowers graduating in 2009: $30,112. Proportion who borrowed: 57%.

CAMPUS LIFE AND EXTRACURRICULAR ACTIVITIES

Campus housing available (% using): women's dorms (7%), men's dorms (3%), apartment for single students (90%). Students who live in college-owned, operated, or affiliated housing: 51%. **Student employment:** During the 2009-2010 academic year, 30% of undergraduates worked on campus. Average per-year earnings: $1,030. **Clubs and organizations:** Number of student organizations: 76. Activities include: campus ministries, choral groups, concert band, dance, drama/theater, international student organization, jazz band, marching band, music ensembles, musical theater, pep band, radio station, student government, student newspaper, symphony orchestra, television station, yearbook. Number of fraternities: 5; sororities: 4. Proportion of men in fraternities: 6%; of women in sororities: 6%. Average proportion of students who stay on campus on weekends: 50%. **Sports program (2009-2010):** Member of NCAA I. *Men's intercollegiate varsity sports:* baseball, basketball, cross country, football, golf, tennis, track and field (indoor), track and field (outdoor). *Women's intercollegiate varsity sports:* basketball, bowling, cross country, golf, soccer, softball, tennis, track and field (indoor), track and field (outdoor), volleyball.

SERVICES AND FACILITIES

Basic services: nonremedial tutoring, placement service, health service, health insurance. **Remedial assistance:** reading, math, writing, study skills. **Counseling services:** career, military, personal, veteran student, academic, psychological. **For learning-disabled students:** School does not offer a structured program with separate admission and additional fees. Total undergraduates in learning-disabled program or receiving services: 246. Services include: remedial math, remedial English, remedial reading, tape recorders, other special classes, untimed tests, note-taking services, oral tests, readers, extended time for tests, tutors, priority seating, other testing accommodations, other. **Library:** Number of titles: 322,995; number of current serial subscriptions: 1,163,073. **Information technology resources:** Students are not required to lease or own a computer. Number of campus computers available to all students: 350. School has a wireless network. Approximate number of users that can be accommodated: 3,000. Proportion of college-owned housing units wired for high-speed internet access: 98%. **Campus safety:** Security services offered: 24-hour foot-and-vehicle patrols, lighted pathways/sidewalks, controlled dormitory access (key, security card, etc).

TRANSFER AND INTERNATIONAL STUDENTS

Transfer students: May apply for admission for the following academic terms: Fall, Spring, Summer. Applicants need a minimum number of credits to apply. For fall 2009: Transfer applications received: 617. Transfer applicants offered admission: 229. Transfer applicants enrolled: 162. **International students:** Number of foreign undergraduates: 435 (10% of student body). Number of countries represented: 40. Minimum TOEFL score required: 500 (paper); 173 (computer). Average TOEFL score: 477 (paper).

Louisiana College

- **Address:** 1140 College Drive, Pineville, LA 71360
- **Website:** http://www.lacollege.edu
- **Private; Religious affiliation:** Southern Baptist Convention
- **Enrollment:** 960 full-time; 77 part-time

KEY STATS

✔ **U.S News College Ranking:** 49, Regional Colleges (South)
✔ **ACT Score:** 22
✔ **Tuition:** 2010-2011: $13,430

Selectivity: Selective	**Room/board:** $4,560
Acceptance rate: 51%	**Average debt:** N/A
Student/faculty ratio: 13/1	**Proportion who borrowed:** 45%

UNDERGRADUATE STUDENT BODY STATS

2009-2010 enrollment: 960 full-time; 77 part-time. Men: 51%; women: 49%. **Ethnic makeup:** African American: 19%; American-Indian: 1%; Asian American: 2%; Hispanic: 2%; White: 76%. **Religious preference:** Roman Catholic: 16%; Protestant: 20%; Hindu: 1%; No preference: 9%; Southern Baptist Convention: 51%; Christian: 2%; Other: 1%.

ADMISSIONS FACTS AND FIGURES

Phone: (318) 487-7259. **Email:** admissions@lacollege.edu. **Website:** http://www.lacollege.edu. **Application deadlines for fall 2011:** Regular decision: August 15. Early decision: Not offered. Early action: Not offered. Admission can be deferred. **Application fee:** $25. **To apply online, go to:** http://www.lacollege.edu/apply/index.aspx. **Admissions requirements/recommendations:** High school units required (recommended): English: 4; Mathematics: 3; Science: 3; Foreign language: (2); Social studies: 2; History: 1; Academic electives: 4; Total units: 17 (17). Tests: The college uses SAT or ACT scores in admissions decisions. Either SAT or ACT required. For admission to the fall 2011 entering class, the school will accept: ACT with or without writing accepted. Campus visit: Recommended. Admissions interview: Neither required nor recommended. Off-campus interview: Not available. **Factors that count in admissions decisions:** *Academic:* Secondary school

record: Very Important. Class rank: Very Important. Letters of recommendation: Considered. Standardized test scores: Very Important. Essay: Not Considered. *Nonacademic:* Interview: Considered. Extracurricular activities: Considered. Talent/ability: Considered. Character/personal qualities: Considered. Alumni/ae relationship: Considered. Geographical residence: Considered. State residency: Considered. Religious affiliation/commitment: Considered. Minority status: Considered. Volunteer work: Considered. Work experience: Considered. **Other schools with the greatest overlap in applicants:** Louisiana State University–Alexandria; Louisiana State University–Baton Rouge; Louisiana Tech University; University of Louisiana–Lafayette; University of Louisiana–Monroe. **Admissions statistics for the fall 2009 entering class:** Total applicants: 1,091. Total accepted: 560. Freshmen enrolled: 254; Overall acceptance rate: 51%. **Average high school grade point average:** 3.2. **First-year students submitting ACT scores:** 100%. Scores (25/75 percentile): English: N/A, Math: N/A, Composite: N/A.

ACADEMICS

Year founded: 1906. **Academic calendar:** Semester. **Degrees offered:** associate, bachelor's, master's. **Major fields of study:** biological and biomedical sciences; business, management, marketing, and related support services; communication, journalism, and related programs; communications technologies/technicians and support services; computer and information sciences and support services; education; engineering; engineering technologies/technicians; English language and literature/letters; foreign languages, literatures, and linguistics; health professions and related clinical sciences; history; legal professions and studies; liberal arts and sciences studies, and humanities; mathematics and statistics; multi/interdisciplinary studies; parks, recreation, leisure, and fitness studies; philosophy and religious studies; physical sciences; psychology; public administration and social service professions; security and protective services; social sciences; theology and religious vocations; visual and performing arts. **Areas of required coursework:** arts/fine arts, humanities, computer literacy, mathematics, English (including composition), philosophy, foreign languages, sciences (biological or physical), history, social science, other. **Pre-professional programs:** pre-law, pre-dentistry, pre-medicine, pre-theology, pre-veterinary science, pre-optometry, pre-pharmacy, other. **Special academic programs (% participation):** double major (5%), honors program (5%), independent study (5%), internships (5%), study abroad (2%), teacher certificate program (10%). **Teacher certification offered in:** special education, elementary, middle/junior high, secondary. **Faculty and instruction (2009-2010):** Total instructional faculty: 63 full-time, 38 part-time (57% men; 43% women). Full-time faculty with Ph.D. or other terminal degree: 57%. Student/faculty ratio: 13/1. Classes of fewer than 20 students: 71%; of 20 to 49 students: 29%; of 50 or more students: 1%. **Advanced Placement and International Baccalaureate credit:** AP tests may be used for: Placement only. Scores accepted: 3, 4, 5. **Freshmen returning for sophomore year:** 59%. **Graduation rates:** Four-year: 23%; five-year: 39%; six-year: 42%.

COSTS AND FINANCIAL AID

Financial aid office: (318) 487-7386. **Expenses (2010-2011):** Tuition and fees 2010-2011: $13,430; room/board: $4,560. Estimated books and supplies: $1,200; transportation: $1,049; personal expenses: $1,819. **Financial aid:** Priority filing date for institution's financial aid form: March 31. In 2009-2010, 92% of undergraduates applied for financial aid. Of those, 88% were determined to have financial need; Average financial aid package (proportion receiving): $5,809 (88%). Average amount of gift aid, such as scholarships or grants (proportion receiving): $2,156 (88%). Average amount of self-help aid, such as work study or loans (proportion receiving): $1,885 (18%). Average need-based loan (excluding PLUS or other private loans): $2,850. Among students who received need-based aid, the average percentage of need met: 34%. Among students who received aid based on merit, the average award (and the proportion receiving): $1,050 (88%). Proportion who borrowed: 45%.

CAMPUS LIFE AND EXTRACURRICULAR ACTIVITIES

Campus housing available (% using): women's dorms (45%), men's dorms (27%), apartments for married students (4%), apartment for single students (24%). **Student employment:** During the 2009-2010 academic year, 5% of undergraduates worked on campus. Average per-year earnings: $2,300. **Clubs and organizations:** Number of student organizations: 40. Activities include: choral groups, concert band, drama/theater, jazz band, literary magazine, marching band, music ensembles, musical theater, opera, pep band, radio station, student government, student newspaper, yearbook. Number of fraternities: 3; sororities: 3. Average proportion of students who stay on campus on weekends: 55%. **Sports program (2009-2010):** Member of NCAA III.

SERVICES AND FACILITIES

Basic services: nonremedial tutoring, placement service, health service. **Counseling services:** career, personal, academic, religious. **For learning-disabled students:** School does not offer a structured program with separate admission and additional fees. Services include: remedial math, remedial English, tape recorders, untimed tests, note-taking services, oral tests, learning center, readers, extended time for tests, tutors, texts on tape, other testing accommodations, other. **Library:** Number of titles: 328,673; number of current serial subscriptions: 402. **Information technology resources:** Students are not required to lease or own a computer. Number of campus computers available to all students: 242. School has a wireless network. Approximate number of users that can be accommodated: 1,000. Proportion of college-owned housing units wired for high-speed internet access: 100%. **Campus safety:** Security services offered: 24-hour foot-and-vehicle patrols, late-night transport/escort service, controlled dormitory access (key, security card, etc).

TRANSFER AND INTERNATIONAL STUDENTS

Transfer students: May apply for admission for the following academic terms: Fall, Spring, Summer. Applicants need a minimum number of credits to apply. **International students:** Number of foreign undergraduates: 7. Number of countries represented: 9. Minimum TOEFL score required: 550 (paper); 213 (computer). Average TOEFL score: 600 (paper).

Louisiana State University–Alexandria

- **Address:** 8100 Highway 71 S, Alexandria, LA 71302
- **Website:** http://www.lsua.edu
- **Public**
- **Enrollment:** N/A

KEY STATS

- ✔ **U.S News College Ranking:** second tier, Regional Colleges (South)
- ✔ **SAT or ACT Score (25th/75th percentile):** N/A
- ✔ **Tuition:** 2009-2010: $3,562 in state, $6,270 out of state

Selectivity: Less selective	**Room/board:** $6,410
Acceptance rate: N/A	**Average debt:** N/A
Student/faculty ratio: N/A	**Proportion who borrowed:** N/A

Louisiana State University–Baton Rouge

- **Address:** 156 Thomas Boyd Hall, Baton Rouge, LA 70803
- **Website:** http://www.lsu.edu
- **Public**
- **Enrollment:** 21,539 full-time; 1,473 part-time

KEY STATS

- ✔ **U.S News College Ranking:** 124, National Universities
- ✔ **ACT Score (25th/75th percentile):** 23-28
- ✔ **Tuition:** 2009-2010: $5,233 in state, $14,383 out of state

Selectivity: More selective	**Room/board:** $7,738
Acceptance rate: 69%	**Average debt:** $18,118
Student/faculty ratio: 20/1	**Proportion who borrowed:** 41%

UNDERGRADUATE STUDENT BODY STATS

2009-2010 enrollment: 21,539 full-time; 1,473 part-time. Men: 49%; women: 51%. **Religious preference:** Roman Catholic: 41%; Protestant: 31%; No preference: 21%.

ADMISSIONS FACTS AND FIGURES

Phone: (225) 578-1175. **Email:** admissions@lsu.edu. **Website:** http://www.lsu.edu. **Application deadlines for fall 2011:** Regular decision: April 15. Early decision: Not offered. Early action: Not offered. Admission can be deferred. **Application fee:** $40. **To apply online, go to:** http://www.lsu.edu/paurec/apply.shtml. **Admissions requirements/recommendations:** High school units required (recommended): English: 4; Mathematics: 3 (4); Science: 3; Foreign language: 2; Social studies: 1; History: 2; Academic electives: 3; Total units: 18. Tests: The college uses SAT or ACT scores in admissions decisions. Either SAT or ACT required. For admission to the fall 2011 entering class, the school will accept: ACT with writing recommended. Campus visit: Recommended. Admissions interview: Neither required nor recommended. Off-campus interview: Not available. **Factors that count in admissions decisions:** *Academic:* Secondary school record: Very Important. Class rank: Important. Letters of recommendation: Considered. Standardized test scores: Very Important. Essay: Considered. *Nonacademic:* Interview: Not Considered. Extracurricular activities: Considered. Talent/ability: Important. Character/personal qualities: Not Considered. Alumni/ae relationship: Considered. Geographical residence: Not Considered. State residency: Not Considered. Religious affiliation/commitment: Not Considered. Minority status: Not Considered. Volunteer work: Not Considered. Work experience: Not Considered. **Other schools with the greatest overlap in applicants:** Southeastern Louisiana University; Texas A&M University–College Station; University of Georgia; University of Louisiana–Lafayette; University of Texas–Austin. **Admissions statistics for the fall 2009 entering class:** Total applicants: 15,917. Total accepted: 11,012. Freshmen enrolled: 4,789; 24% were from out of state. Overall acceptance rate: 69%. **Credentials of fall 2009 freshmen:** 25% ranked in the top 10 percent of their high school class; 53% were in the top 25 percent; 83% were in the top half. (Proportion submitting class standing: 91%.) **Average high school grade point average:** 3.5. **First-year students who submitted SAT scores:** 14%. Scores (25/75 percentile): Critical Reading: 510-630, Math: 540-650, Combined: 1050-1280. **First-year students submitting ACT scores:** 87%. Scores (25/75 percentile): English: 23-29, Math: 22-27, Composite: 23-28.

ACADEMICS

Year founded: 1860. **Academic calendar:** Semester. **Degrees offered:** bachelor's, master's, post-master's certificate, doctorate. **Most popular majors:** 19% business, management, marketing, and related support services, 9% biological and biomedical sciences, 9% liberal arts and sciences studies, and humanities, 9% social sciences, 8% education. **Major fields of study:** agriculture, agriculture operations, and related sciences; architecture and related services; area, ethnic, cultural, and gender studies; biological and biomedical sciences; business, management, marketing, and related support services; communication, journalism, and related programs; computer and information sciences and support services; education; engineering; English language and literature/letters; family and consumer sciences/human sciences; foreign languages, literatures, and linguistics; health professions and related clinical sciences; history; liberal arts and sciences studies, and humanities; mathematics and statistics; multi/interdisciplinary studies; natural resources and conservation; philosophy and religious studies; physical sciences; psychology; social sciences; visual and performing arts. **Areas of required coursework:** arts/fine arts, humanities, computer literacy, mathematics, English (including composition), foreign languages, sciences (biological or physical), social science. **Pre-professional programs:** pre-law, pre-dentistry, pre-medicine, pre-veterinary science. **Special academic programs:** accelerated program, cooperative (work-study plan) program, cross-registration, distance learning, double major, dual enrollment, English as a Second Language (ESL), exchange student program (domestic), honors program, independent study, internships, student-designed major, study abroad, teacher certificate program. **Teacher certification offered in:** early childhood, special education, elementary, vo-tech, secondary. **Cooperative education programs:** agriculture, business, computer science, engineering, natural science, technologies, other. **Reserve Officers Training Corps (ROTC):** Army ROTC: Offered on campus; Navy ROTC: Offered at cooperating institution (Southern University and A&M College); Air Force ROTC: Offered on campus. **Faculty and instruction (2009-2010):** Total instructional faculty: 1,309 full-time, 146 part-time (65% men; 35% women; 14% minorities). Full-time faculty with Ph.D. or other terminal degree: 88%. Student/faculty ratio: 20/1. Classes of fewer than 20 students: 35%; of 20 to 49 students: 46%; of 50 or more students: 19%. **Advanced Placement and International Baccalaureate credit:** AP tests may be used for: Credit only. Scores accepted: 3, 4, 5. International Baccalaureate exams may be used for: Credit only. **Freshmen returning for sophomore year:** 84%. **Graduation rates:** Four-year: 28%; five-year: 54%; six-year: 61%. **Graduate study:** 26% of students pursue further study immediately upon graduation. Fields in which graduates pursue further study: Master of Business Administration (MBA), 10%; law, 17%; medicine, 22%; dentistry, 2%; engineering, 4%; theology (or the seminary), 1%; education, 5%; arts and sciences, 9%; veterinary medicine, 3%.

COSTS AND FINANCIAL AID

Financial aid office: (225) 578-3103. **Expenses (2009-2010):** Tuition and fees 2009-2010: $5,233 in state, $14,383 out of state; room/board: $7,738. Estimated books and supplies: $1,500; transportation: $1,050; personal expenses: $1,820. **Financial aid:** Priority filing date for institution's financial aid form: July 1. In 2009-2010, 51% of undergraduates applied for financial aid. Of those, 35% were determined to have financial need; 19% had their need fully met. Average financial aid package (proportion receiving): $11,518 (35%). Average amount of gift aid, such as scholarships or grants (proportion receiving): $8,505 (30%). Average amount of self-help aid, such as work study or loans (proportion receiving): $4,540 (26%). Average need-based loan (excluding PLUS or other private loans): $4,360. Among students who received need-based aid, the average percentage of need met: 69%. Among students who received aid based on merit, the average award (and the proportion receiving): $5,135 (16%). The average athletic scholarship (and the proportion receiving): $15,376 (2%). Average amount of debt of borrowers graduating in 2009: $18,118. Proportion who borrowed: 41%.

CAMPUS LIFE AND EXTRACURRICULAR ACTIVITIES

Campus housing available: coed dorms, women's dorms, men's dorms, sorority housing, fraternity housing, apartments for married students, apartment for single students, special housing for disabled students. Students who live in college-owned, operated, or affiliated housing: 25%. **Student employment:** During the 2009-2010 academic year, 25% of undergraduates worked on campus. Average per-year earnings: $2,100. **Clubs and organizations:** Number of student organizations: 300. Activities include: campus ministries, choral groups, concert band, dance, drama/theater, international student organization, jazz band, literary magazine, marching band, music ensembles, musical theater, opera, pep band, radio station, student government, student newspaper, student film society, symphony orchestra, television station, yearbook. Number of fraternities: 22; sororities: 16. Proportion of men in fraternities: 13%; of women in sororities: 20%. Average proportion of students who stay on campus on weekends: 50%. **Sports program (2009-2010):** Member of NCAA I. *Men's intercollegiate varsity sports:* baseball, basketball, cross country, football, golf, swimming, tennis, track and field (indoor), track and field (outdoor). *Women's intercollegiate varsity sports:* basketball, cross country, golf, gymnastics, soccer, softball, swimming, tennis, track and field (indoor), track and field (outdoor), volleyball.

SERVICES AND FACILITIES

Basic services: nonremedial tutoring, women's center, placement service, day care, health service, health insurance. **Counseling services:** minority student, career, military, personal, veteran student, academic, older student, psychological. **For learning-disabled students:** School does not offer a structured program with separate admission and additional fees. Services include: tape recorders, other special classes, note-taking services, oral tests, readers, extended time for tests, priority registration, texts on tape, other testing accommodations. **Library:** Number of titles: 4,112,774; number of current serial subscriptions: 104,177. **Information technology resources:** Students are not required to lease or own a computer. Number of campus computers available to all students: 1,500. School has a wireless network. Approximate number of users that can be accommodated: 70,000. Proportion of college-owned housing units wired for high-speed internet access: 95%. **Campus safety:** Security services offered: 24-hour foot-and-vehicle patrols, late-night transport/escort service, 24-hour emergency telephones, lighted pathways/sidewalks, controlled dormitory access (key, security card, etc).

TRANSFER AND INTERNATIONAL STUDENTS

Transfer students: May apply for admission for the following academic terms: Fall, Spring, Summer. Applicants need a minimum number of credits to apply. For fall 2009: Transfer applications received: 2,021. Transfer applicants offered admission: 1,241. Transfer applicants enrolled: 839. **International students:** Number of countries represented: 74. Minimum TOEFL score required: 550 (paper); 213 (computer).

Louisiana State University–Shreveport

- **Address:** 1 University Place, Shreveport, LA 71115
- **Website:** http://www.lsus.edu
- **Public**
- **Enrollment:** 2,511 full-time; 1,709 part-time

KEY STATS

✔ **U.S News College Ranking:** second tier, Regional Universities (South)
✔ **ACT Score (25th/75th percentile):** 20-24
✔ **Tuition:** 2009-2010: $3,733 in state, $8,503 out of state

Selectivity: Selective	**Room/board:** N/A
Acceptance rate: N/A	**Average debt:** N/A
Student/faculty ratio: N/A	**Proportion who borrowed:** N/A

UNDERGRADUATE STUDENT BODY STATS

2009-2010 enrollment: 2,511 full-time; 1,709 part-time. Men: 38%; women: 62%. **Ethnic makeup:** African American: 24%; American-Indian: 1%; Asian American: 2%; Hispanic: 2%; White: 70%; International: 2%.

ADMISSIONS FACTS AND FIGURES

Phone: (318) 797-5061. **Email:** admissions@pilot.lsus.edu. **Website:** http://www.lsus.edu. **Application deadlines for fall 2011:** Regular decision: June 1. Early decision: Not offered. Early action: Not offered. Admission cannot be deferred. **Application fee:** $10. **To apply online, go to:** http://www.lsus.edu/admissions/apply.php. **Admissions requirements/recommendations:** High school units required (recommended): English: 4 (4); Mathematics: 3 (3); Science: 3 (3); Foreign language: 2 (2); Social studies: 2 (2); History: 1 (1); Academic electives: 1 (1); Total units: 17 (17). Tests: The college uses SAT or ACT scores in admissions decisions. Either SAT or ACT required. For admission to the fall 2011 entering class, the school will accept: ACT with or without writing accepted. Campus visit: Recommended. Admissions interview: Neither required nor recommended. Off-campus interview: Not available. **Factors that count in admissions decisions:** *Academic:* Secondary school record: Considered. Class rank: Considered. Letters of recommendation: Not Considered. Standardized test scores: Considered. Essay: Not Considered. *Nonacademic:* Interview: Not Considered. Extracurricular activities: Not Considered. Talent/ability: Not Considered. Character/personal qualities: Not Considered. Alumni/ae relationship: Not Considered. Geographical residence: Not Considered. State residency: Not Considered. Religious affiliation/commitment: Not Considered. Minority status: Not Considered. Volunteer work: Not Considered. Work experience: Not Considered. **Size of waiting list:** 0 applicants; enrolled from waiting list: 0. **Average high school grade point average:** 3.1.

ACADEMICS

Year founded: 1967. **Academic calendar:** Semester. **Degrees offered:** bachelor's, master's, post-master's certificate. **Most popular majors:** 15% general studies, 8% biology/biological sciences, 7% psychology, 6% business/commerce, 5% elementary education and teaching. **Major fields of study:** biological and biomedical sciences; business, management, marketing, and related support services; communication, journalism, and related programs; computer and information sciences and support services; education; English language and literature/letters; foreign languages, literatures, and linguistics; health professions and related clinical sciences; history; liberal arts and sciences studies, and humanities; mathematics and statistics; natural resources and conservation; physical sciences; psychology; security and protective services; social sciences; visual and performing arts. **Areas of required coursework:** arts/fine arts, humanities, mathematics, English (including composition), sciences (biological or physical), history, social science, other. **Pre-professional programs:** pre-law, pre-dentistry, pre-medicine, pre-veterinary science, pre-optometry, pre-pharmacy. **Special academic programs:** accelerated program, cooperative (work-study plan) program, cross-registration, distance learning, double major, dual enrollment, independent study, internships, study abroad, teacher certificate program. **Teacher certification offered in:** early childhood, special education, elementary, middle/junior high, secondary. **Cooperative education programs:** education, health professions. **Reserve Officers Training Corps (ROTC):** Army ROTC: Offered at cooperating institution. **Advanced Placement and International Baccalaureate credit:** AP tests may be used for: Credit only. **Freshmen returning for sophomore year:** 62%. **Graduation rates:** Four-year: 5%; five-year: 13%; six-year: 21%.

COSTS AND FINANCIAL AID

Financial aid office: (318) 797-5363. **Expenses (2009-2010):** Tuition and fees 2009-2010: $3,733 in state, $8,503 out of state. Estimated books and supplies: $1,000.

CAMPUS LIFE AND EXTRACURRICULAR ACTIVITIES

Campus housing available: apartment for single students. Average per-year earnings: $6,240. **Clubs and organizations:** Number of student organizations: 72. Activities include: campus ministries, dance, drama/theater, jazz band, literary magazine, radio station, student government, student newspaper, student film society. Number of fraternities: 5; sororities: 3. Average proportion of students who stay on campus on weekends: 30%. **Sports program (2009-2010):** Member of NAIA. *Men's intercollegiate varsity sports:* baseball, basketball. *Women's intercollegiate varsity sports:* basketball, soccer.

SERVICES AND FACILITIES

Remedial assistance: reading, math, writing, study skills. **Counseling services:** career, personal, academic, older student, psychological. **For learning-disabled students:** School does not offer a structured program with separate admission and additional fees. Services include: remedial math, remedial English. **Information technology resources:** Students are not required to lease or own a computer. Number of campus computers available to all students: 235. School has a wireless network. **Campus safety:** Security services offered: 24-hour foot-and-vehicle patrols, 24-hour emergency telephones, lighted pathways/sidewalks.

TRANSFER AND INTERNATIONAL STUDENTS

Transfer students: May apply for admission for the following academic terms: Fall, Spring, Summer. Applicants need a minimum number of credits to apply. **International students:** Number of foreign undergraduates: 57 (2% of student body). Minimum TOEFL score required: 500 (paper).

Louisiana Tech University

- **Address:** 700 W. California Avenue, Ruston, LA 71272
- **Website:** http://www.latech.edu
- **Public**
- **Enrollment:** 6,484 full-time; 2,264 part-time

KEY STATS

✔ **U.S News College Ranking:** second tier, National Universities
✔ **ACT Score (25th/75th percentile):** 20-26
✔ **Tuition:** 2009-2010: $4,776 in state, $8,760 out of state

Selectivity: Selective	**Room/board:** $5,178
Acceptance rate: 63%	**Average debt:** $12,408
Student/faculty ratio: 21/1	**Proportion who borrowed:** 51%

UNDERGRADUATE STUDENT BODY STATS

2009-2010 enrollment: 6,484 full-time; 2,264 part-time. Men: 52%; women: 48%. **Ethnic makeup:** African American: 14%; Asian American: 1%; Hispanic: 2%; White: 80%; International: 4%.

ADMISSIONS FACTS AND FIGURES

Phone: (318) 257-3036. **Email:** bulldog@latech.edu. **Website:** http://www.latech.edu. **Application deadlines for fall 2011:** Regular decision: July 31. Early decision: Not offered. Early action: Not offered. Admission cannot be deferred. **Application fee:** $20. **To apply online, go to:** http://www.latech.edu/admissions/apply.shtml. **Admissions requirements/recommendations:** High school units required (recommended): English: 4; Mathematics: 3; Science: 3; Foreign language: 2; Social studies: 3; History: 1; Total units: 18. Tests: The college uses SAT or ACT scores in admissions decisions. Either SAT or ACT required. For admission to the fall 2011 entering class, the school will accept: ACT with or without writing accepted. Campus visit: Recommended. Admissions interview: Neither required nor recommended. Off-campus interview: Not available. **Factors that count in admissions decisions:** *Academic:* Secondary school record: Very Important. Class rank: Very Important. Letters of recommendation: Considered. Standardized test scores: Very Important. Essay: Not Considered. *Nonacademic:* Interview: Not Considered. Extracurricular activities: Considered. Talent/ability: Important. Character/personal qualities: Not Considered. Alumni/ae relationship: Considered. Geographical residence: Not Considered. State residency: Not Considered. Religious affiliation/commitment: Not Considered.

Minority status: Not Considered. Volunteer work: Not Considered. Work experience: Not Considered. **Other schools with the greatest overlap in applicants:** Louisiana State University–Baton Rouge; Northwestern State University of Louisiana; Southeastern Louisiana University; University of Louisiana–Monroe; University of New Orleans. **Admissions statistics for the fall 2009 entering class:** Total applicants: 4,734. Total accepted: 2,973. Freshmen enrolled: 1,507; 12% were from out of state. Overall acceptance rate: 63%. **Credentials of fall 2009 freshmen:** 19% ranked in the top 10 percent of their high school class; 48% were in the top 25 percent; 77% were in the top half. (Proportion submitting class standing: 88%.) **Average high school grade point average:** 3.3. **First-year students who submitted SAT scores:** 4%. Scores (25/75 percentile): Critical Reading: 440-550, Math: 460-590, Combined: 900-1140. **First-year students submitting ACT scores:** 96%. Scores (25/75 percentile): English: 19-26, Math: 20-27, Composite: 20-26.

ACADEMICS

Year founded: 1894. **Academic calendar:** Quarter. **Degrees offered:** associate, bachelor's, post-bachelor's certificate, master's, doctorate. **Most popular majors:** 16% business, management, marketing, and related support services, 12% engineering, 9% health professions and related clinical sciences, 8% education, 5% social sciences. **Major fields of study:** agriculture, agriculture operations, and related sciences; architecture and related services; biological and biomedical sciences; business, management, marketing, and related support services; communication, journalism, and related programs; computer and information sciences and support services; education; engineering; engineering technologies/technicians; English language and literature/letters; family and consumer sciences/human sciences; foreign languages, literatures, and linguistics; health professions and related clinical sciences; history; liberal arts and sciences studies, and humanities; mathematics and statistics; natural resources and conservation; parks, recreation, leisure, and fitness studies; physical sciences; psychology; social sciences; transportation and materials moving; visual and performing arts. **Areas of required coursework:** arts/fine arts, humanities, computer literacy, mathematics, English (including composition), sciences (biological or physical), history, social science. **Special academic programs:** distance learning, double major, dual enrollment, honors program, independent study, internships, study abroad, teacher certificate program. **Teacher certification offered in:** early childhood, special education, elementary, middle/junior high, secondary. **Cooperative education programs:** agriculture, engineering, natural science, other. **Reserve Officers Training Corps (ROTC):** Army ROTC: Offered at cooperating institution (Grambling State University); Air Force ROTC: Offered on campus. **Faculty and instruction (2009-2010):** Total instructional faculty: 378 full-time, 98 part-time (57% men; 43% women; 4% minorities). Full-time faculty with Ph.D. or other terminal degree: 78%. Student/faculty ratio: 21/1. Classes of fewer than 20 students: 48%; of 20 to 49 students: 44%; of 50 or more students: 8%. **Advanced Placement and International Baccalaureate credit:** AP tests may be used for: Credit only. International Baccalaureate exams may be used for: Credit only. **Freshmen returning for sophomore year:** 73%. **Graduation rates:** Four-year: 26%; five-year: 42%; six-year: 46%.

COSTS AND FINANCIAL AID

Financial aid office: (318) 257-2643. **Expenses (2009-2010):** Tuition and fees 2009-2010: $4,776 in state, $8,760 out of state; room/board: $5,178. Estimated books and supplies: $1,800; transportation: $1,959; personal expenses: $1,500. **Financial aid:** Priority filing date for institution's financial aid form: April 15. In 2009-2010, 72% of undergraduates applied for financial aid. Of those, 49% were determined to have financial need; 21% had their need fully met. Average financial aid package (proportion receiving): $9,446 (46%). Average amount of gift aid, such as scholarships or grants (proportion receiving): $7,171 (41%). Average amount of self-help aid, such as work study or loans (proportion receiving): $3,931 (37%). Average need-based loan (excluding PLUS or other private loans): $3,745. Among students who received need-based aid, the average percentage of need met: 65%. Among students who received aid based on merit, the average award (and the proportion receiving): $2,370 (16%). The average athletic scholarship (and the proportion receiving): $9,099 (3%). Average amount of debt of borrowers graduating in 2009: $12,408. Proportion who borrowed: 51%.

CAMPUS LIFE AND EXTRACURRICULAR ACTIVITIES

Campus housing available (% using): women's dorms (30%), men's dorms (30%), fraternity housing, apartments for married students, apartment for single students (39%), special housing for disabled students. Students who live in college-owned, operated, or affiliated housing: 15%. **Student employment:** During the 2009-2010 academic year, 16% of undergraduates worked on campus. Average per-year earnings: $2,500. **Clubs and organiza-**

tions: Number of student organizations: 154. Activities include: campus ministries, choral groups, concert band, dance, drama/theater, international student organization, jazz band, marching band, music ensembles, musical theater, pep band, radio station, student government, student newspaper, student film society, television station, yearbook. Number of fraternities: 13; sororities: 7. Proportion of men in fraternities: 5%; of women in sororities: 6%. **Sports program (2009-2010):** Member of NCAA I. *Men's intercollegiate varsity sports:* baseball, basketball, cross country, football, golf, track and field (indoor). *Women's intercollegiate varsity sports:* basketball, bowling, cross country, softball, tennis, track and field (indoor), volleyball.

SERVICES AND FACILITIES

Basic services: nonremedial tutoring, women's center, placement service, health service, health insurance, other. **Remedial assistance:** reading, math, writing, study skills. **Counseling services:** minority student, career, military, personal, veteran student, academic, psychological. **For learning-disabled students:** School does not offer a structured program with separate admission and additional fees. Total undergraduates in learning-disabled program or receiving services: 387. Services include: tape recorders, note-taking services, oral tests, learning center, readers, extended time for tests, tutors, priority registration, priority seating, other testing accommodations. **Library:** Number of titles: 3,645,697; number of current serial subscriptions: 2,633. **Information technology resources:** Students are not required to lease or own a computer. Number of campus computers available to all students: 1,500. School has a wireless network. Approximate number of users that can be accommodated: 3,000. Proportion of college-owned housing units wired for high-speed internet access: 100%. **Campus safety:** Security services offered: 24-hour foot-and-vehicle patrols, late-night transport/escort service, 24-hour emergency telephones, lighted pathways/sidewalks, student patrols, controlled dormitory access (key, security card, etc).

TRANSFER AND INTERNATIONAL STUDENTS

Transfer students: May apply for admission for the following academic terms: Fall, Winter, Spring, Summer. Applicants need a minimum number of credits to apply. For fall 2009: Transfer applications received: 1,061. Transfer applicants offered admission: 515. Transfer applicants enrolled: 364. **International students:** Number of foreign undergraduates: 250 (4% of student body). Number of countries represented: 56. Minimum TOEFL score required: 500 (paper); 173 (computer).

Loyola University New Orleans

- **Address:** 6363 St. Charles Avenue, New Orleans, LA 70118-6195
- **Website:** http://www.loyno.edu
- **Private; Religious affiliation:** Roman Catholic (Jesuit)
- **Enrollment:** 2,463 full-time; 301 part-time

KEY STATS

✔ **U.S News College Ranking:** 7, Regional Universities (South)
✔ **SAT Score (25th/75th percentile):** 1120-1330
✔ **Tuition:** 2010-2011: $31,504

Selectivity: More selective	**Room/board:** $7,160
Acceptance rate: 58%	**Average debt:** $22,320
Student/faculty ratio: 11/1	**Proportion who borrowed:** 64%

UNDERGRADUATE STUDENT BODY STATS

2009-2010 enrollment: 2,463 full-time; 301 part-time. Men: 43%; women: 57%. **Ethnic makeup:** African American: 14%; American-Indian: 1%; Asian American: 5%; Hispanic: 11%; White: 66%; International: 3%. **Religious preference:** Protestant: 4%; Jewish: 1%; Muslim: 1%; Buddhist: 1%; No preference: 4%; Unknown: 27%; Roman Catholic (Jesuit): 46%; Baptist, Episcopal, Lutheran, Methodist, Protestant: 12%; Other: 4%.

ADMISSIONS FACTS AND FIGURES

Phone: (800) 456-9652. **Email:** admit@loyno.edu. **Website:** http://www.loyno.edu. **Application deadlines for fall 2011:** Regular decision: Rolling. Early decision: Not offered. Early action: Not offered. Admission cannot be deferred. **Application fee:** $20. **To apply online, go to:** http://apply.loyno.edu/application/. **Admissions requirements/recommendations:** High school units required (recommended): English: 4 (4); Mathematics: 2 (3); Science: 2 (3); Foreign language: (2); Social studies: 2 (2); Total units: 17 (22). Tests: The college uses SAT or ACT scores in admissions decisions. Either SAT or ACT required. For admission to the fall 2011 entering class, the school will

accept: ACT with or without writing accepted. Campus visit: Recommended. Admissions interview: Recommended. Off-campus interview: May be arranged. **Factors that count in admissions decisions:** *Academic:* Secondary school record: Very Important. Class rank: Considered. Letters of recommendation: Important. Standardized test scores: Very Important. Essay: Important. *Nonacademic:* Interview: Considered. Extracurricular activities: Important. Talent/ability: Important. Character/personal qualities: Considered. Alumni/ae relationship: Considered. Geographical residence: Considered. State residency: Considered. Religious affiliation/commitment: Not Considered. Minority status: Not Considered. Volunteer work: Considered. Work experience: Considered. **Other schools with the greatest overlap in applicants:** Louisiana State University–Baton Rouge; Spring Hill College; Tulane University; University of New Orleans; Xavier University of Louisiana. **Admissions statistics for the fall 2009 entering class:** Total applicants: 4,345. Total accepted: 2,538. Freshmen enrolled: 809; 53% were from out of state. Overall acceptance rate: 58%. **Credentials of fall 2009 freshmen:** 29% ranked in the top 10 percent of their high school class; 60% were in the top 25 percent; 91% were in the top half. (Proportion submitting class standing: 32%.) **Average high school grade point average:** 3.7. **First-year students who submitted SAT scores:** 54%. Scores (25/75 percentile): Critical Reading: 570-670, Math: 550-660, Combined: 1120-1330. **First-year students submitting ACT scores:** 29%. Scores (25/75 percentile): English: 24-30, Math: 22-27, Composite: 24-29.

ACADEMICS

Year founded: 1912. **Academic calendar:** Semester. **Degrees offered:** bachelor's, post-bachelor's certificate, master's, post-master's certificate. **Most popular majors:** 10% communication studies/speech communication and rhetoric, 10% psychology, 6% marketing/marketing management, 6% music, 5% political science and government. **Major fields of study:** biological and biomedical sciences; business, management, marketing, and related support services; communication, journalism, and related programs; education; English language and literature/letters; foreign languages, literatures, and linguistics; health professions and related clinical sciences; history; legal professions and studies; mathematics and statistics; philosophy and religious studies; physical sciences; psychology; security and protective services; social sciences; theology and religious vocations; visual and performing arts. **Areas of required coursework:** arts/fine arts, humanities, mathematics, English (including composition), philosophy, foreign languages, sciences (biological or physical), history, social science, other. **Preprofessional programs:** pre-law, pre-dentistry, pre-medicine, pre-veterinary science, pre-optometry, pre-pharmacy, other. **Special academic programs:** accelerated program, cross-registration, distance learning, double major, dual enrollment, English as a Second Language (ESL), exchange student program (domestic), honors program, independent study, internships, liberal arts/career combination, student-designed major, study abroad, teacher certificate program, other. **Teacher certification offered in:** special education. **Reserve Officers Training Corps (ROTC):** Army ROTC: Offered at cooperating institution (Tulane University); Navy ROTC: Offered at cooperating institution (Tulane University); Air Force ROTC: Offered at cooperating institution (Tulane University). **Faculty and instruction (2009-2010):** Total instructional faculty: 283 full-time, 158 part-time (56% men; 44% women; 12% minorities). Full-time faculty with Ph.D. or other terminal degree: 88%. Student/faculty ratio: 11/1. Classes of fewer than 20 students: 59%; of 20 to 49 students: 40%; of 50 or more students: 1%. **Advanced Placement and International Baccalaureate credit:** AP tests may be used for: Placement only. Scores accepted: 4, 5. International Baccalaureate exams may be used for: Placement only. **Freshmen returning for sophomore year:** 77%. **Graduation rates:** Four-year: 48%; five-year: 58%; six-year: 63%. **Graduate study:** Fields in which graduates pursue further study: Master of Business Administration (MBA), 12%; law, 32%; medicine, 29%; dentistry, 1%; theology (or the seminary), 1%; education, 4%; arts and sciences, 22%.

COSTS AND FINANCIAL AID

Financial aid office: (504) 865-3231. **Expenses (2010-2011):** Tuition and fees 2010-2011: $31,504; room/board: $7,160. Estimated books and supplies: $1,000; transportation: $750; personal expenses: $1,500. **Financial aid:** Priority filing date for institution's financial aid form: February 15; deadline: June 1. In 2009-2010, 77% of undergraduates applied for financial aid. Of those, 64% were determined to have financial need; 24% had their need fully met. Average financial aid package (proportion receiving): $24,349 (64%). Average amount of gift aid, such as scholarships or grants (proportion receiving): $14,571 (63%). Average amount of self-help aid, such as work study or loans (proportion receiving): $5,216 (47%). Average need-based loan (excluding PLUS or other private loans): $4,390. Among students who received need-based aid, the average percentage of need met:

82%. Among students who received aid based on merit, the average award (and the proportion receiving): $15,906 (34%). The average athletic scholarship (and the proportion receiving): $20,806 (1%). Average amount of debt of borrowers graduating in 2009: $22,320. Proportion who borrowed: 64%.

CAMPUS LIFE AND EXTRACURRICULAR ACTIVITIES

Campus housing available (% using): coed dorms (95%), apartment for single students (2%), special housing for disabled students (1%), other housing options (2%). Students who live in college-owned, operated, or affiliated housing: 35%. **Student employment:** During the 2009-2010 academic year, 27% of undergraduates worked on campus. Average per-year earnings: $1,920. **Clubs and organizations:** Number of student organizations: 90. Activities include: campus ministries, choral groups, concert band, dance, drama/theater, international student organization, jazz band, literary magazine, music ensembles, musical theater, opera, pep band, radio station, student government, student newspaper, student film society, symphony orchestra, yearbook. Number of fraternities: 7; sororities: 7. Proportion of men in fraternities: 9%; of women in sororities: 13%. Average proportion of students who stay on campus on weekends: 85%. **Sports program (2009-2010):** Member of NAIA. **Men's intercollegiate varsity sports:** baseball, basketball, cross country, track and field (indoor), track and field (outdoor). **Women's intercollegiate varsity sports:** basketball, cross country, track and field (indoor), track and field (outdoor), volleyball.

SERVICES AND FACILITIES

Basic services: nonremedial tutoring, women's center, placement service, day care, health service, health insurance, other. **Remedial assistance:** math, writing, study skills, other. **Counseling services:** minority student, career, military, personal, veteran student, academic, older student, psychological, religious, other. **For learning-disabled students:** School does not offer a structured program with separate admission and additional fees. Services include: remedial math, reading machines, tape recorders, note-taking services, learning center, readers, extended time for tests, tutors, priority seating, texts on tape, other. **Library:** Number of titles: 623,596; number of current serial subscriptions: 80,410. **Information technology resources:** Students are not required to lease or own a computer. Number of campus computers available to all students: 525. School has a wireless network. Approximate number of users that can be accommodated: 4,000. Proportion of college-owned housing units wired for high-speed internet access: 100%. **Campus safety:** Security services offered: 24-hour foot-and-vehicle patrols, late-night transport/escort service, 24-hour emergency telephones, lighted pathways/sidewalks, student patrols, controlled dormitory access (key, security card, etc.).

TRANSFER AND INTERNATIONAL STUDENTS

Transfer students: May apply for admission for the following academic terms: Fall, Spring, Summer. Applicants need a minimum number of credits to apply. For fall 2009: Transfer applications received: 664. Transfer applicants offered admission: 258. Transfer applicants enrolled: 155. **International students:** Number of foreign undergraduates: 73 (3% of student body). Number of countries represented: 31. Minimum TOEFL score required: 550 (paper); 213 (computer).

McNeese State University

- **Address:** 4205 Ryan Street, Lake Charles, LA 70609
- **Website:** http://www.mcneese.edu
- **Public**
- **Enrollment:** 5,967 full-time; 1,568 part-time

KEY STATS

✔ **U.S News College Ranking:** second tier, Regional Universities (South)
✔ **SAT or ACT Score (25th/75th percentile):** N/A
✔ **Tuition:** 2009-2010: $3,587 in state, $10,259 out of state

Selectivity: Selective	**Room/board:** $5,770
Acceptance rate: 67%	**Average debt:** N/A
Student/faculty ratio: 21/1	**Proportion who borrowed:** N/A

UNDERGRADUATE STUDENT BODY STATS

2009-2010 enrollment: 5,967 full-time; 1,568 part-time. Men: 39%; women: 61%. **Ethnic makeup:** African American: 19%; American-Indian: 1%; Asian American: 1%; Hispanic: 1%; White: 74%; International: 4%.

ADMISSIONS FACTS AND FIGURES

Phone: (337) 475-5356. **Email:** admissions@mcneese.edu. **Website:** http://www.mcneese.edu. **Application deadlines for fall 2011:** Regular decision: Rolling. Early decision: Not offered. Early action: Not offered. Admission can be deferred. **Application fee:** $20. **Admissions requirements/recommendations:** High school units required (recommended): English: 4; Mathematics: 3; Science: 3; Foreign language: 2; Social studies: 1; History: 2; Total units: 18. Tests: The college uses SAT or ACT scores in admissions decisions. Either SAT or ACT required. For admission to the fall 2011 entering class, the school will accept: ACT with or without writing accepted. Campus visit: Recommended. Admissions interview: Neither required nor recommended. Off-campus interview: May be arranged. **Factors that count in admissions decisions: Academic:** Secondary school record: Very Important. Class rank: Very Important. Letters of recommendation: Not Considered. Standardized test scores: Very Important. Essay: Not Considered. **Nonacademic:** Interview: Not Considered. Extracurricular activities: Not Considered. Talent/ability: Not Considered. Character/personal qualities: Not Considered. Alumni/ae relationship: Not Considered. Geographical residence: Not Considered. State residency: Not Considered. Religious affiliation/commitment: Not Considered. Minority status: Not Considered. Volunteer work: Not Considered. Work experience: Not Considered. **Admissions statistics for the fall 2009 entering class:** Total applicants: 2,904. Total accepted: 1,946. Freshmen enrolled: 1,334; 8% were from out of state. Overall acceptance rate: 67%. **Credentials of fall 2009 freshmen:** 19% ranked in the top 10 percent of their high school class; 40% were in the top 25 percent; 72% were in the top half. (Proportion submitting class standing: 92%.) **Average high school grade point average:** 3.2. **First-year students who submitted SAT scores:** 4%. **First-year students submitting ACT scores:** 89%. Scores (25/75 percentile): English: N/A, Math: N/A, Composite: N/A.

ACADEMICS

Year founded: 1939. **Academic calendar:** Semester. **Degrees offered:** associate, transfer-associate, terminal-associate, bachelor's, post-bachelor's certificate, master's, post-master's certificate. **Most popular majors:** 18% general studies, 15% nursing/registered nurse training (R.N., A.S.N., B.S.N., M.S.N.), 8% business administration and management, 5% engineering, 4% accounting. **Major fields of study:** agriculture, agriculture operations, and related sciences; biological and biomedical sciences; business, management, marketing, and related support services; communication, journalism, and related programs; computer and information sciences and support services; education; engineering; engineering technologies/technicians; English language and literature/letters; family and consumer sciences/human sciences; foreign languages, literatures, and linguistics; health professions and related clinical sciences; history; liberal arts and sciences studies, and humanities; mathematics and statistics; natural resources and conservation; parks, recreation, leisure, and fitness studies; physical sciences; psychology; security and protective services; social sciences; visual and performing arts. **Areas of required coursework:** arts/fine arts, humanities, computer literacy, mathematics, English (including composition), sciences (biological or physical), social science, other. **Pre-professional programs:** pre-law, pre-dentistry, pre-medicine, pre-veterinary science. **Special academic programs:** accelerated program, cooperative (work-study plan) program, cross-registration, distance learning, double major, dual enrollment, English as a Second Language (ESL), honors program, independent study, internships, study abroad, teacher certificate program. **Teacher certification offered in:** early childhood, special education, elementary, middle/junior high, secondary. **Cooperative education programs:** engineering, technologies. **Reserve Officers Training Corps (ROTC):** Army ROTC: Offered on campus. **Faculty and instruction (2009-2010):** Total instructional faculty: 307 full-time, 102 part-time (51% men; 49% women). Full-time faculty with Ph.D. or other terminal degree: 66%. Student/faculty ratio: 21/1. Classes of fewer than 20 students: 40%; of 20 to 49 students: 53%; of 50 or more students: 7%. **Advanced Placement and International Baccalaureate credit:** AP tests may be used for: Placement only. Scores accepted: 2, 3, 4, 5. **Freshmen returning for sophomore year:** 67%. **Graduation rates:** Four-year: 12%; five-year: 28%; six-year: 36%.

COSTS AND FINANCIAL AID

Financial aid office: (337) 475-5065. **Expenses (2009-2010):** Tuition and fees 2009-2010: $3,587 in state, $10,259 out of state; room/board: $5,770. Estimated books and supplies: $1,200; transportation: $1,050; personal expenses: $1,820. **Financial aid:** Priority filing date for institution's financial aid form: May 1.

CAMPUS LIFE AND EXTRACURRICULAR ACTIVITIES

Campus housing available: coed dorms, fraternity housing, apartment for single students. **Clubs and organizations:** Number of student organizations: 93. Activities include: campus ministries, choral groups, concert band, dance, drama/theater, international student organization, jazz band, literary magazine, marching band, music ensembles, musical theater, pep band, student government, student newspaper, yearbook. Number of fraternities: 7; sororities: 6. **Sports program (2009-2010):** Member of NCAA I. *Men's intercollegiate varsity sports:* baseball, basketball, cross country, football, golf, track and field (indoor), track and field (outdoor). *Women's intercollegiate varsity sports:* basketball, cross country, golf, soccer, softball, tennis, track and field (indoor), track and field (outdoor), volleyball.

SERVICES AND FACILITIES

Basic services: nonremedial tutoring, women's center, placement service, health service, health insurance. **Remedial assistance:** reading, math, writing, study skills. **Counseling services:** minority student, career, military, personal, veteran student, academic, older student, psychological, birth control, religious. **For learning-disabled students:** School does not offer a structured program with separate admission and additional fees. Services include: remedial math, remedial English, reading machines, remedial reading, tape recorders, other special classes, diagnostic testing service, note-taking services, oral tests, learning center, readers, extended time for tests, tutors, exams on tape or computer, other testing accommodations, other. **Information technology resources:** Students are not required to lease or own a computer. Number of campus computers available to all students: 700. School has a wireless network. **Campus safety:** Security services offered: 24-hour foot-and-vehicle patrols, late-night transport/escort service, 24-hour emergency telephones, lighted pathways/sidewalks, controlled dormitory access (key, security card, etc).

TRANSFER AND INTERNATIONAL STUDENTS

Transfer students: May apply for admission for the following academic terms: Fall, Spring, Summer. Applicants do not need a minimum number of credits to apply. **International students:** Number of foreign undergraduates: 260 (4% of student body). Number of countries represented: 44. Minimum TOEFL score required: 500 (paper); 173 (computer).

Nicholls State University

- **Address:** PO Box 2004, University Station, Thibodaux, LA 70310
- **Website:** http://www.nicholls.edu
- **Public**
- **Enrollment:** 5,177 full-time; 1,347 part-time

KEY STATS

✔ **U.S News College Ranking:** second tier, Regional Universities (South)
✔ **ACT Score (25th/75th percentile):** 20-24
✔ **Tuition:** 2009-2010: $3,965 in state, $10,433 out of state

Selectivity: Selective	**Room/board:** $7,310
Acceptance rate: 78%	**Average debt:** $18,822
Student/faculty ratio: 22/1	**Proportion who borrowed:** 56%

UNDERGRADUATE STUDENT BODY STATS

2009-2010 enrollment: 5,177 full-time; 1,347 part-time. Men: 38%; women: 62%. **Ethnic makeup:** African American: 18%; American-Indian: 2%; Asian American: 1%; Hispanic: 2%; White: 76%; International: 2%.

ADMISSIONS FACTS AND FIGURES

Phone: (985) 448-4507. **Email:** nicholls@nicholls.edu. **Website:** http://www.nicholls.edu. **Application deadlines for fall 2011:** Regular decision: Rolling. Early decision: Not offered. Early action: Not offered. Admission can be deferred. **Application fee:** $20. **To apply online, go to:** http://www.nicholls.edu/apply/. **Admissions requirements/recommendations:** High school units required (recommended): English: 4 (4); Mathematics: 3 (3); Science: 3 (3); Foreign language: 2 (2); Social studies: 1 (1); History: 2 (2); Academic electives: (7); Total units: 17 (23). Tests: The college uses SAT or ACT scores in admissions decisions. Either SAT or ACT required. For admission to the fall 2011 entering class, the school will accept: ACT with or without writing accepted. Campus visit: Required. Admissions interview: Neither required nor recommended. Off-campus interview: May be arranged. **Factors that count in admissions decisions:** *Academic:* Secondary school record: Very Important. Class rank: Not Considered. Letters of recommendation: Not

Considered. Standardized test scores: Important. Essay: Not Considered. *Nonacademic:* Interview: Not Considered. Extracurricular activities: Not Considered. Talent/ability: Considered. Character/personal qualities: Not Considered. Alumni/ae relationship: Not Considered. Geographical residence: Not Considered. State residency: Not Considered. Religious affiliation/commitment: Not Considered. Minority status: Not Considered. Volunteer work: Not Considered. Work experience: Not Considered. **Other schools with the greatest overlap in applicants:** Louisiana State University–Baton Rouge; Southeastern Louisiana University; University of Louisiana–Lafayette. **Admissions statistics for the fall 2009 entering class:** Total applicants: 1,887. Total accepted: 1,478. Freshmen enrolled: 1,247; 4% were from out of state. Overall acceptance rate: 78%. **Credentials of fall 2009 freshmen:** 16% ranked in the top 10 percent of their high school class; 40% were in the top 25 percent; 74% were in the top half. (Proportion submitting class standing: 96%.) **Average high school grade point average:** 3.2. **First-year students submitting ACT scores:** 96%. Scores (25/75 percentile): English: 20-24, Math: 18-23, Composite: 20-24.

ACADEMICS

Year founded: 1948. **Academic calendar:** Semester. **Degrees offered:** associate, transfer-associate, terminal-associate, bachelor's, master's, post-master's certificate. **Most popular majors:** 25% business, management, marketing, and related support services, 23% health professions and related clinical sciences, 12% liberal arts and sciences studies, and humanities, 8% education, 5% family and consumer sciences/human sciences. **Major fields of study:** agriculture, agriculture operations, and related sciences; biological and biomedical sciences; business, management, marketing, and related support services; communication, journalism, and related programs; computer and information sciences and support services; education; engineering technologies/technicians; English language and literature/letters; family and consumer sciences/human sciences; foreign languages, literatures, and linguistics; health professions and related clinical sciences; history; liberal arts and sciences studies, and humanities; mathematics and statistics; personal and culinary services; physical sciences; psychology; social sciences; visual and performing arts. **Areas of required coursework:** arts/fine arts, humanities, computer literacy, mathematics, English (including composition), sciences (biological or physical), history, social science, other. **Pre-professional programs:** pre-law, pre-dentistry, pre-medicine, pre-veterinary science, pre-pharmacy. **Special academic programs:** cross-registration, distance learning, dual enrollment, honors program, independent study, internships, study abroad, teacher certificate program. **Teacher certification offered in:** early childhood, special education, elementary, middle/junior high, secondary. **Faculty and instruction (2009-2010):** Total instructional faculty: 265 full-time, 6 part-time (49% men; 51% women; 11% minorities). Full-time faculty with Ph.D. or other terminal degree: 57%. Student/faculty ratio: 22/1. Classes of fewer than 20 students: 36%; of 20 to 49 students: 52%; of 50 or more students: 12%. **Freshmen returning for sophomore year:** 66%. **Graduation rates:** Four-year: 13%; five-year: 29%; six-year: 31%.

COSTS AND FINANCIAL AID

Financial aid office: (985) 448-4048. **Expenses (2009-2010):** Tuition and fees 2009-2010: $3,965 in state, $10,433 out of state; room/board: $7,310. Estimated books and supplies: $1,500; transportation: $1,400; personal expenses: $2,000. **Financial aid:** Priority filing date for institution's financial aid form: April 15; deadline: June 30. In 2009-2010, 81% of undergraduates applied for financial aid. Of those, 47% were determined to have financial need; 70% had their need fully met. Average financial aid package (proportion receiving): $7,415 (46%). Average amount of gift aid, such as scholarships or grants (proportion receiving): $4,482 (40%). Average amount of self-help aid, such as work study or loans (proportion receiving): $3,701 (32%). Average need-based loan (excluding PLUS or other private loans): $3,532. Among students who received need-based aid, the average percentage of need met: 90%. Among students who received aid based on merit, the average award (and the proportion receiving): $2,811 (6%). The average athletic scholarship (and the proportion receiving): $6,250 (3%). Average amount of debt of borrowers graduating in 2009: $18,822. Proportion who borrowed: 56%.

CAMPUS LIFE AND EXTRACURRICULAR ACTIVITIES

Campus housing available (% using): coed dorms (70%), apartments for married students, apartment for single students (30%), special housing for disabled students (0%), special housing for international students (0%). Students who live in college-owned, operated, or affiliated housing: 20%. **Student employment:** During the 2009-2010 academic year, 13% of undergraduates worked on campus. Average per-year earnings: $1,524. **Clubs and organizations:** Number of student organizations: 69. Activities include:

choral groups, concert band, dance, drama/theater, jazz band, literary magazine, marching band, music ensembles, musical theater, pep band, radio station, student government, student newspaper, student film society, television station, yearbook. Number of fraternities: 9; sororities: 7. Proportion of men in fraternities: 11%; of women in sororities: 6%. Average proportion of students who stay on campus on weekends: 20%. **Sports program (2009-2010):** Member of NCAA I. *Men's intercollegiate varsity sports:* baseball, basketball, cross country, football, golf, tennis. *Women's intercollegiate varsity sports:* basketball, cross country, golf, soccer, softball, tennis, track and field (indoor), track and field (outdoor), volleyball.

SERVICES AND FACILITIES

Basic services: nonremedial tutoring, women's center, placement service, health service, health insurance. **Remedial assistance:** math, writing. **Counseling services:** minority student, career, military, personal, veteran student, academic, older student, psychological, birth control, religious. **For learning-disabled students:** School does not offer a structured program with separate admission and additional fees. Total undergraduates in learning-disabled program or receiving services: 100. Services include: remedial math, remedial English, reading machines, tape recorders, untimed tests, note-taking services, oral tests, learning center, readers, extended time for tests, tutors, priority registration, priority seating, texts on tape, other testing accommodations, other. **Library:** Number of titles: 486,990; number of current serial subscriptions: 1,259. **Information technology resources:** Students are not required to lease or own a computer. Number of campus computers available to all students: 1,000. School has a wireless network. Approximate number of users that can be accommodated: 7,250. Proportion of college-owned housing units wired for high-speed internet access: 100%. **Campus safety:** Security services offered: 24-hour foot-and-vehicle patrols, late-night transport/escort service, 24-hour emergency telephones, lighted pathways/sidewalks, student patrols, controlled dormitory access (key, security card, etc).

TRANSFER AND INTERNATIONAL STUDENTS

Transfer students: May apply for admission for the following academic terms: Fall, Spring, Summer. Applicants need a minimum number of credits to apply. For fall 2009: Transfer applications received: 512. Transfer applicants offered admission: 399. Transfer applicants enrolled: 299. **International students:** Number of foreign undergraduates: 117 (2% of student body). Number of countries represented: 45. Minimum TOEFL score required: 500 (paper); 173 (computer). Average TOEFL score: 567 (paper).

Northwestern State University of Louisiana

- **Address:** College Avenue, Natchitoches, LA 71497
- **Website:** http://www.nsula.edu
- **Public**
- **Enrollment:** 5,411 full-time; 2,730 part-time

KEY STATS

✔ **U.S News College Ranking:** 83, Regional Universities (South)
✔ **ACT Score (25th/75th percentile):** 18-23
✔ **Tuition:** 2009-2010: $3,932 in state, $10,618 out of state
  Selectivity: Selective   **Room/board:** $6,682
  Acceptance rate: 81%   **Average debt:** $21,773
  Student/faculty ratio: 18/1   **Proportion who borrowed:** 68%

UNDERGRADUATE STUDENT BODY STATS

2009-2010 enrollment: 5,411 full-time; 2,730 part-time. Men: 33%; women: 67%. **Ethnic makeup:** African American: 30%; American-Indian: 2%; Asian American: 1%; Hispanic: 2%; White: 64%; International: 1%.

ADMISSIONS FACTS AND FIGURES

Phone: (800) 426-3754. **Email:** admissions@nsula.edu. **Website:** http://www.nsula.edu. **Application deadlines for fall 2011:** Regular decision: July 6. Early decision: Not offered. Early action: Not offered. Admission can be deferred. **Application fee:** $20. **To apply online, go to:** http://www.nsula.edu/applyforadmission.asp. **Admissions requirements/recommendations:** High school units required (recommended): English: 4; Mathematics: 3; Science: 3; Foreign language: 2; Social studies: 1; History: 2; Total units: 18. Tests: The college uses SAT or ACT scores in admissions decisions. Either SAT or ACT required. For admission to the fall 2011 entering class, the school will accept: ACT with or without writing accepted. Campus visit: Recommended.

Admissions interview: Recommended. Off-campus interview: May be arranged. **Factors that count in admissions decisions:** *Academic:* Secondary school record: Very Important. Class rank: Important. Letters of recommendation: Not Considered. Standardized test scores: Very Important. Essay: Not Considered. *Nonacademic:* Interview: Not Considered. Extracurricular activities: Considered. Talent/ability: Considered. Character/personal qualities: Not Considered. Alumni/ae relationship: Considered. Geographical residence: Considered. State residency: Considered. Religious affiliation/commitment: Not Considered. Minority status: Not Considered. Volunteer work: Not Considered. Work experience: Not Considered. **Other schools with the greatest overlap in applicants:** Louisiana Tech University; McNeese State University; Southeastern Louisiana University; University of Louisiana–Lafayette; University of Louisiana–Monroe. **Admissions statistics for the fall 2009 entering class:** Total applicants: 2,781. Total accepted: 2,249. Freshmen enrolled: 1,340; 10% were from out of state. Overall acceptance rate: 81%. **Credentials of fall 2009 freshmen:** 12% ranked in the top 10 percent of their high school class; 36% were in the top 25 percent; 67% were in the top half. (Proportion submitting class standing: 92%.) **Average high school grade point average:** 3.1. **First-year students who submitted SAT scores:** 8%. Scores (25/75 percentile): Critical Reading: 418-530, Math: 430-560, Combined: 848-1090. **First-year students submitting ACT scores:** 88%. Scores (25/75 percentile): English: 19-24, Math: 17-22, Composite: 18-23.

ACADEMICS

Year founded: 1884. **Academic calendar:** Semester. **Degrees offered:** associate, bachelor's, master's, post-master's certificate. **Most popular majors:** 18% health professions and related clinical sciences, 17% liberal arts and sciences studies, and humanities, 14% business, management, marketing, and related support services, 11% psychology, 8% education. **Major fields of study:** biological and biomedical sciences; business, management, marketing, and related support services; communication, journalism, and related programs; computer and information sciences and support services; education; engineering technologies/technicians; English language and literature/letters; family and consumer sciences/human sciences; health professions and related clinical sciences; history; liberal arts and sciences studies, and humanities; mathematics and statistics; multi/interdisciplinary studies; parks, recreation, leisure, and fitness studies; physical sciences; psychology; public administration and social service professions; security and protective services; social sciences; visual and performing arts. **Areas of required coursework:** arts/fine arts, humanities, computer literacy, mathematics, English (including composition), sciences (biological or physical), history, social science, other. **Pre-professional programs:** pre-dentistry, pre-medicine, pre-veterinary science, pre-optometry, pre-pharmacy, other. **Special academic programs (% participation):** cooperative (work-study plan) program (4%), distance learning (96%), double major (19%), dual enrollment (2%), honors program (3%), independent study (38%), internships, study abroad (.2%), teacher certificate program (6%). **Teacher certification offered in:** early childhood, special education, elementary, middle/junior high, adult education, secondary. **Cooperative education programs:** other. **Reserve Officers Training Corps (ROTC):** Army ROTC: Offered on campus; Air Force ROTC: Offered at cooperating institution (Louisiana Tech University). **Faculty and instruction (2009-2010):** Total instructional faculty: 318 full-time, 213 part-time (43% men; 57% women; 12% minorities). Full-time faculty with Ph.D. or other terminal degree: 57%. Student/faculty ratio: 18/1. Classes of fewer than 20 students: 44%; of 20 to 49 students: 47%; of 50 or more students: 9%. **Advanced Placement and International Baccalaureate credit:** AP tests may be used for: Credit and/or placement. Scores accepted: 3, 4, 5. **Freshmen returning for sophomore year:** 68%. **Graduation rates:** Four-year: 18%; five-year: 31%; six-year: 36%. **Graduate study:** 13% of students pursue further study immediately upon graduation; 16% within one year. Fields in which graduates pursue further study: Master of Business Administration (MBA), 5%; law, 4%; medicine, 3%; education, 32%; arts and sciences, 55%.

COSTS AND FINANCIAL AID

Financial aid office: (318) 357-5961. **Expenses (2009-2010):** Tuition and fees 2009-2010: $3,932 in state, $10,618 out of state; room/board: $6,682. Estimated books and supplies: $1,200; transportation: $1,049; personal expenses: $1,819. **Financial aid:** Priority filing date for institution's financial aid form: May 1. In 2009-2010, 77% of undergraduates applied for financial aid. Of those, 63% were determined to have financial need; 37% had their need fully met. Average financial aid package (proportion receiving): $6,741 (60%). Average amount of gift aid, such as scholarships or grants (proportion receiving): $4,672 (43%). Average amount of self-help aid, such as work study or loans (proportion receiving): $3,873 (41%). Average need-based loan (excluding PLUS or other private loans): $6,517. Among students who received need-based aid, the average percentage of need met: 54%.

Among students who received aid based on merit, the average award (and the proportion receiving): $4,874 (27%). The average athletic scholarship (and the proportion receiving): $9,779 (5%). Average amount of debt of borrowers graduating in 2009: $21,773. Proportion who borrowed: 68%.

CAMPUS LIFE AND EXTRACURRICULAR ACTIVITIES

Campus housing available (% using): coed dorms (7%), sorority housing, fraternity housing, apartments for married students (2%), apartment for single students (91%), special housing for disabled students. Students who live in college-owned, operated, or affiliated housing: 18%. **Student employment:** During the 2009-2010 academic year, 6% of undergraduates worked on campus. Average per-year earnings: $1,544. **Clubs and organizations:** Number of student organizations: 87. Activities include: campus ministries, choral groups, concert band, dance, drama/theater, international student organization, jazz band, literary magazine, marching band, music ensembles, musical theater, opera, pep band, radio station, student government, student newspaper, symphony orchestra, television station, yearbook. Number of fraternities: 10; sororities: 7. **Sports program (2009-2010):** Member of NCAA I. *Men's intercollegiate varsity sports:* baseball, basketball, cross country, football, track and field (indoor), track and field (outdoor). *Women's intercollegiate varsity sports:* basketball, cross country, soccer, softball, tennis, track and field (indoor), track and field (outdoor), volleyball.

SERVICES AND FACILITIES

Basic services: nonremedial tutoring, placement service, health service, health insurance. **Remedial assistance:** reading, math, writing, study skills. **Counseling services:** minority student, career, military, personal, veteran student, academic, older student, psychological. **For learning-disabled students:** School does not offer a structured program with separate admission and additional fees. Services include: remedial math, remedial English, reading machines, tape recorders, other special classes, untimed tests, note-taking services, oral tests, learning center, readers, extended time for tests, tutors, priority registration, priority seating, exams on tape or computer. **Library:** Number of titles: 777,027; number of current serial subscriptions: 1,183. **Information technology resources:** Students are not required to lease or own a computer. School has a wireless network. **Campus safety:** Security services offered: 24-hour foot-and-vehicle patrols, late-night transport/escort service, 24-hour emergency telephones, lighted pathways/sidewalks, student patrols, controlled dormitory access (key, security card, etc).

TRANSFER AND INTERNATIONAL STUDENTS

Transfer students: May apply for admission for the following academic terms: Fall, Spring, Summer. Applicants need a minimum number of credits to apply. For fall 2009: Transfer applications received: 1,188. Transfer applicants offered admission: 847. Transfer applicants enrolled: 611. **International students:** Number of foreign undergraduates: 49 (1% of student body). Number of countries represented: 28. Minimum TOEFL score required: 500 (paper); 173 (computer).

Our Lady of Holy Cross College

- **Address:** 4123 Woodland Drive, New Orleans, LA 70131
- **Website:** http://www.olhcc.edu
- **Private; Religious affiliation:** Roman Catholic
- **Enrollment:** 524 full-time; 495 part-time

KEY STATS

✔ **U.S News College Ranking:** 70, Regional Colleges (South)
✔ **SAT or ACT Score (25th/75th percentile):** N/A
✔ **Tuition:** 2010-2011: $10,862

Selectivity: Less selective	**Room/board:** $0
Acceptance rate: 40%	**Average debt:** N/A
Student/faculty ratio: N/A	**Proportion who borrowed:** N/A

UNDERGRADUATE STUDENT BODY STATS

2009-2010 enrollment: 524 full-time; 495 part-time. Men: 19%; women: 81%. **Ethnic makeup:** African American: 21%; American-Indian: 1%; Asian American: 4%; Hispanic: 5%; White: 69%. **Religious preference:** Roman Catholic: 58%; Protestant: 10%; No preference: 15%; Unknown: 14%; Other: 3%.

ADMISSIONS FACTS AND FIGURES

Phone: (504) 398-2175. **Email:** admissions@olhcc.edu. **Website:** http://www.olhcc.edu. **Application deadlines for fall 2011:** Regular decision: July 20. Early decision: Not offered. Early action: Not offered. Admission can be deferred. **Application fee:** $25. **Admissions requirements/recommendations:** Tests: The college uses SAT or ACT scores in admissions decisions. Either SAT or ACT required. For admission to the fall 2011 entering class, the school will accept: ACT with or without writing accepted. Campus visit: Recommended. Admissions interview: Neither required nor recommended. Off-campus interview: Not available. **Factors that count in admissions decisions:** *Academic:* Secondary school record: Very Important. Class rank: Considered. Letters of recommendation: Not Considered. Standardized test scores: Very Important. Essay: Not Considered. *Nonacademic:* Interview: Not Considered. Extracurricular activities: Not Considered. Talent/ability: Not Considered. Character/personal qualities: Not Considered. Alumni/ae relationship: Not Considered. Geographical residence: Not Considered. State residency: Not Considered. Religious affiliation/commitment: Not Considered. Minority status: Not Considered. Volunteer work: Not Considered. Work experience: Not Considered. **Other schools with the greatest overlap in applicants:** Nicholls State University; Southeastern Louisiana University; University of New Orleans. **Admissions statistics for the fall 2009 entering class:** Total applicants: 1,264. Total accepted: 504. Freshmen enrolled: 79; Overall acceptance rate: 40%.

ACADEMICS

Year founded: 1916. **Academic calendar:** Semester. **Degrees offered:** certificate, associate, bachelor's, master's. **Major fields of study:** area, ethnic, cultural, and gender studies; biological and biomedical sciences; business, management, marketing, and related support services; education; English language and literature/letters; health professions and related clinical sciences; history; liberal arts and sciences studies, and humanities; psychology; social sciences. **Areas of required coursework:** arts/fine arts, humanities, computer literacy, mathematics, English (including composition), philosophy, sciences (biological or physical), history, social science. **Pre-professional programs:** pre-law, pre-dentistry, pre-medicine, pre-theology, pre-veterinary science, pre-pharmacy. **Special academic programs (% participation):** honors program (10%), independent study (10%). **Teacher certification offered in:** elementary, middle/junior high, secondary. **Reserve Officers Training Corps (ROTC):** Army ROTC: Offered at cooperating institution; Navy ROTC: Offered at cooperating institution; Air Force ROTC: Offered at cooperating institution. **Advanced Placement and International Baccalaureate credit:** AP tests may be used for: Credit only. **Freshmen returning for sophomore year:** 52%. **Graduation rates:** Four-year: 0%; five-year: 0%; six-year: 31%.

COSTS AND FINANCIAL AID

Financial aid office: (504) 398-2165. **Expenses (2010-2011):** Tuition and fees 2010-2011: $10,862; room/board: $0. Estimated books and supplies: $1,200; transportation: $1,579; personal expenses: $2,019. **Financial aid:** Priority filing date for institution's financial aid form: May 13; deadline: July 23.

CAMPUS LIFE AND EXTRACURRICULAR ACTIVITIES

Student employment: During the 2009-2010 academic year, 1% of undergraduates worked on campus. **Clubs and organizations:** Number of student organizations: 16. Activities include: campus ministries, choral groups, drama/theater, literary magazine, student government, student newspaper. Number of fraternities: 0; sororities: 0.

SERVICES AND FACILITIES

Basic services: nonremedial tutoring, placement service, health service, health insurance. **Remedial assistance:** reading, math, writing. **Counseling services:** minority student, career, military, personal, veteran student, academic, older student, psychological, religious. **For learning-disabled students:** School does not offer a structured program with separate admission and additional fees. Services include: remedial math, remedial English, remedial reading, tape recorders, untimed tests, note-taking services, oral tests, readers, extended time for tests, other. **Information technology resources:** Students are not required to lease or own a computer. Number of campus computers available to all students: 107. School has a wireless network. Proportion of college-owned housing units wired for high-speed internet access: 0%. **Campus safety:** Security services offered: late-night transport/escort service, lighted pathways/sidewalks.

TRANSFER AND INTERNATIONAL STUDENTS

Transfer students: May apply for admission for the following academic terms: Fall, Spring, Summer. Applicants need a minimum number of cred-

its to apply. **International students:** Minimum TOEFL score required: 500 (paper); 200 (computer).

Southeastern Louisiana University

- **Address:** SLU 10752, Hammond, LA 70402
- **Website:** http://www.selu.edu
- **Public**
- **Enrollment:** 11,196 full-time; 2,588 part-time

KEY STATS
✔ **U.S News College Ranking:** second tier, Regional Universities (South)
✔ **ACT Score (25th/75th percentile):** 20-24
✔ **Tuition:** 2009-2010: $3,932 in state, $11,188 out of state

Selectivity: Selective	**Room/board:** $6,450
Acceptance rate: 93%	**Average debt:** $18,947
Student/faculty ratio: 23/1	**Proportion who borrowed:** 60%

UNDERGRADUATE STUDENT BODY STATS
2009-2010 enrollment: 11,196 full-time; 2,588 part-time. Men: 39%; women: 61%. **Ethnic makeup:** African American: 18%; Asian American: 1%; Hispanic: 2%; White: 78%; International: 1%.

ADMISSIONS FACTS AND FIGURES
Phone: (985) 549-5637. **Email:** admissions@selu.edu. **Website:** http://www.selu.edu. **Application deadlines for fall 2011:** Regular decision: August 1. Early decision: Not offered. Early action: Not offered. Admission can be deferred. **Application fee:** $20. **To apply online, go to:** http://www.selu.edu/future_students/apply. **Admissions requirements/recommendations:** High school units required (recommended): English: 4; Mathematics: 3; Science: 3; Foreign language: 2; Social studies: 3; Total units: 17. Tests: The college uses SAT or ACT scores in admissions decisions. Either SAT or ACT required. For admission to the fall 2011 entering class, the school will accept: ACT with or without writing accepted. Campus visit: Recommended. Admissions interview: Neither required nor recommended. Off-campus interview: Not available. **Factors that count in admissions decisions:** *Academic:* Secondary school record: Very Important. Class rank: Very Important. Letters of recommendation: Not Considered. Standardized test scores: Very Important. Essay: Not Considered. *Nonacademic:* Interview: Not Considered. Extracurricular activities: Not Considered. Talent/ability: Not Considered. Character/personal qualities: Not Considered. Alumni/ae relationship: Not Considered. Geographical residence: Not Considered. State residency: Not Considered. Religious affiliation/commitment: Not Considered. Minority status: Not Considered. Volunteer work: Not Considered. Work experience: Not Considered. **Admissions statistics for the fall 2009 entering class:** Total applicants: 3,531. Total accepted: 3,277. Freshmen enrolled: 2,717; 3% were from out of state. Overall acceptance rate: 93%. **Credentials of fall 2009 freshmen:** 11% ranked in the top 10 percent of their high school class; 31% were in the top 25 percent; 64% were in the top half. (Proportion submitting class standing: 92%.) **Average high school grade point average:** 3.1. **First-year students submitting ACT scores:** 100%. Scores (25/75 percentile): English: 20-25, Math: 18-24, Composite: 20-24.

ACADEMICS
Year founded: 1925. **Academic calendar:** Semester. **Degrees offered:** associate, bachelor's, master's, doctorate. **Most popular majors:** 30% business, management, marketing, and related support services, 17% liberal arts and sciences studies, and humanities, 12% education, 12% health professions and related clinical sciences, 4% psychology. **Major fields of study:** agriculture, agriculture operations, and related sciences; biological and biomedical sciences; business, management, marketing, and related support services; communication, journalism, and related programs; computer and information sciences and support services; education; engineering technologies/technicians; English language and literature/letters; family and consumer sciences/human sciences; foreign languages, literatures, and linguistics; health professions and related clinical sciences; history; liberal arts and sciences studies, and humanities; mathematics and statistics; physical sciences; psychology; public administration and social service professions; security and protective services; social sciences; visual and performing arts. **Areas of required coursework:** arts/fine arts, humanities, computer literacy, mathematics, English (including composition), sciences (biological or physical), history, social science. **Special academic programs:** cross-registration,

distance learning, double major, dual enrollment, English as a Second Language (ESL), honors program, independent study, internships, liberal arts/career combination, study abroad, teacher certificate program. **Teacher certification offered in:** early childhood, special education, elementary, middle/junior high, secondary. **Reserve Officers Training Corps (ROTC):** Army ROTC: Offered at cooperating institution (Louisiana State University–Baton Rouge). **Faculty and instruction (2009-2010):** Total instructional faculty: 526 full-time, 116 part-time (43% men; 57% women; 12% minorities). Full-time faculty with Ph.D. or other terminal degree: 63%. Student/faculty ratio: 23/1. Classes of fewer than 20 students: 28%; of 20 to 49 students: 64%; of 50 or more students: 9%. **Advanced Placement and International Baccalaureate credit:** AP tests may be used for: Credit only. Scores accepted: 3, 4, 5. **Freshmen returning for sophomore year:** 65%. **Graduation rates:** Four-year: 9%; five-year: 22%; six-year: 30%.

COSTS AND FINANCIAL AID
Financial aid office: (985) 549-2244. **Expenses (2009-2010):** Tuition and fees 2009-2010: $3,932 in state, $11,188 out of state; room/board: $6,450. Estimated books and supplies: $1,200; transportation: $1,048; personal expenses: $1,818. **Financial aid:** Priority filing date for institution's financial aid form: May 1. Average amount of debt of borrowers graduating in 2009: $18,947. Proportion who borrowed: 60%.

CAMPUS LIFE AND EXTRACURRICULAR ACTIVITIES
Campus housing available (% using): coed dorms (69%), women's dorms (11%), sorority housing (4%), fraternity housing (2%), apartment for single students (14%). Students who live in college-owned, operated, or affiliated housing: 18%. **Clubs and organizations:** Number of student organizations: 105. Activities include: campus ministries, choral groups, concert band, dance, drama/theater, international student organization, jazz band, literary magazine, marching band, music ensembles, musical theater, opera, pep band, radio station, student government, student newspaper, student film society, symphony orchestra, television station, yearbook. Number of fraternities: 11; sororities: 8. Average proportion of students who stay on campus on weekends: 20%. **Sports program (2009-2010):** Member of NCAA I. *Men's intercollegiate varsity sports:* baseball, basketball, cross country, football, golf, track and field (indoor), track and field (outdoor). *Women's intercollegiate varsity sports:* basketball, cross country, soccer, softball, tennis, track and field (indoor), track and field (outdoor), volleyball.

SERVICES AND FACILITIES
Basic services: placement service, health service, health insurance, other. **Remedial assistance:** reading, math, writing, study skills, other. **Counseling services:** minority student, career, personal, veteran student, academic, older student, psychological, birth control, other. **For learning-disabled students:** School does not offer a structured program with separate admission and additional fees. Total undergraduates in learning-disabled program or receiving services: 115. Services include: remedial math, remedial English, reading machines, tape recorders, note-taking services, oral tests, extended time for tests, tutors, priority registration, typist/scribe, other testing accommodations, other. **Library:** Number of titles: 596,078; number of current serial subscriptions: 3,923. **Information technology resources:** Students are not required to lease or own a computer. Number of campus computers available to all students: 1,603. School has a wireless network. Approximate number of users that can be accommodated: 1,080. Proportion of college-owned housing units wired for high-speed internet access: 100%. **Campus safety:** Security services offered: 24-hour foot-and-vehicle patrols, late-night transport/escort service, 24-hour emergency telephones, lighted pathways/sidewalks, student patrols, controlled dormitory access (key, security card, etc).

TRANSFER AND INTERNATIONAL STUDENTS
Transfer students: May apply for admission for the following academic terms: Fall, Spring, Summer. Applicants need a minimum number of credits to apply. For fall 2009: Transfer applications received: 907. Transfer applicants offered admission: 686. Transfer applicants enrolled: 589. **International students:** Number of foreign undergraduates: 178 (1% of student body). Number of countries represented: 55. Minimum TOEFL score required: 500 (paper); 173 (computer).

Southern University and A&M College

- **Address:** PO Box 9374, Baton Rouge, LA 70813
- **Website:** http://www.subr.edu/
- **Public**
- **Enrollment:** N/A

KEY STATS

- ✔ **U.S News College Ranking:** second tier, Regional Universities (South)
- ✔ **ACT Score (25th/75th percentile):** 17-20
- ✔ **Tuition:** 2010-2011: $4,132 in state, $9,924 out of state
- **Selectivity:** Less selective   **Room/board:** $5,666
- **Acceptance rate:** 57%   **Average debt:** N/A
- **Student/faculty ratio:** N/A   **Proportion who borrowed:** N/A

Southern University–New Orleans

- **Address:** 6400 Press Drive, New Orleans, LA 70126
- **Website:** http://www.suno.edu
- **Public**
- **Enrollment:** 2,048 full-time; 542 part-time

KEY STATS

- ✔ **U.S News College Ranking:** second tier, Regional Universities (South)
- ✔ **ACT Score (25th/75th percentile):** 13-16
- ✔ **Tuition:** 2009-2010: $3,161 in state, $6,899 out of state
- **Selectivity:** Less selective   **Room/board:** N/A
- **Acceptance rate:** 48%   **Average debt:** N/A
- **Student/faculty ratio:** 22/1   **Proportion who borrowed:** N/A

UNDERGRADUATE STUDENT BODY STATS

2009-2010 enrollment: 2,048 full-time; 542 part-time. Men: 30%; women: 70%. **Ethnic makeup:** African American: 97%; Asian American: 1%; White: 2%.

ADMISSIONS FACTS AND FIGURES

Phone: (504) 286-5314. **Website:** http://www.suno.edu. **Application deadlines for fall 2011:** Regular decision: Rolling. Early decision: Not offered. Early action: Not offered. Admission cannot be deferred. **Application fee:** $20. **To apply online, go to:** http://www.suno.edu/Enroll/. **Admissions requirements/ recommendations:** Tests: The college uses SAT or ACT scores in admissions decisions. Either SAT or ACT required. For admission to the fall 2011 entering class, the school will accept: ACT with or without writing accepted. Campus visit: Neither required nor recommended. Admissions interview: Neither required nor recommended. Off-campus interview: Not available. **Factors that count in admissions decisions:** *Academic:* Secondary school record: Not Considered. Class rank: Not Considered. Letters of recommendation: Not Considered. Standardized test scores: Not Considered. Essay: Not Considered. *Nonacademic:* Interview: Not Considered. Extracurricular activities: Not Considered. Talent/ability: Not Considered. Character/personal qualities: Not Considered. Alumni/ae relationship: Not Considered. Geographical residence: Not Considered. State residency: Not Considered. Religious affiliation/commitment: Not Considered. Minority status: Not Considered. Volunteer work: Not Considered. Work experience: Not Considered. **Admissions statistics for the fall 2009 entering class:** Total applicants: 1,281. Total accepted: 620. Freshmen enrolled: 437; Overall acceptance rate: 48%. **Credentials of fall 2009 freshmen:** 10% ranked in the top 10 percent of their high school class; 30% were in the top 25 percent; 62% were in the top half. (Proportion submitting class standing: 68%.) **First-year students submitting ACT scores:** 100%. Scores (25/75 percentile): English: 12-16, Math: 15-16, Composite: 13-16.

ACADEMICS

Year founded: 1956. **Academic calendar:** Semester. **Degrees offered:** associate, bachelor's, master's. **Major fields of study:** biological and biomedical sciences; business, management, marketing, and related support services; communication, journalism, and related programs; computer and information sciences and support services; education; engineering; engineering technologies/technicians; English language and literature/letters; foreign languages, literatures, and linguistics; history; liberal arts and sciences studies, and humanities; mathematics and statistics; physical sciences;

psychology; public administration and social service professions; security and protective services; social sciences; visual and performing arts. **Special academic programs:** cross-registration, distance learning, double major, dual enrollment, English as a Second Language (ESL), exchange student program (domestic), external degree program, honors program, independent study, internships, liberal arts/career combination, student-designed major, study abroad, teacher certificate program, weekend college. **Faculty and instruction (2009-2010):** Total instructional faculty: 100 full-time, 2 part-time (59% men; 41% women; 69% minorities). Full-time faculty with Ph.D. or other terminal degree: 75%. Student/faculty ratio: 22/1. Classes of fewer than 20 students: 34%; of 20 to 49 students: 64%; of 50 or more students: 2%. **Freshmen returning for sophomore year:** 43%. **Graduation rates:** Four-year: 2%; five-year: 4%; six-year: 8%.

COSTS AND FINANCIAL AID

Financial aid office: (504) 286-5263. **Expenses (2009-2010):** Tuition and fees 2009-2010: $3,161 in state, $6,899 out of state. Estimated books and supplies: $1,200; transportation: $1,049; personal expenses: $1,819. **Financial aid:** Priority filing date for institution's financial aid form: April 15.

CAMPUS LIFE AND EXTRACURRICULAR ACTIVITIES

Activities include: choral groups, concert band, dance, student government, student newspaper, television station. **Sports program (2009-2010):** Member of NAIA.

SERVICES AND FACILITIES

Basic services: nonremedial tutoring, placement service, health service, health insurance. **Remedial assistance:** reading, math, study skills. **Counseling services:** career, personal, veteran student, academic. **Information technology resources:** Students are not required to lease or own a computer. **Campus safety:** Security services offered: 24-hour foot-and-vehicle patrols, lighted pathways/sidewalks.

TRANSFER AND INTERNATIONAL STUDENTS

Transfer students: May apply for admission for the following academic terms: Fall, Spring, Summer. Applicants do not need a minimum number of credits to apply. For fall 2009: Transfer applications received: 1,010. Transfer applicants offered admission: 436. Transfer applicants enrolled: 345. **International students:** Number of foreign undergraduates: 0.

Tulane University

- **Address:** 6823 St. Charles Avenue, 218 Gibson Hall, New Orleans, LA 70118
- **Website:** http://www.tulane.edu
- **Private**
- **Enrollment:** 5,452 full-time; 1,758 part-time

KEY STATS

- ✔ **U.S News College Ranking:** 51, National Universities
- ✔ **ACT Score (25th/75th percentile):** 29-32
- ✔ **Tuition:** 2010-2011: $41,884
- **Selectivity:** Most selective   **Room/board:** $9,824
- **Acceptance rate:** 26%   **Average debt:** $27,522
- **Student/faculty ratio:** 8/1   **Proportion who borrowed:** 47%

UNDERGRADUATE STUDENT BODY STATS

2009-2010 enrollment: 5,452 full-time; 1,758 part-time. Men: 45%; women: 55%. **Ethnic makeup:** African American: 10%; American-Indian: 2%; Asian American: 4%; Hispanic: 4%; White: 77%; International: 3%.

ADMISSIONS FACTS AND FIGURES

Phone: (504) 865-5731. **Email:** undergrad.admission@tulane.edu. **Website:** http://www.tulane.edu. **Application deadlines for fall 2011:** Regular decision: January 15; decision sent by April 1. Early decision: Not offered. Early action: Send application by: November 1; Decision sent by: December 15. Admission can be deferred. **To apply online, go to:** http://www.tulane-app.org/login/login.asp. **Admissions requirements/recommendations:** High school units required (recommended): English: (4); Mathematics: (4); Science: (4); Foreign language: (3); Social studies: (3); Academic electives: (3). Tests: The college uses SAT or ACT scores in admissions decisions. Either SAT or ACT required. For admission to the fall 2011 entering class, the school will accept: ACT with writing required. Campus visit:

Recommended. Admissions interview: Neither required nor recom-mended. Off-campus interview: May be arranged. **Factors that count in admissions decisions:** *Academic:* Secondary school record: Very Important. Class rank: Very Important. Letters of recommendation: Important. Standardized test scores: Very Important. Essay: Important. *Nonacademic:* Interview: Considered. Extracurricular activities: Considered. Talent/ability: Considered. Character/personal qualities: Important. Alumni/ae relation-ship: Considered. Geographical residence: Not Considered. State residency: Not Considered. Religious affiliation/commitment: Not Considered. Minority status: Not Considered. Volunteer work: Considered. Work expe-rience: Considered. **Other schools with the greatest overlap in applicants:** Duke University; Emory University; Miami University–Oxford; Vanderbilt University; Washington University in St. Louis. **Admissions statistics for the fall 2009 entering class:** Total applicants: 39,887. Total accepted: 10,563. Freshmen enrolled: 1,502; 84% were from out of state. Accepted through early-decision or early-action plans: 68%. Overall acceptance rate: 26%. Non-early acceptance rate: 20%. **Size of waiting list:** 3881 applicants; enrolled from waiting list: 132. **Credentials of fall 2009 freshmen:** 60% ranked in the top 10 percent of their high school class; 88% were in the top 25 percent; 97% were in the top half. (Proportion submitting class stand-ing: 48%.) **Average high school grade point average:** 3.5. **First-year students who submitted SAT scores:** 49%. Scores (25/75 percentile): Critical Reading: 630-700, Math: 620-700, Combined: 1250-1400. **First-year students submit-ting ACT scores:** 52%. Scores (25/75 percentile): English: 28-33, Math: 26-32, Composite: 29-32.

ACADEMICS

Year founded: 1834. **Academic calendar:** Semester. **Degrees offered:** cer-tificate, associate, bachelor's, post-bachelor's certificate, master's, doctor-ate. **Most popular majors:** 20% business, management, marketing, and related support services, 15% social sciences, 8% architecture and related services, 7% biological and biomedical sciences, 6% psychology. **Major fields of study:** architecture and related services; area, ethnic, cultural, and gender studies; biological and biomedical sciences; business, management, marketing, and related support services; communication, journalism, and related programs; computer and information sciences and support services; engineering; English language and literature/letters; foreign languages, literatures, and linguistics; health professions and related clinical sciences; history; legal professions and studies; liberal arts and sciences studies, and humanities; mathematics and statistics; multi/interdisciplinary studies; natural resources and conservation; parks, recreation, leisure, and fitness studies; philosophy and religious studies; physical sciences; psychology; public administration and social service professions; security and protec-tive services; social sciences; visual and performing arts. **Areas of required coursework:** arts/fine arts, humanities, mathematics, English (including composition), foreign languages, sciences (biological or physical), social science, other. **Pre-professional programs:** pre-medicine. **Special academic programs:** accelerated program, cross-registration, distance learning, double major, English as a Second Language (ESL), exchange student program (domestic), honors program, independent study, internships, liberal arts/career combination, student-designed major, study abroad, teacher certifi-cate program. **Teacher certification offered in:** early childhood, secondary. **Reserve Officers Training Corps (ROTC):** Army ROTC: Offered on campus; Navy ROTC: Offered on campus; Air Force ROTC: Offered on campus. **Faculty and instruction (2009-2010):** Total instructional faculty: 572 full-time, 612 part-time (61% men; 39% women; 16% minorities). Full-time faculty with Ph.D. or other terminal degree: 94%. Student/faculty ratio: 8/1. Classes of fewer than 20 students: 65%; of 20 to 49 students: 28%; of 50 or more students: 7%. **Advanced Placement and International Baccalaureate credit:** AP tests may be used for: Placement only. Scores accepted: 3, 4, 5. International Baccalaureate exams may be used for: Placement only. **Freshmen returning for sophomore year:** 89%. **Graduation rates:** Four-year: 60%; five-year: 72%; six-year: 73%.

COSTS AND FINANCIAL AID

Financial aid office: (504) 865-5723. **Expenses (2010-2011):** Tuition and fees 2010-2011: $41,884; room/board: $9,824. Estimated books and sup-plies: $1,200; transportation: $849; personal expenses: $952. **Financial aid:** Priority filing date for institution's financial aid form: February 15; deadline: February 15. In 2009-2010, 54% of undergraduates applied for financial aid. Of those, 40% were determined to have financial need; 67% had their need fully met. Average financial aid package (proportion receiving): $35,519 (40%). Average amount of gift aid, such as scholarships or grants (proportion receiving): $25,138 (39%). Average amount of self-help aid, such as work study or loans (proportion receiving): $8,003 (26%). Average need-based loan (excluding PLUS or other private loans): $7,945. Among

students who received need-based aid, the average percentage of need met: 92%. Among students who received aid based on merit, the average award (and the proportion receiving): $21,207 (39%). The average athletic scholar-ship (and the proportion receiving): $39,201 (3%). Average amount of debt of borrowers graduating in 2009: $27,522. Proportion who borrowed: 47%.

CAMPUS LIFE AND EXTRACURRICULAR ACTIVITIES

Campus housing available: coed dorms, women's dorms, sorority housing, fraternity housing, apartments for married students, apartment for single students, special housing for disabled students, special housing for interna-tional students. Students who live in college-owned, operated, or affiliated housing: 47%. Average per-year earnings: $2,500. **Clubs and organizations:** Number of student organizations: 250. Activities include: choral groups, concert band, dance, drama/theater, jazz band, literary magazine, marching band, music ensembles, musical theater, pep band, radio station, student government, student newspaper, student film society, television station, yearbook. Number of fraternities: 15; sororities: 11. Proportion of men in fraternities: 16%; of women in sororities: 28%. Average proportion of stu-dents who stay on campus on weekends: 85%. **Sports program (2009-2010):** Member of NCAA I. **Men's intercollegiate varsity sports:** baseball, basketball, cross country, football, tennis, track and field (outdoor). **Women's intercolle-giate varsity sports:** basketball, cross country, golf, swimming, tennis, track and field (indoor), track and field (outdoor), volleyball.

SERVICES AND FACILITIES

Basic services: nonremedial tutoring, women's center, placement ser-vice, health service, health insurance. **Remedial assistance:** study skills. **Counseling services:** minority student, career, military, personal, veteran student, academic, older student, psychological, birth control, religious. **For learning-disabled students:** School does not offer a structured pro-gram with separate admission and additional fees. Total undergraduates in learning-disabled program or receiving services: 552. Services include: reading machines, tape recorders, diagnostic testing service, untimed tests, note-taking services, oral tests, learning center, readers, extended time for tests, tutors, priority seating, texts on tape, typist/scribe, other testing accommodations. **Library:** Number of titles: 3,257,609; number of current serial subscriptions: 72,564. **Information technology resources:** Students are not required to lease or own a computer. School has a wireless net-work. Approximate number of users that can be accommodated: 25,000. Proportion of college-owned housing units wired for high-speed internet access: 100%. **Campus safety:** Security services offered: 24-hour foot-and-vehicle patrols, late-night transport/escort service, 24-hour emergency tele-phones, lighted pathways/sidewalks, student patrols, controlled dormitory access (key, security card, etc).

TRANSFER AND INTERNATIONAL STUDENTS

Transfer students: May apply for admission for the following academic terms: Fall, Spring. Applicants do not need a minimum number of cred-its to apply. For fall 2009: Transfer applications received: 2,277. Transfer applicants offered admission: 452. Transfer applicants enrolled: 124. **International students:** Number of foreign undergraduates: 233 (3% of stu-dent body). Number of countries represented: 45. Minimum TOEFL score required: 550 (paper); 84 (computer).

University of Louisiana–Lafayette

■ **Address:** PO Drawer 41008, Lafayette, LA 70504-1008
■ **Website:** http://www.louisiana.edu
■ **Public**
■ **Enrollment:** 12,530 full-time; 2,302 part-time

KEY STATS

✔ **U.S News College Ranking:** second tier, National Universities
✔ **ACT Score (25th/75th percentile):** 20-24
✔ **Tuition:** 2009-2010: $4,004 in state, $10,184 out of state

Selectivity: Selective	**Room/board:** $4,630
Acceptance rate: 67%	**Average debt:** N/A
Student/faculty ratio: 22/1	**Proportion who borrowed:** N/A

UNDERGRADUATE STUDENT BODY STATS

2009-2010 enrollment: 12,530 full-time; 2,302 part-time. Men: 42%; women: 58%. **Ethnic makeup:** African American: 19%; Asian American: 2%;

Hispanic: 2%; White: 75%; International: 2%. **Religious preference:** Roman Catholic: 47%; Protestant: 12%; Hindu: 1%; Unknown: 32%; Other: 8%.

ADMISSIONS FACTS AND FIGURES
Phone: (337) 482-6553. **Email:** enroll@louisiana.edu. **Website:** http://www.louisiana.edu. **Application deadlines for fall 2011:** Regular decision: Rolling. Early decision: Not offered. Early action: Not offered. Admission can be deferred. **Application fee:** $25. **To apply online, go to:** http://www.louisiana.edu/apply. **Admissions requirements/recommendations:** High school units required (recommended): English: 4; Mathematics: 4; Science: 3; Foreign language: 2; Social studies: 1; History: 2; Academic electives: 1. Tests: The college uses SAT or ACT scores in admissions decisions. Either SAT or ACT required. For admission to the fall 2011 entering class, the school will accept: ACT with or without writing accepted. Campus visit: Neither required nor recommended. Admissions interview: Neither required nor recommended. Off-campus interview: Not available. **Factors that count in admissions decisions:** *Academic:* Secondary school record: Very Important. Class rank: Very Important. Letters of recommendation: Not Considered. Standardized test scores: Very Important. Essay: Not Considered. *Nonacademic:* Interview: Not Considered. Extracurricular activities: Not Considered. Talent/ability: Not Considered. Character/personal qualities: Not Considered. Alumni/ae relationship: Not Considered. Geographical residence: Not Considered. State residency: Considered. Religious affiliation/commitment: Not Considered. Minority status: Not Considered. Volunteer work: Not Considered. Work experience: Not Considered. **Other schools with the greatest overlap in applicants:** Louisiana State University–Baton Rouge; Louisiana Tech University; Southeastern Louisiana University; University of New Orleans. **Admissions statistics for the fall 2009 entering class:** Total applicants: 7,561. Total accepted: 5,100. Freshmen enrolled: 2,606; 4% were from out of state. Overall acceptance rate: 67%. **Credentials of fall 2009 freshmen:** 17% ranked in the top 10 percent of their high school class; 42% were in the top 25 percent; 75% were in the top half. (Proportion submitting class standing: 93%.) **Average high school grade point average:** 3.2. **First-year students who submitted SAT scores:** 6%. **First-year students submitting ACT scores:** 96%. Scores (25/75 percentile): English: 20-25, Math: 19-24, Composite: 20-24.

ACADEMICS
Year founded: 1898. **Academic calendar:** Semester. **Degrees offered:** bachelor's, master's, post-master's certificate, doctorate. **Most popular majors:** 23% business, management, marketing, and related support services, 17% liberal arts and sciences studies, and humanities, 13% education, 9% health professions and related clinical sciences, 5% engineering. **Major fields of study:** agriculture, agriculture operations, and related sciences; architecture and related services; biological and biomedical sciences; business, management, marketing, and related support services; communication, journalism, and related programs; computer and information sciences and support services; education; engineering; engineering technologies/technicians; English language and literature/letters; family and consumer sciences/human sciences; foreign languages, literatures, and linguistics; health professions and related clinical sciences; history; liberal arts and sciences studies, and humanities; mathematics and statistics; natural resources and conservation; philosophy and religious studies; physical sciences; psychology; security and protective services; social sciences; visual and performing arts. **Areas of required coursework:** arts/fine arts, humanities, computer literacy, mathematics, English (including composition), sciences (biological or physical), social science, other. **Pre-professional programs:** pre-veterinary science, pre-pharmacy, other. **Special academic programs:** accelerated program, cooperative (work-study plan) program, cross-registration, distance learning, double major, dual enrollment, exchange student program (domestic), honors program, independent study, internships, student-designed major, study abroad, teacher certificate program. **Teacher certification offered in:** early childhood, special education, elementary, vo-tech, middle/junior high, secondary. **Reserve Officers Training Corps (ROTC):** Army ROTC: Offered on campus. **Faculty and instruction (2009-2010):** Total instructional faculty: 600 full-time, 140 part-time (55% men; 45% women; 15% minorities). Full-time faculty with Ph.D. or other terminal degree: 73%. Student/faculty ratio: 22/1. Classes of fewer than 20 students: 28%; of 20 to 49 students: 63%; of 50 or more students: 9%. **Advanced Placement and International Baccalaureate credit:** AP tests may be used for: Placement only. Scores accepted: 3, 4, 5. **Freshmen returning for sophomore year:** 74%. **Graduation rates:** Four-year: 13%; five-year: 33%; six-year: 42%.

COSTS AND FINANCIAL AID
Financial aid office: (337) 482-6506. **Expenses (2009-2010):** Tuition and fees 2009-2010: $4,004 in state, $10,184 out of state; room/board: $4,630.

Estimated books and supplies: $1,200; transportation: $1,049; personal expenses: $1,819. **Financial aid:** Priority filing date for institution's financial aid form: May 1. In 2009-2010, 76% of undergraduates applied for financial aid. Of those, 49% were determined to have financial need; 9% had their need fully met. Average financial aid package (proportion receiving): $7,037 (47%). Average amount of gift aid, such as scholarships or grants (proportion receiving): $5,320 (41%). Average amount of self-help aid, such as work study or loans (proportion receiving): $3,856 (29%). Average need-based loan (excluding PLUS or other private loans): $3,780. Among students who received need-based aid, the average percentage of need met: 57%. Among students who received aid based on merit, the average award (and the proportion receiving): $1,644 (7%). The average athletic scholarship (and the proportion receiving): $5,831 (3%).

CAMPUS LIFE AND EXTRACURRICULAR ACTIVITIES
Campus housing available: women's dorms, men's dorms, fraternity housing, apartments for married students, apartment for single students, other housing options. Students who live in college-owned, operated, or affiliated housing: 11%. **Clubs and organizations:** Number of student organizations: 174. Activities include: choral groups, concert band, dance, drama/theater, jazz band, literary magazine, marching band, music ensembles, musical theater, opera, radio station, student government, student newspaper, symphony orchestra, yearbook. Number of fraternities: 12; sororities: 9. Proportion of men in fraternities: 6%; of women in sororities: 6%. **Sports program (2009-2010):** Member of NCAA I. *Men's intercollegiate varsity sports:* baseball, basketball, cross country, football, golf, tennis, track and field (indoor), track and field (outdoor). *Women's intercollegiate varsity sports:* basketball, cross country, soccer, softball, tennis, track and field (indoor), track and field (outdoor), volleyball.

SERVICES AND FACILITIES
Basic services: nonremedial tutoring, placement service, day care, health service, health insurance. **Remedial assistance:** reading, math, writing, study skills. **Counseling services:** career, personal, academic. **For learning-disabled students:** School does not offer a structured program with separate admission and additional fees. Services include: remedial math, remedial English, reading machines, remedial reading, tape recorders, other special classes, diagnostic testing service, untimed tests, note-taking services, oral tests, learning center, readers, extended time for tests, tutors, priority registration, priority seating. **Library:** Number of titles: 1,044,594; number of current serial subscriptions: 2,391. **Information technology resources:** Students are not required to lease or own a computer. Number of campus computers available to all students: 1,500. School has a wireless network. Approximate number of users that can be accommodated: 725. Proportion of college-owned housing units wired for high-speed internet access: 38%. **Campus safety:** Security services offered: 24-hour foot-and-vehicle patrols, late-night transport/escort service, 24-hour emergency telephones, lighted pathways/sidewalks, controlled dormitory access (key, security card, etc).

TRANSFER AND INTERNATIONAL STUDENTS
Transfer students: May apply for admission for the following academic terms: Fall, Spring, Summer. Applicants need a minimum number of credits to apply. For fall 2009: Transfer applications received: 1,893. Transfer applicants offered admission: 912. Transfer applicants enrolled: 632. **International students:** Number of foreign undergraduates: 224 (2% of student body). Number of countries represented: 69. Minimum TOEFL score required: 525 (paper); 195 (computer). Average TOEFL score: 533 (paper).

University of Louisiana–Monroe

- **Address:** 700 University Avenue, Monroe, LA 71209
- **Website:** http://www.ulm.edu
- **Public**
- **Enrollment:** 6,019 full-time; 1,800 part-time

KEY STATS
✔ **U.S News College Ranking:** second tier, Regional Universities (South)
✔ **ACT Score (25th/75th percentile):** 20-23
✔ **Tuition:** 2009-2010: $3,813 in state, $10,070 out of state

Selectivity: Selective	**Room/board:** $5,890
Acceptance rate: 74%	**Average debt:** N/A
Student/faculty ratio: 19/1	**Proportion who borrowed:** N/A

UNDERGRADUATE STUDENT BODY STATS

2009-2010 enrollment: 6,019 full-time; 1,800 part-time. Men: 37%; women: 63%. **Ethnic makeup:** African American: 28%; Asian American: 2%; Hispanic: 1%; White: 68%; International: 1%.

ADMISSIONS FACTS AND FIGURES

Phone: (318) 342-5430. **Email:** admissions@ulm.edu. **Website:** http://www.ulm.edu. **Application deadlines for fall 2011:** Regular decision: Rolling. Early decision: Not offered. Early action: Not offered. Admission cannot be deferred. **Application fee:** $20. **To apply online, go to:** http://www.ulm.edu/enrollment/applyinginfo.html. **Admissions requirements/recommendations:** High school units required (recommended): English: 4; Mathematics: 3; Science: 3; Foreign language: 2; Social studies: 1; History: 2; Total units: 15. Tests: The college uses SAT or ACT scores in admissions decisions. Either SAT or ACT required. For admission to the fall 2011 entering class, the school will accept: ACT with writing recommended. Campus visit: Neither required nor recommended. Admissions interview: Neither required nor recommended. **Factors that count in admissions decisions:** *Academic:* Secondary school record: Very Important. Class rank: Important. Letters of recommendation: Not Considered. Standardized test scores: Very Important. Essay: Not Considered. *Nonacademic:* Interview: Not Considered. Extracurricular activities: Not Considered. Talent/ability: Not Considered. Character/personal qualities: Not Considered. Alumni/ae relationship: Considered. Geographical residence: Not Considered. State residency: Not Considered. Religious affiliation/commitment: Not Considered. Minority status: Not Considered. Volunteer work: Not Considered. Work experience: Not Considered. **Other schools with the greatest overlap in applicants:** Grambling State University; Louisiana Tech University. **Admissions statistics for the fall 2009 entering class:** Total applicants: 2,585. Total accepted: 1,924. Freshmen enrolled: 1,345; 8% were from out of state. Overall acceptance rate: 74%. **Credentials of fall 2009 freshmen:** 23% ranked in the top 10 percent of their high school class; 50% were in the top 25 percent; 79% were in the top half. (Proportion submitting class standing: 92%.) **Average high school grade point average:** 3.2. **First-year students who submitted SAT scores:** 5%. Scores (25/75 percentile): Critical Reading: 455-570, Math: 410-535, Combined: 865-1105. **First-year students submitting ACT scores:** 91%. Scores (25/75 percentile): English: 20-25, Math: 18-23, Composite: 20-23.

ACADEMICS

Year founded: 1931. **Academic calendar:** Semester. **Degrees offered:** certificate, associate, terminal-associate, bachelor's, master's, post-master's certificate, doctorate. **Most popular majors:** 7% general studies, 7% pharmaceutics and drug design (M.S., Ph.D.), 6% nursing/registered nurse training (R.N., A.S.N., B.S.N., M.S.N.), 4% kinesiology and exercise science, 3% psychology. **Major fields of study:** agriculture, agriculture operations, and related sciences; biological and biomedical sciences; business, management, marketing, and related support services; communication, journalism, and related programs; computer and information sciences and support services; education; engineering technologies/technicians; English language and literature/letters; family and consumer sciences/human sciences; foreign languages, literatures, and linguistics; health professions and related clinical sciences; history; liberal arts and sciences studies, and humanities; mathematics and statistics; physical sciences; psychology; public administration and social service professions; security and protective services; social sciences; transportation and materials moving; visual and performing arts. **Areas of required coursework:** arts/fine arts, humanities, computer literacy, mathematics, English (including composition), philosophy, foreign languages, sciences (biological or physical), history, social science. **Pre-professional programs:** pre-pharmacy. **Special academic programs:** cooperative (work-study plan) program, distance learning, double major, dual enrollment, English as a Second Language (ESL), honors program, independent study, internships, study abroad, teacher certificate program, other. **Teacher certification offered in:** early childhood, special education, elementary, middle/junior high, secondary. **Reserve Officers Training Corps (ROTC):** Army ROTC: Offered on campus. **Faculty and instruction (2009-2010):** Total instructional faculty: 345 full-time, 40 part-time (48% men; 52% women; 10% minorities). Full-time faculty with Ph.D. or other terminal degree: 55%. Student/faculty ratio: 19/1. Classes of fewer than 20 students: 27%; of 20 to 49 students: 58%; of 50 or more students: 15%. **Freshmen returning for sophomore year:** 67%. **Graduation rates:** Four-year: 11%; five-year: 24%; six-year: 30%.

COSTS AND FINANCIAL AID

Financial aid office: (318) 342-5320. **Expenses (2009-2010):** Tuition and fees 2009-2010: $3,813 in state, $10,070 out of state; room/board: $5,890.

Estimated books and supplies: $1,200. **Financial aid:** Priority filing date for institution's financial aid form: April 1.

CAMPUS LIFE AND EXTRACURRICULAR ACTIVITIES

Campus housing available: coed dorms, women's dorms, men's dorms, fraternity housing, other housing options. Students who live in college-owned, operated, or affiliated housing: 24%. Average per-year earnings: $1,701. Activities include: campus ministries, choral groups, concert band, dance, drama/theater, international student organization, jazz band, literary magazine, marching band, music ensembles, musical theater, opera, radio station, student government, student newspaper, symphony orchestra, television station, yearbook. Number of fraternities: 7; sororities: 7. **Sports program (2009-2010):** Member of NCAA I. *Men's intercollegiate varsity sports:* baseball, basketball, cross country, football, golf, track and field (indoor), track and field (outdoor). *Women's intercollegiate varsity sports:* basketball, cross country, golf, soccer, softball, tennis, track and field (indoor), track and field (outdoor), volleyball.

SERVICES AND FACILITIES

Basic services: placement service, day care, health service, health insurance. **Remedial assistance:** reading, math, other. **Counseling services:** career, personal, veteran student, academic, other. **For learning-disabled students:** School does not offer a structured program with separate admission and additional fees. **Library:** Number of titles: 639,133; number of current serial subscriptions: 9,950. **Information technology resources:** Students are not required to lease or own a computer. School has a wireless network. Proportion of college-owned housing units wired for high-speed internet access: 100%. **Campus safety:** Security services offered: 24-hour foot-and-vehicle patrols, late-night transport/escort service, 24-hour emergency telephones, lighted pathways/sidewalks, controlled dormitory access (key, security card, etc).

TRANSFER AND INTERNATIONAL STUDENTS

Transfer students: May apply for admission for the following academic terms: Fall, Winter, Spring, Summer. Applicants need a minimum number of credits to apply. For fall 2009: Transfer applications received: 1,035. Transfer applicants offered admission: 726. Transfer applicants enrolled: 493. **International students:** Number of foreign undergraduates: 100 (1% of student body). Number of countries represented: 17. Minimum TOEFL score required: 500 (paper); 173 (computer).

University of New Orleans

- ■ **Address:** 2000 Lakeshore Drive, New Orleans, LA 70148
- ■ **Website:** http://www.uno.edu
- ■ **Public**
- ■ **Enrollment:** 6,724 full-time; 2,022 part-time

KEY STATS

✔ **U.S News College Ranking:** second tier, National Universities
✔ **ACT Score (25th/75th percentile):** 20-24
✔ **Tuition:** 2010-2011: $4,332 in state, $12,488 out of state

Selectivity: Selective	**Room/board:** $6,700
Acceptance rate: 57%	**Average debt:** $13,623
Student/faculty ratio: 18/1	**Proportion who borrowed:** 16%

UNDERGRADUATE STUDENT BODY STATS

2009-2010 enrollment: 6,724 full-time; 2,022 part-time. Men: 49%; women: 51%. **Ethnic makeup:** African American: 18%; American-Indian: 1%; Asian American: 6%; Hispanic: 7%; White: 64%; International: 4%.

ADMISSIONS FACTS AND FIGURES

Phone: (504) 280-6595. **Email:** admissions@uno.edu. **Website:** http://www.uno.edu. **Application deadlines for fall 2011:** Regular decision: August 20. Early decision: Not offered. Early action: Not offered. Admission can be deferred. **Application fee:** $40. **To apply online, go to:** http://admissions.uno.edu/app.cfm. **Admissions requirements/recommendations:** High school units required (recommended): English: 4; Mathematics: 3; Science: 3; Foreign language: 2; Social studies: 1; History: 2; Total units: 18. Tests: The college uses SAT or ACT scores in admissions decisions. Either SAT or ACT required. For admission to the fall 2011 entering class, the school will accept: ACT with or without writing accepted. Campus visit: Required. Admissions interview: Neither required nor recommended. Off-campus interview: May be arranged. **Factors that count in admissions decisions:** *Academic:* Secondary school record: Very Important. Class rank: Very Important. Letters of recommendation: Considered. Standardized test scores: Very Important. Essay: Not Considered. *Nonacademic:* Interview: Not Considered. Extracurricular activities: Not Considered. Talent/ability: Not Considered. Character/personal qualities: Not Considered. Alumni/ae relationship: Not Considered. Geographical residence: Considered. State residency: Considered. Religious affiliation/commitment: Not Considered. Minority status: Not Considered. Volunteer work: Not Considered. Work experience: Not Considered. **Admissions statistics for the fall 2009 entering class:** Total applicants: 3,764. Total accepted: 2,130. Freshmen enrolled: 1,259; 6% were from out of state. Overall acceptance rate: 57%. **Credentials of fall 2009 freshmen:** 13% ranked in the top 10 percent of their high school class; 33% were in the top 25 percent; 64% were in the top half. (Proportion submitting class standing: 82%.) **Average high school grade point average:** 3.1. **First-year students who submitted SAT scores:** 16%. Scores (25/75 percentile): Critical Reading: 470-600, Math: 480-625, Combined: 950-1225. **First-year students submitting ACT scores:** 90%. Scores (25/75 percentile): English: 20-26, Math: 18-24, Composite: 20-24.

ACADEMICS

Year founded: 1956. **Academic calendar:** Semester. **Degrees offered:** bachelor's, post-bachelor's certificate, master's, doctorate. **Most popular majors:** 39% business, management, marketing, and related support services, 11% liberal arts and sciences studies, and humanities, 8% psychology, 7% communication, journalism, and related programs, 6% social sciences. **Major fields of study:** area, ethnic, cultural, and gender studies; biological and biomedical sciences; business, management, marketing, and related support services; communication, journalism, and related programs; computer and information sciences and support services; education; engineering; English language and literature/letters; foreign languages, literatures, and linguistics; health professions and related clinical sciences; history; liberal arts and sciences studies, and humanities; mathematics and statistics; multi/interdisciplinary studies; natural resources and conservation; philosophy and religious studies; physical sciences; psychology; social sciences; visual and performing arts. **Areas of required coursework:** arts/fine arts, humanities, computer literacy, mathematics, English (including composition), foreign languages, sciences (biological or physical), history, social science. **Preprofessional programs:** pre-dentistry, pre-medicine, pre-veterinary science, pre-pharmacy, other. **Special academic programs:** cooperative (work-study plan) program, cross-registration, distance learning, double major, dual enrollment, English as a Second Language (ESL), exchange student program (domestic), honors program, independent study, internships, student-designed major, study abroad, teacher certificate program, weekend college. **Teacher certification offered in:** early childhood, special education, elementary, middle/junior high, secondary. **Cooperative education programs:** art, business, computer science, education, engineering, humanities, natural science, social/behavioral science. **Reserve Officers Training Corps (ROTC):** Army ROTC: Offered at cooperating institution (Tulane University); Navy ROTC: Offered at cooperating institution (Tulane University); Air Force ROTC: Offered at cooperating institution (Tulane University). **Faculty and instruction (2009-2010):** Total instructional faculty: 442 full-time, 188 part-time (57% men; 43% women; 16% minorities). Full-time faculty with Ph.D. or other terminal degree: 69%. Student/faculty ratio: 18/1. Classes of fewer than 20 students: 35%; of 20 to 49 students: 53%; of 50 or more students: 13%. **Advanced Placement and International Baccalaureate credit:** AP tests may be used for: Credit and/or placement. Scores accepted: 4, 5. International Baccalaureate exams may be used for: Credit only. **Freshmen returning for sophomore year:** 72%. **Graduation rates:** Four-year: 5%; five-year: 14%; six-year: 21%.

COSTS AND FINANCIAL AID

Financial aid office: (504) 280-6603. **Expenses (2010-2011):** Tuition and fees 2010-2011: $4,332 in state, $12,488 out of state; room/board: $6,700. Estimated books and supplies: $1,200; transportation: $1,049; personal expenses: $2,143. **Financial aid:** Priority filing date for institution's financial aid form: May 15. In 2009-2010, 80% of undergraduates applied for financial aid. Of those, 66% were determined to have financial need; 12% had their need fully met. Average financial aid package (proportion receiving): $8,014 (62%). Average amount of gift aid, such as scholarships or grants (proportion receiving): $5,799 (42%). Average amount of self-help aid, such as work study or loans (proportion receiving): $4,171 (31%). Average need-based loan (excluding PLUS or other private loans): $3,925. Among students who received need-based aid, the average percentage of need met: 59%. Among students who received aid based on merit, the average award (and the proportion receiving): $1,627 (4%). The average athletic scholarship (and the proportion receiving): $7,924 (2%). Average amount of debt of borrowers graduating in 2009: $13,623. Proportion who borrowed: 16%.

CAMPUS LIFE AND EXTRACURRICULAR ACTIVITIES

Campus housing available: coed dorms, apartments for married students, apartment for single students, special housing for disabled students. Students who live in college-owned, operated, or affiliated housing: 3%. **Student employment:** During the 2009-2010 academic year, 7% of undergraduates worked on campus. Average per-year earnings: $8,836. **Clubs and organizations:** Number of student organizations: 105. Activities include: campus ministries, choral groups, concert band, dance, drama/theater, international student organization, jazz band, literary magazine, music ensembles, musical theater, opera, pep band, radio station, student government, student newspaper, student film society. Number of fraternities: 7; sororities: 8. Proportion of men in fraternities: 1%; of women in sororities: 1%. **Sports program (2009-2010):** Member of NCAA I. *Men's intercollegiate varsity sports:* baseball, basketball, golf, swimming, tennis. *Women's intercollegiate varsity sports:* basketball, swimming, tennis, volleyball.

SERVICES AND FACILITIES

Basic services: nonremedial tutoring, women's center, day care, health service, health insurance. **Remedial assistance:** math, writing, other. **Counseling services:** career, personal, veteran student, academic, psychological, birth control. **For learning-disabled students:** School does not offer a structured program with separate admission and additional fees. Services include: reading machines, tape recorders, note-taking services, learning center, readers, extended time for tests, texts on tape, exams on tape or computer. **Library:** Number of titles: 951,394; number of current serial subscriptions: 17,648. **Information technology resources:** Students are not required to lease or own a computer. Number of campus computers available to all students: 1,129. School has a wireless network. Approximate number of users that can be accommodated: 1,750. Proportion of college-owned housing units wired for high-speed internet access: 100%. **Campus safety:** Security services offered: 24-hour foot-and-vehicle patrols, late-night transport/escort service, 24-hour emergency telephones, lighted pathways/sidewalks, controlled dormitory access (key, security card, etc).

TRANSFER AND INTERNATIONAL STUDENTS

Transfer students: May apply for admission for the following academic terms: Fall, Spring, Summer. Applicants need a minimum number of credits to apply. For fall 2009: Transfer applications received: 2,047. Transfer applicants offered admission: 1,205. Transfer applicants enrolled: 842. **International students:** Number of foreign undergraduates: 380 (4% of student body). Number of countries represented: 74. Minimum TOEFL score required: 525 (paper); 195 (computer). Average TOEFL score: 602 (paper).

Xavier University of Louisiana

- **Address:** 1 Drexel Drive, New Orleans, LA 70125
- **Website:** http://www.xula.edu
- **Private; Religious affiliation:** Roman Catholic
- **Enrollment:** 2,565 full-time; 101 part-time

KEY STATS

✔ **U.S News College Ranking:** 22, Regional Universities (South)
✔ **ACT Score (25th/75th percentile):** 18-24
✔ **Tuition:** 2010-2011: $16,300

Selectivity: Selective	**Room/board:** $7,000
Acceptance rate: 67%	**Average debt:** $27,586
Student/faculty ratio: 13/1	**Proportion who borrowed:** 88%

UNDERGRADUATE STUDENT BODY STATS

2009-2010 enrollment: 2,565 full-time; 101 part-time. Men: 28%; women: 72%. **Ethnic makeup:** African American: 74%; Asian American: 10%; Hispanic: 1%; White: 13%; International: 2%.

ADMISSIONS FACTS AND FIGURES

Phone: (504) 520-7388. **Email:** apply@xula.edu. **Website:** http://www.xula.edu. **Application deadlines for fall 2011:** Regular decision: July 1; decision sent by April 15. Early decision: Not offered. Early action: Send application by: January 15; Decision sent by: February 15. Admission cannot be deferred. **Application fee:** $25. **To apply online, go to:** http://www.xula.edu/admissions/apply.php. **Admissions requirements/recommendations:**

High school units required (recommended): English: 4; Mathematics: 2 (4); Science: 1 (3); Foreign language: (1); Social studies: 1; History: (1); Academic electives: 8; Total units: 16. Tests: The college uses SAT or ACT scores in admissions decisions. Either SAT or ACT required. For admission to the fall 2011 entering class, the school will accept: ACT with or without writing accepted. Campus visit: Recommended. Admissions interview: Recommended. Off-campus interview: May be arranged. **Factors that count in admissions decisions:** *Academic:* Secondary school record: Very Important. Class rank: Important. Letters of recommendation: Very Important. Standardized test scores: Very Important. Essay: Important. *Nonacademic:* Interview: Considered. Extracurricular activities: Considered. Talent/ability: Considered. Character/personal qualities: Considered. Alumni/ae relationship: Considered. Geographical residence: Not Considered. State residency: Not Considered. Religious affiliation/commitment: Not Considered. Minority status: Not Considered. Volunteer work: Considered. Work experience: Considered. **Other schools with the greatest overlap in applicants:** Dillard University; Howard University; Southern University and A&M College; Spelman College; University of New Orleans. **Admissions statistics for the fall 2009 entering class:** Total applicants: 3,278. Total accepted: 2,193. Freshmen enrolled: 765; 44% were from out of state. Overall acceptance rate: 67%. Non-early acceptance rate: 67%. **Size of waiting list:** 0 applicants; enrolled from waiting list: 0. **Credentials of fall 2009 freshmen:** 20% ranked in the top 10 percent of their high school class; 34% were in the top 25 percent; 53% were in the top half. (Proportion submitting class standing: 81%.) **First-year students who submitted SAT scores:** 32%. Scores (25/75 percentile): Critical Reading: 420-530, Math: 410-530, Combined: 830-1060. **First-year students submitting ACT scores:** 84%. Scores (25/75 percentile): English: 17-23, Math: 18-24, Composite: 18-24.

ACADEMICS

Year founded: 1915. **Academic calendar:** Semester. **Degrees offered:** bachelor's, master's, post-master's certificate. **Most popular majors:** 39% biological and biomedical sciences, 16% physical sciences, 15% psychology, 10% business, management, marketing, and related support services, 6% social sciences. **Major fields of study:** biological and biomedical sciences; business, management, marketing, and related support services; communication, journalism, and related programs; computer and information sciences and support services; education; engineering; English language and literature/letters; foreign languages, literatures, and linguistics; mathematics and statistics; philosophy and religious studies; physical sciences; psychology; social sciences; theology and religious vocations; visual and performing arts. **Areas of required coursework:** arts/fine arts, humanities, computer literacy, mathematics, English (including composition), philosophy, foreign languages, sciences (biological or physical), history, social science, other. **Preprofessional programs:** pre-law, pre-dentistry, pre-medicine, pre-veterinary science, pre-optometry, pre-pharmacy. **Special academic programs:** accelerated program, cooperative (work-study plan) program, cross-registration, double major, dual enrollment, exchange student program (domestic), honors program, independent study, internships, study abroad. **Teacher certification offered in:** early childhood, special education, elementary, middle/junior high, secondary. **Cooperative education programs:** business, other. **Reserve Officers Training Corps (ROTC):** Army ROTC: Offered at cooperating institution (Tulane University); Navy ROTC: Offered at cooperating institution (Tulane University); Air Force ROTC: Offered at cooperating institution (Tulane University). **Faculty and instruction (2009-2010):** Total instructional faculty: 227 full-time, 31 part-time (51% men; 49% women; 52% minorities). Full-time faculty with Ph.D. or other terminal degree: 87%. Student/faculty ratio: 13/1. Classes of fewer than 20 students: 45%; of 20 to 49 students: 48%; of 50 or more students: 7%. **Advanced Placement and International Baccalaureate credit:** AP tests may be used for: Credit only. International Baccalaureate exams may be used for: Credit only. **Freshmen returning for sophomore year:** 75%. **Graduation rates:** Six-year: 43%. **Graduate study:** 38% of students pursue further study immediately upon graduation; 75% within five years. Fields in which graduates pursue further study: Master of Business Administration (MBA), 1%; law, 1%; medicine, 11%; dentistry, 4%; engineering, 1%; theology (or the seminary), 1%; education, 1%; arts and sciences, 13%.

COSTS AND FINANCIAL AID

Financial aid office: (504) 520-7517. **Expenses (2010-2011):** Tuition and fees 2010-2011: $16,300; room/board: $7,000. Estimated books and supplies: $1,200; transportation: $1,049; personal expenses: $1,819. **Financial aid:** Priority filing date for institution's financial aid form: January 1. In 2009-2010, 94% of undergraduates applied for financial aid. Of those, 87% were determined to have financial need; 1% had their need fully met. Average financial aid package (proportion receiving): $16,797 (86%). Average amount of gift aid, such as scholarships or grants (proportion receiving): $6,273 (61%). Average amount of self-help aid, such as work study or loans (proportion receiving): $5,521 (84%). Average need-based loan (excluding PLUS or other private loans): $4,811. Among students who received need-based aid, the average percentage of need met: 14%. Among students who received aid based on merit, the average award (and the proportion receiving): $8,511 (3%). The average athletic scholarship (and the proportion receiving): $17,391 (3%). Average amount of debt of borrowers graduating in 2009: $27,586. Proportion who borrowed: 88%.

CAMPUS LIFE AND EXTRACURRICULAR ACTIVITIES

Campus housing available (% using): coed dorms (32%), women's dorms (57%), men's dorms (11%), special housing for disabled students. Students who live in college-owned, operated, or affiliated housing: 35%. **Student employment:** During the 2009-2010 academic year, 0% of undergraduates worked on campus. Average per-year earnings: $2,000. Activities include: campus ministries, choral groups, concert band, dance, drama/theater, international student organization, jazz band, literary magazine, music ensembles, opera, student government, student newspaper, symphony orchestra, television station, yearbook. Number of fraternities: 4; sororities: 4. Proportion of men in fraternities: 5%; of women in sororities: 1%. Average proportion of students who stay on campus on weekends: 80%. **Sports program (2009-2010):** Member of NAIA. *Men's intercollegiate varsity sports:* basketball, cross country. *Women's intercollegiate varsity sports:* basketball, cross country.

SERVICES AND FACILITIES

Basic services: nonremedial tutoring, placement service, health service, health insurance. **Remedial assistance:** reading, math, writing, study skills. **Counseling services:** career, personal, academic, psychological. **For learning-disabled students:** School does not offer a structured program with separate admission and additional fees. Services include: tape recorders, untimed tests, oral tests, extended time for tests, priority registration, priority seating, texts on tape, other testing accommodations, other. **Library:** Number of titles: 261,000; number of current serial subscriptions: 1,624. **Information technology resources:** Students are not required to lease or own a computer. Number of campus computers available to all students: 325. School has a wireless network. Approximate number of users that can be accommodated: 3,000. Proportion of college-owned housing units wired for high-speed internet access: 100%. **Campus safety:** Security services offered: 24-hour foot-and-vehicle patrols, late-night transport/escort service, 24-hour emergency telephones, lighted pathways/sidewalks, controlled dormitory access (key, security card, etc).

TRANSFER AND INTERNATIONAL STUDENTS

Transfer students: May apply for admission for the following academic terms: Fall, Spring, Summer. Applicants do not need a minimum number of credits to apply. For fall 2009: Transfer applications received: 1,403. Transfer applicants offered admission: 252. Transfer applicants enrolled: 145. **International students:** Number of foreign undergraduates: 60 (2% of student body).

Maine

Bates College

- **Address:** 2 Andrews Road, Lewiston, ME 04240
- **Website:** http://www.bates.edu
- **Private**
- **Enrollment:** 1,738 full-time

....

KEY STATS

✔ **U.S News College Ranking:** 21, National Liberal Arts Colleges
✔ **SAT Score (25th/75th percentile):** 1260-1410
✔ **Tuition:** N/A
   Selectivity: Most selective   **Room/board:** N/A
   Acceptance rate: 27%   **Average debt:** $17,945
   Student/faculty ratio: 10/1   **Proportion who borrowed:** 38%

UNDERGRADUATE STUDENT BODY STATS

2009-2010 enrollment: 1,738 full-time. Men: 47%; women: 53%. **Ethnic makeup:** African American: 5%; American-Indian: 1%; Asian American: 7%; Hispanic: 4%; White: 78%; International: 6%.

ADMISSIONS FACTS AND FIGURES

Phone: (207) 786-6000. **Email:** admissions@bates.edu. **Website:** http://www.bates.edu. **Application deadlines for fall 2011:** Regular decision: January 1; decision sent by March 31. Early decision: Send application by: November 15; Decision sent by: December 20. Early action: Not offered. Admission can be deferred. **Application fee:** $60. **To apply online, go to:** http://www.bates.edu/apply.xml. **Admissions requirements/recommendations:** High school units required (recommended): English: 4 (4); Mathematics: 3 (4); Science: 3 (4); Foreign language: 2 (4); Total units: 17 (23). Tests: The college uses SAT or ACT scores in admissions decisions. Neither SAT nor ACT required. For admission to the fall 2011 entering class, the school will accept: ACT with or without writing accepted. Campus visit: Recommended. Admissions interview: Recommended. Off-campus interview: May be arranged. **Factors that count in admissions decisions:** *Academic:* Secondary school record: Very Important. Class rank: Very Important. Letters of recommendation: Very Important. Standardized test scores: Considered. Essay: Very Important. *Nonacademic:* Interview: Very Important. Extracurricular activities: Very Important. Talent/ability: Very Important. Character/personal qualities: Very Important. Alumni/ae relationship: Considered. Geographical residence: Considered. State residency: Considered. Religious affiliation/commitment: Not Considered. Minority status: Considered. Volunteer work: Considered. Work experience: Considered. **Other schools with the greatest overlap in applicants:** Bowdoin College; Colby College; Dartmouth College; Middlebury College; Wesleyan University. **Admissions statistics for the fall 2009 entering class:** Total applicants: 4,767. Total accepted: 1,284. Freshmen enrolled: 469; 92% were from out of state. Overall acceptance rate: 27%. Early-decision acceptance rate: 48%. Non-early acceptance rate: 24%. **Size of waiting list:** 893 applicants; enrolled from waiting list: 51. **Credentials of fall 2009 freshmen:** 63% ranked in the top 10 percent of their high school class; 91% were in the top 25 percent; 99% were in the top half. (Proportion submitting class standing: 36%.) **First-year students who submitted SAT scores:** 52%. Scores (25/75 percentile): Critical Reading: 620-700, Math: 640-710, Combined: 1260-1410. **First-year students submitting ACT scores:** 17%. Scores (25/75 percentile): English: N/A, Math: N/A, Composite: 29-31.

ACADEMICS

Year founded: 1855. **Academic calendar:** Other. **Degrees offered:** bachelor's. **Most popular majors:** 28% social sciences, 11% psychology, 10% history, 9% foreign languages, literatures, and linguistics, 8% visual and performing arts. **Major fields of study:** area, ethnic, cultural, and gender studies; biological and biomedical sciences; engineering; English language and literature/letters; foreign languages, literatures, and linguistics; history; mathematics and statistics; multi/interdisciplinary studies; natural resources and conservation; philosophy and religious studies; physical sciences; psychology; social sciences; visual and performing arts. **Special academic programs (%**

participation): accelerated program (.2%), cooperative (work-study plan) program, double major (11.9%), exchange student program (domestic), honors program (10.6%), independent study (31.4%), internships, liberal arts/career combination (0%), student-designed major (2.1%), study abroad (69%), teacher certificate program (1.5%). **Teacher certification offered in:** middle/junior high, secondary. **Cooperative education programs:** engineering. **Faculty and instruction (2009-2010):** Total instructional faculty: 163 full-time, 31 part-time (49% men; 51% women; 14% minorities). Full-time faculty with Ph.D. or other terminal degree: 91%. Student/faculty ratio: 10/1. Classes of fewer than 20 students: 64%; of 20 to 49 students: 33%; of 50 or more students: 3%. **Advanced Placement and International Baccalaureate credit:** AP tests may be used for: Credit and/or placement. Scores accepted: 4, 5. International Baccalaureate exams may be used for: Credit and/or placement. **Freshmen returning for sophomore year:** 95%. **Graduation rates:** Four-year: 86%; five-year: 91%; six-year: 91%. **Graduate study:** Fields in which graduates pursue further study: Master of Business Administration (MBA), 15%; law, 12%; medicine, 9%; dentistry, 1%; theology (or the seminary), 2%; education, 9%; arts and sciences, 51%; veterinary medicine, 1%.

COSTS AND FINANCIAL AID

Financial aid office: (207) 786-6096. **Financial aid:** In 2009-2010, 49% of undergraduates applied for financial aid. Of those, 44% were determined to have financial need; 89% had their need fully met. Average financial aid package (proportion receiving): $33,852 (43%). Average amount of gift aid, such as scholarships or grants (proportion receiving): $31,083 (41%). Average amount of self-help aid, such as work study or loans (proportion receiving): $4,326 (40%). Average need-based loan (excluding PLUS or other private loans): $4,371. Among students who received need-based aid, the average percentage of need met: 100%. Average amount of debt of borrowers graduating in 2009: $17,945. Proportion who borrowed: 38%.

CAMPUS LIFE AND EXTRACURRICULAR ACTIVITIES

Campus housing available (% using): coed dorms (81%), women's dorms (1%), men's dorms (1%), other housing options (13%). Students who live in college-owned, operated, or affiliated housing: 93%. **Student employment:** During the 2009-2010 academic year, 47% of undergraduates worked on campus. Average per-year earnings: $2,350. **Clubs and organizations:** Number of student organizations: 128. Activities include: campus ministries, choral groups, concert band, dance, drama/theater, international student organization, jazz band, literary magazine, model UN, music ensembles, pep band, radio station, student government, student newspaper, student film society, symphony orchestra, yearbook. Number of fraternities: 0; sororities: 0. Average proportion of students who stay on campus on weekends: 95%. **Sports program (2009-2010):** Member of NCAA III. *Men's intercollegiate varsity sports:* baseball, basketball, cross country, football, golf, lacrosse, skiing (nordic), skiing (alpine), soccer, swimming, tennis, track and field (indoor), track and field (outdoor). *Women's intercollegiate varsity sports:* basketball, crew (heavyweight), cross country, field hockey, golf, lacrosse, crew (lightweight), skiing (nordic), skiing (alpine), soccer, softball, squash, swimming, tennis, track and field (indoor), track and field (outdoor), volleyball.

SERVICES AND FACILITIES

Basic services: nonremedial tutoring, women's center, placement service, health service, health insurance. **Counseling services:** minority student, career, personal, academic, older student, psychological, birth control, religious. **For learning-disabled students:** School does not offer a structured program with separate admission and additional fees. Services include: reading machines, tape recorders, diagnostic testing service, untimed tests, note-taking services, oral tests, learning center, readers, extended time for tests, tutors, texts on tape, exams on tape or computer, other testing accommodations. **Library:** Number of titles: 609,408; number of current serial subscriptions: 47,436. **Information technology resources:** Students are not required to lease or own a computer. Number of campus computers available to all students: 521. School has a wireless network. Approximate number of users that can be accommodated: 3,500. Proportion of college-owned housing units wired for high-speed internet access: 100%. **Campus safety:**

Security services offered: 24-hour foot-and-vehicle patrols, late-night transport/escort service, 24-hour emergency telephones, lighted pathways/sidewalks, student patrols, controlled dormitory access (key, security card, etc).

TRANSFER AND INTERNATIONAL STUDENTS

Transfer students: May apply for admission for the following academic terms: Fall, Winter. Applicants need a minimum number of credits to apply. For fall 2009: Transfer applications received: 146. Transfer applicants offered admission: 2. Transfer applicants enrolled: 1. **International students:** Number of foreign undergraduates: 98 (6% of student body). Number of countries represented: 65. Minimum TOEFL score required: 600 (paper).

Bowdoin College

- **Address:** 5700 College Station, Brunswick, ME 04011-8448
- **Website:** http://www.bowdoin.edu
- **Private**
- **Enrollment:** 1,771 full-time; 6 part-time

KEY STATS

✔ **U.S News College Ranking:** 6, National Liberal Arts Colleges
✔ **SAT Score (25th/75th percentile):** 1320-1500
✔ **Tuition:** 2010-2011: $41,565

Selectivity: Most selective	**Room/board:** $11,315
Acceptance rate: 19%	**Average debt:** $18,382
Student/faculty ratio: 9/1	**Proportion who borrowed:** 45%

UNDERGRADUATE STUDENT BODY STATS

2009-2010 enrollment: 1,771 full-time; 6 part-time. Men: 49%; women: 51%. **Ethnic makeup:** African American: 6%; American-Indian: 1%; Asian American: 12%; Hispanic: 10%; White: 68%; International: 3%. **Religious preference:** Roman Catholic: 19%; Protestant: 27%; Jewish: 9%; Muslim: 1%; Hindu: 1%; Buddhist: 2%; No preference: 39%; Other: 2%.

ADMISSIONS FACTS AND FIGURES

Phone: (207) 725-3100. **Email:** admissions@bowdoin.edu. **Website:** http://www.bowdoin.edu. **Application deadlines for fall 2011:** Regular decision: January 1. Early decision: Send application by: November 15; Decision sent by: December 15. Early action: Not offered. Admission can be deferred. **Application fee:** $60. **To apply online, go to:** http://www.bowdoin.edu/admissions/apply/. **Admissions requirements/recommendations:** High school units required (recommended): English: (4); Mathematics: (4); Science: (4); Foreign language: (4); Social studies: (4); Total units: (20). Tests: The college uses SAT or ACT scores in admissions decisions. Neither SAT nor ACT required. For admission to the fall 2011 entering class, the school will accept: ACT with or without writing accepted. Campus visit: Recommended. Admissions interview: Recommended. Off-campus interview: May be arranged. **Factors that count in admissions decisions:** *Academic:* Secondary school record: Very Important. Class rank: Very Important. Letters of recommendation: Very Important. Standardized test scores: Important. Essay: Very Important. *Nonacademic:* Interview: Considered. Extracurricular activities: Very Important. Talent/ability: Very Important. Character/personal qualities: Very Important. Alumni/ae relationship: Important. Geographical residence: Considered. State residency: Considered. Religious affiliation/commitment: Not Considered. Minority status: Considered. Volunteer work: Not Considered. Work experience: Not Considered. **Other schools with the greatest overlap in applicants:** Amherst College; Brown University; Dartmouth College; Middlebury College; Williams College. **Admissions statistics for the fall 2009 entering class:** Total applicants: 5,940. Total accepted: 1,153. Freshmen enrolled: 494; 87% were from out of state. Accepted through early-decision or early-action plans: 41%. Overall acceptance rate: 19%. Early-decision acceptance rate: 30%. Non-early acceptance rate: 18%. **Credentials of fall 2009 freshmen:** 82% ranked in the top 10 percent of their high school class; 96% were in the top 25 percent; 100% were in the top half. (Proportion submitting class standing: 52%.) **First-year students who submitted SAT scores:** 75%. Scores (25/75 percentile): Critical Reading: 660-750, Math: 660-750, Combined: 1320-1500. **First-year students submitting ACT scores:** 28%. Scores (25/75 percentile): English: 31-34, Math: 27-33, Composite: 30-33.

ACADEMICS

Year founded: 1794. **Academic calendar:** Semester. **Degrees offered:** bachelor's. **Most popular majors:** 16% political science and government, 15% economics, 11% history, 8% English language and literature, 8% psychology. **Major fields of study:** area, ethnic, cultural, and gender studies; biological and biomedical sciences; computer and information sciences and support services; English language and literature/letters; foreign languages, literatures, and linguistics; history; mathematics and statistics; multi/interdisciplinary studies; natural resources and conservation; philosophy and religious studies; physical sciences; psychology; social sciences; visual and performing arts. **Areas of required coursework:** arts/fine arts, humanities, mathematics, sciences (biological or physical), social science. **Special academic programs (% participation):** accelerated program (5%), double major (21%), exchange student program (domestic) (2%), independent study (54%), liberal arts/career combination (0%), student-designed major (0%), study abroad (51%), teacher certificate program (1%). **Teacher certification offered in:** middle/junior high, secondary. **Faculty and instruction (2009-2010):** Total instructional faculty: 177 full-time, 40 part-time (50% men; 50% women; 19% minorities). Full-time faculty with Ph.D. or other terminal degree: 99%. Student/faculty ratio: 9/1. Classes of fewer than 20 students: 69%; of 20 to 49 students: 29%; of 50 or more students: 1%. **Advanced Placement and International Baccalaureate credit:** AP tests may be used for: Credit and/or placement. Scores accepted: 3, 4, 5. International Baccalaureate exams may be used for: Credit and/or placement. **Freshmen returning for sophomore year:** 98%. **Graduation rates:** Four-year: 89%; five-year: 93%; six-year: 94%. **Graduate study:** 11% of students pursue further study immediately upon graduation; 15% within one year; 20% within five years. Fields in which graduates pursue further study: Master of Business Administration (MBA), 20%; law, 10%; medicine, 13%; dentistry, 5%; engineering, 2%; theology (or the seminary), 1%; education, 15%; arts and sciences, 31%; veterinary medicine, 3%.

COSTS AND FINANCIAL AID

Financial aid office: (207) 725-3273. **Expenses (2010-2011):** Tuition and fees 2010-2011: $41,565; room/board: $11,315. Estimated books and supplies: $820 personal expenses: $1,250. **Financial aid:** In 2009-2010, 52% of undergraduates applied for financial aid. Of those, 43% were determined to have financial need; 100% had their need fully met. Average financial aid package (proportion receiving): $34,960 (43%). Average amount of gift aid, such as scholarships or grants (proportion receiving): $33,832 (43%). Average amount of self-help aid, such as work study or loans (proportion receiving): $1,875 (34%). Among students who received need-based aid, the average percentage of need met: 100%. Among students who received aid based on merit, the average award (and the proportion receiving): $1,000 (4%). Average amount of debt of borrowers graduating in 2009: $18,382. Proportion who borrowed: 45%.

CAMPUS LIFE AND EXTRACURRICULAR ACTIVITIES

Campus housing available (% using): coed dorms (61%), apartment for single students (26%), special housing for disabled students (0%), other housing options (13%). Students who live in college-owned, operated, or affiliated housing: 94%. **Student employment:** During the 2009-2010 academic year, 60% of undergraduates worked on campus. Average per-year earnings: $1,000. **Clubs and organizations:** Number of student organizations: 125. Activities include: choral groups, concert band, dance, drama/theater, international student organization, jazz band, literary magazine, music ensembles, musical theater, radio station, student government, student newspaper, student film society, symphony orchestra, television station, yearbook. Number of fraternities: 0; sororities: 0. Average proportion of students who stay on campus on weekends: 90%. **Sports program (2009-2010):** Member of NCAA III. *Men's intercollegiate varsity sports:* baseball, basketball, cross country, football, golf, ice hockey, lacrosse, skiing (nordic), soccer, swimming, tennis, track and field (indoor), track and field (outdoor). *Women's intercollegiate varsity sports:* basketball, cross country, field hockey, golf, ice hockey, lacrosse, skiing (nordic), rugby, soccer, softball, swimming, tennis, track and field (indoor), track and field (outdoor), volleyball.

SERVICES AND FACILITIES

Basic services: nonremedial tutoring, women's center, placement service, day care, health service, health insurance. **Counseling services:** minority student, career, personal, academic, psychological, birth control, religious. **For learning-disabled students:** School does not offer a structured program with separate admission and additional fees. Total undergraduates in learning-disabled program or receiving services: 108. Services include: reading machines, tape recorders, note-taking services, oral tests, learning center, readers, extended time for tests, tutors. **Library:** Number of titles: 1,034,567; number of current serial subscriptions: 37,206. **Information technology resources:** Students are not required to lease or own a computer. Number of campus computers available to all students: 450. School has a wireless network. Approximate number of users that can be accommodated: 2,500. Proportion of college-owned housing units wired for high-speed internet access: 100%. **Campus safety:** Security services offered: 24-hour foot-and-vehicle patrols, late-night transport/escort service, 24-hour emergency telephones, lighted pathways/sidewalks, controlled dormitory access (key, security card, etc).

TRANSFER AND INTERNATIONAL STUDENTS
Transfer students: May apply for admission for the following academic terms: Fall. Applicants need a minimum number of credits to apply. For fall 2009: Transfer applications received: 161. Transfer applicants offered admission: 8. Transfer applicants enrolled: 3. **International students:** Number of foreign undergraduates: 61 (3% of student body). Number of countries represented: 21. Minimum TOEFL score required: 600 (paper); 250 (computer).

Colby College

- **Address:** 4000 Mayflower Hill, Waterville, ME 04901-8840
- **Website:** http://www.colby.edu
- **Private**
- **Enrollment:** 1,838 full-time

KEY STATS
✔ **U.S News College Ranking:** 23, National Liberal Arts Colleges
✔ **SAT Score (25th/75th percentile):** 1270-1440
✔ **Tuition:** N/A

Selectivity: More selective	**Room/board:** N/A
Acceptance rate: 34%	**Average debt:** $21,697
Student/faculty ratio: 10/1	**Proportion who borrowed:** 41%

UNDERGRADUATE STUDENT BODY STATS
2009-2010 enrollment: 1,838 full-time. Men: 46%; women: 54%. **Ethnic makeup:** African American: 3%; American-Indian: 1%; Asian American: 8%; Hispanic: 3%; White: 80%; International: 5%. **Religious preference:** Roman Catholic: 18%; Protestant: 18%; Jewish: 10%; Hindu: 1%; Buddhist: 1%; No preference: 40%; Other: 10%.

ADMISSIONS FACTS AND FIGURES
Phone: (800) 723-3032. **Email:** admissions@colby.edu. **Website:** http://www.colby.edu. **Application deadlines for fall 2011:** Regular decision: January 1; decision sent by April 1. Early decision: Send application by: November 15; Decision sent by: December 15. Early action: Not offered. Admission can be deferred. **Application fee:** $65. **To apply online, go to:** http://www.colby.edu/admissions. **Admissions requirements/recommendations:** High school units required (recommended): English: 4 (4); Mathematics: 3 (3); Science: 2 (2); Foreign language: 3 (3); Social studies: 0 (0); History: 0 (0); Academic electives: 2 (2); Total units: 16 (16). Tests: The college uses SAT or ACT scores in admissions decisions. Neither SAT nor ACT required. For admission to the fall 2011 entering class, the school will accept: ACT with or without writing accepted. Campus visit: Recommended. Admissions interview: Recommended. Off-campus interview: May be arranged. **Factors that count in admissions decisions:** *Academic:* Secondary school record: Very Important. Class rank: Important. Letters of recommendation: Important. Standardized test scores: Important. Essay: Important. *Nonacademic:* Interview: Considered. Extracurricular activities: Important. Talent/ability: Important. Character/personal qualities: Very Important. Alumni/ae relationship: Considered. Geographical residence: Considered. State residency: Considered. Religious affiliation/commitment: Not Considered. Minority status: Important. Volunteer work: Considered. Work experience: Considered. **Other schools with the greatest overlap in applicants:** Bates College; Bowdoin College; Colgate University; Dartmouth College; Middlebury College. **Admissions statistics for the fall 2009 entering class:** Total applicants: 4,520. Total accepted: 1,544. Freshmen enrolled: 480; 86% were from out of state. Overall acceptance rate: 34%. Non-early acceptance rate: 34%. **Size of waiting list:** 934 applicants; enrolled from waiting list: 21. **Credentials of fall 2009 freshmen:** 59% ranked in the top 10 percent of their high school class; 89% were in the top 25 percent; 97% were in the top half. (Proportion submitting class standing: 49%.) **First-year students**

who submitted SAT scores: 76%. Scores (25/75 percentile): Critical Reading: 630-720, Math: 640-720, Combined: 1270-1440. **First-year students submitting ACT scores:** 35%. Scores (25/75 percentile): English: 27-32, Math: 28-33, Composite: 28-31.

ACADEMICS
Year founded: 1813. **Academic calendar:** 4-1-4. **Degrees offered:** bachelor's. **Most popular majors:** 22% social sciences, 16% area, ethnic, cultural, and gender studies, 9% biological and biomedical sciences, 8% English language and literature/letters, 8% history. **Major fields of study:** area, ethnic, cultural, and gender studies; biological and biomedical sciences; computer and information sciences and support services; English language and literature/letters; foreign languages, literatures, and linguistics; history; mathematics and statistics; multi/interdisciplinary studies; natural resources and conservation; philosophy and religious studies; physical sciences; psychology; social sciences; visual and performing arts. **Areas of required coursework:** arts/fine arts, humanities, mathematics, English (including composition), foreign languages, sciences (biological or physical), history, social science, other. **Pre-professional programs:** pre-law, pre-dentistry, pre-medicine, pre-veterinary science. **Special academic programs (% participation):** double major (29.5%), exchange student program (domestic) (2%), honors program (20%), independent study (67%), internships (43%), student-designed major (1%), study abroad (60%), teacher certificate program (.8%). **Teacher certification offered in:** secondary. **Reserve Officers Training Corps (ROTC):** Army ROTC: Offered at cooperating institution (University of Maine). **Faculty and instruction (2009-2010):** Total instructional faculty: 165 full-time, 37 part-time (53% men; 47% women; 12% minorities). Full-time faculty with Ph.D. or other terminal degree: 95%. Student/faculty ratio: 10/1. Classes of fewer than 20 students: 64%; of 20 to 49 students: 33%; of 50 or more students: 3%. **Advanced Placement and International Baccalaureate credit:** AP tests may be used for: Credit and/or placement. Scores accepted: 4, 5. International Baccalaureate exams may be used for: Credit and/or placement. **Freshmen returning for sophomore year:** 94%. **Graduation rates:** Four-year: 82%; five-year: 88%; six-year: 88%. **Graduate study:** 17% of students pursue further study immediately upon graduation; 25% within one year; 50% within five years. Fields in which graduates pursue further study: Master of Business Administration (MBA), 3%; law, 20%; medicine, 15%; education, 5%; arts and sciences, 57%.

COSTS AND FINANCIAL AID
Financial aid office: (800) 723-3032. **Financial aid:** In 2009-2010, 44% of undergraduates applied for financial aid. Of those, 38% were determined to have financial need; 100% had their need fully met. Average financial aid package (proportion receiving): $32,252 (38%). Average amount of gift aid, such as scholarships or grants (proportion receiving): $31,423 (38%). Average amount of self-help aid, such as work study or loans (proportion receiving): $1,647 (31%). Average need-based loan (excluding PLUS or other private loans): $2,340. Among students who received need-based aid, the average percentage of need met: 100%. Among students who received aid based on merit, the average award (and the proportion receiving): $337 (3%). The average athletic scholarship (and the proportion receiving): $0 (0%). Average amount of debt of borrowers graduating in 2009: $21,697. Proportion who borrowed: 41%.

CAMPUS LIFE AND EXTRACURRICULAR ACTIVITIES
Campus housing available (% using): coed dorms (74%), cooperative housing (1%), other housing options (25%). Students who live in college-owned, operated, or affiliated housing: 93%. **Student employment:** During the 2009-2010 academic year, 62% of undergraduates worked on campus. Average per-year earnings: $1,200. **Clubs and organizations:** Number of student organizations: 91. Activities include: campus ministries, choral groups, concert band, dance, drama/theater, international student organization, jazz band, literary magazine, model UN, music ensembles, musical theater, radio station, student government, student newspaper, student film society, symphony orchestra, yearbook. Number of fraternities: 0; sororities: 0. Average proportion of students who stay on campus on weekends: 90%. **Sports program (2009-2010):** Member of NCAA III. *Men's intercollegiate varsity sports:* baseball, basketball, cross country, football, golf, ice hockey, lacrosse, skiing (nordic), skiing (alpine), soccer, swimming, tennis, track and field (indoor), track and field (outdoor). *Women's intercollegiate varsity sports:* basketball, crew (heavyweight), cross country, field hockey, golf, ice hockey, lacrosse, skiing (nordic), skiing (alpine), soccer, softball, squash, swimming, tennis, track and field (indoor), track and field (outdoor), volleyball.

SERVICES AND FACILITIES

Basic services: nonremedial tutoring, women's center, placement service, health service, health insurance, other. **Counseling services:** minority student, career, military, personal, veteran student, academic, older student, psychological, birth control, religious. **For learning-disabled students:** School does not offer a structured program with separate admission and additional fees. Services include: reading machines, tape recorders, note-taking services, readers, extended time for tests, tutors, texts on tape. **Library:** Number of titles: 926,539; number of current serial subscriptions: 17,809. **Information technology resources:** Students are not required to lease or own a computer. Number of campus computers available to all students: 365. School has a wireless network. Approximate number of users that can be accommodated: 2,000. Proportion of college-owned housing units wired for high-speed internet access: 100%. **Campus safety:** Security services offered: 24-hour foot-and-vehicle patrols, late-night transport/escort service, 24-hour emergency telephones, lighted pathways/sidewalks, student patrols, controlled dormitory access (key, security card, etc).

TRANSFER AND INTERNATIONAL STUDENTS

Transfer students: May apply for admission for the following academic terms: Fall, Spring. Applicants do not need a minimum number of credits to apply. For fall 2009: Transfer applications received: 157. Transfer applicants offered admission: 31. Transfer applicants enrolled: 8. **International students:** Number of foreign undergraduates: 97 (5% of student body). Number of countries represented: 69. Minimum TOEFL score required: 600 (paper); 240 (computer). Average TOEFL score: 632 (paper).

College of the Atlantic

- **Address:** 105 Eden Street, Bar Harbor, ME 04609
- **Website:** http://www.coa.edu/
- **Private**
- **Enrollment:** 312 full-time; 24 part-time

KEY STATS

- ✔ **U.S News College Ranking:** 131, National Liberal Arts Colleges
- ✔ **SAT Score (25th/75th percentile):** 1130-1310
- ✔ **Tuition:** 2010-2011: $34,380

Selectivity: More selective	**Room/board:** $8,250
Acceptance rate: 75%	**Average debt:** $20,170
Student/faculty ratio: 11/1	**Proportion who borrowed:** 54%

UNDERGRADUATE STUDENT BODY STATS

2009-2010 enrollment: 312 full-time; 24 part-time. Men: 32%; women: 68%. **Ethnic makeup:** African American: 1%; American-Indian: 1%; Asian American: 2%; Hispanic: 1%; White: 81%; International: 15%.

ADMISSIONS FACTS AND FIGURES

Phone: (800) 528-0025. **Email:** inquiry@coa.edu. **Website:** http://www.coa.edu/. **Application deadlines for fall 2011:** Regular decision: February 15; decision sent by April 1. Early decision: Send application by: December 1; Decision sent by: December 15. Early action: Not offered. Admission can be deferred. **Application fee:** $45. **To apply online, go to:** http://www.coa.edu/html/applytocoa.htm. **Admissions requirements/recommendations:** High school units required (recommended): English: 4; Mathematics: 3 (4); Science: 2 (3); Foreign language: 0 (2); Social studies: 2; History: 0 (2); Academic electives: 0 (1); Total units: 15 (19). Tests: The college uses SAT or ACT scores in admissions decisions. Neither SAT nor ACT required. For admission to the fall 2011 entering class, the school will accept: ACT with or without writing accepted. Campus visit: Recommended. Admissions interview: Recommended. Off-campus interview: May be arranged. **Factors that count in admissions decisions:** *Academic:* Secondary school record: Very Important. Class rank: Important. Letters of recommendation: Very Important. Standardized test scores: Considered. Essay: Very Important. *Nonacademic:* Interview: Important. Extracurricular activities: Important. Talent/ability: Important. Character/personal qualities: Important. Alumni/ae relationship: Considered. Geographical residence: Considered. State residency: Considered. Religious affiliation/commitment: Not Considered. Minority status: Considered. Volunteer work: Important. Work experience: Important. **Other schools with the greatest overlap in applicants:** Bennington College; Bowdoin College; Colby College; Hampshire College; Middlebury College. **Admissions statistics for the fall 2009 entering class:** Total applicants: 322. Total accepted: 241. Freshmen enrolled: 76; 82%

were from out of state. Accepted through early-decision or early-action plans: 32%. Overall acceptance rate: 75%. Early-decision acceptance rate: 79%. Non-early acceptance rate: 74%. **Size of waiting list:** 11 applicants; enrolled from waiting list: 0. **Credentials of fall 2009 freshmen:** 26% ranked in the top 10 percent of their high school class; 63% were in the top 25 percent; 93% were in the top half. (Proportion submitting class standing: 36%.) **Average high school grade point average:** 3.5. **First-year students who submitted SAT scores:** 54%. Scores (25/75 percentile): Critical Reading: 620-690, Math: 510-620, Combined: 1130-1310. **First-year students submitting ACT scores:** 13%. Scores (25/75 percentile): English: N/A, Math: N/A, Composite: 21-27.

ACADEMICS

Year founded: 1969. **Academic calendar:** Trimester. **Degrees offered:** bachelor's, master's. **Most popular majors:** 100% multi/interdisciplinary studies. **Major fields of study:** multi/interdisciplinary studies. **Areas of required coursework:** arts/fine arts, humanities, mathematics, English (including composition), sciences (biological or physical), history, social science, other. **Special academic programs (% participation):** cross-registration (19%), exchange student program (domestic) (11%), independent study (85%), internships (100%), liberal arts/career combination (37%), student-designed major (100%), study abroad (63%), teacher certificate program (10%). **Teacher certification offered in:** elementary, secondary. **Cooperative education programs:** education. **Faculty and instruction (2009-2010):** Total instructional faculty: 25 full-time, 14 part-time (62% men; 38% women; 5% minorities). Full-time faculty with Ph.D. or other terminal degree: 84%. Student/faculty ratio: 11/1. Classes of fewer than 20 students: 89%; of 20 to 49 students: 11%. **Advanced Placement and International Baccalaureate credit:** AP tests may be used for: Credit only. Scores accepted: 4, 5. International Baccalaureate exams may be used for: Credit only. **Freshmen returning for sophomore year:** 83%. **Graduation rates:** Four-year: 48%; five-year: 61%; six-year: 61%. **Graduate study:** 10% of students pursue further study immediately upon graduation; 10% within one year; 35% within five years. Fields in which graduates pursue further study: Master of Business Administration (MBA), 4%; law, 10%; medicine, 5%; engineering, 1%; theology (or the seminary), 2%; education, 13%; arts and sciences, 40%; veterinary medicine, 2%.

COSTS AND FINANCIAL AID

Financial aid office: (800) 528-0025. **Expenses (2010-2011):** Tuition and fees 2010-2011: $34,380; room/board: $8,250. Estimated books and supplies: $600; transportation: $450; personal expenses: $630. **Financial aid:** Priority filing date for institution's financial aid form: February 15; deadline: February 15. In 2009-2010, 86% of undergraduates applied for financial aid. Of those, 86% were determined to have financial need; 71% had their need fully met. Average financial aid package (proportion receiving): $30,646 (85%). Average amount of gift aid, such as scholarships or grants (proportion receiving): $26,366 (80%). Average amount of self-help aid, such as work study or loans (proportion receiving): $5,617 (80%). Average need-based loan (excluding PLUS or other private loans): $4,830. Among students who received need-based aid, the average percentage of need met: 96%. Among students who received aid based on merit, the average award (and the proportion receiving): $0 (0%). The average athletic scholarship (and the proportion receiving): $0 (0%). Average amount of debt of borrowers graduating in 2009: $20,170. Proportion who borrowed: 54%.

CAMPUS LIFE AND EXTRACURRICULAR ACTIVITIES

Campus housing available (% using): coed dorms (100%), special housing for disabled students (0%), other housing options. Students who live in college-owned, operated, or affiliated housing: 43%. **Student employment:** During the 2009-2010 academic year, 5% of undergraduates worked on campus. Average per-year earnings: $1,000. **Clubs and organizations:** Number of student organizations: 9. Activities include: choral groups, concert band, dance, drama/theater, international student organization, jazz band, literary magazine, music ensembles, student government, student newspaper, student film society, yearbook. Number of fraternities: 0; sororities: 0. Average proportion of students who stay on campus on weekends: 80%.

SERVICES AND FACILITIES

Basic services: nonremedial tutoring, health service, health insurance. **Remedial assistance:** writing, study skills. **Counseling services:** minority student, career, personal, academic, psychological, birth control, religious. **For learning-disabled students:** School does not offer a structured program with separate admission and additional fees. Total undergraduates in learning-disabled program or receiving services: 26. Services include: remedial

English, reading machines, remedial reading, tape recorders, other special classes, untimed tests, note-taking services, oral tests, readers, extended time for tests, tutors, priority seating, texts on tape, other testing accommodations. **Library:** Number of titles: 50,000; number of current serial subscriptions: 230. **Information technology resources:** Students are not required to lease or own a computer. Number of campus computers available to all students: 50. School has a wireless network. Approximate number of users that can be accommodated: 500. Proportion of college-owned housing units wired for high-speed internet access: 100%. **Campus safety:** Security services offered: late-night transport/escort service, 24-hour emergency telephones, lighted pathways/sidewalks, controlled dormitory access (key, security card, etc).

TRANSFER AND INTERNATIONAL STUDENTS

Transfer students: May apply for admission for the following academic terms: Fall, Winter, Spring. Applicants do not need a minimum number of credits to apply. For fall 2009: Transfer applications received: 55. Transfer applicants offered admission: 42. Transfer applicants enrolled: 31. **International students:** Number of foreign undergraduates: 48 (15% of student body). Number of countries represented: 33. Minimum TOEFL score required: 550 (paper); 217 (computer). Average TOEFL score: 600 (paper).

Husson University

- ■ **Address:** 1 College Circle, Bangor, ME 04401
- ■ **Website:** http://www.husson.edu
- ■ **Private**
- ■ **Enrollment:** 1,903 full-time; 568 part-time

KEY STATS

- ✔ **U.S News College Ranking:** second tier, Regional Universities (North)
- ✔ **SAT Score (25th/75th percentile):** 830-1020
- ✔ **Tuition:** 2010-2011: $13,450

Selectivity: Less selective	**Room/board:** $7,240
Acceptance rate: 87%	**Average debt:** $33,010
Student/faculty ratio: 22/1	**Proportion who borrowed:** 88%

UNDERGRADUATE STUDENT BODY STATS

2009-2010 enrollment: 1,903 full-time; 568 part-time. Men: 41%; women: 59%. **Ethnic makeup:** African American: 5%; Asian American: 1%; Hispanic: 1%; White: 92%; International: 1%. **Religious preference:** Roman Catholic: 21%; Protestant: 25%; Muslim: 1%; Buddhist: 1%; No preference: 34%; 0: 0%; Other: 18%.

ADMISSIONS FACTS AND FIGURES

Phone: (207) 941-7100. **Email:** admit@husson.edu. **Website:** http://www.husson.edu. **Application deadlines for fall 2011:** Regular decision: August 30. Early decision: Not offered. Early action: Not offered. Admission can be deferred. **Application fee:** $40. **To apply online, go to:** http://www.husson.edu/?cat_id=343. **Admissions requirements/recommendations:** High school units required (recommended): English: (4); Mathematics: (3); Science: (3); Social studies: (1); History: (1). Tests: The college uses SAT or ACT scores in admissions decisions. Either SAT or ACT required. For admission to the fall 2011 entering class, the school will accept: ACT with writing required. Campus visit: Recommended. Admissions interview: Recommended. Off-campus interview: May be arranged. **Factors that count in admissions decisions:** *Academic:* Secondary school record: Very Important. Class rank: Important. Letters of recommendation: Very Important. Standardized test scores: Important. Essay: Important. *Nonacademic:* Interview: Very Important. Extracurricular activities: Important. Talent/ability: Not Considered. Character/personal qualities: Important. Alumni/ae relationship: Considered. Geographical residence: Not Considered. State residency: Not Considered. Religious affiliation/commitment: Not Considered. Minority status: Not Considered. Volunteer work: Considered. Work experience: Considered. **Other schools with the greatest overlap in applicants:** St. Joseph's College; University of Maine; University of Maine–Farmington; University of New England; University of Southern Maine. **Admissions statistics for the fall 2009 entering class:** Total applicants: 1,280. Total accepted: 1,113. Freshmen enrolled: 532; 18% were from out of state. Overall acceptance rate: 87%. **Size of waiting list:** 39 applicants; enrolled from waiting list: 11. **Credentials of fall 2009 freshmen:** 11% ranked in the top 10 percent of their high school class; 30% were in the top 25 percent; 61% were in the top half. (Proportion submitting class standing: 97%.) **Average high school**

grade point average: 3.1. **First-year students who submitted SAT scores:** 95%. Scores (25/75 percentile): Critical Reading: 410-510, Math: 420-510, Combined: 830-1020. **First-year students submitting ACT scores:** 7%. Scores (25/75 percentile): English: 16-23, Math: 17-23, Composite: 16-22.

ACADEMICS

Year founded: 1898. **Academic calendar:** Semester. **Degrees offered:** associate, bachelor's, master's, post-master's certificate. **Most popular majors:** 42% business/commerce, 24% health professions and related clinical sciences, 11% criminology, 10% psychology, 5% education. **Major fields of study:** biological and biomedical sciences; business, management, marketing, and related support services; computer and information sciences and support services; education; health professions and related clinical sciences; legal professions and studies; liberal arts and sciences studies, and humanities; physical sciences; psychology; security and protective services. **Areas of required coursework:** arts/fine arts, humanities, computer literacy, mathematics, English (including composition), philosophy, foreign languages, sciences (biological or physical), history, social science. **Pre-professional programs:** pre-law, pre-dentistry, pre-medicine, pre-veterinary science, pre-optometry, pre-pharmacy. **Special academic programs (% participation):** cooperative (work-study plan) program (2%), double major, independent study, internships (2%), liberal arts/career combination (9%), student-designed major (7%), teacher certificate program (15%). **Teacher certification offered in:** elementary, middle/junior high, secondary. **Cooperative education programs:** business, computer science, health professions. **Reserve Officers Training Corps (ROTC):** Army ROTC: Offered on campus; Navy ROTC: Offered at cooperating institution (University of Maine). **Faculty and instruction (2009-2010):** Total instructional faculty: 101 full-time, 8 part-time (41% men; 59% women; 6% minorities). Student/faculty ratio: 22/1. Classes of fewer than 20 students: 49%; of 20 to 49 students: 49%; of 50 or more students: 1%. **Advanced Placement and International Baccalaureate credit:** AP tests may be used for: Credit and/or placement. Scores accepted: 3, 4, 5. International Baccalaureate exams may be used for: Credit and/or placement. **Freshmen returning for sophomore year:** 70%. **Graduation rates:** Four-year: 17%; five-year: 37%; six-year: 40%. **Graduate study:** 2% of students pursue further study immediately upon graduation; 5% within one year; 10% within five years. Fields in which graduates pursue further study: Master of Business Administration (MBA), 17%.

COSTS AND FINANCIAL AID

Financial aid office: (207) 941-7156. **Expenses (2010-2011):** Tuition and fees 2010-2011: $13,450; room/board: $7,240. Estimated books and supplies: $1,000; transportation: $550; personal expenses: $1,150. **Financial aid:** Priority filing date for institution's financial aid form: April 15; deadline: April 15. In 2009-2010, 99% of undergraduates applied for financial aid. Of those, 86% were determined to have financial need; 11% had their need fully met. Average financial aid package (proportion receiving): $11,462 (85%). Average amount of gift aid, such as scholarships or grants (proportion receiving): $7,963 (75%). Average amount of self-help aid, such as work study or loans (proportion receiving): $4,721 (79%). Average need-based loan (excluding PLUS or other private loans): $4,076. Among students who received need-based aid, the average percentage of need met: 73%. Among students who received aid based on merit, the average award (and the proportion receiving): $3,687 (6%). The average athletic scholarship (and the proportion receiving): $0 (0%). Average amount of debt of borrowers graduating in 2009: $33,010. Proportion who borrowed: 88%.

CAMPUS LIFE AND EXTRACURRICULAR ACTIVITIES

Campus housing available (% using): coed dorms (100%). Students who live in college-owned, operated, or affiliated housing: 37%. **Student employment:** During the 2009-2010 academic year, 25% of undergraduates worked on campus. Average per-year earnings: $1,600. **Clubs and organizations:** Number of student organizations: 44. Activities include: campus ministries, choral groups, dance, drama/theater, international student organization, literary magazine, pep band, radio station, student government, student newspaper, yearbook. Number of fraternities: 2; sororities: 3. Proportion of men in fraternities: 1%; of women in sororities: 1%. Average proportion of students who stay on campus on weekends: 40%. **Sports program (2009-2010):** Member of NCAA III. *Men's intercollegiate varsity sports:* baseball, basketball, football, golf, lacrosse, soccer. *Women's intercollegiate varsity sports:* basketball, field hockey, golf, lacrosse, soccer, softball, swimming, volleyball.

SERVICES AND FACILITIES

Basic services: nonremedial tutoring, health service, health insurance. **Remedial assistance:** reading, math, writing, study skills. **Counseling ser-**

vices: minority student, career, military, personal, academic, psychological, religious. **For learning-disabled students:** School does not offer a structured program with separate admission and additional fees. Total undergraduates in learning-disabled program or receiving services: 42. Services include: remedial math, remedial English, tape recorders, untimed tests, note-taking services, learning center, extended time for tests, tutors, priority seating, texts on tape. **Library:** Number of titles: 40,814; number of current serial subscriptions: 27,881. **Information technology resources:** Students are not required to lease or own a computer. Number of campus computers available to all students: 110. School has a wireless network. Approximate number of users that can be accommodated: 1,000. Proportion of college-owned housing units wired for high-speed internet access: 100%. **Campus safety:** Security services offered: 24-hour foot-and-vehicle patrols, late-night transport/escort service, lighted pathways/sidewalks, controlled dormitory access (key, security card, etc).

TRANSFER AND INTERNATIONAL STUDENTS

Transfer students: May apply for admission for the following academic terms: Fall, Winter, Spring, Summer. Applicants do not need a minimum number of credits to apply. For fall 2009: Transfer applications received: 340. Transfer applicants offered admission: 215. Transfer applicants enrolled: 151. **International students:** Number of foreign undergraduates: 28 (1% of student body). Minimum TOEFL score required: 500 (paper); 173 (computer).

Maine College of Art

- **Address:** 522 Congress Street, Portland, ME 04101
- **Website:** http://www.meca.edu
- **Private**
- **Enrollment:** 295 full-time; 9 part-time

KEY STATS

✔ **U.S News College Ranking:** Unranked Specialty School–Fine Arts
✔ **SAT Score (25th/75th percentile):** 860-1170
✔ **Tuition:** 2010-2011: $29,675

Selectivity: N/A	Room/board: $9,725
Acceptance rate: 97%	Average debt: N/A
Student/faculty ratio: 10/1	Proportion who borrowed: N/A

UNDERGRADUATE STUDENT BODY STATS

2009-2010 enrollment: 295 full-time; 9 part-time. Men: 31%; women: 69%. **Ethnic makeup:** African American: 1%; American-Indian: 1%; Asian American: 2%; Hispanic: 2%; White: 94%.

ADMISSIONS FACTS AND FIGURES

Phone: (800) 699-1509. **Email:** admissions@meca.edu. **Website:** http://www.meca.edu. **Application deadlines for fall 2011:** Regular decision: Rolling. Early decision: Not offered. Early action: Not offered. Admission can be deferred. **Application fee:** $40. **To apply online, go to:** https://apply.meca.edu/. **Admissions requirements/recommendations:** High school units required (recommended): English: 4 (4); Mathematics: 3 (3); Science: 3 (3); Foreign language: 2 (2); Social studies: 4 (4); History: 4 (4); Academic electives: 3 (3); Total units: 27 (27). Tests: The college uses SAT or ACT scores in admissions decisions. Neither SAT nor ACT required. For admission to the fall 2011 entering class, the school will accept: ACT with or without writing accepted. Campus visit: Recommended. Admissions interview: Recommended. Off-campus interview: May be arranged. **Factors that count in admissions decisions:** *Academic:* Secondary school record: Important. Class rank: Considered. Letters of recommendation: Important. Standardized test scores: Considered. Essay: Important. *Nonacademic:* Interview: Important. Extracurricular activities: Considered. Talent/ability: Very Important. Character/personal qualities: Important. Alumni/ae relationship: Considered. Geographical residence: Not Considered. State residency: Not Considered. Religious affiliation/commitment: Not Considered. Minority status: Not Considered. Volunteer work: Considered. Work experience: Considered. **Other schools with the greatest overlap in applicants:** Maryland Institute College of Art; Massachusetts College of Art and Design; Montserrat College of Art; Rhode Island School of Design; University of Maine. **Admissions statistics for the fall 2009 entering class:** Total applicants: 285. Total accepted: 276. Freshmen enrolled: 69; 72% were from out of state. Overall acceptance rate: 97%. **Credentials of fall 2009 freshmen:** 10% ranked in the top 10 percent of their high school class; 31% were in the

top 25 percent. **First-year students who submitted SAT scores:** 88%. Scores (25/75 percentile): Critical Reading: 440-620, Math: 420-550, Combined: 860-1170. **First-year students submitting ACT scores:** 15%. Scores (25/75 percentile): English: N/A, Math: N/A, Composite: 16-28.

ACADEMICS

Year founded: 1882. **Academic calendar:** Semester. **Degrees offered:** bachelor's, post-bachelor's certificate, master's. **Most popular majors:** 16% sculpture, 15% illustration, 15% photography, 12% graphic design, 11% ceramic arts and ceramics. **Major fields of study:** visual and performing arts. **Areas of required coursework:** arts/fine arts, humanities, mathematics, English (including composition), philosophy, sciences (biological or physical), history, social science. **Special academic programs (% participation):** cross-registration, double major, exchange student program (domestic), independent study, internships, student-designed major (3%), study abroad, teacher certificate program. **Teacher certification offered in:** elementary, middle/junior high, secondary. **Cooperative education programs:** art, education. **Faculty and instruction (2009-2010):** Total instructional faculty: 7 full-time, 46 part-time (45% men; 55% women; 6% minorities). Student/faculty ratio: 10/1. Classes of fewer than 20 students: 74%; of 20 to 49 students: 26%. **Advanced Placement and International Baccalaureate credit:** International Baccalaureate exams may be used for: Credit only. **Freshmen returning for sophomore year:** 69%. **Graduation rates:** Four-year: 35%; five-year: 42%; six-year: 42%.

COSTS AND FINANCIAL AID

Financial aid office: (207) 775-3052. **Expenses (2010-2011):** Tuition and fees 2010-2011: $29,675; room/board: $9,725. Estimated books and supplies: $2,100; transportation: $2,100; personal expenses: $2,100. **Financial aid:** Priority filing date for institution's financial aid form: March 1; deadline: April 15.

CAMPUS LIFE AND EXTRACURRICULAR ACTIVITIES

Campus housing available (% using): coed dorms (100%). Students who live in college-owned, operated, or affiliated housing: 36%. Average per-year earnings: $1,500. Activities include: student government. Number of fraternities: 0; sororities: 0. Average proportion of students who stay on campus on weekends: 80%.

SERVICES AND FACILITIES

Basic services: nonremedial tutoring, health service, health insurance. **Counseling services:** personal, academic, psychological. **For learning-disabled students:** School does not offer a structured program with separate admission and additional fees. Services include: reading machines, tape recorders, untimed tests, note-taking services, oral tests, learning center, readers, extended time for tests, tutors, texts on tape. **Library:** Number of titles: 33,000; number of current serial subscriptions: 101. **Information technology resources:** Students are not required to lease or own a computer. Number of campus computers available to all students: 85. School has a wireless network. Proportion of college-owned housing units wired for high-speed internet access: 100%. **Campus safety:** Security services offered: 24-hour emergency telephones, lighted pathways/sidewalks, controlled dormitory access (key, security card, etc).

TRANSFER AND INTERNATIONAL STUDENTS

Transfer students: May apply for admission for the following academic terms: Fall, Spring. Applicants do not need a minimum number of credits to apply. For fall 2009: Transfer applications received: 47. Transfer applicants offered admission: 47. Transfer applicants enrolled: 28. **International students:** Number of countries represented: 0. Minimum TOEFL score required: 550 (paper); 213 (computer).

Maine Maritime Academy

- **Address:** Pleasant Street, Castine, ME 04420-001
- **Website:** http://www.mainemaritime.edu
- **Public**
- **Enrollment:** 916 full-time; 6 part-time

KEY STATS
- ✔ **U.S News College Ranking:** 9, Regional Colleges (North)
- ✔ **SAT Score (25th/75th percentile):** 900-1100
- ✔ **Tuition:** 2010-2011: $14,665 in state, $19,245 out of state

Selectivity: Selective	Room/board: $8,870
Acceptance rate: 63%	Average debt: $39,237
Student/faculty ratio: 13/1	Proportion who borrowed: 73%

UNDERGRADUATE STUDENT BODY STATS
2009-2010 enrollment: 916 full-time; 6 part-time. Men: 81%; women: 19%. **Ethnic makeup:** African American: 1%; White: 98%; International: 1%.

ADMISSIONS FACTS AND FIGURES
Phone: (207) 326-2206. **Email:** admissions@mma.edu. **Website:** http://www.mainemaritime.edu. **Application deadlines for fall 2011:** Regular decision: May 31; decision sent by June 30. Early decision: Send application by: December 20; Decision sent by: January 20. Early action: Not offered. Admission can be deferred. **Application fee:** $15. **To apply online, go to:** http://mainemaritime.edu/admissions/online_application0405.php. **Admissions requirements/recommendations:** High school units required (recommended): English: 4; Mathematics: 4; Science: 2 (3); Foreign language: (2); Social studies: 2; History: 2. Tests: The college uses SAT or ACT scores in admissions decisions. Either SAT or ACT required. For admission to the fall 2011 entering class, the school will accept: ACT with writing required. Campus visit: Recommended. Admissions interview: Recommended. Off-campus interview: May be arranged. **Factors that count in admissions decisions:** *Academic:* Secondary school record: Very Important. Class rank: Considered. Letters of recommendation: Important. Standardized test scores: Important. Essay: Not Considered. *Nonacademic:* Interview: Considered. Extracurricular activities: Considered. Talent/ability: Not Considered. Character/personal qualities: Very Important. Alumni/ae relationship: Considered. Geographical residence: Not Considered. State residency: Not Considered. Religious affiliation/commitment: Not Considered. Minority status: Not Considered. Volunteer work: Considered. Work experience: Considered. **Other schools with the greatest overlap in applicants:** College of the Atlantic; Husson University; Massachusetts Maritime Academy; University of Maine; University of Southern Maine. **Admissions statistics for the fall 2009 entering class:** Total applicants: 871. Total accepted: 545. Freshmen enrolled: 242; 34% were from out of state. Accepted through early-decision or early-action plans: 24%. Overall acceptance rate: 63%. Early-decision acceptance rate: 96%. Non-early acceptance rate: 60%. **Credentials of fall 2009 freshmen:** 11% ranked in the top 10 percent of their high school class; 34% were in the top 25 percent; 75% were in the top half. (Proportion submitting class standing: 59%.) **Average high school grade point average:** 3.3. **First-year students who submitted SAT scores:** 90%. Scores (25/75 percentile): Critical Reading: 440-540, Math: 460-560, Combined: 900-1100. **First-year students submitting ACT scores:** 24%. Scores (25/75 percentile): English: 16-22, Math: 16-23, Composite: N/A.

ACADEMICS
Year founded: 1941. **Academic calendar:** Semester. **Degrees offered:** associate, bachelor's, master's. **Most popular majors:** 49% engineering technologies/technicians, 34% marine science/merchant marine officer, 7% naval architecture and marine engineering, 5% biological and biomedical sciences, 5% international business/trade/commerce. **Major fields of study:** biological and biomedical sciences; business, management, marketing, and related support services; engineering; engineering technologies/technicians; transportation and materials moving. **Areas of required coursework:** humanities, computer literacy, mathematics, English (including composition), sciences (biological or physical), history, social science. **Special academic programs (% participation):** cooperative (work-study plan) program (92%), distance learning (5%), double major (3%), dual enrollment (1%), exchange student program (domestic) (1%), independent study (5%), internships (3%), study abroad (1%), teacher certificate program (0%). **Teacher certification offered in:** secondary. **Cooperative education programs:** business, engineering, other. **Reserve Officers Training Corps (ROTC):** Navy ROTC: Offered on campus. **Faculty and instruction (2009-2010):** Total instructional faculty: 53 full-time, 32 part-time (66% men; 34% women; 5% minorities). Full-time faculty with Ph.D. or other terminal degree: 57%. Student/faculty ratio: 13/1. Classes of fewer than 20 students: 44%; of 20 to 49 students: 56%; of 50 or more students: 1%. **Advanced Placement and International Baccalaureate credit:** AP tests may be used for: Credit only. Scores accepted: 3, 4, 5. **Freshmen returning for sophomore year:** 83%. **Graduation rates:** Four-year: 44%; five-year: 63%; six-year: 65%. **Graduate study:** 8% of students pursue further study within one year. Fields in which graduates pursue further study: Master of Business Administration (MBA), 6%; arts and sciences, 2%.

COSTS AND FINANCIAL AID
Financial aid office: (207) 326-2339. **Expenses (2010-2011):** Tuition and fees 2010-2011: $14,665 in state, $19,245 out of state; room/board: $8,870. Estimated books and supplies: $1,000. **Financial aid:** Priority filing date for institution's financial aid form: April 15; deadline: April 15. In 2009-2010, 86% of undergraduates applied for financial aid. Of those, 67% were determined to have financial need; 13% had their need fully met. Average financial aid package (proportion receiving): $8,890 (67%). Average amount of gift aid, such as scholarships or grants (proportion receiving): $6,351 (46%). Average amount of self-help aid, such as work study or loans (proportion receiving): $4,496 (66%). Average need-based loan (excluding PLUS or other private loans): $4,370. Among students who received need-based aid, the average percentage of need met: 35%. Among students who received aid based on merit, the average award (and the proportion receiving): $3,373 (6%). The average athletic scholarship (and the proportion receiving): $0 (0%). Average amount of debt of borrowers graduating in 2009: $39,237. Proportion who borrowed: 73%.

CAMPUS LIFE AND EXTRACURRICULAR ACTIVITIES
Campus housing available (% using): coed dorms (94%), apartments for married students (0%), apartment for single students (6%). Students who live in college-owned, operated, or affiliated housing: 73%. **Student employment:** During the 2009-2010 academic year, 42% of undergraduates worked on campus. Average per-year earnings: $900. **Clubs and organizations:** Number of student organizations: 23. Activities include: choral groups, drama/theater, jazz band, marching band, pep band, student government, yearbook. Number of fraternities: 0; sororities: 0. Average proportion of students who stay on campus on weekends: 20%. **Sports program (2009-2010):** Member of NCAA III. *Men's intercollegiate varsity sports:* basketball, cross country, football, golf, lacrosse, soccer. *Women's intercollegiate varsity sports:* basketball, cross country, soccer, softball, volleyball.

SERVICES AND FACILITIES
Basic services: placement service, health service, health insurance. **Remedial assistance:** math, writing, study skills. **Counseling services:** career, military, personal, veteran student, academic, psychological. **For learning-disabled students:** School does not offer a structured program with separate admission and additional fees. Total undergraduates in learning-disabled program or receiving services: 69. Services include: tape recorders, untimed tests, note-taking services, oral tests, readers, extended time for tests, tutors, priority seating, texts on tape, exams on tape or computer, other testing accommodations, other. **Library:** Number of titles: 99,614; number of current serial subscriptions: 326. **Information technology resources:** Students are required to lease or own a computer. Number of campus computers available to all students: 800. School has a wireless network. Approximate number of users that can be accommodated: 1,000. Proportion of college-owned housing units wired for high-speed internet access: 100%. **Campus safety:** Security services offered: 24-hour foot-and-vehicle patrols, late-night transport/escort service, lighted pathways/sidewalks, controlled dormitory access (key, security card, etc).

TRANSFER AND INTERNATIONAL STUDENTS
Transfer students: May apply for admission for the following academic terms: Fall, Spring. Applicants do not need a minimum number of credits to apply. For fall 2009: Transfer applications received: 123. Transfer applicants offered admission: 59. Transfer applicants enrolled: 38. **International students:** Number of foreign undergraduates: 13 (1% of student body). Number of countries represented: 7. Minimum TOEFL score required: 550 (paper); 215 (computer).

St. Joseph's College

- **Address:** 278 Whites Bridge Road, Standish, ME 04084
- **Website:** http://www.sjcme.edu
- **Private; Religious affiliation:** Roman Catholic
- **Enrollment:** N/A

KEY STATS

- ✔ **U.S News College Ranking:** second tier, Regional Universities (North)
- ✔ **SAT or ACT Score (25th/75th percentile):** N/A
- ✔ **Tuition:** 2010-2011: $27,345

Selectivity: Less selective	**Room/board:** $10,550
Acceptance rate: N/A	**Average debt:** $36,071
Student/faculty ratio: N/A	**Proportion who borrowed:** 87%

Thomas College

- **Address:** 180 W. River Road, Waterville, ME 04901
- **Website:** http://www.thomas.edu
- **Private**
- **Enrollment:** N/A

KEY STATS

- ✔ **U.S News College Ranking:** 48, Regional Colleges (North)
- ✔ **SAT or ACT Score (25th/75th percentile):** N/A
- ✔ **Tuition:** 2009-2010: $20,440

Selectivity: Less selective	**Room/board:** $8,410
Acceptance rate: N/A	**Average debt:** N/A
Student/faculty ratio: N/A	**Proportion who borrowed:** N/A

Unity College

- **Address:** 90 Quaker Hill Road, Unity, ME 04988
- **Website:** http://www.unity.edu
- **Private**
- **Enrollment:** N/A

KEY STATS

- ✔ **U.S News College Ranking:** second tier, Regional Colleges (North)
- ✔ **SAT or ACT Score (25th/75th percentile):** N/A
- ✔ **Tuition:** 2009-2010: $21,690

Selectivity: Less selective	**Room/board:** $4,830
Acceptance rate: N/A	**Average debt:** N/A
Student/faculty ratio: N/A	**Proportion who borrowed:** N/A

University of Maine

- **Address:** 168 College Avenue, Orono, ME 04469
- **Website:** http://www.umaine.edu
- **Public**
- **Enrollment:** 8,004 full-time; 1,480 part-time

KEY STATS

- ✔ **U.S News College Ranking:** 159, National Universities
- ✔ **SAT Score (25th/75th percentile):** 950-1170
- ✔ **Tuition:** 2010-2011: $10,150 in state, $25,198 out of state

Selectivity: Selective	**Room/board:** $8,766
Acceptance rate: 80%	**Average debt:** $30,824
Student/faculty ratio: 15/1	**Proportion who borrowed:** 77%

UNDERGRADUATE STUDENT BODY STATS

2009-2010 enrollment: 8,004 full-time; 1,480 part-time. Men: 51%; women: 49%. **Ethnic makeup:** African American: 1%; American-Indian: 2%; Asian American: 1%; Hispanic: 1%; White: 93%; International: 2%.

ADMISSIONS FACTS AND FIGURES

Phone: (877) 486-2364. **Email:** um-admit@maine.edu. **Website:** http://www.umaine.edu. **Application deadlines for fall 2011:** Regular decision: Rolling. Early decision: Not offered. Early action: Send application by: December 15; Decision sent by: January 31. Admission can be deferred. **Application fee:** $40. **To apply online, go to:** http://apply.maine.edu. **Admissions requirements/recommendations:** High school units required (recommended): English: 4 (4); Mathematics: 3 (4); Science: 2 (4); Foreign language: 2 (2); Social studies: 2 (2); History: (1); Academic electives: 4 (4); Total units: 17 (21). Tests: The college uses SAT or ACT scores in admissions decisions. Either SAT or ACT required. For admission to the fall 2011 entering class, the school will accept: ACT with or without writing accepted. Campus visit: Recommended. Admissions interview: Recommended. Off-campus interview: Not available. **Factors that count in admissions decisions:** *Academic:* Secondary school record: Very Important. Class rank: Very Important. Letters of recommendation: Important. Standardized test scores: Very Important. Essay: Important. *Nonacademic:* Interview: Considered. Extracurricular activities: Considered. Talent/ability: Considered. Character/personal qualities: Considered. Alumni/ae relationship: Not Considered. Geographical residence: Considered. State residency: Considered. Religious affiliation/commitment: Not Considered. Minority status: Not Considered. Volunteer work: Considered. Work experience: Considered. **Other schools with the greatest overlap in applicants:** University of Maine–Farmington; University of Massachusetts–Amherst; University of New Hampshire; University of Southern Maine; University of Vermont. **Admissions statistics for the fall 2009 entering class:** Total applicants: 6,786. Total accepted: 5,435. Freshmen enrolled: 1,731; 18% were from out of state. Overall acceptance rate: 80%. Non-early acceptance rate: 80%. **Size of waiting list:** 0 applicants; enrolled from waiting list: 0. **Credentials of fall 2009 freshmen:** 20% ranked in the top 10 percent of their high school class; 49% were in the top 25 percent; 85% were in the top half. (Proportion submitting class standing: 73%.) **Average high school grade point average:** 3.2. **First-year students who submitted SAT scores:** 95%. Scores (25/75 percentile): Critical Reading: 470-580, Math: 480-590, Combined: 950-1170. **First-year students submitting ACT scores:** 10%. Scores (25/75 percentile): English: N/A, Math: N/A, Composite: 20-26.

ACADEMICS

Year founded: 1862. **Academic calendar:** Semester. **Degrees offered:** bachelor's, post-bachelor's certificate, master's, post-master's certificate, doctorate. **Most popular majors:** 14% business, management, marketing, and related support services, 11% education, 10% engineering, 8% health professions and related clinical sciences, 7% social sciences. **Major fields of study:** agriculture, agriculture operations, and related sciences; architecture and related services; area, ethnic, cultural, and gender studies; biological and biomedical sciences; business, management, marketing, and related support services; communication, journalism, and related programs; computer and information sciences and support services; education; engineering; engineering technologies/technicians; English language and literature/letters; family and consumer sciences/human sciences; foreign languages, literatures, and linguistics; health professions and related clinical sciences; history; liberal arts and sciences studies, and humanities; mathematics and statistics; multi/interdisciplinary studies; natural resources and conservation; parks, recreation, leisure, and fitness studies; philosophy and religious studies; physical sciences; psychology; public administration and social service professions; social sciences; visual and performing arts. **Areas of required coursework:** arts/fine arts, humanities, mathematics, English (including composition), sciences (biological or physical), social science, other. **Pre-professional programs:** pre-law, pre-dentistry, pre-medicine, pre-veterinary science, pre-optometry, pre-pharmacy. **Special academic programs:** accelerated program, cooperative (work-study plan) program, distance learning, double major, dual enrollment, English as a Second Language (ESL), exchange student program (domestic), honors program, independent study, internships, liberal arts/career combination, study abroad, teacher certificate program. **Teacher certification offered in:** early childhood, special education, elementary, middle/junior high, adult education, secondary. **Cooperative education programs:** business, education, engineering, health professions, natural science, social/behavioral science. **Reserve Officers Training Corps (ROTC):** Army ROTC: Offered on campus; Navy ROTC: Offered on campus. **Faculty and instruction (2009-2010):** Total instructional faculty: 557 full-time, 236 part-time (58% men; 42% women; 5% minorities). Full-time faculty with Ph.D. or other terminal degree: 75%. Student/faculty ratio: 15/1. Classes of fewer than 20 students: 49%; of 20 to 49 students: 38%; of 50 or more students: 13%. **Advanced Placement and International Baccalaureate credit:** AP tests may be used for: Credit only. Scores accepted: 3, 4, 5. International Baccalaureate exams may be used for:

Credit only. **Freshmen returning for sophomore year:** 79%. **Graduation rates:** Four-year: 34%; five-year: 53%; six-year: 58%. **Graduate study:** 19% of students pursue further study within one year.

COSTS AND FINANCIAL AID

Financial aid office: (207) 581-1324. **Expenses (2010-2011):** Tuition and fees 2010-2011: $10,150 in state, $25,198 out of state; room/board: $8,766. Estimated books and supplies: $1,000; transportation: $500; personal expenses: $1,700. **Financial aid:** Priority filing date for institution's financial aid form: March 1. In 2009-2010, 91% of undergraduates applied for financial aid. Of those, 77% were determined to have financial need; 32% had their need fully met. Average financial aid package (proportion receiving): $10,588 (77%). Average amount of gift aid, such as scholarships or grants (proportion receiving): $6,826 (60%). Average amount of self-help aid, such as work study or loans (proportion receiving): $6,872 (70%). Average need-based loan (excluding PLUS or other private loans): $6,392. Among students who received need-based aid, the average percentage of need met: 74%. Among students who received aid based on merit, the average award (and the proportion receiving): $4,115 (10%). The average athletic scholarship (and the proportion receiving): $20,811 (2%). Average amount of debt of borrowers graduating in 2009: $30,824. Proportion who borrowed: 77%.

CAMPUS LIFE AND EXTRACURRICULAR ACTIVITIES

Campus housing available (% using): coed dorms (86%), sorority housing (1%), fraternity housing (1%), apartments for married students (3%), apartment for single students (9%), special housing for disabled students, special housing for international students, other housing options. Students who live in college-owned, operated, or affiliated housing: 40%. **Student employment:** During the 2009-2010 academic year, 15% of undergraduates worked on campus. Average per-year earnings: $2,550. **Clubs and organizations:** Number of student organizations: 234. Activities include: campus ministries, choral groups, concert band, dance, drama/theater, international student organization, jazz band, literary magazine, marching band, music ensembles, musical theater, opera, pep band, radio station, student government, student newspaper, student film society, symphony orchestra, television station, yearbook. Number of fraternities: 5; sororities: 7. Average proportion of students who stay on campus on weekends: 75%. **Sports program (2009-2010):** Member of NCAA I. *Men's intercollegiate varsity sports:* baseball, basketball, cross country, football, ice hockey, soccer, swimming, track and field (indoor), track and field (outdoor). *Women's intercollegiate varsity sports:* basketball, cross country, field hockey, ice hockey, soccer, softball, swimming, track and field (indoor), track and field (outdoor), volleyball.

SERVICES AND FACILITIES

Basic services: nonremedial tutoring, women's center, placement service, day care, health service, health insurance. **Remedial assistance:** math, writing, study skills. **Counseling services:** minority student, career, military, personal, veteran student, academic, older student, psychological, birth control, religious. **For learning-disabled students:** School does not offer a structured program with separate admission and additional fees. Services include: remedial math, remedial English, remedial reading, tape recorders, untimed tests, note-taking services, oral tests, readers, extended time for tests, tutors, substitution of courses, texts on tape, other testing accommodations. **Library:** Number of titles: 1,326,490; number of current serial subscriptions: 16,988. **Information technology resources:** Students are not required to lease or own a computer. Number of campus computers available to all students: 500. School has a wireless network. Approximate number of users that can be accommodated: 6,000. Proportion of college-owned housing units wired for high-speed internet access: 100%. **Campus safety:** Security services offered: 24-hour foot-and-vehicle patrols, late-night transport/escort service, 24-hour emergency telephones, lighted pathways/sidewalks, student patrols, controlled dormitory access (key, security card, etc).

TRANSFER AND INTERNATIONAL STUDENTS

Transfer students: May apply for admission for the following academic terms: Fall, Spring, Summer. Applicants need a minimum number of credits to apply. For fall 2009: Transfer applications received: 1,021. Transfer applicants offered admission: 717. Transfer applicants enrolled: 501. **International students:** Number of foreign undergraduates: 178 (2% of student body). Number of countries represented: 72. Minimum TOEFL score required: 530 (paper); 197 (computer). Average TOEFL score: 550 (paper).

University of Maine—Augusta

- **Address:** 46 University Drive, Augusta, ME 04330
- **Website:** http://www.uma.edu
- **Public**
- **Enrollment:** 1,699 full-time; 3,355 part-time

KEY STATS

✔ **U.S News College Ranking:** second tier, Regional Colleges (North)
✔ **SAT or ACT Score (25th/75th percentile):** N/A
✔ **Tuition:** 2010-2011: $6,110 in state, $13,858 out of state
   Selectivity: Less selective   **Room/board:** N/A
   Acceptance rate: 96%   **Average debt:** N/A
   Student/faculty ratio: 18/1   **Proportion who borrowed:** N/A

UNDERGRADUATE STUDENT BODY STATS

2009-2010 enrollment: 1,699 full-time; 3,355 part-time. Men: 27%; women: 73%. **Ethnic makeup:** African American: 1%; American-Indian: 3%; Asian American: 1%; Hispanic: 1%; White: 95%.

ADMISSIONS FACTS AND FIGURES

Phone: (207) 621-3465. **Email:** umaadm@maine.edu. **Website:** http://www.uma.edu. **Application deadlines for fall 2011:** Regular decision: August 31. Early decision: Not offered. Early action: Not offered. Admission can be deferred. **Application fee:** $40. **To apply online, go to:** http://www.uma.edu/readytoapply.html. **Admissions requirements/recommendations:** High school units required (recommended): English: 4 (4); Mathematics: 3 (3); Science: 2 (2); Social studies: 2 (2); History: 2 (2); Total units: 15 (15). Tests: The college uses SAT or ACT scores in admissions decisions. Neither SAT nor ACT required. For admission to the fall 2011 entering class, the school will accept: ACT with or without writing accepted. Campus visit: Recommended. Admissions interview: Neither required nor recommended. Off-campus interview: May be arranged. **Factors that count in admissions decisions:** *Academic:* Secondary school record: Important. Class rank: Important. Letters of recommendation: Considered. Standardized test scores: Considered. Essay: Considered. *Nonacademic:* Interview: Considered. Extracurricular activities: Considered. Talent/ability: Considered. Character/personal qualities: Considered. Alumni/ae relationship: Not Considered. Geographical residence: Not Considered. State residency: Not Considered. Religious affiliation/commitment: Not Considered. Minority status: Not Considered. Volunteer work: Considered. Work experience: Considered. **Other schools with the greatest overlap in applicants:** Husson University; Thomas College; University of Maine; University of Maine–Farmington; University of Southern Maine. **Admissions statistics for the fall 2009 entering class:** Total applicants: 1,053. Total accepted: 1,012. Freshmen enrolled: 589; Overall acceptance rate: 96%.

ACADEMICS

Year founded: 1965. **Academic calendar:** Semester. **Degrees offered:** certificate, associate, transfer-associate, terminal-associate, bachelor's, post-bachelor's certificate. **Most popular majors:** 32% health professions and related clinical sciences, 19% business, management, marketing, and related support services, 14% liberal arts and sciences studies, and humanities, 8% library science, 7% social sciences. **Major fields of study:** biological and biomedical sciences; business, management, marketing, and related support services; computer and information sciences and support services; English language and literature/letters; health professions and related clinical sciences; library science; public administration and social service professions; security and protective services; social sciences; visual and performing arts. **Areas of required coursework:** arts/fine arts, humanities, computer literacy, mathematics, English (including composition), sciences (biological or physical), history, social science. **Special academic programs:** cross-registration, distance learning, dual enrollment, honors program, independent study, internships, liberal arts/career combination, student-designed major, study abroad. **Reserve Officers Training Corps (ROTC):** Army ROTC: Offered at cooperating institution; Navy ROTC: Offered at cooperating institution; Air Force ROTC: Offered at cooperating institution. **Faculty and instruction (2009-2010):** Total instructional faculty: 104 full-time, 192 part-time (42% men; 58% women; 0% minorities). Full-time faculty with Ph.D. or other terminal degree: 54%. Student/faculty ratio: 18/1. Classes of fewer than 20 students: 64%; of 20 to 49 students: 34%; of 50 or more students: 2%. **Advanced Placement and International Baccalaureate credit:** AP tests may be used for: Placement only. Scores accepted: 3, 4, 5. International Baccalaureate exams may be used for: Placement only. **Freshmen returning**

for sophomore year: 55%. **Graduation rates:** Four-year: 4%; five-year: 10%; six-year: 15%.

COSTS AND FINANCIAL AID

Financial aid office: (207) 621-3163. **Expenses (2010-2011):** Tuition and fees 2010-2011: $6,110 in state, $13,858 out of state. Estimated books and supplies: $1,040; transportation: $1,800; personal expenses: $1,800. **Financial aid:** Priority filing date for institution's financial aid form: March 1. In 2009-2010, 88% of undergraduates applied for financial aid. Of those, 81% were determined to have financial need; 18% had their need fully met. Average financial aid package (proportion receiving): $10,766 (79%). Average amount of gift aid, such as scholarships or grants (proportion receiving): $2,328 (67%). Average amount of self-help aid, such as work study or loans (proportion receiving): $3,286 (68%). Average need-based loan (excluding PLUS or other private loans): $3,452. Among students who received need-based aid, the average percentage of need met: 73%. Among students who received aid based on merit, the average award (and the proportion receiving): $1,260 (1%). The average athletic scholarship (and the proportion receiving): $0 (0%).

CAMPUS LIFE AND EXTRACURRICULAR ACTIVITIES

Students who live in college-owned, operated, or affiliated housing: 0%. **Student employment:** During the 2009-2010 academic year, 10% of undergraduates worked on campus. Average per-year earnings: $2,000. **Clubs and organizations:** Number of student organizations: 22. Activities include: concert band, drama/theater, international student organization, jazz band, music ensembles, pep band, student government, student newspaper. Number of fraternities: 0; sororities: 0. **Sports program (2009-2010):** *Men's intercollegiate varsity sports:* basketball, golf. *Women's intercollegiate varsity sports:* basketball, golf, soccer.

SERVICES AND FACILITIES

Basic services: nonremedial tutoring, health insurance, other. **Remedial assistance:** reading, math, writing, study skills. **Counseling services:** minority student, career, personal, veteran student, academic, older student, psychological, other. **For learning-disabled students:** School does not offer a structured program with separate admission and additional fees. Services include: remedial math, remedial English, remedial reading, extended time for tests, tutors. **Library:** Number of titles: 94,018; number of current serial subscriptions: 4,541. **Information technology resources:** Students are not required to lease or own a computer. Number of campus computers available to all students: 340. School has a wireless network. Approximate number of users that can be accommodated: 1,080. **Campus safety:** Security services offered: late-night transport/escort service, 24-hour emergency telephones, lighted pathways/sidewalks.

TRANSFER AND INTERNATIONAL STUDENTS

Transfer students: May apply for admission for the following academic terms: Fall, Spring, Summer. Applicants do not need a minimum number of credits to apply. For fall 2009: Transfer applications received: 2,868. Transfer applicants offered admission: 2,173. Transfer applicants enrolled: 1,259. **International students:** Number of foreign undergraduates: 0. Number of countries represented: 6. Minimum TOEFL score required: 500 (paper); 173 (computer). Average TOEFL score: 500 (paper).

University of Maine–Farmington

- **Address:** 111 South Street, Farmington, ME 04938
- **Website:** http://www.farmington.edu
- **Public**
- **Enrollment:** 1,971 full-time; 220 part-time

KEY STATS

✔ **U.S News College Ranking:** 18, Regional Colleges (North)
✔ **SAT Score (25th/75th percentile):** 910-1120
✔ **Tuition:** 2010-2011: $9,022 in state, $17,758 out of state

Selectivity: Selective	**Room/board:** $7,854
Acceptance rate: 80%	**Average debt:** N/A
Student/faculty ratio: 14/1	**Proportion who borrowed:** N/A

UNDERGRADUATE STUDENT BODY STATS

2009-2010 enrollment: 1,971 full-time; 220 part-time. Men: 35%; women: 65%. **Ethnic makeup:** African American: 1%; American-Indian: 1%; Asian American: 1%; Hispanic: 1%; White: 96%.

ADMISSIONS FACTS AND FIGURES

Phone: (207) 778-7050. **Email:** umfadmit@maine.edu. **Website:** http://www.farmington.edu. **Application deadlines for fall 2011:** Regular decision: Rolling. Early decision: Not offered. Early action: Send application by: December 15; Decision sent by: January 15. Admission can be deferred. **Application fee:** $40. **To apply online, go to:** http://www.farmington.edu/admissions. **Admissions requirements/recommendations:** High school units required (recommended): English: 4 (4); Mathematics: 3 (4); Science: 2 (3); Foreign language: 2 (3); Social studies: 2 (3); Academic electives: (3); Total units: 15 (19). Tests: The college uses SAT or ACT scores in admissions decisions. Neither SAT nor ACT required. Campus visit: Recommended. Admissions interview: Recommended. Off-campus interview: May be arranged. **Factors that count in admissions decisions:** *Academic:* Secondary school record: Very Important. Class rank: Very Important. Letters of recommendation: Important. Standardized test scores: Not Considered. Essay: Important. *Nonacademic:* Interview: Important. Extracurricular activities: Important. Talent/ability: Important. Character/personal qualities: Important. Alumni/ae relationship: Considered. Geographical residence: Considered. State residency: Considered. Religious affiliation/commitment: Not Considered. Minority status: Considered. Volunteer work: Important. Work experience: Important. **Other schools with the greatest overlap in applicants:** St. Joseph's College; University of Maine; University of New England; University of New Hampshire; University of Southern Maine. **Admissions statistics for the fall 2009 entering class:** Total applicants: 1,534. Total accepted: 1,232. Freshmen enrolled: 519; 19% were from out of state. Overall acceptance rate: 80%. Non-early acceptance rate: 80%. **Credentials of fall 2009 freshmen:** 13% ranked in the top 10 percent of their high school class; 42% were in the top 25 percent; 82% were in the top half. (Proportion submitting class standing: 79%.) **First-year students who submitted SAT scores:** 94%. Scores (25/75 percentile): Critical Reading: 460-570, Math: 450-550, Combined: 910-1120.

ACADEMICS

Year founded: 1864. **Academic calendar:** Semester. **Degrees offered:** bachelor's, master's. **Most popular majors:** 37% education, 16% health services/allied health/health sciences, 10% psychology, 9% multi/interdisciplinary studies, 6% business/managerial economics. **Major fields of study:** area, ethnic, cultural, and gender studies; biological and biomedical sciences; business, management, marketing, and related support services; computer and information sciences and support services; education; English language and literature/letters; health professions and related clinical sciences; history; liberal arts and sciences studies, and humanities; mathematics and statistics; multi/interdisciplinary studies; natural resources and conservation; philosophy and religious studies; physical sciences; psychology; social sciences; visual and performing arts. **Areas of required coursework:** arts/fine arts, humanities, mathematics, English (including composition), sciences (biological or physical), social science, other. **Pre-professional programs:** pre-law, pre-dentistry, pre-medicine, pre-veterinary science, pre-optometry, pre-pharmacy, other. **Special academic programs (% participation):** cross-registration (5%), double major (3%), dual enrollment (1%), exchange student program (domestic) (4%), honors program (5%), independent study (2%), internships (24%), student-designed major (1%), study abroad (8%), teacher certificate program (38%). **Teacher certification offered in:** early childhood, special education, elementary, middle/junior high, secondary. **Faculty and instruction (2009-2010):** Total instructional faculty: 120 full-time, 49 part-time (46% men; 54% women; 3% minorities). Full-time faculty with Ph.D. or other terminal degree: 91%. Student/faculty ratio: 14/1. Classes of fewer than 20 students: 65%; of 20 to 49 students: 33%; of 50 or more students: 1%. **Advanced Placement and International Baccalaureate credit:** AP tests may be used for: Credit and/or placement. Scores accepted: 3, 4, 5. International Baccalaureate exams may be used for: Credit only. **Freshmen returning for sophomore year:** 73%. **Graduation rates:** Four-year: 46%; five-year: 59%; six-year: 61%. **Graduate study:** 15% of students pursue further study immediately upon graduation; 18% within one year; 25% within five years. Fields in which graduates pursue further study: Master of Business Administration (MBA), 6%; law, 3%; medicine, 1%; dentistry, 1%; engineering, 1%; theology (or the seminary), 2%; education, 60%; arts and sciences, 25%; veterinary medicine, 1%.

COSTS AND FINANCIAL AID

Financial aid office: (207) 778-7100. **Expenses (2010-2011):** Tuition and fees 2010-2011: $9,022 in state, $17,758 out of state; room/board: $7,854. Estimated books and supplies: $720. **Financial aid:** Priority filing date for institution's financial aid form: March 1.

CAMPUS LIFE AND EXTRACURRICULAR ACTIVITIES

Campus housing available (% using): coed dorms (84%), women's dorms (15%), special housing for international students (1%). Students who live in college-owned, operated, or affiliated housing: 48%. **Student employment:** During the 2009-2010 academic year, 40% of undergraduates worked on campus. Average per-year earnings: $1,300. **Clubs and organizations:** Number of student organizations: 58. Activities include: choral groups, dance, drama/theater, literary magazine, music ensembles, radio station, student government, student newspaper, student film society, yearbook. Number of fraternities: 0; sororities: 0. Average proportion of students who stay on campus on weekends: 50%. **Sports program (2009-2010):** Member of NCAA III. *Men's intercollegiate varsity sports:* baseball, basketball, cross country, golf, soccer. *Women's intercollegiate varsity sports:* basketball, cross country, field hockey, golf, soccer, softball, volleyball.

SERVICES AND FACILITIES

Basic services: nonremedial tutoring, placement service, health service, health insurance. **Remedial assistance:** reading, math, writing, study skills. **Counseling services:** minority student, career, military, personal, veteran student, academic, older student, psychological, birth control. **For learning-disabled students:** School does not offer a structured program with separate admission and additional fees. Services include: remedial math, remedial English, reading machines, tape recorders, note-taking services, learning center, extended time for tests, tutors, priority seating, texts on tape, other testing accommodations, other. **Library:** Number of titles: 98,935; number of current serial subscriptions: 498. **Information technology resources:** Students are not required to lease or own a computer. Number of campus computers available to all students: 185. School has a wireless network. Approximate number of users that can be accommodated: 3,000. Proportion of college-owned housing units wired for high-speed internet access: 100%. **Campus safety:** Security services offered: 24-hour foot-and-vehicle patrols, late-night transport/escort service, 24-hour emergency telephones, lighted pathways/sidewalks, controlled dormitory access (key, security card, etc).

TRANSFER AND INTERNATIONAL STUDENTS

Transfer students: May apply for admission for the following academic terms: Fall, Spring. Applicants need a minimum number of credits to apply. For fall 2009: Transfer applications received: 261. Transfer applicants offered admission: 178. Transfer applicants enrolled: 128. **International students:** Number of foreign undergraduates: 10. Number of countries represented: 7. Minimum TOEFL score required: 550 (paper); 213 (computer).

University of Maine—Fort Kent

- ■ **Address:** 23 University Drive, Fort Kent, ME 04743
- ■ **Website:** http://www.umfk.maine.edu
- ■ **Public**
- ■ **Enrollment:** 577 full-time; 549 part-time

KEY STATS

- ✔ **U.S News College Ranking:** 46, Regional Colleges (North)
- ✔ **SAT Score (25th/75th percentile):** 700-947
- ✔ **Tuition:** 2009-2010: $6,803 in state, $15,953 out of state

Selectivity: Less selective	**Room/board:** $7,080
Acceptance rate: 78%	**Average debt:** N/A
Student/faculty ratio: 16/1	**Proportion who borrowed:** N/A

UNDERGRADUATE STUDENT BODY STATS

2009-2010 enrollment: 577 full-time; 549 part-time. Men: 33%; women: 67%. **Ethnic makeup:** African American: 2%; American-Indian: 2%; Hispanic: 1%; White: 83%; International: 12%.

ADMISSIONS FACTS AND FIGURES

Phone: (207) 834-7600. **Email:** umfkadm@maine.edu. **Website:** http://www.umfk.maine.edu. **Application deadlines for fall 2011:** Regular decision: Rolling. Early decision: Not offered. Early action: Not offered. Admission can be deferred. **Application fee:** $40. **To apply online, go to:** http://www.umfk.maine.edu/admissions/apply/. **Admissions requirements/recommendations:** High school units required (recommended): English: 4; Mathematics: 2; Science: 2; Foreign language: (2); Social studies: 2; Total units: 16. Tests: The college uses SAT or ACT scores in admissions decisions. Neither SAT nor ACT required. Campus visit: Recommended. Admissions interview: Recommended. Off-campus interview: May be arranged. **Factors that count in admissions decisions:** *Academic:* Secondary school record: Important. Class rank: Important. Letters of recommendation: Important. Standardized test scores: Considered. Essay: Important. *Nonacademic:* Interview: Considered. Extracurricular activities: Considered. Talent/ability: Important. Character/personal qualities: Important. Alumni/ae relationship: Considered. Geographical residence: Important. State residency: Important. Religious affiliation/commitment: Not Considered. Minority status: Not Considered. Volunteer work: Important. Work experience: Considered. **Other schools with the greatest overlap in applicants:** University of Maine; University of Maine–Presque Isle. **Admissions statistics for the fall 2009 entering class:** Total applicants: 280. Total accepted: 217. Freshmen enrolled: 125; 8% were from out of state. Overall acceptance rate: 78%. **Credentials of fall 2009 freshmen:** 2% ranked in the top 10 percent of their high school class; 19% were in the top 25 percent; 62% were in the top half. (Proportion submitting class standing: 5%.) **Average high school grade point average:** 2.6. **First-year students who submitted SAT scores:** 87%. Scores (25/75 percentile): Critical Reading: 350-482, Math: 350-465, Combined: 700-947. **First-year students submitting ACT scores:** 7%. Scores (25/75 percentile): English: N/A, Math: N/A, Composite: 18-22.

ACADEMICS

Year founded: 1878. **Academic calendar:** Semester. **Degrees offered:** associate, bachelor's. **Most popular majors:** 62% education, 22% health professions and related clinical sciences, 7% business, management, marketing, and related support services, 4% natural resources and conservation, 4% social sciences. **Major fields of study:** biological and biomedical sciences; business, management, marketing, and related support services; computer and information sciences and support services; education; English language and literature/letters; foreign languages, literatures, and linguistics; health professions and related clinical sciences; history; liberal arts and sciences studies, and humanities; natural resources and conservation; physical sciences; social sciences. **Areas of required coursework:** humanities, computer literacy, mathematics, English (including composition), foreign languages, sciences (biological or physical), history, social science. **Special academic programs (% participation):** cross-registration, distance learning (32%), double major (4%), English as a Second Language (ESL), honors program (1%), independent study (13%), internships (15%), liberal arts/career combination, student-designed major (0%), teacher certificate program (52%), other. **Teacher certification offered in:** special education, elementary, middle/junior high, secondary, bilingual/bicultural. **Cooperative education programs:** business, social/behavioral science. **Faculty and instruction (2009-2010):** Total instructional faculty: 36 full-time, 29 part-time (54% men; 46% women; 6% minorities). Full-time faculty with Ph.D. or other terminal degree: 89%. Student/faculty ratio: 16/1. Classes of fewer than 20 students: 45%; of 20 to 49 students: 50%; of 50 or more students: 5%. **Advanced Placement and International Baccalaureate credit:** AP tests may be used for: Credit and/or placement. **Freshmen returning for sophomore year:** 63%. **Graduation rates:** Four-year: 21%; five-year: 31%; six-year: 40%. **Graduate study:** 1% of students pursue further study immediately upon graduation; 3% within one year; 5% within five years. Fields in which graduates pursue further study: Master of Business Administration (MBA), 2%; law, 2%; medicine, 1%; education, 75%; arts and sciences, 20%.

COSTS AND FINANCIAL AID

Financial aid office: (888) 879-8635. **Expenses (2009-2010):** Tuition and fees 2009-2010: $6,803 in state, $15,953 out of state; room/board: $7,080. Estimated books and supplies: $1,100; transportation: $1,400; personal expenses: $1,000. **Financial aid:** Priority filing date for institution's financial aid form: March 1. In 2009-2010, 63% of undergraduates applied for financial aid. Of those, 57% were determined to have financial need; 47% had their need fully met. Average financial aid package (proportion receiving): $5,422 (57%). Average amount of gift aid, such as scholarships or grants (proportion receiving): $2,756 (35%). Average amount of self-help aid, such as work study or loans (proportion receiving): $3,045 (46%). Average need-based loan (excluding PLUS or other private loans): $2,361. Among students who received need-based aid, the average percentage of need met: 82%. Among students who received aid based on merit, the average award (and the proportion receiving): $881 (6%). The average athletic scholarship (and the proportion receiving): $0 (0%).

CAMPUS LIFE AND EXTRACURRICULAR ACTIVITIES

Campus housing available: coed dorms. Students who live in college-owned, operated, or affiliated housing: 20%. **Student employment:** During the 2009-2010 academic year, 3% of undergraduates worked on campus. Average per-year earnings: $1,500. Activities include: choral groups, drama/theater, student government, student newspaper. Number of fraternities: 1; sororities: 1. Proportion of men in fraternities: 2%; of women in sororities: 1%. Average proportion of students who stay on campus on weekends: 75%. **Sports program (2009-2010):** Member of NAIA. *Men's intercollegiate varsity sports:* basketball, skiing (nordic), skiing (alpine), soccer. *Women's intercollegiate varsity sports:* basketball, skiing (nordic), skiing (alpine), soccer, volleyball.

SERVICES AND FACILITIES

Basic services: health service, health insurance. **Remedial assistance:** reading, math, writing, study skills. **Counseling services:** minority student, military, personal, veteran student, academic, older student. **For learning-disabled students:** School does not offer a structured program with separate admission and additional fees. Services include: remedial math, remedial English, remedial reading, tape recorders, videotaped classes, untimed tests, oral tests, readers, extended time for tests, tutors, other. **Library:** Number of titles: 69,189; number of current serial subscriptions: 335. **Information technology resources:** Students are not required to lease or own a computer. Number of campus computers available to all students: 99. School has a wireless network. Proportion of college-owned housing units wired for high-speed internet access: 100%. **Campus safety:** Security services offered: controlled dormitory access (key, security card, etc.).

TRANSFER AND INTERNATIONAL STUDENTS

Transfer students: May apply for admission for the following academic terms: Fall, Spring, Summer. Applicants do not need a minimum number of credits to apply. For fall 2009: Transfer applications received: 298. Transfer applicants offered admission: 238. Transfer applicants enrolled: 81. **International students:** Number of foreign undergraduates: 132 (12% of student body). Minimum TOEFL score required: 500 (paper).

University of Maine—Machias

- **Address:** 9 O'Brien Avenue, Machias, ME 04654
- **Website:** http://www.umm.maine.edu
- **Public**
- **Enrollment:** 452 full-time; 512 part-time

KEY STATS

- ✔ **U.S News College Ranking:** second tier, National Liberal Arts Colleges
- ✔ **SAT Score (25th/75th percentile):** 810-1010
- ✔ **Tuition:** 2009-2010: $6,775 in state, $17,515 out of state

Selectivity: Less selective	**Room/board:** $6,936
Acceptance rate: 74%	**Average debt:** N/A
Student/faculty ratio: 14/1	**Proportion who borrowed:** N/A

UNDERGRADUATE STUDENT BODY STATS

2009-2010 enrollment: 452 full-time; 512 part-time. Men: 30%; women: 70%. **Ethnic makeup:** African American: 3%; American-Indian: 4%; Asian American: 1%; Hispanic: 2%; White: 88%; International: 3%.

ADMISSIONS FACTS AND FIGURES

Phone: (888) 468-6866. **Email:** ummadmissions@maine.edu. **Website:** http://www.umm.maine.edu. **Application deadlines for fall 2011:** Regular decision: August 15. Early decision: Not offered. Early action: Send application by: December 15; Decision sent by: N/A. Admission can be deferred. **Application fee:** $40. **To apply online, go to:** http://apply.maine.edu/. **Admissions requirements/recommendations:** High school units required (recommended): English: 4; Mathematics: 3; Science: 2; Foreign language: (2); Social studies: 2; Academic electives: (3); Total units: 11 (5). Tests: The college uses SAT or ACT scores in admissions decisions. Either SAT or ACT required. For admission to the fall 2011 entering class, the school will accept: ACT with or without writing accepted. Campus visit: Recommended. Admissions interview: Recommended. Off-campus interview: May be arranged. **Factors that count in admissions decisions:** *Academic:* Secondary school record: Important. Class rank: Important. Letters of recommendation: Very Important. Standardized test scores: Important. Essay: Very Important. *Nonacademic:* Interview: Very Important. Extracurricular

activities: Important. Talent/ability: Considered. Character/personal qualities: Considered. Alumni/ae relationship: Not Considered. Geographical residence: Not Considered. State residency: Not Considered. Religious affiliation/commitment: Not Considered. Minority status: Not Considered. Volunteer work: Considered. Work experience: Considered. **Other schools with the greatest overlap in applicants:** University of Maine; University of Maine–Farmington; University of New England. **Admissions statistics for the fall 2009 entering class:** Total applicants: 374. Total accepted: 276. Freshmen enrolled: 105; 29% were from out of state. Overall acceptance rate: 74%. Non-early acceptance rate: 74%. **Credentials of fall 2009 freshmen:** 10% ranked in the top 10 percent of their high school class; 35% were in the top 25 percent. **First-year students who submitted SAT scores:** 83%. Scores (25/75 percentile): Critical Reading: 420-520, Math: 390-490, Combined: 810-1010. **First-year students submitting ACT scores:** 22%. Scores (25/75 percentile): English: 17-22, Math: 16-19, Composite: 17-22.

ACADEMICS

Year founded: 1909. **Academic calendar:** Semester. **Degrees offered:** certificate, associate, bachelor's. **Most popular majors:** 22% behavioral sciences, 22% biology/biological sciences, 12% parks, recreation, and leisure studies, 10% business administration and management, 8% environmental studies. **Major fields of study:** biological and biomedical sciences; business, management, marketing, and related support services; education; English language and literature/letters; history; liberal arts and sciences studies, and humanities; multi/interdisciplinary studies; natural resources and conservation; parks, recreation, leisure, and fitness studies; visual and performing arts. **Areas of required coursework:** arts/fine arts, humanities, mathematics, English (including composition), sciences (biological or physical), history, social science, other. **Pre-professional programs:** other. **Special academic programs:** cooperative (work-study plan) program, distance learning, double major, dual enrollment, independent study, internships, student-designed major, study abroad, teacher certificate program. **Teacher certification offered in:** early childhood, special education, elementary, secondary. **Cooperative education programs:** business, natural science, social/behavioral science, other. **Faculty and instruction (2009-2010):** Total instructional faculty: 30 full-time, 40 part-time (57% men; 43% women; 3% minorities). Full-time faculty with Ph.D. or other terminal degree: 77%. Student/faculty ratio: 14/1. Classes of fewer than 20 students: 73%; of 20 to 49 students: 28%. **Advanced Placement and International Baccalaureate credit:** AP tests may be used for: Credit only. Scores accepted: 3, 4, 5. **Freshmen returning for sophomore year:** 73%. **Graduation rates:** Four-year: 15%; five-year: 30%; six-year: 39%. **Graduate study:** 8% of students pursue further study immediately upon graduation. Fields in which graduates pursue further study: Master of Business Administration (MBA), 18%; theology (or the seminary), 2%; arts and sciences, 79%; veterinary medicine, 1%.

COSTS AND FINANCIAL AID

Financial aid office: (207) 255-1203. **Expenses (2009-2010):** Tuition and fees 2009-2010: $6,775 in state, $17,515 out of state; room/board: $6,936. Estimated books and supplies: $800. **Financial aid:** Priority filing date for institution's financial aid form: March 1.

CAMPUS LIFE AND EXTRACURRICULAR ACTIVITIES

Campus housing available (% using): coed dorms (100%). Students who live in college-owned, operated, or affiliated housing: 44%. **Student employment:** During the 2009-2010 academic year, 60% of undergraduates worked on campus. Average per-year earnings: $1,600. **Clubs and organizations:** Number of student organizations: 33. Activities include: choral groups, concert band, dance, drama/theater, international student organization, jazz band, literary magazine, music ensembles, musical theater, radio station, student government. Number of fraternities: 5; sororities: 4. Proportion of men in fraternities: 17%; of women in sororities: 4%. Average proportion of students who stay on campus on weekends: 50%. **Sports program (2009-2010):** Member of NAIA. *Men's intercollegiate varsity sports:* basketball, soccer. *Women's intercollegiate varsity sports:* basketball, soccer, volleyball.

SERVICES AND FACILITIES

Basic services: nonremedial tutoring, placement service, day care, health service, health insurance. **Remedial assistance:** reading, math, writing, study skills. **Counseling services:** career, personal, veteran student, academic. **For learning-disabled students:** School does not offer a structured program with separate admission and additional fees. Total undergraduates in learning-disabled program or receiving services: 49. Services include: remedial math, remedial English, reading machines, tape recorders, videotaped classes, untimed tests, note-taking services, oral tests, learning center, readers, extended time for tests, tutors, priority seating, substitution of courses, typist/scribe, exams on tape or computer, other testing accommodations, other. **Library:** Number of titles: 87,349; number of current serial subscriptions: 195. **Information technology resources:** Students are not required to lease or own a computer. Number of campus computers available to all students: 110. School has a wireless network. Approximate number of users that can be accommodated: 512. Proportion of college-owned housing units wired for high-speed internet access: 100%. **Campus safety:** Security services offered: late-night transport/escort service, lighted pathways/sidewalks, controlled dormitory access (key, security card, etc).

TRANSFER AND INTERNATIONAL STUDENTS

Transfer students: May apply for admission for the following academic terms: Fall, Spring, Summer. Applicants do not need a minimum number of credits to apply. For fall 2009: Transfer applications received: 98. Transfer applicants offered admission: 70. Transfer applicants enrolled: 48. **International students:** Number of foreign undergraduates: 15 (3% of student body). Number of countries represented: 5. Minimum TOEFL score required: 500 (paper); 61 (computer).

University of Maine—Presque Isle

- **Address:** 181 Main Street, Presque Isle, ME 04769
- **Website:** http://www.umpi.maine.edu
- **Public**
- **Enrollment:** N/A

KEY STATS

✔ **U.S News College Ranking:** Unranked, National Liberal Arts Colleges
✔ **SAT or ACT Score (25th/75th percentile):** N/A
✔ **Tuition:** 2009-2010: $6,835 in state, $15,985 out of state

Selectivity: N/A	**Room/board:** $6,710
Acceptance rate: N/A	**Average debt:** N/A
Student/faculty ratio: N/A	**Proportion who borrowed:** N/A

University of New England

- **Address:** Hills Beach Road, Biddeford, ME 04005
- **Website:** http://www.une.edu
- **Private**
- **Enrollment:** 2,059 full-time; 382 part-time

KEY STATS

✔ **U.S News College Ranking:** 81, Regional Universities (North)
✔ **SAT Score (25th/75th percentile):** 970-1160
✔ **Tuition:** 2010-2011: $29,330

Selectivity: Selective	**Room/board:** $11,410
Acceptance rate: 80%	**Average debt:** N/A
Student/faculty ratio: 13/1	**Proportion who borrowed:** N/A

UNDERGRADUATE STUDENT BODY STATS

2009-2010 enrollment: 2,059 full-time; 382 part-time. Men: 31%; women: 69%. **Ethnic makeup:** African American: 1%; Asian American: 2%; Hispanic: 1%; White: 94%; International: 1%.

ADMISSIONS FACTS AND FIGURES

Phone: (207) 283-0171. **Email:** admissions@une.edu. **Website:** http://www.une.edu. **Application deadlines for fall 2011:** Regular decision: February 15. Early decision: Not offered. Early action: Not offered. Admission can be deferred. **Application fee:** $40. **To apply online, go to:** https://www.une.edu/admissions/application/apply.asp. **Admissions requirements/recommendations:** High school units required (recommended): English: 4 (0); Mathematics: 3 (4); Science: 2 (3); Foreign language: (2); Social studies: 1 (2); History: 1 (2); Academic electives: 2 (4); Total units: 16 (20). Tests: The college uses SAT or ACT scores in admissions decisions. Either SAT or ACT required. For admission to the fall 2011 entering class, the school will accept: ACT with or without writing accepted. Campus visit: Recommended. Admissions interview: Recommended. Off-campus interview: May be arranged. **Factors that count in admissions decisions:** *Academic:* Secondary school record: Very Important. Class rank: Important. Letters of recommendation: Very Important. Standardized test scores: Very Important.

Essay: Considered. *Nonacademic:* Interview: Considered. Extracurricular activities: Considered. Talent/ability: Not Considered. Character/personal qualities: Considered. Alumni/ae relationship: Considered. Geographical residence: Considered. State residency: Not Considered. Religious affiliation/commitment: Considered. Minority status: Not Considered. Volunteer work: Considered. Work experience: Considered. **Other schools with the greatest overlap in applicants:** Quinnipiac University; St. Joseph's College; University of Maine; University of New Hampshire; University of Southern Maine. **Admissions statistics for the fall 2009 entering class:** Total applicants: 3,315. Total accepted: 2,661. Freshmen enrolled: 607; 65% were from out of state. Overall acceptance rate: 80%. **Credentials of fall 2009 freshmen:** 25% ranked in the top 10 percent of their high school class; 59% were in the top 25 percent; 88% were in the top half. (Proportion submitting class standing: 67%.) **Average high school grade point average:** 3.2. **First-year students who submitted SAT scores:** 90%. Scores (25/75 percentile): Critical Reading: 480-570, Math: 490-590, Combined: 970-1160. **First-year students submitting ACT scores:** 8%. Scores (25/75 percentile): English: 21-26, Math: 21-26, Composite: 21-26.

ACADEMICS

Year founded: 1831. **Academic calendar:** Semester. **Degrees offered:** associate, bachelor's, post-bachelor's certificate, master's, post-master's certificate. **Most popular majors:** 29% biological and biomedical sciences, 28% health professions and related clinical sciences, 14% psychology, 11% parks, recreation, leisure, and fitness studies, 5% education. **Major fields of study:** agriculture, agriculture operations, and related sciences; area, ethnic, cultural, and gender studies; biological and biomedical sciences; business, management, marketing, and related support services; communication, journalism, and related programs; education; English language and literature/letters; health professions and related clinical sciences; history; liberal arts and sciences studies, and humanities; mathematics and statistics; natural resources and conservation; parks, recreation, leisure, and fitness studies; physical sciences; psychology; social sciences. **Areas of required coursework:** arts/fine arts, humanities, mathematics, English (including composition), sciences (biological or physical), social science, other. **Pre-professional programs:** pre-dentistry, pre-medicine, pre-pharmacy, other. **Special academic programs:** cross-registration, double major, honors program, independent study, internships, student-designed major, study abroad, teacher certificate program. **Teacher certification offered in:** elementary, secondary. **Reserve Officers Training Corps (ROTC):** Army ROTC: Offered at cooperating institution. **Faculty and instruction (2009-2010):** Total instructional faculty: 197 full-time, 173 part-time (49% men; 51% women; 4% minorities). Full-time faculty with Ph.D. or other terminal degree: 72%. Student/faculty ratio: 13/1. Classes of fewer than 20 students: 43%; of 20 to 49 students: 49%; of 50 or more students: 7%. **Advanced Placement and International Baccalaureate credit:** AP tests may be used for: Credit only. Scores accepted: 3, 4, 5. International Baccalaureate exams may be used for: Credit only. **Freshmen returning for sophomore year:** 76%. **Graduation rates:** Four-year: 40%; five-year: 49%; six-year: 53%.

COSTS AND FINANCIAL AID

Financial aid office: (207) 602-2342. **Expenses (2010-2011):** Tuition and fees 2010-2011: $29,330; room/board: $11,410. Estimated books and supplies: $1,350; transportation: $1,350; personal expenses: $1,400. **Financial aid:** Priority filing date for institution's financial aid form: May 1.

CAMPUS LIFE AND EXTRACURRICULAR ACTIVITIES

Campus housing available (% using): coed dorms (90%), women's dorms (10%). Students who live in college-owned, operated, or affiliated housing: 57%. **Clubs and organizations:** Number of student organizations: 44. Activities include: dance, drama/theater, literary magazine, pep band, radio station, student government, student newspaper, yearbook. Number of fraternities: 0; sororities: 0. Average proportion of students who stay on campus on weekends: 60%. **Sports program (2009-2010):** Member of NCAA III. *Men's intercollegiate varsity sports:* basketball, cross country, golf, ice hockey, lacrosse, soccer. *Women's intercollegiate varsity sports:* basketball, cross country, field hockey, lacrosse, soccer, softball, swimming, volleyball.

SERVICES AND FACILITIES

Basic services: nonremedial tutoring, health service, health insurance. **Remedial assistance:** math, writing, study skills. **Counseling services:** minority student, career, personal, veteran student, academic, older student, psychological, religious. **For learning-disabled students:** School does not offer a structured program with separate admission and additional fees. Services include: remedial math, remedial English, reading machines, tape recorders, other special classes, untimed tests, note-taking services, learning center, readers, extended time for tests, tutors, priority registration, priority seating, texts on tape, typist/scribe, exams on tape or computer, other testing accommodations. **Library:** Number of titles: 156,752; number of current serial subscriptions: 39,705. **Information technology resources:** Students are not required to lease or own a computer. Number of campus computers available to all students: 150. School has a wireless network. Proportion of college-owned housing units wired for high-speed internet access: 100%. **Campus safety:** Security services offered: 24-hour foot-and-vehicle patrols, late-night transport/escort service, 24-hour emergency telephones, lighted pathways/sidewalks, controlled dormitory access (key, security card, etc).

TRANSFER AND INTERNATIONAL STUDENTS

Transfer students: May apply for admission for the following academic terms: Fall, Spring. Applicants need a minimum number of credits to apply. **International students:** Number of foreign undergraduates: 25 (1% of student body). Number of countries represented: 12. Minimum TOEFL score required: 550 (paper); 213 (computer).

University of Southern Maine

- **Address:** 37 College Avenue, Gorham, ME 04038
- **Website:** http://www.usm.maine.edu
- **Public**
- **Enrollment:** 4,831 full-time; 2,787 part-time

KEY STATS

✔ **U.S News College Ranking:** 110, Regional Universities (North)
✔ **SAT Score (25th/75th percentile):** 900-1120
✔ **Tuition:** 2009-2010: $8,174 in state, $20,384 out of state
  Selectivity: Less selective   **Room/board:** $8,762
  Acceptance rate: 84%   **Average debt:** $25,892
  Student/faculty ratio: 15/1   **Proportion who borrowed:** N/A

UNDERGRADUATE STUDENT BODY STATS

2009-2010 enrollment: 4,831 full-time; 2,787 part-time. Men: 43%; women: 57%. **Ethnic makeup:** African American: 2%; American-Indian: 2%; Asian American: 2%; Hispanic: 1%; White: 92%; International: 2%.

ADMISSIONS FACTS AND FIGURES

Phone: (207) 780-5670. **Email:** usmadm@usm.maine.edu. **Website:** http://www.usm.maine.edu. **Application deadlines for fall 2011:** Early decision: Not offered. Early action: Not offered. Admission can be deferred. **Application fee:** $40. **To apply online, go to:** http://apply.maine.edu. **Admissions requirements/recommendations:** High school units required (recommended): English: 4 (0); Mathematics: 3 (4); Science: 2 (3); Foreign language: 2 (3); Social studies: 2 (3); History: 2 (3); Academic electives: 0 (0); Total units: 16 (0). Tests: The college uses SAT or ACT scores in admissions decisions. Either SAT or ACT required. For admission to the fall 2011 entering class, the school will accept: ACT with or without writing accepted. Campus visit: Recommended. Admissions interview: Recommended. Off-campus interview: May be arranged. **Factors that count in admissions decisions:** *Academic:* Secondary school record: Very Important. Class rank: Very Important. Letters of recommendation: Important. Standardized test scores: Very Important. Essay: Important. *Nonacademic:* Interview: Considered. Extracurricular activities: Considered. Talent/ability: Considered. Character/personal qualities: Considered. Alumni/ae relationship: Considered. Geographical residence: Considered. State residency: Considered. Religious affiliation/commitment: Not Considered. Minority status: Considered. Volunteer work: Considered. Work experience: Considered. **Other schools with the greatest overlap in applicants:** St. Joseph's College; University of Maine; University of Maine; University of Maine–Farmington; University of Maine–Farmington; University of New England; University of New England; University of New Hampshire; University of New Hampshire. **Admissions statistics for the fall 2009 entering class:** Total applicants: 4,141. Total accepted: 3,458. Freshmen enrolled: 924; 24% were from out of state. Overall acceptance rate: 84%. **Credentials of fall 2009 freshmen:** 8% ranked in the top 10 percent of their high school class; 29% were in the top 25 percent; 66% were in the top half. (Proportion submitting class standing: 79%.) **Average high school grade point average:** 3.0. **First-year students who submitted SAT scores:** 97%. Scores (25/75 percentile): Critical Reading: 450-560, Math: 450-560, Combined: 900-1120. **First-year students submitting ACT scores:** 7%. Scores (25/75 percentile): English: N/A, Math: N/A, Composite: 18-23.

ACADEMICS

Year founded: 1878. **Academic calendar:** Semester. **Degrees offered:** associate, bachelor's, master's, post-master's certificate, doctorate. **Most popular majors:** 12% business administration and management, 12% nursing/registered nurse training (R.N., A.S.N., B.S.N., M.S.N.), 6% psychology, 6% social sciences, 4% communication studies/speech communication and rhetoric. **Major fields of study:** agriculture, agriculture operations, and related sciences; area, ethnic, cultural, and gender studies; biological and biomedical sciences; business, management, marketing, and related support services; communication, journalism, and related programs; computer and information sciences and support services; education; engineering; English language and literature/letters; foreign languages, literatures, and linguistics; health professions and related clinical sciences; liberal arts and sciences studies, and humanities; mathematics and statistics; natural resources and conservation; parks, recreation, leisure, and fitness studies; philosophy and religious studies; physical sciences; psychology; public administration and social service professions; social sciences; visual and performing arts. **Areas of required coursework:** arts/fine arts, humanities, mathematics, English (including composition), philosophy, sciences (biological or physical), history, social science. **Pre-professional programs:** pre-law, pre-dentistry, pre-medicine, pre-veterinary science. **Special academic programs:** cooperative (work-study plan) program, cross-registration, distance learning, double major, dual enrollment, English as a Second Language (ESL), exchange student program (domestic), honors program, independent study, internships, liberal arts/career combination, student-designed major, study abroad, teacher certificate program, weekend college, other. **Teacher certification offered in:** special education, elementary, middle/junior high, adult education, secondary. **Cooperative education programs:** art, business, computer science, education, engineering, health professions, humanities, natural science, social/behavioral science, technologies, vocational arts. **Reserve Officers Training Corps (ROTC):** Army ROTC: Offered at cooperating institution (University of New England); Air Force ROTC: Offered at cooperating institution (University of New England). **Faculty and instruction (2009-2010):** Total instructional faculty: 370 full-time, 294 part-time (49% men; 51% women; 3% minorities). Full-time faculty with Ph.D. or other terminal degree: 85%. Student/faculty ratio: 15/1. Classes of fewer than 20 students: 40%; of 20 to 49 students: 56%; of 50 or more students: 4%. **Advanced Placement and International Baccalaureate credit:** AP tests may be used for: Credit and/or placement. Scores accepted: 3, 4, 5. International Baccalaureate exams may be used for: Credit and/or placement. **Freshmen returning for sophomore year:** 66%. **Graduation rates:** Four-year: 12%; five-year: 31%; six-year: 34%.

COSTS AND FINANCIAL AID

Financial aid office: (207) 780-5250. **Expenses (2009-2010):** Tuition and fees 2009-2010: $8,174 in state, $20,384 out of state; room/board: $8,762. Estimated books and supplies: $1,200. **Financial aid:** Priority filing date for institution's financial aid form: February 15. In 2009-2010, 93% of undergraduates applied for financial aid. Of those, 82% were determined to have financial need; 60% had their need fully met. Average financial aid package (proportion receiving): $13,618 (82%). Average amount of gift aid, such as scholarships or grants (proportion receiving): $5,518 (59%). Average amount of self-help aid, such as work study or loans (proportion receiving): $8,398 (78%). Average need-based loan (excluding PLUS or other private loans): $7,613. Among students who received need-based aid, the average percentage of need met: 69%. Among students who received aid based on merit, the average award (and the proportion receiving): $3,474 (4%). The average athletic scholarship (and the proportion receiving): $0 (0%). Average amount of debt of borrowers graduating in 2009: $25,892.

CAMPUS LIFE AND EXTRACURRICULAR ACTIVITIES

Campus housing available (% using): coed dorms (76%), apartments for married students (0%), apartment for single students (6%), special housing for disabled students (0%), special housing for international students (2%). Students who live in college-owned, operated, or affiliated housing: 21%. **Clubs and organizations:** Number of student organizations: 75. Activities include: campus ministries, choral groups, concert band, dance, drama/theater, international student organization, jazz band, literary magazine, model UN, music ensembles, musical theater, opera, radio station, student government, student newspaper, student film society, symphony orchestra, television station. Number of fraternities: 4; sororities: 3. Proportion of men in fraternities: 1%; of women in sororities: 1%. Average proportion of students who stay on campus on weekends: 80%. **Sports program (2009-2010):** Member of NCAA III. *Men's intercollegiate varsity sports:* baseball, basketball, cross country, golf, ice hockey, lacrosse, soccer, tennis, track and field (indoor), track and field (outdoor), wrestling. *Women's intercollegiate varsity*

sports: basketball, cross country, field hockey, golf, ice hockey, lacrosse, soccer, softball, tennis, track and field (indoor), track and field (outdoor), volleyball.

SERVICES AND FACILITIES
Basic services: nonremedial tutoring, women's center, placement service, health service, health insurance. **Remedial assistance:** reading, math, writing, study skills. **Counseling services:** minority student, career, military, personal, veteran student, academic, older student, psychological, birth control, religious. **For learning-disabled students:** School does not offer a structured program with separate admission and additional fees. Services include: remedial math, remedial English, reading machines, remedial reading, tape recorders, untimed tests, note-taking services, learning center, readers, extended time for tests, tutors, texts on tape, other testing accommodations. **Library:** Number of titles: 432,430; number of current serial subscriptions: 9,258. **Information technology resources:** Students are not required to lease

or own a computer. Number of campus computers available to all students: 850. School has a wireless network. Approximate number of users that can be accommodated: 1,000. Proportion of college-owned housing units wired for high-speed internet access: 100%. **Campus safety:** Security services offered: 24-hour foot-and-vehicle patrols, late-night transport/escort service, 24-hour emergency telephones, lighted pathways/sidewalks, controlled dormitory access (key, security card, etc).

TRANSFER AND INTERNATIONAL STUDENTS
Transfer students: May apply for admission for the following academic terms: Fall, Spring. Applicants need a minimum number of credits to apply. For fall 2009: Transfer applications received: 1,729. Transfer applicants offered admission: 1,227. Transfer applicants enrolled: 848. **International students:** Number of foreign undergraduates: 110 (2% of student body). Minimum TOEFL score required: 550 (paper); 213 (computer). Average TOEFL score: 558 (paper).

Maryland

Bowie State University

- **Address:** 14000 Jericho Park Road, Bowie, MD 20715-9465
- **Website:** http://www.bowiestate.edu
- **Public**
- **Enrollment:** 3,710 full-time; 690 part-time

KEY STATS
- ✔ **U.S News College Ranking:** second tier, Regional Universities (North)
- ✔ **SAT Score (25th/75th percentile):** 790-950
- ✔ **Tuition:** 2009-2010: $6,038 in state, $16,476 out of state
  - **Selectivity:** Less selective **Room/board:** $8,135
  - **Acceptance rate:** 48% **Average debt:** $17,198
  - **Student/faculty ratio:** 16/1 **Proportion who borrowed:** 66%

UNDERGRADUATE STUDENT BODY STATS
2009-2010 enrollment: 3,710 full-time; 690 part-time. Men: 37%; women: 63%. **Ethnic makeup:** African American: 90%; Asian American: 2%; Hispanic: 2%; White: 5%; International: 1%.

ADMISSIONS FACTS AND FIGURES
Phone: (301) 860-3415. **Email:** ugradadmissions@bowiestate.edu. **Website:** http://www.bowiestate.edu. **Application deadlines for fall 2011:** Regular decision: Rolling. Early decision: Not offered. Early action: Not offered. Admission can be deferred. **Application fee:** $40. **To apply online, go to:** http://www.bowiestate.edu/apply_now/. **Admissions requirements/recommendations:** High school units required (recommended): English: 4 (4); Mathematics: 3 (3); Science: 3 (3); Foreign language: 2 (2); Social studies: 1 (1); History: 2 (2); Total units: 12 (12). Tests: The college uses SAT or ACT scores in admissions decisions. Either SAT or ACT required. For admission to the fall 2011 entering class, the school will accept: ACT with or without writing accepted. Campus visit: Neither required nor recommended. Admissions interview: Neither required nor recommended. Off-campus interview: Not available. **Factors that count in admissions decisions:** *Academic:* Secondary school record: Very Important. Class rank: Not Considered. Letters of recommendation: Considered. Standardized test scores: Very Important. Essay: Considered. *Nonacademic:* Interview: Not Considered. Extracurricular activities: Considered. Talent/ability: Not Considered. Character/personal qualities: Not Considered. Alumni/ae relationship: Not Considered. Geographical residence: Not Considered. State residency: Not Considered. Religious affiliation/commitment: Not Considered. Minority status: Not Considered. Volunteer work: Not Considered. Work experience: Not Considered. **Admissions statistics for the fall 2009 entering class:** Total applicants: 3,526. Total accepted: 1,704. Freshmen enrolled: 642; 3% were from out of state. Overall acceptance rate: 48%. **Size of waiting list:** 0 applicants; enrolled from waiting list: N/A. **Average high school grade point average:** 2.8. **First-year students who submitted SAT scores:** 92%. Scores (25/75 percentile): Critical Reading: 400-480, Math: 390-470, Combined: 790-950. **First-year students submitting ACT scores:** 8%. Scores (25/75 percentile): English: N/A, Math: N/A, Composite: N/A.

ACADEMICS
Year founded: 1865. **Academic calendar:** Semester. **Degrees offered:** bachelor's, post-bachelor's certificate, master's, doctorate. **Most popular majors:** 24% business administration and management, 15% sociology, 14% radio and television broadcasting technology/technician, 9% psychology, 8% elementary education and teaching. **Major fields of study:** biological and biomedical sciences; business, management, marketing, and related support services; communication, journalism, and related programs; computer and information sciences and support services; education; English language and literature/letters; health professions and related clinical sciences; history; mathematics and statistics; multi/interdisciplinary studies; psychology; public administration and social service professions; social sciences; visual and performing arts. **Areas of required coursework:** arts/fine arts, humanities, computer literacy, mathematics, English (including composition), philoso-phy, sciences (biological or physical), history, social science, other. **Special academic programs:** cooperative (work-study plan) program, cross-registration, distance learning, double major, dual enrollment, exchange student program (domestic), honors program, independent study, internships, liberal arts/career combination, study abroad, teacher certificate program. **Teacher certification offered in:** early childhood, elementary, secondary. **Reserve Officers Training Corps (ROTC):** Army ROTC: Offered on campus; Air Force ROTC: Offered at cooperating institution. **Faculty and instruction (2009-2010):** Total instructional faculty: 230 full-time, 176 part-time (53% men; 47% women; 81% minorities). Full-time faculty with Ph.D. or other terminal degree: 92%. Student/faculty ratio: 16/1. Classes of fewer than 20 students: 41%; of 20 to 49 students: 57%; of 50 or more students: 2%. **Advanced Placement and International Baccalaureate credit:** AP tests may be used for: Credit only. Scores accepted: 3, 4, 5. International Baccalaureate exams may be used for: Credit only. **Freshmen returning for sophomore year:** 73%. **Graduation rates:** Four-year: 13%; five-year: 32%; six-year: 38%.

COSTS AND FINANCIAL AID
Financial aid office: (301) 860-3540. **Expenses (2009-2010):** Tuition and fees 2009-2010: $6,038 in state, $16,476 out of state; room/board: $8,135. Estimated books and supplies: $1,400; transportation: $1,354; personal expenses: $1,876. **Financial aid:** Priority filing date for institution's financial aid form: March 1. In 2009-2010, 80% of undergraduates applied for financial aid. Of those, 79% were determined to have financial need; 45% had their need fully met. Average financial aid package (proportion receiving): $8,114 (79%). Average amount of gift aid, such as scholarships or grants (proportion receiving): $6,319 (60%). Average amount of self-help aid, such as work study or loans (proportion receiving): $4,053 (65%). Average need-based loan (excluding PLUS or other private loans): $4,001. Among students who received need-based aid, the average percentage of need met: 48%. Among students who received aid based on merit, the average award (and the proportion receiving): $159 (2%). The average athletic scholarship (and the proportion receiving): $5,502 (4%). Average amount of debt of borrowers graduating in 2009: $17,198. Proportion who borrowed: 66%.

CAMPUS LIFE AND EXTRACURRICULAR ACTIVITIES
Campus housing available (% using): coed dorms (24%), women's dorms (24%), men's dorms (15%), apartment for single students (37%), other housing options (0%). Students who live in college-owned, operated, or affiliated housing: 52%. **Clubs and organizations:** Number of student organizations: 71. Activities include: choral groups, concert band, dance, drama/theater, jazz band, literary magazine, marching band, musical theater, pep band, radio station, student government, student newspaper, television station, yearbook. Number of fraternities: 6; sororities: 5. Proportion of men in fraternities: 8%; of women in sororities: 15%. Average proportion of students who stay on campus on weekends: 45%. **Sports program (2009-2010):** Member of NCAA II. *Men's intercollegiate varsity sports:* basketball, cross country, football, track and field (indoor), track and field (outdoor). *Women's intercollegiate varsity sports:* basketball, bowling, cross country, softball, track and field (indoor), track and field (outdoor), volleyball.

SERVICES AND FACILITIES
Basic services: nonremedial tutoring, placement service, health service. **Remedial assistance:** reading, math, writing, study skills. **Counseling services:** minority student, career, military, personal, academic. **For learning-disabled students:** School does not offer a structured program with separate admission and additional fees. Services include: reading machines, tape recorders, note-taking services, oral tests, learning center, extended time for tests, tutors, priority registration, priority seating, texts on tape, other testing accommodations. **Library:** Number of titles: 266,203; number of current serial subscriptions: 460. **Information technology resources:** Students are not required to lease or own a computer. Number of campus computers available to all students: 3,144. School has a wireless network. Approximate number of users that can be accommodated: 500. **Campus safety:** Security services offered: 24-hour foot-and-vehicle patrols, 24-hour emergency telephones, lighted pathways/sidewalks, controlled dormitory access (key, security card, etc).

TRANSFER AND INTERNATIONAL STUDENTS

Transfer students: May apply for admission for the following academic terms: Fall, Spring. Applicants need a minimum number of credits to apply. For fall 2009: Transfer applications received: 1,421. Transfer applicants offered admission: 862. Transfer applicants enrolled: 428. **International students:** Number of foreign undergraduates: 33 (1% of student body). Minimum TOEFL score required: 500 (paper); 173 (computer).

College of Notre Dame of Maryland

- **Address:** 4701 N. Charles Street, Baltimore, MD 21210
- **Website:** http://www.ndm.edu
- **Private; Religious affiliation:** Roman Catholic
- **Enrollment:** 493 full-time; 761 part-time

....

KEY STATS

✔ **U.S News College Ranking:** 29, Regional Universities (North)
✔ **SAT Score (25th/75th percentile):** 900-1160
✔ **Tuition:** 2010-2011: $28,350

Selectivity: Selective	**Room/board:** $9,500
Acceptance rate: 71%	**Average debt:** $33,882
Student/faculty ratio: 12/1	**Proportion who borrowed:** 72%

UNDERGRADUATE STUDENT BODY STATS

2009-2010 enrollment: 493 full-time; 761 part-time. Men: 6%; women: 94%. **Ethnic makeup:** African American: 29%; Asian American: 3%; Hispanic: 2%; White: 64%; International: 2%.

ADMISSIONS FACTS AND FIGURES

Phone: (410) 532-5330. **Email:** admiss@ndm.edu. **Website:** http://www.ndm.edu. **Application deadlines for fall 2011:** Regular decision: Rolling. Early decision: Not offered. Early action: Not offered. Admission can be deferred. **Application fee:** $45. **To apply online, go to:** http://www.ndm.edu/applynow.cfm. **Admissions requirements/recommendations:** High school units required (recommended): English: 4 (4); Mathematics: 3 (3); Science: 2 (2); Foreign language: 3 (3); Social studies: 2 (2); History: 0 (0); Academic electives: 4 (4); Total units: 18 (18). Tests: The college uses SAT or ACT scores in admissions decisions. Either SAT or ACT required. For admission to the fall 2011 entering class, the school will accept: ACT with or without writing accepted. Campus visit: Recommended. Admissions interview: Recommended. Off-campus interview: May be arranged. **Factors that count in admissions decisions:** *Academic:* Secondary school record: Very Important. Class rank: Considered. Letters of recommendation: Very Important. Standardized test scores: Very Important. Essay: Very Important. *Nonacademic:* Interview: Very Important. Extracurricular activities: Important. Talent/ability: Important. Character/personal qualities: Considered. Alumni/ae relationship: Considered. Geographical residence: Not Considered. State residency: Not Considered. Religious affiliation/commitment: Not Considered. Minority status: Not Considered. Volunteer work: Important. Work experience: Considered. **Other schools with the greatest overlap in applicants:** McDaniel College; Mount St. Mary's University; Stevenson University; Towson University; University of Maryland–Baltimore County. **Admissions statistics for the fall 2009 entering class:** 15% were from out of state. Overall acceptance rate: 71%. **Credentials of fall 2009 freshmen:** 15% ranked in the top 10 percent of their high school class; 39% were in the top 25 percent; 80% were in the top half. (Proportion submitting class standing: 67%.) **Average high school grade point average:** 3.5. **First-year students who submitted SAT scores:** 86%. Scores (25/75 percentile): Critical Reading: 450-590, Math: 450-570, Combined: 900-1160. **First-year students submitting ACT scores:** 9%. Scores (25/75 percentile): English: N/A, Math: N/A, Composite: 19-26.

ACADEMICS

Year founded: 1873. **Academic calendar:** Semester. **Degrees offered:** certificate, bachelor's, post-bachelor's certificate, master's, post-master's certificate, doctorate. **Most popular majors:** 39% nursing, 17% business administration and management, 6% education, 5% liberal arts and sciences studies, and humanities, 4% communication and media studies. **Major fields of study:** biological and biomedical sciences; business, management, marketing, and related support services; communication, journalism, and related programs; computer and information sciences and support services; education; engineering; English language and literature/letters; foreign languages, literatures, and linguistics; health professions and related

clinical sciences; history; liberal arts and sciences studies, and humanities; mathematics and statistics; multi/interdisciplinary studies; philosophy and religious studies; physical sciences; psychology; public administration and social service professions; social sciences; visual and performing arts. **Areas of required coursework:** arts/fine arts, humanities, mathematics, English (including composition), philosophy, foreign languages, sciences (biological or physical), history, social science, other. **Pre-professional programs:** pre-law, pre-dentistry, pre-medicine, pre-veterinary science, pre-pharmacy. **Special academic programs:** accelerated program, cross-registration, double major, English as a Second Language (ESL), honors program, independent study, internships, liberal arts/career combination, student-designed major, study abroad, teacher certificate program, weekend college. **Teacher certification offered in:** early childhood, special education, elementary, middle/junior high, secondary, bilingual/bicultural. **Reserve Officers Training Corps (ROTC):** Army ROTC: Offered at cooperating institution (Loyola University Maryland). **Faculty and instruction (2009-2010):** Total instructional faculty: 101 full-time, 11 part-time (29% men; 71% women; 11% minorities). Full-time faculty with Ph.D. or other terminal degree: 89%. Student/faculty ratio: 12/1. Classes of fewer than 20 students: 85%; of 20 to 49 students: 15%; of 50 or more students: 0%. **Advanced Placement and International Baccalaureate credit:** AP tests may be used for: Credit and/or placement. Scores accepted: 3, 4, 5. International Baccalaureate exams may be used for: Credit and/or placement. **Freshmen returning for sophomore year:** 75%. **Graduation rates:** Four-year: 57%; five-year: 64%; six-year: 63%. **Graduate study:** 47% of students pursue further study within one year. Fields in which graduates pursue further study: Master of Business Administration (MBA), 20%; law, 2%; medicine, 14%; dentistry, 2%; engineering, 2%; theology (or the seminary), 2%; education, 27%; arts and sciences, 30%; veterinary medicine, 1%.

COSTS AND FINANCIAL AID

Financial aid office: (410) 532-5369. **Expenses (2010-2011):** Tuition and fees 2010-2011: $28,350; room/board: $9,500. Estimated books and supplies: $1,200; transportation: $600; personal expenses: $1,000. **Financial aid:** Priority filing date for institution's financial aid form: February 15. In 2009-2010, 90% of undergraduates applied for financial aid. Of those, 84% were determined to have financial need; 18% had their need fully met. Average financial aid package (proportion receiving): $19,708 (84%). Average amount of gift aid, such as scholarships or grants (proportion receiving): $15,921 (81%). Average amount of self-help aid, such as work study or loans (proportion receiving): $4,401 (66%). Average need-based loan (excluding PLUS or other private loans): $4,079. Among students who received need-based aid, the average percentage of need met: 69%. Among students who received aid based on merit, the average award (and the proportion receiving): $14,732 (9%). The average athletic scholarship (and the proportion receiving): $0 (0%). Average amount of debt of borrowers graduating in 2009: $33,882. Proportion who borrowed: 72%.

CAMPUS LIFE AND EXTRACURRICULAR ACTIVITIES

Campus housing available (% using): women's dorms (100%). Students who live in college-owned, operated, or affiliated housing: 51%. Average per-year earnings: $1,500. **Clubs and organizations:** Number of student organizations: 30. Activities include: choral groups, dance, drama/theater, international student organization, literary magazine, music ensembles, radio station, student government, student newspaper, student film society, television station, yearbook. Number of fraternities: 0; sororities: 0. **Sports program (2009-2010):** Member of NCAA III. *Women's intercollegiate varsity sports:* basketball, field hockey, lacrosse, soccer, softball, swimming, tennis, volleyball.

SERVICES AND FACILITIES

Basic services: nonremedial tutoring, health service, health insurance. **Counseling services:** career, personal, academic, older student, psychological. **For learning-disabled students:** School does not offer a structured program with separate admission and additional fees. Services include: reading machines, tape recorders, untimed tests, oral tests, extended time for tests, tutors, priority seating, texts on tape, other testing accommodations. **Library:** Number of titles: 431,697; number of current serial subscriptions: 69,240. **Information technology resources:** Students are not required to lease or own a computer. School has a wireless network. Approximate number of users that can be accommodated: 500. Proportion of college-owned housing units wired for high-speed internet access: 100%. **Campus safety:** Security services offered: 24-hour foot-and-vehicle patrols, late-night transport/escort service, 24-hour emergency telephones, lighted pathways/sidewalks, controlled dormitory access (key, security card, etc).

Transfer students: May apply for admission for the following academic terms: Fall, Spring. Applicants need a minimum number of credits to apply. For fall 2009: Transfer applications received: 152. Transfer applicants offered admission: 125. Transfer applicants enrolled: 58. **International students:** Number of foreign undergraduates: 25 (2% of student body). Number of countries represented: 15. Minimum TOEFL score required: 500 (paper); 173 (computer).

Coppin State University

- **Address:** 2500 W. North Avenue, Baltimore, MD 21216-3698
- **Website:** http://www.coppin.edu
- **Public**
- **Enrollment:** 2,575 full-time; 726 part-time

KEY STATS

✔ **U.S News College Ranking:** second tier, Regional Universities (North)
✔ **SAT Score (25th/75th percentile):** 790-950
✔ **Tuition:** 2009-2010: $7,355 in state, $16,050 out of state

Selectivity: Less selective	**Room/board:** $9,966
Acceptance rate: 55%	**Average debt:** N/A
Student/faculty ratio: 14/1	**Proportion who borrowed:** N/A

UNDERGRADUATE STUDENT BODY STATS

2009-2010 enrollment: 2,575 full-time; 726 part-time. Men: 24%; women: 76%. **Ethnic makeup:** African American: 88%; White: 7%; International: 4%.

ADMISSIONS FACTS AND FIGURES

Phone: (410) 951-3600. **Email:** admissions@coppin.edu. **Website:** http://www.coppin.edu. **Application deadlines for fall 2011:** Regular decision: July 15. Early decision: Not offered. Early action: Not offered. Admission can be deferred. **Application fee:** $35. **To apply online, go to:** http://apply.usmd.edu. **Admissions requirements/recommendations:** High school units required (recommended): English: 4; Mathematics: 3; Science: 2; Foreign language: 2; Social studies: 3; Total units: 16. Tests: The college uses SAT or ACT scores in admissions decisions. Either SAT or ACT required. For admission to the fall 2011 entering class, the school will accept: ACT with or without writing accepted. Campus visit: Recommended. Admissions interview: Neither required nor recommended. Off-campus interview: Not available. **Factors that count in admissions decisions:** *Academic:* Secondary school record: Very Important. Class rank: Considered. Letters of recommendation: Important. Standardized test scores: Important. Essay: Considered. *Nonacademic:* Interview: Considered. Extracurricular activities: Considered. Talent/ability: Important. Character/personal qualities: Considered. Alumni/ae relationship: Considered. Geographical residence: Considered. State residency: Considered. Religious affiliation/commitment: Not Considered. Minority status: Considered. Volunteer work: Considered. Work experience: Considered. **Other schools with the greatest overlap in applicants:** Frostburg State University; Morgan State University; Morgan State University; Towson University; Towson University; University of Maryland–Baltimore County; University of Maryland–Baltimore County; University of Maryland–Eastern Shore; University of Maryland–Eastern Shore. **Admissions statistics for the fall 2009 entering class:** Total applicants: 5,473. Total accepted: 3,031. Freshmen enrolled: 610; Overall acceptance rate: 55%. **Average high school grade point average:** 2.7. **First-year students who submitted SAT scores:** 77%. Scores (25/75 percentile): Critical Reading: 400-480, Math: 390-470, Combined: 790-950.

ACADEMICS

Year founded: 1900. **Academic calendar:** Semester. **Degrees offered:** certificate, bachelor's, master's. **Most popular majors:** 25% nursing, 9% business administration, management, and operations, 8% criminal justice/safety studies, 8% psychology, 5% sport and fitness administration/management. **Major fields of study:** biological and biomedical sciences; business, management, marketing, and related support services; computer and information sciences and support services; education; English language and literature/letters; health professions and related clinical sciences; history; mathematics and statistics; multi/interdisciplinary studies; parks, recreation, leisure, and fitness studies; physical sciences; psychology; public administration and social service professions; security and protective services; social sciences; visual and performing arts. **Areas of required coursework:** arts/fine arts, humanities, computer literacy, mathematics, English (including composition), philosophy, sciences (biological or physical), history, social science. **Pre-professional programs:** pre-dentistry, pre-pharmacy, other. **Special academic programs:** accelerated program, cooperative (work-study plan) program, distance learning, double major, external degree program, honors program, independent study, internships, liberal arts/career combination, study abroad, teacher certificate program, weekend college, other. **Teacher certification offered in:** early childhood, special education, elementary, adult education, secondary. **Cooperative education programs:** business, computer science, natural science, social/behavioral science. **Reserve Officers Training Corps (ROTC):** Army ROTC: Offered on campus. **Faculty and instruction (2009-2010):** Total instructional faculty: 159 full-time, 173 part-time (45% men; 55% women; 90% minorities). Full-time faculty with Ph.D. or other terminal degree: 59%. Student/faculty ratio: 14/1. **Advanced Placement and International Baccalaureate credit:** AP tests may be used for: Placement only. Scores accepted: 3. International Baccalaureate exams may be used for: Placement only. **Freshmen returning for sophomore year:** 61%. **Graduation rates:** Four-year: 5%; five-year: 11%; six-year: 19%.

COSTS AND FINANCIAL AID

Financial aid office: (410) 951-3636. **Expenses (2009-2010):** Tuition and fees 2009-2010: $7,355 in state, $16,050 out of state; room/board: $9,966. Estimated books and supplies: $800; transportation: $600; personal expenses: $2,786. **Financial aid:** Priority filing date for institution's financial aid form: March 1.

CAMPUS LIFE AND EXTRACURRICULAR ACTIVITIES

Campus housing available: coed dorms, special housing for disabled students, other housing options. **Clubs and organizations:** Number of student organizations: 28. Activities include: choral groups, concert band, dance, drama/theater, music ensembles, radio station, student government, student newspaper, student film society, television station, yearbook. Number of fraternities: 3; sororities: 4. Average proportion of students who stay on campus on weekends: 40%. **Sports program (2009-2010):** Member of NCAA I. *Men's intercollegiate varsity sports:* baseball, basketball, cross country, tennis, track and field (indoor), track and field (outdoor). *Women's intercollegiate varsity sports:* basketball, bowling, cross country, softball, tennis, track and field (indoor), track and field (outdoor), volleyball.

SERVICES AND FACILITIES

Basic services: nonremedial tutoring, health service, health insurance. **Remedial assistance:** reading, math, writing, study skills. **Counseling services:** career, personal, academic, psychological. **For learning-disabled students:** Services include: remedial math, remedial reading, untimed tests, extended time for tests. **Information technology resources:** Students are not required to lease or own a computer. Number of campus computers available to all students: 335. School has a wireless network. Proportion of college-owned housing units wired for high-speed internet access: 100%. **Campus safety:** Security services offered: 24-hour foot-and-vehicle patrols, late-night transport/escort service, 24-hour emergency telephones, lighted pathways/sidewalks, controlled dormitory access (key, security card, etc).

TRANSFER AND INTERNATIONAL STUDENTS

Transfer students: May apply for admission for the following academic terms: Fall, Spring. Applicants need a minimum number of credits to apply. For fall 2009: Transfer applications received: 757. Transfer applicants offered admission: 590. Transfer applicants enrolled: 266. **International students:** Number of foreign undergraduates: 132 (4% of student body). Number of countries represented: 23. Minimum TOEFL score required: 500 (paper); 173 (computer).

Frostburg State University

- **Address:** 101 Braddock Road, Frostburg, MD 21532
- **Website:** http://www.frostburg.edu
- **Public**
- **Enrollment:** 4,439 full-time; 316 part-time

KEY STATS

✔ **U.S News College Ranking:** 121, Regional Universities (North)
✔ **SAT Score (25th/75th percentile):** 860-1060
✔ **Tuition:** 2010-2011: $6,904 in state, $16,950 out of state

Selectivity: Less selective	**Room/board:** $8,554
Acceptance rate: 59%	**Average debt:** $18,255
Student/faculty ratio: 16/1	**Proportion who borrowed:** 64%

UNDERGRADUATE STUDENT BODY STATS

2009-2010 enrollment: 4,439 full-time; 316 part-time. Men: 51%; women: 49%. **Ethnic makeup:** African American: 24%; Asian American: 2%; Hispanic: 3%; White: 71%.

ADMISSIONS FACTS AND FIGURES

Phone: (301) 687-4201. **Email:** fsuadmissions@frostburg.edu. **Website:** http://www.frostburg.edu. **Application deadlines for fall 2011:** Regular decision: Rolling. Early decision: Send application by: December 15; Decision sent by: N/A. Early action: Not offered. **Application fee:** $30. **To apply online, go to:** http://www.frostburg.edu/ungrad/admiss/onlineappproc.htm. **Admissions requirements/recommendations:** High school units required (recommended): English: 4; Mathematics: 3; Science: 3; Foreign language: 2; History: 3; Total units: 15. Tests: The college uses SAT or ACT scores in admissions decisions. Either SAT or ACT required. For admission to the fall 2011 entering class, the school will accept: ACT with or without writing accepted. Campus visit: Recommended. **Factors that count in admissions decisions:** *Academic:* Secondary school record: Important. Standardized test scores: Very Important. Essay: Considered. **Admissions statistics for the fall 2009 entering class:** Total applicants: 4,476. Total accepted: 2,624. Freshmen enrolled: 1,041; 7% were from out of state. Overall acceptance rate: 59%. Non-early acceptance rate: 59%. **Credentials of fall 2009 freshmen:** 8% ranked in the top 10 percent of their high school class; 26% were in the top 25 percent; 64% were in the top half. (Proportion submitting class standing: 51%.) **Average high school grade point average:** 3.1. **First-year students who submitted SAT scores:** 97%. Scores (25/75 percentile): Critical Reading: 430-530, Math: 430-530, Combined: 860-1060. **First-year students submitting ACT scores:** 13%. Scores (25/75 percentile): English: 16-22, Math: 16-22, Composite: 17-22.

ACADEMICS

Year founded: 1898. **Academic calendar:** Semester. **Degrees offered:** certificate, bachelor's, post-bachelor's certificate, master's, post-master's certificate. **Most popular majors:** 21% business administration and management, 8% liberal arts and sciences/liberal studies, 7% early childhood education and teaching, 6% psychology, 5% criminal justice/safety studies. **Major fields of study:** architecture and related services; biological and biomedical sciences; business, management, marketing, and related support services; communication, journalism, and related programs; computer and information sciences and support services; education; English language and literature/letters; foreign languages, literatures, and linguistics; health professions and related clinical sciences; history; liberal arts and sciences studies, and humanities; mathematics and statistics; multi/interdisciplinary studies; natural resources and conservation; parks, recreation, leisure, and fitness studies; philosophy and religious studies; physical sciences; psychology; public administration and social service professions; security and protective services; social sciences; visual and performing arts. **Areas of required coursework:** arts/fine arts, humanities, computer literacy, mathematics, English (including composition), sciences (biological or physical), social science. **Pre-professional programs:** pre-law, pre-dentistry, pre-medicine, pre-veterinary science, pre-optometry, pre-pharmacy. **Special academic programs (% participation):** distance learning, double major (3%), dual enrollment, honors program, independent study, internships, study abroad, teacher certificate program. **Teacher certification offered in:** early childhood, special education, elementary, middle/junior high, secondary. **Cooperative education programs:** engineering. **Faculty and instruction (2009-2010):** Total instructional faculty: 242 full-time, 118 part-time (56% men; 44% women; 11% minorities). Full-time faculty with Ph.D. or other terminal degree: 85%. Student/faculty ratio: 16/1. Classes of fewer than 20 students: 47%; of 20 to 49 students: 50%; of 50 or more students: 3%. **Advanced Placement and International Baccalaureate credit:** AP tests may be used for: Credit only. Scores accepted: 3, 4, 5. International Baccalaureate exams may be used for: Credit only. **Freshmen returning for sophomore year:** 72%. **Graduation rates:** Four-year: 25%; five-year: 46%; six-year: 49%. **Graduate study:** 34% of students pursue further study within one year.

COSTS AND FINANCIAL AID

Financial aid office: (301) 687-4301. **Expenses (2010-2011):** Tuition and fees 2010-2011: $6,904 in state, $16,950 out of state; room/board: $8,554. Estimated books and supplies: $1,500; transportation: $500; personal expenses: $850. **Financial aid:** Priority filing date for institution's financial aid form: March 1. In 2009-2010, 79% of undergraduates applied for financial aid. Of those, 56% were determined to have financial need; 25% had their need fully met. Average financial aid package (proportion receiving): $8,927 (56%). Average amount of gift aid, such as scholarships or grants (proportion receiving): $6,538 (40%). Average amount of self-help aid, such as work study or loans (proportion receiving): $3,854 (44%). Average need-based loan (excluding PLUS or other private loans): $3,794. Among students who received need-based aid, the average percentage of need met: 71%. Among students who received aid based on merit, the average award (and the proportion receiving): $2,995 (10%). The average athletic scholarship (and the proportion receiving): $0 (0%). Average amount of debt of borrowers graduating in 2009: $18,255. Proportion who borrowed: 64%.

CAMPUS LIFE AND EXTRACURRICULAR ACTIVITIES

Campus housing available (% using): coed dorms (95%), women's dorms (5%). Students who live in college-owned, operated, or affiliated housing: 34%. **Student employment:** During the 2009-2010 academic year, 17% of undergraduates worked on campus. Average per-year earnings: $800. **Clubs and organizations:** Number of student organizations: 80. Activities include: choral groups, concert band, dance, drama/theater, jazz band, literary magazine, marching band, music ensembles, musical theater, pep band, radio station, student government, student newspaper, television station, yearbook. Number of fraternities: 9; sororities: 6. **Sports program (2009-2010):** Member of NCAA III. ***Men's intercollegiate varsity sports:*** baseball, basketball, cross country, football, soccer, swimming, tennis, track and field (indoor), track and field (outdoor). ***Women's intercollegiate varsity sports:*** basketball, cross country, field hockey, lacrosse, soccer, softball, swimming, tennis, track and field (indoor), track and field (outdoor), volleyball.

SERVICES AND FACILITIES

Basic services: nonremedial tutoring, health service. **Remedial assistance:** math. **Counseling services:** career, personal, veteran student, academic, psychological. **For learning-disabled students:** School does not offer a structured program with separate admission and additional fees. Total undergraduates in learning-disabled program or receiving services: 240. Services include: remedial math, tape recorders, untimed tests, note-taking services, readers, extended time for tests, tutors. **Library:** Number of titles: 336,753; number of current serial subscriptions: 2,848. **Information technology resources:** Students are not required to lease or own a computer. Number of campus computers available to all students: 668. School has a wireless network. Proportion of college-owned housing units wired for high-speed internet access: 100%. **Campus safety:** Security services offered: late-night transport/escort service, 24-hour emergency telephones.

TRANSFER AND INTERNATIONAL STUDENTS

Transfer students: May apply for admission for the following academic terms: Fall, Winter, Spring, Summer. Applicants need a minimum number of credits to apply. For fall 2009: Transfer applications received: 949. Transfer applicants offered admission: 624. Transfer applicants enrolled: 419. **International students:** Number of foreign undergraduates: 20. Number of countries represented: 40. Minimum TOEFL score required: 550 (paper); 213 (computer).

Goucher College

- ■ **Address:** 1021 Dulaney Valley Road, Baltimore, MD 21204
- ■ **Website:** http://www.goucher.edu
- ■ **Private**
- ■ **Enrollment:** 1,446 full-time; 35 part-time

KEY STATS

✔ **U.S News College Ranking:** 111, National Liberal Arts Colleges

✔ **SAT Score (25th/75th percentile):** 1060-1300

✔ **Tuition:** 2010-2011: $35,142

Selectivity: Selective	**Room/board:** $10,284
Acceptance rate: 73%	**Average debt:** $18,465
Student/faculty ratio: 9/1	**Proportion who borrowed:** 74%

UNDERGRADUATE STUDENT BODY STATS

2009-2010 enrollment: 1,446 full-time; 35 part-time. Men: 32%; women: 68%. **Ethnic makeup:** African American: 8%; American-Indian: 1%; Asian American: 3%; Hispanic: 5%; White: 83%; International: 1%.

ADMISSIONS FACTS AND FIGURES

Phone: (410) 337-6100. **Email:** admissions@goucher.edu. **Website:** http://www.goucher.edu. **Application deadlines for fall 2011:** Regular decision: February 1; decision sent by April 1. Early decision: Not offered. Early action: Send application by: December 1; Decision sent by: February 15. Admission can be deferred. **Application fee:** $55. **To apply online, go to:** http://www.goucher.edu/admissions. **Admissions requirements/recommendations:** High school units required (recommended): English: 4 (4); Mathematics: 3 (4); Science: 2 (3); Foreign language: 2 (4); Social studies: 3 (3); Academic electives: 2 (2); Total units: 16 (20). Tests: The college uses SAT or ACT scores in admissions decisions. Neither SAT nor ACT required. For admission to the fall 2011 entering class, the school will accept: ACT with or without writing accepted. Campus visit: Recommended. Admissions interview: Recommended. Off-campus interview: May be arranged. **Factors that count in admissions decisions:** *Academic:* Secondary school record: Very Important. Class rank: Important. Letters of recommendation: Important. Standardized test scores: Considered. Essay: Important. *Nonacademic:* Interview: Considered. Extracurricular activities: Important. Talent/ability: Important. Character/personal qualities: Considered. Alumni/ae relationship: Considered. Geographical residence: Considered. State residency: Considered. Religious affiliation/commitment: Not Considered. Minority status: Considered. Volunteer work: Considered. Work experience: Considered. **Other schools with the greatest overlap in applicants:** American University; Loyola University Maryland; Skidmore College; Towson University; University of Maryland–College Park. **Admissions statistics for the fall 2009 entering class:** Total applicants: 3,651. Total accepted: 2,664. Freshmen enrolled: 400; 76% were from out of state. Accepted through early-decision or early-action plans: 44%. Overall acceptance rate: 73%. Non-early acceptance rate: 69%. **Size of waiting list:** 261 applicants; enrolled from waiting list: 23. **Credentials of fall 2009 freshmen:** 26% ranked in the top 10 percent of their high school class; 52% were in the top 25 percent; 89% were in the top half. (Proportion submitting class standing: 39%.) **Average high school grade point average:** 3.2. **First-year students who submitted SAT scores:** 77%. Scores (25/75 percentile): Critical Reading: 550-670, Math: 510-630, Combined: 1060-1300. **First-year students submitting ACT scores:** 24%. Scores (25/75 percentile): English: 21-27, Math: 23-32, Composite: 23-29.

ACADEMICS

Year founded: 1885. **Academic calendar:** Semester. **Degrees offered:** bachelor's, post-bachelor's certificate, master's. **Most popular majors:** 18% visual and performing arts, 13% psychology, 12% social sciences, 10% English language and literature/letters, 10% communication, journalism, and related programs. **Major fields of study:** area, ethnic, cultural, and gender studies; biological and biomedical sciences; business, management, marketing, and related support services; communication, journalism, and related programs; computer and information sciences and support services; education; English language and literature/letters; foreign languages, literatures, and linguistics; history; mathematics and statistics; multi/interdisciplinary studies; philosophy and religious studies; physical sciences; psychology; social sciences; visual and performing arts. **Areas of required coursework:** arts/fine arts, humanities, computer literacy, mathematics, English (including composition), foreign languages, sciences (biological or physical), history, social science, other. **Pre-professional programs:** pre-law, pre-dentistry,

pre-medicine, pre-veterinary science. **Special academic programs (% participation):** cross-registration (1%), double major (10%), dual enrollment, independent study, internships, student-designed major, study abroad (100%), teacher certificate program (4%). **Teacher certification offered in:** special education, elementary, secondary. **Cooperative education programs:** engineering. **Reserve Officers Training Corps (ROTC):** Army ROTC: Offered at cooperating institution (Loyola University Maryland). **Faculty and instruction (2009-2010):** Total instructional faculty: 130 full-time, 83 part-time (36% men; 64% women; 12% minorities). Full-time faculty with Ph.D. or other terminal degree: 88%. Student/faculty ratio: 9/1. Classes of fewer than 20 students: 74%; of 20 to 49 students: 26%; of 50 or more students: 1%. **Advanced Placement and International Baccalaureate credit:** AP tests may be used for: Placement only. Scores accepted: 4, 5. International Baccalaureate exams may be used for: Placement only. **Freshmen returning for sophomore year:** 80%. **Graduation rates:** Four-year: 60%; five-year: 68%; six-year: 68%. **Graduate study:** 35% of students pursue further study within one year.

COSTS AND FINANCIAL AID

Financial aid office: (410) 337-6141. **Expenses (2010-2011):** Tuition and fees 2010-2011: $35,142; room/board: $10,284. Estimated books and supplies: $800; transportation: $530; personal expenses: $1,020. **Financial aid:** Priority filing date for institution's financial aid form: February 1. In 2009-2010, 67% of undergraduates applied for financial aid. Of those, 57% were determined to have financial need; 25% had their need fully met. Average financial aid package (proportion receiving): $25,518 (57%). Average amount of gift aid, such as scholarships or grants (proportion receiving): $22,271 (54%). Average amount of self-help aid, such as work study or loans (proportion receiving): $5,007 (50%). Average need-based loan (excluding PLUS or other private loans): $4,250. Among students who received need-based aid, the average percentage of need met: 80%. Among students who received aid based on merit, the average award (and the proportion receiving): $12,129 (20%). The average athletic scholarship (and the proportion receiving): $0 (0%). Average amount of debt of borrowers graduating in 2009: $18,465. Proportion who borrowed: 74%.

CAMPUS LIFE AND EXTRACURRICULAR ACTIVITIES

Campus housing available (% using): coed dorms (50%), women's dorms (25%), men's dorms (5%), special housing for disabled students (1%), other housing options (8%). Students who live in college-owned, operated, or affiliated housing: 84%. **Student employment:** During the 2009-2010 academic year, 40% of undergraduates worked on campus. Average per-year earnings: $2,200. **Clubs and organizations:** Number of student organizations: 60. Activities include: campus ministries, choral groups, dance, drama/theater, international student organization, jazz band, literary magazine, model UN, music ensembles, musical theater, opera, radio station, student government, student newspaper, student film society, symphony orchestra, television station, yearbook. Number of fraternities: 0; sororities: 0. Average proportion of students who stay on campus on weekends: 75%. **Sports program (2009-2010):** Member of NCAA III. *Men's intercollegiate varsity sports:* basketball, cross country, lacrosse, soccer, swimming, tennis, track and field (indoor), track and field (outdoor). *Women's intercollegiate varsity sports:* basketball, cross country, equestrian, field hockey, lacrosse, soccer, swimming, tennis, track and field (indoor), track and field (outdoor), volleyball.

SERVICES AND FACILITIES

Basic services: nonremedial tutoring, women's center, placement service, health service, health insurance. **Remedial assistance:** writing, study skills. **Counseling services:** minority student, career, personal, veteran student, academic, older student, psychological, birth control, religious. **For learning-disabled students:** School does not offer a structured program with separate admission and additional fees. **Library:** Number of titles: 298,778; number of current serial subscriptions: 41,432. **Information technology resources:** Students are not required to lease or own a computer. Number of campus computers available to all students: 150. School has a wireless network. Approximate number of users that can be accommodated: 1,100. Proportion of college-owned housing units wired for high-speed internet access: 100%. **Campus safety:** Security services offered: 24-hour foot-and-vehicle patrols, late-night transport/escort service, 24-hour emergency telephones, lighted pathways/sidewalks, controlled dormitory access (key, security card, etc).

TRANSFER AND INTERNATIONAL STUDENTS

Transfer students: May apply for admission for the following academic terms: Fall, Spring. Applicants do not need a minimum number of credits to apply. For fall 2009: Transfer applications received: 161. Transfer applicants offered admission: 96. Transfer applicants enrolled: 35. **International**

students: Number of foreign undergraduates: 13 (1% of student body). Number of countries represented: 22. Minimum TOEFL score required: 550 (paper); 213 (computer). Average TOEFL score: 557 (paper).

Hood College

- **Address:** 401 Rosemont Avenue, Frederick, MD 21701
- **Website:** http://www.hood.edu
- **Private; Religious affiliation:** United Church of Christ
- **Enrollment:** 1,259 full-time; 173 part-time

KEY STATS

✔ **U.S. News College Ranking:** 23, Regional Universities (North)
✔ **SAT Score (25th/75th percentile):** 960-1190
✔ **Tuition:** 2010-2011: $29,860

Selectivity: Selective	**Room/board:** $9,901
Acceptance rate: 72%	**Average debt:** $17,382
Student/faculty ratio: 12/1	**Proportion who borrowed:** 64%

UNDERGRADUATE STUDENT BODY STATS

2009-2010 enrollment: 1,259 full-time; 173 part-time. Men: 32%; women: 68%. **Ethnic makeup:** African American: 11%; Asian American: 2%; Hispanic: 4%; White: 80%; International: 2%. **Religious preference:** Roman Catholic: 12%; Protestant: 18%; Jewish: 1%; Muslim: 1%; No preference: 3%; Unknown: 45%; United Church of Christ: 1%; Christian: 14%; Other: 5%.

ADMISSIONS FACTS AND FIGURES

Phone: (800) 922-1599. **Email:** admissions@hood.edu. **Website:** http://www.hood.edu. **Application deadlines for fall 2011:** Regular decision: Rolling. Early decision: Not offered. Early action: Send application by: December 1; Decision sent by: December 15. Admission can be deferred. **Application fee:** $35. **To apply online, go to:** http://www.hood.edu/admissions/apply.cfm. **Admissions requirements/recommendations:** High school units required (recommended): English: 4 (4); Mathematics: 3 (4); Science: 3 (3); Foreign language: 2 (2); Social studies: 2 (2); History: 1 (1); Academic electives: 1 (1); Total units: 16 (17). Tests: The college uses SAT or ACT scores in admissions decisions. Either SAT or ACT required. For admission to the fall 2011 entering class, the school will accept: ACT with or without writing accepted. Campus visit: Recommended. Admissions interview: Recommended. Off-campus interview: May be arranged. **Factors that count in admissions decisions:** *Academic:* Secondary school record: Very Important. Class rank: Considered. Letters of recommendation: Considered. Standardized test scores: Important. Essay: Considered. *Nonacademic:* Interview: Considered. Extracurricular activities: Considered. Talent/ability: Not Considered. Character/personal qualities: Not Considered. Alumni/ae relationship: Considered. Geographical residence: Not Considered. State residency: Not Considered. Religious affiliation/commitment: Not Considered. Minority status: Not Considered. Volunteer work: Not Considered. Work experience: Not Considered. **Other schools with the greatest overlap in applicants:** McDaniel College; Salisbury University; Towson University; University of Maryland–Baltimore County; University of Maryland–College Park. **Admissions statistics for the fall 2009 entering class:** Total applicants: 1,622. Total accepted: 1,166. Freshmen enrolled: 251; 23% were from out of state. Overall acceptance rate: 72%. Non-early acceptance rate: 72%. **Size of waiting list:** 0 applicants; enrolled from waiting list: 0. **Credentials of fall 2009 freshmen:** 20% ranked in the top 10 percent of their high school class; 51% were in the top 25 percent; 85% were in the top half. (Proportion submitting class standing: 63%.) **Average high school grade point average:** 3.5. **First-year students who submitted SAT scores:** 95%. Scores (25/75 percentile): Critical Reading: 490-600, Math: 470-590, Combined: 960-1190. **First-year students submitting ACT scores:** 19%. Scores (25/75 percentile): English: 20-25, Math: 19-26, Composite: 20-25.

ACADEMICS

Year founded: 1893. **Academic calendar:** Semester. **Degrees offered:** certificate, bachelor's, post-bachelor's certificate, master's. **Most popular majors:** 14% psychology, 13% education, 10% business, management, marketing, and related support services, 9% biological and biomedical sciences, 9% social sciences. **Major fields of study:** area, ethnic, cultural, and gender studies; biological and biomedical sciences; business, management, marketing, and related support services; communication, journalism, and related programs; computer and information sciences and support services; education; English language and literature/letters; foreign languages, literatures, and linguistics; history; legal professions and studies; mathematics and statistics; multi/interdisciplinary studies; natural resources and conservation; philosophy and religious studies; physical sciences; psychology; public administration and social service professions; social sciences; visual and performing arts. **Areas of required coursework:** arts/fine arts, humanities, computer literacy, mathematics, English (including composition), philosophy, foreign languages, sciences (biological or physical), history, social science, other. **Pre-professional programs:** pre-law, pre-dentistry, pre-medicine, pre-veterinary science. **Special academic programs (% participation):** distance learning (1%), double major (10%), honors program (30%), independent study (40%), internships (30%), liberal arts/career combination (2%), student-designed major (0%), study abroad (3%), teacher certificate program (16%). **Teacher certification offered in:** early childhood, special education, elementary, secondary. **Reserve Officers Training Corps (ROTC):** Army ROTC: Offered on campus. **Faculty and instruction (2009-2010):** Total instructional faculty: 80 full-time, 177 part-time (47% men; 53% women; 9% minorities). Full-time faculty with Ph.D. or other terminal degree: 98%. Student/faculty ratio: 12/1. Classes of fewer than 20 students: 62%; of 20 to 49 students: 38%; of 50 or more students: 1%. **Advanced Placement and International Baccalaureate credit:** AP tests may be used for: Credit and/or placement. Scores accepted: 4, 5. International Baccalaureate exams may be used for: Credit and/or placement. **Freshmen returning for sophomore year:** 80%. **Graduation rates:** Four-year: 61%; five-year: 69%; six-year: 70%. **Graduate study:** 37% of students pursue further study immediately upon graduation; 40% within one year; 68% within five years. Fields in which graduates pursue further study: Master of Business Administration (MBA), 22%; law, 4%; medicine, 2%; education, 8%; arts and sciences, 50%.

COSTS AND FINANCIAL AID

Financial aid office: (301) 696-3411. **Expenses (2010-2011):** Tuition and fees 2010-2011: $29,860; room/board: $9,901. Estimated books and supplies: $1,000; transportation: $1,100; personal expenses: $1,100. **Financial aid:** Priority filing date for institution's financial aid form: February 15. In 2009-2010, 93% of undergraduates applied for financial aid. Of those, 83% were determined to have financial need; 23% had their need fully met. Average financial aid package (proportion receiving): $21,899 (82%). Average amount of gift aid, such as scholarships or grants (proportion receiving): $18,444 (81%). Average amount of self-help aid, such as work study or loans (proportion receiving): $4,601 (64%). Average need-based loan (excluding PLUS or other private loans): $4,242. Among students who received need-based aid, the average percentage of need met: 78%. Among students who received aid based on merit, the average award (and the proportion receiving): $18,175 (18%). The average athletic scholarship (and the proportion receiving): $0 (0%). Average amount of debt of borrowers graduating in 2009: $17,382. Proportion who borrowed: 64%.

CAMPUS LIFE AND EXTRACURRICULAR ACTIVITIES

Campus housing available (% using): coed dorms (66%), women's dorms (14%), apartment for single students (17%), special housing for disabled students (0%), other housing options (3%). Students who live in college-owned, operated, or affiliated housing: 54%. **Student employment:** During the 2009-2010 academic year, 11% of undergraduates worked on campus. Average per-year earnings: $1,084. **Clubs and organizations:** Number of student organizations: 79. Activities include: campus ministries, choral groups, dance, drama/theater, international student organization, jazz band, literary magazine, model UN, music ensembles, musical theater, radio station, student government, student newspaper, student film society, yearbook. Number of fraternities: 0; sororities: 0. Average proportion of students who stay on campus on weekends: 75%. **Sports program (2009-2010):** Member of NCAA III. *Men's intercollegiate varsity sports:* basketball, cross country, golf, lacrosse, soccer, swimming, tennis, track and field (outdoor). *Women's intercollegiate varsity sports:* basketball, cross country, field hockey, golf, lacrosse, soccer, softball, swimming, tennis, track and field (outdoor), volleyball.

SERVICES AND FACILITIES

Basic services: nonremedial tutoring, placement service, health service, health insurance. **Remedial assistance:** reading, math, writing, study skills, other. **Counseling services:** minority student, career, military, personal, veteran student, academic, older student, psychological, birth control, religious. **For learning-disabled students:** School does not offer a structured program with separate admission and additional fees. Total undergraduates in learning-disabled program or receiving services: 95. Services include: remedial math, remedial English, reading machines, tape recorders, other special classes, untimed tests, note-taking services, oral tests, extended time for tests, tutors, priority seating, substitution of courses, other testing accommodations, other. **Library:** Number of titles: 208,600; number of current serial subscriptions: 42,224. **Information technology resources:** Students are not required to lease or own a computer. Number of campus computers available to all students: 353. School has a wireless network. Approximate number of users that can be accommodated: 3,200. Proportion of college-owned housing units wired for high-speed internet access: 100%. **Campus safety:** Security services offered: 24-hour foot-and-vehicle patrols, late-night transport/escort service, 24-hour emergency telephones, lighted pathways/sidewalks, controlled dormitory access (key, security card, etc).

TRANSFER AND INTERNATIONAL STUDENTS

Transfer students: May apply for admission for the following academic terms: Fall, Spring, Summer. Applicants need a minimum number of credits to apply. For fall 2009: Transfer applications received: 302. Transfer applicants offered admission: 263. Transfer applicants enrolled: 145. **International students:** Number of foreign undergraduates: 31 (2% of student body). Number of countries represented: 26. Minimum TOEFL score required: 550 (paper); 213 (computer). Average TOEFL score: 550 (paper).

Johns Hopkins University

- ■ **Address:** 3400 N. Charles Street, Baltimore, MD 21218
- ■ **Website:** http://www.jhu.edu
- ■ **Private**
- ■ **Enrollment:** 5,788 full-time; 144 part-time

KEY STATS

✔ **U.S News College Ranking:** 13, National Universities

✔ **SAT Score (25th/75th percentile):** 1300-1500

✔ **Tuition:** 2010-2011: $40,680

Selectivity: Most selective	**Room/board:** $12,510
Acceptance rate: 27%	**Average debt:** $21,859
Student/faculty ratio: 10/1	**Proportion who borrowed:** 46%

UNDERGRADUATE STUDENT BODY STATS

2009-2010 enrollment: 5,788 full-time; 144 part-time. Men: 50%; women: 50%. **Ethnic makeup:** African American: 7%; Asian American: 21%; Hispanic: 7%; White: 57%; International: 8%. **Religious preference:** Roman Catholic: 31%; Protestant: 32%; Jewish: 13%; Muslim: 2%; Hindu: 5%; Buddhist: 2%; No preference: 12%.

ADMISSIONS FACTS AND FIGURES

Phone: (410) 516-8171. **Email:** gotojhu@jhu.edu. **Website:** http://www.jhu.edu. **Application deadlines for fall 2011:** Regular decision: January 1; decision sent by April 1. Early decision: Send application by: November 1; Decision sent by: December 15. Early action: Not offered. Admission can be deferred. **Application fee:** $70. **To apply online, go to:** http://apply.jhu.edu. **Admissions requirements/recommendations:** High school units required (recommended): English: (4); Mathematics: (4); Science: (4); Foreign language: (4); Social studies: (2); History: (2); Total units: (20). Tests: The college uses SAT or ACT scores in admissions decisions. Either SAT or ACT required. For admission to the fall 2011 entering class, the school will accept: ACT with writing required. Campus visit: Recommended. Admissions interview: Recommended. Off-campus interview: May be arranged. **Factors that count in admissions decisions:** *Academic:* Secondary school record: Very Important. Class rank: Important. Letters of recommendation: Very Important. Standardized test scores: Important. Essay: Important. *Nonacademic:* Interview: Considered. Extracurricular activities: Important. Talent/ability: Important. Character/personal qualities: Very Important. Alumni/ae relationship: Considered. Geographical residence: Considered. State residency: Considered. Religious affiliation/commitment: Not Considered. Minority status: Considered. Volunteer work: Important. Work experience: Important. **Other schools with the greatest overlap in applicants:** Cornell University; Duke University; Harvard University; University of Pennsylvania; Yale University. **Admissions statistics for the fall 2009 entering class:** Total applicants: 16,122. Total accepted: 4,308. Freshmen enrolled: 1,349; 89% were from out of state. Overall acceptance rate: 27%. Early-decision acceptance rate: 50%. Non-early acceptance rate: 25%. **Size of waiting list:** 3667 applicants; enrolled from waiting list: 1. **Credentials of fall 2009 freshmen:** 83% ranked in the top 10 percent of their high school class; 97% were in the top 25 percent; 100% were in the top half. (Proportion submitting class standing: 33%.) **Average high school grade point average:** 3.7. **First-year students who submitted SAT scores:**

93%. Scores (25/75 percentile): Critical Reading: 630-730, Math: 670-770, Combined: 1300-1500. **First-year students submitting ACT scores:** 36%. Scores (25/75 percentile): English: 29-34, Math: 25-31, Composite: 29-33.

ACADEMICS

Year founded: 1876. **Academic calendar:** Semester. **Degrees offered:** certificate, diploma, bachelor's, post-bachelor's certificate, master's, post-master's certificate, doctorate. **Most popular majors:** 22% public health (M.P.H., D.P.H.), 17% biomedical/medical engineering, 14% biology/biological sciences, 8% public policy analysis, 6% liberal arts and sciences/liberal studies. **Major fields of study:** area, ethnic, cultural, and gender studies; biological and biomedical sciences; communications technologies/technicians and support services; computer and information sciences and support services; education; engineering; English language and literature/letters; foreign languages, literatures, and linguistics; health professions and related clinical sciences; history; liberal arts and sciences studies, and humanities; mathematics and statistics; multi/interdisciplinary studies; philosophy and religious studies; physical sciences; psychology; social sciences; visual and performing arts. **Areas of required coursework:** humanities, mathematics, English (including composition), sciences (biological or physical), social science. **Pre-professional programs:** pre-law, pre-medicine. **Special academic programs (% participation):** cross-registration, double major (15.5%), dual enrollment, independent study (32%), internships (66%), study abroad (16%). **Teacher certification offered in:** special education, elementary, secondary. **Reserve Officers Training Corps (ROTC):** Army ROTC: Offered on campus; Air Force ROTC: Offered at cooperating institution (University of Maryland–College Park). **Faculty and instruction (2009-2010):** Total instructional faculty: 3,063 full-time, 193 part-time (63% men; 37% women; 19% minorities). Full-time faculty with Ph.D. or other terminal degree: 91%. Student/faculty ratio: 10/1. Classes of fewer than 20 students: 66%; of 20 to 49 students: 22%; of 50 or more students: 11%. **Advanced Placement and International Baccalaureate credit:** AP tests may be used for: Credit only. Scores accepted: 4, 5. International Baccalaureate exams may be used for: Credit only. **Freshmen returning for sophomore year:** 97%. **Graduation rates:** Four-year: 83%; five-year: 90%; six-year: 91%. **Graduate study:** 37% of students pursue further study immediately upon graduation. Fields in which graduates pursue further study: Master of Business Administration (MBA), 7%; law, 14%; medicine, 31%; engineering, 5%; education, 1%; arts and sciences, 31%.

COSTS AND FINANCIAL AID

Financial aid office: (410) 516-8028. **Expenses (2010-2011):** Tuition and fees 2010-2011: $40,680; room/board: $12,510. Estimated books and supplies: $1,200; transportation: $700; personal expenses: $1,000. **Financial aid:** Priority filing date for institution's financial aid form: March 1; deadline: March 1. In 2009-2010, 55% of undergraduates applied for financial aid. Of those, 46% were determined to have financial need; 99% had their need fully met. Average financial aid package (proportion receiving): $31,853 (46%). Average amount of gift aid, such as scholarships or grants (proportion receiving): $28,380 (40%). Average amount of self-help aid, such as work study or loans (proportion receiving): $5,695 (41%). Average need-based loan (excluding PLUS or other private loans): $4,530. Among students who received need-based aid, the average percentage of need met: 98%. Among students who received aid based on merit, the average award (and the proportion receiving): $27,360 (1%). The average athletic scholarship (and the proportion receiving): $29,939 (1%). Average amount of debt of borrowers graduating in 2009: $21,859. Proportion who borrowed: 46%.

CAMPUS LIFE AND EXTRACURRICULAR ACTIVITIES

Campus housing available (% using): coed dorms (85%), women's dorms (1%), men's dorms (1%), sorority housing, apartment for single students (12%), special housing for disabled students (1%), other housing options. Students who live in college-owned, operated, or affiliated housing: 56%. **Student employment:** During the 2009-2010 academic year, 34% of undergraduates worked on campus. Average per-year earnings: $5,801. **Clubs and organizations:** Number of student organizations: 265. Activities include: campus ministries, choral groups, concert band, dance, drama/theater, jazz band, literary magazine, marching band, music ensembles, musical theater, pep band, radio station, student government, student newspaper, student film society, symphony orchestra. Number of fraternities: 13; sororities: 7. Proportion of men in fraternities: 23%; of women in sororities: 22%. Average proportion of students who stay on campus on weekends: 90%. **Sports program (2009-2010):** Member of NCAA III. *Men's intercollegiate varsity sports:* baseball, basketball, cross country, fencing, football, lacrosse, soccer, swimming, tennis, track and field (indoor), track and field (outdoor), water polo, wrestling. *Women's intercollegiate varsity sports:* basketball, crew (heavyweight), crew (lightweight), cross country, fencing, field hockey, lacrosse, soccer, swimming, tennis, track and field (indoor), track and field (outdoor), volleyball.

SERVICES AND FACILITIES

Basic services: nonremedial tutoring, women's center, placement service, health service, health insurance. **Counseling services:** minority student, career, military, personal, academic, psychological, birth control, religious. **For learning-disabled students:** School does not offer a structured program with separate admission and additional fees. Services include: reading machines, tape recorders, untimed tests, note-taking services, oral tests, readers, extended time for tests, tutors, priority registration, priority seating, texts on tape, other testing accommodations. **Library:** Number of titles: 3,730,439; number of current serial subscriptions: 100,074. **Information technology resources:** Students are not required to lease or own a computer. Number of campus computers available to all students: 525. School has a wireless network. Approximate number of users that can be accommodated: 3,000. Proportion of college-owned housing units wired for high-speed internet access: 100%. **Campus safety:** Security services offered: 24-hour foot-and-vehicle patrols, late-night transport/escort service, 24-hour emergency telephones, lighted pathways/sidewalks, student patrols, controlled dormitory access (key, security card, etc).

TRANSFER AND INTERNATIONAL STUDENTS

Transfer students: May apply for admission for the following academic terms: Fall. Applicants need a minimum number of credits to apply. For fall 2009: Transfer applications received: 802. Transfer applicants offered admission: 68. Transfer applicants enrolled: 32. **International students:** Number of foreign undergraduates: 444 (8% of student body). Minimum TOEFL score required: 600 (paper); 250 (computer).

Loyola University Maryland

- **Address:** 4501 N. Charles Street, Baltimore, MD 21210
- **Website:** http://www.loyola.edu
- **Private; Religious affiliation:** Roman Catholic
- **Enrollment:** 3,719 full-time; 38 part-time

KEY STATS

- ✔ **U.S News College Ranking:** 3, Regional Universities (North)
- ✔ **SAT Score (25th/75th percentile):** 1070-1270
- ✔ **Tuition:** 2010-2011: $39,350

Selectivity: More selective	**Room/board:** $11,730
Acceptance rate: 66%	**Average debt:** $26,855
Student/faculty ratio: 12/1	**Proportion who borrowed:** 72%

UNDERGRADUATE STUDENT BODY STATS

2009-2010 enrollment: 3,719 full-time; 38 part-time. Men: 41%; women: 59%. **Ethnic makeup:** African American: 4%; Asian American: 3%; Hispanic: 4%; White: 87%; International: 1%. **Religious preference:** Protestant: 7%; Jewish: 1%; Unknown: 1%; Roman Catholic: 78%; Christian Orthodox: 3%; Other: 10%.

ADMISSIONS FACTS AND FIGURES

Phone: (410) 617-5012. **Website:** http://www.loyola.edu. **Application deadlines for fall 2011:** Regular decision: January 15; decision sent by April 1. Early decision: Not offered. Early action: Send application by: November 1; Decision sent by: January 15. Admission can be deferred. **Application fee:** $50. **To apply online, go to:** http://admissions.loyola.edu/admissions/application/apply.asp. **Admissions requirements/recommendations:** High school units required (recommended): English: 4 (4); Mathematics: 3 (4); Science: 3 (4); Foreign language: 3 (4); Social studies: 2 (3); History: 2 (3); Total units: 17 (22). Tests: The college uses SAT or ACT scores in admissions decisions. Neither SAT nor ACT required. For admission to the fall 2011 entering class, the school will accept: ACT with or without writing accepted. Campus visit: Recommended. Admissions interview: Neither required nor recommended. Off-campus interview: Not available. **Factors that count in admissions decisions:** *Academic:* Secondary school record: Very Important. Class rank: Important. Letters of recommendation: Very Important. Standardized test scores: Considered. Essay: Very Important. *Nonacademic:* Interview: Considered. Extracurricular activities: Important. Talent/ability: Important. Character/personal qualities: Very Important. Alumni/ae relationship: Important. Geographical residence: Considered.

State residency: Not Considered. Religious affiliation/commitment: Not Considered. Minority status: Considered. Volunteer work: Important. Work experience: Considered. **Other schools with the greatest overlap in applicants:** Boston College; Fairfield University; Fordham University; Providence College; Villanova University. **Admissions statistics for the fall 2009 entering class:** Total applicants: 9,117. Total accepted: 6,008. Freshmen enrolled: 968; 84% were from out of state. Accepted through early-decision or early-action plans: 66%. Overall acceptance rate: 66%. Non-early acceptance rate: 49%. **Size of waiting list:** 2491 applicants; enrolled from waiting list: 917. **Credentials of fall 2009 freshmen:** 31% ranked in the top 10 percent of their high school class; 65% were in the top 25 percent; 94% were in the top half. (Proportion submitting class standing: 25%.) **Average high school grade point average:** 3.4. **First-year students who submitted SAT scores:** 88%. Scores (25/75 percentile): Critical Reading: 530-630, Math: 540-640, Combined: 1070-1270. **First-year students submitting ACT scores:** 26%. Scores (25/75 percentile): English: 23-28, Math: 23-28, Composite: 24-28.

ACADEMICS

Year founded: 1852. **Academic calendar:** Semester. **Degrees offered:** certificate, bachelor's, master's, post-master's certificate, doctorate. **Most popular majors:** 37% business/commerce, 11% communication studies/speech communication and rhetoric, 7% biology/biological sciences, 7% psychology, 7% social sciences. **Major fields of study:** biological and biomedical sciences; business, management, marketing, and related support services; communication, journalism, and related programs; computer and information sciences and support services; education; engineering; English language and literature/letters; foreign languages, literatures, and linguistics; health professions and related clinical sciences; history; mathematics and statistics; multi/interdisciplinary studies; philosophy and religious studies; physical sciences; psychology; social sciences; visual and performing arts. **Areas of required coursework:** arts/fine arts, humanities, mathematics, English (including composition), philosophy, foreign languages, sciences (biological or physical), history, social science, other. **Pre-professional programs:** pre-law, pre-dentistry, pre-medicine, pre-veterinary science, pre-optometry, other. **Special academic programs (% participation):** cooperative (work-study plan) program (23%), cross-registration (2%), double major (6%), honors program (6%), independent study, internships (81%), study abroad (81%), teacher certificate program (4%). **Teacher certification offered in:** special education, elementary, middle/junior high, secondary. **Reserve Officers Training Corps (ROTC):** Army ROTC: Offered on campus; Air Force ROTC: Offered at cooperating institution (University of Maryland–College Park). **Faculty and instruction (2009-2010):** Total instructional faculty: 331 full-time, 230 part-time (55% men; 45% women; 11% minorities). Full-time faculty with Ph.D. or other terminal degree: 79%. Student/faculty ratio: 12/1. Classes of fewer than 20 students: 48%; of 20 to 49 students: 51%; of 50 or more students: 1%. **Advanced Placement and International Baccalaureate credit:** AP tests may be used for: Credit and/or placement. Scores accepted: 3, 4, 5. International Baccalaureate exams may be used for: Credit and/or placement. **Freshmen returning for sophomore year:** 90%. **Graduation rates:** Four-year: 77%; five-year: 82%; six-year: 83%. **Graduate study:** 24% of students pursue further study within one year. Fields in which graduates pursue further study: Master of Business Administration (MBA), 13%; law, 11%; medicine, 4%; dentistry, 1%; engineering, 1%; education, 15%; arts and sciences, 54%; veterinary medicine, 1%.

COSTS AND FINANCIAL AID

Financial aid office: (410) 617-2576. **Expenses (2010-2011):** Tuition and fees 2010-2011: $39,350; room/board: $11,730. Estimated books and supplies: $1,130; transportation: $380; personal expenses: $1,080. **Financial aid:** Priority filing date for institution's financial aid form: February 15; deadline: February 15. In 2009-2010, 59% of undergraduates applied for financial aid. Of those, 49% were determined to have financial need; 98% had their need fully met. Average financial aid package (proportion receiving): $27,300 (49%). Average amount of gift aid, such as scholarships or grants (proportion receiving): $19,275 (44%). Average amount of self-help aid, such as work study or loans (proportion receiving): $8,025 (46%). Average need-based loan (excluding PLUS or other private loans): $5,875. Among students who received need-based aid, the average percentage of need met: 97%. Among students who received aid based on merit, the average award (and the proportion receiving): $14,190 (10%). The average athletic scholarship (and the proportion receiving): $26,630 (4%). Average amount of debt of borrowers graduating in 2009: $26,855. Proportion who borrowed: 72%.

CAMPUS LIFE AND EXTRACURRICULAR ACTIVITIES

Campus housing available (% using): coed dorms, apartment for single students (79%), special housing for disabled students (2%), other housing options (19%). Students who live in college-owned, operated, or affiliated housing: 84%. **Student employment:** During the 2009-2010 academic year, 25% of undergraduates worked on campus. Average per-year earnings: $2,800. **Clubs and organizations:** Number of student organizations: 200. Activities include: campus ministries, choral groups, dance, drama/theater, international student organization, jazz band, literary magazine, music ensembles, musical theater, pep band, radio station, student government, student newspaper, television station, yearbook. Number of fraternities: 0; sororities: 0. Average proportion of students who stay on campus on weekends: 83%. **Sports program (2009-2010):** Member of NCAA I. *Men's intercollegiate varsity sports:* basketball, cross country, golf, lacrosse, soccer, swimming, tennis. *Women's intercollegiate varsity sports:* basketball, cross country, lacrosse, crew (lightweight), soccer, swimming, tennis, track and field (indoor), track and field (outdoor), volleyball.

SERVICES AND FACILITIES
Basic services: nonremedial tutoring, women's center, placement service, health service, health insurance, other. **Remedial assistance:** math, writing, study skills, other. **Counseling services:** minority student, career, personal, academic, psychological, religious, other. **For learning-disabled students:** School does not offer a structured program with separate admission and additional fees. Total undergraduates in learning-disabled program or receiving services: 112. Services include: remedial math, reading machines, tape recorders, note-taking services, oral tests, learning center, readers, extended time for tests, tutors, priority seating, texts on tape, typist/scribe, exams on tape or computer, other testing accommodations, other. **Library:** Number of titles: 1,036,963; number of current serial subscriptions: 69,240. **Information technology resources:** Students are not required to lease or own a computer. Number of campus computers available to all students: 575. School has a wireless network. Approximate number of users that can be accommodated: 5,000. Proportion of college-owned housing units wired for high-speed internet access: 100%. **Campus safety:** Security services offered: 24-hour foot-and-vehicle patrols, late-night transport/escort service, 24-hour emergency telephones, lighted pathways/sidewalks, student patrols, controlled dormitory access (key, security card, etc).

TRANSFER AND INTERNATIONAL STUDENTS
Transfer students: May apply for admission for the following academic terms: Fall, Spring, Summer. Applicants do not need a minimum number of credits to apply. For fall 2009: Transfer applications received: 215. Transfer applicants offered admission: 86. Transfer applicants enrolled: 31. **International students:** Number of foreign undergraduates: 23 (1% of student body). Number of countries represented: 15. Minimum TOEFL score required: 550 (paper); 213 (computer).

Maryland Institute College of Art

- **Address:** 1300 Mount Royal Avenue, Baltimore, MD 21217-4134
- **Website:** http://www.mica.edu
- **Private**
- **Enrollment:** 1,678 full-time; 24 part-time

KEY STATS
- ✔ **U.S News College Ranking:** Unranked Specialty School–Fine Arts
- ✔ **SAT Score (25th/75th percentile):** 1040-1280
- ✔ **Tuition:** 2010-2011: $35,690

Selectivity: N/A	**Room/board:** $10,580
Acceptance rate: 47%	**Average debt:** N/A
Student/faculty ratio: 10/1	**Proportion who borrowed:** N/A

UNDERGRADUATE STUDENT BODY STATS
2009-2010 enrollment: 1,678 full-time; 24 part-time. Men: 30%; women: 70%. **Ethnic makeup:** African American: 4%; Asian American: 11%; Hispanic: 4%; White: 77%; International: 4%.

ADMISSIONS FACTS AND FIGURES
Phone: (410) 225-2222. **Email:** admissions@mica.edu. **Website:** http://www.mica.edu. **Application deadlines for fall 2011:** Regular decision: February 13; decision sent by March 13. Early decision: Send application by: November 14; Decision sent by: December 15. Early action: Not offered. Admission can be deferred. **Application fee:** $60. **To apply online, go to:** http://www.mica.edu/ADM/index.cfm?id=1. **Admissions requirements/recommendations:** High school units required (recommended): English: 4 (4); Mathematics: 2

(3); Science: 2 (3); Foreign language: 0 (0); Social studies: 4 (4); History: 3 (4); Academic electives: 6 (0); Total units: 24 (24). Tests: The college uses SAT or ACT scores in admissions decisions. Either SAT or ACT required. For admission to the fall 2011 entering class, the school will accept: ACT with or without writing accepted. Campus visit: Recommended. Admissions interview: Recommended. Off-campus interview: May be arranged. **Factors that count in admissions decisions:** *Academic:* Secondary school record: Very Important. Class rank: Important. Letters of recommendation: Considered. Standardized test scores: Important. Essay: Important. *Nonacademic:* Interview: Important. Extracurricular activities: Important. Talent/ability: Very Important. Character/personal qualities: Considered. Alumni/ae relationship: Considered. Geographical residence: Not Considered. State residency: Not Considered. Religious affiliation/commitment: Not Considered. Minority status: Considered. Volunteer work: Considered. Work experience: Not Considered. **Other schools with the greatest overlap in applicants:** Carnegie Mellon University; Pratt Institute; Rhode Island School of Design; School of the Art Institute of Chicago; Syracuse University. **Admissions statistics for the fall 2009 entering class:** Total applicants: 2,892. Total accepted: 1,348. Freshmen enrolled: 459; 83% were from out of state. Overall acceptance rate: 47%. Non-early acceptance rate: 47%. **Credentials of fall 2009 freshmen:** 30% ranked in the top 10 percent of their high school class; 71% were in the top 25 percent; 93% were in the top half. (Proportion submitting class standing: 53%.) **Average high school grade point average:** 3.5. First-year students who submitted SAT scores: 89%. Scores (25/75 percentile): Critical Reading: 530-660, Math: 510-620, Combined: 1040-1280.

ACADEMICS
Year founded: 1826. **Academic calendar:** Semester. **Degrees offered:** bachelor's, post-bachelor's certificate, master's. **Most popular majors:** 21% painting, 14% illustration, 14% intermedia/multimedia, 10% graphic design, 7% fiber, textile, and weaving arts. **Major fields of study:** education; visual and performing arts. **Areas of required coursework:** arts/fine arts, humanities, computer literacy, English (including composition), sciences (biological or physical), history, social science. **Special academic programs:** accelerated program, cross-registration, distance learning, double major, dual enrollment, exchange student program (domestic), independent study, internships, student-designed major, study abroad, teacher certificate program, other. **Teacher certification offered in:** elementary, middle/junior high, secondary. **Reserve Officers Training Corps (ROTC):** Army ROTC: Offered at cooperating institution (Johns Hopkins University). **Faculty and instruction (2009-2010):** Total instructional faculty: 129 full-time, 168 part-time (46% men; 54% women; 12% minorities). Full-time faculty with Ph.D. or other terminal degree: 83%. Student/faculty ratio: 10/1. Classes of fewer than 20 students: 75%; of 20 to 49 students: 25%; of 50 or more students: 0%. **Advanced Placement and International Baccalaureate credit:** AP tests may be used for: Credit and/or placement. Scores accepted: 4. International Baccalaureate exams may be used for: Credit and/or placement. **Freshmen returning for sophomore year:** 85%. **Graduation rates:** Four-year: 61%; five-year: 67%; six-year: 69%. **Graduate study:** 26% of students pursue further study immediately upon graduation. Fields in which graduates pursue further study: education, 20%; arts and sciences, 80%.

COSTS AND FINANCIAL AID
Financial aid office: (410) 225-2285. **Expenses (2010-2011):** Tuition and fees 2010-2011: $35,690; room/board: $10,580. Estimated books and supplies: $1,450; transportation: $725; personal expenses: $675. **Financial aid:**

CAMPUS LIFE AND EXTRACURRICULAR ACTIVITIES
Campus housing available: coed dorms, apartment for single students, special housing for disabled students, special housing for international students. Students who live in college-owned, operated, or affiliated housing: 88%. **Clubs and organizations:** Number of student organizations: 50. Activities include: choral groups, dance, drama/theater, international student organization, literary magazine, radio station, student government, student film society. Number of fraternities: 0; sororities: 0. Average proportion of students who stay on campus on weekends: 90%.

SERVICES AND FACILITIES
Basic services: nonremedial tutoring, health service, health insurance. **Remedial assistance:** writing, study skills. **Counseling services:** minority student, career, personal, academic, psychological. **For learning-disabled students:** School does not offer a structured program with separate admission and additional fees. Total undergraduates in learning-disabled program or receiving services: 100. Services include: note-taking services, learning center, tutors, other testing accommodations, other. **Library:** Number of titles:

85,100; number of current serial subscriptions: 321. **Information technology resources:** Students are not required to lease or own a computer. Number of campus computers available to all students: 430. School has a wireless network. Proportion of college-owned housing units wired for high-speed internet access: 100%. **Campus safety:** Security services offered: 24-hour foot-and-vehicle patrols, late-night transport/escort service, 24-hour emergency telephones, lighted pathways/sidewalks, student patrols, controlled dormitory access (key, security card, etc).

TRANSFER AND INTERNATIONAL STUDENTS

Transfer students: May apply for admission for the following academic terms: Fall, Spring. Applicants need a minimum number of credits to apply. For fall 2009: Transfer applications received: 300. Transfer applicants offered admission: 118. Transfer applicants enrolled: 57. **International students:** Number of foreign undergraduates: 68 (4% of student body). Number of countries represented: 28. Minimum TOEFL score required: 550 (paper); 213 (computer).

McDaniel College

- **Address:** 2 College Hill, Westminster, MD 21157
- **Website:** http://www.mcdaniel.edu
- **Private**
- **Enrollment:** 1,660 full-time; 47 part-time

KEY STATS

✔ **U.S News College Ranking:** 122, National Liberal Arts Colleges
✔ **SAT Score (25th/75th percentile):** 1000-1240
✔ **Tuition:** 2010-2011: $33,280

Selectivity: Selective	**Room/board:** $7,060
Acceptance rate: 79%	**Average debt:** $25,325
Student/faculty ratio: 12/1	**Proportion who borrowed:** 63%

UNDERGRADUATE STUDENT BODY STATS

2009-2010 enrollment: 1,660 full-time; 47 part-time. Men: 46%; women: 54%. **Ethnic makeup:** African American: 6%; Asian American: 4%; Hispanic: 3%; White: 86%.

ADMISSIONS FACTS AND FIGURES

Phone: (800) 638-5005. **Email:** admissions@mcdaniel.edu. **Website:** http://www.mcdaniel.edu. **Application deadlines for fall 2011:** Regular decision: February 15; decision sent by April 1. Early decision: Not offered. Early action: Send application by: December 1; Decision sent by: January 1. Admission can be deferred. **Application fee:** $50. **To apply online, go to:** http://www.mcdaniel.edu/263.htm. **Admissions requirements/recommendations:** High school units required (recommended): English: 4 (4); Mathematics: 3 (4); Science: 3 (4); Foreign language: 3 (4); Social studies: 3 (3); Total units: 16 (19). Tests: The college uses SAT or ACT scores in admissions decisions. Either SAT or ACT required. For admission to the fall 2011 entering class, the school will accept: ACT with or without writing accepted. Campus visit: Recommended. Admissions interview: Recommended. Off-campus interview: May be arranged. **Factors that count in admissions decisions:** *Academic:* Secondary school record: Very Important. Class rank: Considered. Letters of recommendation: Important. Standardized test scores: Important. Essay: Important. *Nonacademic:* Interview: Considered. Extracurricular activities: Considered. Talent/ability: Considered. Character/personal qualities: Not Considered. Alumni/ae relationship: Considered. Geographical residence: Not Considered. State residency: Not Considered. Religious affiliation/commitment: Not Considered. Minority status: Not Considered. Volunteer work: Considered. Work experience: Considered. **Admissions statistics for the fall 2009 entering class:** Total applicants: 2,532. Total accepted: 2,006. Freshmen enrolled: 425; 40% were from out of state. Accepted through early-decision or early-action plans: 55%. Overall acceptance rate: 79%. Non-early acceptance rate: 78%. **Size of waiting list:** 49 applicants; enrolled from waiting list: 3. **Credentials of fall 2009 freshmen:** 27% ranked in the top 10 percent of their high school class; 52% were in the top 25 percent; 88% were in the top half. (Proportion submitting class standing: 55%.) **Average high school grade point average:** 3.4. **First-year students who submitted SAT scores:** 93%. Scores (25/75 percentile): Critical Reading: 500-620, Math: 500-620, Combined: 1000-1240. **First-year students submitting ACT scores:** 24%. Scores (25/75 percentile): English: N/A, Math: N/A, Composite: 21-26.

ACADEMICS

Year founded: 1867. **Academic calendar:** 4-1-4. **Degrees offered:** bachelor's, post-bachelor's certificate, master's. **Most popular majors:** 23% social sciences, 14% business, management, marketing, and related support services, 12% psychology, 9% communication, journalism, and related programs, 7% English language and literature/letters. **Major fields of study:** biological and biomedical sciences; business, management, marketing, and related support services; communication, journalism, and related programs; computer and information sciences and support services; English language and literature/letters; foreign languages, literatures, and linguistics; history; mathematics and statistics; multi/interdisciplinary studies; natural resources and conservation; parks, recreation, leisure, and fitness studies; philosophy and religious studies; physical sciences; psychology; public administration and social service professions; social sciences; visual and performing arts. **Areas of required coursework:** arts/fine arts, humanities, mathematics, English (including composition), foreign languages, sciences (biological or physical), history, social science, other. **Pre-professional programs:** pre-law, pre-dentistry, pre-medicine, pre-veterinary science, pre-optometry, pre-pharmacy, other. **Special academic programs (% participation):** accelerated program (8%), double major (18%), dual enrollment (2%), exchange student program (domestic) (3%), honors program (9%), independent study (38%), internships (41%), student-designed major (1%), study abroad (32%), teacher certificate program (5%). **Teacher certification offered in:** elementary, secondary. **Reserve Officers Training Corps (ROTC):** Army ROTC: Offered on campus. **Faculty and instruction (2009-2010):** Total instructional faculty: 103 full-time, 266 part-time (46% men; 54% women; 9% minorities). Full-time faculty with Ph.D. or other terminal degree: 98%. Student/faculty ratio: 12/1. Classes of fewer than 20 students: 67%; of 20 to 49 students: 33%; of 50 or more students: 0%. **Advanced Placement and International Baccalaureate credit:** AP tests may be used for: Credit and/or placement. Scores accepted: 4, 5. International Baccalaureate exams may be used for: Credit and/or placement. **Freshmen returning for sophomore year:** 84%. **Graduation rates:** Four-year: 62%; five-year: 70%; six-year: 70%. **Graduate study:** 37% of students pursue further study within one year. Fields in which graduates pursue further study: Master of Business Administration (MBA), 5%; law, 7%; medicine, 7%; theology (or the seminary), 2%; education, 14%; arts and sciences, 12%; veterinary medicine, 2%.

COSTS AND FINANCIAL AID

Financial aid office: (410) 857-2233. **Expenses (2010-2011):** Tuition and fees 2010-2011: $33,280; room/board: $7,060. Estimated books and supplies: $1,200; transportation: $500; personal expenses: $1,000. **Financial aid:** Priority filing date for institution's financial aid form: March 1. In 2009-2010, 78% of undergraduates applied for financial aid. Of those, 69% were determined to have financial need; 30% had their need fully met. Average financial aid package (proportion receiving): $24,842 (69%). Average amount of gift aid, such as scholarships or grants (proportion receiving): $17,794 (67%). Average amount of self-help aid, such as work study or loans (proportion receiving): $5,707 (60%). Average need-based loan (excluding PLUS or other private loans): $4,879. Among students who received need-based aid, the average percentage of need met: 97%. Among students who received aid based on merit, the average award (and the proportion receiving): $12,939 (22%). The average athletic scholarship (and the proportion receiving): $0 (0%). Average amount of debt of borrowers graduating in 2009: $25,325. Proportion who borrowed: 63%.

CAMPUS LIFE AND EXTRACURRICULAR ACTIVITIES

Campus housing available (% using): coed dorms (31%), women's dorms (16%), men's dorms (14%), sorority housing (7%), fraternity housing (3%), apartment for single students (23%), other housing options (6%). Students who live in college-owned, operated, or affiliated housing: 79%. **Student employment:** During the 2009-2010 academic year, 18% of undergraduates worked on campus. Average per-year earnings: $1,442. **Clubs and organizations:** Number of student organizations: 132. Activities include: campus ministries, choral groups, concert band, dance, drama/theater, jazz band, literary magazine, music ensembles, musical theater, radio station, student government, student newspaper, symphony orchestra, television station, yearbook. Number of fraternities: 5; sororities: 4. Proportion of men in fraternities: 13%; of women in sororities: 14%. Average proportion of students who stay on campus on weekends: 75%. **Sports program (2009-2010):** Member of NCAA III. *Men's intercollegiate varsity sports:* baseball, basketball, cross country, football, golf, lacrosse, soccer, swimming, track and field (indoor), track and field (outdoor). *Women's intercollegiate varsity sports:* basketball, cross country, field hockey, golf, lacrosse, soccer, softball, swimming, track and field (indoor), track and field (outdoor), volleyball.

SERVICES AND FACILITIES

Basic services: nonremedial tutoring, placement service, health service, health insurance. **Remedial assistance:** math, writing. **Counseling services:** minority student, career, personal, academic, birth control. **For learning-disabled students:** School does not offer a structured program with separate admission and additional fees. Total undergraduates in learning-disabled program or receiving services: 179. Services include: remedial math, remedial English, reading machines, tape recorders, note-taking services, learning center, readers, extended time for tests, tutors, texts on tape. **Library:** Number of titles: 440,760; number of current serial subscriptions: 21,549. **Information technology resources:** Students are not required to lease or own a computer. Number of campus computers available to all students: 340. School has a wireless network. Approximate number of users that can be accommodated: 600. Proportion of college-owned housing units wired for high-speed internet access: 100%. **Campus safety:** Security services offered: 24-hour foot-and-vehicle patrols, late-night transport/escort service, 24-hour emergency telephones, lighted pathways/sidewalks, controlled dormitory access (key, security card, etc).

TRANSFER AND INTERNATIONAL STUDENTS

Transfer students: May apply for admission for the following academic terms: Fall, Spring. Applicants need a minimum number of credits to apply. For fall 2009: Transfer applications received: 158. Transfer applicants offered admission: 95. Transfer applicants enrolled: 53. **International students:** Number of foreign undergraduates: 7. Number of countries represented: 16. Minimum TOEFL score required: 550 (paper); 213 (computer). Average TOEFL score: 550 (paper).

Morgan State University

- **Address:** 1700 E. Cold Spring Lane, Baltimore, MD 21251
- **Website:** http://www.morgan.edu
- **Public**
- **Enrollment:** 5,572 full-time; 627 part-time

KEY STATS

✔ **U.S News College Ranking:** second tier, National Universities
✔ **SAT Score (25th/75th percentile):** 830-980
✔ **Tuition:** 2009-2010: $6,548 in state, $15,418 out of state

Selectivity: Less selective	Room/board: $8,340
Acceptance rate: 32%	Average debt: $32,582
Student/faculty ratio: 14/1	Proportion who borrowed: 87%

UNDERGRADUATE STUDENT BODY STATS

2009-2010 enrollment: 5,572 full-time; 627 part-time. Men: 44%; women: 56%. **Ethnic makeup:** African American: 93%; Asian American: 1%; Hispanic: 1%; White: 2%; International: 4%.

ADMISSIONS FACTS AND FIGURES

Phone: (800) 332-6674. **Website:** http://www.morgan.edu. **Application deadlines for fall 2011:** Regular decision: Rolling. Early decision: Not offered. Early action: Send application by: N/A; Decision sent by: N/A. Admission can be deferred. **Application fee:** $35. **To apply online, go to:** http://www.morgan.edu/admin/admission/admission.asp. **Admissions requirements/recommendations:** High school units required (recommended): English: 4 (4); Mathematics: 3 (3); Science: 3 (3); Foreign language: 2 (2); Social studies: 3 (3); History: 3 (3); Academic electives: 3 (3); Total units: 21 (21). Tests: The college uses SAT or ACT scores in admissions decisions. Either SAT or ACT required. For admission to the fall 2011 entering class, the school will accept: ACT with or without writing accepted. Campus visit: Recommended. Admissions interview: Neither required nor recommended. Off-campus interview: May be arranged. **Factors that count in admissions decisions:** *Academic:* Secondary school record: Considered. Class rank: Considered. Letters of recommendation: Very Important. Standardized test scores: Considered. Essay: Important. *Nonacademic:* Interview: Not Considered. Extracurricular activities: Considered. Talent/ability: Important. Character/personal qualities: Considered. Alumni/ae relationship: Considered. Geographical residence: Important. State residency: Important. Religious affiliation/commitment: Not Considered. Minority status: Not Considered. Volunteer work: Considered. Work experience: Considered. **Other schools with the greatest overlap in applicants:** Bowie State University; Hampton University; Howard University; North Carolina A&T State University; University of Maryland–Eastern Shore. **Admissions**

statistics for the fall 2009 entering class: Total applicants: 12,154. Total accepted: 3,864. Freshmen enrolled: 1,283; 7% were from out of state. Overall acceptance rate: 32%. Non-early acceptance rate: 32%. **Average high school grade point average:** 2.8. **First-year students who submitted SAT scores:** 89%. Scores (25/75 percentile): Critical Reading: 420-490, Math: 410-490, Combined: 830-980.

ACADEMICS

Year founded: 1867. **Academic calendar:** Semester. **Degrees offered:** bachelor's, master's, doctorate. **Most popular majors:** 26% business, management, marketing, and related support services, 11% communication, journalism, and related programs, 9% engineering, 8% biological and biomedical sciences, 8% education. **Major fields of study:** architecture and related services; area, ethnic, cultural, and gender studies; biological and biomedical sciences; business, management, marketing, and related support services; communication, journalism, and related programs; computer and information sciences and support services; education; engineering; English language and literature/letters; family and consumer sciences/human sciences; history; mathematics and statistics; philosophy and religious studies; physical sciences; psychology; social sciences; visual and performing arts. **Areas of required coursework:** humanities, mathematics, English (including composition), foreign languages, sciences (biological or physical), history, social science. **Pre-professional programs:** pre-law, pre-dentistry, pre-medicine, pre-theology, pre-veterinary science, pre-optometry, pre-pharmacy. **Special academic programs:** cooperative (work-study plan) program, cross-registration, double major, dual enrollment, honors program, independent study, internships, liberal arts/career combination, teacher certificate program, weekend college. **Teacher certification offered in:** elementary, secondary. **Cooperative education programs:** art, business, computer science, education, engineering, health professions, home economics, humanities, natural science, social/behavioral science, technologies. **Reserve Officers Training Corps (ROTC):** Army ROTC: Offered on campus. **Faculty and instruction (2009-2010):** Total instructional faculty: 440 full-time, 109 part-time (58% men; 42% women; 78% minorities). Full-time faculty with Ph.D. or other terminal degree: 67%. Student/faculty ratio: 14/1. **Advanced Placement and International Baccalaureate credit:** AP tests may be used for: Placement only. Scores accepted: 3, 4, 5. International Baccalaureate exams may be used for: Placement only. **Freshmen returning for sophomore year:** 67%. **Graduation rates:** Four-year: 11%; five-year: 26%; six-year: 33%. **Graduate study:** 39% of students pursue further study within one year.

COSTS AND FINANCIAL AID

Financial aid office: (443) 885-3170. **Expenses (2009-2010):** Tuition and fees 2009-2010: $6,548 in state, $15,418 out of state; room/board: $8,340. Estimated books and supplies: $721; transportation: $361; personal expenses: $2,369. **Financial aid:** In 2009-2010, 77% of undergraduates applied for financial aid. Of those, 74% were determined to have financial need; 15% had their need fully met. Average financial aid package (proportion receiving): $17,329 (74%). Average amount of gift aid, such as scholarships or grants (proportion receiving): $3,832 (54%). Average amount of self-help aid, such as work study or loans (proportion receiving): $4,288 (43%). Average need-based loan (excluding PLUS or other private loans): $4,030. Among students who received need-based aid, the average percentage of need met: 49%. Among students who received aid based on merit, the average award (and the proportion receiving): $6,746 (1%). The average athletic scholarship (and the proportion receiving): $12,813 (4%). Average amount of debt of borrowers graduating in 2009: $32,582. Proportion who borrowed: 87%.

CAMPUS LIFE AND EXTRACURRICULAR ACTIVITIES

Campus housing available (% using): coed dorms (43%), women's dorms (29%), men's dorms (23%), apartment for single students, special housing for disabled students (5%). Students who live in college-owned, operated, or affiliated housing: 33%. **Student employment:** During the 2009-2010 academic year, 6% of undergraduates worked on campus. Average per-year earnings: $2,500. **Clubs and organizations:** Number of student organizations: 61. Activities include: choral groups, concert band, dance, drama/theater, jazz band, marching band, music ensembles, musical theater, radio station, student government, student newspaper, student film society, yearbook. Number of fraternities: 4; sororities: 5. Average proportion of students who stay on campus on weekends: 55%. **Sports program (2009-2010):** Member of NCAA I.

SERVICES AND FACILITIES

Basic services: nonremedial tutoring, placement service, day care, health service, health insurance. **Remedial assistance:** reading, math, writing, study skills. **Counseling services:** minority student, career, personal, academic, psychological. **For learning-disabled students:** School does not offer a structured program with separate admission and additional fees. Services include: remedial math, remedial English, remedial reading, tape recorders, other special classes, note-taking services, oral tests, learning center, readers, extended time for tests, tutors, priority registration, priority seating, other testing accommodations. **Library:** Number of titles: 303,917; number of current serial subscriptions: 1,684. **Information technology resources:** Students are not required to lease or own a computer. School has a wireless network. Approximate number of users that can be accommodated: 1,500. Proportion of college-owned housing units wired for high-speed internet access: 100%. **Campus safety:** Security services offered: 24-hour foot-and-vehicle patrols, late-night transport/escort service, 24-hour emergency telephones, lighted pathways/sidewalks, controlled dormitory access (key, security card, etc).

TRANSFER AND INTERNATIONAL STUDENTS

Transfer students: May apply for admission for the following academic terms: Fall, Spring. Applicants need a minimum number of credits to apply. For fall 2009: Transfer applications received: 1,687. Transfer applicants offered admission: 782. Transfer applicants enrolled: 451. **International students:** Number of foreign undergraduates: 218 (4% of student body). Number of countries represented: 32. Minimum TOEFL score required: 550 (paper).

Mount St. Mary's University

- **Address:** 16300 Old Emmitsburg Road, Emmitsburg, MD 21727
- **Website:** http://www.msmary.edu
- **Private; Religious affiliation:** Roman Catholic
- **Enrollment:** 1,501 full-time; 119 part-time

KEY STATS

✔ **U.S News College Ranking:** 22, Regional Universities (North)
✔ **SAT Score (25th/75th percentile):** 930-1170
✔ **Tuition:** 2010-2011: $30,350

Selectivity: Selective	**Room/board:** $10,308
Acceptance rate: 84%	**Average debt:** $26,160
Student/faculty ratio: 13/1	**Proportion who borrowed:** 67%

UNDERGRADUATE STUDENT BODY STATS

2009-2010 enrollment: 1,501 full-time; 119 part-time. Men: 42%; women: 58%. **Ethnic makeup:** African American: 8%; American-Indian: 1%; Asian American: 3%; Hispanic: 6%; White: 82%; International: 1%.

ADMISSIONS FACTS AND FIGURES

Phone: (800) 448-4347. **Email:** admissions@msmary.edu. **Website:** http://www.msmary.edu. **Application deadlines for fall 2011:** Regular decision: Rolling. Early decision: Not offered. Early action: Send application by: December 1; Decision sent by: December 15. Admission can be deferred. **Application fee:** $35. **To apply online, go to:** http://www.msmary.edu/admissions/apply/index.html. **Admissions requirements/recommendations:** High school units required (recommended): English: 4; Mathematics: 3; Science: 3; Foreign language: 2; Social studies: 3; Academic electives: 1; Total units: 16. Tests: The college uses SAT or ACT scores in admissions decisions. Either SAT or ACT required. For admission to the fall 2011 entering class, the school will accept: ACT with or without writing accepted. Campus visit: Recommended. Admissions interview: Recommended. Off-campus interview: May be arranged. **Factors that count in admissions decisions:** *Academic:* Secondary school record: Very Important. Class rank: Important. Letters of recommendation: Considered. Standardized test scores: Important. Essay: Considered. *Nonacademic:* Interview: Considered. Extracurricular activities: Important. Talent/ability: Important. Character/personal qualities: Considered. Alumni/ae relationship: Considered. Geographical residence: Not Considered. State residency: Not Considered. Religious affiliation/commitment: Not Considered. Minority status: Not Considered. Volunteer work: Considered. Work experience: Considered. **Other schools with the greatest overlap in applicants:** Catholic University of America; Loyola University Maryland; Salisbury University; Towson University; University of Maryland–College Park. **Admissions statistics for the fall 2009 entering class:** Total applicants: 2,963. Total accepted: 2,497. Freshmen enrolled: 465; 45% were from out of state. Accepted through early-decision or early-action plans: 14%. Overall acceptance rate: 84%.

Non-early acceptance rate: 84%. **Credentials of fall 2009 freshmen:** 21% ranked in the top 10 percent of their high school class; 45% were in the top 25 percent; 78% were in the top half. (Proportion submitting class standing: 56%.) **Average high school grade point average:** 3.1. **First-year students who submitted SAT scores:** 91%. Scores (25/75 percentile): Critical Reading: 470-580, Math: 460-590, Combined: 930-1170. **First-year students submitting ACT scores:** 8%. Scores (25/75 percentile): English: 19-24, Math: 17-23, Composite: 20-25.

ACADEMICS

Year founded: 1808. **Academic calendar:** Semester. **Degrees offered:** bachelor's, post-bachelor's certificate, master's, post-master's certificate. **Most popular majors:** 18% business/commerce, 10% elementary education and teaching, 8% accounting, 8% biology/biological sciences, 8% communication studies/speech communication and rhetoric. **Major fields of study:** biological and biomedical sciences; business, management, marketing, and related support services; communication, journalism, and related programs; computer and information sciences and support services; education; English language and literature/letters; foreign languages, literatures, and linguistics; history; mathematics and statistics; multi/interdisciplinary studies; parks, recreation, leisure, and fitness studies; philosophy and religious studies; physical sciences; psychology; security and protective services; social sciences; theology and religious vocations; visual and performing arts. **Areas of required coursework:** arts/fine arts, humanities, mathematics, English (including composition), philosophy, foreign languages, sciences (biological or physical), history, social science, other. **Pre-professional programs:** pre-law, pre-medicine, pre-theology. **Special academic programs:** accelerated program, cross-registration, double major, dual enrollment, honors program, independent study, internships, liberal arts/career combination, student-designed major, study abroad, teacher certificate program, weekend college, other. **Teacher certification offered in:** special education, elementary, middle/junior high, secondary. **Reserve Officers Training Corps (ROTC):** Army ROTC: Offered at cooperating institution (McDaniel College). **Faculty and instruction (2009-2010):** Total instructional faculty: 112 full-time, 75 part-time (56% men; 44% women; 5% minorities). Full-time faculty with Ph.D. or other terminal degree: 86%. Student/faculty ratio: 13/1. Classes of fewer than 20 students: 48%; of 20 to 49 students: 51%; of 50 or more students: 1%. **Advanced Placement and International Baccalaureate credit:** AP tests may be used for: Credit and/or placement. Scores accepted: 3, 4, 5. International Baccalaureate exams may be used for: Credit only. **Freshmen returning for sophomore year:** 80%. **Graduation rates:** Four-year: 70%; five-year: 73%; six-year: 68%. **Graduate study:** 30% of students pursue further study within one year. Fields in which graduates pursue further study: Master of Business Administration (MBA), 6%; law, 1%; medicine, 2%; education, 6%; arts and sciences, 15%.

COSTS AND FINANCIAL AID

Financial aid office: (301) 447-5207. **Expenses (2010-2011):** Tuition and fees 2010-2011: $30,350; room/board: $10,308. Estimated books and supplies: $1,000; transportation: $300; personal expenses: $500. **Financial aid:** In 2009-2010, 78% of undergraduates applied for financial aid. Of those, 66% were determined to have financial need; 24% had their need fully met. Average financial aid package (proportion receiving): $18,996 (66%). Average amount of gift aid, such as scholarships or grants (proportion receiving): $14,784 (65%). Average amount of self-help aid, such as work study or loans (proportion receiving): $5,248 (54%). Average need-based loan (excluding PLUS or other private loans): $4,434. Among students who received need-based aid, the average percentage of need met: 72%. Among students who received aid based on merit, the average award (and the proportion receiving): $9,586 (32%). The average athletic scholarship (and the proportion receiving): $10,693 (10%). Average amount of debt of borrowers graduating in 2009: $26,160. Proportion who borrowed: 67%.

CAMPUS LIFE AND EXTRACURRICULAR ACTIVITIES

Campus housing available: coed dorms, apartment for single students, special housing for disabled students, other housing options. Students who live in college-owned, operated, or affiliated housing: 84%. **Student employment:** During the 2009-2010 academic year, 26% of undergraduates worked on campus. Average per-year earnings: $1,068. **Clubs and organizations:** Number of student organizations: 70. Activities include: campus ministries, choral groups, concert band, dance, drama/theater, international student organization, jazz band, literary magazine, music ensembles, musical theater, pep band, radio station, student government, student newspaper, television station, yearbook. Number of fraternities: 0; sororities: 0. Average proportion of students who stay on campus on weekends: 80%. **Sports program (2009-2010):** Member of NCAA I. *Men's intercollegiate varsity* *sports:* baseball, basketball, cross country, golf, lacrosse, soccer, tennis, track and field (indoor), track and field (outdoor). *Women's intercollegiate varsity sports:* basketball, cross country, golf, lacrosse, soccer, softball, swimming, tennis, track and field (indoor), track and field (outdoor).

SERVICES AND FACILITIES

Basic services: nonremedial tutoring, health service, health insurance. **Remedial assistance:** math, writing, study skills. **Counseling services:** minority student, career, personal, academic, psychological, religious. **For learning-disabled students:** School does not offer a structured program with separate admission and additional fees. Services include: remedial math, reading machines, note-taking services, oral tests, learning center, readers, extended time for tests, tutors, priority seating, texts on tape, other testing accommodations. **Library:** Number of titles: 216,740; number of current serial subscriptions: 912. **Information technology resources:** Students are not required to lease or own a computer. Number of campus computers available to all students: 100. School has a wireless network. Approximate number of users that can be accommodated: 2,500. Proportion of college-owned housing units wired for high-speed internet access: 100%. **Campus safety:** Security services offered: 24-hour foot-and-vehicle patrols, late-night transport/escort service, 24-hour emergency telephones, lighted pathways/sidewalks, controlled dormitory access (key, security card, etc).

TRANSFER AND INTERNATIONAL STUDENTS

Transfer students: May apply for admission for the following academic terms: Fall, Spring, Summer. Applicants do not need a minimum number of credits to apply. For fall 2009: Transfer applications received: 145. Transfer applicants offered admission: 79. Transfer applicants enrolled: 35. **International students:** Number of foreign undergraduates: 16 (1% of student body). Number of countries represented: 13. Minimum TOEFL score required: 550 (paper); 213 (computer).

Salisbury University

- Address: 1101 Camden Avenue, Salisbury, MD 21801
- Website: http://www.salisbury.edu/
- Public
- Enrollment: 6,954 full-time; 603 part-time

KEY STATS

✔ U.S News College Ranking: 46, Regional Universities (North)
✔ SAT Score (25th/75th percentile): 1040-1220
✔ Tuition: 2009-2010: $6,618 in state, $15,114 out of state

Selectivity: Selective	Room/board: $7,910
Acceptance rate: 54%	Average debt: $17,521
Student/faculty ratio: 17/1	Proportion who borrowed: 56%

UNDERGRADUATE STUDENT BODY STATS

2009-2010 enrollment: 6,954 full-time; 603 part-time. Men: 45%; women: 55%. **Ethnic makeup:** African American: 11%; American-Indian: 1%; Asian American: 3%; Hispanic: 3%; White: 82%; International: 1%.

ADMISSIONS FACTS AND FIGURES

Phone: (410) 543-6161. **Email:** admissions@salisbury.edu. **Website:** http://www.salisbury.edu/. **Application deadlines for fall 2011:** Regular decision: Rolling; decision sent by March 15. Early decision: Not offered. Early action: Send application by: December 1; Decision sent by: January 15. Admission cannot be deferred. **Application fee:** $45. **To apply online, go to:** http://www.salisbury.edu/admissions/applications/welcome.html. **Admissions requirements/recommendations:** High school units required (recommended): English: 4 (4); Mathematics: 3 (4); Science: 3 (4); Foreign language: 2 (3); Social studies: 3 (3); Academic electives: (3); Total units: 15 (21). Tests: The college uses SAT or ACT scores in admissions decisions. Neither SAT nor ACT required. For admission to the fall 2011 entering class, the school will accept: ACT with or without writing accepted. Campus visit: Recommended. Admissions interview: Neither required nor recommended. Off-campus interview: Not available. **Factors that count in admissions decisions:** *Academic:* Secondary school record: Very Important. Class rank: Important. Letters of recommendation: Considered. Standardized test scores: Important. Essay: Considered. *Nonacademic:* Interview: Not Considered. Extracurricular activities: Very Important. Talent/ability: Very Important. Character/personal qualities: Considered. Alumni/ae relationship: Important. Geographical residence: Important. State residency:

Not Considered. Religious affiliation/commitment: Not Considered. Minority status: Considered. Volunteer work: Important. Work experience: Considered. **Other schools with the greatest overlap in applicants:** Frostburg State University; St. Mary's College of Maryland; Towson University; University of Maryland–Baltimore County; University of Maryland–College Park. **Admissions statistics for the fall 2009 entering class:** Total applicants: 7,525. Total accepted: 4,026. Freshmen enrolled: 1,276; 16% were from out of state. Overall acceptance rate: 54%. Non-early acceptance rate: 54%. **Credentials of fall 2009 freshmen:** 23% ranked in the top 10 percent of their high school class; 58% were in the top 25 percent; 91% were in the top half. (Proportion submitting class standing: 51%.) **Average high school grade point average:** 3.6. **First-year students who submitted SAT scores:** 72%. Scores (25/75 percentile): Critical Reading: 520-600, Math: 520-620, Combined: 1040-1220. **First-year students submitting ACT scores:** 12%. Scores (25/75 percentile): English: 21-25, Math: 20-24, Composite: 21-26.

ACADEMICS

Year founded: 1925. **Academic calendar:** 4-1-4. **Degrees offered:** bachelor's, post-bachelor's certificate, master's, post-master's certificate. **Most popular majors:** 10% communication studies/speech communication and rhetoric, 6% business administration and management, 6% elementary education and teaching, 6% marketing/marketing management, 6% psychology. **Major fields of study:** biological and biomedical sciences; business, management, marketing, and related support services; communication, journalism, and related programs; computer and information sciences and support services; education; English language and literature/letters; foreign languages, literatures, and linguistics; health professions and related clinical sciences; history; liberal arts and sciences studies, and humanities; mathematics and statistics; multi/interdisciplinary studies; natural resources and conservation; parks, recreation, leisure, and fitness studies; philosophy and religious studies; physical sciences; psychology; public administration and social service professions; social sciences; visual and performing arts. **Areas of required coursework:** arts/fine arts, humanities, computer literacy, mathematics, English (including composition), sciences (biological or physical), history, social science, other. **Pre-professional programs:** pre-law, pre-dentistry, pre-medicine, pre-veterinary science, pre-optometry, pre-pharmacy, other. **Special academic programs:** accelerated program, cross-registration, distance learning, double major, dual enrollment, English as a Second Language (ESL), honors program, independent study, internships, liberal arts/career combination, student-designed major, study abroad, teacher certificate program. **Teacher certification offered in:** early childhood, elementary, secondary. **Reserve Officers Training Corps (ROTC):** Army ROTC: Offered on campus; Air Force ROTC: Offered at cooperating institution (University of Delaware). **Faculty and instruction (2009-2010):** Total instructional faculty: 380 full-time, 191 part-time (49% men; 51% women; 10% minorities). Full-time faculty with Ph.D. or other terminal degree: 85%. Student/faculty ratio: 17/1. Classes of fewer than 20 students: 32%; of 20 to 49 students: 64%; of 50 or more students: 4%. **Advanced Placement and International Baccalaureate credit:** AP tests may be used for: Credit and/or placement. Scores accepted: 3. International Baccalaureate exams may be used for: Placement only. **Freshmen returning for sophomore year:** 81%. **Graduation rates:** Four-year: 46%; five-year: 63%; six-year: 68%. **Graduate study:** 24% of students pursue further study within one year. Fields in which graduates pursue further study: Master of Business Administration (MBA), 2%; law, 1%; arts and sciences, 20%.

COSTS AND FINANCIAL AID

Financial aid office: (410) 543-6165. **Expenses (2009-2010):** Tuition and fees 2009-2010: $6,618 in state, $15,114 out of state; room/board: $7,910. Estimated books and supplies: $1,300; transportation: $1,200; personal expenses: $1,500. **Financial aid:** Priority filing date for institution's financial aid form: March 1; deadline: December 31. In 2009-2010, 66% of undergraduates applied for financial aid. Of those, 42% were determined to have financial need; 20% had their need fully met. Average financial aid package (proportion receiving): $7,027 (40%). Average amount of gift aid, such as scholarships or grants (proportion receiving): $5,256 (31%). Average amount of self-help aid, such as work study or loans (proportion receiving): $3,809 (33%). Average need-based loan (excluding PLUS or other private loans): $3,764. Among students who received need-based aid, the average percentage of need met: 60%. Among students who received aid based on merit, the average award (and the proportion receiving): $2,225 (8%). Average amount of debt of borrowers graduating in 2009: $17,521. Proportion who borrowed: 56%.

CAMPUS LIFE AND EXTRACURRICULAR ACTIVITIES

Campus housing available (% using): coed dorms (82%), women's dorms (5%), men's dorms (5%), apartment for single students (8%). Students who live in college-owned, operated, or affiliated housing: 36%. **Student employment:** During the 2009-2010 academic year, 16% of undergraduates worked on campus. Average per-year earnings: $2,500. **Clubs and organizations:** Number of student organizations: 126. Activities include: campus ministries, choral groups, concert band, dance, drama/theater, jazz band, literary magazine, music ensembles, musical theater, pep band, radio station, student government, student newspaper, student film society, symphony orchestra, television station. Number of fraternities: 8; sororities: 4. Proportion of men in fraternities: 6%; of women in sororities: 4%. **Sports program (2009-2010):** Member of NCAA III. *Men's intercollegiate varsity sports:* baseball, basketball, cross country, football, lacrosse, soccer, swimming, tennis, track and field (outdoor). *Women's intercollegiate varsity sports:* basketball, cross country, field hockey, lacrosse, soccer, softball, swimming, tennis, track and field (outdoor), volleyball.

SERVICES AND FACILITIES

Basic services: nonremedial tutoring, health service. **Counseling services:** minority student, career, personal, veteran student, academic, psychological. **For learning-disabled students:** School does not offer a structured program with separate admission and additional fees. Services include: reading machines, tape recorders, note-taking services, oral tests, learning center, readers, extended time for tests, tutors, priority seating. **Library:** Number of titles: 442,682; number of current serial subscriptions: 1,241. **Information technology resources:** Students are not required to lease or own a computer. Number of campus computers available to all students: 423. School has a wireless network. Approximate number of users that can be accommodated: 2,500. Proportion of college-owned housing units wired for high-speed internet access: 100%. **Campus safety:** Security services offered: 24-hour foot-and-vehicle patrols, late-night transport/escort service, 24-hour emergency telephones, lighted pathways/sidewalks, controlled dormitory access (key, security card, etc).

TRANSFER AND INTERNATIONAL STUDENTS

Transfer students: May apply for admission for the following academic terms: Fall, Spring. Applicants need a minimum number of credits to apply. For fall 2009: Transfer applications received: 2,026. Transfer applicants offered admission: 1,495. Transfer applicants enrolled: 866. **International students:** Number of foreign undergraduates: 41 (1% of student body). Number of countries represented: 46. Minimum TOEFL score required: 550 (paper); 213 (computer). Average TOEFL score: 617 (paper).

Sojourner-Douglass College

- **Address:** 500 N. Caroline Street, Baltimore, MD 21205
- **Website:** http://www.sdc.edu/
- **Private**
- **Enrollment:** N/A

KEY STATS
- ✔ **U.S News College Ranking:** Unranked, Regional Colleges (North)
- ✔ **SAT or ACT Score (25th/75th percentile):** N/A
- ✔ **Tuition:** 2009-2010: $7,920

Selectivity: N/A	Room/board: N/A
Acceptance rate: N/A	Average debt: N/A
Student/faculty ratio: N/A	Proportion who borrowed: N/A

Stevenson University

- **Address:** 1525 Greenspring Valley Road, Stevenson, MD 21153
- **Website:** http://www.stevenson.edu/
- **Private**
- **Enrollment:** 2,619 full-time; 557 part-time

KEY STATS
- ✔ **U.S News College Ranking:** 11, Regional Colleges (North)
- ✔ **SAT Score (25th/75th percentile):** 900-1120
- ✔ **Tuition:** 2010-2011: $22,090

Selectivity: Selective	Room/board: $10,826
Acceptance rate: 57%	Average debt: $20,779
Student/faculty ratio: 15/1	Proportion who borrowed: 65%

UNDERGRADUATE STUDENT BODY STATS

2009-2010 enrollment: 2,619 full-time; 557 part-time. Men: 30%; women: 70%. **Ethnic makeup:** African American: 17%; American-Indian: 1%; Asian American: 3%; Hispanic: 2%; White: 78%. **Religious preference:** Roman Catholic: 28%; Jewish: 3%; Muslim: 1%; Hindu: 1%; Buddhist: 1%; No preference: 17%; Other: 49%.

ADMISSIONS FACTS AND FIGURES

Phone: (410) 486-7001. **Email:** admissions@stevenson.edu. **Website:** http://www.stevenson.edu/. **Application deadlines for fall 2011:** Regular decision: Rolling. Early decision: Not offered. Early action: Not offered. Admission can be deferred. **Application fee:** $40. **To apply online, go to:** http://www.stevenson.edu/admissions/application/apply.asp. **Admissions requirements/recommendations:** High school units required (recommended): English: 4 (4); Mathematics: 3 (3); Science: 3 (3); Foreign language: 0 (2); Social studies: 2 (2); History: 1 (1); Academic electives: 4 (4); Total units: 17 (17). Tests: The college uses SAT or ACT scores in admissions decisions. Either SAT or ACT required. For admission to the fall 2011 entering class, the school will accept: ACT with or without writing accepted. Campus visit: Recommended. Admissions interview: Recommended. Off-campus interview: May be arranged. **Factors that count in admissions decisions:** *Academic:* Secondary school record: Very Important. Class rank: Considered. Letters of recommendation: Considered. Standardized test scores: Important. Essay: Important. *Nonacademic:* Interview: Considered. Extracurricular activities: Important. Talent/ability: Important. Character/personal qualities: Considered. Alumni/ae relationship: Considered. Geographical residence: Considered. State residency: Not Considered. Religious affiliation/commitment: Not Considered. Minority status: Not Considered. Volunteer work: Considered. Work experience: Considered. **Other schools with the greatest overlap in applicants:** Frostburg State University; Salisbury University; Towson University; University of Maryland–College Park; York College of Pennsylvania. **Admissions statistics for the fall 2009 entering class:** Total applicants: 4,107. Total accepted: 2,345. Freshmen enrolled: 527; 14% were from out of state. Overall acceptance rate: 57%. **Credentials of fall 2009 freshmen:** 16% ranked in the top 10 percent of their high school class; 39% were in the top 25 percent; 79% were in the top half. (Proportion submitting class standing: 76%.) **Average high school grade point average:** 3.4. **First-year students who submitted SAT scores:** 97%. Scores (25/75 percentile): Critical Reading: 450-560, Math: 450-560, Combined: 900-1120. **First-year students submitting ACT scores:** 14%. Scores (25/75 percentile): English: 16-21, Math: 17-23, Composite: 18-22.

ACADEMICS

Year founded: 1947. **Academic calendar:** Semester. **Degrees offered:** bachelor's, master's. **Most popular majors:** 24% business, management, marketing, and related support services, 19% health professions and related clinical sciences, 9% visual and performing arts, 8% computer and information sciences and support services, 8% education. **Major fields of study:** biological and biomedical sciences; business, management, marketing, and related support services; computer and information sciences and support services; education; English language and literature/letters; family and consumer sciences/human sciences; health professions and related clinical sciences; history; legal professions and studies; mathematics and statistics; multi/interdisciplinary studies; physical sciences; psychology; visual and performing arts. **Areas of required coursework:** arts/fine arts, humanities, computer literacy, mathematics, English (including composition), philosophy, sciences (biological or physical), history, social science. **Pre-professional programs:** pre-law, pre-dentistry, pre-medicine, pre-veterinary science, pre-optometry, pre-pharmacy. **Special academic programs (% participation): accelerated program (20%), cooperative (work-study plan) program, cross-registration, distance learning (15%), double major (2%), dual enrollment, honors program (1%), independent study (7%), internships (91%), liberal arts/career combination (100%), student-designed major (7%), study abroad (1%), teacher certificate program (8%). **Teacher certification offered in:** early childhood, elementary, middle/junior high. **Cooperative education programs:** art, business, computer science, education, health professions, humanities, natural science, social/behavioral science, technologies, other. **Reserve Officers Training Corps (ROTC):** Army ROTC: Offered at cooperating institution (Johns Hopkins University). **Faculty and instruction (2009-2010):** Total instructional faculty: 110 full-time, 239 part-time (48% men; 52% women; 10% minorities). Full-time faculty with Ph.D. or other terminal degree: 65%. Student/faculty ratio: 15/1. Classes of fewer than 20 students: 67%; of 20 to 49 students: 33%; of 50 or more students: 0%. **Advanced Placement and International Baccalaureate credit:** AP tests may be used for: Placement only. Scores accepted: 3, 4, 5. International Baccalaureate exams may be used for: Placement only. **Freshmen returning for sophomore year:** 80%. **Graduation rates:** Four-year: 46%; five-year: 56%; six-year: 62%. **Graduate study:** 17% of students pursue further study within one year. Fields in which graduates pursue further study: Master of Business Administration (MBA), 28%; law, 8%; medicine, 8%; dentistry, 3%; education, 12%; arts and sciences, 41%.

COSTS AND FINANCIAL AID

Financial aid office: (443) 334-2559. **Expenses (2010-2011):** Tuition and fees 2010-2011: $22,090; room/board: $10,826. Estimated books and supplies: $1,250; transportation: $960. **Financial aid:** Priority filing date for institution's financial aid form: February 15. In 2009-2010, 80% of undergraduates applied for financial aid. Of those, 69% were determined to have financial need; 29% had their need fully met. Average financial aid package (proportion receiving): $14,124 (68%). Average amount of gift aid, such as scholarships or grants (proportion receiving): $10,967 (64%). Average amount of self-help aid, such as work study or loans (proportion receiving): $4,435 (51%). Average need-based loan (excluding PLUS or other private loans): $4,095. Among students who received need-based aid, the average percentage of need met: 63%. Among students who received aid based on merit, the average award (and the proportion receiving): $6,920 (21%). The average athletic scholarship (and the proportion receiving): $0 (0%). Average amount of debt of borrowers graduating in 2009: $20,779. Proportion who borrowed: 65%.

CAMPUS LIFE AND EXTRACURRICULAR ACTIVITIES

Campus housing available (% using): apartment for single students (42%), other housing options (58%). Students who live in college-owned, operated, or affiliated housing: 41%. **Student employment:** During the 2009-2010 academic year, 20% of undergraduates worked on campus. Average per-year earnings: $2,000. **Clubs and organizations:** Number of student organizations: 40. Activities include: campus ministries, choral groups, dance, drama/theater, jazz band, literary magazine, music ensembles, pep band, student government, student newspaper, symphony orchestra. Number of fraternities: 0; sororities: 2. of women in sororities: 2%. Average proportion of students who stay on campus on weekends: 40%. **Sports program (2009-2010):** Member of NCAA III. *Men's intercollegiate varsity sports:* baseball, basketball, cross country, golf, lacrosse, soccer, tennis, volleyball. *Women's intercollegiate varsity sports:* basketball, cross country, field hockey, golf, lacrosse, soccer, softball, tennis, volleyball.

SERVICES AND FACILITIES

Basic services: nonremedial tutoring, placement service, health service, other. **Remedial assistance:** reading, math, writing, study skills, other. **Counseling services:** minority student, career, military, personal, veteran student, academic, older student, psychological, birth control. **For learning-disabled students:** School does not offer a structured program with separate admission and additional fees. Services include: remedial math, remedial English, reading machines, remedial reading, tape recorders, untimed tests, note-taking services, oral tests, learning center, readers, extended time for tests, tutors, priority seating, other testing accommodations. **Library:** Number of titles: 81,682; number of current serial subscriptions: 31,973. **Information technology resources:** Students are not required to lease or own a computer. Number of campus computers available to all students: 250. School has a wireless network. Approximate number of users that can be accommodated: 5,000. Proportion of college-owned housing units wired for high-speed internet access: 100%. **Campus safety:** Security services offered: late-night transport/escort service, 24-hour emergency telephones, lighted pathways/sidewalks, controlled dormitory access (key, security card, etc).

TRANSFER AND INTERNATIONAL STUDENTS

Transfer students: May apply for admission for the following academic terms: Fall, Spring, Summer. Applicants do not need a minimum number of credits to apply. For fall 2009: Transfer applications received: 1,538. Transfer applicants offered admission: 749. Transfer applicants enrolled: 393. **International students:** Number of foreign undergraduates: 12. Number of countries represented: 9. Minimum TOEFL score required: 550 (paper); 213 (computer).

St. John's College

- **Address:** PO Box 2800, Annapolis, MD 21404
- **Website:** http://www.sjca.edu
- **Private**
- **Enrollment:** N/A

KEY STATS
✔ **U.S News College Ranking:** 166, National Liberal Arts Colleges
✔ **SAT or ACT Score (25th/75th percentile):** N/A
✔ **Tuition:** 2009-2010: $40,392

Selectivity: Selective	**Room/board:** $9,600
Acceptance rate: N/A	**Average debt:** N/A
Student/faculty ratio: N/A	**Proportion who borrowed:** N/A

St. Mary's College of Maryland

- **Address:** 18952 E. Fisher Road, St. Mary's City, MD 20686-3001
- **Website:** http://www.smcm.edu
- **Public**
- **Enrollment:** 1,952 full-time; 65 part-time

KEY STATS
✔ **U.S. News College Ranking:** 88, National Liberal Arts Colleges
✔ **SAT Score (25th/75th percentile):** 1130-1340
✔ **Tuition:** 2010-2011: $13,630 in state, $25,023 out of state

Selectivity: More selective	**Room/board:** $10,235
Acceptance rate: 57%	**Average debt:** $17,125
Student/faculty ratio: 12/1	**Proportion who borrowed:** 70%

UNDERGRADUATE STUDENT BODY STATS

2009-2010 enrollment: 1,952 full-time; 65 part-time. Men: 42%; women: 58%. **Ethnic makeup:** African American: 8%; American-Indian: 1%; Asian American: 4%; Hispanic: 4%; White: 81%; International: 2%.

ADMISSIONS FACTS AND FIGURES

Phone: (800) 492-7181. **Email:** admissions@smcm.edu. **Website:** http://www.smcm.edu. **Application deadlines for fall 2011:** Regular decision: January 1; decision sent by April 1. Early decision: Send application by: November 1; Decision sent by: December 1. Early action: Not offered. Admission cannot be deferred. **Application fee:** $50. **To apply online, go to:** https://hp1.smcm.edu/cgi-bin/public/ATapplication.cgi. **Admissions requirements/recommendations:** High school units required (recommended): English: 4; Mathematics: 3 (4); Science: 3; Foreign language: 2 (4); Social studies: 2; History: 1 (2); Academic electives: 0; Total units: 20 (24). Tests: The college uses SAT or ACT scores in admissions decisions. Either SAT or ACT required. For admission to the fall 2011 entering class, the school will accept: ACT with or without writing accepted. Campus visit: Recommended. Admissions interview: Recommended. Off-campus interview: Not available. **Factors that count in admissions decisions:** *Academic:* Secondary school record: Very Important. Class rank: Not Considered. Letters of recommendation: Important. Standardized test scores: Important. Essay: Important. *Nonacademic:* Interview: Considered. Extracurricular activities: Important. Talent/ability: Important. Character/personal qualities: Not Considered. Alumni/ae relationship: Considered. Geographical residence: Considered. State residency: Considered. Religious affiliation/commitment: Not Considered. Minority status: Considered. Volunteer work: Important. Work experience: Considered. **Other schools with the greatest overlap in applicants:** College of William and Mary; University of Maryland–Baltimore County; University of Maryland–College Park; Washington College. **Admissions statistics for the fall 2009 entering class:** Total applicants: 2,411. Total accepted: 1,381. Freshmen enrolled: 488; 17% were from out of state. Accepted through early-decision or early-action plans: 34%. Overall acceptance rate: 57%. Early-decision acceptance rate: 78%. Non-early acceptance rate: 55%. **Size of waiting list:** 206 applicants; enrolled from waiting list: 70. **Credentials of fall 2009 freshmen:** 47% ranked in the top 10 percent of their high school class; 78% were in the top 25 percent; 95% were in the top half. (Proportion submitting class standing: 49%.) **Average high school grade point average:** 3.8. **First-year students who submitted SAT scores:** 94%. Scores (25/75 percentile): Critical Reading: 580-690, Math: 550-650, Combined: 1130-1340. **First-year students submitting ACT scores:** 17%. Scores (25/75 percentile): English: 23-28, Math: 23-30, Composite: 24-29.

ACADEMICS

Year founded: 1840. **Academic calendar:** Semester. **Degrees offered:** bachelor's, master's. **Most popular majors:** 13% English language and literature, 11% biology/biological sciences, 10% psychology, 9% economics, 9% history. **Major fields of study:** biological and biomedical sciences; computer and information sciences and support services; English language and literature/letters; foreign languages, literatures, and linguistics; history; mathematics and statistics; multi/interdisciplinary studies; philosophy and religious studies; physical sciences; psychology; public administration and social service professions; social sciences; visual and performing arts. **Areas of required coursework:** arts/fine arts, mathematics, English (including composition), philosophy, foreign languages, sciences (biological or physical), history, social science. **Pre-professional programs:** pre-law, pre-dentistry, pre-medicine, pre-veterinary science, pre-optometry, pre-pharmacy. **Special academic programs (% participation):** cooperative (work-study plan) program, double major (13%), dual enrollment, exchange student program (domestic) (1%), honors program (3%), independent study (83%), internships (7%), student-designed major (2%), study abroad (25%). **Teacher certification offered in:** early childhood, elementary, secondary. **Cooperative education programs:** computer science. **Faculty and instruction (2009-2010):** Total instructional faculty: 142 full-time, 83 part-time (52% men; 48% women; 14% minorities). Full-time faculty with Ph.D. or other terminal degree: 98%. Student/faculty ratio: 12/1. Classes of fewer than 20 students: 65%; of 20 to 49 students: 34%; of 50 or more students: 1%. **Advanced Placement and International Baccalaureate credit:** AP tests may be used for: Credit only. Scores accepted: 4, 5. International Baccalaureate exams may be used for: Credit only. **Freshmen returning for sophomore year:** 90%. **Graduation rates:** Four-year: 71%; five-year: 78%; six-year: 79%. **Graduate study:** 33% of students pursue further study within one year; 59% within five years. Fields in which graduates pursue further study: Master of Business Administration (MBA), 4%; law, 11%; medicine, 2%; dentistry, 4%; education, 9%; arts and sciences, 67%; veterinary medicine, 4%.

COSTS AND FINANCIAL AID

Financial aid office: (240) 895-3000. **Expenses (2010-2011):** Tuition and fees 2010-2011: $13,630 in state, $25,023 out of state; room/board: $10,235. Estimated books and supplies: $1,000; transportation: $1,000; personal expenses: $1,500. **Financial aid:** Priority filing date for institution's financial aid form: February 15; deadline: March 1. In 2009-2010, 62% of undergraduates applied for financial aid. Of those, 44% were determined to have financial need; Average financial aid package (proportion receiving): $6,500 (44%). Average amount of gift aid, such as scholarships or grants (proportion receiving): $4,000 (18%). Average amount of self-help aid, such as work study or loans (proportion receiving): $1,000 (18%). Average need-based loan (excluding PLUS or other private loans): $6,000. Among students who received need-based aid, the average percentage of need met: 62%. Among students who received aid based on merit, the average award (and the proportion receiving): $4,000 (27%). The average athletic scholarship (and the proportion receiving): $0 (0%). Average amount of debt of borrowers graduating in 2009: $17,125. Proportion who borrowed: 70%.

CAMPUS LIFE AND EXTRACURRICULAR ACTIVITIES

Campus housing available (% using): coed dorms (25%), women's dorms (10%), men's dorms (11%), apartment for single students (25%), special housing for disabled students (1%), other housing options (22%). Students who live in college-owned, operated, or affiliated housing: 85%. **Student employment:** During the 2009-2010 academic year, 15% of undergraduates worked on campus. Average per-year earnings: $1,500. **Clubs and organizations:** Number of student organizations: 83. Activities include: choral groups, dance, drama/theater, international student organization, jazz band, literary magazine, music ensembles, musical theater, radio station, student government, student newspaper, student film society, symphony orchestra, television station, yearbook. Number of fraternities: 0; sororities: 0. Average

proportion of students who stay on campus on weekends: 70%. **Sports program (2009-2010):** Member of NCAA III. **Men's intercollegiate varsity sports:** baseball, basketball, cross country, lacrosse, soccer, swimming, tennis. **Women's intercollegiate varsity sports:** basketball, cross country, field hockey, lacrosse, soccer, swimming, tennis, volleyball.

SERVICES AND FACILITIES

Basic services: nonremedial tutoring, women's center, health service, other. **Remedial assistance:** writing. **Counseling services:** minority student, career, military, personal, veteran student, academic, older student, psychological, birth control. **For learning-disabled students:** School does not offer a structured program with separate admission and additional fees. Total undergraduates in learning-disabled program or receiving services: 85. Services include: tape recorders, untimed tests, note-taking services, oral tests, extended time for tests, tutors, priority registration, priority seating, texts on tape, exams on tape or computer, other testing accommodations, waiver of foreign language degree requirement, other. **Library:** Number of titles: 161,866; number of current serial subscriptions: 16,890. **Information technology resources:** Students are not required to lease or own a computer. Number of campus computers available to all students: 400. School has a wireless network. Approximate number of users that can be accommodated: 500. Proportion of college-owned housing units wired for high-speed internet access: 100%. **Campus safety:** Security services offered: 24-hour foot-and-vehicle patrols, late-night transport/escort service, 24-hour emergency telephones, lighted pathways/sidewalks, student patrols, controlled dormitory access (key, security card, etc).

TRANSFER AND INTERNATIONAL STUDENTS

Transfer students: May apply for admission for the following academic terms: Fall, Spring. Applicants need a minimum number of credits to apply. For fall 2009: Transfer applications received: 174. Transfer applicants offered admission: 129. Transfer applicants enrolled: 72. **International students:** Number of foreign undergraduates: 32 (2% of student body). Number of countries represented: 38. Minimum TOEFL score required: 90 (computer).

Towson University

- **Address:** 8000 York Road, Towson, MD 21252-0001
- **Website:** http://www.towson.edu
- **Public**
- **Enrollment:** 15,281 full-time; 1,867 part-time

KEY STATS

✔ **U.S News College Ranking:** 46, Regional Universities (North)
✔ **SAT Score (25th/75th percentile):** 980-1170
✔ **Tuition:** 2010-2011: $7,656 in state, $19,114 out of state
  Selectivity: Selective   **Room/board:** $9,614
  Acceptance rate: 63%   **Average debt:** $13,245
  Student/faculty ratio: 17/1   **Proportion who borrowed:** 23%

UNDERGRADUATE STUDENT BODY STATS

2009-2010 enrollment: 15,281 full-time; 1,867 part-time. Men: 40%; women: 60%. **Ethnic makeup:** African American: 12%; Asian American: 4%; Hispanic: 3%; White: 77%; International: 3%.

ADMISSIONS FACTS AND FIGURES

Phone: (410) 704-2113. **Email:** admissions@towson.edu. **Website:** http://www.towson.edu. **Application deadlines for fall 2011:** Regular decision: February 15. Early decision: Not offered. Early action: Not offered. Admission can be deferred. **Application fee:** $45. **To apply online, go to:** http://apply.usmd.edu. **Admissions requirements/recommendations:** High school units required (recommended): English: 4 (4); Mathematics: 3 (4); Science: 3 (3); Foreign language: 2 (4); Social studies: 3 (4); Academic electives: 6; Total units: 21. Tests: The college uses SAT or ACT scores in admissions decisions. Either SAT or ACT required. For admission to the fall 2011 entering class, the school will accept: ACT with writing exam. Campus visit: Recommended. Admissions interview: Neither required nor recommended. Off-campus interview: Not available. **Factors that count in admissions decisions:** *Academic:* Secondary school record: Important. Class rank: Considered. Letters of recommendation: Considered. Standardized test scores: Important. Essay: Considered. *Nonacademic:* Interview: Not Considered. Extracurricular activities: Not Considered. Talent/ability:

Considered. Character/personal qualities: Not Considered. Alumni/ae relationship: Not Considered. Geographical residence: Not Considered. State residency: Not Considered. Religious affiliation/commitment: Not Considered. Minority status: Not Considered. Volunteer work: Not Considered. Work experience: Not Considered. **Admissions statistics for the fall 2009 entering class:** Total applicants: 15,423. Total accepted: 9,696. Freshmen enrolled: 2,405; 27% were from out of state. Overall acceptance rate: 63%. **Size of waiting list:** 2360 applicants; enrolled from waiting list: 376. **Credentials of fall 2009 freshmen:** 24% ranked in the top 10 percent of their high school class; 56% were in the top 25 percent; 93% were in the top half. (Proportion submitting class standing: 46%.) **Average high school grade point average:** 3.6. **First-year students who submitted SAT scores:** 95%. Scores (25/75 percentile): Critical Reading: 490-580, Math: 490-590, Combined: 980-1170. **First-year students submitting ACT scores:** 14%. Scores (25/75 percentile): English: 20-25, Math: 19-25, Composite: 21-24.

ACADEMICS

Year founded: 1866. **Academic calendar:** Semester. **Degrees offered:** bachelor's, post-bachelor's certificate, master's, post-master's certificate, doctorate. **Most popular majors:** 18% business, management, marketing, and related support services, 11% education, 11% social sciences, 10% communication, journalism, and related programs, 10% health professions and related clinical sciences. **Major fields of study:** area, ethnic, cultural, and gender studies; biological and biomedical sciences; business, management, marketing, and related support services; communication, journalism, and related programs; computer and information sciences and support services; education; English language and literature/letters; foreign languages, literatures, and linguistics; health professions and related clinical sciences; history; mathematics and statistics; multi/interdisciplinary studies; parks, recreation, leisure, and fitness studies; philosophy and religious studies; physical sciences; psychology; social sciences; visual and performing arts. **Areas of required coursework:** arts/fine arts, humanities, computer literacy, mathematics, English (including composition), sciences (biological or physical), history, social science, other. **Pre-professional programs:** pre-law, pre-dentistry, pre-medicine, pre-veterinary science, pre-optometry, pre-pharmacy. **Special academic programs:** cooperative (work-study plan) program, cross-registration, distance learning, double major, dual enrollment, English as a Second Language (ESL), exchange student program (domestic), honors program, independent study, internships, liberal arts/career combination, student-designed major, study abroad, teacher certificate program. **Teacher certification offered in:** early childhood, special education, elementary, middle/junior high, secondary, bilingual/bicultural. **Cooperative education programs:** business, computer science, education, health professions, natural science, technologies. **Reserve Officers Training Corps (ROTC):** Army ROTC: Offered at cooperating institution (Loyola University Maryland); Air Force ROTC: Offered at cooperating institution (University of Maryland–College Park). **Faculty and instruction (2009-2010):** Total instructional faculty: 822 full-time, 723 part-time (47% men; 53% women; 12% minorities). Full-time faculty with Ph.D. or other terminal degree: 74%. Student/faculty ratio: 17/1. Classes of fewer than 20 students: 36%; of 20 to 49 students: 63%; of 50 or more students: 1%. **Advanced Placement and International Baccalaureate credit:** AP tests may be used for: Placement only. Scores accepted: 3, 4, 5. **Freshmen returning for sophomore year:** 82%. **Graduation rates:** Four-year: 46%; five-year: 69%; six-year: 67%. **Graduate study:** 26% of students pursue further study within one year.

COSTS AND FINANCIAL AID

Financial aid office: (410) 704-4236. **Expenses (2010-2011):** Tuition and fees 2010-2011: $7,656 in state, $19,114 out of state; room/board: $9,614. Estimated books and supplies: $1,080; transportation: $1,798; personal expenses: $1,982. **Financial aid:** Priority filing date for institution's financial aid form: January 31; deadline: February 10. In 2009-2010, 65% of undergraduates applied for financial aid. Of those, 48% were determined to have financial need; 17% had their need fully met. Average financial aid package (proportion receiving): $9,182 (45%). Average amount of gift aid, such as scholarships or grants (proportion receiving): $7,429 (31%). Average amount of self-help aid, such as work study or loans (proportion receiving): $4,183 (34%). Average need-based loan (excluding PLUS or other private loans): $4,129. Among students who received need-based aid, the average percentage of need met: 67%. Among students who received aid based on merit, the average award (and the proportion receiving): $5,229 (8%). The average athletic scholarship (and the proportion receiving): $11,535 (1%). Average amount of debt of borrowers graduating in 2009: $13,245. Proportion who borrowed: 23%.

CAMPUS LIFE AND EXTRACURRICULAR ACTIVITIES

Campus housing available (% using): coed dorms (73%), apartment for single students (18%), special housing for disabled students (1%), special housing for international students (3%), other housing options (0%). Students who live in college-owned, operated, or affiliated housing: 25%. Average per-year earnings: $4,800. **Clubs and organizations:** Number of student organizations: 198. Activities include: campus ministries, choral groups, concert band, dance, drama/theater, international student organization, jazz band, literary magazine, marching band, music ensembles, musical theater, pep band, radio station, student government, student newspaper, symphony orchestra, television station, yearbook. Number of fraternities: 14; sororities: 14. Proportion of men in fraternities: 3%; of women in sororities: 2%. Average proportion of students who stay on campus on weekends: 60%. **Sports program (2009-2010):** Member of NCAA I. **Men's intercollegiate varsity sports:** baseball, basketball, cross country, football, golf, lacrosse, soccer, swimming, tennis, track and field (outdoor). **Women's intercollegiate varsity sports:** basketball, cross country, field hockey, gymnastics, lacrosse, soccer, softball, swimming, tennis, track and field (outdoor), volleyball.

SERVICES AND FACILITIES

Basic services: nonremedial tutoring, women's center, day care, health service. **Remedial assistance:** reading, math, writing. **Counseling services:** minority student, career, military, personal, veteran student, academic, psychological, birth control. **For learning-disabled students:** School does not offer a structured program with separate admission and additional fees. Total undergraduates in learning-disabled program or receiving services: 705. Services include: remedial math, remedial English, reading machines, remedial reading, tape recorders, note-taking services, oral tests, learning center, readers, extended time for tests, tutors, early syllabus, priority registration, priority seating, proofreading services, substitution of courses, texts on tape, typist/scribe, exams on tape or computer, other testing accommodations. **Library:** Number of titles: 561,743; number of current serial subscriptions: 8,042. **Information technology resources:** Students are not required to lease or own a computer. Number of campus computers available to all students: 1,876. School has a wireless network. Approximate number of users that can be accommodated: 9,000. Proportion of college-owned housing units wired for high-speed internet access: 100%. **Campus safety:** Security services offered: 24-hour foot-and-vehicle patrols, late-night transport/escort service, 24-hour emergency telephones, lighted pathways/sidewalks, student patrols, controlled dormitory access (key, security card, etc).

TRANSFER AND INTERNATIONAL STUDENTS

Transfer students: May apply for admission for the following academic terms: Fall, Spring. Applicants need a minimum number of credits to apply. For fall 2009: Transfer applications received: 4,218. Transfer applicants offered admission: 2,964. Transfer applicants enrolled: 1,539. **International students:** Number of foreign undergraduates: 511 (3% of student body). Number of countries represented: 94. Minimum TOEFL score required: 500 (paper); 61 (computer). Average TOEFL score: 533 (paper).

United States Naval Academy

- **Address:** 121 Blake Road, Annapolis, MD 21402
- **Website:** http://www.usna.edu
- **Public**
- **Enrollment:** 4,552 full-time

KEY STATS

✔ **U.S News College Ranking:** 16, National Liberal Arts Colleges
✔ **SAT Score (25th/75th percentile):** 1140-1350
✔ **Tuition:** N/A

Selectivity: More selective	**Room/board:** $0
Acceptance rate: 10%	**Average debt:** $0
Student/faculty ratio: 9/1	**Proportion who borrowed:** 0%

UNDERGRADUATE STUDENT BODY STATS

2009-2010 enrollment: 4,552 full-time. Men: 80%; women: 20%. **Ethnic makeup:** African American: 5%; Asian American: 4%; Hispanic: 12%; White: 78%; International: 1%.

ADMISSIONS FACTS AND FIGURES

Phone: (410) 293-4361. **Email:** webmail@usna.edu. **Website:** http://www.usna.edu. **Application deadlines for fall 2011:** Regular decision: January 31. Early decision: Not offered. Early action: Send application by: N/A; Decision sent by: N/A. Admission cannot be deferred. **To apply online, go to:** http://www.usna.edu/Admissions/steps.htm. **Admissions requirements/recommendations:** High school units required (recommended): English: (4); Mathematics: (4); Science: (2); Foreign language: (2); History: (2). Tests: The college uses SAT or ACT scores in admissions decisions. Either SAT or ACT required. For admission to the fall 2011 entering class, the school will accept: ACT with or without writing accepted. Campus visit: Recommended. Admissions interview: Required. Off-campus interview: May be arranged. **Factors that count in admissions decisions: Academic:** Secondary school record: Very Important. Class rank: Very Important. Letters of recommendation: Very Important. Standardized test scores: Very Important. Essay: Very Important. **Nonacademic:** Interview: Very Important. Extracurricular activities: Very Important. Talent/ability: Important. Character/personal qualities: Very Important. Alumni/ae relationship: Considered. Geographical residence: Considered. State residency: Not Considered. Religious affiliation/commitment: Not Considered. Minority status: Considered. Volunteer work: Considered. Work experience: Considered. **Other schools with the greatest overlap in applicants:** United States Air Force Academy; United States Military Academy. **Admissions statistics for the fall 2009 entering class:** Total applicants: 15,342. Total accepted: 1,464. Freshmen enrolled: 1,251; 96% were from out of state. Overall acceptance rate: 10%. Non-early acceptance rate: 10%. **Size of waiting list:** 127 applicants; enrolled from waiting list: 38. **Credentials of fall 2009 freshmen:** 56% ranked in the top 10 percent of their high school class; 81% were in the top 25 percent; 96% were in the top half. (Proportion submitting class standing: 70%.) **First-year students who submitted SAT scores:** 85%. Scores (25/75 percentile): Critical Reading: 550-660, Math: 590-690, Combined: 1140-1350. **First-year students submitting ACT scores:** 65%. Scores (25/75 percentile): English: 23-30, Math: 25-31, Composite: N/A.

ACADEMICS

Year founded: 1845. **Academic calendar:** Semester. **Degrees offered:** bachelor's. **Most popular majors:** 17% political science and government, 12% economics, 9% history, 9% mechanical engineering, 9% systems engineering. **Major fields of study:** computer and information sciences and support services; engineering; English language and literature/letters; foreign languages, literatures, and linguistics; history; mathematics and statistics; physical sciences; social sciences. **Areas of required coursework:** humanities, mathematics, English (including composition), philosophy, sciences (biological or physical), history, social science, other. **Special academic programs (% participation):** accelerated program (2%), double major (1%), exchange student program (domestic) (1%), honors program (1%), independent study (1%), study abroad (1%). **Faculty and instruction (2009-2010):** Total instructional faculty: 523 full-time, 51 part-time (74% men; 26% women; 9% minorities). Full-time faculty with Ph.D. or other terminal degree: 64%. Student/faculty ratio: 9/1. Classes of fewer than 20 students: 59%; of 20 to 49 students: 41%; of 50 or more students: 0%. **Advanced Placement and International Baccalaureate credit:** AP tests may be used for: Credit and/or placement. Scores accepted: 4, 5. **Freshmen returning for sophomore year:** 97%. **Graduation rates:** Four-year: 89%; five-year: 89%; six-year: 89%. **Graduate study:** 2% of students pursue further study immediately upon graduation; 50% within five years. Fields in which graduates pursue further study: medicine, 1%.

COSTS AND FINANCIAL AID

Expenses (N/A):Financial aid: Average financial aid package (proportion receiving): $0 (0%). Average amount of gift aid, such as scholarships or grants (proportion receiving): $0 (0%). Average amount of self-help aid, such as work study or loans (proportion receiving): $0 (0%). Average need-based loan (excluding PLUS or other private loans): $0. Among students who received aid based on merit, the average award (and the proportion receiving): $0 (0%). The average athletic scholarship (and the proportion receiving): $0 (0%). Average amount of debt of borrowers graduating in 2009: $0.

CAMPUS LIFE AND EXTRACURRICULAR ACTIVITIES

Campus housing available (% using): coed dorms (100%). Students who live in college-owned, operated, or affiliated housing: 100%. **Student employment:** During the 2009-2010 academic year, 0% of undergraduates worked on campus. Average per-year earnings: $0. **Clubs and organizations:** Number of student organizations: 86. Activities include: choral groups, concert band, drama/theater, jazz band, literary magazine, marching band, music ensembles, musical theater, pep band, radio station, student government, symphony orchestra, yearbook. Number of fraternities: 0; sororities: 0. Average proportion of students who stay on campus on weekends: 50%. **Sports program (2009-2010):** Member of NCAA I. **Men's intercollegiate varsity sports:** baseball, basketball, cross country, football, golf, gymnastics, lacrosse, rifle, soccer, swimming, tennis, track and field (indoor), track and field (outdoor), water polo, wrestling. **Women's intercollegiate varsity sports:** basketball, cross country, lacrosse, crew (lightweight), soccer, swimming, tennis, track and field (indoor), track and field (outdoor), volleyball.

SERVICES AND FACILITIES

Basic services: nonremedial tutoring, placement service, health service, health insurance. **Remedial assistance:** reading, math, writing, study skills. **Counseling services:** minority student, career, military, personal, veteran student, academic, psychological, religious. **Library:** Number of titles: 701,505; number of current serial subscriptions: 1,979. **Information technology resources:** Students are required to lease or own a computer. Number of campus computers available to all students: 4,500. School has a wireless network. Approximate number of users that can be accommodated: 1,400. Proportion of college-owned housing units wired for high-speed internet access: 100%. **Campus safety:** Security services offered: 24-hour foot-and-vehicle patrols, lighted pathways/sidewalks, student patrols, controlled dormitory access (key, security card, etc).

TRANSFER AND INTERNATIONAL STUDENTS

International students: Number of foreign undergraduates: 53 (1% of student body). Number of countries represented: 28. Minimum TOEFL score required: 500 (paper); 173 (computer).

University of Baltimore

- **Address:** 1420 N. Charles Street, Baltimore, MD 21201
- **Website:** http://www.ubalt.edu
- **Public**
- **Enrollment:** N/A

KEY STATS

✔ **U.S News College Ranking:** second tier, Regional Universities (North)
✔ **SAT or ACT Score (25th/75th percentile):** N/A
✔ **Tuition:** 2009-2010: $7,171 in state, $20,677 out of state
  Selectivity: Less selective   **Room/board:** N/A
  Acceptance rate: N/A   **Average debt:** N/A
  Student/faculty ratio: N/A   **Proportion who borrowed:** N/A

University of Maryland–Baltimore County

- **Address:** 1000 Hilltop Circle, Baltimore, MD 21250
- **Website:** http://www.umbc.edu
- **Public**
- **Enrollment:** 8,614 full-time; 1,333 part-time

KEY STATS

✔ **U.S News College Ranking:** 159, National Universities
✔ **SAT Score (25th/75th percentile):** 1080-1290
✔ **Tuition:** 2010-2011: $9,171 in state, $19,108 out of state
  Selectivity: Selective   **Room/board:** $9,359
  Acceptance rate: 69%   **Average debt:** $19,353
  Student/faculty ratio: 19/1   **Proportion who borrowed:** 50%

UNDERGRADUATE STUDENT BODY STATS

2009-2010 enrollment: 8,614 full-time; 1,333 part-time. Men: 54%; women: 46%. **Ethnic makeup:** African American: 17%; American-Indian: 1%; Asian American: 21%; Hispanic: 4%; White: 54%; International: 4%.

ADMISSIONS FACTS AND FIGURES

Phone: (410) 455-2291. **Email:** admissions@umbc.edu. **Website:** http://www.umbc.edu. **Application deadlines for fall 2011:** Regular decision: February 1. Early decision: Not offered. Early action: Send application by: November 1; Decision sent by: December 15. Admission can be deferred. **Application fee:** $50. **To apply online, go to:** http://www.umbc.edu/undergrad/index.

html?l1=apply&. **Admissions requirements/recommendations:** High school units required (recommended): English: 4 (0); Mathematics: 3 (4); Science: 3 (0); Foreign language: 2 (0); Social studies: 0 (0); History: 0 (0); Academic electives: 0 (0); Total units: 15 (4). Tests: The college uses SAT or ACT scores in admissions decisions. SAT required. For admission to the fall 2011 entering class, the school will accept: ACT with or without writing accepted. Campus visit: Recommended. Admissions interview: Neither required nor recommended. Off-campus interview: Not available. **Factors that count in admissions decisions:** *Academic:* Secondary school record: Very Important. Class rank: Important. Letters of recommendation: Important. Standardized test scores: Very Important. Essay: Important. *Nonacademic:* Interview: Not Considered. Extracurricular activities: Considered. Talent/ability: Important. Character/personal qualities: Considered. Alumni/ae relationship: Not Considered. Geographical residence: Not Considered. State residency: Not Considered. Religious affiliation/commitment: Not Considered. Minority status: Not Considered. Volunteer work: Not Considered. Work experience: Not Considered. **Other schools with the greatest overlap in applicants:** Johns Hopkins University; Pennsylvania State University–University Park; Towson University; University of Maryland–College Park. **Admissions statistics for the fall 2009 entering class:** Total applicants: 6,047. Total accepted: 4,168. Freshmen enrolled: 1,532; 9% were from out of state. Accepted through early-decision or early-action plans: 29%. Overall acceptance rate: 69%. Non-early acceptance rate: 64%. **Size of waiting list:** 246 applicants; enrolled from waiting list: 112. **Credentials of fall 2009 freshmen:** 24% ranked in the top 10 percent of their high school class; 52% were in the top 25 percent; 84% were in the top half. (Proportion submitting class standing: 49%.) **Average high school grade point average:** 3.6. **First-year students who submitted SAT scores:** 93%. Scores (25/75 percentile): Critical Reading: 530-630, Math: 550-660, Combined: 1080-1290. **First-year students submitting ACT scores:** 12%. Scores (25/75 percentile): English: N/A, Math: N/A, Composite: 22-29.

ACADEMICS

Year founded: 1963. **Academic calendar:** 4-1-4. **Degrees offered:** bachelor's, post-bachelor's certificate, master's, doctorate. **Most popular majors:** 17% social sciences, 14% psychology, 13% biological and biomedical sciences, 12% computer and information sciences and support services, 9% engineering. **Major fields of study:** area, ethnic, cultural, and gender studies; biological and biomedical sciences; communication, journalism, and related programs; computer and information sciences and support services; engineering; English language and literature/letters; foreign languages, literatures, and linguistics; health professions and related clinical sciences; history; mathematics and statistics; multi/interdisciplinary studies; natural resources and conservation; philosophy and religious studies; physical sciences; psychology; public administration and social service professions; social sciences; visual and performing arts. **Areas of required coursework:** arts/fine arts, humanities, mathematics, English (including composition), foreign languages, sciences (biological or physical), social science. **Preprofessional programs:** pre-law, pre-dentistry, pre-medicine, pre-veterinary science, pre-optometry, pre-pharmacy, other. **Special academic programs:** accelerated program, cooperative (work-study plan) program, cross-registration, distance learning, double major, dual enrollment, English as a Second Language (ESL), honors program, independent study, internships, liberal arts/career combination, student-designed major, study abroad, teacher certificate program. **Teacher certification offered in:** early childhood, elementary, secondary, bilingual/bicultural. **Cooperative education programs:** computer science, engineering, natural science, social/behavioral science, technologies. **Reserve Officers Training Corps (ROTC):** Army ROTC: Offered at cooperating institution (Johns Hopkins University). **Faculty and instruction (2009-2010):** Total instructional faculty: 480 full-time, 250 part-time (58% men; 42% women; 19% minorities). Full-time faculty with Ph.D. or other terminal degree: 87%. Student/faculty ratio: 19/1. Classes of fewer than 20 students: 40%; of 20 to 49 students: 47%; of 50 or more students: 13%. **Advanced Placement and International Baccalaureate credit:** AP tests may be used for: Credit and/or placement. Scores accepted: 3, 4, 5. International Baccalaureate exams may be used for: Placement only. **Freshmen returning for sophomore year:** 85%. **Graduation rates:** Four-year: 34%; five-year: 53%; six-year: 59%. **Graduate study:** 43% of students pursue further study within one year. Fields in which graduates pursue further study: Master of Business Administration (MBA), 5%; law, 3%; medicine, 6%; dentistry, 2%; theology (or the seminary), 1%; education, 12%; arts and sciences, 64%.

COSTS AND FINANCIAL AID

Financial aid office: (410) 455-2387. **Expenses (2010-2011):** Tuition and fees 2010-2011: $9,171 in state, $19,108 out of state; room/board: $9,359.

Estimated books and supplies: $1,200; transportation: $870; personal expenses: $1,450. **Financial aid:** Priority filing date for institution's financial aid form: February 14. In 2009-2010, 63% of undergraduates applied for financial aid. Of those, 48% were determined to have financial need; 33% had their need fully met. Average financial aid package (proportion receiving): $10,480 (46%). Average amount of gift aid, such as scholarships or grants (proportion receiving): $7,723 (37%). Average amount of self-help aid, such as work study or loans (proportion receiving): $4,240 (32%). Average need-based loan (excluding PLUS or other private loans): $4,061. Among students who received need-based aid, the average percentage of need met: 63%. Among students who received aid based on merit, the average award (and the proportion receiving): $5,240 (32%). The average athletic scholarship (and the proportion receiving): $7,630 (3%). Average amount of debt of borrowers graduating in 2009: $19,353. Proportion who borrowed: 50%.

CAMPUS LIFE AND EXTRACURRICULAR ACTIVITIES

Campus housing available: coed dorms, apartment for single students, special housing for disabled students, other housing options. Students who live in college-owned, operated, or affiliated housing: 37%. **Student employment:** During the 2009-2010 academic year, 25% of undergraduates worked on campus. Average per-year earnings: $3,782. **Clubs and organizations:** Number of student organizations: 250. Activities include: campus ministries, choral groups, dance, drama/theater, international student organization, jazz band, literary magazine, model UN, music ensembles, musical theater, pep band, radio station, student government, student newspaper, student film society, symphony orchestra. Number of fraternities: 11; sororities: 11. Proportion of men in fraternities: 3%; of women in sororities: 3%. Average proportion of students who stay on campus on weekends: 65%. **Sports program (2009-2010):** Member of NCAA I. *Men's intercollegiate varsity sports:* baseball, basketball, cross country, lacrosse, soccer, swimming, tennis, track and field (indoor), track and field (outdoor). *Women's intercollegiate varsity sports:* basketball, cross country, lacrosse, soccer, softball, swimming, tennis, track and field (indoor), track and field (outdoor), volleyball.

SERVICES AND FACILITIES

Basic services: nonremedial tutoring, women's center, placement service, day care, health service, health insurance. **Remedial assistance:** reading, math, writing, study skills. **Counseling services:** career, personal, academic, psychological, birth control. **For learning-disabled students:** School does not offer a structured program with separate admission and additional fees. Services include: remedial math, remedial English, remedial reading, tape recorders, videotaped classes, untimed tests, note-taking services, oral tests, learning center, readers, extended time for tests, tutors, priority registration, priority seating, substitution of courses, typist/scribe, exams on tape or computer, other testing accommodations, waiver of foreign language degree requirement, waiver of math degree requirement, other. **Library:** Number of titles: 1,016,805; number of current serial subscriptions: 3,559. **Information technology resources:** Students are required to lease or own a computer. Number of campus computers available to all students: 875. School has a wireless network. Approximate number of users that can be accommodated: 5,000. Proportion of college-owned housing units wired for high-speed internet access: 100%. **Campus safety:** Security services offered: 24-hour foot-and-vehicle patrols, late-night transport/escort service, 24-hour emergency telephones, lighted pathways/sidewalks, controlled dormitory access (key, security card, etc).

TRANSFER AND INTERNATIONAL STUDENTS

Transfer students: May apply for admission for the following academic terms: Fall, Winter, Spring, Summer. Applicants need a minimum number of credits to apply. For fall 2009: Transfer applications received: 2,088. Transfer applicants offered admission: 1,704. Transfer applicants enrolled: 1,125. **International students:** Number of foreign undergraduates: 383 (4% of student body). Number of countries represented: 81. Minimum TOEFL score required: 550 (paper); 220 (computer). Average TOEFL score: 618 (paper).

University of Maryland—College Park

- **Address:** College Park, MD 20742-5025
- **Website:** http://www.maryland.edu
- **Public**
- **Enrollment:** 24,583 full-time; 1,910 part-time

KEY STATS

- ✔ **U.S News College Ranking:** 56, National Universities
- ✔ **SAT Score (25th/75th percentile):** 1200-1390
- ✔ **Tuition:** 2010-2011: $8,416 in state, $24,831 out of state
- **Selectivity:** More selective
- **Room/board:** N/A
- **Acceptance rate:** 42%
- **Average debt:** $20,256
- **Student/faculty ratio:** 18/1
- **Proportion who borrowed:** 44%

UNDERGRADUATE STUDENT BODY STATS

2009-2010 enrollment: 24,583 full-time; 1,910 part-time. Men: 53%; women: 47%. **Ethnic makeup:** African American: 12%; Asian American: 15%; Hispanic: 6%; White: 64%; International: 2%.

ADMISSIONS FACTS AND FIGURES

Phone: (301) 314-8385. **Email:** um-admit@uga.umd.edu. **Website:** http://www.maryland.edu. **Application deadlines for fall 2011:** Regular decision: January 20; decision sent by April 1. Early decision: Not offered. Early action: Send application by: November 1; Decision sent by: February 15. Admission can be deferred. **Application fee:** $55. **To apply online, go to:** http://www.admissions.umd.edu/admissions. **Admissions requirements/recommendations:** High school units required (recommended): English: 4; Mathematics: 4; Science: 3; Foreign language: 2; Social studies: 3; Total units: 16. Tests: The college uses SAT or ACT scores in admissions decisions. Either SAT or ACT required. For admission to the fall 2011 entering class, the school will accept: ACT with writing required. Campus visit: Recommended. Admissions interview: Neither required nor recommended. Off-campus interview: Not available. **Factors that count in admissions decisions:** *Academic:* Secondary school record: Very Important. Class rank: Important. Letters of recommendation: Important. Standardized test scores: Very Important. Essay: Important. *Nonacademic:* Interview: Not Considered. Extracurricular activities: Considered. Talent/ability: Important. Character/personal qualities: Considered. Alumni/ae relationship: Considered. Geographical residence: Considered. State residency: Important. Religious affiliation/commitment: Not Considered. Minority status: Considered. Volunteer work: Considered. Work experience: Considered. **Other schools with the greatest overlap in applicants:** Pennsylvania State University–University Park; Towson University; University of Delaware; University of Maryland–Baltimore County; University of Virginia. **Admissions statistics for the fall 2009 entering class:** Total applicants: 28,331. Total accepted: 11,870. Freshmen enrolled: 4,202; 33% were from out of state. Overall acceptance rate: 42%. Non-early acceptance rate: 42%. **Size of waiting list:** 857 applicants; enrolled from waiting list: 9. **Credentials of fall 2009 freshmen:** 71% ranked in the top 10 percent of their high school class; 91% were in the top 25 percent; 99% were in the top half. (Proportion submitting class standing: 48%.) **Average high school grade point average:** 3.9. **First-year students who submitted SAT scores:** 94%. Scores (25/75 percentile): Critical Reading: 580-680, Math: 620-710, Combined: 1200-1390.

ACADEMICS

Year founded: 1856. **Academic calendar:** Semester. **Degrees offered:** certificate, bachelor's, post-bachelor's certificate, master's, post-master's certificate, doctorate. **Most popular majors:** 7% criminology, 7% economics, 6% finance, 5% political science and government, 5% psychology. **Major fields of study:** agriculture, agriculture operations, and related sciences; architecture and related services; area, ethnic, cultural, and gender studies; biological and biomedical sciences; business, management, marketing, and related support services; communication, journalism, and related programs; computer and information sciences and support services; education; engineering; English language and literature/letters; family and consumer sciences/human sciences; foreign languages, literatures, and linguistics; health professions and related clinical sciences; history; legal professions and studies; mathematics and statistics; multi/interdisciplinary studies; natural resources and conservation; parks, recreation, leisure, and fitness studies; philosophy and religious studies; physical sciences; psychology; social sciences; visual and performing arts. **Areas of required coursework:** arts/fine arts, humanities, mathematics, English (including composition), sciences (biological or physical), history, social science, other. **Pre-professional**

programs: pre-law, pre-dentistry, pre-medicine, pre-veterinary science, pre-optometry, pre-pharmacy, other. **Special academic programs:** accelerated program, cooperative (work-study plan) program, cross-registration, distance learning, double major, dual enrollment, English as a Second Language (ESL), exchange student program (domestic), external degree program, honors program, independent study, internships, student-designed major, study abroad, teacher certificate program, other. **Teacher certification offered in:** early childhood, special education, elementary, middle/junior high, secondary. **Cooperative education programs:** engineering. **Reserve Officers Training Corps (ROTC):** Army ROTC: Offered on campus; Navy ROTC: Offered at cooperating institution (George Washington University); Air Force ROTC: Offered on campus. **Faculty and instruction (2009-2010):** Total instructional faculty: 1,621 full-time, 630 part-time (63% men; 37% women; 18% minorities). Full-time faculty with Ph.D. or other terminal degree: 94%. Student/faculty ratio: 18/1. Classes of fewer than 20 students: 34%; of 20 to 49 students: 51%; of 50 or more students: 15%. **Advanced Placement and International Baccalaureate credit:** AP tests may be used for: Credit and/or placement. Scores accepted: 3, 4, 5. International Baccalaureate exams may be used for: Credit and/or placement. **Freshmen returning for sophomore year:** 93%. **Graduation rates:** Four-year: 63%; five-year: 80%; six-year: 82%. **Graduate study:** 26% of students pursue further study immediately upon graduation.

COSTS AND FINANCIAL AID

Financial aid office: (301) 314-9000. **Expenses (2010-2011):** Tuition and fees 2010-2011: $8,416 in state, $24,831 out of state. Estimated books and supplies: $1,025; transportation: $756; personal expenses: $2,268. **Financial aid:** Priority filing date for institution's financial aid form: February 15. In 2009-2010, 58% of undergraduates applied for financial aid. Of those, 41% were determined to have financial need; 7% had their need fully met. Average financial aid package (proportion receiving): $9,481 (38%). Average amount of gift aid, such as scholarships or grants (proportion receiving): $6,950 (25%). Average amount of self-help aid, such as work study or loans (proportion receiving): $4,176 (26%). Average need-based loan (excluding PLUS or other private loans): $4,280. Among students who received need-based aid, the average percentage of need met: 60%. Among students who received aid based on merit, the average award (and the proportion receiving): $6,584 (11%). The average athletic scholarship (and the proportion receiving): $14,959 (1%). Average amount of debt of borrowers graduating in 2009: $20,256. Proportion who borrowed: 44%.

CAMPUS LIFE AND EXTRACURRICULAR ACTIVITIES

Campus housing available (% using): coed dorms (72%), women's dorms (1%), sorority housing (5%), fraternity housing (7%), apartment for single students (15%), special housing for disabled students, special housing for international students, other housing options. Students who live in college-owned, operated, or affiliated housing: 42%. **Student employment:** During the 2009-2010 academic year, 19% of undergraduates worked on campus. Average per-year earnings: $5,928. **Clubs and organizations:** Number of student organizations: 620. Activities include: campus ministries, choral groups, concert band, dance, drama/theater, jazz band, literary magazine, marching band, model UN, music ensembles, musical theater, opera, pep band, radio station, student government, student newspaper, student film society, symphony orchestra, television station, yearbook. Number of fraternities: 36; sororities: 27. Proportion of men in fraternities: 13%; of women in sororities: 10%. Average proportion of students who stay on campus on weekends: 50%. **Sports program (2009-2010):** Member of NCAA I. *Men's intercollegiate varsity sports:* baseball, basketball, cross country, football, golf, lacrosse, soccer, swimming, tennis, track and field (indoor), track and field (outdoor), wrestling. *Women's intercollegiate varsity sports:* basketball, cross country, equestrian, field hockey, golf, gymnastics, lacrosse, soccer, softball, swimming, tennis, track and field (indoor), track and field (outdoor), volleyball, water polo.

SERVICES AND FACILITIES

Basic services: nonremedial tutoring, day care, health service, health insurance. **Remedial assistance:** reading, math, writing, study skills, other. **Counseling services:** minority student, career, personal, veteran student, academic, older student, psychological, birth control. **For learning-disabled students:** School does not offer a structured program with separate admission and additional fees. Total undergraduates in learning-disabled program or receiving services: 469. Services include: remedial math, reading machines, tape recorders, other special classes, note-taking services, oral tests, learning center, readers, extended time for tests, early syllabus, priority registration, priority seating, substitution of courses, texts on tape, typist/scribe, exams on tape or computer, other testing accommodations. **Library:**

Number of titles: 3,767,656; number of current serial subscriptions: 51,989. **Information technology resources:** Students are not required to lease or own a computer. Number of campus computers available to all students: 11,637. School has a wireless network. Approximate number of users that can be accommodated: 25,000. Proportion of college-owned housing units wired for high-speed internet access: 100%. **Campus safety:** Security services offered: 24-hour foot-and-vehicle patrols, late-night transport/escort service, 24-hour emergency telephones, lighted pathways/sidewalks, student patrols, controlled dormitory access (key, security card, etc.).

TRANSFER AND INTERNATIONAL STUDENTS

Transfer students: May apply for admission for the following academic terms: Fall, Spring. Applicants need a minimum number of credits to apply. For fall 2009: Transfer applications received: 7,264. Transfer applicants offered admission: 3,453. Transfer applicants enrolled: 2,044. **International students:** Number of foreign undergraduates: 549 (2% of student body). Number of countries represented: 135. Minimum TOEFL score required: 575 (paper).

University of Maryland–Eastern Shore

- **Address:** J.T. Williams Hall, Room 2106, Princess Anne, MD 21853
- **Website:** http://www.umes.edu
- **Public**
- **Enrollment:** 3,605 full-time; 317 part-time

KEY STATS

✔ **U.S News College Ranking:** second tier, Regional Universities (North)
✔ **SAT Score (25th/75th percentile):** 750-930
✔ **Tuition:** 2010-2011: $6,305 in state, $13,746 out of state

Selectivity: Less selective	**Room/board:** $7,480
Acceptance rate: 56%	**Average debt:** $5,290
Student/faculty ratio: 18/1	**Proportion who borrowed:** 89%

UNDERGRADUATE STUDENT BODY STATS

2009-2010 enrollment: 3,605 full-time; 317 part-time. Men: 41%; women: 59%. **Ethnic makeup:** African American: 83%; Asian American: 1%; Hispanic: 1%; White: 12%; International: 3%.

ADMISSIONS FACTS AND FIGURES

Phone: (410) 651-6410. **Email:** umesadmissions@umes.edu. **Website:** http://www.umes.edu. **Application deadlines for fall 2011:** Regular decision: July 15. Early decision: Not offered. Early action: Send application by: November 15; Decision sent by: December 1. Admission can be deferred. **Application fee:** $25. **To apply online, go to:** http://www.acaff.usmh.usmd.edu/umsapp/uindex.html. **Admissions requirements/recommendations:** High school units required (recommended): English: 4; Mathematics: 3; Science: 2; Foreign language: 2; Social studies: 3; Academic electives: 6; Total units: 20. Tests: The college uses SAT or ACT scores in admissions decisions. Either SAT or ACT required. For admission to the fall 2011 entering class, the school will accept: ACT with or without writing accepted. Campus visit: Recommended. Admissions interview: Recommended. Off-campus interview: Not available. **Factors that count in admissions decisions:** *Academic:* Secondary school record: Very Important. Class rank: Very Important. Letters of recommendation: Considered. Standardized test scores: Very Important. Essay: Considered. *Nonacademic:* Interview: Considered. Extracurricular activities: Considered. Talent/ability: Considered. Character/personal qualities: Very Important. Alumni/ae relationship: Not Considered. Geographical residence: Considered. State residency: Considered. Religious affiliation/commitment: Not Considered. Minority status: Not Considered. Volunteer work: Not Considered. Work experience: Not Considered. **Other schools with the greatest overlap in applicants:** Alabama Agricultural and Mechanical University; Albany State University; Alcorn State University; California State University–Bakersfield; Fort Valley State University. **Admissions statistics for the fall 2009 entering class:** Total applicants: 4,317. Total accepted: 2,409. Freshmen enrolled: 921; 71% were from out of state. Overall acceptance rate: 56%. Non-early acceptance rate: 56%. **Size of waiting list:** 0 applicants; enrolled from waiting list: 0. **Average high school grade point average:** 2.8. **First-year students who submitted SAT scores:** 87%. Scores (25/75 percentile): Critical Reading: 380-470, Math: 370-460, Combined: 750-930. **First-year students submitting ACT scores:** 14%. Scores (25/75 percentile): English: 13-17, Math: 15-17, Composite: 15-18.

ACADEMICS

Year founded: 1886. **Academic calendar:** Semester. **Degrees offered:** bachelor's, master's, doctorate. **Most popular majors:** 17% criminal justice/police science, 11% sociology, 8% business administration and management, 8% hotel/motel administration/management, 6% English language and literature. **Major fields of study:** agriculture, agriculture operations, and related sciences; architecture and related services; area, ethnic, cultural, and gender studies; biological and biomedical sciences; business, management, marketing, and related support services; computer and information sciences and support services; construction trades; education; engineering; engineering technologies/technicians; English language and literature/letters; family and consumer sciences/human sciences; health professions and related clinical sciences; history; legal professions and studies; liberal arts and sciences studies, and humanities; mathematics and statistics; multi/interdisciplinary studies; natural resources and conservation; parks, recreation, leisure, and fitness studies; physical sciences; security and protective services; social sciences; transportation and materials moving; visual and performing arts. **Areas of required coursework:** mathematics, English (including composition), social science. **Pre-professional programs:** pre-law, pre-dentistry, pre-medicine, pre-pharmacy, other. **Special academic programs (% participation):** cooperative (work-study plan) program, cross-registration, distance learning (35%), dual enrollment, honors program (1%), independent study (100%), internships, study abroad. **Teacher certification offered in:** special education, vo-tech, middle/junior high, secondary. **Cooperative education programs:** agriculture, art, business, computer science, education, engineering, health professions, home economics, humanities, natural science, social/behavioral science, technologies, vocational arts. **Faculty and instruction (2009-2010):** Total instructional faculty: 178 full-time, 121 part-time (53% men; 47% women; 48% minorities). Full-time faculty with Ph.D. or other terminal degree: 68%. Student/faculty ratio: 18/1. Classes of fewer than 20 students: 48%; of 20 to 49 students: 48%; of 50 or more students: 4%. **Advanced Placement and International Baccalaureate credit:** AP tests may be used for: Placement only. Scores accepted: 3. International Baccalaureate exams may be used for: Placement only. **Freshmen returning for sophomore year:** 67%. **Graduation rates:** Four-year: 18%; five-year: 29%; six-year: 35%. **Graduate study:** 28% of students pursue further study within one year.

COSTS AND FINANCIAL AID

Financial aid office: (410) 651-6172. **Expenses (2010-2011):** Tuition and fees 2010-2011: $6,305 in state, $13,746 out of state; room/board: $7,480. Estimated books and supplies: $1,800; transportation: $1,500; personal expenses: $1,800. **Financial aid:** Priority filing date for institution's financial aid form: March 1. In 2009-2010, 90% of undergraduates applied for financial aid. Of those, 81% were determined to have financial need; 54% had their need fully met. Average financial aid package (proportion receiving): $14,500 (81%). Average amount of gift aid, such as scholarships or grants (proportion receiving): $7,150 (73%). Average amount of self-help aid, such as work study or loans (proportion receiving): $4,590 (73%). Average need-based loan (excluding PLUS or other private loans): $4,950. Among students who received need-based aid, the average percentage of need met: 84%. Among students who received aid based on merit, the average award (and the proportion receiving): $2,875 (6%). The average athletic scholarship (and the proportion receiving): $15,200 (2%). Average amount of debt of borrowers graduating in 2009: $5,290. Proportion who borrowed: 89%.

CAMPUS LIFE AND EXTRACURRICULAR ACTIVITIES

Campus housing available (% using): coed dorms (57%), women's dorms (27%), men's dorms (16%). Students who live in college-owned, operated, or affiliated housing: 54%. **Student employment:** During the 2009-2010 academic year, 12% of undergraduates worked on campus. Average per-year earnings: $4,760. **Clubs and organizations:** Number of student organizations: 75. Activities include: choral groups, concert band, dance, drama/theater, jazz band, music ensembles, radio station, student government, student newspaper, yearbook. Number of fraternities: 4; sororities: 4. Average proportion of students who stay on campus on weekends: 75%. **Sports program (2009-2010):** Member of NCAA I. *Men's intercollegiate varsity sports:* baseball, basketball, cross country, tennis, track and field (indoor), track and field (outdoor). *Women's intercollegiate varsity sports:* basketball, bowling, cross country, softball, tennis, track and field (indoor), track and field (outdoor), volleyball.

SERVICES AND FACILITIES

Basic services: nonremedial tutoring, placement service, day care, health service, health insurance. **Remedial assistance:** reading, math, writing, study skills, other. **Counseling services:** minority student, career, personal, veteran student, academic, psychological, religious. **For learning-disabled students:** School does not offer a structured program with separate admission and additional fees. Total undergraduates in learning-disabled program or receiving services: 60. Services include: tape recorders, untimed tests, note-taking services, learning center, readers, extended time for tests, tutors, priority seating, texts on tape, exams on tape or computer, other. **Library:** Number of titles: 211,876; number of current serial subscriptions: 619. **Information technology resources:** Students are not required to lease or own a computer. Number of campus computers available to all students: 739. School has a wireless network. Proportion of college-owned housing units wired for high-speed internet access: 100%. **Campus safety:** Security services offered: 24-hour foot-and-vehicle patrols, late-night transport/escort service, 24-hour emergency telephones, lighted pathways/sidewalks, student patrols, controlled dormitory access (key, security card, etc).

TRANSFER AND INTERNATIONAL STUDENTS

Transfer students: May apply for admission for the following academic terms: Fall, Winter, Spring, Summer. Applicants do not need a minimum number of credits to apply. For fall 2009: Transfer applications received: 580. Transfer applicants offered admission: 354. Transfer applicants enrolled: 231. **International students:** Number of foreign undergraduates: 97 (3% of student body). Number of countries represented: 39. Minimum TOEFL score required: 500 (paper); 173 (computer). Average TOEFL score: 550 (paper).

University of Maryland—University College

- **Address:** 3501 University Boulevard E, Adelphi, MD 20783
- **Website:** http://www.umuc.edu/
- **Public**
- **Enrollment:** 3,408 full-time; 20,876 part-time

KEY STATS

✔ **U.S News College Ranking:** Unranked, Regional Universities (North)
✔ **SAT or ACT Score (25th/75th percentile):** N/A
✔ **Tuition:** 2009-2010: $5,760 in state, $12,216 out of state

Selectivity: N/A	**Room/board:** N/A
Acceptance rate: 100%	**Average debt:** N/A
Student/faculty ratio: 19/1	**Proportion who borrowed:** N/A

UNDERGRADUATE STUDENT BODY STATS

2009-2010 enrollment: 3,408 full-time; 20,876 part-time. Men: 44%; women: 56%. **Ethnic makeup:** African American: 32%; American-Indian: 1%; Asian American: 4%; Hispanic: 6%; White: 56%; International: 2%.

ADMISSIONS FACTS AND FIGURES

Phone: (800) 888-8682. **Email:** enroll@umuc.edu. **Website:** http://www.umuc.edu/. **Application deadlines for fall 2011:** Regular decision: Rolling. Early decision: Not offered. Early action: Not offered. Admission can be deferred. **Application fee:** $50. **To apply online, go to:** http://www.umuc.edu/admissions/index.shtml. **Admissions requirements/recommendations:** Tests: The college does not use SAT or ACT scores in admissions decisions. Neither SAT nor ACT required. Campus visit: Neither required nor recommended. Admissions interview: Neither required nor recommended. Off-campus interview: Not available. **Factors that count in admissions decisions:** *Academic:* Secondary school record: Not Considered. Class rank: Not Considered. Letters of recommendation: Not Considered. Standardized test scores: Not Considered. Essay: Not Considered. *Nonacademic:* Interview: Not Considered. Extracurricular activities: Not Considered. Talent/ability: Not Considered. Character/personal qualities: Not Considered. Alumni/ae relationship: Not Considered. Geographical residence: Not Considered. State residency: Not Considered. Religious affiliation/commitment: Not Considered. Minority status: Not Considered. Volunteer work: Not Considered. Work experience: Not Considered. **Admissions statistics for the fall 2009 entering class:** Total applicants: 2,949. Total accepted: 2,946. Freshmen enrolled: 999; 36% were from out of state. Overall acceptance rate: 100%.

ACADEMICS

Year founded: 1947. **Academic calendar:** Semester. **Degrees offered:** certificate, transfer-associate, bachelor's, post-bachelor's certificate, master's. **Most popular majors:** 38% business, management, marketing, and related support services, 21% computer and information sciences and support services,

8% multi/interdisciplinary studies, 7% psychology, 5% security and protective services. **Major fields of study:** area, ethnic, cultural, and gender studies; biological and biomedical sciences; business, management, marketing, and related support services; communication, journalism, and related programs; computer and information sciences and support services; English language and literature/letters; history; legal professions and studies; liberal arts and sciences studies, and humanities; multi/interdisciplinary studies; natural resources and conservation; psychology; security and protective services; social sciences. **Areas of required coursework:** humanities, computer literacy, mathematics, English (including composition), sciences (biological or physical), social science. **Special academic programs:** accelerated program, cooperative (work-study plan) program, cross-registration, distance learning, double major, dual enrollment, external degree program, independent study, internships, teacher certificate program, weekend college. **Faculty and instruction (2009-2010):** Total instructional faculty: 228 full-time, 1,730 part-time (59% men; 41% women; 14% minorities). Full-time faculty with Ph.D. or other terminal degree: 83%. Student/faculty ratio: 19/1. Classes of fewer than 20 students: 53%; of 20 to 49 students: 47%. **Advanced Placement and International Baccalaureate credit:** AP tests may be used for: Credit and/or placement. Scores accepted: 3, 4, 5. International Baccalaureate exams may be used for: Credit only. **Graduation rates:** Six-year: 12%.

COSTS AND FINANCIAL AID

Financial aid office: (301) 985-7510. **Expenses (2009-2010):** Tuition and fees 2009-2010: $5,760 in state, $12,216 out of state. Estimated books and supplies: $2,000; transportation: $1,200; personal expenses: $5,500. **Financial aid:** Priority filing date for institution's financial aid form: June 1. In 2009-2010, 67% of undergraduates applied for financial aid. Of those, 64% were determined to have financial need; Average financial aid package (proportion receiving): $6,795 (59%). Average amount of gift aid, such as scholarships or grants (proportion receiving): $3,978 (35%). Average amount of self-help aid, such as work study or loans (proportion receiving): $4,291 (48%). Average need-based loan (excluding PLUS or other private loans): $4,200. Among students who received need-based aid, the average percentage of need met: 23%.

CAMPUS LIFE AND EXTRACURRICULAR ACTIVITIES

Number of fraternities: 0; sororities: 0.

SERVICES AND FACILITIES

Basic services: nonremedial tutoring. **Remedial assistance:** math, writing. **Counseling services:** minority student, career, military, veteran student, academic, older student. **For learning-disabled students:** School does not offer a structured program with separate admission and additional fees. Services include: remedial math, remedial English, reading machines, tape recorders, untimed tests, note-taking services, oral tests, readers, extended time for tests, tutors, early syllabus, priority registration, priority seating, substitution of courses, texts on tape, typist/scribe, exams on tape or computer, other testing accommodations. **Library:** Number of titles: 1,247; number of current serial subscriptions: 76,740. **Information technology resources:** Students are not required to lease or own a computer. Number of campus computers available to all students: 465. School has a wireless network. **Campus safety:** Security services offered: 24-hour emergency telephones, lighted pathways/sidewalks.

TRANSFER AND INTERNATIONAL STUDENTS

Transfer students: May apply for admission for the following academic terms: Fall, Spring, Summer. Applicants do not need a minimum number of credits to apply. For fall 2009: Transfer applications received: 5,906. Transfer applicants offered admission: 5,903. Transfer applicants enrolled: 3,807. **International students:** Number of foreign undergraduates: 426 (2% of student body). Minimum TOEFL score required: 550 (paper); 79 (computer). Average TOEFL score: 550 (paper).

Washington Adventist University

- **Address:** 7600 Flower Avenue, Takoma Park, MD 20912
- **Website:** http://www.cuc.edu
- **Private; Religious affiliation:** Seventh-day Adventist
- **Enrollment:** 805 full-time; 270 part-time

KEY STATS

✔ **U.S News College Ranking:** second tier, Regional Colleges (North)
✔ **SAT or ACT Score (25th/75th percentile):** N/A
✔ **Tuition:** 2010-2011: $19,480

Selectivity: Less selective	Room/board: $7,530
Acceptance rate: 41%	Average debt: $9,799
Student/faculty ratio: 14/1	Proportion who borrowed: 80%

UNDERGRADUATE STUDENT BODY STATS

2009-2010 enrollment: 805 full-time; 270 part-time. Men: 34%; women: 66%. **Ethnic makeup:** African American: 52%; Asian American: 6%; Hispanic: 11%; White: 31%. **Religious preference:** Roman Catholic: 5%; Protestant: 11%; Unknown: 22%; Seventh-day Adventist: 51%; Other: 11%.

ADMISSIONS FACTS AND FIGURES

Phone: (301) 891-4080. **Email:** enroll@cuc.edu. **Website:** http://www.cuc.edu. **Application deadlines for fall 2011:** Regular decision: August 1. Early decision: Not offered. Early action: Not offered. Admission can be deferred. **Application fee:** $25. **To apply online, go to:** https://my.cuc.edu/scripts/trad.cfm. **Admissions requirements/recommendations:** High school units required (recommended): English: 4 (4); Mathematics: 2 (4); Science: 2 (4); Foreign language: 0 (2); Social studies: 0 (2); History: 4 (4); Academic electives: 4 (4); Total units: 18 (29). Tests: The college uses SAT or ACT scores in admissions decisions. Either SAT or ACT required. For admission to the fall 2011 entering class, the school will accept: ACT with or without writing accepted. Campus visit: Recommended. Admissions interview: Neither required nor recommended. Off-campus interview: May be arranged. **Factors that count in admissions decisions:** *Academic:* Secondary school record: Considered. Class rank: Not Considered. Letters of recommendation: Important. Standardized test scores: Very Important. Essay: Considered. *Nonacademic:* Interview: Not Considered. Extracurricular activities: Not Considered. Talent/ability: Considered. Character/personal qualities: Important. Alumni/ae relationship: Not Considered. Geographical residence: Not Considered. State residency: Not Considered. Religious affiliation/commitment: Considered. Minority status: Not Considered. Volunteer work: Not Considered. Work experience: Not Considered. **Other schools with the greatest overlap in applicants:** Andrews University; Southern Adventist University; University of Maryland–College Park. **Admissions statistics for the fall 2009 entering class:** Total applicants: 1,293. Total accepted: 531. Freshmen enrolled: 144; Overall acceptance rate: 41%.

ACADEMICS

Year founded: 1904. **Academic calendar:** Semester. **Degrees offered:** certificate, associate, bachelor's, master's. **Most popular majors:** 31% health professions and related clinical sciences, 18% psychology, 15% business, management, marketing, and related support services, 7% education, 7% liberal arts and sciences studies, and humanities. **Major fields of study:** biological and biomedical sciences; business, management, marketing, and related support services; communication, journalism, and related programs; computer and information sciences and support services; education; English language and literature/letters; health professions and related clinical sciences; history; liberal arts and sciences studies, and humanities; mathematics and statistics; parks, recreation, leisure, and fitness studies; philosophy and religious studies; physical sciences; psychology; theology and religious vocations; visual and performing arts. **Areas of required coursework:** humanities, computer literacy, mathematics, English (including composition), sciences (biological or physical), history, social science, other. **Pre-professional programs:** pre-law, pre-dentistry, pre-medicine, pre-veterinary science, pre-optometry, pre-pharmacy. **Special academic programs (% participation):** accelerated program (40%), cooperative (work-study plan) program (20%), cross-registration, distance learning, double major (8%), dual enrollment, English as a Second Language (ESL), external degree program, honors program, independent study, internships (29%), liberal arts/career combination, student-designed major (12%), study abroad, teacher certificate program (8%), other. **Teacher certification offered in:** special education, elementary, secondary. **Cooperative education programs:** business, computer science, natural science. **Faculty and instruction**

(2009-2010): Total instructional faculty: 41 full-time, 68 part-time (50% men; 50% women). Full-time faculty with Ph.D. or other terminal degree: 51%. Student/faculty ratio: 14/1. Classes of fewer than 20 students: 73%; of 20 to 49 students: 22%; of 50 or more students: 5%. **Advanced Placement and International Baccalaureate credit:** AP tests may be used for: Credit only. Scores accepted: 3, 4, 5. **Freshmen returning for sophomore year:** 65%. **Graduation rates:** Four-year: 13%; five-year: 23%; six-year: 37%.

COSTS AND FINANCIAL AID

Financial aid office: (301) 891-4005. **Expenses (2010-2011):** Tuition and fees 2010-2011: $19,480; room/board: $7,530. Estimated books and supplies: $1,200; transportation: $800; personal expenses: $1,250. **Financial aid:** Priority filing date for institution's financial aid form: March 1. Average amount of debt of borrowers graduating in 2009: $9,799. Proportion who borrowed: 80%.

CAMPUS LIFE AND EXTRACURRICULAR ACTIVITIES

Campus housing available (% using): women's dorms (26%), men's dorms (18%), apartments for married students, apartment for single students. **Student employment:** During the 2009-2010 academic year, 33% of undergraduates worked on campus. Average per-year earnings: $5,500. **Clubs and organizations:** Number of student organizations: 16. Activities include: campus ministries, choral groups, concert band, international student organization, jazz band, literary magazine, music ensembles, pep band, radio station, student government, student newspaper, symphony orchestra, yearbook. **Sports program (2009-2010):** Member of NCAA II. *Men's intercollegiate varsity sports:* baseball, basketball, cross country, soccer, track and field (outdoor). *Women's intercollegiate varsity sports:* soccer, softball.

SERVICES AND FACILITIES

Basic services: nonremedial tutoring, health service, health insurance. **Remedial assistance:** math, writing, study skills. **Counseling services:** career, personal, academic, psychological, religious. **For learning-disabled students:** School does not offer a structured program with separate admission and additional fees. Services include: remedial math, remedial English, untimed tests, learning center, extended time for tests, tutors. **Library:** Number of titles: 142,903; number of current serial subscriptions: 349. **Information technology resources:** Students are not required to lease or own a computer. School has a wireless network. Proportion of college-owned housing units wired for high-speed internet access: 90%. **Campus safety:** Security services offered: 24-hour foot-and-vehicle patrols, late-night transport/escort service, lighted pathways/sidewalks, controlled dormitory access (key, security card, etc).

TRANSFER AND INTERNATIONAL STUDENTS

Transfer students: May apply for admission for the following academic terms: Fall, Spring, Summer. Applicants need a minimum number of credits to apply. For fall 2009: Transfer applications received: 0. Transfer applicants offered admission: 0. Transfer applicants enrolled: 0. **International students:** Number of countries represented: 27. Minimum TOEFL score required: 550 (paper); 213 (computer).

Washington College

- **Address:** 300 Washington Avenue, Chestertown, MD 21620
- **Website:** http://www.washcoll.edu
- **Private**
- **Enrollment:** 1,285 full-time; 29 part-time

KEY STATS

✔ **U.S News College Ranking:** 93, National Liberal Arts Colleges
✔ **SAT Score (25th/75th percentile):** 1030-1230
✔ **Tuition:** 2010-2011: $36,738

Selectivity: More selective	Room/board: $7,834
Acceptance rate: 72%	Average debt: $28,727
Student/faculty ratio: 12/1	Proportion who borrowed: 58%

UNDERGRADUATE STUDENT BODY STATS

2009-2010 enrollment: 1,285 full-time; 29 part-time. Men: 41%; women: 59%. **Ethnic makeup:** African American: 5%; Asian American: 2%; Hispanic: 1%; White: 90%; International: 2%.

ADMISSIONS FACTS AND FIGURES

Phone: (410) 778-7700. **Email:** adm.off@washcoll.edu. **Website:** http://www.washcoll.edu. **Application deadlines for fall 2011:** Regular decision: March 1. Early decision: Send application by: November 1; Decision sent by: December 1. Early action: Send application by: November 15; Decision sent by: December 15. Admission can be deferred. **Application fee:** $55. **To apply online, go to:** https://app.commonapp.org. **Admissions requirements/recommendations:** High school units required (recommended): English: 4 (4); Mathematics: 3 (4); Science: 3 (4); Foreign language: 2 (4); Social studies: 2 (4); History: 2; Total units: 16 (20). Tests: The college uses SAT or ACT scores in admissions decisions. Either SAT or ACT required. For admission to the fall 2011 entering class, the school will accept: ACT with or without writing accepted. Campus visit: Recommended. Admissions interview: Recommended. Off-campus interview: Not available. **Factors that count in admissions decisions:** *Academic:* Secondary school record: Very Important. Class rank: Important. Letters of recommendation: Considered. Standardized test scores: Important. Essay: Considered. *Nonacademic:* Interview: Very Important. Extracurricular activities: Considered. Talent/ability: Considered. Character/personal qualities: Considered. Alumni/ae relationship: Considered. Geographical residence: Considered. State residency: Considered. Religious affiliation/commitment: Not Considered. Minority status: Considered. Volunteer work: Considered. Work experience: Important. **Admissions statistics for the fall 2009 entering class:** Total applicants: 4,498. Total accepted: 3,240. Freshmen enrolled: 378; 50% were from out of state. Accepted through early-decision or early-action plans: 10%. Overall acceptance rate: 72%. Early-decision acceptance rate: 76%. Non-early acceptance rate: 72%. **Size of waiting list:** 402 applicants; enrolled from waiting list: 60. **Credentials of fall 2009 freshmen:** 30% ranked in the top 10 percent of their high school class; 71% were in the top 25 percent; 92% were in the top half. (Proportion submitting class standing: 58%.) **Average high school grade point average:** 3.4. **First-year students who submitted SAT scores:** 91%. Scores (25/75 percentile): Critical Reading: 520-620, Math: 510-610, Combined: 1030-1230. **First-year students submitting ACT scores:** 25%. Scores (25/75 percentile): English: N/A, Math: N/A, Composite: 22-29.

ACADEMICS

Year founded: 1782. **Academic calendar:** Semester. **Degrees offered:** bachelor's, master's. **Most popular majors:** 18% social sciences, 14% business, management, marketing, and related support services, 13% English language and literature/letters, 12% psychology, 9% biological and biomedical sciences. **Major fields of study:** area, ethnic, cultural, and gender studies; biological and biomedical sciences; business, management, marketing, and related support services; computer and information sciences and support services; English language and literature/letters; foreign languages, literatures, and linguistics; history; liberal arts and sciences studies, and humanities; mathematics and statistics; multi/interdisciplinary studies; natural resources and conservation; philosophy and religious studies; physical sciences; psychology; social sciences; visual and performing arts. **Areas of required coursework:** arts/fine arts, humanities, mathematics, English (including composition), foreign languages, sciences (biological or physical), social science, other. **Pre-professional programs:** pre-law, pre-dentistry, pre-medicine, pre-veterinary science, pre-optometry, pre-pharmacy. **Special academic programs (% participation):** cross-registration, double major (11%), dual enrollment, exchange student program (domestic), honors program, independent study (12%), internships (20%), liberal arts/career combination, student-designed major, study abroad (30%), teacher certificate program (3%). **Teacher certification offered in:** elementary, middle/junior high, secondary. **Faculty and instruction (2009-2010):** Total instructional faculty: 87 full-time, 66 part-time (58% men; 42% women; 12% minorities). Full-time faculty with Ph.D. or other terminal degree: 93%. Student/faculty ratio: 12/1. Classes of fewer than 20 students: 67%; of 20 to 49 students: 32%; of 50 or more students: 1%. **Advanced Placement and International Baccalaureate credit:** AP tests may be used for: Credit only. Scores accepted: 4, 5. International Baccalaureate exams may be used for: Credit and/or placement. **Freshmen returning for sophomore year:** 83%. **Graduation rates:** Four-year: 75%; five-year: 77%; six-year: 79%. **Graduate study:** 24% of students pursue further study immediately upon graduation; 30% within one year.

COSTS AND FINANCIAL AID

Financial aid office: (410) 778-7214. **Expenses (2010-2011):** Tuition and fees 2010-2011: $36,738; room/board: $7,834. Estimated books and supplies: $1,250; transportation: $1,000; personal expenses: $1,500. **Financial aid:** Priority filing date for institution's financial aid form: February 15. In 2009-2010, 67% of undergraduates applied for financial aid. Of those, 55% were determined to have financial need; 27% had their need fully met. Average financial aid package (proportion receiving): $21,084 (55%). Average amount of gift aid, such as scholarships or grants (proportion receiving): $18,614 (53%). Average amount of self-help aid, such as work study or loans (proportion receiving): $5,501 (47%). Average need-based loan (excluding PLUS or other private loans): $4,824. Among students who received need-based aid, the average percentage of need met: 71%. Among students who received aid based on merit, the average award (and the proportion receiving): $13,730 (27%). The average athletic scholarship (and the proportion receiving): $0 (0%). Average amount of debt of borrowers graduating in 2009: $28,727. Proportion who borrowed: 58%.

CAMPUS LIFE AND EXTRACURRICULAR ACTIVITIES

Campus housing available (% using): coed dorms (41%), women's dorms (25%), men's dorms (13%), sorority housing (3%), fraternity housing (7%), apartment for single students (0%), special housing for international students (2%). Students who live in college-owned, operated, or affiliated housing: 86%. **Student employment:** During the 2009-2010 academic year, 35% of undergraduates worked on campus. Average per-year earnings: $2,000. **Clubs and organizations:** Number of student organizations: 103. Activities include: campus ministries, choral groups, concert band, dance, drama/theater, international student organization, jazz band, literary magazine, model UN, music ensembles, radio station, student government, student newspaper, student film society, yearbook. Number of fraternities: 4; sororities: 3. Proportion of men in fraternities: 8%; of women in sororities: 14%. Average proportion of students who stay on campus on weekends: 65%. **Sports program (2009-2010):** Member of NCAA III. *Men's intercollegiate varsity sports:* baseball, basketball, lacrosse, soccer, swimming, tennis. *Women's intercollegiate varsity sports:* basketball, crew (heavyweight), field hockey, lacrosse, soccer, softball, swimming, tennis, volleyball.

SERVICES AND FACILITIES

Basic services: nonremedial tutoring, placement service, health service, health insurance. **Remedial assistance:** math, writing, study skills. **Counseling services:** minority student, career, personal, academic, psychological. **For learning-disabled students:** School does not offer a structured program with separate admission and additional fees. Total undergraduates in learning-disabled program or receiving services: 75. Services include: note-taking services, learning center, readers, extended time for tests, tutors, priority seating, substitution of courses, typist/scribe, other testing accommodations. **Library:** Number of titles: 219,461; number of current serial subscriptions: 44,548. **Information technology resources:** Students are not required to lease or own a computer. Number of campus computers available to all students: 150. School has a wireless network. Approximate number of users that can be accommodated: 2,000. Proportion of college-owned housing units wired for high-speed internet access: 100%. **Campus safety:** Security services offered: 24-hour foot-and-vehicle patrols, late-night transport/escort service, 24-hour emergency telephones, lighted pathways/sidewalks, student patrols, controlled dormitory access (key, security card, etc).

TRANSFER AND INTERNATIONAL STUDENTS

Transfer students: May apply for admission for the following academic terms: Fall, Spring. Applicants do not need a minimum number of credits to apply. For fall 2009: Transfer applications received: 77. Transfer applicants offered admission: 48. Transfer applicants enrolled: 18. **International students:** Number of foreign undergraduates: 25 (2% of student body). Number of countries represented: 28. Minimum TOEFL score required: 550 (paper); 213 (computer). Average TOEFL score: 570 (paper).

Massachusetts

American International College

- **Address:** 1000 State Street, Springfield, MA 01109
- **Website:** http://www.aic.edu
- **Private**
- **Enrollment:** 1,581 full-time; 148 part-time

....

KEY STATS

✔ **U.S News College Ranking:** second tier, Regional Universities (North)
✔ **SAT Score (25th/75th percentile):** 840-1030
✔ **Tuition:** 2010-2011: $26,700

Selectivity: Less selective	**Room/board:** $10,930
Acceptance rate: 79%	**Average debt:** $25,693
Student/faculty ratio: 15/1	**Proportion who borrowed:** 100%

UNDERGRADUATE STUDENT BODY STATS

2009-2010 enrollment: 1,581 full-time; 148 part-time. Men: 42%; women: 58%. **Ethnic makeup:** African American: 27%; American-Indian: 1%; Asian American: 3%; Hispanic: 9%; White: 56%; International: 4%.

ADMISSIONS FACTS AND FIGURES

Phone: (413) 205-3201. **Email:** inquiry@aic.edu. **Website:** http://www.aic.edu. **Application deadlines for fall 2011:** Regular decision: Rolling. Early decision: Not offered. Early action: Not offered. Admission can be deferred. **Application fee:** $25. **To apply online, go to:** http://www.aic.edu/pages/251.html. **Admissions requirements/recommendations:** High school units required (recommended): English: 4 (4); Mathematics: 2 (3); Science: 2 (3); Foreign language: 1 (2); Social studies: 1 (2); History: 2 (2); Academic electives: 4 (3); Total units: 16 (18). Tests: The college uses SAT or ACT scores in admissions decisions. Either SAT or ACT required. For admission to the fall 2011 entering class, the school will accept: ACT with writing required. Campus visit: Recommended. Admissions interview: Recommended. Off-campus interview: May be arranged. **Factors that count in admissions decisions:** *Academic:* Secondary school record: Important. Class rank: Important. Letters of recommendation: Considered. Standardized test scores: Important. Essay: Considered. *Nonacademic:* Interview: Considered. Extracurricular activities: Considered. Talent/ability: Not Considered. Character/personal qualities: Important. Alumni/ae relationship: Considered. Geographical residence: Not Considered. State residency: Not Considered. Religious affiliation/commitment: Not Considered. Minority status: Considered. Volunteer work: Considered. Work experience: Considered. **Other schools with the greatest overlap in applicants:** Quinnipiac University; Springfield College; University of Connecticut; Western New England College; Westfield State College. **Admissions statistics for the fall 2009 entering class:** Total applicants: 1,469. Total accepted: 1,162. Freshmen enrolled: 350; 51% were from out of state. Overall acceptance rate: 79%. **Credentials of fall 2009 freshmen:** 22% ranked in the top 10 percent of their high school class; 28% were in the top 25 percent; 73% were in the top half. (Proportion submitting class standing: 80%.) **Average high school grade point average:** 3.0. **First-year students who submitted SAT scores:** 92%. Scores (25/75 percentile): Critical Reading: 420-510, Math: 420-520, Combined: 840-1030. **First-year students submitting ACT scores:** 4%. Scores (25/75 percentile): English: N/A, Math: N/A, Composite: 17-23.

ACADEMICS

Year founded: 1885. **Academic calendar:** Semester. **Degrees offered:** associate, bachelor's, master's, post-master's certificate, doctorate. **Most popular majors:** 25% nursing/registered nurse training (R.N., A.S.N., B.S.N., M.S.N.), 13% criminal justice/safety studies, 8% psychology, 7% business administration and management, 6% accounting. **Major fields of study:** area, ethnic, cultural, and gender studies; biological and biomedical sciences; business, management, marketing, and related support services; communication, journalism, and related programs; computer and information sciences and support services; education; English language and literature/letters; foreign languages, literatures, and linguistics; health professions and related clinical sciences; history; liberal arts and sciences

studies, and humanities; mathematics and statistics; parks, recreation, leisure, and fitness studies; philosophy and religious studies; psychology. **Areas of required coursework:** humanities, computer literacy, mathematics, English (including composition), sciences (biological or physical), social science. **Pre-professional programs:** pre-law, pre-dentistry, pre-medicine, pre-veterinary science, pre-optometry, pre-pharmacy. **Special academic programs (% participation):** accelerated program, cross-registration, distance learning, double major (9%), dual enrollment, honors program (1%), independent study (20%), internships (85%), liberal arts/career combination, study abroad (1%), teacher certificate program (3%), weekend college (1%). **Teacher certification offered in:** early childhood, special education, elementary, middle/junior high, secondary. **Reserve Officers Training Corps (ROTC):** Army ROTC: Offered at cooperating institution (Western New England College); Air Force ROTC: Offered at cooperating institution (Western New England College). **Faculty and instruction (2009-2010):** Total instructional faculty: 89 full-time, 234 part-time (44% men; 56% women; 5% minorities). Full-time faculty with Ph.D. or other terminal degree: 47%. Student/faculty ratio: 15/1. Classes of fewer than 20 students: 53%; of 20 to 49 students: 44%; of 50 or more students: 3%. **Advanced Placement and International Baccalaureate credit:** AP tests may be used for: Credit and/or placement. Scores accepted: 3, 4, 5. International Baccalaureate exams may be used for: Credit and/or placement. **Freshmen returning for sophomore year:** 67%. **Graduation rates:** Four-year: 32%; five-year: 40%; six-year: 45%. **Graduate study:** 50% of students pursue further study immediately upon graduation; 10% within five years. Fields in which graduates pursue further study: Master of Business Administration (MBA), 25%; law, 2%; medicine, 2%; dentistry, 1%; education, 30%; veterinary medicine, 1%.

COSTS AND FINANCIAL AID

Financial aid office: (413) 205-3259. **Expenses (2010-2011):** Tuition and fees 2010-2011: $26,700; room/board: $10,930. Estimated books and supplies: $1,500; transportation: $1,000; personal expenses: $1,000. **Financial aid:** Priority filing date for institution's financial aid form: May 1. In 2009-2010, 93% of undergraduates applied for financial aid. Of those, 89% were determined to have financial need; 12% had their need fully met. Average financial aid package (proportion receiving): $21,229 (88%). Average amount of gift aid, such as scholarships or grants (proportion receiving): $17,033 (88%). Average amount of self-help aid, such as work study or loans (proportion receiving): $4,609 (81%). Average need-based loan (excluding PLUS or other private loans): $4,178. Among students who received need-based aid, the average percentage of need met: 68%. Among students who received aid based on merit, the average award (and the proportion receiving): $10,968 (10%). The average athletic scholarship (and the proportion receiving): $14,607 (8%). Average amount of debt of borrowers graduating in 2009: $25,693. Proportion who borrowed: 100%.

CAMPUS LIFE AND EXTRACURRICULAR ACTIVITIES

Campus housing available (% using): coed dorms (56%), women's dorms (14%), men's dorms (19%), apartment for single students (11%). Students who live in college-owned, operated, or affiliated housing: 47%. **Student employment:** During the 2009-2010 academic year, 25% of undergraduates worked on campus. Average per-year earnings: $2,400. **Clubs and organizations:** Number of student organizations: 40. Activities include: campus ministries, choral groups, dance, drama/theater, international student organization, literary magazine, pep band, radio station, student government, student newspaper, yearbook. Number of fraternities: 4; sororities: 5. Proportion of men in fraternities: 1%; of women in sororities: 1%. Average proportion of students who stay on campus on weekends: 65%. **Sports program (2009-2010):** Member of NCAA II. *Men's intercollegiate varsity sports:* baseball, basketball, cross country, football, golf, ice hockey, lacrosse, soccer, tennis, track and field (indoor), track and field (outdoor), wrestling. *Women's intercollegiate varsity sports:* basketball, cross country, field hockey, lacrosse, soccer, softball, tennis, track and field (indoor), track and field (outdoor), volleyball.

SERVICES AND FACILITIES

Basic services: nonremedial tutoring, placement service, health service, health insurance. **Remedial assistance:** reading, math, writing, study skills.

Counseling services: minority student, career, military, personal, veteran student, academic, psychological, birth control. For learning-disabled students: School does not offer a structured program with separate admission and additional fees. Total undergraduates in learning-disabled program or receiving services: 140. Services include: remedial math, remedial English, reading machines, tape recorders, diagnostic testing service, untimed tests, note-taking services, oral tests, learning center, readers, extended time for tests, tutors, priority registration, priority seating, other testing accommodations. Library: Number of titles: 70,741; number of current serial subscriptions: 269. Information technology resources: Students are not required to lease or own a computer. Number of campus computers available to all students: 175. School has a wireless network. Approximate number of users that can be accommodated: 4,240. Proportion of college-owned housing units wired for high-speed internet access: 100%. Campus safety: Security services offered: 24-hour foot-and-vehicle patrols, late-night transport/escort service, 24-hour emergency telephones, lighted pathways/sidewalks, student patrols, controlled dormitory access (key, security card, etc.).

TRANSFER AND INTERNATIONAL STUDENTS

Transfer students: May apply for admission for the following academic terms: Fall, Spring, Summer. Applicants do not need a minimum number of credits to apply. For fall 2009: Transfer applications received: 579. Transfer applicants offered admission: 366. Transfer applicants enrolled: 220. International students: Number of foreign undergraduates: 76 (4% of student body). Number of countries represented: 46. Minimum TOEFL score required: 550 (paper). Average TOEFL score: 500 (paper).

Amherst College

- Address: PO Box 5000, Amherst, MA 01002-5000
- Website: http://www.amherst.edu
- Private
- Enrollment: 1,744 full-time

KEY STATS

✔ U.S News College Ranking: 2, National Liberal Arts Colleges
✔ SAT Score (25th/75th percentile): 1310-1530
✔ Tuition: 2010-2011: $40,862

Selectivity: Most selective	Room/board: $10,660
Acceptance rate: 16%	Average debt: $11,347
Student/faculty ratio: 8/1	Proportion who borrowed: 41%

UNDERGRADUATE STUDENT BODY STATS

2009-2010 enrollment: 1,744 full-time. Men: 50%; women: 50%. Ethnic makeup: African American: 11%; Asian American: 10%; Hispanic: 11%; White: 60%; International: 8%. Religious preference: Roman Catholic: 19%; Protestant: 18%; Jewish: 11%; Muslim: 1%; Hindu: 1%; Buddhist: 1%; No preference: 30%; Unknown: 9%; others: 10%.

ADMISSIONS FACTS AND FIGURES

Phone: (413) 542-2328. Email: admission@amherst.edu. Website: http://www.amherst.edu. Application deadlines for fall 2011: Regular decision: January 1; decision sent by April 1. Early decision: Send application by: November 15; Decision sent by: December 15. Early action: Not offered. Admission can be deferred. Application fee: $60. To apply online, go to: http://www.amherst.edu/admission/. Admissions requirements/recommendations: High school units required (recommended): English: (4); Mathematics: (4); Science: (3); Foreign language: (4); Social studies: (2); History: (2); Total units: (20). Tests: The college uses SAT or ACT scores in admissions decisions. Either SAT or ACT required. For admission to the fall 2011 entering class, the school will accept: ACT with writing recommended. Campus visit: Recommended. Admissions interview: Neither required nor recommended. Off-campus interview: Not available. Factors that count in admissions decisions: *Academic:* Secondary school record: Very Important. Class rank: Important. Letters of recommendation: Very Important. Standardized test scores: Very Important. Essay: Very Important. *Nonacademic:* Interview: Not Considered. Extracurricular activities: Very Important. Talent/ability: Very Important. Character/personal qualities: Very Important. Alumni/ae relationship: Important. Geographical residence: Considered. State residency: Considered. Religious affiliation/commitment: Not Considered. Minority status: Considered. Volunteer work: Important. Work experience: Considered. Other schools with the greatest overlap in applicants: Brown University; Harvard University; Princeton

University; Williams College; Yale University. Admissions statistics for the fall 2009 entering class: Total applicants: 7,679. Total accepted: 1,227. Freshmen enrolled: 467; 90% were from out of state. Overall acceptance rate: 16%. Non-early acceptance rate: 16%. Size of waiting list: 1217 applicants; enrolled from waiting list: 0. Credentials of fall 2009 freshmen: 85% ranked in the top 10 percent of their high school class; 94% were in the top 25 percent; 100% were in the top half. (Proportion submitting class standing: 58%.) First-year students who submitted SAT scores: 76%. Scores (25/75 percentile): Critical Reading: 660-760, Math: 650-770, Combined: 1310-1530. First-year students submitting ACT scores: 26%. Scores (25/75 percentile): English: 30-34, Math: 29-35, Composite: 30-34.

ACADEMICS

Year founded: 1821. Academic calendar: Semester. Degrees offered: bachelor's. Most popular majors: 20% economics, 12% English language and literature, 12% psychology, 11% political science and government, 8% biology/biological sciences. Major fields of study: area, ethnic, cultural, and gender studies; biological and biomedical sciences; computer and information sciences and support services; English language and literature/letters; foreign languages, literatures, and linguistics; history; legal professions and studies; mathematics and statistics; multi/interdisciplinary studies; philosophy and religious studies; physical sciences; psychology; social sciences; visual and performing arts. Pre-professional programs: pre-law, pre-dentistry, pre-medicine, pre-veterinary science. Special academic programs (% participation): cross-registration (52%), double major (30%), exchange student program (domestic) (5%), honors program (42%), independent study (16%), internships (60%), student-designed major (1%), study abroad (40%), teacher certificate program. Teacher certification offered in: secondary. Reserve Officers Training Corps (ROTC): Air Force ROTC: Offered at cooperating institution (University of Massachusetts–Amherst). Faculty and instruction (2009-2010): Total instructional faculty: 206 full-time, 27 part-time (56% men; 44% women; 20% minorities). Full-time faculty with Ph.D. or other terminal degree: 98%. Student/faculty ratio: 8/1. Classes of fewer than 20 students: 75%; of 20 to 49 students: 22%; of 50 or more students: 3%. Advanced Placement and International Baccalaureate credit: AP tests may be used for: Placement only. Scores accepted: 5. Freshmen returning for sophomore year: 98%. Graduation rates: Four-year: 85%; five-year: 92%; six-year: 94%. Graduate study: 28% of students pursue further study immediately upon graduation. Fields in which graduates pursue further study: Master of Business Administration (MBA), 14%; law, 15%; medicine, 14%; dentistry, 1%; engineering, 3%; theology (or the seminary), 2%; education, 9%; arts and sciences, 14%; veterinary medicine, 1%.

COSTS AND FINANCIAL AID

Financial aid office: (413) 542-2296. Expenses (2010-2011): Tuition and fees 2010-2011: $40,862; room/board: $10,660. Estimated books and supplies: $1,000; transportation: $650; personal expenses: $1,800. Financial aid: Priority filing date for institution's financial aid form: February 15. In 2009-2010, 64% of undergraduates applied for financial aid. Of those, 58% were determined to have financial need; 100% had their need fully met. Average financial aid package (proportion receiving): $41,124 (58%). Average amount of gift aid, such as scholarships or grants (proportion receiving): $39,451 (57%). Average amount of self-help aid, such as work study or loans (proportion receiving): $2,093 (50%). Average need-based loan (excluding PLUS or other private loans): $2,941. Among students who received need-based aid, the average percentage of need met: 100%. Among students who received aid based on merit, the average award (and the proportion receiving): $0 (0%). The average athletic scholarship (and the proportion receiving): $0 (0%). Average amount of debt of borrowers graduating in 2009: $11,347. Proportion who borrowed: 41%.

CAMPUS LIFE AND EXTRACURRICULAR ACTIVITIES

Campus housing available (% using): coed dorms (100%), special housing for disabled students, cooperative housing, other housing options. Students who live in college-owned, operated, or affiliated housing: 97%. Student employment: During the 2009-2010 academic year, 60% of undergraduates worked on campus. Average per-year earnings: $1,600. Clubs and organizations: Number of student organizations: 104. Activities include: campus ministries, choral groups, concert band, dance, drama/theater, international student organization, jazz band, literary magazine, model UN, music ensembles, musical theater, opera, pep band, radio station, student government, student newspaper, student film society, symphony orchestra, yearbook. Number of fraternities: 0; sororities: 0. Average proportion of students who stay on campus on weekends: 95%. Sports program (2009-2010): Member of NCAA III.

SERVICES AND FACILITIES

Basic services: nonremedial tutoring, women's center, placement service, health service, health insurance. **Counseling services:** minority student, career, personal, veteran student, academic, psychological, birth control, religious, other. **For learning-disabled students:** School does not offer a structured program with separate admission and additional fees. Total undergraduates in learning-disabled program or receiving services: 67. Services include: tape recorders, note-taking services, readers, extended time for tests, tutors, other. **Library:** Number of titles: 1,003,887; number of current serial subscriptions: 10,632. **Information technology resources:** Students are not required to lease or own a computer. Number of campus computers available to all students: 550. School has a wireless network. Approximate number of users that can be accommodated: 3,000. Proportion of college-owned housing units wired for high-speed internet access: 100%. **Campus safety:** Security services offered: 24-hour foot-and-vehicle patrols, late-night transport/escort service, 24-hour emergency telephones, lighted pathways/sidewalks, student patrols, controlled dormitory access (key, security card, etc).

TRANSFER AND INTERNATIONAL STUDENTS

Transfer students: May apply for admission for the following academic terms: Fall, Spring. Applicants need a minimum number of credits to apply. For fall 2009: Transfer applications received: 395. Transfer applicants offered admission: 22. Transfer applicants enrolled: 17. **International students:** Number of foreign undergraduates: 142 (8% of student body). Minimum TOEFL score required: 600 (paper); 250 (computer). Average TOEFL score: 650 (paper).

Anna Maria College

- ■ **Address:** Sunset Lane, Paxton, MA 01612
- ■ **Website:** http://www.annamaria.edu
- ■ **Private; Religious affiliation:** Roman Catholic
- ■ **Enrollment:** N/A

KEY STATS
- ✔ **U.S News College Ranking:** second tier, Regional Universities (North)
- ✔ **ACT Score (25th/75th percentile):** 16-21
- ✔ **Tuition:** 2009-2010: $26,620

Selectivity: Less selective	**Room/board:** $9,630
Acceptance rate: 89%	**Average debt:** N/A
Student/faculty ratio: N/A	**Proportion who borrowed:** N/A

Assumption College

- ■ **Address:** 500 Salisbury Street, Worcester, MA 01609
- ■ **Website:** http://www.assumption.edu
- ■ **Private; Religious affiliation:** Roman Catholic
- ■ **Enrollment:** 2,114 full-time; 3 part-time

KEY STATS
- ✔ **U.S News College Ranking:** 36, Regional Universities (North)
- ✔ **SAT Score (25th/75th percentile):** 970-1170
- ✔ **Tuition:** 2010-2011: $31,305

Selectivity: Selective	**Room/board:** $10,260
Acceptance rate: 79%	**Average debt:** $24,382
Student/faculty ratio: 12/1	**Proportion who borrowed:** 83%

UNDERGRADUATE STUDENT BODY STATS

2009-2010 enrollment: 2,114 full-time; 3 part-time. Men: 42%; women: 58%. **Ethnic makeup:** African American: 2%; Asian American: 1%; Hispanic: 3%; White: 93%; International: 1%.

ADMISSIONS FACTS AND FIGURES

Phone: (866) 477-7776. **Email:** admiss@assumption.edu. **Website:** http://www.assumption.edu. **Application deadlines for fall 2011:** Regular decision: February 15. Early decision: Not offered. Early action: Send application by: November 15; Decision sent by: December 15. Admission can be deferred. **Application fee:** $50. **To apply online, go to:** http://www.assumption.edu/admiss/Applying/freshman.html. **Admissions requirements/recommenda-**

tions: High school units required (recommended): English: 4; Mathematics: 3; Science: 2; Foreign language: 2; History: 2; Academic electives: 5; Total units: 18. Tests: The college uses SAT or ACT scores in admissions decisions. Neither SAT nor ACT required. For admission to the fall 2011 entering class, the school will accept: ACT with or without writing accepted. Campus visit: Recommended. Admissions interview: Recommended. Off-campus interview: Not available. **Factors that count in admissions decisions:** *Academic:* Secondary school record: Important. Class rank: Considered. Letters of recommendation: Important. Standardized test scores: Considered. Essay: Very Important. *Nonacademic:* Interview: Important. Extracurricular activities: Considered. Talent/ability: Considered. Character/personal qualities: Considered. Alumni/ae relationship: Considered. Geographical residence: Not Considered. State residency: Not Considered. Religious affiliation/commitment: Not Considered. Minority status: Considered. Volunteer work: Important. Work experience: Not Considered. **Other schools with the greatest overlap in applicants:** Merrimack College; Providence College; St. Anselm College; Stonehill College; University of Massachusetts–Amherst. **Admissions statistics for the fall 2009 entering class:** Total applicants: 3,719. Total accepted: 2,947. Freshmen enrolled: 515; 38% were from out of state. Accepted through early-decision or early-action plans: 43%. Overall acceptance rate: 79%. Non-early acceptance rate: 72%. **Size of waiting list:** 302 applicants; enrolled from waiting list: 73. **Credentials of fall 2009 freshmen:** 14% ranked in the top 10 percent of their high school class; 44% were in the top 25 percent; 85% were in the top half. (Proportion submitting class standing: 55%.) **Average high school grade point average:** 3.4. **First-year students who submitted SAT scores:** 96%. Scores (25/75 percentile): Critical Reading: 480-580, Math: 490-590, Combined: 970-1170. **First-year students submitting ACT scores:** 23%. Scores (25/75 percentile): English: 19-25, Math: 20-25, Composite: 20-25.

ACADEMICS

Year founded: 1904. **Academic calendar:** Semester. **Degrees offered:** bachelor's, post-bachelor's certificate, master's, post-master's certificate. **Most popular majors:** 24% business, management, marketing, and related support services; 11% psychology, 10% communication, journalism, and related programs, 10% social sciences, 8% biological and biomedical sciences. **Major fields of study:** area, ethnic, cultural, and gender studies; biological and biomedical sciences; business, management, marketing, and related support services; communication, journalism, and related programs; computer and information sciences and support services; English language and literature/letters; foreign languages, literatures, and linguistics; health professions and related clinical sciences; history; mathematics and statistics; multi/interdisciplinary studies; natural resources and conservation; philosophy and religious studies; physical sciences; psychology; social sciences; theology and religious vocations; visual and performing arts. **Areas of required coursework:** arts/fine arts, humanities, mathematics, English (including composition), philosophy, foreign languages, sciences (biological or physical), history, social science, other. **Pre-professional programs:** pre-optometry, other. **Special academic programs:** cross-registration, double major, honors program, independent study, internships, student-designed major, study abroad, teacher certificate program. **Teacher certification offered in:** elementary, middle/junior high, secondary. **Reserve Officers Training Corps (ROTC):** Army ROTC: Offered at cooperating institution (Worcester Polytechnic Institute); Air Force ROTC: Offered at cooperating institution (Worcester Polytechnic Institute). **Faculty and instruction (2009-2010):** Total instructional faculty: 154 full-time, 67 part-time (57% men; 43% women; 8% minorities). Full-time faculty with Ph.D. or other terminal degree: 93%. Student/faculty ratio: 12/1. Classes of fewer than 20 students: 47%; of 20 to 49 students: 53%; of 50 or more students: 0%. **Advanced Placement and International Baccalaureate credit:** AP tests may be used for: Credit and/or placement. Scores accepted: 3, 4, 5. International Baccalaureate exams may be used for: Credit and/or placement. **Freshmen returning for sophomore year:** 82%. **Graduation rates:** Four-year: 64%; five-year: 66%; six-year: 70%. **Graduate study:** 26% of students pursue further study within one year.

COSTS AND FINANCIAL AID

Financial aid office: (508) 767-7158. **Expenses (2010-2011):** Tuition and fees 2010-2011: $31,305; room/board: $10,260. Estimated books and supplies: $1,000; transportation: $500; personal expenses: $500. **Financial aid:** Priority filing date for institution's financial aid form: February 1; deadline: February 15. In 2009-2010, 87% of undergraduates applied for financial aid. Of those, 76% were determined to have financial need; 18% had their need fully met. Average financial aid package (proportion receiving): $19,557 (75%). Average amount of gift aid, such as scholarships or grants (proportion receiving): $15,334 (75%). Average amount of self-help aid, such as work study or loans (proportion receiving): $5,011 (64%). Average need-based loan (excluding PLUS or other private loans): $4,723. Among students who received need-based aid, the average percentage of need met: 71%. Among students who received aid based on merit, the average award (and the proportion receiving): $9,517 (19%). The average athletic scholarship (and the proportion receiving): $23,145 (2%). Average amount of debt of borrowers graduating in 2009: $24,382. Proportion who borrowed: 83%.

CAMPUS LIFE AND EXTRACURRICULAR ACTIVITIES
Campus housing available: coed dorms, women's dorms, special housing for disabled students, other housing options. Students who live in college-owned, operated, or affiliated housing: 90%. **Student employment:** During the 2009-2010 academic year, 18% of undergraduates worked on campus. Average per-year earnings: $603. **Clubs and organizations:** Number of student organizations: 60. Activities include: campus ministries, choral groups, concert band, drama/theater, literary magazine, musical theater, pep band, student government, student newspaper, student film society, television station, yearbook. Number of fraternities: 0; sororities: 0. Average proportion of students who stay on campus on weekends: 80%. **Sports program (2009-2010):** Member of NCAA II. *Men's intercollegiate varsity sports:* baseball, basketball, cross country, football, golf, ice hockey, lacrosse, soccer, tennis, track and field (indoor), track and field (outdoor). *Women's intercollegiate varsity sports:* basketball, cross country, field hockey, lacrosse, crew (lightweight), soccer, softball, swimming, tennis, track and field (indoor), track and field (outdoor), volleyball.

SERVICES AND FACILITIES
Basic services: nonremedial tutoring, placement service, health service, health insurance. **Counseling services:** minority student, career, personal, academic, psychological, religious. **For learning-disabled students:** School does not offer a structured program with separate admission and additional fees. Total undergraduates in learning-disabled program or receiving services: 160. **Library:** Number of titles: 217,162; number of current serial subscriptions: 1,273. **Information technology resources:** Students are not required to lease or own a computer. Number of campus computers available to all students: 315. School has a wireless network. Approximate number of users that can be accommodated: 5,000. Proportion of college-owned housing units wired for high-speed internet access: 100%. **Campus safety:** Security services offered: 24-hour foot-and-vehicle patrols, late-night transport/escort service, 24-hour emergency telephones, lighted pathways/sidewalks, controlled dormitory access (key, security card, etc).

TRANSFER AND INTERNATIONAL STUDENTS
Transfer students: May apply for admission for the following academic terms: Fall, Spring. Applicants do not need a minimum number of credits to apply. For fall 2009: Transfer applications received: 146. Transfer applicants offered admission: 77. Transfer applicants enrolled: 32. **International students:** Number of foreign undergraduates: 12 (1% of student body). Number of countries represented: 9. Minimum TOEFL score required: 550 (paper); 213 (computer).

Atlantic Union College

- **Address:** PO Box 1000, South Lancaster, MA 01561
- **Website:** http://www.auc.edu
- **Private; Religious affiliation:** Seventh-day Adventist
- **Enrollment:** 371 full-time; 90 part-time

KEY STATS
✔ **U.S News College Ranking:** second tier, National Liberal Arts Colleges
✔ **SAT Score (25th/75th percentile):** 670-950
✔ **Tuition:** 2010-2011: $17,066

Selectivity: Less selective	**Room/board:** $5,000
Acceptance rate: 59%	**Average debt:** $38,328
Student/faculty ratio: 10/1	**Proportion who borrowed:** 83%

UNDERGRADUATE STUDENT BODY STATS
2009-2010 enrollment: 371 full-time; 90 part-time. Men: 33%; women: 67%. **Ethnic makeup:** African American: 54%; Asian American: 4%; Hispanic: 19%; White: 23%. **Religious preference:** Seventh-day Adventist: 67%; Other: 33%.

ADMISSIONS FACTS AND FIGURES
Phone: (978) 368-2235. **Email:** enroll@auc.edu. **Website:** http://www.auc.edu. **Application deadlines for fall 2011:** Regular decision: August 1. Early decision: Not offered. Early action: Not offered. Admission can be deferred. **Application fee:** $25. **To apply online, go to:** http://www.auc.edu/index.php?id=5. **Admissions requirements/recommendations:** High school units required (recommended): English: 4; Mathematics: (3); Science: 2; Foreign language: 2; Social studies: 2; Total units: 14. Tests: The college uses SAT or ACT scores in admissions decisions. Neither SAT nor ACT required. For admission to the fall 2011 entering class, the school will accept: ACT with writing required. Campus visit: Recommended. Admissions interview: Neither required nor recommended. Off-campus interview: Not available. **Factors that count in admissions decisions:** *Academic:* Secondary school record: Very Important. Class rank: Not Considered. Letters of recommendation: Important. Standardized test scores: Very Important. Essay: Considered. *Nonacademic:* Interview: Considered. Extracurricular activities: Considered. Talent/ability: Important. Character/personal qualities: Very Important. Alumni/ae relationship: Important. Geographical residence: Important. State residency: Important. Religious affiliation/commitment: Very Important. Minority status: Considered. Volunteer work: Considered. Work experience: Important. **Other schools with the greatest overlap in applicants:** Andrews University; La Sierra University; Oakwood University; Southern Adventist University; Washington Adventist University. **Admissions statistics for the fall 2009 entering class:** Total applicants: 224. Total accepted: 133. Freshmen enrolled: 89; Overall acceptance rate: 59%. **First-year students who submitted SAT scores:** 69%. **First-year students submitting ACT scores:** 10%. Scores (25/75 percentile): English: N/A, Math: N/A, Composite: N/A.

ACADEMICS
Year founded: 1882. **Academic calendar:** Semester. **Degrees offered:** certificate, associate, bachelor's, post-bachelor's certificate, master's. **Major fields of study:** biological and biomedical sciences; business, management, marketing, and related support services; computer and information sciences and support services; education; English language and literature/letters; health professions and related clinical sciences; history; liberal arts and sciences studies, and humanities; mathematics and statistics; parks, recreation, leisure, and fitness studies; philosophy and religious studies; psychology; public administration and social service professions; social sciences; theology and religious vocations; visual and performing arts. **Areas of required coursework:** arts/fine arts, humanities, computer literacy, mathematics, English (including composition), foreign languages, sciences (biological or physical), history, social science, other. **Pre-professional programs:** pre-law, pre-dentistry, pre-medicine, pre-veterinary science, pre-pharmacy. **Special academic programs:** cross-registration, distance learning, double major, English as a Second Language (ESL), honors program, independent study, internships, study abroad, teacher certificate program. **Teacher certification offered in:** early childhood, elementary, adult education, secondary. **Faculty and instruction (2009-2010):** Total instruction faculty: 26 full-time, 46 part-time (54% men; 46% women; 19% minorities). Full-time faculty with Ph.D. or other terminal degree: 62%. Student/faculty ratio: 10/1. Classes of fewer than 20 students: 81%; of 20 to 49 students: 18%; of 50 or more students: 1%. **Advanced Placement and International Baccalaureate credit:** AP tests may be used for: Credit only. International Baccalaureate exams may be used for: Credit only. **Freshmen returning for sophomore year:** 54%. **Graduation rates:** Six-year: 37%.

COSTS AND FINANCIAL AID
Financial aid office: (978) 368-2280. **Expenses (2010-2011):** Tuition and fees 2010-2011: $17,066; room/board: $5,000. Estimated books and supplies: $1,500; transportation: $2,000; personal expenses: $400. **Financial aid:** Priority filing date for institution's financial aid form: May 1; deadline: September 9. In 2009-2010, 88% of undergraduates applied for financial aid. Of those, 82% were determined to have financial need; 11% had their need fully met. Average financial aid package (proportion receiving): $12,049 (81%). Average amount of gift aid, such as scholarships or grants (proportion receiving): $6,876 (94%). Average amount of self-help aid, such as work study or loans (proportion receiving): $6,049 (77%). Average need-based loan (excluding PLUS or other private loans): $4,384. Among students who received need-based aid, the average percentage of need met: 65%. Among students who received aid based on merit, the average award (and the proportion receiving): $2,963 (10%). The average athletic scholarship (and the proportion receiving): $0 (0%). Average amount of debt of borrowers graduating in 2009: $38,328. Proportion who borrowed: 83%.

CAMPUS LIFE AND EXTRACURRICULAR ACTIVITIES

Campus housing available: women's dorms, men's dorms, apartments for married students. Students who live in college-owned, operated, or affiliated housing: 50%. **Student employment:** During the 2009-2010 academic year, 54% of undergraduates worked on campus. Average per-year earnings: $2,500. **Clubs and organizations:** Number of student organizations: 23. Activities include: campus ministries, choral groups, concert band, drama/theater, music ensembles, student government, student newspaper, symphony orchestra, yearbook. Average proportion of students who stay on campus on weekends: 50%.

SERVICES AND FACILITIES

Basic services: nonremedial tutoring, health service, health insurance. **Remedial assistance:** reading, math, writing, study skills. **Counseling services:** personal, religious. **For learning-disabled students:** School does not offer a structured program with separate admission and additional fees. Services include: remedial math, remedial reading, diagnostic testing service, note-taking services, learning center, extended time for tests, tutors. **Library:** Number of titles: 157,521; number of current serial subscriptions: 258. **Information technology resources:** Students are not required to lease or own a computer. Number of campus computers available to all students: 74. School has a wireless network. Proportion of college-owned housing units wired for high-speed internet access: 50%. **Campus safety:** Security services offered: 24-hour emergency telephones, student patrols.

TRANSFER AND INTERNATIONAL STUDENTS

Transfer students: May apply for admission for the following academic terms: Fall, Spring, Summer. Applicants do not need a minimum number of credits to apply. For fall 2009: Transfer applications received: 169. Transfer applicants offered admission: 127. Transfer applicants enrolled: 65. **International students:** Number of foreign undergraduates: 0. Number of countries represented: 22. Minimum TOEFL score required: 525 (paper); 195 (computer).

Babson College

- **Address:** 231 Forest Street, Babson Park, MA 02457-0310
- **Website:** http://www.babson.edu
- **Private**
- **Enrollment:** 1,898 full-time

KEY STATS
✔ **U.S News College Ranking:** Unranked Specialty School–Business
✔ **SAT Score (25th/75th percentile):** 1165-1350
✔ **Tuition:** 2010-2011: $39,040

Selectivity: More selective	**Room/board:** $12,876
Acceptance rate: 40%	**Average debt:** $28,164
Student/faculty ratio: 13/1	**Proportion who borrowed:** 49%

UNDERGRADUATE STUDENT BODY STATS

2009-2010 enrollment: 1,898 full-time. Men: 57%; women: 43%. **Ethnic makeup:** African American: 5%; Asian American: 13%; Hispanic: 8%; White: 51%; International: 22%.

ADMISSIONS FACTS AND FIGURES

Phone: (781) 239-5522. **Email:** ugradadmission@babson.edu. **Website:** http://www.babson.edu. **Application deadlines for fall 2011:** Regular decision: January 15; decision sent by April 1. Early decision: Send application by: November 1; Decision sent by: December 7. Early action: Send application by: November 1; Decision sent by: January 1. Admission can be deferred. **Application fee:** $65. **To apply online, go to:** http://www.babson.edu/ugrad/apply. **Admissions requirements/recommendations:** High school units required (recommended): English: (4); Mathematics: (4); Science: (4); Foreign language: (4); Social studies: (2); History: (2); Total units: (20). Tests: The college uses SAT or ACT scores in admissions decisions. Either SAT or ACT required. For admission to the fall 2011 entering class, the school will accept: ACT with writing required. Campus visit: Recommended. Admissions interview: Recommended. Off-campus interview: May be arranged. **Factors that count in admissions decisions:** *Academic:* Secondary school record: Very Important. Class rank: Important. Letters of recommendation: Very Important. Standardized test scores: Very Important. Essay: Very Important. *Nonacademic:* Interview: Considered. Extracurricular activities: Important. Talent/ability: Considered. Character/

personal qualities: Very Important. Alumni/ae relationship: Considered. Geographical residence: Considered. State residency: Considered. Religious affiliation/commitment: Not Considered. Minority status: Considered. Volunteer work: Considered. Work experience: Considered. **Other schools with the greatest overlap in applicants:** Bentley University; Boston College; Boston University; New York University; University of Pennsylvania. **Admissions statistics for the fall 2009 entering class:** Total applicants: 4,150. Total accepted: 1,675. Freshmen enrolled: 471; 79% were from out of state. Accepted through early-decision or early-action plans: 47%. Overall acceptance rate: 40%. Early-decision acceptance rate: 61%. Non-early acceptance rate: 37%. **Size of waiting list:** 489 applicants; enrolled from waiting list: 44. **Credentials of fall 2009 freshmen:** 50% ranked in the top 10 percent of their high school class; 86% were in the top 25 percent; 99% were in the top half. (Proportion submitting class standing: 28%.) **Average high school grade point average:** 3.5. **First-year students who submitted SAT scores:** 91%. Scores (25/75 percentile): Critical Reading: 560-650, Math: 605-700, Combined: 1165-1350. **First-year students submitting ACT scores:** 22%. Scores (25/75 percentile): English: 26-31, Math: 23-29, Composite: 25-29.

ACADEMICS

Year founded: 1919. **Academic calendar:** Semester. **Degrees offered:** bachelor's, master's, post-master's certificate. **Most popular majors:** 100% business, management, marketing, and related support services. **Major fields of study:** business, management, marketing, and related support services; communication, journalism, and related programs; computer and information sciences and support services; history; legal professions and studies; mathematics and statistics; philosophy and religious studies; social sciences. **Areas of required coursework:** humanities, mathematics, English (including composition), sciences (biological or physical), history, social science, other. **Special academic programs:** cross-registration, honors program, independent study, internships, liberal arts/career combination, study abroad. **Reserve Officers Training Corps (ROTC):** Army ROTC: Offered at cooperating institution (Boston University); Navy ROTC: Offered at cooperating institution (Boston University); Air Force ROTC: Offered at cooperating institution (Boston University). **Faculty and instruction (2009-2010):** Total instructional faculty: 174 full-time, 94 part-time (69% men; 31% women; 12% minorities). Full-time faculty with Ph.D. or other terminal degree: 89%. Student/faculty ratio: 13/1. Classes of fewer than 20 students: 19%; of 20 to 49 students: 78%; of 50 or more students: 3%. **Advanced Placement and International Baccalaureate credit:** AP tests may be used for: Placement only. Scores accepted: 4, 5. International Baccalaureate exams may be used for: Placement only. **Freshmen returning for sophomore year:** 94%. **Graduation rates:** Four-year: 87%; five-year: 90%; six-year: 89%. **Graduate study:** 6% of students pursue further study immediately upon graduation.

COSTS AND FINANCIAL AID

Financial aid office: (781) 239-4219. **Expenses (2010-2011):** Tuition and fees 2010-2011: $39,040; room/board: $12,876. Estimated books and supplies: $1,000; transportation: $650; personal expenses: $1,784. **Financial aid:** Priority filing date for institution's financial aid form: February 15; deadline: February 15. In 2009-2010, 47% of undergraduates applied for financial aid. Of those, 44% were determined to have financial need; 68% had their need fully met. Average financial aid package (proportion receiving): $31,719 (44%). Average amount of gift aid, such as scholarships or grants (proportion receiving): $26,193 (41%). Average amount of self-help aid, such as work study or loans (proportion receiving): $5,526 (44%). Average need-based loan (excluding PLUS or other private loans): $4,020. Among students who received need-based aid, the average percentage of need met: 95%. Among students who received aid based on merit, the average award (and the proportion receiving): $17,764 (7%). The average athletic scholarship (and the proportion receiving): $0 (0%). Average amount of debt of borrowers graduating in 2009: $28,164. Proportion who borrowed: 49%.

CAMPUS LIFE AND EXTRACURRICULAR ACTIVITIES

Campus housing available (% using): coed dorms (92%), sorority housing (1%), fraternity housing (1%), apartments for married students (1%), special housing for disabled students (2%), other housing options (0%). Students who live in college-owned, operated, or affiliated housing: 85%. **Student employment:** During the 2009-2010 academic year, 39% of undergraduates worked on campus. Average per-year earnings: $2,640. **Clubs and organizations:** Number of student organizations: 92. Activities include: campus ministries, dance, drama/theater, international student organization, jazz band, literary magazine, radio station, student government, student newspaper. Number of fraternities: 4; sororities: 3. Proportion of men in fraternities: 17%; of women in sororities: 19%. Average proportion of students who stay on campus on weekends: 75%. **Sports program (2009-2010):** Member of NCAA III. **Men's intercollegiate varsity sports:** baseball, basketball, cross country, golf, ice hockey, lacrosse, skiing (alpine), soccer, swimming, tennis, track and field (outdoor). **Women's intercollegiate varsity sports:** basketball, cross country, field hockey, lacrosse, skiing (alpine), soccer, softball, swimming, tennis, track and field (outdoor), volleyball.

SERVICES AND FACILITIES

Basic services: nonremedial tutoring, placement service, health service, other. **Remedial assistance:** study skills. **Counseling services:** minority student, career, personal, academic, psychological, birth control, religious. **For learning-disabled students:** School does not offer a structured program with separate admission and additional fees. Services include: reading machines, tape recorders, note-taking services, extended time for tests, other testing accommodations. **Library:** Number of titles: 114,006; number of current serial subscriptions: 409. **Information technology resources:** Students are required to lease or own a computer. Number of campus computers available to all students: 2,050. School has a wireless network. Approximate number of users that can be accommodated: 10,000. Proportion of college-owned housing units wired for high-speed internet access: 100%. **Campus safety:** Security services offered: 24-hour foot-and-vehicle patrols, late-night transport/escort service, 24-hour emergency telephones, lighted pathways/sidewalks, controlled dormitory access (key, security card, etc).

TRANSFER AND INTERNATIONAL STUDENTS

Transfer students: May apply for admission for the following academic terms: Fall, Spring. Applicants need a minimum number of credits to apply. **International students:** Number of foreign undergraduates: 425 (22% of student body). Number of countries represented: 60. Minimum TOEFL score required: 600 (paper); 250 (computer). Average TOEFL score: 610 (paper).

Bard College at Simon's Rock

- **Address:** 84 Alford Road, Great Barrington, MA 01230
- **Website:** http://www.simons-rock.edu
- **Private**
- **Enrollment:** 421 full-time; 10 part-time

KEY STATS
✔ **U.S News College Ranking:** 20, Regional Colleges (North)
✔ **SAT or ACT Score (25th/75th percentile):** N/A
✔ **Tuition:** 2010-2011: $41,990

Selectivity: Less selective	**Room/board:** $11,450
Acceptance rate: 84%	**Average debt:** $20,000
Student/faculty ratio: N/A	**Proportion who borrowed:** 38%

UNDERGRADUATE STUDENT BODY STATS

2009-2010 enrollment: 421 full-time; 10 part-time. Men: 41%; women: 59%. **Ethnic makeup:** African American: 7%; American-Indian: 1%; Asian American: 5%; Hispanic: 4%; White: 79%; International: 4%.

ADMISSIONS FACTS AND FIGURES

Phone: (413) 528-7312. **Email:** admit@simons-rock.edu. **Website:** http://www.simons-rock.edu. **Application deadlines for fall 2011:** Regular decision: Rolling. Early decision: Not offered. Early action: Not offered. Admission cannot be deferred. **Application fee:** $50. **Admissions requirements/recommendations:** High school units required (recommended): English: 2 (2); Mathematics: 2 (2); Science: 2 (2); Foreign language: 2 (2); Social studies: 2 (2); History: 2 (2); Academic electives: 2 (2); Total units: 15 (15). Tests: The college uses SAT or ACT scores in admissions decisions. Neither SAT nor ACT required. For admission to the fall 2011 entering class, the school will accept: ACT with or without writing accepted. Campus visit: Recommended. Admissions interview: Required. Off-campus interview: May be arranged. **Factors that count in admissions decisions:** *Academic:* Secondary school record: Important. Class rank: Important. Letters of recommendation: Very Important. Standardized test scores: Considered. Essay: Very Important. *Nonacademic:* Interview: Very Important. Extracurricular activities: Important. Talent/ability: Very Important. Character/personal qualities: Very Important. Alumni/ae relationship: Considered. Geographical residence: Considered. State residency: Not Considered. Religious affiliation/commitment: Not Considered. Minority status: Considered. Volunteer work: Considered. Work experience: Considered. **Admissions statistics for the fall**

2009 entering class: Total applicants: 332. Total accepted: 280. Freshmen enrolled: 179; Overall acceptance rate: 84%.

ACADEMICS

Year founded: 1964. **Academic calendar:** Semester. **Degrees offered:** associate, bachelor's. **Most popular majors:** 100% liberal arts and sciences studies, and humanities. **Major fields of study:** area, ethnic, cultural, and gender studies; biological and biomedical sciences; English language and literature/letters; foreign languages, literatures, and linguistics; health professions and related clinical sciences; history; legal professions and studies; liberal arts and sciences studies, and humanities; mathematics and statistics; multi/interdisciplinary studies; natural resources and conservation; philosophy and religious studies; psychology; public administration and social service professions; science technologies/technicians; social sciences; visual and performing arts. **Areas of required coursework:** arts/fine arts, humanities, computer literacy, mathematics, English (including composition), philosophy, foreign languages, sciences (biological or physical), history, social science, other. **Pre-professional programs:** other. **Special academic programs:** accelerated program, cooperative (work-study plan) program, cross-registration, dual enrollment, exchange student program (domestic), independent study, internships, student-designed major, study abroad. **Cooperative education programs:** engineering. **Faculty and instruction (2009-2010):** Total instructional faculty: N/A. Classes of fewer than 20 students: 96%; of 20 to 49 students: 4%; of 50 or more students: 0%. **Advanced Placement and International Baccalaureate credit:** AP tests may be used for: Placement only. **Freshmen returning for sophomore year:** 80%. **Graduation rates:** Four-year: 20%; five-year: 26%; six-year: 28%.

COSTS AND FINANCIAL AID

Financial aid office: (413) 528-7297. **Expenses (2010-2011):** Tuition and fees 2010-2011: $41,990; room/board: $11,450. Estimated books and supplies: $1,000; transportation: $1,000; personal expenses: $0. **Financial aid:** Priority filing date for institution's financial aid form: April 15. In 2009-2010, 69% of undergraduates applied for financial aid. Of those, 62% were determined to have financial need; 15% had their need fully met. Average financial aid package (proportion receiving): $33,639 (62%). Average amount of gift aid, such as scholarships or grants (proportion receiving): $17,567 (53%). Average amount of self-help aid, such as work study or loans (proportion receiving): $6,424 (61%). Average need-based loan (excluding PLUS or other private loans): $4,644. Among students who received need-based aid, the average percentage of need met: 68%. Among students who received aid based on merit, the average award (and the proportion receiving): $14,929 (15%). Average amount of debt of borrowers graduating in 2009: $20,000. Proportion who borrowed: 38%.

CAMPUS LIFE AND EXTRACURRICULAR ACTIVITIES

Campus housing available: coed dorms, women's dorms, men's dorms, apartment for single students. Activities include: choral groups, concert band, dance, drama/theater, international student organization, jazz band, literary magazine, music ensembles, musical theater, radio station, student government, student newspaper, student film society, yearbook. Number of fraternities: 0; sororities: 0. Average proportion of students who stay on campus on weekends: 90%.

SERVICES AND FACILITIES

Basic services: nonremedial tutoring, women's center, health service, health insurance. **Remedial assistance:** reading, math, writing, study skills, other. **Counseling services:** minority student, career, personal, academic, psychological, birth control, religious. **For learning-disabled students:** School does not offer a structured program with separate admission and additional fees. Services include: reading machines, tape recorders, other special classes, videotaped classes, diagnostic testing service, untimed tests, note-taking services, oral tests, learning center, readers, extended time for tests, tutors, priority seating, texts on tape, other testing accommodations, other. **Information technology resources:** Students are not required to lease or own a computer. Number of campus computers available to all students: 75. School has a wireless network. Approximate number of users that can be accommodated: 600. Proportion of college-owned housing units wired for high-speed internet access: 100%. **Campus safety:** Security services offered: late-night transport/escort service, 24-hour emergency telephones, lighted pathways/sidewalks, controlled dormitory access (key, security card, etc).

TRANSFER AND INTERNATIONAL STUDENTS

Transfer students: May apply for admission for the following academic terms: Fall, Spring. Applicants do not need a minimum number of credits to apply. For fall 2009: Transfer applications received: 0. Transfer applicants offered admission: 0. Transfer applicants enrolled: 0. **International students:** Number of foreign undergraduates: 17 (4% of student body). Number of countries represented: 10. Minimum TOEFL score required: 500 (paper).

Bay Path College

- **Address:** 588 Longmeadow Street, Longmeadow, MA 01106
- **Website:** http://www.baypath.edu
- **Private**
- **Enrollment:** 1,199 full-time; 282 part-time

KEY STATS
✔ **U.S News College Ranking:** 27, Regional Colleges (North)
✔ **SAT Score (25th/75th percentile):** 830-1075
✔ **Tuition:** 2009-2010: $24,530

Selectivity: Selective	**Room/board:** $10,035
Acceptance rate: 83%	**Average debt:** N/A
Student/faculty ratio: 15/1	**Proportion who borrowed:** N/A

UNDERGRADUATE STUDENT BODY STATS
2009-2010 enrollment: 1,199 full-time; 282 part-time. Men: 0%; women: 100%. **Ethnic makeup:** African American: 11%; Asian American: 2%; Hispanic: 11%; White: 75%.

ADMISSIONS FACTS AND FIGURES
Phone: (413) 565-1331. **Email:** admiss@baypath.edu. **Website:** http://www.baypath.edu. **Application deadlines for fall 2011:** Regular decision: Rolling. Early decision: Not offered. Early action: Send application by: December 15; Decision sent by: January 2. Admission can be deferred. **Application fee:** $25. **To apply online, go to:** http://mail.baypath.edu/BPC.nsf/Traditional?OpenForm. **Admissions requirements/recommendations:** High school units required (recommended): English: 4; Mathematics: 3 (4); Science: 2 (3); Foreign language: 0 (2); Social studies: 2; History: 1 (2); Total units: 15 (20). Tests: The college uses SAT or ACT scores in admissions decisions. Either SAT or ACT required. For admission to the fall 2011 entering class, the school will accept: ACT with writing recommended. Campus visit: Recommended. Admissions interview: Recommended. Off-campus interview: Not available. **Factors that count in admissions decisions:** *Academic:* Secondary school record: Very Important. Class rank: Considered. Letters of recommendation: Considered. Standardized test scores: Important. Essay: Considered. *Nonacademic:* Interview: Considered. Extracurricular activities: Considered. Talent/ability: Considered. Character/personal qualities: Considered. Alumni/ae relationship: Considered. Geographical residence: Considered. State residency: Not Considered. Religious affiliation/commitment: Not Considered. Minority status: Not Considered. Volunteer work: Considered. Work experience: Considered. **Other schools with the greatest overlap in applicants:** College of Our Lady of the Elms; University of Massachusetts–Amherst; University of New Haven; Western New England College; Westfield State College. **Admissions statistics for the fall 2009 entering class:** Total applicants: 702. Total accepted: 582. Freshmen enrolled: 152; 50% were from out of state. Overall acceptance rate: 83%. Non-early acceptance rate: 83%. **Credentials of fall 2009 freshmen:** 21% ranked in the top 10 percent of their high school class; 43% were in the top 25 percent; 76% were in the top half. (Proportion submitting class standing: 81%.) **Average high school grade point average:** 3.2. **First-year students who submitted SAT scores:** 93%. Scores (25/75 percentile): Critical Reading: 420-550, Math: 410-525, Combined: 830-1075. **First-year students submitting ACT scores:** 12%. Scores (25/75 percentile): English: 17-23, Math: 17-24, Composite: 19-24.

ACADEMICS
Year founded: 1897. **Academic calendar:** Semester. **Degrees offered:** certificate, associate, bachelor's, master's. **Most popular majors:** 33% liberal arts and sciences studies, and humanities, 23% business, management, marketing, and related support services, 17% psychology, 14% security and protective services, 11% legal professions and studies. **Major fields of study:** biological and biomedical sciences; business, management, marketing, and related support services; education; health professions and related clinical sciences; legal professions and studies; liberal arts and sciences studies, and humanities; psychology; security and protective services. **Areas of required coursework:** arts/fine arts, computer literacy, mathematics, English (including composition), sciences (biological or physical), history, social science.

Pre-professional programs: pre-law, pre-medicine, pre-veterinary science. **Special academic programs:** accelerated program, cooperative (work-study plan) program, cross-registration, distance learning, double major, English as a Second Language (ESL), exchange student program (domestic), honors program, independent study, internships, student-designed major, study abroad, teacher certificate program, weekend college. **Teacher certification offered in:** early childhood, elementary, secondary. **Cooperative education programs:** business, other. **Reserve Officers Training Corps (ROTC):** Army ROTC: Offered at cooperating institution (Western New England College); Air Force ROTC: Offered at cooperating institution (Western New England College). **Faculty and instruction (2009-2010):** Total instructional faculty: 43 full-time, 154 part-time (35% men; 65% women; 5% minorities). Full-time faculty with Ph.D. or other terminal degree: 60%. Student/faculty ratio: 15/1. Classes of fewer than 20 students: 63%; of 20 to 49 students: 37%; of 50 or more students: 0%. **Advanced Placement and International Baccalaureate credit:** AP tests may be used for: Placement only. Scores accepted: 3, 4, 5. **Freshmen returning for sophomore year:** 69%. **Graduation rates:** Six-year: 50%.

COSTS AND FINANCIAL AID
Financial aid office: (413) 565-1261. **Expenses (2009-2010):** Tuition and fees 2009-2010: $24,530; room/board: $10,035. Estimated books and supplies: $1,200; transportation: $500; personal expenses: $900. **Financial aid:** Priority filing date for institution's financial aid form: March 15.

CAMPUS LIFE AND EXTRACURRICULAR ACTIVITIES
Campus housing available (% using): women's dorms (100%). Students who live in college-owned, operated, or affiliated housing: 62%. **Clubs and organizations:** Number of student organizations: 32. Activities include: choral groups, dance, drama/theater, international student organization, model UN, musical theater, student government. Number of fraternities: 0; sororities: 0. Average proportion of students who stay on campus on weekends: 55%. **Sports program (2009-2010):** Member of NCAA III. *Women's intercollegiate varsity sports:* basketball, cross country, field hockey, soccer, softball, tennis, volleyball.

SERVICES AND FACILITIES
Basic services: nonremedial tutoring, health service, health insurance, other. **Remedial assistance:** reading, math, writing, study skills, other. **Counseling services:** career, personal, academic, older student, psychological, birth control, other. **For learning-disabled students:** School does not offer a structured program with separate admission and additional fees. Services include: tape recorders, untimed tests, note-taking services, learning center, extended time for tests, tutors, priority seating, texts on tape, other testing accommodations, other. **Information technology resources:** Students are not required to lease or own a computer. Number of campus computers available to all students: 200. School has a wireless network. Approximate number of users that can be accommodated: 750. Proportion of college-owned housing units wired for high-speed internet access: 100%. **Campus safety:** Security services offered: 24-hour foot-and-vehicle patrols, late-night transport/escort service, 24-hour emergency telephones, lighted pathways/sidewalks, controlled dormitory access (key, security card, etc).

TRANSFER AND INTERNATIONAL STUDENTS
Transfer students: May apply for admission for the following academic terms: Fall, Spring. Applicants do not need a minimum number of credits to apply. For fall 2009: Transfer applications received: 151. Transfer applicants offered admission: 107. Transfer applicants enrolled: 45. **International students:** Number of foreign undergraduates: 7. Number of countries represented: 6. Minimum TOEFL score required: 500 (paper); 187 (computer). Average TOEFL score: 520 (paper).

Becker College

- **Address:** 61 Sever Street, Worcester, MA 01609
- **Website:** http://www.beckercollege.edu
- **Private**
- **Enrollment:** 1,432 full-time; 310 part-time

KEY STATS

- ✔ **U.S News College Ranking:** second tier, Regional Colleges (North)
- ✔ **SAT Score (25th/75th percentile):** 780-980
- ✔ **Tuition:** 2010-2011: $26,880

Selectivity: Least selective	**Room/board:** $10,020
Acceptance rate: 78%	**Average debt:** $31,800
Student/faculty ratio: N/A	**Proportion who borrowed:** 98%

UNDERGRADUATE STUDENT BODY STATS

2009-2010 enrollment: 1,432 full-time; 310 part-time. Men: 33%; women: 67%. **Ethnic makeup:** African American: 6%; American-Indian: 1%; Asian American: 2%; Hispanic: 2%; White: 89%.

ADMISSIONS FACTS AND FIGURES

Phone: (877) 523-2537. **Email:** admissions@beckercollege.edu. **Website:** http://www.beckercollege.edu. **Application deadlines for fall 2011:** Regular decision: Rolling. Early decision: Not offered. Early action: Not offered. Admission can be deferred. **Application fee:** $30. **To apply online, go to:** http://admissions.becker.edu/admissions/application/apply.asp. **Admissions requirements/recommendations:** High school units required (recommended): English: 4 (4); Mathematics: 3 (3); Science: 3 (3); Foreign language: 0 (2); Social studies: 2 (2); History: 1 (1); Academic electives: 2 (2); Total units: 17 (20). Tests: The college uses SAT or ACT scores in admissions decisions. Either SAT or ACT required. For admission to the fall 2011 entering class, the school will accept: ACT with writing required. Campus visit: Recommended. Admissions interview: Recommended. Off-campus interview: Not available. **Factors that count in admissions decisions:** *Academic:* Secondary school record: Very Important. Class rank: Considered. Letters of recommendation: Considered. Standardized test scores: Important. Essay: Considered. *Nonacademic:* Interview: Considered. Extracurricular activities: Considered. Talent/ability: Considered. Character/personal qualities: Considered. Alumni/ae relationship: Considered. Geographical residence: Not Considered. State residency: Not Considered. Religious affiliation/commitment: Not Considered. Minority status: Not Considered. Volunteer work: Considered. Work experience: Considered. **Other schools with the greatest overlap in applicants:** Anna Maria College; College of Our Lady of the Elms; Endicott College; Mount Ida College; Newbury College. **Admissions statistics for the fall 2009 entering class:** Total applicants: 2,387. Total accepted: 1,854. Freshmen enrolled: 365; 33% were from out of state. Overall acceptance rate: 78%. **First-year students who submitted SAT scores:** 92%. Scores (25/75 percentile): Critical Reading: 390-490, Math: 390-490, Combined: 780-980. **First-year students submitting ACT scores:** 6%. Scores (25/75 percentile): English: N/A, Math: N/A, Composite: 17-21.

ACADEMICS

Year founded: 1784. **Academic calendar:** Semester. **Degrees offered:** associate, bachelor's. **Major fields of study:** business, management, marketing, and related support services; health professions and related clinical sciences; legal professions and studies; liberal arts and sciences studies, and humanities; parks, recreation, leisure, and fitness studies; psychology; security and protective services; visual and performing arts. **Areas of required coursework:** humanities, computer literacy, mathematics, English (including composition), sciences (biological or physical), history, social science. **Pre-professional programs:** pre-law, pre-veterinary science. **Special academic programs:** accelerated program, cooperative (work-study plan) program, cross-registration, distance learning, dual enrollment, internships, liberal arts/career combination, study abroad, teacher certificate program. **Teacher certification offered in:** early childhood, elementary. **Cooperative education programs:** business, health professions. **Reserve Officers Training Corps (ROTC):** Army ROTC: Offered at cooperating institution (Worcester Polytechnic Institute); Air Force ROTC: Offered at cooperating institution (Worcester Polytechnic Institute). **Advanced Placement and International Baccalaureate credit:** AP tests may be used for: Credit and/or placement. Scores accepted: 3, 4, 5. **Graduation rates:** Six-year: 42%.

COSTS AND FINANCIAL AID

Financial aid office: (508) 791-9241. **Expenses (2010-2011):** Tuition and fees 2010-2011: $26,880; room/board: $10,020. Estimated books and supplies: $1,000; transportation: $1,000; personal expenses: $1,500. **Financial aid:** Priority filing date for institution's financial aid form: March 1. In 2009-2010, 26% of undergraduates applied for financial aid. Of those, 59% were determined to have financial need; 2% had their need fully met. Average financial aid package (proportion receiving): $10,070 (34%). Average amount of gift aid, such as scholarships or grants (proportion receiving): $7,189 (15%). Average amount of self-help aid, such as work study or loans (proportion receiving): $4,029 (10%). Average need-based loan (excluding PLUS or other private loans): $4,031. Among students who received need-based aid, the average percentage of need met: 74%. Among students who received aid based on merit, the average award (and the proportion receiving): $2,114 (24%). The average athletic scholarship (and the proportion receiving): $0 (0%). Average amount of debt of borrowers graduating in 2009: $31,800. Proportion who borrowed: 98%.

CAMPUS LIFE AND EXTRACURRICULAR ACTIVITIES

Campus housing available: coed dorms, women's dorms, men's dorms, apartment for single students. Students who live in college-owned, operated, or affiliated housing: 50%. Average per-year earnings: $3,000. **Clubs and organizations:** Number of student organizations: 60. Activities include: choral groups, dance, drama/theater, literary magazine, student government, student newspaper, yearbook. Number of fraternities: 0; sororities: 0. Average proportion of students who stay on campus on weekends: 70%. **Sports program (2009-2010):** Member of NCAA III. *Men's intercollegiate varsity sports:* baseball, basketball, football, golf, ice hockey, lacrosse, soccer, tennis. *Women's intercollegiate varsity sports:* basketball, equestrian, field hockey, lacrosse, soccer, softball, tennis, volleyball.

SERVICES AND FACILITIES

Basic services: nonremedial tutoring, placement service, health service, health insurance. **Remedial assistance:** reading, math, writing, study skills, other. **Counseling services:** career, personal, academic, older student, psychological. **For learning-disabled students:** School does not offer a structured program with separate admission and additional fees. Services include: remedial math, remedial English, tape recorders, note-taking services, oral tests, learning center, extended time for tests, tutors, proofreading services. **Information technology resources:** Students are not required to lease or own a computer. Number of campus computers available to all students: 75. School has a wireless network. **Campus safety:** Security services offered: 24-hour foot-and-vehicle patrols, late-night transport/escort service, 24-hour emergency telephones, lighted pathways/sidewalks, student patrols, controlled dormitory access (key, security card, etc).

TRANSFER AND INTERNATIONAL STUDENTS

Transfer students: May apply for admission for the following academic terms: Fall, Spring, Summer. Applicants need a minimum number of credits to apply. For fall 2009: Transfer applications received: 511. Transfer applicants offered admission: 308. Transfer applicants enrolled: 149. **International students:** Number of countries represented: 12. Minimum TOEFL score required: 500 (paper); 173 (computer).

Bentley University

- **Address:** 175 Forest Street, Waltham, MA 02452-4705
- **Website:** http://www.bentley.edu
- **Private**
- **Enrollment:** 4,030 full-time; 205 part-time

KEY STATS

- ✔ **U.S News College Ranking:** 4, Regional Universities (North)
- ✔ **SAT Score (25th/75th percentile):** 1140-1310
- ✔ **Tuition:** 2010-2011: $37,058

Selectivity: More selective	**Room/board:** $12,180
Acceptance rate: 43%	**Average debt:** $33,073
Student/faculty ratio: 14/1	**Proportion who borrowed:** 64%

UNDERGRADUATE STUDENT BODY STATS

2009-2010 enrollment: 4,030 full-time; 205 part-time. Men: 60%; women: 40%. **Ethnic makeup:** African American: 3%; Asian American: 7%; Hispanic: 5%; White: 75%; International: 9%.

ADMISSIONS FACTS AND FIGURES

Phone: (781) 891-2244. **Email:** ugadmission@bentley.edu. **Website:** http://www.bentley.edu. **Application deadlines for fall 2011:** Regular decision: January 15; decision sent by April 1. Early decision: Send application by: November 1; Decision sent by: December 18. Early action: Send application by: November 15; Decision sent by: January 23. Admission can be deferred. **Application fee:** $50. **To apply online, go to:** http://www.bentley.edu/undergraduate/applying.cfm. **Admissions requirements/recommendations:** High school units required (recommended): English: 4 (4); Mathematics: 4 (4); Science: 3 (3); Foreign language: 3 (3); Social studies: 3 (3); Total units: 19 (19). Tests: The college uses SAT or ACT scores in admissions decisions. Either SAT or ACT required. For admission to the fall 2011 entering class, the school will accept: ACT with writing required. Campus visit: Recommended. Admissions interview: Recommended. Off-campus interview: May be arranged. **Factors that count in admissions decisions:** *Academic:* Secondary school record: Very Important. Class rank: Considered. Letters of recommendation: Important. Standardized test scores: Very Important. Essay: Important. *Nonacademic:* Interview: Considered. Extracurricular activities: Important. Talent/ability: Considered. Character/personal qualities: Important. Alumni/ae relationship: Considered. Geographical residence: Considered. State residency: Considered. Religious affiliation/commitment: Not Considered. Minority status: Considered. Volunteer work: Important. Work experience: Considered. **Other schools with the greatest overlap in applicants:** Babson College; Boston College; Boston University; Northeastern University; Villanova University. **Admissions statistics for the fall 2009 entering class:** Total applicants: 6,675. Total accepted: 2,842. Freshmen enrolled: 949; 57% were from out of state. Accepted through early-decision or early-action plans: 66%. Overall acceptance rate: 43%. Early-decision acceptance rate: 73%. Non-early acceptance rate: 29%. **Size of waiting list:** 1200 applicants; enrolled from waiting list: 118. **Credentials of fall 2009 freshmen:** 38% ranked in the top 10 percent of their high school class; 79% were in the top 25 percent; 97% were in the top half. (Proportion submitting class standing: 44%.) **First-year students who submitted SAT scores:** 83%. Scores (25/75 percentile): Critical Reading: 540-630, Math: 600-680, Combined: 1140-1310. **First-year students submitting ACT scores:** 28%. Scores (25/75 percentile): English: N/A, Math: N/A, Composite: 25-28.

ACADEMICS

Year founded: 1917. **Academic calendar:** Semester. **Degrees offered:** certificate, associate, transfer-associate, terminal-associate, bachelor's, post-bachelor's certificate, master's, post-master's certificate, doctorate. **Most popular majors:** 19% finance, 15% accounting and related services, 15% business administration and management, 15% marketing/marketing management, 13% accounting. **Major fields of study:** business, management, marketing, and related support services; computer and information sciences and support services; English language and literature/letters; history; legal professions and studies; liberal arts and sciences studies, and humanities; mathematics and statistics; multi/interdisciplinary studies; philosophy and religious studies; public administration and social service professions. **Areas of required coursework:** humanities, computer literacy, mathematics, English (including composition), philosophy, sciences (biological or physical), history, social science, other. **Pre-professional programs:** pre-law. **Special academic programs (% participation):** accelerated program (2.8%), cross-registration, double major (11.6%), honors program (8.06%), independent study (5.27%), internships (94%), liberal arts/career combination (2.87%), student-designed major, study abroad (19.3%). **Reserve Officers Training Corps (ROTC):** Army ROTC: Offered at cooperating institution (Boston University); Air Force ROTC: Offered at cooperating institution (Boston University). **Faculty and instruction (2009-2010):** Total instructional faculty: 279 full-time, 179 part-time (60% men; 40% women; 11% minorities). Full-time faculty with Ph.D. or other terminal degree: 82%. Student/faculty ratio: 14/1. Classes of fewer than 20 students: 29%; of 20 to 49 students: 70%; of 50 or more students: 0%. **Advanced Placement and International Baccalaureate credit:** AP tests may be used for: Credit and/or placement. Scores accepted: 4, 5. International Baccalaureate exams may be used for: Credit only. **Freshmen returning for sophomore year:** 93%. **Graduation rates:** Four-year: 80%; five-year: 87%; six-year: 85%. **Graduate study:** 17% of students pursue further study immediately upon graduation. Fields in which graduates pursue further study: Master of Business Administration (MBA), 95%; law, 4%; arts and sciences, 1%.

COSTS AND FINANCIAL AID

Financial aid office: (781) 891-3441. **Expenses (2010-2011):** Tuition and fees 2010-2011: $37,058; room/board: $12,180. Estimated books and supplies: $1,100 personal expenses: $1,135. **Financial aid:** In 2009-2010, 75% of undergraduates applied for financial aid. Of those, 51% were determined to have financial need; 40% had their need fully met. Average financial aid package (proportion receiving): $29,415 (51%). Average amount of gift aid, such as scholarships or grants (proportion receiving): $21,991 (43%). Average amount of self-help aid, such as work study or loans (proportion receiving): $6,235 (46%). Average need-based loan (excluding PLUS or other private loans): $5,324. Among students who received need-based aid, the average percentage of need met: 92%. Among students who received aid based on merit, the average award (and the proportion receiving): $15,729 (15%). The average athletic scholarship (and the proportion receiving): $31,072 (1%). Average amount of debt of borrowers graduating in 2009: $33,073. Proportion who borrowed: 64%.

CAMPUS LIFE AND EXTRACURRICULAR ACTIVITIES

Campus housing available (% using): coed dorms (30%), apartment for single students (34%), special housing for disabled students, other housing options (34%). Students who live in college-owned, operated, or affiliated housing: 83%. **Student employment:** During the 2009-2010 academic year, 27% of undergraduates worked on campus. Average per-year earnings: $1,422. **Clubs and organizations:** Number of student organizations: 101. Activities include: campus ministries, choral groups, dance, drama/theater, international student organization, jazz band, literary magazine, model UN, music ensembles, pep band, radio station, student government, student newspaper, student film society, television station, yearbook. Number of fraternities: 7; sororities: 4. Proportion of men in fraternities: 12%; of women in sororities: 11%. Average proportion of students who stay on campus on weekends: 85%. **Sports program (2009-2010):** Member of NCAA II. *Men's intercollegiate varsity sports:* baseball, basketball, cross country, football, golf, ice hockey, lacrosse, soccer, swimming, tennis, track and field (indoor), track and field (outdoor). *Women's intercollegiate varsity sports:* basketball, cross country, field hockey, lacrosse, soccer, softball, swimming, tennis, track and field (indoor), track and field (outdoor), volleyball.

SERVICES AND FACILITIES

Basic services: nonremedial tutoring, women's center, placement service, health service, health insurance. **Remedial assistance:** study skills. **Counseling services:** minority student, career, personal, veteran student, academic, older student, psychological, birth control, religious. **For learning-disabled students:** School does not offer a structured program with separate admission and additional fees. Total undergraduates in learning-disabled program or receiving services: 150. Services include: reading machines, tape recorders, note-taking services, oral tests, learning center, readers, extended time for tests, tutors, priority registration, priority seating, substitution of courses, texts on tape, exams on tape or computer, other testing accommodations, other. **Library:** Number of titles: 170,300; number of current serial subscriptions: 39,000. **Information technology resources:** Students are required to lease or own a computer. Number of campus computers available to all students: 4,665. School has a wireless network. Approximate number of users that can be accommodated: 4,000. Proportion of college-owned housing units wired for high-speed internet access: 100%. **Campus safety:** Security services offered: 24-hour foot-and-vehicle patrols, late-night transport/escort service, 24-hour emergency telephones, lighted pathways/sidewalks, student patrols, controlled dormitory access (key, security card, etc).

TRANSFER AND INTERNATIONAL STUDENTS

Transfer students: May apply for admission for the following academic terms: Fall, Spring. Applicants need a minimum number of credits to apply. For fall 2009: Transfer applications received: 534. Transfer applicants offered admission: 264. Transfer applicants enrolled: 142. **International students:** Number of foreign undergraduates: 387 (9% of student body). Number of countries represented: 80. Minimum TOEFL score required: 550 (paper); 213 (computer). Average TOEFL score: 603 (paper).

Berklee College of Music

- **Address:** 1140 Boylston Street, Boston, MA 02215
- **Website:** http://www.berklee.edu
- **Private**
- **Enrollment:** 3,800 full-time; 345 part-time

KEY STATS

✔ **U.S News College Ranking:** Unranked Specialty School–Fine Arts
✔ **SAT or ACT Score (25th/75th percentile):** N/A
✔ **Tuition:** 2009-2010: $33,653

Selectivity: N/A	**Room/board:** $15,080
Acceptance rate: 42%	**Average debt:** N/A
Student/faculty ratio: 12/1	**Proportion who borrowed:** N/A

UNDERGRADUATE STUDENT BODY STATS

2009-2010 enrollment: 3,800 full-time; 345 part-time. Men: 71%; women: 29%. **Ethnic makeup:** African American: 8%; Asian American: 4%; Hispanic: 8%; White: 60%; International: 20%.

ADMISSIONS FACTS AND FIGURES

Phone: (800) 237-5533. **Email:** admissions@berklee.edu. **Website:** http://www.berklee.edu. **Application deadlines for fall 2011:** Regular decision: January 15; decision sent by March 31. Early decision: Not offered. Early action: Send application by: November 1; Decision sent by: January 31. Admission can be deferred. **Application fee:** $150. **To apply online, go to:** https://secure.berklee.edu/AI/prospects/. **Admissions requirements/recommendations:** Tests: The college uses SAT or ACT scores in admissions decisions. Neither SAT nor ACT required. Campus visit: Recommended. Admissions interview: Required. Off-campus interview: May be arranged. **Factors that count in admissions decisions:** *Academic:* Secondary school record: Important. Class rank: Considered. Letters of recommendation: Considered. Standardized test scores: Considered. Essay: Important. *Nonacademic:* Interview: Very Important. Extracurricular activities: Considered. Talent/ability: Very Important. Character/personal qualities: Very Important. Alumni/ae relationship: Considered. Geographical residence: Not Considered. State residency: Not Considered. Religious affiliation/commitment: Not Considered. Minority status: Not Considered. Volunteer work: Considered. Work experience: Considered. **Admissions statistics for the fall 2009 entering class:** Total applicants: 3,636. Total accepted: 1,545. Freshmen enrolled: 863; 85% were from out of state. Overall acceptance rate: 42%. Non-early acceptance rate: 42%. **Size of waiting list:** 296 applicants; enrolled from waiting list: 115.

ACADEMICS

Year founded: 1945. **Academic calendar:** Semester. **Degrees offered:** diploma, bachelor's. **Most popular majors:** 61% visual and performing arts, 17% business, management, marketing, and related support services, 17% engineering, 3% education, 2% health professions and related clinical sciences. **Major fields of study:** visual and performing arts. **Areas of required coursework:** arts/fine arts, computer literacy, English (including composition), sciences (biological or physical), history, social science. **Special academic programs:** cross-registration, distance learning, double major, dual enrollment, English as a Second Language (ESL), exchange student program (domestic), external degree program, independent study, internships, student-designed major, study abroad, teacher certificate program, weekend college, other. **Teacher certification offered in:** early childhood, elementary, middle/junior high, secondary. **Faculty and instruction (2009-2010):** Total instructional faculty: 234 full-time, 296 part-time (74% men; 26% women; 19% minorities). Student/faculty ratio: 12/1. Classes of fewer than 20 students: 94%; of 20 to 49 students: 6%; of 50 or more students: 1%. **Freshmen returning for sophomore year:** 81%. **Graduation rates:** Six-year: 51%.

COSTS AND FINANCIAL AID

Financial aid office: (617) 747-2274. **Expenses (2009-2010):** Tuition and fees 2009-2010: $33,653; room/board: $15,080. Estimated books and supplies: $470; transportation: $941; personal expenses: $2,378. **Financial aid:** Priority filing date for institution's financial aid form: May 1; deadline: May 1.

CAMPUS LIFE AND EXTRACURRICULAR ACTIVITIES

Campus housing available: coed dorms. Students who live in college-owned, operated, or affiliated housing: 19%. **Student employment:** During the 2009-2010 academic year, 30% of undergraduates worked on campus.

Average per-year earnings: $2,000. **Clubs and organizations:** Number of student organizations: 49. Activities include: choral groups, concert band, dance, international student organization, jazz band, literary magazine, music ensembles, musical theater, radio station, student government, student newspaper, student film society. Number of fraternities: 0; sororities: 0.

SERVICES AND FACILITIES

Basic services: nonremedial tutoring, health insurance. **Counseling services:** career, personal, academic. **For learning-disabled students:** School does not offer a structured program with separate admission and additional fees. Services include: untimed tests, learning center, readers, extended time for tests, tutors. **Library:** Number of titles: 47,993; number of current serial subscriptions: 232. **Information technology resources:** Students are required to lease or own a computer. School has a wireless network. Proportion of college-owned housing units wired for high-speed internet access: 100%. **Campus safety:** Security services offered: 24-hour foot-and-vehicle patrols, late-night transport/escort service, 24-hour emergency telephones, controlled dormitory access (key, security card, etc).

TRANSFER AND INTERNATIONAL STUDENTS

Transfer students: May apply for admission for the following academic terms: Fall, Spring, Summer. Applicants need a minimum number of credits to apply. For fall 2009: Transfer applications received: 1,307. Transfer applicants offered admission: 686. Transfer applicants enrolled: 313. **International students:** Number of foreign undergraduates: 696 (20% of student body). Number of countries represented: 73.

Boston Architectural College

- **Address:** 320 Newbury Street, Boston, MA 02115
- **Website:** http://www.the-bac.edu
- **Private**
- **Enrollment:** 620 full-time; 15 part-time

KEY STATS

✔ **U.S News College Ranking:** Unranked Specialty School–Fine Arts
✔ **SAT or ACT Score (25th/75th percentile):** N/A
✔ **Tuition:** 2009-2010: $11,468

Selectivity: N/A	**Room/board:** N/A
Acceptance rate: 73%	**Average debt:** $52,300
Student/faculty ratio: 3/1	**Proportion who borrowed:** 77%

UNDERGRADUATE STUDENT BODY STATS

2009-2010 enrollment: 620 full-time; 15 part-time. Men: 68%; women: 32%. **Ethnic makeup:** African American: 6%; Asian American: 6%; Hispanic: 10%; White: 78%.

ADMISSIONS FACTS AND FIGURES

Phone: (617) 585-0123. **Email:** admissions@the-bac.edu. **Website:** http://www.the-bac.edu. **Application deadlines for fall 2011:** Regular decision: Rolling. Early decision: Not offered. Early action: Not offered. Admission can be deferred. **Application fee:** $50. **To apply online, go to:** https://www.applyweb.com/apply/thebac/menu.html. **Admissions requirements/recommendations:** High school units required (recommended): English: (4); Mathematics: (4); Science: (3); Foreign language: (3); Social studies: (1); History: (2); Academic electives: (0); Total units: (19). Tests: The college does not use SAT or ACT scores in admissions decisions. Neither SAT nor ACT required. Campus visit: Recommended. Admissions interview: Recommended. Off-campus interview: May be arranged. **Factors that count in admissions decisions:** *Academic:* Secondary school record: Not Considered. Class rank: Not Considered. Letters of recommendation: Not Considered. Standardized test scores: Not Considered. Essay: Not Considered. *Nonacademic:* Interview: Not Considered. Extracurricular activities: Not Considered. Talent/ability: Not Considered. Character/personal qualities: Not Considered. Alumni/ae relationship: Not Considered. Geographical residence: Not Considered. State residency: Not Considered. Religious affiliation/commitment: Not Considered. Minority status: Not Considered. Volunteer work: Not Considered. Work experience: Not Considered. **Other schools with the greatest overlap in applicants:** Harvard University; Northeastern University; Rhode Island School of Design; Suffolk University; Wentworth Institute of Technology. **Admissions statistics for the fall 2009 entering class:** Total applicants: 231. Total accepted: 168. Freshmen enrolled: 75; Overall acceptance rate: 73%. **Size of waiting list:** 0 applicants; enrolled from waiting list: 0. **Credentials of fall 2009 freshmen:** 7% ranked in the top 10 percent of their high school class; 28% were in the top 25 percent; 49% were in the top half. (Proportion submitting class standing: 49%.) **Average high school grade point average:** 2.7.

ACADEMICS

Year founded: 1889. **Academic calendar:** Semester. **Degrees offered:** certificate, bachelor's, master's. **Major fields of study:** architecture and related services. **Areas of required coursework:** arts/fine arts, humanities, computer literacy, mathematics, English (including composition), sciences (biological or physical), history, social science. **Special academic programs (% participation):** cross-registration (1%), distance learning (10%), independent study (2%), internships (0%), study abroad (1%). **Cooperative education programs:** art, computer science, technologies. **Faculty and instruction (2009-2010):** Total instructional faculty: 22 full-time, 336 part-time (56% men; 44% women; 8% minorities). Full-time faculty with Ph.D. or other terminal degree: 68%. Student/faculty ratio: 3/1. Classes of fewer than 20 students: 88%; of 20 to 49 students: 11%; of 50 or more students: 1%. **Advanced Placement and International Baccalaureate credit:** AP tests may be used for: Placement only. Scores accepted: 5. **Freshmen returning for sophomore year:** 59%. **Graduation rates:** Four-year: 7%; five-year: 10%; six-year: 24%.

COSTS AND FINANCIAL AID

Financial aid office: (617) 585-0125. **Expenses (2009-2010):** Tuition and fees 2009-2010: $11,468. **Financial aid:** Priority filing date for institution's financial aid form: April 15. In 2009-2010, 100% of undergraduates applied for financial aid. Of those, 90% were determined to have financial need; 3% had their need fully met. Average financial aid package (proportion receiving): $5,149 (82%). Average amount of gift aid, such as scholarships or grants (proportion receiving): $2,900 (40%). Average amount of self-help aid, such as work study or loans (proportion receiving): $3,797 (80%). Average need-based loan (excluding PLUS or other private loans): $3,662. Among students who received need-based aid, the average percentage of need met: 30%. Among students who received aid based on merit, the average award (and the proportion receiving): $1,534 (0%). The average athletic scholarship (and the proportion receiving): $0 (0%). Average amount of debt of borrowers graduating in 2009: $52,300. Proportion who borrowed: 77%.

CAMPUS LIFE AND EXTRACURRICULAR ACTIVITIES

Student employment: During the 2009-2010 academic year, 0% of undergraduates worked on campus. Average per-year earnings: $0. Activities include: student government. Number of fraternities: 0; sororities: 0.

SERVICES AND FACILITIES

Basic services: nonremedial tutoring, placement service, health insurance. **Remedial assistance:** writing, study skills, other. **Counseling services:** minority student, career, military, veteran student, academic, older student. **For learning-disabled students:** School does not offer a structured program with separate admission and additional fees. Services include: tape recorders, videotaped classes, untimed tests, note-taking services, oral tests, learning center, readers, extended time for tests, tutors, early syllabus, priority registration, priority seating, texts on tape, exams on tape or computer, other testing accommodations. **Library:** Number of titles: 27,000; number of current serial subscriptions: 130. **Information technology resources:** Students are not required to lease or own a computer. Number of campus computers available to all students: 70. School has a wireless network. Approximate number of users that can be accommodated: 500. Proportion of college-owned housing units wired for high-speed internet access: 0%. **Campus safety:** Security services offered: 24-hour foot-and-vehicle patrols, late-night transport/escort service, 24-hour emergency telephones, lighted pathways/sidewalks.

TRANSFER AND INTERNATIONAL STUDENTS

Transfer students: May apply for admission for the following academic terms: Fall, Spring. Applicants do not need a minimum number of credits to apply. **International students:** Number of foreign undergraduates: 0. Number of countries represented: 0. Average TOEFL score: 580 (paper).

Boston College

- **Address:** 140 Commonwealth Avenue, Chestnut Hill, MA 02467
- **Website:** http://www.bc.edu
- **Private; Religious affiliation:** Roman Catholic (Jesuit)
- **Enrollment:** 9,171 full-time

KEY STATS

✔ **U.S News College Ranking:** 31, National Universities
✔ **SAT Score (25th/75th percentile):** 1250-1430
✔ **Tuition:** 2010-2011: $40,542

Selectivity: Most selective	**Room/board:** $12,082
Acceptance rate: 30%	**Average debt:** $19,514
Student/faculty ratio: 13/1	**Proportion who borrowed:** 49%

UNDERGRADUATE STUDENT BODY STATS

2009-2010 enrollment: 9,171 full-time. Men: 48%; women: 52%. **Ethnic makeup:** African American: 5%; Asian American: 10%; Hispanic: 8%; White: 74%; International: 3%.

ADMISSIONS FACTS AND FIGURES

Phone: (617) 552-3100. **Website:** http://www.bc.edu. **Application deadlines for fall 2011:** Regular decision: January 1; decision sent by April 15. Early decision: Not offered. Early action: Send application by: November 1; Decision sent by: December 25. Admission can be deferred. **Application fee:** $70. **To apply online, go to:** http://app.commonapp.org/. **Admissions requirements/recommendations:** High school units required (recommended): English: (4); Mathematics: (4); Science: (4); Foreign language: (4); Social studies: (4); History: (4); Total units: (20). Tests: The college uses SAT or ACT scores in admissions decisions. Either SAT or ACT required. For admission to the fall 2011 entering class, the school will accept: ACT with writing required. Campus visit: Recommended. Admissions interview: Neither required nor recommended. Off-campus interview: Not available. **Factors that count in admissions decisions:** *Academic:* Secondary school record: Very Important. Class rank: Important. Letters of recommendation: Important. Standardized test scores: Very Important. Essay: Important. *Nonacademic:* Interview: Not Considered. Extracurricular activities: Important. Talent/ability: Important. Character/personal qualities: Important. Alumni/ae relationship: Important. Geographical residence: Not Considered. State residency: Not Considered. Religious affiliation/commitment: Important. Minority status: Considered. Volunteer work: Important. Work experience: Considered. **Other schools with the greatest overlap in applicants:** Cornell University; Georgetown University; Harvard University; University of Notre Dame; University of Pennsylvania. **Admissions statistics for the fall 2009 entering class:** Total applicants: 29,289. Total accepted: 8,804. Freshmen enrolled: 2,171; 76% were from out of state. Accepted through early-decision or early-action plans: 33%. Overall acceptance rate: 30%. Non-early acceptance rate: 27%. **Size of waiting list:** 4110 applicants; enrolled from waiting list: 407. **Credentials of fall 2009 freshmen:** 79% ranked in the top 10 percent of their high school class; 95% were in the top 25 percent; 99% were in the top half. (Proportion submitting class standing: 29%.) **First-year students who submitted SAT scores:** 86%. Scores (25/75 percentile): Critical Reading: 610-700, Math: 640-730, Combined: 1250-1430. **First-year students submitting ACT scores:** 14%. Scores (25/75 percentile): English: N/A, Math: N/A, Composite: N/A.

ACADEMICS

Year founded: 1863. **Academic calendar:** Semester. **Degrees offered:** bachelor's, master's, post-master's certificate, doctorate. **Most popular majors:** 12% finance, 10% communication studies/speech communication and rhetoric, 8% economics, 7% English language and literature, 7% history. **Major fields of study:** area, ethnic, cultural, and gender studies; biological and biomedical sciences; business, management, marketing, and related support services; communication, journalism, and related programs; computer and information sciences and support services; education; English language and literature/letters; family and consumer sciences/human sciences; foreign languages, literatures, and linguistics; health professions and related clinical sciences; history; mathematics and statistics; multi/interdisciplinary studies; philosophy and religious studies; physical sciences; psychology; social sciences; theology and religious vocations; visual and performing arts. **Areas of required coursework:** arts/fine arts, humanities, mathematics, English (including composition), philosophy, sciences (biological or physical), history, social science, other. **Pre-professional programs:** pre-law, pre-dentistry, pre-medicine, pre-theology, pre-veterinary science. **Special academic pro-**

grams (% participation): accelerated program (1%), cross-registration (9%), distance learning (1%), double major (42%), English as a Second Language (ESL) (1%), exchange student program (domestic) (1%), honors program (13%), independent study (21%), internships (3%), liberal arts/career combination (11%), student-designed major (1%), study abroad (41%), teacher certificate program (9%). **Teacher certification offered in:** early childhood, special education, elementary, secondary. **Reserve Officers Training Corps (ROTC):** Army ROTC: Offered at cooperating institution (Northeastern University); Navy ROTC: Offered at cooperating institution (Boston University); Air Force ROTC: Offered at cooperating institution (Boston University). **Faculty and instruction (2009-2010):** Total instructional faculty: 725 full-time, 669 part-time (50% men; 50% women; 21% minorities). Full-time faculty with Ph.D. or other terminal degree: 98%. Student/faculty ratio: 13/1. Classes of fewer than 20 students: 47%; of 20 to 49 students: 45%; of 50 or more students: 8%. **Advanced Placement and International Baccalaureate credit:** AP tests may be used for: Credit and/or placement. Scores accepted: 3, 4, 5. International Baccalaureate exams may be used for: Credit only. **Freshmen returning for sophomore year:** 95%. **Graduation rates:** Four-year: 88%; five-year: 90%; six-year: 91%. **Graduate study:** 28% of students pursue further study within one year. Fields in which graduates pursue further study: Master of Business Administration (MBA), 5%; law, 28%; medicine, 4%; dentistry, 1%; engineering, 1%; theology (or the seminary), 3%; education, 31%; arts and sciences, 12%.

COSTS AND FINANCIAL AID
Financial aid office: (617) 552-3320. **Expenses (2010-2011):** Tuition and fees 2010-2011: $40,542; room/board: $12,082. Estimated books and supplies: $900; transportation: $200; personal expenses: $1,000. **Financial aid:** Priority filing date for institution's financial aid form: February 1. In 2009-2010, 48% of undergraduates applied for financial aid. Of those, 42% were determined to have financial need; 100% had their need fully met. Average financial aid package (proportion receiving): $30,968 (42%). Average amount of gift aid, such as scholarships or grants (proportion receiving): $26,500 (37%). Average amount of self-help aid, such as work study or loans (proportion receiving): $6,351 (40%). Average need-based loan (excluding PLUS or other private loans): $4,708. Among students who received need-based aid, the average percentage of need met: 100%. Among students who received aid based on merit, the average award (and the proportion receiving): $16,443 (2%). The average athletic scholarship (and the proportion receiving): $40,583 (3%). Average amount of debt of borrowers graduating in 2009: $19,514. Proportion who borrowed: 49%.

CAMPUS LIFE AND EXTRACURRICULAR ACTIVITIES
Campus housing available (% using): coed dorms (98%), special housing for disabled students (2%). Students who live in college-owned, operated, or affiliated housing: 80%. **Student employment:** During the 2009-2010 academic year, 17% of undergraduates worked on campus. Average per-year earnings: $2,400. **Clubs and organizations:** Number of student organizations: 225. Activities include: campus ministries, choral groups, concert band, dance, drama/theater, international student organization, jazz band, literary magazine, marching band, music ensembles, musical theater, pep band, radio station, student government, student newspaper, student film society, symphony orchestra, television station, yearbook. Number of fraternities: 0; sororities: 0. Average proportion of students who stay on campus on weekends: 90%. **Sports program (2009-2010):** Member of NCAA I. **Men's intercollegiate varsity sports:** baseball, basketball, cross country, fencing, football, golf, ice hockey, skiing (alpine), soccer, swimming, tennis, track and field (indoor), track and field (outdoor). **Women's intercollegiate varsity sports:** basketball, crew (heavyweight), cross country, fencing, field hockey, golf, ice hockey, lacrosse, skiing (alpine), soccer, softball, swimming, tennis, track and field (indoor), track and field (outdoor), volleyball.

SERVICES AND FACILITIES
Basic services: nonremedial tutoring, women's center, placement service, day care, health service, health insurance. **Counseling services:** minority student, career, military, personal, veteran student, academic, older student, psychological, religious. **For learning-disabled students:** School does not offer a structured program with separate admission and additional fees. Services include: reading machines, tape recorders, note-taking services, learning center, readers, extended time for tests, tutors, priority registration, texts on tape, other testing accommodations. **Library:** Number of titles: 2,547,714; number of current serial subscriptions: 43,315. **Information technology resources:** Students are not required to lease or own a computer. Number of campus computers available to all students: 1,000. School has a wireless network. Approximate number of users that can be accommodated: 21,654. Proportion of college-owned housing units wired for high-speed

internet access: 100%. **Campus safety:** Security services offered: 24-hour foot-and-vehicle patrols, late-night transport/escort service, 24-hour emergency telephones, lighted pathways/sidewalks, student patrols, controlled dormitory access (key, security card, etc).

TRANSFER AND INTERNATIONAL STUDENTS
Transfer students: May apply for admission for the following academic terms: Fall, Spring. Applicants need a minimum number of credits to apply. For fall 2009: Transfer applications received: 1,542. Transfer applicants offered admission: 329. Transfer applicants enrolled: 146. **International students:** Number of foreign undergraduates: 264 (3% of student body). Number of countries represented: 60. Minimum TOEFL score required: 600 (paper); 250 (computer). Average TOEFL score: 630 (paper).

Boston Conservatory

- **Address:** 8 The Fenway, Boston, MA 02215
- **Website:** http://www.bostonconservatory.edu
- **Private**
- **Enrollment:** 489 full-time

KEY STATS
✔ **U.S News College Ranking:** Unranked Specialty School–Fine Arts
✔ **SAT or ACT Score (25th/75th percentile):** N/A
✔ **Tuition:** 2009-2010: $33,676

Selectivity: N/A	**Room/board:** $16,320
Acceptance rate: 37%	**Average debt:** N/A
Student/faculty ratio: N/A	**Proportion who borrowed:** N/A

UNDERGRADUATE STUDENT BODY STATS
2009-2010 enrollment: 489 full-time. Men: 42%; women: 58%.

ADMISSIONS FACTS AND FIGURES
Phone: (617) 912-9153. **Email:** admissions@bostonconservatory.edu. **Website:** http://www.bostonconservatory.edu. **Application deadlines for fall 2011:** Regular decision: December 1; decision sent by April 1. Early decision: Not offered. Early action: Not offered. Admission can be deferred. **Application fee:** $110. **Admissions requirements/recommendations:** High school units required (recommended): English: 4; Mathematics: 3. Tests: The college uses SAT or ACT scores in admissions decisions. Neither SAT nor ACT required. For admission to the fall 2011 entering class, the school will accept: ACT with writing recommended. Campus visit: Recommended. **Factors that count in admissions decisions:** *Academic:* Secondary school record: Important. Class rank: Considered. Letters of recommendation: Important. Standardized test scores: Considered. Essay: Important. *Nonacademic:* Interview: Very Important. Extracurricular activities: Important. Talent/ability: Very Important. Character/personal qualities: Very Important. Alumni/ae relationship: Not Considered. Geographical residence: Not Considered. State residency: Not Considered. Religious affiliation/commitment: Not Considered. Minority status: Not Considered. Volunteer work: Not Considered. Work experience: Not Considered. **Admissions statistics for the fall 2009 entering class:** Total applicants: 1,814. Total accepted: 680. Freshmen enrolled: 130; Overall acceptance rate: 37%. **Size of waiting list:** N/A applicants; enrolled from waiting list: 8.

ACADEMICS
Year founded: 1867. **Academic calendar:** Semester. **Degrees offered:** diploma, bachelor's, post-bachelor's certificate, master's, post-master's certificate. **Major fields of study:** visual and performing arts. **Areas of required coursework:** English (including composition), history, social science, other. **Special academic programs:** cross-registration, double major, English as a Second Language (ESL), independent study, teacher certificate program. **Freshmen returning for sophomore year:** 74%. **Graduation rates:** Six-year: 31%.

COSTS AND FINANCIAL AID
Financial aid office: (617) 912-9147. **Expenses (2009-2010):** Tuition and fees 2009-2010: $33,676; room/board: $16,320. Estimated books and supplies: $625. **Financial aid:** Priority filing date for institution's financial aid form: February 1; deadline: February 1.

CAMPUS LIFE AND EXTRACURRICULAR ACTIVITIES
Campus housing available: coed dorms, other housing options. Number of fraternities: 1; sororities: 1.

SERVICES AND FACILITIES

Information technology resources: Students are not required to lease or own a computer. School has a wireless network.

TRANSFER AND INTERNATIONAL STUDENTS

Transfer students: May apply for admission for the following academic terms: Fall, Spring. Applicants need a minimum number of credits to apply.

Boston University

- **Address:** 1 Sherborn Street, Boston, MA 02215
- **Website:** http://www.bu.edu
- **Private**
- **Enrollment:** N/A

KEY STATS

- ✔ **U.S News College Ranking:** 56, National Universities
- ✔ **SAT Score (25th/75th percentile):** 1180-1360
- ✔ **Tuition:** 2009-2010: $38,440
  - **Selectivity:** More selective
  - **Acceptance rate:** 54%
  - **Student/faculty ratio:** N/A
  - **Room/board:** $11,848
  - **Average debt:** N/A
  - **Proportion who borrowed:** N/A

Brandeis University

- **Address:** 415 South Street, Waltham, MA 02454-9110
- **Website:** http://www.brandeis.edu
- **Private**
- **Enrollment:** 3,296 full-time; 21 part-time

KEY STATS

- ✔ **U.S News College Ranking:** 34, National Universities
- ✔ **SAT Score (25th/75th percentile):** 1260-1460
- ✔ **Tuition:** 2010-2011: $40,274
  - **Selectivity:** Most selective
  - **Acceptance rate:** 40%
  - **Student/faculty ratio:** 9/1
  - **Room/board:** $11,214
  - **Average debt:** $26,078
  - **Proportion who borrowed:** 58%

UNDERGRADUATE STUDENT BODY STATS

2009-2010 enrollment: 3,296 full-time; 21 part-time. Men: 44%; women: 56%. **Ethnic makeup:** African American: 5%; Asian American: 11%; Hispanic: 5%; White: 70%; International: 10%.

ADMISSIONS FACTS AND FIGURES

Phone: (781) 736-3500. **Email:** admissions@brandeis.edu. **Website:** http://www.brandeis.edu. **Application deadlines for fall 2011:** Regular decision: January 15; decision sent by April 1. Early decision: Send application by: November 15; Decision sent by: December 15. Early action: Not offered. Admission can be deferred. **Application fee:** $55. **To apply online, go to:** http://www.commonapp.org. **Admissions requirements/recommendations:** High school units required (recommended): English: (4); Mathematics: (4); Science: (4); Foreign language: (4); Social studies: (4); Total units: (20). Tests: The college uses SAT or ACT scores in admissions decisions. Either SAT or ACT required. For admission to the fall 2011 entering class, the school will accept: ACT with writing required. Campus visit: Recommended. Admissions interview: Recommended. Off-campus interview: May be arranged. **Factors that count in admissions decisions:** *Academic:* Secondary school record: Very Important. Class rank: Very Important. Letters of recommendation: Important. Standardized test scores: Very Important. Essay: Important. *Nonacademic:* Interview: Considered. Extracurricular activities: Important. Talent/ability: Important. Character/personal qualities: Very Important. Alumni/ae relationship: Considered. Geographical residence: Considered. State residency: Not Considered. Religious affiliation/commitment: Not Considered. Minority status: Considered. Volunteer work: Important. Work experience: Important. **Other schools with the greatest overlap in applicants:** Boston University; Brown University; Cornell University; New York University; Tufts University. **Admissions statistics for the fall 2009 entering class:** Total applicants: 6,815. Total accepted: 2,756. Freshmen enrolled: 781; 71% were from out of state.

Accepted through early-decision or early-action plans: 31%. Overall acceptance rate: 40%. Early-decision acceptance rate: 57%. Non-early acceptance rate: 39%. **Size of waiting list:** 1446 applicants; enrolled from waiting list: 189. **Credentials of fall 2009 freshmen:** 79% ranked in the top 10 percent of their high school class; 97% were in the top 25 percent; 100% were in the top half. (Proportion submitting class standing: 64%.) **Average high school grade point average:** 3.8. **First-year students who submitted SAT scores:** 84%. Scores (25/75 percentile): Critical Reading: 620-730, Math: 640-730, Combined: 1260-1460. **First-year students submitting ACT scores:** 30%. Scores (25/75 percentile): English: 27-33, Math: 26-32, Composite: 27-31.

ACADEMICS

Year founded: 1948. **Academic calendar:** Semester. **Degrees offered:** bachelor's, post-bachelor's certificate, master's, doctorate. **Most popular majors:** 12% economics, 9% biology/biological sciences, 8% political science and government, 8% psychology, 7% history. **Major fields of study:** area, ethnic, cultural, and gender studies; biological and biomedical sciences; computer and information sciences and support services; English language and literature/letters; foreign languages, literatures, and linguistics; health professions and related clinical sciences; history; mathematics and statistics; multi/interdisciplinary studies; philosophy and religious studies; physical sciences; psychology; social sciences; visual and performing arts. **Areas of required coursework:** arts/fine arts, humanities, English (including composition), foreign languages, sciences (biological or physical), social science, other. **Pre-professional programs:** pre-dentistry, pre-medicine, pre-veterinary science, other. **Special academic programs (% participation):** cross-registration (1%), double major (47%), independent study (44%), internships (23%), student-designed major (1%), study abroad (33%), teacher certificate program (2%). **Teacher certification offered in:** elementary, secondary. **Reserve Officers Training Corps (ROTC):** Army ROTC: Offered at cooperating institution (Boston University); Air Force ROTC: Offered at cooperating institution (Boston University). **Faculty and instruction (2009-2010):** Total instructional faculty: 358 full-time, 128 part-time (57% men; 43% women; 10% minorities). Full-time faculty with Ph.D. or other terminal degree: 96%. Student/faculty ratio: 9/1. Classes of fewer than 20 students: 61%; of 20 to 49 students: 30%; of 50 or more students: 9%. **Advanced Placement and International Baccalaureate credit:** AP tests may be used for: Credit and/or placement. Scores accepted: 4, 5. International Baccalaureate exams may be used for: Credit and/or placement. **Freshmen returning for sophomore year:** 94%. **Graduation rates:** Four-year: 84%; five-year: 87%; six-year: 87%. **Graduate study:** 28% of students pursue further study immediately upon graduation; 35% within one year; 50% within five years. Fields in which graduates pursue further study: Master of Business Administration (MBA), 18%; law, 20%; medicine, 19%; dentistry, 1%; engineering, 1%; arts and sciences, 36%; veterinary medicine, 1%.

COSTS AND FINANCIAL AID

Financial aid office: (781) 736-3700. **Expenses (2010-2011):** Tuition and fees 2010-2011: $40,274; room/board: $11,214. Estimated books and supplies: $1,000 personal expenses: $1,500. **Financial aid:** Priority filing date for institution's financial aid form: February 1. In 2009-2010, 58% of undergraduates applied for financial aid. Of those, 51% were determined to have financial need; 15% had their need fully met. Average financial aid package (proportion receiving): $30,397 (51%). Average amount of gift aid, such as scholarships or grants (proportion receiving): $25,790 (48%). Average amount of self-help aid, such as work study or loans (proportion receiving): $6,700 (46%). Average need-based loan (excluding PLUS or other private loans): $5,085. Among students who received need-based aid, the average percentage of need met: 81%. Among students who received aid based on merit, the average award (and the proportion receiving): $23,564 (12%). The average athletic scholarship (and the proportion receiving): $0 (0%). Average amount of debt of borrowers graduating in 2009: $26,078. Proportion who borrowed: 58%.

CAMPUS LIFE AND EXTRACURRICULAR ACTIVITIES

Campus housing available (% using): coed dorms (95%), special housing for disabled students (5%). Students who live in college-owned, operated, or affiliated housing: 83%. **Student employment:** During the 2009-2010 academic year, 20% of undergraduates worked on campus. Average per-year earnings: $2,300. **Clubs and organizations:** Number of student organizations: 226. Activities include: campus ministries, choral groups, concert band, dance, drama/theater, international student organization, jazz band, literary magazine, music ensembles, musical theater, radio station, student government, student newspaper, student film society, television station, yearbook. Number of fraternities: 0; sororities: 0. Average proportion of students who stay on campus on weekends: 80%. **Sports program (2009-**

2010): Member of NCAA III. *Men's intercollegiate varsity sports:* baseball, basketball, cross country, fencing, soccer, tennis, track and field (indoor), track and field (outdoor). *Women's intercollegiate varsity sports:* basketball, cross country, fencing, soccer, softball, tennis, track and field (indoor), track and field (outdoor), volleyball.

SERVICES AND FACILITIES

Basic services: nonremedial tutoring, women's center, placement service, health service, health insurance. **Counseling services:** minority student, career, personal, academic, older student, psychological, birth control, religious. **For learning-disabled students:** School does not offer a structured program with separate admission and additional fees. Total undergraduates in learning-disabled program or receiving services: 195. Services include: reading machines, tape recorders, note-taking services, extended time for tests, texts on tape, exams on tape or computer, other testing accommodations, other. **Library:** Number of titles: 1,208,777; number of current serial subscriptions: 45,505. **Information technology resources:** Students are not required to lease or own a computer. Number of campus computers available to all students: 138. School has a wireless network. Approximate number of users that can be accommodated: 3,000. Proportion of college-owned housing units wired for high-speed internet access: 100%. **Campus safety:** Security services offered: 24-hour foot-and-vehicle patrols, late-night transport/escort service, 24-hour emergency telephones, lighted pathways/sidewalks, controlled dormitory access (key, security card, etc).

TRANSFER AND INTERNATIONAL STUDENTS

Transfer students: May apply for admission for the following academic terms: Fall, Spring. Applicants do not need a minimum number of credits to apply. For fall 2009: Transfer applications received: 378. Transfer applicants offered admission: 139. Transfer applicants enrolled: 55. **International students:** Number of foreign undergraduates: 317 (10% of student body). Number of countries represented: 53. Minimum TOEFL score required: 600 (paper); 100 (computer). Average TOEFL score: 627 (paper).

Bridgewater State College

- **Address:** Boyden Hall, Bridgewater, MA 02325
- **Website:** http://www.bridgew.edu
- **Public**
- **Enrollment:** 7,516 full-time; 1,387 part-time

KEY STATS

✔ **U.S News College Ranking:** second tier, Regional Universities (North)
✔ **SAT Score (25th/75th percentile):** 930-1120
✔ **Tuition:** 2010-2011: $7,054 in state, $13,194 out of state

Selectivity: Selective	**Room/board:** $10,100
Acceptance rate: 61%	**Average debt:** N/A
Student/faculty ratio: 22/1	**Proportion who borrowed:** N/A

UNDERGRADUATE STUDENT BODY STATS

2009-2010 enrollment: 7,516 full-time; 1,387 part-time. Men: 40%; women: 60%. **Ethnic makeup:** African American: 6%; Asian American: 2%; Hispanic: 3%; White: 88%; International: 1%.

ADMISSIONS FACTS AND FIGURES

Phone: (508) 531-1237. **Email:** admission@bridgew.edu. **Website:** http://www.bridgew.edu. **Application deadlines for fall 2011:** Regular decision: Rolling. Early decision: Not offered. Early action: Send application by: November 15; Decision sent by: December 15. Admission can be deferred. **Application fee:** $25. **To apply online, go to:** http://www.bridgew.edu/Admission. **Admissions requirements/recommendations:** High school units required (recommended): English: 4 (4); Mathematics: 3 (3); Science: 3 (3); Foreign language: 2 (2); Social studies: 1 (1); History: 1 (1); Academic electives: 2 (2); Total units: 18 (18). Tests: The college uses SAT or ACT scores in admissions decisions. Either SAT or ACT required. For admission to the fall 2011 entering class, the school will accept: ACT with or without writing accepted. Campus visit: Neither required nor recommended. Admissions interview: Neither required nor recommended. Off-campus interview: Not available. **Factors that count in admissions decisions:** *Academic:* Secondary school record: Very Important. Class rank: Important. Letters of recommendation: Considered. Standardized test scores: Important. Essay: Considered. *Nonacademic:* Interview: Not Considered. Extracurricular activities: Considered. Talent/ability: Considered. Character/personal qualities:

Considered. Alumni/ae relationship: Considered. Geographical residence: Not Considered. State residency: Not Considered. Religious affiliation/commitment: Not Considered. Minority status: Considered. Volunteer work: Considered. Work experience: Considered. **Other schools with the greatest overlap in applicants:** Framingham State College; Northeastern University; University of Massachusetts–Amherst; University of Massachusetts–Dartmouth; Westfield State College. **Admissions statistics for the fall 2009 entering class:** Total applicants: 7,440. Total accepted: 4,559. Freshmen enrolled: 1,479; 4% were from out of state. Overall acceptance rate: 61%. Non-early acceptance rate: 61%. **Size of waiting list:** 500 applicants; enrolled from waiting list: 0. **Credentials of fall 2009 freshmen:** 8% ranked in the top 10 percent of their high school class; 32% were in the top 25 percent; 75% were in the top half. (Proportion submitting class standing: 76%.) **Average high school grade point average:** 3.1. **First-year students who submitted SAT scores:** 94%. Scores (25/75 percentile): Critical Reading: 460-560, Math: 470-560, Combined: 930-1120. **First-year students submitting ACT scores:** 4%. Scores (25/75 percentile): English: N/A, Math: N/A, Composite: 20-24.

ACADEMICS

Year founded: 1840. **Academic calendar:** Semester. **Degrees offered:** bachelor's, post-bachelor's certificate, master's, post-master's certificate. **Most popular majors:** 18% business, management, marketing, and related support services, 14% education, 11% psychology, 9% security and protective services, 8% communication, journalism, and related programs. **Major fields of study:** architecture and related services; area, ethnic, cultural, and gender studies; biological and biomedical sciences; business, management, marketing, and related support services; communication, journalism, and related programs; computer and information sciences and support services; education; English language and literature/letters; foreign languages, literatures, and linguistics; health professions and related clinical sciences; history; legal professions and studies; mathematics and statistics; parks, recreation, leisure, and fitness studies; philosophy and religious studies; physical sciences; psychology; public administration and social service professions; science technologies/technicians; security and protective services; social sciences; transportation and materials moving; visual and performing arts. **Areas of required coursework:** arts/fine arts, humanities, mathematics, English (including composition), philosophy, foreign languages, sciences (biological or physical), history, social science. **Pre-professional programs:** pre-law, pre-dentistry, pre-medicine, pre-veterinary science, other. **Special academic programs (% participation):** accelerated program, cross-registration, distance learning (23%), double major (17%), dual enrollment (2%), English as a Second Language (ESL) (.3%), exchange student program (domestic) (.3%), honors program (6%), independent study (.3%), internships (3%), study abroad (3%), teacher certificate program (15%). **Teacher certification offered in:** early childhood, special education, elementary, middle/junior high, secondary. **Reserve Officers Training Corps (ROTC):** Army ROTC: Offered at cooperating institution (Stonehill College); Air Force ROTC: Offered at cooperating institution (Stonehill College). **Faculty and instruction (2009-2010):** Total instructional faculty: 302 full-time, 260 part-time (52% men; 48% women; 10% minorities). Full-time faculty with Ph.D. or other terminal degree: 90%. Student/faculty ratio: 22/1. Classes of fewer than 20 students: 40%; of 20 to 49 students: 59%; of 50 or more students: 1%. **Advanced Placement and International Baccalaureate credit:** AP tests may be used for: Credit only. Scores accepted: 3. International Baccalaureate exams may be used for: Credit only. **Freshmen returning for sophomore year:** 78%. **Graduation rates:** Four-year: 25%; five-year: 48%; six-year: 51%. **Graduate study:** 19% of students pursue further study within one year.

COSTS AND FINANCIAL AID

Financial aid office: (508) 531-1341. **Expenses (2010-2011):** Tuition and fees 2010-2011: $7,054 in state, $13,194 out of state; room/board: $10,100. Estimated books and supplies: $1,000; transportation: $1,200; personal expenses: $2,000. **Financial aid:** Priority filing date for institution's financial aid form: March 1. In 2009-2010, 78% of undergraduates applied for financial aid. Of those, 62% were determined to have financial need; Average financial aid package (proportion receiving): $7,621 (61%). Average amount of gift aid, such as scholarships or grants (proportion receiving): $4,505 (45%). Average amount of self-help aid, such as work study or loans (proportion receiving): $4,615 (44%). Average need-based loan (excluding PLUS or other private loans): $4,363. Among students who received aid based on merit, the average award (and the proportion receiving): $6,492 (1%).

CAMPUS LIFE AND EXTRACURRICULAR ACTIVITIES

Campus housing available (% using): coed dorms (93%), apartment for single students (7%), special housing for disabled students, other housing options. Students who live in college-owned, operated, or affiliated housing: 32%. **Student employment:** During the 2009-2010 academic year, 24% of undergraduates worked on campus. Average per-year earnings: $3,360. **Clubs and organizations:** Number of student organizations: 67. Activities include: campus ministries, choral groups, concert band, dance, drama/theater, international student organization, jazz band, literary magazine, marching band, music ensembles, musical theater, radio station, student government, student newspaper, yearbook. Number of fraternities: 5; sororities: 3. **Sports program (2009-2010):** Member of NCAA III. **Men's intercollegiate varsity sports:** baseball, basketball, cross country, football, soccer, swimming, tennis, track and field (indoor), track and field (outdoor), wrestling. **Women's intercollegiate varsity sports:** basketball, cross country, field hockey, lacrosse, soccer, softball, swimming, tennis, track and field (indoor), track and field (outdoor), volleyball.

SERVICES AND FACILITIES

Basic services: nonremedial tutoring, women's center, placement service, day care, health service, health insurance. **Remedial assistance:** math, writing, study skills. **Counseling services:** minority student, career, personal, academic, psychological, birth control, religious. **For learning-disabled students:** School does not offer a structured program with separate admission and additional fees. Services include: tape recorders, untimed tests, notetaking services, oral tests, learning center, readers, extended time for tests, tutors, priority seating, texts on tape, other testing accommodations, other. **Library:** Number of titles: 283,269; number of current serial subscriptions: 3,218. **Information technology resources:** Students are required to lease or own a computer. Number of campus computers available to all students: 900. School has a wireless network. Approximate number of users that can be accommodated: 11,250. Proportion of college-owned housing units wired for high-speed internet access: 100%. **Campus safety:** Security services offered: 24-hour foot-and-vehicle patrols, late-night transport/escort service, 24-hour emergency telephones, lighted pathways/sidewalks, controlled dormitory access (key, security card, etc).

TRANSFER AND INTERNATIONAL STUDENTS

Transfer students: May apply for admission for the following academic terms: Fall, Spring. Applicants need a minimum number of credits to apply. For fall 2009: Transfer applications received: 1,628. Transfer applicants offered admission: 1,507. Transfer applicants enrolled: 940. **International students:** Number of foreign undergraduates: 59 (1% of student body). Number of countries represented: 20. Minimum TOEFL score required: 500 (paper); 173 (computer). Average TOEFL score: 520 (paper).

Cambridge College

- ■ **Address:** 1000 Massachusetts Avenue, Cambridge, MA 02138-
- ■ **Website:** http://www.cambridgecollege.edu
- ■ **Private**
- ■ **Enrollment:** 314 full-time; 840 part-time

KEY STATS

✔ **U.S News College Ranking:** Unranked, Regional Universities (North)
✔ **SAT or ACT Score (25th/75th percentile):** N/A
✔ **Tuition:** 2010-2011: $13,240

Selectivity: N/A	**Room/board:** $15,000
Acceptance rate: 100%	**Average debt:** $0
Student/faculty ratio: 16/1	**Proportion who borrowed:** 0%

UNDERGRADUATE STUDENT BODY STATS

2009-2010 enrollment: 314 full-time; 840 part-time. Men: 30%; women: 70%. **Ethnic makeup:** African American: 29%; Asian American: 3%; Hispanic: 19%; White: 48%; International: 1%.

ADMISSIONS FACTS AND FIGURES

Phone: (800) 877-4723. **Website:** http://www.cambridgecollege.edu. **Application deadlines for fall 2011:** Regular decision: Rolling. Early decision: Not offered. Early action: Not offered. Admission can be deferred. **Application fee:** $30. **To apply online, go to:** https://mycc.cambridgecollege.edu/ics/Admissions/Apply_for_admission.jnz. **Admissions requirements/recommendations:** Tests: The college does not use SAT or ACT scores in admissions decisions. Neither SAT nor ACT required. Campus visit: Recommended. Admissions interview: Recommended. Off-campus interview: May be arranged. **Factors that count in admissions decisions:** *Academic:* Secondary school record: Not Considered. Class rank: Not

Considered. Letters of recommendation: Very Important. Standardized test scores: Not Considered. Essay: Very Important. *Nonacademic:* Interview: Very Important. Extracurricular activities: Not Considered. Talent/ability: Important. Character/personal qualities: Important. Alumni/ae relationship: Not Considered. Geographical residence: Not Considered. State residency: Not Considered. Religious affiliation/commitment: Not Considered. Minority status: Not Considered. Volunteer work: Not Considered. Work experience: Important. **Admissions statistics for the fall 2009 entering class:** Total applicants: 120. Total accepted: 120. Freshmen enrolled: 99; 6% were from out of state. Overall acceptance rate: 100%.

ACADEMICS

Year founded: 1971. **Academic calendar:** Trimester. **Degrees offered:** certificate, bachelor's, master's, post-master's certificate, doctorate. **Most popular majors:** 46% liberal arts and sciences/liberal studies, 31% business/commerce, 12% psychology, 11% community psychology. **Areas of required coursework:** arts/fine arts, humanities, computer literacy, mathematics, English (including composition), sciences (biological or physical), social science. **Special academic programs:** accelerated program, distance learning, double major, independent study, internships, weekend college. **Faculty and instruction (2009-2010):** Total instructional faculty: 26 full-time, 545 part-time (40% men; 60% women; 36% minorities). Full-time faculty with Ph.D. or other terminal degree: 69%. Student/faculty ratio: 16/1. Classes of fewer than 20 students: 81%; of 20 to 49 students: 19%; of 50 or more students: 0%. **Advanced Placement and International Baccalaureate credit:** AP tests may be used for: Credit and/or placement. Scores accepted: 5. International Baccalaureate exams may be used for: Placement only. **Freshmen returning for sophomore year:** 46%.

COSTS AND FINANCIAL AID

Financial aid office: (800) 877-4723. **Expenses (2010-2011):** Tuition and fees 2010-2011: $13,240; room/board: $15,000. **Financial aid:** Priority filing date for institution's financial aid form: September 1. In 2009-2010, 81% of undergraduates applied for financial aid. Of those, 76% were determined to have financial need; Average financial aid package (proportion receiving): $8,184 (81%). Average amount of gift aid, such as scholarships or grants (proportion receiving): $5,308 (55%). Average amount of self-help aid, such as work study or loans (proportion receiving): $4,799 (76%). Average need-based loan (excluding PLUS or other private loans): $4,659. Among students who received need-based aid, the average percentage of need met: 31%. Among students who received aid based on merit, the average award (and the proportion receiving): $0 (0%). The average athletic scholarship (and the proportion receiving): $0 (0%). Average amount of debt of borrowers graduating in 2009: $0.

CAMPUS LIFE AND EXTRACURRICULAR ACTIVITIES

Clubs and organizations: Number of student organizations: 1. Activities include: student government. Number of fraternities: 0; sororities: 0.

SERVICES AND FACILITIES

Basic services: nonremedial tutoring. **Remedial assistance:** reading, math, writing, study skills. **Counseling services:** career, academic, older student. **For learning-disabled students:** School does not offer a structured program with separate admission and additional fees. Total undergraduates in learning-disabled program or receiving services: 25. Services include: remedial math, remedial English, reading machines, remedial reading, tape recorders, untimed tests, note-taking services, oral tests, learning center, readers, extended time for tests, tutors, early syllabus, priority registration, priority seating, proofreading services, substitution of courses, texts on tape, typist/scribe, exams on tape or computer, take home exams, other. **Library:** Number of titles: 45,628; number of current serial subscriptions: 14,000. **Information technology resources:** Students are not required to lease or own a computer. School has a wireless network. Approximate number of users that can be accommodated: 1,200. Proportion of college-owned housing units wired for high-speed internet access: 0%. **Campus safety:** Security services offered: 24-hour emergency telephones.

TRANSFER AND INTERNATIONAL STUDENTS

Transfer students: May apply for admission for the following academic terms: Fall, Spring, Summer. Applicants do not need a minimum number of credits to apply. For fall 2009: Transfer applications received: 128. Transfer applicants offered admission: 127. Transfer applicants enrolled: 108. **International students:** Number of foreign undergraduates: 15 (1% of student body). Number of countries represented: 48. Minimum TOEFL score required: 550 (paper); 79 (computer). Average TOEFL score: 550 (paper).

Clark University

- **Address:** 950 Main Street, Worcester, MA 01610-1477
- **Website:** http://www.clarku.edu
- **Private**
- **Enrollment:** 2,206 full-time; 127 part-time

KEY STATS
- ✔ **U.S News College Ranking:** 86, National Universities
- ✔ **SAT Score (25th/75th percentile):** 1080-1290
- ✔ **Tuition:** 2010-2011: $36,420

Selectivity: More selective	**Room/board:** $6,950
Acceptance rate: 64%	**Average debt:** $21,925
Student/faculty ratio: 10/1	**Proportion who borrowed:** 86%

UNDERGRADUATE STUDENT BODY STATS

2009-2010 enrollment: 2,206 full-time; 127 part-time. Men: 39%; women: 61%. **Ethnic makeup:** African American: 2%; Asian American: 4%; Hispanic: 2%; White: 83%; International: 8%. **Religious preference:** Roman Catholic: 17%; Protestant: 27%; Jewish: 13%; Muslim: 1%; Hindu: 1%; Buddhist: 2%; No preference: 39%.

ADMISSIONS FACTS AND FIGURES

Phone: (508) 793-7431. **Email:** admissions@clarku.edu. **Website:** http://www.clarku.edu. **Application deadlines for fall 2011:** Regular decision: January 15; decision sent by April 1. Early decision: Not offered. Early action: Send application by: November 15; Decision sent by: December 23. Admission can be deferred. **Application fee:** $55. **To apply online, go to:** http://www.clarku.edu/admissions/apply/index.cfm. **Admissions requirements/recommendations:** High school units required (recommended): English: (4); Mathematics: (3); Science: (3); Foreign language: (2); Social studies: (2); History: (2); Total units: (16). Tests: The college uses SAT or ACT scores in admissions decisions. Either SAT or ACT required. For admission to the fall 2011 entering class, the school will accept: ACT with or without writing accepted. Campus visit: Recommended. Admissions interview: Recommended. Off-campus interview: May be arranged. **Factors that count in admissions decisions:** *Academic:* Secondary school record: Very Important. Class rank: Considered. Letters of recommendation: Very Important. Standardized test scores: Very Important. Essay: Important. *Nonacademic:* Interview: Considered. Extracurricular activities: Important. Talent/ability: Important. Character/personal qualities: Important. Alumni/ae relationship: Considered. Geographical residence: Considered. State residency: Not Considered. Religious affiliation/commitment: Not Considered. Minority status: Considered. Volunteer work: Important. Work experience: Considered. **Other schools with the greatest overlap in applicants:** American University; Boston University; Northeastern University; University of Massachusetts–Amherst; University of Vermont. **Admissions statistics for the fall 2009 entering class:** Total applicants: 4,271. Total accepted: 2,741. Freshmen enrolled: 550; 60% were from out of state. Overall acceptance rate: 64%. Non-early acceptance rate: 64%. **Size of waiting list:** 145 applicants; enrolled from waiting list: 12. **Credentials of fall 2009 freshmen:** 34% ranked in the top 10 percent of their high school class; 71% were in the top 25 percent; 96% were in the top half. (Proportion submitting class standing: 40%.) **Average high school grade point average:** 3.5. **First-year students who submitted SAT scores:** 89%. Scores (25/75 percentile): Critical Reading: 550-650, Math: 530-640, Combined: 1080-1290. **First-year students submitting ACT scores:** 29%. Scores (25/75 percentile): English: 22-27, Math: 24-30, Composite: 24-29.

ACADEMICS

Year founded: 1887. **Academic calendar:** Semester. **Degrees offered:** bachelor's, post-bachelor's certificate, master's, post-master's certificate, doctorate. **Most popular majors:** 18% psychology, 9% political science and government, 7% business administration, management, and operations, 6% English language and literature, 6% biology. **Major fields of study:** area, ethnic, cultural, and gender studies; biological and biomedical sciences; business, management, marketing, and related support services; communication, journalism, and related programs; English language and literature/letters; foreign languages, literatures, and linguistics; history; mathematics and statistics; multi/interdisciplinary studies; natural resources and conservation; philosophy and religious studies; physical sciences; psychology; social sciences; visual and performing arts. **Areas of required coursework:** arts/fine arts, humanities, mathematics, English (including composition), philosophy, foreign languages, sciences (biological or physical), history,

social science. **Pre-professional programs:** pre-law, pre-dentistry, pre-medicine, pre-veterinary science, pre-optometry. **Special academic programs (% participation):** cross-registration (3%), double major (11%), English as a Second Language (ESL), independent study (44%), internships (43%), liberal arts/career combination (25%), student-designed major (1%), study abroad (32%), teacher certificate program (4%), other. **Teacher certification offered in:** elementary, middle/junior high, secondary. **Reserve Officers Training Corps (ROTC):** Army ROTC: Offered at cooperating institution (Worcester Polytechnic Institute); Navy ROTC: Offered at cooperating institution (College of the Holy Cross); Air Force ROTC: Offered at cooperating institution (Worcester Polytechnic Institute). **Faculty and instruction (2009-2010):** Total instructional faculty: 187 full-time, 105 part-time (58% men; 42% women; 12% minorities). Full-time faculty with Ph.D. or other terminal degree: 96%. Student/faculty ratio: 10/1. Classes of fewer than 20 students: 57%; of 20 to 49 students: 38%; of 50 or more students: 5%. **Advanced Placement and International Baccalaureate credit:** AP tests may be used for: Credit and/or placement. Scores accepted: 4, 5. International Baccalaureate exams may be used for: Credit and/or placement. **Freshmen returning for sophomore year:** 89%. **Graduation rates:** Four-year: 73%; five-year: 78%; six-year: 78%. **Graduate study:** 36% of students pursue further study immediately upon graduation. Fields in which graduates pursue further study: Master of Business Administration (MBA), 20%; law, 8%; medicine, 4%; education, 12%; arts and sciences, 56%.

COSTS AND FINANCIAL AID

Financial aid office: (508) 793-7478. **Expenses (2010-2011):** Tuition and fees 2010-2011: $36,420; room/board: $6,950. Estimated books and supplies: $800; transportation: $250; personal expenses: $700. **Financial aid:** In 2009-2010, 74% of undergraduates applied for financial aid. Of those, 56% were determined to have financial need; 63% had their need fully met. Average financial aid package (proportion receiving): $25,904 (55%). Average amount of gift aid, such as scholarships or grants (proportion receiving): $20,705 (55%). Average amount of self-help aid, such as work study or loans (proportion receiving): $4,844 (46%). Average need-based loan (excluding PLUS or other private loans): $3,288. Among students who received need-based aid, the average percentage of need met: 94%. Among students who received aid based on merit, the average award (and the proportion receiving): $13,013 (34%). Average amount of debt of borrowers graduating in 2009: $21,925. Proportion who borrowed: 86%.

CAMPUS LIFE AND EXTRACURRICULAR ACTIVITIES

Campus housing available (% using): coed dorms (78%), women's dorms (7%), apartment for single students (11%), special housing for disabled students, other housing options (1%). Students who live in college-owned, operated, or affiliated housing: 70%. **Student employment:** During the 2009-2010 academic year, 50% of undergraduates worked on campus. Average per-year earnings: $2,000. **Clubs and organizations:** Number of student organizations: 115. Activities include: choral groups, concert band, dance, drama/theater, jazz band, literary magazine, marching band, music ensembles, musical theater, pep band, radio station, student government, student newspaper, student film society, symphony orchestra, television station, yearbook. Number of fraternities: 0; sororities: 0. Average proportion of students who stay on campus on weekends: 75%. **Sports program (2009-2010):** Member of NCAA III. *Men's intercollegiate varsity sports:* baseball, basketball, cross country, lacrosse, soccer, swimming, tennis. *Women's intercollegiate varsity sports:* basketball, cross country, field hockey, crew (lightweight), soccer, softball, swimming, tennis, volleyball.

SERVICES AND FACILITIES

Basic services: nonremedial tutoring, women's center, placement service, health service, health insurance. **Counseling services:** minority student, career, personal, academic, psychological, birth control. **For learning-disabled students:** School does not offer a structured program with separate admission and additional fees. Total undergraduates in learning-disabled program or receiving services: 141. Services include: oral tests, readers, extended time for tests, texts on tape. **Library:** Number of titles: 625,171; number of current serial subscriptions: 2,487. **Information technology resources:** Students are not required to lease or own a computer. Number of campus computers available to all students: 110. School has a wireless network. Approximate number of users that can be accommodated: 10,000. Proportion of college-owned housing units wired for high-speed internet access: 100%. **Campus safety:** Security services offered: 24-hour foot-and-vehicle patrols, late-night transport/escort service, 24-hour emergency telephones, lighted pathways/sidewalks, student patrols, controlled dormitory access (key, security card, etc).

TRANSFER AND INTERNATIONAL STUDENTS

Transfer students: May apply for admission for the following academic terms: Fall, Spring. Applicants need a minimum number of credits to apply. For fall 2009: Transfer applications received: 240. Transfer applicants offered admission: 128. Transfer applicants enrolled: 27. **International students:** Number of foreign undergraduates: 180 (8% of student body). Number of countries represented: 77. Minimum TOEFL score required: 550 (paper); 80 (computer). Average TOEFL score: 605 (paper).

College of Our Lady of the Elms

- ■ **Address:** 291 Springfield Street, Chicopee, MA 01013
- ■ **Website:** http://www.elms.edu
- ■ **Private; Religious affiliation:** Roman Catholic
- ■ **Enrollment:** N/A

KEY STATS
- ✔ **U.S News College Ranking:** 36, Regional Colleges (North)
- ✔ **SAT or ACT Score (25th/75th percentile):** N/A
- ✔ **Tuition:** 2009-2010: $26,260

Selectivity: Less selective	**Room/board:** $9,446
Acceptance rate: N/A	**Average debt:** N/A
Student/faculty ratio: N/A	**Proportion who borrowed:** N/A

College of the Holy Cross

- ■ **Address:** 1 College Street, Worcester, MA 01610
- ■ **Website:** http://www.holycross.edu
- ■ **Private; Religious affiliation:** Roman Catholic (Jesuit)
- ■ **Enrollment:** 2,897 full-time; 35 part-time

KEY STATS
- ✔ **U.S News College Ranking:** 32, National Liberal Arts Colleges
- ✔ **SAT Score (25th/75th percentile):** 1210-1370
- ✔ **Tuition:** 2010-2011: $39,892

Selectivity: More selective	**Room/board:** $10,940
Acceptance rate: 36%	**Average debt:** $23,785
Student/faculty ratio: 11/1	**Proportion who borrowed:** 57%

UNDERGRADUATE STUDENT BODY STATS

2009-2010 enrollment: 2,897 full-time; 35 part-time. Men: 45%; women: 55%. **Ethnic makeup:** African American: 4%; Asian American: 6%; Hispanic: 8%; White: 80%; International: 1%. **Religious preference:** Roman Catholic: 72%; Protestant: 12%; Buddhist: 1%; No preference: 9%; Christian: 4%; Other: 2%.

ADMISSIONS FACTS AND FIGURES

Phone: (508) 793-2443. **Email:** admissions@holycross.edu. **Website:** http://www.holycross.edu. **Application deadlines for fall 2011:** Regular decision: January 15; decision sent by April 1. Early decision: Send application by: December 15; Decision sent by: January 15. Early action: Not offered. Admission can be deferred. **Application fee:** $60. **To apply online, go to:** http://www.commonapp.org/. **Admissions requirements/recommendations:** High school units required (recommended): English: (4); Mathematics: (4); Science: (4); Foreign language: (4); Social studies: (2); History: (2); Total units: (20). Tests: The college uses SAT or ACT scores in admissions decisions. Neither SAT nor ACT required. For admission to the fall 2011 entering class, the school will accept: ACT with or without writing accepted. Campus visit: Recommended. Admissions interview: Recommended. Off-campus interview: May be arranged. **Factors that count in admissions decisions:** *Academic:* Secondary school record: Very Important. Class rank: Very Important. Letters of recommendation: Very Important. Standardized test scores: Considered. Essay: Important. *Nonacademic:* Interview: Very Important. Extracurricular activities: Important. Talent/ability: Considered. Character/personal qualities: Important. Alumni/ae relationship: Considered. Geographical residence: Considered. State residency: Not Considered. Religious affiliation/commitment: Not Considered. Minority status: Considered. Volunteer work: Considered. Work experience: Considered. **Other schools with the greatest overlap in applicants:** Boston College; Fordham University; Georgetown University; Providence College;

Villanova University. **Admissions statistics for the fall 2009 entering class:** Total applicants: 6,652. Total accepted: 2,426. Freshmen enrolled: 747; 66% were from out of state. Accepted through early-decision or early-action plans: 47%. Overall acceptance rate: 36%. Early-decision acceptance rate: 73%. Non-early acceptance rate: 34%. **Size of waiting list:** 1655 applicants; enrolled from waiting list: 0. **Credentials of fall 2009 freshmen:** 66% ranked in the top 10 percent of their high school class; 93% were in the top 25 percent; 99% were in the top half. (Proportion submitting class standing: 44%.) **Average high school grade point average:** 3.8. **First-year students who submitted SAT scores:** 55%. Scores (25/75 percentile): Critical Reading: 600-680, Math: 610-690, Combined: 1210-1370. **First-year students submitting ACT scores:** 17%. Scores (25/75 percentile): English: 26-32, Math: 26-31, Composite: 26-30.

ACADEMICS

Year founded: 1843. **Academic calendar:** Semester. **Degrees offered:** bachelor's. **Most popular majors:** 34% social sciences, 12% foreign languages, literatures, and linguistics, 11% English language and literature/letters, 11% psychology, 7% history. **Major fields of study:** biological and biomedical sciences; business, management, marketing, and related support services; computer and information sciences and support services; English language and literature/letters; foreign languages, literatures, and linguistics; history; mathematics and statistics; multi/interdisciplinary studies; philosophy and religious studies; physical sciences; psychology; social sciences; visual and performing arts. **Areas of required coursework:** arts/fine arts, humanities, mathematics, English (including composition), philosophy, foreign languages, sciences (biological or physical), history, social science, other. **Pre-professional programs:** pre-dentistry, pre-medicine, pre-veterinary science. **Special academic programs (% participation):** accelerated program (0%), cross-registration (9%), double major (16%), exchange student program (domestic), honors program (6%), independent study (37%), internships (21%), student-designed major (2%), study abroad (33%), teacher certificate program (1%), other (15%). **Teacher certification offered in:** middle/junior high, secondary. **Reserve Officers Training Corps (ROTC):** Army ROTC: Offered at cooperating institution (Worcester Polytechnic Institute); Navy ROTC: Offered on campus; Air Force ROTC: Offered at cooperating institution (Worcester Polytechnic Institute). **Faculty and instruction (2009-2010):** Total instructional faculty: 244 full-time, 62 part-time (54% men; 46% women; 12% minorities). Full-time faculty with Ph.D. or other terminal degree: 98%. Student/faculty ratio: 11/1. Classes of fewer than 20 students: 53%; of 20 to 49 students: 46%; of 50 or more students: 1%. **Advanced Placement and International Baccalaureate credit:** AP tests may be used for: Credit and/or placement. Scores accepted: 4, 5. International Baccalaureate exams may be used for: Credit and/or placement. **Freshmen returning for sophomore year:** 95%. **Graduation rates:** Four-year: 87%; five-year: 89%; six-year: 89%. **Graduate study:** 25% of students pursue further study immediately upon graduation. Fields in which graduates pursue further study: Master of Business Administration (MBA), 5%; law, 19%; medicine, 7%; dentistry, 1%; engineering, 1%; theology (or the seminary), 1%; education, 5%; arts and sciences, 10%; veterinary medicine, 1%.

COSTS AND FINANCIAL AID

Financial aid office: (508) 793-2266. **Expenses (2010-2011):** Tuition and fees 2010-2011: $39,892; room/board: $10,940. Estimated books and supplies: $700; transportation: $300; personal expenses: $900. **Financial aid:** Priority filing date for institution's financial aid form: February 1; deadline: February 1. In 2009-2010, 63% of undergraduates applied for financial aid. Of those, 57% were determined to have financial need; 95% had their need fully met. Average financial aid package (proportion receiving): $29,293 (54%). Average amount of gift aid, such as scholarships or grants (proportion receiving): $27,089 (43%). Average amount of self-help aid, such as work study or loans (proportion receiving): $6,490 (41%). Average need-based loan (excluding PLUS or other private loans): $5,320. Among students who received need-based aid, the average percentage of need met: 100%. Among students who received aid based on merit, the average award (and the proportion receiving): $24,997 (0%). The average athletic scholarship (and the proportion receiving): $34,485 (2%). Average amount of debt of borrowers graduating in 2009: $23,785. Proportion who borrowed: 57%.

CAMPUS LIFE AND EXTRACURRICULAR ACTIVITIES

Campus housing available (% using): coed dorms, apartment for single students (10%), special housing for disabled students, other housing options (60%). Students who live in college-owned, operated, or affiliated housing: 88%. **Student employment:** During the 2009-2010 academic year, 25% of undergraduates worked on campus. Average per-year earnings: $1,590. **Clubs and organizations:** Number of student organizations: 105. Activities include: campus ministries, choral groups, concert band, dance, drama/theater, international student organization, jazz band, literary magazine, marching band, music ensembles, musical theater, pep band, radio station, student government, student newspaper, yearbook. Number of fraternities: 0; sororities: 0. Average proportion of students who stay on campus on weekends: 90%. **Sports program (2009-2010):** Member of NCAA I. *Men's intercollegiate varsity sports:* baseball, basketball, cross country, football, golf, ice hockey, lacrosse, soccer, swimming, tennis, track and field (indoor), track and field (outdoor). *Women's intercollegiate varsity sports:* basketball, crew (heavyweight), cross country, field hockey, golf, ice hockey, lacrosse, soccer, softball, swimming, tennis, track and field (indoor), track and field (outdoor), volleyball.

SERVICES AND FACILITIES
Basic services: nonremedial tutoring, placement service, health service, other. **Counseling services:** minority student, career, military, personal, academic, psychological, religious. **For learning-disabled students:** School does not offer a structured program with separate admission and additional fees. Total undergraduates in learning-disabled program or receiving services: 77. Services include: reading machines, note-taking services, oral tests, learning center, extended time for tests, tutors, priority registration, priority seating, texts on tape, other testing accommodations. **Library:** Number of titles: 627,742; number of current serial subscriptions: 1,334. **Information technology resources:** Students are not required to lease or own a computer. Number of campus computers available to all students: 485. School has a wireless network. Proportion of college-owned housing units wired for high-speed internet access: 100%. **Campus safety:** Security services offered: 24-hour foot-and-vehicle patrols, late-night transport/escort service, 24-hour emergency telephones, lighted pathways/sidewalks, controlled dormitory access (key, security card, etc).

TRANSFER AND INTERNATIONAL STUDENTS
Transfer students: May apply for admission for the following academic terms: Fall, Spring. Applicants need a minimum number of credits to apply. For fall 2009: Transfer applications received: 160. Transfer applicants offered admission: 37. Transfer applicants enrolled: 14. **International students:** Number of foreign undergraduates: 36 (1% of student body). Number of countries represented: 15. Minimum TOEFL score required: 550 (paper); 213 (computer).

Curry College

- **Address:** 1071 Blue Hill Avenue, Milton, MA 02186
- **Website:** http://www.curry.edu
- **Private**
- **Enrollment:** 1,988 full-time; 817 part-time

KEY STATS
✔ **U.S News College Ranking:** 29, Regional Colleges (North)
✔ **SAT Score (25th/75th percentile):** 840-1030
✔ **Tuition:** 2010-2011: $30,750

Selectivity: Less selective	**Room/board:** $11,650
Acceptance rate: 75%	**Average debt:** $38,374
Student/faculty ratio: 11/1	**Proportion who borrowed:** 78%

UNDERGRADUATE STUDENT BODY STATS
2009-2010 enrollment: 1,988 full-time; 817 part-time. Men: 43%; women: 57%. **Ethnic makeup:** African American: 8%; Asian American: 1%; Hispanic: 3%; White: 88%; International: 1%.

ADMISSIONS FACTS AND FIGURES
Phone: (800) 669-0686. **Email:** curryadm@curry.edu. **Website:** http://www.curry.edu. **Application deadlines for fall 2011:** Regular decision: Rolling; decision sent by May 1. Early decision: Send application by: December 1; Decision sent by: N/A. Early action: Not offered. Admission can be deferred. **Application fee:** $50. **To apply online, go to:** http://www.curry.edu/Admissions/Apply/. **Admissions requirements/recommendations:** High school units required (recommended): English: 4; Mathematics: 3; Science: 2; Foreign language: 2; Social studies: 2; History: 2; Total units: 16. Tests: The college uses SAT or ACT scores in admissions decisions. Neither SAT nor ACT required. For admission to the fall 2011 entering class, the school will accept: ACT with or without writing accepted. Campus visit: Recommended. Admissions interview: Recommended. Off-campus

interview: May be arranged. **Factors that count in admissions decisions: Academic:** Secondary school record: Very Important. Class rank: Important. Letters of recommendation: Important. Standardized test scores: Important. Essay: Important. *Nonacademic:* Interview: Considered. Extracurricular activities: Considered. Talent/ability: Considered. Character/personal qualities: Important. Alumni/ae relationship: Not Considered. Geographical residence: Not Considered. State residency: Not Considered. Religious affiliation/commitment: Not Considered. Minority status: Not Considered. Volunteer work: Important. Work experience: Considered. **Other schools with the greatest overlap in applicants:** Lasell College; Regis College; Roger Williams University; Suffolk University; University of Massachusetts–Dartmouth. **Admissions statistics for the fall 2009 entering class:** Total applicants: 4,355. Total accepted: 3,268. Freshmen enrolled: 623; 34% were from out of state. Overall acceptance rate: 75%. Early-decision acceptance rate: 38%. Non-early acceptance rate: 76%. **Size of waiting list:** 212 applicants; enrolled from waiting list: 48. **Credentials of fall 2009 freshmen:** 2% ranked in the top 10 percent of their high school class; 16% were in the top 25 percent; 46% were in the top half. (Proportion submitting class standing: 38%.) **Average high school grade point average:** 2.6. **First-year students who submitted SAT scores:** 70%. Scores (25/75 percentile): Critical Reading: 420-510, Math: 420-520, Combined: 840-1030. **First-year students submitting ACT scores:** 11%. Scores (25/75 percentile): English: N/A, Math: N/A, Composite: 18-22.

ACADEMICS
Year founded: 1879. **Academic calendar:** Semester. **Degrees offered:** bachelor's, master's. **Most popular majors:** 25% nursing/registered nurse training (R.N., A.S.N., B.S.N., M.S.N.), 21% criminal justice/safety studies, 17% communication studies/speech communication and rhetoric, 16% business administration and management, 7% psychology. **Major fields of study:** biological and biomedical sciences; business, management, marketing, and related support services; communication, journalism, and related programs; computer and information sciences and support services; education; English language and literature/letters; health professions and related clinical sciences; liberal arts and sciences studies, and humanities; multi/interdisciplinary studies; natural resources and conservation; philosophy and religious studies; psychology; security and protective services; social sciences; visual and performing arts. **Areas of required coursework:** arts/fine arts, humanities, computer literacy, mathematics, English (including composition), philosophy, sciences (biological or physical), history, social science, other. **Special academic programs (% participation):** cross-registration, double major (4%), honors program (6%), independent study (22%), internships (26%), student-designed major (1%), study abroad (1%), teacher certificate program (1%). **Teacher certification offered in:** early childhood, special education, elementary. **Reserve Officers Training Corps (ROTC):** Army ROTC: Offered at cooperating institution (Stonehill College); Air Force ROTC: Offered at cooperating institution (Boston University). **Faculty and instruction (2009-2010):** Total instructional faculty: 118 full-time, 290 part-time (40% men; 60% women; 7% minorities). Full-time faculty with Ph.D. or other terminal degree: 65%. Student/faculty ratio: 11/1. Classes of fewer than 20 students: 51%; of 20 to 49 students: 49%; of 50 or more students: 0%. **Advanced Placement and International Baccalaureate credit:** AP tests may be used for: Credit and/or placement. Scores accepted: 3, 4, 5. International Baccalaureate exams may be used for: Credit only. **Freshmen returning for sophomore year:** 65%. **Graduation rates:** Four-year: 38%; five-year: 45%; six-year: 48%. **Graduate study:** 10% of students pursue further study immediately upon graduation; 14% within one year. Fields in which graduates pursue further study: Master of Business Administration (MBA), 35%; law, 15%; education, 10%; arts and sciences, 40%.

COSTS AND FINANCIAL AID
Financial aid office: (617) 333-2146. **Expenses (2010-2011):** Tuition and fees 2010-2011: $30,750; room/board: $11,650. Estimated books and supplies: $800; transportation: $1,000; personal expenses: $1,000. **Financial aid:** Priority filing date for institution's financial aid form: March 1. In 2009-2010, 70% of undergraduates applied for financial aid. Of those, 69% were determined to have financial need; 6% had their need fully met. Average financial aid package (proportion receiving): $18,475 (69%). Average amount of gift aid, such as scholarships or grants (proportion receiving): $12,322 (63%). Average amount of self-help aid, such as work study or loans (proportion receiving): $5,345 (66%). Average need-based loan (excluding PLUS or other private loans): $4,360. Among students who received need-based aid, the average percentage of need met: 66%. Among students who received aid based on merit, the average award (and the proportion receiving): $5,293 (4%). The average athletic scholarship (and the proportion

receiving): $0 (0%). Average amount of debt of borrowers graduating in 2009: $38,374. Proportion who borrowed: 78%.

CAMPUS LIFE AND EXTRACURRICULAR ACTIVITIES

Campus housing available (% using): coed dorms (97%), women's dorms (2%), men's dorms (1%), special housing for disabled students. Students who live in college-owned, operated, or affiliated housing: 49%. **Student employment:** During the 2009-2010 academic year, 12% of undergraduates worked on campus. Average per-year earnings: $2,000. **Clubs and organizations:** Number of student organizations: 40. Activities include: campus ministries, choral groups, dance, drama/theater, literary magazine, musical theater, radio station, student government, student newspaper, student film society, television station, yearbook. Number of fraternities: 0; sororities: 0. Average proportion of students who stay on campus on weekends: 55%. **Sports program (2009-2010):** Member of NCAA III. *Men's intercollegiate varsity sports:* baseball, basketball, football, ice hockey, lacrosse, soccer, tennis. *Women's intercollegiate varsity sports:* basketball, cross country, lacrosse, soccer, softball, tennis, volleyball.

SERVICES AND FACILITIES

Basic services: nonremedial tutoring, placement service, day care, health service, health insurance. **Remedial assistance:** reading, math, writing, study skills. **Counseling services:** career, personal, academic, psychological, birth control, religious, other. **For learning-disabled students:** School does not offer a structured program with separate admission and additional fees. Total undergraduates in learning-disabled program or receiving services: 377. Services include: remedial math, remedial English, reading machines, remedial reading, tape recorders, other special classes, diagnostic testing service, untimed tests, note-taking services, oral tests, learning center, readers, extended time for tests, tutors, texts on tape, exams on tape or computer, other testing accommodations, other. **Library:** Number of titles: 98,157; number of current serial subscriptions: 300. **Information technology resources:** Students are not required to lease or own a computer. Number of campus computers available to all students: 215. School has a wireless network. Approximate number of users that can be accommodated: 1,500. Proportion of college-owned housing units wired for high-speed internet access: 100%. **Campus safety:** Security services offered: 24-hour foot-and-vehicle patrols, late-night transport/escort service, 24-hour emergency telephones, lighted pathways/sidewalks, student patrols, controlled dormitory access (key, security card, etc).

TRANSFER AND INTERNATIONAL STUDENTS

Transfer students: May apply for admission for the following academic terms: Fall, Spring. Applicants do not need a minimum number of credits to apply. For fall 2009: Transfer applications received: 451. Transfer applicants offered admission: 194. Transfer applicants enrolled: 84. **International students:** Number of foreign undergraduates: 22 (1% of student body). Number of countries represented: 11. Minimum TOEFL score required: 537 (paper); 75 (computer). Average TOEFL score: 563 (paper).

Eastern Nazarene College

■ **Address:** 23 E. Elm Avenue, Quincy, MA 02170
■ **Website:** http://www.enc.edu
■ **Private; Religious affiliation:** Nazarene
■ **Enrollment:** 823 full-time; 26 part-time

KEY STATS

✔ **U.S News College Ranking:** 31, Regional Colleges (North)
✔ **SAT Score (25th/75th percentile):** 830-1140
✔ **Tuition:** 2010-2011: $23,682

Selectivity: Less selective	**Room/board:** $8,000
Acceptance rate: 64%	**Average debt:** $47,815
Student/faculty ratio: N/A	**Proportion who borrowed:** 83%

UNDERGRADUATE STUDENT BODY STATS

2009-2010 enrollment: 823 full-time; 26 part-time. Men: 41%; women: 59%. **Ethnic makeup:** African American: 18%; American-Indian: 2%; Asian American: 2%; Hispanic: 7%; White: 70%; International: 1%. **Religious preference:** Roman Catholic: 7%; Protestant: 44%; No preference: 1%; Unknown: 10%; Nazarene: 38%.

ADMISSIONS FACTS AND FIGURES

Phone: (617) 745-3711. **Email:** info@enc.edu. **Website:** http://www.enc.edu. **Application deadlines for fall 2011:** Regular decision: Rolling. Early decision: Not offered. Early action: Not offered. Admission can be deferred. **Application fee:** $25. **To apply online, go to:** http://www.enc.edu/undergrad/application.htm. **Admissions requirements/recommendations:** High school units required (recommended): English: 4 (4); Mathematics: 2 (4); Science: (4); Foreign language: 2 (4); Social studies: 1 (2); History: 1 (2); Academic electives: (0); Total units: 16 (16). Tests: The college uses SAT or ACT scores in admissions decisions. Either SAT or ACT required. For admission to the fall 2011 entering class, the school will accept: ACT with writing recommended. Campus visit: Recommended. Admissions interview: Required. Off-campus interview: May be arranged. **Factors that count in admissions decisions:** *Academic:* Secondary school record: Important. Class rank: Important. Letters of recommendation: Very Important. Standardized test scores: Very Important. Essay: Considered. *Nonacademic:* Interview: Considered. Extracurricular activities: Important. Talent/ability: Considered. Character/personal qualities: Very Important. Alumni/ae relationship: Considered. Geographical residence: Not Considered. State residency: Not Considered. Religious affiliation/commitment: Important. Minority status: Not Considered. Volunteer work: Considered. Work experience: Considered. **Other schools with the greatest overlap in applicants:** Eastern University; Gordon College; Northeastern University; University of Massachusetts–Boston. **Admissions statistics for the fall 2009 entering class:** Total applicants: 883. Total accepted: 561. Freshmen enrolled: 190; 47% were from out of state. Overall acceptance rate: 64%. **Credentials of fall 2009 freshmen:** 9% ranked in the top 10 percent of their high school class; 37% were in the top 25 percent; 63% were in the top half. (Proportion submitting class standing: 14%.) **Average high school grade point average:** 2.9. **First-year students who submitted SAT scores:** 76%. Scores (25/75 percentile): Critical Reading: 410-570, Math: 420-570, Combined: 830-1140. **First-year students submitting ACT scores:** 10%. Scores (25/75 percentile): English: 16-28, Math: 15-29, Composite: 17-28.

ACADEMICS

Year founded: 1918. **Academic calendar:** 4-1-4. **Degrees offered:** certificate, diploma, associate, transfer-associate, terminal-associate, bachelor's, master's. **Major fields of study:** biological and biomedical sciences; business, management, marketing, and related support services; communication, journalism, and related programs; computer and information sciences and support services; education; engineering; English language and literature/letters; health professions and related clinical sciences; history; legal professions and studies; liberal arts and sciences studies, and humanities; mathematics and statistics; multi/interdisciplinary studies; natural resources and conservation; parks, recreation, leisure, and fitness studies; philosophy and religious studies; physical sciences; psychology; public administration and social service professions; security and protective services; social sciences; theology and religious vocations; visual and performing arts. **Areas of required coursework:** arts/fine arts, humanities, mathematics, English (including composition), philosophy, foreign languages, sciences (biological or physical), history, social science, other. **Pre-professional programs:** pre-law, pre-dentistry, pre-medicine, pre-theology, pre-veterinary science, pre-pharmacy. **Special academic programs (% participation):** accelerated program, cross-registration (1%), double major (18.2%), dual enrollment, exchange student program (domestic), honors program (9.3%), independent study (2%), internships (13.6%), liberal arts/career combination (8.7%), study abroad (4.2%), teacher certificate program (16.5%). **Teacher certification offered in:** early childhood, special education, elementary, middle/junior high, secondary. **Cooperative education programs:** health professions. **Reserve Officers Training Corps (ROTC):** Army ROTC: Offered at cooperating institution; Air Force ROTC: Offered at cooperating institution. **Faculty and instruction (2009-2010):** Total instructional faculty: 38 full-time, 121 part-time (56% men; 44% women). Full-time faculty with Ph.D. or other terminal degree: 68%. Classes of fewer than 20 students: 83%; of 20 to 49 students: 15%; of 50 or more students: 2%. **Advanced Placement and International Baccalaureate credit:** AP tests may be used for: Placement only. Scores accepted: 3, 4, 5. International Baccalaureate exams may be used for: Placement only. **Freshmen returning for sophomore year:** 70%. **Graduation rates:** Four-year: 32%; five-year: 38%; six-year: 50%. **Graduate study:** Fields in which graduates pursue further study: Master of Business Administration (MBA), 13%; law, 1%; medicine, 3%; engineering, 3%; theology (or the seminary), 32%; education, 23%; arts and sciences, 16%.

COSTS AND FINANCIAL AID

Financial aid office: (617) 745-3869. **Expenses (2010-2011):** Tuition and fees 2010-2011: $23,682; room/board: $8,000. Estimated books and supplies:

$1,100; transportation: $1,600; personal expenses: $2,200. **Financial aid:** Priority filing date for institution's financial aid form: July 1. In 2009-2010, 79% of undergraduates applied for financial aid. Of those, 66% were determined to have financial need; 31% had their need fully met. Average financial aid package (proportion receiving): $20,974 (66%). Average amount of gift aid, such as scholarships or grants (proportion receiving): $8,326 (58%). Average amount of self-help aid, such as work study or loans (proportion receiving): $9,265 (60%). Average need-based loan (excluding PLUS or other private loans): $9,166. Among students who received need-based aid, the average percentage of need met: 72%. Among students who received aid based on merit, the average award (and the proportion receiving): $7,848 (11%). The average athletic scholarship (and the proportion receiving): $0 (0%). Average amount of debt of borrowers graduating in 2009: $47,815. Proportion who borrowed: 83%.

CAMPUS LIFE AND EXTRACURRICULAR ACTIVITIES

Campus housing available (% using): women's dorms (48%), men's dorms (32%), apartments for married students (2%), apartment for single students (17%), special housing for disabled students (1%). Students who live in college-owned, operated, or affiliated housing: 62%. **Student employment:** During the 2009-2010 academic year, 53% of undergraduates worked on campus. Average per-year earnings: $4,800. **Clubs and organizations:** Number of student organizations: 26. Activities include: campus ministries, choral groups, concert band, drama/theater, international student organization, music ensembles, musical theater, radio station, student government, student newspaper, symphony orchestra, yearbook. Number of fraternities: 0; sororities: 0. Average proportion of students who stay on campus on weekends: 70%. **Sports program (2009-2010):** Member of NCAA III. *Men's intercollegiate varsity sports:* baseball, basketball, cross country, soccer, tennis. *Women's intercollegiate varsity sports:* basketball, cross country, soccer, softball, tennis, volleyball.

SERVICES AND FACILITIES

Basic services: nonremedial tutoring, placement service, day care, health service, health insurance. **Remedial assistance:** reading, math, writing, study skills, other. **Counseling services:** minority student, career, personal, academic, older student, psychological, religious, other. **For learning-disabled students:** School does not offer a structured program with separate admission and additional fees. Services include: remedial math, remedial English, reading machines, remedial reading, tape recorders, diagnostic testing service, untimed tests, note-taking services, oral tests, learning center, readers, extended time for tests, tutors, priority seating, texts on tape, other testing accommodations, other. **Library:** Number of titles: 150,756; number of current serial subscriptions: 430. **Information technology resources:** Students are not required to lease or own a computer. Number of campus computers available to all students: 100. School has a wireless network. Approximate number of users that can be accommodated: 500. Proportion of college-owned housing units wired for high-speed internet access: 100%. **Campus safety:** Security services offered: 24-hour foot-and-vehicle patrols, late-night transport/escort service, 24-hour emergency telephones, lighted pathways/sidewalks, student patrols, controlled dormitory access (key, security card, etc).

TRANSFER AND INTERNATIONAL STUDENTS

Transfer students: May apply for admission for the following academic terms: Fall, Winter, Spring, Summer. Applicants need a minimum number of credits to apply. For fall 2009: Transfer applications received: 143. Transfer applicants offered admission: 97. Transfer applicants enrolled: 35. **International students:** Number of foreign undergraduates: 8 (1% of student body). Number of countries represented: 12. Minimum TOEFL score required: 500 (paper); 173 (computer). Average TOEFL score: 550 (paper).

Emerson College

■ **Address:** 120 Boylston Street, Boston, MA 02116-4624
■ **Website:** http://www.emerson.edu
■ **Private**
■ **Enrollment:** 3,422 full-time; 274 part-time

KEY STATS

✔ **U.S News College Ranking:** 14, Regional Universities (North)
✔ **SAT Score (25th/75th percentile):** 1110-1310
✔ **Tuition:** 2010-2011: $31,272

Selectivity: More selective | **Room/board:** $12,881
Acceptance rate: 42% | **Average debt:** $15,262
Student/faculty ratio: 13/1 | **Proportion who borrowed:** 59%

UNDERGRADUATE STUDENT BODY STATS

2009-2010 enrollment: 3,422 full-time; 274 part-time. Men: 40%; women: 60%. **Ethnic makeup:** African American: 3%; Asian American: 5%; Hispanic: 8%; White: 81%; International: 3%.

ADMISSIONS FACTS AND FIGURES

Phone: (617) 824-8600. **Email:** admission@emerson.edu. **Website:** http://www.emerson.edu. **Application deadlines for fall 2011:** Regular decision: January 5; decision sent by April 1. Early decision: Not offered. Early action: Send application by: November 1; Decision sent by: December 15. Admission can be deferred. **Application fee:** $65. **To apply online, go to:** http://www.emerson.edu/undergraduate_admission. **Admissions requirements/recommendations:** High school units required (recommended): English: 4 (4); Mathematics: 3 (3); Foreign language: 3 (3); Social studies: 3 (3); Academic electives: (4); Total units: 16 (20). Tests: The college uses SAT or ACT scores in admissions decisions. Either SAT or ACT required. For admission to the fall 2011 entering class, the school will accept: ACT with writing required. Campus visit: Recommended. Admissions interview: Neither required nor recommended. Off-campus interview: Not available. **Factors that count in admissions decisions:** *Academic:* Secondary school record: Important. Class rank: Important. Letters of recommendation: Important. Standardized test scores: Very Important. Essay: Important. *Nonacademic:* Interview: Not Considered. Extracurricular activities: Important. Talent/ability: Important. Character/personal qualities: Important. Alumni/ae relationship: Considered. Geographical residence: Considered. State residency: Not Considered. Religious affiliation/commitment: Not Considered. Minority status: Considered. Volunteer work: Considered. Work experience: Considered. **Other schools with the greatest overlap in applicants:** Boston University; Ithaca College; New York University; Northeastern University; Syracuse University. **Admissions statistics for the fall 2009 entering class:** Total applicants: 6,943. Total accepted: 2,926. Freshmen enrolled: 766; 80% were from out of state. Accepted through early-decision or early-action plans: 51%. Overall acceptance rate: 42%. Non-early acceptance rate: 36%. **Size of waiting list:** 2089 applicants; enrolled from waiting list: 104. **Credentials of fall 2009 freshmen:** 42% ranked in the top 10 percent of their high school class; 77% were in the top 25 percent; 98% were in the top half. (Proportion submitting class standing: 39%.) **Average high school grade point average:** 3.6. **First-year students who submitted SAT scores:** 90%. Scores (25/75 percentile): Critical Reading: 570-670, Math: 540-640, Combined: 1110-1310. **First-year students submitting ACT scores:** 31%. Scores (25/75 percentile): English: 25-31, Math: 22-27, Composite: 24-29.

ACADEMICS

Year founded: 1880. **Academic calendar:** Semester. **Degrees offered:** certificate, bachelor's, master's. **Most popular majors:** 20% cinematography and film/video production, 20% radio and television, 19% creative writing, 14% marketing/marketing management, 11% drama and dramatics/theater arts. **Major fields of study:** business, management, marketing, and related support services; communication, journalism, and related programs; English language and literature/letters; health professions and related clinical sciences; visual and performing arts. **Areas of required coursework:** arts/fine arts, humanities, mathematics, English (including composition), philosophy, foreign languages, sciences (biological or physical), history, social science. **Special academic programs (% participation):** cross-registration (5%), double major (4%), honors program (5%), independent study (20%), internships (55%), student-designed major (1%), study abroad (20%), teacher certificate program (1%). **Teacher certification offered in:** elementary, middle/junior high, secondary. **Faculty and instruction (2009-2010):** Total instructional faculty: 177 full-time, 254 part-time (57% men; 43% women; 11% minorities). Full-time faculty with Ph.D. or other terminal degree: 71%. Student/faculty ratio: 13/1. Classes of fewer than 20 students: 63%; of 20 to 49 students: 36%; of 50 or more students: 2%. **Advanced Placement and International Baccalaureate credit:** AP tests may be used for: Credit only. Scores accepted: 4, 5. International Baccalaureate exams may be used for: Credit only. **Freshmen returning for sophomore year:** 89%. **Graduation rates:** Four-year: 74%; five-year: 77%; six-year: 75%. **Graduate study:** 10% of students pursue further study immediately upon graduation.

COSTS AND FINANCIAL AID

Financial aid office: (617) 824-8655. **Expenses (2010-2011):** Tuition and fees 2010-2011: $31,272; room/board: $12,881. Estimated books and supplies: $976; transportation: $1,476. **Financial aid:** Priority filing date for institution's financial aid form: March 1. In 2009-2010, 66% of undergraduates applied for financial aid. Of those, 57% were determined to have financial need; 60% had their need fully met. Average financial aid package (proportion receiving): $17,364 (56%). Average amount of gift aid, such as scholarships or grants (proportion receiving): $15,028 (47%). Average amount of self-help aid, such as work study or loans (proportion receiving): $5,070 (54%). Average need-based loan (excluding PLUS or other private loans): $4,509. Among students who received need-based aid, the average percentage of need met: 73%. Among students who received aid based on merit, the average award (and the proportion receiving): $12,327 (5%). The average athletic scholarship (and the proportion receiving): $0 (0%). Average amount of debt of borrowers graduating in 2009: $15,262. Proportion who borrowed: 59%.

CAMPUS LIFE AND EXTRACURRICULAR ACTIVITIES

Campus housing available (% using): coed dorms (99%), special housing for disabled students (1%). Students who live in college-owned, operated, or affiliated housing: 55%. **Student employment:** During the 2009-2010 academic year, 31% of undergraduates worked on campus. Average per-year earnings: $1,300. **Clubs and organizations:** Number of student organizations: 80. Activities include: choral groups, dance, drama/theater, international student organization, literary magazine, musical theater, radio station, student government, student newspaper, student film society, television station, yearbook. Number of fraternities: 4; sororities: 3. Average proportion of students who stay on campus on weekends: 75%. **Sports program (2009-2010):** Member of NCAA III. *Men's intercollegiate varsity sports:* baseball, basketball, cross country, lacrosse, soccer, tennis, volleyball. *Women's intercollegiate varsity sports:* basketball, cross country, lacrosse, soccer, softball, tennis, track and field (indoor), volleyball.

SERVICES AND FACILITIES

Basic services: nonremedial tutoring, health service, health insurance. **Remedial assistance:** reading, math, writing, study skills. **Counseling services:** minority student, career, personal, academic, psychological, birth control. **For learning-disabled students:** School does not offer a structured program with separate admission and additional fees. Total undergraduates in learning-disabled program or receiving services: 200. Services include: remedial math, remedial English, reading machines, remedial reading, tape recorders, note-taking services, oral tests, learning center, extended time for tests, tutors, texts on tape, other. **Library:** Number of titles: 179,000; number of current serial subscriptions: 380. **Information technology resources:** Students are not required to lease or own a computer. Number of campus computers available to all students: 485. School has a wireless network. Approximate number of users that can be accommodated: 2,000. Proportion of college-owned housing units wired for high-speed internet access: 100%. **Campus safety:** Security services offered: 24-hour foot-and-vehicle patrols, late-night transport/escort service, 24-hour emergency telephones, lighted pathways/sidewalks, controlled dormitory access (key, security card, etc).

TRANSFER AND INTERNATIONAL STUDENTS

Transfer students: May apply for admission for the following academic terms: Fall, Spring. Applicants do not need a minimum number of credits to apply. For fall 2009: Transfer applications received: 701. Transfer applicants offered admission: 370. Transfer applicants enrolled: 189. **International students:** Number of foreign undergraduates: 98 (3% of student body). Number of countries represented: 45. Minimum TOEFL score required: 550 (paper); 213 (computer). Average TOEFL score: 610 (paper).

Emmanuel College

- **Address:** 400 The Fenway, Boston, MA 02115
- **Website:** http://www.emmanuel.edu
- **Private; Religious affiliation:** Roman Catholic
- **Enrollment:** 1,648 full-time; 359 part-time

KEY STATS

✔ **U.S News College Ranking:** 51, Regional Universities (North)
✔ **SAT Score (25th/75th percentile):** 990-1160
✔ **Tuition:** 2010-2011: $30,765

Selectivity: Selective	**Room/board:** $12,300
Acceptance rate: 56%	**Average debt:** N/A
Student/faculty ratio: 16/1	**Proportion who borrowed:** N/A

UNDERGRADUATE STUDENT BODY STATS

2009-2010 enrollment: 1,648 full-time; 359 part-time. Men: 26%; women: 74%. **Ethnic makeup:** African American: 7%; Asian American: 3%; Hispanic: 5%; White: 84%; International: 1%.

ADMISSIONS FACTS AND FIGURES

Phone: (617) 735-9715. **Email:** enroll@emmanuel.edu. **Website:** http://www.emmanuel.edu. **Application deadlines for fall 2011:** Regular decision: March 1. Early decision: Send application by: November 1; Decision sent by: December 1. Early action: Send application by: November 15; Decision sent by: December 31. Admission can be deferred. **Application fee:** $40. **To apply online, go to:** http://www.emmanuel.edu/Undergraduate_Admissions/Applications_and_Deadlines.html. **Admissions requirements/recommendations:** High school units required (recommended): English: 4; Mathematics: 3; Science: 2; Foreign language: 2; Social studies: 2. Tests: The college uses SAT or ACT scores in admissions decisions. Either SAT or ACT required. For admission to the fall 2011 entering class, the school will accept: ACT with or without writing accepted. Campus visit: Recommended. Admissions interview: Recommended. Off-campus interview: Not available. **Factors that count in admissions decisions:** *Academic:* Secondary school record: Very Important. Class rank: Considered. Letters of recommendation: Very Important. Standardized test scores: Important. Essay: Very Important. *Nonacademic:* Interview: Considered. Extracurricular activities: Important. Talent/ability: Considered. Character/personal qualities: Important. Alumni/ae relationship: Considered. Geographical residence: Considered. State residency: Not Considered. Religious affiliation/commitment: Considered. Minority status: Not Considered. Volunteer work: Important. Work experience: Considered. **Other schools with the greatest overlap in applicants:** Boston University; Northeastern University; Providence College; Stonehill College; Suffolk University. **Admissions statistics for the fall 2009 entering class:** Total applicants: 5,518. Total accepted: 3,100. Freshmen enrolled: 424; 44% were from out of state. Overall acceptance rate: 56%. Non-early acceptance rate: 56%. **Credentials of fall 2009 freshmen:** 12% ranked in the top 10 percent of their high school class; 41% were in the top 25 percent; 83% were in the top half. (Proportion submitting class standing: 54%.) **Average high school grade point average:** 3.4. **First-year students who submitted SAT scores:** 97%. Scores (25/75 percentile): Critical Reading: 510-590, Math: 480-570, Combined: 990-1160. **First-year students submitting ACT scores:** 20%. Scores (25/75 percentile): English: N/A, Math: N/A, Composite: 20-24.

ACADEMICS

Year founded: 1919. **Academic calendar:** Semester. **Degrees offered:** bachelor's, post-bachelor's certificate, master's, post-master's certificate. **Most popular majors:** 16% business, management, marketing, and related support services, 13% psychology, 9% communication, journalism, and related programs, 9% education, 4% biological and biomedical sciences. **Major fields of study:** area, ethnic, cultural, and gender studies; biological and biomedical sciences; business, management, marketing, and related support services; communication, journalism, and related programs; education; English language and literature/letters; foreign languages, literatures, and linguistics; health professions and related clinical sciences; history; mathematics and statistics; multi/interdisciplinary studies; natural resources and conservation; philosophy and religious studies; physical sciences; psychology; social sciences; visual and performing arts. **Areas of required coursework:** arts/fine arts, humanities, computer literacy, mathematics, English (including composition), foreign languages, sciences (biological or physical), history, social science, other. **Pre-professional programs:** pre-law, pre-dentistry, pre-medicine, pre-veterinary science. **Special academic pro-**

grams: cross-registration, double major, exchange student program (domestic), honors program, independent study, internships, liberal arts/career combination, student-designed major, study abroad, teacher certificate program. **Teacher certification offered in:** elementary, middle/junior high, secondary. **Reserve Officers Training Corps (ROTC):** Army ROTC: Offered at cooperating institution (Boston University). **Faculty and instruction (2009-2010):** Total instructional faculty: 82 full-time, 109 part-time (43% men; 57% women; 10% minorities). Full-time faculty with Ph.D. or other terminal degree: 84%. Student/faculty ratio: 16/1. Classes of fewer than 20 students: 71%; of 20 to 49 students: 29%; of 50 or more students: 0%. **Advanced Placement and International Baccalaureate credit:** AP tests may be used for: Credit and/or placement. Scores accepted: 3, 4, 5. **International** Baccalaureate exams may be used for: Credit and/or placement. **Freshmen returning for sophomore year:** 78%. **Graduation rates:** Four-year: 55%; five-year: 62%; six-year: 60%.

COSTS AND FINANCIAL AID

Financial aid office: (617) 735-9938. **Expenses (2010-2011):** Tuition and fees 2010-2011: $30,765; room/board: $12,300. Estimated books and supplies: $880; transportation: $270; personal expenses: $1,935. **Financial aid:** Priority filing date for institution's financial aid form: April 1. In 2009-2010, 86% of undergraduates applied for financial aid. Of those, 79% were determined to have financial need; 42% had their need fully met. Average financial aid package (proportion receiving): $21,994 (79%). Average amount of gift aid, such as scholarships or grants (proportion receiving): $15,747 (77%). Average amount of self-help aid, such as work study or loans (proportion receiving): $6,115 (77%). Average need-based loan (excluding PLUS or other private loans): $4,975. Among students who received need-based aid, the average percentage of need met: 69%. Among students who received aid based on merit, the average award (and the proportion receiving): $11,671 (10%). The average athletic scholarship (and the proportion receiving): $0 (0%).

CAMPUS LIFE AND EXTRACURRICULAR ACTIVITIES

Campus housing available (% using): coed dorms (100%), special housing for disabled students (0%). Students who live in college-owned, operated, or affiliated housing: 71%. **Student employment:** During the 2009-2010 academic year, 34% of undergraduates worked on campus. Average per-year earnings: $1,462. **Clubs and organizations:** Number of student organizations: 90. Activities include: campus ministries, choral groups, dance, drama/theater, international student organization, jazz band, literary magazine, model UN, music ensembles, musical theater, pep band, radio station, student government, student newspaper, student film society, symphony orchestra, yearbook. Number of fraternities: 0; sororities: 0. Average proportion of students who stay on campus on weekends: 75%. **Sports program (2009-2010):** Member of NCAA III. *Men's intercollegiate varsity sports:* basketball, cross country, golf, soccer, track and field (indoor), track and field (outdoor), volleyball. *Women's intercollegiate varsity sports:* basketball, cross country, lacrosse, soccer, softball, tennis, track and field (indoor), track and field (outdoor), volleyball.

SERVICES AND FACILITIES

Basic services: nonremedial tutoring, placement service, health service. **Remedial assistance:** reading, math, writing, study skills. **Counseling services:** minority student, career, personal, veteran student, academic, psychological, religious. **For learning-disabled students:** School does not offer a structured program with separate admission and additional fees. Services include: reading machines, tape recorders, other special classes, oral tests, learning center, readers, extended time for tests, tutors, early syllabus, take home exams. **Library:** Number of titles: 96,000; number of current serial subscriptions: 1,063. **Information technology resources:** Students are not required to lease or own a computer. Number of campus computers available to all students: 196. School has a wireless network. Approximate number of users that can be accommodated: 1,400. Proportion of college-owned housing units wired for high-speed internet access: 100%. **Campus safety:** Security services offered: 24-hour foot-and-vehicle patrols, late-night transport/escort service, lighted pathways/sidewalks, controlled dormitory access (key, security card, etc).

TRANSFER AND INTERNATIONAL STUDENTS

Transfer students: May apply for admission for the following academic terms: Fall, Spring. Applicants need a minimum number of credits to apply. For fall 2009: Transfer applications received: 452. Transfer applicants offered admission: 171. Transfer applicants enrolled: 62. **International students:** Number of foreign undergraduates: 29 (1% of student body).

Number of countries represented: 23. Minimum TOEFL score required: 550 (paper); 213 (computer).

Endicott College

- **Address:** 376 Hale Street, Beverly, MA 01915
- **Website:** http://www.endicott.edu
- **Private**
- **Enrollment:** 2,115 full-time; 176 part-time

KEY STATS

✔ **U.S News College Ranking:** 10, Regional Colleges (North)
✔ **SAT Score (25th/75th percentile):** 990-1170
✔ **Tuition:** 2010-2011: $26,248

Selectivity: Selective	**Room/board:** $12,388
Acceptance rate: 53%	**Average debt:** $33,783
Student/faculty ratio: 16/1	**Proportion who borrowed:** 69%

UNDERGRADUATE STUDENT BODY STATS

2009-2010 enrollment: 2,115 full-time; 176 part-time. Men: 42%; women: 58%. **Ethnic makeup:** African American: 1%; Asian American: 1%; Hispanic: 2%; White: 94%; International: 2%.

ADMISSIONS FACTS AND FIGURES

Phone: (978) 921-1000. **Email:** admissio@endicott.edu. **Website:** http://www.endicott.edu. **Application deadlines for fall 2011:** Regular decision: February 15. Early decision: Not offered. Early action: Not offered. Admission cannot be deferred. **Application fee:** $40. **To apply online, go to:** https://cars.endicott.edu/cgi-bin/public/apply.cgi. **Admissions requirements/recommendations:** High school units required (recommended): English: (4); Mathematics: (3); Science: (2); Foreign language: (0); Social studies: (2); History: (1); Academic electives: (4); Total units: (16). **Tests:** The college uses SAT or ACT scores in admissions decisions. Either SAT or ACT required. For admission to the fall 2011 entering class, the school will accept: ACT with writing required. Campus visit: Recommended. Admissions interview: Recommended. Off-campus interview: Not available. **Factors that count in admissions decisions:** *Academic:* Secondary school record: Very Important. Class rank: Important. Letters of recommendation: Considered. Standardized test scores: Important. Essay: Important. *Nonacademic:* Interview: Considered. Extracurricular activities: Important. Talent/ability: Important. Character/personal qualities: Very Important. Alumni/ae relationship: Important. Geographical residence: Important. State residency: Considered. Religious affiliation/commitment: Not Considered. Minority status: Considered. Volunteer work: Important. Work experience: Important. **Other schools with the greatest overlap in applicants:** Merrimack College; Quinnipiac University; Roger Williams University; Salve Regina University; University of Massachusetts–Amherst. **Admissions statistics for the fall 2009 entering class:** Total applicants: 3,885. Total accepted: 2,072. Freshmen enrolled: 561; 58% were from out of state. Overall acceptance rate: 53%. **Size of waiting list:** 191 applicants; enrolled from waiting list: 5. **Credentials of fall 2009 freshmen:** 10% ranked in the top 10 percent of their high school class; 41% were in the top 25 percent; 80% were in the top half. (Proportion submitting class standing: 53%.) **First-year students who submitted SAT scores:** 98%. Scores (25/75 percentile): Critical Reading: 490-580, Math: 500-590, Combined: 990-1170. **First-year students submitting ACT scores:** 26%. Scores (25/75 percentile): English: 20-26, Math: 20-25, Composite: 20-25.

ACADEMICS

Year founded: 1939. **Academic calendar:** 4-1-4. **Degrees offered:** associate, bachelor's, post-bachelor's certificate, master's. **Most popular majors:** 32% business, management, marketing, and related support services; 12% parks, recreation, leisure, and fitness studies; 10% communication, journalism, and related programs; 9% visual and performing arts; 8% health professions and related clinical sciences. **Major fields of study:** business, management, marketing, and related support services; communication, journalism, and related programs; education; English language and literature/letters; health professions and related clinical sciences; liberal arts and sciences studies, and humanities; natural resources and conservation; parks, recreation, leisure, and fitness studies; psychology; security and protective services; social sciences; visual and performing arts. **Areas of required coursework:** humanities, mathematics, English (including composition), sciences (biological or physical), social science, other. **Special academic**

programs (% participation): accelerated program, cross-registration, distance learning, exchange student program (domestic), honors program, independent study, internships (100%), liberal arts/career combination, student-designed major, study abroad, teacher certificate program. **Teacher certification offered in:** early childhood, elementary. **Reserve Officers Training Corps (ROTC):** Army ROTC: Offered at cooperating institution (Massachusetts Institute of Technology); Air Force ROTC: Offered at cooperating institution (Massachusetts Institute of Technology). **Faculty and instruction (2009-2010):** Total instructional faculty: 77 full-time, 111 part-time (44% men; 56% women; 6% minorities). Full-time faculty with Ph.D. or other terminal degree: 66%. Student/faculty ratio: 16/1. Classes of fewer than 20 students: 52%; of 20 to 49 students: 48%; of 50 or more students: 0%. **Advanced Placement and International Baccalaureate credit:** AP tests may be used for: Credit only. Scores accepted: 3, 4, 5. International Baccalaureate exams may be used for: Credit only. **Freshmen returning for sophomore year:** 81%. **Graduation rates:** Four-year: 68%; five-year: 71%; six-year: 64%. **Graduate study:** 26% of students pursue further study immediately upon graduation. Fields in which graduates pursue further study: Master of Business Administration (MBA), 26%; law, 9%; education, 27%; arts and sciences, 12%.

COSTS AND FINANCIAL AID

Financial aid office: (978) 232-2070. **Expenses (2010-2011):** Tuition and fees 2010-2011: $26,248; room/board: $12,388. Estimated books and supplies: $1,018; transportation: $1,000; personal expenses: $1,000. **Financial aid:** Priority filing date for institution's financial aid form: March 15. In 2009-2010, 83% of undergraduates applied for financial aid. Of those, 60% were determined to have financial need; 12% had their need fully met. Average financial aid package (proportion receiving): $16,827 (60%). Average amount of gift aid, such as scholarships or grants (proportion receiving): $9,103 (45%). Average amount of self-help aid, such as work study or loans (proportion receiving): $5,300 (57%). Average need-based loan (excluding PLUS or other private loans): $4,594. Among students who received need-based aid, the average percentage of need met: 61%. Among students who received aid based on merit, the average award (and the proportion receiving): $7,007 (17%). The average athletic scholarship (and the proportion receiving): $0 (0%). Average amount of debt of borrowers graduating in 2009: $33,783. Proportion who borrowed: 69%.

CAMPUS LIFE AND EXTRACURRICULAR ACTIVITIES

Campus housing available: coed dorms, women's dorms, apartment for single students, special housing for disabled students, special housing for international students, other housing options. Students who live in college-owned, operated, or affiliated housing: 84%. **Student employment:** During the 2009-2010 academic year, 30% of undergraduates worked on campus. Average per-year earnings: $1,500. **Clubs and organizations:** Number of student organizations: 47. Activities include: campus ministries, choral groups, dance, drama/theater, international student organization, jazz band, literary magazine, model UN, music ensembles, musical theater, radio station, student government, student newspaper, student film society, television station, yearbook. Number of fraternities: 0; sororities: 0. Average proportion of students who stay on campus on weekends: 87%. **Sports program (2009-2010):** Member of NCAA III. *Men's intercollegiate varsity sports:* baseball, basketball, cross country, football, golf, lacrosse, soccer, tennis, volleyball. *Women's intercollegiate varsity sports:* basketball, cross country, equestrian, field hockey, lacrosse, soccer, softball, tennis, volleyball.

SERVICES AND FACILITIES

Basic services: nonremedial tutoring, health service, health insurance, other. **Counseling services:** minority student, career, military, personal, veteran student, academic, older student, psychological, birth control, religious. **For learning-disabled students:** School does not offer a structured program with separate admission and additional fees. Services include: tape recorders, untimed tests, note-taking services, oral tests, learning center, readers, extended time for tests, tutors, priority seating, texts on tape. **Library:** Number of titles: 121,485; number of current serial subscriptions: 47,151. **Information technology resources:** Students are not required to lease or own a computer. Number of campus computers available to all students: 232. School has a wireless network. Approximate number of users that can be accommodated: 1,000. Proportion of college-owned housing units wired for high-speed internet access: 100%. **Campus safety:** Security services offered: 24-hour foot-and-vehicle patrols, late-night transport/escort service, 24-hour emergency telephones, lighted pathways/sidewalks, student patrols, controlled dormitory access (key, security card, etc).

TRANSFER AND INTERNATIONAL STUDENTS

Transfer students: May apply for admission for the following academic terms: Fall, Spring. Applicants do not need a minimum number of credits to apply. For fall 2009: Transfer applications received: 208. Transfer applicants offered admission: 71. Transfer applicants enrolled: 35. **International students:** Number of foreign undergraduates: 45 (2% of student body). Minimum TOEFL score required: 550 (paper); 79 (computer).

Fisher College

- **Address:** 118 Beacon Street, Boston, MA 02116
- **Website:** http://www.fisher.edu
- **Private**
- **Enrollment:** N/A

KEY STATS

✔ **U.S News College Ranking:** second tier, Regional Colleges (North)
✔ **SAT or ACT Score (25th/75th percentile):** N/A
✔ **Tuition:** 2009-2010: $23,450

Selectivity: Less selective	**Room/board:** $12,600
Acceptance rate: N/A	**Average debt:** N/A
Student/faculty ratio: N/A	**Proportion who borrowed:** N/A

Fitchburg State College

- **Address:** 160 Pearl Street, Fitchburg, MA 01420-2697
- **Website:** http://www.fsc.edu
- **Public**
- **Enrollment:** 3,512 full-time; 711 part-time

KEY STATS

✔ **U.S News College Ranking:** 126, Regional Universities (North)
✔ **SAT Score (25th/75th percentile):** 920-1120
✔ **Tuition:** 2010-2011: $7,800 in state, $13,880 out of state

Selectivity: Selective	**Room/board:** $8,064
Acceptance rate: 64%	**Average debt:** $19,902
Student/faculty ratio: 17/1	**Proportion who borrowed:** 67%

UNDERGRADUATE STUDENT BODY STATS

2009-2010 enrollment: 3,512 full-time; 711 part-time. Men: 47%; women: 53%. **Ethnic makeup:** African American: 4%; Asian American: 2%; Hispanic: 4%; White: 91%.

ADMISSIONS FACTS AND FIGURES

Phone: (978) 665-3144. **Email:** admissions@fsc.edu. **Website:** http://www.fsc.edu. **Application deadlines for fall 2011:** Regular decision: Rolling. Early decision: Not offered. Early action: Not offered. Admission can be deferred. **Application fee:** $25. **To apply online, go to:** http://www.fsc.edu/admissions/. **Admissions requirements/recommendations:** High school units required (recommended): English: 4; Mathematics: 3; Science: 3; Foreign language: 2; Social studies: 1; History: 1; Academic electives: 2; Total units: 16. Tests: The college uses SAT or ACT scores in admissions decisions. Either SAT or ACT required. For admission to the fall 2011 entering class, the school will accept: ACT with writing recommended. Campus visit: Recommended. Admissions interview: Neither required nor recommended. Off-campus interview: Not available. **Factors that count in admissions decisions:** *Academic:* Secondary school record: Very Important. Class rank: Not Considered. Letters of recommendation: Considered. Standardized test scores: Important. Essay: Important. *Nonacademic:* Interview: Not Considered. Extracurricular activities: Considered. Talent/ability: Considered. Character/personal qualities: Considered. Alumni/ae relationship: Considered. Geographical residence: Not Considered. State residency: Not Considered. Religious affiliation/commitment: Not Considered. Minority status: Not Considered. Volunteer work: Considered. Work experience: Considered. **Other schools with the greatest overlap in applicants:** Bridgewater State College; University of Massachusetts–Amherst; University of Massachusetts–Dartmouth; University of Massachusetts–Lowell; Worcester State College. **Admissions statistics for the fall 2009 entering class:** Total applicants: 3,809. Total accepted: 2,456. Freshmen enrolled: 783; 9% were from out of state. Overall acceptance rate: 64%.

Size of waiting list: 19 applicants; enrolled from waiting list: 6. **Average high school grade point average:** 3.0. **First-year students who submitted SAT scores:** 98%. Scores (25/75 percentile): Critical Reading: 460-560, Math: 460-560, Combined: 920-1120. **First-year students submitting ACT scores:** 9%. Scores (25/75 percentile): English: N/A, Math: N/A, Composite: 19-23.

ACADEMICS

Year founded: 1894. **Academic calendar:** Semester. **Degrees offered:** certificate, bachelor's, post-bachelor's certificate, master's, post-master's certificate. **Most popular majors:** 15% business administration, management, and operations, 15% film/video and photographic arts, 11% liberal arts and sciences studies, and humanities, 10% teacher education and professional development, 6% criminal justice and corrections. **Major fields of study:** architecture and related services; biological and biomedical sciences; business, management, marketing, and related support services; communication, journalism, and related programs; computer and information sciences and support services; education; engineering technologies/technicians; English language and literature/letters; health professions and related clinical sciences; history; liberal arts and sciences studies, and humanities; mathematics and statistics; parks, recreation, leisure, and fitness studies; psychology; public administration and social service professions; security and protective services; social sciences; visual and performing arts. **Areas of required coursework:** arts/fine arts, humanities, computer literacy, mathematics, English (including composition), philosophy, sciences (biological or physical), history, social science. **Pre-professional programs:** pre-law, pre-dentistry, pre-medicine, pre-veterinary science. **Special academic programs:** cross-registration, distance learning, double major, dual enrollment, honors program, independent study, internships, liberal arts/career combination, student-designed major, study abroad, teacher certificate program. **Teacher certification offered in:** early childhood, special education, elementary, vo-tech, middle/junior high, secondary. **Reserve Officers Training Corps (ROTC):** Army ROTC: Offered on campus. **Faculty and instruction (2009-2010):** Total instructional faculty: 179 full-time, 86 part-time (51% men; 49% women; 11% minorities). Full-time faculty with Ph.D. or other terminal degree: 91%. Student/faculty ratio: 17/1. Classes of fewer than 20 students: 43%; of 20 to 49 students: 57%. **Advanced Placement and International Baccalaureate credit:** AP tests may be used for: Credit only. Scores accepted: 3, 4, 5. **Freshmen returning for sophomore year:** 75%. **Graduation rates:** Four-year: 24%; five-year: 46%; six-year: 51%. **Graduate study:** 15% of students pursue further study immediately upon graduation; 15% within one year.

COSTS AND FINANCIAL AID

Financial aid office: (978) 665-3156. **Expenses (2010-2011):** Tuition and fees 2010-2011: $7,800 in state, $13,880 out of state; room/board: $8,064. Estimated books and supplies: $800; transportation: $350; personal expenses: $1,530. **Financial aid:** Priority filing date for institution's financial aid form: March 1. In 2009-2010, 90% of undergraduates applied for financial aid. Of those, 56% were determined to have financial need; 90% had their need fully met. Average financial aid package (proportion receiving): $8,645 (54%). Average amount of gift aid, such as scholarships or grants (proportion receiving): $4,336 (40%). Average amount of self-help aid, such as work study or loans (proportion receiving): $3,452 (51%). Average need-based loan (excluding PLUS or other private loans): $3,679. Among students who received need-based aid, the average percentage of need met: 93%. Among students who received aid based on merit, the average award (and the proportion receiving): $1,292 (2%). The average athletic scholarship (and the proportion receiving): $0 (0%). Average amount of debt of borrowers graduating in 2009: $19,902. Proportion who borrowed: 67%.

CAMPUS LIFE AND EXTRACURRICULAR ACTIVITIES

Campus housing available (% using): coed dorms (85%), apartment for single students (15%), special housing for disabled students. Students who live in college-owned, operated, or affiliated housing: 42%. **Clubs and organizations:** Number of student organizations: 55. Activities include: choral groups, concert band, dance, drama/theater, jazz band, radio station, student government, student newspaper, student film society. Number of fraternities: 2; sororities: 3. Proportion of men in fraternities: 2%; of women in sororities: 4%. Average proportion of students who stay on campus on weekends: 35%. **Sports program (2009-2010):** Member of NCAA III. *Men's intercollegiate varsity sports:* baseball, basketball, cross country, football, ice hockey, soccer, track and field (indoor), track and field (outdoor). *Women's intercollegiate varsity sports:* basketball, cross country, field hockey, lacrosse, soccer, softball, track and field (indoor), track and field (outdoor).

SERVICES AND FACILITIES

Basic services: nonremedial tutoring, health service, health insurance. **Remedial assistance:** reading, math, writing, study skills. **Counseling services:** minority student, career, personal, academic, psychological. **For learning-disabled students:** School does not offer a structured program with separate admission and additional fees. Total undergraduates in learning-disabled program or receiving services: 245. Services include: remedial math, remedial English, reading machines, remedial reading, tape recorders, note-taking services, oral tests, extended time for tests, tutors, other testing accommodations. **Library:** Number of titles: 224,858; number of current serial subscriptions: 2,229. **Information technology resources:** Students are required to lease or own a computer. Number of campus computers available to all students: 100. School has a wireless network. Approximate number of users that can be accommodated: 200. Proportion of college-owned housing units wired for high-speed internet access: 100%. **Campus safety:** Security services offered: 24-hour foot-and-vehicle patrols, late-night transport/escort service, 24-hour emergency telephones, lighted pathways/sidewalks, controlled dormitory access (key, security card, etc).

TRANSFER AND INTERNATIONAL STUDENTS

Transfer students: May apply for admission for the following academic terms: Fall, Spring. Applicants do not need a minimum number of credits to apply. For fall 2009: Transfer applications received: 755. Transfer applicants offered admission: 691. Transfer applicants enrolled: 375. **International students:** Number of foreign undergraduates: 11. Number of countries represented: 7. Minimum TOEFL score required: 550 (paper); 213 (computer).

Framingham State College

- **Address:** 100 State Street, PO Box 9101, Framingham, MA 01701-9101
- **Website:** http://www.framingham.edu
- **Public**
- **Enrollment:** 3,121 full-time; 726 part-time

KEY STATS

✔ **U.S News College Ranking:** 126, Regional Universities (North)
✔ **SAT Score (25th/75th percentile):** 940-1120
✔ **Tuition:** 2009-2010: $6,540 in state, $12,620 out of state
Selectivity: Selective   **Room/board:** $8,148
Acceptance rate: 63%   **Average debt:** $19,000
Student/faculty ratio: 16/1   **Proportion who borrowed:** 65%

UNDERGRADUATE STUDENT BODY STATS

2009-2010 enrollment: 3,121 full-time; 726 part-time. Men: 35%; women: 65%. **Ethnic makeup:** African American: 5%; Asian American: 2%; Hispanic: 4%; White: 87%; International: 1%.

ADMISSIONS FACTS AND FIGURES

Phone: (508) 626-4500. **Email:** admissions@framingham.edu. **Website:** http://www.framingham.edu. **Application deadlines for fall 2011:** Regular decision: Rolling. Early decision: Not offered. Early action: Send application by: November 15; Decision sent by: December 15. Admission can be deferred. **Application fee:** $50. **To apply online, go to:** http://www.framingham.edu/admissions/apply/index.html. **Admissions requirements/recommendations:** High school units required (recommended): English: 4 (4); Mathematics: 3 (4); Science: 3 (4); Foreign language: 2 (4); Social studies: 1 (1); History: 1 (2); Academic electives: 2 (2); Total units: 16 (21). Tests: The college uses SAT or ACT scores in admissions decisions. Either SAT or ACT required. For admission to the fall 2011 entering class, the school will accept: ACT with writing required. Campus visit: Recommended. Admissions interview: Neither required nor recommended. Off-campus interview: Not available. **Factors that count in admissions decisions:** *Academic:* Secondary school record: Very Important. Class rank: Important. Letters of recommendation: Important. Standardized test scores: Very Important. Essay: Important. *Nonacademic:* Interview: Not Considered. Extracurricular activities: Considered. Talent/ability: Considered. Character/personal qualities: Considered. Alumni/ae relationship: Considered. Geographical residence: Not Considered. State residency: Considered. Religious affiliation/commitment: Not Considered. Minority status: Not Considered. Volunteer work: Considered. Work experience: Considered. **Other schools with the greatest overlap in applicants:** Bridgewater State College; Salem State College; University of Massachusetts–Amherst;

University of Massachusetts–Dartmouth; Westfield State College. **Admissions statistics for the fall 2009 entering class:** Total applicants: 3,384. Total accepted: 2,141. Freshmen enrolled: 724; 5% were from out of state. Accepted through early-decision or early-action plans: 20%. Overall acceptance rate: 63%. Non-early acceptance rate: 62%. **Credentials of fall 2009 freshmen:** 9% ranked in the top 10 percent of their high school class; 32% were in the top 25 percent; 79% were in the top half. (Proportion submitting class standing: 72%.) **Average high school grade point average:** 3.2. **First-year students who submitted SAT scores:** 94%. Scores (25/75 percentile): Critical Reading: 460-560, Math: 480-560, Combined: 940-1120. **First-year students submitting ACT scores:** 4%. Scores (25/75 percentile): English: N/A, Math: N/A, Composite: 20-21.

ACADEMICS

Year founded: 1839. **Academic calendar:** Semester. **Degrees offered:** bachelor's, post-bachelor's certificate, master's. **Most popular majors:** 18% business, management, marketing, and related support services, 12% family and consumer sciences/human sciences, 11% psychology, 11% social sciences, 8% communications technologies/technicians and support services. **Major fields of study:** agriculture, agriculture operations, and related sciences; biological and biomedical sciences; business, management, marketing, and related support services; communications technologies/technicians and support services; computer and information sciences and support services; education; English language and literature/letters; family and consumer sciences/human sciences; foreign languages, literatures, and linguistics; health professions and related clinical sciences; history; liberal arts and sciences studies, and humanities; mathematics and statistics; physical sciences; psychology; social sciences; visual and performing arts. **Areas of required coursework:** arts/fine arts, humanities, mathematics, English (including composition), foreign languages, sciences (biological or physical), history, social science. **Pre-professional programs:** pre-law, pre-medicine, other. **Special academic programs:** cross-registration, distance learning, double major, dual enrollment, honors program, independent study, internships, liberal arts/career combination, study abroad, teacher certificate program. **Teacher certification offered in:** early childhood, elementary, middle/junior high, secondary. **Faculty and instruction (2009-2010):** Total instructional faculty: 164 full-time, 86 part-time (46% men; 54% women; 3% minorities). Full-time faculty with Ph.D. or other terminal degree: 77%. Student/faculty ratio: 16/1. Classes of fewer than 20 students: 36%; of 20 to 49 students: 62%; of 50 or more students: 1%. **Advanced Placement and International Baccalaureate credit:** AP tests may be used for: Credit and/or placement. Scores accepted: 3, 4, 5. International Baccalaureate exams may be used for: Credit and/or placement. **Freshmen returning for sophomore year:** 73%. **Graduation rates:** Four-year: 33%; five-year: 50%; six-year: 49%.

COSTS AND FINANCIAL AID

Financial aid office: (508) 626-4534. **Expenses (2009-2010):** Tuition and fees 2009-2010: $6,540 in state, $12,620 out of state; room/board: $8,148. Estimated books and supplies: $900; transportation: $750; personal expenses: $1,200. **Financial aid:** Priority filing date for institution's financial aid form: March 1. In 2009-2010, 77% of undergraduates applied for financial aid. Of those, 54% were determined to have financial need; 56% had their need fully met. Average financial aid package (proportion receiving): $7,715 (54%). Average amount of gift aid, such as scholarships or grants (proportion receiving): $4,584 (45%). Average amount of self-help aid, such as work study or loans (proportion receiving): $4,417 (53%). Average need-based loan (excluding PLUS or other private loans): $4,196. Among students who received need-based aid, the average percentage of need met: 81%. Among students who received aid based on merit, the average award (and the proportion receiving): $2,290 (2%). The average athletic scholarship (and the proportion receiving): $0 (0%). Average amount of debt of borrowers graduating in 2009: $19,000. Proportion who borrowed: 65%.

CAMPUS LIFE AND EXTRACURRICULAR ACTIVITIES

Campus housing available (% using): coed dorms (75%), women's dorms (20%), other housing options (5%). Students who live in college-owned, operated, or affiliated housing: 50%. **Student employment:** During the 2009-2010 academic year, 12% of undergraduates worked on campus. Average per-year earnings: $1,000. **Clubs and organizations:** Number of student organizations: 57. Activities include: campus ministries, choral groups, dance, drama/theater, international student organization, literary magazine, musical theater, radio station, student government, student newspaper. Number of fraternities: 0; sororities: 0. Average proportion of students who stay on campus on weekends: 45%. **Sports program (2009-2010):** Member of NCAA III. *Men's intercollegiate varsity sports:* baseball, basketball, cross country, football, ice hockey, soccer. *Women's intercollegiate varsity sports:* basketball, cross country, field hockey, lacrosse, soccer, softball, volleyball.

SERVICES AND FACILITIES

Basic services: nonremedial tutoring, placement service, day care, health service, health insurance. **Remedial assistance:** reading, math, writing, study skills. **Counseling services:** minority student, career, military, personal, veteran student, academic, older student, psychological, birth control, religious. **For learning-disabled students:** School does not offer a structured program with separate admission and additional fees. Total undergraduates in learning-disabled program or receiving services: 334. Services include: reading machines, tape recorders, note-taking services, oral tests, learning center, readers, extended time for tests, tutors, priority registration, priority seating, substitution of courses, texts on tape, typist/scribe, exams on tape or computer, other testing accommodations, waiver of foreign language degree requirement, waiver of math degree requirement, other. **Library:** Number of titles: 216,514; number of current serial subscriptions: 423. **Information technology resources:** Students are required to lease or own a computer. Number of campus computers available to all students: 232. School has a wireless network. Approximate number of users that can be accommodated: 5,000. Proportion of college-owned housing units wired for high-speed internet access: 100%. **Campus safety:** Security services offered: 24-hour foot-and-vehicle patrols, late-night transport/escort service, 24-hour emergency telephones, lighted pathways/sidewalks, controlled dormitory access (key, security card, etc).

TRANSFER AND INTERNATIONAL STUDENTS

Transfer students: May apply for admission for the following academic terms: Fall, Spring. Applicants need a minimum number of credits to apply. For fall 2009: Transfer applications received: 581. Transfer applicants offered admission: 376. Transfer applicants enrolled: 310. **International students:** Number of foreign undergraduates: 25 (1% of student body). Number of countries represented: 12. Minimum TOEFL score required: 550 (paper); 213 (computer).

Gordon College

- **Address:** 255 Grapevine Road, Wenham, MA 01984
- **Website:** http://www.gordon.edu
- **Private; Religious affiliation:** nondenominational
- **Enrollment:** 1,554 full-time; 32 part-time

KEY STATS
✔ **U.S News College Ranking:** 131, National Liberal Arts Colleges
✔ **SAT Score (25th/75th percentile):** 1020-1290
✔ **Tuition:** 2010-2011: $29,458

Selectivity: Selective	**Room/board:** $8,100
Acceptance rate: 66%	**Average debt:** $32,405
Student/faculty ratio: 14/1	**Proportion who borrowed:** 81%

UNDERGRADUATE STUDENT BODY STATS

2009-2010 enrollment: 1,554 full-time; 32 part-time. Men: 37%; women: 63%. **Ethnic makeup:** African American: 2%; Asian American: 2%; Hispanic: 3%; White: 88%; International: 4%. **Religious preference:** Roman Catholic: 3%; nondenominational: 97%.

ADMISSIONS FACTS AND FIGURES

Phone: (866) 464-6736. **Email:** admissions@gordon.edu. **Website:** http://www.gordon.edu. **Application deadlines for fall 2011:** Regular decision: Rolling. Early decision: Send application by: November 15; Decision sent by: December 15. Early action: Send application by: December 1; Decision sent by: January 1. Admission can be deferred. **Application fee:** $50. **To apply online, go to:** https://www.gordon.edu/Admissions/Application/NewApplicant.asp. **Admissions requirements/recommendations:** High school units required (recommended): English: 4; Mathematics: 2 (3); Science: 2 (3); Foreign language: 2 (4); Social studies: 2 (3); Academic electives: 5; Total units: 20 (25). Tests: The college uses SAT or ACT scores in admissions decisions. Either SAT or ACT required. For admission to the fall 2011 entering class, the school will accept: ACT with writing required. Campus visit: Recommended. Admissions interview: Required. Off-campus interview: May be arranged. **Factors that count in admissions decisions: Academic:** Secondary school record: Very Important. Class rank: Important. Letters of recommendation: Very Important. Standardized test scores: Very Important. Essay: Very Important. *Nonacademic:* Interview: Very Important. Extracurricular activities: Very Important. Talent/ability: Important. Character/personal qualities: Very Important. Alumni/ae relationship: Considered. Geographical residence: Not Considered. State residency: Not Considered. Religious affiliation/commitment: Very Important. Minority status: Considered. Volunteer work: Considered. Work experience: Considered. **Other schools with the greatest overlap in applicants:** Eastern Nazarene College; Grove City College; Houghton College; Messiah College; Wheaton College. **Admissions statistics for the fall 2009 entering class:** Total applicants: 1,664. Total accepted: 1,106. Freshmen enrolled: 382; 75% were from out of state. Accepted through early-decision or early-action plans: 42%. Overall acceptance rate: 66%. Early-decision acceptance rate: 93%. Non-early acceptance rate: 57%. **Credentials of fall 2009 freshmen:** 32% ranked in the top 10 percent of their high school class; 58% were in the top 25 percent; 86% were in the top half. (Proportion submitting class standing: 51%.) **Average high school grade point average:** 3.5. **First-year students who submitted SAT scores:** 88%. Scores (25/75 percentile): Critical Reading: 520-650, Math: 500-640, Combined: 1020-1290. **First-year students submitting ACT scores:** 17%. Scores (25/75 percentile): English: N/A, Math: N/A, Composite: 24-28.

ACADEMICS
Year founded: 1889. **Academic calendar:** Semester. **Degrees offered:** bachelor's, master's. **Most popular majors:** 13% business administration and management, 9% elementary education and teaching, 8% Christian studies, 8% psychology, 7% communication studies/speech communication and rhetoric. **Major fields of study:** biological and biomedical sciences; business, management, marketing, and related support services; communication, journalism, and related programs; computer and information sciences and support services; education; English language and literature/letters; foreign languages, literatures, and linguistics; history; mathematics and statistics; multi/interdisciplinary studies; parks, recreation, leisure, and fitness studies; philosophy and religious studies; physical sciences; psychology; public administration and social service professions; social sciences; theology and religious vocations; visual and performing arts. **Areas of required coursework:** arts/fine arts, humanities, English (including composition), philosophy, foreign languages, sciences (biological or physical), history, social science, other. **Pre-professional programs:** pre-law, pre-medicine, pre-theology. **Special academic programs:** cooperative (work-study plan) program, cross-registration, double major, exchange student program (domestic), honors program, independent study, internships, liberal arts/career combination, student-designed major, study abroad, teacher certificate program, other. **Teacher certification offered in:** early childhood, special education, elementary, middle/junior high, secondary, bilingual/bicultural. **Cooperative education programs:** art, business, computer science, engineering, health professions, humanities, natural science, social/behavioral science. **Reserve Officers Training Corps (ROTC):** Army ROTC: Offered at cooperating institution (Massachusetts Institute of Technology); Air Force ROTC: Offered at cooperating institution (Massachusetts Institute of Technology). **Faculty and instruction (2009-2010):** Total instructional faculty: 97 full-time, 52 part-time (61% men; 39% women; 7% minorities). Full-time faculty with Ph.D. or other terminal degree: 77%. Student/faculty ratio: 14/1. Classes of fewer than 20 students: 67%; of 20 to 49 students: 30%; of 50 or more students: 3%. **Advanced Placement and International Baccalaureate credit:** AP tests may be used for: Credit only. Scores accepted: 4, 5. International Baccalaureate exams may be used for: Credit only. **Freshmen returning for sophomore year:** 87%. **Graduation rates:** Four-year: 64%; five-year: 70%; six-year: 72%. **Graduate study:** 20% of students pursue further study immediately upon graduation; 25% within one year; 57% within five years. Fields in which graduates pursue further study: Master of Business Administration (MBA), 10%; law, 8%; medicine, 3%; engineering, 3%; theology (or the seminary), 7%; education, 20%; arts and sciences, 10%.

COSTS AND FINANCIAL AID
Financial aid office: (978) 867-4246. **Expenses (2010-2011):** Tuition and fees 2010-2011: $29,458; room/board: $8,100. Estimated books and supplies: $800; transportation: $400; personal expenses: $1,000. **Financial aid:** Priority filing date for institution's financial aid form: March 1. In 2009-2010, 78% of undergraduates applied for financial aid. Of those, 68% were determined to have financial need; 16% had their need fully met. Average financial aid package (proportion receiving): $19,311 (67%). Average amount of gift aid, such as scholarships or grants (proportion receiving): $12,579 (67%). Average amount of self-help aid, such as work study or loans (proportion receiving): $7,851 (59%). Average need-based loan (excluding PLUS or other private loans): $7,043. Among students who received need-based aid, the average percentage of need met: 75%. Among students who received aid based on merit, the average award (and the proportion receiving): $9,343 (24%). Average amount of debt of borrowers graduating in 2009: $32,405. Proportion who borrowed: 81%.

CAMPUS LIFE AND EXTRACURRICULAR ACTIVITIES
Campus housing available (% using): coed dorms (69%), men's dorms (10%), apartments for married students (1%), apartment for single students (20%). Students who live in college-owned, operated, or affiliated housing: 88%. **Student employment:** During the 2009-2010 academic year, 37% of undergraduates worked on campus. Average per-year earnings: $985. **Clubs and organizations:** Number of student organizations: 35. Activities include: campus ministries, choral groups, concert band, dance, drama/theater, international student organization, jazz band, literary magazine, music ensembles, musical theater, student government, student newspaper, symphony orchestra, yearbook. Number of fraternities: 0; sororities: 0. Average proportion of students who stay on campus on weekends: 70%. **Sports program (2009-2010):** Member of NCAA III. *Men's intercollegiate varsity sports:* baseball, basketball, cross country, lacrosse, soccer, swimming, tennis, track and field (indoor), track and field (outdoor). *Women's intercollegiate varsity sports:* basketball, cross country, field hockey, lacrosse, soccer, softball, swimming, tennis, track and field (indoor), track and field (outdoor), volleyball.

SERVICES AND FACILITIES
Basic services: placement service, health service, health insurance. **Remedial assistance:** study skills. **Counseling services:** minority student, career, personal, academic, psychological, religious. **For learning-disabled students:** School does not offer a structured program with separate admission and additional fees. Services include: learning center, tutors, other. **Library:** Number of titles: 148,710; number of current serial subscriptions: 510. **Information technology resources:** Students are not required to lease or own a computer. Number of campus computers available to all students: 180. School has a wireless network. Approximate number of users that can be accommodated: 360. Proportion of college-owned housing units wired for high-speed internet access: 100%. **Campus safety:** Security services offered: 24-hour foot-and-vehicle patrols, late-night transport/escort service, 24-hour emergency telephones, lighted pathways/sidewalks, controlled dormitory access (key, security card, etc).

TRANSFER AND INTERNATIONAL STUDENTS
Transfer students: May apply for admission for the following academic terms: Fall, Spring. Applicants need a minimum number of credits to apply. For fall 2009: Transfer applications received: 114. Transfer applicants offered admission: 90. Transfer applicants enrolled: 45. **International students:** Number of foreign undergraduates: 67 (4% of study body). Number of countries represented: 23. Minimum TOEFL score required: 550 (paper); 213 (computer). Average TOEFL score: 583 (paper).

Hampshire College

■ **Address:** 893 West Street, Amherst, MA 01002
■ **Website:** http://www.hampshire.edu
■ **Private**
■ **Enrollment:** 1,463 full-time

KEY STATS
✔ **U.S News College Ranking:** 119, National Liberal Arts Colleges
✔ **SAT Score (25th/75th percentile):** 1130-1370
✔ **Tuition:** 2010-2011: $41,604

Selectivity: More selective	**Room/board:** $10,798
Acceptance rate: 63%	**Average debt:** $20,669
Student/faculty ratio: 12/1	**Proportion who borrowed:** 51%

UNDERGRADUATE STUDENT BODY STATS
2009-2010 enrollment: 1,463 full-time. Men: 40%; women: 60%. **Ethnic makeup:** African American: 4%; American-Indian: 1%; Asian American: 4%; Hispanic: 8%; White: 78%; International: 4%.

ADMISSIONS FACTS AND FIGURES
Phone: (413) 559-5471. **Email:** admissions@hampshire.edu. **Website:** http://www.hampshire.edu. **Application deadlines for fall 2011:** Regular decision: January 1; decision sent by April 1. Early decision: Send application by: November 15; Decision sent by: December 15. Early action: Send application

by: December 1; Decision sent by: February 15. Admission can be deferred. **Application fee:** $60. **To apply online, go to:** http://www.hampshire.edu/admissions/11845.htm. **Admissions requirements/recommendations:** High school units required (recommended): English: 4 (4); Mathematics: 3 (4); Science: 3 (4); Foreign language: 3 (4); History: 3 (4); Total units: 16 (20). Tests: The college uses SAT or ACT scores in admissions decisions. Neither SAT nor ACT required. For admission to the fall 2011 entering class, the school will accept: ACT with or without writing accepted. Campus visit: Recommended. Admissions interview: Recommended. Off-campus interview: May be arranged. **Factors that count in admissions decisions:** *Academic:* Secondary school record: Important. Class rank: Considered. Letters of recommendation: Important. Standardized test scores: Considered. Essay: Very Important. *Nonacademic:* Interview: Considered. Extracurricular activities: Important. Talent/ability: Important. Character/personal qualities: Very Important. Alumni/ae relationship: Considered. Geographical residence: Not Considered. State residency: Not Considered. Religious affiliation/commitment: Not Considered. Minority status: Considered. Volunteer work: Considered. Work experience: Considered. **Other schools with the greatest overlap in applicants:** Bard College; Bennington College; New York University; Sarah Lawrence College; Smith College. **Admissions statistics for the fall 2009 entering class:** Total applicants: 2,515. Total accepted: 1,578. Freshmen enrolled: 373; 87% were from out of state. Accepted through early-decision or early-action plans: 36%. Overall acceptance rate: 63%. Early-decision acceptance rate: 88%. Non-early acceptance rate: 58%. **Size of waiting list:** 354 applicants; enrolled from waiting list: 3. **Credentials of fall 2009 freshmen:** 27% ranked in the top 10 percent of their high school class; 69% were in the top 25 percent; 89% were in the top half. (Proportion submitting class standing: 43%.) **Average high school grade point average:** 3.5. **First-year students who submitted SAT scores:** 79%. Scores (25/75 percentile): Critical Reading: 600-710, Math: 530-660, Combined: 1130-1370. **First-year students submitting ACT scores:** 28%. Scores (25/75 percentile): English: N/A, Math: N/A, Composite: 25-29.

ACADEMICS

Year founded: 1965. **Academic calendar:** 4-1-4. **Degrees offered:** bachelor's. **Most popular majors:** 12% film/video and photographic arts, 7% drama and dramatics/theater arts, 6% creative writing, 6% fine arts and art studies, 5% area, ethnic, cultural, and gender studies. **Major fields of study:** agriculture, agriculture operations, and related sciences; architecture and related services; area, ethnic, cultural, and gender studies; biological and biomedical sciences; communication, journalism, and related programs; communications technologies/technicians and support services; computer and information sciences and support services; education; engineering technologies/technicians; English language and literature/letters; foreign languages, literatures, and linguistics; history; legal professions and studies; liberal arts and sciences studies, and humanities; mathematics and statistics; multi/interdisciplinary studies; natural resources and conservation; philosophy and religious studies; physical sciences; psychology; social sciences; visual and performing arts. **Areas of required coursework:** arts/fine arts, humanities, sciences (biological or physical), social science, other. **Special academic programs:** exchange student program (domestic), independent study, internships, student-designed major, study abroad, teacher certificate program. **Teacher certification offered in:** early childhood, elementary, middle/junior high, secondary. **Reserve Officers Training Corps (ROTC):** Army ROTC: Offered at cooperating institution (University of Massachusetts–Amherst). **Faculty and instruction (2009-2010):** Total instructional faculty: 99 full-time, 60 part-time (51% men; 49% women; 18% minorities). Full-time faculty with Ph.D. or other terminal degree: 83%. Student/faculty ratio: 12/1. Classes of fewer than 20 students: 68%; of 20 to 49 students: 32%; of 50 or more students: 0%. **Advanced Placement and International Baccalaureate credit:** AP tests may be used for: Credit and/or placement. International Baccalaureate exams may be used for: Credit and/or placement. **Freshmen returning for sophomore year:** 81%. **Graduation rates:** Four-year: 53%; five-year: 61%; six-year: 62%. **Graduate study:** 10% of students pursue further study immediately upon graduation; 40% within five years.

COSTS AND FINANCIAL AID

Financial aid office: (413) 559-5484. **Expenses (2010-2011):** Tuition and fees 2010-2011: $41,604; room/board: $10,798. Estimated books and supplies: $700; personal expenses: $700. **Financial aid:** In 2009-2010, 65% of undergraduates applied for financial aid. Of those, 59% were determined to have financial need; 81% had their need fully met. Average financial aid package (proportion receiving): $35,310 (59%). Average amount of gift aid, such as scholarships or grants (proportion receiving): $28,085 (59%). Average amount of self-help aid, such as work study or loans (proportion receiving): $7,225 (59%). Average need-based loan (excluding PLUS or other

private loans): $4,750. Among students who received need-based aid, the average percentage of need met: 98%. Among students who received aid based on merit, the average award (and the proportion receiving): $6,220 (16%). The average athletic scholarship (and the proportion receiving): $0 (0%). Average amount of debt of borrowers graduating in 2009: $20,669. Proportion who borrowed: 51%.

CAMPUS LIFE AND EXTRACURRICULAR ACTIVITIES

Campus housing available (% using): coed dorms (43%), women's dorms (2%), apartment for single students (55%), special housing for disabled students, special housing for international students. Students who live in college-owned, operated, or affiliated housing: 89%. **Student employment:** During the 2009-2010 academic year, 58% of undergraduates worked on campus. Average per-year earnings: $2,000. **Clubs and organizations:** Number of student organizations: 94. Activities include: choral groups, dance, drama/theater, international student organization, jazz band, student newspaper, student film society. Number of fraternities: 0; sororities: 0. Average proportion of students who stay on campus on weekends: 90%.

SERVICES AND FACILITIES

Basic services: women's center, day care, health service, health insurance. **Remedial assistance:** writing. **Counseling services:** minority student, career, personal, academic, psychological, birth control, religious. **For learning-disabled students:** School does not offer a structured program with separate admission and additional fees. Total undergraduates in learning-disabled program or receiving services: 29. Services include: reading machines, note-taking services, oral tests, readers, extended time for tests, early syllabus, priority seating, proofreading services, texts on tape, typist/scribe, take home exams. **Library:** Number of titles: 133,981; number of current serial subscriptions: 54,558. **Information technology resources:** Students are not required to lease or own a computer. Number of campus computers available to all students: 250. School has a wireless network. Approximate number of users that can be accommodated: 1,000. Proportion of college-owned housing units wired for high-speed internet access: 100%. **Campus safety:** Security services offered: 24-hour foot-and-vehicle patrols, late-night transport/escort service, 24-hour emergency telephones, lighted pathways/sidewalks, student patrols, controlled dormitory access (key, security card, etc).

TRANSFER AND INTERNATIONAL STUDENTS

Transfer students: May apply for admission for the following academic terms: Fall, Spring. Applicants need a minimum number of credits to apply. For fall 2009: Transfer applications received: 219. Transfer applicants offered admission: 105. Transfer applicants enrolled: 44. **International students:** Number of foreign undergraduates: 59 (4% of student body). Number of countries represented: 28. Minimum TOEFL score required: 577 (paper); 233 (computer).

Harvard University

■ **Address:** Undergraduate Admissions Office, 86 Brattle Street, Cambridge, MA 02138
■ **Website:** http://www.college.harvard.edu
■ **Private**
■ **Enrollment:** 6,650 full-time; 5 part-time

KEY STATS

✔ **U.S News College Ranking:** 1, National Universities
✔ **SAT Score (25th/75th percentile):** 1380-1570
✔ **Tuition:** 2010-2011: $38,416

Selectivity: Most selective	Room/board: $12,308
Acceptance rate: 7%	Average debt: $10,871
Student/faculty ratio: 7/1	Proportion who borrowed: 38%

UNDERGRADUATE STUDENT BODY STATS

2009-2010 enrollment: 6,650 full-time; 5 part-time. Men: 49%; women: 51%. **Ethnic makeup:** African American: 8%; American-Indian: 1%; Asian American: 17%; Hispanic: 7%; White: 56%; International: 11%.

ADMISSIONS FACTS AND FIGURES

Phone: (617) 495-1551. **Email:** college@fas.harvard.edu. **Website:** http://www.college.harvard.edu. **Application deadlines for fall 2011:** Regular decision: January 1; decision sent by April 1. Early decision: Not offered. Early action: Not offered. Admission can be deferred. **Application fee:**

$75. **To apply online, go to:** http://www.admissions.college.harvard.edu/. **Admissions requirements/recommendations:** High school units required (recommended): English: (4); Mathematics: (4); Science: (4); Foreign language: (4); Social studies: (3); History: (2). Tests: The college uses SAT or ACT scores in admissions decisions. Either SAT or ACT required. For admission to the fall 2011 entering class, the school will accept: ACT with writing required. Campus visit: Recommended. Admissions interview: Recommended. **Factors that count in admissions decisions:** *Academic:* Secondary school record: Considered. Class rank: Not Considered. Letters of recommendation: Considered. Standardized test scores: Considered. Essay: Considered. *Nonacademic:* Interview: Considered. Extracurricular activities: Considered. Talent/ability: Considered. Character/personal qualities: Considered. Alumni/ae relationship: Considered. Geographical residence: Considered. State residency: Not Considered. Religious affiliation/commitment: Not Considered. Minority status: Considered. Volunteer work: Considered. Work experience: Considered. **Admissions statistics for the fall 2009 entering class:** Total applicants: 29,114. Total accepted: 2,175. Freshmen enrolled: 1,663; 85% were from out of state. Overall acceptance rate: 7%. **Credentials of fall 2009 freshmen:** 95% ranked in the top 10 percent of their high school class; 100% were in the top 25 percent; 100% were in the top half. (Proportion submitting class standing: 75%.) **First-year students who submitted SAT scores:** 96%. Scores (25/75 percentile): Critical Reading: 690-780, Math: 690-790, Combined: 1380-1570. **First-year students submitting ACT scores:** 29%. Scores (25/75 percentile): English: N/A, Math: N/A, Composite: 31-34.

ACADEMICS

Year founded: 1636. **Academic calendar:** Semester. **Degrees offered:** bachelor's, master's, post-master's certificate, doctorate. **Most popular majors:** 14% economics, 10% political science and government, 6% political science and government, 6% sociology, 5% English language and literature. **Major fields of study:** area, ethnic, cultural, and gender studies; biological and biomedical sciences; computer and information sciences and support services; engineering; English language and literature/letters; foreign languages, literatures, and linguistics; history; liberal arts and sciences studies, and humanities; mathematics and statistics; natural resources and conservation; philosophy and religious studies; physical sciences; psychology; social sciences; visual and performing arts. **Areas of required coursework:** humanities, mathematics, English (including composition), foreign languages, sciences (biological or physical), history, social science. **Special academic programs (% participation):** accelerated program (2.4%), cross-registration (18.6%), double major (3.7%), honors program (51.5%), independent study (1.3%), student-designed major (.3%), study abroad (18.1%), teacher certificate program (.1%). **Teacher certification offered in:** middle/junior high, secondary. **Reserve Officers Training Corps (ROTC):** Army ROTC: Offered at cooperating institution (Massachusetts Institute of Technology); Navy ROTC: Offered at cooperating institution (Massachusetts Institute of Technology); Air Force ROTC: Offered at cooperating institution (Massachusetts Institute of Technology). **Faculty and instruction (2009-2010):** Total instructional faculty: 1,863 full-time, 305 part-time (69% men; 31% women; 15% minorities). Full-time faculty with Ph.D. or other terminal degree: 99%. Student/faculty ratio: 7/1. Classes of fewer than 20 students: 80%; of 20 to 49 students: 12%; of 50 or more students: 8%. **Advanced Placement and International Baccalaureate credit:** AP tests may be used for: Placement only. Scores accepted: 5. International Baccalaureate exams may be used for: Placement only. **Freshmen returning for sophomore year:** 97%. **Graduation rates:** Four-year: 88%; five-year: 96%; six-year: 98%.

COSTS AND FINANCIAL AID

Financial aid office: (617) 495-1581. **Expenses (2010-2011):** Tuition and fees 2010-2011: $38,416; room/board: $12,308. Estimated books and supplies: $1,000 personal expenses: $2,226. **Financial aid:** In 2009-2010, 65% of undergraduates applied for financial aid. Of those, 60% were determined to have financial need; 100% had their need fully met. Average financial aid package (proportion receiving): $40,234 (60%). Average amount of gift aid, such as scholarships or grants (proportion receiving): $37,620 (60%). Average amount of self-help aid, such as work study or loans (proportion receiving): $3,328 (49%). Average need-based loan (excluding PLUS or other private loans): $4,461. Among students who received need-based aid, the average percentage of need met: 100%. Among students who received aid based on merit, the average award (and the proportion receiving): $0 (0%). The average athletic scholarship (and the proportion receiving): $0 (0%). Average amount of debt of borrowers graduating in 2009: $10,871. Proportion who borrowed: 38%.

CAMPUS LIFE AND EXTRACURRICULAR ACTIVITIES

Campus housing available: coed dorms, apartments for married students, special housing for disabled students, cooperative housing. Students who live in college-owned, operated, or affiliated housing: 96%. **Clubs and organizations:** Number of student organizations: 393. Activities include: campus ministries, choral groups, concert band, dance, drama/theater, international student organization, jazz band, literary magazine, marching band, model UN, music ensembles, musical theater, opera, pep band, radio station, student government, student newspaper, student film society, symphony orchestra, television station, yearbook. Average proportion of students who stay on campus on weekends: 90%. **Sports program (2009-2010):** Member of NCAA I. *Men's intercollegiate varsity sports:* baseball, basketball, cross country, fencing, football, golf, ice hockey, lacrosse, skiing (nordic), skiing (alpine), soccer, swimming, tennis, track and field (indoor), track and field (outdoor), volleyball, water polo, wrestling. *Women's intercollegiate varsity sports:* basketball, crew (heavyweight), cross country, fencing, field hockey, golf, ice hockey, lacrosse, crew (lightweight), skiing (nordic), skiing (alpine), soccer, softball, squash, swimming, tennis, track and field (indoor), track and field (outdoor), volleyball, water polo.

SERVICES AND FACILITIES

Basic services: nonremedial tutoring, women's center, placement service, health service, health insurance. **Remedial assistance:** writing, study skills. **Counseling services:** minority student, career, military, personal, veteran student, academic, older student, psychological, birth control, religious. **For learning-disabled students:** School does not offer a structured program with separate admission and additional fees. **Library:** Number of titles: 16,254,755; number of current serial subscriptions: 121,791. **Information technology resources:** Students are not required to lease or own a computer. Number of campus computers available to all students: 322. School has a wireless network. **Campus safety:** Security services offered: 24-hour foot-and-vehicle patrols, late-night transport/escort service, 24-hour emergency telephones, lighted pathways/sidewalks, student patrols, controlled dormitory access (key, security card, etc).

TRANSFER AND INTERNATIONAL STUDENTS

International students: Number of foreign undergraduates: 705 (11% of student body). Number of countries represented: 90.

Lasell College

- **Address:** 1844 Commonwealth Avenue, Newton, MA 02466
- **Website:** http://www.lasell.edu
- **Private**
- **Enrollment:** 1,504 full-time; 27 part-time

KEY STATS

✔ **U.S News College Ranking:** 25, Regional Colleges (North)
✔ **SAT Score (25th/75th percentile):** 910-1070
✔ **Tuition:** 2010-2011: $26,000

Selectivity: Less selective   **Room/board:** $11,800
Acceptance rate: 64%   **Average debt:** $38,419
Student/faculty ratio: 14/1   **Proportion who borrowed:** 64%

UNDERGRADUATE STUDENT BODY STATS

2009-2010 enrollment: 1,504 full-time; 27 part-time. Men: 33%; women: 67%. **Ethnic makeup:** African American: 6%; Asian American: 3%; Hispanic: 4%; White: 84%; International: 2%. **Religious preference:** Roman Catholic: 44%; Protestant: 25%; Jewish: 1%; Muslim: 1%; Buddhist: 5%; No preference: 14%; Other: 4%.

ADMISSIONS FACTS AND FIGURES

Phone: (617) 243-2225. **Email:** info@lasell.edu. **Website:** http://www.lasell.edu. **Application deadlines for fall 2011:** Regular decision: Rolling. Early decision: Not offered. Early action: Not offered. Admission can be deferred. **Application fee:** $40. **To apply online, go to:** http://www.lasell.edu/apply. **Admissions requirements/recommendations:** High school units required (recommended): English: 4 (4); Mathematics: 3 (4); Science: 2 (3); Foreign language: 0 (2); Social studies: 2 (3); History: 2 (3); Total units: 15 (21). Tests: The college uses SAT or ACT scores in admissions decisions. Either SAT or ACT required. For admission to the fall 2011 entering class, the school will accept: ACT with or without writing accepted. Campus visit: Recommended. Admissions interview: Recommended. Off-campus interview: May be arranged. **Factors that count in admissions decisions:** *Academic:* Secondary school record: Very Important. Class rank: Considered. Letters of recommendation: Important. Standardized test scores: Very Important. Essay: Important. *Nonacademic:* Interview: Important. Extracurricular activities: Important. Talent/ability: Considered. Character/personal qualities: Important. Alumni/ae relationship: Considered. Geographical residence: Not Considered. State residency: Not Considered. Religious affiliation/commitment: Not Considered. Minority status: Not Considered. Volunteer work: Considered. Work experience: Considered. **Other schools with the greatest overlap in applicants:** Curry College; Endicott College; Fashion Institute of Technology; Northeastern University; Suffolk University. **Admissions statistics for the fall 2009 entering class:** Total applicants: 3,378. Total accepted: 2,156. Freshmen enrolled: 522; 46% were from out of state. Overall acceptance rate: 64%. Size of waiting list: 0 applicants; enrolled from waiting list: 0. **Average high school grade point average:** 2.8. **First-year students who submitted SAT scores:** 88%. Scores (25/75 percentile): Critical Reading: 450-530, Math: 460-540, Combined: 910-1070. **First-year students submitting ACT scores:** 9%. Scores (25/75 percentile): English: N/A, Math: N/A, Composite: 19-23.

ACADEMICS

Year founded: 1851. **Academic calendar:** Semester. **Degrees offered:** bachelor's, post-bachelor's certificate, master's. **Most popular majors:** 35% business administration and management, 20% fashion merchandising, 11% fashion/apparel design, 5% communication and media studies, 5% kinesiology and exercise science. **Major fields of study:** biological and biomedical sciences; business, management, marketing, and related support services; communication, journalism, and related programs; computer and information sciences and support services; education; English language and literature/letters; family and consumer sciences/human sciences; health professions and related clinical sciences; history; legal professions and studies; liberal arts and sciences studies, and humanities; multi/interdisciplinary studies; parks, recreation, leisure, and fitness studies; psychology; public administration and social service professions; security and protective services; social sciences. **Areas of required coursework:** arts/fine arts, mathematics, English (including composition), sciences (biological or physical), history, social science, other. **Pre-professional programs:** pre-law, other. **Special academic programs (% participation):** double major (11%), honors program (21%), independent study (3%), internships (100%), liberal arts/career combination (100%), student-designed major (1%), study abroad (11%), teacher certificate program (3%). **Teacher certification offered in:** early childhood, elementary, secondary. **Faculty and instruction (2009-2010):** Total instructional faculty: 53 full-time, 117 part-time (41% men; 6% minorities). Full-time faculty with Ph.D. or other terminal degree: 83%. Student/faculty ratio: 14/1. Classes of fewer than 20 students: 65%; of 20 to 49 students: 35%; of 50 or more students: 0%. **Advanced Placement and International Baccalaureate credit:** AP tests may be used for: Credit and/or placement. Scores accepted: 3, 4, 5. International Baccalaureate exams may be used for: Credit and/or placement. **Freshmen returning for sophomore year:** 67%. **Graduation rates:** Four-year: 37%; five-year: 44%; six-year: 47%. **Graduate study:** 24% of students pursue further study immediately upon graduation. Fields in which graduates pursue further study: Master of Business Administration (MBA), 33%; law, 4%; education, 7%; arts and sciences, 52%.

COSTS AND FINANCIAL AID

Financial aid office: (617) 243-2227. **Expenses (2010-2011):** Tuition and fees 2010-2011: $26,000; room/board: $11,800. **Financial aid:** Priority filing date for institution's financial aid form: March 1. In 2009-2010, 87% of undergraduates applied for financial aid. Of those, 78% were determined to have financial need; 16% had their need fully met. Average financial aid package (proportion receiving): $20,097 (78%). Average amount of gift aid, such as scholarships or grants (proportion receiving): $14,766 (78%). Average amount of self-help aid, such as work study or loans (proportion receiving): $3,563 (70%). Average need-based loan (excluding PLUS or other private loans): $7,221. Among students who received need-based aid, the average percentage of need met: 89%. Among students who received aid based on merit, the average award (and the proportion receiving): $7,742 (9%). The average athletic scholarship (and the proportion receiving): $0 (0%). Average amount of debt of borrowers graduating in 2009: $38,419. Proportion who borrowed: 64%.

CAMPUS LIFE AND EXTRACURRICULAR ACTIVITIES

Campus housing available (% using): coed dorms (80%), women's dorms (17%), other housing options (2%). Students who live in college-owned, operated, or affiliated housing: 80%. **Student employment:** During the

2009-2010 academic year, 20% of undergraduates worked on campus. Average per-year earnings: $1,500. **Clubs and organizations:** Number of student organizations: 43. Activities include: choral groups, dance, drama/theater, international student organization, jazz band, literary magazine, music ensembles, radio station, student government, student newspaper, yearbook. Number of fraternities: 0; sororities: 0. Average proportion of students who stay on campus on weekends: 45%. **Sports program (2009-2010):** Member of NCAA III. *Men's intercollegiate varsity sports:* baseball, basketball, cross country, lacrosse, soccer, track and field (indoor), volleyball. *Women's intercollegiate varsity sports:* basketball, cross country, field hockey, lacrosse, soccer, softball, track and field (indoor), volleyball.

SERVICES AND FACILITIES

Basic services: nonremedial tutoring, placement service, health service, health insurance. **Counseling services:** career, personal, academic, psychological, birth control, religious. **For learning-disabled students:** School does not offer a structured program with separate admission and additional fees. Services include: remedial math, reading machines, remedial reading, tape recorders, untimed tests, note-taking services, oral tests, learning center, readers, extended time for tests, tutors, texts on tape, other testing accommodations. **Library:** Number of titles: 52,466; number of current serial subscriptions: 221. **Information technology resources:** Students are not required to lease or own a computer. Number of campus computers available to all students: 150. School has a wireless network. Approximate number of users that can be accommodated: 2,000. Proportion of college-owned housing units wired for high-speed internet access: 100%. **Campus safety:** Security services offered: 24-hour foot-and-vehicle patrols, late-night transport/escort service, 24-hour emergency telephones, lighted pathways/sidewalks, controlled dormitory access (key, security card, etc).

TRANSFER AND INTERNATIONAL STUDENTS

Transfer students: May apply for admission for the following academic terms: Fall, Spring. Applicants do not need a minimum number of credits to apply. For fall 2009: Transfer applications received: 382. Transfer applicants offered admission: 155. Transfer applicants enrolled: 60. **International students:** Number of foreign undergraduates: 25 (2% of student body). Number of countries represented: 18. Minimum TOEFL score required: 525 (paper); 73 (computer). Average TOEFL score: 530 (paper).

Lesley University

- **Address:** 29 Everett Street, Cambridge, MA 02138
- **Website:** http://www.lesley.edu
- **Private**
- **Enrollment:** 1,327 full-time; 50 part-time

KEY STATS

✔ **U.S News College Ranking:** 77, Regional Universities (North)
✔ **SAT Score (25th/75th percentile):** 920-1180
✔ **Tuition:** 2010-2011: $29,873

Selectivity: Selective	**Room/board:** $12,800
Acceptance rate: 67%	**Average debt:** $17,000
Student/faculty ratio: 10/1	**Proportion who borrowed:** 90%

UNDERGRADUATE STUDENT BODY STATS

2009-2010 enrollment: 1,327 full-time; 50 part-time. Men: 24%; women: 76%. **Ethnic makeup:** African American: 4%; American-Indian: 1%; Asian American: 3%; Hispanic: 5%; White: 86%; International: 1%.

ADMISSIONS FACTS AND FIGURES

Phone: (617) 349-8800. **Email:** lcadmissions@lesley.edu. **Website:** http://www.lesley.edu. **Application deadlines for fall 2011:** Regular decision: Rolling. Early decision: Not offered. Early action: Send application by: December 1; Decision sent by: December 31. Admission can be deferred. **Application fee:** $50. **To apply online, go to:** http://www.lesley.edu/lc/applying.html. **Admissions requirements/recommendations:** High school units required (recommended): English: 4 (4); Mathematics: 3 (4); Science: 3 (4); Foreign language: 0 (2); Social studies: 1 (2); History: 1 (2); Academic electives: 4 (0); Total units: 18 (20). Tests: The college uses SAT or ACT scores in admissions decisions. Either SAT or ACT required. For admission to the fall 2011 entering class, the school will accept: ACT with writing required. Campus visit: Recommended. Admissions interview: Recommended. Off-campus interview: Not available. **Factors that count in admissions decisions:**

Academic: Secondary school record: Very Important. Class rank: Important. Letters of recommendation: Important. Standardized test scores: Important. Essay: Important. **Nonacademic:** Interview: Important. Extracurricular activities: Important. Talent/ability: Important. Character/personal qualities: Important. Alumni/ae relationship: Considered. Geographical residence: Considered. State residency: Not Considered. Religious affiliation/commitment: Not Considered. Minority status: Considered. Volunteer work: Important. Work experience: Considered. **Other schools with the greatest overlap in applicants:** Boston College; Emmanuel College; Northeastern University; Simmons College; Suffolk University. **Admissions statistics for the fall 2009 entering class:** Total applicants: 2,611. Total accepted: 1,754. Freshmen enrolled: 385; 48% were from out of state. Overall acceptance rate: 67%. Non-early acceptance rate: 67%. **Size of waiting list:** 23 applicants; enrolled from waiting list: 3. **Credentials of fall 2009 freshmen:** 14% ranked in the top 10 percent of their high school class; 43% were in the top 25 percent; 77% were in the top half. (Proportion submitting class standing: 41%.) **First-year students who submitted SAT scores:** 93%. Scores (25/75 percentile): Critical Reading: 470-600, Math: 450-580, Combined: 920-1180. **First-year students submitting ACT scores:** 14%. Scores (25/75 percentile): English: 19-26, Math: 20-28, Composite: 20-26.

ACADEMICS

Year founded: 1909. **Academic calendar:** Semester. **Degrees offered:** associate, bachelor's, master's, post-master's certificate, doctorate. **Most popular majors:** 37% liberal arts and sciences studies, and humanities, 27% visual and performing arts, 14% psychology, 9% education, 7% business, management, marketing, and related support services. **Major fields of study:** area, ethnic, cultural, and gender studies; biological and biomedical sciences; business, management, marketing, and related support services; communications technologies/technicians and support services; education; English language and literature/letters; family and consumer sciences/human sciences; health professions and related clinical sciences; liberal arts and sciences studies, and humanities; mathematics and statistics; natural resources and conservation; psychology; public administration and social service professions; visual and performing arts. **Areas of required coursework:** arts/fine arts, humanities, computer literacy, mathematics, English (including composition), philosophy, sciences (biological or physical), history, social science, other. **Special academic programs:** accelerated program, cross-registration, distance learning, double major, dual enrollment, exchange student program (domestic), honors program, independent study, internships, liberal arts/career combination, student-designed major, study abroad, teacher certificate program. **Teacher certification offered in:** early childhood, special education, elementary, middle/junior high, secondary. **Faculty and instruction (2009-2010):** Total instructional faculty: N/A. Student/faculty ratio: 10/1. Classes of fewer than 20 students: 77%; of 20 to 49 students: 23%; of 50 or more students: 0%. **Advanced Placement and International Baccalaureate credit:** AP tests may be used for: Placement only. Scores accepted: 3, 4, 5. International Baccalaureate exams may be used for: Placement only. **Freshmen returning for sophomore year:** 72%. **Graduation rates:** Four-year: 38%; five-year: 60%; six-year: 53%. **Graduate study:** 32% of students pursue further study immediately upon graduation. Fields in which graduates pursue further study: law, 5%; education, 55%; arts and sciences, 40%.

COSTS AND FINANCIAL AID

Financial aid office: (617) 349-8581. **Expenses (2010-2011):** Tuition and fees 2010-2011: $29,873; room/board: $12,800. Estimated books and supplies: $1,137; transportation: $900; personal expenses: $900. **Financial aid:** Priority filing date for institution's financial aid form: March 1; deadline: March 1. In 2009-2010, 93% of undergraduates applied for financial aid. Of those, 72% were determined to have financial need; 12% had their need fully met. Average financial aid package (proportion receiving): $15,355 (71%). Average amount of gift aid, such as scholarships or grants (proportion receiving): $14,014 (69%). Average amount of self-help aid, such as work study or loans (proportion receiving): $5,166 (61%). Average need-based loan (excluding PLUS or other private loans): $4,028. Among students who received need-based aid, the average percentage of need met: 70%. Among students who received aid based on merit, the average award (and the proportion receiving): $8,885 (18%). The average athletic scholarship (and the proportion receiving): $0 (0%). Average amount of debt of borrowers graduating in 2009: $17,000. Proportion who borrowed: 90%.

CAMPUS LIFE AND EXTRACURRICULAR ACTIVITIES

Campus housing available: coed dorms, women's dorms, other housing options. Students who live in college-owned, operated, or affiliated housing: 54%. **Student employment:** During the 2009-2010 academic year, 10% of undergraduates worked on campus. Average per-year earnings: $2,000. **Clubs and organizations:** Number of student organizations: 20. Activities include: campus ministries, choral groups, dance, drama/theater, international student organization, literary magazine, musical theater, student government, student newspaper. Number of fraternities: 0; sororities: 0. Average proportion of students who stay on campus on weekends: 80%. **Sports program (2009-2010):** Member of NCAA III.

SERVICES AND FACILITIES

Basic services: nonremedial tutoring, placement service, health service, health insurance. **Remedial assistance:** math, writing, study skills. **Counseling services:** minority student, career, personal, veteran student, academic, older student, birth control, religious, other. **For learning-disabled students:** School does not offer a structured program with separate admission and additional fees. Services include: remedial math, reading machines, tape recorders, other special classes, untimed tests, note-taking services, oral tests, learning center, readers, extended time for tests, tutors, other. **Library:** Number of titles: 124,022; number of current serial subscriptions: 3,935. **Information technology resources:** Students are not required to lease or own a computer. Number of campus computers available to all students: 170. School has a wireless network. Approximate number of users that can be accommodated: 500. Proportion of college-owned housing units wired for high-speed internet access: 100%. **Campus safety:** Security services offered: 24-hour foot-and-vehicle patrols, late-night transport/escort service, 24-hour emergency telephones, lighted pathways/sidewalks, controlled dormitory access (key, security card, etc).

TRANSFER AND INTERNATIONAL STUDENTS

Transfer students: May apply for admission for the following academic terms: Fall, Spring. Applicants do not need a minimum number of credits to apply. For fall 2009: Transfer applications received: 440. Transfer applicants offered admission: 219. Transfer applicants enrolled: 96. **International students:** Number of foreign undergraduates: 19 (1% of student body). Minimum TOEFL score required: 173 (computer).

Longy School of Music

- **Address:** 1 Follen Street, Cambridge, MA 02138
- **Website:** http://www.longy.edu
- **Private**
- **Enrollment:** 36 full-time; 11 part-time

KEY STATS

✔ **U.S News College Ranking:** Unranked Specialty School–Fine Arts
✔ **SAT or ACT Score (25th/75th percentile):** N/A
✔ **Tuition:** 2010-2011: $29,300

Selectivity: N/A	Room/board: N/A
Acceptance rate: 73%	Average debt: $21,891
Student/faculty ratio: 6/1	Proportion who borrowed: 57%

UNDERGRADUATE STUDENT BODY STATS

2009-2010 enrollment: 36 full-time; 11 part-time. Men: 49%; women: 51%. **Ethnic makeup:** African American: 9%; Asian American: 2%; Hispanic: 11%; White: 66%; International: 13%.

ADMISSIONS FACTS AND FIGURES

Phone: (617) 876-0956. **Email:** admissions@longy.edu. **Website:** http://www.longy.edu. **Application deadlines for fall 2011:** Regular decision: July 1. Early decision: Not offered. Early action: Not offered. Admission can be deferred. **Application fee:** $100. **To apply online, go to:** http://www.longy.edu/conservatory_admiss/application.htm. **Admissions requirements/recommendations:** Tests: The college does not use SAT or ACT scores in admissions decisions. Neither SAT nor ACT required. Campus visit: Recommended. Admissions interview: Recommended. Off-campus interview: Not available. **Factors that count in admissions decisions:** **Academic:** Secondary school record: Important. Class rank: Not Considered. Letters of recommendation: Very Important. Standardized test scores: Not Considered. Essay: Very Important. **Nonacademic:** Interview: Very Important. Extracurricular activities: Very Important. Talent/ability: Very Important. Character/personal qualities: Very Important. Alumni/ae relationship: Considered. Geographical residence: Not Considered. State residency: Not Considered. Religious affiliation/commitment: Not Considered. Minority status: Not Considered. Volunteer work: Considered. Work experience: Considered. **Other schools with the greatest overlap in applicants:** Boston Conservatory; Boston University; Johns Hopkins University; New England Conservatory of Music; San Francisco Conservatory of Music. **Admissions statistics for the fall 2009 entering class:** Total applicants: 40. Total accepted: 29. Freshmen enrolled: 8; 100% were from out of state. Overall acceptance rate: 73%. **Size of waiting list:** 0 applicants; enrolled from waiting list: 0.

ACADEMICS

Year founded: 1915. **Academic calendar:** Semester. **Degrees offered:** diploma, bachelor's, post-bachelor's certificate, master's. **Most popular majors:** 17% music performance, 16% violin, viola, guitar, and other stringed instruments, 16% voice and opera, 12% piano and organ, 5% music theory and composition. **Major fields of study:** visual and performing arts. **Areas of required coursework:** arts/fine arts. **Faculty and instruction (2009-2010):** Total instructional faculty: 0 full-time, 100 part-time (46% men; 54% women; 12% minorities). Student/faculty ratio: 6/1. Classes of fewer than 20 students: 90%; of 20 to 49 students: 7%; of 50 or more students: 3%. **Freshmen returning for sophomore year:** 82%. **Graduation rates:** Four-year: 22%; five-year: 22%; six-year: 33%. **Graduate study:** 50% of students pursue further study immediately upon graduation; 10% within one year; 30% within five years. Fields in which graduates pursue further study: education, 10%; arts and sciences, 90%.

COSTS AND FINANCIAL AID

Financial aid office: (617) 876-0956. **Expenses (2010-2011):** Tuition and fees 2010-2011: $29,300. Estimated books and supplies: $500; transportation: $928; personal expenses: $2,500. **Financial aid:** Priority filing date for institution's financial aid form: February 27. In 2009-2010, 75% of undergraduates applied for financial aid. Of those, 69% were determined to have financial need; Average financial aid package (proportion receiving): $16,815 (69%). Average amount of gift aid, such as scholarships or grants (proportion receiving): $13,320 (67%). Average amount of self-help aid, such as work study or loans (proportion receiving): $4,179 (53%). Average need-based loan (excluding PLUS or other private loans): $4,179. Among students who received need-based aid, the average percentage of need met: 49%. Among students who received aid based on merit, the average award (and the proportion receiving): $13,811 (31%). The average athletic scholarship (and the proportion receiving): $0 (0%). Average amount of debt of borrowers graduating in 2009: $21,891. Proportion who borrowed: 57%.

CAMPUS LIFE AND EXTRACURRICULAR ACTIVITIES

Campus housing available (% using): coed dorms (100%). Students who live in college-owned, operated, or affiliated housing: 13%. **Student employment:** During the 2009-2010 academic year, 20% of undergraduates worked on campus. Average per-year earnings: $3,300. Activities include: choral groups, dance, jazz band, music ensembles, opera, student government, symphony orchestra. Number of fraternities: 0; sororities: 0.

SERVICES AND FACILITIES

Basic services: nonremedial tutoring, health insurance. **Counseling services:** career, academic, psychological. **For learning-disabled students:** School does not offer a structured program with separate admission and additional fees. Total undergraduates in learning-disabled program or receiving services: 0. **Library:** Number of titles: 20,080; number of current serial subscriptions: 30. **Information technology resources:** Students are not required to lease or own a computer. Number of campus computers available to all students: 9. School has a wireless network. Proportion of college-owned housing units wired for high-speed internet access: 100%. **Campus safety:** Security services offered: controlled dormitory access (key, security card, etc).

TRANSFER AND INTERNATIONAL STUDENTS

Transfer students: May apply for admission for the following academic terms: Fall, Spring. Applicants do not need a minimum number of credits to apply. For fall 2009: Transfer applications received: 22. Transfer applicants offered admission: 19. Transfer applicants enrolled: 13. **International students:** Number of foreign undergraduates: 6 (13% of student body). Number of countries represented: 6. Minimum TOEFL score required: 520 (paper); 190 (computer). Average TOEFL score: 540 (paper).

Massachusetts College of Art and Design

- **Address:** 621 Huntington Avenue, Boston, MA 02115
- **Website:** http://www.massart.edu
- **Public**
- **Enrollment:** 1,593 full-time; 652 part-time

KEY STATS

✔ **U.S News College Ranking:** Unranked Specialty School–Fine Arts
✔ **SAT Score (25th/75th percentile):** 1000-1200
✔ **Tuition:** 2010-2011: $9,000 in state, $25,400 out of state

Selectivity: N/A	Room/board: $11,750
Acceptance rate: 51%	Average debt: N/A
Student/faculty ratio: 13/1	Proportion who borrowed: N/A

UNDERGRADUATE STUDENT BODY STATS

2009-2010 enrollment: 1,593 full-time; 652 part-time. Men: 33%; women: 67%. **Ethnic makeup:** African American: 3%; American-Indian: 1%; Asian American: 6%; Hispanic: 5%; White: 82%; International: 2%.

ADMISSIONS FACTS AND FIGURES

Phone: (617) 879-7222. **Email:** admissions@massart.edu. **Website:** http://www.massart.edu. **Application deadlines for fall 2011:** Regular decision: Rolling; decision sent by April 15. Early decision: Not offered. Early action: Send application by: December 1; Decision sent by: January 5. Admission can be deferred. **Application fee:** $65. **To apply online, go to:** http://www.massart.edu/cgi-bin/frameset.pl?targetPage=http://www.massart.edu/admissions/app.html. **Admissions requirements/recommendations:** High school units required (recommended): English: 4; Mathematics: 2; Science: 2; Foreign language: 2; Social studies: 2; History: 2; Academic electives: 2; Total units: 17. Tests: The college uses SAT or ACT scores in admissions decisions. Either SAT or ACT required. For admission to the fall 2011 entering class, the school will accept ACT with writing required. Campus visit: Recommended. Admissions interview: Neither required nor recommended. Off-campus interview: Not available. **Factors that count in admissions decisions: *Academic:*** Secondary school record: Very Important. Class rank: Considered. Letters of recommendation: Considered. Standardized test scores: Important. Essay: Very Important. ***Nonacademic:*** Interview: Not Considered. Extracurricular activities: Considered. Talent/ability: Very Important. Character/personal qualities: Considered. Alumni/ae relationship: Not Considered. Geographical residence: Considered. State residency: Important. Religious affiliation/commitment: Not Considered. Minority status: Considered. Volunteer work: Considered. Work experience: Considered. **Other schools with the greatest overlap in applicants:** Art Institute of Boston at Lesley University; Pratt Institute; Rhode Island School of Design; University of Massachusetts–Amherst; University of Massachusetts–Dartmouth. **Admissions statistics for the fall 2009 entering class:** Total applicants: 1,631. Total accepted: 837. Freshmen enrolled: 315; 32% were from out of state. Overall acceptance rate: 51%. Non-early acceptance rate: 51%. **Size of waiting list:** 42 applicants; enrolled from waiting list: 27. **Credentials of fall 2009 freshmen:** 18% ranked in the top 10 percent of their high school class; 51% were in the top 25 percent; 85% were in the top half. (Proportion submitting class standing: 43%.) **Average high school grade point average:** 3.3. **First-year students who submitted SAT scores:** 95%. Scores (25/75 percentile): Critical Reading: 510-610, Math: 490-590, Combined: 1000-1200. **First-year students submitting ACT scores:** 9%. Scores (25/75 percentile): English: N/A, Math: N/A, Composite: N/A.

ACADEMICS

Year founded: 1873. **Academic calendar:** Semester. **Degrees offered:** certificate, bachelor's, post-bachelor's certificate, master's. **Major fields of study:** education; visual and performing arts. **Areas of required coursework:** arts/fine arts, humanities, mathematics, English (including composition), sciences (biological or physical), history, social science. **Special academic programs (% participation):** cross-registration, double major (3%), exchange student program (domestic), independent study, internships, student-designed major, study abroad, teacher certificate program. **Teacher certification offered in:** early childhood, elementary, middle/junior high, secondary. **Faculty and instruction (2009-2010):** Total instructional faculty: 101 full-time, 143 part-time. Student/faculty ratio: 13/1. Classes of fewer than 20 students: 85%; of 20 to 49 students: 15%; of 50 or more students: 0%. **Advanced Placement and International Baccalaureate credit:** AP tests may be used for: Placement only. Scores accepted: 4, 5. **Freshmen returning for sophomore year:** 85%. **Graduation rates:** Four-year: 42%; five-year: 60%;

six-year: 65%. **Graduate study:** 2% of students pursue further study within one year.

COSTS AND FINANCIAL AID

Financial aid office: (617) 879-7850. **Expenses (2010-2011):** Tuition and fees 2010-2011: $9,000 in state, $25,400 out of state; room/board: $11,750. Estimated books and supplies: $2,100 personal expenses: $1,350. **Financial aid:** Priority filing date for institution's financial aid form: March 1. In 2009-2010, 75% of undergraduates applied for financial aid. Of those, 60% were determined to have financial need; Average financial aid package (proportion receiving): $8,490 (60%). Average amount of gift aid, such as scholarships or grants (proportion receiving): $6,770 (40%). Average amount of self-help aid, such as work study or loans (proportion receiving): $4,457 (55%). Average need-based loan (excluding PLUS or other private loans): $4,298. Among students who received aid based on merit, the average award (and the proportion receiving): $2,357 (2%).

CAMPUS LIFE AND EXTRACURRICULAR ACTIVITIES

Campus housing available (% using): coed dorms (32%), apartment for single students (68%). Students who live in college-owned, operated, or affiliated housing: 23%. **Clubs and organizations:** Number of student organizations: 30. Activities include: dance, drama/theater, music ensembles, radio station, student government, student newspaper, student film society, television station, yearbook.

SERVICES AND FACILITIES

Basic services: nonremedial tutoring, health service, health insurance. **Remedial assistance:** writing. **Counseling services:** career, personal, academic, psychological. **For learning-disabled students:** School does not offer a structured program with separate admission and additional fees. **Library:** Number of titles: 231,586; number of current serial subscriptions: 557. **Information technology resources:** Students are not required to lease or own a computer. Number of campus computers available to all students: 350. School has a wireless network. Proportion of college-owned housing units wired for high-speed internet access: 100%. **Campus safety:** Security services offered: 24-hour foot-and-vehicle patrols, late-night transport/escort service, 24-hour emergency telephones, lighted pathways/sidewalks, controlled dormitory access (key, security card, etc).

TRANSFER AND INTERNATIONAL STUDENTS

Transfer students: May apply for admission for the following academic terms: Fall, Spring. Applicants do not need a minimum number of credits to apply. For fall 2009: Transfer applications received: 387. Transfer applicants offered admission: 223. Transfer applicants enrolled: 130. **International students:** Number of foreign undergraduates: 36 (2% of student body). Number of countries represented: 30. Minimum TOEFL score required: 550 (paper); 85 (computer).

Massachusetts College of Liberal Arts

- **Address:** 375 Church Street, North Adams, MA 01247
- **Website:** http://www.mcla.edu
- **Public**
- **Enrollment:** 1,467 full-time; 208 part-time

KEY STATS

✔ **U.S News College Ranking:** second tier, National Liberal Arts Colleges
✔ **SAT Score (25th/75th percentile):** 910-1150
✔ **Tuition:** 2009-2010: $6,875 in state, $15,820 out of state

Selectivity: Selective	**Room/board:** $7,868
Acceptance rate: 70%	**Average debt:** $17,297
Student/faculty ratio: 14/1	**Proportion who borrowed:** 51%

UNDERGRADUATE STUDENT BODY STATS

2009-2010 enrollment: 1,467 full-time; 208 part-time. Men: 40%; women: 60%. **Ethnic makeup:** African American: 6%; Asian American: 1%; Hispanic: 5%; White: 88%.

ADMISSIONS FACTS AND FIGURES

Phone: (413) 662-5410. **Email:** admissions@mcla.edu. **Website:** http://www.mcla.edu. **Application deadlines for fall 2011:** Regular decision: Rolling. Early decision: Not offered. Early action: Send application by: December 1; Decision sent by: December 15. Admission can be deferred. **Application**

fee: $35. **To apply online, go to:** http://www.mcla.edu/Admissions/apply. **Admissions requirements/recommendations:** High school units required (recommended): English: 4; Mathematics: 3; Science: 3; Foreign language: 2; Social studies: 2; History: 0; Academic electives: 2; Total units: 16. Tests: The college uses SAT or ACT scores in admissions decisions. Either SAT or ACT required. For admission to the fall 2011 entering class, the school will accept: ACT with or without writing accepted. Campus visit: Recommended. Admissions interview: Recommended. Off-campus interview: May not be arranged. **Factors that count in admissions decisions:** *Academic:* Secondary school record: Very Important. Class rank: Considered. Letters of recommendation: Considered. Standardized test scores: Important. Essay: Important. *Nonacademic:* Interview: Considered. Extracurricular activities: Considered. Talent/ability: Considered. Character/personal qualities: Considered. Alumni/ae relationship: Considered. Geographical residence: Not Considered. State residency: Not Considered. Religious affiliation/commitment: Not Considered. Minority status: Not Considered. Volunteer work: Considered. Work experience: Considered. **Other schools with the greatest overlap in applicants:** Boston University; Northeastern University; Suffolk University; University of Massachusetts–Amherst; Westfield State College. **Admissions statistics for the fall 2009 entering class:** Total applicants: 1,685. Total accepted: 1,187. Freshmen enrolled: 351; 26% were from out of state. Accepted through early-decision or early-action plans: 22%. Overall acceptance rate: 70%. Non-early acceptance rate: 69%. **Credentials of fall 2009 freshmen:** 16% ranked in the top 10 percent of their high school class; 42% were in the top 25 percent; 67% were in the top half. (Proportion submitting class standing: 27%.) **Average high school grade point average:** 3.1. **First-year students who submitted SAT scores:** 96%. Scores (25/75 percentile): Critical Reading: 470-590, Math: 440-560, Combined: 910-1150. **First-year students submitting ACT scores:** 4%. Scores (25/75 percentile): English: N/A, Math: N/A, Composite: 20-24.

ACADEMICS

Year founded: 1894. **Academic calendar:** Semester. **Degrees offered:** certificate, bachelor's, post-bachelor's certificate, master's, post-master's certificate. **Most popular majors:** 21% English language and literature/letters, 19% business, management, marketing, and related support services, 9% psychology, 8% visual and performing arts, 7% history. **Major fields of study:** biological and biomedical sciences; business, management, marketing, and related support services; computer and information sciences and support services; education; English language and literature/letters; history; mathematics and statistics; multi/interdisciplinary studies; natural resources and conservation; philosophy and religious studies; physical sciences; psychology; social sciences; visual and performing arts. **Areas of required coursework:** arts/fine arts, humanities, computer literacy, mathematics, English (including composition), philosophy, foreign languages, sciences (biological or physical), history, social science. **Pre-professional programs:** pre-law, pre-dentistry, pre-medicine, pre-veterinary science, pre-pharmacy. **Special academic programs (% participation):** cross-registration (1%), distance learning, double major (3%), dual enrollment, exchange student program (domestic), honors program (16%), independent study (20%), internships (38%), liberal arts/career combination (3%), student-designed major (8%), study abroad, teacher certificate program. **Teacher certification offered in:** early childhood, special education, elementary, middle/junior high, secondary. **Faculty and instruction (2009-2010):** Total instructional faculty: 84 full-time, 79 part-time (57% men; 43% women; 4% minorities). Full-time faculty with Ph.D. or other terminal degree: 85%. Student/faculty ratio: 14/1. Classes of fewer than 20 students: 65%; of 20 to 49 students: 35%; of 50 or more students: 0%. **Advanced Placement and International Baccalaureate credit:** AP tests may be used for: Placement only. Scores accepted: 3, 4, 5. International Baccalaureate exams may be used for: Credit only. **Freshmen returning for sophomore year:** 74%. **Graduation rates:** Four-year: 38%; five-year: 46%; six-year: 50%. **Graduate study:** 20% of students pursue further study within one year.

COSTS AND FINANCIAL AID

Financial aid office: (413) 662-5219. **Expenses (2009-2010):** Tuition and fees 2009-2010: $6,875 in state, $15,820 out of state; room/board: $7,868. Estimated books and supplies: $950; transportation: $600; personal expenses: $1,409. **Financial aid:** Priority filing date for institution's financial aid form: March 1. In 2009-2010, 86% of undergraduates applied for financial aid. Of those, 67% were determined to have financial need; Average financial aid package (proportion receiving): $9,979 (67%). Average amount of gift aid, such as scholarships or grants (proportion receiving): $5,367 (54%). Average amount of self-help aid, such as work study or loans (proportion receiving): $4,314 (64%). Average need-based loan (excluding PLUS or other private loans): $3,905. Among students who received need-based aid, the average percentage of need met: 86%. Among students who received aid based on merit, the average award (and the proportion receiving): $2,384 (5%). Average amount of debt of borrowers graduating in 2009: $17,297. Proportion who borrowed: 51%.

CAMPUS LIFE AND EXTRACURRICULAR ACTIVITIES
Campus housing available (% using): coed dorms (100%), special housing for disabled students. Students who live in college-owned, operated, or affiliated housing: 68%. **Clubs and organizations:** Number of student organizations: 40. Activities include: choral groups, concert band, dance, drama/theater, jazz band, literary magazine, music ensembles, musical theater, radio station, student government, student newspaper, television station, yearbook. Number of fraternities: 0; sororities: 0. Average proportion of students who stay on campus on weekends: 75%. **Sports program (2009-2010):** Member of NCAA III. *Men's intercollegiate varsity sports:* baseball, basketball, cross country, golf, soccer. *Women's intercollegiate varsity sports:* basketball, cross country, soccer, softball, tennis, volleyball.

SERVICES AND FACILITIES
Basic services: nonremedial tutoring, women's center, placement service, health service, health insurance. **Remedial assistance:** reading, math, writing, study skills. **Counseling services:** minority student, career, personal, veteran student, academic, older student, psychological, birth control. **For learning-disabled students:** School does not offer a structured program with separate admission and additional fees. Services include: remedial math, remedial English, reading machines, remedial reading, tape recorders, untimed tests, note-taking services, oral tests, learning center, readers, extended time for tests, tutors, priority registration, priority seating, texts on tape, other. **Library:** Number of titles: 168,000; number of current serial subscriptions: 106. **Information technology resources:** Students are required to lease or own a computer. Number of campus computers available to all students: 250. School has a wireless network. Proportion of college-owned housing units wired for high-speed internet access: 100%. **Campus safety:** Security services offered: 24-hour foot-and-vehicle patrols, late-night transport/escort service, 24-hour emergency telephones, lighted pathways/sidewalks, controlled dormitory access (key, security card, etc).

TRANSFER AND INTERNATIONAL STUDENTS
Transfer students: May apply for admission for the following academic terms: Fall, Spring. Applicants need a minimum number of credits to apply. For fall 2009: Transfer applications received: 321. Transfer applicants offered admission: 286. Transfer applicants enrolled: 160. **International students:** Number of foreign undergraduates: 1. Number of countries represented: 0. Minimum TOEFL score required: 550 (paper); 213 (computer).

Massachusetts Institute of Technology

- **Address:** 77 Massachusetts Avenue, Cambridge, MA 02139
- **Website:** http://web.mit.edu/
- **Private**
- **Enrollment:** 4,201 full-time; 31 part-time

KEY STATS
✔ **U.S News College Ranking:** 7, National Universities
✔ **SAT Score (25th/75th percentile):** 1370-1560
✔ **Tuition:** 2010-2011: $39,212

Selectivity: Most selective	**Room/board:** $11,234
Acceptance rate: 11%	**Average debt:** $15,043
Student/faculty ratio: 7/1	**Proportion who borrowed:** 45%

UNDERGRADUATE STUDENT BODY STATS
2009-2010 enrollment: 4,201 full-time; 31 part-time. Men: 55%; women: 45%. **Ethnic makeup:** African American: 8%; American-Indian: 1%; Asian American: 26%; Hispanic: 13%; White: 43%; International: 9%.

ADMISSIONS FACTS AND FIGURES
Phone: (617) 253-3400. **Email:** admissions@mit.edu. **Website:** http://web.mit.edu/. **Application deadlines for fall 2011:** Regular decision: January 1; decision sent by March 20. Early decision: Not offered. Early action: Send application by: November 1; Decision sent by: December 20. Admission can be deferred. **Application fee:** $75. **To apply online, go to:** http://my.mit.edu. **Admissions requirements/recommendations:** High school units required (recommended): English: (4); Mathematics: (4); Science: (4); Foreign lan-

guage: (2); Social studies: (2). Tests: The college uses SAT or ACT scores in admissions decisions. Either SAT or ACT required. For admission to the fall 2011 entering class, the school will accept: ACT with writing required. Campus visit: Neither required nor recommended. Admissions interview: Recommended. Off-campus interview: May be arranged. **Factors that count in admissions decisions:** *Academic:* Secondary school record: Important. Class rank: Important. Letters of recommendation: Important. Standardized test scores: Important. Essay: Considered. *Nonacademic:* Interview: Important. Extracurricular activities: Important. Talent/ability: Important. Character/personal qualities: Very Important. Alumni/ae relationship: Considered. Geographical residence: Considered. State residency: Not Considered. Religious affiliation/commitment: Not Considered. Minority status: Considered. Volunteer work: Considered. Work experience: Considered. **Other schools with the greatest overlap in applicants:** California Institute of Technology; Harvard University; Princeton University; Stanford University; Yale University. **Admissions statistics for the fall 2009 entering class:** Total applicants: 15,663. Total accepted: 1,676. Freshmen enrolled: 1,072; 90% were from out of state. Accepted through early-decision or early-action plans: 35%. Overall acceptance rate: 11%. Non-early acceptance rate: 10%. **Size of waiting list:** 455 applicants; enrolled from waiting list: 78. **Credentials of fall 2009 freshmen:** 95% ranked in the top 10 percent of their high school class; 100% were in the top 25 percent; 100% were in the top half. (Proportion submitting class standing: 52%.) **First-year students who submitted SAT scores:** 93%. Scores (25/75 percentile): Critical Reading: 650-760, Math: 720-800, Combined: 1370-1560. **First-year students submitting ACT scores:** 36%. Scores (25/75 percentile): English: 31-35, Math: 33-35, Composite: 32-35.

ACADEMICS
Year founded: 1861. **Academic calendar:** 4-1-4. **Degrees offered:** bachelor's, master's, doctorate. **Most popular majors:** 40% engineering, 15% computer science, 10% physical sciences, 8% mathematics, 6% biology/biological sciences. **Major fields of study:** architecture and related services; biological and biomedical sciences; business, management, marketing, and related support services; communication, journalism, and related programs; computer and information sciences and support services; engineering; English language and literature/letters; foreign languages, literatures, and linguistics; history; liberal arts and sciences studies, and humanities; mathematics and statistics; multi/interdisciplinary studies; philosophy and religious studies; physical sciences; social sciences; visual and performing arts. **Areas of required coursework:** arts/fine arts, humanities, mathematics, sciences (biological or physical), social science, other. **Pre-professional programs:** pre-law, pre-dentistry, pre-medicine, pre-veterinary science, pre-optometry, pre-pharmacy. **Special academic programs (% participation):** cooperative (work-study plan) program (5%), cross-registration (12%), English as a Second Language (ESL) (7%), internships (22%), study abroad (6%), teacher certificate program (4%). **Teacher certification offered in:** middle/junior high, secondary. **Cooperative education programs:** computer science, engineering. **Reserve Officers Training Corps (ROTC):** Army ROTC: Offered on campus; Navy ROTC: Offered on campus; Air Force ROTC: Offered on campus. **Faculty and instruction (2009-2010):** Total instructional faculty: 1,326 full-time, 452 part-time (78% men; 22% women; 13% minorities). Full-time faculty with Ph.D. or other terminal degree: 90%. Student/faculty ratio: 7/1. Classes of fewer than 20 students: 65%; of 20 to 49 students: 23%; of 50 or more students: 13%. **Advanced Placement and International Baccalaureate credit:** AP tests may be used for: Credit and/or placement. Scores accepted: 4, 5. International Baccalaureate exams may be used for: Credit and/or placement. **Freshmen returning for sophomore year:** 98%. **Graduation rates:** Four-year: 83%; five-year: 90%; six-year: 91%. **Graduate study:** 48% of students pursue further study immediately upon graduation. Fields in which graduates pursue further study: Master of Business Administration (MBA), 1%; law, 1%; medicine, 1%; engineering, 53%; arts and sciences, 24%.

COSTS AND FINANCIAL AID
Financial aid office: (617) 253-4971. **Expenses (2010-2011):** Tuition and fees 2010-2011: $39,212; room/board: $11,234. Estimated books and supplies: $1,050 personal expenses: $1,714. **Financial aid:** Priority filing date for institution's financial aid form: February 15; deadline: February 15. In 2009-2010, 83% of undergraduates applied for financial aid. Of those, 63% were determined to have financial need; 100% had their need fully met. Average financial aid package (proportion receiving): $37,696 (63%). Average amount of gift aid, such as scholarships or grants (proportion receiving): $35,470 (62%). Average amount of self-help aid, such as work study or loans (proportion receiving): $2,645 (43%). Average need-based loan (excluding PLUS or other private loans): $3,217. Among students who received need-based aid, the average percentage of need met: 100%.

Average amount of debt of borrowers graduating in 2009: $15,043. Proportion who borrowed: 45%.

CAMPUS LIFE AND EXTRACURRICULAR ACTIVITIES

Campus housing available (% using): coed dorms (73%), women's dorms (6%), sorority housing (4%), fraternity housing (15%), apartments for married students (0%), apartment for single students (0%), special housing for disabled students, cooperative housing (1%), other housing options (1%). Students who live in college-owned, operated, or affiliated housing: 92%. **Student employment:** During the 2009-2010 academic year, 46% of undergraduates worked on campus. Average per-year earnings: $2,643. **Clubs and organizations:** Number of student organizations: 460. Activities include: campus ministries, choral groups, concert band, dance, drama/theater, international student organization, jazz band, literary magazine, marching band, model UN, music ensembles, musical theater, opera, radio station, student government, student newspaper, student film society, symphony orchestra, television station, yearbook. Number of fraternities: 27; sororities: 6. Proportion of men in fraternities: 50%; of women in sororities: 34%. **Sports program (2009-2010):** Member of NCAA III. *Men's intercollegiate varsity sports:* baseball, basketball, cross country, fencing, football, lacrosse, rifle, soccer, swimming, tennis, track and field (indoor), track and field (outdoor), volleyball, water polo. *Women's intercollegiate varsity sports:* basketball, crew (heavyweight), cross country, fencing, field hockey, lacrosse, crew (lightweight), rifle, soccer, softball, swimming, tennis, track and field (indoor), track and field (outdoor), volleyball.

SERVICES AND FACILITIES

Basic services: nonremedial tutoring, placement service, day care, health service, health insurance. **Counseling services:** minority student, career, personal, academic, psychological, religious, other. **For learning-disabled students:** School does not offer a structured program with separate admission and additional fees. Services include: reading machines, tape recorders, note-taking services, readers, extended time for tests, other. **Library:** Number of titles: 3,057,604; number of current serial subscriptions: 60,105. **Information technology resources:** Students are required to lease or own a computer. Number of campus computers available to all students: 1,100. School has a wireless network. Approximate number of users that can be accommodated: 20,000. Proportion of college-owned housing units wired for high-speed internet access: 100%. **Campus safety:** Security services offered: 24-hour foot-and-vehicle patrols, late-night transport/escort service, 24-hour emergency telephones, lighted pathways/sidewalks, controlled dormitory access (key, security card, etc).

TRANSFER AND INTERNATIONAL STUDENTS

Transfer students: May apply for admission for the following academic terms: Fall, Spring. Applicants do not need a minimum number of credits to apply. For fall 2009: Transfer applications received: 401. Transfer applicants offered admission: 24. Transfer applicants enrolled: 21. **International students:** Number of foreign undergraduates: 385 (9% of student body). Number of countries represented: 92. Minimum TOEFL score required: 577 (paper); 90 (computer). Average TOEFL score: 641 (paper).

Massachusetts Maritime Academy

- **Address:** 101 Academy Drive, Buzzards Bay, MA 02532-1803
- **Website:** http://www.maritime.edu
- **Public**
- **Enrollment:** 1,126 full-time; 59 part-time

KEY STATS

✔ **U.S News College Ranking:** 13, Regional Colleges (North)
✔ **SAT Score (25th/75th percentile):** 870-1130
✔ **Tuition:** 2010-2011: $6,609 in state, $20,259 out of state

Selectivity: Less selective	**Room/board:** $9,202
Acceptance rate: 51%	**Average debt:** $26,037
Student/faculty ratio: 18/1	**Proportion who borrowed:** 77%

UNDERGRADUATE STUDENT BODY STATS

2009-2010 enrollment: 1,126 full-time; 59 part-time. Men: 91%; women: 9%. **Ethnic makeup:** African American: 1%; Asian American: 1%; Hispanic: 2%; White: 95%.

ADMISSIONS FACTS AND FIGURES

Phone: (800) 544-3411. **Email:** admissions@maritime.edu. **Website:** http://www.maritime.edu. **Application deadlines for fall 2011:** Regular decision: Rolling. Early decision: Not offered. Early action: Send application by: November 1; Decision sent by: December 15. Admission can be deferred. **Application fee:** $100. **To apply online, go to:** http://www.maritime.edu/pdf/admapp.pdf. **Admissions requirements/recommendations:** High school units required (recommended): English: 4 (0); Mathematics: 3 (0); Science: 3 (0); Foreign language: 2 (0); Social studies: 1 (0); History: 1 (0); Academic electives: 2 (0); Total units: 16 (0). Tests: The college uses SAT or ACT scores in admissions decisions. Either SAT or ACT required. For admission to the fall 2011 entering class, the school will accept: ACT with or without writing accepted. Campus visit: Recommended. Admissions interview: Recommended. Off-campus interview: May be arranged. **Factors that count in admissions decisions:** *Academic:* Secondary school record: Very Important. Class rank: Considered. Letters of recommendation: Important. Standardized test scores: Very Important. Essay: Important. *Nonacademic:* Interview: Important. Extracurricular activities: Important. Talent/ability: Important. Character/personal qualities: Important. Alumni/ae relationship: Considered. Geographical residence: Not Considered. State residency: Considered. Religious affiliation/commitment: Not Considered. Minority status: Not Considered. Volunteer work: Considered. Work experience: Considered. **Admissions statistics for the fall 2009 entering class:** Total applicants: 1,104. Total accepted: 568. Freshmen enrolled: 332; Overall acceptance rate: 51%. Non-early acceptance rate: 51%. **Size of waiting list:** 50 applicants; enrolled from waiting list: 11. **Average high school grade point average:** 2.7. **First-year students who submitted SAT scores:** 97%. Scores (25/75 percentile): Critical Reading: 400-550, Math: 470-580, Combined: 870-1130. **First-year students submitting ACT scores:** 2%. Scores (25/75 percentile): English: N/A, Math: N/A, Composite: 18-23.

ACADEMICS

Year founded: 1891. **Academic calendar:** 4-1-4. **Degrees offered:** certificate, diploma, bachelor's, master's. **Most popular majors:** 36% naval architecture and marine engineering, 20% marine science/merchant marine officer, 18% security and protective services, 15% engineering, 11% environmental science. **Major fields of study:** business, management, marketing, and related support services; engineering; natural resources and conservation; transportation and materials moving. **Areas of required coursework:** humanities, computer literacy, mathematics, English (including composition), sciences (biological or physical), history, social science, other. **Special academic programs (% participation):** cooperative (work-study plan) program (20%), distance learning (3%), double major (5%), dual enrollment (1%), independent study (15%), internships (35%). **Cooperative education programs:** business, engineering, natural science, technologies, other. **Reserve Officers Training Corps (ROTC):** Army ROTC: Offered on campus; Navy ROTC: Offered on campus. **Faculty and instruction (2009-2010):** Total instructional faculty: 63 (83% men; 17% women; 3% minorities). Full-time faculty with Ph.D. or other terminal degree: 54%. Student/faculty ratio: 18/1. **Advanced Placement and International Baccalaureate credit:** AP tests may be used for: Credit and/or placement. **Freshmen returning for sophomore year:** 82%. **Graduation rates:** Four-year: 51%; five-year: 58%; six-year: 63%. **Graduate study:** 4% of students pursue further study immediately upon graduation.

COSTS AND FINANCIAL AID

Financial aid office: (508) 830-5087. **Expenses (2010-2011):** Tuition and fees 2010-2011: $6,609 in state, $20,259 out of state; room/board: $9,202. Estimated books and supplies: $1,000; transportation: $800; personal expenses: $3,688. **Financial aid:** Priority filing date for institution's financial aid form: May 1. Average amount of debt of borrowers graduating in 2009: $26,037. Proportion who borrowed: 77%.

CAMPUS LIFE AND EXTRACURRICULAR ACTIVITIES

Campus housing available (% using): coed dorms (85%), other housing options (15%). **Student employment:** During the 2009-2010 academic year, 20% of undergraduates worked on campus. **Clubs and organizations:** Number of student organizations: 15. Activities include: dance, drama/theater, jazz band, literary magazine, marching band, music ensembles, musical theater, pep band, student government, student newspaper, yearbook. Number of fraternities: 0; sororities: 0. Average proportion of students who stay on campus on weekends: 50%. **Sports program (2009-2010):** Member of NCAA III. *Men's intercollegiate varsity sports:* baseball, cross country, football, lacrosse, rifle, soccer, track and field (outdoor). *Women's intercollegiate varsity sports:* crew (heavyweight), cross country, crew (lightweight), rifle, soccer, softball, track and field (outdoor), volleyball.

SERVICES AND FACILITIES

Basic services: nonremedial tutoring, placement service, health service, health insurance. **Remedial assistance:** reading, math, writing, study skills. **Counseling services:** career, military, personal, academic, birth control, religious. **For learning-disabled students:** School does not offer a structured program with separate admission and additional fees. Services include: remedial math, remedial English, remedial reading, tape recorders, note-taking services, oral tests, learning center, extended time for tests, tutors, priority registration, priority seating, texts on tape, typist/scribe, exams on tape or computer, other testing accommodations. **Library:** Number of titles: 52,874; number of current serial subscriptions: 97. **Information technology resources:** Students are required to lease or own a computer. Number of campus computers available to all students: 125. School has a wireless network. Approximate number of users that can be accommodated: 500. Proportion of college-owned housing units wired for high-speed internet access: 100%. **Campus safety:** Security services offered: 24-hour foot-and-vehicle patrols, late-night transport/escort service, 24-hour emergency telephones, lighted pathways/sidewalks, controlled dormitory access (key, security card, etc).

TRANSFER AND INTERNATIONAL STUDENTS

Transfer students: May apply for admission for the following academic terms: Fall. Applicants need a minimum number of credits to apply. For fall 2009: Transfer applications received: 26. Transfer applicants offered admission: 12. Transfer applicants enrolled: 11. **International students:** Number of foreign undergraduates: 4. Number of countries represented: 5.

Merrimack College

- **Address:** 315 Turnpike Street, North Andover, MA 01845
- **Website:** http://www.merrimack.edu
- **Private; Religious affiliation:** Roman Catholic
- **Enrollment:** 1,884 full-time; 147 part-time

KEY STATS

✔ **U.S News College Ranking:** 174, National Liberal Arts Colleges
✔ **SAT or ACT Score (25th/75th percentile):** N/A
✔ **Tuition:** 2010-2011: $31,380

Selectivity: Selective	**Room/board:** $10,700
Acceptance rate: 79%	**Average debt:** $24,000
Student/faculty ratio: 13/1	**Proportion who borrowed:** 66%

UNDERGRADUATE STUDENT BODY STATS

2009-2010 enrollment: 1,884 full-time; 147 part-time. Men: 52%; women: 48%. **Ethnic makeup:** African American: 2%; Asian American: 2%; Hispanic: 3%; White: 92%; International: 2%.

ADMISSIONS FACTS AND FIGURES

Phone: (978) 837-5100. **Email:** Admission@Merrimack.edu. **Website:** http://www.merrimack.edu. **Application deadlines for fall 2011:** Regular decision: February 1; decision sent by April 1. Early decision: Not offered. Early action: Send application by: November 15; Decision sent by: December 15. Admission can be deferred. **Application fee:** $60. **To apply online, go to:** http://www.merrimack.edu/admission/Applying/Pages/default.aspx. **Admissions requirements/recommendations:** High school units required (recommended): English: 4 (4); Mathematics: 3 (4); Science: 3 (4); Foreign language: 2 (3); Social studies: 2 (3); History: 2 (3); Academic electives: 3 (3); Total units: 19 (24). Tests: The college uses SAT or ACT scores in admissions decisions. Neither SAT nor ACT required. For admission to the fall 2011 entering class, the school will accept: ACT with writing required. Campus visit: Recommended. Admissions interview: Recommended. Off-campus interview: May be arranged. **Factors that count in admissions decisions:** *Academic:* Secondary school record: Very Important. Class rank: Important. Letters of recommendation: Important. Standardized test scores: Not Considered. Essay: Very Important. *Nonacademic:* Interview: Considered. Extracurricular activities: Considered. Talent/ability: Important. Character/personal qualities: Important. Alumni/ae relationship: Considered. Geographical residence: Not Considered. State residency: Not Considered. Religious affiliation/commitment: Not Considered. Minority status: Not Considered. Volunteer work: Considered. Work experience: Considered. **Other schools with the greatest overlap in applicants:** Assumption College; Bentley University; Quinnipiac University; St. Anselm College; Stonehill College. **Admissions statistics for the fall 2009 entering class:** Total applicants: 3,890. Total accepted: 3,075. Freshmen enrolled: 554; Overall acceptance rate: 79%. Non-early acceptance rate: 79%. **Size of waiting list:** 103 applicants; enrolled from waiting list: 3. **Credentials of fall 2009 freshmen:** 10% ranked in the top 10 percent of their high school class; 36% were in the top 25 percent; 73% were in the top half. (Proportion submitting class standing: 67%.)

ACADEMICS

Year founded: 1947. **Academic calendar:** Semester. **Degrees offered:** certificate, associate, bachelor's, master's. **Major fields of study:** biological and bio-medical sciences; business, management, marketing, and related support services; communication, journalism, and related programs; computer and information sciences and support services; engineering; English language and literature/letters; foreign languages, literatures, and linguistics; health professions and related clinical sciences; history; liberal arts and sciences studies, and humanities; mathematics and statistics; natural resources and conservation; philosophy and religious studies; physical sciences; psychology; public administration and social service professions; social sciences; visual and performing arts. **Areas of required coursework:** humanities, mathematics, English (including composition), philosophy, sciences (biological or physical), history, social science, other. **Pre-professional programs:** pre-dentistry, pre-medicine. **Special academic programs:** cooperative (work-study plan) program, cross-registration, double major, English as a Second Language (ESL), honors program, independent study, internships, liberal arts/career combination, student-designed major, study abroad, teacher certificate program. **Teacher certification offered in:** elementary, middle/junior high, secondary. **Cooperative education programs:** business, computer science, engineering, health professions, humanities, natural science, other. **Reserve Officers Training Corps (ROTC):** Air Force ROTC: Offered at cooperating institution. **Faculty and instruction (2009-2010):** Total instructional faculty: 125 full-time, 114 part-time (55% men; 45% women; 7% minorities). Full-time faculty with Ph.D. or other terminal degree: 86%. Student/faculty ratio: 13/1. Classes of fewer than 20 students: 59%; of 20 to 49 students: 40%; of 50 or more students: 1%. **Advanced Placement and International Baccalaureate credit:** AP tests may be used for: Credit only. Scores accepted: 3, 4, 5. International Baccalaureate exams may be used for: Credit only. **Freshmen returning for sophomore year:** 77%. **Graduation rates:** Four-year: 60%; five-year: 69%; six-year: 69%. **Graduate study:** 14% of students pursue further study immediately upon graduation; 20% within one year; 35% within five years. Fields in which graduates pursue further study: Master of Business Administration (MBA), 43%; law, 7%; medicine, 5%; dentistry, 1%; engineering, 6%; theology (or the seminary), 2%; education, 9%; arts and sciences, 27%.

COSTS AND FINANCIAL AID

Financial aid office: (978) 837-5196. **Expenses (2010-2011):** Tuition and fees 2010-2011: $31,380; room/board: $10,700. Estimated books and supplies: $1,000; transportation: $1,500; personal expenses: $450. **Financial aid:** Priority filing date for institution's financial aid form: February 1; deadline: February 1. In 2009-2010, 78% of undergraduates applied for financial aid. Of those, 61% were determined to have financial need; 97% had their need fully met. Average financial aid package (proportion receiving): $15,668 (61%). Average amount of gift aid, such as scholarships or grants (proportion receiving): $9,868 (41%). Average amount of self-help aid, such as work study or loans (proportion receiving): $6,800 (52%). Average need-based loan (excluding PLUS or other private loans): $4,775. Among students who received need-based aid, the average percentage of need met: 70%. Among students who received aid based on merit, the average award (and the proportion receiving): $10,500 (16%). The average athletic scholarship (and the proportion receiving): $14,800 (14%). Average amount of debt of borrowers graduating in 2009: $24,000. Proportion who borrowed: 66%.

CAMPUS LIFE AND EXTRACURRICULAR ACTIVITIES

Campus housing available: coed dorms, women's dorms, men's dorms, apartment for single students, special housing for disabled students, special housing for international students, other housing options. **Clubs and organizations:** Number of student organizations: 50. Activities include: campus ministries, choral groups, dance, drama/theater, international student organization, jazz band, musical theater, pep band, student government, student newspaper, television station, yearbook. Number of fraternities: 2; sororities: 3. **Sports program (2009-2010):** Member of NCAA II. *Men's intercollegiate varsity sports:* baseball, basketball, cross country, football, ice hockey, lacrosse, soccer, tennis, track and field (indoor), track and field (outdoor). *Women's intercollegiate varsity sports:* basketball, cross country, field hockey, lacrosse, soccer, softball, tennis, track and field (indoor), track and field (outdoor).

SERVICES AND FACILITIES

Basic services: nonremedial tutoring, placement service, health service, health insurance. **Remedial assistance:** math, writing, study skills. **Counseling services:** minority student, career, personal, academic, psychological, religious. **For learning-disabled students:** School does not offer a structured program with separate admission and additional fees. Services include: tape recorders, untimed tests, note-taking services, oral tests, learning center, readers, extended time for tests, tutors, other. **Library:** Number of titles: 115,807; number of current serial subscriptions: 39,314. **Information technology resources:** Students are not required to lease or own a computer. Number of campus computers available to all students: 300. School has a wireless network. Approximate number of users that can be accommodated: 4,000. Proportion of college-owned housing units wired for high-speed internet access: 100%. **Campus safety:** Security services offered: 24-hour foot-and-vehicle patrols, late-night transport/escort service, 24-hour emergency telephones, lighted pathways/sidewalks, student patrols, controlled dormitory access (key, security card, etc).

TRANSFER AND INTERNATIONAL STUDENTS

Transfer students: May apply for admission for the following academic terms: Fall, Spring. Applicants do not need a minimum number of credits to apply. For fall 2009: Transfer applications received: 191. Transfer applicants offered admission: 145. Transfer applicants enrolled: 72. **International students:** Number of foreign undergraduates: 30 (2% of student body). Number of countries represented: 17. Minimum TOEFL score required: 550 (paper); 213 (computer). Average TOEFL score: 560 (paper).

Montserrat College of Art

- ■ **Address:** PO Box 26, 23 Essex Street, Beverly, MA 01915
- ■ **Website:** http://www.montserrat.edu
- ■ **Private**
- ■ **Enrollment:** N/A

....

KEY STATS
- ✔ **U.S News College Ranking:** Unranked Specialty School–Fine Arts
- ✔ **SAT or ACT Score (25th/75th percentile):** N/A
- ✔ **Tuition:** 2009-2010: $23,990

Selectivity: N/A	Room/board: $6,180
Acceptance rate: N/A	Average debt: N/A
Student/faculty ratio: N/A	Proportion who borrowed: N/A

Mount Holyoke College

- ■ **Address:** 50 College Street, South Hadley, MA 01075
- ■ **Website:** http://www.mtholyoke.edu
- ■ **Private**
- ■ **Enrollment:** 2,224 full-time; 64 part-time

....

KEY STATS
- ✔ **U.S News College Ranking:** 26, National Liberal Arts Colleges
- ✔ **SAT Score (25th/75th percentile):** 1210-1450
- ✔ **Tuition:** 2010-2011: $40,256

Selectivity: More selective	Room/board: $11,780
Acceptance rate: 58%	Average debt: $23,008
Student/faculty ratio: 9/1	Proportion who borrowed: 61%

UNDERGRADUATE STUDENT BODY STATS

2009-2010 enrollment: 2,224 full-time; 64 part-time. Men: 0%; women: 100%. **Ethnic makeup:** African American: 7%; Asian American: 10%; Hispanic: 6%; White: 58%; International: 20%. **Religious preference:** Roman Catholic: 10%; Protestant: 15%; Jewish: 4%; Muslim: 6%; Hindu: 3%; Buddhist: 4%; No preference: 45%; Other Christian: 6%; Other: 7%.

ADMISSIONS FACTS AND FIGURES

Phone: (413) 538-2023. **Email:** admission@mtholyoke.edu. **Website:** http://www.mtholyoke.edu. **Application deadlines for fall 2011:** Regular deci-

sion: January 15; decision sent by April 1. Early decision: Send application by: November 15; Decision sent by: January 1. Early action: Not offered. Admission can be deferred. **Application fee:** $60. **To apply online, go to:** http://www.mtholyoke.edu/admission/apply.html. **Admissions requirements/recommendations:** High school units required (recommended): English: (4); Mathematics: (3); Science: (3); Foreign language: (3); History: (3); Academic electives: (1); Total units: (17). **Tests:** The college uses SAT or ACT scores in admissions decisions. Neither SAT nor ACT required. For admission to the fall 2011 entering class, the school will accept: ACT with or without writing accepted. Campus visit: Recommended. Admissions interview: Recommended. Off-campus interview: May be arranged. **Factors that count in admissions decisions:** *Academic:* Secondary school record: Very Important. Class rank: Very Important. Letters of recommendation: Very Important. Standardized test scores: Considered. Essay: Very Important. *Nonacademic:* Interview: Important. Extracurricular activities: Important. Talent/ability: Important. Character/personal qualities: Important. Alumni/ae relationship: Considered. Geographical residence: Considered. State residency: Not Considered. Religious affiliation/commitment: Not Considered. Minority status: Considered. Volunteer work: Important. Work experience: Important. **Other schools with the greatest overlap in applicants:** Amherst College; Brown University; Bryn Mawr College; Smith College; Wellesley College. **Admissions statistics for the fall 2009 entering class:** Total applicants: 3,061. Total accepted: 1,771. Freshmen enrolled: 574; 77% were from out of state. Accepted through early-decision or early-action plans: 19%. Overall acceptance rate: 58%. Early-decision acceptance rate: 61%. Non-early acceptance rate: 58%. **Size of waiting list:** 459 applicants; enrolled from waiting list: 0. **Credentials of fall 2009 freshmen:** 62% ranked in the top 10 percent of their high school class; 87% were in the top 25 percent; 99% were in the top half. (Proportion submitting class standing: 35%.) **Average high school grade point average:** 3.7. **First-year students who submitted SAT scores:** 67%. Scores (25/75 percentile): Critical Reading: 610-730; Math: 600-720, Combined: 1210-1450. **First-year students submitting ACT scores:** 20%. Scores (25/75 percentile): English: 28-34, Math: 26-31, Composite: 27-31.

ACADEMICS

Year founded: 1837. **Academic calendar:** Semester. **Degrees offered:** bachelor's, post-bachelor's certificate, master's. **Most popular majors:** 9% English language and literature/letters, 9% biology/biological sciences, 8% economics, 8% international relations and affairs, 8% psychology. **Major fields of study:** architecture and related services; area, ethnic, cultural, and gender studies; biological and biomedical sciences; computer and information sciences and support services; education; engineering; English language and literature/letters; foreign languages, literatures, and linguistics; history; mathematics and statistics; multi/interdisciplinary studies; natural resources and conservation; philosophy and religious studies; physical sciences; psychology; social sciences; visual and performing arts. **Areas of required coursework:** humanities, foreign languages, sciences (biological or physical), social science, other. **Pre-professional programs:** pre-law, pre-dentistry, pre-medicine, pre-veterinary science, pre-optometry, pre-pharmacy, other. **Special academic programs (% participation):** cross-registration (74%), double major (19%), exchange student program (domestic) (16%), independent study (62%), internships (54%), student-designed major (4%), study abroad (44%), teacher certificate program (3%), other. **Teacher certification offered in:** early childhood, elementary, middle/junior high, secondary. **Reserve Officers Training Corps (ROTC):** Army ROTC: Offered at cooperating institution (University of Massachusetts–Amherst); Air Force ROTC: Offered at cooperating institution (University of Massachusetts–Amherst). **Faculty and instruction (2009-2010):** Total instructional faculty: 224 full-time, 63 part-time (44% men; 56% women; 23% minorities). Full-time faculty with Ph.D. or other terminal degree: 95%. Student/faculty ratio: 9/1. Classes of fewer than 20 students: 62%; of 20 to 49 students: 33%; of 50 or more students: 5%. **Advanced Placement and International Baccalaureate credit:** AP tests may be used for: Credit and/or placement. Scores accepted: 4, 5. International Baccalaureate exams may be used for: Credit and/or placement. **Freshmen returning for sophomore year:** 92%. **Graduation rates:** Four-year: 78%; five-year: 83%; six-year: 83%. **Graduate study:** 25% of students pursue further study within one year; 68% within five years. Fields in which graduates pursue further study: Master of Business Administration (MBA), 7%; law, 7%; medicine, 8%; engineering, 2%; arts and sciences, 79%.

COSTS AND FINANCIAL AID

Financial aid office: (413) 538-2291. **Expenses (2010-2011):** Tuition and fees 2010-2011: $40,256; room/board: $11,780. Estimated books and supplies: $1,900. **Financial aid:** Priority filing date for institution's financial aid form:

February 15; deadline: March 1. In 2009-2010, 75% of undergraduates applied for financial aid. Of those, 68% were determined to have financial need; 100% had their need fully met. Average financial aid package (proportion receiving): $33,399 (68%). Average amount of gift aid, such as scholarships or grants (proportion receiving): $28,578 (65%). Average amount of self-help aid, such as work study or loans (proportion receiving): $6,349 (64%). Average need-based loan (excluding PLUS or other private loans): $4,675. Among students who received need-based aid, the average percentage of need met: 100%. Among students who received aid based on merit, the average award (and the proportion receiving): $16,023 (7%). The average athletic scholarship (and the proportion receiving): $0 (0%). Average amount of debt of borrowers graduating in 2009: $23,008. Proportion who borrowed: 61%.

CAMPUS LIFE AND EXTRACURRICULAR ACTIVITIES

Campus housing available (% using): women's dorms (99%), apartment for single students (1%), other housing options (0%). Students who live in college-owned, operated, or affiliated housing: 93%. **Student employment:** During the 2009-2010 academic year, 70% of undergraduates worked on campus. Average per-year earnings: $2,100. **Clubs and organizations:** Number of student organizations: 150. Activities include: choral groups, dance, drama/theater, international student organization, jazz band, literary magazine, model UN, music ensembles, musical theater, radio station, student government, student newspaper, student film society, symphony orchestra, yearbook. Number of fraternities: 0; sororities: 0. Average proportion of students who stay on campus on weekends: 80%. **Sports program (2009-2010):** Member of NCAA III.

SERVICES AND FACILITIES

Basic services: nonremedial tutoring, women's center, health service, health insurance. **Counseling services:** minority student, career, personal, veteran student, academic, older student, psychological, birth control, religious. **For learning-disabled students:** School does not offer a structured program with separate admission and additional fees. Services include: tape recorders, diagnostic testing service, note-taking services, oral tests, readers, extended time for tests, tutors, priority seating, texts on tape, other testing accommodations, other. **Library:** Number of titles: 1,123,338; number of current serial subscriptions: 7,479. **Information technology resources:** Students are not required to lease or own a computer. Number of campus computers available to all students: 700. School has a wireless network. Approximate number of users that can be accommodated: 3,000. Proportion of college-owned housing units wired for high-speed internet access: 100%. **Campus safety:** Security services offered: 24-hour foot-and-vehicle patrols, late-night transport/escort service, 24-hour emergency telephones, lighted pathways/sidewalks, student patrols, controlled dormitory access (key, security card, etc).

TRANSFER AND INTERNATIONAL STUDENTS

Transfer students: May apply for admission for the following academic terms: Fall, Spring. Applicants need a minimum number of credits to apply. For fall 2009: Transfer applications received: 217. Transfer applicants offered admission: 102. Transfer applicants enrolled: 49. **International students:** Number of foreign undergraduates: 439 (20% of student body). Number of countries represented: 69. Minimum TOEFL score required: 600 (paper); 250 (computer). Average TOEFL score: 626 (paper).

Mount Ida College

- **Address:** 777 Dedham Street, Newton, MA 02459
- **Website:** http://www.mountida.edu
- **Private**
- **Enrollment:** 1,399 full-time; 92 part-time

KEY STATS

✔ **U.S News College Ranking:** 41, Regional Colleges (North)
✔ **SAT Score (25th/75th percentile):** 790-980
✔ **Tuition:** 2010-2011: $24,500

Selectivity: Less selective	Room/board: $12,000
Acceptance rate: 74%	Average debt: $43,911
Student/faculty ratio: 12/1	Proportion who borrowed: 89%

UNDERGRADUATE STUDENT BODY STATS

2009-2010 enrollment: 1,399 full-time; 92 part-time. Men: 35%; women: 65%. **Ethnic makeup:** African American: 12%; Asian American: 2%; Hispanic: 6%; White: 74%; International: 5%.

ADMISSIONS FACTS AND FIGURES

Phone: (617) 928-4535. **Email:** admissions@mountida.edu. **Website:** http://www.mountida.edu. **Application deadlines for fall 2011:** Regular decision: Rolling. Early decision: Not offered. Early action: Not offered. Admission can be deferred. **Application fee:** $45. **To apply online, go to:** http://www.mountida.edu/sp.cfm?pageid=413. **Admissions requirements/recommendations:** High school units required (recommended): English: 4 (4); Mathematics: 3 (3); Science: 3 (3); Foreign language: 2 (2); Social studies: 2 (2). Tests: The college uses SAT or ACT scores in admissions decisions. Either SAT or ACT required. For admission to the fall 2011 entering class, the school will accept: ACT with writing recommended. Campus visit: Recommended. Admissions interview: Recommended. Off-campus interview: Not available. **Factors that count in admissions decisions:** *Academic:* Secondary school record: Very Important. Class rank: Not Considered. Letters of recommendation: Very Important. Standardized test scores: Very Important. Essay: Important. *Nonacademic:* Interview: Considered. Extracurricular activities: Considered. Talent/ability: Considered. Character/personal qualities: Considered. Alumni/ae relationship: Not Considered. Geographical residence: Not Considered. State residency: Not Considered. Religious affiliation/commitment: Not Considered. Minority status: Not Considered. Volunteer work: Considered. Work experience: Considered. **Other schools with the greatest overlap in applicants:** Becker College; Curry College; Endicott College; Lasell College; Newbury College. **Admissions statistics for the fall 2009 entering class:** Total applicants: 2,004. Total accepted: 1,477. Freshmen enrolled: 434; 44% were from out of state. Overall acceptance rate: 74%. **Average high school grade point average:** 2.7. **First-year students who submitted SAT scores:** 91%. Scores (25/75 percentile): Critical Reading: 400-490, Math: 390-490, Combined: 790-980. **First-year students submitting ACT scores:** 12%. Scores (25/75 percentile): English: N/A, Math: N/A, Composite: 16-20.

ACADEMICS

Year founded: 1899. **Academic calendar:** Semester. **Degrees offered:** certificate, associate, bachelor's, master's. **Most popular majors:** 22% business administration and management, 12% veterinary/animal health technology/technician and veterinary assistant, 11% interior design, 9% fashion merchandising, 6% criminal justice/law enforcement administration. **Major fields of study:** biological and biomedical sciences; business, management, marketing, and related support services; education; English language and literature/letters; health professions and related clinical sciences; liberal arts and sciences studies, and humanities; psychology; public administration and social service professions. **Areas of required coursework:** humanities, computer literacy, mathematics, English (including composition), philosophy, sciences (biological or physical), history, social science, other. **Pre-professional programs:** pre-law. **Special academic programs (% participation):** distance learning (7%), double major (.6%), English as a Second Language (ESL) (4.5%), honors program, internships (87%), liberal arts/career combination (.5%), study abroad (.6%), teacher certificate program (1%). **Teacher certification offered in:** early childhood. **Faculty and instruction (2009-2010):** Total instructional faculty: 65 full-time, 130 part-time (41% men; 59% women; 8% minorities). Full-time faculty with Ph.D. or other terminal degree: 63%. Student/faculty ratio: 12/1. Classes of fewer than 20 students: 68%; of 20 to 49 students: 32%; of 50 or more students: 0%. **Advanced Placement and International Baccalaureate credit:** AP tests may be used for: Credit only. Scores accepted: 3, 4, 5. International Baccalaureate exams may be used for: Credit only. **Freshmen returning for sophomore year:** 63%. **Graduation rates:** Four-year: 24%; five-year: 32%; six-year: 31%. **Graduate study:** 7% of students pursue further study immediately upon graduation; 8% within one year. Fields in which graduates pursue further study: Master of Business Administration (MBA), 7%; law, 21%; medicine, 7%; arts and sciences, 50%; veterinary medicine, 14%.

COSTS AND FINANCIAL AID

Financial aid office: (617) 928-4785. **Expenses (2010-2011):** Tuition and fees 2010-2011: $24,500; room/board: $12,000. Estimated books and supplies: $1,000; transportation: $1,000; personal expenses: $1,200. **Financial aid:** Priority filing date for institution's financial aid form: May 1. In 2009-2010, 89% of undergraduates applied for financial aid. Of those, 81% were determined to have financial need; 7% had their need fully met. Average financial aid package (proportion receiving): $15,105 (80%). Average amount of gift aid, such as scholarships or grants (proportion receiving):

$11,328 (78%). Average amount of self-help aid, such as work study or loans (proportion receiving): $4,337 (76%). Average need-based loan (excluding PLUS or other private loans): $4,063. Among students who received need-based aid, the average percentage of need met: 58%. Among students who received aid based on merit, the average award (and the proportion receiving): $4,236 (17%). The average athletic scholarship (and the proportion receiving): $0 (0%). Average amount of debt of borrowers graduating in 2009: $43,911. Proportion who borrowed: 89%.

CAMPUS LIFE AND EXTRACURRICULAR ACTIVITIES

Campus housing available (% using): coed dorms (69%), women's dorms (5%), special housing for disabled students (3%). Students who live in college-owned, operated, or affiliated housing: 64%. **Student employment:** During the 2009-2010 academic year, 12% of undergraduates worked on campus. Average per-year earnings: $1,000. **Clubs and organizations:** Number of student organizations: 28. Activities include: choral groups, dance, drama/theater, literary magazine, radio station, student government, student newspaper. Number of fraternities: 0; sororities: 0. Average proportion of students who stay on campus on weekends: 40%. **Sports program (2009-2010):** Member of NCAA III. *Men's intercollegiate varsity sports:* basketball, football, lacrosse, soccer, volleyball. *Women's intercollegiate varsity sports:* basketball, cross country, equestrian, lacrosse, soccer, softball, tennis, volleyball.

SERVICES AND FACILITIES

Basic services: nonremedial tutoring, placement service, health service, health insurance, other. **Remedial assistance:** reading, math, writing, study skills, other. **Counseling services:** minority student, career, personal, academic, psychological, birth control, religious, other. **For learning-disabled students:** School does not offer a structured program with separate admission and additional fees. Total undergraduates in learning-disabled program or receiving services: 89. Services include: remedial math, remedial English, reading machines, tape recorders, learning center, extended time for tests, tutors, priority seating, texts on tape, other testing accommodations, other. **Library:** Number of titles: 94,464; number of current serial subscriptions: 257. **Information technology resources:** Students are not required to lease or own a computer. Number of campus computers available to all students: 122. School has a wireless network. Approximate number of users that can be accommodated: 1,000. Proportion of college-owned housing units wired for high-speed internet access: 100%. **Campus safety:** Security services offered: 24-hour foot-and-vehicle patrols, late-night transport/escort service, 24-hour emergency telephones, lighted pathways/sidewalks, student patrols, controlled dormitory access (key, security card, etc).

TRANSFER AND INTERNATIONAL STUDENTS

Transfer students: May apply for admission for the following academic terms: Fall, Spring. Applicants need a minimum number of credits to apply. For fall 2009: Transfer applications received: 460. Transfer applicants offered admission: 228. Transfer applicants enrolled: 109. **International students:** Number of foreign undergraduates: 72 (5% of student body). Number of countries represented: 27. Minimum TOEFL score required: 470 (paper); 150 (computer).

Newbury College

- **Address:** 129 Fischer Avenue, Brookline, MA 02445-5796
- **Website:** http://www.newbury.edu/
- **Private**
- **Enrollment:** N/A

KEY STATS

✔ **U.S News College Ranking:** Unranked, Regional Colleges (North)
✔ **SAT or ACT Score (25th/75th percentile):** N/A
✔ **Tuition:** 2009-2010: $23,500

Selectivity: N/A	Room/board: $11,230
Acceptance rate: N/A	Average debt: N/A
Student/faculty ratio: N/A	Proportion who borrowed: N/A

New England Conservatory of Music

- **Address:** 290 Huntington Avenue, Boston, MA 02115
- **Website:** http://www.newenglandconservatory.edu
- **Private**
- **Enrollment:** N/A

KEY STATS

✔ **U.S News College Ranking:** Unranked Specialty School—Fine Arts
✔ **SAT or ACT Score (25th/75th percentile):** N/A
✔ **Tuition:** 2010-2011: $34,950

Selectivity: N/A	Room/board: $12,100
Acceptance rate: 31%	Average debt: $38,509
Student/faculty ratio: N/A	Proportion who borrowed: 74%

Nichols College

- **Address:** Box 5000, Dudley, MA 01571
- **Website:** http://www.nichols.edu/
- **Private**
- **Enrollment:** 1,159 full-time; 178 part-time

KEY STATS

✔ **U.S News College Ranking:** Unranked Specialty School—Business
✔ **SAT Score (25th/75th percentile):** 830-1020
✔ **Tuition:** 2009-2010: $28,040

Selectivity: Less selective	Room/board: $9,200
Acceptance rate: 74%	Average debt: $27,112
Student/faculty ratio: 20/1	Proportion who borrowed: 86%

UNDERGRADUATE STUDENT BODY STATS

2009-2010 enrollment: 1,159 full-time; 178 part-time. Men: 59%; women: 41%. **Ethnic makeup:** African American: 5%; Asian American: 2%; Hispanic: 4%; White: 88%; International: 1%.

ADMISSIONS FACTS AND FIGURES

Phone: (800) 470-3379. **Email:** admissions@nichols.edu. **Website:** http://www.nichols.edu/. **Application deadlines for fall 2011:** Regular decision: Rolling. Early decision: Not offered. Early action: Not offered. Admission can be deferred. **Application fee:** $25. **To apply online, go to:** http://www.nichols.edu/highschool/applynow/index.html. **Admissions requirements/recommendations:** High school units required (recommended): English: 4; Mathematics: 2 (3); Science: 2 (3); Foreign language: (2); Social studies: 2 (3); History: 2 (2); Academic electives: (5). Tests: The college uses SAT or ACT scores in admissions decisions. Either SAT or ACT required. For admission to the fall 2011 entering class, the school will accept: ACT with or without writing accepted. Campus visit: Recommended. Admissions interview: Neither required nor recommended. Off-campus interview: Not available. **Factors that count in admissions decisions:** *Academic:* Secondary school record: Very Important. Class rank: Considered. Letters of recommendation: Important. Standardized test scores: Considered. Essay: Important. *Nonacademic:* Interview: Considered. Extracurricular activities: Considered. Talent/ability: Not Considered. Character/personal qualities: Very Important. Alumni/ae relationship: Considered. Geographical residence: Not Considered. State residency: Not Considered. Religious affiliation/commitment: Not Considered. Minority status: Not Considered. Volunteer work: Considered. Work experience: Considered. **Other schools with the greatest overlap in applicants:** Curry College; Endicott College; Western New England College; Westfield State College; Worcester State College. **Admissions statistics for the fall 2009 entering class:** Total applicants: 1,983. Total accepted: 1,463. Freshmen enrolled: 352; 46% were from out of state. Overall acceptance rate: 74%. **Average high school grade point average:** 2.6. **First-year students who submitted SAT scores:** 95%. Scores (25/75 percentile): Critical Reading: 410-500, Math: 420-520, Combined: 830-1020. **First-year students submitting ACT scores:** 14%. Scores (25/75 percentile): English: N/A, Math: N/A, Composite: 17-22.

ACADEMICS

Year founded: 1815. **Academic calendar:** Semester. **Degrees offered:** associate, bachelor's, master's. **Most popular majors:** 23% business administration and management, 22% sport and fitness administration/management, 14%

accounting, 13% marketing/marketing management, 9% criminal justice/law enforcement administration. **Major fields of study:** business, management, marketing, and related support services; education; English language and literature/letters; history; mathematics and statistics; parks, recreation, leisure, and fitness studies; psychology; security and protective services. **Areas of required coursework:** arts/fine arts, humanities, computer literacy, mathematics, English (including composition), philosophy, sciences (biological or physical), history, social science, other. **Special academic programs:** accelerated program, distance learning, double major, dual enrollment, external degree program, honors program, independent study, internships, study abroad, teacher certificate program. **Teacher certification offered in:** middle/junior high, secondary. **Reserve Officers Training Corps (ROTC):** Army ROTC: Offered at cooperating institution (Worcester Polytechnic Institute). **Faculty and instruction (2009-2010):** Total instructional faculty: 36 full-time, 44 part-time (64% men; 36% women; 4% minorities). Full-time faculty with Ph.D. or other terminal degree: 61%. Student/faculty ratio: 20/1. Classes of fewer than 20 students: 41%; of 20 to 49 students: 59%; of 50 or more students: 0%. **Advanced Placement and International Baccalaureate credit:** AP tests may be used for: Credit only. Scores accepted: 3, 4, 5. International Baccalaureate exams may be used for: Credit only. **Freshmen returning for sophomore year:** 65%. **Graduation rates:** Four-year: 45%; five-year: 52%; six-year: 47%. **Graduate study:** 6% of students pursue further study immediately upon graduation; 4% within one year. Fields in which graduates pursue further study: Master of Business Administration (MBA), 90%; law, 5%; arts and sciences, 5%.

COSTS AND FINANCIAL AID
Financial aid office: (508) 213-2278. **Expenses (2009-2010):** Tuition and fees 2009-2010: $28,040; room/board: $9,200. Estimated books and supplies: $1,200; transportation: $1,500; personal expenses: $1,170. **Financial aid:** Priority filing date for institution's financial aid form: March 1; deadline: June 1. In 2009-2010, 99% of undergraduates applied for financial aid. Of those, 90% were determined to have financial need; 6% had their need fully met. Average financial aid package (proportion receiving): $26,532 (90%). Average amount of gift aid, such as scholarships or grants (proportion receiving): $17,143 (85%). Average amount of self-help aid, such as work study or loans (proportion receiving): $5,103 (85%). Average need-based loan (excluding PLUS or other private loans): $3,603. Among students who received need-based aid, the average percentage of need met: 78%. Among students who received aid based on merit, the average award (and the proportion receiving): $9,871 (13%). The average athletic scholarship (and the proportion receiving): $0 (0%). Average amount of debt of borrowers graduating in 2009: $27,112. Proportion who borrowed: 86%.

CAMPUS LIFE AND EXTRACURRICULAR ACTIVITIES
Campus housing available (% using): coed dorms (100%), women's dorms, men's dorms, apartment for single students, special housing for disabled students. Students who live in college-owned, operated, or affiliated housing: 83%. **Student employment:** During the 2009-2010 academic year, 9% of undergraduates worked on campus. Average per-year earnings: $2,500. **Clubs and organizations:** Number of student organizations: 31. Activities include: campus ministries, drama/theater, literary magazine, radio station, student government, student newspaper, yearbook. Number of fraternities: 0; sororities: 0. **Sports program (2009-2010):** Member of NCAA III. *Men's intercollegiate varsity sports:* baseball, basketball, football, golf, ice hockey, lacrosse, soccer, tennis. *Women's intercollegiate varsity sports:* basketball, field hockey, ice hockey, lacrosse, soccer, softball, tennis.

SERVICES AND FACILITIES
Basic services: nonremedial tutoring, placement service, health service, health insurance. **Remedial assistance:** reading, math, writing, study skills. **Counseling services:** minority student, career, military, personal, academic, older student, psychological, birth control, religious. **For learning-disabled students:** School does not offer a structured program with separate admission and additional fees. Services include: remedial math, reading machines, untimed tests, learning center, extended time for tests, tutors. **Library:** Number of titles: 70,046; number of current serial subscriptions: 161. **Information technology resources:** Students are not required to lease or own a computer. Number of campus computers available to all students: 69. School has a wireless network. Approximate number of users that can be accommodated: 200. Proportion of college-owned housing units wired for high-speed internet access: 100%. **Campus safety:** Security services offered: 24-hour foot-and-vehicle patrols, late-night transport/escort service, 24-hour emergency telephones, lighted pathways/sidewalks, controlled dormitory access (key, security card, etc).

TRANSFER AND INTERNATIONAL STUDENTS
Transfer students: May apply for admission for the following academic terms: Fall, Spring. Applicants do not need a minimum number of credits to apply. For fall 2009: Transfer applications received: 162. Transfer applicants offered admission: 87. Transfer applicants enrolled: 40. **International students:** Number of foreign undergraduates: 10 (1% of student body). Minimum TOEFL score required: 550 (paper); 213 (computer).

Northeastern University

- **Address:** 360 Huntington Avenue, Boston, MA 02115
- **Website:** http://www.northeastern.edu/
- **Private**
- **Enrollment:** 12,829 full-time

KEY STATS
- ✔ **U.S News College Ranking:** 69, National Universities
- ✔ **SAT Score (25th/75th percentile):** 1200-1370
- ✔ **Tuition:** 2010-2011: $36,792

Selectivity: More selective	**Room/board:** $12,760
Acceptance rate: 41%	**Average debt:** N/A
Student/faculty ratio: 14/1	**Proportion who borrowed:** N/A

UNDERGRADUATE STUDENT BODY STATS
2009-2010 enrollment: 12,829 full-time. Men: 49%; women: 51%. **Ethnic makeup:** African American: 4%; Asian American: 9%; Hispanic: 5%; White: 73%; International: 8%.

ADMISSIONS FACTS AND FIGURES
Phone: (617) 373-2200. **Email:** admissions@neu.edu. **Website:** http://www.northeastern.edu/. **Application deadlines for fall 2011:** Regular decision: January 15; decision sent by April 1. Early decision: Not offered. Early action: Send application by: November 1; Decision sent by: December 31. Admission can be deferred. **Application fee:** $70. **To apply online, go to:** http://www.northeastern.edu/admissions/. **Admissions requirements/recommendations:** High school units required (recommended): English: 4; Mathematics: 3 (4); Science: 3 (4); Foreign language: 2 (4); Social studies: 3; History: 2; Total units: 17. Tests: The college uses SAT or ACT scores in admissions decisions. Either SAT or ACT required. For admission to the fall 2011 entering class, the school will accept: ACT with writing required. Campus visit: Recommended. Admissions interview: Neither required nor recommended. Off-campus interview: May be arranged. **Factors that count in admissions decisions:** *Academic:* Secondary school record: Very Important. Class rank: Considered. Letters of recommendation: Important. Standardized test scores: Important. Essay: Important. *Nonacademic:* Interview: Considered. Extracurricular activities: Important. Talent/ability: Important. Character/personal qualities: Important. Alumni/ae relationship: Considered. Geographical residence: Considered. State residency: Considered. Religious affiliation/commitment: Not Considered. Minority status: Considered. Volunteer work: Important. Work experience: Considered. **Other schools with the greatest overlap in applicants:** Boston College; Boston University; New York University; University of Connecticut; University of Massachusetts–Amherst. **Admissions statistics for the fall 2009 entering class:** Total applicants: 34,005. Total accepted: 13,948. Freshmen enrolled: 2,833; 68% were from out of state. Accepted through early-decision or early-action plans: 45%. Overall acceptance rate: 41%. Non-early acceptance rate: 36%. **Size of waiting list:** 4790 applicants; enrolled from waiting list: 167. **Credentials of fall 2009 freshmen:** 50% ranked in the top 10 percent of their high school class; 81% were in the top 25 percent; 96% were in the top half. (Proportion submitting class standing: 46%.) **First-year students who submitted SAT scores:** 85%. Scores (25/75 percentile): Critical Reading: 580-670, Math: 620-700, Combined: 1200-1370. **First-year students submitting ACT scores:** 26%. Scores (25/75 percentile): English: N/A, Math: N/A, Composite: 27-31.

ACADEMICS
Year founded: 1898. **Academic calendar:** Semester. **Degrees offered:** bachelor's, master's, post-master's certificate, doctorate. **Most popular majors:** 21% business, management, marketing, and related support services, 13% engineering, 11% health professions and related clinical sciences, 10% social sciences, 7% visual and performing arts. **Major fields of study:** architecture and related services; area, ethnic, cultural, and gender studies; biological and biomedical sciences; business, management, market-

ing, and related support services; communication, journalism, and related programs; computer and information sciences and support services; education; engineering; engineering technologies/technicians; English language and literature/letters; foreign languages, literatures, and linguistics; health professions and related clinical sciences; history; liberal arts and sciences studies, and humanities; mathematics and statistics; multi/interdisciplinary studies; natural resources and conservation; philosophy and religious studies; physical sciences; psychology; public administration and social service professions; security and protective services; social sciences; visual and performing arts. **Areas of required coursework:** arts/fine arts, humanities, mathematics, English (including composition), sciences (biological or physical), history, social science, other. **Pre-professional programs:** pre-law, pre-dentistry, pre-medicine, pre-veterinary science, pre-optometry, pre-pharmacy. **Special academic programs:** accelerated program, cooperative (work-study plan) program, cross-registration, distance learning, double major, English as a Second Language (ESL), exchange student program (domestic), honors program, independent study, internships, liberal arts/career combination, student-designed major, study abroad, teacher certificate program. **Teacher certification offered in:** special education, elementary, middle/junior high, secondary. **Cooperative education programs:** art, business, computer science, education, engineering, health professions, humanities, natural science, social/behavioral science, technologies, other. **Reserve Officers Training Corps (ROTC):** Army ROTC: Offered on campus; Navy ROTC: Offered at cooperating institution (Boston University); Air Force ROTC: Offered at cooperating institution (Boston University). **Faculty and instruction (2009-2010):** Total instructional faculty: 984 full-time, 439 part-time (57% men; 43% women; 12% minorities). Full-time faculty with Ph.D. or other terminal degree: 88%. Student/faculty ratio: 14/1. Classes of fewer than 20 students: 61%; of 20 to 49 students: 32%; of 50 or more students: 7%. **Advanced Placement and International Baccalaureate credit:** AP tests may be used for: Credit and/or placement. Scores accepted: 4, 5. International Baccalaureate exams may be used for: Credit and/or placement. **Freshmen returning for sophomore year:** 91%. **Graduation rates:** Five-year: 69%; six-year: 75%. **Graduate study:** 20% of students pursue further study within one year.

COSTS AND FINANCIAL AID
Financial aid office: (617) 373-3190. **Expenses (2010-2011):** Tuition and fees 2010-2011: $36,792; room/board: $12,760. Estimated books and supplies: $1,000; transportation: $900; personal expenses: $900. **Financial aid:** Priority filing date for institution's financial aid form: February 15. In 2009-2010, 65% of undergraduates applied for financial aid. Of those, 54% were determined to have financial need; 15% had their need fully met. Average financial aid package (proportion receiving): $19,325 (54%). Average amount of gift aid, such as scholarships or grants (proportion receiving): $14,627 (51%). Average amount of self-help aid, such as work study or loans (proportion receiving): $6,183 (47%). Average need-based loan (excluding PLUS or other private loans): $4,910. Among students who received need-based aid, the average percentage of need met: 59%. Among students who received aid based on merit, the average award (and the proportion receiving): $9,139 (23%). The average athletic scholarship (and the proportion receiving): $29,989 (1%).

CAMPUS LIFE AND EXTRACURRICULAR ACTIVITIES
Campus housing available: coed dorms, apartment for single students, special housing for disabled students, special housing for international students, cooperative housing, other housing options. Students who live in college-owned, operated, or affiliated housing: 50%. **Clubs and organizations:** Number of student organizations: 225. Activities include: campus ministries, choral groups, concert band, dance, drama/theater, international student organization, jazz band, literary magazine, model UN, music ensembles, musical theater, pep band, radio station, student government, student newspaper, symphony orchestra, television station, yearbook. Number of fraternities: 9; sororities: 8. Proportion of men in fraternities: 4%; of women in sororities: 4%. **Sports program (2009-2010):** Member of NCAA I. *Men's intercollegiate varsity sports:* baseball, basketball, cross country, ice hockey, soccer, track and field (indoor), track and field (outdoor). *Women's intercollegiate varsity sports:* basketball, crew (heavyweight), cross country, field hockey, ice hockey, crew (lightweight), soccer, swimming, track and field (indoor), track and field (outdoor), volleyball.

SERVICES AND FACILITIES
Basic services: nonremedial tutoring, health service, health insurance. **Remedial assistance:** reading, math, writing, study skills, other. **Counseling services:** minority student, career, personal, academic, older student, psychological, birth control, religious, other. **For learning-disabled students:**

School does not offer a structured program with separate admission and additional fees. Total undergraduates in learning-disabled program or receiving services: 320. Services include: remedial math, remedial English, reading machines, tape recorders, note-taking services, readers, extended time for tests, tutors, substitution of courses, texts on tape, exams on tape or computer, other testing accommodations, other. **Library:** Number of titles: 966,923; number of current serial subscriptions: 41,950. **Information technology resources:** Students are not required to lease or own a computer. Number of campus computers available to all students: 1,993. School has a wireless network. Approximate number of users that can be accommodated: 9,000. Proportion of college-owned housing units wired for high-speed internet access: 100%. **Campus safety:** Security services offered: 24-hour foot-and-vehicle patrols, late-night transport/escort service, 24-hour emergency telephones, lighted pathways/sidewalks, student patrols, controlled dormitory access (key, security card, etc).

TRANSFER AND INTERNATIONAL STUDENTS
Transfer students: May apply for admission for the following academic terms: Fall, Spring. Applicants need a minimum number of credits to apply. For fall 2009: Transfer applications received: 2,508. Transfer applicants offered admission: 1,287. Transfer applicants enrolled: 589. **International students:** Number of foreign undergraduates: 1059 (8% of student body). Number of countries represented: 112. Minimum TOEFL score required: 550 (paper); 79 (computer). Average TOEFL score: 570 (paper).

Pine Manor College

- **Address:** 400 Heath Street, Chestnut Hill, MA 02467
- **Website:** http://www.pmc.edu
- **Private**
- **Enrollment:** 442 full-time; 10 part-time

KEY STATS
✔ **U.S News College Ranking:** second tier, National Liberal Arts Colleges
✔ **SAT or ACT Score (25th/75th percentile):** N/A
✔ **Tuition:** 2009-2010: $20,189

Selectivity: Selective	**Room/board:** $11,670
Acceptance rate: 63%	**Average debt:** N/A
Student/faculty ratio: N/A	**Proportion who borrowed:** N/A

UNDERGRADUATE STUDENT BODY STATS
2009-2010 enrollment: 442 full-time; 10 part-time. Men: 0%; women: 100%. **Ethnic makeup:** African American: 51%; Asian American: 4%; Hispanic: 16%; White: 26%; International: 3%.

ADMISSIONS FACTS AND FIGURES
Phone: (617) 731-7104. **Email:** admission@pmc.edu. **Website:** http://www.pmc.edu. **Application deadlines for fall 2011:** Regular decision: Rolling. Early decision: Not offered. Early action: Not offered. Admission can be deferred. **Application fee:** $25. **To apply online, go to:** http://www.pmc.edu/admissions/apply.html. **Admissions requirements/recommendations:** High school units required (recommended): English: 4 (4); Mathematics: 3 (3); Science: 3 (3); Foreign language: 2 (2); Social studies: 2 (2). Tests: The college uses SAT or ACT scores in admissions decisions. Either SAT or ACT required. For admission to the fall 2011 entering class, the school will accept: ACT with or without writing accepted. Campus visit: Recommended. Admissions interview: Recommended. Off-campus interview: May be arranged. **Factors that count in admissions decisions:** *Academic:* Secondary school record: Important. Class rank: Considered. Letters of recommendation: Very Important. Standardized test scores: Considered. Essay: Very Important. *Nonacademic:* Interview: Very Important. Extracurricular activities: Important. Talent/ability: Important. Character/personal qualities: Important. Alumni/ae relationship: Considered. Geographical residence: Not Considered. State residency: Not Considered. Religious affiliation/commitment: Not Considered. Minority status: Not Considered. Volunteer work: Important. Work experience: Important. **Other schools with the greatest overlap in applicants:** Northeastern University; Regis College; Suffolk University; University of Massachusetts–Amherst; University of Massachusetts–Boston. **Admissions statistics for the fall 2009 entering class:** Total applicants: 611. Total accepted: 385. Freshmen enrolled: 142; Overall acceptance rate: 63%.

ACADEMICS

Year founded: 1911. **Academic calendar:** Semester. **Degrees offered:** associate, bachelor's, master's. **Major fields of study:** biological and biomedical sciences; business, management, marketing, and related support services; communication, journalism, and related programs; English language and literature/letters; history; liberal arts and sciences studies, and humanities; psychology; social sciences; visual and performing arts. **Areas of required coursework:** arts/fine arts, humanities, mathematics, English (including composition), sciences (biological or physical), history, social science, other. **Pre-professional programs:** pre-law, pre-dentistry, pre-medicine, pre-veterinary science. **Special academic programs (% participation):** cross-registration, double major, English as a Second Language (ESL), independent study, internships (100%), liberal arts/career combination, student-designed major, study abroad, teacher certificate program. **Teacher certification offered in:** early childhood, elementary, middle/junior high, secondary. **Faculty and instruction (2009-2010):** Total instructional faculty: 29 full-time, 39 part-time (21% men; 79% women; 15% minorities). Full-time faculty with Ph.D. or other terminal degree: 72%. **Advanced Placement and International Baccalaureate credit:** AP tests may be used for: Placement only. International Baccalaureate exams may be used for: Placement only. **Freshmen returning for sophomore year:** 65%. **Graduation rates:** Four-year: 31%; five-year: 34%; six-year: 35%. **Graduate study:** 20% of students pursue further study immediately upon graduation; 30% within one year; 50% within five years. Fields in which graduates pursue further study: Master of Business Administration (MBA), 10%; law, 20%; medicine, 20%; education, 25%; arts and sciences, 25%.

COSTS AND FINANCIAL AID

Financial aid office: (617) 731-7129. **Expenses (2009-2010):** Tuition and fees 2009-2010: $20,189; room/board: $11,670. Estimated books and supplies: $800; transportation: $800; personal expenses: $800. **Financial aid:** Priority filing date for institution's financial aid form: March 15.

CAMPUS LIFE AND EXTRACURRICULAR ACTIVITIES

Campus housing available (% using): women's dorms (88%), special housing for disabled students (2%). **Student employment:** During the 2009-2010 academic year, 15% of undergraduates worked on campus. Average per-year earnings: $1,800. **Clubs and organizations:** Number of student organizations: 23. Activities include: choral groups, dance, drama/theater, international student organization, literary magazine, model UN, radio station, student government, television station, yearbook. Number of fraternities: 0; sororities: 0. Average proportion of students who stay on campus on weekends: 70%. **Sports program (2009-2010):** Member of NCAA III. *Women's intercollegiate varsity sports:* basketball, cross country, lacrosse, soccer, softball, tennis, volleyball.

SERVICES AND FACILITIES

Basic services: nonremedial tutoring, health service, health insurance. **Remedial assistance:** reading, math, writing, study skills. **Counseling services:** minority student, career, personal, academic, psychological, birth control, religious. **For learning-disabled students:** School does not offer a structured program with separate admission and additional fees. Services include: untimed tests, note-taking services, oral tests, learning center, readers, extended time for tests, tutors, priority seating, texts on tape, other testing accommodations. **Library:** Number of titles: 65,632; number of current serial subscriptions: 272. **Information technology resources:** Students are not required to lease or own a computer. Number of campus computers available to all students: 108. School has a wireless network. Proportion of college-owned housing units wired for high-speed internet access: 100%. **Campus safety:** Security services offered: 24-hour foot-and-vehicle patrols, late-night transport/escort service, 24-hour emergency telephones, lighted pathways/sidewalks, controlled dormitory access (key, security card, etc).

TRANSFER AND INTERNATIONAL STUDENTS

Transfer students: May apply for admission for the following academic terms: Fall, Spring, Summer. Applicants need a minimum number of credits to apply. For fall 2009: Transfer applications received: 34. Transfer applicants offered admission: 23. Transfer applicants enrolled: 18. **International students:** Number of foreign undergraduates: 15 (3% of student body). Number of countries represented: 23. Minimum TOEFL score required: 450 (paper); 133 (computer). Average TOEFL score: 537 (paper).

Regis College

- **Address:** 235 Wellesley Street, Weston, MA 02493-1571
- **Website:** http://www.regiscollege.edu
- **Private; Religious affiliation:** Roman Catholic
- **Enrollment:** N/A

KEY STATS

✔ **U.S News College Ranking:** second tier, Regional Universities (North)
✔ **SAT or ACT Score (25th/75th percentile):** N/A
✔ **Tuition:** 2009-2010: $28,900
   Selectivity: Less selective   **Room/board:** $12,190
   Acceptance rate: N/A   **Average debt:** N/A
   Student/faculty ratio: N/A   **Proportion who borrowed:** N/A

Salem State College

- **Address:** 352 Lafayette Street, Salem, MA 01970
- **Website:** http://www.salemstate.edu
- **Public**
- **Enrollment:** 5,894 full-time; 1,869 part-time

KEY STATS

✔ **U.S News College Ranking:** second tier, Regional Universities (North)
✔ **SAT Score (25th/75th percentile):** 880-1080
✔ **Tuition:** 2009-2010: $6,744 in state, $12,884 out of state
   Selectivity: Less selective   **Room/board:** $9,438
   Acceptance rate: 60%   **Average debt:** N/A
   Student/faculty ratio: 14/1   **Proportion who borrowed:** N/A

UNDERGRADUATE STUDENT BODY STATS

2009-2010 enrollment: 5,894 full-time; 1,869 part-time. Men: 38%; women: 62%. **Ethnic makeup:** African American: 9%; Asian American: 3%; Hispanic: 7%; White: 77%; International: 3%.

ADMISSIONS FACTS AND FIGURES

Phone: (978) 542-6200. **Email:** admissions@salemstate.edu. **Website:** http://www.salemstate.edu. **Application deadlines for fall 2011:** Regular decision: May 1. Early decision: Not offered. Early action: Not offered. Admission can be deferred. **Application fee:** $30. **To apply online, go to:** https://navigator.salemstate.edu:8052/psc/pa88prd/NAVIGATOR/SSC/c/SC_CUSTOM.SC_SA_UG_APPLY.GBL. **Admissions requirements/recommendations:** High school units required (recommended): English: 4 (4); Mathematics: 3 (3); Science: 3 (3); Foreign language: 2 (2); Social studies: 2 (2); History: 1 (3); Academic electives: 2 (2); Total units: 16 (18). Tests: The college uses SAT or ACT scores in admissions decisions. Either SAT or ACT required. For admission to the fall 2011 entering class, the school will accept: ACT with or without writing accepted. Campus visit: Recommended. Admissions interview: Recommended. Off-campus interview: May be arranged. **Factors that count in admissions decisions:** *Academic:* Secondary school record: Very Important. Class rank: Not Considered. Letters of recommendation: Considered. Standardized test scores: Very Important. Essay: Not Considered. *Nonacademic:* Interview: Considered. Extracurricular activities: Considered. Talent/ability: Considered. Character/personal qualities: Considered. Alumni/ae relationship: Not Considered. Geographical residence: Not Considered. State residency: Not Considered. Religious affiliation/commitment: Not Considered. Minority status: Not Considered. Volunteer work: Considered. Work experience: Considered. **Other schools with the greatest overlap in applicants:** Bridgewater State College; University of Massachusetts–Amherst; University of Massachusetts–Dartmouth; University of Massachusetts–Lowell; Westfield State College. **Admissions statistics for the fall 2009 entering class:** Total applicants: 5,835. Total accepted: 3,514. Freshmen enrolled: 994; 3% were from out of state. Overall acceptance rate: 60%. **Average high school grade point average:** 2.9. **First-year students who submitted SAT scores:** 94%. Scores (25/75 percentile): Critical Reading: 440-540, Math: 440-540, Combined: 880-1080.

ACADEMICS

Year founded: 1854. **Academic calendar:** Semester. **Degrees offered:** certificate, bachelor's, post-bachelor's certificate, master's, post-master's certificate. **Most popular majors:** 19% business, management, marketing, and related support services, 15% health professions and related clinical sciences, 9% education, 9% security and protective services, 8% communication, journalism, and related programs. **Major fields of study:** biological and biomedical sciences; business, management, marketing, and related support services; computer and information sciences and support services; education; English language and literature/letters; foreign languages, literatures, and linguistics; health professions and related clinical sciences; history; liberal arts and sciences studies, and humanities; mathematics and statistics; physical sciences; psychology; public administration and social service professions; security and protective services; social sciences; visual and performing arts. **Areas of required coursework:** humanities, computer literacy, mathematics, English (including composition), foreign languages, sciences (biological or physical), history, social science, other. **Special academic programs:** distance learning, double major, dual enrollment, English as a Second Language (ESL), honors program, independent study, internships, study abroad, teacher certificate program. **Teacher certification offered in:** early childhood, special education, elementary, middle/junior high, secondary, bilingual/bicultural. **Reserve Officers Training Corps (ROTC):** Army ROTC: Offered at cooperating institution (Massachusetts Institute of Technology); Air Force ROTC: Offered at cooperating institution (University of Massachusetts–Lowell). **Faculty and instruction (2009-2010):** Total instructional faculty: 331 full-time, 428 part-time (43% men; 57% women; 6% minorities). Student/faculty ratio: 14/1. Classes of fewer than 20 students: 53%; of 20 to 49 students: 47%; of 50 or more students: 1%. **Advanced Placement and International Baccalaureate credit:** AP tests may be used for: Credit and/or placement. Scores accepted: 3, 4, 5. **Freshmen returning for sophomore year:** 73%. **Graduation rates:** Four-year: 13%; five-year: 37%; six-year: 41%. **Graduate study:** 11% of students pursue further study immediately upon graduation.

COSTS AND FINANCIAL AID

Financial aid office: (978) 542-6139. **Expenses (2009-2010):** Tuition and fees 2009-2010: $6,744 in state, $12,884 out of state; room/board: $9,438. Estimated books and supplies: $900; transportation: $650; personal expenses: $1,012. **Financial aid:** Priority filing date for institution's financial aid form: April 1.

CAMPUS LIFE AND EXTRACURRICULAR ACTIVITIES

Campus housing available (% using): coed dorms (97%). Students who live in college-owned, operated, or affiliated housing: 21%. **Student employment:** During the 2009-2010 academic year, 12% of undergraduates worked on campus. **Clubs and organizations:** Number of student organizations: 41. Activities include: campus ministries, choral groups, concert band, dance, drama/theater, international student organization, jazz band, literary magazine, music ensembles, musical theater, radio station, student government, student newspaper. Number of fraternities: 0; sororities: 0. Average proportion of students who stay on campus on weekends: 35%. **Sports program (2009-2010):** Member of NCAA III. *Men's intercollegiate varsity sports:* baseball, basketball, cross country, golf, ice hockey, lacrosse, soccer, tennis. *Women's intercollegiate varsity sports:* basketball, cross country, field hockey, soccer, softball, tennis, volleyball.

SERVICES AND FACILITIES

Basic services: nonremedial tutoring, women's center, placement service, day care, health service, health insurance. **Remedial assistance:** study skills. **Counseling services:** minority student, career, personal, veteran student, academic, older student, psychological, birth control. **For learning-disabled students:** School does not offer a structured program with separate admission and additional fees. Total undergraduates in learning-disabled program or receiving services: 151. Services include: reading machines, tape recorders, note-taking services, learning center, extended time for tests, tutors, priority registration, priority seating, texts on tape, other testing accommodations. **Library:** Number of titles: 305,302; number of current serial subscriptions: 45,441. **Information technology resources:** Students are required to lease or own a computer. Number of campus computers available to all students: 200. School has a wireless network. Approximate number of users that can be accommodated: 5,000. Proportion of college-owned housing units wired for high-speed internet access: 100%. **Campus safety:** Security services offered: 24-hour foot-and-vehicle patrols, late-night transport/escort service, 24-hour emergency telephones, lighted pathways/sidewalks, controlled dormitory access (key, security card, etc).

TRANSFER AND INTERNATIONAL STUDENTS

Transfer students: May apply for admission for the following academic terms: Fall, Spring. Applicants need a minimum number of credits to apply. For fall 2009: Transfer applications received: 1,499. Transfer

applicants offered admission: 1,358. Transfer applicants enrolled: 852. **International students:** Number of foreign undergraduates: 213 (3% of student body). Minimum TOEFL score required: 500 (paper); 197 (computer).

Simmons College

- **Address:** 300 The Fenway, Boston, MA 02115
- **Website:** http://www.simmons.edu
- **Private**
- **Enrollment:** 1,746 full-time; 223 part-time

....

KEY STATS

✔ **U.S News College Ranking:** 14, Regional Universities (North)
✔ **SAT Score (25th/75th percentile):** 990-1190
✔ **Tuition:** 2010-2011: $32,230

Selectivity: Selective	**Room/board:** $12,470
Acceptance rate: 57%	**Average debt:** $45,237
Student/faculty ratio: 13/1	**Proportion who borrowed:** 78%

UNDERGRADUATE STUDENT BODY STATS

2009-2010 enrollment: 1,746 full-time; 223 part-time. Men: 0%; women: 100%. **Ethnic makeup:** African American: 6%; Asian American: 7%; Hispanic: 4%; White: 80%; International: 3%.

ADMISSIONS FACTS AND FIGURES

Phone: (800) 345-8468. **Email:** ugadm@simmons.edu. **Website:** http://www.simmons.edu. **Application deadlines for fall 2011:** Regular decision: February 1; decision sent by April 15. Early decision: Not offered. Early action: Send application by: December 1; Decision sent by: January 20. Admission can be deferred. **Application fee:** $55. **To apply online, go to:** http://www.simmons.edu/undergraduate/admission/apply/. **Admissions requirements/recommendations:** High school units required (recommended): English: 4 (4); Mathematics: 3 (4); Science: 3 (3); Foreign language: 3 (4); Social studies: 3 (4); History: 3 (3); Total units: 19 (22). Tests: The college uses SAT or ACT scores in admissions decisions. Either SAT or ACT required. For admission to the fall 2011 entering class, the school will accept: ACT with or without writing accepted. Campus visit: Recommended. Admissions interview: Recommended. Off-campus interview: May be arranged. **Factors that count in admissions decisions:** *Academic:* Secondary school record: Very Important. Class rank: Important. Letters of recommendation: Important. Standardized test scores: Important. Essay: Important. *Nonacademic:* Interview: Considered. Extracurricular activities: Considered. Talent/ability: Considered. Character/personal qualities: Considered. Alumni/ae relationship: Not Considered. Geographical residence: Not Considered. State residency: Not Considered. Religious affiliation/commitment: Not Considered. Minority status: Not Considered. Volunteer work: Considered. Work experience: Considered. **Other schools with the greatest overlap in applicants:** Boston College; Boston University; Emmanuel College; Mount Holyoke College; Northeastern University. **Admissions statistics for the fall 2009 entering class:** Total applicants: 3,522. Total accepted: 2,013. Freshmen enrolled: 354; 44% were from out of state. Accepted through early-decision or early-action plans: 59%. Overall acceptance rate: 57%. Non-early acceptance rate: 57%. **Size of waiting list:** 0 applicants; enrolled from waiting list: 0. **Credentials of fall 2009 freshmen:** 19% ranked in the top 10 percent of their high school class; 55% were in the top 25 percent; 89% were in the top half. (Proportion submitting class standing: 49%.) **Average high school grade point average:** 3.2. **First-year students who submitted SAT scores:** 95%. Scores (25/75 percentile): Critical Reading: 500-590, Math: 490-600, Combined: 990-1190. **First-year students submitting ACT scores:** 23%. Scores (25/75 percentile): English: 21-27, Math: 19-25, Composite: 22-26.

ACADEMICS

Year founded: 1899. **Academic calendar:** Semester. **Degrees offered:** bachelor's, post-bachelor's certificate, master's, post-master's certificate, doctorate. **Most popular majors:** 35% health professions and related clinical sciences, 11% psychology, 11% social sciences, 9% communication, journalism, and related programs, 8% business, management, marketing, and related support services. **Major fields of study:** area, ethnic, cultural, and gender studies; biological and biomedical sciences; business, management, marketing, and related support services; communication, journalism, and related programs; computer and information sciences and support services; education; English language and literature/letters; foreign languages, literatures, and linguistics; health professions and related clinical sciences; history; mathematics and statistics; multi/interdisciplinary studies; natural resources and conservation; philosophy and religious studies; physical sciences; psychology; social sciences; visual and performing arts. **Areas of required coursework:** arts/fine arts, humanities, computer literacy, mathematics, English (including composition), philosophy, foreign languages, sciences (biological or physical), history, social science, other. **Special academic programs (% participation):** accelerated program (10%), cross-registration (25%), double major (10%), exchange student program (domestic) (10%), honors program (20%), independent study (90%), internships (70%), liberal arts/career combination (100%), student-designed major (1%), study abroad (30%), teacher certificate program (40%). **Teacher certification offered in:** early childhood, special education, elementary, middle/junior high, secondary. **Reserve Officers Training Corps (ROTC):** Army ROTC: Offered at cooperating institution (Northeastern University). **Faculty and instruction (2009-2010):** Total instructional faculty: 231 full-time, 317 part-time (25% men; 75% women; 16% minorities). Full-time faculty with Ph.D. or other terminal degree: 81%. Student/faculty ratio: 13/1. Classes of fewer than 20 students: 68%; of 20 to 49 students: 26%; of 50 or more students: 6%. **Advanced Placement and International Baccalaureate credit:** AP tests may be used for: Credit and/or placement. Scores accepted: 4, 5. International Baccalaureate exams may be used for: Credit and/or placement. **Freshmen returning for sophomore year:** 82%. **Graduation rates:** Four-year: 61%; five-year: 69%; six-year: 74%. **Graduate study:** 26% of students pursue further study immediately upon graduation; 26% within one year. Fields in which graduates pursue further study: Master of Business Administration (MBA), 4%; law, 5%; medicine, 1%; engineering, 1%; education, 21%; arts and sciences, 67%.

COSTS AND FINANCIAL AID

Financial aid office: (617) 521-2001. **Expenses (2010-2011):** Tuition and fees 2010-2011: $32,230; room/board: $12,470. Estimated books and supplies: $1,280; transportation: $800; personal expenses: $1,600. **Financial aid:** Priority filing date for institution's financial aid form: February 15; deadline: March 1. In 2009-2010, 79% of undergraduates applied for financial aid. Of those, 71% were determined to have financial need; 7% had their need fully met. Average financial aid package (proportion receiving): $21,304 (71%). Average amount of gift aid, such as scholarships or grants (proportion receiving): $14,879 (70%). Average amount of self-help aid, such as work study or loans (proportion receiving): $7,089 (67%). Average need-based loan (excluding PLUS or other private loans): $5,140. Among students who received need-based aid, the average percentage of need met: 64%. Among students who received aid based on merit, the average award (and the proportion receiving): $8,520 (19%). The average athletic scholarship (and the proportion receiving): $0 (0%). Average amount of debt of borrowers graduating in 2009: $45,237. Proportion who borrowed: 78%.

CAMPUS LIFE AND EXTRACURRICULAR ACTIVITIES

Campus housing available (% using): women's dorms (100%), special housing for disabled students, other housing options. Students who live in college-owned, operated, or affiliated housing: 48%. **Student employment:** During the 2009-2010 academic year, 33% of undergraduates worked on campus. Average per-year earnings: $2,700. **Clubs and organizations:** Number of student organizations: 79. Activities include: choral groups, dance, drama/theater, literary magazine, radio station, student government, student newspaper, student film society, symphony orchestra, yearbook. Number of fraternities: 0; sororities: 0. Average proportion of students who stay on campus on weekends: 75%. **Sports program (2009-2010):** Member of NCAA III. **Women's intercollegiate varsity sports:** basketball, crew (heavyweight), field hockey, lacrosse, crew (lightweight), soccer, softball, swimming, tennis, volleyball.

SERVICES AND FACILITIES

Basic services: nonremedial tutoring, women's center, placement service, health service, health insurance. **Remedial assistance:** other. **Counseling services:** minority student, career, personal, academic, older student, psychological, birth control, religious. **For learning-disabled students:** School does not offer a structured program with separate admission and additional fees. Total undergraduates in learning-disabled program or receiving services: 79. Services include: reading machines, tape recorders, note-taking services, oral tests, learning center, readers, extended time for tests, tutors, priority seating, substitution of courses, texts on tape, other testing accommodations, other. **Library:** Number of titles: 206,238; number of current serial subscriptions: 49,808. **Information technology resources:** Students are not required to lease or own a computer. Number of campus computers available to all students: 350. School has a wireless network. Approximate

number of users that can be accommodated: 1,000. Proportion of college-owned housing units wired for high-speed internet access: 100%. **Campus safety:** Security services offered: 24-hour foot-and-vehicle patrols, late-night transport/escort service, 24-hour emergency telephones, lighted pathways/sidewalks, controlled dormitory access (key, security card, etc).

TRANSFER AND INTERNATIONAL STUDENTS

Transfer students: May apply for admission for the following academic terms: Fall, Spring. Applicants need a minimum number of credits to apply. For fall 2009: Transfer applications received: 464. Transfer applicants offered admission: 192. Transfer applicants enrolled: 86. **International students:** Number of foreign undergraduates: 63 (3% of student body). Number of countries represented: 59. Minimum TOEFL score required: 560 (paper); 83 (computer). Average TOEFL score: 583 (paper).

Smith College

- **Address:** 7 College Lane, Northampton, MA 01063
- **Website:** http://www.smith.edu
- Private
- **Enrollment:** 2,593 full-time; 21 part-time

KEY STATS

✔ **U.S News College Ranking:** 14, National Liberal Arts Colleges
✔ **SAT Score (25th/75th percentile):** 1190-1400
✔ **Tuition:** 2010-2011: $38,898

Selectivity: More selective	**Room/board:** $13,000
Acceptance rate: 47%	**Average debt:** $21,573
Student/faculty ratio: 9/1	**Proportion who borrowed:** 62%

UNDERGRADUATE STUDENT BODY STATS

2009-2010 enrollment: 2,593 full-time; 21 part-time. Men: 0%; women: 100%. **Ethnic makeup:** African American: 7%; American-Indian: 1%; Asian American: 13%; Hispanic: 7%; White: 67%; International: 6%.

ADMISSIONS FACTS AND FIGURES

Phone: (413) 585-2500. **Email:** admission@smith.edu. **Website:** http://www.smith.edu. **Application deadlines for fall 2011:** Regular decision: January 15. Early decision: Send application by: November 15; Decision sent by: December 15. Early action: Not offered. Admission can be deferred. **Application fee:** $60. **To apply online, go to:** http://www.smith.edu/admission. **Admissions requirements/recommendations:** High school units required (recommended): English: (4); Mathematics: (3); Science: (3); Foreign language: (3); History: (2); Academic electives: (1); Total units: (16). Tests: The college uses SAT or ACT scores in admissions decisions. Neither SAT nor ACT required. For admission to the fall 2011 entering class, the school will accept: ACT with or without writing accepted. Campus visit: Recommended. Admissions interview: Recommended. Off-campus interview: May be arranged. **Factors that count in admissions decisions:** *Academic:* Secondary school record: Very Important. Class rank: Important. Letters of recommendation: Very Important. Standardized test scores: Considered. Essay: Important. *Nonacademic:* Interview: Important. Extracurricular activities: Important. Talent/ability: Important. Character/personal qualities: Very Important. Alumni/ae relationship: Considered. Geographical residence: Not Considered. State residency: Not Considered. Religious affiliation/commitment: Not Considered. Minority status: Considered. Volunteer work: Considered. Work experience: Considered. **Other schools with the greatest overlap in applicants:** Barnard College; Bryn Mawr College; Mount Holyoke College; New York University; Wellesley College. **Admissions statistics for the fall 2009 entering class:** Total applicants: 4,011. Total accepted: 1,904. Freshmen enrolled: 665; 83% were from out of state. Accepted through early-decision or early-action plans: 23%. Overall acceptance rate: 47%. Early-decision acceptance rate: 56%. Non-early acceptance rate: 47%. **Size of waiting list:** 578 applicants; enrolled from waiting list: 96. **Credentials of fall 2009 freshmen:** 66% ranked in the top 10 percent of their high school class; 94% were in the top 25 percent; 100% were in the top half. (Proportion submitting class standing: 44%.) **Average high school grade point average:** 3.9. **First-year students who submitted SAT scores:** 66%. Scores (25/75 percentile): Critical Reading: 610-710, Math: 580-690, Combined: 1190-1400. **First-year students submitting ACT scores:** 23%. Scores (25/75 percentile): English: 28-33, Math: 24-29, Composite: 27-30.

ACADEMICS

Year founded: 1871. **Academic calendar:** Semester. **Degrees offered:** bachelor's, post-bachelor's certificate, master's, post-master's certificate, doctorate. **Most popular majors:** 24% social sciences, 11% psychology, 10% area, ethnic, cultural, and gender studies, 10% visual and performing arts, 9% foreign languages, literatures, and linguistics. **Major fields of study:** architecture and related services; area, ethnic, cultural, and gender studies; biological and biomedical sciences; computer and information sciences and support services; education; engineering; English language and literature/letters; foreign languages, literatures, and linguistics; history; mathematics and statistics; multi/interdisciplinary studies; philosophy and religious studies; physical sciences; psychology; social sciences; visual and performing arts. **Pre-professional programs:** pre-law, pre-dentistry, pre-medicine, pre-theology, pre-veterinary science, pre-optometry, pre-pharmacy. **Special academic programs (% participation):** accelerated program (5%), cross-registration (34%), double major (14%), exchange student program (domestic) (1%), honors program (7%), independent study (38%), internships (63%), student-designed major (.4%), study abroad (42%), teacher certificate program (5%). **Teacher certification offered in:** elementary, middle/junior high, secondary. **Reserve Officers Training Corps (ROTC):** Army ROTC: Offered at cooperating institution (University of Massachusetts–Amherst); Air Force ROTC: Offered at cooperating institution (University of Massachusetts–Amherst). **Faculty and instruction (2009-2010):** Total instructional faculty: 281 full-time, 25 part-time (47% men; 53% women; 16% minorities). Full-time faculty with Ph.D. or other terminal degree: 98%. Student/faculty ratio: 9/1. Classes of fewer than 20 students: 67%; of 20 to 49 students: 28%; of 50 or more students: 5%. **Advanced Placement and International Baccalaureate credit:** AP tests may be used for: Credit and/or placement. Scores accepted: 4, 5. International Baccalaureate exams may be used for: Credit and/or placement. **Freshmen returning for sophomore year:** 91%. **Graduation rates:** Four-year: 78%; five-year: 83%; six-year: 84%. **Graduate study:** 69% of students pursue further study within five years.

COSTS AND FINANCIAL AID

Financial aid office: (413) 585-2530. **Expenses (2010-2011):** Tuition and fees 2010-2011: $38,898; room/board: $13,000. Estimated books and supplies: $800; transportation: $456; personal expenses: $1,220. **Financial aid:** In 2009-2010, 74% of undergraduates applied for financial aid. Of those, 63% were determined to have financial need; 100% had their need fully met. Average financial aid package (proportion receiving): $34,526 (63%). Average amount of gift aid, such as scholarships or grants (proportion receiving): $30,971 (60%). Average amount of self-help aid, such as work study or loans (proportion receiving): $6,273 (62%). Average need-based loan (excluding PLUS or other private loans): $4,567. Among students who received need-based aid, the average percentage of need met: 100%. Among students who received aid based on merit, the average award (and the proportion receiving): $9,805 (5%). The average athletic scholarship (and the proportion receiving): $0 (0%). Average amount of debt of borrowers graduating in 2009: $21,573. Proportion who borrowed: 62%.

CAMPUS LIFE AND EXTRACURRICULAR ACTIVITIES

Campus housing available (% using): women's dorms (98%), cooperative housing (1%), other housing options (1%). Students who live in college-owned, operated, or affiliated housing: 94%. **Student employment:** During the 2009-2010 academic year, 60% of undergraduates worked on campus. Average per-year earnings: $2,526. **Clubs and organizations:** Number of student organizations: 131. Activities include: campus ministries, choral groups, concert band, dance, drama/theater, international student organization, jazz band, literary magazine, music ensembles, musical theater, radio station, student government, student newspaper, television station, yearbook. Number of fraternities: 0; sororities: 0. Average proportion of students who stay on campus on weekends: 90%. **Sports program (2009-2010):** Member of NCAA III. *Women's intercollegiate varsity sports:* basketball, crew (heavyweight), cross country, equestrian, field hockey, lacrosse, skiing (alpine), soccer, softball, squash, swimming, tennis, track and field (indoor), track and field (outdoor), volleyball.

SERVICES AND FACILITIES

Basic services: nonremedial tutoring, women's center, placement service, day care, health service, health insurance, other. **Counseling services:** minority student, career, personal, academic, older student, psychological, birth control, religious. **For learning-disabled students:** School does not offer a structured program with separate admission and additional fees. Total undergraduates in learning-disabled program or receiving services: 160. Services include: reading machines, tape recorders, note-taking services, learning center, readers, extended time for tests, tutors, texts on tape,

exams on tape or computer, other testing accommodations, other. **Library:** Number of titles: 1,520,012; number of current serial subscriptions: 57,094. **Information technology resources:** Students are not required to lease or own a computer. Number of campus computers available to all students: 521. School has a wireless network. Approximate number of users that can be accommodated: 1,000. Proportion of college-owned housing units wired for high-speed internet access: 100%. **Campus safety:** Security services offered: 24-hour foot-and-vehicle patrols, late-night transport/escort service, 24-hour emergency telephones, lighted pathways/sidewalks, controlled dormitory access (key, security card, etc).

TRANSFER AND INTERNATIONAL STUDENTS

Transfer students: May apply for admission for the following academic terms: Fall, Spring. Applicants need a minimum number of credits to apply. For fall 2009: Transfer applications received: 285. Transfer applicants offered admission: 118. Transfer applicants enrolled: 59. **International students:** Number of foreign undergraduates: 123 (6% of student body). Number of countries represented: 60. Minimum TOEFL score required: 600 (paper); 95 (computer).

Springfield College

- **Address:** 263 Alden Street, Springfield, MA 01109
- **Website:** http://www.springfieldcollege.edu
- **Private**
- **Enrollment:** 3,182 full-time; 408 part-time

KEY STATS

✔ **U.S News College Ranking:** 67, Regional Universities (North)
✔ **SAT Score (25th/75th percentile):** 920-1130
✔ **Tuition:** 2010-2011: $27,585

Selectivity: Selective	**Room/board:** $9,915
Acceptance rate: 69%	**Average debt:** $38,689
Student/faculty ratio: 13/1	**Proportion who borrowed:** 88%

UNDERGRADUATE STUDENT BODY STATS

2009-2010 enrollment: 3,182 full-time; 408 part-time. Men: 41%; women: 59%. **Ethnic makeup:** African American: 14%; Hispanic: 4%; White: 82%.

ADMISSIONS FACTS AND FIGURES

Phone: (413) 748-3136. **Email:** admissions@spfldcol.edu. **Website:** http://www.springfieldcollege.edu. **Application deadlines for fall 2011:** Regular decision: April 1. Early decision: Send application by: December 1; Decision sent by: February 1. Early action: Not offered. Admission can be deferred. **Application fee:** $50. **To apply online, go to:** http://www.springfieldcollege.edu/home.nsf/admissions/undergraduate. **Admissions requirements/recommendations:** High school units required (recommended): English: 4; Mathematics: 3 (4); Science: 3 (4); Foreign language: (3); Social studies: 2 (2); History: 1; Academic electives: 1; Total units: 16. **Tests:** The college uses SAT or ACT scores in admissions decisions. Either SAT or ACT required. For admission to the fall 2011 entering class, the school will accept: ACT with writing required. Campus visit: Recommended. Admissions interview: Recommended. Off-campus interview: May be arranged. **Factors that count in admissions decisions:** *Academic:* Secondary school record: Very Important. Class rank: Considered. Letters of recommendation: Very Important. Standardized test scores: Important. Essay: Very Important. *Nonacademic:* Interview: Considered. Extracurricular activities: Very Important. Talent/ability: Considered. Character/personal qualities: Very Important. Alumni/ae relationship: Considered. Geographical residence: Considered. State residency: Not Considered. Religious affiliation/commitment: Not Considered. Minority status: Considered. Volunteer work: Important. Work experience: Important. **Other schools with the greatest overlap in applicants:** Ithaca College; Quinnipiac University; University of Connecticut; University of Massachusetts–Amherst; Western New England College. **Admissions statistics for the fall 2009 entering class:** Total applicants: 2,392. Total accepted: 1,650. Freshmen enrolled: 580; 63% were from out of state. Accepted through early-decision or early-action plans: 10%. Overall acceptance rate: 69%. Early-decision acceptance rate: 65%. Non-early acceptance rate: 69%. **Size of waiting list:** 30 applicants; enrolled from waiting list: 5. **Credentials of fall 2009 freshmen:** 13% ranked in the top 10 percent of their high school class; 38% were in the top 25 percent; 70% were in the top half. (Proportion submitting class standing: 65%.) **First-year**

students who submitted SAT scores: 98%. Scores (25/75 percentile): Critical Reading: 450-550, Math: 470-580, Combined: 920-1130.

ACADEMICS

Year founded: 1885. **Academic calendar:** Semester. **Degrees offered:** certificate, bachelor's, master's, post-master's certificate, doctorate. **Most popular majors:** 34% parks, recreation, leisure, and fitness studies, 26% health professions and related clinical sciences, 9% psychology, 8% business, management, marketing, and related support services, 5% liberal arts and sciences studies, and humanities. **Major fields of study:** area, ethnic, cultural, and gender studies; biological and biomedical sciences; business, management, marketing, and related support services; communication, journalism, and related programs; computer and information sciences and support services; education; English language and literature/letters; health professions and related clinical sciences; liberal arts and sciences studies, and humanities; mathematics and statistics; multi/interdisciplinary studies; natural resources and conservation; parks, recreation, leisure, and fitness studies; physical sciences; psychology; public administration and social service professions; security and protective services; social sciences; visual and performing arts. **Areas of required coursework:** arts/fine arts, humanities, computer literacy, mathematics, English (including composition), philosophy, foreign languages, sciences (biological or physical), history, social science, other. **Special academic programs (% participation):** cross-registration (8%), double major (7%), English as a Second Language (ESL) (0%), independent study (10%), internships (40%), study abroad (4%), teacher certificate program (23%). **Teacher certification offered in:** early childhood, special education, elementary, middle/junior high, secondary. **Reserve Officers Training Corps (ROTC):** Army ROTC: Offered at cooperating institution (Western New England College); Air Force ROTC: Offered at cooperating institution (Western New England College). **Faculty and instruction (2009-2010):** Total instructional faculty: 210 full-time, 461 part-time (44% men; 56% women; 29% minorities). Full-time faculty with Ph.D. or other terminal degree: 83%. Student/faculty ratio: 13/1. Classes of fewer than 20 students: 47%; of 20 to 49 students: 51%; of 50 or more students: 2%. **Advanced Placement and International Baccalaureate credit:** AP tests may be used for: Credit only. Scores accepted: 3, 4, 5. International Baccalaureate exams may be used for: Credit only. **Freshmen returning for sophomore year:** 82%. **Graduation rates:** Four-year: 55%; five-year: 66%; six-year: 66%. **Graduate study:** 49% of students pursue further study immediately upon graduation; 53% within one year; 53% within five years. Fields in which graduates pursue further study: Master of Business Administration (MBA), 2%; law, 1%; medicine, 1%; dentistry, 1%; education, 12%; arts and sciences, 30%.

COSTS AND FINANCIAL AID

Financial aid office: (413) 748-3108. **Expenses (2010-2011):** Tuition and fees 2010-2011: $27,585; room/board: $9,915. Estimated books and supplies: $900; transportation: $700; personal expenses: $1,200. **Financial aid:** Priority filing date for institution's financial aid form: March 15. In 2009-2010, 92% of undergraduates applied for financial aid. Of those, 82% were determined to have financial need; 11% had their need fully met. Average financial aid package (proportion receiving): $19,104 (82%). Average amount of gift aid, such as scholarships or grants (proportion receiving): $14,054 (81%). Average amount of self-help aid, such as work study or loans (proportion receiving): $5,635 (76%). Average need-based loan (excluding PLUS or other private loans): $4,509. Among students who received need-based aid, the average percentage of need met: 75%. Among students who received aid based on merit, the average award (and the proportion receiving): $5,783 (11%). The average athletic scholarship (and the proportion receiving): $0 (0%). Average amount of debt of borrowers graduating in 2009: $38,689. Proportion who borrowed: 88%.

CAMPUS LIFE AND EXTRACURRICULAR ACTIVITIES

Campus housing available (% using): coed dorms (57%), men's dorms (13%), apartment for single students (27%), special housing for disabled students (1%). Students who live in college-owned, operated, or affiliated housing: 54%. **Student employment:** During the 2009-2010 academic year, 22% of undergraduates worked on campus. Average per-year earnings: $1,600. **Clubs and organizations:** Number of student organizations: 50. Activities include: campus ministries, choral groups, dance, drama/theater, international student organization, jazz band, literary magazine, music ensembles, musical theater, radio station, student government, student newspaper, yearbook. Number of fraternities: 0; sororities: 0. Average proportion of students who stay on campus on weekends: 65%. **Sports program (2009-2010):** Member of NCAA III. **Men's intercollegiate varsity sports:** baseball, basketball, cross country, football, golf, gymnastics, lacrosse, soccer, swim-

ming, tennis, track and field (indoor), track and field (outdoor), volleyball, wrestling. **Women's intercollegiate varsity sports:** basketball, cross country, field hockey, gymnastics, lacrosse, soccer, softball, swimming, tennis, track and field (indoor), track and field (outdoor), volleyball.

SERVICES AND FACILITIES

Basic services: nonremedial tutoring, placement service, day care, health service, health insurance, other. **Remedial assistance:** reading, math, writing, study skills, other. **Counseling services:** minority student, career, personal, academic, psychological, birth control, religious. **For learning-disabled students:** School does not offer a structured program with separate admission and additional fees. Total undergraduates in learning-disabled program or receiving services: 98. Services include: remedial math, remedial English, reading machines, tape recorders, untimed tests, note-taking services, learning center, readers, extended time for tests, tutors, texts on tape, other testing accommodations, other. **Library:** Number of titles: 102,928; number of current serial subscriptions: 579. **Information technology resources:** Students are not required to lease or own a computer. Number of campus computers available to all students: 625. School has a wireless network. Approximate number of users that can be accommodated: 1,500. Proportion of college-owned housing units wired for high-speed internet access: 100%. **Campus safety:** Security services offered: 24-hour foot-and-vehicle patrols, late-night transport/escort service, 24-hour emergency telephones, lighted pathways/sidewalks, student patrols, controlled dormitory access (key, security card, etc).

TRANSFER AND INTERNATIONAL STUDENTS

Transfer students: May apply for admission for the following academic terms: Fall, Spring. Applicants do not need a minimum number of credits to apply. For fall 2009: Transfer applications received: 213. Transfer applicants offered admission: 134. Transfer applicants enrolled: 95. **International students:** Number of foreign undergraduates: 2. Number of countries represented: 8. Minimum TOEFL score required: 525 (paper); 69 (computer). Average TOEFL score: 530 (paper).

Stonehill College

- **Address:** 320 Washington Street, Easton, MA 02357
- **Website:** http://www.stonehill.edu
- **Private; Religious affiliation:** Roman Catholic
- **Enrollment:** 2,420 full-time; 48 part-time

KEY STATS

✔ **U.S News College Ranking:** 105, National Liberal Arts Colleges
✔ **SAT Score (25th/75th percentile):** 1120-1280
✔ **Tuition:** 2010-2011: $32,620

Selectivity: More selective	**Room/board:** $12,610	
Acceptance rate: 56%	**Average debt:** $29,163	
Student/faculty ratio: 13/1	**Proportion who borrowed:** 73%	

UNDERGRADUATE STUDENT BODY STATS

2009-2010 enrollment: 2,420 full-time; 48 part-time. Men: 40%; women: 60%. **Ethnic makeup:** African American: 3%; Asian American: 1%; Hispanic: 4%; White: 92%. **Religious preference:** Protestant: 8%; Jewish: 1%; No preference: 13%; Roman Catholic: 71%; Greek Orthodox: 1%; Other: 6%.

ADMISSIONS FACTS AND FIGURES

Phone: (508) 565-1373. **Email:** admissions@stonehill.edu. **Website:** http://www.stonehill.edu. **Application deadlines for fall 2011:** Regular decision: January 15; decision sent by March 15. Early decision: Send application by: November 1; Decision sent by: December 25. Early action: Send application by: November 1; Decision sent by: January 15. Admission can be deferred. **Application fee:** $60. **To apply online, go to:** http://www.commonapp.org/. **Admissions requirements/recommendations:** High school units required (recommended): English: 4 (4); Mathematics: 3 (4); Science: 1 (3); Foreign language: 2 (3); History: 3 (3); Academic electives: 3 (3); Total units: 16 (20). Tests: The college uses SAT or ACT scores in admissions decisions. Neither SAT nor ACT required. For admission to the fall 2011 entering class, the school will accept: ACT with writing recommended. Campus visit: Recommended. Admissions interview: Neither required nor recommended. Off-campus interview: Not available. **Factors that count in admissions decisions: Academic:** Secondary school record: Very Important. Class rank: Very

Important. Letters of recommendation: Important. Standardized test scores: Considered. Essay: Important. *Nonacademic:* Interview: Not Considered. Extracurricular activities: Important. Talent/ability: Very Important. Character/personal qualities: Very Important. Alumni/ae relationship: Considered. Geographical residence: Considered. State residency: Not Considered. Religious affiliation/commitment: Considered. Minority status: Considered. Volunteer work: Important. Work experience: Important. **Other schools with the greatest overlap in applicants:** Bentley University; Boston College; College of the Holy Cross; Northeastern University; Providence College. **Admissions statistics for the fall 2009 entering class:** Total applicants: 5,871. Total accepted: 3,313. Freshmen enrolled: 684; 48% were from out of state. Accepted through early-decision or early-action plans: 48%. Overall acceptance rate: 56%. Early-decision acceptance rate: 80%. Non-early acceptance rate: 52%. **Size of waiting list:** 997 applicants; enrolled from waiting list: 9. Credentials of fall 2009 freshmen: 50% ranked in the top 10 percent of their high school class; 87% were in the top 25 percent; 99% were in the top half. (Proportion submitting class standing: 54%.) **Average high school grade point average:** 3.5. **First-year students who submitted SAT scores:** 58%. Scores (25/75 percentile): Critical Reading: 550-630, Math: 570-650, Combined: 1120-1280. **First-year students submitting ACT scores:** 17%. Scores (25/75 percentile): English: N/A, Math: N/A, Composite: 24-28.

ACADEMICS

Year founded: 1948. **Academic calendar:** Semester. **Degrees offered:** bachelor's. **Most popular majors:** 24% business, management, marketing, and related support services, 15% social sciences, 11% psychology, 8% communication, journalism, and related programs, 7% education. **Major fields of study:** area, ethnic, cultural, and gender studies; biological and biomedical sciences; business, management, marketing, and related support services; communication, journalism, and related programs; computer and information sciences and support services; education; engineering; English language and literature/letters; foreign languages, literatures, and linguistics; health professions and related clinical sciences; history; mathematics and statistics; multi/interdisciplinary studies; philosophy and religious studies; physical sciences; psychology; public administration and social service professions; security and protective services; social sciences; visual and performing arts. **Areas of required coursework:** mathematics, English (including composition), philosophy, foreign languages, sciences (biological or physical), history, social science, other. **Special academic programs (% participation):** cross-registration (4%), double major (19%), dual enrollment (5%), honors program (8%), independent study (19%), internships (51%), liberal arts/career combination (0%), student-designed major (1%), study abroad (40%), teacher certificate program (10%). **Teacher certification offered in:** early childhood, elementary, secondary. **Reserve Officers Training Corps (ROTC):** Army ROTC: Offered on campus. **Faculty and instruction (2009-2010):** Total instructional faculty: 152 full-time, 103 part-time (62% men; 38% women; 8% minorities). Full-time faculty with Ph.D. or other terminal degree: 82%. Student/faculty ratio: 13/1. Classes of fewer than 20 students: 42%; of 20 to 49 students: 57%; of 50 or more students: 0%. **Advanced Placement and International Baccalaureate credit:** AP tests may be used for: Credit only. Scores accepted: 4, 5. International Baccalaureate exams may be used for: Credit only. **Freshmen returning for sophomore year:** 88%. **Graduation rates:** Four-year: 80%; five-year: 82%; six-year: 82%. **Graduate study:** 23% of students pursue further study immediately upon graduation; 32% within one year. Fields in which graduates pursue further study: Master of Business Administration (MBA), 1%; law, 2%; education, 4%; arts and sciences, 23%.

COSTS AND FINANCIAL AID

Financial aid office: (508) 565-1088. **Expenses (2010-2011):** Tuition and fees 2010-2011: $32,620; room/board: $12,610. Estimated books and supplies: $1,200; transportation: $180; personal expenses: $860. **Financial aid:** Priority filing date for institution's financial aid form: February 1; deadline: February 1. In 2009-2010, 81% of undergraduates applied for financial aid. Of those, 67% were determined to have financial need; 18% had their need fully met. Average financial aid package (proportion receiving): $20,972 (67%). Average amount of gift aid, such as scholarships or grants (proportion receiving): $16,617 (64%). Average amount of self-help aid, such as work study or loans (proportion receiving): $5,773 (60%). Average need-based loan (excluding PLUS or other private loans): $4,820. Among students who received need-based aid, the average percentage of need met: 74%. Among students who received aid based on merit, the average award (and the proportion receiving): $8,861 (19%). The average athletic scholarship (and the proportion receiving): $12,127 (3%). Average amount of debt of borrowers graduating in 2009: $29,163. Proportion who borrowed: 73%.

CAMPUS LIFE AND EXTRACURRICULAR ACTIVITIES

Campus housing available (% using): coed dorms (92%), women's dorms (4%), special housing for disabled students, other housing options (4%). Students who live in college-owned, operated, or affiliated housing: 88%. **Student employment:** During the 2009-2010 academic year, 36% of undergraduates worked on campus. Average per-year earnings: $2,235. **Clubs and organizations:** Number of student organizations: 74. Activities include: campus ministries, choral groups, dance, drama/theater, literary magazine, music ensembles, musical theater, pep band, radio station, student government, student newspaper, student film society, yearbook. Number of fraternities: 0; sororities: 0. Average proportion of students who stay on campus on weekends: 80%. **Sports program (2009-2010):** Member of NCAA II. *Men's intercollegiate varsity sports:* baseball, basketball, cross country, football, ice hockey, soccer, tennis, track and field (indoor), track and field (outdoor). *Women's intercollegiate varsity sports:* basketball, cross country, equestrian, field hockey, lacrosse, soccer, softball, tennis, track and field (indoor), track and field (outdoor), volleyball.

SERVICES AND FACILITIES

Basic services: nonremedial tutoring, women's center, placement service, day care, health service, health insurance. **Counseling services:** minority student, career, military, personal, academic, older student, psychological, religious. **For learning-disabled students:** School does not offer a structured program with separate admission and additional fees. Total undergraduates in learning-disabled program or receiving services: 87. Services include: reading machines, tape recorders, diagnostic testing service, note-taking services, learning center, readers, extended time for tests, tutors, priority seating, texts on tape, exams on tape or computer, other testing accommodations, other. **Library:** Number of titles: 247,023; number of current serial subscriptions: 13,488. **Information technology resources:** Students are not required to lease or own a computer. Number of campus computers available to all students: 370. School has a wireless network. Approximate number of users that can be accommodated: 1,000. Proportion of college-owned housing units wired for high-speed internet access: 100%. **Campus safety:** Security services offered: 24-hour foot-and-vehicle patrols, late-night transport/escort service, 24-hour emergency telephones, lighted pathways/sidewalks, controlled dormitory access (key, security card, etc).

TRANSFER AND INTERNATIONAL STUDENTS

Transfer students: May apply for admission for the following academic terms: Fall, Spring. Applicants do not need a minimum number of credits to apply. For fall 2009: Transfer applications received: 136. Transfer applicants offered admission: 72. Transfer applicants enrolled: 23. **International students:** Number of foreign undergraduates: 10. Number of countries represented: 10. Minimum TOEFL score required: 550 (paper); 213 (computer).

Suffolk University

- **Address:** 8 Ashburton Place, Boston, MA 02108
- **Website:** http://www.suffolk.edu
- **Private**
- **Enrollment:** 5,291 full-time; 481 part-time

KEY STATS

✔ **U.S News College Ranking:** 46, Regional Universities (North)
✔ **SAT Score (25th/75th percentile):** 900-1120
✔ **Tuition:** 2010-2011: $28,526

Selectivity: Selective	Room/board: $14,624
Acceptance rate: 85%	Average debt: N/A
Student/faculty ratio: 13/1	Proportion who borrowed: 73%

UNDERGRADUATE STUDENT BODY STATS

2009-2010 enrollment: 5,291 full-time; 481 part-time. Men: 44%; women: 56%. **Ethnic makeup:** African American: 4%; Asian American: 7%; Hispanic: 7%; White: 71%; International: 10%.

ADMISSIONS FACTS AND FIGURES

Phone: (617) 573-8460. **Email:** admission@suffolk.edu. **Website:** http://www.suffolk.edu. **Application deadlines for fall 2011:** Regular decision: March 1. Early decision: Not offered. Early action: Send application by: November 15; Decision sent by: December 20. Admission can be deferred. **Application fee:** $50. **To apply online, go to:** http://www.commonapp.org. **Admissions requirements/recommendations:** High school units required (recommended): English: 4 (4); Mathematics: 3 (4); Science: 2 (4); Foreign language: 2 (3); History: 1 (4); Academic electives: 4 (4); Total units: 17 (22). Tests: The college uses SAT or ACT scores in admissions decisions. Either SAT or ACT required. For admission to the fall 2011 entering class, the school will accept: ACT with writing required. Campus visit: Recommended. Admissions interview: Recommended. Off-campus interview: May be arranged. **Factors that count in admissions decisions:** *Academic:* Secondary school record: Very Important. Class rank: Important. Letters of recommendation: Important. Standardized test scores: Important. Essay: Considered. *Nonacademic:* Interview: Considered. Extracurricular activities: Considered. Talent/ability: Considered. Character/personal qualities: Important. Alumni/ae relationship: Considered. Geographical residence: Considered. State residency: Not Considered. Religious affiliation/commitment: Not Considered. Minority status: Not Considered. Volunteer work: Considered. Work experience: Considered. **Other schools with the greatest overlap in applicants:** Bentley University; Boston University; Emerson College; Emmanuel College; Northeastern University. **Admissions statistics for the fall 2009 entering class:** Total applicants: 9,036. Total accepted: 7,661. Freshmen enrolled: 1,254; 36% were from out of state. Accepted through early-decision or early-action plans: 29%. Overall acceptance rate: 85%. Non-early acceptance rate: 92%. **Size of waiting list:** 163 applicants; enrolled from waiting list: 79. **Credentials of fall 2009 freshmen:** 12% ranked in the top 10 percent of their high school class; 38% were in the top 25 percent; 73% were in the top half. (Proportion submitting class standing: 47%.) **Average high school grade point average:** 3.0. **First-year students who submitted SAT scores:** 92%. Scores (25/75 percentile): Critical Reading: 450-560, Math: 450-560, Combined: 900-1120. **First-year students submitting ACT scores:** 12%. Scores (25/75 percentile): English: N/A, Math: N/A, Composite: 19-24.

ACADEMICS

Year founded: 1906. **Academic calendar:** Semester. **Degrees offered:** certificate, diploma, associate, bachelor's, post-bachelor's certificate, master's, post-master's certificate, doctorate. **Most popular majors:** 39% business, management, marketing, and related support services, 16% social sciences, 15% communication, journalism, and related programs, 6% visual and performing arts, 5% psychology. **Major fields of study:** area, ethnic, cultural, and gender studies; biological and biomedical sciences; business, management, marketing, and related support services; communication, journalism, and related programs; communications technologies/technicians and support services; computer and information sciences and support services; education; engineering; engineering technologies/technicians; English language and literature/letters; foreign languages, literatures, and linguistics; history; legal professions and studies; liberal arts and sciences studies, and humanities; mathematics and statistics; natural resources and conservation; philosophy and religious studies; physical sciences; psychology; public administration and social service professions; security and protective services; social sciences; visual and performing arts. **Areas of required coursework:** humanities, computer literacy, mathematics, English (including composition), philosophy, foreign languages, sciences (biological or physical), social science. **Pre-professional programs:** pre-law, pre-medicine. **Special academic programs (% participation):** accelerated program, cooperative (work-study plan) program (55%), cross-registration, distance learning, double major (10%), dual enrollment, English as a Second Language (ESL), honors program (7%), independent study (20%), internships (73%), liberal arts/career combination, study abroad (12%). **Teacher certification offered in:** elementary, middle/junior high, secondary. **Cooperative education programs:** art, business, computer science, education, engineering, health professions, humanities, natural science, social/behavioral science, other. **Reserve Officers Training Corps (ROTC):** Army ROTC: Offered at cooperating institution (Northeastern University). **Faculty and instruction (2009-2010):** Total instructional faculty: 425 full-time, 564 part-time (59% men; 41% women; 12% minorities). Full-time faculty with Ph.D. or other terminal degree: 91%. Student/faculty ratio: 13/1. Classes of fewer than 20 students: 54%; of 20 to 49 students: 45%; of 50 or more students: 1%. **Advanced Placement and International Baccalaureate credit:** AP tests may be used for: Placement only. Scores accepted: 3, 4, 5. International Baccalaureate exams may be used for: Placement only. **Freshmen returning for sophomore year:** 72%. **Graduation rates:** Four-year: 36%; five-year: 51%; six-year: 52%. **Graduate study:** 33% of students pursue further study immediately upon graduation. Fields in which graduates pursue further study: Master of Business Administration (MBA), 38%; law, 15%; medicine, 7%; education, 5%; arts and sciences, 40%.•

COSTS AND FINANCIAL AID

Financial aid office: (617) 573-8470. **Expenses (2010-2011):** Tuition and fees 2010-2011: $28,526; room/board: $14,624. Estimated books and supplies: $1,200; transportation: $250; personal expenses: $2,233. **Financial aid:** Priority filing date for institution's financial aid form: March 1; deadline: March 1. In 2009-2010, 71% of undergraduates applied for financial aid. Of those, 61% were determined to have financial need; 12% had their need fully met. Average financial aid package (proportion receiving): $19,274 (61%). Average amount of gift aid, such as scholarships or grants (proportion receiving): $11,574 (56%). Average amount of self-help aid, such as work study or loans (proportion receiving): $6,068 (57%). Average need-based loan (excluding PLUS or other private loans): $4,603. Among students who received need-based aid, the average percentage of need met: 70%. Among students who received aid based on merit, the average award (and the proportion receiving): $8,195 (9%). Proportion who borrowed: 73%.

CAMPUS LIFE AND EXTRACURRICULAR ACTIVITIES

Campus housing available (% using): coed dorms (83%), apartment for single students (17%). Students who live in college-owned, operated, or affiliated housing: 23%. **Student employment:** During the 2009-2010 academic year, 16% of undergraduates worked on campus. Average per-year earnings: $2,159. **Clubs and organizations:** Number of student organizations: 75. Activities include: campus ministries, choral groups, dance, drama/theater, international student organization, literary magazine, music ensembles, musical theater, radio station, student government, student newspaper, student film society, television station, yearbook. Number of fraternities: 1; sororities: 1. Proportion of men in fraternities: 1%; of women in sororities: 1%. Average proportion of students who stay on campus on weekends: 50%. **Sports program (2009-2010):** Member of NCAA III. *Men's intercollegiate varsity sports:* baseball, basketball, cross country, golf, ice hockey, soccer, tennis. *Women's intercollegiate varsity sports:* basketball, cross country, soccer, softball, tennis, volleyball.

SERVICES AND FACILITIES

Basic services: nonremedial tutoring, women's center, placement service, health service, health insurance. **Remedial assistance:** reading, math, writing, study skills. **Counseling services:** minority student, career, personal, veteran student, academic, older student, psychological, birth control, religious. **For learning-disabled students:** School does not offer a structured program with separate admission and additional fees. Total undergraduates in learning-disabled program or receiving services: 146. Services include: remedial math, remedial English, reading machines, remedial reading, tape recorders, untimed tests, note-taking services, oral tests, learning center, readers, extended time for tests, tutors, priority registration, priority seating, texts on tape, other testing accommodations, other. **Library:** Number of titles: 134,401; number of current serial subscriptions: 23,743. **Information technology resources:** Students are not required to lease or own a computer. Number of campus computers available to all students: 539. School has a wireless network. Approximate number of users that can be accommodated: 8,300. Proportion of college-owned housing units wired for high-speed internet access: 100%. **Campus safety:** Security services offered: 24-hour foot-and-vehicle patrols, late-night transport/escort service, 24-hour emergency telephones, lighted pathways/sidewalks, controlled dormitory access (key, security card, etc).

TRANSFER AND INTERNATIONAL STUDENTS

Transfer students: May apply for admission for the following academic terms: Fall, Spring, Summer. Applicants do not need a minimum number of credits to apply. For fall 2009: Transfer applications received: 1,369. Transfer applicants offered admission: 965. Transfer applicants enrolled: 418. **International students:** Number of foreign undergraduates: 569 (10% of student body). Number of countries represented: 101. Minimum TOEFL score required: 525 (paper); 197 (computer). Average TOEFL score: 534 (paper).

Tufts University

- **Address:** Medford, MA 02155
- **Website:** http://www.tufts.edu
- **Private**
- **Enrollment:** 5,111 full-time; 53 part-time

KEY STATS

✔ **U.S News College Ranking:** 28, National Universities
✔ **SAT Score (25th/75th percentile):** 1360-1500
✔ **Tuition:** 2010-2011: $41,598

Selectivity: Most selective   **Room/board:** $11,268
Acceptance rate: 27%   **Average debt:** $23,731
Student/faculty ratio: 9/1   **Proportion who borrowed:** 41%

UNDERGRADUATE STUDENT BODY STATS

2009-2010 enrollment: 5,111 full-time; 53 part-time. Men: 49%; women: 51%. **Ethnic makeup:** African American: 5%; Asian American: 13%; Hispanic: 6%; White: 70%; International: 6%.

ADMISSIONS FACTS AND FIGURES

Phone: (617) 627-3170. **Email:** admissions.inquiry@ase.tufts.edu. **Website:** http://www.tufts.edu. **Application deadlines for fall 2011:** Regular decision: January 1; decision sent by April 1. Early decision: Send application by: November 1; Decision sent by: December 15. Early action: Not offered. Admission can be deferred. **Application fee:** $70. **To apply online, go to:** http://admissions.tufts.edu/?pid=122. **Admissions requirements/recommendations:** High school units required (recommended): English: (4); Mathematics: (4); Science: (4); Foreign language: (4); Social studies: (4); History: (4); Total units: (24). Tests: The college uses SAT or ACT scores in admissions decisions. Either SAT or ACT required. For admission to the fall 2011 entering class, the school will accept: ACT with writing required. Campus visit: Recommended. Admissions interview: Recommended. **Factors that count in admissions decisions: *Academic:*** Secondary school record: Very Important. Class rank: Important. Letters of recommendation: Important. Standardized test scores: Important. Essay: Very Important. ***Nonacademic:*** Interview: Considered. Extracurricular activities: Important. Talent/ability: Important. Character/personal qualities: Very Important. Alumni/ae relationship: Considered. Geographical residence: Considered. State residency: Not Considered. Religious affiliation/commitment: Not Considered. Minority status: Considered. Volunteer work: Important. Work experience: Important. **Other schools with the greatest overlap in applicants:** Boston College; Boston College; Brown University; Brown University; Brown University; Brown University; Brown University; Brown University; Cornell University; Cornell University; Cornell University; Cornell University; Cornell University; Cornell University; Georgetown University; Georgetown University; Georgetown University; Georgetown University; Georgetown University; Georgetown University; University of Pennsylvania; University of Pennsylvania; University of Pennsylvania; University of Pennsylvania; University of Pennsylvania; University of Pennsylvania. **Admissions statistics for the fall 2009 entering class:** Total applicants: 15,042. Total accepted: 3,995. Freshmen enrolled: 1,314; 77% were from out of state. Overall acceptance rate: 27%. Non-early acceptance rate: 27%. **Credentials of fall 2009 freshmen:** 85% ranked in the top 10 percent of their high school class; 98% were in the top 25 percent; 100% were in the top half. (Proportion submitting class standing: 51%.) **First-year students who submitted SAT scores:** 73%. Scores (25/75 percentile): Critical Reading: 680-750; Math: 680-750; Combined: 1360-1500. **First-year students submitting ACT scores:** 27%. Scores (25/75 percentile): English: N/A, Math: N/A, Composite: 30-33.

ACADEMICS

Year founded: 1852. **Academic calendar:** Semester. **Degrees offered:** bachelor's, master's, post-master's certificate, doctorate. **Most popular majors:** 13% international relations and affairs, 11% economics, 10% biology, 9% psychology, 8% political science and government. **Major fields of study:** agriculture, agriculture operations, and related sciences; area, ethnic, cultural, and gender studies; biological and biomedical sciences; computer and information sciences and support services; education; engineering; English language and literature/letters; foreign languages, literatures, and linguistics; history; liberal arts and sciences studies, and humanities; mathematics and statistics; multi/interdisciplinary studies; philosophy and religious studies; physical sciences; psychology; social sciences; visual and performing arts. **Areas of required coursework:** arts/fine arts, humanities, mathematics, English (including composition), foreign languages, sciences (biological or physical), social science, other. **Pre-professional programs:** pre-law, pre-medicine. **Special academic programs:** cross-registration, double major, exchange student program (domestic), independent study, internships, liberal arts/career combination, student-designed major, study abroad, teacher certificate program, other. **Teacher certification offered in:** early childhood, special education, elementary, middle/junior high, secondary. **Reserve Officers Training Corps (ROTC):** Army ROTC: Offered at cooperating institution (Massachusetts Institute of Technology); Navy ROTC: Offered at cooperating institution (Massachusetts Institute of Technology); Air Force ROTC: Offered at cooperating institution (Massachusetts Institute of Technology). **Faculty and instruction (2009-2010):** Total instructional faculty: 675 full-time, 422 part-time (56% men; 44% women; 18% minorities). Full-time faculty with Ph.D. or other terminal degree: 95%. Student/faculty ratio: 9/1. Classes of fewer than 20 students: 71%; of 20 to 49 students: 25%; of 50 or more students: 5%. **Advanced Placement and International Baccalaureate credit:** AP tests may be used for: Credit and/or placement. Scores accepted: 4, 5. International Baccalaureate exams may be used for: Credit and/or placement. **Freshmen returning for sophomore year:** 96%. **Graduation rates:** Four-year: 85%; five-year: 89%; six-year: 91%.

COSTS AND FINANCIAL AID

Financial aid office: (617) 627-2000. **Expenses (2010-2011):** Tuition and fees 2010-2011: $41,598; room/board: $11,268. Estimated books and supplies: $800; transportation: $200; personal expenses: $1,334. **Financial aid:** Priority filing date for institution's financial aid form: February 15; deadline: February 15. In 2009-2010, 47% of undergraduates applied for financial aid. Of those, 41% were determined to have financial need; 97% had their need fully met. Average financial aid package (proportion receiving): $30,974 (41%). Average amount of gift aid, such as scholarships or grants (proportion receiving): $28,112 (36%). Average amount of self-help aid, such as work study or loans (proportion receiving): $5,409 (37%). Average need-based loan (excluding PLUS or other private loans): $3,846. Among students who received need-based aid, the average percentage of need met: 100%. Among students who received aid based on merit, the average award (and the proportion receiving): $500 (1%). The average athletic scholarship (and the proportion receiving): $0 (0%). Average amount of debt of borrowers graduating in 2009: $23,731. Proportion who borrowed: 41%.

CAMPUS LIFE AND EXTRACURRICULAR ACTIVITIES

Campus housing available: coed dorms, women's dorms, sorority housing, fraternity housing, apartment for single students, special housing for disabled students, cooperative housing, other housing options. Students who live in college-owned, operated, or affiliated housing: 64%. **Student employment:** During the 2009-2010 academic year, 36% of undergraduates worked on campus. Average per-year earnings: $2,000. **Clubs and organizations:** Number of student organizations: 241. Activities include: campus ministries, choral groups, concert band, dance, drama/theater, international student organization, jazz band, literary magazine, marching band, music ensembles, musical theater, pep band, radio station, student government, student newspaper, student film society, symphony orchestra, television station, yearbook. Number of fraternities: 11; sororities: 5. Proportion of men in fraternities: 20%; of women in sororities: 7%. **Sports program (2009-2010):** Member of NCAA III. ***Men's intercollegiate varsity sports:*** baseball, basketball, cross country, football, ice hockey, lacrosse, soccer, swimming, tennis, track and field (indoor), track and field (outdoor). ***Women's intercollegiate varsity sports:*** basketball, crew (heavyweight), cross country, fencing, field hockey, lacrosse, crew (lightweight), soccer, softball, squash, swimming, tennis, track and field (indoor), track and field (outdoor), volleyball.

SERVICES AND FACILITIES

Basic services: nonremedial tutoring, women's center, placement service, day care, health service, health insurance. **Counseling services:** minority student, career, military, personal, veteran student, academic, older student, psychological, birth control, religious. **For learning-disabled students:** School does not offer a structured program with separate admission and additional fees. Services include: tape recorders, note-taking services, oral tests, learning center, readers, extended time for tests, tutors. **Library:** Number of titles: 3,117,483; number of current serial subscriptions: 2,542. **Information technology resources:** Students are not required to lease or own a computer. School has a wireless network. Proportion of college-owned housing units wired for high-speed internet access: 100%. **Campus safety:** Security services offered: 24-hour foot-and-vehicle patrols, late-night transport/escort service, 24-hour emergency telephones, lighted pathways/sidewalks, controlled dormitory access (key, security card, etc).

TRANSFER AND INTERNATIONAL STUDENTS

Transfer students: May apply for admission for the following academic terms: Fall. Applicants do not need a minimum number of credits to apply. For fall 2009: Transfer applications received: 700. Transfer applicants offered admission: 179. Transfer applicants enrolled: 71. **International students:** Number of foreign undergraduates: 303 (6% of student body). Number of countries represented: 67. Minimum TOEFL score required: 600 (paper); 250 (computer). Average TOEFL score: 643 (paper).

University of Massachusetts—Amherst

- **Address:** University Admissions Center, 37 Mather Drive, Amherst, MA 01003-9313
- **Website:** http://www.umass.edu
- **Public**
- **Enrollment:** 19,315 full-time; 1,558 part-time

KEY STATS

✔ **U.S News College Ranking:** 99, National Universities
✔ **SAT Score (25th/75th percentile):** 1060-1280
✔ **Tuition:** 2010-2011: $12,084 in state, $20,307 out of state
  Selectivity: More selective   **Room/board:** $8,814
  Acceptance rate: 67%   **Average debt:** $23,847
  Student/faculty ratio: 18/1   **Proportion who borrowed:** 67%

UNDERGRADUATE STUDENT BODY STATS

2009-2010 enrollment: 19,315 full-time; 1,558 part-time. Men: 50%; women: 50%. **Ethnic makeup:** African American: 5%; Asian American: 8%; Hispanic: 4%; White: 81%; International: 1%.

ADMISSIONS FACTS AND FIGURES

Phone: (413) 545-0222. **Email:** mail@admissions.umass.edu. **Website:** http://www.umass.edu. **Application deadlines for fall 2011:** Regular decision: January 15. Early decision: Not offered. Early action: Send application by: November 1; Decision sent by: December 15. Admission can be deferred. **Application fee:** $40. **To apply online, go to:** http://www.umass.edu/admissions/applying/. **Admissions requirements/recommendations:** High school units required (recommended): English: 4; Mathematics: 3; Science: 3; Foreign language: 2; Social studies: 2; Academic electives: 2; Total units: 16. Tests: The college uses SAT or ACT scores in admissions decisions. Either SAT or ACT required. For admission to the fall 2011 entering class, the school will accept: ACT with writing recommended. Campus visit: Recommended. Admissions interview: Neither required nor recommended. Off-campus interview: Not available. **Factors that count in admissions decisions:** *Academic:* Secondary school record: Very Important. Class rank: Important. Letters of recommendation: Considered. Standardized test scores: Important. Essay: Considered. *Nonacademic:* Interview: Not Considered. Extracurricular activities: Considered. Talent/ability: Considered. Character/personal qualities: Considered. Alumni/ae relationship: Not Considered. Geographical residence: Considered. State residency: Considered. Religious affiliation/commitment: Not Considered. Minority status: Considered. Volunteer work: Considered. Work experience: Considered. **Other schools with the greatest overlap in applicants:** Boston College; Boston University; University of Connecticut; University of New Hampshire; University of Vermont. **Admissions statistics for the fall 2009 entering class:** Total applicants: 29,452. Total accepted: 19,703. Freshmen enrolled: 4,124; 23% were from out of state. Accepted through early-decision or early-action plans: 31%. Overall acceptance rate: 67%. Non-early acceptance rate: 66%. **Size of waiting list:** 3997 applicants; enrolled from waiting list: 170. **Credentials of fall 2009 freshmen:** 27% ranked in the top 10 percent of their high school class; 67% were in the top 25 percent; 97% were in the top half. (Proportion submitting class standing: 43%.) **Average high school grade point average:** 3.6. **First-year students who submitted SAT scores:** 97%. Scores (25/75 percentile): Critical Reading: 520-630, Math: 540-650, Combined: 1060-1280. **First-year students submitting ACT scores:** 13%. Scores (25/75 percentile): English: N/A, Math: N/A, Composite: 23-28.

ACADEMICS

Year founded: 1863. **Academic calendar:** Semester. **Degrees offered:** certificate, associate, bachelor's, post-bachelor's certificate, master's, post-master's certificate, doctorate. **Most popular majors:** 18% business, management, marketing, and related support services, 12% social sciences, 9% psychology, 8% biological and biomedical sciences, 8% communication, journal-

ism, and related programs. **Major fields of study:** agriculture, agriculture operations, and related sciences; architecture and related services; area, ethnic, cultural, and gender studies; biological and biomedical sciences; business, management, marketing, and related support services; communication, journalism, and related programs; computer and information sciences and support services; education; engineering; English language and literature/letters; family and consumer sciences/human sciences; foreign languages, literatures, and linguistics; health professions and related clinical sciences; history; legal professions and studies; liberal arts and sciences studies, and humanities; mathematics and statistics; multi/interdisciplinary studies; natural resources and conservation; parks, recreation, leisure, and fitness studies; philosophy and religious studies; physical sciences; psychology; social sciences; visual and performing arts. **Areas of required coursework:** arts/fine arts, humanities, mathematics, English (including composition), foreign languages, sciences (biological or physical), history, social science, other. **Pre-professional programs:** pre-law, pre-dentistry, pre-medicine, pre-veterinary science. **Special academic programs (% participation):** cooperative (work-study plan) program, cross-registration, distance learning, double major, dual enrollment, English as a Second Language (ESL), exchange student program (domestic), honors program, independent study, internships (58%), liberal arts/career combination, student-designed major, study abroad (22%), teacher certificate program. **Teacher certification offered in:** early childhood, special education, elementary, middle/junior high, secondary, bilingual/bicultural. **Cooperative education programs:** agriculture, art, business, computer science, education, engineering, health professions, humanities, natural science, social/behavioral science. **Reserve Officers Training Corps (ROTC):** Army ROTC: Offered on campus; Air Force ROTC: Offered on campus. **Faculty and instruction (2009-2010):** Total instructional faculty: 1,170 full-time, 145 part-time (60% men; 40% women; 17% minorities). Full-time faculty with Ph.D. or other terminal degree: 93%. Student/faculty ratio: 18/1. Classes of fewer than 20 students: 35%; of 20 to 49 students: 47%; of 50 or more students: 18%. **Advanced Placement and International Baccalaureate credit:** AP tests may be used for: Placement only. Scores accepted: 4, 5. International Baccalaureate exams may be used for: Credit only. **Freshmen returning for sophomore year:** 85%. **Graduation rates:** Four-year: 49%; five-year: 63%; six-year: 66%. **Graduate study:** 22% of students pursue further study immediately upon graduation. Fields in which graduates pursue further study: Master of Business Administration (MBA), 19%; law, 8%; medicine, 6%; arts and sciences, 64%; veterinary medicine, 3%.

COSTS AND FINANCIAL AID

Financial aid office: (413) 545-0801. **Expenses (2010-2011):** Tuition and fees 2010-2011: $12,084 in state, $20,307 out of state; room/board: $8,814. Estimated books and supplies: $1,000; transportation: $400; personal expenses: $1,000. **Financial aid:** Priority filing date for institution's financial aid form: March 1. In 2009-2010, 80% of undergraduates applied for financial aid. Of those, 58% were determined to have financial need; 27% had their need fully met. Average financial aid package (proportion receiving): $14,606 (57%). Average amount of gift aid, such as scholarships or grants (proportion receiving): $8,848 (53%). Average amount of self-help aid, such as work study or loans (proportion receiving): $4,830 (49%). Average need-based loan (excluding PLUS or other private loans): $4,383. Among students who received need-based aid, the average percentage of need met: 88%. Among students who received aid based on merit, the average award (and the proportion receiving): $2,835 (5%). The average athletic scholarship (and the proportion receiving): $16,717 (1%). Average amount of debt of borrowers graduating in 2009: $23,847. Proportion who borrowed: 67%.

CAMPUS LIFE AND EXTRACURRICULAR ACTIVITIES

Campus housing available (% using): coed dorms (48%), women's dorms (1%), men's dorms (1%), sorority housing (2%), fraternity housing (2%), apartments for married students (2%), apartment for single students (7%), special housing for disabled students (0%), special housing for international students (1%), other housing options (36%). Students who live in college-owned, operated, or affiliated housing: 63%. **Student employment:** During the 2009-2010 academic year, 34% of undergraduates worked on campus. **Clubs and organizations:** Number of student organizations: 298. Activities include: campus ministries, choral groups, concert band, dance, drama/theater, international student organization, jazz band, literary magazine, marching band, model UN, music ensembles, musical theater, opera, pep band, radio station, student government, student newspaper, student film society, symphony orchestra, television station. Number of fraternities: 21; sororities: 15. Proportion of men in fraternities: 5%; of women in sororities: 5%. **Sports program (2009-2010):** Member of NCAA I. *Men's intercollegiate varsity sports:* baseball, basketball, cross country, football, ice hockey, lacrosse, soccer, swimming, track and field (indoor), track and field (outdoor). **Women's intercollegiate varsity sports:** basketball, crew (heavyweight), cross country, field hockey, lacrosse, crew (lightweight), soccer, softball, swimming, tennis, track and field (indoor), track and field (outdoor).

SERVICES AND FACILITIES

Basic services: nonremedial tutoring, women's center, placement service, day care, health service, health insurance, other. **Remedial assistance:** math, writing. **Counseling services:** minority student, career, military, personal, veteran student, academic, psychological, birth control. **For learning-disabled students:** School does not offer a structured program with separate admission and additional fees. Total undergraduates in learning-disabled program or receiving services: 395. Services include: reading machines, tape recorders, other special classes, diagnostic testing service, untimed tests, note-taking services, oral tests, readers, extended time for tests, early syllabus, priority registration, priority seating, proofreading services, substitution of courses, texts on tape, exams on tape or computer, other testing accommodations, other. **Library:** Number of titles: 3,654,181; number of current serial subscriptions: 94,745. **Information technology resources:** Students are not required to lease or own a computer. Number of campus computers available to all students: 424. School has a wireless network. Approximate number of users that can be accommodated: 8,000. Proportion of college-owned housing units wired-for high-speed internet access: 100%. **Campus safety:** Security services offered: 24-hour foot-and-vehicle patrols, late-night transport/escort service, 24-hour emergency telephones, lighted pathways/sidewalks, controlled dormitory access (key, security card, etc).

TRANSFER AND INTERNATIONAL STUDENTS

Transfer students: May apply for admission for the following academic terms: Fall, Spring. Applicants do not need a minimum number of credits to apply. For fall 2009: Transfer applications received: 3,230. Transfer applicants offered admission: 2,012. Transfer applicants enrolled: 1,133. **International students:** Number of foreign undergraduates: 200 (1% of student body). Number of countries represented: 36. Minimum TOEFL score required: 550 (paper); 213 (computer).

University of Massachusetts—Boston

- **Address:** 100 Morrissey Boulevard, Boston, MA 02125-3393
- **Website:** http://www.umb.edu
- **Public**
- **Enrollment:** 7,681 full-time; 3,360 part-time

KEY STATS

✔ **U.S News College Ranking:** second tier, National Universities
✔ **SAT Score (25th/75th percentile):** 950-1150
✔ **Tuition:** 2009-2010: $10,611 in state, $18,655 out of state

Selectivity: Selective	**Room/board:** N/A
Acceptance rate: 61%	**Average debt:** $19,327
Student/faculty ratio: 16/1	**Proportion who borrowed:** 67%

UNDERGRADUATE STUDENT BODY STATS

2009-2010 enrollment: 7,681 full-time; 3,360 part-time. Men: 43%; women: 57%. **Ethnic makeup:** African American: 16%; Asian American: 13%; Hispanic: 9%; White: 57%; International: 4%.

ADMISSIONS FACTS AND FIGURES

Phone: (617) 287-6000. **Email:** enrollment.info@umb.edu. **Website:** http://www.umb.edu. **Application deadlines for fall 2011:** Regular decision: June 1. Early decision: Not offered. Early action: Not offered. Admission can be deferred. **Application fee:** $40. **To apply online, go to:** http://www.umb.edu/admissions/. **Admissions requirements/recommendations:** High school units required (recommended): English: 4; Mathematics: 3; Science: 3; Foreign language: 2; Social studies: 1; History: 1; Academic electives: 2; Total units: 16. **Tests:** The college uses SAT or ACT scores in admissions decisions. SAT required. For admission to the fall 2011 entering class, the school will accept: ACT with or without writing accepted. Campus visit: Neither required nor recommended. Admissions interview: Neither required nor recommended. Off-campus interview: Not available. **Factors that count in admissions decisions: _Academic:_** Secondary school record: Very Important. Class rank: Not Considered. Letters of recommendation: Important. Standardized test scores: Very Important. Essay: Important. **_Nonacademic:_** Interview: Considered. Extracurricular activities: Considered.

Talent/ability: Considered. Character/personal qualities: Very Important. Alumni/ae relationship: Not Considered. Geographical residence: Not Considered. State residency: Not Considered. Religious affiliation/commitment: Not Considered. Minority status: Not Considered. Volunteer work: Considered. Work experience: Considered. **Other schools with the greatest overlap in applicants:** Boston University; Northeastern University; Suffolk University; University of Massachusetts–Amherst; University of Massachusetts–Dartmouth. **Admissions statistics for the fall 2009 entering class:** Total applicants: 6,050. Total accepted: 3,718. Freshmen enrolled: 987; 6% were from out of state. Overall acceptance rate: 61%. **Size of waiting list:** 0 applicants; enrolled from waiting list: N/A. **Average high school grade point average:** 3.0. **First-year students who submitted SAT scores:** 93%. Scores (25/75 percentile): Critical Reading: 460-570, Math: 490-580, Combined: 950-1150.

ACADEMICS

Year founded: 1964. **Academic calendar:** Semester. **Degrees offered:** certificate, bachelor's, post-bachelor's certificate, master's, post-master's certificate, doctorate. **Most popular majors:** 19% business/commerce, 13% health services/allied health/health sciences, 13% psychology, 6% English language and literature, 6% criminal justice/safety studies. **Major fields of study:** area, ethnic, cultural, and gender studies; biological and biomedical sciences; business, management, marketing, and related support services; computer and information sciences and support services; engineering; English language and literature/letters; foreign languages, literatures, and linguistics; health professions and related clinical sciences; history; legal professions and studies; mathematics and statistics; multi/interdisciplinary studies; philosophy and religious studies; physical sciences; psychology; public administration and social service professions; security and protective services; social sciences; visual and performing arts. **Areas of required coursework:** arts/fine arts, humanities, computer literacy, mathematics, English (including composition), philosophy, foreign languages, sciences (biological or physical), history, social science. **Pre-professional programs:** pre-law, pre-medicine. **Special academic programs:** accelerated program, cooperative (work-study plan) program, cross-registration, distance learning, double major, dual enrollment, English as a Second Language (ESL), exchange student program (domestic), honors program, independent study, internships, liberal arts/career combination, student-designed major, study abroad, teacher certificate program. **Teacher certification offered in:** early childhood, special education, elementary, middle/junior high, secondary, bilingual/bicultural. **Reserve Officers Training Corps (ROTC):** Army ROTC: Offered at cooperating institution (Boston University); Navy ROTC: Offered at cooperating institution (Boston University). **Faculty and instruction (2009-2010):** Total instructional faculty: 499 full-time, 465 part-time (45% men; 55% women; 16% minorities). Full-time faculty with Ph.D. or other terminal degree: 93%. Student/faculty ratio: 16/1. Classes of fewer than 20 students: 32%; of 20 to 49 students: 63%; of 50 or more students: 5%. **Advanced Placement and International Baccalaureate credit:** AP tests may be used for: Credit and/or placement. Scores accepted: 3, 4, 5. International Baccalaureate exams may be used for: Placement only. **Freshmen returning for sophomore year:** 74%. **Graduation rates:** Four-year: 11%; five-year: 31%; six-year: 39%.

COSTS AND FINANCIAL AID

Financial aid office: (617) 287-6300. **Expenses (2009-2010):** Tuition and fees 2009-2010: $10,611 in state, $18,655 out of state. Estimated books and supplies: $800; transportation: $1,100; personal expenses: $1,170. **Financial aid:** Priority filing date for institution's financial aid form: March 1. In 2009-2010, 71% of undergraduates applied for financial aid. Of those, 60% were determined to have financial need; 73% had their need fully met. Average financial aid package (proportion receiving): $12,369 (60%). Average amount of gift aid, such as scholarships or grants (proportion receiving): $6,534 (52%). Average amount of self-help aid, such as work study or loans (proportion receiving): $7,152 (58%). Average need-based loan (excluding PLUS or other private loans): $5,965. Among students who received need-based aid, the average percentage of need met: 95%. Among students who received aid based on merit, the average award (and the proportion receiving): $3,539 (4%). Average amount of debt of borrowers graduating in 2009: $19,327. Proportion who borrowed: 67%.

CAMPUS LIFE AND EXTRACURRICULAR ACTIVITIES

Campus housing available: other housing options. Average per-year earnings: $5,000. **Clubs and organizations:** Number of student organizations: 100. Activities include: campus ministries, choral groups, concert band, dance, drama/theater, international student organization, jazz band, literary magazine, model UN, music ensembles, radio station, student government, student newspaper, student film society, symphony orchestra. Number of fraternities: 0; sororities: 0. **Sports program (2009-2010):** Member of NCAA III. *Men's intercollegiate varsity sports:* baseball, basketball, cross country, ice hockey, lacrosse, soccer, tennis, track and field (indoor), track and field (outdoor). *Women's intercollegiate varsity sports:* basketball, cross country, ice hockey, soccer, softball, tennis, volleyball.

SERVICES AND FACILITIES

Basic services: nonremedial tutoring, women's center, placement service, day care, health service, health insurance. **Remedial assistance:** math, writing. **Counseling services:** career, personal, veteran student, academic, psychological. **For learning-disabled students:** School does not offer a structured program with separate admission and additional fees. Services include: reading machines, tape recorders, note-taking services, oral tests, readers, extended time for tests, other. **Information technology resources:** Students are not required to lease or own a computer. Number of campus computers available to all students: 350. School has a wireless network. **Campus safety:** Security services offered: 24-hour foot-and-vehicle patrols, late-night transport/escort service, 24-hour emergency telephones, lighted pathways/sidewalks.

TRANSFER AND INTERNATIONAL STUDENTS

Transfer students: May apply for admission for the following academic terms: Fall, Spring. Applicants do not need a minimum number of credits to apply. For fall 2009: Transfer applications received: 3,245. Transfer applicants offered admission: 2,628. Transfer applicants enrolled: 1,756. **International students:** Number of foreign undergraduates: 355 (4% of student body). Number of countries represented: 100. Minimum TOEFL score required: 550 (paper); 213 (computer).

University of Massachusetts–Dartmouth

- **Address:** 285 Old Westport Road, North Dartmouth, MA 02747-2300
- **Website:** http://www.umassd.edu
- **Public**
- **Enrollment;** 7,068 full-time; 914 part-time

KEY STATS
✔ **U.S News College Ranking:** 81, Regional Universities (North)
✔ **SAT Score (25th/75th percentile):** 960-1160
✔ **Tuition:** 2009-2010: $10,358 in state, $17,040 out of state

Selectivity: Selective	Room/board: $9,370
Acceptance rate: 68%	Average debt: $21,905
Student/faculty ratio: 18/1	Proportion who borrowed: 73%

UNDERGRADUATE STUDENT BODY STATS

2009-2010 enrollment: 7,068 full-time; 914 part-time. Men: 52%; women: 48%. **Ethnic makeup:** African American: 8%; American-Indian: 1%; Asian American: 3%; Hispanic: 3%; White: 85%.

ADMISSIONS FACTS AND FIGURES

Phone: (508) 999-8605. **Email:** admissions@umassd.edu. **Website:** http://www.umassd.edu. **Application deadlines for fall 2011:** Regular decision: Rolling. Early decision: Not offered. Early action: Send application by: November 15; Decision sent by: December 15. Admission can be deferred. **Application fee:** $40. **To apply online, go to:** http://www.umassd.edu/admissions/applyonline.cfm. **Admissions requirements/recommendations:** High school units required (recommended): English: 4; Mathematics: 3; Science: 3; Foreign language: 2; Social studies: 1; History: 1; Academic electives: 2; Total units: 16. Tests: The college uses SAT or ACT scores in admissions decisions. Either SAT or ACT required. For admission to the fall 2011 entering class, the school will accept: ACT with or without writing accepted. Campus visit: Recommended. Admissions interview: Neither required nor recommended. Off-campus interview: Not available. **Factors that count in admissions decisions:** *Academic:* Secondary school record: Very Important. Class rank: Considered. Letters of recommendation: Considered. Standardized test scores: Very Important. Essay: Considered. *Nonacademic:* Interview: Considered. Extracurricular activities: Considered. Talent/ability: Considered. Character/personal qualities: Considered. Alumni/ae relationship: Considered. Geographical residence: Not Considered. State residency: Not Considered. Religious affiliation/commitment: Not Considered. Minority status: Not Considered. Volunteer work: Considered. Work experience: Considered. **Other schools with the greatest overlap in**

applicants: Bridgewater State College; Northeastern University; University of Connecticut; University of Massachusetts–Amherst; University of Rhode Island. **Admissions statistics for the fall 2009 entering class:** Total applicants: 7,149. Total accepted: 4,876. Freshmen enrolled: 1,511; 5% were from out of state. Accepted through early-decision or early-action plans: 2%. Overall acceptance rate: 68%. Non-early acceptance rate: 68%. **Credentials of fall 2009 freshmen:** 14% ranked in the top 10 percent of their high school class; 36% were in the top 25 percent; 75% were in the top half. (Proportion submitting class standing: 64%.) **Average high school grade point average:** 3.1. **First-year students who submitted SAT scores:** 98%. Scores (25/75 percentile): Critical Reading: 470-570, Math: 490-590, Combined: 960-1160. **First-year students submitting ACT scores:** 8%. Scores (25/75 percentile): English: N/A, Math: N/A, Composite: 20-25.

ACADEMICS

Year founded: 1895. **Academic calendar:** Semester. **Degrees offered:** certificate, bachelor's, post-bachelor's certificate, master's, post-master's certificate, doctorate. **Most popular majors:** 34% business, management, marketing, and related support services, 10% health professions and related clinical sciences, 10% social sciences, 8% engineering, 8% psychology. **Major fields of study:** biological and biomedical sciences; business, management, marketing, and related support services; computer and information sciences and support services; education; engineering; English language and literature/letters; foreign languages, literatures, and linguistics; health professions and related clinical sciences; history; liberal arts and sciences studies, and humanities; mathematics and statistics; multi/interdisciplinary studies; philosophy and religious studies; physical sciences; psychology; social sciences; visual and performing arts. **Areas of required coursework:** arts/fine arts, humanities, computer literacy, mathematics, English (including composition), sciences (biological or physical), social science, other. **Pre-professional programs:** pre-law, pre-dentistry, pre-medicine, pre-veterinary science, pre-pharmacy. **Special academic programs (% participation):** cooperative (work-study plan) program (2%), cross-registration (1%), distance learning (3%), double major (3%), dual enrollment (1%), English as a Second Language (ESL) (1%), honors program (12%), independent study (10%), internships (35%), student-designed major (1%), study abroad (4%), teacher certificate program (1%). **Teacher certification offered in:** elementary, middle/junior high, secondary. **Cooperative education programs:** engineering. **Reserve Officers Training Corps (ROTC):** Army ROTC: Offered at cooperating institution (Providence College). **Faculty and instruction (2009-2010):** Total instructional faculty: 369 full-time, 219 part-time (57% men; 43% women; 19% minorities). Full-time faculty with Ph.D. or other terminal degree: 86%. Student/faculty ratio: 18/1. Classes of fewer than 20 students: 32%; of 20 to 49 students: 54%; of 50 or more students: 14%. **Advanced Placement and International Baccalaureate credit:** AP tests may be used for: Placement only. Scores accepted: 3, 4, 5. International Baccalaureate exams may be used for: Placement only. **Freshmen returning for sophomore year:** 75%. **Graduation rates:** Four-year: 32%; five-year: 45%; six-year: 47%. **Graduate study:** 14% of students pursue further study immediately upon graduation; 25% within one year.

COSTS AND FINANCIAL AID

Financial aid office: (508) 999-8632. **Expenses (2009-2010):** Tuition and fees 2009-2010: $10,358 in state, $17,040 out of state; room/board: $9,370. Estimated books and supplies: $1,200; transportation: $650; personal expenses: $1,390. **Financial aid:** Priority filing date for institution's financial aid form: March 1. In 2009-2010, 82% of undergraduates applied for financial aid. Of those, 65% were determined to have financial need; 51% had their need fully met. Average financial aid package (proportion receiving): $13,949 (65%). Average amount of gift aid, such as scholarships or grants (proportion receiving): $6,461 (64%). Average amount of self-help aid, such as work study or loans (proportion receiving): $7,856 (60%). Average need-based loan (excluding PLUS or other private loans): $7,223. Among students who received need-based aid, the average percentage of need met: 90%. Among students who received aid based on merit, the average award (and the proportion receiving): $2,251 (17%). Average amount of debt of borrowers graduating in 2009: $21,905. Proportion who borrowed: 73%.

CAMPUS LIFE AND EXTRACURRICULAR ACTIVITIES

Campus housing available (% using): coed dorms (64%), apartment for single students (35%), special housing for disabled students (1%). Students who live in college-owned, operated, or affiliated housing: 56%. **Student employment:** During the 2009-2010 academic year, 30% of undergraduates worked on campus. Average per-year earnings: $3,000. **Clubs and organizations:** Number of student organizations: 116. Activities include: choral groups, concert band, dance, drama/theater, international student organization, jazz band, literary magazine, music ensembles, musical theater, pep band, radio station, student government, student newspaper, symphony orchestra, yearbook. Number of fraternities: 5; sororities: 3. Average proportion of students who stay on campus on weekends: 40%. **Sports program (2009-2010):** Member of NCAA III. *Men's intercollegiate varsity sports:* baseball, basketball, cross country, football, golf, ice hockey, lacrosse, soccer, swimming, tennis, track and field (indoor), track and field (outdoor). *Women's intercollegiate varsity sports:* basketball, cross country, equestrian, field hockey, lacrosse, soccer, softball, swimming, tennis, track and field (indoor), track and field (outdoor), volleyball.

SERVICES AND FACILITIES

Basic services: nonremedial tutoring, women's center, placement service, day care, health service, health insurance. **Remedial assistance:** reading, math, writing, study skills. **Counseling services:** minority student, career, military, personal, veteran student, academic, older student, psychological, birth control, religious, other. **For learning-disabled students:** School does not offer a structured program with separate admission and additional fees. Services include: remedial math, remedial English, reading machines, tape recorders, untimed tests, note-taking services, oral tests, learning center, readers, extended time for tests, tutors, priority registration, priority seating, substitution of courses, texts on tape, exams on tape or computer, other testing accommodations, other. **Library:** Number of titles: 461,338; number of current serial subscriptions: 2,783. **Information technology resources:** Students are not required to lease or own a computer. Number of campus computers available to all students: 650. School has a wireless network. Approximate number of users that can be accommodated: 2,700. Proportion of college-owned housing units wired for high-speed internet access: 100%. **Campus safety:** Security services offered: 24-hour foot-and-vehicle patrols, late-night transport/escort service, 24-hour emergency telephones, lighted pathways/sidewalks, controlled dormitory access (key, security card, etc).

TRANSFER AND INTERNATIONAL STUDENTS

Transfer students: May apply for admission for the following academic terms: Fall, Spring. Applicants do not need a minimum number of credits to apply. For fall 2009: Transfer applications received: 1,029. Transfer applicants offered admission: 829. Transfer applicants enrolled: 475. **International students:** Number of foreign undergraduates: 24. Number of countries represented: 13. Minimum TOEFL score required: 520 (paper); 68 (computer). Average TOEFL score: 588 (paper).

University of Massachusetts–Lowell

- **Address:** 1 University Avenue, Lowell, MA 01854
- **Website:** http://www.uml.edu
- **Public**
- **Enrollment:** 7,559 full-time; 2,989 part-time

KEY STATS

✔ **U.S News College Ranking:** 183, National Universities
✔ **SAT Score (25th/75th percentile):** 980-1180
✔ **Tuition:** 2009-2010: $10,681 in state, $17,794 out of state

Selectivity: Selective	**Room/board:** $8,635
Acceptance rate: 73%	**Average debt:** $21,542
Student/faculty ratio: 14/1	**Proportion who borrowed:** 73%

UNDERGRADUATE STUDENT BODY STATS

2009-2010 enrollment: 7,559 full-time; 2,989 part-time. Men: 60%; women: 40%. **Ethnic makeup:** African American: 6%; Asian American: 8%; Hispanic: 7%; White: 78%; International: 1%.

ADMISSIONS FACTS AND FIGURES

Phone: (978) 934-3931. **Email:** admissions@uml.edu. **Website:** http://www.uml.edu. **Application deadlines for fall 2011:** Regular decision: Rolling. Early decision: Not offered. Early action: Not offered. Admission can be deferred. **Application fee:** $40. **To apply online, go to:** https://www.umassadmin.net/isis/application/weba_enrl.asp. **Admissions requirements/recommendations:** High school units required (recommended): English: 4; Mathematics: 3; Science: 3; Foreign language: 2; Social studies: 2; Academic electives: 2; Total units: 16. Tests: The college uses SAT or ACT scores in admissions decisions. Either SAT or ACT required. For admission to the fall 2011 entering class, the school will accept: ACT with

or without writing accepted. Campus visit: Recommended. Admissions interview: Recommended. Off-campus interview: Not available. **Factors that count in admissions decisions:** *Academic:* Secondary school record: Very Important. Class rank: Important. Letters of recommendation: Important. Standardized test scores: Very Important. Essay: Important. *Nonacademic:* Interview: Considered. Extracurricular activities: Considered. Talent/ability: Considered. Character/personal qualities: Considered. Alumni/ae relationship: Not Considered. Geographical residence: Not Considered. State residency: Not Considered. Religious affiliation/commitment: Not Considered. Minority status: Not Considered. Volunteer work: Considered. Work experience: Considered. **Other schools with the greatest overlap in applicants:** Northeastern University; University of Massachusetts–Amherst; University of Massachusetts–Boston; University of Massachusetts–Dartmouth; Wentworth Institute of Technology. **Admissions statistics for the fall 2009 entering class:** Total applicants: 5,913. Total accepted: 4,287. Freshmen enrolled: 1,522; 9% were from out of state. Overall acceptance rate: 73%. **Size of waiting list:** 20 applicants; enrolled from waiting list: 3. **Credentials of fall 2009 freshmen:** 15% ranked in the top 10 percent of their high school class; 43% were in the top 25 percent; 78% were in the top half. (Proportion submitting class standing: 63%.) **Average high school grade point average:** 3.3. **First-year students who submitted SAT scores:** 98%. Scores (25/75 percentile): Critical Reading: 480-570, Math: 500-610, Combined: 980-1180.

ACADEMICS

Year founded: 1894. **Academic calendar:** Semester. **Degrees offered:** associate, bachelor's, master's, post-master's certificate, doctorate. **Most popular majors:** 19% business, management, marketing, and related support services, 12% engineering, 12% psychology, 11% health professions and related clinical sciences, 9% computer and information sciences and support services. **Major fields of study:** area, ethnic, cultural, and gender studies; biological and biomedical sciences; business, management, marketing, and related support services; computer and information sciences and support services; education; engineering; engineering technologies/technicians; English language and literature/letters; foreign languages, literatures, and linguistics; health professions and related clinical sciences; history; liberal arts and sciences studies, and humanities; mathematics and statistics; philosophy and religious studies; physical sciences; psychology; security and protective services; social sciences; visual and performing arts. **Areas of required coursework:** humanities, mathematics, English (including composition), sciences (biological or physical), history, social science. **Special academic programs:** accelerated program, cooperative (work-study plan) program, cross-registration, distance learning, double major, dual enrollment, honors program, internships, liberal arts/career combination, study abroad, teacher certification program. **Teacher certification offered in:** elementary, middle/junior high, secondary. **Cooperative education programs:** computer science, engineering. **Reserve Officers Training Corps (ROTC):** Air Force ROTC: Offered on campus. **Faculty and instruction (2009-2010):** Total instructional faculty: 425 full-time, 312 part-time (61% men; 39% women; 12% minorities). Full-time faculty with Ph.D. or other terminal degree: 94%. Student/faculty ratio: 14/1. Classes of fewer than 20 students: 37%; of 20 to 49 students: 57%; of 50 or more students: 6%. **Advanced Placement and International Baccalaureate credit:** AP tests may be used for: Credit only. Scores accepted: 3, 4, 5. **Freshmen returning for sophomore year:** 78%. **Graduation rates:** Four-year: 28%; five-year: 48%; six-year: 53%.

COSTS AND FINANCIAL AID

Financial aid office: (978) 934-4226. **Expenses (2009-2010):** Tuition and fees 2009-2010: $10,681 in state, $17,794 out of state; room/board: $8,635. Estimated books and supplies: $800; transportation: $400; personal expenses: $850. **Financial aid:** Priority filing date for institution's financial aid form: March 1. In 2009-2010, 79% of undergraduates applied for financial aid. Of those, 58% were determined to have financial need; 67% had their need fully met. Average financial aid package (proportion receiving): $12,300 (58%). Average amount of gift aid, such as scholarships or grants (proportion receiving): $5,934 (56%). Average amount of self-help aid, such as work study or loans (proportion receiving): $7,151 (53%). Average need-based loan (excluding PLUS or other private loans): $6,487. Among students who received need-based aid, the average percentage of need met: 94%. Among students who received aid based on merit, the average award (and the proportion receiving): $2,154 (20%). The average athletic scholarship (and the proportion receiving): $8,981 (2%). Average amount of debt of borrowers graduating in 2009: $21,542. Proportion who borrowed: 73%.

CAMPUS LIFE AND EXTRACURRICULAR ACTIVITIES

Campus housing available (% using): coed dorms (95%). Students who live in college-owned, operated, or affiliated housing: 37%. **Student employment:**

During the 2009-2010 academic year, 16% of undergraduates worked on campus. Average per-year earnings: $2,250. **Clubs and organizations:** Number of student organizations: 100. Activities include: campus ministries, choral groups, concert band, dance, drama/theater, international student organization, jazz band, literary magazine, marching band, music ensembles, pep band, radio station, student government, student newspaper, student film society, symphony orchestra, yearbook. Number of fraternities: 0; sororities: 0. Average proportion of students who stay on campus on weekends: 60%. **Sports program (2009-2010):** Member of NCAA II. *Men's intercollegiate varsity sports:* baseball, basketball, cross country, golf, ice hockey, soccer, track and field (indoor), track and field (outdoor). *Women's intercollegiate varsity sports:* basketball, cross country, field hockey, soccer, softball, track and field (indoor), track and field (outdoor), volleyball.

SERVICES AND FACILITIES

Basic services: nonremedial tutoring, women's center, placement service, health service, health insurance. **Remedial assistance:** reading, math, writing, study skills, other. **Counseling services:** minority student, career, military, personal, veteran student, academic, older student, psychological, birth control, religious. **For learning-disabled students:** School does not offer a structured program with separate admission and additional fees. Total undergraduates in learning-disabled program or receiving services: 337. Services include: reading machines, tape recorders, untimed tests, note-taking services, oral tests, learning center, readers, extended time for tests, tutors, priority registration, priority seating, texts on tape, other testing accommodations. **Library:** Number of titles: 382,599; number of current serial subscriptions: 14,353. **Information technology resources:** Students are not required to lease or own a computer. School has a wireless network. Proportion of college-owned housing units wired for high-speed internet access: 100%. **Campus safety:** Security services offered: 24-hour foot-and-vehicle patrols, late-night transport/escort service, 24-hour emergency telephones, lighted pathways/sidewalks, controlled dormitory access (key, security card, etc).

TRANSFER AND INTERNATIONAL STUDENTS

Transfer students: May apply for admission for the following academic terms: Fall, Spring. Applicants need a minimum number of credits to apply. For fall 2009: Transfer applications received: 1,829. Transfer applicants offered admission: 1,470. Transfer applicants enrolled: 935. **International students:** Number of foreign undergraduates: 60 (1% of student body). Number of countries represented: 25. Minimum TOEFL score required: 550 (paper); 213 (computer). Average TOEFL score: 550 (paper).

Wellesley College

- **Address:** 106 Central Street, Wellesley, MA 02481-8203
- **Website:** http://www.wellesley.edu
- **Private**
- **Enrollment:** 2,186 full-time; 138 part-time

KEY STATS

✔ **U.S News College Ranking:** 4, National Liberal Arts Colleges
✔ **SAT Score (25th/75th percentile):** 1280-1470
✔ **Tuition:** 2010-2011: $39,666

Selectivity: Most selective	**Room/board:** $12,284
Acceptance rate: 35%	**Average debt:** $13,324
Student/faculty ratio: 8/1	**Proportion who borrowed:** 56%

UNDERGRADUATE STUDENT BODY STATS

2009-2010 enrollment: 2,186 full-time; 138 part-time. Men: 2%; women: 98%. **Ethnic makeup:** African American: 7%; American-Indian: 1%; Asian American: 26%; Hispanic: 8%; White: 49%; International: 10%. **Religious preference:** Roman Catholic: 17%; Protestant: 35%; Jewish: 9%; Muslim: 3%; Hindu: 2%; Buddhist: 5%; No preference: 28%; Other: 1%.

ADMISSIONS FACTS AND FIGURES

Phone: (781) 283-2270. **Email:** admission@wellesley.edu. **Website:** http://www.wellesley.edu. **Application deadlines for fall 2011:** Regular decision: January 15; decision sent by April 1. Early decision: Send application by: November 1; Decision sent by: December 15. Early action: Not offered. Admission can be deferred. **Application fee:** $50. **To apply online, go to:** https://www.applyweb.com/apply/wellesley/menu.html. **Admissions**

requirements/recommendations: High school units required (recommended): English: (4); Mathematics: (4); Science: (3); Foreign language: (4); Social studies: (4); History: (4). Tests: The college uses SAT or ACT scores in admissions decisions. Either SAT or ACT required. For admission to the fall 2011 entering class, the school will accept: ACT with writing required. Campus visit: Recommended. Admissions interview: Recommended. Off-campus interview: May be arranged. **Factors that count in admissions decisions:** *Academic:* Secondary school record: Very Important. Class rank: Important. Letters of recommendation: Very Important. Standardized test scores: Very Important. Essay: Very Important. *Nonacademic:* Interview: Considered. Extracurricular activities: Important. Talent/ability: Important. Character/personal qualities: Very Important. Alumni/ae relationship: Considered. Geographical residence: Considered. State residency: Considered. Religious affiliation/commitment: Not Considered. Minority status: Considered. Volunteer work: Considered. Work experience: Considered. **Other schools with the greatest overlap in applicants:** Brown University; Columbia University; Harvard University; Princeton University; Stanford University. **Admissions statistics for the fall 2009 entering class:** Total applicants: 4,156. Total accepted: 1,463. Freshmen enrolled: 589; 86% were from out of state. Accepted through early-decision or early-action plans: 20%. Overall acceptance rate: 35%. Early-decision acceptance rate: 59%. Non-early acceptance rate: 34%. **Size of waiting list:** 900 applicants; enrolled from waiting list: 30. **Credentials of fall 2009 freshmen:** 78% ranked in the top 10 percent of their high school class; 96% were in the top 25 percent; 100% were in the top half. (Proportion submitting class standing: 40%.) **First-year students who submitted SAT scores:** 85%. Scores (25/75 percentile): Critical Reading: 640-740, Math: 640-730, Combined: 1280-1470. **First-year students submitting ACT scores:** 38%. Scores (25/75 percentile): English: N/A, Math: N/A, Composite: 29-32.

ACADEMICS

Year founded: 1870. **Academic calendar:** Semester. **Degrees offered:** bachelor's. **Most popular majors:** 16% economics, 13% political science and government, 10% English language and literature, 7% psychology, 5% French language and literature. **Major fields of study:** architecture and related services; area, ethnic, cultural, and gender studies; biological and biomedical sciences; computer and information sciences and support services; education; English language and literature/letters; foreign languages, literatures, and linguistics; history; mathematics and statistics; multi/interdisciplinary studies; natural resources and conservation; philosophy and religious studies; physical sciences; psychology; social sciences; visual and performing arts. **Areas of required coursework:** arts/fine arts, humanities, mathematics, English (including composition), philosophy, foreign languages, sciences (biological or physical), history, social science, other. **Special academic programs (% participation):** cross-registration (53%), double major (34%), dual enrollment (0%), exchange student program (domestic) (.3%), honors program (21%), independent study (61%), internships (70%), student-designed major (.5%), study abroad (51.5%), teacher certificate program (1%). **Teacher certification offered in:** early childhood, elementary, middle/junior high, secondary. **Reserve Officers Training Corps (ROTC):** Army ROTC: Offered at cooperating institution (Massachusetts Institute of Technology); Air Force ROTC: Offered at cooperating institution (Massachusetts Institute of Technology). **Faculty and instruction (2009-2010):** Total instructional faculty: 259 full-time, 55 part-time (41% men; 59% women; 23% minorities). Full-time faculty with Ph.D. or other terminal degree: 96%. Student/faculty ratio: 8/1. Classes of fewer than 20 students: 68%; of 20 to 49 students: 32%; of 50 or more students: 1%. **Advanced Placement and International Baccalaureate credit:** AP tests may be used for: Credit only. Scores accepted: 5. International Baccalaureate exams may be used for: Credit only. **Freshmen returning for sophomore year:** 95%. **Graduation rates:** Four-year: 84%; five-year: 89%; six-year: 90%. **Graduate study:** 20% of students pursue further study immediately upon graduation; 75% within five years. Fields in which graduates pursue further study: Master of Business Administration (MBA), 2%; law, 11%; medicine, 18%; education, 13%; arts and sciences, 53%.

COSTS AND FINANCIAL AID

Financial aid office: (781) 283-2360. **Expenses (2010-2011):** Tuition and fees 2010-2011: $39,666; room/board: $12,284. Estimated books and supplies: $800; transportation: $1,000; personal expenses: $1,250. **Financial aid:** Priority filing date for institution's financial aid form: January 15. In 2009-2010, 71% of undergraduates applied for financial aid. Of those, 62% were determined to have financial need; 100% had their need fully met. Average financial aid package (proportion receiving): $35,951 (62%). Average amount of gift aid, such as scholarships or grants (proportion receiving): $34,014 (60%). Average amount of self-help aid, such as work study or loans (proportion receiving): $3,372 (56%). Average need-based loan (excluding PLUS or other private loans): $3,104. Among students who received need-based aid, the average percentage of need met: 100%. Among students who received aid based on merit, the average award (and the proportion receiving): $0 (0%). The average athletic scholarship (and the proportion receiving): $0 (0%). Average amount of debt of borrowers graduating in 2009: $13,324. Proportion who borrowed: 56%.

CAMPUS LIFE AND EXTRACURRICULAR ACTIVITIES

Campus housing available (% using): coed dorms, women's dorms (99%), apartment for single students (0%), special housing for disabled students (0%), cooperative housing (1%). Students who live in college-owned, operated, or affiliated housing: 92%. **Student employment:** During the 2009-2010 academic year, 22% of undergraduates worked on campus. Average per-year earnings: $1,600. **Clubs and organizations:** Number of student organizations: 150. Activities include: campus ministries, choral groups, dance, drama/theater, international student organization, jazz band, literary magazine, model UN, music ensembles, musical theater, radio station, student government, student newspaper, student film society, yearbook. Number of fraternities: 0; sororities: 0. **Sports program (2009-2010):** Member of NCAA III. *Women's intercollegiate varsity sports:* basketball, crew (heavyweight), cross country, fencing, field hockey, golf, lacrosse, crew (lightweight), soccer, softball, squash, swimming, tennis, volleyball.

SERVICES AND FACILITIES

Basic services: nonremedial tutoring, women's center, health service, health insurance. **Counseling services:** minority student, career, personal, academic, older student, psychological, birth control, religious. **For learning-disabled students:** School does not offer a structured program with separate admission and additional fees. Services include: tape recorders, note-taking services, learning center, readers, extended time for tests, tutors, early syllabus, typist/scribe, exams on tape or computer, other. **Library:** Number of titles: 832,415; number of current serial subscriptions: 13,983. **Information technology resources:** Students are not required to lease or own a computer. Number of campus computers available to all students: 468. School has a wireless network. Approximate number of users that can be accommodated: 2,500. Proportion of college-owned housing units wired for high-speed internet access: 100%. **Campus safety:** Security services offered: 24-hour foot-and-vehicle patrols, late-night transport/escort service, 24-hour emergency telephones, lighted pathways/sidewalks, controlled dormitory access (key, security card, etc).

TRANSFER AND INTERNATIONAL STUDENTS

Transfer students: May apply for admission for the following academic terms: Fall, Spring. Applicants do not need a minimum number of credits to apply. For fall 2009: Transfer applications received: 180. Transfer applicants offered admission: 47. Transfer applicants enrolled: 27. **International students:** Number of foreign undergraduates: 211 (10% of student body). Number of countries represented: 73. Average TOEFL score: 657 (paper).

Western New England College

- **Address:** 1215 Wilbraham Road, Springfield, MA 01119-2684
- **Website:** http://www.wnec.edu
- **Private**
- **Enrollment:** 2,463 full-time; 276 part-time

KEY STATS

✔ **U.S News College Ranking:** 67, Regional Universities (North)
✔ **SAT Score (25th/75th percentile):** 960-1160
✔ **Tuition:** 2010-2011: $29,812

Selectivity: Selective	**Room/board:** $11,336
Acceptance rate: 81%	**Average debt:** N/A
Student/faculty ratio: 15/1	**Proportion who borrowed:** N/A

UNDERGRADUATE STUDENT BODY STATS

2009-2010 enrollment: 2,463 full-time; 276 part-time. Men: 60%; women: 40%. **Ethnic makeup:** African American: 4%; Asian American: 2%; Hispanic: 4%; White: 90%.

ADMISSIONS FACTS AND FIGURES

Phone: (413) 782-1321. **Email:** ugradmis@wnec.edu. **Website:** http://www.wnec.edu. **Application deadlines for fall 2011:** Regular decision: Rolling.

Early decision: Not offered. Early action: Not offered. Admission can be deferred. **Application fee:** $50. **To apply online, go to:** http://www1.wnec.edu/admissions/. **Admissions requirements/recommendations:** High school units required (recommended): English: 4 (4); Mathematics: 2 (4); Science: 1 (2); Foreign language: 0 (2); Social studies: 1 (2); History: 1 (2); Total units: 10 (18). Tests: The college uses SAT or ACT scores in admissions decisions. Either SAT or ACT required. For admission to the fall 2011 entering class, the school will accept: ACT with or without writing accepted. Campus visit: Recommended. Admissions interview: Recommended. Off-campus interview: May be arranged. **Factors that count in admissions decisions:** *Academic:* Secondary school record: Considered. Class rank: Considered. Letters of recommendation: Very Important. Standardized test scores: Very Important. Essay: Considered. *Nonacademic:* Interview: Considered. Extracurricular activities: Considered. Talent/ability: Considered. Character/personal qualities: Considered. Alumni/ae relationship: Considered. Geographical residence: Not Considered. State residency: Not Considered. Religious affiliation/commitment: Not Considered. Minority status: Considered. Volunteer work: Considered. Work experience: Considered. **Admissions statistics for the fall 2009 entering class:** Total applicants: 4,769. Total accepted: 3,861. Freshmen enrolled: 689; 61% were from out of state. Overall acceptance rate: 81%. **Credentials of fall 2009 freshmen:** 14% ranked in the top 10 percent of their high school class; 42% were in the top 25 percent; 77% were in the top half. (Proportion submitting class standing: 63%.) **Average high school grade point average:** 3.2. **First-year students who submitted SAT scores:** 90%. Scores (25/75 percentile): Critical Reading: 470-560, Math: 490-600, Combined: 960-1160. **First-year students submitting ACT scores:** 18%. Scores (25/75 percentile): English: N/A, Math: N/A, Composite: 21-25.

ACADEMICS

Year founded: 1919. **Academic calendar:** Semester. **Degrees offered:** associate, bachelor's, master's, doctorate. **Most popular majors:** 37% business, management, marketing, and related support services, 12% psychology, 11% security and protective services, 9% engineering, 8% sport and fitness administration/management. **Major fields of study:** biological and biomedical sciences; business, management, marketing, and related support services; communication, journalism, and related programs; computer and information sciences and support services; education; engineering; English language and literature/letters; history; legal professions and studies; liberal arts and sciences studies, and humanities; mathematics and statistics; multi/interdisciplinary studies; parks, recreation, leisure, and fitness studies; philosophy and religious studies; physical sciences; psychology; public administration and social service professions; security and protective services; social sciences. **Areas of required coursework:** arts/fine arts, humanities, computer literacy, mathematics, English (including composition), philosophy, sciences (biological or physical), history, social science, other. **Pre-professional programs:** pre-law, pre-dentistry, pre-medicine, pre-pharmacy, other. **Special academic programs:** accelerated program, cross-registration, distance learning, double major, dual enrollment, exchange student program (domestic), honors program, independent study, internships, liberal arts/career combination, student-designed major, study abroad, teacher certificate program, other. **Teacher certification offered in:** elementary, secondary. **Reserve Officers Training Corps (ROTC):** Army ROTC: Offered on campus; Air Force ROTC: Offered at cooperating institution (University of Massachusetts–Amherst). **Faculty and instruction (2009-2010):** Total instructional faculty: 188 full-time, 113 part-time (65% men; 35% women; 6% minorities). Full-time faculty with Ph.D. or other terminal degree: 89%. Student/faculty ratio: 15/1. Classes of fewer than 20 students: 45%; of 20 to 49 students: 55%; of 50 or more students: 0%. **Advanced Placement and International Baccalaureate credit:** AP tests may be used for: Credit and/or placement. Scores accepted: 3, 4, 5. **Freshmen returning for sophomore year:** 76%. **Graduation rates:** Four-year: 43%; five-year: 52%; six-year: 59%.

COSTS AND FINANCIAL AID

Financial aid office: (413) 796-2080. **Expenses (2010-2011):** Tuition and fees 2010-2011: $29,812; room/board: $11,336. Estimated books and supplies: $1,100; transportation: $495; personal expenses: $1,400. **Financial aid:** Priority filing date for institution's financial aid form: April 15; deadline: April 15. In 2009-2010, 85% of undergraduates applied for financial aid. Of those, 75% were determined to have financial need; 12% had their need fully met. Average financial aid package (proportion receiving): $18,654 (75%). Average amount of gift aid, such as scholarships or grants (proportion receiving): $13,383 (74%). Average amount of self-help aid, such as work study or loans (proportion receiving): $5,928 (68%). Average need-based loan (excluding PLUS or other private loans): $4,775. Among students who received need-based aid, the average percentage of need met:

67%. Among students who received aid based on merit, the average award (and the proportion receiving): $9,625 (12%). The average athletic scholarship (and the proportion receiving): $0 (0%).

CAMPUS LIFE AND EXTRACURRICULAR ACTIVITIES

Campus housing available (% using): coed dorms (64%), apartment for single students (35%), special housing for disabled students (1%). Students who live in college-owned, operated, or affiliated housing: 75%. **Student employment:** During the 2009-2010 academic year, 42% of undergraduates worked on campus. Average per-year earnings: $1,700. **Clubs and organizations:** Number of student organizations: 60. Activities include: campus ministries, choral groups, concert band, dance, drama/theater, jazz band, literary magazine, music ensembles, pep band, radio station, student government, student newspaper, yearbook. Number of fraternities: 0; sororities: 0. Average proportion of students who stay on campus on weekends: 75%. **Sports program (2009-2010):** Member of NCAA III. *Men's intercollegiate varsity sports:* baseball, basketball, cross country, football, golf, ice hockey, lacrosse, soccer, tennis, wrestling. *Women's intercollegiate varsity sports:* basketball, cross country, field hockey, lacrosse, soccer, softball, swimming, tennis, volleyball.

SERVICES AND FACILITIES

Basic services: nonremedial tutoring, health service, health insurance, other. **Remedial assistance:** other. **Counseling services:** minority student, career, military, personal, veteran student, academic, older student, psychological, birth control, religious. **For learning-disabled students:** School does not offer a structured program with separate admission and additional fees. Services include: remedial English, reading machines, remedial reading, tape recorders, note-taking services, learning center, readers, extended time for tests, tutors, priority registration, priority seating, texts on tape, other testing accommodations, other. **Library:** Number of titles: 130,900; number of current serial subscriptions: 208. **Information technology resources:** Students are not required to lease or own a computer. School has a wireless network. Proportion of college-owned housing units wired for high-speed internet access: 100%. **Campus safety:** Security services offered: 24-hour foot-and-vehicle patrols, late-night transport/escort service, 24-hour emergency telephones, lighted pathways/sidewalks, student patrols, controlled dormitory access (key, security card, etc).

TRANSFER AND INTERNATIONAL STUDENTS

Transfer students: May apply for admission for the following academic terms: Fall, Spring. Applicants do not need a minimum number of credits to apply. For fall 2009: Transfer applications received: 346. Transfer applicants offered admission: 195. Transfer applicants enrolled: 81. **International students:** Number of foreign undergraduates: 3. Minimum TOEFL score required: 500 (paper); 173 (computer).

Westfield State College

- **Address:** Western Avenue, Westfield, MA 01086
- **Website:** http://www.wsc.mass.edu
- **Public**
- **Enrollment:** 4,543 full-time; 500 part-time

KEY STATS

✔ **U.S News College Ranking:** 112, Regional Universities (North)
✔ **SAT Score (25th/75th percentile):** 930-1110
✔ **Tuition:** 2010-2011: $7,516 in state, $13,596 out of state

Selectivity: Selective	**Room/board:** $8,620
Acceptance rate: 58%	**Average debt:** $18,648
Student/faculty ratio: 17/1	**Proportion who borrowed:** 73%

UNDERGRADUATE STUDENT BODY STATS

2009-2010 enrollment: 4,543 full-time; 500 part-time. Men: 48%; women: 52%. **Ethnic makeup:** African American: 4%; Asian American: 1%; Hispanic: 4%; White: 91%.

ADMISSIONS FACTS AND FIGURES

Phone: (413) 572-5218. **Email:** admission@wsc.ma.edu. **Website:** http://www.wsc.mass.edu. **Application deadlines for fall 2011:** Regular decision: March 15; decision sent by March 31. Early decision: Not offered. Early action: Not offered. Admission can be deferred. **Application fee:** $50. **To apply online, go to:** https://infoweb.wsc.ma.edu:9102/pls/WSCB/bwskalog.P_

DispLoginNon. **Admissions requirements/recommendations:** High school units required (recommended): English: 4; Mathematics: 3; Science: 3; Foreign language: 2; Social studies: 1; History: 1; Academic electives: 2; Total units: 16. Tests: The college uses SAT or ACT scores in admissions decisions. Either SAT or ACT required. For admission to the fall 2011 entering class, the school will accept: ACT with or without writing accepted. Campus visit: Recommended. Admissions interview: Neither required nor recommended. Off-campus interview: Not available. **Factors that count in admissions decisions:** *Academic:* Secondary school record: Very Important. Class rank: Not Considered. Letters of recommendation: Considered. Standardized test scores: Very Important. Essay: Considered. *Nonacademic:* Interview: Not Considered. Extracurricular activities: Important. Talent/ability: Important. Character/personal qualities: Considered. Alumni/ae relationship: Not Considered. Geographical residence: Not Considered. State residency: Not Considered. Religious affiliation/commitment: Not Considered. Minority status: Considered. Volunteer work: Considered. Work experience: Considered. **Other schools with the greatest overlap in applicants:** Bridgewater State College; University of Massachusetts–Amherst; University of Massachusetts–Dartmouth; Western New England College. **Admissions statistics for the fall 2009 entering class:** Total applicants: 5,391. Total accepted: 3,124. Freshmen enrolled: 1,140; 6% were from out of state. Overall acceptance rate: 58%. **Credentials of fall 2009 freshmen:** 8% ranked in the top 10 percent of their high school class; 27% were in the top 25 percent; 72% were in the top half. (Proportion submitting class standing: 66%.) **Average high school grade point average:** 3.0. **First-year students who submitted SAT scores:** 89%. Scores (25/75 percentile): Critical Reading: 460-550, Math: 470-560, Combined: 930-1110. **First-year students submitting ACT scores:** 8%. Scores (25/75 percentile): English: N/A, Math: N/A, Composite: 19-23.

ACADEMICS

Year founded: 1838. **Academic calendar:** Semester. **Degrees offered:** bachelor's, post-bachelor's certificate, master's, post-master's certificate. **Most popular majors:** 17% security and protective services, 14% liberal arts and sciences studies, and humanities, 13% business, management, marketing, and related support services, 11% education, 10% communication, journalism, and related programs. **Major fields of study:** architecture and related services; biological and biomedical sciences; business, management, marketing, and related support services; communication, journalism, and related programs; computer and information sciences and support services; education; English language and literature/letters; history; liberal arts and sciences studies, and humanities; mathematics and statistics; natural resources and conservation; parks, recreation, leisure, and fitness studies; physical sciences; psychology; public administration and social service professions; security and protective services; social sciences; visual and performing arts. **Areas of required coursework:** arts/fine arts, humanities, mathematics, English (including composition), sciences (biological or physical), history, social science, other. **Special academic programs (% participation):** cooperative (work-study plan) program, cross-registration, distance learning (54%), double major (20%), dual enrollment, exchange student program (domestic) (2%), honors program (1.5%), independent study (10%), internships (21%), student-designed major (16%), study abroad (3.5%), teacher certificate program (13%). **Teacher certification offered in:** early childhood, special education, elementary, vo-tech, middle/junior high, secondary. **Cooperative education programs:** art, business, computer science, education, humanities, natural science, social/behavioral science, technologies. **Reserve Officers Training Corps (ROTC):** Army ROTC: Offered on campus; Air Force ROTC: Offered at cooperating institution (University of Massachusetts–Amherst). **Faculty and instruction (2009-2010):** Total instructional faculty: 212 full-time, 250 part-time (54% men; 46% women; 9% minorities). Full-time faculty with Ph.D. or other terminal degree: 87%. Student/faculty ratio: 17/1. Classes of fewer than 20 students: 41%; of 20 to 49 students: 58%; of 50 or more students: 1%. **Advanced Placement and International Baccalaureate credit:** AP tests may be used for: Credit and/or placement. Scores accepted: 3, 4, 5. **Freshmen returning for sophomore year:** 77%. **Graduation rates:** Four-year: 42%; five-year: 56%; six-year: 57%. **Graduate study:** 18% of students pursue further study immediately upon graduation; 21% within one year. Fields in which graduates pursue further study: Master of Business Administration (MBA), 10%; law, 5%; medicine, 3%; education, 19%; arts and sciences, 31%.

COSTS AND FINANCIAL AID

Financial aid office: (413) 572-5218. **Expenses (2010-2011):** Tuition and fees 2010-2011: $7,516 in state, $13,596 out of state; room/board: $8,620. Estimated books and supplies: $950; transportation: $550; personal expenses: $1,200. **Financial aid:** Priority filing date for institution's financial aid form: March 1. In 2009-2010, 80% of undergraduates applied for financial aid. Of those, 54% were determined to have financial need; 20% had their need fully met. Average financial aid package (proportion receiving): $7,812 (53%). Average amount of gift aid, such as scholarships or grants (proportion receiving): $5,058 (34%). Average amount of self-help aid, such as work study or loans (proportion receiving): $4,151 (46%). Average need-based loan (excluding PLUS or other private loans): $3,955. Among students who received need-based aid, the average percentage of need met: 73%. Among students who received aid based on merit, the average award (and the proportion receiving): $4,695 (1%). The average athletic scholarship (and the proportion receiving): $0 (0%). Average amount of debt of borrowers graduating in 2009: $18,648. Proportion who borrowed: 73%.

CAMPUS LIFE AND EXTRACURRICULAR ACTIVITIES

Campus housing available (% using): coed dorms (71%), apartment for single students (26%), special housing for disabled students, other housing options (1%). Students who live in college-owned, operated, or affiliated housing: 56%. **Student employment:** During the 2009-2010 academic year, 9% of undergraduates worked on campus. Average per-year earnings: $1,200. **Clubs and organizations:** Number of student organizations: 72. Activities include: campus ministries, choral groups, concert band, dance, drama/theater, international student organization, jazz band, literary magazine, model UN, music ensembles, musical theater, opera, pep band, radio station, student government, student newspaper, television station, yearbook. Number of fraternities: 0; sororities: 0. Average proportion of students who stay on campus on weekends: 40%. **Sports program (2009-2010):** Member of NCAA III. *Men's intercollegiate varsity sports:* baseball, basketball, cross country, football, golf, ice hockey, soccer, track and field (indoor), track and field (outdoor). *Women's intercollegiate varsity sports:* basketball, cross country, field hockey, golf, lacrosse, soccer, softball, swimming, track and field (indoor), track and field (outdoor), volleyball.

SERVICES AND FACILITIES

Basic services: nonremedial tutoring, placement service, health service. **Counseling services:** minority student, career, military, personal, veteran student, academic, older student, psychological, birth control, religious. **For learning-disabled students:** School does not offer a structured program with separate admission and additional fees. Total undergraduates in learning-disabled program or receiving services: 579. Services include: reading machines, tape recorders, videotaped classes, untimed tests, note-taking services, oral tests, learning center, readers, extended time for tests, tutors, priority registration, priority seating, texts on tape, other testing accommodations. **Library:** Number of titles: 152,067; number of current serial subscriptions: 1,509. **Information technology resources:** Students are not required to lease or own a computer. Number of campus computers available to all students: 275. School has a wireless network. Approximate number of users that can be accommodated: 8,000. Proportion of college-owned housing units wired for high-speed internet access: 100%. **Campus safety:** Security services offered: 24-hour foot-and-vehicle patrols, late-night transport/escort service, 24-hour emergency telephones, lighted pathways/sidewalks, student patrols, controlled dormitory access (key, security card, etc).

TRANSFER AND INTERNATIONAL STUDENTS

Transfer students: May apply for admission for the following academic terms: Fall, Spring. Applicants need a minimum number of credits to apply. For fall 2009: Transfer applications received: 744. Transfer applicants offered admission: 558. Transfer applicants enrolled: 348. **International students:** Number of foreign undergraduates: 6. Number of countries represented: 4. Minimum TOEFL score required: 550 (paper); 80 (computer).

Wheaton College

- ■ **Address:** 26 E. Main Street, Norton, MA 02766
- ■ **Website:** http://www.wheatoncollege.edu
- ■ **Private**
- ■ **Enrollment:** 1,627 full-time; 5 part-time

KEY STATS

✔ **U.S News College Ranking:** 59, National Liberal Arts Colleges
✔ **SAT Score (25th/75th percentile):** 1130-1350
✔ **Tuition:** 2010-2011: $41,084

Selectivity: More selective	**Room/board:** $10,180
Acceptance rate: 59%	**Average debt:** $25,540
Student/faculty ratio: 11/1	**Proportion who borrowed:** 53%

UNDERGRADUATE STUDENT BODY STATS

2009-2010 enrollment: 1,627 full-time; 5 part-time. Men: 38%; women: 62%. **Ethnic makeup:** African American: 5%; Asian American: 2%; Hispanic: 4%; White: 83%; International: 5%.

ADMISSIONS FACTS AND FIGURES

Phone: (508) 286-8251. **Email:** admission@wheatoncollege.edu. **Website:** http://www.wheatoncollege.edu. **Application deadlines for fall 2011:** Regular decision: January 15; decision sent by April 1. Early decision: Send application by: November 15; Decision sent by: December 15. Early action: Not offered. Admission can be deferred. **Application fee:** $55. **To apply online, go to:** http://www.wheatoncollege.edu/Admission/applying.html. **Admissions requirements/recommendations:** High school units required (recommended): English: 4 (4); Mathematics: 4 (4); Science: 3 (3); Foreign language: 4 (4); Social studies: 2 (3); History: 2 (2); Total units: 19 (20). Tests: The college uses SAT or ACT scores in admissions decisions. Neither SAT nor ACT required. For admission to the fall 2011 entering class, the school will accept: ACT with or without writing accepted. Campus visit: Recommended. Admissions interview: Recommended. Off-campus interview: May be arranged. **Factors that count in admissions decisions:** *Academic:* Secondary school record: Very Important. Class rank: Important. Letters of recommendation: Important. Standardized test scores: Not Considered. Essay: Very Important. *Nonacademic:* Interview: Important. Extracurricular activities: Very Important. Talent/ability: Very Important. Character/personal qualities: Very Important. Alumni/ae relationship: Important. Geographical residence: Considered. State residency: Considered. Religious affiliation/commitment: Not Considered. Minority status: Considered. Volunteer work: Important. Work experience: Important. **Other schools with the greatest overlap in applicants:** Bates College; Boston University; Clark University; Connecticut College; Skidmore College. **Admissions statistics for the fall 2009 entering class:** Total applicants: 3,304. Total accepted: 1,947. Freshmen enrolled: 424; 64% were from out of state. Accepted through early-decision or early-action plans: 29%. Overall acceptance rate: 59%. Early-decision acceptance rate: 83%. Non-early acceptance rate: 58%. **Size of waiting list:** 380 applicants; enrolled from waiting list: 18. **Credentials of fall 2009 freshmen:** 53% ranked in the top 10 percent of their high school class; 83% were in the top 25 percent; 98% were in the top half. (Proportion submitting class standing: 33%.) **Average high school grade point average:** 3.5. **First-year students who submitted SAT scores:** 42%. Scores (25/75 percentile): Critical Reading: 570-680, Math: 560-670, Combined: 1130-1350. **First-year students submitting ACT scores:** 12%. Scores (25/75 percentile): English: N/A, Math: N/A, Composite: 27-30.

ACADEMICS

Year founded: 1834. **Academic calendar:** Semester. **Degrees offered:** bachelor's. **Most popular majors:** 15% psychology, 10% English language and literature, 9% economics, 7% political science and government, 5% fine/studio arts. **Major fields of study:** area, ethnic, cultural, and gender studies; biological and biomedical sciences; computer and information sciences and support services; English language and literature/letters; foreign languages, literatures, and linguistics; history; mathematics and statistics; multi/interdisciplinary studies; natural resources and conservation; philosophy and religious studies; physical sciences; psychology; social sciences; visual and performing arts. **Areas of required coursework:** arts/fine arts, humanities, mathematics, English (including composition), foreign languages, sciences (biological or physical), history, social science, other. **Pre-professional programs:** pre-law, pre-dentistry, pre-medicine, pre-veterinary science, pre-optometry. **Special academic programs (% participation):** accelerated program (0%), cross-registration (2%), double major (13%), dual enrollment (0%), exchange student program (domestic) (2%), honors program, independent study (13%), internships (80%), liberal arts/career combination (0%), student-designed major (2%), study abroad (30%), teacher certificate program (7%). **Teacher certification offered in:** early childhood, elementary, secondary. **Reserve Officers Training Corps (ROTC):** Army ROTC: Offered at cooperating institution (Stonehill College). **Faculty and instruction (2009-2010):** Total instructional faculty: 139 full-time, 30 part-time (46% men; 54% women; 20% minorities). Full-time faculty with Ph.D. or other terminal degree: 88%. Student/faculty ratio: 11/1. Classes of fewer than 20 students: 68%; of 20 to 49 students: 28%; of 50 or more students: 4%. **Advanced Placement and International Baccalaureate credit:** AP tests may be used for: Credit and/or placement. Scores accepted: 4, 5. International Baccalaureate exams may be used for: Credit and/or placement. **Freshmen returning for sophomore year:** 86%. **Graduation rates:** Four-year: 73%; five-year: 75%; six-year: 75%. **Graduate study:** 15% of students pursue further study immediately upon graduation; 29% within one year; 55% within five years. Fields in which graduates pursue further study: Master of Business Administration (MBA), 33%; law, 14%; medicine, 13%; dentistry, 3%; theology (or the seminary), 1%; education, 7%; arts and sciences, 40%; veterinary medicine, 5%.

COSTS AND FINANCIAL AID

Financial aid office: (508) 286-8232. **Expenses (2010-2011):** Tuition and fees 2010-2011: $41,084; room/board: $10,180. Estimated books and supplies: $940; transportation: $300; personal expenses: $760. **Financial aid:** Priority filing date for institution's financial aid form: February 1; deadline: February 1. In 2009-2010, 62% of undergraduates applied for financial aid. Of those, 56% were determined to have financial need; 57% had their need fully met. Average financial aid package (proportion receiving): $31,770 (56%). Average amount of gift aid, such as scholarships or grants (proportion receiving): $25,214 (53%). Average amount of self-help aid, such as work study or loans (proportion receiving): $6,556 (55%). Average need-based loan (excluding PLUS or other private loans): $4,614. Among students who received need-based aid, the average percentage of need met: 97%. Among students who received aid based on merit, the average award (and the proportion receiving): $10,725 (13%). The average athletic scholarship (and the proportion receiving): $0 (0%). Average amount of debt of borrowers graduating in 2009: $25,540. Proportion who borrowed: 53%.

CAMPUS LIFE AND EXTRACURRICULAR ACTIVITIES

Campus housing available (% using): coed dorms (83%), women's dorms (14%), men's dorms (3%), special housing for disabled students, special housing for international students, other housing options. Students who live in college-owned, operated, or affiliated housing: 93%. **Student employment:** During the 2009-2010 academic year, 55% of undergraduates worked on campus. Average per-year earnings: $1,175. **Clubs and organizations:** Number of student organizations: 50. Activities include: choral groups, dance, drama/theater, jazz band, literary magazine, music ensembles, musical theater, pep band, radio station, student government, student newspaper, student film society, symphony orchestra, yearbook. Number of fraternities: 0; sororities: 0. Average proportion of students who stay on campus on weekends: 82%. **Sports program (2009-2010):** Member of NCAA III. **Men's intercollegiate varsity sports:** baseball, basketball, cross country, lacrosse, soccer, swimming, tennis, track and field (indoor), track and field (outdoor). **Women's intercollegiate varsity sports:** basketball, cross country, field hockey, lacrosse, soccer, softball, swimming, sync swimming, tennis, track and field (indoor), track and field (outdoor), volleyball.

SERVICES AND FACILITIES

Basic services: nonremedial tutoring, women's center, placement service, health service, health insurance, other. **Remedial assistance:** writing, study skills. **Counseling services:** minority student, career, personal, academic, psychological, birth control, religious. **For learning-disabled students:** School does not offer a structured program with separate admission and additional fees. Services include: reading machines, tape recorders, note-taking services, oral tests, learning center, readers, extended time for tests, tutors, priority seating, substitution of courses, texts on tape, typist/scribe, other. **Library:** Number of titles: 376,616; number of current serial subscriptions: 15,299. **Information technology resources:** Students are not required to lease or own a computer. Number of campus computers available to all students: 356. School has a wireless network. Approximate number of users that can be accommodated: 600. Proportion of college-owned housing units wired for high-speed internet access: 100%. **Campus safety:** Security services offered: 24-hour foot-and-vehicle patrols, late-night transport/escort service,

24-hour emergency telephones, lighted pathways/sidewalks, controlled dormitory access (key, security card, etc).

TRANSFER AND INTERNATIONAL STUDENTS

Transfer students: May apply for admission for the following academic terms: Fall, Spring. Applicants do not need a minimum number of credits to apply. For fall 2009: Transfer applications received: 110. Transfer applicants offered admission: 48. Transfer applicants enrolled: 9. **International students:** Number of foreign undergraduates: 76 (5% of student body). Number of countries represented: 35. Minimum TOEFL score required: 580 (paper); 243 (computer). Average TOEFL score: 595 (paper).

Wheelock College

- **Address:** 200 The Riverway, Boston, MA 02215
- **Website:** http://www.wheelock.edu
- **Private**
- **Enrollment:** 724 full-time; 27 part-time

KEY STATS

✔ **U.S News College Ranking:** 58, Regional Universities (North)
✔ **SAT Score (25th/75th percentile):** 870-1090
✔ **Tuition:** 2010-2011: $28,940

Selectivity: Selective	**Room/board:** $11,900
Acceptance rate: 75%	**Average debt:** $43,319
Student/faculty ratio: 9/1	**Proportion who borrowed:** 96%

UNDERGRADUATE STUDENT BODY STATS

2009-2010 enrollment: 724 full-time; 27 part-time. Men: 9%; women: 91%. **Ethnic makeup:** African American: 9%; American-Indian: 1%; Asian American: 2%; Hispanic: 8%; White: 80%; International: 1%.

ADMISSIONS FACTS AND FIGURES

Phone: (617) 879-2206. **Email:** undergrad@wheelock.edu. **Website:** http://www.wheelock.edu. **Application deadlines for fall 2011:** Regular decision: Rolling. Early decision: Not offered. Early action: Send application by: December 1; Decision sent by: December 22. Admission can be deferred. **Application fee:** $15. **To apply online, go to:** http://www.wheelock.edu/admissions/. **Admissions requirements/recommendations:** High school units required (recommended): English: 4 (4); Mathematics: 3 (3); Science: 2 (3); Foreign language: 0 (2); Social studies: 2 (2); History: 0 (1); Academic electives: 0; Total units: 16 (20). Tests: The college uses SAT or ACT scores in admissions decisions. Either SAT or ACT required. For admission to the fall 2011 entering class, the school will accept: ACT with writing recommended. Campus visit: Recommended. Admissions interview: Recommended. Off-campus interview: May be arranged. **Factors that count in admissions decisions:** *Academic:* Secondary school record: Very Important. Class rank: Important. Letters of recommendation: Important. Standardized test scores: Important. Essay: Very Important. *Nonacademic:* Interview: Considered. Extracurricular activities: Important. Talent/ability: Considered. Character/personal qualities: Important. Alumni/ae relationship: Considered. Geographical residence: Not Considered. State residency: Not Considered. Religious affiliation/commitment: Not Considered. Minority status: Not Considered. Volunteer work: Important. Work experience: Considered. **Other schools with the greatest overlap in applicants:** Bridgewater State College; Emmanuel College; Lesley University; Simmons College; Suffolk University. **Admissions statistics for the fall 2009 entering class:** Total applicants: 1,092. Total accepted: 819. Freshmen enrolled: 191; 33% were from out of state. Accepted through early-decision or early-action plans: 34%. Overall acceptance rate: 75%. Non-early acceptance rate: 71%. **Credentials of fall 2009 freshmen:** 10% ranked in the top 10 percent of their high school class; 35% were in the top 25 percent; 69% were in the top half. (Proportion submitting class standing: 57%.) **Average high school grade point average:** 3.0. **First-year students who submitted SAT scores:** 96%. Scores (25/75 percentile): Critical Reading: 440-550, Math: 430-540, Combined: 870-1090. **First-year students submitting ACT scores:** 17%. Scores (25/75 percentile): English: 17-24, Math: 19-25, Composite: 18-24.

ACADEMICS

Year founded: 1888. **Academic calendar:** Semester. **Degrees offered:** certificate, diploma, associate, bachelor's, post-bachelor's certificate, master's, post-master's certificate. **Most popular majors:** 55% human development and family studies, 15% elementary education and teaching, 10% kindergarten/preschool education and teaching, 10% social work, 9% early childhood education and teaching. **Major fields of study:** area, ethnic, cultural, and gender studies; education; family and consumer sciences/human sciences; liberal arts and sciences studies, and humanities; public administration and social service professions; visual and performing arts. **Areas of required coursework:** arts/fine arts, humanities, mathematics, English (including composition), philosophy, sciences (biological or physical), history, social science, other. **Pre-professional programs:** other. **Special academic programs (% participation):** cross-registration (17%), double major (52%), independent study (42%), internships (100%), liberal arts/career combination (50%), study abroad (5%), teacher certificate program (30%). **Teacher certification offered in:** early childhood, special education, elementary, bilingual/bicultural. **Faculty and instruction (2009-2010):** Total instructional faculty: 59 full-time, 81 part-time (21% men; 79% women; 21% minorities). Full-time faculty with Ph.D. or other terminal degree: 90%. Student/faculty ratio: 9/1. Classes of fewer than 20 students: 63%; of 20 to 49 students: 37%; of 50 or more students: 0%. **Advanced Placement and International Baccalaureate credit:** AP tests may be used for: Credit only. Scores accepted: 4, 5. International Baccalaureate exams may be used for: Placement only. **Freshmen returning for sophomore year:** 70%. **Graduation rates:** Four-year: 53%; five-year: 60%; six-year: 60%. **Graduate study:** 19% of students pursue further study immediately upon graduation; 4% within one year; 6% within five years. Fields in which graduates pursue further study: Master of Business Administration (MBA), 1%; medicine, 1%; education, 37%.

COSTS AND FINANCIAL AID
Financial aid office: (617) 879-2206. **Expenses (2010-2011):** Tuition and fees 2010-2011: $28,940; room/board: $11,900. Estimated books and supplies: $880; transportation: $510; personal expenses: $1,400. **Financial aid:** Priority filing date for institution's financial aid form: February 15. In 2009-2010, 92% of undergraduates applied for financial aid. Of those, 85% were determined to have financial need; 15% had their need fully met. Average financial aid package (proportion receiving): $20,806 (84%). Average amount of gift aid, such as scholarships or grants (proportion receiving): $15,922 (83%). Average amount of self-help aid, such as work study or loans (proportion receiving): $5,678 (75%). Average need-based loan (excluding PLUS or other private loans): $5,097. Among students who received need-based aid, the average percentage of need met: 69%. Among students who received aid based on merit, the average award (and the proportion receiving): $10,010 (13%). The average athletic scholarship (and the proportion receiving): $0 (0%). Average amount of debt of borrowers graduating in 2009: $43,319. Proportion who borrowed: 96%.

CAMPUS LIFE AND EXTRACURRICULAR ACTIVITIES
Campus housing available (% using): coed dorms (83%), women's dorms (14%), special housing for disabled students (3%). Students who live in college-owned, operated, or affiliated housing: 76%. **Student employment:** During the 2009-2010 academic year, 9% of undergraduates worked on campus. Average per-year earnings: $8. **Clubs and organizations:** Number of student organizations: 28. Activities include: choral groups, dance, drama/theater, literary magazine, music ensembles, musical theater, student government, symphony orchestra, yearbook. Number of fraternities: 0; sororities: 0. Average proportion of students who stay on campus on weekends: 60%. **Sports program (2009-2010):** Member of NCAA III. *Men's intercollegiate varsity sports:* basketball, cross country, lacrosse, soccer, tennis. *Women's intercollegiate varsity sports:* basketball, cross country, field hockey, lacrosse, soccer, softball.

SERVICES AND FACILITIES
Basic services: nonremedial tutoring, health service, health insurance. **Remedial assistance:** reading, math, writing, study skills. **Counseling services:** minority student, career, personal, academic, older student, psychological, other. **For learning-disabled students:** School does not offer a structured program with separate admission and additional fees. Total undergraduates in learning-disabled program or receiving services: 76. Services include: reading machines, tape recorders, untimed tests, note-taking services, learning center, readers, extended time for tests, tutors, priority registration, priority seating, texts on tape, typist/scribe, exams on tape or computer, other testing accommodations. **Library:** Number of titles: 79,834; number of current serial subscriptions: 55,896. **Information technology resources:** Students are not required to lease or own a computer. Number of campus computers available to all students: 200. School has a wireless network. Approximate number of users that can be accommodated: 1,000. Proportion of college-owned housing units wired for high-speed internet access: 100%. **Campus safety:** Security services offered: 24-hour foot-and-vehicle patrols, late-night transport/escort service, 24-hour emergency

telephones, lighted pathways/sidewalks, controlled dormitory access (key, security card, etc).

TRANSFER AND INTERNATIONAL STUDENTS
Transfer students: May apply for admission for the following academic terms: Fall, Spring. Applicants need a minimum number of credits to apply. For fall 2009: Transfer applications received: 161. Transfer applicants offered admission: 114. Transfer applicants enrolled: 33. **International students:** Number of foreign undergraduates: 6 (1% of student body). Number of countries represented: 5. Minimum TOEFL score required: 500 (paper); 173 (computer). Average TOEFL score: 550 (paper).

Williams College

- **Address:** 880 Main Street, Williamstown, MA 01267
- **Website:** http://www.williams.edu
- **Private**
- **Enrollment:** 2,033 full-time; 34 part-time

KEY STATS
✔ **U.S News College Ranking:** 1, National Liberal Arts Colleges
✔ **SAT Score (25th/75th percentile):** 1310-1530
✔ **Tuition:** 2010-2011: $41,434

Selectivity: Most selective	**Room/board:** $10,906
Acceptance rate: 20%	**Average debt:** $8,103
Student/faculty ratio: 7/1	**Proportion who borrowed:** 43%

UNDERGRADUATE STUDENT BODY STATS
2009-2010 enrollment: 2,033 full-time; 34 part-time. Men: 48%; women: 52%. **Ethnic makeup:** African American: 10%; Asian American: 12%; Hispanic: 10%; White: 61%; International: 7%.

ADMISSIONS FACTS AND FIGURES
Phone: (413) 597-2211. **Email:** admission@williams.edu. **Website:** http://www.williams.edu. **Application deadlines for fall 2011:** Regular decision: January 1; decision sent by April 1. Early decision: Send application by: November 10; Decision sent by: December 15. Early action: Not offered. Admission can be deferred. **Application fee:** $65. **To apply online, go to:** http://www.williams.edu/Admissions/applying/index.html. **Admissions requirements/recommendations:** High school units required (recommended): English: (4); Mathematics: (4); Science: (3); Foreign language: (4); Social studies: (3). Tests: The college uses SAT or ACT scores in admissions decisions. Either SAT or ACT required. For admission to the fall 2011 entering class, the school will accept: ACT with writing required. Campus visit: Recommended. Admissions interview: Neither required nor recommended. Off-campus interview: May be arranged. **Factors that count in admissions decisions:** *Academic:* Secondary school record: Very Important. Class rank: Important. Letters of recommendation: Very Important. Standardized test scores: Very Important. Essay: Very Important. *Nonacademic:* Interview: Not Considered. Extracurricular activities: Important. Talent/ability: Important. Character/personal qualities: Considered. Alumni/ae relationship: Considered. Geographical residence: Considered. State residency: Not Considered. Religious affiliation/commitment: Not Considered. Minority status: Considered. Volunteer work: Considered. Work experience: Considered. **Other schools with the greatest overlap in applicants:** Amherst College; Dartmouth College; Harvard University; Middlebury College; Yale University. **Admissions statistics for the fall 2009 entering class:** Total applicants: 6,017. Total accepted: 1,229. Freshmen enrolled: 546; 87% were from out of state. Accepted through early-decision or early-action plans: 40%. Overall acceptance rate: 20%. Early-decision acceptance rate: 36%. Non-early acceptance rate: 19%. **Size of waiting list:** 1101 applicants; enrolled from waiting list: 12. **Credentials of fall 2009 freshmen:** 88% ranked in the top 10 percent of their high school class; 99% were in the top 25 percent; 100% were in the top half. (Proportion submitting class standing: 31%.) **First-year students who submitted SAT scores:** 96%. Scores (25/75 percentile): Critical Reading: 660-770, Math: 650-760, Combined: 1310-1530. **First-year students submitting ACT scores:** 30%. Scores (25/75 percentile): English: N/A, Math: N/A, Composite: 30-34.

ACADEMICS
Year founded: 1793. **Academic calendar:** 4-1-4. **Degrees offered:** bachelor's, master's. **Most popular majors:** 14% economics, 13% English language and literature, 12% political science and government, 12% psychology, 11% biol-

ogy/biological sciences. **Major fields of study:** area, ethnic, cultural, and gender studies; biological and biomedical sciences; computer and information sciences and support services; English language and literature/letters; foreign languages, literatures, and linguistics; history; mathematics and statistics; philosophy and religious studies; physical sciences; psychology; social sciences; visual and performing arts. **Special academic programs (% participation):** cross-registration (1%), double major (39%), honors program (25%), independent study (40%), internships (16%), student-designed major (1%), study abroad (50%). **Reserve Officers Training Corps (ROTC):** Air Force ROTC: Offered at cooperating institution (Rochester Institute of Technology). **Faculty and instruction (2009-2010):** Total instructional faculty: 271 full-time, 34 part-time (60% men; 40% women; 20% minorities). Full-time faculty with Ph.D. or other terminal degree: 98%. Student/faculty ratio: 7/1. Classes of fewer than 20 students: 74%; of 20 to 49 students: 23%; of 50 or more students: 4%. **Advanced Placement and International Baccalaureate credit:** AP tests may be used for: Placement only. Scores accepted: 3, 4, 5. International Baccalaureate exams may be used for: Placement only. **Freshmen returning for sophomore year:** 97%. **Graduation rates:** Four-year: 93%; five-year: 96%; six-year: 96%.

COSTS AND FINANCIAL AID

Financial aid office: (413) 597-4181. **Expenses (2010-2011):** Tuition and fees 2010-2011: $41,434; room/board: $10,906. Estimated books and supplies: $800; transportation: $581; personal expenses: $1,200. **Financial aid:** In 2009-2010, 59% of undergraduates applied for financial aid. Of those, 52% were determined to have financial need; 100% had their need fully met. Average financial aid package (proportion receiving): $39,540 (52%). Average amount of gift aid, such as scholarships or grants (proportion receiving): $37,783 (52%). Average amount of self-help aid, such as work study or loans (proportion receiving): $1,757 (52%). Average need-based loan (excluding PLUS or other private loans): $0. Among students who received need-based aid, the average percentage of need met: 100%. Among students who received aid based on merit, the average award (and the proportion receiving): $0 (0%). The average athletic scholarship (and the proportion receiving): $0 (0%). Average amount of debt of borrowers graduating in 2009: $8,103. Proportion who borrowed: 43%.

CAMPUS LIFE AND EXTRACURRICULAR ACTIVITIES

Campus housing available (% using): coed dorms (94%), cooperative housing (6%). Students who live in college-owned, operated, or affiliated housing: 93%. **Student employment:** During the 2009-2010 academic year, 65% of undergraduates worked on campus. Average per-year earnings: $1,950. **Clubs and organizations:** Number of student organizations: 117. Activities include: campus ministries, choral groups, dance, drama/theater, international student organization, jazz band, literary magazine, model UN, music ensembles, musical theater, pep band, radio station, student government, student newspaper, student film society, symphony orchestra, yearbook. Number of fraternities: 0; sororities: 0. Average proportion of students who stay on campus on weekends: 90%. **Sports program (2009-2010):** Member of NCAA III. **Men's intercollegiate varsity sports:** baseball, basketball, cross country, football, golf, ice hockey, lacrosse, skiing (nordic), skiing (alpine), soccer, swimming, tennis, track and field (indoor), track and field (outdoor), wrestling. **Women's intercollegiate varsity sports:** basketball, crew (heavyweight), cross country, field hockey, golf, ice hockey, lacrosse, skiing (nordic), skiing (alpine), soccer, softball, squash, swimming, tennis, track and field (indoor), track and field (outdoor), volleyball.

SERVICES AND FACILITIES

Basic services: nonremedial tutoring, women's center, day care, health service, health insurance. **Remedial assistance:** math, writing, other. **Counseling services:** career, personal, academic, psychological, religious. **For learning-disabled students:** School does not offer a structured program with separate admission and additional fees. Total undergraduates in learning-disabled program or receiving services: 80. Services include: reading machines, tape recorders, note-taking services, readers, extended time for tests, tutors, priority seating, texts on tape, other. **Library:** Number of titles: 955,448; number of current serial subscriptions: 33,016. **Information technology resources:** Students are not required to lease or own a computer. Number of campus computers available to all students: 377. School has a wireless network. Approximate number of users that can be accommodated: 3,000. Proportion of college-owned housing units wired for high-speed internet access: 100%. **Campus safety:** Security services offered: 24-hour foot-and-vehicle patrols, late-night transport/escort service, 24-hour emergency telephones, lighted pathways/sidewalks, controlled dormitory access (key, security card, etc).

TRANSFER AND INTERNATIONAL STUDENTS

Transfer students: May apply for admission for the following academic terms: Fall. Applicants do not need a minimum number of credits to apply. For fall 2009: Transfer applications received: 96. Transfer applicants offered admission: 7. Transfer applicants enrolled: 6. **International students:** Number of foreign undergraduates: 143 (7% of student body). Number of countries represented: 73.

Worcester Polytechnic Institute

- **Address:** 100 Institute Road, Worcester, MA 01609
- **Website:** http://www.wpi.edu
- **Private**
- **Enrollment:** 3,318 full-time; 135 part-time

KEY STATS

✔ **U.S News College Ranking:** 64, National Universities
✔ **SAT Score (25th/75th percentile):** 1190-1380
✔ **Tuition:** 2010-2011: $38,700

Selectivity: More selective	**Room/board:** $11,540
Acceptance rate: 63%	**Average debt:** $44,340
Student/faculty ratio: 14/1	**Proportion who borrowed:** 74%

UNDERGRADUATE STUDENT BODY STATS

2009-2010 enrollment: 3,318 full-time; 135 part-time. Men: 72%; women: 28%. **Ethnic makeup:** African American: 3%; American-Indian: 1%; Asian American: 6%; Hispanic: 6%; White: 75%; International: 9%.

ADMISSIONS FACTS AND FIGURES

Phone: (508) 831-5286. **Email:** admissions@wpi.edu. **Website:** http://www.wpi.edu. **Application deadlines for fall 2011:** Regular decision: February 1; decision sent by April 1. Early decision: Not offered. Early action: Send application by: January 1; Decision sent by: February 1. Admission can be deferred. **Application fee:** $60. To apply online, go to: http://www.admissions.wpi.edu/Admissions/application.html. **Admissions requirements/recommendations:** High school units required (recommended): English: 4; Mathematics: 4; Science: 2 (4); Foreign language: (2); Social studies: (2); History: (1); Total units: 10. Tests: The college uses SAT or ACT scores in admissions decisions. Neither SAT nor ACT required. For admission to the fall 2011 entering class, the school will accept: ACT with or without writing accepted. Campus visit: Recommended. Admissions interview: Neither required nor recommended. Off-campus interview: May be arranged. **Factors that count in admissions decisions:** *Academic:* Secondary school record: Very Important. Class rank: Important. Letters of recommendation: Important. Standardized test scores: Important. Essay: Important. *Nonacademic:* Interview: Considered. Extracurricular activities: Important. Talent/ability: Considered. Character/personal qualities: Important. Alumni/ae relationship: Considered. Geographical residence: Considered. State residency: Not Considered. Religious affiliation/commitment: Not Considered. Minority status: Considered. Volunteer work: Considered. Work experience: Considered. **Other schools with the greatest overlap in applicants:** Boston University; Massachusetts Institute of Technology; Northeastern University; Rensselaer Polytechnic Institute; University of Massachusetts–Amherst. **Admissions statistics for the fall 2009 entering class:** Total applicants: 6,284. Total accepted: 3,989. Freshmen enrolled: 925; 54% were from out of state. Overall acceptance rate: 63%. Non-early acceptance rate: 63%. Size of waiting list: 852 applicants; enrolled from waiting list: 2. **Credentials of fall 2009 freshmen:** 55% ranked in the top 10 percent of their high school class; 88% were in the top 25 percent; 99% were in the top half. (Proportion submitting class standing: 75%.) **Average high school grade point average:** 3.8. **First-year students who submitted SAT scores:** 93%. Scores (25/75 percentile): Critical Reading: 560-660, Math: 630-720, Combined: 1190-1380. **First-year students submitting ACT scores:** 26%. Scores (25/75 percentile): English: N/A, Math: N/A, Composite: 26-31.

ACADEMICS

Year founded: 1865. **Academic calendar:** Quarter. **Degrees offered:** bachelor's, post-bachelor's certificate, master's, post-master's certificate, doctorate. **Most popular majors:** 19% mechanical engineering, 14% electrical, electronics, and communications engineering, 10% computer science, 7% civil engineering, 6% biomedical/medical engineering. **Major fields of study:** biological and biomedical sciences; business, management, marketing, and related support services; computer and information sciences and support services; engineering; English language and literature/letters; liberal arts and sciences studies, and humanities; mathematics and statistics; multi/interdisciplinary studies; physical sciences; social sciences. **Areas of required coursework:** humanities, mathematics, sciences (biological or physical), social science. **Pre-professional programs:** pre-law, pre-dentistry, pre-medicine, pre-veterinary science. **Special academic programs (% participation):** accelerated program (3.4%), cooperative (work-study plan) program (4%), cross-registration (5%), double major (2%), dual enrollment (1%), English as a Second Language (ESL) (.75%), independent study (34%), liberal arts/career combination (1%), student-designed major, study abroad (51%), teacher certificate program, other (60%). **Teacher certification offered in:** middle/junior high, secondary. **Cooperative education programs:** business, computer science, engineering, natural science, social/behavioral science. **Reserve Officers Training Corps (ROTC):** Army ROTC: Offered on campus; Navy ROTC: Offered at cooperating institution (College of the Holy Cross); Air Force ROTC: Offered on campus. **Faculty and instruction (2009-2010):** Total instructional faculty: 263 full-time, 102 part-time (76% men; 24% women; 13% minorities). Full-time faculty with Ph.D. or other terminal degree: 94%. Student/faculty ratio: 14/1. Classes of fewer than 20 students: 67%; of 20 to 49 students: 24%; of 50 or more students: 9%. **Advanced Placement and International Baccalaureate credit:** AP tests may be used for: Credit and/or placement. Scores accepted: 4, 5. International Baccalaureate exams may be used for: Credit and/or placement. **Freshmen returning for sophomore year:** 93%. **Graduation rates:** Four-year: 67%; five-year: 77%; six-year: 80%. **Graduate study:** 31% of students pursue further study immediately upon graduation. Fields in which graduates pursue further study: Master of Business Administration (MBA), 6%; law, 1%; medicine, 6%; dentistry, 1%; engineering, 49%; arts and sciences, 20%; veterinary medicine, 1%.

COSTS AND FINANCIAL AID

Financial aid office: (508) 831-5469. **Expenses (2010-2011):** Tuition and fees 2010-2011: $38,700; room/board: $11,540. Estimated books and supplies: $1,000; transportation: $0; personal expenses: $0. **Financial aid:** Priority filing date for institution's financial aid form: February 1. In 2009-2010, 81% of undergraduates applied for financial aid. Of those, 71% were determined to have financial need; 34% had their need fully met. Average financial aid package (proportion receiving): $25,306 (70%). Average amount of gift aid, such as scholarships or grants (proportion receiving): $17,979 (67%). Average amount of self-help aid, such as work study or loans (proportion receiving): $7,055 (56%). Average need-based loan (excluding PLUS or other private loans): $6,836. Among students who received need-based aid, the average percentage of need met: 70%. Among students who received aid based on merit, the average award (and the proportion receiving): $15,384 (28%). The average athletic scholarship (and the proportion receiving): $0 (0%). Average amount of debt of borrowers graduating in 2009: $44,340. Proportion who borrowed: 74%.

CAMPUS LIFE AND EXTRACURRICULAR ACTIVITIES

Campus housing available (% using): coed dorms (61%), sorority housing (3%), fraternity housing (22%), apartment for single students (11%), special housing for disabled students (0%), special housing for international students (1%), other housing options (2%). Students who live in college-owned, operated, or affiliated housing: 50%. **Student employment:** During the 2009-2010 academic year, 26% of undergraduates worked on campus. Average per-year earnings: $2,640. **Clubs and organizations:** Number of student organizations: 200. Activities include: campus ministries, choral groups, concert band, dance, drama/theater, jazz band, marching band, music ensembles, musical theater, pep band, radio station, student government, student newspaper, symphony orchestra, yearbook. Number of fraternities: 13; sororities: 3. Proportion of men in fraternities: 30%; of women in sororities: 36%. Average proportion of students who stay on campus on weekends: 90%. **Sports program (2009-2010):** Member of NCAA III. *Men's intercollegiate varsity sports:* baseball, basketball, cross country, football, swimming, track and field (indoor), track and field (outdoor), wrestling. *Women's intercollegiate varsity sports:* basketball, crew (heavyweight), cross country, field hockey, crew (lightweight), swimming, track and field (indoor), track and field (outdoor), volleyball.

SERVICES AND FACILITIES

Basic services: nonremedial tutoring, women's center, placement service, health service, health insurance, other. **Counseling services:** minority student, career, military, personal, veteran student, academic, older student, psychological, birth control, religious, other. **For learning-disabled students:** School does not offer a structured program with separate admission and additional fees. Total undergraduates in learning-disabled program or

receiving services: 200. Services include: tape recorders, note-taking services, learning center, extended time for tests, tutors, other testing accommodations. **Library:** Number of titles: 310,722; number of current serial subscriptions: 42,415. **Information technology resources:** Students are not required to lease or own a computer. Number of campus computers available to all students: 700. School has a wireless network. Approximate number of users that can be accommodated: 4,000. Proportion of college-owned housing units wired for high-speed internet access: 100%. **Campus safety:** Security services offered: 24-hour foot-and-vehicle patrols, late-night transport/escort service, 24-hour emergency telephones, lighted pathways/sidewalks, controlled dormitory access (key, security card, etc).

TRANSFER AND INTERNATIONAL STUDENTS

Transfer students: May apply for admission for the following academic terms: Fall, Spring. Applicants do not need a minimum number of credits to apply. For fall 2009: Transfer applications received: 189. Transfer applicants offered admission: 75. Transfer applicants enrolled: 31. **International students:** Number of foreign undergraduates: 308 (9% of student body). Number of countries represented: 61. Minimum TOEFL score required: 550 (paper); 79 (computer). Average TOEFL score: 600 (paper).

Worcester State College

- **Address:** 486 Chandler Street, Worcester, MA 01602-2597
- **Website:** http://www.worcester.edu
- **Public**
- **Enrollment:** 3,494 full-time; 1,209 part-time

KEY STATS

✔ **U.S News College Ranking:** second tier, Regional Universities (North)
✔ **SAT Score (25th/75th percentile):** 930-1110
✔ **Tuition:** 2009-2010: $6,605 in state, $12,685 out of state

Selectivity: Selective	**Room/board:** $9,067
Acceptance rate: 59%	**Average debt:** $17,819
Student/faculty ratio: 17/1	**Proportion who borrowed:** 42%

UNDERGRADUATE STUDENT BODY STATS

2009-2010 enrollment: 3,494 full-time; 1,209 part-time. Men: 40%; women: 60%. **Ethnic makeup:** African American: 6%; American-Indian: 1%; Asian American: 3%; Hispanic: 6%; White: 83%; International: 1%.

ADMISSIONS FACTS AND FIGURES

Phone: (508) 929-8040. **Email:** admissions@worcester.edu. **Website:** http://www.worcester.edu. **Application deadlines for fall 2011:** Regular decision: May 1. Early decision: Not offered. Early action: Not offered. Admission can be deferred. **Application fee:** $40. **To apply online, go to:** https://www.applyweb.com/apply/worcest/menu.html. **Admissions requirements/recommendations:** High school units required (recommended): English: 4; Mathematics: 3; Science: 3; Foreign language: 2; Social studies: 1; History: 1; Academic electives: 2; Total units: 16. Tests: The college uses SAT or ACT scores in admissions decisions. Either SAT or ACT required. For admission to the fall 2011 entering class, the school will accept: ACT with writing required. Campus visit: Recommended. Admissions interview: Neither required nor recommended. Off-campus interview: Not available. **Factors that count in admissions decisions:** *Academic:* Secondary school record: Very Important. Class rank: Important. Letters of recommendation: Considered. Standardized test scores: Very Important. Essay: Considered. *Nonacademic:* Interview: Not Considered. Extracurricular activities: Considered. Talent/ability: Considered. Character/personal qualities: Important. Alumni/ae relationship: Considered. Geographical residence: Considered. State residency: Considered. Religious affiliation/commitment: Not Considered. Minority status: Considered. Volunteer work: Considered. Work experience: Considered. **Other schools with the greatest overlap in applicants:** Anna Maria College; Assumption College; Clark University; Fitchburg State College; University of Massachusetts–Amherst. **Admissions statistics for the fall 2009 entering class:** Total applicants: 3,559. Total accepted: 2,101. Freshmen enrolled: 695; 4% were from out of state. Overall acceptance rate: 59%. **Average high school grade point average:** 3.1. **First-year students who submitted SAT scores:** 94%. Scores (25/75 percentile): Critical Reading: 460-550, Math: 470-560, Combined: 930-1110. **First-year students submitting ACT scores:** 7%. Scores (25/75 percentile): English: N/A, Math: N/A, Composite: 19-24.

ACADEMICS

Year founded: 1874. **Academic calendar:** Semester. **Degrees offered:** certificate, bachelor's, post-bachelor's certificate, master's, post-master's certificate. **Most popular majors:** 22% business, management, marketing, and related support services, 15% health professions and related clinical sciences, 12% psychology, 9% communication, journalism, and related programs, 8% biological and biomedical sciences. **Major fields of study:** biological and biomedical sciences; business, management, marketing, and related support services; communication, journalism, and related programs; computer and information sciences and support services; education; English language and literature/letters; foreign languages, literatures, and linguistics; health professions and related clinical sciences; history; mathematics and statistics; multi/interdisciplinary studies; physical sciences; psychology; security and protective services; social sciences. **Areas of required coursework:** arts/fine arts, humanities, mathematics, English (including composition), sciences (biological or physical), history, social science, other. **Pre-professional programs:** pre-law, pre-dentistry, pre-medicine, pre-veterinary science, pre-pharmacy. **Special academic programs:** cross-registration, distance learning, double major, English as a Second Language (ESL), exchange student program (domestic), honors program, independent study, internships, liberal arts/career combination, study abroad, teacher certificate program, other. **Teacher certification offered in:** early childhood, special education, elementary, middle/junior high, secondary. **Reserve Officers Training Corps (ROTC):** Army ROTC: Offered at cooperating institution (Worcester Polytechnic Institute); Navy ROTC: Offered at cooperating institution (College of the Holy Cross); Air Force ROTC: Offered at cooperating institution (Worcester Polytechnic Institute). **Faculty and instruction (2009-2010):** Total instructional faculty: 179 full-time, 199 part-time (48% men; 52% women; 13% minorities). Full-time faculty with Ph.D. or other terminal degree: 74%. Student/faculty ratio: 17/1. Classes of fewer than 20 students: 49%; of 20 to 49 students: 51%. **Advanced Placement and International Baccalaureate credit:** AP tests may be used for: Credit and/or placement. Scores accepted: 3, 4, 5. International Baccalaureate exams may be used for: Credit only. **Freshmen returning for sophomore year:** 76%. **Graduation rates:** Four-year; 24%; five-year; 41%; six-year; 42%.

COSTS AND FINANCIAL AID

Financial aid office: (508) 929-8056. **Expenses (2009-2010):** Tuition and fees 2009-2010: $6,605 in state, $12,685 out of state; room/board: $9,067. Estimated books and supplies: $984; transportation: $500; personal expenses: $2,200. **Financial aid:** Priority filing date for institution's financial aid form: March 1; deadline: May 1. In 2009-2010, 76% of undergraduates applied for financial aid. Of those, 50% were determined to have financial need; 50% had their need fully met. Average financial aid package (proportion receiving): $9,679 (49%). Average amount of gift aid, such as scholarships or grants (proportion receiving): $4,391 (36%). Average amount of self-help aid, such as work study or loans (proportion receiving): $2,778 (45%). Average need-based loan (excluding PLUS or other private loans): $2,521. Among students who received need-based aid, the average percentage of need met: 85%. Among students who received aid based on merit, the average award (and the proportion receiving): $0 (0%). The average athletic scholarship (and the proportion receiving): $0 (0%). Average amount of debt of borrowers graduating in 2009: $17,819. Proportion who borrowed: 42%.

CAMPUS LIFE AND EXTRACURRICULAR ACTIVITIES

Campus housing available (% using): coed dorms (23%), women's dorms (48%), men's dorms (28%), special housing for disabled students (1%). Students who live in college-owned, operated, or affiliated housing: 24%. **Student employment:** During the 2009-2010 academic year, 3% of undergraduates worked on campus. Average per-year earnings: $3,000. **Clubs and organizations:** Number of student organizations: 44. Activities include: campus ministries, choral groups, concert band, dance, drama/theater, international student organization, jazz band, music ensembles, radio station, student government, student newspaper, television station, yearbook. Number of fraternities: 0; sororities: 0. Average proportion of students who stay on campus on weekends: 40%. **Sports program (2009-2010):** Member of NCAA III. *Men's intercollegiate varsity sports:* baseball, basketball, cross country, football, golf, ice hockey, soccer, track and field (indoor), track and field (outdoor). *Women's intercollegiate varsity sports:* basketball, cross country, field hockey, lacrosse, soccer, softball, tennis, track and field (indoor), track and field (outdoor), volleyball.

SERVICES AND FACILITIES

Basic services: nonremedial tutoring, placement service, health service, health insurance. **Remedial assistance:** reading, math, writing, study skills, other. **Counseling services:** minority student, career, military, personal, veteran student, academic, psychological, birth control, religious. **For learning-disabled students:** School does not offer a structured program with separate admission and additional fees. Total undergraduates in learning-disabled program or receiving services: 87. Services include: remedial math, remedial English, reading machines, remedial reading, tape recorders, note-taking services, oral tests, readers, extended time for tests, priority registration, priority seating, texts on tape, typist/scribe, exams on tape or computer, other. **Library:** Number of titles: 201,975; number of current serial subscriptions: 802. **Information technology resources:** Students are required to lease or own a computer. Number of campus computers available to all students: 500. School has a wireless network. Approximate number of users that can be accommodated: 1,200. Proportion of college-owned housing units wired for high-speed internet access: 100%. **Campus safety:** Security services offered: 24-hour foot-and-vehicle patrols, late-night transport/escort service, 24-hour emergency telephones, lighted pathways/sidewalks, controlled dormitory access (key, security card, etc).

TRANSFER AND INTERNATIONAL STUDENTS

Transfer students: May apply for admission for the following academic terms: Fall, Spring, Summer. Applicants need a minimum number of credits to apply. For fall 2009: Transfer applications received: 1,034. Transfer applicants offered admission: 823. Transfer applicants enrolled: 508. **International students:** Number of foreign undergraduates: 35 (1% of student body). Number of countries represented: 15. Minimum TOEFL score required: 550 (paper); 213 (computer). Average TOEFL score: 560 (paper).

Michigan

Adrian College

- **Address:** 110 S. Madison Street, Adrian, MI 49221
- **Website:** http://www.adrian.edu
- **Private; Religious affiliation:** United Methodist
- **Enrollment:** 1,556 full-time; 53 part-time

KEY STATS

✔ **U.S News College Ranking:** 27, Regional Colleges (Midwest)
✔ **ACT Score (25th/75th percentile):** 20-25
✔ **Tuition:** 2010-2011: $25,900

Selectivity: Selective	**Room/board:** $7,900
Acceptance rate: 62%	**Average debt:** $17,160
Student/faculty ratio: 15/1	**Proportion who borrowed:** 81%

UNDERGRADUATE STUDENT BODY STATS

2009-2010 enrollment: 1,556 full-time; 53 part-time. Men: 53%; women: 47%. **Ethnic makeup:** African American: 4%; Hispanic: 2%; White: 88%; International: 4%. **Religious preference:** Roman Catholic: 18%; Protestant: 23%; Jewish: 1%; Buddhist: 1%; No preference: 48%; United Methodist: 7%; Not Specified: 1%; Other: 1%.

ADMISSIONS FACTS AND FIGURES

Phone: (800) 877-2246. **Email:** admissions@adrian.edu. **Website:** http://www.adrian.edu. **Application deadlines for fall 2011:** Regular decision: Rolling. Early decision: Not offered. Early action: Not offered. Admission can be deferred. **Application fee:** None. **To apply online, go to:** https://www.adrian.edu/apply/. **Admissions requirements/recommendations:** High school units required (recommended): English: 4 (4); Mathematics: 3 (3); Science: 2 (2); Foreign language: 2 (2); Social studies: 1 (1); History: 1 (1); Academic electives: 2 (2); Total units: 15 (15). Tests: The college uses SAT or ACT scores in admissions decisions. Either SAT or ACT required. For admission to the fall 2011 entering class, the school will accept: ACT with or without writing accepted. Campus visit: Recommended. Admissions interview: Recommended. Off-campus interview: May be arranged. **Factors that count in admissions decisions: Academic:** Secondary school record: Very Important. Class rank: Very Important. Letters of recommendation: Not Considered. Standardized test scores: Important. Essay: Not Considered. **Nonacademic:** Interview: Considered. Extracurricular activities: Not Considered. Talent/ability: Important. Character/personal qualities: Considered. Alumni/ae relationship: Considered. Geographical residence: Not Considered. State residency: Not Considered. Religious affiliation/commitment: Not Considered. Minority status: Considered. Volunteer work: Not Considered. Work experience: Not Considered. **Other schools with the greatest overlap in applicants:** Albion College; Central Michigan University; Grand Valley State University; Michigan State University; Wayne State University. **Admissions statistics for the fall 2009 entering class:** Total applicants: 3,888. Total accepted: 2,408. Freshmen enrolled: 480; 24% were from out of state. Overall acceptance rate: 62%. **Credentials of fall 2009 freshmen:** 18% ranked in the top 10 percent of their high school class; 44% were in the top 25 percent; 79% were in the top half. (Proportion submitting class standing: 79%.) **Average high school grade point average:** 3.3. **First-year students who submitted SAT scores:** 8%. **First-year students submitting ACT scores:** 96%. Scores (25/75 percentile): English: 19-25, Math: 19-25, Composite: 20-25.

ACADEMICS

Year founded: 1859. **Academic calendar:** Semester. **Degrees offered:** associate, transfer-associate, bachelor's. **Most popular majors:** 18% business, management, marketing, and related support services, 12% visual and performing arts, 10% biological and biomedical sciences, 10% education, 10% parks, recreation, leisure, and fitness studies. **Major fields of study:** area, ethnic, cultural, and gender studies; biological and biomedical sciences; business, management, marketing, and related support services; communication, journalism, and related programs; education; English language and literature/letters; foreign languages, literatures, and linguistics; health professions and related clinical sciences; history; mathematics and statistics; multi/interdisciplinary studies; natural resources and conservation; parks, recreation, leisure, and fitness studies; philosophy and religious studies; physical sciences; psychology; public administration and social service professions; security and protective services; social sciences; visual and performing arts. **Areas of required coursework:** arts/fine arts, humanities, mathematics, English (including composition), philosophy, foreign languages, sciences (biological or physical), social science, other. **Pre-professional programs:** pre-law, pre-dentistry, pre-medicine, pre-theology, pre-veterinary science, pre-optometry, pre-pharmacy, other. **Special academic programs (% participation):** double major (14%), dual enrollment, honors program (1%), independent study (20%), internships (35%), student-designed major, study abroad (22%), teacher certificate program (12%). **Teacher certification offered in:** early childhood, elementary, middle/junior high, secondary, bilingual/bicultural. **Reserve Officers Training Corps (ROTC):** Army ROTC: Offered at cooperating institution (University of Toledo). **Faculty and instruction (2009-2010):** Total instructional faculty: 81 full-time, 77 part-time (51% men; 49% women; 11% minorities). Full-time faculty with Ph.D. or other terminal degree: 94%. Student/faculty ratio: 15/1. Classes of fewer than 20 students: 67%; of 20 to 49 students: 32%; of 50 or more students: 1%. **Advanced Placement and International Baccalaureate credit:** AP tests may be used for: Placement only. Scores accepted: 4, 5. International Baccalaureate exams may be used for: Placement only. **Freshmen returning for sophomore year:** 73%. **Graduation rates:** Four-year: 46%; five-year: 46%; six-year: 47%. **Graduate study:** 25% of students pursue further study immediately upon graduation; 54% within five years. Fields in which graduates pursue further study: Master of Business Administration (MBA), 9%; law, 9%; medicine, 22%; education, 9%; arts and sciences, 51%.

COSTS AND FINANCIAL AID

Financial aid office: (517) 264-3107. **Expenses (2010-2011):** Tuition and fees 2010-2011: $25,900; room/board: $7,900. Estimated books and supplies: $650; transportation: $756; personal expenses: $916. **Financial aid:** Priority filing date for institution's financial aid form: March 1; deadline: March 1. In 2009-2010, 88% of undergraduates applied for financial aid. Of those, 81% were determined to have financial need; 84% had their need fully met. Average financial aid package (proportion receiving): $21,057 (81%). Average amount of gift aid, such as scholarships or grants (proportion receiving): $9,754 (69%). Average amount of self-help aid, such as work study or loans (proportion receiving): $5,773 (72%). Average need-based loan (excluding PLUS or other private loans): $4,243. Among students who received need-based aid, the average percentage of need met: 79%. Among students who received aid based on merit, the average award (and the proportion receiving): $10,885 (11%). The average athletic scholarship (and the proportion receiving): $0 (0%). Average amount of debt of borrowers graduating in 2009: $17,160. Proportion who borrowed: 81%.

CAMPUS LIFE AND EXTRACURRICULAR ACTIVITIES

Campus housing available (% using): coed dorms (55%), women's dorms (8%), men's dorms (7%), sorority housing (8%), fraternity housing (6%), apartment for single students (12%). Students who live in college-owned, operated, or affiliated housing: 83%. **Student employment:** During the 2009-2010 academic year, 9% of undergraduates worked on campus. Average per-year earnings: $1,000. **Clubs and organizations:** Number of student organizations: 77. Activities include: campus ministries, choral groups, concert band, dance, drama/theater, international student organization, jazz band, literary magazine, marching band, model UN, music ensembles, musical theater, pep band, radio station, student government, student newspaper, symphony orchestra, yearbook. Number of fraternities: 5; sororities: 3. Proportion of men in fraternities: 20%; of women in sororities: 20%. Average proportion of students who stay on campus on weekends: 70%. **Sports program (2009-2010):** Member of NCAA III. **Men's intercollegiate varsity sports:** baseball, basketball, cross country, football, golf, ice hockey, lacrosse, soccer, tennis, track and field (outdoor). **Women's intercollegiate varsity sports:** basketball, bowling, cross country, golf, ice hockey, lacrosse, soccer, softball, tennis, track and field (outdoor), volleyball.

SERVICES AND FACILITIES

Basic services: nonremedial tutoring, placement service, health service, health insurance. **Remedial assistance:** reading, math, study skills. **Counseling services:** minority student, career, personal, veteran student, academic, older student, psychological, birth control, religious. **For learning-disabled students:** School does not offer a structured program with separate admission and additional fees. Total undergraduates in learning-disabled program or receiving services: 27. Services include: remedial math, reading machines, remedial reading, tape recorders, other special classes, diagnostic testing service, note-taking services, oral tests, learning center, readers, extended time for tests, tutors, priority seating, texts on tape, other testing accommodations. **Library:** Number of titles: 145,987; number of current serial subscriptions: 568. **Information technology resources:** Students are not required to lease or own a computer. Number of campus computers available to all students: 180. School has a wireless network. Approximate number of users that can be accommodated: 2,000. Proportion of college-owned housing units wired for high-speed internet access: 100%. **Campus safety:** Security services offered: 24-hour foot-and-vehicle patrols, late-night transport/escort service, 24-hour emergency telephones, lighted pathways/sidewalks, controlled dormitory access (key, security card, etc).

TRANSFER AND INTERNATIONAL STUDENTS

Transfer students: May apply for admission for the following academic terms: Fall, Spring. Applicants do not need a minimum number of credits to apply. For fall 2009: Transfer applications received: 331. Transfer applicants offered admission: 96. Transfer applicants enrolled: 48. **International students:** Number of foreign undergraduates: 69 (4% of student body). Number of countries represented: 4. Minimum TOEFL score required: 500 (paper); 68 (computer).

Albion College

- **Address:** 611 E. Porter, Albion, MI 49224
- **Website:** http://www.albion.edu
- **Private; Religious affiliation:** Methodist
- **Enrollment:** 1,709 full-time; 29 part-time

KEY STATS

✔ **U.S News College Ranking:** 111, National Liberal Arts Colleges
✔ **ACT Score (25th/75th percentile):** 22-28
✔ **Tuition:** 2010-2011: $31,186

Selectivity: More selective	**Room/board:** $8,842
Acceptance rate: 79%	**Average debt:** $30,149
Student/faculty ratio: 13/1	**Proportion who borrowed:** 55%

UNDERGRADUATE STUDENT BODY STATS

2009-2010 enrollment: 1,709 full-time; 29 part-time. Men: 48%; women: 52%. **Ethnic makeup:** African American: 3%; Asian American: 3%; Hispanic: 1%; White: 91%; International: 2%. **Religious preference:** Roman Catholic: 24%; Protestant: 2%; Jewish: 1%; No preference: 2%; Unknown: 46%; Methodist: 8%; Other: 15%.

ADMISSIONS FACTS AND FIGURES

Phone: (800) 858-6770. **Email:** admissions@albion.edu. **Website:** http://www.albion.edu. **Application deadlines for fall 2011:** Regular decision: Rolling. Early decision: Not offered. Early action: Send application by: December 1; Decision sent by: January 1. Admission can be deferred. **Application fee:** $40. **To apply online, go to:** http://www.applyweb.com/apply/albion/. **Admissions requirements/recommendations:** High school units required (recommended): English: 4; Mathematics: 3 (4); Science: 3 (4); Foreign language: 2 (3); Social studies: 3 (4); History: 0 (0); Academic electives: 0 (0); Total units: 15 (19). Tests: The college uses SAT or ACT scores in admissions decisions. Either SAT or ACT required. For admission to the fall 2011 entering class, the school will accept: ACT with or without writing accepted. Campus visit: Required. Admissions interview: Required. Off-campus interview: May be arranged. **Factors that count in admissions decisions: *Academic:*** Secondary school record: Very Important. Class rank: Not Considered. Letters of recommendation: Very Important. Standardized test scores: Very Important. Essay: Very Important. ***Nonacademic:*** Interview: Not Considered. Extracurricular activities: Very Important. Talent/ability: Very Important. Character/personal qualities: Very Important. Alumni/ae relationship: Very Important. Geographical residence: Very Important. State residency: Very Important. Religious

affiliation/commitment: Not Considered. Minority status: Not Considered. Volunteer work: Very Important. Work experience: Very Important. **Other schools with the greatest overlap in applicants:** Grand Valley State University; Hope College; Kalamazoo College; Michigan State University; University of Michigan–Ann Arbor. **Admissions statistics for the fall 2009 entering class:** Total applicants: 1,780. Total accepted: 1,413. Freshmen enrolled: 434; 7% were from out of state. Accepted through early-decision or early-action plans: 52%. Overall acceptance rate: 79%. Non-early acceptance rate: 75%. **Size of waiting list:** 0 applicants; enrolled from waiting list: 0. **Credentials of fall 2009 freshmen:** 27% ranked in the top 10 percent of their high school class; 56% were in the top 25 percent; 86% were in the top half. (Proportion submitting class standing: 73%.) **Average high school grade point average:** 3.5. **First-year students who submitted SAT scores:** 6%. Scores (25/75 percentile): Critical Reading: 530-660, Math: 560-670, Combined: 1090-1330. **First-year students submitting ACT scores:** 97%. Scores (25/75 percentile): English: 21-28, Math: 21-27, Composite: 22-28.

ACADEMICS

Year founded: 1835. **Academic calendar:** Semester. **Degrees offered:** bachelor's. **Most popular majors:** 18% economics, 10% biology/biological sciences, 10% psychology, 8% English language and literature, 7% political science and government. **Major fields of study:** area, ethnic, cultural, and gender studies; biological and biomedical sciences; business, management, marketing, and related support services; communication, journalism, and related programs; computer and information sciences and support services; education; English language and literature/letters; foreign languages, literatures, and linguistics; health professions and related clinical sciences; history; liberal arts and sciences studies, and humanities; mathematics and statistics; multi/interdisciplinary studies; parks, recreation, leisure, and fitness studies; philosophy and religious studies; physical sciences; psychology; public administration and social service professions; social sciences; visual and performing arts. **Areas of required coursework:** arts/fine arts, humanities, sciences (biological or physical), social science. **Pre-professional programs:** pre-law, pre-dentistry, pre-medicine, pre-theology, pre-veterinary science, pre-optometry, pre-pharmacy. **Special academic programs (% participation):** double major (23%), dual enrollment (.22%), honors program (17%), independent study (29.5%), internships (28%), liberal arts/career combination, student-designed major (.88%), study abroad (29.1%), teacher certificate program (4.6%). **Teacher certification offered in:** elementary, secondary. **Faculty and instruction (2009-2010):** Total instructional faculty: 121 full-time, 50 part-time (59% men; 41% women; 5% minorities). Full-time faculty with Ph.D. or other terminal degree: 92%. Student/faculty ratio: 13/1. Classes of fewer than 20 students: 57%; of 20 to 49 students: 42%; of 50 or more students: 1%. **Advanced Placement and International Baccalaureate credit:** AP tests may be used for: Credit only. Scores accepted: 3, 4, 5. International Baccalaureate exams may be used for: Credit only. **Freshmen returning for sophomore year:** 86%. **Graduation rates:** Four-year: 63%; five-year: 74%; six-year: 74%. **Graduate study:** 41% of students pursue further study immediately upon graduation. Fields in which graduates pursue further study: law, 8%; medicine, 12%; arts and sciences, 54%.

COSTS AND FINANCIAL AID

Financial aid office: (517) 629-0440. **Expenses (2010-2011):** Tuition and fees 2010-2011: $31,186; room/board: $8,842. Estimated books and supplies: $900; transportation: $500; personal expenses: $600. **Financial aid:** Priority filing date for institution's financial aid form: March 1. In 2009-2010, 73% of undergraduates applied for financial aid. Of those, 65% were determined to have financial need; 31% had their need fully met. Average financial aid package (proportion receiving): $24,776 (65%). Average amount of gift aid, such as scholarships or grants (proportion receiving): $19,748 (65%). Average amount of self-help aid, such as work study or loans (proportion receiving): $5,774 (52%). Average need-based loan (excluding PLUS or other private loans): $4,912. Among students who received need-based aid, the average percentage of need met: 88%. Among students who received aid based on merit, the average award (and the proportion receiving): $13,179 (33%). The average athletic scholarship (and the proportion receiving): $0 (0%). Average amount of debt of borrowers graduating in 2009: $30,149. Proportion who borrowed: 55%.

CAMPUS LIFE AND EXTRACURRICULAR ACTIVITIES

Campus housing available (% using): coed dorms (76%), women's dorms (7%), men's dorms (0%), fraternity housing (16%), cooperative housing (1%). Students who live in college-owned, operated, or affiliated housing: 90%. **Student employment:** During the 2009-2010 academic year, 28% of undergraduates worked on campus. Average per-year earnings: $3,552. **Clubs and organizations:** Number of student organizations: 113. Activities include: campus ministries, choral groups, concert band, dance, drama/theater, international student organization, jazz band, literary magazine, marching band, model UN, music ensembles, musical theater, pep band, radio station, student government, student newspaper, symphony orchestra, yearbook. Number of fraternities: 6; sororities: 7. Proportion of men in fraternities: 44%; of women in sororities: 43%. **Sports program (2009-2010):** Member of NCAA III. *Men's intercollegiate varsity sports:* baseball, basketball, cross country, football, golf, soccer, swimming, tennis, track and field (indoor), track and field (outdoor). *Women's intercollegiate varsity sports:* basketball, cross country, equestrian, golf, soccer, softball, swimming, tennis, track and field (indoor), track and field (outdoor), volleyball.

SERVICES AND FACILITIES

Basic services: nonremedial tutoring, women's center, placement service, health service, other. **Remedial assistance:** reading, math, writing, study skills. **Counseling services:** minority student, career, military, personal, veteran student, academic, older student, psychological, birth control, religious. **For learning-disabled students:** School does not offer a structured program with separate admission and additional fees. Total undergraduates in learning-disabled program or receiving services: 120. Services include: reading machines, tape recorders, videotaped classes, diagnostic testing service, untimed tests, note-taking services, learning center, extended time for tests, tutors, priority seating, texts on tape, typist/scribe, exams on tape or computer, other testing accommodations. **Library:** Number of titles: 363,870; number of current serial subscriptions: 16,293. **Information technology resources:** Students are not required to lease or own a computer. Number of campus computers available to all students: 508. School has a wireless network. Approximate number of users that can be accommodated: 1,500. Proportion of college-owned housing units wired for high-speed internet access: 100%. **Campus safety:** Security services offered: 24-hour foot-and-vehicle patrols, late-night transport/escort service, 24-hour emergency telephones, lighted pathways/sidewalks, controlled dormitory access (key, security card, etc).

TRANSFER AND INTERNATIONAL STUDENTS

Transfer students: May apply for admission for the following academic terms: Fall, Spring. Applicants do not need a minimum number of credits to apply. For fall 2009: Transfer applications received: 122. Transfer applicants offered admission: 69. Transfer applicants enrolled: 32. **International students:** Number of foreign undergraduates: 36 (2% of student body). Number of countries represented: 17. Minimum TOEFL score required: 550 (paper); 270 (computer). Average TOEFL score: 600 (paper).

Alma College

- **Address:** 614 W. Superior Street, Alma, MI 48801-1599
- **Website:** http://www.alma.edu
- **Private; Religious affiliation:** Presbyterian
- **Enrollment:** 1,377 full-time; 67 part-time

KEY STATS

✔ **U.S News College Ranking:** 137, National Liberal Arts Colleges
✔ **ACT Score (25th/75th percentile):** 21-27
✔ **Tuition:** 2010-2011: $27,580

Selectivity: More selective	**Room/board:** $8,700
Acceptance rate: 75%	**Average debt:** $31,476
Student/faculty ratio: 14/1	**Proportion who borrowed:** 74%

UNDERGRADUATE STUDENT BODY STATS

2009-2010 enrollment: 1,377 full-time; 67 part-time. Men: 44%; women: 56%. **Ethnic makeup:** African American: 2%; American-Indian: 1%; Asian American: 2%; Hispanic: 3%; White: 92%. **Religious preference:** Roman Catholic: 21%; Protestant: 37%; Unknown: 31%; Presbyterian: 7%; Other: 4%.

ADMISSIONS FACTS AND FIGURES

Phone: (800) 321-2562. **Email:** admissions@alma.edu. **Website:** http://www.alma.edu. **Application deadlines for fall 2011:** Regular decision: Rolling. Early decision: Not offered. Early action: Not offered. Admission can be deferred. **Application fee:** $25. **To apply online, go to:** http://www.alma.edu/admissions/apply. **Admissions requirements/recommendations:** High school units required (recommended): English: 4; Mathematics: 3; Science: 3; Foreign language: (2); Social studies: 3; Total units: 16. Tests: The college uses

SAT or ACT scores in admissions decisions. Either SAT or ACT required. For admission to the fall 2011 entering class, the school will accept: ACT with or without writing accepted. Campus visit: Recommended. Admissions interview: Recommended. Off-campus interview: Not available. **Factors that count in admissions decisions:** *Academic:* Secondary school record: Considered. Class rank: Considered. Letters of recommendation: Considered. Standardized test scores: Very Important. Essay: Important. *Nonacademic:* Interview: Considered. Extracurricular activities: Considered. Talent/ability: Considered. Character/personal qualities: Considered. Alumni/ae relationship: Considered. Geographical residence: Considered. State residency: Considered. Religious affiliation/commitment: Not Considered. Minority status: Not Considered. Volunteer work: Considered. Work experience: Considered. **Other schools with the greatest overlap in applicants:** Albion College; Central Michigan University; Grand Valley State University; Hope College; Michigan State University. **Admissions statistics for the fall 2009 entering class:** Total applicants: 1,778. Total accepted: 1,334. Freshmen enrolled: 396; 7% were from out of state. Overall acceptance rate: 75%. **Credentials of fall 2009 freshmen:** 30% ranked in the top 10 percent of their high school class; 57% were in the top 25 percent; 87% were in the top half. (Proportion submitting class standing: 82%.) **Average high school grade point average:** 3.5. **First-year students who submitted SAT scores:** 6%. Scores (25/75 percentile): Critical Reading: 470-708, Math: 483-668, Combined: 953-1376. **First-year students submitting ACT scores:** 98%. Scores (25/75 percentile): English: 20-27, Math: 20-26, Composite: 21-27.

ACADEMICS

Year founded: 1886. **Academic calendar:** Other. **Degrees offered:** bachelor's. **Most popular majors:** 17% business administration and management, 12% biology/biological sciences, 10% health professions and related clinical sciences, 10% social sciences, 10% visual and performing arts. **Major fields of study:** biological and biomedical sciences; business, management, marketing, and related support services; communication, journalism, and related programs; computer and information sciences and support services; education; English language and literature/letters; foreign languages, literatures, and linguistics; health professions and related clinical sciences; history; legal professions and studies; liberal arts and sciences studies, and humanities; mathematics and statistics; multi/interdisciplinary studies; parks, recreation, leisure, and fitness studies; philosophy and religious studies; physical sciences; psychology; social sciences; theology and religious vocations; visual and performing arts. **Areas of required coursework:** humanities, mathematics, English (including composition), foreign languages, sciences (biological or physical), social science. **Pre-professional programs:** pre-law, pre-dentistry, pre-medicine, pre-theology, pre-veterinary science, pre-optometry, other. **Special academic programs (% participation):** double major (12.3%), dual enrollment (13%), honors program (4.2%), independent study (48%), internships (27.2%), student-designed major (1.5%), study abroad (15%), teacher certificate program (16%). **Teacher certification offered in:** early childhood, elementary, secondary. **Reserve Officers Training Corps (ROTC):** Army ROTC: Offered at cooperating institution (Central Michigan University). **Faculty and instruction (2009-2010):** Total instructional faculty: 85 full-time, 55 part-time (58% men; 42% women; 9% minorities). Full-time faculty with Ph.D. or other terminal degree: 91%. Student/faculty ratio: 14/1. Classes of fewer than 20 students: 55%; of 20 to 49 students: 42%; of 50 or more students: 3%. **Advanced Placement and International Baccalaureate credit:** AP tests may be used for: Credit only. Scores accepted: 3, 4, 5. International Baccalaureate exams may be used for: Credit only. **Freshmen returning for sophomore year:** 80%. **Graduation rates:** Four-year: 51%; five-year: 63%; six-year: 63%. **Graduate study:** 35% of students pursue further study immediately upon graduation. Fields in which graduates pursue further study: Master of Business Administration (MBA), 11%; law, 8%; medicine, 18%; dentistry, 2%; engineering, 2%; education, 6%; arts and sciences, 37%.

COSTS AND FINANCIAL AID

Financial aid office: (989) 463-7347. **Expenses (2010-2011):** Tuition and fees 2010-2011: $27,580; room/board: $8,700. Estimated books and supplies: $830; transportation: $756; personal expenses: $736. **Financial aid:** Priority filing date for institution's financial aid form: March 1. In 2009-2010, 91% of undergraduates applied for financial aid. Of those, 81% were determined to have financial need; 19% had their need fully met. Average financial aid package (proportion receiving): $23,085 (81%). Average amount of gift aid, such as scholarships or grants (proportion receiving): $18,926 (81%). Average amount of self-help aid, such as work study or loans (proportion receiving): $4,971 (60%). Average need-based loan (excluding PLUS or other private loans): $4,829. Among students who received need-based aid, the average percentage of need met: 84%. Among students who received aid based on merit, the average award (and the proportion receiving): $11,882 (19%). The average athletic scholarship (and the proportion receiving): $0 (0%). Average amount of debt of borrowers graduating in 2009: $31,476. Proportion who borrowed: 74%.

CAMPUS LIFE AND EXTRACURRICULAR ACTIVITIES

Campus housing available (% using): coed dorms (89%), sorority housing (4%), fraternity housing (5%), other housing options (2%). Students who live in college-owned, operated, or affiliated housing: 87%. **Student employment:** During the 2009-2010 academic year, 31% of undergraduates worked on campus. Average per-year earnings: $1,675. **Clubs and organizations:** Number of student organizations: 75. Activities include: campus ministries, choral groups, concert band, dance, drama/theater, international student organization, jazz band, marching band, model UN, music ensembles, musical theater, radio station, student government, student newspaper, symphony orchestra, yearbook. Number of fraternities: 6; sororities: 5. Proportion of men in fraternities: 16%; of women in sororities: 21%. Average proportion of students who stay on campus on weekends: 65%. **Sports program (2009-2010):** Member of NCAA III. *Men's intercollegiate varsity sports:* baseball, basketball, cross country, football, golf, soccer, swimming, tennis, track and field (outdoor). *Women's intercollegiate varsity sports:* basketball, cross country, golf, soccer, softball, swimming, tennis, track and field (outdoor), volleyball.

SERVICES AND FACILITIES

Basic services: nonremedial tutoring, health service. **Remedial assistance:** reading, math, writing, study skills. **Counseling services:** minority student, career, personal, academic, older student, birth control, religious. **For learning-disabled students:** School does not offer a structured program with separate admission and additional fees. Total undergraduates in learning-disabled program or receiving services: 47. Services include: reading machines, tape recorders, untimed tests, note-taking services, oral tests, learning center, readers, extended time for tests, tutors, priority seating, substitution of courses, texts on tape, typist/scribe, other testing accommodations. **Library:** Number of titles: 279,901; number of current serial subscriptions: 1,500. **Information technology resources:** Students are not required to lease or own a computer. Number of campus computers available to all students: 357. School has a wireless network. Approximate number of users that can be accommodated: 2,000. Proportion of college-owned housing units wired for high-speed internet access: 100%. **Campus safety:** Security services offered: late-night transport/escort service, 24-hour emergency telephones, lighted pathways/sidewalks, controlled dormitory access (key, security card, etc.).

TRANSFER AND INTERNATIONAL STUDENTS

Transfer students: May apply for admission for the following academic terms: Fall, Winter. Applicants need a minimum number of credits to apply. For fall 2009: Transfer applications received: 117. Transfer applicants offered admission: 59. Transfer applicants enrolled: 41. **International students:** Number of foreign undergraduates: 4. Number of countries represented: 10. Minimum TOEFL score required: 525 (paper); 195 (computer).

Andrews University

- **Address:** Berrien Springs, MI 49104
- **Website:** http://www.andrews.edu
- **Private; Religious affiliation:** Seventh-day Adventist
- **Enrollment:** 1,714 full-time; 250 part-time

KEY STATS

✔ **U.S News College Ranking:** 191, National Universities
✔ **ACT Score (25th/75th percentile):** 19-25
✔ **Tuition:** 2010-2011: $22,242

Selectivity: Selective	**Room/board:** $7,140
Acceptance rate: 49%	**Average debt:** $33,931
Student/faculty ratio: 13/1	**Proportion who borrowed:** 73%

UNDERGRADUATE STUDENT BODY STATS

2009-2010 enrollment: 1,714 full-time; 250 part-time. Men: 45%; women: 55%. **Ethnic makeup:** African American: 26%; Asian American: 11%; Hispanic: 12%; White: 39%; International: 12%.

ADMISSIONS FACTS AND FIGURES

Phone: (800) 253-2874. **Email:** enroll@andrews.edu. **Website:** http://www.andrews.edu. **Application deadlines for fall 2011:** Regular decision: Rolling. Early decision: Not offered. Early action: Not offered. Admission can be deferred. **Application fee:** $30. **To apply online, go to:** http://www.andrews.edu/future/apply/index.html. **Admissions requirements/recommendations:** High school units required (recommended): English: 3 (4); Mathematics: 2 (3); Science: 2 (2); Social studies: 1 (1); History: 2 (2); Total units: 13 (15). Tests: The college uses SAT or ACT scores in admissions decisions. Either SAT or ACT required. For admission to the fall 2011 entering class, the school will accept: ACT with or without writing accepted. Campus visit: Recommended. Admissions interview: Neither required nor recommended. **Factors that count in admissions decisions:** *Academic:* Secondary school record: Very Important. Class rank: Not Considered. Letters of recommendation: Very Important. Standardized test scores: Very Important. Essay: Considered. *Nonacademic:* Interview: Considered. Extracurricular activities: Not Considered. Talent/ability: Considered. Character/personal qualities: Very Important. Alumni/ae relationship: Important. Geographical residence: Not Considered. State residency: Not Considered. Religious affiliation/commitment: Important. Minority status: Not Considered. Volunteer work: Not Considered. Work experience: Not Considered. **Admissions statistics for the fall 2009 entering class:** Total applicants: 1,809. Total accepted: 879. Freshmen enrolled: 377; 69% were from out of state. Overall acceptance rate: 49%. **Credentials of fall 2009 freshmen:** 15% ranked in the top 10 percent of their high school class; 21% were in the top 25 percent; 65% were in the top half. (Proportion submitting class standing: 62%.) **Average high school grade point average:** 3.4. **First-year students who submitted SAT scores:** 52%. Scores (25/75 percentile): Critical Reading: 450-580, Math: 430-580, Combined: 880-1160. **First-year students submitting ACT scores:** 68%. Scores (25/75 percentile): English: 19-26, Math: 18-24, Composite: 19-25.

ACADEMICS

Year founded: 1874. **Academic calendar:** Semester. **Degrees offered:** associate, bachelor's, master's, doctorate. **Most popular majors:** 20% health professions and related clinical sciences, 10% business, management, marketing, and related support services, 8% biological and biomedical sciences, 8% foreign languages, literatures, and linguistics, 6% visual and performing arts. **Major fields of study:** agriculture, agriculture operations, and related sciences; architecture and related services; biological and biomedical sciences; business, management, marketing, and related support services; communication, journalism, and related programs; computer and information sciences and support services; education; engineering; engineering technologies/technicians; English language and literature/letters; family and consumer sciences/human sciences; foreign languages, literatures, and linguistics; health professions and related clinical sciences; liberal arts and sciences studies, and humanities; mathematics and statistics; mechanic and repair technologies/technicians; multi/interdisciplinary studies; natural resources and conservation; philosophy and religious studies; physical sciences; psychology; public administration and social service professions; social sciences; theology and religious vocations; visual and performing arts. **Areas of required coursework:** arts/fine arts, humanities, computer literacy, mathematics, English (including composition), sciences (biological or physical), history, social science. **Pre-professional programs:** pre-law, pre-dentistry, pre-medicine, pre-theology, pre-veterinary science, pre-optometry, pre-pharmacy. **Special academic programs:** accelerated program, cooperative (work-study plan) program, cross-registration, distance learning, double major, dual enrollment, English as a Second Language (ESL), external degree program, honors program, independent study, internships, student-designed major, study abroad, teacher certificate program. **Teacher certification offered in:** elementary, secondary. **Cooperative education programs:** agriculture, art, business, computer science, education, engineering, health professions, natural science, technologies. **Faculty and instruction (2009-2010):** Total instructional faculty: 218 full-time, 59 part-time (62% men; 38% women; 27% minorities). Full-time faculty with Ph.D. or other terminal degree: 76%. Student/faculty ratio: 13/1. Classes of fewer than 20 students: 59%; of 20 to 49 students: 33%; of 50 or more students: 8%. **Advanced Placement and International Baccalaureate credit:** AP tests may be used for: Credit and/or placement. Scores accepted: 3, 4, 5. International Baccalaureate exams may be used for: Credit and/or placement. **Freshmen returning for sophomore year:** 80%. **Graduation rates:** Four-year: 34%; five-year: 51%; six-year: 58%.

COSTS AND FINANCIAL AID

Financial aid office: (269) 471-3334. **Expenses (2010-2011):** Tuition and fees 2010-2011: $22,242; room/board: $7,140. Estimated books and supplies:

$1,050; transportation: $1,000; personal expenses: $900. **Financial aid:** Priority filing date for institution's financial aid form: March 15. In 2009-2010, 73% of undergraduates applied for financial aid. Of those, 67% were determined to have financial need; 12% had their need fully met. Average financial aid package (proportion receiving): $23,932 (67%). Average amount of gift aid, such as scholarships or grants (proportion receiving): $8,350 (52%). Average amount of self-help aid, such as work study or loans (proportion receiving): $5,130 (57%). Average need-based loan (excluding PLUS or other private loans): $4,663. Among students who received need-based aid, the average percentage of need met: 86%. Among students who received aid based on merit, the average award (and the proportion receiving): $5,853 (31%). The average athletic scholarship (and the proportion receiving): $0 (0%). Average amount of debt of borrowers graduating in 2009: $33,931. Proportion who borrowed: 73%.

CAMPUS LIFE AND EXTRACURRICULAR ACTIVITIES
Campus housing available (% using): women's dorms (49%), men's dorms (42%), apartments for married students (2%). Students who live in college-owned, operated, or affiliated housing: 59%. **Student employment:** During the 2009-2010 academic year, 58% of undergraduates worked on campus. Average per-year earnings: $2,700. **Clubs and organizations:** Number of student organizations: 45. Activities include: campus ministries, choral groups, concert band, drama/theater, literary magazine, music ensembles, musical theater, radio station, student government, student newspaper, symphony orchestra, yearbook. Number of fraternities: 0; sororities: 0.

SERVICES AND FACILITIES
Basic services: nonremedial tutoring, placement service, day care, health service, health insurance. **Remedial assistance:** reading, math, writing, study skills, other. **Counseling services:** minority student, career, personal, veteran student, academic, older student, psychological, birth control, religious. **For learning-disabled students:** School does not offer a structured program with separate admission and additional fees. Total undergraduates in learning-disabled program or receiving services: 60. Services include: remedial math, remedial English, reading machines, remedial reading, tape recorders, videotaped classes, diagnostic testing service, untimed tests, note-taking services, oral tests, learning center, readers, extended time for tests, tutors, priority seating, texts on tape, other testing accommodations. **Library:** Number of titles: 607,729; number of current serial subscriptions: 53,530. **Information technology resources:** Students are not required to lease or own a computer. Number of campus computers available to all students: 130. School has a wireless network. Approximate number of users that can be accommodated: 2,000. Proportion of college-owned housing units wired for high-speed internet access: 100%. **Campus safety:** Security services offered: 24-hour foot-and-vehicle patrols, late-night transport/escort service, lighted pathways/sidewalks, student patrols, controlled dormitory access (key, security card, etc).

TRANSFER AND INTERNATIONAL STUDENTS
Transfer students: May apply for admission for the following academic terms: Fall, Winter, Spring, Summer. Applicants need a minimum number of credits to apply. For fall 2009: Transfer applications received: 546. Transfer applicants offered admission: 256. Transfer applicants enrolled: 158. **International students:** Number of foreign undergraduates: 211 (12% of student body). Number of countries represented: 68. Minimum TOEFL score required: 550 (paper); 213 (computer).

Aquinas College

- **Address:** 1607 Robinson Road SE, Grand Rapids, MI 49506-1799
- **Website:** http://www.aquinas.edu
- **Private; Religious affiliation:** Roman Catholic
- **Enrollment:** 1,635 full-time; 273 part-time

KEY STATS
✔ **U.S News College Ranking:** 58, Regional Universities (Midwest)
✔ **ACT Score (25th/75th percentile):** 20-26
✔ **Tuition:** 2010-2011: $23,206

Selectivity: Selective	**Room/board:** $7,226
Acceptance rate: 80%	**Average debt:** $14,983
Student/faculty ratio: 13/1	**Proportion who borrowed:** 66%

UNDERGRADUATE STUDENT BODY STATS
2009-2010 enrollment: 1,635 full-time; 273 part-time. Men: 36%; women: 64%. **Ethnic makeup:** African American: 4%; Asian American: 2%; Hispanic: 4%; White: 90%. **Religious preference:** Roman Catholic: 50%; Protestant: 13%; Jewish: 1%; No preference: 11%; Unknown: 12%; Agnostic, Atheist, Eastern Orthodox, Non-Denominational: 7%; Other: 6%.

ADMISSIONS FACTS AND FIGURES
Phone: (616) 732-4460. **Email:** admissions@aquinas.edu. **Website:** http://www.aquinas.edu. **Application deadlines for fall 2011:** Regular decision: Rolling. Early decision: Not offered. Early action: Not offered. Admission can be deferred. **To apply online, go to:** http://www.aquinas.edu/undergraduate/applying/applicat.htm. **Admissions requirements/recommendations:** High school units required (recommended): English: 4; Mathematics: 4; Science: 3; Social studies: 4; Total units: 15. Tests: The college uses SAT or ACT scores in admissions decisions. Either SAT or ACT required. For admission to the fall 2011 entering class, the school will accept: ACT with or without writing accepted. Campus visit: Recommended. Admissions interview: Neither required nor recommended. **Factors that count in admissions decisions:** *Academic:* Secondary school record: Very Important. Class rank: Not Considered. Letters of recommendation: Considered. Standardized test scores: Very Important. Essay: Not Considered. *Nonacademic:* Interview: Not Considered. Extracurricular activities: Considered. Talent/ability: Considered. Character/personal qualities: Considered. Alumni/ae relationship: Not Considered. Geographical residence: Not Considered. State residency: Not Considered. Religious affiliation/commitment: Not Considered. Minority status: Not Considered. Volunteer work: Considered. Work experience: Considered. **Other schools with the greatest overlap in applicants:** Central Michigan University; Grand Valley State University; Michigan State University; University of Michigan–Ann Arbor; Western Michigan University. **Admissions statistics for the fall 2009 entering class:** Total applicants: 2,192. Total accepted: 1,761. Freshmen enrolled: 402; 3% were from out of state. Overall acceptance rate: 80%. **Size of waiting list:** 0 applicants; enrolled from waiting list: 0. **Credentials of fall 2009 freshmen:** 19% ranked in the top 10 percent of their high school class; 48% were in the top 25 percent; 77% were in the top half. (Proportion submitting class standing: 77%.) **Average high school grade point average:** 3.4. **First-year students submitting ACT scores:** 100%. Scores (25/75 percentile): English: 20-26, Math: 19-25, Composite: 20-26.

ACADEMICS
Year founded: 1886. **Academic calendar:** Semester. **Degrees offered:** associate, bachelor's, master's. **Most popular majors:** 31% business, management, marketing, and related support services, 11% education, 9% social sciences, 6% biological and biomedical sciences, 6% communication, journalism, and related programs. **Major fields of study:** biological and biomedical sciences; business, management, marketing, and related support services; communication, journalism, and related programs; computer and information sciences and support services; education; English language and literature/letters; foreign languages, literatures, and linguistics; health professions and related clinical sciences; history; liberal arts and sciences studies, and humanities; mathematics and statistics; natural resources and conservation; parks, recreation, leisure, and fitness studies; philosophy and religious studies; physical sciences; psychology; public administration and social service professions; social sciences; theology and religious vocations; visual and performing arts. **Areas of required coursework:** arts/fine arts, humanities, computer literacy, mathematics, English (including composition), philosophy, foreign languages, sciences (biological or physical), history, social science. **Pre-professional programs:** pre-law, pre-dentistry, pre-medicine, pre-theology, pre-veterinary science, pre-optometry, pre-pharmacy, other. **Special academic programs (% participation):** distance learning (20.5%), double major (15.3%), dual enrollment (.92%), exchange student program (domestic) (1%), honors program (4.6%), independent study (47.2%), internships (46%), liberal arts/career combination (20.8%), student-designed major (.92%), study abroad (14.1%), teacher certificate program (15.6%). **Teacher certification offered in:** early childhood, special education, elementary, middle/junior high, secondary, bilingual/bicultural. **Faculty and instruction (2009-2010):** Total instructional faculty: 94 full-time, 150 part-time (52% men; 48% women; 6% minorities). Full-time faculty with Ph.D. or other terminal degree: 74%. Student/faculty ratio: 13/1. Classes of fewer than 20 students: 57%; of 20 to 49 students: 42%; of 50 or more students: 1%. **Advanced Placement and International Baccalaureate credit:** AP tests may be used for: Credit only. Scores accepted: 3, 4, 5. **Freshmen returning for sophomore year:** 73%. **Graduation rates:** Four-year: 33%; five-year: 50%; six-year: 54%. **Graduate study:** 21% of students pursue further study immediately upon graduation. Fields in which graduates

pursue further study: Master of Business Administration (MBA), 16%; law, 21%; medicine, 11%; dentistry, 5%; education, 5%; arts and sciences, 42%.

COSTS AND FINANCIAL AID

Financial aid office: (616) 632-2893. **Expenses (2010-2011):** Tuition and fees 2010-2011: $23,206; room/board: $7,226. Estimated books and supplies: $798; transportation: $756; personal expenses: $768. **Financial aid:** Priority filing date for institution's financial aid form: March 1. In 2009-2010, 89% of undergraduates applied for financial aid. Of those, 82% were determined to have financial need; 63% had their need fully met. Average financial aid package (proportion receiving): $21,533 (82%). Average amount of gift aid, such as scholarships or grants (proportion receiving): $19,287 (82%). Average amount of self-help aid, such as work study or loans (proportion receiving): $2,246 (82%). Average need-based loan (excluding PLUS or other private loans): $2,216. Among students who received need-based aid, the average percentage of need met: 88%. Among students who received aid based on merit, the average award (and the proportion receiving): $11,267 (21%). The average athletic scholarship (and the proportion receiving): $2,450 (15%). Average amount of debt of borrowers graduating in 2009: $14,983. Proportion who borrowed: 66%.

CAMPUS LIFE AND EXTRACURRICULAR ACTIVITIES

Campus housing available (% using): coed dorms (62%), women's dorms (9%), men's dorms (1%), apartment for single students (21%). Students who live in college-owned, operated, or affiliated housing: 47%. **Student employment:** During the 2009-2010 academic year, 23% of undergraduates worked on campus. Average per-year earnings: $3,454. **Clubs and organizations:** Number of student organizations: 71. Activities include: campus ministries, choral groups, concert band, dance, drama/theater, jazz band, literary magazine, marching band, model UN, music ensembles, musical theater, radio station, student government, student newspaper. Number of fraternities: 0; sororities: 0. Average proportion of students who stay on campus on weekends: 33%. **Sports program (2009-2010):** Member of NAIA.

SERVICES AND FACILITIES

Basic services: nonremedial tutoring, women's center, placement service, day care, health service, health insurance. **Remedial assistance:** reading, math, writing, study skills. **Counseling services:** minority student, career, personal, veteran student, academic, older student, psychological, religious. **For learning-disabled students:** School does not offer a structured program with separate admission and additional fees. Total undergraduates in learning-disabled program or receiving services: 213. Services include: remedial math, remedial English, remedial reading, tape recorders, other special classes, untimed tests, note-taking services, oral tests, learning center, readers, extended time for tests, tutors, priority registration, texts on tape, other testing accommodations, other. **Library:** Number of titles: 100,014; number of current serial subscriptions: 456. **Information technology resources:** Students are not required to lease or own a computer. Number of campus computers available to all students: 531. School has a wireless network. Approximate number of users that can be accommodated: 2,048. Proportion of college-owned housing units wired for high-speed internet access: 100%. **Campus safety:** Security services offered: 24-hour foot-and-vehicle patrols, late-night transport/escort service, 24-hour emergency telephones, lighted pathways/sidewalks, controlled dormitory access (key, security card, etc).

TRANSFER AND INTERNATIONAL STUDENTS

Transfer students: May apply for admission for the following academic terms: Fall, Spring, Summer. Applicants need a minimum number of credits to apply. For fall 2009: Transfer applications received: 280. Transfer applicants offered admission: 154. Transfer applicants enrolled: 85. **International students:** Number of foreign undergraduates: 3. Number of countries represented: 4. Minimum TOEFL score required: 550 (paper); 213 (computer).

Baker College of Flint

- **Address:** 1050 W. Bristol Road, Flint, MI 48507
- **Website:** http://www.baker.edu
- **Private**
- **Enrollment:** N/A

KEY STATS

✔ **U.S News College Ranking:** Unranked, Regional Colleges (Midwest)
✔ **SAT or ACT Score (25th/75th percentile):** N/A
✔ **Tuition:** 2009-2010: $7,020

Selectivity: N/A	Room/board: $2,625
Acceptance rate: N/A	Average debt: N/A
Student/faculty ratio: N/A	Proportion who borrowed: N/A

Calvin College

- **Address:** 3201 Burton Street SE, Grand Rapids, MI 49546
- **Website:** http://www.calvin.edu
- **Private; Religious affiliation:** Christian Reformed
- **Enrollment:** 3,883 full-time; 132 part-time

KEY STATS

✔ **U.S News College Ranking:** 101, National Liberal Arts Colleges
✔ **ACT Score (25th/75th percentile):** 23-29
✔ **Tuition:** 2010-2011: $24,870

Selectivity: More selective	Room/board: $8,525
Acceptance rate: 93%	Average debt: $28,500
Student/faculty ratio: 11/1	Proportion who borrowed: 68%

UNDERGRADUATE STUDENT BODY STATS

2009-2010 enrollment: 3,883 full-time; 132 part-time. Men: 46%; women: 54%. **Ethnic makeup:** African American: 2%; Asian American: 3%; Hispanic: 2%; White: 85%; International: 8%. **Religious preference:** Roman Catholic: 2%; Protestant: 50%; No preference: 2%; Christian Reformed: 46%.

ADMISSIONS FACTS AND FIGURES

Phone: (616) 526-6106. **Email:** admissions@calvin.edu. **Website:** http://www.calvin.edu. **Application deadlines for fall 2011:** Regular decision: August 15. Early decision: Not offered. Early action: Not offered. Admission can be deferred. **Application fee:** $35. **To apply online, go to:** http://www.calvin.edu/admin/admissions/apply.htm. **Admissions requirements/recommendations:** High school units required (recommended): English: 3 (4); Mathematics: 3 (3); Science: 2 (2); Foreign language: 0 (2); Social studies: 2 (3); Academic electives: 3 (3); Total units: 12 (17). Tests: The college uses SAT or ACT scores in admissions decisions. Either SAT or ACT required. For admission to the fall 2011 entering class, the school will accept: ACT with or without writing accepted. Campus visit: Recommended. Admissions interview: Recommended. Off-campus interview: May be arranged. **Factors that count in admissions decisions:** *Academic:* Secondary school record: Very Important. Class rank: Considered. Letters of recommendation: Important. Standardized test scores: Very Important. Essay: Important. *Nonacademic:* Interview: Not Considered. Extracurricular activities: Important. Talent/ability: Not Considered. Character/personal qualities: Important. Alumni/ae relationship: Not Considered. Geographical residence: Not Considered. State residency: Not Considered. Religious affiliation/commitment: Very Important. Minority status: Not Considered. Volunteer work: Considered. Work experience: Considered. **Other schools with the greatest overlap in applicants:** Grand Valley State University; Hope College; Michigan State University; University of Michigan–Ann Arbor; Wheaton College. **Admissions statistics for the fall 2009 entering class:** Total applicants: 2,529. Total accepted: 2,346. Freshmen enrolled: 945; 43% were from out of state. Overall acceptance rate: 93%. **Size of waiting list:** 0 applicants; enrolled from waiting list: 0. **Credentials of fall 2009 freshmen:** 29% ranked in the top 10 percent of their high school class; 57% were in the top 25 percent; 81% were in the top half. (Proportion submitting class standing: 76%.) **Average high school grade point average:** 3.6. **First-year students who submitted SAT scores:** 32%. Scores (25/75 percentile): Critical Reading: 520-670, Math: 550-660, Combined: 1070-1330. **First-year students submitting**

ACT scores: 83%. Scores (25/75 percentile): English: 23-29, Math: 22-30, Composite: 23-29.

ACADEMICS

Year founded: 1876. **Academic calendar:** 4-1-4. **Degrees offered:** bachelor's, master's. **Most popular majors:** 7% business administration and management, 7% engineering, 6% nursing, 5% English language and literature, 5% elementary education and teaching. **Major fields of study:** area, ethnic, cultural, and gender studies; biological and biomedical sciences; business, management, marketing, and related support services; communication, journalism, and related programs; computer and information sciences and support services; education; engineering; English language and literature/letters; foreign languages, literatures, and linguistics; health professions and related clinical sciences; history; legal professions and studies; liberal arts and sciences studies, and humanities; mathematics and statistics; multi/interdisciplinary studies; natural resources and conservation; parks, recreation, leisure, and fitness studies; philosophy and religious studies; physical sciences; psychology; public administration and social service professions; social sciences; theology and religious vocations; visual and performing arts. **Areas of required coursework:** arts/fine arts, humanities, computer literacy, mathematics, English (including composition), philosophy, foreign languages, sciences (biological or physical), history, social science, other. **Pre-professional programs:** pre-law, pre-dentistry, pre-medicine, pre-theology, pre-veterinary science, pre-optometry, pre-pharmacy, other. **Special academic programs (% participation):** accelerated program, double major (14%), dual enrollment, English as a Second Language (ESL), honors program (15%), independent study (5%), internships (76%), student-designed major (3%), study abroad (70%), teacher certificate program (18%), other. **Teacher certification offered in:** early childhood, special education, elementary, middle/junior high, secondary, bilingual/bicultural. **Reserve Officers Training Corps (ROTC):** Army ROTC: Offered at cooperating institution (Western Michigan University). **Faculty and instruction (2009-2010):** Total instructional faculty: 326 full-time, 69 part-time (63% men; 37% women; 9% minorities). Full-time faculty with Ph.D. or other terminal degree: 82%. Student/faculty ratio: 11/1. Classes of fewer than 20 students: 39%; of 20 to 49 students: 60%; of 50 or more students: 1%. **Advanced Placement and International Baccalaureate credit:** AP tests may be used for: Placement only. Scores accepted: 3, 4, 5. International Baccalaureate exams may be used for: Credit only. **Freshmen returning for sophomore year:** 87%. **Graduation rates:** Four-year: 55%; five-year: 73%; six-year: 75%. **Graduate study:** 37% of students pursue further study within one year. Fields in which graduates pursue further study: Master of Business Administration (MBA), 2%; law, 7%; medicine, 15%; engineering, 9%; theology (or the seminary), 8%; education, 6%; arts and sciences, 51%; veterinary medicine, 1%.

COSTS AND FINANCIAL AID

Financial aid office: (616) 526-6137. **Expenses (2010-2011):** Tuition and fees 2010-2011: $24,870; room/board: $8,525. Estimated books and supplies: $1,000; transportation: $1,100; personal expenses: $1,150. **Financial aid:** Priority filing date for institution's financial aid form: February 15. In 2009-2010, 80% of undergraduates applied for financial aid. Of those, 65% were determined to have financial need; 22% had their need fully met. Average financial aid package (proportion receiving): $17,931 (65%). Average amount of gift aid, such as scholarships or grants (proportion receiving): $11,375 (65%). Average amount of self-help aid, such as work study or loans (proportion receiving): $5,492 (60%). Average need-based loan (excluding PLUS or other private loans): $6,270. Among students who received need-based aid, the average percentage of need met: 78%. Among students who received aid based on merit, the average award (and the proportion receiving): $4,509 (29%). The average athletic scholarship (and the proportion receiving): $0 (0%). Average amount of debt of borrowers graduating in 2009: $28,500. Proportion who borrowed: 68%.

CAMPUS LIFE AND EXTRACURRICULAR ACTIVITIES

Campus housing available (% using): women's dorms (40%), men's dorms (33%), apartment for single students (21%). Students who live in college-owned, operated, or affiliated housing: 57%. **Student employment:** During the 2009-2010 academic year, 60% of undergraduates worked on campus. Average per-year earnings: $2,400. **Clubs and organizations:** Number of student organizations: 65. Activities include: campus ministries, choral groups, concert band, dance, drama/theater, international student organization, jazz band, literary magazine, model UN, music ensembles, musical theater, pep band, student government, student newspaper, student film society, symphony orchestra, yearbook. Number of fraternities: 0; sororities: 0. Average proportion of students who stay on campus on weekends: 90%. **Sports program (2009-2010):** Member of NCAA III. *Men's intercollegiate varsity*

sports: baseball, basketball, cross country, golf, soccer, swimming, tennis, track and field (indoor), track and field (outdoor). *Women's intercollegiate varsity sports:* basketball, cross country, golf, soccer, softball, swimming, tennis, track and field (indoor), track and field (outdoor), volleyball.

SERVICES AND FACILITIES

Basic services: nonremedial tutoring, placement service, health service, health insurance. **Remedial assistance:** reading, math, writing, study skills. **Counseling services:** minority student, career, personal, academic, psychological, religious. **For learning-disabled students:** School does not offer a structured program with separate admission and additional fees. Total undergraduates in learning-disabled program or receiving services: 100. Services include: tape recorders, note-taking services, readers, extended time for tests, tutors, priority registration, texts on tape, other testing accommodations, other. **Library:** Number of titles: 493,218; number of current serial subscriptions: 3,694. **Information technology resources:** Students are not required to lease or own a computer. Number of campus computers available to all students: 900. School has a wireless network. Approximate number of users that can be accommodated: 5,000. Proportion of college-owned housing units wired for high-speed internet access: 100%. **Campus safety:** Security services offered: 24-hour foot-and-vehicle patrols, late-night transport/escort service, 24-hour emergency telephones, lighted pathways/sidewalks, controlled dormitory access (key, security card, etc).

TRANSFER AND INTERNATIONAL STUDENTS

Transfer students: May apply for admission for the following academic terms: Fall, Spring, Summer. Applicants do not need a minimum number of credits to apply. For fall 2009: Transfer applications received: 224. Transfer applicants offered admission: 200. Transfer applicants enrolled: 110. **International students:** Number of foreign undergraduates: 310 (8% of student body). Number of countries represented: 65. Minimum TOEFL score required: 550 (paper); 213 (computer). Average TOEFL score: 618 (paper).

Central Michigan University

- **Address:** Warriner Hall, Mount Pleasant, MI 48859
- **Website:** http://www.cmich.edu
- **Public**
- **Enrollment:** 18,253 full-time; 2,327 part-time

KEY STATS

✔ **U.S News College Ranking:** second tier, National Universities
✔ **ACT Score (25th/75th percentile):** 20-25
✔ **Tuition:** 2009-2010: $10,170 in state, $23,670 out of state

Selectivity: Selective	**Room/board:** $7,896
Acceptance rate: 73%	**Average debt:** $26,615
Student/faculty ratio: 21/1	**Proportion who borrowed:** 71%

UNDERGRADUATE STUDENT BODY STATS

2009-2010 enrollment: 18,253 full-time; 2,327 part-time. Men: 45%; women: 55%. **Ethnic makeup:** African American: 6%; American-Indian: 1%; Asian American: 1%; Hispanic: 2%; White: 89%; International: 1%.

ADMISSIONS FACTS AND FIGURES

Phone: (989) 774-3076. **Email:** cmuadmit@cmich.edu. **Website:** http://www.cmich.edu. **Application deadlines for fall 2011:** Regular decision: Rolling. Early decision: Not offered. Early action: Send application by: October 1; Decision sent by: June 30. Admission can be deferred. **Application fee:** $35. **To apply online, go to:** https://apply.cmich.edu. **Admissions requirements/recommendations:** High school units required (recommended): English: (4); Mathematics: (4); Science: (4); Foreign language: (2); Social studies: (2); History: (2); Total units: (20). Tests: The college uses SAT or ACT scores in admissions decisions. Either SAT or ACT required. For admission to the fall 2011 entering class, the school will accept: ACT with or without writing accepted. Campus visit: Recommended. Admissions interview: Recommended. Off-campus interview: Not available. **Factors that count in admissions decisions:** *Academic:* Secondary school record: Very Important. Class rank: Important. Letters of recommendation: Considered. Standardized test scores: Very Important. Essay: Considered. *Nonacademic:* Interview: Considered. Extracurricular activities: Considered. Talent/ability: Important. Character/personal qualities: Considered. Alumni/ae relationship: Considered. Geographical residence: Considered. State residency: Not Considered. Religious affiliation/commitment: Not Considered. Minority status: Not Considered. Volunteer work: Considered. Work experience: Considered. **Other schools with the greatest overlap in applicants:** Eastern Michigan University; Grand Valley State University; Michigan State University; University of Michigan–Ann Arbor; Western Michigan University. **Admissions statistics for the fall 2009 entering class:** Total applicants: 16,859. Total accepted: 12,273. Freshmen enrolled: 3,691; 3% were from out of state. Overall acceptance rate: 73%. Non-early acceptance rate: 73%. **Size of waiting list:** 0 applicants; enrolled from waiting list: 0. **Credentials of fall 2009 freshmen:** 16% ranked in the top 10 percent of their high school class; 41% were in the top 25 percent; 77% were in the top half. (Proportion submitting class standing: 77%.) **Average high school grade point average:** 3.3. **First-year students who submitted SAT scores:** 2%. Scores (25/75 percentile): Critical Reading: 438-560, Math: 450-570, Combined: 888-1130. **First-year students submitting ACT scores:** 98%. Scores (25/75 percentile): English: 18-25, Math: 19-24, Composite: 20-25.

ACADEMICS

Year founded: 1892. **Academic calendar:** Semester. **Degrees offered:** bachelor's, post-bachelor's certificate, master's, post-master's certificate, doctorate. **Most popular majors:** 26% business, management, marketing, and related support services, 17% education, 8% communication, journalism, and related programs, 8% parks, recreation, leisure, and fitness studies, 6% social sciences. **Major fields of study:** architecture and related services; area, ethnic, cultural, and gender studies; biological and biomedical sciences; business, management, marketing, and related support services; communication, journalism, and related programs; computer and information sciences and support services; education; engineering; engineering technologies/technicians; English language and literature/letters; family and consumer sciences/human sciences; foreign languages, literatures, and linguistics; health professions and related clinical sciences; history; liberal arts and sciences studies, and humanities; mathematics and statistics; multi/interdisciplinary studies; natural resources and conservation; parks, recreation, leisure, and fitness studies; philosophy and religious studies; physical sciences; psychology; public administration and social service professions; social sciences; visual and performing arts. **Areas of required coursework:** arts/fine arts, humanities, mathematics, English (including composition), sciences (biological or physical), social science. **Pre-professional programs:** pre-law, pre-dentistry, pre-medicine, pre-veterinary science, pre-optometry, pre-pharmacy, other. **Special academic programs (% participation):** accelerated program, distance learning, double major (12%), dual enrollment, English as a Second Language (ESL), external degree program, honors program (5%), independent study, internships (50%), student-designed major, study abroad, teacher certificate program (13%). **Teacher certification offered in:** early childhood, special education, elementary, vo-tech, middle/junior high, secondary, bilingual/bicultural. **Reserve Officers Training Corps (ROTC):** Army ROTC: Offered on campus. **Faculty and instruction (2009-2010):** Total instructional faculty: 752 full-time, 438 part-time (56% men; 44% women; 15% minorities). Full-time faculty with Ph.D. or other terminal degree: 81%. Student/faculty ratio: 21/1. Classes of fewer than 20 students: 33%; of 20 to 49 students: 56%; of 50 or more students: 11%. **Advanced Placement and International Baccalaureate credit:** AP tests may be used for: Credit and/or placement. Scores accepted: 3, 4, 5. International Baccalaureate exams may be used for: Credit and/or placement. **Freshmen returning for sophomore year:** 77%. **Graduation rates:** Four-year: 21%; five-year: 47%; six-year: 57%. **Graduate study:** 16% of students pursue further study immediately upon graduation. Fields in which graduates pursue further study: Master of Business Administration (MBA), 3%; law, 9%; medicine, 12%; engineering, 2%; education, 2%; arts and sciences, 72%; veterinary medicine, 1%.

COSTS AND FINANCIAL AID

Financial aid office: (989) 774-3674. **Expenses (2009-2010):** Tuition and fees 2009-2010: $10,170 in state, $23,670 out of state; room/board: $7,896. Estimated books and supplies: $1,000; transportation: $1,050. **Financial aid:** Priority filing date for institution's financial aid form: March 1. In 2009-2010, 74% of undergraduates applied for financial aid. Of those, 55% were determined to have financial need; 57% had their need fully met. Average financial aid package (proportion receiving): $10,428 (54%). Average amount of gift aid, such as scholarships or grants (proportion receiving): $4,768 (43%). Average amount of self-help aid, such as work study or loans (proportion receiving): $6,850 (48%). Average need-based loan (excluding PLUS or other private loans): $6,481. Among students who received need-based aid, the average percentage of need met: 83%. Among students who received aid based on merit, the average award (and the proportion receiv-

ing): $3,467 (9%). The average athletic scholarship (and the proportion receiving): $13,687 (1%). Average amount of debt of borrowers graduating in 2009: $26,615. Proportion who borrowed: 71%.

CAMPUS LIFE AND EXTRACURRICULAR ACTIVITIES

Campus housing available (% using): coed dorms (90%), women's dorms (6%), men's dorms (3%), sorority housing (0%), fraternity housing (0%), apartments for married students (1%), apartment for single students (0%), special housing for disabled students (0%), other housing options. Students who live in college-owned, operated, or affiliated housing: 33%. **Student employment:** During the 2009-2010 academic year, 30% of undergraduates worked on campus. Average per-year earnings: $3,500. **Clubs and organizations:** Number of student organizations: 257. Activities include: choral groups, concert band, dance, drama/theater, international student organization, jazz band, literary magazine, marching band, model UN, music ensembles, musical theater, opera, pep band, radio station, student government, student newspaper, student film society, symphony orchestra, television station, yearbook. Number of fraternities: 15; sororities: 15. Proportion of men in fraternities: 5%; of women in sororities: 7%. Average proportion of students who stay on campus on weekends: 40%. **Sports program (2009-2010):** Member of NCAA I. *Men's intercollegiate varsity sports:* baseball, basketball, cross country, football, track and field (indoor), track and field (outdoor), wrestling. *Women's intercollegiate varsity sports:* basketball, cross country, field hockey, gymnastics, soccer, softball, track and field (indoor), track and field (outdoor), volleyball.

SERVICES AND FACILITIES

Basic services: nonremedial tutoring, placement service, health service. **Remedial assistance:** reading, math, writing, study skills. **Counseling services:** minority student, career, military, personal, veteran student, academic, psychological, birth control. **For learning-disabled students:** School does not offer a structured program with separate admission and additional fees. Total undergraduates in learning-disabled program or receiving services: 212. Services include: remedial math, remedial English, reading machines, tape recorders, untimed tests, note-taking services, oral tests, readers, extended time for tests, tutors, priority seating. **Library:** Number of titles: 1,221,815; number of current serial subscriptions: 13,821. **Information technology resources:** Students are not required to lease or own a computer. Number of campus computers available to all students: 3,500. School has a wireless network. Approximate number of users that can be accommodated: 7,000. Proportion of college-owned housing units wired for high-speed internet access: 100%. **Campus safety:** Security services offered: 24-hour foot-and-vehicle patrols, late-night transport/escort service, 24-hour emergency telephones, lighted pathways/sidewalks, student patrols, controlled dormitory access (key, security card, etc).

TRANSFER AND INTERNATIONAL STUDENTS

Transfer students: May apply for admission for the following academic terms: Fall, Winter, Spring, Summer. Applicants need a minimum number of credits to apply. For fall 2009: Transfer applications received: 2,840. Transfer applicants offered admission: 1,852. Transfer applicants enrolled: 1,160. **International students:** Number of foreign undergraduates: 237 (1% of student body). Number of countries represented: 36. Minimum TOEFL score required: 500 (paper); 173 (computer).

Cleary University

■ **Address:** 3601 Plymouth Road, Ann Arbor, MI 48105
■ **Website:** http://www.cleary.edu
■ **Private**
■ **Enrollment:** 413 full-time; 240 part-time

KEY STATS

✔ **U.S News College Ranking:** Unranked Specialty School–Business
✔ **SAT or ACT Score (25th/75th percentile):** N/A
✔ **Tuition:** 2010-2011: $16,560

Selectivity: Least selective	**Room/board:** N/A
Acceptance rate: 85%	**Average debt:** $20,528
Student/faculty ratio: 10/1	**Proportion who borrowed:** 78%

UNDERGRADUATE STUDENT BODY STATS

2009-2010 enrollment: 413 full-time; 240 part-time. Men: 42%; women: 58%. **Ethnic makeup:** African American: 8%; Asian American: 1%; Hispanic: 2%; White: 88%; International: 1%.

ADMISSIONS FACTS AND FIGURES

Phone: (734) 332-4477. **Email:** admissions@cleary.edu. **Website:** http://www.cleary.edu. **Application deadlines for fall 2011:** Regular decision: August 15. Early decision: Not offered. Early action: Send application by: N/A; Decision sent by: N/A. Admission can be deferred. **Application fee:** $25. **To apply online, go to:** https://secure.cleary.edu/apply/default.asp. **Admissions requirements/recommendations:** High school units required (recommended): English: (4); Mathematics: (2); Science: (2); Foreign language: (0); Social studies: (2); History: (2); Academic electives: (12); Total units: (24). Tests: The college uses SAT or ACT scores in admissions decisions. Neither SAT nor ACT required. For admission to the fall 2011 entering class, the school will accept: ACT with or without writing accepted. Campus visit: Recommended. Admissions interview: Recommended. Off-campus interview: May be arranged. **Factors that count in admissions decisions:** *Academic:* Secondary school record: Very Important. Class rank: Considered. Letters of recommendation: Considered. Standardized test scores: Very Important. Essay: Considered. *Nonacademic:* Interview: Important. Extracurricular activities: Not Considered. Talent/ability: Not Considered. Character/personal qualities: Not Considered. Alumni/ae relationship: Not Considered. Geographical residence: Not Considered. State residency: Not Considered. Religious affiliation/commitment: Not Considered. Minority status: Not Considered. Volunteer work: Not Considered. Work experience: Not Considered. **Other schools with the greatest overlap in applicants:** Baker College of Flint; Davenport University; Eastern Michigan University; Walsh College of Accountancy and Business Administration. **Admissions statistics for the fall 2009 entering class:** Total applicants: 78. Total accepted: 66. Freshmen enrolled: 37; Overall acceptance rate: 85%. Non-early acceptance rate: 85%.

ACADEMICS

Year founded: 1883. **Academic calendar:** Quarter. **Degrees offered:** certificate, associate, bachelor's, post-bachelor's certificate, master's. **Major fields of study:** business, management, marketing, and related support services; computer and information sciences and support services. **Areas of required coursework:** humanities, computer literacy, mathematics, English (including composition), philosophy, other. **Special academic programs (% participation):** accelerated program (85%), cooperative (work-study plan) program (2%), distance learning (100%), dual enrollment (4%), independent study (1%), internships (1%). **Cooperative education programs:** business. **Faculty and instruction (2009-2010):** Total instructional faculty: 5 full-time, 146 part-time (60% men; 40% women; 10% minorities). Full-time faculty with Ph.D. or other terminal degree: 40%. Student/faculty ratio: 10/1. Classes of fewer than 20 students: 96%; of 20 to 49 students: 4%. **Advanced Placement and International Baccalaureate credit:** AP tests may be used for: Credit only. International Baccalaureate exams may be used for: Placement only. **Freshmen returning for sophomore year:** 75%.

COSTS AND FINANCIAL AID

Financial aid office: (800) 686-1883. **Expenses (2010-2011):** Tuition and fees 2010-2011: $16,560. **Financial aid:** Priority filing date for institution's financial aid form: July 1; deadline: July 1. In 2009-2010, 61% of undergraduates applied for financial aid. Of those, 60% were determined to have financial need; 1% had their need fully met. Average financial aid package (proportion receiving): $14,623 (60%). Average amount of gift aid, such as scholarships or grants (proportion receiving): $1,285 (53%). Average amount of self-help aid, such as work study or loans (proportion receiving): $1,133 (30%). Average need-based loan (excluding PLUS or other private loans): $1,209. Among students who received need-based aid, the average percentage of need met: 20%. Among students who received aid based on merit, the average award (and the proportion receiving): $2,341 (3%). The average athletic scholarship (and the proportion receiving): $0 (0%). Average amount of debt of borrowers graduating in 2009: $20,528. Proportion who borrowed: 78%.

CAMPUS LIFE AND EXTRACURRICULAR ACTIVITIES

Student employment: During the 2009-2010 academic year, 2% of undergraduates worked on campus. **Clubs and organizations:** Number of student organizations: 5. Number of fraternities: 0; sororities: 0.

SERVICES AND FACILITIES

Basic services: nonremedial tutoring. **Remedial assistance:** math, writing, study skills. **Counseling services:** career, veteran student, academic. **For learning-disabled students:** School does not offer a structured program with separate admission and additional fees. **Library:** Number of titles: 375; number of current serial subscriptions: 20. **Information technology resources:** Students are required to lease or own a computer. Number of campus computers available to all students: 68. School has a wireless network. **Campus safety:** Security services offered: lighted pathways/sidewalks, student patrols.

TRANSFER AND INTERNATIONAL STUDENTS

Transfer students: May apply for admission for the following academic terms: Fall, Winter, Spring. Applicants do not need a minimum number of credits to apply. For fall 2009: Transfer applications received: 224. Transfer applicants offered admission: 200. Transfer applicants enrolled: 110. **International students:** Number of foreign undergraduates: 4 (1% of student body). Number of countries represented: 8. Minimum TOEFL score required: 550 (paper); 213 (computer). Average TOEFL score: 550 (paper).

College for Creative Studies

- **Address:** 201 E. Kirby, Detroit, MI 48202
- **Website:** http://www.collegeforcreativestudies.edu
- **Private**
- **Enrollment:** N/A

KEY STATS

✔ **U.S News College Ranking:** Unranked Specialty School–Fine Arts
✔ **ACT Score (25th/75th percentile):** 18-23
✔ **Tuition:** 2010-2011: $31,275

Selectivity: N/A	**Room/board:** $6,950
Acceptance rate: 39%	**Average debt:** $47,604
Student/faculty ratio: 11/1	**Proportion who borrowed:** 79%

Concordia University

- **Address:** 4090 Geddes Road, Ann Arbor, MI 48105
- **Website:** http://www.cuaa.edu
- **Private; Religious affiliation:** Lutheran Church-Missouri Synod
- **Enrollment:** N/A

KEY STATS

✔ **U.S News College Ranking:** 54, Regional Colleges (Midwest)
✔ **ACT Score (25th/75th percentile):** 20-26
✔ **Tuition:** 2010-2011: $21,082

Selectivity: Selective	**Room/board:** $7,878
Acceptance rate: 63%	**Average debt:** $29,354
Student/faculty ratio: N/A	**Proportion who borrowed:** 93%

Cornerstone University

- **Address:** 1001 E. Beltline NE, Grand Rapids, MI 49525
- **Website:** http://www.cornerstone.edu
- **Private; Religious affiliation:** Evangelical
- **Enrollment:** 1,427 full-time; 465 part-time

KEY STATS

✔ **U.S News College Ranking:** second tier, Regional Universities (Midwest)
✔ **ACT Score (25th/75th percentile):** 20-26
✔ **Tuition:** 2010-2011: $21,178

Selectivity: Selective	**Room/board:** $6,786
Acceptance rate: 79%	**Average debt:** $26,025
Student/faculty ratio: 15/1	**Proportion who borrowed:** 83%

UNDERGRADUATE STUDENT BODY STATS

2009-2010 enrollment: 1,427 full-time; 465 part-time. Men: 41%; women: 59%. **Ethnic makeup:** African American: 10%; Asian American: 1%; Hispanic: 3%; White: 85%; International: 1%. **Religious preference:** Roman Catholic: 1%; Protestant: 1%; Unknown: 3%; Evangelical: 95%.

ADMISSIONS FACTS AND FIGURES

Phone: (616) 222-1426. **Email:** admissions@cornerstone.edu. **Website:** http://www.cornerstone.edu. **Application deadlines for fall 2011:** Regular decision: August 15. Early decision: Not offered. Early action: Not offered. Admission cannot be deferred. **Application fee:** $25. **To apply online, go to:** http://www.cornerstone.edu/future_students/apply. **Admissions requirements/recommendations:** High school units required (recommended): English: 4 (4); Mathematics: 3 (3); Science: 2 (2); Foreign language: 3 (3); Social studies: 3 (3); History: 2 (2); Academic electives: 4 (4); Total units: 22 (22). Tests: The college uses SAT or ACT scores in admissions decisions. Either SAT or ACT required. For admission to the fall 2011 entering class, the school will accept: ACT with or without writing accepted. Campus visit: Recommended. Admissions interview: Neither required nor recommended. Off-campus interview: May be arranged. **Factors that count in admissions decisions:** *Academic:* Secondary school record: Important. Class rank: Important. Letters of recommendation: Very Important. Standardized test scores: Very Important. Essay: Very Important. *Nonacademic:* Interview: Not Considered. Extracurricular activities: Considered. Talent/ability: Important. Character/personal qualities: Very Important. Alumni/ae relationship: Not Considered. Geographical residence: Not Considered. State residency: Not Considered. Religious affiliation/commitment: Very Important. Minority status: Not Considered. Volunteer work: Not Considered. Work experience: Not Considered. **Other schools with the greatest overlap in applicants:** Calvin College; Cedarville University; Grand Valley State University; Spring Arbor University; Taylor University. **Admissions statistics for the fall 2009 entering class:** Total applicants: 1,024. Total accepted: 808. Freshmen enrolled: 337; 14% were from out of state. Overall acceptance rate: 79%. **Average high school grade point average:** 3.5. **First-year students who submitted SAT scores:** 10%. Scores (25/75 percentile): Critical Reading: 490-570, Math: 480-560, Combined: 970-1130. **First-year students submitting ACT scores:** 90%. Scores (25/75 percentile): English: 19-25, Math: 20-26, Composite: 20-26.

ACADEMICS

Year founded: 1941. **Academic calendar:** Semester. **Degrees offered:** associate, bachelor's, master's. **Most popular majors:** 50% business, management, marketing, and related support services, 17% education, 11% theology and religious vocations, 4% security and protective services, 3% psychology. **Major fields of study:** biological and biomedical sciences; business, management, marketing, and related support services; communication, journalism, and related programs; computer and information sciences and support services; education; English language and literature/letters; family and consumer sciences/human sciences; foreign languages, literatures, and linguistics; health professions and related clinical sciences; history; legal professions and studies; multi/interdisciplinary studies; parks, recreation, leisure, and fitness studies; philosophy and religious studies; psychology; public administration and social service professions; social sciences; theology and religious vocations; visual and performing arts. **Areas of required coursework:** arts/fine arts, humanities, computer literacy, mathematics, English (including composition), philosophy, foreign languages, sciences (biological or physical), history, social science, other. **Pre-professional programs:** pre-dentistry, pre-medicine, pre-theology, pre-veterinary science. **Special academic programs (% participation):** accelerated program (1%), distance learning (5%), double major (2%), dual enrollment (1%), English as a Second Language (ESL) (3%), honors program (1%), independent study (1%), internships (85%), liberal arts/career combination (65%), study abroad (2%), teacher certificate program (35%), weekend college (5%). **Teacher certification offered in:** early childhood, special education, elementary, middle/junior high, secondary. **Faculty and instruction (2009-2010):** Total instructional faculty: 58 full-time, 70 part-time (73% men; 27% women; 3% minorities). Full-time faculty with Ph.D. or other terminal degree: 47%. Student/faculty ratio: 15/1. Classes of fewer than 20 students: 61%; of 20 to 49 students: 37%; of 50 or more students: 2%. **Advanced Placement and International Baccalaureate credit:** AP tests may be used for: Placement only. Scores accepted: 3, 4, 5. International Baccalaureate exams may be used for: Placement only. **Freshmen returning for sophomore year:** 70%. **Graduation rates:** Four-year: 34%; five-year: 49%; six-year: 48%. **Graduate study:** 15% of students pursue further study immediately upon graduation; 20% within one year; 35% within five years. Fields in which graduates pursue further study: Master of Business Administration (MBA), 20%; law, 5%; medicine, 5%; theology (or the seminary), 20%; education, 25%; arts and sciences, 25%.

COSTS AND FINANCIAL AID

Financial aid office: (616) 222-1424. **Expenses (2010-2011):** Tuition and fees 2010-2011: $21,178; room/board: $6,786. Estimated books and supplies: $1,000; transportation: $1,444; personal expenses: $1,576. **Financial aid:** Priority filing date for institution's financial aid form: March 1. In 2009-2010, 92% of undergraduates applied for financial aid. Of those, 84% were determined to have financial need; 15% had their need fully met. Average financial aid package (proportion receiving): $18,623 (84%). Average amount of gift aid, such as scholarships or grants (proportion receiving): $11,526 (84%). Average amount of self-help aid, such as work study or loans (proportion receiving): $5,337 (65%). Average need-based loan (excluding PLUS or other private loans): $4,352. Among students who received need-based aid, the average percentage of need met: 85%. Among students who received aid based on merit, the average award (and the proportion receiving): $6,113 (15%). The average athletic scholarship (and the proportion receiving): $6,067 (14%). Average amount of debt of borrowers graduating in 2009: $26,025. Proportion who borrowed: 83%.

CAMPUS LIFE AND EXTRACURRICULAR ACTIVITIES

Campus housing available (% using): women's dorms (54%), men's dorms (40%), apartments for married students (4%), apartment for single students (1%), other housing options (1%). Students who live in college-owned, operated, or affiliated housing: 48%. **Student employment:** During the 2009-2010 academic year, 25% of undergraduates worked on campus. Average per-year earnings: $3,000. **Clubs and organizations:** Number of student organizations: 8. Activities include: campus ministries, choral groups, concert band, dance, drama/theater, jazz band, literary magazine, music ensembles, musical theater, pep band, radio station, student government, student newspaper, student film society, symphony orchestra. Number of fraternities: 0; sororities: 0. Average proportion of students who stay on campus on weekends: 25%. **Sports program (2009-2010):** Member of NAIA. *Men's intercollegiate varsity sports:* basketball, cross country, golf, soccer, track and field (indoor), track and field (outdoor). *Women's intercollegiate varsity sports:* basketball, cross country, golf, soccer, softball, track and field (indoor), track and field (outdoor), volleyball.

SERVICES AND FACILITIES

Basic services: nonremedial tutoring, placement service, health service, health insurance. **Remedial assistance:** reading, math, writing, study skills. **Counseling services:** minority student, career, personal, veteran student, academic, older student, psychological, religious. **For learning-disabled students:** School does not offer a structured program with separate admission and additional fees. Services include: remedial math, remedial English, remedial reading, tape recorders, other special classes, videotaped classes, diagnostic testing service, untimed tests, note-taking services, oral tests, learning center, readers, extended time for tests, tutors, priority seating, texts on tape, other testing accommodations. **Library:** Number of titles: 160,815; number of current serial subscriptions: 2,587. **Information technology resources:** Students are required to lease or own a computer. Number of campus computers available to all students: 1,300. School has a wireless network. Approximate number of users that can be accommodated: 1,200. Proportion of college-owned housing units wired for high-speed internet access: 100%. **Campus safety:** Security services offered: 24-hour foot-and-vehicle patrols, late-night transport/escort service, 24-hour emergency telephones, lighted pathways/sidewalks, student patrols, controlled dormitory access (key, security card, etc).

TRANSFER AND INTERNATIONAL STUDENTS

Transfer students: May apply for admission for the following academic terms: Fall, Spring, Summer. Applicants do not need a minimum number of credits to apply. For fall 2009: Transfer applications received: 177. Transfer applicants offered admission: 99. Transfer applicants enrolled: 52. **International students:** Number of foreign undergraduates: 15 (1% of student body). Number of countries represented: 14. Minimum TOEFL score required: 575 (paper); 235 (computer). Average TOEFL score: 580 (paper).

Davenport University

- **Address:** 6191 Kraft Avenue SE, Grand Rapids, MI 49512
- **Website:** http://www.davenport.edu
- **Private**
- **Enrollment:** 3,359 full-time; 6,672 part-time

KEY STATS

✔ **U.S News College Ranking:** second tier, Regional Universities (Midwest)
✔ **ACT Score:** 21
✔ **Tuition:** 2010-2011: $11,814

Selectivity: Selective	**Room/board:** $8,412
Acceptance rate: 84%	**Average debt:** N/A
Student/faculty ratio: 24/1	**Proportion who borrowed:** N/A

UNDERGRADUATE STUDENT BODY STATS

2009-2010 enrollment: 3,359 full-time; 6,672 part-time. Men: 33%; women: 67%. **Ethnic makeup:** African American: 19%; Asian American: 2%; Hispanic: 3%; White: 75%.

ADMISSIONS FACTS AND FIGURES

Phone: (866) 925-3884. **Email:** Davenport.Admissions@davenport.edu. **Website:** http://www.davenport.edu. **Application deadlines for fall 2011:** Regular decision: Rolling. Early decision: Not offered. Early action: Not offered. Admission can be deferred. **Application fee:** $25. **To apply online,** go to: http://www.davenport.edu/Home/ApplytoDavenport/NewStudents/ApplyNow/tabid/132/Default.aspx. **Admissions requirements/recommendations:** High school units required (recommended): English: 6; Mathematics: 6 (9); Social studies: 9. Tests: The college uses SAT or ACT scores in admissions decisions. Neither SAT nor ACT required. For admission to the fall 2011 entering class, the school will accept: ACT with or without writing accepted. Campus visit: Recommended. Admissions interview: Recommended. Off-campus interview: May be arranged. **Factors that count in admissions decisions: _Academic:_** Secondary school record: Not Considered. Class rank: Not Considered. Letters of recommendation: Not Considered. Standardized test scores: Very Important. Essay: Not Considered. _Nonacademic:_ Interview: Not Considered. Extracurricular activities: Not Considered. Talent/ability: Not Considered. Character/personal qualities: Not Considered. Alumni/ae relationship: Not Considered. Geographical residence: Not Considered. State residency: Not Considered. Religious affiliation/commitment: Not Considered. Minority status: Not Considered. Volunteer work: Not Considered. Work experience: Not Considered. **Admissions statistics for the fall 2009 entering class:** Total applicants: 5,747. Total accepted: 4,848. Freshmen enrolled: 2,052; Overall acceptance rate: 84%.

ACADEMICS

Year founded: 1866. **Academic calendar:** Semester. **Degrees offered:** diploma, associate, bachelor's, post-bachelor's certificate, master's, post-master's certificate. **Most popular majors:** 21% business administration and management, 15% accounting, 13% business/commerce, 9% marketing/marketing management, 6% human resources management/personnel administration. **Major fields of study:** biological and biomedical sciences; business, management, marketing, and related support services; computer and information sciences and support services; health professions and related clinical sciences; legal professions and studies; multi/interdisciplinary studies; security and protective services. **Areas of required coursework:** humanities, computer literacy, mathematics, English (including composition), sciences (biological or physical), social science. **Special academic programs:** accelerated program, distance learning, dual enrollment, English as a Second Language (ESL), independent study, internships, student-designed major, study abroad. **Cooperative education programs:** business, computer science, health professions. **Faculty and instruction (2009-2010):** Total instructional faculty: 157 full-time, 797 part-time (46% men; 54% women; 16% minorities). Full-time faculty with Ph.D. or other terminal degree: 23%. Student/faculty ratio: 24/1. Classes of fewer than 20 students: 57%; of 20 to 49 students: 43%; of 50 or more students: 0%. **Advanced Placement and International Baccalaureate credit:** AP tests may be used for: Credit only. International Baccalaureate exams may be used for: Credit only. **Freshmen returning for sophomore year:** 64%. **Graduation rates:** Four-year: 0%; five-year: 5%; six-year: 20%.

COSTS AND FINANCIAL AID

Financial aid office: (616) 451-3511. **Expenses (2010-2011):** Tuition and fees 2010-2011: $11,814; room/board: $8,412. Estimated books and supplies: $1,200; transportation: $0; personal expenses: $1,350. **Financial aid:** Priority filing date for institution's financial aid form: March 1.

CAMPUS LIFE AND EXTRACURRICULAR ACTIVITIES

Campus housing available: apartment for single students. Students who live in college-owned, operated, or affiliated housing: 3%. Average per-year earnings: $6,864. **Clubs and organizations:** Number of student organizations: 22. Activities include: student government, student newspaper. Number of fraternities: 0; sororities: 0. Average proportion of students who stay on campus on weekends: 1%. **Sports program (2009-2010):** Member of NAIA. _Men's intercollegiate varsity sports:_ baseball, basketball, cross country, golf, ice hockey, lacrosse, soccer, tennis, track and field (indoor). _Women's intercollegiate varsity sports:_ basketball, bowling, cross country, golf, lacrosse, soccer, softball, tennis, track and field (indoor), volleyball.

SERVICES AND FACILITIES

Basic services: nonremedial tutoring. **Remedial assistance:** reading, math, writing, study skills. **Counseling services:** career, personal, academic, older student. **For learning-disabled students:** School does not offer a structured program with separate admission and additional fees. Services include: remedial math, remedial English, remedial reading, learning center, extended time for tests, tutors, other. **Library:** Number of titles: 77,463; number of current serial subscriptions: 571. **Information technology resources:** Students are not required to lease or own a computer. Number of campus computers available to all students: 3,518. School has a wireless network. Proportion of college-owned housing units wired for high-speed internet access: 100%. **Campus safety:** Security services offered: 24-hour foot-and-vehicle patrols, late-night transport/escort service, 24-hour emergency telephones, lighted pathways/sidewalks, controlled dormitory access (key, security card, etc).

TRANSFER AND INTERNATIONAL STUDENTS

Transfer students: May apply for admission for the following academic terms: Fall, Winter, Spring, Summer. Applicants do not need a minimum number of credits to apply. **International students:** Number of foreign undergraduates: 0. Number of countries represented: 49. Minimum TOEFL score required: 500 (paper); 173 (computer).

Eastern Michigan University

- **Address:** Ypsilanti, MI 48197
- **Website:** http://www.emich.edu/
- **Public**
- **Enrollment:** 12,816 full-time; 4,947 part-time

KEY STATS

✔ **U.S News College Ranking:** 81, Regional Universities (Midwest)
✔ **ACT Score (25th/75th percentile):** 18-24
✔ **Tuition:** 2010-2011: $7,368 in state, $19,780 out of state

Selectivity: Selective	**Room/board:** $8,020
Acceptance rate: 71%	**Average debt:** $22,370
Student/faculty ratio: 18/1	**Proportion who borrowed:** 63%

UNDERGRADUATE STUDENT BODY STATS

2009-2010 enrollment: 12,816 full-time; 4,947 part-time. Men: 43%; women: 57%. **Ethnic makeup:** African American: 21%; American-Indian: 1%; Asian American: 2%; Hispanic: 3%; White: 72%; International: 2%.

ADMISSIONS FACTS AND FIGURES

Phone: (734) 487-3060. **Email:** undergraduate.admissions@emich.edu. **Website:** http://www.emich.edu/. **Application deadlines for fall 2011:** Regular decision: Rolling. Early decision: Not offered. Early action: Not offered. Admission can be deferred. **Application fee:** $30. **To apply online, go to:** http://www.emich.edu/admissions/apply.php. **Admissions requirements/recommendations:** High school units required (recommended): English: (4); Mathematics: (4); Science: (4); Foreign language: (2); Social studies: (2); History: (1); Total units: (21). Tests: The college uses SAT or ACT scores in admissions decisions. Either SAT or ACT required. For admission to the fall 2011 entering class, the school will accept: ACT with or without writing accepted. Campus visit: Recommended. Admissions interview:

Neither required nor recommended. Off-campus interview: Not available. **Factors that count in admissions decisions:** *Academic:* Secondary school record: Important. Class rank: Not Considered. Letters of recommendation: Considered. Standardized test scores: Very Important. Essay: Considered. *Nonacademic:* Interview: Not Considered. Extracurricular activities: Not Considered. Talent/ability: Not Considered. Character/personal qualities: Not Considered. Alumni/ae relationship: Not Considered. Geographical residence: Not Considered. State residency: Not Considered. Religious affiliation/commitment: Not Considered. Minority status: Not Considered. Volunteer work: Not Considered. Work experience: Not Considered. **Other schools with the greatest overlap in applicants:** Central Michigan University; Grand Valley State University; Michigan State University; University of Michigan–Ann Arbor; Western Michigan University. **Admissions statistics for the fall 2009 entering class:** Total applicants: 10,341. Total accepted: 7,337. Freshmen enrolled: 2,277; 13% were from out of state. Overall acceptance rate: 71%. **Credentials of fall 2009 freshmen:** 11% ranked in the top 10 percent of their high school class; 36% were in the top 25 percent; 71% were in the top half. (Proportion submitting class standing: 75%.) **Average high school grade point average:** 3.1. **First-year students who submitted SAT scores:** 11%. Scores (25/75 percentile): Critical Reading: 440-580, Math: 450-580, Combined: 890-1160. **First-year students submitting ACT scores:** 94%. Scores (25/75 percentile): English: 17-24, Math: 17-24, Composite: 18-24.

ACADEMICS

Year founded: 1849. **Academic calendar:** Semester. **Degrees offered:** bachelor's, post-bachelor's certificate, master's, post-master's certificate, doctorate. **Most popular majors:** 22% business, management, marketing, and related support services, 20% education, 10% health professions and related clinical sciences, 8% social sciences, 7% visual and performing arts. **Major fields of study:** architecture and related services; area, ethnic, cultural, and gender studies; biological and biomedical sciences; business, management, marketing, and related support services; communication, journalism, and related programs; communications technologies/technicians and support services; computer and information sciences and support services; education; engineering; engineering technologies/technicians; English language and literature/letters; family and consumer sciences/human sciences; foreign languages, literatures, and linguistics; health professions and related clinical sciences; history; legal professions and studies; liberal arts and sciences studies, and humanities; mathematics and statistics; multi/interdisciplinary studies; parks, recreation, leisure, and fitness studies; personal and culinary services; philosophy and religious studies; physical sciences; psychology; public administration and social service professions; security and protective services; social sciences; transportation and materials moving; visual and performing arts. **Areas of required coursework:** arts/fine arts, humanities, computer literacy, mathematics, English (including composition), philosophy, sciences (biological or physical), history, social science, other. **Pre-professional programs:** pre-law, pre-dentistry, pre-medicine, pre-veterinary science, pre-optometry, pre-pharmacy, other. **Special academic programs:** accelerated program, cooperative (work-study plan) program, distance learning, double major, dual enrollment, English as a Second Language (ESL), honors program, independent study, internships, student-designed major, study abroad, teacher certificate program, weekend college. **Teacher certification offered in:** early childhood, special education, elementary, vo-tech, middle/junior high, secondary, bilingual/bicultural. **Cooperative education programs:** art, business, computer science, engineering, health professions, home economics, humanities, natural science, social/behavioral science, technologies. **Reserve Officers Training Corps (ROTC):** Army ROTC: Offered on campus; Navy ROTC: Offered at cooperating institution (University of Michigan–Ann Arbor); Air Force ROTC: Offered at cooperating institution (University of Michigan–Ann Arbor). **Faculty and instruction (2009-2010):** Total instructional faculty: 755 full-time, 535 part-time. Full-time faculty with Ph.D. or other terminal degree: 81%. Student/faculty ratio: 18/1. Classes of fewer than 20 students: 36%; of 20 to 49 students: 59%; of 50 or more students: 5%. **Advanced Placement and International Baccalaureate credit:** AP tests may be used for: Placement only. Scores accepted: 3, 4, 5. International Baccalaureate exams may be used for: Placement only. **Freshmen returning for sophomore year:** 74%. **Graduation rates:** Four-year: 12%; five-year: 30%; six-year: 39%.

COSTS AND FINANCIAL AID

Financial aid office: (734) 487-0455. **Expenses (2010-2011):** Tuition and fees 2010-2011: $7,368 in state, $19,780 out of state; room/board: $8,020. **Financial aid:** Priority filing date for institution's financial aid form: March 1. In 2009-2010, 75% of undergraduates applied for financial aid. Of those, 65% were determined to have financial need; 4% had their need fully met. Average financial aid package (proportion receiving): $8,219 (63%). Average amount of gift aid, such as scholarships or grants (proportion receiving): $4,506 (44%). Average amount of self-help aid, such as work study or loans (proportion receiving): $4,386 (55%). Average need-based loan (excluding PLUS or other private loans): $4,310. Among students who received need-based aid, the average percentage of need met: 54%. Among students who received aid based on merit, the average award (and the proportion receiving): $4,037 (10%). The average athletic scholarship (and the proportion receiving): $15,322 (3%). Average amount of debt of borrowers graduating in 2009: $22,370. Proportion who borrowed: 63%.

CAMPUS LIFE AND EXTRACURRICULAR ACTIVITIES

Campus housing available: coed dorms, sorority housing, apartments for married students, apartment for single students, special housing for disabled students, special housing for international students, other housing options. Students who live in college-owned, operated, or affiliated housing: 16%. **Student employment:** During the 2009-2010 academic year, 10% of undergraduates worked on campus. Average per-year earnings: $3,200. **Clubs and organizations:** Number of student organizations: 220. Activities include: campus ministries, choral groups, concert band, dance, drama/theater, international student organization, literary magazine, marching band, music ensembles, musical theater, pep band, radio station, student government, student newspaper, student film society, symphony orchestra, television station. Number of fraternities: 11; sororities: 13. Proportion of men in fraternities: 4%; of women in sororities: 4%. **Sports program (2009-2010):** Member of NCAA I. *Men's intercollegiate varsity sports:* baseball, basketball, cross country, football, golf, swimming, track and field (indoor), track and field (outdoor), wrestling. *Women's intercollegiate varsity sports:* basketball, cross country, golf, gymnastics, crew (lightweight), soccer, softball, swimming, tennis, track and field (indoor), track and field (outdoor), volleyball.

SERVICES AND FACILITIES

Basic services: nonremedial tutoring, women's center, placement service, day care, health service. **Remedial assistance:** math. **Counseling services:** minority student, career, military, personal, veteran student, academic, psychological. **For learning-disabled students:** School does not offer a structured program with separate admission and additional fees. Total undergraduates in learning-disabled program or receiving services: 110. Services include: remedial math, reading machines, tape recorders, diagnostic testing service, note-taking services, learning center, readers, extended time for tests, tutors, priority registration, priority seating, texts on tape, other testing accommodations. **Library:** Number of titles: 652,983; number of current serial subscriptions: 76,331. **Information technology resources:** Students are not required to lease or own a computer. Number of campus computers available to all students: 1,500. School has a wireless network. Approximate number of users that can be accommodated: 1,800. Proportion of college-owned housing units wired for high-speed internet access: 100%. **Campus safety:** Security services offered: 24-hour foot-and-vehicle patrols, late-night transport/escort service, 24-hour emergency telephones, lighted pathways/sidewalks, student patrols, controlled dormitory access (key, security card, etc).

TRANSFER AND INTERNATIONAL STUDENTS

Transfer students: May apply for admission for the following academic terms: Fall, Winter, Spring, Summer. Applicants need a minimum number of credits to apply. For fall 2009: Transfer applications received: 3,977. Transfer applicants offered admission: 2,999. Transfer applicants enrolled: 1,961. **International students:** Number of foreign undergraduates: 324 (2% of student body). Number of countries represented: 49. Minimum TOEFL score required: 500 (paper); 173 (computer).

Ferris State University

- **Address:** 1201 S. State Street CSS201, Big Rapids, MI 49307
- **Website:** http://www.ferris.edu
- **Public**
- **Enrollment:** 9,203 full-time; 3,389 part-time

KEY STATS

✔ **U.S News College Ranking:** 98, Regional Universities (Midwest)
✔ **ACT Score (25th/75th percentile):** 18-24
✔ **Tuition:** 2009-2010: $9,480 in state, $15,900 out of state

Selectivity: Selective	Room/board: $8,940
Acceptance rate: 55%	Average debt: $34,767
Student/faculty ratio: 16/1	Proportion who borrowed: 76%

UNDERGRADUATE STUDENT BODY STATS

2009-2010 enrollment: 9,203 full-time; 3,389 part-time. Men: 51%; women: 49%. **Ethnic makeup:** African American: 7%; American-Indian: 1%; Asian American: 1%; Hispanic: 2%; White: 88%; International: 1%.

ADMISSIONS FACTS AND FIGURES

Phone: (231) 591-2100. **Email:** admissions@ferris.edu. **Website:** http://www.ferris.edu. **Application deadlines for fall 2011:** Regular decision: August 1. Early decision: Not offered. Early action: Not offered. Admission cannot be deferred. **Application fee:** $30. **To apply online, go to:** http://www.ferris.edu/admissions/application/. **Admissions requirements/recommendations:** High school units required (recommended): English: 0 (4); Mathematics: 0 (4); Science: 0 (4); Foreign language: 0 (3); Social studies: 0 (2); History: 0 (2); Academic electives: 0 (3); Total units: 0 (24). Tests: The college uses SAT or ACT scores in admissions decisions. Either SAT or ACT required. For admission to the fall 2011 entering class, the school will accept: ACT with or without writing accepted. Campus visit: Recommended. Admissions interview: Neither required nor recommended. Off-campus interview: Not available. **Factors that count in admissions decisions:** *Academic:* Secondary school record: Very Important. Class rank: Not Considered. Letters of recommendation: Considered. Standardized test scores: Very Important. Essay: Considered. *Nonacademic:* Interview: Not Considered. Extracurricular activities: Not Considered. Talent/ability: Not Considered. Character/personal qualities: Important. Alumni/ae relationship: Considered. Geographical residence: Considered. State residency: Not Considered. Religious affiliation/commitment: Not Considered. Minority status: Not Considered. Volunteer work: Considered. Work experience: Not Considered. **Other schools with the greatest overlap in applicants:** Central Michigan University; Grand Valley State University; Michigan State University; Northern Michigan University; Western Michigan University. **Admissions statistics for the fall 2009 entering class:** Total applicants: 10,743. Total accepted: 5,942. Freshmen enrolled: 2,242; 6% were from out of state. Overall acceptance rate: 55%. **Average high school grade point average:** 3.2. **First-year students submitting ACT scores:** 98%. Scores (25/75 percentile): English: 17-23, Math: 18-24, Composite: 18-24.

ACADEMICS

Year founded: 1884. **Academic calendar:** Semester. **Degrees offered:** certificate, associate, bachelor's, post-bachelor's certificate, master's. **Most popular majors:** 7% criminal justice/police science, 6% business administration and management, 5% pharmacy (Pharm.D. [U.S.A.] Pharm.D., B.S./B. Pharm. [Canada]), 3% construction management, 3% nursing/registered nurse training (R.N., A.S.N., B.S.N., M.S.N.). **Major fields of study:** biological and biomedical sciences; business, management, marketing, and related support services; communication, journalism, and related programs; communications technologies/technicians and support services; computer and information sciences and support services; education; engineering technologies/technicians; English language and literature/letters; family and consumer sciences/human sciences; health professions and related clinical sciences; history; mathematics and statistics; mechanic and repair technologies/technicians; parks, recreation, leisure, and fitness studies; physical sciences; precision production; psychology; public administration and social service professions; security and protective services; social sciences; visual and performing arts. **Areas of required coursework:** humanities, mathematics, English (including composition), sciences (biological or physical), history, social science, other. **Pre-professional programs:** pre-law, pre-dentistry, pre-medicine, pre-veterinary science, pre-pharmacy. **Special academic programs:** accelerated program, cooperative (work-study plan) program, cross-registration, distance learning, double major, dual enrollment,

exchange student program (domestic), external degree program, honors program, independent study, internships, liberal arts/career combination, student-designed major, study abroad, teacher certificate program. **Teacher certification offered in:** early childhood, special education, elementary, vo-tech, secondary. **Cooperative education programs:** business, other. **Reserve Officers Training Corps (ROTC):** Army ROTC: Offered at cooperating institution (Central Michigan University). **Faculty and instruction (2009-2010):** Total instructional faculty: 613 full-time, 290 part-time (57% men; 43% women; 7% minorities). Full-time faculty with Ph.D. or other terminal degree: 27%. Student/faculty ratio: 16/1. Classes of fewer than 20 students: 33%; of 20 to 49 students: 63%; of 50 or more students: 4%. **Advanced Placement and International Baccalaureate credit:** AP tests may be used for: Credit only. Scores accepted: 3, 4, 5. International Baccalaureate exams may be used for: Credit and/or placement. **Freshmen returning for sophomore year:** 71%. **Graduation rates:** Four-year: 23%; five-year: 44%; six-year: 41%.

COSTS AND FINANCIAL AID

Financial aid office: (231) 591-2110. **Expenses (2009-2010):** Tuition and fees 2009-2010: $9,480 in state, $15,900 out of state; room/board: $8,940. Estimated books and supplies: $1,020; transportation: $870; personal expenses: $690. **Financial aid:** Priority filing date for institution's financial aid form: March 1. In 2009-2010, 91% of undergraduates applied for financial aid. Of those, 72% were determined to have financial need; 14% had their need fully met. Average financial aid package (proportion receiving): $15,531 (71%). Average amount of gift aid, such as scholarships or grants (proportion receiving): $4,830 (50%). Average amount of self-help aid, such as work study or loans (proportion receiving): $4,628 (64%). Average need-based loan (excluding PLUS or other private loans): $4,292. Among students who received need-based aid, the average percentage of need met: 84%. Among students who received aid based on merit, the average award (and the proportion receiving): $3,690 (10%). The average athletic scholarship (and the proportion receiving): $13,367 (1%). Average amount of debt of borrowers graduating in 2009: $34,767. Proportion who borrowed: 76%.

CAMPUS LIFE AND EXTRACURRICULAR ACTIVITIES

Campus housing available: coed dorms, apartments for married students, apartment for single students, special housing for disabled students, special housing for international students, other housing options. Students who live in college-owned, operated, or affiliated housing: 29%. **Student employment:** During the 2009-2010 academic year, 20% of undergraduates worked on campus. Average per-year earnings: $2,775. **Clubs and organizations:** Number of student organizations: 203. Activities include: campus ministries, choral groups, concert band, dance, drama/theater, international student organization, jazz band, literary magazine, music ensembles, musical theater, pep band, radio station, student government, student newspaper, symphony orchestra, television station. Number of fraternities: 9; sororities: 5. Proportion of men in fraternities: 6%; of women in sororities: 5%. **Sports program (2009-2010):** Member of NCAA II. *Men's intercollegiate varsity sports:* basketball, cross country, football, golf, ice hockey, tennis, track and field (outdoor). *Women's intercollegiate varsity sports:* basketball, cross country, golf, soccer, softball, tennis, track and field (outdoor), volleyball.

SERVICES AND FACILITIES

Basic services: nonremedial tutoring, day care, health service, health insurance, other. **Remedial assistance:** reading, math, writing, study skills. **Counseling services:** minority student, career, military, personal, veteran student, academic, psychological, birth control. **For learning-disabled students:** School does not offer a structured program with separate admission and additional fees. Total undergraduates in learning-disabled program or receiving services: 120. Services include: remedial math, remedial English, reading machines, remedial reading, tape recorders, other special classes, note-taking services, learning center, readers, extended time for tests, tutors, substitution of courses, texts on tape, exams on tape or computer, other. **Library:** Number of titles: 411,778; number of current serial subscriptions: 45,000. **Information technology resources:** Students are not required to lease or own a computer. Number of campus computers available to all students: 2,200. School has a wireless network. Proportion of college-owned housing units wired for high-speed internet access: 100%. **Campus safety:** Security services offered: 24-hour foot-and-vehicle patrols, late-night transport/escort service, 24-hour emergency telephones, lighted pathways/sidewalks, student patrols, controlled dormitory access (key, security card, etc).

TRANSFER AND INTERNATIONAL STUDENTS

Transfer students: May apply for admission for the following academic terms: Fall, Spring, Summer. Applicants need a minimum number of cred-

its to apply. For fall 2009: Transfer applications received: 4,161. Transfer applicants offered admission: 2,172. Transfer applicants enrolled: 1,374. **International students:** Number of foreign undergraduates: 86 (1% of student body). Number of countries represented: 36. Minimum TOEFL score required: 500 (paper); 61 (computer). Average TOEFL score: 550 (paper).

Finlandia University

- **Address:** 601 Quincy Street, Hancock, MI 49930
- **Website:** http://www.finlandia.edu
- **Private; Religious affiliation:** ELCA
- **Enrollment:** N/A

KEY STATS
✔ **U.S News College Ranking:** second tier, Regional Colleges (Midwest)
✔ **SAT or ACT Score (25th/75th percentile):** N/A
✔ **Tuition:** 2009-2010: $18,436

Selectivity: Less selective	**Room/board:** $5,974
Acceptance rate: N/A	**Average debt:** N/A
Student/faculty ratio: N/A	**Proportion who borrowed:** N/A

Grace Bible College

- **Address:** 1011 Aldon Street SW, Grand Rapids, MI 49509-9990
- **Website:** http://www.gbcol.edu
- **Private; Religious affiliation:** Grace Gospel Fellowship
- **Enrollment:** N/A

KEY STATS
✔ **U.S News College Ranking:** Unranked, Regional Colleges (Midwest)
✔ **SAT or ACT Score (25th/75th percentile):** N/A
✔ **Tuition:** 2009-2010: $13,920

Selectivity: N/A	**Room/board:** $6,850
Acceptance rate: N/A	**Average debt:** N/A
Student/faculty ratio: N/A	**Proportion who borrowed:** N/A

Grand Valley State University

- **Address:** 1 Campus Drive, Allendale, MI 49401
- **Website:** http://www.gvsu.edu
- **Public**
- **Enrollment:** 18,448 full-time; 2,402 part-time

KEY STATS
✔ **U.S News College Ranking:** 34, Regional Universities (Midwest)
✔ **ACT Score (25th/75th percentile):** 22-26
✔ **Tuition:** 2009-2010: $8,630 in state, $12,944 out of state

Selectivity: Selective	**Room/board:** $7,478
Acceptance rate: 81%	**Average debt:** $24,030
Student/faculty ratio: 17/1	**Proportion who borrowed:** 70%

UNDERGRADUATE STUDENT BODY STATS
2009-2010 enrollment: 18,448 full-time; 2,402 part-time. Men: 41%; women: 59%. **Ethnic makeup:** African American: 5%; American-Indian: 1%; Asian American: 3%; Hispanic: 3%; White: 87%; International: 1%.

ADMISSIONS FACTS AND FIGURES
Phone: (800) 748-0246. **Email:** admissions@gvsu.edu. **Website:** http://www.gvsu.edu. **Application deadlines for fall 2011:** Regular decision: May 1. Early decision: Not offered. Early action: Not offered. Admission cannot be deferred. **Application fee:** $30. **To apply online, go to:** http://admissions.gvsu.edu/admissions/application. **Admissions requirements/recommendations:** High school units required (recommended): English: 4 (4); Mathematics: 3 (4); Science: 3 (4); Foreign language: 2 (2); Social studies: 3 (3); Total units: 16 (20). Tests: The college uses SAT or ACT scores in admissions decisions. Either SAT or ACT required. For admission to the fall 2011 entering class, the school will accept: ACT with writ-

ing recommended. Campus visit: Recommended. Admissions interview: Recommended. Off-campus interview: May be arranged. **Factors that count in admissions decisions:** *Academic:* Secondary school record: Very Important. Class rank: Considered. Letters of recommendation: Considered. Standardized test scores: Important. Essay: Considered. *Nonacademic:* Interview: Not Considered. Extracurricular activities: Considered. Talent/ability: Considered. Character/personal qualities: Not Considered. Alumni/ae relationship: Considered. Geographical residence: Not Considered. State residency: Not Considered. Religious affiliation/commitment: Not Considered. Minority status: Not Considered. Volunteer work: Considered. Work experience: Considered. **Other schools with the greatest overlap in applicants:** Central Michigan University; Hope College; Michigan State University; Western Michigan University. **Admissions statistics for the fall 2009 entering class:** Total applicants: 13,051. Total accepted: 10,520. Freshmen enrolled: 3,727; 5% were from out of state. Overall acceptance rate: 81%. **Credentials of fall 2009 freshmen:** 21% ranked in the top 10 percent of their high school class; 55% were in the top 25 percent; 91% were in the top half. (Proportion submitting class standing: 85%.) **Average high school grade point average:** 3.5. **First-year students who submitted SAT scores:** 5%. Scores (25/75 percentile): Critical Reading: 480-610, Math: 520-640, Combined: 1000-1250. **First-year students submitting ACT scores:** 99%. Scores (25/75 percentile): English: 21-26, Math: 21-27, Composite: 22-26.

ACADEMICS
Year founded: 1960. **Academic calendar:** Semester. **Degrees offered:** certificate, bachelor's, post-bachelor's certificate, master's, post-master's certificate. **Most popular majors:** 20% business, management, marketing, and related support services, 10% health professions and related clinical sciences, 9% biological and biomedical sciences, 9% social sciences, 8% psychology. **Major fields of study:** architecture and related services; area, ethnic, cultural, and gender studies; biological and biomedical sciences; business, management, marketing, and related support services; communication, journalism, and related programs; computer and information sciences and support services; education; engineering; English language and literature/letters; foreign languages, literatures, and linguistics; health professions and related clinical sciences; history; legal professions and studies; liberal arts and sciences studies, and humanities; mathematics and statistics; multi/interdisciplinary studies; natural resources and conservation; parks, recreation, leisure, and fitness studies; philosophy and religious studies; physical sciences; psychology; public administration and social service professions; security and protective services; social sciences; visual and performing arts. **Areas of required coursework:** arts/fine arts, humanities, mathematics, English (including composition), philosophy, sciences (biological or physical), history, social science. **Pre-professional programs:** pre-law, pre-dentistry, pre-medicine, pre-veterinary science, pre-pharmacy. **Special academic programs (% participation):** distance learning (17%), double major (19%), dual enrollment (1%), English as a Second Language (ESL), honors program (6%), independent study (15%), internships (31%), student-designed major (1%), study abroad (16%), teacher certificate program (10%). **Teacher certification offered in:** early childhood, special education, elementary, middle/junior high, secondary. **Cooperative education programs:** education, engineering. **Faculty and instruction (2009-2010):** Total instructional faculty: 1,051 full-time, 536 part-time (52% men; 48% women; 13% minorities). Full-time faculty with Ph.D. or other terminal degree: 70%. Student/faculty ratio: 17/1. Classes of fewer than 20 students: 24%; of 20 to 49 students: 70%; of 50 or more students: 7%. **Advanced Placement and International Baccalaureate credit:** AP tests may be used for: Credit and/or placement. Scores accepted: 3, 4, 5. International Baccalaureate exams may be used for: Placement only. **Freshmen returning for sophomore year:** 84%. **Graduation rates:** Four-year: 26%; five-year: 53%; six-year: 55%. **Graduate study:** 21% of students pursue further study immediately upon graduation.

COSTS AND FINANCIAL AID
Financial aid office: (616) 331-3234. **Expenses (2009-2010):** Tuition and fees 2009-2010: $8,630 in state, $12,944 out of state; room/board: $7,478. Estimated books and supplies: $1,000; transportation: $1,100; personal expenses: $1,100. **Financial aid:** Priority filing date for institution's financial aid form: March 1. In 2009-2010, 80% of undergraduates applied for financial aid. Of those, 62% were determined to have financial need; 10% had their need fully met. Average financial aid package (proportion receiving): $8,485 (61%). Average amount of gift aid, such as scholarships or grants (proportion receiving): $5,572 (47%). Average amount of self-help aid, such as work study or loans (proportion receiving): $4,817 (54%). Average need-based loan (excluding PLUS or other private loans): $4,542. Among students who received need-based aid, the average percentage of need met:

61%. Among students who received aid based on merit, the average award (and the proportion receiving): $3,384 (8%). The average athletic scholarship (and the proportion receiving): $6,313 (1%). Average amount of debt of borrowers graduating in 2009: $24,030. Proportion who borrowed: 70%.

CAMPUS LIFE AND EXTRACURRICULAR ACTIVITIES

Campus housing available: coed dorms, women's dorms, sorority housing, apartments for married students, apartment for single students, special housing for disabled students. Students who live in college-owned, operated, or affiliated housing: 25%. **Student employment:** During the 2009-2010 academic year, 16% of undergraduates worked on campus. Average per-year earnings: $3,800. **Clubs and organizations:** Number of student organizations: 268. Activities include: campus ministries, choral groups, concert band, dance, drama/theater, international student organization, jazz band, literary magazine, marching band, music ensembles, musical theater, pep band, radio station, student government, student newspaper, symphony orchestra, television station. Number of fraternities: 21; sororities: 10. Average proportion of students who stay on campus on weekends: 50%. **Sports program (2009-2010):** Member of NCAA II. *Men's intercollegiate varsity sports:* baseball, basketball, cross country, football, golf, swimming, tennis, track and field (indoor), track and field (outdoor). *Women's intercollegiate varsity sports:* basketball, cross country, golf, soccer, softball, swimming, tennis, track and field (indoor), track and field (outdoor), volleyball.

SERVICES AND FACILITIES

Basic services: nonremedial tutoring, women's center, placement service, day care, health service, health insurance. **Remedial assistance:** math, writing. **Counseling services:** minority student, career, personal, academic, older student, psychological. **For learning-disabled students:** School does not offer a structured program with separate admission and additional fees. Total undergraduates in learning-disabled program or receiving services: 124. Services include: remedial math, remedial English, reading machines, remedial reading, tape recorders, videotaped classes, untimed tests, note-taking services, oral tests, learning center, readers, extended time for tests, tutors, priority registration, priority seating, texts on tape, other testing accommodations. **Library:** Number of titles: 678,488; number of current serial subscriptions: 51,486. **Information technology resources:** Students are not required to lease or own a computer. Number of campus computers available to all students: 2,600. School has a wireless network. Approximate number of users that can be accommodated: 21,500. Proportion of college-owned housing units wired for high-speed internet access: 100%. **Campus safety:** Security services offered: 24-hour foot-and-vehicle patrols, late-night transport/escort service, 24-hour emergency telephones, lighted pathways/sidewalks, student patrols, controlled dormitory access (key, security card, etc).

TRANSFER AND INTERNATIONAL STUDENTS

Transfer students: May apply for admission for the following academic terms: Fall, Winter, Spring, Summer. Applicants do not need a minimum number of credits to apply. For fall 2009: Transfer applications received: 3,533. Transfer applicants offered admission: 2,411. Transfer applicants enrolled: 1,560. **International students:** Number of foreign undergraduates: 191 (1% of student body). Number of countries represented: 66. Minimum TOEFL score required: 550 (paper); 213 (computer). Average TOEFL score: 598 (paper).

Hillsdale College

- **Address:** 33 E. College Street, Hillsdale, MI 49242
- **Website:** http://www.hillsdale.edu
- **Private**
- **Enrollment:** 1,282 full-time; 33 part-time

....

KEY STATS

✔ **U.S News College Ranking:** 88, National Liberal Arts Colleges
✔ **ACT Score (25th/75th percentile):** 26-30
✔ **Tuition:** 2010-2011: $20,500

Selectivity: More selective	**Room/board:** $7,990
Acceptance rate: 62%	**Average debt:** $18,000
Student/faculty ratio: 10/1	**Proportion who borrowed:** 61%

UNDERGRADUATE STUDENT BODY STATS

2009-2010 enrollment: 1,282 full-time; 33 part-time. Men: 47%; women: 53%. **Religious preference:** Roman Catholic: 26%; Protestant: 45%; Jewish: 1%; No preference: 3%; Unknown: 25%.

ADMISSIONS FACTS AND FIGURES

Phone: (517) 607-2327. **Email:** admissions@hillsdale.edu. **Website:** http://www.hillsdale.edu. **Application deadlines for fall 2011:** Regular decision: February 15; decision sent by April 1. Early decision: Send application by: November 15; Decision sent by: December 1. Early action: Send application by: January 1; Decision sent by: December 15. Admission can be deferred. **Application fee:** $35. **To apply online, go to:** http://www.hillsdale.edu/admissions/application/apply.asp. **Admissions requirements/recommendations:** High school units required (recommended): English: 4 (4); Mathematics: 4 (4); Science: 3 (3); Foreign language: 2 (2); Social studies: 1 (1); History: 2 (2); Total units: 16 (16). Tests: The college uses SAT or ACT scores in admissions decisions. Either SAT or ACT required. For admission to the fall 2011 entering class, the school will accept: ACT with or without writing accepted. Campus visit: Recommended. Admissions interview: Recommended. Off-campus interview: May be arranged. **Factors that count in admissions decisions:** *Academic:* Secondary school record: Very Important. Class rank: Important. Letters of recommendation: Important. Standardized test scores: Very Important. Essay: Very Important. *Nonacademic:* Interview: Very Important. Extracurricular activities: Important. Talent/ability: Considered. Character/personal qualities: Very Important. Alumni/ae relationship: Considered. Geographical residence: Not Considered. State residency: Not Considered. Religious affiliation/commitment: Not Considered. Minority status: Not Considered. Volunteer work: Important. Work experience: Important. **Other schools with the greatest overlap in applicants:** Grove City College; Hope College; University of Michigan–Ann Arbor; University of Notre Dame; Wheaton College. **Admissions statistics for the fall 2009 entering class:** Total applicants: 1,632. Total accepted: 1,010. Freshmen enrolled: 375; 59% were from out of state. Overall acceptance rate: 62%. Non-early acceptance rate: 62%. **Size of waiting list:** 30 applicants; enrolled from waiting list: 5. **Credentials of fall 2009 freshmen:** 52% ranked in the top 10 percent of their high school class; 77% were in the top 25 percent; 98% were in the top half. (Proportion submitting class standing: 57%.) **Average high school grade point average:** 3.7. **First-year students who submitted SAT scores:** 45%. Scores (25/75 percentile): Critical Reading: 640-730, Math: 570-670, Combined: 1210-1400. **First-year students submitting ACT scores:** 55%. Scores (25/75 percentile): English: 26-32, Math: 24-30, Composite: 26-30.

ACADEMICS

Year founded: 1844. **Academic calendar:** Semester. **Degrees offered:** bachelor's. **Most popular majors:** 23% business, management, marketing, and related support services, 16% social sciences, 15% history, 11% English language and literature/letters, 11% biological and biomedical sciences. **Major fields of study:** area, ethnic, cultural, and gender studies; biological and biomedical sciences; business, management, marketing, and related support services; communication, journalism, and related programs; education; English language and literature/letters; foreign languages, literatures, and linguistics; history; mathematics and statistics; multi/interdisciplinary studies; philosophy and religious studies; physical sciences; psychology; social sciences; visual and performing arts. **Areas of required coursework:** arts/fine arts, humanities, mathematics, English (including composition), philosophy, foreign languages, sciences (biological or physical), history, social science, other. **Pre-professional programs:** pre-law, pre-dentistry, pre-medicine, pre-theology, pre-veterinary science, pre-optometry, pre-pharmacy. **Special academic programs (% participation):** double major (10%), dual enrollment (1%), honors program (13%), independent study (2%), internships (3%), study abroad (6%), teacher certificate program (15%). **Teacher certification offered in:** early childhood, elementary, secondary. **Faculty and instruction (2009-2010):** Total instructional faculty: 115 full-time, 37 part-time (67% men; 33% women). Full-time faculty with Ph.D. or other terminal degree: 83%. Student/faculty ratio: 10/1. Classes of fewer than 20 students: 77%; of 20 to 49 students: 22%; of 50 or more students: 0%. **Advanced Placement and International Baccalaureate credit:** AP tests may be used for: Credit and/or placement. Scores accepted: 3, 4, 5. International Baccalaureate exams may be used for: Credit and/or placement. **Freshmen returning for sophomore year:** 89%. **Graduation rates:** Four-year: 70%; five-year: 75%; six-year: 75%. **Graduate study:** 30% of students pursue further study immediately upon graduation; 15% within one year; 3% within five years. Fields in which graduates pursue further study: Master of Business Administration (MBA), 24%; law, 21%; medicine, 3%; dentistry, 2%; engineering, 1%; theology (or the seminary), 4%; education, 24%; arts and sciences, 17%; veterinary medicine, 1%.

COSTS AND FINANCIAL AID

Financial aid office: (517) 607-2350. **Expenses (2010-2011):** Tuition and fees 2010-2011: $20,500; room/board: $7,990. Estimated books and supplies: $800; transportation: $1,000; personal expenses: $1,000. **Financial aid:** Priority filing date for institution's financial aid form: February 15; deadline: April 1. In 2009-2010, 64% of undergraduates applied for financial aid. Of those, 53% were determined to have financial need; 32% had their need fully met. Average financial aid package (proportion receiving): $14,046 (47%). Average amount of gift aid, such as scholarships or grants (proportion receiving): $6,900 (28%). Average amount of self-help aid, such as work study or loans (proportion receiving): $4,500 (41%). Average need-based loan (excluding PLUS or other private loans): $4,500. Among students who received need-based aid, the average percentage of need met: 65%. Among students who received aid based on merit, the average award (and the proportion receiving): $5,200 (37%). The average athletic scholarship (and the proportion receiving): $10,916 (16%). Average amount of debt of borrowers graduating in 2009: $18,000. Proportion who borrowed: 61%.

CAMPUS LIFE AND EXTRACURRICULAR ACTIVITIES

Campus housing available (% using): women's dorms (43%), men's dorms (40%), sorority housing (9%), fraternity housing (7%), other housing options (1%). Students who live in college-owned, operated, or affiliated housing: 85%. **Student employment:** During the 2009-2010 academic year, 75% of undergraduates worked on campus. Average per-year earnings: $1,300. **Clubs and organizations:** Number of student organizations: 66. Activities include: campus ministries, choral groups, concert band, dance, drama/theater, international student organization, jazz band, literary magazine, music ensembles, musical theater, pep band, student government, student newspaper, symphony orchestra, yearbook. Number of fraternities: 4; sororities: 3. Proportion of men in fraternities: 36%; of women in sororities: 46%. Average proportion of students who stay on campus on weekends: 90%. **Sports program (2009-2010):** Member of NCAA II.

SERVICES AND FACILITIES

Basic services: nonremedial tutoring, placement service, health service. **Counseling services:** career, personal, academic, psychological, religious. **For learning-disabled students:** Services include: learning center, extended time for tests, tutors. **Library:** Number of titles: 240,000; number of current serial subscriptions: 1,700. **Information technology resources:** Students are not required to lease or own a computer. Number of campus computers available to all students: 270. School has a wireless network. Approximate number of users that can be accommodated: 1,050. Proportion of college-owned housing units wired for high-speed internet access: 100%. **Campus safety:** Security services offered: 24-hour foot-and-vehicle patrols, 24-hour emergency telephones, lighted pathways/sidewalks, controlled dormitory access (key, security card, etc).

TRANSFER AND INTERNATIONAL STUDENTS

Transfer students: May apply for admission for the following academic terms: Fall, Spring, Summer. Applicants do not need a minimum number of credits to apply. For fall 2009: Transfer applications received: 70. Transfer applicants offered admission: 35. Transfer applicants enrolled: 29. **International students:** Number of countries represented: 12. Minimum TOEFL score required: 560 (paper); 83 (computer). Average TOEFL score: 580 (paper).

Hope College

- **Address:** PO Box 9000, Holland, MI 49422-9000
- **Website:** http://www.hope.edu
- **Private; Religious affiliation:** Reformed Church in America
- **Enrollment:** 3,114 full-time; 116 part-time

KEY STATS

✔ **U.S News College Ranking:** 88, National Liberal Arts Colleges
✔ **ACT Score (25th/75th percentile):** 23-29
✔ **Tuition:** 2010-2011: $26,510

Selectivity: More selective	**Room/board:** $8,110
Acceptance rate: 84%	**Average debt:** $28,682
Student/faculty ratio: 12/1	**Proportion who borrowed:** 64%

UNDERGRADUATE STUDENT BODY STATS

2009-2010 enrollment: 3,114 full-time; 116 part-time. Men: 40%; women: 60%. **Ethnic makeup:** African American: 2%; Asian American: 2%; Hispanic: 4%; White: 90%; International: 1%. **Religious preference:** Roman Catholic: 14%; Protestant: 54%; No preference: 1%; Unknown: 15%; Reformed Church in America: 16%; Non-Christian: 0%.

ADMISSIONS FACTS AND FIGURES

Phone: (616) 395-7850. **Email:** admissions@hope.edu. **Website:** http://www.hope.edu. **Application deadlines for fall 2011:** Regular decision: Rolling. Early decision: Not offered. Early action: Not offered. Admission can be deferred. **Application fee:** $35. **To apply online, go to:** http://www.hope.edu/admissions/apply/application.html. **Admissions requirements/recommendations:** High school units required (recommended): English: (4); Mathematics: (3); Science: (2); Foreign language: (2); Social studies: (0); History: (0); Academic electives: (5); Total units: (18). Tests: The college uses SAT or ACT scores in admissions decisions. Either SAT or ACT required. For admission to the fall 2011 entering class, the school will accept: ACT with or without writing accepted. Campus visit: Recommended. Admissions interview: Recommended. Off-campus interview: May be arranged. **Factors that count in admissions decisions:** *Academic:* Secondary school record: Very Important. Class rank: Important. Letters of recommendation: Considered. Standardized test scores: Very Important. Essay: Important. *Nonacademic:* Interview: Considered. Extracurricular activities: Considered. Talent/ability: Considered. Character/personal qualities: Considered. Alumni/ae relationship: Considered. Geographical residence: Considered. State residency: Considered. Religious affiliation/commitment: Considered. Minority status: Considered. Volunteer work: Considered. Work experience: Considered. **Other schools with the greatest overlap in applicants:** Calvin College; Grand Valley State University; Michigan State University; University of Michigan–Ann Arbor; Western Michigan University. **Admissions statistics for the fall 2009 entering class:** Total applicants: 2,941. Total accepted: 2,483. Freshmen enrolled: 803; 30% were from out of state. Overall acceptance rate: 84%. **Size of waiting list:** 0 applicants; enrolled from waiting list: 0. **Credentials of fall 2009 freshmen:** 34% ranked in the top 10 percent of their high school class; 63% were in the top 25 percent; 91% were in the top half. (Proportion submitting class standing: 73%.) **Average high school grade point average:** 3.7. **First-year students who submitted SAT scores:** 18%. Scores (25/75 percentile): Critical Reading: 540-670, Math: 520-660, Combined: 1060-1330. **First-year students submitting ACT scores:** 94%. Scores (25/75 percentile): English: N/A, Math: N/A, Composite: 23-29.

ACADEMICS

Year founded: 1866. **Academic calendar:** Semester. **Degrees offered:** bachelor's. **Most popular majors:** 8% business administration and management, 8% psychology, 7% communication studies/speech communication and rhetoric, 5% English language and literature, 5% nursing/registered nurse training (R.N., A.S.N., B.S.N., M.S.N.). **Major fields of study:** agriculture, agriculture operations, and related sciences; area, ethnic, cultural, and gender studies; biological and biomedical sciences; business, management, marketing, and related support services; communication, journalism, and related programs; computer and information sciences and support services; education; engineering; English language and literature/letters; foreign languages, literatures, and linguistics; health professions and related clinical sciences; history; liberal arts and sciences studies, and humanities; mathematics and statistics; multi/interdisciplinary studies; natural resources and conservation; parks, recreation, leisure, and fitness studies; philosophy and religious studies; physical sciences; psychology; public administration and social service professions; social sciences; visual and performing arts. **Areas**

of required coursework: arts/fine arts, humanities, mathematics, English (including composition), foreign languages, sciences (biological or physical), history, social science, other. **Pre-professional programs:** pre-law, pre-dentistry, pre-medicine, pre-theology, pre-veterinary science, pre-optometry, pre-pharmacy, other. **Special academic programs (% participation):** distance learning, double major (21%), English as a Second Language (ESL), independent study (10%), internships (30%), student-designed major (1%), study abroad (25%), teacher certificate program (10%). **Teacher certification offered in:** special education, elementary, middle/junior high, secondary. **Reserve Officers Training Corps (ROTC):** Army ROTC: Offered at cooperating institution (Western Michigan University). **Faculty and instruction (2009-2010):** Total instructional faculty: 230 full-time, 73 part-time (52% men; 48% women; 8% minorities). Full-time faculty with Ph.D. or other terminal degree: 78%. Student/faculty ratio: 12/1. Classes of fewer than 20 students: 53%; of 20 to 49 students: 45%; of 50 or more students: 2%. **Advanced Placement and International Baccalaureate credit:** AP tests may be used for: Credit only. Scores accepted: 3, 4, 5. International Baccalaureate exams may be used for: Credit only. **Freshmen returning for sophomore year:** 89%. **Graduation rates:** Four-year: 66%; five-year: 79%; six-year: 79%. **Graduate study:** 33% of students pursue further study within one year. Fields in which graduates pursue further study: Master of Business Administration (MBA), 2%; medicine, 10%; dentistry, 1%; engineering, 1%; theology (or the seminary), 2%; education, 2%; arts and sciences, 14%; veterinary medicine, 1%.

COSTS AND FINANCIAL AID
Financial aid office: (616) 395-7765. **Expenses (2010-2011):** Tuition and fees 2010-2011: $26,510; room/board: $8,110. Estimated books and supplies: $800; transportation: $290; personal expenses: $1,230. **Financial aid:** Priority filing date for institution's financial aid form: March 1. In 2009-2010, 75% of undergraduates applied for financial aid. Of those, 62% were determined to have financial need; 35% had their need fully met. Average financial aid package (proportion receiving): $22,419 (62%). Average amount of gift aid, such as scholarships or grants (proportion receiving): $17,144 (53%). Average amount of self-help aid, such as work study or loans (proportion receiving): $5,275 (51%). Average need-based loan (excluding PLUS or other private loans): $4,612. Among students who received need-based aid, the average percentage of need met: 84%. Among students who received aid based on merit, the average award (and the proportion receiving): $7,532 (26%). The average athletic scholarship (and the proportion receiving): $0 (0%). Average amount of debt of borrowers graduating in 2009: $28,682. Proportion who borrowed: 64%.

CAMPUS LIFE AND EXTRACURRICULAR ACTIVITIES
Campus housing available (% using): coed dorms (42%), women's dorms (30%), men's dorms (10%), sorority housing (5%), fraternity housing (4%), apartments for married students (0%), apartment for single students (0%), special housing for disabled students (1%), other housing options (8%). Students who live in college-owned, operated, or affiliated housing: 84%. **Student employment:** During the 2009-2010 academic year, 40% of undergraduates worked on campus. Average per-year earnings: $1,525. **Clubs and organizations:** Number of student organizations: 70. Activities include: campus ministries, choral groups, concert band, dance, drama/theater, international student organization, jazz band, literary magazine, model UN, music ensembles, radio station, student government, student newspaper, symphony orchestra, television station, yearbook. Number of fraternities: 6; sororities: 7. Proportion of men in fraternities: 12%; of women in sororities: 11%. Average proportion of students who stay on campus on weekends: 75%. **Sports program (2009-2010):** Member of NCAA III. *Men's intercollegiate varsity sports:* baseball, basketball, cross country, football, golf, soccer, tennis, track and field (indoor), track and field (outdoor). *Women's intercollegiate varsity sports:* basketball, cross country, golf, soccer, softball, tennis, track and field (indoor), track and field (outdoor), volleyball.

SERVICES AND FACILITIES
Basic services: placement service, health service, health insurance. **Remedial assistance:** reading, math, writing, study skills. **Counseling services:** minority student, career, personal, veteran student, academic, older student, psychological, birth control, religious. **For learning-disabled students:** School does not offer a structured program with separate admission and additional fees. Total undergraduates in learning-disabled program or receiving services: 80. Services include: reading machines, tape recorders, untimed tests, note-taking services, oral tests, learning center, readers, extended time for tests, tutors, priority registration, texts on tape. **Library:** Number of titles: 371,987; number of current serial subscriptions: 12,573. **Information technology resources:** Students are not required to lease or own a computer.

Number of campus computers available to all students: 300. School has a wireless network. Approximate number of users that can be accommodated: 17,500. Proportion of college-owned housing units wired for high-speed internet access: 100%. **Campus safety:** Security services offered: 24-hour foot-and-vehicle patrols, late-night transport/escort service, 24-hour emergency telephones, lighted pathways/sidewalks, controlled dormitory access (key, security card, etc).

TRANSFER AND INTERNATIONAL STUDENTS
Transfer students: May apply for admission for the following academic terms: Fall, Spring. Applicants need a minimum number of credits to apply. For fall 2009: Transfer applications received: 201. Transfer applicants offered admission: 141. Transfer applicants enrolled: 74. **International students:** Number of foreign undergraduates: 39 (1% of student body). Number of countries represented: 28. Minimum TOEFL score required: 550 (paper); 213 (computer).

Kalamazoo College

- **Address:** 1200 Academy Street, Kalamazoo, MI 49006
- **Website:** http://www.kzoo.edu
- **Private**
- **Enrollment:** 1,374 full-time; 10 part-time

KEY STATS
✔ **U.S News College Ranking:** 71, National Liberal Arts Colleges
✔ **ACT Score (25th/75th percentile):** 26-30
✔ **Tuition:** N/A

Selectivity: More selective	**Room/board:** N/A
Acceptance rate: 73%	**Average debt:** N/A
Student/faculty ratio: 12/1	**Proportion who borrowed:** N/A

UNDERGRADUATE STUDENT BODY STATS
2009-2010 enrollment: 1,374 full-time; 10 part-time. Men: 43%; women: 57%. **Ethnic makeup:** African American: 4%; Asian American: 5%; Hispanic: 3%; White: 83%; International: 4%. **Religious preference:** Roman Catholic: 18%; Protestant: 27%; Jewish: 7%; Muslim: 1%; Hindu: 1%; Buddhist: 1%; No preference: 37%; Other: 6%.

ADMISSIONS FACTS AND FIGURES
Phone: (800) 253-3602. **Email:** admission@kzoo.edu. **Website:** http://www.kzoo.edu. **Application deadlines for fall 2011:** Regular decision: February 1; decision sent by April 1. Early decision: Send application by: November 10; Decision sent by: November 20. Early action: Send application by: November 20; Decision sent by: December 20. Admission can be deferred. **Application fee:** $40. **To apply online, go to:** https://www.commonapp.org/CommonApp/default.aspx. **Admissions requirements/recommendations:** High school units required (recommended): English: 4 (4); Mathematics: 3 (4); Science: 3 (4); Foreign language: 3 (4); Social studies: 2 (2); History: 2 (3); Total units: 17 (20). Tests: The college uses SAT or ACT scores in admissions decisions. Either SAT or ACT required. For admission to the fall 2011 entering class, the school will accept: ACT with writing required. Campus visit: Recommended. Admissions interview: Recommended. Off-campus interview: May be arranged. **Factors that count in admissions decisions:** *Academic:* Secondary school record: Very Important. Class rank: Not Considered. Letters of recommendation: Important. Standardized test scores: Important. Essay: Important. *Nonacademic:* Interview: Considered. Extracurricular activities: Very Important. Talent/ability: Important. Character/personal qualities: Important. Alumni/ae relationship: Considered. Geographical residence: Considered. State residency: Considered. Religious affiliation/commitment: Considered. Minority status: Considered. Volunteer work: Very Important. Work experience: Very Important. **Other schools with the greatest overlap in applicants:** Beloit College; College of Wooster; Denison University; Michigan State University; University of Michigan–Ann Arbor. **Admissions statistics for the fall 2009 entering class:** Total applicants: 1,979. Total accepted: 1,449. Freshmen enrolled: 391; 35% were from out of state. Accepted through early-decision or early-action plans: 56%. Overall acceptance rate: 73%. Early-decision acceptance rate: 83%. Non-early acceptance rate: 78%. **Size of waiting list:** 164 applicants; enrolled from waiting list: 3. **Credentials of fall 2009 freshmen:** 46% ranked in the top 10 percent of their high school class; 84% were in the top 25 percent; 98% were in the top half. (Proportion submitting class standing: 51%.) **Average high school grade point average:** 3.6. **First-year**

students who submitted SAT scores: 37%. Scores (25/75 percentile): Critical Reading: 570-690, Math: 560-680, Combined: 1130-1370. **First-year students submitting ACT scores:** 73%. Scores (25/75 percentile): English: 25-31, Math: 24-30, Composite: 26-30.

ACADEMICS

Year founded: 1833. **Academic calendar:** Trimester. **Degrees offered:** bachelor's. **Most popular majors:** 31% social sciences, 13% psychology, 12% biological and biomedical sciences, 10% physical sciences, 8% foreign languages, literatures, and linguistics. **Major fields of study:** area, ethnic, cultural, and gender studies; biological and biomedical sciences; computer and information sciences and support services; English language and literature/letters; foreign languages, literatures, and linguistics; health professions and related clinical sciences; history; liberal arts and sciences studies, and humanities; mathematics and statistics; multi/interdisciplinary studies; philosophy and religious studies; physical sciences; psychology; social sciences; visual and performing arts. **Areas of required coursework:** foreign languages, other. **Pre-professional programs:** pre-law, pre-medicine. **Special academic programs (% participation):** cross-registration, double major (15%), dual enrollment, English as a Second Language (ESL), exchange student program (domestic), independent study, internships (65%), student-designed major, study abroad (83%). **Reserve Officers Training Corps (ROTC):** Army ROTC: Offered at cooperating institution (Western Michigan University). **Faculty and instruction (2009-2010):** Total instructional faculty: 91 full-time, 19 part-time (49% men; 51% women; 22% minorities). Full-time faculty with Ph.D. or other terminal degree: 86%. Student/faculty ratio: 12/1. Classes of fewer than 20 students: 63%; of 20 to 49 students: 37%; of 50 or more students: 1%. **Advanced Placement and International Baccalaureate credit:** AP tests may be used for: Credit only. Scores accepted: 4, 5. International Baccalaureate exams may be used for: Credit only. **Freshmen returning for sophomore year:** 91%. **Graduation rates:** Four-year: 71%; five-year: 74%; six-year: 75%. **Graduate study:** 32% of students pursue further study immediately upon graduation; 30% within one year; 50% within five years.

COSTS AND FINANCIAL AID

Financial aid office: (269) 337-7192. **Financial aid:** Priority filing date for institution's financial aid form: February 15.

CAMPUS LIFE AND EXTRACURRICULAR ACTIVITIES

Campus housing available (% using): coed dorms (89%), special housing for disabled students (1%), other housing options (10%). Students who live in college-owned, operated, or affiliated housing: 75%. **Student employment:** During the 2009-2010 academic year, 26% of undergraduates worked on campus. Average per-year earnings: $715. **Clubs and organizations:** Number of student organizations: 50. Activities include: campus ministries, choral groups, concert band, dance, drama/theater, international student organization, jazz band, literary magazine, music ensembles, musical theater, pep band, radio station, student government, student newspaper, symphony orchestra, yearbook. Number of fraternities: 0; sororities: 0. Average proportion of students who stay on campus on weekends: 75%. **Sports program (2009-2010):** Member of NCAA III. *Men's intercollegiate varsity sports:* baseball, basketball, cross country, football, golf, soccer, swimming, tennis. *Women's intercollegiate varsity sports:* basketball, cross country, golf, soccer, softball, swimming, tennis, volleyball.

SERVICES AND FACILITIES

Basic services: nonremedial tutoring, women's center, placement service, health service, health insurance. **Counseling services:** minority student, career, personal, academic, psychological, birth control, religious. **For learning-disabled students:** School does not offer a structured program with separate admission and additional fees. Total undergraduates in learning-disabled program or receiving services: 22. Services include: tape recorders, diagnostic testing service, note-taking services, oral tests, readers, extended time for tests, priority registration, priority seating, texts on tape. **Library:** Number of titles: 345,295; number of current serial subscriptions: 40,440. **Information technology resources:** Students are not required to lease or own a computer. Number of campus computers available to all students: 202. School has a wireless network. Approximate number of users that can be accommodated: 2,800. Proportion of college-owned housing units wired for high-speed internet access: 100%. **Campus safety:** Security services offered: 24-hour foot-and-vehicle patrols, late-night transport/escort service, 24-hour emergency telephones, lighted pathways/sidewalks, controlled dormitory access (key, security card, etc.).

TRANSFER AND INTERNATIONAL STUDENTS

Transfer students: May apply for admission for the following academic terms: Fall. Applicants do not need a minimum number of credits to apply. For fall 2009: Transfer applications received: 89. Transfer applicants offered admission: 34. Transfer applicants enrolled: 8. **International students:** Number of foreign undergraduates: 58 (4% of student body). Number of countries represented: 7. Minimum TOEFL score required: 550 (paper); 213 (computer). Average TOEFL score: 600 (paper).

Kettering University

- **Address:** 1700 University Avenue, Flint, MI 48504
- **Website:** http://www.kettering.edu
- **Private**
- **Enrollment:** 2,029 full-time; 51 part-time

KEY STATS

✔ **U.S News College Ranking:** Unranked Specialty School–Engineering
✔ **ACT Score (25th/75th percentile):** 24-29
✔ **Tuition:** 2010-2011: $29,096

Selectivity: More selective	**Room/board:** $6,390
Acceptance rate: 64%	**Average debt:** $53,626
Student/faculty ratio: 16/1	**Proportion who borrowed:** 83%

UNDERGRADUATE STUDENT BODY STATS

2009-2010 enrollment: 2,029 full-time; 51 part-time. Men: 83%; women: 17%. **Ethnic makeup:** African American: 4%; American-Indian: 1%; Asian American: 4%; Hispanic: 2%; White: 83%; International: 5%.

ADMISSIONS FACTS AND FIGURES

Phone: (800) 955-4464. **Email:** admissions@kettering.edu. **Website:** http://www.kettering.edu. **Application deadlines for fall 2011:** Regular decision: Rolling. Early decision: Not offered. Early action: Not offered. Admission can be deferred. **Application fee:** $35. **To apply online, go to:** http://admissions.kettering.edu/. **Admissions requirements/recommendations:** High school units required (recommended): English: 3 (4); Mathematics: 4 (4); Science: 2 (3); Foreign language: 0 (2); Social studies: 0 (2); History: 0 (2); Academic electives: 0 (0); Total units: 11 (21). Tests: The college uses SAT or ACT scores in admissions decisions. Either SAT or ACT required. For admission to the fall 2011 entering class, the school will accept: ACT with or without writing accepted. Campus visit: Recommended. Admissions interview: Recommended. Off-campus interview: May be arranged. **Factors that count in admissions decisions:** *Academic:* Secondary school record: Very Important. Class rank: Important. Letters of recommendation: Considered. Standardized test scores: Very Important. Essay: Considered. *Nonacademic:* Interview: Considered. Extracurricular activities: Important. Talent/ability: Not Considered. Character/personal qualities: Not Considered. Alumni/ae relationship: Not Considered. Geographical residence: Not Considered. State residency: Not Considered. Religious affiliation/commitment: Not Considered. Minority status: Considered. Volunteer work: Considered. Work experience: Considered. **Other schools with the greatest overlap in applicants:** Michigan State University; Michigan Technological University; Ohio State University–Columbus; Purdue University–West Lafayette; University of Michigan–Ann Arbor. **Admissions statistics for the fall 2009 entering class:** Total applicants: 3,465. Total accepted: 2,227. Freshmen enrolled: 444; 32% were from out of state. Overall acceptance rate: 64%. **Credentials of fall 2009 freshmen:** 27% ranked in the top 10 percent of their high school class; 67% were in the top 25 percent; 95% were in the top half. (Proportion submitting class standing: 56%.) **Average high school grade point average:** 3.8. **First-year students who submitted SAT scores:** 28%. Scores (25/75 percentile): Critical Reading: 530-650, Math: 600-690, Combined: 1130-1340. **First-year students submitting ACT scores:** 90%. Scores (25/75 percentile): English: 23-29, Math: 26-31, Composite: 24-29.

ACADEMICS

Year founded: 1919. **Academic calendar:** Semester. **Degrees offered:** bachelor's, master's. **Most popular majors:** 90% engineering, 4% business, management, marketing, and related support services, 3% computer and information sciences and support services, 2% physical sciences, 0% mathematics and statistics. **Major fields of study:** business, management, marketing, and related support services; computer and information sciences and support services; engineering; mathematics and statistics; physical sciences. **Areas of required coursework:** humanities, mathematics, sciences (biological or physical), social science, other. **Pre-professional programs:** pre-law, pre-medicine. **Special academic programs (% participation):** accelerated program, cooperative (work-study plan) program (100%), double major (4%), dual enrollment (.24%), independent study (12%), study abroad (20%). **Cooperative education programs:** business, computer science, engineering, natural science, other. **Faculty and instruction (2009-2010):** Total instructional faculty: 116 full-time, 35 part-time (77% men; 23% women; 19% minorities). Full-time faculty with Ph.D. or other terminal degree: 90%. Student/faculty ratio: 16/1. Classes of fewer than 20 students: 52%; of 20 to 49 students: 47%; of 50 or more students: 1%. **Advanced Placement and International Baccalaureate credit:** AP tests may be used for: Credit only. Scores accepted: 3, 4, 5. International Baccalaureate exams may be used for: Credit only. **Freshmen returning for sophomore year:** 89%. **Graduation rates:** Four-year: 8%; five-year: 44%; six-year: 60%. **Graduate study:** 4% of students pursue further study immediately upon graduation; 33% within one year. Fields in which graduates pursue further study: Master of Business Administration (MBA), 4%; medicine, 1%; engineering, 18%; arts and sciences, 6%.

COSTS AND FINANCIAL AID

Financial aid office: (810) 762-7859. **Expenses (2010-2011):** Tuition and fees 2010-2011: $29,096; room/board: $6,390. Estimated books and supplies: $1,111; transportation: $3,659; personal expenses: $2,955. **Financial aid:** Priority filing date for institution's financial aid form: February 14. 19% had their need fully met. Average financial aid package (proportion receiving): $18,194 (N/A). Average amount of gift aid, such as scholarships or grants (proportion receiving): $14,202 (N/A). Average amount of self-help aid, such as work study or loans (proportion receiving): $5,300 (N/A). Average need-based loan (excluding PLUS or other private loans): $4,326. Among students who received need-based aid, the average percentage of need met: 59%. Among students who received aid based on merit, the average award (and the proportion receiving): $11,570 (N/A). The average athletic scholarship (and the proportion receiving): $0 (N/A). Average amount of debt of borrowers graduating in 2009: $53,626. Proportion who borrowed: 83%.

CAMPUS LIFE AND EXTRACURRICULAR ACTIVITIES

Campus housing available (% using): coed dorms (33%), sorority housing (17%), fraternity housing (20%), apartment for single students (6%), other housing options (24%). Students who live in college-owned, operated, or affiliated housing: 28%. **Student employment:** During the 2009-2010 academic year, 1% of undergraduates worked on campus. Average per-year earnings: $4,080. **Clubs and organizations:** Number of student organizations: 39. Activities include: campus ministries, dance, drama/theater, international student organization, jazz band, literary magazine, model UN, music ensembles, radio station, student government, student newspaper, yearbook. Number of fraternities: 13; sororities: 6. Proportion of men in fraternities: 29%; of women in sororities: 23%. Average proportion of students who stay on campus on weekends: 40%.

SERVICES AND FACILITIES

Basic services: nonremedial tutoring, women's center, placement service, health service, health insurance. **Counseling services:** minority student, career, personal, academic, psychological, birth control. **For learning-disabled students:** School does not offer a structured program with separate admission and additional fees. Total undergraduates in learning-disabled program or receiving services: 68. Services include: reading machines, tape recorders, diagnostic testing service, note-taking services, oral tests, readers, extended time for tests, tutors, priority registration, priority seating, texts on tape, other testing accommodations. **Library:** Number of titles: 148,600; number of current serial subscriptions: 400. **Information technology resources:** Students are not required to lease or own a computer. Number of campus computers available to all students: 450. School has a wireless network. Approximate number of users that can be accommodated: 10,000. Proportion of college-owned housing units wired for high-speed internet access: 100%. **Campus safety:** Security services offered: 24-hour foot-and-vehicle patrols, late-night transport/escort service, 24-hour emergency telephones, lighted pathways/sidewalks, controlled dormitory access (key, security card, etc).

TRANSFER AND INTERNATIONAL STUDENTS

Transfer students: May apply for admission for the following academic terms: Fall, Winter, Spring, Summer. Applicants do not need a minimum number of credits to apply. For fall 2009: Transfer applications received: 447. Transfer applicants offered admission: 52. Transfer applicants enrolled: 35. **International students:** Number of foreign undergraduates: 90 (5% of student body). Number of countries represented: 17. Minimum TOEFL score required: 550 (paper); 79 (computer).

Lake Superior State University

- **Address:** 650 W. Easterday Avenue, Sault Ste. Marie, MI 49783-1699
- **Website:** http://www.lssu.edu
- **Public**
- **Enrollment:** 2,097 full-time; 471 part-time

KEY STATS

✔ **U.S News College Ranking:** 64, Regional Colleges (Midwest)
✔ **ACT Score:** 21
✔ **Tuition:** 2009-2010: $8,284 in state, $16,468 out of state

Selectivity: Selective	**Room/board:** $7,994
Acceptance rate: 89%	**Average debt:** N/A
Student/faculty ratio: 16/1	**Proportion who borrowed:** N/A

UNDERGRADUATE STUDENT BODY STATS

2009-2010 enrollment: 2,097 full-time; 471 part-time. Men: 49%; women: 51%. **Ethnic makeup:** African American: 1%; American-Indian: 9%; Hispanic: 1%; White: 80%; International: 9%.

ADMISSIONS FACTS AND FIGURES

Phone: (906) 635-2231. **Email:** admissions@lssu.edu. **Website:** http://www.lssu.edu. **Application deadlines for fall 2011:** Regular decision: August 15. Early decision: Not offered. Early action: Not offered. Admission can be deferred. **Application fee:** $35. **Admissions requirements/recommendations:** High school units required (recommended): English: 0 (4); Mathematics: 0 (3); Science: 0 (3); Foreign language: 0 (2); Social studies: 0 (2); History: 0 (1); Academic electives: 0 (0); Total units: 0 (18). Tests: The college uses SAT or ACT scores in admissions decisions. ACT required. **Factors that count in admissions decisions:** *Academic:* Secondary school record: Very Important. Class rank: Considered. Letters of recommendation: Considered. Standardized test scores: Very Important. Essay: Not Considered. *Nonacademic:* Interview: Considered. Extracurricular activities: Not Considered. Talent/ability: Not Considered. Character/personal qualities: Not Considered. Alumni/ae relationship: Not Considered. Geographical residence: Considered. State residency: Not Considered. Religious affiliation/commitment: Not Considered. Minority status: Not Considered. Volunteer work: Not Considered. Work experience: Not Considered. **Other schools with the greatest overlap in applicants:** Ferris State University; Grand Valley State University; Northern Michigan University. **Admissions statistics for the fall 2009 entering class:** Total applicants: 1,487. Total accepted: 1,322. Freshmen enrolled: 884; 5% were from out of state. Overall acceptance rate: 89%. **Credentials of fall 2009 freshmen:** 14% ranked in the top 10 percent of their high school class; 40% were in the top 25 percent; 74% were in the top half. (Proportion submitting class standing: 93%.) **Average high school grade point average:** 3.0. **First-year students submitting ACT scores:** 90%. Scores (25/75 percentile): English: N/A, Math: N/A, Composite: N/A.

ACADEMICS

Year founded: 1946. **Academic calendar:** Semester. **Degrees offered:** certificate, associate, bachelor's, master's. **Most popular majors:** 20% security and protective services, 19% business, management, marketing, and related support services, 12% health professions and related clinical sciences, 9% education, 9% engineering. **Major fields of study:** biological and biomedical sciences; business, management, marketing, and related support services; communication, journalism, and related programs; computer and information sciences and support services; education; engineering; engineering technologies/technicians; English language and literature/letters; foreign languages, literatures, and linguistics; health professions and related clinical sciences; history; legal professions and studies; liberal arts and sciences studies, and humanities; mathematics and statistics; multi/interdisciplinary studies; natural resources and conservation; parks, recreation, leisure, and fitness studies; physical sciences; psychology; public administration and social service professions; security and protective services; social sciences; visual and performing arts. **Areas of required coursework:** humanities, computer literacy, mathematics, English (including composition), sciences (biological or physical), social science, other. **Special academic programs:** cooperative (work-study plan) program, cross-registration, distance learning, double major, honors program, independent study, internships, student-designed major, teacher certificate program, weekend college. **Faculty and**

instruction (2009-2010): Total instructional faculty: 115 full-time, 69 part-time (52% men; 48% women; 7% minorities). Full-time faculty with Ph.D. or other terminal degree: 55%. Student/faculty ratio: 16/1. Classes of fewer than 20 students: 49%; of 20 to 49 students: 45%; of 50 or more students: 6%. **Freshmen returning for sophomore year:** 65%. **Graduation rates:** Six-year: 39%.

COSTS AND FINANCIAL AID
Financial aid office: (906) 635-2678. **Expenses (2009-2010):** Tuition and fees 2009-2010: $8,284 in state, $16,468 out of state; room/board: $7,994. Estimated books and supplies: $1,150 personal expenses: $2,150. **Financial aid:** Priority filing date for institution's financial aid form: February 21.

CAMPUS LIFE AND EXTRACURRICULAR ACTIVITIES
Campus housing available: coed dorms, women's dorms, men's dorms, sorority housing, fraternity housing, apartments for married students, apartment for single students, other housing options. Students who live in college-owned, operated, or affiliated housing: 30%. Activities include: choral groups, concert band, drama/theater, jazz band, literary magazine, music ensembles, pep band, radio station, student government, student newspaper, symphony orchestra. **Sports program (2009-2010):** Member of NCAA II.

TRANSFER AND INTERNATIONAL STUDENTS
Transfer students: May apply for admission for the following academic terms: Fall, Spring, Summer. Applicants need a minimum number of credits to apply. For fall 2009: Transfer applications received: 429. Transfer applicants offered admission: 411. Transfer applicants enrolled: 228. **International students:** Number of foreign undergraduates: 219 (9% of student body).

Lawrence Technological University

- **Address:** 21000 W. Ten Mile Road, Southfield, MI 48075
- **Website:** http://www.ltu.edu
- **Private**
- **Enrollment:** 1,631 full-time; 1,556 part-time

KEY STATS
✔ **U.S News College Ranking:** 40, Regional Universities (Midwest)
✔ **ACT Score (25th/75th percentile):** 21-27
✔ **Tuition:** 2010-2011: $24,633

Selectivity: More selective	**Room/board:** $9,147
Acceptance rate: 50%	**Average debt:** $42,723
Student/faculty ratio: 11/1	**Proportion who borrowed:** 73%

UNDERGRADUATE STUDENT BODY STATS
2009-2010 enrollment: 1,631 full-time; 1,556 part-time. Men: 77%; women: 23%. **Ethnic makeup:** African American: 13%; Asian American: 4%; Hispanic: 2%; White: 75%; International: 7%.

ADMISSIONS FACTS AND FIGURES
Phone: (248) 204-3160. **Email:** admissions@ltu.edu. **Website:** http://www.ltu.edu. **Application deadlines for fall 2011:** Regular decision: Rolling. Early decision: Not offered. Early action: Not offered. Admission can be deferred. **Application fee:** $30. **To apply online, go to:** http://www.ltu.edu/futurestudents/apply.asp. **Admissions requirements/recommendations:** High school units required (recommended): English: 4 (4); Mathematics: 3 (4); Science: 2 (4); Social studies: 3; History: (2); Total units: 12 (16). Tests: The college uses SAT or ACT scores in admissions decisions. Either SAT or ACT required. For admission to the fall 2011 entering class, the school will accept: ACT with or without writing accepted. Campus visit: Recommended. Admissions interview: Neither required nor recommended. Off-campus interview: May be arranged. **Factors that count in admissions decisions:** *Academic:* Secondary school record: Very Important. Class rank: Not Considered. Letters of recommendation: Considered. Standardized test scores: Very Important. Essay: Considered. *Nonacademic:* Interview: Considered. Extracurricular activities: Not Considered. Talent/ability: Not Considered. Character/personal qualities: Not Considered. Alumni/ae relationship: Not Considered. Geographical residence: Not Considered. State residency: Not Considered. Religious affiliation/commitment: Not Considered. Minority status: Not Considered. Volunteer work: Not Considered. Work experience: Not Considered. **Other schools with the great-**

est **overlap in applicants:** Kettering University; Michigan State University; Michigan Technological University; University of Michigan–Ann Arbor; Wayne State University. **Admissions statistics for the fall 2009 entering class:** Total applicants: 1,698. Total accepted: 845. Freshmen enrolled: 344; 5% were from out of state. Overall acceptance rate: 50%. **Credentials of fall 2009 freshmen:** 26% ranked in the top 10 percent of their high school class; 56% were in the top 25 percent; 85% were in the top half. (Proportion submitting class standing: 86%.) **Average high school grade point average:** 3.3. **First-year students who submitted SAT scores:** 5%. **First-year students submitting ACT scores:** 72%. Scores (25/75 percentile): English: 19-27, Math: 20-27, Composite: 21-27.

ACADEMICS
Year founded: 1932. **Academic calendar:** Semester. **Degrees offered:** certificate, associate, bachelor's, post-bachelor's certificate, master's, doctorate. **Most popular majors:** 22% architecture (B.Arch., B.A./B.S., M.Arch., M.A./M.S., Ph.D.), 21% business administration and management, 14% mechanical engineering, 4% civil engineering, 4% engineering/industrial management. **Major fields of study:** architecture and related services; biological and biomedical sciences; business, management, marketing, and related support services; communication, journalism, and related programs; communications technologies/technicians and support services; computer and information sciences and support services; engineering; engineering technologies/technicians; liberal arts and sciences studies, and humanities; mathematics and statistics; multi/interdisciplinary studies; physical sciences; psychology; visual and performing arts. **Areas of required coursework:** humanities, computer literacy, mathematics, English (including composition), sciences (biological or physical), history, social science, other. **Pre-professional programs:** pre-law, pre-dentistry, pre-medicine. **Special academic programs (% participation):** accelerated program (0%), cooperative (work-study plan) program (9%), distance learning (52%), double major (6.3%), dual enrollment (2%), English as a Second Language (ESL) (2%), honors program (1%), independent study (19%), internships (12%), liberal arts/career combination (0%), study abroad (0%). **Cooperative education programs:** business, computer science, engineering, natural science, technologies. **Reserve Officers Training Corps (ROTC):** Air Force ROTC: Offered at cooperating institution (University of Michigan–Ann Arbor). **Faculty and instruction (2009-2010):** Total instructional faculty: 129 full-time, 301 part-time (77% men; 23% women; 11% minorities). Full-time faculty with Ph.D. or other terminal degree: 78%. Student/faculty ratio: 11/1. Classes of fewer than 20 students: 75%; of 20 to 49 students: 24%; of 50 or more students: 1%. **Advanced Placement and International Baccalaureate credit:** AP tests may be used for: Credit only. Scores accepted: 3, 4. International Baccalaureate exams may be used for: Credit only. **Freshmen returning for sophomore year:** 69%. **Graduation rates:** Four-year: 18%; five-year: 39%; six-year: 46%.

COSTS AND FINANCIAL AID
Financial aid office: (248) 204-2280. **Expenses (2010-2011):** Tuition and fees 2010-2011: $24,633; room/board: $9,147. Estimated books and supplies: $1,319; transportation: $1,781; personal expenses: $2,077. **Financial aid:** Priority filing date for institution's financial aid form: April 1. In 2009-2010, 84% of undergraduates applied for financial aid. Of those, 65% were determined to have financial need; 12% had their need fully met. Average financial aid package (proportion receiving): $18,772 (65%). Average amount of gift aid, such as scholarships or grants (proportion receiving): $10,957 (61%). Average amount of self-help aid, such as work study or loans (proportion receiving): $8,778 (60%). Average need-based loan (excluding PLUS or other private loans): $7,796. Among students who received need-based aid, the average percentage of need met: 69%. Among students who received aid based on merit, the average award (and the proportion receiving): $9,000 (15%). The average athletic scholarship (and the proportion receiving): $0 (0%). Average amount of debt of borrowers graduating in 2009: $42,723. Proportion who borrowed: 73%.

CAMPUS LIFE AND EXTRACURRICULAR ACTIVITIES
Campus housing available (% using): apartments for married students (1%), apartment for single students (98%), special housing for disabled students (1%). Students who live in college-owned, operated, or affiliated housing: 16%. **Student employment:** During the 2009-2010 academic year, 10% of undergraduates worked on campus. Average per-year earnings: $2,399. **Clubs and organizations:** Number of student organizations: 48. Activities include: drama/theater, literary magazine, music ensembles, student government, student newspaper. Number of fraternities: 7; sororities: 4. Proportion of men in fraternities: 5%; of women in sororities: 7%. Average proportion of students who stay on campus on weekends: 35%.

SERVICES AND FACILITIES

Basic services: placement service, health insurance. **Remedial assistance:** math, writing, study skills, other. **Counseling services:** minority student, career, personal, academic, psychological. **For learning-disabled students:** School does not offer a structured program with separate admission and additional fees. Services include: reading machines, tape recorders, untimed tests, note-taking services, oral tests, readers, extended time for tests, tutors, priority seating, texts on tape, typist/scribe, exams on tape or computer, other testing accommodations. **Library:** Number of titles: 80,192; number of current serial subscriptions: 62,157. **Information technology resources:** Students are required to lease or own a computer. Number of campus computers available to all students: 3,532. School has a wireless network. Approximate number of users that can be accommodated: 3,500. Proportion of college-owned housing units wired for high-speed internet access: 100%. **Campus safety:** Security services offered: 24-hour foot-and-vehicle patrols, late-night transport/escort service, 24-hour emergency telephones, lighted pathways/sidewalks, controlled dormitory access (key, security card, etc).

TRANSFER AND INTERNATIONAL STUDENTS

Transfer students: May apply for admission for the following academic terms: Fall, Winter, Spring, Summer. Applicants need a minimum number of credits to apply. For fall 2009: Transfer applications received: 659. Transfer applicants offered admission: 412. Transfer applicants enrolled: 277. **International students:** Number of foreign undergraduates: 156 (7% of student body). Number of countries represented: 13. Minimum TOEFL score required: 550 (paper); 213 (computer).

Madonna University

- **Address:** 36600 Schoolcraft Road, Livonia, MI 48150
- **Website:** http://www.madonna.edu
- **Private; Religious affiliation:** Roman Catholic
- **Enrollment:** 1,667 full-time; 1,466 part-time

KEY STATS

✔ **U.S News College Ranking:** 88, Regional Universities (Midwest)
✔ **ACT Score (25th/75th percentile):** 19-23
✔ **Tuition:** 2010-2011: $13,840

Selectivity: Selective	**Room/board:** $7,120
Acceptance rate: 74%	**Average debt:** $23,323
Student/faculty ratio: 11/1	**Proportion who borrowed:** 59%

UNDERGRADUATE STUDENT BODY STATS

2009-2010 enrollment: 1,667 full-time; 1,466 part-time. Men: 26%; women: 74%. **Ethnic makeup:** African American: 14%; Asian American: 2%; Hispanic: 3%; White: 76%; International: 5%. **Religious preference:** Protestant: 17%; Jewish: 1%; Muslim: 2%; Hindu: 1%; No preference: 5%; Unknown: 20%; Roman Catholic: 41%; Other: 13%.

ADMISSIONS FACTS AND FIGURES

Phone: (734) 432-5339. **Email:** admissions@madonna.edu. **Website:** http://www.madonna.edu. **Application deadlines for fall 2011:** Regular decision: Rolling. Early decision: Not offered. Early action: Not offered. Admission can be deferred. **Application fee:** $25. **To apply online, go to:** http://www.madonna.edu/pages/appon.cfm. **Admissions requirements/recommendations:** High school units required (recommended): English: 3 (4); Mathematics: 2 (4); Science: 3 (4); Foreign language: 0 (2); Social studies: 3 (4); History: 0 (4); Total units: 11 (22). Tests: The college uses SAT or ACT scores in admissions decisions. Either SAT or ACT required. For admission to the fall 2011 entering class, the school will accept: ACT with writing recommended. Campus visit: Recommended. Admissions interview: Recommended. Off-campus interview: May be arranged. **Factors that count in admissions decisions:** *Academic:* Secondary school record: Very Important. Class rank: Important. Letters of recommendation: Important. Standardized test scores: Important. Essay: Important. *Nonacademic:* Interview: Considered. Extracurricular activities: Considered. Talent/ability: Considered. Character/personal qualities: Considered. Alumni/ae relationship: Not Considered. Geographical residence: Not Considered. State residency: Not Considered. Religious affiliation/commitment: Not Considered. Minority status: Not Considered. Volunteer work: Considered. Work experience: Considered. **Other schools with the greatest overlap in applicants:** Eastern Michigan University; University of Detroit Mercy; University of Michigan–Ann Arbor; University of Michigan–Dearborn; Wayne State

University. **Admissions statistics for the fall 2009 entering class:** Total applicants: 702. Total accepted: 516. Freshmen enrolled: 189; Overall acceptance rate: 74%. **Credentials of fall 2009 freshmen:** 16% ranked in the top 10 percent of their high school class; 40% were in the top 25 percent; 70% were in the top half. (Proportion submitting class standing: 61%.) **Average high school grade point average:** 3.2. **First-year students who submitted SAT scores:** 3%. Scores (25/75 percentile): Critical Reading: 480-670, Math: 470-630, Combined: 950-1300. **First-year students submitting ACT scores:** 90%. Scores (25/75 percentile): English: 19-25, Math: 18-24, Composite: 19-23.

ACADEMICS

Year founded: 1947. **Academic calendar:** Semester. **Degrees offered:** certificate, associate, bachelor's, post-bachelor's certificate, master's, post-master's certificate. **Most popular majors:** 21% health professions and related clinical sciences, 14% business, management, marketing, and related support services, 13% security and protective services, 6% family and consumer sciences/human sciences, 5% public administration and social service professions. **Major fields of study:** area, ethnic, cultural, and gender studies; biological and biomedical sciences; business, management, marketing, and related support services; communication, journalism, and related programs; computer and information sciences and support services; education; engineering; engineering technologies/technicians; English language and literature/letters; family and consumer sciences/human sciences; foreign languages, literatures, and linguistics; health professions and related clinical sciences; history; legal professions and studies; liberal arts and sciences studies, and humanities; mathematics and statistics; multi/interdisciplinary studies; natural resources and conservation; parks, recreation, leisure, and fitness studies; personal and culinary services; philosophy and religious studies; physical sciences; psychology; public administration and social service professions; science technologies/technicians; security and protective services; social sciences; theology and religious vocations; visual and performing arts. **Areas of required coursework:** arts/fine arts, humanities, computer literacy, mathematics, English (including composition), philosophy, sciences (biological or physical), history, social science, other. **Pre-professional programs:** pre-law, pre-dentistry, pre-medicine, pre-veterinary science, pre-optometry, other. **Special academic programs (% participation):** accelerated program (0%), cooperative (work-study plan) program (13%), cross-registration (0%), distance learning (87%), double major (1%), dual enrollment (0%), English as a Second Language (ESL) (1%), independent study (16%), internships (4%), liberal arts/career combination (0%), student-designed major (0%), study abroad, teacher certificate program (23%), weekend college (0%). **Teacher certification offered in:** early childhood, special education, elementary, vo-tech, middle/junior high, secondary. **Cooperative education programs:** business, computer science, education, health professions, social/behavioral science, technologies. **Reserve Officers Training Corps (ROTC):** Army ROTC: Offered at cooperating institution (Eastern Michigan University). **Faculty and instruction (2009-2010):** Total instructional faculty: 120 full-time, 210 part-time (41% men; 59% women; 8% minorities). Full-time faculty with Ph.D. or other terminal degree: 100%. Student/faculty ratio: 11/1. Classes of fewer than 20 students: 70%; of 20 to 49 students: 27%; of 50 or more students: 3%. **Advanced Placement and International Baccalaureate credit:** AP tests may be used for: Credit only. Scores accepted: 3, 4, 5. **Freshmen returning for sophomore year:** 83%. **Graduation rates:** Four-year: 18%; five-year: 42%; six-year: 44%. **Graduate study:** 16% of students pursue further study immediately upon graduation. Fields in which graduates pursue further study: Master of Business Administration (MBA), 8%; law, 2%; theology (or the seminary), 2%; education, 35%; arts and sciences, 48%.

COSTS AND FINANCIAL AID

Financial aid office: (734) 432-5662. **Expenses (2010-2011):** Tuition and fees 2010-2011: $13,840; room/board: $7,120. Estimated books and supplies: $1,408; transportation: $886; personal expenses: $1,108. **Financial aid:** Priority filing date for institution's financial aid form: March 1. 11% had their need fully met. Average financial aid package (proportion receiving): $8,902 (N/A). Average amount of gift aid, such as scholarships or grants (proportion receiving): $5,608 (N/A). Average amount of self-help aid, such as work study or loans (proportion receiving): $4,331 (N/A). Average need-based loan (excluding PLUS or other private loans): $4,229. Among students who received need-based aid, the average percentage of need met: 40%. Among students who received aid based on merit, the average award (and the proportion receiving): $3,827 (N/A). The average athletic scholarship (and the proportion receiving): $3,527 (N/A). Average amount of debt of borrowers graduating in 2009: $23,323. Proportion who borrowed: 59%.

CAMPUS LIFE AND EXTRACURRICULAR ACTIVITIES

Campus housing available (% using): women's dorms (57%), men's dorms (43%). **Student employment:** During the 2009-2010 academic year, 14% of undergraduates worked on campus. Average per-year earnings: $2,609. **Clubs and organizations:** Number of student organizations: 19. Activities include: campus ministries, choral groups, international student organization, music ensembles, musical theater, radio station, student government, student newspaper, television station. Number of fraternities: 0; sororities: 0. Average proportion of students who stay on campus on weekends: 2%. **Sports program (2009-2010):** Member of NAIA. *Men's intercollegiate varsity sports:* baseball, basketball, cross country, golf, soccer. *Women's intercollegiate varsity sports:* basketball, cross country, golf, soccer, softball, volleyball.

SERVICES AND FACILITIES

Basic services: nonremedial tutoring, placement service, health insurance. **Remedial assistance:** reading, math, writing, study skills. **Counseling services:** minority student, career, personal, academic, older student, psychological, religious. **For learning-disabled students:** School does not offer a structured program with separate admission and additional fees. Total undergraduates in learning-disabled program or receiving services: 136. Services include: remedial math, remedial English, reading machines, tape recorders, diagnostic testing service, note-taking services, oral tests, learning center, readers, extended time for tests, tutors, priority seating, proofreading services, substitution of courses, texts on tape, typist/scribe, exams on tape or computer, other testing accommodations, other. **Library:** Number of titles: 108,000; number of current serial subscriptions: 515. **Information technology resources:** Students are not required to lease or own a computer. Number of campus computers available to all students: 163. School has a wireless network. Approximate number of users that can be accommodated: 200. Proportion of college-owned housing units wired for high-speed internet access: 100%. **Campus safety:** Security services offered: 24-hour foot-and-vehicle patrols, late-night transport/escort service, 24-hour emergency telephones, lighted pathways/sidewalks, student patrols, controlled dormitory access (key, security card, etc).

TRANSFER AND INTERNATIONAL STUDENTS

Transfer students: May apply for admission for the following academic terms: Fall, Winter, Spring, Summer. Applicants need a minimum number of credits to apply. For fall 2009: Transfer applications received: 822. Transfer applicants offered admission: 686. Transfer applicants enrolled: 420. **International students:** Number of foreign undergraduates: 133 (5% of student body). Number of countries represented: 24. Minimum TOEFL score required: 540 (paper); 76 (computer). Average TOEFL score: 500 (paper).

Marygrove College

- **Address:** 8425 W. McNichols Road, Detroit, MI 48221
- **Website:** http://www.marygrove.edu
- **Private; Religious affiliation:** Roman Catholic
- **Enrollment:** N/A

KEY STATS

✔ **U.S News College Ranking:** second tier, Regional Universities (Midwest)
✔ **SAT or ACT Score (25th/75th percentile):** N/A
✔ **Tuition:** 2009-2010: $16,310

Selectivity: Selective	Room/board: $7,000
Acceptance rate: N/A	Average debt: N/A
Student/faculty ratio: N/A	Proportion who borrowed: N/A

Michigan State University

- **Address:** East Lansing, MI 48824
- **Website:** http://www.msu.edu/
- **Public**
- **Enrollment:** 33,618 full-time; 2,871 part-time

KEY STATS

✔ **U.S News College Ranking:** 79, National Universities
✔ **ACT Score (25th/75th percentile):** 23-27
✔ **Tuition:** 2009-2010: $11,434 in state, $27,832 out of state

Selectivity: More selective	Room/board: $7,444
Acceptance rate: 73%	Average debt: $19,696
Student/faculty ratio: 16/1	Proportion who borrowed: 44%

UNDERGRADUATE STUDENT BODY STATS

2009-2010 enrollment: 33,618 full-time; 2,871 part-time. Men: 48%; women: 52%. **Ethnic makeup:** African American: 8%; American-Indian: 1%; Asian American: 5%; Hispanic: 3%; White: 76%; International: 7%.

ADMISSIONS FACTS AND FIGURES

Phone: (517) 355-8332. **Email:** admis@msu.edu. **Website:** http://www.msu.edu/. **Application deadlines for fall 2011:** Regular decision: Rolling. Early decision: Not offered. Early action: Send application by: October 12; Decision sent by: November 16. Admission cannot be deferred. **Application fee:** $35. **To apply online, go to:** http://admissions.msu.edu/apply.asp. **Admissions requirements/recommendations:** High school units required (recommended): English: 4; Mathematics: 3; Science: 2; Foreign language: 2 (2); Social studies: 2 (2); History: 1 (2). Tests: The college uses SAT or ACT scores in admissions decisions. Either SAT or ACT required. For admission to the fall 2011 entering class, the school will accept: ACT with writing required. Campus visit: Neither required nor recommended. Admissions interview: Neither required nor recommended. Off-campus interview: May be arranged. **Factors that count in admissions decisions:** *Academic:* Secondary school record: Very Important. Class rank: Considered. Letters of recommendation: Considered. Standardized test scores: Very Important. Essay: Important. *Nonacademic:* Interview: Not Considered. Extracurricular activities: Important. Talent/ability: Considered. Character/personal qualities: Considered. Alumni/ae relationship: Considered. Geographical residence: Important. State residency: Considered. Religious affiliation/commitment: Not Considered. Minority status: Not Considered. Volunteer work: Considered. Work experience: Considered. **Other schools with the greatest overlap in applicants:** Central Michigan University; Indiana University–Bloomington; University of Illinois–Urbana-Champaign; University of Michigan–Ann Arbor; Western Michigan University. **Admissions statistics for the fall 2009 entering class:** Total applicants: 25,349. Total accepted: 18,383. Freshmen enrolled: 7,416; 13% were from out of state. Overall acceptance rate: 73%. Non-early acceptance rate: 73%. **Credentials of fall 2009 freshmen:** 31% ranked in the top 10 percent of their high school class; 70% were in the top 25 percent; 96% were in the top half. (Proportion submitting class standing: 61%.) **Average high school grade point average:** 3.6. **First-year students who submitted SAT scores:** 17%. Scores (25/75 percentile): Critical Reading: 470-610, Math: 540-660, Combined: 1010-1270. **First-year students submitting ACT scores:** 85%. Scores (25/75 percentile): English: 22-28, Math: 22-28, Composite: 23-27.

ACADEMICS

Year founded: 1855. **Academic calendar:** Semester. **Degrees offered:** certificate, bachelor's, master's, post-master's certificate, doctorate. **Most popular majors:** 19% business, management, marketing, and related support services, 13% communication, journalism, and related programs, 11% social sciences, 9% biological and biomedical sciences, 7% engineering. **Major fields of study:** agriculture, agriculture operations, and related sciences; architecture and related services; area, ethnic, cultural, and gender studies; biological and biomedical sciences; business, management, marketing, and related support services; communication, journalism, and related programs; computer and information sciences and support services; education; engineering; English language and literature/letters; family and consumer sciences/human sciences; foreign languages, literatures, and linguistics; health professions and related clinical sciences; history; legal professions and studies; liberal arts and sciences studies, and humanities; mathematics and statistics; multi/interdisciplinary studies; natural resources and conservation; parks, recreation, leisure, and fitness studies; philosophy and religious studies; physical sciences; psychology; public administration and social service professions; security and protective services; social sciences; visual and performing arts. **Areas of required coursework:** humanities, mathematics, English (including composition), sciences (biological or physical), social science. **Pre-professional programs:** pre-law, pre-medicine, pre-veterinary science. **Special academic programs:** accelerated program, cooperative (work-study plan) program, distance learning, double major, dual enrollment, English as a Second Language (ESL), exchange student program (domestic), honors program, independent study, internships, liberal arts/career combination, student-designed major, study abroad, teacher certificate program, weekend college. **Teacher certification offered in:** special education, elementary, middle/junior high, secondary. **Cooperative education programs:** engineering. **Reserve Officers Training Corps (ROTC):** Army ROTC: Offered on campus; Air Force ROTC: Offered on campus. **Faculty and instruction (2009-2010):** Total instructional faculty: 2,620 full-time, 352 part-time (62% men; 38% women; 22% minorities). Full-time faculty with Ph.D. or other terminal degree: 93%. Student/faculty ratio: 16/1. Classes of fewer than 20 students: 24%; of 20 to 49 students: 54%; of 50 or more students: 22%. **Advanced Placement and International Baccalaureate credit:** AP tests may be used for: Placement only. Scores accepted: 2. **Freshmen returning for sophomore year:** 91%. **Graduation rates:** Four-year: 49%; five-year: 73%; six-year: 77%. **Graduate study:** 33% of students pursue further study within one year. Fields in which graduates pursue further study: Master of Business Administration (MBA), 19%; law, 17%; medicine, 34%; dentistry, 2%; engineering, 2%; education, 4%; arts and sciences, 18%; veterinary medicine, 4%.

COSTS AND FINANCIAL AID

Financial aid office: (517) 353-5940. **Expenses (2009-2010):** Tuition and fees 2009-2010: $11,434 in state, $27,832 out of state; room/board: $7,444. Estimated books and supplies: $962; transportation: $478; personal expenses: $1,230. **Financial aid:** In 2009-2010, 65% of undergraduates applied for financial aid. Of those, 48% were determined to have financial need; 19% had their need fully met. Average financial aid package (proportion receiving): $10,620 (48%). Average amount of gift aid, such as scholarships or grants (proportion receiving): $8,420 (28%). Average amount of self-help aid, such as work study or loans (proportion receiving): $4,524 (43%). Average need-based loan (excluding PLUS or other private loans): $4,222. Among students who received need-based aid, the average percentage of need met: 66%. Among students who received aid based on merit, the average award (and the proportion receiving): $7,278 (4%). The average athletic scholarship (and the proportion receiving): $16,758 (1%). Average amount of debt of borrowers graduating in 2009: $19,696. Proportion who borrowed: 44%.

CAMPUS LIFE AND EXTRACURRICULAR ACTIVITIES

Campus housing available: coed dorms, women's dorms, sorority housing, fraternity housing, apartments for married students, apartment for single students, special housing for disabled students, special housing for international students, cooperative housing. Students who live in college-owned, operated, or affiliated housing: 40%. **Clubs and organizations:** Number of student organizations: 500. Activities include: campus ministries, choral groups, concert band, dance, drama/theater, international student organization, jazz band, literary magazine, marching band, model UN, music ensembles, musical theater, opera, pep band, radio station, student government, student newspaper, student film society, symphony orchestra, television station, yearbook. Number of fraternities: 31; sororities: 19. Proportion of men in fraternities: 8%; of women in sororities: 7%. Average proportion of students who stay on campus on weekends: 50%. **Sports program (2009-2010):** Member of NCAA I. **Men's intercollegiate varsity sports:** baseball, basketball, cross country, football, golf, ice hockey, soccer, swimming, tennis, track and field (indoor), track and field (outdoor), wrestling. **Women's intercollegiate varsity sports:** basketball, crew (heavyweight), cross country, field hockey, golf, gymnastics, crew (lightweight), soccer, softball, swimming, tennis, track and field (indoor), track and field (outdoor), volleyball.

SERVICES AND FACILITIES

Basic services: nonremedial tutoring, women's center, placement service, day care, health service, health insurance. **Remedial assistance:** reading, math, writing, study skills. **Counseling services:** minority student, career, military, personal, veteran student, academic, older student, psychological, birth control, religious. **For learning-disabled students:** School does not offer a structured program with separate admission and additional fees. Services include: remedial math, remedial English, reading machines, tape recorders, diagnostic testing service, untimed tests, note-taking services, oral tests, learning center, readers, extended time for tests, tutors, priority registration, priority seating, texts on tape, exams on tape or computer, other testing

accommodations, other. **Library:** Number of titles: 5,137,733; number of current serial subscriptions: 91,301. **Information technology resources:** Students are required to lease or own a computer. Number of campus computers available to all students: 2,200. School has a wireless network. Approximate number of users that can be accommodated: 8,000. Proportion of college-owned housing units wired for high-speed internet access: 99%. **Campus safety:** Security services offered: late-night transport/escort service, 24-hour emergency telephones, lighted pathways/sidewalks, controlled dormitory access (key, security card, etc).

TRANSFER AND INTERNATIONAL STUDENTS

Transfer students: May apply for admission for the following academic terms: Fall, Spring, Summer. Applicants do not need a minimum number of credits to apply. For fall 2009: Transfer applications received: 4,786. Transfer applicants offered admission: 2,126. Transfer applicants enrolled: 1,546. **International students:** Number of foreign undergraduates: 2447 (7% of student body). Number of countries represented: 87. Minimum TOEFL score required: 550 (paper); 213 (computer).

Michigan Technological University

- **Address:** 1400 Townsend Drive, Houghton, MI 49931
- **Website:** http://www.mtu.edu
- **Public**
- **Enrollment:** 5,559 full-time; 383 part-time

KEY STATS
✔ **U.S News College Ranking:** 117, National Universities
✔ **ACT Score (25th/75th percentile):** 23-29
✔ **Tuition:** 2010-2011: $12,017 in state, $24,527 out of state
   Selectivity: More selective   **Room/board:** $8,462
   Acceptance rate: 73%   **Average debt:** $26,764
   Student/faculty ratio: 15/1   **Proportion who borrowed:** 68%

UNDERGRADUATE STUDENT BODY STATS
2009-2010 enrollment: 5,559 full-time; 383 part-time. Men: 75%; women: 25%. **Ethnic makeup:** African American: 2%; American-Indian: 1%; Asian American: 1%; Hispanic: 2%; White: 88%; International: 7%.

ADMISSIONS FACTS AND FIGURES
Phone: (906) 487-2335. **Email:** mtu4u@mtu.edu. **Website:** http://www.mtu.edu. **Application deadlines for fall 2011:** Regular decision: Rolling. Early decision: Not offered. Early action: Not offered. Admission can be deferred. **To apply online, go to:** http://www.mtu.edu/apply/. **Admissions requirements/recommendations:** High school units required (recommended): English: 3 (4); Mathematics: 3 (4); Science: 2 (3); Foreign language: 0 (2); Social studies: 0 (3); History: 0 (1); Academic electives: 0 (2); Total units: 8 (20). Tests: The college uses SAT or ACT scores in admissions decisions. Either SAT or ACT required. For admission to the fall 2011 entering class, the school will accept: ACT with or without writing accepted. Campus visit: Recommended. Admissions interview: Recommended. Off-campus interview: May be arranged. **Factors that count in admissions decisions:** *Academic:* Secondary school record: Very Important. Class rank: Important. Letters of recommendation: Considered. Standardized test scores: Very Important. Essay: Considered. *Nonacademic:* Interview: Considered. Extracurricular activities: Considered. Talent/ability: Considered. Character/personal qualities: Considered. Alumni/ae relationship: Considered. Geographical residence: Not Considered. State residency: Not Considered. Religious affiliation/commitment: Not Considered. Minority status: Not Considered. Volunteer work: Considered. Work experience: Considered. **Other schools with the greatest overlap in applicants:** Kettering University; Michigan State University; Milwaukee School of Engineering; University of Michigan–Ann Arbor; Western Michigan University. **Admissions statistics for the fall 2009 entering class:** Total applicants: 4,719. Total accepted: 3,456. Freshmen enrolled: 1,160; 25% were from out of state. Overall acceptance rate: 73%. **Credentials of fall 2009 freshmen:** 28% ranked in the top 10 percent of their high school class; 60% were in the top 25 percent; 90% were in the top half. (Proportion submitting class standing: 85%.) **Average high school grade point average:** 3.6. **First-year students who submitted SAT scores:** 10%. Scores (25/75 percentile): Critical Reading: 510-650, Math: 600-690, Combined: 1110-1340. **First-year students submitting ACT scores:** 94%. Scores (25/75 percentile): English: 22-28, Math: 24-30, Composite: 23-29.

ACADEMICS

Year founded: 1885. **Academic calendar:** Semester. **Degrees offered:** certificate, associate, terminal-associate, bachelor's, post-bachelor's certificate, master's, doctorate. **Most popular majors:** 57% engineering, 11% business, management, marketing, and related support services, 7% computer and information sciences and support services, 4% engineering technologies/technicians, 4% natural resources and conservation. **Major fields of study:** biological and biomedical sciences; business, management, marketing, and related support services; communication, journalism, and related programs; communications technologies/technicians and support services; computer and information sciences and support services; education; engineering; engineering technologies/technicians; health professions and related clinical sciences; history; liberal arts and sciences studies, and humanities; mathematics and statistics; natural resources and conservation; parks, recreation, leisure, and fitness studies; physical sciences; psychology; social sciences; visual and performing arts. **Areas of required coursework:** humanities, computer literacy, mathematics, English (including composition), sciences (biological or physical), social science, other. **Pre-professional programs:** pre-law, pre-dentistry, pre-medicine, pre-veterinary science, pre-optometry, pre-pharmacy, other. **Special academic programs (% participation):** cooperative (work-study plan) program (21%), distance learning (15%), double major (7%), dual enrollment, English as a Second Language (ESL), exchange student program (domestic), honors program, independent study (5%), internships (3%), study abroad (6%), teacher certificate program (2%), other. **Teacher certification offered in:** middle/junior high, secondary. **Cooperative education programs:** agriculture, art, business, computer science, education, engineering, health professions, humanities, natural science, social/behavioral science, technologies, other. **Reserve Officers Training Corps (ROTC):** Army ROTC: Offered on campus; Air Force ROTC: Offered on campus. **Faculty and instruction (2009-2010):** Total instructional faculty: 378 full-time, 67 part-time (69% men; 31% women; 14% minorities). Full-time faculty with Ph.D. or other terminal degree: 86%. Student/faculty ratio: 15/1. Classes of fewer than 20 students: 47%; of 20 to 49 students: 41%; of 50 or more students: 12%. **Advanced Placement and International Baccalaureate credit:** AP tests may be used for: Credit and/or placement. Scores accepted: 3, 4, 5. International Baccalaureate exams may be used for: Credit and/or placement. **Freshmen returning for sophomore year:** 82%. **Graduation rates:** Four-year: 22%; five-year: 59%; six-year: 66%. **Graduate study:** 26% of students pursue further study immediately upon graduation; 30% within one year; 75% within five years. Fields in which graduates pursue further study: Master of Business Administration (MBA), 25%; law, 3%; medicine, 6%; dentistry, 1%; engineering, 60%; arts and sciences, 5%.

COSTS AND FINANCIAL AID

Financial aid office: (906) 487-2622. **Expenses (2010-2011):** Tuition and fees 2010-2011: $12,017 in state, $24,527 out of state; room/board: $8,462. Estimated books and supplies: $1,200; transportation: $1,200; personal expenses: $1,240. **Financial aid:** Priority filing date for institution's financial aid form: March 1. In 2009-2010, 78% of undergraduates applied for financial aid. Of those, 63% were determined to have financial need; 14% had their need fully met. Average financial aid package (proportion receiving): $10,793 (63%). Average amount of gift aid, such as scholarships or grants (proportion receiving): $5,167 (49%). Average amount of self-help aid, such as work study or loans (proportion receiving): $4,456 (55%). Average need-based loan (excluding PLUS or other private loans): $4,386. Among students who received need-based aid, the average percentage of need met: 70%. Among students who received aid based on merit, the average award (and the proportion receiving): $4,162 (23%). The average athletic scholarship (and the proportion receiving): $10,168 (4%). Average amount of debt of borrowers graduating in 2009: $26,764. Proportion who borrowed: 68%.

CAMPUS LIFE AND EXTRACURRICULAR ACTIVITIES

Campus housing available (% using): coed dorms (80%), sorority housing (2%), fraternity housing (6%), apartments for married students (1%), apartment for single students (11%), special housing for disabled students, special housing for international students, other housing options. Students who live in college-owned, operated, or affiliated housing: 44%. **Student employment:** During the 2009-2010 academic year, 23% of undergraduates worked on campus. Average per-year earnings: $4,858. **Clubs and organizations:** Number of student organizations: 210. Activities include: campus ministries, choral groups, concert band, dance, drama/theater, international student organization, jazz band, literary magazine, music ensembles, musical theater, opera, pep band, radio station, student government, student newspaper, student film society, symphony orchestra. Number of fraternities: 13; sororities: 8. Proportion of men in fraternities: 7%; of women in

sororities: 12%. Average proportion of students who stay on campus on weekends: 90%. **Sports program (2009-2010):** Member of NCAA II. **Men's intercollegiate varsity sports:** basketball, cross country, football, ice hockey, skiing (nordic), tennis, track and field (outdoor). **Women's intercollegiate varsity sports:** basketball, cross country, skiing (nordic), soccer, tennis, track and field (outdoor), volleyball.

SERVICES AND FACILITIES

Basic services: nonremedial tutoring, placement service, day care, health service, health insurance, other. **Counseling services:** minority student, career, military, personal, veteran student, academic, older student, psychological, birth control, religious, other. **For learning-disabled students:** School does not offer a structured program with separate admission and additional fees. Services include: reading machines, tape recorders, other special classes, untimed tests, note-taking services, oral tests, learning center, readers, extended time for tests, tutors, priority registration, priority seating, texts on tape. **Library:** Number of titles: 797,416; number of current serial subscriptions: 10,206. **Information technology resources:** Students are not required to lease or own a computer. Number of campus computers available to all students: 1,266. School has a wireless network. Approximate number of users that can be accommodated: 6,000. Proportion of college-owned housing units wired for high-speed internet access: 100%. **Campus safety:** Security services offered: 24-hour foot-and-vehicle patrols, late-night transport/escort service, 24-hour emergency telephones, lighted pathways/sidewalks, student patrols, controlled dormitory access (key, security card, etc).

TRANSFER AND INTERNATIONAL STUDENTS

Transfer students: May apply for admission for the following academic terms: Fall, Spring, Summer. Applicants do not need a minimum number of credits to apply. For fall 2009: Transfer applications received: 733. Transfer applicants offered admission: 403. Transfer applicants enrolled: 236. **International students:** Number of foreign undergraduates: 395 (7% of student body). Number of countries represented: 37. Minimum TOEFL score required: 550 (paper); 79 (computer).

Northern Michigan University

- **Address:** 1401 Presque Isle Avenue, Marquette, MI 49855
- **Website:** http://www.nmu.edu
- **Public**
- **Enrollment:** 7,794 full-time; 784 part-time

KEY STATS

✔ **U.S News College Ranking:** 66, Regional Universities (Midwest)
✔ **ACT Score (25th/75th percentile):** 19-24
✔ **Tuition:** 2009-2010: $7,454 in state, $11,828 out of state

Selectivity: Selective	**Room/board:** $7,846
Acceptance rate: 73%	**Average debt:** $24,074
Student/faculty ratio: 23/1	**Proportion who borrowed:** 67%

UNDERGRADUATE STUDENT BODY STATS

2009-2010 enrollment: 7,794 full-time; 784 part-time. Men: 47%; women: 53%. **Ethnic makeup:** African American: 2%; American-Indian: 3%; Asian American: 1%; Hispanic: 1%; White: 93%; International: 1%.

ADMISSIONS FACTS AND FIGURES

Phone: (906) 227-2650. **Email:** admiss@nmu.edu. **Website:** http://www.nmu.edu. **Application deadlines for fall 2011:** Regular decision: Rolling. Early decision: Not offered. Early action: Not offered. Admission can be deferred. **Application fee:** $30. **To apply online, go to:** http://www.nmu.edu/apply. **Admissions requirements/recommendations:** High school units required (recommended): English: (4); Mathematics: (4); Science: (4); Foreign language: (3); Social studies: (4); Total units: 12 (19). Tests: The college uses SAT or ACT scores in admissions decisions. Either SAT or ACT required. For admission to the fall 2011 entering class, the school will accept: ACT with or without writing accepted. Campus visit: Recommended. Admissions interview: Neither required nor recommended. Off-campus interview: May be arranged. **Factors that count in admissions decisions:** **Academic:** Secondary school record: Not Considered. Class rank: Not Considered. Letters of recommendation: Very Important. Standardized test scores: Not Considered. Essay: Not Considered. **Nonacademic:** Interview: Not Considered. Extracurricular activities: Not Considered. Talent/ability: Not

Considered. Character/personal qualities: Not Considered. Alumni/ae relationship: Not Considered. Geographical residence: Not Considered. State residency: Not Considered. Religious affiliation/commitment: Not Considered. Minority status: Not Considered. Volunteer work: Not Considered. Work experience: Not Considered. **Other schools with the greatest overlap in applicants:** Central Michigan University; Grand Valley State University; Lake Superior State University; Michigan State University; Michigan Technological University. **Admissions statistics for the fall 2009 entering class:** Total applicants: 5,955. Total accepted: 4,338. Freshmen enrolled: 1,772; 27% were from out of state. Overall acceptance rate: 73%. **Average high school grade point average:** 2.9. **First-year students submitting ACT scores:** 94%. Scores (25/75 percentile): English: 17-24, Math: 17-24, Composite: 19-24.

ACADEMICS

Year founded: 1899. **Academic calendar:** Semester. **Degrees offered:** certificate, diploma, associate, transfer-associate, terminal-associate, bachelor's, post-bachelor's certificate, master's, post-master's certificate. **Most popular majors:** 14% business, management, marketing, and related support services, 12% education, 11% health professions and related clinical sciences, 8% visual and performing arts, 7% social sciences. **Major fields of study:** biological and biomedical sciences; business, management, marketing, and related support services; communication, journalism, and related programs; computer and information sciences and support services; construction trades; education; engineering; engineering technologies/technicians; English language and literature/letters; family and consumer sciences/human sciences; foreign languages, literatures, and linguistics; health professions and related clinical sciences; history; legal professions and studies; liberal arts and sciences studies, and humanities; mathematics and statistics; mechanic and repair technologies/technicians; multi/interdisciplinary studies; natural resources and conservation; parks, recreation, leisure, and fitness studies; personal and culinary services; philosophy and religious studies; physical sciences; precision production; psychology; public administration and social service professions; security and protective services; social sciences; transportation and materials moving; visual and performing arts. **Areas of required coursework:** arts/fine arts, humanities, computer literacy, mathematics, English (including composition), foreign languages, sciences (biological or physical), history, social science, other. **Pre-professional programs:** pre-law, pre-dentistry, pre-medicine, pre-veterinary science, pre-optometry, pre-pharmacy, other. **Special academic programs:** distance learning, double major, dual enrollment, English as a Second Language (ESL), exchange student program (domestic), honors program, independent study, internships, liberal arts/career combination, student-designed major, study abroad, teacher certificate program, weekend college. **Teacher certification offered in:** special education, elementary, middle/junior high, secondary, bilingual/bicultural. **Reserve Officers Training Corps (ROTC):** Army ROTC: Offered on campus. **Faculty and instruction (2009-2010):** Total instructional faculty: 317 full-time, 145 part-time (58% men; 42% women; 7% minorities). Full-time faculty with Ph.D. or other terminal degree: 80%. Student/faculty ratio: 23/1. Classes of fewer than 20 students: 23%; of 20 to 49 students: 66%; of 50 or more students: 11%. **Advanced Placement and International Baccalaureate credit:** AP tests may be used for: Credit only. Scores accepted: 3, 4. International Baccalaureate exams may be used for: Credit only. **Freshmen returning for sophomore year:** 73%. **Graduation rates:** Four-year: 18%; five-year: 41%; six-year: 48%. **Graduate study:** 19% of students pursue further study immediately upon graduation.

COSTS AND FINANCIAL AID

Financial aid office: (906) 227-2327. **Expenses (2009-2010):** Tuition and fees 2009-2010: $7,454 in state, $11,828 out of state; room/board: $7,846. Estimated books and supplies: $830; transportation: $440; personal expenses: $1,110. **Financial aid:** Priority filing date for institution's financial aid form: March 1. In 2009-2010, 87% of undergraduates applied for financial aid. Of those, 58% were determined to have financial need; 18% had their need fully met. Average financial aid package (proportion receiving): $7,979 (57%). Average amount of gift aid, such as scholarships or grants (proportion receiving): $4,624 (31%). Average amount of self-help aid, such as work study or loans (proportion receiving): $4,147 (48%). Average need-based loan (excluding PLUS or other private loans): $3,801. Among students who received need-based aid, the average percentage of need met: 64%. Among students who received aid based on merit, the average award (and the proportion receiving): $2,755 (5%). The average athletic scholarship (and the proportion receiving): $7,782 (0%). Average amount of debt of borrowers graduating in 2009: $24,074. Proportion who borrowed: 67%.

CAMPUS LIFE AND EXTRACURRICULAR ACTIVITIES

Campus housing available (% using): coed dorms (31%), apartments for married students (1%), apartment for single students (6%), special housing for disabled students, other housing options (62%). Students who live in college-owned, operated, or affiliated housing: 36%. **Student employment:** During the 2009-2010 academic year, 16% of undergraduates worked on campus. Average per-year earnings: $3,500. **Clubs and organizations:** Number of student organizations: 318. Activities include: campus ministries, choral groups, concert band, dance, drama/theater, international student organization, jazz band, marching band, model UN, music ensembles, musical theater, opera, pep band, radio station, student government, student newspaper, student film society, television station. Number of fraternities: 4; sororities: 4. Average proportion of students who stay on campus on weekends: 75%. **Sports program (2009-2010):** Member of NCAA II. *Men's intercollegiate varsity sports:* basketball, football, golf, ice hockey, skiing (nordic). *Women's intercollegiate varsity sports:* basketball, cross country, skiing (nordic), soccer, swimming, track and field (indoor), track and field (outdoor), volleyball.

SERVICES AND FACILITIES

Basic services: nonremedial tutoring, placement service, health service. **Remedial assistance:** reading, math, writing, study skills. **Counseling services:** minority student, career, military, personal, veteran student, academic, older student, psychological, birth control, religious. **For learning-disabled students:** School does not offer a structured program with separate admission and additional fees. Services include: note-taking services, oral tests, readers, extended time for tests, texts on tape, typist/scribe, other testing accommodations, other. **Library:** Number of titles: 828,516; number of current serial subscriptions: 20,657. **Information technology resources:** Students are not required to lease or own a computer. Number of campus computers available to all students: 10,250. School has a wireless network. Approximate number of users that can be accommodated: 10,000. Proportion of college-owned housing units wired for high-speed internet access: 100%. **Campus safety:** Security services offered: 24-hour foot-and-vehicle patrols, late-night transport/escort service, 24-hour emergency telephones, lighted pathways/sidewalks, controlled dormitory access (key, security card, etc).

TRANSFER AND INTERNATIONAL STUDENTS

Transfer students: May apply for admission for the following academic terms: Fall, Winter, Summer. Applicants need a minimum number of credits to apply. For fall 2009: Transfer applications received: 1,293. Transfer applicants offered admission: 780. Transfer applicants enrolled: 524. **International students:** Number of foreign undergraduates: 78 (1% of student body). Number of countries represented: 24. Minimum TOEFL score required: 500 (paper); 173 (computer).

Northwood University

■ **Address:** 4000 Whiting Drive, Midland, MI 48640
■ **Website:** http://www.northwood.edu
■ **Private**
■ **Enrollment:** 1,764 full-time; 55 part-time

KEY STATS

✔ **U.S News College Ranking:** Unranked Specialty School–Business
✔ **ACT Score (25th/75th percentile):** 18-23
✔ **Tuition:** 2010-2011: $19,272

Selectivity: Selective	**Room/board:** $8,160
Acceptance rate: 73%	**Average debt:** $28,634
Student/faculty ratio: 27/1	**Proportion who borrowed:** 72%

UNDERGRADUATE STUDENT BODY STATS

2009-2010 enrollment: 1,764 full-time; 55 part-time. Men: 61%; women: 39%. **Ethnic makeup:** African American: 12%; American-Indian: 1%; Asian American: 1%; Hispanic: 2%; White: 75%; International: 9%.

ADMISSIONS FACTS AND FIGURES

Phone: (989) 837-4273. **Email:** miadmit@northwood.edu. **Website:** http://www.northwood.edu. **Application deadlines for fall 2011:** Regular decision: Rolling. Early decision: Not offered. Early action: Not offered. Admission can be deferred. **Application fee:** $25. **To apply online, go to:** https://admissions.northwood.edu/. **Admissions requirements/recommendations:**

High school units required (recommended): English: (4); Mathematics: (3); Science: (3); Foreign language: (1); Social studies: (3); Total units: (17). Tests: The college uses SAT or ACT scores in admissions decisions. Either SAT or ACT required. For admission to the fall 2011 entering class, the school will accept: ACT with or without writing accepted. Campus visit: Recommended. Admissions interview: Recommended. Off-campus interview: May be arranged. **Factors that count in admissions decisions:** *Academic:* Secondary school record: Considered. Class rank: Considered. Letters of recommendation: Important. Standardized test scores: Very Important. Essay: Considered. *Nonacademic:* Interview: Considered. Extracurricular activities: Considered. Talent/ability: Considered. Character/personal qualities: Considered. Alumni/ae relationship: Not Considered. Geographical residence: Not Considered. State residency: Not Considered. Religious affiliation/commitment: Not Considered. Minority status: Not Considered. Volunteer work: Not Considered. Work experience: Not Considered. **Admissions statistics for the fall 2009 entering class:** Total applicants: 1,527. Total accepted: 1,122. Freshmen enrolled: 343; 9% were from out of state. Overall acceptance rate: 73%. **Credentials of fall 2009 freshmen:** 9% ranked in the top 10 percent of their high school class; 28% were in the top 25 percent; 63% were in the top half. (Proportion submitting class standing: 12%.) **Average high school grade point average:** 3.1. **First-year students who submitted SAT scores:** 9%. Scores (25/75 percentile): Critical Reading: 410-480, Math: 430-570, Combined: 840-1050. **First-year students submitting ACT scores:** 96%. Scores (25/75 percentile): English: 18-24, Math: 17-23, Composite: 18-23.

ACADEMICS

Year founded: 1959. **Academic calendar:** Semester. **Degrees offered:** bachelor's, master's. **Most popular majors:** 18% marketing/marketing management, 13% business administration and management, 10% accounting, 10% vehicle and vehicle parts and accessories marketing operations. **Major fields of study:** business, management, marketing, and related support services; communication, journalism, and related programs; computer and information sciences and support services; parks, recreation, leisure, and fitness studies. **Areas of required coursework:** humanities, computer literacy, mathematics, English (including composition), philosophy, history, social science. **Special academic programs:** accelerated program, double major, dual enrollment, English as a Second Language (ESL), honors program, independent study, internships, study abroad, weekend college. **Cooperative education programs:** business. **Faculty and instruction (2009-2010):** Total instructional faculty: 50 full-time, 51 part-time (64% men; 36% women; 8% minorities). Full-time faculty with Ph.D. or other terminal degree: 32%. Student/faculty ratio: 27/1. Classes of fewer than 20 students: 35%; of 20 to 49 students: 64%; of 50 or more students: 1%. **Advanced Placement and International Baccalaureate credit:** AP tests may be used for: Credit and/or placement. Scores accepted: 3, 4, 5. International Baccalaureate exams may be used for: Credit and/or placement. **Freshmen returning for sophomore year:** 74%. **Graduation rates:** Four-year: 39%; five-year: 51%; six-year: 51%. **Graduate study:** 10% of students pursue further study immediately upon graduation. Fields in which graduates pursue further study: Master of Business Administration (MBA), 9%; law, 1%.

COSTS AND FINANCIAL AID

Financial aid office: (989) 837-4230. **Expenses (2010-2011):** Tuition and fees 2010-2011: $19,272; room/board: $8,160. Estimated books and supplies: $1,116; transportation: $850; personal expenses: $1,510. **Financial aid:** In 2009-2010, 78% of undergraduates applied for financial aid. Of those, 71% were determined to have financial need; 23% had their need fully met. Average financial aid package (proportion receiving): $15,831 (71%). Average amount of gift aid, such as scholarships or grants (proportion receiving): $5,585 (61%). Average amount of self-help aid, such as work study or loans (proportion receiving): $4,597 (63%). Average need-based loan (excluding PLUS or other private loans): $4,356. Among students who received need-based aid, the average percentage of need met: 54%. Among students who received aid based on merit, the average award (and the proportion receiving): $6,197 (14%). The average athletic scholarship (and the proportion receiving): $10,489 (6%). Average amount of debt of borrowers graduating in 2009: $28,634. Proportion who borrowed: 72%.

CAMPUS LIFE AND EXTRACURRICULAR ACTIVITIES

Campus housing available (% using): women's dorms (22%), men's dorms (37%), apartment for single students (40%). Students who live in college-owned, operated, or affiliated housing: 51%. **Student employment:** During the 2009-2010 academic year, 12% of undergraduates worked on campus. Average per-year earnings: $1,500. **Clubs and organizations:** Number of student organizations: 37. Activities include: choral groups, dance, drama/

theater, international student organization, pep band, student government, student newspaper, yearbook. Number of fraternities: 7; sororities: 4. Proportion of men in fraternities: 8%; of women in sororities: 7%. Average proportion of students who stay on campus on weekends: 40%. **Sports program (2009-2010):** Member of NCAA II. *Men's intercollegiate varsity sports:* baseball, basketball, cross country, football, golf, soccer, tennis, track and field (indoor), track and field (outdoor). *Women's intercollegiate varsity sports:* basketball, cross country, golf, soccer, softball, tennis, track and field (indoor), track and field (outdoor), volleyball.

SERVICES AND FACILITIES

Basic services: nonremedial tutoring, placement service, health service. **Remedial assistance:** reading, math, writing, study skills. **Counseling services:** career, personal, academic, psychological. **For learning-disabled students:** School does not offer a structured program with separate admission and additional fees. Services include: remedial math, remedial English, reading machines, untimed tests, oral tests, learning center, readers, extended time for tests, tutors, priority registration. **Library:** Number of titles: 40,063; number of current serial subscriptions: 335. **Information technology resources:** Students are not required to lease or own a computer. Number of campus computers available to all students: 215. School has a wireless network. Approximate number of users that can be accommodated: 5,000. Proportion of college-owned housing units wired for high-speed internet access: 100%. **Campus safety:** Security services offered: 24-hour foot-and-vehicle patrols, late-night transport/escort service, 24-hour emergency telephones, lighted pathways/sidewalks, student patrols, controlled dormitory access (key, security card, etc).

TRANSFER AND INTERNATIONAL STUDENTS

Transfer students: May apply for admission for the following academic terms: Fall, Winter, Spring, Summer. Applicants need a minimum number of credits to apply. For fall 2009: Transfer applications received: 489. Transfer applicants offered admission: 365. Transfer applicants enrolled: 217. **International students:** Number of foreign undergraduates: 161 (9% of student body). Number of countries represented: 34. Minimum TOEFL score required: 500 (paper); 173 (computer). Average TOEFL score: 538 (paper).

Oakland University

- **Address:** Rochester, MI 48309-4401
- **Website:** http://www.oakland.edu
- **Public**
- **Enrollment:** 11,335 full-time; 3,940 part-time

KEY STATS
✔ **U.S News College Ranking:** second tier, National Universities
✔ **ACT Score (25th/75th percentile):** 19-25
✔ **Tuition:** 2010-2011: $8,783 in state, $20,498 out of state

Selectivity: Selective	**Room/board:** $7,680
Acceptance rate: 69%	**Average debt:** $21,330
Student/faculty ratio: 21/1	**Proportion who borrowed:** 56%

UNDERGRADUATE STUDENT BODY STATS

2009-2010 enrollment: 11,335 full-time; 3,940 part-time. Men: 39%; women: 61%. **Ethnic makeup:** African American: 9%; Asian American: 4%; Hispanic: 2%; White: 84%; International: 1%.

ADMISSIONS FACTS AND FIGURES

Phone: (248) 370-3360. **Email:** ouinfo@oakland.edu. **Website:** http://www.oakland.edu. **Application deadlines for fall 2011:** Regular decision: Rolling. Early decision: Not offered. Early action: Not offered. Admission can be deferred. **To apply online, go to:** http://www.oakland.edu/admissions/index.html. **Admissions requirements/recommendations:** High school units required (recommended): English: 4; Mathematics: 3; Science: 3; Foreign language: (2); Social studies: 3; Total units: 13 (2). Tests: The college uses SAT or ACT scores in admissions decisions. Neither SAT nor ACT required. For admission to the fall 2011 entering class, the school will accept: ACT with or without writing accepted. Campus visit: Recommended. Admissions interview: Neither required nor recommended. Off-campus interview: May be arranged. **Factors that count in admissions decisions:** *Academic:* Secondary school record: Very Important. Class rank: Very Important. Letters of recommendation: Important.

Standardized test scores: Considered. Essay: Considered. **Nonacademic:** Interview: Considered. Extracurricular activities: Important. Talent/ability: Important. Character/personal qualities: Important. Alumni/ae relationship: Considered. Geographical residence: Not Considered. State residency: Not Considered. Religious affiliation/commitment: Not Considered. Minority status: Not Considered. Volunteer work: Important. Work experience: Considered. **Other schools with the greatest overlap in applicants:** Central Michigan University; Grand Valley State University; Michigan State University; University of Michigan–Ann Arbor; Wayne State University. **Admissions statistics for the fall 2009 entering class:** Total applicants: 10,070. Total accepted: 6,912. Freshmen enrolled: 2,466; 2% were from out of state. Overall acceptance rate: 69%. **Credentials of fall 2009 freshmen:** 11% ranked in the top 10 percent of their high school class; 46% were in the top 25 percent; 88% were in the top half. (Proportion submitting class standing: 36%.) **Average high school grade point average:** 3.3. **First-year students submitting ACT scores:** 97%. Scores (25/75 percentile): English: 19-25, Math: 18-25, Composite: 19-25.

ACADEMICS

Year founded: 1957. **Academic calendar:** Semester. **Degrees offered:** bachelor's, post-bachelor's certificate, master's, post-master's certificate, doctorate. **Most popular majors:** 20% business, management, marketing, and related support services, 18% health professions and related clinical sciences, 10% communication, journalism, and related programs, 10% education, 7% social sciences. **Major fields of study:** area, ethnic, cultural, and gender studies; biological and biomedical sciences; business, management, marketing, and related support services; communication, journalism, and related programs; computer and information sciences and support services; education; engineering; English language and literature/letters; foreign languages, literatures, and linguistics; health professions and related clinical sciences; history; liberal arts and sciences studies, and humanities; mathematics and statistics; philosophy and religious studies; physical sciences; psychology; public administration and social service professions; social sciences; visual and performing arts. **Areas of required coursework:** arts/fine arts, humanities, computer literacy, mathematics, English (including composition), philosophy, foreign languages, sciences (biological or physical), history, social science, other. **Pre-professional programs:** pre-law, pre-dentistry, pre-medicine, pre-veterinary science, pre-optometry. **Special academic programs:** accelerated program, cooperative (work-study plan) program, distance learning, double major, dual enrollment, English as a Second Language (ESL), honors program, independent study, internships, student-designed major, study abroad, teacher certificate program. **Teacher certification offered in:** early childhood, special education, elementary, secondary. **Cooperative education programs:** business, computer science, engineering, social/behavioral science. **Reserve Officers Training Corps (ROTC):** Air Force ROTC: Offered at cooperating institution (University of Michigan–Ann Arbor). **Faculty and instruction (2009-2010):** Total instructional faculty: 509 full-time, 528 part-time (48% men; 52% women; 15% minorities). Full-time faculty with Ph.D. or other terminal degree: 90%. Student/faculty ratio: 21/1. Classes of fewer than 20 students: 39%; of 20 to 49 students: 49%; of 50 or more students: 12%. **Advanced Placement and International Baccalaureate credit:** AP tests may be used for: Credit and/or placement. Scores accepted: 3, 4, 5. International Baccalaureate exams may be used for: Credit and/or placement. **Freshmen returning for sophomore year:** 72%. **Graduation rates:** Four-year: 12%; five-year: 32%; six-year: 41%. **Graduate study:** 23% of students pursue further study immediately upon graduation.

COSTS AND FINANCIAL AID

Financial aid office: (248) 370-2550. **Expenses (2010-2011):** Tuition and fees 2010-2011: $8,783 in state, $20,498 out of state; room/board: $7,680. Estimated books and supplies: $1,226; transportation: $0; personal expenses: $2,315. **Financial aid:** Priority filing date for institution's financial aid form: February 15. In 2009-2010, 72% of undergraduates applied for financial aid. Of those, 56% were determined to have financial need; 24% had their need fully met. Average financial aid package (proportion receiving): $7,730 (54%). Average amount of gift aid, such as scholarships or grants (proportion receiving): $4,985 (39%). Average amount of self-help aid, such as work study or loans (proportion receiving): $3,843 (54%). Average need-based loan (excluding PLUS or other private loans): $3,992. Among students who received need-based aid, the average percentage of need met: 73%. Among students who received aid based on merit, the average award (and the proportion receiving): $2,696 (26%). The average athletic scholarship (and the proportion receiving): $11,003 (2%). Average amount of debt of borrowers graduating in 2009: $21,330. Proportion who borrowed: 56%.

CAMPUS LIFE AND EXTRACURRICULAR ACTIVITIES

Campus housing available: coed dorms, sorority housing, fraternity housing, apartments for married students, apartment for single students, special housing for disabled students, special housing for international students, cooperative housing, other housing options. Students who live in college-owned, operated, or affiliated housing: 14%. **Clubs and organizations:** Number of student organizations: 170. Activities include: campus ministries, choral groups, concert band, dance, drama/theater, international student organization, jazz band, literary magazine, music ensembles, musical theater, pep band, radio station, student government, student newspaper, student film society, symphony orchestra, television station. Number of fraternities: 4; sororities: 6. Proportion of men in fraternities: 2%; of women in sororities: 2%. Average proportion of students who stay on campus on weekends: 45%. **Sports program (2009-2010):** Member of NCAA I. **Men's intercollegiate varsity sports:** baseball, basketball, cross country, golf, soccer, swimming, track and field (indoor), track and field (outdoor). **Women's intercollegiate varsity sports:** basketball, cross country, golf, soccer, softball, swimming, tennis, track and field (indoor), track and field (outdoor), volleyball.

SERVICES AND FACILITIES

Basic services: nonremedial tutoring, women's center, placement service, day care, health service, other. **Remedial assistance:** reading, math, writing, study skills. **Counseling services:** minority student, career, personal, veteran student, academic, psychological, birth control. **For learning-disabled students:** School does not offer a structured program with separate admission and additional fees. Total undergraduates in learning-disabled program or receiving services: 208. Services include: remedial math, remedial English, reading machines, tape recorders, videotaped classes, diagnostic testing service, note-taking services, learning center, readers, extended time for tests, tutors, priority registration, priority seating, texts on tape, exams on tape or computer, other. **Library:** Number of titles: 856,760; number of current serial subscriptions: 20,490. **Information technology resources:** Students are not required to lease or own a computer. School has a wireless network. **Campus safety:** Security services offered: 24-hour foot-and-vehicle patrols, late-night transport/escort service, 24-hour emergency telephones, lighted pathways/sidewalks, student patrols, controlled dormitory access (key, security card, etc).

TRANSFER AND INTERNATIONAL STUDENTS

Transfer students: May apply for admission for the following academic terms: Fall, Winter, Spring, Summer. Applicants need a minimum number of credits to apply. For fall 2009: Transfer applications received: 4,478. Transfer applicants offered admission: 2,678. Transfer applicants enrolled: 1,677. **International students:** Number of foreign undergraduates: 113 (1% of student body). Number of countries represented: 48. Minimum TOEFL score required: 550 (paper); 213 (computer).

Olivet College

- **Address:** 320 S. Main Street, Olivet, MI 49076
- **Website:** http://www.olivetcollege.edu
- **Private; Religious affiliation:** United Church of Christ
- **Enrollment:** 1,010 full-time; 141 part-time

KEY STATS

✔ **U.S News College Ranking:** second tier, National Liberal Arts Colleges
✔ **ACT Score (25th/75th percentile):** 17-22
✔ **Tuition:** 2010-2011: $20,500

Selectivity: Selective	**Room/board:** $6,900
Acceptance rate: 64%	**Average debt:** $24,690
Student/faculty ratio: 19/1	**Proportion who borrowed:** 87%

UNDERGRADUATE STUDENT BODY STATS

2009-2010 enrollment: 1,010 full-time; 141 part-time. Men: 55%; women: 45%. **Ethnic makeup:** African American: 12%; American-Indian: 1%; Hispanic: 3%; White: 83%.

ADMISSIONS FACTS AND FIGURES

Phone: (269) 749-7635. **Email:** admissions@olivetcollege.edu. **Website:** http://www.olivetcollege.edu. **Application deadlines for fall 2011:** Regular decision: Rolling. Early decision: Not offered. Early action: Not offered. Admission can be deferred. **Application fee:** $25. **To apply online, go to:**

http://www.olivetcollege.edu/enrollment/admissions.htm. **Admissions requirements/recommendations:** Tests: The college uses SAT or ACT scores in admissions decisions. Either SAT or ACT required. For admission to the fall 2011 entering class, the school will accept: ACT with or without writing accepted. Campus visit: Recommended. Admissions interview: Recommended. Off-campus interview: May be arranged. **Factors that count in admissions decisions:** *Academic:* Secondary school record: Important. Class rank: Not Considered. Letters of recommendation: Important. Standardized test scores: Very Important. Essay: Not Considered. *Nonacademic:* Interview: Important. Extracurricular activities: Not Considered. Talent/ability: Not Considered. Character/personal qualities: Considered. Alumni/ae relationship: Not Considered. Geographical residence: Not Considered. State residency: Not Considered. Religious affiliation/commitment: Not Considered. Minority status: Not Considered. Volunteer work: Important. Work experience: Not Considered. **Other schools with the greatest overlap in applicants:** Albion College; Alma College; Calvin College; Hope College; Kalamazoo College. **Admissions statistics for the fall 2009 entering class:** Total applicants: 1,479. Total accepted: 951. Freshmen enrolled: 285; 4% were from out of state. Overall acceptance rate: 64%. **Average high school grade point average:** 2.8. **First-year students submitting ACT scores:** 98%. Scores (25/75 percentile): English: 15-21, Math: 16-22, Composite: 17-22.

ACADEMICS

Year founded: 1844. **Academic calendar:** Other. **Degrees offered:** certificate, bachelor's, master's. **Most popular majors:** 18% insurance, 15% biology/biological sciences, 11% health and physical education, 9% business administration and management, 5% criminal justice/safety studies. **Major fields of study:** biological and biomedical sciences; business, management, marketing, and related support services; communication, journalism, and related programs; computer and information sciences and support services; education; English language and literature/letters; history; liberal arts and sciences studies, and humanities; mathematics and statistics; multi/interdisciplinary studies; natural resources and conservation; parks, recreation, leisure, and fitness studies; physical sciences; psychology; security and protective services; social sciences; visual and performing arts. **Areas of required coursework:** arts/fine arts, humanities, mathematics, English (including composition), sciences (biological or physical), history. **Pre-professional programs:** pre-law, pre-dentistry, pre-medicine, pre-veterinary science, pre-pharmacy. **Special academic programs (% participation):** cooperative (work-study plan) program (15%), double major (9%), dual enrollment (1%), honors program (3%), independent study (63%), internships (60%), student-designed major (2%), teacher certificate program (33%). **Teacher certification offered in:** special education, elementary, secondary. **Cooperative education programs:** business, education, natural science, social/behavioral science. **Reserve Officers Training Corps (ROTC):** Air Force ROTC: Offered at cooperating institution (Michigan State University). **Faculty and instruction (2009-2010):** Total instructional faculty: 42 full-time, 42 part-time (48% men; 52% women; 7% minorities). Student/faculty ratio: 19/1. Classes of fewer than 20 students: 55%; of 20 to 49 students: 44%; of 50 or more students: 1%. **Advanced Placement and International Baccalaureate credit:** AP tests may be used for: Placement only. Scores accepted: 3, 4, 5. International Baccalaureate exams may be used for: Placement only. **Freshmen returning for sophomore year:** 65%. **Graduation rates:** Four-year: 37%; five-year: 40%; six-year: 40%. **Graduate study:** 10% of students pursue further study immediately upon graduation; 17% within one year. Fields in which graduates pursue further study: law, 11%; medicine, 55%; education, 11%.

COSTS AND FINANCIAL AID

Financial aid office: (269) 749-7102. **Expenses (2010-2011):** Tuition and fees 2010-2011: $20,500; room/board: $6,900. Estimated books and supplies: $900; transportation: $1,560; personal expenses: $1,000. **Financial aid:** Priority filing date for institution's financial aid form: March 1. In 2009-2010, 98% of undergraduates applied for financial aid. Of those, 92% were determined to have financial need; 19% had their need fully met. Average financial aid package (proportion receiving): $17,155 (92%). Average amount of gift aid, such as scholarships or grants (proportion receiving): $11,655 (92%). Average amount of self-help aid, such as work study or loans (proportion receiving): $5,561 (87%). Average need-based loan (excluding PLUS or other private loans): $4,554. Among students who received need-based aid, the average percentage of need met: 82%. Among students who received aid based on merit, the average award (and the proportion receiving): $10,450 (12%). The average athletic scholarship (and the proportion receiving): $0 (0%). Average amount of debt of borrowers graduating in 2009: $24,690. Proportion who borrowed: 87%.

CAMPUS LIFE AND EXTRACURRICULAR ACTIVITIES

Campus housing available (% using): coed dorms (48%), women's dorms (18%), men's dorms (24%), sorority housing (2%), fraternity housing (5%), apartments for married students (1%), special housing for international students (1%), other housing options (1%). Students who live in college-owned, operated, or affiliated housing: 41%. **Student employment:** During the 2009-2010 academic year, 54% of undergraduates worked on campus. Average per-year earnings: $1,600. **Clubs and organizations:** Number of student organizations: 65. Activities include: campus ministries, choral groups, concert band, drama/theater, international student organization, jazz band, literary magazine, marching band, music ensembles, musical theater, pep band, radio station, student government, student newspaper, yearbook. Number of fraternities: 6; sororities: 5. Proportion of men in fraternities: 19%; of women in sororities: 23%. Average proportion of students who stay on campus on weekends: 25%. **Sports program (2009-2010):** Member of NCAA III. *Men's intercollegiate varsity sports:* baseball, basketball, cross country, football, golf, soccer, swimming, track and field (outdoor), wrestling. *Women's intercollegiate varsity sports:* basketball, cross country, golf, lacrosse, soccer, swimming, tennis, track and field (outdoor), volleyball.

SERVICES AND FACILITIES

Basic services: nonremedial tutoring, women's center, placement service, health service, health insurance, other. **Remedial assistance:** reading, math, writing, other. **Counseling services:** minority student, career, personal, academic, older student, psychological, birth control, religious. **For learning-disabled students:** School does not offer a structured program with separate admission and additional fees. Services include: reading machines, tape recorders, other special classes, videotaped classes, untimed tests, note-taking services, oral tests, learning center, readers, extended time for tests, tutors, early syllabus, priority registration, priority seating, proofreading services, substitution of courses, texts on tape, typist/scribe, exams on tape or computer, take home exams, other testing accommodations, other. **Library:** Number of titles: 7,500; number of current serial subscriptions: 250. **Information technology resources:** Students are not required to lease or own a computer. Number of campus computers available to all students: 155. School has a wireless network. Approximate number of users that can be accommodated: 2,500. Proportion of college-owned housing units wired for high-speed internet access: 100%. **Campus safety:** Security services offered: 24-hour foot-and-vehicle patrols, late-night transport/escort service, 24-hour emergency telephones, lighted pathways/sidewalks, student patrols, controlled dormitory access (key, security card, etc.).

TRANSFER AND INTERNATIONAL STUDENTS

Transfer students: May apply for admission for the following academic terms: Fall, Spring, Summer. Applicants do not need a minimum number of credits to apply. For fall 2009: Transfer applications received: 244. Transfer applicants offered admission: 133. Transfer applicants enrolled: 84. **International students:** Number of foreign undergraduates: 4. Number of countries represented: 16. Minimum TOEFL score required: 500 (paper); 200 (computer). Average TOEFL score: 570 (paper).

Rochester College

- **Address:** 800 W. Avon Road, Rochester Hills, MI 48307
- **Website:** http://www.rc.edu
- **Private; Religious affiliation:** Church of Christ
- **Enrollment:** N/A

KEY STATS

✔ **U.S News College Ranking:** second tier, Regional Colleges (Midwest)
✔ **SAT or ACT Score (25th/75th percentile):** N/A
✔ **Tuition:** 2009-2010: $17,362

Selectivity: Less selective	**Room/board:** $5,496
Acceptance rate: N/A	**Average debt:** N/A
Student/faculty ratio: N/A	**Proportion who borrowed:** N/A

Saginaw Valley State University

- **Address:** 7400 Bay Road, University Center, MI 48710
- **Website:** http://www.svsu.edu
- **Public**
- **Enrollment:** N/A

KEY STATS

- ✔ **U.S News College Ranking:** second tier, Regional Universities (Midwest)
- ✔ **ACT Score (25th/75th percentile):** 18-24
- ✔ **Tuition:** 2009-2010: $7,312 in state, $13,205 out of state

Selectivity: Selective	**Room/board:** $7,487
Acceptance rate: 88%	**Average debt:** N/A
Student/faculty ratio: N/A	**Proportion who borrowed:** N/A

Siena Heights University

- **Address:** 1247 E. Siena Heights Drive, Adrian, MI 49221
- **Website:** http://www.sienaheights.edu
- **Private; Religious affiliation:** Roman Catholic
- **Enrollment:** 997 full-time; 1,031 part-time

KEY STATS

- ✔ **U.S News College Ranking:** second tier, Regional Universities (Midwest)
- ✔ **ACT Score:** 21
- ✔ **Tuition:** 2009-2010: $19,210

Selectivity: Selective	**Room/board:** $7,070
Acceptance rate: 69%	**Average debt:** N/A
Student/faculty ratio: N/A	**Proportion who borrowed:** N/A

UNDERGRADUATE STUDENT BODY STATS

2009-2010 enrollment: 997 full-time; 1,031 part-time. Men: 42%; women: 58%. **Ethnic makeup:** African American: 11%; Asian American: 1%; Hispanic: 4%; White: 83%; International: 2%.

ADMISSIONS FACTS AND FIGURES

Phone: (517) 264-7180. **Email:** admissions@sienaheights.edu. **Website:** http://www.sienaheights.edu. **Application deadlines for fall 2011:** Regular decision: Rolling. Early decision: Not offered. Early action: Not offered. Admission can be deferred. **Application fee:** $25. **To apply online, go to:** https://www.sienaheights.edu/ApplicationForm.aspx. **Admissions requirements/recommendations:** High school units required (recommended): English: 4 (4); Mathematics: 4 (4); Science: 3 (3); Foreign language: 1 (2); Social studies: 3 (3); History: 2 (2). Tests: The college uses SAT or ACT scores in admissions decisions. Either SAT or ACT required. For admission to the fall 2011 entering class, the school will accept: ACT with or without writing accepted. Campus visit: Recommended. Admissions interview: Neither required nor recommended. Off-campus interview: May be arranged. **Factors that count in admissions decisions:** *Academic:* Secondary school record: Important. Class rank: Important. Letters of recommendation: Important. Standardized test scores: Very Important. Essay: Considered. *Nonacademic:* Interview: Considered. Extracurricular activities: Considered. Talent/ability: Very Important. Character/personal qualities: Considered. Alumni/ae relationship: Considered. Geographical residence: Not Considered. State residency: Not Considered. Religious affiliation/commitment: Not Considered. Minority status: Not Considered. Volunteer work: Not Considered. Work experience: Not Considered. **Admissions statistics for the fall 2009 entering class:** Total applicants: 957. Total accepted: 659. Freshmen enrolled: 208; 5% were from out of state. Overall acceptance rate: 69%.

ACADEMICS

Year founded: 1919. **Academic calendar:** Semester. **Degrees offered:** associate, terminal-associate, bachelor's, post-bachelor's certificate, master's. **Areas of required coursework:** arts/fine arts, mathematics, English (including composition), philosophy, sciences (biological or physical), history, social science. **Pre-professional programs:** pre-law, pre-medicine, pre-veterinary science. **Special academic programs:** distance learning, double major, dual enrollment, English as a Second Language (ESL), independent study, internships, study abroad, teacher certificate program. **Teacher certification offered in:** early childhood, special education, elementary, middle/

junior high, secondary. **Advanced Placement and International Baccalaureate credit:** AP tests may be used for: Credit and/or placement. International Baccalaureate exams may be used for: Credit and/or placement. **Freshmen returning for sophomore year:** 64%. **Graduation rates:** Six-year: 43%. **Graduate study:** 32% of students pursue further study immediately upon graduation. Fields in which graduates pursue further study: Master of Business Administration (MBA), 30%; law, 14%.

COSTS AND FINANCIAL AID

Financial aid office: (517) 264-7130. **Expenses (2009-2010):** Tuition and fees 2009-2010: $19,210; room/board: $7,070. Estimated books and supplies: $750.

CAMPUS LIFE AND EXTRACURRICULAR ACTIVITIES

Campus housing available (% using): coed dorms (65%), apartment for single students (35%). Students who live in college-owned, operated, or affiliated housing: 50%. **Student employment:** During the 2009-2010 academic year, 5% of undergraduates worked on campus. Average per-year earnings: $1,000. **Clubs and organizations:** Number of student organizations: 28. Activities include: campus ministries, choral groups, dance, drama/theater, international student organization, jazz band, literary magazine, music ensembles, musical theater, student government, student newspaper. Number of fraternities: 1; sororities: 2. Proportion of men in fraternities: 1%; of women in sororities: 1%. Average proportion of students who stay on campus on weekends: 35%. **Sports program (2009-2010):** Member of NAIA. *Men's intercollegiate varsity sports:* baseball, basketball, cross country, golf, lacrosse, soccer, track and field (outdoor), volleyball. *Women's intercollegiate varsity sports:* basketball, cross country, golf, soccer, softball, track and field (outdoor), volleyball.

SERVICES AND FACILITIES

Basic services: nonremedial tutoring, health service. **Remedial assistance:** reading, math, writing, study skills. **Counseling services:** career, personal, academic, psychological. **For learning-disabled students:** School does not offer a structured program with separate admission and additional fees. Services include: remedial math, remedial English. **Library:** Number of titles: 142,000; number of current serial subscriptions: 300. **Information technology resources:** Students are not required to lease or own a computer. Number of campus computers available to all students: 207. School has a wireless network. Approximate number of users that can be accommodated: 500. Proportion of college-owned housing units wired for high-speed internet access: 100%. **Campus safety:** Security services offered: 24-hour foot-and-vehicle patrols, late-night transport/escort service, lighted pathways/sidewalks, controlled dormitory access (key, security card, etc).

TRANSFER AND INTERNATIONAL STUDENTS

Transfer students: May apply for admission for the following academic terms: Fall, Winter, Spring, Summer. Applicants need a minimum number of credits to apply. For fall 2009: Transfer applications received: 327. Transfer applicants offered admission: 213. Transfer applicants enrolled: 110. **International students:** Number of foreign undergraduates: 30 (2% of student body). Number of countries represented: 27. Minimum TOEFL score required: 500 (paper); 63 (computer).

Spring Arbor University

- **Address:** 106 E. Main Street, Spring Arbor, MI 49283-9799
- **Website:** http://www.arbor.edu
- **Private; Religious affiliation:** Free Methodist
- **Enrollment:** 1,978 full-time; 888 part-time

KEY STATS

- ✔ **U.S News College Ranking:** 66, Regional Universities (Midwest)
- ✔ **ACT Score (25th/75th percentile):** 20-26
- ✔ **Tuition:** 2010-2011: $20,536

Selectivity: Selective	**Room/board:** $7,254
Acceptance rate: 78%	**Average debt:** $26,077
Student/faculty ratio: 15/1	**Proportion who borrowed:** 86%

UNDERGRADUATE STUDENT BODY STATS

2009-2010 enrollment: 1,978 full-time; 888 part-time. Men: 32%; women: 68%. **Ethnic makeup:** African American: 11%; American-Indian: 1%; Asian American: 1%; Hispanic: 2%; White: 85%; International: 1%. **Religious**

preference: Roman Catholic: 3%; Protestant: 44%; Unknown: 19%; Free Methodist: 14%; Baptist: 11%; Other: 9%.

ADMISSIONS FACTS AND FIGURES

Phone: (800) 968-0011. **Email:** admissions@arbor.edu. **Website:** http://www.arbor.edu. **Application deadlines for fall 2011:** Regular decision: August 1. Early decision: Not offered. Early action: Not offered. Admission can be deferred. **Application fee:** $30. **To apply online, go to:** http://mysau.arbor.edu/wps/portal/onlineapp. **Admissions requirements/recommendations:** High school units required (recommended): English: 4; Mathematics: 3; Science: 3; Foreign language: (2); History: 3; Total units: 14 (3). Tests: The college uses SAT or ACT scores in admissions decisions. Either SAT or ACT required. For admission to the fall 2011 entering class, the school will accept: ACT with or without writing accepted. Campus visit: Recommended. Admissions interview: Neither required nor recommended. Off-campus interview: May be arranged. **Factors that count in admissions decisions:** *Academic:* Secondary school record: Very Important. Class rank: Considered. Letters of recommendation: Considered. Standardized test scores: Very Important. Essay: Considered. *Nonacademic:* Interview: Considered. Extracurricular activities: Considered. Talent/ability: Considered. Character/personal qualities: Very Important. Alumni/ae relationship: Not Considered. Geographical residence: Not Considered. State residency: Not Considered. Religious affiliation/commitment: Considered. Minority status: Not Considered. Volunteer work: Not Considered. Work experience: Not Considered. **Other schools with the greatest overlap in applicants:** Central Michigan University; Cornerstone University; Grand Valley State University; Michigan State University; Western Michigan University. **Admissions statistics for the fall 2009 entering class:** Total applicants: 2,022. Total accepted: 1,583. Freshmen enrolled: 381; 16% were from out of state. Overall acceptance rate: 78%. **Credentials of fall 2009 freshmen:** 25% ranked in the top 10 percent of their high school class; 49% were in the top 25 percent; 78% were in the top half. (Proportion submitting class standing: 89%.) **Average high school grade point average:** 3.4. **First-year students who submitted SAT scores:** 12%. Scores (25/75 percentile): Critical Reading: 475-595, Math: 470-595, Combined: 945-1190. **First-year students submitting ACT scores:** 95%. Scores (25/75 percentile): English: 19-26, Math: 18-25, Composite: 20-26.

ACADEMICS

Year founded: 1873. **Academic calendar:** Semester. **Degrees offered:** associate, bachelor's, post-bachelor's certificate, master's. **Most popular majors:** 21% elementary education and teaching, 16% business administration, management, and operations, 13% youth ministry, 8% social work, 5% psychology. **Major fields of study:** biological and biomedical sciences; business, management, marketing, and related support services; communication, journalism, and related programs; computer and information sciences and support services; education; engineering; English language and literature/letters; family and consumer sciences/human sciences; foreign languages, literatures, and linguistics; health professions and related clinical sciences; history; mathematics and statistics; parks, recreation, leisure, and fitness studies; philosophy and religious studies; physical sciences; psychology; public administration and social service professions; social sciences; theology and religious vocations; visual and performing arts. **Areas of required coursework:** arts/fine arts, humanities, computer literacy, mathematics, English (including composition), philosophy, sciences (biological or physical), history, social science, other. **Pre-professional programs:** pre-law, pre-dentistry, pre-medicine, pre-veterinary science, other. **Special academic programs (% participation):** accelerated program (70%), cross-registration (10%), distance learning (49%), double major (4%), dual enrollment (0%), English as a Second Language (ESL) (0%), honors program (0%), independent study (5%), internships (26%), student-designed major (0%), study abroad (10%), teacher certificate program (10%), weekend college (49%). **Teacher certification offered in:** early childhood, special education, elementary, secondary. **Reserve Officers Training Corps (ROTC):** Army ROTC: Offered on campus; Air Force ROTC: Offered at cooperating institution (University of Michigan–Ann Arbor). **Faculty and instruction (2009-2010):** Total instructional faculty: 83 full-time, 57 part-time (56% men; 44% women; 6% minorities). Full-time faculty with Ph.D. or other terminal degree: 60%. Student/faculty ratio: 15/1. Classes of fewer than 20 students: 60%; of 20 to 49 students: 38%; of 50 or more students: 2%. **Advanced Placement and International Baccalaureate credit:** AP tests may be used for: Placement only. International Baccalaureate exams may be used for: Placement only. **Freshmen returning for sophomore year:** 73%. **Graduation rates:** Four-year: 40%; five-year: 54%; six-year: 59%. **Graduate study:** 23% of students pursue further study immediately upon graduation; 29% within one year; 41% within five years. Fields in which graduates pursue further

study: Master of Business Administration (MBA), 19%; medicine, 2%; dentistry, 1%; engineering, 1%; theology (or the seminary), 25%; education, 32%; arts and sciences, 20%.

COSTS AND FINANCIAL AID

Financial aid office: (517) 750-6463. **Expenses (2010-2011):** Tuition and fees 2010-2011: $20,536; room/board: $7,254. Estimated books and supplies: $800; transportation: $738; personal expenses: $880. **Financial aid:** Priority filing date for institution's financial aid form: March 1. In 2009-2010, 94% of undergraduates applied for financial aid. Of those, 86% were determined to have financial need; 50% had their need fully met. Average financial aid package (proportion receiving): $22,445 (86%). Average amount of gift aid, such as scholarships or grants (proportion receiving): $12,196 (85%). Average amount of self-help aid, such as work study or loans (proportion receiving): $4,402 (74%). Average need-based loan (excluding PLUS or other private loans): $4,406. Among students who received need-based aid, the average percentage of need met: 91%. Among students who received aid based on merit, the average award (and the proportion receiving): $3,374 (0%). The average athletic scholarship (and the proportion receiving): $6,645 (14%). Average amount of debt of borrowers graduating in 2009: $26,077. Proportion who borrowed: 86%.

CAMPUS LIFE AND EXTRACURRICULAR ACTIVITIES

Campus housing available (% using): women's dorms (48%), men's dorms (31%), apartments for married students (1%), apartment for single students (12%), special housing for disabled students, special housing for international students, other housing options (8%). Students who live in college-owned, operated, or affiliated housing: 71%. **Student employment:** During the 2009-2010 academic year, 42% of undergraduates worked on campus. Average per-year earnings: $2,200. Activities include: campus ministries, choral groups, concert band, drama/theater, international student organization, jazz band, literary magazine, model UN, music ensembles, musical theater, pep band, radio station, student government, student newspaper, student film society, symphony orchestra, television station, yearbook. Number of fraternities: 0; sororities: 0. Average proportion of students who stay on campus on weekends: 60%. **Sports program (2009-2010):** Member of NAIA. *Men's intercollegiate varsity sports:* baseball, basketball, cross country, golf, soccer, tennis, track and field (indoor), track and field (outdoor). *Women's intercollegiate varsity sports:* basketball, cross country, soccer, softball, tennis, track and field (indoor), track and field (outdoor), volleyball.

SERVICES AND FACILITIES

Basic services: nonremedial tutoring, placement service, health service, other. **Remedial assistance:** reading, math, writing, study skills. **Counseling services:** minority student, career, military, personal, veteran student, academic, older student, psychological, birth control, religious. **For learning-disabled students:** School does not offer a structured program with separate admission and additional fees. Total undergraduates in learning-disabled program or receiving services: 32. Services include: remedial math, remedial English, reading machines, remedial reading, tape recorders, untimed tests, note-taking services, oral tests, learning center, readers, extended time for tests, tutors, priority seating, other testing accommodations. **Library:** Number of titles: 115,987; number of current serial subscriptions: 523. **Information technology resources:** Students are not required to lease or own a computer. Number of campus computers available to all students: 441. School has a wireless network. Approximate number of users that can be accommodated: 4,000. Proportion of college-owned housing units wired for high-speed internet access: 100%. **Campus safety:** Security services offered: late-night transport/escort service, 24-hour emergency telephones, lighted pathways/sidewalks, student patrols, controlled dormitory access (key, security card, etc).

TRANSFER AND INTERNATIONAL STUDENTS

Transfer students: May apply for admission for the following academic terms: Fall, Winter, Spring, Summer. Applicants need a minimum number of credits to apply. For fall 2009: Transfer applications received: 305. Transfer applicants offered admission: 172. Transfer applicants enrolled: 79. **International students:** Number of foreign undergraduates: 26 (1% of student body). Number of countries represented: 7. Minimum TOEFL score required: 525 (paper); 197 (computer).

University of Detroit Mercy

- **Address:** 4001 W. McNichols, Detroit, MI 48221-3038
- **Website:** http://www.udmercy.edu
- **Private; Religious affiliation:** Roman Catholic (Jesuit/Sisters of Mercy)
- **Enrollment:** 2,366 full-time; 783 part-time

KEY STATS

✔ **U.S News College Ranking:** 30, Regional Universities (Midwest)
✔ **ACT Score (25th/75th percentile):** 21-26
✔ **Tuition:** 2010-2011: $30,660

Selectivity: More selective	**Room/board:** $8,930
Acceptance rate: 62%	**Average debt:** N/A
Student/faculty ratio: 13/1	**Proportion who borrowed:** N/A

UNDERGRADUATE STUDENT BODY STATS

2009-2010 enrollment: 2,366 full-time; 783 part-time. Men: 36%; women: 64%. **Ethnic makeup:** African American: 19%; Asian American: 2%; Hispanic: 4%; White: 71%; International: 4%. **Religious preference:** Roman Catholic: 31%; Protestant: 10%; Unknown: 28%.

ADMISSIONS FACTS AND FIGURES

Phone: (313) 993-1245. **Email:** admissions@udmercy.edu. **Website:** http://www.udmercy.edu. **Application deadlines for fall 2011:** Regular decision: Rolling. Early decision: Not offered. Early action: Not offered. Admission can be deferred. **Application fee:** $25. **To apply online, go to:** https://jackson.udmercy.edu/apply/apply.jsp. **Admissions requirements/recommendations:** High school units required (recommended): English: (4); Mathematics: (3); Science: (2); Foreign language: (1); Social studies: (2); History: (2); Academic electives: (2). Tests: The college uses SAT or ACT scores in admissions decisions. Either SAT or ACT required. For admission to the fall 2011 entering class, the school will accept: ACT with or without writing accepted. Campus visit: Recommended. Admissions interview: Neither required nor recommended. Off-campus interview: May be arranged. **Factors that count in admissions decisions:** *Academic:* Secondary school record: Very Important. Class rank: Considered. Letters of recommendation: Considered. Standardized test scores: Very Important. Essay: Considered. *Nonacademic:* Interview: Considered. Extracurricular activities: Considered. Talent/ability: Considered. Character/personal qualities: Considered. Alumni/ae relationship: Considered. Geographical residence: Considered. State residency: Considered. Religious affiliation/commitment: Considered. Minority status: Considered. Volunteer work: Considered. Work experience: Considered. **Admissions statistics for the fall 2009 entering class:** Total applicants: 3,241. Total accepted: 2,010. Freshmen enrolled: 552; Overall acceptance rate: 62%. **Credentials of fall 2009 freshmen:** 27% ranked in the top 10 percent of their high school class; 61% were in the top 25 percent; 88% were in the top half. (Proportion submitting class standing: 60%.) **Average high school grade point average:** 3.4. **First-year students submitting ACT scores:** 92%. Scores (25/75 percentile): English: 20-26, Math: 20-26, Composite: 21-26.

ACADEMICS

Year founded: 1877. **Academic calendar:** Semester. **Degrees offered:** certificate, bachelor's, post-bachelor's certificate, master's, post-master's certificate, doctorate. **Most popular majors:** 34% nursing, 8% business administration and management, 6% architecture, 5% biology, 5% dental hygiene/hygienist. **Major fields of study:** architecture and related services; biological and biomedical sciences; business, management, marketing, and related support services; communication, journalism, and related programs; computer and information sciences and support services; education; engineering; English language and literature/letters; health professions and related clinical sciences; legal professions and studies; liberal arts and sciences studies, and humanities; mathematics and statistics; philosophy and religious studies; physical sciences; psychology; public administration and social service professions; security and protective services; social sciences; visual and performing arts. **Areas of required coursework:** humanities, computer literacy, mathematics, English (including composition), philosophy, sciences (biological or physical), social science, other. **Pre-professional programs:** pre-law, pre-dentistry, pre-medicine, other. **Special academic programs:** cooperative (work-study plan) program, distance learning, double major, English as a Second Language (ESL), honors program, independent study, internships, liberal arts/career combination, study abroad, teacher certificate program, weekend college. **Teacher certification offered in:** early childhood, special education, elementary, middle/junior high, secondary.

Cooperative education programs: business, computer science, engineering, health professions, humanities, natural science, social/behavioral science. **Faculty and instruction (2009-2010):** Total instructional faculty: 316 full-time, 379 part-time (51% men; 49% women; 16% minorities). Student/faculty ratio: 13/1. Classes of fewer than 20 students: 57%; of 20 to 49 students: 40%; of 50 or more students: 3%. **Freshmen returning for sophomore year:** 77%. **Graduation rates:** Four-year: 31%; five-year: 47%; six-year: 53%.

COSTS AND FINANCIAL AID

Financial aid office: (313) 993-3350. **Expenses (2010-2011):** Tuition and fees 2010-2011: $30,660; room/board: $8,930. Estimated books and supplies: $1,568; transportation: $1,240; personal expenses: $3,167. **Financial aid:** Priority filing date for institution's financial aid form: March 1. In 2009-2010, 86% of undergraduates applied for financial aid. Of those, 82% were determined to have financial need; 18% had their need fully met. Average financial aid package (proportion receiving): $25,795 (82%). Average amount of gift aid, such as scholarships or grants (proportion receiving): $21,741 (74%). Average amount of self-help aid, such as work study or loans (proportion receiving): $4,054 (79%). Average need-based loan (excluding PLUS or other private loans): $3,636. Among students who received need-based aid, the average percentage of need met: 86%. Among students who received aid based on merit, the average award (and the proportion receiving): $10,224 (12%). The average athletic scholarship (and the proportion receiving): $1,101 (51%).

CAMPUS LIFE AND EXTRACURRICULAR ACTIVITIES

Campus housing available: coed dorms, apartments for married students. **Clubs and organizations:** Number of student organizations: 50. Activities include: campus ministries, drama/theater, international student organization, literary magazine, pep band, radio station, student government, student newspaper. **Sports program (2009-2010):** Member of NCAA I.

SERVICES AND FACILITIES

Basic services: nonremedial tutoring, placement service, health service, health insurance. **Remedial assistance:** reading, math, writing, study skills. **Counseling services:** career, personal, veteran student, academic, psychological, religious. **Library:** Number of titles: 762,247; number of current serial subscriptions: 69,865. **Information technology resources:** Students are not required to lease or own a computer. Number of campus computers available to all students: 250. School has a wireless network. Approximate number of users that can be accommodated: 4,500. Proportion of college-owned housing units wired for high-speed internet access: 100%. **Campus safety:** Security services offered: lighted pathways/sidewalks.

TRANSFER AND INTERNATIONAL STUDENTS

Transfer students: May apply for admission for the following academic terms: Fall, Winter, Spring, Summer. Applicants do not need a minimum number of credits to apply. For fall 2009: Transfer applications received: 2,237. Transfer applicants offered admission: 633. Transfer applicants enrolled: 243. **International students:** Number of foreign undergraduates: 123 (4% of student body).

University of Michigan–Ann Arbor

- **Address:** Ann Arbor, MI 48109
- **Website:** http://www.umich.edu
- **Public**
- **Enrollment:** 25,342 full-time; 866 part-time

KEY STATS

✔ **U.S News College Ranking:** 29, National Universities
✔ **ACT Score (25th/75th percentile):** 27-31
✔ **Tuition:** 2010-2011: $12,400 in state, $36,163 out of state

Selectivity: Most selective	**Room/board:** $8,924
Acceptance rate: 50%	**Average debt:** $26,819
Student/faculty ratio: 15/1	**Proportion who borrowed:** 46%

UNDERGRADUATE STUDENT BODY STATS

2009-2010 enrollment: 25,342 full-time; 866 part-time. Men: 51%; women: 49%. **Ethnic makeup:** African American: 6%; American-Indian: 1%; Asian American: 12%; Hispanic: 4%; White: 72%; International: 5%.

ADMISSIONS FACTS AND FIGURES

Phone: (734) 764-7433. **Website:** http://www.umich.edu. **Application deadlines for fall 2011:** Regular decision: February 1. Early decision: Not offered. Early action: Send application by: November 1; Decision sent by: December 24. Admission can be deferred. **Application fee:** $40. **To apply online, go to:** https://apply.embark.com/ugrad/umich/64. **Admissions requirements/recommendations:** High school units required (recommended): English: 4 (4); Mathematics: 3 (4); Science: 3 (4); Foreign language: 2 (4); Social studies: 3 (3); History: 3 (3); Academic electives: 1 (1); Total units: 16 (20). Tests: The college uses SAT or ACT scores in admissions decisions. Either SAT or ACT required. For admission to the fall 2011 entering class, the school will accept: ACT with writing required. Campus visit: Recommended. Admissions interview: Neither required nor recommended. **Factors that count in admissions decisions:** *Academic:* Secondary school record: Very Important. Class rank: Considered. Letters of recommendation: Important. Standardized test scores: Important. Essay: Important. *Nonacademic:* Interview: Not Considered. Extracurricular activities: Considered. Talent/ability: Considered. Character/personal qualities: Important. Alumni/ae relationship: Considered. Geographical residence: Considered. State residency: Considered. Religious affiliation/commitment: Not Considered. Minority status: Not Considered. Volunteer work: Considered. Work experience: Considered. **Other schools with the greatest overlap in applicants:** Cornell University; Michigan State University; Northwestern University; University of Pennsylvania; University of Wisconsin–Madison. **Admissions statistics for the fall 2009 entering class:** Total applicants: 29,965. Total accepted: 14,970. Freshmen enrolled: 6,079; 33% were from out of state. Overall acceptance rate: 50%. Non-early acceptance rate: 50%. **Size of waiting list:** 8926 applicants; enrolled from waiting list: 100. **Credentials of fall 2009 freshmen:** 92% ranked in the top 10 percent of their high school class; 99% were in the top 25 percent; 100% were in the top half. (Proportion submitting class standing: 96%.) **Average high school grade point average:** 3.8. **First-year students who submitted SAT scores:** 36%. Scores (25/75 percentile): Critical Reading: 590-690, Math: 640-740, Combined: 1230-1430. **First-year students submitting ACT scores:** 80%. Scores (25/75 percentile): English: 27-33, Math: 27-32, Composite: 27-31.

ACADEMICS

Year founded: 1817. **Academic calendar:** Trimester. **Degrees offered:** bachelor's, post-bachelor's certificate, master's, post-master's certificate, doctorate. **Most popular majors:** 7% economics, 7% political science and government, 7% psychology, 5% English literature (British and Commonwealth), 5% business administration and management. **Major fields of study:** architecture and related services; area, ethnic, cultural, and gender studies; biological and biomedical sciences; business, management, marketing, and related support services; communication, journalism, and related programs; computer and information sciences and support services; education; engineering; English language and literature/letters; foreign languages, literatures, and linguistics; health professions and related clinical sciences; history; liberal arts and sciences studies, and humanities; mathematics and statistics; multi/interdisciplinary studies; natural resources and conservation; parks, recreation, leisure, and fitness studies; philosophy and religious studies; physical sciences; psychology; social sciences; visual and performing arts. **Areas of required coursework:** humanities, mathematics, English (including composition), foreign languages, sciences (biological or physical), social science. **Special academic programs (% participation):** accelerated program, cooperative (work-study plan) program, cross-registration, distance learning, double major (13%), dual enrollment (2%), English as a Second Language (ESL), exchange student program (domestic), external degree program, honors program, independent study, internships, liberal arts/career combination, student-designed major, study abroad, teacher certificate program. **Teacher certification offered in:** elementary, secondary. **Cooperative education programs:** engineering. **Reserve Officers Training Corps (ROTC):** Army ROTC: Offered on campus; Navy ROTC: Offered on campus; Air Force ROTC: Offered on campus. **Faculty and instruction (2009-2010):** Total instructional faculty: 2,479 full-time, 595 part-time (60% men; 40% women; 22% minorities). Full-time faculty with Ph.D. or other terminal degree: 91%. Student/faculty ratio: 15/1. Classes of fewer than 20 students: 46%; of 20 to 49 students: 37%; of 50 or more students: 17%. **Advanced Placement and International Baccalaureate credit:** AP tests may be used for: Credit and/or placement. Scores accepted: 3, 4, 5. International Baccalaureate exams may be used for: Credit only. **Freshmen returning for sophomore year:** 96%. **Graduation rates:** Four-year: 73%; five-year: 87%; six-year: 89%. **Graduate study:** Fields in which graduates pursue further study: Master of Business Administration (MBA), 8%; law, 10%; medicine, 4%; engineering, 4%; education, 4%; arts and sciences, 39%.

COSTS AND FINANCIAL AID

Financial aid office: (734) 763-4119. **Expenses (2010-2011):** Tuition and fees 2010-2011: $12,400 in state, $36,163 out of state; room/board: $8,924. Estimated books and supplies: $1,048 personal expenses: $2,090. **Financial aid:** Priority filing date for institution's financial aid form: April 30; deadline: May 31. In 2009-2010, 60% of undergraduates applied for financial aid. Of those, 46% were determined to have financial need; 90% had their need fully met. Average financial aid package (proportion receiving): $11,511 (46%). Average amount of gift aid, such as scholarships or grants (proportion receiving): $9,529 (25%). Average amount of self-help aid, such as work study or loans (proportion receiving): $5,392 (46%). Average need-based loan (excluding PLUS or other private loans): $4,305. Among students who received need-based aid, the average percentage of need met: 90%. Among students who received aid based on merit, the average award (and the proportion receiving): $6,479 (34%). The average athletic scholarship (and the proportion receiving): $27,467 (2%). Average amount of debt of borrowers graduating in 2009: $26,819. Proportion who borrowed: 46%.

CAMPUS LIFE AND EXTRACURRICULAR ACTIVITIES

Campus housing available (% using): coed dorms (34%), women's dorms (1%), sorority housing (3%), fraternity housing (2%), apartments for married students, apartment for single students (2%), special housing for disabled students, cooperative housing (1%), other housing options (57%). Students who live in college-owned, operated, or affiliated housing: 37%. **Clubs and organizations:** Number of student organizations: 999. Activities include: campus ministries, choral groups, concert band, dance, drama/theater, international student organization, jazz band, literary magazine, marching band, model UN, music ensembles, musical theater, opera, pep band, radio station, student government, student newspaper, student film society, symphony orchestra, television station, yearbook. Number of fraternities: 39; sororities: 27. Proportion of men in fraternities: 15%; of women in sororities: 19%. **Sports program (2009-2010):** Member of NCAA I. *Men's intercollegiate varsity sports:* baseball, basketball, cross country, football, golf, gymnastics, ice hockey, soccer, swimming, tennis, track and field (indoor), track and field (outdoor), wrestling. *Women's intercollegiate varsity sports:* basketball, cross country, field hockey, golf, gymnastics, crew (lightweight), soccer, softball, swimming, tennis, track and field (indoor), track and field (outdoor), volleyball, water polo.

SERVICES AND FACILITIES

Basic services: nonremedial tutoring, women's center, placement service, day care, health service, health insurance, other. **Counseling services:** minority student, career, military, personal, veteran student, academic, psychological. **For learning-disabled students:** School does not offer a structured program with separate admission and additional fees. Services include: reading machines, tape recorders, videotaped classes, diagnostic testing service, untimed tests, note-taking services, oral tests, extended time for tests, tutors, priority registration, priority seating, texts on tape, typist/scribe, other. **Library:** Number of titles: 9,559,140; number of current serial subscriptions: 70,047. **Information technology resources:** Students are not required to lease or own a computer. Number of campus computers available to all students: 2,072. School has a wireless network. Proportion of college-owned housing units wired for high-speed internet access: 100%. **Campus safety:** Security services offered: 24-hour foot-and-vehicle patrols, late-night transport/escort service, 24-hour emergency telephones, lighted pathways/sidewalks, controlled dormitory access (key, security card, etc).

TRANSFER AND INTERNATIONAL STUDENTS

Transfer students: May apply for admission for the following academic terms: Fall, Winter, Spring, Summer. Applicants do not need a minimum number of credits to apply. For fall 2009: Transfer applications received: 2,921. Transfer applicants offered admission: 1,276. Transfer applicants enrolled: 910. **International students:** Number of foreign undergraduates: 1431 (6% of student body). Number of countries represented: 83. Minimum TOEFL score required: 570 (paper); 230 (computer).

University of Michigan–Dearborn

- **Address:** 4901 Evergreen, Dearborn, MI 48128-1491
- **Website:** http://www.umd.umich.edu
- **Public**
- **Enrollment:** 4,729 full-time; 2,049 part-time

KEY STATS

- ✔ **U.S News College Ranking:** 32, Regional Universities (Midwest)
- ✔ **ACT Score (25th/75th percentile):** 21-27
- ✔ **Tuition:** 2009-2010: $8,809 in state, $19,297 out of state

Selectivity: More selective	**Room/board:** N/A
Acceptance rate: 67%	**Average debt:** $29,564
Student/faculty ratio: 17/1	**Proportion who borrowed:** 22%

UNDERGRADUATE STUDENT BODY STATS

2009-2010 enrollment: 4,729 full-time; 2,049 part-time. Men: 48%; women: 52%. **Ethnic makeup:** African American: 11%; Asian American: 6%; Hispanic: 3%; White: 79%; International: 1%.

ADMISSIONS FACTS AND FIGURES

Phone: (313) 593-5100. **Email:** admissions@umd.umich.edu. **Website:** http://www.umd.umich.edu. **Application deadlines for fall 2011:** Regular decision: Rolling. Early decision: Not offered. Early action: Not offered. Admission can be deferred. **Application fee:** $30. **To apply online, go to:** https://web-sis.umd.umich.edu/pls/prod/bwskalog.P_DispLoginNon. **Admissions requirements/recommendations:** High school units required (recommended): English: (4); Mathematics: (4); Science: (2); Foreign language: (2); Social studies: (4); History: (4); Total units: 15 (20). Tests: The college uses SAT or ACT scores in admissions decisions. Either SAT or ACT required. For admission to the fall 2011 entering class, the school will accept: ACT with or without writing accepted. Campus visit: Recommended. Admissions interview: Neither required nor recommended. Off-campus interview: Not available. **Factors that count in admissions decisions:** *Academic:* Secondary school record: Not Considered. Class rank: Not Considered. Letters of recommendation: Not Considered. Standardized test scores: Very Important. Essay: Considered. *Nonacademic:* Interview: Considered. Extracurricular activities: Not Considered. Talent/ability: Not Considered. Character/personal qualities: Not Considered. Alumni/ae relationship: Considered. Geographical residence: Not Considered. State residency: Not Considered. Religious affiliation/commitment: Not Considered. Minority status: Not Considered. Volunteer work: Not Considered. Work experience: Not Considered. **Other schools with the greatest overlap in applicants:** Eastern Michigan University; Michigan State University; Oakland University; University of Michigan–Ann Arbor; Wayne State University. **Admissions statistics for the fall 2009 entering class:** Total applicants: 3,711. Total accepted: 2,492. Freshmen enrolled: 922; 1% were from out of state. Overall acceptance rate: 67%. **Credentials of fall 2009 freshmen:** 26% ranked in the top 10 percent of their high school class; 60% were in the top 25 percent; 88% were in the top half. (Proportion submitting class standing: 70%.) **Average high school grade point average:** 3.4. **First-year students who submitted SAT scores:** 5%. **First-year students submitting ACT scores:** 98%. Scores (25/75 percentile): English: 20-27, Math: 21-27, Composite: 21-27.

ACADEMICS

Year founded: 1959. **Academic calendar:** Semester. **Degrees offered:** bachelor's, post-bachelor's certificate, master's. **Most popular majors:** 21% business, management, marketing, and related support services, 16% education, 16% engineering, 10% psychology, 6% social sciences. **Major fields of study:** area, ethnic, cultural, and gender studies; biological and biomedical sciences; business, management, marketing, and related support services; communication, journalism, and related programs; computer and information sciences and support services; education; engineering; English language and literature/letters; foreign languages, literatures, and linguistics; health professions and related clinical sciences; history; liberal arts and sciences studies, and humanities; mathematics and statistics; multi/interdisciplinary studies; natural resources and conservation; philosophy and religious studies; physical sciences; psychology; security and protective services; social sciences; visual and performing arts. **Areas of required coursework:** humanities, mathematics, English (including composition), sciences (biological or physical), history, social science. **Pre-professional programs:** pre-law, pre-medicine. **Special academic programs:** cooperative (work-study plan) program, cross-registration, distance learning, double major, dual enrollment, honors program, independent study, internships, liberal arts/

career combination, student-designed major, study abroad, teacher certificate program. **Teacher certification offered in:** early childhood, special education, elementary, middle/junior high, secondary. **Cooperative education programs:** art, business, computer science, education, engineering, health professions, humanities, natural science, social/behavioral science. **Reserve Officers Training Corps (ROTC):** Army ROTC: Offered at cooperating institution; Navy ROTC: Offered at cooperating institution; Air Force ROTC: Offered at cooperating institution. **Faculty and instruction (2009-2010):** Total instructional faculty: 306 full-time, 201 part-time (62% men; 38% women; 21% minorities). Full-time faculty with Ph.D. or other terminal degree: 86%. Student/faculty ratio: 17/1. Classes of fewer than 20 students: 23%; of 20 to 49 students: 71%; of 50 or more students: 6%. **Freshmen returning for sophomore year:** 79%. **Graduation rates:** Four-year: 18%; five-year: 44%; six-year: 53%.

COSTS AND FINANCIAL AID

Financial aid office: (313) 593-5300. **Expenses (2009-2010):** Tuition and fees 2009-2010: $8,809 in state, $19,297 out of state. Estimated books and supplies: $960; transportation: $1,465; personal expenses: $1,815. **Financial aid:** Priority filing date for institution's financial aid form: February 15. In 2009-2010, 84% of undergraduates applied for financial aid. Of those, 60% were determined to have financial need; 18% had their need fully met. Average financial aid package (proportion receiving): $8,515 (56%). Average amount of gift aid, such as scholarships or grants (proportion receiving): $4,035 (41%). Average amount of self-help aid, such as work study or loans (proportion receiving): $5,530 (55%). Average need-based loan (excluding PLUS or other private loans): $4,330. Among students who received need-based aid, the average percentage of need met: 33%. Among students who received aid based on merit, the average award (and the proportion receiving): $3,256 (44%). The average athletic scholarship (and the proportion receiving): $2,367 (1%). Average amount of debt of borrowers graduating in 2009: $29,564. Proportion who borrowed: 22%.

CAMPUS LIFE AND EXTRACURRICULAR ACTIVITIES

Clubs and organizations: Number of student organizations: 125. Activities include: choral groups, dance, drama/theater, international student organization, literary magazine, pep band, radio station, student government, student newspaper, student film society, television station. Number of fraternities: 4; sororities: 5. Proportion of men in fraternities: 2%; of women in sororities: 2%. **Sports program (2009-2010):** Member of NAIA. *Men's intercollegiate varsity sports:* basketball. *Women's intercollegiate varsity sports:* basketball, softball, volleyball.

SERVICES AND FACILITIES

Basic services: nonremedial tutoring, women's center, placement service, health insurance, other. **Remedial assistance:** reading, math, writing, study skills. **Counseling services:** career, personal, academic, older student, psychological. **For learning-disabled students:** School does not offer a structured program with separate admission and additional fees. Total undergraduates in learning-disabled program or receiving services: 30. Services include: remedial math, remedial English, reading machines, tape recorders, note-taking services, oral tests, readers, extended time for tests, tutors, priority registration, priority seating, texts on tape. **Library:** Number of titles: 382,065; number of current serial subscriptions: 576. **Information technology resources:** Students are not required to lease or own a computer. Number of campus computers available to all students: 695. School has a wireless network. Approximate number of users that can be accommodated: 5,000. **Campus safety:** Security services offered: 24-hour foot-and-vehicle patrols, late-night transport/escort service, 24-hour emergency telephones, lighted pathways/sidewalks.

TRANSFER AND INTERNATIONAL STUDENTS

Transfer students: May apply for admission for the following academic terms: Fall, Winter, Summer. Applicants need a minimum number of credits to apply. For fall 2009: Transfer applications received: 1,478. Transfer applicants offered admission: 1,057. Transfer applicants enrolled: 729. **International students:** Number of foreign undergraduates: 54 (1% of student body). Number of countries represented: 34. Minimum TOEFL score required: 550 (paper); 213 (computer). Average TOEFL score: 570 (paper).

University of Michigan–Flint

- **Address:** 303 E. Kearsley, Flint, MI 48502-1950
- **Website:** http://www.umflint.edu
- **Public**
- **Enrollment:** 4,358 full-time; 2,223 part-time

KEY STATS

✔ **U.S News College Ranking:** 88, Regional Universities (Midwest)
✔ **ACT Score (25th/75th percentile):** 18-24
✔ **Tuition:** 2009-2010: $8,279 in state, $15,793 out of state

Selectivity: Selective	**Room/board:** $6,874
Acceptance rate: 82%	**Average debt:** N/A
Student/faculty ratio: 15/1	**Proportion who borrowed:** N/A

UNDERGRADUATE STUDENT BODY STATS

2009-2010 enrollment: 4,358 full-time; 2,223 part-time. Men: 39%; women: 61%. **Ethnic makeup:** African American: 14%; American-Indian: 1%; Asian American: 2%; Hispanic: 3%; White: 79%; International: 1%.

ADMISSIONS FACTS AND FIGURES

Phone: (810) 762-3300. **Email:** admissions@umflint.edu. **Website:** http://www.umflint.edu. **Application deadlines for fall 2011:** Regular decision: Rolling. Early decision: Not offered. Early action: Not offered. Admission can be deferred. **Application fee:** $30. **To apply online, go to:** http://www.umflint.edu/resources/offices/admissions/applicationforms.php. **Admissions requirements/recommendations:** High school units required (recommended): English: 4 (4); Mathematics: 3 (4); Science: 2 (4); Foreign language: 0 (2); Social studies: 3 (3); History: 0 (3); Academic electives: 0 (0); Total units: 9 (22). Tests: The college uses SAT or ACT scores in admissions decisions. Either SAT or ACT required. For admission to the fall 2011 entering class, the school will accept: ACT with or without writing accepted. Campus visit: Neither required nor recommended. Admissions interview: Neither required nor recommended. Off-campus interview: Not available. **Factors that count in admissions decisions:** *Academic:* Secondary school record: Very Important. Class rank: Considered. Letters of recommendation: Considered. Standardized test scores: Very Important. Essay: Considered. *Nonacademic:* Interview: Considered. Extracurricular activities: Important. Talent/ability: Considered. Character/personal qualities: Not Considered. Alumni/ae relationship: Not Considered. Geographical residence: Not Considered. State residency: Not Considered. Religious affiliation/commitment: Not Considered. Minority status: Not Considered. Volunteer work: Not Considered. Work experience: Not Considered. **Other schools with the greatest overlap in applicants:** Baker College of Flint; Oakland University; Saginaw Valley State University; University of Michigan–Dearborn. **Admissions statistics for the fall 2009 entering class:** Total applicants: 2,693. Total accepted: 2,213. Freshmen enrolled: 768; 1% were from out of state. Overall acceptance rate: 82%. **Credentials of fall 2009 freshmen:** 19% ranked in the top 10 percent of their high school class; 43% were in the top 25 percent; 76% were in the top half. (Proportion submitting class standing: 88%.) **Average high school grade point average:** 3.2. **First-year students who submitted SAT scores:** 2%. Scores (25/75 percentile): Critical Reading: 385-568, Math: 425-548, Combined: 810-1116. **First-year students submitting ACT scores:** 94%. Scores (25/75 percentile): English: 17-24, Math: 17-24, Composite: 18-24.

ACADEMICS

Year founded: 1956. **Academic calendar:** Semester. **Degrees offered:** bachelor's, master's. **Most popular majors:** 20% education, 17% business, management, marketing, and related support services, 17% health professions and related clinical sciences, 5% biological and biomedical sciences, 4% visual and performing arts. **Major fields of study:** area, ethnic, cultural, and gender studies; biological and biomedical sciences; business, management, marketing, and related support services; communication, journalism, and related programs; computer and information sciences and support services; education; engineering; English language and literature/letters; foreign languages, literatures, and linguistics; health professions and related clinical sciences; history; liberal arts and sciences studies, and humanities; mathematics and statistics; multi/interdisciplinary studies; natural resources and conservation; philosophy and religious studies; physical sciences; psychology; public administration and social service professions; security and protective services; social sciences; visual and performing arts. **Areas of required coursework:** arts/fine arts, humanities, English (including composition), philosophy, sciences (biological or physical), history, social science.

Pre-professional programs: pre-law, pre-dentistry, pre-medicine, pre-veterinary science, pre-pharmacy, other. **Special academic programs:** cooperative (work-study plan) program, distance learning, double major, dual enrollment, English as a Second Language (ESL), honors program, independent study, internships, student-designed major, study abroad, teacher certificate program. **Teacher certification offered in:** early childhood, special education, elementary, secondary. **Cooperative education programs:** art, business, computer science, education, engineering, health professions, humanities, natural science, social/behavioral science, technologies. **Reserve Officers Training Corps (ROTC):** Army ROTC: Offered at cooperating institution (University of Michigan–Ann Arbor); Navy ROTC: Offered at cooperating institution (University of Michigan–Ann Arbor); Air Force ROTC: Offered at cooperating institution (University of Michigan–Ann Arbor). **Faculty and instruction (2009-2010):** Total instructional faculty: 257 full-time, 237 part-time (45% men; 55% women; 13% minorities). Full-time faculty with Ph.D. or other terminal degree: 70%. Student/faculty ratio: 15/1. Classes of fewer than 20 students: 39%; of 20 to 49 students: 56%; of 50 or more students: 5%. **Freshmen returning for sophomore year:** 72%. **Graduation rates:** Four-year: 14%; five-year: 36%; six-year: 38%. **Graduate study:** 25% of students pursue further study immediately upon graduation. Fields in which graduates pursue further study: Master of Business Administration (MBA), 16%; education, 21%.

COSTS AND FINANCIAL AID

Financial aid office: (810) 762-3444. **Expenses (2009-2010):** Tuition and fees 2009-2010: $8,279 in state, $15,793 out of state; room/board: $6,874. Estimated books and supplies: $1,000; transportation: $2,148; personal expenses: $1,380. **Financial aid:** Priority filing date for institution's financial aid form: March 1.

CAMPUS LIFE AND EXTRACURRICULAR ACTIVITIES

Campus housing available (% using): coed dorms (100%). Students who live in college-owned, operated, or affiliated housing: 5%. **Clubs and organizations:** Number of student organizations: 89. Activities include: choral groups, concert band, dance, drama/theater, international student organization, jazz band, literary magazine, music ensembles, musical theater, student government, student newspaper, television station. Number of fraternities: 4; sororities: 5. Proportion of men in fraternities: 2%; of women in sororities: 2%. Average proportion of students who stay on campus on weekends: 55%.

SERVICES AND FACILITIES

Basic services: nonremedial tutoring, women's center, placement service, day care, health service. **Remedial assistance:** reading, math, writing, study skills. **Counseling services:** minority student, career, personal, veteran student, academic, older student, psychological, other. **For learning-disabled students:** School does not offer a structured program with separate admission and additional fees. Services include: remedial math, remedial English, reading machines, remedial reading, tape recorders, diagnostic testing service, note-taking services, oral tests, learning center, readers, extended time for tests, tutors, priority seating, texts on tape, other testing accommodations. **Library:** Number of titles: 235,557; number of current serial subscriptions: 905. **Information technology resources:** Students are not required to lease or own a computer. Number of campus computers available to all students: 740. School has a wireless network. Proportion of college-owned housing units wired for high-speed internet access: 100%. **Campus safety:** Security services offered: 24-hour foot-and-vehicle patrols, late-night transport/escort service, 24-hour emergency telephones, lighted pathways/sidewalks, student patrols, controlled dormitory access (key, security card, etc).

TRANSFER AND INTERNATIONAL STUDENTS

Transfer students: May apply for admission for the following academic terms: Fall, Winter, Spring, Summer. Applicants need a minimum number of credits to apply. For fall 2009: Transfer applications received: 1,804. Transfer applicants offered admission: 1,408. Transfer applicants enrolled: 860. **International students:** Number of foreign undergraduates: 87 (1% of student body). Number of countries represented: 40. Minimum TOEFL score required: 500 (paper); 61 (computer). Average TOEFL score: 519 (paper).

Walsh Coll. of Account. and Bus. Admin.

- **Address:** PO Box 7006, Troy, MI 48007-7006
- **Website:** http://www.walshcollege.edu
- **Private**
- **Enrollment:** 151 full-time; 971 part-time

KEY STATS
✔ **U.S News College Ranking:** Unranked Specialty School–Business
✔ **SAT or ACT Score (25th/75th percentile):** N/A
✔ **Tuition:** 2009-2010: $13,605
  Selectivity: Least selective   **Room/board:** N/A
  Acceptance rate: N/A   **Average debt:** N/A
  Student/faculty ratio: N/A   **Proportion who borrowed:** N/A

UNDERGRADUATE STUDENT BODY STATS
2009-2010 enrollment: 151 full-time; 971 part-time. Men: 48%; women: 52%. **Ethnic makeup:** African American: 5%; Asian American: 3%; Hispanic: 1%; White: 88%; International: 3%.

ADMISSIONS FACTS AND FIGURES
Phone: (248) 823-1610. **Email:** admissions@walshcollege.edu. **Website:** http://www.walshcollege.edu. **Application deadlines for fall 2011:** Regular decision: Rolling. Early decision: Not offered. Early action: Not offered. Admission cannot be deferred. **Application fee:** $25. **To apply online, go to:** https://www-secure.walshcollege.edu/forms/admissionsforms/underGraduateApplication.aspx. **Admissions requirements/recommendations:** Tests: The college does not use SAT or ACT scores in admissions decisions. Neither SAT nor ACT required. Campus visit: Neither required nor recommended. Admissions interview: Neither required nor recommended.

ACADEMICS
Year founded: 1922. **Academic calendar:** Semester. **Degrees offered:** certificate, bachelor's, post-bachelor's certificate, master's, doctorate. **Most popular majors:** 70% business administration and management, 28% accounting, 2% management information systems. **Major fields of study:** business, management, marketing, and related support services. **Special academic programs (% participation):** distance learning (40%), internships (3%). **Faculty and instruction (2009-2010):** Total instructional faculty: 18 full-time, 258 part-time (72% men; 28% women; 7% minorities). Classes of fewer than 20 students: 25%; of 20 to 49 students: 75%.

COSTS AND FINANCIAL AID
Financial aid office: (248) 823-1665. **Expenses (2009-2010):** Tuition and fees 2009-2010: $13,605. Estimated books and supplies: $2,520. **Financial aid:** Priority filing date for institution's financial aid form: March 21; deadline: March 21.

CAMPUS LIFE AND EXTRACURRICULAR ACTIVITIES
Activities include: international student organization, student government. Number of fraternities: 0; sororities: 0.

SERVICES AND FACILITIES
Basic services: placement service. **Remedial assistance:** math, writing, study skills. **Counseling services:** academic. **For learning-disabled students:** School does not offer a structured program with separate admission and additional fees. Services include: tape recorders, note-taking services, extended time for tests. **Library:** Number of titles: 26,000; number of current serial subscriptions: 300. **Information technology resources:** Students are not required to lease or own a computer. Number of campus computers available to all students: 450. School has a wireless network. **Campus safety:** Security services offered: lighted pathways/sidewalks.

TRANSFER AND INTERNATIONAL STUDENTS
Transfer students: May apply for admission for the following academic terms: Fall, Winter, Spring, Summer. Applicants need a minimum number of credits to apply. For fall 2009: Transfer applications received: 453. Transfer applicants enrolled: 293. **International students:** Number of foreign undergraduates: 34 (3% of student body). Minimum TOEFL score required: 550 (paper); 213 (computer).

Wayne State University

- **Address:** 656 W. Kirby, Detroit, MI 48202
- **Website:** http://www.wayne.edu/
- **Public**
- **Enrollment:** 13,202 full-time; 7,563 part-time

KEY STATS
✔ **U.S News College Ranking:** second tier, National Universities
✔ **ACT Score (25th/75th percentile):** 17-24
✔ **Tuition:** 2009-2010: $8,643 in state, $18,412 out of state
  Selectivity: Selective   **Room/board:** $7,659
  Acceptance rate: 75%   **Average debt:** $20,507
  Student/faculty ratio: 16/1   **Proportion who borrowed:** 57%

UNDERGRADUATE STUDENT BODY STATS
2009-2010 enrollment: 13,202 full-time; 7,563 part-time. Men: 42%; women: 58%. **Ethnic makeup:** African American: 32%; American-Indian: 1%; Asian American: 7%; Hispanic: 3%; White: 55%; International: 3%.

ADMISSIONS FACTS AND FIGURES
Phone: (313) 577-3577. **Email:** admissions@wayne.edu. **Website:** http://www.wayne.edu/. **Application deadlines for fall 2011:** Regular decision: Rolling. Early decision: Not offered. Early action: Not offered. Admission can be deferred. **Application fee:** $30. **To apply online, go to:** http://www.admissions.wayne.edu/ugrad/appl/index.html. **Admissions requirements/recommendations:** High school units required (recommended): English: (4); Mathematics: (4); Science: (3); Foreign language: (2); Social studies: (3); Academic electives: (2); Total units: (18). Tests: The college uses SAT or ACT scores in admissions decisions. Either SAT or ACT required. For admission to the fall 2011 entering class, the school will accept: ACT with or without writing accepted. Campus visit: Recommended. Admissions interview: Neither required nor recommended. Off-campus interview: May be arranged. **Factors that count in admissions decisions:** *Academic:* Secondary school record: Considered. Class rank: Not Considered. Letters of recommendation: Not Considered. Standardized test scores: Very Important. Essay: Not Considered. *Nonacademic:* Interview: Not Considered. Extracurricular activities: Not Considered. Talent/ability: Not Considered. Character/personal qualities: Not Considered. Alumni/ae relationship: Not Considered. Geographical residence: Not Considered. State residency: Not Considered. Religious affiliation/commitment: Not Considered. Minority status: Not Considered. Volunteer work: Not Considered. Work experience: Not Considered. **Other schools with the greatest overlap in applicants:** Central Michigan University; Eastern Michigan University; Michigan State University; Oakland University; University of Michigan–Ann Arbor. **Admissions statistics for the fall 2009 entering class:** Total applicants: 10,689. Total accepted: 8,063. Freshmen enrolled: 3,046; 1% were from out of state. Overall acceptance rate: 75%. **Average high school grade point average:** 3.1. **First-year students submitting ACT scores:** 95%. Scores (25/75 percentile): English: 16-24, Math: 16-24, Composite: 17-24.

ACADEMICS
Year founded: 1868. **Academic calendar:** Semester. **Degrees offered:** bachelor's, post-bachelor's certificate, master's, post-master's certificate, doctorate. **Most popular majors:** 8% biology/biological sciences, 8% psychology, 6% nursing/registered nurse training (R.N., A.S.N., B.S.N., M.S.N.), 5% organizational behavior studies, 4% elementary education and teaching. **Major fields of study:** area, ethnic, cultural, and gender studies; biological and biomedical sciences; business, management, marketing, and related support services; communication, journalism, and related programs; computer and information sciences and support services; education; engineering; engineering technologies/technicians; English language and literature/letters; family and consumer sciences/human sciences; foreign languages, literatures, and linguistics; health professions and related clinical sciences; history; mathematics and statistics; multi/interdisciplinary studies; natural resources and conservation; personal and culinary services; philosophy and religious studies; physical sciences; psychology; public administration and social service professions; security and protective services; social sciences; visual and performing arts. **Areas of required coursework:** arts/fine arts, humanities, computer literacy, mathematics, English (including composition), foreign languages, sciences (biological or physical), history, social science. **Pre-professional programs:** pre-law, pre-dentistry, pre-medicine, pre-veterinary science, pre-optometry, pre-pharmacy. **Special academic programs:** accelerated program, cooperative (work-study plan) program, cross-

registration, distance learning, double major, dual enrollment, English as a Second Language (ESL), external degree program, honors program, independent study, internships, liberal arts/career combination, study abroad, teacher certificate program, weekend college. **Teacher certification offered in:** early childhood, special education, elementary, vo-tech, middle/junior high, secondary, bilingual/bicultural. **Cooperative education programs:** art, business, computer science, education, engineering, health professions, humanities, natural science, social/behavioral science, technologies. **Reserve Officers Training Corps (ROTC):** Air Force ROTC: Offered at cooperating institution (University of Michigan–Ann Arbor). **Faculty and instruction (2009-2010):** Total instructional faculty: 1,055 full-time, 988 part-time (52% men; 48% women; 27% minorities). Full-time faculty with Ph.D. or other terminal degree: 76%. Student/faculty ratio: 16/1. Classes of fewer than 20 students: 44%; of 20 to 49 students: 46%; of 50 or more students: 10%. **Advanced Placement and International Baccalaureate credit:** AP tests may be used for: Placement only. Scores accepted: 3, 4, 5. International Baccalaureate exams may be used for: Credit only. **Freshmen returning for sophomore year:** 71%. **Graduation rates:** Four-year: 10%; five-year: 23%; six-year: 32%. **Graduate study:** 22% of students pursue further study immediately upon graduation; 26% within one year.

COSTS AND FINANCIAL AID

Financial aid office: (313) 577-3378. **Expenses (2009-2010):** Tuition and fees 2009-2010: $8,643 in state, $18,412 out of state; room/board: $7,659. Estimated books and supplies: $972; transportation: $1,569; personal expenses: $1,841. **Financial aid:** Priority filing date for institution's financial aid form: February 15; deadline: April 30. In 2009-2010, 78% of undergraduates applied for financial aid. Of those, 68% were determined to have financial need; 46% had their need fully met. Average financial aid package (proportion receiving): $15,020 (68%). Average amount of gift aid, such as scholarships or grants (proportion receiving): $6,378 (54%). Average amount of self-help aid, such as work study or loans (proportion receiving): $4,458 (57%). Average need-based loan (excluding PLUS or other private loans): $4,150. Among students who received need-based aid, the average percentage of need met: 83%. Among students who received aid based on merit, the average award (and the proportion receiving): $5,483 (10%). The average athletic scholarship (and the proportion receiving): $8,696 (1%). Average amount of debt of borrowers graduating in 2009: $20,507. Proportion who borrowed: 57%.

CAMPUS LIFE AND EXTRACURRICULAR ACTIVITIES

Campus housing available: coed dorms, fraternity housing, apartments for married students, apartment for single students, special housing for disabled students. Students who live in college-owned, operated, or affiliated housing: 10%. **Student employment:** During the 2009-2010 academic year, 6% of undergraduates worked on campus. Average per-year earnings: $10,148. **Clubs and organizations:** Number of student organizations: 230. Activities include: choral groups, concert band, dance, drama/theater, jazz band, literary magazine, marching band, music ensembles, musical theater, opera, pep band, radio station, student government, student newspaper, student film society, symphony orchestra. Number of fraternities: 11; sororities: 12. Proportion of men in fraternities: 2%; of women in sororities: 2%. **Sports program (2009-2010):** Member of NCAA II. *Men's intercollegiate varsity sports:* baseball, basketball, cross country, fencing, football, golf, ice hockey, swimming, tennis. *Women's intercollegiate varsity sports:* basketball, cross country, fencing, ice hockey, softball, swimming, tennis, volleyball.

SERVICES AND FACILITIES

Basic services: nonremedial tutoring, placement service, day care, health service, health insurance. **Remedial assistance:** reading, math, writing, study skills, other. **Counseling services:** career, personal, veteran student, academic, older student, psychological, religious. **For learning-disabled students:** School does not offer a structured program with separate admission and additional fees. Total undergraduates in learning-disabled program or receiving services: 177. Services include: reading machines, tape recorders, diagnostic testing service, untimed tests, note-taking services, learning center, extended time for tests, tutors, priority registration, priority seating, texts on tape, other. **Library:** Number of titles: 3,665,628; number of current serial subscriptions: 16,068. **Information technology resources:** Students are not required to lease or own a computer. Number of campus computers available to all students: 1,800. School has a wireless network. Approximate number of users that can be accommodated: 3,500. Proportion of college-owned housing units wired for high-speed internet access: 100%. **Campus safety:** Security services offered: 24-hour foot-and-vehicle patrols, 24-hour emergency telephones, lighted pathways/sidewalks, controlled dormitory access (key, security card, etc).

TRANSFER AND INTERNATIONAL STUDENTS

Transfer students: May apply for admission for the following academic terms: Fall, Winter, Spring, Summer. Applicants need a minimum number of credits to apply. For fall 2009: Transfer applications received: 3,403. Transfer applicants offered admission: 3,234. Transfer applicants enrolled: 1,889. **International students:** Number of foreign undergraduates: 556 (3% of student body). Number of countries represented: 39. Minimum TOEFL score required: 550 (paper); 213 (computer). Average TOEFL score: 571 (paper).

Western Michigan University

- **Address:** 1903 W. Michigan Avenue, Kalamazoo, MI 49008
- **Website:** http://www.wmich.edu
- **Public**
- **Enrollment:** 17,043 full-time; 2,504 part-time

KEY STATS
✔ **U.S News College Ranking:** 179, National Universities
✔ **ACT Score (25th/75th percentile):** 20-25
✔ **Tuition:** 2009-2010: $8,382 in state, $19,502 out of state

Selectivity: Selective	**Room/board:** $7,784
Acceptance rate: 83%	**Average debt:** $20,000
Student/faculty ratio: 19/1	**Proportion who borrowed:** 66%

UNDERGRADUATE STUDENT BODY STATS

2009-2010 enrollment: 17,043 full-time; 2,504 part-time. Men: 51%; women: 49%. **Ethnic makeup:** African American: 8%; American-Indian: 1%; Asian American: 2%; Hispanic: 3%; White: 84%; International: 3%.

ADMISSIONS FACTS AND FIGURES

Phone: (269) 387-2000. **Email:** ask-wmu@wmich.edu. **Website:** http://www.wmich.edu. **Application deadlines for fall 2011:** Early decision: Not offered. Early action: Not offered. Admission can be deferred. **Application fee:** $35. **To apply online, go to:** http://www.wmich.edu/admissions/undergradapp/index.html. **Admissions requirements/recommendations:** High school units required (recommended): English: 4 (4); Mathematics: 3 (3); Science: 2 (2); Foreign language: 0 (1); Social studies: 2 (2); History: 1 (1); Academic electives: 2 (1); Total units: 15 (17). Tests: The college uses SAT or ACT scores in admissions decisions. Either SAT or ACT required. For admission to the fall 2011 entering class, the school will accept: ACT with writing recommended. Campus visit: Recommended. Admissions interview: Neither required nor recommended. Off-campus interview: Not available. **Factors that count in admissions decisions:** *Academic:* Secondary school record: Important. Class rank: Not Considered. Letters of recommendation: Considered. Standardized test scores: Important. Essay: Considered. *Nonacademic:* Interview: Not Considered. Extracurricular activities: Not Considered. Talent/ability: Not Considered. Character/personal qualities: Not Considered. Alumni/ae relationship: Not Considered. Geographical residence: Not Considered. State residency: Not Considered. Religious affiliation/commitment: Not Considered. Minority status: Not Considered. Volunteer work: Not Considered. Work experience: Not Considered. **Other schools with the greatest overlap in applicants:** Central Michigan University; Eastern Michigan University; Grand Valley State University; Michigan State University; University of Michigan–Ann Arbor. **Admissions statistics for the fall 2009 entering class:** Total applicants: 12,379. Total accepted: 10,253. Freshmen enrolled: 3,193; 10% were from out of state. Overall acceptance rate: 83%. **Credentials of fall 2009 freshmen:** 12% ranked in the top 10 percent of their high school class; 32% were in the top 25 percent; 71% were in the top half. (Proportion submitting class standing: 80%.) **Average high school grade point average:** 3.2. **First-year students submitting ACT scores:** 97%. Scores (25/75 percentile): English: 19-25, Math: 19-25, Composite: 20-25.

ACADEMICS

Year founded: 1903. **Academic calendar:** Semester. **Degrees offered:** bachelor's, post-bachelor's certificate, master's, post-master's certificate, doctorate. **Most popular majors:** 25% business, management, marketing, and related support services, 14% education, 8% health professions and related clinical sciences, 7% communication, journalism, and related programs, 6% visual and performing arts. **Major fields of study:** area, ethnic, cultural, and gender studies; biological and biomedical sciences; business, management, marketing, and related support services; communication, journalism, and related programs; computer and information sciences and support services; education; engineering; engineering technologies/technicians; English language and literature/letters; family and consumer sciences/human sciences; foreign languages, literatures, and linguistics; health professions and related clinical sciences; history; liberal arts and sciences studies, and humanities; mathematics and statistics; mechanic and repair technologies/technicians; multi/interdisciplinary studies; natural resources and conservation; parks, recreation, leisure, and fitness studies; philosophy and religious studies; physical sciences; psychology; public administration and social service professions; security and protective services; social sciences; transportation and materials moving; visual and performing arts. **Areas of required coursework:** arts/fine arts, humanities, mathematics, English (including composition), sciences (biological or physical), social science, other. **Pre-professional programs:** pre-law, pre-dentistry, pre-medicine. **Special academic programs:** accelerated program, cooperative (work-study plan) program, cross-registration, distance learning, double major, dual enrollment, English as a Second Language (ESL), exchange student program (domestic), honors program, independent study, internships, student-designed major, study abroad, teacher certificate program. **Teacher certification offered in:** early childhood, special education, elementary, middle/junior high, secondary. **Cooperative education programs:** engineering. **Reserve Officers Training Corps (ROTC):** Army ROTC: Offered on campus. **Faculty and instruction (2009-2010):** Total instructional faculty: 908 full-time, 527 part-time (55% men; 45% women; 9% minorities). Full-time faculty with Ph.D. or other terminal degree: 80%. Student/faculty ratio: 19/1. Classes of fewer than 20 students: 37%; of 20 to 49 students: 52%; of 50 or more students: 11%. **Advanced Placement and International Baccalaureate credit:** AP tests may be used for: Credit and/or placement. Scores accepted: 3, 4, 5. International Baccalaureate exams may be used for: Credit only. **Freshmen returning for sophomore year:** 74%. **Graduation rates:** Four-year: 22%; five-year: 47%; six-year: 54%.

COSTS AND FINANCIAL AID

Financial aid office: (269) 387-6000. **Expenses (2009-2010):** Tuition and fees 2009-2010: $8,382 in state, $19,502 out of state; room/board: $7,784. Estimated books and supplies: $1,000; transportation: $1,072; personal expenses: $2,060. **Financial aid:** Priority filing date for institution's financial aid form: March 15. In 2009-2010, 67% of undergraduates applied for financial aid. Of those, 62% were determined to have financial need; 37% had their need fully met. Average financial aid package (proportion receiving): $11,000 (62%). Average amount of gift aid, such as scholarships or grants (proportion receiving): $4,800 (28%). Average amount of self-help aid, such as work study or loans (proportion receiving): $1,200 (47%). Average need-based loan (excluding PLUS or other private loans): $4,000. Among students who received need-based aid, the average percentage of need met: 85%. Among students who received aid based on merit, the average award (and the proportion receiving): $3,500 (12%). The average athletic scholarship (and the proportion receiving): $16,000 (2%). Average amount of debt of borrowers graduating in 2009: $20,000. Proportion who borrowed: 66%.

CAMPUS LIFE AND EXTRACURRICULAR ACTIVITIES

Campus housing available: coed dorms, women's dorms, men's dorms, sorority housing, fraternity housing, apartments for married students, apartment for single students, special housing for disabled students, special housing for international students, other housing options. Students who live in college-owned, operated, or affiliated housing: 24%. Average per-year earnings: $4,832. **Clubs and organizations:** Number of student organizations: 277. Activities include: campus ministries, choral groups, concert band, dance, drama/theater, international student organization, jazz band, literary magazine, marching band, music ensembles, musical theater, opera, pep band, radio station, student government, student newspaper, student film society, symphony orchestra. Number of fraternities: 16; sororities: 11. Proportion of men in fraternities: 5%; of women in sororities: 6%. **Sports program (2009-2010):** Member of NCAA I. *Men's intercollegiate varsity sports:* baseball, basketball, football, ice hockey, soccer, tennis. *Women's intercollegiate varsity sports:* basketball, cross country, golf, gymnastics, soccer, softball, tennis, track and field (indoor), track and field (outdoor), volleyball.

SERVICES AND FACILITIES

Basic services: nonremedial tutoring, women's center, placement service, day care, health service, health insurance, other. **Remedial assistance:** reading, math, writing, study skills. **Counseling services:** minority student, career, personal, veteran student, academic, psychological, birth control, religious. **For learning-disabled students:** School does not offer a structured program with separate admission and additional fees. Services include: remedial math, remedial English, reading machines, remedial reading, tape recorders, learning center, readers, extended time for tests, priority registration, priority seating, substitution of courses, texts on tape, typist/scribe, exams on tape or computer, other testing accommodations, other. **Library:** Number of titles: 2,169,724; number of current serial subscriptions: 47,147. **Information technology resources:** Students are not required to lease or own a computer. Number of campus computers available to all students: 2,000. School has a wireless network. Approximate number of users that can be accommodated: 25,500. Proportion of college-owned housing units wired for high-speed internet access: 100%. **Campus safety:** Security services offered: 24-hour foot-and-vehicle patrols, late-night transport/escort service, 24-hour emergency telephones, lighted pathways/sidewalks, student patrols, controlled dormitory access (key, security card, etc).

TRANSFER AND INTERNATIONAL STUDENTS

Transfer students: May apply for admission for the following academic terms: Fall, Winter, Spring, Summer. Applicants do not need a minimum number of credits to apply. For fall 2009: Transfer applications received: 3,178. Transfer applicants offered admission: 2,454. Transfer applicants enrolled: 1,623. **International students:** Number of foreign undergraduates: 580 (3% of student body). Number of countries represented: 66. Minimum TOEFL score required: 500 (paper); 61 (computer).

Minnesota

Augsburg College

- **Address:** 2211 Riverside Avenue S, Minneapolis, MN 55454
- **Website:** http://www.augsburg.edu
- **Private; Religious affiliation:** Lutheran
- **Enrollment:** 2,574 full-time; 549 part-time

KEY STATS
✔ **U.S News College Ranking:** 22, Regional Universities (Midwest)
✔ **ACT Score (25th/75th percentile):** 19-25
✔ **Tuition:** 2010-2011: $28,864

Selectivity: Selective	**Room/board:** $7,760
Acceptance rate: 52%	**Average debt:** $28,988
Student/faculty ratio: 13/1	**Proportion who borrowed:** 93%

UNDERGRADUATE STUDENT BODY STATS
2009-2010 enrollment: 2,574 full-time; 549 part-time. Men: 46%; women: 54%. **Ethnic makeup:** African American: 8%; American-Indian: 2%; Asian American: 6%; Hispanic: 3%; White: 80%; International: 1%. **Religious preference:** Roman Catholic: 20%; Protestant: 1%; Jewish: 1%; Muslim: 2%; No preference: 4%; Unknown: 31%; Lutheran: 31%; Christian : 4%; Other: 6%.

ADMISSIONS FACTS AND FIGURES
Phone: (612) 330-1001. **Email:** admissions@augsburg.edu. **Website:** http://www.augsburg.edu. **Application deadlines for fall 2011:** Regular decision: August 15. Early decision: Not offered. Early action: Not offered. Admission can be deferred. **Application fee:** $25. **To apply online, go to:** http://www.augsburg.edu/day/application/apply.html. **Admissions requirements/recommendations:** High school units required (recommended): English: 4; Mathematics: 4; Science: 4; Foreign language: 3; Social studies: 4; History: (4); Academic electives: (2); Total units: 19. Tests: The college uses SAT or ACT scores in admissions decisions. Either SAT or ACT required. For admission to the fall 2011 entering class, the school will accept: ACT with or without writing accepted. Campus visit: Recommended. Admissions interview: Recommended. Off-campus interview: May be arranged. **Factors that count in admissions decisions:** *Academic:* Secondary school record: Very Important. Class rank: Important. Letters of recommendation: Important. Standardized test scores: Important. Essay: Very Important. *Nonacademic:* Interview: Considered. Extracurricular activities: Important. Talent/ability: Considered. Character/personal qualities: Important. Alumni/ae relationship: Considered. Geographical residence: Not Considered. State residency: Not Considered. Religious affiliation/commitment: Not Considered. Minority status: Important. Volunteer work: Considered. Work experience: Considered. **Other schools with the greatest overlap in applicants:** Hamline University; Minnesota State University–Mankato; University of Minnesota–Duluth; University of Minnesota–Twin Cities; University of St. Thomas. **Admissions statistics for the fall 2009 entering class:** Total applicants: 2,330. Total accepted: 1,211. Freshmen enrolled: 465; 13% were from out of state. Overall acceptance rate: 52%. **Credentials of fall 2009 freshmen:** 11% ranked in the top 10 percent of their high school class; 37% were in the top 25 percent; 70% were in the top half. (Proportion submitting class standing: 82%.) **Average high school grade point average:** 3.1. **First-year students who submitted SAT scores:** 9%. Scores (25/75 percentile): Critical Reading: 450-590, Math: 473-628, Combined: 923-1218. **First-year students submitting ACT scores:** 94%. Scores (25/75 percentile): English: 18-24, Math: 18-25, Composite: 19-25.

ACADEMICS
Year founded: 1869. **Academic calendar:** Semester. **Degrees offered:** certificate, bachelor's, master's, post-master's certificate. **Most popular majors:** 31% business, management, marketing, and related support services, 10% health professions and related clinical sciences, 9% communication, journalism, and related programs, 9% education, 6% visual and performing arts. **Major fields of study:** area, ethnic, cultural, and gender studies; biological and biomedical sciences; business, management, marketing, and related support services; communication, journalism, and related programs; computer and information sciences and support services; education; engineering; English language and literature/letters; foreign languages, literatures, and linguistics; health professions and related clinical sciences; history; liberal arts and sciences studies, and humanities; mathematics and statistics; philosophy and religious studies; physical sciences; psychology; public administration and social service professions; social sciences; theology and religious vocations; visual and performing arts. **Areas of required coursework:** arts/fine arts, humanities, mathematics, English (including composition), foreign languages, sciences (biological or physical), history, social science, other. **Pre-professional programs:** pre-law, pre-dentistry, pre-medicine, pre-theology, pre-veterinary science, pre-pharmacy, other. **Special academic programs (% participation):** accelerated program, cooperative (work-study plan) program, cross-registration (23%), double major (10%), English as a Second Language (ESL) (1%), honors program (9%), independent study (11%), internships (35%), liberal arts/career combination (0%), student-designed major (1%), study abroad (20%), teacher certificate program (13%), weekend college (61%). **Teacher certification offered in:** special education, elementary, middle/junior high, secondary. **Cooperative education programs:** engineering, health professions. **Reserve Officers Training Corps (ROTC):** Army ROTC: Offered at cooperating institution (University of Minnesota–Twin Cities); Navy ROTC: Offered at cooperating institution (University of Minnesota–Twin Cities); Air Force ROTC: Offered at cooperating institution (University of St. Thomas). **Faculty and instruction (2009-2010):** Total instructional faculty: 200 full-time, 209 part-time (50% men; 50% women; 10% minorities). Full-time faculty with Ph.D. or other terminal degree: 72%. Student/faculty ratio: 13/1. Classes of fewer than 20 students: 62%; of 20 to 49 students: 38%; of 50 or more students: 0%. **Advanced Placement and International Baccalaureate credit:** AP tests may be used for: Credit and/or placement. Scores accepted: 3, 4, 5. International Baccalaureate exams may be used for: Credit and/or placement. **Freshmen returning for sophomore year:** 82%. **Graduation rates:** Four-year: 37%; five-year: 56%; six-year: 58%. **Graduate study:** 15% of students pursue further study within one year.

COSTS AND FINANCIAL AID
Financial aid office: (612) 330-1046. **Expenses (2010-2011):** Tuition and fees 2010-2011: $28,864; room/board: $7,760. Estimated books and supplies: $1,000 personal expenses: $1,670. **Financial aid:** Priority filing date for institution's financial aid form: May 1; deadline: August 1. In 2009-2010, 100% of undergraduates applied for financial aid. Of those, 82% were determined to have financial need; 12% had their need fully met. Average financial aid package (proportion receiving): $18,744 (82%). Average amount of gift aid, such as scholarships or grants (proportion receiving): $14,459 (74%). Average amount of self-help aid, such as work study or loans (proportion receiving): $6,006 (70%). Average need-based loan (excluding PLUS or other private loans): $4,695. Among students who received need-based aid, the average percentage of need met: 63%. Among students who received aid based on merit, the average award (and the proportion receiving): $7,532 (5%). The average athletic scholarship (and the proportion receiving): $0 (0%). Average amount of debt of borrowers graduating in 2009: $28,988. Proportion who borrowed: 93%.

CAMPUS LIFE AND EXTRACURRICULAR ACTIVITIES
Campus housing available (% using): coed dorms (80%), apartment for single students (5%), special housing for disabled students (10%), other housing options (5%). Students who live in college-owned, operated, or affiliated housing: 54%. **Student employment:** During the 2009-2010 academic year, 37% of undergraduates worked on campus. Average per-year earnings: $1,495. **Clubs and organizations:** Number of student organizations: 60. Activities include: campus ministries, choral groups, concert band, dance, drama/theater, international student organization, jazz band, literary magazine, music ensembles, musical theater, radio station, student government, student newspaper, student film society, symphony orchestra, yearbook. Number of fraternities: 0; sororities: 0. Average proportion of students who stay on campus on weekends: 55%. **Sports program (2009-2010):** Member of NCAA III.

SERVICES AND FACILITIES

Basic services: nonremedial tutoring, women's center, placement service, health insurance. **Remedial assistance:** math, writing, study skills. **Counseling services:** minority student, career, personal, academic, psychological, religious. **For learning-disabled students:** School does not offer a structured program with separate admission and additional fees. Services include: reading machines, tape recorders, note-taking services, oral tests, learning center, readers, extended time for tests, tutors, texts on tape, other testing accommodations. **Library:** Number of titles: 189,284; number of current serial subscriptions: 1,307. **Information technology resources:** Students are not required to lease or own a computer. Number of campus computers available to all students: 280. School has a wireless network. Approximate number of users that can be accommodated: 1,800. Proportion of college-owned housing units wired for high-speed internet access: 100%. **Campus safety:** Security services offered: 24-hour foot-and-vehicle patrols, late-night transport/escort service, 24-hour emergency telephones, lighted pathways/sidewalks, student patrols, controlled dormitory access (key, security card, etc).

TRANSFER AND INTERNATIONAL STUDENTS

Transfer students: May apply for admission for the following academic terms: Fall, Winter, Spring. Applicants need a minimum number of credits to apply. For fall 2009: Transfer applications received: 630. Transfer applicants offered admission: 339. Transfer applicants enrolled: 169. **International students:** Number of foreign undergraduates: 36 (1% of student body). Number of countries represented: 20. Minimum TOEFL score required: 550 (paper); 213 (computer). Average TOEFL score: 550 (paper).

Bemidji State University

- **Address:** 1500 Birchmont Drive NE, Bemidji, MN 56601
- **Website:** http://www.bemidjistate.edu
- **Public**
- **Enrollment:** 3,582 full-time; 1,148 part-time

KEY STATS

✔ **U.S News College Ranking:** 92, Regional Universities (Midwest)
✔ **ACT Score (25th/75th percentile):** 11-25
✔ **Tuition:** 2010-2011: $7,496 in state, $7,496 out of state

Selectivity: Selective	**Room/board:** $6,500
Acceptance rate: 81%	**Average debt:** $24,474
Student/faculty ratio: 20/1	**Proportion who borrowed:** 80%

UNDERGRADUATE STUDENT BODY STATS

2009-2010 enrollment: 3,582 full-time; 1,148 part-time. Men: 47%; women: 53%. **Ethnic makeup:** African American: 1%; American-Indian: 4%; Asian American: 1%; Hispanic: 1%; White: 90%; International: 3%.

ADMISSIONS FACTS AND FIGURES

Phone: (218) 755-2040. **Email:** admissions@bemidjistate.edu. **Website:** http://www.bemidjistate.edu. **Application deadlines for fall 2011:** Regular decision: Rolling. Early decision: Not offered. Early action: Not offered. Admission can be deferred. **Application fee:** $20. **To apply online, go to:** http://www.bemidjistate.edu/admissions/undergrad/submit/applynow/. **Admissions requirements/recommendations:** High school units required (recommended): English: 4 (4); Mathematics: 3 (3); Science: 3 (3); Foreign language: 2 (2); Social studies: 3 (3); History: 1 (1); Academic electives: 1 (1); Total units: 16 (16). **Tests:** The college uses SAT or ACT scores in admission's decisions. ACT required. For admission to the fall 2011 entering class, the school will accept: ACT with or without writing accepted. Campus visit: Recommended. Admissions interview: Recommended. Off-campus interview: May be arranged. **Factors that count in admissions decisions:** *Academic:* Secondary school record: Very Important. Class rank: Very Important. Letters of recommendation: Important. Standardized test scores: Very Important. Essay: Considered. *Nonacademic:* Interview: Not Considered. Extracurricular activities: Important. Talent/ability: Important. Character/personal qualities: Not Considered. Alumni/ae relationship: Not Considered. Geographical residence: Not Considered. State residency: Not Considered. Religious affiliation/commitment: Not Considered. Minority status: Not Considered. Volunteer work: Not Considered. Work experience: Not Considered. **Other schools with the greatest overlap in applicants:** Minnesota State University–Moorhead; St. Cloud State University; University of Minnesota–Duluth; University of North Dakota. **Admissions**

statistics for the fall 2009 entering class: Total applicants: 2,167. Total accepted: 1,747. Freshmen enrolled: 810; 6% were from out of state. Overall acceptance rate: 81%. **Credentials of fall 2009 freshmen:** 7% ranked in the top 10 percent of their high school class; 25% were in the top 25 percent; 56% were in the top half. (Proportion submitting class standing: 95%.) **Average high school grade point average:** 3.1.

ACADEMICS

Year founded: 1919. **Academic calendar:** Semester. **Degrees offered:** associate, bachelor's, master's. **Most popular majors:** 24% education, 16% business, management, marketing, and related support services, 9% engineering technologies/technicians, 9% psychology, 7% security and protective services. **Major fields of study:** biological and biomedical sciences; business, management, marketing, and related support services; communication, journalism, and related programs; computer and information sciences and support services; education; engineering technologies/technicians; English language and literature/letters; foreign languages, literatures, and linguistics; health professions and related clinical sciences; history; liberal arts and sciences studies, and humanities; mathematics and statistics; natural resources and conservation; parks, recreation, leisure, and fitness studies; philosophy and religious studies; psychology; public administration and social service professions; security and protective services; social sciences; visual and performing arts. **Areas of required coursework:** arts/fine arts, humanities, mathematics, English (including composition), sciences (biological or physical), history, social science. **Pre-professional programs:** pre-law, pre-dentistry, pre-medicine, pre-veterinary science, pre-optometry, pre-pharmacy. **Special academic programs:** accelerated program, cooperative (work-study plan) program, distance learning, double major, dual enrollment, English as a Second Language (ESL), external degree program, honors program, independent study, internships, liberal arts/career combination, study abroad, teacher certificate program. **Teacher certification offered in:** early childhood, special education, elementary, vo-tech, middle/junior high, secondary. **Cooperative education programs:** education, health professions, technologies. **Faculty and instruction (2009-2010):** Total instructional faculty: 182 full-time, 94 part-time (54% men; 46% women; 5% minorities). Full-time faculty with Ph.D. or other terminal degree: 69%. Student/faculty ratio: 20/1. Classes of fewer than 20 students: 45%; of 20 to 49 students: 50%; of 50 or more students: 5%. **Advanced Placement and International Baccalaureate credit:** AP tests may be used for: Credit only. Scores accepted: 4, 5. International Baccalaureate exams may be used for: Credit only. **Freshmen returning for sophomore year:** 70%. **Graduation rates:** Four-year: 23%; five-year: 42%; six-year: 46%. **Graduate study:** 17% of students pursue further study immediately upon graduation. Fields in which graduates pursue further study: Master of Business Administration (MBA), 5%; law, 1%; medicine, 1%; dentistry, 1%; education, 17%; arts and sciences, 27%.

COSTS AND FINANCIAL AID

Financial aid office: (218) 755-4143. **Expenses (2010-2011):** Tuition and fees 2010-2011: $7,496 in state, $7,496 out of state; room/board: $6,500. Estimated books and supplies: $840; transportation: $1,050; personal expenses: $1,350. **Financial aid:** Priority filing date for institution's financial aid form: May 15. In 2009-2010, 81% of undergraduates applied for financial aid. Of those, 64% were determined to have financial need; 34% had their need fully met. Average financial aid package (proportion receiving): $9,118 (64%). Average amount of gift aid, such as scholarships or grants (proportion receiving): $5,408 (48%). Average amount of self-help aid, such as work study or loans (proportion receiving): $4,153 (56%). Average need-based loan (excluding PLUS or other private loans): $3,726. Among students who received need-based aid, the average percentage of need met: 72%. Among students who received aid based on merit, the average award (and the proportion receiving): $9,121 (16%). The average athletic scholarship (and the proportion receiving): $4,222 (5%). Average amount of debt of borrowers graduating in 2009: $24,474. Proportion who borrowed: 80%.

CAMPUS LIFE AND EXTRACURRICULAR ACTIVITIES

Campus housing available (% using): coed dorms (1%), women's dorms (25%), men's dorms (25%), fraternity housing, apartments for married students, apartment for single students, other housing options (49%). Students who live in college-owned, operated, or affiliated housing: 28%. **Student employment:** During the 2009-2010 academic year, 70% of undergraduates worked on campus. Average per-year earnings: $2,500. **Clubs and organizations:** Number of student organizations: 80. Activities include: choral groups, concert band, dance, drama/theater, international student organization, jazz band, literary magazine, model UN, music ensembles, musical theater, pep band, radio station, student government, student newspaper, student film society, symphony orchestra, television station. Number of fraternities: 2; sororities: 2. Average proportion of students who stay on campus on weekends: 30%. **Sports program (2009-2010):** Member of NCAA II. *Men's intercollegiate varsity sports:* baseball, basketball, football, golf, ice hockey, track and field (indoor), track and field (outdoor). *Women's intercollegiate varsity sports:* basketball, cross country, golf, ice hockey, soccer, softball, tennis, track and field (indoor), track and field (outdoor), volleyball.

SERVICES AND FACILITIES

Basic services: nonremedial tutoring, women's center, placement service, day care, health service, health insurance. **Remedial assistance:** reading, math, writing, study skills. **Counseling services:** minority student, career, personal, veteran student, academic, older student, psychological, birth control. **For learning-disabled students:** School does not offer a structured program with separate admission and additional fees. Services include: remedial math, remedial English, reading machines, remedial reading, tape recorders, untimed tests, note-taking services, oral tests, learning center, readers, extended time for tests, tutors, priority registration, priority seating, texts on tape, other testing accommodations. **Library:** Number of titles: 461,755; number of current serial subscriptions: 3,528. **Information technology resources:** Students are not required to lease or own a computer. Number of campus computers available to all students: 1,600. School has a wireless network. Approximate number of users that can be accommodated: 4,000. Proportion of college-owned housing units wired for high-speed internet access: 100%. **Campus safety:** Security services offered: 24-hour foot-and-vehicle patrols, late-night transport/escort service, 24-hour emergency telephones, lighted pathways/sidewalks, student patrols, controlled dormitory access (key, security card, etc).

TRANSFER AND INTERNATIONAL STUDENTS

Transfer students: May apply for admission for the following academic terms: Fall, Spring, Summer. Applicants do not need a minimum number of credits to apply. For fall 2009: Transfer applications received: 957. Transfer applicants offered admission: 705. Transfer applicants enrolled: 447. **International students:** Number of foreign undergraduates: 123 (3% of student body). Number of countries represented: 41. Minimum TOEFL score required: 550 (paper); 61 (computer).

Bethany Lutheran College

- ■ **Address:** 700 Luther Drive, Mankato, MN 56001
- ■ **Website:** http://www.blc.edu
- ■ **Private**
- ■ **Enrollment:** N/A

....

KEY STATS
✔ **U.S News College Ranking:** second tier, Regional Colleges (Midwest)
✔ **SAT or ACT Score (25th/75th percentile):** N/A
✔ **Tuition:** 2009-2010: $19,650

Selectivity: Less selective	**Room/board:** $6,400
Acceptance rate: N/A	**Average debt:** N/A
Student/faculty ratio: N/A	**Proportion who borrowed:** N/A

Bethel University

- ■ **Address:** 3900 Bethel Drive, St. Paul, MN 55112
- ■ **Website:** http://www.bethel.edu
- ■ **Private; Religious affiliation:** Converge Worldwide (former Baptist General Conference)
- ■ **Enrollment:** 2,773 full-time; 648 part-time

....

KEY STATS
✔ **U.S News College Ranking:** 17, Regional Universities (Midwest)
✔ **ACT Score (25th/75th percentile):** 21-28
✔ **Tuition:** 2010-2011: $28,080

Selectivity: More selective	**Room/board:** $8,220
Acceptance rate: 80%	**Average debt:** $30,496
Student/faculty ratio: 12/1	**Proportion who borrowed:** 80%

UNDERGRADUATE STUDENT BODY STATS

2009-2010 enrollment: 2,773 full-time; 648 part-time. Men: 39%; women: 61%. **Ethnic makeup:** African American: 4%; Asian American: 2%; Hispanic: 1%; White: 92%. **Religious preference:** Roman Catholic: 3%; Protestant: 66%; Unknown: 7%; Converge Worldwide (former Baptist General Conference): 24%.

ADMISSIONS FACTS AND FIGURES

Phone: (800) 255-8706. **Email:** BUadmissions-cas@bethel.edu. **Website:** http://www.bethel.edu. **Application deadlines for fall 2011:** Regular decision: Rolling. Early decision: Not offered. Early action: Not offered. Admission can be deferred. **To apply online, go to:** http://cas.bethel.edu/admissions/application-details. **Admissions requirements/recommendations:** High school units required (recommended): English: 4; Mathematics: 3; Science: 3; Foreign language: (2); Social studies: 4; History: (1); Total units: 14 (5). Tests: The college uses SAT or ACT scores in admissions decisions. Either SAT or ACT required. For admission to the fall 2011 entering class, the school will accept: ACT with or without writing accepted. Campus visit: Recommended. Admissions interview: Recommended. Off-campus interview: Not available. **Factors that count in admissions decisions:** *Academic:* Secondary school record: Very Important. Class rank: Important. Letters of recommendation: Considered. Standardized test scores: Very Important. Essay: Important. *Nonacademic:* Interview: Considered. Extracurricular activities: Important. Talent/ability: Considered. Character/personal qualities: Very Important. Alumni/ae relationship: Considered. Geographical residence: Considered. State residency: Considered. Religious affiliation/commitment: Very Important. Minority status: Considered. Volunteer work: Considered. Work experience: Not Considered. **Other schools with the greatest overlap in applicants:** Gustavus Adolphus College; Northwestern College; University of Minnesota–Twin Cities; University of St. Thomas; Wheaton College. **Admissions statistics for the fall 2009 entering class:** Total applicants: 2,179. Total accepted: 1,734. Freshmen enrolled: 727; 22% were from out of state. Overall acceptance rate: 80%. **Size of waiting list:** 43 applicants; enrolled from waiting list: 10. **Credentials of fall 2009 freshmen:** 31% ranked in the top 10 percent of their high school class; 55% were in the top 25 percent; 84% were in the top half. (Proportion submitting class standing: 76%.) **Average high school grade point average:** 3.5. **First-year students who submitted SAT scores:** 10%. Scores (25/75 percentile): Critical Reading: 513-678, Math: 510-668, Combined: 1023-1346. **First-year students submitting ACT scores:** 94%. Scores (25/75 percentile): English: 21-28, Math: 21-28, Composite: 21-28.

ACADEMICS

Year founded: 1871. **Academic calendar:** 4-1-4. **Degrees offered:** associate, bachelor's, post-bachelor's certificate, master's, post-master's certificate, doctorate. **Most popular majors:** 16% education, 14% business, management, marketing, and related support services, 11% health professions and related clinical sciences, 9% communication, journalism, and related programs, 6% psychology. **Major fields of study:** agriculture, agriculture operations, and related sciences; area, ethnic, cultural, and gender studies; biological and biomedical sciences; business, management, marketing, and related support services; communication, journalism, and related programs; computer and information sciences and support services; education; engineering; English language and literature/letters; foreign languages, literatures, and linguistics; health professions and related clinical sciences; history; liberal arts and sciences studies, and humanities; mathematics and statistics; multi/interdisciplinary studies; natural resources and conservation; parks, recreation, leisure, and fitness studies; philosophy and religious studies; physical sciences; psychology; public administration and social service professions; social sciences; theology and religious vocations; visual and performing arts. **Areas of required coursework:** arts/fine arts, humanities, mathematics, English (including composition), foreign languages, sciences (biological or physical), history, social science, other. **Pre-professional programs:** pre-law, pre-dentistry, pre-medicine, pre-theology, pre-veterinary science, pre-optometry, pre-pharmacy. **Special academic programs (% participation):** distance learning, double major (12%), exchange student program (domestic), honors program (1%), independent study, internships (26%), liberal arts/career combination, student-designed major (2%), study abroad (50%), teacher certificate program. **Teacher certification offered in:** early childhood, elementary, middle/junior high, secondary. **Reserve Officers Training Corps (ROTC):** Army ROTC: Offered at cooperating institution (University of Minnesota–Twin Cities); Air Force ROTC: Offered at cooperating institution (University of St. Thomas). **Faculty and instruction (2009-2010):** Total instructional faculty: 188 full-time, 105 part-time (51% men; 49% women; 9% minorities). Full-time faculty with Ph.D. or other terminal degree: 78%. Student/faculty ratio: 12/1. Classes of fewer than

20 students: 52%; of 20 to 49 students: 45%; of 50 or more students: 3%. **Advanced Placement and International Baccalaureate credit:** AP tests may be used for: Credit only. Scores accepted: 3, 4, 5. International Baccalaureate exams may be used for: Credit only. **Freshmen returning for sophomore year:** 85%. **Graduation rates:** Four-year: 63%; five-year: 73%; six-year: 74%. **Graduate study:** 21% of students pursue further study within one year; 53% within five years. Fields in which graduates pursue further study: Master of Business Administration (MBA), 11%; law, 2%; medicine, 13%; theology (or the seminary), 7%; education, 11%.

COSTS AND FINANCIAL AID

Financial aid office: (800) 255-8706. **Expenses (2010-2011):** Tuition and fees 2010-2011: $28,080; room/board: $8,220. Estimated books and supplies: $1,010; transportation: $400; personal expenses: $1,690. **Financial aid:** Priority filing date for institution's financial aid form: April 15. In 2009-2010, 84% of undergraduates applied for financial aid. Of those, 73% were determined to have financial need; 19% had their need fully met. Average financial aid package (proportion receiving): $20,421 (73%). Average amount of gift aid, such as scholarships or grants (proportion receiving): $14,570 (73%). Average amount of self-help aid, such as work study or loans (proportion receiving): $5,340 (66%). Average need-based loan (excluding PLUS or other private loans): $4,601. Among students who received need-based aid, the average percentage of need met: 79%. Among students who received aid based on merit, the average award (and the proportion receiving): $5,888 (23%). The average athletic scholarship (and the proportion receiving): $0 (0%). Average amount of debt of borrowers graduating in 2009: $30,496. Proportion who borrowed: 80%.

CAMPUS LIFE AND EXTRACURRICULAR ACTIVITIES

Campus housing available (% using): coed dorms (98%), apartment for single students (1%), special housing for disabled students (1%). Students who live in college-owned, operated, or affiliated housing: 70%. **Student employment:** During the 2009-2010 academic year, 45% of undergraduates worked on campus. Average per-year earnings: $1,460. **Clubs and organizations:** Number of student organizations: 55. Activities include: campus ministries, choral groups, concert band, dance, drama/theater, international student organization, jazz band, literary magazine, music ensembles, musical theater, radio station, student government, student newspaper, student film society, symphony orchestra. Number of fraternities: 0; sororities: 0. Average proportion of students who stay on campus on weekends: 70%. **Sports program (2009-2010):** Member of NCAA III. *Men's intercollegiate varsity sports:* baseball, basketball, cross country, football, golf, ice hockey, soccer, tennis, track and field (indoor), track and field (outdoor). *Women's intercollegiate varsity sports:* basketball, cross country, golf, ice hockey, soccer, softball, tennis, track and field (indoor), track and field (outdoor), volleyball.

SERVICES AND FACILITIES

Basic services: nonremedial tutoring, placement service, day care, health service, health insurance. **Remedial assistance:** writing, study skills. **Counseling services:** minority student, career, military, personal, academic, older student, psychological, birth control, religious. **For learning-disabled students:** School does not offer a structured program with separate admission and additional fees. Services include: remedial math, reading machines, tape recorders, note-taking services, oral tests, learning center, readers, extended time for tests, tutors, priority registration, priority seating, texts on tape, other testing accommodations. **Library:** Number of titles: 194,000; number of current serial subscriptions: 38,080. **Information technology resources:** Students are not required to lease or own a computer. Number of campus computers available to all students: 420. School has a wireless network. Approximate number of users that can be accommodated: 3,000. Proportion of college-owned housing units wired for high-speed internet access: 100%. **Campus safety:** Security services offered: 24-hour foot-and-vehicle patrols, late-night transport/escort service, 24-hour emergency telephones, lighted pathways/sidewalks, student patrols, controlled dormitory access (key, security card, etc).

TRANSFER AND INTERNATIONAL STUDENTS

Transfer students: May apply for admission for the following academic terms: Fall, Winter, Spring. Applicants do not need a minimum number of credits to apply. For fall 2009: Transfer applications received: 378. Transfer applicants offered admission: 256. Transfer applicants enrolled: 148. **International students:** Number of foreign undergraduates: 12. Number of countries represented: 6. Minimum TOEFL score required: 525 (paper); 195 (computer).

Carleton College

- **Address:** 1 N. College Street, Northfield, MN 55057
- **Website:** http://www.carleton.edu
- **Private**
- **Enrollment:** 1,996 full-time; 13 part-time

KEY STATS
- ✔ **U.S News College Ranking:** 8, National Liberal Arts Colleges
- ✔ **SAT Score (25th/75th percentile):** 1320-1500
- ✔ **Tuition:** 2010-2011: $41,304

Selectivity: Most selective	**Room/board:** $10,806
Acceptance rate: 31%	**Average debt:** $18,601
Student/faculty ratio: 9/1	**Proportion who borrowed:** 54%

UNDERGRADUATE STUDENT BODY STATS

2009-2010 enrollment: 1,996 full-time; 13 part-time. Men: 48%; women: 52%. **Ethnic makeup:** African American: 5%; American-Indian: 1%; Asian American: 10%; Hispanic: 6%; White: 72%; International: 7%. **Religious preference:** Roman Catholic: 11%; Protestant: 28%; Jewish: 9%; Muslim: 1%; Hindu: 1%; Buddhist: 2%; No preference: 40%; Other: 8%.

ADMISSIONS FACTS AND FIGURES

Phone: (507) 222-4190. **Email:** admissions@carleton.edu. **Website:** http://www.carleton.edu. **Application deadlines for fall 2011:** Regular decision: January 15; decision sent by April 15. Early decision: Send application by: November 15; Decision sent by: December 15. Early action: Not offered. Admission can be deferred. **Application fee:** $30. **To apply online, go to:** http://apps.carleton.edu/admissions/overview/apply. **Admissions requirements/recommendations:** High school units required (recommended): English: (4); Mathematics: (3); Science: (3); Foreign language: (3); Social studies: (3). Tests: The college uses SAT or ACT scores in admissions decisions. Either SAT or ACT required. For admission to the fall 2011 entering class, the school will accept: ACT with writing required. Campus visit: Recommended. Admissions interview: Recommended. Off-campus interview: May be arranged. **Factors that count in admissions decisions:** *Academic:* Secondary school record: Very Important. Class rank: Very Important. Letters of recommendation: Important. Standardized test scores: Important. Essay: Important. *Nonacademic:* Interview: Considered. Extracurricular activities: Important. Talent/ability: Important. Character/personal qualities: Important. Alumni/ae relationship: Important. Geographical residence: Considered. State residency: Considered. Religious affiliation/commitment: Not Considered. Minority status: Important. Volunteer work: Important. Work experience: Important. **Other schools with the greatest overlap in applicants:** Brown University; Harvard University; Macalester College; Williams College; Yale University. **Admissions statistics for the fall 2009 entering class:** Total applicants: 4,784. Total accepted: 1,459. Freshmen enrolled: 529; 77% were from out of state. Accepted through early-decision or early-action plans: 39%. Overall acceptance rate: 31%. Early-decision acceptance rate: 53%. Non-early acceptance rate: 28%. **Size of waiting list:** N/A applicants; enrolled from waiting list: 0. **Credentials of fall 2009 freshmen:** 78% ranked in the top 10 percent of their high school class; 96% were in the top 25 percent; 100% were in the top half. (Proportion submitting class standing: 45%.) **First-year students who submitted SAT scores:** 69%. Scores (25/75 percentile): Critical Reading: 660-760, Math: 660-740, Combined: 1320-1500. **First-year students submitting ACT scores:** 59%. Scores (25/75 percentile): English: N/A, Math: N/A, Composite: 29-33.

ACADEMICS

Year founded: 1866. **Academic calendar:** Trimester. **Degrees offered:** bachelor's. **Most popular majors:** 22% social sciences, 14% physical sciences, 12% biological and biomedical sciences, 8% English language and literature/letters, 8% history. **Major fields of study:** area, ethnic, cultural, and gender studies; biological and biomedical sciences; computer and information sciences and support services; English language and literature/letters; foreign languages, literatures, and linguistics; history; mathematics and statistics; philosophy and religious studies; physical sciences; psychology; social sciences; visual and performing arts. **Areas of required coursework:** arts/fine arts, humanities, mathematics, English (including composition), foreign languages, sciences (biological or physical), social science, other. **Preprofessional programs:** pre-law, pre-dentistry, pre-medicine, pre-theology, pre-veterinary science, pre-optometry, pre-pharmacy. **Special academic programs (% participation):** accelerated program (10%), cross-registration

(3%), double major (7%), independent study (100%), internships (44%), student-designed major (3%), study abroad (71%), teacher certificate program (2%). **Teacher certification offered in:** elementary, middle/junior high, secondary. **Cooperative education programs:** education, engineering, other. **Faculty and instruction (2009-2010):** Total instructional faculty: 217 full-time, 21 part-time (56% men; 44% women; 21% minorities). Full-time faculty with Ph.D. or other terminal degree: 95%. Student/faculty ratio: 9/1. Classes of fewer than 20 students: 60%; of 20 to 49 students: 38%; of 50 or more students: 1%. **Advanced Placement and International Baccalaureate credit:** AP tests may be used for: Credit and/or placement. Scores accepted: 3, 4, 5. International Baccalaureate exams may be used for: Credit and/or placement. **Freshmen returning for sophomore year:** 97%. **Graduation rates:** Four-year: 89%; five-year: 92%; six-year: 92%. **Graduate study:** 21% of students pursue further study immediately upon graduation; 74% within five years. Fields in which graduates pursue further study: Master of Business Administration (MBA), 7%; law, 10%; medicine, 6%; dentistry, 1%; engineering, 3%; theology (or the seminary), 1%; education, 1%; arts and sciences, 47%; veterinary medicine, 1%.

COSTS AND FINANCIAL AID

Financial aid office: (507) 646-4138. **Expenses (2010-2011):** Tuition and fees 2010-2011: $41,304; room/board: $10,806. Estimated books and supplies: $728; transportation: $700; personal expenses: $727. **Financial aid:** Priority filing date for institution's financial aid form: February 15; deadline: February 15. In 2009-2010, 87% of undergraduates applied for financial aid. Of those, 56% were determined to have financial need; 100% had their need fully met. Average financial aid package (proportion receiving): $34,141 (56%). Average amount of gift aid, such as scholarships or grants (proportion receiving): $27,989 (56%). Average amount of self-help aid, such as work study or loans (proportion receiving): $6,453 (55%). Average need-based loan (excluding PLUS or other private loans): $4,802. Among students who received need-based aid, the average percentage of need met: 100%. Among students who received aid based on merit, the average award (and the proportion receiving): $2,644 (7%). The average athletic scholarship (and the proportion receiving): $0 (0%). Average amount of debt of borrowers graduating in 2009: $18,601. Proportion who borrowed: 54%.

CAMPUS LIFE AND EXTRACURRICULAR ACTIVITIES

Campus housing available (% using): coed dorms (80%), apartment for single students (6%), special housing for disabled students (0%), other housing options (5%). Students who live in college-owned, operated, or affiliated housing: 95%. **Student employment:** During the 2009-2010 academic year, 79% of undergraduates worked on campus. Average per-year earnings: $1,747. **Clubs and organizations:** Number of student organizations: 196. Activities include: campus ministries, choral groups, concert band, dance, drama/theater, international student organization, jazz band, literary magazine, model UN, music ensembles, musical theater, radio station, student government, student newspaper, student film society, symphony orchestra, yearbook. Number of fraternities: 0; sororities: 0. Average proportion of students who stay on campus on weekends: 97%. **Sports program (2009-2010):** Member of NCAA III. **Men's intercollegiate varsity sports:** baseball, basketball, cross country, football, golf, soccer, swimming, tennis, track and field (outdoor). **Women's intercollegiate varsity sports:** basketball, cross country, golf, soccer, softball, swimming, tennis, track and field (outdoor), volleyball.

SERVICES AND FACILITIES

Basic services: nonremedial tutoring, women's center, placement service, health service, health insurance. **Counseling services:** minority student, career, personal, academic, psychological, birth control, religious, other. **For learning-disabled students:** School does not offer a structured program with separate admission and additional fees. Services include: reading machines, tape recorders, note-taking services, learning center, extended time for tests, tutors, texts on tape, other testing accommodations. **Library:** Number of titles: 1,055,151; number of current serial subscriptions: 22,035. **Information technology resources:** Students are not required to lease or own a computer. Number of campus computers available to all students: 565. School has a wireless network. Approximate number of users that can be accommodated: 1,000. Proportion of college-owned housing units wired for high-speed internet access: 100%. **Campus safety:** Security services offered: 24-hour foot-and-vehicle patrols, late-night transport/escort service, 24-hour emergency telephones, lighted pathways/sidewalks, student patrols, controlled dormitory access (key, security card, etc).

TRANSFER AND INTERNATIONAL STUDENTS

Transfer students: May apply for admission for the following academic terms: Fall. Applicants need a minimum number of credits to apply. For fall 2009: Transfer applications received: 215. Transfer applicants offered admission: 19. Transfer applicants enrolled: 10. **International students:** Number of foreign undergraduates: 142 (7% of student body). Number of countries represented: 32. Minimum TOEFL score required: 600 (paper); 100 (computer).

College of St. Benedict

- **Address:** 37 S. College Avenue, St. Joseph, MN 56374
- **Website:** http://www.csbsju.edu
- **Private; Religious affiliation:** Roman Catholic (Benedictine)
- **Enrollment:** 2,057 full-time; 49 part-time

KEY STATS

✔ **U.S News College Ranking:** 81, National Liberal Arts Colleges
✔ **ACT Score (25th/75th percentile):** 23-28
✔ **Tuition:** 2010-2011: $32,246

Selectivity: More selective	**Room/board:** $8,652
Acceptance rate: 85%	**Average debt:** N/A
Student/faculty ratio: 12/1	**Proportion who borrowed:** N/A

UNDERGRADUATE STUDENT BODY STATS

2009-2010 enrollment: 2,057 full-time; 49 part-time. Men: 0%; women: 100%. **Ethnic makeup:** African American: 1%; Asian American: 4%; Hispanic: 2%; White: 87%; International: 6%. **Religious preference:** Protestant: 19%; No preference: 17%; Roman Catholic (Benedictine): 63%; Other: 1%.

ADMISSIONS FACTS AND FIGURES

Phone: (320) 363-2196. **Email:** admissions@csbsju.edu. **Website:** http://www.csbsju.edu. **Application deadlines for fall 2011:** Regular decision: Rolling. Early decision: Not offered. Early action: Send application by: November 15; Decision sent by: December 15. Admission can be deferred. **To apply online, go to:** http://www.csbsju.edu/admission/. **Admissions requirements/recommendations:** High school units required (recommended): English: 4 (0); Mathematics: 3 (0); Science: 2 (0); Foreign language: 0 (2); Social studies: 2 (0); History: 0 (0); Academic electives: 4 (0); Total units: 15 (2). Tests: The college uses SAT or ACT scores in admissions decisions. Either SAT or ACT required. For admission to the fall 2011 entering class, the school will accept: ACT with or without writing accepted. Campus visit: Recommended. Admissions interview: Recommended. Off-campus interview: May be arranged. **Factors that count in admissions decisions: *Academic:*** Secondary school record: Very Important. Class rank: Considered. Letters of recommendation: Important. Standardized test scores: Very Important. Essay: Very Important. ***Nonacademic:*** Interview: Considered. Extracurricular activities: Important. Talent/ability: Considered. Character/personal qualities: Considered. Alumni/ae relationship: Considered. Geographical residence: Considered. State residency: Not Considered. Religious affiliation/commitment: Not Considered. Minority status: Considered. Volunteer work: Considered. Work experience: Considered. **Other schools with the greatest overlap in applicants:** Gustavus Adolphus College; St. Olaf College; University of Minnesota–Duluth; University of Minnesota–Twin Cities; University of St. Thomas. **Admissions statistics for the fall 2009 entering class:** Total applicants: 1,604. Total accepted: 1,369. Freshmen enrolled: 551; 19% were from out of state. Accepted through early-decision or early-action plans: 86%. Overall acceptance rate: 85%. Non-early acceptance rate: 66%. **Size of waiting list:** 0 applicants; enrolled from waiting list: 0. **Credentials of fall 2009 freshmen:** 40% ranked in the top 10 percent of their high school class; 76% were in the top 25 percent; 97% were in the top half. (Proportion submitting class standing: 75%.) **Average high school grade point average:** 3.7. **First-year students who submitted SAT scores:** 14%. Scores (25/75 percentile): Critical Reading: 510-660, Math: 510-670, Combined: 1020-1330. **First-year students submitting ACT scores:** 96%. Scores (25/75 percentile): English: 23-29, Math: 23-28, Composite: 23-28.

ACADEMICS

Year founded: 1887. **Academic calendar:** Semester. **Degrees offered:** bachelor's. **Most popular majors:** 11% biology/biological sciences, 11% speech and rhetorical studies, 10% psychology, 8% business administration and management, 8% nursing/registered nurse training (R.N., A.S.N., B.S.N., M.S.N.). **Major fields of study:** area, ethnic, cultural, and gender studies; biological and biomedical sciences; business, management, marketing, and related support services; computer and information sciences and support services; education; English language and literature/letters; foreign languages, literatures, and linguistics; health professions and related clinical sciences; history; liberal arts and sciences studies, and humanities; mathematics and statistics; multi/interdisciplinary studies; natural resources and conservation; philosophy and religious studies; physical sciences; psychology; public administration and social service professions; social sciences; theology and religious vocations; visual and performing arts. **Areas of required coursework:** arts/fine arts, humanities, mathematics, English (including composition), foreign languages, sciences (biological or physical), social science. **Pre-professional programs:** pre-law, pre-dentistry, pre-medicine, pre-theology, pre-veterinary science, pre-optometry, pre-pharmacy, other. **Special academic programs (% participation):** cross-registration (100%), double major (11%), dual enrollment (1%), English as a Second Language (ESL) (3%), honors program (15%), independent study (19%), internships (66%), liberal arts/career combination (33%), student-designed major (1%), study abroad (64%), teacher certificate program (12%). **Teacher certification offered in:** elementary, middle/junior high, secondary. **Reserve Officers Training Corps (ROTC):** Army ROTC: Offered at cooperating institution (St. John's University). **Faculty and instruction (2009-2010):** Total instructional faculty: 159 full-time, 34 part-time (53% men; 47% women; 8% minorities). Full-time faculty with Ph.D. or other terminal degree: 84%. Student/faculty ratio: 12/1. Classes of fewer than 20 students: 53%; of 20 to 49 students: 47%; of 50 or more students: 0%. **Advanced Placement and International Baccalaureate credit:** AP tests may be used for: Credit and/or placement. Scores accepted: 3, 4, 5. International Baccalaureate exams may be used for: Credit and/or placement. **Freshmen returning for sophomore year:** 90%. **Graduation rates:** Four-year: 73%; five-year: 78%; six-year: 78%. **Graduate study:** 21% of students pursue further study within one year. Fields in which graduates pursue further study: Master of Business Administration (MBA), 2%; law, 7%; medicine, 11%; dentistry, 5%; engineering, 1%; theology (or the seminary), 1%; education, 3%; arts and sciences, 70%.

COSTS AND FINANCIAL AID

Financial aid office: (320) 363-5388. **Expenses (2010-2011):** Tuition and fees 2010-2011: $32,246; room/board: $8,652. Estimated books and supplies: $1,000; transportation: $400; personal expenses: $900. **Financial aid:** Priority filing date for institution's financial aid form: March 15. In 2009-2010, 75% of undergraduates applied for financial aid. Of those, 66% were determined to have financial need; 39% had their need fully met. Average financial aid package (proportion receiving): $23,152 (66%). Average amount of gift aid, such as scholarships or grants (proportion receiving): $17,595 (65%). Average amount of self-help aid, such as work study or loans (proportion receiving): $6,435 (61%). Average need-based loan (excluding PLUS or other private loans): $4,405. Among students who received need-based aid, the average percentage of need met: 88%. Among students who received aid based on merit, the average award (and the proportion receiving): $10,821 (29%). The average athletic scholarship (and the proportion receiving): $0 (0%).

CAMPUS LIFE AND EXTRACURRICULAR ACTIVITIES

Campus housing available (% using): women's dorms (67%), apartment for single students (33%), special housing for disabled students. Students who live in college-owned, operated, or affiliated housing: 80%. **Student employment:** During the 2009-2010 academic year, 60% of undergraduates worked on campus. Average per-year earnings: $2,600. **Clubs and organizations:** Number of student organizations: 80. Activities include: campus ministries, choral groups, concert band, dance, drama/theater, international student organization, jazz band, literary magazine, model UN, music ensembles, musical theater, opera, pep band, radio station, student government, student newspaper, symphony orchestra. Number of fraternities: 0; sororities: 0. **Sports program (2009-2010):** Member of NCAA III. *Women's intercollegiate varsity sports:* basketball, cross country, golf, ice hockey, skiing (nordic), soccer, softball, swimming, tennis, track and field (indoor), track and field (outdoor), volleyball.

SERVICES AND FACILITIES

Basic services: nonremedial tutoring, women's center, placement service, health service, health insurance. **Remedial assistance:** math, study skills, other. **Counseling services:** minority student, career, personal, academic, psychological, religious. **For learning-disabled students:** School does not offer a structured program with separate admission and additional fees. Total undergraduates in learning-disabled program or receiving services: 53. Services include: reading machines, note-taking services, extended time for tests, tutors, priority registration, priority seating, substitution of courses,

texts on tape, typist/scribe, exams on tape or computer, other testing accommodations, other. **Library:** Number of titles: 658,438; number of current serial subscriptions: 71,720. **Information technology resources:** Students are not required to lease or own a computer. Number of campus computers available to all students: 860. School has a wireless network. Approximate number of users that can be accommodated: 2,000. Proportion of college-owned housing units wired for high-speed internet access: 100%. **Campus safety:** Security services offered: 24-hour foot-and-vehicle patrols, late-night transport/escort service, 24-hour emergency telephones, lighted pathways/sidewalks, student patrols, controlled dormitory access (key, security card, etc).

TRANSFER AND INTERNATIONAL STUDENTS

Transfer students: May apply for admission for the following academic terms: Fall, Spring. Applicants do not need a minimum number of credits to apply. For fall 2009: Transfer applications received: 71. Transfer applicants offered admission: 48. Transfer applicants enrolled: 28. **International students:** Number of foreign undergraduates: 130 (6% of student body). Number of countries represented: 29. Minimum TOEFL score required: 500 (paper); 173 (computer). Average TOEFL score: 500 (paper).

College of St. Scholastica

- ■ **Address:** 1200 Kenwood Avenue, Duluth, MN 55811
- ■ **Website:** http://www.css.edu
- ■ **Private; Religious affiliation:** Roman Catholic
- ■ **Enrollment:** 2,566 full-time; 255 part-time

KEY STATS
- ✔ **U.S News College Ranking:** 24, Regional Universities (Midwest)
- ✔ **ACT Score (25th/75th percentile):** 21-26
- ✔ **Tuition:** 2010-2011: $28,370

Selectivity: Selective	**Room/board:** $7,498
Acceptance rate: 85%	**Average debt:** $40,401
Student/faculty ratio: 14/1	**Proportion who borrowed:** 81%

UNDERGRADUATE STUDENT BODY STATS

2009-2010 enrollment: 2,566 full-time; 255 part-time. Men: 31%; women: 69%. **Ethnic makeup:** African American: 2%; American-Indian: 3%; Asian American: 1%; Hispanic: 1%; White: 90%; International: 3%. **Religious preference:** Protestant: 22%; No preference: 28%; Roman Catholic: 30%.

ADMISSIONS FACTS AND FIGURES

Phone: (218) 723-6046. **Email:** admissions@css.edu. **Website:** http://www.css.edu. **Application deadlines for fall 2011:** Regular decision: Rolling. Early decision: Not offered. Early action: Not offered. Admission can be deferred. **Application fee:** $25. **To apply online, go to:** https://www2.css.edu/app/admissions/new_apply.cfm. **Admissions requirements/recommendations:** High school units required (recommended): English: (4); Mathematics: (2); Science: (3); Foreign language: (3); Social studies: (3); History: (3); Total units: (18). Tests: The college uses SAT or ACT scores in admissions decisions. Either SAT or ACT required. For admission to the fall 2011 entering class, the school will accept: ACT with or without writing accepted. Campus visit: Recommended. Admissions interview: Recommended. Off-campus interview: May be arranged. **Factors that count in admissions decisions:** *Academic:* Secondary school record: Important. Class rank: Important. Letters of recommendation: Considered. Standardized test scores: Very Important. Essay: Considered. *Nonacademic:* Interview: Considered. Extracurricular activities: Not Considered. Talent/ability: Not Considered. Character/personal qualities: Not Considered. Alumni/ae relationship: Not Considered. Geographical residence: Not Considered. State residency: Not Considered. Religious affiliation/commitment: Not Considered. Minority status: Not Considered. Volunteer work: Not Considered. Work experience: Not Considered. **Other schools with the greatest overlap in applicants:** College of St. Benedict; Concordia College–Moorhead; St. John's University; University of Minnesota–Duluth; University of St. Thomas. **Admissions statistics for the fall 2009 entering class:** Total applicants: 1,864. Total accepted: 1,581. Freshmen enrolled: 536; 14% were from out of state. Overall acceptance rate: 85%. **Credentials of fall 2009 freshmen:** 23% ranked in the top 10 percent of their high school class; 54% were in the top 25 percent; 85% were in the top half. (Proportion submitting class standing: 81%.) **Average high school grade point average:** 3.5. **First-year students who submitted SAT scores:** 3%. Scores (25/75 percentile): Critical Reading:

460-610, Math: 490-670, Combined: 950-1280. **First-year students submitting ACT scores:** 90%. Scores (25/75 percentile): English: N/A, Math: N/A, Composite: 21-26.

ACADEMICS

Year founded: 1912. **Academic calendar:** Semester. **Degrees offered:** certificate, bachelor's, post-bachelor's certificate, master's, post-master's certificate. **Major fields of study:** biological and biomedical sciences; business, management, marketing, and related support services; communication, journalism, and related programs; computer and information sciences and support services; education; English language and literature/letters; health professions and related clinical sciences; history; liberal arts and sciences studies, and humanities; mathematics and statistics; multi/interdisciplinary studies; philosophy and religious studies; physical sciences; psychology; public administration and social service professions; social sciences; visual and performing arts. **Areas of required coursework:** arts/fine arts, mathematics, English (including composition), philosophy, foreign languages, sciences (biological or physical), history, social science, other. **Pre-professional programs:** pre-law, pre-dentistry, pre-medicine, pre-veterinary science, pre-optometry, pre-pharmacy, other. **Special academic programs:** accelerated program, cross-registration, distance learning, double major, dual enrollment, honors program, independent study, internships, liberal arts/career combination, student-designed major, study abroad, teacher certificate program. **Teacher certification offered in:** elementary, middle/junior high, secondary. **Reserve Officers Training Corps (ROTC):** Air Force ROTC: Offered at cooperating institution (University of Minnesota–Duluth). **Faculty and instruction (2009-2010):** Total instructional faculty: 166 full-time, 199 part-time (42% men; 58% women). Full-time faculty with Ph.D. or other terminal degree: 57%. Student/faculty ratio: 14/1. Classes of fewer than 20 students: 60%; of 20 to 49 students: 37%; of 50 or more students: 3%. **Advanced Placement and International Baccalaureate credit:** AP tests may be used for: Credit and/or placement. Scores accepted: 3, 4, 5. International Baccalaureate exams may be used for: Credit and/or placement. **Freshmen returning for sophomore year:** 80%. **Graduation rates:** Four-year: 62%; five-year: 69%; six-year: 67%. **Graduate study:** 27% of students pursue further study immediately upon graduation.

COSTS AND FINANCIAL AID

Financial aid office: (218) 723-6047. **Expenses (2010-2011):** Tuition and fees 2010-2011: $28,370; room/board: $7,498. Estimated books and supplies: $1,100; transportation: $690; personal expenses: $1,094. **Financial aid:** Priority filing date for institution's financial aid form: March 1. In 2009-2010, 92% of undergraduates applied for financial aid. Of those, 79% were determined to have financial need; 14% had their need fully met. Average financial aid package (proportion receiving): $21,625 (78%). Average amount of gift aid, such as scholarships or grants (proportion receiving): $7,011 (65%). Average amount of self-help aid, such as work study or loans (proportion receiving): $5,209 (61%). Average need-based loan (excluding PLUS or other private loans): $4,381. Among students who received need-based aid, the average percentage of need met: 77%. Among students who received aid based on merit, the average award (and the proportion receiving): $10,496 (8%). Average amount of debt of borrowers graduating in 2009: $40,401. Proportion who borrowed: 81%.

CAMPUS LIFE AND EXTRACURRICULAR ACTIVITIES

Campus housing available (% using): coed dorms (39%), apartment for single students (61%), special housing for disabled students (0%), special housing for international students (0%), other housing options (0%). Students who live in college-owned, operated, or affiliated housing: 49%. **Student employment:** During the 2009-2010 academic year, 29% of undergraduates worked on campus. Average per-year earnings: $2,363. **Clubs and organizations:** Number of student organizations: 68. Activities include: campus ministries, choral groups, concert band, dance, drama/theater, international student organization, jazz band, literary magazine, music ensembles, pep band, student government, student newspaper, television station. Number of fraternities: 0; sororities: 0. Average proportion of students who stay on campus on weekends: 51%. **Sports program (2009-2010):** Member of NCAA III. **Men's intercollegiate varsity sports:** baseball, basketball, cross country, football, ice hockey, skiing (nordic), soccer, tennis, track and field (indoor), track and field (outdoor). **Women's intercollegiate varsity sports:** basketball, cross country, ice hockey, skiing (nordic), soccer, softball, tennis, track and field (indoor), track and field (outdoor), volleyball.

SERVICES AND FACILITIES

Basic services: nonremedial tutoring, placement service, health service, health insurance. **Remedial assistance:** study skills. **Counseling services:**

minority student, career, military, personal, veteran student, academic, older student, psychological, religious. **For learning-disabled students:** School does not offer a structured program with separate admission and additional fees. Total undergraduates in learning-disabled program or receiving services: 22. Services include: reading machines, tape recorders, note-taking services, oral tests, readers, extended time for tests, tutors, priority registration, texts on tape, other testing accommodations, other. **Library:** Number of titles: 152,843; number of current serial subscriptions: 48,087. **Information technology resources:** Students are not required to lease or own a computer. Number of campus computers available to all students: 407. School has a wireless network. Approximate number of users that can be accommodated: 1,400. Proportion of college-owned housing units wired for high-speed internet access: 100%. **Campus safety:** Security services offered: 24-hour foot-and-vehicle patrols, late-night transport/escort service, 24-hour emergency telephones, lighted pathways/sidewalks, controlled dormitory access (key, security card, etc).

TRANSFER AND INTERNATIONAL STUDENTS

Transfer students: May apply for admission for the following academic terms: Fall, Spring, Summer. Applicants need a minimum number of credits to apply. For fall 2009: Transfer applications received: 359. Transfer applicants offered admission: 250. Transfer applicants enrolled: 131. **International students:** Number of foreign undergraduates: 97 (4% of student body). Number of countries represented: 34. Minimum TOEFL score required: 550 (paper); 213 (computer). Average TOEFL score: 552 (paper).

College of Visual Arts

- **Address:** 344 Summit Avenue, St. Paul, MN 55102
- **Website:** http://www.cva.edu
- **Private**
- **Enrollment:** 180 full-time; 6 part-time

KEY STATS

✔ **U.S News College Ranking:** Unranked Specialty School–Fine Arts
✔ **ACT Score (25th/75th percentile):** 18-24
✔ **Tuition:** 2010-2011: $23,988

Selectivity: N/A	**Room/board:** N/A
Acceptance rate: 67%	**Average debt:** $38,402
Student/faculty ratio: N/A	**Proportion who borrowed:** 88%

UNDERGRADUATE STUDENT BODY STATS

2009-2010 enrollment: 180 full-time; 6 part-time. Men: 34%; women: 66%. **Ethnic makeup:** African American: 1%; American-Indian: 1%; Asian American: 4%; Hispanic: 1%; White: 90%; International: 1%.

ADMISSIONS FACTS AND FIGURES

Phone: (651) 757-4000. **Email:** admissions@cva.edu. **Website:** http://www.cva.edu. **Application deadlines for fall 2011:** Regular decision: Rolling. Early decision: Not offered. Early action: Not offered. Admission can be deferred. **Application fee:** $40. **To apply online, go to:** https://secure.factorof4.net/cva/application_form.htm. **Admissions requirements/recommendations:** High school units required (recommended): English: (4); Mathematics: (3); Science: (3); Foreign language: (2); Social studies: (3); History: (3). Tests: The college uses SAT or ACT scores in admissions decisions. Either SAT or ACT required. For admission to the fall 2011 entering class, the school will accept: ACT with or without writing accepted. Campus visit: Recommended. Admissions interview: Recommended. Off-campus interview: May be arranged. **Factors that count in admissions decisions:** *Academic:* Secondary school record: Important. Class rank: Considered. Letters of recommendation: Considered. Standardized test scores: Considered. Essay: Considered. *Nonacademic:* Interview: Not Considered. Extracurricular activities: Not Considered. Talent/ability: Very Important. Character/personal qualities: Considered. Alumni/ae relationship: Considered. Geographical residence: Considered. State residency: Not Considered. Religious affiliation/commitment: Not Considered. Minority status: Considered. Volunteer work: Considered. Work experience: Considered. **Other schools with the greatest overlap in applicants:** Minneapolis College of Art and Design; University of Minnesota–Twin Cities; University of Wisconsin–Stout. **Admissions statistics for the fall 2009 entering class:** Total applicants: 139. Total accepted: 93. Freshmen enrolled: 51; Overall acceptance rate: 67%. **Credentials of fall 2009 freshmen:** 14% ranked in the top 25 percent of their high school class. **First-year students who submitted SAT scores:** 2%. **First-year students**

submitting ACT scores: 98%. Scores (25/75 percentile): English: N/A, Math: N/A, Composite: N/A.

ACADEMICS

Year founded: 1924. **Academic calendar:** Semester. **Degrees offered:** bachelor's. **Most popular majors:** 32% graphic design, 30% fine/studio arts, 19% illustration, 19% photography. **Major fields of study:** visual and performing arts. **Areas of required coursework:** arts/fine arts, humanities, computer literacy, mathematics, English (including composition), sciences (biological or physical), social science, other. **Special academic programs (% participation):** honors program (8%), independent study (0%), internships (100%), study abroad (0%). **Faculty and instruction (2009-2010):** Total instructional faculty: N/A. Classes of fewer than 20 students: 91%; of 20 to 49 students: 9%. **Advanced Placement and International Baccalaureate credit:** AP tests may be used for: Credit and/or placement. Scores accepted: 4, 5. **Freshmen returning for sophomore year:** 69%. **Graduation rates:** Four-year: 24%; five-year: 26%; six-year: 29%.

COSTS AND FINANCIAL AID

Financial aid office: (651) 224-3416. **Expenses (2010-2011):** Tuition and fees 2010-2011: $23,988. **Financial aid:** Priority filing date for institution's financial aid form: April 15; deadline: June 1. In 2009-2010, 94% of undergraduates applied for financial aid. Of those, 87% were determined to have financial need; 2% had their need fully met. Average financial aid package (proportion receiving): $14,826 (87%). Average amount of gift aid, such as scholarships or grants (proportion receiving): $9,863 (87%). Average amount of self-help aid, such as work study or loans (proportion receiving): $4,488 (87%). Average need-based loan (excluding PLUS or other private loans): $4,488. Among students who received need-based aid, the average percentage of need met: 53%. Among students who received aid based on merit, the average award (and the proportion receiving): $2,431 (7%). The average athletic scholarship (and the proportion receiving): $0 (0%). Average amount of debt of borrowers graduating in 2009: $38,402. Proportion who borrowed: 88%.

CAMPUS LIFE AND EXTRACURRICULAR ACTIVITIES

Student employment: During the 2009-2010 academic year, 28% of undergraduates worked on campus. Average per-year earnings: $2,000. **Clubs and organizations:** Number of student organizations: 4. Activities include: student government. Number of fraternities: 0; sororities: 0.

SERVICES AND FACILITIES

Remedial assistance: reading, writing, study skills. **Counseling services:** minority student, career, academic, older student. **For learning-disabled students:** School does not offer a structured program with separate admission and additional fees. Services include: remedial English, tape recorders, learning center, extended time for tests, priority seating, other testing accommodations. **Library:** Number of titles: 9,258; number of current serial subscriptions: 40. **Information technology resources:** Students are not required to lease or own a computer. Number of campus computers available to all students: 60. School does not have a wireless network. **Campus safety:** Security services offered: late-night transport/escort service.

TRANSFER AND INTERNATIONAL STUDENTS

Transfer students: May apply for admission for the following academic terms: Fall, Spring, Summer. Applicants do not need a minimum number of credits to apply. **International students:** Number of foreign undergraduates: 2 (1% of student body). Number of countries represented: 2. Minimum TOEFL score required: 500 (paper); 173 (computer).

Concordia College—Moorhead

- **Address:** 901 Eighth Street S, Moorhead, MN 56562
- **Website:** http://www.cord.edu
- **Private; Religious affiliation:** Evangelical Lutheran Church in America
- **Enrollment:** 2,740 full-time; 48 part-time

KEY STATS

- ✔ **U.S News College Ranking:** 137, National Liberal Arts Colleges
- ✔ **ACT Score (25th/75th percentile):** 22-28
- ✔ **Tuition:** 2010-2011: $27,160

Selectivity: More selective	**Room/board:** $6,510
Acceptance rate: 79%	**Average debt:** $30,720
Student/faculty ratio: 13/1	**Proportion who borrowed:** 83%

UNDERGRADUATE STUDENT BODY STATS

2009-2010 enrollment: 2,740 full-time; 48 part-time. Men: 39%; women: 61%. **Ethnic makeup:** African American: 1%; Asian American: 1%; Hispanic: 1%; White: 94%; International: 3%. **Religious preference:** Roman Catholic: 17%; Protestant: 9%; No preference: 5%; Unknown: 8%; Evangelical Lutheran Church in America: 51%; Baptist: 2%; Other: 8%.

ADMISSIONS FACTS AND FIGURES

Phone: (800) 699-9897. **Email:** admissions@cord.edu. **Website:** http://www.cord.edu. **Application deadlines for fall 2011:** Regular decision: Rolling. Early decision: Not offered. Early action: Not offered. Admission can be deferred. **Application fee:** $20. **To apply online, go to:** https://www.cord.edu/dept/admissions/apply/application/index.php. **Admissions requirements/recommendations:** High school units required (recommended): English: (4); Mathematics: (3); Science: (3); Foreign language: (2); Social studies: (3); Total units: 15 (17). Tests: The college uses SAT or ACT scores in admissions decisions. Either SAT or ACT required. For admission to the fall 2011 entering class, the school will accept: ACT with or without writing accepted. Campus visit: Recommended. Admissions interview: Recommended. Off-campus interview: May be arranged. **Factors that count in admissions decisions:** *Academic:* Secondary school record: Very Important. Class rank: Considered. Letters of recommendation: Important. Standardized test scores: Important. Essay: Considered. *Nonacademic:* Interview: Considered. Extracurricular activities: Considered. Talent/ability: Considered. Character/personal qualities: Considered. Alumni/ae relationship: Considered. Geographical residence: Not Considered. State residency: Not Considered. Religious affiliation/commitment: Considered. Minority status: Considered. Volunteer work: Considered. Work experience: Considered. **Other schools with the greatest overlap in applicants:** Gustavus Adolphus College; Minnesota State University–Moorhead; North Dakota State University; University of Minnesota–Twin Cities; University of North Dakota. **Admissions statistics for the fall 2009 entering class:** Total applicants: 2,851. Total accepted: 2,254. Freshmen enrolled: 726; 34% were from out of state. Overall acceptance rate: 79%. **Credentials of fall 2009 freshmen:** 32% ranked in the top 10 percent of their high school class; 66% were in the top 25 percent; 91% were in the top half. (Proportion submitting class standing: 86%.) **Average high school grade point average:** 3.6. **First-year students who submitted SAT scores:** 10%. Scores (25/75 percentile): Critical Reading: 510-680, Math: 523-658, Combined: 1033-1338. **First-year students submitting ACT scores:** 95%. Scores (25/75 percentile): English: 22-29, Math: 22-28, Composite: 22-28.

ACADEMICS

Year founded: 1891. **Academic calendar:** Semester. **Degrees offered:** bachelor's, master's. **Most popular majors:** 10% education, 9% communication and media studies, 8% biology, 6% business administration, management, and operations, 4% Romance languages, literatures, and linguistics. **Major fields of study:** biological and biomedical sciences; business, management, marketing, and related support services; communication, journalism, and related programs; computer and information sciences and support services; education; English language and literature/letters; family and consumer sciences/human sciences; foreign languages, literatures, and linguistics; health professions and related clinical sciences; history; mathematics and statistics; parks, recreation, leisure, and fitness studies; philosophy and religious studies; physical sciences; psychology; public administration and social service professions; social sciences; theology and religious vocations; visual and performing arts. **Areas of required coursework:** arts/fine arts, humanities, mathematics, English (including composition), foreign languages, sciences (biological or physical), social science, other. **Pre-professional programs:**

pre-law, pre-dentistry, pre-medicine, pre-veterinary science, pre-optometry, pre-pharmacy, other. **Special academic programs (% participation):** cooperative (work-study plan) program (37%), double major (29%), exchange student program (domestic), honors program (12%), independent study (31%), internships (30%), study abroad (40%), teacher certificate program (16%). **Teacher certification offered in:** early childhood, elementary, middle/junior high, secondary. **Cooperative education programs:** art, business, computer science, education, health professions, humanities, natural science, social/behavioral science. **Reserve Officers Training Corps (ROTC):** Army ROTC: Offered at cooperating institution (North Dakota State University); Air Force ROTC: Offered at cooperating institution (North Dakota State University). **Faculty and instruction (2009-2010):** Total instructional faculty: 194 full-time, 54 part-time (52% men; 48% women; 6% minorities). Full-time faculty with Ph.D. or other terminal degree: 81%. Student/faculty ratio: 13/1. Classes of fewer than 20 students: 48%; of 20 to 49 students: 50%; of 50 or more students: 2%. **Advanced Placement and International Baccalaureate credit:** AP tests may be used for: Credit and/or placement. Scores accepted: 3, 4, 5. International Baccalaureate exams may be used for: Credit only. **Freshmen returning for sophomore year:** 82%. **Graduation rates:** Four-year: 56%; five-year: 64%; six-year: 67%. **Graduate study:** 20% of students pursue further study immediately upon graduation; 24% within one year. Fields in which graduates pursue further study: Master of Business Administration (MBA), 3%; law, 5%; medicine, 12%; dentistry, 6%; engineering, 2%; theology (or the seminary), 6%; education, 1%; arts and sciences, 5%.

COSTS AND FINANCIAL AID

Financial aid office: (218) 299-3010. **Expenses (2010-2011):** Tuition and fees 2010-2011: $27,160; room/board: $6,510. Estimated books and supplies: $900; transportation: $850; personal expenses: $1,170. **Financial aid:** Priority filing date for institution's financial aid form: April 15. In 2009-2010, 83% of undergraduates applied for financial aid. Of those, 71% were determined to have financial need; 15% had their need fully met. Average financial aid package (proportion receiving): $20,465 (71%). Average amount of gift aid, such as scholarships or grants (proportion receiving): $14,278 (69%). Average amount of self-help aid, such as work study or loans (proportion receiving): $5,592 (62%). Average need-based loan (excluding PLUS or other private loans): $4,708. Among students who received need-based aid, the average percentage of need met: 76%. Among students who received aid based on merit, the average award (and the proportion receiving): $9,005 (19%). The average athletic scholarship (and the proportion receiving): $0 (0%). Average amount of debt of borrowers graduating in 2009: $30,720. Proportion who borrowed: 83%.

CAMPUS LIFE AND EXTRACURRICULAR ACTIVITIES

Campus housing available (% using): coed dorms (59%), women's dorms (15%), apartment for single students (20%). Students who live in college-owned, operated, or affiliated housing: 67%. **Student employment:** During the 2009-2010 academic year, 47% of undergraduates worked on campus. Average per-year earnings: $1,172. **Clubs and organizations:** Number of student organizations: 108. Activities include: campus ministries, choral groups, concert band, dance, drama/theater, international student organization, jazz band, literary magazine, music ensembles, musical theater, pep band, radio station, student government, student newspaper, symphony orchestra, television station, yearbook. Number of fraternities: 0; sororities: 0. **Sports program (2009-2010):** Member of NCAA III. *Men's intercollegiate varsity sports:* baseball, basketball, cross country, football, golf, ice hockey, soccer, tennis, track and field (indoor), track and field (outdoor), wrestling. *Women's intercollegiate varsity sports:* basketball, cross country, golf, ice hockey, soccer, softball, swimming, tennis, track and field (indoor), track and field (outdoor), volleyball.

SERVICES AND FACILITIES

Basic services: nonremedial tutoring, women's center, placement service, day care, health service, health insurance, other. **Remedial assistance:** study skills. **Counseling services:** minority student, career, personal, veteran student, academic, older student, psychological, birth control, religious. **For learning-disabled students:** School does not offer a structured program with separate admission and additional fees. Total undergraduates in learning-disabled program or receiving services: 9. Services include: tape recorders, note-taking services, learning center, readers, extended time for tests, tutors, priority registration, priority seating, texts on tape. **Library:** Number of titles: 346,108; number of current serial subscriptions: 3,425. **Information technology resources:** Students are not required to lease or own a computer. Number of campus computers available to all students: 570. School has a wireless network. Approximate number of users that can be accommodated: 1,300. Proportion of college-owned housing units wired for high-speed

internet access: 100%. **Campus safety:** Security services offered: 24-hour foot-and-vehicle patrols, late-night transport/escort service, 24-hour emergency telephones, lighted pathways/sidewalks, controlled dormitory access (key, security card, etc.).

TRANSFER AND INTERNATIONAL STUDENTS

Transfer students: May apply for admission for the following academic terms: Fall, Spring, Summer. Applicants do not need a minimum number of credits to apply. For fall 2009: Transfer applications received: 186. Transfer applicants offered admission: 106. Transfer applicants enrolled: 67. **International students:** Number of foreign undergraduates: 83 (3% of student body). Number of countries represented: 34. Minimum TOEFL score required: 533 (paper); 73 (computer). Average TOEFL score: 583 (paper).

Concordia University–St. Paul

- **Address:** 275 Syndicate Street N, St. Paul, MN 55104-5494
- **Website:** http://www.csp.edu
- **Private; Religious affiliation:** Lutheran Church-Missouri Synod
- **Enrollment:** 1,423 full-time; 367 part-time

KEY STATS

✔ **U.S News College Ranking:** 95, Regional Universities (Midwest)
✔ **ACT Score (25th/75th percentile):** 18-24
✔ **Tuition:** 2010-2011: $27,400

Selectivity: Selective	**Room/board:** $7,500
Acceptance rate: 56%	**Average debt:** $32,444
Student/faculty ratio: 17/1	**Proportion who borrowed:** 85%

UNDERGRADUATE STUDENT BODY STATS

2009-2010 enrollment: 1,423 full-time; 367 part-time. Men: 42%; women: 58%. **Ethnic makeup:** African American: 10%; American-Indian: 1%; Asian American: 7%; Hispanic: 2%; White: 80%. **Religious preference:** Roman Catholic: 12%; Protestant: 39%; Muslim: 1%; No preference: 4%; Unknown: 25%; Lutheran Church-Missouri Synod: 15%; Other: 4%.

ADMISSIONS FACTS AND FIGURES

Phone: (651) 641-8230. **Email:** admission@csp.edu. **Website:** http://www.csp.edu. **Application deadlines for fall 2011:** Regular decision: Rolling. Early decision: Not offered. Early action: Not offered. Admission can be deferred. **Application fee:** $30. **To apply online, go to:** http://www.csp.edu/Admission/Undergraduate/Application_Process/. **Admissions requirements/recommendations:** High school units required (recommended): English: 4 (4); Mathematics: 2 (3); Science: 2 (3); Social studies: 2 (2); History: 2 (2); Total units: 15 (17). Tests: The college uses SAT or ACT scores in admissions decisions. ACT required. For admission to the fall 2011 entering class, the school will accept: ACT with or without writing accepted. Campus visit: Recommended. Admissions interview: Neither required nor recommended. Off-campus interview: Not available. **Factors that count in admissions decisions:** *Academic:* Secondary school record: Important. Class rank: Important. Letters of recommendation: Important. Standardized test scores: Important. Essay: Considered. *Nonacademic:* Interview: Not Considered. Extracurricular activities: Considered. Talent/ability: Considered. Character/personal qualities: Not Considered. Alumni/ae relationship: Not Considered. Geographical residence: Not Considered. State residency: Not Considered. Religious affiliation/commitment: Not Considered. Minority status: Not Considered. Volunteer work: Considered. Work experience: Considered. **Other schools with the greatest overlap in applicants:** Hamline University; St. Cloud State University; University of Minnesota–Duluth; University of Minnesota–Twin Cities; University of St. Thomas. **Admissions statistics for the fall 2009 entering class:** Total applicants: 1,106. Total accepted: 621. Freshmen enrolled: 184; 21% were from out of state. Overall acceptance rate: 56%. **Credentials of fall 2009 freshmen:** 6% ranked in the top 10 percent of their high school class; 24% were in the top 25 percent; 56% were in the top half. (Proportion submitting class standing: 82%.) **Average high school grade point average:** 3.1. **First-year students who submitted SAT scores:** 6%. **First-year students submitting ACT scores:** 95%. Scores (25/75 percentile): English: 16-23, Math: 17-24, Composite: 18-24.

ACADEMICS

Year founded: 1893. **Academic calendar:** Semester. **Degrees offered:** certificate, associate, bachelor's, post-bachelor's certificate, master's. **Most popular**

majors: 43% business, management, marketing, and related support services, 12% family and consumer sciences/human sciences, 8% computer and information sciences and support services, 7% security and protective services, 5% education. **Major fields of study:** biological and biomedical sciences; business, management, marketing, and related support services; communication, journalism, and related programs; education; English language and literature/letters; family and consumer sciences/human sciences; history; mathematics and statistics; parks, recreation, leisure, and fitness studies; physical sciences; psychology; public administration and social service professions; social sciences; theology and religious vocations; visual and performing arts. **Areas of required coursework:** arts/fine arts, humanities, mathematics, English (including composition), sciences (biological or physical), history, social science, other. **Pre-professional programs:** pre-law, pre-dentistry, pre-medicine, pre-theology, pre-veterinary science, pre-pharmacy. **Special academic programs (% participation):** accelerated program (63%), distance learning (40%), double major (3%), honors program, internships (20%), student-designed major, study abroad (2%), teacher certificate program (5%). **Teacher certification offered in:** early childhood, special education, elementary, middle/junior high, secondary, bilingual/bicultural. **Reserve Officers Training Corps (ROTC):** Army ROTC: Offered at cooperating institution (University of Minnesota–Twin Cities); Navy ROTC: Offered at cooperating institution (University of Minnesota–Twin Cities); Air Force ROTC: Offered at cooperating institution (University of St. Thomas). **Faculty and instruction (2009-2010):** Total instructional faculty: 70 full-time, 242 part-time (48% men; 52% women; 6% minorities). Full-time faculty with Ph.D. or other terminal degree: 67%. Student/faculty ratio: 17/1. Classes of fewer than 20 students: 73%; of 20 to 49 students: 27%. **Advanced Placement and International Baccalaureate credit:** AP tests may be used for: Placement only. Scores accepted: 3, 4, 5. International Baccalaureate exams may be used for: Placement only. **Freshmen returning for sophomore year:** 72%. **Graduation rates:** Four-year: 35%; five-year: 48%; six-year: 47%.

COSTS AND FINANCIAL AID

Financial aid office: (651) 603-6300. **Expenses (2010-2011):** Tuition and fees 2010-2011: $27,400; room/board: $7,500. Estimated books and supplies: $768; transportation: $996; personal expenses: $1,131. **Financial aid:** Priority filing date for institution's financial aid program: May 1. In 2009-2010, 84% of undergraduates applied for financial aid. Of those, 71% were determined to have financial need; 14% had their need fully met. Average financial aid package (proportion receiving): $17,022 (71%). Average amount of gift aid, such as scholarships or grants (proportion receiving): $13,962 (61%). Average amount of self-help aid, such as work study or loans (proportion receiving): $5,749 (60%). Average need-based loan (excluding PLUS or other private loans): $4,888. Among students who received need-based aid, the average percentage of need met: 67%. Among students who received aid based on merit, the average award (and the proportion receiving): $6,867 (9%). The average athletic scholarship (and the proportion receiving): $10,224 (3%). Average amount of debt of borrowers graduating in 2009: $32,444. Proportion who borrowed: 85%.

CAMPUS LIFE AND EXTRACURRICULAR ACTIVITIES

Campus housing available (% using): coed dorms (62%), women's dorms (19%), men's dorms (17%), apartments for married students (2%). Students who live in college-owned, operated, or affiliated housing: 28%. Activities include: campus ministries, choral groups, concert band, dance, drama/theater, jazz band, music ensembles, musical theater, student government, student newspaper, television station. Number of fraternities: 0; sororities: 0. **Sports program (2009-2010):** Member of NCAA II. *Men's intercollegiate varsity sports:* baseball, basketball, cross country, football, golf, track and field (indoor), track and field (outdoor). *Women's intercollegiate varsity sports:* basketball, cross country, golf, soccer, softball, track and field (indoor), track and field (outdoor), volleyball.

SERVICES AND FACILITIES

Basic services: nonremedial tutoring, day care, health service, health insurance. **Remedial assistance:** reading, math, writing, study skills. **Counseling services:** minority student, career, military, personal, veteran student, academic, older student, psychological, religious. **For learning-disabled students:** School does not offer a structured program with separate admission and additional fees. Services include: remedial math, remedial English, reading machines, remedial reading, tape recorders, note-taking services, oral tests, learning center, readers, extended time for tests, tutors, substitution of courses, texts on tape, typist/scribe, exams on tape or computer, other testing accommodations. **Library:** Number of titles: 154,742; number of current serial subscriptions: 27,757. **Information technology resources:** Students are required to lease or own a computer. School has a wireless

network. **Campus safety:** Security services offered: 24-hour foot-and-vehicle patrols, late-night transport/escort service, 24-hour emergency telephones, lighted pathways/sidewalks, student patrols, controlled dormitory access (key, security card, etc.).

TRANSFER AND INTERNATIONAL STUDENTS

Transfer students: May apply for admission for the following academic terms: Fall, Winter, Spring, Summer. Applicants need a minimum number of credits to apply. For fall 2009: Transfer applications received: 285. Transfer applicants offered admission: 155. Transfer applicants enrolled: 94. **International students:** Number of foreign undergraduates: 6. Number of countries represented: 3. Minimum TOEFL score required: 500 (paper); 173 (computer). Average TOEFL score: 530 (paper).

Crown College

- **Address:** 8700 College View Drive, St. Bonifacius, MN 55375
- **Website:** http://www.crown.edu
- **Private; Religious affiliation:** Christian and Missionary Alliance
- **Enrollment:** 819 full-time; 242 part-time

KEY STATS

✔ **U.S News College Ranking:** 46, Regional Colleges (Midwest)
✔ **ACT Score (25th/75th percentile):** 20-24
✔ **Tuition:** 2010-2011: $20,870

Selectivity: Selective	**Room/board:** $7,180
Acceptance rate: 66%	**Average debt:** $31,804
Student/faculty ratio: 14/1	**Proportion who borrowed:** 88%

UNDERGRADUATE STUDENT BODY STATS

2009-2010 enrollment: 819 full-time; 242 part-time. Men: 41%; women: 59%. **Ethnic makeup:** African American: 4%; American-Indian: 1%; Asian American: 8%; Hispanic: 3%; White: 85%. **Religious preference:** Roman Catholic: 2%; Protestant: 55%; Unknown: 3%; Christian and Missionary Alliance: 40%.

ADMISSIONS FACTS AND FIGURES

Phone: (952) 446-4142. **Email:** info@crown.edu. **Website:** http://www.crown.edu. **Application deadlines for fall 2011:** Regular decision: Rolling. Early decision: Not offered. Early action: Not offered. Admission can be deferred. **Application fee:** $35. **To apply online, go to:** http://www.crown.edu/admissions/apply-now.html. **Admissions requirements/recommendations:** High school units required (recommended): English: (4); Mathematics: (3); Science: (3); Foreign language: (2); Social studies: (3). Tests: The college uses SAT or ACT scores in admissions decisions. Either SAT or ACT required. For admission to the fall 2011 entering class, the school will accept: ACT with or without writing accepted. Campus visit: Recommended. Admissions interview: Neither required nor recommended. Off-campus interview: May be arranged. **Factors that count in admissions decisions:** *Academic:* Secondary school record: Very Important. Class rank: Important. Letters of recommendation: Very Important. Standardized test scores: Very Important. Essay: Very Important. *Nonacademic:* Interview: Considered. Extracurricular activities: Considered. Talent/ability: Considered. Character/personal qualities: Important. Alumni/ae relationship: Not Considered. Geographical residence: Not Considered. State residency: Not Considered. Religious affiliation/commitment: Very Important. Minority status: Not Considered. Volunteer work: Considered. Work experience: Considered. **Other schools with the greatest overlap in applicants:** Bethel University; Northwestern College; Nyack College; Toccoa Falls College; Trinity International University. **Admissions statistics for the fall 2009 entering class:** Total applicants: 457. Total accepted: 303. Freshmen enrolled: 149; 30% were from out of state. Overall acceptance rate: 66%. **Credentials of fall 2009 freshmen:** 11% ranked in the top 10 percent of their high school class; 44% were in the top 25 percent; 68% were in the top half. (Proportion submitting class standing: 64%.) **Average high school grade point average:** 3.2. **First-year students who submitted SAT scores:** 15%. Scores (25/75 percentile): Critical Reading: 500-655, Math: 470-635, Combined: 970-1290. **First-year students submitting ACT scores:** 92%. Scores (25/75 percentile): English: 18-24, Math: 20-25, Composite: 20-24.

ACADEMICS

Year founded: 1916. **Academic calendar:** Semester. **Degrees offered:** certificate, associate, bachelor's, master's. **Most popular majors:** 33% nursing/

registered nurse training (R.N., A.S.N., B.S.N., M.S.N.), 20% religious education, 11% business administration and management, 11% elementary education and teaching, 8% psychology. **Major fields of study:** biological and biomedical sciences; business, management, marketing, and related support services; communication, journalism, and related programs; computer and information sciences and support services; education; English language and literature/letters; foreign languages, literatures, and linguistics; health professions and related clinical sciences; history; legal professions and studies; liberal arts and sciences studies, and humanities; parks, recreation, leisure, and fitness studies; psychology; theology and religious vocations; visual and performing arts. **Areas of required coursework:** arts/fine arts, humanities, mathematics, English (including composition), sciences (biological or physical), history, social science, other. **Pre-professional programs:** pre-law. **Special academic programs (% participation):** distance learning (11%), double major (3%), dual enrollment, honors program (4%), independent study (23%), internships (19%), liberal arts/career combination (0%), study abroad (2%), teacher certificate program (0%), weekend college (0%). **Teacher certification offered in:** early childhood, elementary, middle/junior high, secondary. **Reserve Officers Training Corps (ROTC):** Army ROTC: Offered at cooperating institution (University of Minnesota–Twin Cities). **Faculty and instruction (2009-2010):** Total instructional faculty: 35 full-time, 110 part-time (54% men; 46% women; 1% minorities). Full-time faculty with Ph.D. or other terminal degree: 57%. Student/faculty ratio: 14/1. Classes of fewer than 20 students: 68%; of 20 to 49 students: 29%; of 50 or more students: 3%. **Advanced Placement and International Baccalaureate credit:** AP tests may be used for: Credit only. Scores accepted: 3, 4, 5. International Baccalaureate exams may be used for: Credit only. **Freshmen returning for sophomore year:** 69%. **Graduation rates:** Four-year: 32%; five-year: 46%; six-year: 51%.

COSTS AND FINANCIAL AID

Financial aid office: (952) 446-4177. **Expenses (2010-2011):** Tuition and fees 2010-2011: $20,870; room/board: $7,180. Estimated books and supplies: $1,660; transportation: $1,000; personal expenses: $2,500. **Financial aid:** Priority filing date for institution's financial aid form: April 15; deadline: August 1. In 2009-2010, 77% of undergraduates applied for financial aid. Of those, 66% were determined to have financial need; 13% had their need fully met. Average financial aid package (proportion receiving): $15,394 (66%). Average amount of gift aid, such as scholarships or grants (proportion receiving): $6,232 (48%). Average amount of self-help aid, such as work study or loans (proportion receiving): $4,947 (54%). Average need-based loan (excluding PLUS or other private loans): $4,364. Among students who received need-based aid, the average percentage of need met: 61%. Among students who received aid based on merit, the average award (and the proportion receiving): $7,375 (9%). The average athletic scholarship (and the proportion receiving): $0 (0%). Average amount of debt of borrowers graduating in 2009: $31,804. Proportion who borrowed: 88%.

CAMPUS LIFE AND EXTRACURRICULAR ACTIVITIES

Campus housing available (% using): women's dorms (44%), men's dorms (35%), apartments for married students (5%), apartment for single students (13%), special housing for disabled students (3%). Students who live in college-owned, operated, or affiliated housing: 68%. **Clubs and organizations:** Number of student organizations: 19. Activities include: campus ministries, choral groups, concert band, dance, drama/theater, jazz band, literary magazine, music ensembles, musical theater, pep band, radio station, student government, student newspaper, student film society, symphony orchestra, yearbook. Number of fraternities: 0; sororities: 0. Average proportion of students who stay on campus on weekends: 30%. **Sports program (2009-2010):** Member of NCAA III. *Men's intercollegiate varsity sports:* baseball, basketball, cross country, football, golf, soccer. *Women's intercollegiate varsity sports:* basketball, cross country, soccer, softball, volleyball.

SERVICES AND FACILITIES

Basic services: nonremedial tutoring, placement service, health service, health insurance. **Remedial assistance:** reading, math, writing, study skills. **Counseling services:** minority student, career, military, personal, veteran student, academic, older student, psychological, religious. **For learning-disabled students:** School does not offer a structured program with separate admission and additional fees. Total undergraduates in learning-disabled program or receiving services: 34. Services include: remedial math, remedial English, remedial reading, tape recorders, untimed tests, note-taking services, oral tests, learning center, readers, extended time for tests, tutors, priority registration, priority seating, texts on tape, other testing accommodations, other. **Library:** Number of titles: 101,468; number of current serial subscriptions: 28,000. **Information technology resources:** Students are not required to lease or own a computer. Number of campus computers available to all students: 105. School has a wireless network. Approximate number of users that can be accommodated: 500. Proportion of college-owned housing units wired for high-speed internet access: 95%. **Campus safety:** Security services offered: late-night transport/escort service, 24-hour emergency telephones, lighted pathways/sidewalks, student patrols, controlled dormitory access (key, security card, etc).

TRANSFER AND INTERNATIONAL STUDENTS

Transfer students: May apply for admission for the following academic terms: Fall, Spring, Summer. Applicants need a minimum number of credits to apply. For fall 2009: Transfer applications received: 457. Transfer applicants offered admission: 303. Transfer applicants enrolled: 149. **International students:** Number of foreign undergraduates: 1. Number of countries represented: 6. Minimum TOEFL score required: 500 (paper); 80 (computer).

Gustavus Adolphus College

- **Address:** 800 W. College Avenue, St. Peter, MN 56082
- **Website:** http://www.gac.edu
- **Private; Religious affiliation:** Lutheran
- **Enrollment:** 2,442 full-time; 33 part-time

KEY STATS

✔ **U.S News College Ranking:** 79, National Liberal Arts Colleges
✔ **ACT Score (25th/75th percentile):** 24-29
✔ **Tuition:** 2010-2011: $33,458

Selectivity: More selective	**Room/board:** $8,400
Acceptance rate: 74%	**Average debt:** $27,297
Student/faculty ratio: 11/1	**Proportion who borrowed:** 70%

UNDERGRADUATE STUDENT BODY STATS

2009-2010 enrollment: 2,442 full-time; 33 part-time. Men: 42%; women: 58%. **Ethnic makeup:** African American: 3%; Asian American: 6%; Hispanic: 2%; White: 87%; International: 2%. **Religious preference:** Roman Catholic: 18%; Protestant: 11%; No preference: 5%; Unknown: 6%; Lutheran: 50%; Other: 10%.

ADMISSIONS FACTS AND FIGURES

Phone: (507) 933-7676. **Email:** admission@gac.edu. **Website:** http://www.gac.edu. **Application deadlines for fall 2011:** Regular decision: Rolling. Early decision: Not offered. Early action: Send application by: November 1; Decision sent by: November 20. Admission can be deferred. **Application fee:** None. **To apply online, go to:** http://www.collegenet.com. **Admissions requirements/recommendations:** High school units required (recommended): English: 4; Mathematics: 3 (4); Science: 2 (3); Foreign language: 2 (3); Social studies: 2; History: 2; Academic electives: (2); Total units: 17 (22). **Tests:** The college uses SAT or ACT scores in admissions decisions. Neither SAT nor ACT required. For admission to the fall 2011 entering class, the school will accept: ACT with or without writing accepted. Campus visit: Recommended. Admissions interview: Recommended. Off-campus interview: Not available. **Factors that count in admissions decisions:** *Academic:* Secondary school record: Very Important. Class rank: Not Considered. Letters of recommendation: Important. Standardized test scores: Important. Essay: Important. *Nonacademic:* Interview: Considered. Extracurricular activities: Considered. Talent/ability: Considered. Character/personal qualities: Not Considered. Alumni/ae relationship: Considered. Geographical residence: Considered. State residency: Considered. Religious affiliation/commitment: Considered. Minority status: Considered. Volunteer work: Considered. Work experience: Considered. **Other schools with the greatest overlap in applicants:** Luther College; St. John's University; St. Olaf College; St. Thomas University; University of Minnesota–Twin Cities. **Admissions statistics for the fall 2009 entering class:** Total applicants: 2,929. Total accepted: 2,154. Freshmen enrolled: 620; 19% were from out of state. Overall acceptance rate: 74%. Non-early acceptance rate: 74%. **Size of waiting list:** 0 applicants; enrolled from waiting list: 0. **Credentials of fall 2009 freshmen:** 32% ranked in the top 10 percent of their high school class; 82% were in the top 25 percent; 95% were in the top half. (Proportion submitting class standing: 82%.) **Average high school grade point average:** 3.6. **First-year students who submitted SAT scores:** 11%. **First-year students submitting ACT scores:** 78%. Scores (25/75 percentile): English: 24-29, Math: 24-29, Composite: 24-29.

ACADEMICS

Year founded: 1862. **Academic calendar:** 4-1-4. **Degrees offered:** bachelor's. **Most popular majors:** 11% communication studies/speech communication and rhetoric, 9% business/commerce, 8% psychology, 7% biology/biological sciences, 7% political science and government. **Major fields of study:** area, ethnic, cultural, and gender studies; biological and biomedical sciences; business, management, marketing, and related support services; communication, journalism, and related programs; computer and information sciences and support services; education; English language and literature/letters; foreign languages, literatures, and linguistics; health professions and related clinical sciences; history; mathematics and statistics; multi/interdisciplinary studies; natural resources and conservation; parks, recreation, leisure, and fitness studies; philosophy and religious studies; physical sciences; psychology; security and protective services; social sciences; visual and performing arts. **Areas of required coursework:** arts/fine arts, humanities, mathematics, English (including composition), foreign languages, sciences (biological or physical), history, social science, other. **Pre-professional programs:** pre-law, pre-dentistry, pre-medicine, pre-theology, pre-veterinary science, pre-optometry, pre-pharmacy, other. **Special academic programs (% participation):** double major (14%), dual enrollment (4%), honors program (4%), independent study (16%), internships (57%), liberal arts/career combination (12%), student-designed major (1%), study abroad (44%), teacher certificate program (8%). **Teacher certification offered in:** elementary, middle/junior high, secondary, bilingual/bicultural. **Reserve Officers Training Corps (ROTC):** Army ROTC: Offered at cooperating institution (Minnesota State University–Mankato). **Faculty and instruction (2009-2010):** Total instructional faculty: 199 full-time, 87 part-time (53% men; 47% women; 13% minorities). Full-time faculty with Ph.D. or other terminal degree: 89%. Student/faculty ratio: 11/1. Classes of fewer than 20 students: 52%; of 20 to 49 students: 45%; of 50 or more students: 2%. **Advanced Placement and International Baccalaureate credit:** AP tests may be used for: Credit and/or placement. Scores accepted: 4, 5. International Baccalaureate exams may be used for: Credit and/or placement. **Freshmen returning for sophomore year:** 90%. **Graduation rates:** Four-year: 80%; five-year: 82%; six-year: 82%. **Graduate study:** 28% of students pursue further study immediately upon graduation; 32% within one year; 59% within five years. Fields in which graduates pursue further study: Master of Business Administration (MBA), 1%; law, 5%; medicine, 5%; dentistry, 1%; engineering, 2%; theology (or the seminary), 2%; education, 9%; arts and sciences, 33%; veterinary medicine, 1%.

COSTS AND FINANCIAL AID

Financial aid office: (507) 933-7527. **Expenses (2010-2011):** Tuition and fees 2010-2011: $33,458; room/board: $8,400. Estimated books and supplies: $900; transportation: $3,000; personal expenses: $580. **Financial aid:** Priority filing date for institution's financial aid form: February 15; deadline: April 15. In 2009-2010, 76% of undergraduates applied for financial aid. Of those, 65% were determined to have financial need; 66% had their need fully met. Average financial aid package (proportion receiving): $23,652 (65%). Average amount of gift aid, such as scholarships or grants (proportion receiving): $17,264 (65%). Average amount of self-help aid, such as work study or loans (proportion receiving): $5,021 (65%). Average need-based loan (excluding PLUS or other private loans): $4,812. Among students who received need-based aid, the average percentage of need met: 90%. Among students who received aid based on merit, the average award (and the proportion receiving): $7,352 (32%). The average athletic scholarship (and the proportion receiving): $0 (0%). Average amount of debt of borrowers graduating in 2009: $27,297. Proportion who borrowed: 70%.

CAMPUS LIFE AND EXTRACURRICULAR ACTIVITIES

Campus housing available (% using): coed dorms (97%), apartment for single students (2%), other housing options (1%). Students who live in college-owned, operated, or affiliated housing: 81%. **Student employment:** During the 2009-2010 academic year, 80% of undergraduates worked on campus. Average per-year earnings: $1,800. **Clubs and organizations:** Number of student organizations: 130. Activities include: campus ministries, choral groups, concert band, dance, drama/theater, international student organization, jazz band, literary magazine, model UN, music ensembles, musical theater, pep band, radio station, student government, student newspaper, symphony orchestra, television station, yearbook. Number of fraternities: 4; sororities: 6. Proportion of men in fraternities: 7%; of women in sororities: 5%. Average proportion of students who stay on campus on weekends: 85%. **Sports program (2009-2010):** Member of NCAA III. *Men's intercollegiate varsity sports:* baseball, basketball, cross country, football, golf, ice hockey, skiing (nordic), soccer, swimming, tennis, track and field (indoor), track and field (outdoor). *Women's intercollegiate varsity sports:* basketball, cross coun-

try, golf, gymnastics, ice hockey, skiing (nordic), soccer, softball, swimming, tennis, track and field (indoor), track and field (outdoor), volleyball.

SERVICES AND FACILITIES

Basic services: nonremedial tutoring, women's center, placement service, health service, health insurance. **Counseling services:** minority student, career, personal, academic, psychological, birth control, religious. **For learning-disabled students:** School does not offer a structured program with separate admission and additional fees. Services include: reading machines, tape recorders, note-taking services, special bookstore section, oral tests, learning center, readers, extended time for tests, tutors, early syllabus, priority registration, priority seating, typist/scribe, other testing accommodations, other. **Library:** Number of titles: 387,023; number of current serial subscriptions: 1,721. **Information technology resources:** Students are not required to lease or own a computer. Number of campus computers available to all students: 440. School has a wireless network. Approximate number of users that can be accommodated: 2,000. Proportion of college-owned housing units wired for high-speed internet access: 100%. **Campus safety:** Security services offered: 24-hour foot-and-vehicle patrols, late-night transport/escort service, 24-hour emergency telephones, lighted pathways/sidewalks, student patrols, controlled dormitory access (key, security card, etc).

TRANSFER AND INTERNATIONAL STUDENTS

Transfer students: May apply for admission for the following academic terms: Fall, Spring. Applicants do not need a minimum number of credits to apply. For fall 2009: Transfer applications received: 138. Transfer applicants offered admission: 78. Transfer applicants enrolled: 45. **International students:** Number of foreign undergraduates: 46 (2% of student body). Number of countries represented: 15. Minimum TOEFL score required: 550 (paper); 213 (computer). Average TOEFL score: 593 (paper).

Hamline University

- **Address:** 1536 Hewitt Avenue, St. Paul, MN 55104-1284
- **Website:** http://www.hamline.edu
- **Private; Religious affiliation:** Methodist
- **Enrollment:** 1,808 full-time; 113 part-time

KEY STATS
✔ **U.S News College Ranking:** 9, Regional Universities (Midwest)
✔ **ACT Score (25th/75th percentile):** 21-27
✔ **Tuition:** 2010-2011: $30,503

Selectivity: Selective	**Room/board:** $8,396
Acceptance rate: 75%	**Average debt:** $34,598
Student/faculty ratio: 12/1	**Proportion who borrowed:** 79%

UNDERGRADUATE STUDENT BODY STATS

2009-2010 enrollment: 1,808 full-time; 113 part-time. Men: 44%; women: 56%. **Ethnic makeup:** African American: 7%; American-Indian: 1%; Asian American: 5%; Hispanic: 3%; White: 81%; International: 3%. **Religious preference:** Roman Catholic: 17%; Protestant: 8%; Jewish: 1%; Muslim: 1%; No preference: 9%; Unknown: 32%; Methodist: 5%; Lutheran (all synods): 17%; Other: 10%.

ADMISSIONS FACTS AND FIGURES

Phone: (651) 523-2207. **Email:** admission@hamline.edu. **Website:** http://www.hamline.edu. **Application deadlines for fall 2011:** Regular decision: Rolling. Early decision: Not offered. Early action: Send application by: December 1; Decision sent by: December 15. Admission can be deferred. **To apply online, go to:** http://www.hamline.edu/undergraduate/admission/. **Admissions requirements/recommendations:** High school units required (recommended): English: (4); Mathematics: (3); Science: (3); Foreign language: (2); Social studies: (4); History: (0); Academic electives: (4); Total units: 0 (20). Tests: The college uses SAT or ACT scores in admissions decisions. Either SAT or ACT required. For admission to the fall 2011 entering class, the school will accept: ACT with or without writing accepted. Campus visit: Recommended. Admissions interview: Recommended. Off-campus interview: May be arranged. **Factors that count in admissions decisions:** *Academic:* Secondary school record: Very Important. Class rank: Very Important. Letters of recommendation: Important. Standardized test scores: Important. Essay: Important. *Nonacademic:* Interview: Important. Extracurricular activities: Important. Talent/ability: Important. Character/personal qualities: Considered. Alumni/ae relationship: Considered.

Geographical residence: Considered. State residency: Not Considered. Religious affiliation/commitment: Not Considered. Minority status: Considered. Volunteer work: Considered. Work experience: Considered. **Other schools with the greatest overlap in applicants:** Augsburg College; Gustavus Adolphus College; St. Olaf College; University of Minnesota–Twin Cities; University of St. Thomas. **Admissions statistics for the fall 2009 entering class:** Total applicants: 2,176. Total accepted: 1,637. Freshmen enrolled: 400; 23% were from out of state. Accepted through early-decision or early-action plans: 44%. Overall acceptance rate: 75%. Non-early acceptance rate: 69%. **Size of waiting list:** 0 applicants; enrolled from waiting list: 0. **Credentials of fall 2009 freshmen:** 21% ranked in the top 10 percent of their high school class; 50% were in the top 25 percent; 80% were in the top half. (Proportion submitting class standing: 84%.) **Average high school grade point average:** 3.4. **First-year students who submitted SAT scores:** 11%. Scores (25/75 percentile): Critical Reading: 505-630, Math: 480-590, Combined: 985-1220. **First-year students submitting ACT scores:** 91%. Scores (25/75 percentile): English: 20-28, Math: 20-27, Composite: 21-27.

ACADEMICS

Year founded: 1854. **Academic calendar:** 4-1-4. **Degrees offered:** certificate, bachelor's, post-bachelor's certificate, master's, post-master's certificate, doctorate. **Most popular majors:** 20% social sciences, 12% business, management, marketing, and related support services, 12% psychology, 8% legal professions and studies, 8% security and protective services. **Major fields of study:** area, ethnic, cultural, and gender studies; biological and biomedical sciences; business, management, marketing, and related support services; communication, journalism, and related programs; English language and literature/letters; foreign languages, literatures, and linguistics; history; legal professions and studies; mathematics and statistics; multi/interdisciplinary studies; natural resources and conservation; parks, recreation, leisure, and fitness studies; philosophy and religious studies; physical sciences; psychology; security and protective services; social sciences; visual and performing arts. **Areas of required coursework:** arts/fine arts, humanities, computer literacy, English (including composition), sciences (biological or physical), social science, other. **Pre-professional programs:** pre-law, pre-dentistry, pre-medicine, pre-veterinary science, pre-pharmacy, other. **Special academic programs (% participation):** cross-registration (24%), double major (25%), dual enrollment (1%), English as a Second Language (ESL) (2%), honors program (3%), independent study (22%), internships (52%), student-designed major (2%), study abroad (27%), teacher certificate program (8%). **Teacher certification offered in:** elementary, middle/junior high, adult education, secondary, bilingual/bicultural. **Reserve Officers Training Corps (ROTC):** Army ROTC: Offered at cooperating institution (University of Minnesota–Twin Cities); Air Force ROTC: Offered at cooperating institution (University of St. Thomas). **Faculty and instruction (2009-2010):** Total instructional faculty: 192 full-time, 339 part-time (44% men; 56% women; 10% minorities). Full-time faculty with Ph.D. or other terminal degree: 90%. Student/faculty ratio: 12/1. Classes of fewer than 20 students: 56%; of 20 to 49 students: 41%; of 50 or more students: 4%. **Advanced Placement and International Baccalaureate credit:** AP tests may be used for: Credit and/or placement. Scores accepted: 3, 4, 5. International Baccalaureate exams may be used for: Credit and/or placement. **Freshmen returning for sophomore year:** 80%. **Graduation rates:** Four-year: 58%; five-year: 64%; six-year: 67%. **Graduate study:** 20% of students pursue further study immediately upon graduation; 25% within one year. Fields in which graduates pursue further study: Master of Business Administration (MBA), 9%; law, 30%; medicine, 5%; engineering, 5%; theology (or the seminary), 7%; education, 12%; arts and sciences, 33%.

COSTS AND FINANCIAL AID

Financial aid office: (651) 523-3000. **Expenses (2010-2011):** Tuition and fees 2010-2011: $30,503; room/board: $8,396. Estimated books and supplies: $1,200 personal expenses: $1,000. **Financial aid:** Priority filing date for institution's financial aid form: March 15. In 2009-2010, 89% of undergraduates applied for financial aid. Of those, 79% were determined to have financial need; 19% had their need fully met. Average financial aid package (proportion receiving): $22,477 (79%). Average amount of gift aid, such as scholarships or grants (proportion receiving): $16,092 (78%). Average amount of self-help aid, such as work study or loans (proportion receiving): $6,203 (71%). Average need-based loan (excluding PLUS or other private loans): $4,736. Among students who received need-based aid, the average percentage of need met: 81%. Among students who received aid based on merit, the average award (and the proportion receiving): $10,309 (15%). Average amount of debt of borrowers graduating in 2009: $34,598. Proportion who borrowed: 79%.

CAMPUS LIFE AND EXTRACURRICULAR ACTIVITIES

Campus housing available (% using): coed dorms (82%), sorority housing (0%), fraternity housing (2%), apartments for married students (0%), apartment for single students (14%), special housing for international students (0%), other housing options (2%). Students who live in college-owned, operated, or affiliated housing: 41%. **Student employment:** During the 2009-2010 academic year, 24% of undergraduates worked on campus. Average per-year earnings: $2,500. **Clubs and organizations:** Number of student organizations: 85. Activities include: campus ministries, choral groups, concert band, dance, drama/theater, international student organization, jazz band, literary magazine, model UN, music ensembles, musical theater, pep band, radio station, student government, student newspaper, symphony orchestra, television station, yearbook. Number of fraternities: 1; sororities: 1. Proportion of men in fraternities: 3%; of women in sororities: 2%. Average proportion of students who stay on campus on weekends: 75%. **Sports program (2009-2010):** Member of NCAA III. *Men's intercollegiate varsity sports:* baseball, basketball, cross country, football, ice hockey, soccer, swimming, tennis, track and field (indoor), track and field (outdoor). *Women's intercollegiate varsity sports:* basketball, cross country, gymnastics, ice hockey, soccer, softball, swimming, tennis, track and field (indoor), track and field (outdoor), volleyball.

SERVICES AND FACILITIES

Basic services: nonremedial tutoring, women's center, placement service, health service, health insurance. **Remedial assistance:** math, writing, study skills. **Counseling services:** minority student, career, personal, academic, psychological, birth control, religious. **For learning-disabled students:** School does not offer a structured program with separate admission and additional fees. Total undergraduates in learning-disabled program or receiving services: 36. Services include: reading machines, tape recorders, untimed tests, note-taking services, oral tests, learning center, readers, extended time for tests, tutors, early syllabus, priority registration, priority seating, texts on tape, typist/scribe, exams on tape or computer, take home exams, other testing accommodations. **Library:** Number of titles: 488,099; number of current serial subscriptions: 5,971. **Information technology resources:** Students are not required to lease or own a computer. Number of campus computers available to all students: 300. School has a wireless network. Approximate number of users that can be accommodated: 3,000. Proportion of college-owned housing units wired for high-speed internet access: 99%. **Campus safety:** Security services offered: 24-hour foot-and-vehicle patrols, late-night transport/escort service, 24-hour emergency telephones, lighted pathways/sidewalks, controlled dormitory access (key, security card, etc).

TRANSFER AND INTERNATIONAL STUDENTS

Transfer students: May apply for admission for the following academic terms: Fall, Spring. Applicants do not need a minimum number of credits to apply. For fall 2009: Transfer applications received: 329. Transfer applicants offered admission: 222. Transfer applicants enrolled: 110. **International students:** Number of foreign undergraduates: 54 (3% of student body). Number of countries represented: 26. Minimum TOEFL score required: 550 (paper); 79 (computer).

Macalester College

- **Address:** 1600 Grand Avenue, St. Paul, MN 55105
- **Website:** http://www.macalester.edu
- **Private; Religious affiliation:** Presbyterian
- **Enrollment:** 1,958 full-time; 38 part-time

KEY STATS

✔ **U.S News College Ranking:** 26, National Liberal Arts Colleges
✔ **SAT Score (25th/75th percentile):** 1290-1450
✔ **Tuition:** 2010-2011: $40,046

Selectivity: Most selective	**Room/board:** $9,078
Acceptance rate: 46%	**Average debt:** $17,275
Student/faculty ratio: 11/1	**Proportion who borrowed:** 76%

UNDERGRADUATE STUDENT BODY STATS

2009-2010 enrollment: 1,958 full-time; 38 part-time. Men: 42%; women: 58%. **Ethnic makeup:** African American: 4%; American-Indian: 1%; Asian American: 9%; Hispanic: 4%; White: 70%; International: 12%.

ADMISSIONS FACTS AND FIGURES

Phone: (651) 696-6357. **Email:** admissions@macalester.edu. **Website:** http://www.macalester.edu. **Application deadlines for fall 2011:** Regular decision: January 15; decision sent by March 30. Early decision: Send application by: November 15; Decision sent by: December 15. Early action: Not offered. Admission can be deferred. **Application fee:** $40. **To apply online, go to:** http://www.macalester.edu/admissions/apply. **Admissions requirements/recommendations:** High school units required (recommended): English: (4); Mathematics: (3); Science: (3); Foreign language: (3); History: (3); Total units: (19). Tests: The college uses SAT or ACT scores in admissions decisions. Either SAT or ACT required. For admission to the fall 2011 entering class, the school will accept: ACT with or without writing accepted. Campus visit: Recommended. Admissions interview: Recommended. Off-campus interview: May be arranged. **Factors that count in admissions decisions:** *Academic:* Secondary school record: Very Important. Class rank: Considered. Letters of recommendation: Important. Standardized test scores: Important. Essay: Important. *Nonacademic:* Interview: Considered. Extracurricular activities: Important. Talent/ability: Considered. Character/personal qualities: Important. Alumni/ae relationship: Considered. Geographical residence: Not Considered. State residency: Not Considered. Religious affiliation/commitment: Not Considered. Minority status: Considered. Volunteer work: Considered. Work experience: Considered. **Other schools with the greatest overlap in applicants:** Brown University; Carleton College; Grinnell College; Oberlin College; Washington University in St. Louis. **Admissions statistics for the fall 2009 entering class:** Total applicants: 4,565. Total accepted: 2,109. Freshmen enrolled: 565; 80% were from out of state. Accepted through early-decision or early-action plans: 20%. Overall acceptance rate: 46%. Early-decision acceptance rate: 53%. Non-early acceptance rate: 46%. **Size of waiting list:** 534 applicants; enrolled from waiting list: 0. **Credentials of fall 2009 freshmen:** 67% ranked in the top 10 percent of their high school class; 92% were in the top 25 percent; 100% were in the top half. (Proportion submitting class standing: 50%.)
First-year students who submitted SAT scores: 72%. Scores (25/75 percentile): Critical Reading: 660-740, Math: 630-710, Combined: 1290-1450.
First-year students submitting ACT scores: 55%. Scores (25/75 percentile): English: 27-32, Math: 30-34, Composite: 29-32.

ACADEMICS

Year founded: 1874. **Academic calendar:** Semester. **Degrees offered:** bachelor's. **Most popular majors:** 14% economics, 13% political science and government, 10% psychology, 8% international/global studies, 7% biology/biological sciences. **Major fields of study:** area, ethnic, cultural, and gender studies; biological and biomedical sciences; computer and information sciences and support services; English language and literature/letters; foreign languages, literatures, and linguistics; history; liberal arts and sciences studies, and humanities; mathematics and statistics; multi/interdisciplinary studies; natural resources and conservation; philosophy and religious studies; physical sciences; psychology; social sciences; visual and performing arts. **Areas of required coursework:** arts/fine arts, humanities, mathematics, English (including composition), foreign languages, sciences (biological or physical), social science, other. **Pre-professional programs:** pre-law, pre-medicine. **Special academic programs (% participation):** cross-registration (18%), double major (36%), honors program (20%), independent study (45%), internships (38%), student-designed major (1%), study abroad (59%), other (1%). **Cooperative education programs:** engineering, other. **Reserve Officers Training Corps (ROTC):** Army ROTC: Offered at cooperating institution (University of Minnesota–Twin Cities); Navy ROTC: Offered at cooperating institution (University of Minnesota–Twin Cities); Air Force ROTC: Offered at cooperating institution (University of St. Thomas). **Faculty and instruction (2009-2010):** Total instructional faculty: 163 full-time, 73 part-time (51% men; 49% women; 19% minorities). Full-time faculty with Ph.D. or other terminal degree: 96%. Student/faculty ratio: 11/1. Classes of fewer than 20 students: 67%; of 20 to 49 students: 32%; of 50 or more students: 1%. **Advanced Placement and International Baccalaureate credit:** AP tests may be used for: Credit and/or placement. Scores accepted: 3, 4, 5. International Baccalaureate exams may be used for: Credit and/or placement. **Freshmen returning for sophomore year:** 93%. **Graduation rates:** Four-year: 82%; five-year: 85%; six-year: 86%. **Graduate study:** 18% of students pursue further study immediately upon graduation; 37% within one year. Fields in which graduates pursue further study: Master of Business Administration (MBA), 4%; law, 12%; medicine, 7%; engineering, 1%; theology (or the seminary), 2%; education, 8%; arts and sciences, 67%.

COSTS AND FINANCIAL AID

Financial aid office: (651) 696-6214. **Expenses (2010-2011):** Tuition and fees 2010-2011: $40,046; room/board: $9,078. Estimated books and supplies: $990; transportation: $500; personal expenses: $870. **Financial aid:** Priority filing date for institution's financial aid form: February 8; deadline: March 1. In 2009-2010, 75% of undergraduates applied for financial aid. Of those, 67% were determined to have financial need; 100% had their need fully met. Average financial aid package (proportion receiving): $32,258 (67%). Average amount of gift aid, such as scholarships or grants (proportion receiving): $27,111 (67%). Average amount of self-help aid, such as work study or loans (proportion receiving): $5,455 (63%). Average need-based loan (excluding PLUS or other private loans): $3,644. Among students who received need-based aid, the average percentage of need met: 100%. Among students who received aid based on merit, the average award (and the proportion receiving): $6,293 (4%). The average athletic scholarship (and the proportion receiving): $0 (0%). Average amount of debt of borrowers graduating in 2009: $17,275. Proportion who borrowed: 76%.

CAMPUS LIFE AND EXTRACURRICULAR ACTIVITIES

Campus housing available (% using): coed dorms (90%), apartment for single students (2%), cooperative housing (1%). Students who live in college-owned, operated, or affiliated housing: 66%. **Student employment:** During the 2009-2010 academic year, 63% of undergraduates worked on campus. Average per-year earnings: $2,182. **Clubs and organizations:** Number of student organizations: 87. Activities include: campus ministries, choral groups, concert band, dance, drama/theater, international student organization, jazz band, literary magazine, model UN, music ensembles, radio station, student government, student newspaper, symphony orchestra. Number of fraternities: 0; sororities: 0. Average proportion of students who stay on campus on weekends: 93%. **Sports program (2009-2010):** Member of NCAA III. *Men's intercollegiate varsity sports:* baseball, basketball, cross country, football, golf, soccer, swimming, tennis, track and field (indoor), track and field (outdoor). *Women's intercollegiate varsity sports:* basketball, cross country, golf, soccer, softball, swimming, tennis, track and field (indoor), track and field (outdoor), volleyball, water polo.

SERVICES AND FACILITIES

Basic services: nonremedial tutoring, placement service, health service, health insurance. **Remedial assistance:** reading, math, writing, study skills, other. **Counseling services:** minority student, career, personal, academic, psychological, birth control, religious, other. **For learning-disabled students:** School does not offer a structured program with separate admission and additional fees. Total undergraduates in learning-disabled program or receiving services: 40. Services include: reading machines, tape recorders, note-taking services, oral tests, learning center, readers, extended time for tests, tutors, priority seating, substitution of courses, texts on tape, exams on tape or computer, other testing accommodations. **Library:** Number of titles: 434,215; number of current serial subscriptions: 3,387. **Information technology resources:** Students are not required to lease or own a computer. Number of campus computers available to all students: 500. School has a wireless network. Approximate number of users that can be accommodated: 1,500. Proportion of college-owned housing units wired for high-speed internet access: 100%. **Campus safety:** Security services offered: 24-hour foot-and-vehicle patrols, late-night transport/escort service, 24-hour emergency telephones, lighted pathways/sidewalks, controlled dormitory access (key, security card, etc).

TRANSFER AND INTERNATIONAL STUDENTS

Transfer students: May apply for admission for the following academic terms: Fall, Spring. Applicants do not need a minimum number of credits to apply. For fall 2009: Transfer applications received: 194. Transfer applicants offered admission: 52. Transfer applicants enrolled: 20. **International students:** Number of foreign undergraduates: 231 (12% of student body). Number of countries represented: 68. Minimum TOEFL score required: 570 (paper); 67 (computer). Average TOEFL score: 622 (paper).

Metropolitan State University

- **Address:** 700 E. Seventh Street, St. Paul, MN 55106
- **Website:** http://www.metrostate.edu
- **Public**
- **Enrollment:** N/A

KEY STATS

- ✔ **U.S News College Ranking:** second tier, Regional Universities (Midwest)
- ✔ **SAT or ACT Score (25th/75th percentile):** N/A
- ✔ **Tuition:** 2009-2010: $5,627 in state, $11,173 out of state

Selectivity: Selective	Room/board: N/A
Acceptance rate: N/A	Average debt: N/A
Student/faculty ratio: N/A	Proportion who borrowed: N/A

Minneapolis College of Art and Design

- **Address:** 2501 Stevens Avenue, Minneapolis, MN 55404
- **Website:** http://www.mcad.edu
- **Private**
- **Enrollment:** 631 full-time; 24 part-time

KEY STATS

- ✔ **U.S News College Ranking:** Unranked Specialty School–Fine Arts
- ✔ **ACT Score (25th/75th percentile):** 20-26
- ✔ **Tuition:** 2010-2011: $29,700

Selectivity: N/A	Room/board: $4,430
Acceptance rate: 66%	Average debt: $54,100
Student/faculty ratio: 12/1	Proportion who borrowed: 85%

UNDERGRADUATE STUDENT BODY STATS

2009-2010 enrollment: 631 full-time; 24 part-time. Men: 43%; women: 57%. **Ethnic makeup:** African American: 2%; American-Indian: 1%; Asian American: 4%; Hispanic: 5%; White: 86%.

ADMISSIONS FACTS AND FIGURES

Phone: (612) 874-3760. **Email:** admissions@mcad.edu. **Website:** http://www.mcad.edu. **Application deadlines for fall 2011:** Regular decision: May 1. Early decision: Not offered. Early action: Not offered. Admission can be deferred. **Application fee:** $50. **To apply online, go to:** http://www.mcad.edu/apply. **Admissions requirements/recommendations:** High school units required (recommended): English: 4 (4); Social studies: 4 (4); History: 4 (4); Total units: 16 (16). Tests: The college uses SAT or ACT scores in admissions decisions. Either SAT or ACT required. For admission to the fall 2011 entering class, the school will accept: ACT with or without writing accepted. Campus visit: Recommended. Admissions interview: Recommended. Off-campus interview: May be arranged. **Factors that count in admissions decisions:** *Academic:* Secondary school record: Very Important. Class rank: Not Considered. Letters of recommendation: Important. Standardized test scores: Very Important. Essay: Very Important. *Nonacademic:* Interview: Considered. Extracurricular activities: Considered. Talent/ability: Very Important. Character/personal qualities: Considered. Alumni/ae relationship: Not Considered. Geographical residence: Not Considered. State residency: Not Considered. Religious affiliation/commitment: Not Considered. Minority status: Not Considered. Volunteer work: Considered. Work experience: Considered. **Other schools with the greatest overlap in applicants:** College of Visual Arts; Kansas City Art Institute; Milwaukee Institute of Art and Design; School of the Art Institute of Chicago; University of Minnesota–Twin Cities. **Admissions statistics for the fall 2009 entering class:** Total applicants: 444. Total accepted: 293. Freshmen enrolled: 109; 30% were from out of state. Overall acceptance rate: 66%. **Size of waiting list:** 0 applicants; enrolled from waiting list: 0. **Average high school grade point average:** 3.3. **First-year students who submitted SAT scores:** 20%. Scores (25/75 percentile): Critical Reading: 513-647, Math: 462-608, Combined: 975-1255. **First-year students submitting ACT scores:** 80%. Scores (25/75 percentile): English: 20-28, Math: 18-25, Composite: 20-26.

ACADEMICS

Year founded: 1886. **Academic calendar:** Semester. **Degrees offered:** bachelor's, post-bachelor's certificate, master's. **Most popular majors:** 25% commercial and advertising art, 23% visual and performing arts, 22% fine/studio arts, 20% film/video and photographic arts, 10% design and visual communications. **Major fields of study:** communications technologies/technicians and support services; visual and performing arts. **Areas of required coursework:** arts/fine arts, computer literacy. **Special academic programs (% participation):** cooperative (work-study plan) program (35%), distance learning (20%), double major (2%), exchange student program (domestic) (2%), internships (89%), study abroad (12%). **Faculty and instruction (2009-2010):** Total instructional faculty: 43 full-time, 74 part-time (54% men; 46% women; 5% minorities). Full-time faculty with Ph.D. or other terminal degree: 12%. Student/faculty ratio: 12/1. Classes of fewer than 20 students: 77%; of 20 to 49 students: 22%; of 50 or more students: 1%. **Advanced Placement and International Baccalaureate credit:** AP tests may be used for: Credit only. Scores accepted: 4, 5. International Baccalaureate exams may be used for: Credit only. **Freshmen returning for sophomore year:** 84%. **Graduation rates:** Four-year: 73%; five-year: 73%; six-year: 64%. **Graduate study:** 16% of students pursue further study immediately upon graduation; 19% within one year; 25% within five years. Fields in which graduates pursue further study: Master of Business Administration (MBA), 2%; engineering, 2%; education, 2%; arts and sciences, 94%.

COSTS AND FINANCIAL AID

Financial aid office: (612) 874-3782. **Expenses (2010-2011):** Tuition and fees 2010-2011: $29,700; room/board: $4,430. Estimated books and supplies: $2,600; transportation: $420; personal expenses: $750. **Financial aid:** Priority filing date for institution's financial aid form: March 15; deadline: April 1. In 2009-2010, 89% of undergraduates applied for financial aid. Of those, 80% were determined to have financial need; 8% had their need fully met. Average financial aid package (proportion receiving): $16,229 (80%). Average amount of gift aid, such as scholarships or grants (proportion receiving): $11,679 (76%). Average amount of self-help aid, such as work study or loans (proportion receiving): $5,365 (77%). Average need-based loan (excluding PLUS or other private loans): $4,616. Among students who received need-based aid, the average percentage of need met: 60%. Among students who received aid based on merit, the average award (and the proportion receiving): $7,879 (8%). The average athletic scholarship (and the proportion receiving): $0 (0%). Average amount of debt of borrowers graduating in 2009: $54,100. Proportion who borrowed: 85%.

CAMPUS LIFE AND EXTRACURRICULAR ACTIVITIES

Campus housing available (% using): apartment for single students (100%). Students who live in college-owned, operated, or affiliated housing: 40%. **Student employment:** During the 2009-2010 academic year, 20% of undergraduates worked on campus. Average per-year earnings: $1,700. **Clubs and organizations:** Number of student organizations: 10. Activities include: student government, student film society. Number of fraternities: 0; sororities: 0. Average proportion of students who stay on campus on weekends: 95%.

SERVICES AND FACILITIES

Basic services: nonremedial tutoring, health insurance. **Remedial assistance:** writing, study skills. **Counseling services:** career, personal, academic, psychological. **For learning-disabled students:** School does not offer a structured program with separate admission and additional fees. Services include: tape recorders, note-taking services, learning center, readers, extended time for tests, tutors. **Library:** Number of titles: 55,649; number of current serial subscriptions: 126. **Information technology resources:** Students are required to lease or own a computer. Number of campus computers available to all students: 150. School has a wireless network. Approximate number of users that can be accommodated: 500. Proportion of college-owned housing units wired for high-speed internet access: 100%. **Campus safety:** Security services offered: 24-hour foot-and-vehicle patrols, late-night transport/escort service, lighted pathways/sidewalks, controlled dormitory access (key, security card, etc).

TRANSFER AND INTERNATIONAL STUDENTS

Transfer students: May apply for admission for the following academic terms: Fall, Spring. Applicants need a minimum number of credits to apply. For fall 2009: Transfer applications received: 166. Transfer applicants offered admission: 113. Transfer applicants enrolled: 63. **International students:** Number of foreign undergraduates: 0. Number of countries represented: 5. Minimum TOEFL score required: 550 (paper); 213 (computer). Average TOEFL score: 550 (paper).

Minnesota State University–Mankato

- **Address:** 228 Wiecking Center, Mankato, MN 56001
- **Website:** http://www.mnsu.edu
- **Public**
- **Enrollment:** 11,557 full-time; 1,478 part-time

KEY STATS

✔ **U.S News College Ranking:** 65, Regional Universities (Midwest)
✔ **ACT Score (25th/75th percentile):** 20-24
✔ **Tuition:** 2010-2011: $6,724 in state, $13,472 out of state

Selectivity: Selective	**Room/board:** $6,730
Acceptance rate: 89%	**Average debt:** $25,667
Student/faculty ratio: 23/1	**Proportion who borrowed:** 82%

UNDERGRADUATE STUDENT BODY STATS

2009-2010 enrollment: 11,557 full-time; 1,478 part-time. Men: 49%; women: 51%. **Ethnic makeup:** African American: 4%; Asian American: 3%; Hispanic: 2%; White: 88%; International: 3%.

ADMISSIONS FACTS AND FIGURES

Phone: (507) 389-1822. **Email:** admissions@mnsu.edu. **Website:** http://www.mnsu.edu. **Application deadlines for fall 2011:** Regular decision: Rolling. Early decision: Not offered. Early action: Not offered. Admission can be deferred. **Application fee:** $20. **To apply online, go to:** https://secure.mnsu.edu/admapplication/default.zspx. **Admissions requirements/recommendations:** High school units required (recommended): English: 4; Mathematics: 3; Science: 3; Foreign language: 2; Social studies: 2; History: 1; Total units: 16. Tests: The college uses SAT or ACT scores in admissions decisions. ACT required. For admission to the fall 2011 entering class, the school will accept: ACT with or without writing accepted. Campus visit: Recommended. Admissions interview: Neither required nor recommended. Off-campus interview: Not available. **Factors that count in admissions decisions:** *Academic:* Secondary school record: Very Important. Class rank: Very Important. Letters of recommendation: Considered. Standardized test scores: Important. Essay: Not Considered. *Nonacademic:* Interview: Not Considered. Extracurricular activities: Not Considered. Talent/ability: Not Considered. Character/personal qualities: Not Considered. Alumni/ae relationship: Not Considered. Geographical residence: Not Considered. State residency: Not Considered. Religious affiliation/commitment: Not Considered. Minority status: Not Considered. Volunteer work: Not Considered. Work experience: Not Considered. **Other schools with the greatest overlap in applicants:** St. Cloud State University; University of Minnesota–Duluth; University of Minnesota–Twin Cities; University of Wisconsin–Eau Claire; Winona State University. **Admissions statistics for the fall 2009 entering class:** Total applicants: 6,196. Total accepted: 5,489. Freshmen enrolled: 2,287; 16% were from out of state. Overall acceptance rate: 89%. **Credentials of fall 2009 freshmen:** 7% ranked in the top 10 percent of their high school class; 29% were in the top 25 percent; 70% were in the top half. (Proportion submitting class standing: 88%.) **First-year students submitting ACT scores:** 97%. Scores (25/75 percentile): English: 18-23, Math: 19-25, Composite: 20-24.

ACADEMICS

Year founded: 1867. **Academic calendar:** Semester. **Degrees offered:** certificate, associate, bachelor's, master's, post-master's certificate. **Most popular majors:** 21% business, management, marketing, and related support services, 12% education, 12% health professions and related clinical sciences, 7% security and protective services, 6% social sciences. **Major fields of study:** agriculture, agriculture operations, and related sciences; area, ethnic, cultural, and gender studies; biological and biomedical sciences; business, management, marketing, and related support services; communication, journalism, and related programs; computer and information sciences and support services; education; engineering; engineering technologies/technicians; English language and literature/letters; family and consumer sciences/human sciences; foreign languages, literatures, and linguistics; health professions and related clinical sciences; history; legal professions and studies; liberal arts and sciences studies, and humanities; mathematics and statistics; natural resources and conservation; parks, recreation, leisure, and fitness studies; philosophy and religious studies; physical sciences; psychology; public administration and social service professions; security and protective services; social sciences; transportation and materials moving; visual and performing arts. **Areas of required coursework:** arts/fine arts, humanities, mathematics, English (including composition), sciences (bio-

logical or physical), social science, other. **Pre-professional programs:** pre-law, pre-dentistry, pre-medicine, pre-theology, pre-veterinary science, pre-optometry, pre-pharmacy, other. **Special academic programs:** accelerated program, cross-registration, distance learning, double major, dual enrollment, English as a Second Language (ESL), exchange student program (domestic), honors program, independent study, internships, student-designed major, study abroad, teacher certificate program. **Teacher certification offered in:** early childhood, special education, elementary, middle/junior high, secondary. **Reserve Officers Training Corps (ROTC):** Army ROTC: Offered on campus. **Faculty and instruction (2009-2010):** Total instructional faculty: 496 full-time, 235 part-time (50% men; 50% women; 6% minorities). Full-time faculty with Ph.D. or other terminal degree: 82%. Student/faculty ratio: 23/1. Classes of fewer than 20 students: 32%; of 20 to 49 students: 57%; of 50 or more students: 11%. **Advanced Placement and International Baccalaureate credit:** AP tests may be used for: Credit only. Scores accepted: 3, 4, 5. International Baccalaureate exams may be used for: Credit only. **Freshmen returning for sophomore year:** 78%. **Graduation rates:** Four-year: 20%; five-year: 46%; six-year: 50%. **Graduate study:** 13% of students pursue further study within one year.

COSTS AND FINANCIAL AID

Financial aid office: (507) 389-1866. **Expenses (2010-2011):** Tuition and fees 2010-2011: $6,724 in state, $13,472 out of state; room/board: $6,730. Estimated books and supplies: $860; transportation: $410; personal expenses: $1,590. **Financial aid:** Priority filing date for institution's financial aid form: March 15. In 2009-2010, 79% of undergraduates applied for financial aid. Of those, 53% were determined to have financial need; 38% had their need fully met. Average financial aid package (proportion receiving): $8,130 (52%). Average amount of gift aid, such as scholarships or grants (proportion receiving): $5,236 (40%). Average amount of self-help aid, such as work study or loans (proportion receiving): $4,289 (50%). Average need-based loan (excluding PLUS or other private loans): $3,806. Among students who received need-based aid, the average percentage of need met: 86%. Among students who received aid based on merit, the average award (and the proportion receiving): $2,273 (4%). The average athletic scholarship (and the proportion receiving): $4,116 (1%). Average amount of debt of borrowers graduating in 2009: $25,667. Proportion who borrowed: 82%.

CAMPUS LIFE AND EXTRACURRICULAR ACTIVITIES

Campus housing available (% using): coed dorms (100%). Students who live in college-owned, operated, or affiliated housing: 25%. **Student employment:** During the 2009-2010 academic year, 19% of undergraduates worked on campus. Average per-year earnings: $2,140. **Clubs and organizations:** Number of student organizations: 204. Activities include: campus ministries, choral groups, concert band, dance, drama/theater, international student organization, jazz band, literary magazine, model UN, music ensembles, musical theater, opera, radio station, student government, student newspaper, symphony orchestra. Number of fraternities: 7; sororities: 4. Proportion of men in fraternities: 3%; of women in sororities: 3%. Average proportion of students who stay on campus on weekends: 40%. **Sports program (2009-2010):** Member of NCAA II. *Men's intercollegiate varsity sports:* baseball, basketball, cross country, football, golf, ice hockey, swimming, tennis, track and field (indoor), track and field (outdoor), wrestling. *Women's intercollegiate varsity sports:* basketball, bowling, cross country, golf, ice hockey, soccer, softball, swimming, tennis, track and field (indoor), track and field (outdoor), volleyball.

SERVICES AND FACILITIES

Basic services: nonremedial tutoring, women's center, placement service, day care, health service, health insurance, other. **Remedial assistance:** reading, math, writing, study skills, other. **Counseling services:** minority student, career, personal, veteran student, academic, older student, psychological, birth control. **For learning-disabled students:** School does not offer a structured program with separate admission and additional fees. Services include: reading machines, tape recorders, note-taking services, oral tests, learning center, readers, extended time for tests, tutors, priority registration, priority seating, texts on tape, exams on tape or computer. **Library:** Number of titles: 817,409; number of current serial subscriptions: 90,131. **Information technology resources:** Students are not required to lease or own a computer. Number of campus computers available to all students: 1,200. School has a wireless network. Approximate number of users that can be accommodated: 15,000. Proportion of college-owned housing units wired for high-speed internet access: 100%. **Campus safety:** Security services offered: 24-hour foot-and-vehicle patrols, late-night transport/escort service,

24-hour emergency telephones, lighted pathways/sidewalks, student patrols, controlled dormitory access (key, security card, etc).

TRANSFER AND INTERNATIONAL STUDENTS

Transfer students: May apply for admission for the following academic terms: Fall, Spring, Summer. Applicants do not need a minimum number of credits to apply. For fall 2009: Transfer applications received: 1,769. Transfer applicants offered admission: 1,604. Transfer applicants enrolled: 1,020. **International students:** Number of foreign undergraduates: 396 (3% of student body). Number of countries represented: 56. Minimum TOEFL score required: 500 (paper); 61 (computer). Average TOEFL score: 574 (paper).

Minnesota State University–Moorhead

- **Address:** 1104 Seventh Avenue S, Moorhead, MN 56563
- **Website:** http://www.mnstate.edu
- **Public**
- **Enrollment:** 5,773 full-time; 1,177 part-time

KEY STATS

- ✔ **U.S News College Ranking:** 84, Regional Universities (Midwest)
- ✔ **ACT Score (25th/75th percentile):** 19-24
- ✔ **Tuition:** 2010-2011: $6,918 in state, $6,918 out of state

Selectivity: Selective	**Room/board:** $6,468
Acceptance rate: 77%	**Average debt:** $28,149
Student/faculty ratio: 18/1	**Proportion who borrowed:** 80%

UNDERGRADUATE STUDENT BODY STATS

2009-2010 enrollment: 5,773 full-time; 1,177 part-time. Men: 43%; women: 57%. **Ethnic makeup:** African American: 3%; American-Indian: 1%; Asian American: 1%; Hispanic: 1%; White: 88%; International: 5%.

ADMISSIONS FACTS AND FIGURES

Phone: (800) 593-7246. **Email:** dragon@mnstate.edu. **Website:** http://www.mnstate.edu. **Application deadlines for fall 2011:** Regular decision: August 1. Early decision: Not offered. Early action: Not offered. Admission can be deferred. **Application fee:** $20. **To apply online, go to:** http://www.mnstate.edu/admissions/apply_online.cfm. **Admissions requirements/recommendations:** High school units required (recommended): English: 4; Mathematics: 3; Science: 3; Foreign language: 2; Social studies: 3; History: 0; Total units: 16. Tests: The college uses SAT or ACT scores in admissions decisions. Either SAT or ACT required. For admission to the fall 2011 entering class, the school will accept: ACT with or without writing accepted. Campus visit: Recommended. Admissions interview: Neither required nor recommended. Off-campus interview: Not available. **Factors that count in admissions decisions:** *Academic:* Secondary school record: Very Important. Class rank: Very Important. Letters of recommendation: Not Considered. Standardized test scores: Very Important. Essay: Not Considered. *Nonacademic:* Interview: Not Considered. Extracurricular activities: Not Considered. Talent/ability: Not Considered. Character/personal qualities: Not Considered. Alumni/ae relationship: Not Considered. Geographical residence: Not Considered. State residency: Not Considered. Religious affiliation/commitment: Not Considered. Minority status: Not Considered. Volunteer work: Not Considered. Work experience: Not Considered. **Admissions statistics for the fall 2009 entering class:** Total applicants: 2,900. Total accepted: 2,241. Freshmen enrolled: 1,055; 37% were from out of state. Overall acceptance rate: 77%. **Credentials of fall 2009 freshmen:** 9% ranked in the top 10 percent of their high school class; 27% were in the top 25 percent; 64% were in the top half. (Proportion submitting class standing: 88%.) **First-year students submitting ACT scores:** 94%. Scores (25/75 percentile): English: 18-24, Math: 18-24, Composite: 19-24.

ACADEMICS

Year founded: 1887. **Academic calendar:** Semester. **Degrees offered:** certificate, associate, transfer-associate, bachelor's, post-bachelor's certificate, master's, post-master's certificate. **Most popular majors:** 7% elementary education and teaching, 6% journalism, 6% social work, 5% biology/biological sciences, 5% nursing/registered nurse training (R.N., A.S.N., B.S.N., M.S.N.). **Major fields of study:** area, ethnic, cultural, and gender studies; biological and biomedical sciences; business, management, marketing, and related support services; communication, journalism, and related programs; computer and information sciences and support services; education;

engineering technologies/technicians; English language and literature/letters; foreign languages, literatures, and linguistics; health professions and related clinical sciences; history; legal professions and studies; mathematics and statistics; multi/interdisciplinary studies; parks, recreation, leisure, and fitness studies; philosophy and religious studies; physical sciences; psychology; public administration and social service professions; security and protective services; social sciences; visual and performing arts. **Areas of required coursework:** humanities, mathematics, English (including composition), sciences (biological or physical), social science, other. **Pre-professional programs:** pre-law, pre-dentistry, pre-medicine, pre-veterinary science, pre-optometry, pre-pharmacy, other. **Special academic programs:** cross-registration, distance learning, double major, dual enrollment, exchange student program (domestic), external degree program, honors program, independent study, internships, student-designed major, study abroad, teacher certificate program. **Teacher certification offered in:** early childhood, special education, elementary, middle/junior high, secondary. **Reserve Officers Training Corps (ROTC):** Army ROTC: Offered at cooperating institution (North Dakota State University); Air Force ROTC: Offered at cooperating institution (North Dakota State University). **Faculty and instruction (2009-2010):** Total instructional faculty: 294 full-time, 187 part-time (50% men; 50% women; 4% minorities). Full-time faculty with Ph.D. or other terminal degree: 75%. Student/faculty ratio: 18/1. Classes of fewer than 20 students: 41%; of 20 to 49 students: 53%; of 50 or more students: 7%. **Advanced Placement and International Baccalaureate credit:** AP tests may be used for: Credit only. Scores accepted: 3, 4, 5. International Baccalaureate exams may be used for: Placement only. **Freshmen returning for sophomore year:** 69%. **Graduation rates:** Four-year: 20%; five-year: 37%; six-year: 43%. **Graduate study:** 17% of students pursue further study within one year.

COSTS AND FINANCIAL AID

Financial aid office: (218) 477-2251. **Expenses (2010-2011):** Tuition and fees 2010-2011: $6,918 in state, $6,918 out of state; room/board: $6,468. Estimated books and supplies: $800; transportation: $1,000; personal expenses: $1,614. **Financial aid:** Priority filing date for institution's financial aid form: February 15. In 2009-2010, 74% of undergraduates applied for financial aid. Of those, 55% were determined to have financial need; 100% had their need fully met. Average financial aid package (proportion receiving): $8,172 (55%). Average amount of gift aid, such as scholarships or grants (proportion receiving): $4,001 (37%). Average amount of self-help aid, such as work study or loans (proportion receiving): $4,641 (48%). Average need-based loan (excluding PLUS or other private loans): $4,307. The average athletic scholarship (and the proportion receiving): $2,614 (3%). Average amount of debt of borrowers graduating in 2009: $28,149. Proportion who borrowed: 80%.

CAMPUS LIFE AND EXTRACURRICULAR ACTIVITIES

Campus housing available: coed dorms, women's dorms, men's dorms, sorority housing, apartment for single students, special housing for disabled students, other housing options. Students who live in college-owned, operated, or affiliated housing: 22%. **Student employment:** During the 2009-2010 academic year, 13% of undergraduates worked on campus. Average per-year earnings: $2,200. **Clubs and organizations:** Number of student organizations: 130. Activities include: campus ministries, choral groups, concert band, dance, drama/theater, international student organization, jazz band, literary magazine, model UN, music ensembles, musical theater, radio station, student government, student newspaper, student film society, symphony orchestra, television station. Number of fraternities: 0; sororities: 2. of women in sororities: 2%. Average proportion of students who stay on campus on weekends: 25%. **Sports program (2009-2010):** Member of NCAA II. *Men's intercollegiate varsity sports:* basketball, cross country, football, track and field (indoor), track and field (outdoor), wrestling. *Women's intercollegiate varsity sports:* basketball, cross country, golf, soccer, softball, swimming, tennis, track and field (indoor), track and field (outdoor), volleyball.

SERVICES AND FACILITIES

Basic services: nonremedial tutoring, women's center, placement service, day care, health service, health insurance, other. **Remedial assistance:** math, study skills. **Counseling services:** minority student, career, personal, veteran student, academic, older student, psychological, birth control. **For learning-disabled students:** School does not offer a structured program with separate admission and additional fees. **Library:** Number of titles: 645,544; number of current serial subscriptions: 7,894. **Information technology resources:** Students are not required to lease or own a computer. Number of campus computers available to all students: 1,088. School has a wireless network. Approximate number of users that can be accommodated: 2,000.

Proportion of college-owned housing units wired for high-speed internet access: 100%. **Campus safety:** Security services offered: 24-hour foot-and-vehicle patrols, late-night transport/escort service, 24-hour emergency telephones, lighted pathways/sidewalks, student patrols, controlled dormitory access (key, security card, etc).

TRANSFER AND INTERNATIONAL STUDENTS

Transfer students: May apply for admission for the following academic terms: Fall, Spring, Summer. Applicants need a minimum number of credits to apply. For fall 2009: Transfer applications received: 1,506. Transfer applicants offered admission: 1,040. Transfer applicants enrolled: 734. **International students:** Number of foreign undergraduates: 346 (5% of student body). Number of countries represented: 56. Minimum TOEFL score required: 500 (paper); 173 (computer).

North Central University

■ **Address:** 910 Elliot Avenue S, Minneapolis, MN 55404
■ **Website:** http://www.northcentral.edu
■ **Private; Religious affiliation:** Assemblies of God
■ **Enrollment:** 1,124 full-time; 120 part-time

KEY STATS

✔ **U.S News College Ranking:** 70, Regional Colleges (Midwest)
✔ **ACT Score:** 21
✔ **Tuition:** 2009-2010: $15,236

Selectivity: Selective	**Room/board:** $5,300
Acceptance rate: 99%	**Average debt:** N/A
Student/faculty ratio: 17/1	**Proportion who borrowed:** N/A

UNDERGRADUATE STUDENT BODY STATS

2009-2010 enrollment: 1,124 full-time; 120 part-time. Men: 43%; women: 57%. **Religious preference:** Assemblies of God: 67%; Other: 33%.

ADMISSIONS FACTS AND FIGURES

Phone: (800) 289-6222. **Email:** admissions@northcentral.edu. **Website:** http://www.northcentral.edu. **Application deadlines for fall 2011:** Regular decision: June 1. Early decision: Not offered. Early action: Not offered. Admission can be deferred. **Application fee:** $25. **To apply online, go to:** https://www.applyweb.com/apply/ncuug/index.html. **Admissions requirements/recommendations:** High school units required (recommended): English: (4); Mathematics: (2); Science: (2); Foreign language: (1); Social studies: (2); History: (2); Academic electives: (4); Total units: (18). Tests: The college uses SAT or ACT scores in admissions decisions. Either SAT or ACT required. For admission to the fall 2011 entering class, the school will accept: ACT with or without writing accepted. Campus visit: Recommended. Admissions interview: Neither required nor recommended. Off-campus interview: May be arranged. **Factors that count in admissions decisions:** *Academic:* Secondary school record: Very Important. Class rank: Not Considered. Letters of recommendation: Very Important. Standardized test scores: Very Important. Essay: Very Important. *Nonacademic:* Interview: Not Considered. Extracurricular activities: Very Important. Talent/ability: Considered. Character/personal qualities: Very Important. Alumni/ae relationship: Not Considered. Geographical residence: Not Considered. State residency: Not Considered. Religious affiliation/commitment: Very Important. Minority status: Not Considered. Volunteer work: Very Important. Work experience: Not Considered. **Other schools with the greatest overlap in applicants:** Bethel College; Evangel University; Northwestern College; Oral Roberts University; Southeastern University. **Admissions statistics for the fall 2009 entering class:** Total applicants: 598. Total accepted: 592. Freshmen enrolled: 296; Overall acceptance rate: 99%. **First-year students who submitted SAT scores:** 5%. **First-year students submitting ACT scores:** 95%. Scores (25/75 percentile): English: N/A, Math: N/A, Composite: N/A.

ACADEMICS

Year founded: 1930. **Academic calendar:** Semester. **Degrees offered:** certificate, diploma, associate, bachelor's. **Major fields of study:** business, management, marketing, and related support services; communication, journalism, and related programs; education; English language and literature/letters; foreign languages, literatures, and linguistics; multi/interdisciplinary studies; psychology; social sciences; theology and religious vocations; visual and performing arts. **Areas of required coursework:** arts/fine arts, humanities,

mathematics, English (including composition), philosophy, sciences (biological or physical), history, social science, other. **Special academic programs (% participation):** cooperative (work-study plan) program (16%), cross-registration, double major, dual enrollment, internships, liberal arts/career combination, study abroad, teacher certificate program. **Teacher certification offered in:** elementary, middle/junior high. **Cooperative education programs:** education. **Reserve Officers Training Corps (ROTC):** Army ROTC: Offered at cooperating institution (University of Minnesota–Twin Cities); Air Force ROTC: Offered at cooperating institution (University of Minnesota–Twin Cities). **Faculty and instruction (2009-2010):** Total instructional faculty: 46 full-time, 24 part-time. Student/faculty ratio: 17/1. **Advanced Placement and International Baccalaureate credit:** AP tests may be used for: Placement only. Scores accepted: 3, 4, 5. International Baccalaureate exams may be used for: Placement only. **Freshmen returning for sophomore year:** 70%. **Graduation rates:** Six-year: 41%.

COSTS AND FINANCIAL AID

Financial aid office: (612) 343-4485. **Expenses (2009-2010):** Tuition and fees 2009-2010: $15,236; room/board: $5,300. Estimated books and supplies: $1,082.

CAMPUS LIFE AND EXTRACURRICULAR ACTIVITIES

Campus housing available (% using): women's dorms (40%), men's dorms (27%), apartments for married students (3%), apartment for single students (14%). **Student employment:** During the 2009-2010 academic year, 31% of undergraduates worked on campus. Average per-year earnings: $2,400. **Clubs and organizations:** Number of student organizations: 20. Activities include: campus ministries, choral groups, concert band, drama/theater, jazz band, music ensembles, musical theater, radio station, student government, student newspaper. Number of fraternities: 0; sororities: 0. Average proportion of students who stay on campus on weekends: 85%. **Sports program (2009-2010):** Member of NCAA III. *Men's intercollegiate varsity sports:* baseball, basketball, cross country, golf, soccer, track and field (outdoor). *Women's intercollegiate varsity sports:* basketball, cross country, soccer, softball, track and field (outdoor), volleyball.

SERVICES AND FACILITIES

Basic services: nonremedial tutoring, placement service, health insurance. **Remedial assistance:** study skills. **Counseling services:** minority student, career, military, personal, veteran student, academic, older student, psychological, religious. **For learning-disabled students:** School does not offer a structured program with separate admission and additional fees. Services include: reading machines, tape recorders, other special classes, untimed tests, note-taking services, oral tests, learning center, readers, extended time for tests, tutors, priority registration, priority seating, texts on tape, other testing accommodations. **Library:** Number of titles: 73,367; number of current serial subscriptions: 196. **Information technology resources:** Students are not required to lease or own a computer. Number of campus computers available to all students: 83. School has a wireless network. Proportion of college-owned housing units wired for high-speed internet access: 92%. **Campus safety:** Security services offered: 24-hour foot-and-vehicle patrols, late-night transport/escort service, 24-hour emergency telephones, lighted pathways/sidewalks, student patrols, controlled dormitory access (key, security card, etc).

TRANSFER AND INTERNATIONAL STUDENTS

Transfer students: May apply for admission for the following academic terms: Fall, Spring. Applicants do not need a minimum number of credits to apply. For fall 2009: Transfer applications received: 264. Transfer applicants offered admission: 259. Transfer applicants enrolled: 116. **International students:** Number of countries represented: 3. Minimum TOEFL score required: 500 (paper); 200 (computer).

Northwestern College

- **Address:** 3003 Snelling Avenue N, St. Paul, MN 55113-1598
- **Website:** http://www.nwc.edu
- **Private; Religious affiliation:** Christian nondenominational
- **Enrollment:** 1,805 full-time; 53 part-time

KEY STATS

✔ **U.S News College Ranking:** 15, Regional Colleges (Midwest)
✔ **ACT Score (25th/75th percentile):** 21-27
✔ **Tuition:** 2010-2011: $24,570

Selectivity: Selective	**Room/board:** $7,720
Acceptance rate: 98%	**Average debt:** $26,259
Student/faculty ratio: 14/1	**Proportion who borrowed:** 84%

UNDERGRADUATE STUDENT BODY STATS

2009-2010 enrollment: 1,805 full-time; 53 part-time. Men: 43%; women: 57%. **Ethnic makeup:** African American: 2%; Asian American: 4%; Hispanic: 2%; White: 90%. **Religious preference:** Roman Catholic: 1%; Protestant: 99%.

ADMISSIONS FACTS AND FIGURES

Phone: (800) 827-6827. **Email:** admissions@nwc.edu. **Website:** http://www.nwc.edu. **Application deadlines for fall 2011:** Regular decision: August 1. Early decision: Not offered. Early action: Not offered. Admission can be deferred. **Application fee:** $30. **To apply online, go to:** http://www.nwc.edu/web/admission/apply-online. **Admissions requirements/recommendations:** High school units required (recommended): English: 4 (4); Mathematics: 3 (3); Science: 3 (3); Foreign language: 2 (2); Social studies: 3 (3); History: 0 (0); Academic electives: 1 (1); Total units: 16 (16). Tests: The college uses SAT or ACT scores in admissions decisions. Either SAT or ACT required. For admission to the fall 2011 entering class, the school will accept: ACT with or without writing accepted. Campus visit: Recommended. Admissions interview: Recommended. Off-campus interview: May be arranged. **Factors that count in admissions decisions: Academic:** Secondary school record: Very Important. Class rank: Important. Letters of recommendation: Very Important. Standardized test scores: Very Important. Essay: Very Important. **Nonacademic:** Interview: Considered. Extracurricular activities: Important. Talent/ability: Considered. Character/personal qualities: Very Important. Alumni/ae relationship: Considered. Geographical residence: Considered. State residency: Not Considered. Religious affiliation/commitment: Very Important. Minority status: Important. Volunteer work: Important. Work experience: Considered. **Other schools with the greatest overlap in applicants:** Bethel University; Crown College; North Central University; University of Minnesota–Duluth; University of Minnesota–Twin Cities. **Admissions statistics for the fall 2009 entering class:** Total applicants: 1,053. Total accepted: 1,032. Freshmen enrolled: 439; 29% were from out of state. Overall acceptance rate: 98%. **Size of waiting list:** 0 applicants; enrolled from waiting list: 0. **Credentials of fall 2009 freshmen:** 21% ranked in the top 10 percent of their high school class; 47% were in the top 25 percent; 78% were in the top half. (Proportion submitting class standing: 77%.) **Average high school grade point average:** 3.5. **First-year students who submitted SAT scores:** 9%. Scores (25/75 percentile): Critical Reading: 520-650, Math: 460-610, Combined: 980-1260. **First-year students submitting ACT scores:** 94%. Scores (25/75 percentile): English: 21-28, Math: 20-26, Composite: 21-27.

ACADEMICS

Year founded: 1902. **Academic calendar:** Semester. **Degrees offered:** certificate, associate, bachelor's, post-bachelor's certificate, master's. **Most popular majors:** 15% psychology, 11% business administration and management, 9% theological and ministerial studies, 6% elementary education and teaching, 5% communication studies/speech communication and rhetoric. **Major fields of study:** biological and biomedical sciences; business, management, marketing, and related support services; communication, journalism, and related programs; communications technologies/technicians and support services; education; English language and literature/letters; history; mathematics and statistics; multi/interdisciplinary studies; parks, recreation, leisure, and fitness studies; psychology; security and protective services; theology and religious vocations; visual and performing arts. **Areas of required coursework:** arts/fine arts, computer literacy, mathematics, English (including composition), philosophy, sciences (biological or physical), history, social science, other. **Pre-professional programs:** pre-medicine, pre-theology. **Special academic programs (% participation):** distance learning (61%), dou-

ble major (71%), exchange student program (domestic) (1%), honors program (2%), independent study (10%), internships (62%), student-designed major (1%), study abroad (5%), teacher certificate program (17%). **Teacher certification offered in:** early childhood, elementary, middle/junior high, secondary. **Reserve Officers Training Corps (ROTC):** Army ROTC: Offered at cooperating institution (University of Minnesota–Twin Cities); Air Force ROTC: Offered at cooperating institution (University of St. Thomas). **Faculty and instruction (2009-2010):** Total instructional faculty: 101 full-time, 81 part-time (56% men; 44% women; 8% minorities). Full-time faculty with Ph.D. or other terminal degree: 61%. Student/faculty ratio: 14/1. Classes of fewer than 20 students: 52%; of 20 to 49 students: 43%; of 50 or more students: 4%. **Advanced Placement and International Baccalaureate credit:** AP tests may be used for: Credit only. Scores accepted: 3, 4, 5. International Baccalaureate exams may be used for: Credit only. **Freshmen returning for sophomore year:** 81%. **Graduation rates:** Four-year: 45%; five-year: 58%; six-year: 59%. **Graduate study:** 8% of students pursue further study immediately upon graduation. Fields in which graduates pursue further study: theology (or the seminary), 38%; education, 8%; arts and sciences, 54%.

COSTS AND FINANCIAL AID

Financial aid office: (651) 631-5212. **Expenses (2010-2011):** Tuition and fees 2010-2011: $24,570; room/board: $7,720. Estimated books and supplies: $610; transportation: $900; personal expenses: $1,600. **Financial aid:** Priority filing date for institution's financial aid form: March 1. In 2009-2010, 91% of undergraduates applied for financial aid. Of those, 82% were determined to have financial need; 11% had their need fully met. Average financial aid package (proportion receiving): $16,842 (82%). Average amount of gift aid, such as scholarships or grants (proportion receiving): $12,088 (80%). Average amount of self-help aid, such as work study or loans (proportion receiving): $5,006 (69%). Average need-based loan (excluding PLUS or other private loans): $4,365. Among students who received need-based aid, the average percentage of need met: 70%. Among students who received aid based on merit, the average award (and the proportion receiving): $5,383 (14%). The average athletic scholarship (and the proportion receiving): $0 (0%). Average amount of debt of borrowers graduating in 2009: $26,259. Proportion who borrowed: 84%.

CAMPUS LIFE AND EXTRACURRICULAR ACTIVITIES

Campus housing available (% using): women's dorms (49%), men's dorms (33%), apartment for single students (16%). Students who live in college-owned, operated, or affiliated housing: 67%. **Student employment:** During the 2009-2010 academic year, 34% of undergraduates worked on campus. Average per-year earnings: $2,516. **Clubs and organizations:** Number of student organizations: 19. Activities include: campus ministries, choral groups, concert band, drama/theater, jazz band, literary magazine, music ensembles, musical theater, opera, pep band, radio station, student government, student newspaper, symphony orchestra, television station, yearbook. Number of fraternities: 0; sororities: 0. Average proportion of students who stay on campus on weekends: 70%. **Sports program (2009-2010):** Member of NCAA III. **Men's intercollegiate varsity sports:** baseball, basketball, cross country, football, golf, soccer, tennis, track and field (indoor), track and field (outdoor). **Women's intercollegiate varsity sports:** basketball, cross country, golf, soccer, softball, tennis, track and field (indoor), track and field (outdoor), volleyball.

SERVICES AND FACILITIES

Basic services: nonremedial tutoring, placement service, health service, health insurance. **Remedial assistance:** reading, math, writing, study skills, other. **Counseling services:** minority student, career, personal, veteran student, academic, psychological, religious, other. **For learning-disabled students:** School does not offer a structured program with separate admission and additional fees. Total undergraduates in learning-disabled program or receiving services: 22. Services include: remedial math, remedial English, reading machines, remedial reading, tape recorders, other special classes, videotaped classes, untimed tests, note-taking services, oral tests, learning center, readers, extended time for tests, tutors, early syllabus, priority registration, priority seating, texts on tape, typist/scribe, exams on tape or computer, take home exams, other testing accommodations, other. **Library:** Number of titles: 107,716; number of current serial subscriptions: 1,263. **Information technology resources:** Students are required to lease or own a computer. Number of campus computers available to all students: 100. School has a wireless network. Approximate number of users that can be accommodated: 2,400. Proportion of college-owned housing units wired for high-speed internet access: 100%. **Campus safety:** Security services offered: 24-hour foot-and-vehicle patrols, late-night transport/escort service, lighted pathways/sidewalks, controlled dormitory access (key, security card, etc).

TRANSFER AND INTERNATIONAL STUDENTS

Transfer students: May apply for admission for the following academic terms: Fall, Spring, Summer. Applicants do not need a minimum number of credits to apply. For fall 2009: Transfer applications received: 208. Transfer applicants offered admission: 195. Transfer applicants enrolled: 109. **International students:** Number of foreign undergraduates: 9. Number of countries represented: 9. Minimum TOEFL score required: 530 (paper); 71 (computer). Average TOEFL score: 551 (paper).

Southwest Minnesota State University

- **Address:** 1501 State Street, Marshall, MN 56258
- **Website:** http://www.smsu.edu
- **Public**
- **Enrollment:** 2,388 full-time; 3,833 part-time

KEY STATS

✔ **U.S News College Ranking:** 104, Regional Universities (Midwest)
✔ **ACT Score (25th/75th percentile):** 19-24
✔ **Tuition:** 2010-2011: $7,240 in state, $7,240 out of state

Selectivity: Selective	**Room/board:** $6,846
Acceptance rate: 65%	**Average debt:** $18,830
Student/faculty ratio: 20/1	**Proportion who borrowed:** 82%

UNDERGRADUATE STUDENT BODY STATS

2009-2010 enrollment: 2,388 full-time; 3,833 part-time. Men: 42%; women: 58%. **Ethnic makeup:** African American: 3%; Asian American: 3%; Hispanic: 2%; White: 83%; International: 8%.

ADMISSIONS FACTS AND FIGURES

Phone: (507) 537-6286. **Website:** http://www.smsu.edu. **Application deadlines for fall 2011:** Regular decision: September 1. Early decision: Not offered. Early action: Not offered. Admission can be deferred. **Application fee:** $20. **To apply online, go to:** https://www.applyweb.com/apply/swsu/menu.html. **Admissions requirements/recommendations:** High school units required (recommended): English: 4 (4); Mathematics: 3 (3); Science: 3 (3); Foreign language: 2 (2); Social studies: 3 (3); Total units: 16 (16). Tests: The college uses SAT or ACT scores in admissions decisions. ACT required. For admission to the fall 2011 entering class, the school will accept: ACT with or without writing accepted. Campus visit: Required. Admissions interview: Recommended. Off-campus interview: May be arranged. **Factors that count in admissions decisions:** *Academic:* Secondary school record: Very Important. Class rank: Very Important. Letters of recommendation: Important. Standardized test scores: Very Important. Essay: Considered. *Nonacademic:* Interview: Considered. Extracurricular activities: Considered. Talent/ability: Considered. Character/personal qualities: Considered. Alumni/ae relationship: Considered. Geographical residence: Considered. State residency: Considered. Religious affiliation/commitment: Not Considered. Minority status: Considered. Volunteer work: Considered. Work experience: Considered. **Other schools with the greatest overlap in applicants:** Bemidji State University; Minnesota State University–Mankato; Minnesota State University–Moorhead; South Dakota State University; St. Cloud State University. **Admissions statistics for the fall 2009 entering class:** Total applicants: 2,054. Total accepted: 1,336. Freshmen enrolled: 461; 22% were from out of state. Overall acceptance rate: 65%. **Credentials of fall 2009 freshmen:** 13% ranked in the top 10 percent of their high school class; 20% were in the top 25 percent; 52% were in the top half. (Proportion submitting class standing: 69%.) **Average high school grade point average:** 3.4. **First-year students submitting ACT scores:** 92%. Scores (25/75 percentile): English: 19-24, Math: 19-25, Composite: 19-24.

ACADEMICS

Year founded: 1963. **Academic calendar:** Semester. **Degrees offered:** associate, bachelor's, master's. **Most popular majors:** 19% business administration and management, 16% education, 6% finance, 6% health and physical education, 6% marketing/marketing management. **Major fields of study:** agriculture, agriculture operations, and related sciences; biological and biomedical sciences; business, management, marketing, and related support services; communication, journalism, and related programs; computer and information sciences and support services; education; English language and literature/letters; foreign languages, literatures, and linguistics; history; liberal arts and sciences studies, and humanities; mathematics and statistics; natural resources and conservation; parks, recreation, leisure, and fitness studies; philosophy and religious studies; physical sciences; psychology; public administration and social service professions; security and protective services; social sciences; visual and performing arts. **Areas of required coursework:** arts/fine arts, humanities, mathematics, English (including composition), foreign languages, sciences (biological or physical), social science, other. **Pre-professional programs:** pre-law, pre-dentistry, pre-medicine, pre-theology, pre-veterinary science, pre-optometry, pre-pharmacy, other. **Special academic programs:** accelerated program, cross-registration, distance learning, double major, dual enrollment, English as a Second Language (ESL), exchange student program (domestic), external degree program, honors program, independent study, internships, liberal arts/career combination, student-designed major, study abroad, teacher certificate program, other. **Teacher certification offered in:** early childhood, special education, elementary, middle/junior high, adult education, secondary. **Cooperative education programs:** business, education. **Faculty and instruction (2009-2010):** Total instructional faculty: 121 full-time, 113 part-time (52% men; 48% women; 9% minorities). Full-time faculty with Ph.D. or other terminal degree: 83%. Student/faculty ratio: 20/1. Classes of fewer than 20 students: 41%; of 20 to 49 students: 55%; of 50 or more students: 3%. **Advanced Placement and International Baccalaureate credit:** AP tests may be used for: Credit only. Scores accepted: 3. International Baccalaureate exams may be used for: Placement only. **Freshmen returning for sophomore year:** 68%. **Graduation rates:** Four-year: 24%; five-year: 39%; six-year: 43%. **Graduate study:** 6% of students pursue further study immediately upon graduation; 6% within one year. Fields in which graduates pursue further study: Master of Business Administration (MBA), 28%; law, 1%; medicine, 3%; engineering, 2%; education, 15%; arts and sciences, 20%.

COSTS AND FINANCIAL AID

Financial aid office: (507) 537-6281. **Expenses (2010-2011):** Tuition and fees 2010-2011: $7,240 in state, $7,240 out of state; room/board: $6,846. Estimated books and supplies: $1,200; transportation: $1,200; personal expenses: $1,600. **Financial aid:** Priority filing date for institution's financial aid form: March 1. In 2009-2010, 81% of undergraduates applied for financial aid. Of those, 65% were determined to have financial need; 18% had their need fully met. Average financial aid package (proportion receiving): $8,541 (65%). Average amount of gift aid, such as scholarships or grants (proportion receiving): $5,128 (48%). Average amount of self-help aid, such as work study or loans (proportion receiving): $4,288 (55%). Average need-based loan (excluding PLUS or other private loans): $3,946. Among students who received need-based aid, the average percentage of need met: 57%. Among students who received aid based on merit, the average award (and the proportion receiving): $349 (15%). The average athletic scholarship (and the proportion receiving): $3,306 (10%). Average amount of debt of borrowers graduating in 2009: $18,830. Proportion who borrowed: 82%.

CAMPUS LIFE AND EXTRACURRICULAR ACTIVITIES

Campus housing available (% using): coed dorms (92%), women's dorms (7%), men's dorms (0%), special housing for disabled students (1%). Students who live in college-owned, operated, or affiliated housing: 22%. **Student employment:** During the 2009-2010 academic year, 22% of undergraduates worked on campus. Average per-year earnings: $1,500. **Clubs and organizations:** Number of student organizations: 100. Activities include: campus ministries, choral groups, concert band, dance, drama/theater, international student organization, jazz band, literary magazine, marching band, model UN, music ensembles, musical theater, pep band, radio station, student government, student newspaper, symphony orchestra, television station. Number of fraternities: 0; sororities: 0. Average proportion of students who stay on campus on weekends: 33%. **Sports program (2009-2010):** Member of NCAA II. *Men's intercollegiate varsity sports:* baseball, basketball, football, wrestling. *Women's intercollegiate varsity sports:* basketball, golf, soccer, softball, tennis, volleyball.

SERVICES AND FACILITIES

Basic services: women's center, placement service, day care, health service, health insurance. **Remedial assistance:** reading, math, writing, study skills. **Counseling services:** minority student, career, military, personal, veteran student, academic, psychological, birth control. **For learning-disabled students:** School does not offer a structured program with separate admission and additional fees. Total undergraduates in learning-disabled program or receiving services: 27. Services include: remedial math, remedial English, reading machines, other special classes, videotaped classes, diagnostic testing service, note-taking services, oral tests, learning center, extended time for tests, tutors, priority registration, priority seating, texts on tape, exams on tape or computer, other testing accommodations. **Library:** Number of titles: 402,933; number of current serial subscriptions: 32,341. **Information**

technology resources: Students are not required to lease or own a computer. Number of campus computers available to all students: 310. School has a wireless network. Approximate number of users that can be accommodated: 600. Proportion of college-owned housing units wired for high-speed internet access: 100%. **Campus safety:** Security services offered: 24-hour foot-and-vehicle patrols, late-night transport/escort service, 24-hour emergency telephones, lighted pathways/sidewalks, student patrols, controlled dormitory access (key, security card, etc.).

TRANSFER AND INTERNATIONAL STUDENTS

Transfer students: May apply for admission for the following academic terms: Fall, Spring, Summer. Applicants need a minimum number of credits to apply. For fall 2009: Transfer applications received: 302. Transfer applicants offered admission: 300. Transfer applicants enrolled: 279. **International students:** Number of foreign undergraduates: 218 (8% of student body). Number of countries represented: 26. Minimum TOEFL score required: 500 (paper); 173 (computer). Average TOEFL score: 563 (paper).

St. Catherine University

■ **Address:** 2004 Randolph Avenue, St. Paul, MN 55105
■ **Website:** http://www.stkate.edu
■ **Private; Religious affiliation:** Roman Catholic
■ **Enrollment:** 2,468 full-time; 1,329 part-time

KEY STATS

✔ **U.S News College Ranking:** 17, Regional Universities (Midwest)
✔ **ACT Score (25th/75th percentile):** 21-26
✔ **Tuition:** 2010-2011: $28,300

Selectivity: More selective	**Room/board:** $6,746
Acceptance rate: 67%	**Average debt:** $24,400
Student/faculty ratio: 12/1	**Proportion who borrowed:** 96%

UNDERGRADUATE STUDENT BODY STATS

2009-2010 enrollment: 2,468 full-time; 1,329 part-time. Men: 3%; women: 97%. **Ethnic makeup:** African American: 11%; American-Indian: 1%; Asian American: 10%; Hispanic: 3%; White: 74%; International: 1%. **Religious preference:** Protestant: 20%; Jewish: 1%; Muslim: 1%; Buddhist: 1%; No preference: 1%; Roman Catholic: 43%; unspecified Christian: 22%; Other: 11%.

ADMISSIONS FACTS AND FIGURES

Phone: (800) 945-4599. **Email:** admissions@stkate.edu. **Website:** http://www.stkate.edu. **Application deadlines for fall 2011:** Regular decision: Rolling. Early decision: Not offered. Early action: Not offered. Admission can be deferred. **To apply online, go to:** http://www.stkate.edu/admissions/apply_home.html. **Admissions requirements/recommendations:** High school units required (recommended): English: (4); Mathematics: (3); Science: (2); Foreign language: (4); Social studies: (2); Total units: (15). Tests: The college uses SAT or ACT scores in admissions decisions. Either SAT or ACT required. For admission to the fall 2011 entering class, the school will accept: ACT with or without writing accepted. Campus visit: Recommended. Admissions interview: Recommended. Off-campus interview: May be arranged. **Factors that count in admissions decisions:** *Academic:* Secondary school record: Very Important. Class rank: Important. Letters of recommendation: Important. Standardized test scores: Important. Essay: Important. *Nonacademic:* Interview: Considered. Extracurricular activities: Important. Talent/ability: Considered. Character/personal qualities: Considered. Alumni/ae relationship: Considered. Geographical residence: Not Considered. State residency: Not Considered. Religious affiliation/commitment: Considered. Minority status: Considered. Volunteer work: Considered. Work experience: Considered. **Other schools with the greatest overlap in applicants:** College of St. Benedict; Hamline University; University of Minnesota–Twin Cities; University of St. Thomas. **Admissions statistics for the fall 2009 entering class:** Total applicants: 2,151. Total accepted: 1,445. Freshmen enrolled: 414; 11% were from out of state. Overall acceptance rate: 67%. **Credentials of fall 2009 freshmen:** 26% ranked in the top 10 percent of their high school class; 60% were in the top 25 percent; 91% were in the top half. (Proportion submitting class standing: 84%.) **Average high school grade point average:** 3.6. **First-year students who submitted SAT scores:** 4%. **First-year students submitting ACT scores:** 94%. Scores (25/75 percentile): English: 21-26, Math: 20-26, Composite: 21-26.

ACADEMICS

Year founded: 1905. **Academic calendar:** 4-1-4. **Degrees offered:** certificate, associate, bachelor's, post-bachelor's certificate, master's, post-master's certificate. **Most popular majors:** 20% nursing/registered nurse training (R.N., A.S.N., B.S.N., M.S.N.), 7% business administration and management, 6% elementary education and teaching, 5% psychology, 5% social work. **Major fields of study:** area, ethnic, cultural, and gender studies; biological and biomedical sciences; business, management, marketing, and related support services; communication, journalism, and related programs; computer and information sciences and support services; education; English language and literature/letters; family and consumer sciences/human sciences; foreign languages, literatures, and linguistics; health professions and related clinical sciences; history; mathematics and statistics; multi/interdisciplinary studies; parks, recreation, leisure, and fitness studies; philosophy and religious studies; physical sciences; psychology; public administration and social service professions; security and protective services; social sciences; theology and religious vocations; visual and performing arts. **Areas of required coursework:** arts/fine arts, computer literacy, mathematics, English (including composition), philosophy, foreign languages, sciences (biological or physical), history, social science, other. **Pre-professional programs:** pre-law, pre-dentistry, pre-medicine, pre-theology, pre-veterinary science, pre-optometry, pre-pharmacy, other. **Special academic programs (% participation):** cross-registration (1%), double major (9%), dual enrollment (2%), English as a Second Language (ESL) (1%), exchange student program (domestic) (0%), honors program (6%), independent study (17%), internships (44%), student-designed major (1%), study abroad (22%), weekend college (13%). **Teacher certification offered in:** early childhood, elementary, middle/junior high, secondary. **Cooperative education programs:** engineering. **Reserve Officers Training Corps (ROTC):** Army ROTC: Offered at cooperating institution (University of Minnesota–Twin Cities); Air Force ROTC: Offered at cooperating institution (University of St. Thomas). **Faculty and instruction (2009-2010):** Total instructional faculty: 286 full-time, 161 part-time (20% men; 80% women; 8% minorities). Full-time faculty with Ph.D. or other terminal degree: 83%. Student/faculty ratio: 12/1. Classes of fewer than 20 students: 57%; of 20 to 49 students: 40%; of 50 or more students: 3%. **Advanced Placement and International Baccalaureate credit:** AP tests may be used for: Credit only. Scores accepted: 3, 4, 5. International Baccalaureate exams may be used for: Credit only. **Freshmen returning for sophomore year:** 78%. **Graduation rates:** Four-year: 45%; five-year: 60%; six-year: 59%. **Graduate study:** 22% of students pursue further study immediately upon graduation; 25% within one year; 33% within five years. Fields in which graduates pursue further study: Master of Business Administration (MBA), 5%; law, 7%; medicine, 7%; education, 5%; veterinary medicine, 2%.

COSTS AND FINANCIAL AID

Financial aid office: (651) 690-6540. **Expenses (2010-2011):** Tuition and fees 2010-2011: $28,300; room/board: $6,746. Estimated books and supplies: $800; transportation: $350; personal expenses: $3,250. **Financial aid:** Priority filing date for institution's financial aid form: April 15. In 2009-2010, 93% of undergraduates applied for financial aid. Of those, 85% were determined to have financial need; 11% had their need fully met. Average financial aid package (proportion receiving): $26,870 (85%). Average amount of gift aid, such as scholarships or grants (proportion receiving): $10,925 (76%). Average amount of self-help aid, such as work study or loans (proportion receiving): $4,760 (77%). Average need-based loan (excluding PLUS or other private loans): $4,610. Among students who received need-based aid, the average percentage of need met: 83%. Among students who received aid based on merit, the average award (and the proportion receiving): $7,170 (6%). Average amount of debt of borrowers graduating in 2009: $24,400. Proportion who borrowed: 96%.

CAMPUS LIFE AND EXTRACURRICULAR ACTIVITIES

Campus housing available (% using): women's dorms (76%), apartment for single students (21%), other housing options (3%). Students who live in college-owned, operated, or affiliated housing: 40%. **Student employment:** During the 2009-2010 academic year, 34% of undergraduates worked on campus. Average per-year earnings: $2,800. **Clubs and organizations:** Number of student organizations: 58. Activities include: campus ministries, choral groups, dance, drama/theater, international student organization, literary magazine, marching band, music ensembles, musical theater, student government, student newspaper, symphony orchestra. ; sororities: 1. Average proportion of students who stay on campus on weekends: 38%. **Sports program (2009-2010):** Member of NCAA III. *Women's intercollegiate varsity sports:* basketball, cross country, ice hockey, soccer, softball, swimming, tennis, track and field (indoor), track and field (outdoor), volleyball.

SERVICES AND FACILITIES

Basic services: nonremedial tutoring, women's center, placement service, day care, health service, health insurance. **Remedial assistance:** math, writing, study skills. **Counseling services:** minority student, career, personal, academic, older student, psychological, religious. **For learning-disabled students:** School does not offer a structured program with separate admission and additional fees. Services include: remedial math, reading machines, tape recorders, note-taking services, oral tests, learning center, readers, extended time for tests, tutors, priority registration, priority seating, texts on tape, other testing accommodations, other. **Library:** Number of titles: 252,107; number of current serial subscriptions: 14,526. **Information technology resources:** Students are not required to lease or own a computer. Number of campus computers available to all students: 180. School has a wireless network. Proportion of college-owned housing units wired for high-speed internet access: 100%. **Campus safety:** Security services offered: 24-hour foot-and-vehicle patrols, late-night transport/escort service, 24-hour emergency telephones, lighted pathways/sidewalks, controlled dormitory access (key, security card, etc).

TRANSFER AND INTERNATIONAL STUDENTS

Transfer students: May apply for admission for the following academic terms: Fall, Winter, Spring, Summer. Applicants do not need a minimum number of credits to apply. For fall 2009: Transfer applications received: 2,380. Transfer applicants offered admission: 1,495. Transfer applicants enrolled: 810. **International students:** Number of foreign undergraduates: 32 (1% of student body). Number of countries represented: 26. Minimum TOEFL score required: 500 (paper); 173 (computer).

St. Cloud State University

- **Address:** 720 Fourth Avenue S, St. Cloud, MN 56301
- **Website:** http://www.stcloudstate.edu
- **Public**
- **Enrollment:** 12,233 full-time; 3,547 part-time

KEY STATS

✔ **U.S News College Ranking:** 81, Regional Universities (Midwest)
✔ **ACT Score (25th/75th percentile):** 19-24
✔ **Tuition:** 2009-2010: $6,606 in state, $13,234 out of state
  Selectivity: Less selective **Room/board:** $3,008
  Acceptance rate: 87% **Average debt:** $24,373
  Student/faculty ratio: N/A **Proportion who borrowed:** 68%

UNDERGRADUATE STUDENT BODY STATS

2009-2010 enrollment: 12,233 full-time; 3,547 part-time. Men: 48%; women: 52%. **Ethnic makeup:** African American: 4%; American-Indian: 1%; Asian American: 3%; Hispanic: 1%; White: 85%; International: 6%.

ADMISSIONS FACTS AND FIGURES

Phone: (320) 308-2244. **Email:** scsu4u@stcloudstate.edu. **Website:** http://www.stcloudstate.edu. **Application deadlines for fall 2011:** Regular decision: June 1. Early decision: Not offered. Early action: Not offered. Admission can be deferred. **Application fee:** $20. **To apply online, go to:** http://www.stcloudstate.edu/apply/default.asp. **Admissions requirements/recommendations:** High school units required (recommended): English: 4; Mathematics: 3; Science: 3; Foreign language: 2; Social studies: 2; History: 1; Total units: 16. **Tests:** The college uses SAT or ACT scores in admissions decisions. Either SAT or ACT required. For admission to the fall 2011 entering class, the school will accept: ACT with or without writing accepted. Campus visit: Recommended. Admissions interview: Neither required nor recommended. Off-campus interview: Not available. **Factors that count in admissions decisions:** *Academic:* Secondary school record: Very Important. Class rank: Very Important. Letters of recommendation: Considered. Standardized test scores: Considered. Essay: Considered. *Nonacademic:* Interview: Not Considered. Extracurricular activities: Considered. Talent/ability: Considered. Character/personal qualities: Not Considered. Alumni/ae relationship: Not Considered. Geographical residence: Not Considered. State residency: Not Considered. Religious affiliation/commitment: Not Considered. Minority status: Not Considered. Volunteer work: Not Considered. Work experience: Not Considered. **Admissions statistics for the fall 2009 entering class:** Total applicants: 6,016. Total accepted: 5,234. Freshmen enrolled: 2,390; 10% were from out of state. Overall acceptance rate: 87%. **Credentials of fall 2009 freshmen:** 6% ranked in the top 10 per-

cent of their high school class; 23% were in the top 25 percent. **First-year students submitting ACT scores:** 89%. Scores (25/75 percentile): English: 17-23, Math: 18-25, Composite: 19-24.

ACADEMICS

Year founded: 1869. **Academic calendar:** Semester. **Degrees offered:** certificate, associate, bachelor's, post-bachelor's certificate, master's, post-master's certificate. **Most popular majors:** 27% business, management, marketing, and related support services, 12% education, 9% communication, journalism, and related programs, 8% social sciences, 7% psychology. **Major fields of study:** area, ethnic, cultural, and gender studies; biological and biomedical sciences; business, management, marketing, and related support services; computer and information sciences and support services; education; engineering; engineering technologies/technicians; English language and literature/letters; foreign languages, literatures, and linguistics; health professions and related clinical sciences; liberal arts and sciences studies, and humanities; mathematics and statistics; multi/interdisciplinary studies; natural resources and conservation; parks, recreation, leisure, and fitness studies; philosophy and religious studies; physical sciences; psychology; public administration and social service professions; security and protective services; social sciences; transportation and materials moving; visual and performing arts. **Areas of required coursework:** arts/fine arts, humanities, computer literacy, mathematics, English (including composition), philosophy, sciences (biological or physical), history, social science. **Preprofessional programs:** pre-law, pre-dentistry, pre-medicine, pre-veterinary science, pre-optometry, pre-pharmacy, other. **Special academic programs (% participation):** accelerated program, cross-registration, distance learning (53%), double major (5%), dual enrollment (7%), English as a Second Language (ESL) (5%), honors program (4%), independent study (17%), internships (27%), student-designed major (7%), study abroad (6%), teacher certificate program (13%). **Teacher certification offered in:** early childhood, special education, elementary, middle/junior high, secondary, bilingual/bicultural. **Reserve Officers Training Corps (ROTC):** Army ROTC: Offered on campus. **Faculty and instruction (2009-2010):** Total instructional faculty: 668 full-time, 271 part-time. Full-time faculty with Ph.D. or other terminal degree: 82%. Classes of fewer than 20 students: 43%; of 20 to 49 students: 53%; of 50 or more students: 5%. **Advanced Placement and International Baccalaureate credit:** AP tests may be used for: Credit and/or placement. Scores accepted: 3, 4, 5. International Baccalaureate exams may be used for: Credit and/or placement. **Freshmen returning for sophomore year:** 72%. **Graduation rates:** Four-year: 17%; five-year: 40%; six-year: 48%. **Graduate study:** 15% of students pursue further study within one year.

COSTS AND FINANCIAL AID

Financial aid office: (320) 308-2047. **Expenses (2009-2010):** Tuition and fees 2009-2010: $6,606 in state, $13,234 out of state; room/board: $3,008. Estimated books and supplies: $1,200. **Financial aid:** In 2009-2010, 58% of undergraduates applied for financial aid. Of those, 44% were determined to have financial need; 69% had their need fully met. Average financial aid package (proportion receiving): $14,317 (44%). Average amount of gift aid, such as scholarships or grants (proportion receiving): $4,801 (34%). Average amount of self-help aid, such as work study or loans (proportion receiving): $7,372 (43%). Average need-based loan (excluding PLUS or other private loans): $6,776. Among students who received need-based aid, the average percentage of need met: 69%. Among students who received aid based on merit, the average award (and the proportion receiving): $2,021 (2%). The average athletic scholarship (and the proportion receiving): $2,623 (1%). Average amount of debt of borrowers graduating in 2009: $24,373. Proportion who borrowed: 68%.

CAMPUS LIFE AND EXTRACURRICULAR ACTIVITIES

Campus housing available (% using): coed dorms (86%), women's dorms (5%), men's dorms (6%), apartment for single students (3%), special housing for disabled students, special housing for international students. Students who live in college-owned, operated, or affiliated housing: 18%. **Clubs and organizations:** Number of student organizations: 257. Activities include: choral groups, concert band, dance, drama/theater, international student organization, jazz band, literary magazine, marching band, music ensembles, musical theater, opera, pep band, radio station, student government, student newspaper, student film society, symphony orchestra, television station. Number of fraternities: 9; sororities: 4. Average proportion of students who stay on campus on weekends: 37%. **Sports program (2009-2010):** Member of NCAA II. *Men's intercollegiate varsity sports:* baseball, basketball, cross country, football, golf, ice hockey, swimming, tennis, track and field (indoor), track and field (outdoor), wrestling. *Women's intercollegiate varsity sports:* basketball, cross country, golf, ice hockey, skiing (nordic), soccer, softball, swimming, tennis, track and field (indoor), track and field (outdoor), volleyball.

SERVICES AND FACILITIES

Basic services: nonremedial tutoring, women's center, placement service, day care, health service, health insurance, other. **Remedial assistance:** reading, math, writing, study skills. **Counseling services:** minority student, career, military, personal, veteran student, academic, older student, psychological, birth control, religious. **For learning-disabled students:** School does not offer a structured program with separate admission and additional fees. Total undergraduates in learning-disabled program or receiving services: 157. Services include: note-taking services, readers, extended time for tests, priority registration, priority seating, texts on tape, exams on tape or computer, other testing accommodations. **Library:** Number of titles: 947,582; number of current serial subscriptions: 29,740. **Information technology resources:** Students are not required to lease or own a computer. Number of campus computers available to all students: 1,489. School has a wireless network. Approximate number of users that can be accommodated: 6,160. Proportion of college-owned housing units wired for high-speed internet access: 100%. **Campus safety:** Security services offered: 24-hour foot-and-vehicle patrols, late-night transport/escort service, 24-hour emergency telephones, lighted pathways/sidewalks, student patrols, controlled dormitory access (key, security card, etc).

TRANSFER AND INTERNATIONAL STUDENTS

Transfer students: May apply for admission for the following academic terms: Fall, Spring, Summer. Applicants need a minimum number of credits to apply. For fall 2009: Transfer applications received: 2,174. Transfer applicants offered admission: 2,040. Transfer applicants enrolled: 1,323. **International students:** Number of foreign undergraduates: 777 (6% of student body). Number of countries represented: 87. Minimum TOEFL score required: 500 (paper); 173 (computer).

St. John's University

- **Address:** PO Box 7155, Collegeville, MN 56321
- **Website:** http://www.csbsju.edu
- **Private; Religious affiliation:** Roman Catholic (Benedictine)
- **Enrollment:** 1,867 full-time; 48 part-time

KEY STATS

- ✔ **U.S News College Ranking:** 62, National Liberal Arts Colleges
- ✔ **ACT Score (25th/75th percentile):** 23-29
- ✔ **Tuition:** 2010-2011: $31,576

Selectivity: More selective	**Room/board:** $8,044
Acceptance rate: 84%	**Average debt:** N/A
Student/faculty ratio: 12/1	**Proportion who borrowed:** N/A

UNDERGRADUATE STUDENT BODY STATS

2009-2010 enrollment: 1,867 full-time; 48 part-time. Men: 100%; women: 0%. **Ethnic makeup:** African American: 2%; Asian American: 3%; Hispanic: 2%; White: 86%; International: 7%. **Religious preference:** Protestant: 20%; No preference: 21%; Roman Catholic (Benedictine): 58%; Other: 1%.

ADMISSIONS FACTS AND FIGURES

Phone: (320) 363-2196. **Email:** admissions@csbsju.edu. **Website:** http://www.csbsju.edu. **Application deadlines for fall 2011:** Regular decision: Rolling. Early decision: Not offered. Early action: Send application by: November 15; Decision sent by: December 15. Admission can be deferred. **To apply online, go to:** http://www.csbsju.edu/admission/. **Admissions requirements/recommendations:** High school units required (recommended): English: 4 (0); Mathematics: 3 (0); Science: 2 (0); Foreign language: 0 (2); Social studies: 2 (0); History: 0 (0); Academic electives: 4 (0); Total units: 15 (2). Tests: The college uses SAT or ACT scores in admissions decisions. Either SAT or ACT required. For admission to the fall 2011 entering class, the school will accept: ACT with or without writing accepted. Campus visit: Recommended. Admissions interview: Recommended. Off-campus interview: May be arranged. **Factors that count in admissions decisions:** *Academic:* Secondary school record: Very Important. Class rank: Considered. Letters of recommendation: Important. Standardized test scores: Very Important. Essay: Very Important. *Nonacademic:* Interview: Considered. Extracurricular activities: Important. Talent/ability: Considered. Character/personal qualities: Considered. Alumni/ae relation-

ship: Considered. Geographical residence: Considered. State residency: Not Considered. Religious affiliation/commitment: Not Considered. Minority status: Considered. Volunteer work: Considered. Work experience: Considered. **Other schools with the greatest overlap in applicants:** Gustavus Adolphus College; St. Olaf College; University of Minnesota–Duluth; University of Minnesota–Twin Cities; University of St. Thomas. **Admissions statistics for the fall 2009 entering class:** Total applicants: 1,344. Total accepted: 1,125. Freshmen enrolled: 461; 18% were from out of state. Accepted through early-decision or early-action plans: 75%. Overall acceptance rate: 84%. Non-early acceptance rate: 72%. **Size of waiting list:** 0 applicants; enrolled from waiting list: 0. **Credentials of fall 2009 freshmen:** 23% ranked in the top 10 percent of their high school class; 58% were in the top 25 percent; 89% were in the top half. (Proportion submitting class standing: 70%.) **Average high school grade point average:** 3.5. **First-year students who submitted SAT scores:** 18%. Scores (25/75 percentile): Critical Reading: 493-648, Math: 523-675, Combined: 1016-1323. **First-year students submitting ACT scores:** 95%. Scores (25/75 percentile): English: 24-29, Math: 21-28, Composite: 23-29.

ACADEMICS

Year founded: 1857. **Academic calendar:** Semester. **Degrees offered:** bachelor's, master's. **Most popular majors:** 19% business administration and management, 12% accounting, 8% biology/biological sciences, 7% political science and government, 6% speech and rhetorical studies. **Major fields of study:** area, ethnic, cultural, and gender studies; biological and biomedical sciences; business, management, marketing, and related support services; computer and information sciences and support services; education; English language and literature/letters; foreign languages, literatures, and linguistics; health professions and related clinical sciences; history; liberal arts and sciences studies, and humanities; mathematics and statistics; multi/interdisciplinary studies; natural resources and conservation; philosophy and religious studies; physical sciences; psychology; public administration and social service professions; social sciences; theology and religious vocations; visual and performing arts. **Areas of required coursework:** arts/fine arts, humanities, mathematics, English (including composition), foreign languages, sciences (biological or physical), social science. **Pre-professional programs:** pre-law, pre-dentistry, pre-medicine, pre-theology, pre-veterinary science, pre-optometry, pre-pharmacy, other. **Special academic programs (% participation):** cross-registration (100%), double major (8%), dual enrollment (1%), English as a Second Language (ESL) (2%), exchange student program (domestic) (0%), honors program (13%), independent study (19%), internships (53%), liberal arts/career combination (34%), student-designed major (1%), study abroad (54%), teacher certificate program (6%). **Teacher certification offered in:** elementary, middle/junior high, secondary. **Reserve Officers Training Corps (ROTC):** Army ROTC: Offered on campus. **Faculty and instruction (2009-2010):** Total instructional faculty: 147 full-time, 30 part-time (53% men; 47% women; 8% minorities). Full-time faculty with Ph.D. or other terminal degree: 84%. Student/faculty ratio: 12/1. Classes of fewer than 20 students: 53%; of 20 to 49 students: 47%; of 50 or more students: 0%. **Advanced Placement and International Baccalaureate credit:** AP tests may be used for: Credit and/or placement. Scores accepted: 3, 4, 5. International Baccalaureate exams may be used for: Credit and/or placement. **Freshmen returning for sophomore year:** 90%. **Graduation rates:** Four-year: 71%; five-year: 78%; six-year: 80%. **Graduate study:** 15% of students pursue further study within one year. Fields in which graduates pursue further study: Master of Business Administration (MBA), 3%; law, 11%; medicine, 13%; dentistry, 3%; engineering, 2%; theology (or the seminary), 5%; education, 3%; arts and sciences, 58%; veterinary medicine, 2%.

COSTS AND FINANCIAL AID

Financial aid office: (320) 363-3664. **Expenses (2010-2011):** Tuition and fees 2010-2011: $31,576; room/board: $8,044. Estimated books and supplies: $1,000; transportation: $400; personal expenses: $900. **Financial aid:** Priority filing date for institution's financial aid form: March 15. In 2009-2010, 70% of undergraduates applied for financial aid. Of those, 59% were determined to have financial need; 46% had their need fully met. Average financial aid package (proportion receiving): $22,414 (59%). Average amount of gift aid, such as scholarships or grants (proportion receiving): $17,654 (57%). Average amount of self-help aid, such as work study or loans (proportion receiving): $5,996 (54%). Average need-based loan (excluding PLUS or other private loans): $4,692. Among students who received need-based aid, the average percentage of need met: 90%. Among students who received aid based on merit, the average award (and the proportion receiving): $10,628 (34%). The average athletic scholarship (and the proportion receiving): $0 (0%).

CAMPUS LIFE AND EXTRACURRICULAR ACTIVITIES

Campus housing available (% using): men's dorms (67%), apartment for single students (33%), special housing for disabled students. Students who live in college-owned, operated, or affiliated housing: 78%. **Student employment:** During the 2009-2010 academic year, 60% of undergraduates worked on campus. Average per-year earnings: $2,600. **Clubs and organizations:** Number of student organizations: 80. Activities include: campus ministries, choral groups, concert band, dance, drama/theater, international student organization, jazz band, literary magazine, model UN, music ensembles, musical theater, opera, pep band, radio station, student government, student newspaper, symphony orchestra. Number of fraternities: 0; sororities: 0. **Sports program (2009-2010):** Member of NCAA III. *Men's intercollegiate varsity sports:* baseball, basketball, cross country, football, golf, ice hockey, skiing (nordic), soccer, swimming, tennis, track and field (indoor), track and field (outdoor), wrestling.

SERVICES AND FACILITIES

Basic services: nonremedial tutoring, placement service, health service, health insurance. **Remedial assistance:** math, study skills, other. **Counseling services:** minority student, career, personal, academic, psychological, religious. **For learning-disabled students:** School does not offer a structured program with separate admission and additional fees. Total undergraduates in learning-disabled program or receiving services: 59. Services include: reading machines, note-taking services, extended time for tests, tutors, priority registration, priority seating, substitution of courses, texts on tape, typist/scribe, exams on tape or computer, other testing accommodations, other. **Library:** Number of titles: 658,438; number of current serial subscriptions: 71,720. **Information technology resources:** Students are not required to lease or own a computer. Number of campus computers available to all students: 860. School has a wireless network. Approximate number of users that can be accommodated: 2,000. Proportion of college-owned housing units wired for high-speed internet access: 100%. **Campus safety:** Security services offered: 24-hour foot-and-vehicle patrols, late-night transport/escort service, 24-hour emergency telephones, lighted pathways/sidewalks, student patrols, controlled dormitory access (key, security card, etc).

TRANSFER AND INTERNATIONAL STUDENTS

Transfer students: May apply for admission for the following academic terms: Fall, Spring. Applicants do not need a minimum number of credits to apply. For fall 2009: Transfer applications received: 62. Transfer applicants offered admission: 48. Transfer applicants enrolled: 32. **International students:** Number of foreign undergraduates: 132 (7% of student body). Number of countries represented: 39. Minimum TOEFL score required: 500 (paper); 173 (computer). Average TOEFL score: 550 (paper).

St. Mary's University of Minnesota

- **Address:** 700 Terrace Heights, Winona, MN 55987-1399
- **Website:** http://www.smumn.edu
- **Private; Religious affiliation:** Roman Catholic
- **Enrollment:** 1,455 full-time; 658 part-time

KEY STATS

✔ **U.S News College Ranking:** 183, National Universities
✔ **ACT Score (25th/75th percentile):** 19-26
✔ **Tuition:** 2010-2011: $26,090

Selectivity: Selective	**Room/board:** $6,940
Acceptance rate: 72%	**Average debt:** $32,166
Student/faculty ratio: 12/1	**Proportion who borrowed:** 77%

UNDERGRADUATE STUDENT BODY STATS

2009-2010 enrollment: 1,455 full-time; 658 part-time. Men: 48%; women: 52%. **Ethnic makeup:** African American: 3%; Asian American: 2%; Hispanic: 3%; White: 89%; International: 3%. **Religious preference:** Protestant: 16%; Muslim: 1%; No preference: 6%; Unknown: 13%; Roman Catholic: 60%; Other: 4%.

ADMISSIONS FACTS AND FIGURES

Phone: (507) 457-1700. **Email:** admissions@smumn.edu. **Website:** http://www.smumn.edu. **Application deadlines for fall 2011:** Regular decision: May 1; decision sent by May 1. Early decision: Not offered. Early action: Not offered. Admission can be deferred. **Application fee:** $25. **To apply online, go to:** http://smumn.gotoextinguisher.com/application/login/

index.php. **Admissions requirements/recommendations:** High school units required (recommended): English: 4; Mathematics: 3; Science: 3; Foreign language: 0 (2); Social studies: 2; History: 0; Academic electives: 6; Total units: 18. Tests: The college uses SAT or ACT scores in admissions decisions. Either SAT or ACT required. For admission to the fall 2011 entering class, the school will accept: ACT with or without writing accepted. Campus visit: Recommended. Admissions interview: Recommended. Off-campus interview: May be arranged. **Factors that count in admissions decisions:** *Academic:* Secondary school record: Very Important. Class rank: Important. Letters of recommendation: Considered. Standardized test scores: Very Important. Essay: Considered. *Nonacademic:* Interview: Important. Extracurricular activities: Considered. Talent/ability: Important. Character/personal qualities: Important. Alumni/ae relationship: Considered. Geographical residence: Not Considered. State residency: Not Considered. Religious affiliation/commitment: Not Considered. Minority status: Not Considered. Volunteer work: Considered. Work experience: Not Considered. **Other schools with the greatest overlap in applicants:** Gustavus Adolphus College; Minnesota State University–Mankato; University of Minnesota–Twin Cities; University of St. Thomas; Winona State University. **Admissions statistics for the fall 2009 entering class:** Total applicants: 1,408. Total accepted: 1,020. Freshmen enrolled: 330; 35% were from out of state. Overall acceptance rate: 72%. **Credentials of fall 2009 freshmen:** 18% ranked in the top 10 percent of their high school class; 41% were in the top 25 percent; 71% were in the top half. (Proportion submitting class standing: 72%.) **Average high school grade point average:** 3.2. **First-year students who submitted SAT scores:** 8%. Scores (25/75 percentile): Critical Reading: 503-560, Math: 463-605, Combined: 966-1165. **First-year students submitting ACT scores:** 90%. Scores (25/75 percentile): English: 19-25, Math: 18-25, Composite: 19-26.

ACADEMICS

Year founded: 1912. **Academic calendar:** Semester. **Degrees offered:** certificate, diploma, bachelor's, post-bachelor's certificate, master's, post-master's certificate, doctorate. **Most popular majors:** 20% business/commerce, 10% marketing/marketing management, 6% criminal justice/police science, 6% human resources management/personnel administration, 5% accounting. **Major fields of study:** biological and biomedical sciences; business, management, marketing, and related support services; communication, journalism, and related programs; computer and information sciences and support services; education; engineering; engineering technologies/technicians; English language and literature/letters; foreign languages, literatures, and linguistics; health professions and related clinical sciences; history; mathematics and statistics; multi/interdisciplinary studies; philosophy and religious studies; physical sciences; psychology; public administration and social service professions; security and protective services; social sciences; theology and religious vocations; visual and performing arts. **Areas of required coursework:** arts/fine arts, humanities, mathematics, English (including composition), philosophy, sciences (biological or physical), history, social science, other. **Pre-professional programs:** pre-law, pre-dentistry, pre-medicine, pre-theology, pre-veterinary science, other. **Special academic programs (% participation):** cross-registration (5%), double major (13%), dual enrollment (7%), English as a Second Language (ESL) (1%), honors program (15%), independent study (13%), internships (29%), student-designed major (2%), study abroad (18%), teacher certificate program (10%). **Teacher certification offered in:** early childhood, elementary, middle/junior high, secondary. **Cooperative education programs:** health professions. **Reserve Officers Training Corps (ROTC):** Army ROTC: Offered at cooperating institution (University of Wisconsin–La Crosse). **Faculty and instruction (2009-2010):** Total instructional faculty: 103 full-time, 482 part-time (50% men; 50% women; 6% minorities). Full-time faculty with Ph.D. or other terminal degree: 84%. Student/faculty ratio: 12/1. Classes of fewer than 20 students: 51%; of 20 to 49 students: 49%. **Advanced Placement and International Baccalaureate credit:** AP tests may be used for: Credit and/or placement. Scores accepted: 3, 4, 5. International Baccalaureate exams may be used for: Credit and/or placement. **Freshmen returning for sophomore year:** 75%. **Graduation rates:** Four-year: 46%; five-year: 54%; six-year: 55%. **Graduate study:** 22% of students pursue further study immediately upon graduation. Fields in which graduates pursue further study: Master of Business Administration (MBA), 12%; law, 1%; medicine, 28%; theology (or the seminary), 18%; education, 12%; arts and sciences, 22%.

COSTS AND FINANCIAL AID

Financial aid office: (507) 457-1438. **Expenses (2010-2011):** Tuition and fees 2010-2011: $26,090; room/board: $6,940. Estimated books and supplies: $1,300; transportation: $550; personal expenses: $820. **Financial aid:** Priority filing date for institution's financial aid form: March 15. In 2009-2010, 81%

of undergraduates applied for financial aid. Of those, 73% were determined to have financial need; 21% had their need fully met. Average financial aid package (proportion receiving): $19,846 (73%). Average amount of gift aid, such as scholarships or grants (proportion receiving): $15,012 (73%). Average amount of self-help aid, such as work study or loans (proportion receiving): $5,848 (59%). Average need-based loan (excluding PLUS or other private loans): $4,884. Among students who received need-based aid, the average percentage of need met: 76%. Among students who received aid based on merit, the average award (and the proportion receiving): $9,361 (25%). Average amount of debt of borrowers graduating in 2009: $32,166. Proportion who borrowed: 77%.

CAMPUS LIFE AND EXTRACURRICULAR ACTIVITIES

Campus housing available (% using): coed dorms (59%), women's dorms (9%), men's dorms (10%), apartment for single students (20%), special housing for disabled students (2%). Students who live in college-owned, operated, or affiliated housing: 83%. **Student employment:** During the 2009-2010 academic year, 29% of undergraduates worked on campus. Average per-year earnings: $1,630. **Clubs and organizations:** Number of student organizations: 85. Activities include: campus ministries, choral groups, concert band, dance, drama/theater, international student organization, jazz band, literary magazine, music ensembles, musical theater, radio station, student government, student newspaper, yearbook. Number of fraternities: 0; sororities: 0. Proportion of men in fraternities: 4%; of women in sororities: 3%. Average proportion of students who stay on campus on weekends: 75%. **Sports program (2009-2010):** Member of NCAA III. *Men's intercollegiate varsity sports:* baseball, basketball, cross country, golf, ice hockey, soccer, swimming, tennis, track and field (indoor), track and field (outdoor). *Women's intercollegiate varsity sports:* basketball, cross country, golf, ice hockey, soccer, softball, swimming, tennis, track and field (indoor), track and field (outdoor), volleyball.

SERVICES AND FACILITIES

Basic services: nonremedial tutoring, health service, health insurance. **Remedial assistance:** study skills. **Counseling services:** career, personal, academic, psychological, religious. **For learning-disabled students:** School does not offer a structured program with separate admission and additional fees. Total undergraduates in learning-disabled program or receiving services: 25. Services include: remedial math, remedial English, reading machines, tape recorders, note-taking services, oral tests, learning center, readers, extended time for tests, tutors, priority registration, texts on tape, typist/scribe, exams on tape or computer, other testing accommodations. **Library:** Number of titles: 202,719; number of current serial subscriptions: 840. **Information technology resources:** Students are not required to lease or own a computer. Number of campus computers available to all students: 250. School has a wireless network. Approximate number of users that can be accommodated: 1,000. Proportion of college-owned housing units wired for high-speed internet access: 100%. **Campus safety:** Security services offered: 24-hour foot-and-vehicle patrols, late-night transport/escort service, 24-hour emergency telephones, lighted pathways/sidewalks, student patrols, controlled dormitory access (key, security card, etc).

TRANSFER AND INTERNATIONAL STUDENTS

Transfer students: May apply for admission for the following academic terms: Fall, Spring, Summer. Applicants need a minimum number of credits to apply. For fall 2009: Transfer applications received: 358. Transfer applicants offered admission: 251. Transfer applicants enrolled: 176. **International students:** Number of foreign undergraduates: 55 (3% of student body). Number of countries represented: 18. Minimum TOEFL score required: 550 (paper); 213 (computer). Average TOEFL score: 550 (paper).

St. Olaf College

- **Address:** 1520 St. Olaf Avenue, Northfield, MN 55057
- **Website:** http://www.stolaf.edu
- **Private; Religious affiliation:** Lutheran
- **Enrollment:** 3,028 full-time; 71 part-time

KEY STATS

✔ **U.S News College Ranking:** 51, National Liberal Arts Colleges
✔ **ACT Score (25th/75th percentile):** 26-31
✔ **Tuition:** 2010-2011: $36,800

Selectivity: More selective	**Room/board:** $8,500
Acceptance rate: 57%	**Average debt:** $25,853
Student/faculty ratio: 12/1	**Proportion who borrowed:** 66%

UNDERGRADUATE STUDENT BODY STATS

2009-2010 enrollment: 3,028 full-time; 71 part-time. Men: 45%; women: 55%. **Ethnic makeup:** African American: 2%; Asian American: 5%; Hispanic: 2%; White: 89%; International: 2%. **Religious preference:** Roman Catholic: 15%; Protestant: 16%; Muslim: 1%; Buddhist: 1%; No preference: 5%; Unknown: 16%; Lutheran: 37%; Christian, Other: 8%; Other: 1%.

ADMISSIONS FACTS AND FIGURES

Phone: (507) 786-3025. **Email:** admissions@stolaf.edu. **Website:** http://www.stolaf.edu. **Application deadlines for fall 2011:** Regular decision: January 15; decision sent by March 20. Early decision: Send application by: November 15; Decision sent by: December 15. Early action: Not offered. Admission can be deferred. **Application fee:** $40. **To apply online, go to:** http://www.stolaf.edu/admissions/onlineapp/index.html. **Admissions requirements/recommendations:** High school units required (recommended): English: (4); Mathematics: (4); Science: (4); Foreign language: (4); Social studies: (4); Academic electives: (4); Total units: (24). Tests: The college uses SAT or ACT scores in admissions decisions. Either SAT or ACT required. For admission to the fall 2011 entering class, the school will accept: ACT with or without writing accepted. Campus visit: Recommended. Admissions interview: Recommended. Off-campus interview: Not available. **Factors that count in admissions decisions:** *Academic:* Secondary school record: Very Important. Class rank: Important. Letters of recommendation: Important. Standardized test scores: Important. Essay: Very Important. *Nonacademic:* Interview: Considered. Extracurricular activities: Important. Talent/ability: Considered. Character/personal qualities: Important. Alumni/ae relationship: Considered. Geographical residence: Considered. State residency: Considered. Religious affiliation/commitment: Considered. Minority status: Considered. Volunteer work: Considered. Work experience: Considered. **Other schools with the greatest overlap in applicants:** Carleton College; Gustavus Adolphus College; Macalester College; University of Minnesota–Twin Cities; University of Wisconsin–Madison. **Admissions statistics for the fall 2009 entering class:** Total applicants: 3,882. Total accepted: 2,230. Freshmen enrolled: 778; 51% were from out of state. Overall acceptance rate: 57%. Early-decision acceptance rate: 88%. Non-early acceptance rate: 56%. **Size of waiting list:** 576 applicants; enrolled from waiting list: 17. **Credentials of fall 2009 freshmen:** 53% ranked in the top 10 percent of their high school class; 82% were in the top 25 percent; 98% were in the top half. (Proportion submitting class standing: 67%.) **Average high school grade point average:** 3.6. **First-year students who submitted SAT scores:** 46%. Scores (25/75 percentile): Critical Reading: 590-710, Math: 590-690, Combined: 1180-1400. **First-year students submitting ACT scores:** 83%. Scores (25/75 percentile): English: 25-31, Math: 26-33, Composite: 26-31.

ACADEMICS

Year founded: 1874. **Academic calendar:** 4-1-4. **Degrees offered:** bachelor's. **Most popular majors:** 13% biology/biological sciences, 8% economics, 7% English language and literature, 7% psychology, 4% mathematics. **Major fields of study:** area, ethnic, cultural, and gender studies; biological and biomedical sciences; computer and information sciences and support services; education; English language and literature/letters; family and consumer sciences/human sciences; foreign languages, literatures, and linguistics; health professions and related clinical sciences; history; liberal arts and sciences studies, and humanities; mathematics and statistics; multi/interdisciplinary studies; natural resources and conservation; parks, recreation, leisure, and fitness studies; philosophy and religious studies; physical sciences; psychology; public administration and social service professions; social sciences; visual and performing arts. **Areas of required coursework:** arts/fine arts, humanities, mathematics, English (including composition), philosophy, foreign languages, sciences (biological or physical), history, social science, other. **Pre-professional programs:** pre-law, pre-dentistry, pre-medicine, pre-theology, pre-veterinary science, pre-pharmacy, other. **Special academic programs (% participation):** cross-registration (1%), double major (30%), dual enrollment (1%), independent study (46%), internships (21%), student-designed major (2%), study abroad (63%), teacher certificate program (7%). **Teacher certification offered in:** elementary, middle/junior high, secondary. **Faculty and instruction (2009-2010):** Total instructional faculty: 207 full-time, 120 part-time (55% men; 45% women; 8% minorities). Full-time faculty with Ph.D. or other terminal degree: 90%. Student/faculty ratio: 12/1. Classes of fewer than 20 students: 60%; of 20 to 49 students: 36%; of 50 or more students: 4%. **Advanced Placement and International Baccalaureate credit:** AP tests may be used for: Credit and/or placement. Scores accepted: 4, 5. International Baccalaureate exams may be used for: Credit and/or placement. **Freshmen returning for sophomore year:** 93%. **Graduation rates:** Four-year: 82%; five-year: 87%; six-year: 87%. **Graduate study:** 33% of students pursue further study immediately upon graduation; 48% within five years. Fields in which graduates pursue further study: Master of Business Administration (MBA), 4%; law, 9%; medicine, 12%; dentistry, 1%; engineering, 1%; theology (or the seminary), 2%; education, 4%; arts and sciences, 45%.

COSTS AND FINANCIAL AID

Financial aid office: (507) 646-3019. **Expenses (2010-2011):** Tuition and fees 2010-2011: $36,800; room/board: $8,500. Estimated books and supplies: $1,000; transportation: $450; personal expenses: $900. **Financial aid:** Priority filing date for institution's financial aid form: February 1; deadline: April 15. In 2009-2010, 89% of undergraduates applied for financial aid. Of those, 66% were determined to have financial need; 100% had their need fully met. Average financial aid package (proportion receiving): $26,401 (66%). Average amount of gift aid, such as scholarships or grants (proportion receiving): $21,228 (66%). Average amount of self-help aid, such as work study or loans (proportion receiving): $7,289 (66%). Average need-based loan (excluding PLUS or other private loans): $6,575. Among students who received need-based aid, the average percentage of need met: 100%. Among students who received aid based on merit, the average award (and the proportion receiving): $8,611 (17%). The average athletic scholarship (and the proportion receiving): $0 (0%). Average amount of debt of borrowers graduating in 2009: $25,853. Proportion who borrowed: 66%.

CAMPUS LIFE AND EXTRACURRICULAR ACTIVITIES

Campus housing available (% using): coed dorms (92%), special housing for disabled students (1%), other housing options (7%). Students who live in college-owned, operated, or affiliated housing: 96%. **Clubs and organizations:** Number of student organizations: 168. Activities include: campus ministries, choral groups, concert band, dance, drama/theater, international student organization, jazz band, literary magazine, model UN, music ensembles, musical theater, opera, pep band, radio station, student government, student newspaper, student film society, symphony orchestra, television station. Number of fraternities: 0; sororities: 0. Average proportion of students who stay on campus on weekends: 85%. **Sports program (2009-2010):** Member of NCAA III. **Men's intercollegiate varsity sports:** baseball, basketball, cross country, football, golf, ice hockey, skiing (nordic), skiing (alpine), soccer, swimming, tennis, track and field (indoor), track and field (outdoor), wrestling. **Women's intercollegiate varsity sports:** basketball, cross country, golf, ice hockey, skiing (nordic), skiing (alpine), soccer, softball, swimming, tennis, track and field (indoor), track and field (outdoor), volleyball.

SERVICES AND FACILITIES

Basic services: nonremedial tutoring, placement service, health service, health insurance, other. **Counseling services:** minority student, career, personal, academic, older student, psychological, birth control, religious. **For learning-disabled students:** School does not offer a structured program with separate admission and additional fees. Total undergraduates in learning-disabled program or receiving services: 155. Services include: reading machines, tape recorders, note-taking services, oral tests, learning center, readers, extended time for tests, tutors, priority registration, substitution of courses, texts on tape, typist/scribe, exams on tape or computer, other testing accommodations, other. **Library:** Number of titles: 751,464; number of current serial subscriptions: 4,610. **Information technology resources:** Students are not required to lease or own a computer. Number of campus computers available to all students: 855. School has a wireless network. Approximate number of users that can be accommodated: 4,000. Proportion of college-owned housing units wired for high-speed internet access: 100%. **Campus safety:** Security services offered: 24-hour foot-and-

vehicle patrols, late-night transport/escort service, 24-hour emergency telephones, lighted pathways/sidewalks, controlled dormitory access (key, security card, etc).

TRANSFER AND INTERNATIONAL STUDENTS

Transfer students: May apply for admission for the following academic terms: Fall, Winter, Spring. Applicants need a minimum number of credits to apply. For fall 2009: Transfer applications received: 138. Transfer applicants offered admission: 49. Transfer applicants enrolled: 26. **International students:** Number of foreign undergraduates: 67 (2% of student body). Number of countries represented: 26. Minimum TOEFL score required: 550 (paper); 213 (computer). Average TOEFL score: 600 (paper).

University of Minnesota—Crookston

- **Address:** 2900 University Avenue, Crookston, MN 56716
- **Website:** http://www.crk.umn.edu
- **Public**
- **Enrollment:** 1,152 full-time; 1,127 part-time

KEY STATS
✔ **U.S News College Ranking:** 50, Regional Colleges (Midwest)
✔ **ACT Score (25th/75th percentile):** 19-24
✔ **Tuition:** 2010-2011: $10,647 in state, $10,647 out of state

Selectivity: Selective	**Room/board:** $6,568
Acceptance rate: 83%	**Average debt:** $26,199
Student/faculty ratio: 17/1	**Proportion who borrowed:** 86%

UNDERGRADUATE STUDENT BODY STATS

2009-2010 enrollment: 1,152 full-time; 1,127 part-time. Men: 50%; women: 50%. **Ethnic makeup:** African American: 5%; American-Indian: 1%; Asian American: 2%; Hispanic: 3%; White: 81%; International: 8%.

ADMISSIONS FACTS AND FIGURES

Phone: (800) 232-6466. **Email:** UMCinfo@umn.edu. **Website:** http://www.crk.umn.edu. **Application deadlines for fall 2011:** Regular decision: Rolling. Early decision: Not offered. Early action: Not offered. Admission can be deferred. **Application fee:** $30. **To apply online, go to:** http://www2.crk.umn.edu/admissions/requirements/applyonline.htm. **Admissions requirements/recommendations:** High school units required (recommended): English: 4; Mathematics: 3; Science: 3; Foreign language: (2); Social studies: 3; Total units: 13 (2). Tests: The college uses SAT or ACT scores in admissions decisions. Either SAT or ACT required. For admission to the fall 2011 entering class, the school will accept: ACT with or without writing accepted. Campus visit: Recommended. Admissions interview: Neither required nor recommended. Off-campus interview: May be arranged. **Factors that count in admissions decisions:** *Academic:* Secondary school record: Very Important. Class rank: Very Important. Letters of recommendation: Considered. Standardized test scores: Very Important. Essay: Considered. *Nonacademic:* Interview: Not Considered. Extracurricular activities: Not Considered. Talent/ability: Not Considered. Character/personal qualities: Not Considered. Alumni/ae relationship: Not Considered. Geographical residence: Not Considered. State residency: Not Considered. Religious affiliation/commitment: Not Considered. Minority status: Not Considered. Volunteer work: Not Considered. Work experience: Not Considered. **Other schools with the greatest overlap in applicants:** Bemidji State University; Minnesota State University–Moorhead; North Dakota State University; University of Minnesota–Twin Cities; University of North Dakota. **Admissions statistics for the fall 2009 entering class:** Total applicants: 769. Total accepted: 635. Freshmen enrolled: 285; 38% were from out of state. Overall acceptance rate: 83%. **Credentials of fall 2009 freshmen:** 10% ranked in the top 10 percent of their high school class; 27% were in the top 25 percent; 59% were in the top half. (Proportion submitting class standing: 73%.) **Average high school grade point average:** 3.1. **First-year students who submitted SAT scores:** 9%. Scores (25/75 percentile): Critical Reading: 410-560, Math: 420-590, Combined: 830-1150. **First-year students submitting ACT scores:** 84%. Scores (25/75 percentile): English: 18-25, Math: 17-23, Composite: 19-24.

ACADEMICS

Year founded: 1966. **Academic calendar:** Semester. **Degrees offered:** certificate, bachelor's. **Most popular majors:** 20% natural resources/conservation, 13% business administration and management, 9% industrial engineering,

8% agronomy and crop science, 5% horse husbandry/equine science and management. **Major fields of study:** agriculture, agriculture operations, and related sciences; business, management, marketing, and related support services; communication, journalism, and related programs; education; engineering; engineering technologies/technicians; health professions and related clinical sciences; multi/interdisciplinary studies; natural resources and conservation; parks, recreation, leisure, and fitness studies; transportation and materials moving. **Areas of required coursework:** humanities, computer literacy, mathematics, English (including composition), sciences (biological or physical), social science, other. **Pre-professional programs:** pre-dentistry, pre-medicine, pre-veterinary science, pre-optometry, pre-pharmacy. **Special academic programs (% participation):** cross-registration, distance learning (40%), double major, dual enrollment, English as a Second Language (ESL), external degree program, honors program, independent study, internships (85%), student-designed major, study abroad (10%), teacher certificate program (5%). **Teacher certification offered in:** early childhood, secondary. **Reserve Officers Training Corps (ROTC):** Air Force ROTC: Offered at cooperating institution (University of North Dakota). **Faculty and instruction (2009-2010):** Total instructional faculty: 55 full-time, 46 part-time (54% men; 46% women; 8% minorities). Full-time faculty with Ph.D. or other terminal degree: 42%. Student/faculty ratio: 17/1. Classes of fewer than 20 students: 54%; of 20 to 49 students: 43%; of 50 or more students: 3%. **Advanced Placement and International Baccalaureate credit:** AP tests may be used for: Credit only. Scores accepted: 3, 4. International Baccalaureate exams may be used for: Credit only. **Freshmen returning for sophomore year:** 69%. **Graduation rates:** Four-year: 21%; five-year: 36%; six-year: 33%. **Graduate study:** 8% of students pursue further study immediately upon graduation; 8% within one year; 0% within five years. Fields in which graduates pursue further study: Master of Business Administration (MBA), 1%; medicine, 2%; education, 1%.

COSTS AND FINANCIAL AID

Financial aid office: (218) 281-8576. **Expenses (2010-2011):** Tuition and fees 2010-2011: $10,647 in state, $10,647 out of state; room/board: $6,568. Estimated books and supplies: $800; transportation: $1,000; personal expenses: $1,040. **Financial aid:** Priority filing date for institution's financial aid form: March 1. In 2009-2010, 82% of undergraduates applied for financial aid. Of those, 68% were determined to have financial need; 28% had their need fully met. Average financial aid package (proportion receiving): $11,016 (68%). Average amount of gift aid, such as scholarships or grants (proportion receiving): $7,088 (65%). Average amount of self-help aid, such as work study or loans (proportion receiving): $4,941 (60%). Average need-based loan (excluding PLUS or other private loans): $4,764. Among students who received need-based aid, the average percentage of need met: 74%. Among students who received aid based on merit, the average award (and the proportion receiving): $2,254 (8%). Average amount of debt of borrowers graduating in 2009: $26,199. Proportion who borrowed: 86%.

CAMPUS LIFE AND EXTRACURRICULAR ACTIVITIES

Campus housing available (% using): coed dorms (69%), apartment for single students (31%). Students who live in college-owned, operated, or affiliated housing: 41%. **Student employment:** During the 2009-2010 academic year, 10% of undergraduates worked on campus. Average per-year earnings: $1,700. **Clubs and organizations:** Number of student organizations: 42. Activities include: campus ministries, choral groups, drama/theater, international student organization, music ensembles, pep band, student government. Number of fraternities: 2; sororities: 1. Proportion of men in fraternities: 2%; of women in sororities: 1%. Average proportion of students who stay on campus on weekends: 38%. **Sports program (2009-2010):** Member of NCAA II. *Men's intercollegiate varsity sports:* baseball, basketball, football, golf. *Women's intercollegiate varsity sports:* basketball, equestrian, golf, soccer, softball, tennis, volleyball.

SERVICES AND FACILITIES

Basic services: nonremedial tutoring, placement service, day care, health service, health insurance. **Remedial assistance:** math, writing, study skills. **Counseling services:** minority student, career, military, personal, veteran student, academic, older student, birth control, religious. **For learning-disabled students:** School does not offer a structured program with separate admission and additional fees. Total undergraduates in learning-disabled program or receiving services: 15. Services include: remedial math, reading machines, tape recorders, diagnostic testing service, untimed tests, note-taking services, oral tests, learning center, readers, extended time for tests, tutors, priority registration, priority seating, proofreading services, texts on tape, typist/scribe, exams on tape or computer, other testing accommodations, other. **Library:** Number of titles: 55,923; number of current serial

subscriptions: 655. **Information technology resources:** Students are required to lease or own a computer. Number of campus computers available to all students: 20. School has a wireless network. Approximate number of users that can be accommodated: 1,500. Proportion of college-owned housing units wired for high-speed internet access: 100%. **Campus safety:** Security services offered: late-night transport/escort service, 24-hour emergency telephones, lighted pathways/sidewalks, student patrols, controlled dormitory access (key, security card, etc).

TRANSFER AND INTERNATIONAL STUDENTS

Transfer students: May apply for admission for the following academic terms: Fall, Spring, Summer. Applicants need a minimum number of credits to apply. For fall 2009: Transfer applications received: 283. Transfer applicants offered admission: 221. Transfer applicants enrolled: 178. **International students:** Number of foreign undergraduates: 99 (8% of student body). Number of countries represented: 17. Minimum TOEFL score required: 520 (paper); 190 (computer). Average TOEFL score: 550 (paper).

University of Minnesota—Duluth

- **Address:** 1049 University Drive, Duluth, MN 55812-2496
- **Website:** http://www.d.umn.edu
- **Public**
- **Enrollment:** 9,212 full-time; 1,294 part-time

KEY STATS

- ✔ **U.S News College Ranking:** 34, Regional Universities (Midwest)
- ✔ **ACT Score (25th/75th percentile):** 20-26
- ✔ **Tuition:** 2009-2010: $11,193 in state, $13,193 out of state

Selectivity: Selective	**Room/board:** $6,176
Acceptance rate: 71%	**Average debt:** $27,931
Student/faculty ratio: 22/1	**Proportion who borrowed:** 72%

UNDERGRADUATE STUDENT BODY STATS

2009-2010 enrollment: 9,212 full-time; 1,294 part-time. Men: 54%; women: 46%. **Ethnic makeup:** African American: 1%; American-Indian: 1%; Asian American: 3%; Hispanic: 1%; White: 92%; International: 1%.

ADMISSIONS FACTS AND FIGURES

Phone: (218) 726-7171. **Email:** umdadmis@d.umn.edu. **Website:** http://www.d.umn.edu. **Application deadlines for fall 2011:** Regular decision: August 1. Early decision: Not offered. Early action: Not offered. Admission can be deferred. **Application fee:** $35. **To apply online, go to:** http://www.d.umn.edu/admissions/online.html. **Admissions requirements/recommendations:** High school units required (recommended): English: 4; Mathematics: 3; Science: 3; Foreign language: 2; Social studies: 1; History: 1; Total units: 15. Tests: The college uses SAT or ACT scores in admissions decisions. Either SAT or ACT required. For admission to the fall 2011 entering class, the school will accept: ACT with writing required. Campus visit: Recommended. Admissions interview: Neither required nor recommended. Off-campus interview: Not available. **Factors that count in admissions decisions:** *Academic:* Secondary school record: Important. Class rank: Very Important. Letters of recommendation: Considered. Standardized test scores: Very Important. Essay: Considered. *Nonacademic:* Interview: Not Considered. Extracurricular activities: Considered. Talent/ability: Considered. Character/personal qualities: Not Considered. Alumni/ae relationship: Considered. Geographical residence: Considered. State residency: Considered. Religious affiliation/commitment: Not Considered. Minority status: Considered. Volunteer work: Not Considered. Work experience: Not Considered. **Other schools with the greatest overlap in applicants:** Minnesota State University–Mankato; St. Cloud State University; University of Minnesota–Twin Cities; University of St. Thomas; Winona State University. **Admissions statistics for the fall 2009 entering class:** Total applicants: 7,936. Total accepted: 5,669. Freshmen enrolled: 2,118; 12% were from out of state. Overall acceptance rate: 71%. **Credentials of fall 2009 freshmen:** 16% ranked in the top 10 percent of their high school class; 42% were in the top 25 percent; 85% were in the top half. (Proportion submitting class standing: 99%.) **First-year students who submitted SAT scores:** 3%. Scores (25/75 percentile): Critical Reading: 480-590, Math: 480-620, Combined: 960-1210. **First-year students submitting ACT scores:** 98%. Scores (25/75 percentile): English: 21-26, Math: 20-25, Composite: 20-26.

ACADEMICS

Year founded: 1947. **Academic calendar:** Semester. **Degrees offered:** bachelor's, post-bachelor's certificate, master's. **Most popular majors:** 20% business, management, marketing, and related support services, 13% social sciences, 11% education, 10% biological and biomedical sciences, 8% psychology. **Major fields of study:** area, ethnic, cultural, and gender studies; biological and biomedical sciences; business, management, marketing, and related support services; communication, journalism, and related programs; computer and information sciences and support services; education; engineering; English language and literature/letters; foreign languages, literatures, and linguistics; health professions and related clinical sciences; history; mathematics and statistics; multi/interdisciplinary studies; natural resources and conservation; parks, recreation, leisure, and fitness studies; philosophy and religious studies; physical sciences; psychology; social sciences; visual and performing arts. **Areas of required coursework:** arts/fine arts, humanities, computer literacy, mathematics, English (including composition), philosophy, foreign languages, sciences (biological or physical), history, social science. **Pre-professional programs:** pre-law, pre-dentistry, pre-medicine, pre-veterinary science, pre-optometry, pre-pharmacy, other. **Special academic programs:** accelerated program, cross-registration, distance learning, double major, dual enrollment, exchange student program (domestic), external degree program, honors program, independent study, internships, liberal arts/career combination, study abroad, teacher certificate program, weekend college. **Teacher certification offered in:** early childhood, special education, elementary, middle/junior high, secondary. **Reserve Officers Training Corps (ROTC):** Air Force ROTC: Offered on campus. **Faculty and instruction (2009-2010):** Total instructional faculty: 427 full-time, 88 part-time (55% men; 45% women; 17% minorities). Full-time faculty with Ph.D. or other terminal degree: 74%. Student/faculty ratio: 22/1. Classes of fewer than 20 students: 29%; of 20 to 49 students: 55%; of 50 or more students: 16%. **Advanced Placement and International Baccalaureate credit:** AP tests may be used for: Credit and/or placement. Scores accepted: 3, 4, 5. International Baccalaureate exams may be used for: Credit and/or placement. **Freshmen returning for sophomore year:** 80%. **Graduation rates:** Four-year: 26%; five-year: 53%; six-year: 52%. **Graduate study:** 15% of students pursue further study immediately upon graduation.

COSTS AND FINANCIAL AID

Financial aid office: (218) 726-8000. **Expenses (2009-2010):** Tuition and fees 2009-2010: $11,193 in state, $13,193 out of state; room/board: $6,176. Estimated books and supplies: $1,348 personal expenses: $2,850. **Financial aid:** Priority filing date for institution's financial aid form: March 1. In 2009-2010, 78% of undergraduates applied for financial aid. Of those, 58% were determined to have financial need; 34% had their need fully met. Average financial aid package (proportion receiving): $11,087 (58%). Average amount of gift aid, such as scholarships or grants (proportion receiving): $6,432 (57%). Average amount of self-help aid, such as work study or loans (proportion receiving): $5,846 (50%). Average need-based loan (excluding PLUS or other private loans): $5,705. Among students who received need-based aid, the average percentage of need met: 76%. Among students who received aid based on merit, the average award (and the proportion receiving): $2,752 (10%). Average amount of debt of borrowers graduating in 2009: $27,931. Proportion who borrowed: 72%.

CAMPUS LIFE AND EXTRACURRICULAR ACTIVITIES

Campus housing available (% using): coed dorms (46%), women's dorms (4%), men's dorms (2%), apartment for single students (48%), special housing for disabled students. Students who live in college-owned, operated, or affiliated housing: 27%. **Student employment:** During the 2009-2010 academic year, 18% of undergraduates worked on campus. Average per-year earnings: $2,721. **Clubs and organizations:** Number of student organizations: 186. Activities include: campus ministries, choral groups, concert band, dance, drama/theater, international student organization, jazz band, literary magazine, marching band, model UN, music ensembles, musical theater, opera, pep band, radio station, student government, student newspaper, student film society, symphony orchestra. Number of fraternities: 4; sororities: 3. Proportion of men in fraternities: 2%; of women in sororities: 3%. Average proportion of students who stay on campus on weekends: 45%. **Sports program (2009-2010):** Member of NCAA II. *Men's intercollegiate varsity sports:* baseball, basketball, cross country, football, ice hockey, lacrosse, track and field (indoor), track and field (outdoor). *Women's intercollegiate varsity sports:* basketball, cross country, ice hockey, lacrosse, soccer, softball, tennis, track and field (indoor), track and field (outdoor), volleyball.

SERVICES AND FACILITIES

Basic services: nonremedial tutoring, women's center, placement service, day care, health service, health insurance. **Remedial assistance:** math, writing, study skills. **Counseling services:** minority student, career, military, personal, veteran student, academic, older student, psychological, birth control, religious. **For learning-disabled students:** School does not offer a structured program with separate admission and additional fees. Services include: remedial math, remedial English, reading machines, tape recorders, diagnostic testing service, note-taking services, readers, extended time for tests, tutors, priority registration, texts on tape, other testing accommodations. **Library:** Number of titles: 588,408; number of current serial subscriptions: 33,794. **Information technology resources:** Students are not required to lease or own a computer. Number of campus computers available to all students: 551. School has a wireless network. Approximate number of users that can be accommodated: 9,000. Proportion of college-owned housing units wired for high-speed internet access: 100%. **Campus safety:** Security services offered: 24-hour foot-and-vehicle patrols, late-night transport/escort service, 24-hour emergency telephones, lighted pathways/sidewalks, student patrols, controlled dormitory access (key, security card, etc).

TRANSFER AND INTERNATIONAL STUDENTS

Transfer students: May apply for admission for the following academic terms: Fall, Spring. Applicants do not need a minimum number of credits to apply. For fall 2009: Transfer applications received: 1,147. Transfer applicants offered admission: 729. Transfer applicants enrolled: 477. **International students:** Number of foreign undergraduates: 129 (1% of student body). Number of countries represented: 40. Minimum TOEFL score required: 550 (paper); 213 (computer).

University of Minnesota–Morris

- **Address:** 600 E. Fourth Street, Morris, MN 56267
- **Website:** http://www.morris.umn.edu
- **Public**
- **Enrollment:** 1,592 full-time; 113 part-time

KEY STATS
- ✔ **U.S News College Ranking:** 152, National Liberal Arts Colleges
- ✔ **ACT Score (25th/75th percentile):** 22-28
- ✔ **Tuition:** 2010-2011: $11,512 in state, $11,512 out of state
  - **Selectivity:** More selective
  - **Acceptance rate:** 74%
  - **Student/faculty ratio:** 14/1
  - **Room/board:** $7,332
  - **Average debt:** $25,855
  - **Proportion who borrowed:** 77%

UNDERGRADUATE STUDENT BODY STATS

2009-2010 enrollment: 1,592 full-time; 113 part-time. Men: 43%; women: 57%. **Ethnic makeup:** African American: 3%; American-Indian: 12%; Asian American: 3%; Hispanic: 2%; White: 77%; International: 4%. **Religious preference:** Roman Catholic: 24%; Protestant: 44%; No preference: 22%; Other: 10%.

ADMISSIONS FACTS AND FIGURES

Phone: (888) 866-3382. **Email:** admissions@morris.umn.edu. **Website:** http://www.morris.umn.edu. **Application deadlines for fall 2011:** Regular decision: March 15. Early decision: Not offered. Early action: Not offered. Admission can be deferred. **Application fee:** $35. **To apply online, go to:** http://www.morris.umn.edu/apply. **Admissions requirements/recommendations:** High school units required (recommended): English: 4; Mathematics: 3; Science: 3; Foreign language: 2; Social studies: 2; History: 1. **Tests:** The college uses SAT or ACT scores in admissions decisions. Either SAT or ACT required. For admission to the fall 2011 entering class, the school will accept: ACT with writing required. Campus visit: Recommended. Admissions interview: Recommended. Off-campus interview: May be arranged. **Factors that count in admissions decisions:** *Academic:* Secondary school record: Very Important. Class rank: Very Important. Letters of recommendation: Considered. Standardized test scores: Very Important. Essay: Considered. *Nonacademic:* Interview: Considered. Extracurricular activities: Important. Talent/ability: Important. Character/personal qualities: Important. Alumni/ae relationship: Not Considered. Geographical residence: Not Considered. State residency: Not Considered. Religious affiliation/commitment: Not Considered. Minority status: Not Considered. Volunteer work: Important. Work experience: Important. **Other schools with the greatest overlap in applicants:** Concordia College–Moorhead;

Gustavus Adolphus College; St. Olaf College; University of Minnesota–Twin Cities; University of Wisconsin–Madison. **Admissions statistics for the fall 2009 entering class:** Total applicants: 1,453. Total accepted: 1,077. Freshmen enrolled: 405; 10% were from out of state. Overall acceptance rate: 74%. **Credentials of fall 2009 freshmen:** 30% ranked in the top 10 percent of their high school class; 56% were in the top 25 percent; 88% were in the top half. (Proportion submitting class standing: 91%.) **First-year students who submitted SAT scores:** 8%. Scores (25/75 percentile): Critical Reading: 520-710, Math: 520-710, Combined: 1040-1420. **First-year students submitting ACT scores:** 96%. Scores (25/75 percentile): English: 21-29, Math: 21-27, Composite: 22-28.

ACADEMICS

Year founded: 1959. **Academic calendar:** Semester. **Degrees offered:** bachelor's. **Most popular majors:** 8% English language and literature, 8% business administration and management, 8% psychology, 6% human services, 6% political science and government. **Major fields of study:** agriculture, agriculture operations, and related sciences; area, ethnic, cultural, and gender studies; biological and biomedical sciences; business, management, marketing, and related support services; computer and information sciences and support services; education; English language and literature/letters; foreign languages, literatures, and linguistics; history; liberal arts and sciences studies, and humanities; mathematics and statistics; multi/interdisciplinary studies; philosophy and religious studies; physical sciences; psychology; public administration and social service professions; social sciences; visual and performing arts. **Areas of required coursework:** arts/fine arts, humanities, mathematics, English (including composition), philosophy, foreign languages, sciences (biological or physical), history, social science. **Pre-professional programs:** pre-law, pre-dentistry, pre-medicine, pre-veterinary science, pre-optometry, pre-pharmacy, other. **Special academic programs (% participation):** distance learning (2%), double major (21%), exchange student program (domestic) (1%), honors program (4%), independent study (15%), internships (42%), student-designed major (4%), study abroad (56%), teacher certificate program (16%). **Teacher certification offered in:** elementary, middle/junior high, secondary. **Faculty and instruction (2009-2010):** Total instructional faculty: 113 full-time, 55 part-time (52% men; 48% women; 10% minorities). Full-time faculty with Ph.D. or other terminal degree: 86%. Student/faculty ratio: 14/1. Classes of fewer than 20 students: 54%; of 20 to 49 students: 41%; of 50 or more students: 5%. **Advanced Placement and International Baccalaureate credit:** AP tests may be used for: Credit and/or placement. Scores accepted: 3, 4, 5. International Baccalaureate exams may be used for: Credit and/or placement. **Freshmen returning for sophomore year:** 86%. **Graduation rates:** Four-year: 45%; five-year: 63%; six-year: 66%. **Graduate study:** 25% of students pursue further study immediately upon graduation; 30% within one year; 45% within five years. Fields in which graduates pursue further study: Master of Business Administration (MBA), 3%; law, 11%; medicine, 4%; dentistry, 2%; engineering, 2%; theology (or the seminary), 1%; education, 35%; arts and sciences, 40%; veterinary medicine, 2%.

COSTS AND FINANCIAL AID

Financial aid office: (320) 589-6035. **Expenses (2010-2011):** Tuition and fees 2010-2011: $11,512 in state, $11,512 out of state; room/board: $7,332. Estimated books and supplies: $1,000; transportation: $500; personal expenses: $1,600. **Financial aid:** Priority filing date for institution's financial aid form: March 1. In 2009-2010, 83% of undergraduates applied for financial aid. Of those, 66% were determined to have financial need; 44% had their need fully met. Average financial aid package (proportion receiving): $14,261 (66%). Average amount of gift aid, such as scholarships or grants (proportion receiving): $9,147 (65%). Average amount of self-help aid, such as work study or loans (proportion receiving): $6,701 (52%). Average need-based loan (excluding PLUS or other private loans): $6,633. Among students who received need-based aid, the average percentage of need met: 83%. Among students who received aid based on merit, the average award (and the proportion receiving): $3,589 (16%). Average amount of debt of borrowers graduating in 2009: $25,855. Proportion who borrowed: 77%.

CAMPUS LIFE AND EXTRACURRICULAR ACTIVITIES

Campus housing available (% using): coed dorms (74%), apartment for single students (26%), special housing for disabled students. Students who live in college-owned, operated, or affiliated housing: 47%. **Student employment:** During the 2009-2010 academic year, 45% of undergraduates worked on campus. Average per-year earnings: $1,500. **Clubs and organizations:** Number of student organizations: 80. Activities include: campus ministries, choral groups, concert band, dance, drama/theater, international student organization, jazz band, literary magazine, music ensembles, musi-

cal theater, opera, radio station, student government, student newspaper, student film society, symphony orchestra, television station. Number of fraternities: 0; sororities: 0. Average proportion of students who stay on campus on weekends: 75%. **Sports program (2009-2010):** Member of NCAA III. *Men's intercollegiate varsity sports:* baseball, basketball, cross country, football, golf, soccer, tennis, track and field (indoor), track and field (outdoor). *Women's intercollegiate varsity sports:* basketball, cross country, golf, soccer, softball, swimming, tennis, track and field (indoor), track and field (outdoor), volleyball.

SERVICES AND FACILITIES

Basic services: nonremedial tutoring, women's center, placement service, health service, health insurance. **Remedial assistance:** study skills. **Counseling services:** minority student, career, personal, veteran student, academic, psychological, birth control. **For learning-disabled students:** School does not offer a structured program with separate admission and additional fees. Total undergraduates in learning-disabled program or receiving services: 23. Services include: reading machines, tape recorders, other special classes, videotaped classes, untimed tests, note-taking services, oral tests, learning center, readers, extended time for tests, tutors, priority registration, priority seating, texts on tape, typist/scribe, exams on tape or computer, other testing accommodations. **Library:** Number of titles: 206,447; number of current serial subscriptions: 23,963. **Information technology resources:** Students are not required to lease or own a computer. Number of campus computers available to all students: 240. School has a wireless network. Approximate number of users that can be accommodated: 1,000. Proportion of college-owned housing units wired for high-speed internet access: 100%. **Campus safety:** Security services offered: 24-hour foot-and-vehicle patrols, late-night transport/escort service, 24-hour emergency telephones, lighted pathways/sidewalks, controlled dormitory access (key, security card, etc).

TRANSFER AND INTERNATIONAL STUDENTS

Transfer students: May apply for admission for the following academic terms: Fall, Spring, Summer. Applicants do not need a minimum number of credits to apply. For fall 2009: Transfer applications received: 249. Transfer applicants offered admission: 147. Transfer applicants enrolled: 103. **International students:** Number of foreign undergraduates: 60 (4% of student body). Number of countries represented: 16. Minimum TOEFL score required: 550 (paper); 79 (computer).

University of Minnesota–Twin Cities

- **Address:** 100 Church Street SE, Minneapolis, MN 55455-0213
- **Website:** http://www.umn.edu
- **Public**
- **Enrollment:** 28,539 full-time; 4,697 part-time

KEY STATS

✔ **U.S News College Ranking:** 64, National Universities
✔ **ACT Score (25th/75th percentile):** 24-29
✔ **Tuition:** 2009-2010: $11,293 in state, $15,293 out of state
Selectivity: More selective   **Room/board:** $7,582
Acceptance rate: 50%   **Average debt:** $26,516
Student/faculty ratio: 21/1   **Proportion who borrowed:** 63%

UNDERGRADUATE STUDENT BODY STATS

2009-2010 enrollment: 28,539 full-time; 4,697 part-time. Men: 48%; women: 52%. **Ethnic makeup:** African American: 5%; American-Indian: 1%; Asian American: 10%; Hispanic: 2%; White: 77%; International: 5%.

ADMISSIONS FACTS AND FIGURES

Phone: (800) 752-1000. **Website:** http://www.umn.edu. **Application deadlines for fall 2011:** Regular decision: Rolling. Early decision: Not offered. Early action: Not offered. Admission can be deferred. **Application fee:** $45. **To apply online, go to:** http://admissions.tc.umn.edu/. **Admissions requirements/recommendations:** High school units required (recommended): English: 4 (4); Mathematics: 3 (3); Science: 3 (3); Foreign language: 2 (2); Social studies: 3 (3); History: 1 (1); Total units: 16 (16). Tests: The college uses SAT or ACT scores in admissions decisions. Either SAT or ACT required. For admission to the fall 2011 entering class, the school will accept: ACT with writing required. Campus visit: Recommended. Admissions interview: Neither required nor recommended. Off-campus interview: Not available. **Factors that count in admissions decisions: Academic:** Secondary school record: Very Important. Class rank: Very Important. Letters of recommendation: Not Considered. Standardized test scores: Very Important. Essay: Not Considered. **Nonacademic:** Interview: Not Considered. Extracurricular activities: Considered. Talent/ability: Considered. Character/personal qualities: Considered. Alumni/ae relationship: Considered. Geographical residence: Considered. State residency: Not Considered. Religious affiliation/commitment: Not Considered. Minority status: Considered. Volunteer work: Considered. Work experience: Considered. **Other schools with the greatest overlap in applicants:** Iowa State University; University of Michigan–Ann Arbor; University of Minnesota–Duluth; University of St. Thomas; University of Wisconsin–Madison. **Admissions statistics for the fall 2009 entering class:** Total applicants: 33,910. Total accepted: 16,960. Freshmen enrolled: 5,400; 29% were from out of state. Overall acceptance rate: 50%. **Credentials of fall 2009 freshmen:** 43% ranked in the top 10 percent of their high school class; 83% were in the top 25 percent; 99% were in the top half. (Proportion submitting class standing: 80%.) **First-year students who submitted SAT scores:** 15%. Scores (25/75 percentile): Critical Reading: 520-670, Math: 600-710, Combined: 1120-1380. **First-year students submitting ACT scores:** 91%. Scores (25/75 percentile): English: 23-30, Math: 24-30, Composite: 24-29.

ACADEMICS

Year founded: 1851. **Academic calendar:** Semester. **Degrees offered:** certificate, diploma, bachelor's, post-bachelor's certificate, master's, post-master's certificate, doctorate. **Most popular majors:** 12% social sciences, 10% engineering, 8% biological and biomedical sciences, 8% business, management, marketing, and related support services, 7% psychology. **Major fields of study:** agriculture, agriculture operations, and related sciences; architecture and related services; area, ethnic, cultural, and gender studies; biological and biomedical sciences; business, management, marketing, and related support services; communication, journalism, and related programs; computer and information sciences and support services; construction trades; education; engineering; English language and literature/letters; family and consumer sciences/human sciences; foreign languages, literatures, and linguistics; health professions and related clinical sciences; history; mathematics and statistics; multi/interdisciplinary studies; natural resources and conservation; parks, recreation, leisure, and fitness studies; personal and culinary services; philosophy and religious studies; physical sciences; psychology; social sciences; visual and performing arts. **Areas of required coursework:** arts/fine arts, humanities, mathematics, English (including composition), foreign languages, sciences (biological or physical), history, social science. **Pre-professional programs:** pre-law, pre-dentistry, pre-medicine, pre-veterinary science, pre-pharmacy, other. **Special academic programs:** accelerated program, cooperative (work-study plan) program, cross-registration, distance learning, double major, dual enrollment, English as a Second Language (ESL), exchange student program (domestic), external degree program, honors program, independent study, internships, liberal arts/career combination, student-designed major, study abroad, teacher certificate program. **Teacher certification offered in:** early childhood, special education, elementary, vo-tech, middle/junior high, adult education, secondary. **Cooperative education programs:** computer science, engineering. **Reserve Officers Training Corps (ROTC):** Army ROTC: Offered on campus; Navy ROTC: Offered on campus; Air Force ROTC: Offered on campus. **Faculty and instruction (2009-2010):** Total instructional faculty: 1,834 full-time, 937 part-time (60% men; 40% women; 13% minorities). Full-time faculty with Ph.D. or other terminal degree: 82%. Student/faculty ratio: 21/1. Classes of fewer than 20 students: 40%; of 20 to 49 students: 43%; of 50 or more students: 17%. **Advanced Placement and International Baccalaureate credit:** AP tests may be used for: Credit only. Scores accepted: 3, 4, 5. International Baccalaureate exams may be used for: Credit only. **Freshmen returning for sophomore year:** 88%. **Graduation rates:** Four-year: 45%; five-year: 65%; six-year: 68%.

COSTS AND FINANCIAL AID

Financial aid office: (612) 624-1111. **Expenses (2009-2010):** Tuition and fees 2009-2010: $11,293 in state, $15,293 out of state; room/board: $7,582. Estimated books and supplies: $1,000; transportation: $194; personal expenses: $2,000. **Financial aid:** In 2009-2010, 71% of undergraduates applied for financial aid. Of those, 53% were determined to have financial need; 44% had their need fully met. Average financial aid package (proportion receiving): $13,189 (53%). Average amount of gift aid, such as scholarships or grants (proportion receiving): $7,832 (50%). Average amount of self-help aid, such as work study or loans (proportion receiving): $6,837 (46%). Average need-based loan (excluding PLUS or other private loans): $6,073. Among students who received need-based aid, the average percent-age of need met: 83%. Among students who received aid based on merit, the average award (and the proportion receiving): $5,020 (13%). Average amount of debt of borrowers graduating in 2009: $26,516. Proportion who borrowed: 63%.

CAMPUS LIFE AND EXTRACURRICULAR ACTIVITIES

Campus housing available: coed dorms, sorority housing, fraternity housing, apartments for married students, apartment for single students, special housing for disabled students, special housing for international students, cooperative housing, other housing options. Students who live in college-owned, operated, or affiliated housing: 21%. **Student employment:** During the 2009-2010 academic year, 28% of undergraduates worked on campus. **Clubs and organizations:** Number of student organizations: 680. Activities include: choral groups, concert band, dance, drama/theater, jazz band, literary magazine, marching band, music ensembles, musical theater, opera, pep band, radio station, student government, student newspaper, student film society, symphony orchestra, television station. Number of fraternities: 29; sororities: 15. **Sports program (2009-2010):** Member of NCAA I. **Men's intercollegiate varsity sports:** baseball, basketball, cross country, football, golf, gymnastics, ice hockey, skiing (nordic), swimming, tennis, track and field (outdoor), wrestling. **Women's intercollegiate varsity sports:** basketball, crew (heavyweight), crew (lightweight), cross country, golf, gymnastics, ice hockey, skiing (nordic), soccer, softball, swimming, tennis, track and field (outdoor), volleyball.

SERVICES AND FACILITIES

Basic services: nonremedial tutoring, women's center, placement service, day care, health service, health insurance. **Remedial assistance:** reading, math, writing, study skills. **Counseling services:** minority student, career, military, personal, veteran student, academic, older student, psychological, birth control. **For learning-disabled students:** School does not offer a structured program with separate admission and additional fees. Total undergraduates in learning-disabled program or receiving services: 178. Services include: reading machines, note-taking services, readers, extended time for tests, tutors, texts on tape. **Library:** Number of titles: 6,586,737; number of current serial subscriptions: 88,309. **Information technology resources:** Students are not required to lease or own a computer. Number of campus computers available to all students: 20,000. School has a wireless network. Approximate number of users that can be accommodated: 20,000. Proportion of college-owned housing units wired for high-speed internet access: 100%. **Campus safety:** Security services offered: 24-hour foot-and-vehicle patrols, late-night transport/escort service, 24-hour emergency telephones, lighted pathways/sidewalks, student patrols, controlled dormitory access (key, security card, etc).

TRANSFER AND INTERNATIONAL STUDENTS

Transfer students: May apply for admission for the following academic terms: Fall, Spring. Applicants need a minimum number of credits to apply. For fall 2009; Transfer applications received: 8,944. Transfer applicants offered admission: 3,828. Transfer applicants enrolled: 2,513. **International students:** Number of foreign undergraduates: 1448 (5% of student body). Number of countries represented: 77. Minimum TOEFL score required: 550 (paper); 213 (computer).

University of St. Thomas

- **Address:** 2115 Summit Avenue, St. Paul, MN 55105-1096
- **Website:** http://www.stthomas.edu
- **Private; Religious affiliation:** Roman Catholic
- **Enrollment:** 5,796 full-time; 350 part-time

KEY STATS
✔ **U.S News College Ranking:** 124, National Universities
✔ **ACT Score (25th/75th percentile):** 23-28
✔ **Tuition:** 2010-2011: $29,183

Selectivity: Selective	**Room/board:** $8,320
Acceptance rate: 87%	**Average debt:** $32,132
Student/faculty ratio: 15/1	**Proportion who borrowed:** 67%

UNDERGRADUATE STUDENT BODY STATS

2009-2010 enrollment: 5,796 full-time; 350 part-time. Men: 54%; women: 46%. **Ethnic makeup:** African American: 3%; Asian American: 5%; Hispanic: 4%; White: 87%; International: 1%. **Religious preference:**

Protestant: 26%; Muslim: 1%; No preference: 3%; Roman Catholic: 53%; Other: 17%.

ADMISSIONS FACTS AND FIGURES

Phone: (651) 962-6150. **Email:** admissions@stthomas.edu. **Website:** http://www.stthomas.edu. **Application deadlines for fall 2011:** Regular decision: Rolling. Early decision: Not offered. Early action: Not offered. Admission can be deferred. **To apply online, go to:** http://www.stthomas.edu/admissions/undergraduate/apply/. **Admissions requirements/recommendations:** High school units required (recommended): English: (4); Mathematics: 3 (4); Science: (2); Foreign language: (4); Social studies: (2); Total units: 3 (18). Tests: The college uses SAT or ACT scores in admissions decisions. Either SAT or ACT required. For admission to the fall 2011 entering class, the school will accept: ACT with or without writing accepted. Campus visit: Recommended. Admissions interview: Recommended. Off-campus interview: May be arranged. **Factors that count in admissions decisions:** *Academic:* Secondary school record: Very Important. Class rank: Important. Letters of recommendation: Considered. Standardized test scores: Important. Essay: Important. *Nonacademic:* Interview: Not Considered. Extracurricular activities: Considered. Talent/ability: Considered. Character/personal qualities: Considered. Alumni/ae relationship: Considered. Geographical residence: Considered. State residency: Not Considered. Religious affiliation/commitment: Not Considered. Minority status: Considered. Volunteer work: Considered. Work experience: Not Considered. **Other schools with the greatest overlap in applicants:** College of St. Benedict; St. John's University; University of Minnesota–Duluth; University of Minnesota–Twin Cities; University of Wisconsin–Madison. **Admissions statistics for the fall 2009 entering class:** Total applicants: 5,065. Total accepted: 4,389. Freshmen enrolled: 1,352; 20% were from out of state. Overall acceptance rate: 87%. **Credentials of fall 2009 freshmen:** 21% ranked in the top 10 percent of their high school class; 50% were in the top 25 percent; 87% were in the top half. (Proportion submitting class standing: 69%.) **Average high school grade point average:** 3.5. **First-year students who submitted SAT scores:** 11%. Scores (25/75 percentile): Critical Reading: 520-630, Math: 540-650, Combined: 1060-1280. **First-year students submitting ACT scores:** 97%. Scores (25/75 percentile): English: 23-28, Math: 22-28, Composite: 23-28.

ACADEMICS

Year founded: 1885. **Academic calendar:** 4-1-4. **Degrees offered:** certificate, bachelor's, post-bachelor's certificate, master's, post-master's certificate, doctorate. **Most popular majors:** 44% business, management, marketing, and related support services, 10% communication, journalism, and related programs, 8% social sciences, 6% biological and biomedical sciences, 6% philosophy and religious studies. **Major fields of study:** area, ethnic, cultural, and gender studies; biological and biomedical sciences; business, management, marketing, and related support services; communication, journalism, and related programs; computer and information sciences and support services; education; engineering; English language and literature/letters; foreign languages, literatures, and linguistics; health professions and related clinical sciences; history; legal professions and studies; liberal arts and sciences studies, and humanities; mathematics and statistics; multi/interdisciplinary studies; natural resources and conservation; parks, recreation, leisure, and fitness studies; philosophy and religious studies; physical sciences; psychology; public administration and social service professions; social sciences; theology and religious vocations; visual and performing arts. **Areas of required coursework:** arts/fine arts, computer literacy, mathematics, English (including composition), philosophy, foreign languages, sciences (biological or physical), history, social science, other. **Pre-professional programs:** pre-law, pre-dentistry, pre-medicine, pre-veterinary science, pre-pharmacy, other. **Special academic programs:** cross-registration, double major, English as a Second Language (ESL), exchange student program (domestic), honors program, independent study, internships, student-designed major, study abroad, teacher certificate program. **Teacher certification offered in:** special education, elementary, middle/junior high, secondary. **Cooperative education programs:** engineering. **Reserve Officers Training Corps (ROTC):** Army ROTC: Offered at cooperating institution (University of Minnesota–Twin Cities); Navy ROTC: Offered at cooperating institution (University of Minnesota–Twin Cities); Air Force ROTC: Offered on campus. **Faculty and instruction (2009-2010):** Total instructional faculty: 420 full-time, 470 part-time (59% men; 41% women; 10% minorities). Full-time faculty with Ph.D. or other terminal degree: 87%. Student/faculty ratio: 15/1. Classes of fewer than 20 students: 42%; of 20 to 49 students: 56%; of 50 or more students: 2%. **Advanced Placement and International Baccalaureate credit:** AP tests may be used for: Credit and/or placement. Scores accepted: 3, 4, 5. International Baccalaureate exams may be used for: Placement only.

Freshmen returning for sophomore year: 88%. **Graduation rates:** Four-year: 56%; five-year: 71%; six-year: 72%. **Graduate study:** 23% of students pursue further study immediately upon graduation; 38% within five years. Fields in which graduates pursue further study: Master of Business Administration (MBA), 15%; law, 7%; medicine, 22%; engineering, 5%; theology (or the seminary), 9%; education, 9%; arts and sciences, 33%.

COSTS AND FINANCIAL AID

Financial aid office: (651) 962-6550. **Expenses (2010-2011):** Tuition and fees 2010-2011: $29,183; room/board: $8,320. Estimated books and supplies: $1,440; transportation: $1,036; personal expenses: $2,518. **Financial aid:** Priority filing date for institution's financial aid form: April 1. In 2009-2010, 72% of undergraduates applied for financial aid. Of those, 58% were determined to have financial need; 66% had their need fully met. Average financial aid package (proportion receiving): $23,858 (58%). Average amount of gift aid, such as scholarships or grants (proportion receiving): $15,779 (57%). Average amount of self-help aid, such as work study or loans (proportion receiving): $9,095 (49%). Average need-based loan (excluding PLUS or other private loans): $7,447. Among students who received need-based aid, the average percentage of need met: 92%. Among students who received aid based on merit, the average award (and the proportion receiving): $11,065 (11%). The average athletic scholarship (and the proportion receiving): $0 (0%). Average amount of debt of borrowers graduating in 2009: $32,132. Proportion who borrowed: 67%.

CAMPUS LIFE AND EXTRACURRICULAR ACTIVITIES

Campus housing available (% using): women's dorms (49%), men's dorms (51%), apartments for married students, apartment for single students, special housing for disabled students. Students who live in college-owned, operated, or affiliated housing: 43%. **Student employment:** During the 2009-2010 academic year, 33% of undergraduates worked on campus. Average per-year earnings: $2,900. **Clubs and organizations:** Number of student organizations: 101. Activities include: campus ministries, choral groups, concert band, dance, drama/theater, international student organization, jazz band, literary magazine, music ensembles, pep band, radio station, student government, student newspaper, student film society, yearbook. Number of fraternities: 0; sororities: 0. Average proportion of students who stay on campus on weekends: 75%. **Sports program (2009-2010):** Member of NCAA III. *Men's intercollegiate varsity sports:* baseball, basketball, cross country, football, golf, ice hockey, soccer, swimming, tennis, track and field (indoor), track and field (outdoor). *Women's intercollegiate varsity sports:* basketball, cross country, golf, ice hockey, soccer, softball, swimming, tennis, track and field (indoor), track and field (outdoor), volleyball.

SERVICES AND FACILITIES

Basic services: nonremedial tutoring, women's center, placement service, day care, health service, health insurance. **Remedial assistance:** reading, math, writing, study skills. **Counseling services:** minority student, career, personal, veteran student, academic, older student, psychological, religious, other. **For learning-disabled students:** School does not offer a structured program with separate admission and additional fees. Total undergraduates in learning-disabled program or receiving services: 300. Services include: reading machines, tape recorders, note-taking services, oral tests, learning center, readers, extended time for tests, early syllabus, priority registration, priority seating, substitution of courses, texts on tape, typist/scribe, exams on tape or computer, other testing accommodations, waiver of foreign language degree requirement, waiver of math degree requirement, other. **Library:** Number of titles: 736,431; number of current serial subscriptions: 42,269. **Information technology resources:** Students are not required to lease or own a computer. Number of campus computers available to all students: 1,633. School has a wireless network. Approximate number of users that can be accommodated: 25,500. Proportion of college-owned housing units wired for high-speed internet access: 100%. **Campus safety:** Security services offered: 24-hour foot-and-vehicle patrols, late-night transport/escort service, 24-hour emergency telephones, lighted pathways/sidewalks, controlled dormitory access (key, security card, etc).

TRANSFER AND INTERNATIONAL STUDENTS

Transfer students: May apply for admission for the following academic terms: Fall, Spring, Summer. Applicants do not need a minimum number of credits to apply. For fall 2009: Transfer applications received: 557. Transfer applicants offered admission: 454. Transfer applicants enrolled: 285. **International students:** Number of foreign undergraduates: 88 (1% of student body). Number of countries represented: 63. Minimum TOEFL score required: 550 (paper); 80 (computer). Average TOEFL score: 535 (paper).

Winona State University

- **Address:** PO Box 5838, Winona, MN 55987-5838
- **Website:** http://www.winona.edu
- **Public**
- **Enrollment:** 7,471 full-time; 573 part-time

KEY STATS

✔ **U.S News College Ranking:** 49, Regional Universities (Midwest)
✔ **ACT Score (25th/75th percentile):** 21-25
✔ **Tuition:** 2010-2011: $7,000 in state, $11,980 out of state

Selectivity: Selective	**Room/board:** $7,330
Acceptance rate: 71%	**Average debt:** $27,190
Student/faculty ratio: 18/1	**Proportion who borrowed:** 74%

UNDERGRADUATE STUDENT BODY STATS

2009-2010 enrollment: 7,471 full-time; 573 part-time. Men: 40%; women: 60%. **Ethnic makeup:** African American: 1%; Asian American: 2%; Hispanic: 1%; White: 92%; International: 3%.

ADMISSIONS FACTS AND FIGURES

Phone: (507) 457-5100. **Email:** admissions@winona.edu. **Website:** http://www.winona.edu. **Application deadlines for fall 2011:** Regular decision: Rolling. Early decision: Not offered. Early action: Not offered. Admission can be deferred. **Application fee:** $20. **To apply online, go to:** http://www.winona.edu/admissions/6772.asp. **Admissions requirements/recommendations:** High school units required (recommended): English: 4; Mathematics: 3; Science: 3; Foreign language: 2; Social studies: 2; History: 1; Academic electives: 1; Total units: 16. Tests: The college uses SAT or ACT scores in admissions decisions. Either SAT or ACT required. For admission to the fall 2011 entering class, the school will accept: ACT with or without writing accepted. **Factors that count in admissions decisions:** *Academic:* Secondary school record: Very Important. Class rank: Very Important. Letters of recommendation: Considered. Standardized test scores: Very Important. Essay: Not Considered. *Nonacademic:* Interview: Not Considered. Extracurricular activities: Not Considered. Talent/ability: Not Considered. Character/personal qualities: Not Considered. Alumni/ae relationship: Not Considered. Geographical residence: Not Considered. State residency: Not Considered. Religious affiliation/commitment: Not Considered. Minority status: Not Considered. Volunteer work: Not Considered. Work experience: Not Considered. **Other schools with the greatest overlap in applicants:** University of Minnesota–Duluth; University of Minnesota–Twin Cities; University of Wisconsin–Eau Claire; University of Wisconsin–La Crosse; University of Wisconsin–Madison. **Admissions statistics for the fall 2009 entering class:** Total applicants: 6,500. Total accepted: 4,607. Freshmen enrolled: 1,813; 37% were from out of state. Overall acceptance rate: 71%. **Size of waiting list:** 0 applicants; enrolled from waiting list: 0. **Credentials of fall 2009 freshmen:** 10% ranked in the top 10 percent of their high school class; 33% were in the top 25 percent; 73% were in the top half. (Proportion submitting class standing: 88%.) **Average high school grade point average:** 3.3. **First-year students who submitted SAT scores:** 1%. Scores (25/75 percentile): Critical Reading: 440-600, Math: 510-640, Combined: 950-1240. **First-year students submitting ACT scores:** 98%. Scores (25/75 percentile): English: 20-25, Math: 20-25, Composite: 21-25.

ACADEMICS

Year founded: 1858. **Academic calendar:** Semester. **Degrees offered:** certificate, associate, bachelor's, master's, post-master's certificate. **Most popular majors:** 21% business, management, marketing, and related support services, 18% education, 11% health professions and related clinical sciences, 7% communication, journalism, and related programs, 6% biological and biomedical sciences. **Major fields of study:** biological and biomedical sciences; business, management, marketing, and related support services; communication, journalism, and related programs; computer and information sciences and support services; education; engineering; English language and literature/letters; health professions and related clinical sciences; history; legal professions and studies; mathematics and statistics; multi/interdisciplinary studies; natural resources and conservation; parks, recreation, leisure, and fitness studies; public administration and social service professions; security and protective services; visual and performing arts. **Areas of required coursework:** arts/fine arts, humanities, mathematics, English (including composition), sciences (biological or physical), history, social science. **Pre-professional programs:** pre-law, pre-dentistry, pre-medicine, pre-veterinary science, pre-optometry, pre-pharmacy, other. **Special academic programs:** accelerated program, cross-registration, distance learning, double major, dual enrollment, English as a Second Language (ESL), external degree program, independent study, internships, student-designed major, study abroad, teacher certificate program. **Teacher certification offered in:** early childhood, special education, elementary, middle/junior high, adult education, secondary. **Cooperative education programs:** art, business, computer science, education, engineering, health professions, humanities, natural science, social/behavioral science, technologies, other. **Reserve Officers Training Corps (ROTC):** Army ROTC: Offered at cooperating institution; Navy ROTC: Offered at cooperating institution; Air Force ROTC: Offered at cooperating institution. **Faculty and instruction (2009-2010):** Total instructional faculty: 345 full-time, 269 part-time (47% men; 53% women; 7% minorities). Full-time faculty with Ph.D. or other terminal degree: 84%. Student/faculty ratio: 18/1. Classes of fewer than 20 students: 27%; of 20 to 49 students: 65%; of 50 or more students: 8%. **Advanced Placement and International Baccalaureate credit:** AP tests may be used for: Placement only. Scores accepted: 4, 5. International Baccalaureate exams may be used for: Placement only. **Freshmen returning for sophomore year:** 73%. **Graduation rates:** Four-year: 26%; five-year: 48%; six-year: 55%. **Graduate study:** 12% of students pursue further study within one year. Fields in which graduates pursue further study: Master of Business Administration (MBA), 5%; law, 50%; engineering, 6%; education, 78%.

COSTS AND FINANCIAL AID

Financial aid office: (507) 457-5090. **Expenses (2010-2011):** Tuition and fees 2010-2011: $7,000 in state, $11,980 out of state; room/board: $7,330. Estimated books and supplies: $1,200; transportation: $640; personal expenses: $2,160. **Financial aid:** In 2009-2010, 74% of undergraduates applied for financial aid. Of those, 53% were determined to have financial need; 12% had their need fully met. Average financial aid package (proportion receiving): $6,728 (52%). Average amount of gift aid, such as scholarships or grants (proportion receiving): $4,078 (26%). Average amount of self-help aid, such as work study or loans (proportion receiving): $4,281 (46%). Average need-based loan (excluding PLUS or other private loans): $4,045. Among students who received need-based aid, the average percentage of need met: 44%. Among students who received aid based on merit, the average award (and the proportion receiving): $2,557 (12%). Average amount of debt of borrowers graduating in 2009: $27,190. Proportion who borrowed: 74%.

CAMPUS LIFE AND EXTRACURRICULAR ACTIVITIES

Campus housing available (% using): coed dorms (71%), women's dorms (16%), men's dorms (0%), apartment for single students (13%), special housing for disabled students. Students who live in college-owned, operated, or affiliated housing: 31%. **Student employment:** During the 2009-2010 academic year, 36% of undergraduates worked on campus. Average per-year earnings: $3,780. **Clubs and organizations:** Number of student organizations: 210. Activities include: choral groups, concert band, dance, drama/theater, international student organization, jazz band, literary magazine, model UN, music ensembles, musical theater, pep band, radio station, student government, student newspaper, student film society, symphony orchestra, television station. Number of fraternities: 3; sororities: 3. Average proportion of students who stay on campus on weekends: 65%. **Sports program (2009-2010):** Member of NCAA II. *Men's intercollegiate varsity sports:* baseball, basketball, cross country, football, golf. *Women's intercollegiate varsity sports:* basketball, cross country, golf, gymnastics, soccer, softball, tennis, track and field (indoor), track and field (outdoor), volleyball.

SERVICES AND FACILITIES

Basic services: nonremedial tutoring, women's center, placement service, day care, health service, health insurance. **Remedial assistance:** math, writing, study skills. **Counseling services:** minority student, career, military, personal, veteran student, academic, older student, psychological, birth control. **For learning-disabled students:** School does not offer a structured program with separate admission and additional fees. Total undergraduates in learning-disabled program or receiving services: 153. Services include: remedial math, remedial English, reading machines, note-taking services, oral tests, learning center, readers, extended time for tests, tutors, priority registration, priority seating, texts on tape, exams on tape or computer, other testing accommodations. **Library:** Number of titles: 220,000; number of current serial subscriptions: 1,000. **Information technology resources:** Students are required to lease or own a computer. Number of campus computers available to all students: 400. School has a wireless network. Approximate number of users that can be accommodated: 10,000. Proportion of college-owned housing units wired for high-speed internet access: 100%. **Campus safety:** Security services offered: 24-hour foot-and-vehicle patrols, late-night transport/escort service, 24-hour emergency telephones, lighted pathways/sidewalks, student patrols, controlled dormitory access (key, security card, etc).

TRANSFER AND INTERNATIONAL STUDENTS
Transfer students: May apply for admission for the following academic terms: Fall, Spring, Summer. Applicants need a minimum number of cred-its to apply. For fall 2009: Transfer applications received: 1,394. Transfer applicants offered admission: 933. Transfer applicants enrolled: 521.
International students: Number of foreign undergraduates: 261 (3% of student body). Number of countries represented: 54. Minimum TOEFL score required: 520 (paper); 190 (computer). Average TOEFL score: 568 (paper).

Mississippi

Alcorn State University

- **Address:** 1000 ASU Drive #359, Alcorn State, MS 39096
- **Website:** http://www.alcorn.edu
- **Public**
- **Enrollment:** 2,436 full-time; 264 part-time

KEY STATS

✔ **U.S News College Ranking:** 74, Regional Universities (South)
✔ **ACT Score (25th/75th percentile):** 16-19
✔ **Tuition:** 2009-2010: $4,498 in state, $11,064 out of state
   Selectivity: Less selective   **Room/board:** $5,384
   Acceptance rate: 40%   **Average debt:** $19,290
   Student/faculty ratio: 15/1   **Proportion who borrowed:** 50%

UNDERGRADUATE STUDENT BODY STATS

2009-2010 enrollment: 2,436 full-time; 264 part-time. Men: 33%; women: 67%. **Ethnic makeup:** African American: 93%; Hispanic: 1%; White: 5%; International: 1%.

ADMISSIONS FACTS AND FIGURES

Phone: (601) 877-6147. **Email:** ebarnes@alcorn.edu. **Website:** http://www.alcorn.edu. **Application deadlines for fall 2011:** Regular decision: Rolling. Early decision: Not offered. Early action: Not offered. Admission can be deferred. **To apply online, go to:** https://selfserve1og.alcorn.edu/pls/prod/bwskalog.P_DispLoginNon. **Admissions requirements/recommendations:** High school units required (recommended): English: 4; Mathematics: 3; Science: 3; Foreign language: (1); Social studies: 3; Academic electives: 2; Total units: 15. Tests: The college uses SAT or ACT scores in admissions decisions. Either SAT or ACT required. For admission to the fall 2011 entering class, the school will accept: ACT with or without writing accepted. Campus visit: Recommended. Admissions interview: Neither required nor recommended. Off-campus interview: May be arranged. **Factors that count in admissions decisions:** *Academic:* Secondary school record: Very Important. Class rank: Very Important. Letters of recommendation: Considered. Standardized test scores: Important. Essay: Not Considered. *Nonacademic:* Interview: Considered. Extracurricular activities: Not Considered. Talent/ability: Not Considered. Character/personal qualities: Not Considered. Alumni/ae relationship: Not Considered. Geographical residence: Not Considered. State residency: Not Considered. Religious affiliation/commitment: Not Considered. Minority status: Not Considered. Volunteer work: Not Considered. Work experience: Not Considered. **Admissions statistics for the fall 2009 entering class:** Total applicants: 3,195. Total accepted: 1,291. Freshmen enrolled: 464; 21% were from out of state. Overall acceptance rate: 40%. **Credentials of fall 2009 freshmen:** 71% ranked in the top half of their high school class. (Proportion submitting class standing: 61%.) **Average high school grade point average:** 2.8. **First-year students who submitted SAT scores:** 6%. Scores (25/75 percentile): Critical Reading: 390-470, Math: 400-460, Combined: 790-930. **First-year students submitting ACT scores:** 94%. Scores (25/75 percentile): English: 16-21, Math: 16-18, Composite: 16-19.

ACADEMICS

Year founded: 1871. **Academic calendar:** Semester. **Degrees offered:** associate, bachelor's, master's, post-master's certificate. **Most popular majors:** 20% liberal arts and sciences studies, and humanities, 13% biological and biomedical sciences, 13% health professions and related clinical sciences, 9% business, management, marketing, and related support services, 6% social sciences. **Major fields of study:** agriculture, agriculture operations, and related sciences; biological and biomedical sciences; business, management, marketing, and related support services; communication, journalism, and related programs; computer and information sciences and support services; education; engineering technologies/technicians; English language and literature/letters; family and consumer sciences/human sciences; health professions and related clinical sciences; history; liberal arts and sciences studies, and humanities; mathematics and statistics; parks, recreation, lei-

sure, and fitness studies; physical sciences; psychology; security and protective services; social sciences; visual and performing arts. **Areas of required coursework:** arts/fine arts, humanities, computer literacy, mathematics, English (including composition), sciences (biological or physical), history, social science, other. **Pre-professional programs:** pre-law, pre-dentistry, pre-medicine, pre-veterinary science, pre-optometry, pre-pharmacy, other. **Special academic programs:** accelerated program, cooperative (work-study plan) program, distance learning, double major, honors program, independent study, internships, liberal arts/career combination, study abroad, teacher certificate program. **Teacher certification offered in:** early childhood, special education, elementary, secondary. **Cooperative education programs:** agriculture, business, education, health professions, home economics, natural science, social/behavioral science, technologies, other. **Reserve Officers Training Corps (ROTC):** Army ROTC: Offered on campus. **Faculty and instruction (2009-2010):** Total instructional faculty: 183 full-time, 37 part-time (49% men; 51% women; 78% minorities). Full-time faculty with Ph.D. or other terminal degree: 63%. Student/faculty ratio: 15/1. **Advanced Placement and International Baccalaureate credit:** AP tests may be used for: Placement only. Scores accepted: 3, 4, 5. **Freshmen returning for sophomore year:** 64%. **Graduation rates:** Four-year: 22%; five-year: 34%; six-year: 42%. **Graduate study:** 45% of students pursue further study immediately upon graduation.

COSTS AND FINANCIAL AID

Financial aid office: (601) 877-6190. **Expenses (2009-2010):** Tuition and fees 2009-2010: $4,498 in state, $11,064 out of state; room/board: $5,384. Estimated books and supplies: $1,452; transportation: $2,419; personal expenses: $2,419. **Financial aid:** Priority filing date for institution's financial aid form: April 1. In 2009-2010, 93% of undergraduates applied for financial aid. Of those, 93% were determined to have financial need; 98% had their need fully met. Average financial aid package (proportion receiving): $9,494 (93%). Average amount of gift aid, such as scholarships or grants (proportion receiving): $3,529 (84%). Average amount of self-help aid, such as work study or loans (proportion receiving): $4,166 (74%). Average need-based loan (excluding PLUS or other private loans): $4,033. Among students who received need-based aid, the average percentage of need met: 90%. Among students who received aid based on merit, the average award (and the proportion receiving): $2,470 (21%). The average athletic scholarship (and the proportion receiving): $7,556 (8%). Average amount of debt of borrowers graduating in 2009: $19,290. Proportion who borrowed: 50%.

CAMPUS LIFE AND EXTRACURRICULAR ACTIVITIES

Campus housing available (% using): women's dorms (57%), men's dorms (43%). Students who live in college-owned, operated, or affiliated housing: 51%. **Clubs and organizations:** Number of student organizations: 78. Activities include: choral groups, concert band, dance, drama/theater, jazz band, marching band, music ensembles, radio station, student government, student newspaper, television station, yearbook. Number of fraternities: 4; sororities: 4. Proportion of men in fraternities: 7%; of women in sororities: 10%. **Sports program (2009-2010):** Member of NCAA I. *Men's intercollegiate varsity sports:* baseball, basketball, cross country, football, golf, tennis, track and field (indoor). *Women's intercollegiate varsity sports:* basketball, cross country, golf, soccer, softball, tennis, track and field (indoor), volleyball.

SERVICES AND FACILITIES

Basic services: placement service. **Remedial assistance:** reading, math, other. **Counseling services:** career, academic, psychological, other. **For learning-disabled students:** School does not offer a structured program with separate admission and additional fees. Services include: remedial math, remedial English, remedial reading, extended time for tests, tutors, priority seating. **Library:** Number of titles: 335,252; number of current serial subscriptions: 1,046. **Information technology resources:** Students are not required to lease or own a computer. Number of campus computers available to all students: 600. School has a wireless network. Approximate number of users that can be accommodated: 5,000. Proportion of college-owned housing units wired for high-speed internet access: 100%. **Campus safety:** Security services offered: 24-hour foot-and-vehicle patrols, 24-hour emergency telephones, lighted pathways/sidewalks, controlled dormitory access (key, security card, etc).

TRANSFER AND INTERNATIONAL STUDENTS

Transfer students: May apply for admission for the following academic terms: Fall, Spring, Summer. Applicants need a minimum number of credits to apply. For fall 2009: Transfer applications received: 3,195. Transfer applicants offered admission: 1,291. Transfer applicants enrolled: 464. **International students:** Number of foreign undergraduates: 31 (1% of student body). Minimum TOEFL score required: 525 (paper); 195 (computer).

Belhaven University

- **Address:** 1500 Peachtree Street, Jackson, MS 39202
- **Website:** http://www.belhaven.edu
- **Private; Religious affiliation:** Presbyterian
- **Enrollment:** 2,190 full-time; 140 part-time

KEY STATS

✔ **U.S News College Ranking:** 66, Regional Universities (South)
✔ **ACT Score (25th/75th percentile):** 19-24
✔ **Tuition:** 2010-2011: $17,700

Selectivity: Selective	**Room/board:** $6,500
Acceptance rate: 52%	**Average debt:** $32,728
Student/faculty ratio: 10/1	**Proportion who borrowed:** 100%

UNDERGRADUATE STUDENT BODY STATS

2009-2010 enrollment: 2,190 full-time; 140 part-time. Men: 35%; women: 65%. **Ethnic makeup:** African American: 22%; American-Indian: 1%; Asian American: 2%; Hispanic: 3%; White: 71%; International: 1%. **Religious preference:** Roman Catholic: 6%; Protestant: 61%; No preference: 1%; Unknown: 15%; Presbyterian: 17%.

ADMISSIONS FACTS AND FIGURES

Phone: (601) 968-5940. **Email:** admission@belhaven.edu. **Website:** http://www.belhaven.edu. **Application deadlines for fall 2011:** Regular decision: Rolling. Early decision: Not offered. Early action: Not offered. Admission can be deferred. **Application fee:** $25. **To apply online, go to:** http://www.belhaven.edu/apply.htm. **Admissions requirements/recommendations:** High school units required (recommended): English: 4; Mathematics: 2; Science: 1; History: 1; Academic electives: 8; Total units: 16. Tests: The college uses SAT or ACT scores in admissions decisions. Either SAT or ACT required. For admission to the fall 2011 entering class, the school will accept: ACT with or without writing accepted. Campus visit: Recommended. Admissions interview: Neither required nor recommended. Off-campus interview: May be arranged. **Factors that count in admissions decisions:** *Academic:* Secondary school record: Very Important. Class rank: Considered. Letters of recommendation: Considered. Standardized test scores: Very Important. Essay: Considered. *Nonacademic:* Interview: Considered. Extracurricular activities: Not Considered. Talent/ability: Not Considered. Character/personal qualities: Not Considered. Alumni/ae relationship: Not Considered. Geographical residence: Not Considered. State residency: Not Considered. Religious affiliation/commitment: Not Considered. Minority status: Not Considered. Volunteer work: Not Considered. Work experience: Not Considered. **Admissions statistics for the fall 2009 entering class:** Total applicants: 1,380. Total accepted: 712. Freshmen enrolled: 191; 62% were from out of state. Overall acceptance rate: 52%. **Credentials of fall 2009 freshmen:** 35% ranked in the top 10 percent of their high school class; 55% were in the top 25 percent; 80% were in the top half. (Proportion submitting class standing: 70%.) **Average high school grade point average:** 3.3. **First-year students who submitted SAT scores:** 39%. Scores (25/75 percentile): Critical Reading: 490-610, Math: 460-570, Combined: 950-1180. **First-year students submitting ACT scores:** 85%. Scores (25/75 percentile): English: 20-26, Math: 17-23, Composite: 19-24.

ACADEMICS

Year founded: 1883. **Academic calendar:** Semester. **Degrees offered:** certificate, associate, bachelor's, master's. **Most popular majors:** 22% visual and performing arts, 17% business, management, marketing, and related support services, 11% health and physical education/fitness, 9% education, 8% psychology. **Major fields of study:** biological and biomedical sciences; business, management, marketing, and related support services; communication, journalism, and related programs; computer and information sciences

and support services; education; English language and literature/letters; history; liberal arts and sciences studies, and humanities; mathematics and statistics; multi/interdisciplinary studies; parks, recreation, leisure, and fitness studies; philosophy and religious studies; physical sciences; psychology; social sciences; visual and performing arts. **Areas of required coursework:** arts/fine arts, mathematics, English (including composition), foreign languages, sciences (biological or physical), history, other. **Pre-professional programs:** pre-law, pre-dentistry, pre-medicine, pre-theology, pre-pharmacy, other. **Special academic programs:** accelerated program, cooperative (work-study plan) program, distance learning, double major, dual enrollment, English as a Second Language (ESL), honors program, independent study, internships, student-designed major, study abroad, teacher certificate program. **Teacher certification offered in:** early childhood, special education, elementary, middle/junior high, secondary. **Reserve Officers Training Corps (ROTC):** Army ROTC: Offered at cooperating institution (Jackson State University); Air Force ROTC: Offered at cooperating institution (Jackson State University). **Faculty and instruction (2009-2010):** Total instructional faculty: 63 full-time, 84 part-time (53% men; 47% women). Full-time faculty with Ph.D. or other terminal degree: 73%. Student/faculty ratio: 10/1. Classes of fewer than 20 students: 71%; of 20 to 49 students: 29%; of 50 or more students: 1%. **Advanced Placement and International Baccalaureate credit:** AP tests may be used for: Credit only. Scores accepted: 3, 4, 5. International Baccalaureate exams may be used for: Credit only. **Freshmen returning for sophomore year:** 67%. **Graduation rates:** Four-year: 35%; five-year: 47%; six-year: 41%. **Graduate study:** 13% of students pursue further study immediately upon graduation; 25% within one year; 25% within five years. Fields in which graduates pursue further study: Master of Business Administration (MBA), 10%; law, 1%; medicine, 16%; theology (or the seminary), 5%; education, 10%; arts and sciences, 26%.

COSTS AND FINANCIAL AID

Financial aid office: (601) 968-5934. **Expenses (2010-2011):** Tuition and fees 2010-2011: $17,700; room/board: $6,500. Estimated books and supplies: $1,400; transportation: $900. **Financial aid:** Priority filing date for institution's financial aid form: March 1. In 2009-2010, 82% of undergraduates applied for financial aid. Of those, 73% were determined to have financial need; 12% had their need fully met. Average financial aid package (proportion receiving): $14,653 (72%). Average amount of gift aid, such as scholarships or grants (proportion receiving): $10,710 (72%). Average amount of self-help aid, such as work study or loans (proportion receiving): $4,849 (60%). Average need-based loan (excluding PLUS or other private loans): $4,342. Among students who received need-based aid, the average percentage of need met: 61%. Among students who received aid based on merit, the average award (and the proportion receiving): $6,318 (10%). The average athletic scholarship (and the proportion receiving): $6,294 (9%). Average amount of debt of borrowers graduating in 2009: $32,728. Proportion who borrowed: 100%.

CAMPUS LIFE AND EXTRACURRICULAR ACTIVITIES

Campus housing available (% using): women's dorms (59%), men's dorms (40%), special housing for disabled students (1%). Students who live in college-owned, operated, or affiliated housing: 47%. **Student employment:** During the 2009-2010 academic year, 9% of undergraduates worked on campus. Average per-year earnings: $1,432. **Clubs and organizations:** Number of student organizations: 26. Activities include: campus ministries, choral groups, dance, drama/theater, jazz band, literary magazine, marching band, music ensembles, musical theater, pep band, student government, student newspaper, yearbook. Number of fraternities: 0; sororities: 0. Average proportion of students who stay on campus on weekends: 68%. **Sports program (2009-2010):** Member of NAIA. *Men's intercollegiate varsity sports:* baseball, basketball, cross country, football, golf, soccer, tennis. *Women's intercollegiate varsity sports:* basketball, cross country, golf, soccer, softball, tennis, volleyball.

SERVICES AND FACILITIES

Basic services: nonremedial tutoring, health service. **Remedial assistance:** reading, math, writing, study skills. **Counseling services:** career, personal, academic, older student, psychological, religious. **For learning-disabled students:** School does not offer a structured program with separate admission and additional fees. Total undergraduates in learning-disabled program or receiving services: 20. Services include: remedial math, remedial English, remedial reading, tape recorders, untimed tests, extended time for tests, priority registration, priority seating, other. **Library:** Number of titles: 13,201; number of current serial subscriptions: 329. **Information technology resources:** Students are not required to lease or own a computer. Number of campus computers available to all students: 36. School has a wireless network. Approximate number of users that can be accommodated: 400. Proportion of college-owned housing units wired for high-speed internet access: 100%. **Campus safety:** Security services offered: 24-hour foot-and-vehicle patrols, late-night transport/escort service, 24-hour emergency telephones, lighted pathways/sidewalks, controlled dormitory access (key, security card, etc).

TRANSFER AND INTERNATIONAL STUDENTS

Transfer students: May apply for admission for the following academic terms: Fall, Winter, Spring, Summer. Applicants need a minimum number of credits to apply. For fall 2009: Transfer applications received: 642. Transfer applicants offered admission: 261. Transfer applicants enrolled: 174. **International students:** Number of foreign undergraduates: 9 (1% of student body). Number of countries represented: 19. Minimum TOEFL score required: 500 (paper); 173 (computer). Average TOEFL score: 550 (paper).

Blue Mountain College

- **Address:** PO Box 160, Blue Mountain, MS 38610-0160
- **Website:** http://www.bmc.edu
- **Private; Religious affiliation:** Southern Baptist Convention
- **Enrollment:** 422 full-time; 72 part-time

KEY STATS

✔ **U.S News College Ranking:** 25, Regional Colleges (South)
✔ **ACT Score (25th/75th percentile):** 18-24
✔ **Tuition:** 2010-2011: $8,870

Selectivity: Selective	**Room/board:** $3,900
Acceptance rate: 44%	**Average debt:** $16,300
Student/faculty ratio: 14/1	**Proportion who borrowed:** 80%

UNDERGRADUATE STUDENT BODY STATS

2009-2010 enrollment: 422 full-time; 72 part-time. Men: 32%; women: 68%. **Ethnic makeup:** African American: 15%; Hispanic: 1%; White: 83%. **Religious preference:** Protestant: 36%; No preference: 4%; Southern Baptist Convention: 60%; 0: 0%.

ADMISSIONS FACTS AND FIGURES

Phone: (662) 685-4161. **Email:** admissions@bmc.edu. **Website:** http://www.bmc.edu. **Application deadlines for fall 2011:** Regular decision: Rolling. Early decision: Not offered. Early action: Not offered. Admission can be deferred. **Application fee:** $10. **To apply online, go to:** http://www.bmc.edu/onlineapp.asp. **Admissions requirements/recommendations:** High school units required (recommended): English: 4 (4); Mathematics: 3 (3); Science: 3 (3); Foreign language: 2 (2); Social studies: 1 (1); History: 2 (2); Total units: 15 (15). Tests: The college uses SAT or ACT scores in admissions decisions. Either SAT or ACT required. For admission to the fall 2011 entering class, the school will accept: ACT with or without writing accepted. Campus visit: Recommended. Admissions interview: Recommended. Off-campus interview: May be arranged. **Factors that count in admissions decisions:** *Academic:* Secondary school record: Important. Class rank: Important. Letters of recommendation: Considered. Standardized test scores: Important. Essay: Not Considered. *Nonacademic:* Interview: Not Considered. Extracurricular activities: Not Considered. Talent/ability: Not Considered. Character/personal qualities: Considered. Alumni/ae relationship: Considered. Geographical residence: Not Considered. State residency: Not Considered. Religious affiliation/commitment: Not Considered. Minority status: Not Considered. Volunteer work: Not Considered. Work experience: Not Considered. **Other schools with the greatest overlap in applicants:** Mississippi College; Mississippi State University; Union University; University of Mississippi. **Admissions statistics for the fall 2009 entering class:** Total applicants: 272. Total accepted: 119. Freshmen enrolled: 75; 29% were from out of state. Overall acceptance rate: 44%. **Credentials of fall 2009 freshmen:** 27% ranked in the top 10 percent of their high school class; 52% were in the top 25 percent; 73% were in the top half. (Proportion submitting class standing: 75%.) **Average high school grade point average:** 3.4. **First-year students who submitted SAT scores:** 3%. **First-year students submitting ACT scores:** 93%. Scores (25/75 percentile): English: 17-25, Math: 17-22, Composite: 18-24.

ACADEMICS

Year founded: 1873. **Academic calendar:** Semester. **Degrees offered:** bachelor's, master's. **Most popular majors:** 51% education, 16% Bible/biblical studies, 14% psychology, 7% business administration and management, 5% English language and literature. **Major fields of study:** biological and biomedical sciences; business, management, marketing, and related support services; education; English language and literature/letters; foreign languages, literatures, and linguistics; health professions and related clinical sciences; history; mathematics and statistics; multi/interdisciplinary studies; parks, recreation, leisure, and fitness studies; psychology; social sciences; theology and religious vocations; visual and performing arts. **Areas of required coursework:** arts/fine arts, humanities, computer literacy, mathematics, English (including composition), sciences (biological or physical), history, social science, other. **Pre-professional programs:** pre-law, pre-dentistry, pre-medicine, pre-theology, pre-veterinary science, pre-optometry, pre-pharmacy. **Special academic programs (% participation):** distance learning (10%), double major (3%), internships (8%), teacher certificate program (50%). **Teacher certification offered in:** special education, elementary, secondary. **Faculty and instruction (2009-2010):** Total instructional faculty: 27 full-time, 17 part-time (39% men; 61% women; 2% minorities). Full-time faculty with Ph.D. or other terminal degree: 70%. Student/faculty ratio: 14/1. Classes of fewer than 20 students: 67%; of 20 to 49 students: 31%; of 50 or more students: 2%. **Advanced Placement and International Baccalaureate credit:** AP tests may be used for: Credit and/or placement. Scores accepted: 3, 4, 5. **Freshmen returning for sophomore year:** 70%. **Graduation rates:** Four-year: 40%; five-year: 50%; six-year: 54%. **Graduate study:** 15% of students pursue further study immediately upon graduation. Fields in which graduates pursue further study: Master of Business Administration (MBA), 1%; medicine, 2%; theology (or the seminary), 5%; education, 5%.

COSTS AND FINANCIAL AID

Financial aid office: (662) 685-4771. **Expenses (2010-2011):** Tuition and fees 2010-2011: $8,870; room/board: $3,900. Estimated books and supplies: $750; transportation: $1,152; personal expenses: $500. **Financial aid:** Priority filing date for institution's financial aid form: March 31; deadline: July 15. In 2009-2010, 84% of undergraduates applied for financial aid. Of those, 41% were determined to have financial need; 48% had their need fully met. Average financial aid package (proportion receiving): $5,656 (41%). Average amount of gift aid, such as scholarships or grants (proportion receiving): $3,456 (25%). Average amount of self-help aid, such as work study or loans (proportion receiving): $4,198 (36%). Average need-based loan (excluding PLUS or other private loans): $6,000. Among students who received need-based aid, the average percentage of need met: 48%. Among students who received aid based on merit, the average award (and the proportion receiving): $8,445 (11%). The average athletic scholarship (and the proportion receiving): $14,145 (8%). Average amount of debt of borrowers graduating in 2009: $16,300. Proportion who borrowed: 80%.

CAMPUS LIFE AND EXTRACURRICULAR ACTIVITIES

Campus housing available (% using): women's dorms (59%), men's dorms (41%), special housing for disabled students (0%). Students who live in college-owned, operated, or affiliated housing: 39%. **Student employment:** During the 2009-2010 academic year, 0% of undergraduates worked on campus. Average per-year earnings: $0. **Clubs and organizations:** Number of student organizations: 32. Activities include: choral groups, drama/theater, literary magazine, music ensembles, musical theater, student government, yearbook. Number of fraternities: 0; sororities: 0. Average proportion of students who stay on campus on weekends: 15%. **Sports program (2009-2010):** Member of NAIA. *Men's intercollegiate varsity sports:* baseball, basketball, cross country, golf. *Women's intercollegiate varsity sports:* basketball, cross country, softball.

SERVICES AND FACILITIES

Basic services: nonremedial tutoring, placement service, health service, health insurance. **Remedial assistance:** reading, math, writing, study skills. **Counseling services:** career, personal, academic, psychological, religious. **For learning-disabled students:** School does not offer a structured program with separate admission and additional fees. Total undergraduates in learning-disabled program or receiving services: 4. Services include: remedial math, remedial English, remedial reading, tape recorders, untimed tests, note-taking services, oral tests, learning center, readers, extended time for tests, tutors. **Library:** Number of titles: 77,557; number of current serial subscriptions: 116. **Information technology resources:** Students are not required to lease or own a computer. Number of campus computers available to all students: 41. School has a wireless network. Approximate number of users that can be accommodated: 350. Proportion of college-owned housing units wired for high-speed internet access: 100%. **Campus safety:** Security services offered: late-night transport/escort service, lighted pathways/sidewalks, controlled dormitory access (key, security card, etc).

TRANSFER AND INTERNATIONAL STUDENTS

Transfer students: May apply for admission for the following academic terms: Fall, Spring, Summer. Applicants need a minimum number of credits to apply. For fall 2009: Transfer applications received: 180. Transfer applicants offered admission: 111. Transfer applicants enrolled: 86. **International students:** Number of foreign undergraduates: 1. Number of countries represented: 1. Minimum TOEFL score required: 500 (paper); 173 (computer).

Delta State University

- ■ **Address:** Highway 8 W, Cleveland, MS 38733
- ■ **Website:** http://www.deltastate.edu
- ■ **Public**
- ■ **Enrollment:** 2,495 full-time; 620 part-time

KEY STATS

✔ **U.S News College Ranking:** 63, Regional Universities (South)
✔ **ACT Score (25th/75th percentile):** 18-22
✔ **Tuition:** 2009-2010: $4,450 in state, $11,520 out of state

Selectivity: Selective	**Room/board:** $5,778
Acceptance rate: 24%	**Average debt:** $19,840
Student/faculty ratio: 15/1	**Proportion who borrowed:** 65%

UNDERGRADUATE STUDENT BODY STATS

2009-2010 enrollment: 2,495 full-time; 620 part-time. Men: 39%; women: 61%. **Ethnic makeup:** African American: 39%; Asian American: 1%; Hispanic: 1%; White: 58%; International: 2%.

ADMISSIONS FACTS AND FIGURES

Phone: (662) 846-4018. **Email:** admissions@deltastate.edu. **Website:** http://www.deltastate.edu. **Application deadlines for fall 2011:** Regular decision: August 1. Early decision: Not offered. Early action: Not offered. Admission can be deferred. **Application fee:** $25. **To apply online, go to:** https://rapids.deltastate.edu/pls/dsu/bwskalog.P_DispLoginNon. **Admissions requirements/recommendations:** High school units required (recommended): English: 4; Mathematics: 3; Science: 3; Foreign language: 0; Social studies: 3; Academic electives: 2; Total units: 15. Tests: The college uses SAT or ACT scores in admissions decisions. ACT required. For admission to the fall 2011 entering class, the school will accept: ACT with or without writing accepted. Campus visit: Recommended. Admissions interview: Neither required nor recommended. Off-campus interview: Not available. **Factors that count in admissions decisions:** *Academic:* Secondary school record: Very Important. Class rank: Very Important. Letters of recommendation: Not Considered. Standardized test scores: Very Important. Essay: Not Considered. *Nonacademic:* Interview: Not Considered. Extracurricular activities: Important. Talent/ability: Important. Character/personal qualities: Important. Alumni/ae relationship: Important. Geographical residence: Important. State residency: Important. Religious affiliation/commitment: Not Considered. Minority status: Not Considered. Volunteer work: Not Considered. Work experience: Not Considered. **Other schools with the greatest overlap in applicants:** Jackson State University; Mississippi State University; Mississippi Valley State University; University of Mississippi; University of Southern Mississippi. **Admissions statistics for the fall 2009 entering class:** Total applicants: 1,919. Total accepted: 469. Freshmen enrolled: 373; 16% were from out of state. Overall acceptance rate: 24%. **Credentials of fall 2009 freshmen:** 17% ranked in the top 10 percent of their high school class; 42% were in the top 25 percent; 77% were in the top half. (Proportion submitting class standing: 76%.) **Average high school grade point average:** 3.2. **First-year students submitting ACT scores:** 100%. Scores (25/75 percentile): English: 17-23, Math: 16-22, Composite: 18-22.

ACADEMICS

Year founded: 1924. **Academic calendar:** Semester. **Degrees offered:** bachelor's, master's, post-master's certificate, doctorate. **Most popular majors:** 9% nursing/registered nurse training (R.N., A.S.N., B.S.N., M.S.N.), 8% family and consumer sciences/human sciences, 7% elementary education and teaching, 6% physical education teaching and coaching, 5% business

administration and management. **Major fields of study:** biological and biomedical sciences; business, management, marketing, and related support services; communication, journalism, and related programs; education; English language and literature/letters; family and consumer sciences/human sciences; foreign languages, literatures, and linguistics; health professions and related clinical sciences; history; liberal arts and sciences studies, and humanities; mathematics and statistics; multi/interdisciplinary studies; physical sciences; psychology; public administration and social service professions; security and protective services; social sciences; transportation and materials moving; visual and performing arts. **Areas of required coursework:** arts/fine arts, computer literacy, mathematics, English (including composition), foreign languages, sciences (biological or physical), history, social science. **Pre-professional programs:** pre-law, pre-dentistry, pre-medicine, pre-veterinary science, pre-optometry, pre-pharmacy. **Special academic programs:** distance learning, double major, dual enrollment, honors program, independent study, internships, teacher certificate program. **Teacher certification offered in:** early childhood, special education, secondary. **Reserve Officers Training Corps (ROTC):** Army ROTC: Offered at cooperating institution (Mississippi Valley State University). **Faculty and instruction (2009-2010):** Total instructional faculty: 193 full-time, 66 part-time (48% men; 52% women; 12% minorities). Full-time faculty with Ph.D. or other terminal degree: 70%. Student/faculty ratio: 15/1. Classes of fewer than 20 students: 66%; of 20 to 49 students: 33%; of 50 or more students: 1%. **Advanced Placement and International Baccalaureate credit:** AP tests may be used for: Credit only. Scores accepted: 3, 4, 5. **Freshmen returning for sophomore year:** 64%. **Graduation rates:** Four-year: 17%; five-year: 39%; six-year: 45%. **Graduate study:** 14% of students pursue further study immediately upon graduation.

COSTS AND FINANCIAL AID

Financial aid office: (662) 846-4670. **Expenses (2009-2010):** Tuition and fees 2009-2010: $4,450 in state, $11,520 out of state; room/board: $5,778. Estimated books and supplies: $800 personal expenses: $3,222. **Financial aid:** Priority filing date for institution's financial aid form: March 1. Average amount of debt of borrowers graduating in 2009: $19,840. Proportion who borrowed: 65%.

CAMPUS LIFE AND EXTRACURRICULAR ACTIVITIES

Campus housing available (% using): women's dorms (59%), men's dorms (39%), apartments for married students (2%). Students who live in college-owned, operated, or affiliated housing: 30%. **Student employment:** During the 2009-2010 academic year, 8% of undergraduates worked on campus. Average per-year earnings: $1,850. **Clubs and organizations:** Number of student organizations: 120. Activities include: campus ministries, choral groups, concert band, dance, drama/theater, international student organization, jazz band, literary magazine, marching band, music ensembles, musical theater, opera, pep band, student government, student newspaper, symphony orchestra, yearbook. Number of fraternities: 8; sororities: 6. Proportion of men in fraternities: 18%; of women in sororities: 14%. **Sports program (2009-2010):** Member of NCAA II. *Men's intercollegiate varsity sports:* baseball, basketball, football, golf, soccer, swimming, tennis. *Women's intercollegiate varsity sports:* basketball, cross country, soccer, softball, swimming, tennis.

SERVICES AND FACILITIES

Basic services: nonremedial tutoring, placement service, day care, health service, health insurance. **Remedial assistance:** reading, math, writing, study skills. **Counseling services:** career, personal, veteran student, academic, psychological, birth control. **For learning-disabled students:** School does not offer a structured program with separate admission and additional fees. Services include: remedial math, remedial English, remedial reading, tape recorders, learning center, extended time for tests, tutors. **Library:** Number of titles: 367,817; number of current serial subscriptions: 1,180. **Information technology resources:** Students are not required to lease or own a computer. Number of campus computers available to all students: 263. School has a wireless network. Approximate number of users that can be accommodated: 2,800. Proportion of college-owned housing units wired for high-speed internet access: 100%. **Campus safety:** Security services offered: 24-hour foot-and-vehicle patrols, late-night transport/escort service, 24-hour emergency telephones, lighted pathways/sidewalks, student patrols, controlled dormitory access (key, security card, etc).

TRANSFER AND INTERNATIONAL STUDENTS

Transfer students: May apply for admission for the following academic terms: Fall, Spring, Summer. Applicants need a minimum number of credits to apply. For fall 2009: Transfer applications received: 1,357. Transfer

applicants offered admission: 598. Transfer applicants enrolled: 492.
International students: Number of foreign undergraduates: 52 (2% of student body). Number of countries represented: 17. Minimum TOEFL score required: 525 (paper); 196 (computer). Average TOEFL score: 530 (paper).

Jackson State University

- **Address:** 1400 J.R. Lynch Street, Jackson, MS 39217
- **Website:** http://www.jsums.edu
- **Public**
- **Enrollment:** 5,835 full-time; 970 part-time

KEY STATS

✔ **U.S News College Ranking:** second tier, National Universities
✔ **ACT Score (25th/75th percentile):** 17-20
✔ **Tuition:** 2009-2010: $4,634 in state, $11,358 out of state
   Selectivity: Selective   **Room/board:** $5,693
   Acceptance rate: 54%   **Average debt:** N/A
   Student/faculty ratio: 16/1   **Proportion who borrowed:** N/A

UNDERGRADUATE STUDENT BODY STATS

2009-2010 enrollment: 5,835 full-time; 970 part-time. Men: 38%; women: 62%. **Ethnic makeup:** African American: 95%; White: 4%.

ADMISSIONS FACTS AND FIGURES

Phone: (601) 979-2100. **Email:** admappl@jsums.edu. **Website:** http://www.jsums.edu. **Application deadlines for fall 2011:** Regular decision: August 1. Early decision: Not offered. Early action: Not offered. Admission can be deferred. **To apply online, go to:** https://osiris.jsums.edu:4446/pls/PROD/bwskalog.P_DispLoginNon. **Admissions requirements/recommendations:** High school units required (recommended): English: 4 (4); Mathematics: 3 (4); Science: 3 (4); Foreign language: 1 (2); Social studies: 1 (2); History: 2 (2); Academic electives: 2 (2); Total units: 16 (21). Tests: The college uses SAT or ACT scores in admissions decisions. Either SAT or ACT required. For admission to the fall 2011 entering class, the school will accept: ACT with or without writing accepted. Campus visit: Neither required nor recommended. Admissions interview: Neither required nor recommended. Off-campus interview: Not available. **Factors that count in admissions decisions:** *Academic:* Secondary school record: Very Important. Class rank: Not Considered. Letters of recommendation: Not Considered. Standardized test scores: Very Important. Essay: Not Considered. *Nonacademic:* Interview: Not Considered. Extracurricular activities: Considered. Talent/ability: Important. Character/personal qualities: Important. Alumni/ae relationship: Important. Geographical residence: Not Considered. State residency: Not Considered. Religious affiliation/commitment: Not Considered. Minority status: Not Considered. Volunteer work: Not Considered. Work experience: Not Considered. **Admissions statistics for the fall 2009 entering class:** Total applicants: 8,002. Total accepted: 4,290. Freshmen enrolled: 853; 33% were from out of state. Overall acceptance rate: 54%. **Credentials of fall 2009 freshmen:** 33% ranked in the top 25 percent of their high school class. **Average high school grade point average:** 2.9. **First-year students submitting ACT scores:** 98%. Scores (25/75 percentile): English: 16-22, Math: 16-19, Composite: 17-20.

ACADEMICS

Year founded: 1877. **Academic calendar:** Semester. **Degrees offered:** bachelor's, master's, post-master's certificate, doctorate. **Most popular majors:** 11% multi/interdisciplinary studies, 10% biology/biological sciences, 6% accounting, 6% business administration and management, 6% education. **Major fields of study:** architecture and related services; biological and biomedical sciences; business, management, marketing, and related support services; communication, journalism, and related programs; computer and information sciences and support services; education; engineering; engineering technologies/technicians; English language and literature/letters; foreign languages, literatures, and linguistics; health professions and related clinical sciences; history; mathematics and statistics; multi/interdisciplinary studies; natural resources and conservation; physical sciences; psychology; public administration and social service professions; security and protective services; social sciences; visual and performing arts. **Areas of required coursework:** arts/fine arts, humanities, computer literacy, mathematics, English (including composition), philosophy, foreign languages, sciences (biological or physical), history, social science. **Special academic programs:** cooperative (work-study plan) program, distance learning, double

major, dual enrollment, English as a Second Language (ESL), exchange student program (domestic), honors program, independent study, internships, study abroad, teacher certificate program. **Teacher certification offered in:** early childhood, special education, elementary, secondary. **Reserve Officers Training Corps (ROTC):** Army ROTC: Offered on campus; Air Force ROTC: Offered on campus. **Faculty and instruction (2009-2010):** Total instructional faculty: 406 full-time, 119 part-time (53% men; 47% women; 82% minorities). Full-time faculty with Ph.D. or other terminal degree: 74%. Student/faculty ratio: 16/1. Classes of fewer than 20 students: 35%; of 20 to 49 students: 61%; of 50 or more students: 5%. **Freshmen returning for sophomore year:** 73%. **Graduation rates:** Four-year: 15%; five-year: 26%; six-year: 33%. **Graduate study:** 11% of students pursue further study immediately upon graduation; 0% within one year. Fields in which graduates pursue further study: law, 7%; medicine, 13%.

COSTS AND FINANCIAL AID

Financial aid office: (601) 979-2227. **Expenses (2009-2010):** Tuition and fees 2009-2010: $4,634 in state, $11,358 out of state; room/board: $5,693. Estimated books and supplies: $2,100. **Financial aid:** Priority filing date for institution's financial aid form: April 15; deadline: April 15.

CAMPUS LIFE AND EXTRACURRICULAR ACTIVITIES

Campus housing available (% using): women's dorms (58%), men's dorms (42%), other housing options. Students who live in college-owned, operated, or affiliated housing: 25%. **Clubs and organizations:** Number of student organizations: 116. Activities include: choral groups, dance, drama/theater, international student organization, jazz band, marching band, music ensembles, pep band, radio station, student government, student newspaper, television station, yearbook. Number of fraternities: 5; sororities: 4. Proportion of men in fraternities: 3%; of women in sororities: 3%. **Sports program (2009-2010):** Member of NCAA I. *Men's intercollegiate varsity sports:* baseball, basketball, cross country, football, golf, tennis, track and field (indoor), track and field (outdoor). *Women's intercollegiate varsity sports:* basketball, bowling, cross country, golf, soccer, softball, tennis, track and field (indoor), track and field (outdoor), volleyball.

SERVICES AND FACILITIES

Basic services: nonremedial tutoring, placement service, day care, health service, health insurance. **Remedial assistance:** reading, math, writing, study skills. **Counseling services:** career, military, personal, academic, psychological, birth control. **For learning-disabled students:** School does not offer a structured program with separate admission and additional fees. Services include: remedial math, remedial English, reading machines, remedial reading, tape recorders, other special classes, diagnostic testing service, note-taking services, oral tests, learning center, readers, extended time for tests, tutors, priority seating, typist/scribe. **Library:** Number of titles: 499,325; number of current serial subscriptions: 59,781. **Information technology resources:** Students are not required to lease or own a computer. Number of campus computers available to all students: 300. School has a wireless network. Approximate number of users that can be accommodated: 1,500. Proportion of college-owned housing units wired for high-speed internet access: 100%. **Campus safety:** Security services offered: 24-hour foot-and-vehicle patrols, late-night transport/escort service, 24-hour emergency telephones, lighted pathways/sidewalks, controlled dormitory access (key, security card, etc).

TRANSFER AND INTERNATIONAL STUDENTS

Transfer students: May apply for admission for the following academic terms: Fall, Spring, Summer. Applicants need a minimum number of credits to apply. For fall 2009: Transfer applicants enrolled: 508. **International students:** Number of foreign undergraduates: 0. Number of countries represented: 22. Minimum TOEFL score required: 525 (paper); 197 (computer). Average TOEFL score: 525 (paper).

Millsaps College

- **Address:** 1701 N. State Street, Jackson, MS 39210-0001
- **Website:** http://www.millsaps.edu
- **Private; Religious affiliation:** Methodist
- **Enrollment:** 998 full-time; 19 part-time

KEY STATS

✔ **U.S News College Ranking:** 93, National Liberal Arts Colleges
✔ **ACT Score (25th/75th percentile):** 23-29
✔ **Tuition:** 2010-2011: $27,812

Selectivity: More selective	**Room/board:** $9,728
Acceptance rate: 74%	**Average debt:** $29,848
Student/faculty ratio: 10/1	**Proportion who borrowed:** 59%

UNDERGRADUATE STUDENT BODY STATS

2009-2010 enrollment: 998 full-time; 19 part-time. Men: 50%; women: 50%. **Ethnic makeup:** African American: 11%; Asian American: 4%; Hispanic: 2%; White: 81%; International: 2%. **Religious preference:** Roman Catholic: 16%; Protestant: 24%; Jewish: 1%; Hindu: 1%; Unknown: 42%; Methodist: 14%; non-denominational: 1%; Other: 1%.

ADMISSIONS FACTS AND FIGURES

Phone: (601) 974-1050. **Email:** admissions@millsaps.edu. **Website:** http://www.millsaps.edu. **Application deadlines for fall 2011:** Regular decision: Rolling. Early decision: Not offered. Early action: Send application by: January 12; Decision sent by: N/A. Admission can be deferred. **Application fee:** None. **To apply online, go to:** http://millsaps.edu/admissions/new_freshmen.php. **Admissions requirements/recommendations:** High school units required (recommended): English: 4 (4); Mathematics: 3 (4); Science: 3 (4); Foreign language: (2); Social studies: 2 (2); History: 2 (2); Academic electives: (2); Total units: 14 (20). Tests: The college uses SAT or ACT scores in admissions decisions. Either SAT or ACT required. For admission to the fall 2011 entering class, the school will accept: ACT with or without writing accepted. Campus visit: Recommended. Admissions interview: Recommended. Off-campus interview: May be arranged. **Factors that count in admissions decisions:** *Academic:* Secondary school record: Very Important. Class rank: Important. Letters of recommendation: Important. Standardized test scores: Very Important. Essay: Important. *Nonacademic:* Interview: Important. Extracurricular activities: Important. Talent/ability: Important. Character/personal qualities: Very Important. Alumni/ae relationship: Not Considered. Geographical residence: Not Considered. State residency: Not Considered. Religious affiliation/commitment: Not Considered. Minority status: Not Considered. Volunteer work: Important. Work experience: Considered. **Other schools with the greatest overlap in applicants:** Birmingham-Southern College; Hendrix College; Louisiana State University–Baton Rouge; Rhodes College; University of Mississippi. **Admissions statistics for the fall 2009 entering class:** Total applicants: 1,348. Total accepted: 992. Freshmen enrolled: 283; 56% were from out of state. Overall acceptance rate: 74%. Non-early acceptance rate: 74%. **Credentials of fall 2009 freshmen:** 33% ranked in the top 10 percent of their high school class; 50% were in the top 25 percent; 81% were in the top half. (Proportion submitting class standing: 35%.) **Average high school grade point average:** 3.5. **First-year students who submitted SAT scores:** 37%. Scores (25/75 percentile): Critical Reading: 510-640, Math: 520-640, Combined: 1030-1280. **First-year students submitting ACT scores:** 90%. Scores (25/75 percentile): English: 21-28, Math: 23-31, Composite: 23-29.

ACADEMICS

Year founded: 1890. **Academic calendar:** Semester. **Degrees offered:** bachelor's, master's. **Most popular majors:** 24% business administration and management, 13% social sciences, 12% psychology, 11% biological and biomedical sciences, 6% English language and literature/letters. **Major fields of study:** area, ethnic, cultural, and gender studies; biological and biomedical sciences; business, management, marketing, and related support services; computer and information sciences and support services; education; English language and literature/letters; foreign languages, literatures, and linguistics; history; mathematics and statistics; multi/interdisciplinary studies; philosophy and religious studies; physical sciences; psychology; social sciences; visual and performing arts. **Areas of required coursework:** arts/fine arts, humanities, mathematics, English (including composition), sciences (biological or physical), history, social science, other. **Pre-professional programs:** pre-law, pre-dentistry, pre-medicine, pre-theology, pre-veterinary science, pre-optometry, pre-pharmacy, other. **Special academic programs**

(% participation): accelerated program (2%), double major (10%), honors program (29%), independent study (38%), internships (71%), liberal arts/career combination (3%), student-designed major (0%), study abroad (37%), teacher certificate program (8%). **Teacher certification offered in:** special education, elementary, secondary. **Reserve Officers Training Corps (ROTC):** Army ROTC: Offered at cooperating institution (Jackson State University). **Faculty and instruction (2009-2010):** Total instructional faculty: 96 full-time, 20 part-time (53% men; 47% women; 11% minorities). Full-time faculty with Ph.D. or other terminal degree: 94%. Student/faculty ratio: 10/1. Classes of fewer than 20 students: 66%; of 20 to 49 students: 33%; of 50 or more students: 0%. **Advanced Placement and International Baccalaureate credit:** AP tests may be used for: Placement only. Scores accepted: 4, 5. International Baccalaureate exams may be used for: Placement only. **Freshmen returning for sophomore year:** 79%. **Graduation rates:** Four-year: 59%; five-year: 63%; six-year: 66%. **Graduate study:** 48% of students pursue further study immediately upon graduation; 52% within one year; 70% within five years. Fields in which graduates pursue further study: Master of Business Administration (MBA), 30%; law, 15%; medicine, 8%; dentistry, 2%; engineering, 1%; theology (or the seminary), 2%; education, 5%; arts and sciences, 36%; veterinary medicine, 1%.

COSTS AND FINANCIAL AID

Financial aid office: (601) 974-1220. **Expenses (2010-2011):** Tuition and fees 2010-2011: $27,812; room/board: $9,728. Estimated books and supplies: $1,100; transportation: $550; personal expenses: $1,100. **Financial aid:** Priority filing date for institution's financial aid form: March 1. In 2009-2010, 71% of undergraduates applied for financial aid. Of those, 58% were determined to have financial need; 39% had their need fully met. Average financial aid package (proportion receiving): $24,659 (58%). Average amount of gift aid, such as scholarships or grants (proportion receiving): $18,969 (57%). Average amount of self-help aid, such as work study or loans (proportion receiving): $5,011 (41%). Average need-based loan (excluding PLUS or other private loans): $4,359. Among students who received need-based aid, the average percentage of need met: 84%. Among students who received aid based on merit, the average award (and the proportion receiving): $15,127 (39%). The average athletic scholarship (and the proportion receiving): $0 (0%). Average amount of debt of borrowers graduating in 2009: $29,848. Proportion who borrowed: 59%.

CAMPUS LIFE AND EXTRACURRICULAR ACTIVITIES

Campus housing available (% using): coed dorms (54%), women's dorms (21%), men's dorms (18%), fraternity housing (7%), special housing for disabled students. Students who live in college-owned, operated, or affiliated housing: 86%. **Student employment:** During the 2009-2010 academic year, 33% of undergraduates worked on campus. Average per-year earnings: $979. **Clubs and organizations:** Number of student organizations: 89. Activities include: campus ministries, choral groups, dance, drama/theater, international student organization, literary magazine, model UN, music ensembles, musical theater, pep band, student government, student newspaper, student film society, yearbook. Number of fraternities: 6; sororities: 6. Proportion of men in fraternities: 43%; of women in sororities: 54%. Average proportion of students who stay on campus on weekends: 75%. **Sports program (2009-2010):** Member of NCAA III. *Men's intercollegiate varsity sports:* baseball, basketball, cross country, football, golf, lacrosse, soccer, tennis, track and field (indoor), track and field (outdoor). *Women's intercollegiate varsity sports:* basketball, cross country, golf, lacrosse, soccer, softball, tennis, track and field (indoor), track and field (outdoor), volleyball.

SERVICES AND FACILITIES

Basic services: nonremedial tutoring, placement service, health service. **Counseling services:** minority student, career, personal, academic, older student, birth control, religious, other. **For learning-disabled students:** School does not offer a structured program with separate admission and additional fees. Total undergraduates in learning-disabled program or receiving services: 18. Services include: tape recorders, note-taking services, oral tests, readers, extended time for tests, tutors, priority seating, other. **Library:** Number of titles: 196,277; number of current serial subscriptions: 877. **Information technology resources:** Students are not required to lease or own a computer. Number of campus computers available to all students: 150. School has a wireless network. Approximate number of users that can be accommodated: 1,500. Proportion of college-owned housing units wired for high-speed internet access: 100%. **Campus safety:** Security services offered: 24-hour foot-and-vehicle patrols, late-night transport/escort service, 24-hour emergency telephones, lighted pathways/sidewalks, student patrols, controlled dormitory access (key, security card, etc).

TRANSFER AND INTERNATIONAL STUDENTS

Transfer students: May apply for admission for the following academic terms: Fall, Spring. Applicants need a minimum number of credits to apply. For fall 2009: Transfer applications received: 168. Transfer applicants offered admission: 80. Transfer applicants enrolled: 40. **International students:** Number of foreign undergraduates: 19 (2% of student body). Number of countries represented: 10. Minimum TOEFL score required: 550 (paper); 83 (computer).

Mississippi College

- **Address:** MC Box 4001, Clinton, MS 39058
- **Website:** http://www.mc.edu
- **Private; Religious affiliation:** Southern Baptist Convention
- **Enrollment:** 2,686 full-time; 406 part-time

KEY STATS

✔ **U.S News College Ranking:** 35, Regional Universities (South)
✔ **ACT Score (25th/75th percentile):** 20-27
✔ **Tuition:** 2010-2011: $13,550

Selectivity: More selective	**Room/board:** $6,150
Acceptance rate: 61%	**Average debt:** $26,323
Student/faculty ratio: 16/1	**Proportion who borrowed:** 73%

UNDERGRADUATE STUDENT BODY STATS

2009-2010 enrollment: 2,686 full-time; 406 part-time. Men: 40%; women: 60%. **Ethnic makeup:** African American: 25%; Asian American: 1%; Hispanic: 1%; White: 70%; International: 2%. **Religious preference:** Roman Catholic: 4%; Protestant: 27%; Unknown: 7%; Southern Baptist Convention: 62%.

ADMISSIONS FACTS AND FIGURES

Phone: (601) 925-3800. **Email:** enrollment-services@mc.edu. **Website:** http://www.mc.edu. **Application deadlines for fall 2011:** Regular decision: Rolling. Early decision: Send application by: December 1; Decision sent by: December 15. Early action: Not offered. Admission can be deferred. **To apply online, go to:** http://www.mc.edu/admissions. **Admissions requirements/recommendations:** High school units required (recommended): English: (4); Mathematics: (4); Science: (4); Foreign language: (1); Social studies: (2); History: (2); Academic electives: (4); Total units: (22). Tests: The college uses SAT or ACT scores in admissions decisions. Either SAT or ACT required. For admission to the fall 2011 entering class, the school will accept: ACT with or without writing accepted. Campus visit: Recommended. Admissions interview: Neither required nor recommended. Off-campus interview: May be arranged. **Factors that count in admissions decisions:** *Academic:* Secondary school record: Important. Class rank: Considered. Letters of recommendation: Considered. Standardized test scores: Very Important. Essay: Not Considered. *Nonacademic:* Interview: Considered. Extracurricular activities: Important. Talent/ability: Considered. Character/personal qualities: Important. Alumni/ae relationship: Considered. Geographical residence: Not Considered. State residency: Not Considered. Religious affiliation/commitment: Not Considered. Minority status: Not Considered. Volunteer work: Considered. Work experience: Considered. **Other schools with the greatest overlap in applicants:** Jackson State University; Millsaps College; Millsaps College; Mississippi State University; Mississippi State University; University of Mississippi; University of Mississippi; University of Southern Mississippi; University of Southern Mississippi. **Admissions statistics for the fall 2009 entering class:** Total applicants: 1,763. Total accepted: 1,080. Freshmen enrolled: 466; 35% were from out of state. Overall acceptance rate: 61%. Non-early acceptance rate: 61%. **Credentials of fall 2009 freshmen:** 24% ranked in the top 10 percent of their high school class; 50% were in the top 25 percent; 77% were in the top half. (Proportion submitting class standing: 72%.) **Average high school grade point average:** 3.4. **First-year students who submitted SAT scores:** 11%. Scores (25/75 percentile): Critical Reading: 450-600, Math: 470-600, Combined: 920-1200. **First-year students submitting ACT scores:** 95%. Scores (25/75 percentile): English: 20-29, Math: 18-25, Composite: 20-27.

ACADEMICS

Year founded: 1826. **Academic calendar:** Semester. **Degrees offered:** bachelor's, post-bachelor's certificate, master's, post-master's certificate, doctorate. **Most popular majors:** 15% business administration and management,

11% nursing/registered nurse training (R.N., A.S.N., B.S.N., M.S.N.), 10% biology/biological sciences, 8% elementary education and teaching, 6% accounting. **Major fields of study:** biological and biomedical sciences; business, management, marketing, and related support services; communication, journalism, and related programs; computer and information sciences and support services; education; engineering; English language and literature/letters; foreign languages, literatures, and linguistics; health professions and related clinical sciences; history; legal professions and studies; liberal arts and sciences studies, and humanities; mathematics and statistics; parks, recreation, leisure, and fitness studies; philosophy and religious studies; physical sciences; psychology; public administration and social service professions; security and protective services; social sciences; theology and religious vocations; visual and performing arts. **Areas of required coursework:** arts/fine arts, humanities, computer literacy, mathematics, English (including composition), philosophy, sciences (biological or physical), history, social science, other. **Pre-professional programs:** pre-law, pre-dentistry, pre-medicine, pre-theology, pre-veterinary science, pre-optometry, pre-pharmacy, other. **Special academic programs:** accelerated program, distance learning, double major, dual enrollment, English as a Second Language (ESL), honors program, independent study, internships, study abroad, teacher certificate program. **Teacher certification offered in:** early childhood, special education, elementary, secondary. **Reserve Officers Training Corps (ROTC):** Army ROTC: Offered on campus; Air Force ROTC: Offered on campus. **Faculty and instruction (2009-2010):** Total instructional faculty: 180 full-time, 244 part-time (52% men; 48% women; 9% minorities). Full-time faculty with Ph.D. or other terminal degree: 77%. Student/faculty ratio: 16/1. Classes of fewer than 20 students: 50%; of 20 to 49 students: 48%; of 50 or more students: 2%. **Advanced Placement and International Baccalaureate credit:** AP tests may be used for: Credit only. Scores accepted: 3, 4. International Baccalaureate exams may be used for: Credit only. **Freshmen returning for sophomore year:** 70%. **Graduation rates:** Four-year: 36%; five-year: 50%; six-year: 59%. **Graduate study:** 37% of students pursue further study within one year.

COSTS AND FINANCIAL AID

Financial aid office: (601) 925-3319. **Expenses (2010-2011):** Tuition and fees 2010-2011: $13,550; room/board: $6,150. Estimated books and supplies: $1,000; transportation: $1,440; personal expenses: $1,775. **Financial aid:** Priority filing date for institution's financial aid form: March 1. In 2009-2010, 98% of undergraduates applied for financial aid. Of those, 62% were determined to have financial need; 33% had their need fully met. Average financial aid package (proportion receiving): $16,013 (62%). Average amount of gift aid, such as scholarships or grants (proportion receiving): $9,484 (48%). Average amount of self-help aid, such as work study or loans (proportion receiving): $8,088 (46%). Average need-based loan (excluding PLUS or other private loans): $7,582. Among students who received need-based aid, the average percentage of need met: 78%. Among students who received aid based on merit, the average award (and the proportion receiving): $10,104 (35%). The average athletic scholarship (and the proportion receiving): $0 (0%). Average amount of debt of borrowers graduating in 2009: $26,323. Proportion who borrowed: 73%.

CAMPUS LIFE AND EXTRACURRICULAR ACTIVITIES

Campus housing available (% using): women's dorms (50%), men's dorms (47%), apartment for single students (3%), special housing for disabled students. Students who live in college-owned, operated, or affiliated housing: 55%. **Student employment:** During the 2009-2010 academic year, 20% of undergraduates worked on campus. Average per-year earnings: $2,900. **Clubs and organizations:** Number of student organizations: 66. Activities include: campus ministries, choral groups, concert band, dance, drama/theater, international student organization, jazz band, literary magazine, marching band, music ensembles, musical theater, opera, radio station, student government, student newspaper, yearbook. Number of fraternities: 5; sororities: 4. Average proportion of students who stay on campus on weekends: 50%. **Sports program (2009-2010):** Member of NCAA III. *Men's intercollegiate varsity sports:* baseball, basketball, cross country, football, golf, soccer, tennis, track and field (outdoor). *Women's intercollegiate varsity sports:* basketball, cross country, equestrian, soccer, softball, tennis, track and field (outdoor), volleyball.

SERVICES AND FACILITIES

Basic services: nonremedial tutoring, placement service, health service. **Remedial assistance:** math, study skills, other. **Counseling services:** career, academic, psychological. **For learning-disabled students:** School does not offer a structured program with separate admission and additional fees. Services include: remedial math, remedial English, tape recorders, note-taking services, oral tests, readers, extended time for tests, tutors, other. **Library:** Number of titles: 382,586; number of current serial subscriptions: 1,258. **Information technology resources:** Students are not required to lease or own a computer. Number of campus computers available to all students: 390. School has a wireless network. Approximate number of users that can be accommodated: 5,000. Proportion of college-owned housing units wired for high-speed internet access: 100%. **Campus safety:** Security services offered: 24-hour foot-and-vehicle patrols, late-night transport/escort service, 24-hour emergency telephones, lighted pathways/sidewalks, controlled dormitory access (key, security card, etc).

TRANSFER AND INTERNATIONAL STUDENTS

Transfer students: May apply for admission for the following academic terms: Fall, Spring, Summer. Applicants need a minimum number of credits to apply. For fall 2009: Transfer applications received: 1,282. Transfer applicants offered admission: 565. Transfer applicants enrolled: 411. **International students:** Number of foreign undergraduates: 75 (2% of student body). Number of countries represented: 12.

Mississippi State University

- **Address:** PO Box 6334, Mississippi State, MS 39762
- **Website:** http://www.msstate.edu
- **Public**
- **Enrollment:** 13,206 full-time; 1,396 part-time

KEY STATS

✔ **U.S News College Ranking:** 151, National Universities
✔ **ACT Score (25th/75th percentile):** 20-27
✔ **Tuition:** 2009-2010: $5,151 in state, $13,021 out of state

Selectivity: Selective	**Room/board:** $7,520
Acceptance rate: 65%	**Average debt:** $23,413
Student/faculty ratio: 18/1	**Proportion who borrowed:** 51%

UNDERGRADUATE STUDENT BODY STATS

2009-2010 enrollment: 13,206 full-time; 1,396 part-time. Men: 52%; women: 48%. **Ethnic makeup:** African American: 20%; American-Indian: 1%; Asian American: 1%; Hispanic: 1%; White: 75%; International: 2%.

ADMISSIONS FACTS AND FIGURES

Phone: (662) 325-2224. **Email:** admit@admissions.msstate.edu. **Website:** http://www.msstate.edu. **Application deadlines for fall 2011:** Regular decision: Rolling. Early decision: Not offered. Early action: Not offered. Admission cannot be deferred. **Application fee:** $35. **To apply online, go to:** http://www.admissions.msstate.edu/apply/. **Admissions requirements/ recommendations:** High school units required (recommended): English: 4 (4); Mathematics: 3 (4); Science: 3 (4); Foreign language: 0 (1); Social studies: 1 (2); History: 2 (2); Academic electives: 2 (2); Total units: 16 (21). Tests: The college uses SAT or ACT scores in admissions decisions. Either SAT or ACT required. For admission to the fall 2011 entering class, the school will accept: ACT with or without writing accepted. Campus visit: Recommended. Admissions interview: Neither required nor recommended. Off-campus interview: May be arranged. **Factors that count in admissions decisions:** *Academic:* Secondary school record: Considered. Class rank: Important. Letters of recommendation: Not Considered. Standardized test scores: Very Important. Essay: Not Considered. *Nonacademic:* Interview: Not Considered. Extracurricular activities: Not Considered. Talent/ability: Considered. Character/personal qualities: Not Considered. Alumni/ ae relationship: Not Considered. Geographical residence: Not Considered. State residency: Not Considered. Religious affiliation/commitment: Not Considered. Minority status: Not Considered. Volunteer work: Not Considered. Work experience: Not Considered. **Admissions statistics for the fall 2009 entering class:** Total applicants: 7,839. Total accepted: 5,109. Freshmen enrolled: 2,450; 29% were from out of state. Overall acceptance rate: 65%. **Credentials of fall 2009 freshmen:** 27% ranked in the top 10 percent of their high school class; 27% were in the top 25 percent; 83% were in the top half. (Proportion submitting class standing: 99%.) **Average high school grade point average:** 3.1. **First-year students who submitted SAT scores:** 16%. Scores (25/75 percentile): Critical Reading: 470-610, Math: 490-640, Combined: 960-1250. **First-year students submitting ACT scores:** 96%. Scores (25/75 percentile): English: 21-29, Math: 1-27, Composite: 20-27.

ACADEMICS

Year founded: 1878. **Academic calendar:** Semester. **Degrees offered:** bachelor's, master's. **Most popular majors:** 22% business, management, marketing, and related support services, 20% education, 12% engineering, 6% agriculture, agriculture operations, and related sciences, 6% multi/ interdisciplinary studies. **Major fields of study:** agriculture, agriculture operations, and related sciences; architecture and related services; biological and biomedical sciences; business, management, marketing, and related support services; communication, journalism, and related programs; computer and information sciences and support services; education; engineering; engineering technologies/technicians; English language and literature/ letters; family and consumer sciences/human sciences; foreign languages, literatures, and linguistics; health professions and related clinical sciences; history; liberal arts and sciences studies, and humanities; mathematics and statistics; multi/interdisciplinary studies; natural resources and conservation; philosophy and religious studies; physical sciences; psychology; public administration and social service professions; social sciences; visual and performing arts. **Areas of required coursework:** arts/fine arts, humanities, computer literacy, mathematics, English (including composition), sciences (biological or physical), history, social science. **Pre-professional programs:** pre-law, pre-dentistry, pre-medicine, pre-veterinary science, pre-optometry, pre-pharmacy, other. **Special academic programs:** cooperative (work-study plan) program, distance learning, double major, dual enrollment, English as a Second Language (ESL), exchange student program (domestic), external degree program, honors program, independent study, internships, liberal arts/career combination, student-designed major, study abroad, teacher certificate program, weekend college. **Teacher certification offered in:** special education, elementary, vo-tech, middle/junior high, adult education, secondary. **Cooperative education programs:** agriculture, art, business, computer science, education, engineering, technologies, other. **Reserve Officers Training Corps (ROTC):** Army ROTC: Offered on campus; Air Force ROTC: Offered on campus. **Faculty and instruction (2009-2010):** Total instructional faculty: 844 full-time, 124 part-time (63% men; 37% women; 13% minorities). Full-time faculty with Ph.D. or other terminal degree: 80%. Student/ faculty ratio: 18/1. Classes of fewer than 20 students: 40%; of 20 to 49 students: 47%; of 50 or more students: 13%. **Advanced Placement and International Baccalaureate credit:** AP tests may be used for: Credit only. International Baccalaureate exams may be used for: Credit only. **Freshmen returning for sophomore year:** 83%. **Graduation rates:** Four-year: 31%; five-year: 54%; six-year: 61%. **Graduate study:** 22% of students pursue further study immediately upon graduation. Fields in which graduates pursue further study: Master of Business Administration (MBA), 32%; law, 3%; medicine, 9%; engineering, 17%; education, 8%; arts and sciences, 18%; veterinary medicine, 2%.

COSTS AND FINANCIAL AID

Financial aid office: (662) 325-2450. **Expenses (2009-2010):** Tuition and fees 2009-2010: $5,151 in state, $13,021 out of state; room/board: $7,520. Estimated books and supplies: $1,200; transportation: $1,750; personal expenses: $2,250. **Financial aid:** Priority filing date for institution's financial aid form: April 1. In 2009-2010, 67% of undergraduates applied for financial aid. Of those, 56% were determined to have financial need; 28% had their need fully met. Average financial aid package (proportion receiving): $10,551 (55%). Average amount of gift aid, such as scholarships or grants (proportion receiving): $5,422 (50%). Average amount of self-help aid, such as work study or loans (proportion receiving): $4,122 (43%). Average need-based loan (excluding PLUS or other private loans): $3,641. Among students who received need-based aid, the average percentage of need met: 67%. Among students who received aid based on merit, the average award (and the proportion receiving): $2,829 (20%). The average athletic scholarship (and the proportion receiving): $10,814 (3%). Average amount of debt of borrowers graduating in 2009: $23,413. Proportion who borrowed: 51%.

CAMPUS LIFE AND EXTRACURRICULAR ACTIVITIES

Campus housing available (% using): women's dorms (7%), men's dorms (13%), sorority housing (20%), fraternity housing (12%), apartments for married students (7%), apartment for single students (3%), special housing for disabled students (1%), other housing options (20%). Students who live in college-owned, operated, or affiliated housing: 26%. **Student employment:** During the 2009-2010 academic year, 15% of undergraduates worked on campus. Average per-year earnings: $7,960. Activities include: campus ministries, choral groups, concert band, dance, drama/theater, jazz band, marching band, model UN, music ensembles, musical theater, pep band, radio station, student government, student newspaper, symphony orchestra, television station. Number of fraternities: 23; sororities: 9. Proportion of men in fraternities: 5%; of women in sororities: 6%. Average proportion of students who stay on campus on weekends: 20%. **Sports program (2009-2010):** Member of NCAA I. *Men's intercollegiate varsity sports:* baseball, basketball, cross country, football, golf, tennis, track and field (indoor), track and field (outdoor). *Women's intercollegiate varsity sports:* basketball, cross country, golf, soccer, softball, tennis, track and field (indoor), track and field (outdoor), volleyball.

SERVICES AND FACILITIES

Basic services: nonremedial tutoring, day care, health service, health insurance, other. **Remedial assistance:** reading, math, writing, study skills, other. **Counseling services:** minority student, career, military, personal, veteran student, academic, psychological. **For learning-disabled students:** School does not offer a structured program with separate admission and additional fees. Services include: remedial math, remedial English, reading machines, remedial reading, tape recorders, other special classes, note-taking services, oral tests, learning center, readers, extended time for tests, tutors, early syllabus, priority registration, priority seating, substitution of courses, texts on tape, typist/scribe, exams on tape or computer, other testing accommodations. **Library:** Number of titles: 2,191,856; number of current serial subscriptions: 88,003. **Information technology resources:** Students are not required to lease or own a computer. Number of campus computers available to all students: 1,000. School has a wireless network. Approximate number of users that can be accommodated: 10,000. Proportion of college-owned housing units wired for high-speed internet access: 100%. **Campus safety:** Security services offered: 24-hour foot-and-vehicle patrols, late-night transport/escort service, 24-hour emergency telephones, lighted pathways/sidewalks, student patrols, controlled dormitory access (key, security card, etc).

TRANSFER AND INTERNATIONAL STUDENTS

Transfer students: May apply for admission for the following academic terms: Fall, Spring, Summer. Applicants do not need a minimum number of credits to apply. For fall 2009: Transfer applications received: 2,855. Transfer applicants offered admission: 1,588. Transfer applicants enrolled: 1,552. **International students:** Number of foreign undergraduates: 224 (2% of student body). Number of countries represented: 46. Minimum TOEFL score required: 525 (paper); 71 (computer).

Mississippi University for Women

- **Address:** 1100 College Street, Columbus, MS 39701
- **Website:** http://www.muw.edu
- **Public**
- **Enrollment:** 1,758 full-time; 514 part-time

....

KEY STATS

✔ **U.S News College Ranking:** 44, Regional Universities (South)
✔ **ACT Score (25th/75th percentile):** 18-24
✔ **Tuition:** 2010-2011: $4,423 in state, $12,051 out of state

Selectivity: Selective	**Room/board:** $5,164
Acceptance rate: 42%	**Average debt:** $18,363
Student/faculty ratio: 13/1	**Proportion who borrowed:** 64%

UNDERGRADUATE STUDENT BODY STATS

2009-2010 enrollment: 1,758 full-time; 514 part-time. Men: 19%; women: 81%. **Ethnic makeup:** African American: 40%; Asian American: 1%; Hispanic: 1%; White: 57%; International: 1%.

ADMISSIONS FACTS AND FIGURES

Phone: (662) 329-7106. **Email:** admissions@muw.edu. **Website:** http://www.muw.edu. **Application deadlines for fall 2011:** Regular decision: Rolling. Early decision: Not offered. Early action: Not offered. Admission cannot be deferred. **Application fee:** None. **To apply online, go to:** https://www.muw.edu/admissions2/undergrad-app.php. **Admissions requirements/recommendations:** High school units required (recommended): English: 4; Mathematics: 3; Science: 3; Social studies: 3; Academic electives: 2; Total units: 16. Tests: The college uses SAT or ACT scores in admissions decisions. Either SAT or ACT required. For admission to the fall 2011 entering class, the school will accept: ACT with or without writing accepted. Campus visit: Recommended. Admissions interview: Neither required nor recommended. Off-campus interview: Not available. **Factors that count in admissions decisions:** *Academic:* Secondary school record: Very Important. Class rank: Very Important. Letters of recommendation:

Not Considered. Standardized test scores: Very Important. Essay: Not Considered. *Nonacademic:* Interview: Considered. Extracurricular activities: Considered. Talent/ability: Considered. Character/personal qualities: Considered. Alumni/ae relationship: Considered. Geographical residence: Considered. State residency: Not Considered. Religious affiliation/commitment: Not Considered. Minority status: Not Considered. Volunteer work: Considered. Work experience: Considered. **Other schools with the greatest overlap in applicants:** Mississippi State University; University of Mississippi; University of Southern Mississippi. **Admissions statistics for the fall 2009 entering class:** Total applicants: 1,376. Total accepted: 580. Freshmen enrolled: 212; 23% were from out of state. Overall acceptance rate: 42%. **Credentials of fall 2009 freshmen:** 30% ranked in the top 10 percent of their high school class; 61% were in the top 25 percent; 87% were in the top half. (Proportion submitting class standing: 71%.) **Average high school grade point average:** 3.3. **First-year students who submitted SAT scores:** 3%. Scores (25/75 percentile): Critical Reading: 410-640, Math: 390-530, Combined: 800-1170. **First-year students submitting ACT scores:** 96%. Scores (25/75 percentile): English: 19-25, Math: 16-22, Composite: 18-24.

ACADEMICS

Year founded: 1884. **Academic calendar:** Semester. **Degrees offered:** associate, bachelor's, master's, post-master's certificate. **Most popular majors:** 22% nursing/registered nurse training (R.N., A.S.N., B.S.N., M.S.N.), 13% elementary education and teaching, 6% business administration and management, 6% health and physical education, 5% psychology. **Major fields of study:** biological and biomedical sciences; business, management, marketing, and related support services; communication, journalism, and related programs; education; English language and literature/letters; family and consumer sciences/human sciences; foreign languages, literatures, and linguistics; health professions and related clinical sciences; history; legal professions and studies; mathematics and statistics; parks, recreation, leisure, and fitness studies; personal and culinary services; physical sciences; psychology; social sciences; visual and performing arts. **Areas of required coursework:** arts/fine arts, humanities, mathematics, English (including composition), philosophy, sciences (biological or physical), history, social science, other. **Pre-professional programs:** pre-law, pre-dentistry, pre-medicine, pre-theology, pre-veterinary science, pre-optometry, pre-pharmacy, other. **Special academic programs:** cross-registration, distance learning, double major, dual enrollment, honors program, independent study, internships, student-designed major, study abroad, teacher certificate program. **Teacher certification offered in:** special education, elementary, middle/junior high, secondary. **Reserve Officers Training Corps (ROTC):** Army ROTC: Offered at cooperating institution (Mississippi State University); Air Force ROTC: Offered at cooperating institution (Mississippi State University). **Faculty and instruction (2009-2010):** Total instructional faculty: 134 full-time, 51 part-time (38% men; 62% women; 8% minorities). Full-time faculty with Ph.D. or other terminal degree: 56%. Student/faculty ratio: 13/1. Classes of fewer than 20 students: 58%; of 20 to 49 students: 39%; of 50 or more students: 3%. **Advanced Placement and International Baccalaureate credit:** AP tests may be used for: Placement only. Scores accepted: 3, 4, 5. International Baccalaureate exams may be used for: Credit only. **Freshmen returning for sophomore year:** 68%. **Graduation rates:** Four-year: 26%; five-year: 37%; six-year: 41%. **Graduate study:** 25% of students pursue further study immediately upon graduation.

COSTS AND FINANCIAL AID

Financial aid office: (662) 329-7114. **Expenses (2010-2011):** Tuition and fees 2010-2011: $4,423 in state, $12,051 out of state; room/board: $5,164. Estimated books and supplies: $900; transportation: $2,200; personal expenses: $1,115. **Financial aid:** Priority filing date for institution's financial aid form: March 1. In 2009-2010, 85% of undergraduates applied for financial aid. Of those, 74% were determined to have financial need; 67% had their need fully met. Average financial aid package (proportion receiving): $8,408 (74%). Average amount of gift aid, such as scholarships or grants (proportion receiving): $5,201 (57%). Average amount of self-help aid, such as work study or loans (proportion receiving): $4,596 (55%). Average need-based loan (excluding PLUS or other private loans): $4,494. Among students who received need-based aid, the average percentage of need met: 63%. Among students who received aid based on merit, the average award (and the proportion receiving): $4,732 (16%). The average athletic scholarship (and the proportion receiving): $0 (0%). Average amount of debt of borrowers graduating in 2009: $18,363. Proportion who borrowed: 64%.

CAMPUS LIFE AND EXTRACURRICULAR ACTIVITIES

Campus housing available (% using): women's dorms (50%), men's dorms (20%), special housing for disabled students (1%), other housing options

(29%). Students who live in college-owned, operated, or affiliated housing: 25%. **Student employment:** During the 2009-2010 academic year, 11% of undergraduates worked on campus. Average per-year earnings: $1,483. **Clubs and organizations:** Number of student organizations: 72. Activities include: campus ministries, choral groups, dance, drama/theater, international student organization, jazz band, literary magazine, music ensembles, musical theater, radio station, student government, student newspaper, student film society. Number of fraternities: 3; sororities: 15. Proportion of men in fraternities: 8%; of women in sororities: 14%. Average proportion of students who stay on campus on weekends: 50%.

SERVICES AND FACILITIES

Basic services: nonremedial tutoring, women's center, placement service, day care, health service, health insurance. **Remedial assistance:** reading, math, writing, study skills. **Counseling services:** minority student, career, military, personal, veteran student, academic, older student, psychological, birth control, religious. **For learning-disabled students:** School does not offer a structured program with separate admission and additional fees. Total undergraduates in learning-disabled program or receiving services: 15. Services include: remedial math, remedial English, remedial reading, tape recorders, note-taking services, oral tests, learning center, readers, extended time for tests, tutors, priority seating. **Library:** Number of titles: 21,859; number of current serial subscriptions: 3,603. **Information technology resources:** Students are not required to lease or own a computer. Number of campus computers available to all students: 350. School has a wireless network. Approximate number of users that can be accommodated: 500. Proportion of college-owned housing units wired for high-speed internet access: 100%. **Campus safety:** Security services offered: 24-hour foot-and-vehicle patrols, late-night transport/escort service, 24-hour emergency telephones, lighted pathways/sidewalks, controlled dormitory access (key, security card, etc).

TRANSFER AND INTERNATIONAL STUDENTS

Transfer students: May apply for admission for the following academic terms: Fall, Spring, Summer. Applicants do not need a minimum number of credits to apply. For fall 2009: Transfer applications received: 1,117. Transfer applicants offered admission: 542. Transfer applicants enrolled: 337. **International students:** Number of foreign undergraduates: 21 (1% of student body). Number of countries represented: 12. Minimum TOEFL score required: 525 (paper); 71 (computer).

Mississippi Valley State University

- **Address:** 14000 Highway 82 W, Itta Bena, MS 38941-1400
- **Website:** http://www.mvsu.edu
- **Public**
- **Enrollment:** 2,194 full-time; 240 part-time

KEY STATS

✔ **U.S News College Ranking:** second tier, Regional Universities (South)
✔ **ACT Score (25th/75th percentile):** 16-19
✔ **Tuition:** 2009-2010: $4,877 in state, $11,460 out of state

Selectivity: Less selective	**Room/board:** $5,081
Acceptance rate: 30%	**Average debt:** N/A
Student/faculty ratio: 17/1	**Proportion who borrowed:** N/A

UNDERGRADUATE STUDENT BODY STATS

2009-2010 enrollment: 2,194 full-time; 240 part-time. Men: 37%; women: 63%. **Ethnic makeup:** African American: 93%; Hispanic: 1%; White: 6%.

ADMISSIONS FACTS AND FIGURES

Phone: (662) 254-3344. **Email:** admsn@mvsu.edu. **Website:** http://www.mvsu.edu. **Application deadlines for fall 2011:** Regular decision: Rolling. Early decision: Not offered. Early action: Not offered. Admission can be deferred. **To apply online, go to:** http://sutton2.mvsu.edu:7800/prod/bwskalog.P_DispLoginNon. **Admissions requirements/recommendations:** High school units required (recommended): English: 4; Mathematics: 3; Science: 3; Foreign language: 1; Social studies: 3; History: 0; Academic electives: 2; Total units: 16 (18). Tests: The college uses SAT or ACT scores in admissions decisions. ACT required. For admission to the fall 2011 entering class, the school will accept: ACT with or without writing accepted. Campus visit: Neither required nor recommended. Admissions interview: Recommended. Off-campus interview: May be arranged. **Factors**

that count in admissions decisions: **Academic:** Secondary school record: Very Important. Class rank: Very Important. Letters of recommendation: Considered. Standardized test scores: Very Important. Essay: Not Considered. **Nonacademic:** Interview: Considered. Extracurricular activities: Considered. Talent/ability: Considered. Character/personal qualities: Not Considered. Alumni/ae relationship: Not Considered. Geographical residence: Not Considered. State residency: Very Important. Religious affiliation/commitment: Not Considered. Minority status: Not Considered. Volunteer work: Not Considered. Work experience: Not Considered. **Admissions statistics for the fall 2009 entering class:** Total applicants: 6,086. Total accepted: 1,796. Freshmen enrolled: 415; 25% were from out of state. Overall acceptance rate: 30%. **Credentials of fall 2009 freshmen:** 25% ranked in the top 25 percent of their high school class. **Average high school grade point average:** 2.6.

ACADEMICS

Year founded: 1950. **Academic calendar:** Semester. **Degrees offered:** bachelor's, master's. **Most popular majors:** 26% education, 22% security and protective services, 19% public administration and social service professions, 14% business, management, marketing, and related support services. **Major fields of study:** biological and biomedical sciences; business, management, marketing, and related support services; communication, journalism, and related programs; computer and information sciences and support services; education; engineering technologies/technicians; English language and literature/letters; health professions and related clinical sciences; mathematics and statistics; physical sciences; public administration and social service professions; security and protective services; social sciences; visual and performing arts. **Areas of required coursework:** arts/fine arts, mathematics, English (including composition), foreign languages, sciences (biological or physical), history, social science. **Special academic programs:** cooperative (work-study plan) program, distance learning, dual enrollment, honors program, independent study, internships, teacher certificate program. **Teacher certification offered in:** early childhood, special education, elementary, secondary. **Reserve Officers Training Corps (ROTC):** Army ROTC: Offered on campus. **Faculty and instruction (2009-2010):** Total instructional faculty: 133 full-time, 46 part-time (49% men; 51% women). Full-time faculty with Ph.D. or other terminal degree: 36%. Student/faculty ratio: 17/1. Classes of fewer than 20 students: 56%; of 20 to 49 students: 42%; of 50 or more students: 2%. **Freshmen returning for sophomore year:** 62%. **Graduation rates:** Four-year: 18%; five-year: 30%; six-year: 34%. **Graduate study:** 15% of students pursue further study immediately upon graduation; 20% within one year; 30% within five years. Fields in which graduates pursue further study: Master of Business Administration (MBA), 13%; education, 12%; arts and sciences, 71%.

COSTS AND FINANCIAL AID

Financial aid office: (662) 254-3335. **Expenses (2009-2010):** Tuition and fees 2009-2010: $4,877 in state, $11,460 out of state; room/board: $5,081. Estimated books and supplies: $1,400.

CAMPUS LIFE AND EXTRACURRICULAR ACTIVITIES

Campus housing available (% using): women's dorms (65%), men's dorms (35%), apartments for married students, apartment for single students. Students who live in college-owned, operated, or affiliated housing: 38%. **Clubs and organizations:** Number of student organizations: 46. Activities include: choral groups, concert band, dance, drama/theater, jazz band, marching band, music ensembles, pep band, radio station, student government, student newspaper, television station, yearbook. Number of fraternities: 5; sororities: 4. Average proportion of students who stay on campus on weekends: 15%. **Sports program (2009-2010):** Member of NCAA I. **Men's intercollegiate varsity sports:** baseball, basketball, cross country, football, golf, tennis, track and field (indoor), track and field (outdoor). **Women's intercollegiate varsity sports:** basketball, bowling, cross country, golf, soccer, softball, tennis, track and field (indoor), track and field (outdoor), volleyball.

SERVICES AND FACILITIES

Basic services: placement service, health service. **Remedial assistance:** reading, math, writing, study skills. **Counseling services:** career, personal. **Library:** Number of titles: 118,496; number of current serial subscriptions: 402. **Information technology resources:** Students are not required to lease or own a computer. Number of campus computers available to all students: 250. School does not have a wireless network. **Campus safety:** Security services offered: 24-hour emergency telephones, lighted pathways/sidewalks, controlled dormitory access (key, security card, etc).

Transfer students: May apply for admission for the following academic terms: Fall, Spring, Summer. Applicants need a minimum number of credits to apply. For fall 2009: Transfer applicants enrolled: 210. **International students:** Number of countries represented: 5. Minimum TOEFL score required: 525 (paper). Average TOEFL score: 560 (paper).

Rust College

- ■ **Address:** 150 Rust Avenue, Holly Springs, MS 38635
- ■ **Website:** http://www.rustcollege.edu
- ■ **Private; Religious affiliation:** Methodist
- ■ **Enrollment:** 950 full-time; 122 part-time

KEY STATS

✔ **U.S News College Ranking:** second tier, National Liberal Arts Colleges
✔ **ACT Score (25th/75th percentile):** 14-18
✔ **Tuition:** 2009-2010: $7,410

Selectivity: Less selective	**Room/board:** $3,220
Acceptance rate: 61%	**Average debt:** $13,055
Student/faculty ratio: 18/1	**Proportion who borrowed:** 71%

UNDERGRADUATE STUDENT BODY STATS

2009-2010 enrollment: 950 full-time; 122 part-time. Men: 38%; women: 62%. **Ethnic makeup:** African American: 97%; White: 3%. **Religious preference:** Roman Catholic: 2%; Protestant: 70%; Muslim: 1%; No preference: 27%.

ADMISSIONS FACTS AND FIGURES

Phone: (662) 252-8000. **Email:** admissions@rustcollege.edu. **Website:** http://www.rustcollege.edu. **Application deadlines for fall 2011:** Regular decision: Rolling; decision sent by August 15. Early decision: Not offered. Early action: Not offered. Admission can be deferred. **Application fee:** $10. **To apply online, go to:** http://www.rustcollege.edu/rust/rust2/onlineapp.html. **Admissions requirements/recommendations:** High school units required (recommended): English: 4; Mathematics: 3; Science: 3; Foreign language: 0; Social studies: 3; Academic electives: 6; Total units: 19. Tests: The college uses SAT or ACT scores in admissions decisions. ACT required. For admission to the fall 2011 entering class, the school will accept: ACT with or without writing accepted. Campus visit: Recommended. Admissions interview: Recommended. **Factors that count in admissions decisions:** *Academic:* Secondary school record: Important. Class rank: Important. Letters of recommendation: Very Important. Standardized test scores: Important. Essay: Not Considered. *Nonacademic:* Interview: Considered. Extracurricular activities: Considered. Talent/ability: Very Important. Character/personal qualities: Important. Alumni/ae relationship: Not Considered. Geographical residence: Not Considered. State residency: Considered. Religious affiliation/commitment: Not Considered. Minority status: Not Considered. Volunteer work: Not Considered. Work experience: Not Considered. **Admissions statistics for the fall 2009 entering class:** Total applicants: 1,702. Total accepted: 1,033. Freshmen enrolled: 389; Overall acceptance rate: 61%. **First-year students submitting ACT scores:** 90%. Scores (25/75 percentile): English: N/A, Math: N/A, Composite: 14-18.

ACADEMICS

Year founded: 1866. **Academic calendar:** Semester. **Degrees offered:** associate, bachelor's. **Most popular majors:** 21% biology/biological sciences, 10% computer science, 7% social work, 6% sociology. **Major fields of study:** biological and biomedical sciences; business, management, marketing, and related support services; communication, journalism, and related programs; computer and information sciences and support services; education; English language and literature/letters; mathematics and statistics; physical sciences; public administration and social service professions; social sciences; visual and performing arts. **Areas of required coursework:** arts/fine arts, humanities, computer literacy, mathematics, English (including composition), philosophy, sciences (biological or physical), history, social science. **Special academic programs (% participation):** distance learning (10%), double major (1%), honors program (12%), independent study (5%), internships (47%), liberal arts/career combination, study abroad (3%), teacher certificate program (3%). **Teacher certification offered in:** early childhood, elementary. **Faculty and instruction (2009-2010):** Total instructional faculty: N/A. Student/faculty ratio: 18/1. **Advanced Placement and International Baccalaureate credit:** AP tests may be used for: Credit only. Scores accepted:

2, 3, 4, 5. International Baccalaureate exams may be used for: Credit only. **Freshmen returning for sophomore year:** 54%. **Graduation rates:** Four-year: 18%; five-year: 24%; six-year: 31%. **Graduate study:** 15% of students pursue further study immediately upon graduation; 20% within one year; 30% within five years. Fields in which graduates pursue further study: Master of Business Administration (MBA), 2%; medicine, 1%; education, 50%.

COSTS AND FINANCIAL AID

Financial aid office: (662) 252-8000. **Expenses (2009-2010):** Tuition and fees 2009-2010: $7,410; room/board: $3,220. Estimated personal expenses: $70. **Financial aid:** Priority filing date for institution's financial aid form: March 1. In 2009-2010, 86% of undergraduates applied for financial aid. Of those, 88% were determined to have financial need; 88% had their need fully met. Average financial aid package (proportion receiving): $6,533 (88%). Average amount of gift aid, such as scholarships or grants (proportion receiving): $3,260 (86%). Average amount of self-help aid, such as work study or loans (proportion receiving): N/A (88%). Average need-based loan (excluding PLUS or other private loans): $3,873. Among students who received need-based aid, the average percentage of need met: 89%. Among students who received aid based on merit, the average award (and the proportion receiving): N/A (22%). The average athletic scholarship (and the proportion receiving): $0 (N/A). Average amount of debt of borrowers graduating in 2009: $13,055. Proportion who borrowed: 71%.

CAMPUS LIFE AND EXTRACURRICULAR ACTIVITIES

Campus housing available (% using): women's dorms (64%), men's dorms (35%), apartments for married students (1%). **Student employment:** During the 2009-2010 academic year, 54% of undergraduates worked on campus. Average per-year earnings: $1,152. **Clubs and organizations:** Number of student organizations: 38. Activities include: choral groups, concert band, dance, drama/theater, marching band, music ensembles, pep band, radio station, student government, student newspaper, television station, yearbook. Number of fraternities: 2; sororities: 3. Average proportion of students who stay on campus on weekends: 50%. **Sports program (2009-2010):** Member of NCAA III. *Men's intercollegiate varsity sports:* basketball, cross country, track and field (outdoor). *Women's intercollegiate varsity sports:* basketball, cross country, softball, track and field (outdoor), volleyball.

SERVICES AND FACILITIES

Basic services: day care, health service. **Remedial assistance:** reading, math, writing, study skills, other. **Counseling services:** minority student, career, academic, religious. **For learning-disabled students:** Services include: remedial math, remedial English, diagnostic testing service, tutors. **Information technology resources:** Students are not required to lease or own a computer. Number of campus computers available to all students: 220. School has a wireless network. Proportion of college-owned housing units wired for high-speed internet access: 90%. **Campus safety:** Security services offered: 24-hour foot-and-vehicle patrols, late-night transport/escort service, 24-hour emergency telephones, lighted pathways/sidewalks, controlled dormitory access (key, security card, etc).

TRANSFER AND INTERNATIONAL STUDENTS

Transfer students: May apply for admission for the following academic terms: Fall, Spring, Summer. Applicants need a minimum number of credits to apply. **International students:** Minimum TOEFL score required: 540 (paper). Average TOEFL score: 570 (paper).

Tougaloo College

- ■ **Address:** 500 W. County Line Road, Tougaloo, MS 39174
- ■ **Website:** http://www.tougaloo.edu
- ■ **Private; Religious affiliation:** Christian Church (Disciples of Christ)
- ■ **Enrollment:** 905 full-time; 34 part-time

KEY STATS

✔ **U.S News College Ranking:** 166, National Liberal Arts Colleges
✔ **ACT Score (25th/75th percentile):** 24-28
✔ **Tuition:** 2010-2011: $9,710

Selectivity: More selective	**Room/board:** $6,330
Acceptance rate: 25%	**Average debt:** $18,806
Student/faculty ratio: 9/1	**Proportion who borrowed:** 80%

UNDERGRADUATE STUDENT BODY STATS

2009-2010 enrollment: 905 full-time; 34 part-time. Men: 33%; women: 67%. **Ethnic makeup:** African American: 98%; White: 1%.

ADMISSIONS FACTS AND FIGURES

Phone: (601) 977-7765. **Email:** information@mail.tougaloo.edu. **Website:** http://www.tougaloo.edu. **Application deadlines for fall 2011:** Regular decision: Rolling. Early decision: Not offered. Early action: Send application by: November 1; Decision sent by: December 1. Admission can be deferred. **Application fee:** $25. **To apply online, go to:** http://www.tougaloo.edu/content/Admissions/application.pdf. **Admissions requirements/recommendations:** High school units required (recommended): English: 3 (4); Mathematics: 2 (4); Science: 2 (2); Foreign language: (2); Social studies: (2); History: 2; Academic electives: 5; Total units: 16 (14). Tests: The college uses SAT or ACT scores in admissions decisions. Either SAT or ACT required. For admission to the fall 2011 entering class, the school will accept: ACT with or without writing accepted. Campus visit: Recommended. Admissions interview: Recommended. Off-campus interview: May be arranged. **Factors that count in admissions decisions:** *Academic:* Secondary school record: Very Important. Class rank: Very Important. Letters of recommendation: Very Important. Standardized test scores: Important. Essay: Not Considered. *Nonacademic:* Interview: Not Considered. Extracurricular activities: Not Considered. Talent/ability: Not Considered. Character/personal qualities: Not Considered. Alumni/ae relationship: Not Considered. Geographical residence: Not Considered. State residency: Not Considered. Religious affiliation/commitment: Not Considered. Minority status: Not Considered. Volunteer work: Not Considered. Work experience: Not Considered. **Other schools with the greatest overlap in applicants:** Alcorn State University; Dillard University; Jackson State University; Mississippi State University; Xavier University of Louisiana. **Admissions statistics for the fall 2009 entering class:** Total applicants: 4,818. Total accepted: 1,187. Freshmen enrolled: 234; 19% were from out of state. Overall acceptance rate: 25%. Non-early acceptance rate: 25%. **Average high school grade point average:** 3.0. **First-year students who submitted SAT scores:** 30%. Scores (25/75 percentile): Critical Reading: 480-550, Math: 500-510, Combined: 980-1060. **First-year students submitting ACT scores:** 96%. Scores (25/75 percentile): English: 26-29, Math: 23-25, Composite: 24-28.

ACADEMICS

Year founded: 1869. **Academic calendar:** Semester. **Degrees offered:** associate, bachelor's. **Most popular majors:** 27% sociology, 20% biological and biomedical sciences, 11% psychology, 9% education, 8% speech and rhetorical studies. **Major fields of study:** biological and biomedical sciences; business, management, marketing, and related support services; communication, journalism, and related programs; education; English language and literature/letters; history; legal professions and studies; liberal arts and sciences studies, and humanities; psychology; social sciences. **Areas of required coursework:** arts/fine arts, humanities, computer literacy, mathematics, English (including composition), philosophy, foreign languages, sciences (biological or physical), history, social science, other. **Pre-professional programs:** pre-law, pre-dentistry, pre-medicine, pre-theology, pre-veterinary science, pre-pharmacy. **Special academic programs (% participation):** double major (12%), dual enrollment, English as a Second Language (ESL), exchange student program (domestic), honors program (25%), independent study (10%), internships (50%), liberal arts/career combination (20%), student-designed major (10%), study abroad (5%), teacher certificate program (15%), weekend college (2%). **Teacher certification offered in:** early childhood, special education, elementary, middle/junior high, secondary. **Cooperative education programs:** art, business, computer science, education, health professions, humanities, natural science, social/behavioral science. **Reserve Officers Training Corps (ROTC):** Army ROTC: Offered at cooperating institution (Jackson State University); Air Force ROTC: Offered at cooperating institution (Jackson State University). **Faculty and instruction (2009-2010):** Total instructional faculty: 76 full-time, 22 part-time (; 52% minorities). Full-time faculty with Ph.D. or other terminal degree: 66%. Student/faculty ratio: 9/1. Classes of fewer than 20 students: 64%; of 20 to 49 students: 35%; of 50 or more students: 1%. **Advanced Placement and International Baccalaureate credit:** AP tests may be used for: Placement only. Scores accepted: 3, 4, 5. International Baccalaureate exams may be used for: Credit only. **Freshmen returning for sophomore year:** 72%. **Graduation rates:** Four-year: 24%; five-year: 36%; six-year: 41%. **Graduate study:** 66% of students pursue further study immediately upon graduation; 15% within one year; 10% within five years. Fields in which graduates pursue further study: Master of Business Administration (MBA), 15%; law, 20%; medicine, 15%; dentistry, 10%; engineering, 10%; education, 10%; arts and sciences, 20%.

COSTS AND FINANCIAL AID

Financial aid office: (601) 977-7769. **Expenses (2010-2011):** Tuition and fees 2010-2011: $9,710; room/board: $6,330. **Financial aid:** In 2009-2010, 97% of undergraduates applied for financial aid. Of those, 94% were determined to have financial need; 92% had their need fully met. Average financial aid package (proportion receiving): $14,500 (93%). Average amount of gift aid, such as scholarships or grants (proportion receiving): $2,500 (21%). Average amount of self-help aid, such as work study or loans (proportion receiving): $1,100 (9%). Average need-based loan (excluding PLUS or other private loans): $3,375. Among students who received need-based aid, the average percentage of need met: 25%. Among students who received aid based on merit, the average award (and the proportion receiving): $16,524 (0%). The average athletic scholarship (and the proportion receiving): $10,000 (8%). Average amount of debt of borrowers graduating in 2009: $18,806. Proportion who borrowed: 80%.

CAMPUS LIFE AND EXTRACURRICULAR ACTIVITIES

Campus housing available (% using): women's dorms (55%), men's dorms (45%), special housing for disabled students. Students who live in college-owned, operated, or affiliated housing: 65%. **Student employment:** During the 2009-2010 academic year, 10% of undergraduates worked on campus. Average per-year earnings: $3,000. **Clubs and organizations:** Number of student organizations: 52. Activities include: choral groups, concert band, dance, drama/theater, jazz band, literary magazine, music ensembles, musical theater, opera, pep band, student government, student newspaper, student film society, television station, yearbook. Number of fraternities: 4; sororities: 4. Proportion of men in fraternities: 2%; of women in sororities: 6%. Average proportion of students who stay on campus on weekends: 50%. **Sports program (2009-2010):** Member of NAIA. *Men's intercollegiate varsity sports:* baseball, basketball, cross country, golf, tennis. *Women's intercollegiate varsity sports:* basketball, cross country, tennis, volleyball.

SERVICES AND FACILITIES

Basic services: nonremedial tutoring, placement service, health service, health insurance. **Remedial assistance:** reading, math, writing, study skills. **Counseling services:** minority student, career, military, personal, veteran student, academic, older student, psychological, birth control, religious. **For learning-disabled students:** School does not offer a structured program with separate admission and additional fees. Services include: remedial math, remedial English, remedial reading, note-taking services, oral tests, learning center, readers, extended time for tests, tutors, priority registration, priority seating, other testing accommodations. **Library:** Number of titles: 190,258; number of current serial subscriptions: 221. **Information technology resources:** Students are not required to lease or own a computer. Number of campus computers available to all students: 200. School has a wireless network. Approximate number of users that can be accommodated: 300. Proportion of college-owned housing units wired for high-speed internet access: 75%. **Campus safety:** Security services offered: 24-hour foot-and-vehicle patrols, late-night transport/escort service, 24-hour emergency telephones, lighted pathways/sidewalks, student patrols, controlled dormitory access (key, security card, etc.).

TRANSFER AND INTERNATIONAL STUDENTS

Transfer students: May apply for admission for the following academic terms: Fall, Spring, Summer. Applicants do not need a minimum number of credits to apply. For fall 2009: Transfer applications received: 145. Transfer applicants offered admission: 67. Transfer applicants enrolled: 58. **International students:** Number of foreign undergraduates: 4. Number of countries represented: 2. Minimum TOEFL score required: 500 (paper); 250 (computer). Average TOEFL score: 500 (paper).

UNDERGRADUATE STUDENT BODY STATS

2009-2010 enrollment: 12,109 full-time; 1,095 part-time. Men: 47%; women: 53%.

ADMISSIONS FACTS AND FIGURES

Phone: (662) 915-7226. **Email:** admissions@olemiss.edu. **Website:** http://www.olemiss.edu. **Application deadlines for fall 2011:** Regular decision: July 20. Early decision: Not offered. Early action: Not offered. Admission cannot be deferred. **Application fee:** $35. **To apply online, go to:** http://www.olemiss.edu/prospective/index.html. **Admissions requirements/recommendations:** High school units required (recommended): English: 4; Mathematics: 3 (4); Science: 3 (4); Foreign language: 1 (2); Social studies: 1 (2); History: 2; Academic electives: 1; Total units: 15. Tests: The college uses SAT or ACT scores in admissions decisions. Neither SAT nor ACT required. For admission to the fall 2011 entering class, the school will accept: ACT with or without writing accepted. Campus visit: Recommended. **Factors that count in admissions decisions:** *Academic:* Secondary school record: Considered. Class rank: Considered. Letters of recommendation: Not Considered. Standardized test scores: Important. Essay: Not Considered. *Nonacademic:* Interview: Not Considered. Extracurricular activities: Not Considered. Talent/ability: Not Considered. Character/personal qualities: Not Considered. Alumni/ae relationship: Not Considered. Geographical residence: Not Considered. State residency: Not Considered. Religious affiliation/commitment: Not Considered. Minority status: Not Considered. Volunteer work: Not Considered. Work experience: Not Considered. **Admissions statistics for the fall 2009 entering class:** Total applicants: 8,595. Total accepted: 6,833. Freshmen enrolled: 2,576; 46% were from out of state. Overall acceptance rate: 80%. **Credentials of fall 2009 freshmen:** 26% ranked in the top 10 percent of their high school class; 48% were in the top 25 percent; 76% were in the top half. (Proportion submitting class standing: 59%.) **Average high school grade point average:** 3.3. **First-year students who submitted SAT scores:** 29%. Scores (25/75 percentile): Critical Reading: 460-580, Math: 460-600, Combined: 920-1180. **First-year students submitting ACT scores:** 88%. Scores (25/75 percentile): English: 20-28, Math: 18-25, Composite: 20-26.

ACADEMICS

Year founded: 1844. **Academic calendar:** Semester. **Degrees offered:** bachelor's, master's, doctorate. **Most popular majors:** 9% elementary education and teaching, 9% marketing/marketing management, 6% business administration and management, 6% psychology, 5% accounting. **Major fields of study:** architecture and related services; area, ethnic, cultural, and gender studies; biological and biomedical sciences; business, management, marketing, and related support services; communication, journalism, and related programs; computer and information sciences and support services; education; engineering; English language and literature/letters; family and consumer sciences/human sciences; foreign languages, literatures, and linguistics; health professions and related clinical sciences; history; legal professions and studies; liberal arts and sciences studies, and humanities; mathematics and statistics; parks, recreation, leisure, and fitness studies; philosophy and religious studies; physical sciences; psychology; public administration and social service professions; security and protective services; social sciences; visual and performing arts. **Areas of required coursework:** arts/fine arts, humanities, mathematics, English (including composition), foreign languages, sciences (biological or physical), history, social science. **Pre-professional programs:** pre-law, pre-dentistry, pre-medicine, pre-veterinary science, pre-optometry, pre-pharmacy, other. **Special academic programs:** accelerated program, cooperative (work-study plan) program, distance learning, double major, dual enrollment, English as a

Second Language (ESL), honors program, independent study, internships, study abroad, teacher certificate program. **Teacher certification offered in:** special education, elementary, secondary. **Cooperative education programs:** engineering. **Reserve Officers Training Corps (ROTC):** Army ROTC: Offered on campus; Navy ROTC: Offered on campus; Air Force ROTC: Offered on campus. **Faculty and instruction (2009-2010):** Total instructional faculty: 729 full-time, 148 part-time. Full-time faculty with Ph.D. or other terminal degree: 84%. Student/faculty ratio: 17/1. Classes of fewer than 20 students: 49%; of 20 to 49 students: 37%; of 50 or more students: 14%. **Advanced Placement and International Baccalaureate credit:** AP tests may be used for: Credit only. Scores accepted: 3, 4, 5. **Freshmen returning for sophomore year:** 80%. **Graduation rates:** Four-year: 36%; five-year: 56%; six-year: 60%.

COSTS AND FINANCIAL AID

Financial aid office: (662) 915-7175. **Expenses (2009-2010):** Tuition and fees 2009-2010: $5,106 in state, $13,050 out of state; room/board: $6,562. Estimated books and supplies: $1,200; transportation: $2,780; personal expenses: $1,880. **Financial aid:** Priority filing date for institution's financial aid form: March 15. In 2009-2010, 60% of undergraduates applied for financial aid. Of those, 45% were determined to have financial need; 12% had their need fully met. Average financial aid package (proportion receiving): $7,677 (44%). Average amount of gift aid, such as scholarships or grants (proportion receiving): $6,278 (38%). Average amount of self-help aid, such as work study or loans (proportion receiving): $7,710 (33%). Average need-based loan (excluding PLUS or other private loans): $4,661. Among students who received need-based aid, the average percentage of need met: 76%. Among students who received aid based on merit, the average award (and the proportion receiving): $4,106 (20%). The average athletic scholarship (and the proportion receiving): $14,236 (3%). Average amount of debt of borrowers graduating in 2009: $22,866. Proportion who borrowed: 39%.

CAMPUS LIFE AND EXTRACURRICULAR ACTIVITIES

Campus housing available: women's dorms, men's dorms, sorority housing, fraternity housing, apartments for married students, apartment for single students, special housing for international students, other housing options. Students who live in college-owned, operated, or affiliated housing: 27%. Activities include: campus ministries, choral groups, concert band, dance, drama/theater, international student organization, jazz band, marching band, model UN, music ensembles, musical theater, opera, pep band, radio station, student government, student newspaper, symphony orchestra, television station, yearbook. Number of fraternities: 16; sororities: 12. Proportion of men in fraternities: 36%; of women in sororities: 34%. **Sports program (2009-2010):** Member of NCAA I. *Men's intercollegiate varsity sports:* baseball, basketball, cross country, football, golf, tennis, track and field (indoor), track and field (outdoor). *Women's intercollegiate varsity sports:* basketball, cross country, golf, rifle, soccer, softball, tennis, track and field (indoor), track and field (outdoor), volleyball.

SERVICES AND FACILITIES

Basic services: women's center, health service, health insurance. **Remedial assistance:** reading, math, writing. **Counseling services:** personal, academic, psychological. **For learning-disabled students:** School does not offer a structured program with separate admission and additional fees. **Library:** Number of titles: 1,840,496; number of current serial subscriptions: 231,703. **Information technology resources:** Students are not required to lease or own a computer. School has a wireless network. Approximate number of users that can be accommodated: 1,100. Proportion of college-owned housing units wired for high-speed internet access: 100%. **Campus safety:** Security services offered: 24-hour foot-and-vehicle patrols, late-night transport/escort service, 24-hour emergency telephones, lighted pathways/sidewalks, controlled dormitory access (key, security card, etc).

TRANSFER AND INTERNATIONAL STUDENTS

Transfer students: May apply for admission for the following academic terms: Fall, Spring, Summer. Applicants need a minimum number of credits to apply. For fall 2009: Transfer applications received: 2,207. Transfer applicants offered admission: 1,713. Transfer applicants enrolled: 1,263. **International students:** Number of foreign undergraduates: 142. Number of countries represented: 72. Minimum TOEFL score required: 550 (paper); 79 (computer). Average TOEFL score: 565 (paper).

University of Southern Mississippi

- **Address:** 118 College Drive, Hattiesburg, MS 39406-0001
- **Website:** http://www.usm.edu
- **Public**
- **Enrollment:** 10,664 full-time; 1,719 part-time

KEY STATS

- ✔ **U.S News College Ranking:** second tier, National Universities
- ✔ **ACT Score (25th/75th percentile):** 18-24
- ✔ **Tuition:** 2009-2010: $5,296 in state, $12,946 out of state
  - **Selectivity:** Selective
  - **Room/board:** $6,200
  - **Acceptance rate:** 56%
  - **Average debt:** $18,878
  - **Student/faculty ratio:** 16/1
  - **Proportion who borrowed:** 64%

UNDERGRADUATE STUDENT BODY STATS

2009-2010 enrollment: 10,664 full-time; 1,719 part-time. Men: 39%; women: 61%. **Ethnic makeup:** African American: 30%; Asian American: 1%; Hispanic: 2%; White: 66%; International: 1%.

ADMISSIONS FACTS AND FIGURES

Phone: (601) 266-5000. **Email:** admissions@usm.edu. **Website:** http://www.usm.edu. **Application deadlines for fall 2011:** Regular decision: Rolling. Early decision: Not offered. Early action: Not offered. Admission cannot be deferred. **Application fee:** $35. **To apply online, go to:** https://www4.usm.edu/ugapp/. **Admissions requirements/recommendations:** High school units required (recommended): English: 4 (4); Mathematics: 3 (3); Science: 3 (3); Foreign language: 0 (2); Social studies: 3 (3); History: 0 (0); Academic electives: 2 (2); Total units: 1 (17). Tests: The college uses SAT or ACT scores in admissions decisions. Either SAT or ACT required. For admission to the fall 2011 entering class, the school will accept: ACT with or without writing accepted. Campus visit: Neither required nor recommended. Admissions interview: Neither required nor recommended. Off-campus interview: Not available. **Factors that count in admissions decisions:** *Academic:* Secondary school record: Not Considered. Class rank: Considered. Letters of recommendation: Not Considered. Standardized test scores: Very Important. Essay: Not Considered. *Nonacademic:* Interview: Not Considered. Extracurricular activities: Not Considered. Talent/ability: Not Considered. Character/personal qualities: Not Considered. Alumni/ae relationship: Not Considered. Geographical residence: Not Considered. State residency: Not Considered. Religious affiliation/commitment: Not Considered. Minority status: Not Considered. Volunteer work: Not Considered. Work experience: Not Considered. **Other schools with the greatest overlap in applicants:** Mississippi State University; University of Mississippi. **Admissions statistics for the fall 2009 entering class:** Total applicants: 5,081. Total accepted: 2,860. Freshmen enrolled: 1,602; 22% were from out of state. Overall acceptance rate: 56%. **Credentials of fall 2009 freshmen:** 15% ranked in the top 10 percent of their high school class; 41% were in the top 25 percent; 74% were in the top half. (Proportion submitting class standing: 34%.) **Average high school grade point average:** 3.1. **First-year students who submitted SAT scores:** 4%. Scores (25/75 percentile): Critical Reading: 460-560, Math: 450-565, Combined: 910-1125. **First-year students submitting ACT scores:** 96%. Scores (25/75 percentile): English: 19-26, Math: 17-23, Composite: 18-24.

ACADEMICS

Year founded: 1910. **Academic calendar:** Semester. **Degrees offered:** certificate, bachelor's, master's, post-master's certificate, doctorate. **Most popular majors:** 22% business administration and management, 13% nursing/registered nurse training (R.N., A.S.N., B.S.N., M.S.N.), 10% elementary education and teaching, 8% psychology, 5% communication studies/speech communication and rhetoric. **Major fields of study:** architecture and related services; area, ethnic, cultural, and gender studies; biological and biomedical sciences; business, management, marketing, and related support services; communication, journalism, and related programs; computer and information sciences and support services; education; engineering technologies/technicians; English language and literature/letters; family and consumer sciences/human sciences; foreign languages, literatures, and linguistics; health professions and related clinical sciences; history; legal professions and studies; library science; mathematics and statistics; parks, recreation, leisure, and fitness studies; philosophy and religious studies; physical sciences; psychology; public administration and social service professions; security and protective services; social sciences; visual and performing arts. **Areas of required coursework:** arts/fine arts, humanities,

mathematics, English (including composition), sciences (biological or physical), history, social science. **Pre-professional programs:** pre-law, pre-dentistry, pre-medicine, pre-veterinary science, pre-optometry, pre-pharmacy, other. **Special academic programs (% participation):** distance learning (74%), double major (2%), dual enrollment (.2%), English as a Second Language (ESL) (4%), honors program (7%), independent study (3%), internships (39%), study abroad (9%), teacher certificate program (10%). **Teacher certification offered in:** early childhood, special education, elementary, vo-tech, middle/junior high, secondary, bilingual/bicultural. **Cooperative education programs:** computer science, engineering, other. **Reserve Officers Training Corps (ROTC):** Army ROTC: Offered on campus; Air Force ROTC: Offered on campus. **Faculty and instruction (2009-2010):** Total instructional faculty: 758 full-time, 185 part-time (52% men; 48% women; 13% minorities). Full-time faculty with Ph.D. or other terminal degree: 75%. Student/faculty ratio: 16/1. Classes of fewer than 20 students: 46%; of 20 to 49 students: 43%; of 50 or more students: 11%. **Advanced Placement and International Baccalaureate credit:** AP tests may be used for: Credit only. Scores accepted: 3, 4, 5. International Baccalaureate exams may be used for: Credit only. **Freshmen returning for sophomore year:** 73%. **Graduation rates:** Four-year: 21%; five-year: 38%; six-year: 45%.

COSTS AND FINANCIAL AID

Financial aid office: (601) 266-4774. **Expenses (2009-2010):** Tuition and fees 2009-2010: $5,296 in state, $12,946 out of state; room/board: $6,200. Estimated books and supplies: $1,400; transportation: $1,000; personal expenses: $3,576. **Financial aid:** Priority filing date for institution's financial aid form: March 15. In 2009-2010, 75% of undergraduates applied for financial aid. Of those, 64% were determined to have financial need; 27% had their need fully met. Average financial aid package (proportion receiving): $9,117 (63%). Average amount of gift aid, such as scholarships or grants (proportion receiving): $3,982 (42%). Average amount of self-help aid, such as work study or loans (proportion receiving): $4,981 (53%). Average need-based loan (excluding PLUS or other private loans): $4,901. Among students who received need-based aid, the average percentage of need met: 82%. Among students who received aid based on merit, the average award (and the proportion receiving): $3,590 (8%). The average athletic scholarship (and the proportion receiving): $6,651 (4%). Average amount of debt of borrowers graduating in 2009: $18,878. Proportion who borrowed: 64%.

CAMPUS LIFE AND EXTRACURRICULAR ACTIVITIES

Campus housing available (% using): women's dorms (50%), men's dorms (28%), sorority housing (10%), fraternity housing (6%), apartments for married students (6%), special housing for disabled students (0%). Students who live in college-owned, operated, or affiliated housing: 45%. **Student employment:** During the 2009-2010 academic year, 8% of undergraduates worked on campus. Average per-year earnings: $5,665. **Clubs and organizations:** Number of student organizations: 285. Activities include: campus ministries, choral groups, concert band, dance, drama/theater, international student organization, jazz band, literary magazine, marching band, music ensembles, musical theater, opera, pep band, radio station, student government, student newspaper, student film society, symphony orchestra, yearbook. Number of fraternities: 15; sororities: 11. Proportion of men in fraternities: 11%; of women in sororities: 10%. Average proportion of students who stay on campus on weekends: 15%. **Sports program (2009-2010):** Member of NCAA I. *Men's intercollegiate varsity sports:* baseball, basketball, football, golf, tennis, track and field (indoor), track and field (outdoor). *Women's intercollegiate varsity sports:* basketball, cross country, golf, soccer, softball, tennis, track and field (indoor), track and field (outdoor), volleyball.

SERVICES AND FACILITIES

Basic services: nonremedial tutoring, women's center, placement service, day care, health service, health insurance. **Remedial assistance:** reading, math, writing, study skills, other. **Counseling services:** minority student, career, military, personal, veteran student, academic, older student, psychological, birth control, religious. **For learning-disabled students:** School does not offer a structured program with separate admission and additional fees. Services include: remedial math, remedial English, reading machines, remedial reading, tape recorders, other special classes, note-taking services, special bookstore section, oral tests, learning center, readers, extended time for tests, tutors, priority seating, texts on tape, exams on tape or computer, other testing accommodations, other. **Library:** Number of titles: 1,655,628; number of current serial subscriptions: 15,449. **Information technology resources:** Students are not required to lease or own a computer. Number of campus computers available to all students: 203. School has a wireless network. Approximate number of users that can be accommodated: 9,000.

Proportion of college-owned housing units wired for high-speed internet access: 100%. **Campus safety:** Security services offered: 24-hour foot-and-vehicle patrols, late-night transport/escort service, 24-hour emergency telephones, lighted pathways/sidewalks, controlled dormitory access (key, security card, etc).

TRANSFER AND INTERNATIONAL STUDENTS

Transfer students: May apply for admission for the following academic terms: Fall, Spring, Summer. Applicants need a minimum number of credits to apply. For fall 2009: Transfer applications received: 3,409. Transfer applicants offered admission: 2,308. Transfer applicants enrolled: 1,644. **International students:** Number of foreign undergraduates: 77 (1% of student body). Number of countries represented: 65. Minimum TOEFL score required: 525 (paper); 197 (computer). Average TOEFL score: 525 (paper).

William Carey University

- **Address:** 498 Tuscan Avenue, Hattiesburg, MS 39401-5499
- **Website:** http://www.wmcarey.edu
- **Private; Religious affiliation:** Baptist
- **Enrollment:** 1,763 full-time; 327 part-time

KEY STATS
✔ **U.S News College Ranking:** second tier, Regional Universities (South)
✔ **ACT Score (25th/75th percentile):** 21-28
✔ **Tuition:** 2010-2011: $10,350

Selectivity: Selective	**Room/board:** $4,000
Acceptance rate: 95%	**Average debt:** $17,500
Student/faculty ratio: N/A	**Proportion who borrowed:** 85%

UNDERGRADUATE STUDENT BODY STATS

2009-2010 enrollment: 1,763 full-time; 327 part-time. Men: 27%; women: 73%. **Ethnic makeup:** African American: 31%; Asian American: 1%; Hispanic: 2%; White: 63%; International: 3%. **Religious preference:** Roman Catholic: 12%; Protestant: 73%; Other: 15%.

ADMISSIONS FACTS AND FIGURES

Phone: (601) 318-6103. **Email:** admissions@wmcarey.edu. **Website:** http://www.wmcarey.edu. **Application deadlines for fall 2011:** Regular decision: Rolling. Early decision: Not offered. Early action: Not offered. Admission can be deferred. **Application fee:** $40. **To apply online, go to:** https://indigo.wmcarey.edu/prospects/ceportalprospect.asp. **Admissions requirements/recommendations:** High school units required (recommended): English: 8 (8); Mathematics: 6 (6); Science: 6 (6); Social studies: 5 (5). Tests: The college uses SAT or ACT scores in admissions decisions. Either SAT or ACT required. For admission to the fall 2011 entering class, the school will accept: ACT with or without writing accepted. Campus visit: Recommended. Admissions interview: Neither required nor recommended. Off-campus interview: Not available. **Factors that count in admissions decisions:** *Academic:* Secondary school record: Very Important. Class rank: Considered. Letters of recommendation: Considered. Standardized test scores: Very Important. Essay: Not Considered. *Nonacademic:* Interview: Not Considered. Extracurricular activities: Not Considered. Talent/ability: Not Considered. Character/personal qualities: Not Considered. Alumni/ae relationship: Not Considered. Geographical residence: Not Considered. State residency: Not Considered. Religious affiliation/commitment: Not Considered. Minority status: Not Considered. Volunteer work: Not Considered. Work experience: Not Considered. **Admissions statistics for the fall 2009 entering class:** Total applicants: 550. Total accepted: 525. Freshmen enrolled: 136; 14% were from out of state. Overall acceptance rate: 95%. **First-year students who submitted SAT scores:** 20%. Scores (25/75 percentile): Critical Reading: 420-490, Math: 490-650, Combined: 910-1140. **First-year students submitting ACT scores:** 80%. Scores (25/75 percentile): English: 22-29, Math: 18-26, Composite: 21-28.

ACADEMICS

Year founded: 1906. **Academic calendar:** Trimester. **Degrees offered:** bachelor's, master's. **Major fields of study:** biological and biomedical sciences; business, management, marketing, and related support services; communication, journalism, and related programs; education; English language and literature/letters; health professions and related clinical sciences; history; liberal arts and sciences studies, and humanities; mathematics and statistics; parks, recreation, leisure, and fitness studies; physical sciences; psychology; social sciences; theology and religious vocations; visual and performing arts. **Areas of required coursework:** arts/fine arts, humanities, computer literacy, mathematics, English (including composition), sciences (biological or physical), history, social science, other. **Pre-professional programs:** pre-law, pre-dentistry, pre-medicine, pre-veterinary science, pre-optometry, pre-pharmacy. **Special academic programs (% participation):** accelerated program (10%), cross-registration (20%), double major (1.6%), dual enrollment (0%), honors program (1%), independent study (33.8%), internships (19%), study abroad (1%), teacher certificate program (16.8%). **Teacher certification offered in:** elementary, secondary. **Reserve Officers Training Corps (ROTC):** Army ROTC: Offered at cooperating institution; Air Force ROTC: Offered at cooperating institution. **Advanced Placement and International Baccalaureate credit:** AP tests may be used for: Credit and/or placement. Scores accepted: 3. International Baccalaureate exams may be used for: Credit only. **Freshmen returning for sophomore year:** 74%. **Graduation rates:** Four-year: 37%; five-year: 45%; six-year: 42%.

COSTS AND FINANCIAL AID

Financial aid office: (601) 318-6153. **Expenses (2010-2011):** Tuition and fees 2010-2011: $10,350; room/board: $4,000. Estimated books and supplies: $2,850; transportation: $2,850; personal expenses: $3,165. **Financial aid:** Priority filing date for institution's financial aid form: April 1. In 2009-2010, 91% of undergraduates applied for financial aid. Of those, 90% were determined to have financial need; 94% had their need fully met. Average financial aid package (proportion receiving): $15,000 (90%). Average amount of gift aid, such as scholarships or grants (proportion receiving): $8,000 (90%). Average amount of self-help aid, such as work study or loans (proportion receiving): $8,000 (89%). Average need-based loan (excluding PLUS or other private loans): $7,000. Among students who received need-based aid, the average percentage of need met: 90%. Among students who received aid based on merit, the average award (and the proportion receiving): $7,400 (13%). The average athletic scholarship (and the proportion receiving): $8,500 (1%). Average amount of debt of borrowers graduating in 2009: $17,500. Proportion who borrowed: 85%.

CAMPUS LIFE AND EXTRACURRICULAR ACTIVITIES

Campus housing available (% using): women's dorms (49%), men's dorms (42%), apartment for single students (9%). Students who live in college-owned, operated, or affiliated housing: 36%. **Student employment:** During the 2009-2010 academic year, 20% of undergraduates worked on campus. Average per-year earnings: $2,100. **Clubs and organizations:** Number of student organizations: 40. Activities include: campus ministries, choral groups, drama/theater, international student organization, music ensembles, musical theater, pep band, student government, student newspaper, yearbook. Number of fraternities: 2; sororities: 2. Proportion of men in fraternities: 1%; of women in sororities: 1%. Average proportion of students who stay on campus on weekends: 25%. **Sports program (2009-2010):** Member of NAIA. *Men's intercollegiate varsity sports:* baseball, basketball, golf, soccer, tennis. *Women's intercollegiate varsity sports:* basketball, soccer, softball, tennis.

SERVICES AND FACILITIES

Basic services: nonremedial tutoring, placement service, health insurance. **Remedial assistance:** math, writing, study skills. **Counseling services:** career, personal, academic, older student. **For learning-disabled students:** School does not offer a structured program with separate admission and additional fees. Total undergraduates in learning-disabled program or receiving services: 19. Services include: remedial math, remedial English, reading machines, remedial reading, tape recorders, diagnostic testing service, untimed tests, note-taking services, oral tests, extended time for tests, tutors. **Library:** Number of titles: 97,998; number of current serial subscriptions: 772. **Information technology resources:** Students are not required to lease or own a computer. Number of campus computers available to all students: 199. School has a wireless network. Approximate number of users that can be accommodated: 3,400. Proportion of college-owned housing units wired for high-speed internet access: 100%. **Campus safety:** Security services offered: 24-hour foot-and-vehicle patrols, late-night transport/escort service, 24-hour emergency telephones, lighted pathways/sidewalks, controlled dormitory access (key, security card, etc).

TRANSFER AND INTERNATIONAL STUDENTS

Transfer students: May apply for admission for the following academic terms: Fall, Winter, Spring, Summer. Applicants need a minimum number of credits to apply. For fall 2009: Transfer applications received: 645. Transfer applicants offered admission: 598. Transfer applicants enrolled:

377. International students: Number of foreign undergraduates: 73 (3% of student body). Number of countries represented: 19. Minimum TOEFL score required: 523 (paper); 70 (computer). Average TOEFL score: 523 (paper).

Missouri

Avila University

- **Address:** 11901 Wornall Road, Kansas City, MO 64145
- **Website:** http://www.Avila.edu
- **Private; Religious affiliation:** Roman Catholic
- **Enrollment:** 950 full-time; 201 part-time

KEY STATS

✔ **U.S News College Ranking:** 99, Regional Universities (Midwest)
✔ **ACT Score (25th/75th percentile):** 20-25
✔ **Tuition:** 2010-2011: $21,800

Selectivity: Selective	**Room/board:** $6,350
Acceptance rate: 43%	**Average debt:** $18,526
Student/faculty ratio: 14/1	**Proportion who borrowed:** 82%

UNDERGRADUATE STUDENT BODY STATS

2009-2010 enrollment: 950 full-time; 201 part-time. Men: 34%; women: 66%. **Ethnic makeup:** African American: 11%; American-Indian: 1%; Asian American: 1%; Hispanic: 5%; White: 76%; International: 5%. **Religious preference:** Roman Catholic: 25%; Other: 75%.

ADMISSIONS FACTS AND FIGURES

Phone: (816) 501-2400. **Email:** admissions@mail.avila.edu. **Website:** http://www.Avila.edu. **Application deadlines for fall 2011:** Regular decision: Rolling. Early decision: Not offered. Early action: Not offered. Admission can be deferred. **To apply online, go to:** http://www.avila.edu/admission/apply.asp. **Admissions requirements/recommendations:** High school units required (recommended): English: (4); Mathematics: (3); Science: (3); Foreign language: (2); Social studies: (3); Academic electives: (0); Total units: (16). Tests: The college uses SAT or ACT scores in admissions decisions. Either SAT or ACT required. For admission to the fall 2011 entering class, the school will accept: ACT with or without writing accepted. Campus visit: Recommended. Admissions interview: Recommended. Off-campus interview: May be arranged. **Factors that count in admissions decisions:** *Academic:* Secondary school record: Very Important. Class rank: Not Considered. Letters of recommendation: Considered. Standardized test scores: Very Important. Essay: Considered. *Nonacademic:* Interview: Considered. Extracurricular activities: Considered. Talent/ability: Considered. Character/personal qualities: Considered. Alumni/ae relationship: Not Considered. Geographical residence: Not Considered. State residency: Not Considered. Religious affiliation/commitment: Not Considered. Minority status: Not Considered. Volunteer work: Considered. Work experience: Not Considered. **Other schools with the greatest overlap in applicants:** Rockhurst University; University of Central Missouri; University of Kansas; University of Missouri–Kansas City; William Jewell College. **Admissions statistics for the fall 2009 entering class:** Total applicants: 1,036. Total accepted: 446. Freshmen enrolled: 118; 21% were from out of state. Overall acceptance rate: 43%. **Credentials of fall 2009 freshmen:** 22% ranked in the top 10 percent of their high school class; 58% were in the top 25 percent; 86% were in the top half. (Proportion submitting class standing: 77%.) **Average high school grade point average:** 3.4. **First-year students who submitted SAT scores:** 3%. Scores (25/75 percentile): Critical Reading: 535-560, Math: 480-542, Combined: 1015-1102. **First-year students submitting ACT scores:** 93%. Scores (25/75 percentile): English: 20-26, Math: 18-25, Composite: 20-25.

ACADEMICS

Year founded: 1916. **Academic calendar:** Semester. **Degrees offered:** certificate, bachelor's, post-bachelor's certificate, master's. **Most popular majors:** 31% health professions and related clinical sciences, 24% business, management, marketing, and related support services, 11% visual and performing arts, 8% psychology, 6% education. **Major fields of study:** biological and biomedical sciences; business, management, marketing, and related support services; communication, journalism, and related programs; computer and information sciences and support services; education; English language and literature/letters; health professions and related clinical sciences; history; legal professions and studies; liberal arts and sciences studies, and

humanities; mathematics and statistics; multi/interdisciplinary studies; parks, recreation, leisure, and fitness studies; philosophy and religious studies; physical sciences; psychology; public administration and social service professions; social sciences; visual and performing arts. **Areas of required coursework:** arts/fine arts, humanities, computer literacy, mathematics, English (including composition), philosophy, sciences (biological or physical), history, social science, other. **Pre-professional programs:** pre-law, pre-dentistry, pre-medicine, pre-veterinary science, pre-optometry, pre-pharmacy, other. **Special academic programs (% participation):** accelerated program (2%), cooperative (work-study plan) program (0%), cross-registration (64%), distance learning (33%), double major (2%), dual enrollment (0%), English as a Second Language (ESL) (4%), honors program (1%), independent study (9%), internships (59%), liberal arts/career combination (100%), study abroad (1%), teacher certificate program (9%), weekend college (11%). **Teacher certification offered in:** special education, elementary, middle/junior high, secondary. **Cooperative education programs:** health professions. **Reserve Officers Training Corps (ROTC):** Army ROTC: Offered at cooperating institution (University of Missouri–Kansas City). **Faculty and instruction (2009-2010):** Total instructional faculty: 65 full-time, 149 part-time (44% men; 56% women; 6% minorities). Full-time faculty with Ph.D. or other terminal degree: 74%. Student/faculty ratio: 14/1. Classes of fewer than 20 students: 71%; of 20 to 49 students: 28%; of 50 or more students: 0%. **Advanced Placement and International Baccalaureate credit:** AP tests may be used for: Credit only. Scores accepted: 3, 4, 5. International Baccalaureate exams may be used for: Credit only. **Freshmen returning for sophomore year:** 69%. **Graduation rates:** Four-year: 22%; five-year: 39%; six-year: 40%. **Graduate study:** 22% of students pursue further study immediately upon graduation; 30% within one year; 40% within five years.

COSTS AND FINANCIAL AID

Financial aid office: (816) 501-3600. **Expenses (2010-2011):** Tuition and fees 2010-2011: $21,800; room/board: $6,350. Estimated books and supplies: $800; transportation: $600; personal expenses: $2,000. **Financial aid:** Priority filing date for institution's financial aid form: April 1. In 2009-2010, 68% of undergraduates applied for financial aid. Of those, 68% were determined to have financial need; 60% had their need fully met. Average financial aid package (proportion receiving): $13,105 (68%). Average amount of gift aid, such as scholarships or grants (proportion receiving): $7,852 (27%). Average amount of self-help aid, such as work study or loans (proportion receiving): $5,898 (8%). Average need-based loan (excluding PLUS or other private loans): $5,650. Among students who received need-based aid, the average percentage of need met: 52%. Among students who received aid based on merit, the average award (and the proportion receiving): $8,510 (30%). The average athletic scholarship (and the proportion receiving): $5,915 (5%). Average amount of debt of borrowers graduating in 2009: $18,526. Proportion who borrowed: 82%.

CAMPUS LIFE AND EXTRACURRICULAR ACTIVITIES

Campus housing available (% using): coed dorms (100%). Students who live in college-owned, operated, or affiliated housing: 29%. **Student employment:** During the 2009-2010 academic year, 20% of undergraduates worked on campus. Average per-year earnings: $1,200. **Clubs and organizations:** Number of student organizations: 40. Activities include: campus ministries, choral groups, dance, drama/theater, international student organization, literary magazine, musical theater, student government, student newspaper, student film society. Number of fraternities: 0; sororities: 0. Average proportion of students who stay on campus on weekends: 65%. **Sports program (2009-2010):** Member of NAIA. *Men's intercollegiate varsity sports:* baseball, basketball, cross country, football, golf, soccer. *Women's intercollegiate varsity sports:* basketball, cross country, golf, soccer, softball, volleyball.

SERVICES AND FACILITIES

Basic services: nonremedial tutoring, health service, health insurance. **Remedial assistance:** reading, math, writing, study skills, other. **Counseling services:** career, personal, academic, psychological, religious. **For learning-disabled students:** School does not offer a structured program with separate admission and additional fees. Total undergraduates in learning-disabled program or receiving services: 29. Services include: remedial math, remedial English, tape recorders, other special classes, note-taking services, oral tests, learning center, readers, extended time for tests, tutors, priority seating, texts on tape, other testing accommodations. **Library:** Number of titles: 74,300; number of current serial subscriptions: 445. **Information technology resources:** Students are not required to lease or own a computer. Number of campus computers available to all students: 250. School has a wireless network. Approximate number of users that can be accommodated: 630. Proportion of college-owned housing units wired for high-speed internet access: 100%. **Campus safety:** Security services offered: 24-hour foot-and-vehicle patrols, late-night transport/escort service, 24-hour emergency telephones, lighted pathways/sidewalks, controlled dormitory access (key, security card, etc).

TRANSFER AND INTERNATIONAL STUDENTS

Transfer students: May apply for admission for the following academic terms: Fall, Spring, Summer. Applicants do not need a minimum number of credits to apply. For fall 2009: Transfer applications received: 658. Transfer applicants offered admission: 321. Transfer applicants enrolled: 171. **International students:** Number of foreign undergraduates: 46 (5% of student body). Number of countries represented: 34. Minimum TOEFL score required: 500 (paper); 173 (computer). Average TOEFL score: 526 (paper).

Baptist Bible College

- **Address:** 628 E. Kearney Street, Springfield, MO 65803
- **Website:** http://www.gobbc.edu/
- **Private**
- **Enrollment:** N/A

KEY STATS

✔ **U.S News College Ranking:** Unranked, National Liberal Arts Colleges
✔ **SAT or ACT Score (25th/75th percentile):** N/A
✔ **Tuition:** 2009-2010: $13,710

Selectivity: N/A	Room/board: $5,400
Acceptance rate: N/A	Average debt: N/A
Student/faculty ratio: N/A	Proportion who borrowed: N/A

Central Methodist University

- **Address:** 411 Central Methodist Square, Fayette, MO 65248
- **Website:** http://www.centralmethodist.edu
- **Private; Religious affiliation:** United Methodist
- **Enrollment:** 1,013 full-time; 38 part-time

KEY STATS

✔ **U.S News College Ranking:** 56, Regional Colleges (Midwest)
✔ **ACT Score (25th/75th percentile):** 19-24
✔ **Tuition:** 2010-2011: $19,390

Selectivity: Selective	Room/board: $6,240
Acceptance rate: 67%	Average debt: $23,437
Student/faculty ratio: 14/1	Proportion who borrowed: 79%

UNDERGRADUATE STUDENT BODY STATS

2009-2010 enrollment: 1,013 full-time; 38 part-time. Men: 49%; women: 51%. **Ethnic makeup:** African American: 8%; American-Indian: 1%; Asian American: 1%; Hispanic: 2%; White: 86%; International: 3%. **Religious preference:** Roman Catholic: 12%; Protestant: 1%; No preference: 27%; Unknown: 1%; United Methodist : 21%; Baptist: 10%; Other: 28%.

ADMISSIONS FACTS AND FIGURES

Phone: (660) 248-6251. **Email:** admissions@centralmethodist.edu. **Website:** http://www.centralmethodist.edu. **Application deadlines for fall 2011:** Regular decision: Rolling. Early decision: Not offered. Early action: Not offered. Admission can be deferred. **Application fee:** $20. **To apply online, go to:** http://www.centralmethodist.edu/forms/admit/fayette_addmap.html. **Admissions requirements/recommendations:** High school units required (recommended): English: 4 (4); Mathematics: 3 (3); Science: 3 (3); Foreign language: 2 (2); Social studies: 3 (3); Total units: 24 (24). Tests: The col-

lege uses SAT or ACT scores in admissions decisions. Either SAT or ACT required. For admission to the fall 2011 entering class, the school will accept: ACT with or without writing accepted. Campus visit: Recommended. Admissions interview: Recommended. Off-campus interview: May be arranged. **Factors that count in admissions decisions: Academic:** Secondary school record: Important. Class rank: Very Important. Letters of recommendation: Considered. Standardized test scores: Very Important. Essay: Not Considered. **Nonacademic:** Interview: Considered. Extracurricular activities: Very Important. Talent/ability: Important. Character/personal qualities: Very Important. Alumni/ae relationship: Considered. Geographical residence: Considered. State residency: Considered. Religious affiliation/commitment: Important. Minority status: Important. Volunteer work: Considered. Work experience: Considered. **Other schools with the greatest overlap in applicants:** Columbia College; Missouri State University; Missouri Valley College; University of Central Missouri; University of Missouri. **Admissions statistics for the fall 2009 entering class:** Total applicants: 1,146. Total accepted: 764. Freshmen enrolled: 260; 5% were from out of state. Overall acceptance rate: 67%. **Credentials of fall 2009 freshmen:** 11% ranked in the top 10 percent of their high school class; 36% were in the top 25 percent; 74% were in the top half. (Proportion submitting class standing: 97%.) **Average high school grade point average:** 3.3. **First-year students submitting ACT scores:** 97%. Scores (25/75 percentile): English: 19-24, Math: 19-24, Composite: 19-24.

ACADEMICS

Year founded: 1854. **Academic calendar:** Semester. **Degrees offered:** associate, bachelor's. **Most popular majors:** 23% education, 20% health professions and related clinical sciences, 14% business, management, marketing, and related support services, 10% biological and biomedical sciences, 5% communication, journalism, and related programs. **Major fields of study:** biological and biomedical sciences; business, management, marketing, and related support services; communication, journalism, and related programs; computer and information sciences and support services; education; English language and literature/letters; foreign languages, literatures, and linguistics; health professions and related clinical sciences; history; mathematics and statistics; multi/interdisciplinary studies; natural resources and conservation; parks, recreation, leisure, and fitness studies; philosophy and religious studies; physical sciences; psychology; public administration and social service professions; security and protective services; social sciences; visual and performing arts. **Areas of required coursework:** arts/fine arts, humanities, computer literacy, mathematics, English (including composition), sciences (biological or physical), history, social science. **Preprofessional programs:** pre-law, pre-dentistry, pre-medicine, pre-theology, pre-veterinary science, pre-optometry, pre-pharmacy. **Special academic programs (% participation):** accelerated program (0%), distance learning (2%), double major (10%), dual enrollment (1%), honors program (5%), independent study (5%), internships (15%), student-designed major (7%), study abroad (1%), teacher certificate program (37%). **Teacher certification offered in:** early childhood, special education, elementary, middle/junior high, secondary. **Reserve Officers Training Corps (ROTC):** Army ROTC: Offered on campus; Air Force ROTC: Offered at cooperating institution (University of Missouri). **Faculty and instruction (2009-2010):** Total instructional faculty: 59 full-time, 34 part-time (54% men; 46% women; 2% minorities). Full-time faculty with Ph.D. or other terminal degree: 59%. Student/faculty ratio: 14/1. Classes of fewer than 20 students: 37%; of 20 to 49 students: 49%; of 50 or more students: 14%. **Advanced Placement and International Baccalaureate credit:** AP tests may be used for: Credit only. Scores accepted: 3, 4, 5. International Baccalaureate exams may be used for: Credit only. **Freshmen returning for sophomore year:** 62%. **Graduation rates:** Four-year: 27%; five-year: 36%; six-year: 40%. **Graduate study:** 22% of students pursue further study immediately upon graduation; 30% within one year; 50% within five years. Fields in which graduates pursue further study: Master of Business Administration (MBA), 10%; law, 1%; medicine, 1%; theology (or the seminary), 5%; education, 20%; arts and sciences, 1%.

COSTS AND FINANCIAL AID

Financial aid office: (660) 248-6244. **Expenses (2010-2011):** Tuition and fees 2010-2011: $19,390; room/board: $6,240. Estimated books and supplies: $900; transportation: $800; personal expenses: $2,250. **Financial aid:** Priority filing date for institution's financial aid form: March 15. In 2009-2010, 100% of undergraduates applied for financial aid. Of those, 68% were determined to have financial need; 12% had their need fully met. Average financial aid package (proportion receiving): $15,394 (68%). Average amount of gift aid, such as scholarships or grants (proportion receiving): $5,634 (57%). Average amount of self-help aid, such as work study or loans (proportion receiving): $4,130 (68%). Average need-based loan (excluding PLUS or other private loans): $4,022. Among students who received need-based aid, the average percentage of need met: 64%. Among students who received aid based on merit, the average award (and the proportion receiving): $9,190 (10%). The average athletic scholarship (and the proportion receiving): $4,055 (49%). Average amount of debt of borrowers graduating in 2009: $23,437. Proportion who borrowed: 79%.

CAMPUS LIFE AND EXTRACURRICULAR ACTIVITIES

Campus housing available (% using): coed dorms (40%), women's dorms (28%), men's dorms (30%), fraternity housing (1%), apartments for married students (1%). Students who live in college-owned, operated, or affiliated housing: 80%. **Student employment:** During the 2009-2010 academic year, 0% of undergraduates worked on campus. Average per-year earnings: $0. **Clubs and organizations:** Number of student organizations: 40. Activities include: campus ministries, choral groups, concert band, dance, drama/theater, international student organization, jazz band, literary magazine, marching band, music ensembles, musical theater, opera, pep band, radio station, student government, student newspaper, student film society, yearbook. Number of fraternities: 6; sororities: 4. Proportion of men in fraternities: 20%; of women in sororities: 20%. Average proportion of students who stay on campus on weekends: 50%. **Sports program (2009-2010):** Member of NAIA. *Men's intercollegiate varsity sports:* baseball, basketball, cross country, football, soccer, track and field (outdoor). *Women's intercollegiate varsity sports:* basketball, cross country, soccer, softball, track and field (outdoor), volleyball.

SERVICES AND FACILITIES

Basic services: nonremedial tutoring, placement service, health service, health insurance. **Remedial assistance:** math, writing, study skills, other. **Counseling services:** career, personal, academic, psychological, religious. **For learning-disabled students:** School does not offer a structured program with separate admission and additional fees. Total undergraduates in learning-disabled program or receiving services: 25. Services include: remedial math, remedial English, untimed tests, note-taking services, oral tests, learning center, readers, extended time for tests, tutors, proofreading services, exams on tape or computer, other testing accommodations, other. **Library:** Number of titles: 101,856; number of current serial subscriptions: 196. **Information technology resources:** Students are not required to lease or own a computer. Number of campus computers available to all students: 380. School has a wireless network. Approximate number of users that can be accommodated: 1,000. Proportion of college-owned housing units wired for high-speed internet access: 100%. **Campus safety:** Security services offered: 24-hour foot-and-vehicle patrols, late-night transport/escort service, 24-hour emergency telephones, lighted pathways/sidewalks, controlled dormitory access (key, security card, etc).

TRANSFER AND INTERNATIONAL STUDENTS

Transfer students: May apply for admission for the following academic terms: Fall, Winter, Spring, Summer. Applicants need a minimum number of credits to apply. For fall 2009: Transfer applications received: 347. Transfer applicants offered admission: 210. Transfer applicants enrolled: 107. **International students:** Number of foreign undergraduates: 32 (3% of student body). Number of countries represented: 12. Minimum TOEFL score required: 500 (paper); 173 (computer).

College of the Ozarks

- ■ **Address:** PO Box 17, Point Lookout, MO 65726
- ■ **Website:** http://www.cofo.edu
- ■ **Private; Religious affiliation:** Christian interdenominational
- ■ **Enrollment:** 1,334 full-time; 22 part-time

KEY STATS

- ✔ U.S News College Ranking: 7, Regional Colleges (Midwest)
- ✔ ACT Score (25th/75th percentile): 20-25
- ✔ Tuition: 2010-2011: $17,310

Selectivity: Selective	Room/board: $5,300
Acceptance rate: 9%	Average debt: N/A
Student/faculty ratio: 13/1	Proportion who borrowed: N/A

UNDERGRADUATE STUDENT BODY STATS

2009-2010 enrollment: 1,334 full-time; 22 part-time. Men: 43%; women: 57%. **Ethnic makeup:** African American: 1%; American-Indian: 1%; Asian American: 1%; Hispanic: 1%; White: 95%; International: 1%. **Religious preference:** Roman Catholic: 4%; Protestant: 70%; Unknown: 14%; Christian interdenominational: 10%; Other: 1%.

ADMISSIONS FACTS AND FIGURES

Phone: (800) 222-0525. **Email:** admiss4@cofo.edu. **Website:** http://www.cofo.edu. **Application deadlines for fall 2011:** Regular decision: February 15. Early decision: Not offered. Early action: Not offered. Admission cannot be deferred. **Application fee:** None. **To apply online, go to:** https://www.cofo.edu/admissions/applyonline/AppForm.asp?Mode=Inquire. **Admissions requirements/recommendations:** High school units required (recommended): English: 4 (4); Mathematics: 3 (3); Science: 2 (2); Foreign language: 2 (2); Social studies: 3 (3); Total units: 14 (14). Tests: The college uses SAT or ACT scores in admissions decisions. Either SAT or ACT required. For admission to the fall 2011 entering class, the school will accept: ACT with or without writing accepted. Campus visit: Recommended. Admissions interview: Required. Off-campus interview: Not available. **Factors that count in admissions decisions:** *Academic:* Secondary school record: Very Important. Class rank: Very Important. Letters of recommendation: Important. Standardized test scores: Important. Essay: Not Considered. *Nonacademic:* Interview: Very Important. Extracurricular activities: Considered. Talent/ability: Considered. Character/personal qualities: Very Important. Alumni/ae relationship: Considered. Geographical residence: Important. State residency: Considered. Religious affiliation/commitment: Considered. Minority status: Not Considered. Volunteer work: Important. Work experience: Important. **Other schools with the greatest overlap in applicants:** Arkansas Tech University; Drury University; Evangel University; Missouri State University; Southwest Baptist University. **Admissions statistics for the fall 2009 entering class:** Total applicants: 3,025. Total accepted: 263. Freshmen enrolled: 245; 16% were from out of state. Overall acceptance rate: 9%. **Size of waiting list:** 424 applicants; enrolled from waiting list: 15. **Credentials of fall 2009 freshmen:** 22% ranked in the top 10 percent of their high school class; 59% were in the top 25 percent; 91% were in the top half. (Proportion submitting class standing: 81%.) **Average high school grade point average:** 3.5. **First-year students who submitted SAT scores:** 4%. **First-year students submitting ACT scores:** 96%. Scores (25/75 percentile): English: N/A, Math: N/A, Composite: 20-25.

ACADEMICS

Year founded: 1906. **Academic calendar:** Semester. **Degrees offered:** bachelor's. **Most popular majors:** 19% business, management, marketing, and related support services, 19% education, 7% visual and performing arts, 6% English language and literature, 5% psychology. **Major fields of study:** agriculture, agriculture operations, and related sciences; business, management, marketing, and related support services; communication, journalism, and related programs; communications technologies/technicians and support services; computer and information sciences and support services; education; English language and literature/letters; family and consumer sciences/human sciences; foreign languages, literatures, and linguistics; health professions and related clinical sciences; history; legal professions and studies; mathematics and statistics; mechanic and repair technologies/technicians; multi/interdisciplinary studies; parks, recreation, leisure, and fitness studies; philosophy and religious studies; physical sciences; psychology; public administration and social service professions; security and protective services; social sciences; theology and religious vocations; transportation and materials moving; visual and performing arts. **Areas of required coursework:** arts/fine arts, humanities, computer literacy, mathematics, English (including composition), philosophy, foreign languages, sciences (biological or physical), history, social science, other. **Pre-professional programs:** pre-law, pre-medicine, pre-veterinary science, pre-pharmacy, other. **Special academic programs (% participation):** double major (10%), dual enrollment (1%), exchange student program (domestic) (1%), independent study (1%), internships (50%), student-designed major (1%), teacher certificate program (15%), other (1%). **Teacher certification offered in:** early childhood, elementary, vo-tech, middle/junior high, secondary. **Reserve Officers Training Corps (ROTC):** Army ROTC: Offered on campus. **Faculty and instruction (2009-2010):** Total instructional faculty: 95 full-time, 35 part-time (62% men; 38% women; 2% minorities). Full-time faculty with Ph.D. or other terminal degree: 57%. Student/faculty ratio: 13/1. Classes of fewer than 20 students: 62%; of 20 to 49 students: 35%; of 50 or more students: 2%. **Advanced Placement and International Baccalaureate credit:** AP tests may be used for: Credit and/or placement. Scores accepted: 4, 5. International Baccalaureate exams may be used for: Credit and/or placement. **Freshmen returning for sophomore year:** 82%. **Graduation rates:** Four-year: 36%; five-year: 55%; six-year: 60%. **Graduate study:** 13% of students pursue further study immediately upon graduation; 17% within one year; 28% within five years. Fields in which graduates pursue further study: Master of Business Administration (MBA), 16%; law, 3%; medicine, 2%; engineering, 1%; theology (or the seminary), 10%; education, 31%; arts and sciences, 27%.

COSTS AND FINANCIAL AID
Financial aid office: (417) 334-6411. **Expenses (2010-2011):** Tuition and fees 2010-2011: $17,310; room/board: $5,300. Estimated books and supplies: $800; transportation: $2,185; personal expenses: $410. **Financial aid:** Priority filing date for institution's financial aid form: February 15. In 2009-2010, 96% of undergraduates applied for financial aid. Of those, 90% were determined to have financial need; 31% had their need fully met. Average financial aid package (proportion receiving): $15,783 (90%). Average amount of gift aid, such as scholarships or grants (proportion receiving): $12,613 (75%). Average amount of self-help aid, such as work study or loans (proportion receiving): $3,841 (75%). Average need-based loan (excluding PLUS or other private loans): $0. Among students who received need-based aid, the average percentage of need met: 82%. Among students who received aid based on merit, the average award (and the proportion receiving): $10,299 (10%). The average athletic scholarship (and the proportion receiving): $2,919 (3%).

CAMPUS LIFE AND EXTRACURRICULAR ACTIVITIES
Campus housing available (% using): women's dorms (57%), men's dorms (43%). Students who live in college-owned, operated, or affiliated housing: 80%. **Student employment:** During the 2009-2010 academic year, 0% of undergraduates worked on campus. **Clubs and organizations:** Number of student organizations: 45. Activities include: campus ministries, choral groups, concert band, drama/theater, jazz band, literary magazine, music ensembles, musical theater, pep band, radio station, student government, student newspaper, yearbook. Number of fraternities: 0; sororities: 0. Average proportion of students who stay on campus on weekends: 80%. **Sports program (2009-2010):** Member of NAIA. *Men's intercollegiate varsity sports:* baseball, basketball. *Women's intercollegiate varsity sports:* basketball, volleyball.

SERVICES AND FACILITIES
Basic services: nonremedial tutoring, placement service, health service, health insurance. **Remedial assistance:** study skills. **Counseling services:** career, personal, academic, psychological, religious. **For learning-disabled students:** School does not offer a structured program with separate admission and additional fees. Total undergraduates in learning-disabled program or receiving services: 5. Services include: remedial reading, tape recorders, note-taking services, extended time for tests, tutors, texts on tape, other testing accommodations, other. **Library:** Number of titles: 112,550; number of current serial subscriptions: 441. **Information technology resources:** Students are not required to lease or own a computer. Number of campus computers available to all students: 164. School has a wireless network. Approximate number of users that can be accommodated: 1,185. Proportion of college-owned housing units wired for high-speed internet access: 100%. **Campus safety:** Security services offered: 24-hour foot-and-vehicle patrols, late-night transport/escort service, 24-hour emergency telephones, lighted pathways/sidewalks, student patrols, controlled dormitory access (key, security card, etc).

TRANSFER AND INTERNATIONAL STUDENTS
Transfer students: May apply for admission for the following academic terms: Fall, Spring. Applicants do not need a minimum number of credits to apply. For fall 2009: Transfer applications received: 735. Transfer applicants offered admission: 67. Transfer applicants enrolled: 34. **International students:** Number of foreign undergraduates: 19 (1% of student body). Number of countries represented: 15. Minimum TOEFL score required: 550 (paper); 213 (computer). Average TOEFL score: 555 (paper).

Columbia College

- **Address:** 1001 Rogers Street, Columbia, MO 65216
- **Website:** http://www.ccis.edu
- **Private; Religious affiliation:** Christian Church (Disciples of Christ)
- **Enrollment:** 848 full-time; 234 part-time

KEY STATS
✔ **U.S News College Ranking:** 40, Regional Universities (Midwest)
✔ **ACT Score (25th/75th percentile):** 20-26
✔ **Tuition:** 2010-2011: $15,596

Selectivity: Selective	**Room/board:** $6,074
Acceptance rate: 47%	**Average debt:** $13,948
Student/faculty ratio: 14/1	**Proportion who borrowed:** 63%

UNDERGRADUATE STUDENT BODY STATS
2009-2010 enrollment: 848 full-time; 234 part-time. Men: 41%; women: 59%. **Ethnic makeup:** African American: 6%; American-Indian: 1%; Asian American: 1%; Hispanic: 2%; White: 82%; International: 9%. **Religious preference:** Roman Catholic: 6%; Unknown: 82%; Christian Church (Disciples of Christ): 2%; Other: 10%.

ADMISSIONS FACTS AND FIGURES
Phone: (573) 875-7352. **Email:** admissions@ccis.edu. **Website:** http://www.ccis.edu. **Application deadlines for fall 2011:** Regular decision: August 14. Early decision: Not offered. Early action: Not offered. Admission can be deferred. **Application fee:** $35. **To apply online, go to:** http://www.ccis.edu/apply/. **Admissions requirements/recommendations:** High school units required (recommended): English: 0 (4); Mathematics: 0 (3); Science: 0 (3); Foreign language: 0 (2); Social studies: 0 (2); History: 0 (0); Academic electives: 0 (0); Total units: 0 (14). Tests: The college uses SAT or ACT scores in admissions decisions. Either SAT or ACT required. For admission to the fall 2011 entering class, the school will accept: ACT with or without writing accepted. Campus visit: Recommended. Admissions interview: Neither required nor recommended. Off-campus interview: Not available. **Factors that count in admissions decisions:** *Academic:* Secondary school record: Considered. Class rank: Very Important. Letters of recommendation: Not Considered. Standardized test scores: Very Important. Essay: Not Considered. *Nonacademic:* Interview: Not Considered. Extracurricular activities: Not Considered. Talent/ability: Not Considered. Character/personal qualities: Considered. Alumni/ae relationship: Not Considered. Geographical residence: Not Considered. State residency: Not Considered. Religious affiliation/commitment: Not Considered. Minority status: Not Considered. Volunteer work: Not Considered. Work experience: Not Considered. **Other schools with the greatest overlap in applicants:** Drury University; Maryville University of St. Louis; Rockhurst University; Truman State University; Webster University. **Admissions statistics for the fall 2009 entering class:** Total applicants: 1,137. Total accepted: 536. Freshmen enrolled: 174; 11% were from out of state. Overall acceptance rate: 47%. **Size of waiting list:** 0 applicants; enrolled from waiting list: 0. **Credentials of fall 2009 freshmen:** 24% ranked in the top 10 percent of their high school class; 50% were in the top 25 percent; 71% were in the top half. (Proportion submitting class standing: 83%.) **Average high school grade point average:** 3.3. **First-year students who submitted SAT scores:** 9%. Scores (25/75 percentile): Critical Reading: 430-570, Math: 550-680, Combined: 980-1250. **First-year students submitting ACT scores:** 87%. Scores (25/75 percentile): English: 20-26, Math: 18-25, Composite: 20-26.

ACADEMICS
Year founded: 1851. **Academic calendar:** Semester. **Degrees offered:** certificate, associate, bachelor's, post-bachelor's certificate, master's. **Most popular majors:** 15% business administration and management, 11% biology/biological sciences, 9% psychology, 7% marketing/marketing management, 6% English language and literature. **Major fields of study:** area, ethnic, cultural, and gender studies; biological and biomedical sciences; business, management, marketing, and related support services; communication, journalism, and related programs; computer and information sciences and support services; English language and literature/letters; history; mathematics and statistics; multi/interdisciplinary studies; natural resources and conservation; parks, recreation, leisure, and fitness studies; philosophy and religious studies; physical sciences; psychology; public administration and social service professions; security and protective services; social sciences; visual and performing arts. **Areas of required coursework:** humanities, computer literacy, mathematics, English (including composition), sciences (biologi-

cal or physical), history, social science; other. **Pre-professional programs:** pre-law, pre-dentistry, pre-medicine, pre-veterinary science, other. **Special academic programs (% participation):** cross-registration (0%), distance learning (61%), double major (24%), dual enrollment (2%), English as a Second Language (ESL) (2%), honors program (20%), independent study (4%), internships (28%), student-designed major (14%), study abroad (0%), teacher certificate program (7%). **Teacher certification offered in:** special education, elementary, middle/junior high, secondary. **Reserve Officers Training Corps (ROTC):** Army ROTC: Offered at cooperating institution (University of Missouri); Navy ROTC: Offered at cooperating institution (University of Missouri); Air Force ROTC: Offered at cooperating institution (University of Missouri). **Faculty and instruction (2009-2010):** Total instructional faculty: 66 full-time, 45 part-time (51% men; 49% women; 4% minorities). Full-time faculty with Ph.D. or other terminal degree: 79%. Student/faculty ratio: 14/1. Classes of fewer than 20 students: 76%; of 20 to 49 students: 24%. **Advanced Placement and International Baccalaureate credit:** AP tests may be used for: Credit only. Scores accepted: 3, 4, 5. International Baccalaureate exams may be used for: Credit only. **Freshmen returning for sophomore year:** 61%. **Graduation rates:** Four-year: 31%; five-year: 39%; six-year: 44%. **Graduate study:** 29% of students pursue further study within one year. Fields in which graduates pursue further study: Master of Business Administration (MBA), 23%; law, 4%; medicine, 4%; theology (or the seminary), 2%; education, 30%.

COSTS AND FINANCIAL AID
Financial aid office: (573) 875-7390. **Expenses (2010-2011):** Tuition and fees 2010-2011: $15,596; room/board: $6,074. Estimated books and supplies: $856; transportation: $2,916; personal expenses: $5,468. **Financial aid:** Priority filing date for institution's financial aid form: March 1. In 2009-2010, 56% of undergraduates applied for financial aid. Of those, 54% were determined to have financial need; 7% had their need fully met. Average financial aid package (proportion receiving): $11,935 (54%). Average amount of gift aid, such as scholarships or grants (proportion receiving): $5,213 (42%). Average amount of self-help aid, such as work study or loans (proportion receiving): $4,083 (45%). Average need-based loan (excluding PLUS or other private loans): $3,956. Among students who received need-based aid, the average percentage of need met: 54%. Among students who received aid based on merit, the average award (and the proportion receiving): $7,566 (12%). The average athletic scholarship (and the proportion receiving): $15,085 (4%). Average amount of debt of borrowers graduating in 2009: $13,948. Proportion who borrowed: 63%.

CAMPUS LIFE AND EXTRACURRICULAR ACTIVITIES
Campus housing available (% using): coed dorms (67%), women's dorms (18%), apartment for single students (15%), special housing for disabled students. Students who live in college-owned, operated, or affiliated housing: 33%. **Student employment:** During the 2009-2010 academic year, 16% of undergraduates worked on campus. Average per-year earnings: $1,450. **Clubs and organizations:** Number of student organizations: 41. Activities include: campus ministries, choral groups, dance, drama/theater, international student organization, literary magazine, model UN, music ensembles, musical theater, student government, student newspaper. Number of fraternities: 0; sororities: 0. Average proportion of students who stay on campus on weekends: 31%. **Sports program (2009-2010):** Member of NAIA. *Men's intercollegiate varsity sports:* basketball, soccer. *Women's intercollegiate varsity sports:* basketball, softball, volleyball.

SERVICES AND FACILITIES
Basic services: nonremedial tutoring, health service. **Remedial assistance:** math, writing, study skills. **Counseling services:** career, personal, veteran student, academic, psychological, birth control. **For learning-disabled students:** School does not offer a structured program with separate admission and additional fees. Total undergraduates in learning-disabled program or receiving services: 42. Services include: tape recorders, note-taking services, oral tests, readers, extended time for tests, tutors, typist/scribe, other. **Library:** Number of titles: 73,388; number of current serial subscriptions: 200. **Information technology resources:** Students are not required to lease or own a computer. Number of campus computers available to all students: 83. School has a wireless network. Approximate number of users that can be accommodated: 900. Proportion of college-owned housing units wired for high-speed internet access: 100%. **Campus safety:** Security services offered: 24-hour foot-and-vehicle patrols, late-night transport/escort service, 24-hour emergency telephones, lighted pathways/sidewalks, student patrols, controlled dormitory access (key, security card, etc).

TRANSFER AND INTERNATIONAL STUDENTS
Transfer students: May apply for admission for the following academic terms: Fall, Winter, Spring, Summer. Applicants need a minimum number of credits to apply. For fall 2009: Transfer applications received: 643. Transfer applicants offered admission: 186. Transfer applicants enrolled: 180. **International students:** Number of foreign undergraduates: 89 (9% of student body). Number of countries represented: 36. Minimum TOEFL score required: 500 (paper); 61 (computer). Average TOEFL score: 563 (paper).

Culver-Stockton College

- **Address:** 1 College Hill, Canton, MO 63435
- **Website:** http://www.culver.edu
- **Private; Religious affiliation:** Christian Church (Disciples of Christ)
- **Enrollment:** 699 full-time; 55 part-time

KEY STATS
✔ **U.S News College Ranking:** 33, Regional Colleges (Midwest)
✔ **ACT Score (25th/75th percentile):** 19-24
✔ **Tuition:** 2010-2011: $22,550

Selectivity: Selective	Room/board: $7,400
Acceptance rate: 60%	Average debt: $23,761
Student/faculty ratio: 13/1	Proportion who borrowed: 90%

UNDERGRADUATE STUDENT BODY STATS
2009-2010 enrollment: 699 full-time; 55 part-time. Men: 45%; women: 55%. **Ethnic makeup:** African American: 9%; American-Indian: 1%; Asian American: 1%; Hispanic: 2%; White: 84%; International: 3%. **Religious preference:** Roman Catholic: 16%; Protestant: 52%; Jewish: 1%; Buddhist: 1%; No preference: 9%; Unknown: 14%; Christian Church (Disciples of Christ): 7%.

ADMISSIONS FACTS AND FIGURES
Phone: (800) 537-1883. **Email:** admissions@culver.edu. **Website:** http://www.culver.edu. **Application deadlines for fall 2011:** Regular decision: Rolling. Early decision: Not offered. Early action: Not offered. Admission can be deferred. **To apply online, go to:** http://www.culver.edu/enrollment/app/. **Admissions requirements/recommendations:** High school units required (recommended): English: 0 (4); Mathematics: 0 (2); Science: 0 (4); Foreign language: 0 (0); Social studies: 0 (3); History: 0 (0); Academic electives: 0 (2); Total units: (15). Tests: The college uses SAT or ACT scores in admissions decisions. Either SAT or ACT required. For admission to the fall 2011 entering class, the school will accept: ACT with or without writing accepted. Campus visit: Recommended. Admissions interview: Recommended. Off-campus interview: May be arranged. **Factors that count in admissions decisions:** *Academic:* Secondary school record: Important. Class rank: Not Considered. Letters of recommendation: Considered. Standardized test scores: Very Important. Essay: Considered. *Nonacademic:* Interview: Not Considered. Extracurricular activities: Not Considered. Talent/ability: Not Considered. Character/personal qualities: Not Considered. Alumni/ae relationship: Considered. Geographical residence: Not Considered. State residency: Not Considered. Religious affiliation/commitment: Not Considered. Minority status: Not Considered. Volunteer work: Not Considered. Work experience: Not Considered. **Other schools with the greatest overlap in applicants:** Central Methodist University; Lindenwood University; Quincy University; Truman State University; University of Missouri. **Admissions statistics for the fall 2009 entering class:** Total applicants: 1,263. Total accepted: 762. Freshmen enrolled: 148; 44% were from out of state. Overall acceptance rate: 60%. **Credentials of fall 2009 freshmen:** 14% ranked in the top 10 percent of their high school class; 36% were in the top 25 percent; 72% were in the top half. (Proportion submitting class standing: 91%.) **Average high school grade point average:** 3.3. **First-year students who submitted SAT scores:** 5%. Scores (25/75 percentile): Critical Reading: 410-750, Math: 460-700, Combined: 870-1450. **First-year students submitting ACT scores:** 93%. Scores (25/75 percentile): English: 18-24, Math: 18-24, Composite: 19-24.

ACADEMICS
Year founded: 1853. **Academic calendar:** Semester. **Degrees offered:** bachelor's. **Most popular majors:** 19% nursing/registered nurse training (R.N., A.S.N., B.S.N., M.S.N.), 15% business administration and management, 9% criminal justice/law enforcement administration, 9% psychology, 8%

elementary education and teaching. **Major fields of study:** biological and biomedical sciences; business, management, marketing, and related support services; communication, journalism, and related programs; education; English language and literature/letters; health professions and related clinical sciences; history; mathematics and statistics; parks, recreation, leisure, and fitness studies; philosophy and religious studies; psychology; security and protective services; visual and performing arts. **Areas of required coursework:** arts/fine arts, humanities, mathematics, English (including composition), sciences (biological or physical), social science, other. **Pre-professional programs:** pre-law, pre-dentistry, pre-medicine, pre-theology, pre-veterinary science, pre-optometry, pre-pharmacy, other. **Special academic programs (% participation):** accelerated program (3%), distance learning (2%), double major (17%), dual enrollment (16%), honors program (8%), independent study (17%), internships (45%), liberal arts/career combination (100%), student-designed major (0%), study abroad (9%), teacher certificate program (24%). **Teacher certification offered in:** elementary, middle/junior high, secondary. **Faculty and instruction (2009-2010):** Total instructional faculty: 45 full-time, 39 part-time (61% men; 39% women; 10% minorities). Full-time faculty with Ph.D. or other terminal degree: 76%. Student/faculty ratio: 13/1. Classes of fewer than 20 students: 71%; of 20 to 49 students: 28%; of 50 or more students: 0%. **Advanced Placement and International Baccalaureate credit:** AP tests may be used for: Credit and/or placement. Scores accepted: 3, 4, 5. International Baccalaureate exams may be used for: Credit and/or placement. **Freshmen returning for sophomore year:** 64%. **Graduation rates:** Four-year: 43%; five-year: 49%; six-year: 48%. **Graduate study:** 19% of students pursue further study immediately upon graduation. Fields in which graduates pursue further study: Master of Business Administration (MBA), 5%; law, 2%; medicine, 1%; theology (or the seminary), 1%; education, 2%; arts and sciences, 7%.

COSTS AND FINANCIAL AID

Financial aid office: (573) 288-6307. **Expenses (2010-2011):** Tuition and fees 2010-2011: $22,550; room/board: $7,400. Estimated books and supplies: $1,000; transportation: $2,440; personal expenses: $340. **Financial aid:** Priority filing date for institution's financial aid form: March 1; deadline: June 1. In 2009-2010, 92% of undergraduates applied for financial aid. Of those, 87% were determined to have financial need; 19% had their need fully met. Average financial aid package (proportion receiving): $20,481 (87%). Average amount of gift aid, such as scholarships or grants (proportion receiving): $15,634 (87%). Average amount of self-help aid, such as work study or loans (proportion receiving): $5,518 (76%). Average need-based loan (excluding PLUS or other private loans): $4,939. Among students who received need-based aid, the average percentage of need met: 79%. Among students who received aid based on merit, the average award (and the proportion receiving): $11,829 (13%). The average athletic scholarship (and the proportion receiving): $2,820 (10%). Average amount of debt of borrowers graduating in 2009: $23,761. Proportion who borrowed: 90%.

CAMPUS LIFE AND EXTRACURRICULAR ACTIVITIES

Campus housing available (% using): coed dorms (71%), women's dorms, men's dorms, sorority housing (15%), fraternity housing (14%). Students who live in college-owned, operated, or affiliated housing: 78%. **Student employment:** During the 2009-2010 academic year, 48% of undergraduates worked on campus. Average per-year earnings: $1,328. **Clubs and organizations:** Number of student organizations: 44. Activities include: campus ministries, choral groups, concert band, dance, drama/theater, international student organization, jazz band, literary magazine, model UN, music ensembles, musical theater, opera, pep band, radio station, student government, student newspaper. Number of fraternities: 4; sororities: 3. Proportion of men in fraternities: 49%; of women in sororities: 46%. Average proportion of students who stay on campus on weekends: 50%. **Sports program (2009-2010):** Member of NAIA. *Men's intercollegiate varsity sports:* baseball, basketball, cross country, football, golf, soccer, track and field (indoor), track and field (outdoor). *Women's intercollegiate varsity sports:* basketball, cross country, golf, soccer, softball, track and field (indoor), track and field (outdoor), volleyball.

SERVICES AND FACILITIES

Basic services: nonremedial tutoring, placement service. **Remedial assistance:** other. **Counseling services:** career, personal, veteran student, academic, psychological, religious. **For learning-disabled students:** School does not offer a structured program with separate admission and additional fees. Total undergraduates in learning-disabled program or receiving services: 4. Services include: tape recorders, videotaped classes, untimed tests, notetaking services, oral tests, learning center, readers, extended time for tests, tutors. **Library:** Number of titles: 172,705; number of current serial subscriptions: 32,982. **Information technology resources:** Students are not required to lease or own a computer. Number of campus computers available to all students: 100. School has a wireless network. Approximate number of users that can be accommodated: 5,120. Proportion of college-owned housing units wired for high-speed internet access: 100%. **Campus safety:** Security services offered: 24-hour foot-and-vehicle patrols, late-night transport/escort service, 24-hour emergency telephones, lighted pathways/sidewalks, student patrols, controlled dormitory access (key, security card, etc).

TRANSFER AND INTERNATIONAL STUDENTS

Transfer students: May apply for admission for the following academic terms: Fall, Spring, Summer. Applicants do not need a minimum number of credits to apply. For fall 2009: Transfer applications received: 381. Transfer applicants offered admission: 189. Transfer applicants enrolled: 70. **International students:** Number of foreign undergraduates: 23 (3% of student body). Number of countries represented: 10. Minimum TOEFL score required: 500 (paper); 61 (computer).

Drury University

- ■ **Address:** 900 N. Benton Avenue, Springfield, MO 65802
- ■ **Website:** http://www.drury.edu
- ■ **Private; Religious affiliation:** Christian Church (Disciples of Christ)
- ■ **Enrollment:** 1,518 full-time; 32 part-time

KEY STATS
- ✔ **U.S News College Ranking:** 11, Regional Universities (Midwest)
- ✔ **ACT Score (25th/75th percentile):** 22-28
- ✔ **Tuition:** 2010-2011: $19,854

Selectivity: More selective	**Room/board:** $6,971
Acceptance rate: 70%	**Average debt:** $20,500
Student/faculty ratio: 12/1	**Proportion who borrowed:** 67%

UNDERGRADUATE STUDENT BODY STATS
2009-2010 enrollment: 1,518 full-time; 32 part-time. Men: 47%; women: 53%. **Ethnic makeup:** African American: 3%; Asian American: 2%; Hispanic: 2%; White: 87%; International: 6%.

ADMISSIONS FACTS AND FIGURES
Phone: (417) 873-7205. **Email:** druryad@drury.edu. **Website:** http://www.drury.edu. **Application deadlines for fall 2011:** Regular decision: August 1. Early decision: Not offered. Early action: Not offered. Admission can be deferred. **Application fee:** $25. **To apply online, go to:** http://www.drury.edu/admission/freshmen. **Admissions requirements/recommendations:** High school units required (recommended): English: 4 (4); Mathematics: 3 (4); Science: 3 (3); Foreign language: 2 (2); Social studies: 3 (3); Total units: 12 (12). Tests: The college uses SAT or ACT scores in admissions decisions. Either SAT or ACT required. For admission to the fall 2011 entering class, the school will accept: ACT with or without writing accepted. Campus visit: Recommended. Admissions interview: Recommended. Off-campus interview: May be arranged. **Factors that count in admissions decisions:** *Academic:* Secondary school record: Considered. Class rank: Important. Letters of recommendation: Important. Standardized test scores: Important. Essay: Important. *Nonacademic:* Interview: Important. Extracurricular activities: Considered. Talent/ability: Considered. Character/personal qualities: Important. Alumni/ae relationship: Considered. Geographical residence: Considered. State residency: Not Considered. Religious affiliation/commitment: Not Considered. Minority status: Considered. Volunteer work: Considered. Work experience: Considered. **Other schools with the greatest overlap in applicants:** Missouri State University; Truman State University; University of Missouri; Washington University in St. Louis. **Admissions statistics for the fall 2009 entering class:** Total applicants: 1,184. Total accepted: 832. Freshmen enrolled: 338; Overall acceptance rate: 70%. **Credentials of fall 2009 freshmen:** 35% ranked in the top 10 percent of their high school class; 67% were in the top 25 percent; 89% were in the top half. (Proportion submitting class standing: 86%.) **Average high school grade point average:** 3.7. **First-year students who submitted SAT scores:** 4%. **First-year students submitting ACT scores:** 95%. Scores (25/75 percentile): English: N/A, Math: N/A, Composite: 22-28.

ACADEMICS
Year founded: 1873. **Academic calendar:** Semester. **Degrees offered:** bachelor's, master's. **Most popular majors:** 16% psychology, 13% business,

management, marketing, and related support services, 10% security and protective services, 9% biological and biomedical sciences, 8% education. **Major fields of study:** agriculture, agriculture operations, and related sciences; biological and biomedical sciences; business, management, marketing, and related support services; communication, journalism, and related programs; computer and information sciences and support services; education; English language and literature/letters; foreign languages, literatures, and linguistics; health professions and related clinical sciences; history; legal professions and studies; liberal arts and sciences studies, and humanities; mathematics and statistics; natural resources and conservation; parks, recreation, leisure, and fitness studies; philosophy and religious studies; physical sciences; psychology; security and protective services; social sciences; visual and performing arts. **Areas of required coursework:** arts/fine arts, humanities, computer literacy, mathematics, English (including composition), philosophy, foreign languages, sciences (biological or physical), history, social science, other. **Pre-professional programs:** pre-law, pre-dentistry, pre-medicine, pre-veterinary science, pre-optometry, pre-pharmacy, other. **Special academic programs (% participation):** accelerated program, cooperative (work-study plan) program (55%), distance learning (12%), double major (27%), dual enrollment, English as a Second Language (ESL), honors program (10%), independent study, internships (75%), liberal arts/career combination (100%), student-designed major, study abroad (40%), teacher certificate program (35%), other. **Teacher certification offered in:** early childhood, elementary, middle/junior high, secondary. **Cooperative education programs:** other. **Reserve Officers Training Corps (ROTC):** Army ROTC: Offered at cooperating institution. **Faculty and instruction (2009-2010):** Total instructional faculty: 131 full-time, 48 part-time (59% men; 41% women; 8% minorities). Full-time faculty with Ph.D. or other terminal degree: 92%. Student/faculty ratio: 12/1. Classes of fewer than 20 students: 65%; of 20 to 49 students: 34%; of 50 or more students: 0%. **Advanced Placement and International Baccalaureate credit:** AP tests may be used for: Placement only. Scores accepted: 3, 4, 5. International Baccalaureate exams may be used for: Placement only. **Freshmen returning for sophomore year:** 82%. **Graduation rates:** Four-year: 55%; five-year: 62%; six-year: 63%. **Graduate study:** 36% of students pursue further study within one year. Fields in which graduates pursue further study: Master of Business Administration (MBA), 15%; law, 8%; medicine, 15%; dentistry, 2%; engineering, 2%; theology (or the seminary), 3%; education, 5%; arts and sciences, 48%; veterinary medicine, 2%.

COSTS AND FINANCIAL AID

Financial aid office: (417) 873-7312. **Expenses (2010-2011):** Tuition and fees 2010-2011: $19,854; room/board: $6,971. Estimated books and supplies: $1,500; transportation: $1,000; personal expenses: $1,500. **Financial aid:** Priority filing date for institution's financial aid form: March 1. In 2009-2010, 96% of undergraduates applied for financial aid. Of those, 95% were determined to have financial need; 86% had their need fully met. Average financial aid package (proportion receiving): $7,985 (95%). Average amount of gift aid, such as scholarships or grants (proportion receiving): $6,990 (88%). Average amount of self-help aid, such as work study or loans (proportion receiving): $6,850 (86%). Average need-based loan (excluding PLUS or other private loans): $5,500. Among students who received need-based aid, the average percentage of need met: 86%. Among students who received aid based on merit, the average award (and the proportion receiving): $3,585 (14%). The average athletic scholarship (and the proportion receiving): $9,795 (6%). Average amount of debt of borrowers graduating in 2009: $20,500. Proportion who borrowed: 67%.

CAMPUS LIFE AND EXTRACURRICULAR ACTIVITIES

Campus housing available (% using): coed dorms (45%), fraternity housing (9%), apartments for married students (0%), apartment for single students (42%), special housing for disabled students (0%), other housing options (4%). Students who live in college-owned, operated, or affiliated housing: 56%. **Student employment:** During the 2009-2010 academic year, 13% of undergraduates worked on campus. Average per-year earnings: $3,000. **Clubs and organizations:** Number of student organizations: 86. Activities include: campus ministries, choral groups, concert band, dance, drama/theater, international student organization, jazz band, literary magazine, music ensembles, musical theater, opera, pep band, radio station, student government, student newspaper, student film society, symphony orchestra, television station. Number of fraternities: 4; sororities: 4. Proportion of men in fraternities: 33%; of women in sororities: 36%. Average proportion of students who stay on campus on weekends: 50%. **Sports program (2009-2010):** Member of NCAA II. ***Men's intercollegiate varsity sports:*** baseball, basketball, cross country, golf, soccer, swimming, tennis, track and field (outdoor).

Women's intercollegiate varsity sports: basketball, cross country, golf, soccer, swimming, tennis, track and field (outdoor), volleyball.

SERVICES AND FACILITIES

Basic services: placement service, health service. **Remedial assistance:** math, writing, other. **Counseling services:** career, personal, academic, psychological, birth control, religious. **For learning-disabled students:** School does not offer a structured program with separate admission and additional fees. Total undergraduates in learning-disabled program or receiving services: 10. Services include: remedial math, remedial English, reading machines, tape recorders, other special classes, videotaped classes, untimed tests, note-taking services, oral tests, readers, extended time for tests, tutors, early syllabus, priority registration, priority seating, proofreading services, texts on tape, exams on tape or computer, other testing accommodations, other. **Library:** Number of titles: 189,598; number of current serial subscriptions: 496. **Information technology resources:** Students are not required to lease or own a computer. Number of campus computers available to all students: 389. School has a wireless network. Approximate number of users that can be accommodated: 2,000. Proportion of college-owned housing units wired for high-speed internet access: 100%. **Campus safety:** Security services offered: 24-hour foot-and-vehicle patrols, late-night transport/escort service, 24-hour emergency telephones, lighted pathways/sidewalks, controlled dormitory access (key, security card, etc).

TRANSFER AND INTERNATIONAL STUDENTS

Transfer students: May apply for admission for the following academic terms: Fall, Winter, Spring, Summer. Applicants do not need a minimum number of credits to apply. For fall 2009: Transfer applications received: 262. Transfer applicants offered admission: 164. Transfer applicants enrolled: 111. **International students:** Number of foreign undergraduates: 90 (6% of student body). Number of countries represented: 35. Minimum TOEFL score required: 530 (paper); 71 (computer). Average TOEFL score: 603 (paper).

Evangel University

- **Address:** 1111 N. Glenstone, Springfield, MO 65802
- **Website:** http://www.evangel.edu
- **Private; Religious affiliation:** Assemblies of God
- **Enrollment:** 1,624 full-time; 111 part-time

KEY STATS

✔ **U.S News College Ranking:** second tier, National Liberal Arts Colleges
✔ **ACT Score (25th/75th percentile):** 20-25
✔ **Tuition:** 2010-2011: $16,920

Selectivity: Selective	**Room/board:** $6,000
Acceptance rate: 74%	**Average debt:** $30,506
Student/faculty ratio: 18/1	**Proportion who borrowed:** 77%

UNDERGRADUATE STUDENT BODY STATS

2009-2010 enrollment: 1,624 full-time; 111 part-time. Men: 44%; women: 56%. **Ethnic makeup:** African American: 4%; American-Indian: 1%; Asian American: 1%; Hispanic: 4%; White: 89%; International: 1%.

ADMISSIONS FACTS AND FIGURES

Phone: (800) 382-6435. **Email:** admissions@evangel.edu. **Website:** http://www.evangel.edu. **Application deadlines for fall 2011:** Regular decision: August 15. Early decision: Not offered. Early action: Not offered. Admission can be deferred. **Application fee:** $25. **To apply online, go to:** http://www.evangel.edu/FutureStudents/Apply/index.asp. **Admissions requirements/recommendations:** High school units required (recommended): English: 3 (3); Mathematics: 2 (2); Science: 3 (3); Foreign language: 0 (0); Social studies: 2 (2); History: 0 (0); Academic electives: 0 (0); Total units: 11 (11). Tests: The college uses SAT or ACT scores in admissions decisions. Either SAT or ACT required. For admission to the fall 2011 entering class, the school will accept: ACT with writing required. Campus visit: Recommended. Admissions interview: Recommended. **Factors that count in admissions decisions:** *Academic:* Secondary school record: Considered. Class rank: Considered. Letters of recommendation: Important. Standardized test scores: Important. Essay: Important. *Nonacademic:* Interview: Important. Extracurricular activities: Important. Talent/ability: Considered. Character/personal qualities: Very Important. Alumni/ae relationship: Important. Geographical residence: Considered. State residency: Not Considered.

Religious affiliation/commitment: Very Important. Minority status: Not Considered. Volunteer work: Considered. Work experience: Considered. **Other schools with the greatest overlap in applicants:** College of the Ozarks; Drury University; Missouri State University; Southwest Baptist University. **Admissions statistics for the fall 2009 entering class:** Total applicants: 1,163. Total accepted: 857. Freshmen enrolled: 432; 66% were from out of state. Overall acceptance rate: 74%. **First-year students who submitted SAT scores:** 31%. Scores (25/75 percentile): Critical Reading: 470-590, Math: 460-580, Combined: 930-1170. **First-year students submitting ACT scores:** 80%. Scores (25/75 percentile): English: 19-26, Math: 18-25, Composite: 20-25.

ACADEMICS

Year founded: 1955. **Academic calendar:** Semester. **Degrees offered:** associate, bachelor's, master's. **Major fields of study:** biological and biomedical sciences; business, management, marketing, and related support services; communication, journalism, and related programs; computer and information sciences and support services; education; English language and literature/letters; foreign languages, literatures, and linguistics; health professions and related clinical sciences; history; mathematics and statistics; multi/interdisciplinary studies; parks, recreation, leisure, and fitness studies; philosophy and religious studies; physical sciences; psychology; social sciences; visual and performing arts. **Areas of required coursework:** arts/fine arts, humanities, computer literacy, mathematics, English (including composition), sciences (biological or physical), history, social science. **Pre-professional programs:** pre-law, pre-dentistry, pre-medicine, pre-theology, pre-veterinary science, pre-optometry, pre-pharmacy. **Special academic programs:** double major, internships. **Teacher certification offered in:** early childhood, elementary, middle/junior high, secondary. **Cooperative education programs:** engineering. **Reserve Officers Training Corps (ROTC):** Army ROTC: Offered at cooperating institution (Missouri State University). **Faculty and instruction (2009-2010):** Total instructional faculty: 103 full-time, 22 part-time. Student/faculty ratio: 18/1. **Advanced Placement and International Baccalaureate credit:** International Baccalaureate exams may be used for: Credit only. **Freshmen returning for sophomore year:** 69%. **Graduation rates:** Four-year: 32%; five-year: 44%; six-year: 45%.

COSTS AND FINANCIAL AID

Financial aid office: (417) 865-2815. **Expenses (2010-2011):** Tuition and fees 2010-2011: $16,920; room/board: $6,000. Estimated books and supplies: $1,500; transportation: $2,200; personal expenses: $5,130. **Financial aid:** Priority filing date for institution's financial aid form: March 1. In 2009-2010, 94% of undergraduates applied for financial aid. Of those, 84% were determined to have financial need; 9% had their need fully met. Average financial aid package (proportion receiving): $11,981 (83%). Average amount of gift aid, such as scholarships or grants (proportion receiving): $7,873 (75%). Average amount of self-help aid, such as work study or loans (proportion receiving): $5,264 (77%). Average need-based loan (excluding PLUS or other private loans): $4,392. Among students who received need-based aid, the average percentage of need met: 56%. Among students who received aid based on merit, the average award (and the proportion receiving): $3,381 (9%). The average athletic scholarship (and the proportion receiving): $6,022 (4%). Average amount of debt of borrowers graduating in 2009: $30,506. Proportion who borrowed: 77%.

CAMPUS LIFE AND EXTRACURRICULAR ACTIVITIES

Campus housing available: coed dorms, women's dorms, men's dorms, apartments for married students. Students who live in college-owned, operated, or affiliated housing: 75%. **Student employment:** During the 2009-2010 academic year, 44% of undergraduates worked on campus. Average per-year earnings: $1,700. **Clubs and organizations:** Number of student organizations: 40. Activities include: campus ministries, choral groups, concert band, drama/theater, jazz band, literary magazine, music ensembles, musical theater, pep band, radio station, student government, student newspaper, symphony orchestra, television station, yearbook. Number of fraternities: 0; sororities: 0. Average proportion of students who stay on campus on weekends: 80%. **Sports program (2009-2010):** Member of NAIA. **Men's intercollegiate varsity sports:** baseball, basketball, cross country, football, golf, tennis, track and field (indoor), track and field (outdoor). **Women's intercollegiate varsity sports:** basketball, cross country, golf, softball, tennis, track and field (indoor), track and field (outdoor), volleyball.

SERVICES AND FACILITIES

Basic services: nonremedial tutoring, placement service, health service. **Remedial assistance:** reading, math, writing, study skills. **Counseling services:** career, personal, academic, religious. **For learning-disabled students:** School does not offer a structured program with separate admission and additional fees. Services include: remedial math, remedial English, remedial reading, tape recorders, diagnostic testing service, untimed tests, oral tests, learning center, readers, extended time for tests, tutors, other testing accommodations. **Library:** Number of titles: 91,867; number of current serial subscriptions: 1,063. **Information technology resources:** Students are not required to lease or own a computer. Number of campus computers available to all students: 407. School does not have a wireless network. Proportion of college-owned housing units wired for high-speed internet access: 100%. **Campus safety:** Security services offered: 24-hour foot-and-vehicle patrols, late-night transport/escort service, 24-hour emergency telephones, lighted pathways/sidewalks, student patrols, controlled dormitory access (key, security card, etc).

TRANSFER AND INTERNATIONAL STUDENTS

Transfer students: May apply for admission for the following academic terms: Fall, Spring, Summer. Applicants need a minimum number of credits to apply. For fall 2009: Transfer applications received: 201. Transfer applicants offered admission: 143. Transfer applicants enrolled: 96. **International students:** Number of foreign undergraduates: 9 (1% of student body). Number of countries represented: 7. Minimum TOEFL score required: 490 (paper); 163 (computer).

Fontbonne University

- **Address:** 6800 Wydown Boulevard, St. Louis, MO 63105
- **Website:** http://www.fontbonne.edu
- **Private; Religious affiliation:** Roman Catholic
- **Enrollment:** 1,463 full-time; 480 part-time

KEY STATS

✔ **U.S News College Ranking:** 66, Regional Universities (Midwest)
✔ **ACT Score (25th/75th percentile):** 20-25
✔ **Tuition:** 2010-2011: $20,380

Selectivity: Selective	**Room/board:** $7,600
Acceptance rate: 85%	**Average debt:** $25,712
Student/faculty ratio: 14/1	**Proportion who borrowed:** 85%

UNDERGRADUATE STUDENT BODY STATS

2009-2010 enrollment: 1,463 full-time; 480 part-time. Men: 30%; women: 70%. **Ethnic makeup:** African American: 33%; Asian American: 1%; Hispanic: 2%; White: 63%; International: 2%. **Religious preference:** Roman Catholic: 21%; Protestant: 12%; Jewish: 1%; No preference: 12%; Unknown: 54%.

ADMISSIONS FACTS AND FIGURES

Phone: (314) 889-1400. **Email:** admissions@fontbonne.edu. **Website:** http://www.fontbonne.edu. **Application deadlines for fall 2011:** Regular decision: Rolling. Early decision: Not offered. Early action: Not offered. Admission can be deferred. **Application fee:** $25. **To apply online, go to:** https://www.fontbonne.edu/admissions/applyonline/undergraduateapplication.htm. **Admissions requirements/recommendations:** High school units required (recommended): English: 4; Mathematics: 3; Science: 3; Social studies: 3; Academic electives: 3; Total units: 16. Tests: The college uses SAT or ACT scores in admissions decisions. Either SAT or ACT required. For admission to the fall 2011 entering class, the school will accept: ACT with or without writing accepted. Campus visit: Recommended. Admissions interview: Recommended. Off-campus interview: May be arranged. **Factors that count in admissions decisions:** *Academic:* Secondary school record: Very Important. Class rank: Very Important. Letters of recommendation: Considered. Standardized test scores: Very Important. Essay: Considered. *Nonacademic:* Interview: Considered. Extracurricular activities: Considered. Talent/ability: Considered. Character/personal qualities: Very Important. Alumni/ae relationship: Important. Geographical residence: Not Considered. State residency: Not Considered. Religious affiliation/commitment: Not Considered. Minority status: Not Considered. Volunteer work: Considered. Work experience: Considered. **Other schools with the greatest overlap in applicants:** Lindenwood University; Maryville University of St. Louis; Missouri Baptist University; St. Louis University; Webster University. **Admissions statistics for the fall 2009 entering class:** Total applicants: 517. Total accepted: 442. Freshmen enrolled: 180; 21% were from out of state. Overall acceptance rate: 85%. **Credentials of fall 2009 freshmen:** 18% ranked in the top 10 percent of their high school class; 38% were in the top 25 percent; 74% were in the top half. (Proportion submitting class standing:

70%.) **Average high school grade point average:** 3.2. **First-year students submitting ACT scores:** 85%. Scores (25/75 percentile): English: 19-25, Math: 18-25, Composite: 20-25.

ACADEMICS

Year founded: 1923. **Academic calendar:** Semester. **Degrees offered:** certificate, bachelor's, post-bachelor's certificate, master's. **Most popular majors:** 31% business administration and management, 13% organizational behavior studies, 8% special education and teaching, 4% communication studies/speech communication and rhetoric, 3% elementary education and teaching. **Major fields of study:** biological and biomedical sciences; business, management, marketing, and related support services; communication, journalism, and related programs; computer and information sciences and support services; education; English language and literature/letters; family and consumer sciences/human sciences; health professions and related clinical sciences; history; legal professions and studies; liberal arts and sciences studies, and humanities; mathematics and statistics; parks, recreation, leisure, and fitness studies; psychology; public administration and social service professions; visual and performing arts. **Areas of required coursework:** arts/fine arts, humanities, computer literacy, mathematics, English (including composition), philosophy, sciences (biological or physical), history, social science, other. **Pre-professional programs:** pre-law, other. **Special academic programs (% participation):** accelerated program (38%), cooperative (work-study plan) program, cross-registration (0%), distance learning (3%), double major (2%), English as a Second Language (ESL) (8%), exchange student program (domestic) (0%), honors program (2%), independent study (2%), internships, liberal arts/career combination, student-designed major (1%), study abroad (3%), teacher certificate program (14%). **Teacher certification offered in:** early childhood, special education, elementary, middle/junior high, secondary. **Cooperative education programs:** business, engineering, social/behavioral science. **Reserve Officers Training Corps (ROTC):** Army ROTC: Offered at cooperating institution (Washington University in St. Louis); Air Force ROTC: Offered at cooperating institution (Washington University in St. Louis). **Faculty and instruction (2009-2010):** Total instructional faculty: 75 full-time, 240 part-time (37% men; 63% women; 10% minorities). Full-time faculty with Ph.D. or other terminal degree: 71%. Student/faculty ratio: 14/1. Classes of fewer than 20 students: 84%; of 20 to 49 students: 16%; of 50 or more students: 0%. **Advanced Placement and International Baccalaureate credit:** AP tests may be used for: Credit only. Scores accepted: 4, 5. **Freshmen returning for sophomore year:** 62%. **Graduation rates:** Four-year: 31%; five-year: 49%; six-year: 53%. **Graduate study:** 20% of students pursue further study within one year.

COSTS AND FINANCIAL AID

Financial aid office: (314) 889-1414. **Expenses (2010-2011):** Tuition and fees 2010-2011: $20,380; room/board: $7,600. Estimated books and supplies: $1,000. **Financial aid:** Priority filing date for institution's financial aid form: April 1. In 2009-2010, 93% of undergraduates applied for financial aid. Of those, 86% were determined to have financial need; 40% had their need fully met. Average financial aid package (proportion receiving): $10,972 (86%). Average amount of gift aid, such as scholarships or grants (proportion receiving): $4,731 (72%). Average amount of self-help aid, such as work study or loans (proportion receiving): $3,431 (68%). Average need-based loan (excluding PLUS or other private loans): $3,430. Among students who received need-based aid, the average percentage of need met: 74%. Among students who received aid based on merit, the average award (and the proportion receiving): $6,584 (7%). The average athletic scholarship (and the proportion receiving): $0 (0%). Average amount of debt of borrowers graduating in 2009: $25,712. Proportion who borrowed: 85%.

CAMPUS LIFE AND EXTRACURRICULAR ACTIVITIES

Campus housing available (% using): coed dorms (77%), apartment for single students (12%), special housing for international students (8%), other housing options (3%). Students who live in college-owned, operated, or affiliated housing: 10%. **Student employment:** During the 2009-2010 academic year, 1% of undergraduates worked on campus. Average per-year earnings: $1,500. **Clubs and organizations:** Number of student organizations: 34. Activities include: campus ministries, choral groups, dance, drama/theater, international student organization, literary magazine, student government, student newspaper. Number of fraternities: 0; sororities: 0. Average proportion of students who stay on campus on weekends: 50%. **Sports program (2009-2010):** Member of NCAA III. *Men's intercollegiate varsity sports:* baseball, basketball, cross country, golf, lacrosse, soccer, volleyball. *Women's intercollegiate varsity sports:* basketball, bowling, cross country, field hockey, golf, lacrosse, soccer, softball, volleyball.

SERVICES AND FACILITIES

Basic services: nonremedial tutoring. **Remedial assistance:** reading, math, writing, study skills. **Counseling services:** career, personal, academic. **For learning-disabled students:** School does not offer a structured program with separate admission and additional fees. Total undergraduates in learning-disabled program or receiving services: 74. Services include: remedial math, remedial English, reading machines, remedial reading, tape recorders, other special classes, untimed tests, note-taking services, oral tests, learning center, readers, extended time for tests, tutors, priority registration, priority seating, proofreading services, texts on tape, typist/scribe, exams on tape or computer. **Library:** Number of titles: 91,172; number of current serial subscriptions: 19,532. **Information technology resources:** Students are not required to lease or own a computer. Number of campus computers available to all students: 285. School has a wireless network. Approximate number of users that can be accommodated: 3,000. Proportion of college-owned housing units wired for high-speed internet access: 100%. **Campus safety:** Security services offered: 24-hour foot-and-vehicle patrols, late-night transport/escort service, 24-hour emergency telephones, lighted pathways/sidewalks, controlled dormitory access (key, security card, etc).

TRANSFER AND INTERNATIONAL STUDENTS

Transfer students: May apply for admission for the following academic terms: Fall, Spring, Summer. Applicants do not need a minimum number of credits to apply. For fall 2009: Transfer applications received: 322. Transfer applicants offered admission: 298. Transfer applicants enrolled: 225. **International students:** Number of foreign undergraduates: 30 (2% of student body). Number of countries represented: 23. Minimum TOEFL score required: 500 (paper); 173 (computer). Average TOEFL score: 500 (paper).

Hannibal-LaGrange College

- **Address:** 2800 Palmyra Road, Hannibal, MO 63401
- **Website:** http://www.hlg.edu
- **Private; Religious affiliation:** Southern Baptist Convention
- **Enrollment:** 850 full-time; 172 part-time

KEY STATS

✔ **U.S News College Ranking:** 61, Regional Colleges (Midwest)
✔ **ACT Score (25th/75th percentile):** 21-26
✔ **Tuition:** 2010-2011: $15,946

Selectivity: Selective	**Room/board:** $6,180
Acceptance rate: 87%	**Average debt:** N/A
Student/faculty ratio: 12/1	**Proportion who borrowed:** N/A

UNDERGRADUATE STUDENT BODY STATS

2009-2010 enrollment: 850 full-time; 172 part-time. Men: 37%; women: 63%. **Ethnic makeup:** African American: 3%; Asian American: 1%; Hispanic: 2%; White: 86%; International: 9%. **Religious preference:** Roman Catholic: 3%; Protestant: 19%; Southern Baptist Convention: 65%.

ADMISSIONS FACTS AND FIGURES

Phone: (800) 454-1119. **Email:** admissions@hlg.edu. **Website:** http://www.hlg.edu. **Application deadlines for fall 2011:** Regular decision: August 26. Early decision: Not offered. Early action: Not offered. Admission cannot be deferred. **Application fee:** $25. **To apply online, go to:** http://www.hlg.edu/admiss/appcover.php. **Admissions requirements/recommendations:** High school units required (recommended): English: (4); Mathematics: (3); Science: (3); History: (2). Tests: The college uses SAT or ACT scores in admissions decisions. ACT required. For admission to the fall 2011 entering class, the school will accept: ACT with or without writing accepted. Campus visit: Recommended. Admissions interview: Recommended. Off-campus interview: May be arranged. **Factors that count in admissions decisions:** *Academic:* Secondary school record: Important. Class rank: Considered. Letters of recommendation: Considered. Standardized test scores: Very Important. Essay: Not Considered. *Nonacademic:* Interview: Considered. Extracurricular activities: Considered. Talent/ability: Considered. Character/personal qualities: Important. Alumni/ae relationship: Considered. Geographical residence: Not Considered. State residency: Not Considered. Religious affiliation/commitment: Not Considered. Minority status: Not Considered. Volunteer work: Considered. Work experience: Not Considered. **Other schools with the greatest overlap in applicants:** Culver-Stockton College; Missouri Baptist University; Quincy University; Southwest Baptist

University; University of Missouri. **Admissions statistics for the fall 2009 entering class:** Total applicants: 646. Total accepted: 562. Freshmen enrolled: 187; 33% were from out of state. Overall acceptance rate: 87%. **Credentials of fall 2009 freshmen:** 17% ranked in the top 10 percent of their high school class; 49% were in the top 25 percent; 74% were in the top half. (Proportion submitting class standing: 68%.) **First-year students submitting ACT scores:** 100%. Scores (25/75 percentile): English: 20-27, Math: 19-25, Composite: 21-26.

ACADEMICS

Year founded: 1858. **Academic calendar:** Semester. **Degrees offered:** certificate, associate, bachelor's, master's. **Most popular majors:** 30% business, management, marketing, and related support services, 20% elementary education and teaching, 17% education, 12% criminal justice and corrections, 10% nursing/registered nurse training (R.N., A.S.N., B.S.N., M.S.N.). **Major fields of study:** agriculture, agriculture operations, and related sciences; biological and biomedical sciences; communication, journalism, and related programs; computer and information sciences and support services; education; English language and literature/letters; health professions and related clinical sciences; liberal arts and sciences studies, and humanities; mathematics and statistics; parks, recreation, leisure, and fitness studies; psychology; public administration and social service professions; security and protective services; theology and religious vocations; visual and performing arts. **Areas of required coursework:** arts/fine arts, humanities, mathematics, English (including composition), sciences (biological or physical), history, social science, other. **Pre-professional programs:** pre-law, pre-dentistry, pre-medicine, pre-pharmacy. **Special academic programs (% participation):** accelerated program (27%), distance learning, double major (10%), dual enrollment, English as a Second Language (ESL), honors program (6%), independent study, internships, student-designed major, study abroad (6%), teacher certificate program (20%), weekend college. **Teacher certification offered in:** early childhood, elementary, middle/junior high, secondary. **Cooperative education programs:** engineering. **Faculty and instruction (2009-2010):** Total instructional faculty: 62 full-time, 41 part-time (44% men; 56% women; 2% minorities). Full-time faculty with Ph.D. or other terminal degree: 29%. Student/faculty ratio: 12/1. **Advanced Placement and International Baccalaureate credit:** AP tests may be used for: Credit only. Scores accepted: 3. International Baccalaureate exams may be used for: Credit and/or placement. **Freshmen returning for sophomore year:** 66%. **Graduation rates:** Four-year: 8%; five-year: 39%; six-year: 47%. **Graduate study:** 21% of students pursue further study immediately upon graduation.

COSTS AND FINANCIAL AID

Financial aid office: (573) 221-3675. **Expenses (2010-2011):** Tuition and fees 2010-2011: $15,946; room/board: $6,180. Estimated books and supplies: $950; transportation: $3,310. **Financial aid:** Priority filing date for institution's financial aid form: July 1. In 2009-2010, 88% of undergraduates applied for financial aid. Of those, 88% were determined to have financial need; 11% had their need fully met. Average financial aid package (proportion receiving): $9,792 (67%). Average amount of gift aid, such as scholarships or grants (proportion receiving): $7,356 (63%). Average amount of self-help aid, such as work study or loans (proportion receiving): $4,135 (45%). Average need-based loan (excluding PLUS or other private loans): $3,889. Among students who received need-based aid, the average percentage of need met: 59%. Among students who received aid based on merit, the average award (and the proportion receiving): $6,180 (13%). The average athletic scholarship (and the proportion receiving): $4,380 (8%).

CAMPUS LIFE AND EXTRACURRICULAR ACTIVITIES

Campus housing available (% using): women's dorms (45%), men's dorms (41%), apartment for single students (14%), special housing for disabled students (0%). Students who live in college-owned, operated, or affiliated housing: 37%. **Student employment:** During the 2009-2010 academic year, 20% of undergraduates worked on campus. Average per-year earnings: $1,500. **Clubs and organizations:** Number of student organizations: 24. Activities include: choral groups, concert band, drama/theater, jazz band, music ensembles, student government, student newspaper, yearbook. Number of fraternities: 0; sororities: 0. Average proportion of students who stay on campus on weekends: 65%. **Sports program (2009-2010):** Member of NAIA. **Men's intercollegiate varsity sports:** baseball, basketball, cross country, golf, soccer, swimming, track and field (outdoor), volleyball, wrestling. **Women's intercollegiate varsity sports:** cross country, golf, soccer, softball, swimming, track and field (outdoor), volleyball.

SERVICES AND FACILITIES

Basic services: nonremedial tutoring, health insurance, other. **Remedial assistance:** math, writing. **Counseling services:** career, personal, academic. **For learning-disabled students:** School does not offer a structured program with separate admission and additional fees. Services include: remedial math, remedial English, tape recorders, untimed tests, extended time for tests, tutors, priority seating, texts on tape, other testing accommodations. **Library:** Number of titles: 103,244; number of current serial subscriptions: 287. **Information technology resources:** Students are not required to lease or own a computer. Number of campus computers available to all students: 161. School has a wireless network. Approximate number of users that can be accommodated: 256. Proportion of college-owned housing units wired for high-speed internet access: 100%. **Campus safety:** Security services offered: 24-hour emergency telephones, lighted pathways/sidewalks, student patrols, controlled dormitory access (key, security card, etc).

TRANSFER AND INTERNATIONAL STUDENTS

Transfer students: May apply for admission for the following academic terms: Fall, Spring, Summer. Applicants do not need a minimum number of credits to apply. **International students:** Number of foreign undergraduates: 77 (9% of student body). Number of countries represented: 7. Minimum TOEFL score required: 520 (paper); 190 (computer). Average TOEFL score: 520 (paper).

Harris-Stowe State University

- **Address:** 3026 Laclede Avenue, St. Louis, MO 63103
- **Website:** http://www.hssu.edu
- **Public**
- **Enrollment:** 1,408 full-time; 478 part-time

KEY STATS

✔ **U.S News College Ranking:** second tier, Regional Colleges (Midwest)
✔ **ACT Score (25th/75th percentile):** 14-17
✔ **Tuition:** 2009-2010: $4,336 in state, $8,154 out of state

Selectivity: Least selective	**Room/board:** $7,860
Acceptance rate: 96%	**Average debt:** N/A
Student/faculty ratio: 16/1	**Proportion who borrowed:** N/A

UNDERGRADUATE STUDENT BODY STATS

2009-2010 enrollment: 1,408 full-time; 478 part-time. Men: 33%; women: 67%. **Ethnic makeup:** African American: 92%; Hispanic: 1%; White: 7%; International: 1%.

ADMISSIONS FACTS AND FIGURES

Phone: (314) 340-3300. **Email:** admissions@hssu.edu. **Website:** http://www.hssu.edu. **Application deadlines for fall 2011:** Regular decision: Rolling. Early decision: Not offered. Early action: Not offered. Admission can be deferred. **Application fee:** $15. To apply online, go to: http://www.hssu.edu/spcontent.cfm?DeptID=2&pID=14. **Admissions requirements/recommendations:** High school units required (recommended): English: 4; Mathematics: 3; Science: 2; Foreign language: (2); Social studies: 2; History: 1; Academic electives: 3; Total units: 16. Tests: The college uses SAT or ACT scores in admissions decisions. ACT required. For admission to the fall 2011 entering class, the school will accept: ACT with or without writing accepted. Campus visit: Recommended. Admissions interview: Recommended. Off-campus interview: Not available. **Factors that count in admissions decisions:** *Academic:* Secondary school record: Very Important. Class rank: Very Important. Letters of recommendation: Considered. Standardized test scores: Very Important. Essay: Important. *Nonacademic:* Interview: Considered. Extracurricular activities: Considered. Talent/ability: Considered. Character/personal qualities: Not Considered. Alumni/ae relationship: Not Considered. Geographical residence: Not Considered. State residency: Not Considered. Religious affiliation/commitment: Not Considered. Minority status: Not Considered. Volunteer work: Not Considered. Work experience: Not Considered. **Other schools with the greatest overlap in applicants:** Lincoln University; Lindenwood University; University of Missouri–St. Louis. **Admissions statistics for the fall 2009 entering class:** Total applicants: 1,594. Total accepted: 1,535. Freshmen enrolled: 411; 10% were from out of state. Overall acceptance rate: 96%. **Credentials of fall 2009 freshmen:** 2% ranked in the top 10 percent of their high school class; 11% were in the top 25 percent; 40% were in the top half. (Proportion submitting class standing: 64%.) **Average high school grade point average:** 2.3. **First-year students**

submitting ACT scores: 60%. Scores (25/75 percentile): English: 12-17, Math: 15-17, Composite: 14-17.

ACADEMICS

Year founded: 1857. **Academic calendar:** Semester. **Degrees offered:** certificate, bachelor's. **Most popular majors:** 22% business administration and management, 18% elementary education and teaching, 15% accounting, 10% criminal justice/safety studies. **Major fields of study:** business, management, marketing, and related support services; computer and information sciences and support services; education; health professions and related clinical sciences; public administration and social service professions; security and protective services; social sciences. **Areas of required coursework:** arts/fine arts, humanities, computer literacy, mathematics, English (including composition), philosophy, sciences (biological or physical), history, social science. **Special academic programs:** accelerated program, dual enrollment, internships, teacher certificate program. **Teacher certification offered in:** early childhood, elementary, middle/junior high, secondary. **Reserve Officers Training Corps (ROTC):** Army ROTC: Offered at cooperating institution (Washington University in St. Louis); Air Force ROTC: Offered at cooperating institution (St. Louis University). **Faculty and instruction (2009-2010):** Total instructional faculty: 55 full-time, 137 part-time (47% men; 53% women; 65% minorities). Full-time faculty with Ph.D. or other terminal degree: 65%. Student/faculty ratio: 16/1. Classes of fewer than 20 students: 74%; of 20 to 49 students: 26%; of 50 or more students: 0%. **Advanced Placement and International Baccalaureate credit:** AP tests may be used for: Credit only. Scores accepted: 3, 4, 5. **Freshmen returning for sophomore year:** 44%. **Graduation rates:** Four-year: 8%; five-year: 17%; six-year: 20%.

COSTS AND FINANCIAL AID

Financial aid office: (314) 340-3500. **Expenses (2009-2010):** Tuition and fees 2009-2010: $4,336 in state, $8,154 out of state; room/board: $7,860. Estimated books and supplies: $1,000. **Financial aid:** Priority filing date for institution's financial aid form: April 1; deadline: August 1.

CAMPUS LIFE AND EXTRACURRICULAR ACTIVITIES

Campus housing available (% using): coed dorms (100%). Students who live in college-owned, operated, or affiliated housing: 12%. **Clubs and organizations:** Number of student organizations: 41. Activities include: choral groups, dance, drama/theater, student government. Number of fraternities: 7; sororities: 4. Average proportion of students who stay on campus on weekends: 75%. **Sports program (2009-2010):** Member of NAIA. *Men's intercollegiate varsity sports:* baseball, basketball, soccer. *Women's intercollegiate varsity sports:* basketball, soccer, softball, volleyball.

SERVICES AND FACILITIES

Basic services: nonremedial tutoring, day care, health service. **Remedial assistance:** reading, math, writing, study skills. **Counseling services:** career, personal, academic, older student. **For learning-disabled students:** School does not offer a structured program with separate admission and additional fees. Services include: remedial math, remedial English, remedial reading, tape recorders, note-taking services, oral tests, learning center, readers, extended time for tests, tutors, priority seating, substitution of courses, texts on tape, typist/scribe, other testing accommodations, other. **Library:** Number of titles: 76,000; number of current serial subscriptions: 350. **Information technology resources:** Students are not required to lease or own a computer. Number of campus computers available to all students: 327. School has a wireless network. Approximate number of users that can be accommodated: 300. Proportion of college-owned housing units wired for high-speed internet access: 100%. **Campus safety:** Security services offered: 24-hour foot-and-vehicle patrols, late-night transport/escort service, 24-hour emergency telephones, lighted pathways/sidewalks, student patrols, controlled dormitory access (key, security card, etc).

TRANSFER AND INTERNATIONAL STUDENTS

Transfer students: May apply for admission for the following academic terms: Fall, Spring, Summer. Applicants need a minimum number of credits to apply. For fall 2009: Transfer applications received: 466. Transfer applicants offered admission: 312. Transfer applicants enrolled: 229. **International students:** Number of foreign undergraduates: 11 (1% of student body). Number of countries represented: 11. Minimum TOEFL score required: 500 (paper); 173 (computer).

Kansas City Art Institute

- **Address:** 4415 Warwick Boulevard, Kansas City, MO 64111
- **Website:** http://www.kcai.edu
- **Private**
- **Enrollment:** 671 full-time; 19 part-time

KEY STATS

✔ **U.S News College Ranking:** Unranked Specialty School–Fine Arts
✔ **ACT Score (25th/75th percentile):** 21-27
✔ **Tuition:** 2010-2011: $29,866

Selectivity: N/A	**Room/board:** $9,100
Acceptance rate: 67%	**Average debt:** $23,446
Student/faculty ratio: 11/1	**Proportion who borrowed:** 93%

UNDERGRADUATE STUDENT BODY STATS

2009-2010 enrollment: 671 full-time; 19 part-time. Men: 41%; women: 59%.

ADMISSIONS FACTS AND FIGURES

Phone: (800) 522-5224. **Email:** admiss@kcai.edu. **Website:** http://www.kcai.edu. **Application deadlines for fall 2011:** Regular decision: Rolling. Early decision: Not offered. Early action: Not offered. Admission can be deferred. **Application fee:** $35. **To apply online, go to:** https://apply.kcai.edu/apply/authentication.do?cmd=login-check. **Admissions requirements/recommendations:** High school units required (recommended): English: 4 (4); Mathematics: 3 (3); Science: 3 (3); Foreign language: 2 (2); Social studies: 3 (3); History: 1 (1); Total units: 20 (20). Tests: The college uses SAT or ACT scores in admissions decisions. Either SAT or ACT required. For admission to the fall 2011 entering class, the school will accept: ACT with or without writing accepted. Campus visit: Recommended. Admissions interview: Required. Off-campus interview: May be arranged. **Factors that count in admissions decisions:** *Academic:* Secondary school record: Very Important. Class rank: Considered. Letters of recommendation: Very Important. Standardized test scores: Very Important. Essay: Very Important. *Nonacademic:* Interview: Important. Extracurricular activities: Considered. Talent/ability: Very Important. Character/personal qualities: Important. Alumni/ae relationship: Considered. Geographical residence: Not Considered. State residency: Not Considered. Religious affiliation/commitment: Not Considered. Minority status: Not Considered. Volunteer work: Considered. Work experience: Considered. **Other schools with the greatest overlap in applicants:** Cooper Union; Maryland Institute College of Art; Milwaukee Institute of Art and Design; Rhode Island School of Design; School of the Art Institute of Chicago. **Admissions statistics for the fall 2009 entering class:** Total applicants: 701. Total accepted: 470. Freshmen enrolled: 189; 40% were from out of state. Overall acceptance rate: 67%. **Credentials of fall 2009 freshmen:** 9% ranked in the top 10 percent of their high school class; 41% were in the top 25 percent; 76% were in the top half. (Proportion submitting class standing: 78%.) **Average high school grade point average:** 3.3. **First-year students who submitted SAT scores:** 16%. Scores (25/75 percentile): Critical Reading: 480-610, Math: 440-560, Combined: 920-1170. **First-year students submitting ACT scores:** 83%. Scores (25/75 percentile): English: 21-28, Math: 18-24, Composite: 21-27.

ACADEMICS

Year founded: 1885. **Academic calendar:** Semester. **Degrees offered:** bachelor's. **Major fields of study:** visual and performing arts. **Areas of required coursework:** arts/fine arts, humanities, English (including composition), philosophy, sciences (biological or physical), history, social science. **Special academic programs (% participation):** double major (13%), dual enrollment (7%), exchange student program (domestic) (1%), independent study (30%), internships (47%), liberal arts/career combination (13%), study abroad (6%). **Faculty and instruction (2009-2010):** Total instructional faculty: 48 full-time, 48 part-time (56% men; 44% women; 2% minorities). Full-time faculty with Ph.D. or other terminal degree: 90%. Student/faculty ratio: 11/1. Classes of fewer than 20 students: 79%; of 20 to 49 students: 21%. **Advanced Placement and International Baccalaureate credit:** AP tests may be used for: Credit only. Scores accepted: 4, 5. International Baccalaureate exams may be used for: Credit only. **Freshmen returning for sophomore year:** 78%. **Graduation rates:** Four-year: 50%; five-year: 59%; six-year: 66%. **Graduate study:** 15% of students pursue further study immediately upon graduation. Fields in which graduates pursue further study: education, 20%; arts and sciences, 80%.

COSTS AND FINANCIAL AID

Financial aid office: (816) 802-3448. **Expenses (2010-2011):** Tuition and fees 2010-2011: $29,866; room/board: $9,100. Estimated books and supplies: $1,500; transportation: $1,500; personal expenses: $2,000. **Financial aid:** Priority filing date for institution's financial aid form: March 1; deadline: August 1. In 2009-2010, 99% of undergraduates applied for financial aid. Of those, 92% were determined to have financial need; 13% had their need fully met. Average financial aid package (proportion receiving): $18,706 (89%). Average amount of gift aid, such as scholarships or grants (proportion receiving): $14,326 (89%). Average amount of self-help aid, such as work study or loans (proportion receiving): $5,476 (88%). Average need-based loan (excluding PLUS or other private loans): $5,219. Among students who received need-based aid, the average percentage of need met: 58%. Among students who received aid based on merit, the average award (and the proportion receiving): $11,204 (20%). The average athletic scholarship (and the proportion receiving): $0 (0%). Average amount of debt of borrowers graduating in 2009: $23,446. Proportion who borrowed: 93%.

CAMPUS LIFE AND EXTRACURRICULAR ACTIVITIES

Campus housing available (% using): coed dorms (20%), apartment for single students (5%). **Student employment:** During the 2009-2010 academic year, 42% of undergraduates worked on campus. Average per-year earnings: $1,000. **Clubs and organizations:** Number of student organizations: 6. Activities include: dance, literary magazine, student government, student film society. Number of fraternities: 0; sororities: 0. Average proportion of students who stay on campus on weekends: 75%.

SERVICES AND FACILITIES

Basic services: nonremedial tutoring, health insurance. **Remedial assistance:** reading, writing, study skills, other. **Counseling services:** career, personal, academic, psychological. **For learning-disabled students:** School does not offer a structured program with separate admission and additional fees. Services include: remedial English, remedial reading, tape recorders, untimed tests, note-taking services, oral tests, learning center, readers, extended time for tests, tutors, priority registration, priority seating, other testing accommodations. **Library:** Number of titles: 33,958; number of current serial subscriptions: 97. **Information technology resources:** Students are not required to lease or own a computer. Number of campus computers available to all students: 145. School has a wireless network. Approximate number of users that can be accommodated: 250. Proportion of college-owned housing units wired for high-speed internet access: 100%. **Campus safety:** Security services offered: 24-hour foot-and-vehicle patrols, late-night transport/escort service, 24-hour emergency telephones, lighted pathways/sidewalks, controlled dormitory access (key, security card, etc).

TRANSFER AND INTERNATIONAL STUDENTS

Transfer students: May apply for admission for the following academic terms: Fall, Spring. Applicants need a minimum number of credits to apply. For fall 2009: Transfer applications received: 159. Transfer applicants offered admission: 95. Transfer applicants enrolled: 60. **International students:** Number of foreign undergraduates: 0. Number of countries represented: 6. Minimum TOEFL score required: 550 (paper); 215 (computer). Average TOEFL score: 649 (paper).

Lincoln University

- **Address:** PO Box 29, Jefferson City, MO 65102-0029
- **Website:** http://www.lincolnu.edu
- **Public**
- **Enrollment:** N/A

KEY STATS
✔ **U.S News College Ranking:** Unranked, Regional Universities (Midwest)
✔ **SAT or ACT Score (25th/75th percentile):** N/A
✔ **Tuition:** 2009-2010: $4,948 in state, $8,716 out of state

Selectivity: N/A	Room/board: $4,660
Acceptance rate: N/A	Average debt: N/A
Student/faculty ratio: N/A	Proportion who borrowed: N/A

Lindenwood University

- **Address:** 209 S. Kingshighway, St. Charles, MO 63301-1695
- **Website:** http://www.lindenwood.edu
- **Private; Religious affiliation:** Presbyterian
- **Enrollment:** 6,153 full-time; 636 part-time

KEY STATS
✔ **U.S News College Ranking:** second tier, Regional Universities (Midwest)
✔ **ACT Score (25th/75th percentile):** 20-24
✔ **Tuition:** 2010-2011: $13,600

Selectivity: Selective	Room/board: $7,210
Acceptance rate: 57%	Average debt: N/A
Student/faculty ratio: 20/1	Proportion who borrowed: N/A

UNDERGRADUATE STUDENT BODY STATS

2009-2010 enrollment: 6,153 full-time; 636 part-time. Men: 44%; women: 56%. **Ethnic makeup:** African American: 10%; Asian American: 1%; Hispanic: 3%; White: 76%; International: 10%.

ADMISSIONS FACTS AND FIGURES

Phone: (636) 949-4949. **Email:** admissions@lindenwood.edu. **Website:** http://www.lindenwood.edu. **Application deadlines for fall 2011:** Regular decision: Rolling. Early decision: Not offered. Early action: Not offered. Admission can be deferred. **Application fee:** $30. **To apply online, go to:** http://www.lindenwood.edu/admissions/ug_ad.asp. **Admissions requirements/recommendations:** High school units required (recommended): English: (4); Mathematics: (3); Science: (3); Foreign language: (2); Social studies: (3); History: (3); Academic electives: (0); Total units: (19). Tests: The college uses SAT or ACT scores in admissions decisions. Either SAT or ACT required. For admission to the fall 2011 entering class, the school will accept: ACT with or without writing accepted. Campus visit: Recommended. Admissions interview: Recommended. Off-campus interview: May be arranged. **Factors that count in admissions decisions:** *Academic:* Secondary school record: Important. Class rank: Important. Letters of recommendation: Important. Standardized test scores: Very Important. Essay: Important. *Nonacademic:* Interview: Important. Extracurricular activities: Important. Talent/ability: Important. Character/personal qualities: Important. Alumni/ae relationship: Considered. Geographical residence: Not Considered. State residency: Not Considered. Religious affiliation/commitment: Not Considered. Minority status: Not Considered. Volunteer work: Considered. Work experience: Not Considered. **Admissions statistics for the fall 2009 entering class:** Total applicants: 3,261. Total accepted: 1,852. Freshmen enrolled: 1,105; 27% were from out of state. Overall acceptance rate: 57%. **Size of waiting list:** 0 applicants; enrolled from waiting list: 0. **Credentials of fall 2009 freshmen:** 8% ranked in the top 10 percent of their high school class; 26% were in the top 25 percent; 63% were in the top half. (Proportion submitting class standing: 88%.) **Average high school grade point average:** 3.0. **First-year students who submitted SAT scores:** 7%. Scores (25/75 percentile): Critical Reading: 450-570, Math: 480-590, Combined: 930-1160. **First-year students submitting ACT scores:** 70%. Scores (25/75 percentile): English: 19-24, Math: 18-24, Composite: 20-24.

ACADEMICS

Year founded: 1827. **Academic calendar:** 4-1-4. **Degrees offered:** bachelor's, post-bachelor's certificate, master's, post-master's certificate. **Most popular majors:** 30% business/commerce, 8% criminal justice/safety studies, 6% elementary education and teaching, 4% human resources management/personnel administration, 4% mass communication/media studies. **Major fields of study:** area, ethnic, cultural, and gender studies; biological and biomedical sciences; business, management, marketing, and related support services; communication, journalism, and related programs; computer and information sciences and support services; education; English language and literature/letters; foreign languages, literatures, and linguistics; health professions and related clinical sciences; history; legal professions and studies; liberal arts and sciences studies, and humanities; mathematics and statistics; multi/interdisciplinary studies; parks, recreation, leisure, and fitness studies; personal and culinary services; philosophy and religious studies; physical sciences; psychology; public administration and social service professions; security and protective services; social sciences; theology and religious vocations; visual and performing arts. **Areas of required coursework:** arts/fine arts, humanities, mathematics, English (including composition), philosophy, sciences (biological or physical), history, social science, other. **Pre-professional programs:** pre-law, pre-dentistry, pre-medicine, pre-veterinary science, pre-optometry, pre-pharmacy, other. **Special academic programs:** accelerated program, distance learning, double major, dual enrollment, English as a Second Language (ESL), external degree program, honors program, independent study, internships, student-designed major, study abroad, teacher certificate program. **Teacher certification offered in:** early childhood, special education, elementary, middle/junior high, secondary. **Cooperative education programs:** business, computer science, education, health professions, humanities, natural science, social/behavioral science, technologies. **Reserve Officers Training Corps (ROTC):** Army ROTC: Offered on campus. **Faculty and instruction (2009-2010):** Total instructional faculty: 210 full-time, 310 part-time (58% men; 42% women; 10% minorities). Full-time faculty with Ph.D. or other terminal degree: 70%. Student/faculty ratio: 20/1. Classes of fewer than 20 students: 64%; of 20 to 49 students: 36%; of 50 or more students: 0%. **Advanced Placement and International Baccalaureate credit:** AP tests may be used for: Credit only. Scores accepted: 3, 4, 5. International Baccalaureate exams may be used for: Credit only. **Freshmen returning for sophomore year:** 67%. **Graduation rates:** Four-year: 28%; five-year: 41%; six-year: 43%.

COSTS AND FINANCIAL AID

Financial aid office: (636) 949-4923. **Expenses (2010-2011):** Tuition and fees 2010-2011: $13,600; room/board: $7,210. Estimated books and supplies: $3,000; transportation: $3,400; personal expenses: $9,000. **Financial aid:** Priority filing date for institution's financial aid form: April 1. In 2009-2010, 71% of undergraduates applied for financial aid. Of those, 64% were determined to have financial need; 42% had their need fully met. Average financial aid package (proportion receiving): $5,855 (64%). Average amount of gift aid, such as scholarships or grants (proportion receiving): $3,662 (41%). Average amount of self-help aid, such as work study or loans (proportion receiving): $1,984 (60%). Average need-based loan (excluding PLUS or other private loans): $1,984. Among students who received need-based aid, the average percentage of need met: 91%. Among students who received aid based on merit, the average award (and the proportion receiving): $4,685 (15%). The average athletic scholarship (and the proportion receiving): $0 (0%).

CAMPUS LIFE AND EXTRACURRICULAR ACTIVITIES

Campus housing available (% using): women's dorms (30%), men's dorms (35%), sorority housing, fraternity housing, apartments for married students (1%), apartment for single students (32%), special housing for disabled students (1%), other housing options (1%). Students who live in college-owned, operated, or affiliated housing: 57%. **Student employment:** During the 2009-2010 academic year, 50% of undergraduates worked on campus. Average per-year earnings: $2,400. **Clubs and organizations:** Number of student organizations: 72. Activities include: campus ministries, choral groups, concert band, dance, drama/theater, international student organization, jazz band, literary magazine, marching band, music ensembles, musical theater, pep band, radio station, student government, student newspaper, student film society, symphony orchestra, television station. Number of fraternities: 1; sororities: 1. Proportion of men in fraternities: 1%; of women in sororities: 1%. Average proportion of students who stay on campus on weekends: 59%. **Sports program (2009-2010):** Member of NAIA. *Men's intercollegiate varsity sports:* baseball, basketball, cross country, football, golf, ice hockey, lacrosse, rifle, soccer, swimming, tennis, track and field (indoor), track and field (outdoor), volleyball, water polo, wrestling. *Women's intercollegiate varsity sports:* basketball, cross country, field hockey, golf, ice hockey, lacrosse, rifle, soccer, softball, swimming, sync swimming, tennis, track and field (indoor), track and field (outdoor), volleyball, water polo.

SERVICES AND FACILITIES

Basic services: nonremedial tutoring, placement service, health service, health insurance. **Remedial assistance:** reading, math, writing. **Counseling services:** career, military, personal, academic, psychological, religious. **For learning-disabled students:** School does not offer a structured program with separate admission and additional fees. Total undergraduates in learning-disabled program or receiving services: 74. Services include: remedial math, remedial English, diagnostic testing service, note-taking services, oral tests, readers, extended time for tests, tutors, priority registration, priority seating, typist/scribe. **Library:** Number of titles: 172,695; number of current serial subscriptions: 224. **Information technology resources:** Students are not required to lease or own a computer. Number of campus computers available to all students: 160. School has a wireless network. Approximate number of users that can be accommodated: 300. Proportion of college-owned housing units wired for high-speed internet access: 70%. **Campus safety:** Security services offered: 24-hour foot-and-vehicle patrols, late-night

transport/escort service, 24-hour emergency telephones, lighted pathways/sidewalks, controlled dormitory access (key, security card, etc).

TRANSFER AND INTERNATIONAL STUDENTS

Transfer students: May apply for admission for the following academic terms: Fall, Winter, Spring, Summer. Applicants need a minimum number of credits to apply. For fall 2009: Transfer applications received: 1,442. Transfer applicants offered admission: 874. Transfer applicants enrolled: 775. **International students:** Number of foreign undergraduates: 655 (10% of student body). Number of countries represented: 73. Minimum TOEFL score required: 500 (paper); 173 (computer). Average TOEFL score: 523 (paper).

Maryville University of St. Louis

- **Address:** 650 Maryville University Drive, St Louis, MO 63141-7299
- **Website:** http://www.maryville.edu
- **Private**
- **Enrollment:** 1,669 full-time; 1,265 part-time

....

KEY STATS

✔ **U.S News College Ranking:** 30, Regional Universities (Midwest)
✔ **ACT Score (25th/75th percentile):** 22-27
✔ **Tuition:** 2010-2011: $21,910

Selectivity: More selective	**Room/board:** $8,500
Acceptance rate: 66%	**Average debt:** $18,341
Student/faculty ratio: 12/1	**Proportion who borrowed:** 73%

UNDERGRADUATE STUDENT BODY STATS

2009-2010 enrollment: 1,669 full-time; 1,265 part-time. Men: 24%; women: 76%. **Ethnic makeup:** African American: 7%; Asian American: 2%; Hispanic: 2%; White: 88%; International: 1%.

ADMISSIONS FACTS AND FIGURES

Phone: (800) 627-9855. **Email:** admissions@maryville.edu. **Website:** http://www.maryville.edu. **Application deadlines for fall 2011:** Regular decision: August 15. Early decision: Not offered. Early action: Not offered. Admission can be deferred. **Application fee:** $30. **To apply online, go to:** http://www.maryville.edu/admissions/adm_apply.asp. **Admissions requirements/recommendations:** High school units required (recommended): English: 4; Mathematics: 3; Science: 2; Foreign language: (3); Social studies: 2; Academic electives: 8; Total units: 22. Tests: The college uses SAT or ACT scores in admissions decisions. Either SAT or ACT required. For admission to the fall 2011 entering class, the school will accept: ACT with or without writing accepted. Campus visit: Recommended. Admissions interview: Recommended. Off-campus interview: May be arranged. **Factors that count in admissions decisions:** *Academic:* Secondary school record: Important. Class rank: Considered. Letters of recommendation: Considered. Standardized test scores: Very Important. Essay: Important. *Nonacademic:* Interview: Considered. Extracurricular activities: Important. Talent/ability: Considered. Character/personal qualities: Considered. Alumni/ae relationship: Not Considered. Geographical residence: Not Considered. State residency: Not Considered. Religious affiliation/commitment: Not Considered. Minority status: Not Considered. Volunteer work: Not Considered. Work experience: Not Considered. **Other schools with the greatest overlap in applicants:** St. Louis University; Truman State University; University of Missouri; University of Missouri–St. Louis; Webster University. **Admissions statistics for the fall 2009 entering class:** Total applicants: 1,154. Total accepted: 764. Freshmen enrolled: 374; 20% were from out of state. Overall acceptance rate: 66%. **Credentials of fall 2009 freshmen:** 26% ranked in the top 10 percent of their high school class; 56% were in the top 25 percent; 79% were in the top half. (Proportion submitting class standing: 72%.) **Average high school grade point average:** 3.5. **First-year students who submitted SAT scores:** 5%. Scores (25/75 percentile): Critical Reading: 450-570, Math: 490-520, Combined: 940-1090. **First-year students submitting ACT scores:** 89%. Scores (25/75 percentile): English: 21-27, Math: 21-26, Composite: 22-27.

ACADEMICS

Year founded: 1872. **Academic calendar:** Semester. **Degrees offered:** certificate, bachelor's, post-bachelor's certificate, master's, post-master's certificate, doctorate. **Most popular majors:** 20% nursing/registered nurse training (R.N., A.S.N., B.S.N., M.S.N.), 10% business/commerce, 8%

accounting, 7% health professions and related clinical sciences, 5% health/medical preparatory programs. **Major fields of study:** biological and biomedical sciences; business, management, marketing, and related support services; communication, journalism, and related programs; computer and information sciences and support services; education; engineering; English language and literature/letters; health professions and related clinical sciences; history; legal professions and studies; liberal arts and sciences studies, and humanities; mathematics and statistics; multi/interdisciplinary studies; natural resources and conservation; physical sciences; psychology; social sciences; visual and performing arts. **Areas of required coursework:** arts/fine arts, humanities, mathematics, English (including composition), philosophy, sciences (biological or physical), history, social science, other. **Pre-professional programs:** pre-law, pre-dentistry, pre-medicine, pre-optometry. **Special academic programs:** accelerated program, cooperative (work-study plan) program, cross-registration, distance learning, double major, dual enrollment, honors program, independent study, internships, liberal arts/career combination, student-designed major, study abroad, teacher certificate program, weekend college, other. **Teacher certification offered in:** early childhood, elementary, middle/junior high, secondary. **Cooperative education programs:** business, humanities, natural science, social/behavioral science, technologies, other. **Reserve Officers Training Corps (ROTC):** Army ROTC: Offered at cooperating institution (Washington University in St. Louis). **Faculty and instruction (2009-2010):** Total instructional faculty: 111 full-time, 282 part-time (38% men; 62% women; 10% minorities). Full-time faculty with Ph.D. or other terminal degree: 86%. Student/faculty ratio: 12/1. Classes of fewer than 20 students: 67%; of 20 to 49 students: 33%; of 50 or more students: 0%. **Advanced Placement and International Baccalaureate credit:** AP tests may be used for: Credit only. Scores accepted: 3, 4, 5. International Baccalaureate exams may be used for: Credit only. **Freshmen returning for sophomore year:** 81%. **Graduation rates:** Four-year: 51%; five-year: 59%; six-year: 62%. **Graduate study:** 20% of students pursue further study immediately upon graduation; 20% within one year; 20% within five years. Fields in which graduates pursue further study: Master of Business Administration (MBA), 20%; law, 2%; medicine, 3%; education, 20%; arts and sciences, 20%.

COSTS AND FINANCIAL AID

Financial aid office: (314) 529-9360. **Expenses (2010-2011):** Tuition and fees 2010-2011: $21,910; room/board: $8,500. Estimated books and supplies: $1,600; transportation: $2,900; personal expenses: $2,520. **Financial aid:** Priority filing date for institution's financial aid form: March 1. In 2009-2010, 88% of undergraduates applied for financial aid. Of those, 78% were determined to have financial need; 12% had their need fully met. Average financial aid package (proportion receiving): $17,959 (78%). Average amount of gift aid, such as scholarships or grants (proportion receiving): $10,244 (75%). Average amount of self-help aid, such as work study or loans (proportion receiving): $4,653 (71%). Average need-based loan (excluding PLUS or other private loans): $4,021. Among students who received need-based aid, the average percentage of need met: 70%. Among students who received aid based on merit, the average award (and the proportion receiving): $6,609 (19%). The average athletic scholarship (and the proportion receiving): $11,797 (0%). Average amount of debt of borrowers graduating in 2009: $18,341. Proportion who borrowed: 73%.

CAMPUS LIFE AND EXTRACURRICULAR ACTIVITIES

Campus housing available (% using): coed dorms (60%), apartment for single students (40%). Students who live in college-owned, operated, or affiliated housing: 21%. **Student employment:** During the 2009-2010 academic year, 9% of undergraduates worked on campus. Average per-year earnings: $1,685. **Clubs and organizations:** Number of student organizations: 50. Activities include: campus ministries, choral groups, dance, drama/theater, literary magazine, music ensembles, pep band, student government, student newspaper, symphony orchestra. Number of fraternities: 0; sororities: 0. Average proportion of students who stay on campus on weekends: 70%. **Sports program (2009-2010):** Member of NCAA III. *Men's intercollegiate varsity sports:* baseball, basketball, cross country, golf, soccer, tennis, track and field (indoor), track and field (outdoor). *Women's intercollegiate varsity sports:* basketball, cross country, golf, soccer, softball, tennis, track and field (indoor), track and field (outdoor), volleyball.

SERVICES AND FACILITIES

Basic services: nonremedial tutoring, placement service, health service, health insurance. **Remedial assistance:** study skills, other. **Counseling services:** minority student, career, military, personal, veteran student, academic, older student, psychological, birth control, religious, other. **For learning-disabled students:** School does not offer a structured program with

separate admission and additional fees. Total undergraduates in learning-disabled program or receiving services: 64. Services include: tape recorders, untimed tests, note-taking services, oral tests, learning center, readers, extended time for tests, tutors, priority seating, texts on tape. **Library:** Number of titles: 158,930; number of current serial subscriptions: 42,582. **Information technology resources:** Students are not required to lease or own a computer. Number of campus computers available to all students: 514. School has a wireless network. Approximate number of users that can be accommodated: 2,000. Proportion of college-owned housing units wired for high-speed internet access: 100%. **Campus safety:** Security services offered: 24-hour foot-and-vehicle patrols, late-night transport/escort service, 24-hour emergency telephones, lighted pathways/sidewalks, controlled dormitory access (key, security card, etc).

TRANSFER AND INTERNATIONAL STUDENTS

Transfer students: May apply for admission for the following academic terms: Fall, Spring, Summer. Applicants do not need a minimum number of credits to apply. For fall 2009: Transfer applications received: 872. Transfer applicants offered admission: 396. Transfer applicants enrolled: 192. **International students:** Number of foreign undergraduates: 16 (1% of student body). Number of countries represented: 11. Minimum TOEFL score required: 550 (paper); 79 (computer).

Missouri Baptist University

- **Address:** 1 College Park Drive, St. Louis, MO 63141
- **Website:** http://www.mobap.edu
- **Private; Religious affiliation:** Southern Baptist
- **Enrollment:** N/A

KEY STATS

- ✔ **U.S News College Ranking:** second tier, Regional Universities (Midwest)
- ✔ **SAT or ACT Score (25th/75th percentile):** N/A
- ✔ **Tuition:** 2009-2010: $17,860

Selectivity: Selective	**Room/board:** $7,090
Acceptance rate: 67%	**Average debt:** N/A
Student/faculty ratio: N/A	**Proportion who borrowed:** N/A

Missouri Southern State University

- **Address:** 3950 E. Newman Road, Joplin, MO 64801-1595
- **Website:** http://www.mssu.edu
- **Public**
- **Enrollment:** 4,110 full-time; 1,529 part-time

KEY STATS

- ✔ **U.S News College Ranking:** 71, Regional Colleges (Midwest)
- ✔ **ACT Score (25th/75th percentile):** 18-23
- ✔ **Tuition:** 2010-2011: $5,116 in state, $9,406 out of state

Selectivity: Less selective	**Room/board:** $5,220
Acceptance rate: 95%	**Average debt:** $10,006
Student/faculty ratio: 19/1	**Proportion who borrowed:** 51%

UNDERGRADUATE STUDENT BODY STATS

2009-2010 enrollment: 4,110 full-time; 1,529 part-time. Men: 42%; women: 58%.

ADMISSIONS FACTS AND FIGURES

Phone: (417) 625-9378. **Email:** admissions@mssu.edu. **Website:** http://www.mssu.edu. **Application deadlines for fall 2011:** Regular decision: Rolling. Early decision: Not offered. Early action: Not offered. Admission can be deferred. **Application fee:** $15. **To apply online, go to:** http://www.mssu.edu/admissions/forms/online-app.shtml. **Admissions requirements/recommendations:** High school units required (recommended): English: 4; Mathematics: 3; Science: 2; Foreign language: (2); Academic electives: (3); Total units: 16. Tests: The college uses SAT or ACT scores in admissions decisions. Either SAT or ACT required. For admission to the fall 2011 entering class, the school will accept: ACT with or without writing accepted. Campus visit: Recommended. Admissions interview: Neither required nor recommended. Off-campus interview: Not available. **Factors that count in**

admissions decisions: *Academic:* Secondary school record: Very Important. Class rank: Very Important. Letters of recommendation: Considered. Standardized test scores: Very Important. Essay: Not Considered. *Nonacademic:* Interview: Not Considered. Extracurricular activities: Not Considered. Talent/ability: Not Considered. Character/personal qualities: Not Considered. Alumni/ae relationship: Not Considered. Geographical residence: Not Considered. State residency: Not Considered. Religious affiliation/commitment: Not Considered. Minority status: Not Considered. Volunteer work: Not Considered. Work experience: Not Considered. **Other schools with the greatest overlap in applicants:** Columbia College; Missouri State University; Missouri Western State University; Ozark Christian College; Pittsburg State University. **Admissions statistics for the fall 2009 entering class:** Total applicants: 1,568. Total accepted: 1,483. Freshmen enrolled: 858; 2% were from out of state. Overall acceptance rate: 95%. **Credentials of fall 2009 freshmen:** 11% ranked in the top 10 percent of their high school class; 22% were in the top 25 percent; 75% were in the top half. (Proportion submitting class standing: 99%.) **First-year students submitting ACT scores:** 89%. Scores (25/75 percentile): English: 17-24, Math: 17-24, Composite: 18-23.

ACADEMICS

Year founded: 1937. **Academic calendar:** Semester. **Degrees offered:** certificate, associate, bachelor's, master's. **Most popular majors:** 25% business, management, marketing, and related support services, 14% engineering technologies/technicians, 12% security and protective services, 10% health professions and related clinical sciences, 7% liberal arts and sciences studies, and humanities. **Major fields of study:** biological and biomedical sciences; business, management, marketing, and related support services; communication, journalism, and related programs; computer and information sciences and support services; education; English language and literature/letters; foreign languages, literatures, and linguistics; health professions and related clinical sciences; history; mathematics and statistics; parks, recreation, leisure, and fitness studies; physical sciences; psychology; social sciences; visual and performing arts. **Areas of required coursework:** arts/fine arts, humanities, computer literacy, mathematics, English (including composition), philosophy, foreign languages, sciences (biological or physical), history, social science. **Pre-professional programs:** pre-law, pre-dentistry, pre-medicine, pre-veterinary science, pre-optometry, pre-pharmacy, other. **Special academic programs:** accelerated program, cooperative (work-study plan) program, distance learning, double major, dual enrollment, English as a Second Language (ESL), exchange student program (domestic), honors program, independent study, internships, liberal arts/career combination, study abroad, teacher certificate program, weekend college. **Teacher certification offered in:** elementary, middle/junior high, secondary. **Cooperative education programs:** education, health professions, technologies. **Faculty and instruction (2009-2010):** Total instructional faculty: 208 full-time, 87 part-time (57% men; 43% women; 7% minorities). Full-time faculty with Ph.D. or other terminal degree: 58%. Student/faculty ratio: 19/1. Classes of fewer than 20 students: 46%; of 20 to 49 students: 54%; of 50 or more students: 0%. **Advanced Placement and International Baccalaureate credit:** AP tests may be used for: Credit only. Scores accepted: 3, 4, 5. International Baccalaureate exams may be used for: Placement only. **Freshmen returning for sophomore year:** 63%. **Graduation rates:** Six-year: 34%. **Graduate study:** 11% of students pursue further study immediately upon graduation.

COSTS AND FINANCIAL AID

Financial aid office: (417) 625-9325. **Expenses (2010-2011):** Tuition and fees 2010-2011: $5,116 in state, $9,406 out of state; room/board: $5,220. Estimated books and supplies: $300; transportation: $1,800; personal expenses: $1,950. **Financial aid:** Priority filing date for institution's financial aid form: May 1. In 2009-2010, 99% of undergraduates applied for financial aid. Of those, 77% were determined to have financial need; 17% had their need fully met. Average financial aid package (proportion receiving): $14,602 (74%). Average amount of gift aid, such as scholarships or grants (proportion receiving): $5,953 (58%). Average amount of self-help aid, such as work study or loans (proportion receiving): $2,775 (53%). Average need-based loan (excluding PLUS or other private loans): $4,283. Among students who received need-based aid, the average percentage of need met: 55%. Among students who received aid based on merit, the average award (and the proportion receiving): $4,122 (9%). The average athletic scholarship (and the proportion receiving): $6,529 (5%). Average amount of debt of borrowers graduating in 2009: $10,006. Proportion who borrowed: 51%.

CAMPUS LIFE AND EXTRACURRICULAR ACTIVITIES

Campus housing available (% using): coed dorms (56%), women's dorms (14%), men's dorms (26%), apartment for single students (4%). Students who live in college-owned, operated, or affiliated housing: 30%. **Student employment:** During the 2009-2010 academic year, 6% of undergraduates worked on campus. Average per-year earnings: $4,000. **Clubs and organizations:** Number of student organizations: 81. Activities include: campus ministries, choral groups, concert band, dance, drama/theater, international student organization, jazz band, literary magazine, marching band, model UN, music ensembles, musical theater, pep band, radio station, student government, student newspaper, student film society, symphony orchestra, television station. Number of fraternities: 2; sororities: 2. Average proportion of students who stay on campus on weekends: 20%. **Sports program (2009-2010):** Member of NCAA II. **Men's intercollegiate varsity sports:** baseball, basketball, cross country, football, golf, soccer, track and field (indoor), track and field (outdoor). **Women's intercollegiate varsity sports:** basketball, cross country, soccer, tennis, track and field (indoor), track and field (outdoor), volleyball.

SERVICES AND FACILITIES

Basic services: nonremedial tutoring, placement service, day care, health service, health insurance. **Remedial assistance:** reading, math, writing, study skills. **Counseling services:** career, personal, veteran student, academic. **For learning-disabled students:** School does not offer a structured program with separate admission and additional fees. Services include: remedial math, remedial English, tape recorders, note-taking services, oral tests, learning center, readers, extended time for tests, tutors, priority registration, priority seating, texts on tape, other testing accommodations. **Library:** Number of titles: 274,672; number of current serial subscriptions: 480. **Information technology resources:** Students are not required to lease or own a computer. Number of campus computers available to all students: 560. School has a wireless network. Approximate number of users that can be accommodated: 1,000. Proportion of college-owned housing units wired for high-speed internet access: 100%. **Campus safety:** Security services offered: 24-hour foot-and-vehicle patrols, late-night transport/escort service, 24-hour emergency telephones, controlled dormitory access (key, security card, etc).

TRANSFER AND INTERNATIONAL STUDENTS

Transfer students: May apply for admission for the following academic terms: Fall, Spring, Summer. Applicants do not need a minimum number of credits to apply. For fall 2009: Transfer applications received: 1,100. Transfer applicants offered admission: 1,064. Transfer applicants enrolled: 589. **International students:** Number of countries represented: 34. Minimum TOEFL score required: 535 (paper); 200 (computer).

Missouri State University

- **Address:** 901 S. National Avenue, Springfield, MO 65897
- **Website:** http://www.missouristate.edu
- **Public**
- **Enrollment:** 13,319 full-time; 3,705 part-time

KEY STATS

✔ **U.S News College Ranking:** 52, Regional Universities (Midwest)
✔ **ACT Score (25th/75th percentile):** 21-27
✔ **Tuition:** 2010-2011: $6,276 in state, $11,856 out of state

Selectivity: Selective	**Room/board:** $6,394
Acceptance rate: 83%	**Average debt:** N/A
Student/faculty ratio: 21/1	**Proportion who borrowed:** N/A

UNDERGRADUATE STUDENT BODY STATS

2009-2010 enrollment: 13,319 full-time; 3,705 part-time. Men: 44%; women: 56%. **Ethnic makeup:** African American: 4%; American-Indian: 1%; Asian American: 2%; Hispanic: 2%; White: 88%; International: 3%.

ADMISSIONS FACTS AND FIGURES

Phone: (800) 492-7900. **Email:** info@missouristate.edu. **Website:** http://www.missouristate.edu. **Application deadlines for fall 2011:** Regular decision: July 20. Early decision: Not offered. Early action: Not offered. Admission can be deferred. **Application fee:** $35. **To apply online, go to:** http://www.missouristate.edu/apply.asp. **Admissions requirements/recommendations:** High school units required (recommended): English: 4; Mathematics: 3; Science: 3; Foreign language: (2); Social studies: 2; History: 1; Academic electives: 3;

Total units: 24. Tests: The college uses SAT or ACT scores in admissions decisions. Either SAT or ACT required. For admission to the fall 2011 entering class, the school will accept: ACT with or without writing accepted. Campus visit: Recommended. Admissions interview: Neither required nor recommended. **Factors that count in admissions decisions:** *Academic:* Secondary school record: Considered. Class rank: Very Important. Letters of recommendation: Considered. Standardized test scores: Very Important. Essay: Considered. *Nonacademic:* Interview: Considered. Extracurricular activities: Considered. Talent/ability: Considered. Character/personal qualities: Considered. Alumni/ae relationship: Not Considered. Geographical residence: Not Considered. State residency: Not Considered. Religious affiliation/commitment: Not Considered. Minority status: Not Considered. Volunteer work: Considered. Work experience: Considered. **Other schools with the greatest overlap in applicants:** Drury University; Southeast Missouri State University; Truman State University; University of Central Missouri; University of Missouri. **Admissions statistics for the fall 2009 entering class:** Total applicants: 7,079. Total accepted: 5,875. Freshmen enrolled: 2,655; 11% were from out of state. Overall acceptance rate: 83%. **Credentials of fall 2009 freshmen:** 23% ranked in the top 10 percent of their high school class; 51% were in the top 25 percent; 81% were in the top half. (Proportion submitting class standing: 87%.) **Average high school grade point average:** 3.5. **First-year students submitting ACT scores:** 95%. Scores (25/75 percentile): English: 20-26, Math: 21-28, Composite: 21-27.

ACADEMICS

Year founded: 1906. **Academic calendar:** Semester. **Degrees offered:** bachelor's, post-bachelor's certificate, master's, post-master's certificate. **Most popular majors:** 9% finance and financial management services, 8% marketing, 7% business administration, management, and operations, 7% teacher education and professional development, 5% psychology. **Major fields of study:** agriculture, agriculture operations, and related sciences; architecture and related services; biological and biomedical sciences; business, management, marketing, and related support services; communication, journalism, and related programs; computer and information sciences and support services; education; engineering; engineering technologies/technicians; English language and literature/letters; family and consumer sciences/human sciences; foreign languages, literatures, and linguistics; health professions and related clinical sciences; history; liberal arts and sciences studies, and humanities; mathematics and statistics; multi/interdisciplinary studies; natural resources and conservation; parks, recreation, leisure, and fitness studies; philosophy and religious studies; physical sciences; psychology; public administration and social service professions; science technologies/technicians; security and protective services; social sciences; visual and performing arts. **Areas of required coursework:** arts/fine arts, humanities, computer literacy, mathematics, English (including composition), sciences (biological or physical), history, social science. **Preprofessional programs:** pre-law, pre-dentistry, pre-medicine, pre-veterinary science, pre-optometry, pre-pharmacy. **Special academic programs:** accelerated program, cooperative (work-study plan) program, distance learning, double major, dual enrollment, English as a Second Language (ESL), exchange student program (domestic), honors program, independent study, internships, liberal arts/career combination, student-designed major, study abroad, teacher certificate program. **Teacher certification offered in:** early childhood, special education, elementary, middle/junior high, secondary. **Reserve Officers Training Corps (ROTC):** Army ROTC: Offered on campus. **Faculty and instruction (2009-2010):** Total instructional faculty: 721 full-time, 306 part-time (52% men; 48% women; 7% minorities). Full-time faculty with Ph.D. or other terminal degree: 78%. Student/faculty ratio: 21/1. Classes of fewer than 20 students: 28%; of 20 to 49 students: 60%; of 50 or more students: 12%. **Advanced Placement and International Baccalaureate credit:** AP tests may be used for: Placement only. Scores accepted: 3, 4, 5. International Baccalaureate exams may be used for: Credit only. **Freshmen returning for sophomore year:** 74%. **Graduation rates:** Four-year: 28%; five-year: 49%; six-year: 53%. **Graduate study:** 23% of students pursue further study immediately upon graduation; 4% within one year. Fields in which graduates pursue further study: Master of Business Administration (MBA), 55%; law, 7%; medicine, 11%; dentistry, 1%; engineering, 3%; theology (or the seminary), 3%; education, 14%; arts and sciences, 5%; veterinary medicine, 1%.

COSTS AND FINANCIAL AID

Financial aid office: (417) 836-5262. **Expenses (2010-2011):** Tuition and fees 2010-2011: $6,276 in state, $11,856 out of state; room/board: $6,394. Estimated books and supplies: $900. **Financial aid:** Priority filing date for institution's financial aid form: May 31. In 2009-2010, 75% of undergraduates applied for financial aid. Of those, 57% were determined to have financial need; 17% had their need fully met. Average financial aid package (proportion receiving): $8,018 (56%). Average amount of gift aid, such as scholarships or grants (proportion receiving): $5,132 (45%). Average amount of self-help aid, such as work study or loans (proportion receiving): $4,072 (45%). Average need-based loan (excluding PLUS or other private loans): $3,997. Among students who received need-based aid, the average percentage of need met: 67%. Among students who received aid based on merit, the average award (and the proportion receiving): $4,266 (11%). The average athletic scholarship (and the proportion receiving): N/A (2%).

CAMPUS LIFE AND EXTRACURRICULAR ACTIVITIES

Campus housing available: coed dorms, sorority housing, fraternity housing, apartments for married students, apartment for single students, special housing for disabled students, special housing for international students. Students who live in college-owned, operated, or affiliated housing: 26%. **Student employment:** During the 2009-2010 academic year, 16% of undergraduates worked on campus. Average per-year earnings: $2,300. **Clubs and organizations:** Number of student organizations: 300. Activities include: campus ministries, choral groups, concert band, dance, drama/theater, international student organization, jazz band, literary magazine, marching band, model UN, music ensembles, musical theater, opera, pep band, radio station, student government, student newspaper, student film society, symphony orchestra, television station. Number of fraternities: 14; sororities: 10. Proportion of men in fraternities: 11%; of women in sororities: 13%. Average proportion of students who stay on campus on weekends: 50%. **Sports program (2009-2010):** Member of NCAA I. *Men's intercollegiate varsity sports:* baseball, basketball, cross country, football, golf, soccer, swimming, track and field (outdoor). *Women's intercollegiate varsity sports:* basketball, cross country, field hockey, golf, soccer, softball, swimming, track and field (outdoor), volleyball.

SERVICES AND FACILITIES

Basic services: placement service, health service, health insurance. **Counseling services:** minority student, career, personal, veteran student, academic, older student, psychological, birth control. **For learning-disabled students:** School does not offer a structured program with separate admission and additional fees. Services include: diagnostic testing service, untimed tests, note-taking services, oral tests, learning center, readers, extended time for tests, other. **Information technology resources:** Students are not required to lease or own a computer. School has a wireless network. Proportion of college-owned housing units wired for high-speed internet access: 100%. **Campus safety:** Security services offered: 24-hour foot-and-vehicle patrols, late-night transport/escort service, 24-hour emergency telephones, lighted pathways/sidewalks, controlled dormitory access (key, security card, etc).

TRANSFER AND INTERNATIONAL STUDENTS

Transfer students: May apply for admission for the following academic terms: Fall, Spring, Summer. Applicants need a minimum number of credits to apply. For fall 2009: Transfer applications received: 2,010. Transfer applicants offered admission: 1,818. Transfer applicants enrolled: 1,431. **International students:** Number of foreign undergraduates: 471 (3% of student body). Minimum TOEFL score required: 500 (paper); 173 (computer).

Missouri Univ. of Science & Technology

- **Address:** 106 Parker Hall, 300 W. 13th Street, Rolla, MO 65409-0910
- **Website:** http://www.mst.edu
- **Public**
- **Enrollment:** 4,885 full-time; 321 part-time

KEY STATS

✔ **U.S News College Ranking:** 129, National Universities
✔ **ACT Score (25th/75th percentile):** 25-31
✔ **Tuition:** 2010-2011: $8,498 in state, $19,589 out of state
  Selectivity: More selective   **Room/board:** $7,595
  Acceptance rate: 93%   **Average debt:** $24,235
  Student/faculty ratio: 16/1   **Proportion who borrowed:** 83%

UNDERGRADUATE STUDENT BODY STATS

2009-2010 enrollment: 4,885 full-time; 321 part-time. Men: 78%; women: 22%. **Ethnic makeup:** African American: 5%; American-Indian: 1%; Asian American: 2%; Hispanic: 2%; White: 86%; International: 3%.

ADMISSIONS FACTS AND FIGURES

Phone: (573) 341-4165. **Email:** admissions@mst.edu. **Website:** http://www.mst.edu. **Application deadlines for fall 2011:** Regular decision: July 1. Early decision: Not offered. Early action: Not offered. Admission can be deferred. **Application fee:** $45. **To apply online, go to:** http://futurestudents.mst.edu/index.html. **Admissions requirements/recommendations:** High school units required (recommended): English: 4; Mathematics: 4; Science: 3; Foreign language: 2; Social studies: 3; Total units: 17. Tests: The college uses SAT or ACT scores in admissions decisions. Either SAT or ACT required. For admission to the fall 2011 entering class, the school will accept: ACT with or without writing accepted. Campus visit: Recommended. Admissions interview: Neither required nor recommended. Off-campus interview: Not available. **Factors that count in admissions decisions:** *Academic:* Secondary school record: Very Important. Class rank: Very Important. Letters of recommendation: Important. Standardized test scores: Very Important. Essay: Considered. *Nonacademic:* Interview: Considered. Extracurricular activities: Considered. Talent/ability: Considered. Character/personal qualities: Considered. Alumni/ae relationship: Not Considered. Geographical residence: Not Considered. State residency: Not Considered. Religious affiliation/commitment: Not Considered. Minority status: Not Considered. Volunteer work: Considered. Work experience: Considered. **Other schools with the greatest overlap in applicants:** Massachusetts Institute of Technology; Purdue University–West Lafayette; Truman State University; University of Missouri; Washington University in St. Louis. **Admissions statistics for the fall 2009 entering class:** Total applicants: 2,620. Total accepted: 2,430. Freshmen enrolled: 1,108; 19% were from out of state. Overall acceptance rate: 93%. **Credentials of fall 2009 freshmen:** 43% ranked in the top 10 percent of their high school class; 71% were in the top 25 percent; 94% were in the top half. (Proportion submitting class standing: 83%.) **Average high school grade point average:** 3.6. **First-year students who submitted SAT scores:** 6%. Scores (25/75 percentile): Critical Reading: 550-670, Math: 610-700, Combined: 1160-1370. **First-year students submitting ACT scores:** 96%. Scores (25/75 percentile): English: 24-30, Math: 25-31, Composite: 25-31.

ACADEMICS

Year founded: 1870. **Academic calendar:** Semester. **Degrees offered:** certificate, bachelor's, post-bachelor's certificate, master's, doctorate. **Most popular majors:** 75% engineering, 6% computer and information sciences and support services, 4% biological and biomedical sciences, 3% business, management, marketing, and related support services, 3% physical sciences. **Major fields of study:** agriculture, agriculture operations, and related sciences; biological and biomedical sciences; business, management, marketing, and related support services; computer and information sciences and support services; education; engineering; English language and literature/letters; health professions and related clinical sciences; history; legal professions and studies; mathematics and statistics; philosophy and religious studies; physical sciences; psychology; social sciences. **Areas of required coursework:** humanities, computer literacy, mathematics, English (including composition), sciences (biological or physical), history, social science. **Pre-professional programs:** pre-law, pre-medicine. **Special academic programs (% participation):** cooperative (work-study plan) program (25%), distance learning (27%), double major (5%), dual enrollment (3%), honors program (3%), independent study (50%), internships (5%), liberal arts/career combination, study abroad (1%), teacher certificate program (2%). **Teacher certification offered in:** elementary, middle/junior high, secondary. **Cooperative education programs:** business, computer science, engineering, humanities, natural science, social/behavioral science. **Reserve Officers Training Corps (ROTC):** Army ROTC: Offered on campus; Air Force ROTC: Offered on campus. **Faculty and instruction (2009-2010):** Total instructional faculty: 360 full-time, 96 part-time (79% men; 21% women; 27% minorities). Full-time faculty with Ph.D. or other terminal degree: 89%. Student/faculty ratio: 16/1. Classes of fewer than 20 students: 33%; of 20 to 49 students: 52%; of 50 or more students: 16%. **Advanced Placement and International Baccalaureate credit:** AP tests may be used for: Credit only. Scores accepted: 3, 4, 5. International Baccalaureate exams may be used for: Credit only. **Freshmen returning for sophomore year:** 87%. **Graduation rates:** Four-year: 25%; five-year: 55%; six-year: 63%. **Graduate study:** 20% of students pursue further study immediately upon graduation.

COSTS AND FINANCIAL AID

Financial aid office: (573) 341-4282. **Expenses (2010-2011):** Tuition and fees 2010-2011: $8,498 in state, $19,589 out of state; room/board: $7,595. Estimated books and supplies: $960 personal expenses: $3,366. **Financial aid:** Priority filing date for institution's financial aid form: March 1. In 2009-2010, 92% of undergraduates applied for financial aid. Of those, 76% were determined to have financial need; 60% had their need fully met. Average financial aid package (proportion receiving): $13,362 (76%). Average amount of gift aid, such as scholarships or grants (proportion receiving): $4,370 (42%). Average amount of self-help aid, such as work study or loans (proportion receiving): $5,076 (45%). Average need-based loan (excluding PLUS or other private loans): $5,640. Among students who received need-based aid, the average percentage of need met: 44%. Among students who received aid based on merit, the average award (and the proportion receiving): $4,889 (12%). The average athletic scholarship (and the proportion receiving): $5,462 (1%). Average amount of debt of borrowers graduating in 2009: $24,235. Proportion who borrowed: 83%.

CAMPUS LIFE AND EXTRACURRICULAR ACTIVITIES

Campus housing available (% using): coed dorms (61%), sorority housing (5%), fraternity housing (30%), apartments for married students, apartment for single students, special housing for disabled students (1%), cooperative housing (3%), other housing options. Students who live in college-owned, operated, or affiliated housing: 51%. **Student employment:** During the 2009-2010 academic year, 25% of undergraduates worked on campus. Average per-year earnings: $6,047. **Clubs and organizations:** Number of student organizations: 202. Activities include: campus ministries, choral groups, concert band, dance, drama/theater, international student organization, jazz band, literary magazine, marching band, music ensembles, musical theater, pep band, radio station, student government, student newspaper, symphony orchestra, yearbook. Number of fraternities: 21; sororities: 4. Proportion of men in fraternities: 22%; of women in sororities: 20%. Average proportion of students who stay on campus on weekends: 50%. **Sports program (2009-2010):** Member of NCAA II. *Men's intercollegiate varsity sports:* baseball, basketball, cross country, football, soccer, swimming, track and field (indoor), track and field (outdoor). *Women's intercollegiate varsity sports:* basketball, cross country, soccer, softball, track and field (indoor), track and field (outdoor), volleyball.

SERVICES AND FACILITIES

Basic services: nonremedial tutoring, placement service, health service, health insurance. **Counseling services:** minority student, career, personal, veteran student, academic, psychological, birth control, religious. **For learning-disabled students:** School does not offer a structured program with separate admission and additional fees. Services include: reading machines, tape recorders, note-taking services, oral tests, learning center, readers, extended time for tests, tutors, early syllabus, priority registration, priority seating, proofreading services, substitution of courses, texts on tape, typist/scribe, exams on tape or computer, other testing accommodations, other. **Library:** Number of titles: 477,201; number of current serial subscriptions: 2,593. **Information technology resources:** Students are not required to lease or own a computer. Number of campus computers available to all students: 980. School has a wireless network. Approximate number of users that can be accommodated: 6,000. Proportion of college-owned housing units wired for high-speed internet access: 100%. **Campus safety:** Security services offered: 24-hour foot-and-vehicle patrols, late-night transport/escort service, 24-hour emergency telephones, lighted pathways/sidewalks, student patrols, controlled dormitory access (key, security card, etc).

TRANSFER AND INTERNATIONAL STUDENTS

Transfer students: May apply for admission for the following academic terms: Fall, Spring, Summer. Applicants need a minimum number of credits to apply. For fall 2009: Transfer applications received: 568. Transfer applicants offered admission: 483. Transfer applicants enrolled: 313. **International students:** Number of foreign undergraduates: 175 (3% of student body). Number of countries represented: 39. Minimum TOEFL score required: 550 (paper); 213 (computer). Average TOEFL score: 573 (paper).

Missouri Valley College

- **Address:** 500 E. College, Marshall, MO 65340
- **Website:** http://www.moval.edu
- **Private; Religious affiliation:** Presbyterian
- **Enrollment:** N/A

KEY STATS
✔ **U.S News College Ranking:** second tier, Regional Colleges (Midwest)
✔ **SAT or ACT Score (25th/75th percentile):** N/A
✔ **Tuition:** 2010-2011: $17,170

Selectivity: Less selective	Room/board: $6,450
Acceptance rate: N/A	Average debt: $23,200
Student/faculty ratio: N/A	Proportion who borrowed: 82%

Missouri Western State University

- **Address:** 4525 Downs Drive, St. Joseph, MO 64507
- **Website:** http://www.missouriwestern.edu
- **Public**
- **Enrollment:** 4,072 full-time; 1,562 part-time

KEY STATS
✔ **U.S News College Ranking:** 66, Regional Colleges (Midwest)
✔ **ACT Score (25th/75th percentile):** 17-22
✔ **Tuition:** 2010-2011: $5,560 in state, $9,688 out of state

Selectivity: Less selective	Room/board: $6,532
Acceptance rate: 100%	Average debt: $17,989
Student/faculty ratio: 19/1	Proportion who borrowed: 67%

UNDERGRADUATE STUDENT BODY STATS
2009-2010 enrollment: 4,072 full-time; 1,562 part-time. Men: 42%; women: 58%. **Ethnic makeup:** African American: 11%; American-Indian: 1%; Asian American: 1%; Hispanic: 2%; White: 85%.

ADMISSIONS FACTS AND FIGURES
Phone: (816) 271-4266. **Email:** admission@missouriwestern.edu. **Website:** http://www.missouriwestern.edu. **Application deadlines for fall 2011:** Regular decision: May 1. Early decision: Not offered. Early action: Not offered. Admission cannot be deferred. **Application fee:** $15. **Admissions requirements/recommendations:** High school units required (recommended): English: 4; Mathematics: 3; Science: 3; Foreign language: (2); Social studies: 3; Academic electives: 3; Total units: 17. Tests: The college uses SAT or ACT scores in admissions decisions. Neither SAT nor ACT required. For admission to the fall 2011 entering class, the school will accept: ACT with or without writing accepted. Campus visit: Recommended. Admissions interview: Recommended. Off-campus interview: May be arranged. **Factors that count in admissions decisions:** *Academic:* Secondary school record: Not Considered. Class rank: Not Considered. Letters of recommendation: Not Considered. Standardized test scores: Not Considered. Essay: Not Considered. *Nonacademic:* Interview: Not Considered. Extracurricular activities: Not Considered. Talent/ability: Not Considered. Character/personal qualities: Not Considered. Alumni/ae relationship: Not Considered. Geographical residence: Not Considered. State residency: Not Considered. Religious affiliation/commitment: Not Considered. Minority status: Not Considered. Volunteer work: Not Considered. Work experience: Not Considered. **Other schools with the greatest overlap in applicants:** Missouri Southern State University; Missouri State University; Northwest Missouri State University; University of Central Missouri; University of Missouri. **Admissions statistics for the fall 2009 entering class:** Total applicants: 2,606. Total accepted: 2,606. Freshmen enrolled: 1,192; 10% were from out of state. Overall acceptance rate: 100%. **Credentials of fall 2009 freshmen:** 8% ranked in the top 10 percent of their high school class; 26% were in the top 25 percent; 59% were in the top half. (Proportion submitting class standing: 83%.) **First-year students submitting ACT scores:** 87%. Scores (25/75 percentile): English: 16-23, Math: 16-22, Composite: 17-22.

ACADEMICS
Year founded: 1969. **Academic calendar:** Semester. **Degrees offered:** certificate, associate, bachelor's, post-bachelor's certificate, master's. **Most popular majors:** 14% nursing/registered nurse training (R.N., A.S.N., B.S.N.,

M.S.N.), 9% elementary education and teaching, 8% criminal justice/safety studies, 6% business administration and management, 6% health and physical education. **Major fields of study:** biological and biomedical sciences; business, management, marketing, and related support services; computer and information sciences and support services; education; engineering technologies/technicians; English language and literature/letters; foreign languages, literatures, and linguistics; health professions and related clinical sciences; history; mathematics and statistics; multi/interdisciplinary studies; parks, recreation, leisure, and fitness studies; physical sciences; psychology; public administration and social service professions; security and protective services; social sciences; visual and performing arts. **Areas of required coursework:** arts/fine arts, humanities, computer literacy, mathematics, English (including composition), sciences (biological or physical), history, social science, other. **Pre-professional programs:** pre-law, pre-dentistry, pre-medicine, pre-veterinary science, pre-pharmacy. **Special academic programs:** distance learning, double major, dual enrollment, English as a Second Language (ESL), honors program, independent study, internships, liberal arts/career combination, study abroad, teacher certificate program. **Teacher certification offered in:** early childhood, special education, elementary, middle/junior high, secondary. **Cooperative education programs:** education, health professions. **Reserve Officers Training Corps (ROTC):** Army ROTC: Offered on campus. **Faculty and instruction (2009-2010):** Total instructional faculty: 192 full-time, 156 part-time (53% men; 47% women; 5% minorities). Full-time faculty with Ph.D. or other terminal degree: 84%. Student/faculty ratio: 19/1. Classes of fewer than 20 students: 44%; of 20 to 49 students: 50%; of 50 or more students: 6%. **Advanced Placement and International Baccalaureate credit:** AP tests may be used for: Credit only. Scores accepted: 3, 4, 5. International Baccalaureate exams may be used for: Credit only. **Freshmen returning for sophomore year:** 63%. **Graduation rates:** Four-year: 12%; five-year: 23%; six-year: 28%. **Graduate study:** 14% of students pursue further study immediately upon graduation; 66% within one year. Fields in which graduates pursue further study: Master of Business Administration (MBA), 38%; law, 1%; medicine, 1%; dentistry, 1%; engineering, 1%; education, 20%; arts and sciences, 38%.

COSTS AND FINANCIAL AID
Financial aid office: (816) 271-4361. **Expenses (2010-2011):** Tuition and fees 2010-2011: $5,560 in state, $9,688 out of state; room/board: $6,532. Estimated books and supplies: $800; transportation: $1,120; personal expenses: $3,000. **Financial aid:** Priority filing date for institution's financial aid form: March 1. In 2009-2010, 92% of undergraduates applied for financial aid. Of those, 73% were determined to have financial need; 8% had their need fully met. Average financial aid package (proportion receiving): $7,432 (72%). Average amount of gift aid, such as scholarships or grants (proportion receiving): $5,501 (66%). Average amount of self-help aid, such as work study or loans (proportion receiving): $3,646 (51%). Average need-based loan (excluding PLUS or other private loans): $3,581. Among students who received need-based aid, the average percentage of need met: 62%. Among students who received aid based on merit, the average award (and the proportion receiving): $4,162 (8%). The average athletic scholarship (and the proportion receiving): $5,011 (6%). Average amount of debt of borrowers graduating in 2009: $17,989. Proportion who borrowed: 67%.

CAMPUS LIFE AND EXTRACURRICULAR ACTIVITIES
Campus housing available (% using): coed dorms (84%), special housing for disabled students (1%). Students who live in college-owned, operated, or affiliated housing: 20%. **Student employment:** During the 2009-2010 academic year, 9% of undergraduates worked on campus. Average per-year earnings: $3,480. **Clubs and organizations:** Number of student organizations: 60. Activities include: campus ministries, choral groups, concert band, dance, drama/theater, international student organization, jazz band, marching band, music ensembles, musical theater, pep band, student government, student newspaper, student film society, symphony orchestra, yearbook. Number of fraternities: 4; sororities: 5. Proportion of men in fraternities: 5%; of women in sororities: 5%. Average proportion of students who stay on campus on weekends: 50%. **Sports program (2009-2010):** Member of NCAA II. *Men's intercollegiate varsity sports:* baseball, basketball, football, golf. *Women's intercollegiate varsity sports:* basketball, golf, soccer, softball, tennis, volleyball.

SERVICES AND FACILITIES
Basic services: nonremedial tutoring, placement service, day care, health service, health insurance. **Remedial assistance:** reading, math, writing, study skills. **Counseling services:** minority student, career, personal, veteran student, academic, older student, psychological. **For learning-disabled students:** Services include: remedial math, remedial English, reading machines,

remedial reading, tutors. **Library:** Number of titles: 220,695; number of current serial subscriptions: 1,558. **Information technology resources:** Students are not required to lease or own a computer. Number of campus computers available to all students: 400. School has a wireless network. Approximate number of users that can be accommodated: 2,500. Proportion of college-owned housing units wired for high-speed internet access: 100%. **Campus safety:** Security services offered: 24-hour foot-and-vehicle patrols, late-night transport/escort service, 24-hour emergency telephones, lighted pathways/sidewalks, controlled dormitory access (key, security card, etc).

TRANSFER AND INTERNATIONAL STUDENTS

Transfer students: May apply for admission for the following academic terms: Fall, Spring, Summer. Applicants need a minimum number of credits to apply. For fall 2009: Transfer applications received: 581. Transfer applicants offered admission: 576. Transfer applicants enrolled: 310. **International students:** Number of foreign undergraduates: 23. Number of countries represented: 5. Minimum TOEFL score required: 500 (paper); 61 (computer).

Northwest Missouri State University

- **Address:** 800 University Drive, Maryville, MO 64468
- **Website:** http://www.nwmissouri.edu
- **Public**
- **Enrollment:** N/A

KEY STATS

- ✔ **U.S News College Ranking:** 104, Regional Universities (Midwest)
- ✔ **SAT or ACT Score (25th/75th percentile):** N/A
- ✔ **Tuition:** 2009-2010: $6,911 in state, $8,543 out of state
  - **Selectivity:** Selective
  - **Acceptance rate:** N/A
  - **Student/faculty ratio:** N/A
  - **Room/board:** $7,408
  - **Average debt:** N/A
  - **Proportion who borrowed:** N/A

Park University

- **Address:** 8700 N.W. River Park Drive, Parkville, MO 64152
- **Website:** http://www.park.edu
- **Private**
- **Enrollment:** 1,321 full-time; 10,740 part-time

KEY STATS

- ✔ **U.S News College Ranking:** second tier, Regional Universities (Midwest)
- ✔ **ACT Score (25th/75th percentile):** 18-25
- ✔ **Tuition:** 2010-2011: $8,898
  - **Selectivity:** Selective
  - **Acceptance rate:** 70%
  - **Student/faculty ratio:** N/A
  - **Room/board:** $8,800
  - **Average debt:** N/A
  - **Proportion who borrowed:** N/A

UNDERGRADUATE STUDENT BODY STATS

2009-2010 enrollment: 1,321 full-time; 10,740 part-time. Men: 48%; women: 52%. **Ethnic makeup:** African American: 22%; American-Indian: 1%; Asian American: 2%; Hispanic: 15%; White: 56%; International: 3%.

ADMISSIONS FACTS AND FIGURES

Phone: (800) 745-7275. **Email:** admissions@mail.park.edu. **Website:** http://www.park.edu. **Application deadlines for fall 2011:** Regular decision: August 1. Early decision: Not offered. Early action: Not offered. **Application fee:** $25. **To apply online, go to:** https://www.park.edu/apply/apply.asp. **Admissions requirements/recommendations:** High school units required (recommended): English: (3); Mathematics: (2); Science: (2); Foreign language: (2); Social studies: (3); History: (1); Academic electives: (6); Total units: (19). Tests: The college uses SAT or ACT scores in admissions decisions. ACT required. **Factors that count in admissions decisions:** *Academic:* Secondary school record: Very Important. Class rank: Very Important. Letters of recommendation: Considered. Standardized test scores: Very Important. Essay: Considered. *Nonacademic:* Interview: Not Considered. Extracurricular activities: Not Considered. Talent/ability: Not Considered. Character/personal qualities: Not Considered. Alumni/ae relationship: Not Considered. Geographical residence: Not Considered. State residency: Not Considered. Religious affiliation/commitment: Not Considered. Minority status: Not Considered. Volunteer work: Not Considered. Work experience: Not Considered. **Admissions statistics for the fall 2009 entering class:** Total applicants: 554. Total accepted: 389. Freshmen enrolled: 205; Overall acceptance rate: 70%. **Credentials of fall 2009 freshmen:** 24% ranked in the top 10 percent of their high school class; 49% were in the top 25 percent; 81% were in the top half. (Proportion submitting class standing: 67%.) **First-year students submitting ACT scores:** 81%. Scores (25/75 percentile): English: N/A, Math: N/A, Composite: 18-25.

ACADEMICS

Year founded: 1875. **Academic calendar:** Semester. **Degrees offered:** associate, bachelor's, master's. **Major fields of study:** biological and biomedical sciences; business, management, marketing, and related support services; communication, journalism, and related programs; computer and information sciences and support services; education; engineering; English language and literature/letters; foreign languages, literatures, and linguistics; health professions and related clinical sciences; history; legal professions and studies; liberal arts and sciences studies, and humanities; multi/interdisciplinary studies; physical sciences; psychology; public administration and social service professions; security and protective services; social sciences; transportation and materials moving; visual and performing arts. **Areas of required coursework:** arts/fine arts, humanities, mathematics, English (including composition), foreign languages, sciences (biological or physical), social science. **Pre-professional programs:** pre-law. **Special academic programs:** accelerated program, distance learning, double major, English as a Second Language (ESL), honors program, independent study, student-designed major, study abroad, teacher certificate program, weekend college, other. **Teacher certification offered in:** early childhood, special education, elementary, middle/junior high, secondary. **Reserve Officers Training Corps (ROTC):** Army ROTC: Offered on campus. **Freshmen returning for sophomore year:** 62%. **Graduation rates:** Four-year: 16%; five-year: 34%; six-year: 39%.

COSTS AND FINANCIAL AID

Financial aid office: (816) 584-6190. **Expenses (2010-2011):** Tuition and fees 2010-2011: $8,898; room/board: $8,800. Estimated books and supplies: $1,200. **Financial aid:** Priority filing date for institution's financial aid form: April 1.

CAMPUS LIFE AND EXTRACURRICULAR ACTIVITIES

Campus housing available: coed dorms, apartments for married students, apartment for single students. **Clubs and organizations:** Number of student organizations: 36. Number of fraternities: 0; sororities: 0. **Sports program (2009-2010):** Member of NAIA. *Men's intercollegiate varsity sports:* baseball, basketball, cross country, soccer, track and field (indoor), track and field (outdoor). *Women's intercollegiate varsity sports:* basketball, cross country, golf, soccer, softball, track and field (indoor), track and field (outdoor).

SERVICES AND FACILITIES

Basic services: nonremedial tutoring, placement service, health service, health insurance. **Remedial assistance:** reading, math, writing, study skills. **Counseling services:** personal. **For learning-disabled students:** School does not offer a structured program with separate admission and additional fees. Services include: remedial math, remedial English, reading machines, remedial reading, tape recorders, other special classes, videotaped classes, untimed tests, note-taking services, oral tests, learning center, readers, extended time for tests, tutors, texts on tape, other testing accommodations. **Library:** Number of titles: 50,307; number of current serial subscriptions: 591. **Information technology resources:** Students are not required to lease or own a computer. Number of campus computers available to all students: 702. School does not have a wireless network. Proportion of college-owned housing units wired for high-speed internet access: 50%.

TRANSFER AND INTERNATIONAL STUDENTS

Transfer students: May apply for admission for the following academic terms: Fall, Winter, Spring, Summer. Applicants do not need a minimum number of credits to apply. For fall 2009: Transfer applications received: 520. Transfer applicants offered admission: 386. Transfer applicants enrolled: 269. **International students:** Number of foreign undergraduates: 336 (3% of student body). Minimum TOEFL score required: 500 (paper); 173 (computer).

Rockhurst University

- **Address:** 1100 Rockhurst Road, Kansas City, MO 64110-2561
- **Website:** http://www.rockhurst.edu
- **Private; Religious affiliation:** Roman Catholic (Jesuit)
- **Enrollment:** 1,409 full-time; 711 part-time

KEY STATS

✔ **U.S News College Ranking:** 24, Regional Universities (Midwest)
✔ **ACT Score (25th/75th percentile):** 22-28
✔ **Tuition:** 2010-2011: $27,390

Selectivity: More selective	**Room/board:** $7,490
Acceptance rate: 76%	**Average debt:** $21,950
Student/faculty ratio: 13/1	**Proportion who borrowed:** 79%

UNDERGRADUATE STUDENT BODY STATS

2009-2010 enrollment: 1,409 full-time; 711 part-time. Men: 39%; women: 61%. **Ethnic makeup:** African American: 6%; Asian American: 3%; Hispanic: 6%; White: 84%; International: 1%. **Religious preference:** Roman Catholic: 54%; Protestant: 2%; No preference: 1%; Unknown: 24%; Other: 19%.

ADMISSIONS FACTS AND FIGURES

Phone: (816) 501-4100. **Email:** admissions@rockhurst.edu. **Website:** http://www.rockhurst.edu. **Application deadlines for fall 2011:** Regular decision: Rolling. Early decision: Not offered. Early action: Not offered. Admission can be deferred. **Application fee:** $25. **To apply online, go to:** http://www.rockhurst.edu/admission/ugrad/process/index.asp. **Admissions requirements/recommendations:** High school units required (recommended): English: 4 (4); Mathematics: 3 (3); Science: 3 (3); Academic electives: 4 (4); Total units: 16 (16). Tests: The college uses SAT or ACT scores in admissions decisions. Either SAT or ACT required. For admission to the fall 2011 entering class, the school will accept: ACT with or without writing accepted. Campus visit: Recommended. Admissions interview: Recommended. Off-campus interview: May be arranged. **Factors that count in admissions decisions:** *Academic:* Secondary school record: Important. Class rank: Important. Letters of recommendation: Important. Standardized test scores: Important. Essay: Not Considered. *Nonacademic:* Interview: Considered. Extracurricular activities: Considered. Talent/ability: Considered. Character/personal qualities: Important. Alumni/ae relationship: Considered. Geographical residence: Not Considered. State residency: Not Considered. Religious affiliation/commitment: Considered. Minority status: Not Considered. Volunteer work: Considered. Work experience: Not Considered. **Other schools with the greatest overlap in applicants:** Creighton University; St. Louis University; University of Kansas; University of Missouri; University of Missouri–Kansas City. **Admissions statistics for the fall 2009 entering class:** Total applicants: 2,107. Total accepted: 1,611. Freshmen enrolled: 419; 67% were from out of state. Overall acceptance rate: 76%. **Credentials of fall 2009 freshmen:** 22% ranked in the top 10 percent of their high school class; 57% were in the top 25 percent. (Proportion submitting class standing: 69%.) **Average high school grade point average:** 3.5. **First-year students who submitted SAT scores:** 6%. Scores (25/75 percentile): Critical Reading: 530-650, Math: 530-640, Combined: 1060-1290. **First-year students submitting ACT scores:** 98%. Scores (25/75 percentile): English: N/A, Math: N/A, Composite: 22-28.

ACADEMICS

Year founded: 1910. **Academic calendar:** Semester. **Degrees offered:** certificate, bachelor's, post-bachelor's certificate, master's, doctorate. **Major fields of study:** biological and biomedical sciences; business, management, marketing, and related support services; communication, journalism, and related programs; computer and information sciences and support services; education; English language and literature/letters; foreign languages, literatures, and linguistics; health professions and related clinical sciences; history; mathematics and statistics; multi/interdisciplinary studies; philosophy and religious studies; physical sciences; psychology; public administration and social service professions; social sciences. **Areas of required coursework:** arts/fine arts, humanities, computer literacy, mathematics, English (including composition), philosophy, sciences (biological or physical), history, other. **Pre-professional programs:** pre-law, pre-dentistry, pre-medicine, pre-veterinary science, pre-optometry, pre-pharmacy, other. **Special academic programs:** accelerated program, cooperative (work-study plan) program, cross-registration, double major, dual enrollment, exchange student program (domestic), honors program, independent study, internships, study abroad, teacher certificate program. **Teacher certification offered in:** elementary, secondary. **Cooperative education programs:** art, business, computer science, education, health professions, humanities, natural science, social/behavioral science, technologies, other. **Reserve Officers Training Corps (ROTC):** Army ROTC: Offered at cooperating institution (University of Missouri–Kansas City). **Faculty and instruction (2009-2010):** Total instructional faculty: 127 full-time, 101 part-time (45% men; 55% women; 8% minorities). Full-time faculty with Ph.D. or other terminal degree: 81%. Student/faculty ratio: 13/1. Classes of fewer than 20 students: 36%; of 20 to 49 students: 59%; of 50 or more students: 5%. **Advanced Placement and International Baccalaureate credit:** AP tests may be used for: Credit and/or placement. International Baccalaureate exams may be used for: Placement only. **Freshmen returning for sophomore year:** 84%. **Graduation rates:** Four-year: 58%; five-year: 65%; six-year: 64%. **Graduate study:** 24% of students pursue further study immediately upon graduation. Fields in which graduates pursue further study: Master of Business Administration (MBA), 20%; law, 13%; medicine, 4%; dentistry, 1%; education, 6%; arts and sciences, 36%.

COSTS AND FINANCIAL AID

Financial aid office: (816) 501-4100. **Expenses (2010-2011):** Tuition and fees 2010-2011: $27,390; room/board: $7,490. Estimated books and supplies: $1,400; transportation: $1,833; personal expenses: $1,625. **Financial aid:** Priority filing date for institution's financial aid form: March 1; deadline: June 30. In 2009-2010, 96% of undergraduates applied for financial aid. Of those, 81% were determined to have financial need; 14% had their need fully met. Average financial aid package (proportion receiving): $25,772 (77%). Average amount of gift aid, such as scholarships or grants (proportion receiving): $8,021 (64%). Average amount of self-help aid, such as work study or loans (proportion receiving): $4,303 (47%). Average need-based loan (excluding PLUS or other private loans): $3,739. Among students who received need-based aid, the average percentage of need met: 100%. Among students who received aid based on merit, the average award (and the proportion receiving): $12,904 (10%). The average athletic scholarship (and the proportion receiving): $13,570 (10%). Average amount of debt of borrowers graduating in 2009: $21,950. Proportion who borrowed: 79%.

CAMPUS LIFE AND EXTRACURRICULAR ACTIVITIES

Campus housing available (% using): coed dorms (46%), women's dorms (24%), men's dorms (0%), apartment for single students (20%), special housing for disabled students (1%), other housing options (9%). Students who live in college-owned, operated, or affiliated housing: 59%. **Student employment:** During the 2009-2010 academic year, 15% of undergraduates worked on campus. Average per-year earnings: $2,500. **Clubs and organizations:** Number of student organizations: 42. Activities include: campus ministries, choral groups, dance, drama/theater, international student organization, literary magazine, musical theater, student government, student newspaper, yearbook. Number of fraternities: 4; sororities: 4. Average proportion of students who stay on campus on weekends: 60%. **Sports program (2009-2010):** Member of NCAA II. *Men's intercollegiate varsity sports:* baseball, basketball, golf, soccer, tennis. *Women's intercollegiate varsity sports:* basketball, golf, soccer, softball, tennis, volleyball.

SERVICES AND FACILITIES

Basic services: nonremedial tutoring, health service, health insurance. **Remedial assistance:** reading, math, writing, study skills. **Counseling services:** minority student, career, personal, veteran student, academic, older student, psychological, birth control, religious. **For learning-disabled students:** School does not offer a structured program with separate admission and additional fees. Services include: reading machines, note-taking services, learning center, readers, extended time for tests, priority seating, other testing accommodations. **Library:** Number of titles: 189,527; number of current serial subscriptions: 42,563. **Information technology resources:** Students are not required to lease or own a computer. Number of campus computers available to all students: 247. School has a wireless network. Proportion of college-owned housing units wired for high-speed internet access: 100%. **Campus safety:** Security services offered: 24-hour foot-and-vehicle patrols, late-night transport/escort service, 24-hour emergency telephones, lighted pathways/sidewalks, controlled dormitory access (key, security card, etc).

TRANSFER AND INTERNATIONAL STUDENTS

Transfer students: May apply for admission for the following academic terms: Fall, Spring, Summer. Applicants need a minimum number of credits to apply. For fall 2009: Transfer applications received: 358. Transfer applicants offered admission: 180. Transfer applicants enrolled: 68.

International students: Number of foreign undergraduates: 14 (1% of student body). Number of countries represented: 17. Minimum TOEFL score required: 550 (paper); 213 (computer).

Southeast Missouri State University

- **Address:** 1 University Plaza, Cape Girardeau, MO 63701
- **Website:** http://www.semo.edu
- **Public**
- **Enrollment:** 7,281 full-time; 2,307 part-time

KEY STATS

✔ **U.S News College Ranking:** 76, Regional Universities (Midwest)
✔ **ACT Score (25th/75th percentile):** 20-25
✔ **Tuition:** 2010-2011: $6,255 in state, $11,190 out of state

Selectivity: Selective	Room/board: $6,510
Acceptance rate: 92%	Average debt: $20,350
Student/faculty ratio: 18/1	Proportion who borrowed: 69%

UNDERGRADUATE STUDENT BODY STATS

2009-2010 enrollment: 7,281 full-time; 2,307 part-time. Men: 41%; women: 59%. **Ethnic makeup:** African American: 9%; Asian American: 1%; Hispanic: 1%; White: 87%; International: 2%.

ADMISSIONS FACTS AND FIGURES

Phone: (573) 651-2590. **Email:** admissions@semo.edu. **Website:** http://www.semo.edu. **Application deadlines for fall 2011:** Regular decision: July 1. Early decision: Not offered. Early action: Not offered. Admission cannot be deferred. **Application fee:** $25. **To apply online, go to:** http://www.semo.edu/admissions/apply.htm. **Admissions requirements/recommendations:** High school units required (recommended): English: 4; Mathematics: 3; Science: 3; Social studies: 2; History: 1; Academic electives: 3; Total units: 17. Tests: The college uses SAT or ACT scores in admissions decisions. Either SAT or ACT required. For admission to the fall 2011 entering class, the school will accept: ACT with or without writing accepted. Campus visit: Recommended. Admissions interview: Neither required nor recommended. Off-campus interview: May be arranged. **Factors that count in admissions decisions:** *Academic:* Secondary school record: Very Important. Class rank: Considered. Letters of recommendation: Not Considered. Standardized test scores: Very Important. Essay: Not Considered. *Nonacademic:* Interview: Not Considered. Extracurricular activities: Not Considered. Talent/ability: Not Considered. Character/personal qualities: Not Considered. Alumni/ae relationship: Not Considered. Geographical residence: Not Considered. State residency: Not Considered. Religious affiliation/commitment: Not Considered. Minority status: Not Considered. Volunteer work: Not Considered. Work experience: Not Considered. **Other schools with the greatest overlap in applicants:** Missouri State University; Truman State University; University of Missouri; University of Missouri–St. Louis. **Admissions statistics for the fall 2009 entering class:** Total applicants: 4,164. Total accepted: 3,835. Freshmen enrolled: 1,805; 15% were from out of state. Overall acceptance rate: 92%. **Credentials of fall 2009 freshmen:** 16% ranked in the top 10 percent of their high school class; 41% were in the top 25 percent; 71% were in the top half. (Proportion submitting class standing: 82%.) **Average high school grade point average:** 3.3. **First-year students who submitted SAT scores:** 3%. **First-year students submitting ACT scores:** 89%. Scores (25/75 percentile): English: 20-26, Math: 18-25, Composite: 20-25.

ACADEMICS

Year founded: 1873. **Academic calendar:** Semester. **Degrees offered:** certificate, associate, terminal-associate, bachelor's, master's, post-master's certificate. **Most popular majors:** 12% liberal arts and sciences studies, and humanities, 9% teacher education and professional development, 7% teacher education and professional development, 6% business administration, management, and operations, 6% family and consumer sciences/human sciences. **Major fields of study:** agriculture, agriculture operations, and related sciences; biological and biomedical sciences; business, management, marketing, and related support services; communication, journalism, and related programs; computer and information sciences and support services; education; engineering; engineering technologies/technicians; English language and literature/letters; family and consumer sciences/human sciences; foreign languages, literatures, and linguistics; health professions and related clinical sciences; history; liberal arts and sciences studies, and humanities; mathematics and statistics; multi/interdisciplinary

studies; natural resources and conservation; parks, recreation, leisure, and fitness studies; philosophy and religious studies; physical sciences; psychology; public administration and social service professions; security and protective services; social sciences; visual and performing arts. **Areas of required coursework:** arts/fine arts, humanities, mathematics, English (including composition), sciences (biological or physical), history. **Pre-professional programs:** pre-law, pre-dentistry, pre-medicine, pre-veterinary science, pre-optometry, pre-pharmacy, other. **Special academic programs (% participation):** accelerated program, distance learning (84.3%), double major (19.2%), dual enrollment (12.1%), English as a Second Language (ESL) (1.2%), honors program (17.2%), independent study (14.7%), internships (34.1%), liberal arts/career combination, student-designed major (15.7%), study abroad (3.5%), teacher certificate program (25.5%), other (96.7%). **Teacher certification offered in:** early childhood, special education, elementary, middle/junior high, secondary. **Reserve Officers Training Corps (ROTC):** Air Force ROTC: Offered on campus. **Faculty and instruction (2009-2010):** Total instructional faculty: 419 full-time, 172 part-time (51% men; 49% women; 11% minorities). Full-time faculty with Ph.D. or other terminal degree: 75%. Student/faculty ratio: 18/1. Classes of fewer than 20 students: 40%; of 20 to 49 students: 58%; of 50 or more students: 1%. **Advanced Placement and International Baccalaureate credit:** AP tests may be used for: Credit only. Scores accepted: 3, 4, 5. International Baccalaureate exams may be used for: Credit only. **Freshmen returning for sophomore year:** 72%. **Graduation rates:** Four-year: 24%; five-year: 42%; six-year: 50%.

COSTS AND FINANCIAL AID

Financial aid office: (573) 651-2253. **Expenses (2010-2011):** Tuition and fees 2010-2011: $6,255 in state, $711 out of state; room/board: $6,510. **Financial aid:** Priority filing date for institution's financial aid form: March 1. In 2009-2010, 78% of undergraduates applied for financial aid. Of those, 59% were determined to have financial need; 21% had their need fully met. Average financial aid package (proportion receiving): $8,384 (58%). Average amount of gift aid, such as scholarships or grants (proportion receiving): $5,269 (52%). Average amount of self-help aid, such as work study or loans (proportion receiving): $4,045 (44%). Average need-based loan (excluding PLUS or other private loans): $3,836. Among students who received need-based aid, the average percentage of need met: 70%. Among students who received aid based on merit, the average award (and the proportion receiving): $4,227 (15%). The average athletic scholarship (and the proportion receiving): $10,288 (2%). Average amount of debt of borrowers graduating in 2009: $20,350. Proportion who borrowed: 69%.

CAMPUS LIFE AND EXTRACURRICULAR ACTIVITIES

Campus housing available (% using): coed dorms (86%), sorority housing (5%), fraternity housing (5%), apartments for married students (1%), apartment for single students (1%), special housing for disabled students. Students who live in college-owned, operated, or affiliated housing: 29%. **Student employment:** During the 2009-2010 academic year, 17% of undergraduates worked on campus. Average per-year earnings: $1,423. **Clubs and organizations:** Number of student organizations: 127. Activities include: campus ministries, choral groups, concert band, dance, drama/theater, international student organization, jazz band, literary magazine, marching band, model UN, music ensembles, musical theater, opera, pep band, radio station, student government, student newspaper, symphony orchestra. Number of fraternities: 10; sororities: 6. Proportion of men in fraternities: 13%; of women in sororities: 9%. Average proportion of students who stay on campus on weekends: 72%. **Sports program (2009-2010):** Member of NCAA I. *Men's intercollegiate varsity sports:* baseball, basketball, cross country, football, track and field (indoor), track and field (outdoor). *Women's intercollegiate varsity sports:* basketball, cross country, gymnastics, soccer, softball, tennis, track and field (indoor), track and field (outdoor), volleyball.

SERVICES AND FACILITIES

Basic services: nonremedial tutoring, placement service, day care, health service. **Remedial assistance:** reading, math, writing, study skills. **Counseling services:** minority student, career, personal, academic, older student, psychological, birth control. **For learning-disabled students:** School does not offer a structured program with separate admission and additional fees. Total undergraduates in learning-disabled program or receiving services: 60. Services include: remedial math, remedial English, reading machines, tape recorders, untimed tests, note-taking services, oral tests, learning center, readers, extended time for tests, tutors, priority registration, priority seating, texts on tape, typist/scribe, exams on tape or computer, other testing accommodations, other. **Library:** Number of titles: 507,176; number of current serial subscriptions: 48,748. **Information technology resources:** Students are not required to lease or own a computer. Number of campus computers available to all students: 1,311. School has a wireless network. Proportion of college-owned housing units wired for high-speed internet access: 100%. **Campus safety:** Security services offered: 24-hour foot-and-vehicle patrols, late-night transport/escort service, 24-hour emergency telephones, lighted pathways/sidewalks, controlled dormitory access (key, security card, etc).

TRANSFER AND INTERNATIONAL STUDENTS

Transfer students: May apply for admission for the following academic terms: Fall, Spring, Summer. Applicants need a minimum number of credits to apply. For fall 2009: Transfer applications received: 953. Transfer applicants offered admission: 919. Transfer applicants enrolled: 611. **International students:** Number of foreign undergraduates: 180 (2% of student body). Number of countries represented: 36. Minimum TOEFL score required: 500 (paper); 61 (computer).

Southwest Baptist University

- **Address:** 1600 University Avenue, Bolivar, MO 65613
- **Website:** http://www.sbuniv.edu
- **Private; Religious affiliation:** Southern Baptist Convention
- **Enrollment:** N/A

KEY STATS

✔ **U.S News College Ranking:** 99, Regional Universities (Midwest)
✔ **ACT Score (25th/75th percentile):** 20-26
✔ **Tuition:** 2009-2010: $16,530

Selectivity: Selective	**Room/board:** $5,470
Acceptance rate: 74%	**Average debt:** N/A
Student/faculty ratio: N/A	**Proportion who borrowed:** N/A

Stephens College

- **Address:** 1200 E. Broadway, Columbia, MO 65215
- **Website:** http://www.stephens.edu
- **Private**
- **Enrollment:** 785 full-time; 197 part-time

KEY STATS

✔ **U.S News College Ranking:** second tier, National Liberal Arts Colleges
✔ **ACT Score (25th/75th percentile):** 19-25
✔ **Tuition:** 2010-2011: $25,400

Selectivity: Selective	**Room/board:** $8,070
Acceptance rate: 72%	**Average debt:** $22,942
Student/faculty ratio: 12/1	**Proportion who borrowed:** 78%

UNDERGRADUATE STUDENT BODY STATS

2009-2010 enrollment: 785 full-time; 197 part-time. Men: 3%; women: 97%. **Ethnic makeup:** African American: 13%; American-Indian: 1%; Asian American: 1%; Hispanic: 3%; White: 82%.

ADMISSIONS FACTS AND FIGURES

Phone: (800) 876-7207. **Email:** apply@stephens.edu. **Website:** http://www.stephens.edu. **Application deadlines for fall 2011:** Regular decision: Rolling. Early decision: Not offered. Early action: Not offered. Admission can be deferred. **Application fee:** $25. **To apply online, go to:** https://www.stephens.edu/admission/apply/freshman/index.php. **Admissions requirements/recommendations:** High school units required (recommended): English: 4; Mathematics: 3; Science: 2; Foreign language: 2; Social studies: 1; Total units: 12 (2). Tests: The college uses SAT or ACT scores in admissions decisions. Either SAT or ACT required. For admission to the fall 2011 entering class, the school will accept: ACT with or without writing accepted. Campus visit: Recommended. Admissions interview: Recommended. Off-campus interview: May be arranged. **Factors that count in admissions decisions:** *Academic:* Secondary school record: Very Important. Class rank: Considered. Letters of recommendation: Important. Standardized test scores: Very Important. Essay: Very Important. *Nonacademic:* Interview: Considered. Extracurricular activities: Important. Talent/ability: Considered. Character/personal qualities: Considered. Alumni/ae relationship: Not Considered. Geographical residence: Not Considered. State residency: Not Considered. Religious affiliation/commitment: Not Considered. Minority status: Not Considered. Volunteer work: Considered. Work experience: Considered. **Other schools with the greatest overlap in applicants:** Drake University; Missouri State University; Sweet Briar College; University of Missouri; William Woods University. **Admissions statistics for the fall 2009 entering class:** Total applicants: 675. Total accepted: 486. Freshmen enrolled: 269; 44% were from out of state. Overall acceptance rate: 72%. **Credentials of fall 2009 freshmen:** 11% ranked in the top 10 percent of their high school class; 33% were in the top 25 percent; 69% were in the top half. (Proportion submitting class standing: 84%.) **Average high school grade point average:** 3.3. **First-year students who submitted SAT scores:** 18%. Scores (25/75 percentile): Critical Reading: 510-600, Math: 460-548, Combined: 970-1148. **First-year students submitting ACT scores:** 80%. Scores (25/75 percentile): English: 20-25, Math: 17-23, Composite: 19-25.

ACADEMICS

Year founded: 1833. **Academic calendar:** Semester. **Degrees offered:** associate, bachelor's, post-bachelor's certificate, master's. **Most popular majors:** 19% health information/medical records administration/administrator, 13% drama and dramatics/theater arts, 12% fashion merchandising, 10% fashion/apparel design, 6% dance. **Major fields of study:** biological and biomedical sciences; business, management, marketing, and related support services; communication, journalism, and related programs; education; English language and literature/letters; family and consumer sciences/human sciences; health professions and related clinical sciences; legal professions and studies; liberal arts and sciences studies, and humanities; psychology; social sciences; visual and performing arts. **Areas of required coursework:** humanities, computer literacy, mathematics, English (including composition), sciences (biological or physical), history, social science, other. **Pre-professional programs:** pre-law, pre-dentistry, pre-medicine, pre-veterinary science, pre-pharmacy. **Special academic programs (% participation):** cooperative (work-study plan) program, cross-registration, distance learning (19%), double major (3%), dual enrollment (1%), external degree program (19%), independent study (30%), internships (85%), liberal arts/career combination, student-designed major (1%), study abroad (1%), teacher certificate program (1%). **Teacher certification offered in:** early childhood, elementary. **Cooperative education programs:** agriculture, business, health professions, other. **Reserve Officers Training Corps (ROTC):** Army ROTC: Offered at cooperating institution (University of Missouri); Navy ROTC: Offered at cooperating institution (University of Missouri); Air Force ROTC: Offered at cooperating institution (University of Missouri). **Faculty and instruction (2009-2010):** Total instructional faculty: 60 full-time, 64 part-time (26% men; 74% women; 6% minorities). Full-time faculty with Ph.D. or other terminal degree: 43%. Student/faculty ratio: 12/1. Classes of fewer than 20 students: 75%; of 20 to 49 students: 24%; of 50 or more students: 1%. **Advanced Placement and International Baccalaureate credit:** AP tests may be used for: Credit and/or placement. Scores accepted: 3, 4, 5. International Baccalaureate exams may be used for: Credit only. **Freshmen returning for sophomore year:** 70%. **Graduation rates:** Four-year: 43%; five-year: 50%; six-year: 51%. **Graduate study:** 16% of students pursue further study within one year; 26% within five years. Fields in which graduates pursue further study: Master of Business Administration (MBA), 29%; law, 6%; medicine, 12%; education, 6%; arts and sciences, 41%; veterinary medicine, 6%.

COSTS AND FINANCIAL AID

Financial aid office: (573) 876-7106. **Expenses (2010-2011):** Tuition and fees 2010-2011: $25,400; room/board: $8,070. Estimated books and supplies: $1,400; transportation: $965; personal expenses: $2,150. **Financial aid:** Priority filing date for institution's financial aid form: March 15. In 2009-2010, 86% of undergraduates applied for financial aid. Of those, 77% were determined to have financial need; 20% had their need fully met. Average financial aid package (proportion receiving): $20,787 (77%). Average amount of gift aid, such as scholarships or grants (proportion receiving): $16,735 (77%). Average amount of self-help aid, such as work study or loans (proportion receiving): $5,041 (62%). Average need-based loan (excluding PLUS or other private loans): $4,334. Among students who received need-based aid, the average percentage of need met: 78%. Among students who received aid based on merit, the average award (and the proportion receiving): $8,629 (23%). The average athletic scholarship (and the proportion receiving): $6,273 (3%). Average amount of debt of borrowers graduating in 2009: $22,942. Proportion who borrowed: 78%.

CAMPUS LIFE AND EXTRACURRICULAR ACTIVITIES

Campus housing available (% using): women's dorms (93%), sorority housing (3%), apartment for single students (4%). Students who live in college-owned, operated, or affiliated housing: 66%. **Student employment:** During the 2009-2010 academic year, 25% of undergraduates worked on campus. Average per-year earnings: $1,550. **Clubs and organizations:** Number of student organizations: 28. Activities include: choral groups, dance, drama/theater, literary magazine, music ensembles, musical theater, radio station, student government, student newspaper, student film society, television station, yearbook. Number of fraternities: 0; sororities: 2. of women in sororities: 7%. Average proportion of students who stay on campus on weekends: 85%. **Sports program (2009-2010):** Member of NCAA III. *Women's intercollegiate varsity sports:* basketball, cross country, softball, swimming, tennis, volleyball.

SERVICES AND FACILITIES

Basic services: nonremedial tutoring, placement service, health service. **Remedial assistance:** reading, math, writing, study skills. **Counseling services:** career, personal, academic, psychological, birth control. **For learning-disabled students:** School does not offer a structured program with separate admission and additional fees. Services include: untimed tests, special bookstore section, oral tests, learning center, extended time for tests, tutors, priority seating. **Library:** Number of titles: 135,389; number of current serial subscriptions: 21,500. **Information technology resources:** Students are not required to lease or own a computer. Number of campus computers available to all students: 107. School has a wireless network. Approximate number of users that can be accommodated: 7,500. Proportion of college-owned housing units wired for high-speed internet access: 100%. **Campus safety:** Security services offered: 24-hour foot-and-vehicle patrols, late-night transport/escort service, 24-hour emergency telephones, lighted pathways/sidewalks, controlled dormitory access (key, security card, etc).

TRANSFER AND INTERNATIONAL STUDENTS

Transfer students: May apply for admission for the following academic terms: Fall, Spring, Summer. Applicants need a minimum number of credits to apply. For fall 2009: Transfer applications received: 283. Transfer applicants offered admission: 175. Transfer applicants enrolled: 118. **International students:** Number of foreign undergraduates: 3. Number of countries represented: 3. Minimum TOEFL score required: 550 (paper); 213 (computer).

St. Louis University

- ■ **Address:** 1 Grand Boulevard, St. Louis, MO 63103
- ■ **Website:** http://www.slu.edu
- ■ **Private; Religious affiliation:** Roman Catholic
- ■ **Enrollment:** 7,307 full-time; 812 part-time

KEY STATS

✔ **U.S News College Ranking:** 86, National Universities
✔ **ACT Score (25th/75th percentile):** 24-30
✔ **Tuition:** 2010-2011: $32,656

Selectivity: More selective	**Room/board:** $9,170
Acceptance rate: 71%	**Average debt:** $33,747
Student/faculty ratio: 13/1	**Proportion who borrowed:** 64%

UNDERGRADUATE STUDENT BODY STATS

2009-2010 enrollment: 7,307 full-time; 812 part-time. Men: 41%; women: 59%. **Ethnic makeup:** African American: 8%; Asian American: 6%; Hispanic: 3%; White: 75%; International: 7%. **Religious preference:** Protestant: 17%; Jewish: 1%; Muslim: 1%; No preference: 17%; Unknown: 17%; Roman Catholic: 41%; Other: 6%.

ADMISSIONS FACTS AND FIGURES

Phone: (314) 977-2500. **Email:** admitme@slu.edu. **Website:** http://www.slu.edu. **Application deadlines for fall 2011:** Early decision: Not offered. Early action: Not offered. Admission can be deferred. **Application fee:** None. **To apply online, go to:** http://www.slu.edu/admissions/. **Admissions requirements/recommendations:** High school units required (recommended): English: 4 (4); Mathematics: 4 (4); Science: 3 (3); Foreign language: 3 (3); Social studies: 3 (3); History: 0 (0); Academic electives: 3 (3); Total units: 20 (20). Tests: The college uses SAT or ACT scores in admissions decisions. Either SAT or ACT required. For admission to the fall 2011 entering class, the school will accept: ACT with or without writing accepted. Campus visit: Recommended. Admissions interview: Recommended. Off-campus interview: May be arranged. **Factors that count in admissions decisions:**

Academic: Secondary school record: Important. Class rank: Not Considered. Letters of recommendation: Considered. Standardized test scores: Very Important. Essay: Important. *Nonacademic:* Interview: Considered. Extracurricular activities: Important. Talent/ability: Important. Character/personal qualities: Important. Alumni/ae relationship: Considered. Geographical residence: Not Considered. State residency: Not Considered. Religious affiliation/commitment: Not Considered. Minority status: Not Considered. Volunteer work: Considered. Work experience: Not Considered. **Other schools with the greatest overlap in applicants:** Marquette University; Truman State University; University of Illinois–Urbana-Champaign; University of Missouri; University of Notre Dame. **Admissions statistics for the fall 2009 entering class:** Total applicants: 10,707. Total accepted: 7,616. Freshmen enrolled: 1,597; 65% were from out of state. Overall acceptance rate: 71%. **Credentials of fall 2009 freshmen:** 39% ranked in the top 10 percent of their high school class; 71% were in the top 25 percent; 90% were in the top half. (Proportion submitting class standing: 53%.) **Average high school grade point average:** 3.7. **First-year students who submitted SAT scores:** 29%. Scores (25/75 percentile): Critical Reading: 540-650, Math: 540-670, Combined: 1080-1320. **First-year students submitting ACT scores:** 90%. Scores (25/75 percentile): English: 24-30, Math: 24-31, Composite: 24-30.

ACADEMICS

Year founded: 1818. **Academic calendar:** Semester. **Degrees offered:** certificate, bachelor's, post-bachelor's certificate, master's, post-master's certificate, doctorate. **Most popular majors:** 7% biology/biological sciences, 7% nursing/registered nurse training (R.N., A.S.N., B.S.N., M.S.N.), 6% business administration and management, 4% physical therapy/therapist, 4% psychology. **Major fields of study:** area, ethnic, cultural, and gender studies; biological and biomedical sciences; business, management, marketing, and related support services; communication, journalism, and related programs; computer and information sciences and support services; education; engineering; engineering technologies/technicians; English language and literature/letters; family and consumer sciences/human sciences; foreign languages, literatures, and linguistics; health professions and related clinical sciences; history; liberal arts and sciences studies, and humanities; mathematics and statistics; natural resources and conservation; parks, recreation, leisure, and fitness studies; philosophy and religious studies; physical sciences; psychology; public administration and social service professions; security and protective services; social sciences; theology and religious vocations; transportation and materials moving; visual and performing arts. **Areas of required coursework:** arts/fine arts, humanities, mathematics, English (including composition), philosophy, sciences (biological or physical), history, social science, other. **Pre-professional programs:** pre-law, pre-dentistry, pre-medicine, pre-theology, pre-optometry, pre-pharmacy, other. **Special academic programs:** accelerated program, cooperative (work-study plan) program, cross-registration, distance learning, double major, dual enrollment, English as a Second Language (ESL), honors program, independent study, internships, liberal arts/career combination, student-designed major, study abroad, teacher certificate program. **Teacher certification offered in:** early childhood, special education, elementary, middle/junior high, secondary. **Cooperative education programs:** engineering, other. **Reserve Officers Training Corps (ROTC):** Army ROTC: Offered at cooperating institution (Washington University in St. Louis); Air Force ROTC: Offered on campus. **Faculty and instruction (2009-2010):** Total instructional faculty: 639 full-time, 437 part-time (51% men; 49% women; 9% minorities). Full-time faculty with Ph.D. or other terminal degree: 90%. Student/faculty ratio: 13/1. Classes of fewer than 20 students: 55%; of 20 to 49 students: 40%; of 50 or more students: 6%. **Advanced Placement and International Baccalaureate credit:** AP tests may be used for: Credit and/or placement. Scores accepted: 3, 4, 5. International Baccalaureate exams may be used for: Credit only. **Freshmen returning for sophomore year:** 84%. **Graduation rates:** Four-year: 60%; five-year: 72%; six-year: 73%. **Graduate study:** 35% of students pursue further study immediately upon graduation. Fields in which graduates pursue further study: Master of Business Administration (MBA), 20%; law, 16%; medicine, 22%; dentistry, 1%; engineering, 4%; theology (or the seminary), 1%; education, 6%; arts and sciences, 30%.

COSTS AND FINANCIAL AID

Financial aid office: (314) 977-2350. **Expenses (2010-2011):** Tuition and fees 2010-2011: $32,656; room/board: $9,170. Estimated books and supplies: $1,660; transportation: $2,176; personal expenses: $3,618. **Financial aid:** Priority filing date for institution's financial aid form: March 1. In 2009-2010, 63% of undergraduates applied for financial aid. Of those, 55% were determined to have financial need; 12% had their need fully met. Average

financial aid package (proportion receiving): $21,747 (55%). Average amount of gift aid, such as scholarships or grants (proportion receiving): $15,711 (52%). Average amount of self-help aid, such as work study or loans (proportion receiving): $5,464 (44%). Average need-based loan (excluding PLUS or other private loans): $5,126. Among students who received need-based aid, the average percentage of need met: 64%. Among students who received aid based on merit, the average award (and the proportion receiving): $10,408 (28%). The average athletic scholarship (and the proportion receiving): $13,373 (2%). Average amount of debt of borrowers graduating in 2009: $33,747. Proportion who borrowed: 64%.

CAMPUS LIFE AND EXTRACURRICULAR ACTIVITIES

Campus housing available (% using): coed dorms (38%), women's dorms (6%), men's dorms (5%), sorority housing (3%), fraternity housing (2%), apartment for single students (30%), special housing for disabled students (0%), other housing options (1%). Students who live in college-owned, operated, or affiliated housing: 53%. **Student employment:** During the 2009-2010 academic year, 27% of undergraduates worked on campus. Average per-year earnings: $4,800. **Clubs and organizations:** Number of student organizations: 170. Activities include: campus ministries, choral groups, dance, drama/theater, international student organization, jazz band, literary magazine, model UN, music ensembles, musical theater, pep band, radio station, student government, student newspaper, student film society, television station, yearbook. Number of fraternities: 11; sororities: 6. Proportion of men in fraternities: 16%; of women in sororities: 24%. Average proportion of students who stay on campus on weekends: 80%. **Sports program (2009-2010):** Member of NCAA I. *Men's intercollegiate varsity sports:* baseball, basketball, cross country, soccer, swimming, tennis, track and field (indoor), track and field (outdoor). *Women's intercollegiate varsity sports:* basketball, cross country, field hockey, soccer, softball, swimming, tennis, track and field (indoor), track and field (outdoor), volleyball.

SERVICES AND FACILITIES

Basic services: nonremedial tutoring, women's center, health service, health insurance, other. **Remedial assistance:** reading, math, writing, study skills. **Counseling services:** minority student, career, military, personal, academic, older student, psychological, religious, other. **For learning-disabled students:** School does not offer a structured program with separate admission and additional fees. Total undergraduates in learning-disabled program or receiving services: 62. Services include: remedial math, remedial English, remedial reading, tape recorders, diagnostic testing service, note-taking services, readers, extended time for tests, tutors, early syllabus, priority registration, priority seating, texts on tape, exams on tape or computer, other testing accommodations, other. **Library:** Number of titles: 1,832,105; number of current serial subscriptions: 18,018. **Information technology resources:** Students are not required to lease or own a computer. Number of campus computers available to all students: 300. School has a wireless network. Approximate number of users that can be accommodated: 24,000. Proportion of college-owned housing units wired for high-speed internet access: 100%. **Campus safety:** Security services offered: 24-hour foot-and-vehicle patrols, late-night transport/escort service, 24-hour emergency telephones, lighted pathways/sidewalks, controlled dormitory access (key, security card, etc).

TRANSFER AND INTERNATIONAL STUDENTS

Transfer students: May apply for admission for the following academic terms: Fall, Spring, Summer. Applicants need a minimum number of credits to apply. For fall 2009: Transfer applications received: 2,135. Transfer applicants offered admission: 741. Transfer applicants enrolled: 311. **International students:** Number of foreign undergraduates: 584 (7% of student body). Number of countries represented: 46. Minimum TOEFL score required: 550 (paper); 213 (computer).

Truman State University

- **Address:** 100 E. Normal Street, Kirksville, MO 63501
- **Website:** http://www.truman.edu
- **Public**
- **Enrollment:** 5,359 full-time; 109 part-time

KEY STATS

✔ **U.S News College Ranking:** 8, Regional Universities (Midwest)
✔ **ACT Score (25th/75th percentile):** 25-30
✔ **Tuition:** 2010-2011: $6,692 in state, $11,543 out of state
  Selectivity: More selective **Room/board:** $7,096
  Acceptance rate: 72% **Average debt:** $21,858
  Student/faculty ratio: 16/1 **Proportion who borrowed:** 52%

UNDERGRADUATE STUDENT BODY STATS

2009-2010 enrollment: 5,359 full-time; 109 part-time. Men: 42%; women: 58%. **Ethnic makeup:** African American: 4%; American-Indian: 1%; Asian American: 2%; Hispanic: 2%; White: 85%; International: 5%. **Religious preference:** Roman Catholic: 24%; Protestant: 33%; Jewish: 1%; No preference: 2%; Other: 39%.

ADMISSIONS FACTS AND FIGURES

Phone: (660) 785-4114. **Email:** admissions@truman.edu. **Website:** http://www.truman.edu. **Application deadlines for fall 2011:** Regular decision: Rolling. Early decision: Not offered. Early action: Not offered. Admission can be deferred. **Application fee:** None. **To apply online, go to:** http://admissions.truman.edu/apply/index.asp. **Admissions requirements/recommendations:** High school units required (recommended): English: 4 (4); Mathematics: 3 (4); Science: 3 (3); Foreign language: 2 (2); Social studies: 2 (2); History: 1 (1); Total units: 16 (17). Tests: The college uses SAT or ACT scores in admissions decisions. Either SAT or ACT required. For admission to the fall 2011 entering class, the school will accept: ACT with or without writing accepted. Campus visit: Recommended. Admissions interview: Recommended. Off-campus interview: May be arranged. **Factors that count in admissions decisions:** *Academic:* Secondary school record: Very Important. Class rank: Very Important. Letters of recommendation: Considered. Standardized test scores: Very Important. Essay: Important. *Nonacademic:* Interview: Not Considered. Extracurricular activities: Considered. Talent/ability: Considered. Character/personal qualities: Considered. Alumni/ae relationship: Considered. Geographical residence: Considered. State residency: Considered. Religious affiliation/commitment: Not Considered. Minority status: Considered. Volunteer work: Considered. Work experience: Considered. **Other schools with the greatest overlap in applicants:** Missouri State University; St. Louis University; University of Illinois–Urbana-Champaign; University of Missouri; Washington University in St. Louis. **Admissions statistics for the fall 2009 entering class:** Total applicants: 4,608. Total accepted: 3,333. Freshmen enrolled: 1,342; 20% were from out of state. Overall acceptance rate: 72%. **Credentials of fall 2009 freshmen:** 46% ranked in the top 10 percent of their high school class; 95% were in the top 25 percent; 98% were in the top half. (Proportion submitting class standing: 98%.) **Average high school grade point average:** 3.7. **First-year students who submitted SAT scores:** 10%. Scores (25/75 percentile): Critical Reading: 540-660, Math: 560-660, Combined: 1100-1320. **First-year students submitting ACT scores:** 97%. Scores (25/75 percentile): English: 24-32, Math: 23-29, Composite: 25-30.

ACADEMICS

Year founded: 1867. **Academic calendar:** Semester. **Degrees offered:** bachelor's, master's. **Most popular majors:** 10% business administration and management, 9% English language and literature, 9% biology/biological sciences, 9% psychology, 6% communication studies/speech communication and rhetoric. **Major fields of study:** agriculture, agriculture operations, and related sciences; biological and biomedical sciences; business, management, marketing, and related support services; communication, journalism, and related programs; computer and information sciences and support services; English language and literature/letters; foreign languages, literatures, and linguistics; health professions and related clinical sciences; history; mathematics and statistics; multi/interdisciplinary studies; parks, recreation, leisure, and fitness studies; philosophy and religious studies; physical sciences; psychology; security and protective services; social sciences; visual and performing arts. **Areas of required coursework:** arts/fine arts, humanities, computer literacy, mathematics, English (including composition), philosophy, foreign languages, sciences (biological or physical), history, social science. **Pre-professional programs:** pre-law, pre-dentistry, pre-medicine, pre-veterinary science, pre-optometry, pre-pharmacy, other. **Special academic programs (% participation):** double major (.066%), dual enrollment (.01%), English as a Second Language (ESL), honors program (2%), independent study, internships, student-designed major, study abroad (24.25%). **Teacher certification offered in:** special education, elementary, middle/junior high, secondary. **Reserve Officers Training Corps (ROTC):** Army ROTC: Offered on campus. **Faculty and instruction (2009-2010):** Total instructional faculty: 345 full-time, 27 part-time (60% men; 40% women; 11% minorities). Full-time faculty with Ph.D. or other terminal degree: 82%. Student/faculty ratio: 16/1. Classes of fewer than 20 students: 37%; of 20 to 49 students: 61%; of 50 or more students: 2%. **Advanced Placement and International Baccalaureate credit:** AP tests may be used for: Credit and/or placement. Scores accepted: 3, 4, 5. International Baccalaureate exams may be used for: Credit and/or placement. **Freshmen returning for sophomore year:** 86%. **Graduation rates:** Four-year: 47%; five-year: 66%; six-year: 69%. **Graduate study:** 46% of students pursue further study immediately upon graduation. Fields in which graduates pursue further study: Master of Business Administration (MBA), 8%; law, 8%; medicine, 15%; theology (or the seminary), 1%; education, 27%; arts and sciences, 34%; veterinary medicine, 1%.

COSTS AND FINANCIAL AID

Financial aid office: (660) 785-4130. **Expenses (2010-2011):** Tuition and fees 2010-2011: $6,692 in state, $11,543 out of state; room/board: $7,096. Estimated books and supplies: $1,000; transportation: $1,500; personal expenses: $2,500. **Financial aid:** Priority filing date for institution's financial aid form: April 1. In 2009-2010, 70% of undergraduates applied for financial aid. Of those, 49% were determined to have financial need; 63% had their need fully met. Average financial aid package (proportion receiving): $9,996 (48%). Average amount of gift aid, such as scholarships or grants (proportion receiving): $3,820 (31%). Average amount of self-help aid, such as work study or loans (proportion receiving): $3,194 (31%). Average need-based loan (excluding PLUS or other private loans): $3,516. Among students who received need-based aid, the average percentage of need met: 83%. Among students who received aid based on merit, the average award (and the proportion receiving): $2,332 (17%). The average athletic scholarship (and the proportion receiving): $4,116 (6%). Average amount of debt of borrowers graduating in 2009: $21,858. Proportion who borrowed: 52%.

CAMPUS LIFE AND EXTRACURRICULAR ACTIVITIES

Campus housing available (% using): coed dorms (90%), sorority housing (2%), apartments for married students (0%), apartment for single students (7%), special housing for disabled students (0%). Students who live in college-owned, operated, or affiliated housing: 48%. **Student employment:** During the 2009-2010 academic year, 15% of undergraduates worked on campus. Average per-year earnings: $1,667. **Clubs and organizations:** Number of student organizations: 276. Activities include: campus ministries, choral groups, concert band, dance, drama/theater, international student organization, jazz band, literary magazine, marching band, model UN, music ensembles, musical theater, opera, pep band, radio station, student government, student newspaper, student film society, symphony orchestra, television station. Number of fraternities: 18; sororities: 11. Proportion of men in fraternities: 25%; of women in sororities: 17%. Average proportion of students who stay on campus on weekends: 95%. **Sports program (2009-2010):** Member of NCAA II. *Men's intercollegiate varsity sports:* baseball, basketball, cross country, football, golf, soccer, swimming, tennis, track and field (indoor), track and field (outdoor), wrestling. *Women's intercollegiate varsity sports:* basketball, cross country, golf, soccer, softball, swimming, tennis, track and field (indoor), track and field (outdoor), volleyball.

SERVICES AND FACILITIES

Basic services: nonremedial tutoring, women's center, placement service, health service, health insurance. **Counseling services:** minority student, career, military, personal, veteran student, academic, psychological, birth control, religious, other. **For learning-disabled students:** School does not offer a structured program with separate admission and additional fees. Total undergraduates in learning-disabled program or receiving services: 22. Services include: reading machines, tape recorders, videotaped classes, note-taking services, special bookstore section, oral tests, learning center, readers, extended time for tests, tutors, early syllabus, priority registration, priority seating, proofreading services, texts on tape, typist/scribe, exams on tape or computer, other testing accommodations, other. **Library:** Number of titles: 498,237; number of current serial subscriptions: 3,770. **Information technology resources:** Students are not required to lease or own a computer. Number of campus computers available to all students: 965. School has a

wireless network. Approximate number of users that can be accommodated: 2,400. Proportion of college-owned housing units wired for high-speed internet access: 100%. **Campus safety:** Security services offered: 24-hour foot-and-vehicle patrols, late-night transport/escort service, 24-hour emergency telephones, lighted pathways/sidewalks, student patrols, controlled dormitory access (key, security card, etc).

TRANSFER AND INTERNATIONAL STUDENTS

Transfer students: May apply for admission for the following academic terms: Fall, Spring, Summer. Applicants need a minimum number of credits to apply. For fall 2009: Transfer applications received: 395. Transfer applicants offered admission: 251. Transfer applicants enrolled: 155. **International students:** Number of foreign undergraduates: 252 (5% of student body). Number of countries represented: 43. Minimum TOEFL score required: 550 (paper); 79 (computer). Average TOEFL score: 577 (paper).

University of Central Missouri

- **Address:** Administration Building, Suite 304, Warrensburg, MO 64093
- **Website:** http://www.ucmo.edu
- **Public**
- **Enrollment:** 7,565 full-time; 1,523 part-time

KEY STATS

✔ **U.S News College Ranking:** 76, Regional Universities (Midwest)
✔ **ACT Score (25th/75th percentile):** 19-24
✔ **Tuition:** 2009-2010: $6,585 in state, $12,444 out of state

Selectivity: Selective	**Room/board:** $6,320
Acceptance rate: 85%	**Average debt:** $18,272
Student/faculty ratio: 18/1	**Proportion who borrowed:** 69%

UNDERGRADUATE STUDENT BODY STATS

2009-2010 enrollment: 7,565 full-time; 1,523 part-time. Men: 45%; women: 55%. **Ethnic makeup:** African American: 8%; American-Indian: 1%; Asian American: 1%; Hispanic: 2%; White: 86%; International: 2%.

ADMISSIONS FACTS AND FIGURES

Phone: (660) 543-4290. **Email:** admit@ucmo.edu. **Website:** http://www.ucmo.edu. **Application deadlines for fall 2011:** Regular decision: August 19. Early decision: Not offered. Early action: Not offered. Admission can be deferred. **Application fee:** $30. **To apply online, go to:** http://www.ucmo.edu/admit/online_app.htm. **Admissions requirements/recommendations:** High school units required (recommended): English: 4; Mathematics: 3; Science: 2; Foreign language: (2); Social studies: 3; Academic electives: 3; Total units: 16 (2). Tests: The college uses SAT or ACT scores in admissions decisions. Either SAT or ACT required. For admission to the fall 2011 entering class, the school will accept: ACT with or without writing accepted. Campus visit: Recommended. Admissions interview: Neither required nor recommended. Off-campus interview: May be arranged. **Factors that count in admissions decisions:** *Academic:* Secondary school record: Considered. Class rank: Very Important. Letters of recommendation: Considered. Standardized test scores: Very Important. Essay: Not Considered. *Nonacademic:* Interview: Not Considered. Extracurricular activities: Considered. Talent/ability: Considered. Character/personal qualities: Considered. Alumni/ae relationship: Considered. Geographical residence: Not Considered. State residency: Not Considered. Religious affiliation/commitment: Not Considered. Minority status: Not Considered. Volunteer work: Not Considered. Work experience: Not Considered. **Other schools with the greatest overlap in applicants:** Missouri State University; Northwest Missouri State University; University of Missouri; University of Missouri–Kansas City. **Admissions statistics for the fall 2009 entering class:** Total applicants: 3,653. Total accepted: 3,091. Freshmen enrolled: 1,504; 9% were from out of state. Overall acceptance rate: 85%. **Credentials of fall 2009 freshmen:** 14% ranked in the top 10 percent of their high school class; 38% were in the top 25 percent; 73% were in the top half. (Proportion submitting class standing: 69%.) **Average high school grade point average:** 3.3. **First-year students submitting ACT scores:** 95%. Scores (25/75 percentile): English: 19-24, Math: 17-24, Composite: 19-24.

ACADEMICS

Year founded: 1871. **Academic calendar:** Semester. **Degrees offered:** bachelor's, post-bachelor's certificate, master's, post-master's certificate. **Most popular majors:** 7% criminal justice and corrections, 6% nursing, 3% air transportation, 3% psychology, 3% teacher education and professional development. **Major fields of study:** agriculture, agriculture operations, and related sciences; architecture and related services; area, ethnic, cultural, and gender studies; biological and biomedical sciences; business, management, marketing, and related support services; communication, journalism, and related programs; communications technologies/technicians and support services; computer and information sciences and support services; education; engineering; engineering technologies/technicians; English language and literature/letters; family and consumer sciences/human sciences; foreign languages, literatures, and linguistics; health professions and related clinical sciences; history; liberal arts and sciences studies, and humanities; mathematics and statistics; parks, recreation, leisure, and fitness studies; psychology; public administration and social service professions; security and protective services; social sciences; transportation and materials moving; visual and performing arts. **Areas of required coursework:** arts/fine arts, humanities, computer literacy, mathematics, English (including composition), sciences (biological or physical), history, social science, other. **Preprofessional programs:** pre-law, pre-dentistry, pre-medicine, pre-veterinary science, pre-optometry, pre-pharmacy, other. **Special academic programs:** cooperative (work-study plan) program, cross-registration, distance learning, double major, dual enrollment, English as a Second Language (ESL), honors program, independent study, internships, student-designed major, study abroad, teacher certificate program, weekend college. **Teacher certification offered in:** early childhood, special education, elementary, vo-tech, middle/junior high, adult education, secondary, bilingual/bicultural. **Cooperative education programs:** education, technologies, other. **Reserve Officers Training Corps (ROTC):** Army ROTC: Offered on campus; Air Force ROTC: Offered at cooperating institution (University of Missouri). **Faculty and instruction (2009-2010):** Total instructional faculty: 460 full-time, 175 part-time (54% men; 46% women; 12% minorities). Full-time faculty with Ph.D. or other terminal degree: 73%. Student/faculty ratio: 18/1. Classes of fewer than 20 students: 49%; of 20 to 49 students: 48%; of 50 or more students: 3%. **Advanced Placement and International Baccalaureate credit:** AP tests may be used for: Credit only. Scores accepted: 3. International Baccalaureate exams may be used for: Credit only. **Freshmen returning for sophomore year:** 72%. **Graduation rates:** Four-year: 24%; five-year: 44%; six-year: 51%. **Graduate study:** 17% of students pursue further study immediately upon graduation. Fields in which graduates pursue further study: Master of Business Administration (MBA), 16%; law, 2%; education, 17%; arts and sciences, 12%.

COSTS AND FINANCIAL AID
Financial aid office: (660) 543-4040. **Expenses (2009-2010):** Tuition and fees 2009-2010: $6,585 in state, $12,444 out of state; room/board: $6,320. Estimated books and supplies: $700; transportation: $600. **Financial aid:** Priority filing date for institution's financial aid form: April 1. In 2009-2010, 73% of undergraduates applied for financial aid. Of those, 34% were determined to have financial need; 16% had their need fully met. Average financial aid package (proportion receiving): $9,426 (34%). Average amount of gift aid, such as scholarships or grants (proportion receiving): $3,361 (17%). Average amount of self-help aid, such as work study or loans (proportion receiving): $0 (28%). Average need-based loan (excluding PLUS or other private loans): $4,543. Among students who received need-based aid, the average percentage of need met: 90%. Among students who received aid based on merit, the average award (and the proportion receiving): $8,345 (14%). The average athletic scholarship (and the proportion receiving): $5,560 (3%). Average amount of debt of borrowers graduating in 2009: $18,272. Proportion who borrowed: 69%.

CAMPUS LIFE AND EXTRACURRICULAR ACTIVITIES
Campus housing available (% using): coed dorms (79%), women's dorms (3%), sorority housing (6%), fraternity housing (5%), apartments for married students (3%), apartment for single students (4%), special housing for disabled students (0%), special housing for international students (0%), other housing options (0%). Students who live in college-owned, operated, or affiliated housing: 28%. **Student employment:** During the 2009-2010 academic year, 7% of undergraduates worked on campus. Average per-year earnings: $1,242. **Clubs and organizations:** Number of student organizations: 225. Activities include: campus ministries, choral groups, concert band, dance, drama/theater, jazz band, literary magazine, marching band, music ensembles, musical theater, pep band, radio station, student government, student newspaper, student film society, symphony orchestra, television station. Number of fraternities: 9; sororities: 7. Proportion of men in fraternities: 8%; of women in sororities: 8%. Average proportion of students who stay on campus on weekends: 54%. **Sports program (2009-2010):** Member of NCAA II. **Men's intercollegiate varsity sports:** baseball, basket-ball, cross country, football, golf, rifle, track and field (indoor), track and field (outdoor), wrestling. **Women's intercollegiate varsity sports:** basketball, bowling, cross country, rifle, softball, track and field (indoor), track and field (outdoor), volleyball.

SERVICES AND FACILITIES
Basic services: nonremedial tutoring, women's center, placement service, day care, health service, health insurance. **Remedial assistance:** reading, math, writing, study skills. **Counseling services:** minority student, career, personal, academic, psychological, birth control, religious. **For learning-disabled students:** School does not offer a structured program with separate admission and additional fees. Total undergraduates in learning-disabled program or receiving services: 135. Services include: remedial math, remedial English, reading machines, remedial reading, tape recorders, other special classes, videotaped classes, note-taking services, special bookstore section, oral tests, learning center, readers, extended time for tests, tutors, priority registration, priority seating, texts on tape, other testing accommodations, other. **Library:** Number of titles: 1,289,493; number of current serial subscriptions: 39,063. **Information technology resources:** Students are not required to lease or own a computer. Number of campus computers available to all students: 10,000. School has a wireless network. Approximate number of users that can be accommodated: 9,825. Proportion of college-owned housing units wired for high-speed internet access: 100%. **Campus safety:** Security services offered: 24-hour foot-and-vehicle patrols, late-night transport/escort service, 24-hour emergency telephones, lighted pathways/sidewalks, student patrols, controlled dormitory access (key, security card, etc).

TRANSFER AND INTERNATIONAL STUDENTS
Transfer students: May apply for admission for the following academic terms: Fall, Spring, Summer. Applicants need a minimum number of credits to apply. For fall 2009: Transfer applications received: 1,435. Transfer applicants offered admission: 1,000. Transfer applicants enrolled: 836. **International students:** Number of foreign undergraduates: 204 (2% of student body). Number of countries represented: 55. Minimum TOEFL score required: 500 (paper); 173 (computer). Average TOEFL score: 527 (paper).

University of Missouri

- **Address:** 105 Jesse Hall, Columbia, MO 65211
- **Website:** http://www.missouri.edu
- **Public**
- **Enrollment:** 22,382 full-time; 1,487 part-time

KEY STATS
✔ **U.S News College Ranking:** 94, National Universities
✔ **ACT Score (25th/75th percentile):** 23-28
✔ **Tuition:** 2010-2011: $8,501 in state, $19,592 out of state

Selectivity: More selective	**Room/board:** $8,150
Acceptance rate: 83%	**Average debt:** $20,689
Student/faculty ratio: 19/1	**Proportion who borrowed:** 57%

UNDERGRADUATE STUDENT BODY STATS
2009-2010 enrollment: 22,382 full-time; 1,487 part-time. Men: 48%; women: 52%. **Ethnic makeup:** African American: 7%; American-Indian: 1%; Asian American: 2%; Hispanic: 2%; White: 86%; International: 2%.

ADMISSIONS FACTS AND FIGURES
Phone: (573) 882-7786. **Email:** mu4u@missouri.edu. **Website:** http://www.missouri.edu. **Application deadlines for fall 2011:** Regular decision: Rolling; decision sent by June 1. Early decision: Not offered. Early action: Not offered. Admission can be deferred. **Application fee:** $45. **To apply online, go to:** http://admissions.missouri.edu/howtoapply/index.php. **Admissions requirements/recommendations:** High school units required (recommended): English: 4; Mathematics: 4; Science: 3; Foreign language: 2; Social studies: 3; Total units: 17. Tests: The college uses SAT or ACT scores in admissions decisions. Either SAT or ACT required. For admission to the fall 2011 entering class, the school will accept: ACT with or without writing accepted. Campus visit: Recommended. Admissions interview: Neither required nor recommended. Off-campus interview: Not available. **Factors that count in admissions decisions:** *Academic:* Secondary school record: Important. Class rank: Very Important. Letters of recommendation: Considered. Standardized test scores: Very Important. Essay: Considered.

Nonacademic: Interview: Not Considered. Extracurricular activities: Not Considered. Talent/ability: Considered. Character/personal qualities: Not Considered. Alumni/ae relationship: Not Considered. Geographical residence: Not Considered. State residency: Not Considered. Religious affiliation/commitment: Not Considered. Minority status: Considered. Volunteer work: Considered. Work experience: Considered. **Admissions statistics for the fall 2009 entering class:** Total applicants: 16,436. Total accepted: 13,659. Freshmen enrolled: 5,593; 27% were from out of state. Overall acceptance rate: 83%. **Credentials of fall 2009 freshmen:** 25% ranked in the top 10 percent of their high school class; 55% were in the top 25 percent; 86% were in the top half. (Proportion submitting class standing: 80%.) **First-year students who submitted SAT scores:** 11%. Scores (25/75 percentile): Critical Reading: 530-650, Math: 530-650, Combined: 1060-1300. **First-year students submitting ACT scores:** 95%. Scores (25/75 percentile): English: 22-27, Math: 23-29, Composite: 23-28.

ACADEMICS

Year founded: 1839. **Academic calendar:** Semester. **Degrees offered:** bachelor's, master's, post-master's certificate, doctorate. **Most popular majors:** 19% business, management, marketing, and related support services; 13% communication, journalism, and related programs; 7% engineering; 7% health professions and related clinical sciences; 6% social sciences. **Major fields of study:** agriculture, agriculture operations, and related sciences; area, ethnic, cultural, and gender studies; biological and biomedical sciences; business, management, marketing, and related support services; communication, journalism, and related programs; computer and information sciences and support services; education; engineering; English language and literature/letters; family and consumer sciences/human sciences; foreign languages, literatures, and linguistics; health professions and related clinical sciences; history; liberal arts and sciences studies, and humanities; mathematics and statistics; multi/interdisciplinary studies; natural resources and conservation; parks, recreation, leisure, and fitness studies; philosophy and religious studies; physical sciences; psychology; public administration and social service professions; social sciences; visual and performing arts. **Areas of required coursework:** humanities, mathematics, English (including composition), sciences (biological or physical), social science, other. **Preprofessional programs:** pre-law, pre-dentistry, pre-medicine, pre-veterinary science, pre-pharmacy, other. **Special academic programs:** accelerated program, cooperative (work-study plan) program, cross-registration, distance learning, double major, dual enrollment, English as a Second Language (ESL), exchange student program (domestic), external degree program, honors program, independent study, internships, student-designed major, study abroad, teacher certificate program, other. **Teacher certification offered in:** early childhood, special education, elementary, middle/junior high, secondary. **Cooperative education programs:** education, engineering, health professions, social/behavioral science. **Reserve Officers Training Corps (ROTC):** Army ROTC: Offered on campus; Navy ROTC: Offered on campus; Air Force ROTC: Offered on campus. **Faculty and instruction (2009-2010):** Total instructional faculty: 1,266 full-time, 75 part-time (64% men; 36% women; 17% minorities). Full-time faculty with Ph.D. or other terminal degree: 93%. Student/faculty ratio: 19/1. Classes of fewer than 20 students: 44%; of 20 to 49 students: 41%; of 50 or more students: 15%. **Advanced Placement and International Baccalaureate credit:** AP tests may be used for: Credit and/or placement. Scores accepted: 3, 4, 5. International Baccalaureate exams may be used for: Credit only. **Freshmen returning for sophomore year:** 85%. **Graduation rates:** Four-year: 43%; five-year: 65%; six-year: 68%. **Graduate study:** 31% of students pursue further study immediately upon graduation.

COSTS AND FINANCIAL AID

Financial aid office: (573) 882-7506. **Expenses (2010-2011):** Tuition and fees 2010-2011: $8,501 in state, $19,592 out of state; room/board: $8,150. Estimated books and supplies: $1,040; transportation: $1,515; personal expenses: $1,515. **Financial aid:** Priority filing date for institution's financial aid form: March 1. In 2009-2010, 67% of undergraduates applied for financial aid. Of those, 48% were determined to have financial need; 18% had their need fully met. Average financial aid package (proportion receiving): $13,136 (47%). Average amount of gift aid, such as scholarships or grants (proportion receiving): $7,152 (39%). Average amount of self-help aid, such as work study or loans (proportion receiving): $4,592 (37%). Average need-based loan (excluding PLUS or other private loans): $4,441. Among students who received need-based aid, the average percentage of need met: 84%. Among students who received aid based on merit, the average award (and the proportion receiving): $3,531 (17%). The average athletic scholarship (and the proportion receiving): $9,713 (1%). Average amount of debt of borrowers graduating in 2009: $20,689. Proportion who borrowed: 57%.

CAMPUS LIFE AND EXTRACURRICULAR ACTIVITIES

Campus housing available: coed dorms, women's dorms, men's dorms, sorority housing, fraternity housing, apartments for married students, other housing options. Students who live in college-owned, operated, or affiliated housing: 30%. **Clubs and organizations:** Number of student organizations: 639. Activities include: choral groups, concert band, dance, drama/theater, jazz band, literary magazine, marching band, music ensembles, musical theater, opera, pep band, radio station, student government, student newspaper, student film society, symphony orchestra, television station, yearbook. Number of fraternities: 32; sororities: 19. Proportion of men in fraternities: 18%; of women in sororities: 25%. **Sports program (2009-2010):** Member of NCAA I. **Men's intercollegiate varsity sports:** baseball, basketball, cross country, football, golf, swimming, track and field (indoor), track and field (outdoor), wrestling. **Women's intercollegiate varsity sports:** basketball, cross country, golf, gymnastics, soccer, softball, swimming, tennis, track and field (indoor), track and field (outdoor), volleyball.

SERVICES AND FACILITIES

Basic services: nonremedial tutoring, women's center, placement service, day care, health service, health insurance. **Counseling services:** minority student, career, military, personal, veteran student, academic, older student, psychological, birth control, religious. **For learning-disabled students:** School does not offer a structured program with separate admission and additional fees. Total undergraduates in learning-disabled program or receiving services: 124. Services include: reading machines, tape recorders, diagnostic testing service, note-taking services, oral tests, learning center, readers, extended time for tests, tutors, priority registration, priority seating, proofreading services, substitution of courses, texts on tape, typist/scribe, exams on tape or computer, other testing accommodations, other. **Library:** Number of titles: 3,523,795; number of current serial subscriptions: 46,543. **Information technology resources:** Students are not required to lease or own a computer. Number of campus computers available to all students: 1,200. School has a wireless network. Approximate number of users that can be accommodated: 30,000. Proportion of college-owned housing units wired for high-speed internet access: 95%. **Campus safety:** Security services offered: 24-hour foot-and-vehicle patrols, late-night transport/escort service, 24-hour emergency telephones, lighted pathways/sidewalks, student patrols, controlled dormitory access (key, security card, etc).

TRANSFER AND INTERNATIONAL STUDENTS

Transfer students: May apply for admission for the following academic terms: Fall, Winter, Spring, Summer. Applicants need a minimum number of credits to apply. For fall 2009: Transfer applications received: 3,085. Transfer applicants offered admission: 2,151. Transfer applicants enrolled: 1,423. **International students:** Number of foreign undergraduates: 430 (2% of student body). Number of countries represented: 50. Minimum TOEFL score required: 500 (paper); 61 (computer).

University of Missouri–Kansas City

- **Address:** 5100 Rockhill Road, Kansas City, MO 64110
- **Website:** http://www.umkc.edu
- **Public**
- **Enrollment:** 6,264 full-time; 3,134 part-time

KEY STATS

✔ **U.S News College Ranking:** second tier, National Universities
✔ **ACT Score (25th/75th percentile):** 21-28
✔ **Tuition:** 2009-2010: $8,273 in state, $19,364 out of state

Selectivity: More selective	**Room/board:** $9,560
Acceptance rate: 62%	**Average debt:** $20,512
Student/faculty ratio: 13/1	**Proportion who borrowed:** 65%

UNDERGRADUATE STUDENT BODY STATS

2009-2010 enrollment: 6,264 full-time; 3,134 part-time. Men: 42%; women: 58%. **Ethnic makeup:** African American: 15%; American-Indian: 1%; Asian American: 6%; Hispanic: 5%; White: 70%; International: 3%.

ADMISSIONS FACTS AND FIGURES

Phone: (816) 235-1111. **Email:** admit@umkc.edu. **Website:** http://www.umkc.edu. **Application deadlines for fall 2011:** Regular decision: Rolling. Early decision: Not offered. Early action: Not offered. Admission can be deferred. **Application fee:** $45. **To apply online, go to:** http://www.umkc.

edu/admissions. **Admissions requirements/recommendations:** High school units required (recommended): English: 4 (4); Mathematics: 4 (4); Science: 3 (3); Foreign language: 2 (2); Social studies: 3 (3); Total units: 17. Tests: The college uses SAT or ACT scores in admissions decisions. Either SAT or ACT required. For admission to the fall 2011 entering class, the school will accept: ACT with or without writing accepted. Campus visit: Recommended. Admissions interview: Neither required nor recommended. Off-campus interview: Not available. **Factors that count in admissions decisions:** *Academic:* Secondary school record: Very Important. Class rank: Very Important. Letters of recommendation: Considered. Standardized test scores: Very Important. Essay: Considered. *Nonacademic:* Interview: Considered. Extracurricular activities: Considered. Talent/ability: Considered. Character/personal qualities: Considered. Alumni/ae relationship: Not Considered. Geographical residence: Not Considered. State residency: Not Considered. Religious affiliation/commitment: Not Considered. Minority status: Not Considered. Volunteer work: Considered. Work experience: Considered. **Other schools with the greatest overlap in applicants:** Missouri State University; Truman State University; University of Central Missouri; University of Kansas; University of Missouri. **Admissions statistics for the fall 2009 entering class:** Total applicants: 4,117. Total accepted: 2,564. Freshmen enrolled: 1,004; 23% were from out of state. Overall acceptance rate: 62%. **Credentials of fall 2009 freshmen:** 31% ranked in the top 10 percent of their high school class; 58% were in the top 25 percent; 89% were in the top half. (Proportion submitting class standing: 67%.) **Average high school grade point average:** 3.3. **First-year students who submitted SAT scores:** 11%. Scores (25/75 percentile): Critical Reading: 520-650, Math: 550-690, Combined: 1070-1340. **First-year students submitting ACT scores:** 94%. Scores (25/75 percentile): English: 20-28, Math: 19-27, Composite: 21-28.

ACADEMICS

Year founded: 1929. **Academic calendar:** Semester. **Degrees offered:** bachelor's, master's, post-master's certificate, doctorate. **Most popular majors:** 17% liberal arts and sciences studies, and humanities, 13% business, management, marketing, and related support services, 9% education, 9% health professions and related clinical sciences, 7% psychology. **Major fields of study:** architecture and related services; area, ethnic, cultural, and gender studies; biological and biomedical sciences; business, management, marketing, and related support services; communication, journalism, and related programs; computer and information sciences and support services; education; engineering; English language and literature/letters; foreign languages, literatures, and linguistics; health professions and related clinical sciences; history; liberal arts and sciences studies, and humanities; mathematics and statistics; multi/interdisciplinary studies; natural resources and conservation; philosophy and religious studies; physical sciences; psychology; security and protective services; social sciences; visual and performing arts. **Areas of required coursework:** humanities, computer literacy, mathematics, English (including composition), foreign languages, sciences (biological or physical), history, social science. **Pre-professional programs:** pre-law, pre-dentistry, pre-medicine, pre-pharmacy, other. **Special academic programs:** accelerated program, cooperative (work-study plan) program, distance learning, double major, dual enrollment, English as a Second Language (ESL), honors program, independent study, internships, study abroad, teacher certificate program. **Teacher certification offered in:** early childhood, special education, elementary, middle/junior high, secondary, bilingual/bicultural. **Cooperative education programs:** computer science, education, engineering, health professions, other. **Reserve Officers Training Corps (ROTC):** Army ROTC: Offered on campus; Air Force ROTC: Offered at cooperating institution (University of Missouri). **Faculty and instruction (2009-2010):** Total instructional faculty: 721 full-time, 416 part-time (55% men; 45% women; 17% minorities). Full-time faculty with Ph.D. or other terminal degree: 75%. Student/faculty ratio: 13/1. Classes of fewer than 20 students: 56%; of 20 to 49 students: 36%; of 50 or more students: 8%. **Advanced Placement and International Baccalaureate credit:** AP tests may be used for: Credit and/or placement. Scores accepted: 3, 4, 5. International Baccalaureate exams may be used for: Credit and/or placement. **Freshmen returning for sophomore year:** 72%. **Graduation rates:** Four-year: 19%; five-year: 33%; six-year: 45%. **Graduate study:** 49% of students pursue further study immediately upon graduation.

COSTS AND FINANCIAL AID

Financial aid office: (816) 235-1154. **Expenses (2009-2010):** Tuition and fees 2009-2010: $8,273 in state, $19,364 out of state; room/board: $9,560. Estimated books and supplies: $1,180; transportation: $1,091; personal expenses: $5,930. **Financial aid:** Priority filing date for institution's financial aid form: March 1. In 2009-2010, 77% of undergraduates applied for financial aid. Of those, 68% were determined to have financial need; 7% had their need fully met. Average financial aid package (proportion receiving): $9,704 (65%). Average amount of gift aid, such as scholarships or grants (proportion receiving): $6,675 (53%). Average amount of self-help aid, such as work study or loans (proportion receiving): $8,905 (54%). Average need-based loan (excluding PLUS or other private loans): $8,436. Among students who received need-based aid, the average percentage of need met: 51%. Among students who received aid based on merit, the average award (and the proportion receiving): $5,101 (13%). The average athletic scholarship (and the proportion receiving): $11,022 (2%). Average amount of debt of borrowers graduating in 2009: $20,512. Proportion who borrowed: 65%.

CAMPUS LIFE AND EXTRACURRICULAR ACTIVITIES

Campus housing available (% using): coed dorms (67%), sorority housing (1%), fraternity housing (1%), apartment for single students (30%), other housing options (1%). Students who live in college-owned, operated, or affiliated housing: 16%. **Student employment:** During the 2009-2010 academic year, 15% of undergraduates worked on campus. Average per-year earnings: $6,600. **Clubs and organizations:** Number of student organizations: 175. Activities include: campus ministries, choral groups, concert band, dance, drama/theater, international student organization, jazz band, literary magazine, model UN, music ensembles, musical theater, opera, pep band, radio station, student government, student newspaper, student film society, symphony orchestra. Number of fraternities: 8; sororities: 9. Proportion of men in fraternities: 6%; of women in sororities: 7%. Average proportion of students who stay on campus on weekends: 18%. **Sports program (2009-2010):** Member of NCAA I. *Men's intercollegiate varsity sports:* basketball, cross country, golf, soccer, tennis, track and field (indoor), track and field (outdoor). *Women's intercollegiate varsity sports:* basketball, cross country, golf, soccer, softball, tennis, track and field (indoor), track and field (outdoor), volleyball.

SERVICES AND FACILITIES

Basic services: nonremedial tutoring, women's center, placement service, day care, health service, health insurance. **Remedial assistance:** reading, math, writing, study skills. **Counseling services:** minority student, career, personal, veteran student, academic, older student, psychological, birth control, religious. **For learning-disabled students:** School does not offer a structured program with separate admission and additional fees. Services include: tape recorders, diagnostic testing service, note-taking services, readers, extended time for tests, priority registration, priority seating, texts on tape, other testing accommodations, other. **Library:** Number of titles: 1,827,162; number of current serial subscriptions: 41,949. **Information technology resources:** Students are not required to lease or own a computer. Number of campus computers available to all students: 600. School has a wireless network. Approximate number of users that can be accommodated: 9,000. Proportion of college-owned housing units wired for high-speed internet access: 100%. **Campus safety:** Security services offered: 24-hour foot-and-vehicle patrols, late-night transport/escort service, 24-hour emergency telephones, lighted pathways/sidewalks, controlled dormitory access (key, security card, etc.).

TRANSFER AND INTERNATIONAL STUDENTS

Transfer students: May apply for admission for the following academic terms: Fall, Winter, Spring, Summer. Applicants need a minimum number of credits to apply. For fall 2009: Transfer applications received: 2,793. Transfer applicants offered admission: 1,904. Transfer applicants enrolled: 1,449. **International students:** Number of foreign undergraduates: 213 (3% of student body). Number of countries represented: 55. Minimum TOEFL score required: 500 (paper); 173 (computer). Average TOEFL score: 593 (paper).

University of Missouri–St. Louis

- **Address:** 1 University Boulevard, St. Louis, MO 63121-4400
- **Website:** http://www.umsl.edu
- **Public**
- **Enrollment:** 6,029 full-time; 6,953 part-time

KEY STATS

✔ **U.S News College Ranking:** second tier, National Universities
✔ **ACT Score (25th/75th percentile):** 20-26
✔ **Tuition:** 2010-2011: $8,631 in state, $20,220 out of state

Selectivity: Selective	**Room/board:** $8,620
Acceptance rate: 79%	**Average debt:** $25,776
Student/faculty ratio: 17/1	**Proportion who borrowed:** 65%

UNDERGRADUATE STUDENT BODY STATS

2009-2010 enrollment: 6,029 full-time; 6,953 part-time. Men: 39%; women: 61%. **Ethnic makeup:** African American: 21%; Asian American: 3%; Hispanic: 2%; White: 71%; International: 3%.

ADMISSIONS FACTS AND FIGURES

Phone: (314) 516-5451. **Email:** admissions@umsl.edu. **Website:** http://www.umsl.edu. **Application deadlines for fall 2011:** Regular decision: August 23. Early decision: Not offered. Early action: Not offered. Admission cannot be deferred. **Application fee:** $35. **To apply online, go to:** http://www.umsl.edu/admission/apply/index.html. **Admissions requirements/recommendations:** High school units required (recommended): English: 4; Mathematics: 4; Science: 3; Foreign language: 2; Social studies: 3; Total units: 17. Tests: The college uses SAT or ACT scores in admissions decisions. Either SAT or ACT required. For admission to the fall 2011 entering class, the school will accept: ACT with or without writing accepted. Campus visit: Recommended. Admissions interview: Neither required nor recommended. Off-campus interview: Not available. **Factors that count in admissions decisions:** *Academic:* Secondary school record: Very Important. Class rank: Very Important. Letters of recommendation: Considered. Standardized test scores: Very Important. Essay: Considered. *Nonacademic:* Interview: Not Considered. Extracurricular activities: Not Considered. Talent/ability: Not Considered. Character/personal qualities: Not Considered. Alumni/ae relationship: Not Considered. Geographical residence: Not Considered. State residency: Not Considered. Religious affiliation/commitment: Not Considered. Minority status: Not Considered. Volunteer work: Not Considered. Work experience: Not Considered. **Other schools with the greatest overlap in applicants:** Lindenwood University; Missouri State University; Southeast Missouri State University; St. Louis University; University of Missouri. **Admissions statistics for the fall 2009 entering class:** Total applicants: 1,619. Total accepted: 1,278. Freshmen enrolled: 525; 15% were from out of state. Overall acceptance rate: 79%. **Credentials of fall 2009 freshmen:** 22% ranked in the top 10 percent of their high school class; 48% were in the top 25 percent; 81% were in the top half. (Proportion submitting class standing: 74%.) **First-year students who submitted SAT scores:** 4%. Scores (25/75 percentile): Critical Reading: 500-670, Math: 470-670, Combined: 970-1340. **First-year students submitting ACT scores:** 90%. Scores (25/75 percentile): English: 19-26, Math: 18-25, Composite: 20-26.

ACADEMICS

Year founded: 1963. **Academic calendar:** Semester. **Degrees offered:** bachelor's, post-bachelor's certificate, master's, post-master's certificate, doctorate. **Most popular majors:** 28% business, management, marketing, and related support services, 14% education, 9% health professions and related clinical sciences, 9% social sciences, 6% psychology. **Major fields of study:** biological and biomedical sciences; business, management, marketing, and related support services; communication, journalism, and related programs; computer and information sciences and support services; education; engineering; English language and literature/letters; foreign languages, literatures, and linguistics; health professions and related clinical sciences; history; liberal arts and sciences studies, and humanities; mathematics and statistics; multi/interdisciplinary studies; philosophy and religious studies; physical sciences; psychology; public administration and social service professions; social sciences; visual and performing arts. **Areas of required coursework:** humanities, mathematics, English (including composition), foreign languages, sciences (biological or physical), history, social science. **Preprofessional programs:** pre-law, pre-dentistry, pre-medicine, pre-veterinary science, pre-optometry, pre-pharmacy, other. **Special academic programs:** accelerated program, cooperative (work-study plan) program, cross-registra-

tion, distance learning, double major, dual enrollment, English as a Second Language (ESL), exchange student program (domestic), honors program, independent study, internships, student-designed major, study abroad, teacher certificate program, other. **Teacher certification offered in:** early childhood, special education, elementary, middle/junior high, secondary. **Cooperative education programs:** business, computer science, health professions, other. **Reserve Officers Training Corps (ROTC):** Army ROTC: Offered at cooperating institution (Washington University in St. Louis); Air Force ROTC: Offered at cooperating institution (St. Louis University). **Faculty and instruction (2009-2010):** Total instructional faculty: 480 full-time, 378 part-time (46% men; 54% women; 16% minorities). Full-time faculty with Ph.D. or other terminal degree: 76%. Student/faculty ratio: 17/1. Classes of fewer than 20 students: 44%; of 20 to 49 students: 47%; of 50 or more students: 9%. **Advanced Placement and International Baccalaureate credit:** AP tests may be used for: Credit and/or placement. Scores accepted: 3, 4, 5. International Baccalaureate exams may be used for: Credit only. **Freshmen returning for sophomore year:** 70%. **Graduation rates:** Four-year: 21%; five-year: 35%; six-year: 41%. **Graduate study:** 13% of students pursue further study immediately upon graduation; 21% within one year; 37% within five years. Fields in which graduates pursue further study: Master of Business Administration (MBA), 20%; law, 1%; engineering, 2%; education, 25%; arts and sciences, 39%; veterinary medicine, 1%.

COSTS AND FINANCIAL AID

Financial aid office: (314) 516-5526. **Expenses (2010-2011):** Tuition and fees 2010-2011: $8,631 in state, $20,220 out of state; room/board: $8,620. Estimated books and supplies: $950; transportation: $3,250; personal expenses: $6,140. **Financial aid:** Priority filing date for institution's financial aid form: April 1. In 2009-2010, 77% of undergraduates applied for financial aid. Of those, 69% were determined to have financial need; 6% had their need fully met. Average financial aid package (proportion receiving): $8,707 (67%). Average amount of gift aid, such as scholarships or grants (proportion receiving): $5,815 (54%). Average amount of self-help aid, such as work study or loans (proportion receiving): $4,625 (56%). Average need-based loan (excluding PLUS or other private loans): $4,543. Among students who received need-based aid, the average percentage of need met: 48%. Among students who received aid based on merit, the average award (and the proportion receiving): $4,315 (9%). The average athletic scholarship (and the proportion receiving): $11,178 (1%). Average amount of debt of borrowers graduating in 2009: $25,776. Proportion who borrowed: 65%.

CAMPUS LIFE AND EXTRACURRICULAR ACTIVITIES

Campus housing available (% using): coed dorms (38%), sorority housing (1%), apartments for married students (1%), apartment for single students (59%), special housing for disabled students (1%), other housing options. Students who live in college-owned, operated, or affiliated housing: 8%. **Student employment:** During the 2009-2010 academic year, 6% of undergraduates worked on campus. Average per-year earnings: $2,069. **Clubs and organizations:** Number of student organizations: 124. Activities include: campus ministries, choral groups, dance, drama/theater, international student organization, jazz band, literary magazine, model UN, music ensembles, musical theater, opera, pep band, radio station, student government, student newspaper, student film society. Number of fraternities: 3; sororities: 3. Proportion of men in fraternities: 1%; of women in sororities: 1%. **Sports program (2009-2010):** Member of NCAA II. *Men's intercollegiate varsity sports:* baseball, basketball, golf, soccer, tennis. *Women's intercollegiate varsity sports:* basketball, golf, soccer, softball, tennis, volleyball.

SERVICES AND FACILITIES

Basic services: nonremedial tutoring, women's center, placement service, day care, health service, health insurance. **Counseling services:** minority student, career, personal, veteran student, academic, older student, psychological, birth control. **For learning-disabled students:** School does not offer a structured program with separate admission and additional fees. Services include: remedial math, tape recorders, note-taking services, oral tests, readers, extended time for tests, priority seating, texts on tape, other. **Library:** Number of titles: 1,212,610; number of current serial subscriptions: 3,149. **Information technology resources:** Students are not required to lease or own a computer. Number of campus computers available to all students: 1,300. School has a wireless network. Approximate number of users that can be accommodated: 1,500. Proportion of college-owned housing units wired for high-speed internet access: 80%. **Campus safety:** Security services offered: 24-hour foot-and-vehicle patrols, late-night transport/escort service, 24-hour emergency telephones, lighted pathways/sidewalks, controlled dormitory access (key, security card, etc).

Transfer students: May apply for admission for the following academic terms: Fall, Spring, Summer. Applicants need a minimum number of credits to apply. For fall 2009: Transfer applications received: 2,400. Transfer applicants offered admission: 2,218. Transfer applicants enrolled: 1,685. **International students:** Number of foreign undergraduates: 250 (3% of student body). Number of countries represented: 68. Minimum TOEFL score required: 500 (paper); 61 (computer). Average TOEFL score: 567 (paper).

Washington University in St. Louis

- **Address:** Campus Box 1089, 1 Brookings Drive, St. Louis, MO 63130-4899
- **Website:** http://www.wustl.edu
- **Private**
- **Enrollment:** 6,135 full-time; 911 part-time

KEY STATS
✔ **U.S News College Ranking:** 13, National Universities
✔ **SAT Score (25th/75th percentile):** 1390-1530
✔ **Tuition:** 2010-2011: $40,374

Selectivity: Most selective	**Room/board:** $12,941
Acceptance rate: 22%	**Average debt:** N/A
Student/faculty ratio: 7/1	**Proportion who borrowed:** 39%

UNDERGRADUATE STUDENT BODY STATS
2009-2010 enrollment: 6,135 full-time; 911 part-time. Men: 49%; women: 51%. **Ethnic makeup:** African American: 9%; Asian American: 14%; Hispanic: 3%; White: 69%; International: 6%.

ADMISSIONS FACTS AND FIGURES
Phone: (800) 638-0700. **Email:** admissions@wustl.edu. **Website:** http://www.wustl.edu. **Application deadlines for fall 2011:** Regular decision: January 15; decision sent by April 1. Early decision: Send application by: November 15; Decision sent by: December 15. Early action: Not offered. Admission can be deferred. **Application fee:** $55. **To apply online, go to:** http://admissions.wustl.edu. **Admissions requirements/recommendations:** High school units required (recommended): English: (4); Mathematics: (4); Science: (4); Foreign language: (2); Social studies: (4); History: (4); Total units: (20). Tests: The college uses SAT or ACT scores in admissions decisions. Either SAT or ACT required. For admission to the fall 2011 entering class, the school will accept: ACT with or without writing accepted. Campus visit: Recommended. Admissions interview: Neither required nor recommended. Off-campus interview: May be arranged. **Factors that count in admissions decisions:** *Academic:* Secondary school record: Very Important. Class rank: Very Important. Letters of recommendation: Very Important. Standardized test scores: Very Important. Essay: Very Important. *Nonacademic:* Interview: Considered. Extracurricular activities: Very Important. Talent/ability: Very Important. Character/personal qualities: Very Important. Alumni/ae relationship: Considered. Geographical residence: Not Considered. State residency: Not Considered. Religious affiliation/commitment: Not Considered. Minority status: Considered. Volunteer work: Very Important. Work experience: Very Important. **Other schools with the greatest overlap in applicants:** Duke University; Harvard University; Northwestern University; Stanford University; Yale University. **Admissions statistics for the fall 2009 entering class:** Total applicants: 23,105. Total accepted: 5,128. Freshmen enrolled: 1,510; 92% were from out of state. Overall acceptance rate: 22%. Non-early acceptance rate: 22%. **Credentials of fall 2009 freshmen:** 96% ranked in the top 10 percent of their high school class; 100% were in the top 25 percent; 100% were in the top half. (Proportion submitting class standing: 58%.) **First-year students who submitted SAT scores:** 70%. Scores (25/75 percentile): Critical Reading: 680-750, Math: 710-780, Combined: 1390-1530. **First-year students submitting ACT scores:** 61%. Scores (25/75 percentile): English: 32-35, Math: 31-34, Composite: 32-34.

ACADEMICS
Year founded: 1853. **Academic calendar:** Semester. **Degrees offered:** certificate, bachelor's, post-bachelor's certificate, master's, post-master's certificate, doctorate. **Most popular majors:** 17% social sciences, 14% engineering, 13% business, management, marketing, and related support services, 9% pre-medicine/pre-medical studies, 9% psychology. **Major fields of study:** architecture and related services; area, ethnic, cultural, and gender studies; biological and biomedical sciences; business, management, marketing, and related support services; communication, journalism, and related programs; computer and information sciences and support services; education; engineering; English language and literature/letters; foreign languages, literatures, and linguistics; history; liberal arts and sciences studies, and humanities; mathematics and statistics; multi/interdisciplinary studies; natural resources and conservation; philosophy and religious studies; physical sciences; psychology; social sciences; visual and performing arts. **Areas of required coursework:** English (including composition), other. **Pre-professional programs:** pre-law, pre-dentistry, pre-medicine, pre-veterinary science. **Special academic programs:** accelerated program, cooperative (work-study plan) program, cross-registration, double major, dual enrollment, English as a Second Language (ESL), exchange student program (domestic), independent study, internships, liberal arts/career combination, student-designed major, study abroad, teacher certificate program, other. **Teacher certification offered in:** elementary, middle/junior high, secondary. **Cooperative education programs:** business, engineering. **Reserve Officers Training Corps (ROTC):** Army ROTC: Offered on campus; Air Force ROTC: Offered at cooperating institution (St. Louis University). **Faculty and instruction (2009-2010):** Total instructional faculty: 916 full-time, 176 part-time (64% men; 36% women). Full-time faculty with Ph.D. or other terminal degree: 98%. Student/faculty ratio: 7/1. Classes of fewer than 20 students: 70%; of 20 to 49 students: 21%; of 50 or more students: 10%. **Advanced Placement and International Baccalaureate credit:** AP tests may be used for: Placement only. Scores accepted: 4, 5. International Baccalaureate exams may be used for: Credit only. **Freshmen returning for sophomore year:** 97%. **Graduation rates:** Four-year: 84%; five-year: 92%; six-year: 93%. **Graduate study:** 33% of students pursue further study immediately upon graduation; 66% within five years.

COSTS AND FINANCIAL AID
Financial aid office: (888) 547-6670. **Expenses (2010-2011):** Tuition and fees 2010-2011: $40,374; room/board: $12,941. Estimated books and supplies: $1,300; transportation: $1,245; personal expenses: $2,290. **Financial aid:** In 2009-2010, 70% of undergraduates applied for financial aid. Of those, 42% were determined to have financial need; 99% had their need fully met. Average financial aid package (proportion receiving): $32,350 (42%). Average amount of gift aid, such as scholarships or grants (proportion receiving): $28,649 (41%). Average amount of self-help aid, such as work study or loans (proportion receiving): $6,245 (29%). Average need-based loan (excluding PLUS or other private loans): $6,193. Among students who received need-based aid, the average percentage of need met: 100%. Among students who received aid based on merit, the average award (and the proportion receiving): $7,865 (15%). The average athletic scholarship (and the proportion receiving): $0 (0%). Proportion who borrowed: 39%.

CAMPUS LIFE AND EXTRACURRICULAR ACTIVITIES
Campus housing available: coed dorms, fraternity housing, apartments for married students, apartment for single students, cooperative housing, other housing options. Students who live in college-owned, operated, or affiliated housing: 75%. **Student employment:** During the 2009-2010 academic year, 16% of undergraduates worked on campus. Average per-year earnings: $2,000. **Clubs and organizations:** Number of student organizations: 200. Activities include: campus ministries, choral groups, concert band, dance, drama/theater, international student organization, jazz band, literary magazine, model UN, music ensembles, musical theater, opera, pep band, radio station, student government, student newspaper, student film society, symphony orchestra, television station. Number of fraternities: 12; sororities: 6. Proportion of men in fraternities: 25%; of women in sororities: 25%. Average proportion of students who stay on campus on weekends: 97%. **Sports program (2009-2010):** Member of NCAA III. *Men's intercollegiate varsity sports:* baseball, basketball, cross country, football, soccer, swimming, tennis, track and field (indoor), track and field (outdoor). *Women's intercollegiate varsity sports:* basketball, cross country, golf, soccer, softball, swimming, tennis, track and field (indoor), track and field (outdoor), volleyball.

SERVICES AND FACILITIES
Basic services: nonremedial tutoring, women's center, placement service, day care, health service, health insurance, other. **Remedial assistance:** study skills. **Counseling services:** minority student, career, personal, academic, older student, psychological, birth control, religious. **For learning-disabled students:** School does not offer a structured program with separate admission and additional fees. Services include: tape recorders, note-taking services, learning center, readers, extended time for tests, tutors, texts on tape, other testing accommodations. **Library:** Number of titles: 4,281,213;

number of current serial subscriptions: 71,905. **Information technology resources:** Students are not required to lease or own a computer. Number of campus computers available to all students: 2,500. School has a wireless network. Approximate number of users that can be accommodated: 4,500. Proportion of college-owned housing units wired for high-speed internet access: 90%. **Campus safety:** Security services offered: 24-hour foot-and-vehicle patrols, late-night transport/escort service, 24-hour emergency telephones, lighted pathways/sidewalks, student patrols, controlled dormitory access (key, security card, etc).

TRANSFER AND INTERNATIONAL STUDENTS

Transfer students: May apply for admission for the following academic terms: Fall, Spring. Applicants need a minimum number of credits to apply. For fall 2009: Transfer applications received: 1,170. Transfer applicants offered admission: 210. Transfer applicants enrolled: 107. **International students:** Number of foreign undergraduates: 359 (6% of student body). Number of countries represented: 55. Minimum TOEFL score required: 550 (paper); 213 (computer).

Webster University

- **Address:** 470 E. Lockwood Avenue, St. Louis, MO 63119
- **Website:** http://www.webster.edu
- **Private**
- **Enrollment:** 3,331 full-time; 1,407 part-time

KEY STATS

✔ **U.S News College Ranking:** 24, Regional Universities (Midwest)
✔ **ACT Score (25th/75th percentile):** 21-28
✔ **Tuition:** 2010-2011: $21,688
  Selectivity: More selective   **Room/board:** $9,290
  Acceptance rate: 52%   **Average debt:** $26,184
  Student/faculty ratio: 12/1   **Proportion who borrowed:** 57%

UNDERGRADUATE STUDENT BODY STATS

2009-2010 enrollment: 3,331 full-time; 1,407 part-time. Men: 41%; women: 59%. **Ethnic makeup:** African American: 12%; Asian American: 2%; Hispanic: 3%; White: 72%; International: 11%. **Religious preference:** Roman Catholic: 22%; Protestant: 36%; Jewish: 1%; Muslim: 5%; Buddhist: 2%; No preference: 28%; Other: 6%.

ADMISSIONS FACTS AND FIGURES

Phone: (314) 968-6991. **Email:** admit@webster.edu. **Website:** http://www. webster.edu. **Application deadlines for fall 2011:** Regular decision: June 1. Early decision: Not offered. Early action: Not offered. Admission can be deferred. **Application fee:** $35. **To apply online, go to:** https://explore.webster. edu/admissions/undergraduate/application/apply.asp. **Admissions requirements/recommendations:** High school units required (recommended): English: (4); Mathematics: (3); Science: (3); Foreign language: (2); Social studies: (3); Academic electives: (4); Total units: (21). Tests: The college uses SAT or ACT scores in admissions decisions. Either SAT or ACT required. For admission to the fall 2011 entering class, the school will accept: ACT with writing recommended. Campus visit: Recommended. Admissions interview: Recommended. Off-campus interview: May be arranged. **Factors that count in admissions decisions: Academic:** Secondary school record: Important. Class rank: Important. Letters of recommendation: Important. Standardized test scores: Very Important. Essay: Important. **Nonacademic:** Interview: Considered. Extracurricular activities: Considered. Talent/ability: Very Important. Character/personal qualities: Not Considered. Alumni/ae relationship: Not Considered. Geographical residence: Considered. State residency: Not Considered. Religious affiliation/commitment: Not Considered. Minority status: Considered. Volunteer work: Considered. Work experience: Not Considered. **Other schools with the greatest overlap in applicants:** Southeast Missouri State University; Southern Illinois University–Edwardsville; St. Louis University; University of Missouri; University of Missouri–St. Louis. **Admissions statistics for the fall 2009 entering class:** Total applicants: 1,584. Total accepted: 828. Freshmen enrolled: 494; 30% were from out of state. Overall acceptance rate: 52%. **Credentials of fall 2009 freshmen:** 24% ranked in the top 10 percent of their high school class; 55% were in the top 25 percent; 82% were in the top half. (Proportion submitting class standing: 76%.) **Average high school grade point average:** 3.5. **First-year students who submitted SAT scores:** 14%. Scores (25/75 percentile): Critical Reading: 520-640, Math: 490-630,

Combined: 1010-1270. **First-year students submitting ACT scores:** 87%. Scores (25/75 percentile): English: N/A, Math: N/A, Composite: 21-28.

ACADEMICS

Year founded: 1915. **Academic calendar:** Semester. **Degrees offered:** certificate, bachelor's, post-bachelor's certificate, master's, post-master's certificate, doctorate. **Most popular majors:** 30% business administration and management, 6% communication studies/speech communication and rhetoric, 6% psychology, 5% nursing/registered nurse training (R.N., A.S.N., B.S.N., M.S.N.), 4% international relations and affairs. **Major fields of study:** biological and biomedical sciences; business, management, marketing, and related support services; communication, journalism, and related programs; computer and information sciences and support services; education; English language and literature/letters; foreign languages, literatures, and linguistics; health professions and related clinical sciences; history; legal professions and studies; mathematics and statistics; natural resources and conservation; philosophy and religious studies; psychology; social sciences; visual and performing arts. **Areas of required coursework:** arts/fine arts, humanities, mathematics, English (including composition), philosophy, sciences (biological or physical), history, social science, other. **Pre-professional programs:** pre-law, pre-dentistry, pre-medicine, pre-veterinary science, other. **Special academic programs (% participation):** accelerated program (1.3%), cooperative (work-study plan) program (38.3%), distance learning (3.1%), double major (5%), dual enrollment, English as a Second Language (ESL) (18.7%), independent study (7.3%), internships (26.7%), student-designed major, study abroad (27%), teacher certificate program (2.9%). **Teacher certification offered in:** early childhood, special education, elementary, middle/junior high, secondary, bilingual/bicultural. **Cooperative education programs:** computer science. **Reserve Officers Training Corps (ROTC):** Army ROTC: Offered at cooperating institution (Washington University in St. Louis); Air Force ROTC: Offered at cooperating institution (St. Louis University). **Faculty and instruction (2009-2010):** Total instructional faculty: 175 full-time, 718 part-time (59% men; 41% women; 9% minorities). Full-time faculty with Ph.D. or other terminal degree: 78%. Student/faculty ratio: 12/1. Classes of fewer than 20 students: 86%; of 20 to 49 students: 14%; of 50 or more students: 0%. **Advanced Placement and International Baccalaureate credit:** AP tests may be used for: Credit only. Scores accepted: 3, 4, 5. International Baccalaureate exams may be used for: Credit only. **Freshmen returning for sophomore year:** 79%. **Graduation rates:** Four-year: 48%; five-year: 64%; six-year: 62%. **Graduate study:** 16% of students pursue further study within one year. Fields in which graduates pursue further study: Master of Business Administration (MBA), 24%; law, 4%; medicine, 2%; education, 8%; arts and sciences, 26%.

COSTS AND FINANCIAL AID

Financial aid office: (314) 968-6992. **Expenses (2010-2011):** Tuition and fees 2010-2011: $21,688; room/board: $9,290. Estimated books and supplies: $800; transportation: $1,300. **Financial aid:** Priority filing date for institution's financial aid form: April 1. In 2009-2010, 77% of undergraduates applied for financial aid. Of those, 68% were determined to have financial need; Average financial aid package (proportion receiving): $22,542 (68%). Average amount of gift aid, such as scholarships or grants (proportion receiving): $7,033 (55%). Average amount of self-help aid, such as work study or loans (proportion receiving): $5,665 (63%). Average need-based loan (excluding PLUS or other private loans): $4,475. Among students who received aid based on merit, the average award (and the proportion receiving): $8,343 (17%). The average athletic scholarship (and the proportion receiving): $0 (0%). Average amount of debt of borrowers graduating in 2009: $26,184. Proportion who borrowed: 57%.

CAMPUS LIFE AND EXTRACURRICULAR ACTIVITIES

Campus housing available (% using): coed dorms (45%), apartment for single students (55%). Students who live in college-owned, operated, or affiliated housing: 15%. **Student employment:** During the 2009-2010 academic year, 5% of undergraduates worked on campus. Average per-year earnings: $2,730. **Clubs and organizations:** Number of student organizations: 62. Activities include: campus ministries, choral groups, dance, drama/theater, international student organization, jazz band, literary magazine, music ensembles, musical theater, opera, radio station, student government, student newspaper, student film society, symphony orchestra, television station, yearbook. Number of fraternities: 1; sororities: 1. Average proportion of students who stay on campus on weekends: 60%. **Sports program (2009-2010):** Member of NCAA III. **Men's intercollegiate varsity sports:** baseball, basketball, cross country, golf, soccer, tennis, track and field (outdoor). **Women's intercollegiate varsity sports:** basketball, cross country, soccer, softball, tennis, track and field (outdoor), volleyball.

SERVICES AND FACILITIES

Basic services: nonremedial tutoring, health service, health insurance. **Remedial assistance:** reading, math, writing, study skills. **Counseling services:** minority student, career, personal, academic. **For learning-disabled students:** School does not offer a structured program with separate admission and additional fees. Total undergraduates in learning-disabled program or receiving services: 58. Services include: remedial math, remedial English, reading machines, tape recorders, untimed tests, note-taking services, oral tests, learning center, readers, extended time for tests, tutors, priority seating, texts on tape, other testing accommodations. **Library:** Number of titles: 279,298; number of current serial subscriptions: 1,536. **Information technology resources:** Students are not required to lease or own a computer. Number of campus computers available to all students: 450. School has a wireless network. Proportion of college-owned housing units wired for high-speed internet access: 100%. **Campus safety:** Security services offered: 24-hour foot-and-vehicle patrols, late-night transport/escort service, 24-hour emergency telephones, lighted pathways/sidewalks, controlled dormitory access (key, security card, etc).

TRANSFER AND INTERNATIONAL STUDENTS

Transfer students: May apply for admission for the following academic terms: Fall, Spring, Summer. Applicants do not need a minimum number of credits to apply. For fall 2009: Transfer applications received: 605. Transfer applicants offered admission: 457. Transfer applicants enrolled: 322. **International students:** Number of foreign undergraduates: 523 (11% of student body). Number of countries represented: 22. Minimum TOEFL score required: 550 (paper). Average TOEFL score: 560 (paper).

Westminster College

- **Address:** 501 Westminster Avenue, Fulton, MO 65251
- **Website:** http://www.westminster-mo.edu
- **Private; Religious affiliation:** Presbyterian
- **Enrollment:** 1,076 full-time; 11 part-time

KEY STATS

✔ **U.S News College Ranking:** 166, National Liberal Arts Colleges
✔ **ACT Score (25th/75th percentile):** 21-28
✔ **Tuition:** 2010-2011: $19,740

Selectivity: Selective	**Room/board:** $7,610
Acceptance rate: 78%	**Average debt:** $20,018
Student/faculty ratio: 15/1	**Proportion who borrowed:** 58%

UNDERGRADUATE STUDENT BODY STATS

2009-2010 enrollment: 1,076 full-time; 11 part-time. Men: 55%; women: 45%. **Ethnic makeup:** African American: 6%; American-Indian: 1%; Asian American: 2%; Hispanic: 2%; White: 73%; International: 16%. **Religious preference:** Roman Catholic: 27%; Protestant: 36%; Jewish: 1%; Muslim: 4%; Hindu: 3%; Buddhist: 4%; No preference: 9%; Unknown: 1%; Presbyterian: 12%; Other: 3%.

ADMISSIONS FACTS AND FIGURES

Phone: (800) 475-3361. **Email:** admissions@westminster-mo.edu. **Website:** http://www.westminster-mo.edu. **Application deadlines for fall 2011:** Regular decision: Rolling. Early decision: Not offered. Early action: Not offered. Admission can be deferred. **To apply online, go to:** http://www.westminster-mo.edu/application/index.asp. **Admissions requirements/recommendations:** High school units required (recommended): English: 4; Mathematics: 3; Science: 2; Foreign language: (2); Social studies: (2); Academic electives: (2); Total units: 16. Tests: The college uses SAT or ACT scores in admissions decisions. Either SAT or ACT required. For admission to the fall 2011 entering class, the school will accept: ACT with or without writing accepted. Campus visit: Recommended. Admissions interview: Recommended. Off-campus interview: May be arranged. **Factors that count in admissions decisions:** *Academic:* Secondary school record: Very Important. Class rank: Important. Letters of recommendation: Very Important. Standardized test scores: Considered. Essay: Important. *Nonacademic:* Interview: Considered. Extracurricular activities: Important. Talent/ability: Considered. Character/personal qualities: Very Important. Alumni/ae relationship: Considered. Geographical residence: Not Considered. State residency: Not Considered. Religious affiliation/commitment: Not Considered. Minority status: Not Considered. Volunteer work: Important. Work experience: Considered. **Other schools with the greatest overlap in applicants:** Missouri State

University; Truman State University; University of Missouri; William Jewell College; William Woods University. **Admissions statistics for the fall 2009 entering class:** Total applicants: 1,356. Total accepted: 1,057. Freshmen enrolled: 311; 29% were from out of state. Overall acceptance rate: 78%. **Credentials of fall 2009 freshmen:** 16% ranked in the top 10 percent of their high school class; 45% were in the top 25 percent; 78% were in the top half. (Proportion submitting class standing: 71%.) **Average high school grade point average:** 3.4. **First-year students who submitted SAT scores:** 22%. Scores (25/75 percentile): Critical Reading: 440-620, Math: 490-625, Combined: 930-1245. **First-year students submitting ACT scores:** 92%. Scores (25/75 percentile): English: 21-29, Math: 20-27, Composite: 21-28.

ACADEMICS

Year founded: 1851. **Academic calendar:** Semester. **Degrees offered:** bachelor's. **Most popular majors:** 28% business, management, marketing, and related support services, 13% biological and biomedical sciences, 12% education, 9% social sciences, 8% English language and literature/letters. **Major fields of study:** agriculture, agriculture operations, and related sciences; biological and biomedical sciences; business, management, marketing, and related support services; communication, journalism, and related programs; computer and information sciences and support services; education; English language and literature/letters; foreign languages, literatures, and linguistics; history; mathematics and statistics; natural resources and conservation; philosophy and religious studies; physical sciences; psychology; social sciences. **Areas of required coursework:** arts/fine arts, humanities, mathematics, English (including composition), philosophy, foreign languages, sciences (biological or physical), history, social science, other. **Pre-professional programs:** pre-law, pre-dentistry, pre-medicine, pre-theology, pre-veterinary science, pre-optometry, pre-pharmacy. **Special academic programs (% participation):** cooperative (work-study plan) program, cross-registration (1%), double major (25%), dual enrollment, English as a Second Language (ESL), exchange student program (domestic), honors program, independent study (5%), internships (45%), liberal arts/career combination, student-designed major (10%), study abroad (5%), teacher certificate program (12%). **Teacher certification offered in:** early childhood, elementary, middle/junior high, secondary. **Reserve Officers Training Corps (ROTC):** Army ROTC: Offered at cooperating institution (University of Missouri); Air Force ROTC: Offered at cooperating institution (University of Missouri). **Faculty and instruction (2009-2010):** Total instructional faculty: 61 full-time, 30 part-time (59% men; 41% women). Full-time faculty with Ph.D. or other terminal degree: 77%. Student/faculty ratio: 15/1. Classes of fewer than 20 students: 61%; of 20 to 49 students: 39%. **Advanced Placement and International Baccalaureate credit:** AP tests may be used for: Placement only. Scores accepted: 4, 5. International Baccalaureate exams may be used for: Placement only. **Freshmen returning for sophomore year:** 82%. **Graduation rates:** Four-year: 40%; five-year: 55%; six-year: 58%. **Graduate study:** 20% of students pursue further study immediately upon graduation; 25% within one year; 35% within five years. Fields in which graduates pursue further study: Master of Business Administration (MBA), 20%; law, 15%; medicine, 4%; dentistry, 5%; engineering, 2%; theology (or the seminary), 3%; education, 20%; arts and sciences, 30%; veterinary medicine, 1%.

COSTS AND FINANCIAL AID

Financial aid office: (573) 592-5364. **Expenses (2010-2011):** Tuition and fees 2010-2011: $19,740; room/board: $7,610. Estimated books and supplies: $1,000 personal expenses: $2,650. **Financial aid:** Priority filing date for institution's financial aid form: February 15. In 2009-2010, 72% of undergraduates applied for financial aid. Of those, 57% were determined to have financial need; 56% had their need fully met. Average financial aid package (proportion receiving): $17,676 (57%). Average amount of gift aid, such as scholarships or grants (proportion receiving): $13,156 (57%). Average amount of self-help aid, such as work study or loans (proportion receiving): $5,063 (47%). Average need-based loan (excluding PLUS or other private loans): $3,849. Among students who received need-based aid, the average percentage of need met: 80%. Among students who received aid based on merit, the average award (and the proportion receiving): $9,144 (41%). Average amount of debt of borrowers graduating in 2009: $20,018. Proportion who borrowed: 58%.

CAMPUS LIFE AND EXTRACURRICULAR ACTIVITIES

Campus housing available (% using): coed dorms (47%), women's dorms (6%), men's dorms (6%), fraternity housing (22%), apartment for single students (12%), other housing options (7%). Students who live in college-owned, operated, or affiliated housing: 84%. **Student employment:** During the 2009-2010 academic year, 35% of undergraduates worked on campus. Average per-year earnings: $2,115. **Clubs and organizations:** Number of student organizations: 60. Activities include: campus ministries, choral groups, drama/theater, international student organization, literary magazine, model UN, music ensembles, pep band, radio station, student government, student newspaper, yearbook. Number of fraternities: 6; sororities: 3. Proportion of men in fraternities: 54%; of women in sororities: 41%. Average proportion of students who stay on campus on weekends: 60%. **Sports program (2009-2010):** Member of NCAA III. *Men's intercollegiate varsity sports:* baseball, basketball, cross country, football, golf, soccer, tennis, track and field (outdoor). *Women's intercollegiate varsity sports:* basketball, cross country, golf, soccer, softball, tennis, track and field (outdoor), volleyball.

SERVICES AND FACILITIES

Basic services: nonremedial tutoring, women's center, placement service, health service, health insurance. **Remedial assistance:** reading, math, writing, study skills. **Counseling services:** minority student, career, personal, academic, psychological, birth control. **For learning-disabled students:** School does not offer a structured program with separate admission and additional fees. Total undergraduates in learning-disabled program or receiving services: 47. Services include: remedial math, reading machines, tape recorders, other special classes, untimed tests, note-taking services, oral tests, learning center, readers, extended time for tests, tutors, texts on tape, other testing accommodations, other. **Library:** Number of titles: 98,840; number of current serial subscriptions: 219. **Information technology resources:** Students are not required to lease or own a computer. Number of campus computers available to all students: 197. School has a wireless network. Approximate number of users that can be accommodated: 100. Proportion of college-owned housing units wired for high-speed internet access: 95%. **Campus safety:** Security services offered: 24-hour foot-and-vehicle patrols, late-night transport/escort service, 24-hour emergency telephones, lighted pathways/sidewalks, student patrols, controlled dormitory access (key, security card, etc).

TRANSFER AND INTERNATIONAL STUDENTS

Transfer students: May apply for admission for the following academic terms: Fall, Spring. Applicants do not need a minimum number of credits to apply. For fall 2009: Transfer applications received: 121. Transfer applicants offered admission: 88. Transfer applicants enrolled: 50. **International students:** Number of foreign undergraduates: 124 (16% of student body). Number of countries represented: 67. Minimum TOEFL score required: 550 (paper); 213 (computer). Average TOEFL score: 680 (paper).

William Jewell College

- **Address:** 500 College Hill, Liberty, MO 64068
- **Website:** http://www.jewell.edu
- **Private**
- **Enrollment:** 1,030 full-time; 53 part-time

KEY STATS

✔ **U.S News College Ranking:** 131, National Liberal Arts Colleges
✔ **ACT Score (25th/75th percentile):** 23-29
✔ **Tuition:** 2010-2011: $25,825

Selectivity: More selective	**Room/board:** $7,200
Acceptance rate: 55%	**Average debt:** $24,102
Student/faculty ratio: 11/1	**Proportion who borrowed:** 75%

UNDERGRADUATE STUDENT BODY STATS

2009-2010 enrollment: 1,030 full-time; 53 part-time. Men: 40%; women: 60%. **Ethnic makeup:** African American: 4%; American-Indian: 1%; Asian American: 2%; Hispanic: 3%; White: 89%; International: 2%. **Religious preference:** Roman Catholic: 11%; Protestant: 49%; No preference: 3%; Unknown: 32%; Other: 3%.

ADMISSIONS FACTS AND FIGURES

Phone: (888) 253-9355. **Email:** admission@william.jewell.edu. **Website:** http://www.jewell.edu. **Application deadlines for fall 2011:** Regular decision: August 15. Early decision: Not offered. Early action: Not offered. Admission can be deferred. **Application fee:** $25. **To apply online, go to:** http://www.jewell.edu/apply/. **Admissions requirements/recommendations:** High school units required (recommended): English: 4 (4); Mathematics: 3 (4); Science: 3 (3); Foreign language: 2 (3); Social studies: 3 (3); Academic electives: (2); Total units: 15 (19). Tests: The college uses SAT or ACT scores in admis-

sions decisions. Either SAT or ACT required. For admission to the fall 2011 entering class, the school will accept: ACT with writing recommended. Campus visit: Recommended. Admissions interview: Recommended. Off-campus interview: May be arranged. **Factors that count in admissions decisions:** *Academic:* Secondary school record: Very Important. Class rank: Important. Letters of recommendation: Important. Standardized test scores: Important. Essay: Considered. *Nonacademic:* Interview: Considered. Extracurricular activities: Considered. Talent/ability: Considered. Character/personal qualities: Considered. Alumni/ae relationship: Considered. Geographical residence: Not Considered. State residency: Not Considered. Religious affiliation/commitment: Not Considered. Minority status: Not Considered. Volunteer work: Considered. Work experience: Considered. **Other schools with the greatest overlap in applicants:** Missouri State University; Northwest Missouri State University; Rockhurst University; Truman State University; University of Missouri. **Admissions statistics for the fall 2009 entering class:** Total applicants: 2,497. Total accepted: 1,374. Freshmen enrolled: 282; 36% were from out of state. Overall acceptance rate: 55%. **Credentials of fall 2009 freshmen:** 34% ranked in the top 10 percent of their high school class; 68% were in the top 25 percent; 92% were in the top half. (Proportion submitting class standing: 83%.) **Average high school grade point average:** 3.7. **First-year students who submitted SAT scores:** 16%. Scores (25/75 percentile): Critical Reading: 490-640, Math: 510-650, Combined: 1000-1290. **First-year students submitting ACT scores:** 94%. Scores (25/75 percentile): English: 23-30, Math: 22-28, Composite: 23-29.

ACADEMICS

Year founded: 1849. **Academic calendar:** Semester. **Degrees offered:** bachelor's. **Most popular majors:** 22% business administration and management, 17% nursing/registered nurse training (R.N., A.S.N., B.S.N., M.S.N.), 11% psychology, 8% education, 6% biology/biological sciences. **Major fields of study:** area, ethnic, cultural, and gender studies; biological and biomedical sciences; business, management, marketing, and related support services; communication, journalism, and related programs; computer and information sciences and support services; education; English language and literature/letters; foreign languages, literatures, and linguistics; health professions and related clinical sciences; history; legal professions and studies; liberal arts and sciences studies, and humanities; mathematics and statistics; multi/interdisciplinary studies; parks, recreation, leisure, and fitness studies; philosophy and religious studies; physical sciences; psychology; science technologies/technicians; social sciences; theology and religious vocations; visual and performing arts. **Areas of required coursework:** arts/fine arts, humanities, mathematics, English (including composition), philosophy, foreign languages, sciences (biological or physical), social science, other. **Pre-professional programs:** pre-law, pre-dentistry, pre-medicine, pre-veterinary science, pre-optometry. **Special academic programs (% participation):** accelerated program (9%), double major (35%), dual enrollment (39%), honors program (5%), independent study (30%), internships (40%), student-designed major (1%), study abroad (18%), teacher certificate program (0%). **Teacher certification offered in:** elementary, secondary. **Cooperative education programs:** engineering. **Reserve Officers Training Corps (ROTC):** Army ROTC: Offered at cooperating institution (Missouri Western State University). **Faculty and instruction (2009-2010):** Total instructional faculty: 70 full-time, 77 part-time (46% men; 54% women; 5% minorities). Full-time faculty with Ph.D. or other terminal degree: 86%. Student/faculty ratio: 11/1. Classes of fewer than 20 students: 67%; of 20 to 49 students: 33%; of 50 or more students: 0%. **Advanced Placement and International Baccalaureate credit:** AP tests may be used for: Credit only. Scores accepted: 4. International Baccalaureate exams may be used for: Credit only. **Freshmen returning for sophomore year:** 78%. **Graduation rates:** Four-year: 51%; five-year: 61%; six-year: 63%. **Graduate study:** 25% of students pursue further study immediately upon graduation; 2% within one year. Fields in which graduates pursue further study: Master of Business Administration (MBA), 18%; law, 13%; medicine, 13%; dentistry, 3%; theology (or the seminary), 5%; education, 15%; arts and sciences, 13%; veterinary medicine, 2%.

COSTS AND FINANCIAL AID

Financial aid office: (888) 253-9355. **Expenses (2010-2011):** Tuition and fees 2010-2011: $25,825; room/board: $7,200. Estimated books and supplies: $1,100; transportation: $1,620; personal expenses: $2,520. **Financial aid:** Priority filing date for institution's financial aid form: March 1. In 2009-2010, 83% of undergraduates applied for financial aid. Of those, 71% were determined to have financial need; 22% had their need fully met. Average financial aid package (proportion receiving): $20,258 (71%). Average amount of gift aid, such as scholarships or grants (proportion receiving): $15,963 (70%). Average amount of self-help aid, such as work study or loans (proportion receiving): $6,635 (54%). Average need-based loan (excluding PLUS or other private loans): $5,335. Among students who received need-based aid, the average percentage of need met: 79%. Among students who received aid based on merit, the average award (and the proportion receiving): $9,994 (16%). The average athletic scholarship (and the proportion receiving): $8,060 (11%). Average amount of debt of borrowers graduating in 2009: $24,102. Proportion who borrowed: 75%.

CAMPUS LIFE AND EXTRACURRICULAR ACTIVITIES

Campus housing available (% using): coed dorms (33%), women's dorms (24%), men's dorms (17%), sorority housing (16%), fraternity housing (10%), special housing for disabled students (0%). Students who live in college-owned, operated, or affiliated housing: 71%. **Student employment:** During the 2009-2010 academic year, 18% of undergraduates worked on campus. Average per-year earnings: $968. **Clubs and organizations:** Number of student organizations: 60. Activities include: campus ministries, choral groups, concert band, dance, drama/theater, jazz band, literary magazine, music ensembles, musical theater, opera, pep band, radio station, student government, student newspaper, symphony orchestra. Number of fraternities: 3; sororities: 4. Proportion of men in fraternities: 31%; of women in sororities: 34%. Average proportion of students who stay on campus on weekends: 65%. **Sports program (2009-2010):** Member of NAIA. *Men's intercollegiate varsity sports:* baseball, basketball, cross country, football, golf, soccer, tennis, track and field (indoor), track and field (outdoor). *Women's intercollegiate varsity sports:* basketball, cross country, golf, soccer, softball, tennis, track and field (indoor), track and field (outdoor), volleyball.

SERVICES AND FACILITIES

Basic services: nonremedial tutoring, placement service, health service. **Remedial assistance:** math, writing, study skills. **Counseling services:** minority student, career, personal, academic, older student, psychological, birth control, religious. **For learning-disabled students:** School does not offer a structured program with separate admission and additional fees. Total undergraduates in learning-disabled program or receiving services: 28. Services include: tape recorders, untimed tests, note-taking services, learning center, extended time for tests, tutors, priority seating. **Library:** Number of titles: 231,031; number of current serial subscriptions: 323. **Information technology resources:** Students are not required to lease or own a computer. Number of campus computers available to all students: 240. School has a wireless network. Approximate number of users that can be accommodated: 300. Proportion of college-owned housing units wired for high-speed internet access: 100%. **Campus safety:** Security services offered: 24-hour foot-and-vehicle patrols, late-night transport/escort service, 24-hour emergency telephones, lighted pathways/sidewalks, controlled dormitory access (key, security card, etc).

TRANSFER AND INTERNATIONAL STUDENTS

Transfer students: May apply for admission for the following academic terms: Fall, Spring, Summer. Applicants need a minimum number of credits to apply. For fall 2009: Transfer applications received: 206. Transfer applicants offered admission: 79. Transfer applicants enrolled: 51. **International students:** Number of foreign undergraduates: 22 (2% of student body). Number of countries represented: 7. Minimum TOEFL score required: 550 (paper); 81 (computer).

William Woods University

■ **Address:** 1 University Avenue, Fulton, MO 65251
■ **Website:** http://www.williamwoods.edu
■ **Private; Religious affiliation:** Christian Church (Disciples of Christ)
■ **Enrollment:** 864 full-time; 229 part-time

....

KEY STATS

✔ **U.S News College Ranking:** 99, Regional Universities (Midwest)
✔ **ACT Score (25th/75th percentile):** 19-26
✔ **Tuition:** 2010-2011: $18,000

Selectivity: Selective	**Room/board:** $7,200
Acceptance rate: 77%	**Average debt:** $18,997
Student/faculty ratio: 13/1	**Proportion who borrowed:** 75%

UNDERGRADUATE STUDENT BODY STATS

2009-2010 enrollment: 864 full-time; 229 part-time. Men: 24%; women: 76%. **Ethnic makeup:** African American: 5%; American-Indian: 1%; Asian American: 1%; Hispanic: 1%; White: 93%; International: 1%. **Religious preference:** Roman Catholic: 16%; Protestant: 1%; No preference: 18%; Unknown: 14%; Christian Church (Disciples of Christ): 1%; Christian: 21%; Other: 29%.

ADMISSIONS FACTS AND FIGURES

Phone: (573) 592-4221. **Email:** admissions@williamwoods.edu. **Website:** http://www.williamwoods.edu. **Application deadlines for fall 2011:** Regular decision: August 15. Early decision: Not offered. Early action: Not offered. Admission can be deferred. **Application fee:** $25. **To apply online, go to:** http://www.williamwoods.edu/Info.asp?1895. **Admissions requirements/ recommendations:** High school units required (recommended): English: (4); Mathematics: (3); Science: (3); Foreign language: (1); Social studies: (3); History: (2); Academic electives: (4); Total units: 16 (20). Tests: The college uses SAT or ACT scores in admissions decisions. Either SAT or ACT required. For admission to the fall 2011 entering class, the school will accept: ACT with or without writing accepted. Campus visit: Recommended. Admissions interview: Neither required nor recommended. Off-campus interview: May be arranged. **Factors that count in admissions decisions:** *Academic:* Secondary school record: Very Important. Class rank: Very Important. Letters of recommendation: Important. Standardized test scores: Important. Essay: Not Considered. *Nonacademic:* Interview: Considered. Extracurricular activities: Important. Talent/ability: Considered. Character/personal qualities: Considered. Alumni/ae relationship: Considered. Geographical residence: Not Considered. State residency: Not Considered. Religious affiliation/commitment: Not Considered. Minority status: Not Considered. Volunteer work: Considered. Work experience: Not Considered. **Other schools with the greatest overlap in applicants:** Columbia College; Culver-Stockton College; Stephens College; Westminster College; William Jewell College. **Admissions statistics for the fall 2009 entering class:** Total applicants: 877. Total accepted: 672. Freshmen enrolled: 243; 36% were from out of state. Overall acceptance rate: 77%. **Size of waiting list:** 0 applicants; enrolled from waiting list: 0. **Credentials of fall 2009 freshmen:** 18% ranked in the top 10 percent of their high school class; 39% were in the top 25 percent; 75% were in the top half. (Proportion submitting class standing: 89%.) **Average high school grade point average:** 3.5. **First-year students who submitted SAT scores:** 18%. Scores (25/75 percentile): Critical Reading: 490-610, Math: 475-580, Combined: 965-1190. **First-year students submitting ACT scores:** 93%. Scores (25/75 percentile): English: 19-26, Math: 18-24, Composite: 19-26.

ACADEMICS

Year founded: 1870. **Academic calendar:** Semester. **Degrees offered:** associate, bachelor's, master's, post-master's certificate. **Most popular majors:** 29% business administration and management, 16% education, 16% equestrian/equine studies, 6% foreign languages and literatures, 5% visual and performing arts. **Major fields of study:** agriculture, agriculture operations, and related sciences; biological and biomedical sciences; business, management, marketing, and related support services; communication, journalism, and related programs; computer and information sciences and support services; education; English language and literature/letters; foreign languages, literatures, and linguistics; health professions and related clinical sciences; history; legal professions and studies; mathematics and statistics; multi/ interdisciplinary studies; parks, recreation, leisure, and fitness studies; psychology; public administration and social service professions; security and protective services; social sciences; visual and performing arts. **Areas of required coursework:** arts/fine arts, humanities, mathematics, English (including composition), sciences (biological or physical), history, social science. **Pre-professional programs:** pre-law, pre-medicine, pre-veterinary science. **Special academic programs:** accelerated program, cross-registration, double major, dual enrollment, English as a Second Language (ESL), exchange student program (domestic), honors program, independent study, internships, liberal arts/career combination, student-designed major, study abroad, teacher certificate program. **Teacher certification offered in:** early childhood, special education, elementary, middle/junior high, secondary. **Reserve Officers Training Corps (ROTC):** Army ROTC: Offered at cooperating institution (University of Missouri); Navy ROTC: Offered at cooperating institution (University of Missouri); Air Force ROTC: Offered at cooperating institution (University of Missouri). **Faculty and instruction (2009-2010):** Total instructional faculty: 70 full-time, 266 part-time (63% men; 37% women; 8% minorities). Full-time faculty with Ph.D. or other terminal degree: 47%. Student/faculty ratio: 13/1. Classes of fewer than 20 students: 76%; of 20 to 49 students: 24%; of 50 or more students: 0%. **Advanced**

Placement and International Baccalaureate credit: AP tests may be used for: Credit only. Scores accepted: 3, 4, 5. International Baccalaureate exams may be used for: Credit only. **Freshmen returning for sophomore year:** 78%. **Graduation rates:** Four-year: 41%; five-year: 47%; six-year: 45%.

COSTS AND FINANCIAL AID

Financial aid office: (573) 592-4232. **Expenses (2010-2011):** Tuition and fees 2010-2011: $18,000; room/board: $7,200. Estimated books and supplies: $1,200; transportation: $2,000; personal expenses: $3,000. **Financial aid:** Priority filing date for institution's financial aid form: March 1. In 2009-2010, 100% of undergraduates applied for financial aid. Of those, 71% were determined to have financial need; 24% had their need fully met. Average financial aid package (proportion receiving): $14,901 (70%). Average amount of gift aid, such as scholarships or grants (proportion receiving): $11,340 (68%). Average amount of self-help aid, such as work study or loans (proportion receiving): $4,778 (55%). Average need-based loan (excluding PLUS or other private loans): $3,751. Among students who received need-based aid, the average percentage of need met: 74%. Among students who received aid based on merit, the average award (and the proportion receiving): $7,178 (29%). The average athletic scholarship (and the proportion receiving): $5,902 (3%). Average amount of debt of borrowers graduating in 2009: $18,997. Proportion who borrowed: 75%.

CAMPUS LIFE AND EXTRACURRICULAR ACTIVITIES

Campus housing available (% using): coed dorms (35%), women's dorms (20%), sorority housing (35%), fraternity housing (10%). Students who live in college-owned, operated, or affiliated housing: 63%. **Student employment:** During the 2009-2010 academic year, 25% of undergraduates worked on campus. Average per-year earnings: $845. **Clubs and organizations:** Number of student organizations: 47. Activities include: campus ministries, choral groups, dance, drama/theater, literary magazine, musical theater, radio station, student government, student newspaper. Number of fraternities: 2; sororities: 4. Proportion of men in fraternities: 22%; of women in sororities: 30%. Average proportion of students who stay on campus on weekends: 65%. **Sports program (2009-2010):** Member of NAIA.

SERVICES AND FACILITIES

Basic services: nonremedial tutoring, placement service, health service. **Remedial assistance:** math, writing. **Counseling services:** minority student, career, personal, academic, psychological, birth control, religious. **For learning-disabled students:** School does not offer a structured program with separate admission and additional fees. Total undergraduates in learning-disabled program or receiving services: 16. Services include: remedial math, remedial English, tape recorders, untimed tests, note-taking services, oral tests, readers, extended time for tests, tutors, texts on tape, other testing accommodations, other. **Library:** Number of titles: 157,938; number of current serial subscriptions: 38,382. **Information technology resources:** Students are not required to lease or own a computer. Number of campus computers available to all students: 150. School has a wireless network. Approximate number of users that can be accommodated: 400. Proportion of college-owned housing units wired for high-speed internet access: 100%. **Campus safety:** Security services offered: 24-hour foot-and-vehicle patrols, late-night transport/escort service, 24-hour emergency telephones, lighted pathways/sidewalks, controlled dormitory access (key, security card, etc).

TRANSFER AND INTERNATIONAL STUDENTS

Transfer students: May apply for admission for the following academic terms: Fall, Winter, Spring, Summer. Applicants need a minimum number of credits to apply. For fall 2009: Transfer applications received: 302. Transfer applicants offered admission: 185. Transfer applicants enrolled: 114. **International students:** Number of foreign undergraduates: 6 (1% of student body). Number of countries represented: 8. Minimum TOEFL score required: 525 (paper); 195 (computer). Average TOEFL score: 550 (paper).

Montana

Carroll College

- **Address:** 1601 N. Benton Avenue, Helena, MT 59625-0002
- **Website:** http://www.carroll.edu
- **Private; Religious affiliation:** Roman Catholic
- **Enrollment:** N/A

KEY STATS

✔ **U.S News College Ranking:** 181, National Liberal Arts Colleges
✔ **ACT Score (25th/75th percentile):** 21-26
✔ **Tuition:** 2009-2010: $22,384

Selectivity: More selective	**Room/board:** $7,190
Acceptance rate: 76%	**Average debt:** N/A
Student/faculty ratio: N/A	**Proportion who borrowed:** N/A

Montana State University

- **Address:** Bozeman, MT 59717
- **Website:** http://www.montana.edu
- **Public**
- **Enrollment:** 8,962 full-time; 1,878 part-time

KEY STATS

✔ **U.S News College Ranking:** 183, National Universities
✔ **ACT Score (25th/75th percentile):** 21-27
✔ **Tuition:** 2010-2011: $6,212 in state, $18,248 out of state

Selectivity: Selective	**Room/board:** $7,900
Acceptance rate: 64%	**Average debt:** $21,571
Student/faculty ratio: 16/1	**Proportion who borrowed:** 64%

UNDERGRADUATE STUDENT BODY STATS

2009-2010 enrollment: 8,962 full-time; 1,878 part-time. Men: 55%; women: 45%. **Ethnic makeup:** African American: 1%; American-Indian: 3%; Asian American: 2%; Hispanic: 2%; White: 91%; International: 2%.

ADMISSIONS FACTS AND FIGURES

Phone: (406) 994-2452. **Email:** admissions@montana.edu. **Website:** http://www.montana.edu. **Application deadlines for fall 2011:** Regular decision: Rolling. Early decision: Not offered. Early action: Not offered. Admission can be deferred. **Application fee:** $30. **To apply online, go to:** http://www.montana.edu/wwwcat/appopts.html. **Admissions requirements/recommendations:** High school units required (recommended): English: 4; Mathematics: 3; Science: 2; Social studies: 3; Total units: 14. Tests: The college uses SAT or ACT scores in admissions decisions. Either SAT or ACT required. For admission to the fall 2011 entering class, the school will accept: ACT with writing required. Campus visit: Recommended. Admissions interview: Recommended. Off-campus interview: May be arranged. **Factors that count in admissions decisions:** *Academic:* Secondary school record: Very Important. Class rank: Very Important. Standardized test scores: Very Important. *Nonacademic:* Interview: Not Considered. Extracurricular activities: Not Considered. Talent/ability: Not Considered. Character/personal qualities: Not Considered. Alumni/ae relationship: Not Considered. Geographical residence: Not Considered. State residency: Not Considered. Religious affiliation/commitment: Not Considered. Minority status: Not Considered. Volunteer work: Not Considered. Work experience: Not Considered. **Other schools with the greatest overlap in applicants:** Carroll University; Montana State University–Billings; Montana Tech of the University of Montana; University of Montana. **Admissions statistics for the fall 2009 entering class:** Total applicants: 8,033. Total accepted: 5,106. Freshmen enrolled: 2,316; 38% were from out of state. Overall acceptance rate: 64%. **Credentials of fall 2009 freshmen:** 17% ranked in the top 10 percent of their high school class; 41% were in the top 25 percent; 69% were in the top half. (Proportion submitting class standing: 72%.) **Average**

high school grade point average: 3.3. **First-year students who submitted SAT scores:** 41%. Scores (25/75 percentile): Critical Reading: 500-620, Math: 500-640, Combined: 1000-1260. **First-year students submitting ACT scores:** 68%. Scores (25/75 percentile): English: 20-27, Math: 20-28, Composite: 21-27.

ACADEMICS

Year founded: 1893. **Academic calendar:** Semester. **Degrees offered:** certificate, bachelor's, master's, post-master's certificate, doctorate. **Most popular majors:** 11% business, management, marketing, and related support services, 11% engineering, 9% health professions and related clinical sciences, 8% biological and biomedical sciences, 6% education. **Major fields of study:** agriculture, agriculture operations, and related sciences; architecture and related services; biological and biomedical sciences; business, management, marketing, and related support services; computer and information sciences and support services; education; engineering; engineering technologies/technicians; English language and literature/letters; family and consumer sciences/human sciences; foreign languages, literatures, and linguistics; health professions and related clinical sciences; history; liberal arts and sciences studies, and humanities; mathematics and statistics; multi/interdisciplinary studies; natural resources and conservation; parks, recreation, leisure, and fitness studies; philosophy and religious studies; physical sciences; psychology; social sciences; visual and performing arts. **Areas of required coursework:** arts/fine arts, humanities, mathematics, English (including composition), sciences (biological or physical), social science. **Pre-professional programs:** pre-law, pre-dentistry, pre-medicine, pre-veterinary science, pre-optometry, other. **Special academic programs:** cooperative (work-study plan) program, cross-registration, distance learning, double major, English as a Second Language (ESL), exchange student program (domestic), honors program, independent study, internships, student-designed major, study abroad, teacher certificate program. **Teacher certification offered in:** elementary, secondary. **Reserve Officers Training Corps (ROTC):** Army ROTC: Offered on campus; Air Force ROTC: Offered on campus. **Faculty and instruction (2009-2010):** Total instructional faculty: 569 full-time, 239 part-time (58% men; 42% women; 2% minorities). Full-time faculty with Ph.D. or other terminal degree: 78%. Student/faculty ratio: 16/1. Classes of fewer than 20 students: 43%; of 20 to 49 students: 44%; of 50 or more students: 13%. **Advanced Placement and International Baccalaureate credit:** AP tests may be used for: Placement only. Scores accepted: 3, 4, 5. International Baccalaureate exams may be used for: Credit only. **Freshmen returning for sophomore year:** 72%. **Graduation rates:** Four-year: 19%; five-year: 41%; six-year: 48%. **Graduate study:** 17% of students pursue further study within one year. Fields in which graduates pursue further study: Master of Business Administration (MBA), 5%; law, 3%; medicine, 5%; dentistry, 2%; engineering, 5%; theology (or the seminary), 1%; education, 3%; arts and sciences, 24%; veterinary medicine, 1%.

COSTS AND FINANCIAL AID

Financial aid office: (406) 994-2845. **Expenses (2010-2011):** Tuition and fees 2010-2011: $6,212 in state, $18,248 out of state; room/board: $7,900. Estimated books and supplies: $1,130; transportation: $1,170; personal expenses: $1,830. **Financial aid:** Priority filing date for institution's financial aid form: March 1. In 2009-2010, 63% of undergraduates applied for financial aid. Of those, 50% were determined to have financial need; 4% had their need fully met. Average financial aid package (proportion receiving): $10,268 (48%). Average amount of gift aid, such as scholarships or grants (proportion receiving): $4,530 (33%). Average amount of self-help aid, such as work study or loans (proportion receiving): $4,592 (41%). Average need-based loan (excluding PLUS or other private loans): $4,422. Among students who received need-based aid, the average percentage of need met: 72%. Among students who received aid based on merit, the average award (and the proportion receiving): $2,039 (4%). The average athletic scholarship (and the proportion receiving): $6,264 (2%). Average amount of debt of borrowers graduating in 2009: $21,571. Proportion who borrowed: 64%.

CAMPUS LIFE AND EXTRACURRICULAR ACTIVITIES

Campus housing available (% using): coed dorms (61%), women's dorms (18%), men's dorms (12%), sorority housing, fraternity housing, apartments for married students, apartment for single students, special housing for disabled students, special housing for international students, other housing options (5%). Students who live in college-owned, operated, or affiliated housing: 25%. **Student employment:** During the 2009-2010 academic year, 25% of undergraduates worked on campus. Average per-year earnings: $4,000. **Clubs and organizations:** Number of student organizations: 140. Activities include: campus ministries, choral groups, concert band, dance, drama/theater, international student organization, jazz band, literary magazine, marching band, music ensembles, musical theater, pep band, radio station, student government, student newspaper, student film society, television station. Number of fraternities: 9; sororities: 4. Proportion of men in fraternities: 2%; of women in sororities: 2%. **Sports program (2009-2010):** Member of NCAA I. *Men's intercollegiate varsity sports:* basketball, cross country, football, skiing (nordic), skiing (alpine), tennis, track and field (indoor). *Women's intercollegiate varsity sports:* basketball, cross country, golf, skiing (nordic), skiing (alpine), tennis, track and field (indoor), volleyball.

SERVICES AND FACILITIES

Basic services: nonremedial tutoring, women's center, placement service, day care, health service, health insurance. **Remedial assistance:** reading, math, writing. **Counseling services:** minority student, career, military, personal, veteran student, academic, older student, psychological. **For learning-disabled students:** School does not offer a structured program with separate admission and additional fees. Services include: remedial math, remedial English, reading machines, remedial reading, tape recorders, note-taking services, oral tests, learning center, readers, extended time for tests, tutors, priority registration, priority seating, texts on tape, other testing accommodations, other. **Library:** Number of titles: 614,548; number of current serial subscriptions: 10,131. **Information technology resources:** Students are not required to lease or own a computer. Number of campus computers available to all students: 850. **Campus safety:** Security services offered: 24-hour foot-and-vehicle patrols, late-night transport/escort service, 24-hour emergency telephones, lighted pathways/sidewalks, controlled dormitory access (key, security card, etc).

TRANSFER AND INTERNATIONAL STUDENTS

Transfer students: May apply for admission for the following academic terms: Fall, Spring, Summer. Applicants need a minimum number of credits to apply. For fall 2009: Transfer applications received: 1,375. Transfer applicants offered admission: 1,053. Transfer applicants enrolled: 688. **International students:** Number of foreign undergraduates: 238 (2% of student body). Number of countries represented: 69. Minimum TOEFL score required: 525 (paper); 195 (computer). Average TOEFL score: 565 (paper).

Montana State University–Billings

- **Address:** 1500 University Drive, Billings, MT 59101
- **Website:** http://www.msubillings.edu
- **Public**
- **Enrollment:** 3,210 full-time; 1,337 part-time

KEY STATS

✔ **U.S News College Ranking:** 77, Regional Universities (West)
✔ **ACT Score (25th/75th percentile):** 18-24
✔ **Tuition:** 2009-2010: $5,207 in state, $10,555 out of state

Selectivity: Selective	Room/board: $5,310
Acceptance rate: 100%	Average debt: $23,189
Student/faculty ratio: 20/1	Proportion who borrowed: 73%

UNDERGRADUATE STUDENT BODY STATS

2009-2010 enrollment: 3,210 full-time; 1,337 part-time. Men: 38%; women: 62%. **Ethnic makeup:** African American: 1%; American-Indian: 6%; Asian American: 1%; Hispanic: 4%; White: 88%.

ADMISSIONS FACTS AND FIGURES

Phone: (406) 657-2158. **Email:** admissions@msubillings.edu. **Website:** http://www.msubillings.edu. **Application deadlines for fall 2011:** Regular decision: July 1. Early decision: Not offered. Early action: Not offered. Admission cannot be deferred. **Application fee:** $30. **To apply online, go to:** http://www.msubillings.edu/future/apply/. **Admissions requirements/ recommendations:** High school units required (recommended): English: 4 (4); Mathematics: 3 (3); Science: 2 (2); Social studies: 3 (3); Total units: 14

(14). Tests: The college uses SAT or ACT scores in admissions decisions. Either SAT or ACT required. For admission to the fall 2011 entering class, the school will accept: ACT with or without writing accepted. Campus visit: Recommended. Admissions interview: Neither required nor recommended. Off-campus interview: May be arranged. **Factors that count in admissions decisions:** *Academic:* Secondary school record: Very Important. Class rank: Very Important. Letters of recommendation: Not Considered. Standardized test scores: Very Important. Essay: Not Considered. *Nonacademic:* Interview: Not Considered. Extracurricular activities: Not Considered. Talent/ability: Not Considered. Character/personal qualities: Considered. Alumni/ae relationship: Not Considered. Geographical residence: Not Considered. State residency: Not Considered. Religious affiliation/commitment: Not Considered. Minority status: Not Considered. Volunteer work: Not Considered. Work experience: Considered. **Other schools with the greatest overlap in applicants:** Montana State University; Montana State University–Northern; Montana Tech of the University of Montana; Rocky Mountain College; University of Montana. **Admissions statistics for the fall 2009 entering class:** Total applicants: 1,384. Total accepted: 1,381. Freshmen enrolled: 900; 8% were from out of state. Overall acceptance rate: 100%. **Credentials of fall 2009 freshmen:** 11% ranked in the top 10 percent of their high school class; 25% were in the top 25 percent; 59% were in the top half. (Proportion submitting class standing: 79%.) **Average high school grade point average:** 3.0. **First-year students who submitted SAT scores:** 12%. Scores (25/75 percentile): Critical Reading: 460-580, Math: 460-590, Combined: 920-1170. **First-year students submitting ACT scores:** 67%. Scores (25/75 percentile): English: 17-23, Math: 17-24, Composite: 18-24.

ACADEMICS

Year founded: 1927. **Academic calendar:** Semester. **Degrees offered:** certificate, associate, transfer-associate, terminal-associate, bachelor's, post-bachelor's certificate, master's. **Most popular majors:** 26% business/ commerce, 24% elementary education and teaching, 9% liberal arts and sciences/liberal studies, 9% psychology, 5% biology/biological sciences. **Major fields of study:** biological and biomedical sciences; business, management, marketing, and related support services; communication, journalism, and related programs; education; English language and literature/letters; foreign languages, literatures, and linguistics; health professions and related clinical sciences; history; liberal arts and sciences studies, and humanities; mathematics and statistics; multi/interdisciplinary studies; natural resources and conservation; parks, recreation, leisure, and fitness studies; physical sciences; psychology; social sciences; visual and performing arts. **Areas of required coursework:** arts/fine arts, humanities, mathematics, English (including composition), sciences (biological or physical), history, social science, other. **Pre-professional programs:** pre-law, pre-medicine, pre-pharmacy, other. **Special academic programs (% participation):** accelerated program (2%), cooperative (work-study plan) program (33%), cross-registration (1%), distance learning (58%), double major (17%), dual enrollment (3%), English as a Second Language (ESL), external degree program (2%), honors program (1%), independent study (12%), internships (13%), study abroad (1%), teacher certificate program (4%), weekend college (1%), other (27%). **Teacher certification offered in:** early childhood, special education, elementary, middle/junior high, secondary. **Cooperative education programs:** art, business, computer science, education, health professions, humanities, natural science, social/behavioral science, technologies, vocational arts. **Reserve Officers Training Corps (ROTC):** Army ROTC: Offered on campus. **Faculty and instruction (2009-2010):** Total instructional faculty: 154 full-time, 136 part-time (49% men; 51% women; 4% minorities). Full-time faculty with Ph.D. or other terminal degree: 72%. Student/faculty ratio: 20/1. Classes of fewer than 20 students: 44%; of 20 to 49 students: 51%; of 50 or more students: 5%. **Advanced Placement and International Baccalaureate credit:** AP tests may be used for: Credit only. Scores accepted: 3. International Baccalaureate exams may be used for: Credit only. **Freshmen returning for sophomore year:** 60%. **Graduation rates:** Four-year: 14%; five-year: 25%; six-year: 29%. **Graduate study:** 10% of students pursue further study immediately upon graduation; 10% within one year. Fields in which graduates pursue further study: Master of Business Administration (MBA), 8%; medicine, 8%; education, 9%; arts and sciences, 75%.

COSTS AND FINANCIAL AID

Financial aid office: (406) 657-2188. **Expenses (2009-2010):** Tuition and fees 2009-2010: $5,207 in state, $10,555 out of state; room/board: $5,310. Estimated books and supplies: $1,000; transportation: $400; personal expenses: $3,400. **Financial aid:** Priority filing date for institution's financial aid form: March 1; deadline: July 1. In 2009-2010, 76% of undergraduates applied for financial aid. Of those, 62% were determined to have financial need; 3% had their need fully met. Average financial aid package (proportion receiving): $8,806 (59%). Average amount of gift aid, such as scholarships or grants (proportion receiving): $4,392 (45%). Average amount of self-help aid, such as work study or loans (proportion receiving): $3,675 (49%). Average need-based loan (excluding PLUS or other private loans): $3,500. Among students who received need-based aid, the average percentage of need met: 68%. Among students who received aid based on merit, the average award (and the proportion receiving): $2,071 (3%). The average athletic scholarship (and the proportion receiving): $3,878 (2%). Average amount of debt of borrowers graduating in 2009: $23,189. Proportion who borrowed: 73%.

CAMPUS LIFE AND EXTRACURRICULAR ACTIVITIES

Campus housing available (% using): coed dorms (95%), apartments for married students (5%). Students who live in college-owned, operated, or affiliated housing: 12%. **Student employment:** During the 2009-2010 academic year, 11% of undergraduates worked on campus. Average per-year earnings: $1,236. **Clubs and organizations:** Number of student organizations: 53. Activities include: campus ministries, choral groups, concert band, drama/theater, international student organization, jazz band, literary magazine, music ensembles, pep band, radio station, student government, student newspaper, symphony orchestra. Number of fraternities: 0; sororities: 0. Average proportion of students who stay on campus on weekends: 50%. **Sports program (2009-2010):** Member of NCAA II. *Men's intercollegiate varsity sports:* baseball, basketball, cross country, golf, soccer, tennis, track and field (outdoor). *Women's intercollegiate varsity sports:* basketball, cross country, golf, soccer, softball, tennis, track and field (outdoor), volleyball.

SERVICES AND FACILITIES

Basic services: nonremedial tutoring, placement service, day care, health service, health insurance. **Remedial assistance:** reading, math, writing, study skills. **Counseling services:** minority student, career, military, personal, veteran student, academic, older student, psychological, birth control, religious. **For learning-disabled students:** School does not offer a structured program with separate admission and additional fees. Total undergraduates in learning-disabled program or receiving services: 166. Services include: remedial math, remedial English, reading machines, remedial reading, tape recorders, note-taking services, oral tests, learning center, readers, extended time for tests, tutors, priority registration, priority seating, texts on tape, other testing accommodations. **Library:** Number of titles: 365,212; number of current serial subscriptions: 1,600. **Information technology resources:** Students are not required to lease or own a computer. Number of campus computers available to all students: 1,300. School has a wireless network. Approximate number of users that can be accommodated: 300. Proportion of college-owned housing units wired for high-speed internet access: 98%. **Campus safety:** Security services offered: 24-hour foot-and-vehicle patrols, late-night transport/escort service, 24-hour emergency telephones, lighted pathways/sidewalks, controlled dormitory access (key, security card, etc).

TRANSFER AND INTERNATIONAL STUDENTS

Transfer students: May apply for admission for the following academic terms: Fall, Spring, Summer. Applicants need a minimum number of credits to apply. For fall 2009: Transfer applications received: 530. Transfer applicants offered admission: 530. Transfer applicants enrolled: 530. **International students:** Number of foreign undergraduates: 12. Number of countries represented: 20. Minimum TOEFL score required: 500 (paper); 173 (computer). Average TOEFL score: 500 (paper).

Montana State University—Northern

- **Address:** PO Box 7751, Havre, MT 59501
- **Website:** http://www.msun.edu
- **Public**
- **Enrollment:** N/A

KEY STATS

✔ **U.S News College Ranking:** 26, Regional Colleges (West)
✔ **SAT or ACT Score (25th/75th percentile):** N/A
✔ **Tuition:** 2009-2010: $5,080 in state, $14,070 out of state
  Selectivity: Less selective   **Room/board:** $8,000
  Acceptance rate: N/A   **Average debt:** N/A
  Student/faculty ratio: N/A   **Proportion who borrowed:** N/A

Montana Tech of the Univ. of Montana

- **Address:** 1300 W. Park Street, Butte, MT 59701
- **Website:** http://www.mtech.edu
- **Public**
- **Enrollment:** 2,169 full-time; 391 part-time

KEY STATS

✔ **U.S News College Ranking:** 10, Regional Colleges (West)
✔ **ACT Score (25th/75th percentile):** 21-26
✔ **Tuition:** 2009-2010: $6,005 in state, $16,820 out of state
  Selectivity: Selective   **Room/board:** $6,602
  Acceptance rate: 91%   **Average debt:** $23,000
  Student/faculty ratio: 15/1   **Proportion who borrowed:** 85%

UNDERGRADUATE STUDENT BODY STATS

2009-2010 enrollment: 2,169 full-time; 391 part-time. Men: 61%; women: 39%. **Ethnic makeup:** African American: 1%; American-Indian: 2%; Asian American: 1%; Hispanic: 2%; White: 86%; International: 9%.

ADMISSIONS FACTS AND FIGURES

Phone: (406) 496-4256. **Email:** enrollment@mtech.edu. **Website:** http://www.mtech.edu. **Application deadlines for fall 2011:** Regular decision: Rolling. Early decision: Not offered. Early action: Not offered. Admission can be deferred. **Application fee:** $30. **To apply online, go to:** http://www.mtech.edu/onestop/admission/apply_online.htm. **Admissions requirements/recommendations:** High school units required (recommended): English: 4; Mathematics: 3 (4); Science: 2; Social studies: 3; Total units: 14. Tests: The college uses SAT or ACT scores in admissions decisions. Either SAT or ACT required. For admission to the fall 2011 entering class, the school will accept: ACT with writing recommended. Campus visit: Recommended. Admissions interview: Neither required nor recommended. Off-campus interview: Not available. **Factors that count in admissions decisions:** *Academic:* Secondary school record: Not Considered. Class rank: Very Important. Letters of recommendation: Not Considered. Standardized test scores: Very Important. Essay: Not Considered. *Nonacademic:* Interview: Not Considered. Extracurricular activities: Not Considered. Talent/ability: Not Considered. Character/personal qualities: Not Considered. Alumni/ae relationship: Not Considered. Geographical residence: Not Considered. State residency: Not Considered. Religious affiliation/commitment: Not Considered. Minority status: Not Considered. Volunteer work: Not Considered. Work experience: Not Considered. **Other schools with the greatest overlap in applicants:** Colorado School of Mines; Michigan Technological University; Montana State University; New Mexico Institute of Mining and Technology; University of Montana. **Admissions statistics for the fall 2009 entering class:** Total applicants: 821. Total accepted: 746. Freshmen enrolled: 490; 11% were from out of state. Overall acceptance rate: 91%. **Credentials of fall 2009 freshmen:** 14% ranked in the top 10 percent of their high school class; 47% were in the top 25 percent; 76% were in the top half. (Proportion submitting class standing: 74%.) **Average high school grade point average:** 3.4. **First-year students who submitted SAT scores:** 29%. Scores (25/75 percentile): Critical Reading: 450-580, Math: 490-620, Combined: 940-1200. **First-year students submitting ACT scores:** 74%. Scores (25/75 percentile): English: 19-25, Math: 20-27, Composite: 21-26.

ACADEMICS

Year founded: 1893. **Academic calendar:** Semester. **Degrees offered:** certificate, associate, transfer-associate, terminal-associate, bachelor's, post-bachelor's certificate, master's. **Most popular majors:** 20% petroleum engineering, 16% engineering, 13% business/commerce, 7% environmental/environmental health engineering, 6% geological/geophysical engineering. **Major fields of study:** biological and biomedical sciences; business, management, marketing, and related support services; computer and information sciences and support services; engineering; English language and literature/letters; health professions and related clinical sciences; liberal arts and sciences studies, and humanities; mathematics and statistics; physical sciences. **Areas of required coursework:** humanities, mathematics, English (including composition), sciences (biological or physical), social science. **Pre-professional programs:** pre-dentistry, pre-medicine, pre-veterinary science, pre-pharmacy. **Special academic programs:** cooperative (work-study plan) program, cross-registration, distance learning, double major, dual enrollment, external degree program, honors program, independent study, internships, teacher certificate program. **Teacher certification offered in:**

elementary, secondary. **Cooperative education programs:** business, education, engineering, health professions, technologies, vocational arts. **Faculty and instruction (2009-2010):** Total instructional faculty: 127 full-time, 74 part-time (62% men; 38% women; 8% minorities). Full-time faculty with Ph.D. or other terminal degree: 57%. Student/faculty ratio: 15/1. Classes of fewer than 20 students: 59%; of 20 to 49 students: 31%; of 50 or more students: 11%. **Advanced Placement and International Baccalaureate credit:** AP tests may be used for: Credit and/or placement. Scores accepted: 3, 4, 5. International Baccalaureate exams may be used for: Credit and/or placement. **Freshmen returning for sophomore year:** 71%. **Graduation rates:** Four-year: 16%; five-year: 38%; six-year: 40%. **Graduate study:** 16% of students pursue further study immediately upon graduation; 17% within one year. Fields in which graduates pursue further study: medicine, 7%; dentistry, 4%; engineering, 41%; arts and sciences, 41%.

COSTS AND FINANCIAL AID

Financial aid office: (406) 496-4212. **Expenses (2009-2010):** Tuition and fees 2009-2010: $6,005 in state, $16,820 out of state; room/board: $6,602. Estimated books and supplies: $1,000 personal expenses: $1,600. **Financial aid:** Priority filing date for institution's financial aid form: February 1. In 2009-2010, 70% of undergraduates applied for financial aid. Of those, 54% were determined to have financial need; 28% had their need fully met. Average financial aid package (proportion receiving): $9,086 (54%). Average amount of gift aid, such as scholarships or grants (proportion receiving): $4,425 (48%). Average amount of self-help aid, such as work study or loans (proportion receiving): $3,677 (43%). Average need-based loan (excluding PLUS or other private loans): $3,699. Among students who received need-based aid, the average percentage of need met: 76%. Among students who received aid based on merit, the average award (and the proportion receiving): $2,862 (14%). The average athletic scholarship (and the proportion receiving): $5,458 (3%). Average amount of debt of borrowers graduating in 2009: $23,000. Proportion who borrowed: 85%.

CAMPUS LIFE AND EXTRACURRICULAR ACTIVITIES

Campus housing available: coed dorms, apartments for married students, apartment for single students, special housing for disabled students. Students who live in college-owned, operated, or affiliated housing: 15%. Activities include: campus ministries, international student organization, pep band, radio station, student government, student newspaper. Number of fraternities: 0; sororities: 0. Average proportion of students who stay on campus on weekends: 77%. **Sports program (2009-2010):** Member of NAIA. **Men's intercollegiate varsity sports:** basketball, football, golf. **Women's intercollegiate varsity sports:** basketball, golf, volleyball.

SERVICES AND FACILITIES

Basic services: nonremedial tutoring, placement service, health service, health insurance. **Remedial assistance:** math, writing, study skills. **Counseling services:** minority student, career, military, personal, veteran student, academic, older student. **For learning-disabled students:** School does not offer a structured program with separate admission and additional fees. Services include: remedial math, remedial English, note-taking services, oral tests, learning center, extended time for tests, tutors, priority registration, priority seating, proofreading services, other testing accommodations, other. **Library:** Number of titles: 174,528; number of current serial subscriptions: 32,770. **Information technology resources:** Students are not required to lease or own a computer. Number of campus computers available to all students: 491. School has a wireless network. Approximate number of users that can be accommodated: 1,500. Proportion of college-owned housing units wired for high-speed internet access: 100%. **Campus safety:** Security services offered: 24-hour foot-and-vehicle patrols, late-night transport/escort service, 24-hour emergency telephones, lighted pathways/sidewalks, controlled dormitory access (key, security card, etc).

TRANSFER AND INTERNATIONAL STUDENTS

Transfer students: May apply for admission for the following academic terms: Fall, Spring, Summer. Applicants do not need a minimum number of credits to apply. For fall 2009: Transfer applications received: 375. Transfer applicants offered admission: 311. Transfer applicants enrolled: 236. **International students:** Number of foreign undergraduates: 202 (9% of student body). Number of countries represented: 17. Minimum TOEFL score required: 525 (paper); 195 (computer).

Rocky Mountain College

- **Address:** 1511 Poly Drive, Billings, MT 59102
- **Website:** http://www.rocky.edu
- **Private; Religious affiliation:** United Church of Christ, Methodist, and Presbyterian
- **Enrollment:** 781 full-time; 33 part-time

KEY STATS

✔ **U.S News College Ranking:** 7, Regional Colleges (West)
✔ **ACT Score (25th/75th percentile):** 20-26
✔ **Tuition:** 2010-2011: $21,100

Selectivity: Selective	**Room/board:** $6,678
Acceptance rate: 63%	**Average debt:** $24,361
Student/faculty ratio: 11/1	**Proportion who borrowed:** 68%

UNDERGRADUATE STUDENT BODY STATS

2009-2010 enrollment: 781 full-time; 33 part-time. Men: 50%; women: 50%. **Ethnic makeup:** African American: 2%; American-Indian: 4%; Asian American: 1%; Hispanic: 3%; White: 85%; International: 5%. **Religious preference:** Roman Catholic: 14%; Protestant: 23%; No preference: 45%; United Church of Christ, Methodist, and Presbyterian: 9%; Mormon: 2%; Other: 7%.

ADMISSIONS FACTS AND FIGURES

Phone: (406) 657-1026. **Email:** admissions@rocky.edu. **Website:** http://www.rocky.edu. **Application deadlines for fall 2011:** Regular decision: Rolling. Early decision: Not offered. Early action: Send application by: February 15; Decision sent by: February 15. Admission can be deferred. **Application fee:** $35. **To apply online, go to:** http://admissions.rocky.edu/index.php?topgroupid=18&groupid=88. **Admissions requirements/recommendations:** High school units required (recommended): English: 4; Mathematics: 4; Science: 3; Social studies: 3; History: 2; Academic electives: 3; Total units: 19. Tests: The college uses SAT or ACT scores in admissions decisions. Either SAT or ACT required. For admission to the fall 2011 entering class, the school will accept: ACT with or without writing accepted. Campus visit: Recommended. Admissions interview: Recommended. Off-campus interview: May be arranged. **Factors that count in admissions decisions:** *Academic:* Secondary school record: Important. Class rank: Considered. Letters of recommendation: Important. Standardized test scores: Very Important. Essay: Important. *Nonacademic:* Interview: Considered. Extracurricular activities: Considered. Talent/ability: Considered. Character/personal qualities: Considered. Alumni/ae relationship: Considered. Geographical residence: Not Considered. State residency: Not Considered. Religious affiliation/commitment: Not Considered. Minority status: Not Considered. Volunteer work: Not Considered. Work experience: Not Considered. **Other schools with the greatest overlap in applicants:** Carroll College; Montana State University; Montana State University–Billings; University of Montana; University of Montana–Western. **Admissions statistics for the fall 2009 entering class:** Total applicants: 927. Total accepted: 587. Freshmen enrolled: 234; 39% were from out of state. Overall acceptance rate: 63%. Non-early acceptance rate: 63%. **Average high school grade point average:** 3.4. **First-year students who submitted SAT scores:** 40%. Scores (25/75 percentile): Critical Reading: 440-550, Math: 450-550, Combined: 890-1100. **First-year students submitting ACT scores:** 69%. Scores (25/75 percentile): English: 19-25, Math: 18-25, Composite: 20-26.

ACADEMICS

Year founded: 1878. **Academic calendar:** Semester. **Degrees offered:** associate, bachelor's, master's. **Most popular majors:** 22% business administration and management, 14% athletic training/trainer, 12% airline/commercial/professional pilot and flight crew, 10% biology/biological sciences, 10% sociology. **Major fields of study:** agriculture, agriculture operations, and related sciences; biological and biomedical sciences; business, management, marketing, and related support services; communication, journalism, and related programs; computer and information sciences and support services; education; English language and literature/letters; health professions and related clinical sciences; history; mathematics and statistics; multi/interdisciplinary studies; natural resources and conservation; parks, recreation, leisure, and fitness studies; philosophy and religious studies; physical sciences; psychology; social sciences; transportation and materials moving; visual and performing arts. **Areas of required coursework:** arts/fine arts, humanities, mathematics, English (including composition), philosophy, sciences (biological or physical), history, social science, other. **Pre-professional programs:** pre-law, pre-dentistry, pre-medicine, pre-theology, pre-veterinary science, pre-optometry, pre-pharmacy, other. **Special academic programs:** accelerated program, distance learning, double major, dual enrollment, English as a Second Language (ESL), honors program, independent study, internships, student-designed major, study abroad, teacher certificate program. **Teacher certification offered in:** elementary, middle/junior high, secondary. **Reserve Officers Training Corps (ROTC):** Army ROTC: Offered on campus. **Faculty and instruction (2009-2010):** Total instructional faculty: 66 full-time, 39 part-time (59% men; 41% women; 1% minorities). Full-time faculty with Ph.D. or other terminal degree: 70%. Student/faculty ratio: 11/1. Classes of fewer than 20 students: 71%; of 20 to 49 students: 24%; of 50 or more students: 5%. **Advanced Placement and International Baccalaureate credit:** AP tests may be used for: Credit and/or placement. Scores accepted: 3, 4. International Baccalaureate exams may be used for: Credit and/or placement. **Freshmen returning for sophomore year:** 64%. **Graduation rates:** Four-year: 32%; five-year: 43%; six-year: 49%. **Graduate study:** 18% of students pursue further study immediately upon graduation; 5% within one year. Fields in which graduates pursue further study: Master of Business Administration (MBA), 15%; law, 1%; medicine, 40%; dentistry, 1%; arts and sciences, 40%; veterinary medicine, 1%.

COSTS AND FINANCIAL AID

Financial aid office: (406) 657-1031. **Expenses (2010-2011):** Tuition and fees 2010-2011: $21,100; room/board: $6,678. Estimated books and supplies: $1,200 personal expenses: $2,800. **Financial aid:** Priority filing date for institution's financial aid form: April 1. In 2009-2010, 82% of undergraduates applied for financial aid. Of those, 73% were determined to have financial need; 22% had their need fully met. Average financial aid package (proportion receiving): $17,118 (73%). Average amount of gift aid, such as scholarships or grants (proportion receiving): $11,959 (46%). Average amount of self-help aid, such as work study or loans (proportion receiving): $4,941 (63%). Average need-based loan (excluding PLUS or other private loans): $3,905. Among students who received need-based aid, the average percentage of need met: 69%. Among students who received aid based on merit, the average award (and the proportion receiving): $6,891 (20%). The average athletic scholarship (and the proportion receiving): $10,298 (12%). Average amount of debt of borrowers graduating in 2009: $24,361. Proportion who borrowed: 68%.

CAMPUS LIFE AND EXTRACURRICULAR ACTIVITIES

Campus housing available (% using): coed dorms (47%), apartments for married students (11%), apartment for single students (2%), special housing for disabled students (0%). Students who live in college-owned, operated, or affiliated housing: 55%. **Student employment:** During the 2009-2010 academic year, 70% of undergraduates worked on campus. Average per-year earnings: $1,500. **Clubs and organizations:** Number of student organizations: 15. Activities include: choral groups, concert band, drama/theater, international student organization, jazz band, musical theater, pep band, student government, student newspaper, symphony orchestra. Number of fraternities: 0; sororities: 0. Average proportion of students who stay on campus on weekends: 50%. **Sports program (2009-2010):** Member of NAIA. **Men's intercollegiate varsity sports:** basketball, cross country, football, golf, skiing (alpine), soccer. **Women's intercollegiate varsity sports:** basketball, cross country, golf, skiing (alpine), soccer, volleyball.

SERVICES AND FACILITIES

Basic services: nonremedial tutoring, placement service, day care, health service. **Remedial assistance:** reading, math, writing, study skills. **Counseling services:** minority student, career, personal, academic, psychological, religious. **For learning-disabled students:** School does not offer a structured program with separate admission and additional fees. Services include: remedial math, remedial English, remedial reading, tape recorders, other special classes, untimed tests, note-taking services, readers, extended time for tests, tutors, texts on tape, other testing accommodations. **Library:** Number of titles: 10,120; number of current serial subscriptions: 378. **Information technology resources:** Students are not required to lease or own a computer. Number of campus computers available to all students: 124. School has a wireless network. Approximate number of users that can be accommodated: 400. Proportion of college-owned housing units wired for high-speed internet access: 100%. **Campus safety:** Security services offered: late-night transport/escort service, lighted pathways/sidewalks, student patrols, controlled dormitory access (key, security card, etc).

TRANSFER AND INTERNATIONAL STUDENTS

Transfer students: May apply for admission for the following academic terms: Fall, Spring, Summer. Applicants need a minimum number of credits to apply. For fall 2009: Transfer applications received: 224. Transfer applicants offered admission: 137. Transfer applicants enrolled: 79. **International students:** Number of foreign undergraduates: 39 (5% of student body). Number of countries represented: 15. Minimum TOEFL score required: 525 (paper); 72 (computer). Average TOEFL score: 525 (paper).

University of Great Falls

- **Address:** 1301 20th Street S, Great Falls, MT 59405
- **Website:** http://www.ugf.edu
- **Private; Religious affiliation:** Roman Catholic
- **Enrollment:** 588 full-time; 194 part-time

KEY STATS
✔ **U.S News College Ranking:** second tier, Regional Universities (West)
✔ **ACT Score (25th/75th percentile):** 18-22
✔ **Tuition:** 2009-2010: $18,212

Selectivity: Less selective	**Room/board:** $6,610
Acceptance rate: 83%	**Average debt:** N/A
Student/faculty ratio: 12/1	**Proportion who borrowed:** 67%

UNDERGRADUATE STUDENT BODY STATS

2009-2010 enrollment: 588 full-time; 194 part-time. Men: 37%; women: 63%. **Ethnic makeup:** African American: 4%; American-Indian: 4%; Asian American: 1%; Hispanic: 5%; White: 84%; International: 2%. **Religious preference:** Roman Catholic: 28%; Unknown: 72%.

ADMISSIONS FACTS AND FIGURES

Phone: (406) 791-5200. **Email:** enroll@ugf.edu. **Website:** http://www.ugf.edu. **Application deadlines for fall 2011:** Regular decision: September 1. Early decision: Not offered. Early action: Not offered. Admission can be deferred. **Application fee:** $35. **To apply online, go to:** https://ugf.myadmissionsapp.com/apply/authentication.do?cmd=login-check. **Admissions requirements/recommendations:** High school units required (recommended): English: 4; Mathematics: 3; Science: 3; Foreign language: 0; Social studies: 1 (2); History: 3; Academic electives: 5; Total units: 20 (22). Tests: The college uses SAT or ACT scores in admissions decisions. Neither SAT nor ACT required. For admission to the fall 2011 entering class, the school will accept: ACT with or without writing accepted. Campus visit: Recommended. Admissions interview: Recommended. Off-campus interview: May be arranged. **Factors that count in admissions decisions:** *Academic:* Secondary school record: Very Important. Class rank: Considered. Letters of recommendation: Considered. Standardized test scores: Considered. Essay: Important. *Nonacademic:* Interview: Very Important. Extracurricular activities: Important. Talent/ability: Important. Character/personal qualities: Very Important. Alumni/ae relationship: Considered. Geographical residence: Not Considered. State residency: Not Considered. Religious affiliation/commitment: Important. Minority status: Not Considered. Volunteer work: Important. Work experience: Considered. **Other schools with the greatest overlap in applicants:** Carroll College; Montana State University; Montana State University–Northern; Montana Tech of the University of Montana; University of Montana. **Admissions statistics for the fall 2009 entering class:** 42% were from out of state. Overall acceptance rate: 83%. **First-year students who submitted SAT scores:** 25%. Scores (25/75 percentile): Critical Reading: 440-520, Math: 440-520, Combined: 880-1040. **First-year students submitting ACT scores:** 34%. Scores (25/75 percentile): English: 17-24, Math: 16-22, Composite: 18-22.

ACADEMICS

Year founded: 1932. **Academic calendar:** Semester. **Degrees offered:** certificate, associate, transfer-associate, bachelor's, post-bachelor's certificate, master's. **Most popular majors:** 31% education, 17% business, management, marketing, and related support services, 17% psychology, 5% social sciences, 4% computer and information sciences and support services. **Major fields of study:** biological and biomedical sciences; business, management, marketing, and related support services; computer and information sciences and support services; education; English language and literature/letters; history; legal professions and studies; mathematics and statistics; parks, recreation, leisure, and fitness studies; physical sciences; psychology; security and protective services; social sciences; theology and religious vocations;

visual and performing arts. **Areas of required coursework:** arts/fine arts, humanities, computer literacy, mathematics, English (including composition), philosophy, sciences (biological or physical), history, social science, other. **Pre-professional programs:** pre-medicine. **Special academic programs (% participation):** cooperative (work-study plan) program (6%), distance learning (16%), double major (15%), dual enrollment (0%), exchange student program (domestic), honors program, independent study (10%), internships (15%), liberal arts/career combination, study abroad, teacher certificate program (5%), weekend college. **Teacher certification offered in:** special education, elementary, middle/junior high, secondary. **Cooperative education programs:** art, business, computer science, education, social/behavioral science. **Faculty and instruction (2009-2010):** Total instructional faculty: 41 full-time, 72 part-time (44% men; 56% women; 4% minorities). Full-time faculty with Ph.D. or other terminal degree: 85%. Student/faculty ratio: 12/1. Classes of fewer than 20 students: 79%; of 20 to 49 students: 21%. **Advanced Placement and International Baccalaureate credit:** AP tests may be used for: Credit only. Scores accepted: 5. International Baccalaureate exams may be used for: Placement only. **Freshmen returning for sophomore year:** 58%. **Graduation rates:** Six-year: 23%. **Graduate study:** 30% of students pursue further study immediately upon graduation. Fields in which graduates pursue further study: law, 5%; medicine, 1%; education, 10%; arts and sciences, 5%.

COSTS AND FINANCIAL AID

Financial aid office: (406) 791-5235. **Expenses (2009-2010):** Tuition and fees 2009-2010: $18,212; room/board: $6,610. **Financial aid:** Priority filing date for institution's financial aid form: May 1. In 2009-2010, 73% of undergraduates applied for financial aid. Of those, 73% were determined to have financial need; 2% had their need fully met. Average financial aid package (proportion receiving): N/A (73%). Average amount of gift aid, such as scholarships or grants (proportion receiving): $5,238 (49%). Average amount of self-help aid, such as work study or loans (proportion receiving): $4,997 (65%). Average need-based loan (excluding PLUS or other private loans): $4,364. Among students who received need-based aid, the average percentage of need met: 60%. Among students who received aid based on merit, the average award (and the proportion receiving): $9,542 (4%). The average athletic scholarship (and the proportion receiving): $6,095 (44%). Proportion who borrowed: 67%.

CAMPUS LIFE AND EXTRACURRICULAR ACTIVITIES

Campus housing available (% using): coed dorms (44%), apartment for single students (56%). Students who live in college-owned, operated, or affiliated housing: 30%. **Student employment:** During the 2009-2010 academic year, 15% of undergraduates worked on campus. Average per-year earnings: $2,000. **Clubs and organizations:** Number of student organizations: 14. Activities include: campus ministries, choral groups, concert band, dance, drama/theater, jazz band, music ensembles, musical theater, pep band, student government, student newspaper, student film society, symphony orchestra. Number of fraternities: 0; sororities: 0. Average proportion of students who stay on campus on weekends: 25%. **Sports program (2009-2010):** Member of NAIA.

SERVICES AND FACILITIES

Basic services: nonremedial tutoring, placement service, health service, health insurance. **Remedial assistance:** reading, math, writing, study skills. **Counseling services:** minority student, career, personal, veteran student, academic, older student, psychological, religious. **For learning-disabled students:** School does not offer a structured program with separate admission and additional fees. Services include: remedial math, remedial English, reading machines, remedial reading, tape recorders, videotaped classes, diagnostic testing service, untimed tests, note-taking services, oral tests, learning center, readers, extended time for tests, tutors, texts on tape, other testing accommodations. **Library:** Number of titles: 109,264; number of current serial subscriptions: 279. **Information technology resources:** Students are not required to lease or own a computer. Number of campus computers available to all students: 73. School has a wireless network. Proportion of college-owned housing units wired for high-speed internet access: 75%. **Campus safety:** Security services offered: 24-hour foot-and-vehicle patrols, late-night transport/escort service, 24-hour emergency telephones, lighted pathways/sidewalks, controlled dormitory access (key, security card, etc).

TRANSFER AND INTERNATIONAL STUDENTS

Transfer students: May apply for admission for the following academic terms: Fall, Spring, Summer. Applicants need a minimum number of credits to apply. For fall 2009: Transfer applications received: 242. Transfer applicants offered admission: 202. Transfer applicants enrolled: 185.

International students: Number of foreign undergraduates: 15 (2% of student body). Number of countries represented: 5. Minimum TOEFL score required: 500 (paper); 173 (computer).

University of Montana

- **Address:** 32 Campus Drive, Missoula, MT 59812
- **Website:** http://www.umt.edu
- **Public**
- **Enrollment:** 9,205 full-time; 1,515 part-time

KEY STATS
- ✔ **U.S News College Ranking:** 191, National Universities
- ✔ **ACT Score (25th/75th percentile):** 20-26
- ✔ **Tuition:** 2010-2011: $5,685 in state, $19,834 out of state
- **Selectivity:** Selective
- **Room/board:** $6,860
- **Acceptance rate:** 83%
- **Average debt:** $20,223
- **Student/faculty ratio:** 20/1
- **Proportion who borrowed:** 61%

UNDERGRADUATE STUDENT BODY STATS

2009-2010 enrollment: 9,205 full-time; 1,515 part-time. Men: 48%; women: 52%. **Ethnic makeup:** African American: 1%; American-Indian: 4%; Asian American: 2%; Hispanic: 2%; White: 91%; International: 2%.

ADMISSIONS FACTS AND FIGURES

Phone: (800) 462-8636. **Email:** admiss@umontana.edu. **Website:** http://www.umt.edu. **Application deadlines for fall 2011:** Regular decision: Rolling. Early decision: Not offered. Early action: Not offered. Admission can be deferred. **Application fee:** $36. **To apply online, go to:** http://admissions.umt.edu/hottopics/academics/applying.htm. **Admissions requirements/recommendations:** High school units required (recommended): English: 4; Mathematics: 3; Science: 2; Foreign language: (2); Social studies: 3; History: (2); Academic electives: 2. Tests: The college uses SAT or ACT scores in admissions decisions. Either SAT or ACT required. For admission to the fall 2011 entering class, the school will accept: ACT with writing recommended. Campus visit: Recommended. Admissions interview: Neither required nor recommended. **Factors that count in admissions decisions:** *Academic:* Secondary school record: Very Important. Class rank: Very Important. Letters of recommendation: Considered. Standardized test scores: Very Important. Essay: Considered. *Nonacademic:* Interview: Not Considered. Extracurricular activities: Important. Talent/ability: Important. Character/personal qualities: Not Considered. Alumni/ae relationship: Not Considered. Geographical residence: Not Considered. State residency: Not Considered. Religious affiliation/commitment: Not Considered. Minority status: Not Considered. Volunteer work: Not Considered. Work experience: Not Considered. **Other schools with the greatest overlap in applicants:** Colorado State University; Gonzaga University; Montana State University; University of Colorado–Boulder; University of Oregon. **Admissions statistics for the fall 2009 entering class:** Total applicants: 4,630. Total accepted: 3,864. Freshmen enrolled: 1,886; 22% were from out of state. Overall acceptance rate: 83%. **Credentials of fall 2009 freshmen:** 16% ranked in the top 10 percent of their high school class; 39% were in the top 25 percent; 71% were in the top half. (Proportion submitting class standing: 75%.) **Average high school grade point average:** 3.2. **First-year students who submitted SAT scores:** 45%. Scores (25/75 percentile): Critical Reading: 490-610, Math: 480-590, Combined: 970-1200. **First-year students submitting ACT scores:** 67%. Scores (25/75 percentile): English: 19-25, Math: 19-25, Composite: 20-26.

ACADEMICS

Year founded: 1893. **Academic calendar:** Semester. **Degrees offered:** certificate, associate, terminal-associate, bachelor's, master's, post-master's certificate, doctorate. **Most popular majors:** 20% business, management, marketing, and related support services, 9% communication, journalism, and related programs, 8% natural resources and conservation, 6% psychology, 6% visual and performing arts. **Major fields of study:** area, ethnic, cultural, and gender studies; biological and biomedical sciences; business, management, marketing, and related support services; communication, journalism, and related programs; computer and information sciences and support services; education; English language and literature/letters; foreign languages, literatures, and linguistics; health professions and related clinical sciences; history; liberal arts and sciences studies, and humanities; mathematics and statistics; multi/interdisciplinary studies; natural resources and conservation; parks, recreation, leisure, and fitness studies; philosophy and religious studies; physical sciences; public administration and social service professions; social sciences; visual and performing arts. **Areas of required coursework:** arts/fine arts, mathematics, English (including composition), sciences (biological or physical), history, social science, other. **Pre-professional programs:** pre-law, pre-dentistry, pre-medicine, pre-veterinary science, pre-optometry, pre-pharmacy, other. **Special academic programs:** distance learning, double major, English as a Second Language (ESL), exchange student program (domestic), external degree program, honors program, independent study, internships, study abroad, teacher certificate program, other. **Teacher certification offered in:** early childhood, special education, elementary, middle/junior high, secondary, bilingual/bicultural. **Cooperative education programs:** art, business, computer science, education, health professions, humanities, natural science, social/behavioral science, technologies, other. **Reserve Officers Training Corps (ROTC):** Army ROTC: Offered on campus. **Faculty and instruction (2009-2010):** Total instructional faculty: 557 full-time, 262 part-time (58% men; 42% women; 12% minorities). Full-time faculty with Ph.D. or other terminal degree: 83%. Student/faculty ratio: 20/1. Classes of fewer than 20 students: 45%; of 20 to 49 students: 45%; of 50 or more students: 11%. **Advanced Placement and International Baccalaureate credit:** AP tests may be used for: Credit only. Scores accepted: 3, 4, 5. International Baccalaureate exams may be used for: Credit only. **Freshmen returning for sophomore year:** 72%. **Graduation rates:** Four-year: 20%; five-year: 38%; six-year: 44%. **Graduate study:** 21% of students pursue further study immediately upon graduation; 21% within one year.

COSTS AND FINANCIAL AID

Financial aid office: (406) 243-5373. **Expenses (2010-2011):** Tuition and fees 2010-2011: $5,685 in state, $19,834 out of state; room/board: $6,860. Estimated books and supplies: $900; transportation: $1,500; personal expenses: $3,114. **Financial aid:** Priority filing date for institution's financial aid form: February 15. In 2009-2010, 79% of undergraduates applied for financial aid. Of those, 58% were determined to have financial need; 8% had their need fully met. Average financial aid package (proportion receiving): $8,638 (57%). Average amount of gift aid, such as scholarships or grants (proportion receiving): $3,899 (41%). Average amount of self-help aid, such as work study or loans (proportion receiving): $4,429 (50%). Average need-based loan (excluding PLUS or other private loans): $3,931. Among students who received need-based aid, the average percentage of need met: 74%. Among students who received aid based on merit, the average award (and the proportion receiving): $6,352 (22%). The average athletic scholarship (and the proportion receiving): $5,639 (2%). Average amount of debt of borrowers graduating in 2009: $20,223. Proportion who borrowed: 61%.

CAMPUS LIFE AND EXTRACURRICULAR ACTIVITIES

Campus housing available (% using): coed dorms (70%), women's dorms (4%), men's dorms (3%), sorority housing, fraternity housing, apartments for married students (15%), apartment for single students (4%), special housing for disabled students (1%), special housing for international students (2%), other housing options (1%). Students who live in college-owned, operated, or affiliated housing: 27%. **Clubs and organizations:** Number of student organizations: 150. Activities include: choral groups, concert band, dance, drama/theater, international student organization, jazz band, literary magazine, marching band, model UN, music ensembles, musical theater, opera, pep band, radio station, student government, student newspaper, symphony orchestra, television station. Number of fraternities: 6; sororities: 4. Average proportion of students who stay on campus on weekends: 90%. **Sports program (2009-2010):** Member of NCAA I.

SERVICES AND FACILITIES

Basic services: nonremedial tutoring, placement service, health service, health insurance, other. **Remedial assistance:** math, writing, study skills. **Counseling services:** minority student, career, military, personal, veteran student, academic, older student, psychological, birth control. **For learning-disabled students:** School does not offer a structured program with separate admission and additional fees. Services include: reading machines, tape recorders, note-taking services, readers, extended time for tests, tutors, priority registration, substitution of courses, texts on tape, exams on tape or computer, other testing accommodations, other. **Library:** Number of titles: 1,174,948; number of current serial subscriptions: 28,362. **Information technology resources:** Students are not required to lease or own a computer. Number of campus computers available to all students: 500. School has a wireless network. Approximate number of users that can be accommodated: 1,728. Proportion of college-owned housing units wired for high-speed

internet access: 100%. **Campus safety:** Security services offered: 24-hour foot-and-vehicle patrols, late-night transport/escort service, 24-hour emergency telephones, lighted pathways/sidewalks, controlled dormitory access (key, security card, etc).

TRANSFER AND INTERNATIONAL STUDENTS

Transfer students: May apply for admission for the following academic terms: Fall, Spring, Summer. Applicants need a minimum number of credits to apply. For fall 2009: Transfer applications received: 2,348. Transfer applicants offered admission: 2,074. Transfer applicants enrolled: 1,209. **International students:** Number of foreign undergraduates: 184 (2% of student body). Number of countries represented: 65. Minimum TOEFL score required: 500 (paper); 173 (computer). Average TOEFL score: 525 (paper).

University of Montana—Western

- **Address:** 710 S. Atlantic Street, Dillon, MT 59725
- **Website:** http://www.umwestern.edu
- **Public**
- **Enrollment:** 1,041 full-time; 214 part-time

KEY STATS

✔ **U.S News College Ranking:** 12, Regional Colleges (West)
✔ **ACT Score (25th/75th percentile):** 17-22
✔ **Tuition:** 2010-2011: $4,837 in state, $13,381 out of state
  Selectivity: Less selective   **Room/board:** $5,820
  Acceptance rate: 68%   **Average debt:** $22,009
  Student/faculty ratio: 16/1   **Proportion who borrowed:** 82%

UNDERGRADUATE STUDENT BODY STATS

2009-2010 enrollment: 1,041 full-time; 214 part-time. Men: 45%; women: 55%. **Ethnic makeup:** African American: 1%; American-Indian: 2%; Asian American: 3%; Hispanic: 2%; White: 92%.

ADMISSIONS FACTS AND FIGURES

Phone: (406) 683-7331. **Email:** admissions@umwestern.edu. **Website:** http://www.umwestern.edu. **Application deadlines for fall 2011:** Regular decision: Rolling. Early decision: Not offered. Early action: Not offered. Admission can be deferred. **Application fee:** $30. **To apply online, go to:** https://www.applyweb.com/apply/wmc/index.html. **Admissions requirements/recommendations:** High school units required (recommended): English: 4; Mathematics: 3; Science: 2; Foreign language: 0; Social studies: 3; History: 0; Academic electives: 2; Total units: 14. Tests: The college uses SAT or ACT scores in admissions decisions. Either SAT or ACT required. For admission to the fall 2011 entering class, the school will accept: ACT with writing required. Campus visit: Recommended. Admissions interview: Neither required nor recommended. Off-campus interview: Not available. **Factors that count in admissions decisions: Academic:** Secondary school record: Very Important. Class rank: Very Important. Letters of recommendation: Not Considered. Standardized test scores: Very Important. Essay: Not Considered. **Nonacademic:** Interview: Not Considered. Extracurricular activities: Considered. Talent/ability: Considered. Character/personal qualities: Not Considered. Alumni/ae relationship: Considered. Geographical residence: Not Considered. State residency: Considered. Religious affiliation/commitment: Not Considered. Minority status: Not Considered. Volunteer work: Not Considered. Work experience: Not Considered. **Other schools with the greatest overlap in applicants:** Idaho State University; Montana State University; Montana State University–Billings; Montana Tech of the University of Montana; University of Montana. **Admissions statistics for the fall 2009 entering class:** Total applicants: 474. Total accepted: 321. Freshmen enrolled: 240; 22% were from out of state. Overall acceptance rate: 68%. **Credentials of fall 2009 freshmen:** 6% ranked in the top 10 percent of their high school class; 19% were in the top 25 percent; 49% were in the top half. (Proportion submitting class standing: 89%.) **Average high school grade point average:** 3.0. **First-year students who submitted SAT scores:** 27%. Scores (25/75 percentile): Critical Reading: 400-540, Math: 400-550, Combined: 800-1090. **First-year students submitting ACT scores:** 78%. Scores (25/75 percentile): English: 16-21, Math: 16-22, Composite: 17-22.

ACADEMICS

Year founded: 1893. **Academic calendar:** Semester. **Degrees offered:** certificate, associate, bachelor's. **Most popular majors:** 21% liberal arts and sciences/liberal studies, 19% secondary education and teaching, 17% business/commerce, 15% teacher education, 9% child care and support services management. **Major fields of study:** education; liberal arts and sciences studies, and humanities; multi/interdisciplinary studies. **Areas of required coursework:** arts/fine arts, humanities, computer literacy, mathematics, English (including composition), sciences (biological or physical), history, social science. **Pre-professional programs:** pre-law, pre-medicine, pre-veterinary science, pre-pharmacy. **Special academic programs (% participation):** cooperative (work-study plan) program (10%), double major (5%), dual enrollment (10%), honors program (5%), independent study (2%), internships (20%), teacher certificate program (65%). **Teacher certification offered in:** special education, elementary, middle/junior high, secondary. **Cooperative education programs:** business, natural science, social/behavioral science. **Faculty and instruction (2009-2010):** Total instructional faculty: 62 full-time, 25 part-time (47% men; 53% women; 2% minorities). Full-time faculty with Ph.D. or other terminal degree: 73%. Student/faculty ratio: 16/1. Classes of fewer than 20 students: 70%; of 20 to 49 students: 30%; of 50 or more students: 0%. **Advanced Placement and International Baccalaureate credit:** International Baccalaureate exams may be used for: Credit and/or placement. **Freshmen returning for sophomore year:** 68%. **Graduation rates:** Four-year: 12%; five-year: 26%; six-year: 31%. **Graduate study:** 6% of students pursue further study immediately upon graduation; 10% within one year.

COSTS AND FINANCIAL AID
Financial aid office: (406) 683-7511. **Expenses (2010-2011):** Tuition and fees 2010-2011: $4,837 in state, $13,381 out of state; room/board: $5,820. Estimated books and supplies: $925; transportation: $2,320; personal expenses: $1,710. **Financial aid:** Priority filing date for institution's financial aid form: March 1. In 2009-2010, 92% of undergraduates applied for financial aid. Of those, 79% were determined to have financial need; 3% had their need fully met. Average financial aid package (proportion receiving): $3,282 (87%). Average amount of gift aid, such as scholarships or grants (proportion receiving): $2,980 (64%). Average amount of self-help aid, such as work study or loans (proportion receiving): $3,101 (70%). Average need-based loan (excluding PLUS or other private loans): $4,102. Among students who received need-based aid, the average percentage of need met: 17%. Among students who received aid based on merit, the average award (and the proportion receiving): $1,041 (7%). The average athletic scholarship (and the proportion receiving): $1,833 (38%). Average amount of debt of borrowers graduating in 2009: $22,009. Proportion who borrowed: 82%.

CAMPUS LIFE AND EXTRACURRICULAR ACTIVITIES
Campus housing available (% using): coed dorms (48%), women's dorms (23%), men's dorms (24%), apartments for married students (5%), apart-

ment for single students (0%), special housing for disabled students (0%). Students who live in college-owned, operated, or affiliated housing: 36%. **Student employment:** During the 2009-2010 academic year, 10% of undergraduates worked on campus. Average per-year earnings: $2,000. **Clubs and organizations:** Number of student organizations: 30. Activities include: campus ministries, choral groups, drama/theater, literary magazine, music ensembles, musical theater, pep band, radio station, student government, student newspaper. Number of fraternities: 0; sororities: 0. Average proportion of students who stay on campus on weekends: 20%. **Sports program (2009-2010):** Member of NAIA. *Men's intercollegiate varsity sports:* basketball, football, golf. *Women's intercollegiate varsity sports:* basketball, golf, volleyball.

SERVICES AND FACILITIES
Basic services: nonremedial tutoring, placement service, health service, health insurance, other. **Remedial assistance:** reading, math, writing, study skills. **Counseling services:** career, personal, academic, psychological, birth control. **For learning-disabled students:** School does not offer a structured program with separate admission and additional fees. Services include: remedial math, remedial English, reading machines, tape recorders, videotaped classes, untimed tests, note-taking services, oral tests, learning center, readers, extended time for tests, tutors, priority registration, priority seating, proofreading services, texts on tape, typist/scribe, exams on tape or computer. **Library:** Number of titles: 57,467; number of current serial subscriptions: 472. **Information technology resources:** Students are not required to lease or own a computer. Number of campus computers available to all students: 200. School has a wireless network. Approximate number of users that can be accommodated: 150. Proportion of college-owned housing units wired for high-speed internet access: 100%. **Campus safety:** Security services offered: late-night transport/escort service, 24-hour emergency telephones, lighted pathways/sidewalks, controlled dormitory access (key, security card, etc).

TRANSFER AND INTERNATIONAL STUDENTS
Transfer students: May apply for admission for the following academic terms: Fall, Spring, Summer. Applicants need a minimum number of credits to apply. For fall 2009: Transfer applications received: 229. Transfer applicants offered admission: 146. Transfer applicants enrolled: 124. **International students:** Number of foreign undergraduates: 3. Number of countries represented: 5. Minimum TOEFL score required: 500 (paper); 173 (computer).

Nebraska

Bellevue University

- **Address:** 1000 Galvin Road S, Bellevue, NE 68005
- **Website:** http://www.bellevue.edu
- **Private**
- **Enrollment:** 2,842 full-time; 3,934 part-time

KEY STATS

✔ **U.S News College Ranking:** Unranked, Regional Universities (Midwest)
✔ **SAT or ACT Score (25th/75th percentile):** N/A
✔ **Tuition:** 2009-2010: $11,526

Selectivity: N/A	Room/board: $10,350
Acceptance rate: N/A	Average debt: N/A
Student/faculty ratio: N/A	Proportion who borrowed: N/A

UNDERGRADUATE STUDENT BODY STATS

2009-2010 enrollment: 2,842 full-time; 3,934 part-time. Men: 53%; women: 47%. **Ethnic makeup:** African American: 12%; American-Indian: 2%; Asian American: 2%; Hispanic: 8%; White: 73%; International: 2%.

ADMISSIONS FACTS AND FIGURES

Phone: (800) 756-7920. **Email:** info@bellevue.edu. **Website:** http://www.bellevue.edu. **Application deadlines for fall 2011:** Regular decision: Rolling. Early decision: Not offered. Early action: Not offered. Admission can be deferred. **Application fee:** $50. **To apply online, go to:** http://www.bellevue.edu/getstarted/application2.asp. **Admissions requirements/recommendations:** High school units required (recommended): English: (3); Mathematics: (3); Science: (3); Foreign language: (3); Social studies: (3); History: (3); Academic electives: (3). Tests: The college does not use SAT or ACT scores in admissions decisions. Neither SAT nor ACT required. Campus visit: Neither required nor recommended. Admissions interview: Neither required nor recommended. Off-campus interview: Not available. **Factors that count in admissions decisions:** *Academic:* Secondary school record: Not Considered. Class rank: Not Considered. Letters of recommendation: Not Considered. Standardized test scores: Not Considered. Essay: Not Considered. *Nonacademic:* Interview: Not Considered. Extracurricular activities: Not Considered. Talent/ability: Not Considered. Character/personal qualities: Not Considered. Alumni/ae relationship: Not Considered. Geographical residence: Not Considered. State residency: Not Considered. Religious affiliation/commitment: Not Considered. Minority status: Not Considered. Volunteer work: Not Considered. Work experience: Not Considered. **Other schools with the greatest overlap in applicants:** Capella University; Nebraska Wesleyan University; University of Nebraska–Lincoln; University of Nebraska–Omaha; University of Phoenix. **Admissions statistics for the fall 2009 entering class:** Freshmen enrolled: 122;

ACADEMICS

Year founded: 1966. **Academic calendar:** Semester. **Degrees offered:** bachelor's, master's, doctorate. **Major fields of study:** biological and biomedical sciences; business, management, marketing, and related support services; communication, journalism, and related programs; communications technologies/technicians and support services; computer and information sciences and support services; education; health professions and related clinical sciences; history; liberal arts and sciences studies, and humanities; psychology; public administration and social service professions; security and protective services; social sciences; visual and performing arts. **Areas of required coursework:** English (including composition). **Special academic programs (% participation):** accelerated program (48%), distance learning (80%), English as a Second Language (ESL) (4%). **Reserve Officers Training Corps (ROTC):** Army ROTC: Offered at cooperating institution (Creighton University); Air Force ROTC: Offered at cooperating institution (University of Nebraska–Omaha). **Advanced Placement and International Baccalaureate credit:** AP tests may be used for: Placement only. Scores accepted: 3. International Baccalaureate exams may be used for: Placement only. **Graduation rates:** Six-year: 21%.

COSTS AND FINANCIAL AID

Financial aid office: (402) 293-3763. **Expenses (2009-2010):** Tuition and fees 2009-2010: $11,526; room/board: $10,350. Estimated books and supplies: $1,500; transportation: $900; personal expenses: $2,250. **Financial aid:** Priority filing date for institution's financial aid form: April 1.

CAMPUS LIFE AND EXTRACURRICULAR ACTIVITIES

Student employment: During the 2009-2010 academic year, 1% of undergraduates worked on campus. Average per-year earnings: $2,000. **Clubs and organizations:** Number of student organizations: 13. Activities include: student government. Number of fraternities: 0; sororities: 0. **Sports program (2009-2010):** Member of NAIA. *Men's intercollegiate varsity sports:* baseball, basketball, soccer. *Women's intercollegiate varsity sports:* soccer, softball, volleyball.

SERVICES AND FACILITIES

Basic services: nonremedial tutoring, health insurance. **Remedial assistance:** reading, math, writing, study skills, other. **Counseling services:** career, academic. **For learning-disabled students:** School does not offer a structured program with separate admission and additional fees. Services include: tape recorders, videotaped classes, note-taking services, oral tests, readers, extended time for tests, priority seating, texts on tape, other testing accommodations, other. **Library:** Number of titles: 85,314; number of current serial subscriptions: 38,372. **Information technology resources:** Students are not required to lease or own a computer. Number of campus computers available to all students: 600. School has a wireless network. Approximate number of users that can be accommodated: 40. **Campus safety:** Security services offered: 24-hour emergency telephones, lighted pathways/sidewalks.

TRANSFER AND INTERNATIONAL STUDENTS

Transfer students: May apply for admission for the following academic terms: Fall, Winter, Spring, Summer. Applicants do not need a minimum number of credits to apply. **International students:** Number of foreign undergraduates: 162 (3% of student body). Minimum TOEFL score required: 500 (paper); 173 (computer).

Chadron State College

- **Address:** 1000 Main Street, Chadron, NE 69337
- **Website:** http://www.csc.edu
- **Public**
- **Enrollment:** 1,709 full-time; 526 part-time

KEY STATS

✔ **U.S News College Ranking:** 66, Regional Colleges (Midwest)
✔ **ACT Score (25th/75th percentile):** 19-25
✔ **Tuition:** 2009-2010: $4,730 in state, $8,400 out of state

Selectivity: Selective	Room/board: $4,900
Acceptance rate: N/A	Average debt: N/A
Student/faculty ratio: 19/1	Proportion who borrowed: N/A

UNDERGRADUATE STUDENT BODY STATS

2009-2010 enrollment: 1,709 full-time; 526 part-time. Men: 42%; women: 58%. **Ethnic makeup:** African American: 3%; American-Indian: 2%; Asian American: 1%; Hispanic: 4%; White: 88%; International: 2%.

ADMISSIONS FACTS AND FIGURES

Phone: (308) 432-6263. **Email:** inquire@csc.edu. **Website:** http://www.csc.edu. **Application deadlines for fall 2011:** Regular decision: Rolling. Early decision: Not offered. Early action: Not offered. Admission cannot be deferred. **Application fee:** $15. **To apply online, go to:** http://www.csc.edu/apply/onlineApp.csc. **Admissions requirements/recommendations:** High school units required (recommended): English: 4 (4); Mathematics: 3 (3); Science: 3 (3); Social studies: 3 (3); History: 1 (1). Tests: The college uses SAT or

ACT scores in admissions decisions. Neither SAT nor ACT required. For admission to the fall 2011 entering class, the school will accept: ACT with or without writing accepted. Campus visit: Recommended. Admissions interview: Neither required nor recommended. Off-campus interview: Not available. **Factors that count in admissions decisions:** *Academic:* Secondary school record: Considered. Class rank: Considered. Letters of recommendation: Considered. Standardized test scores: Considered. Essay: Not Considered. *Nonacademic:* Interview: Not Considered. Extracurricular activities: Considered. Talent/ability: Considered. Character/personal qualities: Not Considered. Alumni/ae relationship: Not Considered. Geographical residence: Not Considered. State residency: Not Considered. Religious affiliation/commitment: Not Considered. Minority status: Not Considered. Volunteer work: Not Considered. Work experience: Not Considered. **Other schools with the greatest overlap in applicants:** University of Nebraska–Kearney; University of Nebraska–Lincoln; University of Wyoming. **Admissions statistics for the fall 2009 entering class:** Freshmen enrolled: 422; **Credentials of fall 2009 freshmen:** 15% ranked in the top 10 percent of their high school class; 37% were in the top 25 percent; 71% were in the top half. (Proportion submitting class standing: 86%.) **Average high school grade point average:** 3.2. **First-year students submitting ACT scores:** 90%. Scores (25/75 percentile): English: 18-25, Math: 18-25, Composite: 19-25.

ACADEMICS

Year founded: 1911. **Academic calendar:** Semester. **Degrees offered:** bachelor's, master's, post-master's certificate. **Most popular majors:** 22% elementary education and teaching, 21% business administration and management, 12% biology/biological sciences, 8% corrections and criminal justice, 4% psychology. **Major fields of study:** agriculture, agriculture operations, and related sciences; biological and biomedical sciences; business, management, marketing, and related support services; computer and information sciences and support services; education; engineering technologies/technicians; English language and literature/letters; family and consumer sciences/human sciences; foreign languages, literatures, and linguistics; health professions and related clinical sciences; history; liberal arts and sciences studies, and humanities; library science; mathematics and statistics; parks, recreation, leisure, and fitness studies; physical sciences; psychology; public administration and social service professions; security and protective services; social sciences; visual and performing arts. **Areas of required coursework:** arts/fine arts, humanities, mathematics, English (including composition), sciences (biological or physical), history, social science, other. **Pre-professional programs:** pre-law, pre-dentistry, pre-medicine, pre-veterinary science, pre-optometry, pre-pharmacy, other. **Special academic programs:** accelerated program, cooperative (work-study plan) program, distance learning, double major, dual enrollment, independent study, internships, student-designed major, study abroad, teacher certificate program. **Teacher certification offered in:** early childhood, special education, elementary, vo-tech, middle/junior high, secondary. **Reserve Officers Training Corps (ROTC):** Army ROTC: Offered on campus. **Faculty and instruction (2009-2010):** Total instructional faculty: 93 full-time, 41 part-time (56% men; 44% women; 4% minorities). Full-time faculty with Ph.D. or other terminal degree: 75%. Student/faculty ratio: 19/1. Classes of fewer than 20 students: 42%; of 20 to 49 students: 54%; of 50 or more students: 3%. **Advanced Placement and International Baccalaureate credit:** AP tests may be used for: Placement only. **Freshmen returning for sophomore year:** 67%. **Graduation rates:** Four-year: 17%; five-year: 33%; six-year: 44%.

COSTS AND FINANCIAL AID

Financial aid office: (308) 432-6230. **Expenses (2009-2010):** Tuition and fees 2009-2010: $4,730 in state, $8,400 out of state; room/board: $4,900. Estimated books and supplies: $1,050. **Financial aid:** Priority filing date for institution's financial aid form: June 1.

CAMPUS LIFE AND EXTRACURRICULAR ACTIVITIES

Campus housing available: coed dorms, women's dorms, men's dorms, apartments for married students, apartment for single students, special housing for disabled students. Activities include: choral groups, concert band, dance, drama/theater, international student organization, jazz band, literary magazine, music ensembles, pep band, student government, student newspaper. Number of fraternities: 0; sororities: 0. **Sports program (2009-2010):** Member of NCAA II. *Men's intercollegiate varsity sports:* basketball, football, track and field (indoor), track and field (outdoor). *Women's intercollegiate varsity sports:* basketball, golf, softball, track and field (indoor), track and field (outdoor), volleyball.

SERVICES AND FACILITIES

Basic services: nonremedial tutoring, placement service, day care, health service, health insurance. **Remedial assistance:** reading, math, writing, study skills. **Counseling services:** minority student, career, personal, academic, older student, psychological. **For learning-disabled students:** Services include: remedial math, remedial English, remedial reading, untimed tests, oral tests, readers, tutors. **Information technology resources:** Students are not required to lease or own a computer. Number of campus computers available to all students: 75. School has a wireless network. Proportion of college-owned housing units wired for high-speed internet access: 100%. **Campus safety:** Security services offered: 24-hour foot-and-vehicle patrols, late-night transport/escort service, lighted pathways/sidewalks, controlled dormitory access (key, security card, etc).

TRANSFER AND INTERNATIONAL STUDENTS

Transfer students: May apply for admission for the following academic terms: Fall, Spring, Summer. Applicants do not need a minimum number of credits to apply. For fall 2009: Transfer applicants enrolled: 113. **International students:** Number of foreign undergraduates: 35 (2% of student body). Number of countries represented: 25. Minimum TOEFL score required: 550 (paper); 213 (computer). Average TOEFL score: 570 (paper).

College of St. Mary

- **Address:** 7000 Mercy Road, Omaha, NE 68106
- **Website:** http://www.csm.edu
- **Private; Religious affiliation:** Roman Catholic
- **Enrollment:** 687 full-time; 168 part-time

KEY STATS
- ✔ **U.S News College Ranking:** 44, Regional Colleges (Midwest)
- ✔ **ACT Score (25th/75th percentile):** 18-23
- ✔ **Tuition:** 2009-2010: $22,164

Selectivity: Selective	**Room/board:** $6,400
Acceptance rate: 42%	**Average debt:** N/A
Student/faculty ratio: 13/1	**Proportion who borrowed:** N/A

UNDERGRADUATE STUDENT BODY STATS

2009-2010 enrollment: 687 full-time; 168 part-time. Men: 0%; women: 100%. **Ethnic makeup:** African American: 12%; American-Indian: 1%; Asian American: 1%; Hispanic: 9%; White: 76%; International: 1%. **Religious preference:** Roman Catholic: 38%; Other: 62%.

ADMISSIONS FACTS AND FIGURES

Phone: (402) 399-2407. **Email:** enroll@csm.edu. **Website:** http://www.csm.edu. **Application deadlines for fall 2011:** Regular decision: Rolling. Early decision: Not offered. Early action: Not offered. Admission can be deferred. **Application fee:** $30. **To apply online, go to:** http://www.watchmebloom.com. **Admissions requirements/recommendations:** High school units required (recommended): English: (4); Mathematics: (3); Science: (3); Foreign language: (1); Social studies: (2); History: (2); Total units: (16). Tests: The college uses SAT or ACT scores in admissions decisions. Neither SAT nor ACT required. For admission to the fall 2011 entering class, the school will accept: ACT with or without writing accepted. Campus visit: Recommended. Admissions interview: Recommended. Off-campus interview: May be arranged. **Factors that count in admissions decisions:** *Academic:* Secondary school record: Considered. Class rank: Very Important. Letters of recommendation: Considered. Standardized test scores: Very Important. Essay: Considered. *Nonacademic:* Interview: Considered. Extracurricular activities: Considered. Talent/ability: Considered. Character/personal qualities: Considered. Alumni/ae relationship: Considered. Geographical residence: Not Considered. State residency: Not Considered. Religious affiliation/commitment: Not Considered. Minority status: Not Considered. Volunteer work: Not Considered. Work experience: Not Considered. **Other schools with the greatest overlap in applicants:** Bellevue University; Creighton University; Nebraska Methodist College; University of Nebraska–Lincoln; University of Nebraska–Omaha. **Admissions statistics for the fall 2009 entering class:** Total applicants: 510. Total accepted: 216. Freshmen enrolled: 108; 7% were from out of state. Overall acceptance rate: 42%. **Size of waiting list:** 0 applicants; enrolled from waiting list: 0. **Credentials of fall 2009 freshmen:** 14% ranked in the top 10 percent of their high school class; 42% were in the top 25 percent; 76% were in the top half. (Proportion submitting class standing: 80%.)

Average high school grade point average: 3.4. **First-year students submitting ACT scores:** 87%. Scores (25/75 percentile): English: 18-24, Math: 17-22, Composite: 18-23.

ACADEMICS

Year founded: 1923. **Academic calendar:** Semester. **Degrees offered:** certificate, associate, bachelor's, post-bachelor's certificate, master's, doctorate. **Most popular majors:** 37% health professions and related clinical sciences, 21% business/commerce, 14% psychology, 8% general studies, 7% elementary education and teaching. **Major fields of study:** biological and biomedical sciences; business, management, marketing, and related support services; education; English language and literature/letters; health professions and related clinical sciences; legal professions and studies; liberal arts and sciences studies, and humanities; mathematics and statistics; physical sciences; psychology; public administration and social service professions; visual and performing arts. **Areas of required coursework:** arts/fine arts, humanities, computer literacy, mathematics, English (including composition), philosophy, sciences (biological or physical), history, social science, other. **Pre-professional programs:** pre-law, pre-dentistry, pre-medicine, pre-veterinary science, pre-pharmacy. **Special academic programs (% participation):** accelerated program (16%), double major (1%), honors program (1%), independent study (5%), internships (7%), study abroad (1%), teacher certificate program (10%), weekend college (6%). **Teacher certification offered in:** early childhood, special education, elementary, middle/junior high, secondary, bilingual/bicultural. **Cooperative education programs:** engineering. **Reserve Officers Training Corps (ROTC):** Army ROTC: Offered at cooperating institution (Creighton University); Air Force ROTC: Offered at cooperating institution (University of Nebraska–Omaha). **Faculty and instruction (2009-2010):** Total instructional faculty: 54 full-time, 109 part-time (21% men; 79% women; 8% minorities). Full-time faculty with Ph.D. or other terminal degree: 61%. Student/faculty ratio: 13/1. Classes of fewer than 20 students: 73%; of 20 to 49 students: 25%; of 50 or more students: 2%. **Advanced Placement and International Baccalaureate credit:** AP tests may be used for: Credit only. Scores accepted: 3, 4, 5. International Baccalaureate exams may be used for: Credit only. **Freshmen returning for sophomore year:** 62%. **Graduation rates:** Four-year: 42%; five-year: 42%; six-year: 52%. **Graduate study:** 40% of students pursue further study immediately upon graduation; 60% within one year. Fields in which graduates pursue further study: Master of Business Administration (MBA), 20%; law, 20%; medicine, 15%; arts and sciences, 15%.

COSTS AND FINANCIAL AID

Financial aid office: (402) 399-2362. **Expenses (2009-2010):** Tuition and fees 2009-2010: $22,164; room/board: $6,400. Estimated books and supplies: $1,200. **Financial aid:** Priority filing date for institution's financial aid form: March 15.

CAMPUS LIFE AND EXTRACURRICULAR ACTIVITIES

Campus housing available (% using): women's dorms (84%), other housing options (16%). Students who live in college-owned, operated, or affiliated housing: 24%. **Student employment:** During the 2009-2010 academic year, 9% of undergraduates worked on campus. Average per-year earnings: $8. **Clubs and organizations:** Number of student organizations: 21. Activities include: campus ministries, choral groups, dance, drama/theater, music ensembles, student government. Number of fraternities: 0; sororities: 0. Average proportion of students who stay on campus on weekends: 30%. **Sports program (2009-2010):** Member of NAIA. *Women's intercollegiate varsity sports:* basketball, cross country, soccer, softball, swimming, volleyball.

SERVICES AND FACILITIES

Basic services: nonremedial tutoring, placement service, day care, health service, health insurance. **Remedial assistance:** reading, math, writing, study skills. **Counseling services:** minority student, career, personal, academic, older student, psychological, religious. **For learning-disabled students:** School does not offer a structured program with separate admission and additional fees. Total undergraduates in learning-disabled program or receiving services: 22. Services include: remedial math, remedial English, reading machines, remedial reading, tape recorders, diagnostic testing service, untimed tests, note-taking services, oral tests, learning center, readers, extended time for tests, tutors, priority seating, texts on tape, exams on tape or computer, other testing accommodations. **Library:** Number of titles: 74,229; number of current serial subscriptions: 173. **Information technology resources:** Students are not required to lease or own a computer. Number of campus computers available to all students: 215. School has a wireless network. Approximate number of users that can be accommodated: 1,500. Proportion of college-owned housing units wired for high-speed internet

access: 100%. **Campus safety:** Security services offered: 24-hour foot-and-vehicle patrols, late-night transport/escort service, lighted pathways/sidewalks, controlled dormitory access (key, security card, etc).

TRANSFER AND INTERNATIONAL STUDENTS

Transfer students: May apply for admission for the following academic terms: Fall, Spring, Summer. Applicants need a minimum number of credits to apply. For fall 2009: Transfer applications received: 859. Transfer applicants offered admission: 407. Transfer applicants enrolled: 244. **International students:** Number of foreign undergraduates: 7 (1% of student body). Number of countries represented: 4. Minimum TOEFL score required: 550 (paper); 80 (computer). Average TOEFL score: 560 (paper).

Concordia University

- **Address:** 800 N. Columbia Avenue, Seward, NE 68434
- **Website:** http://www.cune.edu
- **Private; Religious affiliation:** Lutheran Church-Missouri Synod
- **Enrollment:** 1,062 full-time; 195 part-time

KEY STATS

✔ **U.S News College Ranking:** 16, Regional Colleges (Midwest)
✔ **ACT Score (25th/75th percentile):** 21-28
✔ **Tuition:** 2010-2011: $22,115

Selectivity: Selective	**Room/board:** $5,820
Acceptance rate: 75%	**Average debt:** $21,941
Student/faculty ratio: 13/1	**Proportion who borrowed:** 79%

UNDERGRADUATE STUDENT BODY STATS

2009-2010 enrollment: 1,062 full-time; 195 part-time. Men: 48%; women: 52%. **Ethnic makeup:** African American: 4%; Asian American: 1%; Hispanic: 2%; White: 93%; International: 1%. **Religious preference:** Roman Catholic: 7%; Protestant: 15%; Unknown: 7%; Lutheran Church-Missouri Synod: 68%; Lutheran-other: 3%.

ADMISSIONS FACTS AND FIGURES

Phone: (800) 535-5494. **Email:** admiss@cune.edu. **Website:** http://www.cune.edu. **Application deadlines for fall 2011:** Regular decision: August 1. Early decision: Not offered. Early action: Not offered. Admission can be deferred. **To apply online, go to:** http://www.cune.edu/apply. **Admissions requirements/recommendations:** High school units required (recommended): English: (4); Mathematics: (3); Science: (2); Foreign language: (1); Social studies: (3); Total units: (16). Tests: The college uses SAT or ACT scores in admissions decisions. Either SAT or ACT required. For admission to the fall 2011 entering class, the school will accept: ACT with or without writing accepted. Campus visit: Recommended. Admissions interview: Recommended. Off-campus interview: May be arranged. **Factors that count in admissions decisions:** *Academic:* Secondary school record: Important. Class rank: Important. Letters of recommendation: Considered. Standardized test scores: Very Important. Essay: Not Considered. *Nonacademic:* Interview: Considered. Extracurricular activities: Considered. Talent/ability: Not Considered. Character/personal qualities: Important. Alumni/ae relationship: Considered. Geographical residence: Not Considered. State residency: Not Considered. Religious affiliation/commitment: Considered. Minority status: Not Considered. Volunteer work: Not Considered. Work experience: Not Considered. **Other schools with the greatest overlap in applicants:** Doane College; Hastings College; Nebraska Wesleyan University; University of Nebraska–Kearney; University of Nebraska–Lincoln. **Admissions statistics for the fall 2009 entering class:** Total applicants: 1,281. Total accepted: 962. Freshmen enrolled: 288; 57% were from out of state. Overall acceptance rate: 75%. **Credentials of fall 2009 freshmen:** 25% ranked in the top 10 percent of their high school class; 51% were in the top 25 percent; 76% were in the top half. (Proportion submitting class standing: 90%.) **Average high school grade point average:** 3.5. **First-year students who submitted SAT scores:** 16%. Scores (25/75 percentile): Critical Reading: 440-590, Math: 430-640, Combined: 870-1230. **First-year students submitting ACT scores:** 93%. Scores (25/75 percentile): English: 20-29, Math: 19-28, Composite: 21-28.

ACADEMICS

Year founded: 1894. **Academic calendar:** Semester. **Degrees offered:** bachelor's, post-bachelor's certificate, master's. **Most popular majors:** 38% education, 12% business, management, marketing, and related support services, 10% theology and religious vocations, 9% psychology, 7% visual and performing arts. **Major fields of study:** biological and biomedical sciences; business, management, marketing, and related support services; communication, journalism, and related programs; computer and information sciences and support services; education; English language and literature/letters; family and consumer sciences/human sciences; foreign languages, literatures, and linguistics; health professions and related clinical sciences; history; legal professions and studies; mathematics and statistics; multi/interdisciplinary studies; parks, recreation, leisure, and fitness studies; physical sciences; psychology; social sciences; theology and religious vocations; visual and performing arts. **Areas of required coursework:** arts/fine arts, humanities, mathematics, English (including composition), foreign languages, sciences (biological or physical), history, social science, other. **Pre-professional programs:** pre-law, pre-dentistry, pre-medicine, pre-theology, pre-veterinary science, pre-optometry, pre-pharmacy. **Special academic programs (% participation):** accelerated program (5%), distance learning (10%), double major (15%), English as a Second Language (ESL) (1%), exchange student program (domestic) (4%), independent study (20%), internships (70%), study abroad (2%), teacher certificate program (40%). **Teacher certification offered in:** early childhood, special education, elementary, middle/junior high, secondary, bilingual/bicultural. **Cooperative education programs:** agriculture. **Reserve Officers Training Corps (ROTC):** Army ROTC: Offered at cooperating institution (University of Nebraska–Lincoln); Air Force ROTC: Offered at cooperating institution (University of Nebraska–Lincoln). **Faculty and instruction (2009-2010):** Total instructional faculty: 55 full-time, 88 part-time (54% men; 46% women; 3% minorities). Full-time faculty with Ph.D. or other terminal degree: 65%. Student/faculty ratio: 13/1. Classes of fewer than 20 students: 50%; of 20 to 49 students: 50%; of 50 or more students: 1%. **Advanced Placement and International Baccalaureate credit:** AP tests may be used for: Credit and/or placement. Scores accepted: 3, 4, 5. International Baccalaureate exams may be used for: Credit and/or placement. **Freshmen returning for sophomore year:** 77%. **Graduation rates:** Four-year: 39%; five-year: 59%; six-year: 61%. **Graduate study:** 20% of students pursue further study immediately upon graduation; 30% within one year; 70% within five years. Fields in which graduates pursue further study: Master of Business Administration (MBA), 5%; law, 2%; medicine, 11%; theology (or the seminary), 15%; education, 18%; arts and sciences, 25%; veterinary medicine, 2%.

COSTS AND FINANCIAL AID

Financial aid office: (402) 643-7270. **Expenses (2010-2011):** Tuition and fees 2010-2011: $22,115; room/board: $5,820. Estimated books and supplies: $800; transportation: $900; personal expenses: $1,300. **Financial aid:** Priority filing date for institution's financial aid form: March 1. In 2009-2010, 91% of undergraduates applied for financial aid. Of those, 78% were determined to have financial need; 29% had their need fully met. Average financial aid package (proportion receiving): $17,208 (77%). Average amount of gift aid, such as scholarships or grants (proportion receiving): $13,086 (77%). Average amount of self-help aid, such as work study or loans (proportion receiving): $4,569 (54%). Average need-based loan (excluding PLUS or other private loans): $4,374. Among students who received need-based aid, the average percentage of need met: 79%. Among students who received aid based on merit, the average award (and the proportion receiving): $8,914 (11%). The average athletic scholarship (and the proportion receiving): $4,292 (11%). Average amount of debt of borrowers graduating in 2009: $21,941. Proportion who borrowed: 79%.

CAMPUS LIFE AND EXTRACURRICULAR ACTIVITIES

Campus housing available (% using): women's dorms (50%), men's dorms (48%), apartments for married students (1%), apartment for single students (1%), special housing for disabled students. Students who live in college-owned, operated, or affiliated housing: 76%. **Student employment:** During the 2009-2010 academic year, 50% of undergraduates worked on campus. Average per-year earnings: $1,700. **Clubs and organizations:** Number of student organizations: 33. Activities include: campus ministries, choral groups, concert band, dance, drama/theater, jazz band, literary magazine, music ensembles, musical theater, pep band, student government, student newspaper, symphony orchestra, yearbook. Number of fraternities: 0; sororities: 0. Average proportion of students who stay on campus on weekends: 80%. **Sports program (2009-2010):** Member of NAIA. *Men's intercollegiate varsity sports:* baseball, basketball, cross country, football, golf, soccer, tennis, track and field (indoor), track and field (outdoor), volleyball, wrestling. *Women's intercollegiate varsity sports:* basketball, cross country, golf, soccer, softball, tennis, track and field (indoor), track and field (outdoor), volleyball.

SERVICES AND FACILITIES

Basic services: nonremedial tutoring, placement service, health service, health insurance. **Remedial assistance:** study skills, other. **Counseling services:** career, personal, academic, psychological, religious. **For learning-disabled students:** School does not offer a structured program with separate admission and additional fees. Services include: tape recorders, note-taking services, learning center, readers, extended time for tests, tutors, priority seating, exams on tape or computer, other testing accommodations, other. **Library:** Number of titles: 170,000; number of current serial subscriptions: 325. **Information technology resources:** Students are not required to lease or own a computer. Number of campus computers available to all students: 199. School has a wireless network. Approximate number of users that can be accommodated: 1,250. Proportion of college-owned housing units wired for high-speed internet access: 100%. **Campus safety:** Security services offered: 24-hour foot-and-vehicle patrols, 24-hour emergency telephones, lighted pathways/sidewalks, controlled dormitory access (key, security card, etc).

TRANSFER AND INTERNATIONAL STUDENTS

Transfer students: May apply for admission for the following academic terms: Fall, Spring. Applicants do not need a minimum number of credits to apply. For fall 2009: Transfer applications received: 241. Transfer applicants offered admission: 121. Transfer applicants enrolled: 81. **International students:** Number of foreign undergraduates: 6 (1% of student body). Number of countries represented: 6. Minimum TOEFL score required: 500 (paper); 173 (computer). Average TOEFL score: 525 (paper).

Creighton University

- **Address:** 2500 California Plaza, Omaha, NE 68178
- **Website:** http://www.creighton.edu
- **Private; Religious affiliation:** Roman Catholic (Jesuit)
- **Enrollment:** 3,869 full-time; 264 part-time

KEY STATS
✔ **U.S News College Ranking:** 1, Regional Universities (Midwest)
✔ **ACT Score (25th/75th percentile):** 24-29
✔ **Tuition:** 2010-2011: $30,578

Selectivity: More selective	**Room/board:** $9,164
Acceptance rate: 82%	**Average debt:** $32,888
Student/faculty ratio: 11/1	**Proportion who borrowed:** 70%

UNDERGRADUATE STUDENT BODY STATS

2009-2010 enrollment: 3,869 full-time; 264 part-time. Men: 41%; women: 59%. **Ethnic makeup:** African American: 3%; American-Indian: 1%; Asian American: 10%; Hispanic: 4%; White: 80%; International: 2%.

ADMISSIONS FACTS AND FIGURES

Phone: (800) 282-5835. **Email:** admissions@creighton.edu. **Website:** http://www.creighton.edu. **Application deadlines for fall 2011:** Regular decision: February 15. Early decision: Not offered. Early action: Not offered. Admission can be deferred. **Application fee:** $40. **To apply online, go to:** http://admissions.creighton.edu/onlineapp.html. **Admissions requirements/recommendations:** High school units required (recommended): English: 4 (4); Mathematics: 3 (4); Science: 2 (3); Foreign language: 2 (3); Social studies: 2 (3); History: 0 (1); Academic electives: 3 (3); Total units: 16 (21). Tests: The college uses SAT or ACT scores in admissions decisions. Either SAT or ACT required. For admission to the fall 2011 entering class, the school will accept: ACT with or without writing accepted. Campus visit: Recommended. Admissions interview: Recommended. Off-campus interview: May be arranged. **Factors that count in admissions decisions:** *Academic:* Secondary school record: Very Important. Class rank: Considered. Letters of recommendation: Considered. Standardized test scores: Important. Essay: Important. *Nonacademic:* Interview: Not Considered. Extracurricular activities: Considered. Talent/ability: Considered. Character/personal qualities: Considered. Alumni/ae relationship: Not Considered. Geographical residence: Not Considered. State residency: Not Considered. Religious affiliation/commitment: Not Considered. Minority status: Considered. Volunteer work: Considered. Work experience: Not Considered. **Other schools with the greatest overlap in applicants:** Drake University; Loyola University Chicago; Marquette University; St. Louis University; University of Nebraska–Lincoln. **Admissions statistics for the fall 2009 entering class:** Total applicants: 4,752. Total accepted: 3,888. Freshmen enrolled: 1,054; 72% were from out of state. Overall acceptance rate: 82%. **Size of waiting list:** 87 applicants; enrolled from waiting list: 18. **Credentials of fall 2009 freshmen:** 41% ranked in the top 10 percent of their high school class; 73% were in the top 25 percent; 93% were in the top half. (Proportion submitting class standing: 65%.) **Average high school grade point average:** 3.8. **First-year students who submitted SAT scores:** 33%. Scores (25/75 percentile): Critical Reading: 520-640, Math: 540-650, Combined: 1060-1290. **First-year students submitting ACT scores:** 90%. Scores (25/75 percentile): English: 24-31, Math: 23-29, Composite: 24-29.

ACADEMICS

Year founded: 1878. **Academic calendar:** Semester. **Degrees offered:** certificate, associate, bachelor's, master's, doctorate. **Most popular majors:** 21% business, management, marketing, and related support services, 20% health professions and related clinical sciences, 12% biological and biomedical sciences, 8% psychology, 7% communication, journalism, and related programs. **Major fields of study:** area, ethnic, cultural, and gender studies; biological and biomedical sciences; business, management, marketing, and related support services; communication, journalism, and related programs; computer and information sciences and support services; education; English language and literature/letters; foreign languages, literatures, and linguistics; health professions and related clinical sciences; history; legal professions and studies; mathematics and statistics; multi/interdisciplinary studies; natural resources and conservation; parks, recreation, leisure, and fitness studies; philosophy and religious studies; physical sciences; psychology; public administration and social service professions; social sciences; visual and performing arts. **Areas of required coursework:** arts/fine arts, humanities, mathematics, English (including composition), philosophy, foreign languages, sciences (biological or physical), history, social science, other. **Pre-professional programs:** pre-law, pre-dentistry, pre-medicine, pre-theology, pre-veterinary science, pre-optometry, pre-pharmacy, other. **Special academic programs (% participation):** accelerated program, cross-registration, distance learning, double major (19%), dual enrollment, English as a Second Language (ESL), honors program (7%), independent study, internships, study abroad (17%), teacher certificate program. **Teacher certification offered in:** special education, elementary, middle/junior high, secondary, bilingual/bicultural. **Reserve Officers Training Corps (ROTC):** Army ROTC: Offered on campus; Air Force ROTC: Offered at cooperating institution (University of Nebraska–Omaha). **Faculty and instruction (2009-2010):** Total instructional faculty: 532 full-time, 203 part-time (56% men; 44% women; 12% minorities). Full-time faculty with Ph.D. or other terminal degree: 83%. Student/faculty ratio: 11/1. Classes of fewer than 20 students: 45%; of 20 to 49 students: 51%; of 50 or more students: 5%. **Advanced Placement and International Baccalaureate credit:** AP tests may be used for: Credit and/or placement. Scores accepted: 3, 4, 5. International Baccalaureate exams may be used for: Credit and/or placement. **Freshmen returning for sophomore year:** 87%. **Graduation rates:** Four-year: 64%; five-year: 74%; six-year: 75%. **Graduate study:** 45% of students pursue further study immediately upon graduation; 10% within one year. Fields in which graduates pursue further study: Master of Business Administration (MBA), 15%; law, 10%; medicine, 20%; dentistry, 3%; theology (or the seminary), 1%; education, 5%; arts and sciences, 35%.

COSTS AND FINANCIAL AID

Financial aid office: (402) 280-2731. **Expenses (2010-2011):** Tuition and fees 2010-2011: $30,578; room/board: $9,164. Estimated books and supplies: $1,200; transportation: $600; personal expenses: $2,000. **Financial aid:** Priority filing date for institution's financial aid form: March 1. In 2009-2010, 60% of undergraduates applied for financial aid. Of those, 50% were determined to have financial need; 51% had their need fully met. Average financial aid package (proportion receiving): $25,003 (50%). Average amount of gift aid, such as scholarships or grants (proportion receiving): $19,497 (49%). Average amount of self-help aid, such as work study or loans (proportion receiving): $7,507 (37%). Average need-based loan (excluding PLUS or other private loans): $6,649. Among students who received need-based aid, the average percentage of need met: 91%. Among students who received aid based on merit, the average award (and the proportion receiving): $11,594 (27%). The average athletic scholarship (and the proportion receiving): $18,453 (4%). Average amount of debt of borrowers graduating in 2009: $32,888. Proportion who borrowed: 70%.

CAMPUS LIFE AND EXTRACURRICULAR ACTIVITIES

Campus housing available (% using): coed dorms (67%), women's dorms (8%), apartments for married students (4%), apartment for single students (21%), special housing for disabled students (0%). Students who live in college-owned, operated, or affiliated housing: 60%. **Student employment:**

During the 2009-2010 academic year, 30% of undergraduates worked on campus. Average per-year earnings: $1,700. **Clubs and organizations:** Number of student organizations: 203. Activities include: campus ministries, choral groups, concert band, dance, drama/theater, international student organization, jazz band, literary magazine, model UN, music ensembles, musical theater, pep band, student government, student newspaper, symphony orchestra, television station, yearbook. Number of fraternities: 5; sororities: 8. Proportion of men in fraternities: 26%; of women in sororities: 34%. Average proportion of students who stay on campus on weekends: 80%. **Sports program (2009-2010):** Member of NCAA I. *Men's intercollegiate varsity sports:* baseball, basketball, cross country, golf, soccer, tennis. *Women's intercollegiate varsity sports:* basketball, cross country, golf, crew (lightweight), soccer, softball, tennis, volleyball.

SERVICES AND FACILITIES

Basic services: nonremedial tutoring, women's center, placement service, day care, health service, health insurance. **Remedial assistance:** reading, math, writing, study skills. **Counseling services:** minority student, career, military, personal, veteran student, academic, older student, psychological, religious. **For learning-disabled students:** School does not offer a structured program with separate admission and additional fees. Total undergraduates in learning-disabled program or receiving services: 120. Services include: reading machines, tape recorders, diagnostic testing service, note-taking services, oral tests, readers, extended time for tests, tutors, priority registration, priority seating, substitution of courses, texts on tape, typist/scribe, exams on tape or computer, other testing accommodations, other. **Library:** Number of titles: 925,385; number of current serial subscriptions: 42,374. **Information technology resources:** Students are not required to lease or own a computer. Number of campus computers available to all students: 1,000. School has a wireless network. Approximate number of users that can be accommodated: 4,000. Proportion of college-owned housing units wired for high-speed internet access: 100%. **Campus safety:** Security services offered: 24-hour foot-and-vehicle patrols, late-night transport/escort service, 24-hour emergency telephones, lighted pathways/sidewalks, student patrols, controlled dormitory access (key, security card, etc).

TRANSFER AND INTERNATIONAL STUDENTS

Transfer students: May apply for admission for the following academic terms: Fall, Spring. Applicants need a minimum number of credits to apply. For fall 2009: Transfer applications received: 303. Transfer applicants offered admission: 117. Transfer applicants enrolled: 72. **International students:** Number of foreign undergraduates: 68 (2% of student body). Number of countries represented: 30. Minimum TOEFL score required: 550 (paper); 80 (computer). Average TOEFL score: 580 (paper).

Dana College

- **Address:** 2848 College Drive, Blair, NE 68008-1099
- **Website:** http://www.dana.edu
- **Private; Religious affiliation:** Lutheran
- **Enrollment:** 576 full-time; 20 part-time

KEY STATS

✔ **U.S News College Ranking:** second tier, Regional Colleges (Midwest)
✔ **ACT Score (25th/75th percentile):** 20-25
✔ **Tuition:** 2009-2010: $21,100

Selectivity: Selective	**Room/board:** $6,690
Acceptance rate: 66%	**Average debt:** N/A
Student/faculty ratio: 14/1	**Proportion who borrowed:** N/A

UNDERGRADUATE STUDENT BODY STATS

2009-2010 enrollment: 576 full-time; 20 part-time. Men: 54%; women: 46%. **Ethnic makeup:** African American: 6%; American-Indian: 1%; Asian American: 2%; Hispanic: 5%; White: 86%. **Religious preference:** Roman Catholic: 23%; Protestant: 31%; No preference: 9%; Unknown: 16%; Lutheran: 19%; Other: 2%.

ADMISSIONS FACTS AND FIGURES

Phone: (800) 444-3262. **Email:** admissions@dana.edu. **Website:** http://www.dana.edu. **Application deadlines for fall 2011:** Regular decision: Rolling. Early decision: Not offered. Early action: Not offered. Admission cannot be deferred. **To apply online, go to:** https://www.dana.edu/admission_application/admission_application.html. **Admissions requirements/**

recommendations: High school units required (recommended): English: 4 (4); Mathematics: 3 (3); Science: 3 (3); Foreign language: 2 (2); Social studies: 4 (4); Total units: 16 (16). Tests: The college uses SAT or ACT scores in admissions decisions. Either SAT or ACT required. For admission to the fall 2011 entering class, the school will accept: ACT with or without writing accepted. Campus visit: Recommended. Admissions interview: Neither required nor recommended. Off-campus interview: Not available. **Factors that count in admissions decisions:** *Academic:* Secondary school record: Very Important. Class rank: Very Important. Letters of recommendation: Considered. Standardized test scores: Very Important. Essay: Considered. *Nonacademic:* Interview: Considered. Extracurricular activities: Considered. Talent/ability: Not Considered. Character/personal qualities: Not Considered. Alumni/ae relationship: Not Considered. Geographical residence: Not Considered. State residency: Not Considered. Religious affiliation/commitment: Not Considered. Minority status: Not Considered. Volunteer work: Considered. Work experience: Considered. **Other schools with the greatest overlap in applicants:** Midland Lutheran College; Morningside College; Nebraska Wesleyan University; University of Nebraska–Lincoln; University of Nebraska–Omaha. **Admissions statistics for the fall 2009 entering class:** Total applicants: 1,087. Total accepted: 721. Freshmen enrolled: 174; 42% were from out of state. Overall acceptance rate: 66%. **Credentials of fall 2009 freshmen:** 8% ranked in the top 10 percent of their high school class; 31% were in the top 25 percent; 67% were in the top half. (Proportion submitting class standing: 97%.) **Average high school grade point average:** 3.3. **First-year students who submitted SAT scores:** 9%. Scores (25/75 percentile): Critical Reading: 390-480, Math: 410-520, Combined: 800-1000. **First-year students submitting ACT scores:** 95%. Scores (25/75 percentile): English: 17-24, Math: 19-25, Composite: 20-25.

ACADEMICS

Year founded: 1884. **Academic calendar:** 4-1-4. **Degrees offered:** bachelor's. **Most popular majors:** 28% business, management, marketing, and related support services, 21% education, 9% parks, recreation, leisure, and fitness studies, 6% security and protective services, 5% biological and biomedical sciences. **Major fields of study:** biological and biomedical sciences; business, management, marketing, and related support services; communication, journalism, and related programs; computer and information sciences and support services; education; English language and literature/letters; foreign languages, literatures, and linguistics; history; mathematics and statistics; multi/interdisciplinary studies; parks, recreation, leisure, and fitness studies; philosophy and religious studies; physical sciences; psychology; public administration and social service professions; security and protective services; social sciences; visual and performing arts. **Areas of required coursework:** arts/fine arts, humanities, mathematics, English (including composition), foreign languages, sciences (biological or physical), social science, other. **Pre-professional programs:** pre-law, pre-dentistry, pre-medicine, pre-theology, pre-veterinary science, pre-optometry, pre-pharmacy, other. **Special academic programs (% participation):** cross-registration (4%), double major (24%), honors program (11%), independent study (43%), internships (61%), study abroad (11%), teacher certificate program (27%). **Teacher certification offered in:** special education, elementary, secondary. **Reserve Officers Training Corps (ROTC)** Army ROTC: Offered at cooperating institution (Creighton University); Air Force ROTC: Offered at cooperating institution (University of Nebraska–Omaha). **Faculty and instruction (2009-2010):** Total instructional faculty: 32 full-time, 24 part-time (55% men; 45% women; 5% minorities). Full-time faculty with Ph.D. or other terminal degree: 69%. Student/faculty ratio: 14/1. Classes of fewer than 20 students: 63%; of 20 to 49 students: 36%; of 50 or more students: 1%. **Advanced Placement and International Baccalaureate credit:** International Baccalaureate exams may be used for: Credit only. **Freshmen returning for sophomore year:** 60%. **Graduation rates:** Four-year: 33%; five-year: 48%; six-year: 48%. **Graduate study:** 16% of students pursue further study within one year.

COSTS AND FINANCIAL AID

Financial aid office: (402) 426-7226. **Expenses (2009-2010):** Tuition and fees 2009-2010: $21,100; room/board: $6,690. Estimated books and supplies: $1,280; transportation: $900; personal expenses: $1,500. **Financial aid:** Priority filing date for institution's financial aid form: March 15.

CAMPUS LIFE AND EXTRACURRICULAR ACTIVITIES

Campus housing available (% using): coed dorms (69%), women's dorms (19%), apartment for single students (12%). Students who live in college-owned, operated, or affiliated housing: 66%. **Student employment:** During the 2009-2010 academic year, 21% of undergraduates worked on campus. Average per-year earnings: $600. **Clubs and organizations:** Number of student organizations: 16. Activities include: campus ministries, choral groups, concert band, dance, drama/theater, jazz band, literary magazine, music ensembles, musical theater, radio station, student government, student newspaper, television station, yearbook. Number of fraternities: 0; sororities: 0. Average proportion of students who stay on campus on weekends: 70%. **Sports program (2009-2010):** Member of NAIA. *Men's intercollegiate varsity sports:* baseball, basketball, cross country, football, soccer, track and field (indoor), track and field (outdoor), wrestling. *Women's intercollegiate varsity sports:* basketball, bowling, cross country, golf, soccer, softball, track and field (indoor), track and field (outdoor), volleyball.

SERVICES AND FACILITIES

Basic services: placement service, health service, health insurance. **Remedial assistance:** study skills. **Counseling services:** career, personal, academic, religious. **For learning-disabled students:** School does not offer a structured program with separate admission and additional fees. Services include: tape recorders, untimed tests, note-taking services, oral tests, learning center, readers, extended time for tests, tutors, priority seating, texts on tape, other testing accommodations. **Library:** Number of titles: 158,752; number of current serial subscriptions: 6,155. **Information technology resources:** Students are not required to lease or own a computer. Number of campus computers available to all students: 110. School has a wireless network. Approximate number of users that can be accommodated: 1,000. Proportion of college-owned housing units wired for high-speed internet access: 100%. **Campus safety:** Security services offered: 24-hour foot-and-vehicle patrols, late-night transport/escort service, 24-hour emergency telephones, lighted pathways/sidewalks, student patrols, controlled dormitory access (key, security card, etc).

TRANSFER AND INTERNATIONAL STUDENTS

Transfer students: May apply for admission for the following academic terms: Fall, Winter, Spring, Summer. Applicants need a minimum number of credits to apply. For fall 2009: Transfer applications received: 223. Transfer applicants offered admission: 118. Transfer applicants enrolled: 56. **International students:** Number of foreign undergraduates: 2. Number of countries represented: 1. Minimum TOEFL score required: 500 (paper); 173 (computer).

Doane College

- **Address:** 1014 Boswell Avenue, Crete, NE 68333
- **Website:** http://www.doane.edu
- **Private; Religious affiliation:** United Church of Christ
- **Enrollment:** 958 full-time; 6 part-time

KEY STATS
- ✔ **U.S News College Ranking:** 152, National Liberal Arts Colleges
- ✔ **ACT Score (25th/75th percentile):** 20-26
- ✔ **Tuition:** 2010-2011: $22,170

Selectivity: Selective	**Room/board:** $6,460
Acceptance rate: 76%	**Average debt:** $19,196
Student/faculty ratio: 12/1	**Proportion who borrowed:** 83%

UNDERGRADUATE STUDENT BODY STATS

2009-2010 enrollment: 958 full-time; 6 part-time. Men: 51%; women: 49%. **Ethnic makeup:** African American: 3%; American-Indian: 1%; Asian American: 1%; Hispanic: 4%; White: 91%; International: 1%. **Religious preference:** Roman Catholic: 22%; Protestant: 1%; No preference: 1%; Unknown: 37%; United Church of Christ: 3%; Lutheran: 11%; Other: 25%.

ADMISSIONS FACTS AND FIGURES

Phone: (402) 826-8222. **Email:** admissions@doane.edu. **Website:** http://www.doane.edu. **Application deadlines for fall 2011:** Regular decision: Rolling. Early decision: Not offered. Early action: Not offered. Admission can be deferred. **To apply online, go to:** http://www.doane.edu/apply. **Admissions requirements/recommendations:** High school units required (recommended): English: 4 (4); Mathematics: 3 (3); Science: 3 (4); Foreign language: (2); Social studies: 3 (3); Total units: 13 (16). Tests: The college uses SAT or ACT scores in admissions decisions. ACT required. For admission to the fall 2011 entering class, the school will accept: ACT with or without writing accepted. Campus visit: Recommended. Admissions interview: Recommended. Off-campus interview: May be arranged. **Factors that count in admissions decisions:** *Academic:* Secondary school record: Important. Class rank: Considered. Letters of recommendation: Considered. Standardized test scores: Very Important. Essay: Not Considered. *Nonacademic:* Interview: Considered. Extracurricular activities: Considered. Talent/ability: Considered. Character/personal qualities: Important. Alumni/ae relationship: Important. Geographical residence: Not Considered. State residency: Not Considered. Religious affiliation/commitment: Not Considered. Minority status: Considered. Volunteer work: Considered. Work experience: Considered. **Other schools with the greatest overlap in applicants:** Hastings College; Nebraska Wesleyan University; University of Nebraska–Lincoln. **Admissions statistics for the fall 2009 entering class:** Total applicants: 1,379. Total accepted: 1,048. Freshmen enrolled: 312; 21% were from out of state. Overall acceptance rate: 76%. **Credentials of fall 2009 freshmen:** 15% ranked in the top 10 percent of their high school class; 42% were in the top 25 percent; 74% were in the top half. (Proportion submitting class standing: 96%.) **Average high school grade point average:** 3.4. **First-year students submitting ACT scores:** 97%. Scores (25/75 percentile): English: 20-26, Math: 19-26, Composite: 20-26.

ACADEMICS

Year founded: 1872. **Academic calendar:** 4-1-4. **Degrees offered:** bachelor's. **Most popular majors:** 25% education, 16% business, management, marketing, and related support services, 11% social sciences, 9% biological and biomedical sciences, 9% visual and performing arts. **Major fields of study:** biological and biomedical sciences; communication, journalism, and related programs; computer and information sciences and support services; education; English language and literature/letters; foreign languages, literatures, and linguistics; history; mathematics and statistics; multi/interdisciplinary studies; parks, recreation, leisure, and fitness studies; philosophy and religious studies; physical sciences; psychology; public administration and social service professions; social sciences; visual and performing arts. **Areas of required coursework:** arts/fine arts, humanities, mathematics, English (including composition), sciences (biological or physical), history, social science. **Pre-professional programs:** pre-law, pre-dentistry, pre-medicine, pre-theology, pre-veterinary science, pre-optometry, pre-pharmacy, other. **Special academic programs (% participation):** double major (24%), English as a Second Language (ESL) (2%), honors program (1%), independent study (35%), internships (39%), student-designed major (1%), study abroad (8%), teacher certificate program (23%). **Teacher certification offered in:** early childhood, special education, elementary, middle/junior high, secondary. **Cooperative education programs:** engineering, health professions. **Reserve Officers Training Corps (ROTC):** Army ROTC: Offered at cooperating institution (University of Nebraska–Lincoln); Air Force ROTC: Offered at cooperating institution (University of Nebraska–Lincoln). **Faculty and instruction (2009-2010):** Total instructional faculty: 70 full-time, 33 part-time (51% men; 49% women; 2% minorities). Full-time faculty with Ph.D. or other terminal degree: 79%. Student/faculty ratio: 12/1. Classes of fewer than 20 students: 79%; of 20 to 49 students: 20%; of 50 or more students: 1%. **Advanced Placement and International Baccalaureate credit:** AP tests may be used for: Credit only. Scores accepted: 3, 4, 5. International Baccalaureate exams may be used for: Credit only. **Freshmen returning for sophomore year:** 77%. **Graduation rates:** Four-year: 60%; five-year: 63%; six-year: 64%. **Graduate study:** 24% of students pursue further study immediately upon graduation. Fields in which graduates pursue further study: Master of Business Administration (MBA), 3%; medicine, 2%; dentistry, 2%; engineering, 3%; theology (or the seminary), 2%; education, 13%; arts and sciences, 36%; veterinary medicine, 2%.

COSTS AND FINANCIAL AID

Financial aid office: (402) 826-8260. **Expenses (2010-2011):** Tuition and fees 2010-2011: $22,170; room/board: $6,460. Estimated books and supplies: $900; transportation: $1,000; personal expenses: $1,500. **Financial aid:** Priority filing date for institution's financial aid form: March 1. In 2009-2010, 90% of undergraduates applied for financial aid. Of those, 79% were determined to have financial need; 40% had their need fully met. Average financial aid package (proportion receiving): $17,462 (79%). Average amount of gift aid, such as scholarships or grants (proportion receiving): $13,506 (78%). Average amount of self-help aid, such as work study or loans (proportion receiving): $5,789 (65%). Average need-based loan (excluding PLUS or other private loans): $4,464. Among students who received need-based aid, the average percentage of need met: 91%. Among students who received aid based on merit, the average award (and the proportion receiving): $10,924 (8%). Average amount of debt of borrowers graduating in 2009: $19,196. Proportion who borrowed: 83%.

CAMPUS LIFE AND EXTRACURRICULAR ACTIVITIES

Campus housing available (% using): coed dorms (43%), women's dorms (40%), men's dorms (17%). Students who live in college-owned, operated,

or affiliated housing: 77%. **Student employment:** During the 2009-2010 academic year, 29% of undergraduates worked on campus. Average per-year earnings: $6,500. **Clubs and organizations:** Number of student organizations: 77. Activities include: choral groups, concert band, dance, drama/theater, jazz band, literary magazine, marching band, music ensembles, pep band, radio station, student government, student newspaper, television station, yearbook. Number of fraternities: 5; sororities: 4. Proportion of men in fraternities: 25%; of women in sororities: 23%. Average proportion of students who stay on campus on weekends: 74%. **Sports program (2009-2010):** Member of NAIA.

SERVICES AND FACILITIES

Basic services: nonremedial tutoring, placement service, health service. **Remedial assistance:** reading, math, writing, study skills. **Counseling services:** minority student, career, personal, academic, psychological, birth control. **For learning-disabled students:** School does not offer a structured program with separate admission and additional fees. Total undergraduates in learning-disabled program or receiving services: 9. Services include: remedial math, tape recorders, note-taking services, learning center, extended time for tests, tutors, texts on tape, other testing accommodations, other. **Library:** Number of titles: 332,788; number of current serial subscriptions: 16,424. **Information technology resources:** Students are not required to lease or own a computer. Number of campus computers available to all students: 370. School has a wireless network. Approximate number of users that can be accommodated: 550. Proportion of college-owned housing units wired for high-speed internet access: 100%. **Campus safety:** Security services offered: 24-hour foot-and-vehicle patrols, lighted pathways/sidewalks, controlled dormitory access (key, security card, etc).

TRANSFER AND INTERNATIONAL STUDENTS

Transfer students: May apply for admission for the following academic terms: Fall, Winter, Spring. Applicants need a minimum number of credits to apply. For fall 2009: Transfer applications received: 142. Transfer applicants offered admission: 75. Transfer applicants enrolled: 43. **International students:** Number of foreign undergraduates: 6 (1% of student body). Number of countries represented: 1. Minimum TOEFL score required: 525 (paper); 196 (computer). Average TOEFL score: 525 (paper).

Hastings College

- **Address:** 710 N. Turner Avenue, Hastings, NE 68901-7621
- **Website:** http://www.hastings.edu
- **Private; Religious affiliation:** Presbyterian Church (USA)
- **Enrollment:** 1,083 full-time; 21 part-time

KEY STATS

✔ **U.S News College Ranking:** 174, National Liberal Arts Colleges
✔ **ACT Score (25th/75th percentile):** 20-26
✔ **Tuition:** 2010-2011: $22,620

Selectivity: Selective	**Room/board:** $6,300
Acceptance rate: 74%	**Average debt:** $21,329
Student/faculty ratio: 11/1	**Proportion who borrowed:** 84%

UNDERGRADUATE STUDENT BODY STATS

2009-2010 enrollment: 1,083 full-time; 21 part-time. Men: 52%; women: 48%. **Ethnic makeup:** African American: 3%; Asian American: 2%; Hispanic: 4%; White: 89%; International: 1%. **Religious preference:** Roman Catholic: 21%; Protestant: 31%; Jewish: 1%; No preference: 34%; Presbyterian Church (USA): 7%; Other: 6%.

ADMISSIONS FACTS AND FIGURES

Phone: (800) 532-7642. **Email:** mmolliconi@hastings.edu. **Website:** http://www.hastings.edu. **Application deadlines for fall 2011:** Regular decision: Rolling. Early decision: Not offered. Early action: Not offered. Admission cannot be deferred. **To apply online, go to:** http://www.hastings.edu/igsbase/igstemplate.cfm?SRC=DB&SRCN=&GnavID=16&SnavID=33. **Admissions requirements/recommendations:** High school units required (recommended): English: 3 (4); Mathematics: 2 (3); Science: 2 (3); Foreign language: 0 (2); Social studies: 3 (4); History: 3 (4); Academic electives: 0 (4); Total units: 13 (28). Tests: The college uses SAT or ACT scores in admissions decisions. Either SAT or ACT required. For admission to the fall 2011 entering class, the school will accept: ACT with writing recommended. Campus visit: Recommended. Admissions interview: Neither required nor recommended. Off-campus interview: May be arranged. **Factors that count in admissions decisions:** *Academic:* Secondary school record: Very Important. Class rank: Very Important. Letters of recommendation: Important. Standardized test scores: Very Important. Essay: Not Considered. *Nonacademic:* Interview: Very Important. Extracurricular activities: Very Important. Talent/ability: Very Important. Character/personal qualities: Very Important. Alumni/ae relationship: Very Important. Geographical residence: Not Considered. State residency: Not Considered. Religious affiliation/commitment: Not Considered. Minority status: Considered. Volunteer work: Very Important. Work experience: Considered. **Other schools with the greatest overlap in applicants:** Doane College; Nebraska Wesleyan University; University of Nebraska–Lincoln. **Admissions statistics for the fall 2009 entering class:** Total applicants: 1,511. Total accepted: 1,123. Freshmen enrolled: 332; 30% were from out of state. Overall acceptance rate: 74%. **Credentials of fall 2009 freshmen:** 12% ranked in the top 10 percent of their high school class; 30% were in the top 25 percent; 75% were in the top half. (Proportion submitting class standing: 95%.) **First-year students who submitted SAT scores:** 9%. Scores (25/75 percentile): Critical Reading: 460-600, Math: 490-590, Combined: 950-1190. **First-year students submitting ACT scores:** 91%. Scores (25/75 percentile): English: 20-26, Math: 20-27, Composite: 20-26.

ACADEMICS
Year founded: 1882. **Academic calendar:** 4-1-4. **Degrees offered:** bachelor's, master's. **Most popular majors:** 9% business administration and management, 9% psychology, 8% biology. **Major fields of study:** business, management, marketing, and related support services; education; parks, recreation, leisure, and fitness studies; psychology; social sciences. **Areas of required coursework:** arts/fine arts, humanities, computer literacy, English (including composition), philosophy, foreign languages, sciences (biological or physical), history, social science, other. **Pre-professional programs:** pre-law, pre-dentistry, pre-medicine, pre-theology, pre-veterinary science, pre-pharmacy, other. **Special academic programs (% participation):** cross-registration (2.16%), double major (28%), dual enrollment (0%), independent study (2.6%), internships (19%), student-designed major (1.29%), study abroad (1.8%), teacher certificate program (33.5%). **Teacher certification offered in:** early childhood, special education, elementary, middle/junior high, secondary. **Cooperative education programs:** agriculture, business, engineering, health professions, vocational arts. **Faculty and instruction (2009-2010):** Total instructional faculty: 86 full-time, 42 part-time (61% men; 39% women; 2% minorities). Full-time faculty with Ph.D. or other terminal degree: 72%. Student/faculty ratio: 11/1. Classes of fewer than 20 students: 63%; of 20 to 49 students: 37%; of 50 or more students: 0%. **Advanced Placement and International Baccalaureate credit:** AP tests may be used for: Credit and/or placement. Scores accepted: 4, 5. International Baccalaureate exams may be used for: Credit and/or placement. **Freshmen returning for sophomore year:** 71%. **Graduation rates:** Four-year: 55%; five-year: 61%; six-year: 62%. **Graduate study:** 19% of students pursue further study immediately upon graduation. Fields in which graduates pursue further study: Master of Business Administration (MBA), 1%; law, 1%; medicine, 1%; engineering, 1%; theology (or the seminary), 1%; education, 3%; arts and sciences, 13%.

COSTS AND FINANCIAL AID
Financial aid office: (402) 461-7391. **Expenses (2010-2011):** Tuition and fees 2010-2011: $22,620; room/board: $6,300. Estimated books and supplies: $830; transportation: $766; personal expenses: $2,250. **Financial aid:** Priority filing date for institution's financial aid form: May 1. In 2009-2010, 83% of undergraduates applied for financial aid. Of those, 74% were determined to have financial need; 24% had their need fully met. Average financial aid package (proportion receiving): $16,744 (74%). Average amount of gift aid, such as scholarships or grants (proportion receiving): $12,964 (72%). Average amount of self-help aid, such as work study or loans (proportion receiving): $5,034 (58%). Average need-based loan (excluding PLUS or other private loans): $4,747. Among students who received need-based aid, the average percentage of need met: 76%. Among students who received aid based on merit, the average award (and the proportion receiving): $8,671 (23%). The average athletic scholarship (and the proportion receiving): $6,019 (15%). Average amount of debt of borrowers graduating in 2009: $21,329. Proportion who borrowed: 84%.

CAMPUS LIFE AND EXTRACURRICULAR ACTIVITIES
Campus housing available (% using): coed dorms (18%), women's dorms (24%), men's dorms (27%), apartment for single students (24%), other housing options (7%). Students who live in college-owned, operated, or affiliated housing: 75%. **Student employment:** During the 2009-2010 aca-

demic year, 25% of undergraduates worked on campus. Average per-year earnings: $1,000. **Clubs and organizations:** Number of student organizations: 80. Activities include: campus ministries, choral groups, concert band, dance, drama/theater, jazz band, literary magazine, marching band, music ensembles, musical theater, pep band, radio station, student government, student newspaper, symphony orchestra, television station, yearbook. Number of fraternities: 4; sororities: 4. Proportion of men in fraternities: 3%; of women in sororities: 4%. Average proportion of students who stay on campus on weekends: 60%. **Sports program (2009-2010):** Member of NAIA. *Men's intercollegiate varsity sports:* baseball, basketball, cross country, football, golf, soccer, tennis, track and field (indoor), track and field (outdoor), wrestling. *Women's intercollegiate varsity sports:* basketball, cross country, golf, soccer, softball, tennis, track and field (indoor), track and field (outdoor), volleyball.

SERVICES AND FACILITIES
Basic services: nonremedial tutoring, health service. **Remedial assistance:** reading, math, writing, study skills. **Counseling services:** minority student, career, personal, academic, psychological, birth control, religious. **For learning-disabled students:** School does not offer a structured program with separate admission and additional fees. Total undergraduates in learning-disabled program or receiving services: 29. Services include: note-taking services, learning center, extended time for tests, tutors, proofreading services, other testing accommodations, waiver of foreign language degree requirement. **Library:** Number of titles: 135,450; number of current serial subscriptions: 1,050. **Information technology resources:** Students are not required to lease or own a computer. Number of campus computers available to all students: 180. School has a wireless network. Approximate number of users that can be accommodated: 450. Proportion of college-owned housing units wired for high-speed internet access: 100%. **Campus safety:** Security services offered: 24-hour foot-and-vehicle patrols, late-night transport/escort service, 24-hour emergency telephones, lighted pathways/sidewalks, controlled dormitory access (key, security card, etc).

TRANSFER AND INTERNATIONAL STUDENTS
Transfer students: May apply for admission for the following academic terms: Fall, Winter, Spring, Summer. Applicants need a minimum number of credits to apply. For fall 2009: Transfer applications received: 195. Transfer applicants offered admission: 103. Transfer applicants enrolled: 68. **International students:** Number of foreign undergraduates: 11 (1% of student body). Number of countries represented: 8. Minimum TOEFL score required: 320 (paper); 47 (computer).

Midland Lutheran College

- **Address:** 900 N. Clarkson Street, Fremont, NE 68025
- **Website:** http://www.mlc.edu
- **Private; Religious affiliation:** Lutheran
- **Enrollment:** 676 full-time; 33 part-time

KEY STATS
- ✔ U.S News College Ranking: 63, Regional Colleges (Midwest)
- ✔ ACT Score (25th/75th percentile): 19-24
- ✔ Tuition: 2009-2010: $22,984

Selectivity: Selective	Room/board: $5,612
Acceptance rate: 64%	Average debt: N/A
Student/faculty ratio: 11/1	Proportion who borrowed: N/A

UNDERGRADUATE STUDENT BODY STATS
2009-2010 enrollment: 676 full-time; 33 part-time. Men: 43%; women: 57%. **Ethnic makeup:** African American: 8%; Asian American: 2%; Hispanic: 3%; White: 85%; International: 1%. **Religious preference:** Roman Catholic: 23%; Protestant: 1%; No preference: 16%; Lutheran: 35%; Other: 25%.

ADMISSIONS FACTS AND FIGURES
Phone: (402) 941-6501. **Email:** admissions@mlc.edu. **Website:** http://www.mlc.edu. **Application deadlines for fall 2011:** Regular decision: August 7. Early decision: Not offered. Early action: Not offered. Admission cannot be deferred. **Application fee:** $30. **To apply online, go to:** http://www.mlc.edu/s/290/midlandlutheran.aspx?sid=290&gid=1&pgid=1330. **Admissions requirements/recommendations:** High school units required (recommended): English: (3); Mathematics: (2); Science: (2); Foreign language: (2); Academic electives: (10); Total units: (17). Tests: The college uses SAT

or ACT scores in admissions decisions. Either SAT or ACT required. For admission to the fall 2011 entering class, the school will accept: ACT with or without writing accepted. Campus visit: Recommended. Off-campus interview: May be arranged. **Factors that count in admissions decisions:** *Academic:* Secondary school record: Considered. Class rank: Very Important. Letters of recommendation: Considered. Standardized test scores: Important. Essay: Not Considered. *Nonacademic:* Interview: Not Considered. Extracurricular activities: Not Considered. Talent/ability: Not Considered. Character/personal qualities: Not Considered. Alumni/ae relationship: Not Considered. Geographical residence: Not Considered. State residency: Not Considered. Religious affiliation/commitment: Not Considered. Minority status: Not Considered. Volunteer work: Not Considered. Work experience: Not Considered. **Other schools with the greatest overlap in applicants:** Dana College; Nebraska Wesleyan University; University of Nebraska–Kearney; University of Nebraska–Lincoln; University of Nebraska–Omaha. **Admissions statistics for the fall 2009 entering class:** Total applicants: 726. Total accepted: 466. Freshmen enrolled: 113; Overall acceptance rate: 64%. **Credentials of fall 2009 freshmen:** 14% ranked in the top 10 percent of their high school class; 32% were in the top 25 percent. **First-year students who submitted SAT scores:** 19%. Scores (25/75 percentile): Critical Reading: 410-500, Math: 420-500, Combined: 830-1000. **First-year students submitting ACT scores:** 81%. Scores (25/75 percentile): English: 18-23, Math: 17-24, Composite: 19-24.

ACADEMICS

Year founded: 1883. **Academic calendar:** 4-1-4. **Degrees offered:** bachelor's, master's. **Most popular majors:** 15% business administration and management, 14% accounting, 14% nursing/registered nurse training (R.N., A.S.N., B.S.N., M.S.N.), 11% education, 9% business/commerce. **Major fields of study:** biological and biomedical sciences; business, management, marketing, and related support services; communication, journalism, and related programs; computer and information sciences and support services; education; English language and literature/letters; foreign languages, literatures, and linguistics; health professions and related clinical sciences; history; mathematics and statistics; parks, recreation, leisure, and fitness studies; philosophy and religious studies; psychology; social sciences; theology and religious vocations; visual and performing arts. **Areas of required coursework:** arts/fine arts, humanities, computer literacy, mathematics, English (including composition), philosophy, foreign languages, sciences (biological or physical), history, social science. **Pre-professional programs:** pre-law, pre-dentistry, pre-medicine, pre-theology, pre-veterinary science, pre-optometry, pre-pharmacy, other. **Special academic programs (% participation):** cooperative (work-study plan) program (1%), cross-registration (1%), distance learning (1%), double major (14%), external degree program (.01%), independent study (10%), internships (57%), liberal arts/career combination (70%), student-designed major (0%), study abroad (1%), teacher certificate program (1%), weekend college (1%). **Teacher certification offered in:** early childhood, special education, elementary, secondary. **Cooperative education programs:** health professions. **Reserve Officers Training Corps (ROTC):** Army ROTC: Offered at cooperating institution (Creighton University). **Faculty and instruction (2009-2010):** Total instructional faculty: 48 full-time, 54 part-time (51% men; 49% women; 3% minorities). Full-time faculty with Ph.D. or other terminal degree: 52%. Student/faculty ratio: 11/1. Classes of fewer than 20 students: 77%; of 20 to 49 students: 22%; of 50 or more students: 0%. **Advanced Placement and International Baccalaureate credit:** AP tests may be used for: Credit only. Scores accepted: 3, 4, 5. International Baccalaureate exams may be used for: Credit only. **Freshmen returning for sophomore year:** 64%. **Graduation rates:** Four-year: 43%; five-year: 49%; six-year: 55%. **Graduate study:** 19% of students pursue further study immediately upon graduation. Fields in which graduates pursue further study: Master of Business Administration (MBA), 1%; law, 2%; medicine, 8%; education, 2%.

COSTS AND FINANCIAL AID

Financial aid office: (402) 941-6520. **Expenses (2009-2010):** Tuition and fees 2009-2010: $22,984; room/board: $5,612. Estimated books and supplies: $1,000; transportation: $700; personal expenses: $1,200.

CAMPUS LIFE AND EXTRACURRICULAR ACTIVITIES

Campus housing available (% using): coed dorms (100%). **Student employment:** During the 2009-2010 academic year, 35% of undergraduates worked on campus. Average per-year earnings: $1,000. **Clubs and organizations:** Number of student organizations: 36. Activities include: choral groups, concert band, drama/theater, jazz band, literary magazine, music ensembles, pep band, student government, student newspaper. Number of fraternities: 3; sororities: 3. Proportion of men in fraternities: 20%; of women in

sororities: 20%. Average proportion of students who stay on campus on weekends: 40%. **Sports program (2009-2010):** Member of NAIA. *Men's intercollegiate varsity sports:* basketball, cross country, football, golf, soccer, tennis, track and field (indoor), track and field (outdoor). *Women's intercollegiate varsity sports:* cross country, golf, soccer, softball, tennis, track and field (indoor), track and field (outdoor), volleyball.

SERVICES AND FACILITIES

Basic services: nonremedial tutoring, placement service, health service, health insurance. **Remedial assistance:** reading, math, writing, study skills. **Counseling services:** career, personal, academic, older student, psychological, religious. **For learning-disabled students:** School does not offer a structured program with separate admission and additional fees. Total undergraduates in learning-disabled program or receiving services: 11. Services include: remedial math, remedial reading, tape recorders, videotaped classes, diagnostic testing service, untimed tests, note-taking services, oral tests, learning center, readers, extended time for tests, tutors, other testing accommodations, other. **Library:** Number of titles: 105,500; number of current serial subscriptions: 11,400. **Information technology resources:** Students are not required to lease or own a computer. Number of campus computers available to all students: 147. School has a wireless network. Approximate number of users that can be accommodated: 1,000. Proportion of college-owned housing units wired for high-speed internet access: 100%. **Campus safety:** Security services offered: 24-hour foot-and-vehicle patrols, 24-hour emergency telephones, lighted pathways/sidewalks, student patrols, controlled dormitory access (key, security card, etc).

TRANSFER AND INTERNATIONAL STUDENTS

Transfer students: May apply for admission for the following academic terms: Fall, Spring. Applicants do not need a minimum number of credits to apply. **International students:** Number of foreign undergraduates: 9 (1% of student body). Number of countries represented: 3. Minimum TOEFL score required: 500 (paper); 173 (computer).

Nebraska Wesleyan University

- **Address:** 5000 St. Paul Avenue, Lincoln, NE 68504-2794
- **Website:** http://www.nebrwesleyan.edu
- **Private; Religious affiliation:** United Methodist
- **Enrollment:** 1,622 full-time; 230 part-time

KEY STATS

✔ **U.S News College Ranking:** 152, National Liberal Arts Colleges
✔ **ACT Score (25th/75th percentile):** 23-27
✔ **Tuition:** 2010-2011: $23,474

Selectivity: More selective	**Room/board:** $6,300
Acceptance rate: 82%	**Average debt:** $21,931
Student/faculty ratio: 13/1	**Proportion who borrowed:** 78%

UNDERGRADUATE STUDENT BODY STATS

2009-2010 enrollment: 1,622 full-time; 230 part-time. Men: 42%; women: 58%. **Ethnic makeup:** African American: 2%; Asian American: 2%; Hispanic: 1%; White: 94%. **Religious preference:** Roman Catholic: 24%; Protestant: 38%; No preference: 12%; Unknown: 2%; United Methodist: 19%; Other: 1%.

ADMISSIONS FACTS AND FIGURES

Phone: (402) 465-2218. **Email:** admissions@nebrwesleyan.edu. **Website:** http://www.nebrwesleyan.edu. **Application deadlines for fall 2011:** Regular decision: August 15. Early decision: Not offered. Early action: Send application by: November 15; Decision sent by: December 15. Admission can be deferred. **Application fee:** $20. **To apply online, go to:** http://admissions.nebrwesleyan.edu/how-to-apply/apply.php. **Admissions requirements/recommendations:** High school units required (recommended): English: (4); Mathematics: (3); Science: (3); Foreign language: (2); Social studies: (3). Tests: The college uses SAT or ACT scores in admissions decisions. Either SAT or ACT required. For admission to the fall 2011 entering class, the school will accept: ACT with or without writing accepted. Campus visit: Recommended. Admissions interview: Neither required nor recommended. Off-campus interview: Not available. **Factors that count in admissions decisions:** *Academic:* Secondary school record: Considered. Class rank: Very Important. Letters of recommendation: Considered. Standardized test scores: Very Important. Essay: Considered. *Nonacademic:*

Interview: Considered. Extracurricular activities: Important. Talent/ability: Important. Character/personal qualities: Important. Alumni/ae relationship: Considered. Geographical residence: Considered. State residency: Not Considered. Religious affiliation/commitment: Not Considered. Minority status: Considered. Volunteer work: Considered. Work experience: Not Considered. **Other schools with the greatest overlap in applicants:** Doane College; Hastings College; University of Nebraska–Kearney; University of Nebraska–Lincoln; University of Nebraska–Omaha. **Admissions statistics for the fall 2009 entering class:** Total applicants: 1,428. Total accepted: 1,178. Freshmen enrolled: 393; 12% were from out of state. Accepted through early-decision or early-action plans: 52%. Overall acceptance rate: 82%. Non-early acceptance rate: 79%. **Credentials of fall 2009 freshmen:** 25% ranked in the top 10 percent of their high school class; 60% were in the top 25 percent; 87% were in the top half. (Proportion submitting class standing: 96%.) **First-year students submitting ACT scores:** 99%. Scores (25/75 percentile): English: 22-28, Math: 21-27, Composite: 23-27.

ACADEMICS

Year founded: 1887. **Academic calendar:** Semester. **Degrees offered:** certificate, bachelor's, post-bachelor's certificate, master's, post-master's certificate. **Most popular majors:** 23% business, management, marketing, and related support services, 19% biological and biomedical sciences, 9% health professions and related clinical sciences, 8% parks, recreation, leisure, and fitness studies, 8% psychology. **Major fields of study:** area, ethnic, cultural, and gender studies; biological and biomedical sciences; business, management, marketing, and related support services; communication, journalism, and related programs; computer and information sciences and support services; education; English language and literature/letters; foreign languages, literatures, and linguistics; health professions and related clinical sciences; history; mathematics and statistics; multi/interdisciplinary studies; parks, recreation, leisure, and fitness studies; philosophy and religious studies; physical sciences; psychology; public administration and social service professions; social sciences; visual and performing arts. **Areas of required coursework:** arts/fine arts, humanities, mathematics, English (including composition), foreign languages, sciences (biological or physical), social science, other. **Pre-professional programs:** pre-law, pre-dentistry, pre-medicine, pre-theology, pre-veterinary science, pre-optometry, pre-pharmacy, other. **Special academic programs (% participation):** accelerated program, double major (11.7%), dual enrollment (5.9%), independent study (27.8%), internships (64.2%), study abroad (22.8%), teacher certificate program (11.7%). **Teacher certification offered in:** special education, elementary, middle/junior high, secondary. **Reserve Officers Training Corps (ROTC):** Army ROTC: Offered at cooperating institution (University of Nebraska–Lincoln); Air Force ROTC: Offered at cooperating institution (University of Nebraska–Lincoln). **Faculty and instruction (2009-2010):** Total instructional faculty: 103 full-time, 65 part-time (49% men; 51% women; 2% minorities). Full-time faculty with Ph.D. or other terminal degree: 88%. Student/faculty ratio: 13/1. Classes of fewer than 20 students: 57%; of 20 to 49 students: 41%; of 50 or more students: 2%. **Advanced Placement and International Baccalaureate credit:** AP tests may be used for: Credit only. Scores accepted: 3, 4, 5. International Baccalaureate exams may be used for: Credit only. **Freshmen returning for sophomore year:** 81%. **Graduation rates:** Four-year: 52%; five-year: 63%; six-year: 66%. **Graduate study:** 25% of students pursue further study immediately upon graduation; 65% within five years.

COSTS AND FINANCIAL AID

Financial aid office: (402) 465-2212. **Expenses (2010-2011):** Tuition and fees 2010-2011: $23,474; room/board: $6,300. Estimated books and supplies: $1,400 personal expenses: $3,000. **Financial aid:** In 2009-2010, 82% of undergraduates applied for financial aid. Of those, 72% were determined to have financial need; 19% had their need fully met. Average financial aid package (proportion receiving): $16,199 (71%). Average amount of gift aid, such as scholarships or grants (proportion receiving): $11,649 (71%). Average amount of self-help aid, such as work study or loans (proportion receiving): $4,805 (60%). Average need-based loan (excluding PLUS or other private loans): $4,636. Among students who received need-based aid, the average percentage of need met: 71%. Among students who received aid based on merit, the average award (and the proportion receiving): $6,800 (28%). The average athletic scholarship (and the proportion receiving): $0 (0%). Average amount of debt of borrowers graduating in 2009: $21,931. Proportion who borrowed: 78%.

CAMPUS LIFE AND EXTRACURRICULAR ACTIVITIES

Campus housing available (% using): coed dorms (36%), women's dorms (10%), sorority housing (9%), fraternity housing (5%), apartment for single students (6%), special housing for disabled students, other housing options

(34%). Students who live in college-owned, operated, or affiliated housing: 60%. **Student employment:** During the 2009-2010 academic year, 36% of undergraduates worked on campus. Average per-year earnings: $1,300. **Clubs and organizations:** Number of student organizations: 80. Activities include: campus ministries, choral groups, concert band, drama/theater, international student organization, jazz band, literary magazine, music ensembles, musical theater, opera, pep band, student government, student newspaper, symphony orchestra, yearbook. Number of fraternities: 4; sororities: 4. Proportion of men in fraternities: 15%; of women in sororities: 19%. Average proportion of students who stay on campus on weekends: 70%. **Sports program (2009-2010):** Member of NCAA III. **Men's intercollegiate varsity sports:** baseball, basketball, cross country, football, golf, soccer, tennis, track and field (indoor), track and field (outdoor). **Women's intercollegiate varsity sports:** basketball, cross country, golf, soccer, softball, tennis, track and field (indoor), track and field (outdoor), volleyball.

SERVICES AND FACILITIES

Basic services: nonremedial tutoring, women's center, placement service, health service, health insurance. **Counseling services:** minority student, career, personal, academic, older student, psychological, birth control, religious. **For learning-disabled students:** School does not offer a structured program with separate admission and additional fees. Services include: tape recorders, videotaped classes, untimed tests, note-taking services, oral tests, learning center, readers, extended time for tests, tutors, early syllabus, priority registration, priority seating, texts on tape, typist/scribe, exams on tape or computer, other testing accommodations, other. **Library:** Number of titles: 221,084; number of current serial subscriptions: 832. **Information technology resources:** Students are not required to lease or own a computer. Number of campus computers available to all students: 405. School has a wireless network. Approximate number of users that can be accommodated: 630. Proportion of college-owned housing units wired for high-speed internet access: 100%. **Campus safety:** Security services offered: 24-hour foot-and-vehicle patrols, 24-hour emergency telephones, lighted pathways/sidewalks, controlled dormitory access (key, security card, etc).

TRANSFER AND INTERNATIONAL STUDENTS

Transfer students: May apply for admission for the following academic terms: Fall, Spring. Applicants do not need a minimum number of credits to apply. For fall 2009: Transfer applications received: 199. Transfer applicants offered admission: 111. Transfer applicants enrolled: 70. **International students:** Number of foreign undergraduates: 7. Number of countries represented: 14. Minimum TOEFL score required: 525 (paper); 195 (computer).

Peru State College

- **Address:** Box 10, Peru, NE 68421-0010
- **Website:** http://www.peru.edu
- **Public**
- **Enrollment:** 1,245 full-time; 897 part-time

KEY STATS

✔ **U.S News College Ranking:** second tier, Regional Colleges (Midwest)
✔ **ACT Score (25th/75th percentile):** 17-24
✔ **Tuition:** 2009-2010: $4,946 in state, $4,946 out of state

Selectivity: Selective	Room/board: $4,804
Acceptance rate: 48%	Average debt: N/A
Student/faculty ratio: 24/1	Proportion who borrowed: N/A

UNDERGRADUATE STUDENT BODY STATS

2009-2010 enrollment: 1,245 full-time; 897 part-time. Men: 42%; women: 58%. **Ethnic makeup:** African American: 3%; American-Indian: 1%; Asian American: 1%; Hispanic: 2%; White: 93%.

ADMISSIONS FACTS AND FIGURES

Phone: (402) 872-2221. **Email:** admissions@peru.edu. **Website:** http://www.peru.edu. **Application deadlines for fall 2011:** Regular decision: Rolling. Early decision: Not offered. Early action: Not offered. Admission can be deferred. **Application fee:** None. **To apply online, go to:** http://www.hpcnet.org/peru/admissionsoffice. **Admissions requirements/recommendations:** High school units required (recommended): English: (4); Mathematics: (3); Science: (3); Foreign language: (2); Social studies: (3); Total units: (0). Tests: The college uses SAT or ACT scores in admissions decisions. Either SAT or ACT required. For admission to the fall 2011 entering class, the school will accept: ACT with or without writing accepted. Campus visit: Recommended. Admissions interview: Neither required nor recommended. Off-campus interview: Not available. **Factors that count in admissions decisions:** *Academic:* Secondary school record: Not Considered. Class rank: Not Considered. Letters of recommendation: Not Considered. Standardized test scores: Not Considered. Essay: Not Considered. *Nonacademic:* Interview: Not Considered. Extracurricular activities: Not Considered. Talent/ability: Not Considered. Character/personal qualities: Not Considered. Alumni/ae relationship: Not Considered. Geographical residence: Not Considered. State residency: Not Considered. Religious affiliation/commitment: Not Considered. Minority status: Not Considered. Volunteer work: Not Considered. Work experience: Not Considered. **Other schools with the greatest overlap in applicants:** Doane College; Northwest Missouri State University; University of Nebraska–Kearney; University of Nebraska–Lincoln; University of Nebraska–Omaha. **Admissions statistics for the fall 2009 entering class:** Total applicants: 1,170. Total accepted: 566. Freshmen enrolled: 235; Overall acceptance rate: 48%. **Size of waiting list:** 0 applicants; enrolled from waiting list: 0. **Credentials of fall 2009 freshmen:** 17% ranked in the top 25 percent of their high school class; 54% were in the top half. (Proportion submitting class standing: 96%.) **Average high school grade point average:** 3.0. **First-year students submitting ACT scores:** 92%. Scores (25/75 percentile): English: N/A, Math: N/A, Composite: 17-24.

ACADEMICS

Year founded: 1867. **Academic calendar:** Semester. **Degrees offered:** certificate, bachelor's, post-bachelor's certificate, master's. **Most popular majors:** 27% education, 24% business administration, management, and operations, 15% business administration and management, 6% psychology, 5% physical education teaching and coaching. **Major fields of study:** agriculture, agriculture operations, and related sciences; biological and biomedical sciences; business, management, marketing, and related support services; computer and information sciences and support services; education; English language and literature/letters; liberal arts and sciences studies, and humanities; mathematics and statistics; psychology; security and protective services. **Areas of required coursework:** arts/fine arts, humanities, computer literacy, mathematics, English (including composition), sciences (biological or physical), history, social science, other. **Pre-professional programs:** pre-law, pre-dentistry, pre-medicine, pre-veterinary science, pre-optometry, pre-pharmacy, other. **Special academic programs:** accelerated program, cooperative (work-study plan) program, cross-registration, distance learning, double major, dual enrollment, external degree program, honors program, independent study, internships, liberal arts/career combination, teacher certificate program. **Teacher certification offered in:** early childhood, special education, elementary, middle/junior high, secondary. **Cooperative education programs:** art, business, computer science, education, humanities, natural science, social/behavioral science, other. **Reserve Officers Training Corps (ROTC):** Army ROTC: Offered at cooperating institution; Air Force ROTC: Offered at cooperating institution. **Faculty and instruction (2009-2010):** Total instructional faculty: 38 full-time, 67 part-time (55% men; 45% women; 1% minorities). Full-time faculty with Ph.D. or other terminal degree: 97%. Student/faculty ratio: 24/1. **Advanced Placement and International Baccalaureate credit:** AP tests may be used for: Placement only. Scores accepted: 3. International Baccalaureate exams may be used for: Placement only. **Freshmen returning for sophomore year:** 57%. **Graduation rates:** Four-year: 15%; five-year: 31%; six-year: 33%. **Graduate study:** 14% of students pursue further study immediately upon graduation. Fields in which graduates pursue further study: Master of Business Administration (MBA), 21%; law, 7%; education, 71%.

COSTS AND FINANCIAL AID

Financial aid office: (402) 872-2228. **Expenses (2009-2010):** Tuition and fees 2009-2010: $4,946 in state, $4,946 out of state; room/board: $4,804. Estimated books and supplies: $850. **Financial aid:** Priority filing date for institution's financial aid form: March 1.

CAMPUS LIFE AND EXTRACURRICULAR ACTIVITIES

Campus housing available (% using): coed dorms (34%), women's dorms (20%), men's dorms (31%), apartments for married students (3%), apartment for single students, special housing for disabled students (1%), other housing options (11%). **Student employment:** During the 2009-2010 academic year, 10% of undergraduates worked on campus. Average per-year earnings: $1,600. **Clubs and organizations:** Number of student organizations: 31. Activities include: campus ministries, choral groups, concert band, dance, drama/theater, jazz band, literary magazine, marching band, music ensembles, musical theater, pep band, radio station, student government, student newspaper, student film society, yearbook. Number of fraterni-

ties: 0; sororities: 0. Average proportion of students who stay on campus on weekends: 25%. **Sports program (2009-2010):** Member of NAIA. *Men's intercollegiate varsity sports:* baseball, basketball, football. *Women's intercollegiate varsity sports:* basketball, cross country, golf, softball, volleyball.

SERVICES AND FACILITIES

Basic services: nonremedial tutoring, placement service, day care, health service, health insurance. **Remedial assistance:** study skills. **Counseling services:** minority student, career, veteran student, academic, older student, birth control. **For learning-disabled students:** School does not offer a structured program with separate admission and additional fees. Total undergraduates in learning-disabled program or receiving services: 55. Services include: tape recorders, videotaped classes, note-taking services, oral tests, learning center, readers, extended time for tests, tutors, priority seating, texts on tape, typist/scribe, other testing accommodations. **Library:** Number of titles: 122,923; number of current serial subscriptions: 246. **Information technology resources:** Students are not required to lease or own a computer. Number of campus computers available to all students: 163. School has a wireless network. Proportion of college-owned housing units wired for high-speed internet access: 100%. **Campus safety:** Security services offered: 24-hour foot-and-vehicle patrols, late-night transport/escort service, 24-hour emergency telephones, lighted pathways/sidewalks.

TRANSFER AND INTERNATIONAL STUDENTS

Transfer students: May apply for admission for the following academic terms: Fall, Spring, Summer. Applicants do not need a minimum number of credits to apply. For fall 2009: Transfer applications received: 663. Transfer applicants offered admission: 347. Transfer applicants enrolled: 257. **International students:** Number of foreign undergraduates: 0. Number of countries represented: 0. Minimum TOEFL score required: 550 (paper); 230 (computer).

Union College

- **Address:** 3800 S. 48th Street, Lincoln, NE 68506
- **Website:** http://www.ucollege.edu
- **Private; Religious affiliation:** Seventh-day Adventist
- **Enrollment:** 664 full-time; 149 part-time

KEY STATS

✔ **U.S News College Ranking:** 35, Regional Colleges (Midwest)
✔ **ACT Score (25th/75th percentile):** 19-26
✔ **Tuition:** 2010-2011: $18,150

Selectivity: Selective	**Room/board:** $6,350
Acceptance rate: 41%	**Average debt:** $23,000
Student/faculty ratio: 12/1	**Proportion who borrowed:** 65%

UNDERGRADUATE STUDENT BODY STATS

2009-2010 enrollment: 664 full-time; 149 part-time. Men: 41%; women: 59%. **Ethnic makeup:** African American: 3%; American-Indian: 1%; Asian American: 3%; Hispanic: 8%; White: 77%; International: 7%. **Religious preference:** Protestant: 1%; No preference: 3%; Seventh-day Adventist: 96%.

ADMISSIONS FACTS AND FIGURES

Phone: (800) 228-4600. **Email:** ucenroll@ucollege.edu. **Website:** http://www.ucollege.edu. **Application deadlines for fall 2011:** Regular decision: Rolling. Early decision: Not offered. Early action: Not offered. Admission can be deferred. **To apply online, go to:** http://www.ucollege.edu/ucscripts/public/template/default.asp?DivID=2&PGID=6. **Admissions requirements/recommendations:** High school units required (recommended): English: 3 (4); Mathematics: 2 (3); Science: 2 (3); Foreign language: (1); Social studies: 1; History: 1; Academic electives: 3; Total units: 20. Tests: The college uses SAT or ACT scores in admissions decisions. Either SAT or ACT required. For admission to the fall 2011 entering class, the school will accept: ACT with or without writing accepted. Campus visit: Recommended. Admissions interview: Recommended. Off-campus interview: May be arranged. **Factors that count in admissions decisions:** *Academic:* Secondary school record: Very Important. Class rank: Important. Letters of recommendation: Very Important. Standardized test scores: Very Important. Essay: Considered. *Nonacademic:* Interview: Important. Extracurricular activities: Important. Talent/ability: Considered. Character/personal qualities: Very Important. Alumni/ae relationship: Not Considered. Geographical residence: Not Considered. State residency: Not Considered. Religious affiliation/commitment: Important. Minority status: Not Considered. Volunteer work: Considered. Work experience: Not Considered. **Other schools with the greatest overlap in applicants:** Andrews University; Pacific Union College; Southern Adventist University; Southwestern Adventist University; Walla Walla University. **Admissions statistics for the fall 2009 entering class:** Total applicants: 392. Total accepted: 162. Freshmen enrolled: 117; 79% were from out of state. Overall acceptance rate: 41%. **Credentials of fall 2009 freshmen:** 13% ranked in the top 10 percent of their high school class; 18% were in the top 25 percent; 69% were in the top half. (Proportion submitting class standing: 60%.) **Average high school grade point average:** 3.4. **First-year students who submitted SAT scores:** 27%. Scores (25/75 percentile): Critical Reading: 540-660, Math: 480-590, Combined: 1020-1250. **First-year students submitting ACT scores:** 83%. Scores (25/75 percentile): English: 19-27, Math: 17-25, Composite: 19-26.

ACADEMICS

Year founded: 1891. **Academic calendar:** Semester. **Degrees offered:** associate, bachelor's, master's. **Most popular majors:** 16% nursing/registered nurse training (R.N., A.S.N., B.S.N., M.S.N.), 15% business administration and management, 10% international public health/international health, 9% elementary education and teaching, 7% communication studies/speech communication and rhetoric. **Major fields of study:** biological and biomedical sciences; business, management, marketing, and related support services; communication, journalism, and related programs; computer and information sciences and support services; education; English language and literature/letters; foreign languages, literatures, and linguistics; health professions and related clinical sciences; history; liberal arts and sciences studies, and humanities; mathematics and statistics; parks, recreation, leisure, and fitness studies; philosophy and religious studies; physical sciences; psychology; public administration and social service professions; social sciences; theology and religious vocations; visual and performing arts. **Areas of required coursework:** arts/fine arts, humanities, computer literacy, mathematics, English (including composition), sciences (biological or physical), history, social science, other. **Pre-professional programs:** pre-law, pre-dentistry, pre-medicine, pre-theology, pre-pharmacy, other. **Special academic programs:** distance learning, double major, English as a Second Language (ESL), honors program, independent study, internships, student-designed major, study abroad, teacher certificate program. **Teacher certification offered in:** elementary, secondary. **Faculty and instruction (2009-2010):** Total instructional faculty: 56 full-time, 35 part-time (55% men; 45% women; 10% minorities). Full-time faculty with Ph.D. or other terminal degree: 43%. Student/faculty ratio: 12/1. Classes of fewer than 20 students: 74%; of 20 to 49 students: 24%; of 50 or more students: 2%. **Advanced Placement and International Baccalaureate credit:** AP tests may be used for: Placement only. Scores accepted: 4, 5. International Baccalaureate exams may be used for: Credit and/or placement. **Freshmen returning for sophomore year:** 69%. **Graduation rates:** Four-year: 27%; five-year: 45%; six-year: 51%.

COSTS AND FINANCIAL AID

Financial aid office: (402) 486-2505. **Expenses (2010-2011):** Tuition and fees 2010-2011: $18,150; room/board: $6,350. Estimated books and supplies: $1,000; transportation: $1,306; personal expenses: $4,094. **Financial aid:** Priority filing date for institution's financial aid form: April 1. In 2009-2010, 74% of undergraduates applied for financial aid. Of those, 74% were determined to have financial need; 3% had their need fully met. Average financial aid package (proportion receiving): $13,000 (74%). Average amount of gift aid, such as scholarships or grants (proportion receiving): $3,000 (45%). Average need-based loan (excluding PLUS or other private loans): $4,500. Among students who received need-based aid, the average percentage of need met: 63%. Among students who received aid based on merit, the average award (and the proportion receiving): $4,000 (25%). Average amount of debt of borrowers graduating in 2009: $23,000. Proportion who borrowed: 65%.

CAMPUS LIFE AND EXTRACURRICULAR ACTIVITIES

Campus housing available (% using): women's dorms (49%), men's dorms (40%), apartments for married students (2%), apartment for single students (9%). Students who live in college-owned, operated, or affiliated housing: 68%. **Student employment:** During the 2009-2010 academic year, 60% of undergraduates worked on campus. Average per-year earnings: $2,200. **Clubs and organizations:** Number of student organizations: 21. Activities include: choral groups, concert band, drama/theater, music ensembles, student government, student newspaper, symphony orchestra, yearbook. Number of fraternities: 0; sororities: 0. Average proportion of students who stay on campus on weekends: 45%.

SERVICES AND FACILITIES

Basic services: nonremedial tutoring, placement service, health service, health insurance. **Remedial assistance:** reading, math, writing, study skills. **Counseling services:** career, personal, academic, psychological, religious. **For learning-disabled students:** School does not offer a structured program with separate admission and additional fees. Total undergraduates in learning-disabled program or receiving services: 25. Services include: remedial math, remedial English, reading machines, tape recorders, videotaped classes, diagnostic testing service, untimed tests, note-taking services, oral tests, learning center, readers, extended time for tests, tutors, priority seating, texts on tape, other testing accommodations, other. **Library:** Number of titles: 170,677; number of current serial subscriptions: 494. **Information technology resources:** Students are not required to lease or own a computer. Number of campus computers available to all students: 85. School has a wireless network. Approximate number of users that can be accommodated: 1,000. Proportion of college-owned housing units wired for high-speed internet access: 85%. **Campus safety:** Security services offered: 24-hour foot-and-vehicle patrols, late-night transport/escort service, 24-hour emergency telephones, lighted pathways/sidewalks, student patrols.

TRANSFER AND INTERNATIONAL STUDENTS

Transfer students: May apply for admission for the following academic terms: Fall, Spring. Applicants need a minimum number of credits to apply. For fall 2009: Transfer applicants enrolled: 75. **International students:** Number of foreign undergraduates: 53 (7% of student body). Number of countries represented: 26. Minimum TOEFL score required: 550 (paper); 213 (computer).

University of Nebraska–Kearney

- **Address:** 905 W. 25th Street, Kearney, NE 68849
- **Website:** http://www.unk.edu
- **Public**
- **Enrollment:** 4,522 full-time; 509 part-time

KEY STATS

✔ **U.S News College Ranking:** 43, Regional Universities (Midwest)
✔ **ACT Score (25th/75th percentile):** 20-25
✔ **Tuition:** 2009-2010: $5,635 in state, $10,397 out of state

Selectivity: Selective	**Room/board:** $6,830
Acceptance rate: 77%	**Average debt:** $19,160
Student/faculty ratio: 16/1	**Proportion who borrowed:** 73%

UNDERGRADUATE STUDENT BODY STATS

2009-2010 enrollment: 4,522 full-time; 509 part-time. Men: 48%; women: 52%. **Ethnic makeup:** African American: 1%; Asian American: 1%; Hispanic: 5%; White: 85%; International: 8%.

ADMISSIONS FACTS AND FIGURES

Phone: (308) 865-8526. **Email:** admissionsug@unk.edu. **Website:** http://www.unk.edu. **Application deadlines for fall 2011:** Regular decision: Rolling. Early decision: Not offered. Early action: Not offered. Admission cannot be deferred. **Application fee:** $45. **To apply online, go to:** http://webeasi.unk.edu/. **Admissions requirements/recommendations:** High school units required (recommended): English: 4; Mathematics: 3; Science: 3; Foreign language: 2; Social studies: 3; Academic electives: 1; Total units: 16. Tests: The college uses SAT or ACT scores in admissions decisions. Either SAT or ACT required. For admission to the fall 2011 entering class, the school will accept: ACT with or without writing accepted. Campus visit: Recommended. Admissions interview: Neither required nor recommended. Off-campus interview: May be arranged. **Factors that count in admissions decisions:** *Academic:* Secondary school record: Considered. Class rank: Very Important. Letters of recommendation: Considered. Standardized test scores: Very Important. Essay: Not Considered. *Nonacademic:* Interview: Not Considered. Extracurricular activities: Considered. Talent/ability: Considered. Character/personal qualities: Not Considered. Alumni/ae relationship: Considered. Geographical residence: Considered. State residency: Considered. Religious affiliation/commitment: Not Considered. Minority status: Considered. Volunteer work: Not Considered. Work experience: Not Considered. **Other schools with the greatest overlap in applicants:** Hastings College; Nebraska Wesleyan University; University of Nebraska–Lincoln; University of Nebraska–Omaha; Wayne State College. **Admissions statistics for the fall 2009 entering class:** Total applicants: 2,895. Total accepted:

2,215. Freshmen enrolled: 983; 7% were from out of state. Overall acceptance rate: 77%. **Credentials of fall 2009 freshmen:** 17% ranked in the top 10 percent of their high school class; 42% were in the top 25 percent; 73% were in the top half. (Proportion submitting class standing: 92%.) **Average high school grade point average:** 3.3. **First-year students who submitted SAT scores:** 1%. Scores (25/75 percentile): Critical Reading: 440-660, Math: 370-700, Combined: 810-1360. **First-year students submitting ACT scores:** 93%. Scores (25/75 percentile): English: 18-25, Math: 19-25, Composite: 20-25.

ACADEMICS

Year founded: 1903. **Academic calendar:** Semester. **Degrees offered:** bachelor's, master's, post-master's certificate. **Most popular majors:** 15% business administration and management, 12% elementary education and teaching, 11% operations management and supervision, 6% parks, recreation, and leisure studies, 4% psychology. **Major fields of study:** agriculture, agriculture operations, and related sciences; biological and biomedical sciences; business, management, marketing, and related support services; communication, journalism, and related programs; computer and information sciences and support services; education; English language and literature/letters; family and consumer sciences/human sciences; foreign languages, literatures, and linguistics; health professions and related clinical sciences; history; liberal arts and sciences studies, and humanities; mathematics and statistics; parks, recreation, leisure, and fitness studies; philosophy and religious studies; physical sciences; psychology; public administration and social service professions; security and protective services; social sciences; visual and performing arts. **Areas of required coursework:** humanities, mathematics, English (including composition), sciences (biological or physical), history, social science, other. **Pre-professional programs:** pre-law, pre-dentistry, pre-medicine, pre-veterinary science, pre-optometry, pre-pharmacy, other. **Special academic programs:** cooperative (work-study plan) program, distance learning, double major, dual enrollment, English as a Second Language (ESL), exchange student program (domestic), honors program, independent study, internships, study abroad, teacher certificate program. **Teacher certification offered in:** early childhood, special education, elementary, middle/junior high, secondary, bilingual/bicultural. **Cooperative education programs:** health professions. **Reserve Officers Training Corps (ROTC):** Army ROTC: Offered on campus. **Faculty and instruction (2009-2010):** Total instructional faculty: 305 full-time, 101 part-time (50% men; 50% women; 7% minorities). Full-time faculty with Ph.D. or other terminal degree: 78%. Student/faculty ratio: 16/1. Classes of fewer than 20 students: 44%; of 20 to 49 students: 51%; of 50 or more students: 5%. **Advanced Placement and International Baccalaureate credit:** International Baccalaureate exams may be used for: Placement only. **Freshmen returning for sophomore year:** 80%. **Graduation rates:** Four-year: 23%; five-year: 52%; six-year: 57%.

COSTS AND FINANCIAL AID

Financial aid office: (308) 865-8520. **Expenses (2009-2010):** Tuition and fees 2009-2010: $5,635 in state, $10,397 out of state; room/board: $6,830. Estimated books and supplies: $952; transportation: $774; personal expenses: $2,556. **Financial aid:** Priority filing date for institution's financial aid form: April 1. In 2009-2010, 74% of undergraduates applied for financial aid. Of those, 61% were determined to have financial need; 30% had their need fully met. Average financial aid package (proportion receiving): $9,443 (60%). Average amount of gift aid, such as scholarships or grants (proportion receiving): $5,582 (39%). Average amount of self-help aid, such as work study or loans (proportion receiving): $3,908 (58%). Average need-based loan (excluding PLUS or other private loans): $3,512. Among students who received need-based aid, the average percentage of need met: 80%. Among students who received aid based on merit, the average award (and the proportion receiving): $2,200 (12%). The average athletic scholarship (and the proportion receiving): $1,477 (4%). Average amount of debt of borrowers graduating in 2009: $19,160. Proportion who borrowed: 73%.

CAMPUS LIFE AND EXTRACURRICULAR ACTIVITIES

Campus housing available: coed dorms, sorority housing, fraternity housing, apartments for married students. Students who live in college-owned, operated, or affiliated housing: 37%. **Clubs and organizations:** Number of student organizations: 155. Activities include: campus ministries, choral groups, concert band, dance, drama/theater, international student organization, jazz band, marching band, model UN, music ensembles, musical theater, pep band, radio station, student government, student newspaper, symphony orchestra, television station. Number of fraternities: 7; sororities: 5. Proportion of men in fraternities: 6%; of women in sororities: 5%. **Sports program (2009-2010):** Member of NCAA II. *Men's intercollegiate varsity sports:* baseball, basketball, cross country, football, golf, tennis, track and field (indoor), track and field (outdoor), wrestling. *Women's intercollegiate*

varsity sports: basketball, cross country, golf, soccer, softball, swimming, tennis, track and field (indoor), track and field (outdoor), volleyball.

SERVICES AND FACILITIES

Basic services: nonremedial tutoring, women's center, placement service, day care, health service, health insurance. **Remedial assistance:** math, study skills. **Counseling services:** minority student, career, personal, veteran student, academic, other. **For learning-disabled students:** School does not offer a structured program with separate admission and additional fees. Services include: remedial math, reading machines, tape recorders, videotaped classes, note-taking services, learning center, tutors, priority seating. **Library:** Number of titles: 637,288; number of current serial subscriptions: 2,191. **Information technology resources:** Students are not required to lease or own a computer. Number of campus computers available to all students: 800. School has a wireless network. Approximate number of users that can be accommodated: 12,000. Proportion of college-owned housing units wired for high-speed internet access: 91%. **Campus safety:** Security services offered: 24-hour foot-and-vehicle patrols, 24-hour emergency telephones, lighted pathways/sidewalks, controlled dormitory access (key, security card, etc).

TRANSFER AND INTERNATIONAL STUDENTS

Transfer students: May apply for admission for the following academic terms: Fall, Spring, Summer. Applicants do not need a minimum number of credits to apply. For fall 2009: Transfer applications received: 528. Transfer applicants offered admission: 367. Transfer applicants enrolled: 334. **International students:** Number of foreign undergraduates: 381 (8% of student body). Number of countries represented: 46. Minimum TOEFL score required: 500 (paper); 61 (computer). Average TOEFL score: 541 (paper).

University of Nebraska—Lincoln

- **Address:** 14th and R Streets, Lincoln, NE 68588
- **Website:** http://www.unl.edu
- **Public**
- **Enrollment:** 17,737 full-time; 1,218 part-time

KEY STATS

✔ **U.S News College Ranking:** 104, National Universities
✔ **ACT Score (25th/75th percentile):** 22-29
✔ **Tuition:** 2010-2011: $7,252 in state, $18,846 out of state

Selectivity: More selective	**Room/board:** $8,196
Acceptance rate: 63%	**Average debt:** $19,128
Student/faculty ratio: 20/1	**Proportion who borrowed:** 60%

UNDERGRADUATE STUDENT BODY STATS

2009-2010 enrollment: 17,737 full-time; 1,218 part-time. Men: 54%; women: 46%. **Ethnic makeup:** African American: 3%; American-Indian: 1%; Asian American: 3%; Hispanic: 4%; White: 88%; International: 3%.

ADMISSIONS FACTS AND FIGURES

Phone: (800) 742-8800. **Email:** Admissions@unl.edu. **Website:** http://www.unl.edu. **Application deadlines for fall 2011:** Regular decision: May 1. Early decision: Not offered. Early action: Not offered. Admission cannot be deferred. **Application fee:** $45. **To apply online, go to:** http://nebraska.unl.edu/apply/. **Admissions requirements/recommendations:** High school units required (recommended): English: 4; Mathematics: 4; Science: 3; Foreign language: 2; Social studies: 3; History: (1); Total units: 16 (1). Tests: The college uses SAT or ACT scores in admissions decisions. Either SAT or ACT required. For admission to the fall 2011 entering class, the school will accept: ACT with or without writing accepted. Campus visit: Recommended. Admissions interview: Neither required nor recommended. Off-campus interview: Not available. **Factors that count in admissions decisions:** *Academic:* Secondary school record: Important. Class rank: Very Important. Letters of recommendation: Considered. Standardized test scores: Very Important. Essay: Not Considered. *Nonacademic:* Interview: Not Considered. Extracurricular activities: Not Considered. Talent/ability: Considered. Character/personal qualities: Not Considered. Alumni/ae relationship: Not Considered. Geographical residence: Not Considered. State residency: Not Considered. Religious affiliation/commitment: Not Considered. Minority status: Not Considered. Volunteer work: Not Considered. Work experience: Not Considered. **Other schools with**

the greatest overlap in applicants: Iowa State University; University of Kansas; University of Nebraska–Kearney; University of Nebraska–Omaha; Washington University in St. Louis. **Admissions statistics for the fall 2009 entering class:** Total applicants: 9,455. Total accepted: 5,943. Freshmen enrolled: 3,986; 19% were from out of state. Overall acceptance rate: 63%. **Credentials of fall 2009 freshmen:** 27% ranked in the top 10 percent of their high school class; 54% were in the top 25 percent; 84% were in the top half. (Proportion submitting class standing: 93%.) **First-year students who submitted SAT scores:** 10%. Scores (25/75 percentile): Critical Reading: 510-670, Math: 530-680, Combined: 1040-1350. **First-year students submitting ACT scores:** 95%. Scores (25/75 percentile): English: 21-29, Math: 21-28, Composite: 22-29.

ACADEMICS

Year founded: 1869. **Academic calendar:** Semester. **Degrees offered:** associate, bachelor's, post-bachelor's certificate, master's, post-master's certificate, doctorate. **Most popular majors:** 22% business, management, marketing, and related support services, 10% education, 9% engineering, 8% family and consumer sciences/human sciences, 6% communication, journalism, and related programs. **Major fields of study:** agriculture, agriculture operations, and related sciences; architecture and related services; area, ethnic, cultural, and gender studies; biological and biomedical sciences; business, management, marketing, and related support services; communication, journalism, and related programs; communications technologies/technicians and support services; computer and information sciences and support services; education; engineering; engineering technologies/technicians; English language and literature/letters; family and consumer sciences/human sciences; foreign languages, literatures, and linguistics; health professions and related clinical sciences; history; legal professions and studies; liberal arts and sciences studies, and humanities; mathematics and statistics; multi/interdisciplinary studies; natural resources and conservation; philosophy and religious studies; physical sciences; psychology; security and protective services; social sciences; visual and performing arts. **Areas of required coursework:** arts/fine arts, humanities, mathematics, English (including composition), foreign languages, sciences (biological or physical), history, social science, other. **Pre-professional programs:** pre-law, pre-dentistry, pre-medicine, pre-veterinary science, pre-optometry, pre-pharmacy, other. **Special academic programs:** accelerated program, cooperative (work-study plan) program, cross-registration, distance learning, double major, dual enrollment, English as a Second Language (ESL), exchange student program (domestic), honors program, independent study, internships, liberal arts/career combination, student-designed major, study abroad, teacher certificate program. **Teacher certification offered in:** early childhood, special education, elementary, vo-tech, secondary, bilingual/bicultural. **Cooperative education programs:** agriculture, business, computer science, engineering. **Reserve Officers Training Corps (ROTC):** Army ROTC: Offered on campus; Navy ROTC: Offered on campus; Air Force ROTC: Offered on campus. **Faculty and instruction (2009-2010):** Total instructional faculty: 1,102 full-time, 9 part-time (71% men; 29% women; 18% minorities). Full-time faculty with Ph.D. or other terminal degree: 96%. Student/faculty ratio: 20/1. Classes of fewer than 20 students: 38%; of 20 to 49 students: 48%; of 50 or more students: 14%. **Advanced Placement and International Baccalaureate credit:** AP tests may be used for: Credit only. Scores accepted: 3, 4, 5. International Baccalaureate exams may be used for: Credit only. **Freshmen returning for sophomore year:** 84%. **Graduation rates:** Four-year: 25%; five-year: 56%; six-year: 63%. **Graduate study:** 26% of students pursue further study immediately upon graduation.

COSTS AND FINANCIAL AID

Financial aid office: (402) 472-2030. **Expenses (2010-2011):** Tuition and fees 2010-2011: $7,252 in state, $18,846 out of state; room/board: $8,196. Estimated books and supplies: $1,010; transportation: $1,221; personal expenses: $2,147. **Financial aid:** Priority filing date for institution's financial aid form: April 1. In 2009-2010, 62% of undergraduates applied for financial aid. Of those, 44% were determined to have financial need; 25% had their need fully met. Average financial aid package (proportion receiving): $10,060 (43%). Average amount of gift aid, such as scholarships or grants (proportion receiving): $6,784 (32%). Average amount of self-help aid, such as work study or loans (proportion receiving): $4,367 (33%). Average need-based loan (excluding PLUS or other private loans): $4,016. Among students who received need-based aid, the average percentage of need met: 86%. Among students who received aid based on merit, the average award (and the proportion receiving): $5,325 (8%). The average athletic scholarship (and the proportion receiving): $11,142 (3%). Average amount of debt of borrowers graduating in 2009: $19,128. Proportion who borrowed: 60%.

CAMPUS LIFE AND EXTRACURRICULAR ACTIVITIES

Campus housing available (% using): coed dorms (62%), women's dorms (1%), sorority housing (10%), fraternity housing (11%), apartments for married students (2%), apartment for single students (12%), special housing for disabled students (1%), special housing for international students, cooperative housing (1%). Students who live in college-owned, operated, or affiliated housing: 39%. Average per-year earnings: $3,120. **Clubs and organizations:** Number of student organizations: 526. Activities include: campus ministries, choral groups, concert band, dance, drama/theater, international student organization, jazz band, literary magazine, marching band, music ensembles, musical theater, opera, pep band, radio station, student government, student newspaper, student film society, symphony orchestra, television station. Number of fraternities: 28; sororities: 18. Proportion of men in fraternities: 16%; of women in sororities: 18%. **Sports program (2009-2010):** Member of NCAA I. *Men's intercollegiate varsity sports:* baseball, basketball, cross country, football, golf, gymnastics, tennis, track and field (indoor), track and field (outdoor), wrestling. *Women's intercollegiate varsity sports:* basketball, bowling, cross country, golf, gymnastics, rifle, soccer, softball, swimming, tennis, track and field (indoor), track and field (outdoor), volleyball.

SERVICES AND FACILITIES

Basic services: nonremedial tutoring, women's center, placement service, day care, health service, health insurance, other. **Remedial assistance:** reading, math, writing, study skills. **Counseling services:** minority student, career, military, personal, veteran student, academic, older student, psychological, birth control. **For learning-disabled students:** School does not offer a structured program with separate admission and additional fees. Total undergraduates in learning-disabled program or receiving services: 149. Services include: reading machines, tape recorders, note-taking services, oral tests, readers, extended time for tests, priority registration, priority seating, substitution of courses, texts on tape, typist/scribe, other testing accommodations. **Library:** Number of titles: 3,246,483; number of current serial subscriptions: 39,318. **Information technology resources:** Students are not required to lease or own a computer. Number of campus computers available to all students: 600. School has a wireless network. Approximate number of users that can be accommodated: 20,000. Proportion of college-owned housing units wired for high-speed internet access: 100%. **Campus safety:** Security services offered: 24-hour foot-and-vehicle patrols, late-night transport/escort service, 24-hour emergency telephones, lighted pathways/sidewalks, controlled dormitory access (key, security card, etc).

TRANSFER AND INTERNATIONAL STUDENTS

Transfer students: May apply for admission for the following academic terms: Fall, Spring, Summer. Applicants need a minimum number of credits to apply. For fall 2009: Transfer applications received: 2,136. Transfer applicants offered admission: 1,345. Transfer applicants enrolled: 1,008. **International students:** Number of foreign undergraduates: 569 (3% of student body). Number of countries represented: 79. Minimum TOEFL score required: 523 (paper); 193 (computer). Average TOEFL score: 568 (paper).

University of Nebraska–Omaha

- **Address:** 6001 Dodge Street, Omaha, NE 68182
- **Website:** http://www.unomaha.edu
- **Public**
- **Enrollment:** 9,064 full-time; 2,490 part-time

KEY STATS

✔ **U.S News College Ranking:** 61, Regional Universities (Midwest)
✔ **ACT Score (25th/75th percentile):** 20-26
✔ **Tuition:** 2010-2011: $6,229 in state, $16,189 out of state

Selectivity: Selective	**Room/board:** $7,230
Acceptance rate: 80%	**Average debt:** N/A
Student/faculty ratio: 19/1	**Proportion who borrowed:** N/A

UNDERGRADUATE STUDENT BODY STATS

2009-2010 enrollment: 9,064 full-time; 2,490 part-time. Men: 49%; women: 51%. **Ethnic makeup:** African American: 6%; American-Indian: 1%; Asian American: 3%; Hispanic: 4%; White: 84%; International: 2%.

ADMISSIONS FACTS AND FIGURES

Phone: (402) 554-2393. **Email:** unoadm@unomaha.edu. **Website:** http://www.unomaha.edu. **Application deadlines for fall 2011:** Regular decision: August 1. Early decision: Not offered. Early action: Not offered. Admission cannot be deferred. **Application fee:** $45. **To apply online, go to:** http://www.ses.unomaha.edu/admissions/. **Admissions requirements/recommendations:** High school units required (recommended): English: 4; Mathematics: 3; Science: 3; Foreign language: 2; Social studies: 1; History: 2; Academic electives: 1; Total units: 16. Tests: The college uses SAT or ACT scores in admissions decisions. Either SAT or ACT required. For admission to the fall 2011 entering class, the school will accept: ACT with or without writing accepted. Campus visit: Neither required nor recommended. Admissions interview: Neither required nor recommended. Off-campus interview: Not available. **Factors that count in admissions decisions:** *Academic:* Secondary school record: Very Important. Class rank: Very Important. Letters of recommendation: Not Considered. Standardized test scores: Very Important. Essay: Not Considered. *Nonacademic:* Interview: Not Considered. Extracurricular activities: Not Considered. Talent/ability: Not Considered. Character/personal qualities: Considered. Alumni/ae relationship: Not Considered. Geographical residence: Not Considered. State residency: Not Considered. Religious affiliation/commitment: Not Considered. Minority status: Not Considered. Volunteer work: Not Considered. Work experience: Not Considered. **Other schools with the greatest overlap in applicants:** Creighton University; University of Nebraska–Lincoln. **Admissions statistics for the fall 2009 entering class:** Total applicants: 4,845. Total accepted: 3,896. Freshmen enrolled: 1,816; 8% were from out of state. Overall acceptance rate: 80%. **Credentials of fall 2009 freshmen:** 11% ranked in the top 10 percent of their high school class; 35% were in the top 25 percent; 71% were in the top half. (Proportion submitting class standing: 92%.) **Average high school grade point average:** 3.3. **First-year students submitting ACT scores:** 95%. Scores (25/75 percentile): English: 19-26, Math: 18-25, Composite: 20-26.

ACADEMICS

Year founded: 1908. **Academic calendar:** Semester. **Degrees offered:** certificate, bachelor's, post-bachelor's certificate, master's, post-master's certificate, doctorate. **Most popular majors:** 22% business, management, marketing, and related support services, 13% education, 8% security and protective services, 6% communication, journalism, and related programs, 6% psychology. **Major fields of study:** area, ethnic, cultural, and gender studies; biological and biomedical sciences; business, management, marketing, and related support services; communication, journalism, and related programs; computer and information sciences and support services; education; engineering; English language and literature/letters; foreign languages, literatures, and linguistics; health professions and related clinical sciences; history; liberal arts and sciences studies, and humanities; library science; mathematics and statistics; multi/interdisciplinary studies; natural resources and conservation; parks, recreation, leisure, and fitness studies; philosophy and religious studies; physical sciences; psychology; public administration and social service professions; security and protective services; social sciences; transportation and materials moving; visual and performing arts. **Areas of required coursework:** arts/fine arts, humanities, mathematics, English (including composition), philosophy, sciences (biological or physical), history, social science, other. **Pre-professional programs:** pre-law, pre-dentistry, pre-medicine, pre-veterinary science, pre-optometry, pre-pharmacy, other. **Special academic programs (% participation):** cooperative (work-study plan) program (10%), cross-registration (.5%), distance learning (26%), double major (3%), dual enrollment (2%), English as a Second Language (ESL) (2%), honors program (10%), independent study (14%), internships (23%), student-designed major (.05%), study abroad (9%), teacher certificate program (9%). **Teacher certification offered in:** early childhood, special education, elementary, middle/junior high, secondary, bilingual/bicultural. **Cooperative education programs:** agriculture, engineering, health professions, home economics. **Reserve Officers Training Corps (ROTC):** Army ROTC: Offered at cooperating institution (Creighton University); Air Force ROTC: Offered on campus. **Faculty and instruction (2009-2010):** Total instructional faculty: 483 full-time, 392 part-time (55% men; 45% women; 16% minorities). Full-time faculty with Ph.D. or other terminal degree: 85%. Student/faculty ratio: 19/1. Classes of fewer than 20 students: 32%; of 20 to 49 students: 55%; of 50 or more students: 13%. **Advanced Placement and International Baccalaureate credit:** AP tests may be used for: Credit only. Scores accepted: 3. International Baccalaureate exams may be used for: Placement only. **Freshmen returning for sophomore year:** 72%. **Graduation rates:** Four-year: 13%; five-year: 35%; six-year: 42%. **Graduate study:** 18% of students pursue further study immediately upon graduation.

COSTS AND FINANCIAL AID

Financial aid office: (402) 554-2327. **Expenses (2010-2011):** Tuition and fees 2010-2011: $6,229 in state, $16,189 out of state; room/board: $7,230. Estimated books and supplies: $900; transportation: $1,290; personal expenses: $2,110. **Financial aid:** Priority filing date for institution's financial aid form: March 1. In 2009-2010, 65% of undergraduates applied for financial aid. Of those, 47% were determined to have financial need; Average financial aid package (proportion receiving): $2,458 (45%). Average amount of gift aid, such as scholarships or grants (proportion receiving): $2,075 (31%). Average amount of self-help aid, such as work study or loans (proportion receiving): $3,120 (35%). Average need-based loan (excluding PLUS or other private loans): $3,251. Among students who received aid based on merit, the average award (and the proportion receiving): $2,261 (5%). The average athletic scholarship (and the proportion receiving): $2,981 (0%).

CAMPUS LIFE AND EXTRACURRICULAR ACTIVITIES

Campus housing available (% using): coed dorms (100%). Students who live in college-owned, operated, or affiliated housing: 11%. **Student employment:** During the 2009-2010 academic year, 9% of undergraduates worked on campus. Average per-year earnings: $5,915. **Clubs and organizations:** Number of student organizations: 126. Activities include: campus ministries, choral groups, concert band, dance, drama/theater, international student organization, jazz band, literary magazine, marching band, model UN, music ensembles, musical theater, opera, pep band, radio station, student government, student newspaper, student film society, symphony orchestra, television station. Number of fraternities: 6; sororities: 7. Proportion of men in fraternities: 2%; of women in sororities: 2%. Average proportion of students who stay on campus on weekends: 15%. **Sports program (2009-2010):** Member of NCAA II. *Men's intercollegiate varsity sports:* baseball, basketball, football, ice hockey, tennis, wrestling. *Women's intercollegiate varsity sports:* basketball, cross country, golf, soccer, softball, swimming, tennis, track and field (outdoor), volleyball.

SERVICES AND FACILITIES

Basic services: nonremedial tutoring, women's center, placement service, day care, health service, health insurance. **Counseling services:** minority student, career, personal, academic, older student, psychological, birth control. **For learning-disabled students:** School does not offer a structured program with separate admission and additional fees. Total undergraduates in learning-disabled program or receiving services: 54. **Library:** Number of titles: 1,442,970; number of current serial subscriptions: 63,076. **Information technology resources:** Students are not required to lease or own a computer. Number of campus computers available to all students: 2,200. School has a wireless network. Approximate number of users that can be accommodated: 3,500. Proportion of college-owned housing units wired for high-speed internet access: 100%. **Campus safety:** Security services offered: 24-hour foot-and-vehicle patrols, late-night transport/escort service, 24-hour emergency telephones, lighted pathways/sidewalks, controlled dormitory access (key, security card, etc).

TRANSFER AND INTERNATIONAL STUDENTS

Transfer students: May apply for admission for the following academic terms: Fall, Spring, Summer. Applicants need a minimum number of credits to apply. For fall 2009: Transfer applications received: 2,212. Transfer applicants offered admission: 1,854. Transfer applicants enrolled: 1,297. **International students:** Number of foreign undergraduates: 283 (3% of student body). Number of countries represented: 63. Minimum TOEFL score required: 487 (paper); 163 (computer). Average TOEFL score: 487 (paper).

Wayne State College

- **Address:** 1111 Main Street, Wayne, NE 68787
- **Website:** http://www.wsc.edu
- **Public**
- **Enrollment:** 2,696 full-time; 243 part-time

KEY STATS

✔ **U.S News College Ranking:** 88, Regional Universities (Midwest)
✔ **ACT Score (25th/75th percentile):** 18-24
✔ **Tuition:** 2009-2010: $4,805 in state, $8,480 out of state

Selectivity: Selective	**Room/board:** $5,280
Acceptance rate: 100%	**Average debt:** N/A
Student/faculty ratio: 20/1	**Proportion who borrowed:** N/A

UNDERGRADUATE STUDENT BODY STATS

2009-2010 enrollment: 2,696 full-time; 243 part-time. Men: 46%; women: 54%. **Ethnic makeup:** African American: 3%; American-Indian: 1%; Asian American: 1%; Hispanic: 2%; White: 93%; International: 1%.

ADMISSIONS FACTS AND FIGURES

Phone: (800) 228-9972. **Email:** admit1@wsc.edu. **Website:** http://www.wsc.edu. **Application deadlines for fall 2011:** Regular decision: Rolling. Early decision: Not offered. Early action: Not offered. Admission can be deferred. **Application fee:** $30. **To apply online, go to:** http://www.wsc.edu/admission/. **Admissions requirements/recommendations:** High school units required (recommended): English: (4); Mathematics: (3); Science: (2); Foreign language: (2); Social studies: (3); Total units: (18). Tests: The college uses SAT or ACT scores in admissions decisions. ACT required. For admission to the fall 2011 entering class, the school will accept: ACT with or without writing accepted. Campus visit: Recommended. Admissions interview: Neither required nor recommended. Off-campus interview: May be arranged. **Factors that count in admissions decisions:** *Academic:* Secondary school record: Not Considered. Class rank: Not Considered. Letters of recommendation: Not Considered. Standardized test scores: Not Considered. Essay: Not Considered. *Nonacademic:* Interview: Not Considered. Extracurricular activities: Not Considered. Talent/ability: Not Considered. Character/personal qualities: Not Considered. Alumni/ae relationship: Not Considered. Geographical residence: Not Considered. State residency: Not Considered. Religious affiliation/commitment: Not Considered. Minority status: Not Considered. Volunteer work: Not Considered. Work experience: Not Considered. **Admissions statistics for the fall 2009 entering class:** Total applicants: 2,055. Total accepted: 2,055. Freshmen enrolled: 665; 14% were from out of state. Overall acceptance rate: 100%. **Credentials of fall 2009 freshmen:** 11% ranked in the top 10 percent of their high school class; 30% were in the top 25 percent; 61% were in the top half. (Proportion submitting class standing: 95%.) **Average high school grade point average:** 3.2. **First-year students submitting ACT scores:** 94%. Scores (25/75 percentile): English: 17-24, Math: 17-24, Composite: 18-24.

ACADEMICS

Year founded: 1909. **Academic calendar:** Semester. **Degrees offered:** bachelor's, master's, post-master's certificate. **Most popular majors:** 22% business, management, marketing, and related support services, 22% education, 8% parks, recreation, leisure, and fitness studies, 8% psychology, 6% security and protective services. **Major fields of study:** biological and biomedical sciences; business, management, marketing, and related support services; communication, journalism, and related programs; computer and information sciences and support services; education; engineering technologies/technicians; English language and literature/letters; family and consumer sciences/human sciences; foreign languages, literatures, and linguistics; health professions and related clinical sciences; history; mathematics and statistics; multi/interdisciplinary studies; parks, recreation, leisure, and fitness studies; physical sciences; psychology; security and protective services; social sciences; visual and performing arts. **Areas of required coursework:** arts/fine arts, humanities, mathematics, English (including composition), philosophy, foreign languages, sciences (biological or physical), history, social science, other. **Pre-professional programs:** pre-law, pre-dentistry, pre-medicine, pre-veterinary science, pre-optometry, pre-pharmacy, other. **Special academic programs:** cooperative (work-study plan) program, distance learning, double major, dual enrollment, honors program, independent study, internships, student-designed major, study abroad, teacher certificate program. **Teacher certification offered in:** early childhood, special education, elementary, vo-tech, middle/junior high, secondary, bilingual/bicultural. **Cooperative education programs:** agriculture, art, business, computer science, education, health professions, home economics, humanities, natural science, social/behavioral science, technologies. **Reserve Officers Training Corps (ROTC):** Army ROTC: Offered at cooperating institution (University of South Dakota). **Faculty and instruction (2009-2010):** Total instructional faculty: 122 full-time, 98 part-time (42% men; 58% women; 6% minorities). Full-time faculty with Ph.D. or other terminal degree: 76%. Student/faculty ratio: 20/1. Classes of fewer than 20 students: 42%; of 20 to 49 students: 57%; of 50 or more students: 1%. **Advanced Placement and International Baccalaureate credit:** AP tests may be used for: Credit and/or placement. Scores accepted: 3. **Freshmen returning for sophomore year:** 69%. **Graduation rates:** Four-year: 27%; five-year: 46%; six-year: 49%.

COSTS AND FINANCIAL AID

Financial aid office: (402) 375-7230. **Expenses (2009-2010):** Tuition and fees 2009-2010: $4,805 in state, $8,480 out of state; room/board: $5,280. Estimated books and supplies: $1,000; transportation: $1,365; personal expenses: $900. **Financial aid:** Priority filing date for institution's financial aid form: April 1. In 2009-2010, 84% of undergraduates applied for financial aid. Of those, 67% were determined to have financial need; 36% had their need fully met. Average financial aid package (proportion receiving): $6,771 (67%). Average amount of gift aid, such as scholarships or grants (proportion receiving): $3,797 (49%). Average amount of self-help aid, such as work study or loans (proportion receiving): $3,822 (53%). Average need-based loan (excluding PLUS or other private loans): $3,747. Among students who received need-based aid, the average percentage of need met: 73%. Among students who received aid based on merit, the average award (and the proportion receiving): $2,805 (12%). The average athletic scholarship (and the proportion receiving): $1,875 (4%).

CAMPUS LIFE AND EXTRACURRICULAR ACTIVITIES

Campus housing available (% using): coed dorms (100%). Students who live in college-owned, operated, or affiliated housing: 46%. **Clubs and organizations:** Number of student organizations: 100. Activities include: campus ministries, choral groups, concert band, dance, drama/theater, international student organization, jazz band, literary magazine, marching band, music ensembles, musical theater, pep band, radio station, student government, student newspaper, television station. Number of fraternities: 1; sororities: 2. **Sports program (2009-2010):** Member of NCAA II. *Men's intercollegiate varsity sports:* baseball, basketball, cross country, football, golf, track and field (indoor), track and field (outdoor). *Women's intercollegiate varsity sports:* basketball, cross country, golf, soccer, softball, track and field (indoor), track and field (outdoor), volleyball.

SERVICES AND FACILITIES

Basic services: placement service, health service. **Counseling services:** minority student, career, personal, academic, psychological. **For learning-disabled students:** School does not offer a structured program with separate admission and additional fees. Services include: tape recorders, diagnostic testing service, untimed tests, note-taking services, oral tests, learning center, readers, extended time for tests, tutors, priority registration, priority seating, texts on tape, typist/scribe, exams on tape or computer, other testing accommodations. **Library:** Number of titles: 238,801; number of current serial subscriptions: 445. **Information technology resources:** Students are not required to lease or own a computer. Number of campus computers available to all students: 280. School has a wireless network. Approximate number of users that can be accommodated: 2,500. Proportion of college-owned housing units wired for high-speed internet access: 100%. **Campus safety:** Security services offered: 24-hour emergency telephones, lighted pathways/sidewalks, controlled dormitory access (key, security card, etc).

TRANSFER AND INTERNATIONAL STUDENTS

Transfer students: May apply for admission for the following academic terms: Fall, Spring, Summer. Applicants do not need a minimum number of credits to apply. For fall 2009: Transfer applications received: 399. Transfer applicants offered admission: 399. Transfer applicants enrolled: 242. **International students:** Number of foreign undergraduates: 22 (1% of student body). Number of countries represented: 14. Minimum TOEFL score required: 550 (paper); 213 (computer).

York College

- **Address:** 1125 E. Eighth Street, York, NE 68467
- **Website:** http://www.york.edu
- **Private; Religious affiliation:** Church of Christ
- **Enrollment:** 416 full-time; 14 part-time

KEY STATS

✔ **U.S News College Ranking:** 55, Regional Colleges (Midwest)
✔ **ACT Score (25th/75th percentile):** 18-24
✔ **Tuition:** 2010-2011: $14,998

Selectivity: Selective	**Room/board:** $5,680
Acceptance rate: 60%	**Average debt:** $22,020
Student/faculty ratio: 11/1	**Proportion who borrowed:** 78%

UNDERGRADUATE STUDENT BODY STATS

2009-2010 enrollment: 416 full-time; 14 part-time. Men: 56%; women: 44%. **Ethnic makeup:** African American: 9%; American-Indian: 1%; Asian American: 1%; Hispanic: 5%; White: 82%; International: 2%. **Religious**

preference: Roman Catholic: 10%; Protestant: 25%; No preference: 1%; Unknown: 14%; Church of Christ: 50%.

ADMISSIONS FACTS AND FIGURES

Phone: (800) 950-9675. **Email:** enroll@york.edu. **Website:** http://www.york.edu. **Application deadlines for fall 2011:** Regular decision: August 31. Early decision: Not offered. Early action: Not offered. Admission can be deferred. **Application fee:** $20. **To apply online, go to:** http://www.york.edu/admissions/apply.asp. **Admissions requirements/recommendations:** High school units required (recommended): English: 3 (4); Mathematics: 2 (4); Science: 2 (4); Foreign language: (3); Social studies: 1 (4); History: 1 (4); Total units: 15 (21). Tests: The college uses SAT or ACT scores in admissions decisions. Either SAT or ACT required. For admission to the fall 2011 entering class, the school will accept: ACT with or without writing accepted. Campus visit: Recommended. Admissions interview: Neither required nor recommended. Off-campus interview: Not available. **Factors that count in admissions decisions:** *Academic:* Secondary school record: Very Important. Class rank: Very Important. Letters of recommendation: Very Important. Standardized test scores: Very Important. Essay: Considered. *Nonacademic:* Interview: Considered. Extracurricular activities: Not Considered. Talent/ability: Not Considered. Character/personal qualities: Considered. Alumni/ae relationship: Not Considered. Geographical residence: Not Considered. State residency: Not Considered. Religious affiliation/commitment: Not Considered. Minority status: Not Considered. Volunteer work: Considered. Work experience: Considered. **Other schools with the greatest overlap in applicants:** Abilene Christian University; Harding University; Oklahoma Christian University; University of Nebraska–Kearney; University of Nebraska–Lincoln. **Admissions statistics for the fall 2009 entering class:** Total applicants: 485. Total accepted: 291. Freshmen enrolled: 117; 75% were from out of state. Overall acceptance rate: 60%. **Credentials of fall 2009 freshmen:** 9% ranked in the top 10 percent of their high school class; 24% were in the top 25 percent; 47% were in the top half. (Proportion submitting class standing: 90%.) **Average high school grade point average:** 3.0. **First-year students who submitted SAT scores:** 7%. Scores (25/75 percentile): Critical Reading: 330-470, Math: 330-460, Combined: 660-930. **First-year students submitting ACT scores:** 87%. Scores (25/75 percentile): English: 17-24, Math: 17-23, Composite: 18-24.

ACADEMICS

Year founded: 1890. **Academic calendar:** Semester. **Degrees offered:** associate, bachelor's. **Most popular majors:** 33% education, 30% business, management, marketing, and related support services, 20% psychology, 8% biological and biomedical sciences, 5% history. **Major fields of study:** biological and biomedical sciences; business, management, marketing, and related support services; education; English language and literature/letters; history; liberal arts and sciences studies, and humanities; psychology; theology and religious vocations; visual and performing arts. **Areas of required coursework:** arts/fine arts, humanities, mathematics, English (including composition), philosophy, sciences (biological or physical), history, social science, other. **Pre-professional programs:** pre-law, pre-dentistry, pre-medicine, pre-veterinary science, pre-optometry, pre-pharmacy, other. **Special academic programs (% participation):** double major (2%), dual enrollment (1%), student-designed major (4%). **Teacher certification offered in:** early childhood, special education, elementary, middle/junior high, secondary. **Reserve Officers Training Corps (ROTC):** Army ROTC: Offered at cooperating institution (University of Nebraska–Lincoln); Navy ROTC: Offered at cooperating institution (University of Nebraska–Lincoln); Air Force ROTC: Offered at cooperating institution (University of Nebraska–Lincoln). **Faculty and instruction (2009-2010):** Total instructional faculty: 22 full-time, 16 part-time (61% men; 39% women; 5% minorities). Full-time faculty with Ph.D. or other terminal degree: 68%. Student/faculty ratio: 11/1. Classes of fewer than 20 students: 82%; of 20 to 49 students: 18%; of 50 or more students: 1%. **Advanced Placement and International Baccalaureate credit:** AP tests may be used for: Credit only. Scores accepted: 3. International Baccalaureate exams may be used for: Credit only. **Freshmen returning for sophomore year:** 72%. **Graduation rates:** Four-year: 18%; five-year: 30%; six-year: 41%. **Graduate study:** 9% of students pursue further study immediately upon graduation; 3% within one year; 15% within five years. Fields in which graduates pursue further study: Master of Business Administration (MBA), 3%; medicine, 9%; education, 15%; arts and sciences, 6%.

COSTS AND FINANCIAL AID

Financial aid office: (402) 363-5624. **Expenses (2010-2011):** Tuition and fees 2010-2011: $14,998; room/board: $5,680. Estimated books and supplies: $1,500; transportation: $800; personal expenses: $2,000. **Financial aid:** Priority filing date for institution's financial aid form: May 31. In 2009-2010, 94% of undergraduates applied for financial aid. Of those, 85% were determined to have financial need; 17% had their need fully met. Average financial aid package (proportion receiving): $13,265 (85%). Average amount of gift aid, such as scholarships or grants (proportion receiving): $9,266 (83%). Average amount of self-help aid, such as work study or loans (proportion receiving): $5,127 (67%). Average need-based loan (excluding PLUS or other private loans): $4,352. Among students who received need-based aid, the average percentage of need met: 77%. Among students who received aid based on merit, the average award (and the proportion receiving): $4,207 (7%). The average athletic scholarship (and the proportion receiving): $6,086 (8%). Average amount of debt of borrowers graduating in 2009: $22,020. Proportion who borrowed: 78%.

CAMPUS LIFE AND EXTRACURRICULAR ACTIVITIES

Campus housing available (% using): women's dorms (35%), men's dorms (21%), apartments for married students (4%), apartment for single students (40%). Students who live in college-owned, operated, or affiliated housing: 80%. **Student employment:** During the 2009-2010 academic year, 0% of undergraduates worked on campus. Average per-year earnings: $0. **Clubs and organizations:** Number of student organizations: 23. Activities include: campus ministries, choral groups, drama/theater, music ensembles, student government, student newspaper, yearbook. Number of fraternities: 4; sororities: 4. Proportion of men in fraternities: 60%; of women in sororities: 72%. Average proportion of students who stay on campus on weekends: 85%. **Sports program (2009-2010):** Member of NAIA. *Men's intercollegiate varsity sports:* baseball, basketball, cross country, soccer, track and field (indoor), track and field (outdoor), wrestling. *Women's intercollegiate varsity sports:* basketball, cross country, soccer, softball, track and field (indoor), track and field (outdoor), volleyball.

SERVICES AND FACILITIES

Basic services: nonremedial tutoring, placement service. **Remedial assistance:** reading, math, writing, study skills. **Counseling services:** career, personal, veteran student, academic, psychological, religious. **For learning-disabled students:** School does not offer a structured program with separate admission and additional fees. Total undergraduates in learning-disabled program or receiving services: 39. Services include: remedial math, remedial English, remedial reading, tape recorders, diagnostic testing service, untimed tests, note-taking services, oral tests, learning center, readers, extended time for tests, tutors, priority seating, texts on tape, other testing accommodations. **Library:** Number of titles: 134,708; number of current serial subscriptions: 292. **Information technology resources:** Students are not required to lease or own a computer. Number of campus computers available to all students: 57. School has a wireless network. Approximate number of users that can be accommodated: 300. Proportion of college-owned housing units wired for high-speed internet access: 100%. **Campus safety:** Security services offered: lighted pathways/sidewalks, student patrols, controlled dormitory access (key, security card, etc).

TRANSFER AND INTERNATIONAL STUDENTS

Transfer students: May apply for admission for the following academic terms: Fall, Spring, Summer. Applicants do not need a minimum number of credits to apply. For fall 2009: Transfer applications received: 170. Transfer applicants offered admission: 129. Transfer applicants enrolled: 63. **International students:** Number of foreign undergraduates: 7 (2% of student body). Number of countries represented: 4. Minimum TOEFL score required: 500 (paper); 173 (computer).

Nevada

Great Basin College

- **Address:** 1500 College Parkway, Elko, NV 89801
- **Website:** http://www.gbcnv.edu
- **Public**
- **Enrollment:** N/A

. . . .

KEY STATS

- ✔ **U.S News College Ranking:** Unranked, Regional Colleges (West)
- ✔ **SAT or ACT Score (25th/75th percentile):** N/A
- ✔ **Tuition:** 2009-2010: $2,010 in state, $8,198 out of state

Selectivity: N/A	Room/board: $4,790
Acceptance rate: N/A	Average debt: N/A
Student/faculty ratio: N/A	Proportion who borrowed: N/A

Sierra Nevada College

- **Address:** 999 Tahoe Boulevard, Incline Village, NV 89451
- **Website:** http://www.sierranevada.edu
- **Private**
- **Enrollment:** 368 full-time; 10 part-time

. . . .

KEY STATS

- ✔ **U.S News College Ranking:** second tier, National Liberal Arts Colleges
- ✔ **SAT or ACT Score (25th/75th percentile):** N/A
- ✔ **Tuition:** 2010-2011: $24,515

Selectivity: Selective	Room/board: $9,750
Acceptance rate: 93%	Average debt: $16,500
Student/faculty ratio: 8/1	Proportion who borrowed: 75%

UNDERGRADUATE STUDENT BODY STATS

2009-2010 enrollment: 368 full-time; 10 part-time. Men: 58%; women: 42%. **Ethnic makeup:** African American: 2%; American-Indian: 4%; Asian American: 2%; Hispanic: 6%; White: 84%; International: 3%.

ADMISSIONS FACTS AND FIGURES

Phone: (800) 332-8666. **Email:** admissions@sierranevada.edu. **Website:** http://www.sierranevada.edu. **Application deadlines for fall 2011:** Regular decision: Rolling. Early decision: Not offered. Early action: Not offered. Admission can be deferred. **To apply online, go to:** https://www.applyweb.com/apply/sierra/menu.html. **Admissions requirements/recommendations:** High school units required (recommended): English: (4); Mathematics: (3); Science: (2); Foreign language: (2); Social studies: (2); History: (2). Tests: The college uses SAT or ACT scores in admissions decisions. Neither SAT nor ACT required. For admission to the fall 2011 entering class, the school will accept: ACT with or without writing accepted. Campus visit: Recommended. Admissions interview: Recommended. Off-campus interview: May be arranged. **Factors that count in admissions decisions:** *Academic:* Secondary school record: Important. Class rank: Considered. Letters of recommendation: Important. Standardized test scores: Considered. Essay: Important. *Nonacademic:* Interview: Considered. Extracurricular activities: Considered. Talent/ability: Considered. Character/personal qualities: Considered. Alumni/ae relationship: Considered. Geographical residence: Not Considered. State residency: Not Considered. Religious affiliation/commitment: Considered. Minority status: Considered. Volunteer work: Considered. Work experience: Considered. **Other schools with the greatest overlap in applicants:** Evergreen State College; Prescott College; Sonoma State University; University of Nevada–Reno; Westminster College. **Admissions statistics for the fall 2009 entering class:** Total applicants: 298. Total accepted: 277. Freshmen enrolled: 88; 0% were from out of state. Overall acceptance rate: 93%. **Size of waiting list:** 0 applicants; enrolled from waiting list: 0.

ACADEMICS

Year founded: 1969. **Academic calendar:** Semester. **Degrees offered:** bachelor's, post-bachelor's certificate, master's. **Most popular majors:** 56% business administration and management, 16% humanities/humanistic studies, 14% fine/studio arts, 12% environmental science. **Major fields of study:** biological and biomedical sciences; business, management, marketing, and related support services; computer and information sciences and support services; education; English language and literature/letters; liberal arts and sciences studies, and humanities; psychology; visual and performing arts. **Areas of required coursework:** arts/fine arts, humanities, computer literacy, mathematics, English (including composition), philosophy, foreign languages, sciences (biological or physical), history, social science, other. **Pre-professional programs:** pre-medicine. **Special academic programs (% participation):** double major (5%), honors program (15%), independent study, internships (38%), study abroad (22%). **Teacher certification offered in:** special education, elementary, secondary. **Reserve Officers Training Corps (ROTC):** Army ROTC: Offered at cooperating institution. **Faculty and instruction (2009-2010):** Total instructional faculty: N/A. Student/faculty ratio: 8/1. **Advanced Placement and International Baccalaureate credit:** AP tests may be used for: Credit only. Scores accepted: 3, 4, 5. International Baccalaureate exams may be used for: Credit only. **Freshmen returning for sophomore year:** 66%. **Graduation rates:** Four-year: 23%; five-year: 32%; six-year: 38%.

COSTS AND FINANCIAL AID

Financial aid office: (775) 831-1314. **Expenses (2010-2011):** Tuition and fees 2010-2011: $24,515; room/board: $9,750. Estimated books and supplies: $1,454; transportation: $838; personal expenses: $2,958. **Financial aid:** Priority filing date for institution's financial aid form: April 1; deadline: August 20. In 2009-2010, 75% of undergraduates applied for financial aid. Of those, 68% were determined to have financial need; 39% had their need fully met. Average financial aid package (proportion receiving): $19,500 (68%). Average amount of gift aid, such as scholarships or grants (proportion receiving): $16,500 (68%). Average amount of self-help aid, such as work study or loans (proportion receiving): $6,500 (68%). Average need-based loan (excluding PLUS or other private loans): $4,500. Among students who received need-based aid, the average percentage of need met: 60%. Among students who received aid based on merit, the average award (and the proportion receiving): $8,000 (7%). The average athletic scholarship (and the proportion receiving): $8,866 (6%). Average amount of debt of borrowers graduating in 2009: $16,500. Proportion who borrowed: 75%.

CAMPUS LIFE AND EXTRACURRICULAR ACTIVITIES

Campus housing available (% using): coed dorms (100%). Students who live in college-owned, operated, or affiliated housing: 46%. **Student employment:** During the 2009-2010 academic year, 70% of undergraduates worked on campus. Average per-year earnings: $2,000. **Clubs and organizations:** Number of student organizations: 25. Activities include: choral groups, dance, drama/theater, international student organization, literary magazine, music ensembles, student government, student newspaper. Number of fraternities: 0; sororities: 0. Average proportion of students who stay on campus on weekends: 80%.

SERVICES AND FACILITIES

Basic services: nonremedial tutoring, health insurance. **Remedial assistance:** math, writing, study skills. **Counseling services:** minority student, career, personal, academic, psychological. **For learning-disabled students:** School does not offer a structured program with separate admission and additional fees. Services include: remedial math, remedial English, remedial reading, tape recorders, videotaped classes, diagnostic testing service, untimed tests, note-taking services, oral tests, learning center, readers, extended time for tests, tutors, priority seating, texts on tape, other testing accommodations. **Library:** Number of titles: 24,750; number of current serial subscriptions: 150. **Information technology resources:** Students are required to lease or own a computer. Number of campus computers available to all students: 50. School has a wireless network. Proportion of college-owned housing units wired for high-speed internet access: 100%. **Campus safety:** Security services offered: late-night transport/escort service, lighted pathways/sidewalks, student patrols, controlled dormitory access (key, security card, etc).

TRANSFER AND INTERNATIONAL STUDENTS

Transfer students: May apply for admission for the following academic terms: Fall, Spring, Summer. Applicants need a minimum number of credits to apply. For fall 2009: Transfer applications received: 133. Transfer applicants offered admission: 131. Transfer applicants enrolled: 70. **International students:** Number of foreign undergraduates: 11 (3% of student body). Minimum TOEFL score required: 550 (paper); 172 (computer).

University of Nevada–Las Vegas

- **Address:** 4505 Maryland Parkway, Las Vegas, NV 89154
- **Website:** http://www.unlv.edu
- **Public**
- **Enrollment:** 16,391 full-time; 6,317 part-time

KEY STATS

✔ **U.S News College Ranking:** second tier, National Universities
✔ **SAT Score (25th/75th percentile):** 890-1140
✔ **Tuition:** 2010-2011: $5,465 in state, $18,755 out of state
    Selectivity: Selective   **Room/board:** $10,456
    Acceptance rate: 78%   **Average debt:** $17,256
    Student/faculty ratio: 21/1   **Proportion who borrowed:** 37%

UNDERGRADUATE STUDENT BODY STATS

2009-2010 enrollment: 16,391 full-time; 6,317 part-time. Men: 45%; women: 55%. **Ethnic makeup:** African American: 8%; American-Indian: 1%; Asian American: 18%; Hispanic: 17%; White: 53%; International: 3%.

ADMISSIONS FACTS AND FIGURES

Phone: (702) 774-8658. **Email:** undergraduate.recruitment@unlv.edu. **Website:** http://www.unlv.edu. **Application deadlines for fall 2011:** Regular decision: Rolling. Early decision: Not offered. Early action: Not offered. Admission can be deferred. **Application fee:** $60. **To apply online, go to:** http://www.unlv.edu/admissions/apply.html. **Admissions requirements/recommendations:** High school units required (recommended): English: 4; Mathematics: 3; Science: 3; Social studies: 3; Total units: 13. Tests: The college uses SAT or ACT scores in admissions decisions. Neither SAT nor ACT required. For admission to the fall 2011 entering class, the school will accept: ACT with or without writing accepted. Campus visit: Recommended. Admissions interview: Neither required nor recommended. Off-campus interview: Not available. **Factors that count in admissions decisions: Academic:** Secondary school record: Very Important. Class rank: Not Considered. Letters of recommendation: Considered. Standardized test scores: Very Important. Essay: Considered. **Nonacademic:** Interview: Not Considered. Extracurricular activities: Not Considered. Talent/ability: Not Considered. Character/personal qualities: Not Considered. Alumni/ae relationship: Not Considered. Geographical residence: Not Considered. State residency: Not Considered. Religious affiliation/commitment: Not Considered. Minority status: Not Considered. Volunteer work: Not Considered. Work experience: Not Considered. **Other schools with the greatest overlap in applicants:** Arizona State University; San Diego State University; University of California–Los Angeles; University of Nevada–Reno; University of Southern California. **Admissions statistics for the fall 2009 entering class:** Total applicants: 7,800. Total accepted: 6,057. Freshmen enrolled: 3,236; 16% were from out of state. Overall acceptance rate: 78%. **Credentials of fall 2009 freshmen:** 22% ranked in the top 10 percent of their high school class; 54% were in the top 25 percent; 86% were in the top half. (Proportion submitting class standing: 80%.) **Average high school grade point average:** 3.3. **First-year students who submitted SAT scores:** 75%. Scores (25/75 percentile): Critical Reading: 440-560, Math: 450-580, Combined: 890-1140. **First-year students submitting ACT scores:** 36%. Scores (25/75 percentile): English: 18-24, Math: 18-25, Composite: 19-24.

ACADEMICS

Year founded: 1957. **Academic calendar:** Semester. **Degrees offered:** certificate, bachelor's, post-bachelor's certificate, master's, post-master's certificate, doctorate. **Most popular majors:** 31% business, management, marketing, and related support services, 9% education, 7% psychology, 6% health professions and related clinical sciences, 6% social sciences. **Major**

fields of study: architecture and related services; area, ethnic, cultural, and gender studies; biological and biomedical sciences; business, management, marketing, and related support services; communication, journalism, and related programs; computer and information sciences and support services; education; engineering; engineering technologies/technicians; English language and literature/letters; foreign languages, literatures, and linguistics; health professions and related clinical sciences; history; legal professions and studies; liberal arts and sciences studies, and humanities; mathematics and statistics; multi/interdisciplinary studies; natural resources and conservation; parks, recreation, leisure, and fitness studies; personal and culinary services; philosophy and religious studies; physical sciences; psychology; public administration and social service professions; security and protective services; social sciences; visual and performing arts. **Areas of required coursework:** arts/fine arts, humanities, computer literacy, mathematics, English (including composition), philosophy, sciences (biological or physical), history, social science. **Pre-professional programs:** pre-law, pre-dentistry, pre-medicine, pre-theology, pre-veterinary science, pre-optometry, pre-pharmacy, other. **Special academic programs:** accelerated program, cooperative (work-study plan) program, cross-registration, distance learning, double major, dual enrollment, English as a Second Language (ESL), exchange student program (domestic), honors program, independent study, internships, student-designed major, study abroad, teacher certificate program. **Teacher certification offered in:** early childhood, special education, elementary, vo-tech, adult education, secondary. **Cooperative education programs:** business, education, engineering, health professions, natural science, social/behavioral science, other. **Reserve Officers Training Corps (ROTC):** Army ROTC: Offered on campus; Air Force ROTC: Offered on campus. **Faculty and instruction (2009-2010):** Total instructional faculty: 897 full-time, 490 part-time. Full-time faculty with Ph.D. or other terminal degree: 88%. Student/faculty ratio: 21/1. Classes of fewer than 20 students: 28%; of 20 to 49 students: 56%; of 50 or more students: 16%. **Advanced Placement and International Baccalaureate credit:** AP tests may be used for: Credit and/or placement. Scores accepted: 3, 4, 5. International Baccalaureate exams may be used for: Placement only. **Freshmen returning for sophomore year:** 74%. **Graduation rates:** Four-year: 12%; five-year: 30%; six-year: 39%. **Graduate study:** 24% of students pursue further study immediately upon graduation.

COSTS AND FINANCIAL AID

Financial aid office: (702) 895-3424. **Expenses (2010-2011):** Tuition and fees 2010-2011: $5,465 in state, $18,755 out of state; room/board: $10,456. Estimated books and supplies: $1,000; transportation: $770; personal expenses: $1,800. **Financial aid:** Priority filing date for institution's financial aid form: February 1. In 2009-2010, 59% of undergraduates applied for financial aid. Of those, 49% were determined to have financial need; 17% had their need fully met. Average financial aid package (proportion receiving): $9,706 (48%). Average amount of gift aid, such as scholarships or grants (proportion receiving): $5,123 (32%). Average amount of self-help aid, such as work study or loans (proportion receiving): $4,480 (43%). Average need-based loan (excluding PLUS or other private loans): $4,146. Among students who received need-based aid, the average percentage of need met: 56%. Among students who received aid based on merit, the average award (and the proportion receiving): $3,194 (2%). The average athletic scholarship (and the proportion receiving): $17,110 (2%). Average amount of debt of borrowers graduating in 2009: $17,256. Proportion who borrowed: 37%.

CAMPUS LIFE AND EXTRACURRICULAR ACTIVITIES

Campus housing available: coed dorms, special housing for disabled students, special housing for international students, other housing options. Students who live in college-owned, operated, or affiliated housing: 5%. **Student employment:** During the 2009-2010 academic year, 15% of undergraduates worked on campus. Average per-year earnings: $4,000. **Clubs and organizations:** Number of student organizations: 180. Activities include: campus ministries, choral groups, concert band, dance, drama/theater, international student organization, jazz band, literary magazine, marching band, music ensembles, musical theater, opera, pep band, radio station, student government, student newspaper, student film society, symphony orchestra, television station, yearbook. Number of fraternities: 18; sororities: 9. Proportion of men in fraternities: 5%; of women in sororities: 3%. Average proportion of students who stay on campus on weekends: 10%. **Sports program (2009-2010):** Member of NCAA I. *Men's intercollegiate varsity sports:* baseball, basketball, football, golf, soccer, swimming, tennis. *Women's intercollegiate varsity sports:* basketball, cross country, equestrian, golf, soccer, softball, swimming, tennis, track and field (indoor), track and field (outdoor), volleyball.

SERVICES AND FACILITIES

Basic services: nonremedial tutoring, women's center, placement service, day care, health service, health insurance. **Remedial assistance:** reading, math, writing, study skills. **Counseling services:** minority student, career, personal, veteran student, academic, older student, psychological, birth control, religious. **For learning-disabled students:** School does not offer a structured program with separate admission and additional fees. Total undergraduates in learning-disabled program or receiving services: 159. Services include: reading machines, tape recorders, diagnostic testing service, note-taking services, oral tests, learning center, readers, extended time for tests, tutors, priority registration, priority seating, substitution of courses, texts on tape, other testing accommodations, other. **Library:** Number of titles: 1,511,496; number of current serial subscriptions: 31,847. **Information technology resources:** Students are not required to lease or own a computer. Number of campus computers available to all students: 2,300. School has a wireless network. Approximate number of users that can be accommodated: 10,000. Proportion of college-owned housing units wired for high-speed internet access: 100%. **Campus safety:** Security services offered: 24-hour foot-and-vehicle patrols, late-night transport/escort service, 24-hour emergency telephones, lighted pathways/sidewalks, controlled dormitory access (key, security card, etc).

TRANSFER AND INTERNATIONAL STUDENTS

Transfer students: May apply for admission for the following academic terms: Fall, Spring, Summer. Applicants need a minimum number of credits to apply. For fall 2009: Transfer applications received: 5,094. Transfer applicants offered admission: 3,554. Transfer applicants enrolled: 2,191. **International students:** Number of foreign undergraduates: 699 (3% of student body). Number of countries represented: 56. Minimum TOEFL score required: 500 (paper); 173 (computer).

University of Nevada–Reno

- **Address:** Reno, NV 89557
- **Website:** http://www.unr.edu
- **Public**
- **Enrollment:** 10,650 full-time; 2,677 part-time

KEY STATS

✔ **U.S News College Ranking:** 191, National Universities
✔ **SAT Score (25th/75th percentile):** 935-1180
✔ **Tuition:** 2010-2011: $5,269 in state, $18,559 out of state

Selectivity: Selective	**Room/board:** $9,765
Acceptance rate: 88%	**Average debt:** $15,854
Student/faculty ratio: 23/1	**Proportion who borrowed:** 36%

UNDERGRADUATE STUDENT BODY STATS

2009-2010 enrollment: 10,650 full-time; 2,677 part-time. Men: 47%; women: 53%. **Ethnic makeup:** African American: 3%; American-Indian: 1%; Asian American: 7%; Hispanic: 10%; White: 77%; International: 2%.

ADMISSIONS FACTS AND FIGURES

Phone: (775) 784-4700. **Email:** asknevada@unr.edu. **Website:** http://www.unr.edu. **Application deadlines for fall 2011:** Regular decision: Rolling. Early decision: Not offered. Early action: Not offered. Admission can be deferred. **Application fee:** $60. **To apply online, go to:** http://www.ss.unr.edu/admissions. **Admissions requirements/recommendations:** High school units required (recommended): English: 4; Mathematics: 3; Science: 3; Foreign language: 0; Social studies: 3; History: 0; Academic electives: 0; Total units: 13. Tests: The college uses SAT or ACT scores in admissions decisions. Neither SAT nor ACT required. For admission to the fall 2011 entering class, the school will accept: ACT with or without writing accepted. Campus visit: Recommended. Admissions interview: Neither required nor recommended. Off-campus interview: Not available. **Factors that count in admissions decisions:** *Academic:* Secondary school record: Very Important. Class rank: Not Considered. Letters of recommendation: Not Considered. Standardized test scores: Considered. Essay: Not Considered. *Nonacademic:* Interview: Not Considered. Extracurricular activities: Not Considered. Talent/ability: Not Considered. Character/personal qualities: Not Considered. Alumni/ae relationship: Not Considered. Geographical residence: Not Considered. State residency: Not Considered. Religious affiliation/commitment: Not Considered. Minority status: Not Considered. Volunteer work: Not Considered. Work experience: Not Considered. **Other**

schools with the greatest overlap in applicants: Arizona State University; San Diego State University; University of Arizona; University of California–Davis; University of Nevada–Las Vegas. **Admissions statistics for the fall 2009 entering class:** Total applicants: 5,045. Total accepted: 4,457. Freshmen enrolled: 2,172; 16% were from out of state. Overall acceptance rate: 88%. **Credentials of fall 2009 freshmen:** 28% ranked in the top 10 percent of their high school class; 57% were in the top 25 percent; 89% were in the top half. (Proportion submitting class standing: 70%.) **Average high school grade point average:** 3.4. **First-year students who submitted SAT scores:** 76%. Scores (25/75 percentile): Critical Reading: 465-580, Math: 470-600, Combined: 935-1180. **First-year students submitting ACT scores:** 54%. Scores (25/75 percentile): English: 19-26, Math: 19-26, Composite: 20-26.

ACADEMICS

Year founded: 1864. **Academic calendar:** Semester. **Degrees offered:** bachelor's, post-bachelor's certificate, master's, post-master's certificate, doctorate. **Most popular majors:** 18% business, management, marketing, and related support services, 11% social sciences, 10% health professions and related clinical sciences, 8% biological and biomedical sciences, 8% engineering. **Major fields of study:** agriculture, agriculture operations, and related sciences; area, ethnic, cultural, and gender studies; biological and biomedical sciences; business, management, marketing, and related support services; communication, journalism, and related programs; computer and information sciences and support services; education; engineering; engineering technologies/technicians; English language and literature/letters; family and consumer sciences/human sciences; foreign languages, literatures, and linguistics; health professions and related clinical sciences; history; liberal arts and sciences studies, and humanities; mathematics and statistics; natural resources and conservation; philosophy and religious studies; physical sciences; psychology; public administration and social service professions; social sciences; visual and performing arts. **Areas of required coursework:** arts/fine arts, humanities, mathematics, English (including composition), sciences (biological or physical), social science, other. **Pre-professional programs:** pre-law, pre-veterinary science, other. **Special academic programs (% participation):** distance learning, double major (5%), dual enrollment, English as a Second Language (ESL) (1%), honors program (5%), independent study (22%), internships (15%), study abroad (11%), teacher certificate program (8%). **Teacher certification offered in:** early childhood, special education, elementary, middle/junior high, secondary, bilingual/bicultural. **Cooperative education programs:** agriculture, business, education, health professions, home economics, natural science, social/behavioral science. **Reserve Officers Training Corps (ROTC):** Army ROTC: Offered on campus. **Faculty and instruction (2009-2010):** Total instructional faculty: 585 full-time, 19 part-time (62% men; 38% women; 17% minorities). Full-time faculty with Ph.D. or other terminal degree: 94%. Student/faculty ratio: 23/1. Classes of fewer than 20 students: 38%; of 20 to 49 students: 47%; of 50 or more students: 15%. **Advanced Placement and International Baccalaureate credit:** AP tests may be used for: Credit and/or placement. Scores accepted: 4, 5. International Baccalaureate exams may be used for: Credit and/or placement. **Freshmen returning for sophomore year:** 78%. **Graduation rates:** Four-year: 13%; five-year: 38%; six-year: 47%. **Graduate study:** 34% of students pursue further study immediately upon graduation; 27% within one year. Fields in which graduates pursue further study: Master of Business Administration (MBA), 10%; law, 7%; medicine, 4%; dentistry, 3%; engineering, 7%; theology (or the seminary), 1%; education, 19%; arts and sciences, 24%; veterinary medicine, 2%.

COSTS AND FINANCIAL AID

Financial aid office: (775) 784-4666. **Expenses (2010-2011):** Tuition and fees 2010-2011: $5,269 in state, $18,559 out of state; room/board: $9,765. Estimated books and supplies: $1,300; transportation: $1,600; personal expenses: $2,578. **Financial aid:** Priority filing date for institution's financial aid form: March 1. In 2009-2010, 55% of undergraduates applied for financial aid. Of those, 41% were determined to have financial need; 14% had their need fully met. Average financial aid package (proportion receiving): $7,598 (40%). Average amount of gift aid, such as scholarships or grants (proportion receiving): $6,034 (34%). Average amount of self-help aid, such as work study or loans (proportion receiving): $4,407 (27%). Average need-based loan (excluding PLUS or other private loans): $4,310. Among students who received need-based aid, the average percentage of need met: 59%. Among students who received aid based on merit, the average award (and the proportion receiving): $2,880 (38%). The average athletic scholarship (and the proportion receiving): $13,473 (3%). Average amount of debt of borrowers graduating in 2009: $15,854. Proportion who borrowed: 36%.

CAMPUS LIFE AND EXTRACURRICULAR ACTIVITIES

Campus housing available (% using): coed dorms (63%), men's dorms (4%), apartments for married students (2%), apartment for single students (13%). Students who live in college-owned, operated, or affiliated housing: 14%. **Student employment:** During the 2009-2010 academic year, 20% of undergraduates worked on campus. Average per-year earnings: $5,310.
Clubs and organizations: Number of student organizations: 240. Activities include: choral groups, concert band, dance, drama/theater, jazz band, literary magazine, marching band, music ensembles, musical theater, pep band, radio station, student government, student newspaper, yearbook. Number of fraternities: 10; sororities: 8. Proportion of men in fraternities: 7%; of women in sororities: 7%. Average proportion of students who stay on campus on weekends: 90%. **Sports program (2009-2010):** Member of NCAA I.
Men's intercollegiate varsity sports: baseball, basketball, football, golf, skiing (nordic), rifle, skiing (alpine), tennis. *Women's intercollegiate varsity sports:* basketball, cross country, golf, skiing (nordic), rifle, skiing (alpine), soccer, softball, swimming, tennis, track and field (outdoor), volleyball.

SERVICES AND FACILITIES

Basic services: day care, health service, health insurance. **Remedial assistance:** reading, math, writing, study skills. **Counseling services:** minority student, career, military, personal, veteran student, academic, older student, psychological, birth control, religious. **For learning-disabled students:** School does not offer a structured program with separate admission and additional fees. Total undergraduates in learning-disabled program or receiving services: 402. Services include: remedial math, remedial English, reading machines, tape recorders, other special classes, diagnostic testing service, note-taking services, oral tests, readers, extended time for tests, tutors, early syllabus, priority seating, substitution of courses, texts on tape, typist/scribe, exams on tape or computer, other testing accommodations, waiver of foreign language degree requirement. **Library:** Number of titles: 1,188,319; number of current serial subscriptions: 34,244. **Information technology resources:** Students are not required to lease or own a computer. Number of campus computers available to all students: 400. School has a wireless network. Approximate number of users that can be accommodated: 1,024. Proportion of college-owned housing units wired for high-speed internet access: 100%. **Campus safety:** Security services offered: 24-hour foot-and-vehicle patrols, late-night transport/escort service, 24-hour emergency telephones, lighted pathways/sidewalks, controlled dormitory access (key, security card, etc).

TRANSFER AND INTERNATIONAL STUDENTS

Transfer students: May apply for admission for the following academic terms: Fall, Spring, Summer. Applicants need a minimum number of credits to apply. For fall 2009: Transfer applications received: 2,046. Transfer applicants offered admission: 1,701. Transfer applicants enrolled: 1,023.
International students: Number of foreign undergraduates: 223 (2% of student body). Number of countries represented: 41. Minimum TOEFL score required: 500 (paper); 173 (computer). Average TOEFL score: 563 (paper).

New Hampshire

Chester College of New England

- **Address:** 40 Chester Street, Chester, NH 03036
- **Website:** http://www.chestercollege.edu
- **Private**
- **Enrollment:** N/A

....

KEY STATS
- ✔ **U.S News College Ranking:** Unranked Specialty School–Fine Arts
- ✔ **SAT or ACT Score (25th/75th percentile):** N/A
- ✔ **Tuition:** 2009-2010: $17,600

Selectivity: N/A	**Room/board:** $8,211
Acceptance rate: N/A	**Average debt:** N/A
Student/faculty ratio: N/A	**Proportion who borrowed:** N/A

Colby-Sawyer College

- **Address:** 541 Main Street, New London, NH 03257-7818
- **Website:** http://www.colby-sawyer.edu
- **Private**
- **Enrollment:** N/A

KEY STATS
- ✔ **U.S News College Ranking:** 25, Regional Colleges (North)
- ✔ **SAT or ACT Score (25th/75th percentile):** N/A
- ✔ **Tuition:** 2009-2010: $31,090

Selectivity: Less selective	**Room/board:** $10,860
Acceptance rate: N/A	**Average debt:** N/A
Student/faculty ratio: N/A	**Proportion who borrowed:** N/A

Daniel Webster College

- **Address:** 20 University Drive, Nashua, NH 03063
- **Website:** http://www.dwc.edu
- **Private**
- **Enrollment:** N/A

....

KEY STATS
- ✔ **U.S News College Ranking:** second tier, Regional Colleges (North)
- ✔ **SAT or ACT Score (25th/75th percentile):** N/A
- ✔ **Tuition:** 2009-2010: $28,615

Selectivity: Less selective	**Room/board:** $9,700
Acceptance rate: N/A	**Average debt:** N/A
Student/faculty ratio: N/A	**Proportion who borrowed:** N/A

Dartmouth College

- **Address:** 6016 McNutt Hall, Hanover, NH 03755
- **Website:** http://www.dartmouth.edu
- **Private**
- **Enrollment:** 4,145 full-time; 51 part-time

....

KEY STATS
- ✔ **U.S News College Ranking:** 9, National Universities
- ✔ **SAT Score (25th/75th percentile):** 1340-1550
- ✔ **Tuition:** 2010-2011: $40,437

Selectivity: Most selective	**Room/board:** $11,838
Acceptance rate: 13%	**Average debt:** $19,081
Student/faculty ratio: 8/1	**Proportion who borrowed:** 48%

UNDERGRADUATE STUDENT BODY STATS
2009-2010 enrollment: 4,145 full-time; 51 part-time. Men: 51%; women: 49%. **Ethnic makeup:** African American: 8%; American-Indian: 4%; Asian American: 15%; Hispanic: 7%; White: 59%; International: 7%.

ADMISSIONS FACTS AND FIGURES
Phone: (603) 646-2875. **Email:** admissions.office@dartmouth.edu. **Website:** http://www.dartmouth.edu. **Application deadlines for fall 2011:** Regular decision: January 1; decision sent by April 10. Early decision: Send application by: November 1; Decision sent by: December 15. Early action: Not offered. Admission can be deferred. **Application fee:** $70. **To apply online, go to:** http://www.apply.embark.com/ugrad/dartmouth. **Admissions requirements/recommendations:** High school units required (recommended): English: 4 (4); Mathematics: 4 (4); Science: 3 (3); Social studies: 3 (3); History: 3 (3); Total units: 17 (17). Tests: The college uses SAT or ACT scores in admissions decisions. Either SAT or ACT required. For admission to the fall 2011 entering class, the school will accept: ACT with writing required. Campus visit: Neither required nor recommended. Admissions interview: Neither required nor recommended. Off-campus interview: Not available. **Factors that count in admissions decisions:** *Academic:* Secondary school record: Very Important. Class rank: Very Important. Letters of recommendation: Very Important. Standardized test scores: Very Important. Essay: Very Important. *Nonacademic:* Interview: Considered. Extracurricular activities: Very Important. Talent/ability: Important. Character/personal qualities: Very Important. Alumni/ae relationship: Considered. Geographical residence: Considered. State residency: Not Considered. Religious affiliation/commitment: Not Considered. Minority status: Considered. Volunteer work: Important. Work experience: Considered. **Other schools with the greatest overlap in applicants:** Brown University; Harvard University; Princeton University; Stanford University; Yale University. **Admissions statistics for the fall 2009 entering class:** Total applicants: 18,132. Total accepted: 2,279. Freshmen enrolled: 1,094; 98% were from out of state. Accepted through early-decision or early-action plans: 36%. Overall acceptance rate: 13%. Early-decision acceptance rate: 26%. Non-early acceptance rate: 11%. **Size of waiting list:** 1532 applicants; enrolled from waiting list: 81. **Credentials of fall 2009 freshmen:** 91% ranked in the top 10 percent of their high school class; 99% were in the top 25 percent; 100% were in the top half. (Proportion submitting class standing: 40%.) **First-year students who submitted SAT scores:** 75%. Scores (25/75 percentile): Critical Reading: 660-770, Math: 680-780, Combined: 1340-1550. **First-year students submitting ACT scores:** 25%. Scores (25/75 percentile): English: N/A, Math: N/A, Composite: 30-34.

ACADEMICS
Year founded: 1769. **Academic calendar:** Quarter. **Degrees offered:** bachelor's, master's, doctorate. **Most popular majors:** 14% economics, 11% political science and government, 9% psychology, 7% biology/biological sciences, 6% English language and literature. **Major fields of study:** area, ethnic, cultural, and gender studies; biological and biomedical sciences; computer and information sciences and support services; engineering; English language and literature/letters; foreign languages, literatures, and linguistics; history; liberal arts and sciences studies, and humanities; mathematics and

statistics; multi/interdisciplinary studies; natural resources and conservation; philosophy and religious studies; physical sciences; psychology; social sciences; visual and performing arts. **Areas of required coursework:** arts/fine arts, humanities, mathematics, English (including composition), foreign languages, sciences (biological or physical), social science, other. **Special academic programs (% participation):** double major (19%), exchange student program (domestic) (2%), honors program, independent study, internships (62%), student-designed major (1%), study abroad (61%), teacher certificate program (1%). **Teacher certification offered in:** elementary, secondary. **Reserve Officers Training Corps (ROTC):** Army ROTC: Offered at cooperating institution (Norwich University). **Faculty and instruction (2009-2010):** Total instructional faculty: 539 full-time, 136 part-time (62% men; 38% women; 14% minorities). Full-time faculty with Ph.D. or other terminal degree: 95%. Student/faculty ratio: 8/1. Classes of fewer than 20 students: 64%; of 20 to 49 students: 27%; of 50 or more students: 9%. **Advanced Placement and International Baccalaureate credit:** AP tests may be used for: Placement only. Scores accepted: 4, 5. International Baccalaureate exams may be used for: Credit and/or placement. **Freshmen returning for sophomore year:** 98%. **Graduation rates:** Four-year: 85%; five-year: 93%; six-year: 94%. **Graduate study:** 18% of students pursue further study immediately upon graduation; 13% within one year.

COSTS AND FINANCIAL AID

Financial aid office: (603) 646-2451. **Expenses (2010-2011):** Tuition and fees 2010-2011: $40,437; room/board: $11,838. Estimated books and supplies: $1,730; transportation: $775; personal expenses: $1,381. **Financial aid:** In 2009-2010, 63% of undergraduates applied for financial aid. Of those, 55% were determined to have financial need; 100% had their need fully met. Average financial aid package (proportion receiving): $38,449 (55%). Average amount of gift aid, such as scholarships or grants (proportion receiving): $35,209 (53%). Average amount of self-help aid, such as work study or loans (proportion receiving): $4,618 (50%). Average need-based loan (excluding PLUS or other private loans): $3,340. Among students who received need-based aid, the average percentage of need met: 100%. Among students who received aid based on merit, the average award (and the proportion receiving): $450 (0%). The average athletic scholarship (and the proportion receiving): $0 (0%). Average amount of debt of borrowers graduating in 2009: $19,081. Proportion who borrowed: 48%.

CAMPUS LIFE AND EXTRACURRICULAR ACTIVITIES

Campus housing available (% using): coed dorms (81%), sorority housing (4%), fraternity housing (8%), apartment for single students (4%), special housing for international students, cooperative housing, other housing options (3%). Students who live in college-owned, operated, or affiliated housing: 87%. **Student employment:** During the 2009-2010 academic year, 36% of undergraduates worked on campus. Average per-year earnings: $2,450. **Clubs and organizations:** Number of student organizations: 330. Activities include: campus ministries, choral groups, concert band, dance, drama/theater, international student organization, jazz band, literary magazine, marching band, model UN, music ensembles, musical theater, opera, pep band, radio station, student government, student newspaper, student film society, symphony orchestra, television station, yearbook. Number of fraternities: 15; sororities: 8. Proportion of men in fraternities: 47%; of women in sororities: 42%. **Sports program (2009-2010):** Member of NCAA I. **Men's intercollegiate varsity sports:** baseball, basketball, cross country, football, golf, ice hockey, lacrosse, skiing (nordic), skiing (alpine), soccer, swimming, tennis, track and field (indoor), track and field (outdoor). **Women's intercollegiate varsity sports:** basketball, crew (heavyweight), cross country, equestrian, field hockey, golf, ice hockey, lacrosse, skiing (nordic), skiing (alpine), soccer, softball, squash, swimming, tennis, track and field (indoor), track and field (outdoor), volleyball.

SERVICES AND FACILITIES

Basic services: nonremedial tutoring, women's center, placement service, health service, health insurance, other. **Counseling services:** minority student, career, personal, academic, psychological, birth control, religious. **For learning-disabled students:** School does not offer a structured program with separate admission and additional fees. Total undergraduates in learning-disabled program or receiving services: 93. Services include: reading machines, tape recorders, note-taking services, oral tests, learning center, readers, extended time for tests, tutors, priority registration, priority seating, texts on tape, typist/scribe, other testing accommodations, other. **Library:** Number of titles: 2,848,521; number of current serial subscriptions: 67,005. **Information technology resources:** Students are required to lease or own a computer. Number of campus computers available to all students: 271. School has a wireless network. Approximate number of users that can be

accommodated: 20,000. Proportion of college-owned housing units wired for high-speed internet access: 100%. **Campus safety:** Security services offered: 24-hour foot-and-vehicle patrols, late-night transport/escort service, 24-hour emergency telephones, lighted pathways/sidewalks, controlled dormitory access (key, security card, etc.).

TRANSFER AND INTERNATIONAL STUDENTS

Transfer students: May apply for admission for the following academic terms: Fall. Applicants need a minimum number of credits to apply. For fall 2009: Transfer applications received: 640. Transfer applicants offered admission: 38. Transfer applicants enrolled: 27. **International students:** Number of foreign undergraduates: 288 (7% of student body). Number of countries represented: 67.

Franklin Pierce University

■ **Address:** 40 University Drive, Rindge, NH 03461
■ **Website:** http://www.franklinpierce.edu/
■ **Private**
■ **Enrollment:** 1,600 full-time; 292 part-time

KEY STATS

✔ **U.S News College Ranking:** second tier, National Liberal Arts Colleges
✔ **SAT Score (25th/75th percentile):** 880-1080
✔ **Tuition:** 2010-2011: $28,800

Selectivity: Less selective	**Room/board:** $10,100
Acceptance rate: 93%	**Average debt:** $41,848
Student/faculty ratio: 14/1	**Proportion who borrowed:** 85%

UNDERGRADUATE STUDENT BODY STATS

2009-2010 enrollment: 1,600 full-time; 292 part-time. Men: 46%; women: 54%. **Ethnic makeup:** African American: 3%; Asian American: 1%; Hispanic: 3%; White: 91%; International: 2%. **Religious preference:** Roman Catholic: 32%; Protestant: 29%; Jewish: 3%; Muslim: 1%; Buddhist: 1%; No preference: 32%; Unknown: 2%.

ADMISSIONS FACTS AND FIGURES

Phone: (800) 437-0048. **Email:** admissions@franklinpierce.edu. **Website:** http://www.franklinpierce.edu/. **Application deadlines for fall 2011:** Regular decision: Rolling. Early decision: Not offered. Early action: Not offered. Admission can be deferred. **Application fee:** $40. **To apply online, go to:** http://www.franklinpierce.edu/admissions/index.htm. **Admissions requirements/recommendations:** High school units required (recommended): English: 4; Mathematics: 3; Science: 2; Foreign language: 0; Social studies: 3; History: 0; Academic electives: 4; Total units: 16. Tests: The college uses SAT or ACT scores in admissions decisions. Either SAT or ACT required. For admission to the fall 2011 entering class, the school will accept: ACT with writing required. Campus visit: Recommended. Admissions interview: Recommended. Off-campus interview: Not available. **Factors that count in admissions decisions: *Academic:*** Secondary school record: Important. Class rank: Considered. Letters of recommendation: Very Important. Standardized test scores: Important. Essay: Important. ***Nonacademic:*** Interview: Considered. Extracurricular activities: Considered. Talent/ability: Considered. Character/personal qualities: Very Important. Alumni/ae relationship: Not Considered. Geographical residence: Not Considered. State residency: Not Considered. Religious affiliation/commitment: Not Considered. Minority status: Not Considered. Volunteer work: Considered. Work experience: Considered. **Other schools with the greatest overlap in applicants:** Colby-Sawyer College; Keene State College; Quinnipiac University; Roger Williams University; Southern New Hampshire University. **Admissions statistics for the fall 2009 entering class:** Total applicants: 2,376. Total accepted: 2,219. Freshmen enrolled: 388; 80% were from out of state. Overall acceptance rate: 93%. **Size of waiting list:** 0 applicants; enrolled from waiting list: 0. **Credentials of fall 2009 freshmen:** 5% ranked in the top 10 percent of their high school class; 29% were in the top 25 percent; 47% were in the top half. (Proportion submitting class standing: 54%.) **Average high school grade point average:** 2.8. **First-year students who submitted SAT scores:** 90%. Scores (25/75 percentile): Critical Reading: 440-540, Math: 440-540, Combined: 880-1080. **First-year students submitting ACT scores:** 10%. Scores (25/75 percentile): English: 17-22, Math: 17-22, Composite: 18-21.

ACADEMICS

Year founded: 1962. **Academic calendar:** Semester. **Degrees offered:** certificate, associate, bachelor's, post-bachelor's certificate, master's, post-master's certificate, doctorate. **Most popular majors:** 15% business administration, management, and operations, 11% criminal justice/law enforcement administration, 8% accounting and finance, 6% marketing/marketing management, 6% mass communication/media studies. **Major fields of study:** area, ethnic, cultural, and gender studies; biological and biomedical sciences; business, management, marketing, and related support services; communication, journalism, and related programs; computer and information sciences and support services; English language and literature/letters; history; liberal arts and sciences studies, and humanities; mathematics and statistics; natural resources and conservation; parks, recreation, leisure, and fitness studies; psychology; public administration and social service professions; security and protective services; social sciences; visual and performing arts. **Areas of required coursework:** arts/fine arts, humanities, mathematics, English (including composition), sciences (biological or physical), history, social science, other. **Pre-professional programs:** pre-law, pre-medicine, other. **Special academic programs (% participation):** accelerated program (3%), cross-registration (10%), distance learning (10%), double major (25%), dual enrollment (2%), English as a Second Language (ESL) (1%), exchange student program (domestic) (0%), honors program (6%), independent study (8%), internships (30%), liberal arts/career combination (35%), student-designed major (5%), study abroad (18%), teacher certificate program (5%), other. **Teacher certification offered in:** early childhood, elementary, secondary. **Reserve Officers Training Corps (ROTC):** Army ROTC: Offered at cooperating institution (University of New Hampshire); Air Force ROTC: Offered at cooperating institution (University of New Hampshire). **Faculty and instruction (2009-2010):** Total instructional faculty: 101 full-time, 141 part-time (53% men; 47% women; 5% minorities). Full-time faculty with Ph.D. or other terminal degree: 73%. Student/faculty ratio: 14/1. Classes of fewer than 20 students: 75%; of 20 to 49 students: 25%; of 50 or more students: 0%. **Advanced Placement and International Baccalaureate credit:** AP tests may be used for: Credit and/or placement. Scores accepted: 3, 4, 5. International Baccalaureate exams may be used for: Placement only. **Freshmen returning for sophomore year:** 65%. **Graduation rates:** Four-year: 33%; five-year: 42%; six-year: 45%. **Graduate study:** 28% of students pursue further study immediately upon graduation; 34% within one year; 46% within five years. Fields in which graduates pursue further study: Master of Business Administration (MBA), 34%; law, 11%; medicine, 7%; dentistry, 1%; education, 32%; arts and sciences, 14%; veterinary medicine, 1%.

COSTS AND FINANCIAL AID

Financial aid office: (603) 899-4186. **Expenses (2010-2011):** Tuition and fees 2010-2011: $28,800; room/board: $10,100. Estimated books and supplies: $1,000; transportation: $600; personal expenses: $600. **Financial aid:** Priority filing date for institution's financial aid form: March 1. In 2009-2010, 83% of undergraduates applied for financial aid. Of those, 74% were determined to have financial need; 17% had their need fully met. Average financial aid package (proportion receiving): $18,733 (74%). Average amount of gift aid, such as scholarships or grants (proportion receiving): $14,047 (73%). Average amount of self-help aid, such as work study or loans (proportion receiving): $5,437 (66%). Average need-based loan (excluding PLUS or other private loans): $4,921. Among students who received need-based aid, the average percentage of need met: 63%. Among students who received aid based on merit, the average award (and the proportion receiving): $8,615 (18%). The average athletic scholarship (and the proportion receiving): $18,834 (5%). Average amount of debt of borrowers graduating in 2009: $41,848. Proportion who borrowed: 85%.

CAMPUS LIFE AND EXTRACURRICULAR ACTIVITIES

Campus housing available (% using): coed dorms (56%), apartment for single students (20%), special housing for disabled students (4%), other housing options (18%). Students who live in college-owned, operated, or affiliated housing: 84%. **Student employment:** During the 2009-2010 academic year, 50% of undergraduates worked on campus. Average per-year earnings: $1,500. **Clubs and organizations:** Number of student organizations: 40. Activities include: campus ministries, choral groups, concert band, dance, drama/theater, international student organization, jazz band, literary magazine, music ensembles, musical theater, radio station, student government, student newspaper, student film society, television station, yearbook. Number of fraternities: 0; sororities: 0. Average proportion of students who stay on campus on weekends: 75%. **Sports program (2009-2010):** Member of NCAA II. *Men's intercollegiate varsity sports:* baseball, basketball, golf, ice hockey, lacrosse, soccer, tennis. *Women's intercollegiate varsity*

sports: basketball, crew (heavyweight), cross country, field hockey, lacrosse, crew (lightweight), soccer, softball, tennis, volleyball.

SERVICES AND FACILITIES

Basic services: nonremedial tutoring, health service, health insurance. **Remedial assistance:** reading, math, writing, study skills, other. **Counseling services:** minority student, career, personal, veteran student, academic, older student, psychological, birth control, religious. **For learning-disabled students:** School does not offer a structured program with separate admission and additional fees. Total undergraduates in learning-disabled program or receiving services: 108. Services include: remedial math, remedial English, untimed tests, oral tests, learning center, readers, extended time for tests, tutors, early syllabus, exams on tape or computer, other testing accommodations, waiver of foreign language degree requirement, other. **Library:** Number of titles: 142,317; number of current serial subscriptions: 161. **Information technology resources:** Students are not required to lease or own a computer. Number of campus computers available to all students: 290. School has a wireless network. Approximate number of users that can be accommodated: 500. Proportion of college-owned housing units wired for high-speed internet access: 100%. **Campus safety:** Security services offered: 24-hour foot-and-vehicle patrols, late-night transport/escort service, 24-hour emergency telephones, lighted pathways/sidewalks, student patrols, controlled dormitory access (key, security card, etc).

TRANSFER AND INTERNATIONAL STUDENTS

Transfer students: May apply for admission for the following academic terms: Fall, Spring, Summer. Applicants do not need a minimum number of credits to apply. For fall 2009: Transfer applications received: 145. Transfer applicants offered admission: 103. Transfer applicants enrolled: 48. **International students:** Number of foreign undergraduates: 38 (2% of student body). Number of countries represented: 12. Minimum TOEFL score required: 500 (paper); 173 (computer).

Granite State College

- **Address:** 8 Old Suncook Road, Concord, NH 03301
- **Website:** http://www.granite.edu
- **Public**
- **Enrollment:** 687 full-time; 831 part-time

KEY STATS

✔ **U.S News College Ranking:** Unranked, National Liberal Arts Colleges
✔ **SAT or ACT Score (25th/75th percentile):** N/A
✔ **Tuition:** 2009-2010: $6,195 in state, $6,555 out of state

Selectivity: N/A	**Room/board:** $6,400
Acceptance rate: 100%	**Average debt:** $23,658
Student/faculty ratio: 10/1	**Proportion who borrowed:** N/A

UNDERGRADUATE STUDENT BODY STATS

2009-2010 enrollment: 687 full-time; 831 part-time. Men: 27%; women: 73%. **Ethnic makeup:** African American: 1%; American-Indian: 1%; Asian American: 1%; Hispanic: 2%; White: 95%.

ADMISSIONS FACTS AND FIGURES

Phone: (603) 513-1391. **Email:** ruth.nawn@granite.edu. **Website:** http://www.granite.edu. **Application deadlines for fall 2011:** Regular decision: Rolling. Early decision: Not offered. Early action: Not offered. Admission can be deferred. **Application fee:** $45. **To apply online, go to:** http://www.granite.edu/admit. **Admissions requirements/recommendations:** Tests: The college does not use SAT or ACT scores in admissions decisions. Neither SAT nor ACT required. Campus visit: Neither required nor recommended. Admissions interview: Recommended. Off-campus interview: May be arranged. **Factors that count in admissions decisions:** *Academic:* Secondary school record: Not Considered. Class rank: Not Considered. Letters of recommendation: Not Considered. Standardized test scores: Not Considered. Essay: Considered. *Nonacademic:* Interview: Considered. Extracurricular activities: Not Considered. Talent/ability: Not Considered. Character/personal qualities: Not Considered. Alumni/ae relationship: Not Considered. Geographical residence: Not Considered. State residency: Not Considered. Religious affiliation/commitment: Not Considered. Minority status: Not Considered. Volunteer work: Not Considered. Work experience: Not Considered. **Other schools with the greatest overlap in applicants:** Daniel Webster College; Franklin Pierce University; Hesser College; Rivier College;

Southern New Hampshire University. **Admissions statistics for the fall 2009 entering class:** Total applicants: 95. Total accepted: 95. Freshmen enrolled: 52; 9% were from out of state. Overall acceptance rate: 100%.

ACADEMICS

Year founded: 1972. **Academic calendar:** Trimester. **Degrees offered:** associate, transfer-associate, bachelor's, post-bachelor's certificate. **Most popular majors:** 31% liberal arts and sciences/liberal studies, 30% behavioral sciences, 27% business administration and management, 5% criminal justice/safety studies, 5% early childhood education and teaching. **Major fields of study:** business, management, marketing, and related support services; computer and information sciences and support services; education; liberal arts and sciences studies, and humanities; multi/interdisciplinary studies; security and protective services. **Areas of required coursework:** arts/fine arts, humanities, computer literacy, mathematics, English (including composition), sciences (biological or physical), history, social science, other. **Special academic programs (% participation):** accelerated program, cooperative (work-study plan) program, cross-registration, distance learning (55%), double major, dual enrollment, independent study, internships, liberal arts/career combination, student-designed major, teacher certificate program. **Teacher certification offered in:** special education. **Cooperative education programs:** education. **Reserve Officers Training Corps (ROTC):** Army ROTC: Offered at cooperating institution (University of New Hampshire). **Faculty and instruction (2009-2010):** Total instructional faculty: 0 full-time, 166 part-time (33% men; 67% women; 1% minorities). Student/faculty ratio: 10/1. Classes of fewer than 20 students: 98%; of 20 to 49 students: 3%. **Advanced Placement and International Baccalaureate credit:** AP tests may be used for: Credit and/or placement. Scores accepted: 3, 4, 5. International Baccalaureate exams may be used for: Placement only. **Freshmen returning for sophomore year:** 51%. **Graduation rates:** Four-year: 43%; five-year: 57%; six-year: 60%.

COSTS AND FINANCIAL AID

Financial aid office: (603) 228-3000. **Expenses (2009-2010):** Tuition and fees 2009-2010: $6,195 in state, $6,555 out of state; room/board: $6,400. Estimated books and supplies: $900 personal expenses: $2,475. Average amount of debt of borrowers graduating in 2009: $23,658.

CAMPUS LIFE AND EXTRACURRICULAR ACTIVITIES

Student employment: During the 2009-2010 academic year, 2% of undergraduates worked on campus. Average per-year earnings: $1,453. **Clubs and organizations:** Number of student organizations: 2. Number of fraternities: 0; sororities: 0.

SERVICES AND FACILITIES

Basic services: nonremedial tutoring. **Remedial assistance:** other. **Counseling services:** career, veteran student, academic, other. **For learning-disabled students:** School does not offer a structured program with separate admission and additional fees. Services include: tape recorders, note-taking services, readers, extended time for tests, tutors, texts on tape, other. **Library:** Number of titles: 0; number of current serial subscriptions: 21. **Information technology resources:** Students are not required to lease or own a computer. Number of campus computers available to all students: 139. School has a wireless network. Approximate number of users that can be accommodated: 100. **Campus safety:** Security services offered: lighted pathways/sidewalks.

TRANSFER AND INTERNATIONAL STUDENTS

Transfer students: May apply for admission for the following academic terms: Fall, Winter, Spring, Summer. Applicants need a minimum number of credits to apply. For fall 2009: Transfer applications received: 200. Transfer applicants offered admission: 200. Transfer applicants enrolled: 136. **International students:** Number of foreign undergraduates: 0. Number of countries represented: 0. Minimum TOEFL score required: 550 (paper); 120 (computer).

Keene State College

- **Address:** 229 Main Street, Keene, NH 03435
- **Website:** http://www.keene.edu
- **Public**
- **Enrollment:** 4,890 full-time; 345 part-time

KEY STATS
- ✔ **U.S News College Ranking:** 88, Regional Universities (North)
- ✔ **SAT Score (25th/75th percentile):** 900-1100
- ✔ **Tuition:** 2009-2010: $9,334 in state, $17,504 out of state

  Selectivity: Less selective   **Room/board:** $8,444

  Acceptance rate: 71%   **Average debt:** $27,785

  Student/faculty ratio: 18/1   **Proportion who borrowed:** 78%

UNDERGRADUATE STUDENT BODY STATS

2009-2010 enrollment: 4,890 full-time; 345 part-time. Men: 44%; women: 56%. **Ethnic makeup:** Hispanic: 1%; White: 97%.

ADMISSIONS FACTS AND FIGURES

Phone: (603) 358-2276. **Email:** admissions@keene.edu. **Website:** http://www.keene.edu. **Application deadlines for fall 2011:** Regular decision: April 1. Early decision: Not offered. Early action: Not offered. Admission can be deferred. **Application fee:** $40. **To apply online, go to:** http://www.keene.edu/admissions/applying.cfm. **Admissions requirements/recommendations:** High school units required (recommended): English: 4; Mathematics: 3; Science: 3; Social studies: 2; Academic electives: 2; Total units: 14. Tests: The college uses SAT or ACT scores in admissions decisions. Either SAT or ACT required. For admission to the fall 2011 entering class, the school will accept: ACT with writing recommended. Campus visit: Recommended. Admissions interview: Neither required nor recommended. Off-campus interview: Not available. **Factors that count in admissions decisions:** *Academic:* Secondary school record: Very Important. Class rank: Considered. Letters of recommendation: Important. Standardized test scores: Important. Essay: Important. *Nonacademic:* Interview: Not Considered. Extracurricular activities: Considered. Talent/ability: Considered. Character/personal qualities: Considered. Alumni/ae relationship: Considered. Geographical residence: Not Considered. State residency: Not Considered. Religious affiliation/commitment: Not Considered. Minority status: Considered. Volunteer work: Considered. Work experience: Considered. **Other schools with the greatest overlap in applicants:** Franklin Pierce University; Plymouth State University; University of New Hampshire; University of Vermont; Westfield State College. **Admissions statistics for the fall 2009 entering class:** Total applicants: 4,997. Total accepted: 3,537. Freshmen enrolled: 1,188; 55% were from out of state. Overall acceptance rate: 71%. **Credentials of fall 2009 freshmen:** 5% ranked in the top 10 percent of their high school class; 22% were in the top 25 percent; 67% were in the top half. (Proportion submitting class standing: 72%.) **Average high school grade point average:** 3.0. **First-year students who submitted SAT scores:** 96%. Scores (25/75 percentile): Critical Reading: 450-550, Math: 450-550, Combined: 900-1100.

ACADEMICS

Year founded: 1909. **Academic calendar:** Semester. **Degrees offered:** certificate, associate, bachelor's, post-bachelor's certificate, master's, post-master's certificate. **Most popular majors:** 17% education, 15% psychology, 12% social sciences, 9% business, management, marketing, and related support services, 9% engineering technologies/technicians. **Major fields of study:** architecture and related services; area, ethnic, cultural, and gender studies; biological and biomedical sciences; business, management, and related support services; communication, journalism, and related programs; computer and information sciences and support services; education; engineering technologies/technicians; English language and literature/letters; foreign languages, literatures, and linguistics; health professions and related clinical sciences; history; liberal arts and sciences studies, and humanities; mathematics and statistics; multi/interdisciplinary studies; natural resources and conservation; parks, recreation, leisure, and fitness studies; physical sciences; psychology; social sciences; visual and performing arts. **Areas of required coursework:** arts/fine arts, humanities, mathematics, English (including composition), sciences (biological or physical), history, social science, other. **Special academic programs (% participation):** cooperative (work-study plan) program (6%), double major (5%), English as a Second Language (ESL) (4%), exchange student program (domestic) (7%), honors program (0%), independent study (27%), internships (9%), liberal arts/career combination (5%), student-designed major (2%), study abroad (9%), teacher certificate program (17%). **Teacher certification offered in:** early childhood, special education, elementary, middle/junior high, secondary. **Cooperative education programs:** business, computer science, humanities, natural science, social/behavioral science, technologies, other. **Reserve Officers Training Corps (ROTC):** Air Force ROTC: Offered at cooperating institution (University of Massachusetts–Lowell). **Faculty and instruction (2009-2010):** Total instructional faculty: 194 full-time, 265 part-time (48% men; 52% women; 2% minorities). Full-time faculty with Ph.D. or other terminal degree: 85%. Student/faculty ratio: 18/1. Classes of fewer than 20 students: 53%; of 20 to 49 students: 46%; of 50 or more students: 1%. **Advanced Placement and International Baccalaureate credit:** AP tests may be used for: Placement only. Scores accepted: 3, 4, 5. **Freshmen returning for sophomore year:** 79%. **Graduation rates:** Four-year: 36%; five-year: 54%; six-year: 56%. **Graduate study:** 28% of students pursue further study immediately upon graduation. Fields in which graduates pursue further study: Master of Business Administration (MBA), 7%; law, 4%; medicine, 5%; engineering, 3%; education, 24%; arts and sciences, 32%.

COSTS AND FINANCIAL AID

Financial aid office: (603) 358-2280. **Expenses (2009-2010):** Tuition and fees 2009-2010: $9,334 in state, $17,504 out of state; room/board: $8,444. Estimated books and supplies: $800; transportation: $1,100; personal expenses: $750. **Financial aid:** In 2009-2010, 76% of undergraduates applied for financial aid. Of those, 53% were determined to have financial need; 19% had their need fully met. Average financial aid package (proportion receiving): $8,603 (52%). Average amount of gift aid, such as scholarships or grants (proportion receiving): $5,091 (32%). Average amount of self-help aid, such as work study or loans (proportion receiving): $6,012 (49%). Average need-based loan (excluding PLUS or other private loans): $4,085. Among students who received need-based aid, the average percentage of need met: 68%. Among students who received aid based on merit, the average award (and the proportion receiving): $3,026 (7%). Average amount of debt of borrowers graduating in 2009: $27,785. Proportion who borrowed: 78%.

CAMPUS LIFE AND EXTRACURRICULAR ACTIVITIES

Campus housing available (% using): coed dorms (85%), women's dorms (5%), apartment for single students (10%). Students who live in college-owned, operated, or affiliated housing: 55%. **Student employment:** During the 2009-2010 academic year, 15% of undergraduates worked on campus. Average per-year earnings: $956. **Clubs and organizations:** Number of student organizations: 100. Activities include: campus ministries, choral groups, concert band, dance, drama/theater, international student organization, jazz band, literary magazine, music ensembles, musical theater, radio station, student government, student newspaper, student film society, television station, yearbook. Number of fraternities: 4; sororities: 5. Proportion of men in fraternities: 3%; of women in sororities: 3%. Average proportion of students who stay on campus on weekends: 65%. **Sports program (2009-2010):** Member of NCAA III. *Men's intercollegiate varsity sports:* baseball, basketball, cross country, lacrosse, soccer, swimming, track and field (outdoor). *Women's intercollegiate varsity sports:* basketball, cross country, field hockey, lacrosse, soccer, softball, swimming, track and field (outdoor), volleyball.

SERVICES AND FACILITIES

Basic services: nonremedial tutoring, health service. **Remedial assistance:** reading, math, writing, study skills. **Counseling services:** minority student, career, personal, veteran student, academic, older student, psychological, birth control, religious. **For learning-disabled students:** School does not offer a structured program with separate admission and additional fees. Services include: reading machines, tape recorders, note-taking services, oral tests, readers, extended time for tests, tutors, priority registration, texts on tape. **Library:** Number of titles: 330,017; number of current serial subscriptions: 830. **Information technology resources:** Students are not required to lease or own a computer. Number of campus computers available to all students: 600. School has a wireless network. Approximate number of users that can be accommodated: 5,000. Proportion of college-owned housing units wired for high-speed internet access: 100%. **Campus safety:** Security services offered: 24-hour foot-and-vehicle patrols, late-night transport/escort service, 24-hour emergency telephones, lighted pathways/sidewalks, controlled dormitory access (key, security card, etc).

TRANSFER AND INTERNATIONAL STUDENTS

Transfer students: May apply for admission for the following academic terms: Fall, Spring. Applicants do not need a minimum number of cred-

its to apply. For fall 2009: Transfer applications received: 568. Transfer applicants offered admission: 364. Transfer applicants enrolled: 236. **International students:** Number of foreign undergraduates: 7. Number of countries represented: 4. Minimum TOEFL score required: 500 (paper); 173 (computer).

New England College

■ **Address:** 15 Main Street, Henniker, NH 03242
■ **Website:** http://www.nec.edu
■ **Private**
■ **Enrollment:** 939 full-time; 75 part-time

KEY STATS

✔ **U.S News College Ranking:** 31, Regional Colleges (North)
✔ **SAT Score (25th/75th percentile):** 780-1000
✔ **Tuition:** 2010-2011: $29,054

Selectivity: Less selective	**Room/board:** $10,170
Acceptance rate: 81%	**Average debt:** $33,466
Student/faculty ratio: 12/1	**Proportion who borrowed:** 77%

UNDERGRADUATE STUDENT BODY STATS

2009-2010 enrollment: 939 full-time; 75 part-time. Men: 50%; women: 50%. **Ethnic makeup:** African American: 6%; Asian American: 1%; Hispanic: 3%; White: 86%; International: 5%.

ADMISSIONS FACTS AND FIGURES

Phone: (800) 521-7642. **Email:** admission@nec.edu. **Website:** http://www.nec.edu. **Application deadlines for fall 2011:** Regular decision: Rolling. Early decision: Not offered. Early action: Not offered. Admission can be deferred. **Application fee:** $30. **To apply online, go to:** http://www.nec.edu/admissions/admissions.html#apply. **Admissions requirements/recommendations:** High school units required (recommended): English: 4 (4); Mathematics: 2 (3); Science: 2 (3); Foreign language: 0 (2); Social studies: 2 (3); History: 0 (0); Academic electives: 0 (0); Total units: 12 (12). Tests: The college uses SAT or ACT scores in admissions decisions. Neither SAT nor ACT required. For admission to the fall 2011 entering class, the school will accept: ACT with or without writing accepted. Campus visit: Recommended. Admissions interview: Recommended. Off-campus interview: May be arranged. **Factors that count in admissions decisions:** *Academic:* Secondary school record: Very Important. Class rank: Considered. Letters of recommendation: Very Important. Standardized test scores: Considered. Essay: Very Important. *Nonacademic:* Interview: Very Important. Extracurricular activities: Very Important. Talent/ability: Very Important. Character/personal qualities: Important. Alumni/ae relationship: Considered. Geographical residence: Not Considered. State residency: Not Considered. Religious affiliation/commitment: Not Considered. Minority status: Not Considered. Volunteer work: Considered. Work experience: Considered. **Other schools with the greatest overlap in applicants:** Colby-Sawyer College; Franklin Pierce University; Keene State College; Plymouth State University; University of New Hampshire. **Admissions statistics for the fall 2009 entering class:** Total applicants: 1,767. Total accepted: 1,428. Freshmen enrolled: 258; 70% were from out of state. Overall acceptance rate: 81%. **Credentials of fall 2009 freshmen:** 2% ranked in the top 10 percent of their high school class; 6% were in the top 25 percent; 37% were in the top half. (Proportion submitting class standing: 56%.) **Average high school grade point average:** 2.7. **First-year students who submitted SAT scores:** 64%. Scores (25/75 percentile): Critical Reading: 390-500, Math: 390-500, Combined: 780-1000. **First-year students submitting ACT scores:** 4%. Scores (25/75 percentile): English: 13-20, Math: 17-20, Composite: 17-23.

ACADEMICS

Year founded: 1946. **Academic calendar:** Semester. **Degrees offered:** associate, bachelor's, master's. **Most popular majors:** 20% business, management, marketing, and related support services, 15% parks, recreation, leisure, and fitness studies, 11% education, 11% psychology, 11% visual and performing arts. **Major fields of study:** business, management, marketing, and related support services; communication, journalism, and related programs; education; engineering; health professions and related clinical sciences; history; legal professions and studies; mathematics and statistics; natural resources and conservation; philosophy and religious studies; psychology; social sciences; visual and performing arts. **Areas of required coursework:** arts/fine arts, humanities, computer literacy, mathematics, English (including composition), sciences (biological or physical), history, social science. **Pre-professional programs:** pre-law, pre-medicine, other. **Special academic programs (% participation):** cross-registration (2%), distance learning (4%), double major (7%), English as a Second Language (ESL) (3%), honors program (2%), independent study (11%), internships (23%), student-designed major (2%), study abroad (10%), teacher certificate program (11%). **Teacher certification offered in:** special education, elementary, secondary. **Cooperative education programs:** engineering, health professions. **Reserve Officers Training Corps (ROTC):** Army ROTC: Offered at cooperating institution (University of New Hampshire); Air Force ROTC: Offered at cooperating institution (University of New Hampshire). **Faculty and instruction (2009-2010):** Total instructional faculty: 65 full-time, 115 part-time (48% men; 52% women; 2% minorities). Full-time faculty with Ph.D. or other terminal degree: 69%. Student/faculty ratio: 12/1. Classes of fewer than 20 students: 78%; of 20 to 49 students: 22%; of 50 or more students: 0%. **Advanced Placement and International Baccalaureate credit:** AP tests may be used for: Credit and/or placement. Scores accepted: 3, 4, 5. International Baccalaureate exams may be used for: Credit only. **Freshmen returning for sophomore year:** 60%. **Graduation rates:** Four-year: 30%; five-year: 41%; six-year: 44%. **Graduate study:** 12% of students pursue further study immediately upon graduation; 15% within one year. Fields in which graduates pursue further study: Master of Business Administration (MBA), 8%; law, 17%; medicine, 17%; education, 8%; arts and sciences, 50%.

COSTS AND FINANCIAL AID

Financial aid office: (603) 428-2414. **Expenses (2010-2011):** Tuition and fees 2010-2011: $29,054; room/board: $10,170. Estimated books and supplies: $1,000; transportation: $1,000; personal expenses: $1,500. **Financial aid:** Priority filing date for institution's financial aid form: February 15; deadline: September 1. In 2009-2010, 79% of undergraduates applied for financial aid. Of those, 72% were determined to have financial need; 22% had their need fully met. Average financial aid package (proportion receiving): $23,584 (71%). Average amount of gift aid, such as scholarships or grants (proportion receiving): $15,259 (69%). Average amount of self-help aid, such as work study or loans (proportion receiving): $9,283 (66%). Average need-based loan (excluding PLUS or other private loans): $8,253. Among students who received need-based aid, the average percentage of need met: 81%. Among students who received aid based on merit, the average award (and the proportion receiving): $10,846 (23%). The average athletic scholarship (and the proportion receiving): $0 (0%). Average amount of debt of borrowers graduating in 2009: $33,466. Proportion who borrowed: 77%.

CAMPUS LIFE AND EXTRACURRICULAR ACTIVITIES

Campus housing available (% using): coed dorms (80%), apartment for single students (10%). Students who live in college-owned, operated, or affiliated housing: 60%. **Student employment:** During the 2009-2010 academic year, 5% of undergraduates worked on campus. Average per-year earnings: $3,000. **Clubs and organizations:** Number of student organizations: 35. Activities include: dance, drama/theater, international student organization, literary magazine, radio station, student government, student newspaper. Number of fraternities: 3; sororities: 2. Proportion of men in fraternities: 10%; of women in sororities: 5%. Average proportion of students who stay on campus on weekends: 75%. **Sports program (2009-2010):** Member of NCAA III. **Men's intercollegiate varsity sports:** baseball, basketball, cross country, ice hockey, lacrosse, soccer. **Women's intercollegiate varsity sports:** basketball, cross country, field hockey, ice hockey, lacrosse, soccer, softball.

SERVICES AND FACILITIES

Basic services: nonremedial tutoring, placement service, health service, health insurance. **Remedial assistance:** math, writing, study skills. **Counseling services:** career, military, personal, veteran student, academic, older student, psychological, birth control. **For learning-disabled students:** School does not offer a structured program with separate admission and additional fees. Services include: remedial math, tape recorders, untimed tests, note-taking services, oral tests, learning center, extended time for tests, tutors, proofreading services, exams on tape or computer, other testing accommodations. **Library:** Number of titles: 106,100; number of current serial subscriptions: 275. **Information technology resources:** Students are required to lease or own a computer. Number of campus computers available to all students: 148. School has a wireless network. Approximate number of users that can be accommodated: 5,000. Proportion of college-owned housing units wired for high-speed internet access: 100%. **Campus safety:** Security services offered: 24-hour foot-and-vehicle patrols, late-night transport/escort service, 24-hour emergency telephones, lighted pathways/sidewalks, controlled dormitory access (key, security card, etc).

TRANSFER AND INTERNATIONAL STUDENTS

Transfer students: May apply for admission for the following academic terms: Fall, Spring, Summer. Applicants do not need a minimum number of credits to apply. For fall 2009: Transfer applications received: 150. Transfer applicants offered admission: 149. Transfer applicants enrolled: 62. **International students:** Number of foreign undergraduates: 45 (5% of student body). Number of countries represented: 23. Minimum TOEFL score required: 550 (paper); 213 (computer).

Plymouth State University

- **Address:** 17 High Street, Plymouth, NH 03264-1595
- **Website:** http://www.plymouth.edu
- **Public**
- **Enrollment:** 4,025 full-time; 236 part-time

KEY STATS

✔ **U.S News College Ranking:** 117, Regional Universities (North)
✔ **SAT Score (25th/75th percentile):** 903-1095
✔ **Tuition:** 2010-2011: $9,970 in state, $18,140 out of state
   Selectivity: Less selective   **Room/board:** $8,690
   Acceptance rate: 70%   **Average debt:** $29,709
   Student/faculty ratio: 16/1   **Proportion who borrowed:** 82%

UNDERGRADUATE STUDENT BODY STATS

2009-2010 enrollment: 4,025 full-time; 236 part-time. Men: 54%; women: 46%. **Ethnic makeup:** Hispanic: 1%; White: 98%.

ADMISSIONS FACTS AND FIGURES

Phone: (603) 535-2237. **Email:** plymouthadmit@plymouth.edu. **Website:** http://www.plymouth.edu. **Application deadlines for fall 2011:** Regular decision: April 1. Early decision: Not offered. Early action: Not offered. Admission can be deferred. **Application fee:** $45. **To apply online, go to:** http://www.plymouth.edu/admit/apply/. **Admissions requirements/recommendations:** High school units required (recommended): English: 4 (4); Mathematics: 3 (3); Science: 2 (3); Foreign language: 0 (2); Social studies: 2 (3); History: 1 (2); Academic electives: 0 (0); Total units: 13 (18). Tests: The college uses SAT or ACT scores in admissions decisions. Either SAT or ACT required. For admission to the fall 2011 entering class, the school will accept: ACT with writing required. Campus visit: Neither required nor recommended. Admissions interview: Neither required nor recommended. Off-campus interview: May be arranged. **Factors that count in admissions decisions: Academic:** Secondary school record: Very Important. Class rank: Important. Letters of recommendation: Important. Standardized test scores: Important. Essay: Important. **Nonacademic:** Interview: Not Considered. Extracurricular activities: Considered. Talent/ability: Important. Character/personal qualities: Important. Alumni/ae relationship: Considered. Geographical residence: Not Considered. State residency: Not Considered. Religious affiliation/commitment: Not Considered. Minority status: Considered. Volunteer work: Considered. Work experience: Considered. **Other schools with the greatest overlap in applicants:** Bridgewater State College; Keene State College; Southern New Hampshire University; University of Massachusetts–Amherst; University of New Hampshire. **Admissions statistics for the fall 2009 entering class:** Total applicants: 4,239. Total accepted: 2,957. Freshmen enrolled: 969; 45% were from out of state. Overall acceptance rate: 70%. **Size of waiting list:** 0 applicants; enrolled from waiting list: 0. **Credentials of fall 2009 freshmen:** 4% ranked in the top 10 percent of their high school class; 17% were in the top 25 percent; 53% were in the top half. (Proportion submitting class standing: 77%.) **Average high school grade point average:** 2.9. **First-year students who submitted SAT scores:** 97%. Scores (25/75 percentile): Critical Reading: 450-550, Math: 453-545, Combined: 903-1095. **First-year students submitting ACT scores:** 7%. Scores (25/75 percentile): English: N/A, Math: N/A, Composite: 19-23.

ACADEMICS

Year founded: 1871. **Academic calendar:** Semester. **Degrees offered:** bachelor's, post-bachelor's certificate, master's, post-master's certificate, doctorate. **Most popular majors:** 27% business, management, marketing, and related support services, 16% education, 8% parks, recreation, leisure, and fitness studies, 8% visual and performing arts, 7% security and protective services. **Major fields of study:** architecture and related services; biological and biomedical sciences; business, management, marketing, and related support services; communication, journalism, and related programs; computer and information sciences and support services; education; English language and literature/letters; foreign languages, literatures, and linguistics; health professions and related clinical sciences; history; liberal arts and sciences studies, and humanities; mathematics and statistics; multi/interdisciplinary studies; parks, recreation, leisure, and fitness studies; philosophy and religious studies; physical sciences; psychology; public administration and social service professions; security and protective services; social sciences; visual and performing arts. **Areas of required coursework:** arts/fine arts, humanities, computer literacy, mathematics, English (including composition), sciences (biological or physical), history, social science, other. **Special academic programs (% participation):** double major (1%), English as a Second Language (ESL), exchange student program (domestic) (1%), honors program (15%), independent study (12%), internships (46%), student-designed major (2%), study abroad (6%), teacher certificate program (16%). **Teacher certification offered in:** early childhood, special education, elementary, middle/junior high, secondary. **Reserve Officers Training Corps (ROTC):** Army ROTC: Offered on campus; Air Force ROTC: Offered on campus. **Faculty and instruction (2009-2010):** Total instructional faculty: 186 full-time, 230 part-time (49% men; 51% women; 3% minorities). Full-time faculty with Ph.D. or other terminal degree: 82%. Student/faculty ratio: 16/1. Classes of fewer than 20 students: 48%; of 20 to 49 students: 51%; of 50 or more students: 1%. **Advanced Placement and International Baccalaureate credit:** AP tests may be used for: Credit and/or placement. Scores accepted: 3, 4, 5. **Freshmen returning for sophomore year:** 78%. **Graduation rates:** Four-year: 34%; five-year: 52%; six-year: 54%. **Graduate study:** 41% of students pursue further study immediately upon graduation.

COSTS AND FINANCIAL AID

Financial aid office: (603) 535-2338. **Expenses (2010-2011):** Tuition and fees 2010-2011: $9,970 in state, $18,140 out of state; room/board: $8,690. Estimated books and supplies: $1,202; transportation: $836; personal expenses: $1,202. **Financial aid:** Priority filing date for institution's financial aid form: March 1. In 2009-2010, 83% of undergraduates applied for financial aid. Of those, 60% were determined to have financial need; 18% had their need fully met. Average financial aid package (proportion receiving): $9,403 (60%). Average amount of gift aid, such as scholarships or grants (proportion receiving): $5,042 (45%). Average amount of self-help aid, such as work study or loans (proportion receiving): $5,647 (59%). Average need-based loan (excluding PLUS or other private loans): $4,225. Among students who received need-based aid, the average percentage of need met: 62%. Among students who received aid based on merit, the average award (and the proportion receiving): $2,567 (8%). The average athletic scholarship (and the proportion receiving): $0 (0%). Average amount of debt of borrowers graduating in 2009: $29,709. Proportion who borrowed: 82%.

CAMPUS LIFE AND EXTRACURRICULAR ACTIVITIES

Campus housing available (% using): coed dorms (74%), apartments for married students (1%), apartment for single students (24%), special housing for disabled students (1%), other housing options (0%). Students who live in college-owned, operated, or affiliated housing: 57%. **Student employment:** During the 2009-2010 academic year, 23% of undergraduates worked on campus. Average per-year earnings: $8. **Clubs and organizations:** Number of student organizations: 107. Activities include: campus ministries, choral groups, concert band, dance, drama/theater, international student organization, jazz band, literary magazine, model UN, music ensembles, musical theater, radio station, student government, student newspaper, student film society, symphony orchestra, yearbook. Number of fraternities: 0; sororities: 3. of women in sororities: 3%. Average proportion of students who stay on campus on weekends: 70%. **Sports program (2009-2010):** Member of NCAA III. **Men's intercollegiate varsity sports:** baseball, basketball, football, ice hockey, lacrosse, skiing (alpine), soccer, wrestling. **Women's intercollegiate varsity sports:** basketball, field hockey, ice hockey, lacrosse, skiing (alpine), soccer, softball, swimming, tennis, volleyball.

SERVICES AND FACILITIES

Basic services: nonremedial tutoring, women's center, placement service, day care, health service. **Counseling services:** minority student, career, military, personal, veteran student, academic, older student, psychological, birth control, religious. **For learning-disabled students:** School does not offer a structured program with separate admission and additional fees. Services include: note-taking services, readers, extended time for tests, tutors, priority registration, substitution of courses, texts on tape, exams on tape or computer. **Library:** Number of titles: 349,394; number of current serial subscriptions: 55,641. **Information technology resources:** Students are not required to lease or own a computer. Number of campus computers available to all students: 500. School has a wireless network. Approximate num-

ber of users that can be accommodated: 1,000. Proportion of college-owned housing units wired for high-speed internet access: 100%. **Campus safety:** Security services offered: 24-hour foot-and-vehicle patrols, late-night transport/escort service, 24-hour emergency telephones, lighted pathways/sidewalks, student patrols, controlled dormitory access (key, security card, etc).

TRANSFER AND INTERNATIONAL STUDENTS

Transfer students: May apply for admission for the following academic terms: Fall, Spring. Applicants do not need a minimum number of credits to apply. For fall 2009: Transfer applications received: 555. Transfer applicants offered admission: 407. Transfer applicants enrolled: 243. **International students:** Number of foreign undergraduates: 17. Number of countries represented: 11. Minimum TOEFL score required: 520 (paper); 190 (computer). Average TOEFL score: 540 (paper).

Rivier College

- **Address:** 420 Main Street, Nashua, NH 03060
- **Website:** http://www.rivier.edu
- **Private; Religious affiliation:** Roman Catholic
- **Enrollment:** 967 full-time; 519 part-time

KEY STATS
- ✔ **U.S News College Ranking:** second tier, Regional Universities (North)
- ✔ **SAT Score (25th/75th percentile):** 850-1040
- ✔ **Tuition:** 2009-2010: $25,050

Selectivity: Less selective	**Room/board:** $9,428
Acceptance rate: 81%	**Average debt:** $36,389
Student/faculty ratio: 15/1	**Proportion who borrowed:** 94%

UNDERGRADUATE STUDENT BODY STATS

2009-2010 enrollment: 967 full-time; 519 part-time. Men: 18%; women: 82%. **Ethnic makeup:** African American: 2%; American-Indian: 1%; Asian American: 2%; Hispanic: 4%; White: 92%.

ADMISSIONS FACTS AND FIGURES

Phone: (603) 888-1311. **Email:** rivadmit@rivier.edu. **Website:** http://www.rivier.edu. **Application deadlines for fall 2011:** Regular decision: Rolling. Early decision: Not offered. Early action: Send application by: November 15; Decision sent by: December 1. Admission can be deferred. **Application fee:** $25. **To apply online, go to:** https://www.applyweb.com/apply/rivier/menu.html. **Admissions requirements/recommendations:** High school units required (recommended): English: 4; Mathematics: 3; Science: 1; Foreign language: 2; Social studies: 2; History: 1; Academic electives: 3; Total units: 16. Tests: The college uses SAT or ACT scores in admissions decisions. Neither SAT nor ACT required. For admission to the fall 2011 entering class, the school will accept: ACT with or without writing accepted. Campus visit: Recommended. Admissions interview: Recommended. Off-campus interview: May be arranged. **Factors that count in admissions decisions:** Academic: Secondary school record: Very Important. Class rank: Important. Letters of recommendation: Important. Standardized test scores: Very Important. Essay: Important. **Nonacademic:** Interview: Considered. Extracurricular activities: Considered. Talent/ability: Considered. Character/personal qualities: Considered. Alumni/ae relationship: Considered. Geographical residence: Not Considered. State residency: Not Considered. Religious affiliation/commitment: Not Considered. Minority status: Not Considered. Volunteer work: Not Considered. Work experience: Not Considered. **Other schools with the greatest overlap in applicants:** Keene State College; Plymouth State University; Southern New Hampshire University; St. Anselm College; University of New Hampshire. **Admissions statistics for the fall 2009 entering class:** Total applicants: 878. Total accepted: 713. Freshmen enrolled: 236; Overall acceptance rate: 81%. Non-early acceptance rate: 81%. **Average high school grade point average:** 2.8. **First-year students who submitted SAT scores:** 98%. Scores (25/75 percentile): Critical Reading: 430-510, Math: 420-530, Combined: 850-1040. **First-year students submitting ACT scores:** 17%. Scores (25/75 percentile): English: N/A, Math: N/A, Composite: 17-22.

ACADEMICS

Year founded: 1933. **Academic calendar:** Semester. **Degrees offered:** certificate, associate, bachelor's, post-bachelor's certificate, master's, post-master's certificate, doctorate. **Most popular majors:** 31% nursing, 21% business, management, marketing, and related support services, 14% special education and teaching, 8% psychology, 6% legal professions and studies. **Major fields of study:** biological and biomedical sciences; business, management, marketing, and related support services; communication, journalism, and related programs; computer and information sciences and support services; education; English language and literature/letters; foreign languages, literatures, and linguistics; health professions and related clinical sciences; history; liberal arts and sciences studies, and humanities; mathematics and statistics; multi/interdisciplinary studies; psychology; security and protective services; social sciences; visual and performing arts. **Areas of required coursework:** arts/fine arts, humanities, English (including composition), philosophy, foreign languages, sciences (biological or physical), history, social science. **Pre-professional programs:** pre-law, pre-dentistry, pre-medicine, pre-theology, pre-veterinary science, pre-pharmacy. **Special academic programs (% participation):** cross-registration (1%), distance learning (1%), double major (1%), dual enrollment (1%), English as a Second Language (ESL) (1%), honors program (2%), independent study (7%), internships (7%), student-designed major (2%), study abroad (1%), teacher certificate program (22%), weekend college (1%). **Teacher certification offered in:** early childhood, special education, elementary, middle/junior high, secondary. **Reserve Officers Training Corps (ROTC):** Air Force ROTC: Offered at cooperating institution (University of Massachusetts–Lowell). **Faculty and instruction (2009-2010):** Total instructional faculty: 71 full-time, 122 part-time (33% men; 67% women). Full-time faculty with Ph.D. or other terminal degree: 76%. Student/faculty ratio: 15/1. Classes of fewer than 20 students: 49%; of 20 to 49 students: 49%; of 50 or more students: 2%. **Advanced Placement and International Baccalaureate credit:** AP tests may be used for: Credit only. **Freshmen returning for sophomore year:** 74%. **Graduation rates:** Four-year: 41%; five-year: 50%; six-year: 53%.

COSTS AND FINANCIAL AID

Financial aid office: (603) 897-8533. **Expenses (2009-2010):** Tuition and fees 2009-2010: $25,050; room/board: $9,428. Estimated books and supplies: $1,200; transportation: $450; personal expenses: $1,500. **Financial aid:** Priority filing date for institution's financial aid form: March 1; deadline: May 1. In 2009-2010, 93% of undergraduates applied for financial aid. Of those, 82% were determined to have financial need; 9% had their need fully met. Average financial aid package (proportion receiving): $14,344 (82%). Average amount of gift aid, such as scholarships or grants (proportion receiving): $10,255 (79%). Average amount of self-help aid, such as work study or loans (proportion receiving): $4,819 (77%). Average need-based loan (excluding PLUS or other private loans): $4,362. Among students who received need-based aid, the average percentage of need met: 60%. Among students who received aid based on merit, the average award (and the proportion receiving): $4,849 (14%). The average athletic scholarship (and the proportion receiving): $0 (0%). Average amount of debt of borrowers graduating in 2009: $36,389. Proportion who borrowed: 94%.

CAMPUS LIFE AND EXTRACURRICULAR ACTIVITIES

Campus housing available (% using): coed dorms (100%). **Student employment:** During the 2009-2010 academic year, 28% of undergraduates worked on campus. Average per-year earnings: $650. **Clubs and organizations:** Number of student organizations: 40. Activities include: dance, drama/theater, music ensembles, student government, student newspaper, yearbook. Number of fraternities: 0; sororities: 0. Average proportion of students who stay on campus on weekends: 40%. **Sports program (2009-2010):** Member of NCAA III.

SERVICES AND FACILITIES

Basic services: placement service, health service, health insurance. **Remedial assistance:** reading, math, writing, study skills. **Counseling services:** career, personal, academic, psychological, religious. **For learning-disabled students:** School does not offer a structured program with separate admission and additional fees. Total undergraduates in learning-disabled program or receiving services: 93. Services include: remedial math, remedial English, reading machines, tape recorders, untimed tests, note-taking services, oral tests, learning center, readers, extended time for tests, tutors, priority registration, priority seating, substitution of courses, texts on tape, typist/scribe, exams on tape or computer, other testing accommodations, waiver of foreign language degree requirement. **Library:** Number of titles: 140,000; number of current serial subscriptions: 405. **Information technology resources:** Students are not required to lease or own a computer. Number of campus computers available to all students: 100. School has a wireless network. Approximate number of users that can be accommodated: 500. Proportion of college-owned housing units wired for high-speed internet access: 100%. **Campus safety:** Security services offered: 24-hour foot-and-vehicle patrols, late-night transport/escort service, 24-hour emergency telephones, lighted pathways/sidewalks, controlled dormitory access (key, security card, etc).

TRANSFER AND INTERNATIONAL STUDENTS

Transfer students: May apply for admission for the following academic terms: Fall, Spring. Applicants do not need a minimum number of credits to apply. For fall 2009: Transfer applications received: 222. Transfer applicants offered admission: 94. Transfer applicants enrolled: 66. **International students:** Number of foreign undergraduates: 1. Minimum TOEFL score required: 500 (paper); 173 (computer).

Southern New Hampshire University

- **Address:** 2500 N. River Road, Manchester, NH 03106
- **Website:** http://www.snhu.edu
- **Private**
- **Enrollment:** 1,896 full-time; 58 part-time

KEY STATS

✔ **U.S News College Ranking:** 99, Regional Universities (North)
✔ **SAT Score (25th/75th percentile):** 880-1060
✔ **Tuition:** 2009-2010: $26,442

Selectivity: Less selective	**Room/board:** $10,176
Acceptance rate: 87%	**Average debt:** N/A
Student/faculty ratio: 16/1	**Proportion who borrowed:** N/A

UNDERGRADUATE STUDENT BODY STATS

2009-2010 enrollment: 1,896 full-time; 58 part-time. Men: 48%; women: 52%. **Ethnic makeup:** African American: 1%; Asian American: 1%; Hispanic: 2%; White: 91%; International: 5%. **Religious preference:** Roman Catholic: 32%; No preference: 31%; Other Christian: 23%; Other: 14%.

ADMISSIONS FACTS AND FIGURES

Phone: (603) 645-9611. **Email:** admission@snhu.edu. **Website:** http://www.snhu.edu. **Application deadlines for fall 2011:** Regular decision: Rolling. Early decision: Not offered. Early action: Send application by: November 15; Decision sent by: December 15. Admission can be deferred. **Application fee:** $40. **To apply online, go to:** https://emasweb.snhu.edu/EMASOnline/Default.aspx?tabid=71. **Admissions requirements/recommendations:** High school units required (recommended): English: 4; Mathematics: 3; Science: 3; Foreign language: 2; Social studies: 2; History: 2; Total units: 12 (2). **Tests:** The college uses SAT or ACT scores in admissions decisions. Either SAT or ACT required. For admission to the fall 2011 entering class, the school will accept: ACT with writing required. Campus visit: Recommended. Admissions interview: Recommended. Off-campus interview: May be arranged. **Factors that count in admissions decisions:** *Academic:* Secondary school record: Very Important. Class rank: Considered. Letters of recommendation: Important. Standardized test scores: Important. Essay: Important. *Nonacademic:* Interview: Considered. Extracurricular activities: Important. Talent/ability: Considered. Character/personal qualities: Important. Alumni/ae relationship: Considered. Geographical residence: Not Considered. State residency: Not Considered. Religious affiliation/commitment: Not Considered. Minority status: Not Considered. Volunteer work: Considered. Work experience: Considered. **Other schools with the greatest overlap in applicants:** Johnson and Wales University; Keene State College; Plymouth State University; University of Massachusetts–Amherst; University of New Hampshire. **Admissions statistics for the fall 2009 entering class:** Total applicants: 3,036. Total accepted: 2,631. Freshmen enrolled: 471; 60% were from out of state. Overall acceptance rate: 87%. Non-early acceptance rate: 87%. **Credentials of fall 2009 freshmen:** 8% ranked in the top 10 percent of their high school class; 25% were in the top 25 percent. **Average high school grade point average:** 3.0. **First-year students who submitted SAT scores:** 87%. Scores (25/75 percentile): Critical Reading: 440-520, Math: 440-540, Combined: 880-1060. **First-year students submitting ACT scores:** 11%. Scores (25/75 percentile): English: 17-24, Math: 16-24, Composite: 18-24.

ACADEMICS

Year founded: 1932. **Academic calendar:** Other. **Degrees offered:** certificate, associate, bachelor's, post-bachelor's certificate, master's, post-master's certificate, doctorate. **Major fields of study:** agriculture, agriculture operations, and related sciences; business, management, marketing, and related support services; communication, journalism, and related programs; computer and information sciences and support services; education; English language and literature/letters; family and consumer sciences/human sciences; history; liberal arts and sciences studies, and humanities; multi/interdisciplinary studies; natural resources and conservation; parks, recreation, leisure, and fitness studies; personal and culinary services; psychology; public administration and social service professions; security and protective services; social sciences; visual and performing arts. **Areas of required coursework:** arts/fine arts, humanities, computer literacy, mathematics, English (including composition), philosophy, sciences (biological or physical), history, social science. **Pre-professional programs:** pre-law. **Special academic programs (% participation):** accelerated program (3.3%), cooperative (work-study plan) program, distance learning, double major, dual enrollment, English as a Second Language (ESL) (.9%), honors program (.8%), independent study (5.7%), internships, student-designed major, study abroad, teacher certificate program (4.4%), weekend college. **Teacher certification offered in:** early childhood, special education, elementary, middle/junior high, secondary. **Cooperative education programs:** business, computer science, social/behavioral science. **Reserve Officers Training Corps (ROTC):** Army ROTC: Offered at cooperating institution (University of New Hampshire); Air Force ROTC: Offered at cooperating institution (University of New Hampshire). **Faculty and instruction (2009-2010):** Total instructional faculty: 120 full-time, 303 part-time (57% men; 43% women; 3% minorities). Full-time faculty with Ph.D. or other terminal degree: 76%. Student/faculty ratio: 16/1. Classes of fewer than 20 students: 58%; of 20 to 49 students: 42%; of 50 or more students: 0%. **Advanced Placement and International Baccalaureate credit:** AP tests may be used for: Credit and/or placement. Scores accepted: 3, 4, 5. International Baccalaureate exams may be used for: Credit and/or placement. **Freshmen returning for sophomore year:** 74%. **Graduation rates:** Four-year: 49%; five-year: 57%; six-year: 50%. **Graduate study:** 12% of students pursue further study within one year.

COSTS AND FINANCIAL AID
Financial aid office: (603) 645-9645. **Expenses (2009-2010):** Tuition and fees 2009-2010: $26,442; room/board: $10,176. Estimated books and supplies: $1,000; transportation: $550; personal expenses: $1,000. **Financial aid:** Priority filing date for institution's financial aid form: March 15.

CAMPUS LIFE AND EXTRACURRICULAR ACTIVITIES
Campus housing available (% using): coed dorms (60%), women's dorms (1%), apartment for single students (39%), special housing for disabled students (0%), other housing options (0%). Students who live in college-owned, operated, or affiliated housing: 78%. **Student employment:** During the 2009-2010 academic year, 10% of undergraduates worked on campus. Average per-year earnings: $2,325. **Clubs and organizations:** Number of student organizations: 58. Activities include: campus ministries, choral groups, dance, drama/theater, international student organization, literary magazine, model UN, musical theater, radio station, student government, student newspaper, television station, yearbook. Number of fraternities: 3; sororities: 3. Proportion of men in fraternities: 6%; of women in sororities: 5%. Average proportion of students who stay on campus on weekends: 65%. **Sports program (2009-2010):** Member of NCAA II. *Men's intercollegiate varsity sports:* baseball, basketball, cross country, golf, ice hockey, lacrosse, soccer, tennis. *Women's intercollegiate varsity sports:* basketball, cross country, lacrosse, soccer, softball, tennis, volleyball.

SERVICES AND FACILITIES
Basic services: nonremedial tutoring, health service, health insurance. **Remedial assistance:** math, writing, study skills. **Counseling services:** minority student, career, personal, veteran student, academic, older student, psychological. **For learning-disabled students:** School does not offer a structured program with separate admission and additional fees. Services include: tape recorders, note-taking services, oral tests, learning center, readers, extended time for tests, tutors, priority registration, priority seating, texts on tape, exams on tape or computer, other testing accommodations. **Library:** Number of titles: 94,580; number of current serial subscriptions: 42,135. **Information technology resources:** Students are required to lease or own a computer. Number of campus computers available to all students: 557. School has a wireless network. Approximate number of users that can be accommodated: 2,500. Proportion of college-owned housing units wired for high-speed internet access: 100%. **Campus safety:** Security services offered: 24-hour foot-and-vehicle patrols, late-night transport/escort service, 24-hour emergency telephones, lighted pathways/sidewalks, student patrols, controlled dormitory access (key, security card, etc).

TRANSFER AND INTERNATIONAL STUDENTS
Transfer students: May apply for admission for the following academic terms: Fall, Spring. Applicants need a minimum number of credits to apply. For fall 2009: Transfer applications received: 370. Transfer applicants offered admission: 277. Transfer applicants enrolled: 130. **International students:** Number of foreign undergraduates: 98 (5% of student body). Number of countries represented: 28. Minimum TOEFL score required: 530 (paper); 197 (computer).

St. Anselm College

- **Address:** 100 St. Anselm Drive, Manchester, NH 03102-1310
- **Website:** http://www.anselm.edu
- **Private; Religious affiliation:** Roman Catholic (Benedictine)
- **Enrollment:** 1,879 full-time; 36 part-time

KEY STATS
✔ **U.S News College Ranking:** 122, National Liberal Arts Colleges
✔ **SAT Score (25th/75th percentile):** 1010-1170
✔ **Tuition:** 2010-2011: $31,575

Selectivity: Selective	**Room/board:** $11,630
Acceptance rate: 77%	**Average debt:** $36,823
Student/faculty ratio: 11/1	**Proportion who borrowed:** 75%

UNDERGRADUATE STUDENT BODY STATS
2009-2010 enrollment: 1,879 full-time; 36 part-time. Men: 43%; women: 57%. **Ethnic makeup:** African American: 1%; American-Indian: 1%; Asian American: 1%; Hispanic: 2%; White: 94%. **Religious preference:** Roman Catholic: 72%; Protestant: 8%; No preference: 2%; Unknown: 15%; Other: 3%.

ADMISSIONS FACTS AND FIGURES
Phone: (603) 641-7500. **Email:** admission@anselm.edu. **Website:** http://www.anselm.edu. **Application deadlines for fall 2011:** Regular decision: March 1. Early decision: Not offered. Early action: Send application by: November 15; Decision sent by: January 15. Admission can be deferred. **Application fee:** $55. To apply online, go to: http://www.anselm.edu/admission/applying/Application.htm. **Admissions requirements/recommendations:** High school units required (recommended): English: 4; Mathematics: 3 (4); Science: 3 (4); Foreign language: 2; Social studies: 2. Tests: The college uses SAT or ACT scores in admissions decisions. Neither SAT nor ACT required. For admission to the fall 2011 entering class, the school will accept: ACT with or without writing accepted. Campus visit: Recommended. Admissions interview: Recommended. Off-campus interview: May be arranged. **Factors that count in admissions decisions:** *Academic:* Secondary school record: Very Important. Class rank: Considered. Letters of recommendation: Very Important. Standardized test scores: Considered. Essay: Very Important. *Nonacademic:* Interview: Not Considered. Extracurricular activities: Considered. Talent/ability: Considered. Character/personal qualities: Considered. Alumni/ae relationship: Considered. Geographical residence: Considered. State residency: Considered. Religious affiliation/commitment: Not Considered. Minority status: Considered. Volunteer work: Considered. Work experience: Considered. **Other schools with the greatest overlap in applicants:** Assumption College; Providence College; Stonehill College; University of Massachusetts–Amherst; University of New Hampshire. **Admissions statistics for the fall 2009 entering class:** Total applicants: 3,664. Total accepted: 2,830. Freshmen enrolled: 531; 80% were from out of state. Overall acceptance rate: 77%. Non-early acceptance rate: 77%. **Size of waiting list:** 562 applicants; enrolled from waiting list: 175. **Credentials of fall 2009 freshmen:** 23% ranked in the top 10 percent of their high school class; 56% were in the top 25 percent. (Proportion submitting class standing: 20%.) **Average high school grade point average:** 3.1. **First-year students who submitted SAT scores:** 94%. Scores (25/75 percentile): Critical Reading: 500-590, Math: 510-580, Combined: 1010-1170. **First-year students submitting ACT scores:** 26%. Scores (25/75 percentile): English: 20-26, Math: 19-25, Composite: 20-26.

ACADEMICS
Year founded: 1889. **Academic calendar:** Semester. **Degrees offered:** bachelor's. **Most popular majors:** 16% nursing, 13% criminology, 13% business/commerce, 8% English language and literature, 7% psychology. **Major fields of study:** biological and biomedical sciences; business, management, marketing, and related support services; computer and information sci-

ences and support services; engineering; English language and literature/letters; foreign languages, literatures, and linguistics; health professions and related clinical sciences; history; liberal arts and sciences studies, and humanities; mathematics and statistics; multi/interdisciplinary studies; philosophy and religious studies; physical sciences; psychology; social sciences; theology and religious vocations; visual and performing arts. **Areas of required coursework:** humanities, English (including composition), philosophy, foreign languages, sciences (biological or physical), other. **Preprofessional programs:** pre-law, pre-dentistry, pre-medicine, pre-theology, pre-veterinary science, pre-optometry, pre-pharmacy. **Special academic programs (% participation):** cross-registration (1%), dual enrollment, exchange student program (domestic) (1%), honors program (13%), independent study (11%), internships (35%), liberal arts/career combination (3%), study abroad (12%), teacher certificate program (3%). **Teacher certification offered in:** early childhood, elementary, middle/junior high, secondary. **Cooperative education programs:** engineering. **Reserve Officers Training Corps (ROTC):** Army ROTC: Offered at cooperating institution (University of New Hampshire). **Faculty and instruction (2009-2010):** Total instructional faculty: 144 full-time, 64 part-time (50% men; 50% women; 7% minorities). Full-time faculty with Ph.D. or other terminal degree: 92%. Student/faculty ratio: 11/1. Classes of fewer than 20 students: 56%; of 20 to 49 students: 41%; of 50 or more students: 4%. **Advanced Placement and International Baccalaureate credit:** AP tests may be used for: Credit and/or placement. Scores accepted: 3, 4, 5. International Baccalaureate exams may be used for: Credit and/or placement. **Freshmen returning for sophomore year:** 85%. **Graduation rates:** Four-year: 71%; five-year: 73%; six-year: 73%. **Graduate study:** 17% of students pursue further study immediately upon graduation.

COSTS AND FINANCIAL AID
Financial aid office: (603) 641-7110. **Expenses (2010-2011):** Tuition and fees 2010-2011: $31,575; room/board: $11,630. Estimated books and supplies: $1,000; transportation: $500; personal expenses: $1,000. **Financial aid:** Priority filing date for institution's financial aid form: March 15; deadline: March 15. In 2009-2010, 84% of undergraduates applied for financial aid. Of those, 72% were determined to have financial need; 17% had their need fully met. Average financial aid package (proportion receiving): $23,195 (72%). Average amount of gift aid, such as scholarships or grants (proportion receiving): $16,967 (72%). Average amount of self-help aid, such as work study or loans (proportion receiving): $7,066 (65%). Average need-based loan (excluding PLUS or other private loans): $5,788. Among students who received need-based aid, the average percentage of need met: 82%. Among students who received aid based on merit, the average award (and the proportion receiving): $8,216 (17%). The average athletic scholarship (and the proportion receiving): $28,592 (1%). Average amount of debt of borrowers graduating in 2009: $36,823. Proportion who borrowed: 75%.

CAMPUS LIFE AND EXTRACURRICULAR ACTIVITIES
Campus housing available (% using): coed dorms (13%), women's dorms (33%), men's dorms (24%), apartment for single students (29%), special housing for disabled students (0%). Students who live in college-owned, operated, or affiliated housing: 91%. **Student employment:** During the 2009-2010 academic year, 15% of undergraduates worked on campus. Average per-year earnings: $825. **Clubs and organizations:** Number of student organizations: 63. Activities include: campus ministries, choral groups, drama/theater, international student organization, jazz band, literary magazine, model UN, musical theater, radio station, student government, student newspaper, yearbook. Number of fraternities: 0; sororities: 0. Average proportion of students who stay on campus on weekends: 70%. **Sports program (2009-2010):** Member of NCAA II. *Men's intercollegiate varsity sports:* baseball, basketball, cross country, football, golf, ice hockey, lacrosse, skiing (alpine), soccer, tennis. *Women's intercollegiate varsity sports:* basketball, cross country, field hockey, ice hockey, lacrosse, skiing (alpine), soccer, softball, tennis, volleyball.

SERVICES AND FACILITIES
Basic services: nonremedial tutoring, health service, health insurance. **Counseling services:** minority student, career, personal, academic, psychological, religious. **For learning-disabled students:** School does not offer a structured program with separate admission and additional fees. Total undergraduates in learning-disabled program or receiving services: 18. Services include: tape recorders, learning center, readers, extended time for tests, tutors, priority seating, texts on tape, other testing accommodations, other. **Library:** Number of titles: 238,994; number of current serial subscriptions: 37,042. **Information technology resources:** Students are not required to lease or own a computer. Number of campus computers available to all students: 145. School has a wireless network. Approximate number of users

that can be accommodated: 2,500. Proportion of college-owned housing units wired for high-speed internet access: 100%. **Campus safety:** Security services offered: 24-hour foot-and-vehicle patrols, late-night transport/escort service, 24-hour emergency telephones, lighted pathways/sidewalks, controlled dormitory access (key, security card, etc).

TRANSFER AND INTERNATIONAL STUDENTS
Transfer students: May apply for admission for the following academic terms: Fall, Spring. Applicants do not need a minimum number of credits to apply. For fall 2009: Transfer applications received: 73. Transfer applicants offered admission: 42. Transfer applicants enrolled: 23. **International students:** Number of foreign undergraduates: 8. Number of countries represented: 9. Minimum TOEFL score required: 550 (paper); 250 (computer).

Thomas More College of Liberal Arts

- **Address:** 6 Manchester Street, Merrimack, NH 03054
- **Website:** http://www.thomasmorecollege.edu
- **Private; Religious affiliation:** Roman Catholic
- **Enrollment:** 64 full-time

KEY STATS
✔ **U.S. News College Ranking:** Unranked, National Liberal Arts Colleges
✔ **SAT or ACT Score (25th/75th percentile):** N/A
✔ **Tuition:** 2010-2011: $16,100

Selectivity: N/A	**Room/board:** $9,100
Acceptance rate: 90%	**Average debt:** $21,133
Student/faculty ratio: 11/1	**Proportion who borrowed:** 77%

UNDERGRADUATE STUDENT BODY STATS
2009-2010 enrollment: 64 full-time. Men: 50%; women: 50%. **Ethnic makeup:** African American: 2%; American-Indian: 2%; Asian American: 2%; Hispanic: 5%; White: 89%; International: 2%. **Religious preference:** Roman Catholic: 85%; Jewish: 3%; Other: 12%.

ADMISSIONS FACTS AND FIGURES
Phone: (800) 880-8308. **Email:** admissions@thomasmorecollege.edu. **Website:** http://www.thomasmorecollege.edu. **Application deadlines for fall 2011:** Regular decision: Rolling. Early decision: Not offered. Early action: Not offered. Admission cannot be deferred. **To apply online, go to:** http://www.thomasmorecollege.edu/index.php?/content/view/60/156/. **Admissions requirements/recommendations:** High school units required (recommended): English: 4; Mathematics: 3; Science: 2; Foreign language: 2; Social studies: 2; History: 2; Total units: 17. Tests: The college uses SAT or ACT scores in admissions decisions. Neither SAT nor ACT required. For admission to the fall 2011 entering class, the school will accept: ACT with or without writing accepted. Campus visit: Recommended. Admissions interview: Required. Off-campus interview: May be arranged. **Factors that count in admissions decisions:** *Academic:* Secondary school record: Considered. Class rank: Considered. Letters of recommendation: Very Important. Standardized test scores: Considered. Essay: Very Important. *Nonacademic:* Interview: Very Important. Extracurricular activities: Considered. Talent/ability: Important. Character/personal qualities: Very Important. Alumni/ae relationship: Not Considered. Geographical residence: Not Considered. State residency: Not Considered. Religious affiliation/commitment: Considered. Minority status: Not Considered. Volunteer work: Considered. Work experience: Not Considered. **Admissions statistics for the fall 2009 entering class:** Total applicants: 59. Total accepted: 53. Freshmen enrolled: 24; 83% were from out of state. Overall acceptance rate: 90%.

ACADEMICS
Year founded: 1978. **Academic calendar:** Semester. **Degrees offered:** bachelor's. **Most popular majors:** 38% philosophy, 38% political science and government, 24% English language and literature. **Major fields of study:** biological and biomedical sciences; English language and literature/letters; philosophy and religious studies; social sciences. **Areas of required coursework:** arts/fine arts, humanities, mathematics, English (including composition), philosophy, foreign languages, sciences (biological or physical), history, social science. **Special academic programs (% participation):** study abroad (100%). **Faculty and instruction (2009-2010):** Total instructional faculty: 6 (100% men). Full-time faculty with Ph.D. or other terminal degree: 83%. Student/faculty ratio: 11/1. Classes of fewer than 20 students: 65%; of 20 to 49 students: 29%; of 50 or more students: 6%. **Freshmen returning**

for sophomore year: 72%. **Graduation rates:** Four-year: 62%; five-year: 62%; six-year: 54%. **Graduate study:** 33% of students pursue further study immediately upon graduation; 55% within five years. Fields in which graduates pursue further study: Master of Business Administration (MBA), 2%; law, 15%; dentistry, 1%; theology (or the seminary), 5%; education, 3%; arts and sciences, 96%; veterinary medicine, 1%.

COSTS AND FINANCIAL AID

Financial aid office: (800) 880-8308. **Expenses (2010-2011):** Tuition and fees 2010-2011: $16,100; room/board: $9,100. Estimated books and supplies: $700; transportation: $600; personal expenses: $900. **Financial aid:** Priority filing date for institution's financial aid form: April 15. In 2009-2010, 80% of undergraduates applied for financial aid. Of those, 69% were determined to have financial need; 11% had their need fully met. Average financial aid package (proportion receiving): $13,172 (69%). Average amount of gift aid, such as scholarships or grants (proportion receiving): $9,794 (66%). Average amount of self-help aid, such as work study or loans (proportion receiving): $5,472 (69%). Average need-based loan (excluding PLUS or other private loans): $4,290. Among students who received need-based aid, the average percentage of need met: 87%. Among students who received aid based on merit, the average award (and the proportion receiving): $3,000 (8%). The average athletic scholarship (and the proportion receiving): $0 (0%). Average amount of debt of borrowers graduating in 2009: $21,133. Proportion who borrowed: 77%.

CAMPUS LIFE AND EXTRACURRICULAR ACTIVITIES

Campus housing available (% using): women's dorms (47%), men's dorms (53%). Students who live in college-owned, operated, or affiliated housing: 92%. **Clubs and organizations:** Number of student organizations: 0. Activities include: choral groups. Number of fraternities: 0; sororities: 0. Average proportion of students who stay on campus on weekends: 98%. **Sports program (2009-2010):** Member of NCAA III.

SERVICES AND FACILITIES

Library: Number of titles: 55,000; number of current serial subscriptions: 5. **Information technology resources:** Students are not required to lease or own a computer. Number of campus computers available to all students: 25. School has a wireless network. Approximate number of users that can be accommodated: 20. Proportion of college-owned housing units wired for high-speed internet access: 0%. **Campus safety:** Security services offered: 24-hour emergency telephones, lighted pathways/sidewalks, student patrols, controlled dormitory access (key, security card, etc).

TRANSFER AND INTERNATIONAL STUDENTS

Transfer students: May apply for admission for the following academic terms: Fall, Spring. Applicants need a minimum number of credits to apply. **International students:** Number of foreign undergraduates: 1 (2% of student body).

University of New Hampshire

- **Address:** 4 Garrison Avenue, Durham, NH 03824
- **Website:** http://www.unh.edu
- **Public**
- **Enrollment:** 12,035 full-time; 556 part-time

KEY STATS

✔ **U.S News College Ranking:** 104, National Universities
✔ **SAT Score (25th/75th percentile):** 1030-1240
✔ **Tuition:** 2010-2011: $13,675 in state, $27,645 out of state

Selectivity: Selective	**Room/board:** $9,052
Acceptance rate: 72%	**Average debt:** $30,760
Student/faculty ratio: 19/1	**Proportion who borrowed:** 74%

UNDERGRADUATE STUDENT BODY STATS

2009-2010 enrollment: 12,035 full-time; 556 part-time. Men: 45%; women: 55%. **Ethnic makeup:** African American: 2%; Asian American: 2%; Hispanic: 2%; White: 93%; International: 1%. **Religious preference:** Roman Catholic: 30%; Protestant: 29%; Jewish: 2%; Buddhist: 1%; No preference: 35%; other religion: 3%.

ADMISSIONS FACTS AND FIGURES

Phone: (603) 862-1360. **Email:** admissions@unh.edu. **Website:** http://www.unh.edu. **Application deadlines for fall 2011:** Regular decision: February 1; decision sent by April 15. Early decision: Not offered. Early action: Send application by: November 15; Decision sent by: January 15. Admission can be deferred. **Application fee:** $50. **To apply online, go to:** https://webcat.unh.edu/index_adm.html. **Admissions requirements/recommendations:** High school units required (recommended): English: 4 (4); Mathematics: 3 (4); Science: 3 (4); Foreign language: 2 (3); Social studies: 3 (3); Total units: 17 (22). Tests: The college uses SAT or ACT scores in admissions decisions. Either SAT or ACT required. For admission to the fall 2011 entering class, the school will accept: ACT with writing required. Campus visit: Recommended. Admissions interview: Neither required nor recommended. Off-campus interview: Not available. **Factors that count in admissions decisions:** *Academic:* Secondary school record: Very Important. Class rank: Very Important. Letters of recommendation: Important. Standardized test scores: Considered. Essay: Considered. *Nonacademic:* Interview: Not Considered. Extracurricular activities: Considered. Talent/ability: Considered. Character/personal qualities: Considered. Alumni/ae relationship: Considered. Geographical residence: Considered. State residency: Considered. Religious affiliation/commitment: Not Considered. Minority status: Considered. Volunteer work: Considered. Work experience: Considered. **Other schools with the greatest overlap in applicants:** Boston University; Northeastern University; University of Connecticut; University of Massachusetts–Amherst; University of Vermont. **Admissions statistics for the fall 2009 entering class:** Total applicants: 16,132. Total accepted: 11,583. Freshmen enrolled: 3,004; 46% were from out of state. Accepted through early-decision or early-action plans: 36%. Overall acceptance rate: 72%. Non-early acceptance rate: 78%. **Credentials of fall 2009 freshmen:** 25% ranked in the top 10 percent of their high school class; 71% were in the top 25 percent; 97% were in the top half. (Proportion submitting class standing: 73%.) **First-year students who submitted SAT scores:** 94%. Scores (25/75 percentile): Critical Reading: 510-610, Math: 520-630, Combined: 1030-1240. **First-year students submitting ACT scores:** 3%. Scores (25/75 percentile): English: N/A, Math: N/A, Composite: N/A.

ACADEMICS

Year founded: 1866. **Academic calendar:** Semester. **Degrees offered:** certificate, associate, bachelor's, post-bachelor's certificate, master's, post-master's certificate, doctorate. **Most popular majors:** 13% business administration and management, 8% psychology, 6% communication studies/speech communication and rhetoric, 5% political science and government, 3% biology/biological sciences. **Major fields of study:** agriculture, agriculture operations, and related sciences; architecture and related services; area, ethnic, cultural, and gender studies; biological and biomedical sciences; business, management, marketing, and related support services; communication, journalism, and related programs; computer and information sciences and support services; education; engineering; English language and literature/letters; family and consumer sciences/human sciences; foreign languages, literatures, and linguistics; health professions and related clinical sciences; history; liberal arts and sciences studies, and humanities; mathematics and statistics; multi/interdisciplinary studies; natural resources and conservation; parks, recreation, leisure, and fitness studies; personal and culinary services; philosophy and religious studies; physical sciences; psychology; public administration and social service professions; social sciences; visual and performing arts. **Areas of required coursework:** arts/fine arts, humanities, mathematics, English (including composition), philosophy, foreign languages, sciences (biological or physical), history, social science, other. **Pre-professional programs:** pre-law, pre-dentistry, pre-medicine, pre-veterinary science, pre-optometry, pre-pharmacy. **Special academic programs (% participation):** cross-registration (1%), double major (11%), English as a Second Language (ESL) (.02%), exchange student program (domestic) (4%), honors program (11%), independent study (8%), internships, student-designed major, study abroad (17%), teacher certificate program (2%), other (30%). **Teacher certification offered in:** early childhood, special education, elementary, vo-tech, middle/junior high, adult education, secondary, bilingual/bicultural. **Cooperative education programs:** natural science. **Reserve Officers Training Corps (ROTC):** Army ROTC: Offered on campus; Air Force ROTC: Offered on campus. **Faculty and instruction (2009-2010):** Total instructional faculty: 618 full-time, 358 part-time (54% men; 46% women; 6% minorities). Full-time faculty with Ph.D. or other terminal degree: 84%. Student/faculty ratio: 19/1. Classes of fewer than 20 students: 41%; of 20 to 49 students: 42%; of 50 or more students: 16%. **Advanced Placement and International Baccalaureate credit:** AP tests may be used for: Placement only. International Baccalaureate exams may be used for: Credit only. **Freshmen returning for sophomore year:** 87%. **Graduation rates:** Four-year:

60%; five-year: 74%; six-year: 75%. **Graduate study:** 30% of students pursue further study immediately upon graduation; 35% within one year. Fields in which graduates pursue further study: Master of Business Administration (MBA), 3%; law, 1%; medicine, 1%; engineering, 1%; education, 5%; arts and sciences, 15%; veterinary medicine, 1%.

COSTS AND FINANCIAL AID
Financial aid office: (603) 862-3600. **Expenses (2010-2011):** Tuition and fees 2010-2011: $13,675 in state, $27,645 out of state; room/board: $9,052. Estimated books and supplies: $1,200; transportation: $300; personal expenses: $2,231. **Financial aid:** In 2009-2010, 76% of undergraduates applied for financial aid. Of those, 60% were determined to have financial need; 22% had their need fully met. Average financial aid package (proportion receiving): $18,346 (59%). Average amount of gift aid, such as scholarships or grants (proportion receiving): $3,223 (37%). Average amount of self-help aid, such as work study or loans (proportion receiving): $3,134 (57%). Average need-based loan (excluding PLUS or other private loans): $3,456. Among students who received need-based aid, the average percentage of need met: 80%. Among students who received aid based on merit, the average award (and the proportion receiving): $8,640 (21%). The average athletic scholarship (and the proportion receiving): $25,707 (2%). Average amount of debt of borrowers graduating in 2009: $30,760. Proportion who borrowed: 74%.

CAMPUS LIFE AND EXTRACURRICULAR ACTIVITIES
Campus housing available (% using): coed dorms (79%), apartments for married students (1%), apartment for single students (19%), special housing for international students (1%). Students who live in college-owned, operated, or affiliated housing: 59%. **Student employment:** During the 2009-2010 academic year, 33% of undergraduates worked on campus. Average per-year earnings: $1,823. **Clubs and organizations:** Number of student organizations: 187. Activities include: campus ministries, choral groups, concert band, dance, drama/theater, international student organization, jazz band, literary magazine, marching band, model UN, music ensembles, musical theater, pep band, radio station, student government, student newspaper, student film society, symphony orchestra, television station, yearbook. Number of fraternities: 11; sororities: 7. Proportion of men in fraternities: 9%; of women in sororities: 9%. Average proportion of students who stay on campus on weekends: 65%. **Sports program (2009-2010):** Member of NCAA I. *Men's intercollegiate varsity sports:* basketball, cross country, football, ice hockey, skiing (nordic), skiing (alpine), soccer, track and field (indoor), track and field (outdoor). *Women's intercollegiate varsity sports:* basketball, cross country, field hockey, gymnastics, ice hockey, lacrosse, skiing (nordic), skiing (alpine), soccer, swimming, track and field (indoor), track and field (outdoor), volleyball.

SERVICES AND FACILITIES
Basic services: nonremedial tutoring, women's center, placement service, day care, health service, health insurance, other. **Counseling services:** minority student, career, military, personal, veteran student, academic, older student, psychological, birth control, religious. **For learning-disabled students:** School does not offer a structured program with separate admission and additional fees. Total undergraduates in learning-disabled program or receiving services: 340. Services include: reading machines, tape recorders, untimed tests, note-taking services, oral tests, learning center, readers, extended time for tests, tutors, priority registration, priority seating, texts on tape, typist/scribe, other testing accommodations, other. **Library:** Number of titles: 2,129,271; number of current serial subscriptions: 70,923. **Information technology resources:** Students are not required to lease or own a computer. Number of campus computers available to all students: 448. School has a wireless network. Approximate number of users that can be accommodated: 15,000. Proportion of college-owned housing units wired for high-speed internet access: 100%. **Campus safety:** Security services offered: 24-hour foot-and-vehicle patrols, late-night transport/escort service, 24-hour emergency telephones, lighted pathways/sidewalks, student patrols, controlled dormitory access (key, security card, etc).

TRANSFER AND INTERNATIONAL STUDENTS
Transfer students: May apply for admission for the following academic terms: Fall, Spring. Applicants need a minimum number of credits to apply. For fall 2009: Transfer applications received: 1,483. Transfer applicants offered admission: 1,041. Transfer applicants enrolled: 572. **International students:** Number of foreign undergraduates: 75 (1% of student body). Number of countries represented: 29. Minimum TOEFL score required: 550 (paper); 213 (computer). Average TOEFL score: 604 (paper).

New Jersey

Bloomfield College

- **Address:** 467 Franklin Street, Bloomfield, NJ 07003
- **Website:** http://www.bloomfield.edu
- **Private; Religious affiliation:** Presbyterian
- **Enrollment:** 1,731 full-time; 411 part-time

KEY STATS

✔ **U.S News College Ranking:** second tier, National Liberal Arts Colleges
✔ **SAT Score (25th/75th percentile):** 730-910
✔ **Tuition:** 2010-2011: $22,400

Selectivity: Less selective	**Room/board:** $10,600
Acceptance rate: 77%	**Average debt:** $28,310
Student/faculty ratio: 15/1	**Proportion who borrowed:** 87%

UNDERGRADUATE STUDENT BODY STATS

2009-2010 enrollment: 1,731 full-time; 411 part-time. Men: 35%; women: 65%. **Ethnic makeup:** African American: 50%; Asian American: 3%; Hispanic: 20%; White: 26%; International: 1%.

ADMISSIONS FACTS AND FIGURES

Phone: (800) 848-4555. **Email:** admission@bloomfield.edu. **Website:** http://www.bloomfield.edu. **Application deadlines for fall 2011:** Regular decision: August 1. Early decision: Not offered. Early action: Send application by: January 7; Decision sent by: January 21. Admission can be deferred. **Application fee:** $40. **To apply online, go to:** http://www.bloomfield.edu/admissions. **Admissions requirements/recommendations:** High school units required (recommended): Total units: 14. Tests: The college uses SAT or ACT scores in admissions decisions. Either SAT or ACT required. For admission to the fall 2011 entering class, the school will accept: ACT with or without writing accepted. Campus visit: Recommended. Admissions interview: Recommended. Off-campus interview: May be arranged. **Factors that count in admissions decisions:** *Academic:* Secondary school record: Very Important. Class rank: Important. Letters of recommendation: Very Important. Standardized test scores: Very Important. Essay: Very Important. *Nonacademic:* Interview: Important. Extracurricular activities: Important. Talent/ability: Important. Character/personal qualities: Not Considered. Alumni/ae relationship: Considered. Geographical residence: Not Considered. State residency: Not Considered. Religious affiliation/commitment: Not Considered. Minority status: Not Considered. Volunteer work: Important. Work experience: Considered. **Other schools with the greatest overlap in applicants:** Fairleigh Dickinson University; Kean University; Montclair State University; New Jersey City University; William Paterson University of New Jersey. **Admissions statistics for the fall 2009 entering class:** Total applicants: 2,549. Total accepted: 1,961. Freshmen enrolled: 483; 4% were from out of state. Accepted through early-decision or early-action plans: 6%. Overall acceptance rate: 77%. Non-early acceptance rate: 78%. **Credentials of fall 2009 freshmen:** 8% ranked in the top 10 percent of their high school class; 24% were in the top 25 percent; 60% were in the top half. (Proportion submitting class standing: 73%.) **Average high school grade point average:** 2.6. **First-year students who submitted SAT scores:** 92%. Scores (25/75 percentile): Critical Reading: 370-450, Math: 360-460, Combined: 730-910.

ACADEMICS

Year founded: 1868. **Academic calendar:** Semester. **Degrees offered:** certificate, bachelor's, post-bachelor's certificate, master's. **Most popular majors:** 17% business, management, marketing, and related support services, 17% social sciences, 15% psychology, 12% health professions and related clinical sciences, 10% visual and performing arts. **Major fields of study:** biological and biomedical sciences; business, management, marketing, and related support services; communication, journalism, and related programs; computer and information sciences and support services; education; English language and literature/letters; health professions and related clinical sciences; history; mathematics and statistics; multi/interdisciplinary studies; philosophy and religious studies; physical sciences; psychology; social sciences; visual and performing arts. **Areas of required coursework:** arts/fine arts, humanities, computer literacy, mathematics, English (including composition), philosophy, sciences (biological or physical), history, social science. **Pre-professional programs:** pre-medicine, other. **Special academic programs (% participation):** accelerated program (12%), distance learning (0%), double major (0%), dual enrollment (0%), English as a Second Language (ESL) (5%), honors program (.3%), independent study (20%), internships (33%), liberal arts/career combination (0%), student-designed major (0%), study abroad (0%), teacher certificate program (10%), weekend college (10%). **Teacher certification offered in:** early childhood, special education, elementary, secondary. **Reserve Officers Training Corps (ROTC):** Army ROTC: Offered at cooperating institution (Seton Hall University). **Faculty and instruction (2009-2010):** Total instructional faculty: 68 full-time, 171 part-time (48% men; 52% women; 32% minorities). Full-time faculty with Ph.D. or other terminal degree: 74%. Student/faculty ratio: 15/1. Classes of fewer than 20 students: 74%; of 20 to 49 students: 25%; of 50 or more students: 0%. **Advanced Placement and International Baccalaureate credit:** AP tests may be used for: Credit and/or placement. Scores accepted: 3, 4, 5. International Baccalaureate exams may be used for: Credit only. **Freshmen returning for sophomore year:** 69%. **Graduation rates:** Four-year: 11%; five-year: 23%; six-year: 26%. **Graduate study:** 7% of students pursue further study within one year.

COSTS AND FINANCIAL AID

Financial aid office: (973) 748-9000. **Expenses (2010-2011):** Tuition and fees 2010-2011: $22,400; room/board: $10,600. Estimated books and supplies: $1,000; transportation: $1,000; personal expenses: $1,800. **Financial aid:** Priority filing date for institution's financial aid form: March 15; deadline: June 1. In 2009-2010, 98% of undergraduates applied for financial aid. Of those, 88% were determined to have financial need; 2% had their need fully met. Average financial aid package (proportion receiving): $16,544 (87%). Average amount of gift aid, such as scholarships or grants (proportion receiving): $13,844 (83%). Average amount of self-help aid, such as work study or loans (proportion receiving): $8,749 (25%). Average need-based loan (excluding PLUS or other private loans): $8,289. Among students who received need-based aid, the average percentage of need met: 56%. Among students who received aid based on merit, the average award (and the proportion receiving): $9,892 (9%). The average athletic scholarship (and the proportion receiving): $19,071 (2%). Average amount of debt of borrowers graduating in 2009: $28,310. Proportion who borrowed: 87%.

CAMPUS LIFE AND EXTRACURRICULAR ACTIVITIES

Campus housing available (% using): coed dorms (37%), apartment for single students (17%), other housing options (44%). Students who live in college-owned, operated, or affiliated housing: 24%. **Student employment:** During the 2009-2010 academic year, 14% of undergraduates worked on campus. Average per-year earnings: $2,000. **Clubs and organizations:** Number of student organizations: 43. Activities include: campus ministries, dance, drama/theater, international student organization, radio station, student government. Number of fraternities: 6; sororities: 7. Proportion of men in fraternities: 3%; of women in sororities: 1%. Average proportion of students who stay on campus on weekends: 20%. **Sports program (2009-2010):** Member of NCAA II. *Men's intercollegiate varsity sports:* baseball, basketball, cross country, soccer, tennis. *Women's intercollegiate varsity sports:* basketball, cross country, soccer, softball, volleyball.

SERVICES AND FACILITIES

Basic services: nonremedial tutoring, placement service, health service, health insurance. **Remedial assistance:** reading, math, writing, study skills. **Counseling services:** career, personal, academic, older student, psychological, birth control, religious. **For learning-disabled students:** School does not offer a structured program with separate admission and additional fees. Total undergraduates in learning-disabled program or receiving services: 51. Services include: remedial math, remedial English, remedial reading, tape recorders, untimed tests, note-taking services, oral tests, learning center, readers, extended time for tests, tutors, priority registration, priority seating, substitution of courses, texts on tape, typist/scribe, exams on tape or computer, take home exams, other testing accommodations, other. **Library:**

Number of titles: 65,000; number of current serial subscriptions: 560. **Information technology resources:** Students are not required to lease or own a computer. Number of campus computers available to all students: 200. School has a wireless network. Approximate number of users that can be accommodated: 300. Proportion of college-owned housing units wired for high-speed internet access: 100%. **Campus safety:** Security services offered: 24-hour foot-and-vehicle patrols, late-night transport/escort service, 24-hour emergency telephones, lighted pathways/sidewalks, controlled dormitory access (key, security card, etc).

TRANSFER AND INTERNATIONAL STUDENTS

Transfer students: May apply for admission for the following academic terms: Fall, Spring, Summer. Applicants need a minimum number of credits to apply. For fall 2009: Transfer applications received: 841. Transfer applicants offered admission: 535. Transfer applicants enrolled: 267. **International students:** Number of foreign undergraduates: 29 (1% of student body). Number of countries represented: 3. Minimum TOEFL score required: 550 (paper); 213 (computer). Average TOEFL score: 565 (paper).

Caldwell College

- **Address:** 9 Ryerson Avenue, Caldwell, NJ 07006
- **Website:** hftp://www.caldwell.edu
- **Private; Religious affiliation:** Roman Catholic
- **Enrollment:** 1,143 full-time; 466 part-time

KEY STATS

✔ **U.S News College Ranking:** 105, Regional Universities (North)
✔ **SAT Score (25th/75th percentile):** 900-1160
✔ **Tuition:** 2010-2011: $25,602

Selectivity: Selective	**Room/board:** $10,000
Acceptance rate: 57%	**Average debt:** $24,500
Student/faculty ratio: 13/1	**Proportion who borrowed:** 87%

UNDERGRADUATE STUDENT BODY STATS

2009-2010 enrollment: 1,143 full-time; 466 part-time. Men: 34%; women: 66%. **Ethnic makeup:** African American: 12%; American-Indian: 1%; Asian American: 2%; Hispanic: 16%; White: 61%; International: 8%. **Religious preference:** Protestant: 25%; Jewish: 5%; Unknown: 3%; Roman Catholic: 67%.

ADMISSIONS FACTS AND FIGURES

Phone: (973) 618-3500. **Email:** admissions@caldwell.edu. **Website:** http://www.caldwell.edu. **Application deadlines for fall 2011:** Regular decision: Rolling. Early decision: Not offered. Early action: Send application by: January 1; Decision sent by: January 15. Admission can be deferred. **Application fee:** $40. **To apply online, go to:** http://www.collegeboard.org. **Admissions requirements/recommendations:** High school units required (recommended): English: 4; Mathematics: 2; Science: 2; Foreign language: 2; History: 1; Academic electives: 5; Total units: 16. Tests: The college uses SAT or ACT scores in admissions decisions. Either SAT or ACT required. For admission to the fall 2011 entering class, the school will accept: ACT with writing required. Campus visit: Recommended. Admissions interview: Recommended. Off-campus interview: May be arranged. **Factors that count in admissions decisions:** *Academic:* Secondary school record: Very Important. Class rank: Important. Letters of recommendation: Considered. Standardized test scores: Important. Essay: Considered. *Nonacademic:* Interview: Considered. Extracurricular activities: Very Important. Talent/ability: Important. Character/personal qualities: Important. Alumni/ae relationship: Considered. Geographical residence: Not Considered. State residency: Not Considered. Religious affiliation/commitment: Not Considered. Minority status: Not Considered. Volunteer work: Considered. Work experience: Considered. **Other schools with the greatest overlap in applicants:** Kean University; Montclair State University; Rutgers, the State University of New Jersey–New Brunswick; Seton Hall University; William Paterson University of New Jersey. **Admissions statistics for the fall 2009 entering class:** Total applicants: 1,740. Total accepted: 995. Freshmen enrolled: 272; Overall acceptance rate: 57%. Non-early acceptance rate: 57%. **Credentials of fall 2009 freshmen:** 12% ranked in the top 10 percent of their high school class; 31% were in the top 25 percent; 70% were in the top half. (Proportion submitting class standing: 75%.) **Average high school grade point average:** 3.0. **First-year students who submitted SAT scores:** 98%. Scores (25/75 percentile): Critical Reading: 460-565, Math: 440-595, Combined: 900-1160.

First-year students submitting ACT scores: 2%. Scores (25/75 percentile): English: N/A, Math: N/A, Composite: N/A.

ACADEMICS

Year founded: 1939. **Academic calendar:** Semester. **Degrees offered:** certificate, bachelor's, post-bachelor's certificate, master's, post-master's certificate, doctorate. **Most popular majors:** 22% psychology, 12% business administration and management, 8% criminal justice/safety studies, 8% education, 8% English language and literature. **Major fields of study:** area, ethnic, cultural, and gender studies; biological and biomedical sciences; business, management, marketing, and related support services; communication, journalism, and related programs; computer and information sciences and support services; education; English language and literature/letters; foreign languages, literatures, and linguistics; history; mathematics and statistics; multi/interdisciplinary studies; physical sciences; psychology; security and protective services; social sciences; visual and performing arts. **Areas of required coursework:** arts/fine arts, humanities, computer literacy, mathematics, English (including composition), philosophy, foreign languages, sciences (biological or physical), history, social science, other. **Preprofessional programs:** pre-law, pre-dentistry, pre-medicine, pre-theology, pre-veterinary science, pre-optometry. **Special academic programs (% participation):** accelerated program, cooperative (work-study plan) program (21%), distance learning, double major (23%), English as a Second Language (ESL), external degree program, honors program, independent study, internships (32%), liberal arts/career combination, student-designed major (0%), study abroad (7%), teacher certificate program (18%), weekend college. **Teacher certification offered in:** early childhood, special education, elementary, middle/junior high, secondary. **Cooperative education programs:** art, business, computer science, education, humanities, social/behavioral science. **Faculty and instruction (2009-2010):** Total instructional faculty: 82 full-time, 129 part-time (37% men; 63% women). Full-time faculty with Ph.D. or other terminal degree: 84%. Student/faculty ratio: 13/1. Classes of fewer than 20 students: 79%; of 20 to 49 students: 21%. **Advanced Placement and International Baccalaureate credit:** AP tests may be used for: Placement only. Scores accepted: 3, 4, 5. International Baccalaureate exams may be used for: Credit only. **Freshmen returning for sophomore year:** 73%. **Graduation rates:** Four-year: 29%; five-year: 45%; six-year: 49%. **Graduate study:** 35% of students pursue further study immediately upon graduation; 45% within one year; 50% within five years. Fields in which graduates pursue further study: Master of Business Administration (MBA), 20%; law, 3%; medicine, 2%; theology (or the seminary), 1%; education, 30%; arts and sciences, 10%.

COSTS AND FINANCIAL AID

Financial aid office: (973) 618-3221. **Expenses (2010-2011):** Tuition and fees 2010-2011: $25,602; room/board: $10,000. Estimated books and supplies: $1,600; transportation: $750; personal expenses: $1,000. **Financial aid:** Priority filing date for institution's financial aid form: April 15. In 2009-2010, 85% of undergraduates applied for financial aid. Of those, 76% were determined to have financial need; 15% had their need fully met. Average financial aid package (proportion receiving): N/A (76%). Average amount of gift aid, such as scholarships or grants (proportion receiving): $14,070 (71%). Average amount of self-help aid, such as work study or loans (proportion receiving): $4,752 (63%). Average need-based loan (excluding PLUS or other private loans): $4,563. Among students who received need-based aid, the average percentage of need met: 74%. Among students who received aid based on merit, the average award (and the proportion receiving): $11,940 (12%). The average athletic scholarship (and the proportion receiving): $6,840 (10%). Average amount of debt of borrowers graduating in 2009: $24,500. Proportion who borrowed: 87%.

CAMPUS LIFE AND EXTRACURRICULAR ACTIVITIES

Campus housing available (% using): coed dorms (100%). Students who live in college-owned, operated, or affiliated housing: 43%. **Student employment:** During the 2009-2010 academic year, 15% of undergraduates worked on campus. Average per-year earnings: $1,000. **Clubs and organizations:** Number of student organizations: 23. Activities include: choral groups, concert band, dance, drama/theater, jazz band, literary magazine, music ensembles, musical theater, student government, student newspaper, yearbook. Number of fraternities: 0; sororities: 0. Average proportion of students who stay on campus on weekends: 35%. **Sports program (2009-2010):** Member of NCAA II.

SERVICES AND FACILITIES

Basic services: nonremedial tutoring, placement service, health service, other. **Remedial assistance:** reading, math, writing, study skills. **Counseling services:** minority student, career, personal, academic, older student, psychological, religious, other. **For learning-disabled students:** School does not offer a structured program with separate admission and additional fees. Services include: remedial math, remedial English, reading machines, remedial reading, tape recorders, other special classes, untimed tests, note-taking services, oral tests, learning center, readers, extended time for tests, tutors. **Library:** Number of titles: 149,200; number of current serial subscriptions: 450. **Information technology resources:** Students are not required to lease or own a computer. Number of campus computers available to all students: 234. School has a wireless network. Approximate number of users that can be accommodated: 50. Proportion of college-owned housing units wired for high-speed internet access: 100%. **Campus safety:** Security services offered: 24-hour foot-and-vehicle patrols, late-night transport/escort service, 24-hour emergency telephones, lighted pathways/sidewalks, controlled dormitory access (key, security card, etc).

TRANSFER AND INTERNATIONAL STUDENTS

Transfer students: May apply for admission for the following academic terms: Fall, Spring. Applicants need a minimum number of credits to apply. For fall 2009: Transfer applications received: 210. Transfer applicants offered admission: 87. Transfer applicants enrolled: 31. **International students:** Number of foreign undergraduates: 95 (8% of student body). Minimum TOEFL score required: 450 (paper); 133 (computer). Average TOEFL score: 550 (paper).

Centenary College

- **Address:** 400 Jefferson Street, Hackettstown, NJ 07840
- **Website:** http://www.centenarycollege.edu
- **Private; Religious affiliation:** United Methodist
- **Enrollment:** 1,963 full-time; 177 part-time

KEY STATS

✔ **U.S News College Ranking:** second tier, Regional Universities (North)
✔ **SAT Score (25th/75th percentile):** 830-1020
✔ **Tuition:** 2010-2011: $28,054

Selectivity: Less selective	**Room/board:** $9,434
Acceptance rate: 89%	**Average debt:** $28,104
Student/faculty ratio: 16/1	**Proportion who borrowed:** 83%

UNDERGRADUATE STUDENT BODY STATS

2009-2010 enrollment: 1,963 full-time; 177 part-time. Men: 37%; women: 63%. **Ethnic makeup:** African American: 6%; Asian American: 6%; Hispanic: 5%; White: 82%; International: 1%. **Religious preference:** Roman Catholic: 45%; Jewish: 2%; No preference: 15%; Unknown: 30%; United Methodist: 8%.

ADMISSIONS FACTS AND FIGURES

Phone: (800) 236-8679. **Email:** admissions@centenarycollege.edu. **Website:** http://www.centenarycollege.edu. **Application deadlines for fall 2011:** Regular decision: August 15. Early decision: Not offered. Early action: Not offered. Admission can be deferred. **Application fee:** $30. **To apply online, go to:** https://secure.centenarycollege.edu/application.php?current_step=start&WT.mc_id=. **Admissions requirements/recommendations:** High school units required (recommended): English: 4 (4); Mathematics: 3 (4); Science: 2 (4); Foreign language: (2); Social studies: (4); Total units: 16 (20). Tests: The college uses SAT or ACT scores in admissions decisions. Either SAT or ACT required. Campus visit: Recommended. Admissions interview: Recommended. Off-campus interview: Not available. **Factors that count in admissions decisions:** *Academic:* Secondary school record: Important. Class rank: Considered. Letters of recommendation: Important. Standardized test scores: Very Important. Essay: Very Important. *Nonacademic:* Interview: Very Important. Extracurricular activities: Important. Talent/ability: Important. Character/personal qualities: Important. Alumni/ae relationship: Considered. Geographical residence: Not Considered. State residency: Not Considered. Religious affiliation/commitment: Considered. Minority status: Not Considered. Volunteer work: Important. Work experience: Considered. **Other schools with the greatest overlap in applicants:** Caldwell College; Monmouth University; Montclair State University; Rutgers, the State University of New Jersey–New Brunswick; William Paterson University of New Jersey. **Admissions statistics for the fall 2009 entering class:** Total applicants: 754. Total accepted: 673. Freshmen enrolled: 271; 24% were from out of state. Overall acceptance rate: 89%. **Credentials of fall 2009 freshmen:** 14% ranked in the top 10 percent of their high school class;

30% were in the top 25 percent; 69% were in the top half. (Proportion submitting class standing: 51%.) **Average high school grade point average:** 2.7. **First-year students who submitted SAT scores:** 90%. Scores (25/75 percentile): Critical Reading: 410-510, Math: 420-510, Combined: 830-1020. **First-year students submitting ACT scores:** 7%. Scores (25/75 percentile): English: N/A, Math: N/A, Composite: N/A.

ACADEMICS

Year founded: 1867. **Academic calendar:** Semester. **Degrees offered:** associate, bachelor's, master's. **Most popular majors:** 49% business, management, marketing, and related support services, 10% psychology, 7% security and protective services, 6% history. **Major fields of study:** agriculture, agriculture operations, and related sciences; business, management, marketing, and related support services; communication, journalism, and related programs; English language and literature/letters; history; liberal arts and sciences studies, and humanities; mathematics and statistics; psychology; security and protective services; social sciences; visual and performing arts. **Areas of required coursework:** arts/fine arts, humanities, computer literacy, mathematics, English (including composition), sciences (biological or physical), history, social science. **Special academic programs (% participation):** accelerated program (31%), double major (15%), English as a Second Language (ESL) (5%), exchange student program (domestic) (2%), honors program (2%), independent study (7%), internships (35%), liberal arts/career combination (10%), student-designed major (1%), study abroad (5%), teacher certificate program (14%), weekend college (1%). **Teacher certification offered in:** special education, elementary, middle/junior high, secondary. **Faculty and instruction (2009-2010):** Total instructional faculty: 69 full-time, 270 part-time (47% men; 53% women; 1% minorities). Full-time faculty with Ph.D. or other terminal degree: 57%. Student/faculty ratio: 16/1. Classes of fewer than 20 students: 61%; of 20 to 49 students: 39%. **Advanced Placement and International Baccalaureate credit:** AP tests may be used for: Credit only. Scores accepted: 3, 4, 5. International Baccalaureate exams may be used for: Credit only. **Freshmen returning for sophomore year:** 75%. **Graduation rates:** Four-year: 51%; five-year: 52%; six-year: 49%. **Graduate study:** 5% of students pursue further study immediately upon graduation; 8% within one year; 10% within five years.

COSTS AND FINANCIAL AID

Financial aid office: (908) 852-1400. **Expenses (2010-2011):** Tuition and fees 2010-2011: $28,054; room/board: $9,434. Estimated books and supplies: $1,000. **Financial aid:** Priority filing date for institution's financial aid form: April 1. In 2009-2010, 54% of undergraduates applied for financial aid. Of those, 48% were determined to have financial need; 19% had their need fully met. Average financial aid package (proportion receiving): $17,867 (48%). Average amount of gift aid, such as scholarships or grants (proportion receiving): $13,118 (47%). Average amount of self-help aid, such as work study or loans (proportion receiving): $5,620 (41%). Average need-based loan (excluding PLUS or other private loans): $4,493. Among students who received need-based aid, the average percentage of need met: 70%. Among students who received aid based on merit, the average award (and the proportion receiving): $7,470 (18%). The average athletic scholarship (and the proportion receiving): $0 (0%). Average amount of debt of borrowers graduating in 2009: $28,104. Proportion who borrowed: 83%.

CAMPUS LIFE AND EXTRACURRICULAR ACTIVITIES

Campus housing available (% using): coed dorms (75%), apartment for single students (25%). Students who live in college-owned, operated, or affiliated housing: 53%. **Clubs and organizations:** Number of student organizations: 30. Activities include: campus ministries, choral groups, dance, drama/theater, international student organization, literary magazine, model UN, music ensembles, musical theater, radio station, student government, student newspaper, student film society, television station, yearbook. Number of fraternities: 2; sororities: 3. Proportion of men in fraternities: 10%; of women in sororities: 10%. Average proportion of students who stay on campus on weekends: 75%. **Sports program (2009-2010):** Member of NCAA III. *Men's intercollegiate varsity sports:* baseball, basketball, cross country, golf, lacrosse, soccer, wrestling. *Women's intercollegiate varsity sports:* basketball, cross country, equestrian, lacrosse, soccer, softball, volleyball.

SERVICES AND FACILITIES

Basic services: nonremedial tutoring, women's center, placement service, health service. **Remedial assistance:** reading, math, writing, study skills. **Counseling services:** minority student, career, personal, academic, older student, psychological. **For learning-disabled students:** School does not offer a structured program with separate admission and additional fees.

Services include: remedial math, remedial English, reading machines, tape recorders, note-taking services, oral tests, learning center, readers, extended time for tests, tutors, texts on tape, typist/scribe, exams on tape or computer, other testing accommodations, other. **Library:** Number of titles: 72,606; number of current serial subscriptions: 84. **Information technology resources:** Students are required to lease or own a computer. School has a wireless network. Approximate number of users that can be accommodated: 12,000. Proportion of college-owned housing units wired for high-speed internet access: 100%. **Campus safety:** Security services offered: 24-hour foot-and-vehicle patrols, late-night transport/escort service, 24-hour emergency telephones, lighted pathways/sidewalks, student patrols, controlled dormitory access (key, security card, etc).

TRANSFER AND INTERNATIONAL STUDENTS

Transfer students: May apply for admission for the following academic terms: Fall, Spring. Applicants do not need a minimum number of credits to apply. For fall 2009: Transfer applications received: 295. Transfer applicants offered admission: 202. Transfer applicants enrolled: 138. **International students:** Number of foreign undergraduates: 12 (1% of student body). Minimum TOEFL score required: 450 (paper); 133 (computer). Average TOEFL score: 480 (paper).

College of New Jersey

- ■ **Address:** PO Box 7718, 2000 Pennington Road, Ewing, NJ 08628-0718
- ■ **Website:** http://www.tcnj.edu
- ■ **Public**
- ■ **Enrollment:** 6,080 full-time; 157 part-time

KEY STATS

✔ **U.S News College Ranking:** 4, Regional Universities (North)
✔ **SAT Score (25th/75th percentile):** 1150-1350
✔ **Tuition:** 2009-2010: $12,722 in state, $21,408 out of state
Selectivity: More selective   **Room/board:** $9,996
Acceptance rate: 46%   **Average debt:** $24,801
Student/faculty ratio: 13/1   **Proportion who borrowed:** 58%

UNDERGRADUATE STUDENT BODY STATS

2009-2010 enrollment: 6,080 full-time; 157 part-time. Men: 41%; women: 59%. **Ethnic makeup:** African American: 6%; Asian American: 6%; Hispanic: 9%; White: 77%; International: 1%. **Religious preference:** Roman Catholic: 45%; Protestant: 14%; Jewish: 5%; Muslim: 1%; Hindu: 3%; Buddhist: 1%; No preference: 17%; Christian: 9%; Other: 5%.

ADMISSIONS FACTS AND FIGURES

Phone: (609) 771-2131. **Email:** admiss@tcnj.edu. **Website:** http://www.tcnj. edu. **Application deadlines for fall 2011:** Regular decision: January 15. Early decision: Send application by: November 15; Decision sent by: December 15. Early action: Not offered. Admission can be deferred. **Application fee:** $70. **To apply online, go to:** http://www.tcnj.edu/~admiss/apply/. **Admissions requirements/recommendations:** High school units required (recommended): English: 4 (4); Mathematics: 3 (3); Science: 3 (3); Foreign language: 2 (3); Social studies: 2 (3); Total units: 18 (20). Tests: The college uses SAT or ACT scores in admissions decisions. Either SAT or ACT required. For admission to the fall 2011 entering class, the school will accept: ACT with or without writing accepted. Campus visit: Recommended. Admissions interview: Recommended. Off-campus interview: May be arranged. **Factors that count in admissions decisions:** *Academic:* Secondary school record: Very Important. Class rank: Very Important. Letters of recommendation: Important. Standardized test scores: Very Important. Essay: Important. *Nonacademic:* Interview: Not Considered. Extracurricular activities: Very Important. Talent/ability: Important. Character/personal qualities: Important. Alumni/ae relationship: Considered. Geographical residence: Important. State residency: Important. Religious affiliation/commitment: Not Considered. Minority status: Considered. Volunteer work: Very Important. Work experience: Considered. **Other schools with the greatest overlap in applicants:** Boston College; New York University; Rutgers, the State University of New Jersey–New Brunswick; University of Delaware; Villanova University. **Admissions statistics for the fall 2009 entering class:** Total applicants: 9,283. Total accepted: 4,267. Freshmen enrolled: 1,284; 6% were from out of state. Accepted through early-decision or early-action plans: 9%. Overall acceptance rate: 46%. Early-decision acceptance rate: 47%. Non-early acceptance rate: 46%. **Size of waiting list:** 1116 applicants;

enrolled from waiting list: 288. **Credentials of fall 2009 freshmen:** 61% ranked in the top 10 percent of their high school class; 92% were in the top 25 percent; 99% were in the top half. (Proportion submitting class standing: 68%.) **First-year students who submitted SAT scores:** 97%. Scores (25/75 percentile): Critical Reading: 560-660, Math: 590-690, Combined: 1150-1350.

ACADEMICS

Year founded: 1855. **Academic calendar:** Semester. **Degrees offered:** bachelor's, post-bachelor's certificate, master's, post-master's certificate. **Most popular majors:** 14% business administration and management, 8% psychology, 7% biology/biological sciences, 6% elementary education and teaching, 6% physical education teaching and coaching. **Major fields of study:** area, ethnic, cultural, and gender studies; biological and biomedical sciences; business, management, marketing, and related support services; computer and information sciences and support services; education; engineering; English language and literature/letters; foreign languages, literatures, and linguistics; health professions and related clinical sciences; history; mathematics and statistics; philosophy and religious studies; physical sciences; psychology; security and protective services; social sciences; visual and performing arts. **Areas of required coursework:** arts/fine arts, humanities, mathematics, English (including composition), philosophy, foreign languages, sciences (biological or physical), history, social science, other. **Pre-professional programs:** pre-law, pre-dentistry, pre-medicine, pre-optometry. **Special academic programs (% participation):** double major (13%), exchange student program (domestic) (1%), honors program (10%), independent study (29%), internships (77%), study abroad (20%), teacher certificate program (25%). **Teacher certification offered in:** early childhood, special education, elementary, middle/junior high, secondary, bilingual/bicultural. **Reserve Officers Training Corps (ROTC):** Army ROTC: Offered at cooperating institution (Princeton University); Air Force ROTC: Offered at cooperating institution (Rutgers, the State University of New Jersey–New Brunswick). **Faculty and instruction (2009-2010):** Total instructional faculty: 348 full-time, 402 part-time (48% men; 52% women; 15% minorities). Full-time faculty with Ph.D. or other terminal degree: 89%. Student/faculty ratio: 13/1. Classes of fewer than 20 students: 42%; of 20 to 49 students: 58%; of 50 or more students: 0%. **Advanced Placement and International Baccalaureate credit:** AP tests may be used for: Credit only. Scores accepted: 4, 5. International Baccalaureate exams may be used for: Credit only. **Freshmen returning for sophomore year:** 95%. **Graduation rates:** Four-year: 73%; five-year: 84%; six-year: 85%. **Graduate study:** 33% of students pursue further study immediately upon graduation; 27% within one year; 51% within five years. Fields in which graduates pursue further study: Master of Business Administration (MBA), 5%; law, 14%; medicine, 20%; dentistry, 1%; engineering, 5%; theology (or the seminary), 1%; education, 22%; arts and sciences, 31%; veterinary medicine, 1%.

COSTS AND FINANCIAL AID

Financial aid office: (609) 771-2211. **Expenses (2009-2010):** Tuition and fees 2009-2010: $12,722 in state, $21,408 out of state; room/board: $9,996. Estimated books and supplies: $1,000; transportation: $1,000; personal expenses: $1,500. **Financial aid:** Priority filing date for institution's financial aid form: March 1. In 2009-2010, 72% of undergraduates applied for financial aid. Of those, 49% were determined to have financial need; 20% had their need fully met. Average financial aid package (proportion receiving): $10,088 (47%). Average amount of gift aid, such as scholarships or grants (proportion receiving): N/A (19%). Average amount of self-help aid, such as work study or loans (proportion receiving): $4,483 (34%). Average need-based loan (excluding PLUS or other private loans): $4,326. Among students who received need-based aid, the average percentage of need met: 52%. Among students who received aid based on merit, the average award (and the proportion receiving): $4,777 (18%). The average athletic scholarship (and the proportion receiving): $0 (0%). Average amount of debt of borrowers graduating in 2009: $24,801. Proportion who borrowed: 58%.

CAMPUS LIFE AND EXTRACURRICULAR ACTIVITIES

Campus housing available (% using): coed dorms (96%), apartment for single students, special housing for disabled students (1%), special housing for international students (1%), other housing options (2%). Students who live in college-owned, operated, or affiliated housing: 58%. **Student employment:** During the 2009-2010 academic year, 25% of undergraduates worked on campus. Average per-year earnings: $1,870. **Clubs and organizations:** Number of student organizations: 205. Activities include: campus ministries, choral groups, concert band, dance, drama/theater, international student organization, jazz band, literary magazine, music ensembles, musical theater, opera, pep band, radio station, student government, student newspaper, symphony orchestra, television station, yearbook. Number of fraternities: 12; sororities: 16. Proportion of men in fraternities: 16%; of women in sororities: 13%. Average proportion of students who stay on campus on weekends: 65%. **Sports program (2009-2010):** Member of NCAA III. *Men's intercollegiate varsity sports:* baseball, basketball, cross country, football, soccer, swimming, tennis, track and field (indoor), track and field (outdoor), wrestling. *Women's intercollegiate varsity sports:* basketball, cross country, field hockey, lacrosse, soccer, softball, swimming, tennis, track and field (indoor), track and field (outdoor).

SERVICES AND FACILITIES

Basic services: nonremedial tutoring, women's center, placement service, health service, health insurance. **Remedial assistance:** math, writing, study skills. **Counseling services:** minority student, career, personal, academic, psychological, birth control, religious. **For learning-disabled students:** School does not offer a structured program with separate admission and additional fees. Services include: tape recorders, note-taking services, readers, extended time for tests, other. **Library:** Number of titles: 674,051; number of current serial subscriptions: 6,194. **Information technology resources:** Students are not required to lease or own a computer. Number of campus computers available to all students: 649. School has a wireless network. Approximate number of users that can be accommodated: 2,000. Proportion of college-owned housing units wired for high-speed internet access: 100%. **Campus safety:** Security services offered: 24-hour foot-and-vehicle patrols, late-night transport/escort service, 24-hour emergency telephones, lighted pathways/sidewalks, student patrols, controlled dormitory access (key, security card, etc).

TRANSFER AND INTERNATIONAL STUDENTS

Transfer students: May apply for admission for the following academic terms: Fall, Spring. Applicants need a minimum number of credits to apply. For fall 2009: Transfer applications received: 1,027. Transfer applicants offered admission: 536. Transfer applicants enrolled: 324. **International students:** Number of foreign undergraduates: 59 (1% of student body). Number of countries represented: 25. Minimum TOEFL score required: 550 (paper); 90 (computer).

College of St. Elizabeth

- **Address:** 2 Convent Road, Morristown, NJ 07960-6989
- **Website:** http://www.cse.edu
- **Private; Religious affiliation:** Roman Catholic
- **Enrollment:** N/A

....

KEY STATS
✔ **U.S News College Ranking:** 126, Regional Universities (North)
✔ **SAT or ACT Score (25th/75th percentile):** N/A
✔ **Tuition:** 2009-2010: $25,058

Selectivity: Less selective	**Room/board:** $10,904
Acceptance rate: N/A	**Average debt:** N/A
Student/faculty ratio: N/A	**Proportion who borrowed:** N/A

Drew University

- **Address:** 36 Madison Avenue, Madison, NJ 07940-1493
- **Website:** http://www.drew.edu
- **Private; Religious affiliation:** Methodist
- **Enrollment:** 1,679 full-time; 60 part-time

....

KEY STATS
✔ **U.S News College Ranking:** 79, National Liberal Arts Colleges
✔ **SAT Score (25th/75th percentile):** 1010-1248
✔ **Tuition:** 2010-2011: $39,573

Selectivity: More selective	**Room/board:** $10,772
Acceptance rate: 74%	**Average debt:** $17,444
Student/faculty ratio: 11/1	**Proportion who borrowed:** 61%

UNDERGRADUATE STUDENT BODY STATS

2009-2010 enrollment: 1,679 full-time; 60 part-time. Men: 40%; women: 60%. **Ethnic makeup:** African American: 8%; Asian American: 6%; Hispanic: 10%; White: 74%; International: 2%.

ADMISSIONS FACTS AND FIGURES

Phone: (973) 408-3739. **Email:** cadm@drew.edu. **Website:** http://www.drew.edu. **Application deadlines for fall 2011:** Regular decision: February 15; decision sent by March 31. Early decision: Send application by: December 1; Decision sent by: December 24. Early action: Not offered. Admission can be deferred. **Application fee:** $50. **To apply online, go to:** http://www.drew.edu/cla/admissions.aspx?id=24689. **Admissions requirements/recommendations:** High school units required (recommended): English: (4); Mathematics: (3); Science: (2); Foreign language: (2); Social studies: (2); History: (2); Academic electives: (3); Total units: (18). Tests: The college uses SAT or ACT scores in admissions decisions. Neither SAT nor ACT required. For admission to the fall 2011 entering class, the school will accept: ACT with writing recommended. Campus visit: Recommended. Admissions interview: Recommended. Off-campus interview: May be arranged. **Factors that count in admissions decisions:** *Academic:* Secondary school record: Very Important. Class rank: Considered. Letters of recommendation: Important. Standardized test scores: Considered. Essay: Important. *Nonacademic:* Interview: Important. Extracurricular activities: Important. Talent/ability: Very Important. Character/personal qualities: Considered. Alumni/ae relationship: Considered. Geographical residence: Considered. State residency: Not Considered. Religious affiliation/commitment: Not Considered. Minority status: Considered. Volunteer work: Considered. Work experience: Considered. **Other schools with the greatest overlap in applicants:** Boston University; College of New Jersey; Muhlenberg College; New York University; Rutgers, the State University of New Jersey–New Brunswick. **Admissions statistics for the fall 2009 entering class:** Total applicants: 5,392. Total accepted: 3,991. Freshmen enrolled: 506; 44% were from out of state. Accepted through early-decision or early-action plans: 7%. Overall acceptance rate: 74%. Early-decision acceptance rate: 95%. Non-early acceptance rate: 74%. **Credentials of fall 2009 freshmen:** 38% ranked in the top 10 percent of their high school class; 67% were in the top 25 percent; 86% were in the top half. (Proportion submitting class standing: 41%.) **Average high school grade point average:** 3.3. **First-year students who submitted SAT scores:** 78%. Scores (25/75 percentile): Critical Reading: 510-630, Math: 500-618, Combined: 1010-1248. **First-year students submitting ACT scores:** 15%. Scores (25/75 percentile): English: 21-28, Math: 21-27, Composite: 21-27.

ACADEMICS

Year founded: 1867. **Academic calendar:** Semester. **Degrees offered:** bachelor's, post-bachelor's certificate, master's, post-master's certificate, doctorate. **Most popular majors:** 15% economics, 11% psychology, 9% political science and government, 7% history, 6% English language and literature. **Major fields of study:** area, ethnic, cultural, and gender studies; biological and biomedical sciences; computer and information sciences and support services; English language and literature/letters; foreign languages, literatures, and linguistics; history; mathematics and statistics; multi/interdisciplinary studies; philosophy and religious studies; physical sciences; psychology; social sciences; visual and performing arts. **Areas of required coursework:** arts/fine arts, humanities, computer literacy, English (including composition), foreign languages, sciences (biological or physical), social science. **Pre-professional programs:** pre-law, pre-medicine. **Special academic programs (% participation):** accelerated program, cross-registration, double major (19%), exchange student program (domestic), honors program, independent study, internships (50%), student-designed major, study abroad, teacher certificate program, other. **Cooperative education programs:** other. **Faculty and instruction (2009-2010):** Total instructional faculty: 159 full-time, 99 part-time. Full-time faculty with Ph.D. or other terminal degree: 96%. Student/faculty ratio: 11/1. Classes of fewer than 20 students: 71%; of 20 to 49 students: 27%; of 50 or more students: 2%. **Advanced Placement and International Baccalaureate credit:** AP tests may be used for: Credit and/or placement. Scores accepted: 4, 5. International Baccalaureate exams may be used for: Credit and/or placement. **Freshmen returning for sophomore year:** 82%. **Graduation rates:** Four-year: 69%; five-year: 74%; six-year: 76%. **Graduate study:** 27% of students pursue further study immediately upon graduation. Fields in which graduates pursue further study: Master of Business Administration (MBA), 1%; law, 13%; medicine, 8%; theology (or the seminary), 1%; education, 25%; arts and sciences, 51%; veterinary medicine, 1%.

COSTS AND FINANCIAL AID

Financial aid office: (973) 408-3112. **Expenses (2010-2011):** Tuition and fees 2010-2011: $39,573; room/board: $10,772. Estimated books and supplies: $1,228 personal expenses: $2,180. **Financial aid:** In 2009-2010, 71% of undergraduates applied for financial aid. Of those, 58% were determined to have financial need; 26% had their need fully met. Average financial aid package (proportion receiving): $30,067 (58%). Average amount of gift aid, such as scholarships or grants (proportion receiving): $24,393 (58%). Average amount of self-help aid, such as work study or loans (proportion receiving): $5,768 (47%). Average need-based loan (excluding PLUS or other private loans): $4,923. Among students who received need-based aid, the average percentage of need met: 80%. Among students who received aid based on merit, the average award (and the proportion receiving): $11,697 (37%). Average amount of debt of borrowers graduating in 2009: $17,444. Proportion who borrowed: 61%.

CAMPUS LIFE AND EXTRACURRICULAR ACTIVITIES

Campus housing available: coed dorms, special housing for disabled students. Students who live in college-owned, operated, or affiliated housing: 83%. **Student employment:** During the 2009-2010 academic year, 35% of undergraduates worked on campus. Average per-year earnings: $1,250. **Clubs and organizations:** Number of student organizations: 86. Activities include: choral groups, dance, drama/theater, literary magazine, model UN, music ensembles, radio station, student government, student newspaper, student film society, symphony orchestra, television station, yearbook. Number of fraternities: 0; sororities: 0. Average proportion of students who stay on campus on weekends: 67%. **Sports program (2009-2010):** Member of NCAA III. *Men's intercollegiate varsity sports:* baseball, basketball, cross country, fencing, football, lacrosse, soccer, swimming, tennis. *Women's intercollegiate varsity sports:* basketball, cross country, fencing, field hockey, lacrosse, soccer, softball, swimming, tennis.

SERVICES AND FACILITIES

Basic services: nonremedial tutoring, placement service, day care, health service, health insurance. **Remedial assistance:** math, writing, study skills. **Counseling services:** minority student, career, personal, academic, older student, psychological, birth control, religious. **For learning-disabled students:** School does not offer a structured program with separate admission and additional fees. Total undergraduates in learning-disabled program or receiving services: 115. Services include: tape recorders, note-taking services, extended time for tests, tutors, texts on tape, exams on tape or computer, other testing accommodations. **Library:** Number of titles: 615,743; number of current serial subscriptions: 41,161. **Information technology resources:** Students are required to lease or own a computer. Number of campus computers available to all students: 155. School has a wireless network. Approximate number of users that can be accommodated: 1,000. Proportion of college-owned housing units wired for high-speed internet access: 100%. **Campus safety:** Security services offered: 24-hour foot-and-vehicle patrols, late-night transport/escort service, 24-hour emergency telephones, lighted pathways/sidewalks, controlled dormitory access (key, security card, etc).

TRANSFER AND INTERNATIONAL STUDENTS

Transfer students: May apply for admission for the following academic terms: Fall, Spring. Applicants need a minimum number of credits to apply. For fall 2009: Transfer applications received: 186. Transfer applicants offered admission: 131. Transfer applicants enrolled: 58. **International students:** Number of foreign undergraduates: 28 (2% of student body). Number of countries represented: 19. Minimum TOEFL score required: 550 (paper); 213 (computer).

Fairleigh Dickinson University

- **Address:** 1000 River Road, Teaneck, NJ 07666
- **Website:** http://www.fdu.edu
- **Private**
- **Enrollment:** 4,752 full-time; 3,772 part-time

KEY STATS

✔ **U.S News College Ranking:** 57, Regional Universities (North)
✔ **SAT Score (25th/75th percentile):** 890-1100
✔ **Tuition:** 2009-2010: $28,976

Selectivity: Selective	**Room/board:** $12,858
Acceptance rate: 61%	**Average debt:** N/A
Student/faculty ratio: 16/1	**Proportion who borrowed:** N/A

UNDERGRADUATE STUDENT BODY STATS

2009-2010 enrollment: 4,752 full-time; 3,772 part-time. Men: 44%; women: 56%. **Ethnic makeup:** African American: 12%; Asian American: 5%; Hispanic: 19%; White: 60%; International: 4%.

ADMISSIONS FACTS AND FIGURES

Phone: (800) 338-8803. **Email:** admissions@fdu.edu. **Website:** http://www.fdu.edu. **Application deadlines for fall 2011:** Regular decision: Rolling. Early decision: Not offered. Early action: Not offered. Admission can be deferred. **Application fee:** $40. **To apply online, go to:** http://view.fdu.edu/default.aspx?id=355. **Admissions requirements/recommendations:** High school units required (recommended): English: 4; Mathematics: 3 (3); Science: 2 (3); Foreign language: 2 (2); Social studies: 2 (2); History: 2 (2); Academic electives: 3 (3); Total units: 16. Tests: The college uses SAT or ACT scores in admissions decisions. Either SAT or ACT required. For admission to the fall 2011 entering class, the school will accept: ACT with or without writing accepted. Campus visit: Recommended. Admissions interview: Recommended. Off-campus interview: May be arranged. **Factors that count in admissions decisions:** *Academic:* Secondary school record: Very Important. Class rank: Considered. Letters of recommendation: Considered. Standardized test scores: Important. Essay: Not Considered. *Nonacademic:* Interview: Considered. Extracurricular activities: Considered. Talent/ability: Not Considered. Character/personal qualities: Not Considered. Alumni/ae relationship: Not Considered. Geographical residence: Not Considered. State residency: Not Considered. Religious affiliation/commitment: Not Considered. Minority status: Not Considered. Volunteer work: Considered. Work experience: Considered. **Admissions statistics for the fall 2009 entering class:** Total applicants: 9,015. Total accepted: 5,517. Freshmen enrolled: 1,357; 16% were from out of state. Overall acceptance rate: 61%. **Credentials of fall 2009 freshmen:** 17% ranked in the top 10 percent of their high school class; 42% were in the top 25 percent; 77% were in the top half. (Proportion submitting class standing: 44%.) **Average high school grade point average:** 3.1. **First-year students who submitted SAT scores:** 95%. Scores (25/75 percentile): Critical Reading: 440-540, Math: 450-560, Combined: 890-1100.

ACADEMICS

Year founded: 1942. **Academic calendar:** Semester. **Degrees offered:** certificate, associate, terminal-associate, bachelor's, post-bachelor's certificate, master's, post-master's certificate. **Most popular majors:** 10% psychology, 7% business administration and management, 4% business/managerial economics, 3% criminal justice/law enforcement administration, 3% nursing/registered nurse training (R.N., A.S.N., B.S.N., M.S.N.). **Major fields of study:** biological and biomedical sciences; business, management, marketing, and related support services; communication, journalism, and related programs; computer and information sciences and support services; engineering; engineering technologies/technicians; English language and literature/letters; foreign languages, literatures, and linguistics; health professions and related clinical sciences; history; liberal arts and sciences studies, and humanities; mathematics and statistics; multi/interdisciplinary studies; natural resources and conservation; philosophy and religious studies; physical sciences; psychology; security and protective services; social sciences; visual and performing arts. **Areas of required coursework:** arts/fine arts, humanities, computer literacy, mathematics, English (including composition), foreign languages, sciences (biological or physical), social science, other. **Pre-professional programs:** pre-law, pre-dentistry, pre-medicine, pre-veterinary science, pre-optometry, pre-pharmacy, other. **Special academic programs:** accelerated program, cooperative (work-study plan) program, distance learning, double major, English as a Second Language (ESL), external degree program, honors program, independent study, internships, liberal arts/career combination, student-designed major, study abroad, teacher certificate program, weekend college. **Teacher certification offered in:** special education, elementary, bilingual/bicultural. **Cooperative education programs:** other. **Reserve Officers Training Corps (ROTC):** Army ROTC: Offered at cooperating institution (Seton Hall University); Air Force ROTC: Offered at cooperating institution (New Jersey Institute of Technology). **Faculty and instruction (2009-2010):** Total instructional faculty: 309 full-time, 630 part-time (; 6% minorities). Full-time faculty with Ph.D. or other terminal degree: 79%. Student/faculty ratio: 16/1. Classes of fewer than 20 students: 69%; of 20 to 49 students: 31%; of 50 or more students: 1%. **Advanced Placement and International Baccalaureate credit:** AP tests may be used for: Credit only. Scores accepted: 3, 4, 5. International Baccalaureate exams may be used for: Credit only. **Freshmen returning for sophomore year:** 74%. **Graduation rates:** Four-year: 29%; five-year: 43%; six-year: 47%.

COSTS AND FINANCIAL AID

Financial aid office: (201) 692-2823. **Expenses (2009-2010):** Tuition and fees 2009-2010: $28,976; room/board: $12,858. Estimated books and supplies: $908. **Financial aid:** Priority filing date for institution's financial aid form: February 15; deadline: February 15.

CAMPUS LIFE AND EXTRACURRICULAR ACTIVITIES

Campus housing available: coed dorms, special housing for disabled students, other housing options. Students who live in college-owned, operated, or affiliated housing: 38%. Activities include: campus ministries, choral groups, dance, drama/theater, international student organization, literary magazine, model UN, pep band, radio station, student government, student newspaper, student film society, yearbook. Number of fraternities: 9; sororities: 10. **Sports program (2009-2010):** Member of NCAA I. *Men's intercollegiate varsity sports:* baseball, basketball, cross country, golf, soccer, tennis, track and field (indoor). *Women's intercollegiate varsity sports:* basketball, bowling, cross country, fencing, golf, soccer, softball, tennis, track and field (indoor), volleyball.

SERVICES AND FACILITIES

Basic services: nonremedial tutoring, women's center, health service, health insurance. **Remedial assistance:** reading, math, writing, study skills. **Counseling services:** career, veteran student, academic, psychological, birth control. **For learning-disabled students:** School does not offer a structured program with separate admission and additional fees. Total undergraduates in learning-disabled program or receiving services: 134. Services include: remedial math, remedial English, reading machines, remedial reading, tape recorders, other special classes, oral tests, learning center, extended time for tests, tutors, priority registration, substitution of courses, texts on tape, exams on tape or computer, other testing accommodations. **Information technology resources:** Students are not required to lease or own a computer. Number of campus computers available to all students: 400. School has a wireless network. Proportion of college-owned housing units wired for high-speed internet access: 100%. **Campus safety:** Security services offered: 24-hour foot-and-vehicle patrols, late-night transport/escort service, 24-hour emergency telephones, lighted pathways/sidewalks, controlled dormitory access (key, security card, etc).

TRANSFER AND INTERNATIONAL STUDENTS

Transfer students: May apply for admission for the following academic terms: Fall, Winter, Spring, Summer. Applicants need a minimum number of credits to apply. For fall 2009: Transfer applications received: 2,111. Transfer applicants offered admission: 1,484. Transfer applicants enrolled: 630. **International students:** Number of foreign undergraduates: 259 (4% of student body). Minimum TOEFL score required: 550 (paper); 213 (computer).

Felician College

■ **Address:** 262 S. Main Street, Lodi, NJ 07644
■ **Website:** http://www.felician.edu
■ **Private; Religious affiliation:** Roman Catholic
■ **Enrollment:** 1,351 full-time; 407 part-time

KEY STATS

✔ **U.S News College Ranking:** 48, Regional Colleges (North)
✔ **SAT Score (25th/75th percentile):** 740-960
✔ **Tuition:** 2010-2011: $26,425

Selectivity: Less selective	**Room/board:** $10,150
Acceptance rate: 84%	**Average debt:** $17,026
Student/faculty ratio: 12/1	**Proportion who borrowed:** 62%

UNDERGRADUATE STUDENT BODY STATS

2009-2010 enrollment: 1,351 full-time; 407 part-time. Men: 23%; women: 77%. **Ethnic makeup:** African American: 12%; Asian American: 8%; Hispanic: 18%; White: 59%; International: 2%.

ADMISSIONS FACTS AND FIGURES

Phone: (201) 559-6131. **Email:** admissions@felician.edu. **Website:** http://www.felician.edu. **Application deadlines for fall 2011:** Regular decision: Rolling. Early decision: Not offered. Early action: Not offered. Admission can be deferred. **Application fee:** $30. **Admissions requirements/recommendations:** High school units required (recommended): English: (4); Mathematics: (2); Science: (2); Social studies: (2); Academic electives: (3); Total units: (13). Tests: The college uses SAT or ACT scores in admissions decisions. SAT required. For admission to the fall 2011 entering class, the school will accept: ACT with or without writing accepted. Campus visit: Neither required nor recommended. Admissions interview: Neither required nor recommended. Off-campus interview: Not available. **Factors that count in admissions decisions:** *Academic:* Secondary school record: Important. Class rank: Considered. Letters of recommendation: Considered. Standardized test scores: Very Important. Essay: Important. *Nonacademic:* Interview: Considered. Extracurricular activities: Considered. Talent/ability: Not Considered. Character/personal qualities: Considered. Alumni/ae relationship: Considered. Geographical residence: Not Considered. State residency: Not Considered. Religious affiliation/commitment: Not Considered. Minority status: Not Considered. Volunteer work: Considered. Work experience: Considered. **Other schools with the greatest overlap in applicants:** College of New Jersey; Fairleigh Dickinson University. **Admissions statistics for the fall 2009 entering class:** Total applicants: 1,618. Total accepted: 1,358. Freshmen enrolled: 254. Overall acceptance rate: 84%. **Credentials of fall 2009 freshmen:** 10% ranked in the top 10 percent of their high school class; 27% were in the top 25 percent; 59% were in the top half. (Proportion submitting class standing: 63%.) **Average high school grade point average:** 3.0. **First-year students who submitted SAT scores:** 97%. Scores (25/75 percentile): Critical Reading: 370-490, Math: 370-470, Combined: 740-960.

ACADEMICS

Year founded: 1942. **Academic calendar:** Semester. **Degrees offered:** certificate, associate, bachelor's, post-bachelor's certificate, master's, post-master's certificate. **Most popular majors:** 31% business, management, marketing, and related support services, 27% health professions and related clinical sciences, 17% education, 5% biological and biomedical sciences, 5% psychology. **Major fields of study:** biological and biomedical sciences; business, management, marketing, and related support services; computer and information sciences and support services; education; English language and literature/letters; health professions and related clinical sciences; history; liberal arts and sciences studies, and humanities; mathematics and statistics; psychology; theology and religious vocations; visual and performing arts. **Areas of required coursework:** arts/fine arts, humanities, computer literacy, mathematics, English (including composition), philosophy, sciences (biological or physical), history, social science. **Pre-professional programs:** pre-law, pre-medicine, pre-theology. **Special academic programs:** accelerated program, cooperative (work-study plan) program, cross-registration, distance learning, double major, dual enrollment, English as a Second Language (ESL), honors program, independent study, internships, liberal arts/career combination, student-designed major, study abroad, teacher certificate program, weekend college. **Teacher certification offered in:** early childhood, special education, elementary, middle/junior high. **Cooperative education programs:** business, education, health professions, humanities, natural science, social/behavioral science. **Faculty and instruction (2009-2010):** Total instructional faculty: 112

full-time, 88 part-time (37% men; 63% women; 6% minorities). Student/ faculty ratio: 12/1. **Freshmen returning for sophomore year:** 65%. **Graduation rates:** Four-year: 15%; five-year: 29%; six-year: 35%.

COSTS AND FINANCIAL AID

Financial aid office: (201) 559-6010. **Expenses (2010-2011):** Tuition and fees 2010-2011: $26,425; room/board: $10,150. Estimated books and supplies: $1,200; transportation: $1,000; personal expenses: $1,975. **Financial aid:** In 2009-2010, 87% of undergraduates applied for financial aid. Of those, 81% were determined to have financial need; 10% had their need fully met. Average financial aid package (proportion receiving): $18,560 (78%). Average amount of gift aid, such as scholarships or grants (proportion receiving): $12,359 (52%). Average amount of self-help aid, such as work study or loans (proportion receiving): $4,407 (64%). Average need-based loan (excluding PLUS or other private loans): $4,246. Among students who received need-based aid, the average percentage of need met: 56%. Among students who received aid based on merit, the average award (and the proportion receiving): $10,963 (6%). The average athletic scholarship (and the proportion receiving): $13,619 (9%). Average amount of debt of borrowers graduating in 2009: $17,026. Proportion who borrowed: 62%.

CAMPUS LIFE AND EXTRACURRICULAR ACTIVITIES

Campus housing available: coed dorms, women's dorms, men's dorms, special housing for disabled students. **Student employment:** During the 2009-2010 academic year, 9% of undergraduates worked on campus. Average per-year earnings: $2,160. **Clubs and organizations:** Number of student organizations: 24. Activities include: choral groups, drama/theater, literary magazine, radio station, student government. Number of fraternities: 1; sororities: 2. **Sports program (2009-2010):** Member of NCAA II. **Men's intercollegiate varsity sports:** baseball, basketball, cross country, golf, soccer. **Women's intercollegiate varsity sports:** basketball, cross country, soccer, softball, volleyball.

SERVICES AND FACILITIES

Basic services: nonremedial tutoring, health service, health insurance. **Remedial assistance:** reading, math, writing, study skills. **Counseling services:** career, personal, academic, religious. **For learning-disabled students:** School does not offer a structured program with separate admission and additional fees. Services include: extended time for tests. **Library:** Number of titles: 101,040; number of current serial subscriptions: 563. **Information technology resources:** Students are not required to lease or own a computer. Number of campus computers available to all students: 150. School has a wireless network. Approximate number of users that can be accommodated: 500. Proportion of college-owned housing units wired for high-speed internet access: 100%. **Campus safety:** Security services offered: 24-hour foot-and-vehicle patrols, 24-hour emergency telephones, lighted pathways/ sidewalks, controlled dormitory access (key, security card, etc).

TRANSFER AND INTERNATIONAL STUDENTS

Transfer students: May apply for admission for the following academic terms: Fall, Spring, Summer. Applicants do not need a minimum number of credits to apply. **International students:** Number of foreign undergraduates: 38 (2% of student body).

Georgian Court University

- **Address:** 900 Lakewood Avenue, Lakewood, NJ 08701-2697
- **Website:** http://www.georgian.edu
- **Private; Religious affiliation:** Roman Catholic
- **Enrollment:** 1,516 full-time; 454 part-time

KEY STATS

✔ **U.S News College Ranking:** 88, Regional Universities (North)
✔ **SAT or ACT Score (25th/75th percentile):** N/A
✔ **Tuition:** 2010-2011: $26,176

Selectivity: Selective	**Room/board:** $9,856
Acceptance rate: 62%	**Average debt:** $33,729
Student/faculty ratio: 15/1	**Proportion who borrowed:** 85%

UNDERGRADUATE STUDENT BODY STATS

2009-2010 enrollment: 1,516 full-time; 454 part-time. Men: 9%; women: 91%. **Ethnic makeup:** African American: 11%; Asian American: 2%;

Hispanic: 8%; White: 78%. **Religious preference:** Protestant: 9%; Jewish: 1%; No preference: 2%; Unknown: 42%; Roman Catholic: 41%; Other: 5%.

ADMISSIONS FACTS AND FIGURES

Phone: (732) 987-2760. **Email:** admissions@georgian.edu. **Website:** http:// www.georgian.edu. **Application deadlines for fall 2011:** Regular decision: August 1. Early decision: Not offered. Early action: Send application by: November 15; Decision sent by: December 30. Admission can be deferred. **Application fee:** $40. **To apply online, go to:** http://registrar.georgian. edu/IQWeb/Secure/Guest/Onlineapp.asp. **Admissions requirements/ recommendations:** High school units required (recommended): English: 4; Mathematics: 2; Science: 1; Foreign language: 2; History: 1; Academic electives: 6; Total units: 16. Tests: The college uses SAT or ACT scores in admissions decisions. Neither SAT nor ACT required. For admission to the fall 2011 entering class, the school will accept: ACT with or without writing accepted. Campus visit: Recommended. Admissions interview: Recommended. Off-campus interview: May be arranged. **Factors that count in admissions decisions:** *Academic:* Secondary school record: Very Important. Class rank: Considered. Letters of recommendation: Considered. Standardized test scores: Considered. Essay: Considered. *Nonacademic:* Interview: Considered. Extracurricular activities: Considered. Talent/ability: Considered. Character/personal qualities: Considered. Alumni/ae relationship: Considered. Geographical residence: Not Considered. State residency: Not Considered. Religious affiliation/commitment: Not Considered. Minority status: Not Considered. Volunteer work: Considered. Work experience: Considered. **Other schools with the greatest overlap in applicants:** College of New Jersey; Monmouth University; Richard Stockton College of New Jersey; Rowan University; Rutgers, the State University of New Jersey– New Brunswick. **Admissions statistics for the fall 2009 entering class:** Total applicants: 1,008. Total accepted: 624. Freshmen enrolled: 253; 6% were from out of state. Overall acceptance rate: 62%. Non-early acceptance rate: 62%. **Credentials of fall 2009 freshmen:** 16% ranked in the top 10 percent of their high school class; 41% were in the top 25 percent; 79% were in the top half. (Proportion submitting class standing: 42%.) **Average high school grade point average:** 3.1.

ACADEMICS

Year founded: 1908. **Academic calendar:** Semester. **Degrees offered:** certificate, bachelor's, post-bachelor's certificate, master's, post-master's certificate. **Most popular majors:** 25% elementary education and teaching, 23% psychology, 12% business administration and management, 9% English language and literature, 7% history. **Major fields of study:** biological and biomedical sciences; business, management, marketing, and related support services; communication, journalism, and related programs; computer and information sciences and support services; education; English language and literature/letters; foreign languages, literatures, and linguistics; health professions and related clinical sciences; history; liberal arts and sciences studies, and humanities; mathematics and statistics; multi/interdisciplinary studies; philosophy and religious studies; physical sciences; psychology; public administration and social service professions; security and protective services; social sciences; visual and performing arts. **Areas of required coursework:** arts/fine arts, humanities, English (including composition), philosophy, foreign languages, sciences (biological or physical), social science, other. **Special academic programs:** accelerated program, distance learning, double major, dual enrollment, honors program, independent study, internships, liberal arts/career combination, study abroad, teacher certificate program. **Teacher certification offered in:** early childhood, special education, elementary, middle/junior high, secondary, bilingual/bicultural. **Faculty and instruction (2009-2010):** Total instructional faculty: 103 full-time, 186 part-time (39% men; 61% women; 9% minorities). Full-time faculty with Ph.D. or other terminal degree: 87%. Student/faculty ratio: 15/1. Classes of fewer than 20 students: 75%; of 20 to 49 students: 25%. **Advanced Placement and International Baccalaureate credit:** AP tests may be used for: Placement only. Scores accepted: 3, 4, 5. **Freshmen returning for sophomore year:** 74%. **Graduation rates:** Four-year: 24%; five-year: 46%; six-year: 58%.

COSTS AND FINANCIAL AID

Financial aid office: (732) 364-2200. **Expenses (2010-2011):** Tuition and fees 2010-2011: $26,176; room/board: $9,856. Estimated books and supplies: $1,350; transportation: $1,000; personal expenses: $1,200. **Financial aid:** Priority filing date for institution's financial aid form: April 15. In 2009-2010, 94% of undergraduates applied for financial aid. Of those, 86% were determined to have financial need; 11% had their need fully met. Average financial aid package (proportion receiving): $17,906 (86%). Average amount of gift aid, such as scholarships or grants (proportion receiving):

$14,262 (82%). Average amount of self-help aid, such as work study or loans (proportion receiving): $5,031 (71%). Average need-based loan (excluding PLUS or other private loans): $4,667. Among students who received need-based aid, the average percentage of need met: 67%. Among students who received aid based on merit, the average award (and the proportion receiving): $7,232 (7%). The average athletic scholarship (and the proportion receiving): $6,514 (2%). Average amount of debt of borrowers graduating in 2009: $33,729. Proportion who borrowed: 85%.

CAMPUS LIFE AND EXTRACURRICULAR ACTIVITIES

Campus housing available (% using): women's dorms (100%). Students who live in college-owned, operated, or affiliated housing: 30%. **Clubs and organizations:** Number of student organizations: 44. Activities include: campus ministries, choral groups, concert band, dance, jazz band, literary magazine, model UN, music ensembles, student government, student newspaper, yearbook. Number of fraternities: 0; sororities: 0. Average proportion of students who stay on campus on weekends: 30%. **Sports program (2009-2010):** Member of NCAA II. *Women's intercollegiate varsity sports:* basketball, cross country, lacrosse, soccer, softball, tennis, track and field (outdoor), volleyball.

SERVICES AND FACILITIES

Basic services: nonremedial tutoring, placement service, health service, health insurance. **Remedial assistance:** reading, math, writing, study skills. **Counseling services:** career, personal, veteran student, academic, religious. **For learning-disabled students:** School does not offer a structured program with separate admission and additional fees. Services include: remedial math, remedial English, remedial reading, tape recorders, diagnostic testing service, untimed tests, note-taking services, oral tests, learning center, readers, extended time for tests, tutors, priority registration, texts on tape, other testing accommodations. **Library:** Number of titles: 148,026; number of current serial subscriptions: 1,808. **Information technology resources:** Students are not required to lease or own a computer. Number of campus computers available to all students: 197. School has a wireless network. Approximate number of users that can be accommodated: 1,000. Proportion of college-owned housing units wired for high-speed internet access: 100%. **Campus safety:** Security services offered: 24-hour foot-and-vehicle patrols, late-night transport/escort service, 24-hour emergency telephones, lighted pathways/sidewalks, controlled dormitory access (key, security card, etc).

TRANSFER AND INTERNATIONAL STUDENTS

Transfer students: May apply for admission for the following academic terms: Fall, Spring. Applicants need a minimum number of credits to apply. For fall 2009: Transfer applications received: 613. Transfer applicants offered admission: 362. Transfer applicants enrolled: 237. **International students:** Number of foreign undergraduates: 7. Number of countries represented: 10. Minimum TOEFL score required: 550 (paper); 213 (computer).

Kean University

- **Address:** PO Box 411, Union, NJ 07083
- **Website:** http://www.kean.edu
- **Public**
- **Enrollment:** 9,355 full-time; 2,717 part-time

KEY STATS

✔ **U.S News College Ranking:** 105, Regional Universities (North)
✔ **SAT Score (25th/75th percentile):** 830-1010
✔ **Tuition:** 2009-2010: $9,446 in state, $14,081 out of state

Selectivity: Less selective	**Room/board:** $12,264
Acceptance rate: 62%	**Average debt:** $19,698
Student/faculty ratio: 17/1	**Proportion who borrowed:** 68%

UNDERGRADUATE STUDENT BODY STATS

2009-2010 enrollment: 9,355 full-time; 2,717 part-time. Men: 38%; women: 62%. **Ethnic makeup:** African American: 19%; Asian American: 7%; Hispanic: 21%; White: 51%; International: 2%.

ADMISSIONS FACTS AND FIGURES

Phone: (908) 737-7100. **Email:** admitme@kean.edu. **Website:** http://www. kean.edu. **Application deadlines for fall 2011:** Regular decision: May 31. Early decision: Not offered. Early action: Not offered. Admission cannot be deferred. **Application fee:** $50. **To apply online, go to:** https://web4.kean.

edu/adm/ug/default.asp. **Admissions requirements/recommendations:** High school units required (recommended): English: 4; Mathematics: 3; Science: 2; Foreign language: (2); Social studies: (2); History: 2; Academic electives: 5; Total units: 16. Tests: The college uses SAT or ACT scores in admissions decisions. Either SAT or ACT required. For admission to the fall 2011 entering class, the school will accept: ACT with or without writing accepted. Campus visit: Recommended. Admissions interview: Neither required nor recommended. Off-campus interview: Not available. **Factors that count in admissions decisions:** *Academic:* Secondary school record: Very Important. Class rank: Considered. Letters of recommendation: Considered. Standardized test scores: Important. Essay: Considered. *Nonacademic:* Interview: Considered. Extracurricular activities: Considered. Talent/ability: Considered. Character/personal qualities: Considered. Alumni/ae relationship: Considered. Geographical residence: Not Considered. State residency: Not Considered. Religious affiliation/commitment: Not Considered. Minority status: Not Considered. Volunteer work: Considered. Work experience: Considered. **Other schools with the greatest overlap in applicants:** Montclair State University; Rutgers, the State University of New Jersey–New Brunswick; William Paterson University of New Jersey. **Admissions statistics for the fall 2009 entering class:** Total applicants: 5,955. Total accepted: 3,693. Freshmen enrolled: 1,548; 3% were from out of state. Overall acceptance rate: 62%. **Credentials of fall 2009 freshmen:** 8% ranked in the top 10 percent of their high school class; 26% were in the top 25 percent; 66% were in the top half. (Proportion submitting class standing: 65%.) **Average high school grade point average:** 3.0. **First-year students who submitted SAT scores:** 92%. Scores (25/75 percentile): Critical Reading: 410-500, Math: 420-510, Combined: 830-1010.

ACADEMICS

Year founded: 1855. **Academic calendar:** Semester. **Degrees offered:** bachelor's, master's, post-master's certificate, doctorate. **Most popular majors:** 10% business administration and management, 10% psychology, 6% accounting, 6% criminal justice/law enforcement administration, 5% kindergarten/preschool education and teaching. **Major fields of study:** biological and biomedical sciences; business, management, marketing, and related support services; communication, journalism, and related programs; communications technologies/technicians and support services; computer and information sciences and support services; education; engineering technologies/technicians; English language and literature/letters; foreign languages, literatures, and linguistics; health professions and related clinical sciences; history; liberal arts and sciences studies, and humanities; mathematics and statistics; parks, recreation, leisure, and fitness studies; philosophy and religious studies; physical sciences; psychology; public administration and social service professions; science technologies/technicians; security and protective services; social sciences; visual and performing arts. **Areas of required coursework:** arts/fine arts, humanities, computer literacy, mathematics, English (including composition), sciences (biological or physical), history, social science, other. **Pre-professional programs:** pre-medicine, other. **Special academic programs:** accelerated program, cooperative (work-study plan) program, distance learning, double major, dual enrollment, English as a Second Language (ESL), honors program, independent study, internships, liberal arts/career combination, study abroad, teacher certificate program, weekend college, other. **Teacher certification offered in:** early childhood, special education, elementary, middle/junior high, secondary, bilingual/bicultural. **Cooperative education programs:** art, business, computer science, humanities, natural science, social/behavioral science, technologies. **Reserve Officers Training Corps (ROTC):** Army ROTC: Offered at cooperating institution (Seton Hall University); Air Force ROTC: Offered at cooperating institution (New Jersey Institute of Technology). **Faculty and instruction (2009-2010):** Total instructional faculty: 352 full-time, 977 part-time (49% men; 51% women; 24% minorities). Full-time faculty with Ph.D. or other terminal degree: 91%. Student/faculty ratio: 17/1. Classes of fewer than 20 students: 38%; of 20 to 49 students: 62%; of 50 or more students: 0%. **Advanced Placement and International Baccalaureate credit:** AP tests may be used for: Credit only. Scores accepted: 3, 4, 5. International Baccalaureate exams may be used for: Credit only. **Freshmen returning for sophomore year:** 78%. **Graduation rates:** Four-year: 19%; five-year: 38%; six-year: 44%.

COSTS AND FINANCIAL AID

Financial aid office: (908) 737-3190. **Expenses (2009-2010):** Tuition and fees 2009-2010: $9,446 in state, $14,081 out of state; room/board: $12,264. Estimated books and supplies: $1,800 personal expenses: $1,674. **Financial aid:** Priority filing date for institution's financial aid form: March 15. In 2009-2010, 77% of undergraduates applied for financial aid. Of those,

65% were determined to have financial need; 15% had their need fully met. Average financial aid package (proportion receiving): $9,810 (62%). Average amount of gift aid, such as scholarships or grants (proportion receiving): $7,731 (62%). Average amount of self-help aid, such as work study or loans (proportion receiving): $4,585 (61%). Average need-based loan (excluding PLUS or other private loans): $4,454. Among students who received need-based aid, the average percentage of need met: 56%. Among students who received aid based on merit, the average award (and the proportion receiving): $2,703 (1%). Average amount of debt of borrowers graduating in 2009: $19,698. Proportion who borrowed: 68%.

CAMPUS LIFE AND EXTRACURRICULAR ACTIVITIES

Campus housing available (% using): coed dorms (34%), apartment for single students (65%), special housing for disabled students (1%). Students who live in college-owned, operated, or affiliated housing: 15%. **Student employment:** During the 2009-2010 academic year, 6% of undergraduates worked on campus. Average per-year earnings: $4,640. **Clubs and organizations:** Number of student organizations: 143. Activities include: campus ministries, choral groups, concert band, dance, drama/theater, international student organization, jazz band, literary magazine, music ensembles, musical theater, pep band, radio station, student government, student newspaper, student film society, symphony orchestra, television station, yearbook. Number of fraternities: 16; sororities: 17. **Sports program (2009-2010):** Member of NCAA III. *Men's intercollegiate varsity sports:* baseball, basketball, football, lacrosse, soccer, track and field (indoor), track and field (outdoor). *Women's intercollegiate varsity sports:* basketball, field hockey, lacrosse, soccer, softball, tennis, track and field (indoor), track and field (outdoor), volleyball.

SERVICES AND FACILITIES

Basic services: nonremedial tutoring, placement service, day care, health service, health insurance. **Remedial assistance:** reading, math, writing, study skills. **Counseling services:** minority student, career, military, personal, veteran student, academic, older student, psychological, birth control. **For learning-disabled students:** School does not offer a structured program with separate admission and additional fees. Total undergraduates in learning-disabled program or receiving services: 163. Services include: remedial math, remedial English, reading machines, remedial reading, tape recorders, other special classes, videotaped classes, diagnostic testing service, note-taking services, oral tests, learning center, readers, extended time for tests, tutors, priority registration, priority seating, texts on tape, other testing accommodations. **Library:** Number of titles: 374,186; number of current serial subscriptions: 32,675. **Information technology resources:** Students are not required to lease or own a computer. Number of campus computers available to all students: 1,700. School has a wireless network. Approximate number of users that can be accommodated: 2,000. Proportion of college-owned housing units wired for high-speed internet access: 100%. **Campus safety:** Security services offered: 24-hour foot-and-vehicle patrols, late-night transport/escort service, 24-hour emergency telephones, lighted pathways/sidewalks, student patrols, controlled dormitory access (key, security card, etc).

TRANSFER AND INTERNATIONAL STUDENTS

Transfer students: May apply for admission for the following academic terms: Fall, Spring, Summer. Applicants need a minimum number of credits to apply. For fall 2009: Transfer applications received: 2,956. Transfer applicants offered admission: 2,709. Transfer applicants enrolled: 1,733. **International students:** Number of foreign undergraduates: 218 (2% of student body). Number of countries represented: 63.

Monmouth University

- **Address:** 400 Cedar Avenue, West Long Branch, NJ 07764-1898
- **Website:** http://www.monmouth.edu
- **Private**
- **Enrollment:** 4,306 full-time; 375 part-time

KEY STATS

✔ **U.S News College Ranking:** 40, Regional Universities (North)
✔ **SAT Score (25th/75th percentile):** 1000-1170
✔ **Tuition:** 2010-2011: $26,356

Selectivity: Selective	**Room/board:** $9,936
Acceptance rate: 62%	**Average debt:** $25,000
Student/faculty ratio: 15/1	**Proportion who borrowed:** 73%

UNDERGRADUATE STUDENT BODY STATS

2009-2010 enrollment: 4,306 full-time; 375 part-time. Men: 42%; women: 58%. **Ethnic makeup:** African American: 4%; Asian American: 2%; Hispanic: 6%; White: 87%; International: 1%.

ADMISSIONS FACTS AND FIGURES

Phone: (800) 543-9671. **Email:** admission@monmouth.edu. **Website:** http://www.monmouth.edu. **Application deadlines for fall 2011:** Regular decision: March 1; decision sent by April 1. Early decision: Not offered. Early action: Send application by: December 1; Decision sent by: January 15. Admission can be deferred. **Application fee:** $50. **To apply online, go to:** http://www.monmouth.edu/apply. **Admissions requirements/recommendations:** High school units required (recommended): English: 4; Mathematics: 3; Science: 2; Foreign language: (2); Social studies: (2); History: 2; Academic electives: 5; Total units: 16. Tests: The college uses SAT or ACT scores in admissions decisions. Either SAT or ACT required. For admission to the fall 2011 entering class, the school will accept: ACT with writing required. Campus visit: Recommended. Admissions interview: Neither required nor recommended. Off-campus interview: Not available. **Factors that count in admissions decisions:** *Academic:* Secondary school record: Very Important. Class rank: Not Considered. Letters of recommendation: Considered. Standardized test scores: Very Important. Essay: Considered. *Nonacademic:* Interview: Not Considered. Extracurricular activities: Important. Talent/ability: Not Considered. Character/personal qualities: Not Considered. Alumni/ae relationship: Considered. Geographical residence: Not Considered. State residency: Not Considered. Religious affiliation/commitment: Not Considered. Minority status: Not Considered. Volunteer work: Important. Work experience: Important. **Other schools with the greatest overlap in applicants:** College of New Jersey; Montclair State University; Rider University; Rowan University; Rutgers, the State University of New Jersey–New Brunswick. **Admissions statistics for the fall 2009 entering class:** Total applicants: 6,738. Total accepted: 4,160. Freshmen enrolled: 998; 19% were from out of state. Accepted through early-decision or early-action plans: 51%. Overall acceptance rate: 62%. Non-early acceptance rate: 56%. **Size of waiting list:** 0 applicants; enrolled from waiting list: 0. **Credentials of fall 2009 freshmen:** 18% ranked in the top 10 percent of their high school class; 46% were in the top 25 percent; 83% were in the top half. (Proportion submitting class standing: 53%.) **Average high school grade point average:** 3.3. **First-year students who submitted SAT scores:** 89%. Scores (25/75 percentile): Critical Reading: 490-570, Math: 510-600, Combined: 1000-1170. **First-year students submitting ACT scores:** 11%. Scores (25/75 percentile): English: N/A, Math: N/A, Composite: 22-26.

ACADEMICS

Year founded: 1933. **Academic calendar:** Semester. **Degrees offered:** certificate, associate, bachelor's, post-bachelor's certificate, master's, post-master's certificate. **Most popular majors:** 32% business, management, marketing, and related support services, 15% education, 14% communication, journalism, and related programs, 6% security and protective services, 5% psychology. **Major fields of study:** biological and biomedical sciences; business, management, marketing, and related support services; communication, journalism, and related programs; computer and information sciences and support services; education; engineering; English language and literature/letters; foreign languages, literatures, and linguistics; health professions and related clinical sciences; history; mathematics and statistics; physical sciences; psychology; public administration and social service professions; security and protective services; social sciences; visual and performing arts. **Areas of required coursework:** arts/fine arts, humanities, computer literacy, mathematics, English (including composition), sciences (biological or physical), history, social science, other. **Pre-professional programs:** pre-law, pre-dentistry, pre-medicine, pre-veterinary science, pre-pharmacy. **Special academic programs (% participation):** cooperative (work-study plan) program (4.1%), distance learning (20%), double major (15%), honors program (9.4%), independent study (18.3%), internships (56.6%), study abroad (9.7%), teacher certificate program (14.6%). **Teacher certification offered in:** special education, elementary, middle/junior high, secondary. **Reserve Officers Training Corps (ROTC):** Air Force ROTC: Offered at cooperating institution (Rutgers, the State University of New Jersey–New Brunswick). **Faculty and instruction (2009-2010):** Total instructional faculty: 249 full-time, 326 part-time (48% men; 52% women; 10% minorities). Full-time faculty with Ph.D. or other terminal degree: 82%. Student/faculty ratio: 15/1. Classes of fewer than 20 students: 47%; of 20 to 49 students: 53%. **Advanced Placement and International Baccalaureate credit:** AP tests may be used for: Credit and/or placement. Scores accepted: 3, 4, 5. International Baccalaureate exams may be used for: Credit and/or placement. **Freshmen returning for sophomore year:** 78%. **Graduation rates:** Four-year: 40%; five-year: 59%; six-year: 60%. **Graduate study:** 20% of students pursue further study immediately upon graduation.

COSTS AND FINANCIAL AID

Financial aid office: (732) 571-3463. **Expenses (2010-2011):** Tuition and fees 2010-2011: $26,356; room/board: $9,936. Estimated books and supplies: $1,200; transportation: $556; personal expenses: $1,996. **Financial aid:** Priority filing date for institution's financial aid form: February 15. In 2009-2010, 65% of undergraduates applied for financial aid. Of those, 65% were determined to have financial need; 7% had their need fully met. Average financial aid package (proportion receiving): $17,601 (65%). Average amount of gift aid, such as scholarships or grants (proportion receiving): $12,348 (26%). Average amount of self-help aid, such as work study or loans (proportion receiving): $5,458 (53%). Average need-based loan (excluding PLUS or other private loans): $4,828. Among students who received need-based aid, the average percentage of need met: 68%. Among students who received aid based on merit, the average award (and the proportion receiving): $6,689 (30%). The average athletic scholarship (and the proportion receiving): $14,481 (2%). Average amount of debt of borrowers graduating in 2009: $25,000. Proportion who borrowed: 73%.

CAMPUS LIFE AND EXTRACURRICULAR ACTIVITIES

Campus housing available (% using): coed dorms (66%), apartment for single students (29%), other housing options (2%). Students who live in college-owned, operated, or affiliated housing: 44%. **Student employment:** During the 2009-2010 academic year, 9% of undergraduates worked on campus. Average per-year earnings: $1,549. **Clubs and organizations:** Number of student organizations: 65. Activities include: campus ministries, choral groups, concert band, dance, drama/theater, international student organization, jazz band, literary magazine, model UN, music ensembles, musical theater, pep band, radio station, student government, student newspaper, television station, yearbook. Number of fraternities: 6; sororities: 7. Proportion of men in fraternities: 14%; of women in sororities: 14%. **Sports program (2009-2010):** Member of NCAA I. **Men's intercollegiate varsity sports:** baseball, basketball, cross country, football, golf, soccer, tennis, track and field (indoor), track and field (outdoor). **Women's intercollegiate varsity sports:** basketball, bowling, cross country, field hockey, golf, lacrosse, soccer, softball, tennis, track and field (indoor), track and field (outdoor).

SERVICES AND FACILITIES

Basic services: nonremedial tutoring, women's center, placement service, health service, health insurance. **Remedial assistance:** reading, math, writing, study skills. **Counseling services:** minority student, career, military, personal, veteran student, academic, older student, psychological, birth control, religious, other. **For learning-disabled students:** School does not offer a structured program with separate admission and additional fees. Services include: remedial math, remedial English, reading machines, remedial reading, tape recorders, note-taking services, readers, extended time for tests, tutors, priority registration, priority seating, texts on tape, typist/scribe, other testing accommodations, other. **Library:** Number of titles: 263,000; number of current serial subscriptions: 38,200. **Information technology resources:** Students are not required to lease or own a computer. Number of campus computers available to all students: 444. School has a wireless network. Approximate number of users that can be accommodated: 3,000. Proportion of college-owned housing units wired for high-speed internet access: 86%. **Campus safety:** Security services offered: 24-hour foot-and-vehicle patrols, late-night transport/escort service, 24-hour emergency telephones, lighted pathways/sidewalks, controlled dormitory access (key, security card, etc).

TRANSFER AND INTERNATIONAL STUDENTS

Transfer students: May apply for admission for the following academic terms: Fall, Spring, Summer. Applicants need a minimum number of credits to apply. For fall 2009: Transfer applications received: 1,054. Transfer applicants offered admission: 592. Transfer applicants enrolled: 298. **International students:** Number of foreign undergraduates: 26 (1% of student body). Number of countries represented: 18. Minimum TOEFL score required: 550 (paper); 79 (computer).

Montclair State University

- **Address:** 1 Normal Avenue, Montclair, NJ 07043
- **Website:** http://www.montclair.edu
- **Public**
- **Enrollment:** 12,113 full-time; 2,026 part-time

KEY STATS
✔ **U.S News College Ranking:** 61, Regional Universities (North)
✔ **SAT Score (25th/75th percentile):** 900-1090
✔ **Tuition:** 2009-2010: $10,003 in state, $16,636 out of state

Selectivity: Selective	**Room/board:** $10,886
Acceptance rate: 47%	**Average debt:** $24,226
Student/faculty ratio: 17/1	**Proportion who borrowed:** 77%

UNDERGRADUATE STUDENT BODY STATS

2009-2010 enrollment: 12,113 full-time; 2,026 part-time. Men: 39%; women: 61%. **Ethnic makeup:** African American: 9%; Asian American: 6%; Hispanic: 20%; White: 63%; International: 2%.

ADMISSIONS FACTS AND FIGURES

Phone: (973) 655-4444. **Email:** undergraduate.admissions@montclair.edu. **Website:** http://www.montclair.edu. **Application deadlines for fall 2011:** Regular decision: March 1; decision sent by October 1. Early decision: Not offered. Early action: Not offered. Admission can be deferred. **Application fee:** $60. **To apply online, go to:** http://www.montclair.edu/admissions/apply.html. **Admissions requirements/recommendations:** High school units required (recommended): English: 4; Mathematics: 3; Science: 2; Foreign language: 2; Social studies: 2; Academic electives: 3; Total units: 16. Tests: The college uses SAT or ACT scores in admissions decisions. SAT required. For admission to the fall 2011 entering class, the school will accept: ACT with writing required. Campus visit: Recommended. Admissions interview: Neither required nor recommended. Off-campus interview: Not available. **Factors that count in admissions decisions:** *Academic:* Secondary school record: Very Important. Class rank: Not Considered. Letters of recommendation: Considered. Standardized test scores: Important. Essay: Considered. *Nonacademic:* Interview: Not Considered. Extracurricular activities: Considered. Talent/ability: Considered. Character/personal qualities: Not Considered. Alumni/ae relationship: Not Considered. Geographical residence: Not Considered. State residency: Not Considered. Religious affiliation/commitment: Not Considered. Minority status: Not Considered. Volunteer work: Considered. Work experience: Considered. **Other schools with the greatest overlap in applicants:** College of New Jersey; Ramapo College of New Jersey; Rowan University; Rutgers, the State University of New Jersey–New Brunswick; William Paterson University of New Jersey. **Admissions statistics for the fall 2009 entering class:** Total applicants: 13,469. Total accepted: 6,332. Freshmen enrolled: 2,117; 3% were from out of state. Overall acceptance rate: 47%. **Credentials of fall 2009 freshmen:** 10% ranked in the top 10 percent of their high school class; 40% were in the top 25 percent; 83% were in the top half. (Proportion submitting class standing: 54%.) **Average high school grade point average:** 3.2. **First-year students who submitted SAT scores:** 98%. Scores (25/75 percentile): Critical Reading: 440-540, Math: 460-550, Combined: 900-1090.

ACADEMICS

Year founded: 1908. **Academic calendar:** Semester. **Degrees offered:** certificate, bachelor's, post-bachelor's certificate, master's, doctorate. **Most popular majors:** 17% business administration and management, 13% family and consumer sciences/human sciences, 9% psychology, 6% English language and literature, 6% multi/interdisciplinary studies. **Major fields of study:** area, ethnic, cultural, and gender studies; biological and biomedical sciences; business, management, marketing, and related support services; communication, journalism, and related programs; computer and information sciences and support services; education; English language and literature/

letters; family and consumer sciences/human sciences; foreign languages, literatures, and linguistics; health professions and related clinical sciences; history; legal professions and studies; liberal arts and sciences studies, and humanities; mathematics and statistics; multi/interdisciplinary studies; philosophy and religious studies; physical sciences; psychology; social sciences; visual and performing arts. **Areas of required coursework:** arts/fine arts, humanities, mathematics, English (including composition), philosophy, foreign languages, sciences (biological or physical), history, social science. **Pre-professional programs:** pre-law, pre-medicine, pre-pharmacy. **Special academic programs:** cooperative (work-study plan) program, double major, English as a Second Language (ESL), honors program, independent study, internships, study abroad, teacher certificate program. **Teacher certification offered in:** early childhood, special education, elementary, middle/junior high, secondary. **Cooperative education programs:** art, business, computer science, education, health professions, home economics, humanities, natural science, social/behavioral science, technologies, other. **Reserve Officers Training Corps (ROTC):** Army ROTC: Offered on campus; Navy ROTC: Offered on campus; Air Force ROTC: Offered on campus. **Faculty and instruction (2009-2010):** Total instructional faculty: 553 full-time, 936 part-time (47% men; 53% women; 16% minorities). Full-time faculty with Ph.D. or other terminal degree: 92%. Student/faculty ratio: 17/1. Classes of fewer than 20 students: 34%; of 20 to 49 students: 64%; of 50 or more students: 3%. **Advanced Placement and International Baccalaureate credit:** AP tests may be used for: Credit only. Scores accepted: 3, 4, 5. **Freshmen returning for sophomore year:** 82%. **Graduation rates:** Four-year: 30%; five-year: 55%; six-year: 61%. **Graduate study:** 18% of students pursue further study within one year. Fields in which graduates pursue further study: Master of Business Administration (MBA), 7%; law, 7%; medicine, 1%; education, 28%; arts and sciences, 33%.

COSTS AND FINANCIAL AID

Financial aid office: (973) 655-4461. **Expenses (2009-2010):** Tuition and fees 2009-2010: $10,003 in state, $16,636 out of state; room/board: $10,886. Estimated books and supplies: $1,200; transportation: $1,206; personal expenses: $4,062. **Financial aid:** Priority filing date for institution's financial aid form: March 1. In 2009-2010, 76% of undergraduates applied for financial aid. Of those, 65% were determined to have financial need; 24% had their need fully met. Average financial aid package (proportion receiving): $9,153 (63%). Average amount of gift aid, such as scholarships or grants (proportion receiving): $3,573 (35%). Average amount of self-help aid, such as work study or loans (proportion receiving): $3,930 (54%). Average need-based loan (excluding PLUS or other private loans): $4,154. Among students who received need-based aid, the average percentage of need met: 60%. Among students who received aid based on merit, the average award (and the proportion receiving): $6,473 (2%). The average athletic scholarship (and the proportion receiving): $0 (0%). Average amount of debt of borrowers graduating in 2009: $24,226. Proportion who borrowed: 77%.

CAMPUS LIFE AND EXTRACURRICULAR ACTIVITIES

Campus housing available: coed dorms, women's dorms, apartment for single students, special housing for disabled students, special housing for international students, other housing options. Students who live in college-owned, operated, or affiliated housing: 26%. **Student employment:** During the 2009-2010 academic year, 16% of undergraduates worked on campus. Average per-year earnings: $2,297. **Clubs and organizations:** Number of student organizations: 125. Activities include: campus ministries, choral groups, concert band, dance, drama/theater, international student organization, jazz band, literary magazine, marching band, music ensembles, musical theater, opera, pep band, radio station, student government, student newspaper, symphony orchestra, television station, yearbook. Number of fraternities: 18; sororities: 22. **Sports program (2009-2010):** Member of NCAA III. **Men's intercollegiate varsity sports:** baseball, basketball, football, lacrosse, soccer, swimming, track and field (indoor), track and field (outdoor). **Women's intercollegiate varsity sports:** basketball, field hockey, lacrosse, soccer, softball, swimming, track and field (indoor), track and field (outdoor), volleyball.

SERVICES AND FACILITIES

Basic services: women's center, placement service, day care, health service, health insurance, other. **Remedial assistance:** reading, math, writing, other. **Counseling services:** minority student, personal, academic, older student, psychological, other. **For learning-disabled students:** School does not offer a structured program with separate admission and additional fees. Total undergraduates in learning-disabled program or receiving services: 195. Services include: remedial math, remedial English, reading machines, tape recorders, untimed tests, note-taking services, oral tests, learning center, readers, extended time for tests, tutors, priority registration, priority seating, proofreading services, substitution of courses, texts on tape, typist/scribe, exams on tape or computer, other testing accommodations, other. **Library:** Number of titles: 495,462; number of current serial subscriptions: 3,094. **Information technology resources:** Students are not required to lease or own a computer. Number of campus computers available to all students: 700. School has a wireless network. Approximate number of users that can be accommodated: 16,100. Proportion of college-owned housing units wired for high-speed internet access: 100%. **Campus safety:** Security services offered: 24-hour emergency telephones, lighted pathways/sidewalks, controlled dormitory access (key, security card, etc).

TRANSFER AND INTERNATIONAL STUDENTS

Transfer students: May apply for admission for the following academic terms: Fall, Spring. Applicants need a minimum number of credits to apply. For fall 2009: Transfer applications received: 4,655. Transfer applicants offered admission: 2,204. Transfer applicants enrolled: 1,315. **International students:** Number of foreign undergraduates: 266 (2% of student body). Number of countries represented: 97. Minimum TOEFL score required: 80 (computer). Average TOEFL score: 547 (paper).

New Jersey City University

- **Address:** 2039 Kennedy Boulevard, Jersey City, NJ 07305
- **Website:** http://www.njcu.edu/
- **Public**
- **Enrollment:** 4,695 full-time; 1,672 part-time

KEY STATS

✔ **U.S News College Ranking:** second tier, Regional Universities (North)
✔ **SAT Score (25th/75th percentile):** 850-1020
✔ **Tuition:** 2009-2010: $2,446 in state, $16,266 out of state

Selectivity: Less selective	**Room/board:** $9,043
Acceptance rate: 35%	**Average debt:** N/A
Student/faculty ratio: 15/1	**Proportion who borrowed:** N/A

UNDERGRADUATE STUDENT BODY STATS

2009-2010 enrollment: 4,695 full-time; 1,672 part-time. Men: 39%; women: 61%. **Ethnic makeup:** African American: 20%; Asian American: 7%; Hispanic: 35%; White: 36%; International: 1%.

ADMISSIONS FACTS AND FIGURES

Phone: (888) 441-6528. **Email:** admissions@njcu.edu. **Website:** http://www.njcu.edu/. **Application deadlines for fall 2011:** Regular decision: April 1; decision sent by January 1. Early decision: Not offered. Early action: Not offered. Admission can be deferred. **Application fee:** $35. **To apply online, go to:** http://www.njcu.edu/i2e/home/index.asp. **Admissions requirements/recommendations:** High school units required (recommended): English: 4 (4); Mathematics: 4 (4); Science: 4 (4); Foreign language: 0 (2); Social studies: 4 (4); Total units: 16 (21). Tests: The college uses SAT or ACT scores in admissions decisions. Either SAT or ACT required. Campus visit: Recommended. Admissions interview: Recommended. Off-campus interview: May be arranged. **Factors that count in admissions decisions:** *Academic:* Secondary school record: Very Important. Class rank: Very Important. Letters of recommendation: Important. Standardized test scores: Very Important. Essay: Important. *Nonacademic:* Interview: Considered. Extracurricular activities: Important. Talent/ability: Considered. Character/personal qualities: Considered. Alumni/ae relationship: Not Considered. Geographical residence: Not Considered. State residency: Not Considered. Religious affiliation/commitment: Not Considered. Minority status: Not Considered. Volunteer work: Very Important. Work experience: Not Considered. **Admissions statistics for the fall 2009 entering class:** Total applicants: 4,339. Total accepted: 1,509. Freshmen enrolled: 763; 2% were from out of state. Overall acceptance rate: 35%. **Credentials of fall 2009 freshmen:** 9% ranked in the top 10 percent of their high school class; 33% were in the top 25 percent; 73% were in the top half. (Proportion submitting class standing: 56%.) **First-year students who submitted SAT scores:** 100%. Scores (25/75 percentile): Critical Reading: 420-500, Math: 430-520, Combined: 850-1020.

ACADEMICS

Year founded: 1927. **Academic calendar:** Semester. **Degrees offered:** bachelor's, master's, post-master's certificate. **Most popular majors:** 23% business administration and management, 10% psychology, 9% corrections and criminal justice, 7% English language and literature, 7% organizational behavior studies. **Major fields of study:** biological and biomedical sciences; business, management, marketing, and related support services; communication, journalism, and related programs; computer and information sciences and support services; education; English language and literature/letters; family and consumer sciences/human sciences; foreign languages, literatures, and linguistics; health professions and related clinical sciences; history; mathematics and statistics; philosophy and religious studies; physical sciences; psychology; security and protective services; social sciences; visual and performing arts. **Areas of required coursework:** arts/fine arts, humanities, computer literacy, mathematics, English (including composition), sciences (biological or physical), social science. **Pre-professional programs:** pre-law. **Special academic programs:** accelerated program, cooperative (work-study plan) program, distance learning, double major, English as a Second Language (ESL), honors program, independent study, internships, study abroad, teacher certificate program, weekend college. **Teacher certification offered in:** early childhood, special education, elementary, secondary. **Cooperative education programs:** art, business, computer science, education, health professions, humanities, natural science, social/behavioral science, technologies. **Faculty and instruction (2009-2010):** Total instructional faculty: 246 full-time, 461 part-time (55% men; 45% women; 21% minorities). Full-time faculty with Ph.D. or other terminal degree: 89%. Student/faculty ratio: 15/1. Classes of fewer than 20 students: 47%; of 20 to 49 students: 51%; of 50 or more students: 3%. **Advanced Placement and International Baccalaureate credit:** AP tests may be used for: Credit only. Scores accepted: 3, 4, 5. **Freshmen returning for sophomore year:** 73%. **Graduation rates:** Four-year: 7%; five-year: 26%; six-year: 34%. **Graduate study:** 40% of students pursue further study immediately upon graduation; 45% within one year.

COSTS AND FINANCIAL AID

Financial aid office: (201) 200-3173. **Expenses (2009-2010):** Tuition and fees 2009-2010: $2,446 in state, $16,266 out of state; room/board: $9,043. Estimated books and supplies: $1,988; transportation: $1,890; personal expenses: $2,251. **Financial aid:** Priority filing date for institution's financial aid form: April 15. In 2009-2010, 81% of undergraduates applied for financial aid. Of those, 76% were determined to have financial need; 7% had their need fully met. Average financial aid package (proportion receiving): $8,440 (72%). Average amount of gift aid, such as scholarships or grants (proportion receiving): $6,727 (54%). Average amount of self-help aid, such as work study or loans (proportion receiving): $4,275 (43%). Average need-based loan (excluding PLUS or other private loans): $4,280. Among students who received need-based aid, the average percentage of need met: 59%. Among students who received aid based on merit, the average award (and the proportion receiving): $4,982 (1%).

CAMPUS LIFE AND EXTRACURRICULAR ACTIVITIES

Campus housing available (% using): coed dorms (100%). Activities include: choral groups, concert band, dance, drama/theater, jazz band, literary magazine, music ensembles, musical theater, opera, radio station, student government, student newspaper, symphony orchestra, yearbook. Number of fraternities: 5; sororities: 7. Average proportion of students who stay on campus on weekends: 5%. **Sports program (2009-2010):** Member of NCAA III. **Men's intercollegiate varsity sports:** baseball, basketball, soccer, track and field (indoor), volleyball. **Women's intercollegiate varsity sports:** basketball, bowling, soccer, softball, track and field (indoor), volleyball.

SERVICES AND FACILITIES

Basic services: women's center, placement service, day care, health service, health insurance. **Remedial assistance:** reading, math, writing, study skills. **Counseling services:** career, veteran student, psychological. **For learning-disabled students:** School does not offer a structured program with separate admission and additional fees. Services include: remedial math, remedial English, remedial reading, diagnostic testing service, untimed tests, note-taking services, extended time for tests. **Library:** Number of titles: 319,360; number of current serial subscriptions: 25,214. **Information technology resources:** Students are not required to lease or own a computer. School has a wireless network. Proportion of college-owned housing units wired for high-speed internet access: 100%. **Campus safety:** Security services offered: 24-hour foot-and-vehicle patrols, late-night transport/escort service, 24-hour emergency telephones, lighted pathways/sidewalks.

TRANSFER AND INTERNATIONAL STUDENTS

Transfer students: May apply for admission for the following academic terms: Fall, Winter, Spring, Summer. Applicants need a minimum num-

ber of credits to apply. For fall 2009: Transfer applicants enrolled: 906. **International students:** Number of foreign undergraduates: 85 (1% of student body). Minimum TOEFL score required: 500 (paper); 173 (computer).

New Jersey Institute of Technology

- **Address:** University Heights, Newark, NJ 07102-1982
- **Website:** http://www.njit.edu
- **Public**
- **Enrollment:** 4,790 full-time; 1,134 part-time

KEY STATS
✔ **U.S News College Ranking:** 139, National Universities
✔ **SAT Score (25th/75th percentile):** 1040-1250
✔ **Tuition:** 2010-2011: $12,856 in state, $22,600 out of state

Selectivity: Selective	Room/board: N/A
Acceptance rate: 67%	Average debt: $25,408
Student/faculty ratio: 15/1	Proportion who borrowed: 39%

UNDERGRADUATE STUDENT BODY STATS

2009-2010 enrollment: 4,790 full-time; 1,134 part-time. Men: 79%; women: 21%. **Ethnic makeup:** African American: 10%; American-Indian: 1%; Asian American: 21%; Hispanic: 20%; White: 44%; International: 4%.

ADMISSIONS FACTS AND FIGURES

Phone: (973) 596-3300. **Email:** admissions@njit.edu. **Website:** http://www.njit.edu. **Application deadlines for fall 2011:** Regular decision: March 1. Early decision: Not offered. Early action: Not offered. Admission can be deferred. **Application fee:** $50. **To apply online, go to:** http://www.njit.edu/admissions/apply-online.php. **Admissions requirements/recommendations:** High school units required (recommended): English: 4; Mathematics: 4; Science: 2; Foreign language: (2); Social studies: (1); History: (1); Academic electives: (2); Total units: 16. Tests: The college uses SAT or ACT scores in admissions decisions. Either SAT or ACT required. For admission to the fall 2011 entering class, the school will accept: ACT with or without writing accepted. Campus visit: Recommended. Admissions interview: Neither required nor recommended. Off-campus interview: May be arranged. **Factors that count in admissions decisions:** *Academic:* Secondary school record: Very Important. Class rank: Very Important. Letters of recommendation: Considered. Standardized test scores: Very Important. Essay: Considered. *Nonacademic:* Interview: Considered. Extracurricular activities: Considered. Talent/ability: Considered. Character/personal qualities: Considered. Alumni/ae relationship: Considered. Geographical residence: Considered. State residency: Considered. Religious affiliation/commitment: Not Considered. Minority status: Considered. Volunteer work: Considered. Work experience: Considered. **Other schools with the greatest overlap in applicants:** Drexel University; Rowan University; Rutgers, the State University of New Jersey–New Brunswick; Rutgers, the State University of New Jersey–Newark; Stevens Institute of Technology. **Admissions statistics for the fall 2009 entering class:** Total applicants: 4,315. Total accepted: 2,874. Freshmen enrolled: 994; 6% were from out of state. Overall acceptance rate: 67%. **Size of waiting list:** 203 applicants; enrolled from waiting list: 50. **Credentials of fall 2009 freshmen:** 26% ranked in the top 10 percent of their high school class; 55% were in the top 25 percent; 83% were in the top half. (Proportion submitting class standing: 57%.) **First-year students who submitted SAT scores:** 99%. Scores (25/75 percentile): Critical Reading: 490-590, Math: 550-660, Combined: 1040-1250.

ACADEMICS

Year founded: 1881. **Academic calendar:** Semester. **Degrees offered:** bachelor's, post-bachelor's certificate, master's, doctorate. **Most popular majors:** 14% engineering technology, 13% architecture (B.Arch., B.A./B.S., M.Arch., M.A./M.S., Ph.D.), 12% business administration and management, 8% information technology, 8% mechanical engineering. **Major fields of study:** architecture and related services; biological and biomedical sciences; business, management, marketing, and related support services; computer and information sciences and support services; engineering; engineering technologies/technicians; English language and literature/letters; history; mathematics and statistics; multi/interdisciplinary studies; natural resources and conservation; physical sciences. **Areas of required coursework:** humanities, computer literacy, mathematics, English (including composition), sciences (biological or physical), history, social science, other. **Pre-professional programs:** pre-law, pre-dentistry, pre-medicine, pre-veterinary science, pre-optometry, pre-pharmacy. **Special academic programs (% participation):** accelerated program (8%), cooperative (work-study plan) program (18%), cross-registration (5%), distance learning (10%), double major (5%), dual enrollment (1%), English as a Second Language (ESL) (8%), honors program (20%), independent study (10%), internships (5%), liberal arts/career combination (1%), study abroad (1%), teacher certificate program (2%), weekend college (5%). **Teacher certification offered in:** elementary, middle/junior high, secondary. **Cooperative education programs:** business, computer science, education, engineering, humanities, natural science, social/behavioral science, technologies. **Reserve Officers Training Corps (ROTC):** Army ROTC: Offered at cooperating institution (Seton Hall University); Air Force ROTC: Offered on campus. **Faculty and instruction (2009-2010):** Total instructional faculty: 406 full-time, 249 part-time (81% men; 19% women; 23% minorities). Full-time faculty with Ph.D. or other terminal degree: 100%. Student/faculty ratio: 15/1. Classes of fewer than 20 students: 39%; of 20 to 49 students: 57%; of 50 or more students: 4%. **Advanced Placement and International Baccalaureate credit:** AP tests may be used for: Credit only. Scores accepted: 3, 4, 5. International Baccalaureate exams may be used for: Credit only. **Freshmen returning for sophomore year:** 82%. **Graduation rates:** Four-year: 17%; five-year: 45%; six-year: 55%. **Graduate study:** 18% of students pursue further study immediately upon graduation; 40% within one year; 67% within five years. Fields in which graduates pursue further study: Master of Business Administration (MBA), 17%; law, 1%; medicine, 4%; dentistry, 2%; engineering, 57%; education, 2%; arts and sciences, 6%.

COSTS AND FINANCIAL AID

Financial aid office: (973) 596-3479. **Expenses (2010-2011):** Tuition and fees 2010-2011: $12,856 in state, $22,600 out of state. Estimated books and supplies: $2,700; transportation: $3,000; personal expenses: $1,200. **Financial aid:** Priority filing date for institution's financial aid form: March 15; deadline: May 15. In 2009-2010, 75% of undergraduates applied for financial aid. Of those, 67% were determined to have financial need; 9% had their need fully met. Average financial aid package (proportion receiving): $13,059 (67%). Average amount of gift aid, such as scholarships or grants (proportion receiving): $11,735 (52%). Average amount of self-help aid, such as work study or loans (proportion receiving): $4,308 (45%). Average need-based loan (excluding PLUS or other private loans): $4,281. Among students who received need-based aid, the average percentage of need met: 61%. Among students who received aid based on merit, the average award (and the proportion receiving): $10,574 (11%). The average athletic scholarship (and the proportion receiving): $15,673 (3%). Average amount of debt of borrowers graduating in 2009: $25,408. Proportion who borrowed: 39%.

CAMPUS LIFE AND EXTRACURRICULAR ACTIVITIES

Campus housing available (% using): coed dorms (60%), sorority housing (7%), fraternity housing (12%), other housing options (21%). Students who live in college-owned, operated, or affiliated housing: 27%. **Student employment:** During the 2009-2010 academic year, 25% of undergraduates worked on campus. Average per-year earnings: $4,000. **Clubs and organizations:** Number of student organizations: 70. Activities include: concert band, dance, drama/theater, international student organization, literary magazine, marching band, radio station, student government, student newspaper, yearbook. Number of fraternities: 15; sororities: 8. Proportion of men in fraternities: 5%; of women in sororities: 3%. Average proportion of students who stay on campus on weekends: 30%. **Sports program (2009-2010):** Member of NCAA I. *Men's intercollegiate varsity sports:* baseball, basketball, cross country, fencing, soccer, swimming, tennis, track and field (indoor), track and field (outdoor), volleyball. *Women's intercollegiate varsity sports:* basketball, cross country, fencing, soccer, swimming, tennis, track and field (indoor), track and field (outdoor), volleyball.

SERVICES AND FACILITIES

Basic services: nonremedial tutoring, women's center, placement service, day care, health service, health insurance. **Remedial assistance:** reading, math, writing, study skills. **Counseling services:** minority student, career, military, personal, veteran student, academic, older student, psychological, birth control. **For learning-disabled students:** School does not offer a structured program with separate admission and additional fees. Services include: remedial math, remedial English, reading machines, remedial reading, tape recorders, videotaped classes, note-taking services, oral tests, readers, extended time for tests, tutors, texts on tape, other testing accommodations. **Library:** Number of titles: 223,998; number of current serial subscriptions: 31,656. **Information technology resources:** Students are required to lease or own a computer. Number of campus computers available to all students: 1,938. School has a wireless network. Approximate number of users that can be accommodated: 1,500. Proportion of college-owned housing units wired for high-speed internet access: 100%. **Campus safety:** Security services offered: 24-hour foot-and-vehicle patrols, late-night transport/escort service, 24-hour emergency telephones, lighted pathways/sidewalks, controlled dormitory access (key, security card, etc).

TRANSFER AND INTERNATIONAL STUDENTS

Transfer students: May apply for admission for the following academic terms: Fall, Spring. Applicants do not need a minimum number of credits to apply. For fall 2009: Transfer applications received: 1,442. Transfer applicants offered admission: 784. Transfer applicants enrolled: 472. **International students:** Number of foreign undergraduates: 245 (4% of student body). Number of countries represented: 63. Minimum TOEFL score required: 550 (paper); 79 (computer). Average TOEFL score: 591 (paper).

Princeton University

- **Address:** Princeton, NJ 08544
- **Website:** http://www.princeton.edu
- **Private**
- **Enrollment:** 5,044 full-time; 69 part-time

KEY STATS

✔ **U.S News College Ranking:** 2, National Universities
✔ **SAT Score (25th/75th percentile):** 1390-1580
✔ **Tuition:** 2010-2011: $36,640

Selectivity: Most selective	**Room/board:** $11,940
Acceptance rate: 10%	**Average debt:** $5,667
Student/faculty ratio: 6/1	**Proportion who borrowed:** 22%

UNDERGRADUATE STUDENT BODY STATS

2009-2010 enrollment: 5,044 full-time; 69 part-time. Men: 51%; women: 49%. **Ethnic makeup:** African American: 8%; Asian American: 16%; Hispanic: 8%; White: 58%; International: 10%.

ADMISSIONS FACTS AND FIGURES

Phone: (609) 258-3060. **Email:** uaoffice@princeton.edu. **Website:** http://www.princeton.edu. **Application deadlines for fall 2011:** Regular decision: January 1; decision sent by March 31. Early decision: Not offered. Early action: Not offered. Admission can be deferred. **Application fee:** $65. **To apply online, go to:** http://www.princeton.edu/pr/admissions/u/appl. **Admissions requirements/recommendations:** High school units required (recommended): English: (4); Mathematics: (4); Science: (4); Foreign language: (4); Social studies: (2); History: (2); Total units: (21). Tests: The college uses SAT or ACT scores in admissions decisions. Either SAT or ACT required. For admission to the fall 2011 entering class, the school will accept: ACT with writing required. Campus visit: Recommended. Admissions interview: Recommended. Off-campus interview: May be arranged. **Factors that count in admissions decisions:** *Academic:* Secondary school record: Very Important. Class rank: Very Important. Letters of recommendation: Very Important. Standardized test scores: Very Important. Essay: Very Important. *Nonacademic:* Interview: Considered. Extracurricular activities: Important. Talent/ability: Very Important. Character/personal qualities: Very Important. Alumni/ae relationship: Considered. Geographical residence: Considered. State residency: Not Considered. Religious affiliation/commitment: Not Considered. Minority status: Considered. Volunteer work: Considered. Work experience: Considered. **Other schools with the greatest overlap in applicants:** Columbia University; Harvard University; Stanford University; University of Pennsylvania; Yale University. **Admissions statistics for the fall 2009 entering class:** Total applicants: 21,963. Total accepted: 2,209. Freshmen enrolled: 1,320; 81% were from out of state. Overall acceptance rate: 10%. **Size of waiting list:** 1332 applicants; enrolled from waiting list: 60. **Credentials of fall 2009 freshmen:** 95% ranked in the top 10 percent of their high school class; 100% were in the top 25 percent; 100% were in the top half. (Proportion submitting class standing: 30%.) **Average high school grade point average:** 3.9. **First-year students who submitted SAT scores:** 96%. Scores (25/75 percentile): Critical Reading: 690-790, Math: 700-790, Combined: 1390-1580. **First-year students submitting ACT scores:** 25%. Scores (25/75 percentile): English: 32-35, Math: 31-35, Composite: 31-35.

ACADEMICS

Year founded: 1746. **Academic calendar:** Semester. **Degrees offered:** bachelor's, master's, doctorate. **Most popular majors:** 11% economics, 10%

political science and government, 8% history, 7% public policy analysis, 5% psychology. **Major fields of study:** architecture and related services; area, ethnic, cultural, and gender studies; biological and biomedical sciences; business, management, marketing, and related support services; engineering; English language and literature/letters; foreign languages, literatures, and linguistics; history; mathematics and statistics; multi/interdisciplinary studies; philosophy and religious studies; physical sciences; psychology; public administration and social service professions; social sciences; visual and performing arts. **Areas of required coursework:** humanities, English (including composition), foreign languages, sciences (biological or physical), social science. **Pre-professional programs:** pre-medicine. **Special academic programs:** cross-registration, exchange student program (domestic), independent study, student-designed major, study abroad, teacher certificate program. **Teacher certification offered in:** elementary, secondary. **Reserve Officers Training Corps (ROTC):** Army ROTC: Offered on campus; Navy ROTC: Offered at cooperating institution (Rutgers, the State University of New Jersey–New Brunswick). **Faculty and instruction (2009-2010):** Total instructional faculty: 846 full-time, 212 part-time (69% men; 31% women; 18% minorities). Full-time faculty with Ph.D. or other terminal degree: 93%. Student/faculty ratio: 6/1. Classes of fewer than 20 students: 73%; of 20 to 49 students: 16%; of 50 or more students: 11%. **Advanced Placement and International Baccalaureate credit:** AP tests may be used for: Credit and/or placement. Scores accepted: 4, 5. International Baccalaureate exams may be used for: Credit and/or placement. **Freshmen returning for sophomore year:** 98%. **Graduation rates:** Four-year: 90%; five-year: 95%; six-year: 96%. **Graduate study:** 21% of students pursue further study immediately upon graduation. Fields in which graduates pursue further study: law, 17%; medicine, 17%; dentistry, 1%; engineering, 16%; theology (or the seminary), 1%; arts and sciences, 50%.

COSTS AND FINANCIAL AID

Financial aid office: (609) 258-3330. **Expenses (2010-2011):** Tuition and fees 2010-2011: $36,640; room/board: $11,940. Estimated books and supplies: $1,260 personal expenses: $2,340. **Financial aid:** Priority filing date for institution's financial aid form: February 1. In 2009-2010, 63% of undergraduates applied for financial aid. Of those, 59% were determined to have financial need; 100% had their need fully met. Average financial aid package (proportion receiving): $36,495 (59%). Average amount of gift aid, such as scholarships or grants (proportion receiving): $34,828 (59%). Average amount of self-help aid, such as work study or loans (proportion receiving): $1,667 (41%). Average need-based loan (excluding PLUS or other private loans): $0. Among students who received need-based aid, the average percentage of need met: 100%. Average amount of debt of borrowers graduating in 2009: $5,667. Proportion who borrowed: 22%.

CAMPUS LIFE AND EXTRACURRICULAR ACTIVITIES

Campus housing available (% using): coed dorms (100%), special housing for disabled students. Students who live in college-owned, operated, or affiliated housing: 98%. **Student employment:** During the 2009-2010 academic year, 46% of undergraduates worked on campus. Average per-year earnings: $1,330. **Clubs and organizations:** Number of student organizations: 250. Activities include: campus ministries, choral groups, concert band, dance, drama/theater, international student organization, jazz band, literary magazine, marching band, model UN, music ensembles, musical theater, opera, pep band, radio station, student government, student newspaper, student film society, symphony orchestra, yearbook. Number of fraternities: 0; sororities: 0. **Sports program (2009-2010):** Member of NCAA I. *Men's intercollegiate varsity sports:* baseball, basketball, cross country, fencing, football, golf, ice hockey, lacrosse, soccer, swimming, tennis, track and field (indoor), track and field (outdoor), volleyball, water polo, wrestling. *Women's intercollegiate varsity sports:* basketball, crew (heavyweight), cross country, fencing, field hockey, golf, ice hockey, lacrosse, crew (lightweight), soccer, softball, squash, swimming, tennis, track and field (indoor), track and field (outdoor), volleyball, water polo.

SERVICES AND FACILITIES

Basic services: women's center, health service, health insurance. **Remedial assistance:** math, writing, other. **Counseling services:** minority student, career, personal, academic, psychological, birth control, religious. **For learning-disabled students:** School does not offer a structured program with separate admission and additional fees. Total undergraduates in learning-disabled program or receiving services: 108. Services include: tape recorders, note-taking services, learning center, readers, extended time for tests, tutors, substitution of courses, texts on tape, typist/scribe, exams on tape or computer, other testing accommodations. **Library:** Number of titles: 6,941,254; number of current serial subscriptions: 56,711. **Information tech-**

nology resources: Students are not required to lease or own a computer. Number of campus computers available to all students: 750. School has a wireless network. Approximate number of users that can be accommodated: 16,299. Proportion of college-owned housing units wired for high-speed internet access: 99%. **Campus safety:** Security services offered: 24-hour foot-and-vehicle patrols, late-night transport/escort service, 24-hour emergency telephones, lighted pathways/sidewalks, controlled dormitory access (key, security card, etc).

TRANSFER AND INTERNATIONAL STUDENTS

International students: Number of foreign undergraduates: 518 (10% of student body). Number of countries represented: 100.

Ramapo College of New Jersey

- ■ **Address:** 505 Ramapo Valley Road, Mahwah, NJ 07430-1680
- ■ **Website:** http://www.ramapo.edu
- ■ **Public**
- ■ **Enrollment:** 5,224 full-time; 552 part-time

KEY STATS

✔ **U.S News College Ranking:** 25, Regional Universities (North)
✔ **SAT Score (25th/75th percentile):** 1070-1230
✔ **Tuition:** 2010-2011: $11,874 in state, $19,679 out of state

Selectivity: Selective	**Room/board:** $11,730
Acceptance rate: 51%	**Average debt:** $19,789
Student/faculty ratio: 18/1	**Proportion who borrowed:** 55%

UNDERGRADUATE STUDENT BODY STATS

2009-2010 enrollment: 5,224 full-time; 552 part-time. Men: 42%; women: 58%. **Ethnic makeup:** African American: 5%; Asian American: 5%; Hispanic: 9%; White: 79%; International: 2%.

ADMISSIONS FACTS AND FIGURES

Phone: (201) 684-7300. **Email:** admissions@ramapo.edu. **Website:** http://www.ramapo.edu. **Application deadlines for fall 2011:** Regular decision: March 1. Early decision: Not offered. Early action: Send application by: November 15; Decision sent by: December 15. Admission can be deferred. **Application fee:** $60. **To apply online, go to:** http://www.ramapo.edu/admissions/apply.html. **Admissions requirements/recommendations:** High school units required (recommended): English: 4; Mathematics: 3; Science: 3; Foreign language: 2; Social studies: 3; History: 0; Academic electives: 3; Total units: 18. Tests: The college uses SAT or ACT scores in admissions decisions. SAT required. For admission to the fall 2011 entering class, the school will accept: ACT with writing recommended. Campus visit: Recommended. Admissions interview: Recommended. Off-campus interview: May be arranged. **Factors that count in admissions decisions:** *Academic:* Secondary school record: Very Important. Class rank: Very Important. Letters of recommendation: Important. Standardized test scores: Very Important. Essay: Important. *Nonacademic:* Interview: Not Considered. Extracurricular activities: Important. Talent/ability: Important. Character/personal qualities: Not Considered. Alumni/ae relationship: Considered. Geographical residence: Considered. State residency: Considered. Religious affiliation/commitment: Not Considered. Minority status: Not Considered. Volunteer work: Considered. Work experience: Considered. **Other schools with the greatest overlap in applicants:** College of New Jersey; Montclair State University; Richard Stockton College of New Jersey; Rowan University; Rutgers, the State University of New Jersey–New Brunswick. **Admissions statistics for the fall 2009 entering class:** Total applicants: 5,121. Total accepted: 2,628. Freshmen enrolled: 937; 3% were from out of state. Overall acceptance rate: 51%. Non-early acceptance rate: 51%. **Size of waiting list:** 505 applicants; enrolled from waiting list: 104. **Credentials of fall 2009 freshmen:** 24% ranked in the top 10 percent of their high school class; 62% were in the top 25 percent; 94% were in the top half. (Proportion submitting class standing: 41%.) **Average high school grade point average:** 3.4. First-year students who submitted SAT scores: 97%. Scores (25/75 percentile): Critical Reading: 520-600, Math: 550-630, Combined: 1070-1230.

ACADEMICS

Year founded: 1969. **Academic calendar:** Semester. **Degrees offered:** certificate, bachelor's, master's. **Most popular majors:** 15% business administration and management, 15% psychology, 11% communication studies/speech communication and rhetoric, 8% nursing science (M.S., Ph.D.), 6% history. **Major fields of study:** area, ethnic, cultural, and gender studies; biological and biomedical sciences; business, management, marketing, and related support services; communication, journalism, and related programs; computer and information sciences and support services; foreign languages, literatures, and linguistics; health professions and related clinical sciences; history; legal professions and studies; liberal arts and sciences studies, and humanities; mathematics and statistics; multi/interdisciplinary studies; natural resources and conservation; physical sciences; psychology; public administration and social service professions; social sciences; visual and performing arts. **Areas of required coursework:** humanities, mathematics, English (including composition), sciences (biological or physical), history, social science. **Pre-professional programs:** pre-law, pre-dentistry, pre-medicine, pre-optometry, other. **Special academic programs:** accelerated program, cooperative (work-study plan) program, distance learning, double major, dual enrollment, exchange student program (domestic), external degree program, honors program, independent study, internships, liberal arts/career combination, student-designed major, study abroad, teacher certificate program. **Teacher certification offered in:** elementary, secondary. **Cooperative education programs:** art, business, computer science, education, health professions, humanities, natural science, social/behavioral science, vocational arts. **Reserve Officers Training Corps (ROTC):** Air Force ROTC: Offered at cooperating institution. **Faculty and instruction (2009-2010):** Total instructional faculty: 213 full-time, 195 part-time. Full-time faculty with Ph.D. or other terminal degree: 95%. Student/faculty ratio: 18/1. Classes of fewer than 20 students: 24%; of 20 to 49 students: 76%. **Advanced Placement and International Baccalaureate credit:** AP tests may be used for: Credit only. Scores accepted: 4, 5. International Baccalaureate exams may be used for: Credit only. **Freshmen returning for sophomore year:** 88%. **Graduation rates:** Four-year: 59%; five-year: 73%; six-year: 69%.

COSTS AND FINANCIAL AID

Financial aid office: (201) 684-7549. **Expenses (2010-2011):** Tuition and fees 2010-2011: $11,874 in state, $19,679 out of state; room/board: $11,730. Estimated books and supplies: $1,200; transportation: $500; personal expenses: $2,250. **Financial aid:** Priority filing date for institution's financial aid form: March 1. In 2009-2010, 63% of undergraduates applied for financial aid. Of those, 46% were determined to have financial need; 4% had their need fully met. Average financial aid package (proportion receiving): $12,053 (45%). Average amount of gift aid, such as scholarships or grants (proportion receiving): $10,678 (21%). Average amount of self-help aid, such as work study or loans (proportion receiving): $4,661 (39%). Average need-based loan (excluding PLUS or other private loans): $4,563. Among students who received need-based aid, the average percentage of need met: 69%. Among students who received aid based on merit, the average award (and the proportion receiving): $12,174 (5%). The average athletic scholarship (and the proportion receiving): $0 (0%). Average amount of debt of borrowers graduating in 2009: $19,789. Proportion who borrowed: 55%.

CAMPUS LIFE AND EXTRACURRICULAR ACTIVITIES

Campus housing available (% using): coed dorms (100%), apartment for single students. Students who live in college-owned, operated, or affiliated housing: 55%. **Student employment:** During the 2009-2010 academic year, 13% of undergraduates worked on campus. Average per-year earnings: $3,800. **Clubs and organizations:** Number of student organizations: 92. Activities include: campus ministries, choral groups, dance, drama/theater, international student organization, literary magazine, model UN, music ensembles, musical theater, radio station, student government, student newspaper, student film society, television station, yearbook. Number of fraternities: 13; sororities: 11. Proportion of men in fraternities: 10%; of women in sororities: 9%. **Sports program (2009-2010):** Member of NCAA III. *Men's intercollegiate varsity sports:* baseball, basketball, cross country, soccer, tennis, track and field (indoor), track and field (outdoor), volleyball. *Women's intercollegiate varsity sports:* basketball, cross country, field hockey, lacrosse, soccer, softball, tennis, track and field (indoor), track and field (outdoor), volleyball.

SERVICES AND FACILITIES

Basic services: nonremedial tutoring, women's center, placement service, health service, health insurance, other. **Remedial assistance:** reading, math, writing, study skills. **Counseling services:** minority student, career, personal, veteran student, academic, older student, psychological, birth control. **For learning-disabled students:** School does not offer a structured program with separate admission and additional fees. Services include: remedial math, remedial English, reading machines, remedial reading, tape recorders, other special classes, note-taking services, learning center, extended time for tests,

tutors, early syllabus, priority registration, priority seating, texts on tape, other testing accommodations, other. **Library:** Number of titles: 177,487; number of current serial subscriptions: 487. **Information technology resources:** Students are not required to lease or own a computer. Number of campus computers available to all students: 1,058. School has a wireless network. Approximate number of users that can be accommodated: 1,500. Proportion of college-owned housing units wired for high-speed internet access: 100%. **Campus safety:** Security services offered: 24-hour foot-and-vehicle patrols, late-night transport/escort service, 24-hour emergency telephones, lighted pathways/sidewalks, student patrols, controlled dormitory access (key, security card, etc.).

TRANSFER AND INTERNATIONAL STUDENTS

Transfer students: May apply for admission for the following academic terms: Fall, Spring. Applicants do not need a minimum number of credits to apply. For fall 2009: Transfer applications received: 1,458. Transfer applicants offered admission: 1,007. Transfer applicants enrolled: 608. **International students:** Number of foreign undergraduates: 91 (2% of student body). Number of countries represented: 46. Minimum TOEFL score required: 550 (paper); 213 (computer). Average TOEFL score: 580 (paper).

Richard Stockton College of New Jersey

- ■ **Address:** PO Box 195, Pomona, NJ 08240-0195
- ■ **Website:** http://www.stockton.edu
- ■ **Public**
- ■ **Enrollment:** 6,068 full-time; 745 part-time

KEY STATS
- ✔ **U.S News College Ranking:** 51, Regional Universities (North)
- ✔ **SAT Score (25th/75th percentile):** 1000-1200
- ✔ **Tuition:** 2010-2011: $11,455 in state, $17,309 out of state

Selectivity: Selective	**Room/board:** $10,495
Acceptance rate: 61%	**Average debt:** $27,847
Student/faculty ratio: 19/1	**Proportion who borrowed:** 69%

UNDERGRADUATE STUDENT BODY STATS

2009-2010 enrollment: 6,068 full-time; 745 part-time. Men: 43%; women: 57%. **Ethnic makeup:** African American: 8%; Asian American: 6%; Hispanic: 7%; White: 78%.

ADMISSIONS FACTS AND FIGURES

Phone: (609) 652-4261. **Email:** admissions@stockton.edu. **Website:** http://www.stockton.edu. **Application deadlines for fall 2011:** Regular decision: May 1. Early decision: Not offered. Early action: Not offered. Admission can be deferred. **Application fee:** $50. **To apply online, go to:** http://intraweb.stockton.edu/eyos/page.cfm?siteID=64&pageID=5. **Admissions requirements/ recommendations:** High school units required (recommended): English: 4; Mathematics: 3; Science: 2; Foreign language: 0; Social studies: 2; Academic electives: 5; Total units: 16. Tests: The college uses SAT or ACT scores in admissions decisions. Either SAT or ACT required. For admission to the fall 2011 entering class, the school will accept: ACT with writing recommended. Campus visit: Recommended. Admissions interview: Neither required nor recommended. Off-campus interview: Not available. **Factors that count in admissions decisions:** *Academic:* Secondary school record: Very Important. Class rank: Very Important. Letters of recommendation: Considered. Standardized test scores: Very Important. Essay: Considered. *Nonacademic:* Interview: Not Considered. Extracurricular activities: Considered. Talent/ability: Considered. Character/personal qualities: Considered. Alumni/ae relationship: Considered. Geographical residence: Not Considered. State residency: Not Considered. Religious affiliation/commitment: Not Considered. Minority status: Not Considered. Volunteer work: Considered. Work experience: Considered. **Other schools with the greatest overlap in applicants:** College of New Jersey; Rowan University; Rutgers, the State University of New Jersey–New Brunswick; Temple University; University of Delaware. **Admissions statistics for the fall 2009 entering class:** Total applicants: 4,547. Total accepted: 2,783. Freshmen enrolled: 870; 1% were from out of state. Overall acceptance rate: 61%. **Size of waiting list:** 466 applicants; enrolled from waiting list: 105. **Credentials of fall 2009 freshmen:** 26% ranked in the top 10 percent of their high school class; 60% were in the top 25 percent; 96% were in the top half. (Proportion submitting class standing: 83%.) **First-year students who submitted SAT scores:** 94%. Scores (25/75 percentile): Critical Reading: 490-590, Math: 510-610,

Combined: 1000-1200. **First-year students submitting ACT scores:** 6%. Scores (25/75 percentile): English: 18-23, Math: 18-25, Composite: 19-23.

ACADEMICS

Year founded: 1969. **Academic calendar:** Semester. **Degrees offered:** certificate, bachelor's, master's, doctorate. **Most popular majors:** 19% business administration and management, 11% psychology, 11% teacher education, 9% biology/biological sciences, 8% criminology. **Major fields of study:** biological and biomedical sciences; business, management, marketing, and related support services; communication, journalism, and related programs; computer and information sciences and support services; education; English language and literature/letters; foreign languages, literatures, and linguistics; health professions and related clinical sciences; history; liberal arts and sciences studies, and humanities; mathematics and statistics; natural resources and conservation; philosophy and religious studies; physical sciences; psychology; public administration and social service professions; social sciences; visual and performing arts. **Areas of required coursework:** arts/fine arts, humanities, mathematics, English (including composition), sciences (biological or physical), history, social science, other. **Pre-professional programs:** pre-law, pre-dentistry, pre-medicine, pre-veterinary science, pre-pharmacy. **Special academic programs (% participation):** accelerated program, distance learning (18%), double major (5%), English as a Second Language (ESL), honors program, independent study (50%), internships (25%), liberal arts/career combination (5%), study abroad (1%), teacher certificate program (7%). **Teacher certification offered in:** special education, elementary, middle/junior high, secondary. **Faculty and instruction (2009-2010):** Total instructional faculty: 264 full-time, 255 part-time (52% men; 48% women; 16% minorities). Full-time faculty with Ph.D. or other terminal degree: 95%. Student/faculty ratio: 19/1. Classes of fewer than 20 students: 22%; of 20 to 49 students: 75%; of 50 or more students: 2%. **Advanced Placement and International Baccalaureate credit:** AP tests may be used for: Credit only. Scores accepted: 3, 4, 5. International Baccalaureate exams may be used for: Credit only. **Freshmen returning for sophomore year:** 82%. **Graduation rates:** Four-year: 39%; five-year: 59%; six-year: 66%. **Graduate study:** 29% of students pursue further study within one year. Fields in which graduates pursue further study: Master of Business Administration (MBA), 9%; engineering, 6%; education, 11%; arts and sciences, 71%; veterinary medicine, 3%.

COSTS AND FINANCIAL AID

Financial aid office: (609) 652-4201. **Expenses (2010-2011):** Tuition and fees 2010-2011: $11,455 in state, $17,309 out of state; room/board: $10,495. Estimated books and supplies: $1,600; transportation: $2,900; personal expenses: $2,700. **Financial aid:** Priority filing date for institution's financial aid form: March 1. In 2009-2010, 79% of undergraduates applied for financial aid. Of those, 67% were determined to have financial need; 27% had their need fully met. Average financial aid package (proportion receiving): $15,435 (66%). Average amount of gift aid, such as scholarships or grants (proportion receiving): $8,353 (33%). Average amount of self-help aid, such as work study or loans (proportion receiving): $4,645 (55%). Average need-based loan (excluding PLUS or other private loans): $4,569. Among students who received need-based aid, the average percentage of need met: 70%. Among students who received aid based on merit, the average award (and the proportion receiving): $6,019 (20%). The average athletic scholarship (and the proportion receiving): $0 (0%). Average amount of debt of borrowers graduating in 2009: $27,847. Proportion who borrowed: 69%.

CAMPUS LIFE AND EXTRACURRICULAR ACTIVITIES

Campus housing available (% using): coed dorms (48%), special housing for disabled students (2%), other housing options (39%). Students who live in college-owned, operated, or affiliated housing: 37%. **Student employment:** During the 2009-2010 academic year, 6% of undergraduates worked on campus. Average per-year earnings: $1,305. **Clubs and organizations:** Number of student organizations: 112. Activities include: campus ministries, choral groups, concert band, dance, drama/theater, international student organization, literary magazine, music ensembles, musical theater, radio station, student government, student newspaper, television station, yearbook. Number of fraternities: 11; sororities: 9. Proportion of men in fraternities: 5%; of women in sororities: 5%. Average proportion of students who stay on campus on weekends: 45%. **Sports program (2009-2010):** Member of NCAA III. **Men's intercollegiate varsity sports:** baseball, basketball, cross country, lacrosse, soccer, track and field (indoor), track and field (outdoor). **Women's intercollegiate varsity sports:** basketball, crew (heavyweight), cross country, field hockey, crew (lightweight), soccer, softball, tennis, track and field (indoor), track and field (outdoor), volleyball.

SERVICES AND FACILITIES

Basic services: nonremedial tutoring, day care, health service, health insurance, other. **Remedial assistance:** reading, math, writing, study skills. **Counseling services:** minority student, career, personal, veteran student, academic, older student, psychological, birth control, religious. **For learning-disabled students:** School does not offer a structured program with separate admission and additional fees. Services include: reading machines, tape recorders, note-taking services, oral tests, readers, extended time for tests, priority registration, priority seating, texts on tape, other testing accommodations, other. **Library:** Number of titles: 281,155; number of current serial subscriptions: 37,050. **Information technology resources:** Students are not required to lease or own a computer. Number of campus computers available to all students: 850. School has a wireless network. Approximate number of users that can be accommodated: 1,300. Proportion of college-owned housing units wired for high-speed internet access: 100%. **Campus safety:** Security services offered: 24-hour foot-and-vehicle patrols, late-night transport/escort service, 24-hour emergency telephones, lighted pathways/sidewalks, student patrols, controlled dormitory access (key, security card, etc).

TRANSFER AND INTERNATIONAL STUDENTS

Transfer students: May apply for admission for the following academic terms: Fall, Spring. Applicants do not need a minimum number of credits to apply. For fall 2009: Transfer applications received: 1,762. Transfer applicants offered admission: 1,506. Transfer applicants enrolled: 1,005. **International students:** Number of foreign undergraduates: 20. Number of countries represented: 36. Minimum TOEFL score required: 525 (paper); 213 (computer). Average TOEFL score: 550 (paper).

Rider University

- **Address:** 2083 Lawrenceville Road, Lawrenceville, NJ 08648-3099
- **Website:** http://www.rider.edu
- **Private**
- **Enrollment:** 4,074 full-time; 817 part-time

KEY STATS

✔ **U.S News College Ranking:** 36, Regional Universities (North)
✔ **SAT Score (25th/75th percentile):** 930-1140
✔ **Tuition:** 2010-2011: $30,470

Selectivity: Selective	**Room/board:** $11,200
Acceptance rate: 75%	**Average debt:** $35,042
Student/faculty ratio: 13/1	**Proportion who borrowed:** 72%

UNDERGRADUATE STUDENT BODY STATS

2009-2010 enrollment: 4,074 full-time; 817 part-time. Men: 40%; women: 60%. **Ethnic makeup:** African American: 10%; Asian American: 3%; Hispanic: 6%; White: 77%; International: 3%.

ADMISSIONS FACTS AND FIGURES

Phone: (609) 896-5042. **Email:** admissions@rider.edu. **Website:** http://www.rider.edu. **Application deadlines for fall 2011:** Regular decision: Rolling. Early decision: Send application by: November 15; Decision sent by: December 15. Early action: Send application by: November 15; Decision sent by: December 15. Admission can be deferred. **Application fee:** $50. **To apply online, go to:** http://www.rider.edu/160_15590.htm. **Admissions requirements/recommendations:** High school units required (recommended): English: 4; Mathematics: 3 (4); Science: (4); Foreign language: (2); Social studies: (2); History: (2); Total units: 16. Tests: The college uses SAT or ACT scores in admissions decisions. Either SAT or ACT required. For admission to the fall 2011 entering class, the school will accept: ACT with writing required. Campus visit: Recommended. Admissions interview: Recommended. Off-campus interview: Not available. **Factors that count in admissions decisions:** *Academic:* Secondary school record: Very Important. Class rank: Considered. Letters of recommendation: Very Important. Standardized test scores: Very Important. Essay: Very Important. *Nonacademic:* Interview: Considered. Extracurricular activities: Considered. Talent/ability: Considered. Character/personal qualities: Considered. Alumni/ae relationship: Considered. Geographical residence: Considered. State residency: Considered. Religious affiliation/commitment: Not Considered. Minority status: Not Considered. Volunteer work: Considered. Work experience: Considered. **Other schools with the greatest overlap in applicants:** College of New Jersey; Monmouth University; Montclair State University; Rowan University; Rutgers, the State University of New Jersey–New Brunswick. **Admissions statistics for the fall 2009 entering class:** Total applicants: 7,372. Total accepted: 5,534. Freshmen enrolled: 1,026; 28% were from out of state. Accepted through early-decision or early-action plans: 19%. Overall acceptance rate: 75%. Early-decision acceptance rate: 52%. Non-early acceptance rate: 77%. **Size of waiting list:** 50 applicants; enrolled from waiting list: 4. **Credentials of fall 2009 freshmen:** 16% ranked in the top 10 percent of their high school class; 45% were in the top 25 percent; 79% were in the top half. (Proportion submitting class standing: 50%.) **Average high school grade point average:** 3.3. **First-year students who submitted SAT scores:** 96%. Scores (25/75 percentile): Critical Reading: 460-560, Math: 470-580, Combined: 930-1140. **First-year students submitting ACT scores:** 18%. Scores (25/75 percentile): English: N/A, Math: N/A, Composite: 19-24.

ACADEMICS

Year founded: 1865. **Academic calendar:** Semester. **Degrees offered:** certificate, associate, transfer-associate, bachelor's, master's, post-master's certificate. **Most popular majors:** 11% speech and rhetorical studies, 10% adult and continuing education and teaching, 9% liberal arts and sciences/liberal studies, 7% accounting, 7% finance. **Major fields of study:** area, ethnic, cultural, and gender studies; biological and biomedical sciences; business, management, marketing, and related support services; communication, journalism, and related programs; computer and information sciences and support services; education; English language and literature/letters; foreign languages, literatures, and linguistics; history; liberal arts and sciences studies, and humanities; mathematics and statistics; multi/interdisciplinary studies; natural resources and conservation; philosophy and religious studies; physical sciences; psychology; social sciences; theology and religious vocations; visual and performing arts. **Areas of required coursework:** humanities, mathematics, English (including composition), sciences (biological or physical), history, social science. **Pre-professional programs:** pre-law, pre-dentistry, pre-medicine, pre-veterinary science, other. **Special academic programs (% participation):** distance learning (20%), double major (21%), honors program (5%), independent study (16%), internships (26%), study abroad (9%), teacher certificate program (13%), weekend college (9%). **Teacher certification offered in:** early childhood, special education, elementary, middle/junior high, secondary, bilingual/bicultural. **Cooperative education programs:** business. **Reserve Officers Training Corps (ROTC):** Army ROTC: Offered at cooperating institution (Princeton University). **Faculty and instruction (2009-2010):** Total instructional faculty: 243 full-time, 383 part-time (53% men; 47% women; 17% minorities). Full-time faculty with Ph.D. or other terminal degree: 97%. Student/faculty ratio: 13/1. Classes of fewer than 20 students: 50%; of 20 to 49 students: 49%; of 50 or more students: 1%. **Advanced Placement and International Baccalaureate credit:** AP tests may be used for: Credit and/or placement. Scores accepted: 3, 4, 5. International Baccalaureate exams may be used for: Credit and/or placement. **Freshmen returning for sophomore year:** 81%. **Graduation rates:** Four-year: 47%; five-year: 58%; six-year: 59%. **Graduate study:** 16% of students pursue further study within one year. Fields in which graduates pursue further study: Master of Business Administration (MBA), 27%; law, 7%; medicine, 3%; engineering, 1%; education, 16%; arts and sciences, 18%.

COSTS AND FINANCIAL AID

Financial aid office: (609) 896-5360. **Expenses (2010-2011):** Tuition and fees 2010-2011: $30,470; room/board: $11,200. Estimated books and supplies: $1,500; transportation: $2,000; personal expenses: $875. **Financial aid:** Priority filing date for institution's financial aid form: March 1. In 2009-2010, 80% of undergraduates applied for financial aid. Of those, 70% were determined to have financial need; 19% had their need fully met. Average financial aid package (proportion receiving): $21,152 (70%). Average amount of gift aid, such as scholarships or grants (proportion receiving): $15,320 (68%). Average amount of self-help aid, such as work study or loans (proportion receiving): $7,154 (51%). Average need-based loan (excluding PLUS or other private loans): $4,178. Among students who received need-based aid, the average percentage of need met: 72%. Among students who received aid based on merit, the average award (and the proportion receiving): $10,703 (20%). The average athletic scholarship (and the proportion receiving): $12,646 (6%). Average amount of debt of borrowers graduating in 2009: $35,042. Proportion who borrowed: 72%.

CAMPUS LIFE AND EXTRACURRICULAR ACTIVITIES

Campus housing available (% using): coed dorms (69%), women's dorms (5%), sorority housing (7%), fraternity housing (4%), apartment for single students (4%), other housing options (11%). Students who live in college-owned, operated, or affiliated housing: 56%. **Student employment:** During the 2009-2010 academic year, 21% of undergraduates worked on campus.

Average per-year earnings: $2,096. **Clubs and organizations:** Number of student organizations: 90. Activities include: campus ministries, choral groups, concert band, dance, drama/theater, international student organization, literary magazine, model UN, music ensembles, musical theater, opera, pep band, radio station, student government, student newspaper, student film society, symphony orchestra, television station, yearbook. Number of fraternities: 4; sororities: 8. Proportion of men in fraternities: 4%; of women in sororities: 9%. Average proportion of students who stay on campus on weekends: 50%. **Sports program (2009-2010):** Member of NCAA I. **Men's intercollegiate varsity sports:** baseball, basketball, cross country, golf, soccer, swimming, tennis, track and field (indoor), track and field (outdoor), wrestling. **Women's intercollegiate varsity sports:** basketball, cross country, field hockey, soccer, softball, swimming, tennis, track and field (indoor), track and field (outdoor), volleyball.

SERVICES AND FACILITIES

Basic services: nonremedial tutoring, women's center, placement service, health service. **Remedial assistance:** reading, math, writing, study skills. **Counseling services:** minority student, career, personal, veteran student, academic, older student, psychological, birth control, religious. **For learning-disabled students:** School does not offer a structured program with separate admission and additional fees. Services include: remedial math, reading machines, remedial reading, tape recorders, other special classes, note-taking services, oral tests, learning center, readers, extended time for tests, tutors, priority registration, priority seating, texts on tape, other testing accommodations, other. **Library:** Number of titles: 481,958; number of current serial subscriptions: 42,085. **Information technology resources:** Students are not required to lease or own a computer. Number of campus computers available to all students: 500. School has a wireless network. Approximate number of users that can be accommodated: 150. Proportion of college-owned housing units wired for high-speed internet access: 100%. **Campus safety:** Security services offered: 24-hour foot-and-vehicle patrols, late-night transport/escort service, 24-hour emergency telephones, lighted pathways/sidewalks, student patrols, controlled dormitory access (key, security card, etc).

TRANSFER AND INTERNATIONAL STUDENTS

Transfer students: May apply for admission for the following academic terms: Fall, Spring, Summer. Applicants do not need a minimum number of credits to apply. For fall 2009: Transfer applications received: 687. Transfer applicants offered admission: 500. Transfer applicants enrolled: 241. **International students:** Number of foreign undergraduates: 154 (3% of student body). Number of countries represented: 58. Minimum TOEFL score required: 550 (paper); 213 (computer).

Rowan University

- **Address:** 201 Mullica Hill Road, Glassboro, NJ 08028
- **Website:** http://www.rowan.edu
- **Public**
- **Enrollment:** 8,335 full-time; 1,330 part-time

KEY STATS

✔ **U.S News College Ranking:** 23, Regional Universities (North)
✔ **SAT Score (25th/75th percentile):** 960-1170
✔ **Tuition:** 2010-2011: $11,676 in state, $19,034 out of state

Selectivity: Selective	**Room/board:** $10,348
Acceptance rate: 68%	**Average debt:** $26,092
Student/faculty ratio: 15/1	**Proportion who borrowed:** 73%

UNDERGRADUATE STUDENT BODY STATS

2009-2010 enrollment: 8,335 full-time; 1,330 part-time. Men: 47%; women: 53%. **Ethnic makeup:** African American: 9%; Asian American: 3%; Hispanic: 7%; White: 79%; International: 1%. **Religious preference:** Roman Catholic: 44%; Protestant: 20%; Jewish: 3%; Muslim: 1%; Buddhist: 1%; No preference: 15%; Unknown: 5%; Eastern Orthodox and other Christian: 9%; Other: 2%.

ADMISSIONS FACTS AND FIGURES

Phone: (856) 256-4200. **Email:** admissions@rowan.edu. **Website:** http://www.rowan.edu. **Application deadlines for fall 2011:** Regular decision: March 1; decision sent by April 15. Early decision: Not offered. Early action: Not offered. Admission can be deferred. **Application fee:** $50. **To apply**

online, go to: http://www.rowan.edu/provost/academic_affairs/admissions/applications/index.cfm. **Admissions requirements/recommendations:** High school units required (recommended): English: 4; Mathematics: 3 (4); Science: 2 (3); Foreign language: (2); Social studies: 2; Total units: 16 (18). Tests: The college uses SAT or ACT scores in admissions decisions. Either SAT or ACT required. For admission to the fall 2011 entering class, the school will accept: ACT with or without writing accepted. Campus visit: Recommended. Admissions interview: Neither required nor recommended. Off-campus interview: Not available. **Factors that count in admissions decisions:** *Academic:* Secondary school record: Very Important. Class rank: Important. Letters of recommendation: Considered. Standardized test scores: Important. Essay: Not Considered. *Nonacademic:* Interview: Not Considered. Extracurricular activities: Considered. Talent/ability: Considered. Character/personal qualities: Considered. Alumni/ae relationship: Not Considered. Geographical residence: Not Considered. State residency: Not Considered. Religious affiliation/commitment: Not Considered. Minority status: Not Considered. Volunteer work: Considered. Work experience: Considered. **Other schools with the greatest overlap in applicants:** College of New Jersey; Drexel University; Richard Stockton College of New Jersey; Rutgers, the State University of New Jersey–New Brunswick; University of Delaware. **Admissions statistics for the fall 2009 entering class:** Total applicants: 7,486. Total accepted: 5,073. Freshmen enrolled: 1,602; 3% were from out of state. Overall acceptance rate: 68%. **Size of waiting list:** 300 applicants; enrolled from waiting list: 60. **Credentials of fall 2009 freshmen:** 16% ranked in the top 10 percent of their high school class; 45% were in the top 25 percent; 86% were in the top half. (Proportion submitting class standing: 58%.) **Average high school grade point average:** 3.4. **First-year students who submitted SAT scores:** 97%. Scores (25/75 percentile): Critical Reading: 470-570, Math: 490-600, Combined: 960-1170.

ACADEMICS

Year founded: 1923. **Academic calendar:** Semester. **Degrees offered:** bachelor's, master's, doctorate. **Most popular majors:** 18% education, 16% business, management, marketing, and related support services, 11% communication, journalism, and related programs, 7% security and protective services, 6% social sciences. **Major fields of study:** biological and biomedical sciences; business, management, marketing, and related support services; communication, journalism, and related programs; communications technologies/technicians and support services; computer and information sciences and support services; education; engineering; English language and literature/letters; foreign languages, literatures, and linguistics; health professions and related clinical sciences; history; liberal arts and sciences studies, and humanities; library science; mathematics and statistics; natural resources and conservation; physical sciences; psychology; security and protective services; social sciences; visual and performing arts. **Areas of required coursework:** arts/fine arts, humanities, computer literacy, mathematics, English (including composition), philosophy, sciences (biological or physical), history, social science, other. **Pre-professional programs:** pre-dentistry, pre-medicine, pre-veterinary science, pre-optometry, pre-pharmacy, other. **Special academic programs:** accelerated program, distance learning, double major, dual enrollment, English as a Second Language (ESL), exchange student program (domestic), honors program, independent study, internships, study abroad, teacher certificate program, weekend college. **Teacher certification offered in:** early childhood, special education, elementary, middle/junior high, secondary, bilingual/bicultural. **Cooperative education programs:** business. **Reserve Officers Training Corps (ROTC):** Army ROTC: Offered at cooperating institution (Drexel University). **Faculty and instruction (2009-2010):** Total instructional faculty: 400 full-time, 616 part-time (55% men; 45% women; 14% minorities). Full-time faculty with Ph.D. or other terminal degree: 84%. Student/faculty ratio: 15/1. Classes of fewer than 20 students: 41%; of 20 to 49 students: 58%; of 50 or more students: 1%. **Advanced Placement and International Baccalaureate credit:** AP tests may be used for: Credit and/or placement. Scores accepted: 3, 4, 5. International Baccalaureate exams may be used for: Credit and/or placement. **Freshmen returning for sophomore year:** 84%. **Graduation rates:** Four-year: 43%; five-year: 62%; six-year: 66%. **Graduate study:** 36% of students pursue further study immediately upon graduation; 18% within one year. Fields in which graduates pursue further study: Master of Business Administration (MBA), 14%; law, 6%; medicine, 12%; engineering, 8%; education, 20%; arts and sciences, 37%; veterinary medicine, 4%.

COSTS AND FINANCIAL AID

Financial aid office: (856) 256-4250. **Expenses (2010-2011):** Tuition and fees 2010-2011: $11,676 in state, $19,034 out of state; room/board: $10,348. Estimated books and supplies: $1,500; transportation: $900; personal expenses: $1,000. **Financial aid:** Priority filing date for institution's financial aid form: March 15. In 2009-2010, 78% of undergraduates applied for financial aid. Of those, 58% were determined to have financial need; 24% had their need fully met. Average financial aid package (proportion receiving): $8,793 (56%). Average amount of gift aid, such as scholarships or grants (proportion receiving): $8,507 (28%). Average amount of self-help aid, such as work study or loans (proportion receiving): $4,398 (49%). Average need-based loan (excluding PLUS or other private loans): $4,303. Among students who received need-based aid, the average percentage of need met: 81%. Among students who received aid based on merit, the average award (and the proportion receiving): $3,927 (8%). Average amount of debt of borrowers graduating in 2009: $26,092. Proportion who borrowed: 73%.

CAMPUS LIFE AND EXTRACURRICULAR ACTIVITIES

Campus housing available: coed dorms, apartment for single students, special housing for disabled students, special housing for international students, other housing options. Students who live in college-owned, operated, or affiliated housing: 34%. **Student employment:** During the 2009-2010 academic year, 6% of undergraduates worked on campus. Average per-year earnings: $4,634. **Clubs and organizations:** Number of student organizations: 135. Activities include: campus ministries, choral groups, concert band, dance, drama/theater, jazz band, literary magazine, music ensembles, pep band, radio station, student government, student newspaper, student film society, symphony orchestra, television station, yearbook. Number of fraternities: 10; sororities: 10. Proportion of men in fraternities: 5%; of women in sororities: 6%. Average proportion of students who stay on campus on weekends: 66%. **Sports program (2009-2010):** Member of NCAA III. *Men's intercollegiate varsity sports:* baseball, basketball, cross country, football, soccer, swimming, track and field (indoor), track and field (outdoor). *Women's intercollegiate varsity sports:* basketball, cross country, field hockey, lacrosse, soccer, softball, swimming, track and field (indoor), track and field (outdoor), volleyball.

SERVICES AND FACILITIES

Basic services: nonremedial tutoring, day care, health service, health insurance. **Remedial assistance:** reading, math, writing, study skills. **Counseling services:** minority student, career, personal, veteran student, academic, psychological, birth control. **For learning-disabled students:** School does not offer a structured program with separate admission and additional fees. Services include: remedial math, remedial English, reading machines, remedial reading, tape recorders, untimed tests, note-taking services, oral tests, learning center, readers, extended time for tests, tutors, early syllabus, priority registration, priority seating, substitution of courses, texts on tape, typist/scribe, exams on tape or computer. **Library:** Number of titles: 448,026; number of current serial subscriptions: 29,126. **Information technology resources:** Students are not required to lease or own a computer. Number of campus computers available to all students: 1,500. School has a wireless network. Approximate number of users that can be accommodated: 5,000. Proportion of college-owned housing units wired for high-speed internet access: 100%. **Campus safety:** Security services offered: 24-hour foot-and-vehicle patrols, late-night transport/escort service, 24-hour emergency telephones, lighted pathways/sidewalks, student patrols, controlled dormitory access (key, security card, etc).

TRANSFER AND INTERNATIONAL STUDENTS

Transfer students: May apply for admission for the following academic terms: Fall, Spring. Applicants need a minimum number of credits to apply. For fall 2009: Transfer applications received: 2,149. Transfer applicants offered admission: 1,497. Transfer applicants enrolled: 962. **International students:** Number of foreign undergraduates: 117 (1% of student body). Number of countries represented: 30. Minimum TOEFL score required: 550 (paper); 79 (computer). Average TOEFL score: 550 (paper).

Rutgers–Camden

- **Address:** 406 Penn Street, Camden, NJ 08102
- **Website:** http://www.rutgers.edu/
- **Public**
- **Enrollment:** 3,342 full-time; 779 part-time

KEY STATS
- ✔ **U.S News College Ranking:** 29, Regional Universities (North)
- ✔ **SAT Score (25th/75th percentile):** 1000-1200
- ✔ **Tuition:** 2010-2011: $12,364 in state, $23,423 out of state

Selectivity: Selective	**Room/board:** $10,362
Acceptance rate: 49%	**Average debt:** $22,552
Student/faculty ratio: 12/1	**Proportion who borrowed:** 70%

UNDERGRADUATE STUDENT BODY STATS
2009-2010 enrollment: 3,342 full-time; 779 part-time. Men: 45%; women: 55%. **Ethnic makeup:** African American: 16%; Asian American: 8%; Hispanic: 9%; White: 66%; International: 1%.

ADMISSIONS FACTS AND FIGURES
Phone: (856) 225-6104. **Email:** camden@ugadm.rutgers.edu. **Website:** http://www.rutgers.edu/. **Application deadlines for fall 2011:** Regular decision: Rolling; decision sent by February 28. Early decision: Not offered. Early action: Not offered. Admission cannot be deferred. **Application fee:** $65. **To apply online, go to:** http://admissions.rutgers.edu. **Admissions requirements/recommendations:** High school units required (recommended): English: 4; Mathematics: 3 (4); Science: 2; Foreign language: 2; Academic electives: 5; Total units: 16. Tests: The college uses SAT or ACT scores in admissions decisions. Either SAT or ACT required. For admission to the fall 2011 entering class, the school will accept: ACT with writing required. Campus visit: Recommended. Admissions interview: Neither required nor recommended. Off-campus interview: Not available. **Factors that count in admissions decisions:** *Academic:* Secondary school record: Very Important. Class rank: Very Important. Letters of recommendation: Considered. Standardized test scores: Very Important. Essay: Considered. *Nonacademic:* Interview: Not Considered. Extracurricular activities: Considered. Talent/ability: Not Considered. Character/personal qualities: Not Considered. Alumni/ae relationship: Not Considered. Geographical residence: Considered. State residency: Considered. Religious affiliation/commitment: Not Considered. Minority status: Considered. Volunteer work: Considered. Work experience: Considered. **Other schools with the greatest overlap in applicants:** College of New Jersey; Drexel University; Pennsylvania State University–University Park; Rowan University; University of Delaware. **Admissions statistics for the fall 2009 entering class:** Total applicants: 5,529. Total accepted: 2,683. Freshmen enrolled: 435; 6% were from out of state. Overall acceptance rate: 49%. **Size of waiting list:** N/A applicants; enrolled from waiting list: 0. **Credentials of fall 2009 freshmen:** 17% ranked in the top 10 percent of their high school class; 40% were in the top 25 percent; 74% were in the top half. (Proportion submitting class standing: 73%.) **First-year students who submitted SAT scores:** 99%. Scores (25/75 percentile): Critical Reading: 490-600, Math: 510-600, Combined: 1000-1200. **First-year students submitting ACT scores:** 1%. Scores (25/75 percentile): English: N/A, Math: N/A, Composite: N/A.

ACADEMICS
Year founded: 1927. **Academic calendar:** Semester. **Degrees offered:** bachelor's, master's. **Most popular majors:** 25% business, management, marketing, and related support services, 13% psychology, 11% social sciences, 8% English language and literature/letters, 6% security and protective services. **Major fields of study:** area, ethnic, cultural, and gender studies; biological and biomedical sciences; business, management, marketing, and related support services; computer and information sciences and support services; English language and literature/letters; foreign languages, literatures, and linguistics; health professions and related clinical sciences; history; liberal arts and sciences studies, and humanities; mathematics and statistics; multi/interdisciplinary studies; natural resources and conservation; philosophy and religious studies; physical sciences; psychology; public administration and social service professions; security and protective services; social sciences; visual and performing arts. **Areas of required coursework:** arts/fine arts, humanities, mathematics, English (including composition), foreign languages, sciences (biological or physical), history, social science. **Pre-professional programs:** pre-law, pre-dentistry, pre-medicine, pre-pharmacy. **Special academic programs:** accelerated program,

cooperative (work-study plan) program, cross-registration, distance learning, double major, dual enrollment, English as a Second Language (ESL), honors program, liberal arts/career combination, student-designed major, study abroad, teacher certificate program, other. **Reserve Officers Training Corps (ROTC):** Army ROTC: Offered at cooperating institution (University of Pennsylvania); Air Force ROTC: Offered at cooperating institution (University of Pennsylvania). **Faculty and instruction (2009-2010):** Total instructional faculty: 252 full-time, 182 part-time (61% men; 39% women; 15% minorities). Full-time faculty with Ph.D. or other terminal degree: 99%. Student/faculty ratio: 12/1. Classes of fewer than 20 students: 45%; of 20 to 49 students: 47%; of 50 or more students: 7%. **Advanced Placement and International Baccalaureate credit:** AP tests may be used for: Credit and/or placement. Scores accepted: 4, 5. **Freshmen returning for sophomore year:** 81%. **Graduation rates:** Four-year: 30%; five-year: 52%; six-year: 59%.

COSTS AND FINANCIAL AID
Financial aid office: (856) 225-6039. **Expenses (2010-2011):** Tuition and fees 2010-2011: $12,364 in state, $23,423 out of state; room/board: $10,362. **Financial aid:** Priority filing date for institution's financial aid form: March 15. In 2009-2010, 88% of undergraduates applied for financial aid. Of those, 74% were determined to have financial need; 43% had their need fully met. Average financial aid package (proportion receiving): $12,413 (72%). Average amount of gift aid, such as scholarships or grants (proportion receiving): $10,049 (50%). Average amount of self-help aid, such as work study or loans (proportion receiving): $4,709 (53%). Average need-based loan (excluding PLUS or other private loans): $4,316. Among students who received need-based aid, the average percentage of need met: 64%. Among students who received aid based on merit, the average award (and the proportion receiving): $5,544 (4%). The average athletic scholarship (and the proportion receiving): $0 (0%). Average amount of debt of borrowers graduating in 2009: $22,552. Proportion who borrowed: 70%.

CAMPUS LIFE AND EXTRACURRICULAR ACTIVITIES
Campus housing available: coed dorms, apartment for single students, special housing for disabled students. Students who live in college-owned, operated, or affiliated housing: 11%. **Student employment:** During the 2009-2010 academic year, 8% of undergraduates worked on campus. Average per-year earnings: $2,450. **Clubs and organizations:** Number of student organizations: 70. Activities include: drama/theater, literary magazine, radio station, student government, student newspaper, yearbook. Number of fraternities: 2; sororities: 5. **Sports program (2009-2010):** Member of NCAA III. **Men's intercollegiate varsity sports:** baseball, basketball, cross country, golf, soccer, track and field (indoor), track and field (outdoor). **Women's intercollegiate varsity sports:** basketball, crew (heavyweight), cross country, crew (lightweight), soccer, softball, track and field (indoor), track and field (outdoor), volleyball.

SERVICES AND FACILITIES
Basic services: nonremedial tutoring, women's center, placement service, health service, health insurance. **Remedial assistance:** reading, math, writing, study skills. **Counseling services:** minority student, career, personal, academic, psychological. **For learning-disabled students:** Services include: remedial math, remedial English, remedial reading, tape recorders, note-taking services, learning center, extended time for tests, tutors. **Library:** Number of titles: 729,987; number of current serial subscriptions: 15,013. **Information technology resources:** Students are not required to lease or own a computer. Number of campus computers available to all students: 205. School has a wireless network. Approximate number of users that can be accommodated: 300. Proportion of college-owned housing units wired for high-speed internet access: 100%. **Campus safety:** Security services offered: 24-hour foot-and-vehicle patrols, late-night transport/escort service, 24-hour emergency telephones, lighted pathways/sidewalks, student patrols, controlled dormitory access (key, security card, etc).

TRANSFER AND INTERNATIONAL STUDENTS
Transfer students: May apply for admission for the following academic terms: Fall, Spring. Applicants need a minimum number of credits to apply. For fall 2009: Transfer applications received: 2,800. Transfer applicants offered admission: 1,467. Transfer applicants enrolled: 531. **International students:** Number of foreign undergraduates: 21 (1% of student body). Number of countries represented: 11. Minimum TOEFL score required: 550 (paper); 213 (computer).

Rutgers—Newark

- **Address:** 249 University Avenue, Newark, NJ 07102-1896
- **Website:** http://rutgers-newark.rutgers.edu
- **Public**
- **Enrollment:** 5,754 full-time; 1,553 part-time

KEY STATS

✔ **U.S News College Ranking:** 143, National Universities
✔ **SAT Score (25th/75th percentile):** 980-1190
✔ **Tuition:** 2010-2011: $12,069 in state, $23,531 out of state

Selectivity: Selective	**Room/board:** $11,653
Acceptance rate: 60%	**Average debt:** $19,500
Student/faculty ratio: 12/1	**Proportion who borrowed:** 55%

UNDERGRADUATE STUDENT BODY STATS

2009-2010 enrollment: 5,754 full-time; 1,553 part-time. Men: 47%; women: 53%. **Ethnic makeup:** African American: 19%; Asian American: 24%; Hispanic: 21%; White: 34%; International: 2%.

ADMISSIONS FACTS AND FIGURES

Phone: (973) 353-5205. **Email:** admissions@ugadm.rutgers.edu. **Website:** http://rutgers-newark.rutgers.edu. **Application deadlines for fall 2011:** Regular decision: Rolling; decision sent by February 28. Early decision: Not offered. Early action: Not offered. **Application fee:** $65. **To apply online, go to:** http://admissions.rutgers.edu/. **Admissions requirements/recommendations:** High school units required (recommended): English: 4; Mathematics: 3 (4); Science: 2; Foreign language: 2; Academic electives: 5; Total units: 16. Tests: The college uses SAT or ACT scores in admissions decisions. Either SAT or ACT required. For admission to the fall 2011 entering class, the school will accept: ACT with writing required. Campus visit: Recommended. Admissions interview: Neither required nor recommended. Off-campus interview: Not available. **Factors that count in admissions decisions:** *Academic:* Secondary school record: Very Important. Class rank: Very Important. Letters of recommendation: Considered. Standardized test scores: Very Important. Essay: Considered. *Nonacademic:* Interview: Not Considered. Extracurricular activities: Considered. Talent/ability: Not Considered. Character/personal qualities: Not Considered. Alumni/ae relationship: Not Considered. Geographical residence: Considered. State residency: Considered. Religious affiliation/commitment: Not Considered. Minority status: Considered. Volunteer work: Considered. Work experience: Considered. **Other schools with the greatest overlap in applicants:** College of New Jersey; Montclair State University; New York University; Ramapo College of New Jersey; William Paterson University of New Jersey. **Admissions statistics for the fall 2009 entering class:** Total applicants: 12,462. Total accepted: 7,430. Freshmen enrolled: 914; 4% were from out of state. Overall acceptance rate: 60%. **Credentials of fall 2009 freshmen:** 29% ranked in the top 10 percent of their high school class; 59% were in the top 25 percent; 89% were in the top half. (Proportion submitting class standing: 61%.) **First-year students who submitted SAT scores:** 99%. Scores (25/75 percentile): Critical Reading: 470-570, Math: 510-620, Combined: 980-1190. **First-year students submitting ACT scores:** 1%. Scores (25/75 percentile): English: N/A, Math: N/A, Composite: N/A.

ACADEMICS

Year founded: 1908. **Academic calendar:** Semester. **Degrees offered:** bachelor's, master's, doctorate. **Most popular majors:** 11% psychology, 9% nursing/registered nurse training (R.N., A.S.N., B.S.N., M.S.N.), 8% accounting, 8% biology/biological sciences, 8% finance. **Major fields of study:** area, ethnic, cultural, and gender studies; biological and biomedical sciences; business, management, marketing, and related support services; communication, journalism, and related programs; computer and information sciences and support services; engineering; English language and literature/letters; foreign languages, literatures, and linguistics; health professions and related clinical sciences; history; mathematics and statistics; multi/interdisciplinary studies; natural resources and conservation; philosophy and religious studies; physical sciences; psychology; public administration and social service professions; security and protective services; social sciences; visual and performing arts. **Areas of required coursework:** arts/fine arts, humanities, computer literacy, mathematics, sciences (biological or physical), social science. **Pre-professional programs:** pre-law, pre-dentistry, pre-medicine, pre-pharmacy. **Special academic programs:** accelerated program, cross-registration, distance learning, double major, dual enrollment, English as a Second Language (ESL), honors program, independent study,

internships, liberal arts/career combination, student-designed major, study abroad, teacher certificate program, weekend college, other. **Reserve Officers Training Corps (ROTC):** Army ROTC: Offered at cooperating institution (Rutgers, the State University of New Jersey–New Brunswick); Air Force ROTC: Offered at cooperating institution (Rutgers, the State University of New Jersey–New Brunswick). **Faculty and instruction (2009-2010):** Total instructional faculty: 447 full-time, 257 part-time (57% men; 43% women; 21% minorities). Full-time faculty with Ph.D. or other terminal degree: 99%. Student/faculty ratio: 12/1. Classes of fewer than 20 students: 29%; of 20 to 49 students: 55%; of 50 or more students: 17%. **Advanced Placement and International Baccalaureate credit:** AP tests may be used for: Credit and/or placement. **Freshmen returning for sophomore year:** 87%. **Graduation rates:** Four-year: 34%; five-year: 56%; six-year: 65%.

COSTS AND FINANCIAL AID

Financial aid office: (973) 353-5151. **Expenses (2010-2011):** Tuition and fees 2010-2011: $12,069 in state, $23,531 out of state; room/board: $11,653. **Financial aid:** Priority filing date for institution's financial aid form: March 15. In 2009-2010, 79% of undergraduates applied for financial aid. Of those, 71% were determined to have financial need; 27% had their need fully met. Average financial aid package (proportion receiving): $13,090 (68%). Average amount of gift aid, such as scholarships or grants (proportion receiving): $10,680 (53%). Average amount of self-help aid, such as work study or loans (proportion receiving): $4,600 (50%). Average need-based loan (excluding PLUS or other private loans): $4,474. Among students who received need-based aid, the average percentage of need met: 77%. Among students who received aid based on merit, the average award (and the proportion receiving): $6,000 (2%). The average athletic scholarship (and the proportion receiving): $9,500 (0%). Average amount of debt of borrowers graduating in 2009: $19,500. Proportion who borrowed: 55%.

CAMPUS LIFE AND EXTRACURRICULAR ACTIVITIES

Campus housing available: coed dorms, sorority housing, fraternity housing, apartment for single students, special housing for disabled students. Students who live in college-owned, operated, or affiliated housing: 17%. **Student employment:** During the 2009-2010 academic year, 13% of undergraduates worked on campus. Average per-year earnings: $1,600. **Clubs and organizations:** Number of student organizations: 85. Activities include: choral groups, drama/theater, literary magazine, radio station, student government, student newspaper, yearbook. Number of fraternities: 9; sororities: 9. **Sports program (2009-2010):** Member of NCAA I. *Men's intercollegiate varsity sports:* baseball, basketball, cross country, soccer, tennis, track and field (indoor), track and field (outdoor), volleyball. *Women's intercollegiate varsity sports:* basketball, cross country, soccer, softball, tennis, track and field (indoor), track and field (outdoor), volleyball.

SERVICES AND FACILITIES

Basic services: nonremedial tutoring, women's center, placement service, day care, health service, health insurance. **Remedial assistance:** reading, math, writing, study skills. **Counseling services:** minority student, career, military, personal, veteran student, academic, older student, psychological, birth control, religious. **For learning-disabled students:** Services include: remedial math, remedial English, remedial reading, learning center, extended time for tests. **Library:** Number of titles: 1,042,620; number of current serial subscriptions: 16,498. **Information technology resources:** Students are not required to lease or own a computer. Number of campus computers available to all students: 708. School has a wireless network. Approximate number of users that can be accommodated: 5,200. Proportion of college-owned housing units wired for high-speed internet access: 100%. **Campus safety:** Security services offered: 24-hour foot-and-vehicle patrols, late-night transport/escort service, 24-hour emergency telephones, lighted pathways/sidewalks, student patrols, controlled dormitory access (key, security card, etc).

TRANSFER AND INTERNATIONAL STUDENTS

Transfer students: May apply for admission for the following academic terms: Fall, Spring. Applicants need a minimum number of credits to apply. For fall 2009: Transfer applications received: 4,115. Transfer applicants offered admission: 1,792. Transfer applicants enrolled: 664. **International students:** Number of foreign undergraduates: 129 (2% of student body). Number of countries represented: 35. Minimum TOEFL score required: 550 (paper); 213 (computer).

Rutgers–New Brunswick

■ **Address:** 65 Davidson Road, Room 202, Piscataway, NJ 08854-8097
■ **Website:** http://www.rutgers.edu
■ **Public**
■ **Enrollment:** 27,588 full-time; 1,507 part-time

KEY STATS
✔ **U.S News College Ranking:** 64, National Universities
✔ **SAT Score (25th/75th percentile):** 1090-1310
✔ **Tuition:** 2010-2011: $12,582 in state, $24,044 out of state
   Selectivity: More selective   **Room/board:** $11,216
   Acceptance rate: 61%   **Average debt:** $19,760
   Student/faculty ratio: 14/1   **Proportion who borrowed:** 52%

UNDERGRADUATE STUDENT BODY STATS
2009-2010 enrollment: 27,588 full-time; 1,507 part-time. Men: 52%; women: 48%. **Ethnic makeup:** African American: 8%; Asian American: 25%; Hispanic: 10%; White: 55%; International: 2%.

ADMISSIONS FACTS AND FIGURES
Phone: (732) 932-4636. **Email:** admissions@ugadm.rutgers.edu. **Website:** http://www.rutgers.edu. **Application deadlines for fall 2011:** Regular decision: Rolling; decision sent by February 28. Early decision: Not offered. Early action: Not offered. Admission can be deferred. **Application fee:** $65. **To apply online, go to:** http://admissions.rutgers.edu. **Admissions requirements/recommendations:** High school units required (recommended): English: 4 (4); Mathematics: 3 (4); Science: 2 (2); Foreign language: 2 (2); Academic electives: 5 (5); Total units: 16 (16). Tests: The college uses SAT or ACT scores in admissions decisions. Either SAT or ACT required. For admission to the fall 2011 entering class, the school will accept: ACT with writing required. Campus visit: Recommended. Admissions interview: Neither required nor recommended. Off-campus interview: Not available. **Factors that count in admissions decisions:** *Academic:* Secondary school record: Very Important. Class rank: Very Important. Letters of recommendation: Considered. Standardized test scores: Very Important. Essay: Considered. *Nonacademic:* Interview: Not Considered. Extracurricular activities: Considered. Talent/ability: Considered. Character/personal qualities: Considered. Alumni/ae relationship: Not Considered. Geographical residence: Considered. State residency: Considered. Religious affiliation/commitment: Not Considered. Minority status: Considered. Volunteer work: Considered. Work experience: Considered. **Other schools with the greatest overlap in applicants:** Cornell University; New York University; Pennsylvania State University–University Park; Princeton University; University of Pennsylvania. **Admissions statistics for the fall 2009 entering class:** Total applicants: 28,624. Total accepted: 17,598. Freshmen enrolled: 5,835; 8% were from out of state. Overall acceptance rate: 61%. **Credentials of fall 2009 freshmen:** 42% ranked in the top 10 percent of their high school class; 80% were in the top 25 percent; 98% were in the top half. (Proportion submitting class standing: 59%.) **First-year students who submitted SAT scores:** 99%. Scores (25/75 percentile): Critical Reading: 530-630, Math: 560-680, Combined: 1090-1310. **First-year students submitting ACT scores:** 1%. Scores (25/75 percentile): English: N/A, Math: N/A, Composite: N/A.

ACADEMICS
Year founded: 1766. **Academic calendar:** Semester. **Degrees offered:** bachelor's, master's, doctorate. **Most popular majors:** 17% social sciences, 11% psychology, 10% biological and biomedical sciences, 10% communication, journalism, and related programs, 8% engineering. **Major fields of study:** agriculture, agriculture operations, and related sciences; architecture and related services; area, ethnic, cultural, and gender studies; biological and biomedical sciences; business, management, marketing, and related support services; communication, journalism, and related programs; computer and information sciences and support services; education; engineering; English language and literature/letters; foreign languages, literatures, and linguistics; health professions and related clinical sciences; history; mathematics and statistics; multi/interdisciplinary studies; natural resources and conservation; philosophy and religious studies; physical sciences; psychology; public administration and social service professions; security and protective services; social sciences; visual and performing arts. **Areas of required coursework:** arts/fine arts, humanities, mathematics, English (including composition), sciences (biological or physical), social science. **Pre-professional programs:** pre-law, pre-dentistry, pre-medicine, pre-veterinary science. **Special academic programs:** accelerated program, cooperative

(work-study plan) program, cross-registration, distance learning, double major, dual enrollment, English as a Second Language (ESL), honors program, independent study, internships, liberal arts/career combination, student-designed major, study abroad, teacher certificate program. **Teacher certification offered in:** early childhood, special education, elementary, middle/junior high, secondary, bilingual/bicultural. **Cooperative education programs:** agriculture, art, business, computer science, health professions, natural science, technologies. **Reserve Officers Training Corps (ROTC):** Army ROTC: Offered on campus; Air Force ROTC: Offered on campus. **Faculty and instruction (2009-2010):** Total instructional faculty: 1,678 full-time, 867 part-time (58% men; 42% women; 17% minorities). Full-time faculty with Ph.D. or other terminal degree: 99%. Student/faculty ratio: 14/1. Classes of fewer than 20 students: 42%; of 20 to 49 students: 39%; of 50 or more students: 19%. **Advanced Placement and International Baccalaureate credit:** AP tests may be used for: Credit and/or placement. International Baccalaureate exams may be used for: Credit and/or placement. **Freshmen returning for sophomore year:** 91%. **Graduation rates:** Four-year: 52%; five-year: 71%; six-year: 77%.

COSTS AND FINANCIAL AID
Financial aid office: (732) 932-7057. **Expenses (2010-2011):** Tuition and fees 2010-2011: $12,582 in state, $24,044 out of state; room/board: $11,216. **Financial aid:** Priority filing date for institution's financial aid form: March 15. In 2009-2010, 72% of undergraduates applied for financial aid. Of those, 58% were determined to have financial need; 39% had their need fully met. Average financial aid package (proportion receiving): $14,415 (56%). Average amount of gift aid, such as scholarships or grants (proportion receiving): $11,354 (34%). Average amount of self-help aid, such as work study or loans (proportion receiving): $4,850 (43%). Average need-based loan (excluding PLUS or other private loans): $4,440. Among students who received need-based aid, the average percentage of need met: 65%. Among students who received aid based on merit, the average award (and the proportion receiving): $6,098 (3%). The average athletic scholarship (and the proportion receiving): $22,600 (1%). Average amount of debt of borrowers graduating in 2009: $19,760. Proportion who borrowed: 52%.

CAMPUS LIFE AND EXTRACURRICULAR ACTIVITIES
Campus housing available: coed dorms, women's dorms, men's dorms, sorority housing, fraternity housing, apartments for married students, apartment for single students, cooperative housing, other housing options. Students who live in college-owned, operated, or affiliated housing: 50%. **Student employment:** During the 2009-2010 academic year, 26% of undergraduates worked on campus. Average per-year earnings: $1,600. **Clubs and organizations:** Number of student organizations: 400. Activities include: choral groups, concert band, dance, drama/theater, jazz band, literary magazine, marching band, music ensembles, opera, pep band, radio station, student government, student newspaper, student film society, symphony orchestra, television station, yearbook. Number of fraternities: 27; sororities: 17. **Sports program (2009-2010):** Member of NCAA I. *Men's intercollegiate varsity sports:* baseball, basketball, cross country, football, golf, lacrosse, soccer, track and field (indoor), track and field (outdoor), wrestling. *Women's intercollegiate varsity sports:* basketball, crew (heavyweight), cross country, field hockey, golf, gymnastics, lacrosse, crew (lightweight), soccer, softball, swimming, tennis, track and field (indoor), track and field (outdoor), volleyball.

SERVICES AND FACILITIES
Basic services: women's center, placement service, health service, health insurance. **Remedial assistance:** reading, math, writing. **Counseling services:** minority student, career, personal, veteran student, academic, psychological. **For learning-disabled students:** Services include: remedial math, remedial English, remedial reading, extended time for tests. **Library:** Number of titles: 5,080,676; number of current serial subscriptions: 74,031. **Information technology resources:** Students are not required to lease or own a computer. Number of campus computers available to all students: 1,450. School has a wireless network. Approximate number of users that can be accommodated: 4,000. Proportion of college-owned housing units wired for high-speed internet access: 100%. **Campus safety:** Security services offered: 24-hour foot-and-vehicle patrols, late-night transport/escort service, 24-hour emergency telephones, lighted pathways/sidewalks, student patrols, controlled dormitory access (key, security card, etc).

TRANSFER AND INTERNATIONAL STUDENTS
Transfer students: May apply for admission for the following academic terms: Fall, Spring. Applicants need a minimum number of credits to apply. For fall 2009: Transfer applications received: 7,818. Transfer

applicants offered admission: 3,473. Transfer applicants enrolled: 1,908.
International students: Number of foreign undergraduates: 536 (2% of student body). Number of countries represented: 65. Minimum TOEFL score required: 550 (paper); 213 (computer).

Seton Hall University

- **Address:** 400 S. Orange Avenue, South Orange, NJ 07079
- **Website:** http://www.shu.edu
- **Private; Religious affiliation:** Roman Catholic
- **Enrollment:** 4,671 full-time; 542 part-time

KEY STATS

✔ **U.S News College Ranking:** 136, National Universities
✔ **SAT Score (25th/75th percentile):** 940-1150
✔ **Tuition:** 2010-2011: $31,890

Selectivity: Selective	**Room/board:** $12,050
Acceptance rate: 79%	**Average debt:** N/A
Student/faculty ratio: 14/1	**Proportion who borrowed:** N/A

UNDERGRADUATE STUDENT BODY STATS

2009-2010 enrollment: 4,671 full-time; 542 part-time. Men: 42%; women: 58%. **Ethnic makeup:** African American: 14%; Asian American: 7%; Hispanic: 12%; White: 65%; International: 2%. **Religious preference:** Protestant: 11%; Jewish: 1%; Muslim: 2%; Hindu: 1%; Buddhist: 1%; No preference: 12%; Roman Catholic: 62%; Other Christian: 9%; Other: 1%.

ADMISSIONS FACTS AND FIGURES

Phone: (973) 761-9332. **Email:** thehall@shu.edu. **Website:** http://www.shu.edu. **Application deadlines for fall 2011:** Regular decision: Rolling. Early decision: Not offered. Early action: Send application by: November 15; Decision sent by: December 30. Admission can be deferred. **Application fee:** $55. **To apply online, go to:** http://www.shu.edu/applying/. **Admissions requirements/recommendations:** High school units required (recommended): English: 4; Mathematics: 3; Science: 1; Foreign language: 2; Social studies: 2; History: 0; Academic electives: 4; Total units: 16. Tests: The college uses SAT or ACT scores in admissions decisions. Either SAT or ACT required. For admission to the fall 2011 entering class, the school will accept: ACT with or without writing accepted. Campus visit: Recommended. Admissions interview: Recommended. Off-campus interview: Not available. **Factors that count in admissions decisions:** *Academic:* Secondary school record: Very Important. Class rank: Not Considered. Letters of recommendation: Very Important. Standardized test scores: Very Important. Essay: Very Important. *Nonacademic:* Interview: Considered. Extracurricular activities: Important. Talent/ability: Considered. Character/personal qualities: Considered. Alumni/ae relationship: Not Considered. Geographical residence: Not Considered. State residency: Not Considered. Religious affiliation/commitment: Not Considered. Minority status: Not Considered. Volunteer work: Important. Work experience: Important. **Other schools with the greatest overlap in applicants:** Quinnipiac University; Rutgers, the State University of New Jersey–New Brunswick; Sacred Heart University; St. Peter's College; Villanova University. **Admissions statistics for the fall 2009 entering class:** Total applicants: 10,851. Total accepted: 8,602. Freshmen enrolled: 1,139; 29% were from out of state. Overall acceptance rate: 79%. Non-early acceptance rate: 79%. **Credentials of fall 2009 freshmen:** 22% ranked in the top 10 percent of their high school class; 50% were in the top 25 percent; 83% were in the top half. (Proportion submitting class standing: 46%.) **Average high school grade point average:** 3.1. **First-year students who submitted SAT scores:** 94%. Scores (25/75 percentile): Critical Reading: 470-570, Math: 470-580, Combined: 940-1150. **First-year students submitting ACT scores:** 19%. Scores (25/75 percentile): English: 19-25, Math: 20-26, Composite: 20-25.

ACADEMICS

Year founded: 1856. **Academic calendar:** Semester. **Degrees offered:** bachelor's, post-bachelor's certificate, master's, post-master's certificate, doctorate. **Most popular majors:** 14% nursing/registered nurse training (R.N., A.S.N., B.S.N., M.S.N.), 7% finance, 6% biology/biological sciences, 6% criminal justice/safety studies, 5% international relations and affairs. **Major fields of study:** area, ethnic, cultural, and gender studies; biological and biomedical sciences; business, management, marketing, and related support services; communication, journalism, and related programs; computer and information sciences and support services; education; English language

and literature/letters; foreign languages, literatures, and linguistics; health professions and related clinical sciences; history; liberal arts and sciences studies, and humanities; mathematics and statistics; natural resources and conservation; parks, recreation, leisure, and fitness studies; philosophy and religious studies; physical sciences; psychology; public administration and social service professions; security and protective services; social sciences; theology and religious vocations; visual and performing arts. **Areas of required coursework:** humanities, mathematics, English (including composition), philosophy, sciences (biological or physical), social science. **Preprofessional programs:** pre-law, pre-dentistry, pre-medicine, pre-theology. **Special academic programs (% participation):** accelerated program (4%), cooperative (work-study plan) program, cross-registration, distance learning (0%), double major (18%), dual enrollment, English as a Second Language (ESL), honors program (1%), independent study, internships (76%), liberal arts/career combination (1%), study abroad (25%), teacher certificate program (9%). **Teacher certification offered in:** special education, elementary, middle/junior high, secondary. **Cooperative education programs:** art, business, computer science, education, health professions, humanities, natural science, social/behavioral science. **Reserve Officers Training Corps (ROTC):** Army ROTC: Offered on campus. **Faculty and instruction (2009-2010):** Total instructional faculty: 460 full-time, 419 part-time (52% men; 48% women; 16% minorities). Full-time faculty with Ph.D. or other terminal degree: 88%. Student/faculty ratio: 14/1. Classes of fewer than 20 students: 45%; of 20 to 49 students: 52%; of 50 or more students: 2%. **Advanced Placement and International Baccalaureate credit:** AP tests may be used for: Placement only. Scores accepted: 4, 5. International Baccalaureate exams may be used for: Placement only. **Freshmen returning for sophomore year:** 83%. **Graduation rates:** Four-year: 50%; five-year: 61%; six-year: 63%. **Graduate study:** 23% of students pursue further study immediately upon graduation; 28% within one year. Fields in which graduates pursue further study: Master of Business Administration (MBA), 6%; law, 20%; medicine, 3%; dentistry, 1%; theology (or the seminary), 5%; education, 7%; arts and sciences, 57%; veterinary medicine, 1%.

COSTS AND FINANCIAL AID

Financial aid office: (973) 761-9350. **Expenses (2010-2011):** Tuition and fees 2010-2011: $31,890; room/board: $12,050. Estimated books and supplies: $1,300; transportation: $1,800; personal expenses: $1,800. **Financial aid:** Priority filing date for institution's financial aid form: February 15.

CAMPUS LIFE AND EXTRACURRICULAR ACTIVITIES

Campus housing available (% using): coed dorms (88%), apartment for single students (7%), special housing for disabled students (0%), other housing options (0%). Students who live in college-owned, operated, or affiliated housing: 43%. **Student employment:** During the 2009-2010 academic year, 26% of undergraduates worked on campus. Average per-year earnings: $2,962. **Clubs and organizations:** Number of student organizations: 99. Activities include: campus ministries, choral groups, dance, drama/theater, international student organization, literary magazine, model UN, pep band, radio station, student government, student newspaper, television station. Number of fraternities: 13; sororities: 14. Proportion of men in fraternities: 8%; of women in sororities: 7%. Average proportion of students who stay on campus on weekends: 65%. **Sports program (2009-2010):** Member of NCAA I. *Men's intercollegiate varsity sports:* baseball, basketball, golf, soccer, swimming. *Women's intercollegiate varsity sports:* basketball, golf, soccer, softball, swimming, tennis, volleyball.

SERVICES AND FACILITIES

Basic services: nonremedial tutoring, health service, health insurance. **Remedial assistance:** reading, math, writing, study skills. **Counseling services:** career, personal, academic, psychological, religious. **For learning-disabled students:** School does not offer a structured program with separate admission and additional fees. Services include: remedial math, reading machines, remedial reading, tape recorders, untimed tests, note-taking services, learning center, extended time for tests, tutors, priority seating, substitution of courses, texts on tape, exams on tape or computer, other testing accommodations, other. **Library:** Number of titles: 629,978; number of current serial subscriptions: 29,000. **Information technology resources:** Students are required to lease or own a computer. Number of campus computers available to all students: 8,000. School has a wireless network. Approximate number of users that can be accommodated: 5,000. Proportion of college-owned housing units wired for high-speed internet access: 100%. **Campus safety:** Security services offered: 24-hour foot-and-vehicle patrols, late-night transport/escort service, 24-hour emergency telephones, lighted pathways/sidewalks, controlled dormitory access (key, security card, etc).

TRANSFER AND INTERNATIONAL STUDENTS

Transfer students: May apply for admission for the following academic terms: Fall, Spring. Applicants do not need a minimum number of credits to apply. For fall 2009: Transfer applications received: 1,377. Transfer applicants offered admission: 919. Transfer applicants enrolled: 338. **International students:** Number of foreign undergraduates: 86 (2% of student body). Number of countries represented: 36. Minimum TOEFL score required: 280 (computer).

Stevens Institute of Technology

- **Address:** Castle Point on Hudson, Hoboken, NJ 07030
- **Website:** http://www.stevens.edu
- **Private**
- **Enrollment:** 2,233 full-time; 1 part-time

KEY STATS

✔ **U.S News College Ranking:** 86, National Universities
✔ **SAT Score (25th/75th percentile):** 1170-1360
✔ **Tuition:** 2010-2011: $39,976

Selectivity: More selective	**Room/board:** $12,550
Acceptance rate: 51%	**Average debt:** N/A
Student/faculty ratio: 7/1	**Proportion who borrowed:** N/A

UNDERGRADUATE STUDENT BODY STATS

2009-2010 enrollment: 2,233 full-time; 1 part-time. Men: 74%; women: 26%. **Ethnic makeup:** African American: 3%; Asian American: 11%; Hispanic: 10%; White: 72%; International: 4%.

ADMISSIONS FACTS AND FIGURES

Phone: (201) 216-5194. **Email:** admissions@stevens.edu. **Website:** http://www.stevens.edu. **Application deadlines for fall 2011:** Regular decision: February 1. Early decision: Send application by: November 15; Decision sent by: December 15. Early action: Not offered. Admission can be deferred. **Application fee:** $55. **To apply online, go to:** http://www.stevens.edu/undergrad/instructions.html. **Admissions requirements/recommendations:** High school units required (recommended): English: 4; Mathematics: 4; Science: 3 (4); Foreign language: (2); Social studies: (2); History: (2); Academic electives: (4); Total units: 14 (18). Tests: The college uses SAT or ACT scores in admissions decisions. Either SAT or ACT required. For admission to the fall 2011 entering class, the school will accept: ACT with or without writing accepted. Campus visit: Recommended. Admissions interview: Required. Off-campus interview: May be arranged. **Factors that count in admissions decisions: *Academic:*** Secondary school record: Very Important. Class rank: Considered. Letters of recommendation: Very Important. Standardized test scores: Very Important. Essay: Very Important. ***Nonacademic:*** Interview: Very Important. Extracurricular activities: Very Important. Talent/ability: Important. Character/personal qualities: Very Important. Alumni/ae relationship: Considered. Geographical residence: Not Considered. State residency: Not Considered. Religious affiliation/commitment: Not Considered. Minority status: Not Considered. Volunteer work: Very Important. Work experience: Very Important. **Other schools with the greatest overlap in applicants:** Carnegie Mellon University; Cornell University; Massachusetts Institute of Technology; Rensselaer Polytechnic Institute; Rutgers, the State University of New Jersey–New Brunswick. **Admissions statistics for the fall 2009 entering class:** Total applicants: 2,972. Total accepted: 1,514. Freshmen enrolled: 561; 40% were from out of state. Accepted through early-decision or early-action plans: 44%. Overall acceptance rate: 51%. Early-decision acceptance rate: 67%. Non-early acceptance rate: 48%. **Size of waiting list:** 481 applicants; enrolled from waiting list: 30. **Credentials of fall 2009 freshmen:** 58% ranked in the top 10 percent of their high school class; 85% were in the top 25 percent; 98% were in the top half. (Proportion submitting class standing: 49%.) **Average high school grade point average:** 3.8. **First-year students who submitted SAT scores:** 87%. Scores (25/75 percentile): Critical Reading: 550-650; Math: 620-710, Combined: 1170-1360. **First-year students submitting ACT scores:** 26%. Scores (25/75 percentile): English: N/A, Math: N/A, Composite: 24-29.

ACADEMICS

Year founded: 1870. **Academic calendar:** Semester. **Degrees offered:** certificate, bachelor's, post-bachelor's certificate, master's, doctorate. **Most popular majors:** 62% engineering, 13% business, management, marketing, and related support services, 8% biological and biomedical sciences, 6%

engineering technologies/technicians, 5% computer and information sciences and support services. **Major fields of study:** biological and biomedical sciences; business, management, marketing, and related support services; computer and information sciences and support services; engineering; engineering technologies/technicians; liberal arts and sciences studies, and humanities; mathematics and statistics; multi/interdisciplinary studies; physical sciences; social sciences; visual and performing arts. **Areas of required coursework:** humanities, computer literacy, mathematics, English (including composition), philosophy, sciences (biological or physical), history, social science, other. **Pre-professional programs:** pre-law, pre-dentistry, pre-medicine, pre-veterinary science, pre-pharmacy. **Special academic programs (% participation):** accelerated program (1%), cooperative (work-study plan) program (41%), cross-registration (5%), distance learning (0%), double major (15%), dual enrollment (5%), honors program (12%), independent study (4%), internships (42%), study abroad (5%). **Cooperative education programs:** computer science, engineering, natural science. **Reserve Officers Training Corps (ROTC):** Army ROTC: Offered at cooperating institution (Seton Hall University); Air Force ROTC: Offered at cooperating institution (New Jersey Institute of Technology). **Faculty and instruction (2009-2010):** Total instructional faculty: 249 full-time, 212 part-time (82% men; 18% women; 17% minorities). Full-time faculty with Ph.D. or other terminal degree: 90%. Student/faculty ratio: 7/1. Classes of fewer than 20 students: 43%; of 20 to 49 students: 49%; of 50 or more students: 8%. **Advanced Placement and International Baccalaureate credit:** AP tests may be used for: Credit and/or placement. Scores accepted: 4, 5. International Baccalaureate exams may be used for: Placement only. **Freshmen returning for sophomore year:** 90%. **Graduation rates:** Four-year: 30%; five-year: 71%; six-year: 75%. **Graduate study:** 24% of students pursue further study immediately upon graduation. Fields in which graduates pursue further study: Master of Business Administration (MBA), 4%; law, 10%; medicine, 24%; dentistry, 7%; engineering, 29%; arts and sciences, 26%.

COSTS AND FINANCIAL AID

Financial aid office: (201) 216-5555. **Expenses (2010-2011):** Tuition and fees 2010-2011: $39,976; room/board: $12,550. Estimated books and supplies: $950; transportation: $500; personal expenses: $750. **Financial aid:** Priority filing date for institution's financial aid form: February 15; deadline: April 1. In 2009-2010, 83% of undergraduates applied for financial aid. Of those, 74% were determined to have financial need; 16% had their need fully met. Average financial aid package (proportion receiving): $27,104 (73%). Average amount of gift aid, such as scholarships or grants (proportion receiving): $14,655 (57%). Average amount of self-help aid, such as work study or loans (proportion receiving): $5,170 (58%). Average need-based loan (excluding PLUS or other private loans): $4,841. Among students who received need-based aid, the average percentage of need met: 72%. Among students who received aid based on merit, the average award (and the proportion receiving): $13,102 (11%). The average athletic scholarship (and the proportion receiving): $0 (0%).

CAMPUS LIFE AND EXTRACURRICULAR ACTIVITIES

Campus housing available (% using): coed dorms (71%), women's dorms (1%), sorority housing (3%), fraternity housing (13%), apartments for married students, apartment for single students (12%), special housing for disabled students (0%). Students who live in college-owned, operated, or affiliated housing: 85%. **Student employment:** During the 2009-2010 academic year, 25% of undergraduates worked on campus. Average per-year earnings: $1,000. **Clubs and organizations:** Number of student organizations: 120. Activities include: campus ministries, choral groups, concert band, dance, drama/theater, international student organization, jazz band, literary magazine, music ensembles, musical theater, pep band, radio station, student government, student newspaper, student film society, television station, yearbook. Number of fraternities: 11; sororities: 4. Proportion of men in fraternities: 19%; of women in sororities: 20%. Average proportion of students who stay on campus on weekends: 70%. **Sports program (2009-2010):** Member of NCAA III. ***Men's intercollegiate varsity sports:*** baseball, basketball, cross country, fencing, golf, lacrosse, soccer, swimming, tennis, track and field (indoor), track and field (outdoor), volleyball, wrestling. ***Women's intercollegiate varsity sports:*** basketball, cross country, equestrian, fencing, field hockey, golf, lacrosse, soccer, swimming, tennis, track and field (indoor), track and field (outdoor), volleyball.

SERVICES AND FACILITIES

Basic services: nonremedial tutoring, women's center, placement service, health service, health insurance. **Counseling services:** minority student, career, personal, veteran student, academic, psychological. **For learning-disabled students:** School does not offer a structured program with separate admission and additional fees. Services include: tape recorders, untimed tests, oral tests, extended time for tests, tutors. **Library:** Number of titles: 123,063; number of current serial subscriptions: 39,500. **Information technology resources:** Students are not required to lease or own a computer. Number of campus computers available to all students: 2,150. School has a wireless network. Approximate number of users that can be accommodated: 3,000. Proportion of college-owned housing units wired for high-speed internet access: 100%. **Campus safety:** Security services offered: 24-hour foot-and-vehicle patrols, late-night transport/escort service, 24-hour emergency telephones, lighted pathways/sidewalks, controlled dormitory access (key, security card, etc).

TRANSFER AND INTERNATIONAL STUDENTS

Transfer students: May apply for admission for the following academic terms: Fall, Spring. Applicants need a minimum number of credits to apply. For fall 2009: Transfer applications received: 263. Transfer applicants offered admission: 94. Transfer applicants enrolled: 52. **International students:** Number of foreign undergraduates: 92 (4% of student body). Number of countries represented: 39. Minimum TOEFL score required: 550 (paper); 213 (computer). Average TOEFL score: 555 (paper).

St. Peter's College

- **Address:** 2641 Kennedy Boulevard, Jersey City, NJ 07306-5997
- **Website:** http://www.spc.edu
- **Private; Religious affiliation:** Roman Catholic (Jesuit)
- **Enrollment:** 2,100 full-time; 312 part-time

KEY STATS

✔ **U.S News College Ranking:** 104, Regional Universities (North)
✔ **SAT Score (25th/75th percentile):** 840-1040
✔ **Tuition:** 2010-2011: $28,332

Selectivity: Selective	**Room/board:** $11,510
Acceptance rate: 49%	**Average debt:** $19,744
Student/faculty ratio: 13/1	**Proportion who borrowed:** 68%

UNDERGRADUATE STUDENT BODY STATS

2009-2010 enrollment: 2,100 full-time; 312 part-time. Men: 43%; women: 57%. **Ethnic makeup:** African American: 25%; Asian American: 11%; Hispanic: 28%; White: 33%; International: 3%. **Religious preference:** Roman Catholic: 60%; Protestant: 5%; Muslim: 2%; No preference: 10%; Hindu and Buddhist: 1%; Other: 22%.

ADMISSIONS FACTS AND FIGURES

Phone: (201) 915-9213. **Email:** admissions@spc.edu. **Website:** http://www.spc.edu. **Application deadlines for fall 2011:** Regular decision: August 15. Early decision: Not offered. Early action: Not offered. Admission can be deferred. **To apply online, go to:** https://www.spcadmission.org/secure/8953/preview_app.asp?wcc=sp2. **Admissions requirements/recommendations:** High school units required (recommended): English: 4 (4); Mathematics: 3 (4); Science: 2 (3); Foreign language: 2 (3); Social studies: (3); History: 2 (3); Academic electives: 3 (3); Total units: 17 (24). Tests: The college uses SAT or ACT scores in admissions decisions. Either SAT or ACT required. For admission to the fall 2011 entering class, the school will accept: ACT with or without writing accepted. Campus visit: Recommended. Admissions interview: Recommended. Off-campus interview: May be arranged. **Factors that count in admissions decisions:** *Academic:* Secondary school record: Very Important. Class rank: Important. Letters of recommendation: Important. Standardized test scores: Very Important. Essay: Important. *Nonacademic:* Interview: Considered. Extracurricular activities: Important. Talent/ability: Considered. Character/personal qualities: Important. Alumni/ae relationship: Considered. Geographical residence: Not Considered. State residency: Not Considered. Religious affiliation/commitment: Not Considered. Minority status: Not Considered. Volunteer work: Considered. Work experience: Considered. **Admissions statistics for the fall 2009 entering class:** Total applicants: 6,547. Total accepted: 3,181. Freshmen enrolled: 539; 22% were from out of state. Overall acceptance rate: 49%. **Size of waiting list:** 332 applicants; enrolled from waiting list: 75. **Credentials of fall 2009 freshmen:** 14% ranked in the top 10 percent of their high school class; 41% were in the top 25 percent; 70% were in the top half. (Proportion submitting class standing: 61%.) **Average high school grade point average:** 3.2. **First-year students who submitted SAT scores:** 99%. Scores (25/75 percentile): Critical

Reading: 420-510, Math: 420-530, Combined: 840-1040. **First-year students submitting ACT scores:** 9%. Scores (25/75 percentile): English: N/A, Math: N/A, Composite: 17-24.

ACADEMICS

Year founded: 1872. **Academic calendar:** Semester. **Degrees offered:** certificate, associate, bachelor's, master's. **Most popular majors:** 13% business administration and management, 11% criminal justice/safety studies, 8% accounting, 7% elementary education and teaching, 7% nursing/registered nurse training (R.N., A.S.N., B.S.N., M.S.N.). **Major fields of study:** area, ethnic, cultural, and gender studies; biological and biomedical sciences; business, management, marketing, and related support services; communication, journalism, and related programs; computer and information sciences and support services; education; English language and literature/letters; foreign languages, literatures, and linguistics; health professions and related clinical sciences; history; liberal arts and sciences studies, and humanities; mathematics and statistics; multi/interdisciplinary studies; philosophy and religious studies; physical sciences; psychology; public administration and social service professions; security and protective services; social sciences; visual and performing arts. **Areas of required coursework:** arts/fine arts, humanities, computer literacy, mathematics, English (including composition), philosophy, foreign languages, sciences (biological or physical), history, social science, other. **Pre-professional programs:** pre-law, pre-dentistry, pre-medicine, pre-theology, pre-pharmacy. **Special academic programs:** cooperative (work-study plan) program, distance learning, double major, English as a Second Language (ESL), honors program, independent study, internships, student-designed major, study abroad, teacher certificate program. **Teacher certification offered in:** elementary, secondary. **Cooperative education programs:** art, business, computer science, education, humanities, natural science, social/behavioral science, other. **Reserve Officers Training Corps (ROTC):** Army ROTC: Offered at cooperating institution (Seton Hall University); Air Force ROTC: Offered at cooperating institution (New Jersey Institute of Technology). **Faculty and instruction (2009-2010):** Total instructional faculty: 115 full-time, 171 part-time (61% men; 39% women; 15% minorities). Full-time faculty with Ph.D. or other terminal degree: 80%. Student/faculty ratio: 13/1. Classes of fewer than 20 students: 55%; of 20 to 49 students: 45%; of 50 or more students: 0%. **Advanced Placement and International Baccalaureate credit:** AP tests may be used for: Credit and/or placement. Scores accepted: 3, 4, 5. International Baccalaureate exams may be used for: Credit only. **Freshmen returning for sophomore year:** 74%. **Graduation rates:** Four-year: 33%; five-year: 46%; six-year: 48%.

COSTS AND FINANCIAL AID

Financial aid office: (201) 915-4929. **Expenses (2010-2011):** Tuition and fees 2010-2011: $28,332; room/board: $11,510. Estimated books and supplies: $800; transportation: $700; personal expenses: $600. **Financial aid:** In 2009-2010, 98% of undergraduates applied for financial aid. Of those, 85% were determined to have financial need; 4% had their need fully met. Average financial aid package (proportion receiving): $19,780 (85%). Average amount of gift aid, such as scholarships or grants (proportion receiving): $17,051 (83%). Average amount of self-help aid, such as work study or loans (proportion receiving): $4,134 (61%). Average need-based loan (excluding PLUS or other private loans): $3,805. Among students who received need-based aid, the average percentage of need met: 68%. Among students who received aid based on merit, the average award (and the proportion receiving): $14,670 (11%). The average athletic scholarship (and the proportion receiving): $17,096 (2%). Average amount of debt of borrowers graduating in 2009: $19,744. Proportion who borrowed: 68%.

CAMPUS LIFE AND EXTRACURRICULAR ACTIVITIES

Campus housing available (% using): coed dorms (94%), other housing options (6%). Students who live in college-owned, operated, or affiliated housing: 42%. **Student employment:** During the 2009-2010 academic year, 20% of undergraduates worked on campus. Average per-year earnings: $2,000. **Clubs and organizations:** Number of student organizations: 42. Activities include: campus ministries, choral groups, drama/theater, international student organization, literary magazine, model UN, pep band, radio station, student government, student newspaper, yearbook. Number of fraternities: 0; sororities: 0. Average proportion of students who stay on campus on weekends: 40%. **Sports program (2009-2010):** Member of NCAA I. *Men's intercollegiate varsity sports:* baseball, basketball, cross country, golf, soccer, swimming, tennis, track and field (indoor), volleyball. *Women's intercollegiate varsity sports:* basketball, bowling, cross country, soccer, softball, swimming, tennis, track and field (indoor), track and field (outdoor), volleyball.

SERVICES AND FACILITIES

Basic services: nonremedial tutoring, placement service, health service, health insurance. **Remedial assistance:** reading, math, writing, study skills. **Counseling services:** minority student, career, personal, veteran student, academic, older student, psychological, birth control, religious. **For learning-disabled students:** School does not offer a structured program with separate admission and additional fees. Total undergraduates in learning-disabled program or receiving services: 50. Services include: remedial math, remedial English, reading machines, remedial reading, tape recorders, diagnostic testing service, untimed tests, note-taking services, oral tests, learning center, readers, extended time for tests, tutors, priority registration, priority seating, other testing accommodations. **Library:** Number of titles: 250,000; number of current serial subscriptions: 1,594. **Information technology resources:** Students are not required to lease or own a computer. Number of campus computers available to all students: 325. School has a wireless network. Approximate number of users that can be accommodated: 1,800. Proportion of college-owned housing units wired for high-speed internet access: 90%. **Campus safety:** Security services offered: 24-hour foot-and-vehicle patrols, late-night transport/escort service, 24-hour emergency telephones, lighted pathways/sidewalks, controlled dormitory access (key, security card, etc).

TRANSFER AND INTERNATIONAL STUDENTS

Transfer students: May apply for admission for the following academic terms: Fall, Winter, Spring, Summer. Applicants need a minimum number of credits to apply. For fall 2009: Transfer applications received: 306. Transfer applicants offered admission: 283. Transfer applicants enrolled: 113. **International students:** Number of foreign undergraduates: 80 (3% of student body). Number of countries represented: 15. Minimum TOEFL score required: 520 (paper); 190 (computer).

Thomas Edison State College

- **Address:** 101 W. State Street, Trenton, NJ 08608-1176
- **Website:** http://www.tesc.edu
- **Public**
- **Enrollment:** N/A; 17,320 part-time

KEY STATS
✔ **U.S News College Ranking:** Unranked, National Liberal Arts Colleges
✔ **SAT or ACT Score (25th/75th percentile):** N/A
✔ **Tuition:** 2009-2010: $4,798 in state, $6,823 out of state

Selectivity: N/A	**Room/board:** N/A
Acceptance rate: N/A	**Average debt:** N/A
Student/faculty ratio: N/A	**Proportion who borrowed:** N/A

UNDERGRADUATE STUDENT BODY STATS
2009-2010 enrollment: N/A full-time; 17,320 part-time. Men: 62%; women: 38%. **Ethnic makeup:** African American: 16%; American-Indian: 1%; Asian American: 3%; Hispanic: 8%; White: 70%; International: 1%.

ADMISSIONS FACTS AND FIGURES
Phone: (888) 442-8372. **Email:** admissions@tesc.edu. **Website:** http://www.tesc.edu. **Application deadlines for fall 2011:** Regular decision: Rolling. Early decision: Not offered. Early action: Not offered. Admission cannot be deferred. **Application fee:** $75. **To apply online, go to:** http://www.tesc.edu/223.php. **Admissions requirements/recommendations:** Tests: The college does not use SAT or ACT scores in admissions decisions. Neither SAT nor ACT required. Campus visit: Neither required nor recommended. Admissions interview: Neither required nor recommended. Off-campus interview: Not available.

ACADEMICS
Year founded: 1972. **Academic calendar:** Continuous. **Degrees offered:** certificate, associate, bachelor's, post-bachelor's certificate, master's, post-master's certificate. **Most popular majors:** 21% liberal arts and sciences/liberal studies, 13% nuclear engineering technology/technician, 6% business administration and management, 6% psychology, 6% social sciences. **Major fields of study:** agriculture, agriculture operations, and related sciences; biological and biomedical sciences; business, management, marketing, and related support services; communication, journalism, and related programs; computer and information sciences and support services; engineering technologies/technicians; English language and literature/letters; family

and consumer sciences/human sciences; foreign languages, literatures, and linguistics; health professions and related clinical sciences; history; legal professions and studies; liberal arts and sciences studies, and humanities; mathematics and statistics; mechanic and repair technologies/technicians; multi/interdisciplinary studies; natural resources and conservation; parks, recreation, leisure, and fitness studies; philosophy and religious studies; psychology; public administration and social service professions; security and protective services; social sciences; transportation and materials moving; visual and performing arts. **Areas of required coursework:** humanities, mathematics, English (including composition), sciences (biological or physical), social science. **Special academic programs (% participation):** distance learning (100%), dual enrollment, external degree program, independent study, student-designed major, other. **Advanced Placement and International Baccalaureate credit:** AP tests may be used for: Credit only. Scores accepted: 3, 4, 5. International Baccalaureate exams may be used for: Credit only.

COSTS AND FINANCIAL AID
Financial aid office: (609) 633-9658. **Expenses (2009-2010):** Tuition and fees 2009-2010: $4,798 in state, $6,823 out of state.

SERVICES AND FACILITIES
Counseling services: military, veteran student, academic, older student, other. **For learning-disabled students:** School does not offer a structured program with separate admission and additional fees. Total undergraduates in learning-disabled program or receiving services: 39. Services include: extended time for tests, texts on tape, exams on tape or computer, other testing accommodations, other. **Information technology resources:** Students are not required to lease or own a computer. School has a wireless network. Approximate number of users that can be accommodated: 100. **Campus safety:** Security services offered: late-night transport/escort service, 24-hour emergency telephones, lighted pathways/sidewalks.

TRANSFER AND INTERNATIONAL STUDENTS
Transfer students: May apply for admission for the following academic terms: Fall, Winter, Spring, Summer. Applicants do not need a minimum number of credits to apply. **International students:** Number of foreign undergraduates: 222 (1% of student body). Number of countries represented: 73. Minimum TOEFL score required: 500 (paper).

William Paterson University of New Jersey

- **Address:** 300 Pompton Road, Wayne, NJ 07470
- **Website:** http://www.wpunj.edu/
- **Public**
- **Enrollment:** 7,768 full-time; 1,411 part-time

KEY STATS
✔ **U.S News College Ranking:** 93, Regional Universities (North)
✔ **SAT Score (25th/75th percentile):** 890-1080
✔ **Tuition:** 2009-2010: $10,838 in state, $17,592 out of state

Selectivity: Selective	**Room/board:** $10,280
Acceptance rate: 65%	**Average debt:** $25,893
Student/faculty ratio: 15/1	**Proportion who borrowed:** 64%

UNDERGRADUATE STUDENT BODY STATS
2009-2010 enrollment: 7,768 full-time; 1,411 part-time. Men: 45%; women: 55%. **Ethnic makeup:** African American: 14%; Asian American: 6%; Hispanic: 19%; White: 60%; International: 1%. **Religious preference:** Roman Catholic: 41%; Protestant: 13%; Jewish: 3%; Muslim: 4%; Hindu: 1%; Buddhist: 1%; No preference: 13%; Unknown: 4%; Other: 7%.

ADMISSIONS FACTS AND FIGURES
Phone: (973) 720-2125. **Email:** admissions@wpunj.edu. **Website:** http://www.wpunj.edu/. **Application deadlines for fall 2011:** Regular decision: May 1. Early decision: Not offered. Early action: Not offered. Admission can be deferred. **Application fee:** $50. **To apply online, go to:** http://ww2.wpunj.edu/admissn/apply_now.cfm. **Admissions requirements/recommendations:** High school units required (recommended): English: 4; Mathematics: 3; Science: 2; Social studies: 2; Total units: 16. Tests: The college uses SAT or ACT scores in admissions decisions. Either SAT or ACT required. For admission to the fall 2011 entering class, the school will accept: ACT with or without writing accepted. Campus visit: Recommended. Admissions interview: Neither required nor recommended. Off-campus interview: May be

arranged. **Factors that count in admissions decisions:** *Academic:* Secondary school record: Very Important. Class rank: Very Important. Letters of recommendation: Considered. Standardized test scores: Very Important. Essay: Considered. *Nonacademic:* Interview: Considered. Extracurricular activities: Considered. Talent/ability: Considered. Character/personal qualities: Considered. Alumni/ae relationship: Considered. Geographical residence: Considered. State residency: Not Considered. Religious affiliation/commitment: Not Considered. Volunteer work: Considered. Work experience: Not Considered. **Other schools with the greatest overlap in applicants:** Kean University; Montclair State University; Ramapo College of New Jersey; Rutgers, the State University of New Jersey–New Brunswick. **Admissions statistics for the fall 2009 entering class:** Total applicants: 6,969. Total accepted: 4,552. Freshmen enrolled: 1,453; 3% were from out of state. Overall acceptance rate: 65%. **Credentials of fall 2009 freshmen:** 9% ranked in the top 10 percent of their high school class; 29% were in the top 25 percent; 63% were in the top half. (Proportion submitting class standing: 62%.) **First-year students who submitted SAT scores:** 98%. Scores (25/75 percentile): Critical Reading: 440-530, Math: 450-550, Combined: 890-1080.

ACADEMICS

Year founded: 1855. **Academic calendar:** Semester. **Degrees offered:** bachelor's, post-bachelor's certificate, master's, post-master's certificate. **Most popular majors:** 21% business, management, marketing, and related support services, 15% education, 11% communication, journalism, and related programs, 11% psychology, 10% social sciences. **Major fields of study:** area, ethnic, cultural, and gender studies; biological and biomedical sciences; business, management, marketing, and related support services; communication, journalism, and related programs; computer and information sciences and support services; education; English language and literature/letters; foreign languages, literatures, and linguistics; health professions and related clinical sciences; history; mathematics and statistics; natural resources and conservation; philosophy and religious studies; physical sciences; psychology; social sciences; visual and performing arts. **Areas of required coursework:** arts/fine arts, humanities, mathematics, English (including composition), philosophy, foreign languages, sciences (biological or physical), history, social science, other. **Pre-professional programs:** pre-law, pre-dentistry, pre-medicine, pre-veterinary science. **Special academic programs:** accelerated program, cross-registration, distance learning, double major, dual enrollment, English as a Second Language (ESL), exchange student program (domestic), honors program, independent study, internships, study abroad, teacher certificate program, other. **Teacher certification offered in:** early childhood, special education, elementary, middle/junior high, secondary, bilingual/bicultural. **Reserve Officers Training Corps (ROTC):** Air Force ROTC: Offered at cooperating institution (New Jersey Institute of Technology). **Faculty and instruction (2009-2010):** Total instructional faculty: 371 full-time, 650 part-time (49% men; 51% women; 25% minorities). Full-time faculty with Ph.D. or other terminal degree: 93%. Student/faculty ratio: 15/1. Classes of fewer than 20 students: 48%; of 20 to 49 students: 51%; of 50 or more students: 1%. **Advanced Placement and International Baccalaureate credit:** AP tests may be used for: Credit only. Scores accepted: 3, 4, 5. **Freshmen returning for sophomore year:** 77%. **Graduation rates:** Four-year: 21%; five-year: 46%; six-year: 49%. **Graduate study:** 21% of students pursue further study immediately upon graduation; 19% within one year. Fields in which graduates pursue further study: Master of Business Administration (MBA), 9%; law, 9%; medicine, 9%; education, 15%; arts and sciences, 26%.

COSTS AND FINANCIAL AID

Financial aid office: (973) 720-2202. **Expenses (2009-2010):** Tuition and fees 2009-2010: $10,838 in state, $17,592 out of state; room/board: $10,280. Estimated books and supplies: $1,600; transportation: $2,673; personal expenses: $2,250. **Financial aid:** Priority filing date for institution's financial aid form: April 1. In 2009-2010, 80% of undergraduates applied for financial aid. Of those, 66% were determined to have financial need; 32% had their need fully met. Average financial aid package (proportion receiving): $14,598 (65%). Average amount of gift aid, such as scholarships or grants (proportion receiving): $8,850 (37%). Average amount of self-help aid, such as work study or loans (proportion receiving): $4,518 (55%). Average need-based loan (excluding PLUS or other private loans): $4,405. Among students who received aid based on merit, the average award (and the proportion receiving): $6,271 (5%). The average athletic scholarship (and the proportion receiving): $0 (0%). Average amount of debt of borrowers graduating in 2009: $25,893. Proportion who borrowed: 64%.

CAMPUS LIFE AND EXTRACURRICULAR ACTIVITIES

Campus housing available (% using): coed dorms (78%), apartment for single students (19%), special housing for disabled students (1%), other housing options (1%). Students who live in college-owned, operated, or affiliated housing: 24%. **Student employment:** During the 2009-2010 academic year, 3% of undergraduates worked on campus. Average per-year earnings: $3,480. **Clubs and organizations:** Number of student organizations: 83. Activities include: campus ministries, choral groups, concert band, dance, drama/theater, international student organization, jazz band, literary magazine, model UN, music ensembles, musical theater, radio station, student government, student newspaper, student film society, television station, yearbook. Number of fraternities: 7; sororities: 9. Proportion of men in fraternities: 2%; of women in sororities: 2%. Average proportion of students who stay on campus on weekends: 65%. **Sports program (2009-2010):** Member of NCAA III. *Men's intercollegiate varsity sports:* baseball, basketball, football, soccer, swimming. *Women's intercollegiate varsity sports:* basketball, field hockey, soccer, softball, swimming, tennis, volleyball.

SERVICES AND FACILITIES

Basic services: nonremedial tutoring, women's center, placement service, day care, health service, health insurance. **Remedial assistance:** reading, math, writing, study skills. **Counseling services:** minority student, career, personal, veteran student, academic, older student, psychological, birth control, religious. **For learning-disabled students:** School does not offer a structured program with separate admission and additional fees. Services include: remedial math, remedial English, reading machines, remedial reading, tape recorders, note-taking services, oral tests, readers, extended time for tests, tutors, texts on tape, other testing accommodations. **Library:** Number of titles: 351,704; number of current serial subscriptions: 6,478. **Information technology resources:** Students are not required to lease or own a computer. Number of campus computers available to all students: 1,100. School has a wireless network. Approximate number of users that can be accommodated: 500. Proportion of college-owned housing units wired for high-speed internet access: 100%. **Campus safety:** Security services offered: 24-hour foot-and-vehicle patrols, late-night transport/escort service, 24-hour emergency telephones, lighted pathways/sidewalks, student patrols, controlled dormitory access (key, security card, etc).

TRANSFER AND INTERNATIONAL STUDENTS

Transfer students: May apply for admission for the following academic terms: Fall, Spring. Applicants need a minimum number of credits to apply. For fall 2009: Transfer applications received: 2,222. Transfer applicants offered admission: 1,835. Transfer applicants enrolled: 1,030. **International students:** Number of foreign undergraduates: 71 (1% of student body). Number of countries represented: 43. Minimum TOEFL score required: 550 (paper); 80 (computer). Average TOEFL score: 550 (paper).

New Mexico

College of Santa Fe

- **Address:** 1600 St. Michael's Drive, Santa Fe, NM 87505
- **Website:** http://www.csf.edu
- **Private**
- **Enrollment:** 166 full-time; 29 part-time

KEY STATS
✔ **U.S News College Ranking:** 80, Regional Universities (West)
✔ **SAT or ACT Score (25th/75th percentile):** N/A
✔ **Tuition:** 2010-2011: $30,358

Selectivity: Less selective	**Room/board:** $8,338
Acceptance rate: N/A	**Average debt:** N/A
Student/faculty ratio: 22/1	**Proportion who borrowed:** N/A

UNDERGRADUATE STUDENT BODY STATS
2009-2010 enrollment: 166 full-time; 29 part-time. Men: 49%; women: 51%. **Ethnic makeup:** African American: 2%; American-Indian: 3%; Asian American: 2%; Hispanic: 19%; White: 74%; International: 1%. **Religious preference:** Roman Catholic: 2%; Protestant: 1%; No preference: 97%.

ADMISSIONS FACTS AND FIGURES
Phone: (505) 473-6133. **Email:** admissions@csf.edu. **Website:** http://www.csf.edu. **Application deadlines for fall 2011:** Regular decision: Rolling. Early decision: Not offered. Early action: Not offered. Admission can be deferred. **Application fee:** $35. **To apply online, go to:** http://www.csf.edu/prospective_students/apply/onlineapp. **Admissions requirements/recommendations:** High school units required (recommended): English: 4 (4); Mathematics: 2 (3); Science: 2 (3); Foreign language: 0 (2); Social studies: 2 (2); History: 0 (2); Academic electives: 6 (6); Total units: 16 (22). Tests: The college uses SAT or ACT scores in admissions decisions. Either SAT or ACT required. For admission to the fall 2011 entering class, the school will accept: ACT with writing recommended. Campus visit: Recommended. Admissions interview: Required. Off-campus interview: May be arranged. **Factors that count in admissions decisions:** *Academic:* Secondary school record: Very Important. Class rank: Important. Letters of recommendation: Important. Standardized test scores: Important. Essay: Important. *Nonacademic:* Interview: Very Important. Extracurricular activities: Important. Talent/ability: Very Important. Character/personal qualities: Very Important. Alumni/ae relationship: Important. Geographical residence: Not Considered. State residency: Not Considered. Religious affiliation/commitment: Not Considered. Minority status: Not Considered. Volunteer work: Important. Work experience: Considered. **Other schools with the greatest overlap in applicants:** Chapman University; Emerson College; Ithaca College; New York University; Savannah College of Art and Design. **Admissions statistics for the fall 2009 entering class:** Total applicants: 0. Total accepted: 0. Freshmen enrolled: 0; **Average high school grade point average:** 0.0.

ACADEMICS
Year founded: 1874. **Academic calendar:** Semester. **Degrees offered:** bachelor's, master's. **Most popular majors:** 20% art/art studies, 19% film/cinema studies, 14% theater/theater arts management, 8% music, 5% education. **Major fields of study:** area, ethnic, cultural, and gender studies; biological and biomedical sciences; business, management, marketing, and related support services; communication, journalism, and related programs; computer and information sciences and support services; education; English language and literature/letters; health professions and related clinical sciences; liberal arts and sciences studies, and humanities; multi/interdisciplinary studies; natural resources and conservation; philosophy and religious studies; psychology; public administration and social service professions; security and protective services; social sciences; visual and performing arts. **Areas of required coursework:** arts/fine arts, humanities, English (including composition), philosophy, sciences (biological or physical), social science. **Special academic programs:** accelerated program, cooperative (work-study plan) program, double major, dual enrollment, exchange student program (domestic), independent study, internships, student-designed major, study abroad, teacher certificate program. **Teacher certification offered in:** special education, elementary, middle/junior high, secondary, bilingual/bicultural. **Cooperative education programs:** art, other. **Faculty and instruction (2009-2010):** Total instructional faculty: 7 full-time, 19 part-time (69% men; 31% women; 35% minorities). Full-time faculty with Ph.D. or other terminal degree: 86%. Student/faculty ratio: 22/1. Classes of fewer than 20 students: 55%; of 20 to 49 students: 45%. **Advanced Placement and International Baccalaureate credit:** AP tests may be used for: Credit and/or placement. Scores accepted: 3, 4, 5. International Baccalaureate exams may be used for: Placement only. **Freshmen returning for sophomore year:** 69%. **Graduation rates:** Four-year: 37%; five-year: 45%; six-year: 43%.

COSTS AND FINANCIAL AID
Financial aid office: (505) 473-6454. **Expenses (2010-2011):** Tuition and fees 2010-2011: $30,358; room/board: $8,338. Estimated books and supplies: $1,224; transportation: $840; personal expenses: $1,400. **Financial aid:** Priority filing date for institution's financial aid form: March 1. In 2009-2010, 100% of undergraduates applied for financial aid. Of those, 100% were determined to have financial need; Average financial aid package (proportion receiving): N/A (100%). Average amount of gift aid, such as scholarships or grants (proportion receiving): $6,526 (38%). Average amount of self-help aid, such as work study or loans (proportion receiving): $5,712 (59%). Average need-based loan (excluding PLUS or other private loans): $4,504. Among students who received aid based on merit, the average award (and the proportion receiving): $0 (0%). The average athletic scholarship (and the proportion receiving): $0 (0%).

CAMPUS LIFE AND EXTRACURRICULAR ACTIVITIES
Campus housing available (% using): coed dorms (46%), women's dorms (0%), men's dorms (0%), apartment for single students (54%), special housing for disabled students (0%). Students who live in college-owned, operated, or affiliated housing: 44%. **Student employment:** During the 2009-2010 academic year, 40% of undergraduates worked on campus. Average per-year earnings: $2,000. **Clubs and organizations:** Number of student organizations: 9. Activities include: choral groups, dance, drama/theater, literary magazine, music ensembles, musical theater, student government, television station, yearbook. Number of fraternities: 0; sororities: 0. Average proportion of students who stay on campus on weekends: 75%.

SERVICES AND FACILITIES
Basic services: nonremedial tutoring, placement service, health service, health insurance. **Remedial assistance:** writing, study skills. **Counseling services:** career, personal, veteran student, academic, older student, psychological, birth control, religious. **For learning-disabled students:** School does not offer a structured program with separate admission and additional fees. Services include: reading machines, tape recorders, other special classes, note-taking services, oral tests, learning center, readers, extended time for tests, tutors, texts on tape, typist/scribe, waiver of foreign language degree requirement. **Library:** Number of titles: 186,000; number of current serial subscriptions: 117. **Information technology resources:** Students are not required to lease or own a computer. Number of campus computers available to all students: 84. School has a wireless network. Proportion of college-owned housing units wired for high-speed internet access: 100%. **Campus safety:** Security services offered: 24-hour foot-and-vehicle patrols, late-night transport/escort service, lighted pathways/sidewalks, controlled dormitory access (key, security card, etc).

TRANSFER AND INTERNATIONAL STUDENTS
Transfer students: May apply for admission for the following academic terms: Fall, Spring. Applicants need a minimum number of credits to apply. For fall 2009: Transfer applications received: 0. **International students:** Number of foreign undergraduates: 1 (1% of student body). Minimum TOEFL score required: 550 (paper); 213 (computer). Average TOEFL score: 550 (paper).

Eastern New Mexico University

- **Address:** Station 2, Portales, NM 88130
- **Website:** http://www.enmu.edu
- **Public**
- **Enrollment:** N/A

KEY STATS

✔ **U.S News College Ranking:** second tier, Regional Universities (West)
✔ **ACT Score (25th/75th percentile):** 17-22
✔ **Tuition:** 2009-2010: $3,552 in state, $9,102 out of state

Selectivity: Selective	**Room/board:** $5,374
Acceptance rate: 67%	**Average debt:** N/A
Student/faculty ratio: N/A	**Proportion who borrowed:** N/A

New Mexico Highlands University

- **Address:** Box 9000, Las Vegas, NM 87701
- **Website:** http://www.nmhu.edu
- **Public**
- **Enrollment:** 1,634 full-time; 624 part-time

KEY STATS

✔ **U.S News College Ranking:** second tier, Regional Universities (West)
✔ **ACT Score (25th/75th percentile):** 16-20
✔ **Tuition:** 2009-2010: $2,761 in state, $4,328 out of state

Selectivity: Less selective	**Room/board:** $7,555
Acceptance rate: 56%	**Average debt:** N/A
Student/faculty ratio: N/A	**Proportion who borrowed:** N/A

UNDERGRADUATE STUDENT BODY STATS

2009-2010 enrollment: 1,634 full-time; 624 part-time. Men: 41%; women: 59%.

ADMISSIONS FACTS AND FIGURES

Phone: (505) 454-3439. **Email:** admissions@nmhu.edu. **Website:** http://www.nmhu.edu. **Application deadlines for fall 2011:** Regular decision: Rolling. Early decision: Not offered. Early action: Not offered. Admission can be deferred. **Application fee:** $15. **To apply online, go to:** http://www.nmhu.edu/future/apply.html. **Admissions requirements/recommendations:** Tests: The college uses SAT or ACT scores in admissions decisions. ACT required. Campus visit: Recommended. Admissions interview: Recommended. Off-campus interview: May be arranged. **Factors that count in admissions decisions:** *Academic:* Secondary school record: Not Considered. Class rank: Not Considered. Letters of recommendation: Not Considered. Standardized test scores: Not Considered. Essay: Not Considered. *Nonacademic:* Interview: Not Considered. Extracurricular activities: Not Considered. Talent/ability: Not Considered. Character/personal qualities: Not Considered. Alumni/ae relationship: Not Considered. Geographical residence: Not Considered. State residency: Not Considered. Religious affiliation/commitment: Not Considered. Minority status: Not Considered. Volunteer work: Not Considered. Work experience: Not Considered. **Other schools with the greatest overlap in applicants:** Adams State College; Eastern New Mexico University; Fort Lewis College; New Mexico State University; University of New Mexico. **Admissions statistics for the fall 2009 entering class:** Total applicants: 3,228. Total accepted: 1,803. Freshmen enrolled: 398; Overall acceptance rate: 56%. **Size of waiting list:** 0 applicants; enrolled from waiting list: 0. **Credentials of fall 2009 freshmen:** 6% ranked in the top 10 percent of their high school class; 28% were in the top 25 percent; 62% were in the top half. (Proportion submitting class standing: 83%.) **First-year students submitting ACT scores:** 70%. Scores (25/75 percentile): English: N/A, Math: N/A, Composite: 16-20.

ACADEMICS

Year founded: 1893. **Academic calendar:** Semester. **Degrees offered:** associate, bachelor's, master's. **Major fields of study:** biological and biomedical sciences; business, management, marketing, and related support services; communication, journalism, and related programs; computer and information sciences and support services; education; engineering; English language and literature/letters; family and consumer sciences/human sci-ences; foreign languages, literatures, and linguistics; health professions and related clinical sciences; history; mathematics and statistics; natural resources and conservation; parks, recreation, leisure, and fitness studies; physical sciences; psychology; security and protective services; social sciences; visual and performing arts. **Areas of required coursework:** arts/fine arts, humanities, computer literacy, mathematics, English (including composition), foreign languages, sciences (biological or physical), history, social science. **Pre-professional programs:** pre-law, pre-medicine. **Special academic programs:** cooperative (work-study plan) program, distance learning, double major, dual enrollment, honors program, independent study, internships, study abroad, teacher certificate program. **Teacher certification offered in:** early childhood, special education, elementary, secondary, bilingual/bicultural. **Cooperative education programs:** business, natural science. **Faculty and instruction (2009-2010):** Total instructional faculty: 146 (51% men; 49% women). **Advanced Placement and International Baccalaureate credit:** AP tests may be used for: Placement only. Scores accepted: 3, 4, 5. **Freshmen returning for sophomore year:** 47%. **Graduation rates:** Six-year: 22%.

COSTS AND FINANCIAL AID

Financial aid office: (505) 454-3430. **Expenses (2009-2010):** Tuition and fees 2009-2010: $2,761 in state, $4,328 out of state; room/board: $7,555. Estimated books and supplies: $850. **Financial aid:** Priority filing date for institution's financial aid form: March 1.

CAMPUS LIFE AND EXTRACURRICULAR ACTIVITIES

Campus housing available (% using): coed dorms (91%), apartments for married students (9%). **Student employment:** During the 2009-2010 academic year, 20% of undergraduates worked on campus. Average per-year earnings: $4,000. **Clubs and organizations:** Number of student organizations: 47. Activities include: choral groups, concert band, dance, drama/theater, international student organization, jazz band, literary magazine, marching band, music ensembles, musical theater, pep band, radio station, student government, student newspaper, television station. Number of fraternities: 1; sororities: 1. Average proportion of students who stay on campus on weekends: 30%. **Sports program (2009-2010):** Member of NCAA II. **Men's intercollegiate varsity sports:** baseball, basketball, cross country, football. **Women's intercollegiate varsity sports:** basketball, cross country, soccer, softball, track and field (indoor), volleyball.

SERVICES AND FACILITIES

Basic services: nonremedial tutoring, women's center, placement service, day care, health service, health insurance. **Remedial assistance:** reading, math, writing, study skills. **Counseling services:** minority student, career, military, personal, academic, psychological. **For learning-disabled students:** School does not offer a structured program with separate admission and additional fees. Services include: remedial math, remedial English, reading machines, remedial reading, tape recorders, other special classes, videotaped classes, diagnostic testing service, untimed tests, note-taking services, oral tests, learning center, readers, extended time for tests, tutors, priority seating, proofreading services, texts on tape, typist/scribe, exams on tape or computer, other testing accommodations. **Library:** Number of titles: 616,333; number of current serial subscriptions: 729. **Information technology resources:** Students are not required to lease or own a computer. Number of campus computers available to all students: 350. School has a wireless network. Proportion of college-owned housing units wired for high-speed internet access: 99%. **Campus safety:** Security services offered: 24-hour foot-and-vehicle patrols, lighted pathways/sidewalks, controlled dormitory access (key, security card, etc).

TRANSFER AND INTERNATIONAL STUDENTS

Transfer students: May apply for admission for the following academic terms: Fall, Spring, Summer. Applicants need a minimum number of credits to apply. For fall 2009: Transfer applications received: 785. Transfer applicants offered admission: 498. Transfer applicants enrolled: 346. **International students:** Number of countries represented: 7. Minimum TOEFL score required: 540 (paper); 207 (computer). Average TOEFL score: 500 (paper).

New Mexico Institute of Mining and Tech.

- ■ **Address:** 801 Leroy Place, Socorro, NM 87801
- ■ **Website:** http://www.nmt.edu
- ■ **Public**
- ■ **Enrollment:** 1,095 full-time; 227 part-time

KEY STATS
- ✔ **U.S News College Ranking:** 17, Regional Universities (West)
- ✔ **ACT Score (25th/75th percentile):** 23-28
- ✔ **Tuition:** 2010-2011: $4,942 in state, $14,620 out of state
- **Selectivity:** More selective **Room/board:** $5,874
- **Acceptance rate:** 79% **Average debt:** $7,894
- **Student/faculty ratio:** 11/1 **Proportion who borrowed:** 90%

UNDERGRADUATE STUDENT BODY STATS
2009-2010 enrollment: 1,095 full-time; 227 part-time. Men: 66%; women: 34%. **Ethnic makeup:** African American: 1%; American-Indian: 3%; Asian American: 3%; Hispanic: 25%; White: 65%; International: 2%.

ADMISSIONS FACTS AND FIGURES
Phone: (505) 835-5424. **Email:** admission@admin.nmt.edu. **Website:** http://www.nmt.edu. **Application deadlines for fall 2011:** Regular decision: August 1. Early decision: Not offered. Early action: Not offered. Admission can be deferred. **Application fee:** $15. **To apply online, go to:** http://www.nmt.edu/mainpage/admission/appform/homepage.html. **Admissions requirements/recommendations:** High school units required (recommended): English: 4 (4); Mathematics: 3 (4); Science: 2 (4); Foreign language: 0 (2); Social studies: 2 (3); History: 1 (1); Academic electives: 3 (0); Total units: 15 (18). Tests: The college uses SAT or ACT scores in admissions decisions. Either SAT or ACT required. For admission to the fall 2011 entering class, the school will accept: ACT with or without writing accepted. Campus visit: Recommended. Admissions interview: Neither required nor recommended. Off-campus interview: Not available. **Factors that count in admissions decisions:** *Academic:* Secondary school record: Very Important. Class rank: Considered. Letters of recommendation: Not Considered. Standardized test scores: Very Important. Essay: Not Considered. *Nonacademic:* Interview: Not Considered. Extracurricular activities: Considered. Talent/ability: Considered. Character/personal qualities: Not Considered. Alumni/ae relationship: Not Considered. Geographical residence: Not Considered. State residency: Not Considered. Religious affiliation/commitment: Not Considered. Minority status: Not Considered. Volunteer work: Not Considered. Work experience: Not Considered. **Other schools with the greatest overlap in applicants:** Colorado School of Mines; Massachusetts Institute of Technology; New Mexico State University; Texas Tech University; University of New Mexico. **Admissions statistics for the fall 2009 entering class:** Total applicants: 445. Total accepted: 353. Freshmen enrolled: 255; 20% were from out of state. Overall acceptance rate: 79%. **Credentials of fall 2009 freshmen:** 36% ranked in the top 10 percent of their high school class; 67% were in the top 25 percent; 89% were in the top half. (Proportion submitting class standing: 76%.) **Average high school grade point average:** 3.6. **First-year students who submitted SAT scores:** 39%. Scores (25/75 percentile): Critical Reading: 530-650, Math: 570-680, Combined: 1100-1330. **First-year students submitting ACT scores:** 89%. Scores (25/75 percentile): English: 21-28, Math: 23-28, Composite: 23-28.

ACADEMICS
Year founded: 1889. **Academic calendar:** Semester. **Degrees offered:** associate, terminal-associate, bachelor's, master's, doctorate. **Most popular majors:** 43% engineering, 14% computer and information sciences and support services, 11% physical sciences, 10% biological and biomedical sciences, 6% liberal arts and sciences studies, and humanities. **Major fields of study:** biological and biomedical sciences; business, management, marketing, and related support services; computer and information sciences and support services; engineering; English language and literature/letters; liberal arts and sciences studies, and humanities; mathematics and statistics; physical sciences; psychology. **Areas of required coursework:** humanities, computer literacy, mathematics, English (including composition), sciences (biological or physical), social science. **Pre-professional programs:** pre-dentistry, pre-medicine, pre-veterinary science, pre-pharmacy. **Special academic programs:** accelerated program, cooperative (work-study plan) program, distance learning, double major, dual enrollment, exchange student program (domestic), independent study, internships, student-designed major, study abroad, teacher certificate program. **Teacher certification offered in:** second-

ary. **Faculty and instruction (2009-2010):** Total instructional faculty: 124 full-time, 29 part-time (80% men; 20% women; 14% minorities). Full-time faculty with Ph.D. or other terminal degree: 97%. Student/faculty ratio: 11/1. Classes of fewer than 20 students: 63%; of 20 to 49 students: 34%; of 50 or more students: 4%. **Advanced Placement and International Baccalaureate credit:** AP tests may be used for: Placement only. Scores accepted: 3, 4, 5. **Freshmen returning for sophomore year:** 70%. **Graduation rates:** Four-year: 21%; five-year: 39%; six-year: 48%.

COSTS AND FINANCIAL AID
Financial aid office: (505) 835-5333. **Expenses (2010-2011):** Tuition and fees 2010-2011: $4,942 in state, $14,620 out of state; room/board: $5,874. Estimated personal expenses: $3,850. **Financial aid:** Priority filing date for institution's financial aid form: June 1. In 2009-2010, 91% of undergraduates applied for financial aid. Of those, 45% were determined to have financial need; 42% had their need fully met. Average financial aid package (proportion receiving): $10,397 (44%). Average amount of gift aid, such as scholarships or grants (proportion receiving): $6,463 (26%). Average amount of self-help aid, such as work study or loans (proportion receiving): $5,665 (30%). Average need-based loan (excluding PLUS or other private loans): $5,089. Among students who received need-based aid, the average percentage of need met: 89%. Among students who received aid based on merit, the average award (and the proportion receiving): $5,226 (38%). The average athletic scholarship (and the proportion receiving): $0 (0%). Average amount of debt of borrowers graduating in 2009: $7,894. Proportion who borrowed: 90%.

CAMPUS LIFE AND EXTRACURRICULAR ACTIVITIES
Campus housing available: coed dorms, women's dorms, men's dorms, apartments for married students, apartment for single students. **Clubs and organizations:** Number of student organizations: 65. Activities include: choral groups, concert band, dance, drama/theater, jazz band, music ensembles, musical theater, radio station, student government, student newspaper. Number of fraternities: 0; sororities: 0.

SERVICES AND FACILITIES
Basic services: nonremedial tutoring, placement service, day care, health service, health insurance. **Remedial assistance:** study skills. **Counseling services:** career, personal, academic. **For learning-disabled students:** School does not offer a structured program with separate admission and additional fees. Services include: tape recorders, untimed tests, note-taking services, oral tests, readers, extended time for tests, tutors. **Library:** Number of titles: 321,829; number of current serial subscriptions: 884. **Information technology resources:** Students are not required to lease or own a computer. Number of campus computers available to all students: 200. School has a wireless network. **Campus safety:** Security services offered: 24-hour foot-and-vehicle patrols.

TRANSFER AND INTERNATIONAL STUDENTS
Transfer students: May apply for admission for the following academic terms: Fall, Spring, Summer. Applicants need a minimum number of credits to apply. For fall 2009: Transfer applications received: 172. Transfer applicants offered admission: 72. Transfer applicants enrolled: 59. **International students:** Number of foreign undergraduates: 20 (2% of student body). Number of countries represented: 25. Minimum TOEFL score required: 540 (paper); 207 (computer).

New Mexico State University

- ■ **Address:** Box 30001, MSC 3004, Las Cruces, NM 88003-8001
- ■ **Website:** http://www.nmsu.edu
- ■ **Public**
- ■ **Enrollment:** 12,621 full-time; 2,077 part-time

KEY STATS
- ✔ **U.S News College Ranking:** second tier, National Universities
- ✔ **ACT Score (25th/75th percentile):** 18-23
- ✔ **Tuition:** 2009-2010: $4,998 in state, $15,150 out of state
- **Selectivity:** Selective **Room/board:** $6,338
- **Acceptance rate:** 96% **Average debt:** $23,262
- **Student/faculty ratio:** 20/1 **Proportion who borrowed:** 51%

UNDERGRADUATE STUDENT BODY STATS

2009-2010 enrollment: 12,621 full-time; 2,077 part-time. Men: 45%; women: 55%. **Ethnic makeup:** African American: 3%; American-Indian: 4%; Asian American: 1%; Hispanic: 44%; White: 43%; International: 5%.

ADMISSIONS FACTS AND FIGURES

Phone: (505) 646-3121. **Email:** admissions@nmsu.edu. **Website:** http://www.nmsu.edu. **Application deadlines for fall 2011:** Regular decision: August 28. Early decision: Not offered. Early action: Not offered. Admission can be deferred. **Application fee:** $20. **To apply online, go to:** http://www.nmsu.edu/~admision/admit-form.html. **Admissions requirements/recommendations:** High school units required (recommended): English: 4; Mathematics: 3; Science: 2; Foreign language: 1; Total units: 10. Tests: The college uses SAT or ACT scores in admissions decisions. Either SAT or ACT required. For admission to the fall 2011 entering class, the school will accept: ACT with or without writing accepted. Campus visit: Recommended. Admissions interview: Neither required nor recommended. Off-campus interview: May be arranged. **Factors that count in admissions decisions: Academic:** Secondary school record: Very Important. Class rank: Not Considered. Letters of recommendation: Not Considered. Standardized test scores: Very Important. Essay: Not Considered. *Nonacademic:* Interview: Not Considered. Extracurricular activities: Not Considered. Talent/ability: Not Considered. Character/personal qualities: Not Considered. Alumni/ae relationship: Not Considered. Geographical residence: Not Considered. State residency: Not Considered. Religious affiliation/commitment: Not Considered. Minority status: Not Considered. Volunteer work: Not Considered. Work experience: Not Considered. **Other schools with the greatest overlap in applicants:** Arizona State University; Texas Tech University; University of Arizona; University of New Mexico; University of Texas–El Paso. **Admissions statistics for the fall 2009 entering class:** Total applicants: 6,650. Total accepted: 6,404. Freshmen enrolled: 2,878; 23% were from out of state. Overall acceptance rate: 96%. **Credentials of fall 2009 freshmen:** 15% ranked in the top 10 percent of their high school class; 42% were in the top 25 percent; 75% were in the top half. (Proportion submitting class standing: 81%.) **Average high school grade point average:** 3.3. **First-year students who submitted SAT scores:** 24%. Scores (25/75 percentile): Critical Reading: 420-540, Math: 430-550, Combined: 850-1090. **First-year students submitting ACT scores:** 75%. Scores (25/75 percentile): English: 17-23, Math: 16-24, Composite: 18-23.

ACADEMICS

Year founded: 1888. **Academic calendar:** Semester. **Degrees offered:** associate, bachelor's, post-bachelor's certificate, master's, post-master's certificate, doctorate. **Most popular majors:** 7% elementary education and teaching, 6% criminal justice/safety studies, 6% nursing/registered nurse training (R.N., A.S.N., B.S.N., M.S.N.), 4% foreign languages and literatures, 3% marketing/marketing management. **Major fields of study:** agriculture, agriculture operations, and related sciences; architecture and related services; area, ethnic, cultural, and gender studies; biological and biomedical sciences; business, management, marketing, and related support services; communication, journalism, and related programs; computer and information sciences and support services; education; engineering; engineering technologies/technicians; English language and literature/letters; family and consumer sciences/human sciences; foreign languages, literatures, and linguistics; health professions and related clinical sciences; history; liberal arts and sciences studies, and humanities; mathematics and statistics; natural resources and conservation; parks, recreation, leisure, and fitness studies; philosophy and religious studies; physical sciences; psychology; public administration and social service professions; security and protective services; social sciences; visual and performing arts. **Areas of required coursework:** arts/fine arts, humanities, computer literacy, mathematics, English (including composition), philosophy, sciences (biological or physical), history, social science. **Pre-professional programs:** pre-law, pre-dentistry, pre-medicine, pre-veterinary science, pre-pharmacy, other. **Special academic programs:** accelerated program, cooperative (work-study plan) program, cross-registration, distance learning, double major, dual enrollment, English as a Second Language (ESL), exchange student program (domestic), external degree program, honors program, independent study, internships, student-designed major, study abroad, teacher certificate program, weekend college. **Teacher certification offered in:** early childhood, special education, elementary, vo-tech, middle/junior high, adult education, secondary, bilingual/bicultural. **Cooperative education programs:** agriculture, business, computer science, education, engineering, home economics, natural science, technologies. **Reserve Officers Training Corps (ROTC):** Army ROTC: Offered on campus; Air Force ROTC: Offered on campus. **Faculty and instruction (2009-2010):** Total instructional faculty: 699 full-time, 324 part-time (55% men; 45% women; 18% minorities). Full-time faculty with Ph.D. or other

terminal degree: 75%. Student/faculty ratio: 20/1. Classes of fewer than 20 students: 45%; of 20 to 49 students: 45%; of 50 or more students: 11%. **Advanced Placement and International Baccalaureate credit:** International Baccalaureate exams may be used for: Placement only. **Freshmen returning for sophomore year:** 76%. **Graduation rates:** Four-year: 13%; five-year: 37%; six-year: 45%.

COSTS AND FINANCIAL AID

Financial aid office: (505) 646-4105. **Expenses (2009-2010):** Tuition and fees 2009-2010: $4,998 in state, $15,150 out of state; room/board: $6,338. Estimated books and supplies: $1,032; transportation: $1,666; personal expenses: $2,212. **Financial aid:** Priority filing date for institution's financial aid form: March 1. In 2009-2010, 73% of undergraduates applied for financial aid. Of those, 64% were determined to have financial need; 5% had their need fully met. Average financial aid package (proportion receiving): $7,539 (56%). Average amount of gift aid, such as scholarships or grants (proportion receiving): $5,125 (48%). Average amount of self-help aid, such as work study or loans (proportion receiving): $4,203 (41%). Average need-based loan (excluding PLUS or other private loans): $4,130. Among students who received need-based aid, the average percentage of need met: 48%. Among students who received aid based on merit, the average award (and the proportion receiving): $315 (1%). The average athletic scholarship (and the proportion receiving): $8,728 (1%). Average amount of debt of borrowers graduating in 2009: $23,262. Proportion who borrowed: 51%.

CAMPUS LIFE AND EXTRACURRICULAR ACTIVITIES

Campus housing available (% using): coed dorms (55%), sorority housing (2%), fraternity housing (3%), apartments for married students (16%), apartment for single students (23%), special housing for disabled students (1%). **Student employment:** During the 2009-2010 academic year, 18% of undergraduates worked on campus. Average per-year earnings: $6,400. **Clubs and organizations:** Number of student organizations: 234. Activities include: choral groups, concert band, dance, drama/theater, jazz band, literary magazine, marching band, music ensembles, musical theater, opera, pep band, radio station, student government, student newspaper, symphony orchestra, television station. Number of fraternities: 13; sororities: 6. Average proportion of students who stay on campus on weekends: 79%. **Sports program (2009-2010):** Member of NCAA I. *Men's intercollegiate varsity sports:* baseball, basketball, cross country, football, golf, tennis. *Women's intercollegiate varsity sports:* basketball, cross country, equestrian, golf, soccer, softball, swimming, tennis, track and field (indoor), track and field (outdoor), volleyball.

SERVICES AND FACILITIES

Basic services: nonremedial tutoring, women's center, placement service, health service, health insurance. **Remedial assistance:** math. **Counseling services:** minority student, career, military, personal, veteran student, academic, older student, psychological, birth control, religious. **For learning-disabled students:** School does not offer a structured program with separate admission and additional fees. Total undergraduates in learning-disabled program or receiving services: 105. Services include: remedial math, remedial English, remedial reading, tape recorders, note-taking services, oral tests, learning center, readers, extended time for tests, priority registration, priority seating, typist/scribe, exams on tape or computer, other testing accommodations, other. **Library:** Number of titles: 1,799,043; number of current serial subscriptions: 4,402. **Information technology resources:** Students are not required to lease or own a computer. Number of campus computers available to all students: 471. School has a wireless network. Approximate number of users that can be accommodated: 38,000. Proportion of college-owned housing units wired for high-speed internet access: 100%. **Campus safety:** Security services offered: 24-hour foot-and-vehicle patrols, late-night transport/escort service, 24-hour emergency telephones, lighted pathways/sidewalks, controlled dormitory access (key, security card, etc).

TRANSFER AND INTERNATIONAL STUDENTS

Transfer students: May apply for admission for the following academic terms: Fall, Spring, Summer. Applicants need a minimum number of credits to apply. For fall 2009: Transfer applications received: 1,152. Transfer applicants offered admission: 1,048. Transfer applicants enrolled: 721. **International students:** Number of foreign undergraduates: 691 (5% of student body). Number of countries represented: 45. Minimum TOEFL score required: 500 (paper); 61 (computer). Average TOEFL score: 550 (paper).

St. John's College

- **Address:** 1160 Camino Cruz Blanca, Santa Fe, NM 87505
- **Website:** http://www.sjcsf.edu
- **Private**
- **Enrollment:** N/A

KEY STATS

✔ **U.S News College Ranking:** 187, National Liberal Arts Colleges
✔ **SAT or ACT Score (25th/75th percentile):** N/A
✔ **Tuition:** 2009-2010: $40,396

Selectivity: Selective	**Room/board:** $9,600
Acceptance rate: N/A	**Average debt:** N/A
Student/faculty ratio: N/A	**Proportion who borrowed:** N/A

University of New Mexico

- **Address:** 1 University of New Mexico, Albuquerque, NM 87131-0001
- **Website:** http://www.unm.edu
- **Public**
- **Enrollment:** 16,050 full-time; 5,282 part-time

KEY STATS

✔ **U.S News College Ranking:** second tier, National Universities
✔ **ACT Score (25th/75th percentile):** 19-25
✔ **Tuition:** 2009-2010: $5,101 in state, $17,254 out of state

Selectivity: Selective	**Room/board:** $7,746
Acceptance rate: 62%	**Average debt:** N/A
Student/faculty ratio: 21/1	**Proportion who borrowed:** N/A

UNDERGRADUATE STUDENT BODY STATS

2009-2010 enrollment: 16,050 full-time; 5,282 part-time. Men: 44%; women: 56%. **Ethnic makeup:** African American: 3%; American-Indian: 7%; Asian American: 4%; Hispanic: 37%; White: 48%; International: 1%.

ADMISSIONS FACTS AND FIGURES

Phone: (505) 277-8900. **Email:** apply@unm.edu. **Website:** http://www.unm.edu. **Application deadlines for fall 2011:** Early decision: Not offered. Early action: Not offered. Admission can be deferred. **Application fee:** $20. **To apply online, go to:** http://www.unm.edu/apply/. **Admissions requirements/recommendations:** High school units required (recommended): English: 4; Mathematics: 3; Science: 2; Foreign language: 2; Social studies: 1; History: 1; Total units: 13. Tests: The college uses SAT or ACT scores in admissions decisions. Either SAT or ACT required. For admission to the fall 2011 entering class, the school will accept: ACT with writing recommended. Campus visit: Recommended. Admissions interview: Neither required nor recommended. Off-campus interview: Not available. **Factors that count in admissions decisions: *Academic:*** Secondary school record: Very Important. Class rank: Important. Letters of recommendation: Not Considered. Standardized test scores: Important. Essay: Considered. ***Nonacademic:*** Interview: Not Considered. Extracurricular activities: Considered. Talent/ability: Considered. Character/personal qualities: Considered. Alumni/ae relationship: Not Considered. Geographical residence: Not Considered. State residency: Not Considered. Religious affiliation/commitment: Not Considered. Minority status: Not Considered. Volunteer work: Considered. Work experience: Considered. **Other schools with the greatest overlap in applicants:** Arizona State University; New Mexico Institute of Mining and Technology; New Mexico State University. **Admissions statistics for the fall 2009 entering class:** Total applicants: 10,743. Total accepted: 6,614. Freshmen enrolled: 3,409; 11% were from out of state. Overall acceptance rate: 62%. **Credentials of fall 2009 freshmen:** 21% ranked in the top 10 percent of their high school class; 47% were in the top 25 percent; 79% were in the top half. (Proportion submitting class standing: 85%.) **Average high school grade point average:** 3.3. **First-year students who submitted SAT scores:** 21%. Scores (25/75 percentile): Critical Reading: 480-610, Math: 480-610, Combined: 960-1220. **First-year students submitting ACT scores:** 90%. Scores (25/75 percentile): English: N/A, Math: N/A, Composite: 19-25.

ACADEMICS

Year founded: 1889. **Academic calendar:** Semester. **Degrees offered:** certificate, associate, bachelor's, master's, post-master's certificate, doctorate.

Most popular majors: 15% business, management, marketing, and related support services, 13% education, 9% social sciences, 8% health professions and related clinical sciences, 8% psychology. **Major fields of study:** architecture and related services; area, ethnic, cultural, and gender studies; biological and biomedical sciences; business, management, marketing, and related support services; communication, journalism, and related programs; computer and information sciences and support services; education; engineering; English language and literature/letters; family and consumer sciences/human sciences; foreign languages, literatures, and linguistics; health professions and related clinical sciences; history; liberal arts and sciences studies, and humanities; mathematics and statistics; natural resources and conservation; philosophy and religious studies; physical sciences; psychology; public administration and social service professions; security and protective services; social sciences; visual and performing arts. **Areas of required coursework:** arts/fine arts, humanities, mathematics, English (including composition), foreign languages, sciences (biological or physical), social science. **Special academic programs:** accelerated program, cooperative (work-study plan) program, distance learning, double major, dual enrollment, English as a Second Language (ESL), exchange student program (domestic), honors program, independent study, internships, student-designed major, study abroad, teacher certificate program, weekend college. **Teacher certification offered in:** early childhood, special education, elementary, adult education, secondary, bilingual/bicultural. **Cooperative education programs:** art, business, engineering, other. **Reserve Officers Training Corps (ROTC):** Army ROTC: Offered on campus; Navy ROTC: Offered on campus; Air Force ROTC: Offered on campus. **Faculty and instruction (2009-2010):** Total instructional faculty: 957 full-time, 524 part-time (52% men; 48% women; 21% minorities). Full-time faculty with Ph.D. or other terminal degree: 84%. Student/faculty ratio: 21/1. Classes of fewer than 20 students: 41%; of 20 to 49 students: 45%; of 50 or more students: 14%. **Advanced Placement and International Baccalaureate credit:** AP tests may be used for: Credit and/or placement. Scores accepted: 3, 4, 5. International Baccalaureate exams may be used for: Credit and/or placement. **Freshmen returning for sophomore year:** 77%. **Graduation rates:** Four-year: 11%; five-year: 34%; six-year: 43%.

COSTS AND FINANCIAL AID

Financial aid office: (505) 277-3012. **Expenses (2009-2010):** Tuition and fees 2009-2010: $5,101 in state, $17,254 out of state; room/board: $7,746. Estimated books and supplies: $920. **Financial aid:** Priority filing date for institution's financial aid form: March 1.

CAMPUS LIFE AND EXTRACURRICULAR ACTIVITIES

Campus housing available: coed dorms, sorority housing, fraternity housing, apartments for married students, apartment for single students, special housing for disabled students, special housing for international students, other housing options. Students who live in college-owned, operated, or affiliated housing: 10%. **Clubs and organizations:** Number of student organizations: 375. Activities include: campus ministries, choral groups, concert band, dance, drama/theater, international student organization, jazz band, literary magazine, marching band, model UN, music ensembles, musical theater, opera, pep band, radio station, student government, student newspaper, student film society, symphony orchestra, television station. Number of fraternities: 9; sororities: 10. Proportion of men in fraternities: 2%; of women in sororities: 2%. **Sports program (2009-2010):** Member of NCAA I. ***Men's intercollegiate varsity sports:*** baseball, basketball, cross country, football, golf, skiing (nordic), soccer, tennis, track and field (indoor). ***Women's intercollegiate varsity sports:*** basketball, cross country, golf, skiing (nordic), soccer, softball, swimming, tennis, track and field (indoor), volleyball.

SERVICES AND FACILITIES

Basic services: nonremedial tutoring, women's center, placement service, day care, health service, health insurance. **Remedial assistance:** reading, math, writing, study skills. **Counseling services:** minority student, career, personal, veteran student, academic, psychological. **For learning-disabled students:** School does not offer a structured program with separate admission and additional fees. Total undergraduates in learning-disabled program or receiving services: 155. Services include: remedial math, remedial English, reading machines, remedial reading, tape recorders, videotaped classes, note-taking services, learning center, readers, extended time for tests, tutors, priority seating, texts on tape, typist/scribe, exams on tape or computer, other testing accommodations, other. **Library:** Number of titles: 3,117,590; number of current serial subscriptions: 77,094. **Information technology resources:** Students are not required to lease or own a computer. Number of campus computers available to all students: 766. School has a wireless network. Proportion of college-owned housing units wired for high-speed internet access: 100%. **Campus safety:** Security services offered: 24-hour foot-and-vehicle patrols, late-night transport/escort service, 24-hour emergency telephones, lighted pathways/sidewalks, student patrols, controlled dormitory access (key, security card, etc.).

TRANSFER AND INTERNATIONAL STUDENTS

Transfer students: May apply for admission for the following academic terms: Fall, Spring, Summer. Applicants need a minimum number of credits to apply. For fall 2009: Transfer applications received: 3,228. Transfer applicants offered admission: 2,063. Transfer applicants enrolled: 1,293. **International students:** Number of foreign undergraduates: 190 (1% of student body). Number of countries represented: 49. Minimum TOEFL score required: 520 (paper); 190 (computer).

University of the Southwest

- **Address:** 6610 Lovington Highway, Hobbs, NM 88240
- **Website:** http://www.csw.edu
- **Private**
- **Enrollment:** 266 full-time; 51 part-time

KEY STATS
- ✔ **U.S News College Ranking:** 84, Regional Universities (West)
- ✔ **SAT Score (25th/75th percentile):** 770-940
- ✔ **Tuition:** 2010-2011: $13,633

Selectivity: Less selective	**Room/board:** $6,530
Acceptance rate: 60%	**Average debt:** $22,200
Student/faculty ratio: 10/1	**Proportion who borrowed:** 86%

UNDERGRADUATE STUDENT BODY STATS

2009-2010 enrollment: 266 full-time; 51 part-time. Men: 51%; women: 49%. **Ethnic makeup:** African American: 7%; Asian American: 2%; Hispanic: 38%; White: 50%; International: 3%.

ADMISSIONS FACTS AND FIGURES

Phone: (505) 392-6563. **Email:** admissions@csw.edu. **Website:** http://www.csw.edu. **Application deadlines for fall 2011:** Regular decision: Rolling. Early decision: Not offered. Early action: Not offered. Admission can be deferred. **Application fee:** $25. **To apply online, go to:** http://www.csw.edu/204021.ihtml. **Admissions requirements/recommendations:** Tests: The college uses SAT or ACT scores in admissions decisions. Either SAT or ACT required. For admission to the fall 2011 entering class, the school will accept: ACT with or without writing accepted. Campus visit: Recommended. Admissions interview: Recommended. Off-campus interview: May be arranged. **Factors that count in admissions decisions:** *Academic:* Secondary school record: Very Important. Class rank: Very Important. Letters of recommendation: Considered. Standardized test scores: Very Important. Essay: Not Considered. *Nonacademic:* Interview: Important. Extracurricular activities: Important. Talent/ability: Very Important. Character/personal qualities: Important. Alumni/ae relationship: Not Considered. Geographical residence: Not Considered. State residency: Not Considered. Religious affiliation/commitment: Not Considered. Minority status: Not Considered. Volunteer work: Not Considered. Work experience: Not Considered. **Other schools with the greatest overlap in applicants:** Eastern New Mexico University; New Mexico State University; Texas Tech University. **Admissions statistics for the fall 2009 entering class:** Total applicants: 213. Total accepted: 128. Freshmen enrolled: 51; Overall acceptance rate: 60%. **Credentials of fall 2009 freshmen:** 17% ranked in the top 10 percent of their high school class; 41% were in the top 25 percent; 68% were in the top half. (Proportion submitting class standing: 84%.) **Average high school grade point average:** 3.2. **First-year students who submitted SAT scores:** 57%. Scores (25/75 percentile): Critical Reading: 360-450, Math: 410-490, Combined: 770-940. **First-year students submitting ACT scores:** 41%. Scores (25/75 percentile): English: 16-22, Math: 14-21, Composite: 24-27.

ACADEMICS

Year founded: 1962. **Academic calendar:** Semester. **Degrees offered:** bachelor's, master's. **Major fields of study:** biological and biomedical sciences; business, management, marketing, and related support services; computer and information sciences and support services; education; English language and literature/letters; history; liberal arts and sciences studies, and humanities; mathematics and statistics; psychology; public administration and social service professions; security and protective services; social sci-

ences. **Areas of required coursework:** arts/fine arts, humanities, computer literacy, mathematics, English (including composition), sciences (biological or physical), history, social science, other. **Special academic programs (% participation):** distance learning (31%), double major (1%), dual enrollment (2%), internships (35%), teacher certificate program (32%). **Teacher certification offered in:** early childhood, special education, elementary, middle/junior high, secondary, bilingual/bicultural. **Cooperative education programs:** other. **Faculty and instruction (2009-2010):** Total instructional faculty: 17 full-time, 33 part-time (40% men; 60% women; 12% minorities). Full-time faculty with Ph.D. or other terminal degree: 65%. Student/faculty ratio: 10/1. Classes of fewer than 20 students: 88%; of 20 to 49 students: 12%; of 50 or more students: 0%. **Advanced Placement and International Baccalaureate credit:** AP tests may be used for: Credit only. Scores accepted: 3, 4, 5. International Baccalaureate exams may be used for: Credit only. **Freshmen returning for sophomore year:** 77%. **Graduation rates:** Six-year: 45%.

COSTS AND FINANCIAL AID

Financial aid office: (505) 392-6561. **Expenses (2010-2011):** Tuition and fees 2010-2011: $13,633; room/board: $6,530. Estimated books and supplies: $1,200; transportation: $1,500; personal expenses: $1,000. **Financial aid:** Priority filing date for institution's financial aid form: April 1. In 2009-2010, 98% of undergraduates applied for financial aid. Of those, 86% were determined to have financial need; 12% had their need fully met. Average financial aid package (proportion receiving): $3,877 (86%). Average amount of gift aid, such as scholarships or grants (proportion receiving): $2,534 (57%). Average amount of self-help aid, such as work study or loans (proportion receiving): $1,725 (54%). Average need-based loan (excluding PLUS or other private loans): $1,585. Among students who received need-based aid, the average percentage of need met: 70%. Among students who received aid based on merit, the average award (and the proportion receiving): $1,240 (6%). The average athletic scholarship (and the proportion receiving): $1,807 (54%). Average amount of debt of borrowers graduating in 2009: $22,200. Proportion who borrowed: 86%.

CAMPUS LIFE AND EXTRACURRICULAR ACTIVITIES

Campus housing available (% using): coed dorms (15%), women's dorms (29%), apartment for single students (25%), special housing for disabled students. Students who live in college-owned, operated, or affiliated housing: 44%. **Student employment:** During the 2009-2010 academic year, 21% of undergraduates worked on campus. Average per-year earnings: $1,482. **Clubs and organizations:** Number of student organizations: 7. Activities include: campus ministries, drama/theater, literary magazine, student government. Number of fraternities: 0; sororities: 0. Average proportion of students who stay on campus on weekends: 56%. **Sports program (2009-2010):** Member of NAIA. *Men's intercollegiate varsity sports:* baseball, basketball, cross country, golf, soccer, tennis, track and field (outdoor). *Women's intercollegiate varsity sports:* basketball, cross country, golf, soccer, softball, tennis, track and field (outdoor).

SERVICES AND FACILITIES

Basic services: placement service. **Remedial assistance:** math, writing, study skills, other. **Counseling services:** personal, academic, psychological. **For learning-disabled students:** School does not offer a structured program with separate admission and additional fees. Total undergraduates in learning-disabled program or receiving services: 5. Services include: remedial math, remedial English, tape recorders, diagnostic testing service, untimed tests, note-taking services, oral tests, learning center, readers, extended time for tests, tutors, priority seating, texts on tape, other testing accommodations. **Library:** Number of titles: 54,485; number of current serial subscriptions: 198. **Information technology resources:** Students are not required to lease or own a computer. Number of campus computers available to all students: 80. School has a wireless network. Approximate number of users that can be accommodated: 70. Proportion of college-owned housing units wired for high-speed internet access: 100%. **Campus safety:** Security services offered: late-night transport/escort service, lighted pathways/sidewalks, controlled dormitory access (key, security card, etc.).

TRANSFER AND INTERNATIONAL STUDENTS

Transfer students: May apply for admission for the following academic terms: Fall, Winter, Spring, Summer. Applicants need a minimum number of credits to apply. **International students:** Number of foreign undergraduates: 7 (3% of student body). Number of countries represented: 7. Minimum TOEFL score required: 550 (paper); 213 (computer). Average TOEFL score: 550 (paper).

Western New Mexico University

- **Address:** Box 680, Silver City, NM 88062
- **Website:** http://www.wnmu.edu
- **Public**
- **Enrollment:** 1,586 full-time; 1,162 part-time

....

KEY STATS

✔ **U.S News College Ranking:** Unranked, Regional Universities (West)

✔ **SAT or ACT Score (25th/75th percentile):** N/A

✔ **Tuition:** 2009-2010: $3,589 in state, $12,825 out of state

Selectivity: N/A	Room/board: $7,750
Acceptance rate: 100%	Average debt: $5,500
Student/faculty ratio: 15/1	Proportion who borrowed: 40%

UNDERGRADUATE STUDENT BODY STATS

2009-2010 enrollment: 1,586 full-time; 1,162 part-time. Men: 40%; women: 60%. **Ethnic makeup:** African American: 4%; American-Indian: 2%; Asian American: 2%; Hispanic: 51%; White: 39%; International: 2%.

ADMISSIONS FACTS AND FIGURES

Phone: (575) 538-6106. **Email:** admissions@wnmu.edu. **Website:** http://www.wnmu.edu. **Application deadlines for fall 2011:** Regular decision: August 1. Early decision: Not offered. Early action: Not offered. Admission cannot be deferred. **Application fee:** None. **To apply online, go to:** http://www.wnmu.edu/onlineapps.htm. **Admissions requirements/recommendations:** High school units required (recommended): English: 0 (4); Mathematics: 0 (3); Science: 0 (2); Foreign language: 0 (0); Social studies: 0 (2); History: 0 (1); Academic electives: 0 (0); Total units: 0 (12). Tests: The college does not use SAT or ACT scores in admissions decisions. Neither SAT nor ACT required. For admission to the fall 2011 entering class, the school will accept: ACT with or without writing accepted. Campus visit: Recommended. Admissions interview: Neither required nor recommended. Off-campus interview: May be arranged. **Factors that count in admissions decisions:** *Academic:* Secondary school record: Not Considered. Class rank: Not Considered. Letters of recommendation: Not Considered. Standardized test scores: Considered. Essay: Not Considered. *Nonacademic:* Interview: Not Considered. Extracurricular activities: Not Considered. Talent/ability: Not Considered. Character/personal qualities: Not Considered. Alumni/ae relationship: Not Considered. Geographical residence: Not Considered. State residency: Not Considered. Religious affiliation/commitment: Not Considered. Minority status: Not Considered. Volunteer work: Not Considered. Work experience: Not Considered. **Other schools with the greatest overlap in applicants:** New Mexico State University; University of New Mexico. **Admissions statistics for the fall 2009 entering class:** Total applicants: 1,108. Total accepted: 1,108. Freshmen enrolled: 466; 14% were from out of state. Overall acceptance rate: 100%. **Size of waiting list:** 0 applicants; enrolled from waiting list: 0.

ACADEMICS

Year founded: 1893. **Academic calendar:** Semester. **Degrees offered:** certificate, associate, bachelor's, post-bachelor's certificate, master's. **Most popular majors:** 12% criminal justice/safety studies, 10% operations management and supervision, 9% business administration and management, 8% elementary education and teaching, 6% general studies. **Major fields of study:** biological and biomedical sciences; business, management, marketing, and related support services; computer and information sciences and support services; education; English language and literature/letters; foreign languages, literatures, and linguistics; health professions and related clinical sciences; history; liberal arts and sciences studies, and humanities; mathematics and statistics; natural resources and conservation; parks, recreation, leisure, and fitness studies; physical sciences; psychology; public administration and social service professions; security and protective services; social sciences; visual and performing arts. **Areas of required coursework:** arts/fine arts, humanities, computer literacy, mathematics, English (including composition), foreign languages, sciences (biological or physical), history, social science. **Pre-professional programs:** pre-law, pre-dentistry, pre-medicine, pre-pharmacy. **Special academic programs (% participation):** cooperative (work-study plan) program (10%), distance learning (90%), double major (9%), dual enrollment (6%), honors program (6%), independent study (41%), internships (28%), teacher certificate program. **Teacher certification offered in:** early childhood, special education, elementary, vo-tech, secondary, bilingual/bicultural. **Cooperative education programs:** art, business, computer science, education, social/behavioral science, technologies, vocational arts. **Faculty and instruction (2009-2010):** Total instructional faculty: 104 full-time, 128 part-time (45% men; 55% women; 21% minorities). Full-time faculty with Ph.D. or other terminal degree: 84%. Student/faculty ratio: 15/1. Classes of fewer than 20 students: 75%; of 20 to 49 students: 25%; of 50 or more students: 1%. **Advanced Placement and International Baccalaureate credit:** AP tests may be used for: Placement only. Scores accepted: 4, 5. **Freshmen returning for sophomore year:** 48%. **Graduation rates:** Six-year: 21%. **Graduate study:** 3% of students pursue further study immediately upon graduation; 6% within one year; 11% within five years. Fields in which graduates pursue further study: Master of Business Administration (MBA), 9%; education, 51%; arts and sciences, 40%.

COSTS AND FINANCIAL AID

Financial aid office: (575) 538-6173. **Expenses (2009-2010):** Tuition and fees 2009-2010: $3,589 in state, $12,825 out of state; room/board: $7,750. Estimated books and supplies: $1,000; transportation: $1,768; personal expenses: $2,102. **Financial aid:** Priority filing date for institution's financial aid form: April 1. In 2009-2010, 89% of undergraduates applied for financial aid. Of those, 76% were determined to have financial need; 11% had their need fully met. Average financial aid package (proportion receiving): $8,662 (76%). Average amount of gift aid, such as scholarships or grants (proportion receiving): $4,412 (67%). Average amount of self-help aid, such as work study or loans (proportion receiving): $3,848 (49%). Average need-based loan (excluding PLUS or other private loans): $3,863. Among students who received need-based aid, the average percentage of need met: 75%. Among students who received aid based on merit, the average award (and the proportion receiving): $4,019 (5%). The average athletic scholarship (and the proportion receiving): $2,800 (5%). Average amount of debt of borrowers graduating in 2009: $5,500. Proportion who borrowed: 40%.

CAMPUS LIFE AND EXTRACURRICULAR ACTIVITIES

Campus housing available: coed dorms, women's dorms, men's dorms, apartments for married students, apartment for single students. Students who live in college-owned, operated, or affiliated housing: 10%. **Student employment:** During the 2009-2010 academic year, 3% of undergraduates worked on campus. Average per-year earnings: $2,500. **Clubs and organizations:** Number of student organizations: 27. Activities include: marching band, student government, student newspaper, student film society. Number of fraternities: 1; sororities: 1. Proportion of men in fraternities: 3%; of women in sororities: 2%. Average proportion of students who stay on campus on weekends: 25%. **Sports program (2009-2010):** Member of NCAA II. *Men's intercollegiate varsity sports:* basketball, cross country, football, golf, tennis. *Women's intercollegiate varsity sports:* basketball, cross country, golf, softball, tennis, volleyball.

SERVICES AND FACILITIES

Basic services: nonremedial tutoring, placement service, day care, health service, health insurance. **Remedial assistance:** reading, math, writing. **Counseling services:** career, personal, academic, birth control. **For learning-disabled students:** School does not offer a structured program with separate admission and additional fees. Total undergraduates in learning-disabled program or receiving services: 4. Services include: remedial math, remedial English, remedial reading, tape recorders, note-taking services, oral tests, learning center, readers, extended time for tests, tutors, texts on tape. **Library:** Number of titles: 142,262; number of current serial subscriptions: 630. **Information technology resources:** Students are not required to lease or own a computer. Number of campus computers available to all students: 1,200. School has a wireless network. Approximate number of users that can be accommodated: 200. Proportion of college-owned housing units wired for high-speed internet access: 100%. **Campus safety:** Security services offered: 24-hour emergency telephones, lighted pathways/sidewalks, controlled dormitory access (key, security card, etc).

TRANSFER AND INTERNATIONAL STUDENTS

Transfer students: May apply for admission for the following academic terms: Fall, Spring, Summer. Applicants do not need a minimum number of credits to apply. For fall 2009: Transfer applications received: 394. Transfer applicants offered admission: 394. Transfer applicants enrolled: 159. **International students:** Number of foreign undergraduates: 41 (2% of student body). Number of countries represented: 16. Minimum TOEFL score required: 550 (paper); 79 (computer).

New York

Adelphi University

- **Address:** 1 South Avenue, Garden City, NY 11530
- **Website:** http://www.adelphi.edu
- **Private**
- **Enrollment:** 4,300 full-time; 654 part-time

KEY STATS

✔ **U.S News College Ranking:** 159, National Universities
✔ **SAT Score (25th/75th percentile):** 980-1180
✔ **Tuition:** 2010-2011: $27,400

Selectivity: Selective	**Room/board:** $11,000
Acceptance rate: 70%	**Average debt:** $28,307
Student/faculty ratio: 9/1	**Proportion who borrowed:** 69%

UNDERGRADUATE STUDENT BODY STATS

2009-2010 enrollment: 4,300 full-time; 654 part-time. Men: 29%; women: 71%. **Ethnic makeup:** African American: 11%; Asian American: 6%; Hispanic: 7%; White: 72%; International: 3%. **Religious preference:** Roman Catholic: 47%; Protestant: 25%; Jewish: 6%; Muslim: 1%; Hindu: 2%; Buddhist: 1%; No preference: 14%; Other: 4%.

ADMISSIONS FACTS AND FIGURES

Phone: (800) 233-5744. **Email:** admissions@adelphi.edu. **Website:** http://www.adelphi.edu. **Application deadlines for fall 2011:** Regular decision: Rolling. Early decision: Not offered. Early action: Send application by: December 1; Decision sent by: December 31. Admission can be deferred. **Application fee:** $35. **To apply online, go to:** http://www.adelphi.edu/prepare/admis. **Admissions requirements/recommendations:** High school units required (recommended): English: 4 (4); Mathematics: 3 (3); Science: 3 (3); Foreign language: 2 (2); Total units: 16 (16). Tests: The college uses SAT or ACT scores in admissions decisions. Neither SAT nor ACT required. For admission to the fall 2011 entering class, the school will accept: ACT with writing required. Campus visit: Recommended. Admissions interview: Recommended. Off-campus interview: Not available. **Factors that count in admissions decisions:** *Academic:* Secondary school record: Very Important. Class rank: Important. Letters of recommendation: Considered. Standardized test scores: Important. Essay: Important. *Nonacademic:* Interview: Considered. Extracurricular activities: Important. Talent/ability: Important. Character/personal qualities: Important. Alumni/ae relationship: Considered. Geographical residence: Not Considered. State residency: Not Considered. Religious affiliation/commitment: Not Considered. Minority status: Not Considered. Volunteer work: Important. Work experience: Considered. **Other schools with the greatest overlap in applicants:** Fordham University; Hofstra University; Long Island University–C.W. Post Campus; SUNY–Stony Brook; St. John's University. **Admissions statistics for the fall 2009 entering class:** Total applicants: 7,359. Total accepted: 5,125. Freshmen enrolled: 1,005; 11% were from out of state. Accepted through early-decision or early-action plans: 33%. Overall acceptance rate: 70%. Non-early acceptance rate: 65%. **Credentials of fall 2009 freshmen:** 24% ranked in the top 10 percent of their high school class; 60% were in the top 25 percent; 87% were in the top half. (Proportion submitting class standing: 40%.) **Average high school grade point average:** 3.4. **First-year students who submitted SAT scores:** 76%. Scores (25/75 percentile): Critical Reading: 480-580, Math: 500-600, Combined: 980-1180. **First-year students submitting ACT scores:** 15%. Scores (25/75 percentile): English: 20-26, Math: 20-26, Composite: 20-26.

ACADEMICS

Year founded: 1896. **Academic calendar:** Semester. **Degrees offered:** associate, bachelor's, post-bachelor's certificate, master's, post-master's certificate, doctorate. **Most popular majors:** 31% nursing/registered nurse training (R.N., A.S.N., B.S.N., M.S.N.), 13% business, management, marketing, and related support services, 11% social sciences, 7% psychology, 7% visual and performing arts. **Major fields of study:** area, ethnic, cultural, and gender studies; biological and biomedical sciences; business, management, market-ing, and related support services; communication, journalism, and related programs; computer and information sciences and support services; education; English language and literature/letters; foreign languages, literatures, and linguistics; health professions and related clinical sciences; history; liberal arts and sciences studies, and humanities; mathematics and statistics; multi/interdisciplinary studies; natural resources and conservation; philosophy and religious studies; physical sciences; psychology; public administration and social service professions; security and protective services; social sciences; visual and performing arts. **Areas of required coursework:** arts/fine arts, humanities, mathematics, English (including composition), sciences (biological or physical), social science, other. **Pre-professional programs:** pre-law, pre-dentistry, pre-medicine, pre-veterinary science, pre-optometry, other. **Special academic programs (% participation):** accelerated program (15%), cross-registration, distance learning, double major (2%), dual enrollment, English as a Second Language (ESL), honors program (5.6%), independent study (4.1%), internships (25%), liberal arts/career combination, student-designed major, study abroad (5%), teacher certificate program (13%), weekend college, other. **Teacher certification offered in:** early childhood, special education, elementary, middle/junior high, secondary, bilingual/bicultural. **Reserve Officers Training Corps (ROTC):** Army ROTC: Offered at cooperating institution (Hofstra University); Air Force ROTC: Offered at cooperating institution (New York Institute of Technology). **Faculty and instruction (2009-2010):** Total instructional faculty: 308 full-time, 585 part-time (38% men; 62% women; 18% minorities). Full-time faculty with Ph.D. or other terminal degree: 87%. Student/faculty ratio: 9/1. Classes of fewer than 20 students: 46%; of 20 to 49 students: 53%; of 50 or more students: 1%. **Advanced Placement and International Baccalaureate credit:** AP tests may be used for: Placement only. Scores accepted: 3, 4, 5. International Baccalaureate exams may be used for: Credit only. **Freshmen returning for sophomore year:** 79%. **Graduation rates:** Four-year: 52%; five-year: 60%; six-year: 62%. **Graduate study:** 41% of students pursue further study immediately upon graduation.

COSTS AND FINANCIAL AID

Financial aid office: (516) 877-3365. **Expenses (2010-2011):** Tuition and fees 2010-2011: $27,400; room/board: $11,000. Estimated books and supplies: $1,000; transportation: $1,100; personal expenses: $1,200. **Financial aid:** Priority filing date for institution's financial aid form: March 1. In 2009-2010, 80% of undergraduates applied for financial aid. Of those, 69% were determined to have financial need; 2% had their need fully met. Average financial aid package (proportion receiving): $17,850 (61%). Average amount of gift aid, such as scholarships or grants (proportion receiving): $6,469 (45%). Average amount of self-help aid, such as work study or loans (proportion receiving): $5,533 (54%). Average need-based loan (excluding PLUS or other private loans): $4,509. Among students who received need-based aid, the average percentage of need met: 38%. Among students who received aid based on merit, the average award (and the proportion receiving): $8,353 (64%). The average athletic scholarship (and the proportion receiving): $11,400 (2%). Average amount of debt of borrowers graduating in 2009: $28,307. Proportion who borrowed: 69%.

CAMPUS LIFE AND EXTRACURRICULAR ACTIVITIES

Campus housing available (% using): coed dorms (79%), special housing for disabled students (2%), other housing options (14%). Students who live in college-owned, operated, or affiliated housing: 23%. **Student employment:** During the 2009-2010 academic year, 19% of undergraduates worked on campus. Average per-year earnings: $2,156. **Clubs and organizations:** Number of student organizations: 80. Activities include: campus ministries, choral groups, concert band, dance, drama/theater, international student organization, jazz band, literary magazine, model UN, music ensembles, musical theater, opera, radio station, student government, student newspaper, student film society, symphony orchestra, yearbook. Number of fraternities: 2; sororities: 5. Proportion of men in fraternities: 8%; of women in sororities: 11%. Average proportion of students who stay on campus on weekends: 45%. **Sports program (2009-2010):** Member of NCAA II. *Men's intercollegiate varsity sports:* baseball, basketball, cross country, golf, lacrosse, soccer, swimming, tennis, track and field (outdoor). *Women's intercollegiate varsity sports:* basketball, bowling, cross country, field hockey, lacrosse, soccer, softball, swimming, tennis, track and field (outdoor), volleyball.

SERVICES AND FACILITIES

Basic services: nonremedial tutoring, placement service, day care, health service, other. **Remedial assistance:** reading, math, writing, study skills, other. **Counseling services:** minority student, career, personal, veteran student, academic, older student, psychological, birth control, religious. **For learning-disabled students:** School does not offer a structured program with separate admission and additional fees. Total undergraduates in learning-disabled program or receiving services: 134. Services include: remedial English, reading machines, tape recorders, note-taking services, oral tests, learning center, readers, extended time for tests, tutors, priority registration, texts on tape, typist/scribe, exams on tape or computer, other testing accommodations, waiver of foreign language degree requirement, other. **Library:** Number of titles: 593,920; number of current serial subscriptions: 31,688. **Information technology resources:** Students are not required to lease or own a computer. Number of campus computers available to all students: 772. School has a wireless network. Approximate number of users that can be accommodated: 2,000. Proportion of college-owned housing units wired for high-speed internet access: 100%. **Campus safety:** Security services offered: 24-hour foot-and-vehicle patrols, late-night transport/escort service, 24-hour emergency telephones, lighted pathways/sidewalks, student patrols, controlled dormitory access (key, security card, etc).

TRANSFER AND INTERNATIONAL STUDENTS

Transfer students: May apply for admission for the following academic terms: Fall, Spring. Applicants do not need a minimum number of credits to apply. For fall 2009: Transfer applications received: 2,219. Transfer applicants offered admission: 934. Transfer applicants enrolled: 511. **International students:** Number of foreign undergraduates: 136 (3% of student body). Number of countries represented: 49. Minimum TOEFL score required: 550 (paper); 80 (computer). Average TOEFL score: 626 (paper).

Alfred University

- **Address:** 1 Saxon Drive, Alfred, NY 14802-1205
- **Website:** http://www.alfred.edu
- **Private**
- **Enrollment:** N/A

KEY STATS
✔ **U.S News College Ranking:** 20, Regional Universities (North)
✔ **ACT Score (25th/75th percentile):** 21-26
✔ **Tuition:** 2010-2011: $25,976

Selectivity: Selective	Room/board: $11,364
Acceptance rate: 76%	Average debt: $26,750
Student/faculty ratio: N/A	Proportion who borrowed: 83%

Bard College

- **Address:** PO Box 5000, Annandale on Hudson, NY 12504
- **Website:** http://www.bard.edu
- **Private**
- **Enrollment:** 1,866 full-time; 73 part-time

KEY STATS
✔ **U.S News College Ranking:** 38, National Liberal Arts Colleges
✔ **SAT Score (25th/75th percentile):** 1330-1420
✔ **Tuition:** 2010-2011: $41,670

Selectivity: Most selective	Room/board: $11,810
Acceptance rate: 33%	Average debt: $26,131
Student/faculty ratio: 10/1	Proportion who borrowed: 52%

UNDERGRADUATE STUDENT BODY STATS
2009-2010 enrollment: 1,866 full-time; 73 part-time. Men: 43%; women: 57%. **Ethnic makeup:** African American: 2%; American-Indian: 1%; Asian American: 3%; Hispanic: 3%; White: 80%; International: 12%.

ADMISSIONS FACTS AND FIGURES

Phone: (845) 758-7472. **Email:** admission@bard.edu. **Website:** http://www.bard.edu. **Application deadlines for fall 2011:** Regular decision: January 15; decision sent by April 1. Early decision: Not offered. Early action: Send application by: November 1; Decision sent by: January 1. Admission can be deferred. **Application fee:** $50. **To apply online, go to:** http://www.bard.edu/admission/applying/. **Admissions requirements/recommendations:** High school units required (recommended): English: (4); Mathematics: (4); Science: (4); Foreign language: (4); Social studies: (4); History: (4); Total units: (24). Tests: The college uses SAT or ACT scores in admissions decisions. Neither SAT nor ACT required. For admission to the fall 2011 entering class, the school will accept: ACT with or without writing accepted. Campus visit: Recommended. Admissions interview: Neither required nor recommended. Off-campus interview: May be arranged. **Factors that count in admissions decisions:** *Academic:* Secondary school record: Very Important. Class rank: Considered. Letters of recommendation: Very Important. Standardized test scores: Considered. Essay: Very Important. *Nonacademic:* Interview: Considered. Extracurricular activities: Very Important. Talent/ability: Very Important. Character/personal qualities: Very Important. Alumni/ae relationship: Considered. Geographical residence: Considered. State residency: Considered. Religious affiliation/commitment: Considered. Minority status: Considered. Volunteer work: Important. Work experience: Important. **Other schools with the greatest overlap in applicants:** New York University; Oberlin College; Reed College; Vassar College; Wesleyan University. **Admissions statistics for the fall 2009 entering class:** Total applicants: 5,510. Total accepted: 1,826. Freshmen enrolled: 505; 70% were from out of state. Overall acceptance rate: 33%. Non-early acceptance rate: 33%. **Size of waiting list:** 565 applicants; enrolled from waiting list: 10. **Credentials of fall 2009 freshmen:** 64% ranked in the top 10 percent of their high school class; 95% were in the top 25 percent; 100% were in the top half. (Proportion submitting class standing: 41%.) **Average high school grade point average:** 3.5. **First-year students who submitted SAT scores:** 52%. Scores (25/75 percentile): Critical Reading: 680-740, Math: 650-680, Combined: 1330-1420.

ACADEMICS

Year founded: 1860. **Academic calendar:** Semester. **Degrees offered:** associate, bachelor's, master's, doctorate. **Most popular majors:** 32% visual and performing arts, 15% English language and literature/letters, 15% social sciences, 9% history, 8% foreign languages, literatures, and linguistics. **Major fields of study:** English language and literature/letters; liberal arts and sciences studies, and humanities; multi/interdisciplinary studies; social sciences; visual and performing arts. **Areas of required coursework:** arts/fine arts, humanities, mathematics, English (including composition), sciences (biological or physical), history, social science, other. **Pre-professional programs:** pre-law, pre-medicine. **Special academic programs (% participation):** cross-registration (1%), double major (4%), dual enrollment, independent study (10%), internships (10%), student-designed major (1%), study abroad (42%). **Teacher certification offered in:** secondary. **Faculty and instruction (2009-2010):** Total instructional faculty: 145 full-time, 92 part-time (52% men; 48% women; 15% minorities). Full-time faculty with Ph.D. or other terminal degree: 96%. Student/faculty ratio: 10/1. Classes of fewer than 20 students: 77%; of 20 to 49 students: 23%. **Advanced Placement and International Baccalaureate credit:** AP tests may be used for: Credit only. Scores accepted: 5. International Baccalaureate exams may be used for: Credit only. **Freshmen returning for sophomore year:** 86%. **Graduation rates:** Four-year: 71%; five-year: 77%; six-year: 79%.

COSTS AND FINANCIAL AID

Financial aid office: (845) 758-7525. **Expenses (2010-2011):** Tuition and fees 2010-2011: $41,670; room/board: $11,810. Estimated books and supplies: $850; transportation: $750; personal expenses: $700. **Financial aid:** Priority filing date for institution's financial aid form: February 1; deadline: February 15. In 2009-2010, 68% of undergraduates applied for financial aid. Of those, 62% were determined to have financial need; 51% had their need fully met. Average financial aid package (proportion receiving): $34,643 (62%). Average amount of gift aid, such as scholarships or grants (proportion receiving): $28,319 (56%). Average amount of self-help aid, such as work study or loans (proportion receiving): $5,931 (48%). Average need-based loan (excluding PLUS or other private loans): $4,501. Among students who received need-based aid, the average percentage of need met: 92%. Among students who received aid based on merit, the average award (and the proportion receiving): $13,098 (2%). The average athletic scholarship (and the proportion receiving): $0 (0%). Average amount of debt of borrowers graduating in 2009: $26,131. Proportion who borrowed: 52%.

CAMPUS LIFE AND EXTRACURRICULAR ACTIVITIES

Campus housing available (% using): coed dorms (97%), women's dorms (1%), apartment for single students (1%), cooperative housing (1%). Students who live in college-owned, operated, or affiliated housing: 64%. **Student employment:** During the 2009-2010 academic year, 30% of undergraduates worked on campus. Average per-year earnings: $2,000. **Clubs and organizations:** Number of student organizations: 127. Activities include: campus ministries, choral groups, concert band, dance, drama/theater, international student organization, jazz band, literary magazine, model UN, music ensembles, musical theater, opera, radio station, student government, student newspaper, student film society, symphony orchestra. Number of fraternities: 0; sororities: 0. Average proportion of students who stay on campus on weekends: 80%. **Sports program (2009-2010):** Member of NCAA III. *Men's intercollegiate varsity sports:* basketball, cross country, soccer, tennis, track and field (outdoor), volleyball. *Women's intercollegiate varsity sports:* basketball, cross country, soccer, tennis, track and field (outdoor), volleyball.

SERVICES AND FACILITIES

Basic services: nonremedial tutoring, placement service, health service, health insurance. **Remedial assistance:** math, writing, study skills. **Counseling services:** minority student, career, personal, academic, older student, psychological, birth control, religious. **For learning-disabled students:** School does not offer a structured program with separate admission and additional fees. Total undergraduates in learning-disabled program or receiving services: 67. Services include: reading machines, tape recorders, note-taking services, oral tests, learning center, extended time for tests, tutors, texts on tape, exams on tape or computer, other testing accommodations. **Library:** Number of titles: 351,163; number of current serial subscriptions: 32,413. **Information technology resources:** Students are not required to lease or own a computer. Number of campus computers available to all students: 425. School has a wireless network. Approximate number of users that can be accommodated: 500. Proportion of college-owned housing units wired for high-speed internet access: 10%. **Campus safety:** Security services offered: 24-hour foot-and-vehicle patrols, late-night transport/escort service, 24-hour emergency telephones, lighted pathways/sidewalks, student patrols, controlled dormitory access (key, security card, etc).

TRANSFER AND INTERNATIONAL STUDENTS

Transfer students: May apply for admission for the following academic terms: Fall, Spring. Applicants need a minimum number of credits to apply. For fall 2009: Transfer applications received: 239. Transfer applicants offered admission: 132. Transfer applicants enrolled: 79. **International students:** Number of foreign undergraduates: 224 (12% of student body). Number of countries represented: 52. Minimum TOEFL score required: 600 (paper); 100 (computer). Average TOEFL score: 620 (paper).

Barnard College

- **Address:** 3009 Broadway, New York, NY 10027
- **Website:** http://www.barnard.edu
- **Private**
- **Enrollment:** 2,356 full-time; 61 part-time

KEY STATS

- ✔ **U.S News College Ranking:** 26, National Liberal Arts Colleges
- ✔ **SAT Score (25th/75th percentile):** 1250-1440
- ✔ **Tuition:** 2010-2011: $40,546

Selectivity: Most selective	**Room/board:** $12,950
Acceptance rate: 31%	**Average debt:** $14,706
Student/faculty ratio: 9/1	**Proportion who borrowed:** 44%

UNDERGRADUATE STUDENT BODY STATS

2009-2010 enrollment: 2,356 full-time; 61 part-time. Men: 0%; women: 100%. **Ethnic makeup:** African American: 4%; Asian American: 16%; Hispanic: 9%; White: 66%; International: 5%. **Religious preference:** Roman Catholic: 16%; Jewish: 30%; Muslim: 2%; Hindu: 2%; Buddhist: 3%; No preference: 20%; Other: 27%.

ADMISSIONS FACTS AND FIGURES

Phone: (212) 854-2014. **Email:** admissions@barnard.edu. **Website:** http://www.barnard.edu. **Application deadlines for fall 2011:** Regular decision: January 1; decision sent by April 1. Early decision: Send application by:

November 15; Decision sent by: December 15. Early action: Not offered. Admission can be deferred. **Application fee:** $55. **To apply online, go to:** http://www.barnard.edu/admiss/applying/. **Admissions requirements/recommendations:** High school units required (recommended): English: 4 (4); Mathematics: 3 (3); Science: 3 (3); Foreign language: 3 (3); History: 3 (3); Total units: 16 (16). Tests: The college uses SAT or ACT scores in admissions decisions. Either SAT or ACT required. For admission to the fall 2011 entering class, the school will accept: ACT with writing required. Campus visit: Recommended. Admissions interview: Recommended. Off-campus interview: May be arranged. **Factors that count in admissions decisions:** *Academic:* Secondary school record: Very Important. Class rank: Important. Letters of recommendation: Very Important. Standardized test scores: Important. Essay: Very Important. *Nonacademic:* Interview: Considered. Extracurricular activities: Very Important. Talent/ability: Important. Character/personal qualities: Very Important. Alumni/ae relationship: Considered. Geographical residence: Considered. State residency: Not Considered. Religious affiliation/commitment: Not Considered. Minority status: Considered. Volunteer work: Important. Work experience: Considered. **Other schools with the greatest overlap in applicants:** Brown University; Columbia University; New York University; Princeton University; Wellesley College. **Admissions statistics for the fall 2009 entering class:** Total applicants: 4,174. Total accepted: 1,295. Freshmen enrolled: 577; 67% were from out of state. Accepted through early-decision or early-action plans: 32%. Overall acceptance rate: 31%. Early-decision acceptance rate: 52%. Non-early acceptance rate: 29%. **Size of waiting list:** 784 applicants; enrolled from waiting list: 54. **Credentials of fall 2009 freshmen:** 75% ranked in the top 10 percent of their high school class; 93% were in the top 25 percent; 98% were in the top half. (Proportion submitting class standing: 35%.) **Average high school grade point average:** 3.8. **First-year students who submitted SAT scores:** 83%. Scores (25/75 percentile): Critical Reading: 630-730, Math: 620-710, Combined: 1250-1440. **First-year students submitting ACT scores:** 33%. Scores (25/75 percentile): English: N/A, Math: N/A, Composite: 28-32.

ACADEMICS

Year founded: 1889. **Academic calendar:** Semester. **Degrees offered:** bachelor's. **Most popular majors:** 29% social sciences, 13% visual and performing arts, 12% English language and literature/letters, 10% area, ethnic, cultural, and gender studies, 8% biological and biomedical sciences. **Major fields of study:** architecture and related services; area, ethnic, cultural, and gender studies; biological and biomedical sciences; computer and information sciences and support services; engineering; English language and literature/letters; foreign languages, literatures, and linguistics; history; mathematics and statistics; multi/interdisciplinary studies; natural resources and conservation; philosophy and religious studies; physical sciences; psychology; social sciences; visual and performing arts. **Areas of required coursework:** arts/fine arts, humanities, mathematics, English (including composition), philosophy, foreign languages, sciences (biological or physical), history, social science, other. **Pre-professional programs:** pre-law, pre-medicine, other. **Special academic programs:** accelerated program, cross-registration, double major, dual enrollment, exchange student program (domestic), honors program, independent study, internships, liberal arts/career combination, student-designed major, study abroad, teacher certificate program. **Teacher certification offered in:** early childhood, elementary, middle/junior high, secondary. **Faculty and instruction (2009-2010):** Total instructional faculty: 208 full-time, 141 part-time (35% men; 65% women; 14% minorities). Full-time faculty with Ph.D. or other terminal degree: 94%. Student/faculty ratio: 9/1. Classes of fewer than 20 students: 71%; of 20 to 49 students: 22%; of 50 or more students: 7%. **Advanced Placement and International Baccalaureate credit:** AP tests may be used for: Placement only. Scores accepted: 4, 5. International Baccalaureate exams may be used for: Placement only. **Freshmen returning for sophomore year:** 95%. **Graduation rates:** Four-year: 83%; five-year: 90%; six-year: 91%. **Graduate study:** 21% of students pursue further study immediately upon graduation. Fields in which graduates pursue further study: Master of Business Administration (MBA), 1%; law, 4%; medicine, 3%; education, 4%; arts and sciences, 6%.

COSTS AND FINANCIAL AID

Financial aid office: (212) 854-2154. **Expenses (2010-2011):** Tuition and fees 2010-2011: $40,546; room/board: $12,950. Estimated books and supplies: $1,146; transportation: $0; personal expenses: $1,407. **Financial aid:** In 2009-2010, 52% of undergraduates applied for financial aid. Of those, 44% were determined to have financial need; 100% had their need fully met. Average financial aid package (proportion receiving): $35,365 (44%). Average amount of gift aid, such as scholarships or grants (proportion receiving): $30,538 (42%). Average amount of self-help aid, such as work study or loans (proportion receiving): $5,838 (44%). Average need-based loan (excluding PLUS or other private loans): $4,692. Among students who received need-based aid, the average percentage of need met: 100%. Among students who received aid based on merit, the average award (and the proportion receiving): $0 (0%). The average athletic scholarship (and the proportion receiving): $0 (0%). Average amount of debt of borrowers graduating in 2009: $14,706. Proportion who borrowed: 44%.

CAMPUS LIFE AND EXTRACURRICULAR ACTIVITIES

Campus housing available: coed dorms, women's dorms, apartment for single students, special housing for disabled students. Students who live in college-owned, operated, or affiliated housing: 90%. **Student employment:** During the 2009-2010 academic year, 35% of undergraduates worked on campus. Average per-year earnings: $3,500. **Clubs and organizations:** Number of student organizations: 100. Activities include: campus ministries, choral groups, concert band, dance, drama/theater, jazz band, literary magazine, marching band, music ensembles, musical theater, opera, pep band, radio station, student government, student newspaper, student film society, symphony orchestra, television station, yearbook. Number of fraternities: 0; sororities: 0. Average proportion of students who stay on campus on weekends: 71%. **Sports program (2009-2010):** Member of NCAA I. *Women's intercollegiate varsity sports:* archery, basketball, crew (heavyweight), cross country, fencing, field hockey, golf, lacrosse, crew (lightweight), soccer, softball, swimming, tennis, track and field (indoor), track and field (outdoor), volleyball.

SERVICES AND FACILITIES

Basic services: nonremedial tutoring, women's center, health service, health insurance. **Counseling services:** career, personal, academic, psychological. **For learning-disabled students:** School does not offer a structured program with separate admission and additional fees. Services include: reading machines, tape recorders, diagnostic testing service, note-taking services, readers, extended time for tests, tutors, other. **Library:** Number of titles: 206,500; number of current serial subscriptions: 500. **Information technology resources:** Students are not required to lease or own a computer. Number of campus computers available to all students: 220. School has a wireless network. Approximate number of users that can be accommodated: 255. Proportion of college-owned housing units wired for high-speed internet access: 100%. **Campus safety:** Security services offered: 24-hour foot-and-vehicle patrols, late-night transport/escort service, 24-hour emergency telephones, lighted pathways/sidewalks, controlled dormitory access (key, security card, etc).

TRANSFER AND INTERNATIONAL STUDENTS

Transfer students: May apply for admission for the following academic terms: Fall, Spring. Applicants need a minimum number of credits to apply. **International students:** Number of foreign undergraduates: 111 (5% of student body). Number of countries represented: 30. Minimum TOEFL score required: 600 (paper); 250 (computer). Average TOEFL score: 620 (paper).

Binghamton University–SUNY

- **Address:** PO Box 6000, Binghamton, NY 13902-6000
- **Website:** http://www.binghamton.edu
- **Public**
- **Enrollment:** 11,279 full-time; 425 part-time

KEY STATS

✔ **U.S News College Ranking:** 86, National Universities
✔ **SAT Score (25th/75th percentile):** 1200-1380
✔ **Tuition:** 2010-2011: $6,815 in state, $14,715 out of state

Selectivity: More selective	**Room/board:** $11,246
Acceptance rate: 33%	**Average debt:** $14,560
Student/faculty ratio: 20/1	**Proportion who borrowed:** 49%

UNDERGRADUATE STUDENT BODY STATS

2009-2010 enrollment: 11,279 full-time; 425 part-time. Men: 53%; women: 47%. **Ethnic makeup:** African American: 5%; Asian American: 12%; Hispanic: 7%; White: 66%; International: 10%. **Religious preference:** Roman Catholic: 28%; Protestant: 18%; Jewish: 22%; Muslim: 1%; Hindu: 1%; Buddhist: 1%; No preference: 26%; Other: 3%.

ADMISSIONS FACTS AND FIGURES

Phone: (607) 777-2171. **Email:** admit@binghamton.edu. **Website:** http://www.binghamton.edu. **Application deadlines for fall 2011:** Regular decision: Rolling; decision sent by April 1. Early decision: Not offered. Early action: Send application by: November 15; Decision sent by: January 15. Admission can be deferred. **Application fee:** $50. **To apply online, go to:** http://www.suny.edu/student/. **Admissions requirements/recommendations:** High school units required (recommended): English: 4 (4); Mathematics: 3 (4); Science: 2 (4); Foreign language: 3 (4); Social studies: 2 (4); History: (4); Total units: 16. Tests: The college uses SAT or ACT scores in admissions decisions. Either SAT or ACT required. For admission to the fall 2011 entering class, the school will accept: ACT with writing required. Campus visit: Recommended. Admissions interview: Neither required nor recommended. Off-campus interview: Not available. **Factors that count in admissions decisions:** *Academic:* Secondary school record: Very Important. Class rank: Important. Letters of recommendation: Important. Standardized test scores: Very Important. Essay: Important. *Nonacademic:* Interview: Not Considered. Extracurricular activities: Important. Talent/ability: Considered. Character/personal qualities: Considered. Alumni/ae relationship: Considered. Geographical residence: Considered. State residency: Considered. Religious affiliation/commitment: Not Considered. Minority status: Considered. Volunteer work: Considered. Work experience: Considered. **Other schools with the greatest overlap in applicants:** Boston College; Boston University; Cornell University; New York University; Syracuse University. **Admissions statistics for the fall 2009 entering class:** Total applicants: 29,061. Total accepted: 9,692. Freshmen enrolled: 2,123; 17% were from out of state. Accepted through early-decision or early-action plans: 37%. Overall acceptance rate: 33%. Non-early acceptance rate: 30%. **Size of waiting list:** 1137 applicants; enrolled from waiting list: 45. **Credentials of fall 2009 freshmen:** 51% ranked in the top 10 percent of their high school class; 84% were in the top 25 percent; 97% were in the top half. (Proportion submitting class standing: 41%.) **Average high school grade point average:** 3.6. **First-year students who submitted SAT scores:** 93%. Scores (25/75 percentile): Critical Reading: 580-670, Math: 620-710, Combined: 1200-1380. **First-year students submitting ACT scores:** 30%. Scores (25/75 percentile): English: N/A, Math: N/A, Composite: 27-30.

ACADEMICS

Year founded: 1946. **Academic calendar:** Semester. **Degrees offered:** bachelor's, post-bachelor's certificate, master's, post-master's certificate, doctorate. **Most popular majors:** 14% business administration and management, 9% English language and literature, 9% engineering, 9% psychology, 8% biology/biological sciences. **Major fields of study:** architecture and related services; area, ethnic, cultural, and gender studies; biological and biomedical sciences; business, management, marketing, and related support services; computer and information sciences and support services; engineering; English language and literature/letters; foreign languages, literatures, and linguistics; health professions and related clinical sciences; history; liberal arts and sciences studies, and humanities; mathematics and statistics; multi/interdisciplinary studies; philosophy and religious studies; physical sciences; psychology; social sciences; visual and performing arts. **Areas of required coursework:** arts/fine arts, humanities, mathematics, English (including composition), foreign languages, sciences (biological or physical), history, social science, other. **Pre-professional programs:** pre-law, pre-dentistry, pre-medicine, pre-veterinary science, pre-optometry, pre-pharmacy, other. **Special academic programs (% participation):** accelerated program, cross-registration, distance learning, double major (7%), dual enrollment, English as a Second Language (ESL), exchange student program (domestic), honors program, independent study, internships (44%), liberal arts/career combination, student-designed major, study abroad (16%). **Reserve Officers Training Corps (ROTC):** Army ROTC: Offered at cooperating institution (Cornell University); Air Force ROTC: Offered at cooperating institution (Cornell University). **Faculty and instruction (2009-2010):** Total instructional faculty: 596 full-time, 275 part-time (57% men; 43% women; 20% minorities). Full-time faculty with Ph.D. or other terminal degree: 91%. Student/faculty ratio: 20/1. Classes of fewer than 20 students: 40%; of 20 to 49 students: 46%; of 50 or more students: 15%. **Advanced Placement and International Baccalaureate credit:** AP tests may be used for: Credit and/or placement. Scores accepted: 3, 4, 5. International Baccalaureate exams may be used for: Credit and/or placement. **Freshmen returning for sophomore year:** 90%. **Graduation rates:** Four-year: 70%; five-year: 80%; six-year: 81%. **Graduate study:** 42% of students pursue further study immediately upon graduation. Fields in which graduates pursue further study: Master of Business Administration (MBA), 19%; law, 6%; medicine, 17%; dentistry, 1%; engineering, 8%; education, 20%; arts and sciences, 28%.

COSTS AND FINANCIAL AID

Financial aid office: (607) 777-2428. **Expenses (2010-2011):** Tuition and fees 2010-2011: $6,815 in state, $14,715 out of state; room/board: $11,246. Estimated books and supplies: $1,000; transportation: $250; personal expenses: $750. **Financial aid:** Priority filing date for institution's financial aid form: February 1. In 2009-2010, 70% of undergraduates applied for financial aid. Of those, 46% were determined to have financial need; 22% had their need fully met. Average financial aid package (proportion receiving): $11,940 (46%). Average amount of gift aid, such as scholarships or grants (proportion receiving): $6,643 (40%). Average amount of self-help aid, such as work study or loans (proportion receiving): $5,943 (45%). Average need-based loan (excluding PLUS or other private loans): $5,358. Among students who received need-based aid, the average percentage of need met: 79%. Among students who received aid based on merit, the average award (and the proportion receiving): $4,311 (3%). The average athletic scholarship (and the proportion receiving): $9,938 (3%). Average amount of debt of borrowers graduating in 2009: $14,560. Proportion who borrowed: 49%.

CAMPUS LIFE AND EXTRACURRICULAR ACTIVITIES

Campus housing available (% using): coed dorms (74%), apartment for single students (16%), special housing for disabled students (1%). Students who live in college-owned, operated, or affiliated housing: 61%. **Student employment:** During the 2009-2010 academic year, 6% of undergraduates worked on campus. Average per-year earnings: $1,862. **Clubs and organizations:** Number of student organizations: 329. Activities include: campus ministries, choral groups, concert band, dance, drama/theater, international student organization, jazz band, literary magazine, model UN, music ensembles, musical theater, opera, pep band, radio station, student government, student newspaper, student film society, symphony orchestra, television station, yearbook. Number of fraternities: 26; sororities: 21. Proportion of men in fraternities: 10%; of women in sororities: 11%. Average proportion of students who stay on campus on weekends: 80%. **Sports program (2009-2010):** Member of NCAA I. *Men's intercollegiate varsity sports:* baseball, basketball, cross country, golf, lacrosse, soccer, swimming, tennis, track and field (indoor), track and field (outdoor), wrestling. *Women's intercollegiate varsity sports:* basketball, cross country, lacrosse, soccer, softball, swimming, tennis, track and field (indoor), track and field (outdoor), volleyball.

SERVICES AND FACILITIES

Basic services: nonremedial tutoring, women's center, placement service, day care, health service, health insurance, other. **Remedial assistance:** math, writing, study skills, other. **Counseling services:** minority student, career, military, personal, veteran student, academic, older student, psychological, birth control, religious. **For learning-disabled students:** School does not offer a structured program with separate admission and additional fees. Total undergraduates in learning-disabled program or receiving services: 172. Services include: reading machines, note-taking services, readers, extended time for tests, tutors, texts on tape, exams on tape or computer, other testing accommodations, other. **Library:** Number of titles: 2,380,358; number of current serial subscriptions: 81,959. **Information technology resources:** Students are not required to lease or own a computer. Number of campus computers available to all students: 1,116. School has a wireless network. Approximate number of users that can be accommodated: 40,000. Proportion of college-owned housing units wired for high-speed internet access: 100%. **Campus safety:** Security services offered: 24-hour foot-and-vehicle patrols, late-night transport/escort service, 24-hour emergency telephones, lighted pathways/sidewalks, student patrols, controlled dormitory access (key, security card, etc).

TRANSFER AND INTERNATIONAL STUDENTS

Transfer students: May apply for admission for the following academic terms: Fall, Spring. Applicants do not need a minimum number of credits to apply. For fall 2009: Transfer applications received: 4,651. Transfer applicants offered admission: 1,617. Transfer applicants enrolled: 734. **International students:** Number of foreign undergraduates: 1117 (10% of student body). Number of countries represented: 70. Minimum TOEFL score required: 550 (paper); 213 (computer). Average TOEFL score: 600 (paper).

Boricua College

- **Address:** 3755 Broadway, New York, NY 10032
- **Website:** http://www.boricuacollege.edu/
- **Private**
- **Enrollment:** N/A

KEY STATS

✔ **U.S News College Ranking:** Unranked, Regional Colleges (North)
✔ **SAT or ACT Score (25th/75th percentile):** N/A
✔ **Tuition:** 2009-2010: $9,500

Selectivity: N/A	**Room/board:** N/A
Acceptance rate: N/A	**Average debt:** N/A
Student/faculty ratio: N/A	**Proportion who borrowed:** N/A

Buffalo State College—SUNY

- **Address:** 1300 Elmwood Avenue, Buffalo, NY 14222
- **Website:** http://www.buffalostate.edu
- **Public**
- **Enrollment:** 8,780 full-time; 1,042 part-time

KEY STATS

✔ **U.S News College Ranking:** 97, Regional Universities (North)
✔ **SAT Score (25th/75th percentile):** 890-1070
✔ **Tuition:** 2010-2011: $6,007 in state, $13,907 out of state

Selectivity: Selective	**Room/board:** $10,168
Acceptance rate: 43%	**Average debt:** $18,350
Student/faculty ratio: 16/1	**Proportion who borrowed:** 71%

UNDERGRADUATE STUDENT BODY STATS

2009-2010 enrollment: 8,780 full-time; 1,042 part-time. Men: 41%; women: 59%. **Ethnic makeup:** African American: 13%; Asian American: 1%; Hispanic: 5%; White: 79%; International: 1%.

ADMISSIONS FACTS AND FIGURES

Phone: (716) 878-4017. **Email:** admissions@buffalostate.edu. **Website:** http://www.buffalostate.edu. **Application deadlines for fall 2011:** Regular decision: Rolling. Early decision: Send application by: November 15; Decision sent by: December 15. Early action: Not offered. Admission can be deferred. **Application fee:** $40. **To apply online, go to:** http://www.buffalostate.edu/admissions/applying/. **Admissions requirements/recommendations:** High school units required (recommended): English: (4); Mathematics: 2 (3); Science: 2 (3); Foreign language: (3); Academic electives: (4); Total units: (17). Tests: The college uses SAT or ACT scores in admissions decisions. SAT required. For admission to the fall 2011 entering class, the school will accept: ACT with or without writing accepted. Campus visit: Recommended. Admissions interview: Neither required nor recommended. Off-campus interview: May not be arranged. **Factors that count in admissions decisions:** *Academic:* Secondary school record: Very Important. Class rank: Important. Letters of recommendation: Considered. Standardized test scores: Very Important. Essay: Considered. *Nonacademic:* Interview: Considered. Extracurricular activities: Considered. Talent/ability: Considered. Character/personal qualities: Considered. Alumni/ae relationship: Not Considered. Geographical residence: Not Considered. State residency: Not Considered. Religious affiliation/commitment: Not Considered. Minority status: Not Considered. Volunteer work: Considered. Work experience: Considered. **Other schools with the greatest overlap in applicants:** College at Brockport—SUNY; SUNY—Fredonia; University at Buffalo—SUNY. **Admissions statistics for the fall 2009 entering class:** Total applicants: 11,132. Total accepted: 4,750. Freshmen enrolled: 1,524; 2% were from out of state. Accepted through early-decision or early-action plans: 4%. Overall acceptance rate: 43%. Early-decision acceptance rate: 58%. Non-early acceptance rate: 43%. **Credentials of fall 2009 freshmen:** 8% ranked in the top 10 percent of their high school class; 35% were in the top 25 percent; 82% were in the top half. (Proportion submitting class standing: 87%.) **Average high school grade point average:** 3.1. **First-year students who submitted SAT scores:** 94%. Scores (25/75 percentile): Critical Reading: 440-530, Math: 450-540, Combined: 890-1070.

ACADEMICS

Year founded: 1871. **Academic calendar:** Semester. **Degrees offered:** bachelor's, master's, post-master's certificate. **Most popular majors:** 15% education, 8% business, management, marketing, and related support services, 5% communication, journalism, and related programs, 5% social sciences, 4% visual and performing arts. **Major fields of study:** biological and biomedical sciences; business, management, marketing, and related support services; communication, journalism, and related programs; computer and information sciences and support services; education; engineering technologies/technicians; English language and literature/letters; family and consumer sciences/human sciences; foreign languages, literatures, and linguistics; health professions and related clinical sciences; history; liberal arts and sciences studies, and humanities; mathematics and statistics; multi/interdisciplinary studies; philosophy and religious studies; physical sciences; psychology; public administration and social service professions; security and protective services; social sciences; visual and performing arts. **Areas of required coursework:** arts/fine arts, humanities, computer literacy, mathematics, English (including composition), philosophy, foreign languages, sciences (biological or physical), history, social science. **Pre-professional programs:** pre-law, pre-medicine, other. **Special academic programs (% participation):** cooperative (work-study plan) program (1%), cross-registration (1%), distance learning (1%), double major (1%), dual enrollment (1%), English as a Second Language (ESL) (1%), exchange student program (domestic) (1%), honors program (2%), independent study (3.7%), internships (5%), liberal arts/career combination, student-designed major (2%), study abroad (1%), teacher certificate program (1%). **Teacher certification offered in:** early childhood, special education, elementary, vo-tech, middle/junior high, adult education, secondary, bilingual/bicultural. **Reserve Officers Training Corps (ROTC):** Army ROTC: Offered at cooperating institution (Canisius College). **Faculty and instruction (2009-2010):** Total instructional faculty: 425 full-time, 412 part-time (51% men; 49% women; 14% minorities). Full-time faculty with Ph.D. or other terminal degree: 84%. Student/faculty ratio: 16/1. Classes of fewer than 20 students: 45%; of 20 to 49 students: 46%; of 50 or more students: 8%. **Advanced Placement and International Baccalaureate credit:** AP tests may be used for: Credit only. Scores accepted: 3, 4, 5. International Baccalaureate exams may be used for: Credit only. **Freshmen returning for sophomore year:** 76%. **Graduation rates:** Four-year: 21%; five-year: 43%; six-year: 44%. **Graduate study:** 28% of students pursue further study immediately upon graduation; 44% within one year; 55% within five years. Fields in which graduates pursue further study: Master of Business Administration (MBA), 2%; law, 8%; education, 20%; arts and sciences, 18%.

COSTS AND FINANCIAL AID

Financial aid office: (716) 878-4901. **Expenses (2010-2011):** Tuition and fees 2010-2011: $6,007 in state, $13,907 out of state; room/board: $10,168. Estimated books and supplies: $990; transportation: $1,100; personal expenses: $1,000. **Financial aid:** Priority filing date for institution's financial aid form: March 15; deadline: May 1. In 2009-2010, 95% of undergraduates applied for financial aid. Of those, 88% were determined to have financial need; 54% had their need fully met. Average financial aid package (proportion receiving): $9,450 (88%). Average amount of gift aid, such as scholarships or grants (proportion receiving): $4,150 (71%). Average amount of self-help aid, such as work study or loans (proportion receiving): $4,320 (67%). Average need-based loan (excluding PLUS or other private loans): $3,902. Among students who received need-based aid, the average percentage of need met: 66%. Among students who received aid based on merit, the average award (and the proportion receiving): $2,200 (4%). Average amount of debt of borrowers graduating in 2009: $18,350. Proportion who borrowed: 71%.

CAMPUS LIFE AND EXTRACURRICULAR ACTIVITIES

Campus housing available (% using): coed dorms (80%), other housing options (20%). Students who live in college-owned, operated, or affiliated housing: 25%. **Student employment:** During the 2009-2010 academic year, 7% of undergraduates worked on campus. Average per-year earnings: $4,500. **Clubs and organizations:** Number of student organizations: 85. Activities include: choral groups, concert band, dance, drama/theater, international student organization, jazz band, literary magazine, music ensembles, radio station, student government, student newspaper, student film society, yearbook. Number of fraternities: 11; sororities: 13. Proportion of men in fraternities: 1%; of women in sororities: 1%. Average proportion of students who stay on campus on weekends: 55%. **Sports program (2009-2010):** Member of NCAA III. *Men's intercollegiate varsity sports:* basketball, cross country, football, ice hockey, soccer, swimming, track and field (indoor), track and field (outdoor). *Women's intercollegiate varsity sports:* basketball, cross country, ice hockey, rifle, soccer, softball, swimming, track and field (indoor), track and field (outdoor), volleyball.

SERVICES AND FACILITIES

Basic services: women's center, day care, health service, health insurance. **Remedial assistance:** other. **Counseling services:** minority student, career, personal, veteran student, academic, older student, psychological, birth control, other. **For learning-disabled students:** School does not offer a structured program with separate admission and additional fees. Services include: remedial math, remedial English, reading machines, tape recorders, note-taking services, oral tests, learning center, readers, extended time for tests, tutors. **Library:** Number of titles: 671,388; number of current serial subscriptions: 2,676. **Information technology resources:** Students are not required to lease or own a computer. Number of campus computers available to all students: 1,700. School has a wireless network. Approximate number of users that can be accommodated: 125. Proportion of college-owned housing units wired for high-speed internet access: 100%. **Campus safety:** Security services offered: 24-hour foot-and-vehicle patrols, late-night transport/escort service, 24-hour emergency telephones, lighted pathways/sidewalks, student patrols, controlled dormitory access (key, security card, etc).

TRANSFER AND INTERNATIONAL STUDENTS

Transfer students: May apply for admission for the following academic terms: Fall, Spring, Summer. Applicants need a minimum number of credits to apply. For fall 2009: Transfer applications received: 3,541. Transfer applicants offered admission: 2,013. Transfer applicants enrolled: 1,288. **International students:** Number of foreign undergraduates: 87 (1% of student body). Number of countries represented: 21. Minimum TOEFL score required: 500 (paper); 173 (computer).

Canisius College

- **Address:** 2001 Main Street, Buffalo, NY 14208-1098
- **Website:** http://www.canisius.edu
- **Private; Religious affiliation:** Roman Catholic
- **Enrollment:** 3,050 full-time; 146 part-time

KEY STATS

✔ **U.S News College Ranking:** 20, Regional Universities (North)
✔ **SAT Score (25th/75th percentile):** 990-1220
✔ **Tuition:** 2010-2011: $30,077

Selectivity: Selective	**Room/board:** $10,980
Acceptance rate: 77%	**Average debt:** $33,645
Student/faculty ratio: 11/1	**Proportion who borrowed:** 77%

UNDERGRADUATE STUDENT BODY STATS

2009-2010 enrollment: 3,050 full-time; 146 part-time. Men: 48%; women: 52%. **Ethnic makeup:** African American: 6%; Asian American: 1%; Hispanic: 2%; White: 86%; International: 4%. **Religious preference:** Protestant: 21%; Jewish: 1%; Muslim: 1%; No preference: 15%; Roman Catholic: 58%; Other: 2%.

ADMISSIONS FACTS AND FIGURES

Phone: (800) 843-1517. **Email:** admissions@canisius.edu. **Website:** http://www.canisius.edu. **Application deadlines for fall 2011:** Regular decision: May 1. Early decision: Not offered. Early action: Not offered. Admission can be deferred. **Application fee:** $40. **To apply online, go to:** http://www.canisius.edu/canhp/departments/admissions/index.html. **Admissions requirements/recommendations:** High school units required (recommended): English: 4 (4); Mathematics: 3 (4); Science: 2 (4); Foreign language: 2 (4); Social studies: 4 (4); History: 0 (0); Academic electives: 0 (4); Total units: 17 (26). Tests: The college uses SAT or ACT scores in admissions decisions. Either SAT or ACT required. For admission to the fall 2011 entering class, the school will accept: ACT with or without writing accepted. Campus visit: Recommended. Admissions interview: Recommended. Off-campus interview: May be arranged. **Factors that count in admissions decisions:** *Academic:* Secondary school record: Very Important. Class rank: Considered. Letters of recommendation: Important. Standardized test scores: Important. Essay: Important. *Nonacademic:* Interview: Considered. Extracurricular activities: Considered. Talent/ability: Considered. Character/personal qualities: Considered. Alumni/ae relationship: Considered. Geographical residence: Not Considered. State residency: Not Considered. Religious affiliation/commitment: Not Considered. Minority status: Not

Considered. Volunteer work: Considered. Work experience: Considered. **Other schools with the greatest overlap in applicants:** Niagara University; SUNY–Fredonia; SUNY–Geneseo; St. Bonaventure University; University at Buffalo–SUNY. **Admissions statistics for the fall 2009 entering class:** Total applicants: 3,996. Total accepted: 3,084. Freshmen enrolled: 708; 8% were from out of state. Overall acceptance rate: 77%. **Credentials of fall 2009 freshmen:** 28% ranked in the top 10 percent of their high school class; 57% were in the top 25 percent; 87% were in the top half. (Proportion submitting class standing: 67%.) **Average high school grade point average:** 3.5. **First-year students who submitted SAT scores:** 96%. Scores (25/75 percentile): Critical Reading: 490-600, Math: 500-620, Combined: 990-1220. **First-year students submitting ACT scores:** 38%. Scores (25/75 percentile): English: 21-28, Math: 22-27, Composite: 21-27.

ACADEMICS

Year founded: 1870. **Academic calendar:** Semester. **Degrees offered:** associate, bachelor's, master's, post-master's certificate. **Most popular majors:** 9% communication studies/speech communication and rhetoric, 9% psychology, 8% marketing/marketing management, 7% finance, 6% business administration and management. **Major fields of study:** area, ethnic, cultural, and gender studies; biological and biomedical sciences; business, management, marketing, and related support services; communication, journalism, and related programs; computer and information sciences and support services; education; English language and literature/letters; foreign languages, literatures, and linguistics; health professions and related clinical sciences; history; liberal arts and sciences studies, and humanities; mathematics and statistics; natural resources and conservation; philosophy and religious studies; physical sciences; psychology; security and protective services; social sciences; visual and performing arts. **Areas of required coursework:** arts/fine arts, humanities, computer literacy, mathematics, English (including composition), philosophy, sciences (biological or physical), history, social science. **Pre-professional programs:** pre-law, pre-dentistry, pre-medicine, pre-veterinary science, pre-optometry, pre-pharmacy. **Special academic programs (% participation):** cooperative (work-study plan) program, cross-registration (1%), distance learning, double major (10%), dual enrollment (2%), English as a Second Language (ESL), honors program (9%), independent study, internships, study abroad, teacher certificate program. **Teacher certification offered in:** early childhood, special education, elementary, middle/junior high, secondary. **Reserve Officers Training Corps (ROTC):** Army ROTC: Offered on campus. **Faculty and instruction (2009-2010):** Total instructional faculty: 230 full-time, 233 part-time (56% men; 44% women; 7% minorities). Full-time faculty with Ph.D. or other terminal degree: 94%. Student/faculty ratio: 11/1. Classes of fewer than 20 students: 46%; of 20 to 49 students: 53%; of 50 or more students: 1%. **Advanced Placement and International Baccalaureate credit:** AP tests may be used for: Credit only. Scores accepted: 3, 4, 5. International Baccalaureate exams may be used for: Credit only. **Freshmen returning for sophomore year:** 82%. **Graduation rates:** Four-year: 57%; five-year: 66%; six-year: 66%. **Graduate study:** 25% of students pursue further study within one year. Fields in which graduates pursue further study: Master of Business Administration (MBA), 12%; law, 3%; medicine, 7%; dentistry, 4%; theology (or the seminary), 1%; education, 45%; arts and sciences, 27%; veterinary medicine, 1%.

COSTS AND FINANCIAL AID

Financial aid office: (716) 888-2300. **Expenses (2010-2011):** Tuition and fees 2010-2011: $30,077; room/board: $10,980. Estimated books and supplies: $700; transportation: $250; personal expenses: $630. **Financial aid:** Priority filing date for institution's financial aid form: February 15. In 2009-2010, 82% of undergraduates applied for financial aid. Of those, 76% were determined to have financial need; 28% had their need fully met. Average financial aid package (proportion receiving): $24,558 (76%). Average amount of gift aid, such as scholarships or grants (proportion receiving): $18,092 (75%). Average amount of self-help aid, such as work study or loans (proportion receiving): $5,352 (63%). Average need-based loan (excluding PLUS or other private loans): $4,228. Among students who received need-based aid, the average percentage of need met: 81%. Among students who received aid based on merit, the average award (and the proportion receiving): $13,797 (20%). The average athletic scholarship (and the proportion receiving): $21,063 (3%). Average amount of debt of borrowers graduating in 2009: $33,645. Proportion who borrowed: 77%.

CAMPUS LIFE AND EXTRACURRICULAR ACTIVITIES

Campus housing available (% using): coed dorms (49%), apartment for single students (48%), special housing for disabled students (1%), special housing for international students (1%). Students who live in college-owned, operated, or affiliated housing: 46%. **Student employment:** During

the 2009-2010 academic year, 25% of undergraduates worked on campus. Average per-year earnings: $3,600. **Clubs and organizations:** Number of student organizations: 100. Activities include: campus ministries, choral groups, concert band, dance, drama/theater, international student organization, jazz band, literary magazine, music ensembles, musical theater, pep band, radio station, student government, student newspaper, student film society, television station, yearbook. Number of fraternities: 1Proportion of men in fraternities: 1%; of women in sororities: 1%. Average proportion of students who stay on campus on weekends: 85%. **Sports program (2009-2010):** Member of NCAA I. **Men's intercollegiate varsity sports:** baseball, basketball, cross country, golf, ice hockey, lacrosse, soccer, swimming. **Women's intercollegiate varsity sports:** basketball, cross country, lacrosse, soccer, softball, swimming, sync swimming, volleyball.

SERVICES AND FACILITIES

Basic services: nonremedial tutoring, placement service, health service, health insurance. **Remedial assistance:** reading, math, writing, study skills. **Counseling services:** minority student, career, military, personal, veteran student, academic, older student, psychological, religious. **For learning-disabled students:** School does not offer a structured program with separate admission and additional fees. Services include: remedial math, remedial English, remedial reading, tape recorders, note-taking services, readers, extended time for tests, tutors, priority seating, texts on tape. **Library:** Number of titles: 379,124; number of current serial subscriptions: 17,712. **Information technology resources:** Students are not required to lease or own a computer. Number of campus computers available to all students: 300. School has a wireless network. Approximate number of users that can be accommodated: 5,000. Proportion of college-owned housing units wired for high-speed internet access: 100%. **Campus safety:** Security services offered: 24-hour foot-and-vehicle patrols, late-night transport/escort service, 24-hour emergency telephones, lighted pathways/sidewalks, controlled dormitory access (key, security card, etc).

TRANSFER AND INTERNATIONAL STUDENTS

Transfer students: May apply for admission for the following academic terms: Fall, Spring, Summer. Applicants need a minimum number of credits to apply. For fall 2009: Transfer applications received: 422. Transfer applicants offered admission: 270. Transfer applicants enrolled: 124. **International students:** Number of foreign undergraduates: 116 (4% of student body). Number of countries represented: 25. Minimum TOEFL score required: 500 (paper); 173 (computer).

Cazenovia College

- ■ **Address:** 22 Sullivan Street, Cazenovia, NY 13035-1804
- ■ **Website:** http://www.cazenovia.edu
- ■ **Private**
- ■ **Enrollment:** 966 full-time; 153 part-time

KEY STATS

✔ **U.S News College Ranking:** 21, Regional Colleges (North)
✔ **SAT Score (25th/75th percentile):** 880-1090
✔ **Tuition:** 2010-2011: $25,482

Selectivity: Selective	**Room/board:** $10,825
Acceptance rate: 70%	**Average debt:** N/A
Student/faculty ratio: 12/1	**Proportion who borrowed:** 85%

UNDERGRADUATE STUDENT BODY STATS

2009-2010 enrollment: 966 full-time; 153 part-time. Men: 26%; women: 74%. **Ethnic makeup:** African American: 4%; Hispanic: 3%; White: 92%.

ADMISSIONS FACTS AND FIGURES

Phone: (800) 654-3210. **Email:** admission@cazenovia.edu. **Website:** http://www.cazenovia.edu. **Application deadlines for fall 2011:** Regular decision: Rolling. Early decision: Not offered. Early action: Not offered. Admission can be deferred. **Application fee:** $30. **To apply online, go to:** http://www.cazenovia.edu/apply-online. **Admissions requirements/recommendations:** High school units required (recommended): English: 4 (4); Mathematics: 2 (2); Science: 2 (2); Foreign language: 0 (2); Social studies: 4 (4); History: 0 (0); Academic electives: (2); Total units: 12 (16). Tests: The college uses SAT or ACT scores in admissions decisions. Neither SAT nor ACT required. For admission to the fall 2011 entering class, the school will accept: ACT with or without writing accepted. Campus visit: Recommended. Admissions interview: Recommended. Off-campus interview: May be arranged. **Factors that count in admissions decisions:** *Academic:* Secondary school record: Very Important. Class rank: Important. Letters of recommendation: Important. Standardized test scores: Important. Essay: Considered. *Nonacademic:* Interview: Important. Extracurricular activities: Very Important. Talent/ability: Considered. Character/personal qualities: Considered. Alumni/ae relationship: Considered. Volunteer work: Considered. Work experience: Considered. **Admissions statistics for the fall 2009 entering class:** Total applicants: 2,362. Total accepted: 1,663. Freshmen enrolled: 272; 21% were from out of state. Overall acceptance rate: 70%. **Credentials of fall 2009 freshmen:** 12% ranked in the top 10 percent of their high school class; 32% were in the top 25 percent; 77% were in the top half. (Proportion submitting class standing: 98%.) **Average high school grade point average:** 3.2. **First-year students who submitted SAT scores:** 83%. Scores (25/75 percentile): Critical Reading: 440-540, Math: 440-550, Combined: 880-1090. **First-year students submitting ACT scores:** 22%. Scores (25/75 percentile): English: N/A, Math: N/A, Composite: 17-24.

ACADEMICS

Year founded: 1824. **Academic calendar:** Semester. **Degrees offered:** certificate, associate, bachelor's. **Most popular majors:** 33% visual and performing arts, 31% business, management, marketing, and related support services, 8% security and protective services, 7% public administration and social service professions, 6% education. **Major fields of study:** business, management, marketing, and related support services; communication, journalism, and related programs; education; English language and literature/letters; liberal arts and sciences studies, and humanities; natural resources and conservation; psychology; public administration and social service professions; social sciences; visual and performing arts. **Areas of required coursework:** arts/fine arts, humanities, computer literacy, mathematics, English (including composition), sciences (biological or physical), other. **Pre-professional programs:** pre-law. **Special academic programs (% participation):** accelerated program, distance learning, double major, honors program, independent study, internships (97%), study abroad, teacher certificate program. **Teacher certification offered in:** early childhood, special education. **Reserve Officers Training Corps (ROTC):** Army ROTC: Offered at cooperating institution (Syracuse University); Air Force ROTC: Offered at cooperating institution (Syracuse University). **Faculty and instruction (2009-2010):** Total instructional faculty: 56 full-time, 90 part-time (40% men; 60% women; 3% minorities). Full-time faculty with Ph.D. or other terminal degree: 79%. Student/faculty ratio: 12/1. Classes of fewer than 20 students: 75%; of 20 to 49 students: 24%; of 50 or more students: 1%. **Advanced Placement and International Baccalaureate credit:** AP tests may be used for: Placement only. Scores accepted: 3, 4, 5. International Baccalaureate exams may be used for: Placement only. **Freshmen returning for sophomore year:** 68%. **Graduation rates:** Four-year: 35%; five-year: 39%; six-year: 43%. **Graduate study:** 15% of students pursue further study immediately upon graduation; 20% within one year; 30% within five years.

COSTS AND FINANCIAL AID

Financial aid office: (315) 655-7887. **Expenses (2010-2011):** Tuition and fees 2010-2011: $25,482; room/board: $10,825. Estimated books and supplies: $1,000; transportation: $1,000; personal expenses: $100. **Financial aid:** Priority filing date for institution's financial aid form: March 1. In 2009-2010, 92% of undergraduates applied for financial aid. Of those, 85% were determined to have financial need; 18% had their need fully met. Average financial aid package (proportion receiving): $20,838 (85%). Average amount of gift aid, such as scholarships or grants (proportion receiving): $16,422 (85%). Average amount of self-help aid, such as work study or loans (proportion receiving): $4,506 (71%). Average need-based loan (excluding PLUS or other private loans): $4,068. Among students who received need-based aid, the average percentage of need met: 77%. Among students who received aid based on merit, the average award (and the proportion receiving): $11,444 (11%). The average athletic scholarship (and the proportion receiving): $0 (0%). Proportion who borrowed: 85%.

CAMPUS LIFE AND EXTRACURRICULAR ACTIVITIES

Campus housing available: coed dorms, women's dorms, apartment for single students, special housing for disabled students, other housing options. Students who live in college-owned, operated, or affiliated housing: 92%. **Student employment:** During the 2009-2010 academic year, 6% of undergraduates worked on campus. **Clubs and organizations:** Number of student organizations: 54. Activities include: campus ministries, choral groups, concert band, dance, drama/theater, jazz band, literary magazine, musical theater, radio station, student government, student newspaper, student film society, yearbook. Number of fraternities: 0; sororities: 0. Average

proportion of students who stay on campus on weekends: 70%. **Sports program (2009-2010):** Member of NCAA III. *Men's intercollegiate varsity sports:* baseball, basketball, cross country, golf, lacrosse, soccer, swimming. *Women's intercollegiate varsity sports:* basketball, cross country, equestrian, lacrosse, soccer, softball, swimming, volleyball.

SERVICES AND FACILITIES

Basic services: nonremedial tutoring, placement service, health service, health insurance. **Remedial assistance:** reading, math, writing, study skills. **Counseling services:** minority student, career, personal, academic, older student, psychological, birth control, religious, other. **For learning-disabled students:** School does not offer a structured program with separate admission and additional fees. Services include: remedial math, remedial reading, tape recorders, untimed tests, note-taking services, oral tests, learning center, readers, extended time for tests, tutors, priority registration, other testing accommodations. **Library:** Number of titles: 87,465; number of current serial subscriptions: 27,732. **Information technology resources:** Students are not required to lease or own a computer. Number of campus computers available to all students: 356. School has a wireless network. Proportion of college-owned housing units wired for high-speed internet access: 100%. **Campus safety:** Security services offered: 24-hour foot-and-vehicle patrols, late-night transport/escort service, 24-hour emergency telephones, lighted pathways/sidewalks, controlled dormitory access (key, security card, etc).

TRANSFER AND INTERNATIONAL STUDENTS

Transfer students: May apply for admission for the following academic terms: Fall, Spring. Applicants need a minimum number of credits to apply. For fall 2009: Transfer applications received: 246. Transfer applicants offered admission: 120. Transfer applicants enrolled: 54. **International students:** Number of foreign undergraduates: 0. Number of countries represented: 3. Minimum TOEFL score required: 550 (paper); 213 (computer).

Clarkson University

- **Address:** Box 5605, Potsdam, NY 13699
- **Website:** http://www.clarkson.edu
- **Private**
- **Enrollment:** 2,735 full-time; 11 part-time

KEY STATS

✔ **U.S News College Ranking:** 124, National Universities
✔ **SAT Score (25th/75th percentile):** 1060-1270
✔ **Tuition:** 2010-2011: $34,760

Selectivity: More selective	**Room/board:** $11,906
Acceptance rate: 73%	**Average debt:** $32,125
Student/faculty ratio: 15/1	**Proportion who borrowed:** 85%

UNDERGRADUATE STUDENT BODY STATS

2009-2010 enrollment: 2,735 full-time; 11 part-time. Men: 72%; women: 28%. **Ethnic makeup:** African American: 3%; American-Indian: 1%; Asian American: 4%; Hispanic: 3%; White: 86%; International: 3%.

ADMISSIONS FACTS AND FIGURES

Phone: (800) 527-6577. **Email:** admission@clarkson.edu. **Website:** http://www.clarkson.edu. **Application deadlines for fall 2011:** Regular decision: January 15. Early decision: Send application by: December 1; Decision sent by: January 1. Early action: Not offered. Admission can be deferred. **Application fee:** $50. **To apply online, go to:** http://www.clarkson.edu/admission/highschool/apply.html. **Admissions requirements/recommendations:** High school units required (recommended): English: 4; Mathematics: 3 (4); Science: 3 (4); Total units: 16. Tests: The college uses SAT or ACT scores in admissions decisions. Either SAT or ACT required. For admission to the fall 2011 entering class, the school will accept: ACT with or without writing accepted. Campus visit: Recommended. Admissions interview: Recommended. Off-campus interview: May be arranged. **Factors that count in admissions decisions:** *Academic:* Secondary school record: Very Important. Class rank: Important. Letters of recommendation: Important. Standardized test scores: Important. Essay: Considered. *Nonacademic:* Interview: Not Considered. Extracurricular activities: Important. Talent/ability: Considered. Character/personal qualities: Considered. Alumni/ae relationship: Considered. Geographical residence: Not Considered. State residency: Not Considered. Religious affiliation/commitment: Not Considered. Minority status: Not Considered. Volunteer work: Important.

Work experience: Considered. **Other schools with the greatest overlap in applicants:** Lehigh University; Rensselaer Polytechnic Institute; Rochester Institute of Technology; University of Rochester; Worcester Polytechnic Institute. **Admissions statistics for the fall 2009 entering class:** Total applicants: 4,125. Total accepted: 2,998. Freshmen enrolled: 777; 30% were from out of state. Accepted through early-decision or early-action plans: 13%. Overall acceptance rate: 73%. Early-decision acceptance rate: 88%. Non-early acceptance rate: 72%. **Size of waiting list:** 149 applicants; enrolled from waiting list: 16. **Credentials of fall 2009 freshmen:** 34% ranked in the top 10 percent of their high school class; 67% were in the top 25 percent; 94% were in the top half. (Proportion submitting class standing: 72%.) **Average high school grade point average:** 3.5. **First-year students who submitted SAT scores:** 95%. Scores (25/75 percentile): Critical Reading: 500-610, Math: 560-660, Combined: 1060-1270. **First-year students submitting ACT scores:** 35%. Scores (25/75 percentile): English: 20-26, Math: 24-29, Composite: 23-27.

ACADEMICS

Year founded: 1896. **Academic calendar:** Semester. **Degrees offered:** bachelor's, master's, doctorate. **Most popular majors:** 45% engineering, 30% business administration and management, 7% biology/biological sciences, 4% psychology. **Major fields of study:** biological and biomedical sciences; business, management, marketing, and related support services; communication, journalism, and related programs; computer and information sciences and support services; engineering; history; liberal arts and sciences studies, and humanities; mathematics and statistics; multi/interdisciplinary studies; physical sciences; psychology; social sciences. **Areas of required coursework:** humanities, computer literacy, mathematics, sciences (biological or physical), social science, other. **Pre-professional programs:** pre-law, pre-dentistry, pre-medicine, pre-veterinary science, other. **Special academic programs (% participation):** accelerated program (2%), cooperative (work-study plan) program (8%), cross-registration (12%), distance learning (6%), double major (5%), dual enrollment (4%), English as a Second Language (ESL) (.2%), honors program (4%), independent study (9%), liberal arts/career combination (.3%), student-designed major (1%), study abroad (7%). **Cooperative education programs:** business, computer science, engineering, humanities, natural science. **Reserve Officers Training Corps (ROTC):** Army ROTC: Offered on campus; Air Force ROTC: Offered on campus. **Faculty and instruction (2009-2010):** Total instructional faculty: 204 full-time, 22 part-time (72% men; 28% women; 19% minorities). Full-time faculty with Ph.D. or other terminal degree: 86%. Student/faculty ratio: 15/1. Classes of fewer than 20 students: 47%; of 20 to 49 students: 35%; of 50 or more students: 18%. **Advanced Placement and International Baccalaureate credit:** AP tests may be used for: Credit and/or placement. Scores accepted: 4, 5. International Baccalaureate exams may be used for: Credit only. **Freshmen returning for sophomore year:** 85%. **Graduation rates:** Four-year: 54%; five-year: 69%; six-year: 72%. **Graduate study:** 29% of students pursue further study immediately upon graduation; 32% within one year. Fields in which graduates pursue further study: Master of Business Administration (MBA), 10%; law, 3%; medicine, 5%; engineering, 31%; education, 3%; arts and sciences, 46%; veterinary medicine, 1%.

COSTS AND FINANCIAL AID

Financial aid office: (315) 268-6479. **Expenses (2010-2011):** Tuition and fees 2010-2011: $34,760; room/board: $11,906. Estimated books and supplies: $1,100; transportation: $1,042; personal expenses: $1,000. **Financial aid:** Priority filing date for institution's financial aid form: February 15. In 2009-2010, 90% of undergraduates applied for financial aid. Of those, 81% were determined to have financial need; 22% had their need fully met. Average financial aid package (proportion receiving): $31,447 (81%). Average amount of gift aid, such as scholarships or grants (proportion receiving): $21,803 (79%). Average amount of self-help aid, such as work study or loans (proportion receiving): $9,133 (67%). Average need-based loan (excluding PLUS or other private loans): $5,218. Among students who received need-based aid, the average percentage of need met: 87%. Among students who received aid based on merit, the average award (and the proportion receiving): $14,547 (10%). The average athletic scholarship (and the proportion receiving): $38,916 (1%). Average amount of debt of borrowers graduating in 2009: $32,125. Proportion who borrowed: 85%.

CAMPUS LIFE AND EXTRACURRICULAR ACTIVITIES

Campus housing available (% using): coed dorms (69%), sorority housing (1%), fraternity housing (3%), apartment for single students (27%). Students who live in college-owned, operated, or affiliated housing: 80%. **Student employment:** During the 2009-2010 academic year, 22% of undergraduates worked on campus. Average per-year earnings: $1,020. **Clubs and organizations:** Number of student organizations: 117. Activities include: choral groups, drama/theater, international student organization, jazz band, literary magazine, musical theater, pep band, radio station, student government, student newspaper, symphony orchestra, television station, yearbook. Number of fraternities: 11; sororities: 3. Proportion of men in fraternities: 11%; of women in sororities: 9%. Average proportion of students who stay on campus on weekends: 90%. **Sports program (2009-2010):** Member of NCAA III. *Men's intercollegiate varsity sports:* baseball, basketball, cross country, golf, ice hockey, lacrosse, skiing (nordic), skiing (alpine), soccer, swimming. *Women's intercollegiate varsity sports:* basketball, cross country, ice hockey, lacrosse, skiing (nordic), skiing (alpine), soccer, swimming, volleyball.

SERVICES AND FACILITIES

Basic services: nonremedial tutoring, placement service, health service, health insurance. **Remedial assistance:** writing, study skills. **Counseling services:** minority student, career, military, personal, veteran student, academic, older student, psychological, birth control, religious. **For learning-disabled students:** School does not offer a structured program with separate admission and additional fees. Total undergraduates in learning-disabled program or receiving services: 44. Services include: reading machines, tape recorders, videotaped classes, note-taking services, oral tests, learning center, readers, extended time for tests, tutors, early syllabus, priority registration, priority seating, texts on tape, exams on tape or computer, other testing accommodations. **Library:** Number of titles: 314,892; number of current serial subscriptions: 3,127. **Information technology resources:** Students are not required to lease or own a computer. Number of campus computers available to all students: 350. School has a wireless network. Approximate number of users that can be accommodated: 2,500. Proportion of college-owned housing units wired for high-speed internet access: 100%. **Campus safety:** Security services offered: 24-hour foot-and-vehicle patrols, late-night transport/escort service, 24-hour emergency telephones, lighted pathways/sidewalks, controlled dormitory access (key, security card, etc).

TRANSFER AND INTERNATIONAL STUDENTS

Transfer students: May apply for admission for the following academic terms: Fall, Spring. Applicants do not need a minimum number of credits to apply. For fall 2009: Transfer applications received: 222. Transfer applicants offered admission: 160. Transfer applicants enrolled: 92. **International students:** Number of foreign undergraduates: 78 (3% of student body). Number of countries represented: 44. Minimum TOEFL score required: 550 (paper); 80 (computer).

Colgate University

- **Address:** 13 Oak Drive, Hamilton, NY 13346
- **Website:** http://www.colgate.edu
- **Private**
- **Enrollment:** 2,800 full-time; 25 part-time

KEY STATS

✔ **U.S News College Ranking:** 21, National Liberal Arts Colleges
✔ **SAT Score (25th/75th percentile):** 1270-1440
✔ **Tuition:** 2010-2011: $41,870

Selectivity: Most selective	**Room/board:** $10,190
Acceptance rate: 32%	**Average debt:** $19,202
Student/faculty ratio: 10/1	**Proportion who borrowed:** 30%

UNDERGRADUATE STUDENT BODY STATS

2009-2010 enrollment: 2,800 full-time; 25 part-time. Men: 47%; women: 53%. **Ethnic makeup:** African American: 6%; American-Indian: 1%; Asian American: 5%; Hispanic: 6%; White: 77%; International: 5%. **Religious preference:** Roman Catholic: 21%; Protestant: 18%; Jewish: 13%; Muslim: 1%; Hindu: 1%; Buddhist: 1%; No preference: 26%; Unknown: 6%; None: 4%; None: 8%; Other: 1%.

ADMISSIONS FACTS AND FIGURES

Phone: (315) 228-7401. **Email:** admission@mail.colgate.edu. **Website:** http://www.colgate.edu. **Application deadlines for fall 2011:** Regular decision: January 15; decision sent by April 1. Early decision: Send application by: November 15; Decision sent by: December 15. Early action: Not offered. Admission can be deferred. **Application fee:** $60. **To apply online, go to:** http://www.colgate.edu/DesktopDefault1.aspx?tabid=610. **Admissions**

requirements/recommendations: High school units required (recommended): English: 4 (4); Mathematics: 3 (4); Science: 3 (4); Foreign language: 3 (4); Social studies: 3 (4); History: 0 (0); Academic electives: 0 (0); Total units: 16 (20). Tests: The college uses SAT or ACT scores in admissions decisions. Either SAT or ACT required. For admission to the fall 2011 entering class, the school will accept: ACT with or without writing accepted. Campus visit: Recommended. Admissions interview: Neither required nor recommended. Off-campus interview: May be arranged. **Factors that count in admissions decisions:** *Academic:* Secondary school record: Very Important. Class rank: Very Important. Letters of recommendation: Important. Standardized test scores: Important. Essay: Important. *Nonacademic:* Interview: Not Considered. Extracurricular activities: Important. Talent/ability: Important. Character/personal qualities: Important. Alumni/ae relationship: Considered. Geographical residence: Considered. State residency: Not Considered. Religious affiliation/commitment: Not Considered. Minority status: Considered. Volunteer work: Considered. Work experience: Considered. **Other schools with the greatest overlap in applicants:** Boston College; Cornell University; Dartmouth College; Middlebury College; Williams College. **Admissions statistics for the fall 2009 entering class:** Total applicants: 7,816. Total accepted: 2,464. Freshmen enrolled: 750; 68% were from out of state. Accepted through early-decision or early-action plans: 47%. Overall acceptance rate: 32%. Early-decision acceptance rate: 56%. Non-early acceptance rate: 29%. **Size of waiting list:** 1510 applicants; enrolled from waiting list: 22. **Credentials of fall 2009 freshmen:** 68% ranked in the top 10 percent of their high school class; 91% were in the top 25 percent; 100% were in the top half. (Proportion submitting class standing: 37%.) **Average high school grade point average:** 3.6. **First-year students who submitted SAT scores:** 65%. Scores (25/75 percentile): Critical Reading: 630-710, Math: 640-730, Combined: 1270-1440. **First-year students submitting ACT scores:** 35%. Scores (25/75 percentile): English: 29-34, Math: 28-33, Composite: 29-32.

ACADEMICS

Year founded: 1819. **Academic calendar:** Semester. **Degrees offered:** bachelor's, master's. **Most popular majors:** 11% economics, 11% history, 9% English language and literature, 9% political science and government, 9% sociology. **Major fields of study:** agriculture, agriculture operations, and related sciences; area, ethnic, cultural, and gender studies; biological and biomedical sciences; computer and information sciences and support services; education; English language and literature/letters; foreign languages, literatures, and linguistics; history; liberal arts and sciences studies, and humanities; mathematics and statistics; multi/interdisciplinary studies; natural resources and conservation; philosophy and religious studies; physical sciences; psychology; social sciences; visual and performing arts. **Areas of required coursework:** humanities, sciences (biological or physical), social science, other. **Special academic programs (% participation):** double major (19.2%), honors program (19%), independent study (39%), internships (8%), student-designed major (.3%), study abroad (58%), teacher certificate program (0%). **Teacher certification offered in:** elementary, secondary. **Reserve Officers Training Corps (ROTC):** Army ROTC: Offered at cooperating institution (Syracuse University). **Faculty and instruction (2009-2010):** Total instructional faculty: 264 full-time, 52 part-time (57% men; 43% women; 20% minorities). Full-time faculty with Ph.D. or other terminal degree: 97%. Student/faculty ratio: 10/1. Classes of fewer than 20 students: 62%; of 20 to 49 students: 36%; of 50 or more students: 3%. **Advanced Placement and International Baccalaureate credit:** AP tests may be used for: Credit and/or placement. Scores accepted: 3, 4, 5. International Baccalaureate exams may be used for: Credit and/or placement. **Freshmen returning for sophomore year:** 94%. **Graduation rates:** Four-year: 85%; five-year: 89%; six-year: 90%. **Graduate study:** 23% of students pursue further study immediately upon graduation; 45% within five years. Fields in which graduates pursue further study: Master of Business Administration (MBA), 3%; law, 22%; medicine, 23%; engineering, 3%; theology (or the seminary), 2%; education, 3%; arts and sciences, 43%; veterinary medicine, 1%.

COSTS AND FINANCIAL AID

Financial aid office: (315) 228-7431. **Expenses (2010-2011):** Tuition and fees 2010-2011: $41,870; room/board: $10,190. Estimated books and supplies: $980; transportation: $100; personal expenses: $890. **Financial aid:** Priority filing date for institution's financial aid form: January 15; deadline: January 15. In 2009-2010, 37% of undergraduates applied for financial aid. Of those, 35% were determined to have financial need; 100% had their need fully met. Average financial aid package (proportion receiving): $37,738 (35%). Average amount of gift aid, such as scholarships or grants (proportion receiving): $33,211 (35%). Average amount of self-help aid, such as work study or loans (proportion receiving): $5,612 (28%). Average need-based loan (excluding PLUS or other private loans): $4,505. Among students who received need-based aid, the average percentage of need met: 100%. Among students who received aid based on merit, the average award (and the proportion receiving): $0 (0%). The average athletic scholarship (and the proportion receiving): $35,168 (6%). Average amount of debt of borrowers graduating in 2009: $19,202. Proportion who borrowed: 30%.

CAMPUS LIFE AND EXTRACURRICULAR ACTIVITIES

Campus housing available (% using): coed dorms (47%), sorority housing (3%), fraternity housing (6%), apartment for single students (15%). Students who live in college-owned, operated, or affiliated housing: 90%. **Student employment:** During the 2009-2010 academic year, 27% of undergraduates worked on campus. Average per-year earnings: $1,850. **Clubs and organizations:** Number of student organizations: 122. Activities include: choral groups, concert band, dance, drama/theater, international student organization, jazz band, literary magazine, model UN, music ensembles, musical theater, pep band, radio station, student government, student newspaper, symphony orchestra, television station, yearbook. Number of fraternities: 6; sororities: 3. Proportion of men in fraternities: 40%; of women in sororities: 40%. Average proportion of students who stay on campus on weekends: 95%. **Sports program (2009-2010):** Member of NCAA I. *Men's intercollegiate varsity sports:* basketball, cross country, football, golf, ice hockey, lacrosse, soccer, swimming, tennis, track and field (indoor), track and field (outdoor). *Women's intercollegiate varsity sports:* basketball, crew (heavyweight), cross country, crew (lightweight), field hockey, ice hockey, lacrosse, soccer, softball, swimming, tennis, track and field (indoor), track and field (outdoor), volleyball.

SERVICES AND FACILITIES

Basic services: nonremedial tutoring, women's center, placement service, health service, health insurance. **Counseling services:** minority student, career, personal, academic, psychological, birth control, religious. **For learning-disabled students:** School does not offer a structured program with separate admission and additional fees. Total undergraduates in learning-disabled program or receiving services: 184. **Library:** Number of titles: 1,303,217; number of current serial subscriptions: 47,967. **Information technology resources:** Students are not required to lease or own a computer. Number of campus computers available to all students: 850. School has a wireless network. Approximate number of users that can be accommodated: 3,000. Proportion of college-owned housing units wired for high-speed internet access: 100%. **Campus safety:** Security services offered: 24-hour foot-and-vehicle patrols, late-night transport/escort service, 24-hour emergency telephones, lighted pathways/sidewalks, student patrols, controlled dormitory access (key, security card, etc).

TRANSFER AND INTERNATIONAL STUDENTS

Transfer students: May apply for admission for the following academic terms: Fall, Spring. Applicants do not need a minimum number of credits to apply. For fall 2009: Transfer applications received: 236. Transfer applicants offered admission: 44. Transfer applicants enrolled: 18. **International students:** Number of foreign undergraduates: 139 (5% of student body). Number of countries represented: 35.

College at Brockport—SUNY

- **Address:** 350 New Campus Drive, Brockport, NY 14420
- **Website:** http://www.brockport.edu
- **Public**
- **Enrollment:** 6,474 full-time; 645 part-time

KEY STATS

✔ **U.S News College Ranking:** 67, Regional Universities (North)
✔ **SAT Score (25th/75th percentile):** 970-1150
✔ **Tuition:** 2010-2011: $6,108 in state, $14,008 out of state

Selectivity: Selective	**Room/board:** $9,700
Acceptance rate: 45%	**Average debt:** $26,095
Student/faculty ratio: 18/1	**Proportion who borrowed:** 81%

UNDERGRADUATE STUDENT BODY STATS

2009-2010 enrollment: 6,474 full-time; 645 part-time. Men: 43%; women: 57%. **Ethnic makeup:** African American: 6%; Asian American: 2%; Hispanic: 3%; White: 88%.

ADMISSIONS FACTS AND FIGURES

Phone: (585) 395-2751. **Email:** admit@brockport.edu. **Website:** http://www.brockport.edu. **Application deadlines for fall 2011:** Regular decision: Rolling. Early decision: Not offered. Early action: Not offered. Admission can be deferred. **Application fee:** $40. **To apply online, go to:** http://www.suny.edu/student/oas. **Admissions requirements/recommendations:** High school units required (recommended): English: 4; Mathematics: 3; Science: 3; Foreign language: (3); Social studies: 4; Academic electives: 3; Total units: 18. Tests: The college uses SAT or ACT scores in admissions decisions. Either SAT or ACT required. For admission to the fall 2011 entering class, the school will accept: ACT with writing recommended. Campus visit: Recommended. Admissions interview: Recommended. Off-campus interview: Not available. **Factors that count in admissions decisions:** *Academic:* Secondary school record: Very Important. Class rank: Important. Letters of recommendation: Important. Standardized test scores: Important. Essay: Important. *Nonacademic:* Interview: Considered. Extracurricular activities: Important. Talent/ability: Important. Character/personal qualities: Important. Alumni/ae relationship: Not Considered. Geographical residence: Not Considered. State residency: Not Considered. Religious affiliation/commitment: Not Considered. Minority status: Considered. Volunteer work: Important. Work experience: Important. **Other schools with the greatest overlap in applicants:** SUNY College–Cortland; SUNY–Fredonia; SUNY–Geneseo; SUNY–Oswego; University at Buffalo–SUNY. **Admissions statistics for the fall 2009 entering class:** Total applicants: 8,671. Total accepted: 3,875. Freshmen enrolled: 1,090; 2% were from out of state. Overall acceptance rate: 45%. **Size of waiting list:** 220 applicants; enrolled from waiting list: 0. **Credentials of fall 2009 freshmen:** 15% ranked in the top 10 percent of their high school class; 50% were in the top 25 percent; 88% were in the top half. (Proportion submitting class standing: 77%.) **Average high school grade point average:** 3.5. **First-year students who submitted SAT scores:** 95%. Scores (25/75 percentile): Critical Reading: 470-560, Math: 500-590, Combined: 970-1150. **First-year students submitting ACT scores:** 43%. Scores (25/75 percentile): English: 19-25, Math: 21-26, Composite: 21-25.

ACADEMICS

Year founded: 1835. **Academic calendar:** Semester. **Degrees offered:** bachelor's, master's, post-master's certificate. **Most popular majors:** 17% business administration and management, 12% health professions and related clinical sciences, 12% physical education teaching and coaching, 8% English language and literature, 8% psychology. **Major fields of study:** area, ethnic, cultural, and gender studies; biological and biomedical sciences; business, management, marketing, and related support services; communication, journalism, and related programs; computer and information sciences and support services; education; English language and literature/letters; foreign languages, literatures, and linguistics; health professions and related clinical sciences; history; mathematics and statistics; natural resources and conservation; parks, recreation, leisure, and fitness studies; philosophy and religious studies; physical sciences; psychology; public administration and social service professions; security and protective services; social sciences; visual and performing arts. **Areas of required coursework:** arts/fine arts, humanities, computer literacy, mathematics, English (including composition), foreign languages, sciences (biological or physical), history, social science, other. **Pre-professional programs:** pre-law, pre-dentistry, pre-medicine, pre-veterinary science, pre-optometry. **Special academic programs:** accelerated program, cross-registration, distance learning, double major, dual enrollment, honors program, independent study, internships, student-designed major, study abroad, teacher certificate program. **Teacher certification offered in:** special education, elementary, middle/junior high, secondary, bilingual/bicultural. **Cooperative education programs:** art, business, computer science, education, health professions, humanities, natural science, social/behavioral science, technologies. **Reserve Officers Training Corps (ROTC):** Army ROTC: Offered on campus; Navy ROTC: Offered at cooperating institution; Air Force ROTC: Offered at cooperating institution. **Faculty and instruction (2009-2010):** Total instructional faculty: 328 full-time, 269 part-time (51% men; 49% women; 13% minorities). Full-time faculty with Ph.D. or other terminal degree: 87%. Student/faculty ratio: 18/1. Classes of fewer than 20 students: 41%; of 20 to 49 students: 53%; of 50 or more students: 5%. **Advanced Placement and International Baccalaureate credit:** AP tests may be used for: Credit only. Scores accepted: 3, 4, 5. International Baccalaureate exams may be used for: Credit only. **Freshmen returning for sophomore year:** 84%. **Graduation rates:** Four-year: 40%; five-year: 58%; six-year: 60%. **Graduate study:** 23% of students pursue further study within one year. Fields in which graduates pursue further study: Master of Business Administration (MBA), 3%; law, 4%; medicine, 1%; education, 36%; arts and sciences, 12%.

COSTS AND FINANCIAL AID

Financial aid office: (585) 395-2501. **Expenses (2010-2011):** Tuition and fees 2010-2011: $6,108 in state, $14,008 out of state; room/board: $9,700. Estimated books and supplies: $1,200; transportation: $200; personal expenses: $1,630. **Financial aid:** Priority filing date for institution's financial aid form: February 15. In 2009-2010, 89% of undergraduates applied for financial aid. Of those, 70% were determined to have financial need; 28% had their need fully met. Average financial aid package (proportion receiving): $9,606 (70%). Average amount of gift aid, such as scholarships or grants (proportion receiving): $5,045 (61%). Average amount of self-help aid, such as work study or loans (proportion receiving): $4,888 (61%). Average need-based loan (excluding PLUS or other private loans): $4,605. Among students who received need-based aid, the average percentage of need met: 74%. Among students who received aid based on merit, the average award (and the proportion receiving): $4,245 (3%). The average athletic scholarship (and the proportion receiving): $0 (0%). Average amount of debt of borrowers graduating in 2009: $26,095. Proportion who borrowed: 81%.

CAMPUS LIFE AND EXTRACURRICULAR ACTIVITIES

Campus housing available (% using): coed dorms (92%), apartment for single students (8%), special housing for disabled students, special housing for international students, other housing options. Students who live in college-owned, operated, or affiliated housing: 38%. **Student employment:** During the 2009-2010 academic year, 30% of undergraduates worked on campus. Average per-year earnings: $1,349. **Clubs and organizations:** Number of student organizations: 71. Activities include: campus ministries, choral groups, dance, drama/theater, international student organization, literary magazine, model UN, musical theater, radio station, student government, student newspaper, television station. Number of fraternities: 6; sororities: 3. Proportion of men in fraternities: 1%; of women in sororities: 2%. Average proportion of students who stay on campus on weekends: 50%. **Sports program (2009-2010):** Member of NCAA III. *Men's intercollegiate varsity sports:* baseball, basketball, cross country, football, ice hockey, lacrosse, soccer, swimming, track and field (indoor), track and field (outdoor), wrestling. *Women's intercollegiate varsity sports:* basketball, cross country, field hockey, gymnastics, lacrosse, soccer, softball, swimming, tennis, track and field (indoor), track and field (outdoor), volleyball.

SERVICES AND FACILITIES

Basic services: nonremedial tutoring, women's center, placement service, day care, health service, health insurance. **Counseling services:** minority student, career, military, personal, veteran student, academic, older student, psychological, birth control, other. **For learning-disabled students:** School does not offer a structured program with separate admission and additional fees. Total undergraduates in learning-disabled program or receiving services: 204. Services include: remedial math, remedial English, reading machines, tape recorders, note-taking services, learning center, extended time for tests, tutors, priority registration, priority seating, texts on tape, other testing accommodations. **Library:** Number of titles: 826,619; number of current serial subscriptions: 1,604. **Information technology resources:** Students are not required to lease or own a computer. Number of campus computers available to all students: 850. School has a wireless network. Approximate number of users that can be accommodated: 3,000. Proportion of college-owned housing units wired for high-speed internet access: 100%. **Campus safety:** Security services offered: 24-hour foot-and-vehicle patrols, late-night transport/escort service, 24-hour emergency telephones, lighted pathways/sidewalks, student patrols, controlled dormitory access (key, security card, etc).

TRANSFER AND INTERNATIONAL STUDENTS

Transfer students: May apply for admission for the following academic terms: Fall, Spring. Applicants do not need a minimum number of credits to apply. For fall 2009: Transfer applications received: 3,286. Transfer applicants offered admission: 1,783. Transfer applicants enrolled: 961. **International students:** Number of countries represented: 21. Minimum TOEFL score required: 530 (paper); 71 (computer).

College of Mount St. Vincent

- **Address:** 6301 Riverdale Avenue, Riverdale, NY 10471
- **Website:** http://www.mountsaintvincent.edu
- **Private; Religious affiliation:** Roman Catholic
- **Enrollment:** 1,350 full-time; 205 part-time

KEY STATS

✔ **U.S News College Ranking:** 117, Regional Universities (North)

✔ **SAT Score (25th/75th percentile):** 810-1030

✔ **Tuition:** 2010-2011: $26,910

Selectivity: Less selective	**Room/board:** $10,380
Acceptance rate: 72%	**Average debt:** N/A
Student/faculty ratio: 12/1	**Proportion who borrowed:** 90%

UNDERGRADUATE STUDENT BODY STATS

2009-2010 enrollment: 1,350 full-time; 205 part-time. Men: 25%; women: 75%. **Ethnic makeup:** African American: 12%; Asian American: 10%; Hispanic: 30%; White: 48%. **Religious preference:** Protestant: 3%; Muslim: 2%; No preference: 1%; Roman Catholic: 80%; Other: 14%.

ADMISSIONS FACTS AND FIGURES

Phone: (718) 405-3267. **Email:** admissions.office@mountsaintvincent.edu. **Website:** http://www.mountsaintvincent.edu. **Application deadlines for fall 2011:** Regular decision: Rolling. Early decision: Not offered. Early action: Send application by: November 1; Decision sent by: December 1. Admission can be deferred. **Application fee:** $35. **To apply online, go to:** https://www.mountsaintvincent.edu/application.htm. **Admissions requirements/recommendations:** High school units required (recommended): English: 4 (4); Mathematics: 3 (4); Science: 2 (3); Foreign language: 2 (3); Social studies: 3 (4); History: 0 (0); Academic electives: 2 (3); Total units: 16 (20). Tests: The college uses SAT or ACT scores in admissions decisions. Either SAT or ACT required. For admission to the fall 2011 entering class, the school will accept: ACT with writing recommended. Campus visit: Recommended. Admissions interview: Recommended. Off-campus interview: May be arranged. **Factors that count in admissions decisions:** *Academic:* Secondary school record: Very Important. Class rank: Considered. Letters of recommendation: Important. Standardized test scores: Important. Essay: Important. *Nonacademic:* Interview: Important. Extracurricular activities: Important. Talent/ability: Not Considered. Character/personal qualities: Important. Alumni/ae relationship: Considered. Geographical residence: Considered. State residency: Considered. Religious affiliation/commitment: Not Considered. Minority status: Not Considered. Volunteer work: Considered. Work experience: Considered. **Other schools with the greatest overlap in applicants:** Fordham University; Iona College; Manhattan College; St. John's University. **Admissions statistics for the fall 2009 entering class:** Total applicants: 2,057. Total accepted: 1,472. Freshmen enrolled: 390; 11% were from out of state. Overall acceptance rate: 72%. Non-early acceptance rate: 72%. **Size of waiting list:** 130 applicants; enrolled from waiting list: 6. **Credentials of fall 2009 freshmen:** (Proportion submitting class standing: 13%.) **Average high school grade point average:** 2.8. **First-year students who submitted SAT scores:** 100%. Scores (25/75 percentile): Critical Reading: 410-520, Math: 400-510, Combined: 810-1030.

ACADEMICS

Year founded: 1847. **Academic calendar:** Semester. **Degrees offered:** certificate, associate, bachelor's, master's, post-master's certificate. **Most popular majors:** 23% nursing/registered nurse training (R.N., A.S.N., B.S.N., M.S.N.), 18% business/commerce, 13% communication studies/speech communication and rhetoric, 12% liberal arts and sciences/liberal studies, 10% psychology. **Major fields of study:** biological and biomedical sciences; business, management, marketing, and related support services; communication, journalism, and related programs; English language and literature/letters; foreign languages, literatures, and linguistics; health professions and related clinical sciences; history; liberal arts and sciences studies, and humanities; mathematics and statistics; philosophy and religious studies; physical sciences; psychology; social sciences. **Areas of required coursework:** arts/fine arts, humanities, computer literacy, mathematics, English (including composition), philosophy, foreign languages, sciences (biological or physical), history, social science, other. **Pre-professional programs:** pre-law, pre-dentistry, pre-medicine, pre-veterinary science, pre-pharmacy, other. **Special academic programs (% participation):** cross-registration (31%), double major (1%), honors program (14%), independent study (28%), internships (47%), teacher certificate program (8%). **Teacher certification offered in:** early childhood, special education, elementary, middle/junior high, secondary. **Reserve Officers Training Corps (ROTC):** Air Force ROTC: Offered at cooperating institution (Manhattan College). **Faculty and instruction (2009-2010):** Total instructional faculty: 73 full-time, 123 part-time (36% men; 64% women; 33% minorities). Full-time faculty with Ph.D. or other terminal degree: 84%. Student/faculty ratio: 12/1. Classes of fewer than 20 students: 50%; of 20 to 49 students: 50%; of 50 or more students: 0%. **Advanced Placement and International Baccalaureate credit:** AP tests may be used for: Placement only. Scores accepted: 3, 4, 5. International Baccalaureate exams may be used for: Placement only. **Freshmen returning for sophomore year:** 74%. **Graduation rates:** Four-year: 40%; five-year: 53%; six-year: 54%. **Graduate study:** 10% of students pursue further study immediately upon graduation; 20% within one year; 35% within five years. Fields in which graduates pursue further study: Master of Business Administration (MBA), 22%; law, 3%; education, 28%; arts and sciences, 34%; veterinary medicine, 3%.

COSTS AND FINANCIAL AID

Financial aid office: (718) 405-3290. **Expenses (2010-2011):** Tuition and fees 2010-2011: $26,910; room/board: $10,380. Estimated books and supplies: $900; transportation: $200; personal expenses: $900. **Financial aid:** Priority filing date for institution's financial aid form: February 15. In 2009-2010, 88% of undergraduates applied for financial aid. Of those, 82% were determined to have financial need; Average financial aid package (proportion receiving): N/A (82%). Average amount of gift aid, such as scholarships or grants (proportion receiving): $9,800 (N/A). Average amount of self-help aid, such as work study or loans (proportion receiving): $5,000 (82%). Average need-based loan (excluding PLUS or other private loans): $4,800. Among students who received need-based aid, the average percentage of need met: 75%. Proportion who borrowed: 90%.

CAMPUS LIFE AND EXTRACURRICULAR ACTIVITIES

Campus housing available (% using): coed dorms (100%). Students who live in college-owned, operated, or affiliated housing: 47%. **Student employment:** During the 2009-2010 academic year, 15% of undergraduates worked on campus. Average per-year earnings: $800. **Clubs and organizations:** Number of student organizations: 36. Activities include: campus ministries, choral groups, dance, drama/theater, international student organization, literary magazine, musical theater, radio station, student government, student newspaper, television station, yearbook. Number of fraternities: 0; sororities: 0. Average proportion of students who stay on campus on weekends: 55%. **Sports program (2009-2010):** Member of NCAA III. *Men's intercollegiate varsity sports:* baseball, basketball, cross country, lacrosse, soccer, tennis, volleyball. *Women's intercollegiate varsity sports:* basketball, cross country, lacrosse, soccer, softball, swimming, tennis, volleyball.

SERVICES AND FACILITIES

Basic services: nonremedial tutoring, health service. **Remedial assistance:** reading, math, writing, study skills. **Counseling services:** career, personal, academic, psychological, religious. **For learning-disabled students:** School does not offer a structured program with separate admission and additional fees. Total undergraduates in learning-disabled program or receiving services: 37. Services include: remedial math, remedial English, reading machines, remedial reading, tape recorders, untimed tests, note-taking services, oral tests, learning center, readers, extended time for tests, tutors, priority seating, texts on tape, typist/scribe, other testing accommodations, waiver of foreign language degree requirement. **Library:** Number of titles: 110,924; number of current serial subscriptions: 19,823. **Information technology resources:** Students are not required to lease or own a computer. Number of campus computers available to all students: 238. School has a wireless network. Approximate number of users that can be accommodated: 2,000. Proportion of college-owned housing units wired for high-speed internet access: 100%. **Campus safety:** Security services offered: 24-hour foot-and-vehicle patrols, late-night transport/escort service, 24-hour emergency telephones, lighted pathways/sidewalks, controlled dormitory access (key, security card, etc).

TRANSFER AND INTERNATIONAL STUDENTS

Transfer students: May apply for admission for the following academic terms: Fall, Spring. Applicants do not need a minimum number of credits to apply. For fall 2009: Transfer applications received: 859. Transfer applicants offered admission: 243. Transfer applicants enrolled: 52. **International students:** Number of foreign undergraduates: 7. Number of countries represented: 6. Minimum TOEFL score required: 550 (paper); 213 (computer). Average TOEFL score: 550 (paper).

College of New Rochelle

- **Address:** Castle Place, New Rochelle, NY 10805-2338
- **Website:** http://www.cnr.edu
- **Private**
- **Enrollment:** N/A

KEY STATS

✔ **U.S News College Ranking:** second tier, Regional Universities (North)
✔ **SAT or ACT Score (25th/75th percentile):** N/A
✔ **Tuition:** 2009-2010: $26,426

Selectivity: Less selective	**Room/board:** $9,600
Acceptance rate: N/A	**Average debt:** N/A
Student/faculty ratio: N/A	**Proportion who borrowed:** N/A

College of St. Rose

- **Address:** 432 Western Avenue, Albany, NY 12203-1490
- **Website:** http://www.strose.edu
- **Private**
- **Enrollment:** 2,844 full-time; 192 part-time

KEY STATS

✔ **U.S News College Ranking:** 40, Regional Universities (North)
✔ **SAT Score (25th/75th percentile):** 930-1140
✔ **Tuition:** 2010-2011: $24,138

Selectivity: Selective	**Room/board:** $9,880
Acceptance rate: 72%	**Average debt:** $29,391
Student/faculty ratio: 14/1	**Proportion who borrowed:** 84%

UNDERGRADUATE STUDENT BODY STATS

2009-2010 enrollment: 2,844 full-time; 192 part-time. Men: 31%; women: 69%. **Ethnic makeup:** African American: 4%; Asian American: 2%; Hispanic: 5%; White: 88%; International: 1%. **Religious preference:** Roman Catholic: 56%; Protestant: 15%; Jewish: 1%; Buddhist: 1%; No preference: 19%; Other: 8%.

ADMISSIONS FACTS AND FIGURES

Phone: (518) 454-5150. **Email:** admit@mail.strose.edu. **Website:** http://www.strose.edu. **Application deadlines for fall 2011:** Regular decision: Rolling. Early decision: Not offered. Early action: Send application by: December 1; Decision sent by: December 1. Admission can be deferred. **Application fee:** $40. **To apply online, go to:** https://www.saintroseinfo.org/secure/9207/preview_app.asp?wcc=srb. **Admissions requirements/recommendations:** High school units required (recommended): English: 4 (4); Mathematics: 3 (4); Science: 3 (4); Foreign language: 3 (4); Social studies: 4 (4); History: 4 (4); Academic electives: 0 (4); Total units: 45 (58). Tests: The college uses SAT or ACT scores in admissions decisions. Either SAT or ACT required. For admission to the fall 2011 entering class, the school will accept: ACT with or without writing accepted. Campus visit: Recommended. Admissions interview: Recommended. Off-campus interview: May be arranged. **Factors that count in admissions decisions:** *Academic:* Secondary school record: Very Important. Class rank: Considered. Letters of recommendation: Considered. Standardized test scores: Important. Essay: Considered. *Nonacademic:* Interview: Very Important. Extracurricular activities: Important. Talent/ability: Very Important. Character/personal qualities: Important. Alumni/ae relationship: Considered. Geographical residence: Important. State residency: Considered. Religious affiliation/commitment: Not Considered. Minority status: Important. Volunteer work: Important. Work experience: Very Important. **Other schools with the greatest overlap in applicants:** Ithaca College; Le Moyne College; Marist College; Siena College; University at Albany–SUNY. **Admissions statistics for the fall 2009 entering class:** Total applicants: 4,025. Total accepted: 2,882. Freshmen enrolled: 583; 10% were from out of state. Accepted through early-decision or early-action plans: 63%. Overall acceptance rate: 72%. Non-early acceptance rate: 61%. **Credentials of fall 2009 freshmen:** 13% ranked in the top 10 percent of their high school class; 43% were in the top 25 percent; 80% were in the top half. (Proportion submitting class standing: 66%.) **Average high school grade point average:** 3.3. **First-year students who submitted SAT scores:** 96%. Scores (25/75 percentile): Critical Reading: 460-570, Math: 470-

570, Combined: 930-1140. **First-year students submitting ACT scores:** 33%. Scores (25/75 percentile): English: N/A, Math: N/A, Composite: 19-25.

ACADEMICS

Year founded: 1920. **Academic calendar:** Semester. **Degrees offered:** bachelor's, post-bachelor's certificate, master's, post-master's certificate. **Most popular majors:** 46% education, 14% business, management, marketing, and related support services, 7% communications technologies/technicians and support services, 7% psychology, 6% social sciences. **Major fields of study:** agriculture, agriculture operations, and related sciences; area, ethnic, cultural, and gender studies; biological and biomedical sciences; business, management, marketing, and related support services; communications technologies/technicians and support services; computer and information sciences and support services; education; English language and literature/letters; foreign languages, literatures, and linguistics; health professions and related clinical sciences; history; liberal arts and sciences studies, and humanities; mathematics and statistics; natural resources and conservation; philosophy and religious studies; physical sciences; psychology; public administration and social service professions; security and protective services; social sciences; visual and performing arts. **Areas of required coursework:** arts/fine arts, humanities, computer literacy, mathematics, English (including composition), philosophy, foreign languages, sciences (biological or physical), history, social science, other. **Pre-professional programs:** pre-law, pre-dentistry, pre-medicine, pre-veterinary science. **Special academic programs (% participation):** accelerated program (2%), cross-registration, distance learning, double major, independent study, internships, student-designed major (2%), study abroad, teacher certificate program. **Teacher certification offered in:** early childhood, special education, elementary, middle/junior high, secondary, bilingual/bicultural. **Reserve Officers Training Corps (ROTC):** Army ROTC: Offered at cooperating institution (Siena College); Navy ROTC: Offered at cooperating institution (Rensselaer Polytechnic Institute); Air Force ROTC: Offered at cooperating institution (University at Albany–SUNY). **Faculty and instruction (2009-2010):** Total instructional faculty: 213 full-time, 228 part-time (41% men; 59% women; 8% minorities). Full-time faculty with Ph.D. or other terminal degree: 87%. Student/faculty ratio: 14/1. Classes of fewer than 20 students: 65%; of 20 to 49 students: 35%; of 50 or more students: 0%. **Advanced Placement and International Baccalaureate credit:** AP tests may be used for: Credit and/or placement. Scores accepted: 3, 4. International Baccalaureate exams may be used for: Credit and/or placement. **Freshmen returning for sophomore year:** 81%. **Graduation rates:** Four-year: 53%; five-year: 68%; six-year: 71%. **Graduate study:** 48% of students pursue further study immediately upon graduation; 52% within one year. Fields in which graduates pursue further study: Master of Business Administration (MBA), 5%; law, 1%; medicine, 1%; education, 85%; arts and sciences, 8%.

COSTS AND FINANCIAL AID

Financial aid office: (518) 458-5424. **Expenses (2010-2011):** Tuition and fees 2010-2011: $24,138; room/board: $9,880. Estimated books and supplies: $1,200; transportation: $960; personal expenses: $1,500. **Financial aid:** Priority filing date for institution's financial aid form: March 1. In 2009-2010, 99% of undergraduates applied for financial aid. Of those, 98% were determined to have financial need; 2% had their need fully met. Average financial aid package (proportion receiving): $8,897 (97%). Average amount of gift aid, such as scholarships or grants (proportion receiving): $3,453 (81%). Average amount of self-help aid, such as work study or loans (proportion receiving): $2,895 (90%). Average need-based loan (excluding PLUS or other private loans): $2,346. Among students who received need-based aid, the average percentage of need met: 8%. Among students who received aid based on merit, the average award (and the proportion receiving): $2,104 (9%). The average athletic scholarship (and the proportion receiving): $8,844 (2%). Average amount of debt of borrowers graduating in 2009: $29,391. Proportion who borrowed: 84%.

CAMPUS LIFE AND EXTRACURRICULAR ACTIVITIES

Campus housing available (% using): coed dorms (55%), women's dorms (34%), men's dorms (5%), apartment for single students (5%), special housing for disabled students (0%). Students who live in college-owned, operated, or affiliated housing: 38%. **Student employment:** During the 2009-2010 academic year, 3% of undergraduates worked on campus. Average per-year earnings: $1,000. **Clubs and organizations:** Number of student organizations: 33. Activities include: campus ministries, choral groups, concert band, dance, drama/theater, international student organization, jazz band, literary magazine, music ensembles, musical theater, radio station, student government, student newspaper, symphony orchestra, television station, yearbook. Number of fraternities: 0; sororities: 0. Average proportion of students who stay on campus on weekends: 60%. **Sports program (2009-2010):** Member of NCAA II. *Men's intercollegiate varsity sports:* baseball, basketball, cross country, golf, soccer, swimming, track and field (indoor), track and field (outdoor). *Women's intercollegiate varsity sports:* basketball, cross country, soccer, softball, swimming, tennis, track and field (indoor), track and field (outdoor), volleyball.

SERVICES AND FACILITIES

Basic services: nonremedial tutoring, placement service, health service, other. **Remedial assistance:** math, writing, study skills, other. **Counseling services:** minority student, career, military, personal, veteran student, academic, older student, psychological, religious, other. **For learning-disabled students:** School does not offer a structured program with separate admission and additional fees. Services include: reading machines, tape recorders, note-taking services, special bookstore section, oral tests, learning center, readers, extended time for tests, tutors, priority registration, priority seating, proofreading services, substitution of courses, texts on tape, typist/scribe, exams on tape or computer, other testing accommodations. **Library:** Number of titles: 223,218; number of current serial subscriptions: 641. **Information technology resources:** Students are not required to lease or own a computer. Number of campus computers available to all students: 584. School has a wireless network. Proportion of college-owned housing units wired for high-speed internet access: 98%. **Campus safety:** Security services offered: 24-hour foot-and-vehicle patrols, late-night transport/escort service, 24-hour emergency telephones, lighted pathways/sidewalks, student patrols, controlled dormitory access (key, security card, etc).

TRANSFER AND INTERNATIONAL STUDENTS

Transfer students: May apply for admission for the following academic terms: Fall, Spring, Summer. Applicants do not need a minimum number of credits to apply. For fall 2009: Transfer applications received: 827. Transfer applicants offered admission: 584. Transfer applicants enrolled: 285. **International students:** Number of foreign undergraduates: 42 (1% of student body). Number of countries represented: 27. Minimum TOEFL score required: 500 (paper); 80 (computer).

Columbia University

- **Address:** 2960 Broadway, New York, NY 10027
- **Website:** http://www.columbia.edu
- **Private**
- **Enrollment:** 6,762 full-time; 981 part-time

KEY STATS

✔ **U.S News College Ranking:** 4, National Universities
✔ **SAT Score (25th/75th percentile):** 1370-1550
✔ **Tuition:** 2010-2011: $43,304

Selectivity: Most selective	**Room/board:** $10,570
Acceptance rate: 10%	**Average debt:** N/A
Student/faculty ratio: 6/1	**Proportion who borrowed:** N/A

UNDERGRADUATE STUDENT BODY STATS

2009-2010 enrollment: 6,762 full-time; 981 part-time. Men: 50%; women: 50%. **Ethnic makeup:** African American: 9%; American-Indian: 1%; Asian American: 15%; Hispanic: 11%; White: 53%; International: 10%.

ADMISSIONS FACTS AND FIGURES

Phone: (212) 854-2522. **Email:** ugrad-ask@columbia.edu. **Website:** http://www.columbia.edu. **Application deadlines for fall 2011:** Regular decision: January 1; decision sent by April 1. Early decision: Send application by: November 1; Decision sent by: December 15. Early action: Not offered. Admission can be deferred. **Application fee:** $80. **To apply online, go to:** http://www.columbia.edu/cu/admissions/ugrad/. **Admissions requirements/recommendations:** High school units required (recommended): English: 4 (4); Mathematics: 3 (4); Science: 3 (4); Foreign language: 3 (4); History: 3 (4); Academic electives: 3 (4). Tests: The college uses SAT or ACT scores in admissions decisions. Either SAT or ACT required. For admission to the fall 2011 entering class, the school will accept: ACT with writing required. Campus visit: Recommended. Admissions interview: Neither required nor recommended. Off-campus interview: May not be arranged. **Factors that count in admissions decisions:** *Academic:* Secondary school record: Very Important. Class rank: Very Important. Letters of recommendation: Very Important. Standardized test scores: Very Important. Essay:

Very Important. *Nonacademic:* Interview: Considered. Extracurricular activities: Very Important. Talent/ability: Important. Character/personal qualities: Very Important. Alumni/ae relationship: Considered. Geographical residence: Considered. State residency: Not Considered. Religious affiliation/commitment: Not Considered. Minority status: Considered. Volunteer work: Considered. Work experience: Considered. **Other schools with the greatest overlap in applicants:** Harvard University; Massachusetts Institute of Technology; Princeton University; Stanford University; Yale University. **Admissions statistics for the fall 2009 entering class:** Total applicants: 25,427. Total accepted: 2,501. Freshmen enrolled: 1,419; 75% were from out of state. Accepted through early-decision or early-action plans: 45%. Overall acceptance rate: 10%. Early-decision acceptance rate: 23%. Non-early acceptance rate: 8%. **Credentials of fall 2009 freshmen:** 97% ranked in the top 10 percent of their high school class; 99% were in the top 25 percent; 100% were in the top half. (Proportion submitting class standing: 80%.) **First-year students who submitted SAT scores:** 96%. Scores (25/75 percentile): Critical Reading: 680-770, Math: 690-780, Combined: 1370-1550. **First-year students submitting ACT scores:** 28%. Scores (25/75 percentile): English: 31-34, Math: 31-34, Composite: 31-34.

ACADEMICS

Year founded: 1754. **Academic calendar:** Semester. **Degrees offered:** certificate, bachelor's, post-bachelor's certificate, master's, doctorate. **Most popular majors:** 24% social sciences, 22% engineering, 8% history, 6% English language and literature/letters, 6% biological and biomedical sciences. **Major fields of study:** architecture and related services; area, ethnic, cultural, and gender studies; biological and biomedical sciences; computer and information sciences and support services; education; engineering; engineering technologies/technicians; English language and literature/letters; foreign languages, literatures, and linguistics; history; mathematics and statistics; multi/interdisciplinary studies; natural resources and conservation; philosophy and religious studies; physical sciences; psychology; social sciences; visual and performing arts. **Areas of required coursework:** humanities, English (including composition), philosophy, sciences (biological or physical), other. **Pre-professional programs:** pre-law, pre-dentistry, pre-medicine, pre-theology, pre-veterinary science, pre-optometry, pre-pharmacy. **Special academic programs:** accelerated program, cooperative (work-study plan) program, cross-registration, double major, dual enrollment, English as a Second Language (ESL), exchange student program (domestic), independent study, internships, liberal arts/career combination, student-designed major, study abroad, teacher certificate program, other. **Teacher certification offered in:** early childhood, elementary, middle/junior high, secondary. **Reserve Officers Training Corps (ROTC):** Army ROTC: Offered at cooperating institution; Navy ROTC: Offered at cooperating institution; Air Force ROTC: Offered at cooperating institution. **Faculty and instruction (2009-2010):** Total instructional faculty: 1,422 full-time, 352 part-time (67% men; 33% women; 18% minorities). Full-time faculty with Ph.D. or other terminal degree: 100%. Student/faculty ratio: 6/1. Classes of fewer than 20 students: 79%; of 20 to 49 students: 14%; of 50 or more students: 7%. **Advanced Placement and International Baccalaureate credit:** AP tests may be used for: Credit and/or placement. Scores accepted: 4, 5. International Baccalaureate exams may be used for: Credit and/or placement. **Freshmen returning for sophomore year:** 99%. **Graduation rates:** Four-year: 87%; five-year: 94%; six-year: 96%.

COSTS AND FINANCIAL AID

Financial aid office: (212) 854-3711. **Expenses (2010-2011):** Tuition and fees 2010-2011: $43,304; room/board: $10,570. Estimated books and supplies: $2,807. **Financial aid:** In 2009-2010, 57% of undergraduates applied for financial aid. Of those, 50% were determined to have financial need; 100% had their need fully met. Average financial aid package (proportion receiving): $37,490 (50%). Average amount of gift aid, such as scholarships or grants (proportion receiving): $35,705 (49%). Average amount of self-help aid, such as work study or loans (proportion receiving): $2,449 (42%). Average need-based loan (excluding PLUS or other private loans): $2,541. Among students who received need-based aid, the average percentage of need met: 100%.

CAMPUS LIFE AND EXTRACURRICULAR ACTIVITIES

Campus housing available (% using): coed dorms (83%), sorority housing (1%), fraternity housing (4%), apartment for single students (6%), special housing for disabled students (5%), other housing options (1%). Students who live in college-owned, operated, or affiliated housing: 95%. **Student employment:** During the 2009-2010 academic year, 43% of undergraduates worked on campus. **Clubs and organizations:** Number of student organizations: 500. Activities include: campus ministries, choral groups, concert band, dance, drama/theater, international student organization, jazz band, literary magazine, marching band, model UN, music ensembles, musical theater, opera, pep band, radio station, student government, student newspaper, student film society, symphony orchestra, television station, yearbook. Number of fraternities: 17; sororities: 11. Proportion of men in fraternities: 10%; of women in sororities: 10%. Average proportion of students who stay on campus on weekends: 95%. **Sports program (2009-2010):** Member of NCAA I. *Men's intercollegiate varsity sports:* baseball, basketball, cross country, fencing, football, golf, soccer, swimming, tennis, track and field (indoor), track and field (outdoor), wrestling. *Women's intercollegiate varsity sports:* archery, basketball, crew (heavyweight), cross country, fencing, field hockey, golf, lacrosse, crew (lightweight), soccer, softball, squash, swimming, tennis, track and field (indoor), track and field (outdoor), volleyball.

SERVICES AND FACILITIES

Basic services: nonremedial tutoring, placement service, health service, health insurance. **Counseling services:** career, personal, academic, psychological, birth control. **For learning-disabled students:** School does not offer a structured program with separate admission and additional fees. Total undergraduates in learning-disabled program or receiving services: 350. Services include: reading machines, tape recorders, note-taking services, learning center, readers, extended time for tests, early syllabus, priority registration, priority seating, substitution of courses, texts on tape, exams on tape or computer, other testing accommodations, waiver of foreign language degree requirement, other. **Library:** Number of titles: 10,449,223; number of current serial subscriptions: 144,787. **Information technology resources:** Students are not required to lease or own a computer. Number of campus computers available to all students: 540. School has a wireless network. Approximate number of users that can be accommodated: 20,000. Proportion of college-owned housing units wired for high-speed internet access: 100%. **Campus safety:** Security services offered: 24-hour foot-and-vehicle patrols, late-night transport/escort service, 24-hour emergency telephones, lighted pathways/sidewalks, controlled dormitory access (key, security card, etc).

TRANSFER AND INTERNATIONAL STUDENTS

Transfer students: May apply for admission for the following academic terms: Fall. Applicants need a minimum number of credits to apply. For fall 2009: Transfer applications received: 2,349. Transfer applicants offered admission: 143. Transfer applicants enrolled: 104. **International students:** Number of foreign undergraduates: 802 (10% of student body). Number of countries represented: 86. Minimum TOEFL score required: 600 (paper); 250 (computer).

Concordia College

■ **Address:** 171 White Plains Road, Bronxville, NY 10708
■ **Website:** http://www.concordia-ny.edu
■ **Private; Religious affiliation:** Lutheran
■ **Enrollment:** N/A

KEY STATS

✔ **U.S News College Ranking:** second tier, National Liberal Arts Colleges
✔ **ACT Score (25th/75th percentile):** 16-20
✔ **Tuition:** 2009-2010: $24,700
    Selectivity: Less selective   **Room/board:** $9,125
    Acceptance rate: 68%   **Average debt:** N/A
    Student/faculty ratio: N/A   **Proportion who borrowed:** N/A

Cooper Union

■ **Address:** 30 Cooper Square, New York, NY 10003
■ **Website:** http://www.cooper.edu
■ **Private**
■ **Enrollment:** 895 full-time; 2 part-time

KEY STATS

✔ **U.S News College Ranking:** 2, Regional Colleges (North)
✔ **SAT Score (25th/75th percentile):** 1200-1480
✔ **Tuition:** 2010-2011: $36,650
    Selectivity: Most selective   **Room/board:** $9,700
    Acceptance rate: 7%   **Average debt:** $12,700
    Student/faculty ratio: 9/1   **Proportion who borrowed:** 33%

UNDERGRADUATE STUDENT BODY STATS

2009-2010 enrollment: 895 full-time; 2 part-time. Men: 63%; women: 37%. **Ethnic makeup:** African American: 5%; American-Indian: 1%; Asian American: 19%; Hispanic: 8%; White: 52%; International: 15%.

ADMISSIONS FACTS AND FIGURES

Phone: (212) 353-4120. **Email:** admissions@cooper.edu. **Website:** http://www.cooper.edu. **Application deadlines for fall 2011:** Regular decision: January 1; decision sent by April 1. Early decision: Send application by: December 1; Decision sent by: December 22. Early action: Not offered. Admission can be deferred. **Application fee:** $65. **To apply online, go to:** http://www.cooper.edu/administration/admissions/apply.html. **Admissions requirements/recommendations:** High school units required (recommended): English: 4 (4); Mathematics: 4 (4); Science: 2 (3); Foreign language: 0 (0); Social studies: 2 (4); History: 0 (0); Academic electives: 8 (10); Total units: 16 (18). Tests: The college uses SAT or ACT scores in admissions decisions. Either SAT or ACT required. For admission to the fall 2011 entering class, the school will accept: ACT with writing recommended. Campus visit: Recommended. Admissions interview: Neither required nor recommended. Off-campus interview: Not available. **Factors that count in admissions decisions: *Academic:*** Secondary school record: Very Important. Class rank: Considered. Letters of recommendation: Considered. Standardized test scores: Very Important. Essay: Important. *Nonacademic:* Interview: Considered. Extracurricular activities: Important. Talent/ability: Very Important. Character/personal qualities: Important. Alumni/ae relationship: Not Considered. Geographical residence: Not Considered. State residency: Not Considered. Religious affiliation/commitment: Not Considered. Minority status: Considered. Volunteer work: Important. Work experience: Considered. **Other schools with the greatest overlap in applicants:** Binghamton University–SUNY; Carnegie Mellon University; Columbia University; Cornell University; New York University. **Admissions statistics for the fall 2009 entering class:** Total applicants: 3,387. Total accepted: 249. Freshmen enrolled: 193; 50% were from out of state. Accepted through early-decision or early-action plans: 39%. Overall acceptance rate: 7%. Early-decision acceptance rate: 13%. Non-early acceptance rate: 6%. **Size of waiting list:** 100 applicants; enrolled from waiting list: 11. **Credentials of fall 2009 freshmen:** 93% ranked in the top 10 percent of their high school class; 98% were in the top 25 percent; 99% were in the top half. (Proportion submitting class standing: 65%.) **Average high school grade point average:** 3.6. **First-year students who submitted SAT scores:** 99%. Scores (25/75 percentile): Critical Reading: 600-710, Math: 600-770, Combined: 1200-1480. **First-year students submitting ACT scores:** 1%. Scores (25/75 percentile): English: N/A, Math: N/A, Composite: 29-33.

ACADEMICS

Year founded: 1859. **Academic calendar:** Semester. **Degrees offered:** certificate, bachelor's, master's. **Most popular majors:** 27% fine/studio arts, 14% architecture (B.Arch., B.A./B.S., M.Arch., M.A./M.S., Ph.D.), 13% chemical engineering, 13% civil engineering, 13% electrical, electronics, and communications engineering. **Major fields of study:** architecture and related services; engineering; visual and performing arts. **Areas of required coursework:** humanities, computer literacy, mathematics, sciences (biological or physical), history, social science. **Pre-professional programs:** other. **Special academic programs (% participation):** cross-registration (20%), English as a Second Language (ESL) (5%), exchange student program (domestic) (10%), honors program (100%), independent study (25%), internships (90%), liberal arts/career combination (100%), study abroad (25%). **Faculty and instruction (2009-2010):** Total instructional faculty: 55 full-time, 174 part-time (73% men; 27% women; 15% minorities). Full-time faculty with

Ph.D. or other terminal degree: 91%. Student/faculty ratio: 9/1. Classes of fewer than 20 students: 72%; of 20 to 49 students: 28%; of 50 or more students: 0%. **Advanced Placement and International Baccalaureate credit:** AP tests may be used for: Credit and/or placement. Scores accepted: 4, 5. International Baccalaureate exams may be used for: Placement only. **Freshmen returning for sophomore year:** 94%. **Graduation rates:** Four-year: 70%; five-year: 83%; six-year: 85%. **Graduate study:** 50% of students pursue further study immediately upon graduation. Fields in which graduates pursue further study: Master of Business Administration (MBA), 14%; law, 9%; medicine, 2%; dentistry, 1%; engineering, 74%.

COSTS AND FINANCIAL AID
Financial aid office: (212) 353-4113. **Expenses (2010-2011):** Tuition and fees 2010-2011: $36,650; room/board: $9,700. Estimated books and supplies: $1,400; transportation: $700; personal expenses: $1,575. **Financial aid:** Priority filing date for institution's financial aid form: May 1; deadline: May 1. In 2009-2010, 34% of undergraduates applied for financial aid. Of those, 32% were determined to have financial need; 53% had their need fully met. Average financial aid package (proportion receiving): $35,000 (32%). Average amount of gift aid, such as scholarships or grants (proportion receiving): $5,000 (32%). Average amount of self-help aid, such as work study or loans (proportion receiving): $3,400 (17%). Average need-based loan (excluding PLUS or other private loans): $3,100. Among students who received need-based aid, the average percentage of need met: 92%. Among students who received aid based on merit, the average award (and the proportion receiving): $35,000 (68%). The average athletic scholarship (and the proportion receiving): $0 (0%). Average amount of debt of borrowers graduating in 2009: $12,700. Proportion who borrowed: 33%.

CAMPUS LIFE AND EXTRACURRICULAR ACTIVITIES
Campus housing available (% using): coed dorms (100%). Students who live in college-owned, operated, or affiliated housing: 17%. **Student employment:** During the 2009-2010 academic year, 78% of undergraduates worked on campus. Average per-year earnings: $1,113. **Clubs and organizations:** Number of student organizations: 85. Activities include: choral groups, dance, drama/theater, literary magazine, music ensembles, student government, student newspaper, student film society, yearbook. Number of fraternities: 1; sororities: 1. Proportion of men in fraternities: 3%; of women in sororities: 1%. Average proportion of students who stay on campus on weekends: 35%.

SERVICES AND FACILITIES
Basic services: nonremedial tutoring, placement service, health insurance. **Remedial assistance:** writing. **Counseling services:** career, academic. **For learning-disabled students:** School does not offer a structured program with separate admission and additional fees. Total undergraduates in learning-disabled program or receiving services: 8. Services include: tape recorders, untimed tests, readers, extended time for tests, tutors, texts on tape, other testing accommodations. **Library:** Number of titles: 108,097; number of current serial subscriptions: 2,829. **Information technology resources:** Students are not required to lease or own a computer. Number of campus computers available to all students: 350. School has a wireless network. Approximate number of users that can be accommodated: 500. Proportion of college-owned housing units wired for high-speed internet access: 100%. **Campus safety:** Security services offered: controlled dormitory access (key, security card, etc).

TRANSFER AND INTERNATIONAL STUDENTS
Transfer students: May apply for admission for the following academic terms: Fall. Applicants need a minimum number of credits to apply. For fall 2009: Transfer applications received: 657. Transfer applicants offered admission: 35. Transfer applicants enrolled: 31. **International students:** Number of foreign undergraduates: 135 (15% of student body). Number of countries represented: 27. Minimum TOEFL score required: 600 (paper); 100 (computer). Average TOEFL score: 650 (paper).

Cornell University

- **Address:** Ithaca, NY 14853
- **Website:** http://www.cornell.edu
- **Private**
- **Enrollment:** 13,931 full-time

KEY STATS
✔ **U.S News College Ranking:** 15, National Universities
✔ **SAT Score (25th/75th percentile):** 1290-1500
✔ **Tuition:** 2010-2011: $39,666

Selectivity: Most selective	**Room/board:** $12,650
Acceptance rate: 19%	**Average debt:** $21,951
Student/faculty ratio: 11/1	**Proportion who borrowed:** 46%

UNDERGRADUATE STUDENT BODY STATS
2009-2010 enrollment: 13,931 full-time. Men: 51%; women: 49%. **Ethnic makeup:** African American: 5%; Asian American: 17%; Hispanic: 6%; White: 63%; International: 8%.

ADMISSIONS FACTS AND FIGURES
Phone: (607) 255-5241. **Email:** admissions@cornell.edu. **Website:** http://www.cornell.edu. **Application deadlines for fall 2011:** Regular decision: January 2. Early decision: Send application by: November 1; Decision sent by: December 15. Early action: Not offered. Admission can be deferred. **Application fee:** $70. **To apply online, go to:** http://admissions.cornell.edu/apply. **Admissions requirements/recommendations:** High school units required (recommended): English: 4; Mathematics: 3; Science: (3); Foreign language: (3); Social studies: (3); History: (3); Total units: 16. Tests: The college uses SAT or ACT scores in admissions decisions. Either SAT or ACT required. For admission to the fall 2011 entering class, the school will accept: ACT with writing required. Campus visit: Recommended. Admissions interview: Neither required nor recommended. Off-campus interview: Not available. **Factors that count in admissions decisions:** *Academic:* Secondary school record: Very Important. Class rank: Important. Letters of recommendation: Very Important. Standardized test scores: Very Important. Essay: Very Important. *Nonacademic:* Interview: Considered. Extracurricular activities: Very Important. Talent/ability: Very Important. Character/personal qualities: Considered. Alumni/ae relationship: Considered. Geographical residence: Considered. State residency: Considered. Religious affiliation/commitment: Not Considered. Minority status: Considered. Volunteer work: Considered. Work experience: Considered. **Admissions statistics for the fall 2009 entering class:** Total applicants: 34,371. Total accepted: 6,565. Freshmen enrolled: 3,181; 69% were from out of state. Accepted through early-decision or early-action plans: 39%. Overall acceptance rate: 19%. Early-decision acceptance rate: 37%. Non-early acceptance rate: 17%. **Size of waiting list:** 3308 applicants; enrolled from waiting list: 0. **Credentials of fall 2009 freshmen:** 86% ranked in the top 10 percent of their high school class; 98% were in the top 25 percent; 100% were in the top half. (Proportion submitting class standing: 34%.) **First-year students who submitted SAT scores:** 94%. Scores (25/75 percentile): Critical Reading: 630-730, Math: 660-770, Combined: 1290-1500. **First-year students submitting ACT scores:** 34%. Scores (25/75 percentile): English: N/A, Math: N/A, Composite: 29-33.

ACADEMICS
Year founded: 1865. **Academic calendar:** Semester. **Degrees offered:** bachelor's, master's, doctorate. **Most popular majors:** 18% engineering, 14% business, management, marketing, and related support services, 13% agriculture, agriculture operations, and related sciences, 12% biological and biomedical sciences, 10% social sciences. **Major fields of study:** agriculture, agriculture operations, and related sciences; architecture and related services; area, ethnic, cultural, and gender studies; biological and biomedical sciences; business, management, marketing, and related support services; communication, journalism, and related programs; computer and information sciences and support services; education; engineering; English language and literature/letters; family and consumer sciences/human sciences; foreign languages, literatures, and linguistics; health professions and related clinical sciences; history; liberal arts and sciences studies, and humanities; mathematics and statistics; multi/interdisciplinary studies; natural resources and conservation; philosophy and religious studies; physical sciences; psychology; public administration and social service professions; social sciences; visual and performing arts. **Areas of required coursework:** humanities, mathematics, English (including composition),

sciences (biological or physical), social science. **Pre-professional programs:** pre-law, pre-medicine, pre-veterinary science. **Special academic programs:** accelerated program, cooperative (work-study plan) program, cross-registration, distance learning, double major, English as a Second Language (ESL), exchange student program (domestic), honors program, independent study, internships, liberal arts/career combination, student-designed major, study abroad, teacher certificate program, other. **Cooperative education programs:** agriculture, engineering. **Reserve Officers Training Corps (ROTC):** Army ROTC: Offered on campus; Navy ROTC: Offered on campus; Air Force ROTC: Offered on campus. **Faculty and instruction (2009-2010):** Total instructional faculty: 1,458 full-time, 73 part-time (74% men; 26% women; 16% minorities). Full-time faculty with Ph.D. or other terminal degree: 99%. Student/faculty ratio: 11/1. Classes of fewer than 20 students: 56%; of 20 to 49 students: 26%; of 50 or more students: 18%. **Advanced Placement and International Baccalaureate credit:** AP tests may be used for: Credit and/or placement. Scores accepted: 4, 5. International Baccalaureate exams may be used for: Credit and/or placement. **Freshmen returning for sophomore year:** 96%. **Graduation rates:** Four-year: 85%; five-year: 91%; six-year: 92%. **Graduate study:** 34% of students pursue further study immediately upon graduation. Fields in which graduates pursue further study: Master of Business Administration (MBA), 4%; law, 17%; medicine, 15%; dentistry, 1%; engineering, 23%; education, 3%; veterinary medicine, 4%.

COSTS AND FINANCIAL AID

Financial aid office: (607) 255-5145. **Expenses (2010-2011):** Tuition and fees 2010-2011: $39,666; room/board: $12,650. Estimated books and supplies: $780 personal expenses: $1,580. **Financial aid:** In 2009-2010, 46% of undergraduates applied for financial aid. Of those, 46% were determined to have financial need; 100% had their need fully met. Average financial aid package (proportion receiving): $36,812 (46%). Average amount of gift aid, such as scholarships or grants (proportion receiving): $31,911 (45%). Average amount of self-help aid, such as work study or loans (proportion receiving): $4,900 (42%). Average need-based loan (excluding PLUS or other private loans): $3,327. Among students who received need-based aid, the average percentage of need met: 100%. Average amount of debt of borrowers graduating in 2009: $21,951. Proportion who borrowed: 46%.

CAMPUS LIFE AND EXTRACURRICULAR ACTIVITIES

Campus housing available (% using): coed dorms (60%), women's dorms (6%), men's dorms (0%), sorority housing (5%), fraternity housing (13%), apartments for married students (0%), apartment for single students (2%), special housing for disabled students (1%), special housing for international students (2%), cooperative housing (0%), other housing options (0%). Students who live in college-owned, operated, or affiliated housing: 56%. **Student employment:** During the 2009-2010 academic year, 50% of undergraduates worked on campus. Average per-year earnings: $2,100. **Clubs and organizations:** Number of student organizations: 814. Activities include: campus ministries, choral groups, concert band, dance, drama/theater, international student organization, jazz band, literary magazine, marching band, model UN, music ensembles, musical theater, pep band, radio station, student government, student newspaper, student film society, symphony orchestra, television station, yearbook. Number of fraternities: 50; sororities: 19. Proportion of men in fraternities: 32%; of women in sororities: 23%. Average proportion of students who stay on campus on weekends: 90%. **Sports program (2009-2010):** Member of NCAA I. *Men's intercollegiate varsity sports:* baseball, basketball, cross country, football, golf, ice hockey, lacrosse, soccer, swimming, tennis, track and field (indoor), track and field (outdoor), wrestling. *Women's intercollegiate varsity sports:* basketball, crew (heavyweight), cross country, equestrian, fencing, field hockey, gymnastics, ice hockey, lacrosse, crew (lightweight), soccer, softball, squash, swimming, tennis, track and field (indoor), track and field (outdoor), volleyball.

SERVICES AND FACILITIES

Basic services: nonremedial tutoring, women's center, placement service, health service, health insurance, other. **Counseling services:** minority student, career, personal, veteran student, academic, psychological, birth control, religious. **For learning-disabled students:** School does not offer a structured program with separate admission and additional fees. Total undergraduates in learning-disabled program or receiving services: 274. Services include: learning center, extended time for tests, other testing accommodations, other. **Library:** Number of titles: 7,518,029; number of current serial subscriptions: 93,000. **Information technology resources:** Students are not required to lease or own a computer. Number of campus computers available to all students: 2,650. School has a wireless network. Approximate number of users that can be accommodated: 35,000.

Proportion of college-owned housing units wired for high-speed internet access: 100%. **Campus safety:** Security services offered: 24-hour foot-and-vehicle patrols, late-night transport/escort service, 24-hour emergency telephones, lighted pathways/sidewalks, controlled dormitory access (key, security card, etc).

TRANSFER AND INTERNATIONAL STUDENTS

Transfer students: May apply for admission for the following academic terms: Fall, Spring. Applicants need a minimum number of credits to apply. For fall 2009: Transfer applications received: 3,240. Transfer applicants offered admission: 727. Transfer applicants enrolled: 567. **International students:** Number of foreign undergraduates: 1177 (8% of student body). Number of countries represented: 77. Minimum TOEFL score required: 600 (paper); 100 (computer).

CUNY–Baruch College

- **Address:** 1 Bernard Baruch Way, New York, NY 10010
- **Website:** http://www.baruch.cuny.edu
- **Public**
- **Enrollment:** 9,473 full-time; 2,859 part-time

KEY STATS

✔ **U.S News College Ranking:** 25, Regional Universities (North)
✔ **SAT Score (25th/75th percentile):** 1050-1260
✔ **Tuition:** 2010-2011: $4,920 in state, $12,770 out of state

Selectivity: More selective	**Room/board:** N/A
Acceptance rate: 23%	**Average debt:** $14,676
Student/faculty ratio 17/1	**Proportion who borrowed:** 37%

UNDERGRADUATE STUDENT BODY STATS

2009-2010 enrollment: 9,473 full-time; 2,859 part-time. Men: 49%; women: 51%. **Ethnic makeup:** African American: 10%; Asian American: 32%; Hispanic: 16%; White: 30%; International: 12%.

ADMISSIONS FACTS AND FIGURES

Phone: (646) 312-1400. **Email:** admissions@baruch.cuny.edu. **Website:** http://www.baruch.cuny.edu. **Application deadlines for fall 2011:** Regular decision: Rolling. Early decision: Send application by: December 13; Decision sent by: January 7. Early action: Not offered. Admission can be deferred. **Application fee:** $65. **To apply online, go to:** https://portal.cuny.edu/cms/id/cuny/documents/informationpage/006373.htm. **Admissions requirements/recommendations:** High school units required (recommended): English: 4; Mathematics: 3 (4); Science: 2; Foreign language: 2 (2); Social studies: 4; History: 0 (0); Academic electives: 0 (1); Total units: 16. Tests: The college uses SAT or ACT scores in admissions decisions. SAT required. For admission to the fall 2011 entering class, the school will accept: ACT with or without writing accepted. Campus visit: Neither required nor recommended. Admissions interview: Neither required nor recommended. Off-campus interview: Not available. **Factors that count in admissions decisions:** *Academic:* Secondary school record: Very Important. Class rank: Considered. Letters of recommendation: Important. Standardized test scores: Very Important. Essay: Important. *Nonacademic:* Interview: Considered. Extracurricular activities: Considered. Talent/ability: Considered. Character/personal qualities: Considered. Alumni/ae relationship: Considered. Geographical residence: Not Considered. State residency: Not Considered. Religious affiliation/commitment: Not Considered. Minority status: Not Considered. Volunteer work: Not Considered. Work experience: Considered. **Other schools with the greatest overlap in applicants:** Binghamton University–SUNY; Fordham University; New York University; SUNY–Stony Brook; St. John's University. **Admissions statistics for the fall 2009 entering class:** Total applicants: 19,775. Total accepted: 4,476. Freshmen enrolled: 1,442; 4% were from out of state. Overall acceptance rate: 23%. Non-early acceptance rate: 23%. **Credentials of fall 2009 freshmen:** 34% ranked in the top 10 percent of their high school class; 61% were in the top 25 percent; 91% were in the top half. (Proportion submitting class standing: 94%.) **Average high school grade point average:** 3.1. **First-year students who submitted SAT scores:** 94%. Scores (25/75 percentile): Critical Reading: 490-590, Math: 560-670, Combined: 1050-1260.

ACADEMICS

Year founded: 1919. **Academic calendar:** Semester. **Degrees offered:** bachelor's, master's, post-master's certificate. **Most popular majors:** 32%

investments and securities, 20% accounting, 11% sales, distribution, and marketing operations, 10% business administration and management, 6% communication, journalism, and related programs. **Major fields of study:** biological and biomedical sciences; business, management, marketing, and related support services; communication, journalism, and related programs; computer and information sciences and support services; engineering; English language and literature/letters; foreign languages, literatures, and linguistics; history; liberal arts and sciences studies, and humanities; mathematics and statistics; multi/interdisciplinary studies; philosophy and religious studies; psychology; public administration and social service professions; social sciences; visual and performing arts. **Areas of required coursework:** arts/fine arts, humanities, computer literacy, mathematics, English (including composition), philosophy, foreign languages, sciences (biological or physical), history, social science, other. **Pre-professional programs:** pre-law, pre-dentistry, pre-medicine, pre-veterinary science. **Special academic programs (% participation):** accelerated program (1%), cross-registration (1%), distance learning (0%), double major (1%), English as a Second Language (ESL) (2%), exchange student program (domestic) (1%), honors program (3%), independent study (4%), internships (50%), student-designed major (3%), study abroad (5%). **Cooperative education programs:** business. **Reserve Officers Training Corps (ROTC):** Army ROTC: Offered at cooperating institution (Fordham University). **Faculty and instruction (2009-2010):** Total instructional faculty: 498 full-time, 668 part-time (61% men; 39% women; 28% minorities). Full-time faculty with Ph.D. or other terminal degree: 91%. Student/faculty ratio: 17/1. Classes of fewer than 20 students: 27%; of 20 to 49 students: 61%; of 50 or more students: 12%. **Advanced Placement and International Baccalaureate credit:** AP tests may be used for: Placement only. Scores accepted: 4, 5. International Baccalaureate exams may be used for: Credit only. **Freshmen returning for sophomore year:** 89%. **Graduation rates:** Four-year: 33%; five-year: 55%; six-year: 59%. **Graduate study:** 7% of students pursue further study within one year.

COSTS AND FINANCIAL AID

Financial aid office: (646) 312-1360. **Expenses (2010-2011):** Tuition and fees 2010-2011: $4,920 in state, $12,770 out of state. Estimated books and supplies: $1,070. **Financial aid:** Priority filing date for institution's financial aid form: March 15; deadline: April 30. In 2009-2010, 79% of undergraduates applied for financial aid. Of those, 72% were determined to have financial need; 15% had their need fully met. Average financial aid package (proportion receiving): $6,598 (65%). Average amount of gift aid, such as scholarships or grants (proportion receiving): $4,958 (65%). Average amount of self-help aid, such as work study or loans (proportion receiving): $3,526 (63%). Average need-based loan (excluding PLUS or other private loans): $5,000. Among students who received need-based aid, the average percentage of need met: 76%. Among students who received aid based on merit, the average award (and the proportion receiving): $4,600 (1%). The average athletic scholarship (and the proportion receiving): $0 (0%). Average amount of debt of borrowers graduating in 2009: $14,676. Proportion who borrowed: 37%.

CAMPUS LIFE AND EXTRACURRICULAR ACTIVITIES

Student employment: During the 2009-2010 academic year, 6% of undergraduates worked on campus. Average per-year earnings: $2,500. **Clubs and organizations:** Number of student organizations: 150. Activities include: campus ministries, choral groups, dance, drama/theater, literary magazine, musical theater, radio station, student government, student newspaper, yearbook. Number of fraternities: 9; sororities: 7. Proportion of men in fraternities: 3%; of women in sororities: 5%. Average proportion of students who stay on campus on weekends: 5%. **Sports program (2009-2010):** Member of NCAA III. *Men's intercollegiate varsity sports:* baseball, basketball, cross country, soccer, swimming, tennis, volleyball. *Women's intercollegiate varsity sports:* basketball, cross country, softball, swimming, tennis, volleyball.

SERVICES AND FACILITIES

Basic services: nonremedial tutoring, placement service, day care, health service. **Remedial assistance:** other. **Counseling services:** career, personal, veteran student, academic, psychological. **For learning-disabled students:** School does not offer a structured program with separate admission and additional fees. Total undergraduates in learning-disabled program or receiving services: 107. Services include: reading machines, tape recorders, videotaped classes, diagnostic testing service, note-taking services, special bookstore section, oral tests, learning center, readers, extended time for tests, tutors, priority registration, priority seating, texts on tape, exams on tape or computer, other testing accommodations, other. **Library:** Number of titles: 566,509; number of current serial subscriptions: 70,269. **Information**

technology resources: Students are not required to lease or own a computer. Number of campus computers available to all students: 1,300. School has a wireless network. Approximate number of users that can be accommodated: 1,200. **Campus safety:** Security services offered: 24-hour foot-and-vehicle patrols, 24-hour emergency telephones, lighted pathways/sidewalks.

TRANSFER AND INTERNATIONAL STUDENTS

Transfer students: May apply for admission for the following academic terms: Fall, Spring. Applicants do not need a minimum number of credits to apply. For fall 2009: Transfer applications received: 8,368. Transfer applicants offered admission: 1,844. Transfer applicants enrolled: 1,260. **International students:** Number of foreign undergraduates: 1468 (12% of student body). Number of countries represented: 137. Minimum TOEFL score required: 620 (paper); 105 (computer). Average TOEFL score: 650 (paper).

CUNY–Brooklyn College

- **Address:** 2900 Bedford Avenue, Brooklyn, NY 11210
- **Website:** http://www.brooklyn.cuny.edu
- **Public**
- **Enrollment:** 9,268 full-time; 3,801 part-time

KEY STATS

✔ **U.S News College Ranking:** 61, Regional Universities (North)
✔ **SAT Score (25th/75th percentile):** 980-1190
✔ **Tuition:** 2010-2011: $5,051 in state, $12,901 out of state

Selectivity: Selective	**Room/board:** N/A
Acceptance rate: 28%	**Average debt:** $17,000
Student/faculty ratio: 15/1	**Proportion who borrowed:** 42%

UNDERGRADUATE STUDENT BODY STATS

2009-2010 enrollment: 9,268 full-time; 3,801 part-time. Men: 40%; women: 60%. **Ethnic makeup:** African American: 25%; Asian American: 16%; Hispanic: 12%; White: 41%; International: 6%.

ADMISSIONS FACTS AND FIGURES

Phone: (718) 951-5001. **Email:** adminqry@brooklyn.cuny.edu. **Website:** http://www.brooklyn.cuny.edu. **Application deadlines for fall 2011:** Early decision: Not offered. Early action: Not offered. Admission cannot be deferred. **Application fee:** $65. **To apply online, go to:** http://www.brooklyn.cuny.edu/pub/apply.htm. **Admissions requirements/recommendations:** High school units required (recommended): English: 4 (4); Mathematics: 3 (3); Science: 3 (3); Foreign language: 3 (3); Social studies: 4 (4); Academic electives: 4 (4); Total units: 21 (21). Tests: The college uses SAT or ACT scores in admissions decisions. Either SAT or ACT required. For admission to the fall 2011 entering class, the school will accept: ACT with or without writing accepted. Campus visit: Recommended. Admissions interview: Neither required nor recommended. Off-campus interview: Not available. **Factors that count in admissions decisions:** *Academic:* Secondary school record: Very Important. Class rank: Not Considered. Letters of recommendation: Not Considered. Standardized test scores: Very Important. Essay: Not Considered. *Nonacademic:* Interview: Not Considered. Extracurricular activities: Not Considered. Talent/ability: Not Considered. Character/personal qualities: Not Considered. Alumni/ae relationship: Not Considered. Geographical residence: Not Considered. State residency: Not Considered. Religious affiliation/commitment: Not Considered. Minority status: Not Considered. Volunteer work: Not Considered. Work experience: Not Considered. **Other schools with the greatest overlap in applicants:** CUNY–Baruch College; CUNY–Hunter College; SUNY–Stony Brook; University at Albany–SUNY; University at Buffalo–SUNY. **Admissions statistics for the fall 2009 entering class:** Total applicants: 17,497. Total accepted: 4,873. Freshmen enrolled: 977; 1% were from out of state. Overall acceptance rate: 28%. **Credentials of fall 2009 freshmen:** 19% ranked in the top 10 percent of their high school class; 56% were in the top 25 percent; 85% were in the top half. (Proportion submitting class standing: 54%.) **Average high school grade point average:** 3.4. **First-year students who submitted SAT scores:** 88%. Scores (25/75 percentile): Critical Reading: 470-580, Math: 510-610, Combined: 980-1190.

ACADEMICS

Year founded: 1930. **Academic calendar:** Semester. **Degrees offered:** certificate, bachelor's, post-bachelor's certificate, master's, post-master's certificate. **Most popular majors:** 33% business, management, marketing, and related support services, 13% education, 12% psychology, 7% health professions and related clinical sciences, 6% social sciences. **Major fields of study:** area, ethnic, cultural, and gender studies; biological and biomedical sciences; business, management, marketing, and related support services; communication, journalism, and related programs; communications technologies/technicians and support services; computer and information sciences and support services; education; English language and literature/letters; foreign languages, literatures, and linguistics; health professions and related clinical sciences; history; liberal arts and sciences studies, and humanities; mathematics and statistics; natural resources and conservation; parks, recreation, leisure, and fitness studies; philosophy and religious studies; physical sciences; psychology; social sciences; visual and performing arts. **Areas of required coursework:** arts/fine arts, humanities, computer literacy, mathematics, English (including composition), philosophy, foreign languages, sciences (biological or physical), history, social science, other. **Pre-professional programs:** pre-law, pre-medicine. **Special academic programs:** accelerated program, cooperative (work-study plan) program, cross-registration, distance learning, double major, dual enrollment, English as a Second Language (ESL), honors program, independent study, internships, study abroad, teacher certificate program, weekend college. **Teacher certification offered in:** early childhood, special education, elementary, middle/junior high, secondary, bilingual/bicultural. **Cooperative education programs:** education, health professions. **Faculty and instruction (2009-2010):** Total instructional faculty: 557 full-time, 844 part-time (53% men; 47% women; 22% minorities). Full-time faculty with Ph.D. or other terminal degree: 93%. Student/faculty ratio: 15/1. Classes of fewer than 20 students: 40%; of 20 to 49 students: 58%; of 50 or more students: 2%. **Advanced Placement and International Baccalaureate credit:** AP tests may be used for: Credit only. Scores accepted: 3, 4, 5. International Baccalaureate exams may be used for: Credit only. **Freshmen returning for sophomore year:** 78%. **Graduation rates:** Four-year: 17%; five-year: 36%; six-year: 45%.

COSTS AND FINANCIAL AID

Financial aid office: (718) 951-5045. **Expenses (2010-2011):** Tuition and fees 2010-2011: $5,051 in state, $12,901 out of state. **Financial aid:** Priority filing date for institution's financial aid form: April 1. In 2009-2010, 79% of undergraduates applied for financial aid. Of those, 75% were determined to have financial need; 98% had their need fully met. Average financial aid package (proportion receiving): $6,100 (74%). Average amount of gift aid, such as scholarships or grants (proportion receiving): $3,600 (68%). Average amount of self-help aid, such as work study or loans (proportion receiving): $3,500 (70%). Average need-based loan (excluding PLUS or other private loans): $3,500. Among students who received need-based aid, the average percentage of need met: 99%. Among students who received aid based on merit, the average award (and the proportion receiving): $1,700 (11%). The average athletic scholarship (and the proportion receiving): $0 (0%). Average amount of debt of borrowers graduating in 2009: $17,000. Proportion who borrowed: 42%.

CAMPUS LIFE AND EXTRACURRICULAR ACTIVITIES

Average per-year earnings: $8. **Clubs and organizations:** Number of student organizations: 171. Activities include: dance, drama/theater, international student organization, literary magazine, music ensembles, musical theater, radio station, student government, student newspaper, student film society, symphony orchestra, television station, yearbook. Number of fraternities: 7; sororities: 9. Proportion of men in fraternities: 3%; of women in sororities: 3%. **Sports program (2009-2010):** Member of NCAA III. *Men's intercollegiate varsity sports:* basketball, cross country, soccer, tennis, volleyball. *Women's intercollegiate varsity sports:* basketball, cross country, softball, tennis, volleyball.

SERVICES AND FACILITIES

Basic services: nonremedial tutoring, women's center, day care, health service, health insurance. **Counseling services:** minority student, career, military, personal, veteran student, academic, older student, psychological, birth control, religious. **For learning-disabled students:** School does not offer a structured program with separate admission and additional fees. Services include: reading machines, tape recorders, untimed tests, note-taking services, learning center, readers, extended time for tests, priority registration, priority seating, texts on tape. **Library:** Number of titles: 1,461,646; number of current serial subscriptions: 57,235. **Information technology resources:** Students are not required to lease or own a computer. Number of campus computers available to all students: 1,200. School has a wireless network. Approximate number of users that can be accommodated: 400. Proportion of college-owned housing units wired for high-speed internet access: 0%.

Campus safety: Security services offered: 24-hour foot-and-vehicle patrols, late-night transport/escort service, 24-hour emergency telephones, lighted pathways/sidewalks.

TRANSFER AND INTERNATIONAL STUDENTS

Transfer students: May apply for admission for the following academic terms: Fall, Spring. Applicants do not need a minimum number of credits to apply. For fall 2009: Transfer applicants enrolled: 1,759. **International students:** Number of foreign undergraduates: 685 (6% of student body). Number of countries represented: 86. Minimum TOEFL score required: 500 (paper); 173 (computer).

CUNY–City College

- **Address:** 160 Convent Avenue, New York, NY 10031
- **Website:** http://www.ccny.cuny.edu
- **Public**
- **Enrollment:** 9,641 full-time; 3,319 part-time

KEY STATS

✔ U.S News College Ranking: 61, Regional Universities (North)
✔ SAT Score (25th/75th percentile): 910-1150
✔ Tuition: 2010-2011: $4,929 in state, $10,289 out of state

Selectivity: Selective	Room/board: $7,875
Acceptance rate: 29%	Average debt: $16,821
Student/faculty ratio: 11/1	Proportion who borrowed: 31%

UNDERGRADUATE STUDENT BODY STATS

2009-2010 enrollment: 9,641 full-time; 3,319 part-time. Men: 49%; women: 51%. **Ethnic makeup:** African American: 23%; Asian American: 20%; Hispanic: 36%; White: 11%; International: 11%.

ADMISSIONS FACTS AND FIGURES

Phone: (212) 650-6977. **Email:** admissions@ccny.cuny.edu. **Website:** http://www.ccny.cuny.edu. **Application deadlines for fall 2011:** Regular decision: Rolling. Early decision: Not offered. Early action: Not offered. Admission cannot be deferred. **Application fee:** $65. **To apply online, go to:** http://www.applyto.uapc.cuny.edu/. **Admissions requirements/recommendations:** High school units required (recommended): English: 4 (4); Mathematics: 3 (3); Science: 2 (2); Foreign language: 3 (3); Social studies: 4 (4); Academic electives: 1 (1); Total units: 19 (19). Tests: The college uses SAT or ACT scores in admissions decisions. SAT required. Campus visit: Neither required nor recommended. Admissions interview: Neither required nor recommended. Off-campus interview: Not available. **Factors that count in admissions decisions:** *Academic:* Secondary school record: Very Important. Class rank: Not Considered. Letters of recommendation: Not Considered. Standardized test scores: Very Important. Essay: Not Considered. *Nonacademic:* Interview: Not Considered. Extracurricular activities: Not Considered. Talent/ability: Not Considered. Character/personal qualities: Not Considered. Alumni/ae relationship: Not Considered. Geographical residence: Not Considered. State residency: Not Considered. Religious affiliation/commitment: Not Considered. Minority status: Not Considered. Volunteer work: Not Considered. Work experience: Not Considered. **Other schools with the greatest overlap in applicants:** CUNY–Baruch College; CUNY–Brooklyn College; CUNY–Hunter College; CUNY–Lehman College; CUNY–Queens College. **Admissions statistics for the fall 2009 entering class:** Total applicants: 22,574. Total accepted: 6,551. Freshmen enrolled: 1,770; 9% were from out of state. Overall acceptance rate: 29%. **Credentials of fall 2009 freshmen:** 29% ranked in the top 10 percent of their high school class; 31% were in the top 25 percent; 88% were in the top half. (Proportion submitting class standing: 42%.) **Average high school grade point average:** 3.0. **First-year students who submitted SAT scores:** 89%. Scores (25/75 percentile): Critical Reading: 440-550, Math: 470-600, Combined: 910-1150.

ACADEMICS

Year founded: 1847. **Academic calendar:** Semester. **Degrees offered:** bachelor's, post-bachelor's certificate, master's, post-master's certificate, doctorate. **Most popular majors:** 16% engineering, 13% psychology, 12% visual and performing arts, 11% social sciences, 10% liberal arts and sciences studies, and humanities. **Major fields of study:** architecture and related services; area, ethnic, cultural, and gender studies; biological and biomedical sciences; business, management, marketing, and related support services; communication, journalism, and related programs; computer and information sciences and support services; education; engineering; English language and literature/letters; foreign languages, literatures, and linguistics; health professions and related clinical sciences; history; liberal arts and sciences studies, and humanities; mathematics and statistics; philosophy and religious studies; physical sciences; psychology; social sciences; visual and performing arts. **Areas of required coursework:** arts/fine arts, humanities, computer literacy, mathematics, English (including composition), philosophy, foreign languages, sciences (biological or physical), history, social science. **Pre-professional programs:** pre-law, pre-dentistry, pre-medicine. **Special academic programs:** accelerated program, cooperative (work-study plan) program, distance learning, double major, dual enrollment, English as a Second Language (ESL), honors program, independent study, internships, study abroad, teacher certificate program. **Teacher certification offered in:** early childhood, special education, elementary, middle/junior high, secondary, bilingual/bicultural. **Cooperative education programs:** art, computer science, engineering, health professions, social/behavioral science. **Faculty and instruction (2009-2010):** Total instructional faculty: 574 full-time, 1,009 part-time (56% men; 44% women; 20% minorities). Full-time faculty with Ph.D. or other terminal degree: 84%. Student/faculty ratio: 11/1. Classes of fewer than 20 students: 38%; of 20 to 49 students: 60%; of 50 or more students: 2%. **Advanced Placement and International Baccalaureate credit:** AP tests may be used for: Credit only. Scores accepted: 4, 5. International Baccalaureate exams may be used for: Credit only. **Freshmen returning for sophomore year:** 80%. **Graduation rates:** Four-year: 4%; five-year: 23%; six-year: 37%. **Graduate study:** 35% of students pursue further study immediately upon graduation. Fields in which graduates pursue further study: Master of Business Administration (MBA), 1%; law, 1%; medicine, 3%; engineering, 2%; education, 14%; arts and sciences, 14%.

COSTS AND FINANCIAL AID

Financial aid office: (212) 650-5819. **Expenses (2010-2011):** Tuition and fees 2010-2011: $4,929 in state, $10,289 out of state; room/board: $7,875. Estimated books and supplies: $1,016; transportation: $960; personal expenses: $1,200. **Financial aid:** Priority filing date for institution's financial aid form: April 1. In 2009-2010, 94% of undergraduates applied for financial aid. Of those, 90% were determined to have financial need; 59% had their need fully met. Average financial aid package (proportion receiving): $10,085 (87%). Average amount of gift aid, such as scholarships or grants (proportion receiving): $6,672 (77%). Average amount of self-help aid, such as work study or loans (proportion receiving): $6,934 (60%). Average need-based loan (excluding PLUS or other private loans): $3,774. Among students who received need-based aid, the average percentage of need met: 81%. Among students who received aid based on merit, the average award (and the proportion receiving): $2,630 (4%). The average athletic scholarship (and the proportion receiving): $0 (0%). Average amount of debt of borrowers graduating in 2009: $16,821. Proportion who borrowed: 31%.

CAMPUS LIFE AND EXTRACURRICULAR ACTIVITIES

Campus housing available: apartments for married students, apartment for single students, other housing options. Students who live in college-owned, operated, or affiliated housing: 3%. **Student employment:** During the 2009-2010 academic year, 9% of undergraduates worked on campus. Average per-year earnings: $1,000. **Clubs and organizations:** Number of student organizations: 120. Activities include: choral groups, dance, drama/theater, international student organization, jazz band, literary magazine, model UN, music ensembles, musical theater, radio station, student government, student newspaper, student film society, television station, yearbook. Number of fraternities: 3; sororities: 2. Average proportion of students who stay on campus on weekends: 37%. **Sports program (2009-2010):** Member of NCAA III. *Men's intercollegiate varsity sports:* basketball, track and field (indoor), track and field (outdoor). *Women's intercollegiate varsity sports:* basketball, track and field (indoor), track and field (outdoor).

SERVICES AND FACILITIES

Basic services: nonremedial tutoring, placement service, day care, health service. **Remedial assistance:** reading, math, writing, study skills. **Counseling services:** minority student, career, personal, veteran student, academic, psychological, birth control, religious. **For learning-disabled students:** School does not offer a structured program with separate admission and additional fees. Total undergraduates in learning-disabled program or receiving services: 82. Services include: reading machines, tape recorders, note-taking services, oral tests, learning center, readers, extended time for tests, tutors. **Library:** Number of titles: 1,446,663; number of current serial subscriptions: 50,096. **Information technology resources:** Students are not required to lease or own a computer. Number of campus computers available to all students: 1,989. School has a wireless network. Approximate number of users

that can be accommodated: 1,000. Proportion of college-owned housing units wired for high-speed internet access: 100%. **Campus safety:** Security services offered: 24-hour foot-and-vehicle patrols, late-night transport/escort service, 24-hour emergency telephones, lighted pathways/sidewalks, controlled dormitory access (key, security card, etc).

TRANSFER AND INTERNATIONAL STUDENTS

Transfer students: May apply for admission for the following academic terms: Fall, Winter, Spring, Summer. Applicants do not need a minimum number of credits to apply. For fall 2009: Transfer applications received: 6,924. Transfer applicants offered admission: 2,615. Transfer applicants enrolled: 1,536. **International students:** Number of foreign undergraduates: 1112 (11% of student body). Number of countries represented: 153. Minimum TOEFL score required: 500 (paper); 173 (computer). Average TOEFL score: 558 (paper).

CUNY–College of Staten Island

- **Address:** 2800 Victory Boulevard, Staten Island, NY 10314
- **Website:** http://www.csi.cuny.edu
- **Public**
- **Enrollment:** 9,231 full-time; 3,655 part-time

KEY STATS
✔ **U.S News College Ranking:** second tier, Regional Universities (North)
✔ **SAT Score (25th/75th percentile):** 895-1080
✔ **Tuition:** 2009-2010: $4,978 in state, $11,178 out of state
  Selectivity: Less selective   **Room/board:** N/A
  Acceptance rate: 100%   **Average debt:** N/A
  Student/faculty ratio: 18/1   **Proportion who borrowed:** N/A

UNDERGRADUATE STUDENT BODY STATS

2009-2010 enrollment: 9,231 full-time; 3,655 part-time. Men: 42%; women: 58%. **Ethnic makeup:** African American: 6%; Asian American: 6%; Hispanic: 8%; White: 77%; International: 3%.

ADMISSIONS FACTS AND FIGURES

Phone: (718) 982-2010. **Email:** admissions@mail.csi.cuny.edu. **Website:** http://www.csi.cuny.edu. **Application deadlines for fall 2011:** Regular decision: Rolling; decision sent by December 15. Early decision: Not offered. Early action: Not offered. Admission can be deferred. **Application fee:** $65. **To apply online, go to:** http://www.cuny.edu/apply. **Admissions requirements/recommendations:** High school units required (recommended): English: 4 (4); Mathematics: 2 (3); Science: 2 (3); Foreign language: 2 (3); Social studies: 4 (4); Total units: 15 (16). Tests: The college uses SAT or ACT scores in admissions decisions. Neither SAT nor ACT required. For admission to the fall 2011 entering class, the school will accept: ACT with or without writing accepted. Campus visit: Recommended. Off-campus interview: Not available. **Factors that count in admissions decisions:** *Academic:* Secondary school record: Very Important. Class rank: Not Considered. Letters of recommendation: Not Considered. Standardized test scores: Important. Essay: Not Considered. *Nonacademic:* Interview: Not Considered. Extracurricular activities: Not Considered. Talent/ability: Not Considered. Character/personal qualities: Not Considered. Alumni/ae relationship: Not Considered. Geographical residence: Not Considered. State residency: Not Considered. Religious affiliation/commitment: Not Considered. Minority status: Not Considered. Volunteer work: Not Considered. Work experience: Not Considered. **Other schools with the greatest overlap in applicants:** CUNY–Baruch College; CUNY–Brooklyn College; CUNY–Hunter College; CUNY–John Jay College of Criminal Justice; CUNY–New York City College of Technology. **Admissions statistics for the fall 2009 entering class:** Total applicants: 9,730. Total accepted: 9,730. Freshmen enrolled: 2,685; 1% were from out of state. Overall acceptance rate: 100%. **Average high school grade point average:** 3.0. **First-year students who submitted SAT scores:** 99%. Scores (25/75 percentile): Critical Reading: 440-530, Math: 455-550, Combined: 895-1080.

ACADEMICS

Year founded: 1955. **Academic calendar:** Semester. **Degrees offered:** certificate, associate, terminal-associate, bachelor's, master's, post-master's certificate, doctorate. **Most popular majors:** 24% business, management, marketing, and related support services, 18% social sciences, 10% liberal arts and sciences studies, and humanities, 10% psychology, 6% English language and literature/letters. **Major fields of study:** architecture and related services; area, ethnic, cultural, and gender studies; biological and biomedical sciences; business, management, marketing, and related support services; communication, journalism, and related programs; computer and information sciences and support services; education; engineering; English language and literature/letters; foreign languages, literatures, and linguistics; health professions and related clinical sciences; history; liberal arts and sciences studies, and humanities; mathematics and statistics; philosophy and religious studies; physical sciences; psychology; public administration and social service professions; social sciences; visual and performing arts. **Areas of required coursework:** arts/fine arts, humanities, mathematics, English (including composition), philosophy, foreign languages, sciences (biological or physical), history, social science, other. **Pre-professional programs:** pre-law, pre-dentistry, pre-medicine, pre-veterinary science, pre-optometry, other. **Special academic programs:** accelerated program, cooperative (work-study plan) program, cross-registration, distance learning, double major, dual enrollment, English as a Second Language (ESL), exchange student program (domestic), honors program, independent study, internships, liberal arts/career combination, study abroad, teacher certificate program, weekend college. **Teacher certification offered in:** early childhood, elementary, secondary, bilingual/bicultural. **Faculty and instruction (2009-2010):** Total instructional faculty: 368 full-time, 680 part-time (53% men; 47% women; 19% minorities). Full-time faculty with Ph.D. or other terminal degree: 76%. Student/faculty ratio: 18/1. Classes of fewer than 20 students: 31%; of 20 to 49 students: 66%; of 50 or more students: 3%. **Advanced Placement and International Baccalaureate credit:** AP tests may be used for: Credit and/or placement. Scores accepted: 3, 4, 5. International Baccalaureate exams may be used for: Placement only. **Freshmen returning for sophomore year:** 81%. **Graduation rates:** Four-year: 23%; five-year: 39%; six-year: 47%. **Graduate study:** 15% of students pursue further study immediately upon graduation; 19% within one year; 30% within five years.

COSTS AND FINANCIAL AID

Financial aid office: (718) 982-2030. **Expenses (2009-2010):** Tuition and fees 2009-2010: $4,978 in state, $11,178 out of state. **Financial aid:** Priority filing date for institution's financial aid form: March 31. In 2009-2010, 77% of undergraduates applied for financial aid. Of those, 59% were determined to have financial need; 6% had their need fully met. Average financial aid package (proportion receiving): $7,520 (57%). Average amount of gift aid, such as scholarships or grants (proportion receiving): $6,695 (56%). Average amount of self-help aid, such as work study or loans (proportion receiving): $2,657 (17%). Average need-based loan (excluding PLUS or other private loans): $4,143. Among students who received need-based aid, the average percentage of need met: 60%. Among students who received aid based on merit, the average award (and the proportion receiving): $1,545 (5%).

CAMPUS LIFE AND EXTRACURRICULAR ACTIVITIES

Student employment: During the 2009-2010 academic year, 2% of undergraduates worked on campus. **Clubs and organizations:** Number of student organizations: 47. Activities include: campus ministries, choral groups, dance, drama/theater, international student organization, jazz band, literary magazine, music ensembles, radio station, student government, student newspaper, student film society, yearbook. Number of fraternities: 0; sororities: 0. **Sports program (2009-2010):** Member of NCAA III. *Men's intercollegiate varsity sports:* baseball, basketball, cross country, soccer, swimming, tennis. *Women's intercollegiate varsity sports:* basketball, cross country, soccer, softball, swimming, tennis, volleyball.

SERVICES AND FACILITIES

Basic services: nonremedial tutoring, women's center, placement service, day care, health service, health insurance. **Remedial assistance:** reading, math, writing, other. **Counseling services:** minority student, career, military, personal, veteran student, academic, older student, psychological, birth control, religious. **For learning-disabled students:** School does not offer a structured program with separate admission and additional fees. Total undergraduates in learning-disabled program or receiving services: 197. Services include: remedial math, remedial English, reading machines, remedial reading, tape recorders, note-taking services, oral tests, readers, extended time for tests, tutors, early syllabus, priority registration, texts on tape, typist/scribe, exams on tape or computer, take home exams. **Library:** Number of titles: 243,000; number of current serial subscriptions: 44,000. **Information technology resources:** Students are not required to lease or own a computer. Number of campus computers available to all students: 1,254. School has a wireless network. Approximate number of users that can be accommodated: 1,024. **Campus safety:** Security services offered: 24-hour foot-and-vehicle patrols, late-night transport/escort service, 24-hour emergency telephones, lighted pathways/sidewalks.

TRANSFER AND INTERNATIONAL STUDENTS

Transfer students: May apply for admission for the following academic terms: Fall, Spring, Summer. Applicants do not need a minimum number of credits to apply. For fall 2009: Transfer applicants offered admission: 1,022. Transfer applicants enrolled: 678. **International students:** Number of foreign undergraduates: 369 (3% of student body). Number of countries represented: 105. Minimum TOEFL score required: 450 (paper); 133 (computer). Average TOEFL score: 526 (paper).

CUNY–Hunter College

- **Address:** 695 Park Avenue, New York, NY 10021
- **Website:** http://www.hunter.cuny.edu
- **Public**
- **Enrollment:** 11,171 full-time; 4,713 part-time

KEY STATS

✔ **U.S News College Ranking:** 39, Regional Universities (North)
✔ **SAT Score (25th/75th percentile):** 1030-1230
✔ **Tuition:** 2010-2011: $4,999 in state, $10,359 out of state

Selectivity: More selective	**Room/board:** $3,300
Acceptance rate: 26%	**Average debt:** $7,500
Student/faculty ratio: 15/1	**Proportion who borrowed:** 53%

UNDERGRADUATE STUDENT BODY STATS

2009-2010 enrollment: 11,171 full-time; 4,713 part-time. Men: 33%; women: 67%. **Ethnic makeup:** African American: 12%; Asian American: 21%; Hispanic: 19%; White: 39%; International: 9%.

ADMISSIONS FACTS AND FIGURES

Phone: (212) 772-4490. **Email:** admissions@hunter.cuny.edu. **Website:** http://www.hunter.cuny.edu. **Application deadlines for fall 2011:** Regular decision: March 15. Early decision: Not offered. Early action: Not offered. Admission can be deferred. **Application fee:** $65. **To apply online, go to:** https://portal.cuny.edu/cms/id/cuny/documents/informationpage/006373.htm. **Admissions requirements/recommendations:** High school units required (recommended): English: 2 (4); Mathematics: 2 (3); Science: 1 (2); Foreign language: (2); Social studies: (4); Total units: (16). Tests: The college uses SAT or ACT scores in admissions decisions. Either SAT or ACT required. For admission to the fall 2011 entering class, the school will accept: ACT with or without writing accepted. Campus visit: Recommended. Admissions interview: Neither required nor recommended. **Factors that count in admissions decisions:** *Academic:* Secondary school record: Very Important. Class rank: Not Considered. Letters of recommendation: Not Considered. Standardized test scores: Very Important. Essay: Not Considered. *Nonacademic:* Interview: Not Considered. Extracurricular activities: Not Considered. Talent/ability: Not Considered. Character/personal qualities: Not Considered. Alumni/ae relationship: Not Considered. Geographical residence: Not Considered. State residency: Not Considered. Religious affiliation/commitment: Not Considered. Minority status: Not Considered. Volunteer work: Not Considered. Work experience: Not Considered. **Other schools with the greatest overlap in applicants:** Binghamton University–SUNY; Fordham University; New York University; SUNY–Stony Brook. **Admissions statistics for the fall 2009 entering class:** Total applicants: 30,528. Total accepted: 7,892. Freshmen enrolled: 2,028; 5% were from out of state. Overall acceptance rate: 26%. **Credentials of fall 2009 freshmen:** 23% ranked in the top 10 percent of their high school class; 52% were in the top 25 percent; 83% were in the top half. (Proportion submitting class standing: 86%.) **Average high school grade point average:** 3.1. **First-year students who submitted SAT scores:** 100%. Scores (25/75 percentile): Critical Reading: 510-610, Math: 520-620, Combined: 1030-1230.

ACADEMICS

Year founded: 1870. **Academic calendar:** Semester. **Degrees offered:** bachelor's, master's, post-master's certificate. **Most popular majors:** 23% social sciences, 15% English language and literature/letters, 15% psychology, 9% visual and performing arts, 8% communication, journalism, and related programs. **Major fields of study:** area, ethnic, cultural, and gender studies; biological and biomedical sciences; business, management, marketing, and related support services; communication, journalism, and related programs; computer and information sciences and support services; education; English language and literature/letters; family and consumer sciences/human sciences; foreign languages, literatures, and linguistics; health professions and related clinical sciences; history; liberal arts and sciences studies, and humanities; mathematics and statistics; multi/interdisciplinary studies; philosophy and religious studies; physical sciences; psychology; social sciences; visual and performing arts. **Areas of required coursework:** arts/fine arts, humanities, mathematics, English (including composition), foreign languages, sciences (biological or physical), history, social science, other. **Pre-professional programs:** pre-law, pre-dentistry, pre-medicine, pre-veterinary science, pre-optometry, pre-pharmacy, other. **Special academic programs:** accelerated program, cross-registration, distance learning, double major, dual enrollment, English as a Second Language (ESL), exchange student program (domestic), honors program, independent study, internships, liberal arts/career combination, student-designed major, study abroad, teacher certificate program, other. **Teacher certification offered in:** early childhood, special education, elementary, middle/junior high, secondary, bilingual/bicultural. **Faculty and instruction (2009-2010):** Total instructional faculty: 694 full-time, 1,086 part-time (42% men; 58% women; 18% minorities). Full-time faculty with Ph.D. or other terminal degree: 88%. Student/faculty ratio: 15/1. Classes of fewer than 20 students: 42%; of 20 to 49 students: 53%; of 50 or more students: 5%. **Advanced Placement and International Baccalaureate credit:** AP tests may be used for: Placement only. Scores accepted: 4, 5. **Freshmen returning for sophomore year:** 83%. **Graduation rates:** Four-year: 17%; five-year: 36%; six-year: 40%.

COSTS AND FINANCIAL AID

Financial aid office: (212) 772-4820. **Expenses (2010-2011):** Tuition and fees 2010-2011: $4,999 in state, $10,359 out of state; room/board: $3,300. Estimated books and supplies: $1,070; transportation: $918; personal expenses: $4,526. **Financial aid:** Priority filing date for institution's financial aid form: May 1. In 2009-2010, 69% of undergraduates applied for financial aid. Of those, 57% were determined to have financial need; 16% had their need fully met. Average financial aid package (proportion receiving): $5,092 (55%). Average amount of gift aid, such as scholarships or grants (proportion receiving): $4,141 (57%). Average amount of self-help aid, such as work study or loans (proportion receiving): $2,174 (17%). Average need-based loan (excluding PLUS or other private loans): $3,179. Among students who received need-based aid, the average percentage of need met: 78%. Among students who received aid based on merit, the average award (and the proportion receiving): $2,368 (7%). Average amount of debt of borrowers graduating in 2009: $7,500. Proportion who borrowed: 53%.

CAMPUS LIFE AND EXTRACURRICULAR ACTIVITIES

Campus housing available (% using): coed dorms (3%), other housing options (97%). **Clubs and organizations:** Number of student organizations: 150. Activities include: concert band, dance, drama/theater, jazz band, literary magazine, music ensembles, musical theater, radio station, student government, student newspaper, student film society, symphony orchestra, television station, yearbook. Number of fraternities: 2; sororities: 2. Proportion of men in fraternities: 1%; **Sports program (2009-2010):** Member of NCAA III. **Men's intercollegiate varsity sports:** basketball, cross country, fencing, soccer, swimming, track and field (indoor), track and field (outdoor), volleyball, wrestling. **Women's intercollegiate varsity sports:** basketball, cross country, fencing, soccer, softball, swimming, track and field (indoor), track and field (outdoor), volleyball.

SERVICES AND FACILITIES

Basic services: nonremedial tutoring, women's center, placement service, day care, health service. **Counseling services:** career, personal, academic, psychological, religious. **For learning-disabled students:** School does not offer a structured program with separate admission and additional fees. Services include: reading machines, tape recorders, diagnostic testing service, untimed tests, note-taking services, learning center, readers, extended time for tests, tutors, priority registration, priority seating, texts on tape, other testing accommodations, other. **Library:** Number of titles: 873,465; number of current serial subscriptions: 4,656. **Information technology resources:** Students are not required to lease or own a computer. Number of campus computers available to all students: 1,280. School has a wireless network. Approximate number of users that can be accommodated: 3,000. Proportion of college-owned housing units wired for high-speed internet access: 100%. **Campus safety:** Security services offered: 24-hour foot-and-vehicle patrols, late-night transport/escort service, 24-hour emergency telephones, lighted pathways/sidewalks, controlled dormitory access (key, security card, etc).

TRANSFER AND INTERNATIONAL STUDENTS

Transfer students: May apply for admission for the following academic terms: Fall, Spring. Applicants do not need a minimum number of credits to apply. For fall 2009: Transfer applications received: 11,148. Transfer applicants offered admission: 2,778. Transfer applicants enrolled: 1,590. **International students:** Number of foreign undergraduates: 1323 (9% of student body). Minimum TOEFL score required: 500 (paper); 173 (computer). Average TOEFL score: 559 (paper).

CUNY–John Jay College of Criminal Justice

- **Address:** 899 10th Avenue, New York, NY 10019
- **Website:** http://www.jjay.cuny.edu/
- **Public**
- **Enrollment:** 10,383 full-time; 2,963 part-time

KEY STATS

✔ **U.S News College Ranking:** 121, Regional Universities (North)
✔ **SAT Score (25th/75th percentile):** 810-1000
✔ **Tuition:** 2009-2010: $4,929 in state, $12,779 out of state

Selectivity: Less selective   **Room/board:** N/A
Acceptance rate: 63%   **Average debt:** $45,000
Student/faculty ratio: 19/1   **Proportion who borrowed:** 49%

UNDERGRADUATE STUDENT BODY STATS

2009-2010 enrollment: 10,383 full-time; 2,963 part-time. Men: 43%; women: 57%. **Ethnic makeup:** African American: 23%; Asian American: 8%; Hispanic: 41%; White: 25%; International: 3%.

ADMISSIONS FACTS AND FIGURES

Phone: (212) 237-8869. **Email:** admiss@jjay.cuny.edu. **Website:** http://www.jjay.cuny.edu/. **Application deadlines for fall 2011:** Regular decision: May 31. Early decision: Not offered. Early action: Not offered. Admission can be deferred. **Application fee:** $65. **To apply online, go to:** http://portal.cuny.edu/cms/id/cuny/documents/informationpage/006373.htm. **Admissions requirements/recommendations:** High school units required (recommended): English: 4; Mathematics: 3 (4); Foreign language: 2 (3); Social studies: 2 (4); Total units: 14 (19). Tests: The college uses SAT or ACT scores in admissions decisions. Either SAT or ACT required. For admission to the fall 2011 entering class, the school will accept: ACT with writing required. Campus visit: Neither required nor recommended. Admissions interview: Neither required nor recommended. Off-campus interview: Not available. **Factors that count in admissions decisions:** *Academic:* Secondary school record: Considered. Class rank: Not Considered. Letters of recommendation: Not Considered. Standardized test scores: Very Important. Essay: Not Considered. *Nonacademic:* Interview: Not Considered. Extracurricular activities: Not Considered. Talent/ability: Not Considered. Character/personal qualities: Not Considered. Alumni/ae relationship: Not Considered. Geographical residence: Not Considered. State residency: Not Considered. Religious affiliation/commitment: Not Considered. Minority status: Not Considered. Volunteer work: Not Considered. Work experience: Not Considered. **Admissions statistics for the fall 2009 entering class:** Total applicants: 11,603. Total accepted: 7,285. Freshmen enrolled: 2,873; 4% were from out of state. Overall acceptance rate: 63%. **Average high school grade point average:** 2.6. **First-year students who submitted SAT scores:** 95%. Scores (25/75 percentile): Critical Reading: 400-490, Math: 410-510, Combined: 810-1000.

ACADEMICS

Year founded: 1965. **Academic calendar:** Semester. **Degrees offered:** certificate, associate, bachelor's, master's. **Most popular majors:** 50% criminal justice/law enforcement administration, 21% forensic psychology, 14% social sciences, 12% public administration, 3% physical sciences. **Major fields of study:** computer and information sciences and support services; physical sciences; psychology; public administration and social service professions; security and protective services; social sciences. **Areas of required coursework:** arts/fine arts, mathematics, English (including composition), philosophy, foreign languages, sciences (biological or physical), history, social science, other. **Pre-professional programs:** pre-law. **Special academic programs:** cooperative (work-study plan) program, cross-registration, distance learning, dual enrollment, English as a Second Language (ESL), exchange student program (domestic), honors program, independent study, internships, liberal arts/career combination, study abroad, weekend college.

Cooperative education programs: other. **Faculty and instruction (2009-2010):** Total instructional faculty: 439 full-time, 662 part-time (55% men; 45% women; 28% minorities). Full-time faculty with Ph.D. or other terminal degree: 81%. Student/faculty ratio: 19/1. Classes of fewer than 20 students: 23%; of 20 to 49 students: 77%; of 50 or more students: 0%. **Advanced Placement and International Baccalaureate credit:** AP tests may be used for: Placement only. Scores accepted: 3. International Baccalaureate exams may be used for: Credit only. **Freshmen returning for sophomore year:** 74%. **Graduation rates:** Four-year: 23%; five-year: 37%; six-year: 42%. **Graduate study:** Fields in which graduates pursue further study: law, 10%; education, 4%; arts and sciences, 86%.

COSTS AND FINANCIAL AID

Financial aid office: (212) 237-8151. **Expenses (2009-2010):** Tuition and fees 2009-2010: $4,929 in state, $12,779 out of state. **Financial aid:** In 2009-2010, 88% of undergraduates applied for financial aid. Of those, 82% were determined to have financial need; Average financial aid package (proportion receiving): $10,150 (77%). Average amount of gift aid, such as scholarships or grants (proportion receiving): $3,175 (71%). Average amount of self-help aid, such as work study or loans (proportion receiving): $2,183 (11%). Average need-based loan (excluding PLUS or other private loans): $3,500. Among students who received need-based aid, the average percentage of need met: 85%. Among students who received aid based on merit, the average award (and the proportion receiving): $0 (0%). The average athletic scholarship (and the proportion receiving): $0 (0%). Average amount of debt of borrowers graduating in 2009: $45,000. Proportion who borrowed: 49%.

CAMPUS LIFE AND EXTRACURRICULAR ACTIVITIES

Student employment: During the 2009-2010 academic year, 22% of undergraduates worked on campus. Average per-year earnings: $10,000. **Clubs and organizations:** Number of student organizations: 38. Activities include: choral groups, dance, drama/theater, musical theater, radio station, student government, student newspaper, yearbook. Number of fraternities: 0; sororities: 0. **Sports program (2009-2010):** Member of NCAA III. *Men's intercollegiate varsity sports:* baseball, basketball, cross country, rifle, soccer, tennis. *Women's intercollegiate varsity sports:* basketball, cross country, rifle, softball, swimming, tennis, volleyball.

SERVICES AND FACILITIES

Basic services: nonremedial tutoring, women's center, placement service, day care. **Remedial assistance:** reading, math, writing, study skills. **Counseling services:** minority student, career, personal, academic, older student, psychological. **For learning-disabled students:** School does not offer a structured program with separate admission and additional fees. Total undergraduates in learning-disabled program or receiving services: 350. Services include: remedial math, remedial English, reading machines, tape recorders, diagnostic testing service, note-taking services, oral tests, learning center, readers, extended time for tests, tutors, priority registration, substitution of courses, texts on tape, typist/scribe, exams on tape or computer, waiver of foreign language degree requirement, waiver of math degree requirement. **Library:** Number of titles: 256,700; number of current serial subscriptions: 14,374. **Information technology resources:** Students are not required to lease or own a computer. Number of campus computers available to all students: 1,900. School has a wireless network. Approximate number of users that can be accommodated: 5,000. Proportion of college-owned housing units wired for high-speed internet access: 0%. **Campus safety:** Security services offered: 24-hour emergency telephones, lighted pathways/sidewalks, student patrols.

TRANSFER AND INTERNATIONAL STUDENTS

Transfer students: May apply for admission for the following academic terms: Fall, Spring. Applicants do not need a minimum number of credits to apply. For fall 2009: Transfer applicants enrolled: 935. **International students:** Number of foreign undergraduates: 350 (3% of student body). Number of countries represented: 68. Minimum TOEFL score required: 500 (paper); 173 (computer).

CUNY–Lehman College

- **Address:** 250 Bedford Park Boulevard W, Bronx, NY 10468
- **Website:** http://www.lehman.cuny.edu
- **Public**
- **Enrollment:** 5,986 full-time; 3,734 part-time

KEY STATS

✔ **U.S News College Ranking:** 121, Regional Universities (North)
✔ **SAT Score (25th/75th percentile):** 900-1050
✔ **Tuition:** 2009-2010: $4,940 in state, $10,300 out of state

Selectivity: Selective	**Room/board:** $10,382
Acceptance rate: 26%	**Average debt:** $13,700
Student/faculty ratio: N/A	**Proportion who borrowed:** 32%

UNDERGRADUATE STUDENT BODY STATS

2009-2010 enrollment: 5,986 full-time; 3,734 part-time. Men: 30%; women: 70%. **Ethnic makeup:** African American: 30%; Asian American: 5%; Hispanic: 51%; White: 10%; International: 4%. **Religious preference:** Roman Catholic: 45%; Protestant: 10%; Muslim: 3%; Hindu: 2%; Buddhist: 1%; No preference: 14%; Other: 25%.

ADMISSIONS FACTS AND FIGURES

Phone: (718) 960-8131. **Email:** undergraduate.admissions@lehman.cuny.edu. **Website:** http://www.lehman.cuny.edu. **Application deadlines for fall 2011:** Regular decision: October 1. Early decision: Not offered. Early action: Not offered. Admission can be deferred. **Application fee:** $65. **To apply online, go to:** http://www.lehman.edu/lehman/services/apply.html. **Admissions requirements/recommendations:** High school units required (recommended): English: 4; Mathematics: 3; Science: 2; Foreign language: 2; Social studies: 4; History: 0; Total units: 16. Tests: The college uses SAT or ACT scores in admissions decisions. Either SAT or ACT required. For admission to the fall 2011 entering class, the school will accept: ACT with or without writing accepted. Campus visit: Recommended. Admissions interview: Neither required nor recommended. Off-campus interview: Not available. **Factors that count in admissions decisions:** *Academic:* Secondary school record: Very Important. Class rank: Not Considered. Letters of recommendation: Considered. Standardized test scores: Very Important. Essay: Considered. *Nonacademic:* Interview: Considered. Extracurricular activities: Considered. Talent/ability: Considered. Character/personal qualities: Not Considered. Alumni/ae relationship: Not Considered. Geographical residence: Not Considered. State residency: Not Considered. Religious affiliation/commitment: Not Considered. Minority status: Not Considered. Volunteer work: Not Considered. Work experience: Not Considered. **Other schools with the greatest overlap in applicants:** CUNY–Baruch College; CUNY–City College; CUNY–Hunter College; New York University; Pace University. **Admissions statistics for the fall 2009 entering class:** Total applicants: 15,291. Total accepted: 3,915. Freshmen enrolled: 774; 3% were from out of state. Overall acceptance rate: 26%. **First-year students who submitted SAT scores:** 76%. Scores (25/75 percentile): Critical Reading: 440-520, Math: 460-530, Combined: 900-1050.

ACADEMICS

Year founded: 1968. **Academic calendar:** Semester. **Degrees offered:** bachelor's, master's, post-master's certificate. **Major fields of study:** area, ethnic, cultural, and gender studies; biological and biomedical sciences; business, management, marketing, and related support services; communication, journalism, and related programs; computer and information sciences and support services; education; English language and literature/letters; family and consumer sciences/human sciences; foreign languages, literatures, and linguistics; health professions and related clinical sciences; history; liberal arts and sciences studies, and humanities; mathematics and statistics; multi/interdisciplinary studies; parks, recreation, leisure, and fitness studies; philosophy and religious studies; physical sciences; psychology; public administration and social service professions; social sciences; visual and performing arts. **Areas of required coursework:** arts/fine arts, humanities, computer literacy, mathematics, English (including composition), philosophy, foreign languages, sciences (biological or physical), history, social science, other. **Pre-professional programs:** pre-law, pre-medicine. **Special academic programs (% participation):** accelerated program (2%), cross-registration (5%), distance learning (7%), double major (2%), dual enrollment (10%), English as a Second Language (ESL) (1%), honors program (1%), independent study (3%), internships (10%), student-designed major (4%), study abroad (1%), teacher certificate program (3%), weekend college (20%). **Teacher certification offered in:** early childhood, special education, elementary, middle/junior high, secondary, bilingual/bicultural. **Cooperative education programs:** agriculture, business, computer science, education, health professions, natural science, social/behavioral science. **Reserve Officers Training Corps (ROTC):** Army ROTC: Offered at cooperating institution. **Faculty and instruction (2009-2010):** Total instructional faculty: 374 full-time, 593 part-time (47% men; 53% women; 35% minorities). Classes of fewer than 20 students: 42%; of 20 to 49 students: 57%; of 50 or more students: 1%. **Advanced Placement and International Baccalaureate credit:** AP tests may be used for: Placement only. Scores accepted: 3, 4, 5. International Baccalaureate exams may be used for: Credit only. **Freshmen returning for sophomore year:** 74%. **Graduation rates:** Four-year: 11%; five-year: 24%; six-year: 32%. **Graduate study:** 29% of students pursue further study immediately upon graduation.

COSTS AND FINANCIAL AID

Financial aid office: (718) 960-8545. **Expenses (2009-2010):** Tuition and fees 2009-2010: $4,940 in state, $10,300 out of state; room/board: $10,382. Estimated books and supplies: $1,070. **Financial aid:** In 2009-2010, 82% of undergraduates applied for financial aid. Of those, 81% were determined to have financial need; 5% had their need fully met. Average financial aid package (proportion receiving): $4,002 (81%). Average amount of gift aid, such as scholarships or grants (proportion receiving): $1,455 (78%). Average amount of self-help aid, such as work study or loans (proportion receiving): $1,371 (28%). Average need-based loan (excluding PLUS or other private loans): $2,006. Among students who received need-based aid, the average percentage of need met: 66%. Among students who received aid based on merit, the average award (and the proportion receiving): $3,243 (1%). The average athletic scholarship (and the proportion receiving): $0 (0%). Average amount of debt of borrowers graduating in 2009: $13,700. Proportion who borrowed: 32%.

CAMPUS LIFE AND EXTRACURRICULAR ACTIVITIES

Campus housing available: other housing options. Students who live in college-owned, operated, or affiliated housing: 0%. **Student employment:** During the 2009-2010 academic year, 2% of undergraduates worked on campus. Average per-year earnings: $3,680. **Clubs and organizations:** Number of student organizations: 36. Activities include: choral groups, concert band, dance, drama/theater, jazz band, literary magazine, music ensembles, musical theater, opera, radio station, student government, student newspaper, student film society, symphony orchestra, television station, yearbook. Number of fraternities: 2; sororities: 2. **Sports program (2009-2010):** Member of NCAA III.

SERVICES AND FACILITIES

Basic services: nonremedial tutoring, day care, health service. **Remedial assistance:** reading, math, writing, study skills. **Counseling services:** career, personal, veteran student, academic, psychological, birth control. **For learning-disabled students:** School does not offer a structured program with separate admission and additional fees. Services include: tape recorders, untimed tests, note-taking services, learning center, extended time for tests, tutors, priority registration, texts on tape, other testing accommodations. **Library:** Number of titles: 599,932; number of current serial subscriptions: 5,043. **Information technology resources:** Students are not required to lease or own a computer. Number of campus computers available to all students: 1,325. School has a wireless network. Approximate number of users that can be accommodated: 1,300. Proportion of college-owned housing units wired for high-speed internet access: 100%. **Campus safety:** Security services offered: 24-hour foot-and-vehicle patrols, late-night transport/escort service, 24-hour emergency telephones, lighted pathways/sidewalks.

TRANSFER AND INTERNATIONAL STUDENTS

Transfer students: May apply for admission for the following academic terms: Fall, Spring. Applicants do not need a minimum number of credits to apply. For fall 2009: Transfer applicants enrolled: 1,255. **International students:** Number of foreign undergraduates: 360 (4% of student body). Number of countries represented: 138. Minimum TOEFL score required: 500 (paper); 173 (computer). Average TOEFL score: 520 (paper).

CUNY–Medgar Evers College

- **Address:** 1650 Bedford Avenue, Brooklyn, NY 11225
- **Website:** http://www.mec.cuny.edu
- **Public**
- **Enrollment:** 4,652 full-time; 2,429 part-time

KEY STATS

✔ **U.S News College Ranking:** second tier, Regional Colleges (North)
✔ **SAT Score (25th/75th percentile):** 670-870
✔ **Tuition:** 2010-2011: $4,982 in state, $10,262 out of state

Selectivity: Least selective	**Room/board:** N/A
Acceptance rate: 100%	**Average debt:** N/A
Student/faculty ratio: 19/1	**Proportion who borrowed:** N/A

UNDERGRADUATE STUDENT BODY STATS

2009-2010 enrollment: 4,652 full-time; 2,429 part-time. Men: 25%; women: 75%. **Ethnic makeup:** African American: 88%; Asian American: 1%; Hispanic: 6%; White: 3%; International: 2%.

ADMISSIONS FACTS AND FIGURES

Phone: (718) 270-6024. **Email:** enroll@mec.cuny.edu. **Website:** http://www.mec.cuny.edu. **Application deadlines for fall 2011:** Regular decision: May 3. Early decision: Not offered. Early action: Not offered. Admission can be deferred. **Application fee:** $65. **To apply online, go to:** http://www1.cuny.edu/admissions/undergraduate/onlineapp-1.html. **Admissions requirements/recommendations:** High school units required (recommended): English: (4); Mathematics: (3); Science: (2); Foreign language: (2); Social studies: (2); Academic electives: (2); Total units: (16). Tests: The college uses SAT or ACT scores in admissions decisions. Neither SAT nor ACT required. Campus visit: Recommended. Admissions interview: Neither required nor recommended. Off-campus interview: Not available. **Factors that count in admissions decisions:** *Academic:* Secondary school record: Considered. Class rank: Not Considered. Letters of recommendation: Not Considered. Standardized test scores: Considered. Essay: Not Considered. *Nonacademic:* Interview: Not Considered. Extracurricular activities: Not Considered. Talent/ability: Not Considered. Character/personal qualities: Not Considered. Alumni/ae relationship: Not Considered. Geographical residence: Not Considered. State residency: Not Considered. Religious affiliation/commitment: Not Considered. Minority status: Not Considered. Volunteer work: Not Considered. Work experience: Not Considered. **Admissions statistics for the fall 2009 entering class:** Total applicants: 7,178. Total accepted: 7,178. Freshmen enrolled: 1,378; 1% were from out of state. Overall acceptance rate: 100%. **Average high school grade point average:** 2.1. **First-year students who submitted SAT scores:** 42%. Scores (25/75 percentile): Critical Reading: 340-440, Math: 330-430, Combined: 670-870.

ACADEMICS

Year founded: 1969. **Academic calendar:** Semester. **Degrees offered:** certificate, associate, bachelor's. **Most popular majors:** 48% business/commerce, 15% psychology, 9% biology/biological sciences, 7% nursing/registered nurse training (R.N., A.S.N., B.S.N., M.S.N.), 5% special education and teaching. **Major fields of study:** biological and biomedical sciences; business, management, marketing, and related support services; education; English language and literature/letters; health professions and related clinical sciences; mathematics and statistics; natural resources and conservation; psychology; public administration and social service professions. **Areas of required coursework:** arts/fine arts, humanities, computer literacy, mathematics, English (including composition), foreign languages, history. **Special academic programs:** cooperative (work-study plan) program, distance learning, English as a Second Language (ESL), honors program, independent study, internships, study abroad, teacher certificate program, weekend college. **Teacher certification offered in:** early childhood, special education, elementary. **Cooperative education programs:** art, business, computer science, education, health professions, natural science, social/behavioral science. **Faculty and instruction (2009-2010):** Total instructional faculty: 189 full-time, 308 part-time (54% men; 46% women; 88% minorities). Full-time faculty with Ph.D. or other terminal degree: 52%. Student/faculty ratio: 19/1. Classes of fewer than 20 students: 18%; of 20 to 49 students: 82%; of 50 or more students: 0%. **Advanced Placement and International Baccalaureate credit:** International Baccalaureate exams may be used for: Placement only. **Freshmen returning for sophomore year:** 59%. **Graduation rates:** Four-year: 0%; five-year: 5%; six-year: 13%.

COSTS AND FINANCIAL AID

Financial aid office: (718) 270-6038. **Expenses (2010-2011):** Tuition and fees 2010-2011: $4,982 in state, $10,262 out of state. Estimated books and supplies: $1,070; transportation: $918; personal expenses: $2,754. **Financial aid:** Priority filing date for institution's financial aid form: April 1. Average financial aid package (proportion receiving): $3,721 (83%). Average amount of gift aid, such as scholarships or grants (proportion receiving): $3,542 (82%). Average amount of self-help aid, such as work study or loans (proportion receiving): $941 (19%). Average need-based loan (excluding PLUS or other private loans): $1,621.

CAMPUS LIFE AND EXTRACURRICULAR ACTIVITIES

Clubs and organizations: Number of student organizations: 32. Activities include: choral groups, dance, drama/theater, international student organization, jazz band, literary magazine, musical theater, radio station, student government, student newspaper, television station, yearbook. Number of fraternities: 2; sororities: 0. **Sports program (2009-2010):** Member of NCAA III. *Men's intercollegiate varsity sports:* basketball, cross country, soccer, track and field (indoor), track and field (outdoor), volleyball. *Women's intercollegiate varsity sports:* basketball, cross country, soccer, tennis, track and field (indoor), track and field (outdoor), volleyball.

SERVICES AND FACILITIES

Basic services: nonremedial tutoring, women's center, placement service, day care, health service. **Remedial assistance:** reading, math, writing, study skills. **Counseling services:** personal, academic. **For learning-disabled students:** School does not offer a structured program with separate admission and additional fees. Services include: reading machines, tape recorders, diagnostic testing service, note-taking services, learning center, readers, extended time for tests, tutors, priority registration, priority seating, proofreading services, substitution of courses, typist/scribe, exams on tape or computer, other testing accommodations, waiver of math degree requirement. **Library:** Number of titles: 120,000; number of current serial subscriptions: 420. **Information technology resources:** Students are not required to lease or own a computer. Number of campus computers available to all students: 175. School has a wireless network. Approximate number of users that can be accommodated: 1,500. **Campus safety:** Security services offered: 24-hour foot-and-vehicle patrols.

TRANSFER AND INTERNATIONAL STUDENTS

Transfer students: May apply for admission for the following academic terms: Fall, Spring, Summer. Applicants need a minimum number of credits to apply. For fall 2009: Transfer applications received: 1,330. Transfer applicants offered admission: 777. Transfer applicants enrolled: 777. **International students:** Number of foreign undergraduates: 112 (2% of student body). Minimum TOEFL score required: 475 (paper). Average TOEFL score: 475 (paper).

CUNY–New York City College of Tech.

- **Address:** 300 Jay Street, Brooklyn, NY 11201
- **Website:** http://www.citytech.cuny.edu
- **Public**
- **Enrollment:** 9,130 full-time; 6,269 part-time

KEY STATS

✔ **U.S News College Ranking:** second tier, Regional Colleges (North)
✔ **SAT Score (25th/75th percentile):** 720-910
✔ **Tuition:** 2010-2011: $4,939 in state, $12,789 out of state

Selectivity: Least selective	**Room/board:** N/A
Acceptance rate: 84%	**Average debt:** N/A
Student/faculty ratio: 17/1	**Proportion who borrowed:** N/A

UNDERGRADUATE STUDENT BODY STATS

2009-2010 enrollment: 9,130 full-time; 6,269 part-time. Men: 52%; women: 48%. **Ethnic makeup:** African American: 37%; Asian American: 16%; Hispanic: 27%; White: 14%; International: 6%.

ADMISSIONS FACTS AND FIGURES

Phone: (718) 260-5500. **Email:** admissions@citytech.cuny.edu. **Website:** http://www.citytech.cuny.edu. **Application deadlines for fall 2011:** Regular decision: Rolling. Early decision: Not offered. Early action: Not offered. Admission can be deferred. **Application fee:** $65. **To apply online, go to:**

https://portal.uapc.cuny.edu. **Admissions requirements/recommendations:** High school units required (recommended): English: 4 (4); Mathematics: 3 (4); Science: 2 (3); Foreign language: 2 (2); Social studies: 3 (4); Academic electives: 1 (2); Total units: 16 (20). Tests: The college uses SAT or ACT scores in admissions decisions. Neither SAT nor ACT required. Campus visit: Neither required nor recommended. Admissions interview: Neither required nor recommended. Off-campus interview: Not available. **Factors that count in admissions decisions:** *Academic:* Secondary school record: Important. Class rank: Considered. Letters of recommendation: Considered. Standardized test scores: Considered. Essay: Considered. *Nonacademic:* Interview: Not Considered. Extracurricular activities: Not Considered. Talent/ability: Not Considered. Character/personal qualities: Not Considered. Alumni/ae relationship: Not Considered. Geographical residence: Not Considered. State residency: Not Considered. Religious affiliation/commitment: Not Considered. Minority status: Not Considered. Volunteer work: Not Considered. Work experience: Not Considered. **Other schools with the greatest overlap in applicants:** CUNY–Baruch College; CUNY–Brooklyn College; CUNY–City College; CUNY–Hunter College; CUNY–Queens College. **Admissions statistics for the fall 2009 entering class:** Total applicants: 14,419. Total accepted: 12,105. Freshmen enrolled: 3,251; 1% were from out of state. Overall acceptance rate: 84%.

ACADEMICS

Year founded: 1946. **Academic calendar:** Semester. **Degrees offered:** certificate, associate, bachelor's. **Most popular majors:** 20% information science/studies, 17% hospitality administration/management, 12% human services, 10% design and visual communications, 8% legal assistant/paralegal. **Major fields of study:** architecture and related services; business, management, marketing, and related support services; computer and information sciences and support services; education; engineering technologies/technicians; family and consumer sciences/human sciences; health professions and related clinical sciences; legal professions and studies; mathematics and statistics; public administration and social service professions; visual and performing arts. **Areas of required coursework:** humanities, computer literacy, mathematics, English (including composition), philosophy, sciences (biological or physical), social science, other. **Special academic programs (% participation):** distance learning, dual enrollment (3%), English as a Second Language (ESL) (35%), honors program (2%), independent study (1%), internships (30%), study abroad (1%), teacher certificate program (4%), weekend college. **Teacher certification offered in:** vo-tech. **Cooperative education programs:** art, business, computer science, education, engineering, health professions, technologies. **Faculty and instruction (2009-2010):** Total instructional faculty: 411 full-time, 790 part-time (57% men; 43% women; 38% minorities). Full-time faculty with Ph.D. or other terminal degree: 64%. Student/faculty ratio: 17/1. Classes of fewer than 20 students: 34%; of 20 to 49 students: 66%; of 50 or more students: 0%. **Advanced Placement and International Baccalaureate credit:** AP tests may be used for: Credit only. Scores accepted: 3, 4, 5. International Baccalaureate exams may be used for: Placement only. **Freshmen returning for sophomore year:** 78%. **Graduation rates:** Four-year: 6%; five-year: 13%; six-year: 14%.

COSTS AND FINANCIAL AID

Financial aid office: (718) 260-5700. **Expenses (2010-2011):** Tuition and fees 2010-2011: $4,939 in state, $12,789 out of state. **Financial aid:** In 2009-2010, 85% of undergraduates applied for financial aid. Of those, 79% were determined to have financial need; 5% had their need fully met. Average financial aid package (proportion receiving): $7,863 (77%). Average amount of gift aid, such as scholarships or grants (proportion receiving): $7,501 (76%). Average amount of self-help aid, such as work study or loans (proportion receiving): $2,479 (19%). Average need-based loan (excluding PLUS or other private loans): $3,859. Among students who received need-based aid, the average percentage of need met: 60%. Among students who received aid based on merit, the average award (and the proportion receiving): $491 (1%).

CAMPUS LIFE AND EXTRACURRICULAR ACTIVITIES

Student employment: During the 2009-2010 academic year, 2% of undergraduates worked on campus. Average per-year earnings: $10,000. **Clubs and organizations:** Number of student organizations: 60. Activities include: drama/theater, musical theater, student government, student newspaper. Number of fraternities: 0; sororities: 0. **Sports program (2009-2010):** Member of NCAA III. *Men's intercollegiate varsity sports:* basketball, cross country, soccer, tennis, track and field (indoor), track and field (outdoor), volleyball. *Women's intercollegiate varsity sports:* basketball, cross country, softball, tennis, track and field (indoor), track and field (outdoor), volleyball.

SERVICES AND FACILITIES

Basic services: nonremedial tutoring, women's center, placement service, day care, health service, health insurance. **Remedial assistance:** reading, math, writing, study skills. **Counseling services:** minority student, career, personal, veteran student, academic, older student, psychological, birth control. **For learning-disabled students:** School does not offer a structured program with separate admission and additional fees. Total undergraduates in learning-disabled program or receiving services: 144. Services include: remedial math, remedial English, reading machines, remedial reading, tape recorders, diagnostic testing service, untimed tests, note-taking services, oral tests, learning center, readers, extended time for tests, tutors, priority registration, priority seating, texts on tape, other testing accommodations, other. **Library:** Number of titles: 179,062; number of current serial subscriptions: 60,000. **Information technology resources:** Students are not required to lease or own a computer. Number of campus computers available to all students: 443. School has a wireless network. **Campus safety:** Security services offered: 24-hour foot-and-vehicle patrols, late-night transport/escort service, 24-hour emergency telephones.

TRANSFER AND INTERNATIONAL STUDENTS

Transfer students: May apply for admission for the following academic terms: Fall, Spring, Summer. Applicants do not need a minimum number of credits to apply. For fall 2009: Transfer applicants enrolled: 1,045. **International students:** Number of foreign undergraduates: 826 (6% of student body). Number of countries represented: 59. Minimum TOEFL score required: 500 (paper); 173 (computer). Average TOEFL score: 525 (paper).

CUNY–Queens College

- ■ **Address:** 65-30 Kissena Boulevard, Flushing, NY 11367
- ■ **Website:** http://www.qc.edu/
- ■ **Public**
- ■ **Enrollment:** 11,762 full-time; 4,297 part-time

KEY STATS

✔ **U.S News College Ranking:** 58, Regional Universities (North)
✔ **SAT Score (25th/75th percentile):** 980-1170
✔ **Tuition:** 2010-2011: $5,116 in state, $10,476 out of state

Selectivity: Selective	**Room/board:** $11,125
Acceptance rate: 33%	**Average debt:** $14,000
Student/faculty ratio: 16/1	**Proportion who borrowed:** 41%

UNDERGRADUATE STUDENT BODY STATS

2009-2010 enrollment: 11,762 full-time; 4,297 part-time. Men: 41%; women: 59%. **Ethnic makeup:** African American: 9%; Asian American: 23%; Hispanic: 18%; White: 44%; International: 6%.

ADMISSIONS FACTS AND FIGURES

Phone: (718) 997-5600. **Email:** applyto@uapc.cuny.edu. **Website:** http://www.qc.edu/. **Application deadlines for fall 2011:** Regular decision: Rolling; decision sent by May 30. Early decision: Not offered. Early action: Not offered. Admission can be deferred. **Application fee:** $65. **To apply online, go to:** http://www.qc.edu/applying.htm. **Admissions requirements/recommendations:** High school units required (recommended): English: 4 (4); Mathematics: 3 (3); Science: 2 (3); Foreign language: 3 (3); Social studies: 4 (4); Total units: 16 (17). Tests: The college uses SAT or ACT scores in admissions decisions. Either SAT or ACT required. For admission to the fall 2011 entering class, the school will accept: ACT with or without writing accepted. Campus visit: Recommended. Admissions interview: Neither required nor recommended. Off-campus interview: Not available. **Factors that count in admissions decisions:** *Academic:* Secondary school record: Very Important. Class rank: Not Considered. Letters of recommendation: Not Considered. Standardized test scores: Very Important. Essay: Not Considered. *Nonacademic:* Interview: Not Considered. Extracurricular activities: Not Considered. Talent/ability: Not Considered. Character/personal qualities: Not Considered. Alumni/ae relationship: Not Considered. Geographical residence: Not Considered. State residency: Not Considered. Religious affiliation/commitment: Not Considered. Minority status: Not Considered. Volunteer work: Not Considered. Work experience: Not Considered. **Other schools with the greatest overlap in applicants:** Binghamton University–SUNY; CUNY–Hunter College; New York University; SUNY–Stony Brook; St. John's University. **Admissions statistics for the fall 2009 entering class:** Total applicants: 18,028. Total accepted:

5,878. Freshmen enrolled: 1,712; 1% were from out of state. Overall acceptance rate: 33%. **Credentials of fall 2009 freshmen:** 18% ranked in the top 10 percent of their high school class; 35% were in the top 25 percent. **Average high school grade point average:** 3.5. **First-year students who submitted SAT scores:** 100%. Scores (25/75 percentile): Critical Reading: 470-570, Math: 510-600, Combined: 980-1170.

ACADEMICS

Year founded: 1937. **Academic calendar:** Semester. **Degrees offered:** bachelor's, post-bachelor's certificate, master's, post-master's certificate. **Most popular majors:** 10% accounting, 8% psychology, 6% sociology, 5% economics, 4% English language and literature. **Major fields of study:** area, ethnic, cultural, and gender studies; biological and biomedical sciences; business, management, marketing, and related support services; communication, journalism, and related programs; computer and information sciences and support services; education; English language and literature/letters; family and consumer sciences/human sciences; foreign languages, literatures, and linguistics; health professions and related clinical sciences; history; mathematics and statistics; multi/interdisciplinary studies; natural resources and conservation; parks, recreation, leisure, and fitness studies; philosophy and religious studies; physical sciences; psychology; social sciences; visual and performing arts. **Areas of required coursework:** humanities, mathematics, English (including composition), foreign languages, sciences (biological or physical), history, social science, other. **Pre-professional programs:** pre-law, pre-dentistry, pre-medicine, other. **Special academic programs:** accelerated program, cross-registration, distance learning, double major, dual enrollment, English as a Second Language (ESL), honors program, independent study, internships, liberal arts/career combination, student-designed major, study abroad, teacher certificate program, weekend college. **Teacher certification offered in:** early childhood, special education, elementary, middle/junior high, secondary, bilingual/bicultural. **Cooperative education programs:** art, business, computer science, education, humanities, natural science, social/behavioral science, other. **Reserve Officers Training Corps (ROTC):** Army ROTC: Offered at cooperating institution (St. John's University); Navy ROTC: Offered at cooperating institution (St. John's University). **Faculty and instruction (2009-2010):** Total instructional faculty: 636 full-time, 766 part-time (53% men; 47% women; 21% minorities). Full-time faculty with Ph.D. or other terminal degree: 77%. Student/faculty ratio: 16/1. Classes of fewer than 20 students: 32%; of 20 to 49 students: 58%; of 50 or more students: 10%. **Advanced Placement and International Baccalaureate credit:** AP tests may be used for: Credit only. Scores accepted: 2, 3. **Freshmen returning for sophomore year:** 84%. **Graduation rates:** Four-year: 25%; five-year: 45%; six-year: 53%. **Graduate study:** 25% of students pursue further study within one year. Fields in which graduates pursue further study: Master of Business Administration (MBA), 1%; law, 2%; medicine, 1%; dentistry, 1%; engineering, 1%; education, 21%; arts and sciences, 5%.

COSTS AND FINANCIAL AID

Financial aid office: (718) 997-5101. **Expenses (2010-2011):** Tuition and fees 2010-2011: $5,116 in state, $10,476 out of state; room/board: $11,125. Estimated books and supplies: $1,146; transportation: $918. **Financial aid:** Priority filing date for institution's financial aid form: February 15. In 2009-2010, 89% of undergraduates applied for financial aid. Of those, 78% were determined to have financial need; 79% had their need fully met. Average financial aid package (proportion receiving): $7,500 (78%). Average amount of gift aid, such as scholarships or grants (proportion receiving): $4,800 (64%). Average amount of self-help aid, such as work study or loans (proportion receiving): $6,500 (28%). Average need-based loan (excluding PLUS or other private loans): $4,900. Among students who received need-based aid, the average percentage of need met: 95%. Among students who received aid based on merit, the average award (and the proportion receiving): $8,300 (1%). The average athletic scholarship (and the proportion receiving): $7,352 (1%). Average amount of debt of borrowers graduating in 2009: $14,000. Proportion who borrowed: 41%.

CAMPUS LIFE AND EXTRACURRICULAR ACTIVITIES

Campus housing available: coed dorms, apartment for single students. Students who live in college-owned, operated, or affiliated housing: 2%. **Student employment:** During the 2009-2010 academic year, 2% of undergraduates worked on campus. Average per-year earnings: $1,000. **Clubs and organizations:** Number of student organizations: 140. Activities include: choral groups, concert band, dance, drama/theater, jazz band, literary magazine, music ensembles, musical theater, radio station, student government, student newspaper, student film society, symphony orchestra, television station, yearbook. Number of fraternities: 2; sororities: 3. Average proportion of students who stay on campus on weekends: 18%. **Sports program (2009-2010):** Member of NCAA II. *Men's intercollegiate varsity sports:* baseball, basketball, cross country, soccer, swimming, tennis, track and field (indoor), water polo. *Women's intercollegiate varsity sports:* basketball, cross country, fencing, lacrosse, soccer, softball, swimming, tennis, track and field (indoor), volleyball.

SERVICES AND FACILITIES

Basic services: nonremedial tutoring, women's center, day care, health service. **Counseling services:** minority student, career, personal, veteran student, academic, psychological, birth control. **For learning-disabled students:** School does not offer a structured program with separate admission and additional fees. Total undergraduates in learning-disabled program or receiving services: 308. Services include: reading machines, tape recorders, note-taking services, special bookstore section, readers, extended time for tests, tutors, priority registration, priority seating, proofreading services, substitution of courses, texts on tape, exams on tape or computer, take home exams, other testing accommodations, other. **Library:** Number of titles: 1,075,178; number of current serial subscriptions: 36,327. **Information technology resources:** Students are not required to lease or own a computer. Number of campus computers available to all students: 2,300. School has a wireless network. Approximate number of users that can be accommodated: 4,000. **Campus safety:** Security services offered: 24-hour foot-and-vehicle patrols, late-night transport/escort service, 24-hour emergency telephones, lighted pathways/sidewalks.

TRANSFER AND INTERNATIONAL STUDENTS

Transfer students: May apply for admission for the following academic terms: Fall, Spring. Applicants need a minimum number of credits to apply. For fall 2009: Transfer applications received: 8,817. Transfer applicants offered admission: 3,370. Transfer applicants enrolled: 2,305. **International students:** Number of foreign undergraduates: 866 (6% of student body). Number of countries represented: 115. Minimum TOEFL score required: 500 (paper); 173 (computer). Average TOEFL score: 550 (paper).

CUNY–York College

- **Address:** 94-20 Guy R. Brewer Boulevard, Jamaica, NY 11451
- **Website:** http://www.york.cuny.edu
- **Public**
- **Enrollment:** N/A

KEY STATS

✔ **U.S News College Ranking:** second tier, Regional Colleges (North)
✔ **SAT Score (25th/75th percentile):** 750-940
✔ **Tuition:** 2009-2010: $4,262 in state, $8,902 out of state
  Selectivity: Least selective   **Room/board:** N/A
  Acceptance rate: N/A   **Average debt:** N/A
  Student/faculty ratio: N/A   **Proportion who borrowed:** N/A

Daemen College

- **Address:** 4380 Main Street, Amherst, NY 14226-3592
- **Website:** http://www.daemen.edu
- **Private**
- **Enrollment:** 1,502 full-time; 537 part-time

KEY STATS

✔ **U.S News College Ranking:** second tier, Regional Universities (North)
✔ **SAT Score (25th/75th percentile):** 890-1130
✔ **Tuition:** 2010-2011: $21,460
  Selectivity: Selective   **Room/board:** $10,340
  Acceptance rate: 62%   **Average debt:** $18,910
  Student/faculty ratio: 15/1   **Proportion who borrowed:** 90%

UNDERGRADUATE STUDENT BODY STATS

2009-2010 enrollment: 1,502 full-time; 537 part-time. Men: 25%; women: 75%. **Ethnic makeup:** African American: 10%; Asian American: 1%; Hispanic: 3%; White: 84%; International: 1%. **Religious preference:** Roman

Catholic: 39%; Protestant: 31%; Jewish: 1%; Buddhist: 1%; No preference: 21%; Morman: 1%; Other: 6%.

ADMISSIONS FACTS AND FIGURES

Phone: (800) 462-7652. **Email:** admissions@daemen.edu. **Website:** http://www.daemen.edu. **Application deadlines for fall 2011:** Regular decision: Rolling. Early decision: Not offered. Early action: Not offered. Admission can be deferred. **Application fee:** $25. **To apply online, go to:** https://apply.embark.com/ugrad/daemen/16/. **Admissions requirements/recommendations:** High school units required (recommended): English: (4); Mathematics: (4); Science: (4); Social studies: (4); Total units: (16). Tests: The college uses SAT or ACT scores in admissions decisions. Neither SAT nor ACT required. For admission to the fall 2011 entering class, the school will accept: ACT with or without writing accepted. Campus visit: Recommended. Admissions interview: Recommended. Off-campus interview: May be arranged. **Factors that count in admissions decisions:** *Academic:* Secondary school record: Important. Class rank: Important. Letters of recommendation: Important. Standardized test scores: Important. Essay: Important. *Nonacademic:* Interview: Important. Extracurricular activities: Considered. Talent/ability: Considered. Character/personal qualities: Considered. Alumni/ae relationship: Considered. Geographical residence: Not Considered. State residency: Not Considered. Religious affiliation/commitment: Not Considered. Minority status: Not Considered. Volunteer work: Considered. Work experience: Considered. **Other schools with the greatest overlap in applicants:** Buffalo State College–SUNY; Canisius College; D'Youville College; Niagara University; University at Buffalo–SUNY. **Admissions statistics for the fall 2009 entering class:** Total applicants: 1,964. Total accepted: 1,219. Freshmen enrolled: 402; Overall acceptance rate: 62%. Size of waiting list: 301 applicants; enrolled from waiting list: 35. **Credentials of fall 2009 freshmen:** 17% ranked in the top 10 percent of their high school class; 51% were in the top 25 percent; 86% were in the top half. (Proportion submitting class standing: 75%.) **Average high school grade point average:** 3.6. **First-year students who submitted SAT scores:** 76%. Scores (25/75 percentile): Critical Reading: 440-550, Math: 450-580, Combined: 890-1130. **First-year students submitting ACT scores:** 40%. Scores (25/75 percentile): English: N/A, Math: N/A, Composite: 19-25.

ACADEMICS

Year founded: 1947. **Academic calendar:** 4-1-4. **Degrees offered:** certificate, bachelor's, master's, post-master's certificate. **Most popular majors:** 11% elementary education and teaching, 8% business administration and management, 7% health/medical preparatory programs, 7% psychology. **Major fields of study:** biological and biomedical sciences; business, management, marketing, and related support services; education; English language and literature/letters; foreign languages, literatures, and linguistics; health professions and related clinical sciences; history; mathematics and statistics; multi/interdisciplinary studies; philosophy and religious studies; psychology; public administration and social service professions; social sciences; visual and performing arts. **Areas of required coursework:** computer literacy, mathematics, English (including composition), other. **Pre-professional programs:** pre-law, other. **Special academic programs (% participation):** accelerated program (0%), cross-registration, double major, dual enrollment, exchange student program (domestic), honors program, independent study, internships (34%), student-designed major (5%), study abroad (0%), teacher certificate program (23%), weekend college (0%). **Teacher certification offered in:** early childhood, special education, elementary, secondary. **Reserve Officers Training Corps (ROTC):** Army ROTC: Offered at cooperating institution (Canisius College). **Faculty and instruction (2009-2010):** Total instructional faculty: 100 full-time, 158 part-time (40% men; 60% women; 8% minorities). Full-time faculty with Ph.D. or other terminal degree: 80%. Student/faculty ratio: 15/1. Classes of fewer than 20 students: 56%; of 20 to 49 students: 41%; of 50 or more students: 2%. **Advanced Placement and International Baccalaureate credit:** AP tests may be used for: Credit only. Scores accepted: 3, 4, 5. International Baccalaureate exams may be used for: Credit only. **Freshmen returning for sophomore year:** 72%. **Graduation rates:** Four-year: 33%; five-year: 48%; six-year: 50%. **Graduate study:** 13% of students pursue further study immediately upon graduation; 30% within one year. Fields in which graduates pursue further study: Master of Business Administration (MBA), 2%; medicine, 2%; education, 26%; arts and sciences, 6%.

COSTS AND FINANCIAL AID

Financial aid office: (716) 839-8254. **Expenses (2010-2011):** Tuition and fees 2010-2011: $21,460; room/board: $10,340. Estimated books and supplies: $800; transportation: $700; personal expenses: $800. **Financial aid:** Priority filing date for institution's financial aid form: February 15. Average amount of debt of borrowers graduating in 2009: $18,910. Proportion who borrowed: 90%.

CAMPUS LIFE AND EXTRACURRICULAR ACTIVITIES
Campus housing available (% using): coed dorms (33%), special housing for disabled students (0%), other housing options (67%). **Student employment:** During the 2009-2010 academic year, 6% of undergraduates worked on campus. Average per-year earnings: $800. **Clubs and organizations:** Number of student organizations: 48. Activities include: campus ministries, choral groups, dance, drama/theater, international student organization, literary magazine, student government, student newspaper, yearbook. Number of fraternities: 1; sororities: 4. Proportion of men in fraternities: 4%; of women in sororities: 3%. Average proportion of students who stay on campus on weekends: 40%. **Sports program (2009-2010):** Member of NAIA. *Men's intercollegiate varsity sports:* basketball, cross country, golf, soccer. *Women's intercollegiate varsity sports:* basketball, cross country, soccer, volleyball.

SERVICES AND FACILITIES
Basic services: nonremedial tutoring, health insurance. **Remedial assistance:** reading, math, writing, study skills. **Counseling services:** career, veteran student, academic, psychological, religious. **For learning-disabled students:** School does not offer a structured program with separate admission and additional fees. Services include: remedial math, remedial English, remedial reading, tape recorders, note-taking services, oral tests, learning center, readers, extended time for tests, tutors, priority registration, priority seating, texts on tape, other. **Library:** Number of titles: 136,883; number of current serial subscriptions: 31,925. **Information technology resources:** Students are not required to lease or own a computer. Number of campus computers available to all students: 68. School has a wireless network. Approximate number of users that can be accommodated: 400. Proportion of college-owned housing units wired for high-speed internet access: 100%. **Campus safety:** Security services offered: 24-hour foot-and-vehicle patrols, late-night transport/escort service, 24-hour emergency telephones, lighted pathways/sidewalks, controlled dormitory access (key, security card, etc).

TRANSFER AND INTERNATIONAL STUDENTS
Transfer students: May apply for admission for the following academic terms: Fall, Spring, Summer. Applicants do not need a minimum number of credits to apply. For fall 2009: Transfer applications received: 706. Transfer applicants offered admission: 434. Transfer applicants enrolled: 264. **International students:** Number of foreign undergraduates: 21 (1% of student body). Number of countries represented: 9. Minimum TOEFL score required: 500 (paper); 173 (computer). Average TOEFL score: 570 (paper).

Dominican College

- **Address:** 470 Western Highway, Orangeburg, NY 10962-1210
- **Website:** http://www.dc.edu
- **Private**
- **Enrollment:** 1,363 full-time; 314 part-time

KEY STATS
✔ **U.S News College Ranking:** second tier, Regional Universities (North)
✔ **SAT Score (25th/75th percentile):** 790-990
✔ **Tuition:** 2010-2011: $21,990

Selectivity: Less selective	**Room/board:** $10,560
Acceptance rate: 73%	**Average debt:** $24,690
Student/faculty ratio: 15/1	**Proportion who borrowed:** 97%

UNDERGRADUATE STUDENT BODY STATS
2009-2010 enrollment: 1,363 full-time; 314 part-time. Men: 32%; women: 68%. **Ethnic makeup:** African American: 11%; Asian American: 10%; Hispanic: 21%; White: 56%; International: 1%. **Religious preference:** Roman Catholic: 49%; Protestant: 38%.

ADMISSIONS FACTS AND FIGURES
Phone: (845) 359-3533. **Email:** admissions@dc.edu. **Website:** http://www.dc.edu. **Application deadlines for fall 2011:** Regular decision: Rolling. Early decision: Not offered. Early action: Not offered. Admission can be deferred. **Application fee:** $35. **To apply online, go to:** http://www.dc.edu/apply.aspx. **Admissions requirements/recommendations:** High school units required (recommended): English: 4 (4); Mathematics: 3 (6); Science: 3 (3); Foreign language: 1 (2); Social studies: 3 (4); History: 3 (4); Academic electives: 2 (2); Total units: 16 (18). Tests: The college uses SAT or ACT scores in admissions decisions. Either SAT or ACT required. For admission to the fall 2011 entering class, the school will accept: ACT with writing required. Campus visit: Recommended. Admissions interview: Recommended. Off-campus interview: Not available. **Factors that count in admissions decisions:** *Academic:* Secondary school record: Important. Class rank: Not Considered. Letters of recommendation: Important. Standardized test scores: Important. Essay: Considered. *Nonacademic:* Interview: Considered. Extracurricular activities: Considered. Talent/ability: Considered. Character/personal qualities: Considered. Alumni/ae relationship: Not Considered. Geographical residence: Not Considered. State residency: Not Considered. Religious affiliation/commitment: Not Considered. Minority status: Not Considered. Volunteer work: Considered. Work experience: Considered. **Other schools with the greatest overlap in applicants:** College of New Rochelle; Iona College; Nyack College; Ramapo College of New Jersey; St. Thomas Aquinas College. **Admissions statistics for the fall 2009 entering class:** Total applicants: 1,474. Total accepted: 1,072. Freshmen enrolled: 375; 33% were from out of state. Overall acceptance rate: 73%. **Size of waiting list:** 29 applicants; enrolled from waiting list: 0. **Average high school grade point average:** 2.7. **First-year students who submitted SAT scores:** 95%. Scores (25/75 percentile): Critical Reading: 390-490, Math: 400-500, Combined: 790-990. **First-year students submitting ACT scores:** 5%. Scores (25/75 percentile): English: N/A, Math: N/A, Composite: 17-22.

ACADEMICS
Year founded: 1952. **Academic calendar:** Semester. **Degrees offered:** certificate, associate, bachelor's, master's. **Most popular majors:** 33% health professions and related clinical sciences, 24% business administration and management, 15% liberal arts and sciences studies, and humanities, 15% social sciences, 7% education. **Major fields of study:** biological and biomedical sciences; business, management, marketing, and related support services; computer and information sciences and support services; education; English language and literature/letters; foreign languages, literatures, and linguistics; health professions and related clinical sciences; history; legal professions and studies; liberal arts and sciences studies, and humanities; mathematics and statistics; parks, recreation, leisure, and fitness studies; psychology; public administration and social service professions; social sciences. **Areas of required coursework:** humanities, computer literacy, mathematics, English (including composition), philosophy, foreign languages, sciences (biological or physical), history, social science, other. **Pre-professional programs:** pre-law, pre-medicine, other. **Special academic programs (% participation):** accelerated program (18%), distance learning (2.5%), dual enrollment (25%), honors program (2%), independent study (27%), internships (1%), teacher certificate program (19%), weekend college (18%). **Teacher certification offered in:** early childhood, special education, elementary, middle/junior high, secondary. **Faculty and instruction (2009-2010):** Total instructional faculty: 72 full-time, 163 part-time (35% men; 65% women; 10% minorities). Full-time faculty with Ph.D. or other terminal degree: 57%. Student/faculty ratio: 15/1. Classes of fewer than 20 students: 56%; of 20 to 49 students: 44%; of 50 or more students: 0%. **Advanced Placement and International Baccalaureate credit:** AP tests may be used for: Credit only. Scores accepted: 3. International Baccalaureate exams may be used for: Credit only. **Freshmen returning for sophomore year:** 67%. **Graduation rates:** Four-year: 19%; five-year: 31%; six-year: 40%.

COSTS AND FINANCIAL AID
Financial aid office: (845) 359-7800. **Expenses (2010-2011):** Tuition and fees 2010-2011: $21,990; room/board: $10,560. Estimated books and supplies: $1,500; transportation: $1,000; personal expenses: $2,000. **Financial aid:** Priority filing date for institution's financial aid form: February 15. In 2009-2010, 94% of undergraduates applied for financial aid. Of those, 91% were determined to have financial need; 12% had their need fully met. Average financial aid package (proportion receiving): $15,918 (91%). Average amount of gift aid, such as scholarships or grants (proportion receiving): $10,619 (80%). Average amount of self-help aid, such as work study or loans (proportion receiving): $4,858 (81%). Average need-based loan (excluding PLUS or other private loans): $4,360. Among students who received need-based aid, the average percentage of need met: 75%. Among students who received aid based on merit, the average award (and the proportion receiving): $6,147 (7%). The average athletic scholarship (and the proportion receiving): $8,117 (4%). Average amount of debt of borrowers graduating in 2009: $24,690. Proportion who borrowed: 97%.

CAMPUS LIFE AND EXTRACURRICULAR ACTIVITIES

Campus housing available (% using): coed dorms (100%), other housing options (0%). Students who live in college-owned, operated, or affiliated housing: 55%. **Student employment:** During the 2009-2010 academic year, 25% of undergraduates worked on campus. Average per-year earnings: $2,000. **Clubs and organizations:** Number of student organizations: 33. Activities include: campus ministries, choral groups, dance, drama/theater, literary magazine, musical theater, student government, student newspaper, yearbook. Number of fraternities: 0; sororities: 0. Average proportion of students who stay on campus on weekends: 60%. **Sports program (2009-2010):** Member of NCAA II.

SERVICES AND FACILITIES

Basic services: nonremedial tutoring, placement service, health service. **Remedial assistance:** reading, math, writing, study skills. **Counseling services:** career, personal, academic, psychological, religious. **For learning-disabled students:** School does not offer a structured program with separate admission and additional fees. Total undergraduates in learning-disabled program or receiving services: 52. Services include: remedial math, remedial English, reading machines, remedial reading, tape recorders, diagnostic testing service, untimed tests, note-taking services, learning center, readers, extended time for tests, tutors, other testing accommodations. **Information technology resources:** Students are not required to lease or own a computer. Number of campus computers available to all students: 150. School has a wireless network. Proportion of college-owned housing units wired for high-speed internet access: 100%. **Campus safety:** Security services offered: 24-hour foot-and-vehicle patrols, late-night transport/escort service, lighted pathways/sidewalks, controlled dormitory access (key, security card, etc).

TRANSFER AND INTERNATIONAL STUDENTS

Transfer students: May apply for admission for the following academic terms: Fall, Spring, Summer. Applicants do not need a minimum number of credits to apply. For fall 2009: Transfer applications received: 513. Transfer applicants offered admission: 277. Transfer applicants enrolled: 155. **International students:** Number of foreign undergraduates: 22 (1% of student body). Number of countries represented: 18. Minimum TOEFL score required: 550 (paper); 213 (computer). Average TOEFL score: 620 (paper).

Dowling College

- **Address:** Idle Hour Boulevard, Oakdale Long Island, NY 11769
- **Website:** http://www.dowling.edu
- **Private**
- **Enrollment:** 2,133 full-time; 1,232 part-time

KEY STATS

✔ **U.S News College Ranking:** second tier, Regional Universities (North)
✔ **SAT Score (25th/75th percentile):** 830-1050
✔ **Tuition:** 2009-2010: $22,850

Selectivity: Less selective	**Room/board:** $10,200
Acceptance rate: 86%	**Average debt:** $31,000
Student/faculty ratio: 16/1	**Proportion who borrowed:** 74%

UNDERGRADUATE STUDENT BODY STATS

2009-2010 enrollment: 2,133 full-time; 1,232 part-time. Men: 45%; women: 55%. **Ethnic makeup:** African American: 8%; Asian American: 2%; Hispanic: 9%; White: 77%; International: 4%.

ADMISSIONS FACTS AND FIGURES

Phone: (631) 244-3030. **Email:** admissions@dowling.edu. **Website:** http://www.dowling.edu. **Application deadlines for fall 2011:** Regular decision: May 15. Early decision: Not offered. Early action: Send application by: November 15; Decision sent by: December 31. Admission can be deferred. **Application fee:** $35. **To apply online, go to:** http://www.dowling.edu/admissions/intro2_ugrad.shtm. **Admissions requirements/recommendations:** High school units required (recommended): English: 4 (4); Mathematics: 3 (3); Science: 2 (2); Foreign language: 2 (2); Social studies: 4 (4); Total units: 16 (16). Tests: The college uses SAT or ACT scores in admissions decisions. Neither SAT nor ACT required. For admission to the fall 2011 entering class, the school will accept: ACT with or without writing accepted. Campus visit: Recommended. Admissions interview: Neither required nor recommended. Off-campus interview: Not available. **Factors that count in admissions decisions:** **Academic:** Secondary school record: Very Important. Class rank: Important. Letters of recommendation: Very Important. Standardized test scores: Considered. Essay: Very Important. **Nonacademic:** Interview: Considered. Extracurricular activities: Important. Talent/ability: Important. Character/personal qualities: Very Important. Alumni/ae relationship: Not Considered. Geographical residence: Not Considered. State residency: Not Considered. Religious affiliation/commitment: Not Considered. Minority status: Not Considered. Volunteer work: Important. Work experience: Important. **Other schools with the greatest overlap in applicants:** Adelphi University; Hofstra University; Long Island University–C.W. Post Campus; SUNY–Stony Brook; St. Joseph's College New York–Suffolk. **Admissions statistics for the fall 2009 entering class:** Total applicants: 2,221. Total accepted: 1,918. Freshmen enrolled: 544; 9% were from out of state. Overall acceptance rate: 86%. Non-early acceptance rate: 86%. **Credentials of fall 2009 freshmen:** 8% ranked in the top 10 percent of their high school class; 28% were in the top 25 percent; 60% were in the top half. (Proportion submitting class standing: 55%.) **Average high school grade point average:** 3.0. **First-year students who submitted SAT scores:** 74%. Scores (25/75 percentile): Critical Reading: 410-510, Math: 420-540, Combined: 830-1050.

ACADEMICS

Year founded: 1955. **Academic calendar:** Semester. **Degrees offered:** bachelor's, post-bachelor's certificate, master's, post-master's certificate. **Most popular majors:** 14% business administration and management, 10% special education and teaching, 10% psychology, 9% elementary education and teaching, 8% accounting. **Major fields of study:** biological and biomedical sciences; business, management, marketing, and related support services; communication, journalism, and related programs; computer and information sciences and support services; education; engineering; English language and literature/letters; foreign languages, literatures, and linguistics; health professions and related clinical sciences; history; liberal arts and sciences studies, and humanities; mathematics and statistics; multi/interdisciplinary studies; philosophy and religious studies; psychology; social sciences; transportation and materials moving; visual and performing arts. **Areas of required coursework:** arts/fine arts, humanities, mathematics, English (including composition), philosophy, sciences (biological or physical), history, social science. **Pre-professional programs:** pre-law, pre-dentistry, pre-medicine, pre-veterinary science. **Special academic programs:** distance learning, double major, English as a Second Language (ESL), honors program, independent study, internships, student-designed major, study abroad, teacher certificate program, weekend college, other. **Teacher certification offered in:** early childhood, special education, elementary, middle/junior high, secondary. **Reserve Officers Training Corps (ROTC):** Army ROTC: Offered at cooperating institution (Hofstra University); Air Force ROTC: Offered at cooperating institution (Manhattan College). **Faculty and instruction (2009-2010):** Total instructional faculty: 119 full-time, 339 part-time (60% men; 40% women; 18% minorities). Full-time faculty with Ph.D. or other terminal degree: 95%. Student/faculty ratio: 16/1. Classes of fewer than 20 students: 65%; of 20 to 49 students: 35%; of 50 or more students: 0%. **Advanced Placement and International Baccalaureate credit:** AP tests may be used for: Placement only. International Baccalaureate exams may be used for: Credit and/or placement. **Freshmen returning for sophomore year:** 64%. **Graduation rates:** Four-year: 16%; five-year: 32%; six-year: 38%.

COSTS AND FINANCIAL AID

Financial aid office: (631) 244-3303. **Expenses (2009-2010):** Tuition and fees 2009-2010: $22,850; room/board: $10,200. Estimated books and supplies: $1,000; transportation: $1,350; personal expenses: $100. **Financial aid:** Priority filing date for institution's financial aid form: March 1. In 2009-2010, 72% of undergraduates applied for financial aid. Of those, 72% were determined to have financial need; 2% had their need fully met. Average financial aid package (proportion receiving): $16,426 (72%). Average amount of gift aid, such as scholarships or grants (proportion receiving): $9,144 (69%). Average amount of self-help aid, such as work study or loans (proportion receiving): $16,864 (64%). Average need-based loan (excluding PLUS or other private loans): $4,406. Among students who received need-based aid, the average percentage of need met: 94%. Among students who received aid based on merit, the average award (and the proportion receiving): $5,478 (7%). The average athletic scholarship (and the proportion receiving): $10,407 (11%). Average amount of debt of borrowers graduating in 2009: $31,000. Proportion who borrowed: 74%.

CAMPUS LIFE AND EXTRACURRICULAR ACTIVITIES

Campus housing available (% using): coed dorms (100%). Students who live in college-owned, operated, or affiliated housing: 8%. **Student employment:** During the 2009-2010 academic year, 4% of undergraduates worked on campus. Average per-year earnings: $3,500. **Clubs and organizations:** Number of student organizations: 30. Activities include: choral groups, drama/theater, international student organization, jazz band, literary magazine, music ensembles, student government, student newspaper, yearbook. Number of fraternities: 0; sororities: 0. Average proportion of students who stay on campus on weekends: 15%. **Sports program (2009-2010):** Member of NCAA II. *Men's intercollegiate varsity sports:* baseball, basketball, cross country, golf, lacrosse, soccer. *Women's intercollegiate varsity sports:* basketball, crew (heavyweight), cross country, lacrosse, soccer, softball, volleyball.

SERVICES AND FACILITIES

Basic services: nonremedial tutoring, placement service, health service, health insurance. **Remedial assistance:** reading, math, writing, study skills. **Counseling services:** minority student, career, personal, veteran student, academic, older student, psychological. **For learning-disabled students:** School does not offer a structured program with separate admission and additional fees. Total undergraduates in learning-disabled program or receiving services: 235. Services include: remedial math, remedial English, untimed tests, note-taking services, readers, extended time for tests, tutors, texts on tape, other testing accommodations. **Library:** Number of titles: 154,031; number of current serial subscriptions: 3,131. **Information technology resources:** Students are not required to lease or own a computer. Number of campus computers available to all students: 324. School has a wireless network. Proportion of college-owned housing units wired for high-speed internet access: 100%. **Campus safety:** Security services offered: 24-hour foot-and-vehicle patrols, late-night transport/escort service, lighted pathways/sidewalks, controlled dormitory access (key, security card, etc).

TRANSFER AND INTERNATIONAL STUDENTS

Transfer students: May apply for admission for the following academic terms: Fall, Winter, Spring, Summer. Applicants do not need a minimum number of credits to apply. For fall 2009: Transfer applications received: 583. Transfer applicants offered admission: 492. Transfer applicants enrolled: 298. **International students:** Number of foreign undergraduates: 148 (4% of student body). Number of countries represented: 60. Minimum TOEFL score required: 550 (paper); 213 (computer).

D'Youville College

- **Address:** 320 Porter Avenue, Buffalo, NY 14201-1084
- **Website:** http://www.dyc.edu
- **Private**
- **Enrollment:** 1,467 full-time; 399 part-time

KEY STATS

✔ **U.S News College Ranking:** 114, Regional Universities (North)
✔ **SAT Score (25th/75th percentile):** 960-1140
✔ **Tuition:** 2010-2011: $21,030

Selectivity: Selective	**Room/board:** $9,800
Acceptance rate: 83%	**Average debt:** $31,401
Student/faculty ratio: 12/1	**Proportion who borrowed:** 100%

UNDERGRADUATE STUDENT BODY STATS

2009-2010 enrollment: 1,467 full-time; 399 part-time. Men: 26%; women: 74%. **Ethnic makeup:** African American: 11%; American-Indian: 1%; Asian American: 2%; Hispanic: 4%; White: 73%; International: 9%. **Religious preference:** Roman Catholic: 26%; Protestant: 5%; Jewish: 1%; Muslim: 1%; No preference: 10%; Unknown: 36%; Other: 4%.

ADMISSIONS FACTS AND FIGURES

Phone: (716) 829-7600. **Email:** admiss@dyc.edu. **Website:** http://www.dyc.edu. **Application deadlines for fall 2011:** Regular decision: Rolling. Early decision: Not offered. Early action: Not offered. Admission can be deferred. **Application fee:** $25. **To apply online, go to:** https://www.dyc.edu/nias/. **Admissions requirements/recommendations:** High school units required (recommended): English: (4); Mathematics: (3); Science: (3); Foreign language: (3); Social studies: (3); Total units: (16). Tests: The college uses SAT or ACT scores in admissions decisions. Either SAT or ACT required. For admission to the fall 2011 entering class, the school will accept: ACT with or without writing accepted. Campus visit: Recommended. Admissions interview: Recommended. Off-campus interview: Not available. **Factors that count in admissions decisions:** *Academic:* Secondary school record: Very Important. Class rank: Important. Letters of recommendation: Considered. Standardized test scores: Very Important. Essay: Not Considered. *Nonacademic:* Interview: Considered. Extracurricular activities: Considered. Talent/ability: Considered. Character/personal qualities: Considered. Alumni/ae relationship: Considered. Geographical residence: Not Considered. State residency: Not Considered. Religious affiliation/commitment: Not Considered. Minority status: Not Considered. Volunteer work: Considered. Work experience: Considered. **Other schools with the greatest overlap in applicants:** Canisius College; Daemen College; Nazareth College; Niagara University; University at Buffalo–SUNY. **Admissions statistics for the fall 2009 entering class:** Total applicants: 949. Total accepted: 791. Freshmen enrolled: 155; 8% were from out of state. Overall acceptance rate: 83%. **Credentials of fall 2009 freshmen:** 13% ranked in the top 10 percent of their high school class; 50% were in the top 25 percent; 88% were in the top half. (Proportion submitting class standing: 56%.) **First-year students who submitted SAT scores:** 97%. Scores (25/75 percentile): Critical Reading: 470-560, Math: 490-580, Combined: 960-1140. **First-year students submitting ACT scores:** 39%. Scores (25/75 percentile): English: N/A, Math: N/A, Composite: 21-25.

ACADEMICS

Year founded: 1908. **Academic calendar:** Semester. **Degrees offered:** bachelor's, post-bachelor's certificate, master's, post-master's certificate, doctorate. **Most popular majors:** 33% nursing/registered nurse training (R.N., A.S.N., B.S.N., M.S.N.), 12% business administration and management, 9% multi/interdisciplinary studies, 9% physician assistant, 8% health services administration. **Major fields of study:** biological and biomedical sciences; business, management, marketing, and related support services; education; English language and literature/letters; health professions and related clinical sciences; history; liberal arts and sciences studies, and humanities; philosophy and religious studies; psychology; social sciences. **Areas of required coursework:** arts/fine arts, humanities, computer literacy, mathematics, English (including composition), philosophy, foreign languages, sciences (biological or physical), history, social science, other. **Pre-professional programs:** pre-law, pre-dentistry, pre-medicine, pre-veterinary science, pre-pharmacy. **Special academic programs (% participation):** accelerated program, cross-registration, distance learning, double major, dual enrollment, independent study, internships, liberal arts/career combination, study abroad (2%), teacher certificate program, weekend college, other. **Teacher certification offered in:** early childhood, special education, elementary, middle/junior high, secondary. **Reserve Officers Training Corps (ROTC):** Army ROTC: Offered at cooperating institution (Canisius College). **Faculty and instruction (2009-2010):** Total instructional faculty: 144 full-time, 178 part-time (50% men; 50% women; 6% minorities). Student/faculty ratio: 12/1. Classes of fewer than 20 students: 65%; of 20 to 49 students: 34%; of 50 or more students: 1%. **Advanced Placement and International Baccalaureate credit:** AP tests may be used for: Credit and/or placement. Scores accepted: 3, 4, 5. International Baccalaureate exams may be used for: Credit only. **Freshmen returning for sophomore year:** 72%. **Graduation rates:** Four-year: 40%; five-year: 63%; six-year: 51%.

COSTS AND FINANCIAL AID

Financial aid office: (716) 829-7500. **Expenses (2010-2011):** Tuition and fees 2010-2011: $21,030; room/board: $9,800. Estimated books and supplies: $1,200; transportation: $1,500; personal expenses: $800. **Financial aid:** Priority filing date for institution's financial aid form: February 15. In 2009-2010, 99% of undergraduates applied for financial aid. Of those, 92% were determined to have financial need; 14% had their need fully met. Average financial aid package (proportion receiving): $15,796 (91%). Average amount of gift aid, such as scholarships or grants (proportion receiving): $10,534 (87%). Average amount of self-help aid, such as work study or loans (proportion receiving): $6,406 (81%). Average need-based loan (excluding PLUS or other private loans): $5,988. Among students who received need-based aid, the average percentage of need met: 63%. Among students who received aid based on merit, the average award (and the proportion receiving): $6,656 (5%). The average athletic scholarship (and the proportion receiving): $0 (0%). Average amount of debt of borrowers graduating in 2009: $31,401. Proportion who borrowed: 100%.

CAMPUS LIFE AND EXTRACURRICULAR ACTIVITIES

Campus housing available (% using): coed dorms (52%), apartment for single students (48%). Students who live in college-owned, operated, or affiliated housing: 14%. **Student employment:** During the 2009-2010 academic year, 25% of undergraduates worked on campus. Average per-year earnings: $1,500. **Clubs and organizations:** Number of student organizations: 32. Activities include: campus ministries, choral groups, drama/theater, literary magazine, student government, student newspaper, yearbook.

Number of fraternities: o; sororities: o. Average proportion of students who stay on campus on weekends: 75%. **Sports program (2009-2010):** Member of NCAA III. *Men's intercollegiate varsity sports:* baseball, basketball, golf, soccer, tennis, volleyball. *Women's intercollegiate varsity sports:* basketball, crew (heavyweight), cross country, golf, crew (lightweight), soccer, softball, tennis, volleyball.

SERVICES AND FACILITIES

Basic services: nonremedial tutoring, placement service, health service, health insurance, other. **Remedial assistance:** reading, math, writing, study skills, other. **Counseling services:** minority student, career, personal, veteran student, academic, older student, birth control, religious. **For learning-disabled students:** School does not offer a structured program with separate admission and additional fees. Services include: remedial math, remedial English, reading machines, remedial reading, tape recorders, videotaped classes, untimed tests, note-taking services, oral tests, learning center, readers, extended time for tests, tutors. **Library:** Number of titles: 99,769; number of current serial subscriptions: 711. **Information technology resources:** Students are not required to lease or own a computer. Number of campus computers available to all students: 120. School has a wireless network. Proportion of college-owned housing units wired for high-speed internet access: 100%. **Campus safety:** Security services offered: late-night transport/escort service, 24-hour emergency telephones, student patrols, controlled dormitory access (key, security card, etc).

TRANSFER AND INTERNATIONAL STUDENTS

Transfer students: May apply for admission for the following academic terms: Fall, Spring, Summer. Applicants need a minimum number of credits to apply. For fall 2009: Transfer applications received: 705. Transfer applicants offered admission: 637. Transfer applicants enrolled: 235. **International students:** Number of foreign undergraduates: 155 (9% of student body). Minimum TOEFL score required: 500 (paper); 173 (computer). Average TOEFL score: 515 (paper).

Elmira College

- **Address:** 1 Park Place, Elmira, NY 14901
- **Website:** http://www.elmira.edu
- **Private**
- **Enrollment:** 1,125 full-time; 234 part-time

KEY STATS

✔ **U.S News College Ranking:** 6, Regional Colleges (North)
✔ **SAT Score (25th/75th percentile):** 960-1190
✔ **Tuition:** 2010-2011: $35,900

Selectivity: Selective	**Room/board:** $11,150
Acceptance rate: 79%	**Average debt:** $26,874
Student/faculty ratio: 12/1	**Proportion who borrowed:** 81%

UNDERGRADUATE STUDENT BODY STATS

2009-2010 enrollment: 1,125 full-time; 234 part-time. Men: 28%; women: 72%. **Ethnic makeup:** African American: 3%; Asian American: 1%; Hispanic: 2%; White: 92%; International: 1%. **Religious preference:** Roman Catholic: 40%; Protestant: 30%; Jewish: 2%; Buddhist: 1%; Unknown: 27%.

ADMISSIONS FACTS AND FIGURES

Phone: (607) 735-1724. **Email:** admissions@elmira.edu. **Website:** http://www.elmira.edu. **Application deadlines for fall 2011:** Regular decision: March 15. Early decision: Send application by: November 15; Decision sent by: December 15. Early action: Not offered. Admission can be deferred. **Application fee:** $50. **To apply online, go to:** http://app.commonapp.org/. **Admissions requirements/recommendations:** High school units required (recommended): English: 4; Mathematics: 3; Science: 3; Foreign language: (2); Social studies: 3; History: 1; Academic electives: 2; Total units: 16. Tests: The college uses SAT or ACT scores in admissions decisions. Either SAT or ACT required. For admission to the fall 2011 entering class, the school will accept: ACT with or without writing accepted. Campus visit: Recommended. Admissions interview: Recommended. Off-campus interview: May be arranged. **Factors that count in admissions decisions:** *Academic:* Secondary school record: Very Important. Class rank: Very Important. Letters of recommendation: Important. Standardized test scores: Important. Essay: Important. *Nonacademic:* Interview: Very Important. Extracurricular activities: Important. Talent/ability: Considered. Character/personal qualities:

Very Important. Alumni/ae relationship: Considered. Geographical residence: Considered. State residency: Not Considered. Religious affiliation/commitment: Not Considered. Minority status: Considered. Volunteer work: Considered. Work experience: Considered. **Other schools with the greatest overlap in applicants:** Hartwick College; Hobart and William Smith Colleges; Ithaca College; Nazareth College; St. Lawrence University. **Admissions statistics for the fall 2009 entering class:** Total applicants: 2,083. Total accepted: 1,648. Freshmen enrolled: 430; 48% were from out of state. Accepted through early-decision or early-action plans: 8%. Overall acceptance rate: 79%. Early-decision acceptance rate: 37%. Non-early acceptance rate: 81%. Size of waiting list: 26 applicants; enrolled from waiting list: 2. **Credentials of fall 2009 freshmen:** 31% ranked in the top 10 percent of their high school class; 56% were in the top 25 percent; 91% were in the top half. (Proportion submitting class standing: 66%.) **Average high school grade point average:** 3.2. **First-year students who submitted SAT scores:** 87%. Scores (25/75 percentile): Critical Reading: 490-600, Math: 470-590, Combined: 960-1190. **First-year students submitting ACT scores:** 30%. Scores (25/75 percentile): English: N/A, Math: N/A, Composite: 21-26.

ACADEMICS

Year founded: 1855. **Academic calendar:** Other. **Degrees offered:** associate, bachelor's, master's. **Most popular majors:** 19% business administration and management, 19% elementary education and teaching, 10% psychology, 5% biology/biological sciences, 4% mathematics. **Major fields of study:** area, ethnic, cultural, and gender studies; biological and biomedical sciences; business, management, marketing, and related support services; computer and information sciences and support services; education; English language and literature/letters; foreign languages, literatures, and linguistics; health professions and related clinical sciences; history; liberal arts and sciences studies, and humanities; mathematics and statistics; multi/interdisciplinary studies; philosophy and religious studies; physical sciences; psychology; public administration and social service professions; security and protective services; social sciences; visual and performing arts. **Areas of required coursework:** arts/fine arts, humanities, mathematics, English (including composition), sciences (biological or physical), history, social science, other. **Pre-professional programs:** pre-law, pre-dentistry, pre-medicine, pre-veterinary science, pre-optometry, pre-pharmacy. **Special academic programs (% participation):** accelerated program (1%), distance learning (1%), double major (22%), English as a Second Language (ESL) (1%), honors program (2%), independent study (12%), internships (100%), liberal arts/career combination (1%), student-designed major (4%), study abroad (42%), teacher certificate program (17%). **Teacher certification offered in:** elementary, middle/junior high, secondary. **Reserve Officers Training Corps (ROTC):** Army ROTC: Offered on campus; Air Force ROTC: Offered at cooperating institution (Cornell University). **Faculty and instruction (2009-2010):** Total instructional faculty: 87 full-time, 24 part-time (46% men; 54% women; 9% minorities). Full-time faculty with Ph.D. or other terminal degree: 100%. Student/faculty ratio: 12/1. Classes of fewer than 20 students: 81%; of 20 to 49 students: 19%; of 50 or more students: 0%. **Advanced Placement and International Baccalaureate credit:** AP tests may be used for: Credit and/or placement. Scores accepted: 3, 4, 5. International Baccalaureate exams may be used for: Credit and/or placement. **Freshmen returning for sophomore year:** 74%. **Graduation rates:** Four-year: 63%; five-year: 66%; six-year: 63%. **Graduate study:** 40% of students pursue further study immediately upon graduation; 64% within one year; 85% within five years. Fields in which graduates pursue further study: Master of Business Administration (MBA), 8%; law, 3%; medicine, 2%; theology (or the seminary), 1%; education, 46%; arts and sciences, 12%.

COSTS AND FINANCIAL AID

Financial aid office: (607) 735-1728. **Expenses (2010-2011):** Tuition and fees 2010-2011: $35,900; room/board: $11,150. Estimated books and supplies: $600; transportation: $550. **Financial aid:** Priority filing date for institution's financial aid form: February 1. In 2009-2010, 84% of undergraduates applied for financial aid. Of those, 78% were determined to have financial need; 16% had their need fully met. Average financial aid package (proportion receiving): $26,317 (78%). Average amount of gift aid, such as scholarships or grants (proportion receiving): $22,110 (78%). Average amount of self-help aid, such as work study or loans (proportion receiving): $5,042 (66%). Average need-based loan (excluding PLUS or other private loans): $4,354. Among students who received need-based aid, the average percentage of need met: 80%. Among students who received aid based on merit, the average award (and the proportion receiving): $17,653 (19%). The average athletic scholarship (and the proportion receiving): $0 (0%). Average amount of debt of borrowers graduating in 2009: $26,874. Proportion who borrowed: 81%.

CAMPUS LIFE AND EXTRACURRICULAR ACTIVITIES

Campus housing available (% using): coed dorms (71%), women's dorms (23%), apartment for single students (6%). Students who live in college-owned, operated, or affiliated housing: 93%. **Student employment:** During the 2009-2010 academic year, 50% of undergraduates worked on campus. Average per-year earnings: $2,000. **Clubs and organizations:** Number of student organizations: 104. Activities include: campus ministries, choral groups, concert band, dance, drama/theater, international student organization, literary magazine, model UN, music ensembles, musical theater, radio station, student government, student newspaper, yearbook. Number of fraternities: 0; sororities: 0. Average proportion of students who stay on campus on weekends: 90%. **Sports program (2009-2010):** Member of NCAA III. *Men's intercollegiate varsity sports:* basketball, golf, ice hockey, lacrosse, soccer, tennis, volleyball. *Women's intercollegiate varsity sports:* basketball, field hockey, golf, ice hockey, lacrosse, skiing (alpine), soccer, softball, tennis, volleyball.

SERVICES AND FACILITIES

Basic services: nonremedial tutoring, placement service, health service, health insurance, other. **Remedial assistance:** math, writing, study skills, other. **Counseling services:** minority student, career, military, personal, veteran student, academic, psychological, birth control, religious. **For learning-disabled students:** School does not offer a structured program with separate admission and additional fees. Total undergraduates in learning-disabled program or receiving services: 54. Services include: remedial math, reading machines, tape recorders, untimed tests, note-taking services, oral tests, readers, extended time for tests, tutors, proofreading services, texts on tape, typist/scribe, exams on tape or computer, other testing accommodations, other. **Library:** Number of titles: 185,229; number of current serial subscriptions: 324. **Information technology resources:** Students are not required to lease or own a computer. Number of campus computers available to all students: 115. School has a wireless network. Approximate number of users that can be accommodated: 500. Proportion of college-owned housing units wired for high-speed internet access: 98%. **Campus safety:** Security services offered: 24-hour foot-and-vehicle patrols, late-night transport/escort service, 24-hour emergency telephones, lighted pathways/sidewalks, controlled dormitory access (key, security card, etc).

TRANSFER AND INTERNATIONAL STUDENTS

Transfer students: May apply for admission for the following academic terms: Fall, Winter, Spring. Applicants need a minimum number of credits to apply. For fall 2009: Transfer applications received: 161. Transfer applicants offered admission: 88. Transfer applicants enrolled: 49. **International students:** Number of foreign undergraduates: 19 (1% of student body). Number of countries represented: 31. Minimum TOEFL score required: 500 (paper); 61 (computer). Average TOEFL score: 550 (paper).

Excelsior College

- **Address:** 7 Columbia Circle, Albany, NY 12203
- **Website:** http://www.excelsior.edu
- **Private**
- **Enrollment:** N/A

KEY STATS
✔ **U.S News College Ranking:** Unranked, National Liberal Arts Colleges
✔ **SAT or ACT Score (25th/75th percentile):** N/A
✔ **Tuition:** N/A

Selectivity: N/A	**Room/board:** N/A
Acceptance rate: N/A	**Average debt:** N/A
Student/faculty ratio: N/A	**Proportion who borrowed:** N/A

Farmingdale State College–SUNY

- **Address:** 2350 Broadhollow Road, Farmingdale, NY 11735-1021
- **Website:** http://www.farmingdale.edu
- **Public**
- **Enrollment:** 5,019 full-time; 1,969 part-time

KEY STATS
✔ **U.S News College Ranking:** 39, Regional Colleges (North)
✔ **SAT Score (25th/75th percentile):** 950-1090
✔ **Tuition:** 2009-2010: $6,030 in state, $13,930 out of state

Selectivity: Selective	**Room/board:** $11,090
Acceptance rate: 40%	**Average debt:** N/A
Student/faculty ratio: 18/1	**Proportion who borrowed:** N/A

UNDERGRADUATE STUDENT BODY STATS

2009-2010 enrollment: 5,019 full-time; 1,969 part-time. Men: 57%; women: 43%. **Ethnic makeup:** African American: 8%; Asian American: 4%; Hispanic: 8%; White: 79%; International: 1%.

ADMISSIONS FACTS AND FIGURES

Phone: (631) 420-2200. **Email:** admissions@farmingdale.edu. **Website:** http://www.farmingdale.edu. **Application deadlines for fall 2011:** Regular decision: Rolling. Early decision: Not offered. Early action: Not offered. Admission cannot be deferred. **Application fee:** $40. **To apply online, go to:** https://www.applyweb.com/aw?suny95ud. **Admissions requirements/recommendations:** High school units required (recommended): English: 3 (4); Mathematics: 2 (3); Science: 1 (2); Total units: 7 (10). Tests: The college uses SAT or ACT scores in admissions decisions. SAT required. For admission to the fall 2011 entering class, the school will accept: ACT with writing required. Campus visit: Recommended. Admissions interview: Required. Off-campus interview: Not available. **Factors that count in admissions decisions:** *Academic:* Secondary school record: Important. Class rank: Important. Letters of recommendation: Important. Standardized test scores: Important. Essay: Considered. *Nonacademic:* Interview: Considered. Extracurricular activities: Considered. Talent/ability: Considered. Character/personal qualities: Considered. Alumni/ae relationship: Considered. Geographical residence: Not Considered. State residency: Not Considered. Religious affiliation/commitment: Not Considered. Minority status: Not Considered. Volunteer work: Considered. Work experience: Considered. **Other schools with the greatest overlap in applicants:** CUNY–New York City College of Technology; Hofstra University; Long Island University–C.W. Post Campus; SUNY College–Old Westbury; SUNY–Stony Brook. **Admissions statistics for the fall 2009 entering class:** Total applicants: 5,714. Total accepted: 2,312. Freshmen enrolled: 1,355; 1% were from out of state. Overall acceptance rate: 40%. **Credentials of fall 2009 freshmen:** 8% ranked in the top 10 percent of their high school class; 31% were in the top 25 percent; 70% were in the top half. (Proportion submitting class standing: 25%.) **First-year students who submitted SAT scores:** 90%. Scores (25/75 percentile): Critical Reading: 440-520, Math: 510-570, Combined: 950-1090.

ACADEMICS

Year founded: 1912. **Academic calendar:** Semester. **Degrees offered:** certificate, associate, bachelor's. **Most popular majors:** 37% business, management, marketing, and related support services, 14% engineering technologies/technicians, 9% biological and biomedical sciences, 9% communication, journalism, and related programs, 8% security and protective services. **Major fields of study:** agriculture, agriculture operations, and related sciences; biological and biomedical sciences; business, management, marketing, and related support services; computer and information sciences and support services; engineering technologies/technicians; English language and literature/letters; health professions and related clinical sciences; mathematics and statistics; multi/interdisciplinary studies; psychology; security and protective services; social sciences; transportation and materials moving; visual and performing arts. **Areas of required coursework:** humanities, computer literacy, mathematics, English (including composition), foreign languages, sciences (biological or physical), history, social science. **Special academic programs:** distance learning, English as a Second Language (ESL), honors program, independent study, internships, study abroad. **Faculty and instruction (2009-2010):** Total instructional faculty: 191 full-time, 364 part-time (53% men; 47% women; 15% minorities). Full-time faculty with Ph.D. or other terminal degree: 56%. Student/faculty ratio: 18/1. Classes of fewer than 20 students: 29%; of 20 to 49 students: 69%; of 50 or more students: 2%. **Advanced Placement and International**

Baccalaureate credit: AP tests may be used for: Placement only. Scores accepted: 3, 4, 5. **Freshmen returning for sophomore year:** 76%. **Graduation rates:** Four-year: 14%; five-year: 31%; six-year: 31%. **Graduate study:** 50% of students pursue further study within one year.

COSTS AND FINANCIAL AID
Financial aid office: (631) 420-2328. **Expenses (2009-2010):** Tuition and fees 2009-2010: $6,030 in state, $13,930 out of state; room/board: $11,090. Estimated books and supplies: $1,245. **Financial aid:** Priority filing date for institution's financial aid form: April 4.

CAMPUS LIFE AND EXTRACURRICULAR ACTIVITIES
Campus housing available (% using): coed dorms (100%). Students who live in college-owned, operated, or affiliated housing: 7%. **Clubs and organizations:** Number of student organizations: 30. Activities include: drama/theater, literary magazine, radio station, student government, student newspaper, yearbook. Average proportion of students who stay on campus on weekends: 5%. **Sports program (2009-2010):** Member of NCAA III.

SERVICES AND FACILITIES
Basic services: nonremedial tutoring, placement service, day care, health service, health insurance. **Remedial assistance:** reading, math, writing, study skills. **Counseling services:** minority student, career, personal, academic, older student, psychological, birth control. **For learning-disabled students:** School does not offer a structured program with separate admission and additional fees. Total undergraduates in learning-disabled program or receiving services: 182. Services include: reading machines, tape recorders, diagnostic testing service, untimed tests, learning center, readers, extended time for tests, tutors. **Library:** Number of titles: 125,000; number of current serial subscriptions: 800. **Information technology resources:** Students are not required to lease or own a computer. Number of campus computers available to all students: 950. School has a wireless network. Approximate number of users that can be accommodated: 4,000. Proportion of college-owned housing units wired for high-speed internet access: 90%. **Campus safety:** Security services offered: 24-hour foot-and-vehicle patrols, 24-hour emergency telephones, lighted pathways/sidewalks, controlled dormitory access (key, security card, etc).

TRANSFER AND INTERNATIONAL STUDENTS
Transfer students: May apply for admission for the following academic terms: Fall, Spring. Applicants do not need a minimum number of credits to apply. For fall 2009: Transfer applications received: 2,237. Transfer applicants offered admission: 1,369. Transfer applicants enrolled: 713. **International students:** Number of foreign undergraduates: 59 (1% of student body). Minimum TOEFL score required: 500 (paper); 173 (computer).

Fashion Institute of Technology

- **Address:** Seventh Avenue at 27th Street, New York, NY 10001-5992
- **Website:** http://www.fitnyc.edu
- **Public**
- **Enrollment:** 7,163 full-time; 3,044 part-time

KEY STATS
- ✔ **U.S News College Ranking:** Unranked, Regional Colleges (North)
- ✔ **SAT or ACT Score (25th/75th percentile):** N/A
- ✔ **Tuition:** 2009-2010: $4,164 in state, $11,592 out of state

Selectivity: N/A	**Room/board:** $11,248
Acceptance rate: 40%	**Average debt:** $24,554
Student/faculty ratio: 17/1	**Proportion who borrowed:** 57%

UNDERGRADUATE STUDENT BODY STATS
2009-2010 enrollment: 7,163 full-time; 3,044 part-time. Men: 16%; women: 84%. **Ethnic makeup:** African American: 6%; Asian American: 7%; Hispanic: 9%; White: 66%; International: 11%.

ADMISSIONS FACTS AND FIGURES
Phone: (212) 217-3760. **Email:** fitinfo@fitsuny.edu. **Website:** http://www.fitnyc.edu. **Application deadlines for fall 2011:** Regular decision: January 1; decision sent by April 1. Early decision: Not offered. Early action: Not offered. Admission cannot be deferred. **Application fee:** $50. **To apply online, go to:** http://fitnyc.edu/html/admissions/HowDoIApply/index.html. **Admissions requirements/recommendations:** High school units required

(recommended): English: (4); Mathematics: (3); Science: (3); Foreign language: (2); Social studies: (2); History: (2). Tests: The college does not use SAT or ACT scores in admissions decisions. Neither SAT nor ACT required. Campus visit: Recommended. Admissions interview: Neither required nor recommended. Off-campus interview: Not available. **Factors that count in admissions decisions:** *Academic:* Secondary school record: Very Important. Class rank: Very Important. Letters of recommendation: Not Considered. Standardized test scores: Not Considered. Essay: Very Important. *Nonacademic:* Interview: Not Considered. Extracurricular activities: Considered. Talent/ability: Very Important. Character/personal qualities: Considered. Alumni/ae relationship: Not Considered. Geographical residence: Not Considered. State residency: Not Considered. Religious affiliation/commitment: Not Considered. Minority status: Not Considered. Volunteer work: Not Considered. Work experience: Not Considered. **Admissions statistics for the fall 2009 entering class:** Total applicants: 3,973. Total accepted: 1,605. Freshmen enrolled: 1,068; 35% were from out of state. Overall acceptance rate: 40%. **Credentials of fall 2009 freshmen:** 15% ranked in the top 10 percent of their high school class; 44% were in the top 25 percent. **Average high school grade point average:** 3.3.

ACADEMICS
Year founded: 1944. **Academic calendar:** Semester. **Degrees offered:** certificate, associate, bachelor's, master's. **Most popular majors:** 27% fashion merchandising, 14% advertising, 13% fashion/apparel design, 7% international marketing, 5% graphic design. **Major fields of study:** business, management, marketing, and related support services; communication, journalism, and related programs; communications technologies/technicians and support services; family and consumer sciences/human sciences; visual and performing arts. **Areas of required coursework:** arts/fine arts, humanities, mathematics, English (including composition), foreign languages, sciences (biological or physical), history, social science. **Special academic programs:** distance learning, English as a Second Language (ESL), honors program, independent study, internships, study abroad. **Faculty and instruction (2009-2010):** Total instructional faculty: 253 full-time, 754 part-time (51% men; 49% women). Student/faculty ratio: 17/1. Classes of fewer than 20 students: 36%; of 20 to 49 students: 64%; of 50 or more students: 0%. **Advanced Placement and International Baccalaureate credit:** AP tests may be used for: Credit and/or placement. Scores accepted: 3, 4, 5. International Baccalaureate exams may be used for: Credit and/or placement. **Freshmen returning for sophomore year:** 85%. **Graduation rates:** Six-year: 54%.

COSTS AND FINANCIAL AID
Financial aid office: (212) 217-7439. **Expenses (2009-2010):** Tuition and fees 2009-2010: $4,164 in state, $11,592 out of state; room/board: $11,248. Estimated books and supplies: $1,750. **Financial aid:** In 2009-2010, 62% of undergraduates applied for financial aid. Of those, 48% were determined to have financial need; 13% had their need fully met. Average financial aid package (proportion receiving): $11,288 (47%). Average amount of gift aid, such as scholarships or grants (proportion receiving): $5,327 (35%). Average amount of self-help aid, such as work study or loans (proportion receiving): $4,559 (37%). Average need-based loan (excluding PLUS or other private loans): $4,292. Among students who received need-based aid, the average percentage of need met: 66%. Among students who received aid based on merit, the average award (and the proportion receiving): $1,641 (2%). Average amount of debt of borrowers graduating in 2009: $24,554. Proportion who borrowed: 57%.

CAMPUS LIFE AND EXTRACURRICULAR ACTIVITIES
Campus housing available: coed dorms, women's dorms, apartment for single students, special housing for disabled students. Students who live in college-owned, operated, or affiliated housing: 23%. **Clubs and organizations:** Number of student organizations: 75. Activities include: campus ministries, choral groups, dance, drama/theater, international student organization, literary magazine, music ensembles, musical theater, radio station, student government, student newspaper, television station, yearbook. Number of fraternities: 0; sororities: 0.

SERVICES AND FACILITIES
Basic services: nonremedial tutoring, placement service, health service, health insurance. **Remedial assistance:** reading, math, writing, study skills. **Counseling services:** other. **For learning-disabled students:** School does not offer a structured program with separate admission and additional fees. Services include: remedial math, remedial English, reading machines, remedial reading, tape recorders, diagnostic testing service, note-taking services, learning center, readers, extended time for tests, tutors, priority seating, substitution of courses, texts on tape, typist/scribe, exams on tape

or computer, waiver of foreign language degree requirement, other. **Library:** Number of titles: 216,388; number of current serial subscriptions: 352. **Information technology resources:** Students are not required to lease or own a computer. Number of campus computers available to all students: 1,300. School has a wireless network. Approximate number of users that can be accommodated: 3,000. Proportion of college-owned housing units wired for high-speed internet access: 100%. **Campus safety:** Security services offered: 24-hour foot-and-vehicle patrols, late-night transport/escort service, 24-hour emergency telephones, lighted pathways/sidewalks, controlled dormitory access (key, security card, etc).

TRANSFER AND INTERNATIONAL STUDENTS

Transfer students: May apply for admission for the following academic terms: Fall, Spring. Applicants do not need a minimum number of credits to apply. For fall 2009: Transfer applications received: 2,235. Transfer applicants offered admission: 1,040. Transfer applicants enrolled: 740. **International students:** Number of foreign undergraduates: 908 (11% of student body). Number of countries represented: 64. Minimum TOEFL score required: 550 (paper); 213 (computer).

Fordham University

- **Address:** 113 W. 60th Street, New York, NY 10023
- **Website:** http://www.fordham.edu
- **Private; Religious affiliation:** Roman Catholic
- **Enrollment:** 7,370 full-time; 580 part-time

KEY STATS

✔ **U.S News College Ranking:** 56, National Universities
✔ **SAT Score (25th/75th percentile):** 1140-1340
✔ **Tuition:** 2010-2011: $38,277

Selectivity: More selective	**Room/board:** $14,491
Acceptance rate: 50%	**Average debt:** N/A
Student/faculty ratio: 13/1	**Proportion who borrowed:** N/A

UNDERGRADUATE STUDENT BODY STATS

2009-2010 enrollment: 7,370 full-time; 580 part-time. Men: 47%; women: 53%. **Ethnic makeup:** African American: 5%; Asian American: 8%; Hispanic: 13%; White: 71%; International: 3%. **Religious preference:** Protestant: 7%; Jewish: 2%; Muslim: 1%; Hindu: 1%; Buddhist: 1%; Unknown: 25%; Roman Catholic: 54%; Greek Orthodox: 2%; Other: 7%.

ADMISSIONS FACTS AND FIGURES

Phone: (800) 367-3426. **Email:** enroll@fordham.edu. **Website:** http://www.fordham.edu. **Application deadlines for fall 2011:** Regular decision: January 15; decision sent by April 1. Early decision: Not offered. Early action: Send application by: November 1; Decision sent by: N/A. Admission can be deferred. **Application fee:** $50. **To apply online, go to:** http://www.fordham.edu/admiss/admiss.htm. **Admissions requirements/recommendations:** High school units required (recommended): English: 4 (4); Mathematics: 3 (4); Science: 3 (4); Foreign language: 2 (3); Social studies: 2 (2); History: 2 (2); Academic electives: 6 (6); Total units: 22 (25). Tests: The college uses SAT or ACT scores in admissions decisions. Either SAT or ACT required. For admission to the fall 2011 entering class, the school will accept: ACT with or without writing accepted. Campus visit: Recommended. Admissions interview: Recommended. Off-campus interview: May be arranged. **Factors that count in admissions decisions:** *Academic:* Secondary school record: Very Important. Class rank: Very Important. Letters of recommendation: Important. Standardized test scores: Very Important. Essay: Important. *Nonacademic:* Interview: Important. Extracurricular activities: Important. Talent/ability: Important. Character/personal qualities: Important. Alumni/ae relationship: Considered. Geographical residence: Considered. State residency: Not Considered. Religious affiliation/commitment: Not Considered. Minority status: Considered. Volunteer work: Considered. Work experience: Considered. **Other schools with the greatest overlap in applicants:** Boston College; Boston University; George Washington University; New York University; Rutgers, the State University of New Jersey–New Brunswick. **Admissions statistics for the fall 2009 entering class:** Total applicants: 24,557. Total accepted: 12,181. Freshmen enrolled: 1,835; 52% were from out of state. Accepted through early-decision or early-action plans: 34%. Overall acceptance rate: 50%. Non-early acceptance rate: 47%. **Size of waiting list:** 3945 applicants; enrolled from waiting list: 135. **Credentials of fall 2009 freshmen:** 42% ranked in the top 10 percent of their high school class; 78%

were in the top 25 percent; 97% were in the top half. (Proportion submitting class standing: 32%.) **Average high school grade point average:** 3.5. **First-year students who submitted SAT scores:** 90%. Scores (25/75 percentile): Critical Reading: 570-670, Math: 570-670, Combined: 1140-1340. **First-year students submitting ACT scores:** 29%. Scores (25/75 percentile): English: 26-32, Math: 24-29, Composite: 26-30.

ACADEMICS

Year founded: 1841. **Academic calendar:** Semester. **Degrees offered:** bachelor's, master's, post-master's certificate, doctorate. **Most popular majors:** 16% business administration and management, 12% communication studies/speech communication and rhetoric, 7% psychology, 6% English language and literature, 6% accounting. **Major fields of study:** area, ethnic, cultural, and gender studies; biological and biomedical sciences; business, management, marketing, and related support services; communication, journalism, and related programs; computer and information sciences and support services; education; engineering; English language and literature/letters; foreign languages, literatures, and linguistics; history; liberal arts and sciences studies, and humanities; mathematics and statistics; multi/interdisciplinary studies; philosophy and religious studies; physical sciences; psychology; public administration and social service professions; social sciences; visual and performing arts. **Areas of required coursework:** arts/fine arts, humanities, mathematics, English (including composition), philosophy, foreign languages, sciences (biological or physical), history, social science, other. **Pre-professional programs:** pre-law, pre-dentistry, pre-medicine, pre-theology, pre-veterinary science, pre-optometry, pre-pharmacy. **Special academic programs (% participation):** distance learning, double major (12.2%), English as a Second Language (ESL), exchange student program (domestic), honors program (2.6%), independent study, internships (75%), student-designed major (1%), study abroad (12.6%), teacher certificate program, weekend college, other. **Teacher certification offered in:** early childhood, elementary, middle/junior high, secondary. **Reserve Officers Training Corps (ROTC):** Army ROTC: Offered on campus; Navy ROTC: Offered at cooperating institution (SUNY Maritime College); Air Force ROTC: Offered at cooperating institution (Manhattan College). **Faculty and instruction (2009-2010):** Total instructional faculty: 699 full-time, 811 part-time (55% men; 45% women; 14% minorities). Full-time faculty with Ph.D. or other terminal degree: 96%. Student/faculty ratio: 13/1. Classes of fewer than 20 students: 50%; of 20 to 49 students: 49%; of 50 or more students: 1%. **Advanced Placement and International Baccalaureate credit:** AP tests may be used for: Credit and/or placement. Scores accepted: 3, 4, 5. International Baccalaureate exams may be used for: Credit and/or placement. **Freshmen returning for sophomore year:** 90%. **Graduation rates:** Four-year: 75%; five-year: 78%; six-year: 79%. **Graduate study:** 25% of students pursue further study immediately upon graduation. Fields in which graduates pursue further study: Master of Business Administration (MBA), 5%; law, 10%; medicine, 4%; dentistry, 1%.

COSTS AND FINANCIAL AID

Financial aid office: (718) 817-3800. **Expenses (2010-2011):** Tuition and fees 2010-2011: $38,277; room/board: $14,491. Estimated books and supplies: $915; transportation: $830; personal expenses: $1,616. **Financial aid:** Priority filing date for institution's financial aid form: February 1; deadline: February 1.

CAMPUS LIFE AND EXTRACURRICULAR ACTIVITIES

Campus housing available (% using): coed dorms (68%), apartment for single students (32%), other housing options. Students who live in college-owned, operated, or affiliated housing: 55%. **Student employment:** During the 2009-2010 academic year, 17% of undergraduates worked on campus. Average per-year earnings: $3,000. **Clubs and organizations:** Number of student organizations: 133. Activities include: campus ministries, choral groups, dance, drama/theater, international student organization, jazz band, literary magazine, marching band, music ensembles, musical theater, pep band, radio station, student government, student newspaper, student film society, television station, yearbook. Number of fraternities: 0; sororities: 0. Average proportion of students who stay on campus on weekends: 80%. **Sports program (2009-2010):** Member of NCAA I. *Men's intercollegiate varsity sports:* baseball, basketball, cross country, football, golf, soccer, swimming, tennis, track and field (indoor), track and field (outdoor), water polo. *Women's intercollegiate varsity sports:* basketball, crew (heavyweight), cross country, crew (lightweight), soccer, softball, swimming, tennis, track and field (indoor), track and field (outdoor), volleyball.

SERVICES AND FACILITIES

Basic services: nonremedial tutoring, placement service, health service, other. **Remedial assistance:** study skills. **Counseling services:** minority student, career, personal, academic, psychological, religious. **For learning-disabled students:** School does not offer a structured program with separate admission and additional fees. Services include: tape recorders, note-taking services, readers, extended time for tests, tutors, priority registration, priority seating, texts on tape, other. **Library:** Number of titles: 2,689,555; number of current serial subscriptions: 40,476. **Information technology resources:** Students are not required to lease or own a computer. Number of campus computers available to all students: 1,500. School has a wireless network. Approximate number of users that can be accommodated: 15,000. Proportion of college-owned housing units wired for high-speed internet access: 100%. **Campus safety:** Security services offered: 24-hour foot-and-vehicle patrols, late-night transport/escort service, 24-hour emergency telephones, lighted pathways/sidewalks, controlled dormitory access (key, security card, etc).

TRANSFER AND INTERNATIONAL STUDENTS

Transfer students: May apply for admission for the following academic terms: Fall, Spring. Applicants do not need a minimum number of credits to apply. For fall 2009: Transfer applications received: 1,523. Transfer applicants offered admission: 834. Transfer applicants enrolled: 363. **International students:** Number of foreign undergraduates: 205 (3% of student body). Number of countries represented: 59. Minimum TOEFL score required: 575 (paper); 231 (computer). Average TOEFL score: 587 (paper).

Hamilton College

- **Address:** 198 College Hill Road, Clinton, NY 13323
- **Website:** http://www.hamilton.edu
- **Private**
- **Enrollment:** 1,851 full-time; 31 part-time

KEY STATS
- ✔ **U.S News College Ranking:** 18, National Liberal Arts Colleges
- ✔ **SAT Score (25th/75th percentile):** 1310-1470
- ✔ **Tuition:** 2010-2011: $41,280

Selectivity: Most selective	**Room/board:** $10,480
Acceptance rate: 30%	**Average debt:** $19,466
Student/faculty ratio: 10/1	**Proportion who borrowed:** 46%

UNDERGRADUATE STUDENT BODY STATS

2009-2010 enrollment: 1,851 full-time; 31 part-time. Men: 47%; women: 53%. **Ethnic makeup:** African American: 4%; American-Indian: 1%; Asian American: 8%; Hispanic: 5%; White: 78%; International: 5%. **Religious preference:** Roman Catholic: 21%; Protestant: 16%; Jewish: 11%; Muslim: 1%; Hindu: 2%; Buddhist: 2%; No preference: 35%; Other: 12%.

ADMISSIONS FACTS AND FIGURES

Phone: (800) 843-2655. **Email:** admission@hamilton.edu. **Website:** http://www.hamilton.edu. **Application deadlines for fall 2011:** Regular decision: January 1; decision sent by April 1. Early decision: Send application by: November 15; Decision sent by: December 15. Early action: Not offered. Admission can be deferred. **Application fee:** $75. **To apply online, go to:** http://www.hamilton.edu/admission/ApplicationProcess/Application.html. **Admissions requirements/recommendations:** High school units required (recommended): English: (4); Mathematics: (3); Science: (3); Foreign language: (3); Social studies: (3); Total units: (16). Tests: The college uses SAT or ACT scores in admissions decisions. Either SAT or ACT required. For admission to the fall 2011 entering class, the school will accept: ACT with or without writing accepted. Campus visit: Recommended. Admissions interview: Recommended. Off-campus interview: May be arranged. **Factors that count in admissions decisions:** *Academic:* Secondary school record: Very Important. Class rank: Very Important. Letters of recommendation: Important. Standardized test scores: Important. Essay: Important. *Nonacademic:* Interview: Important. Extracurricular activities: Important. Talent/ability: Considered. Character/personal qualities: Important. Alumni/ae relationship: Considered. Geographical residence: Considered. State residency: Not Considered. Religious affiliation/commitment: Not Considered. Minority status: Considered. Volunteer work: Considered. Work experience: Considered. **Other schools with the greatest overlap in applicants:** Bates College; Bowdoin College; Colby College; Colgate

University; Middlebury College. **Admissions statistics for the fall 2009 entering class:** Total applicants: 4,661. Total accepted: 1,390. Freshmen enrolled: 466; 65% were from out of state. Accepted through early-decision or early-action plans: 49%. Overall acceptance rate: 30%. Early-decision acceptance rate: 42%. Non-early acceptance rate: 28%. **Size of waiting list:** 1096 applicants; enrolled from waiting list: 17. **Credentials of fall 2009 freshmen:** 80% ranked in the top 10 percent of their high school class; 97% were in the top 25 percent; 100% were in the top half. (Proportion submitting class standing: 46%.) **First-year students who submitted SAT scores:** 60%. Scores (25/75 percentile): Critical Reading: 660-740, Math: 650-730, Combined: 1310-1470. **First-year students submitting ACT scores:** 13%. Scores (25/75 percentile): English: N/A, Math: N/A, Composite: 28-31.

ACADEMICS

Year founded: 1812. **Academic calendar:** Semester. **Degrees offered:** bachelor's. **Most popular majors:** 15% economics, 10% political science and government, 9% psychology, 7% mathematics, 5% communication studies/speech communication and rhetoric. **Major fields of study:** area, ethnic, cultural, and gender studies; biological and biomedical sciences; communication, journalism, and related programs; communications technologies/technicians and support services; computer and information sciences and support services; English language and literature/letters; foreign languages, literatures, and linguistics; history; mathematics and statistics; multi/inter-disciplinary studies; philosophy and religious studies; physical sciences; psychology; science technologies/technicians; social sciences; theology and religious vocations; visual and performing arts. **Pre-professional programs:** pre-law, pre-medicine. **Special academic programs (% participation):** accelerated program, cross-registration, double major (19%), English as a Second Language (ESL), independent study, internships, student-designed major (1%), study abroad (43%). **Reserve Officers Training Corps (ROTC):** Army ROTC: Offered at cooperating institution (Syracuse University); Air Force ROTC: Offered at cooperating institution (Syracuse University). **Faculty and instruction (2009-2010):** Total instructional faculty: 177 full-time, 42 part-time (57% men; 43% women; 15% minorities). Full-time faculty with Ph.D. or other terminal degree: 97%. Student/faculty ratio: 10/1. Classes of fewer than 20 students: 73%; of 20 to 49 students: 27%; of 50 or more students: 1%. **Advanced Placement and International Baccalaureate credit:** AP tests may be used for: Credit and/or placement. Scores accepted: 4, 5. International Baccalaureate exams may be used for: Credit only. **Freshmen returning for sophomore year:** 95%. **Graduation rates:** Four-year: 83%; five-year: 86%; six-year: 86%. **Graduate study:** 18% of students pursue further study immediately upon graduation; 18% within one year.

COSTS AND FINANCIAL AID

Financial aid office: (315) 859-4434. **Expenses (2010-2011):** Tuition and fees 2010-2011: $41,280; room/board: $10,480. Estimated books and supplies: $1,300; transportation: $500; personal expenses: $500. **Financial aid:** Priority filing date for institution's financial aid form: February 8; deadline: February 8. In 2009-2010, 49% of undergraduates applied for financial aid. Of those, 41% were determined to have financial need; 100% had their need fully met. Average financial aid package (proportion receiving): $36,305 (41%). Average amount of gift aid, such as scholarships or grants (proportion receiving): $35,502 (41%). Average amount of self-help aid, such as work study or loans (proportion receiving): $4,910 (35%). Average need-based loan (excluding PLUS or other private loans): $3,835. Among students who received need-based aid, the average percentage of need met: 100%. Among students who received aid based on merit, the average award (and the proportion receiving): $22,205 (2%). The average athletic scholarship (and the proportion receiving): $0 (0%). Average amount of debt of borrowers graduating in 2009: $19,466. Proportion who borrowed: 46%.

CAMPUS LIFE AND EXTRACURRICULAR ACTIVITIES

Campus housing available (% using): coed dorms (90%), apartments for married students, apartment for single students (8%), special housing for disabled students (1%), cooperative housing (1%). Students who live in college-owned, operated, or affiliated housing: 97%. **Student employment:** During the 2009-2010 academic year, 48% of undergraduates worked on campus. Average per-year earnings: $1,200. **Clubs and organizations:** Number of student organizations: 118. Activities include: campus ministries, choral groups, concert band, dance, drama/theater, international student organization, jazz band, literary magazine, model UN, music ensembles, musical theater, radio station, student government, student newspaper, student film society, symphony orchestra, yearbook. Number of fraternities: 11; sororities: 7. Proportion of men in fraternities: 34%; of women in sororities: 16%. Average proportion of students who stay on campus on weekends: 90%. **Sports program (2009-2010):** Member of NCAA

III. **Men's intercollegiate varsity sports:** baseball, basketball, cross country, football, golf, ice hockey, lacrosse, soccer, swimming, tennis, track and field (indoor), track and field (outdoor). **Women's intercollegiate varsity sports:** basketball, crew (heavyweight), cross country, field hockey, ice hockey, lacrosse, soccer, softball, swimming, tennis, track and field (indoor), track and field (outdoor), volleyball.

SERVICES AND FACILITIES

Basic services: nonremedial tutoring, women's center, placement service, day care, health service. **Counseling services:** minority student, career, personal, academic, psychological, birth control, religious. **For learning-disabled students:** School does not offer a structured program with separate admission and additional fees. Services include: tape recorders, note-taking services, oral tests, learning center, readers, extended time for tests, tutors, other testing accommodations. **Library:** Number of titles: 634,831; number of current serial subscriptions: 3,790. **Information technology resources:** Students are not required to lease or own a computer. Number of campus computers available to all students: 800. School has a wireless network. Approximate number of users that can be accommodated: 2,000. Proportion of college-owned housing units wired for high-speed internet access: 100%. **Campus safety:** Security services offered: 24-hour foot-and-vehicle patrols, late-night transport/escort service, 24-hour emergency telephones, lighted pathways/sidewalks, controlled dormitory access (key, security card, etc).

TRANSFER AND INTERNATIONAL STUDENTS

Transfer students: May apply for admission for the following academic terms: Fall, Spring. Applicants do not need a minimum number of credits to apply. For fall 2009: Transfer applications received: 179. Transfer applicants offered admission: 21. Transfer applicants enrolled: 5. **International students:** Number of foreign undergraduates: 92 (5% of student body). Number of countries represented: 40. Average TOEFL score: 630 (paper).

Hartwick College

- **Address:** 1 Hartwick Drive, Oneonta, NY 13820-4020
- **Website:** http://www.hartwick.edu
- **Private**
- **Enrollment:** 1,427 full-time; 46 part-time

KEY STATS

✔ **U.S News College Ranking:** 174, National Liberal Arts Colleges
✔ **SAT Score (25th/75th percentile):** 970-1198
✔ **Tuition:** 2010-2011: $34,630

Selectivity: Selective	**Room/board:** $9,345
Acceptance rate: 91%	**Average debt:** $32,800
Student/faculty ratio: 11/1	**Proportion who borrowed:** 74%

UNDERGRADUATE STUDENT BODY STATS

2009-2010 enrollment: 1,427 full-time; 46 part-time. Men: 41%; women: 59%. **Ethnic makeup:** African American: 4%; Asian American: 2%; Hispanic: 4%; White: 86%; International: 3%. **Religious preference:** Roman Catholic: 30%; Protestant: 27%; Jewish: 6%; Buddhist: 1%; No preference: 29%; Other: 7%.

ADMISSIONS FACTS AND FIGURES

Phone: (607) 431-4150. **Email:** admissions@hartwick.edu. **Website:** http://www.hartwick.edu. **Application deadlines for fall 2011:** Regular decision: Rolling. Early decision: Send application by: November 15; Decision sent by: December 15. Early action: Not offered. Admission can be deferred. **Application fee:** $35. **To apply online, go to:** http://www.hartwick.edu/x2598.xml. **Admissions requirements/recommendations:** High school units required (recommended): English: (4); Mathematics: (3); Science: (3); Foreign language: (3); Social studies: (2); History: (2); Total units: (19). Tests: The college uses SAT or ACT scores in admissions decisions. Neither SAT nor ACT required. For admission to the fall 2011 entering class, the school will accept: ACT with or without writing accepted. Campus visit: Recommended. Admissions interview: Recommended. Off-campus interview: May be arranged. **Factors that count in admissions decisions:** *Academic:* Secondary school record: Very Important. Class rank: Important. Letters of recommendation: Important. Standardized test scores: Considered. Essay: Considered. *Nonacademic:* Interview: Considered. Extracurricular activities: Considered. Talent/ability: Considered. Character/

personal qualities: Considered. Alumni/ae relationship: Considered. Geographical residence: Considered. State residency: Considered. Religious affiliation/commitment: Not Considered. Minority status: Considered. Volunteer work: Considered. Work experience: Considered. **Other schools with the greatest overlap in applicants:** Hobart and William Smith Colleges; Ithaca College; SUNY College–Oneonta; Siena College; University of Vermont. **Admissions statistics for the fall 2009 entering class:** Total applicants: 2,385. Total accepted: 2,177. Freshmen enrolled: 402; 33% were from out of state. Overall acceptance rate: 91%. Early-decision acceptance rate: 92%. Non-early acceptance rate: 91%. **Size of waiting list:** 97 applicants; enrolled from waiting list: 37. **Credentials of fall 2009 freshmen:** 17% ranked in the top 10 percent of their high school class; 42% were in the top 25 percent; 77% were in the top half. (Proportion submitting class standing: 63%.) **Average high school grade point average:** 3.1. **First-year students who submitted SAT scores:** 63%. Scores (25/75 percentile): Critical Reading: 480-598, Math: 490-600, Combined: 970-1198. **First-year students submitting ACT scores:** 20%. Scores (25/75 percentile): English: N/A, Math: N/A, Composite: 23-27.

ACADEMICS

Year founded: 1797. **Academic calendar:** 4-1-4. **Degrees offered:** bachelor's. **Most popular majors:** 22% social sciences, 16% business, management, marketing, and related support services, 10% visual and performing arts, 9% health professions and related clinical sciences, 8% biological and bio-medical sciences. **Major fields of study:** biological and biomedical sciences; business, management, marketing, and related support services; computer and information sciences and support services; education; English language and literature/letters; foreign languages, literatures, and linguistics; health professions and related clinical sciences; history; mathematics and statistics; multi/interdisciplinary studies; philosophy and religious studies; physical sciences; psychology; social sciences; visual and performing arts. **Areas of required coursework:** arts/fine arts, humanities, mathematics, English (including composition), foreign languages, sciences (biological or physical), history, social science, other. **Pre-professional programs:** pre-law, pre-dentistry, pre-medicine, pre-veterinary science, pre-optometry. **Special academic programs (% participation):** accelerated program (2%), cross-registration, double major (1%), exchange student program (domestic), honors program (8%), independent study (.18%), internships (52%), liberal arts/career combination, student-designed major (.01%), study abroad (37%), teacher certificate program (4%). **Teacher certification offered in:** early childhood, elementary, middle/junior high, secondary. **Cooperative education programs:** engineering, other. **Faculty and instruction (2009-2010):** Total instructional faculty: 103 full-time, 92 part-time (54% men; 46% women; 4% minorities). Full-time faculty with Ph.D. or other terminal degree: 97%. Student/faculty ratio: 11/1. Classes of fewer than 20 students: 62%; of 20 to 49 students: 37%; of 50 or more students: 1%. **Advanced Placement and International Baccalaureate credit:** AP tests may be used for: Credit and/or placement. Scores accepted: 3, 4, 5. International Baccalaureate exams may be used for: Credit and/or placement. **Freshmen returning for sophomore year:** 74%. **Graduation rates:** Four-year: 44%; five-year: 53%; six-year: 55%. **Graduate study:** 16% of students pursue further study immediately upon graduation; 22% within five years. Fields in which graduates pursue further study: law, 2%; medicine, 1%; arts and sciences, 17%.

COSTS AND FINANCIAL AID

Financial aid office: (607) 431-4130. **Expenses (2010-2011):** Tuition and fees 2010-2011: $34,630; room/board: $9,345. Estimated books and supplies: $700; transportation: $300; personal expenses: $400. **Financial aid:** In 2009-2010, 81% of undergraduates applied for financial aid. Of those, 74% were determined to have financial need; 11% had their need fully met. Average financial aid package (proportion receiving): $24,206 (74%). Average amount of gift aid, such as scholarships or grants (proportion receiving): $19,972 (74%). Average amount of self-help aid, such as work study or loans (proportion receiving): $5,760 (68%). Average need-based loan (excluding PLUS or other private loans): $4,681. Among students who received need-based aid, the average percentage of need met: 78%. Among students who received aid based on merit, the average award (and the proportion receiving): $10,267 (23%). The average athletic scholarship (and the proportion receiving): $24,355 (2%). Average amount of debt of borrowers graduating in 2009: $32,800. Proportion who borrowed: 74%.

CAMPUS LIFE AND EXTRACURRICULAR ACTIVITIES

Campus housing available (% using): coed dorms (74%), women's dorms (9%), sorority housing (4%), fraternity housing (3%), apartment for single students (7%), other housing options (3%). Students who live in college-owned, operated, or affiliated housing: 86%. **Student employment:** During the 2009-2010 academic year, 55% of undergraduates worked on campus. Average per-year earnings: $1,400. **Clubs and organizations:** Number of student organizations: 70. Activities include: campus ministries, choral groups, dance, drama/theater, international student organization, jazz band, literary magazine, music ensembles, radio station, student government, student newspaper, yearbook. Number of fraternities: 3; sororities: 3. Proportion of men in fraternities: 9%; of women in sororities: 9%. Average proportion of students who stay on campus on weekends: 70%. **Sports program (2009-2010):** Member of NCAA III. *Men's intercollegiate varsity sports:* basketball, cross country, football, lacrosse, soccer, swimming, tennis. *Women's intercollegiate varsity sports:* basketball, cross country, equestrian, field hockey, lacrosse, soccer, swimming, tennis, volleyball, water polo.

SERVICES AND FACILITIES

Basic services: nonremedial tutoring, women's center, placement service, health service, health insurance. **Counseling services:** career, personal, academic, psychological, birth control. **For learning-disabled students:** School does not offer a structured program with separate admission and additional fees. Total undergraduates in learning-disabled program or receiving services: 112. Services include: reading machines, tape recorders, note-taking services, extended time for tests, texts on tape, other. **Library:** Number of titles: 317,781; number of current serial subscriptions: 400. **Information technology resources:** Students are not required to lease or own a computer. Number of campus computers available to all students: 1,500. School has a wireless network. Approximate number of users that can be accommodated: 800. Proportion of college-owned housing units wired for high-speed internet access: 100%. **Campus safety:** Security services offered: 24-hour foot-and-vehicle patrols, late-night transport/escort service, 24-hour emergency telephones, lighted pathways/sidewalks, controlled dormitory access (key, security card, etc).

TRANSFER AND INTERNATIONAL STUDENTS

Transfer students: May apply for admission for the following academic terms: Fall, Spring. Applicants do not need a minimum number of credits to apply. For fall 2009: Transfer applications received: 95. Transfer applicants offered admission: 86. Transfer applicants enrolled: 34. **International students:** Number of foreign undergraduates: 48 (3% of student body). Number of countries represented: 28. Minimum TOEFL score required: 550 (paper); 213 (computer). Average TOEFL score: 550 (paper).

Hilbert College

- Address: 5200 S. Park Avenue, Hamburg, NY 14075-1597
- Website: http://www.hilbert.edu/
- Private; Religious affiliation: Roman Catholic (Franciscan)
- Enrollment: N/A

KEY STATS

✔ **U.S News College Ranking:** 47, Regional Colleges (North)
✔ **SAT or ACT Score (25th/75th percentile):** N/A
✔ **Tuition:** 2009-2010: $17,990

Selectivity: Less selective	**Room/board:** $7,700
Acceptance rate: N/A	**Average debt:** N/A
Student/faculty ratio: N/A	**Proportion who borrowed:** N/A

Hobart and William Smith Colleges

- Address: 337 Pulteney Street, Geneva, NY 14456
- Website: http://www.hws.edu
- Private
- Enrollment: 2,091 full-time; 1 part-time

KEY STATS

✔ **U.S News College Ranking:** 67, National Liberal Arts Colleges
✔ **SAT Score (25th/75th percentile):** 1150-1310
✔ **Tuition:** 2010-2011: $41,710

Selectivity: More selective	**Room/board:** $10,458
Acceptance rate: 56%	**Average debt:** $30,970
Student/faculty ratio: 11/1	**Proportion who borrowed:** 79%

UNDERGRADUATE STUDENT BODY STATS

2009-2010 enrollment: 2,091 full-time; 1 part-time. Men: 46%; women: 54%. **Ethnic makeup:** African American: 4%; American-Indian: 1%; Asian American: 3%; Hispanic: 4%; White: 85%; International: 3%. **Religious preference:** Roman Catholic: 29%; Protestant: 28%; Jewish: 8%; Muslim: 1%; Hindu: 1%; Buddhist: 1%; No preference: 29%; Other: 3%.

ADMISSIONS FACTS AND FIGURES

Phone: (315) 781-3622. **Email:** admissions@hws.edu. **Website:** http://www.hws.edu. **Application deadlines for fall 2011:** Regular decision: February 1; decision sent by April 1. Early decision: Send application by: November 15; Decision sent by: December 15. Early action: Not offered. Admission can be deferred. **Application fee:** $45. **To apply online, go to:** http://www.hws.edu/admissions/apply_application.aspx. **Admissions requirements/recommendations:** High school units required (recommended): English: 4; Mathematics: 3; Science: 3; Foreign language: 2 (3); Social studies: 2 (3); Academic electives: 2 (4); Total units: 18. Tests: The college uses SAT or ACT scores in admissions decisions. Neither SAT nor ACT required. For admission to the fall 2011 entering class, the school will accept: ACT with or without writing accepted. Campus visit: Recommended. Admissions interview: Recommended. Off-campus interview: May be arranged. **Factors that count in admissions decisions:** *Academic:* Secondary school record: Very Important. Class rank: Important. Letters of recommendation: Important. Standardized test scores: Considered. Essay: Important. *Nonacademic:* Interview: Important. Extracurricular activities: Important. Talent/ability: Considered. Character/personal qualities: Important. Alumni/ae relationship: Considered. Geographical residence: Considered. State residency: Considered. Religious affiliation/commitment: Not Considered. Minority status: Considered. Volunteer work: Important. Work experience: Important. **Other schools with the greatest overlap in applicants:** Hamilton College; Skidmore College; St. Lawrence University; Union College; University of Vermont. **Admissions statistics for the fall 2009 entering class:** Total applicants: 5,207. Total accepted: 2,918. Freshmen enrolled: 549; 53% were from out of state. Accepted through early-decision or early-action plans: 29%. Overall acceptance rate: 56%. Early-decision acceptance rate: 72%. Non-early acceptance rate: 55%. **Size of waiting list:** 521 applicants; enrolled from waiting list: 42. **Credentials of fall 2009 freshmen:** 41% ranked in the top 10 percent of their high school class; 73% were in the top 25 percent; 95% were in the top half. (Proportion submitting class standing: 37%.) **Average high school grade point average:** 3.4. **First-year students who submitted SAT scores:** 40%. Scores (25/75 percentile): Critical Reading: 570-660, Math: 580-650, Combined: 1150-1310. **First-year students submitting ACT scores:** 11%. Scores (25/75 percentile): English: N/A, Math: N/A, Composite: 25-30.

ACADEMICS

Year founded: 1822. **Academic calendar:** Semester. **Degrees offered:** bachelor's, master's. **Most popular majors:** 13% economics, 10% psychology, 9% English language and literature, 8% political science and government, 7% environmental science. **Major fields of study:** architecture and related services; area, ethnic, cultural, and gender studies; biological and biomedical sciences; communication, journalism, and related programs; computer and information sciences and support services; English language and literature/letters; foreign languages, literatures, and linguistics; history; liberal arts and sciences studies, and humanities; mathematics and statistics; natural resources and conservation; philosophy and religious studies; physical sciences; psychology; public administration and social service professions; social sciences; visual and performing arts. **Areas of required coursework:** arts/fine arts, humanities, mathematics, sciences (biological or physical), social science, other. **Pre-professional programs:** pre-law, pre-dentistry, pre-medicine, pre-veterinary science, pre-optometry. **Special academic programs (% participation):** double major (21%), English as a Second Language (ESL) (1%), honors program (8%), independent study (53%), internships (17%), student-designed major (3%), study abroad (58%), teacher certificate program (6%). **Teacher certification offered in:** special education, elementary, secondary. **Faculty and instruction (2009-2010):** Total instructional faculty: 181 full-time, 13 part-time (59% men; 41% women; 18% minorities). Full-time faculty with Ph.D. or other terminal degree: 96%. Student/faculty ratio: 11/1. Classes of fewer than 20 students: 64%; of 20 to 49 students: 35%; of 50 or more students: 1%. **Advanced Placement and International Baccalaureate credit:** AP tests may be used for: Credit and/or placement. Scores accepted: 4, 5. International Baccalaureate exams may be used for: Credit and/or placement. **Freshmen returning for sophomore year:** 86%. **Graduation rates:** Four-year: 74%; five-year: 78%; six-year: 79%. **Graduate study:** 20% of students pursue further study immediately upon graduation; 49% within one year; 69% within five years. Fields in which graduates pursue further study: Master of Business Administration (MBA), 9%; law, 14%; medicine, 10%; dentistry, 1%; engineering, 7%; theology (or the seminary), 2%; education, 14%; arts and sciences, 42%; veterinary medicine, 1%.

COSTS AND FINANCIAL AID

Financial aid office: (315) 781-3315. **Expenses (2010-2011):** Tuition and fees 2010-2011: $41,710; room/board: $10,458. Estimated books and supplies: $1,300; transportation: $210; personal expenses: $600. **Financial aid:** Priority filing date for institution's financial aid form: February 15; deadline: March 15. In 2009-2010, 91% of undergraduates applied for financial aid. Of those, 76% were determined to have financial need; 83% had their need fully met. Average financial aid package (proportion receiving): $29,433 (75%). Average amount of gift aid, such as scholarships or grants (proportion receiving): $24,984 (74%). Average amount of self-help aid, such as work study or loans (proportion receiving): $5,376 (63%). Average need-based loan (excluding PLUS or other private loans): $4,190. Among students who received need-based aid, the average percentage of need met: 78%. Among students who received aid based on merit, the average award (and the proportion receiving): $14,177 (23%). The average athletic scholarship (and the proportion receiving): $0 (0%). Average amount of debt of borrowers graduating in 2009: $30,970. Proportion who borrowed: 79%.

CAMPUS LIFE AND EXTRACURRICULAR ACTIVITIES

Campus housing available (% using): coed dorms (39%), women's dorms (14%), men's dorms (15%), fraternity housing (4%), apartment for single students (13%), cooperative housing (7%), other housing options (1%). Students who live in college-owned, operated, or affiliated housing: 90%. **Student employment:** During the 2009-2010 academic year, 53% of undergraduates worked on campus. Average per-year earnings: $1,843. **Clubs and organizations:** Number of student organizations: 80. Activities include: campus ministries, choral groups, dance, drama/theater, international student organization, jazz band, literary magazine, music ensembles, radio station, student government, student newspaper, student film society, yearbook. Number of fraternities: 6; sororities: 0. Proportion of men in fraternities: 21%; Average proportion of students who stay on campus on weekends: 90%. **Sports program (2009-2010):** Member of NCAA III. *Men's intercollegiate varsity sports:* basketball, cross country, football, golf, ice hockey, lacrosse, soccer, tennis. *Women's intercollegiate varsity sports:* basketball, crew (heavyweight), cross country, field hockey, golf, lacrosse, soccer, squash, swimming, tennis.

SERVICES AND FACILITIES

Basic services: nonremedial tutoring, women's center, placement service, health service, health insurance. **Remedial assistance:** math, writing, study skills. **Counseling services:** minority student, career, personal, academic, psychological, birth control, religious. **For learning-disabled students:** School does not offer a structured program with separate admission and additional fees. Total undergraduates in learning-disabled program or receiving services: 187. Services include: reading machines, remedial reading, tape recorders, note-taking services, oral tests, learning center, readers, extended time for tests, tutors, priority seating, texts on tape, exams on tape or computer, other testing accommodations. **Library:** Number of titles: 399,118; number of current serial subscriptions: 3,114. **Information technology resources:** Students are not required to lease or own a computer. Number of campus computers available to all students: 350. School has a wireless network. Approximate number of users that can be accommodated: 10,000. Proportion of college-owned housing units wired for high-speed internet access: 100%. **Campus safety:** Security services offered: 24-hour foot-and-vehicle patrols, late-night transport/escort service, 24-hour emergency telephones, lighted pathways/sidewalks, controlled dormitory access (key, security card, etc).

TRANSFER AND INTERNATIONAL STUDENTS

Transfer students: May apply for admission for the following academic terms: Fall, Spring. Applicants do not need a minimum number of credits to apply. For fall 2009: Transfer applications received: 122. Transfer applicants offered admission: 60. Transfer applicants enrolled: 29. **International students:** Number of foreign undergraduates: 59 (3% of student body). Number of countries represented: 17. Minimum TOEFL score required: 550 (paper); 72 (computer). Average TOEFL score: 600 (paper).

Hofstra University

- **Address:** 100 Hofstra University, Hempstead, NY 11549
- **Website:** http://www.hofstra.edu
- **Private**
- **Enrollment:** 7,327 full-time; 592 part-time

KEY STATS

✔ **U.S News College Ranking:** 139, National Universities
✔ **SAT Score (25th/75th percentile):** 1100-1270
✔ **Tuition:** 2009-2010: $30,130

Selectivity: More selective	**Room/board:** $11,330
Acceptance rate: 57%	**Average debt:** N/A
Student/faculty ratio: 14/1	**Proportion who borrowed:** 64%

UNDERGRADUATE STUDENT BODY STATS

2009-2010 enrollment: 7,327 full-time; 592 part-time. Men: 48%; women: 52%. **Ethnic makeup:** African American: 9%; Asian American: 5%; Hispanic: 9%; White: 75%; International: 2%.

ADMISSIONS FACTS AND FIGURES

Phone: (516) 463-6700. **Email:** admission@hofstra.edu. **Website:** http://www.hofstra.edu. **Application deadlines for fall 2011:** Regular decision: Rolling. Early decision: Not offered. Early action: Send application by: November 15; Decision sent by: December 15. Admission can be deferred. **Application fee:** $70. **To apply online, go to:** http://www.hofstra.edu/application. **Admissions requirements/recommendations:** High school units required (recommended): English: 4; Mathematics: 3 (4); Science: 3 (4); Foreign language: 2 (3); Social studies: 3 (4); Total units: 16. Tests: The college uses SAT or ACT scores in admissions decisions. Neither SAT nor ACT required. For admission to the fall 2011 entering class, the school will accept: ACT with writing required. Campus visit: Recommended. Admissions interview: Recommended. Off-campus interview: May be arranged. **Factors that count in admissions decisions:** *Academic:* Secondary school record: Very Important. Class rank: Very Important. Letters of recommendation: Very Important. Standardized test scores: Very Important. Essay: Very Important. *Nonacademic:* Interview: Important. Extracurricular activities: Important. Talent/ability: Important. Character/personal qualities: Important. Alumni/ae relationship: Considered. Geographical residence: Considered. State residency: Not Considered. Religious affiliation/commitment: Not Considered. Minority status: Considered. Volunteer work: Considered. Work experience: Considered. **Other schools with the greatest overlap in applicants:** Boston University; Fordham University; New York University; Pennsylvania State University–University Park; SUNY–Stony Brook. **Admissions statistics for the fall 2009 entering class:** Total applicants: 20,829. Total accepted: 11,801. Freshmen enrolled: 1,568; 45% were from out of state. Accepted through early-decision or early-action plans: 41%. Overall acceptance rate: 57%. Non-early acceptance rate: 67%. **Size of waiting list:** 948 applicants; enrolled from waiting list: 90. **Credentials of fall 2009 freshmen:** 31% ranked in the top 10 percent of their high school class; 59% were in the top 25 percent; 87% were in the top half. (Proportion submitting class standing: 49%.) **Average high school grade point average:** 3.4. **First-year students who submitted SAT scores:** 71%. Scores (25/75 percentile): Critical Reading: 540-630, Math: 560-640, Combined: 1100-1270. **First-year students submitting ACT scores:** 22%. Scores (25/75 percentile): English: N/A, Math: N/A, Composite: 24-28.

ACADEMICS

Year founded: 1935. **Academic calendar:** 4-1-4. **Degrees offered:** certificate, bachelor's, post-bachelor's certificate, master's, post-master's certificate, doctorate. **Most popular majors:** 10% marketing/marketing management, 9% psychology, 7% accounting, 7% business administration and management, 6% finance. **Major fields of study:** area, ethnic, cultural, and gender studies; biological and biomedical sciences; business, management, marketing, and related support services; communication, journalism, and related programs; computer and information sciences and support services; education; engineering; English language and literature/letters; foreign languages, literatures, and linguistics; health professions and related clinical sciences; history; legal professions and studies; liberal arts and sciences studies, and humanities; mathematics and statistics; multi/interdisciplinary studies; natural resources and conservation; parks, recreation, leisure, and fitness studies; philosophy and religious studies; physical sciences; psychology; security and protective services; social sciences; visual and performing arts. **Areas of required coursework:** humanities, mathematics, English (including composition), foreign languages, sciences (biological or physical), social science. **Pre-professional programs:** pre-law, pre-dentistry, pre-medicine, pre-veterinary science, pre-optometry, pre-pharmacy, other. **Special academic programs:** accelerated program, cross-registration, distance learning, double major, dual enrollment, English as a Second Language (ESL), external degree program, honors program, independent study, internships, liberal arts/career combination, student-designed major, study abroad, teacher certificate program. **Teacher certification offered in:** early childhood, special education, elementary, middle/junior high, secondary, bilingual/bicultural. **Reserve Officers Training Corps (ROTC):** Army ROTC: Offered on campus. **Faculty and instruction (2009-2010):** Total instructional faculty: 544 full-time, 636 part-time (56% men; 44% women; 14% minorities). Full-time faculty with Ph.D. or other terminal degree: 91%. Student/faculty ratio: 14/1. Classes of fewer than 20 students: 48%; of 20 to 49 students: 48%; of 50 or more students: 3%. **Advanced Placement and International Baccalaureate credit:** AP tests may be used for: Credit only. Scores accepted: 3, 4, 5. International Baccalaureate exams may be used for: Credit only. **Freshmen returning for sophomore year:** 78%. **Graduation rates:** Four-year: 41%; five-year: 53%; six-year: 56%. **Graduate study:** 36% of students pursue further study within one year. Fields in which graduates pursue further study: Master of Business Administration (MBA), 14%; law, 10%; medicine, 6%; engineering, 1%; education, 21%; arts and sciences, 21%.

COSTS AND FINANCIAL AID

Financial aid office: (516) 463-6680. **Expenses (2009-2010):** Tuition and fees 2009-2010: $30,130; room/board: $11,330. Estimated books and supplies: $1,000; transportation: $1,580; personal expenses: $1,242. **Financial aid:** Priority filing date for institution's financial aid form: February 15. In 2009-2010, 76% of undergraduates applied for financial aid. Of those, 62% were determined to have financial need; 19% had their need fully met. Average financial aid package (proportion receiving): $18,000 (61%). Average amount of gift aid, such as scholarships or grants (proportion receiving): $11,000 (53%). Average amount of self-help aid, such as work study or loans (proportion receiving): $6,000 (52%). Average need-based loan (excluding PLUS or other private loans): $5,000. Among students who received need-based aid, the average percentage of need met: 56%. Among students who received aid based on merit, the average award (and the proportion receiving): $10,000 (19%). The average athletic scholarship (and the proportion receiving): $25,000 (1%). Proportion who borrowed: 64%.

CAMPUS LIFE AND EXTRACURRICULAR ACTIVITIES

Campus housing available: coed dorms, apartment for single students, special housing for disabled students, other housing options. Students who live in college-owned, operated, or affiliated housing: 46%. **Student employment:** During the 2009-2010 academic year, 32% of undergraduates worked on campus. Average per-year earnings: $3,100. **Clubs and organizations:** Number of student organizations: 135. Activities include: campus ministries, choral groups, concert band, dance, drama/theater, international student organization, jazz band, literary magazine, model UN, music ensembles, musical theater, opera, pep band, radio station, student government, student newspaper, student film society, symphony orchestra, television station, yearbook. Number of fraternities: 13; sororities: 12. Proportion of men in fraternities: 6%; of women in sororities: 8%. **Sports program (2009-2010):** Member of NCAA I. *Men's intercollegiate varsity sports:* baseball, basketball, cross country, golf, lacrosse, soccer, tennis, wrestling. *Women's intercollegiate varsity sports:* basketball, cross country, field hockey, golf, lacrosse, soccer, softball, tennis, volleyball.

SERVICES AND FACILITIES

Basic services: nonremedial tutoring, placement service, day care, health service, health insurance. **Counseling services:** minority student, career, military, personal, veteran student, academic, older student, psychological, birth control, religious. **For learning-disabled students:** School does not offer a structured program with separate admission and additional fees. Total undergraduates in learning-disabled program or receiving services: 83. Services include: reading machines, tape recorders, other special classes, note-taking services, learning center, extended time for tests, tutors, priority registration, priority seating, substitution of courses, texts on tape, typist/scribe, exams on tape or computer, other testing accommodations, other. **Library:** Number of titles: 1,075,361; number of current serial subscriptions: 11,353. **Information technology resources:** Students are not required to lease or own a computer. Number of campus computers available to all students: 1,628. School has a wireless network. Approximate number of users that can be accommodated: 11,140. Proportion of college-owned housing units wired for high-speed internet access: 100%. **Campus safety:** Security services offered: 24-hour foot-and-vehicle patrols, late-night transport/escort service, 24-hour emergency telephones, lighted pathways/sidewalks, student patrols, controlled dormitory access (key, security card, etc).

TRANSFER AND INTERNATIONAL STUDENTS

Transfer students: May apply for admission for the following academic terms: Fall, Spring. Applicants do not need a minimum number of credits to apply. For fall 2009: Transfer applications received: 2,111. Transfer applicants offered admission: 1,449. Transfer applicants enrolled: 526. **International students:** Number of foreign undergraduates: 128 (2% of student body). Number of countries represented: 58. Minimum TOEFL score required: 550 (paper); 213 (computer).

Houghton College

- **Address:** 1 Willard Avenue, Houghton, NY 14744
- **Website:** http://www.houghton.edu
- **Private; Religious affiliation:** Wesleyan Church
- **Enrollment:** 1,252 full-time; 59 part-time

KEY STATS
- ✔ **U.S News College Ranking:** 137, National Liberal Arts Colleges
- ✔ **SAT Score (25th/75th percentile):** 1030-1300
- ✔ **Tuition:** 2010-2011: $24,560
  - **Selectivity:** More selective   **Room/board:** N/A
  - **Acceptance rate:** 82%   **Average debt:** $28,334
  - **Student/faculty ratio:** 12/1   **Proportion who borrowed:** 96%

UNDERGRADUATE STUDENT BODY STATS

2009-2010 enrollment: 1,252 full-time; 59 part-time. Men: 35%; women: 65%. **Ethnic makeup:** African American: 2%; Asian American: 2%; Hispanic: 1%; White: 90%; International: 4%. **Religious preference:** Roman Catholic: 2%; Protestant: 77%; No preference: 2%; Unknown: 1%; Wesleyan Church: 18%.

ADMISSIONS FACTS AND FIGURES

Phone: (800) 777-2556. **Email:** admission@houghton.edu. **Website:** http://www.houghton.edu. **Application deadlines for fall 2011:** Regular decision: Rolling. Early decision: Not offered. Early action: Not offered. Admission can be deferred. **Application fee:** $40. **To apply online, go to:** https://www.applyweb.com/apply/hough/. **Admissions requirements/recommendations:** High school units required (recommended): English: (4); Mathematics: (3); Science: (2); Foreign language: (2); Social studies: (1); History: (2); Total units: (16). Tests: The college uses SAT or ACT scores in admissions decisions. Either SAT or ACT required. For admission to the fall 2011 entering class, the school will accept: ACT with or without writing accepted. Campus visit: Recommended. Admissions interview: Recommended. Off-campus interview: Not available. **Factors that count in admissions decisions:** *Academic:* Secondary school record: Very Important. Class rank: Important. Letters of recommendation: Considered. Standardized test scores: Important. Essay: Considered. *Nonacademic:* Interview: Considered. Extracurricular activities: Considered. Talent/ability: Considered. Character/personal qualities: Important. Alumni/ae relationship: Considered. Geographical residence: Not Considered. State residency: Not Considered. Religious affiliation/commitment: Important. Minority status: Considered. Volunteer work: Considered. Work experience: Considered. **Other schools with the greatest overlap in applicants:** Gordon College; Grove City College; Messiah College; Roberts Wesleyan College; Wheaton College. **Admissions statistics for the fall 2009 entering class:** Total applicants: 1,080. Total accepted: 889. Freshmen enrolled: 287; 47% were from out of state. Overall acceptance rate: 82%. **Credentials of fall 2009 freshmen:** 36% ranked in the top 10 percent of their high school class; 62% were in the top 25 percent; 89% were in the top half. (Proportion submitting class standing: 67%.) **Average high school grade point average:** 3.6. **First-year students who submitted SAT scores:** 88%. Scores (25/75 percentile): Critical Reading: 520-660; Math: 510-640, Combined: 1030-1300. **First-year students submitting ACT scores:** 37%. Scores (25/75 percentile): English: N/A, Math: N/A, Composite: 22-29.

ACADEMICS

Year founded: 1883. **Academic calendar:** Semester. **Degrees offered:** associate, bachelor's, master's. **Most popular majors:** 26% business, management, marketing, and related support services, 16% education, 8% visual and performing arts, 6% English language and literature/letters, 6% biological and biomedical sciences. **Major fields of study:** area, ethnic, cultural, and gender studies; biological and biomedical sciences; business, management, marketing, and related support services; communication, journalism, and related programs; computer and information sciences and support services; education; English language and literature/letters; foreign languages, literatures, and linguistics; history; liberal arts and sciences studies, and humanities; mathematics and statistics; multi/interdisciplinary studies; parks, recreation, leisure, and fitness studies; philosophy and religious studies; physical sciences; psychology; social sciences; theology and religious vocations; visual and performing arts. **Areas of required coursework:** arts/fine arts, humanities, mathematics, English (including composition), philosophy, foreign languages, sciences (biological or physical), history, social science, other. **Pre-professional programs:** pre-law, pre-dentistry, pre-medicine, pre-theology, pre-veterinary science, pre-optometry, pre-pharmacy, other. **Special academic programs (% participation):** cross-registration (1%), double major (20%), exchange student program (domestic) (2%), honors program (16%), independent study (30%), internships (50%), liberal arts/career combination (47%), study abroad (48%), teacher certificate program (24%). **Teacher certification offered in:** special education, elementary, middle/junior high, secondary, bilingual/bicultural. **Reserve Officers Training Corps (ROTC):** Army ROTC: Offered at cooperating institution. **Faculty and instruction (2009-2010):** Total instructional faculty: 88 full-time, 54 part-time (63% men; 37% women; 9% minorities). Full-time faculty with Ph.D. or other terminal degree: 88%. Student/faculty ratio: 12/1. Classes of fewer than 20 students: 65%; of 20 to 49 students: 32%; of 50 or more students: 3%. **Advanced Placement and International Baccalaureate credit:** AP tests may be used for: Credit only. Scores accepted: 4, 5. International Baccalaureate exams may be used for: Credit only. **Freshmen returning for sophomore year:** 84%. **Graduation rates:** Four-year: 61%; five-year: 68%; six-year: 70%. **Graduate study:** 38% of students pursue further study immediately upon graduation; 53% within one year. Fields in which graduates pursue further study: Master of Business Administration (MBA), 4%; law, 1%; medicine, 3%; engineering, 1%; theology (or the seminary), 3%; education, 22%; arts and sciences, 65%; veterinary medicine, 1%.

COSTS AND FINANCIAL AID

Financial aid office: (585) 567-9328. **Expenses (2010-2011):** Tuition and fees 2010-2011: $24,560. Estimated books and supplies: $900; transportation: $750; personal expenses: $2,250. **Financial aid:** Priority filing date for institution's financial aid form: March 1. In 2009-2010, 89% of undergraduates applied for financial aid. Of those, 82% were determined to have financial need; 18% had their need fully met. Average financial aid package (proportion receiving): $20,192 (82%). Average amount of gift aid, such as scholarships or grants (proportion receiving): $14,050 (81%). Average amount of self-help aid, such as work study or loans (proportion receiving): $6,996 (73%). Average need-based loan (excluding PLUS or other private loans): $5,316. Among students who received need-based aid, the average percentage of need met: 78%. Among students who received aid based on merit, the average award (and the proportion receiving): $8,825 (15%). The average athletic scholarship (and the proportion receiving): $5,662 (2%). Average amount of debt of borrowers graduating in 2009: $28,334. Proportion who borrowed: 96%.

CAMPUS LIFE AND EXTRACURRICULAR ACTIVITIES

Campus housing available (% using): women's dorms (42%), men's dorms (24%), apartments for married students (1%), apartment for single students (26%), special housing for disabled students, special housing for international students (5%). Students who live in college-owned, operated, or affiliated housing: 89%. **Clubs and organizations:** Number of student organizations: 40. Activities include: campus ministries, choral groups, concert band, dance, drama/theater, international student organization, jazz band, literary magazine, music ensembles, musical theater, opera, student government, student newspaper, symphony orchestra, yearbook. Number of fraternities: 0; sororities: 0. Average proportion of students who stay on campus on weekends: 67%. **Sports program (2009-2010):** Member of NAIA. *Men's intercollegiate varsity sports:* basketball, cross country, soccer, track and field (indoor), track and field (outdoor). *Women's intercollegiate varsity sports:* basketball, cross country, field hockey, soccer, track and field (indoor), track and field (outdoor), volleyball.

SERVICES AND FACILITIES

Basic services: nonremedial tutoring, placement service, health service, health insurance. **Remedial assistance:** writing, study skills. **Counseling services:** career, personal, veteran student, academic, psychological, religious. **For learning-disabled students:** School does not offer a structured program with separate admission and additional fees. Services include: reading

machines, tape recorders, diagnostic testing service, note-taking services, oral tests, extended time for tests, tutors, priority registration, priority seating, substitution of courses, texts on tape, exams on tape or computer, other testing accommodations. **Library:** Number of titles: 230,070; number of current serial subscriptions: 27,151. **Information technology resources:** Students are not required to lease or own a computer. Number of campus computers available to all students: 53. School has a wireless network. Approximate number of users that can be accommodated: 2,850. Proportion of college-owned housing units wired for high-speed internet access: 100%. **Campus safety:** Security services offered: 24-hour foot-and-vehicle patrols, 24-hour emergency telephones, lighted pathways/sidewalks, controlled dormitory access (key, security card, etc).

TRANSFER AND INTERNATIONAL STUDENTS

Transfer students: May apply for admission for the following academic terms: Fall, Spring. Applicants need a minimum number of credits to apply. For fall 2009: Transfer applications received: 133. Transfer applicants offered admission: 105. Transfer applicants enrolled: 54. **International students:** Number of foreign undergraduates: 55 (4% of student body). Number of countries represented: 23. Minimum TOEFL score required: 550 (paper); 213 (computer).

Iona College

- **Address:** 715 North Avenue, New Rochelle, NY 10801
- **Website:** http://www.iona.edu/info
- **Private; Religious affiliation:** Roman Catholic
- **Enrollment:** 3,245 full-time; 99 part-time

KEY STATS

✔ **U.S News College Ranking:** 33, Regional Universities (North)
✔ **SAT Score (25th/75th percentile):** 1094-1293
✔ **Tuition:** 2010-2011: $28,850

Selectivity: Selective	**Room/board:** $11,800
Acceptance rate: 58%	**Average debt:** $24,213
Student/faculty ratio: 13/1	**Proportion who borrowed:** 68%

UNDERGRADUATE STUDENT BODY STATS

2009-2010 enrollment: 3,245 full-time; 99 part-time. Men: 44%; women: 56%. **Ethnic makeup:** African American: 5%; Asian American: 2%; Hispanic: 12%; White: 80%; International: 1%.

ADMISSIONS FACTS AND FIGURES

Phone: (914) 633-2502. **Email:** admissions@iona.edu. **Website:** http://www.iona.edu/info. **Application deadlines for fall 2011:** Regular decision: February 15; decision sent by March 20. Early decision: Not offered. Early action: Send application by: December 1; Decision sent by: December 21. Admission can be deferred. **Application fee:** $50. **To apply online, go to:** http://www.iona.edu/admis/applyToIona.cfm. **Admissions requirements/recommendations:** High school units required (recommended): English: 4 (4); Mathematics: 3 (4); Science: 2 (3); Foreign language: 2 (2); Social studies: 1 (2); History: 1 (2); Academic electives: 1 (3); Total units: 16 (20). Tests: The college uses SAT or ACT scores in admissions decisions. Either SAT or ACT required. For admission to the fall 2011 entering class, the school will accept: ACT with or without writing accepted. Campus visit: Recommended. Admissions interview: Recommended. Off-campus interview: Not available. **Factors that count in admissions decisions:** *Academic:* Secondary school record: Very Important. Class rank: Important. Letters of recommendation: Considered. Standardized test scores: Important. Essay: Important. *Nonacademic:* Interview: Important. Extracurricular activities: Considered. Talent/ability: Considered. Character/personal qualities: Important. Alumni/ae relationship: Considered. Geographical residence: Considered. State residency: Not Considered. Religious affiliation/commitment: Not Considered. Minority status: Not Considered. Volunteer work: Considered. Work experience: Considered. **Other schools with the greatest overlap in applicants:** Fordham University; Hofstra University; Manhattan College; Marist College; St. John's University. **Admissions statistics for the fall 2009 entering class:** Total applicants: 7,313. Total accepted: 4,242. Freshmen enrolled: 792; 24% were from out of state. Overall acceptance rate: 58%. Non-early acceptance rate: 58%. **Size of waiting list:** 704 applicants; enrolled from waiting list: 120. **Credentials of fall 2009 freshmen:** 31% ranked in the top 10 percent of their high school class; 54% were in the top 25 percent; 93% were in the top half. (Proportion submitting class standing:

43%.) **Average high school grade point average:** 3.5. **First-year students who submitted SAT scores:** 95%. Scores (25/75 percentile): Critical Reading: 541-642, Math: 553-651, Combined: 1094-1293.

ACADEMICS

Year founded: 1940. **Academic calendar:** Semester. **Degrees offered:** certificate, bachelor's, post-bachelor's certificate, master's, post-master's certificate. **Most popular majors:** 33% business, management, marketing, and related support services, 19% communication, journalism, and related programs, 10% psychology, 8% criminal justice/law enforcement administration, 8% education. **Major fields of study:** agriculture, agriculture operations, and related sciences; biological and biomedical sciences; business, management, marketing, and related support services; communication, journalism, and related programs; computer and information sciences and support services; education; English language and literature/letters; foreign languages, literatures, and linguistics; health professions and related clinical sciences; history; liberal arts and sciences studies, and humanities; mathematics and statistics; multi/interdisciplinary studies; philosophy and religious studies; physical sciences; psychology; public administration and social service professions; security and protective services; social sciences; visual and performing arts. **Areas of required coursework:** arts/fine arts, humanities, computer literacy, mathematics, English (including composition), philosophy, foreign languages, sciences (biological or physical), history, social science, other. **Pre-professional programs:** pre-law, pre-dentistry, pre-medicine, pre-veterinary science, pre-optometry, pre-pharmacy, other. **Special academic programs:** accelerated program, distance learning, double major, honors program, independent study, internships, study abroad, teacher certificate program, weekend college. **Teacher certification offered in:** early childhood, elementary, secondary. **Reserve Officers Training Corps (ROTC):** Army ROTC: Offered at cooperating institution (Fordham University); Air Force ROTC: Offered at cooperating institution (Manhattan College). **Faculty and instruction (2009-2010):** Total instructional faculty: 183 full-time, 207 part-time (63% men; 37% women; 14% minorities). Full-time faculty with Ph.D. or other terminal degree: 92%. Student/faculty ratio: 13/1. Classes of fewer than 20 students: 41%; of 20 to 49 students: 58%; of 50 or more students: 0%. **Advanced Placement and International Baccalaureate credit:** AP tests may be used for: Credit and/or placement. Scores accepted: 3, 4, 5. International Baccalaureate exams may be used for: Credit and/or placement. **Freshmen returning for sophomore year:** 85%. **Graduation rates:** Four-year: 50%; five-year: 60%; six-year: 61%. **Graduate study:** 40% of students pursue further study immediately upon graduation; 30% within one year. Fields in which graduates pursue further study: Master of Business Administration (MBA), 36%; law, 6%; medicine, 3%; education, 27%; arts and sciences, 28%.

COSTS AND FINANCIAL AID

Financial aid office: (914) 633-2497. **Expenses (2010-2011):** Tuition and fees 2010-2011: $28,850; room/board: $11,800. Estimated books and supplies: $1,800; transportation: $600; personal expenses: $1,250. **Financial aid:** Priority filing date for institution's financial aid form: February 15; deadline: April 15. In 2009-2010, 97% of undergraduates applied for financial aid. Of those, 75% were determined to have financial need; 24% had their need fully met. Average financial aid package (proportion receiving): $18,067 (75%). Average amount of gift aid, such as scholarships or grants (proportion receiving): $5,153 (49%). Average amount of self-help aid, such as work study or loans (proportion receiving): $3,994 (58%). Average need-based loan (excluding PLUS or other private loans): $2,964. Among students who received need-based aid, the average percentage of need met: 29%. Among students who received aid based on merit, the average award (and the proportion receiving): $11,070 (21%). The average athletic scholarship (and the proportion receiving): $14,314 (7%). Average amount of debt of borrowers graduating in 2009: $24,213. Proportion who borrowed: 68%.

CAMPUS LIFE AND EXTRACURRICULAR ACTIVITIES

Campus housing available (% using): coed dorms (68%), apartment for single students (14%), special housing for disabled students (2%). Students who live in college-owned, operated, or affiliated housing: 31%. **Student employment:** During the 2009-2010 academic year, 8% of undergraduates worked on campus. Average per-year earnings: $871. **Clubs and organizations:** Number of student organizations: 65. Activities include: campus ministries, choral groups, dance, drama/theater, international student organization, literary magazine, model UN, music ensembles, musical theater, pep band, radio station, student government, student newspaper, student film society, television station, yearbook. Number of fraternities: 4; sororities: 6. Proportion of men in fraternities: 4%; of women in sororities: 6%. Average proportion of students who stay on campus on weekends: 65%.

Sports program (2009-2010): Member of NCAA I. *Men's intercollegiate varsity sports:* basketball, golf, soccer, swimming, track and field (indoor), water polo. *Women's intercollegiate varsity sports:* basketball, crew (heavyweight), crew (lightweight), lacrosse, soccer, softball, swimming, track and field (indoor), volleyball, water polo.

SERVICES AND FACILITIES

Basic services: nonremedial tutoring, placement service, health service, health insurance. **Remedial assistance:** reading, math, writing, study skills. **Counseling services:** minority student, career, personal, veteran student, academic, older student, psychological, religious. **For learning-disabled students:** School does not offer a structured program with separate admission and additional fees. Total undergraduates in learning-disabled program or receiving services: 95. Services include: reading machines, tape recorders, note-taking services, oral tests, learning center, readers, extended time for tests, tutors. **Library:** Number of titles: 272,014; number of current serial subscriptions: 744. **Information technology resources:** Students are not required to lease or own a computer. Number of campus computers available to all students: 2,000. School has a wireless network. Approximate number of users that can be accommodated: 10,000. Proportion of college-owned housing units wired for high-speed internet access: 100%. **Campus safety:** Security services offered: 24-hour foot-and-vehicle patrols, late-night transport/escort service, 24-hour emergency telephones, lighted pathways/sidewalks, student patrols, controlled dormitory access (key, security card, etc).

TRANSFER AND INTERNATIONAL STUDENTS

Transfer students: May apply for admission for the following academic terms: Fall, Spring. Applicants do not need a minimum number of credits to apply. For fall 2009: Transfer applications received: 299. Transfer applicants offered admission: 203. Transfer applicants enrolled: 105. **International students:** Number of foreign undergraduates: 44 (1% of student body). Number of countries represented: 35. Minimum TOEFL score required: 550 (paper); 213 (computer). Average TOEFL score: 561 (paper).

Ithaca College

- **Address:** 953 Danby Road, Ithaca, NY 14850-7000
- **Website:** http://www.ithaca.edu
- **Private**
- **Enrollment:** 6,370 full-time; 70 part-time

KEY STATS

✔ **U.S News College Ranking:** 7, Regional Universities (North)
✔ **SAT Score (25th/75th percentile):** 1060-1270
✔ **Tuition:** 2010-2011: $33,630

Selectivity: More selective	**Room/board:** $12,314
Acceptance rate: 79%	**Average debt:** N/A
Student/faculty ratio: 12/1	**Proportion who borrowed:** N/A

UNDERGRADUATE STUDENT BODY STATS

2009-2010 enrollment: 6,370 full-time; 70 part-time. Men: 43%; women: 57%. **Ethnic makeup:** African American: 3%; American-Indian: 1%; Asian American: 4%; Hispanic: 4%; White: 86%; International: 2%.

ADMISSIONS FACTS AND FIGURES

Phone: (800) 429-4274. **Email:** admission@ithaca.edu. **Website:** http://www.ithaca.edu. **Application deadlines for fall 2011:** Regular decision: February 1; decision sent by April 15. Early decision: Send application by: November 1; Decision sent by: December 15. Early action: Not offered. Admission can be deferred. **Application fee:** $60. **To apply online, go to:** http://www.ithaca.edu/admission/. **Admissions requirements/recommendations:** High school units required (recommended): English: 4 (4); Mathematics: 3 (4); Science: 3 (4); Foreign language: 2 (2); Social studies: 3 (4); Academic electives: 1 (1); Total units: 16 (19). Tests: The college uses SAT or ACT scores in admissions decisions. Either SAT or ACT required. For admission to the fall 2011 entering class, the school will accept: ACT with writing required. Campus visit: Recommended. Admissions interview: Neither required nor recommended. Off-campus interview: Not available. **Factors that count in admissions decisions:** *Academic:* Secondary school record: Very Important. Class rank: Important. Letters of recommendation: Important. Standardized test scores: Important. Essay: Important. *Nonacademic:* Interview: Considered. Extracurricular activities: Important.

Talent/ability: Important. Character/personal qualities: Important. Alumni/ae relationship: Considered. Geographical residence: Not Considered. State residency: Not Considered. Religious affiliation/commitment: Not Considered. Minority status: Considered. Volunteer work: Considered. Work experience: Considered. **Other schools with the greatest overlap in applicants:** Boston University; New York University; Syracuse University; University of Massachusetts–Amherst; University of Vermont. **Admissions statistics for the fall 2009 entering class:** Total applicants: 11,916. Total accepted: 9,471. Freshmen enrolled: 2,027; 57% were from out of state. Overall acceptance rate: 79%. Non-early acceptance rate: 79%. **Credentials of fall 2009 freshmen:** 27% ranked in the top 10 percent of their high school class; 67% were in the top 25 percent; 93% were in the top half. (Proportion submitting class standing: 57%.) **First-year students who submitted SAT scores:** 93%. Scores (25/75 percentile): Critical Reading: 530-630, Math: 530-640, Combined: 1060-1270. **First-year students submitting ACT scores:** 34%. Scores (25/75 percentile): English: N/A, Math: N/A, Composite: N/A.

ACADEMICS

Year founded: 1892. **Academic calendar:** Semester. **Degrees offered:** certificate, bachelor's, master's. **Most popular majors:** 19% communication, journalism, and related programs, 19% visual and performing arts, 14% health professions and related clinical sciences, 11% business, management, marketing, and related support services, 7% English language and literature/letters. **Major fields of study:** area, ethnic, cultural, and gender studies; biological and biomedical sciences; business, management, marketing, and related support services; communication, journalism, and related programs; communications technologies/technicians and support services; computer and information sciences and support services; education; English language and literature/letters; foreign languages, literatures, and linguistics; health professions and related clinical sciences; history; legal professions and studies; liberal arts and sciences studies, and humanities; mathematics and statistics; multi/interdisciplinary studies; natural resources and conservation; parks, recreation, leisure, and fitness studies; philosophy and religious studies; physical sciences; psychology; social sciences; visual and performing arts. **Pre-professional programs:** pre-law, pre-dentistry, pre-medicine, pre-veterinary science, pre-optometry, other. **Special academic programs:** accelerated program, cross-registration, distance learning, double major, dual enrollment, honors program, independent study, internships, liberal arts/career combination, student-designed major, study abroad, teacher certificate program, other. **Teacher certification offered in:** special education, elementary, middle/junior high, secondary. **Reserve Officers Training Corps (ROTC):** Army ROTC: Offered at cooperating institution (Cornell University); Air Force ROTC: Offered at cooperating institution (Cornell University). **Faculty and instruction (2009-2010):** Total instructional faculty: 461 full-time, 241 part-time (52% men; 48% women; 8% minorities). Full-time faculty with Ph.D. or other terminal degree: 95%. Student/faculty ratio: 12/1. Classes of fewer than 20 students: 53%; of 20 to 49 students: 43%; of 50 or more students: 4%. **Advanced Placement and International Baccalaureate credit:** International Baccalaureate exams may be used for: Credit only. **Freshmen returning for sophomore year:** 86%. **Graduation rates:** Four-year: 71%; five-year: 77%; six-year: 77%. **Graduate study:** 40% of students pursue further study within one year. Fields in which graduates pursue further study: Master of Business Administration (MBA), 3%; law, 7%; medicine, 3%; education, 11%; arts and sciences, 76%.

COSTS AND FINANCIAL AID

Financial aid office: (607) 274-3131. **Expenses (2010-2011):** Tuition and fees 2010-2011: $33,630; room/board: $12,314. Estimated books and supplies: $1,275; transportation: $0; personal expenses: $1,600. **Financial aid:** Priority filing date for institution's financial aid form: February 1. In 2009-2010, 79% of undergraduates applied for financial aid. Of those, 69% were determined to have financial need; 54% had their need fully met. Average financial aid package (proportion receiving): $28,273 (69%). Average amount of gift aid, such as scholarships or grants (proportion receiving): $18,579 (67%). Average amount of self-help aid, such as work study or loans (proportion receiving): $8,077 (64%). Average need-based loan (excluding PLUS or other private loans): $6,243. Among students who received need-based aid, the average percentage of need met: 90%. Among students who received aid based on merit, the average award (and the proportion receiving): $9,551 (18%).

CAMPUS LIFE AND EXTRACURRICULAR ACTIVITIES

Campus housing available: coed dorms, women's dorms, sorority housing, fraternity housing, apartment for single students, special housing for disabled students. Students who live in college-owned, operated, or affiliated housing: 77%. **Student employment:** During the 2009-2010 academic year,

36% of undergraduates worked on campus. Average per-year earnings: $2,400. **Clubs and organizations:** Number of student organizations: 170. Activities include: campus ministries, choral groups, concert band, dance, drama/theater, international student organization, jazz band, literary magazine, music ensembles, musical theater, opera, pep band, radio station, student government, student newspaper, student film society, symphony orchestra, television station, yearbook. Number of fraternities: 0; sororities: 0. Average proportion of students who stay on campus on weekends: 95%. **Sports program (2009-2010):** Member of NCAA III. *Men's intercollegiate varsity sports:* baseball, basketball, cross country, football, lacrosse, soccer, swimming, tennis, track and field (indoor), track and field (outdoor), wrestling. *Women's intercollegiate varsity sports:* basketball, cross country, field hockey, golf, gymnastics, lacrosse, crew (lightweight), soccer, softball, swimming, tennis, track and field (indoor), track and field (outdoor), volleyball.

SERVICES AND FACILITIES

Basic services: health service, health insurance. **Counseling services:** minority student, career, military, personal, veteran student, academic, older student, psychological, birth control, religious. **For learning-disabled students:** School does not offer a structured program with separate admission and additional fees. Total undergraduates in learning-disabled program or receiving services: 470. Services include: reading machines, tape recorders, untimed tests, note-taking services, oral tests, readers, extended time for tests, priority seating, texts on tape, other testing accommodations, other. **Library:** Number of titles: 304,015; number of current serial subscriptions: 44,425. **Information technology resources:** Students are not required to lease or own a computer. Number of campus computers available to all students: 640. School has a wireless network. Approximate number of users that can be accommodated: 7,000. Proportion of college-owned housing units wired for high-speed internet access: 100%. **Campus safety:** Security services offered: 24-hour foot-and-vehicle patrols, late-night transport/escort service, 24-hour emergency telephones, lighted pathways/sidewalks, student patrols, controlled dormitory access (key, security card, etc).

TRANSFER AND INTERNATIONAL STUDENTS

Transfer students: May apply for admission for the following academic terms: Fall, Spring. Applicants do not need a minimum number of credits to apply. For fall 2009: Transfer applications received: 512. Transfer applicants offered admission: 390. Transfer applicants enrolled: 162. **International students:** Number of foreign undergraduates: 101 (2% of student body). Number of countries represented: 45. Minimum TOEFL score required: 550 (paper); 213 (computer).

Juilliard School

- **Address:** 60 Lincoln Center Plaza, New York, NY 10023-6588
- **Website:** http://www.juilliard.edu
- **Private**
- **Enrollment:** N/A

KEY STATS

✔ **U.S News College Ranking:** Unranked Specialty School–Fine Arts
✔ **SAT or ACT Score (25th/75th percentile):** N/A
✔ **Tuition:** 2009-2010: $28,640

Selectivity: N/A	Room/board: $11,250
Acceptance rate: 8%	Average debt: N/A
Student/faculty ratio: N/A	Proportion who borrowed: N/A

Keuka College

- **Address:** 141 Central Avenue, Keuka Park, NY 14478
- **Website:** http://www.keuka.edu
- **Private; Religious affiliation:** American Baptist
- **Enrollment:** 1,223 full-time; 299 part-time

KEY STATS

✔ **U.S News College Ranking:** 21, Regional Colleges (North)
✔ **SAT Score (25th/75th percentile):** 840-1060
✔ **Tuition:** 2010-2011: $23,760

Selectivity: Less selective	**Room/board:** $9,500
Acceptance rate: 77%	**Average debt:** $16,500
Student/faculty ratio: 14/1	**Proportion who borrowed:** 95%

UNDERGRADUATE STUDENT BODY STATS

2009-2010 enrollment: 1,223 full-time; 299 part-time. Men: 25%; women: 75%. **Ethnic makeup:** African American: 7%; American-Indian: 2%; Asian American: 2%; Hispanic: 3%; White: 86%. **Religious preference:** Roman Catholic: 26%; Protestant: 27%; Jewish: 1%; Unknown: 41%; American Baptist: 4%; 0: 0%; Other: 1%.

ADMISSIONS FACTS AND FIGURES

Phone: (315) 279-5254. **Email:** admissions@mail.keuka.edu. **Website:** http://www.keuka.edu. **Application deadlines for fall 2011:** Regular decision: Rolling. Early decision: Not offered. Early action: Not offered. Admission can be deferred. **Application fee:** $30. **To apply online, go to:** http://apply.keuka.edu/. **Admissions requirements/recommendations:** High school units required (recommended): English: 4 (4); Mathematics: 3 (3); Science: 3 (3); Foreign language: 3 (3); Social studies: 3 (3); History: 2 (2); Total units: 20 (18). Tests: The college uses SAT or ACT scores in admissions decisions. Neither SAT nor ACT required. Campus visit: Recommended. Admissions interview: Recommended. Off-campus interview: May be arranged. **Factors that count in admissions decisions:** *Academic:* Secondary school record: Very Important. Class rank: Important. Letters of recommendation: Important. Standardized test scores: Considered. Essay: Important. *Nonacademic:* Interview: Important. Extracurricular activities: Important. Talent/ability: Considered. Character/personal qualities: Important. Alumni/ae relationship: Considered. Geographical residence: Not Considered. State residency: Not Considered. Religious affiliation/commitment: Not Considered. Minority status: Not Considered. Volunteer work: Considered. Work experience: Considered. **Other schools with the greatest overlap in applicants:** Elmira College; Nazareth College; SUNY–Geneseo; St. Bonaventure University; St. John Fisher College. **Admissions statistics for the fall 2009 entering class:** Total applicants: 867. Total accepted: 666. Freshmen enrolled: 253; 6% were from out of state. Overall acceptance rate: 77%. **Credentials of fall 2009 freshmen:** 11% ranked in the top 10 percent of their high school class; 38% were in the top 25 percent; 65% were in the top half. (Proportion submitting class standing: 79%.) **Average high school grade point average:** 3.1. **First-year students who submitted SAT scores:** 75%. Scores (25/75 percentile): Critical Reading: 410-550, Math: 430-510, Combined: 840-1060. **First-year students submitting ACT scores:** 26%. Scores (25/75 percentile): English: 16-23, Math: 18-24, Composite: 18-21.

ACADEMICS

Year founded: 1890. **Academic calendar:** 4-1-4. **Degrees offered:** bachelor's, master's. **Most popular majors:** 23% health professions and related clinical sciences, 21% business, management, marketing, and related support services, 19% education, 4% psychology, 4% public administration and social service professions. **Major fields of study:** biological and biomedical sciences; business, management, marketing, and related support services; communication, journalism, and related programs; education; English language and literature/letters; foreign languages, literatures, and linguistics; health professions and related clinical sciences; liberal arts and sciences studies, and humanities; mathematics and statistics; physical sciences; psychology; public administration and social service professions; security and protective services; social sciences. **Areas of required coursework:** arts/fine arts, humanities, computer literacy, mathematics, English (including composition), philosophy, sciences (biological or physical), history, social science, other. **Pre-professional programs:** pre-law, pre-dentistry, pre-medicine, pre-veterinary science. **Special academic programs (% participation):** accelerated program (35%), cooperative (work-study plan) program (67%), cross-registration, double major, dual enrollment, independent study, internships (100%), student-designed major, study abroad, teacher certificate program (30%). **Teacher certification offered in:** early childhood, special education, elementary, middle/junior high, secondary. **Faculty and instruction (2009-2010):** Total instructional faculty: 74 full-time, 35 part-time (39% men; 61% women; 9% minorities). Full-time faculty with Ph.D. or other terminal degree: 84%. Student/faculty ratio: 14/1. Classes of fewer than 20 students: 53%; of 20 to 49 students: 47%; of 50 or more students: 0%. **Advanced Placement and International Baccalaureate credit:** AP tests may be used for: Credit only. Scores accepted: 3. International Baccalaureate exams may be used for: Credit only. **Freshmen returning for sophomore year:** 67%. **Graduation rates:** Four-year: 45%; five-year: 52%; six-year: 48%. **Graduate study:** 44% of students pursue further study immediately upon graduation; 44% within one year. Fields in which graduates pursue further study: Master of Business Administration (MBA), 10%; education, 21%; arts and sciences, 69%.

COSTS AND FINANCIAL AID

Financial aid office: (315) 279-5232. **Expenses (2010-2011):** Tuition and fees 2010-2011: $23,760; room/board: $9,500. Estimated books and supplies: $1,000; transportation: $900; personal expenses: $1,100. **Financial aid:** In 2009-2010, 99% of undergraduates applied for financial aid. Of those, 90% were determined to have financial need; 22% had their need fully met. Average financial aid package (proportion receiving): $16,576 (90%). Average amount of gift aid, such as scholarships or grants (proportion receiving): $11,866 (85%). Average amount of self-help aid, such as work study or loans (proportion receiving): $6,028 (80%). Average need-based loan (excluding PLUS or other private loans): $5,811. Among students who received need-based aid, the average percentage of need met: 74%. Among students who received aid based on merit, the average award (and the proportion receiving): $9,185 (7%). The average athletic scholarship (and the proportion receiving): $0 (0%). Average amount of debt of borrowers graduating in 2009: $16,500. Proportion who borrowed: 95%.

CAMPUS LIFE AND EXTRACURRICULAR ACTIVITIES

Campus housing available (% using): coed dorms (81%), women's dorms (18%), special housing for disabled students (0%), cooperative housing (0%), other housing options (0%). Students who live in college-owned, operated, or affiliated housing: 82%. **Student employment:** During the 2009-2010 academic year, 67% of undergraduates worked on campus. Average per-year earnings: $468. **Clubs and organizations:** Number of student organizations: 33. Activities include: choral groups, concert band, dance, drama/theater, literary magazine, musical theater, radio station, student government, student newspaper, student film society, yearbook. Number of fraternities: 0; sororities: 0. Average proportion of students who stay on campus on weekends: 45%. **Sports program (2009-2010):** Member of NCAA III. *Men's intercollegiate varsity sports:* baseball, basketball, cross country, golf, soccer, tennis. *Women's intercollegiate varsity sports:* basketball, cross country, golf, soccer, softball, sync swimming, tennis, volleyball.

SERVICES AND FACILITIES

Basic services: health service, health insurance. **Remedial assistance:** math, writing, study skills, other. **Counseling services:** minority student, career, personal, veteran student, academic. **For learning-disabled students:** School does not offer a structured program with separate admission and additional fees. Total undergraduates in learning-disabled program or receiving services: 111. Services include: remedial math, remedial English, reading machines, remedial reading, tape recorders, note-taking services, learning center, readers, extended time for tests, tutors, priority registration, priority seating, proofreading services, texts on tape, typist/scribe, exams on tape or computer. **Library:** Number of titles: 109,271; number of current serial subscriptions: 246. **Information technology resources:** Students are not required to lease or own a computer. Number of campus computers available to all students: 323. School has a wireless network. Approximate number of users that can be accommodated: 1,024. Proportion of college-owned housing units wired for high-speed internet access: 100%. **Campus safety:** Security services offered: 24-hour foot-and-vehicle patrols, late-night transport/escort service, 24-hour emergency telephones, lighted pathways/sidewalks, student patrols, controlled dormitory access (key, security card, etc).

TRANSFER AND INTERNATIONAL STUDENTS

Transfer students: May apply for admission for the following academic terms: Fall, Spring. Applicants do not need a minimum number of credits to apply. For fall 2009: Transfer applications received: 156. Transfer applicants offered admission: 105. Transfer applicants enrolled: 69. **International students:** Number of foreign undergraduates: 5. Minimum TOEFL score required: 500 (paper); 300 (computer). Average TOEFL score: 520 (paper).

Le Moyne College

- **Address:** 1419 Salt Springs Road, Syracuse, NY 13214-1301
- **Website:** http://www.lemoyne.edu
- **Private; Religious affiliation:** Roman Catholic (Jesuit)
- **Enrollment:** 2,332 full-time; 452 part-time

KEY STATS

✔ **U.S News College Ranking:** 17, Regional Universities (North)
✔ **SAT Score (25th/75th percentile):** 995-1190
✔ **Tuition:** 2010-2011: $27,340

Selectivity: Selective	Room/board: $10,480
Acceptance rate: 67%	Average debt: $27,483
Student/faculty ratio: 13/1	Proportion who borrowed: 84%

UNDERGRADUATE STUDENT BODY STATS

2009-2010 enrollment: 2,332 full-time; 452 part-time. Men: 37%; women: 63%. **Ethnic makeup:** African American: 4%; American-Indian: 1%; Asian American: 2%; Hispanic: 5%; White: 87%; International: 1%. **Religious preference:** Protestant: 5%; Muslim: 1%; Unknown: 60%; Roman Catholic (Jesuit): 31%.

ADMISSIONS FACTS AND FIGURES

Phone: (315) 445-4300. **Email:** admission@lemoyne.edu. **Website:** http://www.lemoyne.edu. **Application deadlines for fall 2011:** Regular decision: Rolling. Early decision: Send application by: December 1; Decision sent by: December 15. Early action: Not offered. Admission can be deferred. **Application fee:** $35. **Admissions requirements/recommendations:** High school units required (recommended): English: 4; Mathematics: 3 (4); Science: 3 (4); Foreign language: 3; Social studies: 4; Total units: 17. Tests: The college uses SAT or ACT scores in admissions decisions. Either SAT or ACT required. For admission to the fall 2011 entering class, the school will accept: ACT with or without writing accepted. Campus visit: Recommended. Admissions interview: Recommended. Off-campus interview: Not available. **Factors that count in admissions decisions:** *Academic:* Secondary school record: Very Important. Class rank: Important. Letters of recommendation: Important. Standardized test scores: Important. Essay: Important. *Nonacademic:* Interview: Important. Extracurricular activities: Important. Talent/ability: Important. Character/personal qualities: Considered. Alumni/ae relationship: Considered. Geographical residence: Considered. State residency: Considered. Religious affiliation/commitment: Not Considered. Minority status: Not Considered. Volunteer work: Considered. Work experience: Important. **Other schools with the greatest overlap in applicants:** Canisius College; SUNY–Geneseo; Siena College; St. John Fisher College; Syracuse University. **Admissions statistics for the fall 2009 entering class:** Total applicants: 4,526. Total accepted: 3,023. Freshmen enrolled: 608; 6% were from out of state. Accepted through early-decision or early-action plans: 6%. Overall acceptance rate: 67%. Early-decision acceptance rate: 85%. Non-early acceptance rate: 67%. **Size of waiting list:** 95 applicants; enrolled from waiting list: 7. **Credentials of fall 2009 freshmen:** 22% ranked in the top 10 percent of their high school class; 58% were in the top 25 percent; 88% were in the top half. (Proportion submitting class standing: 69%.) **Average high school grade point average:** 3.3. **First-year students who submitted SAT scores:** 79%. Scores (25/75 percentile): Critical Reading: 490-580, Math: 505-610, Combined: 995-1190. **First-year students submitting ACT scores:** 46%. Scores (25/75 percentile): English: 19-25, Math: 20-26, Composite: 20-26.

ACADEMICS

Year founded: 1946. **Academic calendar:** Semester. **Degrees offered:** bachelor's, master's, post-master's certificate. **Most popular majors:** 16% psychology, 10% biology/biological sciences, 8% English language and literature, 8% accounting, 7% sociology. **Major fields of study:** biological and biomedical sciences; business, management, marketing, and related support services; communication, journalism, and related programs; English language and literature/letters; foreign languages, literatures, and linguistics; health professions and related clinical sciences; history; mathematics and statistics; multi/interdisciplinary studies; philosophy and religious studies; physical sciences; psychology; social sciences; visual and performing arts. **Areas of required coursework:** humanities, mathematics, English (including composition), philosophy, foreign languages, sciences (biological or physical), history, social science, other. **Pre-professional programs:** pre-law, pre-dentistry, pre-medicine, pre-veterinary science, pre-optometry, pre-pharmacy, other. **Special academic programs (% participation):** accelerated program, double

major (6%), dual enrollment (1%), honors program (5%), independent study (22%), internships (22%), study abroad (10%), teacher certificate program (23%). **Teacher certification offered in:** special education, elementary, middle/junior high, secondary, bilingual/bicultural. **Reserve Officers Training Corps (ROTC):** Army ROTC: Offered at cooperating institution (Syracuse University); Air Force ROTC: Offered at cooperating institution (Syracuse University). **Faculty and instruction (2009-2010):** Total instructional faculty: 158 full-time, 167 part-time (54% men; 46% women; 9% minorities). Full-time faculty with Ph.D. or other terminal degree: 94%. Student/faculty ratio: 13/1. Classes of fewer than 20 students: 41%; of 20 to 49 students: 57%; of 50 or more students: 1%. **Advanced Placement and International Baccalaureate credit:** AP tests may be used for: Credit and/or placement. Scores accepted: 3, 4, 5. International Baccalaureate exams may be used for: Credit only. **Freshmen returning for sophomore year:** 84%. **Graduation rates:** Four-year: 61%; five-year: 68%; six-year: 72%. **Graduate study:** 40% of students pursue further study within one year. Fields in which graduates pursue further study: Master of Business Administration (MBA), 2%; law, 2%; medicine, 3%; education, 11%; arts and sciences, 22%.

COSTS AND FINANCIAL AID

Financial aid office: (315) 445-4400. **Expenses (2010-2011):** Tuition and fees 2010-2011: $27,340; room/board: $10,480. Estimated books and supplies: $1,250; transportation: $530; personal expenses: $900. **Financial aid:** Priority filing date for institution's financial aid form: February 1. In 2009-2010, 92% of undergraduates applied for financial aid. Of those, 85% were determined to have financial need; 25% had their need fully met. Average financial aid package (proportion receiving): $20,065 (85%). Average amount of gift aid, such as scholarships or grants (proportion receiving): $15,652 (85%). Average amount of self-help aid, such as work study or loans (proportion receiving): $4,877 (69%). Average need-based loan (excluding PLUS or other private loans): $4,499. Among students who received need-based aid, the average percentage of need met: 76%. Among students who received aid based on merit, the average award (and the proportion receiving): $5,414 (8%). The average athletic scholarship (and the proportion receiving): $8,602 (7%). Average amount of debt of borrowers graduating in 2009: $27,483. Proportion who borrowed: 84%.

CAMPUS LIFE AND EXTRACURRICULAR ACTIVITIES

Campus housing available (% using): coed dorms (48%), women's dorms (10%), men's dorms (10%), apartment for single students (20%), special housing for disabled students, other housing options (12%). Students who live in college-owned, operated, or affiliated housing: 60%. **Student employment:** During the 2009-2010 academic year, 19% of undergraduates worked on campus. Average per-year earnings: $930. **Clubs and organizations:** Number of student organizations: 70. Activities include: campus ministries, choral groups, concert band, dance, drama/theater, international student organization, jazz band, literary magazine, model UN, music ensembles, musical theater, pep band, radio station, student government, student newspaper, student film society, television station, yearbook. Number of fraternities: 0; sororities: 0. Average proportion of students who stay on campus on weekends: 85%. **Sports program (2009-2010):** Member of NCAA II. *Men's intercollegiate varsity sports:* baseball, basketball, cross country, golf, lacrosse, soccer, swimming, tennis. *Women's intercollegiate varsity sports:* basketball, cross country, golf, lacrosse, soccer, softball, swimming, tennis, volleyball.

SERVICES AND FACILITIES

Basic services: nonremedial tutoring, placement service, health service. **Remedial assistance:** math, writing, study skills, other. **Counseling services:** minority student, career, personal, veteran student, academic, older student, psychological, religious. **For learning-disabled students:** School does not offer a structured program with separate admission and additional fees. Total undergraduates in learning-disabled program or receiving services: 123. Services include: remedial math, remedial English, reading machines, tape recorders, note-taking services, learning center, extended time for tests, tutors, texts on tape, exams on tape or computer, other. **Library:** Number of titles: 270,763; number of current serial subscriptions: 122,165. **Information technology resources:** Students are not required to lease or own a computer. Number of campus computers available to all students: 325. School has a wireless network. Approximate number of users that can be accommodated: 1,500. Proportion of college-owned housing units wired for high-speed internet access: 100%. **Campus safety:** Security services offered: 24-hour foot-and-vehicle patrols, late-night transport/escort service, 24-hour emergency telephones, lighted pathways/sidewalks, controlled dormitory access (key, security card, etc).

TRANSFER AND INTERNATIONAL STUDENTS

Transfer students: May apply for admission for the following academic terms: Fall, Spring. Applicants do not need a minimum number of credits to apply. For fall 2009: Transfer applications received: 346. Transfer applicants offered admission: 256. Transfer applicants enrolled: 169. **International students:** Number of foreign undergraduates: 21 (1% of student body). Number of countries represented: 17. Minimum TOEFL score required: 550 (paper); 213 (computer).

Long Island University—C.W. Post Campus

- **Address:** 720 Northern Boulevard, Brookville, NY 11548-1300
- **Website:** http://www.liu.edu
- **Private**
- **Enrollment:** 4,115 full-time; 4,353 part-time

KEY STATS

✔ **U.S News College Ranking:** second tier, National Universities
✔ **SAT Score (25th/75th percentile):** 880-1090
✔ **Tuition:** 2010-2011: $30,210

Selectivity: Less selective	**Room/board:** $10,980
Acceptance rate: 82%	**Average debt:** N/A
Student/faculty ratio: 14/1	**Proportion who borrowed:** 65%

UNDERGRADUATE STUDENT BODY STATS

2009-2010 enrollment: 4,115 full-time; 4,353 part-time. Men: 29%; women: 71%. **Ethnic makeup:** African American: 9%; Asian American: 8%; Hispanic: 8%; White: 76%.

ADMISSIONS FACTS AND FIGURES

Phone: (516) 299-2900. **Email:** enroll@cwpost.liu.edu. **Website:** http://www.liu.edu. **Application deadlines for fall 2011:** Regular decision: Rolling. Early decision: Not offered. Early action: Not offered. Admission can be deferred. **Application fee:** $30. **To apply online, go to:** http://www.liu.edu/admissions/apply. **Admissions requirements/recommendations:** High school units required (recommended): English: (4); Mathematics: (3); Science: (3); Foreign language: (2); Social studies: (4); Total units: (16). Tests: The college uses SAT or ACT scores in admissions decisions. Either SAT or ACT required. For admission to the fall 2011 entering class, the school will accept: ACT with or without writing accepted. Campus visit: Recommended. Admissions interview: Recommended. Off-campus interview: May be arranged. **Factors that count in admissions decisions:** *Academic:* Secondary school record: Very Important. Class rank: Considered. Letters of recommendation: Very Important. Standardized test scores: Very Important. Essay: Very Important. *Nonacademic:* Interview: Considered. Extracurricular activities: Important. Talent/ability: Considered. Character/personal qualities: Considered. Alumni/ae relationship: Considered. Geographical residence: Not Considered. State residency: Not Considered. Religious affiliation/commitment: Not Considered. Minority status: Not Considered. Volunteer work: Important. Work experience: Important. **Other schools with the greatest overlap in applicants:** Adelphi University; Hofstra University; Molloy College; SUNY–Stony Brook; St. John's University. **Admissions statistics for the fall 2009 entering class:** Total applicants: 4,923. Total accepted: 4,052. Freshmen enrolled: 855; 24% were from out of state. Overall acceptance rate: 82%. **Credentials of fall 2009 freshmen:** 9% ranked in the top 10 percent of their high school class; 26% were in the top 25 percent; 59% were in the top half. (Proportion submitting class standing: 14%.) **Average high school grade point average:** 3.0. **First-year students who submitted SAT scores:** 89%. Scores (25/75 percentile): Critical Reading: 440-530, Math: 440-560, Combined: 880-1090. **First-year students submitting ACT scores:** 21%. Scores (25/75 percentile): English: 18-24, Math: 18-24, Composite: 19-23.

ACADEMICS

Year founded: 1954. **Academic calendar:** Semester. **Degrees offered:** certificate, diploma, bachelor's, post-bachelor's certificate, master's, post-master's certificate, doctorate. **Most popular majors:** 15% business administration and management, 9% elementary education and teaching, 7% criminal justice/law enforcement administration, 7% psychology, 5% accounting. **Major fields of study:** biological and biomedical sciences; business, management, marketing, and related support services; communication, journalism, and related programs; computer and information sciences and support services; education; English language and literature/letters; family and consumer sciences/human sciences; foreign languages, literatures, and linguistics; health professions and related clinical sciences; history; liberal arts and sciences studies, and humanities; mathematics and statistics; multi/interdisciplinary studies; philosophy and religious studies; physical sciences; psychology; public administration and social service professions; security and protective services; social sciences; visual and performing arts. **Areas of required coursework:** arts/fine arts, humanities, computer literacy, mathematics, English (including composition), philosophy, foreign languages, sciences (biological or physical), history, social science. **Pre-professional programs:** pre-law, pre-dentistry, pre-medicine, pre-veterinary science, pre-pharmacy. **Special academic programs:** accelerated program, cooperative (work-study plan) program, cross-registration, double major, dual enrollment, English as a Second Language (ESL), exchange student program (domestic), external degree program, honors program, independent study, internships, liberal arts/career combination, student-designed major, study abroad, teacher certificate program, weekend college. **Teacher certification offered in:** early childhood, special education, elementary, middle/junior high, secondary, bilingual/bicultural. **Cooperative education programs:** art, business, computer science, education, engineering, health professions, humanities, natural science, social/behavioral science, technologies. **Reserve Officers Training Corps (ROTC):** Army ROTC: Offered at cooperating institution (Hofstra University). **Faculty and instruction (2009-2010):** Total instructional faculty: 277 full-time, 464 part-time (52% men; 48% women; 15% minorities). Full-time faculty with Ph.D. or other terminal degree: 92%. Student/faculty ratio: 14/1. Classes of fewer than 20 students: 56%; of 20 to 49 students: 39%; of 50 or more students: 5%. **Advanced Placement and International Baccalaureate credit:** AP tests may be used for: Credit only. Scores accepted: 3, 4, 5. International Baccalaureate exams may be used for: Credit only. **Freshmen returning for sophomore year:** 70%. **Graduation rates:** Four-year: 25%; five-year: 38%; six-year: 41%. **Graduate study:** 33% of students pursue further study within one year. Fields in which graduates pursue further study: Master of Business Administration (MBA), 24%; law, 7%; medicine, 7%; education, 48%; arts and sciences, 7%.

COSTS AND FINANCIAL AID

Financial aid office: (516) 299-2338. **Expenses (2010-2011):** Tuition and fees 2010-2011: $30,210; room/board: $10,980. Estimated books and supplies: $800. **Financial aid:** Priority filing date for institution's financial aid form: March 1; deadline: March 1. In 2009-2010, 83% of undergraduates applied for financial aid. Of those, 68% were determined to have financial need; 15% had their need fully met. Average financial aid package (proportion receiving): $14,500 (66%). Average amount of gift aid, such as scholarships or grants (proportion receiving): $5,800 (47%). Average amount of self-help aid, such as work study or loans (proportion receiving): $6,900 (52%). Average need-based loan (excluding PLUS or other private loans): $5,350. Among students who received need-based aid, the average percentage of need met: 75%. Among students who received aid based on merit, the average award (and the proportion receiving): $6,950 (14%). The average athletic scholarship (and the proportion receiving): $17,332 (6%). Proportion who borrowed: 65%.

CAMPUS LIFE AND EXTRACURRICULAR ACTIVITIES

Campus housing available (% using): coed dorms (84%), special housing for disabled students, other housing options (16%). Students who live in college-owned, operated, or affiliated housing: 35%. **Student employment:** During the 2009-2010 academic year, 20% of undergraduates worked on campus. Average per-year earnings: $1,589. **Clubs and organizations:** Number of student organizations: 68. Activities include: campus ministries, choral groups, concert band, dance, drama/theater, international student organization, jazz band, literary magazine, music ensembles, musical theater, pep band, radio station, student government, student newspaper, television station, yearbook. Number of fraternities: 5; sororities: 10. of women in sororities: 2%. Average proportion of students who stay on campus on weekends: 60%. **Sports program (2009-2010):** Member of NCAA II. *Men's intercollegiate varsity sports:* baseball, basketball, cross country, football, lacrosse, soccer. *Women's intercollegiate varsity sports:* basketball, cross country, field hockey, lacrosse, soccer, softball, swimming, tennis, volleyball.

SERVICES AND FACILITIES

Basic services: nonremedial tutoring, women's center, placement service, health service, health insurance. **Remedial assistance:** reading, math, writing, study skills. **Counseling services:** minority student, career, personal, veteran student, academic, older student, psychological, birth control, religious. **For learning-disabled students:** School does not offer a structured program with separate admission and additional fees. Total undergraduates in learning-disabled program or receiving services: 81. Services include:

reading machines, tape recorders, diagnostic testing service, note-taking services, learning center, readers, extended time for tests, tutors, texts on tape, other testing accommodations. **Library:** Number of titles: 1,193,495; number of current serial subscriptions: 10,718. **Information technology resources:** Students are not required to lease or own a computer. Number of campus computers available to all students: 600. School has a wireless network. Proportion of college-owned housing units wired for high-speed internet access: 100%. **Campus safety:** Security services offered: 24-hour foot-and-vehicle patrols, late-night transport/escort service, 24-hour emergency telephones, lighted pathways/sidewalks, student patrols, controlled dormitory access (key, security card, etc).

TRANSFER AND INTERNATIONAL STUDENTS

Transfer students: May apply for admission for the following academic terms: Fall, Winter, Spring, Summer. Applicants do not need a minimum number of credits to apply. For fall 2009: Transfer applications received: 1,550. Transfer applicants offered admission: 1,085. Transfer applicants enrolled: 457. **International students:** Number of foreign undergraduates: 0. Number of countries represented: 50. Minimum TOEFL score required: 527 (paper); 71 (computer). Average TOEFL score: 567 (paper).

Manhattan College

- **Address:** Manhattan College Parkway, Riverdale, NY 10471
- **Website:** http://www.manhattan.edu
- **Private; Religious affiliation:** Roman Catholic
- **Enrollment:** 2,962 full-time; 90 part-time

KEY STATS

✔ **U.S News College Ranking:** 17, Regional Universities (North)
✔ **SAT Score (25th/75th percentile):** 990-1195
✔ **Tuition:** 2010-2011: $27,105

Selectivity: Selective	**Room/board:** $10,670
Acceptance rate: 65%	**Average debt:** $26,779
Student/faculty ratio: 13/1	**Proportion who borrowed:** 68%

UNDERGRADUATE STUDENT BODY STATS

2009-2010 enrollment: 2,962 full-time; 90 part-time. Men: 53%; women: 47%. **Ethnic makeup:** African American: 3%; Asian American: 3%; Hispanic: 12%; White: 79%; International: 2%. **Religious preference:** Roman Catholic: 73%; Protestant: 20%; Jewish: 1%; Muslim: 2%; Hindu: 1%; Unknown: 3%.

ADMISSIONS FACTS AND FIGURES

Phone: (718) 862-7200. **Email:** admit@manhattan.edu. **Website:** http://www.manhattan.edu. **Application deadlines for fall 2011:** Regular decision: Rolling. Early decision: Send application by: November 15; Decision sent by: December 15. Early action: Not offered. Admission can be deferred. **Application fee:** $60. **To apply online, go to:** http://www.manhattan.edu/admissions/ug/apply.shtml. **Admissions requirements/recommendations:** High school units required (recommended): English: 4 (4); Mathematics: 3 (4); Science: 2 (3); Foreign language: 2 (3); Social studies: 3 (3); History: 3 (3); Academic electives: 2 (2); Total units: 19 (22). Tests: The college uses SAT or ACT scores in admissions decisions. Either SAT or ACT required. For admission to the fall 2011 entering class, the school will accept: ACT with writing required. Campus visit: Recommended. Admissions interview: Recommended. Off-campus interview: Not available. **Factors that count in admissions decisions:** *Academic:* Secondary school record: Very Important. Class rank: Important. Letters of recommendation: Important. Standardized test scores: Very Important. Essay: Important. *Nonacademic:* Interview: Important. Extracurricular activities: Important. Talent/ability: Considered. Character/personal qualities: Considered. Alumni/ae relationship: Considered. Geographical residence: Not Considered. State residency: Not Considered. Religious affiliation/commitment: Not Considered. Minority status: Not Considered. Volunteer work: Considered. Work experience: Considered. **Other schools with the greatest overlap in applicants:** Fordham University; Iona College; Marist College; SUNY–Stony Brook; St. John's University. **Admissions statistics for the fall 2009 entering class:** Total applicants: 5,055. Total accepted: 3,300. Freshmen enrolled: 693; 34% were from out of state. Overall acceptance rate: 65%. Early-decision acceptance rate: 76%. Non-early acceptance rate: 65%. **Size of waiting list:** 232 applicants; enrolled from waiting list: 70. **Credentials of fall 2009 freshmen:** 20% ranked in the top 10 percent of their high school class; 45% were in the top

25 percent; 88% were in the top half. (Proportion submitting class standing: 24%.) **Average high school grade point average:** 3.4. **First-year students who submitted SAT scores:** 94%. Scores (25/75 percentile): Critical Reading: 490-580, Math: 500-615, Combined: 990-1195. **First-year students submitting ACT scores:** 25%. Scores (25/75 percentile): English: N/A, Math: N/A, Composite: 21-25.

ACADEMICS

Year founded: 1853. **Academic calendar:** Semester. **Degrees offered:** certificate, bachelor's, master's, post-master's certificate. **Most popular majors:** 13% finance, 10% marketing, 8% communication, journalism, and related programs, 7% civil engineering, 5% management science. **Major fields of study:** biological and biomedical sciences; business, management, marketing, and related support services; communication, journalism, and related programs; computer and information sciences and support services; education; engineering; English language and literature/letters; foreign languages, literatures, and linguistics; history; liberal arts and sciences studies, and humanities; mathematics and statistics; multi/interdisciplinary studies; philosophy and religious studies; physical sciences; psychology; social sciences. **Areas of required coursework:** arts/fine arts, humanities, computer literacy, mathematics, English (including composition), philosophy, foreign languages, sciences (biological or physical), history, social science. **Pre-professional programs:** pre-law, pre-medicine. **Special academic programs (% participation):** cross-registration (2%), double major (30%), exchange student program (domestic) (1%), honors program (6%), independent study (30%), internships (40%), liberal arts/career combination (30%), study abroad (15%), teacher certificate program (20%). **Teacher certification offered in:** early childhood, special education, elementary, middle/junior high, secondary. **Cooperative education programs:** art, business, computer science, education, engineering, health professions, humanities, natural science, social/behavioral science, technologies. **Reserve Officers Training Corps (ROTC):** Army ROTC: Offered at cooperating institution; Air Force ROTC: Offered on campus. **Faculty and instruction (2009-2010):** Total instructional faculty: 176 full-time, 188 part-time (64% men; 36% women; 11% minorities). Full-time faculty with Ph.D. or other terminal degree: 98%. Student/faculty ratio: 13/1. Classes of fewer than 20 students: 48%; of 20 to 49 students: 52%. **Advanced Placement and International Baccalaureate credit:** AP tests may be used for: Placement only. Scores accepted: 3, 4, 5. International Baccalaureate exams may be used for: Placement only. **Freshmen returning for sophomore year:** 86%. **Graduation rates:** Four-year: 61%; five-year: 67%; six-year: 69%. **Graduate study:** 30% of students pursue further study immediately upon graduation; 10% within one year; 12% within five years. Fields in which graduates pursue further study: Master of Business Administration (MBA), 17%; law, 6%; medicine, 6%; dentistry, 5%; engineering, 17%; theology (or the seminary), 1%; education, 24%; arts and sciences, 24%.

COSTS AND FINANCIAL AID

Financial aid office: (718) 862-7100. **Expenses (2010-2011):** Tuition and fees 2010-2011: $27,105; room/board: $10,670. Estimated books and supplies: $1,200; transportation: $600; personal expenses: $1,200. **Financial aid:** Priority filing date for institution's financial aid form: April 1; deadline: April 1. In 2009-2010, 79% of undergraduates applied for financial aid. Of those, 65% were determined to have financial need; 15% had their need fully met. Average financial aid package (proportion receiving): $16,839 (64%). Average amount of gift aid, such as scholarships or grants (proportion receiving): $7,690 (61%). Average amount of self-help aid, such as work study or loans (proportion receiving): $4,544 (50%). Average need-based loan (excluding PLUS or other private loans): $4,369. Among students who received need-based aid, the average percentage of need met: 67%. Among students who received aid based on merit, the average award (and the proportion receiving): $8,126 (33%). The average athletic scholarship (and the proportion receiving): $16,968 (3%). Average amount of debt of borrowers graduating in 2009: $26,779. Proportion who borrowed: 68%.

CAMPUS LIFE AND EXTRACURRICULAR ACTIVITIES

Campus housing available (% using): coed dorms (100%). Students who live in college-owned, operated, or affiliated housing: 64%. **Student employment:** During the 2009-2010 academic year, 35% of undergraduates worked on campus. Average per-year earnings: $1,375. **Clubs and organizations:** Number of student organizations: 62. Activities include: campus ministries, choral groups, concert band, dance, drama/theater, international student organization, jazz band, literary magazine, model UN, music ensembles, musical theater, pep band, radio station, student government, student newspaper, symphony orchestra, television station, yearbook. Number of fraternities: 3; sororities: 2. Average proportion of students who stay on campus on weekends: 70%. **Sports program (2009-2010):** Member of NCAA I. **Men's intercollegiate varsity sports:** baseball, basketball, cross country, golf, lacrosse, soccer, swimming, track and field (indoor), track and field (outdoor). **Women's intercollegiate varsity sports:** basketball, cross country, lacrosse, soccer, softball, swimming, tennis, track and field (indoor), track and field (outdoor), volleyball.

SERVICES AND FACILITIES

Basic services: nonremedial tutoring, placement service, health service, health insurance. **Remedial assistance:** reading, math, writing, study skills, other. **Counseling services:** minority student, career, military, personal, veteran student, academic, older student, psychological, religious. **For learning-disabled students:** School does not offer a structured program with separate admission and additional fees. Services include: note-taking services, readers, extended time for tests, priority seating, other. **Library:** Number of titles: 243,803; number of current serial subscriptions: 794. **Information technology resources:** Students are not required to lease or own a computer. Number of campus computers available to all students: 545. School has a wireless network. Approximate number of users that can be accommodated: 2,048. Proportion of college-owned housing units wired for high-speed internet access: 100%. **Campus safety:** Security services offered: 24-hour foot-and-vehicle patrols, late-night transport/escort service, 24-hour emergency telephones, lighted pathways/sidewalks, controlled dormitory access (key, security card, etc).

TRANSFER AND INTERNATIONAL STUDENTS

Transfer students: May apply for admission for the following academic terms: Fall, Spring. Applicants do not need a minimum number of credits to apply. For fall 2009: Transfer applications received: 541. Transfer applicants offered admission: 378. Transfer applicants enrolled: 177. **International students:** Number of foreign undergraduates: 55 (2% of student body). Minimum TOEFL score required: 520 (paper); 200 (computer). Average TOEFL score: 540 (paper).

Manhattan School of Music

- ■ **Address:** 120 Claremont Avenue, New York, NY 10027
- ■ **Website:** http://www.msmnyc.edu
- ■ Private
- ■ **Enrollment:** N/A

....

KEY STATS

✔ **U.S News College Ranking:** Unranked Specialty School–Fine Arts
✔ **SAT or ACT Score (25th/75th percentile):** N/A
✔ **Tuition:** 2009-2010: $31,875
   Selectivity: N/A   **Room/board:** $13,550
   Acceptance rate: N/A   **Average debt:** N/A
   Student/faculty ratio: N/A   **Proportion who borrowed:** N/A

Manhattanville College

- ■ **Address:** 2900 Purchase Street, Purchase, NY 10577
- ■ **Website:** http://www.mville.edu
- ■ Private
- ■ **Enrollment:** 1,717 full-time; 118 part-time

....

KEY STATS

✔ **U.S News College Ranking:** 40, Regional Universities (North)
✔ **SAT Score (25th/75th percentile):** 1030-1250
✔ **Tuition:** 2010-2011: $34,350
   Selectivity: Selective   **Room/board:** $13,920
   Acceptance rate: 53%   **Average debt:** $23,292
   Student/faculty ratio: 11/1   **Proportion who borrowed:** 75%

UNDERGRADUATE STUDENT BODY STATS

2009-2010 enrollment: 1,717 full-time; 118 part-time. Men: 35%; women: 65%. **Ethnic makeup:** African American: 8%; Asian American: 2%; Hispanic: 16%; White: 61%; International: 13%.

ADMISSIONS FACTS AND FIGURES

Phone: (800) 328-4553. **Email:** admissions@mville.edu. **Website:** http://www.mville.edu. **Application deadlines for fall 2011:** Regular decision: March 1. Early decision: Send application by: December 1. Decision sent by: December 31. Early action: Not offered. Admission can be deferred. **Application fee:** $70. **To apply online, go to:** http://www.mville.edu/admissions/index.html. **Admissions requirements/recommendations:** High school units required (recommended): English: 4; Mathematics: 3; Science: 2; Social studies: 2; Academic electives: 5; Total units: 16. Tests: The college uses SAT or ACT scores in admissions decisions. Either SAT or ACT required. For admission to the fall 2011 entering class, the school will accept: ACT with or without writing accepted. Campus visit: Recommended. Admissions interview: Recommended. Off-campus interview: May be arranged. **Factors that count in admissions decisions:** *Academic:* Secondary school record: Very Important. Class rank: Not Considered. Letters of recommendation: Important. Standardized test scores: Very Important. Essay: Important. *Nonacademic:* Interview: Important. Extracurricular activities: Important. Talent/ability: Considered. Character/personal qualities: Considered. Alumni/ae relationship: Considered. Geographical residence: Considered. State residency: Not Considered. Religious affiliation/commitment: Not Considered. Minority status: Not Considered. Volunteer work: Considered. Work experience: Considered. **Other schools with the greatest overlap in applicants:** Fordham University; Manhattan College; New York University; Pace University; Purchase College–SUNY. **Admissions statistics for the fall 2009 entering class:** Total applicants: 4,502. Total accepted: 2,370. Freshmen enrolled: 492; 45% were from out of state. Overall acceptance rate: 53%. Non-early acceptance rate: 53%. **Size of waiting list:** 0 applicants; enrolled from waiting list: 20. **Credentials of fall 2009 freshmen:** 23% ranked in the top 10 percent of their high school class; 47% were in the top 25 percent; 80% were in the top half. (Proportion submitting class standing: 76%.) **First-year students who submitted SAT scores:** 86%. Scores (25/75 percentile): Critical Reading: 520-640, Math: 510-610, Combined: 1030-1250. **First-year students submitting ACT scores:** 25%. Scores (25/75 percentile): English: N/A, Math: N/A, Composite: 22-26.

ACADEMICS

Year founded: 1841. **Academic calendar:** Semester. **Degrees offered:** bachelor's, post-bachelor's certificate, master's, post-master's certificate. **Most popular majors:** 17% business administration and management, 11% communication studies/speech communication and rhetoric, 11% psychology, 8% English language and literature, 8% history. **Major fields of study:** area, ethnic, cultural, and gender studies; biological and biomedical sciences; business, management, marketing, and related support services; computer and information sciences and support services; education; English language and literature/letters; foreign languages, literatures, and linguistics; history; liberal arts and sciences studies, and humanities; mathematics and statistics; philosophy and religious studies; physical sciences; psychology; social sciences; visual and performing arts. **Areas of required coursework:** arts/fine arts, humanities, mathematics, English (including composition), foreign languages, sciences (biological or physical), history, social science, other. **Pre-professional programs:** pre-law, pre-medicine. **Special academic programs (% participation):** accelerated program (5%), cross-registration (1%), double major (12%), dual enrollment (1%), exchange student program (domestic) (1%), honors program (5%), independent study (50%), internships (30%), student-designed major (6%), study abroad (9%), teacher certificate program (7%), weekend college. **Teacher certification offered in:** early childhood, special education, elementary, middle/junior high, secondary, bilingual/bicultural. **Faculty and instruction (2009-2010):** Total instructional faculty: 101 full-time, 166 part-time (49% men; 51% women; 12% minorities). Full-time faculty with Ph.D. or other terminal degree: 100%. Student/faculty ratio: 11/1. Classes of fewer than 20 students: 72%; of 20 to 49 students: 28%. **Advanced Placement and International Baccalaureate credit:** AP tests may be used for: Placement only. Scores accepted: 4, 5. International Baccalaureate exams may be used for: Placement only. **Freshmen returning for sophomore year:** 76%. **Graduation rates:** Four-year: 53%; five-year: 57%; six-year: 60%. **Graduate study:** 33% of students pursue further study within one year. Fields in which graduates pursue further study: Master of Business Administration (MBA), 9%; law, 4%; medicine, 13%; education, 46%; arts and sciences, 28%.

COSTS AND FINANCIAL AID

Financial aid office: (914) 323-5357. **Expenses (2010-2011):** Tuition and fees 2010-2011: $34,350; room/board: $13,920. Estimated books and supplies: $800; transportation: $800; personal expenses: $1,500. **Financial aid:** Priority filing date for institution's financial aid form: March 1; deadline: March 1. In 2009-2010, 72% of undergraduates applied for financial aid.

Of those, 66% were determined to have financial need; 14% had their need fully met. Average financial aid package (proportion receiving): $26,779 (66%). Average amount of gift aid, such as scholarships or grants (proportion receiving): $17,427 (62%). Average amount of self-help aid, such as work study or loans (proportion receiving): $5,330 (57%). Average need-based loan (excluding PLUS or other private loans): $4,523. Among students who received need-based aid, the average percentage of need met: 96%. Among students who received aid based on merit, the average award (and the proportion receiving): $18,753 (28%). Average amount of debt of borrowers graduating in 2009: $23,292. Proportion who borrowed: 75%.

CAMPUS LIFE AND EXTRACURRICULAR ACTIVITIES

Campus housing available (% using): coed dorms (100%). Students who live in college-owned, operated, or affiliated housing: 76%. **Student employment:** During the 2009-2010 academic year, 16% of undergraduates worked on campus. Average per-year earnings: $1,750. **Clubs and organizations:** Number of student organizations: 43. Activities include: campus ministries, choral groups, concert band, dance, drama/theater, international student organization, jazz band, literary magazine, music ensembles, musical theater, opera, pep band, radio station, student government, student newspaper, student film society, symphony orchestra, television station, yearbook. Number of fraternities: 0; sororities: 0. Average proportion of students who stay on campus on weekends: 75%. **Sports program (2009-2010):** Member of NCAA III. *Men's intercollegiate varsity sports:* baseball, basketball, golf, ice hockey, lacrosse, soccer, tennis. *Women's intercollegiate varsity sports:* basketball, field hockey, ice hockey, lacrosse, soccer, softball, tennis, volleyball.

SERVICES AND FACILITIES

Basic services: nonremedial tutoring, health service, health insurance. **Remedial assistance:** reading, math, writing, study skills. **Counseling services:** minority student, career, personal, academic, psychological, birth control, religious. **For learning-disabled students:** School does not offer a structured program with separate admission and additional fees. Total undergraduates in learning-disabled program or receiving services: 136. Services include: reading machines, tape recorders, oral tests, learning center, readers, extended time for tests, tutors, priority seating, proofreading services, substitution of courses, texts on tape, typist/scribe, exams on tape or computer, take home exams, other testing accommodations, other. **Library:** Number of titles: 250,209; number of current serial subscriptions: 36,923. **Information technology resources:** Students are not required to lease or own a computer. Number of campus computers available to all students: 400. School has a wireless network. Approximate number of users that can be accommodated: 3,500. Proportion of college-owned housing units wired for high-speed internet access: 100%. **Campus safety:** Security services offered: 24-hour foot-and-vehicle patrols, late-night transport/escort service, 24-hour emergency telephones, lighted pathways/sidewalks, controlled dormitory access (key, security card, etc).

TRANSFER AND INTERNATIONAL STUDENTS

Transfer students: May apply for admission for the following academic terms: Fall, Spring. Applicants do not need a minimum number of credits to apply. For fall 2009: Transfer applicants enrolled: 76. **International students:** Number of foreign undergraduates: 230 (13% of student body). Number of countries represented: 60. Minimum TOEFL score required: 550 (paper); 217 (computer). Average TOEFL score: 595 (paper).

Marist College

- **Address:** 3399 North Road, Poughkeepsie, NY 12601
- **Website:** http://www.marist.edu
- **Private**
- **Enrollment:** 4,542 full-time; 788 part-time

....

KEY STATS

✔ **U.S News College Ranking:** 10, Regional Universities (North)
✔ **SAT Score (25th/75th percentile):** 1060-1260
✔ **Tuition:** 2010-2011: $27,750

Selectivity: More selective	**Room/board:** $12,350
Acceptance rate: 36%	**Average debt:** $29,345
Student/faculty ratio: 15/1	**Proportion who borrowed:** 76%

UNDERGRADUATE STUDENT BODY STATS

2009-2010 enrollment: 4,542 full-time; 788 part-time. Men: 44%; women: 56%. **Ethnic makeup:** African American: 3%; Asian American: 2%; Hispanic: 6%; White: 87%.

ADMISSIONS FACTS AND FIGURES

Phone: (845) 575-3226. **Email:** admissions@marist.edu. **Website:** http://www.marist.edu. **Application deadlines for fall 2011:** Regular decision: February 15; decision sent by March 30. Early decision: Send application by: November 15; Decision sent by: December 15. Early action: Send application by: December 1; Decision sent by: January 30. Admission can be deferred. **Application fee:** $50. **To apply online, go to:** http://www.marist.edu/admissions/freshmen/apply.html. **Admissions requirements/recommendations:** High school units required (recommended): English: 4; Mathematics: 3 (4); Science: 3 (4); Foreign language: 2 (3); Social studies: 2; History: 1; Academic electives: 2; Total units: 17. Tests: The college uses SAT or ACT scores in admissions decisions. Either SAT or ACT required. For admission to the fall 2011 entering class, the school will accept: ACT with writing required. Campus visit: Recommended. Admissions interview: Neither required nor recommended. Off-campus interview: Not available. **Factors that count in admissions decisions:** *Academic:* Secondary school record: Very Important. Class rank: Important. Letters of recommendation: Important. Standardized test scores: Very Important. Essay: Important. *Nonacademic:* Interview: Not Considered. Extracurricular activities: Important. Talent/ability: Important. Character/personal qualities: Important. Alumni/ae relationship: Considered. Geographical residence: Important. State residency: Important. Religious affiliation/commitment: Not Considered. Minority status: Considered. Volunteer work: Important. Work experience: Important. **Other schools with the greatest overlap in applicants:** Boston College; Fairfield University; Providence College; SUNY–Geneseo; Villanova University. **Admissions statistics for the fall 2009 entering class:** Total applicants: 10,004. Total accepted: 3,601. Freshmen enrolled: 1,041; 53% were from out of state. Accepted through early-decision or early-action plans: 67%. Overall acceptance rate: 36%. Early-decision acceptance rate: 85%. Non-early acceptance rate: 26%. **Size of waiting list:** 3053 applicants; enrolled from waiting list: 111. **Credentials of fall 2009 freshmen:** 27% ranked in the top 10 percent of their high school class; 70% were in the top 25 percent; 89% were in the top half. (Proportion submitting class standing: 48%.) **Average high school grade point average:** 3.4. **First-year students who submitted SAT scores:** 90%. Scores (25/75 percentile): Critical Reading: 520-620, Math: 540-640, Combined: 1060-1260. **First-year students submitting ACT scores:** 32%. Scores (25/75 percentile): English: N/A, Math: N/A, Composite: 23-28.

ACADEMICS

Year founded: 1929. **Academic calendar:** Semester. **Degrees offered:** certificate, bachelor's, post-bachelor's certificate, master's. **Most popular majors:** 30% business, management, marketing, and related support services, 20% communication, journalism, and related programs, 13% education, 6% psychology, 5% biological and biomedical sciences. **Major fields of study:** area, ethnic, cultural, and gender studies; biological and biomedical sciences; business, management, marketing, and related support services; communication, journalism, and related programs; computer and information sciences and support services; education; English language and literature/letters; foreign languages, literatures, and linguistics; health professions and related clinical sciences; history; liberal arts and sciences studies, and humanities; mathematics and statistics; natural resources and conservation; philosophy and religious studies; physical sciences; psychology; public administration and social service professions; security and protective services; social sciences; visual and performing arts. **Areas of required coursework:** arts/fine arts, computer literacy, mathematics, English (including composition), philosophy, sciences (biological or physical), history, social science, other. **Pre-professional programs:** pre-law, pre-dentistry, pre-medicine, pre-veterinary science. **Special academic programs:** accelerated program, cooperative (work-study plan) program, cross-registration, distance learning, double major, dual enrollment, English as a Second Language (ESL), honors program, independent study, internships, liberal arts/career combination, study abroad, teacher certificate program, weekend college, other. **Teacher certification offered in:** early childhood, special education, secondary. **Cooperative education programs:** business, computer science. **Reserve Officers Training Corps (ROTC):** Army ROTC: Offered on campus. **Faculty and instruction (2009-2010):** Total instructional faculty: 219 full-time, 377 part-time (54% men; 46% women; 8% minorities). Full-time faculty with Ph.D. or other terminal degree: 77%. Student/faculty ratio: 15/1. Classes of fewer than 20 students: 50%; of 20 to 49 students: 50%; of 50 or more students: 0%. **Advanced Placement and International Baccalaureate**

credit: AP tests may be used for: Credit only. Scores accepted: 3, 4, 5. International Baccalaureate exams may be used for: Credit only. **Freshmen returning for sophomore year:** 90%. **Graduation rates:** Four-year: 76%; five-year: 83%; six-year: 80%. **Graduate study:** 30% of students pursue further study within one year. Fields in which graduates pursue further study: Master of Business Administration (MBA), 18%; law, 10%; medicine, 5%; dentistry, 3%; education, 15%; arts and sciences, 48%; veterinary medicine, 3%.

COSTS AND FINANCIAL AID

Financial aid office: (845) 575-3230. **Expenses (2010-2011):** Tuition and fees 2010-2011: $27,750; room/board: $12,350. Estimated books and supplies: $1,600; transportation: $1,140. **Financial aid:** Priority filing date for institution's financial aid form: February 15; deadline: May 1. In 2009-2010, 76% of undergraduates applied for financial aid. Of those, 61% were determined to have financial need; 16% had their need fully met. Average financial aid package (proportion receiving): $15,387 (61%). Average amount of gift aid, such as scholarships or grants (proportion receiving): $11,209 (57%). Average amount of self-help aid, such as work study or loans (proportion receiving): $5,934 (52%). Average need-based loan (excluding PLUS or other private loans): $5,931. Among students who received need-based aid, the average percentage of need met: 62%. Among students who received aid based on merit, the average award (and the proportion receiving): $7,101 (25%). The average athletic scholarship (and the proportion receiving): $11,099 (6%). Average amount of debt of borrowers graduating in 2009: $29,345. Proportion who borrowed: 76%.

CAMPUS LIFE AND EXTRACURRICULAR ACTIVITIES

Campus housing available (% using): coed dorms (55%), apartment for single students (44%), special housing for disabled students (1%), other housing options. Students who live in college-owned, operated, or affiliated housing: 74%. **Student employment:** During the 2009-2010 academic year, 31% of undergraduates worked on campus. Average per-year earnings: $1,200. **Clubs and organizations:** Number of student organizations: 84. Activities include: campus ministries, choral groups, concert band, dance, drama/theater, international student organization, jazz band, literary magazine, marching band, music ensembles, musical theater, pep band, radio station, student government, student newspaper, student film society, television station, yearbook. Number of fraternities: 3; sororities: 4. Proportion of men in fraternities: 1%; of women in sororities: 3%. Average proportion of students who stay on campus on weekends: 80%. **Sports program (2009-2010):** Member of NCAA I. *Men's intercollegiate varsity sports:* baseball, basketball, cross country, football, lacrosse, soccer, swimming, tennis, track and field (outdoor). *Women's intercollegiate varsity sports:* basketball, crew (heavyweight), cross country, lacrosse, crew (lightweight), soccer, softball, swimming, tennis, track and field (outdoor), volleyball, water polo.

SERVICES AND FACILITIES

Basic services: nonremedial tutoring, placement service, health service, health insurance. **Remedial assistance:** reading, math, writing, study skills. **Counseling services:** career, personal, academic, older student, psychological, birth control, religious. **For learning-disabled students:** School does not offer a structured program with separate admission and additional fees. Total undergraduates in learning-disabled program or receiving services: 106. Services include: reading machines, tape recorders, note-taking services, oral tests, readers, extended time for tests, tutors, priority registration, priority seating, proofreading services, substitution of courses, texts on tape, typist/scribe, exams on tape or computer, other testing accommodations, other. **Library:** Number of titles: 207,750; number of current serial subscriptions: 30,127. **Information technology resources:** Students are not required to lease or own a computer. Number of campus computers available to all students: 761. School has a wireless network. Approximate number of users that can be accommodated: 5,000. Proportion of college-owned housing units wired for high-speed internet access: 100%. **Campus safety:** Security services offered: 24-hour foot-and-vehicle patrols, late-night transport/escort service, 24-hour emergency telephones, lighted pathways/sidewalks, controlled dormitory access (key, security card, etc).

TRANSFER AND INTERNATIONAL STUDENTS

Transfer students: May apply for admission for the following academic terms: Fall, Spring. Applicants need a minimum number of credits to apply. For fall 2009: Transfer applications received: 809. Transfer applicants offered admission: 568. Transfer applicants enrolled: 312. **International students:** Number of foreign undergraduates: 18. Number of countries represented: 12. Minimum TOEFL score required: 550 (paper); 80 (computer). Average TOEFL score: 580 (paper).

Marymount Manhattan College

■ **Address:** 221 E. 71st Street, New York, NY 10021
■ **Website:** http://www.mmm.edu
■ **Private**
■ **Enrollment:** 1,751 full-time; 289 part-time

KEY STATS

✔ **U.S News College Ranking:** second tier, National Liberal Arts Colleges
✔ **SAT Score (25th/75th percentile):** 950-1160
✔ **Tuition:** 2010-2011: $23,536

Selectivity: Selective	**Room/board:** $13,416
Acceptance rate: 70%	**Average debt:** $15,988
Student/faculty ratio: 11/1	**Proportion who borrowed:** 84%

UNDERGRADUATE STUDENT BODY STATS

2009-2010 enrollment: 1,751 full-time; 289 part-time. Men: 24%; women: 76%. **Ethnic makeup:** African American: 12%; Asian American: 3%; Hispanic: 14%; White: 68%; International: 3%.

ADMISSIONS FACTS AND FIGURES

Phone: (212) 517-0430. **Email:** admissions@mmm.edu. **Website:** http://www.mmm.edu. **Application deadlines for fall 2011:** Regular decision: Rolling. Early decision: Not offered. Early action: Not offered. Admission can be deferred. **Application fee:** $60. **To apply online, go to:** http://www.mmm.edu/become/apply/new_apply.html. **Admissions requirements/recommendations:** High school units required (recommended): English: 4; Mathematics: 3; Science: 3 (2); Foreign language: (2); Social studies: 3; Academic electives: 4; Total units: 17 (4). Tests: The college uses SAT or ACT scores in admissions decisions. Either SAT or ACT required. For admission to the fall 2011 entering class, the school will accept: ACT with or without writing accepted. Campus visit: Recommended. Admissions interview: Recommended. Off-campus interview: May be arranged. **Factors that count in admissions decisions:** *Academic:* Secondary school record: Very Important. Class rank: Considered. Letters of recommendation: Important. Standardized test scores: Very Important. Essay: Important. *Nonacademic:* Interview: Considered. Extracurricular activities: Important. Talent/ability: Important. Character/personal qualities: Important. Alumni/ae relationship: Not Considered. Geographical residence: Not Considered. State residency: Not Considered. Religious affiliation/commitment: Not Considered. Minority status: Not Considered. Volunteer work: Considered. Work experience: Considered. **Other schools with the greatest overlap in applicants:** Fordham University; Hofstra University; New York University; Pace University; Purchase College–SUNY. **Admissions statistics for the fall 2009 entering class:** Total applicants: 3,447. Total accepted: 2,419. Freshmen enrolled: 516; 67% were from out of state. Overall acceptance rate: 70%. **Size of waiting list:** 99 applicants; enrolled from waiting list: 64. **Average high school grade point average:** 3.2. **First-year students who submitted SAT scores:** 83%. Scores (25/75 percentile): Critical Reading: 490-600, Math: 460-560, Combined: 950-1160. **First-year students submitting ACT scores:** 11%. Scores (25/75 percentile): English: N/A, Math: N/A, Composite: 22-26.

ACADEMICS

Year founded: 1936. **Academic calendar:** Semester. **Degrees offered:** certificate, associate, bachelor's. **Most popular majors:** 37% visual and performing arts, 27% communication, journalism, and related programs, 12% social sciences, 7% psychology, 5% health professions and related clinical sciences. **Major fields of study:** agriculture, agriculture operations, and related sciences; biological and biomedical sciences; business, management, marketing, and related support services; communication, journalism, and related programs; English language and literature/letters; health professions and related clinical sciences; history; liberal arts and sciences studies, and humanities; philosophy and religious studies; psychology; social sciences; visual and performing arts. **Areas of required coursework:** arts/fine arts, humanities, mathematics, English (including composition), sciences (biological or physical), social science, other. **Pre-professional programs:** pre-law, pre-medicine. **Special academic programs (% participation):** accelerated program (11%), cross-registration (2%), distance learning (12%), double major (16%), dual enrollment (5%), English as a Second Language (ESL) (5%), exchange student program (domestic) (1%), honors program (13%), independent study (22%), internships (27%), study abroad (1%), teacher certificate program (12%). **Teacher certification offered in:** early childhood, special education, elementary, middle/junior high, secondary, bilingual/bicultural. **Faculty and instruction (2009-2010):** Total instructional faculty:

96 full-time, 214 part-time (51% men; 49% women; 14% minorities). Full-time faculty with Ph.D. or other terminal degree: 91%. Student/faculty ratio: 11/1. Classes of fewer than 20 students: 69%; of 20 to 49 students: 31%. **Advanced Placement and International Baccalaureate credit:** AP tests may be used for: Credit only. Scores accepted: 3, 4, 5. International Baccalaureate exams may be used for: Credit only. **Freshmen returning for sophomore year:** 63%. **Graduation rates:** Four-year: 39%; five-year: 48%; six-year: 49%. **Graduate study:** 31% of students pursue further study immediately upon graduation; 40% within one year; 46% within five years. Fields in which graduates pursue further study: Master of Business Administration (MBA), 22%; law, 16%; medicine, 5%; dentistry, 1%; education, 19%; arts and sciences, 37%.

COSTS AND FINANCIAL AID

Financial aid office: (212) 517-0480. **Expenses (2010-2011):** Tuition and fees 2010-2011: $23,536; room/board: $13,416. Estimated books and supplies: $1,000; transportation: $1,000; personal expenses: $2,000. **Financial aid:** Priority filing date for institution's financial aid form: March 15. In 2009-2010, 75% of undergraduates applied for financial aid. Of those, 62% were determined to have financial need; 3% had their need fully met. Average financial aid package (proportion receiving): $13,251 (62%). Average amount of gift aid, such as scholarships or grants (proportion receiving): $9,454 (62%). Average amount of self-help aid, such as work study or loans (proportion receiving): $4,576 (56%). Average need-based loan (excluding PLUS or other private loans): $4,236. Among students who received need-based aid, the average percentage of need met: 47%. Among students who received aid based on merit, the average award (and the proportion receiving): $5,119 (17%). Average amount of debt of borrowers graduating in 2009: $15,988. Proportion who borrowed: 84%.

CAMPUS LIFE AND EXTRACURRICULAR ACTIVITIES

Campus housing available (% using): coed dorms (100%). Students who live in college-owned, operated, or affiliated housing: 36%. **Student employment:** During the 2009-2010 academic year, 17% of undergraduates worked on campus. Average per-year earnings: $1,500. **Clubs and organizations:** Number of student organizations: 43. Activities include: choral groups, dance, drama/theater, international student organization, literary magazine, musical theater, radio station, student government, student newspaper, yearbook. Number of fraternities: 0; sororities: 0. Average proportion of students who stay on campus on weekends: 25%.

SERVICES AND FACILITIES

Basic services: nonremedial tutoring, placement service, health service, health insurance. **Remedial assistance:** reading, math, writing, study skills. **Counseling services:** minority student, career, personal, academic, older student, psychological. **For learning-disabled students:** School does not offer a structured program with separate admission and additional fees. Total undergraduates in learning-disabled program or receiving services: 38. Services include: remedial math, remedial English, remedial reading, tape recorders, diagnostic testing service, extended time for tests, tutors. **Library:** Number of titles: 70,000; number of current serial subscriptions: 21,000. **Information technology resources:** Students are not required to lease or own a computer. Number of campus computers available to all students: 205. School has a wireless network. Approximate number of users that can be accommodated: 300. Proportion of college-owned housing units wired for high-speed internet access: 85%. **Campus safety:** Security services offered: controlled dormitory access (key, security card, etc).

TRANSFER AND INTERNATIONAL STUDENTS

Transfer students: May apply for admission for the following academic terms: Fall, Winter, Spring, Summer. Applicants need a minimum number of credits to apply. For fall 2009: Transfer applications received: 587. Transfer applicants offered admission: 368. Transfer applicants enrolled: 151. **International students:** Number of foreign undergraduates: 57 (3% of student body). Number of countries represented: 37. Minimum TOEFL score required: 550 (paper); 213 (computer). Average TOEFL score: 573 (paper).

Medaille College

- **Address:** 18 Agassiz Circle, Buffalo, NY 14214
- **Website:** http://www.medaille.edu
- **Private**
- **Enrollment:** 1,711 full-time; 100 part-time

KEY STATS

✔ **U.S News College Ranking:** second tier, Regional Universities (North)
✔ **SAT Score (25th/75th percentile):** 820-1020
✔ **Tuition:** 2010-2011: $19,590

Selectivity: Less selective	**Room/board:** $9,288
Acceptance rate: 30%	**Average debt:** $21,000
Student/faculty ratio: 17/1	**Proportion who borrowed:** 95%

UNDERGRADUATE STUDENT BODY STATS

2009-2010 enrollment: 1,711 full-time; 100 part-time. Men: 36%; women: 64%. **Ethnic makeup:** African American: 11%; Hispanic: 1%; White: 87%.

ADMISSIONS FACTS AND FIGURES

Phone: (716) 880-2200. **Email:** admissionsug@medaille.edu. **Website:** http://www.medaille.edu. **Application deadlines for fall 2011:** Regular decision: Rolling; decision sent by September 1. Early decision: Not offered. Early action: Not offered. Admission can be deferred. **Application fee:** $35. **Admissions requirements/recommendations:** High school units required (recommended): English: 4 (4); Mathematics: 2 (3); Science: 2 (3); Foreign language: (2); Social studies: 4 (4); History: (2); Total units: 12 (20). Tests: The college uses SAT or ACT scores in admissions decisions. Either SAT or ACT required. For admission to the fall 2011 entering class, the school will accept: ACT with or without writing accepted. Campus visit: Recommended. Admissions interview: Recommended. Off-campus interview: May be arranged. **Factors that count in admissions decisions:** *Academic:* Secondary school record: Very Important. Class rank: Considered. Letters of recommendation: Important. Standardized test scores: Very Important. Essay: Important. *Nonacademic:* Interview: Very Important. Extracurricular activities: Important. Talent/ability: Considered. Character/personal qualities: Considered. Alumni/ae relationship: Considered. Geographical residence: Not Considered. State residency: Not Considered. Religious affiliation/ commitment: Not Considered. Minority status: Not Considered. Volunteer work: Considered. Work experience: Considered. **Other schools with the greatest overlap in applicants:** Buffalo State College–SUNY; Canisius College; Daemen College; Hilbert College; University at Buffalo–SUNY. **Admissions statistics for the fall 2009 entering class:** Total applicants: 1,341. Total accepted: 402. Freshmen enrolled: 402; 3% were from out of state. Overall acceptance rate: 30%. **First-year students who submitted SAT scores:** 92%. Scores (25/75 percentile): Critical Reading: 400-500, Math: 420-520, Combined: 820-1020. **First-year students submitting ACT scores:** 24%. Scores (25/75 percentile): English: N/A, Math: N/A, Composite: 18-22.

ACADEMICS

Year founded: 1937. **Academic calendar:** Semester. **Degrees offered:** certificate, associate, bachelor's, post-bachelor's certificate, master's. **Most popular majors:** 31% purchasing, procurement/acquisitions, and contracts management, 10% sport and fitness administration/management, 7% elementary education and teaching, 6% veterinary/animal health technology/technician and veterinary assistant, 5% biology/biological sciences. **Major fields of study:** biological and biomedical sciences; business, management, marketing, and related support services; communication, journalism, and related programs; computer and information sciences and support services; education; English language and literature/letters; health professions and related clinical sciences; liberal arts and sciences studies, and humanities; parks, recreation, leisure, and fitness studies; psychology; public administration and social service professions; security and protective services; visual and performing arts. **Areas of required coursework:** arts/fine arts, humanities, computer literacy, mathematics, English (including composition), sciences (biological or physical), history, social science. **Pre-professional programs:** pre-law, pre-medicine, pre-veterinary science. **Special academic programs (% participation):** accelerated program (40%), double major (0%), dual enrollment (0%), honors program (5%), independent study (1%), internships (70%), teacher certificate program (12%), weekend college (1%). **Teacher certification offered in:** special education, elementary, middle/junior high, secondary. **Reserve Officers Training Corps (ROTC):** Army ROTC: Offered at cooperating institution (Canisius College). **Faculty and instruction (2009-2010):** Total instructional faculty: 84 full-time, 238 part-time (51%

men; 49% women; 19% minorities). Full-time faculty with Ph.D. or other terminal degree: 79%. Student/faculty ratio: 17/1. Classes of fewer than 20 students: 40%; of 20 to 49 students: 59%; of 50 or more students: 1%. **Advanced Placement and International Baccalaureate credit:** AP tests may be used for: Credit only. Scores accepted: 3, 4, 5. International Baccalaureate exams may be used for: Credit only. **Freshmen returning for sophomore year:** 70%. **Graduation rates:** Four-year: 50%; five-year: 56%; six-year: 42%. **Graduate study:** 13% of students pursue further study immediately upon graduation; 18% within one year; 25% within five years. Fields in which graduates pursue further study: Master of Business Administration (MBA), 37%; law, 1%; medicine, 1%; education, 45%; arts and sciences, 15%; veterinary medicine, 1%.

COSTS AND FINANCIAL AID

Financial aid office: (716) 880-2256. **Expenses (2010-2011):** Tuition and fees 2010-2011: $19,590; room/board: $9,288. Estimated books and supplies: $1,100; transportation: $2,000; personal expenses: $1,100. **Financial aid:** Priority filing date for institution's financial aid form: April 1. In 2009-2010, 100% of undergraduates applied for financial aid. Of those, 96% were determined to have financial need; 2% had their need fully met. Average financial aid package (proportion receiving): $24,000 (96%). Average amount of gift aid, such as scholarships or grants (proportion receiving): $8,030 (96%). Average amount of self-help aid, such as work study or loans (proportion receiving): $7,000 (96%). Average need-based loan (excluding PLUS or other private loans): $7,000. Among students who received need-based aid, the average percentage of need met: 55%. Among students who received aid based on merit, the average award (and the proportion receiving): $9,000 (1%). Average amount of debt of borrowers graduating in 2009: $21,000. Proportion who borrowed: 95%.

CAMPUS LIFE AND EXTRACURRICULAR ACTIVITIES

Campus housing available (% using): coed dorms (100%). Students who live in college-owned, operated, or affiliated housing: 24%. **Student employment:** During the 2009-2010 academic year, 2% of undergraduates worked on campus. Average per-year earnings: $1,500. **Clubs and organizations:** Number of student organizations: 24. Activities include: drama/theater, literary magazine, musical theater, radio station, student government, student newspaper, television station, yearbook. Number of fraternities: 0; sororities: 0. Average proportion of students who stay on campus on weekends: 25%. **Sports program (2009-2010):** Member of NCAA III. *Men's intercollegiate varsity sports:* baseball, basketball, cross country, golf, lacrosse, soccer, volleyball. *Women's intercollegiate varsity sports:* basketball, bowling, cross country, golf, lacrosse, soccer, softball, volleyball.

SERVICES AND FACILITIES

Basic services: nonremedial tutoring, placement service, health service. **Remedial assistance:** reading, math, writing, study skills. **Counseling services:** career, personal, academic. **For learning-disabled students:** School does not offer a structured program with separate admission and additional fees. Total undergraduates in learning-disabled program or receiving services: 62. Services include: remedial math, remedial English, reading machines, remedial reading, tape recorders, videotaped classes, untimed tests, note-taking services, learning center, readers, extended time for tests, tutors, texts on tape, other. **Library:** Number of titles: 100,313; number of current serial subscriptions: 260. **Information technology resources:** Students are not required to lease or own a computer. Number of campus computers available to all students: 202. School has a wireless network. Approximate number of users that can be accommodated: 600. Proportion of college-owned housing units wired for high-speed internet access: 100%. **Campus safety:** Security services offered: 24-hour foot-and-vehicle patrols, late-night transport/escort service, 24-hour emergency telephones, lighted pathways/sidewalks, controlled dormitory access (key, security card, etc).

TRANSFER AND INTERNATIONAL STUDENTS

Transfer students: May apply for admission for the following academic terms: Fall, Spring, Summer. Applicants do not need a minimum number of credits to apply. For fall 2009: Transfer applications received: 434. Transfer applicants offered admission: 131. Transfer applicants enrolled: 115. **International students:** Number of foreign undergraduates: 0. Number of countries represented: 1. Minimum TOEFL score required: 550 (paper); 213 (computer). Average TOEFL score: 560 (paper).

Mercy College

- **Address:** 555 Broadway, Dobbs Ferry, NY 10522
- **Website:** http://www.mercy.edu
- **Private**
- **Enrollment:** 4,103 full-time; 1,816 part-time

KEY STATS

✔ **U.S News College Ranking:** second tier, Regional Universities (North)
✔ **SAT or ACT Score (25th/75th percentile):** N/A
✔ **Tuition:** 2009-2010: $16,490

Selectivity: Less selective	**Room/board:** $10,812
Acceptance rate: 59%	**Average debt:** N/A
Student/faculty ratio: 17/1	**Proportion who borrowed:** N/A

UNDERGRADUATE STUDENT BODY STATS

2009-2010 enrollment: 4,103 full-time; 1,816 part-time. Men: 33%; women: 67%. **Ethnic makeup:** African American: 27%; Asian American: 3%; Hispanic: 30%; White: 39%; International: 1%.

ADMISSIONS FACTS AND FIGURES

Phone: (877) 637-2946. **Email:** admissions@mercy.edu. **Website:** http://www.mercy.edu. **Application deadlines for fall 2011:** Regular decision: Rolling; decision sent by September 5. Early decision: Not offered. Early action: Send application by: December 1; Decision sent by: January 2. Admission can be deferred. **Application fee:** $40. **To apply online, go to:** http://www.mercy.edu/apply. **Admissions requirements/recommendations:** High school units required (recommended): English: 4 (4); Mathematics: 4 (4); Science: 3 (3); Foreign language: 3 (2); Social studies: 2 (2); History: 2 (2); Academic electives: 3; Total units: 21 (17). Tests: The college uses SAT or ACT scores in admissions decisions. Neither SAT nor ACT required. For admission to the fall 2011 entering class, the school will accept: ACT with writing recommended. Campus visit: Recommended. Admissions interview: Recommended. Off-campus interview: Not available. **Factors that count in admissions decisions:** *Academic:* Secondary school record: Important. Class rank: Important. Letters of recommendation: Important. Standardized test scores: Important. Essay: Important. *Nonacademic:* Interview: Important. Extracurricular activities: Very Important. Talent/ability: Very Important. Character/personal qualities: Very Important. Alumni/ae relationship: Considered. Geographical residence: Not Considered. State residency: Not Considered. Religious affiliation/commitment: Not Considered. Minority status: Not Considered. Volunteer work: Considered. Work experience: Considered. **Other schools with the greatest overlap in applicants:** CUNY–Lehman College; Iona College; Pace University. **Admissions statistics for the fall 2009 entering class:** Total applicants: 4,355. Total accepted: 2,557. Freshmen enrolled: 926; 7% were from out of state. Overall acceptance rate: 59%. Non-early acceptance rate: 59%.

ACADEMICS

Year founded: 1950. **Academic calendar:** Semester. **Degrees offered:** certificate, associate, transfer-associate, bachelor's, post-bachelor's certificate, master's, post-master's certificate. **Most popular majors:** 32% social sciences, 23% business administration and management, 16% health professions and related clinical sciences, 10% cognitive psychology and psycholinguistics, 4% security and protective services. **Major fields of study:** biological and biomedical sciences; business, management, marketing, and related support services; foreign languages, literatures, and linguistics; history; legal professions and studies; mathematics and statistics; multi/interdisciplinary studies; philosophy and religious studies; psychology; public administration and social service professions; security and protective services. **Areas of required coursework:** arts/fine arts, humanities, computer literacy, mathematics, English (including composition), philosophy, foreign languages, sciences (biological or physical), history, social science. **Pre-professional programs:** pre-law, pre-medicine, pre-veterinary science, pre-optometry, other. **Special academic programs:** accelerated program, cooperative (work-study plan) program, distance learning, double major, dual enrollment, honors program, internships, teacher certificate program. **Teacher certification offered in:** early childhood, special education, elementary, middle/junior high, secondary, bilingual/bicultural. **Cooperative education programs:** art, business, computer science, education, health professions, humanities, natural science, social/behavioral science, technologies, vocational arts. **Reserve Officers Training Corps (ROTC):** Army ROTC: Offered at cooperating institution (Fordham University); Air Force ROTC: Offered at cooperating institution (Manhattan College). **Faculty and instruction (2009-2010):** Total instructional faculty: 224 full-time, 597 part-time (50% men; 50% women; 21% minorities). Full-time faculty with Ph.D. or other terminal degree: 68%. Student/faculty ratio: 17/1. Classes of fewer than 20 students: 70%; of 20 to 49 students: 30%; of 50 or more students: 0%. **Advanced Placement and International Baccalaureate credit:** AP tests may be used for: Placement only. Scores accepted: 3. International Baccalaureate exams may be used for: Credit only. **Freshmen returning for sophomore year:** 58%. **Graduation rates:** Four-year: 14%; five-year: 22%; six-year: 27%.

COSTS AND FINANCIAL AID
Financial aid office: (914) 378-3421. **Expenses (2009-2010):** Tuition and fees 2009-2010: $16,490; room/board: $10,812. Estimated books and supplies: $1,320; transportation: $1,054; personal expenses: $1,580. **Financial aid:** Priority filing date for institution's financial aid form: February 15. In 2009-2010, 91% of undergraduates applied for financial aid. Of those, 84% were determined to have financial need; 2% had their need fully met. Average financial aid package (proportion receiving): $12,855 (82%). Average amount of gift aid, such as scholarships or grants (proportion receiving): $8,544 (74%). Average amount of self-help aid, such as work study or loans (proportion receiving): $5,046 (70%). Average need-based loan (excluding PLUS or other private loans): $4,113. Among students who received need-based aid, the average percentage of need met: 56%. Among students who received aid based on merit, the average award (and the proportion receiving): $3,827 (2%). The average athletic scholarship (and the proportion receiving): $6,001 (3%).

CAMPUS LIFE AND EXTRACURRICULAR ACTIVITIES
Campus housing available (% using): coed dorms (100%). Students who live in college-owned, operated, or affiliated housing: 3%. **Student employment:** During the 2009-2010 academic year, 1% of undergraduates worked on campus. Average per-year earnings: $5,000. **Clubs and organizations:** Number of student organizations: 20. Activities include: campus ministries, dance, international student organization, model UN, student government, student newspaper. Number of fraternities: 0; sororities: 0. Average proportion of students who stay on campus on weekends: 5%. **Sports program (2009-2010):** Member of NCAA II. *Men's intercollegiate varsity sports:* baseball, basketball, cross country, lacrosse, soccer, tennis, track and field (indoor). *Women's intercollegiate varsity sports:* basketball, cross country, lacrosse, soccer, softball, track and field (indoor), volleyball.

SERVICES AND FACILITIES
Basic services: nonremedial tutoring, placement service, day care, health service. **Remedial assistance:** reading, math, writing, study skills. **Counseling services:** career, personal, veteran student, psychological. **For learning-disabled students:** School does not offer a structured program with separate admission and additional fees. Total undergraduates in learning-disabled program or receiving services: 18. Services include: tape recorders, video-taped classes, untimed tests, note-taking services, oral tests, learning center, readers, extended time for tests, tutors, priority registration, texts on tape, typist/scribe, exams on tape or computer, other testing accommodations. **Library:** Number of titles: 304,396; number of current serial subscriptions: 642. **Information technology resources:** Students are not required to lease or own a computer. Number of campus computers available to all students: 680. School has a wireless network. Approximate number of users that can be accommodated: 381. Proportion of college-owned housing units wired for high-speed internet access: 100%. **Campus safety:** Security services offered: 24-hour foot-and-vehicle patrols, 24-hour emergency telephones, lighted pathways/sidewalks, controlled dormitory access (key, security card, etc).

TRANSFER AND INTERNATIONAL STUDENTS
Transfer students: May apply for admission for the following academic terms: Fall, Spring, Summer. Applicants need a minimum number of credits to apply. For fall 2009: Transfer applications received: 2,148. Transfer applicants offered admission: 1,473. Transfer applicants enrolled: 899. **International students:** Number of foreign undergraduates: 49 (1% of student body). Number of countries represented: 33. Minimum TOEFL score required: 550 (paper); 213 (computer).

Metropolitan College of New York

- **Address:** 75 Varick Street, New York, NY 10013
- **Website:** http://www.metropolitan.edu/
- **Private**
- **Enrollment:** 631 full-time; 45 part-time

KEY STATS
✔ **U.S News College Ranking:** second tier, Regional Universities (North)
✔ **SAT or ACT Score (25th/75th percentile):** N/A
✔ **Tuition:** 2009-2010: $16,750

Selectivity: Less selective	**Room/board:** $9,600
Acceptance rate: 51%	**Average debt:** N/A
Student/faculty ratio: 13/1	**Proportion who borrowed:** N/A

UNDERGRADUATE STUDENT BODY STATS
2009-2010 enrollment: 631 full-time; 45 part-time. Men: 29%; women: 71%. **Ethnic makeup:** African American: 63%; American-Indian: 1%; Asian American: 1%; Hispanic: 19%; White: 13%; International: 3%.

ADMISSIONS FACTS AND FIGURES
Website: http://www.metropolitan.edu/. **Application deadlines for fall 2011:** Regular decision: Rolling. Early decision: Not offered. Early action: Not offered. Admission can be deferred. **Application fee:** $30. **Admissions requirements/recommendations:** High school units required (recommended): English: (4); Mathematics: (4); Science: (4); Foreign language: (2); Social studies: (3); History: (2). Tests: Neither SAT nor ACT required. Campus visit: Recommended. Admissions interview: Recommended. **Factors that count in admissions decisions:** *Academic:* Secondary school record: Important. Letters of recommendation: Important. Standardized test scores: Important. Essay: Considered. *Nonacademic:* Interview: Important. Volunteer work: Considered. Work experience: Important. **Other schools with the greatest overlap in applicants:** CUNY–Baruch College; CUNY–Hunter College; DeVry Institute of Technology–New York; Mercy College. **Admissions statistics for the fall 2009 entering class:** Total applicants: 650. Total accepted: 330. Freshmen enrolled: 126; Overall acceptance rate: 51%.

ACADEMICS
Academic calendar: Semester. **Most popular majors:** 67% community organization and advocacy, 25% business/commerce. **Areas of required coursework:** arts/fine arts, humanities, computer literacy, mathematics, English (including composition), philosophy, sciences (biological or physical), history. **Pre-professional programs:** pre-law. **Special academic programs (% participation):** accelerated program (95%), cooperative (work-study plan) program (90%), distance learning (2%), honors program, internships (65%), study abroad (10%), teacher certificate program (9%), weekend college (35%). **Teacher certification offered in:** early childhood. **Faculty and instruction (2009-2010):** Total instructional faculty: 26 full-time, 157 part-time. Full-time faculty with Ph.D. or other terminal degree: 85%. Student/faculty ratio: 13/1. **Freshmen returning for sophomore year:** 46%. **Graduation rates:** Six-year: 43%. **Graduate study:** 35% of students pursue further study within five years.

COSTS AND FINANCIAL AID
Expenses (2009-2010): Tuition and fees 2009-2010: $16,750; room/board: $9,600. Estimated books and supplies: $1,000.

CAMPUS LIFE AND EXTRACURRICULAR ACTIVITIES
Activities include: international student organization, student government, student newspaper.

SERVICES AND FACILITIES
Basic services: nonremedial tutoring, placement service. **Remedial assistance:** reading, math, writing. **Counseling services:** minority student, career, veteran student, academic, older student. **For learning-disabled students:** School does not offer a structured program with separate admission and additional fees. Total undergraduates in learning-disabled program or receiving services: 18. Services include: tape recorders, untimed tests, learning center, extended time for tests, other testing accommodations. **Information technology resources:** Students are not required to lease or own a computer. Number of campus computers available to all students: 150. School has a wireless network.

TRANSFER AND INTERNATIONAL STUDENTS

Transfer students: May apply for admission for the following academic terms: Fall, Spring, Summer. Applicants do not need a minimum number of credits to apply. **International students:** Number of foreign undergraduates: 19 (3% of student body).

Molloy College

- ■ **Address:** 1000 Hempstead Avenue, PO Box 5002, Rockville Centre, NY 11571
- ■ **Website:** http://www.molloy.edu
- ■ **Private; Religious affiliation:** Roman Catholic
- ■ **Enrollment:** 2,308 full-time; 729 part-time

KEY STATS

✔ **U.S News College Ranking:** 67, Regional Universities (North)
✔ **SAT Score (25th/75th percentile):** 940-1130
✔ **Tuition:** 2009-2010: $20,960

Selectivity: Selective
Room/board: N/A
Acceptance rate: 59%
Average debt: $29,823
Student/faculty ratio: 10/1
Proportion who borrowed: 77%

UNDERGRADUATE STUDENT BODY STATS

2009-2010 enrollment: 2,308 full-time; 729 part-time. Men: 22%; women: 78%. **Ethnic makeup:** African American: 15%; Asian American: 7%; Hispanic: 11%; White: 65%; International: 1%. **Religious preference:** Roman Catholic: 64%; Protestant: 7%; Jewish: 4%; Muslim: 1%; No preference: 8%; Unknown: 16%.

ADMISSIONS FACTS AND FIGURES

Phone: (888) 466-5569. **Email:** admissions@molloy.edu. **Website:** http://www.molloy.edu. **Application deadlines for fall 2011:** Regular decision: Rolling. Early decision: Not offered. Early action: Send application by: November 15; Decision sent by: November 30. Admission can be deferred. **Application fee:** $30. **To apply online, go to:** https://www.molloy.edu/admissions/apply_online.asp. **Admissions requirements/recommendations:** High school units required (recommended): English: 4 (4); Mathematics: 3 (4); Science: 3 (4); Foreign language: 3 (3); Social studies: 4 (4); Academic electives: 4 (2). Tests: The college uses SAT or ACT scores in admissions decisions. Either SAT or ACT required. For admission to the fall 2011 entering class, the school will accept: ACT with writing required. Campus visit: Recommended. Admissions interview: Recommended. Off-campus interview: Not available. **Factors that count in admissions decisions:** *Academic:* Secondary school record: Very Important. Class rank: Considered. Letters of recommendation: Considered. Standardized test scores: Very Important. Essay: Considered. *Nonacademic:* Interview: Considered. Extracurricular activities: Considered. Talent/ability: Considered. Character/personal qualities: Not Considered. Alumni/ae relationship: Not Considered. Geographical residence: Not Considered. State residency: Not Considered. Religious affiliation/commitment: Not Considered. Minority status: Not Considered. Volunteer work: Considered. Work experience: Considered. **Other schools with the greatest overlap in applicants:** Adelphi University; Long Island University–C.W. Post Campus; St. John's University. **Admissions statistics for the fall 2009 entering class:** Total applicants: 1,803. Total accepted: 1,064. Freshmen enrolled: 420; 0% were from out of state. Overall acceptance rate: 59%. Non-early acceptance rate: 59%. **Credentials of fall 2009 freshmen:** 30% ranked in the top 10 percent of their high school class; 50% were in the top 25 percent; 86% were in the top half. (Proportion submitting class standing: 54%.) **Average high school grade point average:** 2.9. **First-year students who submitted SAT scores:** 95%. Scores (25/75 percentile): Critical Reading: 460-560, Math: 480-570, Combined: 940-1130. **First-year students submitting ACT scores:** 20%. Scores (25/75 percentile): English: N/A, Math: N/A, Composite: 22-27.

ACADEMICS

Year founded: 1955. **Academic calendar:** 4-1-4. **Degrees offered:** associate, bachelor's, master's, post-master's certificate. **Most popular majors:** 48% health professions and related clinical sciences, 14% education, 9% business, management, marketing, and related support services, 4% psychology, 4% security and protective services. **Major fields of study:** biological and biomedical sciences; business, management, marketing, and related support services; communication, journalism, and related programs; computer and information sciences and support services; education; English language and literature/letters; foreign languages, literatures, and linguistics; health professions and related clinical sciences; history; liberal arts and sciences studies, and humanities; mathematics and statistics; multi/interdisciplinary studies; philosophy and religious studies; psychology; public administration and social service professions; security and protective services; social sciences; visual and performing arts. **Areas of required coursework:** arts/fine arts, humanities, mathematics, English (including composition), philosophy, foreign languages, sciences (biological or physical), history, social science, other. **Pre-professional programs:** pre-law, pre-dentistry, pre-medicine, pre-veterinary science, pre-optometry. **Special academic programs:** cross-registration, double major, English as a Second Language (ESL), honors program, independent study, internships, liberal arts/career combination, student-designed major, study abroad, teacher certificate program. **Teacher certification offered in:** special education, elementary, middle/junior high, secondary. **Reserve Officers Training Corps (ROTC):** Army ROTC: Offered at cooperating institution (Hofstra University); Navy ROTC: Offered at cooperating institution. **Faculty and instruction (2009-2010):** Total instructional faculty: 169 full-time, 350 part-time (33% men; 67% women; 15% minorities). Full-time faculty with Ph.D. or other terminal degree: 67%. Student/faculty ratio: 10/1. Classes of fewer than 20 students: 64%; of 20 to 49 students: 36%; of 50 or more students: 0%. **Advanced Placement and International Baccalaureate credit:** AP tests may be used for: Credit only. Scores accepted: 3. International Baccalaureate exams may be used for: Credit only. **Freshmen returning for sophomore year:** 83%. **Graduation rates:** Four-year: 36%; five-year: 60%; six-year: 64%.

COSTS AND FINANCIAL AID

Financial aid office: (516) 256-2217. **Expenses (2009-2010):** Tuition and fees 2009-2010: $20,960. **Financial aid:** Priority filing date for institution's financial aid form: April 15; deadline: May 1. In 2009-2010, 100% of undergraduates applied for financial aid. Of those, 86% were determined to have financial need; 11% had their need fully met. Average financial aid package (proportion receiving): $12,545 (86%). Average amount of gift aid, such as scholarships or grants (proportion receiving): $8,590 (77%). Average amount of self-help aid, such as work study or loans (proportion receiving): $5,848 (72%). Average need-based loan (excluding PLUS or other private loans): $5,598. Among students who received need-based aid, the average percentage of need met: 53%. Among students who received aid based on merit, the average award (and the proportion receiving): $6,352 (7%). The average athletic scholarship (and the proportion receiving): $7,186 (3%). Average amount of debt of borrowers graduating in 2009: $29,823. Proportion who borrowed: 77%.

CAMPUS LIFE AND EXTRACURRICULAR ACTIVITIES

Students who live in college-owned, operated, or affiliated housing: 0%. **Clubs and organizations:** Number of student organizations: 24. Activities include: campus ministries, choral groups, dance, drama/theater, jazz band, literary magazine, music ensembles, student government, student newspaper, yearbook. Number of fraternities: 0; sororities: 0. **Sports program (2009-2010):** Member of NCAA II. *Men's intercollegiate varsity sports:* baseball, basketball, cross country, lacrosse, soccer, track and field (indoor), track and field (outdoor). *Women's intercollegiate varsity sports:* basketball, cross country, equestrian, lacrosse, soccer, softball, tennis, track and field (indoor), track and field (outdoor), volleyball.

SERVICES AND FACILITIES

Basic services: nonremedial tutoring, women's center, placement service, health service, health insurance. **Remedial assistance:** reading, math, writing, study skills. **Counseling services:** minority student, career, older student. **For learning-disabled students:** School does not offer a structured program with separate admission and additional fees. Total undergraduates in learning-disabled program or receiving services: 83. Services include: remedial math, remedial English, reading machines, remedial reading, tape recorders, note-taking services, readers, extended time for tests, tutors, priority registration, priority seating, substitution of courses, texts on tape, other testing accommodations, waiver of foreign language degree requirement, other. **Library:** Number of titles: 115,625; number of current serial subscriptions: 690. **Information technology resources:** Students are not required to lease or own a computer. Number of campus computers available to all students: 361. School has a wireless network. Approximate number of users that can be accommodated: 875. **Campus safety:** Security services offered: 24-hour foot-and-vehicle patrols, late-night transport/escort service, 24-hour emergency telephones, lighted pathways/sidewalks.

TRANSFER AND INTERNATIONAL STUDENTS

Transfer students: May apply for admission for the following academic terms: Fall, Spring. Applicants do not need a minimum number of credits to apply. For fall 2009: Transfer applications received: 1,525. Transfer applicants offered admission: 757. Transfer applicants enrolled: 458. **International students:** Number of foreign undergraduates: 22 (1% of student body). Number of countries represented: 14. Minimum TOEFL score required: 500 (paper); 175 (computer).

Mount St. Mary College

- **Address:** 330 Powell Avenue, Newburgh, NY 12550
- **Website:** http://www.msmc.edu
- **Private; Religious affiliation:** Roman Catholic
- **Enrollment:** 1,867 full-time; 378 part-time

KEY STATS

✔ **U.S News College Ranking:** 126, Regional Universities (North)
✔ **SAT Score (25th/75th percentile):** 910-1100
✔ **Tuition:** 2010-2011: $23,300

Selectivity: Selective	**Room/board:** $11,900
Acceptance rate: 72%	**Average debt:** $32,729
Student/faculty ratio: 17/1	**Proportion who borrowed:** 94%

UNDERGRADUATE STUDENT BODY STATS

2009-2010 enrollment: 1,867 full-time; 378 part-time. Men: 25%; women: 75%. **Ethnic makeup:** African American: 7%; Asian American: 2%; Hispanic: 10%; White: 79%. **Religious preference:** Protestant: 1%; Jewish: 1%; No preference: 10%; Unknown: 11%; Roman Catholic: 60%; Christian: 9%; Other: 8%.

ADMISSIONS FACTS AND FIGURES

Phone: (845) 569-3248. **Email:** admissions@msmc.edu. **Website:** http://www.msmc.edu. **Application deadlines for fall 2011:** Regular decision: August 15. Early decision: Not offered. Early action: Not offered. Admission can be deferred. **Application fee:** $45. **To apply online, go to:** http://www.msmc.edu/admissions/steps_to_apply/online_application.htm. **Admissions requirements/recommendations:** High school units required (recommended): English: 4 (4); Mathematics: 3 (3); Science: 3 (3); Foreign language: 2 (2); Social studies: 3 (3); History: 2 (2); Academic electives: 3 (3); Total units: 21 (21). Tests: The college uses SAT or ACT scores in admissions decisions. Either SAT or ACT required. For admission to the fall 2011 entering class, the school will accept: ACT with writing required. Campus visit: Recommended. Admissions interview: Recommended. Off-campus interview: May be arranged. **Factors that count in admissions decisions:** *Academic:* Secondary school record: Very Important. Class rank: Important. Letters of recommendation: Important. Standardized test scores: Important. Essay: Important. *Nonacademic:* Interview: Important. Extracurricular activities: Considered. Talent/ability: Important. Character/personal qualities: Important. Alumni/ae relationship: Considered. Geographical residence: Not Considered. State residency: Not Considered. Religious affiliation/commitment: Not Considered. Minority status: Not Considered. Volunteer work: Considered. Work experience: Considered. **Other schools with the greatest overlap in applicants:** College of St. Rose; Marist College; SUNY College–Cortland; SUNY College–Oneonta; SUNY–New Paltz. **Admissions statistics for the fall 2009 entering class:** Total applicants: 2,612. Total accepted: 1,877. Freshmen enrolled: 478; 20% were from out of state. Overall acceptance rate: 72%. **Credentials of fall 2009 freshmen:** 9% ranked in the top 10 percent of their high school class; 33% were in the top 25 percent; 76% were in the top half. (Proportion submitting class standing: 64%.) **Average high school grade point average:** 3.2. **First-year students who submitted SAT scores:** 94%. Scores (25/75 percentile): Critical Reading: 450-540, Math: 460-560, Combined: 910-1100. **First-year students submitting ACT scores:** 33%. Scores (25/75 percentile): English: 18-23, Math: 18-24, Composite: 19-23.

ACADEMICS

Year founded: 1959. **Academic calendar:** Semester. **Degrees offered:** certificate, bachelor's, master's, post-master's certificate. **Most popular majors:** 24% business, management, marketing, and related support services, 13% health professions and related clinical sciences, 13% history, 10% English language and literature/letters, 10% psychology. **Major fields of study:** biological and biomedical sciences; business, management, marketing,

and related support services; communication, journalism, and related programs; computer and information sciences and support services; education; English language and literature/letters; foreign languages, literatures, and linguistics; health professions and related clinical sciences; history; mathematics and statistics; multi/interdisciplinary studies; physical sciences; psychology; public administration and social service professions; social sciences. **Areas of required coursework:** arts/fine arts, humanities, computer literacy, mathematics, English (including composition), philosophy, sciences (biological or physical), history, social science. **Pre-professional programs:** pre-law, pre-dentistry, pre-medicine, pre-veterinary science, pre-optometry. **Special academic programs (% participation):** accelerated program (16%), cooperative (work-study plan) program (31%), cross-registration (1%), distance learning (10%), double major (5%), dual enrollment (0%), honors program (7%), independent study (3%), internships (24%), liberal arts/career combination (17%), student-designed major (2%), study abroad (8%), teacher certificate program (17%). **Teacher certification offered in:** early childhood, special education, elementary, middle/junior high, secondary. **Cooperative education programs:** business, computer science, education, health professions, humanities, natural science, social/behavioral science, technologies. **Reserve Officers Training Corps (ROTC):** Army ROTC: Offered at cooperating institution (Fordham University). **Faculty and instruction (2009-2010):** Total instructional faculty: 81 full-time, 138 part-time (44% men; 56% women; 10% minorities). Full-time faculty with Ph.D. or other terminal degree: 85%. Student/faculty ratio: 17/1. Classes of fewer than 20 students: 41%; of 20 to 49 students: 57%; of 50 or more students: 2%. **Advanced Placement and International Baccalaureate credit:** AP tests may be used for: Placement only. Scores accepted: 4, 5. International Baccalaureate exams may be used for: Credit and/or placement. **Freshmen returning for sophomore year:** 71%. **Graduation rates:** Four-year: 39%; five-year: 50%; six-year: 53%. **Graduate study:** 42% of students pursue further study within one year; 80% within five years. Fields in which graduates pursue further study: Master of Business Administration (MBA), 15%; law, 1%; medicine, 1%; education, 39%; arts and sciences, 44%.

COSTS AND FINANCIAL AID

Financial aid office: (845) 569-3298. **Expenses (2010-2011):** Tuition and fees 2010-2011: $23,300; room/board: $11,900. Estimated books and supplies: $1,100; transportation: $550; personal expenses: $1,000. **Financial aid:** Priority filing date for institution's financial aid form: February 15; deadline: March 1. In 2009-2010, 90% of undergraduates applied for financial aid. Of those, 78% were determined to have financial need; 15% had their need fully met. Average financial aid package (proportion receiving): $13,804 (77%). Average amount of gift aid, such as scholarships or grants (proportion receiving): $10,089 (73%). Average amount of self-help aid, such as work study or loans (proportion receiving): $4,643 (71%). Average need-based loan (excluding PLUS or other private loans): $4,171. Among students who received need-based aid, the average percentage of need met: 58%. Among students who received aid based on merit, the average award (and the proportion receiving): $7,667 (12%). The average athletic scholarship (and the proportion receiving): $0 (0%). Average amount of debt of borrowers graduating in 2009: $32,729. Proportion who borrowed: 94%.

CAMPUS LIFE AND EXTRACURRICULAR ACTIVITIES

Campus housing available (% using): coed dorms (91%), women's dorms (8%), special housing for disabled students (1%). Students who live in college-owned, operated, or affiliated housing: 39%. **Student employment:** During the 2009-2010 academic year, 9% of undergraduates worked on campus. Average per-year earnings: $1,000. **Clubs and organizations:** Number of student organizations: 30. Activities include: campus ministries, choral groups, concert band, dance, drama/theater, literary magazine, music ensembles, musical theater, radio station, student government, student newspaper, student film society, yearbook. Number of fraternities: 0; sororities: 0. Average proportion of students who stay on campus on weekends: 84%. **Sports program (2009-2010):** Member of NCAA III. *Men's intercollegiate varsity sports:* baseball, basketball, cross country, lacrosse, soccer, swimming, tennis. *Women's intercollegiate varsity sports:* basketball, cross country, lacrosse, soccer, softball, swimming, tennis, volleyball.

SERVICES AND FACILITIES

Basic services: nonremedial tutoring, placement service, health service, health insurance. **Remedial assistance:** reading, math, writing, study skills. **Counseling services:** career, personal, academic, older student, psychological, religious. **For learning-disabled students:** School does not offer a structured program with separate admission and additional fees. Total undergraduates in learning-disabled program or receiving services: 50. Services include: remedial math, remedial English, remedial reading, tape recorders, other special classes, note-taking services, oral tests, learning center, readers, extended time for tests, tutors, priority registration, priority seating, texts on tape, typist/scribe, other testing accommodations. **Library:** Number of titles: 114,078; number of current serial subscriptions: 29,775. **Information technology resources:** Students are not required to lease or own a computer. Number of campus computers available to all students: 524. School has a wireless network. Approximate number of users that can be accommodated: 2,000. Proportion of college-owned housing units wired for high-speed internet access: 100%. **Campus safety:** Security services offered: 24-hour foot-and-vehicle patrols, late-night transport/escort service, 24-hour emergency telephones, lighted pathways/sidewalks, controlled dormitory access (key, security card, etc.).

TRANSFER AND INTERNATIONAL STUDENTS

Transfer students: May apply for admission for the following academic terms: Fall, Winter, Spring, Summer. Applicants need a minimum number of credits to apply. For fall 2009: Transfer applications received: 568. Transfer applicants offered admission: 359. Transfer applicants enrolled: 258. **International students:** Number of foreign undergraduates: 1. Number of countries represented: 6. Minimum TOEFL score required: 500 (paper); 80 (computer). Average TOEFL score: 550 (paper).

Nazareth College

- ■ **Address:** 4245 East Avenue, Rochester, NY 14618-3790
- ■ **Website:** http://www.naz.edu
- ■ **Private**
- ■ **Enrollment:** 2,070 full-time; 157 part-time

KEY STATS
- ✔ **U.S News College Ranking:** 25, Regional Universities (North)
- ✔ **SAT Score (25th/75th percentile):** 1070-1230
- ✔ **Tuition:** 2010-2011: $26,184

Selectivity: Selective	**Room/board:** $10,716
Acceptance rate: 77%	**Average debt:** $35,010
Student/faculty ratio: 12/1	**Proportion who borrowed:** 90%

UNDERGRADUATE STUDENT BODY STATS

2009-2010 enrollment: 2,070 full-time; 157 part-time. Men: 24%; women: 76%. **Ethnic makeup:** African American: 4%; Asian American: 2%; Hispanic: 4%; White: 89%; International: 1%.

ADMISSIONS FACTS AND FIGURES

Phone: (585) 389-2860. **Email:** admissions@naz.edu. **Website:** http://www.naz.edu. **Application deadlines for fall 2011:** Regular decision: February 15. Early decision: Send application by: November 15; Decision sent by: December 15. Early action: Send application by: December 15; Decision sent by: January 15. Admission can be deferred. **Application fee:** $40. **To apply online, go to:** http://admissions.naz.edu/. **Admissions requirements/recommendations:** High school units required (recommended): English: 4 (4); Mathematics: 3 (4); Science: 3 (4); Foreign language: 3 (4); Social studies: 3 (4); Total units: 16 (20). Tests: The college uses SAT or ACT scores in admissions decisions. Neither SAT nor ACT required. For admission to the fall 2011 entering class, the school will accept: ACT with or without writing accepted. Campus visit: Recommended. Admissions interview: Recommended. Off-campus interview: May be arranged. **Factors that count in admissions decisions: Academic:** Secondary school record: Very Important. Class rank: Very Important. Letters of recommendation: Very Important. Standardized test scores: Considered. Essay: Very Important. **Nonacademic:** Interview: Important. Extracurricular activities: Important. Talent/ability: Important. Character/personal qualities: Important. Alumni/ae relationship: Considered. Geographical residence: Important. State residency: Important. Religious affiliation/commitment: Not Considered. Minority status: Important. Volunteer work: Important. Work experience: Important. **Other schools with the greatest overlap in applicants:** Ithaca College; Le Moyne College; SUNY–Fredonia; SUNY–Geneseo; St. John Fisher College. **Admissions statistics for the fall 2009 entering class:** Total applicants: 2,221. Total accepted: 1,710. Freshmen enrolled: 492; 8% were from out of state. Accepted through early-decision or early-action plans: 60%. Overall acceptance rate: 77%. Early-decision acceptance rate: 92%. Non-early acceptance rate: 71%. **Size of waiting list:** 61 applicants; enrolled from waiting list: 2. **Credentials of fall 2009 freshmen:** 31% ranked in the top 10 percent of their high school class; 64% were in the top 25 percent; 88%

were in the top half. (Proportion submitting class standing: 74%.) **Average high school grade point average:** 3.4. **First-year students who submitted SAT scores:** 61%. Scores (25/75 percentile): Critical Reading: 540-610, Math: 530-620, Combined: 1070-1230. **First-year students submitting ACT scores:** 29%. Scores (25/75 percentile): English: N/A, Math: N/A, Composite: 23-27.

ACADEMICS

Year founded: 1924. **Academic calendar:** Semester. **Degrees offered:** bachelor's, master's, post-master's certificate. **Most popular majors:** 19% health professions and related clinical sciences, 12% business, management, marketing, and related support services, 9% psychology, 9% visual and performing arts, 7% social sciences. **Major fields of study:** area, ethnic, cultural, and gender studies; biological and biomedical sciences; business, management, marketing, and related support services; communication, journalism, and related programs; computer and information sciences and support services; education; English language and literature/letters; foreign languages, literatures, and linguistics; health professions and related clinical sciences; history; mathematics and statistics; multi/interdisciplinary studies; philosophy and religious studies; physical sciences; psychology; public administration and social service professions; social sciences; visual and performing arts. **Areas of required coursework:** arts/fine arts, humanities, computer literacy, mathematics, English (including composition), philosophy, foreign languages, sciences (biological or physical), history, social science. **Pre-professional programs:** pre-law, pre-dentistry, pre-medicine, pre-veterinary science. **Special academic programs (% participation):** cross-registration (2.7%), distance learning (1%), double major (5.5%), honors program (1.4%), independent study (7.9%), internships (73.3%), study abroad (12.3%), teacher certificate program (32.1%). **Teacher certification offered in:** early childhood, special education, elementary, middle/junior high, secondary. **Reserve Officers Training Corps (ROTC):** Army ROTC: Offered at cooperating institution (Rochester Institute of Technology); Air Force ROTC: Offered at cooperating institution (Rochester Institute of Technology). **Faculty and instruction (2009-2010):** Total instructional faculty: 156 full-time, 258 part-time (32% men; 68% women; 10% minorities). Full-time faculty with Ph.D. or other terminal degree: 93%. Student/faculty ratio: 12/1. Classes of fewer than 20 students: 60%; of 20 to 49 students: 40%; of 50 or more students: 0%. **Advanced Placement and International Baccalaureate credit:** AP tests may be used for: Credit and/or placement. Scores accepted: 3, 4, 5. International Baccalaureate exams may be used for: Credit and/or placement. **Freshmen returning for sophomore year:** 84%. **Graduation rates:** Four-year: 62%; five-year: 72%; six-year: 73%. **Graduate study:** 36% of students pursue further study immediately upon graduation. Fields in which graduates pursue further study: Master of Business Administration (MBA), 3%; law, 3%; medicine, 1%; education, 38%; arts and sciences, 20%.

COSTS AND FINANCIAL AID

Financial aid office: (585) 389-2310. **Expenses (2010-2011):** Tuition and fees 2010-2011: $26,184; room/board: $10,716. Estimated books and supplies: $1,100; transportation: $200; personal expenses: $900. **Financial aid:** Priority filing date for institution's financial aid form: February 15. In 2009-2010, 90% of undergraduates applied for financial aid. Of those, 81% were determined to have financial need; 21% had their need fully met. Average financial aid package (proportion receiving): $18,649 (81%). Average amount of gift aid, such as scholarships or grants (proportion receiving): $13,536 (81%). Average amount of self-help aid, such as work study or loans (proportion receiving): $6,013 (69%). Average need-based loan (excluding PLUS or other private loans): $4,922. Among students who received need-based aid, the average percentage of need met: 73%. Among students who received aid based on merit, the average award (and the proportion receiving): $14,045 (17%). The average athletic scholarship (and the proportion receiving): $0 (0%). Average amount of debt of borrowers graduating in 2009: $35,010. Proportion who borrowed: 90%.

CAMPUS LIFE AND EXTRACURRICULAR ACTIVITIES

Campus housing available (% using): coed dorms (69%), women's dorms (0%), apartment for single students (16%), special housing for disabled students (0%), other housing options (15%). Students who live in college-owned, operated, or affiliated housing: 53%. **Student employment:** During the 2009-2010 academic year, 25% of undergraduates worked on campus. Average per-year earnings: $1,020. **Clubs and organizations:** Number of student organizations: 56. Activities include: campus ministries, choral groups, concert band, dance, drama/theater, international student organization, jazz band, literary magazine, music ensembles, musical theater, opera, radio station, student government, student newspaper, symphony orchestra, yearbook. Number of fraternities: 0; sororities: 0. Average proportion of students who stay on campus on weekends: 85%. **Sports program (2009-2010):**

Member of NCAA III. **Men's intercollegiate varsity sports:** basketball, cross country, golf, lacrosse, soccer, swimming, tennis, track and field (indoor), track and field (outdoor), volleyball. **Women's intercollegiate varsity sports:** basketball, cross country, equestrian, field hockey, golf, lacrosse, soccer, softball, swimming, tennis, track and field (indoor), track and field (outdoor), volleyball.

SERVICES AND FACILITIES

Basic services: nonremedial tutoring, placement service, day care, health service, health insurance. **Remedial assistance:** math, writing, study skills. **Counseling services:** minority student, career, personal, veteran student, academic, older student, psychological, birth control, religious. **For learning-disabled students:** School does not offer a structured program with separate admission and additional fees. Total undergraduates in learning-disabled program or receiving services: 136. Services include: reading machines, tape recorders, untimed tests, note-taking services, special bookstore section, oral tests, readers, extended time for tests, tutors, priority seating, texts on tape, typist/scribe, exams on tape or computer, waiver of foreign language degree requirement, waiver of math degree requirement, other. **Library:** Number of titles: 223,544; number of current serial subscriptions: 2,850. **Information technology resources:** Students are not required to lease or own a computer. Number of campus computers available to all students: 233. School has a wireless network. Approximate number of users that can be accommodated: 300. Proportion of college-owned housing units wired for high-speed internet access: 100%. **Campus safety:** Security services offered: 24-hour foot-and-vehicle patrols, late-night transport/escort service, 24-hour emergency telephones, lighted pathways/sidewalks, student patrols, controlled dormitory access (key, security card, etc).

TRANSFER AND INTERNATIONAL STUDENTS

Transfer students: May apply for admission for the following academic terms: Fall, Spring, Summer. Applicants need a minimum number of credits to apply. For fall 2009: Transfer applications received: 422. Transfer applicants offered admission: 245. Transfer applicants enrolled: 154. **International students:** Number of foreign undergraduates: 18 (1% of student body). Number of countries represented: 20. Minimum TOEFL score required: 550 (paper); 213 (computer). Average TOEFL score: 630 (paper).

New School

- **Address:** 66 W. 12th Street, New York, NY 10011
- **Website:** http://www.newschool.edu
- **Private**
- **Enrollment:** 5,796 full-time; 1,086 part-time

KEY STATS

✔ **U.S News College Ranking:** 139, National Universities
✔ **SAT Score (25th/75th percentile):** 970-1220
✔ **Tuition:** 2010-2011: $37,585

Selectivity: Selective	**Room/board:** $15,260
Acceptance rate: 64%	**Average debt:** $30,275
Student/faculty ratio: 10/1	**Proportion who borrowed:** 51%

UNDERGRADUATE STUDENT BODY STATS

2009-2010 enrollment: 5,796 full-time; 1,086 part-time. Men: 29%; women: 71%. **Ethnic makeup:** African American: 5%; Asian American: 12%; Hispanic: 8%; White: 51%; International: 23%.

ADMISSIONS FACTS AND FIGURES

Phone: (877) 528-3321. **Email:** studentinfo@newschool.edu. **Website:** http://www.newschool.edu. **Application deadlines for fall 2011:** Regular decision: Rolling; decision sent by March 15. Early decision: Send application by: November 15; Decision sent by: December 15. Early action: Not offered. Admission can be deferred. **Application fee:** $50. **Admissions requirements/recommendations:** High school units required (recommended): English: 4; Mathematics: (3); Science: (3); Foreign language: (2); Social studies: (3); History: (2); Total units: 16 (18). Tests: The college uses SAT or ACT scores in admissions decisions. Neither SAT nor ACT required. Campus visit: Recommended. Admissions interview: Recommended. Off-campus interview: May be arranged. **Factors that count in admissions decisions:** *Academic:* Secondary school record: Considered. Class rank: Considered. Letters of recommendation: Considered. Standardized test scores: Considered. Essay: Considered. *Nonacademic:* Interview: Considered.

Extracurricular activities: Considered. Talent/ability: Considered. Character/personal qualities: Considered. Alumni/ae relationship: Considered. Geographical residence: Considered. State residency: Not Considered. Religious affiliation/commitment: Not Considered. Minority status: Not Considered. Volunteer work: Considered. Work experience: Considered. **Admissions statistics for the fall 2009 entering class:** Total applicants: 4,997. Total accepted: 3,183. Freshmen enrolled: 1,152; 75% were from out of state. Overall acceptance rate: 64%. Non-early acceptance rate: 64%. **Size of waiting list:** 87 applicants; enrolled from waiting list: 84. **Credentials of fall 2009 freshmen:** 18% ranked in the top 10 percent of their high school class; 44% were in the top 25 percent; 78% were in the top half. (Proportion submitting class standing: 16%.) **Average high school grade point average:** 3.3. **First-year students who submitted SAT scores:** 68%. Scores (25/75 percentile): Critical Reading: 490-620, Math: 480-600, Combined: 970-1220. **First-year students submitting ACT scores:** 17%. Scores (25/75 percentile): English: 19-25, Math: 21-27, Composite: 21-26.

ACADEMICS

Year founded: 1919. **Academic calendar:** Semester. **Degrees offered:** certificate, diploma, associate, bachelor's, post-bachelor's certificate, master's, doctorate. **Most popular majors:** 62% visual and performing arts, 33% liberal arts and sciences studies, and humanities; 3% business, management, marketing, and related support services, 2% architecture and related services. **Major fields of study:** architecture and related services; business, management, marketing, and related support services; communication, journalism, and related programs; education; English language and literature/letters; history; liberal arts and sciences studies, and humanities; multi/interdisciplinary studies; philosophy and religious studies; psychology; social sciences; visual and performing arts. **Areas of required coursework:** humanities, computer literacy, English (including composition), social science. **Special academic programs:** accelerated program, cross-registration, distance learning, double major, dual enrollment, English as a Second Language (ESL), exchange student program (domestic), independent study, internships, liberal arts/career combination, student-designed major, study abroad, other. **Faculty and instruction (2009-2010):** Total instructional faculty: 370 full-time, 1,583 part-time (51% men; 49% women; 16% minorities). Full-time faculty with Ph.D. or other terminal degree: 69%. Student/faculty ratio: 10/1. Classes of fewer than 20 students: 91%; of 20 to 49 students: 8%; of 50 or more students: 1%. **Advanced Placement and International Baccalaureate credit:** AP tests may be used for: Placement only. Scores accepted: 4, 5. International Baccalaureate exams may be used for: Credit only. **Freshmen returning for sophomore year:** 81%. **Graduation rates:** Four-year: 51%; five-year: 63%; six-year: 66%.

COSTS AND FINANCIAL AID

Financial aid office: (212) 229-8930. **Expenses (2010-2011):** Tuition and fees 2010-2011: $37,585; room/board: $15,260. Estimated books and supplies: $2,050; transportation: $729; personal expenses: $1,550. **Financial aid:** Priority filing date for institution's financial aid form: March 1. In 2009-2010, 52% of undergraduates applied for financial aid. Of those, 47% were determined to have financial need; 7% had their need fully met. Average financial aid package (proportion receiving): $25,345 (47%). Average amount of gift aid, such as scholarships or grants (proportion receiving): $13,761 (45%). Average amount of self-help aid, such as work study or loans (proportion receiving): $11,353 (46%). Average need-based loan (excluding PLUS or other private loans): $11,085. Among students who received need-based aid, the average percentage of need met: 65%. Among students who received aid based on merit, the average award (and the proportion receiving): $11,267 (3%). The average athletic scholarship (and the proportion receiving): $0 (0%). Average amount of debt of borrowers graduating in 2009: $30,275. Proportion who borrowed: 51%.

CAMPUS LIFE AND EXTRACURRICULAR ACTIVITIES

Campus housing available (% using): coed dorms (100%), apartment for single students (0%), special housing for disabled students (0%). Students who live in college-owned, operated, or affiliated housing: 22%. **Student employment:** During the 2009-2010 academic year, 15% of undergraduates worked on campus. Average per-year earnings: $6,894. **Clubs and organizations:** Number of student organizations: 30. Activities include: choral groups, dance, drama/theater, international student organization, jazz band, literary magazine, music ensembles, opera, radio station, student government, student newspaper, student film society, symphony orchestra. Number of fraternities: 0; sororities: 0. Average proportion of students who stay on campus on weekends: 75%.

SERVICES AND FACILITIES

Basic services: health service, health insurance. **Remedial assistance:** writing, other. **Counseling services:** career, personal, academic, psychological, birth control. **For learning-disabled students:** School does not offer a structured program with separate admission and additional fees. Total undergraduates in learning-disabled program or receiving services: 260. Services include: reading machines, tape recorders, note-taking services, readers, extended time for tests, priority registration, priority seating, texts on tape, other testing accommodations, other. **Library:** Number of titles: 278,039; number of current serial subscriptions: 41,681. **Information technology resources:** Students are not required to lease or own a computer. Number of campus computers available to all students: 1,057. School has a wireless network. Approximate number of users that can be accommodated: 1,500. Proportion of college-owned housing units wired for high-speed internet access: 100%. **Campus safety:** Security services offered: 24-hour emergency telephones, lighted pathways/sidewalks, controlled dormitory access (key, security card, etc).

TRANSFER AND INTERNATIONAL STUDENTS

Transfer students: May apply for admission for the following academic terms: Fall, Spring. Applicants need a minimum number of credits to apply. For fall 2009: Transfer applications received: 3,011. Transfer applicants offered admission: 2,184. Transfer applicants enrolled: 1,166. **International students:** Number of foreign undergraduates: 1564 (23% of student body). Number of countries represented: 100. Minimum TOEFL score required: 560 (paper); 213 (computer). Average TOEFL score: 584 (paper).

New York Institute of Technology

- **Address:** PO Box 8000, Old Westbury, NY 11568-8000
- **Website:** http://www.nyit.edu
- **Private**
- **Enrollment:** 6,212 full-time; 1,529 part-time

KEY STATS

✔ **U.S News College Ranking:** 81, Regional Universities (North)
✔ **SAT Score (25th/75th percentile):** 1010-1200
✔ **Tuition:** 2010-2011: $25,470

Selectivity: Selective	**Room/board:** $11,100
Acceptance rate: 74%	**Average debt:** N/A
Student/faculty ratio: 15/1	**Proportion who borrowed:** N/A

UNDERGRADUATE STUDENT BODY STATS

2009-2010 enrollment: 6,212 full-time; 1,529 part-time. Men: 62%; women: 38%. **Ethnic makeup:** African American: 7%; Asian American: 8%; Hispanic: 7%; White: 69%; International: 8%.

ADMISSIONS FACTS AND FIGURES

Phone: (516) 686-7520. **Email:** admissions@nyit.edu. **Website:** http://www.nyit.edu. **Application deadlines for fall 2011:** Regular decision: Rolling. Early decision: Not offered. Early action: Not offered. Admission can be deferred. **Application fee:** $50. **To apply online, go to:** http://www.nyit.edu/admissions/apply_to_nyit/. **Admissions requirements/recommendations:** High school units required (recommended): English: 4 (4); Mathematics: 3 (3); Science: 3 (3); Social studies: 3 (4); Academic electives: 7 (7); Total units: 17 (17). Tests: The college uses SAT or ACT scores in admissions decisions. Either SAT or ACT required. For admission to the fall 2011 entering class, the school will accept: ACT with or without writing accepted. Campus visit: Recommended. Admissions interview: Recommended. Off-campus interview: Not available. **Factors that count in admissions decisions: Academic:** Secondary school record: Very Important. Class rank: Considered. Letters of recommendation: Considered. Standardized test scores: Important. Essay: Important. **Nonacademic:** Interview: Important. Extracurricular activities: Considered. Talent/ability: Considered. Character/personal qualities: Considered. Alumni/ae relationship: Not Considered. Geographical residence: Not Considered. State residency: Not Considered. Religious affiliation/commitment: Not Considered. Minority status: Not Considered. Volunteer work: Considered. Work experience: Considered. **Other schools with the greatest overlap in applicants:** Hofstra University; New York University; Rutgers, the State University of New Jersey–New Brunswick; SUNY–Stony Brook; St. John's University. **Admissions statistics for the fall 2009 entering class:** Total applicants: 4,650. Total accepted:

3,455. Freshmen enrolled: 1,103; 12% were from out of state. Overall acceptance rate: 74%. **Credentials of fall 2009 freshmen:** 19% ranked in the top 10 percent of their high school class; 45% were in the top 25 percent; 84% were in the top half. (Proportion submitting class standing: 12%.) **Average high school grade point average:** 3.4. **First-year students who submitted SAT scores:** 88%. Scores (25/75 percentile): Critical Reading: 470-560, Math: 540-640, Combined: 1010-1200. **First-year students submitting ACT scores:** 13%. Scores (25/75 percentile): English: N/A, Math: N/A, Composite: 21-26.

ACADEMICS

Year founded: 1955. **Academic calendar:** Semester. **Degrees offered:** certificate, associate, bachelor's, post-bachelor's certificate, master's, post-master's certificate. **Most popular majors:** 35% business, management, marketing, and related support services, 14% multi/interdisciplinary studies, 8% architecture and related services, 6% visual and performing arts, 5% computer and information sciences and support services. **Major fields of study:** architecture and related services; biological and biomedical sciences; business, management, marketing, and related support services; communication, journalism, and related programs; computer and information sciences and support services; education; engineering; engineering technologies/technicians; English language and literature/letters; health professions and related clinical sciences; multi/interdisciplinary studies; physical sciences; psychology; security and protective services; social sciences; visual and performing arts. **Areas of required coursework:** humanities, computer literacy, mathematics, English (including composition), philosophy, sciences (biological or physical), history, social science, other. **Pre-professional programs:** pre-law, pre-medicine. **Special academic programs:** accelerated program, cooperative (work-study plan) program, cross-registration, distance learning, double major, dual enrollment, English as a Second Language (ESL), honors program, independent study, internships, liberal arts/career combination, study abroad, teacher certificate program, weekend college, other. **Teacher certification offered in:** early childhood, elementary, vo-tech, middle/junior high, secondary. **Reserve Officers Training Corps (ROTC):** Army ROTC: Offered on campus; Air Force ROTC: Offered on campus. **Faculty and instruction (2009-2010):** Total instructional faculty: 300 full-time, 648 part-time (59% men; 41% women; 17% minorities). Student/faculty ratio: 15/1. Classes of fewer than 20 students: 64%; of 20 to 49 students: 34%; of 50 or more students: 2%. **Advanced Placement and International Baccalaureate credit:** AP tests may be used for: Placement only. Scores accepted: 3, 4, 5. International Baccalaureate exams may be used for: Placement only. **Freshmen returning for sophomore year:** 73%. **Graduation rates:** Four-year: 23%; five-year: 44%; six-year: 43%. **Graduate study:** 25% of students pursue further study immediately upon graduation; 13% within one year; 19% within five years. Fields in which graduates pursue further study: Master of Business Administration (MBA), 35%; law, 3%; medicine, 7%; engineering, 20%; education, 13%; arts and sciences, 21%; veterinary medicine, 1%.

COSTS AND FINANCIAL AID

Financial aid office: (516) 686-7680. **Expenses (2010-2011):** Tuition and fees 2010-2011: $25,470; room/board: $11,100. Estimated books and supplies: $1,460; transportation: $500; personal expenses: $2,883. **Financial aid:** Priority filing date for institution's financial aid form: March 1. In 2009-2010, 58% of undergraduates applied for financial aid. Of those, 51% were determined to have financial need; Average financial aid package (proportion receiving): $20,439 (51%). Average amount of gift aid, such as scholarships or grants (proportion receiving): $6,796 (36%). Average amount of self-help aid, such as work study or loans (proportion receiving): $6,702 (38%). Average need-based loan (excluding PLUS or other private loans): $6,226. Among students who received aid based on merit, the average award (and the proportion receiving): $11,506 (10%). The average athletic scholarship (and the proportion receiving): $22,703 (1%).

CAMPUS LIFE AND EXTRACURRICULAR ACTIVITIES

Campus housing available (% using): coed dorms (100%), special housing for disabled students. Students who live in college-owned, operated, or affiliated housing: 9%. **Student employment:** During the 2009-2010 academic year, 1% of undergraduates worked on campus. Average per-year earnings: $1,400. **Clubs and organizations:** Number of student organizations: 95. Activities include: choral groups, dance, drama/theater, international student organization, literary magazine, musical theater, radio station, student government, student newspaper, student film society, television station. Number of fraternities: 6; sororities: 3. Proportion of men in fraternities: 1%; of women in sororities: 1%. Average proportion of students who stay on campus on weekends: 40%. **Sports program (2009-2010):** Member of NCAA II. **Men's intercollegiate varsity sports:** baseball, basketball, cross country, lacrosse, soccer. **Women's intercollegiate varsity sports:** basketball, cross country, soccer, softball, volleyball.

SERVICES AND FACILITIES
Basic services: nonremedial tutoring, placement service, health service, health insurance. **Remedial assistance:** reading, math, writing, study skills. **Counseling services:** minority student, career, personal, veteran student, academic, psychological. **For learning-disabled students:** School does not offer a structured program with separate admission and additional fees. Total undergraduates in learning-disabled program or receiving services: 48. Services include: remedial math, remedial English, reading machines, remedial reading, tape recorders, other special classes, untimed tests, note-taking services, oral tests, learning center, readers, extended time for tests, tutors, early syllabus, priority registration, priority seating, substitution of courses, exams on tape or computer, other testing accommodations. **Library:** Number of titles: 152,397; number of current serial subscriptions: 1,002. **Information technology resources:** Students are required to lease or own a computer. Number of campus computers available to all students: 1,250. School has a wireless network. Approximate number of users that can be accommodated: 600. Proportion of college-owned housing units wired for high-speed internet access: 100%. **Campus safety:** Security services offered: 24-hour foot-and-vehicle patrols, late-night transport/escort service, 24-hour emergency telephones, lighted pathways/sidewalks, controlled dormitory access (key, security card, etc).

TRANSFER AND INTERNATIONAL STUDENTS
Transfer students: May apply for admission for the following academic terms: Fall, Spring, Summer. Applicants need a minimum number of credits to apply. For fall 2009: Transfer applications received: 1,610. Transfer applicants offered admission: 1,165. Transfer applicants enrolled: 566. **International students:** Number of foreign undergraduates: 569 (8% of student body). Number of countries represented: 75. Minimum TOEFL score required: 550 (paper); 213 (computer). Average TOEFL score: 560 (paper).

New York University

- **Address:** 70 Washington Square S, New York, NY 10012
- **Website:** http://www.nyu.edu
- **Private**
- **Enrollment:** 20,281 full-time; 1,357 part-time

KEY STATS
✔ **U.S News College Ranking:** 33, National Universities
✔ **SAT Score (25th/75th percentile):** 1210-1430
✔ **Tuition:** 2009-2010: $38,765

Selectivity: Most selective	**Room/board:** $13,228
Acceptance rate: 38%	**Average debt:** $33,487
Student/faculty ratio: 11/1	**Proportion who borrowed:** 59%

UNDERGRADUATE STUDENT BODY STATS
2009-2010 enrollment: 20,281 full-time; 1,357 part-time. Men: 39%; women: 61%. **Ethnic makeup:** African American: 4%; Asian American: 20%; Hispanic: 8%; White: 60%; International: 8%.

ADMISSIONS FACTS AND FIGURES
Phone: (212) 998-4500. **Email:** admissions@nyu.edu. **Website:** http://www.nyu.edu. **Application deadlines for fall 2011:** Regular decision: January 1; decision sent by April 1. Early decision: Send application by: November 1; Decision sent by: December 15. Early action: Send application by: November 1; Decision sent by: N/A. Admission can be deferred. **Application fee:** $65. **To apply online, go to:** http://admissions.nyu.edu/apply.now. **Admissions requirements/recommendations:** High school units required (recommended): English: 4 (4); Mathematics: 3 (4); Science: 3 (4); Foreign language: 2 (3); History: 4 (4); Total units: 16 (18). Tests: The college uses SAT or ACT scores in admissions decisions. Either SAT or ACT required. For admission to the fall 2011 entering class, the school will accept: ACT with writing required. Campus visit: Recommended. Admissions interview: Neither required nor recommended. Off-campus interview: Not available. **Factors that count in admissions decisions:** *Academic:* Secondary school record: Very Important. Class rank: Important. Letters of recommendation: Very Important. Standardized test scores: Very Important. Essay: Very Important. *Nonacademic:* Interview: Not Considered. Extracurricular activities: Very Important. Talent/ability: Very Important. Character/personal

qualities: Important. Alumni/ae relationship: Important. Geographical residence: Important. State residency: Not Considered. Religious affiliation/commitment: Not Considered. Minority status: Important. Volunteer work: Important. Work experience: Important. **Other schools with the greatest overlap in applicants:** Boston University; Columbia University; Cornell University; Harvard University; University of Pennsylvania. **Admissions statistics for the fall 2009 entering class:** Total applicants: 37,462. Total accepted: 14,159. Freshmen enrolled: 4,998; 72% were from out of state. Overall acceptance rate: 38%. Early-decision acceptance rate: 39%. Non-early acceptance rate: 38%. **Size of waiting list:** 2626 applicants; enrolled from waiting list: 298. **Credentials of fall 2009 freshmen:** 64% ranked in the top 10 percent of their high school class; 92% were in the top 25 percent; 100% were in the top half. (Proportion submitting class standing: 31%.) **Average high school grade point average:** 3.6. **First-year students who submitted SAT scores:** 87%. Scores (25/75 percentile): Critical Reading: 610-710, Math: 600-720, Combined: 1210-1430. **First-year students submitting ACT scores:** 13%. Scores (25/75 percentile): English: N/A, Math: N/A, Composite: 27-31.

ACADEMICS
Year founded: 1831. **Academic calendar:** Semester. **Degrees offered:** certificate, diploma, associate, transfer-associate, terminal-associate, bachelor's, post-bachelor's certificate, master's, post-master's certificate, doctorate. **Most popular majors:** 21% visual and performing arts, 18% business, management, marketing, and related support services, 16% social sciences, 7% communication, journalism, and related programs, 7% liberal arts and sciences studies, and humanities. **Major fields of study:** architecture and related services; area, ethnic, cultural, and gender studies; biological and biomedical sciences; business, management, marketing, and related support services; communication, journalism, and related programs; communications technologies/technicians and support services; computer and information sciences and support services; education; engineering; English language and literature/letters; family and consumer sciences/human sciences; foreign languages, literatures, and linguistics; health professions and related clinical sciences; history; liberal arts and sciences studies, and humanities; mathematics and statistics; multi/interdisciplinary studies; parks, recreation, leisure, and fitness studies; philosophy and religious studies; physical sciences; psychology; public administration and social service professions; social sciences; visual and performing arts. **Areas of required coursework:** arts/fine arts, humanities, mathematics, English (including composition), foreign languages, sciences (biological or physical), history, social science, other. **Pre-professional programs:** pre-dentistry, pre-medicine, pre-veterinary science. **Special academic programs:** accelerated program, cross-registration, distance learning, double major, English as a Second Language (ESL), exchange student program (domestic), honors program, independent study, internships, liberal arts/career combination, student-designed major, study abroad, teacher certificate program, weekend college, other. **Teacher certification offered in:** early childhood, special education, elementary, secondary, bilingual/bicultural. **Reserve Officers Training Corps (ROTC):** Army ROTC: Offered at cooperating institution (Fordham University); Navy ROTC: Offered at cooperating institution (Fordham University). **Faculty and instruction (2009-2010):** Total instructional faculty: 2,315 full-time, 2,845 part-time (53% men; 47% women; 19% minorities). Full-time faculty with Ph.D. or other terminal degree: 92%. Student/faculty ratio: 11/1. Classes of fewer than 20 students: 60%; of 20 to 49 students: 28%; of 50 or more students: 12%. **Advanced Placement and International Baccalaureate credit:** AP tests may be used for: Credit only. International Baccalaureate exams may be used for: Placement only. **Freshmen returning for sophomore year:** 92%. **Graduation rates:** Four-year: 78%; five-year: 84%; six-year: 85%. **Graduate study:** 29% of students pursue further study immediately upon graduation; 34% within one year; 80% within five years. Fields in which graduates pursue further study: Master of Business Administration (MBA), 1%; law, 25%; medicine, 17%; dentistry, 2%; education, 15%; arts and sciences, 4%; veterinary medicine, 1%.

COSTS AND FINANCIAL AID
Financial aid office: (212) 998-4444. **Expenses (2009-2010):** Tuition and fees 2009-2010: $38,765; room/board: $13,228. Estimated books and supplies: $950 personal expenses: $1,000. **Financial aid:** In 2009-2010, 60% of undergraduates applied for financial aid. Of those, 51% were determined to have financial need; Average financial aid package (proportion receiving): $23,900 (49%). Average amount of gift aid, such as scholarships or grants (proportion receiving): $16,870 (47%). Average amount of self-help aid, such as work study or loans (proportion receiving): $8,244 (N/A). Average need-based loan (excluding PLUS or other private loans): $5,583. Among students who received need-based aid, the average percentage of need met: 64%. Among students who received aid based on merit, the average award

(and the proportion receiving): $7,426 (8%). The average athletic scholarship (and the proportion receiving): $0 (0%). Average amount of debt of borrowers graduating in 2009: $33,487. Proportion who borrowed: 59%.

CAMPUS LIFE AND EXTRACURRICULAR ACTIVITIES
Campus housing available: coed dorms, sorority housing, fraternity housing, apartment for single students, special housing for disabled students, other housing options. Students who live in college-owned, operated, or affiliated housing: 51%. **Student employment:** During the 2009-2010 academic year, 23% of undergraduates worked on campus. Average per-year earnings: $4,000. **Clubs and organizations:** Number of student organizations: 454. Activities include: campus ministries, choral groups, concert band, dance, drama/theater, international student organization, jazz band, literary magazine, model UN, music ensembles, musical theater, opera, pep band, radio station, student government, student newspaper, student film society, symphony orchestra, television station, yearbook. Number of fraternities: 17; sororities: 10. Proportion of men in fraternities: 2%; of women in sororities: 2%. **Sports program (2009-2010):** Member of NCAA III. *Men's intercollegiate varsity sports:* basketball, cross country, fencing, golf, soccer, swimming, tennis, track and field (indoor), track and field (outdoor), volleyball, wrestling. *Women's intercollegiate varsity sports:* basketball, cross country, fencing, golf, soccer, swimming, tennis, track and field (indoor), track and field (outdoor), volleyball.

SERVICES AND FACILITIES
Basic services: nonremedial tutoring, women's center, placement service, health service, health insurance. **Remedial assistance:** reading, math, writing, study skills. **Counseling services:** minority student, career, personal, academic, older student, psychological, birth control, religious. **For learning-disabled students:** School does not offer a structured program with separate admission and additional fees. Total undergraduates in learning-disabled program or receiving services: 270. Services include: reading machines, tape recorders, videotaped classes, note-taking services, readers, extended time for tests, priority registration, priority seating, substitution of courses, texts on tape, typist/scribe, exams on tape or computer, other testing accommodations. **Library:** Number of titles: 5,721,018; number of current serial subscriptions: 67,960. **Information technology resources:** Students are not required to lease or own a computer. School has a wireless network. Proportion of college-owned housing units wired for high-speed internet access: 100%. **Campus safety:** Security services offered: 24-hour foot-and-vehicle patrols, late-night transport/escort service, 24-hour emergency telephones, lighted pathways/sidewalks, student patrols, controlled dormitory access (key, security card, etc).

TRANSFER AND INTERNATIONAL STUDENTS
Transfer students: May apply for admission for the following academic terms: Fall, Spring, Summer. Applicants need a minimum number of credits to apply. For fall 2009: Transfer applications received: 5,808. Transfer applicants offered admission: 1,938. Transfer applicants enrolled: 1,115. **International students:** Number of foreign undergraduates: 1598 (8% of student body). Number of countries represented: 133.

Niagara University

- **Address:** Niagara University, NY 14109
- **Website:** http://www.niagara.edu
- **Private; Religious affiliation:** Roman Catholic (Vincentian)
- **Enrollment:** 2,968 full-time; 292 part-time

KEY STATS
✔ **U.S News College Ranking:** 58, Regional Universities (North)
✔ **SAT Score (25th/75th percentile):** 960-1160
✔ **Tuition:** 2010-2011: $25,650

Selectivity: Selective	**Room/board:** $10,650
Acceptance rate: 80%	**Average debt:** $27,215
Student/faculty ratio: 14/1	**Proportion who borrowed:** 78%

UNDERGRADUATE STUDENT BODY STATS
2009-2010 enrollment: 2,968 full-time; 292 part-time. Men: 37%; women: 63%. **Ethnic makeup:** African American: 4%; American-Indian: 1%; Asian American: 1%; Hispanic: 2%; White: 77%; International: 16%. **Religious preference:** Roman Catholic: 35%; Protestant: 9%; No preference: 6%; Unknown: 45%.

ADMISSIONS FACTS AND FIGURES
Phone: (716) 286-8700. **Email:** admissions@niagara.edu. **Website:** http://www.niagara.edu. **Application deadlines for fall 2011:** Regular decision: August 1. Early decision: Not offered. Early action: Send application by: December 10; Decision sent by: December 10. Admission can be deferred. **Application fee:** $30. **To apply online, go to:** http://www.niagara.edu/admissions/pre-app.htm. **Admissions requirements/recommendations:** High school units required (recommended): English: 4; Mathematics: 2; Science: 2; Foreign language: 2; Social studies: 2; Academic electives: 4; Total units: 16. Tests: The college uses SAT or ACT scores in admissions decisions. Either SAT or ACT required. For admission to the fall 2011 entering class, the school will accept: ACT with or without writing accepted. Campus visit: Recommended. Admissions interview: Recommended. Off-campus interview: May be arranged. **Factors that count in admissions decisions:** *Academic:* Secondary school record: Very Important. Class rank: Important. Letters of recommendation: Important. Standardized test scores: Important. Essay: Considered. *Nonacademic:* Interview: Important. Extracurricular activities: Considered. Talent/ability: Considered. Character/personal qualities: Considered. Alumni/ae relationship: Considered. Geographical residence: Not Considered. State residency: Not Considered. Religious affiliation/commitment: Not Considered. Minority status: Not Considered. Volunteer work: Considered. Work experience: Considered. **Other schools with the greatest overlap in applicants:** Canisius College; SUNY–Fredonia; SUNY–Geneseo; St. John Fisher College; University at Buffalo–SUNY. **Admissions statistics for the fall 2009 entering class:** Total applicants: 2,942. Total accepted: 2,362. Freshmen enrolled: 677; 11% were from out of state. Accepted through early-decision or early-action plans: 5%. Overall acceptance rate: 80%. Non-early acceptance rate: 80%. **Credentials of fall 2009 freshmen:** 13% ranked in the top 10 percent of their high school class; 41% were in the top 25 percent; 78% were in the top half. (Proportion submitting class standing: 75%.) **Average high school grade point average:** 3.3. **First-year students who submitted SAT scores:** 95%. Scores (25/75 percentile): Critical Reading: 490-590, Math: 470-570, Combined: 960-1160. **First-year students submitting ACT scores:** 44%. Scores (25/75 percentile): English: 19-25, Math: 20-25, Composite: 20-25.

ACADEMICS
Year founded: 1856. **Academic calendar:** Semester. **Degrees offered:** certificate, associate, bachelor's, post-bachelor's certificate, master's, post-master's certificate. **Most popular majors:** 24% business/commerce, 18% education, 8% security and protective services, 8% social sciences, 5% psychology. **Major fields of study:** biological and biomedical sciences; business, management, marketing, and related support services; communication, journalism, and related programs; computer and information sciences and support services; education; English language and literature/letters; foreign languages, literatures, and linguistics; health professions and related clinical sciences; history; mathematics and statistics; philosophy and religious studies; physical sciences; psychology; security and protective services; social sciences; transportation and materials moving; visual and performing arts. **Areas of required coursework:** humanities, mathematics, English (including composition), philosophy, sciences (biological or physical), history, social science, other. **Pre-professional programs:** pre-law, pre-dentistry, pre-medicine, pre-theology, pre-veterinary science, pre-pharmacy. **Special academic programs (% participation):** cooperative (work-study plan) program (5%), cross-registration (1%), double major (4%), English as a Second Language (ESL), honors program (8%), independent study (5%), internships (4%), liberal arts/career combination (2%), study abroad (18%), teacher certificate program (20%). **Teacher certification offered in:** early childhood, special education, elementary, middle/junior high, secondary. **Cooperative education programs:** business, computer science, social/behavioral science, other. **Reserve Officers Training Corps (ROTC):** Army ROTC: Offered on campus. **Faculty and instruction (2009-2010):** Total instructional faculty: 149 full-time, 205 part-time (56% men; 44% women; 12% minorities). Full-time faculty with Ph.D. or other terminal degree: 95%. Student/faculty ratio: 14/1. Classes of fewer than 20 students: 44%; of 20 to 49 students: 56%; of 50 or more students: 0%. **Advanced Placement and International Baccalaureate credit:** AP tests may be used for: Credit only. Scores accepted: 3, 4, 5. International Baccalaureate exams may be used for: Credit only. **Freshmen returning for sophomore year:** 79%. **Graduation rates:** Four-year: 59%; five-year: 64%; six-year: 64%. **Graduate study:** 8% of students pursue further study immediately upon graduation; 76% within one year; 0% within five years. Fields in which graduates pursue further study: Master of Business Administration (MBA), 19%; law, 5%; medicine, 2%; dentistry, 1%; education, 37%; arts and sciences, 63%.

COSTS AND FINANCIAL AID

Financial aid office: (716) 286-8686. **Expenses (2010-2011):** Tuition and fees 2010-2011: $25,650; room/board: $10,650. Estimated books and supplies: $1,050; transportation: $700; personal expenses: $750. **Financial aid:** Priority filing date for institution's financial aid form: February 15. In 2009-2010, 79% of undergraduates applied for financial aid. Of those, 71% were determined to have financial need; 53% had their need fully met. Average financial aid package (proportion receiving): $19,418 (71%). Average amount of gift aid, such as scholarships or grants (proportion receiving): $15,144 (70%). Average amount of self-help aid, such as work study or loans (proportion receiving): $5,358 (57%). Average need-based loan (excluding PLUS or other private loans): $4,675. Among students who received need-based aid, the average percentage of need met: 82%. Among students who received aid based on merit, the average award (and the proportion receiving): $9,291 (17%). The average athletic scholarship (and the proportion receiving): $20,184 (4%). Average amount of debt of borrowers graduating in 2009: $27,215. Proportion who borrowed: 78%.

CAMPUS LIFE AND EXTRACURRICULAR ACTIVITIES

Campus housing available (% using): coed dorms (97%), apartment for single students (3%). Students who live in college-owned, operated, or affiliated housing: 52%. **Student employment:** During the 2009-2010 academic year, 17% of undergraduates worked on campus. Average per-year earnings: $1,800. **Clubs and organizations:** Number of student organizations: 60. Activities include: campus ministries, choral groups, dance, drama/theater, international student organization, literary magazine, musical theater, pep band, radio station, student government, student newspaper, student film society, television station, yearbook. Number of fraternities: 1; sororities: 2. Average proportion of students who stay on campus on weekends: 54%. **Sports program (2009-2010):** Member of NCAA I. *Men's intercollegiate varsity sports:* baseball, basketball, cross country, golf, ice hockey, soccer, swimming, tennis. *Women's intercollegiate varsity sports:* basketball, cross country, golf, ice hockey, lacrosse, soccer, softball, swimming, tennis, volleyball.

SERVICES AND FACILITIES

Basic services: nonremedial tutoring, placement service, health service, health insurance. **Remedial assistance:** reading, math, writing, study skills. **Counseling services:** minority student, career, military, personal, veteran student, academic, older student, psychological, religious. **For learning-disabled students:** School does not offer a structured program with separate admission and additional fees. Services include: remedial math, remedial English, reading machines, remedial reading, tape recorders, note-taking services, learning center, extended time for tests, tutors, other testing accommodations. **Library:** Number of titles: 272,514; number of current serial subscriptions: 22,000. **Information technology resources:** Students are not required to lease or own a computer. Number of campus computers available to all students: 150. School has a wireless network. Approximate number of users that can be accommodated: 300. Proportion of college-owned housing units wired for high-speed internet access: 100%. **Campus safety:** Security services offered: 24-hour foot-and-vehicle patrols, late-night transport/escort service, 24-hour emergency telephones, lighted pathways/sidewalks, controlled dormitory access (key, security card, etc).

TRANSFER AND INTERNATIONAL STUDENTS

Transfer students: May apply for admission for the following academic terms: Fall, Spring, Summer. Applicants do not need a minimum number of credits to apply. For fall 2009: Transfer applications received: 419. Transfer applicants offered admission: 323. Transfer applicants enrolled: 179. **International students:** Number of foreign undergraduates: 504 (16% of student body). Number of countries represented: 21. Minimum TOEFL score required: 550 (paper); 213 (computer). Average TOEFL score: 575 (paper).

Nyack College

- **Address:** 1 South Boulevard, Nyack, NY 10960-3698
- **Website:** http://www.nyack.edu
- **Private; Religious affiliation:** Christian and Missionary Alliance
- **Enrollment:** N/A

KEY STATS

✔ **U.S News College Ranking:** second tier, Regional Universities (North)
✔ **SAT or ACT Score (25th/75th percentile):** N/A
✔ **Tuition:** 2009-2010: $19,350

Selectivity: Less selective	**Room/board:** $7,900
Acceptance rate: N/A	**Average debt:** N/A
Student/faculty ratio: N/A	**Proportion who borrowed:** N/A

Pace University

- **Address:** 1 Pace Plaza, New York, NY 10038
- **Website:** http://www.pace.edu
- **Private**
- **Enrollment:** 6,498 full-time; 1,473 part-time

KEY STATS

✔ **U.S News College Ranking:** 170, National Universities
✔ **SAT Score (25th/75th percentile):** 990-1190
✔ **Tuition:** 2010-2011: $33,612

Selectivity: Selective	**Room/board:** $11,900
Acceptance rate: 78%	**Average debt:** $34,115
Student/faculty ratio: 15/1	**Proportion who borrowed:** 58%

UNDERGRADUATE STUDENT BODY STATS

2009-2010 enrollment: 6,498 full-time; 1,473 part-time. Men: 40%; women: 60%. **Ethnic makeup:** African American: 11%; Asian American: 9%; Hispanic: 13%; White: 62%; International: 5%.

ADMISSIONS FACTS AND FIGURES

Phone: (212) 346-1323. **Email:** infoctr@pace.edu. **Website:** http://www.pace.edu. **Application deadlines for fall 2011:** Regular decision: February 15. Early decision: Not offered. Early action: Send application by: November 30; Decision sent by: December 31. Admission can be deferred. **Application fee:** $50. **To apply online, go to:** http://apply.pace.edu. **Admissions requirements/recommendations:** High school units required (recommended): English: 4 (4); Mathematics: 3 (4); Science: 2 (2); Foreign language: 2 (3); Social studies: 1 (2); History: 2 (3); Academic electives: 2 (2); Total units: 16 (20). Tests: The college uses SAT or ACT scores in admissions decisions. Either SAT or ACT required. For admission to the fall 2011 entering class, the school will accept: ACT with or without writing accepted. Campus visit: Recommended. Admissions interview: Recommended. Off-campus interview: May be arranged. **Factors that count in admissions decisions:** *Academic:* Secondary school record: Very Important. Class rank: Important. Letters of recommendation: Considered. Standardized test scores: Very Important. Essay: Considered. *Nonacademic:* Interview: Not Considered. Extracurricular activities: Considered. Talent/ability: Considered. Character/personal qualities: Considered. Alumni/ae relationship: Considered. Geographical residence: Not Considered. State residency: Not Considered. Religious affiliation/commitment: Not Considered. Minority status: Not Considered. Volunteer work: Considered. Work experience: Considered. **Other schools with the greatest overlap in applicants:** CUNY–Baruch College; CUNY–Hunter College; Fordham University; New York University; St. John's University. **Admissions statistics for the fall 2009 entering class:** Total applicants: 10,985. Total accepted: 8,587. Freshmen enrolled: 1,672; 40% were from out of state. Accepted through early-decision or early-action plans: 30%. Overall acceptance rate: 78%. Non-early acceptance rate: 74%. **Credentials of fall 2009 freshmen:** 14% ranked in the top 10 percent of their high school class; 39% were in the top 25 percent; 76% were in the top half. (Proportion submitting class standing: 40%.) **Average high school grade point average:** 3.2. First-year students who submitted SAT scores: 94%. Scores (25/75 percentile): Critical Reading: 490-590, Math: 500-600, Combined: 990-1190. **First-year students submitting ACT scores:** 4%. Scores (25/75 percentile): English: N/A, Math: N/A, Composite: 20-26.

ACADEMICS

Year founded: 1906. **Academic calendar:** Semester. **Degrees offered:** certificate, diploma, associate, bachelor's, post-bachelor's certificate, master's, post-master's certificate, doctorate. **Most popular majors:** 34% business, management, marketing, and related support services, 13% health professions and related clinical sciences, 10% communication, journalism, and related programs, 7% computer and information sciences and support services, 6% psychology. **Major fields of study:** area, ethnic, cultural, and gender studies; biological and biomedical sciences; business, management, marketing, and related support services; communication, journalism, and related programs; computer and information sciences and support services; education; English language and literature/letters; foreign languages, literatures, and linguistics; health professions and related clinical sciences; history; liberal arts and sciences studies, and humanities; mathematics and statistics; multi/interdisciplinary studies; natural resources and conservation; philosophy and religious studies; physical sciences; psychology; public administration and social service professions; security and protective services; social sciences; visual and performing arts. **Areas of required coursework:** arts/fine arts, humanities, computer literacy, mathematics, English (including composition), philosophy, sciences (biological or physical), social science, other. **Pre-professional programs:** pre-law, pre-dentistry, pre-medicine, pre-veterinary science, other. **Special academic programs (% participation):** accelerated program (2%), cooperative (work-study plan) program (91%), distance learning (58%), dual enrollment (5%), English as a Second Language (ESL) (1%), honors program (19%), independent study (29%), internships (50%), study abroad (23%), teacher certificate program (2%). **Teacher certification offered in:** early childhood, elementary, middle/junior high, secondary. **Cooperative education programs:** business, computer science, education, health professions, social/behavioral science, other. **Reserve Officers Training Corps (ROTC):** Army ROTC: Offered at cooperating institution (St. John's University); Air Force ROTC: Offered at cooperating institution (Manhattan College). **Faculty and instruction (2009-2010):** Total instructional faculty: 447 full-time, 671 part-time (52% men; 48% women; 15% minorities). Full-time faculty with Ph.D. or other terminal degree: 85%. Student/faculty ratio: 15/1. Classes of fewer than 20 students: 51%; of 20 to 49 students: 47%; of 50 or more students: 2%. **Advanced Placement and International Baccalaureate credit:** AP tests may be used for: Credit only. Scores accepted: 4, 5. International Baccalaureate exams may be used for: Credit and/or placement. **Freshmen returning for sophomore year:** 75%. **Graduation rates:** Four-year: 45%; five-year: 58%; six-year: 60%. **Graduate study:** 20% of students pursue further study immediately upon graduation. Fields in which graduates pursue further study: Master of Business Administration (MBA), 5%; law, 5%; medicine, 1%; engineering, 1%; education, 14%; arts and sciences, 74%.

COSTS AND FINANCIAL AID

Financial aid office: (212) 346-1300. **Expenses (2010-2011):** Tuition and fees 2010-2011: $33,612; room/board: $11,900. Estimated books and supplies: $800; transportation: $600; personal expenses: $1,252. **Financial aid:** Priority filing date for institution's financial aid form: February 15. In 2009-2010, 81% of undergraduates applied for financial aid. Of those, 74% were determined to have financial need; 13% had their need fully met. Average financial aid package (proportion receiving): $28,055 (74%). Average amount of gift aid, such as scholarships or grants (proportion receiving): $23,607 (73%). Average amount of self-help aid, such as work study or loans (proportion receiving): $5,082 (63%). Average need-based loan (excluding PLUS or other private loans): $4,517. Among students who received need-based aid, the average percentage of need met: 78%. Among students who received aid based on merit, the average award (and the proportion receiving): $9,602 (19%). The average athletic scholarship (and the proportion receiving): $14,904 (0%). Average amount of debt of borrowers graduating in 2009: $34,115. Proportion who borrowed: 58%.

CAMPUS LIFE AND EXTRACURRICULAR ACTIVITIES

Campus housing available (% using): coed dorms (84%), other housing options (16%). Students who live in college-owned, operated, or affiliated housing: 45%. **Student employment:** During the 2009-2010 academic year, 8% of undergraduates worked on campus. Average per-year earnings: $2,020. **Clubs and organizations:** Number of student organizations: 90. Activities include: choral groups, dance, drama/theater, literary magazine, model UN, musical theater, radio station, student government, student newspaper, student film society, television station, yearbook. Number of fraternities: 11; sororities: 9. Proportion of men in fraternities: 5%; of women in sororities: 5%. Average proportion of students who stay on campus on weekends: 50%. **Sports program (2009-2010):** Member of NCAA II. **Men's intercollegiate varsity sports:** baseball, basketball, cross country, football,

golf, lacrosse, swimming, tennis, track and field (outdoor). **Women's intercollegiate varsity sports:** basketball, cross country, equestrian, soccer, softball, swimming, tennis, track and field (outdoor), volleyball.

SERVICES AND FACILITIES

Basic services: nonremedial tutoring, placement service, health service. **Remedial assistance:** math, writing. **Counseling services:** minority student, career, academic, psychological, other. **For learning-disabled students:** School does not offer a structured program with separate admission and additional fees. Services include: remedial math, remedial English, reading machines, remedial reading, tape recorders, untimed tests, note-taking services, oral tests, learning center, readers, extended time for tests, tutors, priority registration, priority seating, texts on tape, other testing accommodations, other. **Library:** Number of titles: 806,756; number of current serial subscriptions: 1,673. **Information technology resources:** Students are not required to lease or own a computer. Number of campus computers available to all students: 508. School has a wireless network. Approximate number of users that can be accommodated: 2,500. Proportion of college-owned housing units wired for high-speed internet access: 100%. **Campus safety:** Security services offered: 24-hour foot-and-vehicle patrols, late-night transport/escort service, 24-hour emergency telephones, lighted pathways/sidewalks, controlled dormitory access (key, security card, etc).

TRANSFER AND INTERNATIONAL STUDENTS

Transfer students: May apply for admission for the following academic terms: Fall, Spring, Summer. Applicants need a minimum number of credits to apply. For fall 2009: Transfer applications received: 2,244. Transfer applicants offered admission: 1,643. Transfer applicants enrolled: 563. **International students:** Number of foreign undergraduates: 348 (5% of student body). Number of countries represented: 38. Minimum TOEFL score required: 550 (paper); 88 (computer). Average TOEFL score: 567 (paper).

Paul Smith's College

- **Address:** Routes 30 and 36, Paul Smiths, NY 12970-0265
- **Website:** http://www.paulsmiths.edu
- **Private**
- **Enrollment:** N/A

KEY STATS

✔ **U.S News College Ranking:** second tier, Regional Colleges (North)
✔ **SAT or ACT Score (25th/75th percentile):** N/A
✔ **Tuition:** 2010-2011: $20,865

Selectivity: Less selective	**Room/board:** $9,390
Acceptance rate: N/A	**Average debt:** $16,784
Student/faculty ratio: N/A	**Proportion who borrowed:** 88%

Polytechnic Institute of New York Univ.

- **Address:** 6 Metrotech Center, Brooklyn, NY 11201
- **Website:** http://www.poly.edu/
- **Private**
- **Enrollment:** 1,665 full-time; 67 part-time

KEY STATS

✔ **U.S News College Ranking:** 153, National Universities
✔ **SAT Score (25th/75th percentile):** 1190-1360
✔ **Tuition:** 2010-2011: $36,284

Selectivity: More selective	**Room/board:** $10,080
Acceptance rate: 55%	**Average debt:** $31,035
Student/faculty ratio: 15/1	**Proportion who borrowed:** 74%

UNDERGRADUATE STUDENT BODY STATS

2009-2010 enrollment: 1,665 full-time; 67 part-time. Men: 80%; women: 20%. **Ethnic makeup:** African American: 10%; Asian American: 30%; Hispanic: 12%; White: 35%; International: 12%.

ADMISSIONS FACTS AND FIGURES

Phone: (718) 260-3100. **Email:** uadmit@poly.edu. **Website:** http://www.poly.edu/. **Application deadlines for fall 2011:** Regular decision: Rolling.

Early decision: Not offered. Early action: Not offered. Admission can be deferred. **Application fee:** $50. **To apply online, go to:** http://www.poly.edu/admissions/undergrad/apply/applyonline.php. **Admissions requirements/recommendations:** High school units required (recommended): English: 4; Mathematics: 4; Science: 4; Foreign language: (2); Social studies: 0; Academic electives: 0; Total units: 12 (0). Tests: The college uses SAT or ACT scores in admissions decisions. Either SAT or ACT required. Campus visit: Recommended. Admissions interview: Recommended. Off-campus interview: May be arranged. **Factors that count in admissions decisions:** *Academic:* Secondary school record: Very Important. Class rank: Important. Letters of recommendation: Considered. Standardized test scores: Very Important. Essay: Considered. *Nonacademic:* Interview: Considered. Extracurricular activities: Considered. Talent/ability: Not Considered. Character/personal qualities: Considered. Alumni/ae relationship: Considered. Geographical residence: Not Considered. State residency: Not Considered. Religious affiliation/commitment: Not Considered. Minority status: Not Considered. Volunteer work: Considered. Work experience: Considered. **Other schools with the greatest overlap in applicants:** CUNY–City College; Cooper Union; Rensselaer Polytechnic Institute; Rochester Institute of Technology; Stevens Institute of Technology. **Admissions statistics for the fall 2009 entering class:** Total applicants: 3,897. Total accepted: 2,145. Freshmen enrolled: 366; 27% were from out of state. Overall acceptance rate: 55%. **Size of waiting list:** 0 applicants; enrolled from waiting list: 0. **Credentials of fall 2009 freshmen:** 36% ranked in the top 10 percent of their high school class; 69% were in the top 25 percent; 91% were in the top half. (Proportion submitting class standing: 29%.) **Average high school grade point average:** 3.4. **First-year students who submitted SAT scores:** 93%. Scores (25/75 percentile): Critical Reading: 560-640, Math: 630-720, Combined: 1190-1360. **First-year students submitting ACT scores:** 7%. Scores (25/75 percentile): English: N/A, Math: N/A, Composite: 26-32.

ACADEMICS

Year founded: 1854. **Academic calendar:** Semester. **Degrees offered:** certificate, bachelor's, master's, doctorate. **Most popular majors:** 15% mechanical engineering, 14% electrical, electronics, and communications engineering, 11% civil engineering, 11% computer engineering, 11% computer science. **Major fields of study:** biological and biomedical sciences; business, management, marketing, and related support services; communication, journalism, and related programs; communications technologies/technicians and support services; computer and information sciences and support services; engineering; liberal arts and sciences studies, and humanities; mathematics and statistics; physical sciences. **Areas of required coursework:** humanities, computer literacy, mathematics, English (including composition), sciences (biological or physical), history, social science. **Pre-professional programs:** pre-medicine. **Special academic programs (% participation):** cooperative (work-study plan) program (52.1%), distance learning (3%), double major (3%), honors program (8.9%), internships (31%). **Cooperative education programs:** computer science, engineering. **Reserve Officers Training Corps (ROTC):** Army ROTC: Offered at cooperating institution (Fordham University); Air Force ROTC: Offered at cooperating institution (Manhattan College). **Faculty and instruction (2009-2010):** Total instructional faculty: 152 full-time, 189 part-time (82% men; 18% women; 22% minorities). Full-time faculty with Ph.D. or other terminal degree: 89%. Student/faculty ratio: 15/1. Classes of fewer than 20 students: 52%; of 20 to 49 students: 44%; of 50 or more students: 3%. **Advanced Placement and International Baccalaureate credit:** AP tests may be used for: Placement only. Scores accepted: 4, 5. International Baccalaureate exams may be used for: Credit only. **Freshmen returning for sophomore year:** 82%. **Graduation rates:** Four-year: 36%; five-year: 47%; six-year: 54%. **Graduate study:** 27% of students pursue further study immediately upon graduation. Fields in which graduates pursue further study: Master of Business Administration (MBA), 1%; medicine, 1%; engineering, 97%; education, 1%.

COSTS AND FINANCIAL AID

Financial aid office: (718) 260-3300. **Expenses (2010-2011):** Tuition and fees 2010-2011: $36,284; room/board: $10,080. Estimated books and supplies: $1,500; transportation: $800; personal expenses: $1,900. **Financial aid:** Priority filing date for institution's financial aid form: January 31. In 2009-2010, 95% of undergraduates applied for financial aid. Of those, 72% were determined to have financial need; 55% had their need fully met. Average financial aid package (proportion receiving): $26,211 (72%). Average amount of gift aid, such as scholarships or grants (proportion receiving): $12,353 (65%). Average amount of self-help aid, such as work study or loans (proportion receiving): $4,812 (58%). Average need-based loan (excluding PLUS or other private loans): $4,683. Among students who received need-based aid, the average percentage of need met: 89%. Among students who received aid based on merit, the average award (and the proportion receiving): $18,428 (21%). The average athletic scholarship (and the proportion receiving): $0 (0%). Average amount of debt of borrowers graduating in 2009: $31,035. Proportion who borrowed: 74%.

CAMPUS LIFE AND EXTRACURRICULAR ACTIVITIES

Campus housing available (% using): coed dorms (100%). Students who live in college-owned, operated, or affiliated housing: 26%. **Student employment:** During the 2009-2010 academic year, 9% of undergraduates worked on campus. **Clubs and organizations:** Number of student organizations: 39. Activities include: drama/theater, literary magazine, radio station, student government, student newspaper, student film society, yearbook. Number of fraternities: 3; sororities: 1. Proportion of men in fraternities: 4%; of women in sororities: 2%. Average proportion of students who stay on campus on weekends: 31%. **Sports program (2009-2010):** Member of NCAA III. *Men's intercollegiate varsity sports:* baseball, basketball, golf, soccer, tennis, track and field (outdoor), volleyball. *Women's intercollegiate varsity sports:* basketball, soccer, softball, tennis, track and field (outdoor), volleyball.

SERVICES AND FACILITIES

Basic services: nonremedial tutoring, placement service, health service. **Remedial assistance:** reading, math, writing, study skills. **Counseling services:** career, personal, academic, psychological. **For learning-disabled students:** School does not offer a structured program with separate admission and additional fees. Total undergraduates in learning-disabled program or receiving services: 6. Services include: untimed tests, note-taking services, learning center, extended time for tests, tutors, other testing accommodations. **Library:** Number of titles: 140,000; number of current serial subscriptions: 3,500. **Information technology resources:** Students are required to lease or own a computer. Number of campus computers available to all students: 1,330. School has a wireless network. Approximate number of users that can be accommodated: 5,000. Proportion of college-owned housing units wired for high-speed internet access: 100%. **Campus safety:** Security services offered: 24-hour emergency telephones, lighted pathways/sidewalks, controlled dormitory access (key, security card, etc).

TRANSFER AND INTERNATIONAL STUDENTS

Transfer students: May apply for admission for the following academic terms: Fall, Spring. Applicants need a minimum number of credits to apply. For fall 2009: Transfer applications received: 328. Transfer applicants offered admission: 225. Transfer applicants enrolled: 96. **International students:** Number of foreign undergraduates: 201 (12% of student body). Number of countries represented: 46. Minimum TOEFL score required: 550 (paper); 21 (computer). Average TOEFL score: 605 (paper).

Pratt Institute

- **Address:** 200 Willoughby Avenue, Brooklyn, NY 11205
- **Website:** http://www.pratt.edu
- **Private**
- **Enrollment:** 2,837 full-time; 161 part-time

KEY STATS

✔ **U.S News College Ranking:** Unranked Specialty School–Fine Arts
✔ **SAT Score (25th/75th percentile):** 1050-1290
✔ **Tuition:** 2010-2011: $37,090

Selectivity: N/A	Room/board: $10,020
Acceptance rate: 41%	Average debt: N/A
Student/faculty ratio: 11/1	Proportion who borrowed: N/A

UNDERGRADUATE STUDENT BODY STATS

2009-2010 enrollment: 2,837 full-time; 161 part-time. Men: 38%; women: 62%. **Ethnic makeup:** African American: 5%; Asian American: 15%; Hispanic: 9%; White: 58%; International: 13%.

ADMISSIONS FACTS AND FIGURES

Phone: (718) 636-3514. **Email:** admissions@pratt.edu. **Website:** http://www.pratt.edu. **Application deadlines for fall 2011:** Regular decision: January 5; decision sent by April 1. Early decision: Not offered. Early action: Send application by: November 1; Decision sent by: December 22. Admission can be deferred. **Application fee:** $50. **To apply online, go to:** http://www.pratt.edu/admiss/apply. **Admissions requirements/recommendations:** High school units required (recommended): English: (4); Mathematics:

(4); Science: (2); Social studies: (1); Academic electives: (5); Total units: (16). Tests: The college uses SAT or ACT scores in admissions decisions. Either SAT or ACT required. For admission to the fall 2011 entering class, the school will accept: ACT with writing required. Campus visit: Recommended. Admissions interview: Neither required nor recommended. Off-campus interview: May be arranged. **Factors that count in admissions decisions:** *Academic:* Secondary school record: Very Important. Class rank: Considered. Letters of recommendation: Important. Standardized test scores: Very Important. Essay: Important. *Nonacademic:* Interview: Considered. Extracurricular activities: Considered. Talent/ability: Very Important. Character/personal qualities: Important. Alumni/ae relationship: Important. Geographical residence: Not Considered. State residency: Not Considered. Religious affiliation/commitment: Not Considered. Minority status: Not Considered. Volunteer work: Considered. Work experience: Considered. **Admissions statistics for the fall 2009 entering class:** Total applicants: 5,471. Total accepted: 2,268. Freshmen enrolled: 629; Accepted through early-decision or early-action plans: 28%. Overall acceptance rate: 41%. Non-early acceptance rate: 45%. **Size of waiting list:** 608 applicants; enrolled from waiting list: 30. **Average high school grade point average:** 3.5. **First-year students who submitted SAT scores:** 87%. Scores (25/75 percentile): Critical Reading: 530-640, Math: 520-650, Combined: 1050-1290. **First-year students submitting ACT scores:** 23%. Scores (25/75 percentile): English: N/A, Math: N/A, Composite: 22-28.

ACADEMICS

Year founded: 1887. **Academic calendar:** Semester. **Degrees offered:** associate, transfer-associate, terminal-associate, bachelor's, master's, post-master's certificate. **Major fields of study:** architecture and related services; education; English language and literature/letters; visual and performing arts. **Areas of required coursework:** arts/fine arts, humanities, computer literacy, mathematics, English (including composition), sciences (biological or physical), history, social science. **Special academic programs (% participation):** cross-registration, double major, English as a Second Language (ESL) (16%), exchange student program (domestic) (.1%), independent study (1%), internships (2%), study abroad, teacher certificate program (2%). **Teacher certification offered in:** elementary, middle/junior high, secondary. **Faculty and instruction (2009-2010):** Total instructional faculty: 120 full-time, 877 part-time (59% men; 41% women; 15% minorities). Full-time faculty with Ph.D. or other terminal degree: 68%. Student/faculty ratio: 11/1. Classes of fewer than 20 students: 87%; of 20 to 49 students: 13%; of 50 or more students: 0%. **Advanced Placement and International Baccalaureate credit:** AP tests may be used for: Credit only. Scores accepted: 4, 5. International Baccalaureate exams may be used for: Credit only. **Freshmen returning for sophomore year:** 85%. **Graduation rates:** Four-year: 36%; five-year: 54%; six-year: 54%. **Graduate study:** 3% of students pursue further study immediately upon graduation; 2% within one year; 5% within five years. Fields in which graduates pursue further study: education, 1%; arts and sciences, 3%.

COSTS AND FINANCIAL AID

Financial aid office: (718) 636-3599. **Expenses (2010-2011):** Tuition and fees 2010-2011: $37,090; room/board: $10,020. Estimated books and supplies: $3,000 personal expenses: $1,800. **Financial aid:** Priority filing date for institution's financial aid form: February 1; deadline: February 1. In 2009-2010, 78% of undergraduates applied for financial aid. Of those, 69% were determined to have financial need; Average financial aid package (proportion receiving): $13,039 (69%). Average amount of gift aid, such as scholarships or grants (proportion receiving): $10,896 (63%). Average amount of self-help aid, such as work study or loans (proportion receiving): N/A (60%). Average need-based loan (excluding PLUS or other private loans): $6,956. Among students who received need-based aid, the average percentage of need met: 64%. Among students who received aid based on merit, the average award (and the proportion receiving): $7,432 (12%). The average athletic scholarship (and the proportion receiving): $0 (0%).

CAMPUS LIFE AND EXTRACURRICULAR ACTIVITIES

Campus housing available (% using): coed dorms (97%), apartment for single students (3%). **Student employment:** During the 2009-2010 academic year, 31% of undergraduates worked on campus. Average per-year earnings: $2,170. **Clubs and organizations:** Number of student organizations: 42. Activities include: campus ministries, drama/theater, international student organization, literary magazine, radio station, student government, student newspaper, student film society, television station, yearbook. Number of fraternities: 2; sororities: 2. Average proportion of students who stay on campus on weekends: 80%. **Sports program (2009-2010):** Member of NCAA III. *Men's intercollegiate varsity sports:* basketball, cross country, tennis, track and field (indoor), track and field (outdoor). *Women's intercollegiate varsity*

sports: cross country, tennis, track and field (indoor), track and field (outdoor), volleyball.

SERVICES AND FACILITIES

Basic services: placement service, health service, health insurance. **Remedial assistance:** reading, math, writing, study skills. **Counseling services:** minority student, career, personal, veteran student, academic, psychological, birth control, religious. **For learning-disabled students:** School does not offer a structured program with separate admission and additional fees. Total undergraduates in learning-disabled program or receiving services: 470. Services include: reading machines, tape recorders, diagnostic testing service, note-taking services, learning center, readers, extended time for tests, tutors, priority seating, texts on tape, other testing accommodations. **Library:** Number of titles: 189,898; number of current serial subscriptions: 914. **Information technology resources:** Students are not required to lease or own a computer. Number of campus computers available to all students: 500. School has a wireless network. Approximate number of users that can be accommodated: 500. Proportion of college-owned housing units wired for high-speed internet access: 100%. **Campus safety:** Security services offered: 24-hour foot-and-vehicle patrols, 24-hour emergency telephones, lighted pathways/sidewalks, controlled dormitory access (key, security card, etc).

TRANSFER AND INTERNATIONAL STUDENTS

Transfer students: May apply for admission for the following academic terms: Fall, Spring, Summer. Applicants need a minimum number of credits to apply. For fall 2009: Transfer applications received: 1,145. Transfer applicants offered admission: 494. Transfer applicants enrolled: 150. **International students:** Number of foreign undergraduates: 395 (13% of student body). Number of countries represented: 49. Minimum TOEFL score required: 550 (paper); 80 (computer). Average TOEFL score: 598 (paper).

Purchase College–SUNY

- **Address:** 735 Anderson Hill Road, Purchase, NY 10577
- **Website:** http://www.purchase.edu
- **Public**
- **Enrollment:** 3,698 full-time; 379 part-time

KEY STATS

✔ **U.S News College Ranking:** 187, National Liberal Arts Colleges
✔ **SAT Score (25th/75th percentile):** 1000-1210
✔ **Tuition:** 2010-2011: $6,475 in state, $14,375 out of state

Selectivity: Selective	**Room/board:** $10,270
Acceptance rate: 27%	**Average debt:** $26,275
Student/faculty ratio: 16/1	**Proportion who borrowed:** 58%

UNDERGRADUATE STUDENT BODY STATS

2009-2010 enrollment: 3,698 full-time; 379 part-time. Men: 44%; women: 56%. **Ethnic makeup:** African American: 7%; Asian American: 3%; Hispanic: 12%; White: 76%; International: 2%.

ADMISSIONS FACTS AND FIGURES

Phone: (914) 251-6300. **Email:** admissions@purchase.edu. **Website:** http://www.purchase.edu. **Application deadlines for fall 2011:** Regular decision: July 15. Early decision: Send application by: November 1; Decision sent by: December 5. Early action: Not offered. Admission can be deferred. **Application fee:** $40. **To apply online, go to:** http://www.purchase.edu/admissions/adm_applyonline.asp. **Admissions requirements/recommendations:** High school units required (recommended): English: (4); Mathematics: (4); Science: (3); Foreign language: (3); Social studies: (4); History: (0); Academic electives: (2); Total units: (20). Tests: The college uses SAT or ACT scores in admissions decisions. Either SAT or ACT required. For admission to the fall 2011 entering class, the school will accept: ACT with or without writing accepted. Campus visit: Recommended. Admissions interview: Recommended. Off-campus interview: May be arranged. **Factors that count in admissions decisions:** *Academic:* Secondary school record: Considered. Class rank: Considered. Letters of recommendation: Considered. Standardized test scores: Important. Essay: Very Important. *Nonacademic:* Interview: Considered. Extracurricular activities: Considered. Talent/ability: Very Important. Character/personal qualities: Considered. Alumni/ae relationship: Not Considered. Geographical residence: Not Considered. State residency: Not Considered. Religious affiliation/commitment: Not Considered. Minority status: Not Considered.

Volunteer work: Not Considered. Work experience: Not Considered. **Other schools with the greatest overlap in applicants:** Binghamton University–SUNY; Juilliard School; New York University; SUNY–New Paltz; University at Albany–SUNY. **Admissions statistics for the fall 2009 entering class:** Total applicants: 8,620. Total accepted: 2,300. Freshmen enrolled: 694; 23% were from out of state. Accepted through early-decision or early-action plans: 2%. Overall acceptance rate: 27%. Early-decision acceptance rate: 47%. Non-early acceptance rate: 27%. **Credentials of fall 2009 freshmen:** 11% ranked in the top 10 percent of their high school class; 38% were in the top 25 percent; 81% were in the top half. (Proportion submitting class standing: 42%.) **Average high school grade point average:** 3.2. **First-year students who submitted SAT scores:** 94%. Scores (25/75 percentile): Critical Reading: 510-630, Math: 490-580, Combined: 1000-1210. **First-year students submitting ACT scores:** 19%. Scores (25/75 percentile): English: 22-26, Math: 18-24, Composite: 21-25.

ACADEMICS

Year founded: 1967. **Academic calendar:** Semester. **Degrees offered:** certificate, bachelor's, master's, post-master's certificate. **Most popular majors:** 35% visual and performing arts, 25% liberal arts and sciences studies, and humanities, 10% social sciences, 6% English language and literature/letters, 5% communication, journalism, and related programs. **Major fields of study:** area, ethnic, cultural, and gender studies; biological and biomedical sciences; communication, journalism, and related programs; English language and literature/letters; foreign languages, literatures, and linguistics; history; mathematics and statistics; multi/interdisciplinary studies; philosophy and religious studies; physical sciences; psychology; social sciences; visual and performing arts. **Areas of required coursework:** humanities, mathematics, English (including composition), foreign languages, sciences (biological or physical), history, social science, other. **Special academic programs:** cross-registration, double major, English as a Second Language (ESL), independent study, internships, liberal arts/career combination, student-designed major, study abroad. **Faculty and instruction (2009-2010):** Total instructional faculty: 150 full-time, 234 part-time (52% men; 48% women; 13% minorities). Full-time faculty with Ph.D. or other terminal degree: 69%. Student/faculty ratio: 16/1. Classes of fewer than 20 students: 70%; of 20 to 49 students: 26%; of 50 or more students: 3%. **Freshmen returning for sophomore year:** 80%. **Graduation rates:** Four-year: 30%; five-year: 44%; six-year: 49%. **Graduate study:** 25% of students pursue further study within one year. Fields in which graduates pursue further study: Master of Business Administration (MBA), 8%; law, 8%; medicine, 2%; dentistry, 2%; education, 29%; veterinary medicine, 2%.

COSTS AND FINANCIAL AID

Financial aid office: (914) 251-6350. **Expenses (2010-2011):** Tuition and fees 2010-2011: $6,475 in state, $14,375 out of state; room/board: $10,270. Estimated books and supplies: $1,122; transportation: $1,079; personal expenses: $1,974. **Financial aid:** Priority filing date for institution's financial aid form: February 1. In 2009-2010, 74% of undergraduates applied for financial aid. Of those, 56% were determined to have financial need; 7% had their need fully met. Average financial aid package (proportion receiving): $9,728 (56%). Average amount of gift aid, such as scholarships or grants (proportion receiving): $6,001 (46%). Average amount of self-help aid, such as work study or loans (proportion receiving): $4,955 (55%). Average need-based loan (excluding PLUS or other private loans): $4,787. Among students who received need-based aid, the average percentage of need met: 59%. Among students who received aid based on merit, the average award (and the proportion receiving): $1,989 (3%). The average athletic scholarship (and the proportion receiving): $0 (0%). Average amount of debt of borrowers graduating in 2009: $26,275. Proportion who borrowed: 58%.

CAMPUS LIFE AND EXTRACURRICULAR ACTIVITIES

Campus housing available (% using): coed dorms (49%), apartment for single students (40%), special housing for disabled students (1%), special housing for international students (1%). Students who live in college-owned, operated, or affiliated housing: 67%. **Clubs and organizations:** Number of student organizations: 34. Activities include: choral groups, dance, drama/theater, jazz band, literary magazine, radio station, student government, student newspaper, student film society, television station. Number of fraternities: 0; sororities: 0. Average proportion of students who stay on campus on weekends: 70%. **Sports program (2009-2010):** Member of NCAA III. **Men's intercollegiate varsity sports:** baseball, basketball, cross country, golf, soccer, tennis, volleyball. **Women's intercollegiate varsity sports:** basketball, cross country, soccer, softball, swimming, tennis, volleyball.

SERVICES AND FACILITIES

Basic services: day care, health service, health insurance. **Remedial assistance:** reading, math, writing, study skills. **Counseling services:** career, personal, academic, psychological. **For learning-disabled students:** School does not offer a structured program with separate admission and additional fees. Services include: reading machines, tape recorders, note-taking services, learning center, readers, extended time for tests, tutors, priority seating, substitution of courses, texts on tape, typist/scribe, exams on tape or computer. **Library:** Number of titles: 244,399; number of current serial subscriptions: 47,885. **Information technology resources:** Students are not required to lease or own a computer. Number of campus computers available to all students: 600. School has a wireless network. Proportion of college-owned housing units wired for high-speed internet access: 100%. **Campus safety:** Security services offered: 24-hour foot-and-vehicle patrols, 24-hour emergency telephones, lighted pathways/sidewalks, controlled dormitory access (key, security card, etc).

TRANSFER AND INTERNATIONAL STUDENTS

Transfer students: May apply for admission for the following academic terms: Fall, Spring. Applicants do not need a minimum number of credits to apply. For fall 2009: Transfer applications received: 2,025. Transfer applicants offered admission: 770. Transfer applicants enrolled: 390. **International students:** Number of foreign undergraduates: 62 (2% of student body). Number of countries represented: 27. Minimum TOEFL score required: 550 (paper); 213 (computer).

Rensselaer Polytechnic Institute

- **Address:** 110 Eighth Street, Troy, NY 12180-3590
- **Website:** http://www.rpi.edu
- **Private**
- **Enrollment:** 5,601 full-time; 58 part-time

KEY STATS

✔ **U.S News College Ranking:** 41, National Universities
✔ **SAT Score (25th/75th percentile):** 1270-1450
✔ **Tuition:** 2010-2011: $40,680

Selectivity: More selective   **Room/board:** $11,465
Acceptance rate: 43%   **Average debt:** $30,838
Student/faculty ratio: 16/1   **Proportion who borrowed:** 71%

UNDERGRADUATE STUDENT BODY STATS

2009-2010 enrollment: 5,601 full-time; 58 part-time. Men: 72%; women: 28%. **Ethnic makeup:** African American: 3%; American-Indian: 1%; Asian American: 11%; Hispanic: 6%; White: 76%; International: 3%.

ADMISSIONS FACTS AND FIGURES

Phone: (518) 276-6216. **Email:** admissions@rpi.edu. **Website:** http://www.rpi.edu. **Application deadlines for fall 2011:** Regular decision: January 15; decision sent by March 20. Early decision: Send application by: November 2; Decision sent by: December 5. Early action: Not offered. Admission can be deferred. **Application fee:** $70. **To apply online, go to:** http://admissions.rpi.edu. **Admissions requirements/recommendations:** High school units required (recommended): English: 4; Mathematics: 4; Science: 3 (4); Social studies: 2 (3); Total units: 15. Tests: The college uses SAT or ACT scores in admissions decisions. Either SAT or ACT required. For admission to the fall 2011 entering class, the school will accept: ACT with writing required. Campus visit: Recommended. Admissions interview: Neither required nor recommended. Off-campus interview: Not available. **Factors that count in admissions decisions:** *Academic:* Secondary school record: Very Important. Class rank: Very Important. Letters of recommendation: Important. Standardized test scores: Very Important. Essay: Important. *Nonacademic:* Interview: Considered. Extracurricular activities: Important. Talent/ability: Considered. Character/personal qualities: Important. Alumni/ae relationship: Considered. Geographical residence: Considered. State residency: Not Considered. Religious affiliation/commitment: Not Considered. Minority status: Considered. Volunteer work: Considered. Work experience: Considered. **Other schools with the greatest overlap in applicants:** Carnegie Mellon University; Cornell University; Massachusetts Institute of Technology; University of Rochester; Worcester Polytechnic Institute. **Admissions statistics for the fall 2009 entering class:** Total applicants: 12,350. Total accepted: 5,291. Freshmen enrolled: 1,337; 70% were from out of state. Accepted through early-decision or early-action plans: 27%.

Overall acceptance rate: 43%. Early-decision acceptance rate: 39%. Non-early acceptance rate: 43%. **Size of waiting list:** 3799 applicants; enrolled from waiting list: 186. **Credentials of fall 2009 freshmen:** 61% ranked in the top 10 percent of their high school class; 90% were in the top 25 percent; 98% were in the top half. (Proportion submitting class standing: 63%.) **Average high school grade point average:** 3.7. **First-year students who submitted SAT scores:** 76%. Scores (25/75 percentile): Critical Reading: 610-700, Math: 660-750, Combined: 1270-1450. **First-year students submitting ACT scores:** 24%. Scores (25/75 percentile): English: N/A, Math: N/A, Composite: 25-30.

ACADEMICS

Year founded: 1824. **Academic calendar:** Semester. **Degrees offered:** bachelor's, master's, doctorate. **Most popular majors:** 53% engineering, 10% business, management, marketing, and related support services, 9% computer and information sciences and support services, 6% architecture and related services, 6% biological and biomedical sciences. **Major fields of study:** architecture and related services; biological and biomedical sciences; business, management, marketing, and related support services; communication, journalism, and related programs; computer and information sciences and support services; engineering; health professions and related clinical sciences; legal professions and studies; mathematics and statistics; philosophy and religious studies; physical sciences; psychology; social sciences; visual and performing arts. **Areas of required coursework:** humanities, computer literacy, mathematics, English (including composition), sciences (biological or physical), social science. **Pre-professional programs:** pre-law, pre-medicine. **Special academic programs (% participation):** accelerated program (2%), cooperative (work-study plan) program (10%), cross-registration (2%), double major (20%), dual enrollment, exchange student program (domestic), honors program, independent study, internships (10%), liberal arts/career combination, student-designed major, study abroad (12%). **Cooperative education programs:** art, business, computer science, engineering, humanities, natural science, social/behavioral science, technologies, other. **Reserve Officers Training Corps (ROTC):** Army ROTC: Offered at cooperating institution (Siena College); Navy ROTC: Offered on campus; Air Force ROTC: Offered on campus. **Faculty and instruction (2009-2010):** Total instructional faculty: 386 full-time, 89 part-time (79% men; 21% women; 20% minorities). Full-time faculty with Ph.D. or other terminal degree: 99%. Student/faculty ratio: 16/1. Classes of fewer than 20 students: 53%; of 20 to 49 students: 37%; of 50 or more students: 10%. **Advanced Placement and International Baccalaureate credit:** AP tests may be used for: Placement only. Scores accepted: 4, 5. International Baccalaureate exams may be used for: Placement only. **Freshmen returning for sophomore year:** 93%. **Graduation rates:** Four-year: 64%; five-year: 81%; six-year: 82%. **Graduate study:** 27% of students pursue further study immediately upon graduation; 30% within one year; 40% within five years. Fields in which graduates pursue further study: Master of Business Administration (MBA), 10%; law, 4%; medicine, 16%; dentistry, 1%; engineering, 40%; education, 3%; arts and sciences, 26%.

COSTS AND FINANCIAL AID

Financial aid office: (518) 276-6813. **Expenses (2010-2011):** Tuition and fees 2010-2011: $40,680; room/board: $11,465. Estimated books and supplies: $1,890. **Financial aid:** Priority filing date for institution's financial aid form: February 15. In 2009-2010, 74% of undergraduates applied for financial aid. Of those, 65% were determined to have financial need; 36% had their need fully met. Average financial aid package (proportion receiving): $32,065 (65%). Average amount of gift aid, such as scholarships or grants (proportion receiving): $22,268 (65%). Average amount of self-help aid, such as work study or loans (proportion receiving): $8,167 (53%). Average need-based loan (excluding PLUS or other private loans): $6,068. Among students who received need-based aid, the average percentage of need met: 84%. Among students who received aid based on merit, the average award (and the proportion receiving): $14,086 (32%). The average athletic scholarship (and the proportion receiving): $44,653 (1%). Average amount of debt of borrowers graduating in 2009: $30,838. Proportion who borrowed: 71%.

CAMPUS LIFE AND EXTRACURRICULAR ACTIVITIES

Campus housing available (% using): coed dorms (77%), sorority housing (1%), fraternity housing (1%), apartments for married students (2%), apartment for single students (18%), special housing for disabled students (0%), other housing options (1%). Students who live in college-owned, operated, or affiliated housing: 59%. **Student employment:** During the 2009-2010 academic year, 35% of undergraduates worked on campus. Average per-year earnings: $2,250. **Clubs and organizations:** Number of student organizations: 177. Activities include: campus ministries, choral groups, concert band, dance, drama/theater, international student organization, jazz band,

literary magazine, music ensembles, musical theater, pep band, radio station, student government, student newspaper, student film society, symphony orchestra, television station, yearbook. Number of fraternities: 31; sororities: 5. Proportion of men in fraternities: 25%; of women in sororities: 18%. Average proportion of students who stay on campus on weekends: 75%. **Sports program (2009-2010):** Member of NCAA III. **Men's intercollegiate varsity sports:** baseball, basketball, cross country, football, golf, ice hockey, lacrosse, soccer, swimming, tennis, track and field (indoor), track and field (outdoor). **Women's intercollegiate varsity sports:** basketball, cross country, field hockey, ice hockey, lacrosse, soccer, softball, swimming, tennis, track and field (indoor), track and field (outdoor).

SERVICES AND FACILITIES

Basic services: nonremedial tutoring, placement service, day care, health service, health insurance. **Remedial assistance:** math, writing, study skills. **Counseling services:** minority student, career, military, personal, veteran student, academic, older student, psychological, birth control, religious. **For learning-disabled students:** School does not offer a structured program with separate admission and additional fees. Services include: reading machines, tape recorders, note-taking services, learning center, extended time for tests, tutors, texts on tape, other testing accommodations. **Library:** Number of titles: 348,311; number of current serial subscriptions: 19,075. **Information technology resources:** Students are required to lease or own a computer. Number of campus computers available to all students: 6,818. School has a wireless network. Approximate number of users that can be accommodated: 12,000. Proportion of college-owned housing units wired for high-speed internet access: 100%. **Campus safety:** Security services offered: 24-hour foot-and-vehicle patrols, late-night transport/escort service, 24-hour emergency telephones, lighted pathways/sidewalks, controlled dormitory access (key, security card, etc).

TRANSFER AND INTERNATIONAL STUDENTS

Transfer students: May apply for admission for the following academic terms: Fall, Spring, Summer. Applicants need a minimum number of credits to apply. For fall 2009: Transfer applications received: 307. Transfer applicants offered admission: 189. Transfer applicants enrolled: 103. **International students:** Number of foreign undergraduates: 148 (3% of student body). Number of countries represented: 34. Minimum TOEFL score required: 570 (paper); 230 (computer). Average TOEFL score: 599 (paper).

Roberts Wesleyan College

- **Address:** 2301 Westside Drive, Rochester, NY 14624-1997
- **Website:** http://www.roberts.edu
- **Private; Religious affiliation:** Free Methodist
- **Enrollment:** 1,265 full-time; 123 part-time

KEY STATS

✔ **U.S News College Ranking:** 61, Regional Universities (North)
✔ **SAT Score (25th/75th percentile):** 950-1200
✔ **Tuition:** 2010-2011: $24,360

Selectivity: Selective	**Room/board:** $8,826
Acceptance rate: 65%	**Average debt:** $30,329
Student/faculty ratio: 11/1	**Proportion who borrowed:** 99%

UNDERGRADUATE STUDENT BODY STATS

2009-2010 enrollment: 1,265 full-time; 123 part-time. Men: 31%; women: 69%. **Ethnic makeup:** African American: 9%; Asian American: 1%; Hispanic: 4%; White: 84%; International: 1%. **Religious preference:** Roman Catholic: 10%; Protestant: 67%; Unknown: 11%; Free Methodist: 12%.

ADMISSIONS FACTS AND FIGURES

Phone: (585) 594-6400. **Email:** admissions@roberts.edu. **Website:** http://www.roberts.edu. **Application deadlines for fall 2011:** Regular decision: August 15. Early decision: Not offered. Early action: Not offered. Admission can be deferred. **Application fee:** $35. **To apply online, go to:** http://www.roberts.edu/prospective%20students/apply/index.htm. **Admissions requirements/recommendations:** High school units required (recommended): English: 4; Mathematics: 2 (4); Science: (4); Foreign language: (3); Social studies: 2 (3); History: (3); Total units: 13 (3). Tests: The college uses SAT or ACT scores in admissions decisions. Either SAT or ACT required. For admission to the fall 2011 entering class, the school will accept: ACT with writing recommended. Campus visit: Recommended. Admissions interview: Recommended. Off-campus interview: May be arranged. **Factors that count in admissions decisions:** *Academic:* Secondary school record: Very Important. Class rank: Considered. Letters of recommendation: Important. Standardized test scores: Very Important. Essay: Important. *Nonacademic:* Interview: Very Important. Extracurricular activities: Important. Talent/ability: Considered. Character/personal qualities: Very Important. Alumni/ae relationship: Considered. Geographical residence: Not Considered. State residency: Not Considered. Religious affiliation/commitment: Very Important. Minority status: Not Considered. Volunteer work: Considered. Work experience: Not Considered. **Other schools with the greatest overlap in applicants:** College at Brockport–SUNY; Houghton College; Messiah College; Nazareth College; St. John Fisher College. **Admissions statistics for the fall 2009 entering class:** Total applicants: 1,358. Total accepted: 886. Freshmen enrolled: 264; 12% were from out of state. Overall acceptance rate: 65%. **Credentials of fall 2009 freshmen:** 28% ranked in the top 10 percent of their high school class; 56% were in the top 25 percent; 80% were in the top half. (Proportion submitting class standing: 100%.) **Average high school grade point average:** 3.3. **First-year students who submitted SAT scores:** 88%. Scores (25/75 percentile): Critical Reading: 470-590, Math: 480-610, Combined: 950-1200. **First-year students submitting ACT scores:** 33%. Scores (25/75 percentile): English: 19-26, Math: 20-26, Composite: 21-27.

ACADEMICS

Year founded: 1866. **Academic calendar:** Semester. **Degrees offered:** bachelor's, master's. **Most popular majors:** 25% business, management, marketing, and related support services, 21% health professions and related clinical sciences, 14% education, 7% public administration and social service professions, 6% psychology. **Major fields of study:** biological and biomedical sciences; business, management, marketing, and related support services; communication, journalism, and related programs; computer and information sciences and support services; education; English language and literature/letters; health professions and related clinical sciences; history; liberal arts and sciences studies, and humanities; mathematics and statistics; philosophy and religious studies; physical sciences; psychology; public administration and social service professions; security and protective services; social sciences; theology and religious vocations; visual and performing arts. **Areas of required coursework:** arts/fine arts, humanities, mathematics, English (including composition), philosophy, foreign languages, sciences (biological or physical), history, social science, other. **Pre-professional programs:** pre-law, pre-dentistry, pre-medicine, pre-veterinary science, pre-pharmacy, other. **Special academic programs:** accelerated program, cooperative (work-study plan) program, cross-registration, distance learning, double major, English as a Second Language (ESL), honors program, independent study, internships, study abroad, teacher certificate program. **Teacher certification offered in:** early childhood, special education, elementary, middle/junior high, secondary. **Reserve Officers Training Corps (ROTC):** Army ROTC: Offered at cooperating institution; Air Force ROTC: Offered at cooperating institution (Rochester Institute of Technology). **Faculty and instruction (2009-2010):** Total instructional faculty: 102 full-time, 146 part-time (47% men; 53% women; 8% minorities). Full-time faculty with Ph.D. or other terminal degree: 66%. Student/faculty ratio: 11/1. Classes of fewer than 20 students: 62%; of 20 to 49 students: 36%; of 50 or more students: 2%. **Advanced Placement and International Baccalaureate credit:** AP tests may be used for: Credit only. Scores accepted: 3, 4, 5. International Baccalaureate exams may be used for: Credit only. **Freshmen returning for sophomore year:** 83%. **Graduation rates:** Four-year: 55%; five-year: 65%; six-year: 62%. **Graduate study:** 29% of students pursue further study immediately upon graduation. Fields in which graduates pursue further study: Master of Business Administration (MBA), 5%; law, 5%; medicine, 5%; theology (or the seminary), 10%; education, 65%; arts and sciences, 10%.

COSTS AND FINANCIAL AID

Financial aid office: (585) 594-6150. **Expenses (2010-2011):** Tuition and fees 2010-2011: $24,360; room/board: $8,826. Estimated books and supplies: $1,000; transportation: $900; personal expenses: $1,800. **Financial aid:** Priority filing date for institution's financial aid form: March 15. In 2009-2010, 93% of undergraduates applied for financial aid. Of those, 89% were determined to have financial need; 9% had their need fully met. Average financial aid package (proportion receiving): $17,513 (89%). Average amount of gift aid, such as scholarships or grants (proportion receiving): $11,890 (86%). Average amount of self-help aid, such as work study or loans (proportion receiving): $6,427 (82%). Average need-based loan (excluding PLUS or other private loans): $5,450. Among students who received need-based aid, the average percentage of need met: 69%. Among students who received aid based on merit, the average award (and the proportion receiv-

ing): $4,707 (9%). The average athletic scholarship (and the proportion receiving): $6,124 (2%). Average amount of debt of borrowers graduating in 2009: $30,329. Proportion who borrowed: 99%.

CAMPUS LIFE AND EXTRACURRICULAR ACTIVITIES

Campus housing available (% using): coed dorms (25%), women's dorms (40%), men's dorms (17%), apartments for married students (5%), apartment for single students (12%), special housing for disabled students (1%). Students who live in college-owned, operated, or affiliated housing: 65%. **Student employment:** During the 2009-2010 academic year, 22% of undergraduates worked on campus. Average per-year earnings: $2,000. **Clubs and organizations:** Number of student organizations: 55. Activities include: campus ministries, choral groups, concert band, dance, drama/theater, jazz band, model UN, music ensembles, musical theater, opera, student government, student newspaper, symphony orchestra, yearbook. Number of fraternities: 0; sororities: 0. Average proportion of students who stay on campus on weekends: 60%. **Sports program (2009-2010):** Member of NAIA. *Men's intercollegiate varsity sports:* basketball, cross country, golf, soccer, tennis, track and field (indoor), track and field (outdoor). *Women's intercollegiate varsity sports:* basketball, cross country, soccer, tennis, track and field (indoor), track and field (outdoor), volleyball.

SERVICES AND FACILITIES

Basic services: nonremedial tutoring, placement service, health service, health insurance. **Remedial assistance:** reading, math, writing, study skills. **Counseling services:** minority student, career, military, personal, veteran student, academic, older student, psychological, religious. **For learning-disabled students:** School does not offer a structured program with separate admission and additional fees. Total undergraduates in learning-disabled program or receiving services: 93. Services include: remedial math, remedial English, remedial reading, learning center, tutors, other. **Library:** Number of titles: 134,798; number of current serial subscriptions: 1,871. **Information technology resources:** Students are not required to lease or own a computer. Number of campus computers available to all students: 200. School has a wireless network. Approximate number of users that can be accommodated: 500. Proportion of college-owned housing units wired for high-speed internet access: 100%. **Campus safety:** Security services offered: 24-hour foot-and-vehicle patrols, late-night transport/escort service, 24-hour emergency telephones, lighted pathways/sidewalks, student patrols, controlled dormitory access (key, security card, etc).

TRANSFER AND INTERNATIONAL STUDENTS

Transfer students: May apply for admission for the following academic terms: Fall, Spring, Summer. Applicants need a minimum number of credits to apply. For fall 2009: Transfer applications received: 318. Transfer applicants offered admission: 178. Transfer applicants enrolled: 109. **International students:** Number of foreign undergraduates: 15 (1% of student body). Number of countries represented: 12. Minimum TOEFL score required: 550 (paper); 213 (computer).

Rochester Institute of Technology

- **Address:** 1 Lomb Memorial Drive, Rochester, NY 14623
- **Website:** http://www.rit.edu
- **Private**
- **Enrollment:** 12,367 full-time; 1,678 part-time

KEY STATS

✔ **U.S News College Ranking:** 7, Regional Universities (North)
✔ **SAT Score (25th/75th percentile):** 1090-1310
✔ **Tuition:** 2010-2011: $30,717

Selectivity: More selective	**Room/board:** $10,044
Acceptance rate: 61%	**Average debt:** N/A
Student/faculty ratio: 12/1	**Proportion who borrowed:** N/A

UNDERGRADUATE STUDENT BODY STATS

2009-2010 enrollment: 12,367 full-time; 1,678 part-time. Men: 67%; women: 33%. **Ethnic makeup:** African American: 5%; Asian American: 5%; Hispanic: 4%; White: 75%; International: 11%.

ADMISSIONS FACTS AND FIGURES

Phone: (585) 475-6631. **Email:** admissions@rit.edu. **Website:** http://www.rit.edu. **Application deadlines for fall 2011:** Regular decision: Rolling; decision sent by March 15. Early decision: Send application by: December 1; Decision sent by: January 15. Early action: Not offered. Admission can be deferred. **Application fee:** $50. **To apply online, go to:** http://www.rit.edu/~960www/application/undergraduate/. **Admissions requirements/recommendations:** High school units required (recommended): English: 4 (4); Mathematics: 2 (3); Science: 2 (3); Foreign language: 0 (3); Social studies: 4 (4); Academic electives: 9 (5); Total units: 22 (22). Tests: The college uses SAT or ACT scores in admissions decisions. Either SAT or ACT required. For admission to the fall 2011 entering class, the school will accept: ACT with or without writing accepted. Campus visit: Recommended. Admissions interview: Recommended. Off-campus interview: May be arranged. **Factors that count in admissions decisions:** *Academic:* Secondary school record: Very Important. Class rank: Important. Letters of recommendation: Considered. Standardized test scores: Important. Essay: Considered. *Nonacademic:* Interview: Considered. Extracurricular activities: Considered. Talent/ability: Considered. Character/personal qualities: Considered. Alumni/ae relationship: Considered. Geographical residence: Considered. State residency: Not Considered. Religious affiliation/commitment: Not Considered. Minority status: Considered. Volunteer work: Considered. Work experience: Considered. **Other schools with the greatest overlap in applicants:** Cornell University; Rensselaer Polytechnic Institute; University at Buffalo–SUNY; University of Rochester; Worcester Polytechnic Institute. **Admissions statistics for the fall 2009 entering class:** Total applicants: 12,994. Total accepted: 7,988. Freshmen enrolled: 2,611; 51% were from out of state. Overall acceptance rate: 61%. Non-early acceptance rate: 61%. **Size of waiting list:** 376 applicants; enrolled from waiting list: 344. **Credentials of fall 2009 freshmen:** 33% ranked in the top 10 percent of their high school class; 67% were in the top 25 percent; 92% were in the top half. (Proportion submitting class standing: 68%.) **First-year students who submitted SAT scores:** 76%. Scores (25/75 percentile): Critical Reading: 530-640, Math: 560-670, Combined: 1090-1310. **First-year students submitting ACT scores:** 24%. Scores (25/75 percentile): English: N/A, Math: N/A, Composite: 25-30.

ACADEMICS
Year founded: 1829. **Academic calendar:** Quarter. **Degrees offered:** certificate, diploma, associate, bachelor's, post-bachelor's certificate, master's, doctorate. **Most popular majors:** 18% engineering, 16% computer and information sciences and support services, 15% visual and performing arts, 11% business, management, marketing, and related support services, 9% engineering technologies/technicians. **Major fields of study:** biological and biomedical sciences; business, management, marketing, and related support services; communication, journalism, and related programs; communications technologies/technicians and support services; computer and information sciences and support services; engineering; engineering technologies/technicians; family and consumer sciences/human sciences; foreign languages, literatures, and linguistics; health professions and related clinical sciences; legal professions and studies; mathematics and statistics; multi/interdisciplinary studies; natural resources and conservation; physical sciences; precision production; psychology; public administration and social service professions; security and protective services; social sciences; visual and performing arts. **Areas of required coursework:** arts/fine arts, humanities, computer literacy, mathematics, English (including composition), sciences (biological or physical), social science, other. **Pre-professional programs:** pre-law, pre-dentistry, pre-medicine, pre-veterinary science, pre-optometry, pre-pharmacy. **Special academic programs (% participation):** accelerated program, cooperative (work-study plan) program (70%), cross-registration, distance learning, double major, English as a Second Language (ESL), exchange student program (domestic), honors program, independent study, internships, liberal arts/career combination, student-designed major, study abroad, weekend college. **Cooperative education programs:** business, computer science, engineering, natural science, social/behavioral science, technologies, other. **Reserve Officers Training Corps (ROTC):** Army ROTC: Offered on campus; Navy ROTC: Offered at cooperating institution (University of Rochester); Air Force ROTC: Offered on campus. **Faculty and instruction (2009-2010):** Total instructional faculty: 945 full-time, 481 part-time (65% men; 35% women; 10% minorities). Student/faculty ratio: 12/1. Classes of fewer than 20 students: 38%; of 20 to 49 students: 47%; of 50 or more students: 14%. **Advanced Placement and International Baccalaureate credit:** AP tests may be used for: Credit and/or placement. Scores accepted: 3, 4, 5. International Baccalaureate exams may be used for: Credit and/or placement. **Freshmen returning for sophomore year:** 89%. **Graduation rates:** Four-year: 28%; five-year: 58%; six-year: 64%. **Graduate study:** 18% of students pursue further study immediately upon graduation; 20% within one year. Fields in which graduates pursue further study: Master of Business Administration (MBA), 20%; law, 6%; medicine, 5%; dentistry, 1%; engi-

neering, 60%; education, 1%; arts and sciences, 6%; veterinary medicine, 1%.

COSTS AND FINANCIAL AID
Financial aid office: (585) 475-2186. **Expenses (2010-2011):** Tuition and fees 2010-2011: $30,717; room/board: $10,044. Estimated books and supplies: $1,050; transportation: $300; personal expenses: $675. **Financial aid:** Priority filing date for institution's financial aid form: March 1. In 2009-2010, 80% of undergraduates applied for financial aid. Of those, 72% were determined to have financial need; 87% had their need fully met. Average financial aid package (proportion receiving): $22,500 (72%). Average amount of gift aid, such as scholarships or grants (proportion receiving): $16,000 (66%). Average amount of self-help aid, such as work study or loans (proportion receiving): $6,500 (64%). Average need-based loan (excluding PLUS or other private loans): $5,500. Among students who received need-based aid, the average percentage of need met: 88%. Among students who received aid based on merit, the average award (and the proportion receiving): $8,000 (11%). The average athletic scholarship (and the proportion receiving): $0 (0%).

CAMPUS LIFE AND EXTRACURRICULAR ACTIVITIES
Campus housing available: coed dorms, sorority housing, fraternity housing, apartments for married students, apartment for single students, special housing for disabled students, special housing for international students, other housing options. Students who live in college-owned, operated, or affiliated housing: 60%. **Student employment:** During the 2009-2010 academic year, 30% of undergraduates worked on-campus. Average per-year earnings: $2,900. **Clubs and organizations:** Number of student organizations: 195. Activities include: campus ministries, choral groups, concert band, dance, drama/theater, international student organization, jazz band, literary magazine, music ensembles, musical theater, pep band, radio station, student government, student newspaper, student film society, symphony orchestra, yearbook. Number of fraternities: 17; sororities: 12. Proportion of men in fraternities: 2%; of women in sororities: 2%. **Sports program (2009-2010):** Member of NCAA III.

SERVICES AND FACILITIES
Basic services: nonremedial tutoring, women's center, placement service, day care, health service, health insurance, other. **Remedial assistance:** math, writing, study skills. **Counseling services:** minority student, career, military, personal, veteran student, academic, older student, psychological, birth control, religious. **For learning-disabled students:** School does not offer a structured program with separate admission and additional fees. Services include: reading machines, tape recorders, other special classes, diagnostic testing service, note-taking services, oral tests, learning center, readers, extended time for tests, tutors, priority registration, texts on tape, other testing accommodations. **Library:** Number of titles: 373,425; number of current serial subscriptions: 26,955. **Information technology resources:** Students are not required to lease or own a computer. Number of campus computers available to all students: 3,530. School has a wireless network. Approximate number of users that can be accommodated: 1,500. Proportion of college-owned housing units wired for high-speed internet access: 100%. **Campus safety:** Security services offered: 24-hour foot-and-vehicle patrols, late-night transport/escort service, 24-hour emergency telephones, lighted pathways/sidewalks, controlled dormitory access (key, security card, etc).

TRANSFER AND INTERNATIONAL STUDENTS
Transfer students: May apply for admission for the following academic terms: Fall, Winter, Spring, Summer. Applicants do not need a minimum number of credits to apply. For fall 2009: Transfer applications received: 2,557. Transfer applicants offered admission: 1,115. Transfer applicants enrolled: 735. **International students:** Number of foreign undergraduates: 1559 (11% of student body). Number of countries represented: 95. Minimum TOEFL score required: 550 (paper); 213 (computer). Average TOEFL score: 600 (paper).

Russell Sage College

- **Address:** 45 Ferry Street, Troy, NY 12180-4115
- **Website:** http://www.sage.edu/rsc/index.php
- **Private**
- **Enrollment:** 692 full-time; 57 part-time

KEY STATS

✔ **U.S News College Ranking:** 131, National Liberal Arts Colleges
✔ **SAT Score (25th/75th percentile):** 980-1180
✔ **Tuition:** 2009-2010: $27,990

Selectivity: Selective	**Room/board:** $9,670
Acceptance rate: 76%	**Average debt:** N/A
Student/faculty ratio: 11/1	**Proportion who borrowed:** N/A

UNDERGRADUATE STUDENT BODY STATS

2009-2010 enrollment: 692 full-time; 57 part-time. Men: 1%; women: 99%. **Ethnic makeup:** African American: 7%; Asian American: 3%; Hispanic: 3%; White: 87%.

ADMISSIONS FACTS AND FIGURES

Phone: (888) 837-9724. **Email:** rscadm@sage.edu. **Website:** http://www.sage.edu/rsc/index.php. **Application deadlines for fall 2011:** Regular decision: Rolling. Early decision: Not offered. Early action: Send application by: December 1; Decision sent by: December 15. Admission can be deferred. **Application fee:** $30. **To apply online, go to:** https://www.applyweb.com/apply/rsc/. **Admissions requirements/recommendations:** High school units required (recommended): English: 4 (4); Mathematics: 3 (4); Science: 3 (4); Foreign language: 2 (3); Social studies: 4 (4); Total units: 16. Tests: The college uses SAT or ACT scores in admissions decisions. Neither SAT nor ACT required. For admission to the fall 2011 entering class, the school will accept: ACT with or without writing accepted. Campus visit: Recommended. Admissions interview: Recommended. Off-campus interview: May not be arranged. **Factors that count in admissions decisions:** *Academic:* Secondary school record: Very Important. Class rank: Very Important. Letters of recommendation: Very Important. Standardized test scores: Very Important. Essay: Important. *Nonacademic:* Interview: Important. Extracurricular activities: Important. Talent/ability: Important. Character/personal qualities: Important. Alumni/ae relationship: Important. Geographical residence: Not Considered. State residency: Not Considered. Religious affiliation/commitment: Not Considered. Minority status: Not Considered. Volunteer work: Considered. Work experience: Considered. **Other schools with the greatest overlap in applicants:** College of St. Rose; SUNY College–Oneonta; SUNY–Oswego; Siena College; University at Albany–SUNY. **Admissions statistics for the fall 2009 entering class:** Total applicants: 486. Total accepted: 371. Freshmen enrolled: 128; 16% were from out of state. Accepted through early-decision or early-action plans: 34%. Overall acceptance rate: 76%. Non-early acceptance rate: 70%. **Credentials of fall 2009 freshmen:** 24% ranked in the top 10 percent of their high school class; 69% were in the top 25 percent; 92% were in the top half. (Proportion submitting class standing: 85%.) **Average high school grade point average:** 3.3. **First-year students who submitted SAT scores:** 63%. Scores (25/75 percentile): Critical Reading: 490-590, Math: 490-590, Combined: 980-1180. **First-year students submitting ACT scores:** 24%. Scores (25/75 percentile): English: N/A, Math: N/A, Composite: 22-25.

ACADEMICS

Year founded: 1916. **Academic calendar:** Semester. **Degrees offered:** bachelor's. **Most popular majors:** 39% health professions and related clinical sciences, 9% education, 8% liberal arts and sciences studies, and humanities, 5% psychology, 4% multi/interdisciplinary studies. **Major fields of study:** area, ethnic, cultural, and gender studies; biological and biomedical sciences; business, management, marketing, and related support services; communication, journalism, and related programs; education; English language and literature/letters; foreign languages, literatures, and linguistics; health professions and related clinical sciences; history; mathematics and statistics; multi/interdisciplinary studies; natural resources and conservation; physical sciences; psychology; security and protective services; social sciences; visual and performing arts. **Areas of required coursework:** arts/fine arts, humanities, mathematics, English (including composition), foreign languages, sciences (biological or physical), history, social science, other. **Pre-professional programs:** pre-law, pre-dentistry, pre-medicine, pre-veterinary science, other. **Special academic programs (% participation):** accelerated program (8%), cross-registration (4%), distance learning (6%),

double major (7%), dual enrollment (3%), honors program (32%), independent study (15%), internships (75%), liberal arts/career combination (13%), student-designed major (6%), study abroad (5%), teacher certificate program (13%). **Teacher certification offered in:** elementary, middle/junior high, secondary. **Reserve Officers Training Corps (ROTC):** Army ROTC: Offered at cooperating institution; Air Force ROTC: Offered at cooperating institution. **Faculty and instruction (2009-2010):** Total instructional faculty: 48 full-time, 49 part-time (32% men; 68% women; 3% minorities). Full-time faculty with Ph.D. or other terminal degree: 75%. Student/faculty ratio: 11/1. Classes of fewer than 20 students: 57%; of 20 to 49 students: 43%; of 50 or more students: 0%. **Advanced Placement and International Baccalaureate credit:** AP tests may be used for: Placement only. Scores accepted: 3, 4, 5. International Baccalaureate exams may be used for: Placement only. **Freshmen returning for sophomore year:** 78%. **Graduation rates:** Four-year: 64%; five-year: 70%; six-year: 70%. **Graduate study:** 34% of students pursue further study immediately upon graduation. Fields in which graduates pursue further study: Master of Business Administration (MBA), 5%; education, 25%.

COSTS AND FINANCIAL AID

Financial aid office: (518) 244-2215. **Expenses (2009-2010):** Tuition and fees 2009-2010: $27,990; room/board: $9,670. Estimated books and supplies: $1,200; transportation: $600; personal expenses: $1,225. **Financial aid:** Priority filing date for institution's financial aid form: March 1.

CAMPUS LIFE AND EXTRACURRICULAR ACTIVITIES

Campus housing available (% using): women's dorms (51%), other housing options (49%). Students who live in college-owned, operated, or affiliated housing: 51%. **Student employment:** During the 2009-2010 academic year, 36% of undergraduates worked on campus. Average per-year earnings: $1,900. **Clubs and organizations:** Number of student organizations: 40. Activities include: choral groups, dance, drama/theater, literary magazine, music ensembles, musical theater, student government, student newspaper, yearbook. Number of fraternities: 0; sororities: 0. Average proportion of students who stay on campus on weekends: 50%. **Sports program (2009-2010):** Member of NCAA III. *Women's intercollegiate varsity sports:* basketball, lacrosse, soccer, softball, tennis, volleyball.

SERVICES AND FACILITIES

Basic services: nonremedial tutoring, women's center, placement service, health service, health insurance. **Remedial assistance:** reading, math, writing, study skills. **Counseling services:** minority student, career, personal, academic, older student, psychological, birth control, religious. **For learning-disabled students:** School does not offer a structured program with separate admission and additional fees. Total undergraduates in learning-disabled program or receiving services: 27. Services include: reading machines, tape recorders, untimed tests, note-taking services, oral tests, learning center, readers, extended time for tests, tutors, texts on tape, typist/scribe, exams on tape or computer, other testing accommodations. **Library:** Number of titles: 256,905; number of current serial subscriptions: 65,003. **Information technology resources:** Students are not required to lease or own a computer. Number of campus computers available to all students: 164. School has a wireless network. Approximate number of users that can be accommodated: 300. Proportion of college-owned housing units wired for high-speed internet access: 100%. **Campus safety:** Security services offered: 24-hour foot-and-vehicle patrols, late-night transport/escort service, 24-hour emergency telephones, lighted pathways/sidewalks, controlled dormitory access (key, security card, etc).

TRANSFER AND INTERNATIONAL STUDENTS

Transfer students: May apply for admission for the following academic terms: Fall, Spring. Applicants need a minimum number of credits to apply. For fall 2009: Transfer applications received: 330. Transfer applicants offered admission: 163. Transfer applicants enrolled: 101. **International students:** Number of foreign undergraduates: 1. Number of countries represented: 1. Minimum TOEFL score required: 550 (paper); 213 (computer).

Sage Colleges–Albany

- **Address:** 140 New Scotland Avenue, Albany, NY 12208
- **Website:** http://www.sage.edu
- **Private**
- **Enrollment:** 557 full-time; 291 part-time

KEY STATS

- ✔ **U.S News College Ranking:** second tier, Regional Universities (North)
- ✔ **SAT Score (25th/75th percentile):** 820-1040
- ✔ **Tuition:** 2009-2010: $27,770

Selectivity: Less selective	**Room/board:** $9,830
Acceptance rate: 65%	**Average debt:** N/A
Student/faculty ratio: 13/1	**Proportion who borrowed:** N/A

UNDERGRADUATE STUDENT BODY STATS

2009-2010 enrollment: 557 full-time; 291 part-time. Men: 34%; women: 66%. **Ethnic makeup:** African American: 14%; Asian American: 2%; Hispanic: 4%; White: 79%.

ADMISSIONS FACTS AND FIGURES

Phone: (518) 292-1730. **Email:** scaadm@sage.edu. **Website:** http://www.sage.edu. **Application deadlines for fall 2011:** Regular decision: Rolling. Early decision: Not offered. Early action: Send application by: December 1; Decision sent by: December 15. Admission can be deferred. **Application fee:** $30. **To apply online, go to:** http://www.applyweb.com/apply/sca. **Admissions requirements/recommendations:** High school units required (recommended): English: 4; Mathematics: 3 (3); Science: 3 (3); Foreign language: 2; Social studies: 4; Total units: 16. Tests: The college uses SAT or ACT scores in admissions decisions. Neither SAT nor ACT required. For admission to the fall 2011 entering class, the school will accept: ACT with or without writing accepted. Campus visit: Recommended. Admissions interview: Recommended. Off-campus interview: Not available. **Factors that count in admissions decisions:** *Academic:* Secondary school record: Very Important. Class rank: Very Important. Letters of recommendation: Very Important. Standardized test scores: Very Important. Essay: Important. *Nonacademic:* Interview: Important. Extracurricular activities: Important. Talent/ability: Important. Character/personal qualities: Important. Alumni/ae relationship: Important. Geographical residence: Not Considered. State residency: Not Considered. Religious affiliation/commitment: Not Considered. Minority status: Not Considered. Volunteer work: Important. Work experience: Considered. **Other schools with the greatest overlap in applicants:** College of St. Rose; Mount St. Mary College; Pratt Institute; Siena College; University at Albany–SUNY. **Admissions statistics for the fall 2009 entering class:** Total applicants: 529. Total accepted: 342. Freshmen enrolled: 105; 12% were from out of state. Accepted through early-decision or early-action plans: 8%. Overall acceptance rate: 65%. Non-early acceptance rate: 62%. **Credentials of fall 2009 freshmen:** 7% ranked in the top 10 percent of their high school class; 26% were in the top 25 percent; 60% were in the top half. (Proportion submitting class standing: 83%.) **Average high school grade point average:** 2.8. **First-year students who submitted SAT scores:** 76%. Scores (25/75 percentile): Critical Reading: 410-510, Math: 410-530, Combined: 820-1040. **First-year students submitting ACT scores:** 21%. Scores (25/75 percentile): English: N/A, Math: N/A, Composite: 16-22.

ACADEMICS

Year founded: 1916. **Academic calendar:** Semester. **Degrees offered:** bachelor's, post-bachelor's certificate, master's, post-master's certificate, doctorate. **Most popular majors:** 22% business, management, marketing, and related support services, 15% visual and performing arts, 11% liberal arts and sciences studies, and humanities, 10% education, 10% social sciences. **Major fields of study:** area, ethnic, cultural, and gender studies; business, management, marketing, and related support services; communication, journalism, and related programs; computer and information sciences and support services; education; health professions and related clinical sciences; legal professions and studies; liberal arts and sciences studies, and humanities; psychology; public administration and social service professions; security and protective services; social sciences; visual and performing arts. **Areas of required coursework:** arts/fine arts, humanities, computer literacy, mathematics, English (including composition), foreign languages, sciences (biological or physical), history, social science. **Special academic programs (% participation):** cross-registration (5%), distance learning (31%), dual enrollment (1%), honors program (3%), independent study (5%), internships (100%), student-designed major (10%), study abroad (2%). **Teacher**

certification offered in: special education, elementary, middle/junior high, secondary. **Reserve Officers Training Corps (ROTC):** Army ROTC: Offered at cooperating institution; Air Force ROTC: Offered at cooperating institution. **Faculty and instruction (2009-2010):** Total instructional faculty: 80 full-time, 117 part-time (36% men; 64% women; 3% minorities). Full-time faculty with Ph.D. or other terminal degree: 81%. Student/faculty ratio: 13/1. Classes of fewer than 20 students: 75%; of 20 to 49 students: 25%; of 50 or more students: 0%. **Advanced Placement and International Baccalaureate credit:** AP tests may be used for: Placement only. Scores accepted: 3, 4, 5. International Baccalaureate exams may be used for: Placement only. **Freshmen returning for sophomore year:** 67%. **Graduation rates:** Four-year: 28%; five-year: 42%; six-year: 41%. **Graduate study:** 37% of students pursue further study within one year. Fields in which graduates pursue further study: Master of Business Administration (MBA), 7%; law, 5%; education, 2%.

COSTS AND FINANCIAL AID

Financial aid office: (518) 244-2215. **Expenses (2009-2010):** Tuition and fees 2009-2010: $27,770; room/board: $9,830. Estimated books and supplies: $1,200; transportation: $600; personal expenses: $1,225. **Financial aid:** Priority filing date for institution's financial aid form: March 1.

CAMPUS LIFE AND EXTRACURRICULAR ACTIVITIES

Campus housing available (% using): coed dorms (53%), other housing options (47%). Students who live in college-owned, operated, or affiliated housing: 37%. **Student employment:** During the 2009-2010 academic year, 30% of undergraduates worked on campus. Average per-year earnings: $1,900. Activities include: literary magazine, student government, student newspaper, student film society. Average proportion of students who stay on campus on weekends: 50%. **Sports program (2009-2010):** Member of NCAA III. **Men's intercollegiate varsity sports:** basketball, cross country, golf, soccer, tennis, volleyball. **Women's intercollegiate varsity sports:** basketball, lacrosse, soccer, softball, tennis, volleyball.

SERVICES AND FACILITIES

Basic services: nonremedial tutoring, placement service, health service, health insurance. **Remedial assistance:** reading, math, writing, study skills. **Counseling services:** minority student, career, personal, academic, older student, psychological, birth control, religious. **For learning-disabled students:** School does not offer a structured program with separate admission and additional fees. Total undergraduates in learning-disabled program or receiving services: 24. Services include: reading machines, tape recorders, untimed tests, note-taking services, learning center, readers, extended time for tests, tutors, texts on tape, typist/scribe, exams on tape or computer, other testing accommodations. **Library:** Number of titles: 256,905; number of current serial subscriptions: 65,003. **Information technology resources:** Students are not required to lease or own a computer. Number of campus computers available to all students: 196. School has a wireless network. Approximate number of users that can be accommodated: 300. Proportion of college-owned housing units wired for high-speed internet access: 100%. **Campus safety:** Security services offered: 24-hour foot-and-vehicle patrols, late-night transport/escort service, 24-hour emergency telephones, lighted pathways/sidewalks, controlled dormitory access (key, security card, etc).

TRANSFER AND INTERNATIONAL STUDENTS

Transfer students: May apply for admission for the following academic terms: Fall, Spring, Summer. Applicants need a minimum number of credits to apply. For fall 2009: Transfer applications received: 497. Transfer applicants offered admission: 269. Transfer applicants enrolled: 146. **International students:** Number of foreign undergraduates: 4 (1% of student body). Minimum TOEFL score required: 550 (paper); 213 (computer).

Sarah Lawrence College

- **Address:** 1 Mead Way, Bronxville, NY 10708-5999
- **Website:** http://www.sarahlawrence.edu
- **Private**
- **Enrollment:** 1,318 full-time; 49 part-time

KEY STATS

✔ **U.S News College Ranking:** Unranked, National Liberal Arts Colleges
✔ **SAT or ACT Score (25th/75th percentile):** N/A
✔ **Tuition:** 2010-2011: $43,564

Selectivity: N/A	**Room/board:** $13,370
Acceptance rate: 58%	**Average debt:** $17,246
Student/faculty ratio: 9/1	**Proportion who borrowed:** 52%

UNDERGRADUATE STUDENT BODY STATS

2009-2010 enrollment: 1,318 full-time; 49 part-time. Men: 27%; women: 73%. **Ethnic makeup:** African American: 3%; Asian American: 5%; Hispanic: 5%; White: 83%; International: 4%.

ADMISSIONS FACTS AND FIGURES

Phone: (914) 395-2510. **Email:** slcadmit@sarahlawrence.edu. **Website:** http://www.sarahlawrence.edu. **Application deadlines for fall 2011:** Regular decision: January 1; decision sent by April 1. Early decision: Send application by: November 1; Decision sent by: December 15. Early action: Not offered. Admission can be deferred. **Application fee:** $60. **To apply online, go to:** http://www.slc.edu/index.php?pageID=1437. **Admissions requirements/ recommendations:** High school units required (recommended): English: 4; Mathematics: 2 (4); Science: 2 (4); Foreign language: 2 (4); History: 2 (4). Tests: The college does not use SAT or ACT scores in admissions decisions. Neither SAT nor ACT required. Campus visit: Recommended. Admissions interview: Recommended. Off-campus interview: May be arranged. **Factors that count in admissions decisions:** *Academic:* Secondary school record: Very Important. Class rank: Considered. Letters of recommendation: Very Important. Standardized test scores: Not Considered. Essay: Very Important. *Nonacademic:* Interview: Considered. Extracurricular activities: Important. Talent/ability: Important. Character/personal qualities: Important. Alumni/ae relationship: Considered. Geographical residence: Considered. State residency: Not Considered. Religious affiliation/commitment: Not Considered. Minority status: Considered. Volunteer work: Considered. Work experience: Considered. **Other schools with the greatest overlap in applicants:** Bard College; Brown University; Columbia University; New York University; Vassar College. **Admissions statistics for the fall 2009 entering class:** Total applicants: 2,126. Total accepted: 1,239. Freshmen enrolled: 365; Overall acceptance rate: 58%. Non-early acceptance rate: 58%. **Credentials of fall 2009 freshmen:** 46% ranked in the top 10 percent of their high school class; 79% were in the top 25 percent; 97% were in the top half. (Proportion submitting class standing: 34%.) **Average high school grade point average:** 3.6.

ACADEMICS

Year founded: 1926. **Academic calendar:** Semester. **Degrees offered:** certificate, bachelor's, master's. **Pre-professional programs:** pre-law, pre-medicine. **Special academic programs (% participation):** exchange student program (domestic) (15%), independent study (100%), internships (25%), student-designed major (100%), study abroad (55%). **Teacher certification offered in:** early childhood, elementary. **Faculty and instruction (2009-2010):** Total instructional faculty: 107 full-time, 203 part-time (49% men; 51% women; 38% minorities). Student/faculty ratio: 9/1. Classes of fewer than 20 students: 94%; of 20 to 49 students: 4%; of 50 or more students: 2%. **Advanced Placement and International Baccalaureate credit:** AP tests may be used for: Credit only. Scores accepted: 4, 5. International Baccalaureate exams may be used for: Credit only. **Freshmen returning for sophomore year:** 81%. **Graduation rates:** Four-year: 64%; five-year: 71%; six-year: 75%. **Graduate study:** 10% of students pursue further study immediately upon graduation; 10% within one year; 70% within five years. Fields in which graduates pursue further study: Master of Business Administration (MBA), 15%; law, 10%; medicine, 10%; education, 25%; arts and sciences, 25%.

COSTS AND FINANCIAL AID

Financial aid office: (914) 395-2570. **Expenses (2010-2011):** Tuition and fees 2010-2011: $43,564; room/board: $13,370. Estimated books and supplies: $600 personal expenses: $500. **Financial aid:** Priority filing date for institution's financial aid form: February 1; deadline: February 1. In 2009-2010,

63% of undergraduates applied for financial aid. Of those, 59% were determined to have financial need; 44% had their need fully met. Average financial aid package (proportion receiving): $29,576 (58%). Average amount of gift aid, such as scholarships or grants (proportion receiving): $29,576 (54%). Average amount of self-help aid, such as work study or loans (proportion receiving): $4,805 (56%). Average need-based loan (excluding PLUS or other private loans): $3,465. Among students who received need-based aid, the average percentage of need met: 92%. Among students who received aid based on merit, the average award (and the proportion receiving): $0 (0%). The average athletic scholarship (and the proportion receiving): $0 (0%). Average amount of debt of borrowers graduating in 2009: $17,246. Proportion who borrowed: 52%.

CAMPUS LIFE AND EXTRACURRICULAR ACTIVITIES

Campus housing available: coed dorms, women's dorms, apartment for single students, cooperative housing. **Student employment:** During the 2009-2010 academic year, 45% of undergraduates worked on campus. Average per-year earnings: $1,800. **Clubs and organizations:** Number of student organizations: 61. Activities include: choral groups, dance, drama/theater, jazz band, literary magazine, model UN, music ensembles, musical theater, radio station, student government, student newspaper, student film society, symphony orchestra, yearbook. Number of fraternities: 0; sororities: 0. Average proportion of students who stay on campus on weekends: 90%.

SERVICES AND FACILITIES

Basic services: nonremedial tutoring, health service, health insurance. **Counseling services:** minority student, career, personal, veteran student, academic, older student, psychological, birth control. **For learning-disabled students:** School does not offer a structured program with separate admission and additional fees. Services include: tape recorders, note-taking services, readers, extended time for tests, priority seating, texts on tape. **Library:** Number of titles: 298,611; number of current serial subscriptions: 917. **Information technology resources:** Students are not required to lease or own a computer. Number of campus computers available to all students: 150. School has a wireless network. Approximate number of users that can be accommodated: 243. Proportion of college-owned housing units wired for high-speed internet access: 100%. **Campus safety:** Security services offered: 24-hour foot-and-vehicle patrols, late-night transport/escort service, 24-hour emergency telephones, lighted pathways/sidewalks, controlled dormitory access (key, security card, etc).

TRANSFER AND INTERNATIONAL STUDENTS

Transfer students: May apply for admission for the following academic terms: Fall, Spring. Applicants need a minimum number of credits to apply. **International students:** Number of foreign undergraduates: 45 (4% of student body). Number of countries represented: 44. Minimum TOEFL score required: 600 (paper); 250 (computer). Average TOEFL score: 650 (paper).

Siena College

- **Address:** 515 Loudon Road, Loudonville, NY 12211
- **Website:** http://www.siena.edu
- **Private; Religious affiliation:** Roman Catholic
- **Enrollment:** 3,101 full-time; 184 part-time

KEY STATS

✔ **U.S News College Ranking:** 114, National Liberal Arts Colleges
✔ **SAT Score (25th/75th percentile):** 1030-1230
✔ **Tuition:** 2010-2011: $26,495

Selectivity: More selective	**Room/board:** $10,375
Acceptance rate: 53%	**Average debt:** $28,200
Student/faculty ratio: 13/1	**Proportion who borrowed:** 77%

UNDERGRADUATE STUDENT BODY STATS

2009-2010 enrollment: 3,101 full-time; 184 part-time. Men: 46%; women: 54%. **Ethnic makeup:** African American: 2%; Asian American: 3%; Hispanic: 4%; White: 90%.

ADMISSIONS FACTS AND FIGURES

Phone: (888) 287-4362. **Email:** admit@siena.edu. **Website:** http://www.siena.edu. **Application deadlines for fall 2011:** Regular decision: February 15; decision sent by March 15. Early decision: Send application by: December 1;

Decision sent by: December 15. Early action: Send application by: December 1; Decision sent by: January 1. Admission can be deferred. **Application fee:** $50. **To apply online, go to:** http://www.siena.edu/level3col.aspx?menu_id= 564&id=128&linkidentifier=id&itemid=128. **Admissions requirements/ recommendations:** High school units required (recommended): English: 4 (4); Mathematics: 3 (4); Science: 3 (4); Foreign language: o (3); Social studies: 1 (1); History: 2 (3); Academic electives: o (o); Total units: 13 (19). Tests: The college uses SAT or ACT scores in admissions decisions. Either SAT or ACT required. For admission to the fall 2011 entering class, the school will accept: ACT with writing required. Campus visit: Recommended. Admissions interview: Recommended. Off-campus interview: May be arranged. **Factors that count in admissions decisions:** *Academic:* Secondary school record: Very Important. Class rank: Considered. Letters of recommendation: Important. Standardized test scores: Important. Essay: Considered. *Nonacademic:* Interview: Considered. Extracurricular activities: Considered. Talent/ability: Considered. Character/personal qualities: Considered. Alumni/ae relationship: Considered. Geographical residence: Not Considered. State residency: Not Considered. Religious affiliation/commitment: Not Considered. Minority status: Considered. Volunteer work: Considered. Work experience: Considered. **Other schools with the greatest overlap in applicants:** Binghamton University–SUNY; Fordham University; Marist College; SUNY College–Oneonta; University at Albany–SUNY. **Admissions statistics for the fall 2009 entering class:** Total applicants: 7,282. Total accepted: 3,889. Freshmen enrolled: 783; 22% were from out of state. Overall acceptance rate: 53%. Non-early acceptance rate: 53%. **Size of waiting list:** 1149 applicants; enrolled from waiting list: 25. **Credentials of fall 2009 freshmen:** 28% ranked in the top 10 percent of their high school class; 61% were in the top 25 percent; 93% were in the top half. (Proportion submitting class standing: 66%.) **First-year students who submitted SAT scores:** 81%. Scores (25/75 percentile): Critical Reading: 500-600, Math: 530-630, Combined: 1030-1230. **First-year students submitting ACT scores:** 35%. Scores (25/75 percentile): English: N/A, Math: N/A, Composite: 22-27.

ACADEMICS

Year founded: 1937. **Academic calendar:** Semester. **Degrees offered:** certificate, bachelor's, master's. **Most popular majors:** 21% marketing/marketing management, 13% accounting, 11% finance, 11% psychology, 8% English language and literature. **Major fields of study:** area, ethnic, cultural, and gender studies; biological and biomedical sciences; business, management, marketing, and related support services; computer and information sciences and support services; education; English language and literature/ letters; foreign languages, literatures, and linguistics; history; mathematics and statistics; multi/interdisciplinary studies; philosophy and religious studies; physical sciences; psychology; public administration and social service professions; social sciences; visual and performing arts. **Areas of required coursework:** arts/fine arts, humanities, mathematics, English (including composition), philosophy, sciences (biological or physical), history, social science, other. **Pre-professional programs:** pre-law, pre-dentistry, pre-medicine, pre-veterinary science, pre-optometry, other. **Special academic programs:** accelerated program, cross-registration, double major, English as a Second Language (ESL), honors program, independent study, internships, liberal arts/career combination, study abroad, teacher certificate program, other. **Teacher certification offered in:** middle/junior high, secondary. **Cooperative education programs:** business, computer science, engineering, health professions, natural science, social/behavioral science, other. **Reserve Officers Training Corps (ROTC):** Army ROTC: Offered on campus; Navy ROTC: Offered at cooperating institution (Rensselaer Polytechnic Institute); Air Force ROTC: Offered at cooperating institution (Rensselaer Polytechnic Institute). **Faculty and instruction (2009-2010):** Total instructional faculty: 194 full-time, 136 part-time (60% men; 40% women; 10% minorities). Full-time faculty with Ph.D. or other terminal degree: 91%. Student/faculty ratio: 13/1. Classes of fewer than 20 students: 37%; of 20 to 49 students: 63%; of 50 or more students: 0%. **Advanced Placement and International Baccalaureate credit:** AP tests may be used for: Credit and/or placement. Scores accepted: 4, 5. International Baccalaureate exams may be used for: Credit only. **Freshmen returning for sophomore year:** 87%. **Graduation rates:** Four-year: 68%; five-year: 72%; six-year: 73%. **Graduate study:** 27% of students pursue further study within one year. Fields in which graduates pursue further study: Master of Business Administration (MBA), 20%; law, 10%; medicine, 19%; education, 20%; arts and sciences, 28%.

COSTS AND FINANCIAL AID

Financial aid office: (518) 783-2427. **Expenses (2010-2011):** Tuition and fees 2010-2011: $26,495; room/board: $10,375. Estimated books and supplies: $1,140; transportation: $935; personal expenses: $1,300. **Financial aid:** Priority filing date for institution's financial aid form: February 15;

deadline: May 1. In 2009-2010, 82% of undergraduates applied for financial aid. Of those, 68% were determined to have financial need; 17% had their need fully met. Average financial aid package (proportion receiving): $17,659 (68%). Average amount of gift aid, such as scholarships or grants (proportion receiving): $13,350 (67%). Average amount of self-help aid, such as work study or loans (proportion receiving): $4,598 (56%). Average need-based loan (excluding PLUS or other private loans): $4,510. Among students who received need-based aid, the average percentage of need met: 73%. Among students who received aid based on merit, the average award (and the proportion receiving): $9,154 (12%). The average athletic scholarship (and the proportion receiving): $14,688 (8%). Average amount of debt of borrowers graduating in 2009: $28,200. Proportion who borrowed: 77%.

CAMPUS LIFE AND EXTRACURRICULAR ACTIVITIES

Campus housing available (% using): coed dorms (72%), other housing options (28%). Students who live in college-owned, operated, or affiliated housing: 76%. **Student employment:** During the 2009-2010 academic year, 23% of undergraduates worked on campus. Average per-year earnings: $1,890. **Clubs and organizations:** Number of student organizations: 68. Activities include: campus ministries, choral groups, dance, drama/ theater, literary magazine, model UN, musical theater, opera, pep band, radio station, student government, student newspaper, symphony orchestra, television station, yearbook. Number of fraternities: 0; sororities: 0. **Sports program (2009-2010):** Member of NCAA I. *Men's intercollegiate varsity sports:* baseball, basketball, cross country, golf, lacrosse, soccer, tennis. *Women's intercollegiate varsity sports:* basketball, cross country, field hockey, golf, lacrosse, soccer, softball, swimming, tennis, volleyball, water polo.

SERVICES AND FACILITIES

Basic services: nonremedial tutoring, women's center, placement service, health service, other. **Counseling services:** minority student, career, military, personal, academic, psychological, religious, other. **For learning-disabled students:** School does not offer a structured program with separate admission and additional fees. Services include: reading machines, tape recorders, note-taking services, oral tests, readers, extended time for tests, tutors, priority registration, priority seating, texts on tape. **Library:** Number of titles: 348,389; number of current serial subscriptions: 12,476. **Information technology resources:** Students are not required to lease or own a computer. Number of campus computers available to all students: 456. School has a wireless network. Approximate number of users that can be accommodated: 925. Proportion of college-owned housing units wired for high-speed internet access: 100%. **Campus safety:** Security services offered: 24-hour foot-and-vehicle patrols, late-night transport/escort service, 24-hour emergency telephones, lighted pathways/sidewalks, controlled dormitory access (key, security card, etc).

TRANSFER AND INTERNATIONAL STUDENTS

Transfer students: May apply for admission for the following academic terms: Fall, Spring, Summer. Applicants do not need a minimum number of credits to apply. For fall 2009: Transfer applications received: 303. Transfer applicants offered admission: 233. Transfer applicants enrolled: 120. **International students:** Number of foreign undergraduates: 12. Number of countries represented: 6. Minimum TOEFL score required: 550 (paper); 213 (computer).

Skidmore College

■ **Address:** 815 N. Broadway, Saratoga Springs, NY 12866
■ **Website:** http://www.skidmore.edu
■ **Private**
■ **Enrollment:** 2,591 full-time; 83 part-time

KEY STATS

✔ **U.S News College Ranking:** 41, National Liberal Arts Colleges
✔ **SAT Score (25th/75th percentile):** 1150-1350
✔ **Tuition:** 2010-2011: $41,184

Selectivity: More selective	**Room/board:** $10,986
Acceptance rate: 42%	**Average debt:** $18,303
Student/faculty ratio: 9/1	**Proportion who borrowed:** 51%

UNDERGRADUATE STUDENT BODY STATS

2009-2010 enrollment: 2,591 full-time; 83 part-time. Men: 40%; women: 60%. **Ethnic makeup:** African American: 4%; American-Indian: 1%; Asian American: 9%; Hispanic: 5%; White: 78%; International: 3%.

ADMISSIONS FACTS AND FIGURES

Phone: (518) 580-5570. **Email:** admissions@skidmore.edu. **Website:** http://www.skidmore.edu. **Application deadlines for fall 2011:** Regular decision: January 15; decision sent by April 1. Early decision: Send application by: November 15; Decision sent by: December 15. Early action: Not offered. Admission can be deferred. **Application fee:** $60. **To apply online, go to:** http://www.skidmore.edu/admissions/inquire/apply.htm. **Admissions requirements/recommendations:** High school units required (recommended): English: 0 (4); Mathematics: 0 (4); Science: 0 (4); Foreign language: 0 (4); Social studies: 0 (4); History: 0 (0); Academic electives: 0 (0); Total units: 0 (20). Tests: The college uses SAT or ACT scores in admissions decisions. Either SAT or ACT required. For admission to the fall 2011 entering class, the school will accept: ACT with writing required. Campus visit: Recommended. Admissions interview: Recommended. Off-campus interview: May be arranged. **Factors that count in admissions decisions:** *Academic:* Secondary school record: Very Important. Class rank: Important. Letters of recommendation: Important. Standardized test scores: Considered. Essay: Important. *Nonacademic:* Interview: Considered. Extracurricular activities: Important. Talent/ability: Important. Character/personal qualities: Important. Alumni/ae relationship: Considered. Geographical residence: Considered. State residency: Not Considered. Religious affiliation/commitment: Not Considered. Minority status: Considered. Volunteer work: Important. Work experience: Important. **Other schools with the greatest overlap in applicants:** Brown University; Connecticut College; Tufts University; Vassar College; Wesleyan University. **Admissions statistics for the fall 2009 entering class:** Total applicants: 6,371. Total accepted: 2,693. Freshmen enrolled: 664; 71% were from out of state. Accepted through early-decision or early-action plans: 41%. Overall acceptance rate: 42%. Early-decision acceptance rate: 71%. Non-early acceptance rate: 40%. **Size of waiting list:** 833 applicants; enrolled from waiting list: 67. **Credentials of fall 2009 freshmen:** 39% ranked in the top 10 percent of their high school class; 74% were in the top 25 percent; 94% were in the top half. (Proportion submitting class standing: 30%.) **Average high school grade point average:** 0.0. **First-year students who submitted SAT scores:** 85%. Scores (25/75 percentile): Critical Reading: 570-680, Math: 580-670, Combined: 1150-1350. **First-year students submitting ACT scores:** 31%. Scores (25/75 percentile): English: 25-29, Math: 26-32, Composite: 26-30.

ACADEMICS

Year founded: 1903. **Academic calendar:** Semester. **Degrees offered:** bachelor's, master's. **Most popular majors:** 16% social sciences, 16% visual and performing arts, 12% business, management, marketing, and related support services, 10% psychology, 8% English language and literature/letters. **Major fields of study:** area, ethnic, cultural, and gender studies; biological and biomedical sciences; business, management, marketing, and related support services; computer and information sciences and support services; education; English language and literature/letters; foreign languages, literatures, and linguistics; history; liberal arts and sciences studies, and humanities; mathematics and statistics; natural resources and conservation; parks, recreation, leisure, and fitness studies; philosophy and religious studies; physical sciences; psychology; public administration and social service professions; social sciences; visual and performing arts. **Areas of required coursework:** arts/fine arts, humanities, mathematics, English (including composition), foreign languages, sciences (biological or physical), social science, other. **Pre-professional programs:** pre-law, pre-dentistry, pre-medicine, pre-veterinary science. **Special academic programs (% participation):** accelerated program (.9%), cross-registration (.5%), double major (16.2%), dual enrollment (.2%), exchange student program (domestic) (.8%), honors program (3.9%), independent study (45.4%), internships (17.3%), liberal arts/career combination (33.4%), student-designed major (2%), study abroad (53.4%), teacher certificate program (1.9%). **Teacher certification offered in:** elementary. **Reserve Officers Training Corps (ROTC):** Army ROTC: Offered at cooperating institution (Siena College); Air Force ROTC: Offered at cooperating institution (Rensselaer Polytechnic Institute). **Faculty and instruction (2009-2010):** Total instructional faculty: 248 full-time, 89 part-time (44% men; 56% women), 13% minorities). Full-time faculty with Ph.D. or other terminal degree: 83%. Student/faculty ratio: 9/1. Classes of fewer than 20 students: 72%; of 20 to 49 students: 27%; of 50 or more students: 1%. **Advanced Placement and International Baccalaureate credit:** AP tests may be used for: Credit and/or placement. Scores accepted: 4, 5. International Baccalaureate exams may be used for: Credit only. **Freshmen returning for**

sophomore year: 94%. **Graduation rates:** Four-year: 82%; five-year: 85%; six-year: 85%. **Graduate study:** 19% of students pursue further study within one year; 53% within five years. Fields in which graduates pursue further study: Master of Business Administration (MBA), 4%; law, 10%; medicine, 2%; engineering, 1%; education, 8%; arts and sciences, 28%; veterinary medicine, 5%.

COSTS AND FINANCIAL AID

Financial aid office: (518) 580-5750. **Expenses (2010-2011):** Tuition and fees 2010-2011: $41,184; room/board: $10,986. Estimated books and supplies: $1,300; transportation: $300; personal expenses: $1,080. **Financial aid:** In 2009-2010, 49% of undergraduates applied for financial aid. Of those, 44% were determined to have financial need; 100% had their need fully met. Average financial aid package (proportion receiving): $34,104 (44%). Average amount of gift aid, such as scholarships or grants (proportion receiving): $28,524 (44%). Average amount of self-help aid, such as work study or loans (proportion receiving): $5,171 (37%). Average need-based loan (excluding PLUS or other private loans): $3,878. Among students who received need-based aid, the average percentage of need met: 87%. Among students who received aid based on merit, the average award (and the proportion receiving): $10,000 (0%). The average athletic scholarship (and the proportion receiving): $0 (0%). Average amount of debt of borrowers graduating in 2009: $18,303. Proportion who borrowed: 51%.

CAMPUS LIFE AND EXTRACURRICULAR ACTIVITIES

Campus housing available (% using): coed dorms (64%), women's dorms (2%), apartment for single students (34%), special housing for disabled students. Students who live in college-owned, operated, or affiliated housing: 85%. **Student employment:** During the 2009-2010 academic year, 50% of undergraduates worked on campus. Average per-year earnings: $950. **Clubs and organizations:** Number of student organizations: 80. Activities include: campus ministries, choral groups, concert band, dance, drama/theater, international student organization, jazz band, literary magazine, model UN, music ensembles, musical theater, opera, radio station, student government, student newspaper, symphony orchestra, television station, yearbook. Number of fraternities: 0; sororities: 0. Average proportion of students who stay on campus on weekends: 65%. **Sports program (2009-2010):** Member of NCAA III. *Men's intercollegiate varsity sports:* baseball, basketball, golf, ice hockey, lacrosse, soccer, swimming, tennis. *Women's intercollegiate varsity sports:* basketball, crew (heavyweight), equestrian, field hockey, lacrosse, soccer, softball, swimming, tennis, volleyball.

SERVICES AND FACILITIES

Basic services: nonremedial tutoring, health service, health insurance. **Remedial assistance:** other. **Counseling services:** minority student, career, personal, academic, psychological, birth control, religious. **For learning-disabled students:** School does not offer a structured program with separate admission and additional fees. Total undergraduates in learning-disabled program or receiving services: 167. Services include: reading machines, tape recorders, note-taking services, readers, extended time for tests, tutors, priority registration, texts on tape, other testing accommodations, other. **Library:** Number of titles: 365,133; number of current serial subscriptions: 5,851. **Information technology resources:** Students are not required to lease or own a computer. Number of campus computers available to all students: 400. School has a wireless network. Approximate number of users that can be accommodated: 2,800. Proportion of college-owned housing units wired for high-speed internet access: 100%. **Campus safety:** Security services offered: 24-hour foot-and-vehicle patrols, late-night transport/escort service, 24-hour emergency telephones, lighted pathways/sidewalks, controlled dormitory access (key, security card, etc).

TRANSFER AND INTERNATIONAL STUDENTS

Transfer students: May apply for admission for the following academic terms: Fall, Spring. Applicants do not need a minimum number of credits to apply. For fall 2009: Transfer applications received: 201. Transfer applicants offered admission: 105. Transfer applicants enrolled: 49. **International students:** Number of foreign undergraduates: 89 (3% of student body). Number of countries represented: 46. Minimum TOEFL score required: 590 (paper); 243 (computer).

St. Bonaventure University

- **Address:** Route 417, St. Bonaventure, NY 14778
- **Website:** http://www.sbu.edu
- **Private; Religious affiliation:** Roman Catholic
- **Enrollment:** 1,865 full-time; 102 part-time

KEY STATS

✔ **U.S News College Ranking:** 29, Regional Universities (North)
✔ **SAT Score (25th/75th percentile):** 920-1130
✔ **Tuition:** 2010-2011: $26,895

Selectivity: Selective	**Room/board:** $9,717
Acceptance rate: 84%	**Average debt:** $36,832
Student/faculty ratio: 14/1	**Proportion who borrowed:** 83%

UNDERGRADUATE STUDENT BODY STATS

2009-2010 enrollment: 1,865 full-time; 102 part-time. Men: 48%; women: 52%. **Ethnic makeup:** African American: 4%; Asian American: 2%; Hispanic: 3%; White: 88%; International: 2%. **Religious preference:** Protestant: 23%; Jewish: 1%; No preference: 16%; Roman Catholic: 59%; Other: 1%.

ADMISSIONS FACTS AND FIGURES

Phone: (800) 462-5050. **Email:** admissions@sbu.edu. **Website:** http://www.sbu.edu. **Application deadlines for fall 2011:** Regular decision: July 1. Early decision: Not offered. Early action: Not offered. Admission can be deferred. **Application fee:** $30. **To apply online, go to:** http://www.sbu.edu/admissions/admissions_app.vep. **Admissions requirements/recommendations:** High school units required (recommended): English: (4); Mathematics: (3); Science: (3); Foreign language: (2); Social studies: (4); Total units: (19). Tests: The college uses SAT or ACT scores in admissions decisions. Either SAT or ACT required. For admission to the fall 2011 entering class, the school will accept: ACT with or without writing accepted. Campus visit: Recommended. Admissions interview: Recommended. Off-campus interview: May be arranged. **Factors that count in admissions decisions:** *Academic:* Secondary school record: Very Important. Class rank: Considered. Letters of recommendation: Very Important. Standardized test scores: Important. Essay: Important. *Nonacademic:* Interview: Important. Extracurricular activities: Important. Talent/ability: Important. Character/personal qualities: Very Important. Alumni/ae relationship: Considered. Geographical residence: Considered. State residency: Considered. Religious affiliation/commitment: Not Considered. Minority status: Not Considered. Volunteer work: Important. Work experience: Considered. **Other schools with the greatest overlap in applicants:** Canisius College; Niagara University; SUNY–Fredonia; St. John Fisher College; University at Buffalo–SUNY. **Admissions statistics for the fall 2009 entering class:** Total applicants: 1,927. Total accepted: 1,617. Freshmen enrolled: 466; 24% were from out of state. Overall acceptance rate: 84%. **Credentials of fall 2009 freshmen:** 13% ranked in the top 10 percent of their high school class; 41% were in the top 25 percent; 75% were in the top half. (Proportion submitting class standing: 64%.) **Average high school grade point average:** 3.2. **First-year students who submitted SAT scores:** 96%. Scores (25/75 percentile): Critical Reading: 460-560, Math: 460-570, Combined: 920-1130. **First-year students submitting ACT scores:** 42%. Scores (25/75 percentile): English: 18-25, Math: 19-25, Composite: 20-25.

ACADEMICS

Year founded: 1858. **Academic calendar:** Semester. **Degrees offered:** bachelor's, post-bachelor's certificate, master's, post-master's certificate. **Most popular majors:** 17% journalism, 13% marketing/marketing management, 9% business administration and management, 8% accounting, 7% sociology. **Major fields of study:** area, ethnic, cultural, and gender studies; biological and biomedical sciences; business, management, marketing, and related support services; communication, journalism, and related programs; computer and information sciences and support services; education; English language and literature/letters; family and consumer sciences/human sciences; foreign languages, literatures, and linguistics; history; legal professions and studies; mathematics and statistics; natural resources and conservation; philosophy and religious studies; physical sciences; psychology; social sciences; theology and religious vocations; visual and performing arts. **Areas of required coursework:** arts/fine arts, humanities, computer literacy, mathematics, English (including composition), philosophy, foreign languages, sciences (biological or physical), history, social science. **Pre-professional programs:** pre-law, pre-dentistry, pre-medicine, pre-veterinary science, pre-optometry, pre-pharmacy. **Special academic programs:** cross-registration, double major, honors program, independent study, internships, student-designed major, study abroad, teacher certificate program. **Teacher certification offered in:** early childhood, special education, elementary, secondary. **Reserve Officers Training Corps (ROTC):** Army ROTC: Offered on campus. **Faculty and instruction (2009-2010):** Total instructional faculty: 155 full-time, 61 part-time (63% men; 37% women; 5% minorities). Full-time faculty with Ph.D. or other terminal degree: 81%. Student/faculty ratio: 14/1. Classes of fewer than 20 students: 57%; of 20 to 49 students: 42%; of 50 or more students: 0%. **Advanced Placement and International Baccalaureate credit:** AP tests may be used for: Credit and/or placement. Scores accepted: 3, 4, 5. International Baccalaureate exams may be used for: Credit and/or placement. **Freshmen returning for sophomore year:** 80%. **Graduation rates:** Four-year: 50%; five-year: 65%; six-year: 69%. **Graduate study:** 45% of students pursue further study immediately upon graduation. Fields in which graduates pursue further study: Master of Business Administration (MBA), 18%; law, 6%; medicine, 5%; engineering, 1%; theology (or the seminary), 1%; education, 39%; arts and sciences, 30%.

COSTS AND FINANCIAL AID

Financial aid office: (716) 375-2528. **Expenses (2010-2011):** Tuition and fees 2010-2011: $26,895; room/board: $9,717. Estimated books and supplies: $700; transportation: $605; personal expenses: $650. **Financial aid:** Priority filing date for institution's financial aid form: February 15. In 2009-2010, 86% of undergraduates applied for financial aid. Of those, 76% were determined to have financial need; 29% had their need fully met. Average financial aid package (proportion receiving): $22,000 (76%). Average amount of gift aid, such as scholarships or grants (proportion receiving): $15,935 (76%). Average amount of self-help aid, such as work study or loans (proportion receiving): $5,456 (65%). Average need-based loan (excluding PLUS or other private loans): $4,600. Among students who received need-based aid, the average percentage of need met: 79%. Among students who received aid based on merit, the average award (and the proportion receiving): $10,307 (22%). The average athletic scholarship (and the proportion receiving): $18,100 (5%). Average amount of debt of borrowers graduating in 2009: $36,832. Proportion who borrowed: 83%.

CAMPUS LIFE AND EXTRACURRICULAR ACTIVITIES

Campus housing available (% using): coed dorms (73%), apartment for single students (27%), special housing for disabled students (0%). Students who live in college-owned, operated, or affiliated housing: 80%. **Student employment:** During the 2009-2010 academic year, 24% of undergraduates worked on campus. Average per-year earnings: $1,711. **Clubs and organizations:** Number of student organizations: 61. Activities include: campus ministries, choral groups, concert band, dance, drama/theater, international student organization, jazz band, literary magazine, model UN, music ensembles, pep band, radio station, student government, student newspaper, television station, yearbook. Number of fraternities: 0; sororities: 0. Average proportion of students who stay on campus on weekends: 90%. **Sports program (2009-2010):** Member of NCAA I. *Men's intercollegiate varsity sports:* baseball, basketball, cross country, golf, soccer, swimming, tennis. *Women's intercollegiate varsity sports:* basketball, cross country, lacrosse, soccer, softball, swimming, tennis.

SERVICES AND FACILITIES

Basic services: nonremedial tutoring, placement service, health service, health insurance, other. **Remedial assistance:** reading, math, writing, study skills. **Counseling services:** career, personal, academic, psychological, religious. **For learning-disabled students:** School does not offer a structured program with separate admission and additional fees. Services include: tape recorders, untimed tests, note-taking services, oral tests, learning center, readers, extended time for tests, tutors, texts on tape, typist/scribe, exams on tape or computer. **Library:** Number of titles: 331,219; number of current serial subscriptions: 997. **Information technology resources:** Students are not required to lease or own a computer. Number of campus computers available to all students: 290. School has a wireless network. Approximate number of users that can be accommodated: 3,500. Proportion of college-owned housing units wired for high-speed internet access: 100%. **Campus safety:** Security services offered: 24-hour foot-and-vehicle patrols, late-night transport/escort service, 24-hour emergency telephones, lighted pathways/sidewalks, controlled dormitory access (key, security card, etc).

TRANSFER AND INTERNATIONAL STUDENTS

Transfer students: May apply for admission for the following academic terms: Fall, Spring, Summer. Applicants need a minimum number of credits to apply. For fall 2009: Transfer applications received: 174. Transfer

applicants offered admission: 112. Transfer applicants enrolled: 62.
International students: Number of foreign undergraduates: 34 (2% of student body). Minimum TOEFL score required: 550 (paper); 213 (computer). Average TOEFL score: 561 (paper).

St. Francis College

■ **Address:** 180 Remsen Street, Brooklyn Heights, NY 11201
■ **Website:** http://www.stfranciscollege.edu
■ **Private**
■ **Enrollment:** 2,205 full-time; 276 part-time

KEY STATS
✔ **U.S News College Ranking:** 29, Regional Colleges (North)
✔ **SAT Score (25th/75th percentile):** 820-1030
✔ **Tuition:** 2010-2011: $17,280

Selectivity: Less selective	**Room/board:** $13,500
Acceptance rate: 78%	**Average debt:** N/A
Student/faculty ratio: 18/1	**Proportion who borrowed:** N/A

UNDERGRADUATE STUDENT BODY STATS
2009-2010 enrollment: 2,205 full-time; 276 part-time. Men: 45%; women: 55%. **Ethnic makeup:** African American: 15%; Asian American: 4%; Hispanic: 15%; White: 58%; International: 7%. **Religious preference:** Roman Catholic: 53%; Protestant: 29%; Jewish: 4%; Muslim: 4%; Hindu: 1%; Buddhist: 1%; No preference: 6%; Eastern Orthodox: 2%.

ADMISSIONS FACTS AND FIGURES
Phone: (718) 489-5200. **Email:** admissions@stfranciscollege.edu. **Website:** http://www.stfranciscollege.edu. **Application deadlines for fall 2011:** Regular decision: Rolling. Early decision: Not offered. Early action: Not offered. Admission can be deferred. **Application fee:** $35. **To apply online, go to:** http://www.stfranciscollege.edu/admissions/undergraduate/applying/applicationListing.aspx. **Admissions requirements/recommendations:** High school units required (recommended): English: 4 (4); Mathematics: 2 (2); Science: 2 (2); Social studies: 3 (4); Academic electives: (6); Total units: 16 (19). Tests: The college uses SAT or ACT scores in admissions decisions. Either SAT or ACT required. For admission to the fall 2011 entering class, the school will accept: ACT with writing recommended. Campus visit: Recommended. Admissions interview: Recommended. Off-campus interview: May be arranged. **Factors that count in admissions decisions:** *Academic:* Secondary school record: Important. Class rank: Considered. Letters of recommendation: Important. Standardized test scores: Very Important. Essay: Very Important. *Nonacademic:* Interview: Important. Extracurricular activities: Important. Talent/ability: Important. Character/personal qualities: Important. Alumni/ae relationship: Important. Geographical residence: Not Considered. State residency: Not Considered. Religious affiliation/commitment: Not Considered. Minority status: Not Considered. Volunteer work: Considered. Work experience: Considered. **Other schools with the greatest overlap in applicants:** CUNY–College of Staten Island; CUNY–John Jay College of Criminal Justice; CUNY–Queens College; St. John's University; St. Joseph's College New York. **Admissions statistics for the fall 2009 entering class:** Total applicants: 1,944. Total accepted: 1,513. Freshmen enrolled: 603; 2% were from out of state. Overall acceptance rate: 78%. **Average high school grade point average:** 2.6. **First-year students who submitted SAT scores:** 97%. Scores (25/75 percentile): Critical Reading: 420-510, Math: 400-520, Combined: 820-1030.

ACADEMICS
Year founded: 1884. **Academic calendar:** Semester. **Degrees offered:** associate, bachelor's, master's. **Most popular majors:** 18% business administration, management, and operations, 13% liberal arts and sciences studies, and humanities, 12% dental support services and allied professions, 12% radio, television, and digital communication, 8% economics. **Major fields of study:** area, ethnic, cultural, and gender studies; biological and biomedical sciences; business, management, marketing, and related support services; communication, journalism, and related programs; computer and information sciences and support services; education; English language and literature/letters; foreign languages, literatures, and linguistics; health professions and related clinical sciences; history; liberal arts and sciences studies, and humanities; mathematics and statistics; philosophy and religious studies; physical sciences; psychology; security and protective services; social sciences. **Areas of required coursework:** arts/fine arts, humanities,

computer literacy, mathematics, English (including composition), philosophy, foreign languages, sciences (biological or physical), history, social science, other. **Pre-professional programs:** pre-law, pre-dentistry, pre-medicine, pre-veterinary science, other. **Special academic programs:** accelerated program, cooperative (work-study plan) program, cross-registration, double major, dual enrollment, exchange student program (domestic), honors program, independent study, internships, liberal arts/career combination, student-designed major, study abroad, teacher certificate program. **Teacher certification offered in:** early childhood, elementary, middle/junior high, secondary. **Cooperative education programs:** computer science, education, health professions, other. **Reserve Officers Training Corps (ROTC):** Army ROTC: Offered at cooperating institution (Polytechnic Institute of New York University); Air Force ROTC: Offered at cooperating institution (Manhattan College). **Faculty and instruction (2009-2010):** Total instructional faculty: 77 full-time, 163 part-time (60% men; 40% women; 17% minorities). Full-time faculty with Ph.D. or other terminal degree: 87%. Student/faculty ratio: 18/1. Classes of fewer than 20 students: 47%; of 20 to 49 students: 53%; of 50 or more students: 1%. **Advanced Placement and International Baccalaureate credit:** AP tests may be used for: Credit only. Scores accepted: 3, 4, 5. International Baccalaureate exams may be used for: Credit only. **Freshmen returning for sophomore year:** 75%. **Graduation rates:** Four-year: 17%; five-year: 29%; six-year: 54%.

COSTS AND FINANCIAL AID
Financial aid office: (718) 489-5255. **Expenses (2010-2011):** Tuition and fees 2010-2011: $17,280; room/board: $13,500. Estimated books and supplies: $1,000; transportation: $600; personal expenses: $1,250. **Financial aid:** Priority filing date for institution's financial aid form: February 15. In 2009-2010, 73% of undergraduates applied for financial aid. Of those, 64% were determined to have financial need; 12% had their need fully met. Average financial aid package (proportion receiving): $10,887 (64%). Average amount of gift aid, such as scholarships or grants (proportion receiving): $8,092 (60%). Average amount of self-help aid, such as work study or loans (proportion receiving): $4,314 (43%). Average need-based loan (excluding PLUS or other private loans): $4,314. Among students who received need-based aid, the average percentage of need met: 52%. Among students who received aid based on merit, the average award (and the proportion receiving): $6,917 (4%). The average athletic scholarship (and the proportion receiving): $10,056 (5%).

CAMPUS LIFE AND EXTRACURRICULAR ACTIVITIES
Campus housing available (% using): coed dorms (100%). Students who live in college-owned, operated, or affiliated housing: 3%. **Student employment:** During the 2009-2010 academic year, 11% of undergraduates worked on campus. Average per-year earnings: $2,200. **Clubs and organizations:** Number of student organizations: 35. Activities include: choral groups, dance, drama/theater, literary magazine, student government, student newspaper, yearbook. Number of fraternities: 0; sororities: 0. Average proportion of students who stay on campus on weekends: 20%. **Sports program (2009-2010):** Member of NCAA I. *Men's intercollegiate varsity sports:* basketball, cross country, golf, soccer, swimming, tennis, track and field (indoor), track and field (outdoor), water polo. *Women's intercollegiate varsity sports:* basketball, bowling, cross country, golf, swimming, tennis, track and field (indoor), track and field (outdoor), volleyball, water polo.

SERVICES AND FACILITIES
Basic services: nonremedial tutoring, placement service, health service, health insurance. **Remedial assistance:** reading, math, writing, study skills. **Counseling services:** minority student, career, military, personal, veteran student, academic, older student, psychological, birth control, religious. **For learning-disabled students:** School does not offer a structured program with separate admission and additional fees. Total undergraduates in learning-disabled program or receiving services: 91. Services include: remedial math, remedial English, remedial reading, tape recorders, note-taking services, oral tests, readers, extended time for tests, tutors, priority seating, texts on tape, typist/scribe, exams on tape or computer, other. **Library:** Number of titles: 117,838; number of current serial subscriptions: 30,812. **Information technology resources:** Students are not required to lease or own a computer. Number of campus computers available to all students: 378. School has a wireless network. Approximate number of users that can be accommodated: 1,000. **Campus safety:** Security services offered: 24-hour foot-and-vehicle patrols, 24-hour emergency telephones.

TRANSFER AND INTERNATIONAL STUDENTS
Transfer students: May apply for admission for the following academic terms: Fall, Winter, Spring, Summer. Applicants do not need a minimum

number of credits to apply. For fall 2009: Transfer applications received: 484. Transfer applicants offered admission: 299. Transfer applicants enrolled: 154. **International students:** Number of foreign undergraduates: 186 (7% of student body). Number of countries represented: 57. Minimum TOEFL score required: 500 (paper). Average TOEFL score: 515 (paper).

St. John Fisher College

- **Address:** 3690 East Avenue, Rochester, NY 14618
- **Website:** http://www.sjfc.edu
- **Private; Religious affiliation:** Roman Catholic
- **Enrollment:** 2,628 full-time; 204 part-time

KEY STATS

✔ **U.S News College Ranking:** 36, Regional Universities (North)
✔ **SAT Score (25th/75th percentile):** 990-1170
✔ **Tuition:** 2010-2011: $25,270

Selectivity: Selective	**Room/board:** $10,290
Acceptance rate: 65%	**Average debt:** $30,281
Student/faculty ratio: 14/1	**Proportion who borrowed:** 84%

UNDERGRADUATE STUDENT BODY STATS

2009-2010 enrollment: 2,628 full-time; 204 part-time. Men: 42%; women: 58%. **Ethnic makeup:** African American: 5%; Asian American: 2%; Hispanic: 3%; White: 89%.

ADMISSIONS FACTS AND FIGURES

Phone: (585) 385-8064. **Email:** admissions@sjfc.edu. **Website:** http://www.sjfc.edu. **Application deadlines for fall 2011:** Regular decision: Rolling. Early decision: Send application by: December 1; Decision sent by: January 15. Early action: Not offered. Admission can be deferred. **Application fee:** $30. **To apply online, go to:** http://sjfc.edu/admissions/freshman/apply/. **Admissions requirements/recommendations:** High school units required (recommended): English: (4); Mathematics: (4); Science: (4); Foreign language: (3); Social studies: (4); Total units: 16. Tests: The college uses SAT or ACT scores in admissions decisions. Either SAT or ACT required. For admission to the fall 2011 entering class, the school will accept: ACT with or without writing accepted. Campus visit: Recommended. Admissions interview: Recommended. Off-campus interview: May be arranged. **Factors that count in admissions decisions:** *Academic:* Secondary school record: Very Important. Class rank: Important. Letters of recommendation: Very Important. Standardized test scores: Important. Essay: Important. *Nonacademic:* Interview: Important. Extracurricular activities: Important. Talent/ability: Important. Character/personal qualities: Very Important. Alumni/ae relationship: Very Important. Geographical residence: Considered. State residency: Considered. Religious affiliation/commitment: Not Considered. Minority status: Not Considered. Volunteer work: Important. Work experience: Important. **Other schools with the greatest overlap in applicants:** Canisius College; College at Brockport–SUNY; Le Moyne College; Nazareth College; University at Buffalo–SUNY. **Admissions statistics for the fall 2009 entering class:** Total applicants: 3,440. Total accepted: 2,237. Freshmen enrolled: 558; 3% were from out of state. Accepted through early-decision or early-action plans: 9%. Overall acceptance rate: 65%. Early-decision acceptance rate: 63%. Non-early acceptance rate: 65%. **Credentials of fall 2009 freshmen:** 23% ranked in the top 10 percent of their high school class; 55% were in the top 25 percent; 89% were in the top half. (Proportion submitting class standing: 72%.) **Average high school grade point average:** 3.5. **First-year students who submitted SAT scores:** 97%. Scores (25/75 percentile): Critical Reading: 480-570; Math: 510-600, Combined: 990-1170. **First-year students submitting ACT scores:** 51%. Scores (25/75 percentile): English: 20-25, Math: 21-26, Composite: 22-26.

ACADEMICS

Year founded: 1948. **Academic calendar:** Semester. **Degrees offered:** bachelor's, post-bachelor's certificate, master's, post-master's certificate, doctorate. **Most popular majors:** 26% business, management, marketing, and related support services, 22% education, 11% health professions and related clinical sciences, 9% communication, journalism, and related programs, 7% social sciences. **Major fields of study:** area, ethnic, cultural, and gender studies; biological and biomedical sciences; business, management, marketing, and related support services; communication, journalism, and related programs; computer and information sciences and support services; educa-

tion; English language and literature/letters; foreign languages, literatures, and linguistics; health professions and related clinical sciences; history; liberal arts and sciences studies, and humanities; mathematics and statistics; parks, recreation, leisure, and fitness studies; philosophy and religious studies; physical sciences; psychology; social sciences. **Areas of required coursework:** humanities, mathematics, English (including composition), philosophy, sciences (biological or physical), social science. **Pre-professional programs:** pre-law, pre-dentistry, pre-medicine, pre-veterinary science, pre-optometry, pre-pharmacy, other. **Special academic programs (% participation):** cross-registration (4%), double major (20%), honors program (6%), independent study (9%), internships (27%), liberal arts/career combination, student-designed major (1%), study abroad (6%), teacher certificate program (22%). **Teacher certification offered in:** special education, elementary, middle/junior high, secondary. **Cooperative education programs:** engineering, natural science, other. **Reserve Officers Training Corps (ROTC):** Army ROTC: Offered at cooperating institution (Rochester Institute of Technology); Navy ROTC: Offered at cooperating institution (University of Rochester); Air Force ROTC: Offered at cooperating institution (Rochester Institute of Technology). **Faculty and instruction (2009-2010):** Total instructional faculty: 201 full-time, 174 part-time (42% men; 58% women; 10% minorities). Full-time faculty with Ph.D. or other terminal degree: 89%. Student/faculty ratio: 14/1. Classes of fewer than 20 students: 42%; of 20 to 49 students: 57%; of 50 or more students: 0%. **Advanced Placement and International Baccalaureate credit:** AP tests may be used for: Credit and/or placement. Scores accepted: 3, 4, 5. International Baccalaureate exams may be used for: Credit and/or placement. **Freshmen returning for sophomore year:** 84%. **Graduation rates:** Four-year: 63%; five-year: 73%; six-year: 71%. **Graduate study:** 36% of students pursue further study within one year. Fields in which graduates pursue further study: Master of Business Administration (MBA), 15%; law, 2%; medicine, 5%; education, 50%; arts and sciences, 5%.

COSTS AND FINANCIAL AID

Financial aid office: (585) 385-8042. **Expenses (2010-2011):** Tuition and fees 2010-2011: $25,270; room/board: $10,290. Estimated books and supplies: $900; transportation: $300; personal expenses: $600. **Financial aid:** Priority filing date for institution's financial aid form: February 15. In 2009-2010, 92% of undergraduates applied for financial aid. Of those, 82% were determined to have financial need; 37% had their need fully met. Average financial aid package (proportion receiving): $17,795 (82%). Average amount of gift aid, such as scholarships or grants (proportion receiving): $13,219 (81%). Average amount of self-help aid, such as work study or loans (proportion receiving): $5,279 (77%). Average need-based loan (excluding PLUS or other private loans): $4,594. Among students who received need-based aid, the average percentage of need met: 81%. Among students who received aid based on merit, the average award (and the proportion receiving): $7,634 (16%). The average athletic scholarship (and the proportion receiving): $0 (0%). Average amount of debt of borrowers graduating in 2009: $30,281. Proportion who borrowed: 84%.

CAMPUS LIFE AND EXTRACURRICULAR ACTIVITIES

Campus housing available (% using): coed dorms (96%), women's dorms (4%). Students who live in college-owned, operated, or affiliated housing: 49%. **Student employment:** During the 2009-2010 academic year, 8% of undergraduates worked on campus. Average per-year earnings: $496. **Clubs and organizations:** Number of student organizations: 70. Activities include: campus ministries, choral groups, dance, drama/theater, literary magazine, musical theater, student government, student newspaper, television station, yearbook. Number of fraternities: 0; sororities: 0. Average proportion of students who stay on campus on weekends: 50%. **Sports program (2009-2010):** Member of NCAA III. *Men's intercollegiate varsity sports:* baseball, basketball, football, golf, lacrosse, soccer, tennis. *Women's intercollegiate varsity sports:* basketball, golf, lacrosse, soccer, softball, tennis, volleyball.

SERVICES AND FACILITIES

Basic services: nonremedial tutoring, day care, health service, health insurance, other. **Remedial assistance:** math, writing. **Counseling services:** minority student, career, personal, veteran student, academic, psychological, birth control, religious, other. **For learning-disabled students:** School does not offer a structured program with separate admission and additional fees. Total undergraduates in learning-disabled program or receiving services: 112. Services include: remedial English, tape recorders, note-taking services, readers, extended time for tests, tutors, texts on tape, other. **Library:** Number of titles: 214,834; number of current serial subscriptions: 22,428. **Information technology resources:** Students are not required to lease or own a computer. Number of campus computers available to all students: 525.

School has a wireless network. Approximate number of users that can be accommodated: 800. Proportion of college-owned housing units wired for high-speed internet access: 100%. **Campus safety:** Security services offered: 24-hour foot-and-vehicle patrols, late-night transport/escort service, 24-hour emergency telephones, lighted pathways/sidewalks, controlled dormitory access (key, security card, etc).

TRANSFER AND INTERNATIONAL STUDENTS

Transfer students: May apply for admission for the following academic terms: Fall, Spring, Summer. Applicants need a minimum number of credits to apply. For fall 2009: Transfer applications received: 747. Transfer applicants offered admission: 545. Transfer applicants enrolled: 287. **International students:** Number of foreign undergraduates: 6. Number of countries represented: 6. Minimum TOEFL score required: 550 (paper); 79 (computer).

St. John's University

- **Address:** 8000 Utopia Parkway, Queens, NY 11439
- **Website:** http://www.stjohns.edu/
- **Private; Religious affiliation:** Roman Catholic
- **Enrollment:** 11,824 full-time; 2,984 part-time

KEY STATS

✔ **U.S News College Ranking:** 143, National Universities
✔ **SAT Score (25th/75th percentile):** 970-1210
✔ **Tuition:** 2010-2011: $31,980

Selectivity: Selective	**Room/board:** $13,900
Acceptance rate: 43%	**Average debt:** $30,692
Student/faculty ratio: 19/1	**Proportion who borrowed:** 70%

UNDERGRADUATE STUDENT BODY STATS

2009-2010 enrollment: 11,824 full-time; 2,984 part-time. Men: 45%; women: 55%. **Ethnic makeup:** African American: 18%; Asian American: 18%; Hispanic: 15%; White: 45%; International: 5%. **Religious preference:** Protestant: 13%; Jewish: 2%; Muslim: 4%; Hindu: 3%; Buddhist: 1%; No preference: 8%; Unknown: 7%; Roman Catholic: 51%; Other: 5%.

ADMISSIONS FACTS AND FIGURES

Phone: (718) 990-2000. **Email:** admhelp@stjohns.edu. **Website:** http://www.stjohns.edu/. **Application deadlines for fall 2011:** Regular decision: Rolling. Early decision: Not offered. Early action: Not offered. Admission can be deferred. **Application fee:** $50. **To apply online, go to:** http://www.stjohns.edu/admission/undergraduate/apply/freshmanonline. **Admissions requirements/recommendations:** High school units required (recommended): English: 4; Mathematics: (3); Science: (2); Foreign language: (2); History: (2); Total units: 4 (12). Tests: The college uses SAT or ACT scores in admissions decisions. Either SAT or ACT required. For admission to the fall 2011 entering class, the school will accept: ACT with or without writing accepted. Campus visit: Neither required nor recommended. Admissions interview: Neither required nor recommended. Off-campus interview: May be arranged. **Factors that count in admissions decisions:** *Academic:* Secondary school record: Important. Class rank: Considered. Letters of recommendation: Considered. Standardized test scores: Very Important. Essay: Considered. *Nonacademic:* Interview: Considered. Extracurricular activities: Considered. Talent/ability: Not Considered. Character/personal qualities: Considered. Alumni/ae relationship: Considered. Geographical residence: Considered. State residency: Not Considered. Religious affiliation/commitment: Not Considered. Minority status: Not Considered. Volunteer work: Considered. Work experience: Considered. **Other schools with the greatest overlap in applicants:** CUNY–Baruch College; Fordham University; New York University; Rutgers, the State University of New Jersey–New Brunswick; SUNY–Stony Brook. **Admissions statistics for the fall 2009 entering class:** Total applicants: 52,980. Total accepted: 22,788. Freshmen enrolled: 3,108; 32% were from out of state. Overall acceptance rate: 43%. **Credentials of fall 2009 freshmen:** 24% ranked in the top 10 percent of their high school class; 50% were in the top 25 percent; 79% were in the top half. (Proportion submitting class standing: 9%.) **Average high school grade point average:** 3.3. **First-year students who submitted SAT scores:** 96%. Scores (25/75 percentile): Critical Reading: 480-590, Math: 490-620, Combined: 970-1210.

ACADEMICS

Year founded: 1870. **Academic calendar:** Semester. **Degrees offered:** certificate, diploma, associate, transfer-associate, terminal-associate, bachelor's, post-bachelor's certificate, master's, post-master's certificate, doctorate. **Most popular majors:** 26% business, management, marketing, and related support services, 11% communication, journalism, and related programs, 8% security and protective services, 7% health professions and related clinical sciences, 6% education. **Major fields of study:** area, ethnic, cultural, and gender studies; biological and biomedical sciences; business, management, marketing, and related support services; communication, journalism, and related programs; communications technologies/technicians and support services; computer and information sciences and support services; education; engineering technologies/technicians; English language and literature/letters; foreign languages, literatures, and linguistics; health professions and related clinical sciences; history; legal professions and studies; liberal arts and sciences studies, and humanities; mathematics and statistics; natural resources and conservation; parks, recreation, leisure, and fitness studies; personal and culinary services; philosophy and religious studies; physical sciences; psychology; public administration and social service professions; security and protective services; social sciences; visual and performing arts. **Areas of required coursework:** arts/fine arts, mathematics, English (including composition), philosophy, foreign languages, sciences (biological or physical), history, social science, other. **Pre-professional programs:** pre-law, pre-medicine, pre-theology, pre-optometry, pre-pharmacy. **Special academic programs:** accelerated program, cross-registration, distance learning, double major, dual enrollment, English as a Second Language (ESL), honors program, independent study, internships, liberal arts/career combination, study abroad, teacher certificate program, weekend college. **Teacher certification offered in:** early childhood, special education, elementary, middle/junior high, secondary, bilingual/bicultural. **Reserve Officers Training Corps (ROTC):** Army ROTC: Offered on campus. **Faculty and instruction (2009-2010):** Total instructional faculty: 669 full-time, 771 part-time (60% men; 40% women; 18% minorities). Full-time faculty with Ph.D. or other terminal degree: 87%. Student/faculty ratio: 19/1. Classes of fewer than 20 students: 34%; of 20 to 49 students: 60%; of 50 or more students: 6%. **Advanced Placement and International Baccalaureate credit:** AP tests may be used for: Credit only. Scores accepted: 3, 4, 5. International Baccalaureate exams may be used for: Credit only. **Freshmen returning for sophomore year:** 78%. **Graduation rates:** Four-year: 38%; five-year: 49%; six-year: 58%. **Graduate study:** 20% of students pursue further study immediately upon graduation. Fields in which graduates pursue further study: Master of Business Administration (MBA), 20%; law, 25%; medicine, 7%; theology (or the seminary), 1%; education, 25%; arts and sciences, 22%.

COSTS AND FINANCIAL AID

Financial aid office: (718) 990-2000. **Expenses (2010-2011):** Tuition and fees 2010-2011: $31,980; room/board: $13,900. Estimated books and supplies: $1,000; transportation: $1,100; personal expenses: $2,700. **Financial aid:** Priority filing date for institution's financial aid form: February 1. In 2009-2010, 87% of undergraduates applied for financial aid. Of those, 81% were determined to have financial need; 10% had their need fully met. Average financial aid package (proportion receiving): $20,524 (80%). Average amount of gift aid, such as scholarships or grants (proportion receiving): $10,506 (69%). Average amount of self-help aid, such as work study or loans (proportion receiving): $6,857 (63%). Average need-based loan (excluding PLUS or other private loans): $6,601. Among students who received need-based aid, the average percentage of need met: 62%. Among students who received aid based on merit, the average award (and the proportion receiving): $10,463 (5%). The average athletic scholarship (and the proportion receiving): $24,370 (2%). Average amount of debt of borrowers graduating in 2009: $30,692. Proportion who borrowed: 70%.

CAMPUS LIFE AND EXTRACURRICULAR ACTIVITIES

Campus housing available (% using): coed dorms (70%), apartment for single students (12%), other housing options. Students who live in college-owned, operated, or affiliated housing: 30%. **Student employment:** During the 2009-2010 academic year, 10% of undergraduates worked on campus. Average per-year earnings: $4,250. **Clubs and organizations:** Number of student organizations: 180. Activities include: campus ministries, choral groups, dance, drama/theater, jazz band, literary magazine, model UN, music ensembles, musical theater, pep band, radio station, student government, student newspaper, television station, yearbook. Number of fraternities: 16; sororities: 17. Proportion of men in fraternities: 6%; of women in sororities: 7%. Average proportion of students who stay on campus on weekends: 65%. **Sports program (2009-2010):** Member of NCAA I. *Men's intercollegiate varsity sports:* baseball, basketball, fencing, golf, lacrosse, soccer, tennis. **Women's intercollegiate varsity sports:** basketball, cross country, fencing, golf, soccer, softball, tennis, track and field (indoor), track and field (outdoor), volleyball.

SERVICES AND FACILITIES

Basic services: nonremedial tutoring, health service, health insurance. **Remedial assistance:** reading, math, writing, study skills, other. **Counseling services:** career, personal, veteran student, academic, psychological, religious. **For learning-disabled students:** School does not offer a structured program with separate admission and additional fees. Total undergraduates in learning-disabled program or receiving services: 30. Services include: tape recorders, diagnostic testing service, untimed tests, oral tests, readers, extended time for tests, tutors, priority registration, typist/scribe. **Library:** Number of titles: 812,395; number of current serial subscriptions: 47,068. **Information technology resources:** Students are required to lease or own a computer. Number of campus computers available to all students: 15,200. School has a wireless network. Approximate number of users that can be accommodated: 22,000. Proportion of college-owned housing units wired for high-speed internet access: 100%. **Campus safety:** Security services offered: 24-hour foot-and-vehicle patrols, late-night transport/escort service, 24-hour emergency telephones, lighted pathways/sidewalks, controlled dormitory access (key, security card, etc).

TRANSFER AND INTERNATIONAL STUDENTS

Transfer students: May apply for admission for the following academic terms: Fall, Spring, Summer. Applicants do not need a minimum number of credits to apply. For fall 2009: Transfer applications received: 3,309. Transfer applicants offered admission: 1,226. Transfer applicants enrolled: 448. **International students:** Number of foreign undergraduates: 551 (5% of student body). Number of countries represented: 83. Minimum TOEFL score required: 500 (paper); 61 (computer).

St. Joseph's College New York

- **Address:** 245 Clinton Avenue, Brooklyn, NY 11205-3688
- **Website:** http://www.sjcny.edu
- **Private**
- **Enrollment:** 3,954 full-time; 1,081 part-time

KEY STATS

✔ **U.S News College Ranking:** 15, Regional Colleges (North)
✔ **SAT Score (25th/75th percentile):** 940-1160
✔ **Tuition:** 2010-2011: $17,575

Selectivity: Selective	**Room/board:** N/A
Acceptance rate: 45%	**Average debt:** $20,941
Student/faculty ratio: 16/1	**Proportion who borrowed:** 62%

UNDERGRADUATE STUDENT BODY STATS

2009-2010 enrollment: 3,954 full-time; 1,081 part-time. Men: 27%; women: 73%. **Ethnic makeup:** African American: 11%; Asian American: 2%; Hispanic: 10%; White: 76%.

ADMISSIONS FACTS AND FIGURES

Phone: (718) 940-5800. **Email:** brooklynas@sjcny.edu. **Website:** http://www.sjcny.edu. **Application deadlines for fall 2011:** Regular decision: Rolling. Early decision: Not offered. Early action: Not offered. Admission can be deferred. **To apply online, go to:** https://www.universalcollegeapp.com/. **Admissions requirements/recommendations:** High school units required (recommended): English: 4; Mathematics: 3; Science: 2; Foreign language: 2 (3); Social studies: 4; Academic electives: 3; Total units: 18 (3). Tests: The college uses SAT or ACT scores in admissions decisions. Either SAT or ACT required. For admission to the fall 2011 entering class, the school will accept: ACT with writing required. Campus visit: Recommended. Admissions interview: Recommended. Off-campus interview: May be arranged. **Factors that count in admissions decisions:** *Academic:* Secondary school record: Very Important. Class rank: Important. Letters of recommendation: Important. Standardized test scores: Very Important. Essay: Important. *Nonacademic:* Interview: Important. Extracurricular activities: Important. Talent/ability: Considered. Character/personal qualities: Important. Alumni/ae relationship: Considered. Geographical residence: Not Considered. State residency: Not Considered. Religious affiliation/commitment: Not Considered. Minority status: Not Considered. Volunteer work: Considered. Work experience: Considered. **Other schools with the greatest overlap in applicants:** CUNY–Brooklyn College; CUNY–Hunter College; Hofstra University; Long Island University–C.W. Post Campus; St. John's University. **Admissions statistics for the fall 2009 entering class:** Total applicants: 2,871. Total accepted: 1,300. Freshmen enrolled: 689; 1% were from out of state. Overall acceptance rate: 45%. **Average high school grade point average:** 3.1. **First-year students who submitted SAT scores:** 85%. Scores (25/75 percentile): Critical Reading: 470-580, Math: 470-580, Combined: 940-1160. **First-year students submitting ACT scores:** 24%. Scores (25/75 percentile): English: N/A, Math: N/A, Composite: 22-25.

ACADEMICS

Year founded: 1916. **Academic calendar:** Semester. **Degrees offered:** certificate, bachelor's, master's. **Most popular majors:** 41% education, 19% business, management, marketing, and related support services, 6% psychology, 5% social sciences, 5% speech and rhetorical studies. **Major fields of study:** biological and biomedical sciences; business, management, marketing, and related support services; computer and information sciences and support services; education; English language and literature/letters; family and consumer sciences/human sciences; foreign languages, literatures, and linguistics; health professions and related clinical sciences; history; liberal arts and sciences studies, and humanities; mathematics and statistics; parks, recreation, leisure, and fitness studies; physical sciences; psychology; social sciences. **Areas of required coursework:** humanities, mathematics, English (including composition), foreign languages, sciences (biological or physical), history, social science. **Pre-professional programs:** pre-law, pre-dentistry, pre-medicine, pre-veterinary science, pre-optometry, pre-pharmacy. **Special academic programs:** accelerated program, honors program, independent study, internships, teacher certificate program, weekend college. **Teacher certification offered in:** early childhood, special education, elementary, middle/junior high, secondary. **Cooperative education programs:** business, social/behavioral science. **Faculty and instruction (2009-2010):** Total instructional faculty: 167 full-time, 378 part-time (48% men; 52% women; 12% minorities). Full-time faculty with Ph.D. or other terminal degree: 76%. Student/faculty ratio: 16/1. Classes of fewer than 20 students: 64%; of 20 to 49 students: 36%; of 50 or more students: 0%. **Advanced Placement and International Baccalaureate credit:** AP tests may be used for: Credit and/or placement. Scores accepted: 3, 4, 5. International Baccalaureate exams may be used for: Credit and/or placement. **Freshmen returning for sophomore year:** 81%. **Graduation rates:** Four-year: 59%; five-year: 72%; six-year: 71%. **Graduate study:** 40% of students pursue further study immediately upon graduation; 20% within one year; 20% within five years. Fields in which graduates pursue further study: Master of Business Administration (MBA), 5%; law, 1%; medicine, 1%; dentistry, 1%; education, 62%; arts and sciences, 30%.

COSTS AND FINANCIAL AID

Financial aid office: (718) 636-6808. **Expenses (2010-2011):** Tuition and fees 2010-2011: $17,575. **Financial aid:** Priority filing date for institution's financial aid form: February 25. In 2009-2010, 88% of undergraduates applied for financial aid. Of those, 67% were determined to have financial need; 24% had their need fully met. Average financial aid package (proportion receiving): $10,449 (65%). Average amount of gift aid, such as scholarships or grants (proportion receiving): $7,760 (55%). Average amount of self-help aid, such as work study or loans (proportion receiving): $4,367 (46%). Average need-based loan (excluding PLUS or other private loans): $4,265. Among students who received need-based aid, the average percentage of need met: 69%. Among students who received aid based on merit, the average award (and the proportion receiving): $6,856 (14%). Average amount of debt of borrowers graduating in 2009: $20,941. Proportion who borrowed: 62%.

CAMPUS LIFE AND EXTRACURRICULAR ACTIVITIES

Students who live in college-owned, operated, or affiliated housing: 2%. **Student employment:** During the 2009-2010 academic year, 3% of undergraduates worked on campus. Average per-year earnings: $3,118. **Clubs and organizations:** Number of student organizations: 56. Activities include: campus ministries, choral groups, dance, drama/theater, international student organization, jazz band, literary magazine, music ensembles, musical theater, student government, student newspaper, student film society, yearbook. Number of fraternities: 3; sororities: 4. Proportion of men in fraternities: 1%; of women in sororities: 1%. **Sports program (2009-2010):** Member of NCAA III. **Men's intercollegiate varsity sports:** baseball, basketball, cross country, golf, soccer, tennis, track and field (indoor), track and field (outdoor). **Women's intercollegiate varsity sports:** basketball, cross country, equestrian, soccer, softball, swimming, tennis, track and field (indoor), track and field (outdoor), volleyball.

SERVICES AND FACILITIES

Basic services: nonremedial tutoring, placement service. **Remedial assistance:** math, writing. **Counseling services:** career, personal, academic, psychological, religious, other. **For learning-disabled students:** School does not offer a structured program with separate admission and additional fees. Total undergraduates in learning-disabled program or receiving services: 48. Services include: note-taking services, learning center, extended time for tests, tutors, priority seating, texts on tape, other testing accommodations. **Library:** Number of titles: 265,125; number of current serial subscriptions: 16,104. **Information technology resources:** Students are not required to lease or own a computer. Number of campus computers available to all students: 603. School has a wireless network. Approximate number of users that can be accommodated: 4,096. Proportion of college-owned housing units wired for high-speed internet access: 100%. **Campus safety:** Security services offered: 24-hour foot-and-vehicle patrols, late-night transport/escort service, 24-hour emergency telephones, lighted pathways/sidewalks.

TRANSFER AND INTERNATIONAL STUDENTS

Transfer students: May apply for admission for the following academic terms: Fall, Spring. Applicants need a minimum number of credits to apply. For fall 2009: Transfer applications received: 368. Transfer applicants offered admission: 233. Transfer applicants enrolled: 118. **International students:** Number of foreign undergraduates: 2. Number of countries represented: 14. Minimum TOEFL score required: 550 (paper); 213 (computer). Average TOEFL score: 550 (paper).

St. Lawrence University

- **Address:** 23 Romoda Drive, Canton, NY 13617
- **Website:** http://www.stlawu.edu
- **Private**
- **Enrollment:** 2,274 full-time; 21 part-time

KEY STATS

✔ **U.S News College Ranking:** 55, National Liberal Arts Colleges
✔ **SAT Score (25th/75th percentile):** 1140-1290
✔ **Tuition:** 2010-2011: $41,155

Selectivity: More selective	**Room/board:** $10,615
Acceptance rate: 39%	**Average debt:** $31,653
Student/faculty ratio: 11/1	**Proportion who borrowed:** 74%

UNDERGRADUATE STUDENT BODY STATS

2009-2010 enrollment: 2,274 full-time; 21 part-time. Men: 45%; women: 55%. **Ethnic makeup:** African American: 3%; American-Indian: 1%; Asian American: 2%; Hispanic: 4%; White: 84%; International: 6%.

ADMISSIONS FACTS AND FIGURES

Phone: (315) 229-5261. **Email:** admissions@stlawu.edu. **Website:** http://www.stlawu.edu. **Application deadlines for fall 2011:** Regular decision: February 1. Early decision: Send application by: November 15; Decision sent by: December 15. Early action: Not offered. Admission can be deferred. **Application fee:** $60. **To apply online, go to:** http://web.stlawu.edu/admis/online_app.html. **Admissions requirements/recommendations:** High school units required (recommended): English: (4); Mathematics: (4); Science: (4); Foreign language: (4); Social studies: (2); History: (2); Total units: (20). Tests: The college uses SAT or ACT scores in admissions decisions. Neither SAT nor ACT required. For admission to the fall 2011 entering class, the school will accept: ACT with or without writing accepted. Campus visit: Recommended. Admissions interview: Recommended. Off-campus interview: May be arranged. **Factors that count in admissions decisions:** *Academic:* Secondary school record: Important. Class rank: Important. Letters of recommendation: Very Important. Standardized test scores: Considered. Essay: Very Important. *Nonacademic:* Interview: Important. Extracurricular activities: Important. Talent/ability: Considered. Character/personal qualities: Very Important. Alumni/ae relationship: Considered. Geographical residence: Considered. State residency: Not Considered. Religious affiliation/commitment: Not Considered. Minority status: Important. Volunteer work: Considered. Work experience: Considered. **Other schools with the greatest overlap in applicants:** Colby College; Colgate University; Hamilton College; Ithaca College; University of Vermont. **Admissions statistics for the fall 2009 entering class:** Total applicants: 4,715. Total accepted: 1,848. Freshmen enrolled: 580; 57% were from out of state. Accepted through early-decision or early-action plans: 31%. Overall accep-

tance rate: 39%. Early-decision acceptance rate: 79%. Non-early acceptance rate: 37%. **Size of waiting list:** 444 applicants; enrolled from waiting list: 36. **Credentials of fall 2009 freshmen:** 41% ranked in the top 10 percent of their high school class; 81% were in the top 25 percent; 96% were in the top half. (Proportion submitting class standing: 44%.) **Average high school grade point average:** 3.5. **First-year students who submitted SAT scores:** 56%. Scores (25/75 percentile): Critical Reading: 570-640, Math: 570-650, Combined: 1140-1290. **First-year students submitting ACT scores:** 21%. Scores (25/75 percentile): English: N/A, Math: N/A, Composite: 26-29.

ACADEMICS

Year founded: 1856. **Academic calendar:** Semester. **Degrees offered:** bachelor's, master's, post-master's certificate. **Most popular majors:** 30% social sciences, 14% psychology, 11% visual and performing arts, 7% biological and biomedical sciences, 6% English language and literature/letters. **Major fields of study:** area, ethnic, cultural, and gender studies; biological and biomedical sciences; English language and literature/letters; foreign languages, literatures, and linguistics; history; mathematics and statistics; multi/interdisciplinary studies; philosophy and religious studies; physical sciences; psychology; social sciences; visual and performing arts. **Areas of required coursework:** arts/fine arts, humanities, sciences (biological or physical), social science, other. **Pre-professional programs:** pre-law, pre-dentistry, pre-medicine, pre-veterinary science. **Special academic programs (% participation):** cross-registration (4%), double major (19%), exchange student program (domestic) (0%), independent study (51%), internships (45%), student-designed major (.2%), study abroad (48%), teacher certificate program (3%), other. **Teacher certification offered in:** middle/junior high, secondary. **Reserve Officers Training Corps (ROTC):** Army ROTC: Offered at cooperating institution (Clarkson University); Air Force ROTC: Offered at cooperating institution (Clarkson University). **Faculty and instruction (2009-2010):** Total instructional faculty: 170 full-time, 29 part-time (50% men; 50% women; 13% minorities). Full-time faculty with Ph.D. or other terminal degree: 98%. Student/faculty ratio: 11/1. Classes of fewer than 20 students: 64%; of 20 to 49 students: 35%; of 50 or more students: 1%. **Advanced Placement and International Baccalaureate credit:** AP tests may be used for: Credit and/or placement. Scores accepted: 4, 5. International Baccalaureate exams may be used for: Credit and/or placement. **Freshmen returning for sophomore year:** 89%. **Graduation rates:** Four-year: 79%; five-year: 80%; six-year: 81%. **Graduate study:** 24% of students pursue further study immediately upon graduation. Fields in which graduates pursue further study: Master of Business Administration (MBA), 1%; law, 11%; medicine, 14%; education, 22%; arts and sciences, 52%.

COSTS AND FINANCIAL AID

Financial aid office: (315) 229-5265. **Expenses (2010-2011):** Tuition and fees 2010-2011: $41,155; room/board: $10,615. Estimated books and supplies: $750; transportation: $400; personal expenses: $500. **Financial aid:** Priority filing date for institution's financial aid form: February 1; deadline: February 1. In 2009-2010, 71% of undergraduates applied for financial aid. Of those, 63% were determined to have financial need; 42% had their need fully met. Average financial aid package (proportion receiving): $35,989 (62%). Average amount of gift aid, such as scholarships or grants (proportion receiving): $26,987 (62%). Average amount of self-help aid, such as work study or loans (proportion receiving): $5,402 (49%). Average need-based loan (excluding PLUS or other private loans): $4,282. Among students who received need-based aid, the average percentage of need met: 90%. Among students who received aid based on merit, the average award (and the proportion receiving): $11,335 (16%). The average athletic scholarship (and the proportion receiving): $48,298 (2%). Average amount of debt of borrowers graduating in 2009: $31,653. Proportion who borrowed: 74%.

CAMPUS LIFE AND EXTRACURRICULAR ACTIVITIES

Campus housing available (% using): coed dorms (72%), sorority housing (5%), fraternity housing (0%), apartment for single students (8%), special housing for disabled students (1%), special housing for international students (2%), other housing options. Students who live in college-owned, operated, or affiliated housing: 98%. **Student employment:** During the 2009-2010 academic year, 37% of undergraduates worked on campus. Average per-year earnings: $2,000. **Clubs and organizations:** Number of student organizations: 125. Activities include: campus ministries, choral groups, concert band, dance, drama/theater, international student organization, jazz band, literary magazine, model UN, music ensembles, radio station, student government, student newspaper, student film society, yearbook. Number of fraternities: 2; sororities: 4. Proportion of men in fraternities: 4%; of women in sororities: 19%. Average proportion of students who stay on campus on weekends: 90%. **Sports program (2009-2010):** Member of NCAA III. *Men's intercollegiate varsity sports:* baseball, basketball, cross country, football, golf, ice hockey, lacrosse, skiing (nordic), skiing (alpine), soccer, swimming, tennis, track and field (indoor), track and field (outdoor). *Women's intercollegiate varsity sports:* basketball, cross country, equestrian, field hockey, golf, ice hockey, lacrosse, crew (lightweight), skiing (nordic), skiing (alpine), soccer, softball, squash, swimming, tennis, track and field (indoor), track and field (outdoor), volleyball.

SERVICES AND FACILITIES

Basic services: nonremedial tutoring, women's center, health service, health insurance. **Counseling services:** career, personal, academic, psychological, birth control, religious. **For learning-disabled students:** School does not offer a structured program with separate admission and additional fees. Total undergraduates in learning-disabled program or receiving services: 262. Services include: reading machines, tape recorders, untimed tests, note-taking services, readers, extended time for tests, tutors, priority registration, priority seating, texts on tape, other testing accommodations, other. **Library:** Number of titles: 1,009,885; number of current serial subscriptions: 8,212. **Information technology resources:** Students are not required to lease or own a computer. Number of campus computers available to all students: 608. School has a wireless network. Approximate number of users that can be accommodated: 2,000. Proportion of college-owned housing units wired for high-speed internet access: 100%. **Campus safety:** Security services offered: 24-hour foot-and-vehicle patrols, late-night transport/escort service, 24-hour emergency telephones, lighted pathways/sidewalks, student patrols, controlled dormitory access (key, security card, etc).

TRANSFER AND INTERNATIONAL STUDENTS

Transfer students: May apply for admission for the following academic terms: Fall, Spring. Applicants do not need a minimum number of credits to apply. For fall 2009: Transfer applications received: 265. Transfer applicants offered admission: 49. Transfer applicants enrolled: 24. **International students:** Number of foreign undergraduates: 126 (6% of student body). Number of countries represented: 42.

St. Thomas Aquinas College

- **Address:** 125 Route 340, Sparkill, NY 10976
- **Website:** http://www.stac.edu
- **Private**
- **Enrollment:** 1,340 full-time; 582 part-time

KEY STATS

✔ **U.S News College Ranking:** 112, Regional Universities (North)
✔ **SAT Score (25th/75th percentile):** 840-1050
✔ **Tuition:** 2010-2011: $22,410

Selectivity: Less selective	**Room/board:** $10,300
Acceptance rate: 84%	**Average debt:** N/A
Student/faculty ratio: 15/1	**Proportion who borrowed:** N/A

UNDERGRADUATE STUDENT BODY STATS

2009-2010 enrollment: 1,340 full-time; 582 part-time. Men: 45%; women: 55%. **Ethnic makeup:** African American: 4%; Asian American: 4%; Hispanic: 12%; White: 79%; International: 1%. **Religious preference:** Roman Catholic: 69%; Protestant: 2%; Jewish: 2%; Muslim: 1%; Hindu: 1%; Buddhist: 1%; No preference: 13%; Unknown: 3%; Orthodox: 2%; Other: 6%.

ADMISSIONS FACTS AND FIGURES

Phone: (845) 398-4100. **Email:** admissions@stac.edu. **Website:** http://www.stac.edu. **Application deadlines for fall 2011:** Regular decision: Rolling. Early decision: Send application by: December 15; Decision sent by: March 1. Early action: Not offered. Admission can be deferred. **Application fee:** $30. **To apply online, go to:** http://applyweb.com/aw?stac. **Admissions requirements/recommendations:** High school units required (recommended): English: 4; Mathematics: 3; Science: 3; Foreign language: 3; Social studies: 4; Total units: 20. Tests: The college uses SAT or ACT scores in admissions decisions. Either SAT or ACT required. For admission to the fall 2011 entering class, the school will accept: ACT with or without writing accepted. Campus visit: Recommended. Admissions interview: Recommended. Off-campus interview: May be arranged. **Factors that count in admissions decisions:** *Academic:* Secondary school record: Very Important. Class rank: Not Considered. Letters of recommendation: Important. Standardized test

scores: Important. Essay: Important. *Nonacademic:* Interview: Important. Extracurricular activities: Important. Talent/ability: Important. Character/personal qualities: Not Considered. Alumni/ae relationship: Considered. Geographical residence: Not Considered. State residency: Not Considered. Religious affiliation/commitment: Not Considered. Minority status: Not Considered. Volunteer work: Considered. Work experience: Considered. **Other schools with the greatest overlap in applicants:** Fordham University; Iona College; Marist College; Mount St. Mary College; SUNY–New Paltz. **Admissions statistics for the fall 2009 entering class:** Total applicants: 1,357. Total accepted: 1,140. Freshmen enrolled: 295; 19% were from out of state. Overall acceptance rate: 84%. Non-early acceptance rate: 84%. **Credentials of fall 2009 freshmen:** 5% ranked in the top 10 percent of their high school class; 12% were in the top 25 percent; 40% were in the top half. (Proportion submitting class standing: 35%.) **Average high school grade point average:** 2.6. **First-year students who submitted SAT scores:** 94%. Scores (25/75 percentile): Critical Reading: 420-510, Math: 420-540, Combined: 840-1050. **First-year students submitting ACT scores:** 21%. Scores (25/75 percentile): English: N/A, Math: N/A, Composite: 17-24.

ACADEMICS

Year founded: 1952. **Academic calendar:** Semester. **Degrees offered:** certificate, associate, bachelor's, master's, post-master's certificate. **Major fields of study:** biological and biomedical sciences; business, management, marketing, and related support services; communication, journalism, and related programs; computer and information sciences and support services; education; English language and literature/letters; foreign languages, literatures, and linguistics; history; liberal arts and sciences studies, and humanities; multi/interdisciplinary studies; parks, recreation, leisure, and fitness studies; philosophy and religious studies; psychology; security and protective services; social sciences; visual and performing arts. **Areas of required coursework:** arts/fine arts, humanities, computer literacy, mathematics, English (including composition), philosophy, foreign languages, sciences (biological or physical), history, social science, other. **Pre-professional programs:** pre-law, pre-dentistry, pre-medicine, pre-pharmacy, other. **Special academic programs:** accelerated program, cooperative (work-study plan) program, cross-registration, double major, dual enrollment, English as a Second Language (ESL), exchange student program (domestic), honors program, independent study, internships, liberal arts/career combination, study abroad, teacher certificate program, other. **Teacher certification offered in:** early childhood, special education, elementary, middle/junior high, secondary. **Cooperative education programs:** engineering, health professions, natural science, social/behavioral science. **Faculty and instruction (2009-2010):** Total instructional faculty: 66 full-time, 74 part-time (50% men; 50% women; 9% minorities). Student/faculty ratio: 15/1. Classes of fewer than 20 students: 48%; of 20 to 49 students: 52%. **Advanced Placement and International Baccalaureate credit:** AP tests may be used for: Placement only. Scores accepted: 3, 4, 5. **Freshmen returning for sophomore year:** 74%. **Graduation rates:** Four-year: 28%; five-year: 47%; six-year: 52%. **Graduate study:** 39% of students pursue further study within one year. Fields in which graduates pursue further study: Master of Business Administration (MBA), 12%; law, 3%; education, 44%; arts and sciences, 41%.

COSTS AND FINANCIAL AID

Financial aid office: (845) 398-4097. **Expenses (2010-2011):** Tuition and fees 2010-2011: $22,410; room/board: $10,300. Estimated books and supplies: $1,000; transportation: $1,500; personal expenses: $1,500. **Financial aid:** Priority filing date for institution's financial aid form: February 15. In 2009-2010, 87% of undergraduates applied for financial aid. Of those, 65% were determined to have financial need; 16% had their need fully met. Average financial aid package (proportion receiving): $11,924 (64%). Average amount of gift aid, such as scholarships or grants (proportion receiving): $9,369 (58%). Average amount of self-help aid, such as work study or loans (proportion receiving): $4,295 (48%). Average need-based loan (excluding PLUS or other private loans): $4,295. Among students who received need-based aid, the average percentage of need met: 60%. Among students who received aid based on merit, the average award (and the proportion receiving): $6,044 (13%). The average athletic scholarship (and the proportion receiving): $6,633 (2%).

CAMPUS LIFE AND EXTRACURRICULAR ACTIVITIES

Campus housing available (% using): women's dorms (57%), men's dorms (43%). Students who live in college-owned, operated, or affiliated housing: 42%. **Student employment:** During the 2009-2010 academic year, 12% of undergraduates worked on campus. Average per-year earnings: $1,200. **Clubs and organizations:** Number of student organizations: 27. Activities include: choral groups, dance, drama/theater, literary magazine, music ensembles, musical theater, opera, radio station, student government, student newspaper, television station, yearbook. Number of fraternities: 0; sororities: 0. Average proportion of students who stay on campus on weekends: 50%. **Sports program (2009-2010):** Member of NCAA II. *Men's intercollegiate varsity sports:* baseball, basketball, cross country, golf, soccer, tennis, track and field (indoor), track and field (outdoor). *Women's intercollegiate varsity sports:* basketball, cross country, lacrosse, soccer, softball, tennis, track and field (indoor), track and field (outdoor).

SERVICES AND FACILITIES

Basic services: nonremedial tutoring, placement service, health service, health insurance. **Remedial assistance:** reading, math, writing, study skills. **Counseling services:** career, personal, academic, psychological. **For learning-disabled students:** School does not offer a structured program with separate admission and additional fees. Total undergraduates in learning-disabled program or receiving services: 74. Services include: remedial math, remedial English, reading machines, tape recorders, other special classes, note-taking services, oral tests, learning center, readers, extended time for tests, tutors, priority registration, priority seating, texts on tape, other testing accommodations. **Library:** Number of titles: 93,478; number of current serial subscriptions: 445. **Information technology resources:** Students are not required to lease or own a computer. Number of campus computers available to all students: 200. School has a wireless network. Approximate number of users that can be accommodated: 1,500. Proportion of college-owned housing units wired for high-speed internet access: 100%. **Campus safety:** Security services offered: 24-hour foot-and-vehicle patrols, late-night transport/escort service, 24-hour emergency telephones, lighted pathways/sidewalks, controlled dormitory access (key, security card, etc).

TRANSFER AND INTERNATIONAL STUDENTS

Transfer students: May apply for admission for the following academic terms: Fall, Spring. Applicants need a minimum number of credits to apply. For fall 2009: Transfer applications received: 261. Transfer applicants offered admission: 212. Transfer applicants enrolled: 100. **International students:** Number of foreign undergraduates: 11 (1% of student body). Number of countries represented: 15. Minimum TOEFL score required: 530 (paper); 173 (computer).

SUNY College–Cortland

- **Address:** PO Box 2000, Cortland, NY 13045
- **Website:** http://www.cortland.edu
- **Public**
- **Enrollment:** 6,053 full-time; 205 part-time

KEY STATS

✔ **U.S News College Ranking:** 77, Regional Universities (North)
✔ **SAT Score (25th/75th percentile):** 990-1150
✔ **Tuition:** 2010-2011: $6,215 in state, $14,115 out of state

Selectivity: Selective	**Room/board:** $10,490
Acceptance rate: 39%	**Average debt:** N/A
Student/faculty ratio: 16/1	**Proportion who borrowed:** N/A

UNDERGRADUATE STUDENT BODY STATS

2009-2010 enrollment: 6,053 full-time; 205 part-time. Men: 43%; women: 57%. **Ethnic makeup:** African American: 3%; American-Indian: 1%; Asian American: 2%; Hispanic: 6%; White: 89%; International: 1%.

ADMISSIONS FACTS AND FIGURES

Phone: (607) 753-4711. **Email:** admissions@cortland.edu. **Website:** http://www.cortland.edu. **Application deadlines for fall 2011:** Regular decision: Rolling. Early decision: Send application by: November 15; Decision sent by: December 15. Early action: Not offered. Admission can be deferred. **Application fee:** $40. **To apply online, go to:** https://www.suny.edu/student/oas/welcome.do. **Admissions requirements/recommendations:** High school units required (recommended): English: 4 (4); Mathematics: 3 (4); Science: 3 (4); Foreign language: 3 (4); Social studies: 4 (4). Tests: The college uses SAT or ACT scores in admissions decisions. Either SAT or ACT required. For admission to the fall 2011 entering class, the school will accept: ACT with writing recommended. Campus visit: Recommended. Admissions interview: Recommended. Off-campus interview: Not available. **Factors that count in admissions decisions:** *Academic:* Secondary school record: Very Important. Class rank: Considered. Letters of recommendation: Important.

Standardized test scores: Very Important. Essay: Important. *Nonacademic:* Interview: Considered. Extracurricular activities: Important. Talent/ability: Important. Character/personal qualities: Not Considered. Alumni/ae relationship: Considered. Geographical residence: Considered. State residency: Considered. Religious affiliation/commitment: Not Considered. Minority status: Considered. Volunteer work: Considered. Work experience: Considered. **Other schools with the greatest overlap in applicants:** Binghamton University–SUNY; College at Brockport–SUNY; SUNY College–Oneonta; SUNY–Oswego; University at Albany–SUNY. **Admissions statistics for the fall 2009 entering class:** Total applicants: 11,968. Total accepted: 4,679. Freshmen enrolled: 1,167; 3% were from out of state. Overall acceptance rate: 39%. Non-early acceptance rate: 39%. **Credentials of fall 2009 freshmen:** 17% ranked in the top 10 percent of their high school class; 56% were in the top 25 percent; 89% were in the top half. (Proportion submitting class standing: 9%.) **First-year students who submitted SAT scores:** 89%. Scores (25/75 percentile): Critical Reading: 510-590, Math: 480-560, Combined: 990-1150. **First-year students submitting ACT scores:** 21%. Scores (25/75 percentile): English: N/A, Math: N/A, Composite: N/A.

ACADEMICS

Year founded: 1868. **Academic calendar:** Semester. **Degrees offered:** bachelor's, post-bachelor's certificate, master's, post-master's certificate. **Most popular majors:** 43% education, 16% parks, recreation, leisure, and fitness studies, 13% social sciences, 6% communication, journalism, and related programs, 4% health professions and related clinical sciences. **Major fields of study:** area, ethnic, cultural, and gender studies; biological and biomedical sciences; communication, journalism, and related programs; education; English language and literature/letters; foreign languages, literatures, and linguistics; health professions and related clinical sciences; history; mathematics and statistics; parks, recreation, leisure, and fitness studies; philosophy and religious studies; physical sciences; psychology; social sciences; visual and performing arts. **Areas of required coursework:** arts/fine arts, humanities, mathematics, English (including composition), foreign languages, sciences (biological or physical), history, social science, other. **Special academic programs:** cooperative (work-study plan) program, cross-registration, distance learning, double major, dual enrollment, exchange student program (domestic), honors program, independent study, internships, liberal arts/career combination, student-designed major, study abroad, teacher certificate program. **Cooperative education programs:** engineering, health professions, other. **Reserve Officers Training Corps (ROTC):** Army ROTC: Offered at cooperating institution (Cornell University); Air Force ROTC: Offered at cooperating institution (Cornell University). **Faculty and instruction (2009-2010):** Total instructional faculty: 336 full-time, 261 part-time (49% men; 51% women; 9% minorities). Full-time faculty with Ph.D. or other terminal degree: 63%. Student/faculty ratio: 16/1. Classes of fewer than 20 students: 44%; of 20 to 49 students: 51%; of 50 or more students: 5%. **Advanced Placement and International Baccalaureate credit:** AP tests may be used for: Credit only. Scores accepted: 3, 4, 5. International Baccalaureate exams may be used for: Credit only. **Freshmen returning for sophomore year:** 81%. **Graduation rates:** Four-year: 41%; five-year: 65%; six-year: 61%. **Graduate study:** 33% of students pursue further study within one year. Fields in which graduates pursue further study: Master of Business Administration (MBA), 2%; law, 1%; education, 72%; arts and sciences, 25%.

COSTS AND FINANCIAL AID

Financial aid office: (607) 753-4717. **Expenses (2010-2011):** Tuition and fees 2010-2011: $6,215 in state, $14,115 out of state; room/board: $10,490. Estimated books and supplies: $1,000; transportation: $800; personal expenses: $1,665. **Financial aid:** Priority filing date for institution's financial aid form: March 1; deadline: May 1. In 2009-2010, 84% of undergraduates applied for financial aid. Of those, 61% were determined to have financial need; 17% had their need fully met. Average financial aid package (proportion receiving): $11,858 (59%). Average amount of gift aid, such as scholarships or grants (proportion receiving): $4,673 (49%). Average amount of self-help aid, such as work study or loans (proportion receiving): $3,594 (53%). Average need-based loan (excluding PLUS or other private loans): $4,183. Among students who received need-based aid, the average percentage of need met: 71%. Among students who received aid based on merit, the average award (and the proportion receiving): $8,868 (18%). The average athletic scholarship (and the proportion receiving): $0 (0%).

CAMPUS LIFE AND EXTRACURRICULAR ACTIVITIES

Campus housing available: coed dorms, apartment for single students, special housing for disabled students, special housing for international students, cooperative housing, other housing options. Students who live in college-owned, operated, or affiliated housing: 50%. **Student employment:** During the 2009-2010 academic year, 5% of undergraduates worked on campus. **Clubs and organizations:** Number of student organizations: 80. Activities include: campus ministries, choral groups, dance, drama/theater, international student organization, literary magazine, model UN, music ensembles, musical theater, radio station, student government, student newspaper, student film society, symphony orchestra, television station, yearbook. Number of fraternities: 0; sororities: 0. **Sports program (2009-2010):** Member of NCAA III. **Men's intercollegiate varsity sports:** baseball, basketball, cross country, football, ice hockey, lacrosse, soccer, swimming, track and field (indoor), track and field (outdoor), wrestling. **Women's intercollegiate varsity sports:** basketball, cross country, field hockey, golf, gymnastics, ice hockey, lacrosse, soccer, softball, swimming, tennis, track and field (indoor), track and field (outdoor), volleyball.

SERVICES AND FACILITIES

Basic services: nonremedial tutoring, placement service, day care, health service, health insurance. **Counseling services:** minority student, career, military, personal, veteran student, academic, older student, psychological, birth control, religious. **For learning-disabled students:** School does not offer a structured program with separate admission and additional fees. Services include: reading machines, tape recorders, untimed tests, note-taking services, oral tests, learning center, readers, extended time for tests, priority registration. **Library:** Number of titles: 418,908; number of current serial subscriptions: 52,314. **Information technology resources:** Students are not required to lease or own a computer. Number of campus computers available to all students: 873. School has a wireless network. **Campus safety:** Security services offered: 24-hour foot-and-vehicle patrols, late-night transport/escort service, 24-hour emergency telephones, lighted pathways/sidewalks, controlled dormitory access (key, security card, etc).

TRANSFER AND INTERNATIONAL STUDENTS

Transfer students: May apply for admission for the following academic terms: Fall, Spring. Applicants do not need a minimum number of credits to apply. For fall 2009: Transfer applications received: 2,768. Transfer applicants offered admission: 1,169. Transfer applicants enrolled: 612. **International students:** Number of foreign undergraduates: 32 (1% of student body). Number of countries represented: 5. Minimum TOEFL score required: 550 (paper); 231 (computer).

SUNY Coll. of Agr. and Tech.–Cobleskill

- **Address:** Cobleskill, NY 12043
- **Website:** http://www.cobleskill.edu
- **Public**
- **Enrollment:** 2,556 full-time; 132 part-time

KEY STATS

✔ **U.S News College Ranking:** 43, Regional Colleges (North)
✔ **SAT Score (25th/75th percentile):** 880-1090
✔ **Tuition:** 2010-2011: $6,224 in state, $14,124 out of state

Selectivity: Less selective	**Room/board:** $9,939
Acceptance rate: 71%	**Average debt:** $19,627
Student/faculty ratio: 21/1	**Proportion who borrowed:** 66%

UNDERGRADUATE STUDENT BODY STATS

2009-2010 enrollment: 2,556 full-time; 132 part-time. Men: 52%; women: 48%. **Ethnic makeup:** African American: 8%; American-Indian: 1%; Asian American: 1%; Hispanic: 5%; White: 84%; International: 1%.

ADMISSIONS FACTS AND FIGURES

Phone: (518) 255-5525. **Email:** admissionsoffice@cobleskill.edu. **Website:** http://www.cobleskill.edu. **Application deadlines for fall 2011:** Regular decision: Rolling. Early decision: Not offered. Early action: Not offered. Admission can be deferred. **Application fee:** $40. **To apply online, go to:** http://www.suny.edu/student. **Admissions requirements/recommendations:** High school units required (recommended): English: 3 (4); Mathematics: 2 (3); Science: 2 (3); Foreign language: 0 (1); Social studies: 0 (1); History: 1 (1); Academic electives: 0 (1); Total units: 10 (16). Tests: The college uses SAT or ACT scores in admissions decisions. Neither SAT nor ACT required. For admission to the fall 2011 entering class, the school will accept: ACT with or without writing accepted. Campus visit: Recommended. Admissions interview: Neither required nor recommended. Off-campus interview:

May be arranged. **Factors that count in admissions decisions:** *Academic:* Secondary school record: Very Important. Class rank: Important. Letters of recommendation: Considered. Standardized test scores: Important. Essay: Not Considered. *Nonacademic:* Interview: Considered. Extracurricular activities: Important. Talent/ability: Important. Character/personal qualities: Important. Alumni/ae relationship: Considered. Geographical residence: Not Considered. State residency: Not Considered. Religious affiliation/commitment: Not Considered. Minority status: Not Considered. Volunteer work: Important. Work experience: Not Considered. **Other schools with the greatest overlap in applicants:** SUNY College of Technology–Alfred; SUNY College of Technology–Delhi; SUNY College–Cortland; SUNY College–Oneonta; SUNY–Plattsburgh. **Admissions statistics for the fall 2009 entering class:** Total applicants: 3,103. Total accepted: 2,212. Freshmen enrolled: 1,173; 9% were from out of state. Overall acceptance rate: 71%. **Credentials of fall 2009 freshmen:** 2% ranked in the top 10 percent of their high school class; 2% were in the top 25 percent; 29% were in the top half. (Proportion submitting class standing: 99%.) **Average high school grade point average:** 2.6. **First-year students who submitted SAT scores:** 85%. Scores (25/75 percentile): Critical Reading: 420-540, Math: 460-550, Combined: 880-1090. **First-year students submitting ACT scores:** 26%. Scores (25/75 percentile): English: N/A, Math: N/A, Composite: 20-23.

ACADEMICS

Year founded: 1911. **Academic calendar:** Semester. **Degrees offered:** certificate, associate, transfer-associate, terminal-associate, bachelor's. **Most popular majors:** 31% agriculture, agriculture operations, and related sciences, 16% business, management, marketing, and related support services, 12% family and consumer sciences/human sciences, 11% liberal arts and sciences studies, and humanities, 9% natural resources and conservation. **Major fields of study:** agriculture, agriculture operations, and related sciences; biological and biomedical sciences; business, management, marketing, and related support services; computer and information sciences and support services; family and consumer sciences/human sciences; natural resources and conservation. **Areas of required coursework:** humanities, computer literacy, mathematics, English (including composition), foreign languages, sciences (biological or physical), history, social science. **Pre-professional programs:** pre-veterinary science. **Special academic programs:** cooperative (work-study plan) program, cross-registration, distance learning, honors program, internships, study abroad, weekend college. **Cooperative education programs:** agriculture, business, computer science. **Faculty and instruction (2009-2010):** Total instructional faculty: 101 full-time, 73 part-time (57% men; 43% women; 6% minorities). Full-time faculty with Ph.D. or other terminal degree: 39%. Student/faculty ratio: 21/1. Classes of fewer than 20 students: 35%; of 20 to 49 students: 58%; of 50 or more students: 7%. **Freshmen returning for sophomore year:** 73%. **Graduation rates:** Four-year: 35%; five-year: 44%; six-year: 54%.

COSTS AND FINANCIAL AID

Financial aid office: (518) 255-5623. **Expenses (2010-2011):** Tuition and fees 2010-2011: $6,224 in state, $14,124 out of state; room/board: $9,939. Estimated books and supplies: $1,200. **Financial aid:** Priority filing date for institution's financial aid form: February 15. In 2009-2010, 91% of undergraduates applied for financial aid. Of those, 75% were determined to have financial need; 1% had their need fully met. Average financial aid package (proportion receiving): $7,134 (74%). Average amount of gift aid, such as scholarships or grants (proportion receiving): $4,848 (65%). Average amount of self-help aid, such as work study or loans (proportion receiving): $3,478 (61%). Average need-based loan (excluding PLUS or other private loans): $3,420. Among students who received need-based aid, the average percentage of need met: 81%. Among students who received aid based on merit, the average award (and the proportion receiving): $357 (15%). Average amount of debt of borrowers graduating in 2009: $19,627. Proportion who borrowed: 66%.

CAMPUS LIFE AND EXTRACURRICULAR ACTIVITIES

Campus housing available (% using): coed dorms (100%), special housing for disabled students. Students who live in college-owned, operated, or affiliated housing: 57%. **Student employment:** During the 2009-2010 academic year, 10% of undergraduates worked on campus. Average per-year earnings: $1,750. **Clubs and organizations:** Number of student organizations: 35. Activities include: campus ministries, choral groups, international student organization, student government. Number of fraternities: 0; sororities: 0. Average proportion of students who stay on campus on weekends: 60%. **Sports program (2009-2010):** Member of NCAA III.

SERVICES AND FACILITIES

Basic services: nonremedial tutoring, placement service, day care, health service, health insurance, other. **Remedial assistance:** reading, math, writing, study skills. **Counseling services:** minority student, career, personal, academic, older student, psychological, birth control. **For learning-disabled students:** School does not offer a structured program with separate admission and additional fees. Services include: remedial math, remedial English, reading machines, tape recorders, untimed tests, note-taking services, oral tests, learning center, extended time for tests, tutors, priority registration, priority seating, texts on tape, typist/scribe, other testing accommodations. **Library:** Number of titles: 67,737; number of current serial subscriptions: 34,514. **Information technology resources:** Students are not required to lease or own a computer. Number of campus computers available to all students: 300. School has a wireless network. Approximate number of users that can be accommodated: 1,000. Proportion of college-owned housing units wired for high-speed internet access: 100%. **Campus safety:** Security services offered: 24-hour foot-and-vehicle patrols, late-night transport/escort service, 24-hour emergency telephones, lighted pathways/sidewalks, student patrols, controlled dormitory access (key, security card, etc).

TRANSFER AND INTERNATIONAL STUDENTS

Transfer students: May apply for admission for the following academic terms: Fall, Spring. Applicants need a minimum number of credits to apply. For fall 2009: Transfer applications received: 450. Transfer applicants offered admission: 334. Transfer applicants enrolled: 237. **International students:** Number of foreign undergraduates: 20 (1% of student body). Number of countries represented: 10. Minimum TOEFL score required: 500 (paper); 61 (computer). Average TOEFL score: 500 (paper).

SUNY Coll. of Environ. Sci. and Forestry

- **Address:** 1 Forestry Drive, Syracuse, NY 13210
- **Website:** http://www.esf.edu
- **Public**
- **Enrollment:** 1,525 full-time; 45 part-time

KEY STATS

✔ **U.S News College Ranking:** 79, National Universities
✔ **SAT Score (25th/75th percentile):** 1070-1260
✔ **Tuition:** 2010-2011: $5,946 in state, $13,846 out of state
  Selectivity: More selective   **Room/board:** $12,930
  Acceptance rate: 43%   **Average debt:** $27,000
  Student/faculty ratio: 12/1   **Proportion who borrowed:** 80%

UNDERGRADUATE STUDENT BODY STATS

2009-2010 enrollment: 1,525 full-time; 45 part-time. Men: 60%; women: 40%. **Ethnic makeup:** African American: 1%; American-Indian: 1%; Asian American: 4%; Hispanic: 3%; White: 91%; International: 1%.

ADMISSIONS FACTS AND FIGURES

Phone: (315) 470-6600. **Email:** esfinfo@esf.edu. **Website:** http://www.esf. edu. **Application deadlines for fall 2011:** Regular decision: Rolling; decision sent by April 1. Early decision: Not offered. Early action: Send application by: December 15; Decision sent by: January 2. Admission can be deferred. **Application fee:** $40. **To apply online, go to:** http://www.esf.edu/admissions/undergrad/apply.htm. **Admissions requirements/recommendations:** High school units required (recommended): English: 4; Mathematics: 3 (4); Science: 3 (4); Foreign language: 0 (3); Social studies: 3; History: 1; Total units: 14 (19). Tests: The college uses SAT or ACT scores in admissions decisions. Either SAT or ACT required. For admission to the fall 2011 entering class, the school will accept: ACT with writing recommended. Campus visit: Recommended. Admissions interview: Recommended. Off-campus interview: May be arranged. **Factors that count in admissions decisions:** *Academic:* Secondary school record: Very Important. Class rank: Important. Letters of recommendation: Important. Standardized test scores: Very Important. Essay: Very Important. *Nonacademic:* Interview: Considered. Extracurricular activities: Important. Talent/ability: Important. Character/personal qualities: Not Considered. Alumni/ae relationship: Considered. Geographical residence: Considered. State residency: Considered. Religious affiliation/commitment: Not Considered. Minority status: Considered. Volunteer work: Important. Work experience: Important. **Other schools with the greatest overlap in applicants:** Binghamton University–SUNY; Cornell University; Rensselaer Polytechnic Institute; SUNY–Geneseo;

University at Buffalo–SUNY. **Admissions statistics for the fall 2009 entering class:** Total applicants: 1,677. Total accepted: 723. Freshmen enrolled: 283; 22% were from out of state. Accepted through early-decision or early-action plans: 54%. Overall acceptance rate: 43%. Non-early acceptance rate: 31%. Size of waiting list: 70 applicants; enrolled from waiting list: 20. **Credentials of fall 2009 freshmen:** 39% ranked in the top 10 percent of their high school class; 77% were in the top 25 percent; 96% were in the top half. (Proportion submitting class standing: 68%.) **Average high school grade point average:** 3.8. **First-year students who submitted SAT scores:** 96%. Scores (25/75 percentile): Critical Reading: 530-620, Math: 540-640, Combined: 1070-1260. **First-year students submitting ACT scores:** 39%. Scores (25/75 percentile): English: N/A, Math: N/A, Composite: 23-27.

ACADEMICS

Year founded: 1911. **Academic calendar:** Semester. **Degrees offered:** associate, bachelor's, post-bachelor's certificate, master's, doctorate. **Most popular majors:** 41% environmental biology, 29% natural resources management and policy, 16% engineering. **Major fields of study:** architecture and related services; biological and biomedical sciences; engineering; natural resources and conservation; physical sciences. **Areas of required coursework:** arts/fine arts, humanities, mathematics, English (including composition), sciences (biological or physical), history, social science. **Pre-professional programs:** pre-law, pre-dentistry, pre-medicine, pre-veterinary science. **Special academic programs (% participation):** accelerated program (8%), cooperative (work-study plan) program (8%), cross-registration (100%), distance learning (1%), double major (10%), dual enrollment (5%), English as a Second Language (ESL) (1%), honors program (12%), independent study (60%), internships (35%), study abroad (35%), teacher certificate program (5%). **Teacher certification offered in:** secondary. **Cooperative education programs:** engineering. **Reserve Officers Training Corps (ROTC):** Army ROTC: Offered at cooperating institution (Syracuse University); Air Force ROTC: Offered at cooperating institution (Syracuse University). **Faculty and instruction (2009-2010):** Total instructional faculty: 146 full-time, 27 part-time (73% men; 27% women; 10% minorities). Full-time faculty with Ph.D. or other terminal degree: 96%. Student/faculty ratio: 12/1. Classes of fewer than 20 students: 77%; of 20 to 49 students: 16%; of 50 or more students: 7%. **Advanced Placement and International Baccalaureate credit:** AP tests may be used for: Credit only. Scores accepted: 3, 4, 5. International Baccalaureate exams may be used for: Credit only. **Freshmen returning for sophomore year:** 86%. **Graduation rates:** Four-year: 48%; five-year: 63%; six-year: 65%. **Graduate study:** 22% of students pursue further study immediately upon graduation; 26% within one year; 35% within five years. Fields in which graduates pursue further study: law, 5%; medicine, 3%; dentistry, 2%; engineering, 20%; education, 25%; arts and sciences, 40%; veterinary medicine, 5%.

COSTS AND FINANCIAL AID

Financial aid office: (315) 470-6706. **Expenses (2010-2011):** Tuition and fees 2010-2011: $5,946 in state, $13,846 out of state; room/board: $12,930. Estimated books and supplies: $1,200; transportation: $600; personal expenses: $450. **Financial aid:** Priority filing date for institution's financial aid form: March 1. In 2009-2010, 83% of undergraduates applied for financial aid. Of those, 60% were determined to have financial need; 100% had their need fully met. Average financial aid package (proportion receiving): $13,000 (60%). Average amount of gift aid, such as scholarships or grants (proportion receiving): $5,000 (60%). Average amount of self-help aid, such as work study or loans (proportion receiving): $7,500 (60%). Average need-based loan (excluding PLUS or other private loans): $6,750. Among students who received need-based aid, the average percentage of need met: 100%. Among students who received aid based on merit, the average award (and the proportion receiving): $2,500 (6%). The average athletic scholarship (and the proportion receiving): $0 (0%). Average amount of debt of borrowers graduating in 2009: $27,000. Proportion who borrowed: 80%.

CAMPUS LIFE AND EXTRACURRICULAR ACTIVITIES

Campus housing available: coed dorms, sorority housing, fraternity housing, apartments for married students, apartment for single students, special housing for disabled students, special housing for international students, other housing options. Students who live in college-owned, operated, or affiliated housing: 33%. **Clubs and organizations:** Number of student organizations: 200. Activities include: campus ministries, choral groups, concert band, dance, drama/theater, jazz band, literary magazine, marching band, music ensembles, musical theater, pep band, radio station, student government, student newspaper, student film society, symphony orchestra, yearbook. Number of fraternities: 27; sororities: 20. Proportion of men in fraternities: 5%; of women in sororities: 5%. Average proportion of students who stay on campus on weekends: 50%. **Sports program (2009-2010): Men's**

intercollegiate varsity sports: cross country, golf, soccer. *Women's intercollegiate varsity sports:* cross country, golf, soccer.

SERVICES AND FACILITIES

Basic services: nonremedial tutoring, placement service, day care, health service, health insurance. **Remedial assistance:** writing, study skills. **Counseling services:** minority student, career, military, personal, veteran student, academic, older student, psychological, birth control, religious. **For learning-disabled students:** School does not offer a structured program with separate admission and additional fees. Total undergraduates in learning-disabled program or receiving services: 36. Services include: remedial math, remedial English, diagnostic testing service, note-taking services, oral tests, readers, extended time for tests, tutors, priority seating, other testing accommodations. **Library:** Number of titles: 139,580; number of current serial subscriptions: 2,691. **Information technology resources:** Students are not required to lease or own a computer. Number of campus computers available to all students: 130. School has a wireless network. Proportion of college-owned housing units wired for high-speed internet access: 100%. **Campus safety:** Security services offered: 24-hour foot-and-vehicle patrols, late-night transport/escort service, 24-hour emergency telephones, lighted pathways/sidewalks, controlled dormitory access (key, security card, etc).

TRANSFER AND INTERNATIONAL STUDENTS

Transfer students: May apply for admission for the following academic terms: Fall, Spring. Applicants do not need a minimum number of credits to apply. For fall 2009: Transfer applications received: 859. Transfer applicants offered admission: 359. Transfer applicants enrolled: 231. **International students:** Number of foreign undergraduates: 12 (1% of student body). Number of countries represented: 6. Minimum TOEFL score required: 550 (paper); 213 (computer). Average TOEFL score: 600 (paper).

SUNY College of Technology–Alfred

- **Address:** 10 Upper College Drive, Alfred, NY 14802
- **Website:** http://www.alfredstate.edu/alfred/Default.asp
- **Public**
- **Enrollment:** 3,184 full-time; 346 part-time

KEY STATS

✔ **U.S News College Ranking:** 27, Regional Colleges (North)
✔ **SAT Score (25th/75th percentile):** 880-1120
✔ **Tuition:** 2010-2011: $6,162 in state, $14,062 out of state
  Selectivity: Less selective   **Room/board:** $9,330
  Acceptance rate: 61%   **Average debt:** N/A
  Student/faculty ratio: 19/1   **Proportion who borrowed:** N/A

UNDERGRADUATE STUDENT BODY STATS

2009-2010 enrollment: 3,184 full-time; 346 part-time. Men: 62%; women: 38%. **Ethnic makeup:** African American: 8%; Asian American: 1%; Hispanic: 3%; White: 85%; International: 3%.

ADMISSIONS FACTS AND FIGURES

Phone: (800) 425-3733. **Email:** admissions@alfredstate.edu. **Website:** http://www.alfredstate.edu/alfred/Default.asp. **Application deadlines for fall 2011:** Regular decision: Rolling. Early decision: Not offered. Early action: Not offered. Admission can be deferred. **Application fee:** $40. **To apply online, go to:** http://www.suny.edu/Student/apply_online.cfm. **Admissions requirements/recommendations:** High school units required (recommended): English: (4); Mathematics: (4); Science: (4); Social studies: (4). Tests: The college uses SAT or ACT scores in admissions decisions. Neither SAT nor ACT required. For admission to the fall 2011 entering class, the school will accept: ACT with or without writing accepted. Campus visit: Recommended. Admissions interview: Recommended. Off-campus interview: Not available. **Factors that count in admissions decisions:** *Academic:* Secondary school record: Very Important. Class rank: Considered. Letters of recommendation: Considered. Standardized test scores: Important. Essay: Considered. *Nonacademic:* Interview: Considered. Extracurricular activities: Considered. Talent/ability: Considered. Character/personal qualities: Considered. Alumni/ae relationship: Not Considered. Geographical residence: Not Considered. State residency: Not Considered. Religious affiliation/commitment: Not Considered. Minority status: Not Considered. Volunteer work: Considered. Work experience: Considered. **Other schools with the greatest overlap in applicants:** Rochester Institute of Technology;

SUNY College of Agriculture and Technology–Cobleskill; SUNY College of Technology–Canton; SUNY College of Technology–Delhi; University at Buffalo–SUNY. **Admissions statistics for the fall 2009 entering class:** Total applicants: 5,699. Total accepted: 3,483. Freshmen enrolled: 1,319; Overall acceptance rate: 61%. **Size of waiting list:** 265 applicants; enrolled from waiting list: 136. **First-year students who submitted SAT scores:** 57%. Scores (25/75 percentile): Critical Reading: 420-540, Math: 460-580, Combined: 880-1120. **First-year students submitting ACT scores:** 18%. Scores (25/75 percentile): English: N/A, Math: N/A, Composite: 18-24.

ACADEMICS

Year founded: 1908. **Academic calendar:** Semester. **Degrees offered:** certificate, associate, transfer-associate, terminal-associate, bachelor's. **Most popular majors:** 62% engineering technologies/technicians, 20% computer and information sciences and support services, 18% business, management, marketing, and related support services. **Major fields of study:** architecture and related services; business, management, marketing, and related support services; computer and information sciences and support services; construction trades; engineering; engineering technologies/technicians. **Areas of required coursework:** arts/fine arts, humanities, computer literacy, mathematics, English (including composition), foreign languages, sciences (biological or physical), history, social science. **Special academic programs:** cross-registration, distance learning, English as a Second Language (ESL), honors program, independent study, internships, liberal arts/career combination, student-designed major, study abroad. **Reserve Officers Training Corps (ROTC):** Army ROTC: Offered at cooperating institution (St. Bonaventure University). **Faculty and instruction (2009-2010):** Total instructional faculty: 157 full-time, 46 part-time (67% men; 33% women; 4% minorities). Student/faculty ratio: 19/1. Classes of fewer than 20 students: %; of 20 to 49 students: %; of 50 or more students: %. **Advanced Placement and International Baccalaureate credit:** AP tests may be used for: Credit and/or placement. Scores accepted: 3, 4, 5. International Baccalaureate exams may be used for: Credit and/or placement. **Freshmen returning for sophomore year:** 67%. **Graduation rates:** Four-year: 34%; five-year: 45%; six-year: 40%.

COSTS AND FINANCIAL AID

Financial aid office: (607) 587-4251. **Expenses (2010-2011):** Tuition and fees 2010-2011: $6,162 in state, $14,062 out of state; room/board: $9,330. Estimated books and supplies: $1,200; transportation: $1,650; personal expenses: $800. **Financial aid:** Priority filing date for institution's financial aid form: March 1. In 2009-2010, 90% of undergraduates applied for financial aid. Of those, 80% were determined to have financial need; 3% had their need fully met. Average financial aid package (proportion receiving): $12,452 (79%). Average amount of gift aid, such as scholarships or grants (proportion receiving): $5,248 (69%). Average amount of self-help aid, such as work study or loans (proportion receiving): $6,242 (69%). Average need-based loan (excluding PLUS or other private loans): $7,987. Among students who received need-based aid, the average percentage of need met: 64%. Among students who received aid based on merit, the average award (and the proportion receiving): $4,982 (6%). The average athletic scholarship (and the proportion receiving): $1,080 (1%).

CAMPUS LIFE AND EXTRACURRICULAR ACTIVITIES

Campus housing available (% using): coed dorms (84%), apartment for single students (5%), special housing for disabled students (3%), special housing for international students (3%), other housing options (1%). Students who live in college-owned, operated, or affiliated housing: 67%. **Student employment:** During the 2009-2010 academic year, 8% of undergraduates worked on campus. Average per-year earnings: $1,300. **Clubs and organizations:** Number of student organizations: 74. Activities include: choral groups, concert band, dance, drama/theater, international student organization, jazz band, literary magazine, music ensembles, musical theater, radio station, student government, student newspaper, yearbook. Number of fraternities: 4; sororities: 5. Proportion of men in fraternities: 1%; of women in sororities: 1%. Average proportion of students who stay on campus on weekends: 75%. **Sports program (2009-2010):** *Men's intercollegiate varsity sports:* baseball, basketball, cross country, football, lacrosse, soccer, swimming, track and field (indoor), track and field (outdoor), wrestling. *Women's intercollegiate varsity sports:* basketball, cross country, soccer, softball, swimming, track and field (indoor), track and field (outdoor), volleyball.

SERVICES AND FACILITIES

Basic services: nonremedial tutoring, placement service, day care, health service, health insurance. **Remedial assistance:** reading, math, writing, study skills. **Counseling services:** career, personal, academic, psychological. **For learning-disabled students:** School does not offer a structured program with separate admission and additional fees. Total undergraduates in learning-disabled program or receiving services: 152. Services include: remedial math, remedial English, reading machines, remedial reading, tape recorders, note-taking services, oral tests, learning center, readers, extended time for tests, tutors, priority seating, texts on tape, typist/scribe, exams on tape or computer, other testing accommodations. **Library:** Number of titles: 64,738; number of current serial subscriptions: 64,038. **Information technology resources:** Students are not required to lease or own a computer. Number of campus computers available to all students: 1,200. School has a wireless network. Approximate number of users that can be accommodated: 4,096. Proportion of college-owned housing units wired for high-speed internet access: 100%. **Campus safety:** Security services offered: 24-hour foot-and-vehicle patrols, late-night transport/escort service, 24-hour emergency telephones, lighted pathways/sidewalks, controlled dormitory access (key, security card, etc).

TRANSFER AND INTERNATIONAL STUDENTS

Transfer students: May apply for admission for the following academic terms: Fall, Spring. Applicants do not need a minimum number of credits to apply. For fall 2009: Transfer applications received: 907. Transfer applicants offered admission: 320. Transfer applicants enrolled: 267. **International students:** Number of foreign undergraduates: 62 (3% of student body). Number of countries represented: 13. Minimum TOEFL score required: 500 (paper); 61 (computer). Average TOEFL score: 530 (paper).

SUNY College of Technology–Delhi

- **Address:** 2 Main Street, Delhi, NY 13753
- **Website:** http://www.delhi.edu/
- **Public**
- **Enrollment:** 2,609 full-time; 574 part-time

KEY STATS

✔ **U.S News College Ranking:** 39, Regional Colleges (North)
✔ **SAT Score (25th/75th percentile):** 830-1030
✔ **Tuition:** 2010-2011: $6,230 in state, $14,130 out of state

Selectivity: Less selective	**Room/board:** $9,500
Acceptance rate: 34%	**Average debt:** N/A
Student/faculty ratio: 16/1	**Proportion who borrowed:** 88%

UNDERGRADUATE STUDENT BODY STATS

2009-2010 enrollment: 2,609 full-time; 574 part-time. Men: 51%; women: 49%. **Ethnic makeup:** African American: 12%; Asian American: 2%; Hispanic: 8%; White: 77%; International: 1%.

ADMISSIONS FACTS AND FIGURES

Phone: (607) 746-4550. **Email:** enroll@delhi.edu. **Website:** http://www.delhi.edu/. **Application deadlines for fall 2011:** Regular decision: Rolling. Early decision: Not offered. Early action: Not offered. Admission can be deferred. **Application fee:** $40. **To apply online, go to:** http://www.suny.edu/student/apply_online.cfm. **Admissions requirements/recommendations:** High school units required (recommended): English: 4; Mathematics: 2 (4); Science: 2 (4); Foreign language: 0 (3); Social studies: 4; Total units: 20. Tests: The college uses SAT or ACT scores in admissions decisions. Neither SAT nor ACT required. For admission to the fall 2011 entering class, the school will accept: ACT with or without writing accepted. Campus visit: Recommended. Admissions interview: Recommended. Off-campus interview: Not available. **Factors that count in admissions decisions:** *Academic:* Secondary school record: Important. Class rank: Important. Letters of recommendation: Considered. Standardized test scores: Important. Essay: Considered. *Nonacademic:* Interview: Considered. Extracurricular activities: Considered. Talent/ability: Not Considered. Character/personal qualities: Not Considered. Alumni/ae relationship: Not Considered. Geographical residence: Not Considered. State residency: Not Considered. Religious affiliation/commitment: Not Considered. Minority status: Not Considered. Volunteer work: Considered. Work experience: Considered. **Other schools with the greatest overlap in applicants:** SUNY College of Agriculture and Technology–Cobleskill; SUNY College of Technology–Alfred; SUNY College of Technology–Canton; SUNY College–Cortland; SUNY College–Oneonta. **Admissions statistics for the fall 2009 entering class:** Total applicants: 4,970. Total accepted: 1,698. Freshmen enrolled: 1,027; 2% were from out of state. Overall acceptance rate: 34%. **Size of waiting list:** N/A

applicants; enrolled from waiting list: 8. **Credentials of fall 2009 freshmen:** 3% ranked in the top 10 percent of their high school class; 8% were in the top 25 percent; 41% were in the top half. (Proportion submitting class standing: 67%.) **Average high school grade point average:** 2.7. **First-year students who submitted SAT scores:** 43%. Scores (25/75 percentile): Critical Reading: 410-500, Math: 420-530, Combined: 830-1030. **First-year students submitting ACT scores:** 8%. Scores (25/75 percentile): English: N/A, Math: N/A, Composite: N/A.

ACADEMICS

Year founded: 1913. **Academic calendar:** Semester. **Degrees offered:** certificate, associate, bachelor's. **Most popular majors:** 48% tourism promotion operations, 31% business, management, marketing, and related support services, 13% architecture and related services, 5% computer and information sciences and support services, 2% system, networking, and Lan/Wan management/manager. **Major fields of study:** architecture and related services; business, management, marketing, and related support services; computer and information sciences and support services. **Areas of required coursework:** arts/fine arts, humanities, computer literacy, mathematics, English (including composition), sciences (biological or physical), history, social science. **Special academic programs (% participation):** distance learning (12%), dual enrollment (12%), English as a Second Language (ESL) (10%), honors program (5%), internships (100%), study abroad (1%). **Faculty and instruction (2009-2010):** Total instructional faculty: 122 full-time, 80 part-time (49% men; 51% women; 5% minorities). Full-time faculty with Ph.D. or other terminal degree: 27%. Student/faculty ratio: 16/1. Classes of fewer than 20 students: 57%; of 20 to 49 students: 39%; of 50 or more students: 4%. **Advanced Placement and International Baccalaureate credit:** AP tests may be used for: Credit and/or placement. Scores accepted: 4, 5. International Baccalaureate exams may be used for: Credit and/or placement. **Freshmen returning for sophomore year:** 64%. **Graduation rates:** Four-year: 23%; five-year: 43%; six-year: 43%. **Graduate study:** 65% of students pursue further study immediately upon graduation; 75% within one year; 90% within five years. Fields in which graduates pursue further study: Master of Business Administration (MBA), 60%; engineering, 1%; education, 3%; arts and sciences, 21%; veterinary medicine, 15%.

COSTS AND FINANCIAL AID

Financial aid office: (607) 746-4570. **Expenses (2010-2011):** Tuition and fees 2010-2011: $6,230 in state, $14,130 out of state; room/board: $9,500. Estimated books and supplies: $1,300; transportation: $900; personal expenses: $996. **Financial aid:** Priority filing date for institution's financial aid form: February 15. In 2009-2010, 92% of undergraduates applied for financial aid. Average financial aid package (proportion receiving): N/A (90%). Average amount of gift aid, such as scholarships or grants (proportion receiving): N/A (74%). Average amount of self-help aid, such as work study or loans (proportion receiving): N/A (71%). Proportion who borrowed: 88%.

CAMPUS LIFE AND EXTRACURRICULAR ACTIVITIES

Campus housing available (% using): coed dorms (90%), apartment for single students (5%), special housing for disabled students (1%). Students who live in college-owned, operated, or affiliated housing: 60%. **Student employment:** During the 2009-2010 academic year, 17% of undergraduates worked on campus. Average per-year earnings: $2,145. **Clubs and organizations:** Number of student organizations: 50. Activities include: campus ministries, choral groups, dance, drama/theater, international student organization, jazz band, literary magazine, music ensembles, musical theater, pep band, radio station, student government, student newspaper, television station. Number of fraternities: 5; sororities: 4. Proportion of men in fraternities: 8%; of women in sororities: 7%. Average proportion of students who stay on campus on weekends: 75%. **Sports program (2009-2010):** *Men's intercollegiate varsity sports:* basketball, cross country, golf, lacrosse, soccer, swimming, tennis, track and field (indoor), track and field (outdoor). *Women's intercollegiate varsity sports:* basketball, cross country, golf, soccer, softball, swimming, tennis, track and field (indoor), track and field (outdoor), volleyball.

SERVICES AND FACILITIES

Basic services: nonremedial tutoring, placement service, day care, health service, health insurance. **Remedial assistance:** reading, math, writing, study skills. **Counseling services:** minority student, career, personal, veteran student, academic, psychological, birth control. **For learning-disabled students:** School does not offer a structured program with separate admission and additional fees. Services include: remedial math, remedial English, reading machines, note-taking services, learning center, extended time for tests, tutors, priority seating, texts on tape, exams on tape or computer, other testing accommodations, other. **Library:** Number of titles: 54,109; number of current serial subscriptions: 267. **Information technology resources:** Students are not required to lease or own a computer. School has a wireless network. Approximate number of users that can be accommodated: 3,000. Proportion of college-owned housing units wired for high-speed internet access: 100%. **Campus safety:** Security services offered: 24-hour foot-and-vehicle patrols, late-night transport/escort service, 24-hour emergency telephones, lighted pathways/sidewalks, controlled dormitory access (key, security card, etc).

TRANSFER AND INTERNATIONAL STUDENTS

Transfer students: May apply for admission for the following academic terms: Fall, Spring, Summer. Applicants do not need a minimum number of credits to apply. For fall 2009: Transfer applications received: 1,042. Transfer applicants offered admission: 594. Transfer applicants enrolled: 280. **International students:** Number of foreign undergraduates: 30 (1% of student body). Number of countries represented: 7. Minimum TOEFL score required: 450 (paper); 133 (computer). Average TOEFL score: 500 (paper).

SUNY College–Old Westbury

- **Address:** PO Box 210, Old Westbury, NY 11568
- **Website:** http://www.oldwestbury.edu
- **Public**
- **Enrollment:** 3,205 full-time; 608 part-time

KEY STATS

✔ **U.S News College Ranking:** second tier, National Liberal Arts Colleges
✔ **SAT Score (25th/75th percentile):** 930-1100
✔ **Tuition:** 2010-2011: $5,897 in state, $13,797 out of state

Selectivity: Selective	Room/board: $9,390
Acceptance rate: 51%	Average debt: $17,104
Student/faculty ratio: 20/1	Proportion who borrowed: 46%

UNDERGRADUATE STUDENT BODY STATS

2009-2010 enrollment: 3,205 full-time; 608 part-time. Men: 41%; women: 59%. **Ethnic makeup:** African American: 33%; American-Indian: 1%; Asian American: 8%; Hispanic: 19%; White: 39%; International: 2%.

ADMISSIONS FACTS AND FIGURES

Phone: (516) 876-3073. **Email:** enroll@oldwestbury.edu. **Website:** http://www.oldwestbury.edu. **Application deadlines for fall 2011:** Regular decision: Rolling. Early decision: Send application by: N/A; Decision sent by: N/A. Early action: Not offered. Admission can be deferred. **Application fee:** $40. **To apply online, go to:** http://www.suny.edu/Student/apply_online.cfm. **Admissions requirements/recommendations:** High school units required (recommended): English: 4 (4); Mathematics: 3 (3); Science: 3 (3); Foreign language: 2 (3); Social studies: 2 (2); History: 2 (2); Academic electives: 3 (3); Total units: 19 (21). Tests: The college uses SAT or ACT scores in admissions decisions. Either SAT or ACT required. For admission to the fall 2011 entering class, the school will accept: ACT with writing required. Campus visit: Recommended. Admissions interview: Neither required nor recommended. Off-campus interview: Not available. **Factors that count in admissions decisions:** *Academic:* Secondary school record: Very Important. Class rank: Not Considered. Letters of recommendation: Important. Standardized test scores: Important. Essay: Very Important. *Nonacademic:* Interview: Considered. Extracurricular activities: Considered. Talent/ability: Considered. Character/personal qualities: Considered. Alumni/ae relationship: Not Considered. Geographical residence: Not Considered. State residency: Not Considered. Religious affiliation/commitment: Not Considered. Minority status: Not Considered. Volunteer work: Considered. Work experience: Considered. **Other schools with the greatest overlap in applicants:** Farmingdale State College–SUNY; Hofstra University; SUNY–New Paltz; SUNY–Stony Brook; St. John's University. **Admissions statistics for the fall 2009 entering class:** Total applicants: 3,610. Total accepted: 1,830. Freshmen enrolled: 421; 3% were from out of state. Overall acceptance rate: 51%. Non-early acceptance rate: 51%. **Credentials of fall 2009 freshmen:** 10% ranked in the top 10 percent of their high school class; 37% were in the top 25 percent; 73% were in the top half. (Proportion submitting class standing: 20%.) **Average high school grade point average:** 2.8. **First-year students who submitted SAT scores:** 97%. Scores (25/75 percentile): Critical Reading: 460-550, Math: 470-550, Combined: 930-1100.

ACADEMICS

Year founded: 1965. **Academic calendar:** Semester. **Degrees offered:** certificate, bachelor's, master's. **Most popular majors:** 15% accounting, 11% psychology, 9% elementary education and teaching, 8% business administration and management, 8% communication studies/speech communication and rhetoric. **Major fields of study:** area, ethnic, cultural, and gender studies; biological and biomedical sciences; business, management, marketing, and related support services; communication, journalism, and related programs; computer and information sciences and support services; education; English language and literature/letters; foreign languages, literatures, and linguistics; liberal arts and sciences studies, and humanities; mathematics and statistics; philosophy and religious studies; physical sciences; psychology; social sciences; visual and performing arts. **Areas of required coursework:** arts/fine arts, humanities, computer literacy, mathematics, English (including composition), philosophy, foreign languages, sciences (biological or physical), history, social science. **Pre-professional programs:** pre-law, pre-medicine. **Special academic programs:** cross-registration, distance learning, double major, English as a Second Language (ESL), exchange student program (domestic), honors program, independent study, internships, liberal arts/career combination, study abroad, teacher certificate program, other. **Teacher certification offered in:** early childhood, special education, elementary, middle/junior high, secondary, bilingual/bicultural. **Reserve Officers Training Corps (ROTC):** Army ROTC: Offered at cooperating institution (Hofstra University); Air Force ROTC: Offered at cooperating institution (Manhattan College). **Faculty and instruction (2009-2010):** Total instructional faculty: 131 full-time, 120 part-time (48% men; 52% women; 31% minorities). Full-time faculty with Ph.D. or other terminal degree: 84%. Student/faculty ratio: 20/1. Classes of fewer than 20 students: 23%; of 20 to 49 students: 76%; of 50 or more students: 1%. **Advanced Placement and International Baccalaureate credit:** AP tests may be used for: Credit only. Scores accepted: 3, 4, 5. International Baccalaureate exams may be used for: Credit only. **Freshmen returning for sophomore year:** 74%. **Graduation rates:** Four-year: 18%; five-year: 32%; six-year: 37%. **Graduate study:** 8% of students pursue further study immediately upon graduation; 78% within one year; 0% within five years. Fields in which graduates pursue further study: Master of Business Administration (MBA), 22%; law, 10%; medicine, 7%; dentistry, 1%; engineering, 1%; theology (or the seminary), 1%; education, 20%; arts and sciences, 16%; veterinary medicine, 1%.

COSTS AND FINANCIAL AID

Financial aid office: (516) 876-3222. **Expenses (2010-2011):** Tuition and fees 2010-2011: $5,897 in state, $13,797 out of state; room/board: $9,390. Estimated books and supplies: $1,000; transportation: $750; personal expenses: $1,210. **Financial aid:** Priority filing date for institution's financial aid form: April 12; deadline: May 10. In 2009-2010, 78% of undergraduates applied for financial aid. Of those, 66% were determined to have financial need; Average financial aid package (proportion receiving): $7,115 (78%). Average amount of gift aid, such as scholarships or grants (proportion receiving): $5,785 (61%). Average amount of self-help aid, such as work study or loans (proportion receiving): $2,642 (42%). Average need-based loan (excluding PLUS or other private loans): $2,561. Among students who received need-based aid, the average percentage of need met: 44%. Among students who received aid based on merit, the average award (and the proportion receiving): $0 (0%). The average athletic scholarship (and the proportion receiving): $0 (0%). Average amount of debt of borrowers graduating in 2009: $17,104. Proportion who borrowed: 46%.

CAMPUS LIFE AND EXTRACURRICULAR ACTIVITIES

Campus housing available (% using): coed dorms (100%). Students who live in college-owned, operated, or affiliated housing: 26%. **Student employment:** During the 2009-2010 academic year, 14% of undergraduates worked on campus. Average per-year earnings: $900. **Clubs and organizations:** Number of student organizations: 60. Activities include: campus ministries, choral groups, dance, drama/theater, international student organization, radio station, student government, student newspaper, student film society, yearbook. Number of fraternities: 7; sororities: 6. Proportion of men in fraternities: 2%; of women in sororities: 2%. Average proportion of students who stay on campus on weekends: 38%. **Sports program (2009-2010):** Member of NCAA III. *Men's intercollegiate varsity sports:* baseball, basketball, cross country, golf, soccer, swimming, track and field (indoor), volleyball. *Women's intercollegiate varsity sports:* basketball, cross country, soccer, softball, swimming, volleyball.

SERVICES AND FACILITIES

Basic services: nonremedial tutoring, women's center, placement service, day care, health service, health insurance. **Remedial assistance:** reading, math, writing, study skills. **Counseling services:** minority student, career, personal, veteran student, academic, older student, psychological, birth control. **For learning-disabled students:** School does not offer a structured program with separate admission and additional fees. Services include: remedial math, remedial English, reading machines, tape recorders, note-taking services, oral tests, readers, extended time for tests, tutors, texts on tape, other testing accommodations, other. **Library:** Number of titles: 208,623; number of current serial subscriptions: 696. **Information technology resources:** Students are not required to lease or own a computer. Number of campus computers available to all students: 450. School has a wireless network. Approximate number of users that can be accommodated: 1,000. Proportion of college-owned housing units wired for high-speed internet access: 100%. **Campus safety:** Security services offered: 24-hour foot-and-vehicle patrols, late-night transport/escort service, 24-hour emergency telephones, lighted pathways/sidewalks, student patrols, controlled dormitory access (key, security card, etc).

TRANSFER AND INTERNATIONAL STUDENTS

Transfer students: May apply for admission for the following academic terms: Fall, Spring. Applicants need a minimum number of credits to apply. For fall 2009: Transfer applications received: 1,531. Transfer applicants offered admission: 1,361. Transfer applicants enrolled: 769. **International students:** Number of foreign undergraduates: 59 (2% of student body). Number of countries represented: 24. Minimum TOEFL score required: 500 (paper); 183 (computer). Average TOEFL score: 500 (paper).

SUNY College—Oneonta

- **Address:** Ravine Parkway, Oneonta, NY 13820
- **Website:** http://www.oneonta.edu
- **Public**
- **Enrollment:** 5,580 full-time; 131 part-time

KEY STATS

✔ **U.S News College Ranking:** 45, Regional Universities (North)
✔ **SAT Score (25th/75th percentile):** 1060-1210
✔ **Tuition:** 2010-2011: $6,350 in state, $14,150 out of state

Selectivity: Selective	**Room/board:** $9,150
Acceptance rate: 39%	**Average debt:** $16,490
Student/faculty ratio: 17/1	**Proportion who borrowed:** 75%

UNDERGRADUATE STUDENT BODY STATS

2009-2010 enrollment: 5,580 full-time; 131 part-time. Men: 43%; women: 57%. **Ethnic makeup:** African American: 3%; Asian American: 2%; Hispanic: 5%; White: 88%; International: 2%.

ADMISSIONS FACTS AND FIGURES

Phone: (607) 436-2524. **Email:** admissions@oneonta.edu. **Website:** http://www.oneonta.edu. **Application deadlines for fall 2011:** Regular decision: Rolling. Early decision: Not offered. Early action: Send application by: November 15; Decision sent by: December 15. Admission can be deferred. **Application fee:** $40. **To apply online, go to:** http://www.suny.edu/Student/Apply/Apply.cfm. **Admissions requirements/recommendations:** High school units required (recommended): English: 4 (4); Mathematics: 2 (3); Science: 2 (3); Foreign language: 2 (3); Social studies: 3 (3); History: 0 (0); Academic electives: 0 (0); Total units: 16 (16). Tests: The college uses SAT or ACT scores in admissions decisions. Either SAT or ACT required. For admission to the fall 2011 entering class, the school will accept: ACT with or without writing accepted. Campus visit: Recommended. Admissions interview: Recommended. Off-campus interview: May be arranged. **Factors that count in admissions decisions:** *Academic:* Secondary school record: Very Important. Class rank: Considered. Letters of recommendation: Considered. Standardized test scores: Important. Essay: Important. *Nonacademic:* Interview: Important. Extracurricular activities: Important. Talent/ability: Important. Character/personal qualities: Important. Alumni/ae relationship: Considered. Geographical residence: Not Considered. State residency: Not Considered. Religious affiliation/commitment: Not Considered. Minority status: Considered. Volunteer work: Important. Work experience: Considered. **Other schools with the greatest overlap in applicants:** Binghamton University–SUNY; SUNY–Fredonia; SUNY–Geneseo; SUNY–New Paltz; University at Albany–SUNY. **Admissions statistics for the fall 2009 entering class:** Total applicants: 12,688. Total accepted: 4,972. Freshmen enrolled: 1,109; 2% were from out of state. Accepted through

early-decision or early-action plans: 39%. Overall acceptance rate: 39%. Non-early acceptance rate: 36%. **Size of waiting list:** 379 applicants; enrolled from waiting list: 2. **Credentials of fall 2009 freshmen:** 24% ranked in the top 10 percent of their high school class; 66% were in the top 25 percent; 98% were in the top half. (Proportion submitting class standing: 17%.) **Average high school grade point average:** 3.5. **First-year students who submitted SAT scores:** 87%. Scores (25/75 percentile): Critical Reading: 520-590, Math: 540-620, Combined: 1060-1210. **First-year students submitting ACT scores:** 27%. Scores (25/75 percentile): English: N/A, Math: N/A, Composite: 23-26.

ACADEMICS

Year founded: 1889. **Academic calendar:** Semester. **Degrees offered:** bachelor's, post-bachelor's certificate, master's, post-master's certificate. **Most popular majors:** 18% education, 18% visual and performing arts, 12% communication, journalism, and related programs, 9% family and consumer sciences/human sciences, 8% business, management, marketing, and related support services. **Major fields of study:** area, ethnic, cultural, and gender studies; biological and biomedical sciences; business, management, marketing, and related support services; communication, journalism, and related programs; computer and information sciences and support services; education; English language and literature/letters; family and consumer sciences/human sciences; foreign languages, literatures, and linguistics; health professions and related clinical sciences; history; legal professions and studies; mathematics and statistics; multi/interdisciplinary studies; natural resources and conservation; philosophy and religious studies; physical sciences; psychology; security and protective services; social sciences; visual and performing arts. **Areas of required coursework:** arts/fine arts, humanities, computer literacy, mathematics, English (including composition), foreign languages, sciences (biological or physical), history, social science. **Pre-professional programs:** pre-law, pre-dentistry, pre-medicine, pre-veterinary science. **Special academic programs:** cross-registration, distance learning, double major, English as a Second Language (ESL), honors program, independent study, internships, study abroad, teacher certificate program, other. **Teacher certification offered in:** early childhood, elementary, middle/junior high, secondary. **Faculty and instruction (2009-2010):** Total instructional faculty: 267 full-time, 232 part-time (52% men; 48% women; 15% minorities). Full-time faculty with Ph.D. or other terminal degree: 84%. Student/faculty ratio: 17/1. Classes of fewer than 20 students: %; of 20 to 49 students: %; of 50 or more students: %. **Advanced Placement and International Baccalaureate credit:** AP tests may be used for: Credit and/or placement. Scores accepted: 3, 4, 5. International Baccalaureate exams may be used for: Credit and/or placement. **Freshmen returning for sophomore year:** 82%. **Graduation rates:** Four-year: 50%; five-year: 63%; six-year: 59%. **Graduate study:** 49% of students pursue further study within one year.

COSTS AND FINANCIAL AID

Financial aid office: (607) 436-2532. **Expenses (2010-2011):** Tuition and fees 2010-2011: $6,350 in state, $14,150 out of state; room/board: $9,150. Estimated books and supplies: $1,200; transportation: $935; personal expenses: $1,184. **Financial aid:** Priority filing date for institution's financial aid form: March 15. In 2009-2010, 80% of undergraduates applied for financial aid. Of those, 57% were determined to have financial need; 16% had their need fully met. Average financial aid package (proportion receiving): $11,712 (56%). Average amount of gift aid, such as scholarships or grants (proportion receiving): $5,001 (46%). Average amount of self-help aid, such as work study or loans (proportion receiving): $4,576 (46%). Average need-based loan (excluding PLUS or other private loans): $4,486. Among students who received need-based aid, the average percentage of need met: 63%. Among students who received aid based on merit, the average award (and the proportion receiving): $2,000 (19%). The average athletic scholarship (and the proportion receiving): $0 (0%). Average amount of debt of borrowers graduating in 2009: $16,490. Proportion who borrowed: 75%.

CAMPUS LIFE AND EXTRACURRICULAR ACTIVITIES

Campus housing available (% using): coed dorms (100%). Students who live in college-owned, operated, or affiliated housing: 60%. **Student employment:** During the 2009-2010 academic year, 15% of undergraduates worked on campus. Average per-year earnings: $1,600. **Clubs and organizations:** Number of student organizations: 80. Activities include: campus ministries, choral groups, concert band, dance, drama/theater, international student organization, jazz band, literary magazine, model UN, music ensembles, musical theater, opera, pep band, radio station, student government, student newspaper, student film society, symphony orchestra, television station, yearbook. Number of fraternities: 3; sororities: 7. Proportion of men in fraternities: 2%; of women in sororities: 5%. Average proportion of students who stay on campus on weekends: 60%. **Sports program (2009-2010):** Member of NCAA III. *Men's intercollegiate varsity sports:* baseball, basketball, cross country, lacrosse, soccer, swimming, tennis, track and field (indoor), track and field (outdoor), wrestling. *Women's intercollegiate varsity sports:* basketball, cross country, field hockey, lacrosse, soccer, softball, swimming, tennis, track and field (indoor), track and field (outdoor), volleyball.

SERVICES AND FACILITIES

Basic services: nonremedial tutoring, women's center, placement service, day care, health service, health insurance. **Remedial assistance:** reading, math, writing, study skills. **Counseling services:** minority student, career, personal, academic, older student, psychological, birth control. **For learning-disabled students:** School does not offer a structured program with separate admission and additional fees. Total undergraduates in learning-disabled program or receiving services: 201. Services include: remedial math, remedial English, reading machines, remedial reading, tape recorders, videotaped classes, untimed tests, note-taking services, oral tests, learning center, readers, extended time for tests, tutors, texts on tape. **Library:** Number of titles: 525,850; number of current serial subscriptions: 38,009. **Information technology resources:** Students are not required to lease or own a computer. Number of campus computers available to all students: 760. School has a wireless network. Approximate number of users that can be accommodated: 2,000. Proportion of college-owned housing units wired for high-speed internet access: 100%. **Campus safety:** Security services offered: 24-hour foot-and-vehicle patrols, late-night transport/escort service, 24-hour emergency telephones, lighted pathways/sidewalks, controlled dormitory access (key, security card, etc).

TRANSFER AND INTERNATIONAL STUDENTS

Transfer students: May apply for admission for the following academic terms: Fall, Spring. Applicants do not need a minimum number of credits to apply. For fall 2009: Transfer applications received: 2,324. Transfer applicants offered admission: 1,027. Transfer applicants enrolled: 555. **International students:** Number of foreign undergraduates: 96 (2% of student body). Number of countries represented: 20. Minimum TOEFL score required: 500 (paper); 173 (computer). Average TOEFL score: 525 (paper).

SUNY College–Potsdam

■ **Address:** 44 Pierrepont Avenue, Potsdam, NY 13676
■ **Website:** http://www.potsdam.edu
■ **Public**
■ **Enrollment:** 3,631 full-time; 103 part-time

KEY STATS

✔ **U.S News College Ranking:** 91, Regional Universities (North)
✔ **SAT Score (25th/75th percentile):** 940-1140
✔ **Tuition:** 2010-2011: $6,290 in state, $14,190 out of state

Selectivity: Selective	**Room/board:** $9,630
Acceptance rate: 66%	**Average debt:** $19,220
Student/faculty ratio: 14/1	**Proportion who borrowed:** 80%

UNDERGRADUATE STUDENT BODY STATS

2009-2010 enrollment: 3,631 full-time; 103 part-time. Men: 43%; women: 57%. **Ethnic makeup:** African American: 3%; American-Indian: 1%; Asian American: 1%; Hispanic: 3%; White: 88%; International: 3%.

ADMISSIONS FACTS AND FIGURES

Phone: (315) 267-2180. **Email:** admissions@potsdam.edu. **Website:** http://www.potsdam.edu. **Application deadlines for fall 2011:** Regular decision: Rolling. Early decision: Not offered. Early action: Not offered. Admission can be deferred. **Application fee:** $40. **To apply online, go to:** http://www.suny.edu/student. **Admissions requirements/recommendations:** High school units required (recommended): English: 4 (4); Mathematics: 2 (4); Science: 2 (4); Foreign language: 0 (4); Social studies: 4 (4); Total units: 13 (21). Tests: The college uses SAT or ACT scores in admissions decisions. Neither SAT nor ACT required. For admission to the fall 2011 entering class, the school will accept: ACT with or without writing accepted. Campus visit: Recommended. Admissions interview: Recommended. Off-campus interview: Not available. **Factors that count in admissions decisions:** *Academic:* Secondary school record: Very Important. Class rank: Important. Letters of recommendation: Important. Standardized test scores: Considered. Essay:

Important. *Nonacademic:* Interview: Important. Extracurricular activities: Important. Talent/ability: Important. Character/personal qualities: Important. Alumni/ae relationship: Considered. Geographical residence: Not Considered. State residency: Not Considered. Religious affiliation/commitment: Not Considered. Minority status: Not Considered. Volunteer work: Considered. Work experience: Considered. **Other schools with the greatest overlap in applicants:** Ithaca College; SUNY–Fredonia; SUNY–Oswego; SUNY–Plattsburgh; St. Lawrence University. **Admissions statistics for the fall 2009 entering class:** Total applicants: 4,525. Total accepted: 2,970. Freshmen enrolled: 835; Overall acceptance rate: 66%. **Size of waiting list:** 54 applicants; enrolled from waiting list: 18. **Credentials of fall 2009 freshmen:** 7% ranked in the top 10 percent of their high school class; 31% were in the top 25 percent; 70% were in the top half. (Proportion submitting class standing: 27%.) **Average high school grade point average:** 0.9. **First-year students who submitted SAT scores:** 95%. Scores (25/75 percentile): Critical Reading: 470-570, Math: 470-570, Combined: 940-1140. **First-year students submitting ACT scores:** 32%. Scores (25/75 percentile): English: N/A, Math: N/A, Composite: 20-24.

ACADEMICS

Year founded: 1816. **Academic calendar:** Semester. **Degrees offered:** bachelor's, master's. **Most popular majors:** 11% education, 9% music teacher education, 6% psychology, 5% English language and literature, 5% business administration and management. **Major fields of study:** area, ethnic, cultural, and gender studies; biological and biomedical sciences; business, management, marketing, and related support services; computer and information sciences and support services; education; English language and literature/letters; foreign languages, literatures, and linguistics; health professions and related clinical sciences; history; mathematics and statistics; multi/interdisciplinary studies; natural resources and conservation; philosophy and religious studies; physical sciences; psychology; security and protective services; social sciences; visual and performing arts. **Areas of required coursework:** arts/fine arts, humanities, mathematics, English (including composition), philosophy, foreign languages, sciences (biological or physical), history, social science, other. **Pre-professional programs:** pre-law, pre-dentistry, pre-medicine, pre-veterinary science, pre-optometry, pre-pharmacy, other. **Special academic programs:** cross-registration, distance learning, double major, dual enrollment, exchange student program (domestic), honors program, independent study, internships, liberal arts/career combination, student-designed major, study abroad, teacher certificate program, other. **Teacher certification offered in:** early childhood, special education, elementary, middle/junior high, secondary. **Reserve Officers Training Corps (ROTC):** Army ROTC: Offered at cooperating institution (Clarkson University); Air Force ROTC: Offered at cooperating institution (Clarkson University). **Faculty and instruction (2009-2010):** Total instructional faculty: 262 full-time, 100 part-time (52% men; 48% women; 7% minorities). Full-time faculty with Ph.D. or other terminal degree: 78%. Student/faculty ratio: 14/1. Classes of fewer than 20 students: 64%; of 20 to 49 students: 33%; of 50 or more students: 3%. **Advanced Placement and International Baccalaureate credit:** AP tests may be used for: Credit and/or placement. Scores accepted: 3, 4, 5. International Baccalaureate exams may be used for: Credit and/or placement. **Freshmen returning for sophomore year:** 74%. **Graduation rates:** Four-year: 37%; five-year: 55%; six-year: 52%. **Graduate study:** 42% of students pursue further study within one year. Fields in which graduates pursue further study: Master of Business Administration (MBA), 6%; law, 1%; medicine, 3%; dentistry, 1%; education, 47%; arts and sciences, 41%; veterinary medicine, 1%.

COSTS AND FINANCIAL AID

Financial aid office: (315) 267-2162. **Expenses (2010-2011):** Tuition and fees 2010-2011: $6,290 in state, $14,190 out of state; room/board: $9,630. Estimated books and supplies: $1,200; transportation: $800; personal expenses: $1,100. **Financial aid:** Priority filing date for institution's financial aid form: March 1; deadline: March 1. In 2009-2010, 85% of undergraduates applied for financial aid. Of those, 66% were determined to have financial need; 70% had their need fully met. Average financial aid package (proportion receiving): $14,073 (65%). Average amount of gift aid, such as scholarships or grants (proportion receiving): $5,956 (60%). Average amount of self-help aid, such as work study or loans (proportion receiving): $4,454 (56%). Average need-based loan (excluding PLUS or other private loans): $4,360. Among students who received need-based aid, the average percentage of need met: 71%. Among students who received aid based on merit, the average award (and the proportion receiving): $11,677 (6%). The average athletic scholarship (and the proportion receiving): $0 (0%). Average amount of debt of borrowers graduating in 2009: $19,220. Proportion who borrowed: 80%.

CAMPUS LIFE AND EXTRACURRICULAR ACTIVITIES

Campus housing available: coed dorms, apartment for single students, special housing for disabled students, special housing for international students, other housing options. Students who live in college-owned, operated, or affiliated housing: 40%. **Student employment:** During the 2009-2010 academic year, 13% of undergraduates worked on campus. Average per-year earnings: $900. **Clubs and organizations:** Number of student organizations: 100. Activities include: campus ministries, choral groups, concert band, dance, drama/theater, international student organization, jazz band, literary magazine, music ensembles, musical theater, opera, radio station, student government, student newspaper, symphony orchestra, yearbook. Number of fraternities: 6; sororities: 8. Proportion of men in fraternities: 4%; of women in sororities: 8%. Average proportion of students who stay on campus on weekends: 70%. **Sports program (2009-2010):** Member of NCAA III. *Men's intercollegiate varsity sports:* basketball, cross country, golf, ice hockey, lacrosse, soccer, swimming. *Women's intercollegiate varsity sports:* basketball, cross country, equestrian, ice hockey, lacrosse, soccer, softball, swimming, tennis, volleyball.

SERVICES AND FACILITIES

Basic services: nonremedial tutoring, women's center, placement service, day care, health service, health insurance. **Counseling services:** minority student, career, military, personal, veteran student, academic, older student, psychological, birth control, religious. **For learning-disabled students:** School does not offer a structured program with separate admission and additional fees. Services include: reading machines, tape recorders, other special classes, note-taking services, oral tests, learning center, readers, extended time for tests, tutors, other. **Library:** Number of titles: 458,202; number of current serial subscriptions: 572. **Information technology resources:** Students are not required to lease or own a computer. Number of campus computers available to all students: 541. School has a wireless network. Approximate number of users that can be accommodated: 5,000. Proportion of college-owned housing units wired for high-speed internet access: 100%. **Campus safety:** Security services offered: 24-hour foot-and-vehicle patrols, late-night transport/escort service, 24-hour emergency telephones, lighted pathways/sidewalks, student patrols, controlled dormitory access (key, security card, etc).

TRANSFER AND INTERNATIONAL STUDENTS

Transfer students: May apply for admission for the following academic terms: Fall, Winter, Spring, Summer. Applicants need a minimum number of credits to apply. For fall 2009: Transfer applications received: 1,016. Transfer applicants offered admission: 668. **International students:** Number of foreign undergraduates: 120 (3% of student body). Number of countries represented: 31. Minimum TOEFL score required: 550 (paper); 213 (computer). Average TOEFL score: 573 (paper).

SUNY Empire State College

- ■ **Address:** 2 Union Avenue, Saratoga Springs, NY 12866
- ■ **Website:** http://www.esc.edu
- ■ **Public**
- ■ **Enrollment:** 4,876 full-time; 8,523 part-time

....

KEY STATS

- ✔ **U.S News College Ranking:** Unranked, Regional Universities (North)
- ✔ **SAT or ACT Score (25th/75th percentile):** N/A
- ✔ **Tuition:** 2009-2010: $5,195 in state, $13,095 out of state

Selectivity: N/A	Room/board: N/A
Acceptance rate: 78%	Average debt: N/A
Student/faculty ratio: 13/1	Proportion who borrowed: N/A

UNDERGRADUATE STUDENT BODY STATS

2009-2010 enrollment: 4,876 full-time; 8,523 part-time. Men: 40%; women: 60%. **Ethnic makeup:** African American: 14%; American-Indian: 1%; Asian American: 2%; Hispanic: 8%; White: 71%; International: 5%.

ADMISSIONS FACTS AND FIGURES

Phone: (518) 587-2100. **Email:** admissions@esc.edu. **Website:** http://www.esc.edu. **Application deadlines for fall 2011:** Regular decision: Rolling. Early decision: Not offered. Early action: Not offered. Admission can be deferred. **To apply online, go to:** http://www.esc.edu/apply. **Admissions requirements/recommendations:** Tests: The college does not use SAT or ACT

scores in admissions decisions. Neither SAT nor ACT required. Campus visit: Neither required nor recommended. Admissions interview: Neither required nor recommended. Off-campus interview: Not available. **Factors that count in admissions decisions:** *Academic:* Secondary school record: Not Considered. Class rank: Not Considered. Letters of recommendation: Not Considered. Standardized test scores: Not Considered. Essay: Very Important. *Nonacademic:* Interview: Not Considered. Extracurricular activities: Not Considered. Talent/ability: Not Considered. Character/personal qualities: Not Considered. Alumni/ae relationship: Not Considered. Geographical residence: Not Considered. State residency: Not Considered. Religious affiliation/commitment: Not Considered. Minority status: Not Considered. Volunteer work: Not Considered. Work experience: Not Considered. **Other schools with the greatest overlap in applicants:** Charter Oak State College; Excelsior College; Thomas Edison State College; Union Institute and University. **Admissions statistics for the fall 2009 entering class:** Total applicants: 1,023. Total accepted: 800. Freshmen enrolled: 555; 2% were from out of state. Overall acceptance rate: 78%.

ACADEMICS

Year founded: 1971. **Academic calendar:** Other. **Degrees offered:** associate, bachelor's, master's. **Most popular majors:** 41% business, management, marketing, and related support services, 22% public administration and social service professions, 7% physical sciences, 7% psychology, 6% English language and literature/letters. **Major fields of study:** business, management, marketing, and related support services; education; English language and literature/letters; history; liberal arts and sciences studies, and humanities; multi/interdisciplinary studies; physical sciences; psychology; public administration and social service professions; social sciences; visual and performing arts. **Areas of required coursework:** arts/fine arts, humanities, computer literacy, mathematics, English (including composition), philosophy, foreign languages, sciences (biological or physical), history, social science, other. **Special academic programs:** cross-registration, distance learning, double major, external degree program, independent study, student-designed major, other. **Faculty and instruction (2009-2010):** Total instructional faculty: 181 full-time, 1,264 part-time (45% men; 55% women; 12% minorities). Full-time faculty with Ph.D. or other terminal degree: 97%. Student/faculty ratio: 13/1. **Graduation rates:** Six-year: 14%.

COSTS AND FINANCIAL AID

Financial aid office: (518) 587-2100. **Expenses (2009-2010):** Tuition and fees 2009-2010: $5,195 in state, $13,095 out of state. Estimated books and supplies: $1,502; transportation: $450; personal expenses: $1,901. **Financial aid:** Priority filing date for institution's financial aid form: April 1.

CAMPUS LIFE AND EXTRACURRICULAR ACTIVITIES

Students who live in college-owned, operated, or affiliated housing: 0%. Number of fraternities: 0; sororities: 0.

SERVICES AND FACILITIES

Counseling services: academic. **For learning-disabled students:** School does not offer a structured program with separate admission and additional fees. **Information technology resources:** Students are not required to lease or own a computer.

TRANSFER AND INTERNATIONAL STUDENTS

Transfer students: May apply for admission for the following academic terms: Fall, Winter, Spring, Summer. Applicants do not need a minimum number of credits to apply. For fall 2009: Transfer applications received: 4,919. Transfer applicants offered admission: 3,984. Transfer applicants enrolled: 2,309. **International students:** Number of foreign undergraduates: 540 (5% of student body). Number of countries represented: 12. Minimum TOEFL score required: 550 (paper); 213 (computer).

SUNY–Fredonia

- **Address:** Fredonia, NY 14063-1136
- **Website:** http://www.fredonia.edu
- **Public**
- **Enrollment:** 5,209 full-time; 165 part-time

KEY STATS

- ✔ **U.S News College Ranking:** 46, Regional Universities (North)
- ✔ **SAT Score (25th/75th percentile):** 1010-1190
- ✔ **Tuition:** 2010-2011: $6,458 in state, $14,358 out of state

Selectivity: Selective	**Room/board:** $9,810
Acceptance rate: 49%	**Average debt:** $25,101
Student/faculty ratio: 17/1	**Proportion who borrowed:** 86%

UNDERGRADUATE STUDENT BODY STATS

2009-2010 enrollment: 5,209 full-time; 165 part-time. Men: 44%; women: 56%. **Ethnic makeup:** African American: 3%; American-Indian: 1%; Asian American: 1%; Hispanic: 3%; White: 91%; International: 1%. **Religious preference:** Roman Catholic: 30%; Protestant: 26%; Jewish: 1%; Buddhist: 1%; No preference: 18%; Unknown: 24%.

ADMISSIONS FACTS AND FIGURES

Phone: (800) 252-1212. **Email:** admissions.office@fredonia.edu. **Website:** http://www.fredonia.edu. **Application deadlines for fall 2011:** Regular decision: Rolling. Early decision: Send application by: November 1; Decision sent by: December 1. Early action: Not offered. Admission can be deferred. **Application fee:** $40. **To apply online, go to:** http://www.fredonia.edu/admissions/applying.html. **Admissions requirements/recommendations:** High school units required (recommended): English: 4 (4); Mathematics: 3 (4); Science: 3 (4); Foreign language: 3 (4); Social studies: 4 (4); Academic electives: (1); Total units: 20 (23). Tests: The college uses SAT or ACT scores in admissions decisions. Either SAT or ACT required. For admission to the fall 2011 entering class, the school will accept: ACT with or without writing accepted. Campus visit: Recommended. Admissions interview: Neither required nor recommended. Off-campus interview: Not available. **Factors that count in admissions decisions:** *Academic:* Secondary school record: Very Important. Class rank: Important. Letters of recommendation: Important. Standardized test scores: Important. Essay: Important. *Nonacademic:* Interview: Not Considered. Extracurricular activities: Considered. Talent/ability: Considered. Character/personal qualities: Considered. Alumni/ae relationship: Considered. Geographical residence: Not Considered. State residency: Not Considered. Religious affiliation/commitment: Not Considered. Minority status: Considered. Volunteer work: Considered. Work experience: Considered. **Other schools with the greatest overlap in applicants:** Buffalo State College–SUNY; College at Brockport–SUNY; SUNY–Geneseo; SUNY–Oswego; University at Buffalo–SUNY. **Admissions statistics for the fall 2009 entering class:** Total applicants: 6,632. Total accepted: 3,281. Freshmen enrolled: 1,108; 2% were from out of state. Accepted through early-decision or early-action plans: 7%. Overall acceptance rate: 49%. Early-decision acceptance rate: 82%. Non-early acceptance rate: 49%. **Credentials of fall 2009 freshmen:** 15% ranked in the top 10 percent of their high school class; 49% were in the top 25 percent; 90% were in the top half. (Proportion submitting class standing: 77%.) **Average high school grade point average:** 3.4. **First-year students who submitted SAT scores:** 93%. Scores (25/75 percentile): Critical Reading: 500-590; Math: 510-600, Combined: 1010-1190. **First-year students submitting ACT scores:** 20%. Scores (25/75 percentile): English: N/A, Math: N/A, Composite: 21-25.

ACADEMICS

Year founded: 1826. **Academic calendar:** Semester. **Degrees offered:** bachelor's, post-bachelor's certificate, master's, post-master's certificate. **Most popular majors:** 12% elementary education and teaching, 9% business administration and management, 9% communication and media studies, 6% music teacher education, 6% psychology. **Major fields of study:** biological and biomedical sciences; business, management, marketing, and related support services; communication, journalism, and related programs; communications technologies/technicians and support services; computer and information sciences and support services; education; foreign languages, literatures, and linguistics; health professions and related clinical sciences; liberal arts and sciences studies, and humanities; mathematics and statistics; philosophy and religious studies; physical sciences; psychology; public administration and social service professions; social sciences; visual and performing arts. **Areas of required coursework:** arts/fine arts, humani-

ties, computer literacy, mathematics, English (including composition), foreign languages, sciences (biological or physical), history, social science, other. **Pre-professional programs:** pre-law, pre-medicine, pre-veterinary science, pre-optometry, pre-pharmacy. **Special academic programs:** accelerated program, cooperative (work-study plan) program, cross-registration, distance learning, double major, dual enrollment, English as a Second Language (ESL), honors program, independent study, internships, liberal arts/career combination, student-designed major, study abroad, teacher certificate program. **Teacher certification offered in:** early childhood, special education, elementary, middle/junior high, secondary, bilingual/bicultural. **Cooperative education programs:** engineering. **Reserve Officers Training Corps (ROTC):** Army ROTC: Offered at cooperating institution (St. Bonaventure University). **Faculty and instruction (2009-2010):** Total instructional faculty: 259 full-time, 195 part-time (55% men; 45% women; 11% minorities). Full-time faculty with Ph.D. or other terminal degree: 92%. Student/faculty ratio: 17/1. Classes of fewer than 20 students: 57%; of 20 to 49 students: 37%; of 50 or more students: 6%. **Advanced Placement and International Baccalaureate credit:** AP tests may be used for: Credit and/or placement. Scores accepted: 3, 4, 5. International Baccalaureate exams may be used for: Credit and/or placement. **Freshmen returning for sophomore year:** 85%. **Graduation rates:** Four-year: 45%; five-year: 59%; six-year: 63%. **Graduate study:** 41% of students pursue further study within one year.

COSTS AND FINANCIAL AID

Financial aid office: (716) 673-3253. **Expenses (2010-2011):** Tuition and fees 2010-2011: $6,458 in state, $14,358 out of state; room/board: $9,810. Estimated books and supplies: $1,200; transportation: $1,032; personal expenses: $700. **Financial aid:** Priority filing date for institution's financial aid form: February 1. In 2009-2010, 86% of undergraduates applied for financial aid. Of those, 66% were determined to have financial need; 23% had their need fully met. Average financial aid package (proportion receiving): $8,119 (66%). Average amount of gift aid, such as scholarships or grants (proportion receiving): $4,048 (55%). Average amount of self-help aid, such as work study or loans (proportion receiving): $4,396 (59%). Average need-based loan (excluding PLUS or other private loans): $4,306. Among students who received need-based aid, the average percentage of need met: 65%. Among students who received aid based on merit, the average award (and the proportion receiving): $2,051 (7%). The average athletic scholarship (and the proportion receiving): $0 (0%). Average amount of debt of borrowers graduating in 2009: $25,101. Proportion who borrowed: 86%.

CAMPUS LIFE AND EXTRACURRICULAR ACTIVITIES

Campus housing available (% using): coed dorms (60%), women's dorms (23%), men's dorms (16%). Students who live in college-owned, operated, or affiliated housing: 50%. **Student employment:** During the 2009-2010 academic year, 15% of undergraduates worked on campus. Average per-year earnings: $2,025. **Clubs and organizations:** Number of student organizations: 140. Activities include: campus ministries, choral groups, concert band, dance, drama/theater, international student organization, jazz band, literary magazine, marching band, model UN, music ensembles, musical theater, opera, pep band, radio station, student government, student newspaper, student film society, symphony orchestra, television station. Number of fraternities: 3; sororities: 3. Proportion of men in fraternities: 3%; of women in sororities: 3%. Average proportion of students who stay on campus on weekends: 45%. **Sports program (2009-2010):** Member of NCAA III. *Men's intercollegiate varsity sports:* baseball, basketball, cross country, ice hockey, soccer, swimming, track and field (indoor), track and field (outdoor). *Women's intercollegiate varsity sports:* basketball, cross country, lacrosse, soccer, softball, swimming, tennis, track and field (indoor), track and field (outdoor), volleyball.

SERVICES AND FACILITIES

Basic services: nonremedial tutoring, women's center, placement service, day care, health service, health insurance. **Counseling services:** minority student, career, military, personal, veteran student, academic, older student, psychological, birth control, religious. **For learning-disabled students:** School does not offer a structured program with separate admission and additional fees. Total undergraduates in learning-disabled program or receiving services: 74. Services include: tape recorders, note-taking services, learning center, extended time for tests, tutors, texts on tape, typist/scribe, exams on tape or computer, other testing accommodations, other. **Library:** Number of titles: 449,437; number of current serial subscriptions: 49,636. **Information technology resources:** Students are not required to lease or own a computer. Number of campus computers available to all students: 409. School has a wireless network. Approximate number of users that can be accommodated:

2,000. Proportion of college-owned housing units wired for high-speed internet access: 100%. **Campus safety:** Security services offered: 24-hour foot-and-vehicle patrols, late-night transport/escort service, 24-hour emergency telephones, lighted pathways/sidewalks, student patrols, controlled dormitory access (key, security card, etc).

TRANSFER AND INTERNATIONAL STUDENTS

Transfer students: May apply for admission for the following academic terms: Fall, Winter, Spring, Summer. Applicants do not need a minimum number of credits to apply. For fall 2009: Transfer applications received: 1,491. Transfer applicants offered admission: 794. Transfer applicants enrolled: 455. **International students:** Number of foreign undergraduates: 76 (1% of student body). Number of countries represented: 19. Minimum TOEFL score required: 500 (paper); 64 (computer). Average TOEFL score: 510 (paper).

SUNY–Geneseo

- **Address:** 1 College Circle, Geneseo, NY 14454-1401
- **Website:** http://www.geneseo.edu
- **Public**
- **Enrollment:** 5,395 full-time; 100 part-time

KEY STATS

✔ **U.S News College Ranking:** 12, Regional Universities (North)
✔ **SAT Score (25th/75th percentile):** 1240-1390
✔ **Tuition:** 2009-2010: $6,278 in state, $14,178 out of state

Selectivity: More selective	**Room/board:** $9,170
Acceptance rate: 35%	**Average debt:** $21,000
Student/faculty ratio: 19/1	**Proportion who borrowed:** 63%

UNDERGRADUATE STUDENT BODY STATS

2009-2010 enrollment: 5,395 full-time; 100 part-time. Men: 43%; women: 57%. **Ethnic makeup:** African American: 3%; American-Indian: 1%; Asian American: 8%; Hispanic: 2%; White: 87%. **Religious preference:** Roman Catholic: 44%; Protestant: 15%; Hindu: 1%; Buddhist: 1%; No preference: 20%.

ADMISSIONS FACTS AND FIGURES

Phone: (585) 245-5571. **Email:** admissions@geneseo.edu. **Website:** http://www.geneseo.edu. **Application deadlines for fall 2011:** Regular decision: January 1. Early decision: Send application by: November 15; Decision sent by: December 15. Early action: Not offered. Admission can be deferred. **Application fee:** $40. **To apply online, go to:** http://www.suny.edu/student/apply_online.cfm. **Admissions requirements/recommendations:** High school units required (recommended): English: (4); Mathematics: (4); Science: (4); Foreign language: (4); Social studies: (4); Total units: (20). Tests: The college uses SAT or ACT scores in admissions decisions. Either SAT or ACT required. For admission to the fall 2011 entering class, the school will accept: ACT with or without writing accepted. Campus visit: Recommended. Admissions interview: Neither required nor recommended. Off-campus interview: Not available. **Factors that count in admissions decisions: _Academic:_** Secondary school record: Very Important. Class rank: Important. Letters of recommendation: Important. Standardized test scores: Very Important. Essay: Important. **_Nonacademic:_** Interview: Not Considered. Extracurricular activities: Important. Talent/ability: Important. Character/personal qualities: Considered. Alumni/ae relationship: Considered. Geographical residence: Not Considered. State residency: Not Considered. Religious affiliation/commitment: Not Considered. Minority status: Important. Volunteer work: Considered. Work experience: Considered. **Other schools with the greatest overlap in applicants:** Colgate University; Cornell University; Hamilton College; New York University. **Admissions statistics for the fall 2009 entering class:** Total applicants: 10,412. Total accepted: 3,631. Freshmen enrolled: 948; 2% were from out of state. Accepted through early-decision or early-action plans: 15%. Overall acceptance rate: 35%. Non-early acceptance rate: 32%. **Size of waiting list:** 780 applicants; enrolled from waiting list: 0. **Credentials of fall 2009 freshmen:** 56% ranked in the top 10 percent of their high school class; 88% were in the top 25 percent; 99% were in the top half. (Proportion submitting class standing: 49%.) **Average high school grade point average:** 3.8. **First-year students who submitted SAT scores:** 68%. Scores (25/75 percentile): Critical Reading: 610-700, Math: 630-690, Combined: 1240-1390. **First-year**

students submitting ACT scores: 29%. Scores (25/75 percentile): English: N/A, Math: N/A, Composite: 28-30.

ACADEMICS

Year founded: 1871. **Academic calendar:** Semester. **Degrees offered:** bachelor's, master's. **Most popular majors:** 24% education, 14% social sciences, 13% business, management, marketing, and related support services, 11% biological and biomedical sciences, 9% psychology. **Major fields of study:** area, ethnic, cultural, and gender studies; biological and biomedical sciences; business, management, marketing, and related support services; communication, journalism, and related programs; computer and information sciences and support services; education; English language and literature/letters; foreign languages, literatures, and linguistics; health professions and related clinical sciences; history; mathematics and statistics; multi/interdisciplinary studies; philosophy and religious studies; physical sciences; psychology; social sciences; visual and performing arts. **Areas of required coursework:** arts/fine arts, humanities, mathematics, English (including composition), foreign languages, sciences (biological or physical), history, social science, other. **Pre-professional programs:** pre-law, pre-dentistry, pre-medicine, pre-theology, pre-optometry. **Special academic programs:** cross-registration, double major, dual enrollment, English as a Second Language (ESL), honors program, independent study, internships, study abroad, teacher certificate program, other. **Teacher certification offered in:** early childhood, special education, elementary, secondary. **Reserve Officers Training Corps (ROTC):** Army ROTC: Offered at cooperating institution (Rochester Institute of Technology); Air Force ROTC: Offered at cooperating institution (Rochester Institute of Technology). **Faculty and instruction (2009-2010):** Total instructional faculty: 251 full-time, 102 part-time (56% men; 44% women; 13% minorities). Full-time faculty with Ph.D. or other terminal degree: 89%. Student/faculty ratio: 19/1. Classes of fewer than 20 students: 28%; of 20 to 49 students: 64%; of 50 or more students: 8%. **Advanced Placement and International Baccalaureate credit:** AP tests may be used for: Credit only. Scores accepted: 3, 4, 5. International Baccalaureate exams may be used for: Credit only. **Freshmen returning for sophomore year:** 91%. **Graduation rates:** Four-year: 64%; five-year: 76%; six-year: 80%. **Graduate study:** 42% of students pursue further study immediately upon graduation; 0% within one year; 0% within five years. Fields in which graduates pursue further study: Master of Business Administration (MBA), 2%; law, 8%; medicine, 8%; dentistry, 4%; engineering, 2%; education, 27%; arts and sciences, 19%; veterinary medicine, 1%.

COSTS AND FINANCIAL AID

Financial aid office: (585) 245-5731. **Expenses (2009-2010):** Tuition and fees 2009-2010: $6,278 in state, $14,178 out of state; room/board: $9,170. Estimated books and supplies: $900; transportation: $950; personal expenses: $950. **Financial aid:** In 2009-2010, 70% of undergraduates applied for financial aid. Of those, 44% were determined to have financial need; 72% had their need fully met. Average financial aid package (proportion receiving): $8,041 (44%). Average amount of gift aid, such as scholarships or grants (proportion receiving): $4,018 (44%). Average amount of self-help aid, such as work study or loans (proportion receiving): $4,805 (36%). Average need-based loan (excluding PLUS or other private loans): $4,466. Among students who received need-based aid, the average percentage of need met: 73%. Among students who received aid based on merit, the average award (and the proportion receiving): $2,068 (10%). The average athletic scholarship (and the proportion receiving): $0 (0%). Average amount of debt of borrowers graduating in 2009: $21,000. Proportion who borrowed: 63%.

CAMPUS LIFE AND EXTRACURRICULAR ACTIVITIES

Campus housing available (% using): coed dorms (78%), apartment for single students (7%), special housing for disabled students (1%), special housing for international students (5%). Students who live in college-owned, operated, or affiliated housing: 55%. **Student employment:** During the 2009-2010 academic year, 17% of undergraduates worked on campus. Average per-year earnings: $1,622. **Clubs and organizations:** Number of student organizations: 191. Activities include: campus ministries, choral groups, dance, drama/theater, international student organization, jazz band, literary magazine, model UN, music ensembles, musical theater, pep band, radio station, student government, student newspaper, symphony orchestra, television station. Number of fraternities: 9; sororities: 12. Proportion of men in fraternities: 11%; of women in sororities: 15%. Average proportion of students who stay on campus on weekends: 98%. **Sports program (2009-2010):** Member of NCAA III. **_Men's intercollegiate varsity sports:_** basketball, cross country, ice hockey, lacrosse, soccer, swimming, track and field (indoor), track and field (outdoor). **_Women's intercollegiate varsity sports:_** basketball, cross country, field hockey, lacrosse, soccer, softball, swimming, tennis, track and field (indoor), track and field (outdoor), volleyball.

SERVICES AND FACILITIES

Basic services: nonremedial tutoring, placement service, day care, health service, health insurance. **Counseling services:** minority student, career, military, personal, veteran student, academic, older student, psychological, birth control, religious. **For learning-disabled students:** School does not offer a structured program with separate admission and additional fees. Total undergraduates in learning-disabled program or receiving services: 90. Services include: reading machines, tape recorders, note-taking services, readers, extended time for tests, priority registration, priority seating, texts on tape, exams on tape or computer, other testing accommodations, other. **Library:** Number of titles: 677,184; number of current serial subscriptions: 35,763. **Information technology resources:** Students are required to lease or own a computer. Number of campus computers available to all students: 900. School has a wireless network. Approximate number of users that can be accommodated: 17,000. Proportion of college-owned housing units wired for high-speed internet access: 100%. **Campus safety:** Security services offered: 24-hour foot-and-vehicle patrols, late-night transport/escort service, 24-hour emergency telephones, lighted pathways/sidewalks, student patrols, controlled dormitory access (key, security card, etc).

TRANSFER AND INTERNATIONAL STUDENTS

Transfer students: May apply for admission for the following academic terms: Fall, Spring. Applicants need a minimum number of credits to apply. For fall 2009: Transfer applications received: 1,885. Transfer applicants offered admission: 923. Transfer applicants enrolled: 455. **International students:** Number of countries represented: 29. Minimum TOEFL score required: 525 (paper); 197 (computer). Average TOEFL score: 560 (paper).

SUNY Institute of Technology–Utica/Rome

- **Address:** 100 Seymour Road, Utica, NY 13502
- **Website:** http://www.sunyit.edu
- **Public**
- **Enrollment:** 1,546 full-time; 756 part-time

KEY STATS

✔ **U.S News College Ranking:** 99, Regional Universities (North)
✔ **SAT Score (25th/75th percentile):** 940-1160
✔ **Tuition:** 2009-2010: $6,033 in state, $13,933 out of state

Selectivity: Selective	
Acceptance rate: 38%	**Average debt:** N/A
Student/faculty ratio: 17/1	**Proportion who borrowed:** N/A

Room/board: $9,550

UNDERGRADUATE STUDENT BODY STATS

2009-2010 enrollment: 1,546 full-time; 756 part-time. Men: 52%; women: 48%. **Ethnic makeup:** African American: 8%; Asian American: 2%; Hispanic: 3%; White: 85%; International: 1%.

ADMISSIONS FACTS AND FIGURES

Phone: (315) 792-7500. **Email:** admissions@sunyit.edu. **Website:** http://www.sunyit.edu. **Application deadlines for fall 2011:** Regular decision: August 1. Early decision: Send application by: November 1; Decision sent by: December 15. Early action: Send application by: December 1; Decision sent by: December 15. Admission can be deferred. **Application fee:** $50. **To apply online, go to:** https://www.suny.edu/student/oas/welcome.do. **Admissions requirements/recommendations:** High school units required (recommended): English: 4 (4); Mathematics: 3 (4); Science: 3 (4); Foreign language: (3); Social studies: 2 (2); History: 2 (2); Academic electives: (2); Total units: 14 (21). Tests: The college uses SAT or ACT scores in admissions decisions. Either SAT or ACT required. For admission to the fall 2011 entering class, the school will accept: ACT with or without writing accepted. Campus visit: Recommended. Admissions interview: Recommended. Off-campus interview: May be arranged. **Factors that count in admissions decisions:** *Academic:* Secondary school record: Very Important. Class rank: Considered. Letters of recommendation: Important. Standardized test scores: Very Important. Essay: Considered. *Nonacademic:* Interview: Considered. Extracurricular activities: Important. Talent/ability: Important. Character/personal qualities: Important. Alumni/ae relationship: Not Considered. Geographical residence: Not Considered. State residency: Not Considered. Religious affiliation/commitment: Not Considered. Minority status: Not Considered. Volunteer work: Important. Work experience: Important. **Other schools with the greatest overlap in applicants:** Binghamton University–SUNY; Clarkson University; Rochester Institute of Technology; SUNY–Oswego; University at Buffalo–SUNY. **Admissions statistics for the fall 2009 entering class:** Total applicants: 1,798. Total accepted: 678. Freshmen enrolled: 203; 0% were from out of state. Overall acceptance rate: 38%. Non-early acceptance rate: 38%. **Credentials of fall 2009 freshmen:** 10% ranked in the top 10 percent of their high school class; 33% were in the top 25 percent; 81% were in the top half. (Proportion submitting class standing: 69%.) **Average high school grade point average:** 3.2. **First-year students who submitted SAT scores:** 94%. Scores (25/75 percentile): Critical Reading: 450-560, Math: 490-600, Combined: 940-1160. **First-year students submitting ACT scores:** 18%. Scores (25/75 percentile): English: 18-24, Math: 23-27, Composite: 22-25.

ACADEMICS

Year founded: 1966. **Academic calendar:** Semester. **Degrees offered:** bachelor's, master's, post-master's certificate. **Most popular majors:** 18% business administration and management, 14% nursing/registered nurse training (R.N., A.S.N., B.S.N., M.S.N.), 10% civil engineering technology/technician, 7% information science/studies, 7% psychology. **Major fields of study:** business, management, marketing, and related support services; communication, journalism, and related programs; computer and information sciences and support services; engineering; engineering technologies/technicians; health professions and related clinical sciences; liberal arts and sciences studies, and humanities; mathematics and statistics; psychology; social sciences. **Areas of required coursework:** arts/fine arts, humanities, computer literacy, mathematics, English (including composition), foreign languages, sciences (biological or physical), history, social science. **Pre-professional programs:** pre-law. **Special academic programs (% participation):** accelerated program (4.1%), cooperative (work-study plan) program (2.1%), cross-registration (36.6%), distance learning (8.9%), double major (1.2%), independent study (4.1%), internships (2.5%). **Cooperative education programs:** health professions. **Reserve Officers Training Corps (ROTC):** Army ROTC: Offered at cooperating institution (Utica College); Air Force ROTC: Offered at cooperating institution (Syracuse University). **Faculty and instruction (2009-2010):** Total instructional faculty: 91 full-time, 94 part-time (56% men; 44% women; 15% minorities). Full-time faculty with Ph.D. or other terminal degree: 80%. Student/faculty ratio: 17/1. Classes of fewer than 20 students: 48%; of 20 to 49 students: 51%; of 50 or more students: 0%. **Advanced Placement and International Baccalaureate credit:** AP tests may be used for: Credit and/or placement. Scores accepted: 3, 4, 5. International Baccalaureate exams may be used for: Placement only. **Freshmen returning for sophomore year:** 69%. **Graduation rates:** Four-year: 44%; five-year: 47%; six-year: 50%. **Graduate study:** 8% of students pursue further study immediately upon graduation. Fields in which graduates pursue further study: Master of Business Administration (MBA), 35%; medicine, 18%; engineering, 1%; arts and sciences, 18%.

COSTS AND FINANCIAL AID

Financial aid office: (315) 792-7210. **Expenses (2009-2010):** Tuition and fees 2009-2010: $6,033 in state, $13,933 out of state; room/board: $9,550. Estimated books and supplies: $1,000; transportation: $1,052; personal expenses: $900. **Financial aid:** Priority filing date for institution's financial aid form: March 15. In 2009-2010, 83% of undergraduates applied for financial aid. Of those, 69% were determined to have financial need; Average financial aid package (proportion receiving): N/A (69%). Average amount of gift aid, such as scholarships or grants (proportion receiving): $5,604 (62%). Average amount of self-help aid, such as work study or loans (proportion receiving): $7,183 (56%). Average need-based loan (excluding PLUS or other private loans): $4,168. Among students who received need-based aid, the average percentage of need met: 64%. Among students who received aid based on merit, the average award (and the proportion receiving): $1,747 (3%). The average athletic scholarship (and the proportion receiving): $0 (0%).

CAMPUS LIFE AND EXTRACURRICULAR ACTIVITIES

Campus housing available (% using): coed dorms (90%), special housing for disabled students (1%), cooperative housing (9%). Students who live in college-owned, operated, or affiliated housing: 25%. **Clubs and organizations:** Number of student organizations: 46. Activities include: dance, drama/theater, international student organization, jazz band, literary magazine, music ensembles, radio station, student government, student newspaper, television station, yearbook. Number of fraternities: 0; sororities: 0. Average proportion of students who stay on campus on weekends: 70%. **Sports**

program (2009-2010): Member of NCAA III. **Men's intercollegiate varsity sports:** baseball, basketball, cross country, golf, soccer, swimming, volleyball. **Women's intercollegiate varsity sports:** basketball, bowling, cross country, soccer, softball, swimming, volleyball.

SERVICES AND FACILITIES

Basic services: nonremedial tutoring. **Remedial assistance:** reading, math, writing, study skills, other. **Counseling services:** minority student, career, personal, academic, older student, psychological. **For learning-disabled students:** School does not offer a structured program with separate admission and additional fees. Total undergraduates in learning-disabled program or receiving services: 70. Services include: remedial math, remedial English, reading machines, remedial reading, tape recorders, videotaped classes, note-taking services, learning center, readers, extended time for tests, tutors, priority registration, priority seating, texts on tape, exams on tape or computer, other testing accommodations, other. **Library:** Number of titles: 176,321; number of current serial subscriptions: 22,457. **Information technology resources:** Students are not required to lease or own a computer. Number of campus computers available to all students: 212. School has a wireless network. Approximate number of users that can be accommodated: 1,728. Proportion of college-owned housing units wired for high-speed internet access: 100%. **Campus safety:** Security services offered: 24-hour foot-and-vehicle patrols, 24-hour emergency telephones, lighted pathways/sidewalks, controlled dormitory access (key, security card, etc).

TRANSFER AND INTERNATIONAL STUDENTS

Transfer students: May apply for admission for the following academic terms: Fall, Spring. Applicants do not need a minimum number of credits to apply. For fall 2009: Transfer applications received: 1,128. Transfer applicants offered admission: 675. Transfer applicants enrolled: 439. **International students:** Number of foreign undergraduates: 18 (1% of student body). Number of countries represented: 16. Minimum TOEFL score required: 550 (paper); 79 (computer).

SUNY Maritime College

- **Address:** 6 Pennyfield Avenue, Throggs Neck, NY 10465
- **Website:** http://www.sunymaritime.edu
- **Public**
- **Enrollment:** 1,463 full-time; 112 part-time

KEY STATS

✔ **U.S News College Ranking:** 19, Regional Colleges (North)
✔ **SAT Score (25th/75th percentile):** 970-1150
✔ **Tuition:** 2009-2010: $6,090 in state, $13,990 out of state

Selectivity: Selective	**Room/board:** $9,930
Acceptance rate: 63%	**Average debt:** N/A
Student/faculty ratio: 15/1	**Proportion who borrowed:** N/A

UNDERGRADUATE STUDENT BODY STATS

2009-2010 enrollment: 1,463 full-time; 112 part-time. Men: 90%; women: 10%. **Ethnic makeup:** African American: 6%; Asian American: 4%; Hispanic: 9%; White: 74%; International: 7%.

ADMISSIONS FACTS AND FIGURES

Phone: (718) 409-7221. **Email:** admissions@sunymaritime.edu. **Website:** http://www.sunymaritime.edu. **Application deadlines for fall 2011:** Regular decision: Rolling. Early decision: Not offered. Early action: Not offered. Admission can be deferred. **Application fee:** $40. **To apply online, go to:** http://www.suny.edu/student/apply_online.cfm. **Admissions requirements/recommendations:** High school units required (recommended): English: 3 (4); Mathematics: 3 (4); Science: 3 (4); Foreign language: 1 (3); Social studies: 3; History: 3; Total units: 18. Tests: The college uses SAT or ACT scores in admissions decisions. Either SAT or ACT required. For admission to the fall 2011 entering class, the school will accept: ACT with or without writing accepted. Campus visit: Recommended. Admissions interview: Recommended. Off-campus interview: May be arranged. **Factors that count in admissions decisions:** *Academic:* Secondary school record: Very Important. Class rank: Considered. Letters of recommendation: Important. Standardized test scores: Very Important. Essay: Considered. *Nonacademic:* Interview: Considered. Extracurricular activities: Considered. Talent/ability: Important. Character/personal qualities: Not Considered. Alumni/ae relationship: Considered. Geographical residence: Not Considered. State resi-

dency: Not Considered. Religious affiliation/commitment: Not Considered. Minority status: Not Considered. Volunteer work: Important. Work experience: Important. **Other schools with the greatest overlap in applicants:** Maine Maritime Academy; Massachusetts Maritime Academy; United States Coast Guard Academy; United States Merchant Marine Academy; Webb Institute. **Admissions statistics for the fall 2009 entering class:** Total applicants: 1,386. Total accepted: 874. Freshmen enrolled: 355; 26% were from out of state. Overall acceptance rate: 63%. **Size of waiting list:** 25 applicants; enrolled from waiting list: 5. **Credentials of fall 2009 freshmen:** 12% ranked in the top 10 percent of their high school class; 60% were in the top 25 percent; 92% were in the top half. (Proportion submitting class standing: 7%.) **Average high school grade point average:** 3.0. **First-year students who submitted SAT scores:** 97%. Scores (25/75 percentile): Critical Reading: 460-550, Math: 510-600, Combined: 970-1150. **First-year students submitting ACT scores:** 21%. Scores (25/75 percentile): English: N/A, Math: N/A, Composite: 20-24.

ACADEMICS

Year founded: 1874. **Academic calendar:** Semester. **Degrees offered:** associate, bachelor's, master's. **Most popular majors:** 31% tourism and travel services management, 23% naval architecture and marine engineering, 22% business, management, marketing, and related support services; 7% atmospheric sciences and meteorology, 5% mechanical engineering. **Major fields of study:** biological and biomedical sciences; business, management, marketing, and related support services; engineering; engineering technologies/technicians; multi/interdisciplinary studies; transportation and materials moving. **Areas of required coursework:** humanities, computer literacy, mathematics, English (including composition), sciences (biological or physical), history, social science. **Special academic programs:** accelerated program, cooperative (work-study plan) program, distance learning, double major, dual enrollment, English as a Second Language (ESL), honors program, independent study, internships. **Cooperative education programs:** business, engineering, natural science. **Reserve Officers Training Corps (ROTC):** Army ROTC: Offered at cooperating institution; Navy ROTC: Offered on campus. **Faculty and instruction (2009-2010):** Total instructional faculty: 86 full-time, 54 part-time (79% men; 21% women; 14% minorities). Full-time faculty with Ph.D. or other terminal degree: 65%. Student/faculty ratio: 15/1. Classes of fewer than 20 students: 31%; of 20 to 49 students: 66%; of 50 or more students: 3%. **Advanced Placement and International Baccalaureate credit:** AP tests may be used for: Credit only. Scores accepted: 3, 4, 5. International Baccalaureate exams may be used for: Credit only. **Freshmen returning for sophomore year:** 73%. **Graduation rates:** Four-year: 27%; five-year: 46%; six-year: 52%. **Graduate study:** 6% of students pursue further study immediately upon graduation.

COSTS AND FINANCIAL AID

Financial aid office: (718) 409-7254. **Expenses (2009-2010):** Tuition and fees 2009-2010: $6,090 in state, $13,990 out of state; room/board: $9,930. Estimated books and supplies: $1,260; transportation: $1,000; personal expenses: $2,000. **Financial aid:** Priority filing date for institution's financial aid form: March 1; deadline: July 15. In 2009-2010, 46% of undergraduates applied for financial aid. Of those, 46% were determined to have financial need; 9% had their need fully met. Average financial aid package (proportion receiving): $9,735 (48%). Average amount of gift aid, such as scholarships or grants (proportion receiving): $4,526 (45%). Average amount of self-help aid, such as work study or loans (proportion receiving): $4,607 (42%). Average need-based loan (excluding PLUS or other private loans): $4,576. Among students who received need-based aid, the average percentage of need met: 53%. Among students who received aid based on merit, the average award (and the proportion receiving): $2,611 (3%). The average athletic scholarship (and the proportion receiving): $0 (0%).

CAMPUS LIFE AND EXTRACURRICULAR ACTIVITIES

Campus housing available (% using): coed dorms (100%). Students who live in college-owned, operated, or affiliated housing: 80%. **Student employment:** During the 2009-2010 academic year, 9% of undergraduates worked on campus. Average per-year earnings: $1,100. **Clubs and organizations:** Number of student organizations: 30. Activities include: campus ministries, choral groups, international student organization, jazz band, marching band, music ensembles, pep band, student government, yearbook. Number of fraternities: 0; sororities: 0. Average proportion of students who stay on campus on weekends: 25%. **Sports program (2009-2010):** Member of NCAA III. **Men's intercollegiate varsity sports:** baseball, basketball, cross country, football, ice hockey, lacrosse, rifle, soccer, swimming. **Women's intercollegiate varsity sports:** basketball, crew (heavyweight), cross country, lacrosse, rifle, soccer, softball, swimming, volleyball.

SERVICES AND FACILITIES

Basic services: nonremedial tutoring, placement service, health service, health insurance. **Remedial assistance:** reading, math, writing, study skills. **Counseling services:** minority student, career, military, personal, veteran student, academic, older student, psychological, birth control, religious. **For learning-disabled students:** School does not offer a structured program with separate admission and additional fees. Services include: remedial math, remedial English, remedial reading, tape recorders, other special classes, untimed tests, note-taking services, oral tests, learning center, readers, extended time for tests, tutors, priority seating, texts on tape, typist/scribe, other testing accommodations. **Library:** Number of titles: 66,316; number of current serial subscriptions: 42,449. **Information technology resources:** Students are not required to lease or own a computer. Number of campus computers available to all students: 140. School has a wireless network. Proportion of college-owned housing units wired for high-speed internet access: 100%. **Campus safety:** Security services offered: 24-hour foot-and-vehicle patrols, 24-hour emergency telephones, lighted pathways/sidewalks, controlled dormitory access (key, security card, etc).

TRANSFER AND INTERNATIONAL STUDENTS

Transfer students: May apply for admission for the following academic terms: Fall, Spring. Applicants need a minimum number of credits to apply. For fall 2009: Transfer applications received: 292. Transfer applicants offered admission: 171. Transfer applicants enrolled: 106. **International students:** Number of foreign undergraduates: 107 (7% of student body). Number of countries represented: 34. Minimum TOEFL score required: 550 (paper); 213 (computer).

SUNY–New Paltz

- **Address:** 1 Hawk Drive, New Paltz, NY 12561-2443
- **Website:** http://www.newpaltz.edu
- **Public**
- **Enrollment:** 5,935 full-time; 619 part-time

KEY STATS

✔ **U.S News College Ranking:** 33, Regional Universities (North)
✔ **SAT Score (25th/75th percentile):** 1040-1220
✔ **Tuition:** 2009-2010: $6,081 in state, $13,981 out of state

Selectivity: Selective	Room/board: $9,202
Acceptance rate: 34%	Average debt: $16,823
Student/faculty ratio: 16/1	Proportion who borrowed: 66%

UNDERGRADUATE STUDENT BODY STATS

2009-2010 enrollment: 5,935 full-time; 619 part-time. Men: 34%; women: 66%. **Ethnic makeup:** African American: 5%; American-Indian: 1%; Asian American: 4%; Hispanic: 10%; White: 77%; International: 3%.

ADMISSIONS FACTS AND FIGURES

Phone: (845) 257-3200. **Email:** admissions@newpaltz.edu. **Website:** http://www.newpaltz.edu. **Application deadlines for fall 2011:** Regular decision: April 1. Early decision: Not offered. Early action: Send application by: November 15; Decision sent by: December 15. Admission cannot be deferred. **Application fee:** $40. **To apply online, go to:** http://www.suny.edu/student/apply_online.cfm. **Admissions requirements/recommendations:** High school units required (recommended): English: 4 (4); Mathematics: 3 (4); Science: 3 (4); Foreign language: 2 (4); Social studies: 4 (4); History: 1 (1); Total units: 17 (21). Tests: The college uses SAT or ACT scores in admissions decisions. Either SAT or ACT required. For admission to the fall 2011 entering class, the school will accept: ACT with writing required. Campus visit: Recommended. Admissions interview: Neither required nor recommended. Off-campus interview: Not available. **Factors that count in admissions decisions:** *Academic:* Secondary school record: Very Important. Class rank: Considered. Letters of recommendation: Important. Standardized test scores: Very Important. Essay: Important. *Nonacademic:* Interview: Not Considered. Extracurricular activities: Considered. Talent/ability: Considered. Character/personal qualities: Not Considered. Alumni/ae relationship: Not Considered. Geographical residence: Not Considered. State residency: Not Considered. Religious affiliation/commitment: Not Considered. Minority status: Not Considered. Volunteer work: Considered. Work experience: Considered. **Other schools with the greatest overlap in applicants:** Binghamton University–SUNY; Binghamton University–SUNY; New York University; SUNY College–Oneonta; SUNY College–Oneonta;

SUNY–Stony Brook; SUNY–Stony Brook; University at Albany–SUNY; University at Albany–SUNY. **Admissions statistics for the fall 2009 entering class:** Total applicants: 15,426. Total accepted: 5,240. Freshmen enrolled: 1,055; 6% were from out of state. Overall acceptance rate: 34%. Non-early acceptance rate: 34%. **Size of waiting list:** 634 applicants; enrolled from waiting list: 89. **Credentials of fall 2009 freshmen:** 24% ranked in the top 10 percent of their high school class; 70% were in the top 25 percent; 94% were in the top half. (Proportion submitting class standing: 9%.) **Average high school grade point average:** 3.5. **First-year students who submitted SAT scores:** 94%. Scores (25/75 percentile): Critical Reading: 520-610, Math: 520-610, Combined: 1040-1220. **First-year students submitting ACT scores:** 25%. Scores (25/75 percentile): English: 23-26, Math: 23-28, Composite: 23-27.

ACADEMICS

Year founded: 1828. **Academic calendar:** Semester. **Degrees offered:** bachelor's, master's, post-master's certificate. **Most popular majors:** 34% education, 11% business, management, marketing, and related support services, 10% visual and performing arts, 8% English language and literature/letters, 8% social sciences. **Major fields of study:** area, ethnic, cultural, and gender studies; biological and biomedical sciences; business, management, marketing, and related support services; communication, journalism, and related programs; computer and information sciences and support services; education; engineering; English language and literature/letters; foreign languages, literatures, and linguistics; health professions and related clinical sciences; history; liberal arts and sciences studies, and humanities; mathematics and statistics; philosophy and religious studies; physical sciences; psychology; social sciences; visual and performing arts. **Areas of required coursework:** arts/fine arts, humanities, computer literacy, mathematics, English (including composition), philosophy, foreign languages, sciences (biological or physical), history, social science. **Pre-professional programs:** pre-law, pre-dentistry, pre-medicine, pre-veterinary science, pre-optometry. **Special academic programs:** cooperative (work-study plan) program, cross-registration, distance learning, double major, dual enrollment, English as a Second Language (ESL), exchange student program (domestic), honors program, independent study, internships, liberal arts/career combination, student-designed major, study abroad, teacher certificate program. **Teacher certification offered in:** early childhood, special education, elementary, secondary, bilingual/bicultural. **Cooperative education programs:** art, business, computer science, education, engineering, health professions, humanities, natural science, social/behavioral science, technologies. **Faculty and instruction (2009-2010):** Total instructional faculty: 325 full-time, 343 part-time (45% men; 55% women; 14% minorities). Full-time faculty with Ph.D. or other terminal degree: 83%. Student/faculty ratio: 16/1. Classes of fewer than 20 students: 34%; of 20 to 49 students: 64%; of 50 or more students: 2%. **Advanced Placement and International Baccalaureate credit:** AP tests may be used for: Credit and/or placement. Scores accepted: 3, 4, 5. International Baccalaureate exams may be used for: Credit and/or placement. **Freshmen returning for sophomore year:** 86%. **Graduation rates:** Four-year: 45%; five-year: 64%; six-year: 66%. **Graduate study:** 24% of students pursue further study immediately upon graduation; 37% within one year.

COSTS AND FINANCIAL AID

Financial aid office: (845) 257-3250. **Expenses (2009-2010):** Tuition and fees 2009-2010: $6,081 in state, $13,981 out of state; room/board: $9,202. Estimated books and supplies: $1,250; transportation: $1,158; personal expenses: $1,000. **Financial aid:** Priority filing date for institution's financial aid form: March 15. In 2009-2010, 75% of undergraduates applied for financial aid. Of those, 52% were determined to have financial need; 16% had their need fully met. Average financial aid package (proportion receiving): $9,023 (51%). Average amount of gift aid, such as scholarships or grants (proportion receiving): $4,774 (26%). Average amount of self-help aid, such as work study or loans (proportion receiving): $4,525 (45%). Average need-based loan (excluding PLUS or other private loans): $4,287. Among students who received need-based aid, the average percentage of need met: 59%. Among students who received aid based on merit, the average award (and the proportion receiving): $1,591 (1%). The average athletic scholarship (and the proportion receiving): $0 (0%). Average amount of debt of borrowers graduating in 2009: $16,823. Proportion who borrowed: 66%.

CAMPUS LIFE AND EXTRACURRICULAR ACTIVITIES

Campus housing available: coed dorms, women's dorms, men's dorms, special housing for disabled students, special housing for international students, other housing options. Students who live in college-owned, operated, or affiliated housing: 46%. **Student employment:** During the 2009-2010 academic year, 17% of undergraduates worked on campus. Average per-year earnings: $1,100. **Clubs and organizations:** Number of student organizations: 135. Activities include: campus ministries, choral groups, concert band, dance, drama/theater, international student organization, jazz band, literary magazine, model UN, music ensembles, musical theater, radio station, student government, student newspaper, symphony orchestra, television station. Number of fraternities: 10; sororities: 13. Proportion of men in fraternities: 4%; of women in sororities: 3%. **Sports program (2009-2010):** Member of NCAA III. *Men's intercollegiate varsity sports:* baseball, basketball, cross country, soccer, swimming, tennis, volleyball. *Women's intercollegiate varsity sports:* basketball, cross country, field hockey, lacrosse, soccer, softball, swimming, tennis, volleyball.

SERVICES AND FACILITIES

Basic services: nonremedial tutoring, placement service, day care, health service, health insurance. **Remedial assistance:** math, writing, study skills. **Counseling services:** minority student, career, personal, veteran student, academic, psychological, birth control, religious, other. **For learning-disabled students:** School does not offer a structured program with separate admission and additional fees. Services include: reading machines, remedial reading, tape recorders, note-taking services, oral tests, learning center, readers, extended time for tests, tutors, priority seating, texts on tape. **Library:** Number of titles: 545,719; number of current serial subscriptions: 43,780. **Information technology resources:** Students are not required to lease or own a computer. Number of campus computers available to all students: 950. School has a wireless network. Approximate number of users that can be accommodated: 600. Proportion of college-owned housing units wired for high-speed internet access: 100%. **Campus safety:** Security services offered: 24-hour foot-and-vehicle patrols, late-night transport/escort service, 24-hour emergency telephones, lighted pathways/sidewalks, student patrols, controlled dormitory access (key, security card, etc.)

TRANSFER AND INTERNATIONAL STUDENTS

Transfer students: May apply for admission for the following academic terms: Fall, Spring. Applicants do not need a minimum number of credits to apply. For fall 2009: Transfer applications received: 3,411. Transfer applicants offered admission: 1,236. Transfer applicants enrolled: 648. **International students:** Number of foreign undergraduates: 202 (3% of student body). Number of countries represented: 55. Minimum TOEFL score required: 550 (paper); 80 (computer).

SUNY–Oswego

- **Address:** 7060 State Route 104, Oswego, NY 13126
- **Website:** http://www.oswego.edu
- **Public**
- **Enrollment:** 6,765 full-time; 435 part-time

KEY STATS

✔ **U.S News College Ranking:** 67, Regional Universities (North)
✔ **SAT Score (25th/75th percentile):** 1060-1200
✔ **Tuition:** 2009-2010: $6,651 in state, $14,551 out of state

Selectivity: Selective	**Room/board:** $10,870
Acceptance rate: 47%	**Average debt:** $25,351
Student/faculty ratio: 18/1	**Proportion who borrowed:** 86%

UNDERGRADUATE STUDENT BODY STATS

2009-2010 enrollment: 6,765 full-time; 435 part-time. Men: 48%; women: 52%. **Ethnic makeup:** African American: 4%; Asian American: 2%; Hispanic: 5%; White: 87%; International: 1%.

ADMISSIONS FACTS AND FIGURES

Phone: (315) 312-2250. **Email:** admiss@oswego.edu. **Website:** http://www.oswego.edu. **Application deadlines for fall 2011:** Regular decision: Rolling. Early decision: Send application by: November 15; Decision sent by: December 15. Early action: Not offered. Admission can be deferred. **Application fee:** $40. **To apply online, go to:** http://infostu.suny.edu/. **Admissions requirements/recommendations:** High school units required (recommended): English: 4 (4); Mathematics: 3 (4); Science: 3 (4); Foreign language: 3 (4); Social studies: 4 (4); Total units: 18 (20). Tests: The college uses SAT or ACT scores in admissions decisions. Either SAT or ACT required. For admission to the fall 2011 entering class, the school will

accept: ACT with or without writing accepted. Campus visit: Recommended. Admissions interview: Recommended. Off-campus interview: Not available. **Factors that count in admissions decisions:** *Academic:* Secondary school record: Very Important. Class rank: Important. Letters of recommendation: Considered. Standardized test scores: Important. Essay: Considered. *Nonacademic:* Interview: Considered. Extracurricular activities: Considered. Talent/ability: Considered. Character/personal qualities: Considered. Alumni/ae relationship: Not Considered. Geographical residence: Not Considered. State residency: Not Considered. Religious affiliation/commitment: Not Considered. Minority status: Considered. Volunteer work: Considered. Work experience: Considered. **Other schools with the greatest overlap in applicants:** Binghamton University–SUNY; Ithaca College; SUNY College–Cortland; SUNY College–Oneonta; SUNY–Geneseo. **Admissions statistics for the fall 2009 entering class:** Total applicants: 10,464. Total accepted: 4,899. Freshmen enrolled: 1,391; 2% were from out of state. Overall acceptance rate: 47%. Non-early acceptance rate: 47%. **Credentials of fall 2009 freshmen:** 15% ranked in the top 10 percent of their high school class; 54% were in the top 25 percent; 89% were in the top half. (Proportion submitting class standing: 60%.) **Average high school grade point average:** 3.5. **First-year students who submitted SAT scores:** 97%. Scores (25/75 percentile): Critical Reading: 530-600, Math: 530-600, Combined: 1060-1200. **First-year students submitting ACT scores:** 33%. Scores (25/75 percentile): English: N/A, Math: N/A, Composite: 21-25.

ACADEMICS

Year founded: 1861. **Academic calendar:** Semester. **Degrees offered:** bachelor's, master's, post-master's certificate. **Most popular majors:** 27% education, 20% business, management, marketing, and related support services, 12% communication, journalism, and related programs, 7% psychology, 6% security and protective services. **Major fields of study:** area, ethnic, cultural, and gender studies; biological and biomedical sciences; business, management, marketing, and related support services; communication, journalism, and related programs; computer and information sciences and support services; education; English language and literature/letters; foreign languages, literatures, and linguistics; history; liberal arts and sciences studies, and humanities; mathematics and statistics; multi/interdisciplinary studies; philosophy and religious studies; physical sciences; psychology; security and protective services; social sciences; visual and performing arts. **Areas of required coursework:** arts/fine arts, humanities, computer literacy, mathematics, English (including composition), philosophy, foreign languages, sciences (biological or physical), history, social science, other. **Preprofessional programs:** pre-law, pre-dentistry, pre-medicine, pre-veterinary science, pre-optometry. **Special academic programs (% participation):** cross-registration, distance learning (11%), double major (19%), dual enrollment, English as a Second Language (ESL), exchange student program (domestic), honors program (4%), independent study (30%), internships (20%), liberal arts/career combination, study abroad (17%), teacher certificate program (28%). **Teacher certification offered in:** early childhood, special education, elementary, vo-tech, middle/junior high, secondary, bilingual/bicultural. **Cooperative education programs:** agriculture, art, business, computer science, education, engineering, health professions. **Reserve Officers Training Corps (ROTC):** Army ROTC: Offered at cooperating institution (Syracuse University); Air Force ROTC: Offered at cooperating institution (Syracuse University). **Faculty and instruction (2009-2010):** Total instructional faculty: 312 full-time, 201 part-time (57% men; 43% women; 15% minorities). Full-time faculty with Ph.D. or other terminal degree: 88%. Student/faculty ratio: 18/1. Classes of fewer than 20 students: 51%; of 20 to 49 students: 41%; of 50 or more students: 8%. **Advanced Placement and International Baccalaureate credit:** AP tests may be used for: Credit and/or placement. Scores accepted: 3. International Baccalaureate exams may be used for: Credit and/or placement. **Freshmen returning for sophomore year:** 79%. **Graduation rates:** Four-year: 40%; five-year: 55%; six-year: 56%. **Graduate study:** 26% of students pursue further study immediately upon graduation; 35% within one year. Fields in which graduates pursue further study: Master of Business Administration (MBA), 10%; law, 4%; medicine, 1%; dentistry, 1%; engineering, 1%; theology (or the seminary), 1%; education, 57%; arts and sciences, 30%.

COSTS AND FINANCIAL AID

Financial aid office: (315) 312-2248. **Expenses (2009-2010):** Tuition and fees 2009-2010: $6,651 in state, $14,551 out of state; room/board: $10,870. Estimated books and supplies: $800; transportation: $600; personal expenses: $850. **Financial aid:** Priority filing date for institution's financial aid form: March 1. In 2009-2010, 87% of undergraduates applied for financial aid. Of those, 66% were determined to have financial need; 41% had their need fully met. Average financial aid package (proportion receiving): $10,744 (64%). Average amount of gift aid, such as scholarships or grants (proportion receiving): $4,642 (56%). Average amount of self-help aid, such as work study or loans (proportion receiving): $6,452 (56%). Average need-based loan (excluding PLUS or other private loans): $6,146. Among students who received need-based aid, the average percentage of need met: 84%. Among students who received aid based on merit, the average award (and the proportion receiving): $7,290 (17%). The average athletic scholarship (and the proportion receiving): $0 (0%). Average amount of debt of borrowers graduating in 2009: $25,351. Proportion who borrowed: 86%.

CAMPUS LIFE AND EXTRACURRICULAR ACTIVITIES

Campus housing available (% using): coed dorms (100%), other housing options. Students who live in college-owned, operated, or affiliated housing: 58%. **Student employment:** During the 2009-2010 academic year, 36% of undergraduates worked on campus. Average per-year earnings: $1,458. **Clubs and organizations:** Number of student organizations: 161. Activities include: choral groups, concert band, dance, drama/theater, international student organization, jazz band, literary magazine, music ensembles, musical theater, opera, radio station, student government, student newspaper, student film society, symphony orchestra, television station, yearbook. Number of fraternities: 11; sororities: 9. Proportion of men in fraternities: 7%; of women in sororities: 6%. Average proportion of students who stay on campus on weekends: 70%. **Sports program (2009-2010):** Member of NCAA III. *Men's intercollegiate varsity sports:* baseball, basketball, cross country, golf, ice hockey, lacrosse, soccer, swimming, tennis, track and field (indoor), track and field (outdoor), wrestling. *Women's intercollegiate varsity sports:* basketball, cross country, field hockey, ice hockey, lacrosse, soccer, softball, swimming, tennis, track and field (indoor), track and field (outdoor), volleyball.

SERVICES AND FACILITIES

Basic services: nonremedial tutoring, women's center, placement service, day care, health service, health insurance. **Remedial assistance:** reading, math, writing, study skills. **Counseling services:** career, personal, veteran student, academic, older student. **For learning-disabled students:** School does not offer a structured program with separate admission and additional fees. Total undergraduates in learning-disabled program or receiving services: 279. Services include: reading machines, tape recorders, note-taking services, readers, extended time for tests, tutors, priority registration, priority seating, substitution of courses, texts on tape, exams on tape or computer, other testing accommodations. **Library:** Number of titles: 460,558; number of current serial subscriptions: 36,382. **Information technology resources:** Students are not required to lease or own a computer. Number of campus computers available to all students: 750. School has a wireless network. Approximate number of users that can be accommodated: 5,000. Proportion of college-owned housing units wired for high-speed internet access: 100%. **Campus safety:** Security services offered: 24-hour foot-and-vehicle patrols, 24-hour emergency telephones, lighted pathways/sidewalks, controlled dormitory access (key, security card, etc).

TRANSFER AND INTERNATIONAL STUDENTS

Transfer students: May apply for admission for the following academic terms: Fall, Spring. Applicants need a minimum number of credits to apply. For fall 2009: Transfer applications received: 2,458. Transfer applicants offered admission: 1,365. Transfer applicants enrolled: 775. **International students:** Number of foreign undergraduates: 79 (1% of student body). Number of countries represented: 25. Minimum TOEFL score required: 550 (paper); 213 (computer). Average TOEFL score: 550 (paper).

SUNY–Plattsburgh

- **Address:** 101 Broad Street, Plattsburgh, NY 12901-2697
- **Website:** http://www.plattsburgh.edu
- **Public**
- **Enrollment:** 5,563 full-time; 343 part-time

KEY STATS
- ✔ **U.S News College Ranking:** 84, Regional Universities (North)
- ✔ **SAT Score (25th/75th percentile):** 980-1150
- ✔ **Tuition:** 2010-2011: $6,102 in state, $14,002 out of state

Selectivity: Selective	**Room/board:** $8,860
Acceptance rate: 48%	**Average debt:** $21,010
Student/faculty ratio: 16/1	**Proportion who borrowed:** 72%

UNDERGRADUATE STUDENT BODY STATS
2009-2010 enrollment: 5,563 full-time; 343 part-time. Men: 45%; women: 55%. **Ethnic makeup:** African American: 5%; American-Indian: 1%; Asian American: 2%; Hispanic: 5%; White: 81%; International: 7%.

ADMISSIONS FACTS AND FIGURES
Phone: (888) 673-0012. **Email:** admissions@plattsburgh.edu. **Website:** http://www.plattsburgh.edu. **Application deadlines for fall 2011:** Regular decision: Rolling. Early decision: Send application by: November 15; Decision sent by: December 15. Early action: Not offered. Admission can be deferred. **Application fee:** $40. **To apply online, go to:** http://www.plattsburgh.edu/admissions/apply.php. **Admissions requirements/recommendations:** High school units required (recommended): English: 4 (4); Mathematics: 3 (4); Science: 3 (4); Foreign language: 0 (3); Social studies: 3 (3); History: 1 (1); Academic electives: 0 (2); Total units: 14 (21). Tests: The college uses SAT or ACT scores in admissions decisions. Either SAT or ACT required. For admission to the fall 2011 entering class, the school will accept: ACT with or without writing accepted. Campus visit: Recommended. Admissions interview: Recommended. Off-campus interview: May be arranged. **Factors that count in admissions decisions:** *Academic:* Secondary school record: Very Important. Class rank: Important. Letters of recommendation: Important. Standardized test scores: Very Important. Essay: Important. *Nonacademic:* Interview: Very Important. Extracurricular activities: Important. Talent/ability: Considered. Character/personal qualities: Considered. Alumni/ae relationship: Important. Geographical residence: Considered. State residency: Considered. Religious affiliation/commitment: Not Considered. Minority status: Important. Volunteer work: Considered. Work experience: Considered. **Other schools with the greatest overlap in applicants:** SUNY College–Cortland; SUNY College–Oneonta; SUNY–New Paltz; SUNY–Oswego; University at Albany–SUNY. **Admissions statistics for the fall 2009 entering class:** Total applicants: 6,719. Total accepted: 3,245. Freshmen enrolled: 1,066; 6% were from out of state. Accepted through early-decision or early-action plans: 4%. Overall acceptance rate: 48%. Early-decision acceptance rate: 64%. Non-early acceptance rate: 48%. Size of waiting list: 56 applicants; enrolled from waiting list: 3. **Credentials of fall 2009 freshmen:** 10% ranked in the top 10 percent of their high school class; 34% were in the top 25 percent; 80% were in the top half. (Proportion submitting class standing: 61%.) **Average high school grade point average:** 3.1. **First-year students who submitted SAT scores:** 92%. Scores (25/75 percentile): Critical Reading: 480-570, Math: 500-580, Combined: 980-1150. **First-year students submitting ACT scores:** 32%. Scores (25/75 percentile): English: 19-24, Math: 19-24, Composite: 20-24.

ACADEMICS
Year founded: 1889. **Academic calendar:** Semester. **Degrees offered:** certificate, bachelor's, master's, post-master's certificate. **Most popular majors:** 19% business, management, marketing, and related support services, 13% education, 9% communication, journalism, and related programs, 8% psychology, 8% security and protective services. **Major fields of study:** agriculture, agriculture operations, and related sciences; area, ethnic, cultural, and gender studies; biological and biomedical sciences; business, management, marketing, and related support services; communication, journalism, and related programs; computer and information sciences and support services; education; English language and literature/letters; family and consumer sciences/human sciences; foreign languages, literatures, and linguistics; health professions and related clinical sciences; history; liberal arts and sciences studies, and humanities; mathematics and statistics; natural resources and conservation; philosophy and religious studies; physical sciences; psychology; public administration and social service professions;

security and protective services; social sciences; visual and performing arts. **Areas of required coursework:** arts/fine arts, humanities, computer literacy, mathematics, English (including composition), philosophy, foreign languages, sciences (biological or physical), history, social science, other. **Preprofessional programs:** pre-law, pre-dentistry, pre-medicine, pre-veterinary science, pre-optometry, pre-pharmacy. **Special academic programs (% participation):** cooperative (work-study plan) program (24%), cross-registration (3.5%), distance learning (81.4%), double major (7.5%), dual enrollment (0%), English as a Second Language (ESL) (2.7%), exchange student program (domestic) (1.5%), honors program (11.7%), independent study (15.5%), internships (37.9%), student-designed major (1.7%), study abroad (9%), teacher certificate program (20.8%). **Teacher certification offered in:** early childhood, special education, elementary, middle/junior high, secondary. **Cooperative education programs:** art, business, computer science, education, engineering, health professions, humanities, natural science, social/behavioral science, technologies. **Reserve Officers Training Corps (ROTC):** Army ROTC: Offered on campus. **Faculty and instruction (2009-2010):** Total instructional faculty: 281 full-time, 244 part-time (49% men; 51% women; 9% minorities). Full-time faculty with Ph.D. or other terminal degree: 80%. Student/faculty ratio: 16/1. Classes of fewer than 20 students: 44%; of 20 to 49 students: 50%; of 50 or more students: 6%. **Advanced Placement and International Baccalaureate credit:** AP tests may be used for: Credit and/or placement. Scores accepted: 3, 4, 5. International Baccalaureate exams may be used for: Credit and/or placement. **Freshmen returning for sophomore year:** 80%. **Graduation rates:** Four-year: 43%; five-year: 56%; six-year: 55%. **Graduate study:** 20% of students pursue further study immediately upon graduation; 25% within one year; 30% within five years. Fields in which graduates pursue further study: Master of Business Administration (MBA), 3%; law, 2%; medicine, 2%; education, 60%; arts and sciences, 20%.

COSTS AND FINANCIAL AID

Financial aid office: (518) 564-4061. **Expenses (2010-2011):** Tuition and fees 2010-2011: $6,102 in state, $14,002 out of state; room/board: $8,860. Estimated books and supplies: $975; transportation: $564; personal expenses: $1,494. **Financial aid:** Priority filing date for institution's financial aid form: February 15. In 2009-2010, 80% of undergraduates applied for financial aid. Of those, 60% were determined to have financial need; 31% had their need fully met. Average financial aid package (proportion receiving): $11,140 (59%). Average amount of gift aid, such as scholarships or grants (proportion receiving): $5,723 (52%). Average amount of self-help aid, such as work study or loans (proportion receiving): $7,147 (52%). Average need-based loan (excluding PLUS or other private loans): $6,897. Among students who received need-based aid, the average percentage of need met: 90%. Among students who received aid based on merit, the average award (and the proportion receiving): $6,268 (28%). The average athletic scholarship (and the proportion receiving): $0 (0%). Average amount of debt of borrowers graduating in 2009: $21,010. Proportion who borrowed: 72%.

CAMPUS LIFE AND EXTRACURRICULAR ACTIVITIES

Campus housing available (% using): coed dorms (88%), special housing for disabled students (0%), other housing options (12%). Students who live in college-owned, operated, or affiliated housing: 47%. **Student employment:** During the 2009-2010 academic year, 19% of undergraduates worked on campus. Average per-year earnings: $2,200. **Clubs and organizations:** Number of student organizations: 120. Activities include: campus ministries, choral groups, concert band, dance, drama/theater, international student organization, jazz band, literary magazine, music ensembles, musical theater, radio station, student government, student newspaper, symphony orchestra, television station, yearbook. Number of fraternities: 9; sororities: 7. Proportion of men in fraternities: 6%; of women in sororities: 9%. Average proportion of students who stay on campus on weekends: 80%. **Sports program (2009-2010):** Member of NCAA III. *Men's intercollegiate varsity sports:* baseball, basketball, cross country, ice hockey, lacrosse, soccer, track and field (indoor), track and field (outdoor). *Women's intercollegiate varsity sports:* basketball, cross country, ice hockey, soccer, softball, tennis, track and field (indoor), track and field (outdoor), volleyball.

SERVICES AND FACILITIES

Basic services: nonremedial tutoring, women's center, placement service, health service, health insurance. **Remedial assistance:** reading, math, writing, study skills. **Counseling services:** minority student, career, military, personal, veteran student, academic, older student, psychological, birth control, religious. **For learning-disabled students:** School does not offer a structured program with separate admission and additional fees. Total undergraduates in learning-disabled program or receiving services: 170. Services include: reading machines, tape recorders, other special classes, diagnostic test-

ing service, untimed tests, note-taking services, oral tests, learning center, readers, extended time for tests, tutors, priority seating, texts on tape, other testing accommodations. **Library:** Number of titles: 592,543; number of current serial subscriptions: 3,379. **Information technology resources:** Students are not required to lease or own a computer. Number of campus computers available to all students: 343. School has a wireless network. Approximate number of users that can be accommodated: 300. Proportion of college-owned housing units wired for high-speed internet access: 100%. **Campus safety:** Security services offered: 24-hour foot-and-vehicle patrols, late-night transport/escort service, 24-hour emergency telephones, lighted pathways/sidewalks, controlled dormitory access (key, security card, etc).

TRANSFER AND INTERNATIONAL STUDENTS

Transfer students: May apply for admission for the following academic terms: Fall, Spring. Applicants do not need a minimum number of credits to apply. For fall 2009: Transfer applications received: 1,994. Transfer applicants offered admission: 1,134. Transfer applicants enrolled: 620. **International students:** Number of foreign undergraduates: 385 (7% of student body). Number of countries represented: 63. Minimum TOEFL score required: 450 (paper); 133 (computer). Average TOEFL score: 553 (paper).

SUNY–Stony Brook

- **Address:** Administration Building, Stony Brook, NY 11794
- **Website:** http://www.stonybrook.edu
- **Public**
- **Enrollment:** 15,124 full-time; 1,271 part-time

KEY STATS

✔ **U.S News College Ranking:** 99, National Universities
✔ **SAT Score (25th/75th percentile):** 1100-1290
✔ **Tuition:** 2010-2011: $6,578 in state, $14,478 out of state

Selectivity: More selective	**Room/board:** $10,070
Acceptance rate: 40%	**Average debt:** $17,528
Student/faculty ratio: 19/1	**Proportion who borrowed:** 63%

UNDERGRADUATE STUDENT BODY STATS

2009-2010 enrollment: 15,124 full-time; 1,271 part-time. Men: 52%; women: 48%. **Ethnic makeup:** African American: 7%; Asian American: 23%; Hispanic: 9%; White: 55%; International: 7%.

ADMISSIONS FACTS AND FIGURES

Phone: (631) 632-6868. **Email:** enroll@stonybrook.edu. **Website:** http://www.stonybrook.edu. **Application deadlines for fall 2011:** Regular decision: Rolling; decision sent by April 1. Early decision: Not offered. Early action: Not offered. Admission can be deferred. **Application fee:** $50. **To apply online, go to:** http://www.suny.edu/student/apply_online.cfm. **Admissions requirements/recommendations:** High school units required (recommended): English: 4; Mathematics: 3 (4); Science: 3 (4); Foreign language: 2 (3); Social studies: 4; Total units: 16 (19). Tests: The college uses SAT or ACT scores in admissions decisions. Either SAT or ACT required. For admission to the fall 2011 entering class, the school will accept: ACT with writing required. Campus visit: Recommended. Admissions interview: Recommended. Off-campus interview: May be arranged. **Factors that count in admissions decisions:** *Academic:* Secondary school record: Very Important. Class rank: Considered. Letters of recommendation: Important. Standardized test scores: Very Important. Essay: Important. *Nonacademic:* Interview: Considered. Extracurricular activities: Considered. Talent/ability: Considered. Character/personal qualities: Considered. Alumni/ae relationship: Considered. Geographical residence: Not Considered. State residency: Not Considered. Religious affiliation/commitment: Not Considered. Minority status: Not Considered. Volunteer work: Considered. Work experience: Considered. **Other schools with the greatest overlap in applicants:** Binghamton University–SUNY; Cornell University; New York University; University at Albany–SUNY; University at Buffalo–SUNY. **Admissions statistics for the fall 2009 entering class:** Total applicants: 28,587. Total accepted: 11,411. Freshmen enrolled: 2,806; 11% were from out of state. Overall acceptance rate: 40%. **Size of waiting list:** 2350 applicants; enrolled from waiting list: 130. **Credentials of fall 2009 freshmen:** 38% ranked in the top 10 percent of their high school class; 72% were in the top 25 percent; 95% were in the top half. (Proportion submitting class standing: 38%.) **Average high school grade point average:** 3.6. **First-year students who submitted SAT scores:** 95%. Scores (25/75 percentile): Critical Reading: 520-

620, Math: 580-670, Combined: 1100-1290. **First-year students submitting ACT scores:** 22%. Scores (25/75 percentile): English: 23-28, Math: 24-29, Composite: 24-28.

ACADEMICS
Year founded: 1957. **Academic calendar:** Semester. **Degrees offered:** bachelor's, post-bachelor's certificate, master's, post-master's certificate, doctorate. **Most popular majors:** 13% psychology, 12% health professions and related clinical sciences, 8% business administration and management, 7% biology/biological sciences, 5% political science and government. **Major fields of study:** area, ethnic, cultural, and gender studies; biological and biomedical sciences; business, management, marketing, and related support services; communication, journalism, and related programs; computer and information sciences and support services; engineering; English language and literature/letters; foreign languages, literatures, and linguistics; health professions and related clinical sciences; history; liberal arts and sciences studies, and humanities; mathematics and statistics; multi/interdisciplinary studies; natural resources and conservation; philosophy and religious studies; physical sciences; psychology; public administration and social service professions; social sciences; visual and performing arts. **Areas of required coursework:** arts/fine arts, humanities, mathematics, English (including composition), philosophy, foreign languages, sciences (biological or physical), history, social science. **Pre-professional programs:** pre-law, pre-dentistry, pre-medicine. **Special academic programs:** cross-registration, distance learning, double major, dual enrollment, English as a Second Language (ESL), exchange student program (domestic), honors program, independent study, internships, student-designed major, study abroad, teacher certificate program, other. **Teacher certification offered in:** middle/junior high, secondary. **Reserve Officers Training Corps (ROTC):** Army ROTC: Offered at cooperating institution; Navy ROTC: Offered on campus; Air Force ROTC: Offered at cooperating institution. **Faculty and instruction (2009-2010):** Total instructional faculty: 972 full-time, 510 part-time (63% men; 37% women; 17% minorities). Full-time faculty with Ph.D. or other terminal degree: 98%. Student/faculty ratio: 19/1. Classes of fewer than 20 students: 33%; of 20 to 49 students: 44%; of 50 or more students: 22%. **Advanced Placement and International Baccalaureate credit:** AP tests may be used for: Credit only. Scores accepted: 3. International Baccalaureate exams may be used for: Credit only. **Freshmen returning for sophomore year:** 89%. **Graduation rates:** Four-year: 45%; five-year: 63%; six-year: 67%. **Graduate study:** 34% of students pursue further study within one year.

COSTS AND FINANCIAL AID
Financial aid office: (631) 632-6840. **Expenses (2010-2011):** Tuition and fees 2010-2011: $6,578 in state, $14,478 out of state; room/board: $10,070. Estimated books and supplies: $900; transportation: $500; personal expenses: $1,292. **Financial aid:** Priority filing date for institution's financial aid form: March 1. In 2009-2010, 72% of undergraduates applied for financial aid. Of those, 56% were determined to have financial need; 17% had their need fully met. Average financial aid package (proportion receiving): $11,124 (55%). Average amount of gift aid, such as scholarships or grants (proportion receiving): $6,953 (49%). Average amount of self-help aid, such as work study or loans (proportion receiving): $4,942 (53%). Average need-based loan (excluding PLUS or other private loans): $4,545. Among students who received need-based aid, the average percentage of need met: 71%. Among students who received aid based on merit, the average award (and the proportion receiving): $3,599 (7%). The average athletic scholarship (and the proportion receiving): $19,188 (1%). Average amount of debt of borrowers graduating in 2009: $17,528. Proportion who borrowed: 63%.

CAMPUS LIFE AND EXTRACURRICULAR ACTIVITIES
Campus housing available (% using): coed dorms (71%), apartments for married students (1%), apartment for single students (26%), special housing for disabled students (1%), other housing options (1%). Students who live in college-owned, operated, or affiliated housing: 51%. **Student employment:** During the 2009-2010 academic year, 12% of undergraduates worked on campus. Average per-year earnings: $2,003. **Clubs and organizations:** Number of student organizations: 271. Activities include: campus ministries, choral groups, concert band, dance, drama/theater, international student organization, jazz band, literary magazine, marching band, model UN, music ensembles, pep band, radio station, student government, student newspaper, student film society, television station. Number of fraternities: 16; sororities: 15. Average proportion of students who stay on campus on weekends: 50%. **Sports program (2009-2010):** Member of NCAA I. *Men's intercollegiate varsity sports:* baseball, basketball, cross country, football, lacrosse, soccer, swimming, tennis, track and field (indoor), track and field (outdoor). *Women's intercollegiate varsity sports:* basketball, cross country,

lacrosse, soccer, softball, swimming, tennis, track and field (indoor), track and field (outdoor), volleyball.

SERVICES AND FACILITIES
Basic services: nonremedial tutoring, women's center, placement service, day care, health service, health insurance, other. **Remedial assistance:** other. **Counseling services:** minority student, career, military, personal, veteran student, academic, older student, psychological, birth control, religious. **For learning-disabled students:** School does not offer a structured program with separate admission and additional fees. Total undergraduates in learning-disabled program or receiving services: 200. Services include: reading machines, tape recorders, note-taking services, readers, extended time for tests, priority registration, priority seating, texts on tape, exams on tape or computer, other testing accommodations. **Library:** Number of titles: 2,277,714; number of current serial subscriptions: 95,517. **Information technology resources:** Students are not required to lease or own a computer. Number of campus computers available to all students: 1,500. School has a wireless network. Proportion of college-owned housing units wired for high-speed internet access: 95%. **Campus safety:** Security services offered: 24-hour foot-and-vehicle patrols, late-night transport/escort service, 24-hour emergency telephones, lighted pathways/sidewalks, controlled dormitory access (key, security card, etc.).

TRANSFER AND INTERNATIONAL STUDENTS
Transfer students: May apply for admission for the following academic terms: Fall, Spring. Applicants do not need a minimum number of credits to apply. For fall 2009: Transfer applications received: 5,946. Transfer applicants offered admission: 2,603. Transfer applicants enrolled: 1,449. **International students:** Number of foreign undergraduates: 1121 (7% of student body). Number of countries represented: 87. Minimum TOEFL score required: 550 (paper); 213 (computer).

Syracuse University

- **Address:** Syracuse, NY 13244
- **Website:** http://syr.edu
- **Private**
- **Enrollment:** 13,040 full-time; 696 part-time

KEY STATS
✔ **U.S News College Ranking:** 55, National Universities
✔ **SAT Score (25th/75th percentile):** 1050-1270
✔ **Tuition:** 2010-2011: $36,302
Selectivity: More selective   **Room/board:** $12,850
Acceptance rate: 60%   **Average debt:** $28,358
Student/faculty ratio: 15/1   **Proportion who borrowed:** 65%

UNDERGRADUATE STUDENT BODY STATS
2009-2010 enrollment: 13,040 full-time; 696 part-time. Men: 43%; women: 57%. **Ethnic makeup:** African American: 8%; American-Indian: 1%; Asian American: 9%; Hispanic: 7%; White: 69%; International: 5%. **Religious preference:** Roman Catholic: 20%; Protestant: 12%; Jewish: 11%; Muslim: 1%; Hindu: 1%; Buddhist: 1%; No preference: 52%; Other: 2%.

ADMISSIONS FACTS AND FIGURES
Phone: (315) 443-3611. **Email:** orange@syr.edu. **Website:** http://syr.edu. **Application deadlines for fall 2011:** Regular decision: January 1. Early decision: Send application by: November 15; Decision sent by: December 15. Early action: Not offered. Admission can be deferred. **Application fee:** $70. **To apply online, go to:** http://syr.edu/futurestudents/undergraduate/. **Admissions requirements/recommendations:** High school units required (recommended): English: 4; Mathematics: 4; Science: 4; Foreign language: 3; Social studies: 4; Total units: 19. Tests: The college uses SAT or ACT scores in admissions decisions. Either SAT or ACT required. For admission to the fall 2011 entering class, the school will accept: ACT with writing required. Campus visit: Recommended. Admissions interview: Recommended. Off-campus interview: May be arranged. **Factors that count in admissions decisions:** *Academic:* Secondary school record: Very Important. Class rank: Very Important. Letters of recommendation: Very Important. Standardized test scores: Very Important. Essay: Very Important. *Nonacademic:* Interview: Very Important. Extracurricular activities: Very Important. Talent/ability: Very Important. Character/personal qualities: Very Important. Alumni/ae relationship: Considered. Geographical resi-

dence: Not Considered. State residency: Not Considered. Religious affiliation/commitment: Not Considered. Minority status: Considered. Volunteer work: Important. Work experience: Important. **Other schools with the greatest overlap in applicants:** Boston University; Ithaca College; New York University; Pennsylvania State University–University Park; University of Maryland–College Park. **Admissions statistics for the fall 2009 entering class:** Total applicants: 20,951. Total accepted: 12,596. Freshmen enrolled: 3,261; 55% were from out of state. Accepted through early-decision or early-action plans: 18%. Overall acceptance rate: 60%. Early-decision acceptance rate: 77%. Non-early acceptance rate: 59%. **Size of waiting list:** 3348 applicants; enrolled from waiting list: 501. **Credentials of fall 2009 freshmen:** 39% ranked in the top 10 percent of their high school class; 73% were in the top 25 percent; 96% were in the top half. (Proportion submitting class standing: 44%.) **Average high school grade point average:** 3.6. **First-year students who submitted SAT scores:** 88%. Scores (25/75 percentile): Critical Reading: 510-620, Math: 540-650, Combined: 1050-1270. **First-year students submitting ACT scores:** 35%. Scores (25/75 percentile): English: 23-29, Math: 23-28, Composite: 23-28.

ACADEMICS

Year founded: 1870. **Academic calendar:** Semester. **Degrees offered:** certificate, associate, bachelor's, post-bachelor's certificate, master's, post-master's certificate, doctorate. **Most popular majors:** 21% business, management, marketing, and related support services, 13% social sciences, 12% visual and performing arts, 7% psychology, 6% engineering. **Major fields of study:** architecture and related services; area, ethnic, cultural, and gender studies; biological and biomedical sciences; business, management, marketing, and related support services; communication, journalism, and related programs; communications technologies/technicians and support services; computer and information sciences and support services; education; engineering; engineering technologies/technicians; English language and literature/letters; family and consumer sciences/human sciences; foreign languages, literatures, and linguistics; health professions and related clinical sciences; history; legal professions and studies; liberal arts and sciences studies, and humanities; library science; mathematics and statistics; philosophy and religious studies; physical sciences; psychology; public administration and social service professions; security and protective services; social sciences; transportation and materials moving; visual and performing arts. **Areas of required coursework:** humanities, mathematics, English (including composition), foreign languages, sciences (biological or physical), social science, other. **Pre-professional programs:** pre-law, pre-dentistry, pre-medicine, pre-veterinary science, pre-optometry. **Special academic programs (% participation):** accelerated program, cooperative (work-study plan) program (3%), distance learning, double major (28%), dual enrollment (6%), English as a Second Language (ESL) (3%), exchange student program (domestic), honors program (10%), independent study (21%), internships (50%), liberal arts/career combination (4%), student-designed major, study abroad (43%), teacher certificate program (4%). **Teacher certification offered in:** early childhood, special education, elementary, secondary. **Cooperative education programs:** computer science, education, engineering, other. **Reserve Officers Training Corps (ROTC):** Army ROTC: Offered on campus; Air Force ROTC: Offered on campus. **Faculty and instruction (2009-2010):** Total instructional faculty: 962 full-time, 545 part-time (59% men; 41% women; 15% minorities). Full-time faculty with Ph.D. or other terminal degree: 87%. Student/faculty ratio: 15/1. Classes of fewer than 20 students: 63%; of 20 to 49 students: 30%; of 50 or more students: 8%. **Advanced Placement and International Baccalaureate credit:** AP tests may be used for: Credit and/or placement. Scores accepted: 3, 4, 5. International Baccalaureate exams may be used for: Credit only. **Freshmen returning for sophomore year:** 91%. **Graduation rates:** Four-year: 73%; five-year: 82%; six-year: 83%. **Graduate study:** 18% of students pursue further study within one year. Fields in which graduates pursue further study: Master of Business Administration (MBA), 8%; law, 16%; medicine, 12%; dentistry, 2%; engineering, 15%; education, 10%; arts and sciences, 6%.

COSTS AND FINANCIAL AID

Financial aid office: (315) 443-1513. **Expenses (2010-2011):** Tuition and fees 2010-2011: $36,302; room/board: $12,850. Estimated books and supplies: $1,308; transportation: $600; personal expenses: $900. **Financial aid:** In 2009-2010, 69% of undergraduates applied for financial aid. Of those, 59% were determined to have financial need; 65% had their need fully met. Average financial aid package (proportion receiving): $29,976 (59%). Average amount of gift aid, such as scholarships or grants (proportion receiving): $21,300 (54%). Average amount of self-help aid, such as work study or loans (proportion receiving): $8,950 (59%). Average need-based loan (excluding PLUS or other private loans): $7,225. Among students who

received need-based aid, the average percentage of need met: 86%. Among students who received aid based on merit, the average award (and the proportion receiving): $9,130 (14%). The average athletic scholarship (and the proportion receiving): $38,890 (3%). Average amount of debt of borrowers graduating in 2009: $28,358. Proportion who borrowed: 65%.

CAMPUS LIFE AND EXTRACURRICULAR ACTIVITIES

Campus housing available (% using): coed dorms (66%), sorority housing (5%), fraternity housing (3%), apartments for married students (1%), apartment for single students (19%), special housing for disabled students (1%), other housing options (5%). Students who live in college-owned, operated, or affiliated housing: 75%. **Student employment:** During the 2009-2010 academic year, 50% of undergraduates worked on campus. Average per-year earnings: $2,500. **Clubs and organizations:** Number of student organizations: 347. Activities include: campus ministries, choral groups, concert band, dance, drama/theater, international student organization, jazz band, literary magazine, marching band, music ensembles, musical theater, pep band, radio station, student government, student newspaper, student film society, symphony orchestra, television station, yearbook. Number of fraternities: 29; sororities: 19. Proportion of men in fraternities: 16%; of women in sororities: 24%. Average proportion of students who stay on campus on weekends: 85%. **Sports program (2009-2010):** Member of NCAA I. *Men's intercollegiate varsity sports:* basketball, cross country, football, lacrosse, soccer, swimming, track and field (outdoor). *Women's intercollegiate varsity sports:* basketball, crew (heavyweight), cross country, field hockey, ice hockey, lacrosse, soccer, softball, swimming, tennis, track and field (outdoor), volleyball.

SERVICES AND FACILITIES

Basic services: nonremedial tutoring, women's center, placement service, day care, health service, health insurance. **Counseling services:** minority student, career, military, personal, veteran student, academic, older student, psychological, birth control, religious, other. **For learning-disabled students:** School does not offer a structured program with separate admission and additional fees. Total undergraduates in learning-disabled program or receiving services: 689. Services include: reading machines, tape recorders, diagnostic testing service, note-taking services, learning center, readers, extended time for tests, tutors, priority seating, texts on tape, exams on tape or computer, other testing accommodations. **Library:** Number of titles: 3,201,031; number of current serial subscriptions: 39,703. **Information technology resources:** Students are not required to lease or own a computer. Number of campus computers available to all students: 3,427. School has a wireless network. Approximate number of users that can be accommodated: 100,000. Proportion of college-owned housing units wired for high-speed internet access: 100%. **Campus safety:** Security services offered: 24-hour foot-and-vehicle patrols, late-night transport/escort service, 24-hour emergency telephones, lighted pathways/sidewalks, student patrols, controlled dormitory access (key, security card, etc).

TRANSFER AND INTERNATIONAL STUDENTS

Transfer students: May apply for admission for the following academic terms: Fall, Spring. Applicants need a minimum number of credits to apply. For fall 2009: Transfer applications received: 1,113. Transfer applicants offered admission: 657. Transfer applicants enrolled: 318. **International students:** Number of foreign undergraduates: 704 (5% of student body). Number of countries represented: 70. Minimum TOEFL score required: 550 (paper); 80 (computer). Average TOEFL score: 599 (paper).

Touro College

■ **Address:** 27-33 W. 23rd Street, New York, NY 10001
■ **Website:** http://www.touro.edu/
■ **Private**
■ **Enrollment:** 6,440 full-time; 1,782 part-time

KEY STATS

✔ **U.S News College Ranking:** 97, Regional Universities (North)
✔ **SAT Score (25th/75th percentile):** 1040-1270
✔ **Tuition:** 2010-2011: $14,000

Selectivity: More selective	**Room/board:** $11,340
Acceptance rate: 71%	**Average debt:** N/A
Student/faculty ratio: 13/1	**Proportion who borrowed:** N/A

UNDERGRADUATE STUDENT BODY STATS

2009-2010 enrollment: 6,440 full-time; 1,782 part-time. Men: 31%; women: 69%. **Ethnic makeup:** African American: 16%; Asian American: 5%; Hispanic: 11%; White: 68%.

ADMISSIONS FACTS AND FIGURES

Phone: (718) 252-7800. **Email:** lasadmit@adminm.touro.edu. **Website:** http://www.touro.edu/. **Application deadlines for fall 2011:** Regular decision: Rolling. Early decision: Not offered. Early action: Not offered. Admission can be deferred. **Application fee:** $50. **Admissions requirements/recommendations:** High school units required (recommended): English: 4 (4); Mathematics: 2 (2); Science: 2 (2); Foreign language: 2 (2); Social studies: 0 (0); History: 2 (2); Academic electives: 4 (4); Total units: 16 (16). Tests: The college uses SAT or ACT scores in admissions decisions. Neither SAT nor ACT required. For admission to the fall 2011 entering class, the school will accept: ACT with or without writing accepted. Campus visit: Recommended. Admissions interview: Recommended. Off-campus interview: May be arranged. **Factors that count in admissions decisions:** *Academic:* Secondary school record: Very Important. Class rank: Considered. Letters of recommendation: Considered. Standardized test scores: Very Important. Essay: Important. *Nonacademic:* Interview: Important. Extracurricular activities: Considered. Talent/ability: Considered. Character/personal qualities: Considered. Alumni/ae relationship: Considered. Geographical residence: Not Considered. State residency: Not Considered. Religious affiliation/commitment: Very Important. Minority status: Not Considered. Volunteer work: Considered. Work experience: Considered. **Admissions statistics for the fall 2009 entering class:** Total applicants: 1,338. Total accepted: 947. Freshmen enrolled: 970; Overall acceptance rate: 71%. **Credentials of fall 2009 freshmen:** 67% ranked in the top 10 percent of their high school class; 92% were in the top 25 percent; 95% were in the top half. (Proportion submitting class standing: 40%.) **Average high school grade point average:** 3.6. **First-year students who submitted SAT scores:** 69%. Scores (25/75 percentile): Critical Reading: 530-650, Math: 510-620, Combined: 1040-1270. **First-year students submitting ACT scores:** 6%. Scores (25/75 percentile): English: N/A, Math: N/A, Composite: 22-26.

ACADEMICS

Year founded: 1971. **Academic calendar:** Semester. **Degrees offered:** certificate, associate, bachelor's, master's, doctorate. **Most popular majors:** 22% business administration and management, 22% liberal arts and sciences/liberal studies, 18% psychology, 8% human services, 7% physician assistant. **Major fields of study:** biological and biomedical sciences; business, management, marketing, and related support services; communications technologies/technicians and support services; computer and information sciences and support services; education; English language and literature/letters; foreign languages, literatures, and linguistics; health professions and related clinical sciences; history; liberal arts and sciences studies, and humanities; mathematics and statistics; multi/interdisciplinary studies; philosophy and religious studies; physical sciences; psychology; public administration and social service professions; social sciences. **Areas of required coursework:** humanities, computer literacy, mathematics, English (including composition), sciences (biological or physical). **Pre-professional programs:** pre-law, pre-dentistry, pre-medicine. **Special academic programs (% participation):** accelerated program (5%), cross-registration (1%), distance learning (10%), double major (1%), honors program (8%), independent study (38%), internships (4%), liberal arts/career combination (85%), study abroad (25%), teacher certificate program (6%). **Teacher certification offered in:** early childhood, special education, elementary, middle/junior high, secondary, bilingual/bicultural. **Faculty and instruction (2009-2010):** Total instructional faculty: 495 full-time, 780 part-time (53% men; 47% women; 34% minorities). Full-time faculty with Ph.D. or other terminal degree: 72%. Student/faculty ratio: 13/1. Classes of fewer than 20 students: 84%; of 20 to 49 students: 15%; of 50 or more students: 0%. **Advanced Placement and International Baccalaureate credit:** AP tests may be used for: Placement only. Scores accepted: 4, 5. **Freshmen returning for sophomore year:** 80%. **Graduation rates:** Four-year: 0%; five-year: 0%; six-year: 58%.

COSTS AND FINANCIAL AID

Financial aid office: (718) 252-7800. **Expenses (2010-2011):** Tuition and fees 2010-2011: $14,000; room/board: $11,340. Estimated books and supplies: $975; transportation: $748; personal expenses: $2,307. **Financial aid:** Priority filing date for institution's financial aid form: May 15; deadline: August 15. In 2009-2010, 98% of undergraduates applied for financial aid. Of those, 98% were determined to have financial need; Average financial aid package (proportion receiving): $12,200 (98%). Average amount of gift aid, such as scholarships or grants (proportion receiving): $3,600 (98%). Average amount of self-help aid, such as work study or loans (proportion receiving): $700 (0%). Average need-based loan (excluding PLUS or other private loans): $3,500. Among students who received need-based aid, the average percentage of need met: 90%. Among students who received aid based on merit, the average award (and the proportion receiving): $1,800 (25%). The average athletic scholarship (and the proportion receiving): $0 (0%).

CAMPUS LIFE AND EXTRACURRICULAR ACTIVITIES

Campus housing available (% using): women's dorms (1%), men's dorms (1%). Activities include: choral groups, student government, student newspaper, yearbook. Number of fraternities: 0; sororities: 0. Average proportion of students who stay on campus on weekends: 1%.

SERVICES AND FACILITIES

Basic services: nonremedial tutoring. **Remedial assistance:** reading, math, writing. **For learning-disabled students:** Services include: remedial math, remedial English, remedial reading. **Library:** Number of titles: 342,464; number of current serial subscriptions: 26,083. **Information technology resources:** Students are not required to lease or own a computer. Number of campus computers available to all students: 1,200. School has a wireless network. Proportion of college-owned housing units wired for high-speed internet access: 0%. **Campus safety:** Security services offered: 24-hour foot-and-vehicle patrols.

TRANSFER AND INTERNATIONAL STUDENTS

Transfer students: May apply for admission for the following academic terms: Fall, Spring, Summer. Applicants need a minimum number of credits to apply. For fall 2009: Transfer applications received: 651. Transfer applicants offered admission: 441. Transfer applicants enrolled: 300. **International students:** Number of foreign undergraduates: 2. Minimum TOEFL score required: 500 (paper); 173 (computer).

Union College

- **Address:** 807 Union Street, Schenectady, NY 12308
- **Website:** http://www.union.edu
- **Private**
- **Enrollment:** 2,157 full-time; 37 part-time

KEY STATS

✔ **U.S News College Ranking:** 41, National Liberal Arts Colleges
✔ **SAT Score (25th/75th percentile):** 1210-1370
✔ **Tuition:** N/A

Selectivity: More selective	**Room/board:** N/A
Acceptance rate: 41%	**Average debt:** $24,739
Student/faculty ratio: 10/1	**Proportion who borrowed:** 61%

UNDERGRADUATE STUDENT BODY STATS

2009-2010 enrollment: 2,157 full-time; 37 part-time. Men: 51%; women: 49%. **Ethnic makeup:** African American: 5%; Asian American: 7%; Hispanic: 5%; White: 80%; International: 3%.

ADMISSIONS FACTS AND FIGURES

Phone: (888) 843-6688. **Email:** admissions@union.edu. **Website:** http://www.union.edu. **Application deadlines for fall 2011:** Regular decision: January 15; decision sent by April 1. Early decision: Send application by: November 15; Decision sent by: December 15. Early action: Not offered. Admission can be deferred. **Application fee:** $50. **To apply online, go to:** http://www.union.edu/Admissions/Applying/Applications.php. **Admissions requirements/recommendations:** High school units required (recommended): English: 4 (4); Mathematics: 3 (4); Science: 2 (4); Foreign language: 2 (4); Social studies: 1 (2); History: 1 (2); Total units: 16 (24). Tests: The college uses SAT or ACT scores in admissions decisions. Neither SAT nor ACT required. For admission to the fall 2011 entering class, the school will accept: ACT with or without writing accepted. Campus visit: Recommended. Admissions interview: Recommended. Off-campus interview: May be arranged. **Factors that count in admissions decisions:** *Academic:* Secondary school record: Very Important. Class rank: Very Important. Letters of recommendation: Important. Standardized test scores: Important. Essay: Considered. *Nonacademic:* Interview: Considered. Extracurricular activities: Important. Talent/ability: Important. Character/personal qualities: Important. Alumni/ae relationship: Considered. Geographical residence: Considered. State residency: Considered. Religious affiliation/commitment: Not Considered. Minority status: Considered. Volunteer work: Considered. Work experience: Considered. **Other schools with the greatest overlap in applicants:** Colgate University; Cornell University; Rensselaer Polytechnic Institute; University of Rochester; University of Vermont. **Admissions statistics for the fall 2009 entering class:** Total applicants: 4,829. Total accepted: 1,987. Freshmen enrolled: 520; 57% were from out of state. Accepted through early-decision or early-action plans: 40%. Overall acceptance rate: 41%. Early-decision acceptance rate: 72%. Non-early acceptance rate: 39%. **Size of waiting list:** 840 applicants; enrolled from waiting list: 109. **Credentials of fall 2009 freshmen:** 58% ranked in the top 10 percent of their high school class; 84% were in the top 25 percent; 99% were in the top half. (Proportion submitting class standing: 43%.) **Average high school grade point average:** 3.6. **First-year students who submitted SAT scores:** 53%. Scores (25/75 percentile): Critical Reading: 590-670, Math: 620-700, Combined: 1210-1370. **First-year students submitting ACT scores:** 22%. Scores (25/75 percentile): English: 25-31, Math: 26-32, Composite: 27-30.

ACADEMICS

Year founded: 1795. **Academic calendar:** Trimester. **Degrees offered:** bachelor's. **Most popular majors:** 11% political science and government, 9% economics, 8% English language and literature, 8% mechanical engineering, 8% psychology. **Major fields of study:** area, ethnic, cultural, and gender studies; biological and biomedical sciences; computer and information sciences and support services; engineering; English language and literature/letters; foreign languages, literatures, and linguistics; history; liberal arts and sciences studies, and humanities; mathematics and statistics; multi/interdisciplinary studies; philosophy and religious studies; physical sciences; psychology; social sciences; visual and performing arts. **Areas of required coursework:** humanities, mathematics, English (including composition), sciences (biological or physical), history, social science, other. **Pre-professional programs:** other. **Special academic programs (% participation):** accelerated program (4%), cross-registration, double major (11%), dual enrollment, honors program (10%), independent study (37%), internships (6%), liberal arts/career combination (0%), student-designed major (1%), study abroad (62%), teacher certificate program. **Teacher certification offered in:** secondary. **Reserve Officers Training Corps (ROTC):** Army ROTC: Offered at cooperating institution (Siena College); Navy ROTC: Offered at cooperating institution (Rensselaer Polytechnic Institute); Air Force ROTC: Offered at cooperating institution (Rensselaer Polytechnic Institute). **Faculty and instruction (2009-2010):** Total instructional faculty: 199 full-time, 29 part-time (55% men; 45% women; 12% minorities). Full-time faculty with Ph.D. or other terminal degree: 96%. Student/faculty ratio: 10/1. Classes of fewer than 20 students: 70%; of 20 to 49 students: 29%; of 50 or more students: 1%. **Advanced Placement and International Baccalaureate credit:** AP tests may be used for: Credit and/or placement. Scores accepted: 3, 4, 5. International Baccalaureate exams may be used for: Credit and/or placement. **Freshmen returning for sophomore year:** 92%. **Graduation rates:** Four-year: 80%; five-year: 85%; six-year: 86%. **Graduate study:** 30% of students pursue further study immediately upon graduation. Fields in which graduates pursue further study: Master of Business Administration (MBA), 11%; law, 11%; medicine, 16%; engineering, 7%; education, 13%; arts and sciences, 41%; veterinary medicine, 1%.

COSTS AND FINANCIAL AID

Financial aid office: (518) 388-6123. **Financial aid:** Priority filing date for institution's financial aid form: February 1; deadline: February 1. In 2009-2010, 59% of undergraduates applied for financial aid. Of those, 48% were determined to have financial need; 97% had their need fully met. Average financial aid package (proportion receiving): $33,778 (47%). Average amount of gift aid, such as scholarships or grants (proportion receiving): $28,489 (46%). Average amount of self-help aid, such as work study or loans (proportion receiving): $4,920 (45%). Average need-based loan (excluding PLUS or other private loans): $4,007. Among students who received need-based aid, the average percentage of need met: 99%. Among students who received aid based on merit, the average award (and the proportion receiving): $10,002 (16%). The average athletic scholarship (and the proportion receiving): $0 (0%). Average amount of debt of borrowers graduating in 2009: $24,739. Proportion who borrowed: 61%.

CAMPUS LIFE AND EXTRACURRICULAR ACTIVITIES

Campus housing available (% using): coed dorms (68%), sorority housing (5%), fraternity housing (9%), apartment for single students (9%). Students who live in college-owned, operated, or affiliated housing: 87%. **Student employment:** During the 2009-2010 academic year, 20% of undergraduates worked on campus. Average per-year earnings: $1,532. **Clubs and organiza-**

tions: Number of student organizations: 105. Activities include: campus ministries, choral groups, concert band, dance, drama/theater, international student organization, jazz band, literary magazine, model UN, music ensembles, pep band, radio station, student government, student newspaper, student film society, symphony orchestra, television station, yearbook. Number of fraternities: 12; sororities: 5. Proportion of men in fraternities: 32%; of women in sororities: 31%. Average proportion of students who stay on campus on weekends: 80%. **Sports program (2009-2010):** Member of NCAA III. **Men's intercollegiate varsity sports:** baseball, basketball, cross country, football, ice hockey, lacrosse, soccer, swimming, tennis, track and field (indoor), track and field (outdoor). **Women's intercollegiate varsity sports:** basketball, crew (heavyweight), cross country, field hockey, ice hockey, lacrosse, soccer, softball, swimming, tennis, track and field (indoor), track and field (outdoor), volleyball.

SERVICES AND FACILITIES

Basic services: nonremedial tutoring, women's center, health service, other. **Counseling services:** minority student, career, personal, academic, psychological, religious. **For learning-disabled students:** School does not offer a structured program with separate admission and additional fees. Total undergraduates in learning-disabled program or receiving services: 154. Services include: reading machines, tape recorders, note-taking services, readers, extended time for tests, priority registration, priority seating, texts on tape, other testing accommodations, other. **Library:** Number of titles: 634,183; number of current serial subscriptions: 12,500. **Information technology resources:** Students are not required to lease or own a computer. Number of campus computers available to all students: 491. School has a wireless network. Approximate number of users that can be accommodated: 3,000. Proportion of college-owned housing units wired for high-speed internet access: 100%. **Campus safety:** Security services offered: 24-hour foot-and-vehicle patrols, late-night transport/escort service, 24-hour emergency telephones, lighted pathways/sidewalks, controlled dormitory access (key, security card, etc).

TRANSFER AND INTERNATIONAL STUDENTS

Transfer students: May apply for admission for the following academic terms: Fall, Winter, Spring. Applicants need a minimum number of credits to apply. For fall 2009: Transfer applications received: 139. Transfer applicants offered admission: 60. Transfer applicants enrolled: 21. **International students:** Number of foreign undergraduates: 73 (3% of student body). Number of countries represented: 29. Minimum TOEFL score required: 600 (paper); 250 (computer).

United States Merchant Marine Academy

- **Address:** 300 Steamboat Road, Kings Point, NY 11024
- **Website:** http://www.usmma.edu
- **Public**
- **Enrollment:** 964 full-time

KEY STATS

✔ **U.S News College Ranking:** 3, Regional Colleges (North)
✔ **SAT Score (25th/75th percentile):** 1120-1298
✔ **Tuition:** N/A

Selectivity: Selective	**Room/board:** N/A
Acceptance rate: 25%	**Average debt:** $6,416
Student/faculty ratio: 11/1	**Proportion who borrowed:** 29%

UNDERGRADUATE STUDENT BODY STATS

2009-2010 enrollment: 964 full-time. Men: 89%; women: 11%. **Ethnic makeup:** African American: 2%; American-Indian: 1%; Asian American: 4%; Hispanic: 4%; White: 86%; International: 3%.

ADMISSIONS FACTS AND FIGURES

Phone: (516) 773-5391. **Email:** admissions@usmma.edu. **Website:** http://www.usmma.edu. **Application deadlines for fall 2011:** Regular decision: March 1. Early decision: Not offered. Early action: Not offered. Admission cannot be deferred. **Application fee:** None. **To apply online, go to:** https://info.usmma.edu/applyonline.htm. **Admissions requirements/recommendations:** High school units required (recommended): English: 4; Mathematics: 3 (4); Science: 3 (4); Foreign language: (2); Social studies: (4); Academic electives: 8; Total units: 18. Tests: The college uses SAT or ACT scores in admissions decisions. Either SAT or ACT required. For admission to the fall 2011 entering class, the school will accept: ACT with or without writing accepted. Campus visit: Recommended. Admissions interview: Recommended. Off-campus interview: May be arranged. **Factors that count in admissions decisions:** *Academic:* Secondary school record: Very Important. Class rank: Important. Letters of recommendation: Important. Standardized test scores: Very Important. Essay: Important. *Nonacademic:* Interview: Considered. Extracurricular activities: Important. Talent/ability: Important. Character/personal qualities: Very Important. Alumni/ae relationship: Not Considered. Geographical residence: Not Considered. State residency: Considered. Religious affiliation/commitment: Not Considered. Minority status: Considered. Volunteer work: Considered. Work experience: Considered. **Other schools with the greatest overlap in applicants:** United States Coast Guard Academy; United States Naval Academy. **Admissions statistics for the fall 2009 entering class:** Total applicants: 1,823. Total accepted: 450. Freshmen enrolled: 291; Overall acceptance rate: 25%. **Credentials of fall 2009 freshmen:** 15% ranked in the top 10 percent of their high school class; 42% were in the top 25 percent; 87% were in the top half. (Proportion submitting class standing: 100%.) **Average high school grade point average:** 3.5. **First-year students who submitted SAT scores:** 78%. Scores (25/75 percentile): Critical Reading: 534-635, Math: 586-663, Combined: 1120-1298. **First-year students submitting ACT scores:** 47%. Scores (25/75 percentile): English: 23-28, Math: 25-30, Composite: 24-29.

ACADEMICS
Year founded: 1943. **Academic calendar:** Trimester. **Degrees offered:** bachelor's, master's. **Most popular majors:** 52% marine science/merchant marine officer, 26% systems engineering, 18% naval architecture and marine engineering, 4% naval architecture and marine engineering. **Major fields of study:** engineering; transportation and materials moving. **Areas of required coursework:** humanities, computer literacy, mathematics, English (including composition), sciences (biological or physical), history. **Special academic programs (% participation):** cooperative (work-study plan) program (100%), honors program (2%), independent study (10%), internships (100%). **Cooperative education programs:** other. **Reserve Officers Training Corps (ROTC):** Army ROTC: Offered on campus; Navy ROTC: Offered on campus; Air Force ROTC: Offered on campus. **Faculty and instruction (2009-2010):** Total instructional faculty: 88 (88% men; 13% women; 10% minorities). Student/faculty ratio: 11/1. Classes of fewer than 20 students: 45%; of 20 to 49 students: 54%; of 50 or more students: 1%. **Advanced Placement and International Baccalaureate credit:** AP tests may be used for: Credit and/or placement. Scores accepted: 4, 5. **Freshmen returning for sophomore year:** 89%. **Graduation rates:** Four-year: 65%; five-year: 73%; six-year: 74%. **Graduate study:** 1% of students pursue further study immediately upon graduation.

COSTS AND FINANCIAL AID
Financial aid office: (516) 773-5295. **Financial aid:** In 2009-2010, 55% of undergraduates applied for financial aid. Of those, 24% were determined to have financial need; Average financial aid package (proportion receiving): $3,300 (19%). Average amount of gift aid, such as scholarships or grants (proportion receiving): N/A (19%). Average amount of self-help aid, such as work study or loans (proportion receiving): $1,393 (2%). Average need-based loan (excluding PLUS or other private loans): $1,393. Among students who received need-based aid, the average percentage of need met: 90%. Average amount of debt of borrowers graduating in 2009: $6,416. Proportion who borrowed: 29%.

CAMPUS LIFE AND EXTRACURRICULAR ACTIVITIES
Campus housing available (% using): coed dorms (100%). **Student employment:** During the 2009-2010 academic year, 5% of undergraduates worked on campus. Average per-year earnings: $500. **Clubs and organizations:** Number of student organizations: 27. Activities include: choral groups, concert band, marching band, pep band, student government, student newspaper, yearbook. Number of fraternities: 0; sororities: 0. Average proportion of students who stay on campus on weekends: 60%. **Sports program (2009-2010):** Member of NCAA III. *Men's intercollegiate varsity sports:* baseball, basketball, cross country, football, golf, lacrosse, rifle, soccer, swimming, tennis, track and field (outdoor), wrestling. *Women's intercollegiate varsity sports:* basketball, crew (heavyweight), cross country, crew (lightweight), rifle, softball, swimming, track and field (outdoor), water polo.

SERVICES AND FACILITIES
Basic services: nonremedial tutoring, placement service, health service. **Remedial assistance:** math, writing, study skills, other. **Counseling services:** minority student, career, military, personal, veteran student, academic, psychological, birth control, religious. **Library:** Number of titles: 181,651; num-

ber of current serial subscriptions: 875. **Information technology resources:** Students are required to lease or own a computer. Number of campus computers available to all students: 400. School has a wireless network. Approximate number of users that can be accommodated: 1,500. Proportion of college-owned housing units wired for high-speed internet access: 100%. **Campus safety:** Security services offered: 24-hour foot-and-vehicle patrols, 24-hour emergency telephones, lighted pathways/sidewalks.

TRANSFER AND INTERNATIONAL STUDENTS
Transfer students: May apply for admission for the following academic terms: Fall. Applicants do not need a minimum number of credits to apply. **International students:** Number of foreign undergraduates: 17 (3% of student body). Number of countries represented: 7. Minimum TOEFL score required: 533 (paper); 73 (computer). Average TOEFL score: 570 (paper).

United States Military Academy

- **Address:** 600 Thayer Road, West Point, NY 10996-2101
- **Website:** http://www.usma.edu
- **Public**
- **Enrollment:** 4,621 full-time

KEY STATS
✔ **U.S News College Ranking:** 16, National Liberal Arts Colleges
✔ **SAT Score (25th/75th percentile):** 1140-1330
✔ **Tuition:** N/A

Selectivity: More selective	**Room/board:** $0
Acceptance rate: 15%	**Average debt:** N/A
Student/faculty ratio: 7/1	**Proportion who borrowed:** N/A

UNDERGRADUATE STUDENT BODY STATS
2009-2010 enrollment: 4,621 full-time. Men: 85%; women: 15%. **Ethnic makeup:** African American: 6%; American-Indian: 1%; Asian American: 7%; Hispanic: 9%; White: 76%; International: 1%. **Religious preference:** Roman Catholic: 35%; Protestant: 53%; Jewish: 1%; No preference: 7%; Unitarian, Buddhist, Hindu, not specified: 2%; Other: 2%.

ADMISSIONS FACTS AND FIGURES
Phone: (845) 938-4041. **Email:** admissions@usma.edu. **Website:** http://www.usma.edu. **Application deadlines for fall 2011:** Regular decision: February 28. Early decision: Not offered. Early action: Not offered. Admission cannot be deferred. **To apply online, go to:** https://candidate.usma.edu/guest/cq/dad_pcq_part1.cfm?field1=BW. **Admissions requirements/recommendations:** High school units required (recommended): English: (4); Mathematics: (4); Science: (4); Foreign language: (2); Social studies: (1); History: (1); Academic electives: (3); Total units: (19). Tests: The college uses SAT or ACT scores in admissions decisions. Either SAT or ACT required. For admission to the fall 2011 entering class, the school will accept: ACT with writing recommended. Campus visit: Recommended. Admissions interview: Recommended. Off-campus interview: May be arranged. **Factors that count in admissions decisions:** *Academic:* Secondary school record: Very Important. Class rank: Very Important. Letters of recommendation: Important. Standardized test scores: Very Important. Essay: Important. *Nonacademic:* Interview: Considered. Extracurricular activities: Very Important. Talent/ability: Important. Character/personal qualities: Very Important. Alumni/ae relationship: Not Considered. Geographical residence: Not Considered. State residency: Not Considered. Religious affiliation/commitment: Not Considered. Minority status: Important. Volunteer work: Considered. Work experience: Considered. **Other schools with the greatest overlap in applicants:** United States Air Force Academy; United States Coast Guard Academy; United States Merchant Marine Academy; United States Naval Academy. **Admissions statistics for the fall 2009 entering class:** Total applicants: 11,107. Total accepted: 1,640. Freshmen enrolled: 1,262; 97% were from out of state. Overall acceptance rate: 15%. **Credentials of fall 2009 freshmen:** 42% ranked in the top 10 percent of their high school class; 70% were in the top 25 percent; 94% were in the top half. (Proportion submitting class standing: 100%.) **First-year students who submitted SAT scores:** 86%. Scores (25/75 percentile): Critical Reading: 560-660, Math: 580-670, Combined: 1140-1330. **First-year students submitting ACT scores:** 70%. Scores (25/75 percentile): English: 25-31, Math: 26-30, Composite: 25-29.

ACADEMICS

Year founded: 1802. **Academic calendar:** Semester. **Degrees offered:** bachelor's. **Most popular majors:** 21% engineering, 19% social sciences, 10% foreign languages, literatures, and linguistics, 9% business, management, marketing, and related support services, 6% history. **Major fields of study:** computer and information sciences and support services; engineering; foreign languages, literatures, and linguistics; history; legal professions and studies; mathematics and statistics. **Areas of required coursework:** humanities, computer literacy, mathematics, English (including composition), philosophy, foreign languages, sciences (biological or physical), history, social science, other. **Pre-professional programs:** other. **Special academic programs (% participation):** double major (7%), exchange student program (domestic) (4%), honors program (20%), study abroad (13%). **Faculty and instruction (2009-2010):** Total instructional faculty: 625 (82% men; 18% women; 11% minorities). Full-time faculty with Ph.D. or other terminal degree: 44%. Student/faculty ratio: 7/1. Classes of fewer than 20 students: 96%; of 20 to 49 students: 4%; of 50 or more students: 0%. **Advanced Placement and International Baccalaureate credit:** AP tests may be used for: Placement only. Scores accepted: 4, 5. **Freshmen returning for sophomore year:** 91%. **Graduation rates:** Four-year: 80%; five-year: 81%; six-year: 82%. **Graduate study:** 2% of students pursue further study immediately upon graduation; 0% within one year; 0% within five years. Fields in which graduates pursue further study: medicine, 100%.

COSTS AND FINANCIAL AID

Financial aid office: (845) 938-4262. **Expenses (N/A):**

CAMPUS LIFE AND EXTRACURRICULAR ACTIVITIES

Campus housing available (% using): coed dorms (100%). Students who live in college-owned, operated, or affiliated housing: 100%. **Student employment:** During the 2009-2010 academic year, 0% of undergraduates worked on campus. Average per-year earnings: $0. **Clubs and organizations:** Number of student organizations: 116. Activities include: campus ministries, choral groups, drama/theater, international student organization, jazz band, literary magazine, music ensembles, pep band, radio station, student government, student newspaper, television station, yearbook. Number of fraternities: 0; sororities: 0. Average proportion of students who stay on campus on weekends: 90%. **Sports program (2009-2010):** Member of NCAA I. **Men's intercollegiate varsity sports:** baseball, basketball, cross country, football, golf, gymnastics, ice hockey, lacrosse, rifle, soccer, swimming, tennis, track and field (indoor), track and field (outdoor), wrestling. **Women's intercollegiate varsity sports:** basketball, cross country, rifle, soccer, softball, swimming, tennis, track and field (indoor), track and field (outdoor), volleyball.

SERVICES AND FACILITIES

Basic services: nonremedial tutoring, health service. **Remedial assistance:** reading, math, writing, study skills. **Counseling services:** minority student, military, personal, academic, psychological, birth control, religious. **Library:** Number of titles: 507,775; number of current serial subscriptions: 831. **Information technology resources:** Students are required to lease or own a computer. Number of campus computers available to all students: 5,195. School has a wireless network. Approximate number of users that can be accommodated: 6,000. Proportion of college-owned housing units wired for high-speed internet access: 100%. **Campus safety:** Security services offered: 24-hour foot-and-vehicle patrols, late-night transport/escort service, 24-hour emergency telephones, lighted pathways/sidewalks, controlled dormitory access (key, security card, etc).

TRANSFER AND INTERNATIONAL STUDENTS

International students: Number of foreign undergraduates: 57 (1% of student body). Number of countries represented: 37. Minimum TOEFL score required: 500 (paper); 75 (computer). Average TOEFL score: 588 (paper).

University at Albany–SUNY

- **Address:** 1400 Washington Avenue, Albany, NY 12222
- **Website:** http://www.albany.edu
- **Public**
- **Enrollment:** 12,319 full-time; 795 part-time

KEY STATS

- ✔ **U.S News College Ranking:** 143, National Universities
- ✔ **SAT Score (25th/75th percentile):** 1030-1210
- ✔ **Tuition:** 2009-2010: $6,748 in state, $14,648 out of state
- **Selectivity:** Selective **Room/board:** $10,238
- **Acceptance rate:** 47% **Average debt:** $22,092
- **Student/faculty ratio:** 19/1 **Proportion who borrowed:** 71%

UNDERGRADUATE STUDENT BODY STATS

2009-2010 enrollment: 12,319 full-time; 795 part-time. Men: 52%; women: 48%. **Ethnic makeup:** African American: 10%; Asian American: 6%; Hispanic: 9%; White: 71%; International: 3%.

ADMISSIONS FACTS AND FIGURES

Phone: (518) 442-5435. **Email:** ugadmissions@albany.edu. **Website:** http://www.albany.edu. **Application deadlines for fall 2011:** Regular decision: March 1. Early decision: Not offered. Early action: Send application by: November 15; Decision sent by: January 15. Admission can be deferred. **Application fee:** $50. **To apply online, go to:** http://www.applyweb.com/apply/suny31ud/. **Admissions requirements/recommendations:** High school units required (recommended): English: 4; Mathematics: 2 (4); Science: 2 (3); Foreign language: 1 (3); Social studies: 3; History: 2; Academic electives: 4; Total units: 18. Tests: The college uses SAT or ACT scores in admissions decisions. Either SAT or ACT required. For admission to the fall 2011 entering class, the school will accept: ACT with writing required. Campus visit: Recommended. **Factors that count in admissions decisions:** *Academic:* Secondary school record: Very Important. Class rank: Very Important. Letters of recommendation: Very Important. Standardized test scores: Very Important. Essay: Important. *Nonacademic:* Interview: Not Considered. Extracurricular activities: Considered. Talent/ability: Considered. Character/personal qualities: Very Important. Alumni/ae relationship: Considered. Geographical residence: Considered. State residency: Not Considered. Religious affiliation/commitment: Not Considered. Volunteer work: Considered. Work experience: Considered. **Other schools with the greatest overlap in applicants:** Binghamton University–SUNY; Buffalo State College–SUNY; SUNY–Stony Brook. **Admissions statistics for the fall 2009 entering class:** Total applicants: 22,188. Total accepted: 10,442. Freshmen enrolled: 2,333; 6% were from out of state. Overall acceptance rate: 47%. Non-early acceptance rate: 47%. **Credentials of fall 2009 freshmen:** 21% ranked in the top 10 percent of their high school class; 60% were in the top 25 percent; 94% were in the top half. (Proportion submitting class standing: 54%.) **Average high school grade point average:** 3.4. **First-year students who submitted SAT scores:** 95%. Scores (25/75 percentile): Critical Reading: 500-590, Math: 530-620, Combined: 1030-1210. **First-year students submitting ACT scores:** 26%. Scores (25/75 percentile): English: N/A, Math: N/A, Composite: 22-27.

ACADEMICS

Year founded: 1844. **Academic calendar:** Semester. **Degrees offered:** bachelor's, post-bachelor's certificate, master's, post-master's certificate, doctorate. **Most popular majors:** 23% social sciences, 16% business, management, marketing, and related support services, 12% psychology, 10% communication, journalism, and related programs, 7% history. **Major fields of study:** area, ethnic, cultural, and gender studies; biological and biomedical sciences; business, management, marketing, and related support services; communication, journalism, and related programs; computer and information sciences and support services; education; English language and literature/letters; foreign languages, literatures, and linguistics; history; liberal arts and sciences studies, and humanities; mathematics and statistics; multi/interdisciplinary studies; natural resources and conservation; philosophy and religious studies; physical sciences; psychology; public administration and social service professions; social sciences; visual and performing arts. **Areas of required coursework:** arts/fine arts, humanities, computer literacy, mathematics, foreign languages, sciences (biological or physical), history, social science, other. **Pre-professional programs:** pre-law, pre-dentistry, pre-medicine, pre-optometry, other. **Special academic programs:** accelerated program, cross-registration, distance learning, double major, dual enrollment, English as a Second Language (ESL), honors program, independent study, internships, liberal arts/career combination, student-designed major, study abroad, teacher certificate program, other. **Teacher certification offered in:** special education, elementary, middle/junior high, secondary. **Reserve Officers Training Corps (ROTC):** Army ROTC: Offered on campus; Air Force ROTC: Offered at cooperating institution (Rensselaer Polytechnic Institute). **Faculty and instruction (2009-2010):** Total instructional faculty: 637 full-time, 631 part-time (59% men; 41% women; 15% minorities). Full-time faculty with Ph.D. or other terminal degree: 95%. Student/faculty ratio: 19/1. Classes of fewer than 20 students: 20%; of 20 to 49 students: 55%; of 50 or more students: 24%. **Advanced Placement and International Baccalaureate credit:** AP tests may be used for: Credit and/or placement. Scores accepted: 3. International Baccalaureate exams may be used for: Placement only. **Freshmen returning for sophomore year:** 84%. **Graduation rates:** Four-year: 53%; five-year: 62%; six-year: 63%. **Graduate study:** 41% of students pursue further study immediately upon graduation. Fields in which graduates pursue further study: Master of Business Administration (MBA), 7%; law, 12%; medicine, 5%; education, 18%; arts and sciences, 29%.

COSTS AND FINANCIAL AID
Financial aid office: (518) 442-5757. **Expenses (2009-2010):** Tuition and fees 2009-2010: $6,748 in state, $14,648 out of state; room/board: $10,238. Estimated books and supplies: $1,600 personal expenses: $1,142. **Financial aid:** Priority filing date for institution's financial aid form: March 15. In 2009-2010, 78% of undergraduates applied for financial aid. Of those, 59% were determined to have financial need; 11% had their need fully met. Average financial aid package (proportion receiving): $9,649 (58%). Average amount of gift aid, such as scholarships or grants (proportion receiving): $6,398 (51%). Average amount of self-help aid, such as work study or loans (proportion receiving): $4,706 (48%). Average need-based loan (excluding PLUS or other private loans): $4,408. Among students who received need-based aid, the average percentage of need met: 68%. Among students who received aid based on merit, the average award (and the proportion receiving): $3,528 (5%). The average athletic scholarship (and the proportion receiving): $11,872 (2%). Average amount of debt of borrowers graduating in 2009: $22,092. Proportion who borrowed: 71%.

CAMPUS LIFE AND EXTRACURRICULAR ACTIVITIES
Campus housing available (% using): coed dorms (62%), women's dorms (1%), apartment for single students (22%), special housing for disabled students (2%), special housing for international students (1%). Students who live in college-owned, operated, or affiliated housing: 57%. **Clubs and organizations:** Number of student organizations: 160. Activities include: campus ministries, choral groups, concert band, dance, drama/theater, international student organization, jazz band, literary magazine, music ensembles, musical theater, pep band, radio station, student government, student newspaper, student film society, symphony orchestra, television station, yearbook. Number of fraternities: 14; sororities: 18. Proportion of men in fraternities: 2%; of women in sororities: 4%. Average proportion of students who stay on campus on weekends: 90%. **Sports program (2009-2010):** Member of NCAA I. *Men's intercollegiate varsity sports:* baseball, basketball, cross country, football, lacrosse, soccer, track and field (indoor), track and field (outdoor). *Women's intercollegiate varsity sports:* basketball, cross country, field hockey, golf, lacrosse, soccer, softball, tennis, track and field (indoor), track and field (outdoor), volleyball.

SERVICES AND FACILITIES
Basic services: nonremedial tutoring, placement service, day care, health service, health insurance, other. **Remedial assistance:** reading, math, writing, study skills, other. **Counseling services:** minority student, career, personal, academic, psychological, birth control, religious, other. **For learning-disabled students:** School does not offer a structured program with separate admission and additional fees. **Library:** Number of titles: 2,225,241; number of current serial subscriptions: 54,874. **Information technology resources:** Students are not required to lease or own a computer. Number of campus computers available to all students: 500. School has a wireless network. Approximate number of users that can be accommodated: 12,400. Proportion of college-owned housing units wired for high-speed internet access: 100%. **Campus safety:** Security services offered: 24-hour foot-and-vehicle patrols, late-night transport/escort service, 24-hour emergency telephones, lighted pathways/sidewalks, student patrols, controlled dormitory access (key, security card, etc).

TRANSFER AND INTERNATIONAL STUDENTS
Transfer students: May apply for admission for the following academic terms: Fall, Spring, Summer. Applicants need a minimum number of cred-

its to apply. For fall 2009: Transfer applications received: 5,040. Transfer applicants offered admission: 2,278. Transfer applicants enrolled: 1,369. **International students:** Number of foreign undergraduates: 350 (3% of student body). Number of countries represented: 340. Minimum TOEFL score required: 550 (paper); 79 (computer). Average TOEFL score: 550 (paper).

University at Buffalo–SUNY

- **Address:** 3435 Main Street, Buffalo, NY 14214
- **Website:** http://www.buffalo.edu
- **Public**
- **Enrollment:** 17,966 full-time; 1,402 part-time

KEY STATS
- ✔ **U.S News College Ranking:** 120, National Universities
- ✔ **SAT Score (25th/75th percentile):** 1060-1250
- ✔ **Tuition:** 2010-2011: $7,014 in state, $14,914 out of state

Selectivity: More selective	**Room/board:** $10,442
Acceptance rate: 52%	**Average debt:** $15,911
Student/faculty ratio: 16/1	**Proportion who borrowed:** 85%

UNDERGRADUATE STUDENT BODY STATS
2009-2010 enrollment: 17,966 full-time; 1,402 part-time. Men: 54%; women: 46%. **Ethnic makeup:** African American: 7%; Asian American: 10%; Hispanic: 3%; White: 67%; International: 13%.

ADMISSIONS FACTS AND FIGURES
Phone: (716) 645-6900. **Email:** ub-admissions@buffalo.edu. **Website:** http://www.buffalo.edu. **Application deadlines for fall 2011:** Regular decision: Rolling. Early decision: Send application by: November 1; Decision sent by: December 15. Early action: Not offered. Admission cannot be deferred. **Application fee:** $40. **To apply online, go to:** http://www.admissions.buffalo.edu/apply/. **Admissions requirements/recommendations:** High school units required (recommended): English: (4); Mathematics: (3); Science: (3); Foreign language: (3); Social studies: (4); Total units: (17). Tests: The college uses SAT or ACT scores in admissions decisions. Either SAT or ACT required. For admission to the fall 2011 entering class, the school will accept: ACT with writing required. Campus visit: Recommended. Admissions interview: Neither required nor recommended. Off-campus interview: May be arranged. **Factors that count in admissions decisions:** *Academic:* Secondary school record: Very Important. Class rank: Important. Letters of recommendation: Important. Standardized test scores: Very Important. Essay: Considered. *Nonacademic:* Interview: Important. Extracurricular activities: Considered. Talent/ability: Considered. Character/personal qualities: Considered. Alumni/ae relationship: Not Considered. Geographical residence: Considered. State residency: Not Considered. Religious affiliation/commitment: Not Considered. Minority status: Considered. Volunteer work: Considered. Work experience: Considered. **Other schools with the greatest overlap in applicants:** Binghamton University–SUNY; Cornell University; New York University; SUNY–Stony Brook; University at Albany–SUNY. **Admissions statistics for the fall 2009 entering class:** Total applicants: 21,137. Total accepted: 10,913. Freshmen enrolled: 3,194; 6% were from out of state. Overall acceptance rate: 52%. Non-early acceptance rate: 52%. **Size of waiting list:** 1163 applicants; enrolled from waiting list: 232. **Credentials of fall 2009 freshmen:** 28% ranked in the top 10 percent of their high school class; 65% were in the top 25 percent; 95% were in the top half. (Proportion submitting class standing: 47%.) **Average high school grade point average:** 3.3. **First-year students who submitted SAT scores:** 93%. Scores (25/75 percentile): Critical Reading: 510-600, Math: 550-650, Combined: 1060-1250. **First-year students submitting ACT scores:** 37%. Scores (25/75 percentile): English: N/A, Math: N/A, Composite: 23-28.

ACADEMICS
Year founded: 1846. **Academic calendar:** Semester. **Degrees offered:** certificate, bachelor's, master's, post-master's certificate, doctorate. **Most popular majors:** 21% business, management, marketing, and related support services, 15% social sciences, 10% engineering, 10% psychology, 9% biological and biomedical sciences. **Major fields of study:** architecture and related services; area, ethnic, cultural, and gender studies; biological and biomedical sciences; business, management, marketing, and related support services; communication, journalism, and related programs; computer and information sciences and support services; engineering; English language

and literature/letters; foreign languages, literatures, and linguistics; health professions and related clinical sciences; history; liberal arts and sciences studies, and humanities; mathematics and statistics; multi/interdisciplinary studies; parks, recreation, leisure, and fitness studies; philosophy and religious studies; physical sciences; psychology; social sciences; visual and performing arts. **Areas of required coursework:** arts/fine arts, humanities, computer literacy, mathematics, English (including composition), foreign languages, sciences (biological or physical), history, social science, other. **Pre-professional programs:** pre-law, pre-dentistry, pre-medicine, pre-veterinary science, pre-optometry, pre-pharmacy, other. **Special academic programs (% participation):** accelerated program, cooperative (work-study plan) program (2%), cross-registration (12%), distance learning (22%), double major (8%), dual enrollment (.1%), English as a Second Language (ESL) (9%), exchange student program (domestic), honors program (7%), independent study (16%), internships (22%), liberal arts/career combination, student-designed major (.4%), study abroad (7%), teacher certificate program (5%), other. **Teacher certification offered in:** early childhood, elementary, middle/junior high, secondary, bilingual/bicultural. **Cooperative education programs:** engineering. **Reserve Officers Training Corps (ROTC):** Army ROTC: Offered at cooperating institution (Canisius College). **Faculty and instruction (2009-2010):** Total instructional faculty: 1,209 full-time, 528 part-time (61% men; 39% women; 20% minorities). Full-time faculty with Ph.D. or other terminal degree: 94%. Student/faculty ratio: 16/1. Classes of fewer than 20 students: 38%; of 20 to 49 students: 43%; of 50 or more students: 20%. **Advanced Placement and International Baccalaureate credit:** AP tests may be used for: Credit and/or placement. Scores accepted: 3, 4, 5. International Baccalaureate exams may be used for: Credit and/or placement. **Freshmen returning for sophomore year:** 88%. **Graduation rates:** Four-year: 42%; five-year: 60%; six-year: 66%. **Graduate study:** 40% of students pursue further study within one year. Fields in which graduates pursue further study: Master of Business Administration (MBA), 10%; law, 8%; medicine, 5%; dentistry, 1%; engineering, 12%; education, 20%; arts and sciences, 22%.

COSTS AND FINANCIAL AID

Financial aid office: (866) 838-7257. **Expenses (2010-2011):** Tuition and fees 2010-2011: $7,014 in state, $14,914 out of state; room/board: $10,442. Estimated books and supplies: $1,004; transportation: $765; personal expenses: $1,142. **Financial aid:** Priority filing date for institution's financial aid form: March 1. In 2009-2010, 73% of undergraduates applied for financial aid. Of those, 54% were determined to have financial need; 33% had their need fully met. Average financial aid package (proportion receiving): $9,070 (48%). Average amount of gift aid, such as scholarships or grants (proportion receiving): $4,490 (32%). Average amount of self-help aid, such as work study or loans (proportion receiving): $4,452 (39%). Average need-based loan (excluding PLUS or other private loans): $4,305. Among students who received need-based aid, the average percentage of need met: 65%. Among students who received aid based on merit, the average award (and the proportion receiving): $3,335 (5%). The average athletic scholarship (and the proportion receiving): $12,180 (1%). Average amount of debt of borrowers graduating in 2009: $15,911. Proportion who borrowed: 85%.

CAMPUS LIFE AND EXTRACURRICULAR ACTIVITIES

Campus housing available (% using): coed dorms (85%), apartments for married students (0%), apartment for single students (14%), special housing for disabled students (1%), special housing for international students (0%), other housing options (0%). Students who live in college-owned, operated, or affiliated housing: 34%. **Clubs and organizations:** Number of student organizations: 215. Activities include: campus ministries, choral groups, concert band, dance, drama/theater, international student organization, jazz band, literary magazine, marching band, music ensembles, musical theater, pep band, radio station, student government, student newspaper, student film society, symphony orchestra, television station. Number of fraternities: 22; sororities: 17. Proportion of men in fraternities: 3%; of women in sororities: 4%. **Sports program (2009-2010):** Member of NCAA I. **Men's intercollegiate varsity sports:** baseball, basketball, cross country, football, soccer, swimming, tennis, track and field (indoor), track and field (outdoor), wrestling. **Women's intercollegiate varsity sports:** basketball, crew (heavyweight), cross country, crew (lightweight), soccer, softball, swimming, tennis, track and field (indoor), track and field (outdoor), volleyball.

SERVICES AND FACILITIES

Basic services: nonremedial tutoring, placement service, day care, health service, health insurance. **Remedial assistance:** reading, math, writing, study skills. **Counseling services:** minority student, career, military, personal, veteran student, academic, older student, psychological, birth control, religious.

For learning-disabled students: School does not offer a structured program with separate admission and additional fees. Services include: remedial math, remedial English, reading machines, remedial reading, tape recorders, note-taking services, oral tests, learning center, readers, extended time for tests, tutors, substitution of courses, texts on tape, other testing accommodations, other. **Library:** Number of titles: 3,852,074; number of current serial subscriptions: 79,944. **Information technology resources:** Students are not required to lease or own a computer. Number of campus computers available to all students: 2,000. School has a wireless network. Approximate number of users that can be accommodated: 10,000. Proportion of college-owned housing units wired for high-speed internet access: 100%. **Campus safety:** Security services offered: 24-hour foot-and-vehicle patrols, late-night transport/escort service, 24-hour emergency telephones, lighted pathways/sidewalks, student patrols, controlled dormitory access (key, security card, etc).

TRANSFER AND INTERNATIONAL STUDENTS

Transfer students: May apply for admission for the following academic terms: Fall, Spring. Applicants need a minimum number of credits to apply. For fall 2009: Transfer applications received: 5,535. Transfer applicants offered admission: 3,367. Transfer applicants enrolled: 1,735. **International students:** Number of foreign undergraduates: 2521 (13% of student body). Number of countries represented: 85. Minimum TOEFL score required: 550 (paper); 79 (computer). Average TOEFL score: 550 (paper).

University of Rochester

- **Address:** Wilson Boulevard, Rochester, NY 14627
- **Website:** http://www.rochester.edu
- **Private**
- **Enrollment:** 5,193 full-time; 254 part-time

KEY STATS
- ✔ **U.S News College Ranking:** 37, National Universities
- ✔ **SAT Score (25th/75th percentile):** 1230-1410
- ✔ **Tuition:** 2010-2011: $40,282

Selectivity: Most selective	**Room/board:** $11,640
Acceptance rate: 39%	**Average debt:** $27,121
Student/faculty ratio: 10/1	**Proportion who borrowed:** 55%

UNDERGRADUATE STUDENT BODY STATS

2009-2010 enrollment: 5,193 full-time; 254 part-time. Men: 48%; women: 52%. **Ethnic makeup:** African American: 4%; Asian American: 10%; Hispanic: 4%; White: 74%; International: 8%.

ADMISSIONS FACTS AND FIGURES

Phone: (585) 275-3221. **Email:** admit@admissions.rochester.edu. **Website:** http://www.rochester.edu. **Application deadlines for fall 2011:** Regular decision: January 1; decision sent by April 1. Early decision: Send application by: November 1; Decision sent by: December 15. Early action: Not offered. Admission can be deferred. **Application fee:** $60. **To apply online, go to:** http://enrollment.rochester.edu/admissions. **Admissions requirements/recommendations:** High school units required (recommended): Total units: 32. Tests: The college uses SAT or ACT scores in admissions decisions. Either SAT or ACT required. For admission to the fall 2011 entering class, the school will accept: ACT with or without writing accepted. Campus visit: Recommended. Admissions interview: Recommended. Off-campus interview: May be arranged. **Factors that count in admissions decisions: _Academic:_** Secondary school record: Very Important. Class rank: Considered. Letters of recommendation: Very Important. Standardized test scores: Important. Essay: Important. **_Nonacademic:_** Interview: Important. Extracurricular activities: Important. Talent/ability: Important. Character/personal qualities: Very Important. Alumni/ae relationship: Considered. Geographical residence: Considered. State residency: Not Considered. Religious affiliation/commitment: Not Considered. Minority status: Considered. Volunteer work: Considered. Work experience: Considered. **Other schools with the greatest overlap in applicants:** Binghamton University–SUNY; Boston University; Brown University; Cornell University; Tufts University. **Admissions statistics for the fall 2009 entering class:** Total applicants: 12,111. Total accepted: 4,686. Freshmen enrolled: 1,087; 52% were from out of state. Accepted through early-decision or early-action plans: 25%. Overall acceptance rate: 39%. Early-decision acceptance rate: 39%. Non-early acceptance rate: 39%. **Size of waiting list:** 1243 applicants;

enrolled from waiting list: 71. **Credentials of fall 2009 freshmen:** 76% ranked in the top 10 percent of their high school class; 91% were in the top 25 percent; 99% were in the top half. (Proportion submitting class standing: 41%.) **Average high school grade point average:** 3.8. **First-year students who submitted SAT scores:** 91%. Scores (25/75 percentile): Critical Reading: 590-690, Math: 640-720, Combined: 1230-1410. **First-year students submitting ACT scores:** 46%. Scores (25/75 percentile): English: 27-33, Math: 28-33, Composite: 28-33.

ACADEMICS

Year founded: 1850. **Academic calendar:** Semester. **Degrees offered:** bachelor's, post-bachelor's certificate, master's, post-master's certificate, doctorate. **Most popular majors:** 19% social sciences, 12% biological and biomedical sciences, 12% psychology, 11% visual and performing arts, 9% health professions and related clinical sciences. **Major fields of study:** area, ethnic, cultural, and gender studies; biological and biomedical sciences; computer and information sciences and support services; education; engineering; English language and literature/letters; foreign languages, literatures, and linguistics; health professions and related clinical sciences; history; liberal arts and sciences studies, and humanities; mathematics and statistics; natural resources and conservation; philosophy and religious studies; physical sciences; psychology; social sciences; visual and performing arts. **Areas of required coursework:** humanities, sciences (biological or physical), social science, other. **Pre-professional programs:** pre-dentistry, pre-medicine, pre-veterinary science. **Special academic programs (% participation):** accelerated program (0%), cooperative (work-study plan) program (0%), cross-registration (8%), double major (18%), dual enrollment (2%), English as a Second Language (ESL) (0%), honors program (52%), independent study (36%), internships (13%), liberal arts/career combination (3%), student-designed major (2%), study abroad (23%), teacher certificate program (2%), other (13%). **Teacher certification offered in:** early childhood, special education, elementary, middle/junior high, secondary. **Cooperative education programs:** engineering. **Reserve Officers Training Corps (ROTC):** Army ROTC: Offered at cooperating institution (Rochester Institute of Technology); Navy ROTC: Offered on campus; Air Force ROTC: Offered at cooperating institution (Rochester Institute of Technology). **Faculty and instruction (2009-2010):** Total instructional faculty: 530 full-time, 291 part-time (64% men; 36% women; 11% minorities). Full-time faculty with Ph.D. or other terminal degree: 89%. Student/faculty ratio: 10/1. Classes of fewer than 20 students: 59%; of 20 to 49 students: 28%; of 50 or more students: 13%. **Advanced Placement and International Baccalaureate credit:** AP tests may be used for: Credit and/or placement. Scores accepted: 4, 5. International Baccalaureate exams may be used for: Credit and/or placement. **Freshmen returning for sophomore year:** 95%. **Graduation rates:** Four-year: 69%; five-year: 79%; six-year: 80%. **Graduate study:** 34% of students pursue further study immediately upon graduation; 58% within one year; 92% within five years. Fields in which graduates pursue further study: Master of Business Administration (MBA), 6%; law, 19%; medicine, 19%; dentistry, 2%; engineering, 15%; theology (or the seminary), 2%; education, 4%; arts and sciences, 32%; veterinary medicine, 1%.

COSTS AND FINANCIAL AID

Financial aid office: (585) 275-3226. **Expenses (2010-2011):** Tuition and fees 2010-2011: $40,282; room/board: $11,640. Estimated books and supplies: $1,250; transportation: $500; personal expenses: $1,058. **Financial aid:** Priority filing date for institution's financial aid form: February 1. In 2009-2010, 65% of undergraduates applied for financial aid. Of those, 57% were determined to have financial need; 80% had their need fully met. Average financial aid package (proportion receiving): $32,203 (57%). Average amount of gift aid, such as scholarships or grants (proportion receiving): $26,741 (57%). Average amount of self-help aid, such as work study or loans (proportion receiving): $6,401 (51%). Average need-based loan (excluding PLUS or other private loans): $4,808. Among students who received need-based aid, the average percentage of need met: 96%. Among students who received aid based on merit, the average award (and the proportion receiving): $9,508 (31%). Average amount of debt of borrowers graduating in 2009: $27,121. Proportion who borrowed: 55%.

CAMPUS LIFE AND EXTRACURRICULAR ACTIVITIES

Campus housing available: coed dorms, sorority housing, fraternity housing, apartment for single students, special housing for disabled students, other housing options. Students who live in college-owned, operated, or affiliated housing: 81%. **Student employment:** During the 2009-2010 academic year, 45% of undergraduates worked on campus. Average per-year earnings: $2,500. **Clubs and organizations:** Number of student organizations: 237. Activities include: campus ministries, choral groups, concert band,

dance, drama/theater, international student organization, jazz band, literary magazine, model UN, music ensembles, musical theater, opera, pep band, radio station, student government, student newspaper, student film society, symphony orchestra, television station, yearbook. Number of fraternities: 18; sororities: 14. Proportion of men in fraternities: 8%; of women in sororities: 5%. Average proportion of students who stay on campus on weekends: 90%. **Sports program (2009-2010):** Member of NCAA III. *Men's intercollegiate varsity sports:* baseball, basketball, cross country, football, golf, soccer, swimming, tennis, track and field (indoor), track and field (outdoor). *Women's intercollegiate varsity sports:* basketball, crew (heavyweight), cross country, field hockey, lacrosse, crew (lightweight), soccer, softball, swimming, tennis, track and field (indoor), track and field (outdoor), volleyball.

SERVICES AND FACILITIES

Basic services: nonremedial tutoring, health service, health insurance. **Remedial assistance:** study skills. **Counseling services:** minority student, career, personal, academic, psychological, birth control, religious. **For learning-disabled students:** School does not offer a structured program with separate admission and additional fees. Total undergraduates in learning-disabled program or receiving services: 151. Services include: reading machines, note-taking services, oral tests, learning center, readers, extended time for tests, tutors, early syllabus, priority registration, priority seating, texts on tape, typist/scribe, exams on tape or computer, other testing accommodations, other. **Library:** Number of titles: 3,715,385; number of current serial subscriptions: 36,033. **Information technology resources:** Students are not required to lease or own a computer. Number of campus computers available to all students: 447. School has a wireless network. Approximate number of users that can be accommodated: 4,000. Proportion of college-owned housing units wired for high-speed internet access: 100%. **Campus safety:** Security services offered: 24-hour foot-and-vehicle patrols, late-night transport/escort service, 24-hour emergency telephones, lighted pathways/sidewalks, student patrols, controlled dormitory access (key, security card, etc).

TRANSFER AND INTERNATIONAL STUDENTS

Transfer students: May apply for admission for the following academic terms: Fall, Spring. Applicants do not need a minimum number of credits to apply. For fall 2009: Transfer applications received: 936. Transfer applicants offered admission: 198. Transfer applicants enrolled: 89. **International students:** Number of foreign undergraduates: 400 (8% of student body). Number of countries represented: 40. Minimum TOEFL score required: 600 (paper); 100 (computer). Average TOEFL score: 619 (paper).

Utica College

- **Address:** 1600 Burrstone Road, Utica, NY 13502
- **Website:** http://www.utica.edu
- **Private**
- **Enrollment:** 2,064 full-time; 473 part-time

KEY STATS

✔ **U.S News College Ranking:** 105, Regional Universities (North)
✔ **SAT Score (25th/75th percentile):** 830-1030
✔ **Tuition:** 2010-2011: $28,620

Selectivity: Less selective	**Room/board:** $11,590
Acceptance rate: 78%	**Average debt:** $35,534
Student/faculty ratio: 11/1	**Proportion who borrowed:** 86%

UNDERGRADUATE STUDENT BODY STATS

2009-2010 enrollment: 2,064 full-time; 473 part-time. Men: 43%; women: 57%. **Ethnic makeup:** African American: 11%; American-Indian: 1%; Asian American: 2%; Hispanic: 4%; White: 80%; International: 2%.

ADMISSIONS FACTS AND FIGURES

Phone: (315) 792-3006. **Email:** admiss@utica.edu. **Website:** http://www.utica.edu. **Application deadlines for fall 2011:** Regular decision: Rolling. Early decision: Not offered. Early action: Not offered. Admission can be deferred. **Application fee:** $40. **To apply online, go to:** https://apply.embark.com/ugrad/utica/65/. **Admissions requirements/recommendations:** High school units required (recommended): English: 4; Mathematics: 3; Science: 3; Foreign language: 2; Social studies: 3; Academic electives: 1; Total units: 16. Tests: The college uses SAT or ACT scores in admissions decisions. Neither SAT nor ACT required. For admission to the fall 2011 entering class, the school will accept: ACT with or without writing accepted. Campus visit: Recommended. Admissions interview: Recommended. Off-campus interview: May be arranged. **Factors that count in admissions decisions:** *Academic:* Secondary school record: Very Important. Class rank: Considered. Letters of recommendation: Important. Standardized test scores: Considered. Essay: Important. *Nonacademic:* Interview: Important. Extracurricular activities: Important. Talent/ability: Important. Character/personal qualities: Important. Alumni/ae relationship: Considered. Geographical residence: Not Considered. State residency: Not Considered. Religious affiliation/commitment: Not Considered. Minority status: Not Considered. Volunteer work: Important. Work experience: Important. **Other schools with the greatest overlap in applicants:** Ithaca College; Le Moyne College; Nazareth College; SUNY–Oswego; St. John Fisher College. **Admissions statistics for the fall 2009 entering class:** Total applicants: 2,930. Total accepted: 2,297. Freshmen enrolled: 565; 18% were from out of state. Overall acceptance rate: 78%. **Size of waiting list:** 0 applicants; enrolled from waiting list: 0. **Credentials of fall 2009 freshmen:** 8% ranked in the top 10 percent of their high school class; 30% were in the top 25 percent; 63% were in the top half. (Proportion submitting class standing: 63%.) **Average high school grade point average:** 2.9. **First-year students who submitted SAT scores:** 84%. Scores (25/75 percentile): Critical Reading: 410-510, Math: 420-520, Combined: 830-1030. **First-year students submitting ACT scores:** 18%. Scores (25/75 percentile): English: 16-22, Math: 17-24, Composite: 18-23.

ACADEMICS

Year founded: 1946. **Academic calendar:** Semester. **Degrees offered:** certificate, bachelor's, post-bachelor's certificate, master's. **Most popular majors:** 22% health professions and related clinical sciences, 20% security and protective services, 14% business, management, marketing, and related support services, 11% psychology, 8% communication, journalism, and related programs. **Major fields of study:** biological and biomedical sciences; business, management, marketing, and related support services; communication, journalism, and related programs; computer and information sciences and support services; English language and literature/letters; health professions and related clinical sciences; history; liberal arts and sciences studies, and humanities; mathematics and statistics; philosophy and religious studies; physical sciences; psychology; security and protective services; social sciences. **Areas of required coursework:** arts/fine arts, humanities, mathematics, English (including composition), philosophy, foreign languages, sciences (biological or physical), history, social science. **Pre-professional programs:** pre-law, pre-dentistry, pre-medicine, pre-veterinary science, pre-optometry, other. **Special academic programs (% participation):** accelerated program (1%), cooperative (work-study plan) program (1%), cross-registration (1%), distance learning (2%), double major (1%), dual enrollment (1%), exchange student program (domestic) (1%), honors program (2%), independent study (1%), internships (3%), liberal arts/career combination (1%), study abroad (1%), teacher certificate program (14%), weekend college (1%). **Teacher certification offered in:** early childhood, special education, elementary, middle/junior high, secondary. **Cooperative education programs:** art, business, computer science, education, health professions, humanities, natural science, social/behavioral science, technologies. **Reserve Officers Training Corps (ROTC):** Army ROTC: Offered on campus; Air Force ROTC: Offered at cooperating institution (Syracuse University). **Faculty and instruction (2009-2010):** Total instructional faculty: 131 full-time, 212 part-time (54% men; 46% women). Full-time faculty with Ph.D. or other terminal degree: 86%. Student/faculty ratio: 11/1. Classes of fewer than 20 students: 74%; of 20 to 49 students: 26%; of 50 or more students: 0%. **Advanced Placement and International Baccalaureate credit:** AP tests may be used for: Placement only. Scores accepted: 3, 4, 5. International Baccalaureate exams may be used for: Placement only. **Freshmen returning for sophomore year:** 67%. **Graduation rates:** Four-year: 38%; five-year: 49%; six-year: 49%. **Graduate study:** 13% of students pursue further study within one year. Fields in which graduates pursue further study: medicine, 1%.

COSTS AND FINANCIAL AID

Financial aid office: (315) 792-3179. **Expenses (2010-2011):** Tuition and fees 2010-2011: $28,620; room/board: $11,590. Estimated books and supplies: $1,028; transportation: $858; personal expenses: $870. **Financial aid:** Priority filing date for institution's financial aid form: February 15. In 2009-2010, 97% of undergraduates applied for financial aid. Of those, 91% were determined to have financial need; 11% had their need fully met. Average financial aid package (proportion receiving): $20,690 (91%). Average amount of gift aid, such as scholarships or grants (proportion receiving): $7,886 (90%). Average amount of self-help aid, such as work study or loans (proportion receiving): $4,791 (83%). Average need-based loan (excluding PLUS or other private loans): $4,300. Among students who received need-based aid, the average percentage of need met: 68%. Among students who received aid based on merit, the average award (and the proportion receiving): $9,954 (7%). The average athletic scholarship (and the proportion receiving): $0 (0%). Average amount of debt of borrowers graduating in 2009: $35,534. Proportion who borrowed: 86%.

CAMPUS LIFE AND EXTRACURRICULAR ACTIVITIES

Campus housing available (% using): coed dorms (61%), apartment for single students (8%), special housing for disabled students (2%), special housing for international students (2%), other housing options (27%). Students who live in college-owned, operated, or affiliated housing: 43%. **Student employment:** During the 2009-2010 academic year, 6% of undergraduates worked on campus. Average per-year earnings: $1,309. **Clubs and organizations:** Number of student organizations: 80. Activities include: choral groups, concert band, dance, drama/theater, literary magazine, radio station, student government, student newspaper, student film society, yearbook. Number of fraternities: 4; sororities: 4. Proportion of men in fraternities: 1%; of women in sororities: 1%. Average proportion of students who stay on campus on weekends: 65%. **Sports program (2009-2010):** Member of NCAA III. *Men's intercollegiate varsity sports:* baseball, basketball, cross country, football, golf, ice hockey, lacrosse, soccer, swimming, tennis. *Women's intercollegiate varsity sports:* basketball, cross country, field hockey, golf, ice hockey, lacrosse, soccer, softball, swimming, tennis, volleyball, water polo.

SERVICES AND FACILITIES

Basic services: women's center, placement service, health service, health insurance. **Remedial assistance:** math, writing, study skills. **Counseling services:** minority student, career, military, personal, veteran student, academic, older student, birth control, religious. **For learning-disabled students:** School does not offer a structured program with separate admission and additional fees. Services include: tutors, priority registration. **Library:** Number of titles: 178,804; number of current serial subscriptions: 1,480. **Information technology resources:** Students are not required to lease or own a computer. Number of campus computers available to all students: 246. School has a wireless network. Approximate number of users that can be accommodated: 500. Proportion of college-owned housing units wired for high-speed internet access: 100%. **Campus safety:** Security services offered: 24-hour foot-and-vehicle patrols, late-night transport/escort service, 24-hour emergency telephones, lighted pathways/sidewalks, controlled dormitory access (key, security card, etc.).

TRANSFER AND INTERNATIONAL STUDENTS

Transfer students: May apply for admission for the following academic terms: Fall, Spring, Summer. Applicants need a minimum number of credits to apply. For fall 2009: Transfer applications received: 537. Transfer applicants offered admission: 372. Transfer applicants enrolled: 156. **International students:** Number of foreign undergraduates: 57 (2% of student body). Number of countries represented: 21. Minimum TOEFL score required: 525 (paper); 195 (computer). Average TOEFL score: 620 (paper).

Vassar College

- **Address:** 124 Raymond Avenue, Poughkeepsie, NY 12604
- **Website:** http://www.vassar.edu
- **Private**
- **Enrollment:** 2,394 full-time; 58 part-time

KEY STATS

✔ **U.S News College Ranking:** 12, National Liberal Arts Colleges
✔ **SAT Score (25th/75th percentile):** 1300-1470
✔ **Tuition:** 2010-2011: $43,190

Selectivity: Most selective	**Room/board:** $10,080
Acceptance rate: 25%	**Average debt:** $18,876
Student/faculty ratio: 8/1	**Proportion who borrowed:** 49%

UNDERGRADUATE STUDENT BODY STATS

2009-2010 enrollment: 2,394 full-time; 58 part-time. Men: 41%; women: 59%. **Ethnic makeup:** African American: 5%; Asian American: 11%; Hispanic: 7%; White: 70%; International: 6%.

ADMISSIONS FACTS AND FIGURES

Phone: (845) 437-7300. **Email:** admission@vassar.edu. **Website:** http://www.vassar.edu. **Application deadlines for fall 2011:** Regular decision: January 1; decision sent by April 1. Early decision: Send application by: November 15; Decision sent by: December 15. Early action: Not offered. Admission can be deferred. **Application fee:** $60. **To apply online, go to:** http://admissions.vassar.edu/apply.html. **Admissions requirements/recommendations:** High school units required (recommended): English: (4); Mathematics: (4); Science: (4); Foreign language: (4); Social studies: (2); History: (2); Total units: (20). Tests: The college uses SAT or ACT scores in admissions decisions. Either SAT or ACT required. For admission to the fall 2011 entering class, the school will accept: ACT with writing required. Campus visit: Recommended. Admissions interview: Neither required nor recommended. Off-campus interview: May be arranged. **Factors that count in admissions decisions:** *Academic:* Secondary school record: Very Important. Class rank: Important. Letters of recommendation: Important. Standardized test scores: Important. Essay: Important. *Nonacademic:* Interview: Considered. Extracurricular activities: Considered. Talent/ability: Considered. Character/personal qualities: Important. Alumni/ae relationship: Considered. Geographical residence: Considered. State residency: Not Considered. Religious affiliation/commitment: Not Considered. Minority status: Considered. Volunteer work: Considered. Work experience: Considered. **Other schools with the greatest overlap in applicants:** Brown University; Columbia University; Wellesley College; Wesleyan University. **Admissions statistics for the fall 2009 entering class:** Total applicants: 7,577. Total accepted: 1,873. Freshmen enrolled: 660; 76% were from out of state. Accepted through early-decision or early-action plans: 39%. Overall acceptance rate: 25%. Early-decision acceptance rate: 43%. Non-early acceptance rate: 23%. **Size of waiting list:** 1531 applicants; enrolled from waiting list: 52. **Credentials of fall 2009 freshmen:** 67% ranked in the top 10 percent of their high school class; 95% were in the top 25 percent; 99% were in the top half. (Proportion submitting class standing: 63%.) **Average high school grade point average:** 3.8. **First-year students who submitted SAT scores:** 81%. Scores (25/75 percentile): Critical Reading: 660-750, Math: 640-720, Combined: 1300-1470. **First-year students submitting ACT scores:** 35%. Scores (25/75 percentile): English: N/A, Math: N/A, Composite: 29-32.

ACADEMICS

Year founded: 1861. **Academic calendar:** Semester. **Degrees offered:** bachelor's, master's. **Most popular majors:** 28% social sciences, 13% visual and performing arts, 9% foreign languages, literatures, and linguistics, 8% English language and literature/letters, 8% psychology. **Major fields of study:** area, ethnic, cultural, and gender studies; biological and biomedical sciences; computer and information sciences and support services; education; English language and literature/letters; foreign languages, literatures, and linguistics; history; liberal arts and sciences studies, and humanities; mathematics and statistics; multi/interdisciplinary studies; natural resources and conservation; philosophy and religious studies; physical sciences; psychology; social sciences; visual and performing arts. **Areas of required coursework:** English (including composition), foreign languages, other. **Pre-professional programs:** pre-law, pre-dentistry, pre-medicine, pre-veterinary science. **Special academic programs (% participation):** cross-registration (1%), double major (18%), exchange student program (domestic) (2%), independent study (51%), internships (61%), student-designed major (1%), study abroad (44%), teacher certificate program (1%). **Teacher certification offered in:** elementary, secondary. **Faculty and instruction (2009-2010):** Total instructional faculty: 296 full-time, 32 part-time (51% men; 49% women; 23% minorities). Full-time faculty with Ph.D. or other terminal degree: 89%. Student/faculty ratio: 8/1. Classes of fewer than 20 students: 67%; of 20 to 49 students: 33%; of 50 or more students: 0%. **Advanced Placement and International Baccalaureate credit:** AP tests may be used for: Credit and/or placement. Scores accepted: 4, 5. International Baccalaureate exams may be used for: Credit and/or placement. **Freshmen returning for sophomore year:** 96%. **Graduation rates:** Four-year: 88%; five-year: 92%; six-year: 92%. **Graduate study:** 23% of students pursue further study immediately upon graduation; 55% within five years. Fields in which graduates pursue further study: Master of Business Administration (MBA), 7%; law, 17%; medicine, 10%; dentistry, 1%; engineering, 1%; theology (or the seminary), 1%; education, 8%; arts and sciences, 56%; veterinary medicine, 1%.

COSTS AND FINANCIAL AID

Financial aid office: (845) 437-5320. **Expenses (2010-2011):** Tuition and fees 2010-2011: $43,190; room/board: $10,080. Estimated books and supplies: $860; transportation: $540; personal expenses: $1,290. **Financial aid:** Priority filing date for institution's financial aid form: February 15; deadline: February 15. In 2009-2010, 64% of undergraduates applied for financial aid. Of those, 56% were determined to have financial need; 100% had their need fully met. Average financial aid package (proportion receiving): $37,512 (56%). Average amount of gift aid, such as scholarships or grants (proportion receiving): $33,155 (56%). Average amount of self-help aid, such as work study or loans (proportion receiving): $4,357 (56%). Average need-based loan (excluding PLUS or other private loans): $2,614. Among students who received need-based aid, the average percentage of need met: 100%. Among students who received aid based on merit, the average award (and the proportion receiving): $0 (0%). The average athletic scholarship (and the proportion receiving): $0 (0%). Average amount of debt of borrowers graduating in 2009: $18,876. Proportion who borrowed: 49%.

CAMPUS LIFE AND EXTRACURRICULAR ACTIVITIES

Campus housing available (% using): coed dorms (67%), women's dorms (5%), apartment for single students (20%), special housing for disabled students (0%), cooperative housing (2%). Students who live in college-owned, operated, or affiliated housing: 95%. **Student employment:** During the 2009-2010 academic year, 70% of undergraduates worked on campus. Average per-year earnings: $1,540. **Clubs and organizations:** Number of student organizations: 105. Activities include: campus ministries, choral groups, concert band, dance, drama/theater, international student organization, jazz band, literary magazine, model UN, music ensembles, musical theater, opera, radio station, student government, student newspaper, student film society, symphony orchestra, television station, yearbook. Number of fraternities: 0; sororities: 0. Average proportion of students who stay on campus on weekends: 90%. **Sports program (2009-2010):** Member of NCAA III. *Men's intercollegiate varsity sports:* baseball, basketball, cross country, fencing, lacrosse, soccer, swimming, tennis, volleyball. *Women's intercollegiate varsity sports:* basketball, cross country, fencing, field hockey, golf, lacrosse, crew (lightweight), soccer, squash, swimming, tennis, volleyball.

SERVICES AND FACILITIES

Basic services: nonremedial tutoring, women's center, placement service, health service, health insurance. **Remedial assistance:** reading, math, writing, study skills. **Counseling services:** minority student, career, personal, veteran student, academic, older student, psychological, birth control, religious. **For learning-disabled students:** School does not offer a structured program with separate admission and additional fees. Total undergraduates in learning-disabled program or receiving services: 82. Services include: reading machines, tape recorders, note-taking services, learning center, extended time for tests, early syllabus, priority registration, priority seating, substitution of courses, texts on tape, exams on tape or computer, other testing accommodations. **Library:** Number of titles: 967,820; number of current serial subscriptions: 12,306. **Information technology resources:** Students are not required to lease or own a computer. Number of campus computers available to all students: 350. School has a wireless network. Approximate number of users that can be accommodated: 3,500. Proportion of college-owned housing units wired for high-speed internet access: 100%. **Campus safety:** Security services offered: 24-hour foot-and-vehicle patrols, late-night transport/escort service, 24-hour emergency telephones, lighted pathways/sidewalks, student patrols, controlled dormitory access (key, security card, etc).

TRANSFER AND INTERNATIONAL STUDENTS

Transfer students: May apply for admission for the following academic terms: Fall, Spring. Applicants do not need a minimum number of credits to apply. For fall 2009: Transfer applications received: 315. Transfer applicants offered admission: 28. Transfer applicants enrolled: 3. **International students:** Number of foreign undergraduates: 150 (6% of student body). Number of countries represented: 50. Minimum TOEFL score required: 600 (paper); 250 (computer). Average TOEFL score: 640 (paper).

Vaughn College of Aeronautics and Tech.

- **Address:** 86-01 23rd Avenue, Flushing, NY 11369
- **Website:** http://www.vaughn.edu
- **Private**
- **Enrollment:** 935 full-time; 359 part-time

KEY STATS

✔ **U.S News College Ranking:** 36, Regional Colleges (North)

✔ **SAT Score (25th/75th percentile):** 911-1088

✔ **Tuition:** 2010-2011: $17,595

Selectivity: Less selective	**Room/board:** $11,025
Acceptance rate: 92%	**Average debt:** $21,432
Student/faculty ratio: 15/1	**Proportion who borrowed:** 78%

UNDERGRADUATE STUDENT BODY STATS

2009-2010 enrollment: 935 full-time; 359 part-time. Men: 88%; women: 12%. **Ethnic makeup:** African American: 21%; American-Indian: 1%; Asian American: 12%; Hispanic: 38%; White: 26%; International: 2%.

ADMISSIONS FACTS AND FIGURES

Phone: (718) 429-6600. **Email:** admitme@vaughn.edu. **Website:** http://www.vaughn.edu. **Application deadlines for fall 2011:** Regular decision: Rolling. Early decision: Not offered. Early action: Not offered. Admission can be deferred. **Application fee:** $40. **To apply online, go to:** http://www.vaughn.edu/admissions_app.php. **Admissions requirements/recommendations:** High school units required (recommended): English: 4 (4); Mathematics: 3 (4); Science: 2 (4); Foreign language: 2 (3); Social studies: 2 (4); History: 1 (1); Academic electives: 0 (0); Total units: 14 (18). Tests: The college uses SAT or ACT scores in admissions decisions. SAT required. For admission to the fall 2011 entering class, the school will accept: ACT with writing required. Campus visit: Recommended. Admissions interview: Recommended. Off-campus interview: May be arranged. **Factors that count in admissions decisions:** *Academic:* Secondary school record: Very Important. Class rank: Not Considered. Letters of recommendation: Considered. Standardized test scores: Important. Essay: Considered. *Nonacademic:* Interview: Considered. Extracurricular activities: Considered. Talent/ability: Considered. Character/personal qualities: Considered. Alumni/ae relationship: Considered. Geographical residence: Not Considered. State residency: Not Considered. Religious affiliation/commitment: Not Considered. Minority status: Not Considered. Volunteer work: Considered. Work experience: Considered. **Other schools with the greatest overlap in applicants:** Dowling College; Embry-Riddle Aeronautical University; Farmingdale State College–SUNY; New York Institute of Technology; Polytechnic Institute of New York University. **Admissions statistics for the fall 2009 entering class:** Total applicants: 492. Total accepted: 454. Freshmen enrolled: 262; 10% were from out of state. Overall acceptance rate: 92%. **Average high school grade point average:** 2.9. **First-year students who submitted SAT scores:** 100%. Scores (25/75 percentile): Critical Reading: 440-536, Math: 471-552, Combined: 911-1088.

ACADEMICS

Year founded: 1932. **Academic calendar:** Semester. **Degrees offered:** certificate, associate, bachelor's, master's. **Most popular majors:** 48% aviation/airway management and operations, 30% airframe mechanics and aircraft maintenance technology/technician, 17% electrical and electronic engineering technologies/technicians, 3% computer graphics, 2% business administration and management. **Major fields of study:** engineering technologies/technicians; mechanic and repair technologies/technicians; transportation and materials moving. **Areas of required coursework:** humanities, mathematics, English (including composition), foreign languages, sciences (biological or physical), history. **Special academic programs:** cooperative (work-study plan) program, distance learning, double major, independent study, internships. **Reserve Officers Training Corps (ROTC):** Army ROTC: Offered at cooperating institution (St. John's University); Air Force ROTC: Offered at cooperating institution (Manhattan College). **Faculty and instruction (2009-2010):** Total instructional faculty: 39 full-time, 94 part-time (85% men; 15% women; 42% minorities). Full-time faculty with Ph.D. or other terminal degree: 36%. Student/faculty ratio: 15/1. Classes of fewer than 20 students: 60%; of 20 to 49 students: 40%. **Advanced Placement and International Baccalaureate credit:** AP tests may be used for: Credit and/or placement. Scores accepted: 3, 4, 5. International Baccalaureate exams may be used for: Credit and/or placement. **Freshmen returning for sophomore year:** 75%. **Graduation rates:** Four-year: 31%; five-year: 48%; six-year: 42%.

Graduate study: 5% of students pursue further study immediately upon graduation; 78% within one year. Fields in which graduates pursue further study: Master of Business Administration (MBA), 80%; engineering, 20%.

COSTS AND FINANCIAL AID

Financial aid office: (718) 429-6600. **Expenses (2010-2011):** Tuition and fees 2010-2011: $17,595; room/board: $11,025. Estimated books and supplies: $1,500; transportation: $800; personal expenses: $3,000. **Financial aid:** Priority filing date for institution's financial aid form: January 15. In 2009-2010, 96% of undergraduates applied for financial aid. Of those, 96% were determined to have financial need; 47% had their need fully met. Average financial aid package (proportion receiving): $20,950 (96%). Average amount of gift aid, such as scholarships or grants (proportion receiving): $2,950 (70%). Average amount of self-help aid, such as work study or loans (proportion receiving): $3,250 (89%). Average need-based loan (excluding PLUS or other private loans): $1,750. Among students who received need-based aid, the average percentage of need met: 85%. Among students who received aid based on merit, the average award (and the proportion receiving): $2,200 (27%). Average amount of debt of borrowers graduating in 2009: $21,432. Proportion who borrowed: 78%.

CAMPUS LIFE AND EXTRACURRICULAR ACTIVITIES

Campus housing available (% using): coed dorms (100%). Students who live in college-owned, operated, or affiliated housing: 9%. **Student employment:** During the 2009-2010 academic year, 10% of undergraduates worked on campus. Average per-year earnings: $5,000. **Clubs and organizations:** Number of student organizations: 14. Activities include: dance, drama/theater, international student organization, student government, yearbook. Number of fraternities: 0; sororities: 0. Average proportion of students who stay on campus on weekends: 30%.

SERVICES AND FACILITIES

Basic services: nonremedial tutoring, placement service, health insurance. **Remedial assistance:** reading, math, writing, study skills. **Counseling services:** minority student, career, personal, academic. **For learning-disabled students:** School does not offer a structured program with separate admission and additional fees. Total undergraduates in learning-disabled program or receiving services: 0. Services include: remedial math, remedial English, remedial reading, untimed tests, learning center, extended time for tests, tutors. **Library:** Number of titles: 46,775; number of current serial subscriptions: 135. **Information technology resources:** Students are not required to lease or own a computer. Number of campus computers available to all students: 175. School has a wireless network. Approximate number of users that can be accommodated: 250. Proportion of college-owned housing units wired for high-speed internet access: 100%. **Campus safety:** Security services offered: 24-hour foot-and-vehicle patrols, 24-hour emergency telephones, lighted pathways/sidewalks, controlled dormitory access (key, security card, etc).

TRANSFER AND INTERNATIONAL STUDENTS

Transfer students: May apply for admission for the following academic terms: Fall, Spring, Summer. Applicants do not need a minimum number of credits to apply. For fall 2009: Transfer applications received: 247. Transfer applicants offered admission: 231. Transfer applicants enrolled: 152. **International students:** Number of foreign undergraduates: 32 (2% of student body). Number of countries represented: 12. Minimum TOEFL score required: 560 (paper); 200 (computer). Average TOEFL score: 600 (paper).

Wagner College

- **Address:** 1 Campus Road, Staten Island, NY 10301
- **Website:** http://www.wagner.edu
- **Private**
- **Enrollment:** 1,799 full-time; 71 part-time

KEY STATS

✔ **U.S News College Ranking:** 25, Regional Universities (North)

✔ **SAT Score (25th/75th percentile):** 1050-1290

✔ **Tuition:** 2010-2011: $34,190

Selectivity: Selective	**Room/board:** $10,170
Acceptance rate: 70%	**Average debt:** $36,988
Student/faculty ratio: 13/1	**Proportion who borrowed:** 61%

UNDERGRADUATE STUDENT BODY STATS

2009-2010 enrollment: 1,799 full-time; 71 part-time. Men: 37%; women: 63%. **Ethnic makeup:** African American: 5%; Asian American: 2%; Hispanic: 6%; White: 86%; International: 1%. **Religious preference:** Roman Catholic: 22%; Protestant: 3%; Jewish: 1%; Muslim: 1%; Unknown: 70%; Christian: 3%.

ADMISSIONS FACTS AND FIGURES

Phone: (718) 390-3411. **Email:** adm@wagner.edu. **Website:** http://www.wagner.edu. **Application deadlines for fall 2011:** Regular decision: February 15. Early decision: Send application by: December 1; Decision sent by: December 15. Early action: Not offered. Admission can be deferred. **Application fee:** $50. **To apply online, go to:** http://www.wagner.edu/admissions/apply. **Admissions requirements/recommendations:** High school units required (recommended): English: 4; Mathematics: 3; Science: 2; Foreign language: 2; Social studies: 1; History: 3; Academic electives: 6; Total units: 21. Tests: The college uses SAT or ACT scores in admissions decisions. Either SAT or ACT required. For admission to the fall 2011 entering class, the school will accept: ACT with or without writing accepted. Campus visit: Recommended. Admissions interview: Recommended. Off-campus interview: May be arranged. **Factors that count in admissions decisions:** *Academic:* Secondary school record: Very Important. Class rank: Very Important. Letters of recommendation: Important. Standardized test scores: Important. Essay: Important. *Nonacademic:* Interview: Important. Extracurricular activities: Important. Talent/ability: Important. Character/personal qualities: Important. Alumni/ae relationship: Not Considered. Geographical residence: Not Considered. State residency: Not Considered. Religious affiliation/commitment: Not Considered. Minority status: Not Considered. Volunteer work: Considered. Work experience: Considered. **Other schools with the greatest overlap in applicants:** Drew University; Fairfield University; Fordham University; Marist College; Muhlenberg College. **Admissions statistics for the fall 2009 entering class:** Total applicants: 2,661. Total accepted: 1,853. Freshmen enrolled: 519; 56% were from out of state. Accepted through early-decision or early-action plans: 13%. Overall acceptance rate: 70%. Early-decision acceptance rate: 59%. Non-early acceptance rate: 70%. **Size of waiting list:** 153 applicants; enrolled from waiting list: 27. **Credentials of fall 2009 freshmen:** 15% ranked in the top 10 percent of their high school class; 70% were in the top 25 percent; 92% were in the top half. (Proportion submitting class standing: 61%.) **Average high school grade point average:** 3.6. **First-year students who submitted SAT scores:** 88%. Scores (25/75 percentile): Critical Reading: 520-640, Math: 530-650, Combined: 1050-1290. **First-year students submitting ACT scores:** 12%. Scores (25/75 percentile): English: 23-27, Math: 24-28, Composite: 23-28.

ACADEMICS

Year founded: 1883. **Academic calendar:** Semester. **Degrees offered:** bachelor's, master's, post-master's certificate. **Most popular majors:** 21% business, management, marketing, and related support services, 19% visual and performing arts, 12% health professions and related clinical sciences, 11% psychology, 10% social sciences. **Major fields of study:** biological and biomedical sciences; business, management, marketing, and related support services; computer and information sciences and support services; education; English language and literature/letters; foreign languages, literatures, and linguistics; health professions and related clinical sciences; history; mathematics and statistics; multi/interdisciplinary studies; philosophy and religious studies; physical sciences; psychology; public administration and social service professions; social sciences; visual and performing arts. **Areas of required coursework:** arts/fine arts, humanities, computer literacy, mathematics, English (including composition), philosophy, sciences (biological or physical), history, social science, other. **Pre-professional programs:** pre-law, pre-dentistry, pre-medicine, pre-theology, pre-veterinary science, pre-optometry, pre-pharmacy, other. **Special academic programs (% participation):** double major (10%), exchange student program (domestic) (0%), honors program (7%), independent study, internships (100%), study abroad (4%), teacher certificate program (10%). **Teacher certification offered in:** special education, elementary. **Reserve Officers Training Corps (ROTC):** Army ROTC: Offered at cooperating institution. **Faculty and instruction (2009-2010):** Total instructional faculty: 99 full-time, 139 part-time (53% men; 47% women; 11% minorities). Full-time faculty with Ph.D. or other terminal degree: 94%. Student/faculty ratio: 13/1. Classes of fewer than 20 students: 56%; of 20 to 49 students: 44%; of 50 or more students: 0%. **Advanced Placement and International Baccalaureate credit:** AP tests may be used for: Placement only. Scores accepted: 4, 5. International Baccalaureate exams may be used for: Placement only. **Freshmen returning for sophomore year:** 80%. **Graduation rates:** Four-year: 62%; five-year: 67%; six-year:

66%. **Graduate study:** 47% of students pursue further study within one year. Fields in which graduates pursue further study: Master of Business Administration (MBA), 27%; law, 20%; medicine, 18%; dentistry, 1%; education, 12%; arts and sciences, 29%.

COSTS AND FINANCIAL AID

Financial aid office: (718) 390-3183. **Expenses (2010-2011):** Tuition and fees 2010-2011: $34,190; room/board: $10,170. Estimated books and supplies: $745; transportation: $745; personal expenses: $1,295. **Financial aid:** Priority filing date for institution's financial aid form: February 15. In 2009-2010, 72% of undergraduates applied for financial aid. Of those, 59% were determined to have financial need; 27% had their need fully met. Average financial aid package (proportion receiving): $20,457 (59%). Average amount of gift aid, such as scholarships or grants (proportion receiving): $16,157 (57%). Average amount of self-help aid, such as work study or loans (proportion receiving): $5,622 (46%). Average need-based loan (excluding PLUS or other private loans): $4,643. Among students who received need-based aid, the average percentage of need met: 73%. Among students who received aid based on merit, the average award (and the proportion receiving): $12,072 (31%). The average athletic scholarship (and the proportion receiving): $28,670 (4%). Average amount of debt of borrowers graduating in 2009: $36,988. Proportion who borrowed: 61%.

CAMPUS LIFE AND EXTRACURRICULAR ACTIVITIES

Campus housing available (% using): coed dorms (86%), sorority housing (8%), fraternity housing (6%). Students who live in college-owned, operated, or affiliated housing: 68%. **Student employment:** During the 2009-2010 academic year, 13% of undergraduates worked on campus. Average per-year earnings: $1,200. **Clubs and organizations:** Number of student organizations: 63. Activities include: choral groups, concert band, dance, drama/theater, international student organization, jazz band, literary magazine, music ensembles, musical theater, pep band, radio station, student government, student newspaper, yearbook. Number of fraternities: 5; sororities: 4. Proportion of men in fraternities: 9%; of women in sororities: 13%. Average proportion of students who stay on campus on weekends: 75%. **Sports program (2009-2010):** Member of NCAA I. *Men's intercollegiate varsity sports:* baseball, basketball, cross country, football, golf, lacrosse, tennis, track and field (indoor), track and field (outdoor). *Women's intercollegiate varsity sports:* basketball, cross country, golf, lacrosse, soccer, softball, swimming, tennis, track and field (indoor), track and field (outdoor), water polo.

SERVICES AND FACILITIES

Basic services: nonremedial tutoring, placement service, health service, health insurance. **Remedial assistance:** math, writing. **Counseling services:** career, personal, academic, psychological, birth control, religious. **For learning-disabled students:** School does not offer a structured program with separate admission and additional fees. Total undergraduates in learning-disabled program or receiving services: 83. Services include: tape recorders, untimed tests, learning center, extended time for tests, tutors, priority registration, priority seating, other testing accommodations. **Library:** Number of titles: 175,344; number of current serial subscriptions: 20,600. **Information technology resources:** Students are not required to lease or own a computer. Number of campus computers available to all students: 240. School has a wireless network. Approximate number of users that can be accommodated: 1,500. Proportion of college-owned housing units wired for high-speed internet access: 100%. **Campus safety:** Security services offered: 24-hour foot-and-vehicle patrols, late-night transport/escort service, 24-hour emergency telephones, lighted pathways/sidewalks, controlled dormitory access (key, security card, etc).

TRANSFER AND INTERNATIONAL STUDENTS

Transfer students: May apply for admission for the following academic terms: Fall, Spring. Applicants do not need a minimum number of credits to apply. For fall 2009: Transfer applications received: 215. Transfer applicants offered admission: 94. Transfer applicants enrolled: 45. **International students:** Number of foreign undergraduates: 13 (1% of student body). Number of countries represented: 13. Minimum TOEFL score required: 550 (paper); 217 (computer). Average TOEFL score: 580 (paper).

Webb Institute

- **Address:** 298 Crescent Beach Road, Glen Cove, NY 11542-1398
- **Website:** http://www.webb-institute.edu
- **Private**
- **Enrollment:** 89 full-time

KEY STATS
- ✔ **U.S News College Ranking:** Unranked Specialty School–Engineering
- ✔ **SAT Score (25th/75th percentile):** 1340-1420
- ✔ **Tuition:** 2009-2010: $0

Selectivity: More selective	Room/board: $10,200
Acceptance rate: 35%	Average debt: $8,545
Student/faculty ratio: 7/1	Proportion who borrowed: 33%

UNDERGRADUATE STUDENT BODY STATS
2009-2010 enrollment: 89 full-time. Men: 87%; women: 13%. **Ethnic makeup:** Asian American: 8%; Hispanic: 4%; White: 88%.

ADMISSIONS FACTS AND FIGURES
Phone: (516) 671-2213. **Email:** admissions@webb-institute.edu. **Website:** http://www.webb-institute.edu. **Application deadlines for fall 2011:** Regular decision: February 15. Early decision: Send application by: October 15; Decision sent by: December 15. Early action: Not offered. Admission cannot be deferred. **Application fee:** $25. **Admissions requirements/recommendations:** High school units required (recommended): English: 4; Mathematics: 4; Science: 2; Foreign language: 0; Social studies: 2; History: 0; Academic electives: 4; Total units: 16. **Tests:** The college uses SAT or ACT scores in admissions decisions. SAT required. Campus visit: Recommended. Admissions interview: Required. Off-campus interview: Not available. **Factors that count in admissions decisions:** *Academic:* Secondary school record: Very Important. Class rank: Very Important. Letters of recommendation: Very Important. Standardized test scores: Very Important. Essay: Not Considered. *Nonacademic:* Interview: Very Important. Extracurricular activities: Important. Talent/ability: Important. Character/personal qualities: Very Important. Alumni/ae relationship: Not Considered. Geographical residence: Not Considered. State residency: Not Considered. Religious affiliation/commitment: Not Considered. Minority status: Not Considered. Volunteer work: Considered. Work experience: Considered. **Other schools with the greatest overlap in applicants:** Cooper Union; Massachusetts Institute of Technology; United States Coast Guard Academy; United States Naval Academy; University of Michigan–Ann Arbor. **Admissions statistics for the fall 2009 entering class:** Total applicants: 68. Total accepted: 24. Freshmen enrolled: 19; 74% were from out of state. Accepted through early-decision or early-action plans: 11%. Overall acceptance rate: 35%. Early-decision acceptance rate: 20%. Non-early acceptance rate: 38%. **Credentials of fall 2009 freshmen:** 67% ranked in the top 10 percent of their high school class; 83% were in the top 25 percent; 100% were in the top half. (Proportion submitting class standing: 63%.) **Average high school grade point average:** 3.8. **First-year students who submitted SAT scores:** 100%. Scores (25/75 percentile): Critical Reading: 640-680, Math: 700-740, Combined: 1340-1420.

ACADEMICS
Year founded: 1889. **Academic calendar:** Semester. **Degrees offered:** bachelor's. **Most popular majors:** 100% naval architecture and marine engineering. **Major fields of study:** engineering. **Areas of required coursework:** arts/fine arts, humanities, computer literacy, mathematics, English (including composition), philosophy, sciences (biological or physical), history, social science. **Special academic programs (% participation):** double major (100%), internships (100%), study abroad (4%). **Faculty and instruction (2009-2010):** Total instructional faculty: 11 full-time, 3 part-time (86% men; 14% women; 0% minorities). Full-time faculty with Ph.D. or other terminal degree: 64%. Student/faculty ratio: 7/1. **Freshmen returning for sophomore year:** 90%. **Graduation rates:** Four-year: 77%; five-year: 81%; six-year: 69%. **Graduate study:** 25% of students pursue further study immediately upon graduation; 25% within five years. Fields in which graduates pursue further study: Master of Business Administration (MBA), 5%; engineering, 90%; education, 5%.

COSTS AND FINANCIAL AID
Financial aid office: (516) 671-2213. **Expenses (2009-2010):** Tuition and fees 2009-2010: $0; room/board: $10,200. Estimated books and supplies: $950; transportation: $3,000; personal expenses: $750. **Financial aid:** Priority fil-

ing date for institution's financial aid form: July 1; deadline: August 1. In 2009-2010, 21% of undergraduates applied for financial aid. Of those, 21% were determined to have financial need; 100% had their need fully met. Average financial aid package (proportion receiving): $5,200 (21%). Average amount of gift aid, such as scholarships or grants (proportion receiving): $2,710 (11%). Average amount of self-help aid, such as work-study or loans (proportion receiving): $5,200 (21%). Average need-based loan (excluding PLUS or other private loans): $5,200. Among students who received need-based aid, the average percentage of need met: 53%. Among students who received aid based on merit, the average award (and the proportion receiving): $0 (0%). The average athletic scholarship (and the proportion receiving): $0 (0%). Average amount of debt of borrowers graduating in 2009: $8,545. Proportion who borrowed: 33%.

CAMPUS LIFE AND EXTRACURRICULAR ACTIVITIES
Campus housing available (% using): coed dorms (10%), women's dorms (10%), men's dorms (80%). Students who live in college-owned, operated, or affiliated housing: 100%. Activities include: choral groups, concert band, drama/theater, musical theater, student government, yearbook. Number of fraternities: 0; sororities: 0. Average proportion of students who stay on campus on weekends: 60%.

SERVICES AND FACILITIES
Remedial assistance: study skills. **Counseling services:** personal, academic, psychological. **For learning-disabled students:** School does not offer a structured program with separate admission and additional fees. Services include: extended time for tests, priority seating, other testing accommodations. **Library:** Number of titles: 44,694; number of current serial subscriptions: 230. **Information technology resources:** Students are required to lease or own a computer. Number of campus computers available to all students: 50. School has a wireless network. Approximate number of users that can be accommodated: 130. Proportion of college-owned housing units wired for high-speed internet access: 100%. **Campus safety:** Security services offered: 24-hour foot-and-vehicle patrols, 24-hour emergency telephones, lighted pathways/sidewalks, controlled dormitory access (key, security card, etc).

TRANSFER AND INTERNATIONAL STUDENTS
Transfer students: May apply for admission for the following academic terms: Fall. Applicants do not need a minimum number of credits to apply. For fall 2009: Transfer applications received: 6. Transfer applicants offered admission: 3. Transfer applicants enrolled: 3. **International students:** Number of foreign undergraduates: 0.

Wells College

- **Address:** 170 Main Street, Aurora, NY 13026
- **Website:** http://www.wells.edu
- **Private**
- **Enrollment:** 557 full-time; 11 part-time

KEY STATS
- ✔ **U.S News College Ranking:** 144, National Liberal Arts Colleges
- ✔ **SAT Score (25th/75th percentile):** 980-1230
- ✔ **Tuition:** 2010-2011: $32,180

Selectivity: Selective	Room/board: $11,000
Acceptance rate: 67%	Average debt: $24,180
Student/faculty ratio: 10/1	Proportion who borrowed: 82%

UNDERGRADUATE STUDENT BODY STATS
2009-2010 enrollment: 557 full-time; 11 part-time. Men: 29%; women: 71%. **Ethnic makeup:** African American: 6%; American-Indian: 1%; Asian American: 2%; Hispanic: 4%; White: 85%; International: 2%.

ADMISSIONS FACTS AND FIGURES
Phone: (800) 952-9355. **Email:** admissions@wells.edu. **Website:** http://www.wells.edu. **Application deadlines for fall 2011:** Regular decision: March 1; decision sent by April 1. Early decision: Send application by: December 15; Decision sent by: January 15. Early action: Send application by: December 15; Decision sent by: February 1. Admission can be deferred. **Application fee:** $40. **To apply online, go to:** http://www.commonapp.org. **Admissions requirements/recommendations:** High school units required (recommended): English: 4 (4); Mathematics: 3 (3); Science: 2 (3); Foreign language: 0 (2); Social studies: 1 (2); History: 2 (2); Academic electives: (3);

Total units: (21). Tests: The college uses SAT or ACT scores in admissions decisions. Either SAT or ACT required. For admission to the fall 2011 entering class, the school will accept: ACT with or without writing accepted. Campus visit: Recommended. Admissions interview: Recommended. Off-campus interview: May be arranged. **Factors that count in admissions decisions: Academic:** Secondary school record: Very Important. Class rank: Considered. Letters of recommendation: Very Important. Standardized test scores: Important. Essay: Important. **Nonacademic:** Interview: Important. Extracurricular activities: Very Important. Talent/ability: Important. Character/personal qualities: Important. Alumni/ae relationship: Important. Geographical residence: Not Considered. State residency: Not Considered. Religious affiliation/commitment: Not Considered. Minority status: Considered. Volunteer work: Considered. Work experience: Considered. **Other schools with the greatest overlap in applicants:** Cazenovia College; Elmira College; Hobart and William Smith Colleges; Ithaca College; Le Moyne College. **Admissions statistics for the fall 2009 entering class:** Total applicants: 1,673. Total accepted: 1,124. Freshmen enrolled: 145; 36% were from out of state. Accepted through early-decision or early-action plans: 67%. Overall acceptance rate: 67%. Early-decision acceptance rate: 27%. Non-early acceptance rate: 58%. **Credentials of fall 2009 freshmen:** 31% ranked in the top 10 percent of their high school class; 65% were in the top 25 percent; 91% were in the top half. (Proportion submitting class standing: 68%.) **Average high school grade point average:** 3.5. **First-year students who submitted SAT scores:** 88%. Scores (25/75 percentile): Critical Reading: 500-630, Math: 480-600, Combined: 980-1230. **First-year students submitting ACT scores:** 29%. Scores (25/75 percentile): English: N/A, Math: N/A, Composite: 22-27.

ACADEMICS

Year founded: 1868. **Academic calendar:** Semester. **Degrees offered:** bachelor's. **Most popular majors:** 15% psychology, 14% social sciences, 12% visual and performing arts, 11% English language and literature/letters, 10% biological and biomedical sciences. **Major fields of study:** area, ethnic, cultural, and gender studies; biological and biomedical sciences; business, management, marketing, and related support services; computer and information sciences and support services; English language and literature/letters; foreign languages, literatures, and linguistics; history; liberal arts and sciences studies, and humanities; mathematics and statistics; natural resources and conservation; philosophy and religious studies; physical sciences; psychology; public administration and social service professions; social sciences; visual and performing arts. **Areas of required coursework:** arts/fine arts, humanities, mathematics, foreign languages, sciences (biological or physical), social science, other. **Pre-professional programs:** pre-law, pre-dentistry, pre-medicine, pre-veterinary science, pre-pharmacy, other. **Special academic programs (% participation):** accelerated program (3%), cross-registration (25%), double major (3%), independent study (50%), internships (90%), student-designed major (3%), study abroad (40%), teacher certificate program (12%). **Teacher certification offered in:** elementary, secondary. **Reserve Officers Training Corps (ROTC):** Army ROTC: Offered at cooperating institution (Cornell University); Air Force ROTC: Offered at cooperating institution (Cornell University). **Faculty and instruction (2009-2010):** Total instructional faculty: 39 full-time, 19 part-time (48% men; 52% women; 16% minorities). Full-time faculty with Ph.D. or other terminal degree: 95%. Student/faculty ratio: 10/1. Classes of fewer than 20 students: 85%; of 20 to 49 students: 15%. **Advanced Placement and International Baccalaureate credit:** AP tests may be used for: Placement only. Scores accepted: 4, 5. International Baccalaureate exams may be used for: Credit and/or placement. **Freshmen returning for sophomore year:** 74%. **Graduation rates:** Four-year: 52%; five-year: 57%; six-year: 59%. **Graduate study:** 40% of students pursue further study immediately upon graduation; 10% within one year; 30% within five years. Fields in which graduates pursue further study: Master of Business Administration (MBA), 1%; law, 4%; medicine, 2%; dentistry, 1%; theology (or the seminary), 1%; education, 8%; arts and sciences, 46%; veterinary medicine, 1%.

COSTS AND FINANCIAL AID

Financial aid office: (315) 364-3289. **Expenses (2010-2011):** Tuition and fees 2010-2011: $32,180; room/board: $11,000. Estimated books and supplies: $800; transportation: $0; personal expenses: $800. **Financial aid:** Priority filing date for institution's financial aid form: February 15. In 2009-2010, 90% of undergraduates applied for financial aid. Of those, 83% were determined to have financial need; 21% had their need fully met. Average financial aid package (proportion receiving): $21,009 (83%). Average amount of gift aid, such as scholarships or grants (proportion receiving): $16,271 (83%). Average amount of self-help aid, such as work study or loans (proportion receiving): $5,288 (80%). Average need-based loan (excluding PLUS or other private loans): $4,562. Among students who received need-based aid, the average percentage of need met: 82%. Among students who received aid based on merit, the average award (and the proportion receiving): $8,069 (12%). The average athletic scholarship (and the proportion receiving): $0 (0%). Average amount of debt of borrowers graduating in 2009: $24,180. Proportion who borrowed: 82%.

CAMPUS LIFE AND EXTRACURRICULAR ACTIVITIES

Campus housing available (% using): coed dorms (54%), women's dorms (17%), apartment for single students (5%), other housing options (11%). Students who live in college-owned, operated, or affiliated housing: 84%. **Student employment:** During the 2009-2010 academic year, 63% of undergraduates worked on campus. Average per-year earnings: $1,100. **Clubs and organizations:** Number of student organizations: 40. Activities include: choral groups, dance, drama/theater, international student organization, jazz band, literary magazine, model UN, music ensembles, student government, student newspaper, yearbook. Number of fraternities: 0; sororities: 0. Average proportion of students who stay on campus on weekends: 80%. **Sports program (2009-2010):** Member of NCAA III. **Men's intercollegiate varsity sports:** basketball, cross country, golf, lacrosse, soccer, swimming. **Women's intercollegiate varsity sports:** cross country, field hockey, golf, lacrosse, soccer, softball, swimming, tennis.

SERVICES AND FACILITIES

Basic services: nonremedial tutoring, women's center, health service, health insurance. **Remedial assistance:** math, writing, study skills. **Counseling services:** minority student, career, personal, academic, older student, psychological, birth control, religious. **For learning-disabled students:** School does not offer a structured program with separate admission and additional fees. Services include: reading machines, tape recorders, other special classes, note-taking services, oral tests, extended time for tests, tutors, priority seating, substitution of courses, texts on tape, exams on tape or computer, other testing accommodations, waiver of foreign language degree requirement, other. **Library:** Number of titles: 218,002; number of current serial subscriptions: 371. **Information technology resources:** Students are not required to lease or own a computer. Number of campus computers available to all students: 80. School has a wireless network. Approximate number of users that can be accommodated: 500. Proportion of college-owned housing units wired for high-speed internet access: 100%. **Campus safety:** Security services offered: 24-hour foot-and-vehicle patrols, late-night transport/escort service, 24-hour emergency telephones, lighted pathways/sidewalks, student patrols, controlled dormitory access (key, security card, etc).

TRANSFER AND INTERNATIONAL STUDENTS

Transfer students: May apply for admission for the following academic terms: Fall, Spring. Applicants need a minimum number of credits to apply. For fall 2009: Transfer applications received: 63. Transfer applicants offered admission: 36. Transfer applicants enrolled: 17. **International students:** Number of foreign undergraduates: 13 (2% of student body). Number of countries represented: 13. Minimum TOEFL score required: 550 (paper); 213 (computer). Average TOEFL score: 553 (paper).

Yeshiva University

- **Address:** 500 W. 185th Street, New York, NY 10033
- **Website:** http://www.yu.edu
- **Private**
- **Enrollment:** 2,777 full-time; 76 part-time

KEY STATS
✔ **U.S News College Ranking:** 50, National Universities
✔ **SAT Score (25th/75th percentile):** 1100-1370
✔ **Tuition:** 2010-2011: $33,050

Selectivity: More selective	**Room/board:** $10,905
Acceptance rate: 63%	**Average debt:** $21,665
Student/faculty ratio: 7/1	**Proportion who borrowed:** 47%

UNDERGRADUATE STUDENT BODY STATS
2009-2010 enrollment: 2,777 full-time; 76 part-time. Men: 54%; women: 46%. **Ethnic makeup:** White: 99%. **Religious preference:** Jewish: 100%.

ADMISSIONS FACTS AND FIGURES

Phone: (212) 960-5277. **Email:** yuadmit@ymail.yu.edu. **Website:** http://www.yu.edu. **Application deadlines for fall 2011:** Regular decision: February 15; decision sent by April 1. Early decision: Not offered. Early action: Not offered. Admission can be deferred. **Application fee:** $65. **To apply online, go to:** http://www.yu.edu/admissions/page.aspx?id=470. **Admissions requirements/recommendations:** High school units required (recommended): English: (4); Mathematics: (2); Science: (2); Foreign language: (2); Social studies: (2); History: (2); Total units: (16). Tests: The college uses SAT or ACT scores in admissions decisions. Either SAT or ACT required. For admission to the fall 2011 entering class, the school will accept: ACT with or without writing accepted. Campus visit: Recommended. Admissions interview: Required. Off-campus interview: May be arranged. **Factors that count in admissions decisions:** *Academic:* Secondary school record: Important. Class rank: Considered. Letters of recommendation: Important. Standardized test scores: Important. Essay: Important. *Nonacademic:* Interview: Important. Extracurricular activities: Important. Talent/ability: Important. Character/personal qualities: Not Considered. Alumni/ae relationship: Not Considered. Geographical residence: Not Considered. State residency: Not Considered. Religious affiliation/commitment: Not Considered. Minority status: Not Considered. Volunteer work: Considered. Work experience: Considered. **Other schools with the greatest overlap in applicants:** CUNY–Queens College; New York University; Rutgers, the State University of New Jersey–New Brunswick; Touro College; University of Maryland–College Park. **Admissions statistics for the fall 2009 entering class:** Total applicants: 2,027. Total accepted: 1,269. Freshmen enrolled: 809; 34% were from out of state. Overall acceptance rate: 63%. **Credentials of fall 2009 freshmen:** 51% ranked in the top 10 percent of their high school class; 80% were in the top 25 percent; 96% were in the top half. (Proportion submitting class standing: 50%.) **Average high school grade point average:** 3.5. **First-year students who submitted SAT scores:** 80%. Scores (25/75 percentile): Critical Reading: 550-690, Math: 550-680, Combined: 1100-1370. **First-year students submitting ACT scores:** 16%. Scores (25/75 percentile): English: 21-28, Math: 23-30, Composite: 22-28.

ACADEMICS

Year founded: 1886. **Academic calendar:** Semester. **Degrees offered:** associate, bachelor's, master's, post-master's certificate, doctorate. **Most popular majors:** 16% business administration and management, 16% psychology, 14% biology/biological sciences, 11% accounting, 6% multi/interdisciplinary studies. **Major fields of study:** business, management, marketing, and related support services; communication, journalism, and related programs; computer and information sciences and support services; education; engineering; English language and literature/letters; foreign languages, literatures, and linguistics; health professions and related clinical sciences; history; mathematics and statistics; philosophy and religious studies; physical sciences; psychology; social sciences; visual and performing arts. **Areas of required coursework:** humanities, computer literacy, mathematics, English (including composition), foreign languages, sciences (biological or physical), social science. **Pre-professional programs:** pre-law, pre-dentistry, pre-medicine, pre-veterinary science, pre-optometry, other. **Special academic programs (% participation):** cross-registration (5%), double major (6%), dual enrollment (.7%), English as a Second Language (ESL) (1%), honors program (5%), independent study (2%), internships (15%), student-designed major (7%), study abroad (90%), teacher certificate program (3%). **Teacher certification offered in:** early childhood, elementary. **Faculty and instruction (2009-2010):** Total instructional faculty: 968 full-time, 352 part-time (62% men; 38% women; 16% minorities). Full-time faculty with Ph.D. or other terminal degree: 95%. Student/faculty ratio: 7/1. Classes of fewer than 20 students: 65%; of 20 to 49 students: 34%; of 50 or more students: 1%. **Advanced Placement and International Baccalaureate credit:** AP tests may be used for: Credit and/or placement. Scores accepted: 5. International Baccalaureate exams may be used for: Placement only. **Freshmen returning for sophomore year:** 91%. **Graduation rates:** Four-year: 45%; five-year: 72%; six-year: 85%. **Graduate study:** 53% of students pursue further study immediately upon graduation; 89% within one year; 93% within five years. Fields in which graduates pursue further study: Master of Business Administration (MBA), 12%; law, 13%; medicine, 12%; dentistry, 2%; engineering, 2%; theology (or the seminary), 7%; education, 10%; arts and sciences, 16%.

COSTS AND FINANCIAL AID

Financial aid office: (212) 960-5399. **Expenses (2010-2011):** Tuition and fees 2010-2011: $33,050; room/board: $10,905. Estimated books and supplies: $1,350; transportation: $1,375; personal expenses: $5,750. **Financial aid:** Priority filing date for institution's financial aid form: February 15. In 2009-2010, 65% of undergraduates applied for financial aid. Of those, 53% were determined to have financial need; 22% had their need fully met. Average financial aid package (proportion receiving): $27,297 (50%). Average amount of gift aid, such as scholarships or grants (proportion receiving): $20,958 (46%). Average amount of self-help aid, such as work study or loans (proportion receiving): $5,722 (35%). Average need-based loan (excluding PLUS or other private loans): $6,043. Among students who received need-based aid, the average percentage of need met: 87%. Among students who received aid based on merit, the average award (and the proportion receiving): $18,644 (11%). The average athletic scholarship (and the proportion receiving): $0 (0%). Average amount of debt of borrowers graduating in 2009: $21,665. Proportion who borrowed: 47%.

CAMPUS LIFE AND EXTRACURRICULAR ACTIVITIES

Campus housing available (% using): women's dorms (42%), men's dorms (46%), apartments for married students (2%), apartment for single students (8%). Students who live in college-owned, operated, or affiliated housing: 78%. **Student employment:** During the 2009-2010 academic year, 5% of undergraduates worked on campus. Average per-year earnings: $2,500. **Clubs and organizations:** Number of student organizations: 80. Activities include: choral groups, concert band, drama/theater, jazz band, literary magazine, music ensembles, musical theater, radio station, student government, student newspaper, yearbook. Number of fraternities: 0; sororities: 0. Average proportion of students who stay on campus on weekends: 30%. **Sports program (2009-2010):** Member of NCAA III. *Men's intercollegiate varsity sports:* baseball, basketball, cross country, fencing, golf, soccer, tennis, volleyball, wrestling. *Women's intercollegiate varsity sports:* basketball, cross country, fencing, soccer, tennis, volleyball.

SERVICES AND FACILITIES

Basic services: nonremedial tutoring, placement service, health service, health insurance. **Remedial assistance:** reading, math, writing, study skills. **Counseling services:** career, personal, academic, psychological, religious. **For learning-disabled students:** School does not offer a structured program with separate admission and additional fees. Total undergraduates in learning-disabled program or receiving services: 300. Services include: remedial English, reading machines, tape recorders, untimed tests, oral tests, extended time for tests, priority seating, texts on tape, typist/scribe, exams on tape or computer, other testing accommodations. **Library:** Number of titles: 1,167,457; number of current serial subscriptions: 65,706. **Information technology resources:** Students are not required to lease or own a computer. Number of campus computers available to all students: 850. School has a wireless network. Approximate number of users that can be accommodated: 15,000. Proportion of college-owned housing units wired for high-speed internet access: 100%. **Campus safety:** Security services offered: 24-hour foot-and-vehicle patrols, late-night transport/escort service, 24-hour emergency telephones, lighted pathways/sidewalks, controlled dormitory access (key, security card, etc).

TRANSFER AND INTERNATIONAL STUDENTS

Transfer students: May apply for admission for the following academic terms: Fall, Spring. Applicants do not need a minimum number of credits to apply. For fall 2009: Transfer applications received: 107. Transfer applicants offered admission: 79. Transfer applicants enrolled: 60. **International students:** Number of foreign undergraduates: 0. Number of countries represented: 30. Minimum TOEFL score required: 500 (paper); 173 (computer). Average TOEFL score: 585 (paper).

North Carolina

Appalachian State University

- **Address:** Boone, NC 28608
- **Website:** http://www.appstate.edu
- **Public**
- **Enrollment:** 14,116 full-time; 756 part-time

KEY STATS

- ✔ **U.S News College Ranking:** 9, Regional Universities (South)
- ✔ **SAT Score (25th/75th percentile):** 1070-1250
- ✔ **Tuition:** 2009-2010: $4,491 in state, $15,112 out of state

Selectivity: Selective	**Room/board:** $6,400
Acceptance rate: 63%	**Average debt:** $16,153
Student/faculty ratio: 17/1	**Proportion who borrowed:** 55%

UNDERGRADUATE STUDENT BODY STATS

2009-2010 enrollment: 14,116 full-time; 756 part-time. Men: 48%; women: 52%. **Ethnic makeup:** African American: 3%; Asian American: 1%; Hispanic: 3%; White: 92%.

ADMISSIONS FACTS AND FIGURES

Phone: (828) 262-2120. **Email:** admissions@appstate.edu. **Website:** http://www.appstate.edu. **Application deadlines for fall 2011:** Regular decision: Rolling. Early decision: Not offered. Early action: Not offered. Admission can be deferred. **Application fee:** $50. **To apply online, go to:** http://www.admissions.appstate.edu/apply/index.html. **Admissions requirements/recommendations:** High school units required (recommended): English: 4; Mathematics: 4; Science: 3; Foreign language: 2; Social studies: 1; History: 1; Total units: 13. Tests: The college uses SAT or ACT scores in admissions decisions. Either SAT or ACT required. For admission to the fall 2011 entering class, the school will accept: ACT with writing required. Campus visit: Recommended. Admissions interview: Neither required nor recommended. Off-campus interview: Not available. **Factors that count in admissions decisions: Academic:** Secondary school record: Very Important. Class rank: Very Important. Letters of recommendation: Considered. Standardized test scores: Very Important. Essay: Considered. **Nonacademic:** Interview: Not Considered. Extracurricular activities: Considered. Talent/ability: Considered. Character/personal qualities: Considered. Alumni/ae relationship: Not Considered. Geographical residence: Not Considered. State residency: Not Considered. Religious affiliation/commitment: Not Considered. Minority status: Considered. Volunteer work: Considered. Work experience: Considered. **Other schools with the greatest overlap in applicants:** East Carolina University; North Carolina State University–Raleigh; University of North Carolina–Chapel Hill; University of North Carolina–Charlotte; University of North Carolina–Wilmington. **Admissions statistics for the fall 2009 entering class:** Total applicants: 13,039. Total accepted: 8,224. Freshmen enrolled: 2,743; 12% were from out of state. Overall acceptance rate: 63%. **Size of waiting list:** 1646 applicants; enrolled from waiting list: 0. **Credentials of fall 2009 freshmen:** 22% ranked in the top 10 percent of their high school class; 62% were in the top 25 percent; 93% were in the top half. (Proportion submitting class standing: 87%.) **Average high school grade point average:** 3.9. **First-year students who submitted SAT scores:** 97%. Scores (25/75 percentile): Critical Reading: 530-620, Math: 540-630, Combined: 1070-1250. **First-year students submitting ACT scores:** 23%. Scores (25/75 percentile): English: 21-27, Math: 22-26, Composite: 22-26.

ACADEMICS

Year founded: 1899. **Academic calendar:** Semester. **Degrees offered:** certificate, bachelor's, post-bachelor's certificate, master's, post-master's certificate, doctorate. **Most popular majors:** 7% elementary education and teaching, 5% business administration and management, 5% psychology, 4% accounting, 3% criminal justice/safety studies. **Major fields of study:** architecture and related services; biological and biomedical sciences; business, management, marketing, and related support services; communication, journalism, and related programs; computer and information sciences and support services; education; engineering technologies/technicians;

English language and literature/letters; family and consumer sciences/human sciences; foreign languages, literatures, and linguistics; health professions and related clinical sciences; history; liberal arts and sciences studies, and humanities; mathematics and statistics; parks, recreation, leisure, and fitness studies; philosophy and religious studies; physical sciences; psychology; public administration and social service professions; security and protective services; social sciences; visual and performing arts. **Areas of required coursework:** arts/fine arts, humanities, computer literacy, mathematics, English (including composition), foreign languages, sciences (biological or physical), history, social science, other. **Pre-professional programs:** pre-law, pre-dentistry, pre-medicine, pre-theology, pre-pharmacy, other. **Special academic programs:** distance learning, double major, dual enrollment, English as a Second Language (ESL), exchange student program (domestic), honors program, independent study, internships, liberal arts/career combination, student-designed major, study abroad, teacher certificate program. **Teacher certification offered in:** early childhood, special education, elementary, vo-tech, middle/junior high, secondary, bilingual/bicultural. **Reserve Officers Training Corps (ROTC):** Army ROTC: Offered on campus. **Faculty and instruction (2009-2010):** Total instructional faculty: 824 full-time, 320 part-time (55% men; 45% women; 9% minorities). Full-time faculty with Ph.D. or other terminal degree: 99%. Student/faculty ratio: 17/1. Classes of fewer than 20 students: 38%; of 20 to 49 students: 53%; of 50 or more students: 9%. **Advanced Placement and International Baccalaureate credit:** AP tests may be used for: Credit only. Scores accepted: 3, 4, 5. International Baccalaureate exams may be used for: Credit only. **Freshmen returning for sophomore year:** 86%. **Graduation rates:** Four-year: 37%; five-year: 60%; six-year: 63%.

COSTS AND FINANCIAL AID

Financial aid office: (828) 262-2190. **Expenses (2009-2010):** Tuition and fees 2009-2010: $4,491 in state, $15,112 out of state; room/board: $6,400. Estimated books and supplies: $700; transportation: $1,400; personal expenses: $1,400. **Financial aid:** Priority filing date for institution's financial aid form: March 1. In 2009-2010, 54% of undergraduates applied for financial aid. Of those, 42% were determined to have financial need; 57% had their need fully met. Average financial aid package (proportion receiving): $9,991 (41%). Average amount of gift aid, such as scholarships or grants (proportion receiving): $6,611 (37%). Average amount of self-help aid, such as work study or loans (proportion receiving): $5,484 (30%). Average need-based loan (excluding PLUS or other private loans): $5,494. Among students who received need-based aid, the average percentage of need met: 88%. Among students who received aid based on merit, the average award (and the proportion receiving): $2,837 (8%). The average athletic scholarship (and the proportion receiving): $7,209 (1%). Average amount of debt of borrowers graduating in 2009: $16,153. Proportion who borrowed: 55%.

CAMPUS LIFE AND EXTRACURRICULAR ACTIVITIES

Campus housing available (% using): coed dorms (83%), women's dorms (5%), men's dorms (5%), sorority housing (5%), apartments for married students, special housing for disabled students, special housing for international students, other housing options (2%). Students who live in college-owned, operated, or affiliated housing: 33%. **Student employment:** During the 2009-2010 academic year, 20% of undergraduates worked on campus. Average per-year earnings: $4,650. **Clubs and organizations:** Number of student organizations: 270. Activities include: campus ministries, choral groups, concert band, dance, drama/theater, international student organization, jazz band, literary magazine, marching band, model UN, music ensembles, musical theater, opera, pep band, radio station, student government, student newspaper, student film society, symphony orchestra. Number of fraternities: 18; sororities: 11. Proportion of men in fraternities: 8%; of women in sororities: 11%. Average proportion of students who stay on campus on weekends: 60%. **Sports program (2009-2010):** Member of NCAA I. **Men's intercollegiate varsity sports:** baseball, basketball, cross country, football, golf, soccer, tennis, track and field (indoor), track and field (outdoor), wrestling. **Women's intercollegiate varsity sports:** basketball, cross country, field hockey, golf, soccer, softball, tennis, track and field (indoor), track and field (outdoor), volleyball.

SERVICES AND FACILITIES

Basic services: nonremedial tutoring, women's center, placement service, day care, health service, health insurance. **Remedial assistance:** reading, math, writing, study skills. **Counseling services:** minority student, career, military, personal, veteran student, academic, older student, psychological, birth control. **For learning-disabled students:** School does not offer a structured program with separate admission and additional fees. Total undergraduates in learning-disabled program or receiving services: 200. Services include: remedial math, reading machines, tape recorders, other special classes, diagnostic testing service, untimed tests, note-taking services, oral tests, learning center, readers, extended time for tests, tutors, priority registration, priority seating, proofreading services, substitution of courses, texts on tape, exams on tape or computer, other testing accommodations. **Library:** Number of titles: 955,717; number of current serial subscriptions: 7,448. **Information technology resources:** Students are not required to lease or own a computer. Number of campus computers available to all students: 2,600. School has a wireless network. Approximate number of users that can be accommodated: 18,000. Proportion of college-owned housing units wired for high-speed internet access: 100%. **Campus safety:** Security services offered: 24-hour foot-and-vehicle patrols, late-night transport/escort service, 24-hour emergency telephones, lighted pathways/sidewalks, controlled dormitory access (key, security card, etc.).

TRANSFER AND INTERNATIONAL STUDENTS

Transfer students: May apply for admission for the following academic terms: Fall, Spring, Summer. Applicants need a minimum number of credits to apply. For fall 2009: Transfer applications received: 1,953. Transfer applicants offered admission: 1,515. Transfer applicants enrolled: 1,032. **International students:** Number of foreign undergraduates: 70. Number of countries represented: 28. Minimum TOEFL score required: 500 (paper); 61 (computer).

Barton College

- **Address:** 200 Atlantic Christian College Drive NE, PO Box 5000, Wilson, NC 27893
- **Website:** http://www.barton.edu
- **Private; Religious affiliation:** Christian Church (Disciples of Christ)
- **Enrollment:** 875 full-time; 275 part-time

KEY STATS

✔ **U.S News College Ranking:** 42, Regional Colleges (South)
✔ **SAT Score (25th/75th percentile):** 820-1110
✔ **Tuition:** 2009-2010: $20,648

Selectivity: Less selective	**Room/board:** $7,012
Acceptance rate: 51%	**Average debt:** $28,343
Student/faculty ratio: 12/1	**Proportion who borrowed:** 66%

UNDERGRADUATE STUDENT BODY STATS

2009-2010 enrollment: 875 full-time; 275 part-time. Men: 28%; women: 72%. **Ethnic makeup:** African American: 26%; American-Indian: 1%; Asian American: 2%; Hispanic: 2%; White: 69%; International: 1%. **Religious preference:** Roman Catholic: 7%; Protestant: 63%; No preference: 2%; Unknown: 26%; Christian Church (Disciples of Christ): 2%.

ADMISSIONS FACTS AND FIGURES

Phone: (800) 345-4973. **Email:** enroll@barton.edu. **Website:** http://www.barton.edu. **Application deadlines for fall 2011:** Regular decision: Rolling. Early decision: Not offered. Early action: Not offered. Admission can be deferred. **Application fee:** $25. **To apply online, go to:** http://www.barton.edu/admissions/default.htm. **Admissions requirements/recommendations:** High school units required (recommended): English: 4; Mathematics: 3 (4); Science: 2; Foreign language: (2); Academic electives: 1; Total units: 13. Tests: The college uses SAT or ACT scores in admissions decisions. Either SAT or ACT required. For admission to the fall 2011 entering class, the school will accept: ACT with or without writing accepted. Campus visit: Recommended. Admissions interview: Recommended. Off-campus interview: May be arranged. **Factors that count in admissions decisions:** *Academic:* Secondary school record: Very Important. Class rank: Important. Letters of recommendation: Considered. Standardized test scores: Very Important. Essay: Considered. ***Nonacademic:*** Interview: Important. Extracurricular activities: Considered. Talent/ability: Considered. Character/personal qualities: Considered. Alumni/ae relationship: Considered.

Geographical residence: Not Considered. State residency: Not Considered. Religious affiliation/commitment: Not Considered. Minority status: Not Considered. Volunteer work: Considered. Work experience: Considered. **Other schools with the greatest overlap in applicants:** East Carolina University; North Carolina State University–Raleigh; University of North Carolina–Chapel Hill; University of North Carolina–Greensboro; University of North Carolina–Wilmington. **Admissions statistics for the fall 2009 entering class:** Total applicants: 2,681. Total accepted: 1,360. Freshmen enrolled: 230; 18% were from out of state. Overall acceptance rate: 51%. **Credentials of fall 2009 freshmen:** 7% ranked in the top 10 percent of their high school class; 36% were in the top 25 percent; 68% were in the top half. (Proportion submitting class standing: 93%.) **Average high school grade point average:** 3.0. **First-year students who submitted SAT scores:** 93%. Scores (25/75 percentile): Critical Reading: 400-550, Math: 420-560, Combined: 820-1110. **First-year students submitting ACT scores:** 20%. Scores (25/75 percentile): English: 16-20, Math: 15-21, Composite: 17-20.

ACADEMICS

Year founded: 1902. **Academic calendar:** 4-1-4. **Degrees offered:** bachelor's. **Most popular majors:** 26% business, management, marketing, and related support services, 19% health professions and related clinical sciences, 17% education, 7% social sciences, 6% public administration and social service professions. **Major fields of study:** biological and biomedical sciences; business, management, marketing, and related support services; communication, journalism, and related programs; computer and information sciences and support services; education; English language and literature/letters; foreign languages, literatures, and linguistics; health professions and related clinical sciences; history; liberal arts and sciences studies, and humanities; mathematics and statistics; multi/interdisciplinary studies; natural resources and conservation; parks, recreation, leisure, and fitness studies; philosophy and religious studies; physical sciences; psychology; public administration and social service professions; security and protective services; social sciences; visual and performing arts. **Areas of required coursework:** humanities, computer literacy, mathematics, English (including composition), sciences (biological or physical), history, social science, other. **Pre-professional programs:** pre-law, pre-dentistry, pre-medicine, pre-theology, pre-veterinary science, pre-optometry, pre-pharmacy, other. **Special academic programs (% participation):** cooperative (work-study plan) program, double major (14%), English as a Second Language (ESL), honors program, independent study (28%), internships, study abroad, teacher certificate program (14%), weekend college (18%). **Teacher certification offered in:** early childhood, special education, elementary, middle/junior high, secondary, bilingual/bicultural. **Cooperative education programs:** business, humanities, natural science, social/behavioral science. **Faculty and instruction (2009-2010):** Total instructional faculty: 68 full-time, 49 part-time (42% men; 58% women; 9% minorities). Full-time faculty with Ph.D. or other terminal degree: 69%. Student/faculty ratio: 12/1. Classes of fewer than 20 students: 64%; of 20 to 49 students: 36%; of 50 or more students: 0%. **Advanced Placement and International Baccalaureate credit:** AP tests may be used for: Credit only. Scores accepted: 3, 4, 5. International Baccalaureate exams may be used for: Credit only. **Freshmen returning for sophomore year:** 69%. **Graduation rates:** Four-year: 33%; five-year: 39%; six-year: 39%.

COSTS AND FINANCIAL AID

Financial aid office: (252) 399-6323. **Expenses (2009-2010):** Tuition and fees 2009-2010: $20,648; room/board: $7,012. Estimated books and supplies: $1,100. **Financial aid:** Priority filing date for institution's financial aid form: April 1. In 2009-2010, 90% of undergraduates applied for financial aid. Of those, 84% were determined to have financial need; 10% had their need fully met. Average financial aid package (proportion receiving): $19,289 (84%). Average amount of gift aid, such as scholarships or grants (proportion receiving): $6,134 (64%). Average amount of self-help aid, such as work study or loans (proportion receiving): $1,982 (28%). Average need-based loan (excluding PLUS or other private loans): $5,318. Among students who received need-based aid, the average percentage of need met: 67%. Among students who received aid based on merit, the average award (and the proportion receiving): $4,837 (13%). The average athletic scholarship (and the proportion receiving): $7,242 (5%). Average amount of debt of borrowers graduating in 2009: $28,343. Proportion who borrowed: 66%.

CAMPUS LIFE AND EXTRACURRICULAR ACTIVITIES

Campus housing available (% using): coed dorms (75%), women's dorms (25%), sorority housing, fraternity housing, special housing for disabled students. Students who live in college-owned, operated, or affiliated housing: 52%. **Student employment:** During the 2009-2010 academic year, 5% of undergraduates worked on campus. Average per-year earnings: $2,200.

Clubs and organizations: Number of student organizations: 51. Activities include: campus ministries, choral groups, dance, drama/theater, literary magazine, musical theater, student government, student newspaper, symphony orchestra, television station. Number of fraternities: 3; sororities: 3. Proportion of men in fraternities: 16%; of women in sororities: 11%. Average proportion of students who stay on campus on weekends: 55%. **Sports program (2009-2010):** Member of NCAA II. *Men's intercollegiate varsity sports:* baseball, basketball, cross country, golf, soccer, tennis, track and field (outdoor). *Women's intercollegiate varsity sports:* basketball, cross country, soccer, softball, tennis, track and field (outdoor), volleyball.

SERVICES AND FACILITIES

Basic services: nonremedial tutoring, placement service, health service, health insurance. **Remedial assistance:** reading, math, writing, study skills. **Counseling services:** career, personal, academic, psychological, birth control, religious. **For learning-disabled students:** School does not offer a structured program with separate admission and additional fees. Services include: remedial math, remedial English, reading machines, tape recorders, note-taking services, oral tests, learning center, readers, extended time for tests, tutors, priority seating, texts on tape, other testing accommodations. **Library:** Number of titles: 190,954; number of current serial subscriptions: 13,437. **Information technology resources:** Students are not required to lease or own a computer. Number of campus computers available to all students: 210. School has a wireless network. Approximate number of users that can be accommodated: 350. Proportion of college-owned housing units wired for high-speed internet access: 100%. **Campus safety:** Security services offered: 24-hour foot-and-vehicle patrols, late-night transport/escort service, 24-hour emergency telephones, lighted pathways/sidewalks, controlled dormitory access (key, security card, etc).

TRANSFER AND INTERNATIONAL STUDENTS

Transfer students: May apply for admission for the following academic terms: Fall, Winter, Spring, Summer. Applicants need a minimum number of credits to apply. For fall 2009: Transfer applications received: 469. Transfer applicants offered admission: 249. Transfer applicants enrolled: 81. **International students:** Number of foreign undergraduates: 16 (1% of student body). Number of countries represented: 12. Minimum TOEFL score required: 525 (paper); 195 (computer).

Belmont Abbey College

- **Address:** 100 Belmont-Mount Holly Road, Belmont, NC 28012
- **Website:** http://www.belmontabbeycollege.edu
- **Private; Religious affiliation:** Roman Catholic
- **Enrollment:** 1,520 full-time; 118 part-time

KEY STATS

✔ **U.S News College Ranking:** 39, Regional Colleges (South)
✔ **SAT Score (25th/75th percentile):** 890-1150
✔ **Tuition:** 2010-2011: $23,002

Selectivity: Selective	**Room/board:** $10,094
Acceptance rate: 75%	**Average debt:** $21,000
Student/faculty ratio: 17/1	**Proportion who borrowed:** 73%

UNDERGRADUATE STUDENT BODY STATS

2009-2010 enrollment: 1,520 full-time; 118 part-time. Men: 37%; women: 63%. **Ethnic makeup:** African American: 27%; Asian American: 2%; Hispanic: 5%; White: 64%; International: 3%. **Religious preference:** Roman Catholic: 30%; Protestant: 25%; No preference: 44%.

ADMISSIONS FACTS AND FIGURES

Phone: (704) 825-6665. **Email:** admissions@bac.edu. **Website:** http://www.belmontabbeycollege.edu. **Application deadlines for fall 2011:** Regular decision: August 1. Early decision: Not offered. Early action: Not offered. Admission can be deferred. **Application fee:** $35. **To apply online, go to:** http://www.belmontabbeycollege.edu/admissions/application-process/apply-online.aspx. **Admissions requirements/recommendations:** High school units required (recommended): English: 4; Mathematics: 3 (4); Science: 2; Foreign language: 2 (3); Social studies: 1 (1); History: 1 (1); Academic electives: 3; Total units: 16. Tests: The college uses SAT or ACT scores in admissions decisions. Neither SAT nor ACT required. For admission to the fall 2011 entering class, the school will accept: ACT with or without writing accepted. Campus visit: Recommended. Admissions interview:

Recommended. Off-campus interview: May be arranged. **Factors that count in admissions decisions:** *Academic:* Secondary school record: Very Important. Class rank: Important. Letters of recommendation: Considered. Standardized test scores: Very Important. Essay: Considered. *Nonacademic:* Interview: Important. Extracurricular activities: Considered. Talent/ability: Considered. Character/personal qualities: Not Considered. Alumni/ae relationship: Not Considered. Geographical residence: Not Considered. State residency: Not Considered. Religious affiliation/commitment: Not Considered. Minority status: Not Considered. Volunteer work: Considered. Work experience: Considered. **Other schools with the greatest overlap in applicants:** Appalachian State University; East Carolina University; North Carolina State University–Raleigh; University of North Carolina–Charlotte; Western Carolina University. **Admissions statistics for the fall 2009 entering class:** Total applicants: 1,762. Total accepted: 1,321. Freshmen enrolled: 401; 42% were from out of state. Overall acceptance rate: 75%. **Credentials of fall 2009 freshmen:** 12% ranked in the top 10 percent of their high school class; 22% were in the top 25 percent; 64% were in the top half. (Proportion submitting class standing: 64%.) **First-year students who submitted SAT scores:** 81%. Scores (25/75 percentile): Critical Reading: 440-580, Math: 450-570, Combined: 890-1150. **First-year students submitting ACT scores:** 20%. Scores (25/75 percentile): English: 20-28, Math: 19-25, Composite: 20-28.

ACADEMICS

Year founded: 1876. **Academic calendar:** Semester. **Degrees offered:** bachelor's. **Most popular majors:** 50% business, management, marketing, and related support services, 18% education, 9% biological and biomedical sciences, 7% social sciences, 5% liberal arts and sciences studies, and humanities. **Major fields of study:** biological and biomedical sciences; business, management, marketing, and related support services; computer and information sciences and support services; education; English language and literature/letters; history; liberal arts and sciences studies, and humanities; philosophy and religious studies; psychology; social sciences; theology and religious vocations. **Areas of required coursework:** arts/fine arts, humanities, computer literacy, mathematics, English (including composition), philosophy, sciences (biological or physical), history, social science, other. **Pre-professional programs:** pre-law, pre-dentistry, pre-medicine, pre-theology, pre-veterinary science, pre-optometry, pre-pharmacy. **Special academic programs (% participation):** accelerated program (30%), cooperative (work-study plan) program (2%), double major (5%), dual enrollment (0%), honors program (5%), independent study (10%), internships (55%), study abroad (10%), teacher certificate program (15%), weekend college (5%). **Teacher certification offered in:** elementary. **Reserve Officers Training Corps (ROTC):** Army ROTC: Offered at cooperating institution (University of North Carolina–Charlotte); Navy ROTC: Offered at cooperating institution (University of North Carolina–Charlotte); Air Force ROTC: Offered at cooperating institution (University of North Carolina–Charlotte). **Faculty and instruction (2009-2010):** Total instructional faculty: 69 full-time, 63 part-time (51% men; 49% women; 8% minorities). Full-time faculty with Ph.D. or other terminal degree: 64%. Student/faculty ratio: 17/1. Classes of fewer than 20 students: 62%; of 20 to 49 students: 38%; of 50 or more students: 0%. **Advanced Placement and International Baccalaureate credit:** AP tests may be used for: Credit only. Scores accepted: 3, 4, 5. International Baccalaureate exams may be used for: Credit only. **Freshmen returning for sophomore year:** 59%. **Graduation rates:** Four-year: 29%; five-year: 31%; six-year: 39%. **Graduate study:** 26% of students pursue further study immediately upon graduation; 42% within one year; 77% within five years. Fields in which graduates pursue further study: Master of Business Administration (MBA), 26%; law, 10%; medicine, 3%; dentistry, 2%; theology (or the seminary), 4%; education, 21%; arts and sciences, 18%.

COSTS AND FINANCIAL AID

Financial aid office: (704) 825-6718. **Expenses (2010-2011):** Tuition and fees 2010-2011: $23,002; room/board: $10,094. Estimated books and supplies: $1,000; transportation: $2,600; personal expenses: $2,000. **Financial aid:** Priority filing date for institution's financial aid form: April 1. In 2009-2010, 89% of undergraduates applied for financial aid. Of those, 82% were determined to have financial need; 11% had their need fully met. Average financial aid package (proportion receiving): $13,151 (81%). Average amount of gift aid, such as scholarships or grants (proportion receiving): $9,398 (80%). Average amount of self-help aid, such as work study or loans (proportion receiving): $4,166 (74%). Average need-based loan (excluding PLUS or other private loans): $4,073. Among students who received need-based aid, the average percentage of need met: 56%. Among students who received aid based on merit, the average award (and the proportion receiving): $10,008 (18%). The average athletic scholarship (and the proportion

receiving): $5,598 (7%). Average amount of debt of borrowers graduating in 2009: $21,000. Proportion who borrowed: 73%.

CAMPUS LIFE AND EXTRACURRICULAR ACTIVITIES

Campus housing available (% using): coed dorms (98%), apartment for single students (2%). Students who live in college-owned, operated, or affiliated housing: 40%. **Student employment:** During the 2009-2010 academic year, 25% of undergraduates worked on campus. Average per-year earnings: $2,500. **Clubs and organizations:** Number of student organizations: 31. Activities include: campus ministries, choral groups, dance, drama/theater, international student organization, literary magazine, musical theater, pep band, student government, student newspaper, yearbook. Number of fraternities: 2; sororities: 4. Proportion of men in fraternities: 20%; of women in sororities: 20%. Average proportion of students who stay on campus on weekends: 70%. **Sports program (2009-2010):** Member of NCAA II.

SERVICES AND FACILITIES

Basic services: nonremedial tutoring, placement service, health service. **Remedial assistance:** reading, math, study skills. **Counseling services:** career, personal, academic, older student, psychological, religious. **For learning-disabled students:** School does not offer a structured program with separate admission and additional fees. Services include: remedial math, remedial English, untimed tests, oral tests, learning center, extended time for tests, tutors, priority registration, other testing accommodations, other. **Library:** Number of titles: 119,509; number of current serial subscriptions: 276. **Information technology resources:** Students are not required to lease or own a computer. Number of campus computers available to all students: 75. School has a wireless network. Approximate number of users that can be accommodated: 6,400. Proportion of college-owned housing units wired for high-speed internet access: 100%. **Campus safety:** Security services offered: 24-hour foot-and-vehicle patrols, late-night transport/escort service, 24-hour emergency telephones, lighted pathways/sidewalks, controlled dormitory access (key, security card, etc).

TRANSFER AND INTERNATIONAL STUDENTS

Transfer students: May apply for admission for the following academic terms: Fall, Spring. Applicants need a minimum number of credits to apply. For fall 2009: Transfer applications received: 666. Transfer applicants offered admission: 435. Transfer applicants enrolled: 218. **International students:** Number of foreign undergraduates: 43 (3% of student body). Number of countries represented: 20. Minimum TOEFL score required: 500 (paper); 173 (computer). Average TOEFL score: 620 (paper).

Bennett College

- Address: 900 E. Washington Street, Greensboro, NC 27401
- Website: http://www.bennett.edu
- Private; Religious affiliation: United Methodist
- Enrollment: 709 full-time; 57 part-time

KEY STATS

✔ **U.S News College Ranking:** second tier, National Liberal Arts Colleges
✔ **SAT Score (25th/75th percentile):** 670-870
✔ **Tuition:** 2010-2011: $15,844

Selectivity: Least selective	**Room/board:** $7,006
Acceptance rate: 54%	**Average debt:** $37,667
Student/faculty ratio: 11/1	**Proportion who borrowed:** 98%

UNDERGRADUATE STUDENT BODY STATS

2009-2010 enrollment: 709 full-time; 57 part-time. Men: 0%; women: 100%. **Ethnic makeup:** African American: 96%; Hispanic: 1%; White: 2%; International: 1%. **Religious preference:** Roman Catholic: 3%; Protestant: 70%; Jewish: 1%; No preference: 10%; United Methodist: 9%; Baptist: 7%.

ADMISSIONS FACTS AND FIGURES

Phone: (336) 370-8624. **Email:** admiss@bennett.edu. **Website:** http://www.bennett.edu. **Application deadlines for fall 2011:** Regular decision: Rolling. Early decision: Not offered. Early action: Not offered. Admission can be deferred. **Application fee:** $30. **To apply online, go to:** http://www.ncmentor.org/applications/nc_independents_common_app/apply.html?application_id=1556. **Admissions requirements/recommendations:** High school units required (recommended): English: 4 (4); Mathematics: 3 (3); Science: 3 (3); Foreign language: 2 (2); Social studies: 2 (2); History: 0 (0); Academic elec-

tives: 5 (5); Total units: 19 (19). **Tests:** The college uses SAT or ACT scores in admissions decisions. Neither SAT nor ACT required. For admission to the fall 2011 entering class, the school will accept: ACT with or without writing accepted. Campus visit: Recommended. Admissions interview: Neither required nor recommended. Off-campus interview: Not available. **Factors that count in admissions decisions:** *Academic:* Secondary school record: Very Important. Class rank: Important. Letters of recommendation: Very Important. Standardized test scores: Considered. Essay: Very Important. *Nonacademic:* Interview: Not Considered. Extracurricular activities: Considered. Talent/ability: Considered. Character/personal qualities: Important. Alumni/ae relationship: Important. Geographical residence: Not Considered. State residency: Not Considered. Religious affiliation/commitment: Not Considered. Minority status: Not Considered. Volunteer work: Important. Work experience: Considered. **Other schools with the greatest overlap in applicants:** Greensboro College; Guilford College; North Carolina A&T State University; North Carolina Central University; University of North Carolina–Greensboro. **Admissions statistics for the fall 2009 entering class:** Total applicants: 1,676. Total accepted: 905. Freshmen enrolled: 232; 67% were from out of state. Overall acceptance rate: 54%. **Credentials of fall 2009 freshmen:** 3% ranked in the top 10 percent of their high school class; 10% were in the top 25 percent; 39% were in the top half. (Proportion submitting class standing: 63%.) **Average high school grade point average:** 2.4. **First-year students who submitted SAT scores:** 56%. Scores (25/75 percentile): Critical Reading: 350-450, Math: 320-420, Combined: 670-870. **First-year students submitting ACT scores:** 15%. Scores (25/75 percentile): English: N/A, Math: N/A, Composite: 14-18.

ACADEMICS

Year founded: 1873. **Academic calendar:** Semester. **Degrees offered:** bachelor's. **Most popular majors:** 15% psychology, 15% social work, 11% mass communication/media studies, 9% biology/biological sciences, 8% multi/interdisciplinary studies. **Major fields of study:** biological and biomedical sciences; business, management, marketing, and related support services; communication, journalism, and related programs; computer and information sciences and support services; education; English language and literature/letters; health professions and related clinical sciences; mathematics and statistics; multi/interdisciplinary studies; psychology; public administration and social service professions; social sciences. **Areas of required coursework:** computer literacy, mathematics, English (including composition), foreign languages, sciences (biological or physical). **Special academic programs (% participation):** accelerated program, cooperative (work-study plan) program (10%), cross-registration (2%), double major, exchange student program (domestic), double major, independent study, internships, liberal arts/career combination, student-designed major, study abroad (1%), teacher certificate program. **Teacher certification offered in:** special education, elementary, middle/junior high, secondary. **Cooperative education programs:** engineering. **Reserve Officers Training Corps (ROTC):** Army ROTC: Offered at cooperating institution (North Carolina A&T State University); Air Force ROTC: Offered at cooperating institution (North Carolina A&T State University). **Faculty and instruction (2009-2010):** Total instructional faculty: 56 full-time, 26 part-time (29% men; 71% women; 67% minorities). Full-time faculty with Ph.D. or other terminal degree: 61%. Student/faculty ratio: 11/1. Classes of fewer than 20 students: 68%; of 20 to 49 students: 26%; of 50 or more students: 6%. **Advanced Placement and International Baccalaureate credit:** AP tests may be used for: Credit only. Scores accepted: 4, 5. International Baccalaureate exams may be used for: Placement only. **Freshmen returning for sophomore year:** 67%. **Graduation rates:** Four-year: 28%; five-year: 46%; six-year: 48%. **Graduate study:** 12% of students pursue further study immediately upon graduation.

COSTS AND FINANCIAL AID

Financial aid office: (336) 517-2205. **Expenses (2010-2011):** Tuition and fees 2010-2011: $15,844; room/board: $7,006. Estimated books and supplies: $1,200; transportation: $2,000; personal expenses: $3,000. **Financial aid:** Priority filing date for institution's financial aid form: March 15. In 2009-2010, 96% of undergraduates applied for financial aid. Of those, 93% were determined to have financial need; 2% had their need fully met. Average financial aid package (proportion receiving): $12,120 (91%). Average amount of gift aid, such as scholarships or grants (proportion receiving): $9,326 (82%). Average amount of self-help aid, such as work study or loans (proportion receiving): $3,936 (87%). Average need-based loan (excluding PLUS or other private loans): $3,843. Among students who received need-based aid, the average percentage of need met: 48%. Among students who received aid based on merit, the average award (and the proportion receiving): $6,100 (1%). The average athletic scholarship (and the proportion

receiving): $0 (0%). Average amount of debt of borrowers graduating in 2009: $37,667. Proportion who borrowed: 98%.

CAMPUS LIFE AND EXTRACURRICULAR ACTIVITIES
Campus housing available (% using): women's dorms (100%). Students who live in college-owned, operated, or affiliated housing: 62%. **Clubs and organizations:** Number of student organizations: 52. Activities include: choral groups, dance, drama/theater, music ensembles, radio station, student government, student newspaper, yearbook. Number of fraternities: 0; sororities: 4. of women in sororities: 6%. Average proportion of students who stay on campus on weekends: 45%.

SERVICES AND FACILITIES
Basic services: nonremedial tutoring, women's center, placement service, day care, health service. **Remedial assistance:** reading, math, writing, study skills. **Counseling services:** career, personal, academic, psychological, birth control, religious. **For learning-disabled students:** School does not offer a structured program with separate admission and additional fees. Total undergraduates in learning-disabled program or receiving services: 21. Services include: remedial math, remedial English, reading machines, remedial reading, tape recorders, untimed tests, note-taking services, oral tests, learning center, readers, extended time for tests, tutors, priority registration, priority seating, texts on tape, other testing accommodations. **Library:** Number of titles: 92,830; number of current serial subscriptions: 45. **Information technology resources:** Students are not required to lease or own a computer. Number of campus computers available to all students: 100. School has a wireless network. Approximate number of users that can be accommodated: 1,000. Proportion of college-owned housing units wired for high-speed internet access: 100%. **Campus safety:** Security services offered: 24-hour foot-and-vehicle patrols, late-night transport/escort service, 24-hour emergency telephones, lighted pathways/sidewalks.

TRANSFER AND INTERNATIONAL STUDENTS
Transfer students: May apply for admission for the following academic terms: Fall, Spring. Applicants need a minimum number of credits to apply. For fall 2009: Transfer applications received: 57. Transfer applicants offered admission: 24. Transfer applicants enrolled: 11. **International students:** Number of foreign undergraduates: 5 (1% of student body). Number of countries represented: 5. Minimum TOEFL score required: 500 (paper); 78 (computer).

Brevard College

- **Address:** 1 Brevard College Drive, Brevard, NC 28712
- **Website:** http://www.brevard.edu
- **Private; Religious affiliation:** Methodist
- **Enrollment:** 642 full-time; 16 part-time

KEY STATS
✔ **U.S News College Ranking:** second tier, National Liberal Arts Colleges
✔ **SAT Score (25th/75th percentile):** 850-1090
✔ **Tuition:** 2010-2011: $22,100

Selectivity: Less selective	**Room/board:** $7,950
Acceptance rate: 54%	**Average debt:** $20,770
Student/faculty ratio: 8/1	**Proportion who borrowed:** 59%

UNDERGRADUATE STUDENT BODY STATS
2009-2010 enrollment: 642 full-time; 16 part-time. Men: 57%; women: 43%. **Ethnic makeup:** African American: 11%; American-Indian: 1%; Hispanic: 2%; White: 83%; International: 3%. **Religious preference:** Roman Catholic: 3%; Protestant: 29%; No preference: 55%; Methodist: 12%; Other: 1%.

ADMISSIONS FACTS AND FIGURES
Phone: (828) 884-8300. **Email:** admissions@brevard.edu. **Website:** http://www.brevard.edu. **Application deadlines for fall 2011:** Regular decision: Rolling. Early decision: Not offered. Early action: Not offered. Admission can be deferred. **Application fee:** $30. **To apply online, go to:** http://brevard.edu/admissions/apply.asp. **Admissions requirements/recommendations:** High school units required (recommended): English: (4); Mathematics: (3); Science: (3); Foreign language: (2); Social studies: (4); History: (1); Academic electives: (4); Total units: (22). Tests: The college uses SAT or ACT scores in admissions decisions. Either SAT or ACT required. For admission to the fall 2011 entering class, the school will accept: ACT with

or without writing accepted. Campus visit: Recommended. Admissions interview: Recommended. Off-campus interview: May be arranged. **Factors that count in admissions decisions:** *Academic:* Secondary school record: Very Important. Class rank: Important. Letters of recommendation: Considered. Standardized test scores: Important. Essay: Important. *Nonacademic:* Interview: Important. Extracurricular activities: Important. Talent/ability: Important. Character/personal qualities: Important. Alumni/ae relationship: Considered. Geographical residence: Not Considered. State residency: Not Considered. Religious affiliation/commitment: Considered. Minority status: Not Considered. Volunteer work: Important. Work experience: Considered. **Other schools with the greatest overlap in applicants:** Appalachian State University; Lenoir-Rhyne University; Mars Hill College; University of North Carolina–Asheville; Warren Wilson College. **Admissions statistics for the fall 2009 entering class:** Total applicants: 1,191. Total accepted: 640. Freshmen enrolled: 191; 48% were from out of state. Overall acceptance rate: 54%. **Credentials of fall 2009 freshmen:** 7% ranked in the top 10 percent of their high school class; 22% were in the top 25 percent; 49% were in the top half. (Proportion submitting class standing: 71%.) **Average high school grade point average:** 2.9. **First-year students who submitted SAT scores:** 76%. Scores (25/75 percentile): Critical Reading: 420-540, Math: 430-550, Combined: 850-1090. **First-year students submitting ACT scores:** 37%. Scores (25/75 percentile): English: N/A, Math: N/A, Composite: 16-21.

ACADEMICS
Year founded: 1853. **Academic calendar:** Semester. **Degrees offered:** bachelor's. **Most popular majors:** 28% multi/interdisciplinary studies, 20% business administration and management, 19% parks, recreation, and leisure studies, 11% visual and performing arts, 8% health services/allied health/health sciences. **Major fields of study:** biological and biomedical sciences; business, management, marketing, and related support services; education; English language and literature/letters; health professions and related clinical sciences; history; legal professions and studies; mathematics and statistics; multi/interdisciplinary studies; natural resources and conservation; parks, recreation, leisure, and fitness studies; philosophy and religious studies; psychology; visual and performing arts. **Areas of required coursework:** arts/fine arts, humanities, computer literacy, mathematics, English (including composition), philosophy, sciences (biological or physical), history, social science, other. **Pre-professional programs:** pre-law, pre-dentistry, pre-medicine, pre-theology, pre-veterinary science, other. **Special academic programs:** double major, dual enrollment, honors program, independent study, internships, student-designed major, study abroad, teacher certificate program. **Teacher certification offered in:** elementary, middle/junior high, secondary. **Faculty and instruction (2009-2010):** Total instructional faculty: 55 full-time, 36 part-time (58% men; 42% women; 2% minorities). Full-time faculty with Ph.D. or other terminal degree: 76%. Student/faculty ratio: 8/1. Classes of fewer than 20 students: 75%; of 20 to 49 students: 25%. **Advanced Placement and International Baccalaureate credit:** AP tests may be used for: Credit only. Scores accepted: 3, 4, 5. International Baccalaureate exams may be used for: Credit only. **Freshmen returning for sophomore year:** 57%. **Graduation rates:** Four-year: 23%; five-year: 29%; six-year: 30%.

COSTS AND FINANCIAL AID
Financial aid office: (828) 884-8287. **Expenses (2010-2011):** Tuition and fees 2010-2011: $22,100; room/board: $7,950. Estimated books and supplies: $1,000; transportation: $1,000; personal expenses: $1,000. **Financial aid:** Priority filing date for institution's financial aid form: April 15. In 2009-2010, 80% of undergraduates applied for financial aid. Of those, 72% were determined to have financial need; 28% had their need fully met. Average financial aid package (proportion receiving): $20,500 (72%). Average amount of gift aid, such as scholarships or grants (proportion receiving): $14,200 (72%). Average amount of self-help aid, such as work study or loans (proportion receiving): $4,650 (58%). Average need-based loan (excluding PLUS or other private loans): $4,260. Among students who received need-based aid, the average percentage of need met: 83%. Among students who received aid based on merit, the average award (and the proportion receiving): $2,600 (20%). The average athletic scholarship (and the proportion receiving): $12,250 (10%). Average amount of debt of borrowers graduating in 2009: $20,770. Proportion who borrowed: 59%.

CAMPUS LIFE AND EXTRACURRICULAR ACTIVITIES
Campus housing available (% using): coed dorms (100%), special housing for disabled students (0%), other housing options (0%). Students who live in college-owned, operated, or affiliated housing: 74%. **Student employment:** During the 2009-2010 academic year, 20% of undergraduates worked on campus. Average per-year earnings: $1,500. **Clubs and organizations:**

Number of student organizations: 32. Activities include: campus ministries, choral groups, concert band, dance, drama/theater, jazz band, literary magazine, music ensembles, musical theater, opera, pep band, student government, student newspaper. Number of fraternities: 0; sororities: 0. Average proportion of students who stay on campus on weekends: 50%. **Sports program (2009-2010):** Member of NCAA II. *Men's intercollegiate varsity sports:* baseball, basketball, cross country, football, golf, soccer, tennis, track and field (outdoor). *Women's intercollegiate varsity sports:* basketball, cross country, soccer, softball, tennis, track and field (outdoor), volleyball.

SERVICES AND FACILITIES

Basic services: nonremedial tutoring, health service, health insurance. **Remedial assistance:** reading, math, writing, study skills. **Counseling services:** minority student, career, personal, veteran student, academic, psychological, birth control, religious. **For learning-disabled students:** School does not offer a structured program with separate admission and additional fees. Services include: remedial math, reading machines, remedial reading, tape recorders, note-taking services, oral tests, learning center, readers, extended time for tests, tutors, priority registration, priority seating, texts on tape, typist/scribe, exams on tape or computer, other testing accommodations. **Library:** Number of titles: 59,229; number of current serial subscriptions: 23,951. **Information technology resources:** Students are not required to lease or own a computer. Number of campus computers available to all students: 100. School has a wireless network. Approximate number of users that can be accommodated: 150. Proportion of college-owned housing units wired for high-speed internet access: 100%. **Campus safety:** Security services offered: 24-hour foot-and-vehicle patrols, late-night transport/escort service, 24-hour emergency telephones, controlled dormitory access (key, security card, etc).

TRANSFER AND INTERNATIONAL STUDENTS

Transfer students: May apply for admission for the following academic terms: Fall, Spring. Applicants do not need a minimum number of credits to apply. For fall 2009: Transfer applications received: 193. Transfer applicants offered admission: 112. Transfer applicants enrolled: 38. **International students:** Number of foreign undergraduates: 21 (3% of student body). Number of countries represented: 14. Minimum TOEFL score required: 537 (paper); 203 (computer). Average TOEFL score: 550 (paper).

Campbell University

- **Address:** PO Box 546, Buies Creek, NC 27506
- **Website:** http://www.campbell.edu
- **Private; Religious affiliation:** Baptist
- **Enrollment:** 3,063 full-time; 1,156 part-time

KEY STATS

✔ **U.S News College Ranking:** 37, Regional Universities (South)
✔ **SAT Score (25th/75th percentile):** 910-1150
✔ **Tuition:** 2010-2011: $22,520

Selectivity: Selective	**Room/board:** $8,400
Acceptance rate: 39%	**Average debt:** $38,696
Student/faculty ratio: 19/1	**Proportion who borrowed:** 75%

UNDERGRADUATE STUDENT BODY STATS

2009-2010 enrollment: 3,063 full-time; 1,156 part-time. Men: 49%; women: 51%. **Ethnic makeup:** African American: 13%; American-Indian: 1%; Asian American: 4%; Hispanic: 4%; White: 78%. **Religious preference:** Roman Catholic: 8%; Protestant: 1%; Jewish: 1%; Muslim: 1%; Hindu: 1%; No preference: 13%; Baptist: 35%; Christian: 16%; Other: 24%.

ADMISSIONS FACTS AND FIGURES

Phone: (910) 893-1320. **Email:** adm@mailcenter.campbell.edu. **Website:** http://www.campbell.edu. **Application deadlines for fall 2011:** Regular decision: Rolling. Early decision: Not offered. Early action: Not offered. Admission can be deferred. **Application fee:** $35. **To apply online, go to:** https://www.applyweb.com/apply/campbell/. **Admissions requirements/recommendations:** High school units required (recommended): English: 4; Mathematics: 3; Science: 2; Foreign language: 2; Social studies: 2; Total units: 13. Tests: The college uses SAT or ACT scores in admissions decisions. Either SAT or ACT required. For admission to the fall 2011 entering class, the school will accept: ACT with writing required. Campus visit: Recommended. Admissions interview: Recommended. Off-campus interview: Not available. **Factors that count in admissions decisions:** *Academic:*

Secondary school record: Very Important. Class rank: Important. Letters of recommendation: Considered. Standardized test scores: Very Important. Essay: Considered. *Nonacademic:* Interview: Important. Extracurricular activities: Considered. Talent/ability: Important. Character/personal qualities: Important. Alumni/ae relationship: Considered. Geographical residence: Not Considered. State residency: Not Considered. Religious affiliation/commitment: Not Considered. Minority status: Not Considered. Volunteer work: Considered. Work experience: Considered. **Other schools with the greatest overlap in applicants:** Appalachian State University; East Carolina University; North Carolina State University–Raleigh; University of North Carolina–Chapel Hill; Wake Forest University. **Admissions statistics for the fall 2009 entering class:** Total applicants: 4,102. Total accepted: 1,606. Freshmen enrolled: 739; 19% were from out of state. Overall acceptance rate: 39%. **Credentials of fall 2009 freshmen:** 24% ranked in the top 10 percent of their high school class; 56% were in the top 25 percent; 85% were in the top half. (Proportion submitting class standing: 81%.) **Average high school grade point average:** 3.7. **First-year students who submitted SAT scores:** 94%. Scores (25/75 percentile): Critical Reading: 440-560, Math: 470-590, Combined: 910-1150. **First-year students submitting ACT scores:** 25%. Scores (25/75 percentile): English: N/A, Math: N/A, Composite: 19-24.

ACADEMICS

Year founded: 1887. **Academic calendar:** Semester. **Degrees offered:** associate, bachelor's, master's, doctorate. **Most popular majors:** 22% business administration and management, 16% management information systems, 8% psychology, 8% social sciences, 6% accounting. **Major fields of study:** biological and biomedical sciences; business, management, marketing, and related support services; communication, journalism, and related programs; computer and information sciences and support services; education; English language and literature/letters; family and consumer sciences/human sciences; foreign languages, literatures, and linguistics; health professions and related clinical sciences; legal professions and studies; mathematics and statistics; parks, recreation, leisure, and fitness studies; philosophy and religious studies; psychology; public administration and social service professions; security and protective services; social sciences; theology and religious vocations; visual and performing arts. **Areas of required coursework:** arts/fine arts, humanities, computer literacy, mathematics, English (including composition), foreign languages, sciences (biological or physical), history, social science, other. **Pre-professional programs:** pre-law, pre-dentistry, pre-medicine, pre-veterinary science, pre-pharmacy, other. **Special academic programs:** accelerated program, cooperative (work-study plan) program, distance learning, double major, dual enrollment, honors program, independent study, internships, liberal arts/career combination, study abroad, teacher certificate program. **Teacher certification offered in:** early childhood, elementary, middle/junior high, secondary. **Cooperative education programs:** education. **Reserve Officers Training Corps (ROTC):** Army ROTC: Offered on campus. **Faculty and instruction (2009-2010):** Total instructional faculty: 193 full-time, 99 part-time (56% men; 44% women; 11% minorities). Full-time faculty with Ph.D. or other terminal degree: 92%. Student/faculty ratio: 19/1. Classes of fewer than 20 students: 48%; of 20 to 49 students: 41%; of 50 or more students: 11%. **Advanced Placement and International Baccalaureate credit:** AP tests may be used for: Placement only. Scores accepted: 3, 4, 5. International Baccalaureate exams may be used for: Credit and/or placement. **Freshmen returning for sophomore year:** 71%. **Graduation rates:** Four-year: 36%; five-year: 51%; six-year: 53%. **Graduate study:** 29% of students pursue further study immediately upon graduation. Fields in which graduates pursue further study: Master of Business Administration (MBA), 13%; law, 17%; medicine, 23%; dentistry, 1%; theology (or the seminary), 17%; education, 10%; arts and sciences, 19%.

COSTS AND FINANCIAL AID

Financial aid office: (910) 893-1310. **Expenses (2010-2011):** Tuition and fees 2010-2011: $22,520; room/board: $8,400. Estimated books and supplies: $2,000; transportation: $1,300; personal expenses: $3,640. **Financial aid:** Priority filing date for institution's financial aid form: March 1. In 2009-2010, 89% of undergraduates applied for financial aid. Of those, 79% were determined to have financial need; 90% had their need fully met. Average financial aid package (proportion receiving): $31,629 (79%). Average amount of gift aid, such as scholarships or grants (proportion receiving): $6,504 (69%). Average amount of self-help aid, such as work study or loans (proportion receiving): $4,313 (70%). Average need-based loan (excluding PLUS or other private loans): $3,998. Among students who received need-based aid, the average percentage of need met: 80%. Among students who received aid based on merit, the average award (and the proportion receiving): $4,961 (25%). The average athletic scholarship (and the proportion

receiving): $11,729 (20%). Average amount of debt of borrowers graduating in 2009: $38,696. Proportion who borrowed: 75%.

CAMPUS LIFE AND EXTRACURRICULAR ACTIVITIES

Campus housing available (% using): women's dorms (38%), men's dorms (35%), apartment for single students (27%), special housing for disabled students (0%). Students who live in college-owned, operated, or affiliated housing: 43%. **Student employment:** During the 2009-2010 academic year, 7% of undergraduates worked on campus. Average per-year earnings: $2,500. **Clubs and organizations:** Number of student organizations: 50. Activities include: campus ministries, choral groups, concert band, dance, drama/theater, international student organization, jazz band, literary magazine, music ensembles, musical theater, pep band, student government, student newspaper, symphony orchestra, yearbook. Number of fraternities: 0; sororities: 0. Average proportion of students who stay on campus on weekends: 80%. **Sports program (2009-2010):** Member of NCAA I. *Men's intercollegiate varsity sports:* baseball, basketball, cross country, football, golf, soccer, tennis, track and field (indoor), track and field (outdoor), wrestling. *Women's intercollegiate varsity sports:* basketball, cross country, golf, soccer, softball, swimming, tennis, track and field (indoor), track and field (outdoor), volleyball.

SERVICES AND FACILITIES

Basic services: nonremedial tutoring, placement service, health service, health insurance. **Remedial assistance:** study skills, other. **Counseling services:** minority student, career, military, personal, veteran student, academic, older student, psychological, religious. **For learning-disabled students:** School does not offer a structured program with separate admission and additional fees. Services include: remedial math, remedial English, tape recorders, note-taking services, oral tests, learning center, readers, extended time for tests, tutors, early syllabus, priority seating, substitution of courses, texts on tape, typist/scribe, exams on tape or computer, other testing accommodations. **Library:** Number of titles: 356,169; number of current serial subscriptions: 45,518. **Information technology resources:** Students are not required to lease or own a computer. Number of campus computers available to all students: 250. School has a wireless network. Approximate number of users that can be accommodated: 6,000. Proportion of college-owned housing units wired for high-speed internet access: 100%. **Campus safety:** Security services offered: 24-hour foot-and-vehicle patrols, late-night transport/escort service, 24-hour emergency telephones, lighted pathways/sidewalks, controlled dormitory access (key, security card, etc).

TRANSFER AND INTERNATIONAL STUDENTS

Transfer students: May apply for admission for the following academic terms: Fall, Spring, Summer. Applicants do not need a minimum number of credits to apply. For fall 2009: Transfer applications received: 582. Transfer applicants offered admission: 421. Transfer applicants enrolled: 149. **International students:** Number of foreign undergraduates: 0. Number of countries represented: 42. Minimum TOEFL score required: 500 (paper); 173 (computer). Average TOEFL score: 513 (paper).

Catawba College

- Address: 2300 W. Innes Street, Salisbury, NC 28144
- Website: http://www.catawba.edu
- Private; Religious affiliation: United Church of Christ
- Enrollment: 1,269 full-time; 55 part-time

KEY STATS

✔ **U.S News College Ranking:** 15, Regional Colleges (South)
✔ **SAT Score (25th/75th percentile):** 910-1130
✔ **Tuition:** 2010-2011: $25,160

Selectivity: Selective	**Room/board:** $8,700
Acceptance rate: 70%	**Average debt:** $25,506
Student/faculty ratio: 16/1	**Proportion who borrowed:** 73%

UNDERGRADUATE STUDENT BODY STATS

2009-2010 enrollment: 1,269 full-time; 55 part-time. Men: 48%; women: 52%. **Ethnic makeup:** African American: 18%; Asian American: 1%; Hispanic: 1%; White: 78%; International: 2%. **Religious preference:** Roman Catholic: 11%; Protestant: 56%; Jewish: 1%; No preference: 25%; Unknown: 3%; United Church of Christ: 1%; Other: 1%.

ADMISSIONS FACTS AND FIGURES

Phone: (800) 228-2922. **Email:** admission@catawba.edu. **Website:** http://www.catawba.edu. **Application deadlines for fall 2011:** Regular decision: Rolling. Early decision: Not offered. Early action: Not offered. Admission can be deferred. **Application fee:** $25. **To apply online, go to:** http://www.applyweb.com/aw?catawba. **Admissions requirements/recommendations:** High school units required (recommended): English: 4 (4); Mathematics: 3 (4); Science: 3 (3); Foreign language: (2); Social studies: 2 (2); History: (1); Academic electives: 4 (2); Total units: 16 (18). Tests: The college uses SAT or ACT scores in admissions decisions. Either SAT or ACT required. For admission to the fall 2011 entering class, the school will accept: ACT with writing recommended. Campus visit: Recommended. Admissions interview: Recommended. Off-campus interview: May be arranged. **Factors that count in admissions decisions:** *Academic:* Secondary school record: Important. Class rank: Very Important. Letters of recommendation: Very Important. Standardized test scores: Very Important. Essay: Very Important. *Nonacademic:* Interview: Important. Extracurricular activities: Important. Talent/ability: Important. Character/personal qualities: Important. Alumni/ae relationship: Not Considered. Geographical residence: Not Considered. State residency: Not Considered. Religious affiliation/commitment: Not Considered. Minority status: Not Considered. Volunteer work: Considered. Work experience: Considered. **Other schools with the greatest overlap in applicants:** Appalachian State University; North Carolina State University–Raleigh; University of North Carolina–Charlotte; University of North Carolina–Greensboro; Wingate University. **Admissions statistics for the fall 2009 entering class:** Total applicants: 1,104. Total accepted: 768. Freshmen enrolled: 308; 30% were from out of state. Overall acceptance rate: 70%. **Credentials of fall 2009 freshmen:** 17% ranked in the top 10 percent of their high school class; 43% were in the top 25 percent; 82% were in the top half. (Proportion submitting class standing: 99%.) **Average high school grade point average:** 3.5. **First-year students who submitted SAT scores:** 90%. Scores (25/75 percentile): Critical Reading: 440-560, Math: 470-570, Combined: 910-1130. **First-year students submitting ACT scores:** 16%. Scores (25/75 percentile): English: 17-27, Math: 16-26, Composite: 18-25.

ACADEMICS

Year founded: 1851. **Academic calendar:** Semester. **Degrees offered:** bachelor's, master's. **Most popular majors:** 38% business, management, marketing, and related support services, 14% education, 11% visual and performing arts, 5% natural resources and conservation, 5% parks, recreation, leisure, and fitness studies. **Major fields of study:** biological and biomedical sciences; business, management, marketing, and related support services; communication, journalism, and related programs; computer and information sciences and support services; education; English language and literature/letters; foreign languages, literatures, and linguistics; health professions and related clinical sciences; history; legal professions and studies; mathematics and statistics; natural resources and conservation; parks, recreation, leisure, and fitness studies; philosophy and religious studies; physical sciences; psychology; social sciences; visual and performing arts. **Areas of required coursework:** arts/fine arts, humanities, mathematics, English (including composition), foreign languages, sciences (biological or physical), social science. **Pre-professional programs:** pre-law, pre-medicine. **Special academic programs:** cross-registration, double major, honors program, independent study, internships, liberal arts/career combination, student-designed major, study abroad, teacher certificate program. **Teacher certification offered in:** early childhood, elementary, middle/junior high, secondary. **Reserve Officers Training Corps (ROTC):** Army ROTC: Offered at cooperating institution (University of North Carolina–Charlotte). **Faculty and instruction (2009-2010):** Total instructional faculty: 71 full-time, 35 part-time (55% men; 45% women; 6% minorities). Full-time faculty with Ph.D. or other terminal degree: 87%. Student/faculty ratio: 16/1. Classes of fewer than 20 students: 53%; of 20 to 49 students: 46%; of 50 or more students: 1%. **Advanced Placement and International Baccalaureate credit:** AP tests may be used for: Credit only. Scores accepted: 3, 4, 5. International Baccalaureate exams may be used for: Credit only. **Freshmen returning for sophomore year:** 71%. **Graduation rates:** Four-year: 42%; five-year: 54%; six-year: 46%. **Graduate study:** 5% of students pursue further study immediately upon graduation; 8% within one year; 12% within five years.

COSTS AND FINANCIAL AID

Financial aid office: (704) 637-4416. **Expenses (2010-2011):** Tuition and fees 2010-2011: $25,160; room/board: $8,700. Estimated books and supplies: $1,400; transportation: $1,485; personal expenses: $1,532. **Financial aid:** Priority filing date for institution's financial aid form: March 15. In 2009-2010, 85% of undergraduates applied for financial aid. Of those, 74% were determined to have financial need; 23% had their need fully met. Average

financial aid package (proportion receiving): $18,422 (74%). Average amount of gift aid, such as scholarships or grants (proportion receiving): $5,861 (51%). Average amount of self-help aid, such as work study or loans (proportion receiving): $4,399 (54%). Average need-based loan (excluding PLUS or other private loans): $4,026. Among students who received need-based aid, the average percentage of need met: 70%. Among students who received aid based on merit, the average award (and the proportion receiving): $5,405 (9%). The average athletic scholarship (and the proportion receiving): $5,810 (2%). Average amount of debt of borrowers graduating in 2009: $25,506. Proportion who borrowed: 73%.

CAMPUS LIFE AND EXTRACURRICULAR ACTIVITIES
Campus housing available (% using): coed dorms (79%), women's dorms (9%), men's dorms (12%). Students who live in college-owned, operated, or affiliated housing: 72%. **Student employment:** During the 2009-2010 academic year, 2% of undergraduates worked on campus. Average per-year earnings: $1,700. Activities include: campus ministries, choral groups, concert band, dance, drama/theater, jazz band, literary magazine, music ensembles, musical theater, pep band, student government, student newspaper, symphony orchestra, yearbook. Number of fraternities: 0; sororities: 0. Average proportion of students who stay on campus on weekends: 70%. **Sports program (2009-2010):** Member of NCAA II. *Men's intercollegiate varsity sports:* baseball, basketball, cross country, football, golf, lacrosse, soccer, swimming, tennis. *Women's intercollegiate varsity sports:* basketball, cross country, field hockey, golf, soccer, softball, squash, team handball, volleyball.

SERVICES AND FACILITIES
Basic services: nonremedial tutoring, placement service, health service. **Counseling services:** career, personal, academic, psychological, birth control, religious. **For learning-disabled students:** School does not offer a structured program with separate admission and additional fees. Services include: untimed tests, tutors, other testing accommodations. **Library:** Number of titles: 173,645; number of current serial subscriptions: 1,435. **Information technology resources:** Students are not required to lease or own a computer. Number of campus computers available to all students: 200. School has a wireless network. Proportion of college-owned housing units wired for high-speed internet access: 96%. **Campus safety:** Security services offered: 24-hour foot-and-vehicle patrols, late-night transport/escort service, 24-hour emergency telephones, lighted pathways/sidewalks, controlled dormitory access (key, security card, etc).

TRANSFER AND INTERNATIONAL STUDENTS
Transfer students: May apply for admission for the following academic terms: Fall, Spring, Summer. Applicants do not need a minimum number of credits to apply. For fall 2009: Transfer applications received: 199. Transfer applicants offered admission: 160. Transfer applicants enrolled: 116. **International students:** Number of foreign undergraduates: 26 (2% of student body). Number of countries represented: 18. Minimum TOEFL score required: 525 (paper); 197 (computer).

Chowan University

- **Address:** 1 University Place, Murfreesboro, NC 27855
- **Website:** http://www.chowan.edu
- **Private; Religious affiliation:** Baptist
- **Enrollment:** 1,006 full-time; 74 part-time

KEY STATS
✔ **U.S News College Ranking:** second tier, Regional Colleges (South)
✔ **SAT or ACT Score (25th/75th percentile):** N/A
✔ **Tuition:** 2009-2010: $19,020

Selectivity: Less selective	**Room/board:** $7,310
Acceptance rate: N/A	**Average debt:** N/A
Student/faculty ratio: N/A	**Proportion who borrowed:** N/A

UNDERGRADUATE STUDENT BODY STATS
2009-2010 enrollment: 1,006 full-time; 74 part-time. Men: 66%; women: 34%. **Religious preference:** Roman Catholic: 1%; Protestant: 41%; No preference: 3%; Unknown: 9%; Baptist: 46%.

ADMISSIONS FACTS AND FIGURES
Phone: (252) 398-1236. **Email:** admission@chowan.edu. **Website:** http://www.chowan.edu. **Application deadlines for fall 2011:** Regular decision: Rolling. Early decision: Not offered. Early action: Not offered. Admission can be deferred. **Application fee:** $20. **To apply online, go to:** http://www.chowan.edu/admis/appli_secure.htm. **Admissions requirements/recommendations:** High school units required (recommended): English: (4); Mathematics: (3); Science: (2); Foreign language: (2); Social studies: (2); History: 1; Academic electives: (8); Total units: 1 (21). Tests: The college uses SAT or ACT scores in admissions decisions. Either SAT or ACT required. For admission to the fall 2011 entering class, the school will accept: ACT with or without writing accepted. Campus visit: Recommended. Admissions interview: Recommended. Off-campus interview: May be arranged. **Factors that count in admissions decisions:** *Academic:* Secondary school record: Very Important. Class rank: Considered. Letters of recommendation: Considered. Standardized test scores: Very Important. Essay: Considered. *Nonacademic:* Interview: Considered. Extracurricular activities: Important. Talent/ability: Important. Character/personal qualities: Considered. Alumni/ae relationship: Considered. Geographical residence: Considered. State residency: Not Considered. Religious affiliation/commitment: Not Considered. Minority status: Not Considered. Volunteer work: Considered. Work experience: Considered. **Other schools with the greatest overlap in applicants:** Campbell University; Mars Hill College; Meredith College; North Carolina Wesleyan College; Virginia Wesleyan College.

ACADEMICS
Year founded: 1848. **Academic calendar:** Semester. **Degrees offered:** associate, bachelor's, post-bachelor's certificate, master's. **Major fields of study:** biological and biomedical sciences; business, management, marketing, and related support services; communications technologies/technicians and support services; education; English language and literature/letters; history; liberal arts and sciences studies, and humanities; mathematics and statistics; multi/interdisciplinary studies; parks, recreation, leisure, and fitness studies; philosophy and religious studies; physical sciences; psychology; security and protective services; visual and performing arts. **Areas of required coursework:** arts/fine arts, humanities, computer literacy, mathematics, English (including composition), foreign languages, sciences (biological or physical), history, social science. **Pre-professional programs:** pre-law, pre-medicine, pre-veterinary science. **Special academic programs (% participation):** distance learning (5%), double major (5%), dual enrollment (1%), honors program (1%), independent study (5%), internships (25%), liberal arts/career combination (50%), student-designed major (2%), study abroad (3%), teacher certificate program (3%). **Teacher certification offered in:** early childhood, elementary, middle/junior high, secondary. **Advanced Placement and International Baccalaureate credit:** AP tests may be used for: Credit and/or placement. Scores accepted: 4, 5. International Baccalaureate exams may be used for: Placement only. **Freshmen returning for sophomore year:** 47%. **Graduation rates:** Four-year: 1%; five-year: 17%; six-year: 28%. **Graduate study:** 10% of students pursue further study immediately upon graduation; 12% within one year; 15% within five years. Fields in which graduates pursue further study: Master of Business Administration (MBA), 20%; theology (or the seminary), 20%; education, 40%; arts and sciences, 20%.

COSTS AND FINANCIAL AID
Financial aid office: (252) 398-1229. **Expenses (2009-2010):** Tuition and fees 2009-2010: $19,020; room/board: $7,310. Estimated books and supplies: $864; transportation: $536; personal expenses: $1,000. **Financial aid:** Priority filing date for institution's financial aid form: May 1; deadline: August 1.

CAMPUS LIFE AND EXTRACURRICULAR ACTIVITIES
Campus housing available (% using): women's dorms (60%), men's dorms (40%), special housing for disabled students. **Student employment:** During the 2009-2010 academic year, 5% of undergraduates worked on campus. Average per-year earnings: $1,000. Activities include: choral groups, concert band, drama/theater, jazz band, literary magazine, music ensembles, pep band, student government, yearbook. Number of fraternities: 3; sororities: 2. Average proportion of students who stay on campus on weekends: 50%. **Sports program (2009-2010):** Member of NCAA II. *Men's intercollegiate varsity sports:* baseball, basketball, football, golf, soccer, tennis. *Women's intercollegiate varsity sports:* basketball, golf, soccer, tennis, volleyball.

SERVICES AND FACILITIES
Basic services: nonremedial tutoring, placement service, health service, health insurance. **Remedial assistance:** math, study skills. **Counseling services:** career, academic, religious. **For learning-disabled students:** School

does not offer a structured program with separate admission and additional fees. Services include: remedial math, remedial English, tape recorders, untimed tests, oral tests, learning center, extended time for tests. **Information technology resources:** Students are not required to lease or own a computer. Number of campus computers available to all students: 350. School has a wireless network. Approximate number of users that can be accommodated: 1,000. Proportion of college-owned housing units wired for high-speed internet access: 100%. **Campus safety:** Security services offered: 24-hour foot-and-vehicle patrols, late-night transport/escort service, controlled dormitory access (key, security card, etc).

TRANSFER AND INTERNATIONAL STUDENTS

Transfer students: May apply for admission for the following academic terms: Fall, Spring, Summer. Applicants need a minimum number of credits to apply. **International students:** Number of countries represented: 5. Minimum TOEFL score required: 450 (paper).

Davidson College

- **Address:** 209 Ridge Road, Davidson, NC 28035
- **Website:** http://www.davidson.edu
- **Private; Religious affiliation:** Presbyterian Church (USA)
- **Enrollment:** 1,743 full-time

KEY STATS

✔ **U.S News College Ranking:** 9, National Liberal Arts Colleges
✔ **SAT Score (25th/75th percentile):** 1260-1440
✔ **Tuition:** 2010-2011: $36,683

Selectivity: Most selective	**Room/board:** $10,346
Acceptance rate: 26%	**Average debt:** $20,858
Student/faculty ratio: 11/1	**Proportion who borrowed:** 38%

UNDERGRADUATE STUDENT BODY STATS

2009-2010 enrollment: 1,743 full-time. Men: 49%; women: 51%. **Ethnic makeup:** African American: 7%; American-Indian: 1%; Asian American: 5%; Hispanic: 5%; White: 80%; International: 3%.

ADMISSIONS FACTS AND FIGURES

Phone: (800) 768-0380. **Email:** admission@davidson.edu. **Website:** http://www.davidson.edu. **Application deadlines for fall 2011:** Regular decision: January 2; decision sent by April 1. Early decision: Send application by: November 15; Decision sent by: December 15. Early action: Not offered. Admission can be deferred. **Application fee:** $50. **To apply online, go to:** http://www3.davidson.edu/cms/x7186.xml. **Admissions requirements/recommendations:** High school units required (recommended): English: 4; Mathematics: 3 (4); Science: 2 (4); Foreign language: 2 (4); Total units: 16. Tests: The college uses SAT or ACT scores in admissions decisions. Either SAT or ACT required. For admission to the fall 2011 entering class, the school will accept: ACT with or without writing accepted. Campus visit: Recommended. Admissions interview: Recommended. Off-campus interview: May be arranged. **Factors that count in admissions decisions:** *Academic:* Secondary school record: Very Important. Class rank: Considered. Letters of recommendation: Very Important. Standardized test scores: Important. Essay: Important. *Nonacademic:* Interview: Important. Extracurricular activities: Important. Talent/ability: Important. Character/personal qualities: Very Important. Alumni/ae relationship: Considered. Geographical residence: Not Considered. State residency: Not Considered. Religious affiliation/commitment: Not Considered. Minority status: Not Considered. Volunteer work: Very Important. Work experience: Not Considered. **Other schools with the greatest overlap in applicants:** Duke University; University of North Carolina–Chapel Hill; University of Virginia; Vanderbilt University; Wake Forest University. **Admissions statistics for the fall 2009 entering class:** Total applicants: 4,494. Total accepted: 1,175. Freshmen enrolled: 491; 77% were from out of state. Accepted through early-decision or early-action plans: 45%. Overall acceptance rate: 26%. Early-decision acceptance rate: 49%. Non-early acceptance rate: 23%. **Credentials of fall 2009 freshmen:** 82% ranked in the top 10 percent of their high school class; 97% were in the top 25 percent; 100% were in the top half. (Proportion submitting class standing: 42%.) **Average high school grade point average:** 4.0. **First-year students who submitted SAT scores:** 90%. Scores (25/75 percentile): Critical Reading: 630-730, Math: 630-710, Combined: 1260-1440. **First-year students submitting ACT scores:** 44%. Scores (25/75 percentile): English: N/A, Math: N/A, Composite: 28-32.

ACADEMICS

Year founded: 1837. **Academic calendar:** Semester. **Degrees offered:** bachelor's. **Most popular majors:** 15% political science and government, 12% history, 11% English language and literature, 11% economics, 10% psychology. **Major fields of study:** biological and biomedical sciences; English language and literature/letters; foreign languages, literatures, and linguistics; history; mathematics and statistics; multi/interdisciplinary studies; philosophy and religious studies; physical sciences; psychology; social sciences; visual and performing arts. **Areas of required coursework:** arts/fine arts, mathematics, English (including composition), philosophy, foreign languages, sciences (biological or physical), history, social science, other. **Pre-professional programs:** pre-law, pre-medicine, pre-theology. **Special academic programs:** cross-registration, double major, exchange student program (domestic), honors program, independent study, student-designed major, study abroad, teacher certificate program, other. **Teacher certification offered in:** secondary. **Reserve Officers Training Corps (ROTC):** Army ROTC: Offered on campus; Air Force ROTC: Offered at cooperating institution (University of North Carolina–Charlotte). **Faculty and instruction (2009-2010):** Total instructional faculty: 164 full-time, 5 part-time (61% men; 39% women; 15% minorities). Full-time faculty with Ph.D. or other terminal degree: 97%. Student/faculty ratio: 11/1. Classes of fewer than 20 students: 72%; of 20 to 49 students: 28%; of 50 or more students: 0%. **Advanced Placement and International Baccalaureate credit:** AP tests may be used for: Credit only. Scores accepted: 4, 5. International Baccalaureate exams may be used for: Credit only. **Freshmen returning for sophomore year:** 96%. **Graduation rates:** Four-year: 89%; five-year: 91%; six-year: 91%. **Graduate study:** 26% of students pursue further study immediately upon graduation. Fields in which graduates pursue further study: Master of Business Administration (MBA), 13%; law, 12%; medicine, 19%; engineering, 2%; theology (or the seminary), 1%; education, 7%; arts and sciences, 26%.

COSTS AND FINANCIAL AID

Financial aid office: (704) 894-2232. **Expenses (2010-2011):** Tuition and fees 2010-2011: $36,683; room/board: $10,346. Estimated books and supplies: $1,000; transportation: $450; personal expenses: $1,325. **Financial aid:** In 2009-2010, 52% of undergraduates applied for financial aid. Of those, 44% were determined to have financial need; 97% had their need fully met. Average financial aid package (proportion receiving): $24,121 (43%). Average amount of gift aid, such as scholarships or grants (proportion receiving): $21,962 (37%). Average amount of self-help aid, such as work study or loans (proportion receiving): $3,232 (15%). Average need-based loan (excluding PLUS or other private loans): $3,250. Among students who received need-based aid, the average percentage of need met: 100%. Among students who received aid based on merit, the average award (and the proportion receiving): $17,182 (14%). The average athletic scholarship (and the proportion receiving): $16,395 (10%). Average amount of debt of borrowers graduating in 2009: $20,858. Proportion who borrowed: 38%.

CAMPUS LIFE AND EXTRACURRICULAR ACTIVITIES

Campus housing available: coed dorms, apartment for single students, special housing for disabled students, cooperative housing, other housing options. Students who live in college-owned, operated, or affiliated housing: 93%. **Clubs and organizations:** Number of student organizations: 165. Activities include: campus ministries, choral groups, concert band, dance, drama/theater, international student organization, jazz band, literary magazine, music ensembles, musical theater, pep band, radio station, student government, student newspaper, symphony orchestra, yearbook. Number of fraternities: 9; sororities: 5. Proportion of men in fraternities: 34%; of women in sororities: 44%. **Sports program (2009-2010):** Member of NCAA I. *Men's intercollegiate varsity sports:* baseball, basketball, cross country, football, golf, soccer, swimming, tennis, track and field (indoor), track and field (outdoor), wrestling. *Women's intercollegiate varsity sports:* basketball, cross country, field hockey, lacrosse, soccer, swimming, tennis, track and field (indoor), track and field (outdoor), volleyball.

SERVICES AND FACILITIES

Basic services: nonremedial tutoring, health service, health insurance. **Remedial assistance:** study skills. **Counseling services:** minority student, career, personal, academic, psychological, religious. **For learning-disabled students:** School does not offer a structured program with separate admission and additional fees. Services include: tape recorders, diagnostic testing service, note-taking services, oral tests, readers, extended time for tests, tutors, other testing accommodations. **Library:** Number of titles: 577,604; number of current serial subscriptions: 4,682. **Information technology resources:** Students are not required to lease or own a computer. Number of campus computers available to all students: 142. School has a wireless network. Proportion of college-owned housing units wired for high-speed internet access: 100%. **Campus safety:** Security services offered: 24-hour foot-and-vehicle patrols, late-night transport/escort service, 24-hour emergency telephones, lighted pathways/sidewalks, controlled dormitory access (key, security card, etc).

TRANSFER AND INTERNATIONAL STUDENTS

Transfer students: May apply for admission for the following academic terms: Fall, Spring. Applicants need a minimum number of credits to apply. For fall 2009: Transfer applications received: 111. Transfer applicants offered admission: 36. Transfer applicants enrolled: 14. **International students:** Number of foreign undergraduates: 58 (3% of student body). Number of countries represented: 31. Minimum TOEFL score required: 600 (paper); 100 (computer).

Duke University

- **Address:** 2138 Campus Drive, Box 90586, Durham, NC 27708
- **Website:** http://www.duke.edu/
- **Private; Religious affiliation:** Methodist
- **Enrollment:** 6,550 full-time; 28 part-time

KEY STATS
✔ **U.S News College Ranking:** 9, National Universities
✔ **SAT Score (25th/75th percentile):** 1340-1530
✔ **Tuition:** 2010-2011: $40,472

Selectivity: Most selective	**Room/board:** $11,622
Acceptance rate: 19%	**Average debt:** $23,059
Student/faculty ratio: 8/1	**Proportion who borrowed:** 40%

UNDERGRADUATE STUDENT BODY STATS

2009-2010 enrollment: 6,550 full-time; 28 part-time. Men: 51%; women: 49%. **Ethnic makeup:** African American: 10%; Asian American: 22%; Hispanic: 7%; White: 55%; International: 7%. **Religious preference:** Roman Catholic: 17%; Protestant: 28%; Jewish: 9%; Muslim: 1%; Hindu: 4%; Buddhist: 1%; No preference: 33%; Methodist: 5%; Other: 2%.

ADMISSIONS FACTS AND FIGURES

Phone: (919) 684-3214. **Website:** http://www.duke.edu/. **Application deadlines for fall 2011:** Regular decision: January 2; decision sent by April 1. Early decision: Send application by: November 1; Decision sent by: December 15. Early action: Not offered. Admission can be deferred. **Application fee:** $75. **To apply online, go to:** http://www.admissions.duke.edu/jump/applying/apply.asp. **Admissions requirements/recommendations:** High school units required (recommended): English: (4); Mathematics: (3); Science: (3); Foreign language: (3); Social studies: (3). Tests: The college uses SAT or ACT scores in admissions decisions. Either SAT or ACT required. For admission to the fall 2011 entering class, the school will accept: ACT with writing required. Campus visit: Recommended. Admissions interview: Recommended. Off-campus interview: May be arranged. **Factors that count in admissions decisions:** *Academic:* Secondary school record: Very Important. Class rank: Considered. Letters of recommendation: Very Important. Standardized test scores: Very Important. Essay: Very Important. *Nonacademic:* Interview: Considered. Extracurricular activities: Very Important. Talent/ability: Very Important. Character/personal qualities: Important. Alumni/ae relationship: Considered. Geographical residence: Considered. State residency: Considered. Religious affiliation/commitment: Not Considered. Minority status: Considered. Volunteer work: Considered. Work experience: Considered. **Other schools with the greatest overlap in applicants:** Cornell University; Northwestern University; Princeton University; University of North Carolina–Chapel Hill; University of Pennsylvania. **Admissions statistics for the fall 2009 entering class:** Total applicants: 22,280. Total accepted: 4,219. Freshmen enrolled: 1,723; 86% were from out of state. Accepted through early-decision or early-action plans: 31%. Overall acceptance rate: 19%. Early-decision acceptance rate: 36%. Non-early acceptance rate: 18%. **Credentials of fall 2009 freshmen:** 90% ranked in the top 10 percent of their high school class; 97% were in the top 25 percent; 100% were in the top half. (Proportion submitting class standing: 45%.) **First-year students who submitted SAT scores:** 87%. Scores (25/75 percentile): Critical Reading: 660-750, Math: 680-780, Combined: 1340-1530. **First-year students submitting ACT scores:** 44%. Scores (25/75 percentile): English: 31-35, Math: 29-35, Composite: 30-34.

ACADEMICS

Year founded: 1838. **Academic calendar:** Semester. **Degrees offered:** bachelor's, post-bachelor's certificate, master's, doctorate. **Most popular majors:** 13% economics, 10% psychology, 9% biology, 8% public policy analysis. **Major fields of study:** area, ethnic, cultural, and gender studies; biological and biomedical sciences; computer and information sciences and support services; education; engineering; English language and literature/letters; foreign languages, literatures, and linguistics; history; mathematics and statistics; multi/interdisciplinary studies; natural resources and conservation; philosophy and religious studies; physical sciences; psychology; public administration and social service professions; social sciences; visual and performing arts. **Areas of required coursework:** arts/fine arts, humanities, foreign languages, sciences (biological or physical), history, social science. **Pre-professional programs:** pre-law, pre-medicine. **Special academic programs:** distance learning, double major, honors program, independent study, internships, liberal arts/career combination, student-designed major, study abroad, teacher certificate program. **Teacher certification offered in:** early childhood, elementary, middle/junior high. **Reserve Officers Training Corps (ROTC):** Army ROTC: Offered on campus; Navy ROTC: Offered on campus; Air Force ROTC: Offered on campus. **Faculty and instruction (2009-2010):** Total instructional faculty: 1,058 full-time, 106 part-time (68% men; 32% women; 19% minorities). Full-time faculty with Ph.D. or other terminal degree: 96%. Student/faculty ratio: 8/1. Classes of fewer than 20 students: 71%; of 20 to 49 students: 23%; of 50 or more students: 6%. **Advanced Placement and International Baccalaureate credit:** AP tests may be used for: Credit and/or placement. International Baccalaureate exams may be used for: Placement only. **Freshmen returning for sophomore year:** 97%. **Graduation rates:** Four-year: 89%; five-year: 94%; six-year: 95%. **Graduate study:** 36% of students pursue further study immediately upon graduation; 16% within one year; 17% within five years. Fields in which graduates pursue further study: Master of Business Administration (MBA), 17%; law, 24%; medicine, 18%; engineering, 7%; arts and sciences, 25%.

COSTS AND FINANCIAL AID

Financial aid office: (919) 684-6225. **Expenses (2010-2011):** Tuition and fees 2010-2011: $40,472; room/board: $11,622. Estimated books and supplies: $1,292; transportation: $575; personal expenses: $1,996. **Financial aid:** Priority filing date for institution's financial aid form: March 1; deadline: March 1. In 2009-2010, 47% of undergraduates applied for financial aid. Of those, 42% were determined to have financial need; 100% had their need fully met. Average financial aid package (proportion receiving): $36,576 (42%). Average amount of gift aid, such as scholarships or grants (proportion receiving): $33,810 (41%). Average amount of self-help aid, such as work study or loans (proportion receiving): $4,467 (36%). Average need-based loan (excluding PLUS or other private loans): $2,666. Among students who received need-based aid, the average percentage of need met: 100%. Among students who received aid based on merit, the average award (and the proportion receiving): $23,185 (6%). The average athletic scholarship (and the proportion receiving): $37,188 (5%). Average amount of debt of borrowers graduating in 2009: $23,059. Proportion who borrowed: 40%.

CAMPUS LIFE AND EXTRACURRICULAR ACTIVITIES

Campus housing available (% using): coed dorms (81%), apartment for single students (19%). Students who live in college-owned, operated, or affiliated housing: 83%. **Clubs and organizations:** Number of student organizations: 400. Activities include: campus ministries, choral groups, concert band, dance, drama/theater, international student organization, jazz band, literary magazine, marching band, model UN, music ensembles, musical theater, opera, pep band, radio station, student government, student newspaper, student film society, symphony orchestra, television station, yearbook. Number of fraternities: 15; sororities: 10. Proportion of men in fraternities: 29%; of women in sororities: 42%. Average proportion of students who stay on campus on weekends: 90%. **Sports program (2009-2010):** Member of NCAA I. *Men's intercollegiate varsity sports:* baseball, basketball, soccer, swimming, tennis, wrestling. *Women's intercollegiate varsity sports:* basketball, soccer, swimming, tennis, volleyball.

SERVICES AND FACILITIES

Basic services: women's center, placement service, health service, health insurance. **Counseling services:** minority student, career, personal, academic, psychological. **For learning-disabled students:** School does not offer a structured program with separate admission and additional fees. Services include: tape recorders, oral tests, extended time for tests, tutors, priority seating, other testing accommodations. **Library:** Number of titles: 5,950,442; number of current serial subscriptions: 62,639. **Information technology resources:** Students are not required to lease or own a computer. Number of campus computers available to all students: 450. School has a wireless network. Proportion of college-owned housing units wired for high-speed internet access: 100%. **Campus safety:** Security services offered: 24-hour foot-and-vehicle patrols, late-night transport/escort service, 24-hour emergency telephones, lighted pathways/sidewalks, student patrols, controlled dormitory access (key, security card, etc).

TRANSFER AND INTERNATIONAL STUDENTS

Transfer students: May apply for admission for the following academic terms: Fall, Spring. Applicants need a minimum number of credits to apply. For fall 2009: Transfer applications received: 668. Transfer applicants offered admission: 85. Transfer applicants enrolled: 40. **International students:** Number of foreign undergraduates: 430 (7% of student body). Number of countries represented: 45.

East Carolina University

- **Address:** East Fifth Street, Greenville, NC 27858-4353
- **Website:** http://www.ecu.edu
- **Public**
- **Enrollment:** N/A

KEY STATS

✔ **U.S News College Ranking:** second tier, National Universities
✔ **ACT Score (25th/75th percentile):** 19-23
✔ **Tuition:** 2009-2010: $4,477 in state, $15,311 out of state

Selectivity: Selective	Room/board: N/A
Acceptance rate: 74%	Average debt: N/A
Student/faculty ratio: N/A	Proportion who borrowed: N/A

Elizabeth City State University

- **Address:** 1704 Weeksville Road, Elizabeth City, NC 27909
- **Website:** http://www.ecsu.edu
- **Public**
- **Enrollment:** 2,871 full-time; 337 part-time

KEY STATS

✔ **U.S News College Ranking:** 22, Regional Colleges (South)
✔ **SAT Score (25th/75th percentile):** 730-930
✔ **Tuition:** 2010-2011: $3,707 in state, $12,822 out of state

Selectivity: Least selective	Room/board: $5,639
Acceptance rate: 64%	Average debt: N/A
Student/faculty ratio: 20/1	Proportion who borrowed: N/A

UNDERGRADUATE STUDENT BODY STATS

2009-2010 enrollment: 2,871 full-time; 337 part-time. Men: 39%; women: 61%. **Ethnic makeup:** African American: 81%; Hispanic: 1%; White: 17%; International: 1%. **Religious preference:** Roman Catholic: 2%; Muslim: 3%; No preference: 6%; Unknown: 71%; None: 16%.

ADMISSIONS FACTS AND FIGURES

Phone: (252) 335-3305. **Email:** admissions@mail.ecsu.edu. **Website:** http://www.ecsu.edu. **Application deadlines for fall 2011:** Regular decision: August 1. Early decision: Not offered. Early action: Not offered. Admission can be deferred. **Application fee:** $30. **Admissions requirements/recommendations:** High school units required (recommended): English: 4 (4); Mathematics: 4 (4); Science: 3 (3); Foreign language: 2 (2); Social studies: 2 (2); History: 1 (1); Academic electives: 6 (6); Total units: 23 (23). Tests: The college uses SAT or ACT scores in admissions decisions. Either SAT or ACT required. For admission to the fall 2011 entering class, the school will accept: ACT with writing required. Campus visit: Recommended. Admissions interview: Recommended. Off-campus interview: Not available. **Factors that count in admissions decisions:** *Academic:* Secondary school record: Very Important. Class rank: Considered. Letters of recommendation: Important. Standardized test scores: Very Important. Essay: Not Considered. *Nonacademic:* Interview: Not Considered. Extracurricular activities: Considered. Talent/ability: Important. Character/personal qualities: Important. Alumni/ae relationship: Important. Geographical residence: Very Important. State residency: Important. Religious affiliation/commitment: Not Considered. Minority status: Not Considered. Volunteer work: Not Considered. Work experience: Not Considered. **Other schools with the greatest overlap in applicants:** East Carolina University; Norfolk State University; North Carolina A&T State University; Old Dominion University; University of North Carolina–Wilmington. **Admissions statistics for the fall 2009 entering class:** Total applicants: 1,431. Total accepted: 915. Freshmen enrolled: 664; 17% were from out of state. Overall acceptance rate: 64%. **Credentials of fall 2009 freshmen:** 1% ranked in the top 10 percent of their high school class; 13% were in the top 25 percent; 42% were in the top half. (Proportion submitting class standing: 100%.) **Average high school grade point average:** 2.8. **First-year students who submitted SAT scores:** 92%. Scores (25/75 percentile): Critical Reading: 360-460, Math: 370-470, Combined: 730-930. **First-year students submitting ACT scores:** 14%. Scores (25/75 percentile): English: 12-17, Math: 16-18, Composite: 15-18.

ACADEMICS

Year founded: 1891. **Academic calendar:** Semester. **Degrees offered:** bachelor's, post-bachelor's certificate, master's. **Most popular majors:** 17% business administration and management, 9% criminal justice/safety studies, 7% elementary education and teaching, 7% physical education teaching and coaching, 6% sociology. **Major fields of study:** biological and biomedical sciences; business, management, marketing, and related support services; communication, journalism, and related programs; computer and information sciences and support services; education; engineering technologies/technicians; English language and literature/letters; history; mathematics and statistics; physical sciences; psychology; public administration and social service professions; security and protective services; social sciences; transportation and materials moving; visual and performing arts. **Areas of required coursework:** arts/fine arts, computer literacy, mathematics, English (including composition), sciences (biological or physical), history, social science, other. **Pre-professional programs:** pre-law, pre-dentistry, pre-medicine, pre-pharmacy. **Special academic programs (% participation):** distance learning (20%), double major (16.7%), honors program (4%), independent study, internships, study abroad, teacher certificate program, weekend college (39%), other. **Teacher certification offered in:** early childhood, special education, elementary, middle/junior high, secondary. **Cooperative education programs:** education, technologies. **Reserve Officers Training Corps (ROTC):** Army ROTC: Offered on campus. **Faculty and instruction (2009-2010):** Total instructional faculty: 165 full-time, 82 part-time (56% men; 44% women; 68% minorities). Full-time faculty with Ph.D. or other terminal degree: 70%. Student/faculty ratio: 20/1. Classes of fewer than 20 students: 48%; of 20 to 49 students: 47%; of 50 or more students: 5%. **Advanced Placement and International Baccalaureate credit:** AP tests may be used for: Placement only. Scores accepted: 3, 4, 5. International Baccalaureate exams may be used for: Placement only. **Freshmen returning for sophomore year:** 76%. **Graduation rates:** Four-year: 22%; five-year: 40%; six-year: 47%. **Graduate study:** 17% of students pursue further study immediately upon graduation; 8% within one year; 1% within five years. Fields in which graduates pursue further study: Master of Business Administration (MBA), 5%; law, 2%; medicine, 1%; dentistry, 2%; education, 15%; arts and sciences, 7%.

COSTS AND FINANCIAL AID

Financial aid office: (252) 335-3282. **Expenses (2010-2011):** Tuition and fees 2010-2011: $3,707 in state, $12,822 out of state; room/board: $5,639. Estimated books and supplies: $620; transportation: $1,200; personal expenses: $1,500. **Financial aid:** Priority filing date for institution's financial aid form: March 15; deadline: June 1. Average amount of gift aid, such as scholarships or grants (proportion receiving): N/A (81%). Average amount of self-help aid, such as work study or loans (proportion receiving): N/A (58%). Among students who received need-based aid, the average percentage of need met: 81%.

CAMPUS LIFE AND EXTRACURRICULAR ACTIVITIES

Campus housing available (% using): coed dorms (63%), women's dorms (20%), men's dorms (17%). Students who live in college-owned, operated, or affiliated housing: 55%. **Student employment:** During the 2009-2010 academic year, 3% of undergraduates worked on campus. **Clubs and organizations:** Number of student organizations: 34. Activities include: choral groups, concert band, dance, drama/theater, international student organization, jazz band, literary magazine, marching band, music ensembles, pep band, radio station, student government, student newspaper, television station, yearbook. Number of fraternities: 4; sororities: 4. Proportion of men in fraternities: 15%; of women in sororities: 20%. Average proportion of students who stay on campus on weekends: 80%. **Sports program (2009-2010):** Member of NCAA II. *Men's intercollegiate varsity sports:* baseball, basketball, cross country, football, golf, track and field (outdoor). *Women's*

intercollegiate varsity sports: basketball, bowling, cross country, softball, tennis, track and field (outdoor), volleyball.

SERVICES AND FACILITIES

Basic services: nonremedial tutoring, women's center, placement service, health service, health insurance. **Remedial assistance:** reading, math, writing, study skills, other. **Counseling services:** minority student, career, personal, veteran student, academic, older student, psychological, birth control, religious. **For learning-disabled students:** School does not offer a structured program with separate admission and additional fees. Services include: remedial math, remedial English, remedial reading, tape recorders, untimed tests, note-taking services, learning center, extended time for tests, tutors, priority seating, texts on tape, other. **Library:** Number of titles: 200,226; number of current serial subscriptions: 11,637. **Information technology resources:** Students are not required to lease or own a computer. Number of campus computers available to all students: 425. School has a wireless network. Approximate number of users that can be accommodated: 2,000. Proportion of college-owned housing units wired for high-speed internet access: 100%. **Campus safety:** Security services offered: 24-hour foot-and-vehicle patrols, 24-hour emergency telephones, lighted pathways/sidewalks, controlled dormitory access (key, security card, etc).

TRANSFER AND INTERNATIONAL STUDENTS

Transfer students: May apply for admission for the following academic terms: Fall, Spring, Summer. Applicants need a minimum number of credits to apply. For fall 2009: Transfer applications received: 378. Transfer applicants offered admission: 325. Transfer applicants enrolled: 211. **International students:** Number of foreign undergraduates: 16 (1% of student body). Number of countries represented: 1. Minimum TOEFL score required: 550 (paper); 80 (computer). Average TOEFL score: 550 (paper).

Elon University

- **Address:** 2700 Campus Box, Elon, NC 27244
- **Website:** http://www.elon.edu
- **Private; Religious affiliation:** United Church of Christ
- **Enrollment:** 4,873 full-time; 122 part-time

KEY STATS

✔ **U.S News College Ranking:** 2, Regional Universities (South)
✔ **SAT Score (25th/75th percentile):** 1140-1320
✔ **Tuition:** 2010-2011: $26,827

Selectivity: More selective	**Room/board:** $8,648
Acceptance rate: 48%	**Average debt:** $22,939
Student/faculty ratio: 13/1	**Proportion who borrowed:** 45%

UNDERGRADUATE STUDENT BODY STATS

2009-2010 enrollment: 4,873 full-time; 122 part-time. Men: 41%; women: 59%. **Ethnic makeup:** African American: 6%; Asian American: 1%; Hispanic: 2%; White: 88%; International: 2%. **Religious preference:** Roman Catholic: 23%; Protestant: 36%; Jewish: 4%; No preference: 4%; Unknown: 29%; United Church of Christ: 2%; Other: 2%.

ADMISSIONS FACTS AND FIGURES

Phone: (800) 334-8448. **Email:** admissions@elon.edu. **Website:** http://www.elon.edu. **Application deadlines for fall 2011:** Regular decision: January 10; decision sent by March 15. Early decision: Send application by: November 1; Decision sent by: December 1. Early action: Send application by: November 10; Decision sent by: December 20. Admission can be deferred. **Application fee:** $50. **To apply online, go to:** http://www.elon.edu/admissions/application.asp. **Admissions requirements/recommendations:** High school units required (recommended): English: 4 (4); Mathematics: 3 (4); Science: 3 (3); Foreign language: 2 (3); Social studies: 2 (2); History: 1 (1). Tests: The college uses SAT or ACT scores in admissions decisions. Either SAT or ACT required. For admission to the fall 2011 entering class, the school will accept: ACT with writing required. Campus visit: Recommended. Admissions interview: Neither required nor recommended. Off-campus interview: Not available. **Factors that count in admissions decisions:** *Academic:* Secondary school record: Very Important. Class rank: Considered. Letters of recommendation: Important. Standardized test scores: Very Important. Essay: Important. ***Nonacademic:*** Interview: Not Considered. Extracurricular activities: Important. Talent/ability: Important. Character/personal qualities: Considered. Alumni/ae

relationship: Important. Geographical residence: Considered. State residency: Considered. Religious affiliation/commitment: Not Considered. Minority status: Considered. Volunteer work: Important. Work experience: Important. **Other schools with the greatest overlap in applicants:** Furman University; James Madison University; North Carolina State University–Raleigh; University of North Carolina–Chapel Hill; Wake Forest University. **Admissions statistics for the fall 2009 entering class:** Total applicants: 9,041. Total accepted: 4,367. Freshmen enrolled: 1,291; 75% were from out of state. Accepted through early-decision or early-action plans: 25%. Overall acceptance rate: 48%. Early-decision acceptance rate: 80%. Non-early acceptance rate: 47%. **Size of waiting list:** 2810 applicants; enrolled from waiting list: 148. **Credentials of fall 2009 freshmen:** 32% ranked in the top 10 percent of their high school class; 70% were in the top 25 percent; 92% were in the top half. (Proportion submitting class standing: 48%.) **Average high school grade point average:** 4.0. **First-year students who submitted SAT scores:** 100%. Scores (25/75 percentile): Critical Reading: 570-660, Math: 570-660, Combined: 1140-1320. **First-year students submitting ACT scores:** 41%. Scores (25/75 percentile): English: N/A, Math: N/A, Composite: 25-29.

ACADEMICS

Year founded: 1889. **Academic calendar:** 4-1-4. **Degrees offered:** bachelor's, master's. **Most popular majors:** 20% business/commerce, 16% communication and media studies, 5% biology, 5% psychology, 4% political science and government. **Major fields of study:** biological and biomedical sciences; business, management, marketing, and related support services; communication, journalism, and related programs; computer and information sciences and support services; education; engineering; English language and literature/letters; foreign languages, literatures, and linguistics; health professions and related clinical sciences; history; mathematics and statistics; multi/interdisciplinary studies; natural resources and conservation; parks, recreation, leisure, and fitness studies; philosophy and religious studies; physical sciences; psychology; public administration and social service professions; social sciences; visual and performing arts. **Areas of required coursework:** humanities, mathematics, English (including composition), foreign languages, sciences (biological or physical), social science. **Pre-professional programs:** pre-law, pre-dentistry, pre-medicine, pre-theology, other. **Special academic programs (% participation):** accelerated program (8%), cross-registration (1%), distance learning (6%), double major (10%), dual enrollment (1%), English as a Second Language (ESL) (1%), exchange student program (domestic) (1%), honors program (12%), independent study (15%), internships (76%), liberal arts/career combination (3%), student-designed major (1%), study abroad (71%), teacher certificate program (9%). **Teacher certification offered in:** special education, elementary, middle/junior high, secondary. **Cooperative education programs:** art, business, computer science, education, engineering, health professions, humanities, natural science, social/behavioral science, technologies. **Reserve Officers Training Corps (ROTC):** Army ROTC: Offered at cooperating institution (North Carolina A&T State University); Air Force ROTC: Offered at cooperating institution (North Carolina A&T State University). **Faculty and instruction (2009-2010):** Total instructional faculty: 343 full-time, 143 part-time (55% men; 45% women; 6% minorities). Full-time faculty with Ph.D. or other terminal degree: 87%. Student/faculty ratio: 13/1. Classes of fewer than 20 students: 51%; of 20 to 49 students: 49%; of 50 or more students: 0%. **Advanced Placement and International Baccalaureate credit:** AP tests may be used for: Credit only. Scores accepted: 4, 5. International Baccalaureate exams may be used for: Credit only. **Freshmen returning for sophomore year:** 90%. **Graduation rates:** Four-year: 71%; five-year: 77%; six-year: 75%. **Graduate study:** 15% of students pursue further study immediately upon graduation; 16% within one year; 36% within five years. Fields in which graduates pursue further study: Master of Business Administration (MBA), 25%; law, 5%; medicine, 1%; dentistry, 1%; engineering, 1%; theology (or the seminary), 1%; education, 26%; arts and sciences, 39%; veterinary medicine, 1%.

COSTS AND FINANCIAL AID

Financial aid office: (336) 278-7640. **Expenses (2010-2011):** Tuition and fees 2010-2011: $26,827; room/board: $8,648. Estimated books and supplies: $900; transportation: $1,100; personal expenses: $1,500. **Financial aid:** Priority filing date for institution's financial aid form: February 15. In 2009-2010, 49% of undergraduates applied for financial aid. Of those, 34% were determined to have financial need; Average financial aid package (proportion receiving): $18,939 (34%). Average amount of gift aid, such as scholarships or grants (proportion receiving): $12,840 (31%). Average amount of self-help aid, such as work study or loans (proportion receiving): $6,099 (28%). Average need-based loan (excluding PLUS or other private loans): $4,907. Among students who received need-based aid, the average percentage of need met: 82%. Among students who received aid based on merit, the average award (and the proportion receiving): $5,442 (23%). The average athletic scholarship (and the proportion receiving): $20,982 (6%). Average amount of debt of borrowers graduating in 2009: $22,939. Proportion who borrowed: 45%.

CAMPUS LIFE AND EXTRACURRICULAR ACTIVITIES
Campus housing available (% using): coed dorms (47%), women's dorms (14%), men's dorms (4%), sorority housing (2%), fraternity housing (2%), apartment for single students (30%), special housing for international students (1%). Students who live in college-owned, operated, or affiliated housing: 58%. **Student employment:** During the 2009-2010 academic year, 20% of undergraduates worked on campus. Average per-year earnings: $3,100. **Clubs and organizations:** Number of student organizations: 150. Activities include: campus ministries, choral groups, concert band, dance, drama/theater, international student organization, jazz band, literary magazine, marching band, model UN, music ensembles, musical theater, pep band, radio station, student government, student newspaper, student film society, symphony orchestra, television station, yearbook. Number of fraternities: 11; sororities: 12. Proportion of men in fraternities: 19%; of women in sororities: 29%. Average proportion of students who stay on campus on weekends: 80%. **Sports program (2009-2010):** Member of NCAA I. **Men's intercollegiate varsity sports:** baseball, basketball, cross country, football, golf, soccer, tennis. **Women's intercollegiate varsity sports:** basketball, cross country, golf, soccer, softball, tennis, track and field (indoor), track and field (outdoor), volleyball.

SERVICES AND FACILITIES
Basic services: nonremedial tutoring, placement service, health service. **Remedial assistance:** reading, math, writing. **Counseling services:** minority student, career, personal, veteran student, academic, older student, psychological, birth control, religious, other. **For learning-disabled students:** School does not offer a structured program with separate admission and additional fees. Services include: reading machines, note-taking services, readers, extended time for tests, priority registration, priority seating, substitution of courses, texts on tape, typist/scribe, exams on tape or computer, other. **Library:** Number of titles: 302,630; number of current serial subscriptions: 9,858. **Information technology resources:** Students are not required to lease or own a computer. Number of campus computers available to all students: 1,000. School has a wireless network. Approximate number of users that can be accommodated: 6,000. Proportion of college-owned housing units wired for high-speed internet access: 100%. **Campus safety:** Security services offered: 24-hour foot-and-vehicle patrols, late-night transport/escort service, 24-hour emergency telephones, lighted pathways/sidewalks, controlled dormitory access (key, security card, etc).

TRANSFER AND INTERNATIONAL STUDENTS
Transfer students: May apply for admission for the following academic terms: Fall, Spring. Applicants need a minimum number of credits to apply. For fall 2009: Transfer applications received: 290. Transfer applicants offered admission: 164. Transfer applicants enrolled: 72. **International students:** Number of foreign undergraduates: 116 (2% of student body). Number of countries represented: 45. Minimum TOEFL score required: 550 (paper); 80 (computer).

Fayetteville State University

- **Address:** 1200 Murchison Road, Fayetteville, NC 28301
- **Website:** http://www.uncfsu.edu
- **Public**
- **Enrollment:** 4,246 full-time; 1,340 part-time

KEY STATS
✔ **U.S News College Ranking:** second tier, Regional Universities (South)
✔ **SAT Score (25th/75th percentile):** 760-900
✔ **Tuition:** 2009-2010: $3,457 in state, $13,800 out of state

Selectivity: Least selective	**Room/board:** $5,421
Acceptance rate: 69%	**Average debt:** $20,185
Student/faculty ratio: 16/1	**Proportion who borrowed:** 63%

UNDERGRADUATE STUDENT BODY STATS
2009-2010 enrollment: 4,246 full-time; 1,340 part-time. Men: 33%; women: 67%. **Ethnic makeup:** African American: 78%; American-Indian: 1%; Asian American: 1%; Hispanic: 4%; White: 16%.

ADMISSIONS FACTS AND FIGURES
Phone: (910) 672-1371. **Email:** admissions@uncfsu.edu. **Website:** http://www.uncfsu.edu. **Application deadlines for fall 2011:** Regular decision: July 1. Early decision: Not offered. Early action: Not offered. Admission can be deferred. **Application fee:** $35. **To apply online, go to:** http://www.uncfsu.edu/admissions/. **Admissions requirements/recommendations:** High school units required (recommended): English: 4 (4); Mathematics: 3 (4); Science: 3 (3); Foreign language: 2 (2); Social studies: 2 (2); History: 2 (2); Academic electives: 6 (4); Total units: 21 (21). Tests: The college uses SAT or ACT scores in admissions decisions. Either SAT or ACT required. For admission to the fall 2011 entering class, the school will accept: ACT with writing required. Campus visit: Recommended. Admissions interview: Recommended. Off-campus interview: May be arranged. **Factors that count in admissions decisions:** *Academic:* Secondary school record: Very Important. Class rank: Important. Letters of recommendation: Considered. Standardized test scores: Very Important. Essay: Considered. *Nonacademic:* Interview: Considered. Extracurricular activities: Considered. Talent/ability: Important. Character/personal qualities: Important. Alumni/ae relationship: Not Considered. Geographical residence: Not Considered. State residency: Considered. Religious affiliation/commitment: Not Considered. Minority status: Not Considered. Volunteer work: Not Considered. Work experience: Considered. **Other schools with the greatest overlap in applicants:** North Carolina A&T State University; North Carolina Central University; University of North Carolina–Pembroke; Winston-Salem State University. **Admissions statistics for the fall 2009 entering class:** Total applicants: 3,107. Total accepted: 2,146. Freshmen enrolled: 762; 7% were from out of state. Overall acceptance rate: 69%. **Size of waiting list:** 0 applicants; enrolled from waiting list: 0. **Credentials of fall 2009 freshmen:** 1% ranked in the top 10 percent of their high school class; 12% were in the top 25 percent; 51% were in the top half. (Proportion submitting class standing: 94%.) **Average high school grade point average:** 2.8. **First-year students who submitted SAT scores:** 94%. Scores (25/75 percentile): Critical Reading: 370-440, Math: 390-460, Combined: 760-900. **First-year students submitting ACT scores:** 11%. Scores (25/75 percentile): English: 13-18, Math: 15-18, Composite: 15-19.

ACADEMICS
Year founded: 1867. **Academic calendar:** Semester. **Degrees offered:** bachelor's, master's, doctorate. **Most popular majors:** 15% criminal justice/safety studies, 15% psychology, 11% business administration and management, 10% sociology, 5% nursing/registered nurse training (R.N., A.S.N., B.S.N., M.S.N.). **Major fields of study:** biological and biomedical sciences; business, management, marketing, and related support services; communication, journalism, and related programs; computer and information sciences and support services; education; English language and literature/letters; foreign languages, literatures, and linguistics; history; mathematics and statistics; physical sciences; psychology; security and protective services; social sciences; visual and performing arts. **Areas of required coursework:** arts/fine arts, humanities, computer literacy, mathematics, English (including composition), philosophy, sciences (biological or physical), history, social science. **Pre-professional programs:** pre-dentistry, pre-medicine, pre-veterinary science, pre-pharmacy. **Special academic programs (% participation):** cooperative (work-study plan) program, distance learning, double major (1%), dual enrollment, honors program, independent study, internships, study abroad, teacher certificate program, weekend college, other. **Teacher certification offered in:** early childhood, special education, elementary, middle/junior high, secondary. **Cooperative education programs:** business, natural science, social/behavioral science. **Reserve Officers Training Corps (ROTC):** Army ROTC: Offered on campus; Air Force ROTC: Offered on campus. **Faculty and instruction (2009-2010):** Total instructional faculty: 287 full-time, 1 part-time (59% men; 41% women; 59% minorities). Full-time faculty with Ph.D. or other terminal degree: 85%. Student/faculty ratio: 16/1. Classes of fewer than 20 students: 39%; of 20 to 49 students: 61%; of 50 or more students: 1%. **Advanced Placement and International Baccalaureate credit:** AP tests may be used for: Credit and/or placement. Scores accepted: 3, 4, 5. **Freshmen returning for sophomore year:** 72%. **Graduation rates:** Four-year: 13%; five-year: 25%; six-year: 36%.

COSTS AND FINANCIAL AID
Financial aid office: (910) 672-1325. **Expenses (2009-2010):** Tuition and fees 2009-2010: $3,457 in state, $13,800 out of state; room/board: $5,421.

Estimated books and supplies: $500 personal expenses: $4,300. **Financial aid:** Priority filing date for institution's financial aid form: March 1; deadline: March 1. In 2009-2010, 92% of undergraduates applied for financial aid. Of those, 84% were determined to have financial need; 6% had their need fully met. Average financial aid package (proportion receiving): $9,796 (83%). Average amount of gift aid, such as scholarships or grants (proportion receiving): $5,971 (77%). Average amount of self-help aid, such as work study or loans (proportion receiving): $4,313 (68%). Average need-based loan (excluding PLUS or other private loans): $4,293. Among students who received need-based aid, the average percentage of need met: 77%. Among students who received aid based on merit, the average award (and the proportion receiving): $668 (3%). The average athletic scholarship (and the proportion receiving): $14,391 (2%). Average amount of debt of borrowers graduating in 2009: $20,185. Proportion who borrowed: 63%.

CAMPUS LIFE AND EXTRACURRICULAR ACTIVITIES

Campus housing available (% using): coed dorms (40%), women's dorms (25%), men's dorms (15%), other housing options (20%). Students who live in college-owned, operated, or affiliated housing: 30%. **Clubs and organizations:** Number of student organizations: 100. Activities include: campus ministries, choral groups, concert band, drama/theater, jazz band, marching band, music ensembles, pep band, radio station, student government, student newspaper, yearbook. Number of fraternities: 4; sororities: 1. Proportion of men in fraternities: 1%; of women in sororities: 1%. Average proportion of students who stay on campus on weekends: 60%. **Sports program (2009-2010):** Member of NCAA II. *Men's intercollegiate varsity sports:* basketball, cross country, football, golf. *Women's intercollegiate varsity sports:* basketball, bowling, cross country, softball, tennis, volleyball.

SERVICES AND FACILITIES

Basic services: nonremedial tutoring, placement service, day care, health service, health insurance, other. **Remedial assistance:** math, writing. **Counseling services:** minority student, career, military, personal, veteran student, academic, older student, psychological, other. **For learning-disabled students:** School does not offer a structured program with separate admission and additional fees. **Library:** Number of titles: 317,412; number of current serial subscriptions: 4,725. **Information technology resources:** Students are not required to lease or own a computer. Number of campus computers available to all students: 300. School has a wireless network. Approximate number of users that can be accommodated: 7,500. Proportion of college-owned housing units wired for high-speed internet access: 100%. **Campus safety:** Security services offered: 24-hour foot-and-vehicle patrols, late-night transport/escort service, 24-hour emergency telephones, lighted pathways/sidewalks, student patrols, controlled dormitory access (key, security card, etc).

TRANSFER AND INTERNATIONAL STUDENTS

Transfer students: May apply for admission for the following academic terms: Fall, Winter, Spring, Summer. Applicants do not need a minimum number of credits to apply. For fall 2009: Transfer applications received: 1,191. Transfer applicants offered admission: 984. Transfer applicants enrolled: 599. **International students:** Number of foreign undergraduates: 12. Number of countries represented: 8. Minimum TOEFL score required: 79 (computer). Average TOEFL score: 550 (paper).

Gardner-Webb University

- **Address:** PO Box 997, Boiling Springs, NC 28017
- **Website:** http://www.gardner-webb.edu
- **Private; Religious affiliation:** Baptist
- **Enrollment:** 2,256 full-time; 384 part-time

KEY STATS

✔ **U.S News College Ranking:** 40, Regional Universities (South)
✔ **SAT Score (25th/75th percentile):** 860-1110
✔ **Tuition:** 2010-2011: $22,410

Selectivity: Selective	**Room/board:** $7,220
Acceptance rate: 60%	**Average debt:** N/A
Student/faculty ratio: N/A	**Proportion who borrowed:** N/A

UNDERGRADUATE STUDENT BODY STATS

2009-2010 enrollment: 2,256 full-time; 384 part-time. Men: 35%; women: 65%. **Ethnic makeup:** African American: 18%; American-Indian: 1%; Hispanic: 2%; White: 79%. **Religious preference:** Roman Catholic: 4%; Unknown: 7%; Baptist: 53%; Other: 28%.

ADMISSIONS FACTS AND FIGURES

Phone: (800) 253-6472. **Email:** admissions@gardner-webb.edu. **Website:** http://www.gardner-webb.edu. **Application deadlines for fall 2011:** Regular decision: Rolling. Early decision: Not offered. Early action: Not offered. Admission can be deferred. **Application fee:** $40. **To apply online, go to:** https://gwustream.gardner-webb.edu/Day_Admissions/UndergradApp. aspx. **Admissions requirements/recommendations:** High school units required (recommended): English: 4 (4); Mathematics: 3 (3); Science: 2 (2); Foreign language: 2 (2); Social studies: 2 (2); History: 2 (2); Academic electives: 2 (2); Total units: 18 (18). Tests: The college uses SAT or ACT scores in admissions decisions. Either SAT or ACT required. For admission to the fall 2011 entering class, the school will accept: ACT with or without writing accepted. Campus visit: Recommended. Admissions interview: Recommended. Off-campus interview: May be arranged. **Factors that count in admissions decisions:** *Academic:* Secondary school record: Very Important. Class rank: Very Important. Letters of recommendation: Important. Standardized test scores: Very Important. Essay: Important. *Nonacademic:* Interview: Considered. Extracurricular activities: Important. Talent/ability: Important. Character/personal qualities: Very Important. Alumni/ae relationship: Considered. Geographical residence: Considered. State residency: Not Considered. Religious affiliation/commitment: Considered. Minority status: Not Considered. Volunteer work: Considered. Work experience: Not Considered. **Other schools with the greatest overlap in applicants:** Appalachian State University; Campbell University; Elon University; University of North Carolina–Charlotte; Wingate University. **Admissions statistics for the fall 2009 entering class:** Total applicants: 3,322. Total accepted: 2,006. Freshmen enrolled: 450; 36% were from out of state. Overall acceptance rate: 60%. **Credentials of fall 2009 freshmen:** 33% ranked in the top 10 percent of their high school class; 51% were in the top 25 percent; 75% were in the top half. (Proportion submitting class standing: 96%.) **Average high school grade point average:** 3.5. **First-year students who submitted SAT scores:** 88%. Scores (25/75 percentile): Critical Reading: 440-560, Math: 420-550, Combined: 860-1110. **First-year students submitting ACT scores:** 31%. Scores (25/75 percentile): English: N/A, Math: N/A, Composite: 18-23.

ACADEMICS

Year founded: 1905. **Academic calendar:** Semester. **Degrees offered:** associate, bachelor's, master's, doctorate. **Most popular majors:** 33% business, management, marketing, and related support services; 29% social sciences, 12% health professions and related clinical sciences, 3% education, 3% psychology. **Major fields of study:** biological and biomedical sciences; business, management, marketing, and related support services; communication, journalism, and related programs; computer and information sciences and support services; education; English language and literature/letters; foreign languages, literatures, and linguistics; health professions and related clinical sciences; history; mathematics and statistics; parks, recreation, leisure, and fitness studies; philosophy and religious studies; physical sciences; psychology; social sciences; visual and performing arts. **Areas of required coursework:** arts/fine arts, humanities, computer literacy, mathematics, English (including composition), foreign languages, sciences (biological or physical), history, social science. **Special academic programs (% participation):** distance learning (40%), double major (2%), English as a Second Language (ESL) (1%), honors program (2%), independent study (7%), internships (14%), study abroad (3%), teacher certificate program (5%). **Teacher certification offered in:** early childhood, elementary, middle/junior high, secondary. **Reserve Officers Training Corps (ROTC):** Army ROTC: Offered on campus. **Faculty and instruction (2009-2010):** Total instructional faculty: N/A. Classes of fewer than 20 students: 69%; of 20 to 49 students: 31%; of 50 or more students: 0%. **Advanced Placement and International Baccalaureate credit:** AP tests may be used for: Credit only. International Baccalaureate exams may be used for: Credit only. **Freshmen returning for sophomore year:** 72%. **Graduation rates:** Four-year: 35%; five-year: 44%; six-year: 49%. **Graduate study:** 12% of students pursue further study immediately upon graduation; 15% within one year; 20% within five years. Fields in which graduates pursue further study: Master of Business Administration (MBA), 70%; law, 5%; medicine, 5%; theology (or the seminary), 15%; education, 5%.

COSTS AND FINANCIAL AID

Financial aid office: (704) 406-4243. **Expenses (2010-2011):** Tuition and fees 2010-2011: $22,410; room/board: $7,220. Estimated books and supplies: $1,000; transportation: $1,150; personal expenses: $1,055. **Financial aid:** Priority filing date for institution's financial aid form: March 15; deadline:

June 30. In 2009-2010, 58% of undergraduates applied for financial aid. Of those, 52% were determined to have financial need; 19% had their need fully met. Average financial aid package (proportion receiving): $17,438 (52%). Average amount of gift aid, such as scholarships or grants (proportion receiving): $8,412 (45%). Average amount of self-help aid, such as work study or loans (proportion receiving): $4,622 (39%). Average need-based loan (excluding PLUS or other private loans): $4,266. Among students who received need-based aid, the average percentage of need met: 71%. Among students who received aid based on merit, the average award (and the proportion receiving): $6,860 (12%). The average athletic scholarship (and the proportion receiving): $13,986 (6%).

CAMPUS LIFE AND EXTRACURRICULAR ACTIVITIES

Campus housing available (% using): coed dorms (10%), women's dorms (37%), men's dorms (22%), apartment for single students (31%). Students who live in college-owned, operated, or affiliated housing: 45%. **Student employment:** During the 2009-2010 academic year, 10% of undergraduates worked on campus. Average per-year earnings: $1,600. **Clubs and organizations:** Number of student organizations: 60. Activities include: choral groups, concert band, dance, drama/theater, jazz band, literary magazine, marching band, music ensembles, musical theater, opera, pep band, radio station, student government, student newspaper, student film society, symphony orchestra, television station, yearbook. Number of fraternities: 0; sororities: 0. Average proportion of students who stay on campus on weekends: 45%. **Sports program (2009-2010):** Member of NCAA I.

SERVICES AND FACILITIES

Basic services: nonremedial tutoring, placement service, health insurance. **Remedial assistance:** reading, math, writing. **Counseling services:** career, personal, academic, psychological, religious. **For learning-disabled students:** School does not offer a structured program with separate admission and additional fees. Total undergraduates in learning-disabled program or receiving services: 51. Services include: remedial math, remedial English, reading machines, remedial reading, tape recorders, note-taking services, special bookstore section, oral tests, readers, extended time for tests, tutors, priority registration, priority seating, texts on tape, other testing accommodations, other. **Library:** Number of titles: 230,531; number of current serial subscriptions: 11,143. **Information technology resources:** Students are not required to lease or own a computer. Number of campus computers available to all students: 200. School has a wireless network. Approximate number of users that can be accommodated: 2,960. Proportion of college-owned housing units wired for high-speed internet access: 100%. **Campus safety:** Security services offered: 24-hour foot-and-vehicle patrols, late-night transport/escort service, 24-hour emergency telephones, lighted pathways/sidewalks, student patrols, controlled dormitory access (key, security card, etc.).

TRANSFER AND INTERNATIONAL STUDENTS

Transfer students: May apply for admission for the following academic terms: Fall, Spring, Summer. Applicants need a minimum number of credits to apply. For fall 2009: Transfer applications received: 741. Transfer applicants offered admission: 356. Transfer applicants enrolled: 139. **International students:** Number of foreign undergraduates: 4. Number of countries represented: 21. Minimum TOEFL score required: 500 (paper); 173 (computer). Average TOEFL score: 545 (paper).

Greensboro College

- **Address:** 815 W. Market Street, Greensboro, NC 27401-1875
- **Website:** http://www.gborocollege.edu
- **Private; Religious affiliation:** Methodist
- **Enrollment:** N/A

KEY STATS
- ✔ **U.S News College Ranking:** second tier, National Liberal Arts Colleges
- ✔ **ACT Score (25th/75th percentile):** 16-21
- ✔ **Tuition:** 2009-2010: $23,346

Selectivity: Less selective	**Room/board:** $9,721
Acceptance rate: 63%	**Average debt:** N/A
Student/faculty ratio: N/A	**Proportion who borrowed:** N/A

Guilford College

- **Address:** 5800 W. Friendly Avenue, Greensboro, NC 27410
- **Website:** http://www.guilford.edu
- **Private; Religious affiliation:** Quaker
- **Enrollment:** 2,312 full-time; 521 part-time

KEY STATS
- ✔ **U.S News College Ranking:** 166, National Liberal Arts Colleges
- ✔ **SAT Score (25th/75th percentile):** 960-1190
- ✔ **Tuition:** 2010-2011: $28,800

Selectivity: Selective	**Room/board:** $7,950
Acceptance rate: 62%	**Average debt:** $23,050
Student/faculty ratio: 16/1	**Proportion who borrowed:** 71%

UNDERGRADUATE STUDENT BODY STATS

2009-2010 enrollment: 2,312 full-time; 521 part-time. Men: 41%; women: 59%. **Ethnic makeup:** African American: 25%; American-Indian: 1%; Asian American: 1%; Hispanic: 3%; White: 69%; International: 1%. **Religious preference:** Roman Catholic: 6%; Jewish: 3%; No preference: 45%; Quaker: 5%; Baptist: 9%; Other: 32%.

ADMISSIONS FACTS AND FIGURES

Phone: (800) 992-7759. **Email:** admission@guilford.edu. **Website:** http://www.guilford.edu. **Application deadlines for fall 2011:** Regular decision: August 10. Early decision: Not offered. Early action: Send application by: January 15; Decision sent by: February 15. Admission can be deferred. **Application fee:** $25. **To apply online, go to:** http://www.guilford.edu/admission. **Admissions requirements/recommendations:** High school units required (recommended): English: (4); Mathematics: (3); Science: (3); Foreign language: (2); Social studies: (3); History: (3); Total units: (12). Tests: The college uses SAT or ACT scores in admissions decisions. Neither SAT nor ACT required. For admission to the fall 2011 entering class, the school will accept: ACT with or without writing accepted. Campus visit: Recommended. Admissions interview: Recommended. Off-campus interview: May be arranged. **Factors that count in admissions decisions:** *Academic:* Secondary school record: Very Important. Class rank: Important. Letters of recommendation: Important. Standardized test scores: Important. Essay: Very Important. *Nonacademic:* Interview: Important. Extracurricular activities: Important. Talent/ability: Important. Character/personal qualities: Very Important. Alumni/ae relationship: Considered. Geographical residence: Considered. State residency: Considered. Religious affiliation/commitment: Not Considered. Minority status: Considered. Volunteer work: Important. Work experience: Important. **Other schools with the greatest overlap in applicants:** Appalachian State University; Elon University; Greensboro College; University of North Carolina–Chapel Hill; University of North Carolina–Greensboro. **Admissions statistics for the fall 2009 entering class:** Total applicants: 3,780. Total accepted: 2,356. Freshmen enrolled: 448; 55% were from out of state. Accepted through early-decision or early-action plans: 69%. Overall acceptance rate: 62%. Non-early acceptance rate: 53%. **Size of waiting list:** 51 applicants; enrolled from waiting list: 3. **Credentials of fall 2009 freshmen:** 16% ranked in the top 10 percent of their high school class; 39% were in the top 25 percent; 82% were in the top half. (Proportion submitting class standing: 58%.) **Average high school grade point average:** 3.1. **First-year students who submitted SAT scores:** 87%. Scores (25/75 percentile): Critical Reading: 500-600, Math: 460-590, Combined: 960-1190. **First-year students submitting ACT scores:** 21%. Scores (25/75 percentile): English: N/A, Math: N/A, Composite: 20-26.

ACADEMICS

Year founded: 1837. **Academic calendar:** Semester. **Degrees offered:** certificate, bachelor's. **Most popular majors:** 17% business, management, marketing, and related support services, 12% security and protective services, 11% social sciences, 9% psychology, 7% biological and biomedical sciences. **Major fields of study:** area, ethnic, cultural, and gender studies; biological and biomedical sciences; business, management, marketing, and related support services; computer and information sciences and support services; education; English language and literature/letters; foreign languages, literatures, and linguistics; health professions and related clinical sciences; history; mathematics and statistics; multi/interdisciplinary studies; natural resources and conservation; parks, recreation, leisure, and fitness studies; philosophy and religious studies; physical sciences; psychology; security and protective services; social sciences; visual and performing arts. **Areas of required coursework:** arts/fine arts, humanities, computer literacy, mathematics, English (including composition), philosophy, foreign languages, sciences (biological or physical), history, social science, other. **Pre-professional programs:** pre-law, pre-dentistry, pre-medicine, pre-theology, pre-veterinary science, other. **Special academic programs (% participation):** accelerated program, cooperative (work-study plan) program, cross-registration (5%), double major (29%), English as a Second Language (ESL) (0%), honors program (3%), independent study (69%), internships (36%), student-designed major (1%), study abroad (18%), teacher certificate program (2%). **Teacher certification offered in:** elementary, secondary. **Cooperative education programs:** engineering, other. **Faculty and instruction (2009-2010):** Total instructional faculty: 126 full-time, 87 part-time (50% men; 50% women; 13% minorities). Full-time faculty with Ph.D. or other terminal degree: 86%. Student/faculty ratio: 16/1. Classes of fewer than 20 students: 60%; of 20 to 49 students: 40%; of 50 or more students: 0%. **Advanced Placement and International Baccalaureate credit:** AP tests may be used for: Placement only. Scores accepted: 3, 4, 5. International Baccalaureate exams may be used for: Placement only. **Freshmen returning for sophomore year:** 73%. **Graduation rates:** Four-year: 48%; five-year: 60%; six-year: 61%. **Graduate study:** 18% of students pursue further study immediately upon graduation; 28% within one year; 35% within five years. Fields in which graduates pursue further study: Master of Business Administration (MBA), 23%; law, 10%; medicine, 11%; dentistry, 5%; engineering, 3%; theology (or the seminary), 10%; education, 21%; arts and sciences, 18%; veterinary medicine, 3%.

COSTS AND FINANCIAL AID

Financial aid office: (336) 316-2165. **Expenses (2010-2011):** Tuition and fees 2010-2011: $28,800; room/board: $7,950. Estimated books and supplies: $1,250; transportation: $1,100; personal expenses: $1,220. **Financial aid:** Priority filing date for institution's financial aid form: March 1. In 2009-2010, 91% of undergraduates applied for financial aid. Of those, 73% were determined to have financial need; 23% had their need fully met. Average financial aid package (proportion receiving): $21,918 (73%). Average amount of gift aid, such as scholarships or grants (proportion receiving): $8,113 (53%). Average amount of self-help aid, such as work study or loans (proportion receiving): $7,609 (64%). Average need-based loan (excluding PLUS or other private loans): $5,126. Among students who received need-based aid, the average percentage of need met: 91%. Among students who received aid based on merit, the average award (and the proportion receiving): $7,307 (6%). The average athletic scholarship (and the proportion receiving): $0 (0%). Average amount of debt of borrowers graduating in 2009: $23,050. Proportion who borrowed: 71%.

CAMPUS LIFE AND EXTRACURRICULAR ACTIVITIES

Campus housing available (% using): coed dorms (58%), women's dorms (10%), men's dorms (4%), apartment for single students (23%), special housing for international students (1%), other housing options (4%). Students who live in college-owned, operated, or affiliated housing: 70%. **Student employment:** During the 2009-2010 academic year, 19% of undergraduates worked on campus. Average per-year earnings: $3,455. **Clubs and organizations:** Number of student organizations: 43. Activities include: campus ministries, choral groups, concert band, dance, drama/theater, jazz band, literary magazine, music ensembles, pep band, radio station, student government, student newspaper, student film society, yearbook. Number of fraternities: 0; sororities: 0. Average proportion of students who stay on campus on weekends: 80%. **Sports program (2009-2010):** Member of NCAA III. *Men's intercollegiate varsity sports:* baseball, basketball, cross country, football, golf, lacrosse, soccer, tennis. *Women's intercollegiate varsity sports:* basketball, cross country, lacrosse, rugby, soccer, softball, swimming, tennis, volleyball.

SERVICES AND FACILITIES

Basic services: nonremedial tutoring, women's center, placement service, day care, health service, health insurance. **Remedial assistance:** reading, math, writing, study skills, other. **Counseling services:** minority student, career, personal, veteran student, academic, older student, psychological, birth control, religious, other. **For learning-disabled students:** School does not offer a structured program with separate admission and additional fees. Services include: reading machines, tape recorders, other special classes, untimed tests, note-taking services, oral tests, learning center, readers, extended time for tests, tutors, texts on tape, other testing accommodations. **Library:** Number of titles: 208,696; number of current serial subscriptions: 17,618. **Information technology resources:** Students are not required to lease or own a computer. Number of campus computers available to all students: 275. School has a wireless network. Approximate number of users that can be accommodated: 702. Proportion of college-owned housing units wired for high-speed internet access: 100%. **Campus safety:** Security services

offered: 24-hour foot-and-vehicle patrols, late-night transport/escort service, 24-hour emergency telephones, lighted pathways/sidewalks, controlled dormitory access (key, security card, etc).

TRANSFER AND INTERNATIONAL STUDENTS

Transfer students: May apply for admission for the following academic terms: Fall, Spring. Applicants need a minimum number of credits to apply. For fall 2009: Transfer applications received: 245. Transfer applicants offered admission: 76. Transfer applicants enrolled: 39. **International students:** Number of foreign undergraduates: 20 (1% of student body). Number of countries represented: 17. Minimum TOEFL score required: 550 (paper); 213 (computer). Average TOEFL score: 604 (paper).

High Point University

- **Address:** 833 Montlieu Avenue, High Point, NC 27262-3598
- **Website:** http://www.highpoint.edu
- **Private; Religious affiliation:** United Methodist
- **Enrollment:** 3,149 full-time; 128 part-time

KEY STATS
✔ **U.S News College Ranking:** 3, Regional Colleges (South)
✔ **SAT Score (25th/75th percentile):** 990-1160
✔ **Tuition:** N/A

Selectivity: Selective	**Room/board:** N/A
Acceptance rate: 71%	**Average debt:** $9,437
Student/faculty ratio: 15/1	**Proportion who borrowed:** 69%

UNDERGRADUATE STUDENT BODY STATS

2009-2010 enrollment: 3,149 full-time; 128 part-time. Men: 37%; women: 63%. **Ethnic makeup:** African American: 13%; Asian American: 1%; Hispanic: 2%; White: 82%; International: 2%. **Religious preference:** Roman Catholic: 19%; Protestant: 33%; Jewish: 1%; Buddhist: 1%; No preference: 15%; United Methodist: 16%; Other: 15%.

ADMISSIONS FACTS AND FIGURES

Phone: (800) 345-6993. **Email:** admiss@highpoint.edu. **Website:** http://www.highpoint.edu. **Application deadlines for fall 2011:** Regular decision: August 15. Early decision: Send application by: November 6; Decision sent by: November 27. Early action: Send application by: November 1; Decision sent by: November 15. Admission can be deferred. **Application fee:** $40. **To apply online, go to:** http://www.highpoint.edu/admissions. **Admissions requirements/recommendations:** High school units required (recommended): English: 4; Mathematics: 3; Science: 2; Foreign language: 2; Social studies: 3; History: 2; Academic electives: (2); Total units: 14. Tests: The college uses SAT or ACT scores in admissions decisions. Either SAT or ACT required. For admission to the fall 2011 entering class, the school will accept: ACT with or without writing accepted. Campus visit: Recommended. Admissions interview: Recommended. Off-campus interview: Not available. **Factors that count in admissions decisions:** *Academic:* Secondary school record: Very Important. Class rank: Important. Letters of recommendation: Considered. Standardized test scores: Very Important. Essay: Considered. *Nonacademic:* Interview: Considered. Extracurricular activities: Considered. Talent/ability: Considered. Character/personal qualities: Important. Alumni/ae relationship: Not Considered. Geographical residence: Not Considered. State residency: Not Considered. Religious affiliation/commitment: Not Considered. Minority status: Not Considered. Volunteer work: Considered. Work experience: Considered. **Other schools with the greatest overlap in applicants:** Appalachian State University; Elon University; James Madison University; North Carolina State University–Raleigh; University of North Carolina–Chapel Hill. **Admissions statistics for the fall 2009 entering class:** Total applicants: 4,529. Total accepted: 3,228. Freshmen enrolled: 1,030; 76% were from out of state. Accepted through early-decision or early-action plans: 74%. Overall acceptance rate: 71%. Early-decision acceptance rate: 93%. Non-early acceptance rate: 68%. **Size of waiting list:** 497 applicants; enrolled from waiting list: 284. **Credentials of fall 2009 freshmen:** 17% ranked in the top 10 percent of their high school class; 42% were in the top 25 percent; 77% were in the top half. (Proportion submitting class standing: 58%.) **Average high school grade point average:** 3.1. **First-year students who submitted SAT scores:** 91%. Scores (25/75 percentile): Critical Reading: 490-580, Math: 500-580, Combined: 990-1160. **First-year students submitting ACT scores:** 42%. Scores (25/75 percentile): English: N/A, Math: N/A, Composite: 20-25.

ACADEMICS

Year founded: 1924. **Academic calendar:** Semester. **Degrees offered:** bachelor's, master's. **Most popular majors:** 28% business/commerce, 9% elementary education and teaching, 8% organizational behavior studies, 6% psychology, 5% kinesiology and exercise science. **Major fields of study:** area, ethnic, cultural, and gender studies; biological and biomedical sciences; business, management, marketing, and related support services; communication, journalism, and related programs; computer and information sciences and support services; education; English language and literature/letters; foreign languages, literatures, and linguistics; health professions and related clinical sciences; history; mathematics and statistics; multi/interdisciplinary studies; natural resources and conservation; parks, recreation, leisure, and fitness studies; philosophy and religious studies; physical sciences; psychology; public administration and social service professions; security and protective services; social sciences; visual and performing arts. **Areas of required coursework:** arts/fine arts, humanities, mathematics, English (including composition), philosophy, foreign languages, sciences (biological or physical), history, social science, other. **Pre-professional programs:** pre-law, pre-dentistry, pre-medicine, pre-pharmacy, other. **Special academic programs (% participation):** cross-registration (1.4%), distance learning (.6%), double major (4.6%), English as a Second Language (ESL), honors program (7.2%), independent study (17.8%), internships (9.2%), student-designed major (.2%), study abroad (1.7%), teacher certificate program (5.7%). **Teacher certification offered in:** special education, elementary, middle/junior high, secondary. **Cooperative education programs:** engineering, health professions, other. **Reserve Officers Training Corps (ROTC):** Army ROTC: Offered at cooperating institution; Air Force ROTC: Offered at cooperating institution. **Faculty and instruction (2009-2010):** Total instructional faculty: 159 full-time, 133 part-time (56% men; 44% women; 7% minorities). Full-time faculty with Ph.D. or other terminal degree: 77%. Student/faculty ratio: 15/1. Classes of fewer than 20 students: 74%; of 20 to 49 students: 26%. **Advanced Placement and International Baccalaureate credit:** AP tests may be used for: Placement only. Scores accepted: 3, 4, 5. International Baccalaureate exams may be used for: Placement only. **Freshmen returning for sophomore year:** 80%. **Graduation rates:** Four-year: 47%; five-year: 55%; six-year: 56%. **Graduate study:** 22% of students pursue further study within one year. Fields in which graduates pursue further study: Master of Business Administration (MBA), 19%; law, 4%; medicine, 6%; dentistry, 1%; theology (or the seminary), 6%; education, 23%; arts and sciences, 40%; veterinary medicine, 1%.

COSTS AND FINANCIAL AID

Financial aid office: (336) 841-9128. **Financial aid:** Priority filing date for institution's financial aid form: March 1. In 2009-2010, 93% of undergraduates applied for financial aid. Of those, 66% were determined to have financial need; 57% had their need fully met. Average financial aid package (proportion receiving): $10,995 (66%). Average amount of gift aid, such as scholarships or grants (proportion receiving): $2,884 (47%). Average amount of self-help aid, such as work study or loans (proportion receiving): $5,834 (66%). Average need-based loan (excluding PLUS or other private loans): $5,082. Among students who received need-based aid, the average percentage of need met: 56%. Among students who received aid based on merit, the average award (and the proportion receiving): $2,117 (21%). The average athletic scholarship (and the proportion receiving): $19,026 (5%). Average amount of debt of borrowers graduating in 2009: $9,437. Proportion who borrowed: 69%.

CAMPUS LIFE AND EXTRACURRICULAR ACTIVITIES

Campus housing available (% using): coed dorms (62%), women's dorms (9%), men's dorms (14%), sorority housing (8%), fraternity housing (6%), apartment for single students. Students who live in college-owned, operated, or affiliated housing: 93%. **Student employment:** During the 2009-2010 academic year, 15% of undergraduates worked on campus. Average per-year earnings: $1,500. **Clubs and organizations:** Number of student organizations: 109. Activities include: choral groups, concert band, dance, drama/theater, literary magazine, music ensembles, musical theater, pep band, radio station, student government, student newspaper, symphony orchestra, television station, yearbook. Number of fraternities: 5; sororities: 4. Proportion of men in fraternities: 30%; of women in sororities: 18%. Average proportion of students who stay on campus on weekends: 80%. **Sports program (2009-2010):** Member of NCAA I. *Men's intercollegiate varsity sports:* baseball, basketball, cross country, golf, soccer, tennis, track and field (outdoor). *Women's intercollegiate varsity sports:* basketball, cross country, golf, soccer, tennis, track and field (outdoor), volleyball.

SERVICES AND FACILITIES

Basic services: nonremedial tutoring, placement service, health service, health insurance. **Remedial assistance:** reading, math, writing, study skills. **Counseling services:** minority student, career, military, personal, veteran student, academic, older student, psychological, birth control, religious. **For learning-disabled students:** School does not offer a structured program with separate admission and additional fees. Services include: remedial math, remedial English, reading machines, remedial reading, tape recorders, note-taking services, oral tests, learning center, readers, extended time for tests, tutors, priority registration, priority seating, texts on tape, other testing accommodations. **Library:** Number of titles: 163,075; number of current serial subscriptions: 4,425. **Information technology resources:** Students are not required to lease or own a computer. Number of campus computers available to all students: 1,150. School has a wireless network. Approximate number of users that can be accommodated: 5,000. Proportion of college-owned housing units wired for high-speed internet access: 100%. **Campus safety:** Security services offered: 24-hour foot-and-vehicle patrols, late-night transport/escort service, 24-hour emergency telephones, lighted pathways/sidewalks, student patrols, controlled dormitory access (key, security card, etc).

TRANSFER AND INTERNATIONAL STUDENTS

Transfer students: May apply for admission for the following academic terms: Fall, Spring, Summer. Applicants need a minimum number of credits to apply. For fall 2009: Transfer applications received: 182. Transfer applicants offered admission: 114. Transfer applicants enrolled: 50. **International students:** Number of foreign undergraduates: 56 (2% of student body). Number of countries represented: 50. Minimum TOEFL score required: 500 (paper); 180 (computer). Average TOEFL score: 530 (paper).

Johnson C. Smith University

- **Address:** 100 Beatties Ford Road, Charlotte, NC 28216
- **Website:** http://www.jcsu.edu
- **Private**
- **Enrollment:** 1,415 full-time; 51 part-time

KEY STATS
✔ **U.S News College Ranking:** second tier, National Liberal Arts Colleges
✔ **SAT Score (25th/75th percentile):** 800-930
✔ **Tuition:** 2010-2011: $16,542

Selectivity: Less selective	**Room/board:** $6,439
Acceptance rate: 30%	**Average debt:** $19,000
Student/faculty ratio: 13/1	**Proportion who borrowed:** 81%

UNDERGRADUATE STUDENT BODY STATS

2009-2010 enrollment: 1,415 full-time; 51 part-time. Men: 41%; women: 59%. **Ethnic makeup:** African American: 97%; White: 1%; International: 1%.

ADMISSIONS FACTS AND FIGURES

Phone: (704) 378-1010. **Email:** admissions@jcsu.edu. **Website:** http://www.jcsu.edu. **Application deadlines for fall 2011:** Regular decision: May 2. Early decision: Not offered. Early action: Send application by: December 1; Decision sent by: December 1. Admission can be deferred. **Application fee:** $25. **To apply online, go to:** http://msw23w04.jcsu.edu/ics/Admissions/. **Admissions requirements/recommendations:** High school units required (recommended): English: 4; Mathematics: 3; Science: 2; Foreign language: 2; Social studies: 2; Academic electives: 3; Total units: 16. Tests: The college uses SAT or ACT scores in admissions decisions. Either SAT or ACT required. For admission to the fall 2011 entering class, the school will accept: ACT with or without writing accepted. Campus visit: Recommended. Admissions interview: Recommended. Off-campus interview: May be arranged. **Factors that count in admissions decisions:** *Academic:* Secondary school record: Important. Class rank: Important. Letters of recommendation: Very Important. Standardized test scores: Considered. Essay: Considered. *Nonacademic:* Interview: Not Considered. Extracurricular activities: Considered. Talent/ability: Considered. Character/personal qualities: Considered. Alumni/ae relationship: Not Considered. Geographical residence: Not Considered. State residency: Not Considered. Religious affiliation/commitment: Not Considered. Minority status: Not Considered. Volunteer work: Not Considered. Work experience: Not Considered. **Other schools with the greatest overlap in applicants:** Clark Atlanta University; Delaware State University; Morgan State University; North Carolina Central

University; Shaw University. **Admissions statistics for the fall 2009 entering class:** Total applicants: 5,450. Total accepted: 1,645. Freshmen enrolled: 282; 76% were from out of state. Overall acceptance rate: 30%. Non-early acceptance rate: 30%. **Size of waiting list:** 467 applicants; enrolled from waiting list: 163. **Credentials of fall 2009 freshmen:** 6% ranked in the top 10 percent of their high school class; 21% were in the top 25 percent; 55% were in the top half. (Proportion submitting class standing: 72%.) **Average high school grade point average:** 2.9. **First-year students who submitted SAT scores:** 83%. Scores (25/75 percentile): Critical Reading: 400-460, Math: 400-470, Combined: 800-930. **First-year students submitting ACT scores:** 40%. Scores (25/75 percentile): English: N/A, Math: N/A, Composite: 16-19.

ACADEMICS

Year founded: 1867. **Academic calendar:** Semester. **Degrees offered:** bachelor's. **Most popular majors:** 19% business administration and management, 13% mass communication/media studies, 9% criminal justice/law enforcement administration, 7% sport and fitness administration/management, 6% computer and information sciences. **Major fields of study:** biological and biomedical sciences; business, management, marketing, and related support services; communication, journalism, and related programs; computer and information sciences and support services; education; engineering; English language and literature/letters; foreign languages, literatures, and linguistics; history; liberal arts and sciences studies, and humanities; mathematics and statistics; multi/interdisciplinary studies; parks, recreation, leisure, and fitness studies; physical sciences; psychology; public administration and social service professions; social sciences; visual and performing arts. **Areas of required coursework:** humanities, computer literacy, mathematics, English (including composition), foreign languages, sciences (biological or physical), history, other. **Pre-professional programs:** pre-law, pre-dentistry, pre-medicine. **Special academic programs:** accelerated program, cooperative (work-study plan) program, cross-registration, double major, exchange student program (domestic), honors program, independent study, internships, liberal arts/career combination, study abroad, teacher certificate program. **Teacher certification offered in:** elementary, secondary. **Cooperative education programs:** business, computer science, education, engineering, health professions, humanities, natural science, social/behavioral science. **Reserve Officers Training Corps (ROTC):** Army ROTC: Offered on campus; Air Force ROTC: Offered at cooperating institution (University of North Carolina–Charlotte). **Faculty and instruction (2009-2010):** Total instructional faculty: 100 full-time, 31 part-time (47% men; 53% women; 73% minorities). Full-time faculty with Ph.D. or other terminal degree: 81%. Student/faculty ratio: 13/1. Classes of fewer than 20 students: 49%; of 20 to 49 students: 51%. **Advanced Placement and International Baccalaureate credit:** AP tests may be used for: Credit and/or placement. Scores accepted: 3, 4, 5. International Baccalaureate exams may be used for: Placement only. **Freshmen returning for sophomore year:** 65%. **Graduation rates:** Four-year: 26%; five-year: 36%; six-year: 38%. **Graduate study:** 26% of students pursue further study within one year.

COSTS AND FINANCIAL AID

Financial aid office: (704) 378-1035. **Expenses (2010-2011):** Tuition and fees 2010-2011: $16,542; room/board: $6,439. Estimated books and supplies: $1,750; transportation: $1,750; personal expenses: $3,250. **Financial aid:** Priority filing date for institution's financial aid form: March 1. In 2009-2010, 96% of undergraduates applied for financial aid. Of those, 92% were determined to have financial need; 4% had their need fully met. Average financial aid package (proportion receiving): $12,940 (91%). Average amount of gift aid, such as scholarships or grants (proportion receiving): $8,759 (80%). Average amount of self-help aid, such as work study or loans (proportion receiving): $5,519 (86%). Average need-based loan (excluding PLUS or other private loans): $5,105. Among students who received need-based aid, the average percentage of need met: 51%. Among students who received aid based on merit, the average award (and the proportion receiving): $6,654 (2%). The average athletic scholarship (and the proportion receiving): $10,549 (2%). Average amount of debt of borrowers graduating in 2009: $19,000. Proportion who borrowed: 81%.

CAMPUS LIFE AND EXTRACURRICULAR ACTIVITIES

Campus housing available (% using): coed dorms (22%), women's dorms (44%), men's dorms (34%). Students who live in college-owned, operated, or affiliated housing: 64%. **Clubs and organizations:** Number of student organizations: 55. Activities include: campus ministries, choral groups, concert band, dance, drama/theater, international student organization, jazz band, marching band, music ensembles, pep band, student government, student newspaper, yearbook. Number of fraternities: 5; sororities: 6. Proportion of men in fraternities: 13%; of women in sororities: 6%.

Sports program (2009-2010): Member of NCAA II. *Men's intercollegiate varsity sports:* basketball, cross country, football, golf, tennis, track and field (outdoor). *Women's intercollegiate varsity sports:* basketball, bowling, cross country, softball, tennis, track and field (outdoor), volleyball.

SERVICES AND FACILITIES

Basic services: placement service, health service, health insurance. **Remedial assistance:** reading, math, writing, study skills. **Counseling services:** minority student, career, personal, veteran student, academic, older student, psychological, religious. **For learning-disabled students:** School does not offer a structured program with separate admission and additional fees. Total undergraduates in learning-disabled program or receiving services: 30. Services include: tape recorders, untimed tests, note-taking services, oral tests, learning center, readers, extended time for tests, tutors, priority registration, priority seating, substitution of courses, typist/scribe, exams on tape or computer, other testing accommodations, waiver of math degree requirement. **Library:** Number of titles: 105,249; number of current serial subscriptions: 227. **Information technology resources:** Students are required to lease or own a computer. Number of campus computers available to all students: 1,646. School has a wireless network. Approximate number of users that can be accommodated: 1,500. Proportion of college-owned housing units wired for high-speed internet access: 100%. **Campus safety:** Security services offered: 24-hour foot-and-vehicle patrols, 24-hour emergency telephones, lighted pathways/sidewalks, controlled dormitory access (key, security card, etc).

TRANSFER AND INTERNATIONAL STUDENTS

Transfer students: May apply for admission for the following academic terms: Fall, Spring, Summer. Applicants need a minimum number of credits to apply. For fall 2009: Transfer applications received: 95. Transfer applicants offered admission: 85. Transfer applicants enrolled: 51. **International students:** Number of foreign undergraduates: 11 (1% of student body). Number of countries represented: 1.

Lees-McRae College

■ **Address:** PO Box 128, Banner Elk, NC 28604
■ **Website:** http://www.lmc.edu
■ **Private; Religious affiliation:** Presbyterian
■ **Enrollment:** N/A

KEY STATS

✔ **U.S News College Ranking:** second tier, Regional Colleges (South)
✔ **SAT or ACT Score (25th/75th percentile):** N/A
✔ **Tuition:** 2009-2010: $21,875

Selectivity: Less selective	**Room/board:** $7,400
Acceptance rate: N/A	**Average debt:** N/A
Student/faculty ratio: N/A	**Proportion who borrowed:** N/A

Lenoir-Rhyne University

■ **Address:** PO Box 7163, Hickory, NC 28603-7163
■ **Website:** http://www.lr.edu
■ **Private; Religious affiliation:** Lutheran
■ **Enrollment:** 1,324 full-time; 123 part-time

KEY STATS

✔ **U.S News College Ranking:** 11, Regional Colleges (South)
✔ **SAT Score (25th/75th percentile):** 900-1130
✔ **Tuition:** 2009-2010: $24,200

Selectivity: Selective	**Room/board:** $8,540
Acceptance rate: 77%	**Average debt:** N/A
Student/faculty ratio: 12/1	**Proportion who borrowed:** N/A

UNDERGRADUATE STUDENT BODY STATS

2009-2010 enrollment: 1,324 full-time; 123 part-time. Men: 35%; women: 65%. **Ethnic makeup:** African American: 10%; American-Indian: 1%; Asian American: 2%; Hispanic: 2%; White: 84%; International: 2%. **Religious preference:** Roman Catholic: 6%; Protestant: 41%; No preference: 3%; Unknown: 32%; Lutheran: 12%; Other: 6%.

ADMISSIONS FACTS AND FIGURES

Phone: (828) 328-7300. **Email:** admission@lr.edu. **Website:** http://www. lr.edu. **Application deadlines for fall 2011:** Regular decision: Rolling. Early decision: Not offered. Early action: Send application by: August 15; Decision sent by: September 1. Admission can be deferred. **To apply online, go to:** http://www.lr.edu/admissions/apply.htm. **Admissions requirements/ recommendations:** High school units required (recommended): English: 4; Mathematics: 3; Science: 1; Foreign language: 2; History: 1; Total units: 12. Tests: The college uses SAT or ACT scores in admissions decisions. Either SAT or ACT required. For admission to the fall 2011 entering class, the school will accept: ACT with writing required. Campus visit: Recommended. Admissions interview: Recommended. Off-campus interview: May be arranged. **Factors that count in admissions decisions:** *Academic:* Secondary school record: Very Important. Class rank: Very Important. Letters of recommendation: Considered. Standardized test scores: Important. Essay: Important. *Nonacademic:* Interview: Considered. Extracurricular activities: Considered. Talent/ability: Considered. Character/ personal qualities: Considered. Alumni/ae relationship: Considered. Geographical residence: Considered. State residency: Considered. Religious affiliation/commitment: Considered. Minority status: Considered. Volunteer work: Considered. Work experience: Considered. **Other schools with the greatest overlap in applicants:** Appalachian State University; Gardner-Webb University; Gardner-Webb University; University of North Carolina–Chapel Hill; University of North Carolina–Chapel Hill; University of North Carolina–Charlotte; University of North Carolina–Charlotte; University of North Carolina–Greensboro; University of North Carolina–Greensboro. **Admissions statistics for the fall 2009 entering class:** Total applicants: 2,572. Total accepted: 1,993. Freshmen enrolled: 354; 21% were from out of state. Overall acceptance rate: 77%. Non-early acceptance rate: 77%. **Credentials of fall 2009 freshmen:** 18% ranked in the top 10 percent of their high school class; 46% were in the top 25 percent; 86% were in the top half. (Proportion submitting class standing: 90%.) **First-year students who submitted SAT scores:** 97%. **First-year students submitting ACT scores:** 27%. Scores (25/75 percentile): English: N/A, Math: N/A, Composite: N/A.

ACADEMICS

Year founded: 1891. **Academic calendar:** Semester. **Degrees offered:** bachelor's, post-bachelor's certificate, master's. **Most popular majors:** 22% business, management, marketing, and related support services, 18% health professions and related clinical sciences, 15% education, 7% psychology, 6% social sciences. **Major fields of study:** biological and biomedical sciences; business, management, marketing, and related support services; communication, journalism, and related programs; computer and information sciences and support services; education; English language and literature/ letters; foreign languages, literatures, and linguistics; health professions and related clinical sciences; history; liberal arts and sciences studies, and humanities; mathematics and statistics; natural resources and conservation; parks, recreation, leisure, and fitness studies; philosophy and religious studies; physical sciences; psychology; public administration and social service professions; social sciences; theology and religious vocations; visual and performing arts. **Areas of required coursework:** arts/fine arts, humanities, computer literacy, mathematics, English (including composition), philosophy, foreign languages, sciences (biological or physical), history, social science, other. **Pre-professional programs:** pre-law, pre-medicine, pre-pharmacy. **Special academic programs:** accelerated program, cross-registration, distance learning, double major, dual enrollment, English as a Second Language (ESL), honors program, independent study, internships, liberal arts/career combination, student-designed major, study abroad, teacher certificate program. **Teacher certification offered in:** early childhood, special education, elementary, middle/junior high, secondary, bilingual/bicultural. **Reserve Officers Training Corps (ROTC):** Army ROTC: Offered at cooperating institution (Davidson College); Navy ROTC: Offered at cooperating institution (University of North Carolina–Charlotte). **Faculty and instruction (2009-2010):** Total instructional faculty: 88 full-time, 101 part-time (49% men; 51% women; 7% minorities). Full-time faculty with Ph.D. or other terminal degree: 84%. Student/faculty ratio: 12/1. Classes of fewer than 20 students: 61%; of 20 to 49 students: 39%; of 50 or more students: 0%. **Advanced Placement and International Baccalaureate credit:** AP tests may be used for: Credit and/or placement. Scores accepted: 3, 4, 5. International Baccalaureate exams may be used for: Credit and/or placement. **Freshmen returning for sophomore year:** 70%. **Graduation rates:** Four-year: 40%; five-year: 53%; six-year: 53%.

COSTS AND FINANCIAL AID

Financial aid office: (828) 328-7304. **Expenses (2009-2010):** Tuition and fees 2009-2010: $24,200; room/board: $8,540. Estimated books and supplies:

$1,160. **Financial aid:** Priority filing date for institution's financial aid form: March 1; deadline: September 1.

CAMPUS LIFE AND EXTRACURRICULAR ACTIVITIES

Campus housing available (% using): coed dorms (99%), sorority housing, fraternity housing (1%), special housing for disabled students (0%), other housing options. Students who live in college-owned, operated, or affiliated housing: 55%. **Student employment:** During the 2009-2010 academic year, 9% of undergraduates worked on campus. Average per-year earnings: $750. **Clubs and organizations:** Number of student organizations: 60. Activities include: campus ministries, choral groups, concert band, dance, drama/ theater, jazz band, literary magazine, model UN, music ensembles, musical theater, pep band, radio station, student government, student newspaper, symphony orchestra, yearbook. Number of fraternities: 4; sororities: 4. Proportion of men in fraternities: 11%; of women in sororities: 15%. Average proportion of students who stay on campus on weekends: 30%. **Sports program (2009-2010):** Member of NCAA II. ***Men's intercollegiate varsity sports:*** baseball, basketball, cross country, football, golf, ice hockey, soccer, tennis, track and field (outdoor). ***Women's intercollegiate varsity sports:*** basketball, cross country, golf, soccer, softball, swimming, tennis, track and field (outdoor), volleyball.

SERVICES AND FACILITIES

Basic services: nonremedial tutoring, placement service, health service, health insurance. **Remedial assistance:** reading, math, writing, study skills. **Counseling services:** minority student, career, personal, academic, psychological, religious. **For learning-disabled students:** School does not offer a structured program with separate admission and additional fees. Services include: remedial math, remedial English, reading machines, tape recorders, note-taking services, oral tests, readers, extended time for tests, tutors, priority seating, other testing accommodations. **Library:** Number of titles: 149,674; number of current serial subscriptions: 543. **Information technology resources:** Students are not required to lease or own a computer. Number of campus computers available to all students: 148. School has a wireless network. Approximate number of users that can be accommodated: 500. Proportion of college-owned housing units wired for high-speed internet access: 100%. **Campus safety:** Security services offered: 24-hour foot-and-vehicle patrols, late-night transport/escort service, 24-hour emergency telephones, lighted pathways/sidewalks, controlled dormitory access (key, security card, etc).

TRANSFER AND INTERNATIONAL STUDENTS

Transfer students: May apply for admission for the following academic terms: Fall, Spring, Summer. Applicants need a minimum number of credits to apply. For fall 2009: Transfer applications received: 0. Transfer applicants offered admission: 0. Transfer applicants enrolled: 0. **International students:** Number of foreign undergraduates: 21 (2% of student body). Number of countries represented: 10. Minimum TOEFL score required: 550 (paper); 213 (computer).

Livingstone College

- **Address:** 701 W. Monroe Street, Salisbury, NC 28144
- **Website:** http://www.livingstone.edu/
- **Private; Religious affiliation:** African Methodist Episcopal Zion
- **Enrollment:** 1,078 full-time; 4 part-time

KEY STATS

✔ **U.S News College Ranking:** second tier, Regional Colleges (South)
✔ **SAT Score (25th/75th percentile):** 650-840
✔ **Tuition:** 2010-2011: $13,658

Selectivity: Least selective	**Room/board:** $6,342
Acceptance rate: 67%	**Average debt:** $33,236
Student/faculty ratio: 17/1	**Proportion who borrowed:** 99%

UNDERGRADUATE STUDENT BODY STATS

2009-2010 enrollment: 1,078 full-time; 4 part-time. Men: 55%; women: 45%. **Ethnic makeup:** African American: 98%; White: 2%. **Religious preference:** Roman Catholic: 1%; Protestant: 1%; Muslim: 1%; No preference: 50%; African Methodist Episcopal Zion: 8%.

ADMISSIONS FACTS AND FIGURES

Phone: (704) 216-6001. **Email:** admissions@livingstone.edu. **Website:** http://www.livingstone.edu/. **Application deadlines for fall 2011:** Regular decision: Rolling. Early decision: Not offered. Early action: Not offered. Admission can be deferred. **Application fee:** $25. **To apply online, go to:** http://www.livingstone.edu/admissions/freshman.html. **Admissions requirements/recommendations:** High school units required (recommended): English: 4 (4); Mathematics: 3 (3); Science: 2 (2); Foreign language: 2 (2); Social studies: 2 (2); History: 1 (1); Total units: 13 (13). Tests: The college uses SAT or ACT scores in admissions decisions. Either SAT or ACT required. For admission to the fall 2011 entering class, the school will accept: ACT with or without writing accepted. Campus visit: Recommended. Admissions interview: Neither required nor recommended. Off-campus interview: Not available. **Factors that count in admissions decisions:** *Academic:* Secondary school record: Important. Class rank: Considered. Letters of recommendation: Considered. Standardized test scores: Considered. Essay: Not Considered. *Nonacademic:* Interview: Considered. Extracurricular activities: Considered. Talent/ability: Considered. Character/personal qualities: Important. Alumni/ae relationship: Considered. Geographical residence: Considered. State residency: Not Considered. Religious affiliation/commitment: Not Considered. Minority status: Not Considered. Volunteer work: Considered. Work experience: Considered. **Other schools with the greatest overlap in applicants:** Catawba College; Johnson C. Smith University; North Carolina A&T State University; St. Augustine's College; University of North Carolina–Charlotte. **Admissions statistics for the fall 2009 entering class:** Total applicants: 2,954. Total accepted: 1,968. Freshmen enrolled: 423; 39% were from out of state. Overall acceptance rate: 67%. **Size of waiting list:** 0 applicants; enrolled from waiting list: 0. **Credentials of fall 2009 freshmen:** 5% ranked in the top 10 percent of their high school class; 22% were in the top 25 percent; 32% were in the top half. (Proportion submitting class standing: 98%.) **Average high school grade point average:** 2.2. **First-year students who submitted SAT scores:** 74%. Scores (25/75 percentile): Critical Reading: 330-420, Math: 320-420, Combined: 650-840. **First-year students submitting ACT scores:** 21%. Scores (25/75 percentile): English: 10-15, Math: 15-17, Composite: 13-16.

ACADEMICS

Year founded: 1879. **Academic calendar:** Semester. **Degrees offered:** bachelor's. **Most popular majors:** 21% business administration and management, 13% criminal justice/safety studies, 10% psychology, 10% social work, 8% sociology. **Major fields of study:** biological and biomedical sciences; business, management, marketing, and related support services; computer and information sciences and support services; education; engineering; English language and literature/letters; history; mathematics and statistics; parks, recreation, leisure, and fitness studies; psychology; public administration and social service professions; security and protective services; social sciences; theology and religious vocations; visual and performing arts. **Areas of required coursework:** humanities, computer literacy, mathematics, English (including composition), philosophy, foreign languages, sciences (biological or physical), history, social science, other. **Special academic programs:** accelerated program, cross-registration, double major, internships, teacher certificate program, weekend college, other. **Teacher certification offered in:** early childhood, elementary, secondary. **Reserve Officers Training Corps (ROTC):** Army ROTC: Offered at cooperating institution (University of North Carolina–Charlotte); Air Force ROTC: Offered at cooperating institution (University of North Carolina–Charlotte). **Faculty and instruction (2009-2010):** Total instructional faculty: 52 full-time, 10 part-time (52% men; 48% women; 85% minorities). Full-time faculty with Ph.D. or other terminal degree: 54%. Student/faculty ratio: 17/1. Classes of fewer than 20 students: 55%; of 20 to 49 students: 44%; of 50 or more students: 1%. **Advanced Placement and International Baccalaureate credit:** AP tests may be used for: Credit and/or placement. **Freshmen returning for sophomore year:** 51%. **Graduation rates:** Four-year: 11%; five-year: 21%; six-year: 28%. **Graduate study:** 20% of students pursue further study immediately upon graduation; 20% within one year; 30% within five years. Fields in which graduates pursue further study: Master of Business Administration (MBA), 20%; law, 1%; medicine, 2%; dentistry, 1%; engineering, 1%; theology (or the seminary), 3%; education, 2%; arts and sciences, 15%.

COSTS AND FINANCIAL AID

Financial aid office: (704) 216-6069. **Expenses (2010-2011):** Tuition and fees 2010-2011: $13,658; room/board: $6,342. Estimated books and supplies: $1,300; transportation: $2,000; personal expenses: $2,000. **Financial aid:** Priority filing date for institution's financial aid form: March 15; deadline: June 30. In 2009-2010, 99% of undergraduates applied for financial aid. Of those, 97% were determined to have financial need; 5% had their need fully met. Average financial aid package (proportion receiving): $12,607 (96%). Average amount of gift aid, such as scholarships or grants (proportion receiving): $9,090 (95%). Average amount of self-help aid, such as work study or loans (proportion receiving): $3,872 (91%). Average need-based loan (excluding PLUS or other private loans): $3,685. Among students who received need-based aid, the average percentage of need met: 55%. Among students who received aid based on merit, the average award (and the proportion receiving): $3,785 (2%). The average athletic scholarship (and the proportion receiving): $7,874 (2%). Average amount of debt of borrowers graduating in 2009: $33,236. Proportion who borrowed: 99%.

CAMPUS LIFE AND EXTRACURRICULAR ACTIVITIES

Campus housing available (% using): coed dorms (40%), women's dorms (27%), men's dorms (33%), apartment for single students. Students who live in college-owned, operated, or affiliated housing: 87%. **Student employment:** During the 2009-2010 academic year, 10% of undergraduates worked on campus. Average per-year earnings: $1,000. **Clubs and organizations:** Number of student organizations: 34. Activities include: campus ministries, choral groups, concert band, dance, drama/theater, jazz band, literary magazine, marching band, music ensembles, musical theater, pep band, student government, student film society, yearbook. Number of fraternities: 4; sororities: 4. Proportion of men in fraternities: 2%; of women in sororities: 2%. Average proportion of students who stay on campus on weekends: 75%. **Sports program (2009-2010):** Member of NCAA II. *Men's intercollegiate varsity sports:* basketball, cross country, football, golf, track and field (indoor), track and field (outdoor). *Women's intercollegiate varsity sports:* basketball, bowling, cross country, softball, tennis, track and field (indoor), track and field (outdoor), volleyball.

SERVICES AND FACILITIES

Basic services: nonremedial tutoring, placement service, health service, health insurance. **Remedial assistance:** reading, math, writing, study skills, other. **Counseling services:** minority student, career, personal, academic, older student, psychological, religious. **For learning-disabled students:** School does not offer a structured program with separate admission and additional fees. Services include: remedial math, remedial English, remedial reading, tape recorders, videotaped classes, diagnostic testing service, untimed tests, note-taking services, oral tests, learning center, readers, extended time for tests, tutors, priority seating, texts on tape, other testing accommodations, other. **Library:** Number of titles: 62,332; number of current serial subscriptions: 62. **Information technology resources:** Students are not required to lease or own a computer. Number of campus computers available to all students: 250. School has a wireless network. Approximate number of users that can be accommodated: 75. Proportion of college-owned housing units wired for high-speed internet access: 100%. **Campus safety:** Security services offered: 24-hour foot-and-vehicle patrols, 24-hour emergency telephones, lighted pathways/sidewalks, controlled dormitory access (key, security card, etc).

TRANSFER AND INTERNATIONAL STUDENTS

Transfer students: May apply for admission for the following academic terms: Fall, Spring. Applicants do not need a minimum number of credits to apply. For fall 2009: Transfer applications received: 212. Transfer applicants offered admission: 90. Transfer applicants enrolled: 57. **International students:** Number of foreign undergraduates: 2. Minimum TOEFL score required: 500 (paper); 213 (computer). Average TOEFL score: 500 (paper).

Mars Hill College

- **Address:** 100 Athletic Street, Mars Hill, NC 28754
- **Website:** http://www.mhc.edu
- **Private; Religious affiliation:** Baptist
- **Enrollment:** 1,147 full-time; 90 part-time

KEY STATS

✔ **U.S News College Ranking:** 29, Regional Colleges (South)
✔ **SAT Score (25th/75th percentile):** 850-1060
✔ **Tuition:** 2009-2010: $20,849

Selectivity: Less selective	**Room/board:** $7,285
Acceptance rate: 57%	**Average debt:** N/A
Student/faculty ratio: 12/1	**Proportion who borrowed:** N/A

UNDERGRADUATE STUDENT BODY STATS

2009-2010 enrollment: 1,147 full-time; 90 part-time. Men: 48%; women: 52%. **Ethnic makeup:** African American: 15%; American-Indian: 1%; Asian American: 2%; Hispanic: 3%; White: 76%; International: 3%. **Religious preference:** Roman Catholic: 5%; Protestant: 23%; Unknown: 36%; Baptist: 35%; Other: 1%.

ADMISSIONS FACTS AND FIGURES

Phone: (866) 642-4968. **Email:** admissions@mhc.edu. **Website:** http://www.mhc.edu. **Application deadlines for fall 2011:** Regular decision: Rolling. Early decision: Not offered. Early action: Not offered. Admission can be deferred. **Application fee:** $25. **To apply online, go to:** http://mhc.edu/admissions/apply-now. **Admissions requirements/recommendations:** High school units required (recommended): English: 4 (4); Mathematics: 3 (3); Science: 2 (2); Foreign language: (2); Social studies: (2); History: 2 (2); Academic electives: (4); Total units: 11 (20). Tests: The college uses SAT or ACT scores in admissions decisions. Either SAT or ACT required. For admission to the fall 2011 entering class, the school will accept: ACT with or without writing accepted. Campus visit: Recommended. Admissions interview: Recommended. Off-campus interview: Not available. **Factors that count in admissions decisions:** *Academic:* Secondary school record: Very Important. Class rank: Important. Letters of recommendation: Considered. Standardized test scores: Very Important. Essay: Considered. *Nonacademic:* Interview: Considered. Extracurricular activities: Important. Talent/ability: Considered. Character/personal qualities: Important. Alumni/ae relationship: Important. Geographical residence: Not Considered. State residency: Not Considered. Religious affiliation/commitment: Not Considered. Minority status: Not Considered. Volunteer work: Considered. Work experience: Considered. **Other schools with the greatest overlap in applicants:** Appalachian State University; Gardner-Webb University; University of North Carolina–Asheville; University of North Carolina–Chapel Hill; Western Carolina University. **Admissions statistics for the fall 2009 entering class:** Total applicants: 2,026. Total accepted: 1,155. Freshmen enrolled: 297; 34% were from out of state. Overall acceptance rate: 57%. **Credentials of fall 2009 freshmen:** 6% ranked in the top 10 percent of their high school class; 25% were in the top 25 percent; 59% were in the top half. (Proportion submitting class standing: 77%.) **Average high school grade point average:** 3.2. **First-year students who submitted SAT scores:** 87%. Scores (25/75 percentile): Critical Reading: 420-530, Math: 430-530, Combined: 850-1060. **First-year students submitting ACT scores:** 31%. Scores (25/75 percentile): English: N/A, Math: N/A, Composite: 17-24.

ACADEMICS

Year founded: 1856. **Academic calendar:** Semester. **Degrees offered:** bachelor's. **Most popular majors:** 22% business administration and management, 15% elementary education and teaching, 10% physical education teaching and coaching, 6% psychology, 5% biology/biological sciences. **Major fields of study:** biological and biomedical sciences; business, management, marketing, and related support services; education; English language and literature/letters; family and consumer sciences/human sciences; foreign languages, literatures, and linguistics; health professions and related clinical sciences; history; mathematics and statistics; parks, recreation, leisure, and fitness studies; philosophy and religious studies; physical sciences; psychology; public administration and social service professions; social sciences; visual and performing arts. **Areas of required coursework:** arts/fine arts, humanities, computer literacy, mathematics, English (including composition), foreign languages, sciences (biological or physical), social science. **Pre-professional programs:** pre-law, pre-medicine, pre-theology. **Special academic programs (% participation):** cooperative (work-study plan) program (12%), cross-registration (1%), distance learning (24%), double major (4%), dual enrollment (0%), English as a Second Language (ESL) (1%), independent study (4%), internships (6%), student-designed major (0%), study abroad (8%), teacher certificate program (20%). **Teacher certification offered in:** special education, elementary, middle/junior high, secondary, bilingual/bicultural. **Faculty and instruction (2009-2010):** Total instructional faculty: 70 full-time, 86 part-time. Student/faculty ratio: 12/1. Classes of fewer than 20 students: 71%; of 20 to 49 students: 29%; of 50 or more students: 0%. **Advanced Placement and International Baccalaureate credit:** AP tests may be used for: Placement only. Scores accepted: 3. International Baccalaureate exams may be used for: Placement only. **Freshmen returning for sophomore year:** 63%. **Graduation rates:** Four-year: 25%; five-year: 38%; six-year: 39%. **Graduate study:** 14% of students pursue further study immediately upon graduation.

COSTS AND FINANCIAL AID

Financial aid office: (828) 689-1103. **Expenses (2009-2010):** Tuition and fees 2009-2010: $20,849; room/board: $7,285. Estimated books and supplies: $1,300; transportation: $800; personal expenses: $1,100. **Financial aid:** Priority filing date for institution's financial aid form: March 15.

CAMPUS LIFE AND EXTRACURRICULAR ACTIVITIES

Campus housing available (% using): coed dorms (14%), women's dorms (34%), men's dorms (45%), apartment for single students (7%), special housing for disabled students. Students who live in college-owned, operated, or affiliated housing: 63%. **Student employment:** During the 2009-2010 academic year, 17% of undergraduates worked on campus. Average per-year earnings: $1,500. **Clubs and organizations:** Number of student organizations: 36. Activities include: choral groups, concert band, dance, drama/theater, jazz band, literary magazine, marching band, music ensembles, musical theater, student government, student newspaper, yearbook. Number of fraternities: 6; sororities: 5. Proportion of men in fraternities: 9%; of women in sororities: 12%. Average proportion of students who stay on campus on weekends: 65%. **Sports program (2009-2010):** Member of NCAA II. *Men's intercollegiate varsity sports:* baseball, basketball, cross country, football, golf, lacrosse, soccer, swimming, tennis, track and field (outdoor). *Women's intercollegiate varsity sports:* basketball, cross country, golf, soccer, softball, swimming, tennis, track and field (outdoor), volleyball.

SERVICES AND FACILITIES

Basic services: nonremedial tutoring, placement service, health service, health insurance. **Remedial assistance:** reading, math, writing, study skills. **Counseling services:** career, personal, academic, psychological, religious. **For learning-disabled students:** School does not offer a structured program with separate admission and additional fees. Services include: remedial math, remedial English, remedial reading, tape recorders, note-taking services, oral tests, readers, extended time for tests, tutors, other testing accommodations. **Library:** Number of titles: 189,667; number of current serial subscriptions: 18,821. **Information technology resources:** Students are not required to lease or own a computer. Number of campus computers available to all students: 188. School has a wireless network. Approximate number of users that can be accommodated: 450. Proportion of college-owned housing units wired for high-speed internet access: 100%. **Campus safety:** Security services offered: 24-hour foot-and-vehicle patrols, late-night transport/escort service, 24-hour emergency telephones, lighted pathways/sidewalks, controlled dormitory access (key, security card, etc).

TRANSFER AND INTERNATIONAL STUDENTS

Transfer students: May apply for admission for the following academic terms: Fall, Spring, Summer. Applicants need a minimum number of credits to apply. For fall 2009: Transfer applications received: 238. Transfer applicants offered admission: 125. Transfer applicants enrolled: 79. **International students:** Number of foreign undergraduates: 39 (3% of student body). Number of countries represented: 22. Minimum TOEFL score required: 500 (paper); 176 (computer).

Meredith College

- **Address:** 3800 Hillsborough Street, Raleigh, NC 27607-5298
- **Website:** http://www.meredith.edu
- **Private**
- **Enrollment:** 1,766 full-time; 201 part-time

KEY STATS

✔ **U.S News College Ranking:** 180, National Liberal Arts Colleges
✔ **SAT Score (25th/75th percentile):** 920-1140
✔ **Tuition:** 2009-2010: $24,490

Selectivity: Selective	**Room/board:** $7,020
Acceptance rate: 65%	**Average debt:** $32,300
Student/faculty ratio: 10/1	**Proportion who borrowed:** 76%

UNDERGRADUATE STUDENT BODY STATS

2009-2010 enrollment: 1,766 full-time; 201 part-time. Men: 0%; women: 100%. **Ethnic makeup:** African American: 11%; American-Indian: 1%; Asian American: 3%; Hispanic: 3%; White: 82%; International: 1%.

ADMISSIONS FACTS AND FIGURES

Phone: (919) 760-8581. **Email:** admissions@meredith.edu. **Website:** http://www.meredith.edu. **Application deadlines for fall 2011:** Regular decision: Rolling. Early decision: Send application by: October 15; Decision sent by: November 1. Early action: Not offered. Admission can be deferred. **Application fee:** $40. **To apply online, go to:** http://www.ncmentor.org/applications/nc_independents_common_app/apply.html?application_id=1510. **Admissions requirements/recommendations:** High school units required (recommended): English: 4; Mathematics: 3; Science: 3; Foreign language: 2; Academic electives: 1; Total units: 16. Tests: The college uses SAT or ACT scores in admissions decisions. Either SAT or ACT required. For admission to the fall 2011 entering class, the school will accept: ACT with writing required. Campus visit: Recommended. Admissions interview: Recommended. Off-campus interview: May be arranged. **Factors that count in admissions decisions:** *Academic:* Secondary school record: Very Important. Class rank: Very Important. Letters of recommendation: Important. Standardized test scores: Important. Essay: Considered. *Nonacademic:* Interview: Considered. Extracurricular activities: Considered. Talent/ability: Considered. Character/personal qualities: Important. Alumni/ae relationship: Considered. Geographical residence: Not Considered. State residency: Not Considered. Religious affiliation/commitment: Not Considered. Minority status: Not Considered. Volunteer work: Considered. Work experience: Considered. **Other schools with the greatest overlap in applicants:** Appalachian State University; East Carolina University; Elon University; North Carolina State University–Raleigh; University of North Carolina–Chapel Hill. **Admissions statistics for the fall 2009 entering class:** Total applicants: 1,614. Total accepted: 1,047. Freshmen enrolled: 481; 9% were from out of state. Overall acceptance rate: 65%. Non-early acceptance rate: 65%. **Credentials of fall 2009 freshmen:** 22% ranked in the top 10 percent of their high school class; 50% were in the top 25 percent; 83% were in the top half. (Proportion submitting class standing: 86%.) **Average high school grade point average:** 3.3. **First-year students who submitted SAT scores:** 96%. Scores (25/75 percentile): Critical Reading: 460-570, Math: 460-570, Combined: 920-1140. **First-year students submitting ACT scores:** 19%. Scores (25/75 percentile): English: 17-24, Math: 18-24, Composite: 18-24.

ACADEMICS

Year founded: 1891. **Academic calendar:** Semester. **Degrees offered:** bachelor's, post-bachelor's certificate, master's. **Most popular majors:** 11% psychology, 10% interior design, 7% child development, 6% English language and literature, 5% health/medical preparatory programs. **Major fields of study:** area, ethnic, cultural, and gender studies; biological and biomedical sciences; business, management, marketing, and related support services; communication, journalism, and related programs; computer and information sciences and support services; education; English language and literature/letters; family and consumer sciences/human sciences; foreign languages, literatures, and linguistics; health professions and related clinical sciences; history; mathematics and statistics; multi/interdisciplinary studies; natural resources and conservation; parks, recreation, leisure, and fitness studies; philosophy and religious studies; physical sciences; psychology; public administration and social service professions; social sciences; visual and performing arts. **Areas of required coursework:** arts/fine arts, humanities, computer literacy, mathematics, English (including composition), foreign languages, sciences (biological or physical), history, social science, other. **Pre-professional programs:** pre-law, pre-dentistry, pre-medicine, pre-veterinary science, pre-pharmacy, other. **Special academic programs (% participation):** accelerated program, cooperative (work-study plan) program (1%), cross-registration (10%), double major (2%), dual enrollment, honors program (7%), independent study (11%), internships (34%), student-designed major, study abroad (33%), teacher certificate program (13%), other (3%). **Teacher certification offered in:** early childhood, elementary, middle/junior high, secondary. **Cooperative education programs:** art, business, computer science, home economics, humanities, natural science, social/behavioral science, other. **Reserve Officers Training Corps (ROTC):** Army ROTC: Offered at cooperating institution (North Carolina State University–Raleigh); Air Force ROTC: Offered at cooperating institution (North Carolina State University–Raleigh). **Faculty and instruction (2009-2010):** Total instructional faculty: 138 full-time, 142 part-time (30% men; 70% women; 9% minorities). Full-time faculty with Ph.D. or other terminal degree: 91%. Student/faculty ratio: 10/1. Classes of fewer than 20 students: 63%; of 20 to 49 students: 37%; of 50 or more students: 0%. **Advanced Placement and International Baccalaureate credit:** AP tests may be used for: Credit only. Scores accepted: 3, 4, 5. International Baccalaureate exams may be used for: Credit only. **Freshmen returning for sophomore year:** 75%.

Graduation rates: Four-year: 44%; five-year: 55%; six-year: 57%. **Graduate study:** 19% of students pursue further study within one year.

COSTS AND FINANCIAL AID

Financial aid office: (919) 760-8565. **Expenses (2009-2010):** Tuition and fees 2009-2010: $24,490; room/board: $7,020. Estimated books and supplies: $750; transportation: $550; personal expenses: $1,250. **Financial aid:** Priority filing date for institution's financial aid form: February 15. In 2009-2010, 82% of undergraduates applied for financial aid. Of those, 71% were determined to have financial need; 17% had their need fully met. Average financial aid package (proportion receiving): $18,638 (71%). Average amount of gift aid, such as scholarships or grants (proportion receiving): $14,917 (70%). Average amount of self-help aid, such as work study or loans (proportion receiving): $4,402 (60%). Average need-based loan (excluding PLUS or other private loans): $4,250. Among students who received need-based aid, the average percentage of need met: 78%. Among students who received aid based on merit, the average award (and the proportion receiving): $6,790 (8%). The average athletic scholarship (and the proportion receiving): $0 (0%). Average amount of debt of borrowers graduating in 2009: $32,300. Proportion who borrowed: 76%.

CAMPUS LIFE AND EXTRACURRICULAR ACTIVITIES

Campus housing available (% using): women's dorms (80%), apartment for single students (20%). Students who live in college-owned, operated, or affiliated housing: 60%. **Student employment:** During the 2009-2010 academic year, 28% of undergraduates worked on campus. Average per-year earnings: $1,300. **Clubs and organizations:** Number of student organizations: 90. Activities include: choral groups, concert band, dance, drama/theater, literary magazine, music ensembles, musical theater, student government, student newspaper, yearbook. Number of fraternities: 0; sororities: 0. Average proportion of students who stay on campus on weekends: 55%. **Sports program (2009-2010):** Member of NCAA III. *Women's intercollegiate varsity sports:* basketball, cross country, soccer, softball, tennis, volleyball.

SERVICES AND FACILITIES

Basic services: nonremedial tutoring, health service, health insurance. **Remedial assistance:** math, writing, study skills. **Counseling services:** minority student, career, personal, veteran student, academic, older student, psychological, birth control, religious, other. **For learning-disabled students:** School does not offer a structured program with separate admission and additional fees. Services include: remedial math, remedial English, reading machines, tape recorders, note-taking services, oral tests, learning center, readers, extended time for tests, tutors, priority registration, priority seating, texts on tape, other testing accommodations, other. **Library:** Number of titles: 151,409; number of current serial subscriptions: 3,942. **Information technology resources:** Students are not required to lease or own a computer. School has a wireless network. Proportion of college-owned housing units wired for high-speed internet access: 100%. **Campus safety:** Security services offered: 24-hour foot-and-vehicle patrols, late-night transport/escort service, 24-hour emergency telephones, lighted pathways/sidewalks, controlled dormitory access (key, security card, etc).

TRANSFER AND INTERNATIONAL STUDENTS

Transfer students: May apply for admission for the following academic terms: Fall, Spring. Applicants do not need a minimum number of credits to apply. For fall 2009: Transfer applications received: 292. Transfer applicants offered admission: 158. Transfer applicants enrolled: 86. **International students:** Number of foreign undergraduates: 26 (1% of student body). Number of countries represented: 13. Minimum TOEFL score required: 500 (paper); 173 (computer).

Methodist University

- **Address:** 5400 Ramsey Street, Fayetteville, NC 28311-1498
- **Website:** http://www.methodist.edu
- **Private; Religious affiliation:** United Methodist
- **Enrollment:** 1,728 full-time; 273 part-time

KEY STATS

✔ **U.S News College Ranking:** 35, Regional Colleges (South)
✔ **SAT Score (25th/75th percentile):** 890-1110
✔ **Tuition:** 2010-2011: $24,148

Selectivity: Selective	**Room/board:** $8,836
Acceptance rate: 63%	**Average debt:** $38,820
Student/faculty ratio: N/A	**Proportion who borrowed:** 81%

UNDERGRADUATE STUDENT BODY STATS

2009-2010 enrollment: 1,728 full-time; 273 part-time. Men: 55%; women: 45%. **Ethnic makeup:** African American: 18%; American-Indian: 1%; Asian American: 1%; Hispanic: 5%; White: 70%; International: 4%. **Religious preference:** Roman Catholic: 9%; Protestant: 42%; Jewish: 1%; Unknown: 35%; United Methodist: 13%.

ADMISSIONS FACTS AND FIGURES

Phone: (910) 630-7027. **Email:** admissions@methodist.edu. **Website:** http://www.methodist.edu. **Application deadlines for fall 2011:** Regular decision: Rolling. Early decision: Not offered. Early action: Not offered. Admission can be deferred. **Application fee:** $25. **To apply online, go to:** http://www.methodist.edu/Admissions/application.shtml. **Admissions requirements/recommendations:** High school units required (recommended): English: 4 (4); Mathematics: 3 (4); Science: 3 (4); Foreign language: 0 (2); Social studies: 1 (1); History: 2 (3); Academic electives: 4 (4); Total units: 16 (20). Tests: The college uses SAT or ACT scores in admissions decisions. Either SAT or ACT required. For admission to the fall 2011 entering class, the school will accept: ACT with or without writing accepted. Campus visit: Recommended. Admissions interview: Recommended. Off-campus interview: May not be arranged. **Factors that count in admissions decisions:** *Academic:* Secondary school record: Very Important. Class rank: Considered. Letters of recommendation: Considered. Standardized test scores: Important. Essay: Considered. *Nonacademic:* Interview: Considered. Extracurricular activities: Considered. Talent/ability: Considered. Character/personal qualities: Considered. Alumni/ae relationship: Considered. Geographical residence: Not Considered. State residency: Not Considered. Religious affiliation/commitment: Not Considered. Minority status: Not Considered. Volunteer work: Considered. Work experience: Considered. **Other schools with the greatest overlap in applicants:** Campbell University; Coastal Carolina University; East Carolina University; Elon University; University of North Carolina–Wilmington. **Admissions statistics for the fall 2009 entering class:** Total applicants: 2,904. Total accepted: 1,826. Freshmen enrolled: 490; 47% were from out of state. Overall acceptance rate: 63%. **Size of waiting list:** 0 applicants; enrolled from waiting list: 0. **Credentials of fall 2009 freshmen:** 11% ranked in the top 10 percent of their high school class; 35% were in the top 25 percent; 76% were in the top half. (Proportion submitting class standing: 76%.) **Average high school grade point average:** 3.3. **First-year students who submitted SAT scores:** 76%. Scores (25/75 percentile): Critical Reading: 440-540, Math: 450-570, Combined: 890-1110. **First-year students submitting ACT scores:** 30%. Scores (25/75 percentile): English: 17-22, Math: 18-24, Composite: 18-23.

ACADEMICS

Year founded: 1956. **Academic calendar:** Semester. **Degrees offered:** associate, bachelor's, master's. **Major fields of study:** biological and biomedical sciences; business, management, marketing, and related support services; communication, journalism, and related programs; computer and information sciences and support services; education; English language and literature/letters; foreign languages, literatures, and linguistics; health professions and related clinical sciences; history; mathematics and statistics; parks, recreation, leisure, and fitness studies; philosophy and religious studies; physical sciences; psychology; public administration and social service professions; security and protective services; social sciences; visual and performing arts. **Areas of required coursework:** arts/fine arts, humanities, computer literacy, mathematics, English (including composition), foreign languages, sciences (biological or physical), history, social science, other. **Pre-professional programs:** pre-law, pre-dentistry, pre-medicine, pre-theology, pre-veterinary science, pre-pharmacy, other. **Special academic programs:** distance learning, double major, dual enrollment, English as a Second Language (ESL), honors program, independent study, internships, liberal arts/career combination, study abroad, teacher certificate program, weekend college. **Teacher certification offered in:** special education, elementary, middle/junior high, secondary, bilingual/bicultural. **Reserve Officers Training Corps (ROTC):** Army ROTC: Offered on campus; Air Force ROTC: Offered at cooperating institution. **Advanced Placement and International Baccalaureate credit:** AP tests may be used for: Credit only. Scores accepted: 3, 4, 5. International Baccalaureate exams may be used for: Credit only. **Freshmen returning for sophomore year:** 67%. **Graduation rates:** Four-year: 15%; five-year: 37%; six-year: 38%.

COSTS AND FINANCIAL AID

Financial aid office: (910) 630-7193. **Expenses (2010-2011):** Tuition and fees 2010-2011: $24,148; room/board: $8,836. Estimated books and supplies: $1,200; transportation: $1,500; personal expenses: $4,244. **Financial aid:** Priority filing date for institution's financial aid form: August 1. In 2009-2010, 100% of undergraduates applied for financial aid. Of those, 93% were determined to have financial need; 15% had their need fully met. Average financial aid package (proportion receiving): $15,164 (87%). Average amount of gift aid, such as scholarships or grants (proportion receiving): $7,810 (68%). Average amount of self-help aid, such as work study or loans (proportion receiving): $4,227 (62%). Average need-based loan (excluding PLUS or other private loans): $4,001. Among students who received need-based aid, the average percentage of need met: 67%. Among students who received aid based on merit, the average award (and the proportion receiving): $3,274 (4%). Average amount of debt of borrowers graduating in 2009: $38,820. Proportion who borrowed: 81%.

CAMPUS LIFE AND EXTRACURRICULAR ACTIVITIES

Campus housing available (% using): coed dorms (20%), women's dorms (20%), men's dorms (29%), sorority housing (1%), apartment for single students (30%). Students who live in college-owned, operated, or affiliated housing: 53%. **Clubs and organizations:** Number of student organizations: 74. Activities include: campus ministries, choral groups, concert band, dance, drama/theater, international student organization, jazz band, literary magazine, marching band, model UN, music ensembles, musical theater, pep band, radio station, student government, student newspaper, symphony orchestra, yearbook. Number of fraternities: 3; sororities: 2. Proportion of men in fraternities: 6%; of women in sororities: 6%. Average proportion of students who stay on campus on weekends: 70%. **Sports program (2009-2010):** Member of NCAA III.

SERVICES AND FACILITIES

Basic services: nonremedial tutoring, women's center, placement service, health service, health insurance, other. **Remedial assistance:** math, writing. **Counseling services:** career, military, personal, veteran student, academic, psychological, religious. **For learning-disabled students:** School does not offer a structured program with separate admission and additional fees. Services include: remedial math, remedial English, tape recorders, videotaped classes, untimed tests, note-taking services, oral tests, learning center, readers, extended time for tests, tutors. **Library:** Number of titles: 124,500; number of current serial subscriptions: 571. **Information technology resources:** Students are not required to lease or own a computer. Number of campus computers available to all students: 220. School has a wireless network. Approximate number of users that can be accommodated: 2,000. Proportion of college-owned housing units wired for high-speed internet access: 100%. **Campus safety:** Security services offered: 24-hour foot-and-vehicle patrols, late-night transport/escort service, 24-hour emergency telephones, lighted pathways/sidewalks, controlled dormitory access (key, security card, etc).

TRANSFER AND INTERNATIONAL STUDENTS

Transfer students: May apply for admission for the following academic terms: Fall, Spring, Summer. Applicants need a minimum number of credits to apply. For fall 2009: Transfer applications received: 516. Transfer applicants offered admission: 256. Transfer applicants enrolled: 116. **International students:** Number of foreign undergraduates: 87 (4% of student body). Number of countries represented: 31. Minimum TOEFL score required: 500 (paper); 173 (computer).

Montreat College

- **Address:** PO Box 1267, Montreat, NC 28757-1267
- **Website:** http://www.montreat.edu
- **Private; Religious affiliation:** Presbyterian (U.S.A.)
- **Enrollment:** N/A

....

KEY STATS

✔ **U.S News College Ranking:** 64, Regional Colleges (South)
✔ **SAT or ACT Score (25th/75th percentile):** N/A
✔ **Tuition:** 2010-2011: $22,292

Selectivity: Less selective	**Room/board:** $7,065
Acceptance rate: N/A	**Average debt:** $18,295
Student/faculty ratio: N/A	**Proportion who borrowed:** 81%

Mount Olive College

- **Address:** 634 Henderson Street, Mount Olive, NC 28365
- **Website:** http://www.moc.edu/index.cfm
- **Private; Religious affiliation:** Original Free Will Baptist
- **Enrollment:** N/A

....

KEY STATS

✔ **U.S News College Ranking:** second tier, Regional Colleges (South)
✔ **SAT or ACT Score (25th/75th percentile):** N/A
✔ **Tuition:** 2009-2010: $13,776

Selectivity: Less selective	**Room/board:** $5,540
Acceptance rate: 56%	**Average debt:** N/A
Student/faculty ratio: N/A	**Proportion who borrowed:** N/A

North Carolina A&T State University

- **Address:** 1601 E. Market Street, Greensboro, NC 27411
- **Website:** http://www.ncat.edu
- **Public**
- **Enrollment:** 8,039 full-time; 916 part-time

....

KEY STATS

✔ **U.S News College Ranking:** second tier, National Universities
✔ **SAT Score (25th/75th percentile):** 810-980
✔ **Tuition:** 2010-2011: $3,899 in state, $13,341 out of state

Selectivity: Less selective	**Room/board:** $5,839
Acceptance rate: 65%	**Average debt:** $17,047
Student/faculty ratio: 16/1	**Proportion who borrowed:** N/A

UNDERGRADUATE STUDENT BODY STATS

2009-2010 enrollment: 8,039 full-time; 916 part-time. Men: 47%; women: 53%. **Ethnic makeup:** African American: 90%; Asian American: 1%; Hispanic: 1%; White: 6%; International: 1%.

ADMISSIONS FACTS AND FIGURES

Phone: (336) 334-7946. **Email:** uadmit@ncat.edu. **Website:** http://www.ncat.edu. **Application deadlines for fall 2011:** Regular decision: Rolling. Early decision: Not offered. Early action: Not offered. Admission can be deferred. **Application fee:** $45. **To apply online, go to:** http://www.ncat.edu/admissions.html. **Admissions requirements/recommendations:** High school units required (recommended): English: 4; Mathematics: 4; Science: 3; Foreign language: 2; Social studies: 1; History: 1; Academic electives: 4; Total units: 19. Tests: The college uses SAT or ACT scores in admissions decisions. Either SAT or ACT required. For admission to the fall 2011 entering class, the school will accept: ACT with writing required. Campus visit: Recommended. Admissions interview: Neither required nor recommended. Off-campus interview: Not available. **Factors that count in admissions decisions:** *Academic:* Secondary school record: Very Important. Class rank: Important. Letters of recommendation: Not Considered. Standardized test scores: Important. Essay: Not Considered. *Nonacademic:* Interview: Not Considered. Extracurricular activities: Not Considered. Talent/ability: Not Considered. Character/personal qualities: Not Considered. Alumni/ae relationship: Not Considered. Geographical residence: Considered. State residency: Considered. Religious affiliation/commitment: Not Considered. Minority status: Not Considered. Volunteer work: Not Considered. Work experience: Not Considered. **Admissions statistics for the fall 2009 entering class:** Total applicants: 5,713. Total accepted: 3,728. Freshmen enrolled: 1,898; 18% were from out of state. Overall acceptance rate: 65%. **Credentials of fall 2009 freshmen:** 6% ranked in the top 25 percent of their high school class; 38% were in the top half. (Proportion submitting class standing: 91%.) **Average high school grade point average:** 3.0. **First-year students who submitted SAT scores:** 95%. Scores (25/75 percentile): Critical Reading: 400-480, Math: 410-500, Combined: 810-980. **First-year students submitting ACT scores:** 19%. Scores (25/75 percentile): English: 15-21, Math: 16-21, Composite: 16-21.

ACADEMICS

Year founded: 1891. **Academic calendar:** Semester. **Degrees offered:** bachelor's, master's, doctorate. **Most popular majors:** 14% business, management, marketing, and related support services, 13% engineering, 8% psychology, 7% communication, journalism, and related programs, 7% engineering technologies/technicians. **Major fields of study:** agriculture, agriculture operations, and related sciences; architecture and related services; biological and biomedical sciences; business, management, marketing, and related support services; communication, journalism, and related programs; computer and information sciences and support services; education; engineering; engineering technologies/technicians; English language and literature/letters; family and consumer sciences/human sciences; foreign languages, literatures, and linguistics; health professions and related clinical sciences; history; mathematics and statistics; parks, recreation, leisure, and fitness studies; physical sciences; psychology; public administration and social service professions; social sciences; visual and performing arts. **Special academic programs:** cooperative (work-study plan) program, cross-registration, distance learning, double major, dual enrollment, external degree program, honors program, independent study, internships, liberal arts/career combination, study abroad, teacher certificate program, weekend college. **Reserve Officers Training Corps (ROTC):** Army ROTC: Offered on campus; Air Force ROTC: Offered on campus. **Faculty and instruction (2009-2010):** Total instructional faculty: 518 full-time, 161 part-time (53% men; 47% women; 53% minorities). Full-time faculty with Ph.D. or other terminal degree: 78%. Student/faculty ratio: 16/1. Classes of fewer than 20 students: 32%; of 20 to 49 students: 60%; of 50 or more students: 8%. **Advanced Placement and International Baccalaureate credit:** AP tests may be used for: Credit only. **Freshmen returning for sophomore year:** 73%. **Graduation rates:** Four-year: 18%; five-year: 34%; six-year: 39%.

COSTS AND FINANCIAL AID

Financial aid office: (336) 334-7973. **Expenses (2010-2011):** Tuition and fees 2010-2011: $3,899 in state, $13,341 out of state; room/board: $5,839. Estimated books and supplies: $1,400; transportation: $1,000; personal expenses: $1,500. **Financial aid:** Priority filing date for institution's financial aid form: March 15. In 2009-2010, 92% of undergraduates applied for financial aid. Of those, 84% were determined to have financial need; Average financial aid package (proportion receiving): $11,899 (83%). Average amount of gift aid, such as scholarships or grants (proportion receiving): $4,764 (77%). Average amount of self-help aid, such as work study or loans (proportion receiving): $14,166 (75%). Average need-based loan (excluding PLUS or other private loans): $1,967. Among students who received need-based aid, the average percentage of need met: 84%. Among students who received aid based on merit, the average award (and the proportion receiving): $18,563 (11%). The average athletic scholarship (and the proportion receiving): $3,963 (3%). Average amount of debt of borrowers graduating in 2009: $17,047.

CAMPUS LIFE AND EXTRACURRICULAR ACTIVITIES

Campus housing available: coed dorms, women's dorms, men's dorms, other housing options. Students who live in college-owned, operated, or affiliated housing: 41%. Activities include: campus ministries, choral groups, concert band, dance, drama/theater, international student organization, jazz band, marching band, music ensembles, pep band, radio station, student government, student newspaper, symphony orchestra, television station, yearbook. Number of fraternities: 5; sororities: 4. **Sports program (2009-2010):** Member of NCAA I.

SERVICES AND FACILITIES

Basic services: placement service, health service. **Counseling services:** minority student, career, personal, veteran student, academic, other. **Library:** Number of titles: 618,624; number of current serial subscriptions: 53,195.

Information technology resources: Students are not required to lease or own a computer.

TRANSFER AND INTERNATIONAL STUDENTS

Transfer students: May apply for admission for the following academic terms: Fall, Spring, Summer. Applicants need a minimum number of credits to apply. For fall 2009: Transfer applications received: 1,031. Transfer applicants offered admission: 679. Transfer applicants enrolled: 367. **International students:** Number of foreign undergraduates: 80 (1% of student body). Minimum TOEFL score required: 550 (paper).

North Carolina Central University

■ **Address:** 1801 Fayetteville Street, Durham, NC 27707
■ **Website:** http://www.nccu.edu
■ **Public**
■ **Enrollment:** 5,326 full-time; 1,115 part-time

KEY STATS

✔ **U.S News College Ranking:** 74, Regional Universities (South)
✔ **SAT Score (25th/75th percentile):** 760-920
✔ **Tuition:** 2009-2010: $3,922 in state, $13,991 out of state
Selectivity: Less selective   **Room/board:** $6,530
Acceptance rate: 81%   **Average debt:** N/A
Student/faculty ratio: 15/1   **Proportion who borrowed:** N/A

UNDERGRADUATE STUDENT BODY STATS

2009-2010 enrollment: 5,326 full-time; 1,115 part-time. Men: 34%; women: 66%. **Ethnic makeup:** African American: 87%; Asian American: 1%; Hispanic: 1%; White: 10%; International: 1%.

ADMISSIONS FACTS AND FIGURES

Phone: (919) 530-6298. **Email:** admissions@nccu.edu. **Website:** http://www.nccu.edu. **Application deadlines for fall 2011:** Regular decision: Rolling. Early decision: Not offered. Early action: Not offered. Admission can be deferred. **Application fee:** $40. **To apply online, go to:** http://www1.cfnc.org/Applications/University_of_North_Carolina/apply.html?application_id=1542. **Admissions requirements/recommendations:** High school units required (recommended): English: 4; Mathematics: 4; Science: 3; Foreign language: 2; Social studies: 2; History: 1; Academic electives: 3; Total units: 20. Tests: The college uses SAT or ACT scores in admissions decisions. Either SAT or ACT required. For admission to the fall 2011 entering class, the school will accept: ACT with or without writing accepted. Campus visit: Recommended. Admissions interview: Recommended. Off-campus interview: May be arranged. **Factors that count in admissions decisions: Academic:** Secondary school record: Very Important. Class rank: Important. Letters of recommendation: Considered. Standardized test scores: Important. Essay: Considered. **Nonacademic:** Interview: Considered. Extracurricular activities: Considered. Talent/ability: Considered. Character/personal qualities: Considered. Alumni/ae relationship: Considered. Geographical residence: Considered. State residency: Considered. Religious affiliation/commitment: Considered. Minority status: Not Considered. Volunteer work: Not Considered. Work experience: Not Considered. **Other schools with the greatest overlap in applicants:** Fayetteville State University; North Carolina A&T State University; Shaw University; St. Augustine's College; Winston-Salem State University. **Admissions statistics for the fall 2009 entering class:** Total applicants: 4,402. Total accepted: 3,567. Freshmen enrolled: 1,358; 15% were from out of state. Overall acceptance rate: 81%. **Credentials of fall 2009 freshmen:** 4% ranked in the top 10 percent of their high school class; 17% were in the top 25 percent; 56% were in the top half. (Proportion submitting class standing: 92%.) **Average high school grade point average:** 2.9. **First-year students who submitted SAT scores:** 93%. Scores (25/75 percentile): Critical Reading: 380-460, Math: 380-460, Combined: 760-920. **First-year students submitting ACT scores:** 18%. Scores (25/75 percentile): English: 12-18, Math: 15-18, Composite: 15-18.

ACADEMICS

Year founded: 1910. **Academic calendar:** Semester. **Degrees offered:** bachelor's, master's. **Most popular majors:** 12% business administration and management, 12% criminal justice/safety studies, 8% nursing/registered nurse training (R.N., A.S.N., B.S.N., M.S.N.), 7% political science and government, 6% family and consumer sciences/human sciences. **Major fields of study:** biological and biomedical sciences; business, management,

marketing, and related support services; communication, journalism, and related programs; computer and information sciences and support services; education; English language and literature/letters; family and consumer sciences/human sciences; foreign languages, literatures, and linguistics; health professions and related clinical sciences; history; legal professions and studies; mathematics and statistics; natural resources and conservation; parks, recreation, leisure, and fitness studies; physical sciences; psychology; public administration and social service professions; security and protective services; social sciences; visual and performing arts. **Areas of required coursework:** arts/fine arts, humanities, computer literacy, mathematics, English (including composition), foreign languages, sciences (biological or physical), history, social science. **Special academic programs:** accelerated program, distance learning, double major, dual enrollment, English as a Second Language (ESL), exchange student program (domestic), honors program, independent study, internships, study abroad, teacher certificate program, weekend college. **Teacher certification offered in:** early childhood, special education, elementary, middle/junior high, secondary. **Reserve Officers Training Corps (ROTC):** Army ROTC: Offered on campus; Air Force ROTC: Offered on campus. **Faculty and instruction (2009-2010):** Total instructional faculty: 409 full-time, 199 part-time (48% men; 52% women; 70% minorities). Full-time faculty with Ph.D. or other terminal degree: 73%. Student/faculty ratio: 15/1. Classes of fewer than 20 students: 36%; of 20 to 49 students: 59%; of 50 or more students: 5%. **Advanced Placement and International Baccalaureate credit:** AP tests may be used for: Placement only. International Baccalaureate exams may be used for: Placement only. **Freshmen returning for sophomore year:** 74%. **Graduation rates:** Four-year: 19%; five-year: 38%; six-year: 47%.

COSTS AND FINANCIAL AID

Financial aid office: (919) 530-6180. **Expenses (2009-2010):** Tuition and fees 2009-2010: $3,922 in state, $13,991 out of state; room/board: $6,530. Estimated books and supplies: $1,500; transportation: $600; personal expenses: $1,710. **Financial aid:** Priority filing date for institution's financial aid form: March 1.

CAMPUS LIFE AND EXTRACURRICULAR ACTIVITIES

Campus housing available (% using): coed dorms (97%), women's dorms (3%), men's dorms (0%). Students who live in college-owned, operated, or affiliated housing: 41%. **Clubs and organizations:** Number of student organizations: 83. Activities include: campus ministries, choral groups, concert band, dance, drama/theater, jazz band, literary magazine, marching band, music ensembles, pep band, radio station, student government, student newspaper, yearbook. Number of fraternities: 5; sororities: 4. **Sports program (2009-2010):** Member of NCAA II. **Men's intercollegiate varsity sports:** baseball, basketball, cross country, football, golf, tennis, track and field (indoor), track and field (outdoor). **Women's intercollegiate varsity sports:** basketball, bowling, cross country, golf, softball, tennis, track and field (indoor), track and field (outdoor), volleyball.

SERVICES AND FACILITIES

Basic services: nonremedial tutoring, women's center, placement service, day care, health service, health insurance. **Remedial assistance:** reading, math, writing, study skills. **Counseling services:** minority student, career, personal, veteran student, academic, older student, psychological, birth control, religious. **For learning-disabled students:** School does not offer a structured program with separate admission and additional fees. Services include: reading machines, tape recorders, untimed tests, note-taking services, oral tests, learning center, readers, extended time for tests, tutors, priority registration, priority seating, texts on tape, other testing accommodations. **Library:** Number of titles: 0; number of current serial subscriptions: 2,027. **Information technology resources:** Students are not required to lease or own a computer. Number of campus computers available to all students: 173. School has a wireless network. Approximate number of users that can be accommodated: 1,000. Proportion of college-owned housing units wired for high-speed internet access: 100%. **Campus safety:** Security services offered: 24-hour foot-and-vehicle patrols, late-night transport/escort service, 24-hour emergency telephones, lighted pathways/sidewalks, controlled dormitory access (key, security card, etc).

TRANSFER AND INTERNATIONAL STUDENTS

Transfer students: May apply for admission for the following academic terms: Fall, Spring, Summer. Applicants need a minimum number of credits to apply. For fall 2009: Transfer applications received: 732. Transfer applicants offered admission: 590. Transfer applicants enrolled: 432. **International students:** Number of foreign undergraduates: 32 (1% of student body). Number of countries represented: 20.

North Carolina State University–Raleigh

- **Address:** Box 7001, Raleigh, NC 27695
- **Website:** http://www.ncsu.edu
- **Public**
- **Enrollment:** 22,018 full-time; 3,237 part-time

KEY STATS

✔ **U.S News College Ranking:** 111, National Universities
✔ **SAT Score (25th/75th percentile):** 1080-1280
✔ **Tuition:** 2010-2011: $5,779 in state, $18,314 out of state
   Selectivity: More selective   **Room/board:** $8,154
   Acceptance rate: 55%   **Average debt:** $19,011
   Student/faculty ratio: 17/1   **Proportion who borrowed:** 48%

UNDERGRADUATE STUDENT BODY STATS

2009-2010 enrollment: 22,018 full-time; 3,237 part-time. Men: 56%; women: 44%. **Ethnic makeup:** African American: 9%; American-Indian: 1%; Asian American: 5%; Hispanic: 3%; White: 81%; International: 2%.

ADMISSIONS FACTS AND FIGURES

Phone: (919) 515-2434. **Email:** undergrad_admissions@ncsu.edu. **Website:** http://www.ncsu.edu. **Application deadlines for fall 2011:** Regular decision: February 1. Early decision: Not offered. Early action: Send application by: November 1; Decision sent by: January 30. Admission can be deferred. **Application fee:** $70. **To apply online, go to:** http://www.ncsu.edu/uga. **Admissions requirements/recommendations:** High school units required (recommended): English: 4 (4); Mathematics: 4 (4); Science: 3 (4); Foreign language: 2 (2); Social studies: 1 (1); History: 1 (1); Academic electives: 1 (4); Total units: 16 (20). Tests: The college uses SAT or ACT scores in admissions decisions. Either SAT or ACT required. For admission to the fall 2011 entering class, the school will accept: ACT with writing required. Campus visit: Recommended. Admissions interview: Neither required nor recommended. Off-campus interview: Not available. **Factors that count in admissions decisions:** *Academic:* Secondary school record: Very Important. Class rank: Very Important. Letters of recommendation: Considered. Standardized test scores: Very Important. Essay: Considered. *Nonacademic:* Interview: Not Considered. Extracurricular activities: Considered. Talent/ability: Considered. Character/personal qualities: Considered. Alumni/ae relationship: Considered. Geographical residence: Considered. State residency: Considered. Religious affiliation/commitment: Not Considered. Minority status: Considered. Volunteer work: Considered. Work experience: Considered. **Other schools with the greatest overlap in applicants:** East Carolina University; University of North Carolina–Chapel Hill; University of North Carolina–Charlotte; Virginia Tech; Wake Forest University. **Admissions statistics for the fall 2009 entering class:** Total applicants: 18,782. Total accepted: 10,252. Freshmen enrolled: 4,638; 9% were from out of state. Overall acceptance rate: 55%. Non-early acceptance rate: 55%. **Credentials of fall 2009 freshmen:** 41% ranked in the top 10 percent of their high school class; 83% were in the top 25 percent; 99% were in the top half. (Proportion submitting class standing: 84%.) **Average high school grade point average:** 3.6. **First-year students who submitted SAT scores:** 94%. Scores (25/75 percentile): Critical Reading: 520-620, Math: 560-660, Combined: 1080-1280. **First-year students submitting ACT scores:** 22%. Scores (25/75 percentile): English: 21-28, Math: 24-29, Composite: 23-28.

ACADEMICS

Year founded: 1887. **Academic calendar:** Semester. **Degrees offered:** certificate, associate, bachelor's, post-bachelor's certificate, master's, doctorate. **Most popular majors:** 23% engineering, 15% business/commerce, 10% biology/biological sciences, 7% agriculture, 6% social sciences. **Major fields of study:** agriculture, agriculture operations, and related sciences; architecture and related services; area, ethnic, cultural, and gender studies; biological and biomedical sciences; business, management, marketing, and related support services; communication, journalism, and related programs; computer and information sciences and support services; education; engineering; engineering technologies/technicians; English language and literature/letters; foreign languages, literatures, and linguistics; history; liberal arts and sciences studies, and humanities; mathematics and statistics; multi/interdisciplinary studies; natural resources and conservation; parks, recreation, leisure, and fitness studies; philosophy and religious studies; physical sciences; psychology; public administration and social service professions; social sciences; visual and performing arts. **Areas of required coursework:** arts/fine arts, humanities, computer literacy, mathematics, English (includ-

ing composition), foreign languages, sciences (biological or physical), history, social science. **Pre-professional programs:** pre-law, pre-dentistry, pre-medicine, pre-veterinary science. **Special academic programs (% participation):** accelerated program, cooperative (work-study plan) program (6%), cross-registration, distance learning (38%), double major (9%), dual enrollment, exchange student program (domestic) (1%), honors program (26%), independent study, internships (30%), liberal arts/career combination, student-designed major, study abroad (15%), teacher certificate program (4%). **Teacher certification offered in:** elementary, vo-tech, middle/junior high, secondary. **Cooperative education programs:** agriculture, business, computer science, engineering, humanities, natural science, social/behavioral science. **Reserve Officers Training Corps (ROTC):** Army ROTC: Offered on campus; Navy ROTC: Offered on campus; Air Force ROTC: Offered on campus. **Faculty and instruction (2009-2010):** Total instructional faculty: 1,773 full-time, 172 part-time (68% men; 32% women; 20% minorities). Full-time faculty with Ph.D. or other terminal degree: 87%. Student/faculty ratio: 17/1. Classes of fewer than 20 students: 29%; of 20 to 49 students: 52%; of 50 or more students: 20%. **Advanced Placement and International Baccalaureate credit:** AP tests may be used for: Placement only. Scores accepted: 3, 4, 5. International Baccalaureate exams may be used for: Placement only. **Freshmen returning for sophomore year:** 90%. **Graduation rates:** Six-year: 70%. **Graduate study:** Fields in which graduates pursue further study: Master of Business Administration (MBA), 16%; law, 6%; medicine, 1%; engineering, 20%; theology (or the seminary), 1%; education, 8%; arts and sciences, 46%; veterinary medicine, 2%.

COSTS AND FINANCIAL AID

Financial aid office: (919) 515-2421. **Expenses (2010-2011):** Tuition and fees 2010-2011: $5,779 in state, $18,314 out of state; room/board: $8,154. Estimated books and supplies: $1,000; transportation: $750; personal expenses: $1,994. **Financial aid:** Priority filing date for institution's financial aid form: March 1. In 2009-2010, 64% of undergraduates applied for financial aid. Of those, 45% were determined to have financial need; 51% had their need fully met. Average financial aid package (proportion receiving): $10,594 (44%). Average amount of gift aid, such as scholarships or grants (proportion receiving): $8,678 (42%). Average amount of self-help aid, such as work study or loans (proportion receiving): $3,176 (33%). Average need-based loan (excluding PLUS or other private loans): $2,806. Among students who received need-based aid, the average percentage of need met: 84%. Among students who received aid based on merit, the average award (and the proportion receiving): $5,293 (4%). The average athletic scholarship (and the proportion receiving): $8,576 (1%). Average amount of debt of borrowers graduating in 2009: $19,011. Proportion who borrowed: 48%.

CAMPUS LIFE AND EXTRACURRICULAR ACTIVITIES

Campus housing available (% using): coed dorms (48%), women's dorms (1%), men's dorms (1%), sorority housing (2%), fraternity housing (4%), apartments for married students (3%), apartment for single students (15%), special housing for disabled students, special housing for international students, other housing options (26%). Students who live in college-owned, operated, or affiliated housing: 32%. **Student employment:** During the 2009-2010 academic year, 12% of undergraduates worked on campus. Average per-year earnings: $1,900. **Clubs and organizations:** Number of student organizations: 560. Activities include: campus ministries, choral groups, concert band, dance, drama/theater, international student organization, jazz band, literary magazine, marching band, music ensembles, musical theater, pep band, radio station, student government, student newspaper, student film society, symphony orchestra, television station, yearbook. Number of fraternities: 33; sororities: 17. Proportion of men in fraternities: 10%; of women in sororities: 13%. Average proportion of students who stay on campus on weekends: 60%. **Sports program (2009-2010):** Member of NCAA I. *Men's intercollegiate varsity sports:* baseball, basketball, cross country, football, golf, rifle, soccer, swimming, tennis, track and field (indoor), track and field (outdoor), wrestling. *Women's intercollegiate varsity sports:* basketball, cross country, golf, gymnastics, rifle, soccer, softball, swimming, tennis, track and field (indoor), track and field (outdoor), volleyball.

SERVICES AND FACILITIES

Basic services: nonremedial tutoring, women's center, placement service, health service. **Remedial assistance:** math. **Counseling services:** minority student, career, military, personal, veteran student, academic, older student, psychological, birth control, religious. **For learning-disabled students:** School does not offer a structured program with separate admission and additional fees. Total undergraduates in learning-disabled program or receiving services: 190. Services include: reading machines, tape recorders, note-taking services, readers, extended time for tests, priority registration, priority seating, texts on tape. **Library:** Number of titles: 3,524,653; number of current serial subscriptions: 69,223. **Information technology resources:** Students are not required to lease or own a computer. Number of campus computers available to all students: 3,024. School has a wireless network. Approximate number of users that can be accommodated: 23,750. Proportion of college-owned housing units wired for high-speed internet access: 100%. **Campus safety:** Security services offered: 24-hour foot-and-vehicle patrols, late-night transport/escort service, 24-hour emergency telephones, lighted pathways/sidewalks, student patrols, controlled dormitory access (key, security card, etc).

TRANSFER AND INTERNATIONAL STUDENTS

Transfer students: May apply for admission for the following academic terms: Fall, Spring, Summer. Applicants need a minimum number of credits to apply. For fall 2009: Transfer applications received: 3,868. Transfer applicants offered admission: 1,389. Transfer applicants enrolled: 1,097. **International students:** Number of foreign undergraduates: 351 (2% of student body). Number of countries represented: 57. Minimum TOEFL score required: 550 (paper); 79 (computer). Average TOEFL score: 689 (paper).

North Carolina Wesleyan College

- **Address:** 3400 N. Wesleyan Boulevard, Rocky Mount, NC 27804
- **Website:** http://www.ncwc.edu
- **Private; Religious affiliation:** Methodist
- **Enrollment:** 1,165 full-time; 284 part-time

KEY STATS
✔ **U.S News College Ranking:** 49, Regional Colleges (South)
✔ **SAT Score (25th/75th percentile):** 900-1070
✔ **Tuition:** 2009-2010: $21,780

Selectivity: Less selective	**Room/board:** $7,660
Acceptance rate: 59%	**Average debt:** N/A
Student/faculty ratio: 14/1	**Proportion who borrowed:** N/A

UNDERGRADUATE STUDENT BODY STATS

2009-2010 enrollment: 1,165 full-time; 284 part-time. Men: 41%; women: 59%. **Ethnic makeup:** African American: 55%; American-Indian: 1%; Asian American: 1%; Hispanic: 1%; White: 36%; International: 6%. **Religious preference:** Roman Catholic: 5%; Protestant: 42%; No preference: 53%.

ADMISSIONS FACTS AND FIGURES

Phone: (800) 488-6292. **Email:** adm@ncwc.edu. **Website:** http://www.ncwc.edu. **Application deadlines for fall 2011:** Regular decision: Rolling. Early decision: Not offered. Early action: Not offered. Admission can be deferred. **Application fee:** $25. **To apply online, go to:** http://www.ncwc.edu/Admission/day_apply_inst.htm. **Admissions requirements/recommendations:** High school units required (recommended): English: 4 (4); Mathematics: 3 (3); Science: 2 (2); Foreign language: 2 (2); Social studies: 2 (2). Tests: The college uses SAT or ACT scores in admissions decisions. Neither SAT nor ACT required. For admission to the fall 2011 entering class, the school will accept: ACT with writing required. Campus visit: Neither required nor recommended. Admissions interview: Neither required nor recommended. Off-campus interview: May be arranged. **Factors that count in admissions decisions:** *Academic:* Secondary school record: Very Important. Class rank: Important. Letters of recommendation: Important. Standardized test scores: Important. Essay: Considered. *Nonacademic:* Interview: Important. Extracurricular activities: Important. Talent/ability: Considered. Character/personal qualities: Important. Alumni/ae relationship: Considered. Geographical residence: Not Considered. State residency: Not Considered. Religious affiliation/commitment: Not Considered. Minority status: Not Considered. Volunteer work: Considered. Work experience: Not Considered. **Other schools with the greatest overlap in applicants:** Barton College; Campbell University; East Carolina University; Elon University; North Carolina Central University. **Admissions statistics for the fall 2009 entering class:** Total applicants: 1,741. Total accepted: 1,035. Freshmen enrolled: 305; Overall acceptance rate: 59%. **Credentials of fall 2009 freshmen:** 11% ranked in the top 10 percent of their high school class; 16% were in the top 25 percent; 44% were in the top half. (Proportion submitting class standing: 72%.) **First-year students who submitted SAT scores:** 83%. Scores (25/75 percentile): Critical Reading: 440-520, Math: 460-550, Combined: 900-1070. **First-year students submit-**

ting ACT scores: 17%. Scores (25/75 percentile): English: 15-20, Math: 16-20, Composite: 16-20.

ACADEMICS

Year founded: 1956. **Academic calendar:** Semester. **Degrees offered:** bachelor's. **Most popular majors:** 36% business administration and management, 16% criminal justice/safety studies, 13% psychology, 12% computer and information sciences, 10% accounting. **Major fields of study:** biological and biomedical sciences; business, management, marketing, and related support services; computer and information sciences and support services; education; English language and literature/letters; history; legal professions and studies; mathematics and statistics; multi/interdisciplinary studies; natural resources and conservation; parks, recreation, leisure, and fitness studies; philosophy and religious studies; physical sciences; psychology; security and protective services; social sciences; theology and religious vocations; visual and performing arts. **Areas of required coursework:** humanities, computer literacy, mathematics, English (including composition), sciences (biological or physical), history, social science, other. **Pre-professional programs:** pre-medicine. **Special academic programs (% participation):** accelerated program, cooperative (work-study plan) program, cross-registration, distance learning, double major, dual enrollment, honors program (2%), independent study, internships (2%), liberal arts/career combination, teacher certificate program (5%), weekend college. **Teacher certification offered in:** early childhood, middle/junior high. **Reserve Officers Training Corps (ROTC):** Army ROTC: Offered on campus. **Faculty and instruction:** Total instructional faculty: 45 full-time, 135 part-time (57% men; 43% women; 17% minorities). Full-time faculty with Ph.D. or other terminal degree: 80%. Student/faculty ratio: 14/1. Classes of fewer than 20 students: 76%; of 20 to 49 students: 24%; of 50 or more students: 0%. **Freshmen returning for sophomore year:** 56%. **Graduation rates:** Four-year: 9%; five-year: 29%; six-year: 44%. **Graduate study:** 4% of students pursue further study immediately upon graduation; 7% within one year; 14% within five years.

COSTS AND FINANCIAL AID

Financial aid office: (252) 985-5200. **Expenses (2009-2010):** Tuition and fees 2009-2010: $21,780; room/board: $7,660. Estimated books and supplies: $1,000. **Financial aid:** Priority filing date for institution's financial aid form: March 1.

CAMPUS LIFE AND EXTRACURRICULAR ACTIVITIES

Campus housing available (% using): coed dorms (61%), women's dorms (20%), men's dorms (19%), special housing for disabled students. **Student employment:** During the 2009-2010 academic year, 25% of undergraduates worked on campus. Average per-year earnings: $500. **Clubs and organizations:** Number of student organizations: 34. Activities include: choral groups, drama/theater, international student organization, literary magazine, music ensembles, student government, student newspaper, yearbook. Number of fraternities: 4; sororities: 3. Average proportion of students who stay on campus on weekends: 50%. **Sports program (2009-2010):** Member of NCAA III.

SERVICES AND FACILITIES

Basic services: nonremedial tutoring, placement service, health service. **Remedial assistance:** reading, math, writing, study skills. **Counseling services:** minority student, career, personal, veteran student, academic, older student, psychological, religious. **For learning-disabled students:** School does not offer a structured program with separate admission and additional fees. Services include: remedial math, remedial English, remedial reading, tape recorders, other special classes, diagnostic testing service, untimed tests, note-taking services, special bookstore section, oral tests, learning center, readers, extended time for tests, tutors, priority registration, priority seating, texts on tape, other testing accommodations. **Library:** Number of titles: 93,293; number of current serial subscriptions: 475. **Information technology resources:** Students are not required to lease or own a computer. Number of campus computers available to all students: 100. School does not have a wireless network. Proportion of college-owned housing units wired for high-speed internet access: 100%. **Campus safety:** Security services offered: 24-hour foot-and-vehicle patrols, late-night transport/escort service, 24-hour emergency telephones, lighted pathways/sidewalks, student patrols, controlled dormitory access (key, security card, etc.).

TRANSFER AND INTERNATIONAL STUDENTS

Transfer students: May apply for admission for the following academic terms: Fall, Winter, Spring, Summer. Applicants need a minimum number of credits to apply. **International students:** Number of foreign undergraduates: 71 (6% of student body). Number of countries represented: 4.

Minimum TOEFL score required: 500 (paper); 150 (computer). Average TOEFL score: 500 (paper).

Peace College

- **Address:** 15 E. Peace Street, Raleigh, NC 27604-1194
- **Website:** http://www.peace.edu
- **Private; Religious affiliation:** Presbyterian Church (USA)
- **Enrollment:** 660 full-time; 72 part-time

KEY STATS

✔ **U.S News College Ranking:** second tier, National Liberal Arts Colleges
✔ **SAT Score (25th/75th percentile):** 810-1020
✔ **Tuition:** 2010-2011: $25,232

Selectivity: Less selective	**Room/board:** $8,662
Acceptance rate: 64%	**Average debt:** $23,428
Student/faculty ratio: 14/1	**Proportion who borrowed:** 78%

UNDERGRADUATE STUDENT BODY STATS

2009-2010 enrollment: 660 full-time; 72 part-time. Men: 1%; women: 99%. **Ethnic makeup:** African American: 19%; American-Indian: 2%; Asian American: 2%; Hispanic: 5%; White: 71%; International: 1%. **Religious preference:** Roman Catholic: 8%; Protestant: 53%; Buddhist: 1%; No preference: 4%; Unknown: 23%; Presbyterian Church (USA): 5%; Other: 5%.

ADMISSIONS FACTS AND FIGURES

Phone: (800) 732-2347. **Email:** admissions@peace.edu. **Website:** http://www.peace.edu. **Application deadlines for fall 2011:** Regular decision: Rolling. Early decision: Not offered. Early action: Not offered. Admission can be deferred. **Application fee:** $25. **To apply online, go to:** http://www.peace.edu/content/page/id/510. **Admissions requirements/recommendations:** High school units required (recommended): English: 4 (4); Mathematics: 3 (4); Science: 3 (3); Foreign language: 2 (2); Social studies: 2 (2); History: 2 (2); Total units: 15 (17). Tests: The college uses SAT or ACT scores in admissions decisions. Either SAT or ACT required. For admission to the fall 2011 entering class, the school will accept: ACT with or without writing accepted. Campus visit: Recommended. Admissions interview: Recommended. Off-campus interview: May be arranged. **Factors that count in admissions decisions: Academic:** Secondary school record: Very Important. Class rank: Not Considered. Letters of recommendation: Considered. Standardized test scores: Very Important. Essay: Not Considered. **Nonacademic:** Interview: Important. Extracurricular activities: Considered. Talent/ability: Considered. Character/personal qualities: Considered. Alumni/ae relationship: Considered. Geographical residence: Not Considered. State residency: Not Considered. Religious affiliation/commitment: Not Considered. Minority status: Not Considered. Volunteer work: Considered. Work experience: Considered. **Other schools with the greatest overlap in applicants:** East Carolina University; Meredith College; North Carolina State University–Raleigh; University of North Carolina–Chapel Hill; University of North Carolina–Wilmington. **Admissions statistics for the fall 2009 entering class:** Total applicants: 994. Total accepted: 635. Freshmen enrolled: 151; Overall acceptance rate: 64%. **Credentials of fall 2009 freshmen:** 4% ranked in the top 10 percent of their high school class; 23% were in the top 25 percent; 59% were in the top half. (Proportion submitting class standing: 89%.) **Average high school grade point average:** 3.2. **First-year students who submitted SAT scores:** 93%. Scores (25/75 percentile): Critical Reading: 410-520, Math: 400-500, Combined: 810-1020. **First-year students submitting ACT scores:** 7%. Scores (25/75 percentile): English: N/A, Math: N/A, Composite: 16-18.

ACADEMICS

Year founded: 1857. **Academic calendar:** Semester. **Degrees offered:** bachelor's. **Most popular majors:** 16% psychology, 15% communication studies/speech communication and rhetoric, 12% developmental and child psychology, 12% business administration and management, 8% human resources management/personnel administration. **Major fields of study:** biological and biomedical sciences; business, management, marketing, and related support services; communication, journalism, and related programs; English language and literature/letters; foreign languages, literatures, and linguistics; liberal arts and sciences studies, and humanities; psychology; social sciences; visual and performing arts. **Areas of required coursework:** arts/fine arts, humanities, computer literacy, mathematics, English (including composition), philosophy, foreign languages, sciences (biological or

physical), history, social science, other. **Pre-professional programs:** pre-law, pre-dentistry, pre-medicine, pre-veterinary science, pre-optometry, pre-pharmacy. **Special academic programs (% participation):** cross-registration (10%), distance learning (1%), double major (8%), dual enrollment, honors program (10%), independent study (2%), internships (100%), study abroad (32%), teacher certificate program (5%). **Teacher certification offered in:** special education, elementary. **Reserve Officers Training Corps (ROTC):** Army ROTC: Offered at cooperating institution (North Carolina State University–Raleigh); Navy ROTC: Offered at cooperating institution (North Carolina State University–Raleigh); Air Force ROTC: Offered at cooperating institution (North Carolina State University–Raleigh). **Faculty and instruction (2009-2010):** Total instructional faculty: 45 full-time, 33 part-time (41% men; 59% women; 14% minorities). Full-time faculty with Ph.D. or other terminal degree: 78%. Student/faculty ratio: 14/1. Classes of fewer than 20 students: 74%; of 20 to 49 students: 25%; of 50 or more students: 0%. **Advanced Placement and International Baccalaureate credit:** AP tests may be used for: Credit and/or placement. Scores accepted: 3. International Baccalaureate exams may be used for: Credit and/or placement. **Freshmen returning for sophomore year:** 65%. **Graduation rates:** Four-year: 23%; five-year: 33%; six-year: 35%. **Graduate study:** 9% of students pursue further study immediately upon graduation; 14% within one year. Fields in which graduates pursue further study: Master of Business Administration (MBA), 14%; law, 7%; medicine, 21%; education, 21%; arts and sciences, 37%.

COSTS AND FINANCIAL AID

Financial aid office: (919) 508-2249. **Expenses (2010-2011):** Tuition and fees 2010-2011: $25,232; room/board: $8,662. Estimated books and supplies: $1,300; transportation: $1,000; personal expenses: $2,400. **Financial aid:** Priority filing date for institution's financial aid form: March 15. In 2009-2010, 91% of undergraduates applied for financial aid. Of those, 81% were determined to have financial need; 11% had their need fully met. Average financial aid package (proportion receiving): $19,858 (81%). Average amount of gift aid, such as scholarships or grants (proportion receiving): $15,690 (81%). Average amount of self-help aid, such as work study or loans (proportion receiving): $4,730 (72%). Average need-based loan (excluding PLUS or other private loans): $3,978. Among students who received need-based aid, the average percentage of need met: 72%. Among students who received aid based on merit, the average award (and the proportion receiving): $7,830 (18%). The average athletic scholarship (and the proportion receiving): $0 (0%). Average amount of debt of borrowers graduating in 2009: $23,428. Proportion who borrowed: 78%.

CAMPUS LIFE AND EXTRACURRICULAR ACTIVITIES

Campus housing available (% using): women's dorms (100%). **Student employment:** During the 2009-2010 academic year, 15% of undergraduates worked on campus. Average per-year earnings: $2,000. **Clubs and organizations:** Number of student organizations: 30. Activities include: campus ministries, choral groups, dance, drama/theater, literary magazine, music ensembles, musical theater, student government, student newspaper, yearbook. Number of fraternities: 0; sororities: 0. Average proportion of students who stay on campus on weekends: 35%. **Sports program (2009-2010):** Member of NCAA III. **Women's intercollegiate varsity sports:** basketball, cross country, soccer, softball, tennis, volleyball.

SERVICES AND FACILITIES

Basic services: nonremedial tutoring, placement service, health service. **Remedial assistance:** reading, math, writing, study skills. **Counseling services:** minority student, career, personal, academic, birth control, religious. **For learning-disabled students:** School does not offer a structured program with separate admission and additional fees. Total undergraduates in learning-disabled program or receiving services: 31. Services include: remedial math, remedial English, reading machines, tape recorders, note-taking services, learning center, extended time for tests, tutors, priority seating, texts on tape, exams on tape or computer, other testing accommodations. **Library:** Number of titles: 47,851; number of current serial subscriptions: 4,198. **Information technology resources:** Students are not required to lease or own a computer. Number of campus computers available to all students: 192. School has a wireless network. Approximate number of users that can be accommodated: 800. Proportion of college-owned housing units wired for high-speed internet access: 100%. **Campus safety:** Security services offered: 24-hour foot-and-vehicle patrols, late-night transport/escort service, 24-hour emergency telephones, lighted pathways/sidewalks, controlled dormitory access (key, security card, etc).

TRANSFER AND INTERNATIONAL STUDENTS

Transfer students: May apply for admission for the following academic terms: Fall, Spring, Summer. Applicants need a minimum number of credits to apply. For fall 2009: Transfer applications received: 200. Transfer applicants offered admission: 146. Transfer applicants enrolled: 96. **International students:** Number of foreign undergraduates: 6 (1% of student body). Number of countries represented: 4. Minimum TOEFL score required: 550 (paper); 213 (computer). Average TOEFL score: 560 (paper).

Pfeiffer University

- **Address:** PO Box 960, Misenheimer, NC 28109
- **Website:** http://www.pfeiffer.edu
- **Private; Religious affiliation:** Methodist
- **Enrollment:** 936 full-time; 133 part-time

KEY STATS

✔ **U.S News College Ranking:** 81, Regional Universities (South)
✔ **SAT Score (25th/75th percentile):** 900-1110
✔ **Tuition:** 2009-2010: $19,215

Selectivity: Selective	**Room/board:** $7,928
Acceptance rate: 54%	**Average debt:** N/A
Student/faculty ratio: N/A	**Proportion who borrowed:** N/A

UNDERGRADUATE STUDENT BODY STATS

2009-2010 enrollment: 936 full-time; 133 part-time. Men: 45%; women: 55%. **Ethnic makeup:** African American: 21%; American-Indian: 1%; Asian American: 1%; Hispanic: 3%; White: 70%; International: 4%. **Religious preference:** Roman Catholic: 10%; Protestant: 41%; No preference: 8%; Unknown: 12%; Methodist: 23%; o: 0%; Other: 6%.

ADMISSIONS FACTS AND FIGURES

Phone: (800) 338-2060. **Email:** admissions@pfeiffer.edu. **Website:** http://www.pfeiffer.edu. **Application deadlines for fall 2011:** Regular decision: Rolling. Early decision: Not offered. Early action: Not offered. Admission cannot be deferred. **Application fee:** $25. **To apply online, go to:** http://www.pfeiffer.edu/images/stories/Admissions_Undergrad/pfeifferap_05_07.pdf. **Admissions requirements/recommendations:** High school units required (recommended): English: 4; Mathematics: 3; Science: 2; Foreign language: (2); Social studies: 2; History: 2; Total units: 12. Tests: The college uses SAT or ACT scores in admissions decisions. Either SAT or ACT required. For admission to the fall 2011 entering class, the school will accept: ACT with or without writing accepted. Campus visit: Recommended. Admissions interview: Recommended. Off-campus interview: May be arranged. **Factors that count in admissions decisions:** *Academic:* Secondary school record: Very Important. Class rank: Considered. Letters of recommendation: Important. Standardized test scores: Very Important. Essay: Considered. *Nonacademic:* Interview: Considered. Extracurricular activities: Important. Talent/ability: Important. Character/personal qualities: Very Important. Alumni/ae relationship: Considered. Geographical residence: Not Considered. State residency: Not Considered. Religious affiliation/commitment: Considered. Minority status: Not Considered. Volunteer work: Very Important. Work experience: Considered. **Other schools with the greatest overlap in applicants:** Appalachian State University; East Carolina University; North Carolina State University–Raleigh; University of North Carolina–Charlotte; University of North Carolina–Greensboro. **Admissions statistics for the fall 2009 entering class:** Total applicants: 1,290. Total accepted: 695. Freshmen enrolled: 240; Overall acceptance rate: 54%. **First-year students who submitted SAT scores:** 78%. Scores (25/75 percentile): Critical Reading: 440-540, Math: 460-570, Combined: 900-1110. **First-year students submitting ACT scores:** 25%. Scores (25/75 percentile): English: 15-22, Math: 18-23, Composite: 18-23.

ACADEMICS

Year founded: 1885. **Academic calendar:** Semester. **Degrees offered:** bachelor's, post-bachelor's certificate, master's. **Major fields of study:** area, ethnic, cultural, and gender studies; biological and biomedical sciences; business, management, marketing, and related support services; communication, journalism, and related programs; computer and information sciences and support services; education; engineering; English language and literature/letters; health professions and related clinical sciences; history; legal professions and studies; liberal arts and sciences studies, and humanities; mathematics and statistics; multi/interdisciplinary studies; natural resources and conservation; parks, recreation, leisure, and fitness studies; philosophy and religious studies; physical sciences; psychology; public administration and social service professions; security and protective services; social sciences; theology and religious vocations; visual and performing arts. **Areas of required coursework:** arts/fine arts, humanities, computer literacy, mathematics, English (including composition), philosophy, sciences (biological or physical), history, social science, other. **Pre-professional programs:** pre-law, pre-medicine, pre-theology. **Special academic programs:** accelerated program, cooperative (work-study plan) program, distance learning, double major, dual enrollment, honors program, independent study, internships, liberal arts/career combination, study abroad, teacher certificate program. **Teacher certification offered in:** special education, elementary, secondary. **Cooperative education programs:** art, business, computer science, education, engineering, humanities, natural science, social/behavioral science, technologies. **Reserve Officers Training Corps (ROTC):** Army ROTC: Offered at cooperating institution (Davidson College). **Advanced Placement and International Baccalaureate credit:** AP tests may be used for: Credit only. Scores accepted: 3. International Baccalaureate exams may be used for: Placement only. **Freshmen returning for sophomore year:** 68%. **Graduation rates:** Six-year: 51%.

COSTS AND FINANCIAL AID

Financial aid office: (800) 338-2060. **Expenses (2009-2010):** Tuition and fees 2009-2010: $19,215; room/board: $7,928. Estimated books and supplies: $1,400. **Financial aid:** Priority filing date for institution's financial aid form: April 15.

CAMPUS LIFE AND EXTRACURRICULAR ACTIVITIES

Campus housing available (% using): coed dorms (54%), women's dorms (20%), men's dorms (26%). **Student employment:** During the 2009-2010 academic year, 27% of undergraduates worked on campus. **Clubs and organizations:** Number of student organizations: 30. Activities include: choral groups, concert band, drama/theater, jazz band, literary magazine, music ensembles, musical theater, pep band, student government, student newspaper, yearbook. Number of fraternities: 0; sororities: 0. Average proportion of students who stay on campus on weekends: 75%. **Sports program (2009-2010):** Member of NCAA II. *Men's intercollegiate varsity sports:* baseball, basketball, cross country, golf, lacrosse, soccer, swimming, tennis. *Women's intercollegiate varsity sports:* basketball, cross country, golf, lacrosse, soccer, softball, swimming, tennis, volleyball.

SERVICES AND FACILITIES

Basic services: women's center, health service, health insurance. **Remedial assistance:** reading, math, writing, study skills. **Counseling services:** minority student, career, military, personal, veteran student, academic, older student, psychological, birth control, religious. **For learning-disabled students:** School does not offer a structured program with separate admission and additional fees. Services include: remedial math, reading machines, tape recorders, other special classes, note-taking services, oral tests, learning center, readers, extended time for tests, tutors. **Library:** Number of titles: 128,189; number of current serial subscriptions: 302. **Information technology resources:** Students are not required to lease or own a computer. Number of campus computers available to all students: 100. School has a wireless network. Approximate number of users that can be accommodated: 200. Proportion of college-owned housing units wired for high-speed internet access: 100%. **Campus safety:** Security services offered: 24-hour foot-and-vehicle patrols, late-night transport/escort service, 24-hour emergency telephones, lighted pathways/sidewalks, controlled dormitory access (key, security card, etc).

TRANSFER AND INTERNATIONAL STUDENTS

Transfer students: May apply for admission for the following academic terms: Fall, Spring, Summer. Applicants do not need a minimum number of credits to apply. **International students:** Number of foreign undergraduates: 35 (4% of student body). Number of countries represented: 18. Minimum TOEFL score required: 500 (paper); 173 (computer). Average TOEFL score: 550 (paper).

Queens University of Charlotte

- **Address:** 1900 Selwyn Avenue, Charlotte, NC 28274
- **Website:** http://www.queens.edu
- **Private; Religious affiliation:** Presbyterian
- **Enrollment:** 1,312 full-time; 600 part-time

KEY STATS

✔ **U.S News College Ranking:** 18, Regional Universities (South)
✔ **SAT Score (25th/75th percentile):** 950-1160
✔ **Tuition:** 2010-2011: $23,752

Selectivity: Selective	**Room/board:** $8,724
Acceptance rate: 76%	**Average debt:** $20,108
Student/faculty ratio: 13/1	**Proportion who borrowed:** 79%

UNDERGRADUATE STUDENT BODY STATS

2009-2010 enrollment: 1,312 full-time; 600 part-time. Men: 23%; women: 77%. **Ethnic makeup:** African American: 18%; Asian American: 2%; Hispanic: 5%; White: 70%; International: 5%. **Religious preference:** Roman Catholic: 9%; Protestant: 27%; Jewish: 1%; Muslim: 1%; Hindu: 1%; Buddhist: 1%; Unknown: 32%; Presbyterian: 8%; Christian: 19%; Other: 1%.

ADMISSIONS FACTS AND FIGURES

Phone: (800) 849-0202. **Email:** admissions@queens.edu. **Website:** http://www.queens.edu. **Application deadlines for fall 2011:** Regular decision: Rolling. Early decision: Not offered. Early action: Not offered. Admission can be deferred. **Application fee:** $40. **To apply online, go to:** http://www.queens.edu/admissions/apply.asp. **Admissions requirements/recommendations:** High school units required (recommended): English: 4 (4); Mathematics: 3 (3); Science: 2 (2); Foreign language: 2 (2); Social studies: 2 (2); Total units: 13 (13). Tests: The college uses SAT or ACT scores in admissions decisions. Either SAT or ACT required. For admission to the fall 2011 entering class, the school will accept: ACT with writing required. Campus visit: Recommended. Admissions interview: Recommended. Off-campus interview: May be arranged. **Factors that count in admissions decisions: *Academic:*** Secondary school record: Very Important. Class rank: Important. Letters of recommendation: Considered. Standardized test scores: Very Important. Essay: Considered. ***Nonacademic:*** Interview: Important. Extracurricular activities: Very Important. Talent/ability: Considered. Character/personal qualities: Very Important. Alumni/ae relationship: Considered. Geographical residence: Not Considered. State residency: Not Considered. Religious affiliation/commitment: Not Considered. Minority status: Not Considered. Volunteer work: Important. Work experience: Considered. **Other schools with the greatest overlap in applicants:** Appalachian State University; Elon University; University of North Carolina–Chapel Hill; University of North Carolina–Charlotte; University of North Carolina–Wilmington. **Admissions statistics for the fall 2009 entering class:** Total applicants: 1,701. Total accepted: 1,289. Freshmen enrolled: 316; 43% were from out of state. Overall acceptance rate: 76%. **Credentials of fall 2009 freshmen:** 22% ranked in the top 10 percent of their high school class; 54% were in the top 25 percent; 86% were in the top half. (Proportion submitting class standing: 72%.) **Average high school grade point average:** 3.6. **First-year students who submitted SAT scores:** 92%. Scores (25/75 percentile): Critical Reading: 470-580, Math: 480-580, Combined: 950-1160. **First-year students submitting ACT scores:** 34%. Scores (25/75 percentile): English: 18-25, Math: 19-26, Composite: 20-26.

ACADEMICS

Year founded: 1857. **Academic calendar:** Semester. **Degrees offered:** associate, bachelor's, post-bachelor's certificate, master's, post-master's certificate. **Most popular majors:** 23% health professions and related clinical sciences, 17% business, management, marketing, and related support services, 14% communication, journalism, and related programs, 8% psychology, 7% social sciences. **Major fields of study:** area, ethnic, cultural, and gender studies; biological and biomedical sciences; business, management, marketing, and related support services; communication, journalism, and related programs; computer and information sciences and support services; education; English language and literature/letters; foreign languages, literatures, and linguistics; health professions and related clinical sciences; history; mathematics and statistics; philosophy and religious studies; psychology; social sciences; visual and performing arts. **Areas of required coursework:** arts/fine arts, humanities, mathematics, English (including composition), foreign languages, sciences (biological or physical), history, social science, other. **Pre-professional programs:** pre-law, pre-dentistry, pre-medicine, pre-

veterinary science, pre-pharmacy. **Special academic programs (% participation):** double major (10.1%), honors program (19.1%), independent study (29.8%), internships (100%), liberal arts/career combination (98%), study abroad (92%), teacher certificate program (5.9%). **Teacher certification offered in:** elementary, secondary. **Reserve Officers Training Corps (ROTC):** Army ROTC: Offered at cooperating institution; Air Force ROTC: Offered at cooperating institution. **Faculty and instruction (2009-2010):** Total instructional faculty: 109 full-time, 107 part-time (36% men; 64% women; 10% minorities). Full-time faculty with Ph.D. or other terminal degree: 70%. Student/faculty ratio: 13/1. Classes of fewer than 20 students: 70%; of 20 to 49 students: 29%; of 50 or more students: 1%. **Advanced Placement and International Baccalaureate credit:** AP tests may be used for: Credit and/or placement. Scores accepted: 3, 4, 5. International Baccalaureate exams may be used for: Credit only. **Freshmen returning for sophomore year:** 73%. **Graduation rates:** Four-year: 50%; five-year: 59%; six-year: 60%. **Graduate study:** 16% of students pursue further study immediately upon graduation; 26% within one year. Fields in which graduates pursue further study: law, 3%; medicine, 3%; education, 12%; arts and sciences, 5%.

COSTS AND FINANCIAL AID

Financial aid office: (704) 337-2225. **Expenses (2010-2011):** Tuition and fees 2010-2011: $23,752; room/board: $8,724. Estimated books and supplies: $1,200; transportation: $900; personal expenses: $1,500. **Financial aid:** In 2009-2010, 76% of undergraduates applied for financial aid. Of those, 65% were determined to have financial need; 21% had their need fully met. Average financial aid package (proportion receiving): $16,810 (65%). Average amount of gift aid, such as scholarships or grants (proportion receiving): $12,901 (65%). Average amount of self-help aid, such as work study or loans (proportion receiving): $4,581 (56%). Average need-based loan (excluding PLUS or other private loans): $3,961. Among students who received need-based aid, the average percentage of need met: 71%. Among students who received aid based on merit, the average award (and the proportion receiving): $8,229 (22%). The average athletic scholarship (and the proportion receiving): $7,032 (9%). Average amount of debt of borrowers graduating in 2009: $20,108. Proportion who borrowed: 79%.

CAMPUS LIFE AND EXTRACURRICULAR ACTIVITIES

Campus housing available (% using): coed dorms (89%), apartment for single students (10%), special housing for disabled students (1%). Students who live in college-owned, operated, or affiliated housing: 28%. **Student employment:** During the 2009-2010 academic year, 5% of undergraduates worked on campus. Average per-year earnings: $2,500. **Clubs and organizations:** Number of student organizations: 40. Activities include: campus ministries, choral groups, concert band, dance, drama/theater, international student organization, literary magazine, model UN, music ensembles, pep band, student government, student newspaper, yearbook. Number of fraternities: 2; sororities: 5. Proportion of men in fraternities: 11%; of women in sororities: 11%. Average proportion of students who stay on campus on weekends: 50%. **Sports program (2009-2010):** Member of NCAA II. ***Men's intercollegiate varsity sports:*** basketball, cross country, golf, lacrosse, soccer, tennis, track and field (indoor), track and field (outdoor). ***Women's intercollegiate varsity sports:*** basketball, cross country, golf, lacrosse, soccer, softball, tennis, track and field (indoor), track and field (outdoor), volleyball.

SERVICES AND FACILITIES

Basic services: nonremedial tutoring, placement service, health service, health insurance, other. **Remedial assistance:** reading, math, writing, study skills, other. **Counseling services:** minority student, career, personal, academic, older student, psychological, birth control, religious. **For learning-disabled students:** School does not offer a structured program with separate admission and additional fees. Total undergraduates in learning-disabled program or receiving services: 36. Services include: reading machines, tape recorders, note-taking services, learning center, readers, extended time for tests, tutors, priority seating, substitution of courses, texts on tape, exams on tape or computer, other testing accommodations, other. **Library:** Number of titles: 125,665; number of current serial subscriptions: 304. **Information technology resources:** Students are not required to lease or own a computer. Number of campus computers available to all students: 176. School has a wireless network. Approximate number of users that can be accommodated: 640. Proportion of college-owned housing units wired for high-speed internet access: 100%. **Campus safety:** Security services offered: 24-hour foot-and-vehicle patrols, late-night transport/escort service, 24-hour emergency telephones, lighted pathways/sidewalks, controlled dormitory access (key, security card, etc).

TRANSFER AND INTERNATIONAL STUDENTS

Transfer students: May apply for admission for the following academic terms: Fall, Spring, Summer. Applicants do not need a minimum number of credits to apply. For fall 2009: Transfer applications received: 475. Transfer applicants offered admission: 350. Transfer applicants enrolled: 249. **International students:** Number of foreign undergraduates: 93 (5% of student body). Number of countries represented: 10. Minimum TOEFL score required: 550 (paper); 79 (computer). Average TOEFL score: 560 (paper).

Salem College

- ■ **Address:** 601 S. Church Street, Winston-Salem, NC 27101
- ■ **Website:** http://www.salem.edu
- ■ **Private; Religious affiliation:** Moravian Church in America
- ■ **Enrollment:** N/A

KEY STATS

- ✔ **U.S News College Ranking:** 166, National Liberal Arts Colleges
- ✔ **ACT Score (25th/75th percentile):** 22-28
- ✔ **Tuition:** 2009-2010: $21,380

Selectivity: More selective	**Room/board:** $11,210
Acceptance rate: 59%	**Average debt:** N/A
Student/faculty ratio: N/A	**Proportion who borrowed:** N/A

Shaw University

- ■ **Address:** 118 E. South Street, Raleigh, NC 27601
- ■ **Website:** http://www.shawu.edu
- ■ **Private; Religious affiliation:** Baptist
- ■ **Enrollment:** 2,135 full-time; 207 part-time

KEY STATS

- ✔ **U.S News College Ranking:** second tier, Regional Colleges (South)
- ✔ **SAT Score (25th/75th percentile):** 650-850
- ✔ **Tuition:** 2009-2010: $11,696

Selectivity: Least selective	**Room/board:** $7,200
Acceptance rate: 37%	**Average debt:** N/A
Student/faculty ratio: 16/1	**Proportion who borrowed:** N/A

UNDERGRADUATE STUDENT BODY STATS

2009-2010 enrollment: 2,135 full-time; 207 part-time. Men: 37%; women: 63%. **Ethnic makeup:** African American: 86%; White: 12%; International: 1%.

ADMISSIONS FACTS AND FIGURES

Phone: (800) 214-6683. **Email:** admission@shawu.edu. **Website:** http://www.shawu.edu. **Application deadlines for fall 2011:** Regular decision: July 30. Early decision: Not offered. Early action: Not offered. Admission can be deferred. **Application fee:** $25. **To apply online, go to:** http://www1.cfnc.org/ExternalScripts/Online_Applications/College_Admission/default.asp. **Admissions requirements/recommendations:** High school units required (recommended): English: 3; Mathematics: 2; Science: 2; Social studies: 2; Academic electives: 9; Total units: 18. Tests: The college uses SAT or ACT scores in admissions decisions. Either SAT or ACT required. For admission to the fall 2011 entering class, the school will accept: ACT with or without writing accepted. Campus visit: Recommended. Admissions interview: Recommended. Off-campus interview: May be arranged. **Factors that count in admissions decisions:** *Academic:* Secondary school record: Very Important. Class rank: Important. Letters of recommendation: Very Important. Standardized test scores: Important. Essay: Important. *Nonacademic:* Interview: Not Considered. Extracurricular activities: Important. Talent/ability: Considered. Character/personal qualities: Important. Alumni/ae relationship: Important. Geographical residence: Important. State residency: Important. Religious affiliation/commitment: Not Considered. Minority status: Not Considered. Volunteer work: Not Considered. Work experience: Not Considered. **Other schools with the greatest overlap in applicants:** Johnson C. Smith University; Livingstone College; North Carolina Central University; University of North Carolina–Greensboro; Virginia Union University. **Admissions statistics for the fall**

2009 entering class: 52% were from out of state. Overall acceptance rate: 37%. **Credentials of fall 2009 freshmen:** 3% ranked in the top 10 percent of their high school class; 12% were in the top 25 percent; 37% were in the top half. (Proportion submitting class standing: 26%.) **Average high school grade point average:** 2.4. **First-year students who submitted SAT scores:** 60%. Scores (25/75 percentile): Critical Reading: 330-430, Math: 320-420, Combined: 650-850. **First-year students submitting ACT scores:** 20%. Scores (25/75 percentile): English: N/A, Math: N/A, Composite: 11-16.

ACADEMICS

Year founded: 1865. **Academic calendar:** Semester. **Degrees offered:** associate, bachelor's, master's. **Most popular majors:** 27% business, management, marketing, and related support services, 12% public administration and social service professions, 12% security and protective services, 8% social sciences, 7% communication, journalism, and related programs. **Major fields of study:** biological and biomedical sciences; business, management, marketing, and related support services; communication, journalism, and related programs; computer and information sciences and support services; education; English language and literature/letters; foreign languages, literatures, and linguistics; health professions and related clinical sciences; liberal arts and sciences studies, and humanities; mathematics and statistics; natural resources and conservation; parks, recreation, leisure, and fitness studies; philosophy and religious studies; physical sciences; psychology; public administration and social service professions; security and protective services; social sciences; visual and performing arts. **Areas of required coursework:** humanities, computer literacy, mathematics, English (including composition), sciences (biological or physical), social science, other. **Pre-professional programs:** pre-pharmacy. **Special academic programs:** accelerated program, cross-registration, distance learning, double major, dual enrollment, external degree program, honors program, independent study, liberal arts/career combination, student-designed major, study abroad, teacher certificate program, weekend college. **Teacher certification offered in:** early childhood, special education, elementary, secondary. **Reserve Officers Training Corps (ROTC):** Army ROTC: Offered at cooperating institution (St. Augustine's College); Air Force ROTC: Offered at cooperating institution (North Carolina State University–Raleigh). **Faculty and instruction (2009-2010):** Total instructional faculty: 105 full-time, 131 part-time (61% men; 39% women; 87% minorities). Full-time faculty with Ph.D. or other terminal degree: 72%. Student/faculty ratio: 16/1. Classes of fewer than 20 students: 69%; of 20 to 49 students: 29%; of 50 or more students: 2%. **Advanced Placement and International Baccalaureate credit:** AP tests may be used for: Credit only. **Freshmen returning for sophomore year:** 55%. **Graduation rates:** Four-year: 17%; five-year: 29%; six-year: 31%.

COSTS AND FINANCIAL AID

Financial aid office: (919) 546-8240. **Expenses (2009-2010):** Tuition and fees 2009-2010: $11,696; room/board: $7,200. Estimated books and supplies: $1,300. **Financial aid:** Priority filing date for institution's financial aid form: March 1; deadline: June 1.

CAMPUS LIFE AND EXTRACURRICULAR ACTIVITIES

Campus housing available (% using): women's dorms (53%), men's dorms (47%). Students who live in college-owned, operated, or affiliated housing: 31%. **Student employment:** During the 2009-2010 academic year, 0% of undergraduates worked on campus. Average per-year earnings: $12,000. Activities include: campus ministries, choral groups, concert band, dance, drama/theater, international student organization, jazz band, marching band, model UN, music ensembles, musical theater, opera, pep band, radio station, student government, student newspaper, yearbook. Number of fraternities: 4; sororities: 4. Proportion of men in fraternities: 4%; of women in sororities: 5%. Average proportion of students who stay on campus on weekends: 40%. **Sports program (2009-2010):** Member of NCAA II. *Men's intercollegiate varsity sports:* baseball, basketball, cross country, football, tennis, track and field (outdoor). *Women's intercollegiate varsity sports:* basketball, bowling, cross country, softball, tennis, track and field (outdoor), volleyball.

SERVICES AND FACILITIES

Basic services: nonremedial tutoring, placement service, health service, health insurance. **Counseling services:** minority student, career, military, personal, veteran student, academic, older student, psychological, birth control, religious. **For learning-disabled students:** School does not offer a structured program with separate admission and additional fees. Services include: tape recorders, diagnostic testing service, untimed tests, notetaking services, oral tests, extended time for tests, tutors, priority seating, texts on tape. **Information technology resources:** Students are not required to lease or own a computer. School has a wireless network. Proportion of college-owned housing units wired for high-speed internet access: 100%. **Campus safety:** Security services offered: 24-hour foot-and-vehicle patrols, late-night transport/escort service, 24-hour emergency telephones, lighted pathways/sidewalks, controlled dormitory access (key, security card, etc).

TRANSFER AND INTERNATIONAL STUDENTS

Transfer students: May apply for admission for the following academic terms: Fall, Spring, Summer. Applicants need a minimum number of credits to apply. For fall 2009: Transfer applications received: 281. Transfer applicants offered admission: 248. Transfer applicants enrolled: 156. **International students:** Number of foreign undergraduates: 22 (1% of student body). Number of countries represented: 11.

St. Andrews Presbyterian College

- **Address:** 1700 Dogwood Mile, Laurinburg, NC 28352
- **Website:** http://www.sapc.edu
- **Private; Religious affiliation:** Presbyterian
- **Enrollment:** 559 full-time; 41 part-time

KEY STATS

✔ **U.S News College Ranking:** second tier, National Liberal Arts Colleges
✔ **SAT Score (25th/75th percentile):** 880-1070
✔ **Tuition:** 2010-2011: $21,614

Selectivity: Less selective	**Room/board:** $8,938
Acceptance rate: 74%	**Average debt:** $19,032
Student/faculty ratio: 12/1	**Proportion who borrowed:** 57%

UNDERGRADUATE STUDENT BODY STATS

2009-2010 enrollment: 559 full-time; 41 part-time. Men: 42%; women: 58%. **Ethnic makeup:** African American: 10%; American-Indian: 1%; Asian American: 1%; Hispanic: 3%; White: 84%; International: 2%. **Religious preference:** Roman Catholic: 11%; Protestant: 34%; Jewish: 1%; No preference: 35%; Presbyterian: 11%.

ADMISSIONS FACTS AND FIGURES

Phone: (800) 763-0198. **Email:** admission@sapc.edu. **Website:** http://www.sapc.edu. **Application deadlines for fall 2011:** Regular decision: Rolling. Early decision: Not offered. Early action: Not offered. Admission can be deferred. **Application fee:** $30. **To apply online, go to:** http://www.applyweb.com/aw?andrews. **Admissions requirements/recommendations:** High school units required (recommended): English: 3; Mathematics: 3; Science: 3; Foreign language: 1; Social studies: 3. Tests: The college uses SAT or ACT scores in admissions decisions. Either SAT or ACT required. For admission to the fall 2011 entering class, the school will accept: ACT with or without writing accepted. Campus visit: Recommended. Admissions interview: Recommended. Off-campus interview: Not available. **Factors that count in admissions decisions:** *Academic:* Secondary school record: Considered. Class rank: Considered. Letters of recommendation: Considered. Standardized test scores: Important. Essay: Considered. *Nonacademic:* Interview: Considered. Extracurricular activities: Important. Talent/ability: Considered. Character/personal qualities: Important. Alumni/ae relationship: Not Considered. Geographical residence: Not Considered. State residency: Not Considered. Religious affiliation/commitment: Not Considered. Minority status: Not Considered. Volunteer work: Considered. Work experience: Considered. **Admissions statistics for the fall 2009 entering class:** Total applicants: 763. Total accepted: 566. Freshmen enrolled: 147; 63% were from out of state. Overall acceptance rate: 74%. **Credentials of fall 2009 freshmen:** 12% ranked in the top 10 percent of their high school class; 19% were in the top 25 percent. **First-year students who submitted SAT scores:** 85%. Scores (25/75 percentile): Critical Reading: 430-520, Math: 450-550, Combined: 880-1070. **First-year students submitting ACT scores:** 63%. Scores (25/75 percentile): English: N/A, Math: N/A, Composite: N/A.

ACADEMICS

Year founded: 1896. **Academic calendar:** Semester. **Degrees offered:** bachelor's. **Most popular majors:** 26% business, management, marketing, and related support services, 17% education, 14% psychology, 10% parks, recreation, leisure, and fitness studies, 8% biological and biomedical sciences. **Major fields of study:** area, ethnic, cultural, and gender studies; biological and biomedical sciences; business, management, marketing, and related support services; communication, journalism, and related programs; educa-

tion; English language and literature/letters; health professions and related clinical sciences; history; liberal arts and sciences studies, and humanities; mathematics and statistics; multi/interdisciplinary studies; parks, recreation, leisure, and fitness studies; philosophy and religious studies; physical sciences; psychology; visual and performing arts. **Areas of required coursework:** arts/fine arts, mathematics, English (including composition), philosophy, foreign languages, sciences (biological or physical). **Pre-professional programs:** pre-law, pre-medicine, pre-veterinary science. **Special academic programs (% participation):** double major (5%), honors program (2%), independent study, internships (80%), student-designed major, study abroad (45%), teacher certificate program, weekend college (15%). **Teacher certification offered in:** elementary. **Faculty and instruction (2009-2010):** Total instructional faculty: 33 full-time, 42 part-time (53% men; 47% women; 3% minorities). Full-time faculty with Ph.D. or other terminal degree: 76%. Student/faculty ratio: 12/1. Classes of fewer than 20 students: 74%; of 20 to 49 students: 26%. **Advanced Placement and International Baccalaureate credit:** AP tests may be used for: Credit only. Scores accepted: 3, 4, 5. International Baccalaureate exams may be used for: Credit only. **Freshmen returning for sophomore year:** 65%. **Graduation rates:** Four-year: 34%; five-year: 44%; six-year: 45%. **Graduate study:** 26% of students pursue further study immediately upon graduation; 63% within one year. Fields in which graduates pursue further study: Master of Business Administration (MBA), 10%; law, 2%; medicine, 1%; theology (or the seminary), 10%; education, 10%; arts and sciences, 70%.

COSTS AND FINANCIAL AID

Financial aid office: (910) 277-5560. **Expenses (2010-2011):** Tuition and fees 2010-2011: $21,614; room/board: $8,938. Estimated books and supplies: $1,400; transportation: $2,300; personal expenses: $2,148. **Financial aid:** Priority filing date for institution's financial aid form: April 15. In 2009-2010, 86% of undergraduates applied for financial aid. Of those, 75% were determined to have financial need; 23% had their need fully met. Average financial aid package (proportion receiving): $15,948 (75%). Average amount of gift aid, such as scholarships or grants (proportion receiving): $11,765 (75%). Average amount of self-help aid, such as work study or loans (proportion receiving): $5,117 (62%). Average need-based loan (excluding PLUS or other private loans): $4,327. Among students who received need-based aid, the average percentage of need met: 74%. Among students who received aid based on merit, the average award (and the proportion receiving): $5,228 (21%). The average athletic scholarship (and the proportion receiving): $3,646 (14%). Average amount of debt of borrowers graduating in 2009: $19,032. Proportion who borrowed: 57%.

CAMPUS LIFE AND EXTRACURRICULAR ACTIVITIES

Campus housing available (% using): coed dorms (38%), women's dorms (31%), men's dorms (31%). Students who live in college-owned, operated, or affiliated housing: 81%. **Student employment:** During the 2009-2010 academic year, 13% of undergraduates worked on campus. Average per-year earnings: $600. **Clubs and organizations:** Number of student organizations: 28. Activities include: campus ministries, choral groups, drama/theater, literary magazine, student government, student newspaper, yearbook. Number of fraternities: 0; sororities: 0. Average proportion of students who stay on campus on weekends: 75%. **Sports program (2009-2010):** Member of NCAA II. *Men's intercollegiate varsity sports:* baseball, basketball, cross country, golf, lacrosse, soccer, tennis, track and field (indoor), track and field (outdoor), wrestling. *Women's intercollegiate varsity sports:* basketball, cross country, equestrian, golf, lacrosse, soccer, softball, tennis, track and field (indoor), track and field (outdoor), volleyball.

SERVICES AND FACILITIES

Basic services: health insurance. **Remedial assistance:** math. **Counseling services:** career, personal, academic, psychological, religious. **For learning-disabled students:** School does not offer a structured program with separate admission and additional fees. Services include: reading machines, tape recorders, untimed tests, note-taking services, learning center, extended time for tests, tutors, priority seating, texts on tape, other testing accommodations, other. **Library:** Number of titles: 109,308; number of current serial subscriptions: 21,813. **Information technology resources:** Students are not required to lease or own a computer. Number of campus computers available to all students: 103. School has a wireless network. Proportion of college-owned housing units wired for high-speed internet access: 90%. **Campus safety:** Security services offered: 24-hour foot-and-vehicle patrols, lighted pathways/sidewalks, controlled dormitory access (key, security card, etc).

Transfer students: May apply for admission for the following academic terms: Fall, Spring. Applicants do not need a minimum number of credits to apply. For fall 2009: Transfer applications received: 190. Transfer applicants offered admission: 96. Transfer applicants enrolled: 54. **International students:** Number of foreign undergraduates: 13 (2% of student body). Number of countries represented: 14. Minimum TOEFL score required: 550 (paper); 213 (computer). Average TOEFL score: 597 (paper).

St. Augustine's College

- **Address:** 1315 Oakwood Avenue, Raleigh, NC 27610-2298
- **Website:** http://www.st-aug.edu
- **Private; Religious affiliation:** Episcopal
- **Enrollment:** 1,478 full-time; 51 part-time

KEY STATS
✔ **U.S News College Ranking:** second tier, Regional Colleges (South)
✔ **SAT Score (25th/75th percentile):** 640-840
✔ **Tuition:** 2010-2011: $17,160

Selectivity: Least selective	**Room/board:** $7,126
Acceptance rate: 49%	**Average debt:** $19,347
Student/faculty ratio: 16/1	**Proportion who borrowed:** 91%

UNDERGRADUATE STUDENT BODY STATS
2009-2010 enrollment: 1,478 full-time; 51 part-time. Men: 51%; women: 49%. **Ethnic makeup:** African American: 90%; Hispanic: 1%; White: 7%; International: 2%. **Religious preference:** Roman Catholic: 1%; Protestant: 98%; Episcopal: 1%.

ADMISSIONS FACTS AND FIGURES
Phone: (919) 516-4012. **Email:** admissions@st-aug.edu. **Website:** http://www.st-aug.edu. **Application deadlines for fall 2011:** Regular decision: Rolling. Early decision: Not offered. Early action: Not offered. Admission can be deferred. **Application fee:** $25. **Admissions requirements/recommendations:** High school units required (recommended): English: 4; Mathematics: 2; Science: 2; Social studies: 2; Academic electives: 10; Total units: 20 (2). Tests: The college uses SAT or ACT scores in admissions decisions. Either SAT or ACT required. For admission to the fall 2011 entering class, the school will accept: ACT with or without writing accepted. Campus visit: Recommended. Admissions interview: Neither required nor recommended. Off-campus interview: May be arranged. **Factors that count in admissions decisions:** *Academic:* Secondary school record: Very Important. Class rank: Considered. Letters of recommendation: Important. Standardized test scores: Important. Essay: Considered. *Nonacademic:* Interview: Considered. Extracurricular activities: Considered. Talent/ability: Important. Character/personal qualities: Important. Alumni/ae relationship: Considered. Geographical residence: Considered. State residency: Considered. Religious affiliation/commitment: Considered. Minority status: Important. Volunteer work: Considered. Work experience: Considered. **Other schools with the greatest overlap in applicants:** North Carolina A&T State University; North Carolina Central University; North Carolina State University–Raleigh; Shaw University; Winston-Salem State University. **Admissions statistics for the fall 2009 entering class:** Total applicants: 2,365. Total accepted: 1,157. Freshmen enrolled: 448; 51% were from out of state. Overall acceptance rate: 49%. **Size of waiting list:** 349 applicants; enrolled from waiting list: 107. **Credentials of fall 2009 freshmen:** 6% ranked in the top 10 percent of their high school class; 7% were in the top 25 percent; 15% were in the top half. (Proportion submitting class standing: 40%.) **Average high school grade point average:** 2.4. **First-year students who submitted SAT scores:** 77%. Scores (25/75 percentile): Critical Reading: 320-420, Math: 320-420, Combined: 640-840. **First-year students submitting ACT scores:** 23%. Scores (25/75 percentile): English: 11-17, Math: 14-17, Composite: 13-17.

ACADEMICS
Year founded: 1867. **Academic calendar:** Semester. **Degrees offered:** bachelor's. **Major fields of study:** biological and biomedical sciences; communication, journalism, and related programs; computer and information sciences and support services; education; English language and literature/letters; legal professions and studies; mathematics and statistics; parks, recreation, leisure, and fitness studies; physical sciences; psychology; security and protective services; social sciences; visual and performing arts. **Areas of required coursework:** arts/fine arts, humanities, computer literacy, mathe-

matics, English (including composition), philosophy, foreign languages, sciences (biological or physical), history, social science, other. **Pre-professional programs:** pre-law, pre-medicine. **Special academic programs (% participation):** accelerated program (1%), cooperative (work-study plan) program (1%), cross-registration (1%), double major (1%), honors program (1%), independent study (2%), internships (3%), study abroad (1%), teacher certificate program (1%). **Teacher certification offered in:** elementary. **Reserve Officers Training Corps (ROTC):** Army ROTC: Offered on campus; Air Force ROTC: Offered at cooperating institution (North Carolina State University–Raleigh). **Faculty and instruction (2009-2010):** Total instructional faculty: 79 full-time, 55 part-time (57% men; 43% women). Full-time faculty with Ph.D. or other terminal degree: 46%. Student/faculty ratio: 16/1. **Advanced Placement and International Baccalaureate credit:** AP tests may be used for: Placement only. Scores accepted: 3, 4, 5. International Baccalaureate exams may be used for: Placement only. **Freshmen returning for sophomore year:** 60%. **Graduation rates:** Six-year: 30%. **Graduate study:** 20% of students pursue further study immediately upon graduation; 25% within one year; 30% within five years. Fields in which graduates pursue further study: Master of Business Administration (MBA), 25%; law, 5%; medicine, 2%; theology (or the seminary), 5%; arts and sciences, 1%.

COSTS AND FINANCIAL AID
Financial aid office: (919) 516-4131. **Expenses (2010-2011):** Tuition and fees 2010-2011: $17,160; room/board: $7,126. Estimated books and supplies: $1,650; transportation: $2,000; personal expenses: $3,060. **Financial aid:** Priority filing date for institution's financial aid form: March 15. In 2009-2010, 72% of undergraduates applied for financial aid. Of those, 72% were determined to have financial need; 3% had their need fully met. Average financial aid package (proportion receiving): $1,778 (72%). Average amount of gift aid, such as scholarships or grants (proportion receiving): $1,664 (71%). Average amount of self-help aid, such as work study or loans (proportion receiving): $1,938 (70%). Average need-based loan (excluding PLUS or other private loans): $2,183. Among students who received need-based aid, the average percentage of need met: 50%. Among students who received aid based on merit, the average award (and the proportion receiving): $1,984 (2%). The average athletic scholarship (and the proportion receiving): $3,882 (2%). Average amount of debt of borrowers graduating in 2009: $19,347. Proportion who borrowed: 91%.

CAMPUS LIFE AND EXTRACURRICULAR ACTIVITIES
Campus housing available (% using): women's dorms (45%), men's dorms (55%). Students who live in college-owned, operated, or affiliated housing: 86%. **Student employment:** During the 2009-2010 academic year, 24% of undergraduates worked on campus. Average per-year earnings: $1,500. **Clubs and organizations:** Number of student organizations: 56. Activities include: campus ministries, choral groups, concert band, dance, drama/theater, international student organization, jazz band, marching band, music ensembles, pep band, radio station, student government, student film society, television station. Number of fraternities: 4; sororities: 4. Average proportion of students who stay on campus on weekends: 80%. **Sports program (2009-2010):** Member of NCAA II. *Men's intercollegiate varsity sports:* baseball, basketball, cross country, football, golf, tennis, track and field (indoor), track and field (outdoor). *Women's intercollegiate varsity sports:* basketball, bowling, cross country, softball, tennis, track and field (indoor), track and field (outdoor), volleyball.

SERVICES AND FACILITIES
Basic services: nonremedial tutoring, placement service, health service, health insurance. **Remedial assistance:** reading, math, writing, study skills. **Counseling services:** minority student, career, military, personal, veteran student, academic, older student, psychological, birth control, religious. **For learning-disabled students:** School does not offer a structured program with separate admission and additional fees. Total undergraduates in learning-disabled program or receiving services: 15. Services include: remedial math, remedial English, remedial reading, diagnostic testing service, untimed tests, oral tests, learning center, extended time for tests, tutors, early syllabus, priority seating, substitution of courses, exams on tape or computer, other testing accommodations. **Library:** Number of titles: 100,346; number of current serial subscriptions: 174. **Information technology resources:** Students are not required to lease or own a computer. Number of campus computers available to all students: 250. School has a wireless network. Approximate number of users that can be accommodated: 400. Proportion of college-owned housing units wired for high-speed internet access: 100%. **Campus safety:** Security services offered: 24-hour foot-and-vehicle patrols, late-night transport/escort service, 24-hour emergency telephones, lighted pathways/sidewalks, controlled dormitory access (key, security card, etc).

TRANSFER AND INTERNATIONAL STUDENTS

Transfer students: May apply for admission for the following academic terms: Fall, Spring, Summer. Applicants need a minimum number of credits to apply. For fall 2009: Transfer applications received: 142. Transfer applicants offered admission: 54. Transfer applicants enrolled: 43. **International students:** Number of foreign undergraduates: 32 (2% of student body). Number of countries represented: 9. Minimum TOEFL score required: 500 (paper); 180 (computer). Average TOEFL score: 500 (paper).

University of North Carolina–Asheville

■ **Address:** 1 University Heights, Asheville, NC 28804
■ **Website:** http://www.unca.edu
■ **Public**
■ **Enrollment:** 3,132 full-time; 713 part-time

KEY STATS

✔ **U.S News College Ranking:** 158, National Liberal Arts Colleges
✔ **SAT Score (25th/75th percentile):** 1070-1270
✔ **Tuition:** 2009-2010: $4,411 in state, $16,128 out of state
  Selectivity: Selective   **Room/board:** $6,890
  Acceptance rate: 77%   **Average debt:** $14,596
  Student/faculty ratio: 14/1   **Proportion who borrowed:** 50%

UNDERGRADUATE STUDENT BODY STATS

2009-2010 enrollment: 3,132 full-time; 713 part-time. Men: 43%; women: 57%. **Ethnic makeup:** African American: 2%; Asian American: 1%; Hispanic: 3%; White: 92%; International: 1%.

ADMISSIONS FACTS AND FIGURES

Phone: (828) 251-6481. **Email:** admissions@unca.edu. **Website:** http://www.unca.edu. **Application deadlines for fall 2011:** Regular decision: February 15. Early decision: Not offered. Early action: Send application by: November 15; Decision sent by: December 15. Admission can be deferred. **Application fee:** $50. **To apply online, go to:** http://www.unca.edu/admissions. **Admissions requirements/recommendations:** High school units required (recommended): English: 4; Mathematics: 4; Science: 3; Foreign language: 2; Social studies: 1; History: 1; Academic electives: (4); Total units: 15. Tests: The college uses SAT or ACT scores in admissions decisions. Either SAT or ACT required. For admission to the fall 2011 entering class, the school will accept: ACT with writing required. Campus visit: Recommended. Admissions interview: Recommended. Off-campus interview: Not available. **Factors that count in admissions decisions:** *Academic:* Secondary school record: Very Important. Class rank: Important. Letters of recommendation: Important. Standardized test scores: Important. Essay: Important. *Nonacademic:* Interview: Considered. Extracurricular activities: Considered. Talent/ability: Considered. Character/personal qualities: Not Considered. Alumni/ae relationship: Considered. Geographical residence: Considered. State residency: Considered. Religious affiliation/commitment: Not Considered. Minority status: Considered. Volunteer work: Considered. Work experience: Considered. **Other schools with the greatest overlap in applicants:** Appalachian State University; North Carolina State University–Raleigh; University of North Carolina–Chapel Hill; University of North Carolina–Charlotte; University of North Carolina–Greensboro. **Admissions statistics for the fall 2009 entering class:** Total applicants: 2,510. Total accepted: 1,921. Freshmen enrolled: 641; 17% were from out of state. Overall acceptance rate: 77%. Non-early acceptance rate: 77%. **Credentials of fall 2009 freshmen:** 22% ranked in the top 10 percent of their high school class; 60% were in the top 25 percent; 95% were in the top half. (Proportion submitting class standing: 79%.) **Average high school grade point average:** 3.9. **First-year students who submitted SAT scores:** 95%. Scores (25/75 percentile): Critical Reading: 540-640, Math: 530-630, Combined: 1070-1270. **First-year students submitting ACT scores:** 21%. Scores (25/75 percentile): English: 22-29, Math: 21-27, Composite: 23-27.

ACADEMICS

Year founded: 1927. **Academic calendar:** Semester. **Degrees offered:** bachelor's, post-bachelor's certificate, master's. **Most popular majors:** 14% psychology, 8% English language and literature, 7% natural resources/conservation, 7% sociology, 6% communication studies/speech communication and rhetoric. **Major fields of study:** area, ethnic, cultural, and gender studies; biological and biomedical sciences; business, management, marketing, and related support services; communication, journalism, and related programs;

computer and information sciences and support services; engineering; English language and literature/letters; foreign languages, literatures, and linguistics; health professions and related clinical sciences; history; liberal arts and sciences studies, and humanities; mathematics and statistics; natural resources and conservation; philosophy and religious studies; physical sciences; psychology; social sciences; visual and performing arts. **Areas of required coursework:** arts/fine arts, humanities, computer literacy, mathematics, English (including composition), foreign languages, sciences (biological or physical), social science, other. **Pre-professional programs:** pre-law, pre-dentistry, pre-medicine, pre-veterinary science, pre-pharmacy. **Special academic programs (% participation):** cross-registration, distance learning, double major (8.4%), dual enrollment, exchange student program (domestic), honors program (12.7%), independent study, internships, liberal arts/career combination, student-designed major, study abroad (16.5%), teacher certificate program (6.9%). **Teacher certification offered in:** elementary, middle/junior high, secondary. **Faculty and instruction (2009-2010):** Total instructional faculty: 208 full-time, 92 part-time (53% men; 47% women; 10% minorities). Full-time faculty with Ph.D. or other terminal degree: 85%. Student/faculty ratio: 14/1. Classes of fewer than 20 students: 54%; of 20 to 49 students: 45%; of 50 or more students: 2%. **Advanced Placement and International Baccalaureate credit:** AP tests may be used for: Credit and/or placement. Scores accepted: 3, 4, 5. International Baccalaureate exams may be used for: Placement only. **Freshmen returning for sophomore year:** 80%. **Graduation rates:** Four-year: 29%; five-year: 55%; six-year: 59%. **Graduate study:** 19% of students pursue further study within one year.

COSTS AND FINANCIAL AID

Financial aid office: (828) 251-6535. **Expenses (2009-2010):** Tuition and fees 2009-2010: $4,411 in state, $16,128 out of state; room/board: $6,890. Estimated books and supplies: $850; transportation: $1,500; personal expenses: $1,400. **Financial aid:** Priority filing date for institution's financial aid form: March 1. In 2009-2010, 72% of undergraduates applied for financial aid. Of those, 48% were determined to have financial need; 54% had their need fully met. Average financial aid package (proportion receiving): $10,553 (47%). Average amount of gift aid, such as scholarships or grants (proportion receiving): $6,052 (46%). Average amount of self-help aid, such as work study or loans (proportion receiving): $3,974 (31%). Average need-based loan (excluding PLUS or other private loans): $3,920. Among students who received need-based aid, the average percentage of need met: 85%. Among students who received aid based on merit, the average award (and the proportion receiving): $3,401 (5%). The average athletic scholarship (and the proportion receiving): $7,441 (3%). Average amount of debt of borrowers graduating in 2009: $14,596. Proportion who borrowed: 50%.

CAMPUS LIFE AND EXTRACURRICULAR ACTIVITIES

Campus housing available: coed dorms, women's dorms, men's dorms, special housing for disabled students, other housing options. Students who live in college-owned, operated, or affiliated housing: 35%. **Student employment:** During the 2009-2010 academic year, 20% of undergraduates worked on campus. Average per-year earnings: $1,700. **Clubs and organizations:** Number of student organizations: 69. Activities include: campus ministries, choral groups, concert band, dance, drama/theater, international student organization, jazz band, literary magazine, music ensembles, musical theater, pep band, radio station, student government, student newspaper. Number of fraternities: 1; sororities: 2. Proportion of men in fraternities: 2%; of women in sororities: 3%. Average proportion of students who stay on campus on weekends: 65%. **Sports program (2009-2010):** Member of NCAA I. **Men's intercollegiate varsity sports:** baseball, basketball, cross country, soccer, tennis, track and field (indoor), track and field (outdoor). **Women's intercollegiate varsity sports:** basketball, cross country, soccer, tennis, track and field (indoor), track and field (outdoor), volleyball.

SERVICES AND FACILITIES

Basic services: nonremedial tutoring, women's center, placement service, health service, health insurance. **Counseling services:** minority student, career, personal, veteran student, academic, older student, psychological, birth control. **For learning-disabled students:** School does not offer a structured program with separate admission and additional fees. Total undergraduates in learning-disabled program or receiving services: 100. Services include: reading machines, tape recorders, note-taking services, oral tests, readers, extended time for tests, tutors, priority registration, texts on tape, other. **Library:** Number of titles: 271,741; number of current serial subscriptions: 11,852. **Information technology resources:** Students are not required to lease or own a computer. Number of campus computers available to all students: 216. School has a wireless network. Proportion of college-owned housing units wired for high-speed internet access: 100%. **Campus safety:**

Security services offered: 24-hour foot-and-vehicle patrols, late-night transport/escort service, 24-hour emergency telephones, lighted pathways/sidewalks, controlled dormitory access (key, security card, etc).

TRANSFER AND INTERNATIONAL STUDENTS
Transfer students: May apply for admission for the following academic terms: Fall, Spring. Applicants need a minimum number of credits to apply. For fall 2009: Transfer applications received: 611. Transfer applicants offered admission: 492. Transfer applicants enrolled: 318. **International students:** Number of foreign undergraduates: 22 (1% of student body). Number of countries represented: 18. Minimum TOEFL score required: 550 (paper); 213 (computer).

University of North Carolina–Chapel Hill

- **Address:** South Building, CB #9100, Chapel Hill, NC 27599
- **Website:** http://www.unc.edu
- **Public**
- **Enrollment:** 17,275 full-time; 706 part-time

KEY STATS
✔ **U.S News College Ranking:** 30, National Universities
✔ **SAT Score (25th/75th percentile):** 1210-1410
✔ **Tuition:** 2009-2010: $5,626 in state, $23,514 out of state

Selectivity: Most selective	**Room/board:** $8,670
Acceptance rate: 32%	**Average debt:** $14,262
Student/faculty ratio: 14/1	**Proportion who borrowed:** 29%

UNDERGRADUATE STUDENT BODY STATS
2009-2010 enrollment: 17,275 full-time; 706 part-time. Men: 41%; women: 59%. **Ethnic makeup:** African American: 11%; American-Indian: 1%; Asian American: 7%; Hispanic: 5%; White: 74%; International: 2%.

ADMISSIONS FACTS AND FIGURES
Phone: (919) 966-3621. **Email:** unchelp@admissions.unc.edu. **Website:** http://www.unc.edu. **Application deadlines for fall 2011:** Regular decision: January 31. Early decision: Not offered. Early action: Send application by: November 2; Decision sent by: January 30. Admission can be deferred. **Application fee:** $70. **To apply online, go to:** http://admissions.unc.edu/Apply/Portal.html. **Admissions requirements/recommendations:** High school units required (recommended): English: 4; Mathematics: 4; Science: 3; Foreign language: 2; Social studies: 1; History: 1; Academic electives: 1; Total units: 16. Tests: The college uses SAT or ACT scores in admissions decisions. Either SAT or ACT required. For admission to the fall 2011 entering class, the school will accept: ACT with writing required. Campus visit: Recommended. Admissions interview: Neither required nor recommended. Off-campus interview: Not available. **Factors that count in admissions decisions: Academic:** Secondary school record: Very Important. Class rank: Very Important. Letters of recommendation: Very Important. Standardized test scores: Very Important. Essay: Very Important. **Nonacademic:** Interview: Not Considered. Extracurricular activities: Very Important. Talent/ability: Very Important. Character/personal qualities: Very Important. Alumni/ae relationship: Important. Geographical residence: Not Considered. State residency: Very Important. Religious affiliation/commitment: Not Considered. Minority status: Important. Volunteer work: Important. Work experience: Important. **Other schools with the greatest overlap in applicants:** Duke University; North Carolina State University–Raleigh; University of Virginia; Wake Forest University. **Admissions statistics for the fall 2009 entering class:** Total applicants: 23,224. Total accepted: 7,345. Freshmen enrolled: 3,960; 17% were from out of state. Accepted through early-decision or early-action plans: 78%. Overall acceptance rate: 32%. Non-early acceptance rate: 23%. **Size of waiting list:** 2500 applicants; enrolled from waiting list: 4. **Credentials of fall 2009 freshmen:** 80% ranked in the top 10 percent of their high school class; 96% were in the top 25 percent; 99% were in the top half. (Proportion submitting class standing: 78%.) **Average high school grade point average:** 4.0. **First-year students who submitted SAT scores:** 97%. Scores (25/75 percentile): Critical Reading: 590-700, Math: 620-710, Combined: 1210-1410. **First-year students submitting ACT scores:** 33%. Scores (25/75 percentile): English: 26-33, Math: 26-32, Composite: 26-31.

ACADEMICS
Year founded: 1789. **Academic calendar:** Semester. **Degrees offered:** certificate, bachelor's, post-bachelor's certificate, master's, post-master's certificate, doctorate. **Most popular majors:** 16% social sciences, 12% communication, journalism, and related programs, 9% psychology, 8% biological and biomedical sciences, 8% business, management, marketing, and related support services. **Major fields of study:** area, ethnic, cultural, and gender studies; biological and biomedical sciences; business, management, marketing, and related support services; communication, journalism, and related programs; computer and information sciences and support services; education; English language and literature/letters; family and consumer sciences/human sciences; foreign languages, literatures, and linguistics; health professions and related clinical sciences; history; liberal arts and sciences studies, and humanities; mathematics and statistics; multi/interdisciplinary studies; natural resources and conservation; parks, recreation, leisure, and fitness studies; philosophy and religious studies; physical sciences; psychology; public administration and social service professions; social sciences; visual and performing arts. **Areas of required coursework:** arts/fine arts, humanities, mathematics, English (including composition), philosophy, foreign languages, sciences (biological or physical), history, social science, other. **Pre-professional programs:** pre-law, pre-dentistry, pre-medicine, pre-veterinary science, pre-optometry, pre-pharmacy. **Special academic programs (% participation):** cross-registration (1.3%), distance learning (24.3%), double major (20.2%), dual enrollment, honors program (5.97%), independent study (19.6%), internships, student-designed major (.3%), study abroad (30.3%), teacher certificate program (2.4%). **Teacher certification offered in:** early childhood, special education, elementary, middle/junior high, secondary, bilingual/bicultural. **Reserve Officers Training Corps (ROTC):** Army ROTC: Offered on campus; Navy ROTC: Offered on campus; Air Force ROTC: Offered on campus. **Faculty and instruction (2009-2010):** Total instructional faculty: 1,628 full-time, 136 part-time (58% men; 42% women; 21% minorities). Full-time faculty with Ph.D. or other terminal degree: 91%. Student/faculty ratio: 14/1. Classes of fewer than 20 students: 39%; of 20 to 49 students: 50%; of 50 or more students: 12%. **Advanced Placement and International Baccalaureate credit:** AP tests may be used for: Credit and/or placement. Scores accepted: 3, 4, 5. International Baccalaureate exams may be used for: Credit and/or placement. **Freshmen returning for sophomore year:** 97%. **Graduation rates:** Four-year: 74%; five-year: 86%; six-year: 87%. **Graduate study:** 30% of students pursue further study immediately upon graduation. Fields in which graduates pursue further study: Master of Business Administration (MBA), 1%; law, 18%; medicine, 13%; dentistry, 2%; engineering, 3%; theology (or the seminary), 2%; education, 12%; arts and sciences, 50%; veterinary medicine, 1%.

COSTS AND FINANCIAL AID
Financial aid office: (919) 962-8396. **Expenses (2009-2010):** Tuition and fees 2009-2010: $5,626 in state, $23,514 out of state; room/board: $8,670. Estimated books and supplies: $1,000; transportation: $878; personal expenses: $1,250. **Financial aid:** Priority filing date for institution's financial aid form: March 1. In 2009-2010, 66% of undergraduates applied for financial aid. Of those, 36% were determined to have financial need; 97% had their need fully met. Average financial aid package (proportion receiving): $12,860 (36%). Average amount of gift aid, such as scholarships or grants (proportion receiving): $10,877 (36%). Average amount of self-help aid, such as work study or loans (proportion receiving): $3,306 (18%). Average need-based loan (excluding PLUS or other private loans): $3,990. Among students who received need-based aid, the average percentage of need met: 100%. Among students who received aid based on merit, the average award (and the proportion receiving): $5,348 (14%). The average athletic scholarship (and the proportion receiving): $12,258 (2%). Average amount of debt of borrowers graduating in 2009: $14,262. Proportion who borrowed: 29%.

CAMPUS LIFE AND EXTRACURRICULAR ACTIVITIES
Campus housing available (% using): coed dorms (63%), women's dorms (3%), men's dorms (2%), sorority housing (2%), fraternity housing (5%), apartments for married students (4%), apartment for single students (10%), special housing for disabled students (1%), special housing for international students (2%). Students who live in college-owned, operated, or affiliated housing: 47%. **Student employment:** During the 2009-2010 academic year, 15% of undergraduates worked on campus. Average per-year earnings: $3,570. **Clubs and organizations:** Number of student organizations: 620. Activities include: campus ministries, choral groups, concert band, dance, drama/theater, international student organization, jazz band, literary magazine, marching band, model UN, music ensembles, musical theater, opera, pep band, radio station, student government, student newspaper, student film society, symphony orchestra, television station, yearbook. Number of fraternities: 35; sororities: 23. Proportion of men in fraternities: 16%; of women in sororities: 17%. Average proportion of students who stay on campus on weekends: 80%. **Sports program (2009-2010):** Member of NCAA

I. *Men's intercollegiate varsity sports:* baseball, basketball, cross country, fencing, football, golf, lacrosse, soccer, swimming, tennis, track and field (indoor), track and field (outdoor), wrestling. *Women's intercollegiate varsity sports:* basketball, cross country, fencing, field hockey, golf, gymnastics, lacrosse, crew (lightweight), soccer, softball, swimming, tennis, track and field (indoor), track and field (outdoor), volleyball.

SERVICES AND FACILITIES

Basic services: nonremedial tutoring, women's center, placement service, day care, health service, health insurance. **Counseling services:** minority student, career, personal, veteran student, academic, older student, psychological, birth control, other. **For learning-disabled students:** School does not offer a structured program with separate admission and additional fees. Total undergraduates in learning-disabled program or receiving services: 225. Services include: reading machines, note-taking services, learning center, extended time for tests, substitution of courses, texts on tape, exams on tape or computer, other. **Library:** Number of titles: 6,112,345; number of current serial subscriptions: 80,132. **Information technology resources:** Students are required to lease or own a computer. Number of campus computers available to all students: 800. School has a wireless network. Approximate number of users that can be accommodated: 60,000. Proportion of college-owned housing units wired for high-speed internet access: 100%. **Campus safety:** Security services offered: 24-hour foot-and-vehicle patrols, late-night transport/escort service, 24-hour emergency telephones, lighted pathways/sidewalks, student patrols, controlled dormitory access (key, security card, etc).

TRANSFER AND INTERNATIONAL STUDENTS

Transfer students: May apply for admission for the following academic terms: Fall, Summer. Applicants need a minimum number of credits to apply. For fall 2009: Transfer applications received: 3,316. Transfer applicants offered admission: 1,183. Transfer applicants enrolled: 778. **International students:** Number of foreign undergraduates: 299 (2% of student body). Number of countries represented: 50. Minimum TOEFL score required: 600 (paper); 100 (computer). Average TOEFL score: 620 (paper).

University of North Carolina–Charlotte

- **Address:** 9201 University City Boulevard, Charlotte, NC 28223-0001
- **Website:** http://www.uncc.edu/
- **Public**
- **Enrollment:** 16,494 full-time; 2,925 part-time

KEY STATS

✔ **U.S News College Ranking:** 191, National Universities
✔ **SAT Score (25th/75th percentile):** 960-1140
✔ **Tuition:** 2009-2010: $4,449 in state, $15,061 out of state

Selectivity: Selective	**Room/board:** $7,500
Acceptance rate: 76%	**Average debt:** N/A
Student/faculty ratio: 19/1	**Proportion who borrowed:** N/A

UNDERGRADUATE STUDENT BODY STATS

2009-2010 enrollment: 16,494 full-time; 2,925 part-time. Men: 49%; women: 51%. **Ethnic makeup:** African American: 16%; Asian American: 5%; Hispanic: 5%; White: 71%; International: 3%.

ADMISSIONS FACTS AND FIGURES

Phone: (704) 687-2213. **Email:** unccadm@uncc.edu. **Website:** http://www.uncc.edu/. **Application deadlines for fall 2011:** Regular decision: July 1. Early decision: Not offered. Early action: Not offered. Admission cannot be deferred. **Application fee:** $50. **To apply online, go to:** http://www.admissions.uncc.edu/. **Admissions requirements/recommendations:** High school units required (recommended): English: 4; Mathematics: 4; Science: 3; Foreign language: 2 (3); Social studies: 2; History: 1; Total units: 16. Tests: The college uses SAT or ACT scores in admissions decisions. Either SAT or ACT required. For admission to the fall 2011 entering class, the school will accept: ACT with writing required. Campus visit: Recommended. Admissions interview: Neither required nor recommended. Off-campus interview: Not available. **Factors that count in admissions decisions:** *Academic:* Secondary school record: Very Important. Class rank: Not Considered. Letters of recommendation: Considered. Standardized test scores: Very Important. Essay: Not Considered. *Nonacademic:* Interview: Not Considered. Extracurricular activities: Considered. Talent/ability:

Considered. Character/personal qualities: Considered. Alumni/ae relationship: Not Considered. Geographical residence: Considered. State residency: Considered. Religious affiliation/commitment: Not Considered. Minority status: Not Considered. Volunteer work: Not Considered. Work experience: Not Considered. **Other schools with the greatest overlap in applicants:** Appalachian State University; North Carolina State University–Raleigh; University of North Carolina–Chapel Hill; University of North Carolina–Greensboro; University of North Carolina–Wilmington. **Admissions statistics for the fall 2009 entering class:** Total applicants: 10,702. Total accepted: 8,158. Freshmen enrolled: 3,187; 9% were from out of state. Overall acceptance rate: 76%. **Credentials of fall 2009 freshmen:** 12% ranked in the top 10 percent of their high school class; 41% were in the top 25 percent; 84% were in the top half. (Proportion submitting class standing: 85%.) **Average high school grade point average:** 3.5. **First-year students who submitted SAT scores:** 96%. Scores (25/75 percentile): Critical Reading: 470-550, Math: 490-590, Combined: 960-1140. **First-year students submitting ACT scores:** 17%. Scores (25/75 percentile): English: 18-23, Math: 19-25, Composite: 20-24.

ACADEMICS

Year founded: 1946. **Academic calendar:** Semester. **Degrees offered:** certificate, bachelor's, post-bachelor's certificate, master's, post-master's certificate, doctorate. **Most popular majors:** 21% business, management, marketing, and related support services, 10% education, 8% psychology, 7% engineering, 7% health professions and related clinical sciences. **Major fields of study:** architecture and related services; area, ethnic, cultural, and gender studies; biological and biomedical sciences; business, management, marketing, and related support services; communication, journalism, and related programs; computer and information sciences and support services; education; engineering; engineering technologies/technicians; English language and literature/letters; family and consumer sciences/human sciences; foreign languages, literatures, and linguistics; health professions and related clinical sciences; history; parks, recreation, leisure, and fitness studies; philosophy and religious studies; physical sciences; psychology; public administration and social service professions; security and protective services; social sciences; visual and performing arts. **Areas of required coursework:** arts/fine arts, humanities, computer literacy, mathematics, English (including composition), foreign languages, sciences (biological or physical), history, social science, other. **Pre-professional programs:** pre-law, pre-dentistry, pre-medicine, pre-veterinary science, pre-optometry, pre-pharmacy, other. **Special academic programs (% participation):** accelerated program, cooperative (work-study plan) program (3.5%), cross-registration, distance learning (10.3%), double major (5.1%), dual enrollment, English as a Second Language (ESL) (.001%), honors program (6.3%), independent study (11.9%), internships (40.8%), study abroad (2.6%), teacher certificate program (19.1%), weekend college (10.6%). **Teacher certification offered in:** early childhood, special education, elementary, middle/junior high, secondary, bilingual/bicultural. **Cooperative education programs:** art, business, computer science, education, engineering, health professions, humanities, natural science, social/behavioral science, technologies, other. **Reserve Officers Training Corps (ROTC):** Army ROTC: Offered on campus; Air Force ROTC: Offered on campus. **Faculty and instruction (2009-2010):** Total instructional faculty: 981 full-time, 344 part-time (54% men; 46% women; 16% minorities). Full-time faculty with Ph.D. or other terminal degree: 86%. Student/faculty ratio: 19/1. Classes of fewer than 20 students: 29%; of 20 to 49 students: 50%; of 50 or more students: 21%. **Advanced Placement and International Baccalaureate credit:** AP tests may be used for: Credit only. Scores accepted: 3, 4, 5. International Baccalaureate exams may be used for: Credit only. **Freshmen returning for sophomore year:** 77%. **Graduation rates:** Four-year: 26%; five-year: 48%; six-year: 54%. **Graduate study:** 18% of students pursue further study within one year. Fields in which graduates pursue further study: Master of Business Administration (MBA), 11%; law, 4%; medicine, 11%; engineering, 8%; theology (or the seminary), 2%; education, 20%; arts and sciences, 30%.

COSTS AND FINANCIAL AID

Financial aid office: (704) 687-2461. **Expenses (2009-2010):** Tuition and fees 2009-2010: $4,449 in state, $15,061 out of state; room/board: $7,500. Estimated books and supplies: $1,200; transportation: $1,200; personal expenses: $1,500. **Financial aid:** Priority filing date for institution's financial aid form: April 1. In 2009-2010, 73% of undergraduates applied for financial aid. Of those, 56% were determined to have financial need; 23% had their need fully met. Average financial aid package (proportion receiving): $8,642 (55%). Average amount of gift aid, such as scholarships or grants (proportion receiving): $6,096 (48%). Average amount of self-help aid, such as work study or loans (proportion receiving): $3,772 (44%). Average need-based loan (excluding PLUS or other private loans): $3,724. Among students who received need-based aid, the average percentage of need met: 74%. Among students who received aid based on merit, the average award (and the proportion receiving): $2,427 (1%).

CAMPUS LIFE AND EXTRACURRICULAR ACTIVITIES

Campus housing available (% using): coed dorms (90%), women's dorms (1%), sorority housing (3%), fraternity housing (1%), apartment for single students, special housing for disabled students (4%), special housing for international students (1%). Students who live in college-owned, operated, or affiliated housing: 25%. **Student employment:** During the 2009-2010 academic year, 12% of undergraduates worked on campus. Average per-year earnings: $2,880. **Clubs and organizations:** Number of student organizations: 310. Activities include: campus ministries, choral groups, concert band, dance, drama/theater, international student organization, jazz band, literary magazine, model UN, music ensembles, musical theater, opera, pep band, radio station, student government, student newspaper, television station, yearbook. Number of fraternities: 18; sororities: 10. Proportion of men in fraternities: 7%; of women in sororities: 7%. **Sports program (2009-2010):** Member of NCAA I. **Men's intercollegiate varsity sports:** baseball, basketball, cross country, golf, soccer, tennis, track and field (indoor), track and field (outdoor). **Women's intercollegiate varsity sports:** basketball, cross country, soccer, softball, tennis, track and field (indoor), track and field (outdoor), volleyball.

SERVICES AND FACILITIES

Basic services: nonremedial tutoring, women's center, placement service, health service, health insurance. **Remedial assistance:** reading, math, writing, study skills. **Counseling services:** minority student, career, military, personal, veteran student, academic, older student, psychological, birth control. **For learning-disabled students:** School does not offer a structured program with separate admission and additional fees. Total undergraduates in learning-disabled program or receiving services: 91. Services include: reading machines, tape recorders, videotaped classes, note-taking services, oral tests, learning center, readers, extended time for tests, tutors, priority seating, texts on tape, typist/scribe, other testing accommodations, other. **Library:** Number of titles: 1,073,727; number of current serial subscriptions: 52,621. **Information technology resources:** Students are not required to lease or own a computer. Number of campus computers available to all students: 3,500. School has a wireless network. Approximate number of users that can be accommodated: 4,000. Proportion of college-owned housing units wired for high-speed internet access: 100%. **Campus safety:** Security services offered: 24-hour foot-and-vehicle patrols, late-night transport/escort service, 24-hour emergency telephones, lighted pathways/sidewalks, controlled dormitory access (key, security card, etc).

TRANSFER AND INTERNATIONAL STUDENTS

Transfer students: May apply for admission for the following academic terms: Fall, Spring, Summer. Applicants need a minimum number of credits to apply. For fall 2009: Transfer applications received: 4,132. Transfer applicants offered admission: 3,473. Transfer applicants enrolled: 2,340. **International students:** Number of foreign undergraduates: 498 (3% of student body). Number of countries represented: 80. Minimum TOEFL score required: 507 (paper); 180 (computer). Average TOEFL score: 640 (paper).

University of North Carolina–Greensboro

- ■ **Address:** 1000 Spring Garden Street, Greensboro, NC 27402
- ■ **Website:** http://www.uncg.edu/
- ■ **Public**
- ■ **Enrollment:** 12,855 full-time; 1,783 part-time

....

KEY STATS

✔ **U.S News College Ranking:** 191, National Universities
✔ **SAT Score (25th/75th percentile):** 930-1130
✔ **Tuition:** 2010-2011: $4,520 in state, $16,281 out of state

Selectivity: Selective	**Room/board:** $6,655
Acceptance rate: 73%	**Average debt:** $18,604
Student/faculty ratio: 17/1	**Proportion who borrowed:** 67%

UNDERGRADUATE STUDENT BODY STATS

2009-2010 enrollment: 12,855 full-time; 1,783 part-time. Men: 33%; women: 67%. **Ethnic makeup:** African American: 23%; Asian American: 4%; Hispanic: 4%; White: 69%; International: 1%.

ADMISSIONS FACTS AND FIGURES

Phone: (336) 334-5243. **Email:** undergrad_admissions@uncg.edu. **Website:** http://www.uncg.edu/. **Application deadlines for fall 2011:** Regular decision: August 1. Early decision: Not offered. Early action: Send application by: January 15; Decision sent by: March 1. Admission can be deferred. **Application fee:** $45. **To apply online, go to:** http://web.uncg.edu/adm/applications/. **Admissions requirements/recommendations:** High school units required (recommended): English: 4 (4); Mathematics: 4 (4); Science: 3 (3); Foreign language: 2 (2); Social studies: 2 (2); Total units: 15 (15). Tests: The college uses SAT or ACT scores in admissions decisions. Either SAT or ACT required. For admission to the fall 2011 entering class, the school will accept: ACT with writing required. Campus visit: Neither required nor recommended. Admissions interview: Neither required nor recommended. Off-campus interview: Not available. **Factors that count in admissions decisions:** *Academic:* Secondary school record: Very Important. Class rank: Not Considered. Letters of recommendation: Considered. Standardized test scores: Important. Essay: Not Considered. *Nonacademic:* Interview: Not Considered. Extracurricular activities: Not Considered. Talent/ability: Not Considered. Character/personal qualities: Not Considered. Alumni/ae relationship: Not Considered. Geographical residence: Not Considered. State residency: Not Considered. Religious affiliation/commitment: Not Considered. Minority status: Not Considered. Volunteer work: Not Considered. Work experience: Not Considered. **Admissions statistics for the fall 2009 entering class:** Total applicants: 9,104. Total accepted: 6,616. Freshmen enrolled: 2,511; 7% were from out of state. Overall acceptance rate: 73%. Non-early acceptance rate: 73%. **Credentials of fall 2009 freshmen:** 14% ranked in the top 10 percent of their high school class; 43% were in the top 25 percent; 86% were in the top half. (Proportion submitting class standing: 91%.) **Average high school grade point average:** 3.6. **First-year students who submitted SAT scores:** 97%. Scores (25/75 percentile): Critical Reading: 460-560, Math: 470-570, Combined: 930-1130.

ACADEMICS

Year founded: 1891. **Academic calendar:** Semester. **Degrees offered:** bachelor's, post-bachelor's certificate, master's, post-master's certificate, doctorate. **Most popular majors:** 16% business, management, marketing, and related support services, 13% education, 9% English language and literature/letters, 9% health professions and related clinical sciences, 9% visual and performing arts. **Major fields of study:** area, ethnic, cultural, and gender studies; biological and biomedical sciences; business, management, marketing, and related support services; communication, journalism, and related programs; computer and information sciences and support services; education; English language and literature/letters; family and consumer sciences/human sciences; foreign languages, literatures, and linguistics; health professions and related clinical sciences; history; liberal arts and sciences studies, and humanities; mathematics and statistics; multi/interdisciplinary studies; parks, recreation, leisure, and fitness studies; philosophy and religious studies; physical sciences; psychology; public administration and social service professions; social sciences; visual and performing arts. **Areas of required coursework:** arts/fine arts, humanities, mathematics, English (including composition), philosophy, foreign languages, sciences (biological or physical), history, social science. **Pre-professional programs:** pre-law, pre-dentistry, pre-medicine, pre-veterinary science, pre-pharmacy, other. **Special academic programs:** accelerated program, cross-registration, distance learning, double major, dual enrollment, exchange student program (domestic), honors program, independent study, internships, study abroad, teacher certificate program, other. **Teacher certification offered in:** special education, elementary, middle/junior high, secondary. **Reserve Officers Training Corps (ROTC):** Army ROTC: Offered at cooperating institution (North Carolina A&T State University); Air Force ROTC: Offered at cooperating institution (North Carolina A&T State University). **Faculty and instruction (2009-2010):** Total instructional faculty: 788 full-time, 467 part-time (46% men; 54% women; 35% minorities). Full-time faculty with Ph.D. or other terminal degree: 80%. Student/faculty ratio: 17/1. Classes of fewer than 20 students: 39%; of 20 to 49 students: 47%; of 50 or more students: 14%. **Advanced Placement and International Baccalaureate credit:** AP tests may be used for: Credit and/or placement. Scores accepted: 3, 4, 5. International Baccalaureate exams may be used for: Credit only. **Freshmen returning for sophomore year:** 76%. **Graduation rates:** Four-year: 28%; five-year: 47%; six-year: 52%.

COSTS AND FINANCIAL AID

Financial aid office: (336) 334-5702. **Expenses (2010-2011):** Tuition and fees 2010-2011: $4,520 in state, $16,281 out of state; room/board: $6,655. Estimated books and supplies: $1,282 personal expenses: $2,325. **Financial aid:** Priority filing date for institution's financial aid form: March 1. In 2009-2010, 77% of undergraduates applied for financial aid. Of those, 75% were determined to have financial need; 29% had their need fully met. Average financial aid package (proportion receiving): $9,204 (75%). Average amount of gift aid, such as scholarships or grants (proportion receiving): $6,332 (40%). Average amount of self-help aid, such as work study or loans (proportion receiving): $4,078 (44%). Average need-based loan (excluding PLUS or other private loans): $4,010. Among students who received need-based aid, the average percentage of need met: 59%. Among students who received aid based on merit, the average award (and the proportion receiving): $2,349 (4%). The average athletic scholarship (and the proportion receiving): $8,916 (1%). Average amount of debt of borrowers graduating in 2009: $18,604. Proportion who borrowed: 67%.

CAMPUS LIFE AND EXTRACURRICULAR ACTIVITIES

Campus housing available (% using): coed dorms (85%), women's dorms (7%), apartment for single students (7%), special housing for international students (1%). Students who live in college-owned, operated, or affiliated housing: 30%. **Student employment:** During the 2009-2010 academic year, 2% of undergraduates worked on campus. Average per-year earnings: $1,927. **Clubs and organizations:** Number of student organizations: 200. Activities include: choral groups, concert band, dance, drama/theater, international student organization, jazz band, literary magazine, music ensembles, musical theater, opera, pep band, radio station, student government, student newspaper, student film society, symphony orchestra. Number of fraternities: 12; sororities: 12. **Sports program (2009-2010):** Member of NCAA I. *Men's intercollegiate varsity sports:* baseball, basketball, cross country, golf, soccer, tennis, wrestling. *Women's intercollegiate varsity sports:* basketball, cross country, golf, soccer, softball, tennis, volleyball.

SERVICES AND FACILITIES

Basic services: nonremedial tutoring, placement service, day care, health service, health insurance. **Remedial assistance:** reading, math, writing, study skills. **Counseling services:** minority student, career, personal, academic, psychological, birth control. **For learning-disabled students:** School does not offer a structured program with separate admission and additional fees. Services include: remedial English, reading machines, remedial reading, tape recorders, diagnostic testing service, note-taking services, oral tests, learning center, readers, extended time for tests, tutors, other testing accommodations. **Library:** Number of titles: 3,400,000; number of current serial subscriptions: 4,648. **Information technology resources:** Students are not required to lease or own a computer. Number of campus computers available to all students: 500. School has a wireless network. Proportion of college-owned housing units wired for high-speed internet access: 100%. **Campus safety:** Security services offered: 24-hour foot-and-vehicle patrols, late-night transport/escort service, 24-hour emergency telephones, lighted pathways/sidewalks, student patrols, controlled dormitory access (key, security card, etc).

TRANSFER AND INTERNATIONAL STUDENTS

Transfer students: May apply for admission for the following academic terms: Fall, Spring, Summer. Applicants need a minimum number of credits to apply. For fall 2009: Transfer applications received: 2,828. Transfer applicants offered admission: 2,315. Transfer applicants enrolled: 1,531. **International students:** Number of foreign undergraduates: 135 (1% of student body). Number of countries represented: 20. Minimum TOEFL score required: 550 (paper); 213 (computer).

University of North Carolina–Pembroke

- **Address:** PO Box 1510, Pembroke, NC 28372
- **Website:** http://www.uncp.edu
- **Public**
- **Enrollment:** 4,700 full-time; 1,210 part-time

KEY STATS

✔ **U.S News College Ranking:** second tier, Regional Universities (South)
✔ **SAT Score (25th/75th percentile):** 840-1000
✔ **Tuition:** 2010-2011: $3,890 in state, $13,097 out of state
  Selectivity: Less selective   **Room/board:** $5,990
  Acceptance rate: 79%   **Average debt:** N/A
  Student/faculty ratio: 15/1   **Proportion who borrowed:** N/A

UNDERGRADUATE STUDENT BODY STATS

2009-2010 enrollment: 4,700 full-time; 1,210 part-time. Men: 39%; women: 61%. **Ethnic makeup:** African American: 31%; American-Indian: 15%; Asian American: 2%; Hispanic: 4%; White: 47%; International: 2%.

ADMISSIONS FACTS AND FIGURES

Phone: (910) 521-6262. **Email:** admissions@papa.uncp.edu. **Website:** http://www.uncp.edu. **Application deadlines for fall 2011:** Regular decision: July 31. Early decision: Not offered. Early action: Not offered. Admission can be deferred. **Application fee:** $40. **To apply online, go to:** http://www.uncp.edu/admissions/apply/default.asp. **Admissions requirements/recommendations:** High school units required (recommended): English: 4 (4); Mathematics: 3 (4); Science: 3 (3); Foreign language: 2 (2); Social studies: 1 (1); History: 1 (1); Total units: 14 (15). Tests: The college uses SAT or ACT scores in admissions decisions. Either SAT or ACT required. For admission to the fall 2011 entering class, the school will accept: ACT with writing required. Campus visit: Recommended. Admissions interview: Recommended. Off-campus interview: May be arranged. **Factors that count in admissions decisions:** *Academic:* Secondary school record: Very Important. Class rank: Very Important. Letters of recommendation: Considered. Standardized test scores: Very Important. Essay: Considered. *Nonacademic:* Interview: Considered. Extracurricular activities: Not Considered. Talent/ability: Considered. Character/personal qualities: Considered. Alumni/ae relationship: Not Considered. Geographical residence: Not Considered. State residency: Not Considered. Religious affiliation/commitment: Not Considered. Minority status: Not Considered. Volunteer work: Not Considered. Work experience: Not Considered. **Admissions statistics for the fall 2009 entering class:** Total applicants: 3,031. Total accepted: 2,392. Freshmen enrolled: 1,219; 4% were from out of state. Overall acceptance rate: 79%. **Credentials of fall 2009 freshmen:** 8% ranked in the top 10 percent of their high school class; 25% were in the top 25 percent; 65% were in the top half. (Proportion submitting class standing: 93%.) **Average high school grade point average:** 3.1. **First-year students who submitted SAT scores:** 93%. Scores (25/75 percentile): Critical Reading: 410-490, Math: 430-510, Combined: 840-1000. **First-year students submitting ACT scores:** 13%. Scores (25/75 percentile): English: 15-20, Math: 16-20, Composite: 17-20.

ACADEMICS

Year founded: 1887. **Academic calendar:** Semester. **Degrees offered:** bachelor's, master's. **Most popular majors:** 13% education, 12% biology/biological sciences, 12% business administration and management, 12% sociology, 11% nursing/registered nurse training (R.N., A.S.N., B.S.N., M.S.N.). **Major fields of study:** area, ethnic, cultural, and gender studies; biological and biomedical sciences; business, management, marketing, and related support services; communication, journalism, and related programs; computer and information sciences and support services; education; English language and literature/letters; foreign languages, literatures, and linguistics; health professions and related clinical sciences; history; mathematics and statistics; natural resources and conservation; parks, recreation, leisure, and fitness studies; philosophy and religious studies; physical sciences; psychology; public administration and social service professions; security and protective services; social sciences; visual and performing arts. **Areas of required coursework:** arts/fine arts, humanities, computer literacy, mathematics, English (including composition), philosophy, sciences (biological or physical), history, social science, other. **Special academic programs (% participation):** distance learning (80%), double major (2%), exchange student program (domestic), honors program (3%), independent study (8%), internships (32%), study abroad (2%), teacher certificate program (10%). **Teacher certification offered in:** early childhood, special education, elementary, middle/junior high, secondary. **Reserve Officers Training Corps (ROTC):** Army ROTC: Offered on campus; Air Force ROTC: Offered on campus. **Faculty and instruction (2009-2010):** Total instructional faculty: 323 full-time, 112 part-time (51% men; 49% women; 25% minorities). Full-time faculty with Ph.D. or other terminal degree: 67%. Student/faculty ratio: 15/1. Classes of fewer than 20 students: 39%; of 20 to 49 students: 61%; of 50 or more students: 0%. **Advanced Placement and International Baccalaureate credit:** AP tests may be used for: Credit only. Scores accepted: 3. International Baccalaureate exams may be used for: Credit and/or placement. **Freshmen returning for sophomore year:** 69%. **Graduation rates:** Four-year: 23%; five-year: 33%; six-year: 37%. **Graduate study:** Fields in which graduates pursue further study: arts and sciences, 91%.

COSTS AND FINANCIAL AID

Financial aid office: (910) 521-6255. **Expenses (2010-2011):** Tuition and fees 2010-2011: $3,890 in state, $13,097 out of state; room/board: $5,990. Estimated books and supplies: $1,200; transportation: $1,346; personal expenses: $1,389. **Financial aid:** Priority filing date for institution's financial aid form: March 15. In 2009-2010, 87% of undergraduates applied for financial aid. Of those, 75% were determined to have financial need; 18% had their need fully met. Average financial aid package (proportion receiving): $9,268 (73%). Average amount of gift aid, such as scholarships or grants (proportion receiving): $6,566 (69%). Average amount of self-help aid, such as work study or loans (proportion receiving): $3,712 (57%). Average need-based loan (excluding PLUS or other private loans): $3,647. Among students who received need-based aid, the average percentage of need met: 77%. Among students who received aid based on merit, the average award (and the proportion receiving): $1,050 (0%). The average athletic scholarship (and the proportion receiving): $0 (0%).

CAMPUS LIFE AND EXTRACURRICULAR ACTIVITIES

Campus housing available (% using): coed dorms (21%), women's dorms (28%), men's dorms (23%), other housing options (28%). Students who live in college-owned, operated, or affiliated housing: 27%. **Clubs and organizations:** Number of student organizations: 75. Activities include: campus ministries, choral groups, concert band, dance, drama/theater, international student organization, jazz band, literary magazine, marching band, music ensembles, musical theater, pep band, student government, student newspaper, student film society, television station, yearbook. Number of fraternities: 10; sororities: 8. Proportion of men in fraternities: 7%; of women in sororities: 4%. **Sports program (2009-2010):** Member of NCAA II. *Men's intercollegiate varsity sports:* baseball, basketball, cross country, football, golf, soccer, track and field (indoor), wrestling. *Women's intercollegiate varsity sports:* basketball, cross country, golf, soccer, softball, tennis, track and field (indoor), volleyball.

SERVICES AND FACILITIES

Basic services: nonremedial tutoring, placement service, health service. **Remedial assistance:** reading, math, writing, study skills. **Counseling services:** career, personal, veteran student. **For learning-disabled students:** School does not offer a structured program with separate admission and additional fees. Total undergraduates in learning-disabled program or receiving services: 135. Services include: remedial math, remedial English, reading machines, remedial reading, tape recorders, note-taking services, oral tests, readers, extended time for tests, tutors, priority registration, priority seating, texts on tape, other testing accommodations. **Library:** Number of titles: 367,565; number of current serial subscriptions: 30,199. **Information technology resources:** Students are not required to lease or own a computer. Number of campus computers available to all students: 875. School has a wireless network. Approximate number of users that can be accommodated: 38,000. Proportion of college-owned housing units wired for high-speed internet access: 100%. **Campus safety:** Security services offered: 24-hour foot-and-vehicle patrols, 24-hour emergency telephones, lighted pathways/sidewalks, controlled dormitory access (key, security card, etc).

TRANSFER AND INTERNATIONAL STUDENTS

Transfer students: May apply for admission for the following academic terms: Fall, Spring, Summer. Applicants need a minimum number of credits to apply. For fall 2009: Transfer applications received: 853. Transfer applicants offered admission: 751. Transfer applicants enrolled: 578. **International students:** Number of foreign undergraduates: 76 (2% of student body). Number of countries represented: 23. Minimum TOEFL score required: 500 (paper); 173 (computer).

Univ. of North Carolina School of the Arts

■ **Address:** 1533 S. Main Street, Winston-Salem, NC 27127-2189
■ **Website:** http://www.ncarts.edu
■ **Public**
■ **Enrollment:** 736 full-time; 13 part-time

KEY STATS

✔ **U.S News College Ranking:** Unranked Specialty School–Fine Arts
✔ **SAT Score (25th/75th percentile):** 1010-1220
✔ **Tuition:** 2009-2010: $5,449 in state, $17,395 out of state

Selectivity: N/A	**Room/board:** $7,256
Acceptance rate: 45%	**Average debt:** N/A
Student/faculty ratio: 7/1	**Proportion who borrowed:** N/A

UNDERGRADUATE STUDENT BODY STATS

2009-2010 enrollment: 736 full-time; 13 part-time. Men: 60%; women: 40%. **Ethnic makeup:** African American: 9%; Asian American: 1%; Hispanic: 2%; White: 88%; International: 1%.

ADMISSIONS FACTS AND FIGURES

Phone: (336) 770-3291. **Email:** admissions@ncarts.edu. **Website:** http://www.ncarts.edu. **Application deadlines for fall 2011:** Regular decision: March 1. Early decision: Not offered. Early action: Not offered. Admission can be deferred. **Application fee:** $60. **To apply online, go to:** http://www1.cfnc.org/Applications/University_of_North_Carolina/apply.html?application_id=1543. **Admissions requirements/recommendations:** High school units required (recommended): English: 4; Mathematics: 3; Science: 3; Foreign language: (2); Social studies: 2; History: 1; Academic electives: 4; Total units: 20. Tests: The college uses SAT or ACT scores in admissions decisions. Either SAT or ACT required. For admission to the fall 2011 entering class, the school will accept: ACT with or without writing accepted. Campus visit: Recommended. Admissions interview: Required. Off-campus interview: May be arranged. **Factors that count in admissions decisions:** *Academic:* Secondary school record: Very Important. Class rank: Considered. Letters of recommendation: Very Important. Standardized test scores: Important. Essay: Not Considered. *Nonacademic:* Interview: Very Important. Extracurricular activities: Considered. Talent/ability: Very Important. Character/personal qualities: Considered. Alumni/ae relationship: Not Considered. Geographical residence: Considered. State residency: Considered. Religious affiliation/commitment: Not Considered. Minority status: Considered. Volunteer work: Not Considered. Work experience: Considered. **Other schools with the greatest overlap in applicants:** Boston University; Cornish College of the Arts; Juilliard School; Purchase College–SUNY; Rhode Island School of Design. **Admissions statistics for the fall 2009 entering class:** Total applicants: 676. Total accepted: 305. Freshmen enrolled: 179; Overall acceptance rate: 45%. **Size of waiting list:** 25 applicants; enrolled from waiting list: 7. **First-year students who submitted SAT scores:** 81%. Scores (25/75 percentile): Critical Reading: 520-630, Math: 490-590, Combined: 1010-1220. **First-year students submitting ACT scores:** 26%. Scores (25/75 percentile): English: N/A, Math: N/A, Composite: N/A.

ACADEMICS

Year founded: 1963. **Academic calendar:** Trimester. **Degrees offered:** diploma, bachelor's, master's, post-master's certificate. **Major fields of study:** visual and performing arts. **Areas of required coursework:** arts/fine arts, humanities, computer literacy, mathematics, English (including composition), sciences (biological or physical), history, social science. **Special academic programs:** cooperative (work-study plan) program, English as a Second Language (ESL), independent study, internships. **Faculty and instruction (2009-2010):** Total instructional faculty: N/A. Student/faculty ratio: 7/1. **Advanced Placement and International Baccalaureate credit:** AP tests may be used for: Credit only. International Baccalaureate exams may be used for: Credit only. **Freshmen returning for sophomore year:** 79%. **Graduation rates:** Six-year: 54%.

COSTS AND FINANCIAL AID

Financial aid office: (336) 770-3297. **Expenses (2009-2010):** Tuition and fees 2009-2010: $5,449 in state, $17,395 out of state; room/board: $7,256. Estimated books and supplies: $1,120. **Financial aid:** Priority filing date for institution's financial aid form: March 1. In 2009-2010, 69% of undergraduates applied for financial aid. Of those, 53% were determined to have financial need; 14% had their need fully met. Average financial aid package (proportion receiving): $15,304 (53%). Average amount of gift aid, such as scholarships or grants (proportion receiving): $7,333 (51%). Average amount of self-help aid, such as work study or loans (proportion receiving): $3,830 (46%). Average need-based loan (excluding PLUS or other private loans): $4,016. Among students who received need-based aid, the average percentage of need met: 90%. Among students who received aid based on merit, the average award (and the proportion receiving): $3,527 (17%).

CAMPUS LIFE AND EXTRACURRICULAR ACTIVITIES

Campus housing available: coed dorms, apartment for single students, special housing for disabled students. **Student employment:** During the 2009-2010 academic year, 15% of undergraduates worked on campus. Average per-year earnings: $750. Activities include: campus ministries, student government, student newspaper. Number of fraternities: 0; sororities: 0. Average proportion of students who stay on campus on weekends: 95%.

SERVICES AND FACILITIES

Basic services: health service. **Counseling services:** career, personal, academic, psychological. **For learning-disabled students:** School does not offer a structured program with separate admission and additional fees. **Library:** Number of titles: 105,000; number of current serial subscriptions: 470. **Information technology resources:** Students are not required to lease or own a computer. Number of campus computers available to all students: 60. School has a wireless network. Proportion of college-owned housing units wired for high-speed internet access: 100%. **Campus safety:** Security services offered: 24-hour foot-and-vehicle patrols, late-night transport/escort service, 24-hour emergency telephones, lighted pathways/sidewalks, controlled dormitory access (key, security card, etc).

TRANSFER AND INTERNATIONAL STUDENTS

Transfer students: May apply for admission for the following academic terms: Fall, Winter. Applicants do not need a minimum number of credits to apply. For fall 2009: Transfer applications received: 157. Transfer applicants offered admission: 73. Transfer applicants enrolled: 52. **International students:** Number of foreign undergraduates: 4 (1% of student body). Number of countries represented: 21. Average TOEFL score: 550 (paper).

University of North Carolina–Wilmington

■ **Address:** 601 S. College Road, Wilmington, NC 28403-5963
■ **Website:** http://www.uncw.edu
■ **Public**
■ **Enrollment:** 10,152 full-time; 1,045 part-time

KEY STATS

✔ **U.S News College Ranking:** 13, Regional Universities (South)
✔ **SAT Score (25th/75th percentile):** 1080-1250
✔ **Tuition:** 2010-2011: $5,154 in state, $16,036 out of state
  Selectivity: More selective   **Room/board:** $7,608
  Acceptance rate: 58%   **Average debt:** $16,115
  Student/faculty ratio: 17/1   **Proportion who borrowed:** 54%

UNDERGRADUATE STUDENT BODY STATS

2009-2010 enrollment: 10,152 full-time; 1,045 part-time. Men: 42%; women: 58%. **Ethnic makeup:** African American: 4%; American-Indian: 1%; Asian American: 2%; Hispanic: 4%; White: 88%.

ADMISSIONS FACTS AND FIGURES

Phone: (910) 962-3243. **Email:** admissions@uncw.edu. **Website:** http://www.uncw.edu. **Application deadlines for fall 2011:** Regular decision: February 1; decision sent by April 1. Early decision: Not offered. Early action: Send application by: November 1; Decision sent by: January 20. Admission can be deferred. **Application fee:** $60. **To apply online, go to:** http://www.uncw.edu/admissions. **Admissions requirements/recommendations:** High school units required (recommended): English: 4; Mathematics: 4; Science: 3; Foreign language: 2; Social studies: 1; History: 1; Total units: 15. Tests: The college uses SAT or ACT scores in admissions decisions. Either SAT or ACT required. For admission to the fall 2011 entering class, the school will accept: ACT with writing required. Campus visit: Recommended. Admissions interview: Neither required nor recommended. Off-campus interview: Not available. **Factors that count in admissions decisions:** *Academic:* Secondary school record: Very Important. Class rank: Important. Letters of recommendation: Very Important. Standardized test scores: Very Important. Essay: Very Important. ***Nonacademic:***

Interview: Not Considered. Extracurricular activities: Considered. Talent/ability: Considered. Character/personal qualities: Considered. Alumni/ae relationship: Considered. Geographical residence: Considered. State residency: Considered. Religious affiliation/commitment: Not Considered. Minority status: Considered. Volunteer work: Considered. Work experience: Considered. **Other schools with the greatest overlap in applicants:** Appalachian State University; North Carolina State University–Raleigh; University of North Carolina–Chapel Hill. **Admissions statistics for the fall 2009 entering class:** Total applicants: 9,283. Total accepted: 5,402. Freshmen enrolled: 1,949; 15% were from out of state. Overall acceptance rate: 58%. Non-early acceptance rate: 58%. **Size of waiting list:** 190 applicants; enrolled from waiting list: 11. **Credentials of fall 2009 freshmen:** 24% ranked in the top 10 percent of their high school class; 62% were in the top 25 percent; 99% were in the top half. (Proportion submitting class standing: 84%.) **Average high school grade point average:** 3.8. **First-year students who submitted SAT scores:** 98%. Scores (25/75 percentile): Critical Reading: 530-620, Math: 550-630, Combined: 1080-1250. **First-year students submitting ACT scores:** 29%. Scores (25/75 percentile): English: 21-26, Math: 22-27, Composite: 22-27.

ACADEMICS

Year founded: 1947. **Academic calendar:** Semester. **Degrees offered:** bachelor's, post-bachelor's certificate, master's, post-master's certificate, doctorate. **Most popular majors:** 8% psychology, 7% communication studies/speech communication and rhetoric, 7% marketing/marketing management, 5% finance, 4% biology/biological sciences. **Major fields of study:** biological and biomedical sciences; business, management, marketing, and related support services; communication, journalism, and related programs; computer and information sciences and support services; education; English language and literature/letters; foreign languages, literatures, and linguistics; health professions and related clinical sciences; history; mathematics and statistics; natural resources and conservation; parks, recreation, leisure, and fitness studies; philosophy and religious studies; physical sciences; psychology; public administration and social service professions; security and protective services; social sciences; visual and performing arts. **Areas of required coursework:** arts/fine arts, humanities, mathematics, English (including composition), philosophy, foreign languages, sciences (biological or physical), history, social science, other. **Pre-professional programs:** pre-law, pre-dentistry, pre-medicine, pre-veterinary science, pre-optometry, pre-pharmacy, other. **Special academic programs (% participation):** accelerated program, cooperative (work-study plan) program, cross-registration, distance learning, double major (4%), dual enrollment, exchange student program (domestic) (.003%), honors program (5%), independent study (15%), internships (17%), study abroad (5%), teacher certificate program (12%), other. **Teacher certification offered in:** early childhood, special education, elementary, middle/junior high, secondary. **Faculty and instruction (2009-2010):** Total instructional faculty: 589 full-time, 271 part-time (54% men; 46% women; 17% minorities). Full-time faculty with Ph.D. or other terminal degree: 85%. Student/faculty ratio: 17/1. Classes of fewer than 20 students: 31%; of 20 to 49 students: 62%; of 50 or more students: 7%. **Advanced Placement and International Baccalaureate credit:** AP tests may be used for: Credit only. Scores accepted: 3, 4, 5. International Baccalaureate exams may be used for: Credit only. **Freshmen returning for sophomore year:** 85%. **Graduation rates:** Four-year: 44%; five-year: 65%; six-year: 67%. **Graduate study:** 24% of students pursue further study immediately upon graduation; 14% within one year.

COSTS AND FINANCIAL AID

Financial aid office: (910) 962-3177. **Expenses (2010-2011):** Tuition and fees 2010-2011: $5,154 in state, $16,036 out of state; room/board: $7,608. Estimated books and supplies: $986; transportation: $1,410; personal expenses: $1,173. **Financial aid:** In 2009-2010, 66% of undergraduates applied for financial aid. Of those, 45% were determined to have financial need; 40% had their need fully met. Average financial aid package (proportion receiving): $9,078 (45%). Average amount of gift aid, such as scholarships or grants (proportion receiving): $6,030 (39%). Average amount of self-help aid, such as work study or loans (proportion receiving): $3,605 (31%). Average need-based loan (excluding PLUS or other private loans): $3,547. Among students who received need-based aid, the average percentage of need met: 84%. Among students who received aid based on merit, the average award (and the proportion receiving): $2,272 (3%). The average athletic scholarship (and the proportion receiving): $10,834 (2%). Average amount of debt of borrowers graduating in 2009: $16,115. Proportion who borrowed: 54%.

CAMPUS LIFE AND EXTRACURRICULAR ACTIVITIES

Campus housing available (% using): coed dorms (30%), women's dorms (5%), sorority housing (2%), fraternity housing (0%), apartment for single students (52%), special housing for disabled students (5%), special housing for international students (1%). Students who live in college-owned, operated, or affiliated housing: 38%. **Clubs and organizations:** Number of student organizations: 201. Activities include: campus ministries, choral groups, concert band, dance, drama/theater, international student organization, jazz band, literary magazine, model UN, music ensembles, musical theater, opera, pep band, radio station, student government, student newspaper, student film society, symphony orchestra, television station. Number of fraternities: 13; sororities: 13. Proportion of men in fraternities: 9%; of women in sororities: 8%. Average proportion of students who stay on campus on weekends: 38%. **Sports program (2009-2010):** Member of NCAA I. *Men's intercollegiate varsity sports:* baseball, basketball, cross country, golf, soccer, swimming, tennis, track and field (indoor), track and field (outdoor). *Women's intercollegiate varsity sports:* basketball, cross country, golf, soccer, softball, swimming, tennis, track and field (indoor), track and field (outdoor), volleyball.

SERVICES AND FACILITIES

Basic services: nonremedial tutoring, women's center, placement service, health service. **Remedial assistance:** reading, math, writing, study skills. **Counseling services:** minority student, career, personal, veteran student, academic, older student, psychological, birth control, other. **For learning-disabled students:** School does not offer a structured program with separate admission and additional fees. Total undergraduates in learning-disabled program or receiving services: 235. Services include: reading machines, tape recorders, note-taking services, oral tests, learning center, readers, extended time for tests, tutors, priority registration, priority seating, texts on tape, other testing accommodations, other. **Library:** Number of titles: 1,071,435; number of current serial subscriptions: 30,000. **Information technology resources:** Students are not required to lease or own a computer. Number of campus computers available to all students: 1,315. School has a wireless network. Approximate number of users that can be accommodated: 13,260. Proportion of college-owned housing units wired for high-speed internet access: 100%. **Campus safety:** Security services offered: 24-hour foot-and-vehicle patrols, late-night transport/escort service, 24-hour emergency telephones, lighted pathways/sidewalks, controlled dormitory access (key, security card, etc).

TRANSFER AND INTERNATIONAL STUDENTS

Transfer students: May apply for admission for the following academic terms: Fall, Spring, Summer. Applicants need a minimum number of credits to apply. For fall 2009: Transfer applications received: 2,902. Transfer applicants offered admission: 1,715. Transfer applicants enrolled: 1,224. **International students:** Number of foreign undergraduates: 43. Number of countries represented: 56. Minimum TOEFL score required: 525 (paper); 71 (computer).

Wake Forest University

- **Address:** Box 7305, Reynolda Station, Winston-Salem, NC 27109
- **Website:** http://www.wfu.edu
- **Private**
- **Enrollment:** 4,514 full-time; 55 part-time

KEY STATS

✔ **U.S News College Ranking:** 25, National Universities
✔ **SAT Score (25th/75th percentile):** 1180-1390
✔ **Tuition:** 2010-2011: $39,970

Selectivity: Most selective	**Room/board:** $11,010
Acceptance rate: 38%	**Average debt:** $24,561
Student/faculty ratio: 11/1	**Proportion who borrowed:** 38%

UNDERGRADUATE STUDENT BODY STATS

2009-2010 enrollment: 4,514 full-time; 55 part-time. Men: 49%; women: 51%. **Ethnic makeup:** African American: 7%; Asian American: 6%; Hispanic: 4%; White: 81%; International: 2%. **Religious preference:** Roman Catholic: 24%; Protestant: 48%; Jewish: 2%; Hindu: 1%; Unknown: 23%.

ADMISSIONS FACTS AND FIGURES

Phone: (336) 758-5201. **Email:** admissions@wfu.edu. **Website:** http://www.wfu.edu. **Application deadlines for fall 2011:** Regular decision: January 1; decision sent by April 1. Early decision: Send application by: January 1; Decision sent by: N/A. Early action: Not offered. Admission cannot be deferred. **Application fee:** $50. **To apply online, go to:** http://www.wfu.edu/admissions/apply. **Admissions requirements/recommendations:** High school units required (recommended): English: 4 (4); Mathematics: 3 (4); Science: 1 (4); Foreign language: 2 (4); Social studies: 2 (4); Total units: 16 (20). Tests: The college uses SAT or ACT scores in admissions decisions. Neither SAT nor ACT required. For admission to the fall 2011 entering class, the school will accept: ACT with or without writing accepted. Campus visit: Recommended. Admissions interview: Recommended. Off-campus interview: May be arranged. **Factors that count in admissions decisions:** *Academic:* Secondary school record: Very Important. Class rank: Very Important. Letters of recommendation: Important. Standardized test scores: Considered. Essay: Very Important. *Nonacademic:* Interview: Important. Extracurricular activities: Important. Talent/ability: Important. Character/personal qualities: Very Important. Alumni/ae relationship: Considered. Geographical residence: Considered. State residency: Considered. Religious affiliation/commitment: Considered. Minority status: Considered. Volunteer work: Considered. Work experience: Not Considered. **Other schools with the greatest overlap in applicants:** Duke University; Emory University; University of North Carolina–Chapel Hill; University of Richmond; Vanderbilt University. **Admissions statistics for the fall 2009 entering class:** Total applicants: 10,553. Total accepted: 3,959. Freshmen enrolled: 1,200; 74% were from out of state. Overall acceptance rate: 38%. Early-decision acceptance rate: 42%. Non-early acceptance rate: 37%. **Credentials of fall 2009 freshmen:** 75% ranked in the top 10 percent of their high school class; 89% were in the top 25 percent; 99% were in the top half. (Proportion submitting class standing: 59%.) **First-year students who submitted SAT scores:** 68%. Scores (25/75 percentile): Critical Reading: 580-690, Math: 600-700, Combined: 1180-1390. **First-year students submitting ACT scores:** 39%. Scores (25/75 percentile): English: N/A, Math: N/A, Composite: 27-31.

ACADEMICS

Year founded: 1834. **Academic calendar:** Semester. **Degrees offered:** bachelor's, master's, doctorate. **Most popular majors:** 10% economics, 9% business/commerce, 8% political science and government, 7% communication studies/speech communication and rhetoric, 7% finance. **Major fields of study:** biological and biomedical sciences; business, management, marketing, and related support services; communication, journalism, and related programs; computer and information sciences and support services; education; engineering; English language and literature/letters; foreign languages, literatures, and linguistics; history; mathematics and statistics; parks, recreation, leisure, and fitness studies; philosophy and religious studies; physical sciences; psychology; social sciences; visual and performing arts. **Areas of required coursework:** arts/fine arts, humanities, mathematics, English (including composition), philosophy, foreign languages, sciences (biological or physical), history, social science, other. **Pre-professional programs:** pre-law, pre-medicine. **Special academic programs:** cross-registration, double major, dual enrollment, honors program, independent study, internships, study abroad, teacher certificate program. **Teacher certification offered in:** elementary, middle/junior high, secondary. **Cooperative education programs:** engineering, health professions. **Reserve Officers Training Corps (ROTC):** Army ROTC: Offered on campus. **Faculty and instruction (2009-2010):** Total instructional faculty: 476 full-time, 149 part-time (62% men; 38% women; 14% minorities). Full-time faculty with Ph.D. or other terminal degree: 91%. Student/faculty ratio: 11/1. Classes of fewer than 20 students: 57%; of 20 to 49 students: 40%; of 50 or more students: 3%. **Advanced Placement and International Baccalaureate credit:** AP tests may be used for: Credit only. **Freshmen returning for sophomore year:** 94%. **Graduation rates:** Four-year: 85%; five-year: 90%; six-year: 90%. **Graduate study:** 39% of students pursue further study within one year. Fields in which graduates pursue further study: law, 5%; medicine, 4%; arts and sciences, 26%.

COSTS AND FINANCIAL AID

Financial aid office: (336) 758-5154. **Expenses (2010-2011):** Tuition and fees 2010-2011: $39,970; room/board: $11,010. Estimated books and supplies: $930; transportation: $775; personal expenses: $1,450. **Financial aid:** Priority filing date for institution's financial aid form: February 15; deadline: March 1. In 2009-2010, 42% of undergraduates applied for financial aid. Of those, 38% were determined to have financial need; 64% had their need fully met. Average financial aid package (proportion receiving): $32,965 (38%). Average amount of gift aid, such as scholarships or grants (proportion receiving): $26,473 (35%). Average amount of self-help aid, such as work study or loans (proportion receiving): $12,828 (32%). Average need-based loan (excluding PLUS or other private loans): $11,305. Among students who received need-based aid, the average percentage of need met: 99%. Among students who received aid based on merit, the average award (and the proportion receiving): $13,864 (9%). The average athletic scholarship (and the proportion receiving): $36,616 (4%). Average amount of debt of borrowers graduating in 2009: $24,561. Proportion who borrowed: 38%.

CAMPUS LIFE AND EXTRACURRICULAR ACTIVITIES

Campus housing available: coed dorms, sorority housing, fraternity housing, apartment for single students. Students who live in college-owned, operated, or affiliated housing: 70%. **Student employment:** During the 2009-2010 academic year, 43% of undergraduates worked on campus. Average per-year earnings: $1,200. **Clubs and organizations:** Number of student organizations: 176. Activities include: campus ministries, choral groups, concert band, dance, drama/theater, international student organization, jazz band, literary magazine, marching band, model UN, music ensembles, pep band, radio station, student government, student newspaper, student film society, symphony orchestra, television station, yearbook. Number of fraternities: 14; sororities: 10. Proportion of men in fraternities: 35%; of women in sororities: 50%. Average proportion of students who stay on campus on weekends: 70%. **Sports program (2009-2010):** Member of NCAA I. *Men's intercollegiate varsity sports:* baseball, basketball, cross country, football, golf, soccer, tennis, track and field (outdoor). *Women's intercollegiate varsity sports:* basketball, cross country, field hockey, golf, soccer, tennis, track and field (outdoor), volleyball.

SERVICES AND FACILITIES

Basic services: nonremedial tutoring, other. **Remedial assistance:** study skills. **Counseling services:** minority student, career, military, personal, academic, older student, psychological, birth control, religious. **For learning-disabled students:** School does not offer a structured program with separate admission and additional fees. Total undergraduates in learning-disabled program or receiving services: 157. Services include: learning center, extended time for tests, tutors, other. **Library:** Number of titles: 2,078,070; number of current serial subscriptions: 35,531. **Information technology resources:** Students are required to lease or own a computer. Number of campus computers available to all students: 5,061. School has a wireless network. Approximate number of users that can be accommodated: 23,000. Proportion of college-owned housing units wired for high-speed internet access: 100%. **Campus safety:** Security services offered: 24-hour foot-and-vehicle patrols, late-night transport/escort service, 24-hour emergency telephones, lighted pathways/sidewalks, controlled dormitory access (key, security card, etc).

TRANSFER AND INTERNATIONAL STUDENTS

Transfer students: May apply for admission for the following academic terms: Fall, Spring. Applicants do not need a minimum number of credits to apply. For fall 2009: Transfer applications received: 375. Transfer applicants offered admission: 108. Transfer applicants enrolled: 52. **International students:** Number of foreign undergraduates: 69 (2% of student body). Number of countries represented: 32. Minimum TOEFL score required: 600 (paper); 250 (computer).

Warren Wilson College

- **Address:** PO Box 9000, Asheville, NC 28815
- **Website:** http://www.warren-wilson.edu
- **Private; Religious affiliation:** Presbyterian
- **Enrollment:** N/A

KEY STATS

✔ **U.S News College Ranking:** 183, National Liberal Arts Colleges
✔ **ACT Score (25th/75th percentile):** 23-28
✔ **Tuition:** 2010-2011: $25,626

Selectivity: Selective	Room/board: $8,028
Acceptance rate: 77%	Average debt: $20,441
Student/faculty ratio: N/A	Proportion who borrowed: 34%

Western Carolina University

- **Address:** Cullowhee, NC 28723
- **Website:** http://www.wcu.edu
- **Public**
- **Enrollment:** 6,175 full-time; 1,275 part-time

KEY STATS

✔ **U.S News College Ranking:** 29, Regional Universities (South)
✔ **SAT Score (25th/75th percentile):** 940-1120
✔ **Tuition:** 2010-2011: $4,551 in state, $14,148 out of state

Selectivity: Selective	Room/board: $6,769
Acceptance rate: 44%	Average debt: $11,609
Student/faculty ratio: 15/1	Proportion who borrowed: 51%

UNDERGRADUATE STUDENT BODY STATS

2009-2010 enrollment: 6,175 full-time; 1,275 part-time. Men: 46%; women: 54%. **Ethnic makeup:** African American: 6%; American-Indian: 1%; Asian American: 1%; Hispanic: 2%; White: 87%; International: 3%.

ADMISSIONS FACTS AND FIGURES

Phone: (828) 227-7317. **Email:** admiss@email.wcu.edu. **Website:** http://www.wcu.edu. **Application deadlines for fall 2011:** Regular decision: March 1. Early decision: Not offered. Early action: Send application by: November 15; Decision sent by: December 15. Admission cannot be deferred. **Application fee:** $45. **To apply online, go to:** http://www.wcu.edu/15.asp. **Admissions requirements/recommendations:** High school units required (recommended): English: 4 (4); Mathematics: 4 (4); Science: 3 (3); Foreign language: 2 (2); Social studies: 2 (2); History: 1 (1); Academic electives: 4 (8); Total units: 20 (24). Tests: The college uses SAT or ACT scores in admissions decisions. Either SAT or ACT required. For admission to the fall 2011 entering class, the school will accept: ACT with writing required. Campus visit: Recommended. Admissions interview: Neither required nor recommended. Off-campus interview: Not available. **Factors that count in admissions decisions:** *Academic:* Secondary school record: Very Important. Class rank: Important. Letters of recommendation: Important. Standardized test scores: Very Important. Essay: Important. *Nonacademic:* Interview: Considered. Extracurricular activities: Important. Talent/ability: Very Important. Character/personal qualities: Important. Alumni/ae relationship: Considered. Geographical residence: Considered. State residency: Considered. Religious affiliation/commitment: Not Considered. Minority status: Not Considered. Volunteer work: Important. Work experience: Important. **Other schools with the greatest overlap in applicants:** Appalachian State University; University of North Carolina–Asheville; University of North Carolina–Chapel Hill; University of North Carolina–Charlotte; University of North Carolina–Greensboro. **Admissions statistics for the fall 2009 entering class:** Total applicants: 12,325. Total accepted: 5,441. Freshmen enrolled: 1,555; 8% were from out of state. Accepted through early-decision or early-action plans: 51%. Overall acceptance rate: 44%. Non-early acceptance rate: 50%. **Size of waiting list:** 36 applicants; enrolled from waiting list: 2. **Credentials of fall 2009 freshmen:** 15% ranked in the top 10 percent of their high school class; 43% were in the top 25 percent; 75% were in the top half. (Proportion submitting class standing: 93%.) **Average high school grade point average:** 3.5. **First-year students who submitted SAT scores:** 97%. Scores (25/75 percentile): Critical Reading: 460-560, Math: 480-560, Combined: 940-1120. **First-year students submitting ACT scores:** 16%. Scores (25/75 percentile): English: 18-24, Math: 17-23, Composite: 18-23.

ACADEMICS

Year founded: 1889. **Academic calendar:** Semester. **Degrees offered:** bachelor's, post-bachelor's certificate, master's, post-master's certificate, doctorate. **Major fields of study:** biological and biomedical sciences; business, management, marketing, and related support services; communication, journalism, and related programs; computer and information sciences and support services; education; engineering technologies/technicians; English language and literature/letters; foreign languages, literatures, and linguistics; health professions and related clinical sciences; history; liberal arts and sciences studies, and humanities; mathematics and statistics; natural resources and conservation; parks, recreation, leisure, and fitness studies; philosophy and religious studies; physical sciences; psychology; public administration and social service professions; security and protective services; social sciences; visual and performing arts. **Areas of required coursework:** arts/fine arts, humanities, computer literacy, mathematics, English (including composition), sciences (biological or physical), history, social science, other. **Pre-professional programs:** pre-law, pre-dentistry, pre-medicine, pre-veterinary science, pre-optometry, pre-pharmacy, other. **Special academic programs (% participation):** cooperative (work-study plan) program (13.7%), distance learning (22.6%), double major (10.8%), dual enrollment, honors program (21.7%), independent study, internships, student-designed major, study abroad, teacher certificate program (13%). **Teacher certification offered in:** early childhood, special education, elementary, middle/junior high, secondary, bilingual/bicultural. **Cooperative education programs:** art, business, computer science, education, engineering, health professions, humanities, natural science, social/behavioral science, technologies. **Faculty and instruction (2009-2010):** Total instructional faculty: 473 full-time, 166 part-time (52% men; 48% women; 5% minorities). Full-time faculty with Ph.D. or other terminal degree: 78%. Student/faculty ratio: 15/1. Classes of fewer than 20 students: 33%; of 20 to 49 students: 64%; of 50 or more students: 3%. **Advanced Placement and International Baccalaureate credit:** AP tests may be used for: Credit only. Scores accepted: 3, 4, 5. **Freshmen returning for sophomore year:** 72%. **Graduation rates:** Four-year: 26%; five-year: 45%; six-year: 49%.

COSTS AND FINANCIAL AID

Financial aid office: (828) 227-7290. **Expenses (2010-2011):** Tuition and fees 2010-2011: $4,551 in state, $14,148 out of state; room/board: $6,769. **Financial aid:** Priority filing date for institution's financial aid form: March 15. In 2009-2010, 76% of undergraduates applied for financial aid. Of those, 58% were determined to have financial need; 39% had their need fully met. Average financial aid package (proportion receiving): $8,681 (56%). Average amount of gift aid, such as scholarships or grants (proportion receiving): $6,722 (53%). Average amount of self-help aid, such as work study or loans (proportion receiving): $3,539 (37%). Average need-based loan (excluding PLUS or other private loans): $4,390. Among students who received need-based aid, the average percentage of need met: 81%. Among students who received aid based on merit, the average award (and the proportion receiving): $1,799 (5%). The average athletic scholarship (and the proportion receiving): $9,557 (4%). Average amount of debt of borrowers graduating in 2009: $11,609. Proportion who borrowed: 51%.

CAMPUS LIFE AND EXTRACURRICULAR ACTIVITIES

Campus housing available (% using): coed dorms (81%), women's dorms (10%), men's dorms (6%), sorority housing (1%), fraternity housing (1%), apartments for married students (1%), special housing for disabled students (0%). Students who live in college-owned, operated, or affiliated housing: 48%. **Student employment:** During the 2009-2010 academic year, 9% of undergraduates worked on campus. Average per-year earnings: $4,080. **Clubs and organizations:** Number of student organizations: 103. Activities include: campus ministries, choral groups, concert band, dance, drama/theater, international student organization, jazz band, literary magazine, marching band, model UN, music ensembles, musical theater, pep band, radio station, student government, student newspaper, student film society, television station. Number of fraternities: 11; sororities: 8. Proportion of men in fraternities: 8%; of women in sororities: 6%. Average proportion of students who stay on campus on weekends: 50%. **Sports program (2009-2010):** Member of NCAA I. *Men's intercollegiate varsity sports:* baseball, basketball, cross country, football, golf, track and field (indoor), track and field (outdoor). *Women's intercollegiate varsity sports:* basketball, cross country, golf, soccer, softball, tennis, track and field (indoor), track and field (outdoor), volleyball.

SERVICES AND FACILITIES

Basic services: nonremedial tutoring, women's center, placement service, day care, health service, health insurance. **Counseling services:** minority student, career, military, personal, veteran student, academic, psychological, birth control, religious. **For learning-disabled students:** School does not offer a structured program with separate admission and additional fees. Services include: reading machines, tape recorders, diagnostic testing service, note-taking services, oral tests, learning center, readers, extended time for tests, tutors, priority registration, priority seating, texts on tape, other testing accommodations. **Library:** Number of titles: 625,730; number of current serial subscriptions: 36,372. **Information technology resources:** Students are required to lease or own a computer. Number of campus computers available to all students: 103. School has a wireless network. Approximate number of users that can be accommodated: 2,500. Proportion of college-owned housing units wired for high-speed internet access: 100%. **Campus safety:** Security services offered: 24-hour foot-and-vehicle patrols, late-night transport/escort service, 24-hour emergency telephones, lighted pathways/sidewalks, controlled dormitory access (key, security card, etc).

TRANSFER AND INTERNATIONAL STUDENTS

Transfer students: May apply for admission for the following academic terms: Fall, Spring, Summer. Applicants need a minimum number of credits to apply. For fall 2009: Transfer applications received: 1,718. Transfer applicants offered admission: 1,209. Transfer applicants enrolled: 773. **International students:** Number of foreign undergraduates: 216 (3% of student body). Number of countries represented: 32. Minimum TOEFL score required: 550 (paper); 213 (computer).

Wingate University

- **Address:** PO Box 159, Wingate, NC 28174
- **Website:** http://www.wingate.edu
- **Private; Religious affiliation:** Baptist
- **Enrollment:** 1,372 full-time; 45 part-time

KEY STATS
✔ **U.S News College Ranking:** second tier, National Liberal Arts Colleges
✔ **SAT Score (25th/75th percentile):** 900-1120
✔ **Tuition:** 2010-2011: $21,140

Selectivity: Selective	**Room/board:** $8,350
Acceptance rate: 52%	**Average debt:** $27,616
Student/faculty ratio: 13/1	**Proportion who borrowed:** 75%

UNDERGRADUATE STUDENT BODY STATS

2009-2010 enrollment: 1,372 full-time; 45 part-time. Men: 46%; women: 54%. **Ethnic makeup:** African American: 10%; American-Indian: 1%; Asian American: 2%; Hispanic: 3%; White: 79%; International: 4%.

ADMISSIONS FACTS AND FIGURES

Phone: (800) 755-5550. **Email:** admit@wingate.edu. **Website:** http://www.wingate.edu. **Application deadlines for fall 2011:** Regular decision: Rolling. Early decision: Not offered. Early action: Not offered. Admission can be deferred. **Application fee:** $30. **To apply online, go to:** http://www.wingate.edu/FutureStudents/applynow.asp. **Admissions requirements/recommendations:** High school units required (recommended): English: (4); Mathematics: (3); Science: (2); Foreign language: (2); Social studies: (2); Total units: (13). Tests: The college uses SAT or ACT scores in admissions decisions. Either SAT or ACT required. For admission to the fall 2011 entering class, the school will accept: ACT with or without writing accepted. Campus visit: Recommended. Admissions interview: Recommended. Off-campus interview: May be arranged. **Factors that count in admissions decisions:** *Academic:* Secondary school record: Very Important. Class rank: Very Important. Letters of recommendation: Important. Standardized test scores: Very Important. Essay: Not Considered. *Nonacademic:* Interview: Not Considered. Extracurricular activities: Considered. Talent/ability: Considered. Character/personal qualities: Considered. Alumni/ae relationship: Not Considered. Geographical residence: Not Considered. State residency: Not Considered. Religious affiliation/commitment: Not Considered. Minority status: Not Considered. Volunteer work: Not Considered. Work experience: Not Considered. **Other schools with the greatest overlap in applicants:** Campbell University; Elon University; Gardner-Webb University; High Point University; University of North Carolina–Charlotte. **Admissions statistics for the fall 2009 entering class:** Total applicants: 4,840. Total accepted: 2,519. Freshmen enrolled: 375; 20% were from out of state. Overall acceptance rate: 52%. **Credentials of fall 2009 freshmen:** 23% ranked in the top 10 percent of their high school class; 54% were in the top 25 percent; 88% were in the top half. (Proportion submitting class standing: 85%.) **Average high school grade point average:** 3.6. **First-year students who submitted SAT scores:** 92%. Scores (25/75 percentile): Critical Reading: 440-550, Math: 460-570, Combined: 900-1120. **First-year students submitting ACT scores:** 17%. Scores (25/75 percentile): English: N/A, Math: N/A, Composite: 19-25.

ACADEMICS

Year founded: 1896. **Academic calendar:** Semester. **Degrees offered:** bachelor's, master's. **Most popular majors:** 19% communication studies/speech communication and rhetoric, 18% marketing/marketing management, 9% biology/biological sciences, 7% education, 6% sport and fitness administration/management. **Major fields of study:** area, ethnic, cultural, and gender studies; biological and biomedical sciences; business, management, marketing, and related support services; communication, journalism, and related programs; computer and information sciences and support services; education; English language and literature/letters; foreign languages, literatures, and linguistics; health professions and related clinical sciences; liberal arts and sciences studies, and humanities; mathematics and statistics; multi/interdisciplinary studies; parks, recreation, leisure, and fitness studies; philosophy and religious studies; physical sciences; psychology; public administration and social service professions; social sciences; visual and performing arts. **Areas of required coursework:** arts/fine arts, humanities, computer literacy, mathematics, English (including composition), philosophy, foreign languages, sciences (biological or physical), history, social science, other. **Pre-professional programs:** pre-law, pre-dentistry, pre-medicine, pre-veterinary science, pre-pharmacy, other. **Special academic programs (% participation):** cross-registration, double major (2%), honors program (15%), independent study (7%), internships (50%), study abroad (49%), teacher certificate program. **Teacher certification offered in:** elementary, middle/junior high, secondary. **Reserve Officers Training Corps (ROTC): Army** ROTC: Offered at cooperating institution (University of North Carolina–Charlotte); Air Force ROTC: Offered at cooperating institution (University of North Carolina–Charlotte). **Faculty and instruction (2009-2010):** Total instructional faculty: 119 full-time, 73 part-time (54% men; 46% women; 4% minorities). Full-time faculty with Ph.D. or other terminal degree: 93%. Student/faculty ratio: 13/1. Classes of fewer than 20 students: 59%; of 20 to 49 students: 41%. **Advanced Placement and International Baccalaureate credit:** AP tests may be used for: Credit and/or placement. Scores accepted: 3, 4, 5. International Baccalaureate exams may be used for: Credit only. **Freshmen returning for sophomore year:** 70%. **Graduation rates:** Four-year: 42%; five-year: 51%; six-year: 54%. **Graduate study:** 15% of students pursue further study immediately upon graduation; 20% within one year; 25% within five years. Fields in which graduates pursue further study: Master of Business Administration (MBA), 5%; law, 1%; medicine, 1%; theology (or the seminary), 5%; education, 5%; arts and sciences, 5%.

COSTS AND FINANCIAL AID

Financial aid office: (704) 233-8209. **Expenses (2010-2011):** Tuition and fees 2010-2011: $21,140; room/board: $8,350. Estimated books and supplies: $1,100; transportation: $400; personal expenses: $800. **Financial aid:** Priority filing date for institution's financial aid form: May 1. In 2009-2010, 82% of undergraduates applied for financial aid. Of those, 72% were determined to have financial need; 18% had their need fully met. Average financial aid package (proportion receiving): $17,956 (72%). Average amount of gift aid, such as scholarships or grants (proportion receiving): $7,832 (57%). Average amount of self-help aid, such as work study or loans (proportion receiving): $5,518 (54%). Average need-based loan (excluding PLUS or other private loans): $4,194. Among students who received need-based aid, the average percentage of need met: 79%. Among students who received aid based on merit, the average award (and the proportion receiving): $7,895 (27%). The average athletic scholarship (and the proportion receiving): $7,382 (22%). Average amount of debt of borrowers graduating in 2009: $27,616. Proportion who borrowed: 75%.

CAMPUS LIFE AND EXTRACURRICULAR ACTIVITIES

Campus housing available (% using): coed dorms (13%), women's dorms (13%), men's dorms (16%), sorority housing (3%), fraternity housing (3%), apartment for single students (52%). Students who live in college-owned, operated, or affiliated housing: 80%. **Student employment:** During the 2009-2010 academic year, 25% of undergraduates worked on campus. Average per-year earnings: $700. **Clubs and organizations:** Number of student organizations: 60. Activities include: campus ministries, choral groups, drama/theater, international student organization, jazz band, literary magazine, music ensembles, musical theater, pep band, student government, student newspaper, television station, yearbook. Number of fraternities: 4; sororities: 4. Proportion of men in fraternities: 12%; of women in sororities: 21%. Average proportion of students who stay on campus on weekends: 60%. **Sports program (2009-2010):** Member of NCAA II. *Men's intercollegiate varsity sports:* baseball, basketball, cross country, football, golf, lacrosse, soccer, swimming, tennis. *Women's intercollegiate varsity sports:* basketball, golf, soccer, softball, swimming, tennis, volleyball.

SERVICES AND FACILITIES

Basic services: nonremedial tutoring, health service, other. **Remedial assistance:** study skills. **Counseling services:** minority student, career, personal, academic, psychological, religious. **For learning-disabled students:** School does not offer a structured program with separate admission and additional fees. Services include: note-taking services, extended time for tests, tutors, other. **Library:** Number of titles: 109,279; number of current serial subscriptions: 151. **Information technology resources:** Students are not required to lease or own a computer. Number of campus computers available to

all students: 134. School has a wireless network. Approximate number of users that can be accommodated: 180. Proportion of college-owned housing units wired for high-speed internet access: 100%. **Campus safety:** Security services offered: 24-hour foot-and-vehicle patrols, 24-hour emergency telephones, lighted pathways/sidewalks, controlled dormitory access (key, security card, etc).

TRANSFER AND INTERNATIONAL STUDENTS

Transfer students: May apply for admission for the following academic terms: Fall, Spring, Summer. Applicants do not need a minimum number of credits to apply. For fall 2009: Transfer applications received: 224. Transfer applicants offered admission: 96. Transfer applicants enrolled: 64. **International students:** Number of foreign undergraduates: 59 (4% of student body). Number of countries represented: 13. Minimum TOEFL score required: 550 (paper); 213 (computer).

Winston-Salem State University

- **Address:** 601 Martin Luther King Jr. Drive, Winston-Salem, NC 27110
- **Website:** http://www.wssu.edu
- **Public**
- **Enrollment:** 5,327 full-time; 633 part-time

KEY STATS
✔ **U.S News College Ranking:** 24, Regional Colleges (South)
✔ **SAT Score (25th/75th percentile):** 820-950
✔ **Tuition:** 2009-2010: $3,522 in state, $12,508 out of state
  Selectivity: Less selective   **Room/board:** $6,924
  Acceptance rate: 57%   **Average debt:** $12,560
  Student/faculty ratio: 18/1   **Proportion who borrowed:** 92%

UNDERGRADUATE STUDENT BODY STATS

2009-2010 enrollment: 5,327 full-time; 633 part-time. Men: 30%; women: 70%. **Ethnic makeup:** African American: 81%; Asian American: 1%; Hispanic: 1%; White: 16%; International: 1%.

ADMISSIONS FACTS AND FIGURES

Phone: (336) 750-2070. **Email:** admissions@wssu.edu. **Website:** http://www.wssu.edu. **Application deadlines for fall 2011:** Regular decision: March 15; decision sent by April 1. Early decision: Not offered. Early action: Send application by: December 1; Decision sent by: N/A. Admission can be deferred. **Application fee:** $40. **To apply online, go to:** http://www.wssu.edu/admiss.asp. **Admissions requirements/recommendations:** High school units required (recommended): English: 4; Mathematics: 4; Science: 3; Foreign language: 2; Social studies: 1; History: 1; Total units: 15. Tests: The college uses SAT or ACT scores in admissions decisions. Either SAT or ACT required. For admission to the fall 2011 entering class, the school will accept: ACT with writing required. Campus visit: Neither required nor recommended. Admissions interview: Neither required nor recommended. Off-campus interview: Not available. **Factors that count in admissions decisions:** *Academic:* Secondary school record: Very Important. Class rank: Important. Letters of recommendation: Considered. Standardized test scores: Very Important. Essay: Considered. *Nonacademic:* Interview: Considered. Extracurricular activities: Important. Talent/ability: Considered. Character/personal qualities: Considered. Alumni/ae relationship: Not Considered. Geographical residence: Not Considered. State residency: Not Considered. Religious affiliation/commitment: Not Considered. Minority status: Not Considered. Volunteer work: Not Considered. Work experience: Not Considered. **Admissions statistics for the fall 2009 entering class:** Total applicants: 3,490. Total accepted: 1,979. Freshmen enrolled: 795; 12% were from out of state. Overall acceptance rate: 57%. Non-early acceptance rate: 57%. **Credentials of fall 2009 freshmen:** 2% ranked in the top 10 percent of their high school class; 24% were in the top 25 percent; 65% were in the top half. (Proportion submitting class standing: 92%.) **Average high school grade point average:** 3.0. First-year students who submitted SAT scores: 93%. Scores (25/75 percentile): Critical Reading: 410-470, Math: 410-480, Combined: 820-950.

ACADEMICS

Year founded: 1892. **Academic calendar:** Semester. **Degrees offered:** bachelor's, post-bachelor's certificate, master's. **Most popular majors:** 45% health professions and related clinical sciences, 14% business, management, marketing, and related support services, 6% parks, recreation, leisure, and fitness studies, 6% psychology, 6% social sciences. **Major fields of study:** area, ethnic, cultural, and gender studies; biological and biomedical sciences; business, management, marketing, and related support services; communication, journalism, and related programs; computer and information sciences and support services; education; English language and literature/letters; foreign languages, literatures, and linguistics; health professions and related clinical sciences; history; liberal arts and sciences studies, and humanities; mathematics and statistics; multi/interdisciplinary studies; parks, recreation, leisure, and fitness studies; public administration and social service professions; security and protective services; social sciences; visual and performing arts. **Areas of required coursework:** arts/fine arts, humanities, computer literacy, mathematics, English (including composition), sciences (biological or physical), history, social science. **Preprofessional programs:** pre-dentistry, pre-medicine, pre-pharmacy. **Special academic programs (% participation):** accelerated program (5%), cooperative (work-study plan) program, distance learning (10%), double major (1%), dual enrollment, English as a Second Language (ESL), honors program, independent study, internships, study abroad, teacher certificate program (1%), weekend college. **Teacher certification offered in:** early childhood, special education, elementary, middle/junior high, secondary, bilingual/bicultural. **Cooperative education programs:** business. **Reserve Officers Training Corps (ROTC):** Army ROTC: Offered on campus. **Faculty and instruction (2009-2010):** Total instructional faculty: 334 full-time, 2 part-time (45% men; 55% women; 60% minorities). Full-time faculty with Ph.D. or other terminal degree: 72%. Student/faculty ratio: 18/1. Classes of fewer than 20 students: 50%; of 20 to 49 students: 49%; of 50 or more students: 1%. **Advanced Placement and International Baccalaureate credit:** AP tests may be used for: Placement only. Scores accepted: 3, 4, 5. **Freshmen returning for sophomore year:** 73%. **Graduation rates:** Four-year: 14%; five-year: 30%; six-year: 41%. **Graduate study:** 10% of students pursue further study immediately upon graduation; 15% within one year; 20% within five years. Fields in which graduates pursue further study: Master of Business Administration (MBA), 1%; medicine, 1%; education, 1%; arts and sciences, 1%.

COSTS AND FINANCIAL AID
Financial aid office: (336) 750-3280. **Expenses (2009-2010):** Tuition and fees 2009-2010: $3,522 in state, $12,508 out of state; room/board: $6,924. Estimated books and supplies: $2,000. **Financial aid:** Priority filing date for institution's financial aid form: April 1; deadline: May 1. In 2009-2010, 91% of undergraduates applied for financial aid. Of those, 78% were determined to have financial need; 45% had their need fully met. Average financial aid package (proportion receiving): $9,577 (78%). Average amount of gift aid, such as scholarships or grants (proportion receiving): $6,808 (70%). Average amount of self-help aid, such as work study or loans (proportion receiving): $3,898 (67%). Average need-based loan (excluding PLUS or other private loans): $3,827. Among students who received need-based aid, the average percentage of need met: 73%. Among students who received aid based on merit, the average award (and the proportion receiving): $6,146

(2%). The average athletic scholarship (and the proportion receiving): $9,130 (1%). Average amount of debt of borrowers graduating in 2009: $12,560. Proportion who borrowed: 92%.

CAMPUS LIFE AND EXTRACURRICULAR ACTIVITIES
Campus housing available (% using): coed dorms (34%), women's dorms (34%), men's dorms (32%). Students who live in college-owned, operated, or affiliated housing: 36%. **Student employment:** During the 2009-2010 academic year, 8% of undergraduates worked on campus. **Clubs and organizations:** Number of student organizations: 35. Activities include: choral groups, concert band, drama/theater, international student organization, jazz band, marching band, model UN, music ensembles, pep band, radio station, student government, student newspaper, yearbook. Number of fraternities: 4; sororities: 4. Proportion of men in fraternities: 5%; of women in sororities: 5%. Average proportion of students who stay on campus on weekends: 40%. **Sports program (2009-2010):** Member of NCAA I. *Men's intercollegiate varsity sports:* basketball, cross country, football, golf, tennis, track and field (outdoor). *Women's intercollegiate varsity sports:* basketball, cross country, softball, tennis, track and field (outdoor), volleyball.

SERVICES AND FACILITIES
Basic services: nonremedial tutoring, health service. **Remedial assistance:** reading, math, writing, study skills. **Counseling services:** career, military, personal, veteran student, academic, psychological, birth control. **For learning-disabled students:** School does not offer a structured program with separate admission and additional fees. Total undergraduates in learning-disabled program or receiving services: 31. Services include: remedial math, remedial English, reading machines, remedial reading, tape recorders, untimed tests, note-taking services, oral tests, learning center, readers, extended time for tests, tutors. **Library:** Number of titles: 235,668; number of current serial subscriptions: 1,778. **Information technology resources:** Students are not required to lease or own a computer. Number of campus computers available to all students: 500. School has a wireless network. Approximate number of users that can be accommodated: 5,000. Proportion of college-owned housing units wired for high-speed internet access: 100%. **Campus safety:** Security services offered: 24-hour foot-and-vehicle patrols, late-night transport/escort service, 24-hour emergency telephones, lighted pathways/sidewalks, controlled dormitory access (key, security card, etc).

TRANSFER AND INTERNATIONAL STUDENTS
Transfer students: May apply for admission for the following academic terms: Fall, Spring, Summer. Applicants do not need a minimum number of credits to apply. For fall 2009: Transfer applications received: 1,007. Transfer applicants offered admission: 801. Transfer applicants enrolled: 669. **International students:** Number of foreign undergraduates: 72 (1% of student body). Minimum TOEFL score required: 500 (paper); 200 (computer).

North Dakota

Dickinson State University

- **Address:** 291 Campus Drive, Dickinson, ND 58601
- **Website:** http://www.dickinsonstate.com
- **Public**
- **Enrollment:** 1,797 full-time; 970 part-time

KEY STATS

✔ **U.S News College Ranking:** 66, Regional Colleges (Midwest)
✔ **ACT Score (25th/75th percentile):** 18-23
✔ **Tuition:** 2010-2011: $5,395 in state, $12,585 out of state

Selectivity: Selective	**Room/board:** $4,718
Acceptance rate: 90%	**Average debt:** $18,852
Student/faculty ratio: 15/1	**Proportion who borrowed:** 78%

UNDERGRADUATE STUDENT BODY STATS

2009-2010 enrollment: 1,797 full-time; 970 part-time. Men: 38%; women: 62%. **Ethnic makeup:** African American: 1%; American-Indian: 2%; Asian American: 1%; Hispanic: 2%; White: 80%; International: 14%. **Religious preference:** Roman Catholic: 50%; Protestant: 40%; Muslim: 2%; Unknown: 8%.

ADMISSIONS FACTS AND FIGURES

Phone: (701) 483-2175. **Email:** dsu.hawks@dsu.nodak.edu. **Website:** http://www.dickinsonstate.com. **Application deadlines for fall 2011:** Regular decision: Rolling. Early decision: Not offered. Early action: Not offered. Admission can be deferred. **Application fee:** $35. **To apply online, go to:** http://www.dickinsonstate.com/admissions.asp#apply. **Admissions requirements/recommendations:** High school units required (recommended): English: 4 (4); Mathematics: 3 (3); Science: 3 (3); Social studies: 3 (3); Total units: 13 (13). Tests: The college uses SAT or ACT scores in admissions decisions. Either SAT or ACT required. For admission to the fall 2011 entering class, the school will accept: ACT with writing recommended. Campus visit: Recommended. Admissions interview: Recommended. Off-campus interview: May be arranged. **Factors that count in admissions decisions: *Academic:*** Secondary school record: Important. Class rank: Considered. Letters of recommendation: Not Considered. Standardized test scores: Very Important. Essay: Not Considered. ***Nonacademic:*** Interview: Not Considered. Extracurricular activities: Not Considered. Talent/ability: Not Considered. Character/personal qualities: Not Considered. Alumni/ae relationship: Not Considered. Geographical residence: Not Considered. State residency: Not Considered. Religious affiliation/commitment: Not Considered. Minority status: Not Considered. Volunteer work: Not Considered. Work experience: Not Considered. **Other schools with the greatest overlap in applicants:** Black Hills State University; Dakota State University; Mayville State University; Minot State University; Montana State University–Billings. **Admissions statistics for the fall 2009 entering class:** Total applicants: 639. Total accepted: 574. Freshmen enrolled: 340; 39% were from out of state. Overall acceptance rate: 90%. **First-year students who submitted SAT scores:** 5%. Scores (25/75 percentile): Critical Reading: 358-542, Math: 426-564, Combined: 784-1106. **First-year students submitting ACT scores:** 66%. Scores (25/75 percentile): English: 15-26, Math: 16-20, Composite: 18-23.

ACADEMICS

Year founded: 1918. **Academic calendar:** Semester. **Degrees offered:** certificate, associate, bachelor's. **Most popular majors:** 37% business, management, marketing, and related support services, 18% education, 9% multi/interdisciplinary studies, 5% biological and biomedical sciences, 5% health professions and related clinical sciences. **Major fields of study:** agriculture, agriculture operations, and related sciences; biological and biomedical sciences; business, management, marketing, and related support services; communication, journalism, and related programs; computer and information sciences and support services; education; English language and literature/letters; foreign languages, literatures, and linguistics; health professions and related clinical sciences; history; liberal arts and sciences studies, and humanities; mathematics and statistics; multi/interdisciplinary studies; physical sciences; psychology; social sciences; visual and performing arts. **Areas of required coursework:** arts/fine arts, humanities, computer literacy, mathematics, English (including composition), sciences (biological or physical), history, social science, other. **Pre-professional programs:** pre-law, pre-dentistry, pre-medicine, pre-veterinary science, pre-optometry, pre-pharmacy. **Special academic programs (% participation):** accelerated program (10%), cooperative (work-study plan) program (20%), cross-registration (10%), distance learning (40%), double major (3%), dual enrollment (7%), English as a Second Language (ESL) (8%), honors program (5%), independent study (40%), internships (16%), liberal arts/career combination (40%), student-designed major (1%), study abroad (5%), teacher certificate program (30%), other. **Teacher certification offered in:** early childhood, elementary, vo-tech, middle/junior high, secondary. **Cooperative education programs:** agriculture, business, computer science, health professions, natural science, social/behavioral science. **Faculty and instruction (2009-2010):** Total instructional faculty: 96 full-time, 265 part-time (45% men; 55% women; 3% minorities). Full-time faculty with Ph.D. or other terminal degree: 50%. Student/faculty ratio: 15/1. Classes of fewer than 20 students: 58%; of 20 to 49 students: 40%; of 50 or more students: 2%. **Freshmen returning for sophomore year:** 61%. **Graduation rates:** Four-year: 11%; five-year: 26%; six-year: 31%. **Graduate study:** 14% of students pursue further study immediately upon graduation; 4% within one year; 1% within five years. Fields in which graduates pursue further study: Master of Business Administration (MBA), 23%; law, 3%; medicine, 2%; dentistry, 1%; education, 10%; arts and sciences, 25%.

COSTS AND FINANCIAL AID

Financial aid office: (701) 483-2371. **Expenses (2010-2011):** Tuition and fees 2010-2011: $5,395 in state, $12,585 out of state; room/board: $4,718. Estimated books and supplies: $1,000; transportation: $1,650; personal expenses: $1,650. **Financial aid:** Priority filing date for institution's financial aid form: March 15. In 2009-2010, 65% of undergraduates applied for financial aid. Of those, 48% were determined to have financial need; 96% had their need fully met. Average financial aid package (proportion receiving): $7,914 (46%). Average amount of gift aid, such as scholarships or grants (proportion receiving): $4,257 (40%). Average amount of self-help aid, such as work study or loans (proportion receiving): $3,725 (39%). Average need-based loan (excluding PLUS or other private loans): $3,726. Among students who received need-based aid, the average percentage of need met: 32%. Among students who received aid based on merit, the average award (and the proportion receiving): $1,290 (30%). The average athletic scholarship (and the proportion receiving): $1,356 (9%). Average amount of debt of borrowers graduating in 2009: $18,852. Proportion who borrowed: 78%.

CAMPUS LIFE AND EXTRACURRICULAR ACTIVITIES

Campus housing available (% using): coed dorms (29%), women's dorms (26%), men's dorms (18%), apartments for married students (1%), apartment for single students (25%), other housing options (1%). Students who live in college-owned, operated, or affiliated housing: 30%. **Student employment:** During the 2009-2010 academic year, 17% of undergraduates worked on campus. Average per-year earnings: $1,800. **Clubs and organizations:** Number of student organizations: 55. Activities include: choral groups, concert band, dance, drama/theater, jazz band, literary magazine, marching band, music ensembles, musical theater, pep band, student government, student film society. Number of fraternities: 0; sororities: 0. Average proportion of students who stay on campus on weekends: 60%. **Sports program (2009-2010):** Member of NAIA. ***Men's intercollegiate varsity sports:*** baseball, basketball, cross country, football, golf, track and field (indoor), track and field (outdoor), wrestling. ***Women's intercollegiate varsity sports:*** basketball, cross country, golf, softball, track and field (indoor), track and field (outdoor), volleyball.

SERVICES AND FACILITIES

Basic services: nonremedial tutoring, placement service, health service, health insurance. **Remedial assistance:** math, writing, study skills, other. **Counseling services:** minority student, career, military, personal, veteran student, academic, older student. **For learning-disabled students:** School does not offer a structured program with separate admission and additional fees. Services include: remedial math, remedial English, tape recorders, untimed tests, note-taking services, oral tests, learning center, readers, extended time for tests, tutors, priority registration, priority seating, texts on tape, other testing accommodations, other. **Library:** Number of titles: 168,083; number of current serial subscriptions: 437. **Information technology resources:** Students are not required to lease or own a computer. Number of campus computers available to all students: 247. School has a wireless network. Approximate number of users that can be accommodated: 300. Proportion of college-owned housing units wired for high-speed internet access: 100%. **Campus safety:** Security services offered: 24-hour foot-and-vehicle patrols, late-night transport/escort service, lighted pathways/sidewalks, controlled dormitory access (key, security card, etc).

TRANSFER AND INTERNATIONAL STUDENTS
Transfer students: May apply for admission for the following academic terms: Fall, Spring, Summer. Applicants need a minimum number of credits to apply. For fall 2009: Transfer applications received: 439. Transfer applicants offered admission: 367. Transfer applicants enrolled: 284. **International students:** Number of foreign undergraduates: 393 (14% of student body). Number of countries represented: 31. Minimum TOEFL score required: 525 (paper); 197 (computer).

Jamestown College

- **Address:** 6086 College Lane, Jamestown, ND 58405
- **Website:** http://www.jc.edu
- **Private; Religious affiliation:** Presbyterian
- **Enrollment:** 933 full-time; 77 part-time

KEY STATS
✔ **U.S News College Ranking:** 41, Regional Colleges (Midwest)
✔ **ACT Score (25th/75th percentile):** 20-25
✔ **Tuition:** 2010-2011: $13,870

Selectivity: Selective	**Room/board:** $5,536
Acceptance rate: 67%	**Average debt:** $25,717
Student/faculty ratio: 15/1	**Proportion who borrowed:** 84%

UNDERGRADUATE STUDENT BODY STATS
2009-2010 enrollment: 933 full-time; 77 part-time. Men: 46%; women: 54%. **Ethnic makeup:** African American: 2%; American-Indian: 1%; Asian American: 2%; Hispanic: 2%; White: 90%; International: 4%. **Religious preference:** Roman Catholic: 21%; Protestant: 51%; Unknown: 22%; Presbyterian: 4%; Other: 2%.

ADMISSIONS FACTS AND FIGURES
Phone: (701) 252-3467. **Email:** admissions@jc.edu. **Website:** http://www.jc.edu. **Application deadlines for fall 2011:** Regular decision: Rolling. Early decision: Not offered. Early action: Not offered. Admission can be deferred. **Application fee:** $35. **To apply online, go to:** http://www.jc.edu/admissions/ap.php. **Admissions requirements/recommendations:** High school units required (recommended): English: 4 (4); Mathematics: 3 (3); Science: 4 (4); Foreign language: 0 (2); Social studies: 3 (3); Total units: 14 (16). **Tests:** The college uses SAT or ACT scores in admissions decisions. Either SAT or ACT required. For admission to the fall 2011 entering class, the school will accept: ACT with or without writing accepted. Campus visit: Recommended. Admissions interview: Neither required nor recommended. Off-campus interview: May be arranged. **Factors that count in admissions decisions:** *Academic:* Secondary school record: Important. Class rank: Not Considered. Letters of recommendation: Important. Standardized test scores: Important. Essay: Not Considered. *Nonacademic:* Interview: Considered. Extracurricular activities: Considered. Talent/ability: Considered. Character/personal qualities: Considered. Alumni/ae relationship: Considered. Geographical residence: Not Considered. State residency: Not Considered. Religious affiliation/commitment: Not Considered. Minority status: Not Considered. Volunteer work: Considered. Work experience: Considered. **Other schools with the greatest overlap in applicants:** Dickinson State University; North Dakota State University; University of Mary; University of North Dakota; Valley City State University. **Admissions statistics for the fall 2009 entering class:** Total applicants: 898. Total accepted: 602. Freshmen enrolled: 239; 56% were from out of state. Overall acceptance rate: 67%. **Credentials of fall 2009 freshmen:** 13% ranked

in the top 10 percent of their high school class; 37% were in the top 25 percent; 73% were in the top half. (Proportion submitting class standing: 84%.) Average high school grade point average: 3.3. **First-year students who submitted SAT scores:** 11%. Scores (25/75 percentile): Critical Reading: 400-520, Math: 400-570, Combined: 800-1090. **First-year students submitting ACT scores:** 89%. Scores (25/75 percentile): English: 18-25, Math: 19-25, Composite: 20-25.

ACADEMICS
Year founded: 1884. **Academic calendar:** Semester. **Degrees offered:** bachelor's, master's. **Most popular majors:** 23% nursing, 12% business administration and management, 9% elementary education and teaching, 5% biology/biological sciences, 5% criminal justice/police science. **Major fields of study:** biological and biomedical sciences; business, management, marketing, and related support services; communication, journalism, and related programs; computer and information sciences and support services; education; English language and literature/letters; foreign languages, literatures, and linguistics; health professions and related clinical sciences; history; mathematics and statistics; philosophy and religious studies; physical sciences; psychology; security and protective services; social sciences; visual and performing arts. **Areas of required coursework:** arts/fine arts, humanities, computer literacy, mathematics, English (including composition), philosophy, foreign languages, sciences (biological or physical), history, social science. **Pre-professional programs:** pre-dentistry, pre-medicine, pre-veterinary science, pre-optometry, pre-pharmacy. **Special academic programs (% participation):** double major (22%), dual enrollment (5%), exchange student program (domestic) (1%), honors program (1%), independent study (60%), internships (42%), student-designed major (1%), study abroad (1%), teacher certificate program (15%). **Teacher certification offered in:** early childhood, elementary, middle/junior high, secondary. **Cooperative education programs:** art, business, computer science, education, health professions, humanities, natural science, social/behavioral science. **Faculty and instruction (2009-2010):** Total instructional faculty: 57 full-time, 25 part-time (55% men; 45% women; 5% minorities). Full-time faculty with Ph.D. or other terminal degree: 51%. Student/faculty ratio: 15/1. Classes of fewer than 20 students: 55%; of 20 to 49 students: 43%; of 50 or more students: 2%. **Advanced Placement and International Baccalaureate credit:** AP tests may be used for: Credit and/or placement. Scores accepted: 3. International Baccalaureate exams may be used for: Credit and/or placement. **Freshmen returning for sophomore year:** 74%. **Graduation rates:** Four-year: 31%; five-year: 50%; six-year: 49%. **Graduate study:** 12% of students pursue further study immediately upon graduation; 12% within one year; 28% within five years. Fields in which graduates pursue further study: Master of Business Administration (MBA), 2%; law, 2%; medicine, 1%; dentistry, 1%; education, 4%; arts and sciences, 2%.

COSTS AND FINANCIAL AID
Financial aid office: (701) 252-3467. **Expenses (2010-2011):** Tuition and fees 2010-2011: $13,870; room/board: $5,536. Estimated books and supplies: $1,000; transportation: $1,500; personal expenses: $1,300. **Financial aid:** Priority filing date for institution's financial aid form: March 15. In 2009-2010, 84% of undergraduates applied for financial aid. Of those, 67% were determined to have financial need; 23% had their need fully met. Average financial aid package (proportion receiving): $11,925 (66%). Average amount of gift aid, such as scholarships or grants (proportion receiving): $8,254 (66%). Average amount of self-help aid, such as work study or loans (proportion receiving): $4,685 (53%). Average need-based loan (excluding PLUS or other private loans): $4,270. Among students who received need-based aid, the average percentage of need met: 78%. Among students who received aid based on merit, the average award (and the proportion receiving): $4,784 (29%). The average athletic scholarship (and the proportion receiving): $2,698 (20%). Average amount of debt of borrowers graduating in 2009: $25,717. Proportion who borrowed: 84%.

CAMPUS LIFE AND EXTRACURRICULAR ACTIVITIES
Campus housing available (% using): coed dorms (85%), apartments for married students (4%), apartment for single students (10%), special housing for disabled students (1%). Students who live in college-owned, operated, or affiliated housing: 68%. **Student employment:** During the 2009-2010 academic year, 8% of undergraduates worked on campus. Average per-year earnings: $820. **Clubs and organizations:** Number of student organizations: 33. Activities include: campus ministries, choral groups, concert band, dance, drama/theater, international student organization, jazz band, music ensembles, musical theater, pep band, student government, student newspaper, television station, yearbook. Number of fraternities: 0; sororities: 0. Average proportion of students who stay on campus on

weekends: 60%. **Sports program (2009-2010):** Member of NAIA. *Men's intercollegiate varsity sports:* baseball, basketball, cross country, football, golf, soccer, track and field (indoor), track and field (outdoor), wrestling. *Women's intercollegiate varsity sports:* basketball, cross country, golf, soccer, softball, track and field (indoor), track and field (outdoor), volleyball.

SERVICES AND FACILITIES

Basic services: nonremedial tutoring. **Remedial assistance:** writing, study skills. **Counseling services:** career, personal, academic, psychological, religious. **For learning-disabled students:** School does not offer a structured program with separate admission and additional fees. Total undergraduates in learning-disabled program or receiving services: 4. Services include: untimed tests, note-taking services, oral tests, learning center, extended time for tests, tutors. **Library:** Number of titles: 114,616; number of current serial subscriptions: 23,226. **Information technology resources:** Students are not required to lease or own a computer. Number of campus computers available to all students: 500. School has a wireless network. Approximate number of users that can be accommodated: 1,000. Proportion of college-owned housing units wired for high-speed internet access: 100%. **Campus safety:** Security services offered: late-night transport/escort service, lighted pathways/sidewalks, controlled dormitory access (key, security card, etc).

TRANSFER AND INTERNATIONAL STUDENTS

Transfer students: May apply for admission for the following academic terms: Fall, Spring, Summer. Applicants do not need a minimum number of credits to apply. For fall 2009: Transfer applications received: 172. Transfer applicants offered admission: 87. Transfer applicants enrolled: 72. **International students:** Number of foreign undergraduates: 38 (4% of student body). Number of countries represented: 9. Minimum TOEFL score required: 525 (paper); 197 (computer).

Mayville State University

- **Address:** 330 Third Street NE, Mayville, ND 58257
- **Website:** http://www.mayvillestate.edu
- **Public**
- **Enrollment:** 544 full-time; 343 part-time

KEY STATS

✔ **U.S News College Ranking:** 64, Regional Colleges (Midwest)
✔ **ACT Score (25th/75th percentile):** 16-22
✔ **Tuition:** 2010-2011: $5,937 in state, $8,072 out of state

Selectivity: Less selective	**Room/board:** $4,454
Acceptance rate: 57%	**Average debt:** $25,931
Student/faculty ratio: 14/1	**Proportion who borrowed:** 90%

UNDERGRADUATE STUDENT BODY STATS

2009-2010 enrollment: 544 full-time; 343 part-time. Men: 43%; women: 57%. **Ethnic makeup:** African American: 6%; American-Indian: 2%; Asian American: 1%; Hispanic: 4%; White: 83%; International: 3%.

ADMISSIONS FACTS AND FIGURES

Phone: (701) 788-5222. **Email:** admit@mayvillestate.edu. **Website:** http://www.mayvillestate.edu. **Application deadlines for fall 2011:** Regular decision: Rolling. Early decision: Not offered. Early action: Not offered. Admission can be deferred. **Application fee:** $35. **To apply online, go to:** https://www.mayvillestate.edu/become_a_student/student_form_admit.cfm. **Admissions requirements/recommendations:** High school units required (recommended): English: 4; Mathematics: 3; Science: 3; Foreign language: (2); Social studies: 3; Total units: 17. Tests: The college uses SAT or ACT scores in admissions decisions. Either SAT or ACT required. For admission to the fall 2011 entering class, the school will accept: ACT with or without writing accepted. Campus visit: Neither required nor recommended. Admissions interview: Neither required nor recommended. Off-campus interview: May be arranged. **Factors that count in admissions decisions:** *Academic:* Secondary school record: Very Important. Class rank: Not Considered. Letters of recommendation: Not Considered. Standardized test scores: Considered. Essay: Not Considered. *Nonacademic:* Interview: Not Considered. Extracurricular activities: Not Considered. Talent/ability: Not Considered. Character/personal qualities: Not Considered. Alumni/ae relationship: Not Considered. Geographical residence: Not Considered. State residency: Not Considered. Religious affiliation/commitment: Not Considered. Minority status: Not Considered. Volunteer work: Not

Considered. Work experience: Not Considered. **Other schools with the greatest overlap in applicants:** Minnesota State University–Moorhead; North Dakota State University; University of Minnesota–Crookston; University of North Dakota; Valley City State University. **Admissions statistics for the fall 2009 entering class:** Total applicants: 289. Total accepted: 166. Freshmen enrolled: 147; 50% were from out of state. Overall acceptance rate: 57%. **Credentials of fall 2009 freshmen:** 2% ranked in the top 10 percent of their high school class; 17% were in the top 25 percent; 60% were in the top half. (Proportion submitting class standing: 68%.) **Average high school grade point average:** 3.0. **First-year students who submitted SAT scores:** 12%. **First-year students submitting ACT scores:** 83%. Scores (25/75 percentile): English: 14-21, Math: 16-23, Composite: 16-22.

ACADEMICS

Year founded: 1889. **Academic calendar:** Semester. **Degrees offered:** associate, bachelor's. **Most popular majors:** 36% elementary education and teaching, 31% business administration and management, 9% health and physical education, 8% child care and support services management, 4% psychology. **Major fields of study:** biological and biomedical sciences; business, management, marketing, and related support services; computer and information sciences and support services; education; English language and literature/letters; family and consumer sciences/human sciences; liberal arts and sciences studies, and humanities; mathematics and statistics; parks, recreation, leisure, and fitness studies; physical sciences; psychology; social sciences. **Areas of required coursework:** arts/fine arts, humanities, computer literacy, mathematics, English (including composition), sciences (biological or physical), history, social science, other. **Pre-professional programs:** pre-law, pre-dentistry, pre-medicine, pre-veterinary science, pre-optometry, pre-pharmacy, other. **Special academic programs:** accelerated program, cooperative (work-study plan) program, distance learning, double major, dual enrollment, internships, student-designed major, teacher certificate program. **Teacher certification offered in:** early childhood, elementary, middle/junior high, secondary. **Cooperative education programs:** business, computer science, education, health professions, natural science, social/behavioral science. **Reserve Officers Training Corps (ROTC):** Army ROTC: Offered at cooperating institution (University of North Dakota); Air Force ROTC: Offered at cooperating institution (North Dakota State University). **Faculty and instruction (2009-2010):** Total instructional faculty: 36 full-time, 35 part-time (49% men; 51% women; 4% minorities). Full-time faculty with Ph.D. or other terminal degree: 42%. Student/faculty ratio: 14/1. Classes of fewer than 20 students: 65%; of 20 to 49 students: 35%; of 50 or more students: 0%. **Advanced Placement and International Baccalaureate credit:** AP tests may be used for: Credit only. Scores accepted: 3, 4, 5. **Freshmen returning for sophomore year:** 59%. **Graduation rates:** Four-year: 19%; five-year: 32%; six-year: 35%. **Graduate study:** 5% of students pursue further study immediately upon graduation; 5% within one year. Fields in which graduates pursue further study: Master of Business Administration (MBA), 2%; medicine, 1%; education, 4%; arts and sciences, 2%.

COSTS AND FINANCIAL AID

Financial aid office: (701) 788-4767. **Expenses (2010-2011):** Tuition and fees 2010-2011: $5,937 in state, $8,072 out of state; room/board: $4,454. Estimated books and supplies: $900; transportation: $1,400; personal expenses: $1,400. **Financial aid:** Priority filing date for institution's financial aid form: February 15. In 2009-2010, 84% of undergraduates applied for financial aid. Of those, 63% were determined to have financial need; 16% had their need fully met. Average financial aid package (proportion receiving): $8,594 (63%). Average amount of gift aid, such as scholarships or grants (proportion receiving): $4,425 (54%). Average amount of self-help aid, such as work study or loans (proportion receiving): $3,925 (60%). Average need-based loan (excluding PLUS or other private loans): $3,916. Among students who received need-based aid, the average percentage of need met: 66%. Among students who received aid based on merit, the average award (and the proportion receiving): $878 (46%). The average athletic scholarship (and the proportion receiving): $2,107 (22%). Average amount of debt of borrowers graduating in 2009: $25,931. Proportion who borrowed: 90%.

CAMPUS LIFE AND EXTRACURRICULAR ACTIVITIES

Campus housing available (% using): coed dorms (5%), women's dorms (45%), men's dorms (45%), apartments for married students (1%), apartment for single students (4%). Students who live in college-owned, operated, or affiliated housing: 24%. **Student employment:** During the 2009-2010 academic year, 40% of undergraduates worked on campus. Average per-year earnings: $1,200. **Clubs and organizations:** Number of student organizations: 18. Activities include: choral groups, concert band, drama/theater, international student organization, jazz band, music ensembles, musical theater, pep band, radio station, student government, student newspaper, student film society. Number of fraternities: 0; sororities: 0. Average proportion of students who stay on campus on weekends: 25%. **Sports program (2009-2010):** Member of NAIA. *Men's intercollegiate varsity sports:* baseball, basketball, football. *Women's intercollegiate varsity sports:* basketball, softball, volleyball.

SERVICES AND FACILITIES
Basic services: nonremedial tutoring, placement service, day care, health service, health insurance. **Remedial assistance:** math, writing, study skills. **Counseling services:** career, personal, veteran student, academic. **For learning-disabled students:** School does not offer a structured program with separate admission and additional fees. Total undergraduates in learning-disabled program or receiving services: 22. Services include: remedial math, remedial English, tape recorders, untimed tests, note-taking services, oral tests, learning center, readers, extended time for tests, tutors, texts on tape. **Library:** Number of titles: 93,685; number of current serial subscriptions: 424. **Information technology resources:** Students are required to lease or own a computer. Number of campus computers available to all students: 600. School has a wireless network. Approximate number of users that can be accommodated: 300. Proportion of college-owned housing units wired for high-speed internet access: 100%. **Campus safety:** Security services offered: lighted pathways/sidewalks, controlled dormitory access (key, security card, etc).

TRANSFER AND INTERNATIONAL STUDENTS
Transfer students: May apply for admission for the following academic terms: Fall, Spring, Summer. Applicants do not need a minimum number of credits to apply. For fall 2009: Transfer applications received: 298. Transfer applicants offered admission: 180. Transfer applicants enrolled: 135. **International students:** Number of foreign undergraduates: 31 (3% of student body). Number of countries represented: 4. Minimum TOEFL score required: 520 (paper); 68 (computer).

Minot State University

■ **Address:** 500 University Avenue W, Minot, ND 58707
■ **Website:** http://www.minotstateu.edu
■ **Public**
■ **Enrollment:** 2,300 full-time; 1,045 part-time

KEY STATS
✔ **U.S News College Ranking:** second tier, Regional Universities (Midwest)
✔ **ACT Score (25th/75th percentile):** 19-24
✔ **Tuition:** 2009-2010: $5,410 in state, $5,410 out of state

Selectivity: Selective	**Room/board:** $5,822
Acceptance rate: 82%	**Average debt:** $19,384
Student/faculty ratio: 14/1	**Proportion who borrowed:** 75%

UNDERGRADUATE STUDENT BODY STATS
2009-2010 enrollment: 2,300 full-time; 1,045 part-time. Men: 38%; women: 62%. **Ethnic makeup:** African American: 3%; American-Indian: 5%; Asian American: 1%; Hispanic: 2%; White: 78%; International: 12%.

ADMISSIONS FACTS AND FIGURES
Phone: (701) 858-3350. **Email:** askmsu@minotstateu.edu. **Website:** http://www.minotstateu.edu. **Application deadlines for fall 2011:** Regular decision: Rolling. Early decision: Not offered. Early action: Not offered. Admission can be deferred. **Application fee:** $35. **To apply online, go to:** http://www.rdb.und.nodak.edu/www_ea/plsql/ea_home. **Admissions requirements/recommendations:** High school units required (recommended): English: 4 (4); Mathematics: 3 (3); Science: 3 (3); Social studies: 3 (3); Total units: 13 (13). Tests: The college uses SAT or ACT scores in admissions decisions. Either SAT or ACT required. For admission to the fall 2011 entering class, the school will accept: ACT with writing required. Campus visit: Recommended. Admissions interview: Neither required nor recommended. Off-campus interview: May be arranged. **Factors that count in admissions decisions:** *Academic:* Secondary school record: Very Important. Class rank: Considered. Letters of recommendation: Considered. Standardized test scores: Very Important. Essay: Considered. *Nonacademic:* Interview: Considered. Extracurricular activities: Considered. Talent/ability: Considered. Character/personal qualities: Considered. Alumni/ae relationship: Considered. Geographical residence: Considered. State residency: Considered. Religious affiliation/commitment: Not Considered. Minority status: Considered. Volunteer work: Considered. Work experience: Considered. **Other schools with the greatest overlap in applicants:** North Dakota State University; University of North Dakota. **Admissions statistics for the fall 2009 entering class:** Total applicants: 724. Total accepted: 595. Freshmen enrolled: 438; 12% were from out of state. Overall acceptance rate: 82%. **Size of waiting list:** 0 applicants; enrolled from waiting list: 0. **Average high school grade point average:** 2.0. **First-year students who submitted SAT scores:** 11%. Scores (25/75 percentile): Critical Reading: 430-510, Math: 420-530, Combined: 850-1040. **First-year students submitting ACT scores:** 73%. Scores (25/75 percentile): English: 18-24, Math: 18-23, Composite: 19-24.

ACADEMICS
Year founded: 1913. **Academic calendar:** Semester. **Degrees offered:** certificate, associate, bachelor's, post-bachelor's certificate, master's. **Major fields of study:** biological and biomedical sciences; business, management, marketing, and related support services; communication, journalism, and related programs; communications technologies/technicians and support services; computer and information sciences and support services; education; English language and literature/letters; foreign languages, literatures, and linguistics; health professions and related clinical sciences; history; liberal arts and sciences studies, and humanities; parks, recreation, leisure, and fitness studies; physical sciences; psychology; public administration and social service professions; security and protective services; social sciences; visual and performing arts. **Areas of required coursework:** humanities, mathematics, English (including composition), sciences (biological or physical), history, social science, other. **Pre-professional programs:** pre-law, pre-dentistry, pre-medicine, pre-veterinary science, pre-optometry, pre-pharmacy. **Special academic programs:** cooperative (work-study plan) program, distance learning, double major, dual enrollment, English as a Second Language (ESL), external degree program, honors program, independent study, internships, liberal arts/career combination, student-designed major, study abroad, teacher certificate program. **Teacher certification offered in:** early childhood, special education, elementary, middle/junior high, secondary. **Cooperative education programs:** business, education, health professions. **Faculty and instruction (2009-2010):** Total instructional faculty: 164 full-time, 113 part-time (43% men; 57% women; 3% minorities). Full-time faculty with Ph.D. or other terminal degree: 57%. Student/faculty ratio: 14/1. Classes of fewer than 20 students: %; of 20 to 49 students: %; of 50 or more students: %. **Advanced Placement and International Baccalaureate credit:** International Baccalaureate exams may be used for: Placement only. **Freshmen returning for sophomore year:** 66%. **Graduation rates:** Four-year: 11%; five-year: 18%; six-year: 31%.

COSTS AND FINANCIAL AID
Financial aid office: (701) 858-3375. **Expenses (2009-2010):** Tuition and fees 2009-2010: $5,410 in state, $5,410 out of state; room/board: $5,822. Estimated books and supplies: $1,000; transportation: $0; personal expenses: $3,200. **Financial aid:** Priority filing date for institution's financial aid form: March 15. In 2009-2010, 72% of undergraduates applied for financial aid. Of those, 55% were determined to have financial need; 98% had their need fully met. Average financial aid package (proportion receiving): $7,187 (54%). Average amount of gift aid, such as scholarships or grants (proportion receiving): $3,988 (44%). Average amount of self-help aid, such as work study or loans (proportion receiving): $3,976 (46%). Average need-based loan (excluding PLUS or other private loans): $3,990. Among students who received need-based aid, the average percentage of need met: 64%. Among students who received aid based on merit, the average award (and the proportion receiving): $1,050 (28%). The average athletic scholarship (and the proportion receiving): $1,527 (7%). Average amount of debt of borrowers graduating in 2009: $19,384. Proportion who borrowed: 75%.

CAMPUS LIFE AND EXTRACURRICULAR ACTIVITIES
Campus housing available (% using): coed dorms (35%), women's dorms (33%), men's dorms (19%), apartments for married students (13%), apartment for single students (0%), special housing for disabled students (0%). Students who live in college-owned, operated, or affiliated housing: 84%. **Student employment:** During the 2009-2010 academic year, 4% of undergraduates worked on campus. Average per-year earnings: $2,000. **Clubs and organizations:** Number of student organizations: 59. Activities include: campus ministries, choral groups, concert band, dance, drama/theater, international student organization, jazz band, literary magazine, marching band, music ensembles, musical theater, pep band, radio station, student

government, student newspaper, symphony orchestra, television station. Number of fraternities: 1; sororities: 0. Proportion of men in fraternities: 2%; Average proportion of students who stay on campus on weekends: 10%. **Sports program (2009-2010):** Member of NAIA. *Men's intercollegiate varsity sports:* baseball, basketball, cross country, football, golf, track and field (indoor), track and field (outdoor). *Women's intercollegiate varsity sports:* basketball, cross country, golf, softball, track and field (indoor), track and field (outdoor), volleyball.

SERVICES AND FACILITIES

Basic services: nonremedial tutoring, women's center, placement service, health service, health insurance. **Remedial assistance:** math, writing, study skills, other. **Counseling services:** minority student, career, personal, veteran student, academic, older student, psychological, birth control, religious. **For learning-disabled students:** School does not offer a structured program with separate admission and additional fees. Services include: remedial math, reading machines, tape recorders, videotaped classes, untimed tests, note-taking services, oral tests, learning center, readers, extended time for tests, tutors, priority registration, priority seating, texts on tape. **Library:** Number of titles: 415,361; number of current serial subscriptions: 520. **Information technology resources:** Students are not required to lease or own a computer. Number of campus computers available to all students: 700. School has a wireless network. Approximate number of users that can be accommodated: 800. Proportion of college-owned housing units wired for high-speed internet access: 95%. **Campus safety:** Security services offered: 24-hour emergency telephones, lighted pathways/sidewalks, controlled dormitory access (key, security card, etc).

TRANSFER AND INTERNATIONAL STUDENTS

Transfer students: May apply for admission for the following academic terms: Fall, Spring, Summer. Applicants need a minimum number of credits to apply. For fall 2009: Transfer applications received: 548. Transfer applicants offered admission: 435. Transfer applicants enrolled: 324. **International students:** Number of foreign undergraduates: 274 (12% of student body). Number of countries represented: 22. Minimum TOEFL score required: 525 (paper); 195 (computer). Average TOEFL score: 593 (paper).

North Dakota State University

- ■ **Address:** PO Box 6050, Fargo, ND 58108-6050
- ■ **Website:** http://www.ndsu.edu
- ■ **Public**
- ■ **Enrollment:** 10,658 full-time; 1,075 part-time

KEY STATS

✔ **U.S News College Ranking:** 191, National Universities
✔ **ACT Score (25th/75th percentile):** 20-26
✔ **Tuition:** 2010-2011: $6,661 in state, $16,077 out of state

Selectivity: Selective	**Room/board:** $6,714
Acceptance rate: 79%	**Average debt:** $24,833
Student/faculty ratio: 18/1	**Proportion who borrowed:** 81%

UNDERGRADUATE STUDENT BODY STATS

2009-2010 enrollment: 10,658 full-time; 1,075 part-time. Men: 57%; women: 43%. **Ethnic makeup:** African American: 2%; American-Indian: 1%; Asian American: 1%; Hispanic: 1%; White: 90%; International: 5%.

ADMISSIONS FACTS AND FIGURES

Phone: (701) 231-8643. **Email:** NDSU.Admission@ndsu.edu. **Website:** http://www.ndsu.edu. **Application deadlines for fall 2011:** Regular decision: Rolling. Early decision: Not offered. Early action: Not offered. Admission can be deferred. **Application fee:** $35. **To apply online, go to:** http://apply. ndsu.edu. **Admissions requirements/recommendations:** High school units required (recommended): English: 4 (4); Mathematics: 3 (3); Science: 3 (3); Foreign language: 0 (0); Social studies: 3 (3); History: 0; Academic electives: 0; Total units: 13 (13). Tests: The college uses SAT or ACT scores in admissions decisions. Either SAT or ACT required. For admission to the fall 2011 entering class, the school will accept: ACT with or without writing accepted. Campus visit: Recommended. Admissions interview: Recommended. Off-campus interview: May be arranged. **Factors that count in admissions decisions:** *Academic:* Secondary school record: Very Important. Class rank: Considered. Letters of recommendation: Considered. Standardized test scores: Very Important. Essay: Not Considered. *Nonacademic:* Interview:

Not Considered. Extracurricular activities: Not Considered. Talent/ability: Not Considered. Character/personal qualities: Not Considered. Alumni/ae relationship: Not Considered. Geographical residence: Not Considered. State residency: Not Considered. Religious affiliation/commitment: Not Considered. Minority status: Not Considered. Volunteer work: Not Considered. Work experience: Not Considered. **Other schools with the greatest overlap in applicants:** University of Minnesota–Twin Cities; University of North Dakota. **Admissions statistics for the fall 2009 entering class:** Total applicants: 5,646. Total accepted: 4,473. Freshmen enrolled: 2,459; 60% were from out of state. Overall acceptance rate: 79%. **Credentials of fall 2009 freshmen:** 17% ranked in the top 10 percent of their high school class; 42% were in the top 25 percent; 76% were in the top half. (Proportion submitting class standing: 87%.) **Average high school grade point average:** 3.4. **First-year students who submitted SAT scores:** 3%. Scores (25/75 percentile): Critical Reading: 470-610, Math: 490-650, Combined: 960-1260. **First-year students submitting ACT scores:** 96%. Scores (25/75 percentile): English: 20-26, Math: 19-25, Composite: 20-26.

ACADEMICS

Year founded: 1890. **Academic calendar:** Semester. **Degrees offered:** certificate, bachelor's, master's, post-master's certificate, doctorate. **Most popular majors:** 7% business administration and management, 5% pharmacy, pharmaceutical sciences, and administration, 4% electrical, electronics, and communications engineering, 4% mechanical engineering, 4% nursing/registered nurse training (R.N., A.S.N., B.S.N., M.S.N.). **Major fields of study:** agriculture, agriculture operations, and related sciences; architecture and related services; area, ethnic, cultural, and gender studies; biological and biomedical sciences; business, management, marketing, and related support services; communication, journalism, and related programs; computer and information sciences and support services; education; engineering; English language and literature/letters; family and consumer sciences/ human sciences; foreign languages, literatures, and linguistics; health professions and related clinical sciences; history; liberal arts and sciences studies, and humanities; mathematics and statistics; multi/interdisciplinary studies; natural resources and conservation; parks, recreation, leisure, and fitness studies; philosophy and religious studies; physical sciences; psychology; security and protective services; social sciences; visual and performing arts. **Areas of required coursework:** arts/fine arts, humanities, computer literacy, mathematics, English (including composition), sciences (biological or physical), social science, other. **Pre-professional programs:** pre-law, pre-dentistry, pre-medicine, pre-veterinary science, pre-optometry, pre-pharmacy, other. **Special academic programs:** cooperative (work-study plan) program, cross-registration, distance learning, double major, dual enrollment, English as a Second Language (ESL), honors program, independent study, internships, student-designed major, study abroad, teacher certificate program, other. **Teacher certification offered in:** secondary. **Cooperative education programs:** agriculture, art, business, computer science, education, engineering, health professions, home economics, humanities, natural science, social/behavioral science, technologies. **Reserve Officers Training Corps (ROTC):** Army ROTC: Offered on campus; Air Force ROTC: Offered on campus. **Faculty and instruction (2009-2010):** Total instructional faculty: 647 full-time, 134 part-time (63% men; 37% women; 16% minorities). Full-time faculty with Ph.D. or other terminal degree: 74%. Student/faculty ratio: 18/1. Classes of fewer than 20 students: 42%; of 20 to 49 students: 45%; of 50 or more students: 12%. **Advanced Placement and International Baccalaureate credit:** AP tests may be used for: Credit only. Scores accepted: 3, 4, 5. International Baccalaureate exams may be used for: Credit only. **Freshmen returning for sophomore year:** 80%. **Graduation rates:** Four-year: 22%; five-year: 45%; six-year: 52%. **Graduate study:** 17% of students pursue further study immediately upon graduation. Fields in which graduates pursue further study: Master of Business Administration (MBA), 5%; law, 5%; medicine, 25%; dentistry, 1%; engineering, 8%; arts and sciences, 11%; veterinary medicine, 1%.

COSTS AND FINANCIAL AID

Financial aid office: (800) 726-3188. **Expenses (2010-2011):** Tuition and fees 2010-2011: $6,661 in state, $16,077 out of state; room/board: $6,714. Estimated books and supplies: $1,000; transportation: $1,120; personal expenses: $2,180. **Financial aid:** Priority filing date for institution's financial aid form: March 15. In 2009-2010, 96% of undergraduates applied for financial aid. Of those, 95% were determined to have financial need; 25% had their need fully met. Average financial aid package (proportion receiving): $4,652 (84%). Average amount of gift aid, such as scholarships or grants (proportion receiving): $2,842 (41%). Average amount of self-help aid, such as work study or loans (proportion receiving): $2,895 (67%). Average need-based loan (excluding PLUS or other private loans): $3,672.

Among students who received need-based aid, the average percentage of need met: 51%. Among students who received aid based on merit, the average award (and the proportion receiving): $1,601 (30%). The average athletic scholarship (and the proportion receiving): $8,585 (3%). Average amount of debt of borrowers graduating in 2009: $24,833. Proportion who borrowed: 81%.

CAMPUS LIFE AND EXTRACURRICULAR ACTIVITIES

Campus housing available (% using): coed dorms (41%), women's dorms (17%), men's dorms (23%), apartments for married students (0%), apartment for single students (0%), other housing options (19%). Students who live in college-owned, operated, or affiliated housing: 27%. **Student employment:** During the 2009-2010 academic year, 18% of undergraduates worked on campus. Average per-year earnings: $4,241. **Clubs and organizations:** Number of student organizations: 200. Activities include: choral groups, concert band, dance, drama/theater, international student organization, jazz band, literary magazine, marching band, music ensembles, musical theater, pep band, radio station, student government, student newspaper. Number of fraternities: 10; sororities: 4. Proportion of men in fraternities: 4%; of women in sororities: 2%. Average proportion of students who stay on campus on weekends: 68%. **Sports program (2009-2010):** Member of NCAA I. **Men's intercollegiate varsity sports:** baseball, basketball, cross country, football, golf, track and field (indoor), track and field (outdoor), wrestling. **Women's intercollegiate varsity sports:** basketball, cross country, golf, soccer, softball, track and field (indoor), track and field (outdoor), volleyball.

SERVICES AND FACILITIES

Basic services: nonremedial tutoring, placement service, day care, health service, health insurance. **Remedial assistance:** reading, math, writing, study skills. **Counseling services:** minority student, career, military, personal, veteran student, academic, older student, psychological, religious. **For learning-disabled students:** School does not offer a structured program with separate admission and additional fees. Total undergraduates in learning-disabled program or receiving services: 49. Services include: remedial math, remedial English, remedial reading, tutors. **Library:** Number of titles: 399,775; number of current serial subscriptions: 44,777. **Information technology resources:** Students are not required to lease or own a computer. Number of campus computers available to all students: 550. School has a wireless network. Approximate number of users that can be accommodated: 2,500. Proportion of college-owned housing units wired for high-speed internet access: 100%. **Campus safety:** Security services offered: late-night transport/escort service, 24-hour emergency telephones, lighted pathways/sidewalks, controlled dormitory access (key, security card, etc).

TRANSFER AND INTERNATIONAL STUDENTS

Transfer students: May apply for admission for the following academic terms: Fall, Spring, Summer. Applicants do not need a minimum number of credits to apply. For fall 2009: Transfer applications received: 1,641. Transfer applicants offered admission: 1,123. Transfer applicants enrolled: 802. **International students:** Number of foreign undergraduates: 573 (5% of student body). Number of countries represented: 58. Minimum TOEFL score required: 525 (paper); 193 (computer).

University of Mary

- **Address:** 7500 University Drive, Bismarck, ND 58504
- **Website:** http://www.umary.edu
- **Private; Religious affiliation:** Roman Catholic
- **Enrollment:** 1,554 full-time; 583 part-time

KEY STATS

✔ **U.S News College Ranking:** 104, Regional Universities (Midwest)
✔ **ACT Score (25th/75th percentile):** 20-25
✔ **Tuition:** 2010-2011: $13,088

Selectivity: Selective	**Room/board:** $5,180
Acceptance rate: 78%	**Average debt:** N/A
Student/faculty ratio: 16/1	**Proportion who borrowed:** N/A

UNDERGRADUATE STUDENT BODY STATS

2009-2010 enrollment: 1,554 full-time; 583 part-time. Men: 39%; women: 61%. **Religious preference:** Protestant: 31%; No preference: 5%; Unknown: 10%; Roman Catholic: 43%; Other: 11%.

ADMISSIONS FACTS AND FIGURES

Phone: (701) 355-8030. **Email:** marauder@umary.edu. **Website:** http://www.umary.edu. **Application deadlines for fall 2011:** Regular decision: Rolling. Early decision: Not offered. Early action: Not offered. Admission can be deferred. **Application fee:** $25. **To apply online, go to:** https://forms.umary.edu/UM/Admissions/ApplyNOW/OnlineApp01.htm. **Admissions requirements/recommendations:** High school units required (recommended): English: (4); Mathematics: (3); Science: (3); Social studies: (4); Total units: (14). Tests: The college uses SAT or ACT scores in admissions decisions. Either SAT or ACT required. For admission to the fall 2011 entering class, the school will accept: ACT with or without writing accepted. Campus visit: Recommended. Admissions interview: Neither required nor recommended. Off-campus interview: May be arranged. **Factors that count in admissions decisions:** *Academic:* Secondary school record: Important. Class rank: Important. Letters of recommendation: Considered. Standardized test scores: Important. Essay: Not Considered. *Nonacademic:* Interview: Considered. Extracurricular activities: Considered. Talent/ability: Considered. Character/personal qualities: Considered. Alumni/ae relationship: Considered. Geographical residence: Not Considered. State residency: Not Considered. Religious affiliation/commitment: Not Considered. Minority status: Not Considered. Volunteer work: Considered. Work experience: Considered. **Other schools with the greatest overlap in applicants:** Dickinson State University; Jamestown College; Minnesota State University–Moorhead; North Dakota State University; University of North Dakota. **Admissions statistics for the fall 2009 entering class:** Total applicants: 924. Total accepted: 723. Freshmen enrolled: 312; 38% were from out of state. Overall acceptance rate: 78%. **Credentials of fall 2009 freshmen:** 6% ranked in the top 10 percent of their high school class; 45% were in the top 25 percent; 78% were in the top half. (Proportion submitting class standing: 92%.) **Average high school grade point average:** 3.4. **First-year students who submitted SAT scores:** 9%. **First-year students submitting ACT scores:** 92%. Scores (25/75 percentile): English: 19-25, Math: 18-25, Composite: 20-25.

ACADEMICS

Year founded: 1959. **Academic calendar:** Semester. **Degrees offered:** bachelor's, post-bachelor's certificate, master's, post-master's certificate, doctorate. **Most popular majors:** 39% business, management, marketing, and related support services, 22% health professions and related clinical sciences, 12% education, 8% liberal arts and sciences studies, and humanities, 3% biological and biomedical sciences. **Major fields of study:** biological and biomedical sciences; business, management, marketing, and related support services; communication, journalism, and related programs; computer and information sciences and support services; education; English language and literature/letters; health professions and related clinical sciences; history; liberal arts and sciences studies, and humanities; mathematics and statistics; parks, recreation, leisure, and fitness studies; philosophy and religious studies; psychology; public administration and social service professions; security and protective services; social sciences; theology and religious vocations; visual and performing arts. **Areas of required coursework:** arts/fine arts, humanities, computer literacy, mathematics, English (including composition), philosophy, sciences (biological or physical), social science, other. **Pre-professional programs:** pre-law, pre-dentistry, pre-medicine, pre-theology, pre-veterinary science, pre-optometry, pre-pharmacy, other. **Special academic programs (% participation):** accelerated program (27%), cooperative (work-study plan) program (5%), distance learning (7%), double major (4%), honors program (0%), independent study (35%), internships (16%), student-designed major (0%), study abroad (0%), teacher certificate program (0%). **Teacher certification offered in:** early childhood, special education, elementary, middle/junior high, secondary. **Cooperative education programs:** business, computer science, education, engineering, health professions, natural science, social/behavioral science. **Faculty and instruction (2009-2010):** Total instructional faculty: 95 full-time, 176 part-time (50% men; 50% women; 3% minorities). Full-time faculty with Ph.D. or other terminal degree: 53%. Student/faculty ratio: 16/1. Classes of fewer than 20 students: 57%; of 20 to 49 students: 34%; of 50 or more students: 8%. **Advanced Placement and International Baccalaureate credit:** AP tests may be used for: Credit only. Scores accepted: 3, 4, 5. International Baccalaureate exams may be used for: Credit only. **Freshmen returning for sophomore year:** 73%. **Graduation rates:** Four-year: 38%; five-year: 48%; six-year: 54%. **Graduate study:** 23% of students pursue further study immediately upon graduation; 25% within one year; 30% within five years. Fields in which graduates pursue further study: Master of Business Administration (MBA), 10%; law, 6%; medicine, 67%; dentistry, 4%; engineering, 2%; education, 7%; arts and sciences, 4%.

COSTS AND FINANCIAL AID

Financial aid office: (701) 355-8079. **Expenses (2010-2011):** Tuition and fees 2010-2011: $13,088; room/board: $5,180. Estimated books and supplies: $1,100; transportation: $1,210; personal expenses: $1,055. **Financial aid:** Priority filing date for institution's financial aid form: March 15.

CAMPUS LIFE AND EXTRACURRICULAR ACTIVITIES

Campus housing available (% using): women's dorms (49%), men's dorms (33%), apartment for single students (18%), special housing for disabled students. Students who live in college-owned, operated, or affiliated housing: 32%. **Student employment:** During the 2009-2010 academic year, 11% of undergraduates worked on campus. Average per-year earnings: $900. **Clubs and organizations:** Number of student organizations: 28. Activities include: campus ministries, choral groups, concert band, dance, drama/theater, international student organization, jazz band, music ensembles, musical theater, pep band, student government, student newspaper. Number of fraternities: 0; sororities: 0. Average proportion of students who stay on campus on weekends: 70%. **Sports program (2009-2010):** Member of NCAA II. *Men's intercollegiate varsity sports:* baseball, basketball, cross country, football, golf, soccer, tennis, track and field (indoor), track and field (outdoor), wrestling. *Women's intercollegiate varsity sports:* basketball, cross country, golf, soccer, softball, tennis, track and field (indoor), track and field (outdoor), volleyball.

SERVICES AND FACILITIES

Basic services: nonremedial tutoring, placement service, health service. **Remedial assistance:** reading, math, writing, study skills. **Counseling services:** minority student, career, personal, academic, older student, psychological, birth control, religious. **For learning-disabled students:** School does not offer a structured program with separate admission and additional fees. Total undergraduates in learning-disabled program or receiving services: 64. Services include: remedial math, remedial English, remedial reading, note-taking services, oral tests, learning center, extended time for tests, tutors, priority registration, priority seating, other testing accommodations, waiver of foreign language degree requirement, other. **Library:** Number of titles: 64,524; number of current serial subscriptions: 210. **Information technology resources:** Students are not required to lease or own a computer. Number of campus computers available to all students: 235. School has a wireless network. Approximate number of users that can be accommodated: 500. Proportion of college-owned housing units wired for high-speed internet access: 100%. **Campus safety:** Security services offered: late-night transport/escort service, lighted pathways/sidewalks, controlled dormitory access (key, security card, etc).

TRANSFER AND INTERNATIONAL STUDENTS

Transfer students: May apply for admission for the following academic terms: Fall, Spring, Summer. Applicants do not need a minimum number of credits to apply. For fall 2009: Transfer applications received: 533. Transfer applicants offered admission: 401. Transfer applicants enrolled: 193. **International students:** Number of foreign undergraduates: 0. Number of countries represented: 9. Minimum TOEFL score required: 500 (paper); 175 (computer).

University of North Dakota

- **Address:** University Station, Grand Forks, ND 58202
- **Website:** http://www.go.und.edu
- **Public**
- **Enrollment:** 8,739 full-time; 1,701 part-time

KEY STATS

- ✔ **U.S News College Ranking:** 159, National Universities
- ✔ **ACT Score (25th/75th percentile):** 20-25
- ✔ **Tuition:** 2010-2011: $8,076 in state, $17,195 out of state

Selectivity: Selective	**Room/board:** $6,100
Acceptance rate: 73%	**Average debt:** $36,120
Student/faculty ratio: 18/1	**Proportion who borrowed:** 69%

UNDERGRADUATE STUDENT BODY STATS

2009-2010 enrollment: 8,739 full-time; 1,701 part-time. Men: 55%; women: 45%. **Ethnic makeup:** African American: 1%; American-Indian: 3%; Asian American: 1%; Hispanic: 1%; White: 89%; International: 5%.

ADMISSIONS FACTS AND FIGURES

Phone: (800) 225-5863. **Email:** enrollmentservices@mail.und.edu. **Website:** http://www.go.und.edu. **Application deadlines for fall 2011:** Regular decision: Rolling. Early decision: Not offered. Early action: Not offered. Admission can be deferred. **Application fee:** $35. **To apply online, go to:** http://www.und.edu/enroll/apply.html. **Admissions requirements/recommendations:** High school units required (recommended): English: 4; Mathematics: 3; Science: 3; Foreign language: (1); Social studies: 3; Total units: 13. Tests: The college uses SAT or ACT scores in admissions decisions. Either SAT or ACT required. For admission to the fall 2011 entering class, the school will accept: ACT with or without writing accepted. Campus visit: Recommended. Admissions interview: Recommended. Off-campus interview: May be arranged. **Factors that count in admissions decisions:** *Academic:* Secondary school record: Considered. Class rank: Considered. Letters of recommendation: Not Considered. Standardized test scores: Very Important. Essay: Not Considered. *Nonacademic:* Interview: Not Considered. Extracurricular activities: Not Considered. Talent/ability: Not Considered. Character/personal qualities: Not Considered. Alumni/ae relationship: Not Considered. Geographical residence: Not Considered. State residency: Not Considered. Religious affiliation/commitment: Not Considered. Minority status: Not Considered. Volunteer work: Not Considered. Work experience: Not Considered. **Other schools with the greatest overlap in applicants:** Minnesota State University–Moorhead; North Dakota State University; North Dakota State University; St. Cloud State University; St. Cloud State University; University of Minnesota–Duluth; University of Minnesota–Duluth; University of Minnesota–Twin Cities; University of Minnesota–Twin Cities. **Admissions statistics for the fall 2009 entering class:** Total applicants: 4,111. Total accepted: 3,003. Freshmen enrolled: 1,992; 62% were from out of state. Overall acceptance rate: 73%. **Credentials of fall 2009 freshmen:** 17% ranked in the top 10 percent of their high school class; 40% were in the top 25 percent; 74% were in the top half. (Proportion submitting class standing: 76%.) **Average high school grade point average:** 3.4. **First-year students submitting ACT scores:** 73%. Scores (25/75 percentile): English: 19-25, Math: 20-26, Composite: 20-25.

ACADEMICS

Year founded: 1883. **Academic calendar:** Semester. **Degrees offered:** certificate, diploma, bachelor's, master's, post-master's certificate, doctorate. **Most popular majors:** 8% airline/commercial/professional pilot and flight crew, 8% nursing/registered nurse training (R.N., A.S.N., B.S.N., M.S.N.), 5% air traffic controller, 4% communication studies/speech communication and rhetoric, 4% liberal arts and sciences/liberal studies. **Major fields of study:** area, ethnic, cultural, and gender studies; biological and biomedical sciences; business, management, marketing, and related support services; communication, journalism, and related programs; computer and information sciences and support services; education; engineering; engineering technologies/technicians; English language and literature/letters; foreign languages, literatures, and linguistics; health professions and related clinical sciences; history; liberal arts and sciences studies, and humanities; mathematics and statistics; multi/interdisciplinary studies; parks, recreation, leisure, and fitness studies; philosophy and religious studies; physical sciences; psychology; public administration and social service professions; security and protective services; social sciences; transportation and materials moving; visual and performing arts. **Areas of required coursework:** arts/fine arts, humanities, English (including composition), sciences (biological or physical), social science. **Pre-professional programs:** pre-law, pre-medicine. **Special academic programs:** accelerated program, cooperative (work-study plan) program, cross-registration, distance learning, double major, dual enrollment, English as a Second Language (ESL), exchange student program (domestic), external degree program, honors program, independent study, internships, liberal arts/career combination, student-designed major, study abroad, teacher certificate program, weekend college. **Teacher certification offered in:** early childhood, special education, elementary, middle/junior high, secondary, bilingual/bicultural. **Cooperative education programs:** art, business, computer science, education, engineering, health professions, home economics, humanities, natural science, social/behavioral science, technologies, vocational arts, other. **Reserve Officers Training Corps (ROTC):** Army ROTC: Offered on campus; Air Force ROTC: Offered on campus. **Faculty and instruction (2009-2010):** Total instructional faculty: 594 full-time, 70 part-time (58% men; 42% women; 12% minorities). Full-time faculty with Ph.D. or other terminal degree: 80%. Student/faculty ratio: 18/1. Classes of fewer than 20 students: 39%; of 20 to 49 students: 53%; of 50 or more students: 9%. **Advanced Placement and International Baccalaureate credit:** AP tests may be used for: Credit only. Scores accepted: 3, 4. International Baccalaureate exams may be used for: Credit only. **Freshmen returning for sophomore year:** 77%. **Graduation rates:** Four-year:

23%; five-year: 46%; six-year: 53%. **Graduate study:** 13% of students pursue further study immediately upon graduation; 21% within one year. Fields in which graduates pursue further study: Master of Business Administration (MBA), 1%; law, 1%; medicine, 2%; dentistry, 1%; engineering, 1%; theology (or the seminary), 1%; education, 5%; arts and sciences, 19%.

COSTS AND FINANCIAL AID

Financial aid office: (701) 777-3121. **Expenses (2010-2011):** Tuition and fees 2010-2011: $8,076 in state, $17,195 out of state; room/board: $6,100. Estimated books and supplies: $800; transportation: $1,120; personal expenses: $3,300. **Financial aid:** Priority filing date for institution's financial aid form: March 15. In 2009-2010, 79% of undergraduates applied for financial aid. Of those, 79% were determined to have financial need; 28% had their need fully met. Average financial aid package (proportion receiving): $5,723 (73%). Average amount of gift aid, such as scholarships or grants (proportion receiving): $2,892 (38%). Average amount of self-help aid, such as work study or loans (proportion receiving): $3,500 (63%). Average need-based loan (excluding PLUS or other private loans): $4,130. Among students who received need-based aid, the average percentage of need met: 39%. Among students who received aid based on merit, the average award (and the proportion receiving): $1,469 (29%). The average athletic scholarship (and the proportion receiving): $8,401 (4%). Average amount of debt of borrowers graduating in 2009: $36,120. Proportion who borrowed: 69%.

CAMPUS LIFE AND EXTRACURRICULAR ACTIVITIES

Campus housing available (% using): coed dorms (18%), women's dorms (2%), men's dorms (3%), sorority housing (2%), fraternity housing (2%), apartments for married students (1%), apartment for single students (5%), special housing for disabled students (1%), other housing options (66%). Students who live in college-owned, operated, or affiliated housing: 32%. **Student employment:** During the 2009-2010 academic year, 17% of undergraduates worked on campus. Average per-year earnings: $1,384. **Clubs and organizations:** Number of student organizations: 230. Activities include: campus ministries, choral groups, concert band, dance, drama/theater, international student organization, jazz band, literary magazine, marching band, music ensembles, musical theater, opera, pep band, radio station, student government, student newspaper, student film society, symphony orchestra, television station. Number of fraternities: 13; sororities: 7. Proportion of men in fraternities: 7%; of women in sororities: 8%. Average proportion of students who stay on campus on weekends: 16%. **Sports program (2009-2010):** Member of NCAA II. *Men's intercollegiate varsity sports:* baseball, basketball, cross country, football, golf, ice hockey, swimming, track and field (outdoor). *Women's intercollegiate varsity sports:* basketball, cross country, golf, ice hockey, soccer, softball, swimming, tennis, track and field (outdoor), volleyball.

SERVICES AND FACILITIES

Basic services: nonremedial tutoring, women's center, placement service, day care, health service, health insurance, other. **Remedial assistance:** study skills, other. **Counseling services:** minority student, career, military, personal, veteran student, academic, older student, psychological, birth control, other. **For learning-disabled students:** School does not offer a structured program with separate admission and additional fees. **Library:** Number of titles: 1,083,215; number of current serial subscriptions: 42,291. **Information technology resources:** Students are not required to lease or own a computer. Number of campus computers available to all students: 1,100. School has a wireless network. Approximate number of users that can be accommodated: 10,000. Proportion of college-owned housing units wired for high-speed internet access: 100%. **Campus safety:** Security services offered: 24-hour foot-and-vehicle patrols, late-night transport/escort service, 24-hour emergency telephones, lighted pathways/sidewalks, student patrols, controlled dormitory access (key, security card, etc).

TRANSFER AND INTERNATIONAL STUDENTS

Transfer students: May apply for admission for the following academic terms: Fall, Spring, Summer. Applicants do not need a minimum number of credits to apply. For fall 2009: Transfer applications received: 1,695. Transfer applicants offered admission: 1,237. Transfer applicants enrolled: 811. **International students:** Number of foreign undergraduates: 518 (5% of student body). Number of countries represented: 32. Minimum TOEFL score required: 525 (paper); 195 (computer). Average TOEFL score: 560 (paper).

Valley City State University

■ **Address:** 101 College Street SW, Valley City, ND 58072
■ **Website:** http://www.vcsu.edu
■ **Public**
■ **Enrollment:** 688 full-time; 273 part-time

KEY STATS

✔ **U.S News College Ranking:** 47, Regional Colleges (Midwest)
✔ **ACT Score (25th/75th percentile):** 18-23
✔ **Tuition:** 2010-2011: $6,075 in state, $13,477 out of state
Selectivity: Less selective **Room/board:** $5,017
Acceptance rate: 92% **Average debt:** $25,929
Student/faculty ratio: 12/1 **Proportion who borrowed:** 88%

UNDERGRADUATE STUDENT BODY STATS

2009-2010 enrollment: 688 full-time; 273 part-time. Men: 47%; women: 53%. **Ethnic makeup:** African American: 4%; American-Indian: 2%; Asian American: 1%; Hispanic: 2%; White: 87%; International: 4%.

ADMISSIONS FACTS AND FIGURES

Phone: (701) 845-7101. **Email:** enrollment.services@vcsu.edu. **Website:** http://www.vcsu.edu. **Application deadlines for fall 2011:** Regular decision: Rolling. Early decision: Not offered. Early action: Not offered. Admission can be deferred. **Application fee:** $35. **To apply online, go to:** http://www.vcsu.edu/enrollmentservices/. **Admissions requirements/recommendations:** High school units required (recommended): English: 4; Mathematics: 3; Science: 3; Foreign language: (2); Social studies: 3; Total units: 13 (2). Tests: The college uses SAT or ACT scores in admissions decisions. Either SAT or ACT required. For admission to the fall 2011 entering class, the school will accept ACT with or without writing accepted. Campus visit: Recommended. Admissions interview: Neither required nor recommended. Off-campus interview: Not available. **Factors that count in admissions decisions:** *Academic:* Secondary school record: Very Important. Class rank: Considered. Letters of recommendation: Not Considered. Standardized test scores: Considered. Essay: Not Considered. *Nonacademic:* Interview: Not Considered. Extracurricular activities: Not Considered. Talent/ability: Not Considered. Character/personal qualities: Not Considered. Alumni/ae relationship: Not Considered. Geographical residence: Not Considered. State residency: Not Considered. Religious affiliation/commitment: Not Considered. Minority status: Not Considered. Volunteer work: Not Considered. Work experience: Not Considered. **Other schools with the greatest overlap in applicants:** Jamestown College; Minnesota State University–Moorhead; North Dakota State University; University of North Dakota. **Admissions statistics for the fall 2009 entering class:** Total applicants: 266. Total accepted: 245. Freshmen enrolled: 155; 30% were from out of state. Overall acceptance rate: 92%. **Credentials of fall 2009 freshmen:** 7% ranked in the top 10 percent of their high school class; 24% were in the top 25 percent; 52% were in the top half. (Proportion submitting class standing: 84%.) **Average high school grade point average:** 3.1. **First-year students who submitted SAT scores:** 8%. Scores (25/75 percentile): Critical Reading: 400-540, Math: 430-490, Combined: 830-1030. **First-year students submitting ACT scores:** 85%. Scores (25/75 percentile): English: N/A, Math: N/A, Composite: 18-23.

ACADEMICS

Year founded: 1890. **Academic calendar:** Semester. **Degrees offered:** certificate, bachelor's, master's. **Most popular majors:** 30% elementary education and teaching, 15% business administration and management, 6% wildlife and wildlands science and management, 5% general studies, 5% human resources management/personnel administration. **Major fields of study:** biological and biomedical sciences; business, management, marketing, and related support services; communication, journalism, and related programs; computer and information sciences and support services; education; English language and literature/letters; foreign languages, literatures, and linguistics; health professions and related clinical sciences; history; mathematics and statistics; multi/interdisciplinary studies; natural resources and conservation; parks, recreation, leisure, and fitness studies; physical sciences; psychology; social sciences; visual and performing arts. **Areas of required coursework:** arts/fine arts, humanities, computer literacy, mathematics, English (including composition), sciences (biological or physical), social science. **Pre-professional programs:** pre-law, pre-dentistry, pre-medicine, pre-veterinary science, pre-optometry, pre-pharmacy. **Special academic programs (% participation):** distance learning, double major (10%), independent study (4%), internships (31%), student-designed major (5%), study abroad (1%), teacher certificate program (44%). **Teacher certification offered in:** elementary, vo-tech, middle/junior high, secondary, bilingual/bicultural. **Faculty and instruction (2009-2010):** Total instructional faculty: 58 full-time, 37 part-time (45% men; 55% women; 3% minorities). Full-time faculty with Ph.D. or other terminal degree: 59%. Student/faculty ratio: 12/1. Classes of fewer than 20 students: %; of 20 to 49 students: %; of 50 or more students: %. **Advanced Placement and International Baccalaureate credit:** International Baccalaureate exams may be used for: Credit only. **Freshmen returning for sophomore year:** 66%. **Graduation rates:** Four-year: 23%; five-year: 38%; six-year: 46%. **Graduate study:** 0% of students pursue further study immediately upon graduation. Fields in which graduates pursue further study: education, 6%; veterinary medicine, 14%.

COSTS AND FINANCIAL AID

Financial aid office: (701) 845-7412. **Expenses (2010-2011):** Tuition and fees 2010-2011: $6,075 in state, $13,477 out of state; room/board: $5,017. Estimated books and supplies: $1,000; transportation: $1,369; personal expenses: $1,840. **Financial aid:** Priority filing date for institution's financial aid form: March 15. In 2009-2010, 87% of undergraduates applied for financial aid. Of those, 66% were determined to have financial need; 99% had their need fully met. Average financial aid package (proportion receiving): $8,480 (66%). Average amount of gift aid, such as scholarships or grants (proportion receiving): $4,339 (58%). Average amount of self-help aid, such as work study or loans (proportion receiving): $3,862 (59%). Average need-based loan (excluding PLUS or other private loans): $3,891. Among students who received need-based aid, the average percentage of need met: 76%. Among students who received aid based on merit, the average award (and the proportion receiving): $1,761 (45%). The average athletic scholarship (and the proportion receiving): $1,423 (19%). Average amount of debt of borrowers graduating in 2009: $25,929. Proportion who borrowed: 88%.

CAMPUS LIFE AND EXTRACURRICULAR ACTIVITIES

Campus housing available (% using): coed dorms (32%), women's dorms (21%), men's dorms (40%), apartments for married students (1%), apartment for single students (6%). Students who live in college-owned, operated, or affiliated housing: 32%. **Student employment:** During the 2009-2010 academic year, 29% of undergraduates worked on campus.

Average per-year earnings: $1,600. **Clubs and organizations:** Number of student organizations: 32. Activities include: campus ministries, choral groups, concert band, dance, drama/theater, international student organization, jazz band, literary magazine, music ensembles, musical theater, pep band, student government, student newspaper, yearbook. Number of fraternities: 1; sororities: 1. Proportion of men in fraternities: 2%; of women in sororities: 2%. Average proportion of students who stay on campus on weekends: 40%. **Sports program (2009-2010):** Member of NAIA. *Men's intercollegiate varsity sports:* baseball, basketball, football, golf. *Women's intercollegiate varsity sports:* basketball, golf, softball, volleyball.

SERVICES AND FACILITIES

Basic services: nonremedial tutoring, placement service, health service, health insurance. **Remedial assistance:** writing, study skills, other. **Counseling services:** minority student, career, military, personal, veteran student, academic, older student, psychological, birth control. **For learning-disabled students:** School does not offer a structured program with separate admission and additional fees. Total undergraduates in learning-disabled program or receiving services: 24. Services include: remedial math, remedial English, tape recorders, untimed tests, note-taking services, oral tests, readers, extended time for tests, tutors, priority registration, priority seating, texts on tape, exams on tape or computer, other testing accommodations. **Library:** Number of titles: 100,321; number of current serial subscriptions: 862. **Information technology resources:** Students are required to lease or own a computer. Number of campus computers available to all students: 817. School has a wireless network. Approximate number of users that can be accommodated: 725. Proportion of college-owned housing units wired for high-speed internet access: 100%. **Campus safety:** Security services offered: 24-hour foot-and-vehicle patrols, lighted pathways/sidewalks, student patrols, controlled dormitory access (key, security card, etc).

TRANSFER AND INTERNATIONAL STUDENTS

Transfer students: May apply for admission for the following academic terms: Fall, Spring, Summer. Applicants need a minimum number of credits to apply. For fall 2009: Transfer applications received: 99. Transfer applicants offered admission: 91. Transfer applicants enrolled: 80. **International students:** Number of foreign undergraduates: 38 (4% of student body). Number of countries represented: 9. Minimum TOEFL score required: 525 (paper); 195 (computer).

Ohio

Art Academy of Cincinnati

- **Address:** 1212 Jackson Street, Cincinnati, OH 45202
- **Website:** http://www.artacademy.edu
- **Private**
- **Enrollment:** N/A

KEY STATS

✔ **U.S News College Ranking:** Unranked Specialty School–Fine Arts
✔ **SAT Score (25th/75th percentile):** 900-1170
✔ **Tuition:** 2009-2010: $21,880

Selectivity: N/A	**Room/board:** $6,900
Acceptance rate: 21%	**Average debt:** N/A
Student/faculty ratio: N/A	**Proportion who borrowed:** N/A

Ashland University

- **Address:** 401 College Avenue, Ashland, OH 44805
- **Website:** http://www.ashland.edu
- **Private; Religious affiliation:** Brethren Church
- **Enrollment:** 2,242 full-time; 451 part-time

KEY STATS

✔ **U.S News College Ranking:** 58, Regional Universities (Midwest)
✔ **ACT Score (25th/75th percentile):** 21-25
✔ **Tuition:** 2010-2011: $27,404

Selectivity: Selective	**Room/board:** $9,358
Acceptance rate: 94%	**Average debt:** $36,545
Student/faculty ratio: 16/1	**Proportion who borrowed:** 82%

UNDERGRADUATE STUDENT BODY STATS

2009-2010 enrollment: 2,242 full-time; 451 part-time. Men: 48%; women: 52%. **Ethnic makeup:** African American: 5%; American-Indian: 1%; Asian American: 1%; Hispanic: 2%; White: 89%; International: 2%. **Religious preference:** Roman Catholic: 17%; Protestant: 8%; No preference: 47%; Brethren Church: 3%; Methodist: 8%; Other: 17%.

ADMISSIONS FACTS AND FIGURES

Phone: (419) 289-5052. **Email:** enrollme@ashland.edu. **Website:** http://www.ashland.edu. **Application deadlines for fall 2011:** Regular decision: Rolling; decision sent by August 15. Early decision: Not offered. Early action: Not offered. Admission can be deferred. **To apply online, go to:** http://www.ashland.edu/applynow/apply.php. **Admissions requirements/recommendations:** High school units required (recommended): English: 4 (4); Mathematics: 2 (3); Science: 2 (3); Foreign language: 0 (2); Social studies: 2 (3); History: 1 (1); Total units: 15 (18). Tests: The college uses SAT or ACT scores in admissions decisions. Either SAT or ACT required. For admission to the fall 2011 entering class, the school will accept: ACT with or without writing accepted. Campus visit: Recommended. Admissions interview: Recommended. Off-campus interview: Not available. **Factors that count in admissions decisions:** *Academic:* Secondary school record: Very Important. Class rank: Important. Letters of recommendation: Important. Standardized test scores: Very Important. Essay: Important. *Nonacademic:* Interview: Important. Extracurricular activities: Important. Talent/ability: Important. Character/personal qualities: Important. Alumni/ae relationship: Important. Geographical residence: Important. State residency: Not Considered. Religious affiliation/commitment: Not Considered. Minority status: Not Considered. Volunteer work: Considered. Work experience: Considered. **Other schools with the greatest overlap in applicants:** Bowling Green State University; Kent State University; Ohio State University–Columbus; Ohio University; University of Akron. **Admissions statistics for the fall 2009 entering class:** Total applicants: 2,903. Total accepted: 2,742. Freshmen enrolled: 622; 7% were from out of state. Overall acceptance rate: 94%. **Credentials of fall 2009 freshmen:** 18% ranked in the top 10 percent of their high school class; 47% were in the top 25 percent; 79% were in the top half. (Proportion submitting class standing: 88%.) **Average high school grade point average:** 3.4. **First-year students who submitted SAT scores:** 27%. Scores (25/75 percentile): Critical Reading: 470-570, Math: 490-590, Combined: 960-1160. **First-year students submitting ACT scores:** 91%. Scores (25/75 percentile): English: 21-26, Math: 20-26, Composite: 21-25.

ACADEMICS

Year founded: 1878. **Academic calendar:** Semester. **Degrees offered:** certificate, associate, bachelor's, master's, doctorate. **Most popular majors:** 13% early childhood education and teaching, 7% business administration and management, 7% marketing/marketing management, 6% junior high/intermediate/middle school education and teaching, 4% criminal justice/law enforcement administration. **Major fields of study:** biological and biomedical sciences; business, management, marketing, and related support services; communication, journalism, and related programs; communications technologies/technicians and support services; education; English language and literature/letters; family and consumer sciences/human sciences; foreign languages, literatures, and linguistics; history; mathematics and statistics; parks, recreation, leisure, and fitness studies; philosophy and religious studies; physical sciences; psychology; public administration and social service professions; security and protective services; social sciences; visual and performing arts. **Areas of required coursework:** arts/fine arts, humanities, mathematics, English (including composition), philosophy, sciences (biological or physical), history, social science. **Pre-professional programs:** pre-law, pre-dentistry, pre-medicine, pre-theology, pre-veterinary science, pre-optometry, pre-pharmacy, other. **Special academic programs:** double major, English as a Second Language (ESL), honors program, independent study, internships, student-designed major, study abroad, teacher certificate program, weekend college. **Teacher certification offered in:** early childhood, special education, elementary, vo-tech, middle/junior high, secondary. **Faculty and instruction (2009-2010):** Total instructional faculty: 235 full-time, 347 part-time (52% men; 48% women; 7% minorities). Full-time faculty with Ph.D. or other terminal degree: 92%. Student/faculty ratio: 16/1. Classes of fewer than 20 students: 62%; of 20 to 49 students: 37%; of 50 or more students: 1%. **Advanced Placement and International Baccalaureate credit:** AP tests may be used for: Placement only. Scores accepted: 3, 4, 5. International Baccalaureate exams may be used for: Credit and/or placement. **Freshmen returning for sophomore year:** 71%. **Graduation rates:** Four-year: 46%; five-year: 59%; six-year: 60%. **Graduate study:** 13% of students pursue further study immediately upon graduation; 12% within five years. Fields in which graduates pursue further study: Master of Business Administration (MBA), 2%; law, 1%; medicine, 1%; theology (or the seminary), 1%; education, 1%; arts and sciences, 6%.

COSTS AND FINANCIAL AID

Financial aid office: (419) 289-5002. **Expenses (2010-2011):** Tuition and fees 2010-2011: $27,404; room/board: $9,358. Estimated books and supplies: $900; transportation: $2,268; personal expenses: $1,801. **Financial aid:** Priority filing date for institution's financial aid form: March 15; deadline: March 15. In 2009-2010, 99% of undergraduates applied for financial aid. Of those, 82% were determined to have financial need; Average financial aid package (proportion receiving): $23,254 (82%). Average amount of gift aid, such as scholarships or grants (proportion receiving): $15,366 (82%). Average amount of self-help aid, such as work study or loans (proportion receiving): $6,595 (73%). Average need-based loan (excluding PLUS or other private loans): $4,717. Among students who received need-based aid, the average percentage of need met: 90%. Among students who received aid based on merit, the average award (and the proportion receiving): $8,168 (10%). The average athletic scholarship (and the proportion receiving): $13,608 (3%). Average amount of debt of borrowers graduating in 2009: $36,545. Proportion who borrowed: 82%.

CAMPUS LIFE AND EXTRACURRICULAR ACTIVITIES

Campus housing available (% using): coed dorms (32%), women's dorms (36%), men's dorms (18%), fraternity housing (6%), apartment for single students (8%). **Student employment:** During the 2009-2010 academic year,

28% of undergraduates worked on campus. Average per-year earnings: $1,150. **Clubs and organizations:** Number of student organizations: 96. Activities include: campus ministries, choral groups, concert band, dance, drama/theater, international student organization, jazz band, literary magazine, marching band, music ensembles, musical theater, pep band, radio station, student government, student newspaper, symphony orchestra, television station, yearbook. Number of fraternities: 3; sororities: 5. Proportion of men in fraternities: 22%; of women in sororities: 55%. Average proportion of students who stay on campus on weekends: 50%. **Sports program (2009-2010):** Member of NCAA II. *Men's intercollegiate varsity sports:* baseball, basketball, cross country, football, golf, soccer, swimming, track and field (indoor), track and field (outdoor), wrestling. *Women's intercollegiate varsity sports:* basketball, cross country, golf, soccer, softball, swimming, tennis, track and field (indoor), track and field (outdoor), volleyball.

SERVICES AND FACILITIES

Basic services: nonremedial tutoring, women's center, placement service, health service, health insurance. **Remedial assistance:** reading, math, writing, study skills. **Counseling services:** minority student, career, personal, academic, older student, psychological, birth control, religious. **For learning-disabled students:** School does not offer a structured program with separate admission and additional fees. Total undergraduates in learning-disabled program or receiving services: 132. Services include: remedial math, remedial English, reading machines, tape recorders, untimed tests, note-taking services, oral tests, learning center, readers, extended time for tests, tutors, priority registration, priority seating, texts on tape, typist/scribe, exams on tape or computer, other testing accommodations. **Library:** Number of titles: 336,872; number of current serial subscriptions: 791. **Information technology resources:** Students are not required to lease or own a computer. Number of campus computers available to all students: 2,000. School has a wireless network. Approximate number of users that can be accommodated: 5,000. Proportion of college-owned housing units wired for high-speed internet access: 100%. **Campus safety:** Security services offered: 24-hour foot-and-vehicle patrols, late-night transport/escort service, 24-hour emergency telephones, lighted pathways/sidewalks, student patrols, controlled dormitory access (key, security card, etc).

TRANSFER AND INTERNATIONAL STUDENTS

Transfer students: May apply for admission for the following academic terms: Fall, Spring, Summer. Applicants do not need a minimum number of credits to apply. For fall 2009: Transfer applications received: 352. Transfer applicants offered admission: 174. Transfer applicants enrolled: 88. **International students:** Number of foreign undergraduates: 50 (2% of student body). Number of countries represented: 13. Minimum TOEFL score required: 500 (paper); 65 (computer).

Baldwin-Wallace College

- **Address:** 275 Eastland Road, Berea, OH 44017
- **Website:** http://www.bw.edu
- **Private; Religious affiliation:** United Methodist
- **Enrollment:** 3,180 full-time; 504 part-time

KEY STATS

✔ **U.S News College Ranking:** 13, Regional Universities (Midwest)
✔ **ACT Score (25th/75th percentile):** 21-26
✔ **Tuition:** 2010-2011: $25,260

Selectivity: Selective	**Room/board:** $7,028
Acceptance rate: 67%	**Average debt:** $17,716
Student/faculty ratio: 15/1	**Proportion who borrowed:** 67%

UNDERGRADUATE STUDENT BODY STATS

2009-2010 enrollment: 3,180 full-time; 504 part-time. Men: 42%; women: 58%. **Ethnic makeup:** African American: 7%; Asian American: 1%; Hispanic: 3%; White: 87%; International: 2%. **Religious preference:** Roman Catholic: 39%; Protestant: 46%; Jewish: 1%; Muslim: 1%; United Methodist: 9%; Mormon, Unitarian: 0%; Other: 4%.

ADMISSIONS FACTS AND FIGURES

Phone: (440) 826-2222. **Email:** admission@bw.edu. **Website:** http://www.bw.edu. **Application deadlines for fall 2011:** Regular decision: Rolling. Early decision: Not offered. Early action: Not offered. Admission can be deferred. **Application fee:** $25. **To apply online, go to:** http://www.bw.edu/admission/apply.asp. **Admissions requirements/recommendations:** High school units required (recommended): English: 4 (4); Mathematics: 3 (4); Science: 3 (4); Foreign language: 1 (2); Social studies: 2 (3); History: 1 (1); Academic electives: (3); Total units: 16 (23). Tests: The college uses SAT or ACT scores in admissions decisions. Neither SAT nor ACT required. For admission to the fall 2011 entering class, the school will accept: ACT with or without writing accepted. Campus visit: Recommended. Admissions interview: Recommended. Off-campus interview: May be arranged. **Factors that count in admissions decisions:** *Academic:* Secondary school record: Very Important. Class rank: Important. Letters of recommendation: Considered. Standardized test scores: Considered. Essay: Important. *Nonacademic:* Interview: Considered. Extracurricular activities: Important. Talent/ability: Important. Character/personal qualities: Important. Alumni/ae relationship: Considered. Geographical residence: Considered. State residency: Considered. Religious affiliation/commitment: Not Considered. Minority status: Considered. Volunteer work: Considered. Work experience: Considered. **Other schools with the greatest overlap in applicants:** Bowling Green State University; John Carroll University; Kent State University; University of Akron; University of Mount Union. **Admissions statistics for the fall 2009 entering class:** Total applicants: 3,498. Total accepted: 2,335. Freshmen enrolled: 755; 14% were from out of state. Overall acceptance rate: 67%. **Credentials of fall 2009 freshmen:** 28% ranked in the top 10 percent of their high school class; 54% were in the top 25 percent; 81% were in the top half. (Proportion submitting class standing: 70%.) **Average high school grade point average:** 3.5. **First-year students who submitted SAT scores:** 47%. Scores (25/75 percentile): Critical Reading: 480-610, Math: 490-590, Combined: 970-1200. **First-year students submitting ACT scores:** 83%. Scores (25/75 percentile): English: 21-28, Math: 21-26, Composite: 21-26.

ACADEMICS

Year founded: 1845. **Academic calendar:** Semester. **Degrees offered:** certificate, bachelor's, master's. **Most popular majors:** 30% business, management, marketing, and related support services, 10% education, 10% visual and performing arts, 8% communication, journalism, and related programs, 7% biological and biomedical sciences. **Major fields of study:** biological and biomedical sciences; business, management, marketing, and related support services; communication, journalism, and related programs; computer and information sciences and support services; education; English language and literature/letters; foreign languages, literatures, and linguistics; health professions and related clinical sciences; history; mathematics and statistics; multi/interdisciplinary studies; parks, recreation, leisure, and fitness studies; philosophy and religious studies; physical sciences; psychology; security and protective services; social sciences; visual and performing arts. **Areas of required coursework:** arts/fine arts, humanities, mathematics, English (including composition), sciences (biological or physical), social science, other. **Pre-professional programs:** pre-law, pre-dentistry, pre-medicine, pre-theology, pre-veterinary science, pre-pharmacy, other. **Special academic programs (% participation):** accelerated program (.3%), cross-registration (.3%), distance learning (5%), double major (23%), dual enrollment (1%), English as a Second Language (ESL), exchange student program (domestic) (.3%), honors program (5%), independent study (17%), internships (28%), student-designed major (1%), study abroad (6%), teacher certificate program (12%), weekend college (1%), other (17%). **Teacher certification offered in:** early childhood, special education, middle/junior high, secondary. **Reserve Officers Training Corps (ROTC):** Army ROTC: Offered at cooperating institution (John Carroll University); Air Force ROTC: Offered at cooperating institution (Kent State University). **Faculty and instruction (2009-2010):** Total instructional faculty: 167 full-time, 251 part-time (55% men; 45% women; 9% minorities). Full-time faculty with Ph.D. or other terminal degree: 79%. Student/faculty ratio: 15/1. Classes of fewer than 20 students: 56%; of 20 to 49 students: 43%; of 50 or more students: 1%. **Advanced Placement and International Baccalaureate credit:** AP tests may be used for: Credit and/or placement. Scores accepted: 3, 4, 5. International Baccalaureate exams may be used for: Credit and/or placement. **Freshmen returning for sophomore year:** 83%. **Graduation rates:** Four-year: 50%; five-year: 66%; six-year: 69%. **Graduate study:** 28% of students pursue further study within one year. Fields in which graduates pursue further study: Master of Business Administration (MBA), 18%; law, 2%; medicine, 9%; theology (or the seminary), 2%; education, 23%; arts and sciences, 46%.

COSTS AND FINANCIAL AID

Financial aid office: (440) 826-2108. **Expenses (2010-2011):** Tuition and fees 2010-2011: $25,260; room/board: $7,028. Estimated books and supplies: $1,272 personal expenses: $2,128. **Financial aid:** Priority filing date for institution's financial aid form: May 1; deadline: September 1. In 2009-2010,

90% of undergraduates applied for financial aid. Of those, 80% were determined to have financial need; 48% had their need fully met. Average financial aid package (proportion receiving): $19,838 (80%). Average amount of gift aid, such as scholarships or grants (proportion receiving): $13,687 (80%). Average amount of self-help aid, such as work study or loans (proportion receiving): $6,744 (80%). Average need-based loan (excluding PLUS or other private loans): $4,827. Among students who received need-based aid, the average percentage of need met: 85%. Among students who received aid based on merit, the average award (and the proportion receiving): $10,050 (17%). Average amount of debt of borrowers graduating in 2009: $17,716. Proportion who borrowed: 67%.

CAMPUS LIFE AND EXTRACURRICULAR ACTIVITIES

Campus housing available (% using): coed dorms (63%), women's dorms (7%), men's dorms, sorority housing (6%), fraternity housing (4%), apartment for single students (7%), special housing for disabled students (1%), special housing for international students, other housing options (12%). Students who live in college-owned, operated, or affiliated housing: 61%. **Student employment:** During the 2009-2010 academic year, 17% of undergraduates worked on campus. Average per-year earnings: $1,244. **Clubs and organizations:** Number of student organizations: 136. Activities include: campus ministries, choral groups, concert band, dance, drama/theater, international student organization, jazz band, literary magazine, marching band, model UN, music ensembles, musical theater, opera, pep band, radio station, student government, student newspaper, student film society, symphony orchestra, television station, yearbook. Number of fraternities: 5; sororities: 5. Proportion of men in fraternities: 12%; of women in sororities: 15%. Average proportion of students who stay on campus on weekends: 50%. **Sports program (2009-2010):** Member of NCAA III. *Men's intercollegiate varsity sports:* baseball, basketball, cross country, football, golf, soccer, swimming, tennis, track and field (indoor), track and field (outdoor), wrestling. *Women's intercollegiate varsity sports:* basketball, cross country, golf, soccer, softball, swimming, tennis, track and field (indoor), track and field (outdoor), volleyball.

SERVICES AND FACILITIES

Basic services: nonremedial tutoring, health service, health insurance, other. **Remedial assistance:** reading, math, writing, study skills, other. **Counseling services:** minority student, career, personal, academic, older student, psychological, birth control, religious. **For learning-disabled students:** School does not offer a structured program with separate admission and additional fees. Total undergraduates in learning-disabled program or receiving services: 52. Services include: remedial math, tape recorders, note-taking services, learning center, readers, extended time for tests, tutors, early syllabus, priority registration, priority seating, texts on tape, typist/scribe, other. **Library:** Number of titles: 200,000; number of current serial subscriptions: 44,000. **Information technology resources:** Students are not required to lease or own a computer. Number of campus computers available to all students: 561. School has a wireless network. Approximate number of users that can be accommodated: 4,000. Proportion of college-owned housing units wired for high-speed internet access: 100%. **Campus safety:** Security services offered: 24-hour foot-and-vehicle patrols, late-night transport/escort service, 24-hour emergency telephones, lighted pathways/sidewalks, student patrols, controlled dormitory access (key, security card, etc).

TRANSFER AND INTERNATIONAL STUDENTS

Transfer students: May apply for admission for the following academic terms: Fall, Spring, Summer. Applicants do not need a minimum number of credits to apply. For fall 2009: Transfer applications received: 520. Transfer applicants offered admission: 259. Transfer applicants enrolled: 141. **International students:** Number of foreign undergraduates: 54 (2% of student body). Number of countries represented: 14. Minimum TOEFL score required: 523 (paper); 193 (computer). Average TOEFL score: 576 (paper).

■ **Address:** 1 University Drive, Bluffton, OH 45817
■ **Website:** http://www.bluffton.edu
■ **Private; Religious affiliation:** Mennonite Church USA
■ **Enrollment:** 911 full-time; 94 part-time

KEY STATS

✔ **U.S News College Ranking:** 20, Regional Colleges (Midwest)
✔ **ACT Score (25th/75th percentile):** 19-24
✔ **Tuition:** 2010-2011: $24,930

Selectivity: Selective	**Room/board:** $8,348
Acceptance rate: 66%	**Average debt:** $26,896
Student/faculty ratio: 13/1	**Proportion who borrowed:** 88%

UNDERGRADUATE STUDENT BODY STATS

2009-2010 enrollment: 911 full-time; 94 part-time. Men: 49%; women: 51%. **Ethnic makeup:** African American: 7%; Asian American: 1%; Hispanic: 2%; White: 90%; International: 2%. **Religious preference:** Roman Catholic: 13%; Protestant: 50%; Unknown: 26%; Mennonite Church USA: 11%.

ADMISSIONS FACTS AND FIGURES

Phone: (800) 488-3257. **Email:** admissions@bluffton.edu. **Website:** http://www.bluffton.edu. **Application deadlines for fall 2011:** Regular decision: August 15. Early decision: Not offered. Early action: Not offered. Admission can be deferred. **Application fee:** $20. **To apply online, go to:** http://www.bluffton.edu/admission/apply/index.html. **Admissions requirements/recommendations:** High school units required (recommended): English: (4); Mathematics: (3); Science: (3); Foreign language: (3); Social studies: (3); History: (0); Academic electives: (0); Total units: (16). Tests: The college uses SAT or ACT scores in admissions decisions. Either SAT or ACT required. For admission to the fall 2011 entering class, the school will accept: ACT with or without writing accepted. Campus visit: Recommended. Admissions interview: Recommended. Off-campus interview: May be arranged. **Factors that count in admissions decisions:** *Academic:* Secondary school record: Considered. Class rank: Very Important. Letters of recommendation: Important. Standardized test scores: Very Important. Essay: Considered. *Nonacademic:* Interview: Considered. Extracurricular activities: Considered. Talent/ability: Considered. Character/personal qualities: Considered. Alumni/ae relationship: Not Considered. Geographical residence: Not Considered. State residency: Not Considered. Religious affiliation/commitment: Considered. Minority status: Not Considered. Volunteer work: Considered. Work experience: Not Considered. **Other schools with the greatest overlap in applicants:** Bowling Green State University; Ohio Northern University; Ohio State University–Columbus; University of Findlay; University of Toledo. **Admissions statistics for the fall 2009 entering class:** Total applicants: 1,674. Total accepted: 1,113. Freshmen enrolled: 257; 16% were from out of state. Overall acceptance rate: 66%. **Size of waiting list:** 0 applicants; enrolled from waiting list: 0. **Credentials of fall 2009 freshmen:** 14% ranked in the top 10 percent of their high school class; 33% were in the top 25 percent; 67% were in the top half. (Proportion submitting class standing: 94%.) **Average high school grade point average:** 3.2. **First-year students who submitted SAT scores:** 18%. Scores (25/75 percentile): Critical Reading: 420-570, Math: 450-600, Combined: 870-1170. **First-year students submitting ACT scores:** 92%. Scores (25/75 percentile): English: 17-24, Math: 18-25, Composite: 19-24.

ACADEMICS

Year founded: 1899. **Academic calendar:** Semester. **Degrees offered:** bachelor's, master's. **Most popular majors:** 20% organizational behavior studies, 9% elementary education and teaching, 8% business administration and management, 8% social work, 6% special education and teaching. **Major fields of study:** biological and biomedical sciences; business, management, marketing, and related support services; communication, journalism, and related programs; computer and information sciences and support services; education; English language and literature/letters; family and consumer sciences/human sciences; foreign languages, literatures, and linguistics; health professions and related clinical sciences; history; mathematics and statistics; multi/interdisciplinary studies; parks, recreation, leisure, and fitness studies; philosophy and religious studies; physical sciences; psychology; public administration and social service professions; security and protective services; social sciences; theology and religious vocations; visual and performing arts. **Areas of required coursework:** arts/fine arts, humanities, mathematics, English (including composition), philosophy, sciences (biological or physical), history, social science, other. **Pre-professional programs:** pre-law, pre-dentistry, pre-medicine, pre-theology, pre-optometry. **Special academic programs (% participation):** double major (9%), dual enrollment (2%), honors program (2%), independent study (10%), internships (30%), student-designed major (1%), study abroad (5%), teacher certificate program (23%). **Teacher certification offered in:** early childhood, special education, elementary, vo-tech, middle/junior high, secondary. **Cooperative education programs:** business, education, social/behavioral science, technologies. **Faculty and instruction (2009-2010):** Total instructional faculty: 62 full-time, 47 part-time (61% men; 39% women; 4% minorities). Full-time faculty with Ph.D. or other terminal degree: 73%. Student/faculty ratio: 13/1. Classes of fewer than 20 students: 58%; of 20 to 49 students: 41%; of 50 or more students: 1%. **Advanced Placement and International Baccalaureate credit:** AP tests may be used for: Placement only. Scores accepted: 3, 4, 5. **Freshmen returning for sophomore year:** 74%. **Graduation rates:** Four-year: 56%; five-year: 62%; six-year: 61%. **Graduate study:** 12% of students pursue further study immediately upon graduation; 5% within one year; 45% within five years. Fields in which graduates pursue further study: Master of Business Administration (MBA), 15%; law, 5%; medicine, 4%; dentistry, 1%; theology (or the seminary), 15%; education, 40%; arts and sciences, 5%.

COSTS AND FINANCIAL AID

Financial aid office: (419) 358-3266. **Expenses (2010-2011):** Tuition and fees 2010-2011: $24,930; room/board: $8,348. Estimated books and supplies: $1,400; transportation: $800; personal expenses: $1,500. **Financial aid:** Priority filing date for institution's financial aid form: May 1; deadline: October 1. In 2009-2010, 93% of undergraduates applied for financial aid. Of those, 88% were determined to have financial need; 43% had their need fully met. Average financial aid package (proportion receiving): $21,413 (88%). Average amount of gift aid, such as scholarships or grants (proportion receiving): $15,092 (86%). Average amount of self-help aid, such as work study or loans (proportion receiving): $6,821 (82%). Average need-based loan (excluding PLUS or other private loans): $4,878. Among students who received need-based aid, the average percentage of need met: 89%. Among students who received aid based on merit, the average award (and the proportion receiving): $8,315 (11%). The average athletic scholarship (and the proportion receiving): $0 (0%). Average amount of debt of borrowers graduating in 2009: $26,896. Proportion who borrowed: 88%.

CAMPUS LIFE AND EXTRACURRICULAR ACTIVITIES

Campus housing available (% using): coed dorms (40%), women's dorms (34%), men's dorms (24%). Students who live in college-owned, operated, or affiliated housing: 82%. **Student employment:** During the 2009-2010 academic year, 65% of undergraduates worked on campus. Average per-year earnings: $2,340. **Clubs and organizations:** Number of student organizations: 40. Activities include: campus ministries, choral groups, concert band, dance, drama/theater, international student organization, jazz band, literary magazine, music ensembles, musical theater, pep band, radio station, student government, student newspaper. Number of fraternities: 0; sororities: 0. Average proportion of students who stay on campus on weekends: 60%. **Sports program (2009-2010):** Member of NCAA III. *Men's intercollegiate varsity sports:* baseball, basketball, cross country, football, soccer, track and field (indoor), track and field (outdoor). *Women's intercollegiate varsity sports:* basketball, cross country, soccer, softball, track and field (indoor), track and field (outdoor), volleyball.

SERVICES AND FACILITIES

Basic services: nonremedial tutoring, placement service, health service, health insurance. **Remedial assistance:** reading, math, writing, study skills. **Counseling services:** minority student, career, personal, veteran student, academic, psychological, religious. **For learning-disabled students:** School does not offer a structured program with separate admission and additional fees. Total undergraduates in learning-disabled program or receiving services: 37. Services include: remedial math, remedial English, remedial reading, tape recorders, videotaped classes, untimed tests, note-taking services, oral tests, learning center, readers, extended time for tests, tutors, early syllabus, priority registration, priority seating, substitution of courses, texts on tape, typist/scribe, exams on tape or computer, other testing accommodations. **Library:** Number of titles: 161,372; number of current serial subscriptions: 6,019. **Information technology resources:** Students are not required to lease or own a computer. Number of campus computers available to all students: 175. School has a wireless network. Approximate number of users that can be accommodated: 75. Proportion of college-owned housing units wired for high-speed internet access: 100%. **Campus safety:** Security services offered: 24-hour emergency telephones, lighted pathways/sidewalks, controlled dormitory access (key, security card, etc).

TRANSFER AND INTERNATIONAL STUDENTS

Transfer students: May apply for admission for the following academic terms: Fall, Spring, Summer. Applicants do not need a minimum number of credits to apply. For fall 2009: Transfer applications received: 127. Transfer applicants offered admission: 59. Transfer applicants enrolled: 26. **International students:** Number of foreign undergraduates: 15 (2% of student body). Number of countries represented: 10. Minimum TOEFL score required: 500 (paper); 180 (computer). Average TOEFL score: 535 (paper).

Bowling Green State University

- **Address:** 110 McFall Center, Bowling Green, OH 43403
- **Website:** http://www.bgsu.edu
- **Public**
- **Enrollment:** 13,162 full-time; 1,157 part-time

KEY STATS

✔ **U.S News College Ranking:** 170, National Universities
✔ **ACT Score (25th/75th percentile):** 19-24
✔ **Tuition:** 2010-2011: $9,744 in state, $17,062 out of state

Selectivity: Selective	**Room/board:** $7,810
Acceptance rate: 89%	**Average debt:** $28,542
Student/faculty ratio: 19/1	**Proportion who borrowed:** 72%

UNDERGRADUATE STUDENT BODY STATS

2009-2010 enrollment: 13,162 full-time; 1,157 part-time. Men: 46%; women: 54%. **Ethnic makeup:** African American: 11%; American-Indian: 1%; Asian American: 1%; Hispanic: 3%; White: 83%; International: 2%.

ADMISSIONS FACTS AND FIGURES

Phone: (419) 372-2478. **Email:** choosebgsu@bgsu.edu. **Website:** http://www.bgsu.edu. **Application deadlines for fall 2011:** Regular decision: July 15. Early decision: Not offered. Early action: Not offered. Admission can be deferred. **Application fee:** $40. **To apply online, go to:** http://go2.bgsu.edu/choose/apply/. **Admissions requirements/recommendations:** High school units required (recommended): English: 4 (4); Mathematics: 3 (3); Science: 3 (3); Foreign language: 2 (2); Social studies: 3 (3); Total units: 16 (16). Tests: The college uses SAT or ACT scores in admissions decisions. Either SAT or ACT required. For admission to the fall 2011 entering class, the school will accept: ACT with or without writing accepted. Campus visit: Recommended. Admissions interview: Recommended. Off-campus interview: Not available. **Factors that count in admissions decisions:** *Academic:* Secondary school record: Very Important. Class rank: Important. Letters of recommendation: Considered. Standardized test scores: Very Important. Essay: Considered. *Nonacademic:* Interview: Considered. Extracurricular activities: Considered. Talent/ability: Important. Character/personal qualities: Considered. Alumni/ae relationship: Considered. Geographical residence: Not Considered. State residency: Not Considered. Religious affiliation/commitment: Not Considered. Minority status: Considered. Volunteer work: Considered. Work experience: Considered. **Other schools with the greatest overlap in applicants:** Kent State University; Miami University–Oxford; Ohio State University–Columbus; Ohio University; University of Toledo. **Admissions statistics for the fall 2009 entering class:** Total applicants: 10,418. Total accepted: 9,253. Freshmen enrolled: 3,163; 11% were from out of state. Overall acceptance rate: 89%. **Credentials of fall 2009 freshmen:** 12% ranked in the top 10 percent of their high school class; 35% were in the top 25 percent; 69% were in the top half. (Proportion submitting class standing: 81%.) **Average high school grade point average:** 3.2. **First-year students who submitted SAT scores:** 11%. Scores (25/75 percentile): Critical Reading: 450-580, Math: 450-570, Combined: 900-1150. **First-year students submitting ACT scores:** 92%. Scores (25/75 percentile): English: 19-25, Math: 18-24, Composite: 19-24.

ACADEMICS

Year founded: 1910. **Academic calendar:** Semester. **Degrees offered:** bachelor's, master's, post-master's certificate, doctorate. **Most popular majors:** 6% kindergarten/preschool education and teaching, 5% speech and rhetorical studies, 4% design and visual communications, 4% liberal arts and sciences/liberal studies, 3% sport and fitness administration/management. **Major fields of study:** architecture and related services; area, ethnic, cultural, and gender studies; biological and biomedical sciences; business, management, marketing, and related support services; communication, journalism, and related programs; computer and information sciences and support services; education; engineering technologies/technicians; English language and literature/letters; family and consumer sciences/human sciences; foreign languages, literatures, and linguistics; health professions and related clinical sciences; history; legal professions and studies; liberal arts and sciences studies, and humanities; mathematics and statistics; multi/interdisciplinary studies; natural resources and conservation; parks, recreation, leisure, and fitness studies; philosophy and religious studies; physical sciences; psychology; public administration and social service professions; security and protective services; social sciences; transportation and materials moving; visual and performing arts. **Areas of required coursework:** humanities, English (including composition), sciences (biological or physical), social science, other. **Pre-professional programs:** pre-law, pre-dentistry, pre-medicine, pre-veterinary science, pre-optometry, pre-pharmacy, other. **Special academic programs:** accelerated program, cooperative (work-study plan) program, cross-registration, distance learning, double major, dual enrollment, English as a Second Language (ESL), exchange student program (domestic), honors program, independent study, internships, liberal arts/career combination, student-designed major, study abroad, teacher certificate program. **Teacher certification offered in:** early childhood, special education, elementary, vo-tech, middle/junior high, secondary. **Cooperative education programs:** art, business, computer science, education, health professions, home economics, humanities, natural science, social/behavioral science, technologies. **Reserve Officers Training Corps (ROTC):** Army ROTC: Offered on campus; Air Force ROTC: Offered on campus. **Faculty and instruction (2009-2010):** Total instructional faculty: 795 full-time, 141 part-time (54% men; 46% women; 16% minorities). Full-time faculty with Ph.D. or other terminal degree: 75%. Student/faculty ratio: 19/1. Classes of fewer than 20 students: 32%; of 20 to 49 students: 61%; of 50 or more students: 8%. **Advanced Placement and International Baccalaureate credit:** AP tests may be used for: Credit and/or placement. Scores accepted: 3, 4, 5. International Baccalaureate exams may be used for: Credit and/or placement. **Freshmen returning for sophomore year:** 75%. **Graduation rates:** Four-year: 34%; five-year: 55%; six-year: 60%.

COSTS AND FINANCIAL AID

Financial aid office: (419) 372-2651. **Expenses (2010-2011):** Tuition and fees 2010-2011: $9,744 in state; $17,062 out of state; room/board: $7,810. Estimated books and supplies: $1,216; transportation: $929; personal expenses: $2,616. **Financial aid:** Priority filing date for institution's financial aid form: February 15. In 2009-2010, 74% of undergraduates applied for financial aid. Of those, 62% were determined to have financial need; 14% had their need fully met. Average financial aid package (proportion receiving): $12,886 (62%). Average amount of gift aid, such as scholarships or grants (proportion receiving): $6,327 (45%). Average amount of self-help aid, such as work study or loans (proportion receiving): $7,775 (57%). Average need-based loan (excluding PLUS or other private loans): $7,674. Among students who received need-based aid, the average percentage of need met: 76%. Among students who received aid based on merit, the average award (and the proportion receiving): $4,727 (15%). The average athletic scholarship (and the proportion receiving): $15,945 (2%). Average amount of debt of borrowers graduating in 2009: $28,542. Proportion who borrowed: 72%.

CAMPUS LIFE AND EXTRACURRICULAR ACTIVITIES

Campus housing available (% using): coed dorms (69%), sorority housing (5%), fraternity housing (4%), apartment for single students (1%), special housing for disabled students (2%), special housing for international students (1%), other housing options (18%). Students who live in college-owned, operated, or affiliated housing: 40%. **Student employment:** During the 2009-2010 academic year, 18% of undergraduates worked on campus. Average per-year earnings: $2,068. **Clubs and organizations:** Number of student organizations: 300. Activities include: choral groups, concert band, dance, drama/theater, international student organization, jazz band, literary magazine, marching band, music ensembles, musical theater, pep band, radio station, student government, student newspaper, student film society, symphony orchestra, television station, yearbook. Number of fraternities: 23; sororities: 20. Proportion of men in fraternities: 10%; of women in sororities: 11%. Average proportion of students who stay on campus on weekends: 60%. **Sports program (2009-2010):** Member of NCAA I. ***Men's intercollegiate varsity sports:*** baseball, basketball, cross country, football, golf, ice hockey, soccer. ***Women's intercollegiate varsity sports:*** basketball, cross country, golf, gymnastics, soccer, softball, swimming, tennis, track and field (indoor), track and field (outdoor), volleyball.

SERVICES AND FACILITIES

Basic services: nonremedial tutoring, women's center, placement service, health service, health insurance. **Remedial assistance:** reading, math, writing, study skills. **Counseling services:** minority student, career, military, personal, veteran student, academic, older student, psychological, birth control. **For learning-disabled students:** School does not offer a structured program with separate admission and additional fees. Services include: remedial math, remedial English, reading machines, remedial reading, tape recorders, diagnostic testing service, note-taking services, oral tests, learning center, readers, extended time for tests, tutors, priority registration, priority seating, texts on tape, exams on tape or computer, other testing accommodations, other. **Library:** Number of titles: 2,312,426; number of current serial subscriptions: 50,375. **Information technology resources:** Students are not required to lease or own a computer. Number of campus computers available to all students: 1,400. School has a wireless network. Approximate number of users that can be accommodated: 8,000. Proportion of college-owned housing units wired for high-speed internet access: 100%. **Campus safety:** Security services offered: 24-hour foot-and-vehicle patrols, late-night transport/escort service, 24-hour emergency telephones, lighted pathways/sidewalks, controlled dormitory access (key, security card, etc).

TRANSFER AND INTERNATIONAL STUDENTS

Transfer students: May apply for admission for the following academic terms: Fall, Spring, Summer. Applicants need a minimum number of credits to apply. For fall 2009: Transfer applications received: 1,378. Transfer applicants offered admission: 906. Transfer applicants enrolled: 584. **International students:** Number of foreign undergraduates: 252 (2% of student body). Number of countries represented: 53. Minimum TOEFL score required: 500 (paper); 61 (computer). Average TOEFL score: 543 (paper).

Capital University

- **Address:** 1 College and Main, Columbus, OH 43209-2394
- **Website:** http://www.capital.edu
- **Private; Religious affiliation:** Lutheran
- **Enrollment:** 2,359 full-time; 271 part-time

KEY STATS

✔ **U.S News College Ranking:** 19, Regional Universities (Midwest)
✔ **ACT Score (25th/75th percentile):** 21-27
✔ **Tuition:** 2010-2011: $29,310

Selectivity: Selective	**Room/board:** $7,864
Acceptance rate: 75%	**Average debt:** $21,805
Student/faculty ratio: 11/1	**Proportion who borrowed:** 83%

UNDERGRADUATE STUDENT BODY STATS

2009-2010 enrollment: 2,359 full-time; 271 part-time. Men: 41%; women: 59%. **Ethnic makeup:** African American: 9%; Asian American: 2%; Hispanic: 2%; White: 86%; International: 1%. **Religious preference:** Roman Catholic: 21%; Protestant: 31%; Jewish: 1%; No preference: 14%; Unknown: 8%; Lutheran: 15%; Other: 10%.

ADMISSIONS FACTS AND FIGURES

Phone: (866) 544-6175. **Email:** admissions@capital.edu. **Website:** http://www.capital.edu. **Application deadlines for fall 2011:** Regular decision: Rolling. Early decision: Not offered. Early action: Not offered. Admission can be deferred. **Application fee:** $25. **To apply online, go to:** http://www.applyweb.com/apply/capital/menu.html. **Admissions requirements/recommendations:** High school units required (recommended): English: (4); Mathematics: (3); Science: (3); Foreign language: (2); Social studies: (3); History: (0); Academic electives: (0); Total units: (18). Tests: The college uses SAT or ACT scores in admissions decisions. Either SAT or ACT required. For admission to the fall 2011 entering class, the school will accept: ACT with or without writing accepted. Campus visit: Recommended. Admissions interview: Recommended. Off-campus interview: Not available. **Factors that count in admissions decisions:** *Academic:* Secondary school record: Considered. Class rank: Not Considered. Letters of recommendation: Considered. Standardized test scores: Very Important. Essay: Not Considered. *Nonacademic:* Interview: Considered. Extracurricular activities: Considered. Talent/ability: Very Important. Character/personal qualities: Not Considered. Alumni/ae relationship: Considered. Geographical residence: Considered. State residency: Considered. Religious affiliation/commitment: Considered. Minority status: Considered. Volunteer work:

Not Considered. Work experience: Not Considered. **Other schools with the greatest overlap in applicants:** Bowling Green State University; Ohio Dominican University; Ohio State University–Columbus; Ohio University; Otterbein College. **Admissions statistics for the fall 2009 entering class:** Total applicants: 3,510. Total accepted: 2,631. Freshmen enrolled: 610; 10% were from out of state. Overall acceptance rate: 75%. **Credentials of fall 2009 freshmen:** 22% ranked in the top 10 percent of their high school class; 52% were in the top 25 percent; 85% were in the top half. (Proportion submitting class standing: 86%.) **Average high school grade point average:** 3.5. **First-year students who submitted SAT scores:** 34%. Scores (25/75 percentile): Critical Reading: 480-590, Math: 480-600, Combined: 960-1190. **First-year students submitting ACT scores:** 92%. Scores (25/75 percentile): English: 20-26, Math: 20-26, Composite: 21-27.

ACADEMICS

Year founded: 1830. **Academic calendar:** Semester. **Degrees offered:** bachelor's, master's. **Most popular majors:** 24% health professions and related clinical sciences, 14% education, 13% business, management, marketing, and related support services, 8% public administration and social service professions, 7% social sciences. **Major fields of study:** biological and biomedical sciences; business, management, marketing, and related support services; communication, journalism, and related programs; computer and information sciences and support services; education; engineering; English language and literature/letters; foreign languages, literatures, and linguistics; health professions and related clinical sciences; history; mathematics and statistics; multi/interdisciplinary studies; natural resources and conservation; parks, recreation, leisure, and fitness studies; philosophy and religious studies; physical sciences; psychology; public administration and social service professions; social sciences; visual and performing arts. **Areas of required coursework:** arts/fine arts, humanities, mathematics, English (including composition), foreign languages, sciences (biological or physical), social science, other. **Pre-professional programs:** pre-law, pre-dentistry, pre-medicine, pre-theology, pre-veterinary science, pre-optometry, pre-pharmacy. **Special academic programs (% participation):** accelerated program (5.1%), cross-registration (0%), double major (10.3%), English as a Second Language (ESL) (0%), honors program (11.5%), independent study (12.1%), internships (20.1%), student-designed major (2.6%), study abroad (3.8%). **Teacher certification offered in:** early childhood, special education, elementary, middle/junior high, secondary. **Reserve Officers Training Corps (ROTC):** Army ROTC: Offered on campus; Air Force ROTC: Offered at cooperating institution (Ohio State University–Columbus). **Faculty and instruction (2009-2010):** Total instructional faculty: 203 full-time, 189 part-time (54% men; 46% women; 12% minorities). Full-time faculty with Ph.D. or other terminal degree: 68%. Student/faculty ratio: 11/1. Classes of fewer than 20 students: 60%; of 20 to 49 students: 39%; of 50 or more students: 1%. **Advanced Placement and International Baccalaureate credit:** AP tests may be used for: Credit only. Scores accepted: 3, 4, 5. International Baccalaureate exams may be used for: Credit only. **Freshmen returning for sophomore year:** 75%. **Graduation rates:** Four-year: 52%; five-year: 61%; six-year: 62%. **Graduate study:** 20% of students pursue further study immediately upon graduation. Fields in which graduates pursue further study: Master of Business Administration (MBA), 9%; law, 13%; medicine, 17%; dentistry, 2%; engineering, 1%; theology (or the seminary), 4%; education, 4%; arts and sciences, 49%; veterinary medicine, 1%.

COSTS AND FINANCIAL AID

Financial aid office: (614) 236-6511. **Expenses (2010-2011):** Tuition and fees 2010-2011: $29,310; room/board: $7,864. Estimated books and supplies: $1,000; transportation: $560; personal expenses: $1,730. **Financial aid:** Priority filing date for institution's financial aid form: February 28. In 2009-2010, 87% of undergraduates applied for financial aid. Of those, 80% were determined to have financial need; 21% had their need fully met. Average financial aid package (proportion receiving): $23,895 (80%). Average amount of gift aid, such as scholarships or grants (proportion receiving): $4,405 (63%). Average amount of self-help aid, such as work study or loans (proportion receiving): $5,761 (67%). Average need-based loan (excluding PLUS or other private loans): $5,242. Among students who received need-based aid, the average percentage of need met: 21%. Among students who received aid based on merit, the average award (and the proportion receiving): $12,963 (19%). Average amount of debt of borrowers graduating in 2009: $21,805. Proportion who borrowed: 83%.

CAMPUS LIFE AND EXTRACURRICULAR ACTIVITIES

Campus housing available (% using): coed dorms (88%), sorority housing (2%), fraternity housing (0%), apartment for single students (7%), other housing options (3%). Students who live in college-owned, operated, or affiliated housing: 47%. **Student employment:** During the 2009-2010 academic year, 40% of undergraduates worked on campus. Average per-year earnings: $2,000. **Clubs and organizations:** Number of student organizations: 63. Activities include: campus ministries, choral groups, concert band, dance, drama/theater, international student organization, jazz band, literary magazine, music ensembles, musical theater, radio station, student government, student newspaper, symphony orchestra, television station. Number of fraternities: 5; sororities: 5. Proportion of men in fraternities: 5%; of women in sororities: 4%. Average proportion of students who stay on campus on weekends: 50%. **Sports program (2009-2010):** Member of NCAA III. **Men's intercollegiate varsity sports:** baseball, basketball, cross country, football, golf, soccer, tennis, track and field (indoor), track and field (outdoor). **Women's intercollegiate varsity sports:** basketball, cross country, golf, soccer, softball, tennis, track and field (indoor), track and field (outdoor), volleyball.

SERVICES AND FACILITIES

Basic services: nonremedial tutoring, placement service, health service, health insurance. **Remedial assistance:** reading, math, writing, study skills, other. **Counseling services:** minority student, career, military, personal, academic, older student, psychological, birth control, religious. **For learning-disabled students:** School does not offer a structured program with separate admission and additional fees. Services include: remedial English, reading machines, tape recorders, note-taking services, oral tests, learning center, readers, extended time for tests, tutors, priority registration, priority seating, texts on tape, typist/scribe, exams on tape or computer, other testing accommodations. **Library:** Number of titles: 209,524; number of current serial subscriptions: 8,523. **Information technology resources:** Students are not required to lease or own a computer. Number of campus computers available to all students: 454. School has a wireless network. Approximate number of users that can be accommodated: 1,500. Proportion of college-owned housing units wired for high-speed internet access: 100%. **Campus safety:** Security services offered: 24-hour foot-and-vehicle patrols, late-night transport/escort service, 24-hour emergency telephones, lighted pathways/sidewalks, controlled dormitory access (key, security card, etc.).

TRANSFER AND INTERNATIONAL STUDENTS

Transfer students: May apply for admission for the following academic terms: Fall, Spring, Summer. Applicants need a minimum number of credits to apply. For fall 2009: Transfer applications received: 719. Transfer applicants offered admission: 217. Transfer applicants enrolled: 118. **International students:** Number of foreign undergraduates: 33 (1% of student body). Number of countries represented: 19. Minimum TOEFL score required: 500 (paper); 60 (computer). Average TOEFL score: 550 (paper).

Case Western Reserve University

- **Address:** 10900 Euclid Avenue, Cleveland, OH 44106
- **Website:** http://www.case.edu
- **Private**
- **Enrollment:** 4,095 full-time; 133 part-time

KEY STATS

✔ **U.S News College Ranking:** 41, National Universities
✔ **SAT Score (25th/75th percentile):** 1240-1440
✔ **Tuition:** 2010-2011: $37,648

Selectivity: More selective	**Room/board:** $12,340	
Acceptance rate: 70%	**Average debt:** $37,496	
Student/faculty ratio: 9/1	**Proportion who borrowed:** 64%	

UNDERGRADUATE STUDENT BODY STATS

2009-2010 enrollment: 4,095 full-time; 133 part-time. Men: 56%; women: 44%. **Ethnic makeup:** African American: 5%; Asian American: 16%; Hispanic: 3%; White: 70%; International: 5%.

ADMISSIONS FACTS AND FIGURES

Phone: (216) 368-4450. **Email:** admission@case.edu. **Website:** http://www.case.edu. **Application deadlines for fall 2011:** Regular decision: January 15; decision sent by April 1. Early decision: Not offered. Early action: Send application by: November 1; Decision sent by: December 15. Admission can be deferred. **To apply online, go to:** http://admission.case.edu/admissions/application/default.asp. **Admissions requirements/recommendations:** High school units required (recommended): English: 4; Mathematics: 3 (4); Science: 3; Foreign language: 2 (3); Social studies: 3

(4); Total units: 16. Tests: The college uses SAT or ACT scores in admissions decisions. Either SAT or ACT required. For admission to the fall 2011 entering class, the school will accept: ACT with writing required. Campus visit: Recommended. Admissions interview: Recommended. Off-campus interview: May be arranged. **Factors that count in admissions decisions: *Academic:*** Secondary school record: Very Important. Class rank: Very Important. Letters of recommendation: Important. Standardized test scores: Very Important. Essay: Important. ***Nonacademic:*** Interview: Important. Extracurricular activities: Very Important. Talent/ability: Important. Character/personal qualities: Important. Alumni/ae relationship: Considered. Geographical residence: Not Considered. State residency: Not Considered. Religious affiliation/commitment: Not Considered. Minority status: Considered. Volunteer work: Important. Work experience: Important. **Other schools with the greatest overlap in applicants:** Carnegie Mellon University; Ohio State University–Columbus; University of Michigan–Ann Arbor; University of Pittsburgh; Washington University in St. Louis. **Admissions statistics for the fall 2009 entering class:** Total applicants: 7,998. Total accepted: 5,599. Freshmen enrolled: 966; 53% were from out of state. Accepted through early-decision or early-action plans: 39%. Overall acceptance rate: 70%. Non-early acceptance rate: 66%. **Size of waiting list:** 623 applicants; enrolled from waiting list: 20. **Credentials of fall 2009 freshmen:** 65% ranked in the top 10 percent of their high school class; 87% were in the top 25 percent; 99% were in the top half. (Proportion submitting class standing: 52%.) **First-year students who submitted SAT scores:** 76%. Scores (25/75 percentile): Critical Reading: 590-700, Math: 650-740, Combined: 1240-1440. **First-year students submitting ACT scores:** 58%. Scores (25/75 percentile): English: 27-33, Math: 27-33, Composite: 28-32.

ACADEMICS

Year founded: 1826. **Academic calendar:** Semester. **Degrees offered:** bachelor's, post-bachelor's certificate, master's, doctorate. **Most popular majors:** 14% biology/biological sciences, 10% biomedical/medical engineering, 9% psychology, 8% business administration and management, 7% nursing/registered nurse training (R.N., A.S.N., B.S.N., M.S.N.). **Major fields of study:** area, ethnic, cultural, and gender studies; biological and biomedical sciences; business, management, marketing, and related support services; computer and information sciences and support services; education; engineering; English language and literature/letters; family and consumer sciences/human sciences; foreign languages, literatures, and linguistics; health professions and related clinical sciences; history; mathematics and statistics; multi/interdisciplinary studies; natural resources and conservation; philosophy and religious studies; physical sciences; psychology; social sciences; visual and performing arts. **Areas of required coursework:** humanities, mathematics, English (including composition), sciences (biological or physical), social science. **Pre-professional programs:** pre-law, pre-dentistry, pre-medicine, other. **Special academic programs (% participation):** accelerated program (5%), cooperative (work-study plan) program (10%), cross-registration (5%), double major (24%), dual enrollment, English as a Second Language (ESL), exchange student program (domestic) (1%), honors program (10%), independent study (65%), internships (38%), liberal arts/career combination (1%), student-designed major (1%), study abroad (19%), teacher certificate program (1%). **Teacher certification offered in:** elementary, secondary. **Cooperative education programs:** business, computer science, engineering, natural science. **Reserve Officers Training Corps (ROTC):** Army ROTC: Offered at cooperating institution (John Carroll University); Air Force ROTC: Offered at cooperating institution (Kent State University). **Faculty and instruction (2009-2010):** Total instructional faculty: 746 full-time, 171 part-time (58% men; 42% women; 16% minorities). Full-time faculty with Ph.D. or other terminal degree: 90%. Student/faculty ratio: 9/1. Classes of fewer than 20 students: 61%; of 20 to 49 students: 29%; of 50 or more students: 10%. **Advanced Placement and International Baccalaureate credit:** AP tests may be used for: Credit and/or placement. Scores accepted: 4, 5. International Baccalaureate exams may be used for: Credit and/or placement. **Freshmen returning for sophomore year:** 91%. **Graduation rates:** Four-year: 63%; five-year: 78%; six-year: 81%. **Graduate study:** 44% of students pursue further study immediately upon graduation. Fields in which graduates pursue further study: Master of Business Administration (MBA), 3%; law, 4%; medicine, 9%; dentistry, 2%; engineering, 12%; education, 1%; arts and sciences, 12%; veterinary medicine, 1%.

COSTS AND FINANCIAL AID

Financial aid office: (216) 368-3866. **Expenses (2010-2011):** Tuition and fees 2010-2011: $37,648; room/board: $12,340. Estimated books and supplies: $1,150; transportation: $1,000; personal expenses: $1,325. **Financial aid:** Priority filing date for institution's financial aid form: February 15. In 2009-2010, 72% of undergraduates applied for financial aid. Of those, 64% were determined to have financial need; 92% had their need fully met. Average financial aid package (proportion receiving): $33,478 (64%). Average amount of gift aid, such as scholarships or grants (proportion receiving): $22,793 (62%). Average amount of self-help aid, such as work study or loans (proportion receiving): $9,644 (60%). Average need-based loan (excluding PLUS or other private loans): $7,474. Among students who received need-based aid, the average percentage of need met: 87%. Among students who received aid based on merit, the average award (and the proportion receiving): $18,930 (19%). Average amount of debt of borrowers graduating in 2009: $37,496. Proportion who borrowed: 64%.

CAMPUS LIFE AND EXTRACURRICULAR ACTIVITIES

Campus housing available (% using): coed dorms (61%), sorority housing (5%), fraternity housing (9%), apartment for single students (24%), other housing options (1%). Students who live in college-owned, operated, or affiliated housing: 78%. **Student employment:** During the 2009-2010 academic year, 68% of undergraduates worked on campus. Average per-year earnings: $3,200. **Clubs and organizations:** Number of student organizations: 165. Activities include: campus ministries, choral groups, concert band, dance, drama/theater, international student organization, jazz band, literary magazine, marching band, model UN, music ensembles, musical theater, pep band, radio station, student government, student newspaper, student film society, symphony orchestra, yearbook. Number of fraternities: 16; sororities: 8. Proportion of men in fraternities: 30%; of women in sororities: 31%. **Sports program (2009-2010):** Member of NCAA III. ***Men's intercollegiate varsity sports:*** baseball, basketball, cross country, football, soccer, swimming, tennis, track and field (indoor), track and field (outdoor), volleyball, wrestling. ***Women's intercollegiate varsity sports:*** basketball, cross country, soccer, softball, swimming, tennis, track and field (indoor), track and field (outdoor), volleyball.

SERVICES AND FACILITIES

Basic services: nonremedial tutoring, women's center, placement service, health service, health insurance. **Counseling services:** minority student, career, personal, veteran student, academic, older student, psychological, birth control, religious. **For learning-disabled students:** School does not offer a structured program with separate admission and additional fees. Total undergraduates in learning-disabled program or receiving services: 33. Services include: reading machines, tape recorders, diagnostic testing service, note-taking services, oral tests, learning center, readers, extended time for tests, tutors, priority registration, texts on tape, other testing accommodations. **Library:** Number of titles: 2,777,529; number of current serial subscriptions: 75,083. **Information technology resources:** Students are not required to lease or own a computer. Number of campus computers available to all students: 239. School has a wireless network. Approximate number of users that can be accommodated: 50,000. Proportion of college-owned housing units wired for high-speed internet access: 100%. **Campus safety:** Security services offered: 24-hour foot-and-vehicle patrols, late-night transport/escort service, 24-hour emergency telephones, lighted pathways/sidewalks, controlled dormitory access (key, security card, etc).

TRANSFER AND INTERNATIONAL STUDENTS

Transfer students: May apply for admission for the following academic terms: Fall, Spring, Summer. Applicants do not need a minimum number of credits to apply. For fall 2009: Transfer applications received: 326. Transfer applicants offered admission: 120. Transfer applicants enrolled: 46. **International students:** Number of foreign undergraduates: 211 (5% of student body). Number of countries represented: 22. Minimum TOEFL score required: 550 (paper); 213 (computer).

Cedarville University

- **Address:** 251 N. Main Street, Cedarville, OH 45314
- **Website:** http://www.cedarville.edu
- **Private; Religious affiliation:** Baptist
- **Enrollment:** 2,841 full-time; 188 part-time

KEY STATS

✔ **U.S News College Ranking:** 5, Regional Colleges (Midwest)
✔ **ACT Score (25th/75th percentile):** 23-29
✔ **Tuition:** 2010-2011: $23,038

Selectivity: More selective	**Room/board:** $5,106
Acceptance rate: 76%	**Average debt:** $26,672
Student/faculty ratio: 15/1	**Proportion who borrowed:** 67%

UNDERGRADUATE STUDENT BODY STATS

2009-2010 enrollment: 2,841 full-time; 188 part-time. Men: 46%; women: 54%. **Ethnic makeup:** African American: 2%; Asian American: 1%; Hispanic: 3%; White: 93%; International: 1%.

ADMISSIONS FACTS AND FIGURES

Phone: (800) 233-2784. **Email:** admissions@cedarville.edu. **Website:** http://www.cedarville.edu. **Application deadlines for fall 2011:** Regular decision: Rolling. Early decision: Not offered. Early action: Not offered. Admission can be deferred. **Application fee:** $30. **To apply online, go to:** https://www.cedarville.edu/myapplication/index.cfm. **Admissions requirements/recommendations:** High school units required (recommended): English: 4 (4); Mathematics: 4 (4); Science: 3 (3); Foreign language: 3 (3); Social studies: 3 (3); Total units: 17 (17). Tests: The college uses SAT or ACT scores in admissions decisions. Either SAT or ACT required. For admission to the fall 2011 entering class, the school will accept: ACT with writing recommended. Campus visit: Recommended. Admissions interview: Neither required nor recommended. **Factors that count in admissions decisions:** *Academic:* Secondary school record: Very Important. Class rank: Not Considered. Letters of recommendation: Important. Standardized test scores: Very Important. Essay: Very Important. *Nonacademic:* Interview: Considered. Extracurricular activities: Considered. Talent/ability: Considered. Character/personal qualities: Very Important. Alumni/ae relationship: Considered. Geographical residence: Not Considered. State residency: Not Considered. Religious affiliation/commitment: Very Important. Minority status: Important. Volunteer work: Considered. Work experience: Not Considered. **Other schools with the greatest overlap in applicants:** Indiana Wesleyan University; Liberty University; Ohio State University–Columbus; Taylor University. **Admissions statistics for the fall 2009 entering class:** Total applicants: 2,949. Total accepted: 2,229. Freshmen enrolled: 729; 63% were from out of state. Overall acceptance rate: 76%. **Size of waiting list:** 0 applicants; enrolled from waiting list: 0. **Credentials of fall 2009 freshmen:** 32% ranked in the top 10 percent of their high school class; 53% were in the top 25 percent; 75% were in the top half. (Proportion submitting class standing: 65%.) **Average high school grade point average:** 3.6. **First-year students who submitted SAT scores:** 55%. Scores (25/75 percentile): Critical Reading: 530-650, Math: 530-640, Combined: 1060-1290. **First-year students submitting ACT scores:** 78%. Scores (25/75 percentile): English: 23-30, Math: 22-28, Composite: 23-29.

ACADEMICS

Year founded: 1887. **Academic calendar:** Semester. **Degrees offered:** certificate, bachelor's, master's. **Most popular majors:** 10% nursing/registered nurse training (R.N., A.S.N., B.S.N., M.S.N.), 6% early childhood education and teaching, 5% biology/biological sciences, 5% communication studies/speech communication and rhetoric, 4% mechanical engineering. **Major fields of study:** area, ethnic, cultural, and gender studies; biological and biomedical sciences; business, management, marketing, and related support services; communication, journalism, and related programs; communications technologies/technicians and support services; computer and information sciences and support services; education; engineering; English language and literature/letters; foreign languages, literatures, and linguistics; health professions and related clinical sciences; history; legal professions and studies; mathematics and statistics; multi/interdisciplinary studies; parks, recreation, leisure, and fitness studies; philosophy and religious studies; physical sciences; psychology; public administration and social service professions; security and protective services; social sciences; theology and religious vocations; visual and performing arts. **Areas of required coursework:** arts/fine arts, humanities, mathematics, English

(including composition), sciences (biological or physical), history, social science, other. **Pre-professional programs:** pre-law, pre-dentistry, pre-medicine, pre-veterinary science. **Special academic programs (% participation):** accelerated program (1%), cross-registration (1%), distance learning (46%), double major (9%), honors program (5%), independent study (25%), internships (29%), student-designed major (.1%), study abroad (5%), teacher certificate program (16%). **Teacher certification offered in:** early childhood, special education, middle/junior high, secondary. **Cooperative education programs:** engineering. **Reserve Officers Training Corps (ROTC):** Army ROTC: Offered at cooperating institution; Air Force ROTC: Offered at cooperating institution. **Faculty and instruction (2009-2010):** Total instructional faculty: 195 full-time, 94 part-time (63% men; 37% women; 5% minorities). Full-time faculty with Ph.D. or other terminal degree: 65%. Student/faculty ratio: 15/1. Classes of fewer than 20 students: 64%; of 20 to 49 students: 30%; of 50 or more students: 6%. **Advanced Placement and International Baccalaureate credit:** AP tests may be used for: Placement only. Scores accepted: 3, 4, 5. International Baccalaureate exams may be used for: Credit and/or placement. **Freshmen returning for sophomore year:** 84%. **Graduation rates:** Four-year: 62%; five-year: 75%; six-year: 70%. **Graduate study:** 29% of students pursue further study immediately upon graduation. Fields in which graduates pursue further study: law, 1%; medicine, 1%.

COSTS AND FINANCIAL AID

Financial aid office: (937) 766-7866. **Expenses (2010-2011):** Tuition and fees 2010-2011: $23,038; room/board: $5,106. Estimated books and supplies: $900; transportation: $280; personal expenses: $1,450. **Financial aid:** Priority filing date for institution's financial aid form: March 1. In 2009-2010, 78% of undergraduates applied for financial aid. Of those, 67% were determined to have financial need; 33% had their need fully met. Average financial aid package (proportion receiving): $14,534 (66%). Average amount of gift aid, such as scholarships or grants (proportion receiving): $4,396 (54%). Average amount of self-help aid, such as work study or loans (proportion receiving): $4,421 (59%). Average need-based loan (excluding PLUS or other private loans): $6,372. Among students who received need-based aid, the average percentage of need met: 42%. Among students who received aid based on merit, the average award (and the proportion receiving): $14,395 (21%). The average athletic scholarship (and the proportion receiving): $4,159 (6%). Average amount of debt of borrowers graduating in 2009: $26,672. Proportion who borrowed: 67%.

CAMPUS LIFE AND EXTRACURRICULAR ACTIVITIES

Campus housing available (% using): women's dorms (50%), men's dorms (48%), apartments for married students (2%). Students who live in college-owned, operated, or affiliated housing: 80%. **Student employment:** During the 2009-2010 academic year, 56% of undergraduates worked on campus. Average per-year earnings: $2,940. **Clubs and organizations:** Number of student organizations: 68. Activities include: choral groups, concert band, drama/theater, jazz band, music ensembles, musical theater, pep band, radio station, student government, student newspaper, symphony orchestra, yearbook. Number of fraternities: 0; sororities: 0. Average proportion of students who stay on campus on weekends: 80%. **Sports program (2009-2010):** Member of NAIA. *Men's intercollegiate varsity sports:* baseball, basketball, cross country, golf, soccer, tennis, track and field (indoor), track and field (outdoor). *Women's intercollegiate varsity sports:* basketball, cross country, soccer, softball, team handball, track and field (indoor), track and field (outdoor), volleyball.

SERVICES AND FACILITIES

Basic services: nonremedial tutoring, placement service, health service. **Remedial assistance:** reading, math, writing. **Counseling services:** career, military, personal, veteran student, academic, religious. **For learning-disabled students:** School does not offer a structured program with separate admission and additional fees. Services include: remedial math, remedial English, tape recorders, note-taking services, oral tests, learning center, readers, extended time for tests, tutors, priority registration, priority seating, texts on tape, other testing accommodations, other. **Library:** Number of titles: 184,296; number of current serial subscriptions: 981. **Information technology resources:** Students are not required to lease or own a computer. Number of campus computers available to all students: 1,800. School has a wireless network. Approximate number of users that can be accommodated: 1,000. Proportion of college-owned housing units wired for high-speed internet access: 100%. **Campus safety:** Security services offered: 24-hour foot-and-vehicle patrols, late-night transport/escort service, 24-hour emergency telephones, lighted pathways/sidewalks, controlled dormitory access (key, security card, etc.).

Transfer students: May apply for admission for the following academic terms: Fall, Spring, Summer. Applicants need a minimum number of credits to apply. For fall 2009: Transfer applications received: 336. Transfer applicants offered admission: 199. Transfer applicants enrolled: 97. **International students:** Number of foreign undergraduates: 35 (1% of student body). Number of countries represented: 14. Minimum TOEFL score required: 550 (paper); 213 (computer). Average TOEFL score: 550 (paper).

Central State University

- ■ **Address:** PO Box 1004, Wilberforce, OH 45384
- ■ **Website:** http://www.centralstate.edu
- ■ **Public**
- ■ **Enrollment:** 2,230 full-time; 170 part-time

KEY STATS

✔ **U.S News College Ranking:** second tier, Regional Colleges (Midwest)
✔ **ACT Score (25th/75th percentile):** 14-17
✔ **Tuition:** 2009-2010: $5,294 in state, $11,806 out of state
 Selectivity: Less selective   **Room/board:** $7,920
 Acceptance rate: 39%   **Average debt:** N/A
 Student/faculty ratio: 16/1   **Proportion who borrowed:** N/A

UNDERGRADUATE STUDENT BODY STATS

2009-2010 enrollment: 2,230 full-time; 170 part-time. Men: 51%; women: 49%. **Ethnic makeup:** African American: 96%; Hispanic: 1%; White: 3%.

ADMISSIONS FACTS AND FIGURES

Phone: (937) 376-6348. **Email:** admissions@centralstate.edu. **Website:** http://www.centralstate.edu. **Application deadlines for fall 2011:** Regular decision: Rolling. Early decision: Not offered. Early action: Not offered. Admission can be deferred. **Application fee:** $20. **To apply online, go to:** http://www.centralstate.edu/admissions/apply2.html. **Admissions requirements/recommendations:** High school units required (recommended): English: 4; Mathematics: 3; Science: 3; Foreign language: 2; Social studies: 3; Academic electives: (2); Total units: 16 (2). Tests: The college uses SAT or ACT scores in admissions decisions. Either SAT or ACT required. For admission to the fall 2011 entering class, the school will accept: ACT with or without writing accepted. Campus visit: Neither required nor recommended. Admissions interview: Neither required nor recommended. Off-campus interview: Not available. **Factors that count in admissions decisions:** *Academic:* Secondary school record: Very Important. Class rank: Important. Letters of recommendation: Considered. Standardized test scores: Very Important. Essay: Important. *Nonacademic:* Interview: Considered. Extracurricular activities: Considered. Talent/ability: Considered. Character/personal qualities: Important. Alumni/ae relationship: Not Considered. Geographical residence: Important. State residency: Important. Religious affiliation/commitment: Not Considered. Minority status: Not Considered. Volunteer work: Not Considered. Work experience: Not Considered. **Other schools with the greatest overlap in applicants:** Cleveland State University; Ohio State University–Columbus; University of Cincinnati; Wright State University. **Admissions statistics for the fall 2009 entering class:** Total applicants: 6,948. Total accepted: 2,703. Freshmen enrolled: 713; 50% were from out of state. Overall acceptance rate: 39%. **Credentials of fall 2009 freshmen:** 7% ranked in the top 10 percent of their high school class; 23% were in the top 25 percent; 57% were in the top half. (Proportion submitting class standing: 100%.) **Average high school grade point average:** 2.4. **First-year students who submitted SAT scores:** 14%. Scores (25/75 percentile): Critical Reading: 340-430, Math: 320-420, Combined: 660-850. **First-year students submitting ACT scores:** 87%. Scores (25/75 percentile): English: N/A, Math: N/A, Composite: 14-17.

ACADEMICS

Year founded: 1887. **Academic calendar:** Semester. **Degrees offered:** bachelor's, master's. **Most popular majors:** 29% business, management, marketing, and related support services, 18% education, 14% communication, journalism, and related programs, 7% psychology, 5% engineering. **Major fields of study:** biological and biomedical sciences; business, management, marketing, and related support services; communication, journalism, and related programs; computer and information sciences and support services; education; engineering; engineering technologies/technicians; English language and literature/letters; history; mathematics and statistics; parks,

recreation, leisure, and fitness studies; physical sciences; psychology; public administration and social service professions; social sciences; visual and performing arts. **Areas of required coursework:** arts/fine arts, humanities, computer literacy, mathematics, English (including composition), philosophy, foreign languages, sciences (biological or physical), history, social science. **Pre-professional programs:** pre-law, pre-dentistry, pre-medicine, pre-veterinary science. **Special academic programs:** cooperative (work-study plan) program, cross-registration, double major, English as a Second Language (ESL), honors program, independent study, internships, study abroad, teacher certificate program. **Teacher certification offered in:** early childhood, special education, elementary, middle/junior high, secondary. **Cooperative education programs:** art, business, computer science, education, engineering, humanities, natural science, social/behavioral science, technologies. **Reserve Officers Training Corps (ROTC):** Army ROTC: Offered on campus; Air Force ROTC: Offered at cooperating institution (Wright State University). **Faculty and instruction (2009-2010):** Total instructional faculty: 113 full-time, 81 part-time (59% men; 41% women; 74% minorities). Full-time faculty with Ph.D. or other terminal degree: 69%. Student/faculty ratio: 16/1. Classes of fewer than 20 students: 53%; of 20 to 49 students: 45%; of 50 or more students: 2%. **Advanced Placement and International Baccalaureate credit:** AP tests may be used for: Placement only. Scores accepted: 3, 4, 5. International Baccalaureate exams may be used for: Placement only. **Freshmen returning for sophomore year:** 53%. **Graduation rates:** Four-year: 8%; five-year: 17%; six-year: 24%. **Graduate study:** 10% of students pursue further study immediately upon graduation; 3% within one year; 1% within five years.

COSTS AND FINANCIAL AID

Financial aid office: (937) 376-6579. **Expenses (2009-2010):** Tuition and fees 2009-2010: $5,294 in state, $11,806 out of state; room/board: $7,920. Estimated books and supplies: $1,200; transportation: $900; personal expenses: $1,500. **Financial aid:** Priority filing date for institution's financial aid form: February 15.

CAMPUS LIFE AND EXTRACURRICULAR ACTIVITIES

Campus housing available (% using): coed dorms (66%), women's dorms (14%), men's dorms (20%), other housing options. Students who live in college-owned, operated, or affiliated housing: 57%. **Student employment:** During the 2009-2010 academic year, 20% of undergraduates worked on campus. Average per-year earnings: $4,800. **Clubs and organizations:** Number of student organizations: 40. Activities include: campus ministries, choral groups, concert band, dance, drama/theater, jazz band, marching band, music ensembles, opera, pep band, radio station, student government, student newspaper, television station. Number of fraternities: 8; sororities: 8. Proportion of men in fraternities: 1%; of women in sororities: 1%. Average proportion of students who stay on campus on weekends: 67%. **Sports program (2009-2010):** Member of NCAA II. *Men's intercollegiate varsity sports:* basketball, cross country, football, golf, tennis, track and field (outdoor), volleyball. *Women's intercollegiate varsity sports:* basketball, cross country, golf, tennis, track and field (outdoor), volleyball.

SERVICES AND FACILITIES

Basic services: nonremedial tutoring, placement service, day care, health service, health insurance. **Remedial assistance:** reading, math, writing, study skills. **Counseling services:** career, military, personal, academic, older student, psychological, birth control. **For learning-disabled students:** School does not offer a structured program with separate admission and additional fees. Total undergraduates in learning-disabled program or receiving services: 110. Services include: tape recorders, diagnostic testing service, untimed tests, note-taking services, oral tests, learning center, readers, extended time for tests, tutors, priority seating, other testing accommodations. **Library:** Number of titles: 223,745; number of current serial subscriptions: 41,775. **Information technology resources:** Students are not required to lease or own a computer. Number of campus computers available to all students: 520. School has a wireless network. Approximate number of users that can be accommodated: 300. Proportion of college-owned housing units wired for high-speed internet access: 100%. **Campus safety:** Security services offered: 24-hour foot-and-vehicle patrols, 24-hour emergency telephones, lighted pathways/sidewalks, controlled dormitory access (key, security card, etc).

TRANSFER AND INTERNATIONAL STUDENTS

Transfer students: May apply for admission for the following academic terms: Fall, Spring, Summer. Applicants do not need a minimum number of credits to apply. For fall 2009: Transfer applications received: 666. Transfer applicants offered admission: 229. Transfer applicants enrolled: 152. **International students:** Number of foreign undergraduates: 3. Minimum TOEFL score required: 500 (paper); 173 (computer). Average TOEFL score: 500 (paper).

Chancellor University

- **Address:** 3921 Chester Avenue, Cleveland, OH 44114
- **Website:** http://www.myers.edu
- **Private**
- **Enrollment:** N/A

KEY STATS

✔ **U.S News College Ranking:** second tier, Regional Colleges (Midwest)
✔ **SAT or ACT Score (25th/75th percentile):** N/A
✔ **Tuition:** 2009-2010: $7,800

Selectivity: Less selective	**Room/board:** N/A
Acceptance rate: N/A	**Average debt:** N/A
Student/faculty ratio: N/A	**Proportion who borrowed:** N/A

Cleveland Institute of Art

- **Address:** 11141 East Boulevard, Cleveland, OH 44106
- **Website:** http://www.cia.edu
- **Private**
- **Enrollment:** 493 full-time; 14 part-time

KEY STATS

✔ **U.S News College Ranking:** Unranked Specialty School–Fine Arts
✔ **ACT Score (25th/75th percentile):** 20-26
✔ **Tuition:** 2010-2011: $33,450

Selectivity: N/A	**Room/board:** $10,856
Acceptance rate: 79%	**Average debt:** $60,150
Student/faculty ratio: 8/1	**Proportion who borrowed:** 90%

UNDERGRADUATE STUDENT BODY STATS

2009-2010 enrollment: 493 full-time; 14 part-time. Men: 48%; women: 52%. **Ethnic makeup:** African American: 6%; Asian American: 5%; Hispanic: 5%; White: 82%; International: 2%.

ADMISSIONS FACTS AND FIGURES

Phone: (216) 421-7418. **Email:** admissions@cia.edu. **Website:** http://www.cia.edu. **Application deadlines for fall 2011:** Regular decision: Rolling. Early decision: Not offered. Early action: Send application by: December 1; Decision sent by: December 15. Admission can be deferred. **Application fee:** $30. **To apply online, go to:** https://www.applyweb.com/aw?cia. **Admissions requirements/recommendations:** High school units required (recommended): English: 4 (4); Mathematics: 3 (3); Science: 3 (3); Social studies: 3 (3); Academic electives: 6 (6); Total units: 20 (20). Tests: The college uses SAT or ACT scores in admissions decisions. Either SAT or ACT required. For admission to the fall 2011 entering class, the school will accept: ACT with or without writing accepted. Campus visit: Recommended. Admissions interview: Recommended. Off-campus interview: May be arranged. **Factors that count in admissions decisions: *Academic:*** Secondary school record: Very Important. Class rank: Not Considered. Letters of recommendation: Important. Standardized test scores: Important. Essay: Important. ***Nonacademic:*** Interview: Important. Extracurricular activities: Not Considered. Talent/ability: Very Important. Character/personal qualities: Not Considered. Alumni/ae relationship: Not Considered. Geographical residence: Not Considered. State residency: Not Considered. Religious affiliation/commitment: Not Considered. Minority status: Not Considered. Volunteer work: Not Considered. Work experience: Not Considered. **Other schools with the greatest overlap in applicants:** Columbus College of Art and Design; Maryland Institute College of Art; Pratt Institute; Rhode Island School of Design; School of the Art Institute of Chicago. **Admissions statistics for the fall 2009 entering class:** Total applicants: 457. Total accepted: 362. Freshmen enrolled: 112; 39% were from out of state. Accepted through early-decision or early-action plans: 45%. Overall acceptance rate: 79%. Non-early acceptance rate: 76%. **Credentials of fall 2009 freshmen:** 18% ranked in the top 10 percent of their high school class; 32% were in the top 25 percent; 72% were in the top half. (Proportion submitting class stand-

ing: 50%.) **Average high school grade point average:** 3.2. **First-year students who submitted SAT scores:** 52%. Scores (25/75 percentile): Critical Reading: 490-600, Math: 440-570, Combined: 930-1170. **First-year students submitting ACT scores:** 62%. Scores (25/75 percentile): English: N/A, Math: N/A, Composite: 20-26.

ACADEMICS

Year founded: 1882. **Academic calendar:** Semester. **Degrees offered:** bachelor's. **Major fields of study:** health professions and related clinical sciences; visual and performing arts. **Areas of required coursework:** arts/fine arts, humanities, computer literacy, English (including composition), history, social science, other. **Special academic programs (% participation):** cross-registration (3%), exchange student program (domestic) (3%), independent study (3%), internships (3%), study abroad (3%). **Faculty and instruction (2009-2010):** Total instructional faculty: 47 full-time, 36 part-time (53% men; 47% women; 10% minorities). Full-time faculty with Ph.D. or other terminal degree: 85%. Student/faculty ratio: 8/1. Classes of fewer than 20 students: 74%; of 20 to 49 students: 26%; of 50 or more students: 0%. **Advanced Placement and International Baccalaureate credit:** AP tests may be used for: Credit only. Scores accepted: 3, 4, 5. International Baccalaureate exams may be used for: Credit only. **Freshmen returning for sophomore year:** 80%. **Graduation rates:** Six-year: 62%.

COSTS AND FINANCIAL AID

Financial aid office: (216) 421-7425. **Expenses (2010-2011):** Tuition and fees 2010-2011: $33,450; room/board: $10,856. Estimated books and supplies: $2,000; transportation: $1,400; personal expenses: $1,940. **Financial aid:** Priority filing date for institution's financial aid form: March 15; deadline: June 1. In 2009-2010, 93% of undergraduates applied for financial aid. Of those, 88% were determined to have financial need; 8% had their need fully met. Average financial aid package (proportion receiving): $20,915 (88%). Average amount of gift aid, such as scholarships or grants (proportion receiving): $14,976 (88%). Average amount of self-help aid, such as work study or loans (proportion receiving): $6,375 (82%). Average need-based loan (excluding PLUS or other private loans): $4,760. Among students who received need-based aid, the average percentage of need met: 56%. Among students who received aid based on merit, the average award (and the proportion receiving): $9,538 (12%). The average athletic scholarship (and the proportion receiving): $0 (0%). Average amount of debt of borrowers graduating in 2009: $60,150. Proportion who borrowed: 90%.

CAMPUS LIFE AND EXTRACURRICULAR ACTIVITIES

Campus housing available (% using): coed dorms (80%), sorority housing (1%), apartment for single students (19%). Students who live in college-owned, operated, or affiliated housing: 20%. **Student employment:** During the 2009-2010 academic year, 5% of undergraduates worked on campus. Activities include: campus ministries, student government, student film society. Average proportion of students who stay on campus on weekends: 80%.

SERVICES AND FACILITIES

Basic services: nonremedial tutoring, health service, health insurance. **Remedial assistance:** reading, writing, study skills. **Counseling services:** career, personal, academic. **For learning-disabled students:** School does not offer a structured program with separate admission and additional fees. Total undergraduates in learning-disabled program or receiving services: 43. Services include: remedial English, untimed tests, note-taking services, oral tests, learning center, extended time for tests, tutors, proofreading services, texts on tape, exams on tape or computer. **Library:** Number of titles: 45,000; number of current serial subscriptions: 148. **Information technology resources:** Students are not required to lease or own a computer. Number of campus computers available to all students: 350. School has a wireless network. Approximate number of users that can be accommodated: 350. Proportion of college-owned housing units wired for high-speed internet access: 90%. **Campus safety:** Security services offered: late-night transport/escort service, 24-hour emergency telephones, controlled dormitory access (key, security card, etc).

TRANSFER AND INTERNATIONAL STUDENTS

Transfer students: May apply for admission for the following academic terms: Fall, Spring. Applicants need a minimum number of credits to apply. For fall 2009: Transfer applications received: 78. Transfer applicants offered admission: 53. Transfer applicants enrolled: 34. **International students:** Number of foreign undergraduates: 10 (2% of student body). Number of countries represented: 6. Minimum TOEFL score required: 525 (paper); 195 (computer). Average TOEFL score: 561 (paper).

Cleveland Institute of Music

- **Address:** 11021 East Boulevard, Cleveland, OH 44106
- **Website:** http://www.cim.edu/
- **Private**
- **Enrollment:** N/A

KEY STATS

✔ **U.S News College Ranking:** Unranked Specialty School–Fine Arts
✔ **SAT or ACT Score (25th/75th percentile):** N/A
✔ **Tuition:** 2009-2010: $36,590

Selectivity: N/A	Room/board: $10,576
Acceptance rate: N/A	Average debt: N/A
Student/faculty ratio: N/A	Proportion who borrowed: N/A

Cleveland State University

- **Address:** 2121 Euclid Avenue, Cleveland, OH 44115
- **Website:** http://www.csuohio.edu
- **Public**
- **Enrollment:** 7,563 full-time; 2,868 part-time

KEY STATS

✔ **U.S News College Ranking:** second tier, National Universities
✔ **ACT Score (25th/75th percentile):** 18-23
✔ **Tuition:** 2010-2011: $8,660 in state, $11,580 out of state

Selectivity: Selective	Room/board: $9,470
Acceptance rate: 64%	Average debt: N/A
Student/faculty ratio: 18/1	Proportion who borrowed: N/A

UNDERGRADUATE STUDENT BODY STATS

2009-2010 enrollment: 7,563 full-time; 2,868 part-time. Men: 45%; women: 55%. **Ethnic makeup:** African American: 21%; Asian American: 3%; Hispanic: 4%; White: 70%; International: 2%.

ADMISSIONS FACTS AND FIGURES

Phone: (216) 687-2100. **Email:** admissions@csuohio.edu. **Website:** http://www.csuohio.edu. **Application deadlines for fall 2011:** Regular decision: August 16. Early decision: Not offered. Early action: Send application by: May 1; Decision sent by: N/A. Admission can be deferred. **Application fee:** $30. **To apply online, go to:** http://www.csuohio.edu/admissions/application.html. **Admissions requirements/recommendations:** High school units required (recommended): English: 4; Mathematics: 3; Science: 3; Foreign language: (2); Social studies: 3; Total units: 13 (3). Tests: The college uses SAT or ACT scores in admissions decisions. Either SAT or ACT required. For admission to the fall 2011 entering class, the school will accept: ACT with or without writing accepted. Campus visit: Recommended. Admissions interview: Neither required nor recommended. Off-campus interview: Not available. **Factors that count in admissions decisions:** *Academic:* Secondary school record: Very Important. Class rank: Important. Letters of recommendation: Considered. Standardized test scores: Very Important. Essay: Considered. *Nonacademic:* Interview: Considered. Extracurricular activities: Considered. Talent/ability: Considered. Character/personal qualities: Not Considered. Alumni/ae relationship: Not Considered. Geographical residence: Not Considered. State residency: Not Considered. Religious affiliation/commitment: Not Considered. Minority status: Not Considered. Volunteer work: Considered. Work experience: Considered. **Other schools with the greatest overlap in applicants:** Baldwin-Wallace College; Bowling Green State University; Kent State University; Ohio State University–Columbus; University of Akron. **Admissions statistics for the fall 2009 entering class:** Total applicants: 4,584. Total accepted: 2,946. Freshmen enrolled: 1,185; 6% were from out of state. Overall acceptance rate: 64%. Non-early acceptance rate: 64%. **Credentials of fall 2009 freshmen:** 12% ranked in the top 10 percent of their high school class; 33% were in the top 25 percent; 67% were in the top half. (Proportion submitting class standing: 78%.) **Average high school grade point average:** 3.1. **First-year students who submitted SAT scores:** 33%. Scores (25/75 percentile): Critical Reading: 420-540, Math: 420-550, Combined: 840-1090. **First-year students submitting ACT scores:** 79%. Scores (25/75 percentile): English: 16-23, Math: 17-23, Composite: 18-23.

ACADEMICS

Year founded: 1964. **Academic calendar:** Semester. **Degrees offered:** bachelor's, post-bachelor's certificate, master's, post-master's certificate, doctorate. **Most popular majors:** 21% business, management, marketing, and related support services, 14% health professions and related clinical sciences, 11% social sciences, 8% communication, journalism, and related programs, 8% education. **Major fields of study:** agriculture, agriculture operations, and related sciences; area, ethnic, cultural, and gender studies; biological and biomedical sciences; business, management, marketing, and related support services; communication, journalism, and related programs; computer and information sciences and support services; education; engineering; engineering technologies/technicians; English language and literature/letters; foreign languages, literatures, and linguistics; health professions and related clinical sciences; history; liberal arts and sciences studies, and humanities; mathematics and statistics; multi/interdisciplinary studies; natural resources and conservation; parks, recreation, leisure, and fitness studies; philosophy and religious studies; physical sciences; psychology; public administration and social service professions; social sciences; visual and performing arts. **Areas of required coursework:** arts/fine arts, humanities, computer literacy, mathematics, English (including composition), philosophy, foreign languages, sciences (biological or physical), history, social science, other. **Pre-professional programs:** pre-medicine, pre-pharmacy. **Special academic programs:** accelerated program, cooperative (work-study plan) program, cross-registration, distance learning, double major, dual enrollment, English as a Second Language (ESL), exchange student program (domestic), honors program, independent study, internships, liberal arts/career combination, student-designed major, study abroad, teacher certificate program, weekend college. **Teacher certification offered in:** early childhood, special education, elementary, middle/junior high, adult education, secondary. **Cooperative education programs:** art, business, computer science, education, engineering, health professions, humanities, natural science, social/behavioral science, technologies. **Reserve Officers Training Corps (ROTC):** Army ROTC: Offered at cooperating institution (John Carroll University); Navy ROTC: Offered at cooperating institution (Kent State University). **Faculty and instructional (2009-2010):** Total instructional faculty: 537 full-time, 487 part-time (56% men; 44% women; 19% minorities). Full-time faculty with Ph.D. or other terminal degree: 91%. Student/faculty ratio: 18/1. Classes of fewer than 20 students: 41%; of 20 to 49 students: 51%; of 50 or more students: 8%. **Advanced Placement and International Baccalaureate credit:** AP tests may be used for: Placement only. International Baccalaureate exams may be used for: Placement only. **Freshmen returning for sophomore year:** 61%. **Graduation rates:** Four-year: 7%; five-year: 22%; six-year: 29%.

COSTS AND FINANCIAL AID

Financial aid office: (216) 687-2054. **Expenses (2010-2011):** Tuition and fees 2010-2011: $8,660 in state, $11,580 out of state; room/board: $9,470. Estimated books and supplies: $800; transportation: $1,800; personal expenses: $2,500. **Financial aid:** Priority filing date for institution's financial aid form: February 15. In 2009-2010, 87% of undergraduates applied for financial aid. Of those, 79% were determined to have financial need; 8% had their need fully met. Average financial aid package (proportion receiving): $8,565 (76%). Average amount of gift aid, such as scholarships or grants (proportion receiving): $6,172 (59%). Average amount of self-help aid, such as work study or loans (proportion receiving): $4,389 (66%). Average need-based loan (excluding PLUS or other private loans): $4,157. Among students who received need-based aid, the average percentage of need met: 49%. Among students who received aid based on merit, the average award (and the proportion receiving): $4,242 (5%). The average athletic scholarship (and the proportion receiving): $9,883 (2%).

CAMPUS LIFE AND EXTRACURRICULAR ACTIVITIES

Campus housing available: coed dorms, sorority housing, fraternity housing, special housing for disabled students. Students who live in college-owned, operated, or affiliated housing: 8%. **Student employment:** During the 2009-2010 academic year, 8% of undergraduates worked on campus. Average per-year earnings: $6,720. **Clubs and organizations:** Number of student organizations: 118. Activities include: choral groups, concert band, dance, drama/theater, international student organization, jazz band, literary magazine, music ensembles, musical theater, opera, pep band, radio station, student government, student newspaper, symphony orchestra. Number of fraternities: 8; sororities: 8. Proportion of men in fraternities: 1%; of women in sororities: 1%. Average proportion of students who stay on campus on weekends: 4%. **Sports program (2009-2010):** Member of NCAA I. *Men's intercollegiate varsity sports:* baseball, basketball, fencing, golf, soccer, swimming, tennis, wrestling. *Women's intercollegiate varsity sports:* basketball, fencing, golf, soccer, softball, swimming, tennis, volleyball.

SERVICES AND FACILITIES

Basic services: nonremedial tutoring, women's center, placement service, day care, health service, health insurance. **Remedial assistance:** reading, math, writing, study skills. **Counseling services:** minority student, career, military, personal, veteran student, academic, older student, psychological, birth control. **For learning-disabled students:** School does not offer a structured program with separate admission and additional fees. Services include: remedial math, remedial English, reading machines, tape recorders, note-taking services, oral tests, learning center, readers, extended time for tests, tutors, priority registration, priority seating, texts on tape, other testing accommodations, other. **Library:** Number of titles: 1,215,247; number of current serial subscriptions: 3,065. **Information technology resources:** Students are not required to lease or own a computer. Number of campus computers available to all students: 740. School has a wireless network. Approximate number of users that can be accommodated: 16,000. Proportion of college-owned housing units wired for high-speed internet access: 100%. **Campus safety:** Security services offered: 24-hour foot-and-vehicle patrols, late-night transport/escort service, 24-hour emergency telephones, lighted pathways/sidewalks, student patrols, controlled dormitory access (key, security card, etc).

TRANSFER AND INTERNATIONAL STUDENTS

Transfer students: May apply for admission for the following academic terms: Fall, Spring, Summer. Applicants need a minimum number of credits to apply. For fall 2009: Transfer applications received: 3,182. Transfer applicants offered admission: 2,114. Transfer applicants enrolled: 1,408. **International students:** Number of foreign undergraduates: 245 (3% of student body). Number of countries represented: 52. Minimum TOEFL score required: 525 (paper); 197 (computer). Average TOEFL score: 525 (paper).

College of Mount St. Joseph

- **Address:** 5701 Delhi Road, Cincinnati, OH 45233
- **Website:** http://www.msj.edu
- **Private; Religious affiliation:** Catholic
- **Enrollment:** 1,347 full-time; 556 part-time

KEY STATS

✔ **U.S News College Ranking:** 76, Regional Universities (Midwest)
✔ **ACT Score (25th/75th percentile):** 19-24
✔ **Tuition:** 2010-2011: $23,550

Selectivity: Selective	**Room/board:** $7,392
Acceptance rate: 70%	**Average debt:** $33,648
Student/faculty ratio: 12/1	**Proportion who borrowed:** 84%

UNDERGRADUATE STUDENT BODY STATS

2009-2010 enrollment: 1,347 full-time; 556 part-time. Men: 36%; women: 64%. **Ethnic makeup:** African American: 10%; Hispanic: 1%; White: 88%. **Religious preference:** Protestant: 14%; No preference: 12%; Unknown: 37%; Catholic: 37%.

ADMISSIONS FACTS AND FIGURES

Phone: (513) 244-4531. **Email:** admission@mail.msj.edu. **Website:** http://www.msj.edu. **Application deadlines for fall 2011:** Regular decision: August 15. Early decision: Not offered. Early action: Not offered. Admission can be deferred. **Application fee:** $25. **To apply online, go to:** http://www.msj.edu/view/admissions-apply.aspx. **Admissions requirements/recommendations:** High school units required (recommended): English: 4 (4); Mathematics: 2 (4); Science: 2 (4); Foreign language: 2 (2); Social studies: 1 (2); History: 1 (2); Academic electives: 1 (2); Total units: 13 (22). Tests: The college uses SAT or ACT scores in admissions decisions. Either SAT or ACT required. For admission to the fall 2011 entering class, the school will accept: ACT with writing recommended. Campus visit: Recommended. Admissions interview: Recommended. Off-campus interview: May be arranged. **Factors that count in admissions decisions:** *Academic:* Secondary school record: Very Important. Class rank: Not Considered. Letters of recommendation: Considered. Standardized test scores: Very Important. Essay: Considered. *Nonacademic:* Interview: Considered. Extracurricular activities: Considered. Talent/ability: Considered. Character/personal qualities: Considered. Alumni/ae relationship: Considered. Geographical residence: Considered. State residency: Considered. Religious affiliation/commitment: Considered. Minority status: Considered. Volunteer work: Considered. Work experience: Considered. **Other schools with the greatest overlap in applicants:** Miami

University–Oxford; Northern Kentucky University; Thomas More College; University of Cincinnati; Xavier University. **Admissions statistics for the fall 2009 entering class:** Total applicants: 1,417. Total accepted: 996. Freshmen enrolled: 368; 20% were from out of state. Overall acceptance rate: 70%. **Credentials of fall 2009 freshmen:** 11% ranked in the top 10 percent of their high school class; 35% were in the top 25 percent; 69% were in the top half. (Proportion submitting class standing: 85%.) **Average high school grade point average:** 3.2. **First-year students who submitted SAT scores:** 43%. Scores (25/75 percentile): Critical Reading: 430-520, Math: 430-540, Combined: 860-1060. **First-year students submitting ACT scores:** 84%. Scores (25/75 percentile): English: 18-24, Math: 18-24, Composite: 19-24.

ACADEMICS

Year founded: 1920. **Academic calendar:** Semester. **Degrees offered:** certificate, associate, bachelor's, post-bachelor's certificate, master's. **Most popular majors:** 23% nursing/registered nurse training (R.N., A.S.N., B.S.N., M.S.N.), 14% business administration and management, 7% liberal arts and sciences/liberal studies, 6% criminology, 5% athletic training/trainer. **Major fields of study:** biological and biomedical sciences; business, management, marketing, and related support services; communication, journalism, and related programs; computer and information sciences and support services; education; English language and literature/letters; health professions and related clinical sciences; history; legal professions and studies; liberal arts and sciences studies, and humanities; mathematics and statistics; multi/interdisciplinary studies; philosophy and religious studies; physical sciences; psychology; public administration and social service professions; social sciences; theology and religious vocations; visual and performing arts. **Areas of required coursework:** arts/fine arts, humanities, mathematics, English (including composition), philosophy, sciences (biological or physical), history, social science, other. **Pre-professional programs:** pre-law, pre-dentistry, pre-medicine, pre-theology, pre-veterinary science, pre-optometry, pre-pharmacy. **Special academic programs (% participation):** accelerated program (8%), cooperative (work-study plan) program (25%), cross-registration (7%), distance learning (24%), double major (2%), honors program (10%), independent study (39%), internships (58%), liberal arts/career combination (0%), study abroad (4%), teacher certificate program (10%). **Teacher certification offered in:** early childhood, special education, middle/junior high, secondary. **Cooperative education programs:** art, business, education, health professions, humanities, natural science, social/behavioral science, other. **Reserve Officers Training Corps (ROTC):** Army ROTC: Offered at cooperating institution (Xavier University); Air Force ROTC: Offered at cooperating institution (University of Cincinnati). **Faculty and instruction (2009-2010):** Total instructional faculty: 117 full-time, 119 part-time (36% men; 64% women; 3% minorities). Full-time faculty with Ph.D. or other terminal degree: 74%. Student/faculty ratio: 12/1. Classes of fewer than 20 students: 55%; of 20 to 49 students: 45%; of 50 or more students: 0%. **Advanced Placement and International Baccalaureate credit:** AP tests may be used for: Credit and/or placement. Scores accepted: 3, 4, 5. International Baccalaureate exams may be used for: Credit and/or placement. **Freshmen returning for sophomore year:** 74%. **Graduation rates:** Four-year: 36%; five-year: 51%; six-year: 55%. **Graduate study:** 20% of students pursue further study immediately upon graduation. Fields in which graduates pursue further study: Master of Business Administration (MBA), 13%; law, 3%; education, 13%; arts and sciences, 68%.

COSTS AND FINANCIAL AID

Financial aid office: (513) 244-4418. **Expenses (2010-2011):** Tuition and fees 2010-2011: $23,550; room/board: $7,392. Estimated books and supplies: $800; transportation: $400; personal expenses: $600. **Financial aid:** Priority filing date for institution's financial aid form: March 1. In 2009-2010, 92% of undergraduates applied for financial aid. Of those, 82% were determined to have financial need; 20% had their need fully met. Average financial aid package (proportion receiving): $16,176 (82%). Average amount of gift aid, such as scholarships or grants (proportion receiving): $12,251 (80%). Average amount of self-help aid, such as work study or loans (proportion receiving): $5,030 (69%). Average need-based loan (excluding PLUS or other private loans): $4,518. Among students who received need-based aid, the average percentage of need met: 75%. Among students who received aid based on merit, the average award (and the proportion receiving): $8,166 (13%). The average athletic scholarship (and the proportion receiving): $0 (0%). Average amount of debt of borrowers graduating in 2009: $33,648. Proportion who borrowed: 84%.

CAMPUS LIFE AND EXTRACURRICULAR ACTIVITIES

Campus housing available (% using): coed dorms (100%), special housing for disabled students (0%). Students who live in college-owned, operated, or affiliated housing: 24%. **Student employment:** During the 2009-2010 academic year, 19% of undergraduates worked on campus. Average per-year earnings: $1,500. **Clubs and organizations:** Number of student organizations: 35. Activities include: campus ministries, choral groups, concert band, dance, drama/theater, international student organization, jazz band, literary magazine, music ensembles, musical theater, pep band, student government, student newspaper. Number of fraternities: 0; sororities: 0. **Sports program (2009-2010):** Member of NCAA III. *Men's intercollegiate varsity sports:* baseball, basketball, cross country, football, golf, lacrosse, soccer, tennis, track and field (indoor), track and field (outdoor), volleyball, wrestling. *Women's intercollegiate varsity sports:* basketball, cross country, golf, lacrosse, soccer, softball, tennis, track and field (indoor), track and field (outdoor), volleyball.

SERVICES AND FACILITIES

Basic services: nonremedial tutoring, women's center, placement service, day care, health service, health insurance. **Remedial assistance:** reading, math, writing, study skills. **Counseling services:** minority student, career, military, personal, veteran student, academic, older student, psychological, religious. **For learning-disabled students:** School does not offer a structured program with separate admission and additional fees. Services include: remedial math, remedial English, reading machines, note-taking services, learning center, readers, extended time for tests, tutors, texts on tape, typist/ scribe. **Library:** Number of titles: 97,165; number of current serial subscriptions: 9,214. **Information technology resources:** Students are not required to lease or own a computer. Number of campus computers available to all students: 278. School has a wireless network. Approximate number of users that can be accommodated: 4,500. Proportion of college-owned housing units wired for high-speed internet access: 100%. **Campus safety:** Security services offered: 24-hour foot-and-vehicle patrols, late-night transport/escort service, 24-hour emergency telephones, lighted pathways/sidewalks, student patrols, controlled dormitory access (key, security card, etc).

TRANSFER AND INTERNATIONAL STUDENTS

Transfer students: May apply for admission for the following academic terms: Fall, Winter, Spring, Summer. Applicants need a minimum number of credits to apply. For fall 2009: Transfer applications received: 616. Transfer applicants offered admission: 356. Transfer applicants enrolled: 191. **International students:** Number of foreign undergraduates: 4. Number of countries represented: 6. Minimum TOEFL score required: 510 (paper); 180 (computer).

College of Wooster

- **Address:** 1189 Beall Avenue, Wooster, OH 44691
- **Website:** http://www.wooster.edu/
- **Private**
- **Enrollment:** 1,817 full-time; 17 part-time

KEY STATS

✔ **U.S News College Ranking:** 71, National Liberal Arts Colleges
✔ **ACT Score (25th/75th percentile):** 24-29
✔ **Tuition:** 2010-2011: $36,598

Selectivity: More selective	**Room/board:** $9,070
Acceptance rate: 59%	**Average debt:** $25,140
Student/faculty ratio: 11/1	**Proportion who borrowed:** 58%

UNDERGRADUATE STUDENT BODY STATS

2009-2010 enrollment: 1,817 full-time; 17 part-time. Men: 46%; women: 54%. **Ethnic makeup:** African American: 6%; Asian American: 3%; Hispanic: 2%; White: 83%; International: 5%. **Religious preference:** Roman Catholic: 16%; Protestant: 35%; Jewish: 6%; Muslim: 2%; Buddhist: 1%; No preference: 30%; Baptist: 4%; Other: 6%.

ADMISSIONS FACTS AND FIGURES

Phone: (800) 877-9905. **Email:** admissions@wooster.edu. **Website:** http://www.wooster.edu/. **Application deadlines for fall 2011:** Regular decision: February 15. Early decision: Send application by: December 1; Decision sent by: December 15. Early action: Send application by: January 15; Decision sent by: February 1. Admission can be deferred. **Application fee:** $40. **To apply online, go to:** http://admissions.wooster.edu/apply/default.php. **Admissions requirements/recommendations:** High school units required (recommended): English: 4; Mathematics: 3 (4); Science:

3 (4); Foreign language: 2 (3); Social studies: 3 (4); Academic electives: 2; Total units: 17 (15). Tests: The college uses SAT or ACT scores in admissions decisions. Either SAT or ACT required. For admission to the fall 2011 entering class, the school will accept: ACT with writing required. Campus visit: Recommended. Admissions interview: Recommended. Off-campus interview: May be arranged. **Factors that count in admissions decisions:** *Academic:* Secondary school record: Very Important. Class rank: Very Important. Letters of recommendation: Important. Standardized test scores: Important. Essay: Important. *Nonacademic:* Interview: Considered. Extracurricular activities: Considered. Talent/ability: Important. Character/personal qualities: Important. Alumni/ae relationship: Considered. Geographical residence: Considered. State residency: Considered. Religious affiliation/commitment: Not Considered. Minority status: Considered. Volunteer work: Considered. Work experience: Considered. **Other schools with the greatest overlap in applicants:** Allegheny College; Denison University; Kenyon College; Ohio Wesleyan University; Wittenberg University. **Admissions statistics for the fall 2009 entering class:** Total applicants: 4,752. Total accepted: 2,795. Freshmen enrolled: 481; 58% were from out of state. Accepted through early-decision or early-action plans: 6%. Overall acceptance rate: 59%. Early-decision acceptance rate: 88%. Non-early acceptance rate: 59%. **Credentials of fall 2009 freshmen:** 36% ranked in the top 10 percent of their high school class; 74% were in the top 25 percent; 93% were in the top half. (Proportion submitting class standing: 49%.) **Average high school grade point average:** 3.6. **First-year students who submitted SAT scores:** 65%. Scores (25/75 percentile): Critical Reading: 540-660, Math: 540-650, Combined: 1080-1310. **First-year students submitting ACT scores:** 69%. Scores (25/75 percentile): English: 23-31, Math: 22-28, Composite: 24-29.

ACADEMICS

Year founded: 1866. **Academic calendar:** Semester. **Degrees offered:** bachelor's. **Most popular majors:** 27% social sciences, 9% English language and literature/letters, 9% history, 8% biological and biomedical sciences, 8% philosophy and religious studies. **Major fields of study:** area, ethnic, cultural, and gender studies; biological and biomedical sciences; business, management, marketing, and related support services; communication, journalism, and related programs; computer and information sciences and support services; education; English language and literature/letters; foreign languages, literatures, and linguistics; health professions and related clinical sciences; history; mathematics and statistics; multi/interdisciplinary studies; philosophy and religious studies; physical sciences; psychology; social sciences; visual and performing arts. **Areas of required coursework:** arts/fine arts, humanities, mathematics, English (including composition), foreign languages, sciences (biological or physical), history, social science, other. **Pre-professional programs:** pre-law, pre-medicine, pre-theology, pre-veterinary science, other. **Special academic programs (% participation):** double major (7%), exchange student program (domestic), independent study (100%), internships, student-designed major, study abroad (30%), teacher certificate program. **Teacher certification offered in:** early childhood, elementary, middle/junior high, secondary. **Faculty and instruction (2009-2010):** Total instructional faculty: 131 full-time, 29 part-time (50% men; 50% women). Full-time faculty with Ph.D. or other terminal degree: 99%. Student/faculty ratio: 11/1. Classes of fewer than 20 students: 64%; of 20 to 49 students: 36%; of 50 or more students: 0%. **Advanced Placement and International Baccalaureate credit:** AP tests may be used for: Credit only. Scores accepted: 3, 4, 5. International Baccalaureate exams may be used for: Credit only. **Freshmen returning for sophomore year:** 87%. **Graduation rates:** Four-year: 68%; five-year: 74%; six-year: 76%. **Graduate study:** 43% of students pursue further study within one year; 60% within five years. Fields in which graduates pursue further study: Master of Business Administration (MBA), 5%; law, 12%; medicine, 6%; dentistry, 2%; theology (or the seminary), 5%; education, 10%; arts and sciences, 55%.

COSTS AND FINANCIAL AID

Financial aid office: (330) 263-2317. **Expenses (2010-2011):** Tuition and fees 2010-2011: $36,598; room/board: $9,070. Estimated books and supplies: $1,000; transportation: $150; personal expenses: $600. **Financial aid:** Priority filing date for institution's financial aid form: February 15; deadline: September 1. In 2009-2010, 69% of undergraduates applied for financial aid. Of those, 60% were determined to have financial need; 40% had their need fully met. Average financial aid package (proportion receiving): $27,955 (60%). Average amount of gift aid, such as scholarships or grants (proportion receiving): $22,600 (59%). Average amount of self-help aid, such as work study or loans (proportion receiving): $5,175 (47%). Average need-based loan (excluding PLUS or other private loans): $4,550. Among students who received need-based aid, the average percentage of need met:

86%. Among students who received aid based on merit, the average award (and the proportion receiving): $15,642 (35%). The average athletic scholarship (and the proportion receiving): $0 (0%). Average amount of debt of borrowers graduating in 2009: $25,140. Proportion who borrowed: 58%.

CAMPUS LIFE AND EXTRACURRICULAR ACTIVITIES
Campus housing available (% using): coed dorms (80%), women's dorms (6%), other housing options (14%). Students who live in college-owned, operated, or affiliated housing: 98%. **Student employment:** During the 2009-2010 academic year, 50% of undergraduates worked on campus. Average per-year earnings: $2,200. **Clubs and organizations:** Number of student organizations: 120. Activities include: campus ministries, choral groups, concert band, dance, drama/theater, international student organization, jazz band, literary magazine, marching band, model UN, music ensembles, musical theater, pep band, radio station, student government, student newspaper, student film society, symphony orchestra, yearbook. Number of fraternities: 5; sororities: 6. Proportion of men in fraternities: 10%; of women in sororities: 12%. Average proportion of students who stay on campus on weekends: 90%. **Sports program (2009-2010):** Member of NCAA III. *Men's intercollegiate varsity sports:* baseball, basketball, cross country, football, golf, lacrosse, soccer, swimming, tennis, track and field (indoor), track and field (outdoor). *Women's intercollegiate varsity sports:* basketball, cross country, field hockey, golf, lacrosse, soccer, softball, swimming, tennis, track and field (indoor), track and field (outdoor), volleyball.

SERVICES AND FACILITIES
Basic services: nonremedial tutoring, placement service, health service, health insurance. **Remedial assistance:** reading, math, writing, study skills. **Counseling services:** minority student, career, personal, academic, psychological, birth control, religious, other. **For learning-disabled students:** School does not offer a structured program with separate admission and additional fees. Services include: tape recorders, untimed tests, oral tests, learning center, readers, extended time for tests, tutors. **Library:** Number of titles: 757,789; number of current serial subscriptions: 20,425. **Information technology resources:** Students are not required to lease or own a computer. Number of campus computers available to all students: 500. School has a wireless network. Proportion of college-owned housing units wired for high-speed internet access: 100%. **Campus safety:** Security services offered: 24-hour foot-and-vehicle patrols, late-night transport/escort service, 24-hour emergency telephones, lighted pathways/sidewalks, student patrols, controlled dormitory access (key, security card, etc).

TRANSFER AND INTERNATIONAL STUDENTS
Transfer students: May apply for admission for the following academic terms: Fall, Spring. Applicants do not need a minimum number of credits to apply. For fall 2009: Transfer applications received: 98. Transfer applicants offered admission: 45. Transfer applicants enrolled: 20. **International students:** Number of foreign undergraduates: 90 (5% of student body). Minimum TOEFL score required: 550 (paper); 213 (computer).

Columbus College of Art and Design

- **Address:** 60 Cleveland Avenue, Columbus, OH 43215
- **Website:** http://www.ccad.edu
- **Private**
- **Enrollment:** 1,251 full-time; 174 part-time

KEY STATS
✔ **U.S News College Ranking:** Unranked Specialty School–Fine Arts
✔ **ACT Score (25th/75th percentile):** 18-23
✔ **Tuition:** 2010-2011: $26,522

Selectivity: N/A	Room/board: N/A
Acceptance rate: 70%	Average debt: $44,701
Student/faculty ratio: 12/1	Proportion who borrowed: 87%

UNDERGRADUATE STUDENT BODY STATS
2009-2010 enrollment: 1,251 full-time; 174 part-time. Men: 40%; women: 60%. **Ethnic makeup:** African American: 7%; Asian American: 4%; Hispanic: 4%; White: 82%; International: 3%.

ADMISSIONS FACTS AND FIGURES
Phone: (614) 222-3261. **Email:** admissions@ccad.edu. **Website:** http://www.ccad.edu. **Application deadlines for fall 2011:** Regular decision: Rolling. Early decision: Not offered. Early action: Not offered. Admission can be deferred. **Application fee:** $25. **To apply online, go to:** https://www.applyweb.com/apply/ccad/menu.html. **Admissions requirements/recommendations:** High school units required (recommended): English: (4); Mathematics: (2); Total units: (6). Tests: The college uses SAT or ACT scores in admissions decisions. Either SAT or ACT required. For admission to the fall 2011 entering class, the school will accept: ACT with or without writing accepted. Campus visit: Recommended. Admissions interview: Recommended. Off-campus interview: May be arranged. **Factors that count in admissions decisions:** *Academic:* Secondary school record: Important. Class rank: Not Considered. Letters of recommendation: Important. Standardized test scores: Considered. Essay: Important. *Nonacademic:* Interview: Considered. Extracurricular activities: Considered. Talent/ability: Very Important. Character/personal qualities: Not Considered. Alumni/ae relationship: Considered. Geographical residence: Not Considered. State residency: Not Considered. Religious affiliation/commitment: Not Considered. Minority status: Not Considered. Volunteer work: Considered. Work experience: Considered. **Admissions statistics for the fall 2009 entering class:** Total applicants: 756. Total accepted: 528. Freshmen enrolled: 357; Overall acceptance rate: 70%. **Credentials of fall 2009 freshmen:** 3% ranked in the top 10 percent of their high school class; 15% were in the top 25 percent; 57% were in the top half. (Proportion submitting class standing: 71%.) **Average high school grade point average:** 3.1. **First-year students who submitted SAT scores:** 31%. Scores (25/75 percentile): Critical Reading: 445-580, Math: 420-550, Combined: 865-1130. **First-year students submitting ACT scores:** 69%. Scores (25/75 percentile): English: 18-24, Math: 17-22, Composite: 18-23.

ACADEMICS
Year founded: 1879. **Academic calendar:** Semester. **Degrees offered:** bachelor's. **Most popular majors:** 21% film/video and photographic arts, 20% fine arts and art studies, 19% illustration, 18% commercial and advertising art, 8% fashion/apparel design. **Major fields of study:** visual and performing arts. **Areas of required coursework:** arts/fine arts, humanities, computer literacy, mathematics, English (including composition), philosophy, sciences (biological or physical), history, social science. **Faculty and instruction (2009-2010):** Total instructional faculty: 72 full-time, 108 part-time (59% men; 41% women; 9% minorities). Full-time faculty with Ph.D. or other terminal degree: 56%. Student/faculty ratio: 12/1. Classes of fewer than 20 students: 75%; of 20 to 49 students: 25%; of 50 or more students: 1%. **Advanced Placement and International Baccalaureate credit:** AP tests may be used for: Placement only. Scores accepted: 3, 4, 5. **Freshmen returning for sophomore year:** 78%. **Graduation rates:** Four-year: 47%; five-year: 57%; six-year: 62%.

COSTS AND FINANCIAL AID
Financial aid office: (614) 222-3295. **Expenses (2010-2011):** Tuition and fees 2010-2011: $26,522. Estimated books and supplies: $3,000; transportation: $1,300; personal expenses: $200. **Financial aid:** Priority filing date for institution's financial aid form: March 5; deadline: March 5. In 2009-2010, 95% of undergraduates applied for financial aid. Of those, 84% were determined to have financial need; 14% had their need fully met. Average financial aid package (proportion receiving): $16,572 (83%). Average amount of gift aid, such as scholarships or grants (proportion receiving): $11,054 (83%). Average amount of self-help aid, such as work study or loans (proportion receiving): $6,428 (71%). Average need-based loan (excluding PLUS or other private loans): $5,972. Among students who received need-based aid, the average percentage of need met: 61%. Among students who received aid based on merit, the average award (and the proportion receiving): $7,552 (15%). The average athletic scholarship (and the proportion receiving): $0 (0%). Average amount of debt of borrowers graduating in 2009: $44,701. Proportion who borrowed: 87%.

CAMPUS LIFE AND EXTRACURRICULAR ACTIVITIES
Campus housing available (% using): coed dorms (52%), apartment for single students (48%), special housing for disabled students. Students who live in college-owned, operated, or affiliated housing: 35%. **Student employment:** During the 2009-2010 academic year, 10% of undergraduates worked on campus. Average per-year earnings: $3,240. **Clubs and organizations:** Number of student organizations: 15. Activities include: literary magazine, student government, student film society. Number of fraternities: 0; sororities: 0. Average proportion of students who stay on campus on weekends: 40%.

SERVICES AND FACILITIES
Basic services: placement service, health insurance. **Remedial assistance:** reading, math, writing, study skills. **Counseling services:** career, personal, academic, psychological. **For learning-disabled students:** School does not

offer a structured program with separate admission and additional fees. Total undergraduates in learning-disabled program or receiving services: 90. Services include: remedial English, reading machines, tape recorders, note-taking services, oral tests, learning center, readers, extended time for tests, tutors, priority registration, priority seating, texts on tape, other testing accommodations. **Library:** Number of titles: 56,161; number of current serial subscriptions: 286. **Information technology resources:** Students are required to lease or own a computer. Number of campus computers available to all students: 485. School has a wireless network. Proportion of college-owned housing units wired for high-speed internet access: 100%. **Campus safety:** Security services offered: 24-hour foot-and-vehicle patrols, late-night transport/escort service, 24-hour emergency telephones, lighted pathways/sidewalks, controlled dormitory access (key, security card, etc.).

TRANSFER AND INTERNATIONAL STUDENTS

Transfer students: May apply for admission for the following academic terms: Fall, Spring. Applicants do not need a minimum number of credits to apply. For fall 2009: Transfer applications received: 126. Transfer applicants offered admission: 68. Transfer applicants enrolled: 61. **International students:** Number of foreign undergraduates: 40 (3% of student body). Number of countries represented: 18. Minimum TOEFL score required: 500 (paper); 173 (computer). Average TOEFL score: 550 (paper).

Defiance College

- **Address:** 701 N. Clinton Street, Defiance, OH 43512
- **Website:** http://www.defiance.edu
- **Private; Religious affiliation:** United Church of Christ
- **Enrollment:** 755 full-time; 202 part-time

KEY STATS

✔ **U.S News College Ranking:** 33, Regional Colleges (Midwest)
✔ **ACT Score (25th/75th percentile):** 19-24
✔ **Tuition:** 2010-2011: $24,330

Selectivity: Selective	**Room/board:** $8,120
Acceptance rate: 74%	**Average debt:** $25,388
Student/faculty ratio: 13/1	**Proportion who borrowed:** 90%

UNDERGRADUATE STUDENT BODY STATS

2009-2010 enrollment: 755 full-time; 202 part-time. Men: 48%; women: 52%. **Ethnic makeup:** African American: 7%; American-Indian: 1%; Asian American: 1%; Hispanic: 4%; White: 87%. **Religious preference:** Roman Catholic: 15%; Protestant: 29%; No preference: 36%; United Church of Christ: 4%; Christian Denomination : 16%.

ADMISSIONS FACTS AND FIGURES

Phone: (800) 520-4632. **Email:** admissions@defiance.edu. **Website:** http://www.defiance.edu. **Application deadlines for fall 2011:** Regular decision: Rolling. Early decision: Not offered. Early action: Not offered. Admission can be deferred. **Application fee:** $25. **To apply online, go to:** https://www.defiance.edu/application.html. **Admissions requirements/recommendations:** High school units required (recommended): English: (4); Mathematics: (3); Science: (3); Foreign language: (2); Social studies: (2); Total units: (16). Tests: The college uses SAT or ACT scores in admissions decisions. Either SAT or ACT required. For admission to the fall 2011 entering class, the school will accept: ACT with or without writing accepted. Campus visit: Recommended. Admissions interview: Neither required nor recommended. Off-campus interview: May be arranged. **Factors that count in admissions decisions:** *Academic:* Secondary school record: Very Important. Class rank: Considered. Letters of recommendation: Considered. Standardized test scores: Very Important. Essay: Not Considered. *Nonacademic:* Interview: Important. Extracurricular activities: Not Considered. Talent/ability: Not Considered. Character/personal qualities: Considered. Alumni/ae relationship: Not Considered. Geographical residence: Not Considered. State residency: Not Considered. Religious affiliation/commitment: Not Considered. Minority status: Not Considered. Volunteer work: Considered. Work experience: Not Considered. **Other schools with the greatest overlap in applicants:** Adrian College; Bluffton University; Bowling Green State University; Heidelberg University; University of Toledo. **Admissions statistics for the fall 2009 entering class:** Total applicants: 1,258. Total accepted: 937. Freshmen enrolled: 216; 21% were from out of state. Overall acceptance rate: 74%. **Credentials of fall 2009 freshmen:** 9% ranked in the top 10 percent of their high school class; 25% were in the top 25 percent; 67%

were in the top half. (Proportion submitting class standing: 95%.) **Average high school grade point average:** 3.1. **First-year students who submitted SAT scores:** 17%. Scores (25/75 percentile): Critical Reading: 410-540, Math: 460-550, Combined: 870-1090. **First-year students submitting ACT scores:** 95%. Scores (25/75 percentile): English: 18-25, Math: 18-23, Composite: 19-24.

ACADEMICS

Year founded: 1850. **Academic calendar:** Semester. **Degrees offered:** associate, bachelor's, master's. **Most popular majors:** 24% education, 20% business administration and management, 12% criminal justice/police science, 10% social sciences, 10% sport and fitness administration/management. **Major fields of study:** biological and biomedical sciences; business, management, marketing, and related support services; communication, journalism, and related programs; computer and information sciences and support services; education; health professions and related clinical sciences; history; legal professions and studies; mathematics and statistics; parks, recreation, leisure, and fitness studies; philosophy and religious studies; physical sciences; psychology; public administration and social service professions; security and protective services; theology and religious vocations; visual and performing arts. **Areas of required coursework:** arts/fine arts, humanities, computer literacy, mathematics, English (including composition), philosophy, sciences (biological or physical), history, social science. **Pre-professional programs:** pre-law, pre-dentistry, pre-medicine, pre-theology, pre-veterinary science. **Special academic programs:** accelerated program, cooperative (work-study plan) program, distance learning, double major, honors program, independent study, internships, student-designed major, study abroad, teacher certificate program, weekend college. **Teacher certification offered in:** early childhood, elementary, middle/junior high, secondary. **Cooperative education programs:** art, business, education, health professions, humanities, natural science, social/behavioral science. **Faculty and instruction (2009-2010):** Total instructional faculty: 45 full-time, 50 part-time (61% men; 39% women; 7% minorities). Full-time faculty with Ph.D. or other terminal degree: 60%. Student/faculty ratio: 13/1. Classes of fewer than 20 students: 65%; of 20 to 49 students: 35%; of 50 or more students: 0%. **Advanced Placement and International Baccalaureate credit:** AP tests may be used for: Credit only. Scores accepted: 4, 5. International Baccalaureate exams may be used for: Credit only. **Freshmen returning for sophomore year:** 66%. **Graduation rates:** Four-year: 38%; five-year: 46%; six-year: 52%. **Graduate study:** 38% of students pursue further study immediately upon graduation. Fields in which graduates pursue further study: Master of Business Administration (MBA), 19%; law, 1%; medicine, 1%; dentistry, 1%; theology (or the seminary), 1%; education, 15%; arts and sciences, 40%; veterinary medicine, 1%.

COSTS AND FINANCIAL AID

Financial aid office: (419) 783-2376. **Expenses (2010-2011):** Tuition and fees 2010-2011: $24,330; room/board: $8,120. Estimated books and supplies: $1,350; transportation: $1,000; personal expenses: $2,000. **Financial aid:** Priority filing date for institution's financial aid form: April 1. In 2009-2010, 97% of undergraduates applied for financial aid. Of those, 93% were determined to have financial need; 13% had their need fully met. Average financial aid package (proportion receiving): $18,433 (93%). Average amount of gift aid, such as scholarships or grants (proportion receiving): $6,007 (71%). Average amount of self-help aid, such as work study or loans (proportion receiving): $5,890 (88%). Average need-based loan (excluding PLUS or other private loans): $4,544. Among students who received need-based aid, the average percentage of need met: 75%. Among students who received aid based on merit, the average award (and the proportion receiving): $9,308 (7%). The average athletic scholarship (and the proportion receiving): $0 (0%). Average amount of debt of borrowers graduating in 2009: $25,388. Proportion who borrowed: 90%.

CAMPUS LIFE AND EXTRACURRICULAR ACTIVITIES

Campus housing available (% using): coed dorms (82%), apartment for single students (18%). Students who live in college-owned, operated, or affiliated housing: 51%. **Student employment:** During the 2009-2010 academic year, 44% of undergraduates worked on campus. Average per-year earnings: $400. **Clubs and organizations:** Number of student organizations: 31. Activities include: campus ministries, choral groups, concert band, dance, drama/theater, literary magazine, music ensembles, musical theater, pep band, student government, student newspaper, yearbook. Number of fraternities: 1; sororities: 2. Proportion of men in fraternities: 4%; of women in sororities: 6%. Average proportion of students who stay on campus on weekends: 50%. **Sports program (2009-2010):** Member of NCAA III. *Men's intercollegiate varsity sports:* baseball, basketball, cross country, football, golf, soccer, tennis, track and field (indoor), track and field (outdoor). **Women's intercollegiate varsity sports:** basketball, cross country, golf, soccer, softball, tennis, track and field (indoor), track and field (outdoor), volleyball.

SERVICES AND FACILITIES

Basic services: nonremedial tutoring, placement service, health service, health insurance. **Remedial assistance:** other. **Counseling services:** minority student, career, personal, academic, older student, psychological, religious. **For learning-disabled students:** School does not offer a structured program with separate admission and additional fees. Total undergraduates in learning-disabled program or receiving services: 0. Services include: tape recorders, note-taking services, learning center, readers, tutors. **Library:** Number of titles: 146,344; number of current serial subscriptions: 7,088. **Information technology resources:** Students are not required to lease or own a computer. Number of campus computers available to all students: 200. School has a wireless network. Approximate number of users that can be accommodated: 350. Proportion of college-owned housing units wired for high-speed internet access: 100%. **Campus safety:** Security services offered: late-night transport/escort service, 24-hour emergency telephones, lighted pathways/sidewalks, controlled dormitory access (key, security card, etc).

TRANSFER AND INTERNATIONAL STUDENTS

Transfer students: May apply for admission for the following academic terms: Fall, Spring, Summer. Applicants do not need a minimum number of credits to apply. For fall 2009: Transfer applications received: 162. Transfer applicants offered admission: 101. Transfer applicants enrolled: 63. **International students:** Number of foreign undergraduates: 4. Number of countries represented: 1. Minimum TOEFL score required: 550 (paper); 213 (computer).

Denison University

- **Address:** 1 Main Street, Granville, OH 43023
- **Website:** http://www.denison.edu
- **Private**
- **Enrollment:** 2,237 full-time; 30 part-time

KEY STATS

✔ **U.S News College Ranking:** 51, National Liberal Arts Colleges
✔ **ACT Score (25th/75th percentile):** 27-30
✔ **Tuition:** 2010-2011: $38,220

Selectivity: More selective	**Room/board:** $9,580
Acceptance rate: 50%	**Average debt:** N/A
Student/faculty ratio: 10/1	**Proportion who borrowed:** N/A

UNDERGRADUATE STUDENT BODY STATS

2009-2010 enrollment: 2,237 full-time; 30 part-time. Men: 44%; women: 56%. **Ethnic makeup:** African American: 6%; Asian American: 2%; Hispanic: 3%; White: 83%; International: 6%. **Religious preference:** Roman Catholic: 29%; Protestant: 34%; Jewish: 6%; Muslim: 1%; Hindu: 1%; Buddhist: 1%; No preference: 6%; Other: 20%.

ADMISSIONS FACTS AND FIGURES

Phone: (740) 587-6276. **Email:** admissions@denison.edu. **Website:** http://www.denison.edu. **Application deadlines for fall 2011:** Regular decision: January 15; decision sent by April 1. Early decision: Send application by: December 1; Decision sent by: January 1. Early action: Not offered. Admission can be deferred. **Application fee:** $40. **To apply online, go to:** https://dss.denison.edu/admissions/apppart1ss.php. **Admissions requirements/recommendations:** High school units required (recommended): English: 4; Mathematics: 4; Science: 4; Foreign language: 3; Social studies: 2; History: 1; Academic electives: 1; Total units: 19. Tests: The college uses SAT or ACT scores in admissions decisions. Neither SAT nor ACT required. For admission to the fall 2011 entering class, the school will accept: ACT with or without writing accepted. Campus visit: Recommended. Admissions interview: Recommended. Off-campus interview: May be arranged. **Factors that count in admissions decisions:** *Academic:* Secondary school record: Very Important. Class rank: Considered. Letters of recommendation: Very Important. Standardized test scores: Considered. Essay: Very Important. *Nonacademic:* Interview: Important. Extracurricular activities: Important. Talent/ability: Important. Character/personal qualities: Considered. Alumni/ae relationship: Considered. Geographical residence: Considered. State residency: Considered. Religious affiliation/commit-

ment: Not Considered. Minority status: Not Considered. Volunteer work: Considered. Work experience: Considered. **Other schools with the greatest overlap in applicants:** Allegheny College; College of Wooster; DePauw University; Kenyon College; Ohio Wesleyan University. **Admissions statistics for the fall 2009 entering class:** Total applicants: 5,002. Total accepted: 2,509. Freshmen enrolled: 649; 68% were from out of state. Overall acceptance rate: 50%. Early-decision acceptance rate: 81%. Non-early acceptance rate: 49%. **Size of waiting list:** 466 applicants; enrolled from waiting list: 33. **Credentials of fall 2009 freshmen:** 54% ranked in the top 10 percent of their high school class; 85% were in the top 25 percent; 97% were in the top half. (Proportion submitting class standing: 50%.) **Average high school grade point average:** 3.5. **First-year students who submitted SAT scores:** 34%. Scores (25/75 percentile): Critical Reading: 600-700, Math: 600-680, Combined: 1200-1380. **First-year students submitting ACT scores:** 34%. Scores (25/75 percentile): English: N/A, Math: N/A, Composite: 27-30.

ACADEMICS

Year founded: 1831. **Academic calendar:** Semester. **Degrees offered:** bachelor's. **Most popular majors:** 22% social sciences, 12% communication, journalism, and related programs, 10% biological and biomedical sciences, 10% visual and performing arts, 8% English language and literature/letters. **Major fields of study:** area, ethnic, cultural, and gender studies; biological and biomedical sciences; communication, journalism, and related programs; computer and information sciences and support services; education; English language and literature/letters; foreign languages, literatures, and linguistics; history; mathematics and statistics; natural resources and conservation; philosophy and religious studies; physical sciences; psychology; social sciences; visual and performing arts. **Areas of required coursework:** arts/fine arts, humanities, English (including composition), foreign languages, sciences (biological or physical), social science. **Pre-professional programs:** pre-law, pre-dentistry, pre-medicine, pre-veterinary science, other. **Special academic programs (% participation):** double major (16%), honors program (48%), independent study (52%), internships (30%), student-designed major (1%), study abroad (31%), teacher certificate program, other. **Reserve Officers Training Corps (ROTC):** Army ROTC: Offered at cooperating institution (Capital University). **Faculty and instruction (2009-2010):** Total instructional faculty: 197 full-time, 20 part-time (55% men; 45% women; 17% minorities). Full-time faculty with Ph.D. or other terminal degree: 98%. Student/faculty ratio: 10/1. Classes of fewer than 20 students: 65%; of 20 to 49 students: 35%; of 50 or more students: 0%. **Advanced Placement and International Baccalaureate credit:** AP tests may be used for: Credit and/or placement. Scores accepted: 4, 5. **Freshmen returning for sophomore year:** 90%. **Graduation rates:** Four-year: 80%; five-year: 82%; six-year: 83%. **Graduate study:** 23% of students pursue further study immediately upon graduation; 28% within one year; 40% within five years. Fields in which graduates pursue further study: Master of Business Administration (MBA), 1%; law, 3%; medicine, 2%; arts and sciences, 20%.

COSTS AND FINANCIAL AID

Financial aid office: (740) 587-6279. **Expenses (2010-2011):** Tuition and fees 2010-2011: $38,220; room/board: $9,580. Estimated books and supplies: $650; transportation: $600; personal expenses: $600. **Financial aid:** In 2009-2010, 55% of undergraduates applied for financial aid. Of those, 46% were determined to have financial need; 30% had their need fully met. Average financial aid package (proportion receiving): $32,040 (46%). Average amount of gift aid, such as scholarships or grants (proportion receiving): $26,112 (46%). Average amount of self-help aid, such as work study or loans (proportion receiving): $5,498 (35%). Average need-based loan (excluding PLUS or other private loans): $4,387. Among students who received need-based aid, the average percentage of need met: 96%. Among students who received aid based on merit, the average award (and the proportion receiving): $15,282 (47%). The average athletic scholarship (and the proportion receiving): $0 (0%).

CAMPUS LIFE AND EXTRACURRICULAR ACTIVITIES

Campus housing available (% using): coed dorms (91%), women's dorms (4%), men's dorms (4%), apartment for single students, cooperative housing. Students who live in college-owned, operated, or affiliated housing: 98%. **Student employment:** During the 2009-2010 academic year, 40% of undergraduates worked on campus. Average per-year earnings: $2,100. **Clubs and organizations:** Number of student organizations: 138. Activities include: campus ministries, choral groups, dance, drama/theater, international student organization, jazz band, literary magazine, music ensembles, musical theater, radio station, student government, student newspaper, student film society, television station, yearbook. Number of fraternities: 8; sororities: 6. Proportion of men in fraternities: 19%; of women in sororities:

28%. Average proportion of students who stay on campus on weekends: 90%. **Sports program (2009-2010):** Member of NCAA III. ***Men's intercollegiate varsity sports:*** baseball, basketball, cross country, football, golf, lacrosse, soccer, swimming, tennis, track and field (indoor), track and field (outdoor). ***Women's intercollegiate varsity sports:*** basketball, cross country, field hockey, golf, lacrosse, soccer, swimming, tennis, track and field (indoor), track and field (outdoor), volleyball.

SERVICES AND FACILITIES
Basic services: nonremedial tutoring, women's center, placement service, health service, health insurance. **Counseling services:** minority student, career, personal, academic, psychological, birth control, religious. **For learning-disabled students:** School does not offer a structured program with separate admission and additional fees. Total undergraduates in learning-disabled program or receiving services: 152. Services include: tape recorders, note-taking services, learning center, readers, extended time for tests, tutors, priority seating, texts on tape, other. **Library:** Number of titles: 819,790; number of current serial subscriptions: 6,235. **Information technology resources:** Students are not required to lease or own a computer. Number of campus computers available to all students: 698. School has a wireless network. Approximate number of users that can be accommodated: 1,000. Proportion of college-owned housing units wired for high-speed internet access: 100%. **Campus safety:** Security services offered: 24-hour foot-and-vehicle patrols, late-night transport/escort service, 24-hour emergency telephones, lighted pathways/sidewalks, student patrols, controlled dormitory access (key, security card, etc).

TRANSFER AND INTERNATIONAL STUDENTS
Transfer students: May apply for admission for the following academic terms: Fall, Spring. Applicants do not need a minimum number of credits to apply. For fall 2009: Transfer applications received: 113. Transfer applicants offered admission: 45. Transfer applicants enrolled: 15. **International students:** Number of foreign undergraduates: 124 (6% of student body). Number of countries represented: 28. Minimum TOEFL score required: 550 (paper); 213 (computer). Average TOEFL score: 619 (paper).

Franciscan University of Steubenville

- **Address:** 1235 University Boulevard, Steubenville, OH 43952-1763
- **Website:** http://www.franciscan.edu
- **Private; Religious affiliation:** Roman Catholic
- **Enrollment:** 1,948 full-time; 133 part-time

KEY STATS
✔ **U.S News College Ranking:** 28, Regional Universities (Midwest)
✔ **ACT Score (25th/75th percentile):** 23-28
✔ **Tuition:** 2010-2011: $20,320

Selectivity: More selective	**Room/board:** $6,900
Acceptance rate: 72%	**Average debt:** $30,180
Student/faculty ratio: 15/1	**Proportion who borrowed:** 79%

UNDERGRADUATE STUDENT BODY STATS
2009-2010 enrollment: 1,948 full-time; 133 part-time. Men: 39%; women: 61%. **Ethnic makeup:** Asian American: 2%; Hispanic: 6%; White: 91%; International: 1%. **Religious preference:** Protestant: 3%; Unknown: 6%; Roman Catholic: 91%.

ADMISSIONS FACTS AND FIGURES
Phone: (740) 283-6226. **Email:** admissions@franciscan.edu. **Website:** http://www.franciscan.edu. **Application deadlines for fall 2011:** Regular decision: Rolling. Early decision: Not offered. Early action: Not offered. Admission can be deferred. **Application fee:** $20. **To apply online, go to:** https://jicsweb1.franciscan.edu/ics/Admissions/. **Admissions requirements/recommendations:** High school units required (recommended): English: (4); Mathematics: (3); Science: (3); Foreign language: (3); Social studies: (2); History: (2); Academic electives: (1); Total units: 15. Tests: The college uses SAT or ACT scores in admissions decisions. Either SAT or ACT required. For admission to the fall 2011 entering class, the school will accept: ACT with or without writing accepted. Campus visit: Recommended. Admissions interview: Recommended. Off-campus interview: May be arranged. **Factors that count in admissions decisions:** *Academic:* Secondary school record: Very Important. Class rank: Not Considered. Letters of recommendation: Considered. Standardized test scores: Very Important. Essay: Very

Important. *Nonacademic:* Interview: Very Important. Extracurricular activities: Important. Talent/ability: Important. Character/personal qualities: Very Important. Alumni/ae relationship: Not Considered. Geographical residence: Not Considered. State residency: Not Considered. Religious affiliation/commitment: Not Considered. Minority status: Not Considered. Volunteer work: Not Considered. Work experience: Not Considered. **Other schools with the greatest overlap in applicants:** Catholic University of America; Christendom College; Ohio State University–Columbus; University of Notre Dame. **Admissions statistics for the fall 2009 entering class:** Total applicants: 1,450. Total accepted: 1,040. Freshmen enrolled: 445; 82% were from out of state. Overall acceptance rate: 72%. Size of waiting list: 24 applicants; enrolled from waiting list: 10. **Credentials of fall 2009 freshmen:** 31% ranked in the top 10 percent of their high school class; 60% were in the top 25 percent; 84% were in the top half. (Proportion submitting class standing: 52%.) **Average high school grade point average:** 3.7. **First-year students who submitted SAT scores:** 58%. Scores (25/75 percentile): Critical Reading: 540-650, Math: 500-630, Combined: 1040-1280. **First-year students submitting ACT scores:** 59%. Scores (25/75 percentile): English: 21-27, Math: 23-31, Composite: 23-28.

ACADEMICS
Year founded: 1946. **Academic calendar:** Semester. **Degrees offered:** associate, bachelor's, master's. **Most popular majors:** 22% theology/theological studies, 10% religious education, 9% business administration and management, 7% English language and literature, 7% elementary education and teaching. **Major fields of study:** biological and biomedical sciences; business, management, marketing, and related support services; communication, journalism, and related programs; computer and information sciences and support services; education; English language and literature/letters; foreign languages, literatures, and linguistics; health professions and related clinical sciences; history; legal professions and studies; liberal arts and sciences studies, and humanities; mathematics and statistics; philosophy and religious studies; physical sciences; psychology; public administration and social service professions; social sciences; theology and religious vocations; visual and performing arts. **Areas of required coursework:** humanities, English (including composition), philosophy, foreign languages, sciences (biological or physical), history, social science, other. **Pre-professional programs:** pre-law, pre-dentistry, pre-medicine, pre-theology, pre-veterinary science, pre-optometry, pre-pharmacy, other. **Special academic programs (% participation):** accelerated program (9%), distance learning (3%), double major (24%), honors program (9%), independent study (1%), internships (21%), liberal arts/career combination (3%), study abroad (60%), teacher certificate program (8%). **Teacher certification offered in:** early childhood, special education, elementary, middle/junior high, secondary. **Reserve Officers Training Corps (ROTC):** Army ROTC: Offered on campus; Air Force ROTC: Offered at cooperating institution (University of Pittsburgh). **Faculty and instruction (2009-2010):** Total instructional faculty: 112 full-time, 111 part-time (69% men; 31% women; 0% minorities). Full-time faculty with Ph.D. or other terminal degree: 79%. Student/faculty ratio: 15/1. Classes of fewer than 20 students: 44%; of 20 to 49 students: 54%; of 50 or more students: 3%. **Advanced Placement and International Baccalaureate credit:** AP tests may be used for: Credit and/or placement. Scores accepted: 3, 4, 5. International Baccalaureate exams may be used for: Credit and/or placement. **Freshmen returning for sophomore year:** 84%. **Graduation rates:** Four-year: 63%; five-year: 71%; six-year: 70%. **Graduate study:** 26% of students pursue further study immediately upon graduation. Fields in which graduates pursue further study: Master of Business Administration (MBA), 12%; law, 6%; medicine, 12%; theology (or the seminary), 35%; education, 12%; arts and sciences, 23%.

COSTS AND FINANCIAL AID
Financial aid office: (740) 283-6226. **Expenses (2010-2011):** Tuition and fees 2010-2011: $20,320; room/board: $6,900. Estimated books and supplies: $1,200; transportation: $1,500; personal expenses: $1,200. **Financial aid:** Priority filing date for institution's financial aid form: April 1. In 2009-2010, 81% of undergraduates applied for financial aid. Of those, 68% were determined to have financial need; 14% had their need fully met. Average financial aid package (proportion receiving): $12,549 (68%). Average amount of gift aid, such as scholarships or grants (proportion receiving): $8,177 (65%). Average amount of self-help aid, such as work study or loans (proportion receiving): $4,962 (64%). Average need-based loan (excluding PLUS or other private loans): $4,311. Among students who received need-based aid, the average percentage of need met: 60%. Among students who received aid based on merit, the average award (and the proportion receiving): $4,094 (12%). The average athletic scholarship (and the proportion

receiving): $0 (0%). Average amount of debt of borrowers graduating in 2009: $30,180. Proportion who borrowed: 79%.

CAMPUS LIFE AND EXTRACURRICULAR ACTIVITIES

Campus housing available (% using): women's dorms (52%), men's dorms (31%). Students who live in college-owned, operated, or affiliated housing: 74%. **Student employment:** During the 2009-2010 academic year, 50% of undergraduates worked on campus. Average per-year earnings: $1,500. **Clubs and organizations:** Number of student organizations: 42. Activities include: campus ministries, choral groups, drama/theater, international student organization, literary magazine, music ensembles, radio station, student government, student newspaper, yearbook. Number of fraternities: 0; sororities: 1. Average proportion of students who stay on campus on weekends: 70%. **Sports program (2009-2010):** Member of NCAA III. *Men's intercollegiate varsity sports:* baseball, basketball, cross country, soccer, tennis, track and field (outdoor). *Women's intercollegiate varsity sports:* basketball, cross country, soccer, softball, tennis, track and field (outdoor), volleyball.

SERVICES AND FACILITIES

Basic services: nonremedial tutoring, health service, health insurance. **Remedial assistance:** writing, study skills, other. **Counseling services:** career, personal, veteran student, academic, religious. **For learning-disabled students:** School does not offer a structured program with separate admission and additional fees. Services include: reading machines, tape recorders, untimed tests, note-taking services, oral tests, readers, extended time for tests, tutors, priority registration, other. **Library:** Number of titles: 234,081; number of current serial subscriptions: 410. **Information technology resources:** Students are not required to lease or own a computer. Number of campus computers available to all students: 126. School has a wireless network. Approximate number of users that can be accommodated: 200. Proportion of college-owned housing units wired for high-speed internet access: 100%. **Campus safety:** Security services offered: 24-hour foot-and-vehicle patrols, late-night transport/escort service, 24-hour emergency telephones, lighted pathways/sidewalks, student patrols, controlled dormitory access (key, security card, etc).

TRANSFER AND INTERNATIONAL STUDENTS

Transfer students: May apply for admission for the following academic terms: Fall, Spring, Summer. Applicants do not need a minimum number of credits to apply. For fall 2009: Transfer applications received: 471. Transfer applicants offered admission: 306. Transfer applicants enrolled: 172. **International students:** Number of foreign undergraduates: 15 (1% of student body). Number of countries represented: 11. Minimum TOEFL score required: 550 (paper); 213 (computer). Average TOEFL score: 653 (paper).

Franklin University

- **Address:** 201 S. Grant Avenue, Columbus, OH 43215
- **Website:** http://www.franklin.edu
- **Private**
- **Enrollment:** N/A

KEY STATS
✔ **U.S News College Ranking:** Unranked Specialty School–Business
✔ **SAT or ACT Score (25th/75th percentile):** N/A
✔ **Tuition:** 2009-2010: $7,928

Selectivity: Least selective	**Room/board:** $12,550
Acceptance rate: N/A	**Average debt:** N/A
Student/faculty ratio: N/A	**Proportion who borrowed:** N/A

Heidelberg University

- **Address:** 310 E. Market Street, Tiffin, OH 44883
- **Website:** http://www.heidelberg.edu
- **Private; Religious affiliation:** United Church of Christ
- **Enrollment:** 1,214 full-time; 233 part-time

KEY STATS
✔ **U.S News College Ranking:** 48, Regional Universities (Midwest)
✔ **ACT Score (25th/75th percentile):** 18-24
✔ **Tuition:** 2010-2011: $22,780

Selectivity: Selective	**Room/board:** $8,636
Acceptance rate: 69%	**Average debt:** $35,397
Student/faculty ratio: 13/1	**Proportion who borrowed:** 90%

UNDERGRADUATE STUDENT BODY STATS

2009-2010 enrollment: 1,214 full-time; 233 part-time. Men: 50%; women: 50%. **Ethnic makeup:** African American: 10%; Asian American: 1%; Hispanic: 3%; White: 86%; International: 1%. **Religious preference:** Roman Catholic: 19%; Protestant: 33%; Jewish: 1%; No preference: 3%; Unknown: 41%; United Church of Christ: 3%.

ADMISSIONS FACTS AND FIGURES

Phone: (419) 448-2330. **Email:** adminfo@heidelberg.edu. **Website:** http://www.heidelberg.edu. **Application deadlines for fall 2011:** Regular decision: Rolling. Early decision: Not offered. Early action: Not offered. Admission can be deferred. **Application fee:** $25. **To apply online, go to:** http://www.heidelberg.edu/admissions/applynow. **Admissions requirements/recommendations:** High school units required (recommended): English: (4); Mathematics: (3); Science: (3); Foreign language: (2); Social studies: (3); History: (2); Academic electives: (3); Total units: (21). Tests: The college uses SAT or ACT scores in admissions decisions. Either SAT or ACT required. For admission to the fall 2011 entering class, the school will accept: ACT with or without writing accepted. Campus visit: Recommended. Admissions interview: Recommended. Off-campus interview: May be arranged. **Factors that count in admissions decisions:** *Academic:* Secondary school record: Very Important. Class rank: Important. Letters of recommendation: Considered. Standardized test scores: Very Important. Essay: Considered. *Nonacademic:* Interview: Very Important. Extracurricular activities: Important. Talent/ability: Important. Character/personal qualities: Very Important. Alumni/ae relationship: Considered. Geographical residence: Considered. State residency: Considered. Religious affiliation/commitment: Considered. Minority status: Not Considered. Volunteer work: Important. Work experience: Considered. **Other schools with the greatest overlap in applicants:** Ashland University; Baldwin-Wallace College; Bowling Green State University; Ohio Northern University; Ohio State University–Columbus. **Admissions statistics for the fall 2009 entering class:** Total applicants: 2,209. Total accepted: 1,527. Freshmen enrolled: 381; 20% were from out of state. Overall acceptance rate: 69%. **Credentials of fall 2009 freshmen:** 16% ranked in the top 10 percent of their high school class; 34% were in the top 25 percent; 70% were in the top half. (Proportion submitting class standing: 89%.) **Average high school grade point average:** 3.1. **First-year students who submitted SAT scores:** 25%. Scores (25/75 percentile): Critical Reading: 420-560, Math: 450-560, Combined: 870-1120. **First-year students submitting ACT scores:** 93%. Scores (25/75 percentile): English: 17-24, Math: 17-23, Composite: 18-24.

ACADEMICS

Year founded: 1850. **Academic calendar:** Semester. **Degrees offered:** bachelor's, master's. **Most popular majors:** 23% business, management, marketing, and related support services, 19% education, 13% parks, recreation, leisure, and fitness studies, 10% psychology, 5% biological and biomedical sciences. **Major fields of study:** biological and biomedical sciences; business, management, marketing, and related support services; communication, journalism, and related programs; computer and information sciences and support services; education; English language and literature/letters; foreign languages, literatures, and linguistics; mathematics and statistics; natural resources and conservation; parks, recreation, leisure, and fitness studies; philosophy and religious studies; physical sciences; psychology; security and protective services; social sciences; visual and performing arts. **Areas of required coursework:** arts/fine arts, humanities, computer literacy, mathematics, English (including composition), foreign languages, sciences (biological or physical), history, social science. **Pre-professional programs:** pre-law, pre-dentistry, pre-medicine, pre-theology, pre-veterinary science, pre-optometry. **Special academic programs:** cooperative (work-study plan) program, cross-registration, double major, dual enrollment, English as a Second Language (ESL), exchange student program (domestic), honors program, independent study, internships, liberal arts/career combination, study abroad, teacher certificate program. **Teacher certification offered in:** early childhood, special education, elementary, middle/junior high, secondary, bilingual/bicultural. **Reserve Officers Training Corps (ROTC):** Army ROTC: Offered at cooperating institution (Bowling Green State University); Air Force ROTC: Offered at cooperating institution (Bowling Green State University). **Faculty and instruction (2009-2010):** Total instructional faculty: 70 full-time, 93 part-time (55% men; 45% women; 10% minorities). Full-time faculty with Ph.D. or other terminal degree: 81%. Student/faculty ratio: 13/1. Classes of fewer than 20 students: 61%; of 20 to 49 students: 37%; of 50 or more students: 1%. **Advanced Placement and International Baccalaureate credit:** AP tests may be used for: Credit only. Scores accepted: 3. International Baccalaureate exams may be used for: Credit and/or placement. **Freshmen returning for sophomore year:** 67%. **Graduation rates:** Four-year: 39%; five-year: 53%; six-year: 56%. **Graduate study:** 25% of students pursue further study immediately upon graduation. Fields in which graduates pursue further study: Master of Business Administration (MBA), 20%; law, 1%; medicine, 1%; theology (or the seminary), 1%; education, 1%; arts and sciences, 19%; veterinary medicine, 1%.

COSTS AND FINANCIAL AID

Financial aid office: (419) 448-2293. **Expenses (2010-2011):** Tuition and fees 2010-2011: $22,780; room/board: $8,636. Estimated books and supplies: $1,500; transportation: $750; personal expenses: $750. **Financial aid:** Priority filing date for institution's financial aid form: March 1. In 2009-2010, 90% of undergraduates applied for financial aid. Of those, 71% were determined to have financial need; 24% had their need fully met. Average financial aid package (proportion receiving): $16,911 (71%). Average amount of gift aid, such as scholarships or grants (proportion receiving): $11,834 (70%). Average amount of self-help aid, such as work study or loans (proportion receiving): $5,935 (70%). Average need-based loan (excluding PLUS or other private loans): $4,602. Among students who received need-based aid, the average percentage of need met: 79%. Among students who received aid based on merit, the average award (and the proportion receiving): $8,359 (10%). The average athletic scholarship (and the proportion receiving): $0 (0%). Average amount of debt of borrowers graduating in 2009: $35,397. Proportion who borrowed: 90%.

CAMPUS LIFE AND EXTRACURRICULAR ACTIVITIES

Campus housing available (% using): coed dorms (70%), women's dorms (8%), apartment for single students (13%), special housing for disabled students (1%), cooperative housing (8%). Students who live in college-owned, operated, or affiliated housing: 83%. **Student employment:** During the 2009-2010 academic year, 30% of undergraduates worked on campus. Average per-year earnings: $1,500. **Clubs and organizations:** Number of student organizations: 70. Activities include: campus ministries, choral groups, concert band, dance, drama/theater, international student organization, jazz band, literary magazine, model UN, music ensembles, musical theater, opera, pep band, radio station, student government, student newspaper, student film society, symphony orchestra, television station, yearbook. Number of fraternities: 5; sororities: 4. Proportion of men in fraternities: 17%; of women in sororities: 24%. Average proportion of students who stay on campus on weekends: 65%. **Sports program (2009-2010):** Member of NCAA III. **Men's intercollegiate varsity sports:** baseball, basketball, football, golf, soccer, tennis, track and field (indoor), track and field (outdoor), volleyball, wrestling. **Women's intercollegiate varsity sports:** basketball, golf, soccer, softball, tennis, track and field (indoor), track and field (outdoor), volleyball.

SERVICES AND FACILITIES

Basic services: nonremedial tutoring, placement service, health service, health insurance. **Remedial assistance:** reading, math, writing, study skills. **Counseling services:** minority student, career, personal, academic, older student, psychological, religious. **For learning-disabled students:** School does not offer a structured program with separate admission and additional fees. Total undergraduates in learning-disabled program or receiving services: 22. Services include: remedial math, remedial English, tape recorders, other special classes, untimed tests, note-taking services, oral tests, learning center, readers, extended time for tests, tutors, texts on tape, other testing accommodations. **Library:** Number of titles: 290,595; number of current serial subscriptions: 492. **Information technology resources:** Students are not required to lease or own a computer. Number of campus computers available to all students: 130. School has a wireless network. Approximate number of users that can be accommodated: 200. Proportion of college-owned housing units wired for high-speed internet access: 100%. **Campus safety:** Security services offered: 24-hour foot-and-vehicle patrols, late-night transport/escort service, 24-hour emergency telephones, lighted pathways/sidewalks, student patrols, controlled dormitory access (key, security card, etc).

TRANSFER AND INTERNATIONAL STUDENTS

Transfer students: May apply for admission for the following academic terms: Fall, Spring, Summer. Applicants need a minimum number of credits to apply. For fall 2009: Transfer applications received: 181. Transfer applicants offered admission: 97. Transfer applicants enrolled: 41. **International students:** Number of foreign undergraduates: 19 (1% of student body). Number of countries represented: 12. Minimum TOEFL score required: 550 (paper); 220 (computer).

Hiram College

- **Address:** PO Box 67, Hiram, OH 44234
- **Website:** http://www.hiram.edu
- **Private; Religious affiliation:** Christian Church (Disciples of Christ)
- **Enrollment:** 1,189 full-time; 178 part-time

KEY STATS

✔ **U.S News College Ranking:** 152, National Liberal Arts Colleges
✔ **ACT Score (25th/75th percentile):** 20-26
✔ **Tuition:** 2010-2011: $27,105

Selectivity: Selective	**Room/board:** $9,460
Acceptance rate: 88%	**Average debt:** N/A
Student/faculty ratio: 13/1	**Proportion who borrowed:** N/A

UNDERGRADUATE STUDENT BODY STATS

2009-2010 enrollment: 1,189 full-time; 178 part-time. Men: 45%; women: 55%. **Ethnic makeup:** African American: 10%; Asian American: 1%; Hispanic: 2%; White: 81%; International: 6%. **Religious preference:** Roman Catholic: 26%; Protestant: 45%; Jewish: 2%; Muslim: 1%; Buddhist: 1%; No preference: 21%.

ADMISSIONS FACTS AND FIGURES

Phone: (800) 362-5280. **Email:** admission@hiram.edu. **Website:** http://www.hiram.edu. **Application deadlines for fall 2011:** Regular decision: Rolling. Early decision: Not offered. Early action: Not offered. Admission can be deferred. **To apply online, go to:** http://www.hiram.edu/apply. **Admissions requirements/recommendations:** High school units required (recommended): English: 4 (4); Mathematics: 4 (4); Science: 3 (3); Foreign language: 2 (3); Social studies: 2 (2); History: 1 (1); Academic electives: 2 (2); Total units: 20 (21). Tests: The college uses SAT or ACT scores in admissions decisions. Either SAT or ACT required. For admission to the fall 2011 entering class, the school will accept: ACT with or without writing accepted. Campus visit: Recommended. Admissions interview: Recommended. Off-campus interview: May not be arranged. **Factors that count in admissions decisions:** *Academic:* Secondary school record: Important. Class rank: Considered. Letters of recommendation: Important. Standardized test scores: Important. Essay: Important. *Nonacademic:* Interview: Important. Extracurricular activities: Considered. Talent/ability: Considered. Character/personal qualities: Very Important. Alumni/ae relationship: Considered. Geographical residence: Not Considered. State residency: Not Considered. Religious affiliation/commitment: Not Considered. Minority status: Not Considered. Volunteer work: Considered. Work experience: Not Considered. **Other schools with the greatest overlap in applicants:** Allegheny College; Baldwin-Wallace College; Heidelberg University; John Carroll University; Ohio Wesleyan University. **Admissions statistics for the fall 2009 entering class:** Total applicants: 1,269. Total accepted: 1,112. Freshmen enrolled: 293; 17% were from out of state. Overall acceptance rate: 88%. **Credentials of fall 2009 freshmen:** 20% ranked in the top 10 percent of their high school class; 46% were in the top 25 percent; 74% were in the top half. (Proportion submitting class standing: 81%.) **Average high school grade point average:** 3.3. **First-year students who submitted SAT scores:** 32%. Scores (25/75 percentile): Critical Reading: 440-600, Math: 450-590, Combined: 890-1190. **First-year students submitting ACT scores:** 78%. Scores (25/75 percentile): English: N/A, Math: N/A, Composite: N/A.

ACADEMICS

Year founded: 1850. **Academic calendar:** Other. **Degrees offered:** bachelor's, master's. **Most popular majors:** 22% business, management, marketing, and related support services, 15% biological and biomedical sciences. **Major fields of study:** biological and biomedical sciences; business, management, marketing, and related support services; communication, journalism, and related programs; education; English language and literature/letters; foreign languages, literatures, and linguistics; history; mathematics and statistics; multi/interdisciplinary studies; natural resources and conservation; philosophy and religious studies; physical sciences; psychology; social sciences; visual and performing arts. **Areas of required coursework:** arts/fine arts, humanities, sciences (biological or physical), social science, other. **Pre-professional programs:** pre-law, pre-dentistry, pre-medicine, pre-theology, pre-veterinary science, pre-optometry, pre-pharmacy. **Special academic programs:** accelerated program, cross-registration, double major, dual enrollment, English as a Second Language (ESL), exchange student program (domestic), independent study, internships, student-designed major, study abroad, teacher certificate program, weekend college. **Teacher certification offered in:** early childhood, elementary, middle/junior high, secondary. **Reserve Officers Training Corps (ROTC):** Army ROTC: Offered at cooperating institution (John Carroll University). **Faculty and instruction (2009-2010):** Total instructional faculty: 79 full-time, 60 part-time (52% men; 48% women; 5% minorities). Full-time faculty with Ph.D. or other terminal degree: 96%. Student/faculty ratio: 13/1. Classes of fewer than 20 students: 74%; of 20 to 49 students: 26%; of 50 or more students: 0%. **Advanced Placement and International Baccalaureate credit:** AP tests may be used for: Placement only. Scores accepted: 4, 5. International Baccalaureate exams may be used for: Credit only. **Freshmen returning for sophomore year:** 79%. **Graduation rates:** Four-year: 64%; five-year: 68%; six-year: 69%. **Graduate study:** 23% of students pursue further study immediately upon graduation; 40% within one year; 50% within five years. Fields in which graduates pursue further study: Master of Business Administration (MBA), 1%; law, 2%; medicine, 2%; theology (or the seminary), 1%; education, 1%; arts and sciences, 10%; veterinary medicine, 1%.

COSTS AND FINANCIAL AID

Financial aid office: (330) 569-5107. **Expenses (2010-2011):** Tuition and fees 2010-2011: $27,105; room/board: $9,460. Estimated books and supplies: $700; transportation: $887; personal expenses: $1,408. **Financial aid:** Priority filing date for institution's financial aid form: February 15; deadline: December 15.

CAMPUS LIFE AND EXTRACURRICULAR ACTIVITIES

Campus housing available (% using): coed dorms (90%), women's dorms (9%), apartment for single students, other housing options. Students who live in college-owned, operated, or affiliated housing: 82%. **Student employment:** During the 2009-2010 academic year, 68% of undergraduates worked on campus. Average per-year earnings: $1,251. **Clubs and organizations:** Number of student organizations: 90. Activities include: campus ministries, choral groups, concert band, dance, drama/theater, international student organization, jazz band, literary magazine, marching band, model UN, music ensembles, musical theater, opera, pep band, radio station, student government, student newspaper, television station, yearbook. Number of fraternities: 3; sororities: 3. Average proportion of students who stay on campus on weekends: 60%. **Sports program (2009-2010):** Member of NCAA III. *Men's intercollegiate varsity sports:* baseball, basketball, cross country, football, golf, soccer, swimming, tennis, track and field (indoor), track and field (outdoor). *Women's intercollegiate varsity sports:* basketball, cross country, golf, soccer, swimming, tennis, track and field (indoor), track and field (outdoor), volleyball.

SERVICES AND FACILITIES

Basic services: nonremedial tutoring, placement service, health service, health insurance. **Remedial assistance:** writing, study skills. **Counseling services:** minority student, career, personal, veteran student, academic, older student, psychological, birth control, religious. **For learning-disabled students:** School does not offer a structured program with separate admission and additional fees. Services include: note-taking services, oral tests, extended time for tests, tutors, texts on tape, other testing accommodations. **Library:** Number of titles: 506,792; number of current serial subscriptions: 8,890. **Information technology resources:** Students are not required to lease or own a computer. Number of campus computers available to all students: 120. School has a wireless network. Approximate number of users that can be accommodated: 1,500. Proportion of college-owned housing units wired for high-speed internet access: 100%. **Campus safety:** Security services offered: late-night transport/escort service, 24-hour emergency telephones, lighted pathways/sidewalks, controlled dormitory access (key, security card, etc).

TRANSFER AND INTERNATIONAL STUDENTS

Transfer students: May apply for admission for the following academic terms: Fall, Spring. Applicants do not need a minimum number of credits to apply. For fall 2009: Transfer applications received: 143. Transfer applicants offered admission: 74. Transfer applicants enrolled: 39. **International students:** Number of foreign undergraduates: 80 (6% of student body). Number of countries represented: 35. Minimum TOEFL score required: 500 (paper). Average TOEFL score: 587 (paper).

John Carroll University

- **Address:** 20700 N. Park Boulevard, University Heights, OH 44118
- **Website:** http://www.jcu.edu
- **Private; Religious affiliation:** Roman Catholic (Jesuit)
- **Enrollment:** 2,906 full-time; 81 part-time

KEY STATS

✔ **U.S News College Ranking:** 7, Regional Universities (Midwest)
✔ **ACT Score (25th/75th percentile):** 21-26
✔ **Tuition:** 2010-2011: $30,250

Selectivity: Selective	**Room/board:** $8,750
Acceptance rate: 81%	**Average debt:** $28,830
Student/faculty ratio: 15/1	**Proportion who borrowed:** 74%

UNDERGRADUATE STUDENT BODY STATS

2009-2010 enrollment: 2,906 full-time; 81 part-time. Men: 49%; women: 51%. **Ethnic makeup:** African American: 6%; Asian American: 2%; Hispanic: 3%; White: 88%. **Religious preference:** Protestant: 12%; Jewish: 1%; Muslim: 1%; Buddhist: 1%; No preference: 23%; Roman Catholic (Jesuit): 58%; Eastern Rite: 1%; Other: 3%.

ADMISSIONS FACTS AND FIGURES

Phone: (216) 397-4294. **Email:** admission@jcu.edu. **Website:** http://www.jcu.edu. **Application deadlines for fall 2011:** Regular decision: February 1. Early decision: Not offered. Early action: Not offered. Admission can be deferred. **To apply online, go to:** http://www.jcu.edu/apply. **Admissions requirements/recommendations:** High school units required (recommended): English: 4 (4); Mathematics: 3 (4); Science: 2 (3); Foreign language: 2 (3); Social studies: 2 (4); Academic electives: 3 (3); Total units: 16 (21). Tests: The college uses SAT or ACT scores in admissions decisions. Either SAT or ACT required. For admission to the fall 2011 entering class, the school will accept: ACT with writing recommended. Campus visit: Recommended. Admissions interview: Recommended. Off-campus interview: May be arranged. **Factors that count in admissions decisions:** *Academic:* Secondary school record: Very Important. Class rank: Considered. Letters of recommendation: Considered. Standardized test scores: Important. Essay: Important. *Nonacademic:* Interview: Considered. Extracurricular activities: Important. Talent/ability: Important. Character/personal qualities: Important. Alumni/ae relationship: Considered. Geographical residence: Considered. State residency: Not Considered. Religious affiliation/commitment: Not Considered. Minority status: Not Considered. Volunteer work: Important. Work experience: Important. **Other schools with the greatest overlap in applicants:** Baldwin-Wallace College; Miami University–Oxford; Ohio State University–Columbus; University of Dayton; Xavier University. **Admissions statistics for the fall 2009 entering class:** Total applicants: 3,411. Total accepted: 2,763. Freshmen enrolled: 661; 31% were from out of state. Overall acceptance rate: 81%. **Credentials of fall 2009 freshmen:** 24% ranked in the top 10 percent of their high school class; 50% were in the top 25 percent; 80% were in the top half. (Proportion submitting class standing: 60%.) **Average high school grade point average:** 3.4. **First-year students who submitted SAT scores:** 63%. Scores (25/75 percentile): Critical Reading: 480-580, Math: 480-600, Combined: 960-1180. **First-year students submitting ACT scores:** 81%. Scores (25/75 percentile): English: 20-26, Math: 20-26, Composite: 21-26.

ACADEMICS

Year founded: 1886. **Academic calendar:** Semester. **Degrees offered:** certificate, bachelor's, post-bachelor's certificate, master's. **Most popular majors:** 15% communication studies/speech communication and rhetoric, 9% biology/biological sciences, 9% psychology, 8% accounting, 8%

marketing/marketing management. **Major fields of study:** biological and biomedical sciences; business, management, marketing, and related support services; communication, journalism, and related programs; computer and information sciences and support services; education; engineering; English language and literature/letters; foreign languages, literatures, and linguistics; history; liberal arts and sciences studies, and humanities; mathematics and statistics; philosophy and religious studies; physical sciences; psychology; social sciences; visual and performing arts. **Areas of required coursework:** humanities, mathematics, English (including composition), philosophy, foreign languages, sciences (biological or physical), history, social science, other. **Pre-professional programs:** pre-law, pre-dentistry, pre-medicine, pre-veterinary science, pre-pharmacy. **Special academic programs (% participation):** accelerated program (1%), cooperative (work-study plan) program (10%), cross-registration (1%), double major (8%), exchange student program (domestic) (1%), honors program (7%), independent study (5%), internships (17%), liberal arts/career combination (2%), student-designed major (.2%), study abroad (12%), teacher certificate program (9%). **Teacher certification offered in:** early childhood, middle/junior high, secondary. **Cooperative education programs:** art, business, computer science, humanities, natural science, social/behavioral science, other. **Reserve Officers Training Corps (ROTC):** Army ROTC: Offered on campus. **Faculty and instruction (2009-2010):** Total instructional faculty: 206 full-time, 150 part-time (58% men; 42% women; 9% minorities). Full-time faculty with Ph.D. or other terminal degree: 93%. Student/faculty ratio: 15/1. Classes of fewer than 20 students: 45%; of 20 to 49 students: 55%; of 50 or more students: 0%. **Advanced Placement and International Baccalaureate credit:** AP tests may be used for: Credit only. Scores accepted: 3, 4, 5. International Baccalaureate exams may be used for: Credit only. **Freshmen returning for sophomore year:** 85%. **Graduation rates:** Four-year: 63%; five-year: 74%; six-year: 76%. **Graduate study:** 32% of students pursue further study immediately upon graduation. Fields in which graduates pursue further study: Master of Business Administration (MBA), 22%; law, 10%; medicine, 22%; dentistry, 1%; engineering, 1%; education, 18%; arts and sciences, 26%.

COSTS AND FINANCIAL AID

Financial aid office: (216) 397-4248. **Expenses (2010-2011):** Tuition and fees 2010-2011: $30,250; room/board: $8,750. Estimated books and supplies: $1,200; transportation: $800; personal expenses: $1,000. **Financial aid:** Priority filing date for institution's financial aid form: February 15; deadline: March 15. In 2009-2010, 64% of undergraduates applied for financial aid. Of those, 55% were determined to have financial need; 19% had their need fully met. Average financial aid package (proportion receiving): $23,033 (55%). Average amount of gift aid, such as scholarships or grants (proportion receiving): $15,809 (55%). Average amount of self-help aid, such as work study or loans (proportion receiving): $5,463 (50%). Average need-based loan (excluding PLUS or other private loans): $4,296. Among students who received need-based aid, the average percentage of need met: 81%. Among students who received aid based on merit, the average award (and the proportion receiving): $9,983 (18%). The average athletic scholarship (and the proportion receiving): $0 (0%). Average amount of debt of borrowers graduating in 2009: $28,830. Proportion who borrowed: 74%.

CAMPUS LIFE AND EXTRACURRICULAR ACTIVITIES

Campus housing available (% using): coed dorms (78%), women's dorms (12%), apartment for single students (1%), special housing for disabled students (1%), other housing options (6%). Students who live in college-owned, operated, or affiliated housing: 46%. **Student employment:** During the 2009-2010 academic year, 12% of undergraduates worked on campus. Average per-year earnings: $1,000. **Clubs and organizations:** Number of student organizations: 105. Activities include: campus ministries, choral groups, dance, drama/theater, jazz band, literary magazine, music ensembles, musical theater, pep band, radio station, student government, student newspaper, student film society, television station, yearbook. Number of fraternities: 4; sororities: 5. Proportion of men in fraternities: 8%; of women in sororities: 14%. Average proportion of students who stay on campus on weekends: 60%. **Sports program (2009-2010):** Member of NCAA III. *Men's intercollegiate varsity sports:* baseball, basketball, cross country, football, golf, soccer, swimming, tennis, track and field (indoor), track and field (outdoor), wrestling. *Women's intercollegiate varsity sports:* basketball, cross country, golf, soccer, softball, swimming, tennis, track and field (indoor), track and field (outdoor), volleyball.

SERVICES AND FACILITIES

Basic services: nonremedial tutoring, placement service, health service. **Remedial assistance:** study skills. **Counseling services:** minority student, career, military, personal, veteran student, academic, older student, psy-

chological, religious, other. **For learning-disabled students:** School does not offer a structured program with separate admission and additional fees. Total undergraduates in learning-disabled program or receiving services: 162. Services include: remedial math, remedial English, reading machines, tape recorders, note-taking services, oral tests, readers, extended time for tests, priority registration, priority seating, substitution of courses, texts on tape, typist/scribe, exams on tape or computer, other testing accommodations. **Library:** Number of titles: 768,957; number of current serial subscriptions: 10,801. **Information technology resources:** Students are not required to lease or own a computer. Number of campus computers available to all students: 150. School has a wireless network. Approximate number of users that can be accommodated: 20,000. Proportion of college-owned housing units wired for high-speed internet access: 100%. **Campus safety:** Security services offered: 24-hour foot-and-vehicle patrols, late-night transport/escort service, 24-hour emergency telephones, lighted pathways/sidewalks, controlled dormitory access (key, security card, etc).

TRANSFER AND INTERNATIONAL STUDENTS

Transfer students: May apply for admission for the following academic terms: Fall, Spring. Applicants do not need a minimum number of credits to apply. For fall 2009: Transfer applications received: 419. Transfer applicants offered admission: 233. Transfer applicants enrolled: 120. **International students:** Number of foreign undergraduates: 0. Number of countries represented: 9. Minimum TOEFL score required: 550 (paper); 79 (computer).

Kent State University

- ■ **Address:** PO Box 5190, Kent, OH 44242-0001
- ■ **Website:** http://www.kent.edu
- ■ **Public**
- ■ **Enrollment:** 17,610 full-time; 2,308 part-time

KEY STATS

✔ **U.S News College Ranking:** 183, National Universities
✔ **ACT Score (25th/75th percentile):** 20-25
✔ **Tuition:** 2010-2011: $9,030 in state, $16,990 out of state

Selectivity: Selective	**Room/board:** $8,376
Acceptance rate: 72%	**Average debt:** $26,698
Student/faculty ratio: 20/1	**Proportion who borrowed:** 75%

UNDERGRADUATE STUDENT BODY STATS

2009-2010 enrollment: 17,610 full-time; 2,308 part-time. Men: 42%; women: 58%. **Ethnic makeup:** African American: 9%; American-Indian: 1%; Asian American: 2%; Hispanic: 2%; White: 85%; International: 2%.

ADMISSIONS FACTS AND FIGURES

Phone: (330) 672-2444. **Email:** KENTADM@Admissions.Kent.edu. **Website:** http://www.kent.edu. **Application deadlines for fall 2011:** Regular decision: August 1. Early decision: Not offered. Early action: Not offered. Admission can be deferred. **Application fee:** $40. **To apply online, go to:** https://www.admissions.kent.edu/apply.asp. **Admissions requirements/recommendations:** High school units required (recommended): English: (4); Mathematics: (3); Science: (3); Foreign language: (2); Social studies: (3); Total units: (16). Tests: The college uses SAT or ACT scores in admissions decisions. Either SAT or ACT required. For admission to the fall 2011 entering class, the school will accept: ACT with writing required. Campus visit: Recommended. Admissions interview: Recommended. Off-campus interview: Not available. **Factors that count in admissions decisions:** *Academic:* Secondary school record: Very Important. Class rank: Considered. Letters of recommendation: Considered. Standardized test scores: Very Important. Essay: Not Considered. *Nonacademic:* Interview: Not Considered. Extracurricular activities: Not Considered. Talent/ability: Not Considered. Character/personal qualities: Not Considered. Alumni/ae relationship: Not Considered. Geographical residence: Not Considered. State residency: Not Considered. Religious affiliation/commitment: Not Considered. Minority status: Not Considered. Volunteer work: Not Considered. Work experience: Not Considered. **Other schools with the greatest overlap in applicants:** Bowling Green State University; Ohio State University–Columbus; Ohio University; University of Akron; University of Toledo. **Admissions statistics for the fall 2009 entering class:** Total applicants: 14,933. Total accepted: 10,735. Freshmen enrolled: 4,151; 17% were from out of state. Overall acceptance rate: 72%. **Size of waiting list:** 1135 applicants; enrolled from waiting list: 536. **Credentials of fall 2009 freshmen:** 13% ranked in the top 10 percent of their high school class; 37% were in the top 25 percent; 70% were in the top half. (Proportion submitting class standing: 80%.) **Average high school grade point average:** 3.2. **First-year students who submitted SAT scores:** 33%. Scores (25/75 percentile): Critical Reading: 460-560, Math: 460-580, Combined: 920-1140. **First-year students submitting ACT scores:** 81%. Scores (25/75 percentile): English: 19-25, Math: 18-25, Composite: 20-25.

ACADEMICS

Year founded: 1910. **Academic calendar:** Semester. **Degrees offered:** certificate, associate, transfer-associate, terminal-associate, bachelor's, post-bachelor's certificate, master's, post-master's certificate, doctorate. **Most popular majors:** 21% business, management, marketing, and related support services, 12% health professions and related clinical sciences, 10% education, 8% communication, journalism, and related programs, 7% psychology. **Major fields of study:** architecture and related services; area, ethnic, cultural, and gender studies; biological and biomedical sciences; business, management, marketing, and related support services; communication, journalism, and related programs; computer and information sciences and support services; education; engineering; English language and literature/letters; family and consumer sciences/human sciences; foreign languages, literatures, and linguistics; health professions and related clinical sciences; history; legal professions and studies; liberal arts and sciences studies, and humanities; mathematics and statistics; multi/interdisciplinary studies; natural resources and conservation; parks, recreation, leisure, and fitness studies; philosophy and religious studies; physical sciences; psychology; security and protective services; social sciences; transportation and materials moving; visual and performing arts. **Areas of required coursework:** arts/fine arts, humanities, mathematics, English (including composition), sciences (biological or physical), social science, other. **Pre-professional programs:** pre-law, pre-dentistry, pre-medicine, pre-veterinary science, pre-pharmacy. **Special academic programs:** accelerated program, cooperative (work-study plan) program, cross-registration, distance learning, double major, dual enrollment, English as a Second Language (ESL), exchange student program (domestic), external degree program, honors program, independent study, internships, liberal arts/career combination, student-designed major, study abroad, teacher certificate program, weekend college. **Teacher certification offered in:** early childhood, special education, vo-tech, middle/junior high, secondary, bilingual/bicultural. **Cooperative education programs:** technologies, vocational arts. **Reserve Officers Training Corps (ROTC):** Army ROTC: Offered on campus; Air Force ROTC: Offered on campus. **Faculty and instruction (2009-2010):** Total instructional faculty: 888 full-time, 652 part-time (49% men; 51% women; 15% minorities). Full-time faculty with Ph.D. or other terminal degree: 69%. Student/faculty ratio: 20/1. Classes of fewer than 20 students: 46%; of 20 to 49 students: 46%; of 50 or more students: 8%. **Advanced Placement and International Baccalaureate credit:** AP tests may be used for: Credit and/or placement. Scores accepted: 3, 4, 5. International Baccalaureate exams may be used for: Credit and/or placement. **Freshmen returning for sophomore year:** 74%. **Graduation rates:** Four-year: 25%; five-year: 45%; six-year: 51%.

COSTS AND FINANCIAL AID

Financial aid office: (330) 672-2972. **Expenses (2010-2011):** Tuition and fees 2010-2011: $9,030 in state, $16,990 out of state; room/board: $8,376. Estimated books and supplies: $1,320; transportation: $1,934; personal expenses: $2,520. **Financial aid:** Priority filing date for institution's financial aid form: March 1. In 2009-2010, 76% of undergraduates applied for financial aid. Of those, 64% were determined to have financial need; 36% had their need fully met. Average financial aid package (proportion receiving): $8,820 (64%). Average amount of gift aid, such as scholarships or grants (proportion receiving): $6,152 (46%). Average amount of self-help aid, such as work study or loans (proportion receiving): $4,094 (60%). Average need-based loan (excluding PLUS or other private loans): $3,989. Among students who received need-based aid, the average percentage of need met: 52%. Among students who received aid based on merit, the average award (and the proportion receiving): $3,815 (13%). The average athletic scholarship (and the proportion receiving): $14,591 (1%). Average amount of debt of borrowers graduating in 2009: $26,698. Proportion who borrowed: 75%.

CAMPUS LIFE AND EXTRACURRICULAR ACTIVITIES

Campus housing available (% using): coed dorms (91%), women's dorms (1%), apartments for married students (5%), apartment for single students (2%), special housing for disabled students (1%). Students who live in college-owned, operated, or affiliated housing: 33%. **Student employment:** During the 2009-2010 academic year, 25% of undergraduates worked on campus. Average per-year earnings: $3,500. **Clubs and organizations:** Number of student organizations: 214. Activities include: campus min-

istries, choral groups, concert band, dance, drama/theater, international student organization, jazz band, literary magazine, marching band, music ensembles, musical theater, opera, pep band, radio station, student government, student newspaper, student film society, symphony orchestra, television station. Number of fraternities: 17; sororities: 6. Proportion of men in fraternities: 7%; of women in sororities: 5%. Average proportion of students who stay on campus on weekends: 60%. **Sports program (2009-2010):** Member of NCAA I. **Men's intercollegiate varsity sports:** baseball, basketball, cross country, football, golf, track and field (indoor), track and field (outdoor), wrestling. **Women's intercollegiate varsity sports:** basketball, cross country, field hockey, golf, gymnastics, soccer, softball, track and field (indoor), track and field (outdoor), volleyball.

SERVICES AND FACILITIES

Basic services: nonremedial tutoring, women's center, placement service, day care, health service, health insurance. **Remedial assistance:** reading, math, writing, study skills. **Counseling services:** minority student, career, military, personal, veteran student, academic, older student, psychological, birth control. **For learning-disabled students:** School does not offer a structured program with separate admission and additional fees. Services include: remedial math, remedial English, remedial reading, tape recorders, note-taking services, oral tests, learning center, readers, extended time for tests, tutors, priority registration, priority seating, texts on tape, other testing accommodations. **Library:** Number of titles: 2,367,222; number of current serial subscriptions: 13,357. **Information technology resources:** Students are not required to lease or own a computer. Number of campus computers available to all students: 2,000. School has a wireless network. Approximate number of users that can be accommodated: 5,500. Proportion of college-owned housing units wired for high-speed internet access: 100%. **Campus safety:** Security services offered: 24-hour foot-and-vehicle patrols, late-night transport/escort service, 24-hour emergency telephones, lighted pathways/sidewalks, student patrols, controlled dormitory access (key, security card, etc).

TRANSFER AND INTERNATIONAL STUDENTS

Transfer students: May apply for admission for the following academic terms: Fall, Spring, Summer. Applicants do not need a minimum number of credits to apply. For fall 2009: Transfer applications received: 3,370. Transfer applicants offered admission: 2,160. Transfer applicants enrolled: 1,343. **International students:** Number of foreign undergraduates: 418 (2% of student body). Number of countries represented: 52. Minimum TOEFL score required: 525 (paper); 197 (computer). Average TOEFL score: 525 (paper).

Kenyon College

- **Address:** Ransom Hall, Gambier, OH 43022-9623
- **Website:** http://www.kenyon.edu
- **Private**
- **Enrollment:** 1,618 full-time; 15 part-time

KEY STATS

✔ **U.S News College Ranking:** 32, National Liberal Arts Colleges
✔ **SAT Score (25th/75th percentile):** 1230-1400
✔ **Tuition:** 2010-2011: $40,900

Selectivity: More selective	**Room/board:** $9,500
Acceptance rate: 39%	**Average debt:** $19,934
Student/faculty ratio: 10/1	**Proportion who borrowed:** 58%

UNDERGRADUATE STUDENT BODY STATS

2009-2010 enrollment: 1,618 full-time; 15 part-time. Men: 48%; women: 52%. **Ethnic makeup:** African American: 4%; American-Indian: 1%; Asian American: 6%; Hispanic: 3%; White: 82%; International: 4%.

ADMISSIONS FACTS AND FIGURES

Phone: (740) 427-5776. **Email:** admissions@kenyon.edu. **Website:** http://www.kenyon.edu. **Application deadlines for fall 2011:** Regular decision: January 15; decision sent by April 1. Early decision: Send application by: November 15; Decision sent by: December 15. Early action: Not offered. Admission can be deferred. **Application fee:** $45. **To apply online, go to:** http://www.kenyon.edu/apply.xml. **Admissions requirements/recommendations:** High school units required (recommended): English: 4 (4); Mathematics: 3 (4); Science: 3 (4); Foreign language: 3 (4); Social studies:

1 (1); History: 2 (3); Academic electives: 3 (3); Total units: 21 (24). **Tests:** The college uses SAT or ACT scores in admissions decisions. Either SAT or ACT required. For admission to the fall 2011 entering class, the school will accept: ACT with or without writing accepted. Campus visit: Recommended. Admissions interview: Recommended. Off-campus interview: May be arranged. **Factors that count in admissions decisions:** *Academic:* Secondary school record: Very Important. Class rank: Important. Letters of recommendation: Very Important. Standardized test scores: Important. Essay: Very Important. *Nonacademic:* Interview: Important. Extracurricular activities: Important. Talent/ability: Important. Character/personal qualities: Very Important. Alumni/ae relationship: Considered. Geographical residence: Considered. State residency: Considered. Religious affiliation/commitment: Not Considered. Minority status: Considered. Volunteer work: Considered. Work experience: Considered. **Other schools with the greatest overlap in applicants:** Bowdoin College; Brown University; Carleton College; Middlebury College; Oberlin College. **Admissions statistics for the fall 2009 entering class:** Total applicants: 3,992. Total accepted: 1,538. Freshmen enrolled: 469; 84% were from out of state. Accepted through early-decision or early-action plans: 45%. Overall acceptance rate: 39%. Early-decision acceptance rate: 59%. Non-early acceptance rate: 37%. **Size of waiting list:** 855 applicants; enrolled from waiting list: 15. **Credentials of fall 2009 freshmen:** 56% ranked in the top 10 percent of their high school class; 87% were in the top 25 percent; 99% were in the top half. (Proportion submitting class standing: 28%.) **Average high school grade point average:** 3.8. **First-year students who submitted SAT scores:** 74%. Scores (25/75 percentile): Critical Reading: 630-720, Math: 600-680, Combined: 1230-1400. **First-year students submitting ACT scores:** 44%. Scores (25/75 percentile): English: 28-34, Math: 26-31, Composite: 28-32.

ACADEMICS

Year founded: 1824. **Academic calendar:** Semester. **Degrees offered:** bachelor's. **Most popular majors:** 16% English language and literature, 9% economics, 9% international relations and affairs, 9% political science and government, 8% psychology. **Major fields of study:** area, ethnic, cultural, and gender studies; biological and biomedical sciences; English language and literature/letters; foreign languages, literatures, and linguistics; history; mathematics and statistics; multi/interdisciplinary studies; philosophy and religious studies; physical sciences; psychology; social sciences; visual and performing arts. **Areas of required coursework:** arts/fine arts, humanities, foreign languages, sciences (biological or physical), social science, other. **Pre-professional programs:** pre-law, pre-dentistry, pre-medicine, pre-theology, pre-veterinary science, other. **Special academic programs (% participation):** accelerated program (0%), double major (14%), honors program (11%), independent study (36%), internships (3%), liberal arts/career combination (0%), student-designed major (1%), study abroad (50%). **Faculty and instruction (2009-2010):** Total instructional faculty: 156 full-time, 46 part-time (55% men; 45% women; 14% minorities). Full-time faculty with Ph.D. or other terminal degree: 99%. Student/faculty ratio: 10/1. Classes of fewer than 20 students: 70%; of 20 to 49 students: 29%; of 50 or more students: 2%. **Advanced Placement and International Baccalaureate credit:** AP tests may be used for: Credit and/or placement. Scores accepted: 4, 5. International Baccalaureate exams may be used for: Credit and/or placement. **Freshmen returning for sophomore year:** 93%. **Graduation rates:** Four-year: 85%; five-year: 88%; six-year: 89%. **Graduate study:** 18% of students pursue further study immediately upon graduation; 25% within one year; 70% within five years. Fields in which graduates pursue further study: Master of Business Administration (MBA), 11%; law, 12%; medicine, 6%; dentistry, 1%; engineering, 1%; theology (or the seminary), 1%; education, 18%; arts and sciences, 33%; veterinary medicine, 1%.

COSTS AND FINANCIAL AID

Financial aid office: (740) 427-5430. **Expenses (2010-2011):** Tuition and fees 2010-2011: $40,900; room/board: $9,500. Estimated books and supplies: $1,800; transportation: $1,080; personal expenses: $0. **Financial aid:** Priority filing date for institution's financial aid form: February 15; deadline: February 15. In 2009-2010, 50% of undergraduates applied for financial aid. Of those, 42% were determined to have financial need; 48% had their need fully met. Average financial aid package (proportion receiving): $31,610 (42%). Average amount of gift aid, such as scholarships or grants (proportion receiving): $28,583 (41%). Average amount of self-help aid, such as work study or loans (proportion receiving): $5,186 (33%). Average need-based loan (excluding PLUS or other private loans): $4,500. Among students who received need-based aid, the average percentage of need met: 98%. Among students who received aid based on merit, the average award (and the proportion receiving): $9,496 (10%). The average athletic scholar-

ship (and the proportion receiving): $0 (0%). Average amount of debt of borrowers graduating in 2009: $19,934. Proportion who borrowed: 58%.

CAMPUS LIFE AND EXTRACURRICULAR ACTIVITIES

Campus housing available (% using): coed dorms (64%), women's dorms (3%), fraternity housing (8%), apartment for single students (19%), special housing for disabled students (1%), other housing options (1%). Students who live in college-owned, operated, or affiliated housing: 98%. **Student employment:** During the 2009-2010 academic year, 50% of undergraduates worked on campus. Average per-year earnings: $1,255. **Clubs and organizations:** Number of student organizations: 140. Activities include: campus ministries, choral groups, concert band, dance, drama/theater, international student organization, jazz band, literary magazine, model UN, music ensembles, musical theater, opera, pep band, radio station, student government, student newspaper, student film society, symphony orchestra, yearbook. Number of fraternities: 7; sororities: 4. Proportion of men in fraternities: 26%; of women in sororities: 20%. Average proportion of students who stay on campus on weekends: 99%. **Sports program (2009-2010):** Member of NCAA III. **Men's intercollegiate varsity sports:** baseball, basketball, cross country, football, golf, lacrosse, soccer, swimming, tennis, track and field (indoor), track and field (outdoor). **Women's intercollegiate varsity sports:** basketball, cross country, field hockey, lacrosse, soccer, softball, swimming, tennis, track and field (indoor), track and field (outdoor), volleyball.

SERVICES AND FACILITIES

Basic services: nonremedial tutoring, women's center, placement service, health service, health insurance. **Remedial assistance:** study skills. **Counseling services:** minority student, career, personal, academic, psychological, birth control, religious, other. **For learning-disabled students:** School does not offer a structured program with separate admission and additional fees. Total undergraduates in learning-disabled program or receiving services: 108. Services include: reading machines, tape recorders, note-taking services, readers, extended time for tests, tutors, early syllabus, priority registration, priority seating, texts on tape, exams on tape or computer, other testing accommodations, other. **Library:** Number of titles: 889,142; number of current serial subscriptions: 11,784. **Information technology resources:** Students are not required to lease or own a computer. Number of campus computers available to all students: 450. School has a wireless network. Approximate number of users that can be accommodated: 4,000. Proportion of college-owned housing units wired for high-speed internet access: 100%. **Campus safety:** Security services offered: 24-hour foot-and-vehicle patrols, late-night transport/escort service, 24-hour emergency telephones, lighted pathways/sidewalks, student patrols, controlled dormitory access (key, security card, etc.).

TRANSFER AND INTERNATIONAL STUDENTS

Transfer students: May apply for admission for the following academic terms: Fall, Spring. Applicants do not need a minimum number of credits to apply. For fall 2009: Transfer applications received: 153. Transfer applicants offered admission: 10. Transfer applicants enrolled: 3. **International students:** Number of foreign undergraduates: 69 (4% of student body). Number of countries represented: 42. Minimum TOEFL score required: 600 (paper); 100 (computer).

Lake Erie College

- **Address:** 391 W. Washington Street, Painesville, OH 44077
- **Website:** http://www.lec.edu
- **Private**
- **Enrollment:** 854 full-time; 49 part-time

KEY STATS
- ✔ **U.S News College Ranking:** 58, Regional Colleges (Midwest)
- ✔ **ACT Score (25th/75th percentile):** 18-23
- ✔ **Tuition:** 2010-2011: $25,674

Selectivity: Selective	**Room/board:** $8,192
Acceptance rate: 56%	**Average debt:** N/A
Student/faculty ratio: 15/1	**Proportion who borrowed:** 83%

UNDERGRADUATE STUDENT BODY STATS

2009-2010 enrollment: 854 full-time; 49 part-time. Men: 47%; women: 53%. **Ethnic makeup:** African American: 9%; Asian American: 1%; Hispanic: 2%; White: 87%; International: 1%.

ADMISSIONS FACTS AND FIGURES

Phone: (800) 916-0904. **Email:** admissions@lec.edu. **Website:** http://www.lec.edu. **Application deadlines for fall 2011:** Regular decision: August 1. Early decision: Not offered. Early action: Not offered. Admission can be deferred. **Application fee:** $30. **To apply online, go to:** https://www.lec.edu/undergraduate_application/index.html. **Admissions requirements/recommendations:** High school units required (recommended): English: 4 (4); Mathematics: 4 (4); Science: 3 (3); Foreign language: 2 (2); Social studies: 4 (4); Total units: 17 (17). Tests: The college uses SAT or ACT scores in admissions decisions. Either SAT or ACT required. For admission to the fall 2011 entering class, the school will accept: ACT with or without writing accepted. Campus visit: Recommended. Admissions interview: Recommended. Off-campus interview: May be arranged. **Factors that count in admissions decisions:** *Academic:* Secondary school record: Very Important. Class rank: Important. Letters of recommendation: Very Important. Standardized test scores: Very Important. Essay: Very Important. *Nonacademic:* Interview: Very Important. Extracurricular activities: Important. Talent/ability: Important. Character/personal qualities: Very Important. Alumni/ae relationship: Considered. Geographical residence: Considered. State residency: Considered. Religious affiliation/commitment: Not Considered. Minority status: Not Considered. Volunteer work: Considered. Work experience: Considered. **Other schools with the greatest overlap in applicants:** Ashland University; Kent State University; Notre Dame College of Ohio; Tiffin University; University of Findlay. **Admissions statistics for the fall 2009 entering class:** Total applicants: 1,620. Total accepted: 904. Freshmen enrolled: 388; 25% were from out of state. Overall acceptance rate: 56%. **Size of waiting list:** 74 applicants; enrolled from waiting list: 14. **Credentials of fall 2009 freshmen:** 13% ranked in the top 10 percent of their high school class; 22% were in the top 25 percent; 70% were in the top half. (Proportion submitting class standing: 90%.) **Average high school grade point average:** 3.1. **First-year students who submitted SAT scores:** 24%. Scores (25/75 percentile): Critical Reading: 450-530, Math: 430-550, Combined: 880-1080. **First-year students submitting ACT scores:** 60%. Scores (25/75 percentile): English: 16-22, Math: 17-23, Composite: 18-23.

ACADEMICS

Year founded: 1856. **Academic calendar:** Semester. **Degrees offered:** certificate, transfer-associate, bachelor's, post-bachelor's certificate, master's. **Most popular majors:** 12% farm and ranch management, 10% business administration and management, 5% accounting, 5% early childhood education and teaching, 4% chemistry. **Major fields of study:** agriculture, agriculture operations, and related sciences; biological and biomedical sciences; business, management, marketing, and related support services; communication, journalism, and related programs; education; history; legal professions and studies; mathematics and statistics; multi/interdisciplinary studies; natural resources and conservation; psychology; visual and performing arts. **Areas of required coursework:** arts/fine arts, humanities, computer literacy, mathematics, English (including composition), philosophy, foreign languages, sciences (biological or physical), history, social science, other. **Pre-professional programs:** pre-law, pre-dentistry, pre-medicine, pre-veterinary science, pre-pharmacy. **Special academic programs (% participation):** accelerated program, cross-registration, double major, dual enrollment, honors program (3%), independent study, internships (10%), liberal arts/career combination, student-designed major (1%), study abroad (7%), teacher certificate program, weekend college. **Teacher certification offered in:** early childhood, special education, middle/junior high, secondary. **Faculty and instruction (2009-2010):** Total instructional faculty: N/A. Student/faculty ratio: 15/1. Classes of fewer than 20 students: 68%; of 20 to 49 students: 32%; of 50 or more students: 0%. **Advanced Placement and International Baccalaureate credit:** AP tests may be used for: Placement only. Scores accepted: 3, 4, 5. International Baccalaureate exams may be used for: Credit and/or placement. **Freshmen returning for sophomore year:** 68%. **Graduation rates:** Four-year: 34%; five-year: 40%; six-year: 42%. **Graduate study:** 51% of students pursue further study immediately upon graduation. Fields in which graduates pursue further study: Master of Business Administration (MBA), 20%; law, 2%; medicine, 2%; education, 15%; veterinary medicine, 3%.

COSTS AND FINANCIAL AID

Financial aid office: (440) 375-7100. **Expenses (2010-2011):** Tuition and fees 2010-2011: $25,674; room/board: $8,192. Estimated books and supplies: $900; transportation: $2,282; personal expenses: $1,980. **Financial aid:**

In 2009-2010, 97% of undergraduates applied for financial aid. Of those, 92% were determined to have financial need; 13% had their need fully met. Average financial aid package (proportion receiving): $19,991 (91%). Average amount of gift aid, such as scholarships or grants (proportion receiving): $16,203 (91%). Average amount of self-help aid, such as work study or loans (proportion receiving): $4,503 (79%). Average need-based loan (excluding PLUS or other private loans): $4,238. Among students who received need-based aid, the average percentage of need met: 69%. Among students who received aid based on merit, the average award (and the proportion receiving): $10,714 (8%). The average athletic scholarship (and the proportion receiving): $9,280 (6%). Proportion who borrowed: 83%.

CAMPUS LIFE AND EXTRACURRICULAR ACTIVITIES

Campus housing available (% using): coed dorms (27%), women's dorms (14%), men's dorms (14%). **Student employment:** During the 2009-2010 academic year, 23% of undergraduates worked on campus. Average per-year earnings: $2,000. **Clubs and organizations:** Number of student organizations: 31. Activities include: campus ministries, choral groups, dance, drama/theater, marching band, music ensembles, student government, student newspaper, yearbook. Number of fraternities: 2; sororities: 1. Average proportion of students who stay on campus on weekends: 45%. **Sports program (2009-2010):** Member of NCAA II. *Men's intercollegiate varsity sports:* baseball, basketball, cross country, football, golf, lacrosse, soccer, swimming, tennis, track and field (indoor), track and field (outdoor), wrestling. *Women's intercollegiate varsity sports:* cross country, golf, lacrosse, soccer, softball, swimming, tennis, track and field (indoor), track and field (outdoor), volleyball.

SERVICES AND FACILITIES

Basic services: nonremedial tutoring, placement service, health service. **Remedial assistance:** reading, math, writing, study skills. **Counseling services:** minority student, career, personal, veteran student, academic, older student, birth control, religious, other. **For learning-disabled students:** School does not offer a structured program with separate admission and additional fees. Total undergraduates in learning-disabled program or receiving services: 38. Services include: remedial math, remedial English, other special classes, untimed tests, note-taking services, oral tests, learning center, readers, extended time for tests, tutors, priority seating, texts on tape, typist/scribe, other testing accommodations, other. **Library:** Number of titles: 77,120; number of current serial subscriptions: 10,000. **Information technology resources:** Students are not required to lease or own a computer. Number of campus computers available to all students: 128. School has a wireless network. Approximate number of users that can be accommodated: 1,000. Proportion of college-owned housing units wired for high-speed internet access: 100%. **Campus safety:** Security services offered: 24-hour foot-and-vehicle patrols, late-night transport/escort service, 24-hour emergency telephones, lighted pathways/sidewalks, controlled dormitory access (key, security card, etc).

TRANSFER AND INTERNATIONAL STUDENTS

Transfer students: May apply for admission for the following academic terms: Fall, Spring, Summer. Applicants do not need a minimum number of credits to apply. For fall 2009: Transfer applications received: 234. Transfer applicants offered admission: 114. Transfer applicants enrolled: 71. **International students:** Number of foreign undergraduates: 7 (1% of student body). Number of countries represented: 6. Minimum TOEFL score required: 590 (paper); 225 (computer). Average TOEFL score: 425 (paper).

Lourdes College

- **Address:** 6832 Convent Boulevard, Sylvania, OH 43560-2898
- **Website:** http://www.lourdes.edu
- **Private; Religious affiliation:** Roman Catholic
- **Enrollment:** 1,025 full-time; 928 part-time

KEY STATS

✔ **U.S News College Ranking:** Unranked, Regional Colleges (Midwest)

✔ **SAT or ACT Score (25th/75th percentile):** N/A

✔ **Tuition:** 2010-2011: $15,870

Selectivity: N/A	Room/board: $4,000
Acceptance rate: 80%	Average debt: N/A
Student/faculty ratio: 11/1	Proportion who borrowed: N/A

UNDERGRADUATE STUDENT BODY STATS

2009-2010 enrollment: 1,025 full-time; 928 part-time. Men: 20%; women: 80%. **Ethnic makeup:** African American: 16%; Asian American: 1%; Hispanic: 5%; White: 78%. **Religious preference:** Jewish: 1%; No preference: 10%; Unknown: 19%; Roman Catholic: 30%; Lutheran: 9%; Other: 31%.

ADMISSIONS FACTS AND FIGURES

Phone: (419) 885-5291. **Email:** lcadmits@lourdes.edu. **Website:** http://www.lourdes.edu. **Application deadlines for fall 2011:** Regular decision: Rolling. Early decision: Not offered. Early action: Not offered. Admission can be deferred. **Application fee:** $25. **To apply online, go to:** http://www.lourdes.edu/future_students/?s=9. **Admissions requirements/recommendations:** High school units required (recommended): English: (4); Mathematics: (3); Science: (3); Foreign language: (2); Social studies: (3); Total units: (17). Tests: The college does not use SAT or ACT scores in admissions decisions. Neither SAT nor ACT required. Campus visit: Recommended. Admissions interview: Recommended. Off-campus interview: May be arranged. **Factors that count in admissions decisions:** *Academic:* Secondary school record: Not Considered. Class rank: Not Considered. Letters of recommendation: Not Considered. Standardized test scores: Not Considered. Essay: Not Considered. *Nonacademic:* Interview: Considered. Extracurricular activities: Not Considered. Talent/ability: Not Considered. Character/personal qualities: Not Considered. Alumni/ae relationship: Not Considered. Geographical residence: Not Considered. State residency: Not Considered. Religious affiliation/commitment: Not Considered. Minority status: Not Considered. Volunteer work: Not Considered. Work experience: Not Considered. **Admissions statistics for the fall 2009 entering class:** Total applicants: 390. Total accepted: 312. Freshmen enrolled: 129; 7% were from out of state. Overall acceptance rate: 80%. **Credentials of fall 2009 freshmen:** 7% ranked in the top 10 percent of their high school class; 21% were in the top 25 percent; 53% were in the top half. (Proportion submitting class standing: 67%.) **Average high school grade point average:** 2.9.

ACADEMICS

Year founded: 1958. **Academic calendar:** Semester. **Degrees offered:** certificate, associate, bachelor's, post-bachelor's certificate, master's. **Most popular majors:** 33% nursing, 12% teacher education and professional development, 10% business administration, management, and operations, 9% multi/interdisciplinary studies, 5% social work. **Major fields of study:** biological and biomedical sciences; business, management, marketing, and related support services; education; English language and literature/letters; health professions and related clinical sciences; history; multi/interdisciplinary studies; natural resources and conservation; philosophy and religious studies; psychology; public administration and social service professions; security and protective services; social sciences; visual and performing arts. **Areas of required coursework:** arts/fine arts, humanities, computer literacy, mathematics, English (including composition), philosophy, sciences (biological or physical), history, social science. **Pre-professional programs:** pre-law, pre-dentistry, pre-medicine, pre-veterinary science, other. **Special academic programs:** distance learning, double major, dual enrollment, independent study, internships, liberal arts/career combination, student-designed major, study abroad, teacher certificate program, weekend college. **Teacher certification offered in:** early childhood, elementary, middle/junior high, secondary. **Reserve Officers Training Corps (ROTC):** Army ROTC: Offered at cooperating institution (University of Toledo); Air Force ROTC: Offered at cooperating institution (Bowling Green State University). **Faculty and instruction (2009-2010):** Total instructional faculty: 80 full-time, 153 part-time (29% men; 71% women; 8% minorities). Full-time faculty with Ph.D. or other terminal degree: 51%. Student/faculty ratio: 11/1. Classes of fewer than 20 students: 60%; of 20 to 49 students: 40%; of 50 or more students: 0%. **Freshmen returning for sophomore year:** 60%. **Graduation rates:** Four-year: 3%; five-year: 10%; six-year: 35%.

COSTS AND FINANCIAL AID

Financial aid office: (419) 824-3732. **Expenses (2010-2011):** Tuition and fees 2010-2011: $15,870; room/board: $4,000. Estimated books and supplies: $1,080; transportation: $800; personal expenses: $3,642. **Financial aid:** Priority filing date for institution's financial aid form: March 1. In 2009-2010, 95% of undergraduates applied for financial aid. Of those, 85% were determined to have financial need; Average financial aid package (proportion receiving): $9,732 (85%). Average amount of gift aid, such as scholarships or grants (proportion receiving): $6,590 (63%). Average amount of self-help aid, such as work study or loans (proportion receiving): $4,270 (80%). Average need-based loan (excluding PLUS or other private loans): $4,134. Among students who received aid based on merit, the average

award (and the proportion receiving): $0 (0%). The average athletic scholarship (and the proportion receiving): $0 (0%).

CAMPUS LIFE AND EXTRACURRICULAR ACTIVITIES

Campus housing available: coed dorms, apartment for single students. Students who live in college-owned, operated, or affiliated housing: 0%. **Student employment:** During the 2009-2010 academic year, 10% of undergraduates worked on campus. Average per-year earnings: $1,000. **Clubs and organizations:** Number of student organizations: 25. Activities include: campus ministries, choral groups, drama/theater, literary magazine, student government. Number of fraternities: 0; sororities: 0. **Sports program (2009-2010):** Member of NAIA. *Men's intercollegiate varsity sports:* basketball, golf. *Women's intercollegiate varsity sports:* golf, volleyball.

SERVICES AND FACILITIES

Basic services: nonremedial tutoring. **Remedial assistance:** reading, math, writing, study skills. **Counseling services:** career, personal, academic, religious. **For learning-disabled students:** School does not offer a structured program with separate admission and additional fees. Services include: remedial math, remedial English, remedial reading, tape recorders, untimed tests, note-taking services, oral tests, learning center, readers, extended time for tests, tutors, priority seating, proofreading services, texts on tape, other testing accommodations. **Library:** Number of titles: 66,068; number of current serial subscriptions: 7,340. **Information technology resources:** Students are not required to lease or own a computer. Number of campus computers available to all students: 181. School has a wireless network. Proportion of college-owned housing units wired for high-speed internet access: 100%. **Campus safety:** Security services offered: 24-hour foot-and-vehicle patrols, 24-hour emergency telephones, controlled dormitory access (key, security card, etc).

TRANSFER AND INTERNATIONAL STUDENTS

Transfer students: May apply for admission for the following academic terms: Fall, Spring, Summer. Applicants need a minimum number of credits to apply. For fall 2009: Transfer applications received: 730. Transfer applicants offered admission: 567. Transfer applicants enrolled: 296. **International students:** Number of foreign undergraduates: 2. Minimum TOEFL score required: 500 (paper); 173 (computer).

Malone University

- **Address:** 2600 Cleveland Avenue NW, Canton, OH 44709
- **Website:** http://www.malone.edu
- **Private; Religious affiliation:** Evangelical Friends
- **Enrollment:** 1,857 full-time; 334 part-time

KEY STATS

✔ **U.S News College Ranking:** 61, Regional Universities (Midwest)
✔ **ACT Score (25th/75th percentile):** 19-26
✔ **Tuition:** 2010-2011: $22,444

Selectivity: Selective	**Room/board:** $7,548
Acceptance rate: 71%	**Average debt:** $25,655
Student/faculty ratio: 15/1	**Proportion who borrowed:** 81%

UNDERGRADUATE STUDENT BODY STATS

2009-2010 enrollment: 1,857 full-time; 334 part-time. Men: 41%; women: 59%. **Ethnic makeup:** African American: 8%; Asian American: 1%; Hispanic: 1%; White: 88%; International: 1%. **Religious preference:** Roman Catholic: 7%; Protestant: 78%; No preference: 6%; Unknown: 1%; Evangelical Friends: 8%; 0: 0%.

ADMISSIONS FACTS AND FIGURES

Phone: (330) 471-8145. **Email:** admissions@malone.edu. **Website:** http://www.malone.edu. **Application deadlines for fall 2011:** Regular decision: July 1. Early decision: Not offered. Early action: Not offered. Admission can be deferred. **Application fee:** $20. **To apply online, go to:** http://www3.malone.edu/admissions/apply. **Admissions requirements/recommendations:** High school units required (recommended): English: 4; Mathematics: 3; Science: 3; Foreign language: 2; Social studies: 2; History: 1; Academic electives: 2; Total units: 18. Tests: The college uses SAT or ACT scores in admissions decisions. Either SAT or ACT required. For admission to the fall 2011 entering class, the school will accept: ACT with or without writing accepted. Campus visit: Recommended. Admissions interview: Recommended.

Off-campus interview: Not available. **Factors that count in admissions decisions:** *Academic:* Secondary school record: Very Important. Class rank: Important. Letters of recommendation: Considered. Standardized test scores: Very Important. Essay: Considered. *Nonacademic:* Interview: Considered. Extracurricular activities: Considered. Talent/ability: Important. Character/personal qualities: Very Important. Alumni/ae relationship: Considered. Geographical residence: Not Considered. State residency: Not Considered. Religious affiliation/commitment: Important. Minority status: Considered. Volunteer work: Considered. Work experience: Not Considered. **Other schools with the greatest overlap in applicants:** Indiana Wesleyan University; Kent State University; Mount Vernon Nazarene University; University of Akron; University of Mount Union. **Admissions statistics for the fall 2009 entering class:** Total applicants: 1,641. Total accepted: 1,157. Freshmen enrolled: 481; 16% were from out of state. Overall acceptance rate: 71%. **Credentials of fall 2009 freshmen:** 23% ranked in the top 10 percent of their high school class; 48% were in the top 25 percent; 76% were in the top half. (Proportion submitting class standing: 80%.) **Average high school grade point average:** 3.3. **First-year students who submitted SAT scores:** 19%. Scores (25/75 percentile): Critical Reading: 470-593, Math: 460-590, Combined: 930-1183. **First-year students submitting ACT scores:** 91%. Scores (25/75 percentile): English: 19-25, Math: 18-25, Composite: 19-26.

ACADEMICS

Year founded: 1892. **Academic calendar:** Semester. **Degrees offered:** bachelor's, post-bachelor's certificate, master's. **Most popular majors:** 28% business administration, management, and operations, 18% nursing/registered nurse training (R.N., A.S.N., B.S.N., M.S.N.), 5% early childhood education and teaching, 4% communication, journalism, and related programs, 4% education/teaching of individuals with specific learning disabilities. **Major fields of study:** biological and biomedical sciences; business, management, marketing, and related support services; communication, journalism, and related programs; communications technologies/technicians and support services; computer and information sciences and support services; education; English language and literature/letters; foreign languages, literatures, and linguistics; health professions and related clinical sciences; history; liberal arts and sciences studies, and humanities; mathematics and statistics; parks, recreation, leisure, and fitness studies; philosophy and religious studies; physical sciences; psychology; public administration and social service professions; social sciences; theology and religious vocations; visual and performing arts. **Areas of required coursework:** arts/fine arts, humanities, mathematics, English (including composition), philosophy, sciences (biological or physical), history, social science, other. **Pre-professional programs:** pre-law, pre-dentistry, pre-medicine, pre-theology, pre-veterinary science, other. **Special academic programs (% participation):** accelerated program (5%), cooperative (work-study plan) program (4%), distance learning (69%), double major (14%), dual enrollment (2%), exchange student program (domestic) (5%), honors program (6%), independent study (27%), internships (63%), student-designed major (2%), study abroad (2%), teacher certificate program (10%), other (36%). **Teacher certification offered in:** early childhood, special education, elementary, middle/junior high, secondary. **Cooperative education programs:** other. **Reserve Officers Training Corps (ROTC):** Army ROTC: Offered at cooperating institution (University of Akron); Air Force ROTC: Offered at cooperating institution (University of Akron). **Faculty and instruction (2009-2010):** Total instructional faculty: 110 full-time, 108 part-time (49% men; 51% women; 4% minorities). Full-time faculty with Ph.D. or other terminal degree: 69%. Student/faculty ratio: 15/1. Classes of fewer than 20 students: 52%; of 20 to 49 students: 46%; of 50 or more students: 3%. **Advanced Placement and International Baccalaureate credit:** AP tests may be used for: Credit only. Scores accepted: 3, 4, 5. International Baccalaureate exams may be used for: Placement only. **Freshmen returning for sophomore year:** 74%. **Graduation rates:** Four-year: 44%; five-year: 60%; six-year: 57%. **Graduate study:** 24% of students pursue further study within one year. Fields in which graduates pursue further study: Master of Business Administration (MBA), 31%; law, 1%; medicine, 1%; theology (or the seminary), 8%; education, 21%; arts and sciences, 6%.

COSTS AND FINANCIAL AID

Financial aid office: (330) 471-8159. **Expenses (2010-2011):** Tuition and fees 2010-2011: $22,444; room/board: $7,548. Estimated books and supplies: $930; transportation: $1,100; personal expenses: $1,250. **Financial aid:** Priority filing date for institution's financial aid form: March 1; deadline: July 31. In 2009-2010, 86% of undergraduates applied for financial aid. Of those, 79% were determined to have financial need; 17% had their need fully met. Average financial aid package (proportion receiving):

$15,984 (79%). Average amount of gift aid, such as scholarships or grants (proportion receiving): $12,173 (76%). Average amount of self-help aid, such as work study or loans (proportion receiving): $5,141 (66%). Average need-based loan (excluding PLUS or other private loans): $4,520. Among students who received need-based aid, the average percentage of need met: 72%. Among students who received aid based on merit, the average award (and the proportion receiving): $6,959 (10%). The average athletic scholarship (and the proportion receiving): $6,854 (4%). Average amount of debt of borrowers graduating in 2009: $25,655. Proportion who borrowed: 81%.

CAMPUS LIFE AND EXTRACURRICULAR ACTIVITIES

Campus housing available (% using): women's dorms (52%), men's dorms (41%), special housing for disabled students (3%). Students who live in college-owned, operated, or affiliated housing: 53%. **Student employment:** During the 2009-2010 academic year, 5% of undergraduates worked on campus. Average per-year earnings: $870. **Clubs and organizations:** Number of student organizations: 55. Activities include: campus ministries, choral groups, concert band, dance, drama/theater, international student organization, jazz band, literary magazine, marching band, music ensembles, musical theater, radio station, student government, student newspaper, student film society, television station, yearbook. Number of fraternities: 0; sororities: 0. Average proportion of students who stay on campus on weekends: 40%. **Sports program (2009-2010):** Member of NAIA. *Men's intercollegiate varsity sports:* baseball, basketball, cross country, football, golf, soccer, swimming, tennis, track and field (indoor), track and field (outdoor). *Women's intercollegiate varsity sports:* basketball, cross country, golf, soccer, softball, swimming, tennis, track and field (indoor), track and field (outdoor), volleyball.

SERVICES AND FACILITIES

Basic services: nonremedial tutoring, placement service, health service, health insurance. **Remedial assistance:** reading, math, writing, study skills. **Counseling services:** minority student, career, personal, academic, older student, psychological, religious. **For learning-disabled students:** School does not offer a structured program with separate admission and additional fees. Total undergraduates in learning-disabled program or receiving services: 30. Services include: remedial math, remedial English, reading machines, remedial reading, tape recorders, note-taking services, oral tests, readers, extended time for tests, tutors, priority seating, texts on tape, typist/scribe, exams on tape or computer, other. **Library:** Number of titles: 178,992; number of current serial subscriptions: 47,942. **Information technology resources:** Students are not required to lease or own a computer. Number of campus computers available to all students: 190. School has a wireless network. Approximate number of users that can be accommodated: 1,000. Proportion of college-owned housing units wired for high-speed internet access: 100%. **Campus safety:** Security services offered: 24-hour foot-and-vehicle patrols, late-night transport/escort service, 24-hour emergency telephones, lighted pathways/sidewalks, controlled dormitory access (key, security card, etc).

TRANSFER AND INTERNATIONAL STUDENTS

Transfer students: May apply for admission for the following academic terms: Fall, Spring, Summer. Applicants do not need a minimum number of credits to apply. For fall 2009: Transfer applications received: 428. Transfer applicants offered admission: 265. Transfer applicants enrolled: 133. **International students:** Number of foreign undergraduates: 21 (1% of student body). Number of countries represented: 15. Minimum TOEFL score required: 550 (paper); 213 (computer). Average TOEFL score: 550 (paper).

Marietta College

- **Address:** 215 Fifth Street, Marietta, OH 45750
- **Website:** http://www.marietta.edu
- **Private**
- **Enrollment:** 1,428 full-time; 78 part-time

KEY STATS

✔ **U.S News College Ranking:** 2, Regional Colleges (Midwest)
✔ **ACT Score (25th/75th percentile):** 21-27
✔ **Tuition:** 2010-2011: $28,340

Selectivity: More selective	**Room/board:** $8,440
Acceptance rate: 76%	**Average debt:** $22,623
Student/faculty ratio: 12/1	**Proportion who borrowed:** 87%

UNDERGRADUATE STUDENT BODY STATS

2009-2010 enrollment: 1,428 full-time; 78 part-time. Men: 51%; women: 49%. **Ethnic makeup:** African American: 4%; Asian American: 1%; Hispanic: 1%; White: 84%; International: 10%.

ADMISSIONS FACTS AND FIGURES

Phone: (800) 331-7896. **Email:** admit@marietta.edu. **Website:** http://www.marietta.edu. **Application deadlines for fall 2011:** Regular decision: April 15. Early decision: Not offered. Early action: Not offered. Admission can be deferred. **Application fee:** $25. **To apply online, go to:** http://www.applyweb.com/apply/mar. **Admissions requirements/recommendations:** High school units required (recommended): English: 4 (4); Mathematics: 3 (4); Science: 3 (4); Foreign language: 2 (4); Social studies: 2 (2); History: 2; Academic electives: 3 (3); Total units: 16 (21). Tests: The college uses SAT or ACT scores in admissions decisions. Either SAT or ACT required. For admission to the fall 2011 entering class, the school will accept: ACT with or without writing accepted. Campus visit: Recommended. Admissions interview: Recommended. Off-campus interview: May be arranged. **Factors that count in admissions decisions:** *Academic:* Secondary school record: Very Important. Class rank: Very Important. Letters of recommendation: Important. Standardized test scores: Very Important. Essay: Important. *Nonacademic:* Interview: Important. Extracurricular activities: Considered. Talent/ability: Considered. Character/personal qualities: Important. Alumni/ae relationship: Considered. Geographical residence: Considered. State residency: Considered. Religious affiliation/commitment: Not Considered. Minority status: Considered. Volunteer work: Considered. Work experience: Considered. **Other schools with the greatest overlap in applicants:** John Carroll University; Miami University–Oxford; Ohio State University–Columbus; Ohio University; Otterbein College. **Admissions statistics for the fall 2009 entering class:** Total applicants: 2,521. Total accepted: 1,921. Freshmen enrolled: 388; 28% were from out of state. Overall acceptance rate: 76%. **Credentials of fall 2009 freshmen:** 32% ranked in the top 10 percent of their high school class; 58% were in the top 25 percent; 88% were in the top half. (Proportion submitting class standing: 87%.) **Average high school grade point average:** 3.5. **First-year students who submitted SAT scores:** 38%. Scores (25/75 percentile): Critical Reading: 480-600, Math: 490-610, Combined: 970-1210. **First-year students submitting ACT scores:** 86%. Scores (25/75 percentile): English: N/A, Math: N/A, Composite: 21-27.

ACADEMICS

Year founded: 1797. **Academic calendar:** Semester. **Degrees offered:** certificate, associate, bachelor's, master's. **Most popular majors:** 8% petroleum engineering, 7% advertising, 6% finance, 6% marketing, 6% psychology. **Major fields of study:** biological and biomedical sciences; business, management, marketing, and related support services; communication, journalism, and related programs; computer and information sciences and support services; education; engineering; English language and literature/letters; foreign languages, literatures, and linguistics; health professions and related clinical sciences; history; mathematics and statistics; natural resources and conservation; physical sciences; psychology; social sciences; visual and performing arts. **Areas of required coursework:** arts/fine arts, humanities, computer literacy, mathematics, English (including composition), philosophy, sciences (biological or physical), history, social science, other. **Preprofessional programs:** pre-law, pre-dentistry, pre-medicine, pre-veterinary science. **Special academic programs (% participation):** double major (12%), dual enrollment (1%), English as a Second Language (ESL) (6%), exchange student program (domestic) (0%), honors program (10%), independent study (10%), internships (25%), liberal arts/career combination, student-designed major (0%), study abroad (3%), teacher certificate program (6%).

Teacher certification offered in: early childhood, special education, middle/junior high, secondary. **Cooperative education programs:** engineering. **Faculty and instruction (2009-2010):** Total instructional faculty: 105 full-time, 41 part-time (53% men; 47% women; 5% minorities). Full-time faculty with Ph.D. or other terminal degree: 82%. Student/faculty ratio: 12/1. Classes of fewer than 20 students: 76%; of 20 to 49 students: 24%; of 50 or more students: 0%. **Advanced Placement and International Baccalaureate credit:** AP tests may be used for: Credit and/or placement. Scores accepted: 3, 4, 5. International Baccalaureate exams may be used for: Credit only. **Freshmen returning for sophomore year:** 74%. **Graduation rates:** Four-year: 43%; five-year: 53%; six-year: 60%. **Graduate study:** 30% of students pursue further study immediately upon graduation; 20% within one year. Fields in which graduates pursue further study: Master of Business Administration (MBA), 5%; law, 6%; medicine, 12%; dentistry, 2%; engineering, 5%; theology (or the seminary), 1%; education, 10%; arts and sciences, 58%; veterinary medicine, 1%.

COSTS AND FINANCIAL AID

Financial aid office: (740) 376-4712. **Expenses (2010-2011):** Tuition and fees 2010-2011: $28,340; room/board: $8,440. Estimated books and supplies: $1,088; transportation: $616; personal expenses: $672. **Financial aid:** Priority filing date for institution's financial aid form: March 1; deadline: May 1. In 2009-2010, 95% of undergraduates applied for financial aid. Of those, 77% were determined to have financial need; 50% had their need fully met. Average financial aid package (proportion receiving): $24,875 (77%). Average amount of gift aid, such as scholarships or grants (proportion receiving): $12,858 (74%). Average amount of self-help aid, such as work study or loans (proportion receiving): $5,259 (65%). Average need-based loan (excluding PLUS or other private loans): $3,755. Among students who received need-based aid, the average percentage of need met: 93%. Among students who received aid based on merit, the average award (and the proportion receiving): $8,636 (18%). The average athletic scholarship (and the proportion receiving): $0 (0%). Average amount of debt of borrowers graduating in 2009: $22,623. Proportion who borrowed: 87%.

CAMPUS LIFE AND EXTRACURRICULAR ACTIVITIES

Campus housing available (% using): coed dorms (60%), women's dorms (9%), men's dorms (10%), sorority housing (5%), fraternity housing (3%), apartment for single students (7%), special housing for disabled students (1%), other housing options (0%). Students who live in college-owned, operated, or affiliated housing: 82%. **Student employment:** During the 2009-2010 academic year, 39% of undergraduates worked on campus. Average per-year earnings: $2,000. **Clubs and organizations:** Number of student organizations: 80. Activities include: campus ministries, choral groups, concert band, dance, drama/theater, international student organization, jazz band, literary magazine, model UN, music ensembles, musical theater, radio station, student government, student newspaper, television station, yearbook. Number of fraternities: 3; sororities: 3. Proportion of men in fraternities: 12%; of women in sororities: 22%. Average proportion of students who stay on campus on weekends: 80%. **Sports program (2009-2010):** Member of NCAA III. **Men's intercollegiate varsity sports:** baseball, basketball, cross country, football, soccer, tennis, track and field (indoor), track and field (outdoor). **Women's intercollegiate varsity sports:** basketball, crew (heavyweight), cross country, crew (lightweight), soccer, softball, tennis, track and field (indoor), track and field (outdoor), volleyball.

SERVICES AND FACILITIES

Basic services: nonremedial tutoring, placement service, health service, other. **Remedial assistance:** reading, math, writing, study skills. **Counseling services:** minority student, career, personal, academic, older student, psychological, birth control. **For learning-disabled students:** School does not offer a structured program with separate admission and additional fees. Services include: remedial math, remedial English, reading machines, tape recorders, untimed tests, note-taking services, oral tests, learning center, readers, extended time for tests, tutors, priority seating, texts on tape, other testing accommodations, other. **Library:** Number of titles: 281,750; number of current serial subscriptions: 18,348. **Information technology resources:** Students are not required to lease or own a computer. Number of campus computers available to all students: 350. School has a wireless network. Approximate number of users that can be accommodated: 2,000. Proportion of college-owned housing units wired for high-speed internet access: 100%. **Campus safety:** Security services offered: 24-hour foot-and-vehicle patrols, late-night transport/escort service, 24-hour emergency telephones, lighted pathways/sidewalks, student patrols, controlled dormitory access (key, security card, etc.).

TRANSFER AND INTERNATIONAL STUDENTS

Transfer students: May apply for admission for the following academic terms: Fall, Spring. Applicants need a minimum number of credits to apply. For fall 2009: Transfer applications received: 83. Transfer applicants offered admission: 62. Transfer applicants enrolled: 42. **International students:** Number of foreign undergraduates: 145 (10% of student body). Number of countries represented: 19. Minimum TOEFL score required: 550 (paper); 213 (computer).

Miami University–Oxford

- **Address:** 501 E. High Street, Oxford, OH 45056
- **Website:** http://www.muohio.edu
- **Public**
- **Enrollment:** 14,457 full-time; 214 part-time

KEY STATS

- ✔ **U.S News College Ranking:** 79, National Universities
- ✔ **ACT Score (25th/75th percentile):** 24-29
- ✔ **Tuition:** 2009-2010: $12,312 in state, $26,670 out of state

Selectivity: More selective	**Room/board:** $9,458
Acceptance rate: 79%	**Average debt:** $26,582
Student/faculty ratio: 17/1	**Proportion who borrowed:** 53%

UNDERGRADUATE STUDENT BODY STATS

2009-2010 enrollment: 14,457 full-time; 214 part-time. Men: 47%; women: 53%. **Ethnic makeup:** African American: 4%; American-Indian: 1%; Asian American: 3%; Hispanic: 2%; White: 87%; International: 3%. **Religious preference:** Roman Catholic: 37%; Protestant: 41%; Jewish: 4%; Hindu: 1%; Buddhist: 1%; No preference: 15%; Other: 1%.

ADMISSIONS FACTS AND FIGURES

Phone: (513) 529-2531. **Email:** admission@muohio.edu. **Website:** http://www.muohio.edu. **Application deadlines for fall 2011:** Regular decision: February 1; decision sent by March 15. Early decision: Send application by: November 1; Decision sent by: December 15. Early action: Send application by: December 1; Decision sent by: February 1. Admission can be deferred. **Application fee:** $50. **To apply online, go to:** http://www.muohio.edu/admission/apply. **Admissions requirements/recommendations:** High school units required (recommended): English: (4); Mathematics: (3); Science: (3); Foreign language: (2); Social studies: (2); History: (1); Academic electives: (0); Total units: (16). Tests: The college uses SAT or ACT scores in admissions decisions. Either SAT or ACT required. For admission to the fall 2011 entering class, the school will accept: ACT with writing required. Campus visit: Neither required nor recommended. Admissions interview: Neither required nor recommended. Off-campus interview: Not available. **Factors that count in admissions decisions:** *Academic:* Secondary school record: Very Important. Class rank: Very Important. Letters of recommendation: Very Important. Standardized test scores: Very Important. Essay: Very Important. *Nonacademic:* Interview: Not Considered. Extracurricular activities: Considered. Talent/ability: Very Important. Character/personal qualities: Very Important. Alumni/ae relationship: Considered. Geographical residence: Considered. State residency: Considered. Religious affiliation/commitment: Not Considered. Minority status: Not Considered. Volunteer work: Considered. Work experience: Considered. **Other schools with the greatest overlap in applicants:** Indiana University–Bloomington; Ohio State University–Columbus; Ohio University; University of Dayton; University of Michigan–Ann Arbor. **Admissions statistics for the fall 2009 entering class:** Total applicants: 16,772. Total accepted: 13,223. Freshmen enrolled: 3,236; 30% were from out of state. Accepted through early-decision or early-action plans: 73%. Overall acceptance rate: 79%. Early-decision acceptance rate: 77%. Non-early acceptance rate: 66%. **Size of waiting list:** 1024 applicants; enrolled from waiting list: 802. **Credentials of fall 2009 freshmen:** 39% ranked in the top 10 percent of their high school class; 74% were in the top 25 percent; 97% were in the top half. (Proportion submitting class standing: 54%.) **Average high school grade point average:** 3.7. **First-year students who submitted SAT scores:** 51%. Scores (25/75 percentile): Critical Reading: 530-630, Math: 560-660, Combined: 1090-1290. **First-year students submitting ACT scores:** 83%. Scores (25/75 percentile): English: 23-30, Math: 24-28, Composite: 24-29.

ACADEMICS

Year founded: 1809. **Academic calendar:** Semester. **Degrees offered:** certificate, associate, transfer-associate, terminal-associate, bachelor's, master's, post-master's certificate, doctorate. **Most popular majors:** 26% business, management, marketing, and related support services; 11% social sciences, 10% education, 8% biological and biomedical sciences, 6% psychology. **Major fields of study:** architecture and related services; area, ethnic, cultural, and gender studies; biological and biomedical sciences; business, management, marketing, and related support services; communication, journalism, and related programs; computer and information sciences and support services; education; engineering; engineering technologies/technicians; English language and literature/letters; family and consumer sciences/human sciences; foreign languages, literatures, and linguistics; health professions and related clinical sciences; history; library science; mathematics and statistics; multi/interdisciplinary studies; natural resources and conservation; parks, recreation, leisure, and fitness studies; philosophy and religious studies; physical sciences; psychology; public administration and social service professions; social sciences; visual and performing arts. **Areas of required coursework:** arts/fine arts, humanities, mathematics, English (including composition), philosophy, foreign languages, sciences (biological or physical), history, social science. **Pre-professional programs:** pre-law, pre-dentistry, pre-medicine, pre-veterinary science, pre-optometry, pre-pharmacy, other. **Special academic programs (% participation):** cooperative (work-study plan) program (1%), cross-registration (1%), double major (9%), exchange student program (domestic) (1%), honors program (6%), independent study (60%), internships (30%), liberal arts/career combination (1%), student-designed major (2%), study abroad (33%), teacher certificate program (20%). **Teacher certification offered in:** early childhood, special education, elementary, middle/junior high, secondary. **Cooperative education programs:** computer science, engineering. **Reserve Officers Training Corps (ROTC):** Army ROTC: Offered at cooperating institution (Xavier University); Navy ROTC: Offered on campus; Air Force ROTC: Offered on campus. **Faculty and instruction (2009-2010):** Total instructional faculty: 827 full-time, 361 part-time (57% men; 43% women; 16% minorities). Full-time faculty with Ph.D. or other terminal degree: 89%. Student/faculty ratio: 17/1. Classes of fewer than 20 students: 32%; of 20 to 49 students: 56%; of 50 or more students: 12%. **Advanced Placement and International Baccalaureate credit:** AP tests may be used for: Credit only. Scores accepted: 3, 4. International Baccalaureate exams may be used for: Credit only. **Freshmen returning for sophomore year:** 90%. **Graduation rates:** Four-year: 71%; five-year: 82%; six-year: 83%.

COSTS AND FINANCIAL AID

Financial aid office: (513) 529-8734. **Expenses (2009-2010):** Tuition and fees 2009-2010: $12,312 in state, $26,670 out of state; room/board: $9,458. Estimated books and supplies: $1,460; transportation: $1,170; personal expenses: $5,113. **Financial aid:** Priority filing date for institution's financial aid form: February 15. In 2009-2010, 60% of undergraduates applied for financial aid. Of those, 44% were determined to have financial need; 14% had their need fully met. Average financial aid package (proportion receiving): $11,374 (43%). Average amount of gift aid, such as scholarships or grants (proportion receiving): $6,359 (25%). Average amount of self-help aid, such as work study or loans (proportion receiving): $4,601 (35%). Average need-based loan (excluding PLUS or other private loans): $4,699. Among students who received need-based aid, the average percentage of need met: 59%. Among students who received aid based on merit, the average award (and the proportion receiving): $4,559 (16%). The average athletic scholarship (and the proportion receiving): $20,856 (3%). Average amount of debt of borrowers graduating in 2009: $26,582. Proportion who borrowed: 53%.

CAMPUS LIFE AND EXTRACURRICULAR ACTIVITIES

Campus housing available: coed dorms, women's dorms, men's dorms, sorority housing, fraternity housing, apartments for married students, apartment for single students, special housing for disabled students, special housing for international students, cooperative housing, other housing options. Students who live in college-owned, operated, or affiliated housing: 50%. **Student employment:** During the 2009-2010 academic year, 31% of undergraduates worked on campus. Average per-year earnings: $650. **Clubs and organizations:** Number of student organizations: 304. Activities include: campus ministries, choral groups, concert band, dance, drama/theater, international student organization, jazz band, literary magazine, marching band, model UN, music ensembles, musical theater, opera, pep band, radio station, student government, student newspaper, student film society, symphony orchestra, television station, yearbook. Number of fraternities: 25; sororities: 22. Proportion of men in fraternities: 23%; of women in sororities: 26%. Average proportion of students who stay on campus on weekends: 90%. **Sports program (2009-2010):** Member of NCAA I. *Men's intercollegiate varsity sports:* baseball, basketball, cross country, football, golf, ice hockey, swimming, track and field (outdoor). *Women's intercollegiate varsity sports:* basketball, cross country, field hockey, soccer, softball, swimming, tennis, track and field (outdoor), volleyball.

SERVICES AND FACILITIES

Basic services: nonremedial tutoring, women's center, placement service, day care, health service, health insurance. **Remedial assistance:** reading, math, writing, study skills. **Counseling services:** minority student, career, military, personal, veteran student, academic, older student, psychological, birth control. **For learning-disabled students:** School does not offer a structured program with separate admission and additional fees. Services include: learning center, readers, extended time for tests, tutors, priority registration, priority seating, substitution of courses, texts on tape, exams on tape or computer, other testing accommodations, other. **Library:** Number of titles: 3,848,554; number of current serial subscriptions: 93,876. **Information technology resources:** Students are not required to lease or own a computer. Number of campus computers available to all students: 400. School has a wireless network. Approximate number of users that can be accommodated: 34,000. Proportion of college-owned housing units wired for high-speed internet access: 100%. **Campus safety:** Security services offered: 24-hour foot-and-vehicle patrols, late-night transport/escort service, 24-hour emergency telephones, lighted pathways/sidewalks, student patrols, controlled dormitory access (key, security card, etc).

TRANSFER AND INTERNATIONAL STUDENTS

Transfer students: May apply for admission for the following academic terms: Fall, Spring, Summer. Applicants do not need a minimum number of credits to apply. For fall 2009: Transfer applications received: 791. Transfer applicants offered admission: 522. Transfer applicants enrolled: 266. **International students:** Number of foreign undergraduates: 409 (3% of student body). Number of countries represented: 44. Minimum TOEFL score required: 533 (paper); 72 (computer). Average TOEFL score: 593 (paper).

Mount Vernon Nazarene University

- **Address:** 800 Martinsburg Road, Mount Vernon, OH 43050
- **Website:** http://www.gotomvnu.com
- **Private; Religious affiliation:** Nazarene
- **Enrollment:** 1,736 full-time; 338 part-time

KEY STATS

✔ **U.S News College Ranking:** 26, Regional Colleges (Midwest)
✔ **ACT Score (25th/75th percentile):** 19-25
✔ **Tuition:** 2010-2011: $21,330

Selectivity: Selective	**Room/board:** $6,180
Acceptance rate: 72%	**Average debt:** $29,761
Student/faculty ratio: 14/1	**Proportion who borrowed:** 85%

UNDERGRADUATE STUDENT BODY STATS

2009-2010 enrollment: 1,736 full-time; 338 part-time. Men: 40%; women: 60%. **Ethnic makeup:** African American: 5%; Asian American: 1%; Hispanic: 2%; White: 92%. **Religious preference:** Roman Catholic: 6%; Protestant: 18%; Unknown: 31%; Nazarene: 35%; Baptist (not included in Protestant): 10%.

ADMISSIONS FACTS AND FIGURES

Phone: (866) 462-6868. **Email:** admissions@mvnu.edu. **Website:** http://www.gotomvnu.com. **Application deadlines for fall 2011:** Regular decision: July 15. Early decision: Not offered. Early action: Not offered. Admission can be deferred. **Application fee:** $25. **To apply online, go to:** http://www.gotomvnu.com/application.asp. **Admissions requirements/recommendations:** High school units required (recommended): English: 4 (4); Mathematics: 3 (3); Science: 3 (3); Foreign language: 1 (3); Social studies: 3 (3); Academic electives: 5 (4); Total units: 21 (24). Tests: The college uses SAT or ACT scores in admissions decisions. Either SAT or ACT required. For admission to the fall 2011 entering class, the school will accept: ACT with or without writing accepted. Campus visit: Recommended. Admissions interview: Neither required nor recommended. Off-campus interview: Not available. **Factors that count in admissions decisions:** *Academic:* Secondary school

record: Important. Class rank: Not Considered. Letters of recommendation: Important. Standardized test scores: Very Important. Essay: Considered. *Nonacademic:* Interview: Not Considered. Extracurricular activities: Not Considered. Talent/ability: Not Considered. Character/personal qualities: Important. Alumni/ae relationship: Not Considered. Geographical residence: Not Considered. State residency: Not Considered. Religious affiliation/commitment: Not Considered. Minority status: Not Considered. Volunteer work: Not Considered. Work experience: Not Considered. **Other schools with the greatest overlap in applicants:** Cedarville University; Indiana Wesleyan University; Kent State University; Malone University; Ohio State University–Columbus. **Admissions statistics for the fall 2009 entering class:** Total applicants: 875. Total accepted: 628. Freshmen enrolled: 303; 12% were from out of state. Overall acceptance rate: 72%. **Credentials of fall 2009 freshmen:** 21% ranked in the top 10 percent of their high school class; 47% were in the top 25 percent; 76% were in the top half. (Proportion submitting class standing: 92%.) **Average high school grade point average:** 3.3. **First-year students who submitted SAT scores:** 19%. Scores (25/75 percentile): Critical Reading: 470-570, Math: 470-590, Combined: 940-1160. **First-year students submitting ACT scores:** 100%. Scores (25/75 percentile): English: 19-26, Math: 18-25, Composite: 19-25.

ACADEMICS

Year founded: 1968. **Academic calendar:** 4-1-4. **Degrees offered:** associate, bachelor's, master's. **Most popular majors:** 52% business, management, marketing, and related support services, 9% education, 4% communication, journalism, and related programs, 4% psychology, 4% theology and religious vocations. **Major fields of study:** biological and biomedical sciences; business, management, marketing, and related support services; communication, journalism, and related programs; computer and information sciences and support services; education; English language and literature/letters; family and consumer sciences/human sciences; foreign languages, literatures, and linguistics; history; mathematics and statistics; parks, recreation, leisure, and fitness studies; philosophy and religious studies; physical sciences; psychology; public administration and social service professions; security and protective services; social sciences; theology and religious vocations; visual and performing arts. **Areas of required coursework:** arts/fine arts, humanities, mathematics, English (including composition), philosophy, sciences (biological or physical), history, social science, other. **Pre-professional programs:** pre-law, pre-dentistry, pre-medicine, pre-theology, pre-veterinary science, pre-optometry, pre-pharmacy. **Special academic programs (% participation):** cross-registration (2%), distance learning (9%), double major (15%), dual enrollment (6%), honors program (6%), independent study (12%), internships (20%), liberal arts/career combination, study abroad (10%), teacher certificate program (16%). **Teacher certification offered in:** early childhood, special education, elementary, vo-tech, middle/junior high, secondary. **Cooperative education programs:** engineering, health professions, vocational arts. **Faculty and instruction (2009-2010):** Total instructional faculty: 108 full-time, 159 part-time (60% men; 40% women; 4% minorities). Full-time faculty with Ph.D. or other terminal degree: 64%. Student/faculty ratio: 14/1. Classes of fewer than 20 students: 71%; of 20 to 49 students: 27%; of 50 or more students: 2%. **Advanced Placement and International Baccalaureate credit:** AP tests may be used for: Credit and/or placement. Scores accepted: 3, 4, 5. International Baccalaureate exams may be used for: Credit and/or placement. **Freshmen returning for sophomore year:** 73%. **Graduation rates:** Four-year: 37%; five-year: 49%; six-year: 52%. **Graduate study:** 19% of students pursue further study immediately upon graduation. Fields in which graduates pursue further study: Master of Business Administration (MBA), 10%; medicine, 3%; theology (or the seminary), 1%; education, 1%; arts and sciences, 6%; veterinary medicine, 1%.

COSTS AND FINANCIAL AID

Financial aid office: (740) 392-6868. **Expenses (2010-2011):** Tuition and fees 2010-2011: $21,330; room/board: $6,180. Estimated books and supplies: $1,200; transportation: $1,052; personal expenses: $1,964. **Financial aid:** Priority filing date for institution's financial aid form: March 15. In 2009-2010, 78% of undergraduates applied for financial aid. Of those, 70% were determined to have financial need; 13% had their need fully met. Average financial aid package (proportion receiving): $15,619 (70%). Average amount of gift aid, such as scholarships or grants (proportion receiving): $9,344 (66%). Average amount of self-help aid, such as work study or loans (proportion receiving): $4,517 (63%). Average need-based loan (excluding PLUS or other private loans): $3,984. Among students who received need-based aid, the average percentage of need met: 70%. Among students who received aid based on merit, the average award (and the proportion receiving): $4,102 (6%). The average athletic scholarship (and the proportion

receiving): $4,184 (3%). Average amount of debt of borrowers graduating in 2009: $29,761. Proportion who borrowed: 85%.

CAMPUS LIFE AND EXTRACURRICULAR ACTIVITIES

Campus housing available (% using): women's dorms (27%), men's dorms (17%), apartment for single students (56%), special housing for disabled students. Students who live in college-owned, operated, or affiliated housing: 50%. **Student employment:** During the 2009-2010 academic year, 47% of undergraduates worked on campus. Average per-year earnings: $2,200. **Clubs and organizations:** Number of student organizations: 38. Activities include: campus ministries, choral groups, concert band, drama/theater, international student organization, jazz band, literary magazine, music ensembles, musical theater, opera, pep band, radio station, student government, student newspaper, yearbook. Number of fraternities: 0; sororities: 0. Average proportion of students who stay on campus on weekends: 50%. **Sports program (2009-2010):** Member of NAIA. *Men's intercollegiate varsity sports:* baseball, basketball, cross country, golf, soccer. *Women's intercollegiate varsity sports:* basketball, cross country, soccer, softball, volleyball.

SERVICES AND FACILITIES

Basic services: health service. **Remedial assistance:** reading, math, writing. **Counseling services:** minority student, career, personal, academic, older student, psychological, religious. **For learning-disabled students:** School does not offer a structured program with separate admission and additional fees. Total undergraduates in learning-disabled program or receiving services: 41. Services include: remedial math, remedial English, remedial reading, tape recorders, diagnostic testing service, note-taking services, oral tests, readers, extended time for tests, tutors, priority seating, proofreading services, texts on tape, typist/scribe, exams on tape or computer. **Library:** Number of titles: 100,299; number of current serial subscriptions: 7,399. **Information technology resources:** Students are not required to lease or own a computer. Number of campus computers available to all students: 232. School has a wireless network. Approximate number of users that can be accommodated: 1,000. Proportion of college-owned housing units wired for high-speed internet access: 100%. **Campus safety:** Security services offered: 24-hour foot-and-vehicle patrols, late-night transport/escort service, 24-hour emergency telephones, lighted pathways/sidewalks, controlled dormitory access (key, security card, etc).

TRANSFER AND INTERNATIONAL STUDENTS

Transfer students: May apply for admission for the following academic terms: Fall, Winter, Spring. Applicants do not need a minimum number of credits to apply. For fall 2009: Transfer applications received: 201. Transfer applicants offered admission: 139. Transfer applicants enrolled: 83. **International students:** Number of foreign undergraduates: 8. Number of countries represented: 6. Minimum TOEFL score required: 500 (paper); 80 (computer).

Muskingum University

- **Address:** 163 Stormont Street, New Concord, OH 43762
- **Website:** http://www.muskingum.edu
- **Private; Religious affiliation:** Presbyterian Church (USA)
- **Enrollment:** 1,582 full-time; 143 part-time

KEY STATS

✔ **U.S News College Ranking:** 37, Regional Universities (Midwest)
✔ **ACT Score (25th/75th percentile):** 19-24
✔ **Tuition:** 2010-2011: $20,726

Selectivity: Selective	**Room/board:** $8,170
Acceptance rate: 79%	**Average debt:** $28,343
Student/faculty ratio: 14/1	**Proportion who borrowed:** 79%

UNDERGRADUATE STUDENT BODY STATS

2009-2010 enrollment: 1,582 full-time; 143 part-time. Men: 48%; women: 52%. **Ethnic makeup:** African American: 6%; Asian American: 1%; Hispanic: 1%; White: 89%; International: 2%. **Religious preference:** Roman Catholic: 17%; Protestant: 43%; Jewish: 1%; No preference: 28%; Unknown: 4%; Presbyterian Church (USA): 6%; Other: 1%.

ADMISSIONS FACTS AND FIGURES

Phone: (740) 826-8137. **Email:** adminfo@muskingum.edu. **Website:** http://www.muskingum.edu. **Application deadlines for fall 2011:** Regular decision:

August 1. Early decision: Not offered. Early action: Not offered. Admission can be deferred. **To apply online, go to:** http://www.muskingum.edu/home/admission/applyonline.html. **Admissions requirements/recommendations:** High school units required (recommended): English: 4 (4); Mathematics: 2 (3); Science: 2 (3); Foreign language: 2 (2); Social studies: 1 (1); History: 2 (2); Total units: 10 (15). Tests: The college uses SAT or ACT scores in admissions decisions. Either SAT or ACT required. For admission to the fall 2011 entering class, the school will accept: ACT with or without writing accepted. Campus visit: Recommended. Admissions interview: Recommended. Off-campus interview: Not available. **Factors that count in admissions decisions:** *Academic:* Secondary school record: Very Important. Class rank: Important. Letters of recommendation: Important. Standardized test scores: Important. Essay: Considered. *Nonacademic:* Interview: Considered. Extracurricular activities: Considered. Talent/ability: Considered. Character/personal qualities: Considered. Alumni/ae relationship: Considered. Geographical residence: Considered. State residency: Not Considered. Religious affiliation/commitment: Not Considered. Minority status: Considered. Volunteer work: Not Considered. Work experience: Considered. **Other schools with the greatest overlap in applicants:** Capital University; Marietta College; Ohio State University–Columbus; Ohio University; University of Mount Union. **Admissions statistics for the fall 2009 entering class:** Total applicants: 2,042. Total accepted: 1,603. Freshmen enrolled: 473; 10% were from out of state. Overall acceptance rate: 79%. **Size of waiting list:** 0 applicants; enrolled from waiting list: 0. **Credentials of fall 2009 freshmen:** 28% ranked in the top 10 percent of their high school class; 48% were in the top 25 percent; 76% were in the top half. (Proportion submitting class standing: 90%.) **Average high school grade point average:** 3.2. **First-year students who submitted SAT scores:** 18%. Scores (25/75 percentile): Critical Reading: 430-580, Math: 430-560, Combined: 860-1140. **First-year students submitting ACT scores:** 86%. Scores (25/75 percentile): English: 18-24, Math: 18-25, Composite: 19-24.

ACADEMICS

Year founded: 1837. **Academic calendar:** Semester. **Degrees offered:** bachelor's, master's. **Most popular majors:** 23% education, 21% business, management, marketing, and related support services, 8% psychology, 8% social sciences, 7% biological and biomedical sciences. **Major fields of study:** biological and biomedical sciences; business, management, marketing, and related support services; communication, journalism, and related programs; computer and information sciences and support services; education; English language and literature/letters; foreign languages, literatures, and linguistics; history; liberal arts and sciences studies, and humanities; mathematics and statistics; multi/interdisciplinary studies; philosophy and religious studies; physical sciences; psychology; security and protective services; social sciences; visual and performing arts. **Areas of required coursework:** arts/fine arts, humanities, mathematics, English (including composition), philosophy, sciences (biological or physical), history, social science, other. **Pre-professional programs:** pre-law, pre-dentistry, pre-medicine, pre-theology, pre-veterinary science, pre-optometry, pre-pharmacy. **Special academic programs (% participation):** accelerated program (2%), double major (28%), dual enrollment (1%), English as a Second Language (ESL) (1%), independent study (40%), internships (27%), student-designed major (1%), study abroad (19%), teacher certificate program (31%). **Teacher certification offered in:** early childhood, special education, elementary, middle/junior high, adult education, secondary, bilingual/bicultural. **Faculty and instruction (2009-2010):** Total instructional faculty: 101 full-time, 73 part-time (48% men; 52% women; 8% minorities). Full-time faculty with Ph.D. or other terminal degree: 85%. Student/faculty ratio: 14/1. Classes of fewer than 20 students: 63%; of 20 to 49 students: 37%; of 50 or more students: 0%. **Advanced Placement and International Baccalaureate credit:** AP tests may be used for: Credit only. Scores accepted: 3, 4, 5. International Baccalaureate exams may be used for: Credit only. **Freshmen returning for sophomore year:** 71%. **Graduation rates:** Four-year: 40%; five-year: 53%; six-year: 58%. **Graduate study:** 15% of students pursue further study immediately upon graduation; 20% within one year; 64% within five years. Fields in which graduates pursue further study: Master of Business Administration (MBA), 20%; law, 5%; medicine, 3%; dentistry, 1%; theology (or the seminary), 1%; education, 45%; arts and sciences, 24%; veterinary medicine, 1%.

COSTS AND FINANCIAL AID

Financial aid office: (740) 826-8139. **Expenses (2010-2011):** Tuition and fees 2010-2011: $20,726; room/board: $8,170. Estimated books and supplies: $1,100; transportation: $500; personal expenses: $900. **Financial aid:** Priority filing date for institution's financial aid form: March 1. In 2009-2010, 88% of undergraduates applied for financial aid. Of those, 82% were determined to have financial need; 22% had their need fully

met. Average financial aid package (proportion receiving): $17,950 (82%). Average amount of gift aid, such as scholarships or grants (proportion receiving): $14,040 (82%). Average amount of self-help aid, such as work study or loans (proportion receiving): $4,390 (73%). Average need-based loan (excluding PLUS or other private loans): $4,055. Among students who received need-based aid, the average percentage of need met: 80%. Among students who received aid based on merit, the average award (and the proportion receiving): $5,114 (15%). The average athletic scholarship (and the proportion receiving): $0 (0%). Average amount of debt of borrowers graduating in 2009: $28,343. Proportion who borrowed: 79%.

CAMPUS LIFE AND EXTRACURRICULAR ACTIVITIES

Campus housing available (% using): coed dorms (50%), women's dorms (11%), men's dorms (9%), sorority housing (7%), fraternity housing (8%), apartment for single students (3%), other housing options (12%). Students who live in college-owned, operated, or affiliated housing: 68%. **Student employment:** During the 2009-2010 academic year, 40% of undergraduates worked on campus. Average per-year earnings: $1,000. **Clubs and organizations:** Number of student organizations: 96. Activities include: campus ministries, choral groups, concert band, dance, drama/theater, international student organization, jazz band, literary magazine, marching band, model UN, music ensembles, musical theater, opera, pep band, radio station, student government, student newspaper, student film society, symphony orchestra, television station, yearbook. Number of fraternities: 5; sororities: 6. Proportion of men in fraternities: 25%; of women in sororities: 30%. Average proportion of students who stay on campus on weekends: 60%. **Sports program (2009-2010):** Member of NCAA III. *Men's intercollegiate varsity sports:* baseball, basketball, cross country, football, golf, soccer, tennis, track and field (indoor), track and field (outdoor), wrestling. *Women's intercollegiate varsity sports:* basketball, cross country, golf, soccer, softball, tennis, track and field (indoor), track and field (outdoor), volleyball.

SERVICES AND FACILITIES

Basic services: nonremedial tutoring, women's center, placement service, health service, health insurance. **Remedial assistance:** math, study skills. **Counseling services:** minority student, career, military, personal, veteran student, academic, older student, psychological, birth control, religious. **For learning-disabled students:** School does not offer a structured program with separate admission and additional fees. Total undergraduates in learning-disabled program or receiving services: 167. Services include: reading machines, tape recorders, note-taking services, learning center, readers, extended time for tests, tutors, priority registration, priority seating, proofreading services, texts on tape, typist/scribe, exams on tape or computer, other testing accommodations. **Library:** Number of titles: 211,581; number of current serial subscriptions: 12,879. **Information technology resources:** Students are not required to lease or own a computer. Number of campus computers available to all students: 217. School has a wireless network. Approximate number of users that can be accommodated: 50. Proportion of college-owned housing units wired for high-speed internet access: 100%. **Campus safety:** Security services offered: 24-hour foot-and-vehicle patrols, late-night transport/escort service, 24-hour emergency telephones, lighted pathways/sidewalks, controlled dormitory access (key, security card, etc).

TRANSFER AND INTERNATIONAL STUDENTS

Transfer students: May apply for admission for the following academic terms: Fall, Spring, Summer. Applicants do not need a minimum number of credits to apply. For fall 2009: Transfer applications received: 179. Transfer applicants offered admission: 90. Transfer applicants enrolled: 53. **International students:** Number of foreign undergraduates: 30 (2% of student body). Number of countries represented: 6. Minimum TOEFL score required: 550 (paper); 213 (computer). Average TOEFL score: 510 (paper).

Notre Dame College of Ohio

- **Address:** 4545 College Road, Cleveland, OH 44121
- **Website:** http://www.notredamecollege.edu
- **Private; Religious affiliation:** Roman Catholic
- **Enrollment:** 1,104 full-time; 571 part-time

KEY STATS

✔ **U.S News College Ranking:** 58, Regional Colleges (Midwest)
✔ **ACT Score (25th/75th percentile):** 17-22
✔ **Tuition:** 2010-2011: $23,630

Selectivity: Selective	**Room/board:** $7,820
Acceptance rate: 50%	**Average debt:** N/A
Student/faculty ratio: 16/1	**Proportion who borrowed:** N/A

UNDERGRADUATE STUDENT BODY STATS

2009-2010 enrollment: 1,104 full-time; 571 part-time. Men: 42%; women: 58%. **Ethnic makeup:** African American: 21%; Asian American: 1%; Hispanic: 2%; White: 76%. **Religious preference:** Protestant: 30%; Jewish: 2%; No preference: 3%; Roman Catholic: 53%; Other: 12%.

ADMISSIONS FACTS AND FIGURES

Phone: (216) 373-5355. **Email:** admissions@ndc.edu. **Website:** http://www.notredamecollege.edu. **Application deadlines for fall 2011:** Regular decision: Rolling. Early decision: Not offered. Early action: Not offered. Admission can be deferred. **Application fee:** $30. **To apply online, go to:** http://www.notredamecollege.edu/application/. **Admissions requirements/recommendations:** High school units required (recommended): English: 4 (4); Mathematics: 3 (3); Science: 3 (3); Foreign language: 2 (2); Social studies: 3 (3); History: 0 (0); Academic electives: 0 (0); Total units: 16 (16). Tests: The college uses SAT or ACT scores in admissions decisions. Either SAT or ACT required. For admission to the fall 2011 entering class, the school will accept: ACT with or without writing accepted. Campus visit: Recommended. Admissions interview: Recommended. Off-campus interview: May be arranged. **Factors that count in admissions decisions:** *Academic:* Secondary school record: Very Important. Class rank: Important. Letters of recommendation: Very Important. Standardized test scores: Important. Essay: Considered. *Nonacademic:* Interview: Considered. Extracurricular activities: Considered. Talent/ability: Considered. Character/personal qualities: Considered. Alumni/ae relationship: Considered. Geographical residence: Not Considered. State residency: Not Considered. Religious affiliation/commitment: Not Considered. Minority status: Not Considered. Volunteer work: Considered. Work experience: Considered. **Other schools with the greatest overlap in applicants:** Baldwin-Wallace College; Cleveland State University; John Carroll University; Kent State University; Lake Erie College. **Admissions statistics for the fall 2009 entering class:** Total applicants: 2,386. Total accepted: 1,191. Freshmen enrolled: 344; 5% were from out of state. Overall acceptance rate: 50%. **Credentials of fall 2009 freshmen:** 6% ranked in the top 10 percent of their high school class; 18% were in the top 25 percent; 52% were in the top half. (Proportion submitting class standing: 78%.) **Average high school grade point average:** 2.9. **First-year students who submitted SAT scores:** 18%. Scores (25/75 percentile): Critical Reading: 420-520, Math: 430-560, Combined: 850-1080. **First-year students submitting ACT scores:** 82%. Scores (25/75 percentile): English: 15-21, Math: 16-23, Composite: 17-22.

ACADEMICS

Year founded: 1922. **Academic calendar:** Semester. **Degrees offered:** certificate, associate, bachelor's, post-bachelor's certificate, master's. **Most popular majors:** 11% political science and government, 9% accounting, 9% psychology, 8% business administration and management, 8% education/teaching of individuals with specific learning disabilities. **Major fields of study:** biological and biomedical sciences; business, management, marketing, and related support services; communication, journalism, and related programs; education; English language and literature/letters; health professions and related clinical sciences; history; legal professions and studies; mathematics and statistics; physical sciences; psychology; social sciences; theology and religious vocations; visual and performing arts. **Areas of required coursework:** arts/fine arts, humanities, computer literacy, mathematics, English (including composition), philosophy, sciences (biological or physical), social science, other. **Pre-professional programs:** pre-law, pre-dentistry, pre-medicine, pre-theology, pre-veterinary science, pre-pharmacy. **Special academic programs (% participation):** cooperative (work-study plan) program (95%), cross-registration (1%), distance learning (1%), double major

(3%), dual enrollment (1%), independent study (2%), internships (95%), student-designed major (1%), teacher certificate program (20%), weekend college (5%). **Teacher certification offered in:** early childhood, special education, elementary, middle/junior high, secondary. **Reserve Officers Training Corps (ROTC):** Army ROTC: Offered at cooperating institution (John Carroll University). **Faculty and instruction (2009-2010):** Total instructional faculty: 50 full-time, 85 part-time (37% men; 63% women; 8% minorities). Full-time faculty with Ph.D. or other terminal degree: 56%. Student/faculty ratio: 16/1. Classes of fewer than 20 students: 63%; of 20 to 49 students: 37%. **Advanced Placement and International Baccalaureate credit:** AP tests may be used for: Placement only. Scores accepted: 4, 5. **Freshmen returning for sophomore year:** 65%. **Graduation rates:** Four-year: 36%; five-year: 44%; six-year: 47%.

COSTS AND FINANCIAL AID

Financial aid office: (216) 373-5263. **Expenses (2010-2011):** Tuition and fees 2010-2011: $23,630; room/board: $7,820. Estimated books and supplies: $2,058; transportation: $500; personal expenses: $888.

CAMPUS LIFE AND EXTRACURRICULAR ACTIVITIES

Campus housing available (% using): coed dorms (45%), women's dorms (25%), men's dorms (30%). Students who live in college-owned, operated, or affiliated housing: 63%. **Student employment:** During the 2009-2010 academic year, 50% of undergraduates worked on campus. Average per-year earnings: $2,450. **Clubs and organizations:** Number of student organizations: 33. Activities include: campus ministries, choral groups, concert band, drama/theater, literary magazine, marching band, music ensembles, pep band, student government, student newspaper, student film society, yearbook. Number of fraternities: 0; sororities: 0. Average proportion of students who stay on campus on weekends: 65%. **Sports program (2009-2010):** Member of NAIA. ***Men's intercollegiate varsity sports:*** baseball, basketball, cross country, football, golf, soccer, swimming, tennis, track and field (indoor), track and field (outdoor), water polo, wrestling. ***Women's intercollegiate varsity sports:*** basketball, bowling, cross country, golf, lacrosse, soccer, softball, swimming, track and field (indoor), track and field (outdoor), volleyball, water polo.

SERVICES AND FACILITIES

Basic services: nonremedial tutoring, placement service, health service, health insurance. **Remedial assistance:** reading, math, writing, study skills. **Counseling services:** minority student, career, veteran student, academic, older student, psychological, religious. **For learning-disabled students:** School does not offer a structured program with separate admission and additional fees. Total undergraduates in learning-disabled program or receiving services: 79. Services include: remedial math, remedial English, reading machines, tape recorders, untimed tests, note-taking services, oral tests, learning center, readers, extended time for tests, tutors, priority registration, priority seating, texts on tape, other testing accommodations, other. **Information technology resources:** Students are not required to lease or own a computer. Number of campus computers available to all students: 153. School has a wireless network. Approximate number of users that can be accommodated: 50. Proportion of college-owned housing units wired for high-speed internet access: 100%. **Campus safety:** Security services offered: 24-hour foot-and-vehicle patrols, late-night transport/escort service, 24-hour emergency telephones, lighted pathways/sidewalks, controlled dormitory access (key, security card, etc).

TRANSFER AND INTERNATIONAL STUDENTS

Transfer students: May apply for admission for the following academic terms: Fall, Spring, Summer. Applicants need a minimum number of credits to apply. For fall 2009: Transfer applicants enrolled: 103. **International students:** Number of foreign undergraduates: 4. Number of countries represented: 9. Minimum TOEFL score required: 550 (paper); 213 (computer).

Oberlin College

- **Address:** 247 W. Lorain Street, Suite C, Oberlin, OH 44074
- **Website:** http://www.oberlin.edu
- **Private**
- **Enrollment:** 2,842 full-time; 46 part-time

KEY STATS

✔ **U.S News College Ranking:** 23, National Liberal Arts Colleges
✔ **SAT Score (25th/75th percentile):** 1300-1470
✔ **Tuition:** 2010-2011: $41,577
  Selectivity: Most selective **Room/board:** $11,010
  Acceptance rate: 34% **Average debt:** $18,981
  Student/faculty ratio: 9/1 **Proportion who borrowed:** 54%

UNDERGRADUATE STUDENT BODY STATS

2009-2010 enrollment: 2,842 full-time; 46 part-time. Men: 45%; women: 55%. **Ethnic makeup:** African American: 7%; American-Indian: 1%; Asian American: 7%; Hispanic: 5%; White: 74%; International: 6%. **Religious preference:** Roman Catholic: 10%; Protestant: 20%; Jewish: 12%; No preference: 53%; Other: 5%.

ADMISSIONS FACTS AND FIGURES

Phone: (440) 775-8411. **Email:** college.admissions@oberlin.edu. **Website:** http://www.oberlin.edu. **Application deadlines for fall 2011:** Regular decision: January 15; decision sent by April 1. Early decision: Send application by: November 15; Decision sent by: December 10. Early action: Not offered. Admission can be deferred. **Application fee:** $35. **To apply online, go to:** http://www.oberlin.edu/admissions. **Admissions requirements/recommendations:** High school units required (recommended): English: 4; Mathematics: 4; Science: 3; Foreign language: 3; Social studies: 3. Tests: The college uses SAT or ACT scores in admissions decisions. Either SAT or ACT required. For admission to the fall 2011 entering class, the school will accept: ACT with writing required. Campus visit: Recommended. Admissions interview: Recommended. Off-campus interview: May be arranged. **Factors that count in admissions decisions:** *Academic:* Secondary school record: Very Important. Class rank: Very Important. Letters of recommendation: Important. Standardized test scores: Important. Essay: Important. *Nonacademic:* Interview: Considered. Extracurricular activities: Important. Talent/ability: Important. Character/personal qualities: Important. Alumni/ae relationship: Important. Geographical residence: Considered. State residency: Considered. Religious affiliation/commitment: Not Considered. Minority status: Considered. Volunteer work: Considered. Work experience: Considered. **Other schools with the greatest overlap in applicants:** Brown University; Carleton College; Swarthmore College; Vassar College; Wesleyan University. **Admissions statistics for the fall 2009 entering class:** Total applicants: 7,227. Total accepted: 2,434. Freshmen enrolled: 806; 8% were from out of state. Accepted through early-decision or early-action plans: 26%. Overall acceptance rate: 34%. Early-decision acceptance rate: 65%. Non-early acceptance rate: 32%. **Size of waiting list:** 995 applicants; enrolled from waiting list: 15. **Credentials of fall 2009 freshmen:** 69% ranked in the top 10 percent of their high school class; 90% were in the top 25 percent; 100% were in the top half. (Proportion submitting class standing: 39%.) **Average high school grade point average:** 3.6. **First-year students who submitted SAT scores:** 81%. Scores (25/75 percentile): Critical Reading: 660-750, Math: 640-720, Combined: 1300-1470. **First-year students submitting ACT scores:** 43%. Scores (25/75 percentile): English: N/A, Math: N/A, Composite: 28-32.

ACADEMICS

Year founded: 1833. **Academic calendar:** 4-1-4. **Degrees offered:** diploma, bachelor's, post-bachelor's certificate, master's. **Most popular majors:** 18% music performance, 9% biology, 8% English language and literature, 7% history, 6% psychology. **Major fields of study:** area, ethnic, cultural, and gender studies; biological and biomedical sciences; computer and information sciences and support services; education; engineering; English language and literature/letters; foreign languages, literatures, and linguistics; history; legal professions and studies; mathematics and statistics; multi/interdisciplinary studies; natural resources and conservation; philosophy and religious studies; physical sciences; psychology; social sciences; visual and performing arts. **Areas of required coursework:** social science, other. **Preprofessional programs:** pre-law, pre-dentistry, pre-medicine, pre-veterinary science, other. **Special academic programs:** double major, dual enrollment, English as a Second Language (ESL), exchange student program (domestic), honors program, independent study, internships, student-designed major, study abroad, teacher certificate program. **Teacher certification offered in:** early childhood, elementary, middle/junior high, secondary. **Cooperative education programs:** engineering. **Faculty and instruction (2009-2010):** Total instructional faculty: 295 full-time, 51 part-time (60% men; 40% women; 15% minorities). Full-time faculty with Ph.D. or other terminal degree: 96%. Student/faculty ratio: 9/1. Classes of fewer than 20 students: 72%; of 20 to 49 students: 25%; of 50 or more students: 3%. **Advanced Placement and International Baccalaureate credit:** AP tests may be used for: Credit and/or placement. Scores accepted: 4, 5. International Baccalaureate exams may be used for: Credit and/or placement. **Freshmen returning for sophomore year:** 94%. **Graduation rates:** Four-year: 73%; five-year: 84%; six-year: 86%. **Graduate study:** 22% of students pursue further study immediately upon graduation; 67% within five years. Fields in which graduates pursue further study: Master of Business Administration (MBA), 5%; law, 7%; medicine, 5%.

COSTS AND FINANCIAL AID

Financial aid office: (440) 775-8142. **Expenses (2010-2011):** Tuition and fees 2010-2011: $41,577; room/board: $11,010. Estimated books and supplies: $830; transportation: $750; personal expenses: $978. **Financial aid:** Priority filing date for institution's financial aid form: February 15; deadline: February 15. In 2009-2010, 63% of undergraduates applied for financial aid. Of those, 55% were determined to have financial need; 100% had their need fully met. Average financial aid package (proportion receiving): $32,508 (55%). Average amount of gift aid, such as scholarships or grants (proportion receiving): $27,634 (46%). Average amount of self-help aid, such as work study or loans (proportion receiving): $5,138 (47%). Average need-based loan (excluding PLUS or other private loans): $4,776. Among students who received need-based aid, the average percentage of need met: 100%. Among students who received aid based on merit, the average award (and the proportion receiving): $11,812 (26%). Average amount of debt of borrowers graduating in 2009: $18,981. Proportion who borrowed: 54%.

CAMPUS LIFE AND EXTRACURRICULAR ACTIVITIES

Campus housing available (% using): coed dorms (58%), women's dorms (1%), apartment for single students (6%), special housing for disabled students (2%), cooperative housing (7%). Students who live in college-owned, operated, or affiliated housing: 88%. **Clubs and organizations:** Number of student organizations: 158. Activities include: campus ministries, choral groups, concert band, dance, drama/theater, international student organization, jazz band, literary magazine, marching band, model UN, music ensembles, musical theater, opera, radio station, student government, student newspaper, student film society, symphony orchestra, yearbook. Number of fraternities: 0; sororities: 0. Average proportion of students who stay on campus on weekends: 95%. **Sports program (2009-2010):** Member of NCAA III. *Men's intercollegiate varsity sports:* baseball, basketball, cross country, football, golf, lacrosse, soccer, swimming, tennis, track and field (indoor), track and field (outdoor). *Women's intercollegiate varsity sports:* basketball, cross country, field hockey, lacrosse, soccer, softball, swimming, tennis, track and field (indoor), track and field (outdoor), volleyball.

SERVICES AND FACILITIES

Basic services: nonremedial tutoring, women's center, placement service, health service, health insurance, other. **Remedial assistance:** reading, math, writing, study skills. **Counseling services:** minority student, career, personal, academic, older student, psychological, birth control, religious. **For learning-disabled students:** School does not offer a structured program with separate admission and additional fees. Total undergraduates in learning-disabled program or receiving services: 100. Services include: tape recorders, other special classes, note-taking services, oral tests, learning center, readers, extended time for tests, tutors, priority registration, priority seating, substitution of courses, texts on tape, typist/scribe, exams on tape or computer, other testing accommodations, waiver of foreign language degree requirement, other. **Library:** Number of titles: 1,925,725; number of current serial subscriptions: 30,750. **Information technology resources:** Students are not required to lease or own a computer. Number of campus computers available to all students: 350. School has a wireless network. Approximate number of users that can be accommodated: 4,000. Proportion of college-owned housing units wired for high-speed internet access: 100%. **Campus safety:** Security services offered: 24-hour foot-and-vehicle patrols, late-night transport/escort service, 24-hour emergency telephones, lighted pathways/sidewalks, student patrols, controlled dormitory access (key, security card, etc).

TRANSFER AND INTERNATIONAL STUDENTS

Transfer students: May apply for admission for the following academic terms: Fall, Spring. Applicants need a minimum number of credits to apply. For fall 2009: Transfer applications received: 335. Transfer applicants offered admission: 84. Transfer applicants enrolled: 38. **International students:** Number of foreign undergraduates: 183 (6% of student body). Number of countries represented: 51. Minimum TOEFL score required: 600 (paper); 100 (computer). Average TOEFL score: 641 (paper).

Ohio Dominican University

- **Address:** 1216 Sunbury Road, Columbus, OH 43219
- **Website:** http://www.ohiodominican.edu
- **Private; Religious affiliation:** Roman Catholic
- **Enrollment:** 1,547 full-time; 733 part-time

KEY STATS
✔ **U.S News College Ranking:** 95, Regional Universities (Midwest)
✔ **ACT Score (25th/75th percentile):** 19-23
✔ **Tuition:** 2009-2010: $24,616

Selectivity: Selective	**Room/board:** $8,100
Acceptance rate: 59%	**Average debt:** N/A
Student/faculty ratio: N/A	**Proportion who borrowed:** N/A

UNDERGRADUATE STUDENT BODY STATS

2009-2010 enrollment: 1,547 full-time; 733 part-time. Men: 40%; women: 60%. **Ethnic makeup:** African American: 26%; Asian American: 1%; Hispanic: 2%; White: 70%; International: 1%. **Religious preference:** Protestant: 36%; Jewish: 1%; Muslim: 1%; No preference: 3%; Unknown: 7%; Roman Catholic: 40%; Other: 11%.

ADMISSIONS FACTS AND FIGURES

Phone: (614) 251-4500. **Email:** admissions@ohiodominican.edu. **Website:** http://www.ohiodominican.edu. **Application deadlines for fall 2011:** Regular decision: Rolling. Early decision: Not offered. Early action: Not offered. Admission can be deferred. **Application fee:** $25. **To apply online, go to:** https://www.ohiodominican.edu/admission/apply.asp. **Admissions requirements/recommendations:** High school units required (recommended): English: 4 (4); Mathematics: 3 (4); Science: 3 (3); Foreign language: 3 (3); Social studies: 3 (3); Total units: 16 (17). Tests: The college uses SAT or ACT scores in admissions decisions. Either SAT or ACT required. For admission to the fall 2011 entering class, the school will accept: ACT with or without writing accepted. Campus visit: Recommended. Admissions interview: Recommended. Off-campus interview: May be arranged. **Factors that count in admissions decisions:** *Academic:* Secondary school record: Very Important. Class rank: Considered. Letters of recommendation: Considered. Standardized test scores: Very Important. Essay: Considered. *Nonacademic:* Interview: Considered. Extracurricular activities: Considered. Talent/ability: Considered. Character/personal qualities: Considered. Alumni/ae relationship: Not Considered. Geographical residence: Not Considered. State residency: Not Considered. Religious affiliation/commitment: Not Considered. Minority status: Not Considered. Volunteer work: Considered. Work experience: Considered. **Admissions statistics for the fall 2009 entering class:** Total applicants: 2,367. Total accepted: 1,404. Freshmen enrolled: 283; 7% were from out of state. Overall acceptance rate: 59%. **Credentials of fall 2009 freshmen:** 13% ranked in the top 10 percent of their high school class; 34% were in the top 25 percent; 63% were in the top half. (Proportion submitting class standing: 80%.) **Average high school grade point average:** 3.0. **First-year students submitting ACT scores:** 93%. Scores (25/75 percentile): English: N/A, Math: N/A, Composite: 19-23.

ACADEMICS

Year founded: 1911. **Academic calendar:** Semester. **Degrees offered:** associate, bachelor's, master's. **Most popular majors:** 46% business administration and management, 11% junior high/intermediate/middle school education and teaching, 6% elementary education and teaching, 4% criminal justice/law enforcement administration, 4% sport and fitness administration/management. **Major fields of study:** biological and biomedical sciences; business, management, marketing, and related support services; communication, journalism, and related programs; computer and information sciences and support services; education; English language and literature/letters; history; liberal arts and sciences studies, and humanities; mathematics and statistics; parks, recreation, leisure, and fitness studies; philosophy and religious studies; physical sciences; psychology; public administration and social service professions; security and protective services; social sciences; theology and religious vocations; visual and performing arts. **Areas of required coursework:** arts/fine arts, mathematics, English (including composition), philosophy, foreign languages, sciences (biological or physical), social science, other. **Pre-professional programs:** pre-law, pre-dentistry, pre-medicine, pre-veterinary science, pre-optometry, pre-pharmacy, other. **Special academic programs:** cross-registration, distance learning, double major, dual enrollment, honors program, independent study, internships, study abroad, teacher certificate program, weekend college. **Teacher certification offered in:** early childhood, special education, elementary, middle/junior high, secondary. **Reserve Officers Training Corps (ROTC):** Army ROTC: Offered at cooperating institution (Capital University). **Faculty and instruction (2009-2010):** Total instructional faculty: 75 full-time, 130 part-time (52% men; 48% women; 8% minorities). Full-time faculty with Ph.D. or other terminal degree: 89%. Classes of fewer than 20 students: 62%; of 20 to 49 students: 38%; of 50 or more students: 0%. **Advanced Placement and International Baccalaureate credit:** AP tests may be used for: Credit and/or placement. Scores accepted: 3, 4, 5. International Baccalaureate exams may be used for: Credit and/or placement. **Freshmen returning for sophomore year:** 61%. **Graduation rates:** Four-year: 30%; five-year: 42%; six-year: 44%. **Graduate study:** 20% of students pursue further study immediately upon graduation.

COSTS AND FINANCIAL AID
Financial aid office: (614) 251-4778. **Expenses (2009-2010):** Tuition and fees 2009-2010: $24,616; room/board: $8,100. Estimated books and supplies: $1,000. **Financial aid:** Priority filing date for institution's financial aid form: April 6; deadline: June 6.

CAMPUS LIFE AND EXTRACURRICULAR ACTIVITIES
Campus housing available (% using): coed dorms (100%). Students who live in college-owned, operated, or affiliated housing: 25%. **Student employment:** During the 2009-2010 academic year, 35% of undergraduates worked on campus. Average per-year earnings: $2,500. **Clubs and organizations:** Number of student organizations: 40. Activities include: campus ministries, choral groups, dance, drama/theater, literary magazine, marching band, model UN, music ensembles, musical theater, pep band, radio station, student government, student newspaper. Number of fraternities: 0; sororities: 0. **Sports program (2009-2010):** Member of NAIA. *Men's intercollegiate varsity sports:* baseball, basketball, cross country, football, golf, soccer, tennis. *Women's intercollegiate varsity sports:* basketball, cross country, golf, soccer, softball, tennis, volleyball.

SERVICES AND FACILITIES
Basic services: nonremedial tutoring, placement service, health service. **Remedial assistance:** reading, math, writing, study skills. **Counseling services:** minority student, career, veteran student, academic, older student, psychological, religious. **For learning-disabled students:** School does not offer a structured program with separate admission and additional fees. Services include: remedial math, remedial English, reading machines, remedial reading, tape recorders, videotaped classes, untimed tests, note-taking services, special bookstore section, oral tests, learning center, readers, extended time for tests, tutors, priority seating, texts on tape, exams on tape or computer, other testing accommodations. **Library:** Number of titles: 128,788; number of current serial subscriptions: 8,408. **Information technology resources:** Students are not required to lease or own a computer. Number of campus computers available to all students: 425. School has a wireless network. Proportion of college-owned housing units wired for high-speed internet access: 100%. **Campus safety:** Security services offered: 24-hour foot-and-vehicle patrols, late-night transport/escort service, 24-hour emergency telephones, lighted pathways/sidewalks, controlled dormitory access (key, security card, etc).

TRANSFER AND INTERNATIONAL STUDENTS
Transfer students: May apply for admission for the following academic terms: Fall, Spring, Summer. Applicants need a minimum number of credits to apply. **International students:** Number of foreign undergraduates: 12 (1% of student body). Number of countries represented: 8. Minimum TOEFL score required: 550 (paper); 213 (computer). Average TOEFL score: 550 (paper).

Ohio Northern University

- **Address:** 525 S. Main Street, Ada, OH 45810
- **Website:** http://www.onu.edu
- **Private; Religious affiliation:** Methodist
- **Enrollment:** 2,431 full-time; 254 part-time

KEY STATS
✔ **U.S News College Ranking:** 3, Regional Colleges (Midwest)
✔ **ACT Score (25th/75th percentile):** 23-29
✔ **Tuition:** 2010-2011: $33,099

Selectivity: More selective	**Room/board:** $8,694
Acceptance rate: 76%	**Average debt:** $45,902
Student/faculty ratio: 12/1	**Proportion who borrowed:** 82%

UNDERGRADUATE STUDENT BODY STATS
2009-2010 enrollment: 2,431 full-time; 254 part-time. Men: 54%; women: 46%. **Ethnic makeup:** African American: 4%; American-Indian: 1%; Asian American: 1%; Hispanic: 2%; White: 90%; International: 2%. **Religious preference:** Roman Catholic: 27%; No preference: 28%; Methodist: 13%; Lutheran: 6%; Other: 26%.

ADMISSIONS FACTS AND FIGURES
Phone: (888) 408-4668. **Email:** admissions-ug@onu.edu. **Website:** http://www.onu.edu. **Application deadlines for fall 2011:** Regular decision: August 15. Early decision: Not offered. Early action: Not offered. Admission can be deferred. **Application fee:** $30. **To apply online, go to:** http://www-new.onu.edu/admissions/admission_to_onu/how_to_apply. **Admissions requirements/recommendations:** High school units required (recommended): English: 4 (4); Mathematics: 2 (4); Science: 2 (3); Foreign language: (2); Social studies: 2 (3); History: 2 (2); Academic electives: 4 (4); Total units: 16 (24). Tests: The college uses SAT or ACT scores in admissions decisions. Either SAT or ACT required. For admission to the fall 2011 entering class, the school will accept: ACT with or without writing accepted. Campus visit: Recommended. Admissions interview: Recommended. Off-campus interview: Not available. **Factors that count in admissions decisions:** *Academic:* Secondary school record: Very Important. Class rank: Important. Letters of recommendation: Important. Standardized test scores: Very Important. Essay: Important. *Nonacademic:* Interview: Important. Extracurricular activities: Important. Talent/ability: Considered. Character/personal qualities: Considered. Alumni/ae relationship: Considered. Geographical residence: Not Considered. State residency: Not Considered. Religious affiliation/commitment: Not Considered. Minority status: Not Considered. Volunteer work: Considered. Work experience: Not Considered. **Other schools with the greatest overlap in applicants:** Miami University–Oxford; Ohio State University–Columbus; Ohio University; University of Dayton; Wittenberg University. **Admissions statistics for the fall 2009 entering class:** Total applicants: 3,425. Total accepted: 2,592. Freshmen enrolled: 641; 14% were from out of state. Overall acceptance rate: 76%. **Credentials of fall 2009 freshmen:** 42% ranked in the top 10 percent of their high school class; 66% were in the top 25 percent; 90% were in the top half. (Proportion submitting class standing: 80%.) **Average high school grade point average:** 3.6. **First-year students who submitted SAT scores:** 42%. Scores (25/75 percentile): Critical Reading: 510-630, Math: 560-650, Combined: 1070-1280. **First-year students submitting ACT scores:** 93%. Scores (25/75 percentile): English: 22-29, Math: 24-29, Composite: 23-29.

ACADEMICS
Year founded: 1871. **Academic calendar:** Quarter. **Degrees offered:** bachelor's, post-bachelor's certificate. **Most popular majors:** 22% business, management, marketing, and related support services, 16% engineering, 11% biological and biomedical sciences, 9% health professions and related clinical sciences, 9% visual and performing arts. **Major fields of study:** biological and biomedical sciences; business, management, marketing, and related support services; communication, journalism, and related programs; computer and information sciences and support services; education; engineering; engineering technologies/technicians; English language and literature/letters; foreign languages, literatures, and linguistics; health professions and related clinical sciences; history; legal professions and studies; mathematics and statistics; natural resources and conservation; parks, recreation, leisure, and fitness studies; philosophy and religious studies; physical sciences; psychology; security and protective services; social sciences; theology and religious vocations; visual and performing arts. **Areas of required coursework:** arts/fine arts, humanities, computer literacy, mathematics, English

(including composition), philosophy, sciences (biological or physical), history, social science. **Pre-professional programs:** pre-law, pre-dentistry, pre-medicine, pre-theology, pre-veterinary science, pre-optometry, other. **Special academic programs:** cooperative (work-study plan) program, distance learning, double major, dual enrollment, English as a Second Language (ESL), exchange student program (domestic), honors program, independent study, internships, liberal arts/career combination, study abroad, teacher certificate program. **Teacher certification offered in:** early childhood, middle/junior high. **Cooperative education programs:** computer science, engineering, technologies, other. **Reserve Officers Training Corps (ROTC):** Army ROTC: Offered at cooperating institution (Bowling Green State University); Air Force ROTC: Offered at cooperating institution (Bowling Green State University). **Faculty and instruction (2009-2010):** Total instructional faculty: 242 full-time, 72 part-time (60% men; 40% women; 9% minorities). Full-time faculty with Ph.D. or other terminal degree: 75%. Student/faculty ratio: 12/1. Classes of fewer than 20 students: 57%; of 20 to 49 students: 40%; of 50 or more students: 3%. **Advanced Placement and International Baccalaureate credit:** AP tests may be used for: Credit and/or placement. Scores accepted: 3, 4, 5. International Baccalaureate exams may be used for: Credit and/or placement. **Freshmen returning for sophomore year:** 83%. **Graduation rates:** Four-year: 45%; five-year: 62%; six-year: 66%. **Graduate study:** 18% of students pursue further study immediately upon graduation; 22% within one year. Fields in which graduates pursue further study: Master of Business Administration (MBA), 7%; law, 7%; medicine, 45%; engineering, 7%; theology (or the seminary), 1%; education, 5%; arts and sciences, 26%; veterinary medicine, 1%.

COSTS AND FINANCIAL AID

Financial aid office: (419) 772-2272. **Expenses (2010-2011):** Tuition and fees 2010-2011: $33,099; room/board: $8,694. Estimated books and supplies: $1,800; transportation: $720; personal expenses: $1,200. **Financial aid:** Priority filing date for institution's financial aid form: April 15; deadline: June 1. In 2009-2010, 86% of undergraduates applied for financial aid. Of those, 78% were determined to have financial need; 16% had their need fully met. Average financial aid package (proportion receiving): $25,576 (78%). Average amount of gift aid, such as scholarships or grants (proportion receiving): $19,373 (55%). Average amount of self-help aid, such as work study or loans (proportion receiving): $8,838 (67%). Average need-based loan (excluding PLUS or other private loans): $8,021. Among students who received need-based aid, the average percentage of need met: 79%. Among students who received aid based on merit, the average award (and the proportion receiving): $16,294 (14%). The average athletic scholarship (and the proportion receiving): $0 (0%). Average amount of debt of borrowers graduating in 2009: $45,902. Proportion who borrowed: 82%.

CAMPUS LIFE AND EXTRACURRICULAR ACTIVITIES

Campus housing available (% using): coed dorms (58%), women's dorms (2%), men's dorms (2%), sorority housing (1%), fraternity housing (1%), apartments for married students (1%), apartment for single students (31%), special housing for disabled students (1%), cooperative housing, other housing options (1%). Students who live in college-owned, operated, or affiliated housing: 68%. **Clubs and organizations:** Number of student organizations: 160. Activities include: campus ministries, choral groups, concert band, dance, drama/theater, international student organization, jazz band, literary magazine, marching band, model UN, music ensembles, musical theater, opera, pep band, radio station, student government, student newspaper, symphony orchestra, television station, yearbook. Number of fraternities: 6; sororities: 4. Proportion of men in fraternities: 13%; of women in sororities: 13%. Average proportion of students who stay on campus on weekends: 70%. **Sports program (2009-2010):** Member of NCAA III. *Men's intercollegiate varsity sports:* baseball, basketball, cross country, football, golf, soccer, swimming, tennis, track and field (indoor), track and field (outdoor), wrestling. *Women's intercollegiate varsity sports:* basketball, cross country, golf, soccer, softball, swimming, tennis, track and field (indoor), track and field (outdoor), volleyball.

SERVICES AND FACILITIES

Basic services: nonremedial tutoring, placement service, day care, health service, health insurance. **Remedial assistance:** reading, math, writing, study skills. **Counseling services:** minority student, career, personal, academic, psychological, birth control, religious. **For learning-disabled students:** School does not offer a structured program with separate admission and additional fees. Services include: remedial math, remedial English, remedial reading, tape recorders, other special classes, untimed tests, note-taking services, oral tests, readers, extended time for tests, tutors, other. **Information technology resources:** Students are not required to lease or own a computer.

Number of campus computers available to all students: 503. School has a wireless network. Approximate number of users that can be accommodated: 2,000. Proportion of college-owned housing units wired for high-speed internet access: 100%. **Campus safety:** Security services offered: 24-hour foot-and-vehicle patrols, late-night transport/escort service, 24-hour emergency telephones, lighted pathways/sidewalks, controlled dormitory access (key, security card, etc).

TRANSFER AND INTERNATIONAL STUDENTS

Transfer students: May apply for admission for the following academic terms: Fall, Winter, Spring, Summer. Applicants do not need a minimum number of credits to apply. For fall 2009: Transfer applications received: 172. Transfer applicants offered admission: 80. Transfer applicants enrolled: 49. **International students:** Number of foreign undergraduates: 58 (2% of student body). Number of countries represented: 16. Minimum TOEFL score required: 550 (paper); 213 (computer).

Ohio State University–Columbus

- **Address:** 154 W. 12th Avenue, Columbus, OH 43210
- **Website:** http://www.osu.edu
- **Public**
- **Enrollment:** 37,864 full-time; 3,484 part-time

KEY STATS
✔ **U.S News College Ranking:** 56, National Universities
✔ **ACT Score (25th/75th percentile):** 25-30
✔ **Tuition:** 2009-2010: $8,706 in state, $22,278 out of state
  Selectivity: More selective **Room/board:** $8,409
  Acceptance rate: 76% **Average debt:** $18,426
  Student/faculty ratio: 15/1 **Proportion who borrowed:** 54%

UNDERGRADUATE STUDENT BODY STATS
2009-2010 enrollment: 37,864 full-time; 3,484 part-time. Men: 54%; women: 46%. **Ethnic makeup:** African American: 7%; Asian American: 5%; Hispanic: 3%; White: 81%; International: 4%.

ADMISSIONS FACTS AND FIGURES
Phone: (614) 292-3980. **Email:** askabuckeye@osu.edu. **Website:** http://www.osu.edu. **Application deadlines for fall 2011:** Regular decision: February 1. Early decision: Not offered. Early action: Not offered. Admission cannot be deferred. **Application fee:** $40. **To apply online, go to:** http://www.applyweb.com/apply/osu/index.html. **Admissions requirements/recommendations:** High school units required (recommended): English: 4 (4); Mathematics: 3 (4); Science: 2 (3); Foreign language: 2 (3); Social studies: 2 (3); Academic electives: 1 (1); Total units: 15 (19). Tests: The college uses SAT or ACT scores in admissions decisions. Either SAT or ACT required. For admission to the fall 2011 entering class, the school will accept: ACT with writing required. Campus visit: Recommended. Admissions interview: Neither required nor recommended. Off-campus interview: Not available. **Factors that count in admissions decisions:** *Academic:* Secondary school record: Very Important. Class rank: Very Important. Letters of recommendation: Very Important. Standardized test scores: Important. Essay: Considered. *Nonacademic:* Interview: Not Considered. Extracurricular activities: Important. Talent/ability: Important. Character/personal qualities: Considered. Alumni/ae relationship: Not Considered. Geographical residence: Considered. State residency: Considered. Religious affiliation/commitment: Not Considered. Minority status: Considered. Volunteer work: Important. Work experience: Important. **Other schools with the greatest overlap in applicants:** Case Western Reserve University; Miami University–Oxford; Ohio University; University of Cincinnati; University of Dayton. **Admissions statistics for the fall 2009 entering class:** Total applicants: 18,256. Total accepted: 13,822. Freshmen enrolled: 6,739; 15% were from out of state. Overall acceptance rate: 76%. **Size of waiting list:** 661 applicants; enrolled from waiting list: 10. **Credentials of fall 2009 freshmen:** 49% ranked in the top 10 percent of their high school class; 85% were in the top 25 percent; 99% were in the top half. (Proportion submitting class standing: 69%.) **First-year students who submitted SAT scores:** 51%. Scores (25/75 percentile): Critical Reading: 540-650, Math: 580-690, Combined: 1120-1340. **First-year students submitting ACT scores:** 86%. Scores (25/75 percentile): English: 25-31, Math: 25-30, Composite: 25-30.

ACADEMICS

Year founded: 1870. **Academic calendar:** Quarter. **Degrees offered:** diploma, associate, bachelor's, post-bachelor's certificate, master's, post-master's certificate, doctorate. **Most popular majors:** 6% psychology, 5% communication studies/speech communication and rhetoric, 4% marketing/marketing management, 3% English language and literature, 3% finance. **Major fields of study:** agriculture, agriculture operations, and related sciences; architecture and related services; area, ethnic, cultural, and gender studies; biological and biomedical sciences; business, management, marketing, and related support services; communication, journalism, and related programs; computer and information sciences and support services; education; engineering; engineering technologies/technicians; English language and literature/letters; family and consumer sciences/human sciences; foreign languages, literatures, and linguistics; health professions and related clinical sciences; history; legal professions and studies; liberal arts and sciences studies, and humanities; mathematics and statistics; multi/interdisciplinary studies; natural resources and conservation; parks, recreation, leisure, and fitness studies; philosophy and religious studies; physical sciences; psychology; public administration and social service professions; social sciences; transportation and materials moving; visual and performing arts. **Areas of required coursework:** arts/fine arts, humanities, mathematics, English (including composition), foreign languages, sciences (biological or physical), history, social science, other. **Pre-professional programs:** pre-law, pre-dentistry, pre-medicine, pre-veterinary science, pre-optometry, pre-pharmacy. **Special academic programs (% participation):** accelerated program, cooperative (work-study plan) program, cross-registration (0%), distance learning (46%), double major (6%), dual enrollment (2%), English as a Second Language (ESL) (2%), exchange student program (domestic), honors program (26%), independent study (19%), internships (26%), liberal arts/career combination, student-designed major (1%), study abroad (10%), teacher certificate program, weekend college. **Teacher certification offered in:** early childhood, middle/junior high, secondary, bilingual/bicultural. **Cooperative education programs:** agriculture, art, business, computer science, education, engineering, health professions, humanities, natural science, social/behavioral science, vocational arts. **Reserve Officers Training Corps (ROTC):** Army ROTC: Offered on campus; Navy ROTC: Offered on campus; Air Force ROTC: Offered on campus. **Faculty and instruction (2009-2010):** Total instructional faculty: 3,310 full-time, 1,158 part-time (64% men; 36% women; 19% minorities). Full-time faculty with Ph.D. or other terminal degree: 99%. Student/faculty ratio: 15/1. Classes of fewer than 20 students: 32%; of 20 to 49 students: 47%; of 50 or more students: 20%. **Advanced Placement and International Baccalaureate credit:** AP tests may be used for: Credit only. Scores accepted: 3, 4, 5. International Baccalaureate exams may be used for: Credit only. **Freshmen returning for sophomore year:** 93%. **Graduation rates:** Four-year: 46%; five-year: 71%; six-year: 75%.

COSTS AND FINANCIAL AID

Financial aid office: (614) 292-0300. **Expenses (2009-2010):** Tuition and fees 2009-2010: $8,706 in state, $22,278 out of state; room/board: $8,409. Estimated books and supplies: $1,383; transportation: $144; personal expenses: $3,996. **Financial aid:** Priority filing date for institution's financial aid form: February 15. In 2009-2010, 70% of undergraduates applied for financial aid. Of those, 55% were determined to have financial need; 17% had their need fully met. Average financial aid package (proportion receiving): $10,725 (55%). Average amount of gift aid, such as scholarships or grants (proportion receiving): $8,073 (33%). Average amount of self-help aid, such as work study or loans (proportion receiving): $5,498 (52%). Average need-based loan (excluding PLUS or other private loans): $4,671. Among students who received need-based aid, the average percentage of need met: 57%. Among students who received aid based on merit, the average award (and the proportion receiving): $4,645 (20%). The average athletic scholarship (and the proportion receiving): $18,656 (1%). Average amount of debt of borrowers graduating in 2009: $18,426. Proportion who borrowed: 54%.

CAMPUS LIFE AND EXTRACURRICULAR ACTIVITIES

Campus housing available (% using): coed dorms (80%), women's dorms (1%), sorority housing, fraternity housing, apartments for married students (4%), apartment for single students (10%), special housing for disabled students (2%), special housing for international students (1%), cooperative housing (2%), other housing options. Students who live in college-owned, operated, or affiliated housing: 24%. **Student employment:** During the 2009-2010 academic year, 20% of undergraduates worked on campus. **Clubs and organizations:** Number of student organizations: 950. Activities include: campus ministries, choral groups, concert band, dance, drama/theater, international student organization, jazz band, literary magazine, marching band, music ensembles, musical theater, opera, pep band, radio station, student government, student newspaper, student film society, symphony orchestra, television station, yearbook. Number of fraternities: 42; sororities: 25. Average proportion of students who stay on campus on weekends: 25%. **Sports program (2009-2010):** Member of NCAA I. *Men's intercollegiate varsity sports:* baseball, basketball, cross country, fencing, football, golf, gymnastics, ice hockey, lacrosse, rifle, soccer, swimming, tennis, track and field (outdoor), volleyball, wrestling. *Women's intercollegiate varsity sports:* cross country, fencing, field hockey, golf, gymnastics, ice hockey, lacrosse, rifle, soccer, softball, swimming, sync swimming, tennis, track and field (outdoor), volleyball.

SERVICES AND FACILITIES

Basic services: nonremedial tutoring, women's center, day care, health service, health insurance. **Remedial assistance:** reading, math, writing, study skills. **Counseling services:** minority student, career, military, personal, veteran student, academic, older student, psychological, birth control. **For learning-disabled students:** School does not offer a structured program with separate admission and additional fees. Services include: remedial math, remedial English, reading machines, diagnostic testing service, note-taking services, oral tests, learning center, readers, extended time for tests, tutors, priority registration, priority seating, substitution of courses, texts on tape, typist/scribe, exams on tape or computer, other testing accommodations, other. **Library:** Number of titles: 6,206,443; number of current serial subscriptions: 79,751. **Information technology resources:** Students are not required to lease or own a computer. Number of campus computers available to all students: 675. School has a wireless network. Approximate number of users that can be accommodated: 60,000. Proportion of college-owned housing units wired for high-speed internet access: 100%. **Campus safety:** Security services offered: 24-hour foot-and-vehicle patrols, late-night transport/escort service, 24-hour emergency telephones, lighted pathways/sidewalks, controlled dormitory access (key, security card, etc).

TRANSFER AND INTERNATIONAL STUDENTS

Transfer students: May apply for admission for the following academic terms: Fall, Winter, Spring, Summer. Applicants do not need a minimum number of credits to apply. For fall 2009: Transfer applications received: 3,906. Transfer applicants offered admission: 3,373. Transfer applicants enrolled: 2,072. **International students:** Number of foreign undergraduates: 1516 (4% of student body). Number of countries represented: 76. Minimum TOEFL score required: 527 (paper); 71 (computer). Average TOEFL score: 562 (paper).

Ohio University

- **Address:** Athens, OH 45701
- **Website:** http://www.ohio.edu
- **Public**
- **Enrollment:** 16,523 full-time; 2,066 part-time

KEY STATS

✔ **U.S News College Ranking:** 124, National Universities
✔ **ACT Score (25th/75th percentile):** 21-26
✔ **Tuition:** 2010-2011: $9,537 in state, $18,501 out of state

Selectivity: Selective	**Room/board:** $10,680
Acceptance rate: 82%	**Average debt:** $22,095
Student/faculty ratio: 19/1	**Proportion who borrowed:** 66%

UNDERGRADUATE STUDENT BODY STATS

2009-2010 enrollment: 16,523 full-time; 2,066 part-time. Men: 48%; women: 52%. **Ethnic makeup:** African American: 5%; Asian American: 1%; Hispanic: 2%; White: 88%; International: 3%. **Religious preference:** Roman Catholic: 37%; Protestant: 44%; Jewish: 2%; No preference: 11%.

ADMISSIONS FACTS AND FIGURES

Phone: (740) 593-4100. **Email:** admissions@ohio.edu. **Website:** http://www.ohio.edu. **Application deadlines for fall 2011:** Regular decision: February 1. Early decision: Not offered. Early action: Not offered. Admission can be deferred. **Application fee:** $45. **To apply online, go to:** http://www.applyweb.com/aw?ohiou. **Admissions requirements/recommendations:** High school units required (recommended): English: 4; Mathematics: 3; Science: 3; Foreign language: 2; Social studies: 3; Total units: 16. Tests: The college uses SAT or ACT scores in admissions decisions. Either SAT or ACT required. For admission to the fall 2011 entering class, the school will accept: ACT with or without writing accepted. Campus visit: Recommended. Admissions interview: Neither required nor recommended. Off-campus interview: Not available. **Factors that count in admissions decisions:** *Academic:* Secondary school record: Very Important. Class rank: Important. Letters of recommendation: Considered. Standardized test scores: Important. Essay: Considered. *Nonacademic:* Interview: Not Considered. Extracurricular activities: Considered. Talent/ability: Considered. Character/personal qualities: Considered. Alumni/ae relationship: Considered. Geographical residence: Not Considered. State residency: Not Considered. Religious affiliation/commitment: Not Considered. Minority status: Not Considered. Volunteer work: Considered. Work experience: Considered. **Other schools with the greatest overlap in applicants:** Bowling Green State University; Kent State University; Miami University–Oxford; Ohio State University–Columbus; University of Cincinnati. **Admissions statistics for the fall 2009 entering class:** Total applicants: 14,204. Total accepted: 11,591. Freshmen enrolled: 4,072; 9% were from out of state. Overall acceptance rate: 82%. **Size of waiting list:** 419 applicants; enrolled from waiting list: 131. **Credentials of fall 2009 freshmen:** 16% ranked in the top 10 percent of their high school class; 44% were in the top 25 percent; 83% were in the top half. (Proportion submitting class standing: 76%.) **Average high school grade point average:** 3.4. **First-year students who submitted SAT scores:** 44%. Scores (25/75 percentile): Critical Reading: 480-600, Math: 490-600, Combined: 970-1200. **First-year students submitting ACT scores:** 89%. Scores (25/75 percentile): English: 20-26, Math: 20-26, Composite: 21-26.

ACADEMICS

Year founded: 1804. **Academic calendar:** Quarter. **Degrees offered:** associate, bachelor's, master's, doctorate. **Most popular majors:** 6% journalism, 6% parks, recreation, and leisure studies, 5% speech and rhetorical studies, 4% psychology, 4% radio and television. **Major fields of study:** area, ethnic, cultural, and gender studies; biological and biomedical sciences; business, management, marketing, and related support services; communication, journalism, and related programs; computer and information sciences and support services; education; engineering; engineering technologies/technicians; English language and literature/letters; family and consumer sciences/human sciences; foreign languages, literatures, and linguistics; health professions and related clinical sciences; history; liberal arts and sciences studies, and humanities; mathematics and statistics; parks, recreation, leisure, and fitness studies; philosophy and religious studies; physical sciences; psychology; public administration and social service professions; social sciences; transportation and materials moving; visual and performing arts. **Areas of required coursework:** arts/fine arts, humanities, mathematics, English (including composition), philosophy, foreign languages, sciences (biological or physical), history, social science, other. **Pre-professional programs:** pre-law, pre-dentistry, pre-medicine, pre-theology, pre-veterinary science, pre-optometry, pre-pharmacy, other. **Special academic programs (% participation):** accelerated program (1%), cooperative (work-study plan) program (3%), distance learning (5%), double major (8%), dual enrollment (.4%), English as a Second Language (ESL) (.7%), external degree program (2%), honors program (1%), independent study (1%), internships (11%), liberal arts/career combination (2%), student-designed major (1%), study abroad (18%), teacher certificate program (7%). **Teacher certification offered in:** early childhood, special education, elementary, middle/junior high, secondary. **Cooperative education programs:** business, education, engineering, health professions, home economics. **Reserve Officers Training Corps (ROTC):** Army ROTC: Offered on campus; Air Force ROTC: Offered on campus. **Faculty and instruction (2009-2010):** Total instructional faculty: 907 full-time, 294 part-time (61% men; 39% women; 15% minorities). Full-time faculty with Ph.D. or other terminal degree: 86%. Student/faculty ratio: 19/1. Classes of fewer than 20 students: 45%; of 20 to 49 students: 45%; of 50 or more students: 10%. **Advanced Placement and International Baccalaureate credit:** AP tests may be used for: Placement only. Scores accepted: 3. International Baccalaureate exams may be used for: Credit only. **Freshmen returning for sophomore year:** 80%. **Graduation rates:** Four-year: 48%; five-year: 67%; six-year: 69%. **Graduate study:** 28% of students pursue further study within one year; 36% within five years. Fields in which graduates pursue further study: Master of Business Administration (MBA), 2%; law, 2%; medicine, 2%; engineering, 1%; education, 7%; arts and sciences, 10%.

COSTS AND FINANCIAL AID

Financial aid office: (740) 593-4141. **Expenses (2010-2011):** Tuition and fees 2010-2011: $9,537 in state, $18,501 out of state; room/board: $10,680. Estimated books and supplies: $873; transportation: $1,710; personal expenses: $1,017. **Financial aid:** Priority filing date for institution's finan-

cial aid form: March 15. In 2009-2010, 77% of undergraduates applied for financial aid. Of those, 55% were determined to have financial need; 15% had their need fully met. Average financial aid package (proportion receiving): $8,484 (55%). Average amount of gift aid, such as scholarships or grants (proportion receiving): $7,145 (51%). Average amount of self-help aid, such as work study or loans (proportion receiving): $4,418 (48%). Average need-based loan (excluding PLUS or other private loans): $4,287. Among students who received need-based aid, the average percentage of need met: 58%. Among students who received aid based on merit, the average award (and the proportion receiving): $2,291 (12%). The average athletic scholarship (and the proportion receiving): $17,634 (2%). Average amount of debt of borrowers graduating in 2009: $22,095. Proportion who borrowed: 66%.

CAMPUS LIFE AND EXTRACURRICULAR ACTIVITIES

Campus housing available (% using): coed dorms (79%), women's dorms (2%), sorority housing (5%), fraternity housing (3%), apartments for married students (1%). Students who live in college-owned, operated, or affiliated housing: 45%. **Student employment:** During the 2009-2010 academic year, 42% of undergraduates worked on campus. Average per-year earnings: $1,359. **Clubs and organizations:** Number of student organizations: 323. Activities include: campus ministries, choral groups, concert band, dance, drama/theater, international student organization, jazz band, literary magazine, marching band, music ensembles, musical theater, opera, pep band, radio station, student government, student newspaper, student film society, symphony orchestra, television station, yearbook. Number of fraternities: 17; sororities: 12. Proportion of men in fraternities: 9%; of women in sororities: 13%. Average proportion of students who stay on campus on weekends: 90%. **Sports program (2009-2010):** Member of NCAA I. *Men's intercollegiate varsity sports:* baseball, basketball, cross country, football, golf, wrestling. *Women's intercollegiate varsity sports:* basketball, cross country, field hockey, golf, soccer, softball, swimming, track and field (indoor), track and field (outdoor), volleyball.

SERVICES AND FACILITIES

Basic services: nonremedial tutoring, women's center, placement service, health service, health insurance, other. **Remedial assistance:** reading, math, writing, study skills. **Counseling services:** minority student, career, military, personal, veteran student, academic, psychological, birth control, religious, other. **For learning-disabled students:** School does not offer a structured program with separate admission and additional fees. Total undergraduates in learning-disabled program or receiving services: 857. Services include: remedial math, remedial English, reading machines, remedial reading, tape recorders, diagnostic testing service, note-taking services, oral tests, learning center, readers, extended time for tests, tutors, priority registration, priority seating, texts on tape, typist/scribe, other testing accommodations. **Library:** Number of titles: 2,958,684; number of current serial subscriptions: 46,823. **Information technology resources:** Students are not required to lease or own a computer. Number of campus computers available to all students: 3,000. School has a wireless network. Approximate number of users that can be accommodated: 26,000. Proportion of college-owned housing units wired for high-speed internet access: 100%. **Campus safety:** Security services offered: 24-hour foot-and-vehicle patrols, late-night transport/escort service, 24-hour emergency telephones, lighted pathways/sidewalks, controlled dormitory access (key, security card, etc).

TRANSFER AND INTERNATIONAL STUDENTS

Transfer students: May apply for admission for the following academic terms: Fall, Winter, Spring, Summer. Applicants need a minimum number of credits to apply. For fall 2009: Transfer applications received: 1,416. Transfer applicants offered admission: 1,073. Transfer applicants enrolled: 578. **International students:** Number of foreign undergraduates: 590 (3% of student body). Average TOEFL score: 550 (paper).

Ohio Wesleyan University

- **Address:** 61 S. Sandusky Street, Delaware, OH 43015
- **Website:** http://web.owu.edu
- **Private; Religious affiliation:** Methodist
- **Enrollment:** 1,869 full-time; 24 part-time

KEY STATS
- ✔ **U.S News College Ranking:** 105, National Liberal Arts Colleges
- ✔ **ACT Score (25th/75th percentile):** 23-29
- ✔ **Tuition:** 2010-2011: $36,398
- **Selectivity:** More selective   **Room/board:** $9,276
- **Acceptance rate:** 64%   **Average debt:** $30,954
- **Student/faculty ratio:** 11/1   **Proportion who borrowed:** 74%

UNDERGRADUATE STUDENT BODY STATS
2009-2010 enrollment: 1,869 full-time; 24 part-time. Men: 46%; women: 54%. **Ethnic makeup:** African American: 5%; American-Indian: 1%; Asian American: 2%; Hispanic: 2%; White: 82%; International: 9%.

ADMISSIONS FACTS AND FIGURES
Phone: (740) 368-3020. **Email:** owuadmit@owu.edu. **Website:** http://web.owu.edu. **Application deadlines for fall 2011:** Regular decision: Rolling; decision sent by March 1. Early decision: Not offered. Early action: Send application by: December 15; Decision sent by: January 15. Admission can be deferred. **Application fee:** $35. **To apply online, go to:** http://admission.owu.edu/apps.html. **Admissions requirements/recommendations:** High school units required (recommended): English: 4; Mathematics: 3 (4); Science: 3 (4); Foreign language: 2 (3); Social studies: 3 (4); Total units: 15. Tests: The college uses SAT or ACT scores in admissions decisions. Either SAT or ACT required. For admission to the fall 2011 entering class, the school will accept: ACT with or without writing accepted. Campus visit: Recommended. Admissions interview: Recommended. Off-campus interview: May be arranged. **Factors that count in admissions decisions:** *Academic:* Secondary school record: Very Important. Class rank: Important. Letters of recommendation: Very Important. Standardized test scores: Important. Essay: Very Important. *Nonacademic:* Interview: Very Important. Extracurricular activities: Important. Talent/ability: Important. Character/personal qualities: Very Important. Alumni/ae relationship: Considered. Geographical residence: Considered. State residency: Not Considered. Religious affiliation/commitment: Not Considered. Minority status: Considered. Volunteer work: Considered. Work experience: Considered. **Other schools with the greatest overlap in applicants:** College of Wooster; Denison University; Miami University–Oxford; Ohio State University–Columbus; Wittenberg University. **Admissions statistics for the fall 2009 entering class:** Total applicants: 4,210. Total accepted: 2,691. Freshmen enrolled: 498; 48% were from out of state. Overall acceptance rate: 64%. Non-early acceptance rate: 64%. **Size of waiting list:** 59 applicants; enrolled from waiting list: 12. **Credentials of fall 2009 freshmen:** 38% ranked in the top 10 percent of their high school class; 63% were in the top 25 percent; 88% were in the top half. (Proportion submitting class standing: 51%.) **Average high school grade point average:** 3.5. **First-year students who submitted SAT scores:** 65%. Scores (25/75 percentile): Critical Reading: 520-660; Math: 520-660; Combined: 1040-1320. **First-year students submitting ACT scores:** 67%. Scores (25/75 percentile): English: 23-30, Math: 22-29, Composite: 23-29.

ACADEMICS
Year founded: 1842. **Academic calendar:** Semester. **Degrees offered:** bachelor's. **Most popular majors:** 18% social sciences, 13% biological and biomedical sciences, 11% business, management, marketing, and related support services, 9% psychology, 7% visual and performing arts. **Major fields of study:** area, ethnic, cultural, and gender studies; biological and biomedical sciences; business, management, marketing, and related support services; communication, journalism, and related programs; computer and information sciences and support services; education; English language and literature/letters; foreign languages, literatures, and linguistics; health professions and related clinical sciences; history; legal professions and studies; liberal arts and sciences studies, and humanities; mathematics and statistics; multi/interdisciplinary studies; natural resources and conservation; parks, recreation, leisure, and fitness studies; philosophy and religious studies; physical sciences; psychology; public administration and social service professions; social sciences; theology and religious vocations; visual and performing arts. **Areas of required coursework:** arts/fine arts, humanities, English (including composition), foreign languages, sciences (biological

or physical), social science, other. **Pre-professional programs:** pre-law, pre-dentistry, pre-medicine, pre-theology, pre-veterinary science, pre-optometry, other. **Special academic programs:** double major, dual enrollment, exchange student program (domestic), honors program, independent study, internships, student-designed major, study abroad, teacher certificate program. **Teacher certification offered in:** early childhood, elementary, middle/junior high, secondary. **Reserve Officers Training Corps (ROTC):** Army ROTC: Offered at cooperating institution (Capital University); Air Force ROTC: Offered at cooperating institution (Ohio State University–Columbus). **Faculty and instruction (2009-2010):** Total instructional faculty: 138 full-time, 76 part-time (58% men; 42% women; 6% minorities). Full-time faculty with Ph.D. or other terminal degree: 99%. Student/faculty ratio: 11/1. Classes of fewer than 20 students: 68%; of 20 to 49 students: 32%; of 50 or more students: 0%. **Advanced Placement and International Baccalaureate credit:** AP tests may be used for: Placement only. Scores accepted: 4, 5. International Baccalaureate exams may be used for: Placement only. **Freshmen returning for sophomore year:** 81%. **Graduation rates:** Four-year: 51%; five-year: 58%; six-year: 60%. **Graduate study:** 32% of students pursue further study immediately upon graduation; 32% within one year; 52% within five years. Fields in which graduates pursue further study: Master of Business Administration (MBA), 10%; law, 13%; medicine, 7%; dentistry, 3%; engineering, 4%; education, 7%; arts and sciences, 25%; veterinary medicine, 3%.

COSTS AND FINANCIAL AID
Financial aid office: (740) 368-3050. **Expenses (2010-2011):** Tuition and fees 2010-2011: $36,398; room/board: $9,276. Estimated books and supplies: $2,100; transportation: $306. **Financial aid:** Priority filing date for institution's financial aid form: March 1; deadline: May 1. In 2009-2010, 67% of undergraduates applied for financial aid. Of those, 58% were determined to have financial need; 25% had their need fully met. Average financial aid package (proportion receiving): $28,014 (58%). Average amount of gift aid, such as scholarships or grants (proportion receiving): $22,841 (57%). Average amount of self-help aid, such as work study or loans (proportion receiving): $6,625 (47%). Average need-based loan (excluding PLUS or other private loans): $5,378. Among students who received need-based aid, the average percentage of need met: 85%. Among students who received aid based on merit, the average award (and the proportion receiving): $16,509 (39%). The average athletic scholarship (and the proportion receiving): $0 (0%). Average amount of debt of borrowers graduating in 2009: $30,954. Proportion who borrowed: 74%.

CAMPUS LIFE AND EXTRACURRICULAR ACTIVITIES
Campus housing available: coed dorms, women's dorms, fraternity housing, apartment for single students, special housing for international students, other housing options. Students who live in college-owned, operated, or affiliated housing: 81%. **Student employment:** During the 2009-2010 academic year, 50% of undergraduates worked on campus. Average per-year earnings: $1,500. **Clubs and organizations:** Number of student organizations: 95. Activities include: choral groups, dance, drama/theater, jazz band, literary magazine, music ensembles, musical theater, opera, pep band, radio station, student government, student newspaper, symphony orchestra, yearbook. Number of fraternities: 6; sororities: 7. Proportion of men in fraternities: 21%; of women in sororities: 20%. Average proportion of students who stay on campus on weekends: 75%. **Sports program (2009-2010):** Member of NCAA III. **Men's intercollegiate varsity sports:** baseball, basketball, cross country, football, golf, lacrosse, soccer, swimming, tennis, track and field (indoor), track and field (outdoor). **Women's intercollegiate varsity sports:** basketball, cross country, field hockey, lacrosse, soccer, softball, swimming, tennis, track and field (indoor), track and field (outdoor), volleyball.

SERVICES AND FACILITIES
Basic services: nonremedial tutoring, placement service, health service, health insurance. **Counseling services:** minority student, career, personal, academic, psychological, birth control, religious. **For learning-disabled students:** School does not offer a structured program with separate admission and additional fees. Services include: remedial math, remedial English, tape recorders, other special classes, note-taking services, oral tests, learning center, extended time for tests, tutors, texts on tape, other. **Library:** Number of titles: 460,109; number of current serial subscriptions: 9,045. **Information technology resources:** Students are not required to lease or own a computer. Number of campus computers available to all students: 300. School has a wireless network. Approximate number of users that can be accommodated: 100. Proportion of college-owned housing units wired for high-speed internet access: 100%. **Campus safety:** Security services offered: 24-hour foot-and-vehicle patrols, late-night transport/escort service, 24-hour emergency

telephones, lighted pathways/sidewalks, student patrols, controlled dormitory access (key, security card, etc).

TRANSFER AND INTERNATIONAL STUDENTS
Transfer students: May apply for admission for the following academic terms: Fall, Spring. Applicants need a minimum number of credits to apply. For fall 2009: Transfer applications received: 115. Transfer applicants offered admission: 41. Transfer applicants enrolled: 17. **International students:** Number of foreign undergraduates: 170 (9% of student body). Number of countries represented: 37. Minimum TOEFL score required: 550 (paper); 213 (computer).

Otterbein College

■ **Address:** 1 Otterbein College, Westerville, OH 43081
■ **Website:** http://www.otterbein.edu
■ **Private; Religious affiliation:** United Methodist
■ **Enrollment:** 2,268 full-time; 374 part-time

KEY STATS
✔ **U.S News College Ranking:** 16, Regional Universities (Midwest)
✔ **ACT Score (25th/75th percentile):** 20-26
✔ **Tuition:** 2009-2010: $27,321

Selectivity: Selective	**Room/board:** $7,605
Acceptance rate: 78%	**Average debt:** N/A
Student/faculty ratio: 12/1	**Proportion who borrowed:** N/A

UNDERGRADUATE STUDENT BODY STATS
2009-2010 enrollment: 2,268 full-time; 374 part-time. Men: 36%; women: 64%. **Ethnic makeup:** African American: 7%; Asian American: 1%; Hispanic: 2%; White: 89%. **Religious preference:** Roman Catholic: 22%; Protestant: 4%; Jewish: 1%; Muslim: 1%; Unknown: 25%; United Methodist: 18%; Baptist: 8%; Other: 21%.

ADMISSIONS FACTS AND FIGURES
Phone: (614) 823-1500. **Email:** UOtterB@Otterbein.edu. **Website:** http://www.otterbein.edu. **Application deadlines for fall 2011:** Regular decision: Rolling. Early decision: Not offered. Early action: Not offered. Admission can be deferred. **Application fee:** $25. **To apply online, go to:** http://www.otterbein.edu/Admission/Applying/application.asp. **Admissions requirements/recommendations:** High school units required (recommended): English: 4 (4); Mathematics: 3 (4); Science: 3 (4); Foreign language: 2 (4); Social studies: 3 (4); History: 2 (2); Academic electives: 0 (0); Total units: 17 (22). Tests: The college uses SAT or ACT scores in admissions decisions. Either SAT or ACT required. For admission to the fall 2011 entering class, the school will accept: ACT with or without writing accepted. Campus visit: Recommended. Admissions interview: Recommended. Off-campus interview: May be arranged. **Factors that count in admissions decisions:** *Academic:* Secondary school record: Very Important. Class rank: Important. Letters of recommendation: Important. Standardized test scores: Very Important. Essay: Important. *Nonacademic:* Interview: Considered. Extracurricular activities: Important. Talent/ability: Important. Character/personal qualities: Important. Alumni/ae relationship: Important. Geographical residence: Considered. State residency: Not Considered. Religious affiliation/commitment: Not Considered. Minority status: Not Considered. Volunteer work: Important. Work experience: Considered. **Other schools with the greatest overlap in applicants:** Capital University; Miami University–Oxford; Ohio State University–Columbus; Ohio University. **Admissions statistics for the fall 2009 entering class:** Total applicants: 3,653. Total accepted: 2,859. Freshmen enrolled: 643; 10% were from out of state. Overall acceptance rate: 78%. **Credentials of fall 2009 freshmen:** 27% ranked in the top 10 percent of their high school class; 55% were in the top 25 percent; 82% were in the top half. (Proportion submitting class standing: 81%.) **Average high school grade point average:** 3.4. **First-year students who submitted SAT scores:** 33%. Scores (25/75 percentile): Critical Reading: 470-590, Math: 470-570, Combined: 940-1160. **First-year students submitting ACT scores:** 92%. Scores (25/75 percentile): English: 20-26, Math: 19-26, Composite: 20-26.

ACADEMICS
Year founded: 1847. **Academic calendar:** Quarter. **Degrees offered:** bachelor's, master's, post-master's certificate. **Major fields of study:** agriculture, agriculture operations, and related sciences; biological and biomedical

sciences; business, management, marketing, and related support services; communication, journalism, and related programs; computer and information sciences and support services; English language and literature/letters; foreign languages, literatures, and linguistics; health professions and related clinical sciences; history; liberal arts and sciences studies, and humanities; mathematics and statistics; natural resources and conservation; parks, recreation, leisure, and fitness studies; philosophy and religious studies; physical sciences; psychology; social sciences. **Areas of required coursework:** arts/fine arts, humanities, computer literacy, mathematics, English (including composition), philosophy, foreign languages, sciences (biological or physical), history, social science, other. **Pre-professional programs:** pre-law, pre-dentistry, pre-medicine, pre-theology, pre-veterinary science, pre-optometry. **Special academic programs (% participation):** accelerated program (5%), cross-registration (1%), distance learning (5%), double major (10%), dual enrollment (1%), English as a Second Language (ESL), exchange student program (domestic) (1%), honors program (5%), independent study (3%), internships (2%), liberal arts/career combination (10%), student-designed major (1%), study abroad (2%), teacher certificate program (12%), weekend college (1%). **Teacher certification offered in:** early childhood, elementary, middle/junior high, secondary. **Reserve Officers Training Corps (ROTC):** Army ROTC: Offered at cooperating institution (Capital University); Navy ROTC: Offered at cooperating institution (Capital University); Air Force ROTC: Offered at cooperating institution (Capital University). **Faculty and instruction (2009-2010):** Total instructional faculty: 164 full-time, 157 part-time (44% men; 56% women; 10% minorities). Full-time faculty with Ph.D. or other terminal degree: 96%. Student/faculty ratio: 12/1. Classes of fewer than 20 students: 73%; of 20 to 49 students: 24%; of 50 or more students: 3%. **Advanced Placement and International Baccalaureate credit:** AP tests may be used for: Placement only. Scores accepted: 3, 4, 5. International Baccalaureate exams may be used for: Placement only. **Freshmen returning for sophomore year:** 75%. **Graduation rates:** Four-year: 50%; five-year: 60%; six-year: 62%. **Graduate study:** 21% of students pursue further study immediately upon graduation; 38% within one year; 47% within five years. Fields in which graduates pursue further study: Master of Business Administration (MBA), 10%; law, 5%; medicine, 10%; dentistry, 6%; education, 30%; arts and sciences, 35%; veterinary medicine, 4%.

COSTS AND FINANCIAL AID
Financial aid office: (614) 823-1502. **Expenses (2009-2010):** Tuition and fees 2009-2010: $27,321; room/board: $7,605. Estimated books and supplies: $1,068; transportation: $834; personal expenses: $1,509. **Financial aid:** Priority filing date for institution's financial aid form: April 1; deadline: June 1.

CAMPUS LIFE AND EXTRACURRICULAR ACTIVITIES
Campus housing available (% using): coed dorms (52%), women's dorms (24%), men's dorms (8%), sorority housing (0%), fraternity housing (0%), apartment for single students (13%), special housing for disabled students, other housing options (0%). Students who live in college-owned, operated, or affiliated housing: 52%. **Student employment:** During the 2009-2010 academic year, 12% of undergraduates worked on campus. Average per-year earnings: $880. **Clubs and organizations:** Number of student organizations: 105. Activities include: choral groups, concert band, dance, drama/theater, international student organization, jazz band, literary magazine, marching band, music ensembles, musical theater, opera, pep band, radio station, student government, student newspaper, symphony orchestra, television station, yearbook. Number of fraternities: 7; sororities: 6. Proportion of men in fraternities: 5%; of women in sororities: 5%. Average proportion of students who stay on campus on weekends: 39%. **Sports program (2009-2010):** Member of NCAA III. *Men's intercollegiate varsity sports:* baseball, basketball, cross country, football, golf, soccer, tennis, track and field (indoor). *Women's intercollegiate varsity sports:* basketball, cross country, golf, soccer, softball, tennis, track and field (indoor), volleyball.

SERVICES AND FACILITIES
Basic services: nonremedial tutoring, women's center, placement service, health service, health insurance, other. **Remedial assistance:** reading, math, writing, study skills. **Counseling services:** minority student, career, personal, veteran student, academic, older student, psychological, religious. **For learning-disabled students:** School does not offer a structured program with separate admission and additional fees. Services include: remedial math, remedial reading, tape recorders, note-taking services, oral tests, learning center, readers, extended time for tests, tutors, priority registration, priority seating, texts on tape, other testing accommodations. **Library:** Number of titles: 260,069; number of current serial subscriptions: 9,722. **Information technology resources:** Students are not required to lease or own a computer.

Number of campus computers available to all students: 190. School has a wireless network. Approximate number of users that can be accommodated: 1,000. Proportion of college-owned housing units wired for high-speed internet access: 100%. **Campus safety:** Security services offered: 24-hour foot-and-vehicle patrols, late-night transport/escort service, 24-hour emergency telephones, lighted pathways/sidewalks, controlled dormitory access (key, security card, etc).

TRANSFER AND INTERNATIONAL STUDENTS

Transfer students: May apply for admission for the following academic terms: Fall, Winter, Spring, Summer. Applicants need a minimum number of credits to apply. For fall 2009: Transfer applications received: 391. Transfer applicants offered admission: 160. Transfer applicants enrolled: 60. **International students:** Number of foreign undergraduates: 11. Number of countries represented: 12. Minimum TOEFL score required: 523 (paper); 193 (computer).

Shawnee State University

- **Address:** 940 Second Street, Portsmouth, OH 45662
- **Website:** http://www.shawnee.edu
- **Public**
- **Enrollment:** 3,533 full-time; 687 part-time

KEY STATS

✔ **U.S News College Ranking:** 71, Regional Colleges (Midwest)
✔ **ACT Score (25th/75th percentile):** 17-23
✔ **Tuition:** 2010-2011: $6,546 in state, $11,190 out of state

Selectivity: Selective	**Room/board:** $8,416
Acceptance rate: 84%	**Average debt:** N/A
Student/faculty ratio: 18/1	**Proportion who borrowed:** N/A

UNDERGRADUATE STUDENT BODY STATS

2009-2010 enrollment: 3,533 full-time; 687 part-time. Men: 42%; women: 58%. **Ethnic makeup:** African American: 4%; American-Indian: 1%; White: 94%; International: 1%.

ADMISSIONS FACTS AND FIGURES

Phone: (800) 959-2778. **Email:** To_SSU@shawnee.edu. **Website:** http://www.shawnee.edu. **Application deadlines for fall 2011:** Regular decision: Rolling. Early decision: Not offered. Early action: Not offered. Admission can be deferred. **To apply online, go to:** https://myssu.shawnee.edu/ics/. **Admissions requirements/recommendations:** High school units required (recommended): English: (4); Mathematics: (3); Science: (3); Foreign language: (2); Social studies: (3); Total units: (16). Tests: The college uses SAT or ACT scores in admissions decisions. Neither SAT nor ACT required. For admission to the fall 2011 entering class, the school will accept: ACT with or without writing accepted. Campus visit: Recommended. Admissions interview: Neither required nor recommended. Off-campus interview: Not available. **Factors that count in admissions decisions:** *Academic:* Secondary school record: Not Considered. Class rank: Not Considered. Letters of recommendation: Not Considered. Standardized test scores: Not Considered. Essay: Not Considered. *Nonacademic:* Interview: Not Considered. Extracurricular activities: Not Considered. Talent/ability: Not Considered. Character/personal qualities: Not Considered. Alumni/ae relationship: Not Considered. Geographical residence: Not Considered. State residency: Not Considered. Religious affiliation/commitment: Not Considered. Minority status: Not Considered. Volunteer work: Not Considered. Work experience: Not Considered. **Other schools with the greatest overlap in applicants:** Ohio State University–Columbus; Ohio University. **Admissions statistics for the fall 2009 entering class:** Total applicants: 3,785. Total accepted: 3,179. Freshmen enrolled: 1,130; 8% were from out of state. Overall acceptance rate: 84%. **Credentials of fall 2009 freshmen:** 12% ranked in the top 10 percent of their high school class; 34% were in the top 25 percent; 65% were in the top half. (Proportion submitting class standing: 86%.) **First-year students submitting ACT scores:** 78%. Scores (25/75 percentile): English: 16-23, Math: 16-23, Composite: 17-23.

ACADEMICS

Year founded: 1986. **Academic calendar:** Semester. **Degrees offered:** certificate, associate, bachelor's, master's. **Most popular majors:** 15% business administration and management, 9% nursing/registered nurse training (R.N., A.S.N., B.S.N., M.S.N.), 8% art/art studies, 8% psychology, 8% sport

and fitness administration/management. **Major fields of study:** biological and biomedical sciences; business, management, marketing, and related support services; education; engineering technologies/technicians; English language and literature/letters; health professions and related clinical sciences; history; legal professions and studies; liberal arts and sciences studies, and humanities; mathematics and statistics; parks, recreation, leisure, and fitness studies; physical sciences; psychology; social sciences; visual and performing arts. **Areas of required coursework:** arts/fine arts, humanities, mathematics, English (including composition), philosophy, sciences (biological or physical), social science. **Pre-professional programs:** pre-medicine. **Special academic programs (% participation):** distance learning (2%), double major (10%), dual enrollment (3%), English as a Second Language (ESL), honors program, independent study (2%), internships, student-designed major, study abroad, teacher certificate program. **Faculty and instruction (2009-2010):** Total instructional faculty: 151 full-time, 171 part-time (52% men; 48% women; 4% minorities). Full-time faculty with Ph.D. or other terminal degree: 57%. Student/faculty ratio: 18/1. Classes of fewer than 20 students: 57%; of 20 to 49 students: 40%; of 50 or more students: 4%. **Advanced Placement and International Baccalaureate credit:** AP tests may be used for: Credit and/or placement. Scores accepted: 3, 4, 5. International Baccalaureate exams may be used for: Credit and/or placement. **Freshmen returning for sophomore year:** 57%. **Graduation rates:** Four-year: 15%; five-year: 22%; six-year: 26%. **Graduate study:** 15% of students pursue further study immediately upon graduation; 9% within one year. Fields in which graduates pursue further study: Master of Business Administration (MBA), 10%; law, 6%; medicine, 17%; engineering, 3%; education, 14%; arts and sciences, 27%.

COSTS AND FINANCIAL AID

Financial aid office: (740) 351-4243. **Expenses (2010-2011):** Tuition and fees 2010-2011: $6,546 in state, $11,190 out of state; room/board: $8,416. Estimated books and supplies: $1,440; transportation: $800; personal expenses: $2,260.

CAMPUS LIFE AND EXTRACURRICULAR ACTIVITIES

Campus housing available (% using): coed dorms (100%). Students who live in college-owned, operated, or affiliated housing: 21%. **Student employment:** During the 2009-2010 academic year, 2% of undergraduates worked on campus. Average per-year earnings: $7,400. **Clubs and organizations:** Number of student organizations: 31. Activities include: campus ministries, choral groups, drama/theater, literary magazine, music ensembles, musical theater, student government, student newspaper, symphony orchestra. Number of fraternities: 2; sororities: 2. Proportion of men in fraternities: 1%; of women in sororities: 1%. Average proportion of students who stay on campus on weekends: 80%. **Sports program (2009-2010):** Member of NAIA. **Men's intercollegiate varsity sports:** baseball, basketball, cross country, golf, soccer. **Women's intercollegiate varsity sports:** basketball, cross country, soccer, softball, tennis, volleyball.

SERVICES AND FACILITIES

Basic services: nonremedial tutoring, women's center, placement service, day care, health service. **Remedial assistance:** reading, math, writing, study skills. **Counseling services:** minority student, career, military, personal, veteran student, academic, older student, psychological. **For learning-disabled students:** School does not offer a structured program with separate admission and additional fees. Total undergraduates in learning-disabled program or receiving services: 168. Services include: remedial math, remedial English, reading machines, remedial reading, tape recorders, other special classes, untimed tests, note-taking services, oral tests, learning center, readers, extended time for tests, tutors, priority registration, texts on tape. **Library:** Number of titles: 144,595; number of current serial subscriptions: 8,148. **Information technology resources:** Students are not required to lease or own a computer. Number of campus computers available to all students: 620. School has a wireless network. Approximate number of users that can be accommodated: 1,200. Proportion of college-owned housing units wired for high-speed internet access: 100%. **Campus safety:** Security services offered: 24-hour foot-and-vehicle patrols, late-night transport/escort service, 24-hour emergency telephones, lighted pathways/sidewalks, controlled dormitory access (key, security card, etc).

TRANSFER AND INTERNATIONAL STUDENTS

Transfer students: May apply for admission for the following academic terms: Fall, Spring, Summer. Applicants do not need a minimum number of credits to apply. For fall 2009: Transfer applications received: 695. Transfer applicants offered admission: 424. Transfer applicants enrolled: 214. **International students:** Number of foreign undergraduates: 29 (1% of student body). Number of countries represented: 14. Minimum TOEFL score required: 500 (paper); 207 (computer). Average TOEFL score: 420 (paper).

Tiffin University

- **Address:** 155 Miami Street, Tiffin, OH 44883
- **Website:** http://www.tiffin.edu
- **Private**
- **Enrollment:** 1,853 full-time; 522 part-time

KEY STATS

✔ **U.S News College Ranking:** second tier, Regional Universities (Midwest)
✔ **ACT Score (25th/75th percentile):** 18-23
✔ **Tuition:** 2010-2011: $18,390

Selectivity: Selective	**Room/board:** $8,340
Acceptance rate: 60%	**Average debt:** $26,345
Student/faculty ratio: 19/1	**Proportion who borrowed:** 82%

UNDERGRADUATE STUDENT BODY STATS

2009-2010 enrollment: 1,853 full-time; 522 part-time. Men: 44%; women: 56%. **Ethnic makeup:** African American: 19%; Asian American: 1%; Hispanic: 3%; White: 74%; International: 3%.

ADMISSIONS FACTS AND FIGURES

Phone: (419) 448-3423. **Email:** admiss@tiffin.edu. **Website:** http://www.tiffin.edu. **Application deadlines for fall 2011:** Regular decision: Rolling. Early decision: Not offered. Early action: Not offered. Admission cannot be deferred. **Application fee:** $20. **To apply online, go to:** http://www.tiffin.edu/apply. **Admissions requirements/recommendations:** High school units required (recommended): English: 4; Mathematics: 3; Science: 3; Foreign language: 0; Social studies: 3; History: 0; Academic electives: 0; Total units: 13 (2). Tests: The college uses SAT or ACT scores in admissions decisions. Either SAT or ACT required. For admission to the fall 2011 entering class, the school will accept: ACT with or without writing accepted. Campus visit: Recommended. Admissions interview: Recommended. Off-campus interview: May be arranged. **Factors that count in admissions decisions:** *Academic:* Secondary school record: Very Important. Class rank: Important. Letters of recommendation: Important. Standardized test scores: Very Important. Essay: Important. *Nonacademic:* Interview: Considered. Extracurricular activities: Important. Talent/ability: Considered. Character/personal qualities: Considered. Alumni/ae relationship: Considered. Geographical residence: Important. State residency: Important. Religious affiliation/commitment: Not Considered. Minority status: Considered. Volunteer work: Considered. Work experience: Not Considered. **Other schools with the greatest overlap in applicants:** Ashland University; Bowling Green State University; Ohio State University–Columbus; University of Findlay; University of Toledo. **Admissions statistics for the fall 2009 entering class:** Total applicants: 3,526. Total accepted: 2,101. Freshmen enrolled: 673; 46% were from out of state. Overall acceptance rate: 60%. **Credentials of fall 2009 freshmen:** 8% ranked in the top 10 percent of their high school class; 30% were in the top 25 percent; 64% were in the top half. (Proportion submitting class standing: 82%.) **Average high school grade point average:** 3.1. **First-year students who submitted SAT scores:** 14%. Scores (25/75 percentile): Critical Reading: 430-528, Math: 433-528, Combined: 863-1056. **First-year students submitting ACT scores:** 88%. Scores (25/75 percentile): English: 17-22, Math: 17-23, Composite: 18-23.

ACADEMICS

Year founded: 1888. **Academic calendar:** Semester. **Degrees offered:** certificate, associate, bachelor's, post-bachelor's certificate, master's. **Most popular majors:** 51% business administration and management, 33% criminal justice/law enforcement administration, 6% psychology, 2% computer and information sciences. **Major fields of study:** business, management, marketing, and related support services; communication, journalism, and related programs; computer and information sciences and support services; English language and literature/letters; liberal arts and sciences studies, and humanities; multi/interdisciplinary studies; parks, recreation, leisure, and fitness studies; psychology; public administration and social service professions; security and protective services; social sciences; visual and performing arts. **Areas of required coursework:** arts/fine arts, humanities, computer literacy, mathematics, English (including composition), philosophy, history, social science. **Special academic programs (% participation):** acceler-

ated program (50%), cross-registration, distance learning (50%), double major (4%), dual enrollment, English as a Second Language (ESL), honors program (5%), independent study (4%), internships (35%), study abroad (1%), teacher certificate program (1%). **Cooperative education programs:** education. **Reserve Officers Training Corps (ROTC):** Army ROTC: Offered at cooperating institution (Bowling Green State University); Air Force ROTC: Offered at cooperating institution (Bowling Green State University). **Faculty and instruction (2009-2010):** Total instructional faculty: 66 full-time, 226 part-time (52% men; 48% women; 15% minorities). Full-time faculty with Ph.D. or other terminal degree: 67%. Student/faculty ratio: 19/1. Classes of fewer than 20 students: 67%; of 20 to 49 students: 33%; of 50 or more students: 0%. **Advanced Placement and International Baccalaureate credit:** AP tests may be used for: Credit and/or placement. Scores accepted: 3, 4, 5. International Baccalaureate exams may be used for: Placement only. **Freshmen returning for sophomore year:** 64%. **Graduation rates:** Four-year: 36%; five-year: 41%; six-year: 38%. **Graduate study:** 14% of students pursue further study immediately upon graduation. Fields in which graduates pursue further study: Master of Business Administration (MBA), 25%; law, 1%.

COSTS AND FINANCIAL AID

Financial aid office: (419) 448-3357. **Expenses (2010-2011):** Tuition and fees 2010-2011: $18,390; room/board: $8,340. Estimated books and supplies: $1,500; transportation: $2,000; personal expenses: $2,700. **Financial aid:** Priority filing date for institution's financial aid form: January 15. In 2009-2010, 97% of undergraduates applied for financial aid. Of those, 90% were determined to have financial need; 5% had their need fully met. Average financial aid package (proportion receiving): $13,569 (90%). Average amount of gift aid, such as scholarships or grants (proportion receiving): $5,747 (63%). Average amount of self-help aid, such as work study or loans (proportion receiving): $4,403 (80%). Average need-based loan (excluding PLUS or other private loans): $3,986. Among students who received need-based aid, the average percentage of need met: 5%. Among students who received aid based on merit, the average award (and the proportion receiving): $6,870 (4%). The average athletic scholarship (and the proportion receiving): $5,831 (2%). Average amount of debt of borrowers graduating in 2009: $26,345. Proportion who borrowed: 82%.

CAMPUS LIFE AND EXTRACURRICULAR ACTIVITIES

Campus housing available (% using): coed dorms (55%), women's dorms (10%), men's dorms (15%), sorority housing (2%), fraternity housing (2%), apartments for married students, apartment for single students (3%), special housing for disabled students, special housing for international students (8%), other housing options (5%). Students who live in college-owned, operated, or affiliated housing: 38%. **Student employment:** During the 2009-2010 academic year, 15% of undergraduates worked on campus. Average per-year earnings: $1,000. **Clubs and organizations:** Number of student organizations: 32. Activities include: campus ministries, choral groups, concert band, dance, drama/theater, international student organization, jazz band, literary magazine, marching band, music ensembles, musical theater, pep band, student government, student newspaper, student film society. Number of fraternities: 2; sororities: 3. Proportion of men in fraternities: 1%; of women in sororities: 1%. Average proportion of students who stay on campus on weekends: 65%. **Sports program (2009-2010):** Member of NCAA II. *Men's intercollegiate varsity sports:* baseball, basketball, cross country, football, golf, soccer, tennis, track and field (indoor), track and field (outdoor). *Women's intercollegiate varsity sports:* basketball, cross country, equestrian, golf, lacrosse, soccer, softball, tennis, track and field (indoor), track and field (outdoor), volleyball.

SERVICES AND FACILITIES

Basic services: nonremedial tutoring, women's center, placement service, health service, health insurance. **Remedial assistance:** reading, math, writing, study skills. **Counseling services:** minority student, career, military, personal, academic, older student, psychological, birth control, other. **For learning-disabled students:** School does not offer a structured program with separate admission and additional fees. Total undergraduates in learning-disabled program or receiving services: 39. Services include: remedial math, remedial English, oral tests, learning center, extended time for tests, tutors, other testing accommodations. **Library:** Number of titles: 40,003; number of current serial subscriptions: 155. **Information technology resources:** Students are not required to lease or own a computer. Number of campus computers available to all students: 120. School has a wireless network. Proportion of college-owned housing units wired for high-speed internet access: 100%. **Campus safety:** Security services offered: 24-hour emergency telephones, lighted pathways/sidewalks, student patrols, controlled dormitory access (key, security card, etc).

TRANSFER AND INTERNATIONAL STUDENTS

Transfer students: May apply for admission for the following academic terms: Fall, Spring. Applicants need a minimum number of credits to apply. For fall 2009: Transfer applications received: 722. Transfer applicants offered admission: 373. Transfer applicants enrolled: 340. **International students:** Number of foreign undergraduates: 78 (3% of student body). Number of countries represented: 21. Minimum TOEFL score required: 500 (paper); 61 (computer). Average TOEFL score: 567 (paper).

Union Institute and University

- **Address:** 440 E. McMillan Street, Cincinnati, OH 45206
- **Website:** http://www.myunion.edu
- **Private**
- **Enrollment:** 656 full-time; 306 part-time

KEY STATS

✔ **U.S News College Ranking:** Unranked, National Universities
✔ **SAT or ACT Score (25th/75th percentile):** N/A
✔ **Tuition:** 2009-2010: $11,012

Selectivity: N/A	**Room/board:** $11,508
Acceptance rate: N/A	**Average debt:** N/A
Student/faculty ratio: 12/1	**Proportion who borrowed:** N/A

UNDERGRADUATE STUDENT BODY STATS

2009-2010 enrollment: 656 full-time; 306 part-time. Men: 40%; women: 60%. **Ethnic makeup:** African American: 30%; American-Indian: 1%; Asian American: 2%; Hispanic: 13%; White: 54%.

ADMISSIONS FACTS AND FIGURES

Phone: (513) 487-1239. **Email:** admissions@myunion.edu. **Website:** http://www.myunion.edu. **Application deadlines for fall 2011:** Regular decision: Rolling. Early decision: Not offered. Early action: Not offered. Admission can be deferred. **Application fee:** $35. **To apply online, go to:** http://www.myunion.edu/admissions/index.html. **Admissions requirements/recommendations:** Tests: The college does not use SAT or ACT scores in admissions decisions. Neither SAT nor ACT required. Campus visit: Neither required nor recommended. Admissions interview: Required. Off-campus interview: May be arranged. **Factors that count in admissions decisions:** *Academic:* Secondary school record: Not Considered. Class rank: Not Considered. Letters of recommendation: Important. Standardized test scores: Not Considered. Essay: Very Important. *Nonacademic:* Interview: Very Important. Extracurricular activities: Considered. Talent/ability: Considered. Character/personal qualities: Considered. Alumni/ae relationship: Not Considered. Geographical residence: Not Considered. State residency: Not Considered. Religious affiliation/commitment: Not Considered. Minority status: Not Considered. Volunteer work: Considered. Work experience: Considered. **Admissions statistics for the fall 2009 entering class:** Freshmen enrolled: 28;

ACADEMICS

Year founded: 1964. **Academic calendar:** Trimester. **Degrees offered:** bachelor's, post-bachelor's certificate, master's, post-master's certificate, doctorate. **Most popular majors:** 47% criminal justice/law enforcement administration, 24% liberal arts and sciences/liberal studies. **Major fields of study:** business, management, marketing, and related support services; communication, journalism, and related programs; education; health professions and related clinical sciences; liberal arts and sciences studies, and humanities; psychology; public administration and social service professions; security and protective services; social sciences. **Areas of required coursework:** arts/fine arts, humanities, mathematics, English (including composition), sciences (biological or physical), social science. **Special academic programs (% participation):** cross-registration (0%), distance learning (15%), independent study (85%), teacher certificate program (15%). **Teacher certification offered in:** special education, elementary, secondary. **Faculty and instruction (2009-2010):** Total instructional faculty: 35 full-time, 280 part-time (41% men; 59% women; 19% minorities). Full-time faculty with Ph.D. or other terminal degree: 91%. Student/faculty ratio: 12/1. Classes of fewer than 20 students: 98%; of 20 to 49 students: 1%; of 50 or more students: 0%. **Advanced Placement and International Baccalaureate credit:** AP tests may be used for: Credit only. International Baccalaureate exams may be used for: Credit only. **Freshmen returning for sophomore year:** 73%. **Graduation rates:** Four-year: 21%; five-year: 29%; six-year: 42%.

COSTS AND FINANCIAL AID

Financial aid office: (513) 487-1127. **Expenses (2009-2010):** Tuition and fees 2009-2010: $11,012; room/board: $11,508. Estimated books and supplies: $1,000. **Financial aid:** Priority filing date for institution's financial aid form: March 15; deadline: June 4.

CAMPUS LIFE AND EXTRACURRICULAR ACTIVITIES

Number of fraternities: 0; sororities: 0.

SERVICES AND FACILITIES

Counseling services: career, academic. **For learning-disabled students:** School does not offer a structured program with separate admission and additional fees. Services include: tape recorders, other special classes, untimed tests, oral tests, readers, extended time for tests. **Information technology resources:** Students are not required to lease or own a computer. Number of campus computers available to all students: 75. School does not have a wireless network. **Campus safety:** Security services offered: late-night transport/escort service, lighted pathways/sidewalks.

TRANSFER AND INTERNATIONAL STUDENTS

Transfer students: May apply for admission for the following academic terms: Fall, Winter, Spring, Summer. Applicants do not need a minimum number of credits to apply. For fall 2009: Transfer applicants enrolled: 274. **International students:** Number of foreign undergraduates: 0.

University of Akron

- **Address:** 302 Buchtel Common, Akron, OH 44325
- **Website:** http://www.uakron.edu
- **Public**
- **Enrollment:** 16,632 full-time; 4,695 part-time

KEY STATS

✔ **U.S News College Ranking:** second tier, National Universities
✔ **ACT Score (25th/75th percentile):** 18-24
✔ **Tuition:** 2009-2010: $8,752 in state, $18,000 out of state

Selectivity: Selective	**Room/board:** $8,697
Acceptance rate: 76%	**Average debt:** $19,000
Student/faculty ratio: 20/1	**Proportion who borrowed:** 65%

UNDERGRADUATE STUDENT BODY STATS

2009-2010 enrollment: 16,632 full-time; 4,695 part-time. Men: 51%; women: 49%. **Ethnic makeup:** African American: 15%; Asian American: 2%; Hispanic: 1%; White: 81%; International: 1%.

ADMISSIONS FACTS AND FIGURES

Phone: (330) 972-7077. **Email:** admissions@uakron.edu. **Website:** http://www.uakron.edu. **Application deadlines for fall 2011:** Regular decision: August 9. Early decision: Not offered. Early action: Send application by: November 1; Decision sent by: December 15. Admission can be deferred. **Application fee:** $30. **To apply online, go to:** http://www.uakron.edu/admissions. **Admissions requirements/recommendations:** High school units required (recommended): English: 4 (4); Mathematics: 3 (3); Science: 3 (3); Foreign language: 2 (2); Social studies: 3 (3); Total units: 15 (15). Tests: The college uses SAT or ACT scores in admissions decisions. Either SAT or ACT required. For admission to the fall 2011 entering class, the school will accept: ACT with or without writing accepted. Campus visit: Recommended. Admissions interview: Neither required nor recommended. Off-campus interview: May be arranged. **Factors that count in admissions decisions:** *Academic:* Secondary school record: Very Important. Class rank: Very Important. Letters of recommendation: Not Considered. Standardized test scores: Very Important. Essay: Not Considered. *Nonacademic:* Interview: Not Considered. Extracurricular activities: Not Considered. Talent/ability: Not Considered. Character/personal qualities: Not Considered. Alumni/ae relationship: Not Considered. Geographical residence: Not Considered. State residency: Not Considered. Religious affiliation/commitment: Not Considered. Minority status: Not Considered. Volunteer work: Not Considered. Work experience: Not Considered. **Other schools with the greatest overlap in applicants:** Bowling Green State University; Kent State University; Ohio State University–Columbus; Ohio University; University of Toledo. **Admissions statistics for the fall 2009 entering class:** Total applicants: 13,492. Total accepted: 10,243. Freshmen enrolled: 4,252; 4% were from out of state. Overall acceptance rate: 76%. Non-early acceptance rate:

76%. **Credentials of fall 2009 freshmen:** 11% ranked in the top 10 percent of their high school class; 28% were in the top 25 percent; 57% were in the top half. (Proportion submitting class standing: 74%.) **Average high school grade point average:** 3.0. **First-year students who submitted SAT scores:** 19%. Scores (25/75 percentile): Critical Reading: 430-560, Math: 430-590, Combined: 860-1150. **First-year students submitting ACT scores:** 94%. Scores (25/75 percentile): English: 16-24, Math: 17-24, Composite: 18-24.

ACADEMICS

Year founded: 1870. **Academic calendar:** Semester. **Degrees offered:** certificate, associate, bachelor's, post-bachelor's certificate, master's, post-master's certificate, doctorate. **Most popular majors:** 20% business, management, marketing, and related support services, 16% health professions and related clinical sciences, 11% education, 10% communication, journalism, and related programs, 7% engineering. **Major fields of study:** architecture and related services; biological and biomedical sciences; business, management, marketing, and related support services; communication, journalism, and related programs; computer and information sciences and support services; education; engineering; engineering technologies/technicians; English language and literature/letters; family and consumer sciences/human sciences; foreign languages, literatures, and linguistics; health professions and related clinical sciences; history; liberal arts and sciences studies, and humanities; mathematics and statistics; multi/interdisciplinary studies; parks, recreation, leisure, and fitness studies; philosophy and religious studies; physical sciences; psychology; public administration and social service professions; security and protective services; social sciences; visual and performing arts. **Areas of required coursework:** arts/fine arts, humanities, computer literacy, mathematics, English (including composition), foreign languages, sciences (biological or physical), history, social science, other. **Pre-professional programs:** pre-law, pre-medicine, pre-pharmacy. **Special academic programs (% participation):** accelerated program, cooperative (work-study plan) program (10%), distance learning (30%), double major (4%), dual enrollment (2%), English as a Second Language (ESL), external degree program, honors program (8%), independent study (11%), internships (19%), student-designed major, study abroad, teacher certificate program (18%), weekend college. **Teacher certification offered in:** early childhood, special education, elementary, vo-tech, middle/junior high, secondary. **Cooperative education programs:** art, business, computer science, engineering, health professions, humanities, natural science, social/behavioral science, technologies. **Reserve Officers Training Corps (ROTC):** Army ROTC: Offered on campus; Air Force ROTC: Offered at cooperating institution (Kent State University). **Faculty and instruction (2009-2010):** Total instructional faculty: 768 full-time, 924 part-time (52% men; 48% women; 11% minorities). Full-time faculty with Ph.D. or other terminal degree: 82%. Student/faculty ratio: 20/1. Classes of fewer than 20 students: 39%; of 20 to 49 students: 55%; of 50 or more students: 6%. **Advanced Placement and International Baccalaureate credit:** AP tests may be used for: Credit and/or placement. Scores accepted: 3, 4, 5. International Baccalaureate exams may be used for: Credit only. **Freshmen returning for sophomore year:** 68%. **Graduation rates:** Four-year: 11%; five-year: 26%; six-year: 33%. **Graduate study:** 11% of students pursue further study immediately upon graduation.

COSTS AND FINANCIAL AID

Financial aid office: (330) 972-7032. **Expenses (2009-2010):** Tuition and fees 2009-2010: $8,752 in state, $18,000 out of state; room/board: $8,697. **Financial aid:** Priority filing date for institution's financial aid form: February 1. In 2009-2010, 87% of undergraduates applied for financial aid. Of those, 70% were determined to have financial need; 8% had their need fully met. Average financial aid package (proportion receiving): $7,641 (70%). Average amount of gift aid, such as scholarships or grants (proportion receiving): $5,227 (39%). Average amount of self-help aid, such as work study or loans (proportion receiving): $3,973 (58%). Average need-based loan (excluding PLUS or other private loans): $3,973. Among students who received need-based aid, the average percentage of need met: 52%. Among students who received aid based on merit, the average award (and the proportion receiving): $3,802 (8%). The average athletic scholarship (and the proportion receiving): $8,946 (1%). Average amount of debt of borrowers graduating in 2009: $19,000. Proportion who borrowed: 65%.

CAMPUS LIFE AND EXTRACURRICULAR ACTIVITIES

Campus housing available (% using): coed dorms (54%), women's dorms (4%), men's dorms (0%), sorority housing, fraternity housing, apartment for single students (17%), special housing for disabled students, special housing for international students, other housing options (14%). Students who live in college-owned, operated, or affiliated housing: 15%. **Student employment:** During the 2009-2010 academic year, 11% of undergraduates

worked on campus. Average per-year earnings: $5,800. **Clubs and organizations:** Number of student organizations: 216. Activities include: campus ministries, choral groups, concert band, dance, drama/theater, international student organization, jazz band, marching band, music ensembles, musical theater, pep band, radio station, student government, student newspaper, symphony orchestra, television station, yearbook. Number of fraternities: 15; sororities: 8. Proportion of men in fraternities: 3%; of women in sororities: 3%. Average proportion of students who stay on campus on weekends: 30%. **Sports program (2009-2010):** Member of NCAA I. *Men's intercollegiate varsity sports:* baseball, basketball, cross country, football, golf, rifle, soccer, track and field (indoor), track and field (outdoor). *Women's intercollegiate varsity sports:* basketball, cross country, rifle, soccer, softball, tennis, track and field (indoor), track and field (outdoor), volleyball.

SERVICES AND FACILITIES

Basic services: nonremedial tutoring, women's center, placement service, day care, health service, health insurance. **Remedial assistance:** reading, math, writing, study skills. **Counseling services:** minority student, career, military, personal, veteran student, academic, older student, psychological, birth control, religious. **For learning-disabled students:** School does not offer a structured program with separate admission and additional fees. Services include: remedial math, remedial English, reading machines, remedial reading, tape recorders, diagnostic testing service, note-taking services, oral tests, readers, extended time for tests, priority registration, priority seating, texts on tape, other testing accommodations, other. **Library:** Number of titles: 1,273,976; number of current serial subscriptions: 11,337. **Information technology resources:** Students are not required to lease or own a computer. Number of campus computers available to all students: 3,100. School has a wireless network. Approximate number of users that can be accommodated: 4,080. Proportion of college-owned housing units wired for high-speed internet access: 100%. **Campus safety:** Security services offered: 24-hour foot-and-vehicle patrols, late-night transport/escort service, 24-hour emergency telephones, lighted pathways/sidewalks, student patrols, controlled dormitory access (key, security card, etc).

TRANSFER AND INTERNATIONAL STUDENTS

Transfer students: May apply for admission for the following academic terms: Fall, Spring, Summer. Applicants do not need a minimum number of credits to apply. For fall 2009: Transfer applications received: 2,662. Transfer applicants offered admission: 1,619. Transfer applicants enrolled: 959. **International students:** Number of foreign undergraduates: 209 (1% of student body). Number of countries represented: 50. Minimum TOEFL score required: 500 (paper); 173 (computer).

University of Cincinnati

- ■ **Address:** PO Box 210063, Cincinnati, OH 45221-0063
- ■ **Website:** http://www.uc.edu
- ■ **Public**
- ■ **Enrollment:** 18,247 full-time; 3,637 part-time

KEY STATS

✔ **U.S News College Ranking:** 156, National Universities
✔ **ACT Score (25th/75th percentile):** 22-27
✔ **Tuition:** 2010-2011: $9,399 in state, $23,922 out of state
  Selectivity: More selective   **Room/board:** $9,702
  Acceptance rate: 67%   **Average debt:** $25,878
  Student/faculty ratio: 16/1   **Proportion who borrowed:** 69%

UNDERGRADUATE STUDENT BODY STATS

2009-2010 enrollment: 18,247 full-time; 3,637 part-time. Men: 50%; women: 50%. **Ethnic makeup:** African American: 10%; Asian American: 3%; Hispanic: 2%; White: 83%; International: 2%.

ADMISSIONS FACTS AND FIGURES

Phone: (513) 556-1100. **Email:** admissions@uc.edu. **Website:** http://www.uc.edu. **Application deadlines for fall 2011:** Regular decision: June 1. Early decision: Not offered. Early action: Not offered. Admission can be deferred. **Application fee:** $50. **To apply online, go to:** http://www.admissions.uc.edu/apply/default.html. **Admissions requirements/recommendations:** High school units required (recommended): English: 4; Mathematics: 3 (4); Science: 2 (3); Foreign language: 2; Social studies: 2; History: (1); Academic electives: 2; Total units: 16. Tests: The college uses SAT or ACT scores in admissions decisions. Either SAT or ACT required. For admission to the fall 2011 entering class, the school will accept: ACT with writing required. Campus visit: Recommended. Admissions interview: Neither required nor recommended. Off-campus interview: Not available. **Factors that count in admissions decisions:** *Academic:* Secondary school record: Very Important. Class rank: Very Important. Letters of recommendation: Not Considered. Standardized test scores: Very Important. Essay: Considered. *Nonacademic:* Interview: Not Considered. Extracurricular activities: Considered. Talent/ability: Not Considered. Character/personal qualities: Not Considered. Alumni/ae relationship: Not Considered. Geographical residence: Not Considered. State residency: Not Considered. Religious affiliation/commitment: Not Considered. Minority status: Not Considered. Volunteer work: Not Considered. Work experience: Not Considered. **Admissions statistics for the fall 2009 entering class:** Total applicants: 15,088. Total accepted: 10,086. Freshmen enrolled: 3,647; 8% were from out of state. Overall acceptance rate: 67%. **Credentials of fall 2009 freshmen:** 22% ranked in the top 10 percent of their high school class; 49% were in the top 25 percent; 82% were in the top half. (Proportion submitting class standing: 73%.) **Average high school grade point average:** 3.4. **First-year students who submitted SAT scores:** 53%. Scores (25/75 percentile): Critical Reading: 490-610, Math: 520-640, Combined: 1010-1250. **First-year students submitting ACT scores:** 88%. Scores (25/75 percentile): English: 22-28, Math: 21-27, Composite: 22-27.

ACADEMICS

Year founded: 1819. **Academic calendar:** Quarter. **Degrees offered:** certificate, associate, transfer-associate, terminal-associate, bachelor's, post-bachelor's certificate, master's, post-master's certificate, doctorate. **Most popular majors:** 16% business, management, marketing, and related support services, 16% health professions and related clinical sciences, 10% engineering, 10% visual and performing arts, 7% education. **Major fields of study:** agriculture, agriculture operations, and related sciences; architecture and related services; area, ethnic, cultural, and gender studies; biological and biomedical sciences; business, management, marketing, and related support services; communication, journalism, and related programs; communications technologies/technicians and support services; computer and information sciences and support services; education; engineering; engineering technologies/technicians; English language and literature/letters; family and consumer sciences/human sciences; foreign languages, literatures, and linguistics; health professions and related clinical sciences; history; legal professions and studies; liberal arts and sciences studies, and humanities; mathematics and statistics; multi/interdisciplinary studies; natural resources and conservation; philosophy and religious studies; physical sciences; psychology; public administration and social service professions; security and protective services; social sciences; theology and religious vocations; visual and performing arts. **Pre-professional programs:** pre-law, pre-medicine, pre-pharmacy. **Special academic programs:** accelerated program, cooperative (work-study plan) program, distance learning, double major, English as a Second Language (ESL), honors program, independent study, internships, liberal arts/career combination, study abroad, teacher certificate program, weekend college. **Teacher certification offered in:** early childhood, special education, elementary, vo-tech, middle/junior high, adult education, secondary, bilingual/bicultural. **Cooperative education programs:** art, business, engineering, other. **Reserve Officers Training Corps (ROTC):** Army ROTC: Offered on campus; Air Force ROTC: Offered on campus. **Faculty and instruction (2009-2010):** Total instructional faculty: 1,187 full-time, 38 part-time (58% men; 42% women; 16% minorities). Full-time faculty with Ph.D. or other terminal degree: 55%. Student/faculty ratio: 16/1. Classes of fewer than 20 students: 39%; of 20 to 49 students: 52%; of 50 or more students: 10%. **Advanced Placement and International Baccalaureate credit:** AP tests may be used for: Placement only. International Baccalaureate exams may be used for: Placement only. **Freshmen returning for sophomore year:** 83%. **Graduation rates:** Four-year: 20%; five-year: 49%; six-year: 55%.

COSTS AND FINANCIAL AID

Financial aid office: (513) 556-6982. **Expenses (2010-2011):** Tuition and fees 2010-2011: $9,399 in state, $23,922 out of state; room/board: $9,702. Estimated books and supplies: $1,275 personal expenses: $4,417. **Financial aid:** In 2009-2010, 72% of undergraduates applied for financial aid. Of those, 58% were determined to have financial need; 5% had their need fully met. Average financial aid package (proportion receiving): $7,843 (57%). Average amount of gift aid, such as scholarships or grants (proportion receiving): $5,883 (26%). Average amount of self-help aid, such as work study or loans (proportion receiving): $2,967 (10%). Average need-based loan (excluding PLUS or other private loans): $4,223. Among students who received need-based aid, the average percentage of need met: 63%. Among

students who received aid based on merit, the average award (and the proportion receiving): $4,755 (17%). The average athletic scholarship (and the proportion receiving): $17,049 (1%). Average amount of debt of borrowers graduating in 2009: $25,878. Proportion who borrowed: 69%.

CAMPUS LIFE AND EXTRACURRICULAR ACTIVITIES

Campus housing available: coed dorms, women's dorms, men's dorms, sorority housing, fraternity housing, apartments for married students, apartment for single students. Students who live in college-owned, operated, or affiliated housing: 20%. Activities include: choral groups, concert band, dance, drama/theater, jazz band, marching band, music ensembles, musical theater, opera, pep band, radio station, student government, student newspaper, student film society, symphony orchestra, yearbook. **Sports program (2009-2010):** Member of NCAA I. *Men's intercollegiate varsity sports:* baseball, basketball, cross country, football, golf, soccer, swimming, track and field (outdoor). *Women's intercollegiate varsity sports:* basketball, cross country, golf, lacrosse, soccer, swimming, tennis, track and field (indoor), track and field (outdoor), volleyball.

SERVICES AND FACILITIES

Basic services: women's center, day care, health service, health insurance. **Remedial assistance:** reading, math, writing, study skills. **Counseling services:** career, older student. **For learning-disabled students:** School does not offer a structured program with separate admission and additional fees. Total undergraduates in learning-disabled program or receiving services: 639. Services include: remedial math, remedial English, reading machines, remedial reading, tape recorders, diagnostic testing service, learning center, readers, extended time for tests, early syllabus, priority registration, substitution of courses, texts on tape, typist/scribe, exams on tape or computer, other testing accommodations. **Information technology resources:** Students are not required to lease or own a computer. **Campus safety:** Security services offered: 24-hour foot-and-vehicle patrols, late-night transport/escort service, 24-hour emergency telephones, lighted pathways/sidewalks, controlled dormitory access (key, security card, etc).

TRANSFER AND INTERNATIONAL STUDENTS

Transfer students: May apply for admission for the following academic terms: Fall, Winter, Spring, Summer. Applicants do not need a minimum number of credits to apply. **International students:** Number of foreign undergraduates: 381 (2% of student body). Minimum TOEFL score required: 515 (paper); 185 (computer).

University of Dayton

- **Address:** 300 College Park, Dayton, OH 45469
- **Website:** http://www.udayton.edu
- **Private; Religious affiliation:** Roman Catholic (Marianist)
- **Enrollment:** 6,900 full-time; 506 part-time

KEY STATS

✔ **U.S News College Ranking:** 99, National Universities
✔ **ACT Score (25th/75th percentile):** 23-28
✔ **Tuition:** 2010-2011: $29,930

Selectivity: More selective	**Room/board:** $9,500
Acceptance rate: 73%	**Average debt:** $37,517
Student/faculty ratio: 15/1	**Proportion who borrowed:** 66%

UNDERGRADUATE STUDENT BODY STATS

2009-2010 enrollment: 6,900 full-time; 506 part-time. Men: 51%; women: 49%. **Ethnic makeup:** African American: 3%; Asian American: 1%; Hispanic: 2%; White: 91%; International: 2%. **Religious preference:** Roman Catholic: 59%; Protestant: 14%; No preference: 4%; Unknown: 19%; Other: 4%.

ADMISSIONS FACTS AND FIGURES

Phone: (937) 229-4411. **Email:** admission@udayton.edu. **Website:** http://www.udayton.edu. **Application deadlines for fall 2011:** Regular decision: Rolling. Early decision: Not offered. Early action: Not offered. Admission can be deferred. **Application fee:** $50. **To apply online, go to:** http://admission.udayton.edu/apply/application_login.asp. **Admissions requirements/recommendations:** High school units required (recommended): English: (4); Mathematics: (3); Science: (2); Social studies: (3); Academic electives: (4); Total units: (16). Tests: The college uses SAT or ACT scores in admissions decisions. Either SAT or ACT required. For admission to the fall 2011 entering class, the school will accept: ACT with or without writing accepted. Campus visit: Recommended. Admissions interview: Recommended. Off-campus interview: May be arranged. **Factors that count in admissions decisions: *Academic:*** Secondary school record: Important. Class rank: Important. Letters of recommendation: Considered. Standardized test scores: Important. Essay: Considered. ***Nonacademic:*** Interview: Considered. Extracurricular activities: Considered. Talent/ability: Important. Character/personal qualities: Considered. Alumni/ae relationship: Considered. Geographical residence: Not Considered. State residency: Not Considered. Religious affiliation/commitment: Not Considered. Minority status: Considered. Volunteer work: Considered. Work experience: Considered. **Other schools with the greatest overlap in applicants:** Miami University–Oxford; Ohio State University–Columbus; Ohio University; University of Cincinnati; Xavier University. **Admissions statistics for the fall 2009 entering class:** Total applicants: 12,212. Total accepted: 8,938. Freshmen enrolled: 1,707; 45% were from out of state. Overall acceptance rate: 73%. **Size of waiting list:** 272 applicants; enrolled from waiting list: 113. **Credentials of fall 2009 freshmen:** 27% ranked in the top 10 percent of their high school class; 58% were in the top 25 percent; 87% were in the top half. (Proportion submitting class standing: 47%.) **Average high school grade point average:** 3.6. **First-year students who submitted SAT scores:** 55%. Scores (25/75 percentile): Critical Reading: 510-610, Math: 520-640, Combined: 1030-1250. **First-year students submitting ACT scores:** 86%. Scores (25/75 percentile): English: 23-28, Math: 23-28, Composite: 23-28.

ACADEMICS

Year founded: 1850. **Academic calendar:** Semester. **Degrees offered:** bachelor's, master's, post-master's certificate, doctorate. **Most popular majors:** 24% business, management, marketing, and related support services; 11% communication, journalism, and related programs; 11% education, 9% engineering, 5% psychology. **Major fields of study:** area, ethnic, cultural, and gender studies; biological and biomedical sciences; business, management, marketing, and related support services; communication, journalism, and related programs; computer and information sciences and support services; education; engineering; engineering technologies/technicians; English language and literature/letters; family and consumer sciences/human sciences; foreign languages, literatures, and linguistics; health professions and related clinical sciences; history; legal professions and studies; liberal arts and sciences studies, and humanities; mathematics and statistics; multi/interdisciplinary studies; parks, recreation, leisure, and fitness studies; philosophy and religious studies; physical sciences; psychology; security and protective services; social sciences; visual and performing arts. **Areas of required coursework:** arts/fine arts, humanities, mathematics, English (including composition), philosophy, sciences (biological or physical), history, social science, other. **Pre-professional programs:** pre-law, pre-dentistry, pre-medicine, pre-veterinary science, other. **Special academic programs (% participation):** accelerated program (2%), cooperative (work-study plan) program, cross-registration, distance learning, double major (9%), dual enrollment, English as a Second Language (ESL), exchange student program (domestic), honors program (2%), independent study, internships, liberal arts/career combination, student-designed major, study abroad (41%), teacher certificate program. **Teacher certification offered in:** early childhood, special education, elementary, middle/junior high, secondary, bilingual/bicultural. **Cooperative education programs:** art, business, computer science, engineering, humanities, natural science, social/behavioral science, technologies, other. **Reserve Officers Training Corps (ROTC):** Army ROTC: Offered on campus; Air Force ROTC: Offered at cooperating institution (Wright State University). **Faculty and instruction (2009-2010):** Total instructional faculty: 475 full-time, 462 part-time (61% men; 39% women; 10% minorities). Full-time faculty with Ph.D. or other terminal degree: 91%. Student/faculty ratio: 15/1. Classes of fewer than 20 students: 35%; of 20 to 49 students: 61%; of 50 or more students: 4%. **Advanced Placement and International Baccalaureate credit:** AP tests may be used for: Credit and/or placement. Scores accepted: 3, 4, 5. International Baccalaureate exams may be used for: Placement only. **Freshmen returning for sophomore year:** 87%. **Graduation rates:** Four-year: 58%; five-year: 76%; six-year: 78%. **Graduate study:** 24% of students pursue further study immediately upon graduation; 30% within one year; 15% within five years. Fields in which graduates pursue further study: Master of Business Administration (MBA), 15%; law, 13%; medicine, 9%; dentistry, 1%; engineering, 12%; education, 30%; arts and sciences, 19%.

COSTS AND FINANCIAL AID

Financial aid office: (937) 229-4311. **Expenses (2010-2011):** Tuition and fees 2010-2011: $29,930; room/board: $9,500. Estimated books and supplies: $1,000; transportation: $500; personal expenses: $1,000. **Financial aid:** Priority filing date for institution's financial aid form: March 31. In 2009-2010, 75% of undergraduates applied for financial aid. Of those, 61% were determined to have financial need; 45% had their need fully met. Average financial aid package (proportion receiving): $25,054 (59%). Average amount of gift aid, such as scholarships or grants (proportion receiving): $14,164 (55%). Average amount of self-help aid, such as work study or loans (proportion receiving): $9,691 (59%). Average need-based loan (excluding PLUS or other private loans): $7,402. Among students who received need-based aid, the average percentage of need met: 100%. Among students who received aid based on merit, the average award (and the proportion receiving): $6,328 (40%). The average athletic scholarship (and the proportion receiving): $19,325 (1%). Average amount of debt of borrowers graduating in 2009: $37,517. Proportion who borrowed: 66%.

CAMPUS LIFE AND EXTRACURRICULAR ACTIVITIES

Campus housing available (% using): coed dorms (40%), women's dorms (0%), men's dorms (0%), sorority housing (1%), fraternity housing (1%), apartment for single students (1%), special housing for disabled students (0%), special housing for international students (1%), other housing options (31%). Students who live in college-owned, operated, or affiliated housing: 75%. **Student employment:** During the 2009-2010 academic year, 47% of undergraduates worked on campus. Average per-year earnings: $1,295. **Clubs and organizations:** Number of student organizations: 192. Activities include: campus ministries, choral groups, concert band, dance, drama/theater, international student organization, jazz band, literary magazine, marching band, model UN, music ensembles, musical theater, opera, pep band, radio station, student government, student newspaper, symphony orchestra, television station, yearbook. Number of fraternities: 12; sororities: 7. Proportion of men in fraternities: 8%; of women in sororities: 9%. Average proportion of students who stay on campus on weekends: 85%. **Sports program (2009-2010):** Member of NCAA I. ***Men's intercollegiate varsity sports:*** baseball, basketball, cross country, football, golf, soccer, tennis. ***Women's intercollegiate varsity sports:*** basketball, crew (heavyweight), cross country, golf, crew (lightweight), soccer, softball, tennis, track and field (indoor), track and field (outdoor), volleyball.

SERVICES AND FACILITIES

Basic services: nonremedial tutoring, women's center, placement service, day care, health service, health insurance. **Remedial assistance:** reading, math, writing, study skills. **Counseling services:** minority student, career, military, personal, veteran student, academic, older student, psychological, religious. **For learning-disabled students:** School does not offer a structured program with separate admission and additional fees. Total undergraduates in learning-disabled program or receiving services: 412. Services include: other special classes, note-taking services, oral tests, learning center, extended time for tests, tutors, priority registration, priority seating, texts on tape, exams on tape or computer, other testing accommodations, other. **Library:** Number of titles: 929,704; number of current serial subscriptions: 22,653. **Information technology resources:** Students are required to lease or own a computer. Number of campus computers available to all students: 7,675. School has a wireless network. Approximate number of users that can be accommodated: 12,000. Proportion of college-owned housing units wired for high-speed internet access: 100%. **Campus safety:** Security services offered: 24-hour foot-and-vehicle patrols, late-night transport/escort service, 24-hour emergency telephones, lighted pathways/sidewalks, student patrols, controlled dormitory access (key, security card, etc).

TRANSFER AND INTERNATIONAL STUDENTS

Transfer students: May apply for admission for the following academic terms: Fall, Winter, Summer. Applicants need a minimum number of credits to apply. For fall 2009: Transfer applications received: 833. Transfer applicants offered admission: 298. Transfer applicants enrolled: 173. **International students:** Number of foreign undergraduates: 127 (2% of student body). Number of countries represented: 47. Minimum TOEFL score required: 523 (paper); 193 (computer). Average TOEFL score: 550 (paper).

University of Findlay

- **Address:** 1000 N. Main Street, Findlay, OH 45840
- **Website:** http://www.findlay.edu
- **Private; Religious affiliation:** Churches of God General Conference
- **Enrollment:** 2,632 full-time; 379 part-time

KEY STATS

✔ **U.S News College Ranking:** 52, Regional Universities (Midwest)
✔ **ACT Score (25th/75th percentile):** 20-26
✔ **Tuition:** 2010-2011: $26,798

Selectivity: Selective	**Room/board:** $8,810
Acceptance rate: 68%	**Average debt:** $33,266
Student/faculty ratio: 17/1	**Proportion who borrowed:** 89%

UNDERGRADUATE STUDENT BODY STATS

2009-2010 enrollment: 2,632 full-time; 379 part-time. Men: 36%; women: 64%. **Ethnic makeup:** African American: 3%; Asian American: 1%; Hispanic: 1%; White: 89%; International: 5%. **Religious preference:** Roman Catholic: 31%; Protestant: 35%; Jewish: 1%; No preference: 7%; Unknown: 19%; Churches of God General Conference: 5%.

ADMISSIONS FACTS AND FIGURES

Phone: (800) 548-0932. **Email:** admissions@findlay.edu. **Website:** http://www.findlay.edu. **Application deadlines for fall 2011:** Regular decision: July 1. Early decision: Not offered. Early action: Not offered. Admission can be deferred. **Application fee:** None. **To apply online, go to:** http://www.findlay.edu/admissions/info/undergraduate/apply/default.htm. **Admissions requirements/recommendations:** High school units required (recommended): English: (4); Mathematics: (2); Science: (4); Foreign language: (2); Social studies: (2); History: (1); Academic electives: (1); Total units: (16). Tests: The college uses SAT or ACT scores in admissions decisions. Either SAT or ACT required. For admission to the fall 2011 entering class, the school will accept: ACT with or without writing accepted. Campus visit: Recommended. Admissions interview: Recommended. Off-campus interview: May be arranged. **Factors that count in admissions decisions:** *Academic:* Secondary school record: Very Important. Class rank: Important. Letters of recommendation: Very Important. Standardized test scores: Very Important. Essay: Very Important. *Nonacademic:* Interview: Important. Extracurricular activities: Important. Talent/ability: Considered. Character/personal qualities: Important. Alumni/ae relationship: Considered. Geographical residence: Not Considered. State residency: Not Considered. Religious affiliation/commitment: Not Considered. Minority status: Not Considered. Volunteer work: Important. Work experience: Considered. **Other schools with the greatest overlap in applicants:** Bowling Green State University; Capital University; Ohio Northern University; University of Dayton; University of Toledo. **Admissions statistics for the fall 2009 entering class:** Total applicants: 2,791. Total accepted: 1,902. Freshmen enrolled: 642; 22% were from out of state. Overall acceptance rate: 68%. **Credentials of fall 2009 freshmen:** 30% ranked in the top 10 percent of their high school class; 56% were in the top 25 percent; 82% were in the top half. (Proportion submitting class standing: 85%.) **Average high school grade point average:** 3.4. **First-year students who submitted SAT scores:** 15%. Scores (25/75 percentile): Critical Reading: 460-570, Math: 480-590, Combined: 940-1160. **First-year students submitting ACT scores:** 85%. Scores (25/75 percentile): English: 20-25, Math: 20-25, Composite: 20-26.

ACADEMICS

Year founded: 1882. **Academic calendar:** Semester. **Degrees offered:** certificate, associate, bachelor's, master's. **Most popular majors:** 29% health professions and related clinical sciences, 22% business, management, marketing, and related support services, 10% education, 8% agriculture, agriculture operations, and related sciences, 6% biological and biomedical sciences. **Major fields of study:** agriculture, agriculture operations, and related sciences; biological and biomedical sciences; business, management, marketing, and related support services; communication, journalism, and related programs; communications technologies/technicians and support services; computer and information sciences and support services; education; engineering technologies/technicians; English language and literature/letters; foreign languages, literatures, and linguistics; health professions and related clinical sciences; history; legal professions and studies; mathematics and statistics; parks, recreation, leisure, and fitness studies; philosophy and religious studies; psychology; public administration and social service professions; security and protective services; social sciences; visual and per-

forming arts. **Areas of required coursework:** arts/fine arts, humanities, computer literacy, mathematics, English (including composition), philosophy, foreign languages, sciences (biological or physical), history, social science. **Pre-professional programs:** pre-law, pre-medicine, pre-theology, pre-veterinary science, pre-pharmacy. **Special academic programs (% participation):** accelerated program (6%), cooperative (work-study plan) program, distance learning (12%), double major (19%), dual enrollment (14%), English as a Second Language (ESL) (5%), honors program (5%), independent study (1%), internships (1%), liberal arts/career combination, student-designed major (1%), study abroad (1%), teacher certificate program (2%), weekend college (1%). **Teacher certification offered in:** early childhood, special education, elementary, middle/junior high, adult education, secondary, bilingual/bicultural. **Cooperative education programs:** business, computer science, health professions, social/behavioral science, other. **Reserve Officers Training Corps (ROTC):** Army ROTC: Offered at cooperating institution (Bowling Green State University); Air Force ROTC: Offered at cooperating institution (Bowling Green State University). **Faculty and instruction (2009-2010):** Total instructional faculty: 194 full-time, 88 part-time (49% men; 51% women; 10% minorities). Full-time faculty with Ph.D. or other terminal degree: 62%. Student/faculty ratio: 17/1. Classes of fewer than 20 students: 55%; of 20 to 49 students: 41%; of 50 or more students: 4%. **Advanced Placement and International Baccalaureate credit:** AP tests may be used for: Placement only. Scores accepted: 4. International Baccalaureate exams may be used for: Placement only. **Freshmen returning for sophomore year:** 76%. **Graduation rates:** Four-year: 40%; five-year: 53%; six-year: 54%. **Graduate study:** 37% of students pursue further study within one year.

COSTS AND FINANCIAL AID

Financial aid office: (419) 434-4792. **Expenses (2010-2011):** Tuition and fees 2010-2011: $26,798; room/board: $8,810. Estimated books and supplies: $1,500; transportation: $200. **Financial aid:** Priority filing date for institution's financial aid form: August 1; deadline: September 1. In 2009-2010, 93% of undergraduates applied for financial aid. Of those, 72% were determined to have financial need; 5% had their need fully met. Average financial aid package (proportion receiving): $18,215 (72%). Average amount of gift aid, such as scholarships or grants (proportion receiving): $11,837 (66%). Average amount of self-help aid, such as work study or loans (proportion receiving): $5,342 (66%). Average need-based loan (excluding PLUS or other private loans): $4,755. Among students who received need-based aid, the average percentage of need met: 67%. Among students who received aid based on merit, the average award (and the proportion receiving): $11,300 (11%). The average athletic scholarship (and the proportion receiving): $10,875 (11%). Average amount of debt of borrowers graduating in 2009: $33,266. Proportion who borrowed: 89%.

CAMPUS LIFE AND EXTRACURRICULAR ACTIVITIES

Campus housing available (% using): coed dorms (52%), women's dorms (26%), sorority housing (1%), fraternity housing (1%), apartment for single students (15%), other housing options (5%). Students who live in college-owned, operated, or affiliated housing: 40%. **Student employment:** During the 2009-2010 academic year, 28% of undergraduates worked on campus. Average per-year earnings: $4,200. **Clubs and organizations:** Number of student organizations: 50. Activities include: choral groups, concert band, dance, drama/theater, jazz band, literary magazine, marching band, music ensembles, musical theater, pep band, radio station, student government, student newspaper, television station. Number of fraternities: 2; sororities: 2. Proportion of men in fraternities: 2%; of women in sororities: 2%. Average proportion of students who stay on campus on weekends: 30%. **Sports program (2009-2010):** Member of NCAA II. *Men's intercollegiate varsity sports:* baseball, basketball, cross country, football, golf, soccer, swimming, tennis, track and field (indoor), track and field (outdoor), wrestling. *Women's intercollegiate varsity sports:* basketball, cross country, equestrian, golf, soccer, softball, swimming, tennis, track and field (indoor), track and field (outdoor), volleyball.

SERVICES AND FACILITIES

Basic services: nonremedial tutoring, placement service, health service, health insurance. **Remedial assistance:** reading, math, writing, study skills. **Counseling services:** minority student, career, military, personal, veteran student, academic, older student, psychological, birth control, religious. **For learning-disabled students:** School does not offer a structured program with separate admission and additional fees. Services include: remedial math, remedial English, reading machines, remedial reading, tape recorders, note-taking services, oral tests, learning center, readers, extended time for tests, tutors, priority registration, priority seating, texts on tape, typist/scribe, exams on tape or computer, other testing accommodations. **Library:**

Number of titles: 155,178; number of current serial subscriptions: 6,619. **Information technology resources:** Students are not required to lease or own a computer. Number of campus computers available to all students: 274. School has a wireless network. Proportion of college-owned housing units wired for high-speed internet access: 100%. **Campus safety:** Security services offered: 24-hour foot-and-vehicle patrols, 24-hour emergency telephones, lighted pathways/sidewalks, controlled dormitory access (key, security card, etc).

TRANSFER AND INTERNATIONAL STUDENTS

Transfer students: May apply for admission for the following academic terms: Fall, Spring, Summer. Applicants need a minimum number of credits to apply. For fall 2009: Transfer applications received: 520. Transfer applicants offered admission: 345. Transfer applicants enrolled: 84. **International students:** Number of foreign undergraduates: 150 (5% of student body). Number of countries represented: 24. Minimum TOEFL score required: 500 (paper); 173 (computer). Average TOEFL score: 422 (paper).

University of Mount Union

- **Address:** 1972 Clark Avenue, Alliance, OH 44601
- **Website:** http://www.mountunion.edu/
- **Private; Religious affiliation:** United Methodist
- **Enrollment:** 2,148 full-time; 45 part-time

KEY STATS

✔ **U.S News College Ranking:** 166, National Liberal Arts Colleges
✔ **ACT Score (25th/75th percentile):** 19-25
✔ **Tuition:** 2010-2011: $24,800

Selectivity: Selective	**Room/board:** $7,780
Acceptance rate: 75%	**Average debt:** $25,804
Student/faculty ratio: 14/1	**Proportion who borrowed:** 70%

UNDERGRADUATE STUDENT BODY STATS

2009-2010 enrollment: 2,148 full-time; 45 part-time. Men: 50%; women: 50%. **Ethnic makeup:** African American: 5%; Asian American: 1%; Hispanic: 2%; White: 90%; International: 3%. **Religious preference:** Roman Catholic: 29%; Protestant: 19%; No preference: 35%; United Methodist: 12%.

ADMISSIONS FACTS AND FIGURES

Phone: (330) 823-2590. **Email:** admissions@mountunion.edu. **Website:** http://www.mountunion.edu/. **Application deadlines for fall 2011:** Regular decision: Rolling. Early decision: Not offered. Early action: Not offered. Admission can be deferred. **Application fee:** None. **To apply online, go to:** http://www.mountunion.edu/Admissions/. **Admissions requirements/recommendations:** High school units required (recommended): English: (4); Mathematics: (3); Science: (3); Foreign language: (2); Social studies: (3); History: (0); Academic electives: (1); Total units: (18). Tests: The college uses SAT or ACT scores in admissions decisions. Either SAT or ACT required. For admission to the fall 2011 entering class, the school will accept: ACT with or without writing accepted. Campus visit: Recommended. Admissions interview: Recommended. Off-campus interview: Not available. **Factors that count in admissions decisions:** *Academic:* Secondary school record: Very Important. Class rank: Very Important. Letters of recommendation: Important. Standardized test scores: Very Important. Essay: Considered. *Nonacademic:* Interview: Not Considered. Extracurricular activities: Considered. Talent/ability: Considered. Character/personal qualities: Considered. Alumni/ae relationship: Not Considered. Geographical residence: Not Considered. State residency: Not Considered. Religious affiliation/commitment: Not Considered. Minority status: Considered. Volunteer work: Considered. Work experience: Considered. **Other schools with the greatest overlap in applicants:** Ashland University; Baldwin-Wallace College; Kent State University; Ohio State University–Columbus; University of Akron. **Admissions statistics for the fall 2009 entering class:** Total applicants: 2,320. Total accepted: 1,747. Freshmen enrolled: 578; 14% were from out of state. Overall acceptance rate: 75%. **Credentials of fall 2009 freshmen:** 13% ranked in the top 10 percent of their high school class; 40% were in the top 25 percent; 74% were in the top half. (Proportion submitting class standing: 72%.) **Average high school grade point average:** 3.2. **First-year students who submitted SAT scores:** 31%. Scores (25/75 percentile): Critical Reading: 430-540, Math: 440-590, Combined: 870-1130. **First-year students**

submitting ACT scores: 89%. Scores (25/75 percentile): English: N/A, Math: N/A, Composite: 19-25.

ACADEMICS

Year founded: 1846. **Academic calendar:** Semester. **Degrees offered:** bachelor's, master's. **Most popular majors:** 21% business, management, marketing, and related support services, 13% education, 11% parks, recreation, leisure, and fitness studies, 7% social sciences, 6% biological and biomedical sciences. **Major fields of study:** area, ethnic, cultural, and gender studies; biological and biomedical sciences; business, management, marketing, and related support services; communication, journalism, and related programs; computer and information sciences and support services; education; English language and literature/letters; foreign languages, literatures, and linguistics; health professions and related clinical sciences; history; mathematics and statistics; multi/interdisciplinary studies; parks, recreation, leisure, and fitness studies; philosophy and religious studies; physical sciences; psychology; social sciences; visual and performing arts. **Areas of required coursework:** arts/fine arts, humanities, computer literacy, mathematics, English (including composition), philosophy, foreign languages, sciences (biological or physical), history, social science. **Pre-professional programs:** pre-law, pre-dentistry, pre-medicine, pre-theology, pre-veterinary science, pre-pharmacy. **Special academic programs (% participation):** double major (7.2%), dual enrollment (6%), English as a Second Language (ESL) (.5%), honors program (7%), independent study (17%), internships (20%), student-designed major (0%), study abroad (15%), teacher certificate program (23%). **Teacher certification offered in:** early childhood, special education, elementary, middle/junior high, secondary. **Reserve Officers Training Corps (ROTC):** Army ROTC: Offered on campus; Air Force ROTC: Offered at cooperating institution (Kent State University). **Faculty and instruction (2009-2010):** Total instructional faculty: 124 full-time, 104 part-time (58% men; 42% women; 8% minorities). Full-time faculty with Ph.D. or other terminal degree: 82%. Student/faculty ratio: 14/1. Classes of fewer than 20 students: 54%; of 20 to 49 students: 45%; of 50 or more students: 1%. **Advanced Placement and International Baccalaureate credit:** AP tests may be used for: Credit only. Scores accepted: 3, 4, 5. International Baccalaureate exams may be used for: Credit only. **Freshmen returning for sophomore year:** 78%. **Graduation rates:** Four-year: 50%; five-year: 62%; six-year: 63%. **Graduate study:** 29% of students pursue further study immediately upon graduation; 23% within one year. Fields in which graduates pursue further study: Master of Business Administration (MBA), 7%; law, 14%; medicine, 19%; dentistry, 1%; theology (or the seminary), 2%; education, 13%; arts and sciences, 53%.

COSTS AND FINANCIAL AID

Financial aid office: (877) 543-9185. **Expenses (2010-2011):** Tuition and fees 2010-2011: $24,800; room/board: $7,780. Estimated books and supplies: $1,100; transportation: $835; personal expenses: $800. **Financial aid:** Priority filing date for institution's financial aid form: April 1. In 2009-2010, 88% of undergraduates applied for financial aid. Of those, 80% were determined to have financial need; 10% had their need fully met. Average financial aid package (proportion receiving): $19,313 (79%). Average amount of gift aid, such as scholarships or grants (proportion receiving): $13,935 (79%). Average amount of self-help aid, such as work study or loans (proportion receiving): $5,863 (73%). Average need-based loan (excluding PLUS or other private loans): $4,984. Among students who received need-based aid, the average percentage of need met: 79%. Among students who received aid based on merit, the average award (and the proportion receiving): $7,537 (18%). The average athletic scholarship (and the proportion receiving): $0 (0%). Average amount of debt of borrowers graduating in 2009: $25,804. Proportion who borrowed: 70%.

CAMPUS LIFE AND EXTRACURRICULAR ACTIVITIES

Campus housing available (% using): coed dorms (39%), women's dorms (18%), men's dorms (13%), fraternity housing (5%), apartment for single students (15%), special housing for disabled students (2%), other housing options (1%). Students who live in college-owned, operated, or affiliated housing: 75%. **Student employment:** During the 2009-2010 academic year, 45% of undergraduates worked on campus. Average per-year earnings: $1,831. **Clubs and organizations:** Number of student organizations: 82. Activities include: campus ministries, choral groups, concert band, dance, drama/theater, international student organization, jazz band, literary magazine, marching band, model UN, music ensembles, musical theater, pep band, radio station, student government, student newspaper, symphony orchestra, television station, yearbook. Number of fraternities: 4; sororities: 4. Proportion of men in fraternities: 14%; of women in sororities: 26%. Average proportion of students who stay on campus on weekends: 50%.

Sports program (2009-2010): Member of NCAA III. *Men's intercollegiate varsity sports:* baseball, basketball, cross country, football, golf, soccer, swimming, tennis, track and field (indoor), track and field (outdoor), wrestling. *Women's intercollegiate varsity sports:* basketball, cross country, golf, soccer, softball, swimming, tennis, track and field (indoor), track and field (outdoor), volleyball.

SERVICES AND FACILITIES

Basic services: nonremedial tutoring, placement service, health service, health insurance. **Remedial assistance:** math, writing, study skills. **Counseling services:** minority student, career, military, personal, academic, older student, psychological, religious, other. **For learning-disabled students:** School does not offer a structured program with separate admission and additional fees. Total undergraduates in learning-disabled program or receiving services: 30. Services include: reading machines, tape recorders, note-taking services, oral tests, learning center, readers, extended time for tests, tutors, texts on tape, other testing accommodations. **Library:** Number of titles: 225,813; number of current serial subscriptions: 52,728. **Information technology resources:** Students are not required to lease or own a computer. Number of campus computers available to all students: 250. School has a wireless network. Approximate number of users that can be accommodated: 2,200. Proportion of college-owned housing units wired for high-speed internet access: 100%. **Campus safety:** Security services offered: 24-hour foot-and-vehicle patrols, late-night transport/escort service, 24-hour emergency telephones, lighted pathways/sidewalks, student patrols, controlled dormitory access (key, security card, etc).

TRANSFER AND INTERNATIONAL STUDENTS

Transfer students: May apply for admission for the following academic terms: Fall, Spring, Summer. Applicants do not need a minimum number of credits to apply. For fall 2009: Transfer applications received: 233. Transfer applicants offered admission: 105. Transfer applicants enrolled: 52. **International students:** Number of foreign undergraduates: 62 (3% of student body). Number of countries represented: 21. Minimum TOEFL score required: 450 (paper). Average TOEFL score: 509 (paper).

University of Northwestern Ohio

- **Address:** 1441 N. Cable Road, Lima, OH 45805
- **Website:** http://www.unoh.edu/
- **Private**
- **Enrollment:** N/A

KEY STATS
✔ **U.S News College Ranking:** Unranked, Regional Colleges (Midwest)
✔ **SAT or ACT Score (25th/75th percentile):** N/A
✔ **Tuition:** 2009-2010: $13,400

Selectivity: N/A	Room/board: $6,750
Acceptance rate: N/A	Average debt: N/A
Student/faculty ratio: N/A	Proportion who borrowed: N/A

University of Rio Grande

- **Address:** PO Box 500, Rio Grande, OH 45674
- **Website:** http://www.rio.edu
- **Private**
- **Enrollment:** 1,618 full-time; 420 part-time

KEY STATS
✔ **U.S News College Ranking:** Unranked, Regional Universities (Midwest)
✔ **ACT Score:** 19
✔ **Tuition:** 2009-2010: $18,260

Selectivity: N/A	Room/board: $7,800
Acceptance rate: 80%	Average debt: $18,146
Student/faculty ratio: 18/1	Proportion who borrowed: 76%

UNDERGRADUATE STUDENT BODY STATS

2009-2010 enrollment: 1,618 full-time; 420 part-time. Men: 40%; women: 60%. **Ethnic makeup:** African American: 3%; Asian American: 1%; Hispanic: 1%; White: 95%.

ADMISSIONS FACTS AND FIGURES

Phone: (740) 245-7208. **Email:** admissions@rio.edu. **Website:** http://www.rio.edu. **Application deadlines for fall 2011:** Regular decision: Rolling. Early decision: Not offered. Early action: Not offered. Admission can be deferred. **Application fee:** $25. **To apply online, go to:** https://hope.rio.edu/admissions_application/adapp.aspx. **Admissions requirements/recommendations:** High school units required (recommended): English: 4; Mathematics: 3; Science: 3; Foreign language: 0 (2); Social studies: 3; History: 0 (2); Academic electives: 7 (9); Total units: 20 (21). Tests: The college does not use SAT or ACT scores in admissions decisions. Neither SAT nor ACT required. For admission to the fall 2011 entering class, the school will accept: ACT with or without writing accepted. Campus visit: Recommended. Admissions interview: Recommended. Off-campus interview: May be arranged. **Factors that count in admissions decisions:** *Academic:* Secondary school record: Not Considered. Class rank: Not Considered. Letters of recommendation: Not Considered. Standardized test scores: Not Considered. Essay: Not Considered. *Nonacademic:* Interview: Not Considered. Extracurricular activities: Not Considered. Talent/ability: Not Considered. Character/personal qualities: Not Considered. Alumni/ae relationship: Not Considered. Geographical residence: Not Considered. State residency: Considered. Religious affiliation/commitment: Not Considered. Minority status: Not Considered. Volunteer work: Not Considered. Work experience: Not Considered. **Other schools with the greatest overlap in applicants:** Marshall University; Ohio University; Shawnee State University. **Admissions statistics for the fall 2009 entering class:** Total applicants: 2,733. Total accepted: 2,192. Freshmen enrolled: 488; 2% were from out of state. Overall acceptance rate: 80%. **Credentials of fall 2009 freshmen:** 10% ranked in the top 10 percent of their high school class; 20% were in the top 25 percent; 63% were in the top half. (Proportion submitting class standing: 85%.)

ACADEMICS

Year founded: 1876. **Academic calendar:** Semester. **Degrees offered:** certificate, associate, bachelor's, master's. **Major fields of study:** area, ethnic, cultural, and gender studies; biological and biomedical sciences; business, management, marketing, and related support services; communication, journalism, and related programs; computer and information sciences and support services; education; engineering technologies/technicians; English language and literature/letters; health professions and related clinical sciences; mathematics and statistics; natural resources and conservation; parks, recreation, leisure, and fitness studies; physical sciences; psychology; public administration and social service professions; social sciences; visual and performing arts. **Areas of required coursework:** arts/fine arts, humanities, computer literacy, mathematics, English (including composition), sciences (biological or physical), history, social science. **Special academic programs (% participation):** cooperative (work-study plan) program (10%), distance learning (2%), double major (5%), English as a Second Language (ESL) (1%), honors program (5%), student-designed major (1%), study abroad (1%). **Teacher certification offered in:** early childhood, special education, elementary, vo-tech, middle/junior high, secondary. **Cooperative education programs:** business, technologies. **Faculty and instruction (2009-2010):** Total instructional faculty: 90 full-time, 108 part-time (49% men; 51% women; 4% minorities). Full-time faculty with Ph.D. or other terminal degree: 46%. Student/faculty ratio: 18/1. Classes of fewer than 20 students: 73%; of 20 to 49 students: 25%; of 50 or more students: 2%. **Freshmen returning for sophomore year:** 57%. **Graduation rates:** Six-year: 22%. **Graduate study:** 22% of students pursue further study within one year. Fields in which graduates pursue further study: Master of Business Administration (MBA), 6%; medicine, 11%; education, 4%; arts and sciences, 1%.

COSTS AND FINANCIAL AID

Financial aid office: (740) 245-7218. **Expenses (2009-2010):** Tuition and fees 2009-2010: $18,260; room/board: $7,800. Estimated books and supplies: $1,200; transportation: $1,688; personal expenses: $1,750. **Financial aid:** Priority filing date for institution's financial aid form: March 15; deadline: August 10. In 2009-2010, 89% of undergraduates applied for financial aid. Of those, 64% were determined to have financial need; 19% had their need fully met. Average financial aid package (proportion receiving): $11,695 (62%). Average amount of gift aid, such as scholarships or grants (proportion receiving): N/A (62%). Average amount of self-help aid, such as work study or loans (proportion receiving): $1,832 (51%). Average need-based loan (excluding PLUS or other private loans): $1,875. Among students who received need-based aid, the average percentage of need met: 62%. Among students who received aid based on merit, the average award (and the proportion receiving): $0 (0%). The average athletic scholarship (and the proportion receiving): $0 (0%). Average amount of debt of borrowers graduating in 2009: $18,146. Proportion who borrowed: 76%.

CAMPUS LIFE AND EXTRACURRICULAR ACTIVITIES

Campus housing available (% using): coed dorms (60%), women's dorms (20%), men's dorms (20%). Students who live in college-owned, operated, or affiliated housing: 20%. **Student employment:** During the 2009-2010 academic year, 15% of undergraduates worked on campus. Average per-year earnings: $3,000. **Clubs and organizations:** Number of student organizations: 33. Activities include: choral groups, dance, drama/theater, jazz band, literary magazine, music ensembles, musical theater, pep band, radio station, student government, student newspaper. Number of fraternities: 4; sororities: 5. Proportion of men in fraternities: 2%; of women in sororities: 2%. Average proportion of students who stay on campus on weekends: 20%. **Sports program (2009-2010):** Member of NAIA. *Men's intercollegiate varsity sports:* baseball, basketball, cross country, soccer, track and field (indoor), track and field (outdoor). *Women's intercollegiate varsity sports:* basketball, cross country, soccer, softball, track and field (indoor), track and field (outdoor), volleyball.

SERVICES AND FACILITIES

Basic services: nonremedial tutoring, health service, health insurance. **Remedial assistance:** reading, math, writing, study skills. **Counseling services:** career, personal, veteran student, academic. **For learning-disabled students:** School does not offer a structured program with separate admission and additional fees. Services include: remedial math, remedial English, reading machines, remedial reading, tape recorders, other special classes, untimed tests, note-taking services, oral tests, learning center, readers, extended time for tests, tutors, texts on tape, other testing accommodations. **Library:** Number of titles: 123,318; number of current serial subscriptions: 319. **Information technology resources:** Students are not required to lease or own a computer. Number of campus computers available to all students: 631. School has a wireless network. Approximate number of users that can be accommodated: 760. Proportion of college-owned housing units wired for high-speed internet access: 100%. **Campus safety:** Security services offered: 24-hour foot-and-vehicle patrols, late-night transport/escort service, 24-hour emergency telephones, lighted pathways/sidewalks, controlled dormitory access (key, security card, etc).

TRANSFER AND INTERNATIONAL STUDENTS

Transfer students: May apply for admission for the following academic terms: Fall, Spring, Summer. Applicants do not need a minimum number of credits to apply. For fall 2009: Transfer applications received: 659. Transfer applicants offered admission: 426. Transfer applicants enrolled: 199. **International students:** Number of foreign undergraduates: 6. Minimum TOEFL score required: 400 (paper); 97 (computer). Average TOEFL score: 550 (paper).

University of Toledo

■ **Address:** 2801 W. Bancroft, Toledo, OH 43606
■ **Website:** http://www.utoledo.edu
■ **Public**
■ **Enrollment:** 14,968 full-time; 3,172 part-time

KEY STATS

✔ **U.S News College Ranking:** second tier, National Universities
✔ **ACT Score (25th/75th percentile):** 18-24
✔ **Tuition:** 2010-2011: $8,490 in state, $17,302 out of state
   Selectivity: Selective   **Room/board:** $9,354
   Acceptance rate: 90%   **Average debt:** $27,066
   Student/faculty ratio: 19/1   **Proportion who borrowed:** 71%

UNDERGRADUATE STUDENT BODY STATS

2009-2010 enrollment: 14,968 full-time; 3,172 part-time. Men: 50%; women: 50%. **Ethnic makeup:** African American: 16%; Asian American: 2%; Hispanic: 3%; White: 75%; International: 3%.

ADMISSIONS FACTS AND FIGURES

Phone: (419) 530-8888. **Email:** enroll@utnet.utoledo.edu. **Website:** http://www.utoledo.edu. **Application deadlines for fall 2011:** Regular decision: Rolling. Early decision: Not offered. Early action: Not offered. Admission can be deferred. **Application fee:** $40. **To apply online, go to:** http://under-

gradadmission.utoledo.edu/pages/apply.asp. **Admissions requirements/recommendations:** High school units required (recommended): English: 4; Mathematics: 3; Science: 3; Social studies: 3; Total units: 13. Tests: The college uses SAT or ACT scores in admissions decisions. Either SAT or ACT required. For admission to the fall 2011 entering class, the school will accept: ACT with writing required. Campus visit: Recommended. Admissions interview: Neither required nor recommended. Off-campus interview: May be arranged. **Factors that count in admissions decisions:** *Academic:* Secondary school record: Very Important. Class rank: Not Considered. Letters of recommendation: Not Considered. Standardized test scores: Very Important. Essay: Not Considered. *Nonacademic:* Interview: Not Considered. Extracurricular activities: Not Considered. Talent/ability: Not Considered. Character/personal qualities: Not Considered. Alumni/ae relationship: Not Considered. Geographical residence: Not Considered. State residency: Very Important. Religious affiliation/commitment: Not Considered. Minority status: Not Considered. Volunteer work: Not Considered. Work experience: Not Considered. **Admissions statistics for the fall 2009 entering class:** Total applicants: 12,713. Total accepted: 11,446. Freshmen enrolled: 4,371; 10% were from out of state. Overall acceptance rate: 90%. **Credentials of fall 2009 freshmen:** 15% ranked in the top 10 percent of their high school class; 37% were in the top 25 percent; 65% were in the top half. (Proportion submitting class standing: 85%.) **Average high school grade point average:** 3.1. **First-year students submitting ACT scores:** 87%. Scores (25/75 percentile): English: 16-24, Math: 17-25, Composite: 18-24.

ACADEMICS

Year founded: 1872. **Academic calendar:** Semester. **Degrees offered:** certificate, associate, bachelor's, post-bachelor's certificate, master's, post-master's certificate, doctorate. **Most popular majors:** 20% business, management, marketing, and related support services, 16% health professions and related clinical sciences, 10% engineering, 8% education, 6% multi/interdisciplinary studies. **Major fields of study:** area, ethnic, cultural, and gender studies; biological and biomedical sciences; business, management, marketing, and related support services; communication, journalism, and related programs; computer and information sciences and support services; education; engineering; engineering technologies/technicians; English language and literature/letters; foreign languages, literatures, and linguistics; health professions and related clinical sciences; history; legal professions and studies; liberal arts and sciences studies, and humanities; mathematics and statistics; multi/interdisciplinary studies; natural resources and conservation; parks, recreation, leisure, and fitness studies; philosophy and religious studies; physical sciences; psychology; public administration and social service professions; security and protective services; social sciences; visual and performing arts. **Areas of required coursework:** arts/fine arts, humanities, mathematics, English (including composition), sciences (biological or physical), social science. **Pre-professional programs:** pre-law, pre-dentistry, pre-medicine, pre-veterinary science, pre-pharmacy. **Special academic programs:** accelerated program, cooperative (work-study plan) program, cross-registration, distance learning, double major, dual enrollment, exchange student program (domestic), honors program, independent study, internships, liberal arts/career combination, student-designed major, study abroad, teacher certificate program, weekend college. **Teacher certification offered in:** early childhood, special education, elementary, middle/junior high, secondary, bilingual/bicultural. **Cooperative education programs:** business, education, engineering. **Reserve Officers Training Corps (ROTC):** Army ROTC: Offered on campus; Air Force ROTC: Offered at cooperating institution (Bowling Green State University). **Faculty and instruction (2009-2010):** Total instructional faculty: 809 full-time, 461 part-time (56% men; 44% women). Full-time faculty with Ph.D. or other terminal degree: 89%. Student/faculty ratio: 19/1. Classes of fewer than 20 students: 32%; of 20 to 49 students: 53%; of 50 or more students: 14%. **Advanced Placement and International Baccalaureate credit:** AP tests may be used for: Placement only. Scores accepted: 3. International Baccalaureate exams may be used for: Credit only. **Freshmen returning for sophomore year:** 69%. **Graduation rates:** Four-year: 23%; five-year: 41%; six-year: 45%.

COSTS AND FINANCIAL AID

Financial aid office: (419) 530-8700. **Expenses (2010-2011):** Tuition and fees 2010-2011: $8,490 in state, $17,302 out of state; room/board: $9,354. Estimated books and supplies: $900; transportation: $660; personal expenses: $3,704. **Financial aid:** Priority filing date for institution's financial aid form: April 1. In 2009-2010, 81% of undergraduates applied for financial aid. Of those, 67% were determined to have financial need; 23% had their need fully met. Average financial aid package (proportion receiving): $14,129 (67%). Average amount of gift aid, such as scholarships or grants (proportion receiving): $6,514 (59%). Average amount of self-help aid, such as work study or loans (proportion receiving): $7,672 (59%). Average need-based loan (excluding PLUS or other private loans): $7,599. Among students who received need-based aid, the average percentage of need met: 86%. Among students who received aid based on merit, the average award (and the proportion receiving): $3,921 (22%). The average athletic scholarship (and the proportion receiving): $11,759 (1%). Average amount of debt of borrowers graduating in 2009: $27,066. Proportion who borrowed: 71%.

CAMPUS LIFE AND EXTRACURRICULAR ACTIVITIES

Campus housing available (% using): coed dorms (89%), sorority housing (4%), fraternity housing (4%), special housing for international students (3%). Students who live in college-owned, operated, or affiliated housing: 23%. **Clubs and organizations:** Number of student organizations: 200. Activities include: campus ministries, choral groups, concert band, dance, drama/theater, jazz band, literary magazine, marching band, music ensembles, pep band, radio station, student government, student newspaper, television station. Number of fraternities: 17; sororities: 13. Average proportion of students who stay on campus on weekends: 70%. **Sports program (2009-2010):** Member of NCAA I. *Men's intercollegiate varsity sports:* baseball, basketball, cross country, football, golf, tennis. *Women's intercollegiate varsity sports:* basketball, cross country, golf, soccer, softball, swimming, tennis, track and field (outdoor), volleyball.

SERVICES AND FACILITIES

Basic services: nonremedial tutoring, women's center, placement service, day care, health service, health insurance. **Remedial assistance:** reading, math, writing, study skills. **Counseling services:** minority student, career, military, personal, veteran student, academic, older student, psychological, religious. **For learning-disabled students:** School does not offer a structured program with separate admission and additional fees. Total undergraduates in learning-disabled program or receiving services: 231. Services include: remedial math, remedial English, reading machines, remedial reading, tape recorders, videotaped classes, diagnostic testing service, untimed tests, notetaking services, oral tests, learning center, readers, extended time for tests, tutors, priority registration, texts on tape, other testing accommodations. **Library:** Number of titles: 2,090,789; number of current serial subscriptions: 1,841. **Information technology resources:** Students are not required to lease or own a computer. Number of campus computers available to all students: 5,000. School has a wireless network. Approximate number of users that can be accommodated: 14,000. Proportion of college-owned housing units wired for high-speed internet access: 100%. **Campus safety:** Security services offered: 24-hour foot-and-vehicle patrols, late-night transport/escort service, 24-hour emergency telephones, lighted pathways/sidewalks, student patrols, controlled dormitory access (key, security card, etc).

TRANSFER AND INTERNATIONAL STUDENTS

Transfer students: May apply for admission for the following academic terms: Fall, Spring, Summer. Applicants need a minimum number of credits to apply. For fall 2009: Transfer applications received: 1,960. Transfer applicants offered admission: 1,685. Transfer applicants enrolled: 1,116. **International students:** Number of foreign undergraduates: 544 (3% of student body). Number of countries represented: 60. Minimum TOEFL score required: 500 (paper); 173 (computer).

Urbana University

- ■ **Address:** 579 College Way, Urbana, OH 43078
- ■ **Website:** http://www.urbana.edu
- ■ **Private; Religious affiliation:** Swedenborgian Church
- ■ **Enrollment:** N/A

KEY STATS

✔ **U.S News College Ranking:** second tier, Regional Colleges (Midwest)
✔ **SAT or ACT Score (25th/75th percentile):** N/A
✔ **Tuition:** 2009-2010: $20,130

Selectivity: Less selective	**Room/board:** $7,990
Acceptance rate: N/A	**Average debt:** N/A
Student/faculty ratio: N/A	**Proportion who borrowed:** N/A

Ursuline College

- ■ **Address:** 2550 Lander Road, Pepper Pike, OH 44124
- ■ **Website:** http://www.ursuline.edu
- ■ **Private; Religious affiliation:** Roman Catholic
- ■ **Enrollment:** 690 full-time; 387 part-time

KEY STATS

✔ **U.S News College Ranking:** 72, Regional Universities (Midwest)
✔ **ACT Score (25th/75th percentile):** 19-23
✔ **Tuition:** 2010-2011: $23,940

Selectivity: Selective	**Room/board:** $7,970
Acceptance rate: 90%	**Average debt:** $36,116
Student/faculty ratio: 9/1	**Proportion who borrowed:** 86%

UNDERGRADUATE STUDENT BODY STATS

2009-2010 enrollment: 690 full-time; 387 part-time. Men: 9%; women: 91%. **Ethnic makeup:** African American: 26%; Asian American: 1%; Hispanic: 2%; White: 70%. **Religious preference:** Protestant: 7%; Jewish: 1%; No preference: 42%; Unknown: 3%; Roman Catholic: 28%; Baptist: 3%; Other: 16%.

ADMISSIONS FACTS AND FIGURES

Phone: (440) 449-4203. **Email:** admission@ursuline.edu. **Website:** http://www.ursuline.edu. **Application deadlines for fall 2011:** Regular decision: Rolling. Early decision: Not offered. Early action: Send application by: November 15; Decision sent by: February 15. Admission can be deferred. **Application fee:** $25. **To apply online, go to:** http://admission.ursuline.edu/apply/onlineapp.html. **Admissions requirements/recommendations:** High school units required (recommended): English: 4 (4); Mathematics: 3 (3); Science: 3 (3); Foreign language: 2 (2); Social studies: 3 (3); History: 0 (0); Academic electives: 0 (0); Total units: 17 (17). Tests: The college uses SAT or ACT scores in admissions decisions. Either SAT or ACT required. For admission to the fall 2011 entering class, the school will accept: ACT with or without writing accepted. Campus visit: Recommended. Admissions interview: Recommended. Off-campus interview: May be arranged. **Factors that count in admissions decisions:** *Academic:* Secondary school record: Considered. Class rank: Considered. Letters of recommendation: Important. Standardized test scores: Very Important. Essay: Important. *Nonacademic:* Interview: Considered. Extracurricular activities: Not Considered. Talent/ability: Not Considered. Character/personal qualities: Not Considered. Alumni/ae relationship: Considered. Geographical residence: Not Considered. State residency: Not Considered. Religious affiliation/commitment: Not Considered. Minority status: Not Considered. Volunteer work: Not Considered. Work experience: Not Considered. **Other schools with the greatest overlap in applicants:** Cleveland State University; John Carroll University; Kent State University; Notre Dame College of Ohio; University of Akron. **Admissions statistics for the fall 2009 entering class:** Total applicants: 248. Total accepted: 222. Freshmen enrolled: 95; 8% were from out of state. Accepted through early-decision or early-action plans: 37%. Overall acceptance rate: 90%. **Credentials of fall 2009 freshmen:** 5% ranked in the top 10 percent of their high school class; 34% were in the top 25 percent; 78% were in the top half. (Proportion submitting class standing: 80%.) **Average high school grade point average:** 3.1. **First-year students who submitted SAT scores:** 29%. Scores (25/75 percentile): Critical Reading: 410-510, Math: 400-530, Combined: 810-1040. **First-year students submitting ACT scores:** 86%. Scores (25/75 percentile): English: 17-23, Math: 19-23, Composite: 19-23.

ACADEMICS

Year founded: 1871. **Academic calendar:** Semester. **Degrees offered:** certificate, bachelor's, post-bachelor's certificate, master's, post-master's certificate. **Most popular majors:** 55% health professions and related clinical sciences, 13% business, management, marketing, and related support services, 8% visual and performing arts, 6% psychology, 4% education. **Major fields of study:** area, ethnic, cultural, and gender studies; biological and biomedical sciences; business, management, marketing, and related support services; communication, journalism, and related programs; education; English language and literature/letters; family and consumer sciences/human sciences; health professions and related clinical sciences; history; legal professions and studies; liberal arts and sciences studies, and humanities; mathematics and statistics; multi/interdisciplinary studies; philosophy and religious studies; psychology; public administration and social service professions; social sciences; theology and religious vocations; visual and performing arts. **Areas of required coursework:** arts/fine arts, humanities, mathematics, English (including composition), philosophy, sciences (biological or physical), social science, other. **Pre-professional programs:** pre-law, pre-dentistry, pre-medicine, pre-veterinary science, pre-pharmacy. **Special academic programs (% participation):** accelerated program (26%), cooperative (work-study plan) program, cross-registration, double major, independent study, internships. **Teacher certification offered in:** early childhood, special education, elementary, middle/junior high, secondary. **Reserve Officers Training Corps (ROTC):** Army ROTC: Offered at cooperating institution. **Faculty and instruction (2009-2010):** Total instructional faculty: 70 full-time, 118 part-time (22% men; 78% women; 9% minorities). Full-time faculty with Ph.D. or other terminal degree: 64%. Student/faculty ratio: 9/1. Classes of fewer than 20 students: 80%; of 20 to 49 students: 20%. **Advanced Placement and International Baccalaureate credit:** AP tests may be used for: Credit only. Scores accepted: 3, 4, 5. International Baccalaureate exams may be used for: Credit only. **Freshmen returning for sophomore year:** 72%. **Graduation rates:** Four-year: 30%; five-year: 44%; six-year: 48%. **Graduate study:** 9% of students pursue further study immediately upon graduation; 18% within one year; 7% within five years. Fields in which graduates pursue further study: Master of Business Administration (MBA), 6%; law, 1%; medicine, 1%; education, 9%; arts and sciences, 10%.

COSTS AND FINANCIAL AID

Financial aid office: (440) 646-8309. **Expenses (2010-2011):** Tuition and fees 2010-2011: $23,940; room/board: $7,970. Estimated books and supplies: $1,125; transportation: $630; personal expenses: $700. **Financial aid:** Priority filing date for institution's financial aid form: March 1. In 2009-2010, 95% of undergraduates applied for financial aid. Of those, 89% were determined to have financial need; 12% had their need fully met. Average financial aid package (proportion receiving): $14,705 (87%). Average amount of gift aid, such as scholarships or grants (proportion receiving): $10,414 (77%). Average amount of self-help aid, such as work study or loans (proportion receiving): $5,675 (83%). Average need-based loan (excluding PLUS or other private loans): $5,243. Among students who received need-based aid, the average percentage of need met: 63%. Among students who received aid based on merit, the average award (and the proportion receiving): $5,034 (5%). The average athletic scholarship (and the proportion receiving): $3,811 (3%). Average amount of debt of borrowers graduating in 2009: $36,116. Proportion who borrowed: 86%.

CAMPUS LIFE AND EXTRACURRICULAR ACTIVITIES

Campus housing available (% using): coed dorms (75%), women's dorms (25%). Students who live in college-owned, operated, or affiliated housing: 16%. **Student employment:** During the 2009-2010 academic year, 0% of undergraduates worked on campus. Average per-year earnings: $0. **Clubs and organizations:** Number of student organizations: 20. Activities include: campus ministries, choral groups, drama/theater, literary magazine, student government, student newspaper. Number of fraternities: 0; sororities: 0. Average proportion of students who stay on campus on weekends: 60%. **Sports program (2009-2010):** Member of NAIA. *Women's intercollegiate varsity sports:* basketball, bowling, cross country, golf, soccer, softball, swimming, tennis, track and field (outdoor), volleyball.

SERVICES AND FACILITIES

Basic services: nonremedial tutoring. **Remedial assistance:** reading, math, writing, study skills, other. **Counseling services:** career, personal, psychological, religious. **For learning-disabled students:** School does not offer a structured program with separate admission and additional fees. Total undergraduates in learning-disabled program or receiving services: 48. Services include: remedial math, remedial English, reading machines, remedial reading, tape recorders, other special classes, diagnostic testing service, untimed tests, note-taking services, oral tests, learning center, readers, extended time for tests, tutors, other. **Library:** Number of titles: 136,684; number of current serial subscriptions: 250. **Information technology resources:** Students are not required to lease or own a computer. Number of campus computers available to all students: 72. School has a wireless network. Approximate number of users that can be accommodated: 300. Proportion of college-owned housing units wired for high-speed internet access: 100%. **Campus safety:** Security services offered: 24-hour foot-and-vehicle patrols, late-night transport/escort service, 24-hour emergency telephones, lighted pathways/sidewalks, controlled dormitory access (key, security card, etc).

TRANSFER AND INTERNATIONAL STUDENTS

Transfer students: May apply for admission for the following academic terms: Fall, Spring, Summer. Applicants do not need a minimum number of credits to apply. For fall 2009: Transfer applications received: 242. Transfer applicants offered admission: 236. Transfer applicants enrolled: 185. **International students:** Number of foreign undergraduates: 3. Number of countries represented: 4. Minimum TOEFL score required: 500 (paper); 173 (computer).

Walsh University

- **Address:** 2020 E. Maple Street, North Canton, OH 44720
- **Website:** http://www.walsh.edu
- **Private; Religious affiliation:** Roman Catholic
- **Enrollment:** 1,883 full-time; 409 part-time

KEY STATS
✔ **U.S News College Ranking:** 76, Regional Universities (Midwest)
✔ **ACT Score (25th/75th percentile):** 19-24
✔ **Tuition:** 2010-2011: $22,280

Selectivity: Selective	**Room/board:** $8,360
Acceptance rate: 81%	**Average debt:** $23,446
Student/faculty ratio: 14/1	**Proportion who borrowed:** 92%

UNDERGRADUATE STUDENT BODY STATS

2009-2010 enrollment: 1,883 full-time; 409 part-time. Men: 37%; women: 63%. **Ethnic makeup:** African American: 4%; Asian American: 1%; Hispanic: 1%; White: 93%; International: 1%. **Religious preference:** Protestant: 25%; No preference: 2%; Unknown: 29%; Roman Catholic: 43%.

ADMISSIONS FACTS AND FIGURES

Phone: (800) 362-9846. **Email:** admissions@walsh.edu. **Website:** http://www.walsh.edu. **Application deadlines for fall 2011:** Regular decision: August 15. Early decision: Not offered. Early action: Not offered. Admission can be deferred. **Application fee:** $25. **Admissions requirements/recommendations:** High school units required (recommended): English: 4 (4); Mathematics: 3 (3); Science: 3 (3); Foreign language: (2); Social studies: 2 (3); History: 3; Academic electives: (1); Total units: 16 (16). Tests: The college uses SAT or ACT scores in admissions decisions. Either SAT or ACT required. For admission to the fall 2011 entering class, the school will accept: ACT with or without writing accepted. Campus visit: Recommended. Admissions interview: Recommended. Off-campus interview: May be arranged. **Factors that count in admissions decisions:** *Academic:* Secondary school record: Very Important. Class rank: Considered. Letters of recommendation: Important. Standardized test scores: Very Important. Essay: Considered. *Nonacademic:* Interview: Considered. Extracurricular activities: Not Considered. Talent/ability: Not Considered. Character/personal qualities: Important. Alumni/ae relationship: Not Considered. Geographical residence: Not Considered. State residency: Not Considered. Religious affiliation/commitment: Not Considered. Minority status: Not Considered. Volunteer work: Considered. Work experience: Not Considered. **Other schools with the greatest overlap in applicants:** John Carroll University; Kent State University; Malone University; University of Akron; University of Mount Union. **Admissions statistics for the fall 2009 entering class:** Total applicants: 1,466. Total accepted: 1,191. Freshmen enrolled: 489; 19% were from out of state. Overall acceptance rate: 81%. **Credentials of fall 2009 freshmen:** 16% ranked in the top 10 percent of their high school class; 41% were in the top 25 percent; 75% were in the top half. (Proportion submitting class standing: 90%.) **Average high school grade point average:** 3.3. **First-year students who submitted SAT scores:** 18%. Scores (25/75 percentile): Critical Reading: 440-530, Math: 460-550, Combined: 900-1080. **First-year students submitting ACT scores:** 96%. Scores (25/75 percentile): English: 18-25, Math: 18-25, Composite: 19-24.

ACADEMICS

Year founded: 1958. **Academic calendar:** Semester. **Degrees offered:** associate, bachelor's, master's. **Most popular majors:** 36% business, management, marketing, and related support services, 20% health professions and related clinical sciences, 15% education, 10% biological and biomedical sciences, 5% psychology. **Major fields of study:** biological and biomedical sciences; business, management, marketing, and related support services; communication, journalism, and related programs; computer and information sciences and support services; education; English language and literature/letters; foreign languages, literatures, and linguistics; health professions and related clinical sciences; history; mathematics and statistics; parks, recreation, leisure, and fitness studies; philosophy and religious studies; physical sciences; psychology; social sciences; theology and religious vocations. **Areas of required coursework:** arts/fine arts, humanities, computer literacy, mathematics, English (including composition), philosophy, foreign languages, sciences (biological or physical), history, social science, other. **Pre-professional programs:** pre-law, pre-dentistry, pre-medicine, pre-theology, pre-veterinary science, pre-optometry, pre-pharmacy, other. **Special academic programs (% participation):** accelerated program (17%), cooperative (work-study plan) program (0%), cross-registration (0%), double major (9%), dual enrollment (1%), English as a Second Language (ESL) (0%), exchange student program (domestic) (0%), external degree program (17%), honors program (3%), independent study (2%), internships (14%), study abroad (4%), teacher certificate program (17%). **Teacher certification offered in:** early childhood, special education, middle/junior high, secondary. **Faculty and instruction (2009-2010):** Total instructional faculty: 108 full-time, 158 part-time (50% men; 50% women; 5% minorities). Full-time faculty with Ph.D. or other terminal degree: 75%. Student/faculty ratio: 14/1. Classes of fewer than 20 students: 62%; of 20 to 49 students: 38%; of 50 or more students: 0%. **Advanced Placement and International Baccalaureate credit:** AP tests may be used for: Credit and/or placement. Scores accepted: 3, 4, 5. International Baccalaureate exams may be used for: Placement only. **Freshmen returning for sophomore year:** 76%. **Graduation rates:** Four-year: 51%; five-year: 57%; six-year: 54%. **Graduate study:** 24% of students pursue further study within one year. Fields in which graduates pursue further study: Master of Business Administration (MBA), 25%; law, 5%; medicine, 8%; education, 21%; arts and sciences, 41%.

COSTS AND FINANCIAL AID

Financial aid office: (330) 490-7150. **Expenses (2010-2011):** Tuition and fees 2010-2011: $22,280; room/board: $8,360. Estimated books and supplies: $1,062; transportation: $738; personal expenses: $1,212. **Financial aid:** Priority filing date for institution's financial aid form: February 14. In 2009-2010, 87% of undergraduates applied for financial aid. Of those, 70% were determined to have financial need; 54% had their need fully met. Average financial aid package (proportion receiving): $16,350 (70%). Average amount of gift aid, such as scholarships or grants (proportion receiving): $6,334 (65%). Average amount of self-help aid, such as work study or loans (proportion receiving): $4,865 (56%). Average need-based loan (excluding PLUS or other private loans): $4,701. Among students who received need-based aid, the average percentage of need met: 86%. Among students who received aid based on merit, the average award (and the proportion receiving): $6,334 (14%). The average athletic scholarship (and the proportion receiving): $4,316 (20%). Average amount of debt of borrowers graduating in 2009: $23,446. Proportion who borrowed: 92%.

CAMPUS LIFE AND EXTRACURRICULAR ACTIVITIES

Campus housing available (% using): coed dorms (79%), apartment for single students (20%), special housing for disabled students (1%), special housing for international students. Students who live in college-owned, operated, or affiliated housing: 54%. **Student employment:** During the 2009-2010 academic year, 12% of undergraduates worked on campus. Average per-year earnings: $2,451. **Clubs and organizations:** Number of student organizations: 40. Activities include: campus ministries, choral groups, dance, drama/theater, international student organization, literary magazine, music ensembles, pep band, radio station, student government, student newspaper. Number of fraternities: 0; sororities: 0. Average proportion of students who stay on campus on weekends: 70%. **Sports program (2009-2010):** Member of NAIA. *Men's intercollegiate varsity sports:* baseball, basketball, cross country, football, golf, soccer, tennis, track and field (indoor), track and field (outdoor), volleyball. *Women's intercollegiate varsity sports:* basketball, cross country, golf, soccer, softball, tennis, track and field (indoor), track and field (outdoor), volleyball.

SERVICES AND FACILITIES

Basic services: nonremedial tutoring, placement service, health service, health insurance. **Remedial assistance:** reading, math, writing, study skills. **Counseling services:** minority student, career, personal, veteran student, academic, older student, psychological, other. **For learning-disabled students:** School does not offer a structured program with separate admission and additional fees. Total undergraduates in learning-disabled program or receiving services: 34. Services include: remedial math, remedial English, tape recorders, other special classes, untimed tests, oral tests, learning center, readers, extended time for tests, tutors, priority registration, priority seating, substitution of courses, typist/scribe. **Library:** Number of titles: 139,889; number of current serial subscriptions: 6,257. **Information technology resources:** Students are not required to lease or own a computer.

Number of campus computers available to all students: 335. School has a wireless network. Approximate number of users that can be accommodated: 720. Proportion of college-owned housing units wired for high-speed internet access: 100%. **Campus safety:** Security services offered: 24-hour foot-and-vehicle patrols, late-night transport/escort service, 24-hour emergency telephones, lighted pathways/sidewalks, controlled dormitory access (key, security card, etc).

TRANSFER AND INTERNATIONAL STUDENTS

Transfer students: May apply for admission for the following academic terms: Fall, Spring, Summer. Applicants do not need a minimum number of credits to apply. For fall 2009: Transfer applications received: 236. Transfer applicants offered admission: 208. Transfer applicants enrolled: 157. **International students:** Number of foreign undergraduates: 21 (1% of student body). Number of countries represented: 25. Minimum TOEFL score required: 500 (paper); 61 (computer).

Wilberforce University

- **Address:** PO Box 1001, 1055 N. Beckett Road, Wilberforce, OH 45384
- **Website:** http://www.wilberforce.edu
- **Private; Religious affiliation:** African Methodist Episcopal
- **Enrollment:** N/A

KEY STATS

✔ **U.S News College Ranking:** second tier, Regional Colleges (Midwest)
✔ **SAT or ACT Score (25th/75th percentile):** N/A
✔ **Tuition:** 2009-2010: $12,470

Selectivity: Less selective	**Room/board:** $5,700
Acceptance rate: N/A	**Average debt:** N/A
Student/faculty ratio: N/A	**Proportion who borrowed:** N/A

Wilmington College

- **Address:** 1870 Quaker Way, Wilmington, OH 45177
- **Website:** http://www.wilmington.edu
- **Private; Religious affiliation:** Quaker
- **Enrollment:** 1,267 full-time; 288 part-time

KEY STATS

✔ **U.S News College Ranking:** 31, Regional Colleges (Midwest)
✔ **ACT Score (25th/75th percentile):** 17-23
✔ **Tuition:** 2009-2010: $24,286

Selectivity: Selective	**Room/board:** $8,272
Acceptance rate: 93%	**Average debt:** N/A
Student/faculty ratio: 14/1	**Proportion who borrowed:** N/A

UNDERGRADUATE STUDENT BODY STATS

2009-2010 enrollment: 1,267 full-time; 288 part-time. Men: 46%; women: 54%. **Ethnic makeup:** African American: 9%; American-Indian: 1%; Hispanic: 1%; White: 88%; International: 1%.

ADMISSIONS FACTS AND FIGURES

Phone: (937) 382-6661. **Email:** admission@wilmington.edu. **Website:** http://www.wilmington.edu. **Application deadlines for fall 2011:** Regular decision: August 1. Early decision: Not offered. Early action: Not offered. Admission can be deferred. **Application fee:** $25. **To apply online, go to:** https://app.applyyourself.com/?id=WILM-U. **Admissions requirements/ recommendations:** High school units required (recommended): English: 4; Mathematics: 2; Science: 2; Foreign language: (2); Social studies: (2); History: (0); Academic electives: (0); Total units: 16. Tests: The college uses SAT or ACT scores in admissions decisions. Either SAT or ACT required. For admission to the fall 2011 entering class, the school will accept: ACT with or without writing accepted. Campus visit: Recommended. Admissions interview: Recommended. Off-campus interview: Not available. **Factors that count in admissions decisions:** *Academic:* Secondary school record: Important. Class rank: Important. Letters of recommendation: Considered. Standardized test scores: Important. Essay: Not Considered. *Nonacademic:* Interview: Considered. Extracurricular activities: Considered. Talent/ability: Important. Character/personal qualities: Important. Alumni/ae relationship: Important. Geographical residence: Not Considered. State residency: Not Considered. Religious affiliation/commitment: Not Considered. Minority status: Not Considered. Volunteer work: Considered. Work experience: Not Considered. **Other schools with the greatest overlap in applicants:** Ohio State University–Columbus; Ohio University; Otterbein College; University of Cincinnati; Wright State University. **Admissions statistics for the fall 2009 entering class:** Total applicants: 1,700. Total accepted: 1,577. Freshmen enrolled: 337; 2% were from out of state. Overall acceptance rate: 93%. **Credentials of fall 2009 freshmen:** 13% ranked in the top 10 percent of their high school class; 36% were in the top 25 percent; 66% were in the top half. (Proportion submitting class standing: 100%.) **First-year students who submitted SAT scores:** 22%. Scores (25/75 percentile): Critical Reading: 430-540, Math: 430-570, Combined: 860-1110. **First-year students submitting ACT scores:** 94%. Scores (25/75 percentile): English: 17-23, Math: 15-22, Composite: 17-23.

ACADEMICS

Year founded: 1870. **Academic calendar:** Semester. **Degrees offered:** bachelor's, master's. **Most popular majors:** 28% business, management, marketing, and related support services, 20% education, 7% agriculture, agriculture operations, and related sciences, 7% psychology, 4% history. **Major fields of study:** agriculture, agriculture operations, and related sciences; biological and biomedical sciences; business, management, marketing, and related support services; communication, journalism, and related programs; computer and information sciences and support services; education; English language and literature/letters; foreign languages, literatures, and linguistics; health professions and related clinical sciences; history; liberal arts and sciences studies, and humanities; mathematics and statistics; parks, recreation, leisure, and fitness studies; philosophy and religious studies; physical sciences; psychology; public administration and social service professions; security and protective services; social sciences; visual and performing arts. **Areas of required coursework:** arts/fine arts, humanities, computer literacy, mathematics, English (including composition), sciences (biological or physical), social science. **Special academic programs (% participation):** cross-registration (1%), double major (23%), dual enrollment, honors program (6%), independent study (11%), internships (27%), liberal arts/career combination (100%), student-designed major (.4%), study abroad (10%), teacher certificate program (26%), weekend college (5%). **Teacher certification offered in:** early childhood, elementary, middle/junior high, secondary. **Faculty and instruction (2009-2010):** Total instructional faculty: 65 full-time, 54 part-time (50% men; 50% women). Full-time faculty with Ph.D. or other terminal degree: 77%. Student/faculty ratio: 14/1. Classes of fewer than 20 students: 68%; of 20 to 49 students: 32%; of 50 or more students: 0%. **Advanced Placement and International Baccalaureate credit:** AP tests may be used for: Credit only. Scores accepted: 3, 4, 5. International Baccalaureate exams may be used for: Credit only. **Freshmen returning for sophomore year:** 67%. **Graduation rates:** Four-year: 50%; five-year: 60%; six-year: 57%.

COSTS AND FINANCIAL AID

Financial aid office: (937) 382-6661. **Expenses (2009-2010):** Tuition and fees 2009-2010: $24,286; room/board: $8,272. **Financial aid:** Priority filing date for institution's financial aid form: March 15.

CAMPUS LIFE AND EXTRACURRICULAR ACTIVITIES

Campus housing available: coed dorms, women's dorms, sorority housing, fraternity housing, apartment for single students. Students who live in college-owned, operated, or affiliated housing: 75%. **Student employment:** During the 2009-2010 academic year, 30% of undergraduates worked on campus. Average per-year earnings: $1,000. **Clubs and organizations:** Number of student organizations: 60. Activities include: campus ministries, choral groups, drama/theater, international student organization, literary magazine, music ensembles, musical theater, student government, student newspaper, yearbook. Number of fraternities: 5; sororities: 5. Proportion of men in fraternities: 9%; of women in sororities: 6%. Average proportion of students who stay on campus on weekends: 65%. **Sports program (2009-2010):** Member of NCAA III.

SERVICES AND FACILITIES

Basic services: nonremedial tutoring, placement service, health service, health insurance. **Remedial assistance:** math, writing, study skills. **Counseling services:** minority student, career, personal, academic, psychological, birth control, religious. **For learning-disabled students:** School does not offer a structured program with separate admission and additional fees. Services include: remedial math, remedial English, tape recorders, other special classes, diagnostic testing service, untimed tests, note-taking

services, oral tests, learning center, readers, extended time for tests, tutors. **Information technology resources:** Students are not required to lease or own a computer. Number of campus computers available to all students: 86. School does not have a wireless network. Proportion of college-owned housing units wired for high-speed internet access: 95%. **Campus safety:** Security services offered: 24-hour foot-and-vehicle patrols, late-night transport/escort service, 24-hour emergency telephones, lighted pathways/sidewalks, student patrols, controlled dormitory access (key, security card, etc).

TRANSFER AND INTERNATIONAL STUDENTS

Transfer students: May apply for admission for the following academic terms: Fall, Spring, Summer. Applicants do not need a minimum number of credits to apply. For fall 2009: Transfer applications received: 238. Transfer applicants offered admission: 235. Transfer applicants enrolled: 86. **International students:** Number of foreign undergraduates: 15 (1% of student body). Minimum TOEFL score required: 500 (paper); 173 (computer). Average TOEFL score: 520 (paper).

Wittenberg University

- **Address:** PO Box 720, Springfield, OH 45501
- **Website:** http://www.wittenberg.edu
- **Private; Religious affiliation:** Lutheran
- **Enrollment:** 1,801 full-time; 98 part-time

KEY STATS
- ✔ **U.S News College Ranking:** 114, National Liberal Arts Colleges
- ✔ **ACT Score (25th/75th percentile):** 22-28
- ✔ **Tuition:** 2010-2011: $35,424
  - **Selectivity:** More selective   **Room/board:** $9,032
  - **Acceptance rate:** 72%   **Average debt:** $28,729
  - **Student/faculty ratio:** 12/1   **Proportion who borrowed:** 68%

UNDERGRADUATE STUDENT BODY STATS

2009-2010 enrollment: 1,801 full-time; 98 part-time. Men: 42%; women: 58%. **Ethnic makeup:** African American: 5%; Asian American: 1%; Hispanic: 1%; White: 91%; International: 2%. **Religious preference:** Roman Catholic: 17%; Protestant: 23%; Jewish: 1%; No preference: 31%; Unknown: 7%; Lutheran: 16%; Other: 2%.

ADMISSIONS FACTS AND FIGURES

Phone: (937) 327-6314. **Email:** admission@wittenberg.edu. **Website:** http://www.wittenberg.edu. **Application deadlines for fall 2011:** Regular decision: Rolling. Early decision: Send application by: November 15; Decision sent by: December 15. Early action: Send application by: December 1; Decision sent by: January 1. Admission can be deferred. **Application fee:** $40. **To apply online, go to:** http://www4.wittenberg.edu/admission/apply/. **Admissions requirements/recommendations:** High school units required (recommended): English: 4 (4); Mathematics: 3 (4); Science: 3 (5); Foreign language: 2 (3); Social studies: 0 (0); History: 2 (3); Total units: 16 (20). Tests: The college uses SAT or ACT scores in admissions decisions. Neither SAT nor ACT required. For admission to the fall 2011 entering class, the school will accept: ACT with or without writing accepted. Campus visit: Recommended. Admissions interview: Recommended. Off-campus interview: May be arranged. **Factors that count in admissions decisions:** *Academic:* Secondary school record: Very Important. Class rank: Very Important. Letters of recommendation: Important. Standardized test scores: Considered. Essay: Important. *Nonacademic:* Interview: Considered. Extracurricular activities: Important. Talent/ability: Important. Character/personal qualities: Important. Alumni/ae relationship: Considered. Geographical residence: Not Considered. State residency: Not Considered. Religious affiliation/commitment: Not Considered. Minority status: Not Considered. Volunteer work: Important. Work experience: Considered. **Other schools with the greatest overlap in applicants:** College of Wooster; Denison University; Miami University–Oxford; Ohio Wesleyan University; University of Dayton. **Admissions statistics for the fall 2009 entering class:** Total applicants: 3,222. Total accepted: 2,321. Freshmen enrolled: 488; 30% were from out of state. Accepted through early-decision or early-action plans: 73%. Overall acceptance rate: 72%. Early-decision acceptance rate: 54%. Non-early acceptance rate: 48%. **Credentials of fall 2009 freshmen:** 27% ranked in the top 10 percent of their high school class; 50% were in the top 25 percent; 81% were in the top half. (Proportion submitting class standing: 66%.) **Average high school grade point average:** 3.4. **First-year**

students who submitted SAT scores: 38%. Scores (25/75 percentile): Critical Reading: 500-620, Math: 500-620, Combined: 1000-1240. **First-year students submitting ACT scores:** 63%. Scores (25/75 percentile): English: 21-27, Math: 21-28, Composite: 22-28.

ACADEMICS

Year founded: 1845. **Academic calendar:** Semester. **Degrees offered:** bachelor's, master's. **Most popular majors:** 17% social sciences, 12% business/commerce, 10% English language and literature, 10% biology/biological sciences, 10% education. **Major fields of study:** agriculture, agriculture operations, and related sciences; area, ethnic, cultural, and gender studies; biological and biomedical sciences; business, management, marketing, and related support services; communication, journalism, and related programs; computer and information sciences and support services; education; English language and literature/letters; foreign languages, literatures, and linguistics; history; liberal arts and sciences studies, and humanities; mathematics and statistics; philosophy and religious studies; physical sciences; psychology; social sciences; visual and performing arts. **Areas of required coursework:** arts/fine arts, humanities, computer literacy, mathematics, English (including composition), philosophy, foreign languages, sciences (biological or physical), history, social science. **Pre-professional programs:** pre-law, pre-dentistry, pre-medicine, pre-theology, pre-veterinary science, pre-optometry, pre-pharmacy. **Special academic programs (% participation):** cross-registration (0%), double major (8%), dual enrollment (1%), honors program (12%), independent study (16%), internships (17%), student-designed major (3%), study abroad (22%), teacher certificate program (29%). **Teacher certification offered in:** early childhood, special education, elementary, middle/junior high, secondary. **Reserve Officers Training Corps (ROTC):** Army ROTC: Offered at cooperating institution (Central State University); Air Force ROTC: Offered at cooperating institution (Wright State University). **Faculty and instruction (2009-2010):** Total instructional faculty: 140 full-time, 57 part-time (55% men; 45% women; 8% minorities). Full-time faculty with Ph.D. or other terminal degree: 93%. Student/faculty ratio: 12/1. Classes of fewer than 20 students: 66%; of 20 to 49 students: 33%; of 50 or more students: 1%. **Advanced Placement and International Baccalaureate credit:** AP tests may be used for: Placement only. Scores accepted: 3, 4, 5. International Baccalaureate exams may be used for: Credit only. **Freshmen returning for sophomore year:** 78%. **Graduation rates:** Four-year: 58%; five-year: 65%; six-year: 66%. **Graduate study:** 38% of students pursue further study within one year. Fields in which graduates pursue further study: Master of Business Administration (MBA), 9%; law, 12%; medicine, 14%; education, 10%; arts and sciences, 55%; veterinary medicine, 1%.

COSTS AND FINANCIAL AID

Financial aid office: (937) 327-7321. **Expenses (2010-2011):** Tuition and fees 2010-2011: $35,424; room/board: $9,032. Estimated books and supplies: $1,000; transportation: $800; personal expenses: $1,700. **Financial aid:** Priority filing date for institution's financial aid form: March 1. In 2009-2010, 83% of undergraduates applied for financial aid. Of those, 73% were determined to have financial need; 32% had their need fully met. Average financial aid package (proportion receiving): $27,562 (73%). Average amount of gift aid, such as scholarships or grants (proportion receiving): $21,660 (72%). Average amount of self-help aid, such as work study or loans (proportion receiving): $6,278 (71%). Average need-based loan (excluding PLUS or other private loans): $4,546. Among students who received need-based aid, the average percentage of need met: 85%. Among students who received aid based on merit, the average award (and the proportion receiving): $13,539 (27%). The average athletic scholarship (and the proportion receiving): $0 (0%). Average amount of debt of borrowers graduating in 2009: $28,729. Proportion who borrowed: 68%.

CAMPUS LIFE AND EXTRACURRICULAR ACTIVITIES

Campus housing available (% using): coed dorms (53%), women's dorms (5%), sorority housing (8%), fraternity housing (3%), apartment for single students (6%), special housing for disabled students (1%), special housing for international students (1%), other housing options (23%). Students who live in college-owned, operated, or affiliated housing: 89%. **Student employment:** During the 2009-2010 academic year, 46% of undergraduates worked on campus. Average per-year earnings: $2,754. **Clubs and organizations:** Number of student organizations: 126. Activities include: campus ministries, choral groups, concert band, dance, drama/theater, international student organization, jazz band, literary magazine, model UN, music ensembles, musical theater, opera, radio station, student government, student newspaper, student film society, symphony orchestra. Number of fraternities: 6; sororities: 5. Proportion of men in fraternities: 24%; of women in sororities: 31%. Average proportion of students who stay on campus on

weekends: 81%. **Sports program (2009-2010):** Member of NCAA III. *Men's intercollegiate varsity sports:* baseball, basketball, cross country, football, golf, lacrosse, soccer, swimming, tennis, track and field (indoor), track and field (outdoor). *Women's intercollegiate varsity sports:* basketball, cross country, field hockey, golf, lacrosse, soccer, softball, swimming, tennis, track and field (indoor), track and field (outdoor), volleyball.

SERVICES AND FACILITIES

Basic services: nonremedial tutoring, women's center, placement service, health service, health insurance. **Remedial assistance:** math, writing, study skills. **Counseling services:** minority student, career, personal, academic, psychological, birth control, religious. **For learning-disabled students:** School does not offer a structured program with separate admission and additional fees. Services include: extended time for tests, tutors, substitution of courses, texts on tape. **Library:** Number of titles: 423,930; number of current serial subscriptions: 7,830. **Information technology resources:** Students are not required to lease or own a computer. Number of campus computers available to all students: 500. School has a wireless network. Approximate number of users that can be accommodated: 1,500. Proportion of college-owned housing units wired for high-speed internet access: 76%. **Campus safety:** Security services offered: 24-hour foot-and-vehicle patrols, late-night transport/escort service, 24-hour emergency telephones, lighted pathways/sidewalks, controlled dormitory access (key, security card, etc).

TRANSFER AND INTERNATIONAL STUDENTS

Transfer students: May apply for admission for the following academic terms: Fall, Spring, Summer. Applicants do not need a minimum number of credits to apply. For fall 2009: Transfer applications received: 128. Transfer applicants offered admission: 77. Transfer applicants enrolled: 34. **International students:** Number of foreign undergraduates: 34 (2% of student body). Number of countries represented: 26. Minimum TOEFL score required: 550 (paper); 213 (computer).

Wright State University

- ■ **Address:** 3640 Colonel Glenn Highway, Dayton, OH 45435
- ■ **Website:** http://www.wright.edu
- ■ **Public**
- ■ **Enrollment:** 11,299 full-time; 2,205 part-time

KEY STATS

✔ **U.S News College Ranking:** second tier, National Universities
✔ **ACT Score (25th/75th percentile):** 18-24
✔ **Tuition:** 2009-2010: $7,533 in state, $14,595 out of state

Selectivity: Selective	**Room/board:** $7,925
Acceptance rate: 84%	**Average debt:** $25,357
Student/faculty ratio: 17/1	**Proportion who borrowed:** 73%

UNDERGRADUATE STUDENT BODY STATS

2009-2010 enrollment: 11,299 full-time; 2,205 part-time. Men: 45%; women: 55%. **Ethnic makeup:** African American: 16%; Asian American: 3%; Hispanic: 2%; White: 78%; International: 1%.

ADMISSIONS FACTS AND FIGURES

Phone: (937) 775-5700. **Email:** admissions@wright.edu. **Website:** http://www.wright.edu. **Application deadlines for fall 2011:** Regular decision: Rolling. Early decision: Not offered. Early action: Not offered. Admission can be deferred. **Application fee:** $30. **To apply online, go to:** https://www.applyweb.com/aw?wright. **Admissions requirements/recommendations:** High school units required (recommended): English: 4; Mathematics: 3; Science: 3; Foreign language: 2; Social studies: 3; Total units: 15. Tests: The college uses SAT or ACT scores in admissions decisions. Either SAT or ACT required. For admission to the fall 2011 entering class, the school will accept: ACT with or without writing accepted. Campus visit: Recommended. Admissions interview: Recommended. Off-campus interview: Not available. **Factors that count in admissions decisions:** *Academic:* Secondary school record: Very Important. Class rank: Important. Letters of recommendation: Considered. Standardized test scores: Very Important. Essay: Not Considered. *Nonacademic:* Interview: Not Considered. Extracurricular activities: Not Considered. Talent/ability: Not Considered. Character/personal qualities: Not Considered. Alumni/ae relationship: Not Considered. Geographical residence: Not Considered. State residency: Considered. Religious affiliation/commitment: Not Considered. Minority status: Not Considered. Volunteer work: Not Considered. Work experience: Not Considered. **Other schools with the greatest overlap in applicants:** Ohio State University–Columbus; University of Cincinnati. **Admissions statistics for the fall 2009 entering class:** Total applicants: 6,188. Total accepted: 5,214. Freshmen enrolled: 2,364; 3% were from out of state. Overall acceptance rate: 84%. **Credentials of fall 2009 freshmen:** 15% ranked in the top 10 percent of their high school class; 35% were in the top 25 percent; 65% were in the top half. (Proportion submitting class standing: 86%.) **Average high school grade point average:** 3.1. **First-year students who submitted SAT scores:** 25%. Scores (25/75 percentile): Critical Reading: 440-560, Math: 440-580, Combined: 880-1140. **First-year students submitting ACT scores:** 88%. Scores (25/75 percentile): English: 17-24, Math: 17-24, Composite: 18-24.

ACADEMICS

Year founded: 1964. **Academic calendar:** Quarter. **Degrees offered:** certificate, associate, bachelor's, master's, post-master's certificate, doctorate. **Most popular majors:** 28% business/commerce, 13% chiropractic (D.C.), 10% education, 8% social sciences, 7% psychology. **Major fields of study:** area, ethnic, cultural, and gender studies; biological and biomedical sciences; business, management, marketing, and related support services; communication, journalism, and related programs; computer and information sciences and support services; education; engineering; English language and literature/letters; foreign languages, literatures, and linguistics; health professions and related clinical sciences; history; liberal arts and sciences studies, and humanities; mathematics and statistics; multi/interdisciplinary studies; philosophy and religious studies; physical sciences; psychology; public administration and social service professions; social sciences; visual and performing arts. **Areas of required coursework:** arts/fine arts, humanities, mathematics, English (including composition), sciences (biological or physical), history, social science. **Pre-professional programs:** pre-law, pre-dentistry, pre-medicine. **Special academic programs:** cooperative (work-study plan) program, cross-registration, distance learning, double major, dual enrollment, English as a Second Language (ESL), honors program, independent study, internships, student-designed major, study abroad, teacher certificate program. **Teacher certification offered in:** early childhood, special education, elementary, vo-tech, middle/junior high, secondary. **Cooperative education programs:** art, business, computer science, education, engineering, humanities, technologies, vocational arts. **Reserve Officers Training Corps (ROTC):** Army ROTC: Offered on campus; Air Force ROTC: Offered on campus. **Faculty and instruction (2009-2010):** Total instructional faculty: 853 full-time, 27 part-time (56% men; 44% women). Student/faculty ratio: 17/1. Classes of fewer than 20 students: 41%; of 20 to 49 students: 50%; of 50 or more students: 9%. **Advanced Placement and International Baccalaureate credit:** AP tests may be used for: Placement only. Scores accepted: 3, 4, 5. International Baccalaureate exams may be used for: Placement only. **Freshmen returning for sophomore year:** 70%. **Graduation rates:** Four-year: 19%; five-year: 39%; six-year: 44%.

COSTS AND FINANCIAL AID

Financial aid office: (937) 873-5721. **Expenses (2009-2010):** Tuition and fees 2009-2010: $7,533 in state, $14,595 out of state; room/board: $7,925. Estimated books and supplies: $1,836; transportation: $1,608; personal expenses: $1,389. **Financial aid:** Priority filing date for institution's financial aid form: February 15. In 2009-2010, 79% of undergraduates applied for financial aid. Of those, 69% were determined to have financial need; 9% had their need fully met. Average financial aid package (proportion receiving): $9,177 (68%). Average amount of gift aid, such as scholarships or grants (proportion receiving): $6,113 (50%). Average amount of self-help aid, such as work study or loans (proportion receiving): $4,537 (66%). Average need-based loan (excluding PLUS or other private loans): $4,106. Among students who received need-based aid, the average percentage of need met: 54%. Among students who received aid based on merit, the average award (and the proportion receiving): $4,091 (8%). The average athletic scholarship (and the proportion receiving): $12,472 (1%). Average amount of debt of borrowers graduating in 2009: $25,357. Proportion who borrowed: 73%.

CAMPUS LIFE AND EXTRACURRICULAR ACTIVITIES

Campus housing available: coed dorms, men's dorms, sorority housing, fraternity housing, apartments for married students, apartment for single students, special housing for disabled students, special housing for international students, other housing options. Students who live in college-owned, operated, or affiliated housing: 20%. Average per-year earnings: $7. **Clubs and organizations:** Number of student organizations: 145, Activities include: campus ministries, choral groups, concert band, dance, drama/theater,

international student organization, jazz band, literary magazine, marching band, model UN, music ensembles, musical theater, opera, pep band, radio station, student government, student newspaper, symphony orchestra, television station. Number of fraternities: 11; sororities: 7. Proportion of men in fraternities: 2%; of women in sororities: 2%. **Sports program (2009-2010):** Member of NCAA I.

SERVICES AND FACILITIES

Basic services: nonremedial tutoring, women's center, placement service, day care, health service, other. **Remedial assistance:** reading, math, writing, study skills. **Counseling services:** minority student, career, military, personal, veteran student, academic, psychological, birth control, religious, other. **For learning-disabled students:** School does not offer a structured program with separate admission and additional fees. Services include: remedial math, remedial English, reading machines, remedial reading, tape recorders, other special classes, diagnostic testing service, untimed tests, note-taking services, learning center, readers, extended time for tests, tutors, other. **Library:** Number of titles: 703,000; number of current serial subscriptions: 3,200. **Information technology resources:** Students are not required to lease or own a computer. Number of campus computers available to all students: 3,000. School has a wireless network. Proportion of college-owned housing units wired for high-speed internet access: 100%. **Campus safety:** Security services offered: late-night transport/escort service, 24-hour emergency telephones, lighted pathways/sidewalks.

TRANSFER AND INTERNATIONAL STUDENTS

Transfer students: May apply for admission for the following academic terms: Fall, Winter, Spring, Summer. Applicants need a minimum number of credits to apply. For fall 2009: Transfer applications received: 2,398. Transfer applicants offered admission: 1,786. Transfer applicants enrolled: 1,200. **International students:** Number of foreign undergraduates: 142 (1% of student body). Number of countries represented: 67. Minimum TOEFL score required: 500 (paper); 173 (computer). Average TOEFL score: 550 (paper).

Xavier University

- **Address:** 3800 Victory Parkway, Cincinnati, OH 45207
- **Website:** http://www.xavier.edu
- **Private; Religious affiliation:** Roman Catholic (Jesuit)
- **Enrollment:** 3,729 full-time; 499 part-time

KEY STATS

✔ **U.S News College Ranking:** 3, Regional Universities (Midwest)
✔ **ACT Score (25th/75th percentile):** 23-28
✔ **Tuition:** 2009-2010: $28,570

Selectivity: More selective	**Room/board:** $9,250
Acceptance rate: 73%	**Average debt:** $27,098
Student/faculty ratio: 13/1	**Proportion who borrowed:** 66%

UNDERGRADUATE STUDENT BODY STATS

2009-2010 enrollment: 3,729 full-time; 499 part-time. Men: 45%; women: 55%. **Ethnic makeup:** African American: 12%; Asian American: 2%; Hispanic: 3%; White: 81%; International: 1%. **Religious preference:** Protestant: 12%; Muslim: 1%; Unknown: 23%; Roman Catholic (Jesuit): 53%; Christian denominations: 10%; Other: 1%.

ADMISSIONS FACTS AND FIGURES

Phone: (877) 982-3648. **Email:** xuadmit@xavier.edu. **Website:** http://www.xavier.edu. **Application deadlines for fall 2011:** Regular decision: February 1. Early decision: Not offered. Early action: Not offered. Admission can be deferred. **Application fee:** $35. **To apply online, go to:** http://www.xavier.edu/applyonline. **Admissions requirements/recommendations:** High school units required (recommended): English: (4); Mathematics: (3); Science: (3); Foreign language: (2); Social studies: (3); History: (0); Academic electives: (5); Total units: (21). Tests: The college uses SAT or ACT scores in admissions decisions. Either SAT or ACT required. For admission to the fall 2011 entering class, the school will accept: ACT with or without writing accepted. Campus visit: Recommended. Admissions interview: Recommended. Off-campus interview: May be arranged. **Factors that count in admissions decisions:** *Academic:* Secondary school record: Very Important. Class rank: Important. Letters of recommendation: Important. Standardized test scores: Important. Essay: Important. *Nonacademic:* Interview: Not Considered.

Extracurricular activities: Considered. Talent/ability: Considered. Character/personal qualities: Important. Alumni/ae relationship: Considered. Geographical residence: Not Considered. State residency: Not Considered. Religious affiliation/commitment: Not Considered. Minority status: Not Considered. Volunteer work: Considered. Work experience: Considered. **Other schools with the greatest overlap in applicants:** Miami University–Oxford; Ohio State University–Columbus; Ohio University; University of Cincinnati; University of Dayton. **Admissions statistics for the fall 2009 entering class:** Total applicants: 7,205. Total accepted: 5,272. Freshmen enrolled: 1,183; 47% were from out of state. Overall acceptance rate: 73%. **Size of waiting list:** 71 applicants; enrolled from waiting list: 0. **Credentials of fall 2009 freshmen:** 24% ranked in the top 10 percent of their high school class; 58% were in the top 25 percent; 85% were in the top half. (Proportion submitting class standing: 57%.) **Average high school grade point average:** 3.5. **First-year students who submitted SAT scores:** 66%. Scores (25/75 percentile): Critical Reading: 530-620, Math: 510-610, Combined: 1040-1230. **First-year students submitting ACT scores:** 81%. Scores (25/75 percentile): English: 22-27, Math: 22-29, Composite: 23-28.

ACADEMICS

Year founded: 1831. **Academic calendar:** Semester. **Degrees offered:** certificate, associate, terminal-associate, bachelor's, master's. **Most popular majors:** 25% business, management, marketing, and related support services, 15% liberal arts and sciences studies, and humanities, 8% social sciences, 6% biological and biomedical sciences, 6% health professions and related clinical sciences. **Major fields of study:** biological and biomedical sciences; business, management, marketing, and related support services; communication, journalism, and related programs; computer and information sciences and support services; education; English language and literature/letters; foreign languages, literatures, and linguistics; health professions and related clinical sciences; history; liberal arts and sciences studies, and humanities; mathematics and statistics; multi/interdisciplinary studies; natural resources and conservation; parks, recreation, leisure, and fitness studies; philosophy and religious studies; physical sciences; psychology; public administration and social service professions; security and protective services; social sciences; theology and religious vocations; visual and performing arts. **Areas of required coursework:** arts/fine arts, mathematics, English (including composition), philosophy, foreign languages, sciences (biological or physical), history, social science, other. **Pre-professional programs:** pre-pharmacy, other. **Special academic programs:** cooperative (work-study plan) program, cross-registration, double major, dual enrollment, English as a Second Language (ESL), honors program, independent study, internships, study abroad, teacher certificate program, weekend college. **Teacher certification offered in:** early childhood, special education, elementary, middle/junior high, secondary. **Cooperative education programs:** business, computer science. **Reserve Officers Training Corps (ROTC):** Army ROTC: Offered on campus; Air Force ROTC: Offered at cooperating institution (University of Cincinnati). **Faculty and instruction (2009-2010):** Total instructional faculty: 317 full-time, 308 part-time (49% men; 51% women; 12% minorities). Full-time faculty with Ph.D. or other terminal degree: 77%. Student/faculty ratio: 13/1. Classes of fewer than 20 students: 41%; of 20 to 49 students: 57%; of 50 or more students: 2%. **Advanced Placement and International Baccalaureate credit:** AP tests may be used for: Credit only. Scores accepted: 3, 4, 5. International Baccalaureate exams may be used for: Credit only. **Freshmen returning for sophomore year:** 87%. **Graduation rates:** Four-year: 68%; five-year: 76%; six-year: 78%. **Graduate study:** 25% of students pursue further study within one year. Fields in which graduates pursue further study: Master of Business Administration (MBA), 3%; law, 4%; medicine, 8%; education, 2%; arts and sciences, 4%.

COSTS AND FINANCIAL AID

Financial aid office: (513) 745-3142. **Expenses (2009-2010):** Tuition and fees 2009-2010: $28,570; room/board: $9,250. Estimated books and supplies: $1,000; transportation: $1,200; personal expenses: $1,000. **Financial aid:** Priority filing date for institution's financial aid form: February 15. In 2009-2010, 72% of undergraduates applied for financial aid. Of those, 60% were determined to have financial need; 18% had their need fully met. Average financial aid package (proportion receiving): $17,748 (60%). Average amount of gift aid, such as scholarships or grants (proportion receiving): $12,753 (56%). Average amount of self-help aid, such as work study or loans (proportion receiving): $5,481 (48%). Average need-based loan (excluding PLUS or other private loans): $4,593. Among students who received need-based aid, the average percentage of need met: 70%. Among students who received aid based on merit, the average award (and the proportion receiving): $10,906 (30%). The average athletic scholarship (and the proportion receiving): $13,199 (4%). Average amount of debt of borrowers graduating in 2009: $27,098. Proportion who borrowed: 66%.

CAMPUS LIFE AND EXTRACURRICULAR ACTIVITIES

Campus housing available (% using): coed dorms (68%), apartment for single students (31%), other housing options (1%). Students who live in college-owned, operated, or affiliated housing: 48%. **Student employment:** During the 2009-2010 academic year, 22% of undergraduates worked on campus. Average per-year earnings: $2,200. **Clubs and organizations:** Number of student organizations: 124. Activities include: campus ministries, choral groups, concert band, dance, drama/theater, international student organization, jazz band, literary magazine, music ensembles, musical theater, opera, pep band, radio station, student government, student newspaper, student film society, symphony orchestra, television station. Number of fraternities: 0; sororities: 0. Average proportion of students who stay on campus on weekends: 75%. **Sports program (2009-2010):** Member of NCAA I. *Men's intercollegiate varsity sports:* baseball, basketball, cross country, golf, soccer, swimming, tennis, track and field (indoor), track and field (outdoor). *Women's intercollegiate varsity sports:* basketball, cross country, golf, soccer, swimming, tennis, track and field (indoor), track and field (outdoor), volleyball.

SERVICES AND FACILITIES

Basic services: nonremedial tutoring, women's center, health service, health insurance. **Remedial assistance:** math, study skills. **Counseling services:** career, personal, academic, psychological, religious. **For learning-disabled students:** School does not offer a structured program with separate admission and additional fees. Services include: remedial math, reading machines, remedial reading, tape recorders, diagnostic testing service, note-taking services, learning center, readers, extended time for tests, tutors, early syllabus, priority seating, substitution of courses, texts on tape, typist/scribe, exams on tape or computer. **Library:** Number of titles: 362,152; number of current serial subscriptions: 55,047. **Information technology resources:** Students are not required to lease or own a computer. Number of campus computers available to all students: 250. School has a wireless network. Approximate number of users that can be accommodated: 12,000. Proportion of college-owned housing units wired for high-speed internet access: 100%. **Campus safety:** Security services offered: 24-hour foot-and-vehicle patrols, late-night transport/escort service, 24-hour emergency telephones, lighted pathways/sidewalks, controlled dormitory access (key, security card, etc).

TRANSFER AND INTERNATIONAL STUDENTS

Transfer students: May apply for admission for the following academic terms: Fall, Spring. Applicants need a minimum number of credits to apply. For fall 2009: Transfer applications received: 398. Transfer applicants offered admission: 188. Transfer applicants enrolled: 86. **International students:** Number of foreign undergraduates: 57 (1% of student body). Number of countries represented: 22. Minimum TOEFL score required: 530 (paper); 197 (computer).

Youngstown State University

- **Address:** 1 University Plaza, Youngstown, OH 44555
- **Website:** http://www.ysu.edu
- **Public**
- **Enrollment:** 10,443 full-time; 2,926 part-time

KEY STATS

✔ **U.S News College Ranking:** second tier, Regional Universities (Midwest)
✔ **ACT Score (25th/75th percentile):** 17-23
✔ **Tuition:** 2009-2010: $6,956 in state, $12,629 out of state

Selectivity: Less selective	**Room/board:** $7,400
Acceptance rate: 89%	**Average debt:** N/A
Student/faculty ratio: 19/1	**Proportion who borrowed:** N/A

UNDERGRADUATE STUDENT BODY STATS

2009-2010 enrollment: 10,443 full-time; 2,926 part-time. Men: 47%; women: 53%. **Ethnic makeup:** African American: 16%; Asian American: 1%; Hispanic: 2%; White: 79%; International: 1%.

ADMISSIONS FACTS AND FIGURES

Phone: (877) 468-6978. **Email:** enroll@ysu.edu. **Website:** http://www.ysu.edu. **Application deadlines for fall 2011:** Regular decision: August 15. Early decision: Not offered. Early action: Not offered. Admission can be deferred. **Application fee:** $30. **To apply online, go to:** http://www.ysu.edu/applysu/index.shtml. **Admissions requirements/recommendations:** High school units required (recommended): English: (4); Mathematics: (3); Science: (3); Foreign language: (2); Social studies: (3); Total units: (16). Tests: The college uses SAT or ACT scores in admissions decisions. Either SAT or ACT required. For admission to the fall 2011 entering class, the school will accept: ACT with or without writing accepted. Campus visit: Recommended. Admissions interview: Neither required nor recommended. Off-campus interview: Not available. **Factors that count in admissions decisions:** *Academic:* Secondary school record: Important. Class rank: Important. Letters of recommendation: Not Considered. Standardized test scores: Very Important. Essay: Not Considered. *Nonacademic:* Interview: Not Considered. Extracurricular activities: Not Considered. Talent/ability: Not Considered. Character/personal qualities: Not Considered. Alumni/ae relationship: Not Considered. Geographical residence: Very Important. State residency: Very Important. Religious affiliation/commitment: Not Considered. Minority status: Not Considered. Volunteer work: Not Considered. Work experience: Not Considered. **Admissions statistics for the fall 2009 entering class:** Total applicants: 4,975. Total accepted: 4,419. Freshmen enrolled: 2,637; 10% were from out of state. Overall acceptance rate: 89%. **Credentials of fall 2009 freshmen:** 8% ranked in the top 10 percent of their high school class; 22% were in the top 25 percent; 50% were in the top half. (Proportion submitting class standing: 87%.) **Average high school grade point average:** 2.8. **First-year students who submitted SAT scores:** 13%. Scores (25/75 percentile): Critical Reading: 400-520, Math: 400-540, Combined: 800-1060. **First-year students submitting ACT scores:** 71%. Scores (25/75 percentile): English: 15-22, Math: 16-22, Composite: 17-23.

ACADEMICS

Year founded: 1908. **Academic calendar:** Semester. **Degrees offered:** certificate, diploma, associate, transfer-associate, terminal-associate, bachelor's, post-bachelor's certificate, master's. **Most popular majors:** 6% nursing/registered nurse training (R.N., A.S.N., B.S.N., M.S.N.), 5% criminal justice/safety studies, 5% early childhood education and teaching, 5% general studies, 4% biology/biological sciences. **Major fields of study:** area, ethnic, cultural, and gender studies; biological and biomedical sciences; business, management, marketing, and related support services; communication, journalism, and related programs; computer and information sciences and support services; education; engineering; engineering technologies/technicians; English language and literature/letters; family and consumer sciences/human sciences; foreign languages, literatures, and linguistics; health professions and related clinical sciences; history; legal professions and studies; liberal arts and sciences studies, and humanities; mathematics and statistics; natural resources and conservation; parks, recreation, leisure, and fitness studies; philosophy and religious studies; physical sciences; psychology; public administration and social service professions; security and protective services; social sciences; visual and performing arts. **Areas of required coursework:** arts/fine arts, humanities, mathematics, English (including composition), sciences (biological or physical), social science. **Pre-professional programs:** pre-law, pre-dentistry, pre-medicine, pre-veterinary science, pre-optometry, pre-pharmacy. **Special academic programs:** accelerated program, cooperative (work-study plan) program, cross-registration, distance learning, double major, English as a Second Language (ESL), exchange student program (domestic), honors program, internships, student-designed major, study abroad, teacher certificate program, weekend college. **Teacher certification offered in:** early childhood, special education, vo-tech, middle/junior high, adult education, secondary. **Cooperative education programs:** business, computer science, engineering. **Reserve Officers Training Corps (ROTC):** Army ROTC: Offered on campus; Air Force ROTC: Offered at cooperating institution (Kent State University). **Faculty and instruction (2009-2010):** Total instructional faculty: 447 full-time, 564 part-time (53% men; 47% women; 10% minorities). Full-time faculty with Ph.D. or other terminal degree: 83%. Student/faculty ratio: 19/1. Classes of fewer than 20 students: 34%; of 20 to 49 students: 63%; of 50 or more students: 3%. **Advanced Placement and International Baccalaureate credit:** AP tests may be used for: Credit and/or placement. Scores accepted: 3, 4, 5. International Baccalaureate exams may be used for: Credit only. **Freshmen**

returning for sophomore year: 72%. **Graduation rates:** Four-year: 11%; five-year: 27%; six-year: 36%.

COSTS AND FINANCIAL AID

Financial aid office: (330) 941-3399. **Expenses (2009-2010):** Tuition and fees 2009-2010: $6,956 in state, $12,629 out of state; room/board: $7,400. Estimated books and supplies: $1,212; transportation: $1,559; personal expenses: $619. **Financial aid:** Priority filing date for institution's financial aid form: February 15. In 2009-2010, 84% of undergraduates applied for financial aid. Of those, 75% were determined to have financial need; 4% had their need fully met. Average financial aid package (proportion receiving): $8,308 (75%). Average amount of gift aid, such as scholarships or grants (proportion receiving): $5,546 (55%). Average amount of self-help aid, such as work study or loans (proportion receiving): $3,835 (66%). Average need-based loan (excluding PLUS or other private loans): $3,744. Among students who received need-based aid, the average percentage of need met: 29%. Among students who received aid based on merit, the average award (and the proportion receiving): $2,605 (6%). The average athletic scholarship (and the proportion receiving): $9,950 (3%).

CAMPUS LIFE AND EXTRACURRICULAR ACTIVITIES

Campus housing available (% using): coed dorms (64%), women's dorms (5%), apartment for single students (31%). Students who live in college-owned, operated, or affiliated housing: 7%. **Student employment:** During the 2009-2010 academic year, 11% of undergraduates worked on campus. Average per-year earnings: $7,592. **Clubs and organizations:** Number of student organizations: 165. Activities include: campus ministries, choral groups, concert band, dance, drama/theater, international student organization, jazz band, literary magazine, marching band, model UN, music ensembles, musical theater, opera, pep band, radio station, student government, student newspaper, student film society, symphony orchestra. Number of fraternities: 16; sororities: 4. Proportion of men in fraternities: 2%; of women in sororities: 2%. Average proportion of students who stay on campus on weekends: 30%. **Sports program (2009-2010):** Member of NCAA I. *Men's intercollegiate varsity sports:* baseball, basketball, cross country, football, golf, tennis, track and field (indoor), track and field (outdoor). *Women's intercollegiate varsity sports:* basketball, cross country, golf, soccer, softball, swimming, tennis, track and field (indoor), track and field (outdoor), volleyball.

SERVICES AND FACILITIES

Basic services: nonremedial tutoring, women's center, placement service, day care, health service, health insurance. **Remedial assistance:** reading, math, writing, study skills. **Counseling services:** minority student, career, military, personal, veteran student, academic, older student, psychological. **For learning-disabled students:** School does not offer a structured program with separate admission and additional fees. Total undergraduates in learning-disabled program or receiving services: 231. Services include: remedial math, remedial English, reading machines, remedial reading, tape recorders, note-taking services, oral tests, learning center, readers, extended time for tests, tutors, priority registration, texts on tape, typist/scribe, other testing accommodations, other. **Library:** Number of titles: 873,587; number of current serial subscriptions: 45,721. **Information technology resources:** Students are not required to lease or own a computer. Number of campus computers available to all students: 170. School has a wireless network. Approximate number of users that can be accommodated: 1,016. Proportion of college-owned housing units wired for high-speed internet access: 100%. **Campus safety:** Security services offered: 24-hour foot-and-vehicle patrols, late-night transport/escort service, 24-hour emergency telephones, lighted pathways/sidewalks, student patrols, controlled dormitory access (key, security card, etc).

TRANSFER AND INTERNATIONAL STUDENTS

Transfer students: May apply for admission for the following academic terms: Fall, Spring, Summer. Applicants do not need a minimum number of credits to apply. For fall 2009: Transfer applications received: 1,213. Transfer applicants offered admission: 1,027. Transfer applicants enrolled: 712. **International students:** Number of foreign undergraduates: 74 (1% of student body). Number of countries represented: 49. Minimum TOEFL score required: 500 (paper); 61 (computer). Average TOEFL score: 572 (paper).

Oklahoma

Bacone College

- **Address:** 2299 Old Bacone Road, Muskogee, OK 74403-1568
- **Website:** http://www.bacone.edu/
- **Religious affiliation:** American Baptist Churches USA
- **Enrollment:** 864 full-time; 157 part-time

KEY STATS
✔ **U.S News College Ranking:** second tier, Regional Colleges (West)
✔ **ACT Score (25th/75th percentile):** 16-19
✔ **Tuition:** 2009-2010: $0 in state, $0 out of state

Selectivity: Less selective	**Room/board:** $7,400
Acceptance rate: 28%	**Average debt:** N/A
Student/faculty ratio: N/A	**Proportion who borrowed:** N/A

UNDERGRADUATE STUDENT BODY STATS
2009-2010 enrollment: 864 full-time; 157 part-time. Men: 51%; women: 49%. **Ethnic makeup:** African American: 24%; American-Indian: 30%; Hispanic: 5%; White: 40%.

ADMISSIONS FACTS AND FIGURES
Phone: (888) 682-5514. **Email:** admissions@bacone.edu. **Website:** http://www.bacone.edu/. **Application deadlines for fall 2011:** Regular decision: Rolling. Early decision: Not offered. Early action: Not offered. Admission can be deferred. **Application fee:** $25. **Admissions requirements/recommendations:** Tests: The college uses SAT or ACT scores in admissions decisions. Either SAT or ACT required. For admission to the fall 2011 entering class, the school will accept: ACT with or without writing accepted. Campus visit: Recommended. Admissions interview: Recommended. Off-campus interview: May be arranged. **Factors that count in admissions decisions:** *Academic:* Secondary school record: Important. Class rank: Very Important. Letters of recommendation: Considered. Standardized test scores: Very Important. Essay: Considered. *Nonacademic:* Interview: Considered. Extracurricular activities: Considered. Talent/ability: Considered. Character/personal qualities: Considered. Alumni/ae relationship: Considered. Geographical residence: Considered. State residency: Considered. Religious affiliation/commitment: Considered. Minority status: Considered. Volunteer work: Considered. Work experience: Considered. **Other schools with the greatest overlap in applicants:** Northeastern State University. **Admissions statistics for the fall 2009 entering class:** Total applicants: 1,618. Total accepted: 452. Freshmen enrolled: 207; Overall acceptance rate: 28%. **Credentials of fall 2009 freshmen:** 5% ranked in the top 10 percent of their high school class; 15% were in the top 25 percent; 55% were in the top half. (Proportion submitting class standing: 67%.) **Average high school grade point average:** 2.9. **First-year students who submitted SAT scores:** 18%. Scores (25/75 percentile): Critical Reading: 398-470, Math: 408-483, Combined: 806-953. **First-year students submitting ACT scores:** 65%. Scores (25/75 percentile): English: 14-20, Math: 15-18, Composite: 16-19.

ACADEMICS
Academic calendar: Semester. **Degrees offered:** associate, transfer-associate, bachelor's. **Most popular majors:** 29% nursing/registered nurse training (R.N., A.S.N., B.S.N., M.S.N.), 17% medical radiologic technology/science-radiation therapist, 14% business administration and management, 14% early childhood education and teaching, 8% diagnostic medical sonography/sonographer and ultrasound technician. **Freshmen returning for sophomore year:** 39%. **Graduation rates:** Four-year: 4%; five-year: 10%; six-year: 14%.

COSTS AND FINANCIAL AID
Expenses (2009-2010): Tuition and fees 2009-2010: $0 in state, $0 out of state; room/board: $7,400. Estimated books and supplies: $2,000.

CAMPUS LIFE AND EXTRACURRICULAR ACTIVITIES
Sports program (2009-2010): Member of NAIA. *Men's intercollegiate varsity sports:* baseball, basketball, cross country, football, golf, soccer, track and field (indoor), track and field (outdoor), wrestling. *Women's intercollegiate*

varsity sports: basketball, cross country, golf, soccer, softball, track and field (indoor), track and field (outdoor), volleyball.

SERVICES AND FACILITIES
Basic services: health insurance. **Remedial assistance:** reading, math, writing, study skills. **Counseling services:** career, academic, religious. **Library:** Number of titles: 41,400; number of current serial subscriptions: 0. **Information technology resources:** Students are not required to lease or own a computer. Number of campus computers available to all students: 80. School has a wireless network. Approximate number of users that can be accommodated: 200. Proportion of college-owned housing units wired for high-speed internet access: 80%. **Campus safety:** Security services offered: 24-hour foot-and-vehicle patrols, 24-hour emergency telephones, lighted pathways/sidewalks, controlled dormitory access (key, security card, etc).

TRANSFER AND INTERNATIONAL STUDENTS
Transfer students: May apply for admission for the following academic terms: Fall, Spring, Summer. Applicants need a minimum number of credits to apply. **International students:** Number of foreign undergraduates: 0.

Cameron University

- **Address:** 2800 W. Gore Boulevard, Lawton, OK 73505-6377
- **Website:** http://www.cameron.edu
- **Public**
- **Enrollment:** 3,814 full-time; 1,869 part-time

KEY STATS
✔ **U.S News College Ranking:** second tier, Regional Universities (West)
✔ **ACT Score (25th/75th percentile):** 16-21
✔ **Tuition:** 2009-2010: $4,110 in state, $9,675 out of state

Selectivity: Less selective	**Room/board:** $7,969
Acceptance rate: 100%	**Average debt:** $7,500
Student/faculty ratio: 20/1	**Proportion who borrowed:** 35%

UNDERGRADUATE STUDENT BODY STATS
2009-2010 enrollment: 3,814 full-time; 1,869 part-time. Men: 41%; women: 59%. **Ethnic makeup:** African American: 16%; American-Indian: 8%; Asian American: 3%; Hispanic: 8%; White: 60%; International: 4%.

ADMISSIONS FACTS AND FIGURES
Phone: (580) 581-2289. **Email:** admissions@cameron.edu. **Website:** http://www.cameron.edu. **Application deadlines for fall 2011:** Regular decision: Rolling. Early decision: Not offered. Early action: Not offered. Admission can be deferred. **Application fee:** $15. **To apply online, go to:** http://www.okcollegestart.org/applications/Cameron_University/apply.html. **Admissions requirements/recommendations:** High school units required (recommended): English: 4; Mathematics: 3; Science: 2 (3); Foreign language: 0 (1); Social studies: 0; History: 3; Academic electives: 3; Total units: 15. Tests: The college uses SAT or ACT scores in admissions decisions. Either SAT or ACT required. For admission to the fall 2011 entering class, the school will accept: ACT with or without writing accepted. Campus visit: Recommended. Admissions interview: Neither required nor recommended. Off-campus interview: Not available. **Factors that count in admissions decisions:** *Academic:* Secondary school record: Very Important. Class rank: Very Important. Letters of recommendation: Not Considered. Standardized test scores: Very Important. Essay: Not Considered. *Nonacademic:* Interview: Not Considered. Extracurricular activities: Not Considered. Talent/ability: Considered. Character/personal qualities: Not Considered. Alumni/ae relationship: Not Considered. Geographical residence: Not Considered. State residency: Not Considered. Religious affiliation/commitment: Not Considered. Minority status: Not Considered. Volunteer work: Not Considered. Work experience: Not Considered. **Other schools with the greatest overlap in applicants:** Midwestern State University; Oklahoma State University; University of Central Oklahoma; University of Oklahoma;

University of Science and Arts of Oklahoma. **Admissions statistics for the fall 2009 entering class:** Total applicants: 2,070. Total accepted: 2,067. Freshmen enrolled: 1,150; 16% were from out of state. Overall acceptance rate: 100%. **Credentials of fall 2009 freshmen:** 10% ranked in the top 10 percent of their high school class; 29% were in the top 25 percent; 67% were in the top half. (Proportion submitting class standing: 54%.) **Average high school grade point average:** 3.2. **First-year students submitting ACT scores:** 70%. Scores (25/75 percentile): English: 15-22, Math: 15-21, Composite: 16-21.

ACADEMICS

Year founded: 1908. **Academic calendar:** Semester. **Degrees offered:** associate, bachelor's, master's. **Most popular majors:** 19% business administration and management, 12% elementary education and teaching, 11% criminology, 7% education, 6% psychology. **Major fields of study:** agriculture, agriculture operations, and related sciences; biological and biomedical sciences; business, management, marketing, and related support services; computer and information sciences and support services; education; engineering technologies/technicians; English language and literature/letters; family and consumer sciences/human sciences; foreign languages, literatures, and linguistics; health professions and related clinical sciences; history; mathematics and statistics; multi/interdisciplinary studies; physical sciences; psychology; social sciences; visual and performing arts. **Areas of required coursework:** humanities, computer literacy, mathematics, English (including composition), sciences (biological or physical), history, social science. **Special academic programs:** accelerated program, distance learning, double major, dual enrollment, honors program, independent study, internships, liberal arts/career combination, teacher certificate program, weekend college. **Teacher certification offered in:** early childhood, special education, elementary, middle/junior high, secondary. **Cooperative education programs:** computer science, education, health professions, technologies. **Reserve Officers Training Corps (ROTC):** Army ROTC: Offered on campus. **Faculty and instruction (2009-2010):** Total instructional faculty: 183 full-time, 146 part-time (58% men; 42% women; 17% minorities). Full-time faculty with Ph.D. or other terminal degree: 64%. Student/faculty ratio: 20/1. Classes of fewer than 20 students: 48%; of 20 to 49 students: 49%; of 50 or more students: 3%. **Advanced Placement and International Baccalaureate credit:** AP tests may be used for: Credit only. Scores accepted: 3, 4, 5. **Freshmen returning for sophomore year:** 56%. **Graduation rates:** Four-year: 5%; five-year: 13%; six-year: 25%.

COSTS AND FINANCIAL AID

Financial aid office: (580) 581-2293. **Expenses (2009-2010):** Tuition and fees 2009-2010: $4,110 in state, $9,675 out of state; room/board: $7,969. Estimated books and supplies: $1,350; transportation: $2,522; personal expenses: $1,430. **Financial aid:** Priority filing date for institution's financial aid form: April 1. In 2009-2010, 71% of undergraduates applied for financial aid. Of those, 59% were determined to have financial need; 73% had their need fully met. Average financial aid package (proportion receiving): $10,100 (56%). Average amount of gift aid, such as scholarships or grants (proportion receiving): $3,350 (53%). Average amount of self-help aid, such as work study or loans (proportion receiving): $4,500 (50%). Average need-based loan (excluding PLUS or other private loans): $4,500. Among students who received need-based aid, the average percentage of need met: 82%. Among students who received aid based on merit, the average award (and the proportion receiving): $500 (11%). The average athletic scholarship (and the proportion receiving): $2,750 (2%). Average amount of debt of borrowers graduating in 2009: $7,500. Proportion who borrowed: 35%.

CAMPUS LIFE AND EXTRACURRICULAR ACTIVITIES

Campus housing available (% using): women's dorms (25%), men's dorms (25%), apartment for single students (50%). Students who live in college-owned, operated, or affiliated housing: 9%. **Student employment:** During the 2009-2010 academic year, 8% of undergraduates worked on campus. Average per-year earnings: $2,320. **Clubs and organizations:** Number of student organizations: 70. Activities include: campus ministries, choral groups, concert band, drama/theater, international student organization, jazz band, literary magazine, music ensembles, opera, pep band, radio station, student government, student newspaper, student film society, symphony orchestra, television station. Number of fraternities: 2; sororities: 2. Proportion of men in fraternities: 2%; of women in sororities: 2%. Average proportion of students who stay on campus on weekends: 4%. **Sports program (2009-2010):** Member of NCAA II. *Men's intercollegiate varsity sports:* baseball, basketball, cross country, golf, tennis. *Women's intercollegiate varsity sports:* basketball, golf, softball, tennis, volleyball.

SERVICES AND FACILITIES

Basic services: placement service, health insurance. **Remedial assistance:** reading, math, writing, study skills. **Counseling services:** career, military, veteran student, academic. **For learning-disabled students:** School does not offer a structured program with separate admission and additional fees. Total undergraduates in learning-disabled program or receiving services: 29. Services include: remedial math, remedial English, remedial reading, tape recorders, note-taking services, oral tests, readers, extended time for tests, tutors, priority seating, texts on tape, typist/scribe, other testing accommodations, other. **Library:** Number of titles: 138,426; number of current serial subscriptions: 26,415. **Information technology resources:** Students are not required to lease or own a computer. Number of campus computers available to all students: 568. School has a wireless network. Approximate number of users that can be accommodated: 400. Proportion of college-owned housing units wired for high-speed internet access: 100%. **Campus safety:** Security services offered: 24-hour foot-and-vehicle patrols, late-night transport/escort service, 24-hour emergency telephones, lighted pathways/sidewalks, controlled dormitory access (key, security card, etc).

TRANSFER AND INTERNATIONAL STUDENTS

Transfer students: May apply for admission for the following academic terms: Fall, Spring, Summer. Applicants need a minimum number of credits to apply. For fall 2009: Transfer applications received: 686. Transfer applicants offered admission: 666. Transfer applicants enrolled: 406. **International students:** Number of foreign undergraduates: 238 (4% of student body). Number of countries represented: 44. Minimum TOEFL score required: 500 (paper); 173 (computer). Average TOEFL score: 521 (paper).

East Central University

- **Address:** 14th Street and Francis Avenue, Ada, OK 74820
- **Website:** http://www.ecok.edu
- **Public**
- **Enrollment:** N/A

KEY STATS

✔ **U.S News College Ranking:** second tier, Regional Universities (West)
✔ **SAT or ACT Score (25th/75th percentile):** N/A
✔ **Tuition:** 2009-2010: $4,271 in state, $10,286 out of state

Selectivity: Less selective	**Room/board:** $4,324
Acceptance rate: N/A	**Average debt:** N/A
Student/faculty ratio: N/A	**Proportion who borrowed:** N/A

Langston University

- **Address:** PO Box 907, Langston, OK 73050
- **Website:** http://www.lunet.edu
- **Public**
- **Enrollment:** 2,094 full-time; 340 part-time

KEY STATS

✔ **U.S News College Ranking:** second tier, Regional Colleges (West)
✔ **ACT Score (25th/75th percentile):** 13-19
✔ **Tuition:** 2009-2010: $3,827 in state, $9,407 out of state

Selectivity: Least selective	**Room/board:** $7,040
Acceptance rate: 45%	**Average debt:** $30,186
Student/faculty ratio: N/A	**Proportion who borrowed:** 76%

UNDERGRADUATE STUDENT BODY STATS

2009-2010 enrollment: 2,094 full-time; 340 part-time. Men: 41%; women: 59%. **Ethnic makeup:** African American: 82%; American-Indian: 2%; Asian American: 1%; Hispanic: 1%; White: 12%; International: 2%.

ADMISSIONS FACTS AND FIGURES

Phone: (405) 466-3231. **Email:** admission@speedy.lunet.edu. **Website:** http://www.lunet.edu. **Application deadlines for fall 2011:** Regular decision: August 31; decision sent by August 15. Early decision: Send application by: N/A; Decision sent by: N/A. Early action: Send application by: N/A; Decision sent by: N/A. Admission can be deferred. **Application fee:** $25. **To apply online, go to:** http://www.lunet.edu/index.php?option=com_content&

task=view&id=25&Itemid=39. **Admissions requirements/recommendations:** High school units required (recommended): English: 4 (4); Mathematics: 3 (4); History: 3 (3); Total units: 15 (19). Tests: The college uses SAT or ACT scores in admissions decisions. Either SAT or ACT required. For admission to the fall 2011 entering class, the school will accept: ACT with or without writing accepted. Campus visit: Recommended. Admissions interview: Neither required nor recommended. Off-campus interview: May be arranged. **Factors that count in admissions decisions:** *Academic:* Secondary school record: Very Important. Letters of recommendation: Important. Standardized test scores: Very Important. Essay: Considered. *Nonacademic:* Interview: Considered. Extracurricular activities: Considered. Talent/ability: Important. Alumni/ae relationship: Considered. State residency: Considered. Religious affiliation/commitment: Not Considered. Minority status: Not Considered. **Admissions statistics for the fall 2009 entering class:** Total applicants: 2,609. Total accepted: 1,178. Freshmen enrolled: 889; Overall acceptance rate: 45%. Non-early acceptance rate: 45%. **Credentials of fall 2009 freshmen:** 2% ranked in the top 10 percent of their high school class; 8% were in the top 25 percent; 25% were in the top half. (Proportion submitting class standing: 75%.) **Average high school grade point average:** 2.5. **First-year students who submitted SAT scores:** 20%. **First-year students submitting ACT scores:** 95%. Scores (25/75 percentile): English: 11-17, Math: 14-17, Composite: 13-19.

ACADEMICS

Year founded: 1897. **Academic calendar:** Semester. **Degrees offered:** associate, bachelor's, master's, doctorate. **Major fields of study:** biological and biomedical sciences; communication, journalism, and related programs; education; English language and literature/letters; history; mathematics and statistics; physical sciences; security and protective services; visual and performing arts. **Areas of required coursework:** computer literacy, mathematics, English (including composition), sciences (biological or physical), history, other. **Pre-professional programs:** pre-veterinary science. **Special academic programs:** cooperative (work-study plan) program, distance learning, double major, dual enrollment, honors program, internships, liberal arts/career combination, study abroad, teacher certificate program. **Teacher certification offered in:** early childhood, special education, elementary, secondary. **Cooperative education programs:** agriculture, business, computer science, education, technologies. **Reserve Officers Training Corps (ROTC):** Army ROTC: Offered at cooperating institution. **Freshmen returning for sophomore year:** 52%. **Graduation rates:** Four-year: 6%; five-year: 17%; six-year: 33%.

COSTS AND FINANCIAL AID

Financial aid office: (405) 466-3282. **Expenses (2009-2010):** Tuition and fees 2009-2010: $3,827 in state, $9,407 out of state; room/board: $7,040. **Financial aid:** Priority filing date for institution's financial aid form: March 1; deadline: May 1. In 2009-2010, 94% of undergraduates applied for financial aid. Of those, 85% were determined to have financial need; 27% had their need fully met. Average financial aid package (proportion receiving): $9,611 (84%). Average amount of gift aid, such as scholarships or grants (proportion receiving): $4,726 (73%). Average amount of self-help aid, such as work study or loans (proportion receiving): $3,960 (77%). Average need-based loan (excluding PLUS or other private loans): $3,791. Among students who received need-based aid, the average percentage of need met: 64%. Among students who received aid based on merit, the average award (and the proportion receiving): $3,890 (15%). The average athletic scholarship (and the proportion receiving): $3,100 (4%). Average amount of debt of borrowers graduating in 2009: $30,186. Proportion who borrowed: 76%.

CAMPUS LIFE AND EXTRACURRICULAR ACTIVITIES

Campus housing available (% using): coed dorms, men's dorms, apartments for married students (14%), apartment for single students (86%), special housing for disabled students. Activities include: drama/theater, jazz band, marching band, music ensembles, radio station, student government, student newspaper, yearbook. Number of fraternities: 4; sororities: 4. **Sports program (2009-2010):** Member of NAIA. *Men's intercollegiate varsity sports:* basketball, football, track and field (indoor), track and field (outdoor). *Women's intercollegiate varsity sports:* basketball, softball, track and field (indoor), track and field (outdoor).

SERVICES AND FACILITIES

For learning-disabled students: School does not offer a structured program with separate admission and additional fees. Services include: tape recorders, note-taking services, oral tests, readers, extended time for tests, tutors, texts on tape. **Library:** Number of titles: 85,323; number of current serial subscriptions: 1,444. **Information technology resources:** Students are not required to lease or own a computer. Number of campus computers available to all students: 300. School does not have a wireless network. Proportion of college-owned housing units wired for high-speed internet access: 75%.

TRANSFER AND INTERNATIONAL STUDENTS

Transfer students: May apply for admission for the following academic terms: Fall, Spring, Summer. Applicants need a minimum number of credits to apply. **International students:** Number of foreign undergraduates: 45 (2% of student body). Number of countries represented: 40. Minimum TOEFL score required: 500 (paper); 300 (computer).

Mid-America Christian University

- ■ **Address:** 3500 S.W. 119th Street, Oklahoma City, OK 73170
- ■ **Website:** http://www.macu.edu
- ■ **Private; Religious affiliation:** Church of God, Anderson, IN
- ■ **Enrollment:** N/A

KEY STATS

- ✔ **U.S News College Ranking:** second tier, Regional Colleges (West)
- ✔ **SAT or ACT Score (25th/75th percentile):** N/A
- ✔ **Tuition:** 2009-2010: $13,480

Selectivity: Less selective	**Room/board:** $5,560
Acceptance rate: 43%	**Average debt:** N/A
Student/faculty ratio: N/A	**Proportion who borrowed:** N/A

Northeastern State University

- ■ **Address:** 600 N. Grand, Tahlequah, OK 74464
- ■ **Website:** http://www.nsuok.edu
- ■ **Public**
- ■ **Enrollment:** 5,873 full-time; 2,227 part-time

KEY STATS

- ✔ **U.S News College Ranking:** second tier, Regional Universities (West)
- ✔ **ACT Score (25th/75th percentile):** 18-23
- ✔ **Tuition:** 2009-2010: $4,155 in state, $10,245 out of state

Selectivity: Selective	**Room/board:** $4,966
Acceptance rate: 72%	**Average debt:** $24,143
Student/faculty ratio: 22/1	**Proportion who borrowed:** 68%

UNDERGRADUATE STUDENT BODY STATS

2009-2010 enrollment: 5,873 full-time; 2,227 part-time. Men: 40%; women: 60%. **Ethnic makeup:** African American: 6%; American-Indian: 30%; Asian American: 1%; Hispanic: 2%; White: 59%; International: 3%.

ADMISSIONS FACTS AND FIGURES

Phone: (918) 444-2200. **Email:** nsuinfo@nsuok.edu. **Website:** http://www.nsuok.edu. **Application deadlines for fall 2011:** Regular decision: Rolling. Early decision: Not offered. Early action: Not offered. Admission can be deferred. **To apply online, go to:** http://www.nsuok.edu/applications/index.html. **Admissions requirements/recommendations:** High school units required (recommended): English: 4 (0); Mathematics: 3 (0); Science: 2 (0); Foreign language: 0 (2); Social studies: 2 (0); History: 1 (0); Academic electives: 0 (0); Total units: 15 (0). Tests: The college uses SAT or ACT scores in admissions decisions. ACT required. For admission to the fall 2011 entering class, the school will accept: ACT with or without writing accepted. Campus visit: Recommended. Admissions interview: Neither required nor recommended. Off-campus interview: Not available. **Factors that count in admissions decisions:** *Academic:* Secondary school record: Very Important. Class rank: Very Important. Letters of recommendation: Not Considered. Standardized test scores: Very Important. Essay: Not Considered. *Nonacademic:* Interview: Considered. Extracurricular activities: Considered. Talent/ability: Not Considered. Character/personal qualities: Not Considered. Alumni/ae relationship: Not Considered. Geographical residence: Considered. State residency: Considered. Religious affiliation/commitment: Not Considered. Minority status: Not Considered. Volunteer work: Not Considered. Work experience: Not Considered. **Admissions statistics for the fall 2009 entering class:** Total applicants: 2,604. Total accepted:

1,863. Freshmen enrolled: 1,113; 6% were from out of state. Overall acceptance rate: 72%. **Credentials of fall 2009 freshmen:** 16% ranked in the top 10 percent of their high school class; 39% were in the top 25 percent; 71% were in the top half. (Proportion submitting class standing: 86%.) **Average high school grade point average:** 3.2. **First-year students submitting ACT scores:** 91%. Scores (25/75 percentile): English: 16-23, Math: 16-21, Composite: 18-23.

ACADEMICS

Year founded: 1846. **Academic calendar:** Semester. **Degrees offered:** bachelor's, post-bachelor's certificate, master's, post-master's certificate. **Most popular majors:** 15% elementary education and teaching, 7% accounting, 7% criminal justice/law enforcement administration, 6% psychology, 5% early childhood education and teaching. **Major fields of study:** area, ethnic, cultural, and gender studies; biological and biomedical sciences; business, management, marketing, and related support services; communication, journalism, and related programs; computer and information sciences and support services; education; engineering; engineering technologies/ technicians; English language and literature/letters; family and consumer sciences/human sciences; foreign languages, literatures, and linguistics; health professions and related clinical sciences; history; legal professions and studies; liberal arts and sciences studies, and humanities; mathematics and statistics; natural resources and conservation; parks, recreation, leisure, and fitness studies; physical sciences; psychology; security and protective services; social sciences; visual and performing arts. **Areas of required coursework:** humanities, computer literacy, mathematics, English (including composition), sciences (biological or physical), history, social science, other. **Pre-professional programs:** pre-law, pre-dentistry, pre-medicine, pre-veterinary science, pre-optometry, pre-pharmacy. **Special academic programs (% participation):** cooperative (work-study plan) program (5%), distance learning (67%), double major (1%), dual enrollment (10%), honors program (1%), independent study (2%), internships (46%), student-designed major (.05%), teacher certificate program (28%), weekend college (38%). **Teacher certification offered in:** early childhood, special education, elementary, middle/junior high, secondary. **Cooperative education programs:** business, health professions. **Reserve Officers Training Corps (ROTC):** Army ROTC: Offered on campus. **Faculty and instruction (2009-2010):** Total instructional faculty: 299 full-time, 171 part-time (51% men; 49% women; 13% minorities). Full-time faculty with Ph.D. or other terminal degree: 74%. Student/faculty ratio: 22/1. Classes of fewer than 20 students: 43%; of 20 to 49 students: 52%; of 50 or more students: 5%. **Advanced Placement and International Baccalaureate credit:** AP tests may be used for: Credit only. Scores accepted: 3, 4, 5. International Baccalaureate exams may be used for: Credit only. **Freshmen returning for sophomore year:** 64%. **Graduation rates:** Four-year: 11%; five-year: 24%; six-year: 31%.

COSTS AND FINANCIAL AID

Financial aid office: (918) 456-5511. **Expenses (2009-2010):** Tuition and fees 2009-2010: $4,155 in state, $10,245 out of state; room/board: $4,966. Estimated books and supplies: $1,155; transportation: $1,872; personal expenses: $1,080. **Financial aid:** Priority filing date for institution's financial aid form: March 15. In 2009-2010, 79% of undergraduates applied for financial aid. Of those, 68% were determined to have financial need; 61% had their need fully met. Average financial aid package (proportion receiving): $8,680 (57%). Average amount of gift aid, such as scholarships or grants (proportion receiving): $5,245 (41%). Average amount of self-help aid, such as work study or loans (proportion receiving): $4,326 (37%). Average need-based loan (excluding PLUS or other private loans): $3,825. Among students who received need-based aid, the average percentage of need met: 71%. Among students who received aid based on merit, the average award (and the proportion receiving): $3,374 (3%). The average athletic scholarship (and the proportion receiving): $3,340 (4%). Average amount of debt of borrowers graduating in 2009: $24,143. Proportion who borrowed: 68%.

CAMPUS LIFE AND EXTRACURRICULAR ACTIVITIES

Campus housing available (% using): coed dorms (37%), women's dorms (20%), sorority housing (8%), fraternity housing (4%), apartments for married students (4%), apartment for single students (4%), special housing for disabled students (0%), special housing for international students (4%), cooperative housing (4%). Students who live in college-owned, operated, or affiliated housing: 18%. **Student employment:** During the 2009-2010 academic year, 11% of undergraduates worked on campus. Average per-year earnings: $2,467. **Clubs and organizations:** Number of student organizations: 85. Activities include: campus ministries, choral groups, concert band, dance, drama/theater, international student organization,

jazz band, literary magazine, marching band, model UN, music ensembles, musical theater, pep band, student government, student newspaper, symphony orchestra, television station. Number of fraternities: 9; sororities: 6. Proportion of men in fraternities: 2%; of women in sororities: 2%. **Sports program (2009-2010):** Member of NCAA II. *Men's intercollegiate varsity sports:* baseball, basketball, football, golf, soccer. *Women's intercollegiate varsity sports:* basketball, golf, soccer, softball, tennis.

SERVICES AND FACILITIES

Basic services: nonremedial tutoring, placement service, health service. **Remedial assistance:** reading, math, writing. **Counseling services:** minority student, career, military, personal, veteran student, academic, older student. **For learning-disabled students:** School does not offer a structured program with separate admission and additional fees. Total undergraduates in learning-disabled program or receiving services: 81. Services include: remedial math, remedial English, remedial reading, tape recorders, note-taking services, oral tests, readers, extended time for tests, tutors, texts on tape. **Library:** Number of titles: 422,461; number of current serial subscriptions: 5,732. **Information technology resources:** Students are not required to lease or own a computer. Number of campus computers available to all students: 897. School has a wireless network. Approximate number of users that can be accommodated: 4,000. Proportion of college-owned housing units wired for high-speed internet access: 100%. **Campus safety:** Security services offered: 24-hour foot-and-vehicle patrols, late-night transport/escort service, 24-hour emergency telephones, student patrols, controlled dormitory access (key, security card, etc).

TRANSFER AND INTERNATIONAL STUDENTS

Transfer students: May apply for admission for the following academic terms: Fall, Spring, Summer. Applicants need a minimum number of credits to apply. For fall 2009: Transfer applications received: 2,032. Transfer applicants offered admission: 1,510. Transfer applicants enrolled: 1,041. **International students:** Number of foreign undergraduates: 213 (3% of student body). Number of countries represented: 53. Minimum TOEFL score required: 500 (paper); 61 (computer).

Northwestern Oklahoma State University

- **Address:** 709 Oklahoma Boulevard, Alva, OK 73717
- **Website:** http://www.nwosu.edu
- **Public**
- **Enrollment:** 1,556 full-time; 421 part-time

KEY STATS
✔ **U.S News College Ranking:** 23, Regional Colleges (West)
✔ **ACT Score (25th/75th percentile):** 17-22
✔ **Tuition:** 2010-2011: $4,411 in state, $10,441 out of state
    Selectivity: Less selective   **Room/board:** $3,700
    Acceptance rate: 100%   **Average debt:** $9,381
    Student/faculty ratio: 17/1   **Proportion who borrowed:** 49%

UNDERGRADUATE STUDENT BODY STATS

2009-2010 enrollment: 1,556 full-time; 421 part-time. Men: 44%; women: 56%. **Ethnic makeup:** African American: 5%; American-Indian: 6%; Asian American: 1%; Hispanic: 4%; White: 83%; International: 2%.

ADMISSIONS FACTS AND FIGURES

Phone: (580) 327-8545. **Email:** recruit@nwosu.edu. **Website:** http://www. nwosu.edu. **Application deadlines for fall 2011:** Regular decision: Rolling. Early decision: Not offered. Early action: Not offered. Admission cannot be deferred. **Application fee:** $15. **To apply online, go to:** http://www.okcollegestart.org/Applications/Northwestern_oksu/apply.html. **Admissions requirements/recommendations:** High school units required (recommended): English: 4; Mathematics: 3; Science: 2; Foreign language: (3); History: 2; Academic electives: (3); Total units: 15. Tests: The college uses SAT or ACT scores in admissions decisions. Either SAT or ACT required. For admission to the fall 2011 entering class, the school will accept: ACT with or without writing accepted. Campus visit: Recommended. Admissions interview: Neither required nor recommended. **Factors that count in admissions decisions:** *Academic:* Secondary school record: Very Important. Class rank: Very Important. Letters of recommendation: Not Considered. Standardized test scores: Very Important. Essay: Not Considered. *Nonacademic:* Interview: Not Considered. Extracurricular activities: Not Considered. Talent/ability: Considered. Character/personal qualities: Not Considered. Alumni/ae relationship: Not Considered. Geographical residence: Not Considered. State residency: Not Considered. Religious affiliation/commitment: Not Considered. Minority status: Not Considered. Volunteer work: Not Considered. Work experience: Not Considered. **Other schools with the greatest overlap in applicants:** Oklahoma State University; Southwestern Oklahoma State University; University of Central Oklahoma; University of Oklahoma. **Admissions statistics for the fall 2009 entering class:** Total applicants: 799. Total accepted: 799. Freshmen enrolled: 406; 18% were from out of state. Overall acceptance rate: 100%. **Credentials of fall 2009 freshmen:** 3% ranked in the top 10 percent of their high school class; 21% were in the top 25 percent; 53% were in the top half. (Proportion submitting class standing: 75%.) **Average high school grade point average:** 3.2. **First-year students who submitted SAT scores:** 5%. **First-year students submitting ACT scores:** 94%. Scores (25/75 percentile): English: 15-21, Math: 16-21, Composite: 17-22.

ACADEMICS

Year founded: 1897. **Academic calendar:** Semester. **Degrees offered:** bachelor's, master's. **Most popular majors:** 22% business administration and management, 9% elementary education and teaching, 9% psychology, 6% nursing/registered nurse training (R.N., A.S.N., B.S.N., M.S.N.), 5% accounting. **Major fields of study:** agriculture, agriculture operations, and related sciences; biological and biomedical sciences; business, management, marketing, and related support services; communication, journalism, and related programs; computer and information sciences and support services; construction trades; education; English language and literature/letters; family and consumer sciences/human sciences; foreign languages, literatures, and linguistics; health professions and related clinical sciences; liberal arts and sciences studies, and humanities; library science; mathematics and statistics; parks, recreation, leisure, and fitness studies; physical sciences; psychology; public administration and social service professions; security and protective services; visual and performing arts. **Areas of required coursework:** humanities, computer literacy, mathematics, English (including composition), philosophy, foreign languages, sciences (biological or physical), history, social science. **Pre-professional programs:** pre-law, pre-medicine. **Special academic programs:** distance learning, double major, dual enrollment, honors program, independent study, internships, study abroad, teacher certificate program. **Teacher certification offered in:** early childhood, special education, elementary, middle/junior high, secondary. **Faculty and instruction (2009-2010):** Total instructional faculty: 75 full-time, 70 part-time (45% men; 55% women; 4% minorities). Full-time faculty with Ph.D. or other terminal degree: 57%. Student/faculty ratio: 17/1. **Freshmen returning for sophomore year:** 66%. **Graduation rates:** Four-year: 16%; five-year: 30%; six-year: 31%.

COSTS AND FINANCIAL AID

Financial aid office: (580) 327-8542. **Expenses (2010-2011):** Tuition and fees 2010-2011: $4,411 in state, $10,441 out of state; room/board: $3,700. Estimated books and supplies: $1,200; transportation: $1,600; personal expenses: $2,000. Average amount of debt of borrowers graduating in 2009: $9,381. Proportion who borrowed: 49%.

CAMPUS LIFE AND EXTRACURRICULAR ACTIVITIES

Campus housing available: women's dorms, men's dorms, special housing for disabled students. Students who live in college-owned, operated, or affiliated housing: 44%. **Student employment:** During the 2009-2010 academic year, 13% of undergraduates worked on campus. Activities include: campus ministries, choral groups, concert band, drama/theater, international student organization, jazz band, marching band, music ensembles, pep band, radio station, student government, student newspaper, television station. Number of fraternities: 1; sororities: 2. Proportion of men in fraternities: 1%; of women in sororities: 2%. Average proportion of students who stay on campus on weekends: 18%. **Sports program (2009-2010):** Member of NAIA. *Men's intercollegiate varsity sports:* baseball, basketball, cross country, football, golf. *Women's intercollegiate varsity sports:* basketball, cross country, golf, soccer, softball.

SERVICES AND FACILITIES

Basic services: nonremedial tutoring, placement service. **Remedial assistance:** reading, math, writing. **Counseling services:** career, personal, academic. **Information technology resources:** Students are not required to lease or own a computer. Number of campus computers available to all students: 216. School has a wireless network. Proportion of college-owned housing units wired for high-speed internet access: 100%. **Campus safety:** Security services offered: 24-hour foot-and-vehicle patrols, late-night transport/escort service, 24-hour emergency telephones, lighted pathways/sidewalks, student patrols, controlled dormitory access (key, security card, etc).

TRANSFER AND INTERNATIONAL STUDENTS

Transfer students: May apply for admission for the following academic terms: Fall, Spring, Summer. Applicants need a minimum number of credits to apply. For fall 2009: Transfer applications received: 393. Transfer applicants offered admission: 393. Transfer applicants enrolled: 294. **International students:** Number of foreign undergraduates: 34 (2% of student body). Minimum TOEFL score required: 500 (paper); 173 (computer).

Oklahoma Baptist University

- **Address:** 500 W. University, Shawnee, OK 74804
- **Website:** http://www.okbu.edu
- **Private; Religious affiliation:** Southern Baptist Convention
- **Enrollment:** 1,495 full-time; 219 part-time

KEY STATS

✔ **U.S News College Ranking:** 2, Regional Colleges (West)
✔ **ACT Score (25th/75th percentile):** 21-26
✔ **Tuition:** 2010-2011: $18,670

Selectivity: Selective	**Room/board:** $5,630
Acceptance rate: 66%	**Average debt:** $21,554
Student/faculty ratio: 12/1	**Proportion who borrowed:** 68%

UNDERGRADUATE STUDENT BODY STATS

2009-2010 enrollment: 1,495 full-time; 219 part-time. Men: 43%; women: 57%. **Ethnic makeup:** African American: 7%; American-Indian: 8%; Asian American: 1%; Hispanic: 4%; White: 76%; International: 4%. **Religious preference:** Roman Catholic: 1%; Protestant: 10%; No preference: 17%; Unknown: 5%; Southern Baptist Convention: 64%; Other: 3%.

ADMISSIONS FACTS AND FIGURES

Phone: (405) 878-2023. **Email:** admissions@okbu.edu. **Website:** http://www.okbu.edu. **Application deadlines for fall 2011:** Regular decision: August 1. Early decision: Not offered. Early action: Not offered. Admission can be deferred. **To apply online, go to:** http://www.okbu.edu/admissions/onlineapp.html?section=welcome. **Admissions requirements/recommendations:** High school units required (recommended): English: 4 (4); Mathematics: 3 (3); Science: 3 (3); Foreign language: 2 (2); Social studies: 1 (1); History: 2 (2); Academic electives: 2 (2); Total units: 17 (18). Tests: The college uses SAT or ACT scores in admissions decisions. Either SAT or ACT required. For admission to the fall 2011 entering class, the school will accept: ACT with or without writing accepted. Campus visit: Recommended. Admissions interview: Recommended. Off-campus interview: May be arranged. **Factors that count in admissions decisions:** *Academic:* Secondary school record: Very Important. Class rank: Important. Letters of recommendation: Important. Standardized test scores: Important. Essay: Considered. *Nonacademic:* Interview: Important. Extracurricular activities: Important. Talent/ability: Important. Character/personal qualities: Important. Alumni/ae relationship: Considered. Geographical residence: Considered. State residency: Not Considered. Religious affiliation/commitment: Considered. Minority status: Not Considered. Volunteer work: Considered. Work experience: Considered. **Other schools with the greatest overlap in applicants:** East Central University; Oklahoma State University; Southwestern Oklahoma State University; University of Central Oklahoma; University of Oklahoma. **Admissions statistics for the fall 2009 entering class:** Total applicants: 3,831. Total accepted: 2,515. Freshmen enrolled: 368; 40% were from out of state. Overall acceptance rate: 66%. **Size of waiting list:** 0 applicants; enrolled from waiting list: 0. **Credentials of fall 2009 freshmen:** 30% ranked in the top 10 percent of their high school class; 62% were in the top 25 percent; 87% were in the top half. (Proportion submitting class standing: 85%.) **Average high school grade point average:** 3.6. **First-year students who submitted SAT scores:** 27%. Scores (25/75 percentile): Critical Reading: 480-590, Math: 480-620, Combined: 960-1210. **First-year students submitting ACT scores:** 88%. Scores (25/75 percentile): English: 21-28, Math: 19-26, Composite: 21-26.

ACADEMICS

Year founded: 1910. **Academic calendar:** 4-1-4. **Degrees offered:** associate, bachelor's, master's. **Most popular majors:** 12% elementary education and teaching, 12% nursing/registered nurse training (R.N., A.S.N., B.S.N.,

M.S.N.), 11% Bible/biblical studies, 6% philosophy and religious studies, 5% business, management, marketing, and related support services. **Major fields of study:** biological and biomedical sciences; business, management, marketing, and related support services; communication, journalism, and related programs; computer and information sciences and support services; education; English language and literature/letters; family and consumer sciences/human sciences; foreign languages, literatures, and linguistics; health professions and related clinical sciences; history; legal professions and studies; liberal arts and sciences studies, and humanities; mathematics and statistics; multi/interdisciplinary studies; parks, recreation, leisure, and fitness studies; philosophy and religious studies; physical sciences; psychology; social sciences; theology and religious vocations; visual and performing arts. **Areas of required coursework:** arts/fine arts, humanities, computer literacy, mathematics, English (including composition), philosophy, foreign languages, sciences (biological or physical), history, social science, other. **Pre-professional programs:** pre-law, pre-dentistry, pre-medicine, pre-theology, pre-veterinary science, pre-optometry, pre-pharmacy. **Special academic programs (% participation):** cooperative (work-study plan) program (3%), distance learning (3%), double major (1%), dual enrollment (1%), English as a Second Language (ESL) (3%), exchange student program (domestic) (1%), honors program (5%), independent study (1%), internships (6%), liberal arts/career combination (1%), student-designed major (1%), study abroad (12%), teacher certificate program (19%). **Teacher certification offered in:** early childhood, special education, elementary, middle/junior high, secondary. **Cooperative education programs:** art, business, computer science, education, health professions, social/behavioral science, other. **Reserve Officers Training Corps (ROTC):** Air Force ROTC: Offered at cooperating institution. **Faculty and instruction (2009-2010):** Total instructional faculty: 111 full-time, 57 part-time (51% men; 49% women; 2% minorities). Full-time faculty with Ph.D. or other terminal degree: 71%. Student/faculty ratio: 12/1. Classes of fewer than 20 students: 62%; of 20 to 49 students: 34%; of 50 or more students: 3%. **Advanced Placement and International Baccalaureate credit:** AP tests may be used for: Placement only. Scores accepted: 3. International Baccalaureate exams may be used for: Placement only. **Freshmen returning for sophomore year:** 74%. **Graduation rates:** Four-year: 40%; five-year: 46%; six-year: 57%. **Graduate study:** 27% of students pursue further study immediately upon graduation; 7% within one year; 10% within five years. Fields in which graduates pursue further study: Master of Business Administration (MBA), 20%; law, 5%; medicine, 10%; theology (or the seminary), 26%; education, 10%; arts and sciences, 30%; veterinary medicine, 1%.

COSTS AND FINANCIAL AID
Financial aid office: (405) 878-2016. **Expenses (2010-2011):** Tuition and fees 2010-2011: $18,670; room/board: $5,630. Estimated books and supplies: $1,200; transportation: $1,780; personal expenses: $1,820. **Financial aid:** Priority filing date for institution's financial aid form: April 1. In 2009-2010, 76% of undergraduates applied for financial aid. Of those, 67% were determined to have financial need; 15% had their need fully met. Average financial aid package (proportion receiving): $13,131 (67%). Average amount of gift aid, such as scholarships or grants (proportion receiving): $5,477 (44%). Average amount of self-help aid, such as work study or loans (proportion receiving): $5,456 (40%). Average need-based loan (excluding PLUS or other private loans): $4,882. Among students who received need-based aid, the average percentage of need met: 70%. Among students who received aid based on merit, the average award (and the proportion receiving): $2,704 (17%). The average athletic scholarship (and the proportion receiving): $5,742 (31%). Average amount of debt of borrowers graduating in 2009: $21,554. Proportion who borrowed: 68%.

CAMPUS LIFE AND EXTRACURRICULAR ACTIVITIES
Campus housing available (% using): women's dorms (43%), men's dorms (27%), apartments for married students (2%), apartment for single students (28%), special housing for disabled students. Students who live in college-owned, operated, or affiliated housing: 65%. **Student employment:** During the 2009-2010 academic year, 12% of undergraduates worked on campus. Average per-year earnings: $1,920. **Clubs and organizations:** Number of student organizations: 93. Activities include: campus ministries, choral groups, concert band, drama/theater, international student organization, jazz band, literary magazine, music ensembles, musical theater, opera, pep band, student government, student newspaper, symphony orchestra, yearbook. Number of fraternities: 6; sororities: 3. Proportion of men in fraternities: 12%; of women in sororities: 16%. Average proportion of students who stay on campus on weekends: 55%. **Sports program (2009-2010):** Member of NAIA. **Men's intercollegiate varsity sports:** baseball, basketball, cross country, golf, soccer, tennis, track and field (indoor), track and field (outdoor).

Women's intercollegiate varsity sports: basketball, cross country, golf, soccer, softball, tennis, track and field (indoor), track and field (outdoor), volleyball.

SERVICES AND FACILITIES
Basic services: nonremedial tutoring, placement service, health service. **Remedial assistance:** reading, math, writing, study skills. **Counseling services:** career, personal, academic, psychological, religious. **For learning-disabled students:** School does not offer a structured program with separate admission and additional fees. Services include: reading machines, tape recorders, other special classes, untimed tests, note-taking services, oral tests, readers, extended time for tests, tutors, priority registration, priority seating, texts on tape, other testing accommodations. **Library:** Number of titles: 162,000; number of current serial subscriptions: 336. **Information technology resources:** Students are not required to lease or own a computer. Number of campus computers available to all students: 240. School has a wireless network. Approximate number of users that can be accommodated: 2,000. Proportion of college-owned housing units wired for high-speed internet access: 100%. **Campus safety:** Security services offered: 24-hour foot-and-vehicle patrols, lighted pathways/sidewalks, controlled dormitory access (key, security card, etc).

TRANSFER AND INTERNATIONAL STUDENTS
Transfer students: May apply for admission for the following academic terms: Fall, Winter, Spring, Summer. Applicants do not need a minimum number of credits to apply. For fall 2009: Transfer applications received: 363. Transfer applicants offered admission: 258. Transfer applicants enrolled: 139. **International students:** Number of foreign undergraduates: 68 (4% of student body). Number of countries represented: 13. Minimum TOEFL score required: 500 (paper); 173 (computer). Average TOEFL score: 525 (paper).

Oklahoma Christian University

- **Address:** Box 11000, Oklahoma City, OK 73136-1100
- **Website:** http://www.oc.edu/
- **Private; Religious affiliation:** Church of Christ
- **Enrollment:** 1,865 full-time; 53 part-time

KEY STATS
✔ **U.S News College Ranking:** 44, Regional Universities (West)
✔ **ACT Score (25th/75th percentile):** 20-27
✔ **Tuition:** 2010-2011: $17,456

Selectivity: Selective	**Room/board:** $5,850
Acceptance rate: 56%	**Average debt:** $26,612
Student/faculty ratio: 13/1	**Proportion who borrowed:** 76%

UNDERGRADUATE STUDENT BODY STATS
2009-2010 enrollment: 1,865 full-time; 53 part-time. Men: 52%; women: 48%. **Ethnic makeup:** African American: 7%; American-Indian: 5%; Asian American: 4%; Hispanic: 4%; White: 81%. **Religious preference:** Roman Catholic: 3%; No preference: 5%; Church of Christ: 68%; Baptist: 7%; Other: 17%.

ADMISSIONS FACTS AND FIGURES
Phone: (405) 425-5050. **Email:** info@oc.edu. **Website:** http://www.oc.edu/. **Application deadlines for fall 2011:** Regular decision: Rolling; decision sent by August 7. Early decision: Not offered. Early action: Not offered. Admission can be deferred. **Application fee:** $25. **To apply online, go to:** http://www2.oc.edu/admissions/application/apply.asp. **Admissions requirements/recommendations:** High school units required (recommended): English: 4 (4); Mathematics: 3 (4); Science: 2 (4); Foreign language: (1); Social studies: 1 (2); History: 2 (2); Academic electives: 3 (3); Total units: 16 (22). Tests: The college uses SAT or ACT scores in admissions decisions. Either SAT or ACT required. For admission to the fall 2011 entering class, the school will accept: ACT with or without writing accepted. Campus visit: Recommended. Admissions interview: Recommended. Off-campus interview: May be arranged. **Factors that count in admissions decisions:** *Academic:* Secondary school record: Important. Class rank: Important. Letters of recommendation: Very Important. Standardized test scores: Very Important. Essay: Not Considered. *Nonacademic:* Interview: Important. Extracurricular activities: Important. Talent/ability: Important. Character/personal qualities: Very Important. Alumni/ae relationship: Not Considered. Geographical residence: Not Considered. State residency: Not

Considered. Religious affiliation/commitment: Important. Minority status: Considered. Volunteer work: Important. Work experience: Not Considered. **Other schools with the greatest overlap in applicants:** Abilene Christian University; Harding University; Oklahoma State University; University of Central Oklahoma; University of Oklahoma. **Admissions statistics for the fall 2009 entering class:** Total applicants: 1,718. Total accepted: 970. Freshmen enrolled: 471; 51% were from out of state. Overall acceptance rate: 56%. **Credentials of fall 2009 freshmen:** 30% ranked in the top 10 percent of their high school class; 54% were in the top 25 percent; 79% were in the top half. (Proportion submitting class standing: 61%.) **Average high school grade point average:** 3.4. **First-year students who submitted SAT scores:** 32%. Scores (25/75 percentile): Critical Reading: 470-640, Math: 480-610, Combined: 950-1250. **First-year students submitting ACT scores:** 100%. Scores (25/75 percentile): English: 20-28, Math: 19-27, Composite: 20-27.

ACADEMICS

Year founded: 1950. **Academic calendar:** Semester. **Degrees offered:** bachelor's, master's. **Most popular majors:** 17% business, management, marketing, and related support services, 16% education, 11% communication, journalism, and related programs, 7% theology and religious vocations, 7% visual and performing arts. **Major fields of study:** biological and biomedical sciences; business, management, marketing, and related support services; communication, journalism, and related programs; computer and information sciences and support services; education; engineering; English language and literature/letters; family and consumer sciences/human sciences; foreign languages, literatures, and linguistics; health professions and related clinical sciences; history; legal professions and studies; liberal arts and sciences studies, and humanities; mathematics and statistics; parks, recreation, leisure, and fitness studies; physical sciences; psychology; social sciences; theology and religious vocations; visual and performing arts. **Areas of required coursework:** arts/fine arts, humanities, mathematics, English (including composition), philosophy, sciences (biological or physical), history, social science, other. **Pre-professional programs:** pre-law, pre-dentistry, pre-medicine, pre-theology, pre-veterinary science, pre-optometry, pre-pharmacy, other. **Special academic programs (% participation):** distance learning (4%), double major (6%), dual enrollment (1%), English as a Second Language (ESL) (1%), honors program (6%), independent study (5%), internships (8%), student-designed major (3%), study abroad (22%), teacher certificate program (9%). **Teacher certification offered in:** early childhood, elementary, middle/junior high, secondary. **Cooperative education programs:** other. **Reserve Officers Training Corps (ROTC):** Army ROTC: Offered at cooperating institution (University of Central Oklahoma); Air Force ROTC: Offered at cooperating institution (University of Oklahoma Health Sciences Center). **Faculty and instruction (2009-2010):** Total instructional faculty: 110 full-time, 91 part-time (70% men; 30% women; 7% minorities). Full-time faculty with Ph.D. or other terminal degree: 62%. Student/faculty ratio: 13/1. Classes of fewer than 20 students: 67%; of 20 to 49 students: 30%; of 50 or more students: 3%. **Advanced Placement and International Baccalaureate credit:** AP tests may be used for: Credit and/or placement. Scores accepted: 3. International Baccalaureate exams may be used for: Credit and/or placement. **Freshmen returning for sophomore year:** 71%. **Graduation rates:** Four-year: 40%; five-year: 53%; six-year: 45%. **Graduate study:** 10% of students pursue further study immediately upon graduation; 20% within one year; 30% within five years. Fields in which graduates pursue further study: Master of Business Administration (MBA), 20%; law, 10%; medicine, 10%; dentistry, 3%; engineering, 5%; theology (or the seminary), 15%; education, 15%; arts and sciences, 20%; veterinary medicine, 3%.

COSTS AND FINANCIAL AID

Financial aid office: (405) 425-5190. **Expenses (2010-2011):** Tuition and fees 2010-2011: $17,456; room/board: $5,850. Estimated books and supplies: $1,000; transportation: $1,400; personal expenses: $1,700. **Financial aid:** Priority filing date for institution's financial aid form: April 15; deadline: September 8. In 2009-2010, 98% of undergraduates applied for financial aid. Of those, 66% were determined to have financial need; 21% had their need fully met. Average financial aid package (proportion receiving): $15,488 (65%). Average amount of gift aid, such as scholarships or grants (proportion receiving): $2,445 (36%). Average amount of self-help aid, such as work study or loans (proportion receiving): $4,467 (47%). Average need-based loan (excluding PLUS or other private loans): $3,889. Among students who received need-based aid, the average percentage of need met: 55%. Among students who received aid based on merit, the average award (and the proportion receiving): $3,935 (22%). The average athletic scholarship (and the proportion receiving): $6,670 (10%). Average amount of debt of borrowers graduating in 2009: $26,612. Proportion who borrowed: 76%.

CAMPUS LIFE AND EXTRACURRICULAR ACTIVITIES

Campus housing available (% using): women's dorms (32%), men's dorms (42%), apartments for married students (3%), apartment for single students (23%), special housing for disabled students. Students who live in college-owned, operated, or affiliated housing: 79%. **Student employment:** During the 2009-2010 academic year, 22% of undergraduates worked on campus. Average per-year earnings: $1,750. **Clubs and organizations:** Number of student organizations: 51. Activities include: campus ministries, choral groups, concert band, drama/theater, international student organization, jazz band, literary magazine, model UN, music ensembles, musical theater, opera, pep band, radio station, student government, student newspaper, symphony orchestra, television station, yearbook. Number of fraternities: 6; sororities: 7. Proportion of men in fraternities: 34%; of women in sororities: 36%. Average proportion of students who stay on campus on weekends: 70%. **Sports program (2009-2010):** Member of NAIA. *Men's intercollegiate varsity sports:* baseball, basketball, cross country, golf, soccer, tennis, track and field (indoor), track and field (outdoor). *Women's intercollegiate varsity sports:* basketball, cross country, soccer, softball, tennis, track and field (indoor), track and field (outdoor).

SERVICES AND FACILITIES

Basic services: nonremedial tutoring, placement service, health service, health insurance. **Remedial assistance:** math, writing, study skills. **Counseling services:** minority student, career, personal, veteran student, academic, psychological, religious. **For learning-disabled students:** School does not offer a structured program with separate admission and additional fees. Total undergraduates in learning-disabled program or receiving services: 26. Services include: remedial math, remedial English, reading machines, tape recorders, untimed tests, note-taking services, oral tests, readers, extended time for tests, tutors, early syllabus, priority registration, priority seating, proofreading services, texts on tape, other testing accommodations. **Library:** Number of titles: 141,377; number of current serial subscriptions: 21,639. **Information technology resources:** Students are required to lease or own a computer. Number of campus computers available to all students: 100. School has a wireless network. Approximate number of users that can be accommodated: 2,500. Proportion of college-owned housing units wired for high-speed internet access: 100%. **Campus safety:** Security services offered: 24-hour foot-and-vehicle patrols, late-night transport/escort service, 24-hour emergency telephones, lighted pathways/sidewalks, controlled dormitory access (key, security card, etc).

TRANSFER AND INTERNATIONAL STUDENTS

Transfer students: May apply for admission for the following academic terms: Fall, Spring, Summer. Applicants do not need a minimum number of credits to apply. For fall 2009: Transfer applications received: 252. Transfer applicants offered admission: 232. Transfer applicants enrolled: 98. **International students:** Number of foreign undergraduates: 0. Number of countries represented: 30. Minimum TOEFL score required: 500 (paper); 61 (computer). Average TOEFL score: 504 (paper).

Oklahoma City University

- **Address:** 2501 N. Blackwelder, Oklahoma City, OK 73106-1493
- **Website:** http://www.okcu.edu
- **Private; Religious affiliation:** United Methodist
- **Enrollment:** 1,886 full-time; 397 part-time

KEY STATS

✔ **U.S News College Ranking:** 25, Regional Universities (West)
✔ **ACT Score (25th/75th percentile):** 22-27
✔ **Tuition:** 2010-2011: $26,360

Selectivity: More selective	**Room/board:** $8,760
Acceptance rate: 79%	**Average debt:** $18,532
Student/faculty ratio: 11/1	**Proportion who borrowed:** 48%

UNDERGRADUATE STUDENT BODY STATS

2009-2010 enrollment: 1,886 full-time; 397 part-time. Men: 40%; women: 60%. **Ethnic makeup:** African American: 8%; American-Indian: 4%; Asian American: 3%; Hispanic: 6%; White: 62%; International: 18%. **Religious preference:** Roman Catholic: 11%; Protestant: 15%; Jewish: 1%; Muslim: 2%; Hindu: 1%; Buddhist: 1%; No preference: 24%; Unknown: 15%; United Methodist: 15%.

ADMISSIONS FACTS AND FIGURES

Phone: (405) 208-5050. **Email:** uadmissions@okcu.edu. **Website:** http://www.okcu.edu. **Application deadlines for fall 2011:** Regular decision: August 20. Early decision: Not offered. Early action: Not offered. Admission can be deferred. **Application fee:** $40. **To apply online, go to:** http://www.okcu.edu/admissions/online_menu.asp. **Admissions requirements/recommendations:** High school units required (recommended): English: 4; Mathematics: 3; Science: 3; Foreign language: 2; Social studies: 3; History: 3; Total units: 15. Tests: The college uses SAT or ACT scores in admissions decisions. Either SAT or ACT required. For admission to the fall 2011 entering class, the school will accept: ACT with or without writing accepted. Campus visit: Recommended. Admissions interview: Recommended. Off-campus interview: May be arranged. **Factors that count in admissions decisions:** *Academic:* Secondary school record: Important. Class rank: Very Important. Letters of recommendation: Very Important. Standardized test scores: Very Important. Essay: Very Important. *Nonacademic:* Interview: Not Considered. Extracurricular activities: Important. Talent/ability: Considered. Character/personal qualities: Considered. Alumni/ae relationship: Not Considered. Geographical residence: Not Considered. State residency: Not Considered. Religious affiliation/commitment: Not Considered. Minority status: Not Considered. Volunteer work: Considered. Work experience: Considered. **Other schools with the greatest overlap in applicants:** Baylor University; New York University; Oklahoma State University; Southern Methodist University; University of Oklahoma. **Admissions statistics for the fall 2009 entering class:** Total applicants: 1,185. Total accepted: 931. Freshmen enrolled: 404; 50% were from out of state. Overall acceptance rate: 79%. **Credentials of fall 2009 freshmen:** 32% ranked in the top 10 percent of their high school class; 59% were in the top 25 percent; 86% were in the top half. (Proportion submitting class standing: 82%.) **Average high school grade point average:** 3.5. **First-year students who submitted SAT scores:** 35%. Scores (25/75 percentile): Critical Reading: 490-600, Math: 480-590, Combined: 970-1190. **First-year students submitting ACT scores:** 83%. Scores (25/75 percentile): English: 22-29, Math: 20-26, Composite: 22-27.

ACADEMICS

Year founded: 1904. **Academic calendar:** Semester. **Degrees offered:** bachelor's, master's, doctorate. **Most popular majors:** 26% liberal arts and sciences studies, and humanities, 20% health professions and related clinical sciences, 20% visual and performing arts, 13% business, management, marketing, and related support services. **Major fields of study:** biological and biomedical sciences; business, management, marketing, and related support services; communication, journalism, and related programs; computer and information sciences and support services; education; English language and literature/letters; foreign languages, literatures, and linguistics; health professions and related clinical sciences; history; liberal arts and sciences studies, and humanities; mathematics and statistics; philosophy and religious studies; physical sciences; psychology; social sciences; theology and religious vocations; visual and performing arts. **Areas of required coursework:** arts/fine arts, humanities, computer literacy, mathematics, English (including composition), philosophy, foreign languages, sciences (biological or physical), history, social science. **Pre-professional programs:** pre-law, pre-dentistry, pre-medicine, pre-theology, pre-veterinary science, pre-optometry, pre-pharmacy. **Special academic programs (% participation):** accelerated program, cooperative (work-study plan) program (28%), double major, dual enrollment, English as a Second Language (ESL), exchange student program (domestic), external degree program, honors program (5%), independent study (32%), internships (74%), student-designed major, study abroad (19%), teacher certificate program. **Teacher certification offered in:** early childhood, elementary, middle/junior high, secondary, bilingual/bicultural. **Reserve Officers Training Corps (ROTC):** Army ROTC: Offered at cooperating institution (University of Central Oklahoma); Air Force ROTC: Offered at cooperating institution (University of Oklahoma). **Faculty and instruction (2009-2010):** Total instructional faculty: 198 full-time, 141 part-time (53% men; 47% women; 15% minorities). Full-time faculty with Ph.D. or other terminal degree: 80%. Student/faculty ratio: 11/1. Classes of fewer than 20 students: 72%; of 20 to 49 students: 27%; of 50 or more students: 1%. **Advanced Placement and International Baccalaureate credit:** AP tests may be used for: Placement only. Scores accepted: 3. International Baccalaureate exams may be used for: Credit only. **Freshmen returning for sophomore year:** 78%. **Graduation rates:** Four-year: 40%; five-year: 54%; six-year: 51%. **Graduate study:** 70% of students pursue further study immediately upon graduation.

COSTS AND FINANCIAL AID

Financial aid office: (405) 208-5211. **Expenses (2010-2011):** Tuition and fees 2010-2011: $26,360; room/board: $8,760. Estimated books and supplies: $1,500; transportation: $1,700; personal expenses: $1,000. **Financial aid:** Priority filing date for institution's financial aid form: March 1; deadline: June 30. In 2009-2010, 70% of undergraduates applied for financial aid. Of those, 54% were determined to have financial need; 57% had their need fully met. Average financial aid package (proportion receiving): $18,004 (48%). Average amount of gift aid, such as scholarships or grants (proportion receiving): $12,968 (45%). Average amount of self-help aid, such as work study or loans (proportion receiving): $2,334 (8%). Average need-based loan (excluding PLUS or other private loans): $4,862. Among students who received need-based aid, the average percentage of need met: 78%. Among students who received aid based on merit, the average award (and the proportion receiving): $9,942 (17%). The average athletic scholarship (and the proportion receiving): $15,008 (7%). Average amount of debt of borrowers graduating in 2009: $18,532. Proportion who borrowed: 48%.

CAMPUS LIFE AND EXTRACURRICULAR ACTIVITIES

Campus housing available: coed dorms, women's dorms, men's dorms, fraternity housing, apartments for married students, apartment for single students, special housing for disabled students. Students who live in college-owned, operated, or affiliated housing: 69%. **Clubs and organizations:** Number of student organizations: 47. Activities include: campus ministries, choral groups, concert band, dance, drama/theater, international student organization, jazz band, literary magazine, model UN, music ensembles, musical theater, opera, pep band, student government, student newspaper, symphony orchestra, television station, yearbook. Number of fraternities: 2; sororities: 3. Proportion of men in fraternities: 15%; of women in sororities: 17%. Average proportion of students who stay on campus on weekends: 35%. **Sports program (2009-2010):** Member of NAIA. *Men's intercollegiate varsity sports:* baseball, basketball, cross country, golf, soccer, track and field (outdoor), wrestling. *Women's intercollegiate varsity sports:* basketball, cross country, golf, soccer, softball, track and field (outdoor), volleyball.

SERVICES AND FACILITIES

Basic services: placement service, health service, health insurance. **Remedial assistance:** study skills. **Counseling services:** minority student, career, personal, academic, older student, psychological, birth control, religious. **For learning-disabled students:** School does not offer a structured program with separate admission and additional fees. Services include: remedial math, remedial English, remedial reading, oral tests, learning center, readers, extended time for tests, tutors, priority seating, texts on tape, other testing accommodations. **Library:** Number of titles: 520,953; number of current serial subscriptions: 14,000. **Information technology resources:** Students are not required to lease or own a computer. Number of campus computers available to all students: 477. School has a wireless network. Approximate number of users that can be accommodated: 5,000. Proportion of college-owned housing units wired for high-speed internet access: 100%. **Campus safety:** Security services offered: 24-hour foot-and-vehicle patrols, late-night transport/escort service, 24-hour emergency telephones, lighted pathways/sidewalks, controlled dormitory access (key, security card, etc).

TRANSFER AND INTERNATIONAL STUDENTS

Transfer students: May apply for admission for the following academic terms: Fall, Spring, Summer. Applicants need a minimum number of credits to apply. For fall 2009: Transfer applications received: 669. Transfer applicants offered admission: 449. Transfer applicants enrolled: 197. **International students:** Number of foreign undergraduates: 411 (18% of student body). Number of countries represented: 39. Minimum TOEFL score required: 550 (paper); 213 (computer). Average TOEFL score: 557 (paper).

Oklahoma Panhandle State University

- **Address:** PO Box 430, Goodwell, OK 73939-0430
- **Website:** http://www.opsu.edu
- **Public**
- **Enrollment:** 1,039 full-time; 227 part-time

KEY STATS

- ✔ **U.S News College Ranking:** 26, Regional Colleges (West)
- ✔ **ACT Score (25th/75th percentile):** 17-22
- ✔ **Tuition:** 2009-2010: $5,142 in state, $10,482 out of state
  - **Selectivity:** Less selective **Room/board:** $3,416
  - **Acceptance rate:** 100% **Average debt:** N/A
  - **Student/faculty ratio:** 14/1 **Proportion who borrowed:** N/A

UNDERGRADUATE STUDENT BODY STATS

2009-2010 enrollment: 1,039 full-time; 227 part-time. Men: 52%; women: 48%. **Ethnic makeup:** African American: 7%; American-Indian: 3%; Asian American: 1%; Hispanic: 16%; White: 69%; International: 4%.

ADMISSIONS FACTS AND FIGURES

Phone: (800) 664-6778. **Email:** opsu@opsu.edu. **Website:** http://www.opsu.edu. **Application deadlines for fall 2011:** Regular decision: Rolling. Early decision: Not offered. Early action: Not offered. Admission can be deferred. **To apply online, go to:** http://www.opsu.edu/Admissions/. **Admissions requirements/recommendations:** High school units required (recommended): English: 4 (4); Mathematics: 3 (3); Science: 2 (2); Social studies: 2 (2); History: 1 (1); Academic electives: 3 (3); Total units: 15 (15). Tests: The college uses SAT or ACT scores in admissions decisions. Neither SAT nor ACT required. For admission to the fall 2011 entering class, the school will accept: ACT with writing recommended. Campus visit: Neither required nor recommended. Admissions interview: Neither required nor recommended. Off-campus interview: May be arranged. **Factors that count in admissions decisions: Academic:** Secondary school record: Very Important. Class rank: Very Important. Letters of recommendation: Not Considered. Standardized test scores: Very Important. Essay: Not Considered. **Nonacademic:** Interview: Not Considered. Extracurricular activities: Not Considered. Talent/ability: Not Considered. Character/personal qualities: Not Considered. Alumni/ae relationship: Not Considered. Geographical residence: Not Considered. State residency: Not Considered. Religious affiliation/commitment: Not Considered. Minority status: Not Considered. Volunteer work: Not Considered. Work experience: Not Considered. **Other schools with the greatest overlap in applicants:** Oklahoma City University; Oklahoma State University; Southwestern Oklahoma State University; West Texas A&M University. **Admissions statistics for the fall 2009 entering class:** Total applicants: 317. Total accepted: 317. Freshmen enrolled: 297; 52% were from out of state. Overall acceptance rate: 100%. **Average high school grade point average:** 3.1. **First-year students who submitted SAT scores:** 11%. Scores (25/75 percentile): Critical Reading: 365-478, Math: 410-490, Combined: 775-968. **First-year students submitting ACT scores:** 76%. Scores (25/75 percentile): English: 15-21, Math: 16-20, Composite: 17-22.

ACADEMICS

Year founded: 1909. **Academic calendar:** Semester. **Degrees offered:** associate, bachelor's. **Most popular majors:** 14% biology/biological sciences, 13% health and physical education, 9% business administration and management, 9% psychology, 8% animal sciences. **Major fields of study:** agriculture, agriculture operations, and related sciences; biological and biomedical sciences; business, management, marketing, and related support services; computer and information sciences and support services; education; engineering technologies/technicians; English language and literature/letters; health professions and related clinical sciences; history; liberal arts and sciences studies, and humanities; mathematics and statistics; parks, recreation, leisure, and fitness studies; physical sciences; psychology; social sciences. **Areas of required coursework:** humanities, computer literacy, mathematics, English (including composition), sciences (biological or physical), history, social science. **Special academic programs:** distance learning, double major, dual enrollment, English as a Second Language (ESL), honors program, internships, teacher certificate program. **Faculty and instruction (2009-2010):** Total instructional faculty: 58 full-time, 31 part-time (56% men; 44% women; 2% minorities). Full-time faculty with Ph.D. or other terminal degree: 36%. Student/faculty ratio: 14/1. Classes of fewer than 20 students: 73%; of 20 to 49 students: 25%; of 50 or more students: 3%. **Advanced Placement and International Baccalaureate credit:** AP tests may be

used for: Credit only. Scores accepted: 3, 4, 5. International Baccalaureate exams may be used for: Credit only. **Freshmen returning for sophomore year:** 53%. **Graduation rates:** Four-year: 23%; five-year: 34%; six-year: 40%.

COSTS AND FINANCIAL AID

Financial aid office: (580) 349-1580. **Expenses (2009-2010):** Tuition and fees 2009-2010: $5,142 in state, $10,482 out of state; room/board: $3,416. **Financial aid:** Priority filing date for institution's financial aid form: March 15.

CAMPUS LIFE AND EXTRACURRICULAR ACTIVITIES

Campus housing available: women's dorms, men's dorms, apartments for married students, apartment for single students. Students who live in college-owned, operated, or affiliated housing: 40%. **Student employment:** During the 2009-2010 academic year, 14% of undergraduates worked on campus. Average per-year earnings: $1,311. Activities include: choral groups, concert band, dance, drama/theater, international student organization, jazz band, marching band, music ensembles, musical theater, radio station, student government, student newspaper, yearbook. Number of fraternities: 1; sororities: 0. Average proportion of students who stay on campus on weekends: 40%. **Sports program (2009-2010):** Member of NCAA II. **Men's intercollegiate varsity sports:** baseball, basketball, cross country, football, golf. **Women's intercollegiate varsity sports:** basketball, cross country, golf, softball, volleyball.

SERVICES AND FACILITIES

Basic services: health service. **Remedial assistance:** reading, math, writing, study skills. **For learning-disabled students:** School does not offer a structured program with separate admission and additional fees. Services include: remedial math, remedial English, reading machines, remedial reading, tape recorders, untimed tests, note-taking services, oral tests, learning center, readers, extended time for tests, tutors, priority seating, exams on tape or computer, other testing accommodations. **Library:** Number of titles: 123,026; number of current serial subscriptions: 267. **Information technology resources:** Students are not required to lease or own a computer. School has a wireless network. Approximate number of users that can be accommodated: 250. Proportion of college-owned housing units wired for high-speed internet access: 100%.

TRANSFER AND INTERNATIONAL STUDENTS

Transfer students: May apply for admission for the following academic terms: Fall, Winter, Spring, Summer. Applicants need a minimum number of credits to apply. For fall 2009: Transfer applications received: 264. Transfer applicants offered admission: 264. Transfer applicants enrolled: 249. **International students:** Number of foreign undergraduates: 49 (4% of student body). Number of countries represented: 17. Minimum TOEFL score required: 500 (paper); 173 (computer).

Oklahoma State University

- **Address:** 101 Whitehurst Hall, Stillwater, OK 74078
- **Website:** http://osu.okstate.edu
- **Public**
- **Enrollment:** 15,296 full-time; 2,553 part-time

KEY STATS

- ✔ **U.S News College Ranking:** 132, National Universities
- ✔ **ACT Score (25th/75th percentile):** 22-27
- ✔ **Tuition:** 2009-2010: $6,202 in state, $16,556 out of state
  - **Selectivity:** More selective **Room/board:** $6,402
  - **Acceptance rate:** 86% **Average debt:** $19,468
  - **Student/faculty ratio:** 18/1 **Proportion who borrowed:** 56%

UNDERGRADUATE STUDENT BODY STATS

2009-2010 enrollment: 15,296 full-time; 2,553 part-time. Men: 51%; women: 49%. **Ethnic makeup:** African American: 4%; American-Indian: 9%; Asian American: 2%; Hispanic: 3%; White: 80%; International: 2%.

ADMISSIONS FACTS AND FIGURES

Phone: (405) 744-5358. **Email:** admissions@okstate.edu. **Website:** http://osu.okstate.edu. **Application deadlines for fall 2011:** Regular decision: Rolling. Early decision: Not offered. Early action: Not offered. Admission can be deferred. **Application fee:** $40. **To apply online, go to:** http://admissions.

okstate.edu/AppConcurrent.html. **Admissions requirements/recommendations:** High school units required (recommended): English: 4; Mathematics: 3; Science: 2; Foreign language: (2); Social studies: 2; History: 1; Academic electives: 3; Total units: 15 (3). Tests: The college uses SAT or ACT scores in admissions decisions. Either SAT or ACT required. For admission to the fall 2011 entering class, the school will accept: ACT with or without writing accepted. Campus visit: Recommended. Admissions interview: Recommended. Off-campus interview: Not available. **Factors that count in admissions decisions:** *Academic:* Secondary school record: Considered. Class rank: Very Important. Letters of recommendation: Considered. Standardized test scores: Very Important. Essay: Considered. *Nonacademic:* Interview: Considered. Extracurricular activities: Considered. Talent/ability: Considered. Character/personal qualities: Considered. Alumni/ae relationship: Not Considered. Geographical residence: Not Considered. State residency: Not Considered. Religious affiliation/commitment: Not Considered. Minority status: Not Considered. Volunteer work: Not Considered. Work experience: Not Considered. **Other schools with the greatest overlap in applicants:** University of Oklahoma. **Admissions statistics for the fall 2009 entering class:** Total applicants: 7,561. Total accepted: 6,537. Freshmen enrolled: 3,148; 26% were from out of state. Overall acceptance rate: 86%. **Credentials of fall 2009 freshmen:** 27% ranked in the top 10 percent of their high school class; 55% were in the top 25 percent; 86% were in the top half. (Proportion submitting class standing: 85%.) **Average high school grade point average:** 3.5. **First-year students who submitted SAT scores:** 27%. Scores (25/75 percentile): Critical Reading: 480-600, Math: 500-640, Combined: 980-1240. **First-year students submitting ACT scores:** 93%. Scores (25/75 percentile): English: 21-28, Math: 21-27, Composite: 22-27.

ACADEMICS

Year founded: 1890. **Academic calendar:** Semester. **Degrees offered:** bachelor's, post-bachelor's certificate, master's, post-master's certificate, doctorate. **Most popular majors:** 29% business, management, marketing, and related support services, 8% family and consumer sciences/human sciences, 7% agriculture, agriculture operations, and related sciences, 7% education, 7% engineering. **Major fields of study:** agriculture, agriculture operations, and related sciences; architecture and related services; area, ethnic, cultural, and gender studies; biological and biomedical sciences; business, management, marketing, and related support services; communication, journalism, and related programs; computer and information sciences and support services; education; engineering; engineering technologies/technicians; English language and literature/letters; family and consumer sciences/human sciences; foreign languages, literatures, and linguistics; health professions and related clinical sciences; history; liberal arts and sciences studies, and humanities; mathematics and statistics; natural resources and conservation; parks, recreation, leisure, and fitness studies; philosophy and religious studies; physical sciences; psychology; security and protective services; social sciences; transportation and materials moving; visual and performing arts. **Areas of required coursework:** humanities, mathematics, English (including composition), sciences (biological or physical), history, social science, other. **Pre-professional programs:** pre-law, pre-medicine, pre-veterinary science. **Special academic programs:** accelerated program, cross-registration, distance learning, double major, dual enrollment, English as a Second Language (ESL), exchange student program (domestic), honors program, independent study, internships, student-designed major, study abroad, teacher certificate program. **Teacher certification offered in:** early childhood, special education, elementary, secondary. **Reserve Officers Training Corps (ROTC):** Army ROTC: Offered on campus; Air Force ROTC: Offered on campus. **Faculty and instruction (2009-2010):** Total instructional faculty: 999 full-time, 274 part-time (63% men; 37% women; 10% minorities). Full-time faculty with Ph.D. or other terminal degree: 91%. Student/faculty ratio: 18/1. Classes of fewer than 20 students: 41%; of 20 to 49 students: 46%; of 50 or more students: 13%. **Advanced Placement and International Baccalaureate credit:** International Baccalaureate exams may be used for: Credit and/or placement. **Freshmen returning for sophomore year:** 79%. **Graduation rates:** Four-year: 31%; five-year: 54%; six-year: 60%.

COSTS AND FINANCIAL AID

Financial aid office: (405) 744-6604. **Expenses (2009-2010):** Tuition and fees 2009-2010: $6,202 in state, $16,556 out of state; room/board: $6,402. Estimated books and supplies: $980; transportation: $1,810; personal expenses: $2,440. **Financial aid:** Priority filing date for institution's financial aid form: February 1. In 2009-2010, 65% of undergraduates applied for financial aid. Of those, 50% were determined to have financial need; 15% had their need fully met. Average financial aid package (proportion receiving): $10,788 (50%). Average amount of gift aid, such as scholarships or grants (proportion receiving): $6,022 (36%). Average amount of self-help

aid, such as work study or loans (proportion receiving): $4,199 (34%). Average need-based loan (excluding PLUS or other private loans): $4,161. Among students who received need-based aid, the average percentage of need met: 72%. Among students who received aid based on merit, the average award (and the proportion receiving): $4,305 (23%). The average athletic scholarship (and the proportion receiving): $9,906 (1%). Average amount of debt of borrowers graduating in 2009: $19,468. Proportion who borrowed: 56%.

CAMPUS LIFE AND EXTRACURRICULAR ACTIVITIES

Campus housing available: coed dorms, women's dorms, men's dorms, sorority housing, fraternity housing, apartments for married students, apartment for single students, special housing for disabled students. Students who live in college-owned, operated, or affiliated housing: 39%. Activities include: campus ministries, choral groups, concert band, dance, drama/theater, international student organization, jazz band, literary magazine, marching band, music ensembles, musical theater, opera, pep band, radio station, student government, student newspaper, symphony orchestra, television station. Proportion of men in fraternities: 16%; of women in sororities: 19%. **Sports program (2009-2010):** Member of NCAA I. *Men's intercollegiate varsity sports:* baseball, basketball, cross country, football, golf, tennis, track and field (outdoor), wrestling. *Women's intercollegiate varsity sports:* basketball, cross country, equestrian, golf, soccer, softball, tennis, track and field (outdoor).

SERVICES AND FACILITIES

Basic services: nonremedial tutoring, women's center, placement service, health service, health insurance. **Remedial assistance:** reading, math, writing. **Counseling services:** career, personal, academic, older student, psychological, birth control. **For learning-disabled students:** School does not offer a structured program with separate admission and additional fees. Services include: tape recorders, videotaped classes, note-taking services, readers, priority registration, texts on tape, other testing accommodations. **Library:** Number of titles: 2,866,250; number of current serial subscriptions: 70,493. **Information technology resources:** Students are not required to lease or own a computer. School has a wireless network. Proportion of college-owned housing units wired for high-speed internet access: 100%. **Campus safety:** Security services offered: 24-hour foot-and-vehicle patrols, 24-hour emergency telephones, lighted pathways/sidewalks, controlled dormitory access (key, security card, etc).

TRANSFER AND INTERNATIONAL STUDENTS

Transfer students: May apply for admission for the following academic terms: Fall, Spring, Summer. Applicants need a minimum number of credits to apply. For fall 2009: Transfer applications received: 2,805. Transfer applicants offered admission: 2,229. Transfer applicants enrolled: 1,603. **International students:** Number of foreign undergraduates: 394 (2% of student body). Number of countries represented: 75. Minimum TOEFL score required: 500 (paper); 61 (computer). Average TOEFL score: 511 (paper).

Oklahoma Wesleyan University

■ **Address:** 2201 Silver Lake Road, Bartlesville, OK 74006
■ **Website:** http://www.okwu.edu
■ **Private; Religious affiliation:** The Wesleyan Church
■ **Enrollment:** 540 full-time; 447 part-time

KEY STATS

✔ **U.S News College Ranking:** 6, Regional Colleges (West)
✔ **ACT Score (25th/75th percentile):** 19-27
✔ **Tuition:** 2010-2011: $19,200

Selectivity: More selective	**Room/board:** $6,546
Acceptance rate: 71%	**Average debt:** $21,891
Student/faculty ratio: 16/1	**Proportion who borrowed:** 98%

UNDERGRADUATE STUDENT BODY STATS

2009-2010 enrollment: 540 full-time; 447 part-time. Men: 40%; women: 60%. **Ethnic makeup:** African American: 5%; American-Indian: 10%; Asian American: 1%; Hispanic: 2%; White: 79%; International: 3%. **Religious preference:** Roman Catholic: 3%; Protestant: 52%; Muslim: 1%; No preference: 27%; The Wesleyan Church: 17%.

ADMISSIONS FACTS AND FIGURES

Phone: (866) 222-8226. **Email:** admissions@okwu.edu. **Website:** http://www.okwu.edu. **Application deadlines for fall 2011:** Regular decision: Rolling. Early decision: Not offered. Early action: Not offered. Admission can be deferred. **Application fee:** $25. **To apply online, go to:** https://community.elevatorup.com/Brix?pageID=14531. **Admissions requirements/recommendations:** High school units required (recommended): English: 4 (4); Mathematics: 2 (2); Science: 1 (1); Foreign language: 0 (0); Social studies: 0 (0); History: 2 (2); Academic electives: 6 (6); Total units: 15 (15). Tests: The college uses SAT or ACT scores in admissions decisions. Either SAT or ACT required. For admission to the fall 2011 entering class, the school will accept: ACT with or without writing accepted. Campus visit: Recommended. Admissions interview: Recommended. Off-campus interview: Not available. **Factors that count in admissions decisions:** *Academic:* Secondary school record: Important. Class rank: Very Important. Letters of recommendation: Considered. Standardized test scores: Very Important. Essay: Considered. *Nonacademic:* Interview: Not Considered. Extracurricular activities: Important. Talent/ability: Important. Character/personal qualities: Important. Alumni/ae relationship: Not Considered. Geographical residence: Not Considered. State residency: Not Considered. Religious affiliation/commitment: Considered. Minority status: Not Considered. Volunteer work: Considered. Work experience: Not Considered. **Other schools with the greatest overlap in applicants:** Oklahoma State University; Oral Roberts University; Rogers State University; Southern Nazarene University; University of Oklahoma. **Admissions statistics for the fall 2009 entering class:** Total applicants: 1,385. Total accepted: 985. Freshmen enrolled: 128; 48% were from out of state. Overall acceptance rate: 71%. **Credentials of fall 2009 freshmen:** 25% ranked in the top 10 percent of their high school class; 50% were in the top 25 percent; 59% were in the top half. (Proportion submitting class standing: 96%.) **Average high school grade point average:** 3.3. **First-year students who submitted SAT scores:** 53%. Scores (25/75 percentile): Critical Reading: 421-605, Math: 453-628, Combined: 874-1233. **First-year students submitting ACT scores:** 91%. Scores (25/75 percentile): English: 17-26, Math: 19-28, Composite: 19-27.

ACADEMICS

Year founded: 1972. **Academic calendar:** Semester. **Degrees offered:** certificate, associate, bachelor's, master's. **Major fields of study:** biological and biomedical sciences; business, management, marketing, and related support services; communication, journalism, and related programs; computer and information sciences and support services; education; English language and literature/letters; health professions and related clinical sciences; history; legal professions and studies; mathematics and statistics; parks, recreation, leisure, and fitness studies; philosophy and religious studies; physical sciences; psychology; social sciences; theology and religious vocations; visual and performing arts. **Areas of required coursework:** humanities, computer literacy, mathematics, English (including composition), philosophy, sciences (biological or physical), history, social science, other. **Pre-professional programs:** pre-law, pre-medicine, pre-theology. **Special academic programs (% participation):** accelerated program (80%), double major (9%), independent study (3%), internships (20%), teacher certificate program (4%). **Teacher certification offered in:** early childhood, elementary, middle/junior high, secondary. **Cooperative education programs:** technologies, vocational arts. **Faculty and instruction (2009-2010):** Total instructional faculty: 29. Full-time faculty with Ph.D. or other terminal degree: 48%. Student/faculty ratio: 16/1. **Advanced Placement and International Baccalaureate credit:** Scores accepted: 3. International Baccalaureate exams may be used for: Credit only. **Freshmen returning for sophomore year:** 66%. **Graduation rates:** Four-year: 41%; five-year: 41%; six-year: 41%.

COSTS AND FINANCIAL AID

Financial aid office: (918) 335-6282. **Expenses (2010-2011):** Tuition and fees 2010-2011: $19,200; room/board: $6,546. Estimated books and supplies: $900; transportation: $1,400; personal expenses: $1,900. **Financial aid:** Priority filing date for institution's financial aid form: March 1. In 2009-2010, 92% of undergraduates applied for financial aid. Of those, 78% were determined to have financial need; 14% had their need fully met. Average financial aid package (proportion receiving): $11,318 (77%). Average amount of gift aid, such as scholarships or grants (proportion receiving): $8,196 (68%). Average amount of self-help aid, such as work study or loans (proportion receiving): $4,532 (70%). Average need-based loan (excluding PLUS or other private loans): $4,099. Among students who received need-based aid, the average percentage of need met: 63%. Among students who received aid based on merit, the average award (and the proportion receiving): $5,404 (8%). The average athletic scholarship (and the proportion receiving): $4,636 (7%). Average amount of debt of borrowers graduating in 2009: $21,891. Proportion who borrowed: 98%.

CAMPUS LIFE AND EXTRACURRICULAR ACTIVITIES

Campus housing available (% using): women's dorms (46%), men's dorms (46%). **Student employment:** During the 2009-2010 academic year, 4% of undergraduates worked on campus. Average per-year earnings: $1,680. **Clubs and organizations:** Number of student organizations: 20. Activities include: campus ministries, choral groups, concert band, drama/theater, international student organization, music ensembles, student government, student newspaper, symphony orchestra, yearbook. Number of fraternities: 0; sororities: 0. Average proportion of students who stay on campus on weekends: 80%. **Sports program (2009-2010):** Member of NAIA. *Men's intercollegiate varsity sports:* baseball, basketball, cross country, golf, soccer, tennis, track and field (indoor), track and field (outdoor). *Women's intercollegiate varsity sports:* basketball, cross country, golf, soccer, softball, tennis, track and field (indoor), track and field (outdoor), volleyball.

SERVICES AND FACILITIES

Basic services: nonremedial tutoring, placement service, health service, health insurance. **Remedial assistance:** reading, math, writing, study skills. **Counseling services:** minority student, career, personal, veteran student, academic, older student, religious. **For learning-disabled students:** School does not offer a structured program with separate admission and additional fees. Total undergraduates in learning-disabled program or receiving services: 15. Services include: remedial math, remedial English, reading machines, remedial reading, tape recorders, videotaped classes, untimed tests, note-taking services, oral tests, learning center, readers, extended time for tests, tutors, priority seating, texts on tape, other testing accommodations. **Library:** Number of titles: 59,832; number of current serial subscriptions: 124. **Information technology resources:** Students are not required to lease or own a computer. Number of campus computers available to all students: 60. School has a wireless network. Approximate number of users that can be accommodated: 500. Proportion of college-owned housing units wired for high-speed internet access: 100%. **Campus safety:** Security services offered: late-night transport/escort service, lighted pathways/sidewalks, student patrols, controlled dormitory access (key, security card, etc).

TRANSFER AND INTERNATIONAL STUDENTS

Transfer students: May apply for admission for the following academic terms: Fall, Spring, Summer. Applicants do not need a minimum number of credits to apply. For fall 2009: Transfer applications received: 130. Transfer applicants offered admission: 89. Transfer applicants enrolled: 52. **International students:** Number of foreign undergraduates: 13 (3% of student body). Number of countries represented: 12. Minimum TOEFL score required: 500 (paper); 173 (computer). Average TOEFL score: 523 (paper).

Oral Roberts University

- **Address:** 7777 S. Lewis Avenue, Tulsa, OK 74171
- **Website:** http://www.oru.edu
- **Private; Religious affiliation:** Christian interdenominational
- **Enrollment:** 2,387 full-time; 208 part-time

KEY STATS

✔ **U.S News College Ranking:** second tier, National Universities
✔ **ACT Score (25th/75th percentile):** 20-26
✔ **Tuition:** 2010-2011: $20,044

Selectivity: Selective	**Room/board:** $8,304
Acceptance rate: 65%	**Average debt:** $49,007
Student/faculty ratio: 14/1	**Proportion who borrowed:** 45%

UNDERGRADUATE STUDENT BODY STATS

2009-2010 enrollment: 2,387 full-time; 208 part-time. Men: 41%; women: 59%. **Ethnic makeup:** African American: 15%; American-Indian: 3%; Asian American: 2%; Hispanic: 6%; White: 68%; International: 7%. **Religious preference:** Protestant: 98%; Other: 2%.

ADMISSIONS FACTS AND FIGURES

Phone: (800) 678-8876. **Email:** admissions@oru.edu. **Website:** http://www.oru.edu. **Application deadlines for fall 2011:** Regular decision: Rolling. Early decision: Not offered. Early action: Send application by: September 1; Decision sent by: September 1. Admission can be deferred. **Application fee:**

$35. **To apply online, go to:** https://webapps.oru.edu/new_php/admissions/undergraduate/application/. **Admissions requirements/recommendations:** High school units required (recommended): English: 4 (4); Mathematics: 2 (2); Science: 1 (1); Foreign language: 2 (2); Social studies: 2 (2); Total units: 16 (16). Tests: The college uses SAT or ACT scores in admissions decisions. Either SAT or ACT required. For admission to the fall 2011 entering class, the school will accept: ACT with or without writing accepted. Campus visit: Recommended. Admissions interview: Recommended. Off-campus interview: May be arranged. **Factors that count in admissions decisions:** *Academic:* Secondary school record: Very Important. Class rank: Important. Letters of recommendation: Important. Standardized test scores: Very Important. Essay: Very Important. *Nonacademic:* Interview: Not Considered. Extracurricular activities: Not Considered. Talent/ability: Not Considered. Character/personal qualities: Considered. Alumni/ae relationship: Considered. Geographical residence: Not Considered. State residency: Not Considered. Religious affiliation/commitment: Considered. Minority status: Not Considered. Volunteer work: Not Considered. Work experience: Not Considered. **Other schools with the greatest overlap in applicants:** Northeastern State University; Oklahoma State University; University of Oklahoma; University of Tulsa. **Admissions statistics for the fall 2009 entering class:** Total applicants: 1,268. Total accepted: 827. Freshmen enrolled: 498; 68% were from out of state. Overall acceptance rate: 65%. Non-early acceptance rate: 65%. **Credentials of fall 2009 freshmen:** 21% ranked in the top 10 percent of their high school class; 47% were in the top 25 percent; 78% were in the top half. (Proportion submitting class standing: 65%.) **Average high school grade point average:** 3.3. **First-year students who submitted SAT scores:** 48%. Scores (25/75 percentile): Critical Reading: 466-588, Math: 457-570, Combined: 923-1158. **First-year students submitting ACT scores:** 69%. Scores (25/75 percentile): English: 20-27, Math: 18-25, Composite: 20-26.

ACADEMICS
Year founded: 1963. **Academic calendar:** Semester. **Degrees offered:** bachelor's, master's, doctorate. **Most popular majors:** 25% business, management, marketing, and related support services, 12% communication, journalism, and related programs, 12% theology and religious vocations, 9% education, 6% visual and performing arts. **Major fields of study:** biological and biomedical sciences; business, management, marketing, and related support services; communication, journalism, and related programs; computer and information sciences and support services; education; engineering; English language and literature/letters; foreign languages, literatures, and linguistics; health professions and related clinical sciences; history; legal professions and studies; liberal arts and sciences studies, and humanities; mathematics and statistics; multi/interdisciplinary studies; physical sciences; psychology; public administration and social service professions; social sciences; theology and religious vocations; visual and performing arts. **Areas of required coursework:** arts/fine arts, humanities, computer literacy, mathematics, English (including composition), philosophy, foreign languages, sciences (biological or physical), history, social science, other. **Pre-professional programs:** pre-law, pre-medicine, pre-theology. **Special academic programs (% participation):** distance learning (1%), double major (1%), dual enrollment (1%), English as a Second Language (ESL) (1%), external degree program (1%), honors program (9%), independent study (10%), internships (20%), liberal arts/career combination (5%), student-designed major (2%), study abroad (10%), teacher certificate program (12%). **Teacher certification offered in:** early childhood, special education, elementary, middle/junior high, secondary. **Cooperative education programs:** art, business, computer science, education, engineering, health professions, other. **Reserve Officers Training Corps (ROTC):** Air Force ROTC: Offered at cooperating institution (University of Tulsa). **Faculty and instruction (2009-2010):** Total instructional faculty: 181 full-time, 98 part-time (57% men; 43% women; 15% minorities). Full-time faculty with Ph.D. or other terminal degree: 64%. Student/faculty ratio: 14/1. Classes of fewer than 20 students: 64%; of 20 to 49 students: 31%; of 50 or more students: 5%. **Advanced Placement and International Baccalaureate credit:** AP tests may be used for: Credit and/or placement. Scores accepted: 3. International Baccalaureate exams may be used for: Placement only. **Freshmen returning for sophomore year:** 78%. **Graduation rates:** Four-year: 39%; five-year: 50%; six-year: 52%. **Graduate study:** 60% of students pursue further study immediately upon graduation; 20% within one year; 10% within five years. Fields in which graduates pursue further study: Master of Business Administration (MBA), 1%; medicine, 1%; theology (or the seminary), 2%; education, 1%.

COSTS AND FINANCIAL AID
Financial aid office: (918) 495-7088. **Expenses (2010-2011):** Tuition and fees 2010-2011: $20,044; room/board: $8,304. Estimated books and supplies: $1,680; transportation: $1,786; personal expenses: $1,680. **Financial aid:** Priority filing date for institution's financial aid form: March 15; deadline: April 16. In 2009-2010, 80% of undergraduates applied for financial aid. Of those, 73% were determined to have financial need; 39% had their need fully met. Average financial aid package (proportion receiving): $17,820 (73%). Average amount of gift aid, such as scholarships or grants (proportion receiving): $11,055 (71%). Average amount of self-help aid, such as work study or loans (proportion receiving): $6,216 (63%). Average need-based loan (excluding PLUS or other private loans): $5,621. Among students who received need-based aid, the average percentage of need met: 72%. Among students who received aid based on merit, the average award (and the proportion receiving): $8,811 (18%). The average athletic scholarship (and the proportion receiving): $20,331 (4%). Average amount of debt of borrowers graduating in 2009: $49,007. Proportion who borrowed: 45%.

CAMPUS LIFE AND EXTRACURRICULAR ACTIVITIES
Campus housing available (% using): women's dorms (51%), men's dorms (48%), special housing for disabled students (1%). Students who live in college-owned, operated, or affiliated housing: 75%. **Student employment:** During the 2009-2010 academic year, 29% of undergraduates worked on campus. Average per-year earnings: $2,500. **Clubs and organizations:** Number of student organizations: 60. Activities include: choral groups, concert band, drama/theater, jazz band, literary magazine, music ensembles, musical theater, opera, pep band, radio station, student government, student newspaper, student film society, symphony orchestra, television station, yearbook. Number of fraternities: 0; sororities: 0. Average proportion of students who stay on campus on weekends: 99%. **Sports program (2009-2010):** Member of NCAA I. *Men's intercollegiate varsity sports:* baseball, basketball, cross country, golf, soccer, tennis, track and field (indoor), track and field (outdoor). *Women's intercollegiate varsity sports:* basketball, cross country, golf, soccer, softball, tennis, track and field (indoor), track and field (outdoor), volleyball.

SERVICES AND FACILITIES
Basic services: nonremedial tutoring, placement service, health service, health insurance. **Remedial assistance:** reading, math, writing, study skills. **Counseling services:** career, personal, academic, psychological, religious. **For learning-disabled students:** School does not offer a structured program with separate admission and additional fees. Services include: remedial math, remedial English, reading machines, remedial reading, tape recorders, diagnostic testing service, note-taking services, special bookstore section, oral tests, learning center, readers, extended time for tests, tutors, priority seating, texts on tape, typist/scribe, other testing accommodations. **Library:** Number of titles: 325,000; number of current serial subscriptions: 536. **Information technology resources:** Students are required to lease or own a computer. Number of campus computers available to all students: 507. School has a wireless network. Approximate number of users that can be accommodated: 2,000. Proportion of college-owned housing units wired for high-speed internet access: 100%. **Campus safety:** Security services offered: 24-hour foot-and-vehicle patrols, late-night transport/escort service, 24-hour emergency telephones, lighted pathways/sidewalks, controlled dormitory access (key, security card, etc).

TRANSFER AND INTERNATIONAL STUDENTS
Transfer students: May apply for admission for the following academic terms: Fall, Winter, Spring, Summer. Applicants need a minimum number of credits to apply. For fall 2009: Transfer applications received: 483. Transfer applicants offered admission: 316. Transfer applicants enrolled: 242. **International students:** Number of foreign undergraduates: 171 (7% of student body). Number of countries represented: 58. Minimum TOEFL score required: 500 (paper); 173 (computer). Average TOEFL score: 563 (paper).

Rogers State University

- **Address:** 1701 W. Will Rogers Boulevard, Claremore, OK 74017
- **Website:** http://www.rsu.edu/
- **Public**
- **Enrollment:** 2,613 full-time; 1,541 part-time

KEY STATS

- ✔ **U.S News College Ranking:** second tier, Regional Colleges (West)
- ✔ **ACT Score (25th/75th percentile):** 17-22
- ✔ **Tuition:** 2010-2011: $4,452 in state, $10,316 out of state

Selectivity: Selective	**Room/board:** $6,894
Acceptance rate: 58%	**Average debt:** $11,880
Student/faculty ratio: 21/1	**Proportion who borrowed:** 55%

UNDERGRADUATE STUDENT BODY STATS

2009-2010 enrollment: 2,613 full-time; 1,541 part-time. Men: 37%; women: 63%. **Ethnic makeup:** African American: 3%; American-Indian: 30%; Asian American: 2%; Hispanic: 2%; White: 63%; International: 1%.

ADMISSIONS FACTS AND FIGURES

Phone: (918) 343-7545. **Email:** info@rsu.edu. **Website:** http://www.rsu.edu/. **Application deadlines for fall 2011:** Regular decision: Rolling. Early decision: Not offered. Early action: Not offered. Admission can be deferred. **To apply online, go to:** https://rsuportal.rsu.edu/ics/Admissions/Apply_For_Admission.jnz. **Admissions requirements/recommendations:** High school units required (recommended): English: 4 (4); Mathematics: 3 (4); Science: 2 (3); Foreign language: 0 (2); Social studies: 1 (1); History: 2 (2); Academic electives: 3 (0); Total units: 15 (19). Tests: The college uses SAT or ACT scores in admissions decisions. Either SAT or ACT required. For admission to the fall 2011 entering class, the school will accept: ACT with or without writing accepted. Campus visit: Recommended. Admissions interview: Neither required nor recommended. Off-campus interview: Not available. **Factors that count in admissions decisions:** *Academic:* Secondary school record: Considered. Class rank: Important. Letters of recommendation: Not Considered. Standardized test scores: Important. Essay: Not Considered. *Nonacademic:* Interview: Not Considered. Extracurricular activities: Not Considered. Talent/ability: Not Considered. Character/personal qualities: Not Considered. Alumni/ae relationship: Not Considered. Geographical residence: Not Considered. State residency: Not Considered. Religious affiliation/commitment: Not Considered. Minority status: Not Considered. Volunteer work: Not Considered. Work experience: Not Considered. **Other schools with the greatest overlap in applicants:** Northeastern State University; Oklahoma State University; University of Oklahoma. **Admissions statistics for the fall 2009 entering class:** Total applicants: 1,702. Total accepted: 981. Freshmen enrolled: 849; 3% were from out of state. Overall acceptance rate: 58%. **Credentials of fall 2009 freshmen:** 40% ranked in the top 10 percent of their high school class; 54% were in the top 25 percent; 75% were in the top half. (Proportion submitting class standing: 50%.) **Average high school grade point average:** 3.1. **First-year students submitting ACT scores:** 98%. Scores (25/75 percentile): English: 16-23, Math: 16-21, Composite: 17-22.

ACADEMICS

Year founded: 1909. **Academic calendar:** Semester. **Degrees offered:** associate, transfer-associate, terminal-associate, bachelor's. **Most popular majors:** 36% business administration and management, 16% engineering technologies/technicians, 13% social sciences, 12% biology/biological sciences, 6% criminal justice/law enforcement administration. **Major fields of study:** biological and biomedical sciences; business, management, marketing, and related support services; engineering technologies/technicians; liberal arts and sciences studies, and humanities; social sciences. **Areas of required coursework:** arts/fine arts, humanities, computer literacy, mathematics, English (including composition), philosophy, foreign languages, sciences (biological or physical), history, social science. **Special academic programs (% participation):** distance learning (91%), honors program (2%), independent study (10%), internships (24%), study abroad. **Faculty and instruction (2009-2010):** Total instructional faculty: 104 full-time, 141 part-time (44% men; 56% women; 11% minorities). Full-time faculty with Ph.D. or other terminal degree: 64%. Student/faculty ratio: 21/1. Classes of fewer than 20 students: 38%; of 20 to 49 students: 62%; of 50 or more students: 1%. **Advanced Placement and International Baccalaureate credit:** AP tests may be used for: Credit and/or placement. Scores accepted: 3, 4, 5. International Baccalaureate exams may be used for: Credit and/or placement. **Freshmen**

returning for sophomore year: 50%. **Graduation rates:** Four-year: 4%; five-year: 11%; six-year: 26%. **Graduate study:** 10% of students pursue further study immediately upon graduation.

COSTS AND FINANCIAL AID

Financial aid office: (918) 343-7553. **Expenses (2010-2011):** Tuition and fees 2010-2011: $4,452 in state, $10,316 out of state; room/board: $6,894. Estimated books and supplies: $2,130; transportation: $2,564; personal expenses: $1,800. **Financial aid:** Priority filing date for institution's financial aid form: June 1. In 2009-2010, 79% of undergraduates applied for financial aid. Of those, 67% were determined to have financial need; 10% had their need fully met. Average financial aid package (proportion receiving): $8,004 (66%). Average amount of gift aid, such as scholarships or grants (proportion receiving): $5,267 (51%). Average amount of self-help aid, such as work study or loans (proportion receiving): $3,795 (42%). Average need-based loan (excluding PLUS or other private loans): $3,748. Among students who received need-based aid, the average percentage of need met: 54%. Among students who received aid based on merit, the average award (and the proportion receiving): $2,836 (3%). The average athletic scholarship (and the proportion receiving): $1,737 (1%). Average amount of debt of borrowers graduating in 2009: $11,880. Proportion who borrowed: 55%.

CAMPUS LIFE AND EXTRACURRICULAR ACTIVITIES

Campus housing available (% using): apartments for married students (7%), apartment for single students (93%). Students who live in college-owned, operated, or affiliated housing: 6%. **Student employment:** During the 2009-2010 academic year, 8% of undergraduates worked on campus. Average per-year earnings: $6,960. **Clubs and organizations:** Number of student organizations: 26. Activities include: campus ministries, choral groups, drama/theater, international student organization, jazz band, literary magazine, radio station, student government, student newspaper, television station. Number of fraternities: 2; sororities: 2. Proportion of men in fraternities: 1%; of women in sororities: 1%. Average proportion of students who stay on campus on weekends: 30%. **Sports program (2009-2010):** Member of NAIA. *Men's intercollegiate varsity sports:* baseball, basketball, golf, soccer. *Women's intercollegiate varsity sports:* basketball, golf, soccer, softball.

SERVICES AND FACILITIES

Basic services: nonremedial tutoring, placement service, day care, health service, health insurance. **Remedial assistance:** reading, math, writing, study skills, other. **Counseling services:** minority student, career, personal, veteran student, academic, older student, psychological, birth control. **For learning-disabled students:** School does not offer a structured program with separate admission and additional fees. Total undergraduates in learning-disabled program or receiving services: 98. Services include: remedial math, remedial English, remedial reading, tape recorders, note-taking services, oral tests, learning center, extended time for tests, tutors, priority seating, texts on tape, other testing accommodations. **Library:** Number of titles: 77,650; number of current serial subscriptions: 225. **Information technology resources:** Students are not required to lease or own a computer. Number of campus computers available to all students: 301. School has a wireless network. Approximate number of users that can be accommodated: 456. Proportion of college-owned housing units wired for high-speed internet access: 100%. **Campus safety:** Security services offered: 24-hour foot-and-vehicle patrols, late-night transport/escort service, 24-hour emergency telephones, lighted pathways/sidewalks, student patrols, controlled dormitory access (key, security card, etc.).

TRANSFER AND INTERNATIONAL STUDENTS

Transfer students: May apply for admission for the following academic terms: Fall, Spring, Summer. Applicants need a minimum number of credits to apply. For fall 2009: Transfer applications received: 1,206. Transfer applicants offered admission: 757. Transfer applicants enrolled: 331. **International students:** Number of foreign undergraduates: 22 (1% of student body). Number of countries represented: 11. Minimum TOEFL score required: 500 (paper); 173 (computer).

Southeastern Oklahoma State University

- **Address:** 1405 N. Fourth, PMB 4225, Durant, OK 74701-0609
- **Website:** http://www.se.edu
- **Public**
- **Enrollment:** 2,955 full-time; 819 part-time

KEY STATS

- ✔ **U.S News College Ranking:** second tier, Regional Universities (West)
- ✔ **ACT Score (25th/75th percentile):** 18-23
- ✔ **Tuition:** 2010-2011: $4,316 in state, $10,687 out of state

Selectivity: Selective	**Room/board:** $4,650
Acceptance rate: 82%	**Average debt:** N/A
Student/faculty ratio: 18/1	**Proportion who borrowed:** N/A

UNDERGRADUATE STUDENT BODY STATS

2009-2010 enrollment: 2,955 full-time; 819 part-time. Men: 45%; women: 55%. **Ethnic makeup:** African American: 6%; American-Indian: 30%; Asian American: 1%; Hispanic: 3%; White: 59%; International: 2%.

ADMISSIONS FACTS AND FIGURES

Phone: (580) 745-2060. **Email:** admissions@se.edu. **Website:** http://www.se.edu. **Application deadlines for fall 2011:** Regular decision: Rolling. Early decision: Not offered. Early action: Not offered. Admission cannot be deferred. **Application fee:** $20. **To apply online, go to:** https://campusconnect.se.edu/admission_appl.html. **Admissions requirements/recommendations:** High school units required (recommended): English: 4; Mathematics: 3; Science: 2 (3); Foreign language: (1); Social studies: (1); History: 3; Academic electives: 3; Total units: 15. Tests: The college uses SAT or ACT scores in admissions decisions. Either SAT or ACT required. For admission to the fall 2011 entering class, the school will accept: ACT with or without writing accepted. Campus visit: Recommended. Admissions interview: Neither required nor recommended. Off-campus interview: Not available. **Factors that count in admissions decisions:** *Academic:* Secondary school record: Considered. Class rank: Very Important. Letters of recommendation: Considered. Standardized test scores: Very Important. Essay: Not Considered. *Nonacademic:* Interview: Considered. Extracurricular activities: Not Considered. Talent/ability: Considered. Character/personal qualities: Considered. Alumni/ae relationship: Not Considered. Geographical residence: Not Considered. State residency: Considered. Religious affiliation/commitment: Not Considered. Minority status: Not Considered. Volunteer work: Not Considered. Work experience: Not Considered. **Other schools with the greatest overlap in applicants:** East Central University; Oklahoma State University; University of Central Oklahoma; University of Oklahoma. **Admissions statistics for the fall 2009 entering class:** Total applicants: 1,083. Total accepted: 890. Freshmen enrolled: 669; 24% were from out of state. Overall acceptance rate: 82%. **Credentials of fall 2009 freshmen:** 13% ranked in the top 10 percent of their high school class; 35% were in the top 25 percent; 63% were in the top half. (Proportion submitting class standing: 83%.) **Average high school grade point average:** 3.3. **First-year students who submitted SAT scores:** 7%. **First-year students submitting ACT scores:** 82%. Scores (25/75 percentile): English: 16-22, Math: 17-23, Composite: 18-23.

ACADEMICS

Year founded: 1909. **Academic calendar:** Semester. **Degrees offered:** bachelor's, master's, post-master's certificate. **Most popular majors:** 20% education, 12% liberal arts and sciences studies, and humanities, 10% engineering technologies/technicians, 9% business, management, marketing, and related support services, 8% communication, journalism, and related programs. **Major fields of study:** biological and biomedical sciences; business, management, marketing, and related support services; communication, journalism, and related programs; computer and information sciences and support services; education; engineering technologies/technicians; English language and literature/letters; foreign languages, literatures, and linguistics; history; liberal arts and sciences studies, and humanities; mathematics and statistics; multi/interdisciplinary studies; natural resources and conservation; parks, recreation, leisure, and fitness studies; physical sciences; psychology; security and protective services; social sciences; transportation and materials moving; visual and performing arts. **Areas of required coursework:** computer literacy, mathematics, English (including composition), sciences (biological or physical), history, social science. **Preprofessional programs:** pre-law, pre-dentistry, pre-medicine, pre-veterinary science, pre-optometry, pre-pharmacy. **Special academic programs (% participation):** distance learning (10%), double major (5%), honors program (4%), independent study, internships (14%), teacher certificate program (20%). **Teacher certification offered in:** special education, elementary, middle/junior high, secondary, bilingual/bicultural. **Faculty and instruction (2009-2010):** Total instructional faculty: 143 full-time, 104 part-time (55% men; 45% women; 30% minorities). Full-time faculty with Ph.D. or other terminal degree: 76%. Student/faculty ratio: 18/1. Classes of fewer than 20 students: 47%; of 20 to 49 students: 50%; of 50 or more students: 3%. **Advanced Placement and International Baccalaureate credit:** AP tests may be used for: Credit and/or placement. Scores accepted: 3. International Baccalaureate exams may be used for: Credit and/or placement. **Freshmen returning for sophomore year:** 58%. **Graduation rates:** Four-year: 13%; five-year: 29%; six-year: 31%. **Graduate study:** 11% of students pursue further study immediately upon graduation; 14% within one year; 25% within five years. Fields in which graduates pursue further study: Master of Business Administration (MBA), 9%; law, 1%; medicine, 1%; dentistry, 1%; education, 51%; arts and sciences, 35%; veterinary medicine, 1%.

COSTS AND FINANCIAL AID

Financial aid office: (580) 745-2186. **Expenses (2010-2011):** Tuition and fees 2010-2011: $4,316 in state, $10,687 out of state; room/board: $4,650. Estimated books and supplies: $1,000; transportation: $1,240; personal expenses: $1,641. **Financial aid:** Priority filing date for institution's financial aid form: March 1. In 2009-2010, 83% of undergraduates applied for financial aid. Of those, 72% were determined to have financial need; 21% had their need fully met. Average financial aid package (proportion receiving): $9,675 (70%). Average amount of gift aid, such as scholarships or grants (proportion receiving): $1,575 (55%). Average amount of self-help aid, such as work study or loans (proportion receiving): $1,539 (41%). Average need-based loan (excluding PLUS or other private loans): $1,730. Among students who received need-based aid, the average percentage of need met: 18%. Among students who received aid based on merit, the average award (and the proportion receiving): $860 (5%). The average athletic scholarship (and the proportion receiving): $1,733 (8%).

CAMPUS LIFE AND EXTRACURRICULAR ACTIVITIES

Campus housing available (% using): coed dorms (100%). Students who live in college-owned, operated, or affiliated housing: 18%. **Student employment:** During the 2009-2010 academic year, 20% of undergraduates worked on campus. Average per-year earnings: $2,060. **Clubs and organizations:** Number of student organizations: 62. Activities include: campus ministries, choral groups, concert band, dance, drama/theater, international student organization, jazz band, literary magazine, marching band, music ensembles, musical theater, opera, pep band, radio station, student government, student newspaper, yearbook. Number of fraternities: 2; sororities: 2. Proportion of men in fraternities: 1%; of women in sororities: 1%. Average proportion of students who stay on campus on weekends: 30%. **Sports program (2009-2010):** Member of NCAA II. *Men's intercollegiate varsity sports:* baseball, basketball, golf, tennis. *Women's intercollegiate varsity sports:* basketball, cross country, softball, tennis, volleyball.

SERVICES AND FACILITIES

Basic services: nonremedial tutoring, placement service, health service, other. **Remedial assistance:** reading, math, writing, other. **Counseling services:** minority student, career, personal, veteran student, academic, older student, psychological, birth control. **For learning-disabled students:** School does not offer a structured program with separate admission and additional fees. Total undergraduates in learning-disabled program or receiving services: 38. Services include: remedial math, remedial English, reading machines, remedial reading, tape recorders, other special classes, diagnostic testing service, untimed tests, note-taking services, oral tests, learning center, readers, extended time for tests, tutors, texts on tape, other testing accommodations, other. **Library:** Number of titles: 308,095; number of current serial subscriptions: 1,195. **Information technology resources:** Students are not required to lease or own a computer. Number of campus computers available to all students: 598. School has a wireless network. Approximate number of users that can be accommodated: 100. Proportion of college-owned housing units wired for high-speed internet access: 100%. **Campus safety:** Security services offered: late-night transport/escort service, lighted pathways/sidewalks, controlled dormitory access (key, security card, etc).

TRANSFER AND INTERNATIONAL STUDENTS

Transfer students: May apply for admission for the following academic terms: Fall, Spring, Summer. Applicants need a minimum number of credits to apply. For fall 2009: Transfer applications received: 689. Transfer applicants offered admission: 667. Transfer applicants enrolled: 524. **International students:** Number of foreign undergraduates: 61 (2% of stu-

dent body). Number of countries represented: 30. Minimum TOEFL score required: 500 (paper); 173 (computer).

Southern Nazarene University

- **Address:** 6729 N.W. 39th Expressway, Bethany, OK 73008
- **Website:** http://www.snu.edu
- **Private; Religious affiliation:** Nazarene
- **Enrollment:** 1,602 full-time; 51 part-time

KEY STATS

✔ **U.S News College Ranking:** 68, Regional Universities (West)
✔ **ACT Score (25th/75th percentile):** 19-25
✔ **Tuition:** 2010-2011: $18,282

Selectivity: Selective	**Room/board:** $7,222
Acceptance rate: 98%	**Average debt:** $20,900
Student/faculty ratio: 17/1	**Proportion who borrowed:** 80%

UNDERGRADUATE STUDENT BODY STATS

2009-2010 enrollment: 1,602 full-time; 51 part-time. Men: 47%; women: 53%. **Ethnic makeup:** African American: 11%; American-Indian: 5%; Asian American: 2%; Hispanic: 6%; White: 73%; International: 3%. **Religious preference:** Roman Catholic: 4%; Protestant: 45%; No preference: 4%; Unknown: 15%; Nazarene: 32%; 0: 0%.

ADMISSIONS FACTS AND FIGURES

Phone: (405) 491-6324. **Email:** admissions@snu.edu. **Website:** http://www.snu.edu. **Application deadlines for fall 2011:** Regular decision: August 6. Early decision: Not offered. Early action: Not offered. Admission can be deferred. **Application fee:** $35. **To apply online, go to:** https://my.snu.edu/prospects/. **Admissions requirements/recommendations:** Tests: The college uses SAT or ACT scores in admissions decisions. Neither SAT nor ACT required. For admission to the fall 2011 entering class, the school will accept: ACT with or without writing accepted. Campus visit: Recommended. Admissions interview: Recommended. Off-campus interview: May be arranged. **Factors that count in admissions decisions:** *Academic:* Secondary school record: Considered. Class rank: Very Important. Letters of recommendation: Not Considered. Standardized test scores: Very Important. Essay: Not Considered. *Nonacademic:* Interview: Important. Extracurricular activities: Not Considered. Talent/ability: Considered. Character/personal qualities: Important. Alumni/ae relationship: Considered. Geographical residence: Not Considered. State residency: Not Considered. Religious affiliation/commitment: Considered. Minority status: Not Considered. Volunteer work: Not Considered. Work experience: Not Considered. **Admissions statistics for the fall 2009 entering class:** Total applicants: 420. Total accepted: 413. Freshmen enrolled: 281; 42% were from out of state. Overall acceptance rate: 98%. **Credentials of fall 2009 freshmen:** 22% ranked in the top 10 percent of their high school class; 44% were in the top 25 percent; 73% were in the top half. (Proportion submitting class standing: 85%.) **Average high school grade point average:** 3.4. **First-year students who submitted SAT scores:** 22%. **First-year students submitting ACT scores:** 86%. Scores (25/75 percentile): English: N/A, Math: N/A, Composite: 19-25.

ACADEMICS

Year founded: 1899. **Academic calendar:** Semester. **Degrees offered:** associate, bachelor's, master's. **Most popular majors:** 36% organizational behavior studies, 15% business administration and management, 10% human development and family studies, 6% education, 6% nursing/registered nurse training (R.N., A.S.N., B.S.N., M.S.N.). **Major fields of study:** agriculture, agriculture operations, and related sciences; area, ethnic, cultural, and gender studies; biological and biomedical sciences; business, management, marketing, and related support services; communication, journalism, and related programs; communications technologies/technicians and support services; computer and information sciences and support services; education; English language and literature/letters; family and consumer sciences/human sciences; foreign languages, literatures, and linguistics; health professions and related clinical sciences; history; liberal arts and sciences studies, and humanities; mathematics and statistics; parks, recreation, leisure, and fitness studies; philosophy and religious studies; physical sciences; psychology; social sciences; theology and religious vocations; transportation and materials moving; visual and performing arts. **Areas of required coursework:** arts/fine arts, humanities, computer literacy, mathematics, English (including composition), philosophy, sciences (biological or physical), his-

tory, social science. **Pre-professional programs:** pre-law, pre-dentistry, pre-medicine, pre-pharmacy. **Special academic programs:** accelerated program, cross-registration, distance learning, double major, dual enrollment, English as a Second Language (ESL), honors program, independent study, internships, student-designed major, study abroad, teacher certificate program. **Teacher certification offered in:** early childhood, elementary, middle/junior high, secondary. **Reserve Officers Training Corps (ROTC):** Army ROTC: Offered at cooperating institution (University of Central Oklahoma); Air Force ROTC: Offered at cooperating institution (University of Oklahoma). **Faculty and instruction (2009-2010):** Total instructional faculty: 72 full-time, 129 part-time (49% men; 51% women; 5% minorities). Full-time faculty with Ph.D. or other terminal degree: 76%. Student/faculty ratio: 17/1. Classes of fewer than 20 students: 66%; of 20 to 49 students: 33%; of 50 or more students: 1%. **Advanced Placement and International Baccalaureate credit:** AP tests may be used for: Credit and/or placement. Scores accepted: 3, 4, 5. International Baccalaureate exams may be used for: Credit only. **Freshmen returning for sophomore year:** 68%. **Graduation rates:** Four-year: 32%; five-year: 46%; six-year: 51%.

COSTS AND FINANCIAL AID

Financial aid office: (405) 491-6310. **Expenses (2010-2011):** Tuition and fees 2010-2011: $18,282; room/board: $7,222. Estimated books and supplies: $1,000; transportation: $900; personal expenses: $3,600. **Financial aid:** Priority filing date for institution's financial aid form: March 1. Average amount of debt of borrowers graduating in 2009: $20,900. Proportion who borrowed: 80%.

CAMPUS LIFE AND EXTRACURRICULAR ACTIVITIES

Campus housing available (% using): women's dorms (38%), men's dorms (36%), apartment for single students (26%), special housing for disabled students (0%). Students who live in college-owned, operated, or affiliated housing: 68%. **Student employment:** During the 2009-2010 academic year, 10% of undergraduates worked on campus. Average per-year earnings: $2,500. **Clubs and organizations:** Number of student organizations: 13. Activities include: campus ministries, choral groups, concert band, drama/theater, jazz band, literary magazine, music ensembles, musical theater, opera, pep band, student government, student newspaper, symphony orchestra, television station, yearbook. Number of fraternities: 0; sororities: 0. Average proportion of students who stay on campus on weekends: 50%. **Sports program (2009-2010):** Member of NAIA. *Men's intercollegiate varsity sports:* baseball, basketball, cross country, football, golf, soccer, track and field (indoor), track and field (outdoor). *Women's intercollegiate varsity sports:* basketball, cross country, golf, soccer, softball, tennis, track and field (indoor), track and field (outdoor), volleyball.

SERVICES AND FACILITIES

Basic services: nonremedial tutoring, placement service, health service, health insurance. **Remedial assistance:** reading, math, writing, study skills. **Counseling services:** minority student, career, military, personal, veteran student, academic, older student, psychological, birth control, religious. **For learning-disabled students:** School does not offer a structured program with separate admission and additional fees. Total undergraduates in learning-disabled program or receiving services: 63. Services include: remedial English, reading machines, remedial reading, tape recorders, note-taking services, oral tests, learning center, readers, extended time for tests, tutors, priority seating, texts on tape, other. **Library:** Number of titles: 101,117; number of current serial subscriptions: 41,048. **Information technology resources:** Students are not required to lease or own a computer. Number of campus computers available to all students: 150. School has a wireless network. Approximate number of users that can be accommodated: 2,500. Proportion of college-owned housing units wired for high-speed internet access: 100%. **Campus safety:** Security services offered: 24-hour foot-and-vehicle patrols, late-night transport/escort service, lighted pathways/sidewalks, student patrols, controlled dormitory access (key, security card, etc).

TRANSFER AND INTERNATIONAL STUDENTS

Transfer students: May apply for admission for the following academic terms: Fall, Spring. Applicants do not need a minimum number of credits to apply. For fall 2009: Transfer applications received: 207. Transfer applicants offered admission: 207. Transfer applicants enrolled: 88. **International students:** Number of foreign undergraduates: 52 (3% of student body). Number of countries represented: 29. Minimum TOEFL score required: 500 (paper); 173 (computer). Average TOEFL score: 530 (paper).

Southwestern Oklahoma State University

- **Address:** 100 Campus Drive, Weatherford, OK 73096-3098
- **Website:** http://www.swosu.edu
- **Public**
- **Enrollment:** 3,584 full-time; 686 part-time

KEY STATS

✔ **U.S News College Ranking:** second tier, Regional Universities (West)
✔ **ACT Score (25th/75th percentile):** 18-24
✔ **Tuition:** 2009-2010: $4,110 in state; $9,450 out of state

Selectivity: Selective	**Room/board:** $4,100
Acceptance rate: 92%	**Average debt:** N/A
Student/faculty ratio: 20/1	**Proportion who borrowed:** N/A

UNDERGRADUATE STUDENT BODY STATS

2009-2010 enrollment: 3,584 full-time; 686 part-time. Men: 43%; women: 57%. **Ethnic makeup:** African American: 5%; American-Indian: 6%; Asian American: 2%; Hispanic: 5%; White: 80%; International: 1%.

ADMISSIONS FACTS AND FIGURES

Phone: (580) 774-3782. **Email:** swosuinfo@swosu.edu. **Website:** http://www.swosu.edu. **Application deadlines for fall 2011:** Regular decision: Rolling. Early decision: Not offered. Early action: Not offered. Admission can be deferred. **Application fee:** $15. **To apply online, go to:** http://www.swosu.edu/admissions/apply.asp. **Admissions requirements/recommendations:** High school units required (recommended): English: 4 (4); Mathematics: 3 (3); Science: 2 (2); Social studies: 1 (1); History: 2 (2); Academic electives: 0 (2); Total units: 15 (17). Tests: The college uses SAT or ACT scores in admissions decisions. ACT required. For admission to the fall 2011 entering class, the school will accept: ACT with or without writing accepted. Campus visit: Recommended. Admissions interview: Neither required nor recommended. **Factors that count in admissions decisions:** *Academic:* Secondary school record: Very Important. Class rank: Very Important. Letters of recommendation: Not Considered. Standardized test scores: Very Important. Essay: Not Considered. *Nonacademic:* Interview: Not Considered. Extracurricular activities: Not Considered. Talent/ability: Not Considered. Character/personal qualities: Not Considered. Alumni/ae relationship: Not Considered. Geographical residence: Not Considered. State residency: Not Considered. Religious affiliation/commitment: Not Considered. Minority status: Not Considered. Volunteer work: Not Considered. Work experience: Not Considered. **Other schools with the greatest overlap in applicants:** Oklahoma State University; University of Central Oklahoma; University of Oklahoma. **Admissions statistics for the fall 2009 entering class:** Total applicants: 1,417. Total accepted: 1,305. Freshmen enrolled: 926; 7% were from out of state. Overall acceptance rate: 92%. **Credentials of fall 2009 freshmen:** 18% ranked in the top 10 percent of their high school class; 40% were in the top 25 percent; 72% were in the top half. (Proportion submitting class standing: 81%.) **Average high school grade point average:** 3.3. **First-year students submitting ACT scores:** 91%. Scores (25/75 percentile): English: 17-24, Math: 17-24, Composite: 18-24.

ACADEMICS

Year founded: 1901. **Academic calendar:** Semester. **Degrees offered:** associate, bachelor's, master's. **Most popular majors:** 22% business, management, marketing, and related support services, 20% health professions and related clinical sciences, 17% education, 8% visual and performing arts, 7% parks, recreation, leisure, and fitness studies. **Major fields of study:** biological and biomedical sciences; business, management, marketing, and related support services; computer and information sciences and support services; education; engineering; engineering technologies/technicians; English language and literature/letters; foreign languages; literatures, and linguistics; health professions and related clinical sciences; history; mathematics and statistics; multi/interdisciplinary studies; parks, recreation, leisure, and fitness studies; physical sciences; psychology; public administration and social service professions; security and protective services; social sciences; visual and performing arts. **Areas of required coursework:** arts/fine arts, humanities, computer literacy, mathematics, English (including composition), sciences (biological or physical), history, social science, other. **Pre-professional programs:** pre-law, pre-dentistry, pre-medicine, pre-veterinary science, pre-optometry, pre-pharmacy, other. **Special academic programs:** accelerated program, distance learning, double major, dual enrollment, independent study, internships, student-designed major, study abroad, teacher certificate program, weekend college. **Teacher certification offered in:** early childhood, special education, elementary, middle/junior high, secondary. **Faculty and instruction (2009-2010):** Total instructional faculty: N/A. Student/faculty ratio: 20/1. Classes of fewer than 20 students: 43%; of 20 to 49 students: 51%; of 50 or more students: 5%. **Advanced Placement and International Baccalaureate credit:** AP tests may be used for: Credit only. Scores accepted: 3, 4, 5. **Freshmen returning for sophomore year:** 65%. **Graduation rates:** Four-year: 12%; five-year: 24%; six-year: 36%.

COSTS AND FINANCIAL AID

Financial aid office: (580) 774-3786. **Expenses (2009-2010):** Tuition and fees 2009-2010: $4,110 in state, $9,450 out of state; room/board: $4,100. **Financial aid:** Priority filing date for institution's financial aid form: March 1; deadline: March 1. In 2009-2010, 76% of undergraduates applied for financial aid. Of those, 62% were determined to have financial need; 41% had their need fully met. Average financial aid package (proportion receiving): $4,890 (61%). Average amount of gift aid, such as scholarships or grants (proportion receiving): $1,463 (55%). Average amount of self-help aid, such as work study or loans (proportion receiving): $1,598 (49%). Average need-based loan (excluding PLUS or other private loans): $1,677. Among students who received need-based aid, the average percentage of need met: 89%. Among students who received aid based on merit, the average award (and the proportion receiving): $491 (33%). The average athletic scholarship (and the proportion receiving): $1,043 (7%).

CAMPUS LIFE AND EXTRACURRICULAR ACTIVITIES

Campus housing available (% using): women's dorms (50%), men's dorms (44%), apartments for married students (6%). Students who live in college-owned, operated, or affiliated housing: 25%. **Clubs and organizations:** Number of student organizations: 69. Activities include: campus ministries, choral groups, concert band, drama/theater, international student organization, jazz band, literary magazine, marching band, model UN, music ensembles, musical theater, opera, pep band, student government, student newspaper, symphony orchestra, yearbook. Number of fraternities: 2; sororities: 3. **Sports program (2009-2010):** Member of NCAA II.

SERVICES AND FACILITIES

Basic services: nonremedial tutoring, placement service, health service, health insurance, other. **Remedial assistance:** reading, math, writing, study skills. **Counseling services:** minority student, career, personal, veteran student, academic, older student, psychological, birth control, other. **For learning-disabled students:** School does not offer a structured program with separate admission and additional fees. Services include: remedial math, remedial English, remedial reading, untimed tests, learning center, tutors. **Library:** Number of titles: 299,954; number of current serial subscriptions: 1,136. **Information technology resources:** Students are not required to lease or own a computer. Number of campus computers available to all students: 800. School has a wireless network. Approximate number of users that can be accommodated: 2,000. Proportion of college-owned housing units wired for high-speed internet access: 100%. **Campus safety:** Security services offered: 24-hour emergency telephones, lighted pathways/sidewalks, controlled dormitory access (key, security card, etc).

TRANSFER AND INTERNATIONAL STUDENTS

Transfer students: May apply for admission for the following academic terms: Fall, Spring, Summer. Applicants need a minimum number of credits to apply. For fall 2009: Transfer applications received: 564. Transfer applicants enrolled: 345. **International students:** Number of foreign undergraduates: 55 (1% of student body). Number of countries represented: 33. Minimum TOEFL score required: 500 (paper); 173 (computer).

St. Gregory's University

- **Address:** 1900 W. MacArthur Street, Shawnee, OK 74804
- **Website:** http://www.stgregorys.edu
- **Private; Religious affiliation:** Roman Catholic
- **Enrollment:** N/A

KEY STATS
- ✔ **U.S News College Ranking:** 25, Regional Colleges (West)
- ✔ **SAT Score (25th/75th percentile):** 760-960
- ✔ **Tuition:** 2009-2010: $17,194
  - **Selectivity:** Least selective   **Room/board:** $6,404
  - **Acceptance rate:** 97%   **Average debt:** N/A
  - **Student/faculty ratio:** N/A   **Proportion who borrowed:** N/A

University of Central Oklahoma

- **Address:** 100 N. University Drive, Edmond, OK 73034
- **Website:** http://www.ucok.edu
- **Public**
- **Enrollment:** 9,875 full-time; 4,538 part-time

KEY STATS
- ✔ **U.S News College Ranking:** second tier, Regional Universities (West)
- ✔ **ACT Score (25th/75th percentile):** 19-24
- ✔ **Tuition:** 2010-2011: $4,223 in state, $10,652 out of state
  - **Selectivity:** Selective   **Room/board:** $7,776
  - **Acceptance rate:** 75%   **Average debt:** N/A
  - **Student/faculty ratio:** N/A   **Proportion who borrowed:** N/A

UNDERGRADUATE STUDENT BODY STATS
2009-2010 enrollment: 9,875 full-time; 4,538 part-time. Men: 42%; women: 58%. **Ethnic makeup:** African American: 10%; American-Indian: 6%; Asian American: 4%; Hispanic: 4%; White: 71%; International: 5%.

ADMISSIONS FACTS AND FIGURES
Phone: (405) 974-2338. **Email:** admituco@ucok.edu. **Website:** http://www. ucok.edu. **Application deadlines for fall 2011:** Regular decision: Rolling. Early decision: Not offered. Early action: Not offered. Admission can be deferred. **Application fee:** $25. **To apply online, go to:** https://central.uco.edu/prod/ bwskalog.P_DispLoginNon. **Admissions requirements/recommendations:** High school units required (recommended): English: 4 (4); Mathematics: 3 (4); Science: 2 (3); Foreign language: 0 (2); Social studies: 1 (1); History: 2 (2); Academic electives: 3 (0); Total units: 15 (16). Tests: The college uses SAT or ACT scores in admissions decisions. Either SAT or ACT required. For admission to the fall 2011 entering class, the school will accept: ACT with or without writing accepted. Campus visit: Recommended. Admissions interview: Neither required nor recommended. Off-campus interview: Not available. **Factors that count in admissions decisions:** *Academic:* Secondary school record: Very Important. Class rank: Very Important. Letters of recommendation: Not Considered. Standardized test scores: Very Important. Essay: Not Considered. *Nonacademic:* Interview: Not Considered. Extracurricular activities: Considered. Talent/ability: Considered. Character/personal qualities: Not Considered. Alumni/ae relationship: Not Considered. Geographical residence: Not Considered. State residency: Not Considered. Religious affiliation/commitment: Not Considered. Minority status: Not Considered. Volunteer work: Not Considered. Work experience: Not Considered. **Other schools with the greatest overlap in applicants:** Oklahoma State University; University of Oklahoma. **Admissions statistics for the fall 2009 entering class:** Total applicants: 5,181. Total accepted: 3,907. Freshmen enrolled: 2,208; 2% were from out of state. Overall acceptance rate: 75%. **Credentials of fall 2009 freshmen:** 13% ranked in the top 10 percent of their high school class; 37% were in the top 25 percent; 72% were in the top half. (Proportion submitting class standing: 71%.) **Average high school grade point average:** 3.3. **First-year students submitting ACT scores:** 93%. Scores (25/75 percentile): English: 19-24, Math: 17-23, Composite: 19-24.

ACADEMICS
Year founded: 1890. **Academic calendar:** Semester. **Degrees offered:** certificate, associate, bachelor's, master's. **Major fields of study:** biological and bio-

medical sciences; business, management, marketing, and related support services; communication, journalism, and related programs; computer and information sciences and support services; education; engineering; English language and literature/letters; family and consumer sciences/human sciences; foreign languages, literatures, and linguistics; health professions and related clinical sciences; history; liberal arts and sciences studies, and humanities; mathematics and statistics; personal and culinary services; philosophy and religious studies; physical sciences; psychology; security and protective services; social sciences; visual and performing arts. **Areas of required coursework:** humanities, mathematics, English (including composition), sciences (biological or physical), history. **Pre-professional programs:** pre-dentistry, pre-medicine, pre-veterinary science, pre-optometry, pre-pharmacy, other. **Special academic programs (% participation):** accelerated program, distance learning, double major (1.1%), dual enrollment (0%), English as a Second Language (ESL), honors program, independent study (5.8%), internships (9.8%), teacher certificate program (12.2%). **Teacher certification offered in:** early childhood, special education, elementary, vo-tech, secondary, bilingual/bicultural. **Reserve Officers Training Corps (ROTC):** Army ROTC: Offered on campus. **Faculty and instruction (2009-2010):** Total instructional faculty: N/A. Classes of fewer than 20 students: 31%; of 20 to 49 students: 66%; of 50 or more students: 4%. **Advanced Placement and International Baccalaureate credit:** Scores accepted: 3, 4, 5. International Baccalaureate exams may be used for: Placement only. **Freshmen returning for sophomore year:** 61%. **Graduation rates:** Four-year: 12%; five-year: 29%; six-year: 36%.

COSTS AND FINANCIAL AID
Financial aid office: (405) 974-3334. **Expenses (2010-2011):** Tuition and fees 2010-2011: $4,223 in state, $10,652 out of state; room/board: $7,776. Estimated books and supplies: $1,000. **Financial aid:** Priority filing date for institution's financial aid form: May 31; deadline: May 31. In 2009-2010, 64% of undergraduates applied for financial aid. Of those, 53% were determined to have financial need; 9% had their need fully met. Average financial aid package (proportion receiving): $7,378 (49%). Average amount of gift aid, such as scholarships or grants (proportion receiving): $7,249 (48%). Average amount of self-help aid, such as work study or loans (proportion receiving): $4,413 (49%). Average need-based loan (excluding PLUS or other private loans): $4,339. Among students who received need-based aid, the average percentage of need met: 67%. Among students who received aid based on merit, the average award (and the proportion receiving): $5,549 (54%). The average athletic scholarship (and the proportion receiving): $4,331 (3%).

CAMPUS LIFE AND EXTRACURRICULAR ACTIVITIES
Campus housing available (% using): coed dorms (29%), women's dorms (17%), men's dorms (7%), sorority housing (15%), fraternity housing (12%), apartment for single students (20%). Students who live in college-owned, operated, or affiliated housing: 11%. **Student employment:** During the 2009-2010 academic year, 7% of undergraduates worked on campus. Average per-year earnings: $7,110. **Clubs and organizations:** Number of student organizations: 220. Activities include: choral groups, concert band, dance, drama/theater, international student organization, jazz band, marching band, music ensembles, musical theater, pep band, radio station, student government, student newspaper, symphony orchestra, television station, yearbook. Number of fraternities: 10; sororities: 9. Proportion of men in fraternities: 5%; of women in sororities: 3%. Average proportion of students who stay on campus on weekends: 9%. **Sports program (2009-2010):** Member of NCAA II.

SERVICES AND FACILITIES
Basic services: nonremedial tutoring, placement service, health service, health insurance. **Remedial assistance:** reading, math, writing, study skills. **Counseling services:** minority student, career, personal, academic, older student, psychological, birth control, other. **For learning-disabled students:** School does not offer a structured program with separate admission and additional fees. Services include: remedial math, remedial English, reading machines, remedial reading, tape recorders, note-taking services, special bookstore section, oral tests, readers, extended time for tests, tutors, priority registration, priority seating, texts on tape, other testing accommodations. **Library:** Number of titles: 470,409; number of current serial subscriptions: 3,130. **Information technology resources:** Students are not required to lease or own a computer. Number of campus computers available to all students: 500. School has a wireless network. Approximate number of users that can be accommodated: 350. Proportion of college-owned housing units wired for high-speed internet access: 100%. **Campus safety:** Security services offered: 24-hour foot-and-vehicle patrols, late-night transport/escort service,

24-hour emergency telephones, lighted pathways/sidewalks, controlled dormitory access (key, security card, etc.).

TRANSFER AND INTERNATIONAL STUDENTS

Transfer students: May apply for admission for the following academic terms: Fall, Spring, Summer. Applicants need a minimum number of credits to apply. For fall 2009: Transfer applications received: 2,593. Transfer applicants offered admission: 2,020. Transfer applicants enrolled: 1,643. **International students:** Number of foreign undergraduates: 740 (5% of student body). Number of countries represented: 75. Minimum TOEFL score required: 500 (paper); 173 (computer). Average TOEFL score: 520 (paper).

University of Oklahoma

- ■ **Address:** 660 Parrington Oval, Norman, OK 73019-0390
- ■ **Website:** http://www.ou.edu
- ■ **Public**
- ■ **Enrollment:** 18,167 full-time; 2,892 part-time

KEY STATS

✔ **U.S News College Ranking:** 111, National Universities
✔ **ACT Score (25th/75th percentile):** 23-29
✔ **Tuition:** 2009-2010: $5,245 in state, $13,229 out of state

Selectivity: More selective	**Room/board:** $7,598
Acceptance rate: 93%	**Average debt:** $16,723
Student/faculty ratio: 18/1	**Proportion who borrowed:** 48%

UNDERGRADUATE STUDENT BODY STATS

2009-2010 enrollment: 18,167 full-time; 2,892 part-time. Men: 47%; women: 53%. **Ethnic makeup:** African American: 6%; American-Indian: 7%; Asian American: 6%; Hispanic: 5%; White: 74%; International: 2%.

ADMISSIONS FACTS AND FIGURES

Phone: (405) 325-2252. **Email:** admrec@ou.edu. **Website:** http://www. ou.edu. **Application deadlines for fall 2011:** Regular decision: April 1. Early decision: Not offered. Early action: Not offered. Admission cannot be deferred. **Application fee:** $40. **To apply online, go to:** http://www.go2. ou.edu. **Admissions requirements/recommendations:** High school units required (recommended): English: 4; Mathematics: 3; Science: 3; Foreign language: (2); Social studies: 2; History: 1; Academic electives: 2; Total units: 15. Tests: The college uses SAT or ACT scores in admissions decisions. Either SAT or ACT required. For admission to the fall 2011 entering class, the school will accept: ACT with or without writing accepted. Campus visit: Neither required nor recommended. Admissions interview: Neither required nor recommended. Off-campus interview: Not available. **Factors that count in admissions decisions:** *Academic:* Secondary school record: Very Important. Class rank: Very Important. Letters of recommendation: Considered. Standardized test scores: Very Important. Essay: Considered. *Nonacademic:* Interview: Not Considered. Extracurricular activities: Not Considered. Talent/ability: Not Considered. Character/personal qualities: Not Considered. Alumni/ae relationship: Not Considered. Geographical residence: Not Considered. State residency: Considered. Religious affiliation/commitment: Not Considered. Minority status: Not Considered. Volunteer work: Not Considered. Work experience: Not Considered. **Other schools with the greatest overlap in applicants:** Baylor University; Oklahoma State University; Texas A&M University–College Station; Texas Tech University; University of Texas–Austin. **Admissions statistics for the fall 2009 entering class:** Total applicants: 8,960. Total accepted: 8,312. Freshmen enrolled: 3,760; Overall acceptance rate: 93%. **Size of waiting list:** 1707 applicants; enrolled from waiting list: 1297. **Credentials of fall 2009 freshmen:** 34% ranked in the top 10 percent of their high school class; 68% were in the top 25 percent; 93% were in the top half. (Proportion submitting class standing: 76%.) **Average high school grade point average:** 3.6. **First-year students who submitted SAT scores:** 41%. Scores (25/75 percentile): Critical Reading: 510-640, Math: 530-660, Combined: 1040-1300. **First-year students submitting ACT scores:** 86%. Scores (25/75 percentile): English: 22-29, Math: 22-28, Composite: 23-29.

ACADEMICS

Year founded: 1890. **Academic calendar:** Semester. **Degrees offered:** certificate, bachelor's, post-bachelor's certificate, master's, post-master's certificate, doctorate. **Most popular majors:** 16% business, management, marketing, and related support services, 13% health professions and related

clinical sciences, 10% communication, journalism, and related programs, 9% social sciences, 8% multi/interdisciplinary studies. **Major fields of study:** architecture and related services; area, ethnic, cultural, and gender studies; biological and biomedical sciences; business, management, marketing, and related support services; communication, journalism, and related programs; computer and information sciences and support services; education; engineering; English language and literature/letters; foreign languages, literatures, and linguistics; health professions and related clinical sciences; history; liberal arts and sciences studies, and humanities; mathematics and statistics; multi/interdisciplinary studies; natural resources and conservation; parks, recreation, leisure, and fitness studies; philosophy and religious studies; physical sciences; psychology; public administration and social service professions; social sciences; transportation and materials moving; visual and performing arts. **Areas of required coursework:** arts/fine arts, humanities, computer literacy, mathematics, English (including composition), philosophy, foreign languages, sciences (biological or physical), history, social science, other. **Pre-professional programs:** pre-dentistry, pre-medicine, pre-veterinary science, pre-optometry, pre-pharmacy, other. **Special academic programs:** accelerated program, cooperative (work-study plan) program, distance learning, double major, dual enrollment, English as a Second Language (ESL), external degree program, honors program, independent study, internships, liberal arts/career combination, student-designed major, study abroad, teacher certificate program, weekend college. **Teacher certification offered in:** early childhood, special education, elementary, secondary. **Cooperative education programs:** business, computer science, engineering, natural science, other. **Reserve Officers Training Corps (ROTC):** Army ROTC: Offered on campus; Navy ROTC: Offered on campus; Air Force ROTC: Offered on campus. **Faculty and instruction (2009-2010):** Total instructional faculty: 1,442 full-time, 380 part-time (58% men; 42% women; 17% minorities). Full-time faculty with Ph.D. or other terminal degree: 82%. Student/faculty ratio: 18/1. Classes of fewer than 20 students: 46%; of 20 to 49 students: 43%; of 50 or more students: 11%. **Advanced Placement and International Baccalaureate credit:** AP tests may be used for: Credit and/or placement. Scores accepted: 3, 4, 5. International Baccalaureate exams may be used for: Credit and/or placement. **Freshmen returning for sophomore year:** 84%. **Graduation rates:** Four-year: 29%; five-year: 58%; six-year: 64%.

COSTS AND FINANCIAL AID

Financial aid office: (405) 325-4521. **Expenses (2009-2010):** Tuition and fees 2009-2010: $5,245 in state, $13,229 out of state; room/board: $7,598. Estimated books and supplies: $1,016; transportation: $1,189; personal expenses: $2,504. **Financial aid:** Priority filing date for institution's financial aid form: March 1. In 2009-2010, 61% of undergraduates applied for financial aid. Of those, 57% were determined to have financial need; 78% had their need fully met. Average financial aid package (proportion receiving): $13,072 (57%). Average amount of gift aid, such as scholarships or grants (proportion receiving): $4,453 (23%). Average amount of self-help aid, such as work study or loans (proportion receiving): $5,210 (45%). Average need-based loan (excluding PLUS or other private loans): $4,470. Among students who received need-based aid, the average percentage of need met: 89%. Among students who received aid based on merit, the average award (and the proportion receiving): $4,268 (15%). The average athletic scholarship (and the proportion receiving): $17,635 (1%). Average amount of debt of borrowers graduating in 2009: $16,723. Proportion who borrowed: 48%.

CAMPUS LIFE AND EXTRACURRICULAR ACTIVITIES

Campus housing available (% using): coed dorms (65%), women's dorms, men's dorms, sorority housing, fraternity housing, apartments for married students (2%), apartment for single students (26%), special housing for disabled students (1%), special housing for international students (3%), other housing options (3%). Students who live in college-owned, operated, or affiliated housing: 32%. **Clubs and organizations:** Number of student organizations: 417. Activities include: campus ministries, choral groups, concert band, dance, drama/theater, international student organization, jazz band, literary magazine, marching band, model UN, music ensembles, musical theater, opera, pep band, radio station, student government, student newspaper, student film society, symphony orchestra, television station, yearbook. Number of fraternities: 30; sororities: 20. Proportion of men in fraternities: 20%; of women in sororities: 23%. Average proportion of students who stay on campus on weekends: 80%. **Sports program (2009-2010):** Member of NCAA I. *Men's intercollegiate varsity sports:* baseball, basketball, cross country, football, golf, gymnastics, tennis, track and field (indoor), track and field (outdoor), wrestling. *Women's intercollegiate varsity sports:* basketball, crew (heavyweight), cross country, golf, gymnastics, soccer, softball, tennis, track and field (indoor), track and field (outdoor), volleyball.

SERVICES AND FACILITIES

Basic services: nonremedial tutoring, women's center, placement service, day care, health service, health insurance, other. **Remedial assistance:** reading, math, writing, study skills. **Counseling services:** minority student, career, military, personal, veteran student, academic, older student, psychological, birth control, religious. **For learning-disabled students:** School does not offer a structured program with separate admission and additional fees. Total undergraduates in learning-disabled program or receiving services: 182. Services include: reading machines, note-taking services, readers, extended time for tests, priority registration, typist/scribe, exams on tape or computer. **Library:** Number of titles: 5,433,036; number of current serial subscriptions: 69,621. **Information technology resources:** Students are not required to lease or own a computer. Number of campus computers available to all students: 3,600. School has a wireless network. Approximate number of users that can be accommodated: 40,000. Proportion of college-owned housing units wired for high-speed internet access: 100%. **Campus safety:** Security services offered: 24-hour foot-and-vehicle patrols, late-night transport/escort service, 24-hour emergency telephones, lighted pathways/sidewalks, controlled dormitory access (key, security card, etc).

TRANSFER AND INTERNATIONAL STUDENTS

Transfer students: May apply for admission for the following academic terms: Fall, Spring, Summer. Applicants need a minimum number of credits to apply. For fall 2009: Transfer applications received: 3,684. Transfer applicants offered admission: 2,886. Transfer applicants enrolled: 2,018. **International students:** Number of foreign undergraduates: 438 (2% of student body). Number of countries represented: 75. Minimum TOEFL score required: 550 (paper); 79 (computer). Average TOEFL score: 573 (paper).

Univ. of Science and Arts of Oklahoma

- **Address:** 1727 W. Alabama, Chickasha, OK 73018-5322
- **Website:** http://www.usao.edu
- **Public**
- **Enrollment:** 927 full-time; 160 part-time

KEY STATS
- ✔ **U.S News College Ranking:** 14, Regional Colleges (West)
- ✔ **ACT Score (25th/75th percentile):** 19-26
- ✔ **Tuition:** 2009-2010: $3,552 in state, $8,448 out of state
- **Selectivity:** Selective   **Room/board:** $5,000
- **Acceptance rate:** 74%   **Average debt:** $15,598
- **Student/faculty ratio:** 15/1   **Proportion who borrowed:** 58%

UNDERGRADUATE STUDENT BODY STATS

2009-2010 enrollment: 927 full-time; 160 part-time. Men: 35%; women: 65%. **Ethnic makeup:** African American: 5%; American-Indian: 11%; Asian American: 1%; Hispanic: 5%; White: 73%; International: 6%.

ADMISSIONS FACTS AND FIGURES

Phone: (405) 574-1357. **Email:** usao-admissions@usao.edu. **Website:** http://www.usao.edu. **Application deadlines for fall 2011:** Regular decision: August 31. Early decision: Not offered. Early action: Not offered. Admission can be deferred. **Application fee:** $25. **To apply online, go to:** http://www.usao.edu/apply. **Admissions requirements/recommendations:** High school units required (recommended): English: 4; Mathematics: 3 (4); Science: 3; Foreign language: (2); Social studies: 2; History: 1; Academic electives: 2; Total units: 15 (20). Tests: The college uses SAT or ACT scores in admissions decisions. Either SAT or ACT required. For admission to the fall 2011 entering class, the school will accept: ACT with or without writing accepted. Campus visit: Recommended. Admissions interview: Neither required nor recommended. Off-campus interview: Not available. **Factors that count in admissions decisions:** *Academic:* Secondary school record: Very Important. Class rank: Very Important. Letters of recommendation: Considered. Standardized test scores: Very Important. Essay: Not Considered. *Nonacademic:* Interview: Not Considered. Extracurricular activities: Not Considered. Talent/ability: Important. Character/personal qualities: Considered. Alumni/ae relationship: Not Considered. Geographical residence: Not Considered. State residency: Not Considered. Religious affiliation/commitment: Not Considered. Minority status: Not Considered. Volunteer work: Not Considered. Work experience: Not Considered. **Other schools with the greatest overlap in applicants:** Cameron University; Southwestern Oklahoma State University; University of Central Oklahoma; University of Oklahoma. **Admissions sta-**

tistics for the fall 2009 entering class: Total applicants: 395. Total accepted: 292. Freshmen enrolled: 187; 7% were from out of state. Overall acceptance rate: 74%. **Credentials of fall 2009 freshmen:** 21% ranked in the top 10 percent of their high school class; 52% were in the top 25 percent; 81% were in the top half. (Proportion submitting class standing: 83%.) **Average high school grade point average:** 3.4. **First-year students who submitted SAT scores:** 3%. Scores (25/75 percentile): Critical Reading: 380-480, Math: 480-570, Combined: 860-1050. **First-year students submitting ACT scores:** 87%. Scores (25/75 percentile): English: 19-26, Math: 17-24, Composite: 19-26.

ACADEMICS

Year founded: 1908. **Academic calendar:** Trimester. **Degrees offered:** bachelor's. **Most popular majors:** 22% business, management, marketing, and related support services, 19% education, 9% psychology, 9% visual and performing arts, 7% history. **Major fields of study:** area, ethnic, cultural, and gender studies; biological and biomedical sciences; business, management, marketing, and related support services; communication, journalism, and related programs; computer and information sciences and support services; education; English language and literature/letters; health professions and related clinical sciences; history; mathematics and statistics; multi/interdisciplinary studies; parks, recreation, leisure, and fitness studies; physical sciences; psychology; social sciences; visual and performing arts. **Areas of required coursework:** arts/fine arts, humanities, computer literacy, mathematics, English (including composition), philosophy, sciences (biological or physical), history, social science, other. **Pre-professional programs:** pre-law, pre-dentistry, pre-medicine, pre-veterinary science, pre-optometry, pre-pharmacy, other. **Special academic programs (% participation):** accelerated program (60%), double major (25%), dual enrollment (5%), honors program, independent study (60%), internships (5%), liberal arts/career combination, student-designed major (10%), study abroad, teacher certificate program (25%). **Teacher certification offered in:** early childhood, special education, elementary, middle/junior high, secondary. **Faculty and instruction (2009-2010):** Total instructional faculty: 55 full-time, 33 part-time (50% men; 50% women; 9% minorities). Full-time faculty with Ph.D. or other terminal degree: 89%. Student/faculty ratio: 15/1. Classes of fewer than 20 students: 62%; of 20 to 49 students: 33%; of 50 or more students: 5%. **Advanced Placement and International Baccalaureate credit:** AP tests may be used for: Placement only. Scores accepted: 3, 4, 5. International Baccalaureate exams may be used for: Placement only. **Freshmen returning for sophomore year:** 67%. **Graduation rates:** Four-year: 20%; five-year: 29%; six-year: 28%. **Graduate study:** 20% of students pursue further study immediately upon graduation; 25% within one year; 35% within five years. Fields in which graduates pursue further study: Master of Business Administration (MBA), 20%; law, 15%; medicine, 20%; dentistry, 5%; education, 10%; arts and sciences, 25%; veterinary medicine, 5%.

COSTS AND FINANCIAL AID

Financial aid office: (405) 574-1240. **Expenses (2009-2010):** Tuition and fees 2009-2010: $3,552 in state, $8,448 out of state; room/board: $5,000. Estimated books and supplies: $1,100; transportation: $2,608; personal expenses: $1,506. **Financial aid:** Priority filing date for institution's financial aid form: March 15. In 2009-2010, 74% of undergraduates applied for financial aid. Of those, 62% were determined to have financial need; 20% had their need fully met. Average financial aid package (proportion receiving): $9,044 (61%). Average amount of gift aid, such as scholarships or grants (proportion receiving): $6,991 (58%). Average amount of self-help aid, such as work study or loans (proportion receiving): $3,767 (39%). Average need-based loan (excluding PLUS or other private loans): $3,085. Among students who received need-based aid, the average percentage of need met: 72%. Among students who received aid based on merit, the average award (and the proportion receiving): $1,872 (13%). The average athletic scholarship (and the proportion receiving): $7,869 (9%). Average amount of debt of borrowers graduating in 2009: $15,598. Proportion who borrowed: 58%.

CAMPUS LIFE AND EXTRACURRICULAR ACTIVITIES

Campus housing available (% using): coed dorms (40%), apartment for single students (60%). Students who live in college-owned, operated, or affiliated housing: 47%. **Student employment:** During the 2009-2010 academic year, 4% of undergraduates worked on campus. Average per-year earnings: $5,000. **Clubs and organizations:** Number of student organizations: 45. Activities include: campus ministries, choral groups, concert band, dance, drama/theater, jazz band, literary magazine, music ensembles, musical theater, pep band, student government, student newspaper, television station. Number of fraternities: 1; sororities: 1. Proportion of men in fraternities: 1%; of women in sororities: 2%. Average proportion of students who stay on campus on weekends: 45%. **Sports program (2009-2010):** Member of NAIA. *Men's intercollegiate varsity sports:* baseball, basketball, soccer. *Women's intercollegiate varsity sports:* basketball, soccer, softball.

SERVICES AND FACILITIES

Basic services: nonremedial tutoring, placement service, health service. **Remedial assistance:** reading, math, writing, study skills, other. **Counseling services:** minority student, career, military, personal, veteran student, academic, older student, birth control. **For learning-disabled students:** School does not offer a structured program with separate admission and additional fees. Total undergraduates in learning-disabled program or receiving services: 18. Services include: remedial math, remedial English, reading machines, tape recorders, note-taking services, oral tests, learning center, readers, extended time for tests, tutors, priority seating, texts on tape, typist/scribe, exams on tape or computer, other testing accommodations. **Library:** Number of titles: 74,319; number of current serial subscriptions: 50,000. **Information technology resources:** Students are not required to lease or own a computer. Number of campus computers available to all students: 150. School has a wireless network. Approximate number of users that can be accommodated: 1,500. Proportion of college-owned housing units wired for high-speed internet access: 100%. **Campus safety:** Security services offered: 24-hour foot-and-vehicle patrols, lighted pathways/sidewalks, controlled dormitory access (key, security card, etc).

TRANSFER AND INTERNATIONAL STUDENTS

Transfer students: May apply for admission for the following academic terms: Fall, Spring, Summer. Applicants need a minimum number of credits to apply. For fall 2009: Transfer applications received: 157. Transfer applicants offered admission: 143. Transfer applicants enrolled: 110. **International students:** Number of foreign undergraduates: 56 (6% of student body). Number of countries represented: 16. Minimum TOEFL score required: 500 (paper); 173 (computer). Average TOEFL score: 500 (paper).

University of Tulsa

- ■ **Address:** 800 S. Tucker Drive, Tulsa, OK 74104
- ■ **Website:** http://www.utulsa.edu
- ■ **Private; Religious affiliation:** Presbyterian
- ■ **Enrollment:** 2,929 full-time; 155 part-time

KEY STATS

- ✔ **U.S News College Ranking:** 93, National Universities
- ✔ **ACT Score (25th/75th percentile):** 25-32
- ✔ **Tuition:** 2010-2011: $28,310

Selectivity: Most selective	**Room/board:** $9,018
Acceptance rate: 50%	**Average debt:** $30,086
Student/faculty ratio: 11/1	**Proportion who borrowed:** 48%

UNDERGRADUATE STUDENT BODY STATS

2009-2010 enrollment: 2,929 full-time; 155 part-time. Men: 54%; women: 46%. **Ethnic makeup:** African American: 6%; American-Indian: 4%; Asian American: 3%; Hispanic: 4%; White: 69%; International: 14%. **Religious preference:** Roman Catholic: 13%; Protestant: 31%; Jewish: 1%; Muslim: 3%; No preference: 45%; Presbyterian: 4%; Other: 3%.

ADMISSIONS FACTS AND FIGURES

Phone: (918) 631-2307. **Email:** admission@utulsa.edu. **Website:** http://www.utulsa.edu. **Application deadlines for fall 2011:** Regular decision: Rolling. Early decision: Not offered. Early action: Send application by: November 1; Decision sent by: November 22. Admission can be deferred. **Application fee:** $35. **To apply online, go to:** http://www.utulsa.edu/admission/applying/. **Admissions requirements/recommendations:** High school units required (recommended): English: (4); Mathematics: (3); Science: (3); Foreign language: (2); Social studies: (2); History: (2); Academic electives: (1); Total units: (17). Tests: The college uses SAT or ACT scores in admissions decisions. Either SAT or ACT required. For admission to the fall 2011 entering class, the school will accept: ACT with or without writing accepted. Campus visit: Recommended. Admissions interview: Recommended. Off-campus interview: May be arranged. **Factors that count in admissions decisions:** *Academic:* Secondary school record: Very Important. Class rank: Very Important. Letters of recommendation: Important. Standardized test scores: Very Important. Essay: Important. *Nonacademic:* Interview: Very Important. Extracurricular activities: Important. Talent/ability: Important. Character/

personal qualities: Important. Alumni/ae relationship: Considered. Geographical residence: Not Considered. State residency: Not Considered. Religious affiliation/commitment: Not Considered. Minority status: Considered. Volunteer work: Considered. Work experience: Considered. **Other schools with the greatest overlap in applicants:** Rice University; Southern Methodist University; Texas Christian University; University of Oklahoma; Washington University in St. Louis. **Admissions statistics for the fall 2009 entering class:** Total applicants: 4,698. Total accepted: 2,333. Freshmen enrolled: 690; 48% were from out of state. Overall acceptance rate: 50%. Non-early acceptance rate: 50%. **Size of waiting list:** 317 applicants; enrolled from waiting list: 191. **Credentials of fall 2009 freshmen:** 71% ranked in the top 10 percent of their high school class; 85% were in the top 25 percent; 97% were in the top half. (Proportion submitting class standing: 86%.) **Average high school grade point average:** 3.8. **First-year students who submitted SAT scores:** 40%. Scores (25/75 percentile): Critical Reading: 570-700, Math: 560-690, Combined: 1130-1390. **First-year students submitting ACT scores:** 63%. Scores (25/75 percentile): English: 25-33, Math: 24-32, Composite: 25-32.

ACADEMICS

Year founded: 1894. **Academic calendar:** Semester. **Degrees offered:** bachelor's, post-bachelor's certificate, master's, doctorate. **Most popular majors:** 19% business, management, marketing, and related support services, 14% engineering, 8% visual and performing arts, 6% education, 6% social sciences. **Major fields of study:** biological and biomedical sciences; business, management, marketing, and related support services; communication, journalism, and related programs; computer and information sciences and support services; education; engineering; English language and literature/letters; foreign languages, literatures, and linguistics; health professions and related clinical sciences; history; legal professions and studies; liberal arts and sciences studies, and humanities; mathematics and statistics; natural resources and conservation; parks, recreation, leisure, and fitness studies; philosophy and religious studies; physical sciences; psychology; social sciences; visual and performing arts. **Areas of required coursework:** arts/fine arts, humanities, computer literacy, mathematics, English (including composition), philosophy, foreign languages, sciences (biological or physical), history, social science. **Pre-professional programs:** pre-law, pre-medicine, other. **Special academic programs (% participation):** accelerated program (2%), double major (16%), English as a Second Language (ESL) (7%), honors program (7%), independent study (41%), internships (12%), liberal arts/career combination (5%), student-designed major (0%), study abroad (17%), teacher certificate program (8%). **Teacher certification offered in:** special education, elementary, middle/junior high, secondary. **Reserve Officers Training Corps (ROTC):** Air Force ROTC: Offered at cooperating institution (Oklahoma State University). **Faculty and instruction (2009-2010):** Total instructional faculty: 311 full-time, 78 part-time (65% men; 35% women; 16% minorities). Full-time faculty with Ph.D. or other terminal degree: 96%. Student/faculty ratio: 11/1. Classes of fewer than 20 students: 70%; of 20 to 49 students: 29%; of 50 or more students: 1%. **Advanced Placement and International Baccalaureate credit:** AP tests may be used for: Credit and/or placement. Scores accepted: 3, 4, 5. International Baccalaureate exams may be used for: Credit and/or placement. **Freshmen returning for sophomore year:** 87%. **Graduation rates:** Four-year: 44%; five-year: 60%; six-year: 62%. **Graduate study:** 41% of students pursue further study immediately upon graduation. Fields in which graduates pursue further study: Master of Business Administration (MBA), 17%; law, 4%; medicine, 12%; engineering, 23%; education, 2%; arts and sciences, 42%.

COSTS AND FINANCIAL AID

Financial aid office: (918) 631-2526. **Expenses (2010-2011):** Tuition and fees 2010-2011: $28,310; room/board: $9,018. Estimated books and supplies: $1,200; transportation: $1,508; personal expenses: $3,016. **Financial aid:** Priority filing date for institution's financial aid form: April 1. In 2009-2010, 88% of undergraduates applied for financial aid. Of those, 42% were determined to have financial need; 48% had their need fully met. Average financial aid package (proportion receiving): $26,961 (42%). Average amount of gift aid, such as scholarships or grants (proportion receiving): $5,996 (19%). Average amount of self-help aid, such as work study or loans (proportion receiving): $5,824 (34%). Average need-based loan (excluding PLUS or other private loans): $4,211. Among students who received need-based aid, the average percentage of need met: 85%. Among students who received aid based on merit, the average award (and the proportion receiving): $13,567 (37%). The average athletic scholarship (and the proportion receiving): $24,167 (12%). Average amount of debt of borrowers graduating in 2009: $30,086. Proportion who borrowed: 48%.

CAMPUS LIFE AND EXTRACURRICULAR ACTIVITIES

Campus housing available (% using): coed dorms (13%), women's dorms (11%), men's dorms (12%), sorority housing (7%), fraternity housing (5%), apartments for married students (7%), apartment for single students (43%), other housing options (2%). Students who live in college-owned, operated, or affiliated housing: 80%. **Student employment:** During the 2009-2010 academic year, 22% of undergraduates worked on campus. Average per-year earnings: $4,500. **Clubs and organizations:** Number of student organizations: 160. Activities include: campus ministries, choral groups, concert band, drama/theater, international student organization, jazz band, literary magazine, marching band, model UN, music ensembles, musical theater, opera, pep band, radio station, student government, student newspaper, symphony orchestra, television station, yearbook. Number of fraternities: 9; sororities: 11. Proportion of men in fraternities: 21%; of women in sororities: 23%. Average proportion of students who stay on campus on weekends: 95%. **Sports program (2009-2010):** Member of NCAA I. *Men's intercollegiate varsity sports:* basketball, cross country, football, golf, soccer, tennis, track and field (indoor), track and field (outdoor). *Women's intercollegiate varsity sports:* basketball, crew (heavyweight), cross country, golf, crew (lightweight), soccer, softball, tennis, track and field (indoor), track and field (outdoor), volleyball.

SERVICES AND FACILITIES

Basic services: nonremedial tutoring, women's center, placement service, day care, health service, health insurance. **Counseling services:** minority student, career, personal, veteran student, academic, older student, psychological, birth control, religious. **For learning-disabled students:** School does not offer a structured program with separate admission and additional fees. Services include: reading machines, tape recorders, untimed tests, note-taking services, learning center, readers, extended time for tests, tutors, priority registration, priority seating. **Library:** Number of titles: 1,278,114; number of current serial subscriptions: 36,064. **Information technology resources:** Students are not required to lease or own a computer. Number of campus computers available to all students: 792. School has a wireless network. Approximate number of users that can be accommodated: 1,300. Proportion of college-owned housing units wired for high-speed internet access: 100%. **Campus safety:** Security services offered: 24-hour foot-and-vehicle patrols, late-night transport/escort service, 24-hour emergency telephones, lighted pathways/sidewalks, controlled dormitory access (key, security card, etc).

TRANSFER AND INTERNATIONAL STUDENTS

Transfer students: May apply for admission for the following academic terms: Fall, Spring, Summer. Applicants do not need a minimum number of credits to apply. For fall 2009: Transfer applications received: 519. Transfer applicants offered admission: 301. Transfer applicants enrolled: 161. **International students:** Number of foreign undergraduates: 412 (14% of student body). Number of countries represented: 50. Minimum TOEFL score required: 500 (paper); 173 (computer). Average TOEFL score: 566 (paper).

Oregon

Concordia University

- **Address:** 2811 N.E. Holman Street, Portland, OR 97211
- **Website:** http://www.cu-portland.edu
- **Private; Religious affiliation:** Lutheran Church-Missouri Synod
- **Enrollment:** N/A

KEY STATS

✔ **U.S News College Ranking:** second tier, Regional Universities (West)
✔ **SAT or ACT Score (25th/75th percentile):** N/A
✔ **Tuition:** 2009-2010: $23,110

Selectivity: Less selective	**Room/board:** $6,800
Acceptance rate: N/A	**Average debt:** N/A
Student/faculty ratio: N/A	**Proportion who borrowed:** N/A

Corban University

- **Address:** 5000 Deer Park Drive SE, Salem, OR 97301
- **Website:** http://www.corban.edu
- **Private; Religious affiliation:** Baptist
- **Enrollment:** 758 full-time; 130 part-time

KEY STATS

✔ **U.S News College Ranking:** 5, Regional Colleges (West)
✔ **SAT Score (25th/75th percentile):** 990-1240
✔ **Tuition:** 2010-2011: $24,380

Selectivity: Selective	**Room/board:** $7,720
Acceptance rate: 57%	**Average debt:** $28,537
Student/faculty ratio: 14/1	**Proportion who borrowed:** 91%

UNDERGRADUATE STUDENT BODY STATS

2009-2010 enrollment: 758 full-time; 130 part-time. Men: 40%; women: 60%. **Ethnic makeup:** African American: 1%; American-Indian: 1%; Asian American: 4%; Hispanic: 4%; White: 91%. **Religious preference:** Protestant: 99%; not reported: 1%.

ADMISSIONS FACTS AND FIGURES

Phone: (800) 845-3005. **Email:** admissions@corban.edu. **Website:** http://www.corban.edu. **Application deadlines for fall 2011:** Regular decision: August 1; decision sent by August 1. Early decision: Not offered. Early action: Not offered. Admission cannot be deferred. **Application fee:** $40. **To apply online, go to:** http://www.corban.edu/undergraduate/applyonline.html. **Admissions requirements/recommendations:** High school units required (recommended): English: 4 (4); Mathematics: 3 (3); Science: 2 (2); Foreign language: 2 (2); Social studies: 3 (3); Total units: 14 (14). Tests: The college uses SAT or ACT scores in admissions decisions. Either SAT or ACT required. For admission to the fall 2011 entering class, the school will accept: ACT with writing recommended. Campus visit: Recommended. Admissions interview: Recommended. Off-campus interview: May be arranged. **Factors that count in admissions decisions:** *Academic:* Secondary school record: Important. Class rank: Considered. Letters of recommendation: Very Important. Standardized test scores: Very Important. Essay: Very Important. *Nonacademic:* Interview: Considered. Extracurricular activities: Considered. Talent/ability: Not Considered. Character/personal qualities: Important. Alumni/ae relationship: Considered. Geographical residence: Not Considered. State residency: Not Considered. Religious affiliation/commitment: Very Important. Minority status: Not Considered. Volunteer work: Not Considered. Work experience: Not Considered. **Other schools with the greatest overlap in applicants:** George Fox University; Master's College and Seminary; Northwest Christian University; Northwest University; Seattle Pacific University. **Admissions statistics for the fall 2009 entering class:** Total applicants: 907. Total accepted: 518. Freshmen enrolled: 215; Overall acceptance rate: 57%. **Credentials of fall 2009 freshmen:** 31% ranked in the top 10 percent of their high school class; 61% were in the top 25 percent; 87% were in the top half. (Proportion submitting class standing: 58%.) **Average high school grade point average:** 3.6. **First-year students who submitted SAT scores:** 78%. Scores (25/75 percentile): Critical Reading: 500-630, Math: 490-610, Combined: 990-1240. **First-year students submitting ACT scores:** 30%. Scores (25/75 percentile): English: 19-26, Math: 20-28, Composite: 20-26.

ACADEMICS

Year founded: 1935. **Academic calendar:** Semester. **Degrees offered:** associate, bachelor's, master's. **Most popular majors:** 27% business, management, marketing, and related support services, 26% psychology, 17% education, 9% theology and religious vocations, 7% liberal arts and sciences studies, and humanities. **Major fields of study:** business, management, marketing, and related support services; communication, journalism, and related programs; computer and information sciences and support services; education; English language and literature/letters; health professions and related clinical sciences; legal professions and studies; liberal arts and sciences studies, and humanities; mathematics and statistics; parks, recreation, leisure, and fitness studies; psychology; social sciences; theology and religious vocations; visual and performing arts. **Areas of required coursework:** arts/fine arts, humanities, mathematics, English (including composition), philosophy, sciences (biological or physical), history, social science, other. **Pre-professional programs:** pre-law, pre-dentistry, pre-medicine, pre-theology, pre-veterinary science, pre-optometry, pre-pharmacy. **Special academic programs (% participation):** accelerated program (30%), cross-registration (4%), distance learning (9%), double major (5%), honors program (5%), independent study (10%), internships (66%), student-designed major, study abroad (5%), teacher certificate program (18%), weekend college (70%). **Teacher certification offered in:** elementary, middle/junior high, secondary. **Cooperative education programs:** other. **Reserve Officers Training Corps (ROTC):** Army ROTC: Offered at cooperating institution (Oregon State University); Air Force ROTC: Offered at cooperating institution (Oregon State University). **Faculty and instruction (2009-2010):** Total instructional faculty: 45 full-time, 62 part-time (66% men; 34% women; 2% minorities). Full-time faculty with Ph.D. or other terminal degree: 56%. Student/faculty ratio: 14/1. Classes of fewer than 20 students: 61%; of 20 to 49 students: 37%; of 50 or more students: 2%. **Advanced Placement and International Baccalaureate credit:** AP tests may be used for: Credit only. Scores accepted: 3. International Baccalaureate exams may be used for: Credit only. **Freshmen returning for sophomore year:** 72%. **Graduation rates:** Four-year: 46%; five-year: 56%; six-year: 51%. **Graduate study:** 21% of students pursue further study immediately upon graduation; 32% within one year; 50% within five years. Fields in which graduates pursue further study: Master of Business Administration (MBA), 15%; theology (or the seminary), 13%; education, 48%; arts and sciences, 19%.

COSTS AND FINANCIAL AID

Financial aid office: (503) 375-7006. **Expenses (2010-2011):** Tuition and fees 2010-2011: $24,380; room/board: $7,720. Estimated books and supplies: $900; transportation: $1,600; personal expenses: $1,602. **Financial aid:** Priority filing date for institution's financial aid form: February 15. In 2009-2010, 91% of undergraduates applied for financial aid. Of those, 83% were determined to have financial need; 13% had their need fully met. Average financial aid package (proportion receiving): $17,364 (83%). Average amount of gift aid, such as scholarships or grants (proportion receiving): $13,897 (83%). Average amount of self-help aid, such as work study or loans (proportion receiving): $4,505 (64%). Average need-based loan (excluding PLUS or other private loans): $4,505. Among students who received need-based aid, the average percentage of need met: 65%. Among students who received aid based on merit, the average award (and the proportion receiving): $5,336 (14%). The average athletic scholarship (and the proportion receiving): $7,070 (6%). Average amount of debt of borrowers graduating in 2009: $28,537. Proportion who borrowed: 91%.

CAMPUS LIFE AND EXTRACURRICULAR ACTIVITIES

Campus housing available (% using): women's dorms (60%), men's dorms (32%), apartment for single students (8%). **Student employment:** During the 2009-2010 academic year, 15% of undergraduates worked on campus. Average per-year earnings: $1,500. **Clubs and organizations:** Number of student organizations: 14. Activities include: campus ministries, choral groups, concert band, drama/theater, jazz band, literary magazine, music ensembles, musical theater, pep band, radio station, student government, student newspaper, symphony orchestra, yearbook. Number of fraternities: 0; sororities: 0. Average proportion of students who stay on campus on weekends: 50%. **Sports program (2009-2010):** Member of NAIA. *Men's intercollegiate varsity sports:* baseball, basketball, cross country, golf, soccer, track and field (outdoor). *Women's intercollegiate varsity sports:* basketball, cross country, golf, soccer, softball, track and field (outdoor), volleyball.

SERVICES AND FACILITIES
Basic services: nonremedial tutoring, placement service, health service, health insurance. **Remedial assistance:** study skills. **Counseling services:** career, military, personal, veteran student, academic, older student, psychological, religious. **For learning-disabled students:** School does not offer a structured program with separate admission and additional fees. Services include: tape recorders, note-taking services, oral tests, learning center, readers, extended time for tests, tutors, priority seating, texts on tape. **Library:** Number of titles: 105,769; number of current serial subscriptions: 528. **Information technology resources:** Students are not required to lease or own a computer. Number of campus computers available to all students: 50. School has a wireless network. Approximate number of users that can be accommodated: 400. Proportion of college-owned housing units wired for high-speed internet access: 100%. **Campus safety:** Security services offered: 24-hour foot-and-vehicle patrols, late-night transport/escort service, 24-hour emergency telephones, lighted pathways/sidewalks, student patrols, controlled dormitory access (key, security card, etc.).

TRANSFER AND INTERNATIONAL STUDENTS
Transfer students: May apply for admission for the following academic terms: Fall, Spring, Summer. Applicants need a minimum number of credits to apply. For fall 2009: Transfer applications received: 129. Transfer applicants offered admission: 88. Transfer applicants enrolled: 45. **International students:** Number of foreign undergraduates: 0. Number of countries represented: 2. Minimum TOEFL score required: 500 (paper).

Eastern Oregon University

- **Address:** 1 University Boulevard, La Grande, OR 97850
- **Website:** http://www.eou.edu
- **Public**
- **Enrollment:** 2,098 full-time; 1,391 part-time

KEY STATS
- ✔ **U.S News College Ranking:** second tier, Regional Universities (West)
- ✔ **SAT Score (25th/75th percentile):** 830-1050
- ✔ **Tuition:** 2009-2010: $6,456 in state, $6,456 out of state

Selectivity: Less selective	**Room/board:** $7,435
Acceptance rate: 78%	**Average debt:** $19,881
Student/faculty ratio: 24/1	**Proportion who borrowed:** N/A

UNDERGRADUATE STUDENT BODY STATS
2009-2010 enrollment: 2,098 full-time; 1,391 part-time. Men: 39%; women: 61%. **Ethnic makeup:** African American: 2%; American-Indian: 3%; Asian American: 2%; Hispanic: 4%; White: 87%; International: 1%.

ADMISSIONS FACTS AND FIGURES
Phone: (541) 962-3393. **Email:** admissions@eou.edu. **Website:** http://www.eou.edu. **Application deadlines for fall 2011:** Regular decision: September 15. Early decision: Not offered. Early action: Send application by: December 1; Decision sent by: January 15. Admission can be deferred. **Application fee:** $50. **To apply online, go to:** http://www.eou.edu/admissions/application.htm. **Admissions requirements/recommendations:** High school units required (recommended): English: 4; Mathematics: 3; Science: 2; Foreign language: 2. Tests: The college uses SAT or ACT scores in admissions decisions. Either SAT or ACT required. For admission to the fall 2011 entering class, the school will accept: ACT with or without writing accepted. Campus visit: Recommended. Admissions interview: Neither required nor recommended. Off-campus interview: Not available. **Factors that count in admissions decisions:** *Academic:* Secondary school record: Very Important. Class rank: Considered. Letters of recommendation: Important. Standardized

test scores: Considered. Essay: Considered. *Nonacademic:* Interview: Not Considered. Extracurricular activities: Considered. Talent/ability: Important. Character/personal qualities: Not Considered. Alumni/ae relationship: Not Considered. Geographical residence: Considered. State residency: Not Considered. Religious affiliation/commitment: Not Considered. Minority status: Not Considered. Volunteer work: Considered. Work experience: Considered. **Admissions statistics for the fall 2009 entering class:** Total applicants: 977. Total accepted: 765. Freshmen enrolled: 473; Overall acceptance rate: 78%. Non-early acceptance rate: 78%. **Credentials of fall 2009 freshmen:** 14% ranked in the top 10 percent of their high school class; 31% were in the top 25 percent; 69% were in the top half. (Proportion submitting class standing: 64%.) **Average high school grade point average:** 3.1. **First-year students who submitted SAT scores:** 61%. Scores (25/75 percentile): Critical Reading: 420-530, Math: 410-520, Combined: 830-1050. **First-year students submitting ACT scores:** 23%. Scores (25/75 percentile): English: 16-22, Math: 15-20, Composite: 17-22.

ACADEMICS
Year founded: 1929. **Academic calendar:** Quarter. **Degrees offered:** certificate, associate, bachelor's, master's. **Major fields of study:** agriculture, agriculture operations, and related sciences; biological and biomedical sciences; business, management, marketing, and related support services; computer and information sciences and support services; education; English language and literature/letters; health professions and related clinical sciences; history; liberal arts and sciences studies, and humanities; mathematics and statistics; multi/interdisciplinary studies; physical sciences; psychology; public administration and social service professions; security and protective services; social sciences; visual and performing arts. **Areas of required coursework:** arts/fine arts, humanities, computer literacy, mathematics, English (including composition), foreign languages, sciences (biological or physical), social science, other. **Pre-professional programs:** pre-law, pre-dentistry, pre-medicine, pre-veterinary science, pre-pharmacy. **Special academic programs:** cooperative (work-study plan) program, cross-registration, distance learning, double major, dual enrollment, exchange student program (domestic), external degree program, honors program, independent study, internships, liberal arts/career combination, student-designed major, study abroad, teacher certificate program, weekend college. **Teacher certification offered in:** early childhood, elementary, middle/junior high, secondary. **Cooperative education programs:** agriculture, health professions. **Reserve Officers Training Corps (ROTC):** Army ROTC: Offered on campus. **Faculty and instruction (2009-2010):** Total instructional faculty: 115 full-time, 12 part-time (53% men; 47% women). Full-time faculty with Ph.D. or other terminal degree: 48%. Student/faculty ratio: 24/1. Classes of fewer than 20 students: 66%; of 20 to 49 students: 31%; of 50 or more students: 3%. **Advanced Placement and International Baccalaureate credit:** AP tests may be used for: Placement only. Scores accepted: 3, 4, 5. International Baccalaureate exams may be used for: Placement only. **Freshmen returning for sophomore year:** 65%. **Graduation rates:** Six-year: 30%. **Graduate study:** 23% of students pursue further study immediately upon graduation. Fields in which graduates pursue further study: Master of Business Administration (MBA), 25%; law, 3%; medicine, 7%; education, 47%; arts and sciences, 18%.

COSTS AND FINANCIAL AID
Financial aid office: (541) 962-3551. **Expenses (2009-2010):** Tuition and fees 2009-2010: $6,456 in state, $6,456 out of state; room/board: $7,435. Estimated books and supplies: $1,350; transportation: $900; personal expenses: $1,227. **Financial aid:** Priority filing date for institution's financial aid form: March 1. In 2009-2010, 85% of undergraduates applied for financial aid. Of those, 75% were determined to have financial need; 26% had their need fully met. Average financial aid package (proportion receiving): $9,776 (74%). Average amount of gift aid, such as scholarships or grants (proportion receiving): $6,065 (54%). Average amount of self-help aid, such as work study or loans (proportion receiving): $1,272 (73%). Average need-based loan (excluding PLUS or other private loans): $3,443. Among students who received need-based aid, the average percentage of need met: 57%. Among students who received aid based on merit, the average award (and the proportion receiving): $852 (1%). The average athletic scholarship (and the proportion receiving): $1,963 (9%). Average amount of debt of borrowers graduating in 2009: $19,881.

CAMPUS LIFE AND EXTRACURRICULAR ACTIVITIES
Campus housing available (% using): coed dorms (96%), women's dorms (0%), men's dorms (0%), apartments for married students (4%). **Student employment:** During the 2009-2010 academic year, 19% of undergraduates worked on campus. Average per-year earnings: $1,505. **Clubs and organizations:** Number of student organizations: 48. Activities include: choral

groups, concert band, dance, drama/theater, jazz band, literary magazine, music ensembles, musical theater, radio station, student government, student newspaper, symphony orchestra. Number of fraternities: o; sororities: o. Average proportion of students who stay on campus on weekends: 25%. **Sports program (2009-2010):** Member of NAIA. *Men's intercollegiate varsity sports:* basketball, cross country, football, track and field (indoor), track and field (outdoor). *Women's intercollegiate varsity sports:* basketball, cross country, soccer, softball, track and field (indoor), track and field (outdoor), volleyball.

SERVICES AND FACILITIES

Basic services: women's center, health service, health insurance, other. **Remedial assistance:** math, writing, study skills. **Counseling services:** minority student, career, personal, academic, psychological, birth control. **For learning-disabled students:** School does not offer a structured program with separate admission and additional fees. Services include: remedial math, remedial English, reading machines, remedial reading, tape recorders, videotaped classes, untimed tests, note-taking services, oral tests, learning center, readers, extended time for tests, tutors, priority seating, texts on tape, other testing accommodations. **Library:** Number of titles: 206,149; number of current serial subscriptions: 821. **Information technology resources:** Students are not required to lease or own a computer. Number of campus computers available to all students: 75. School has a wireless network. Approximate number of users that can be accommodated: 90. Proportion of college-owned housing units wired for high-speed internet access: 100%. **Campus safety:** Security services offered: 24-hour foot-and-vehicle patrols, late-night transport/escort service, 24-hour emergency telephones, lighted pathways/sidewalks, controlled dormitory access (key, security card, etc).

TRANSFER AND INTERNATIONAL STUDENTS

Transfer students: May apply for admission for the following academic terms: Fall, Winter, Spring, Summer. Applicants need a minimum number of credits to apply. For fall 2009: Transfer applications received: 898. Transfer applicants offered admission: 765. Transfer applicants enrolled: 554. **International students:** Number of foreign undergraduates: 35 (1% of student body). Number of countries represented: 23. Minimum TOEFL score required: 520 (paper); 190 (computer).

George Fox University

- **Address:** 414 N. Meridian Street, Newberg, OR 97132
- **Website:** http://www.georgefox.edu
- **Private; Religious affiliation:** Evangelical Friends
- **Enrollment:** 1,679 full-time; 288 part-time

KEY STATS

✔ **U.S News College Ranking:** 170, National Universities
✔ **SAT Score (25th/75th percentile):** 980-1220
✔ **Tuition:** 2010-2011: $27,970

Selectivity: Selective	**Room/board:** $8,630
Acceptance rate: 69%	**Average debt:** $24,624
Student/faculty ratio: 11/1	**Proportion who borrowed:** 83%

UNDERGRADUATE STUDENT BODY STATS

2009-2010 enrollment: 1,679 full-time; 288 part-time. Men: 40%; women: 60%. **Ethnic makeup:** African American: 2%; American-Indian: 2%; Asian American: 5%; Hispanic: 5%; White: 80%; International: 5%. **Religious preference:** Roman Catholic: 3%; Protestant: 79%; Unknown: 14%; Evangelical Friends: 4%.

ADMISSIONS FACTS AND FIGURES

Phone: (800) 765-4369. **Email:** admissions@georgefox.edu. **Website:** http://www.georgefox.edu. **Application deadlines for fall 2011:** Regular decision: Rolling. Early decision: Not offered. Early action: Send application by: December 1; Decision sent by: December 15. Admission can be deferred. **Application fee:** $40. **To apply online, go to:** http://apply.georgefox.edu. **Admissions requirements/recommendations:** High school units required (recommended): English: o (4); Mathematics: o (2); Science: o (2); Foreign language: o (2); Social studies: o (3); History: o (2); Academic electives: o (o); Total units: o (16). Tests: The college uses SAT or ACT scores in admissions decisions. Either SAT or ACT required. For admission to the fall 2011 entering class, the school will accept: ACT with or without writing accepted. Campus visit: Recommended. Admissions interview: Recommended.

Off-campus interview: May be arranged. **Factors that count in admissions decisions:** *Academic:* Secondary school record: Very Important. Class rank: Not Considered. Letters of recommendation: Important. Standardized test scores: Important. Essay: Important. *Nonacademic:* Interview: Considered. Extracurricular activities: Considered. Talent/ability: Considered. Character/personal qualities: Considered. Alumni/ae relationship: Not Considered. Geographical residence: Not Considered. State residency: Not Considered. Religious affiliation/commitment: Considered. Minority status: Not Considered. Volunteer work: Considered. Work experience: Considered. **Other schools with the greatest overlap in applicants:** Corban University; Linfield College; Oregon State University; Seattle Pacific University; Whitworth University. **Admissions statistics for the fall 2009 entering class:** Total applicants: 1,528. Total accepted: 1,052. Freshmen enrolled: 413; 38% were from out of state. Accepted through early-decision or early-action plans: 27%. Overall acceptance rate: 69%. Non-early acceptance rate: 71%. **Credentials of fall 2009 freshmen:** 29% ranked in the top 10 percent of their high school class; 60% were in the top 25 percent; 87% were in the top half. (Proportion submitting class standing: 56%.) **Average high school grade point average:** 3.7. **First-year students who submitted SAT scores:** 86%. Scores (25/75 percentile): Critical Reading: 490-610, Math: 490-610, Combined: 980-1220. **First-year students submitting ACT scores:** 35%. Scores (25/75 percentile): English: 20-27, Math: 19-26, Composite: 21-26.

ACADEMICS

Year founded: 1891. **Academic calendar:** Semester. **Degrees offered:** bachelor's, post-bachelor's certificate, master's, post-master's certificate, doctorate. **Most popular majors:** 28% business, management, marketing, and related support services, 13% multi/interdisciplinary studies, 7% health professions and related clinical sciences, 7% visual and performing arts, 5% psychology. **Major fields of study:** biological and biomedical sciences; business, management, marketing, and related support services; communication, journalism, and related programs; computer and information sciences and support services; education; engineering; English language and literature/letters; family and consumer sciences/human sciences; foreign languages, literatures, and linguistics; health professions and related clinical sciences; history; mathematics and statistics; multi/interdisciplinary studies; parks, recreation, leisure, and fitness studies; philosophy and religious studies; physical sciences; psychology; public administration and social service professions; social sciences; theology and religious vocations; visual and performing arts. **Areas of required coursework:** arts/fine arts, humanities, mathematics, English (including composition), philosophy, sciences (biological or physical), history, social science, other. **Pre-professional programs:** pre-law, pre-dentistry, pre-medicine, pre-veterinary science. **Special academic programs (% participation):** accelerated program (5.9%), cross-registration, distance learning (10.9%), double major (10.1%), dual enrollment (1.3%), English as a Second Language (ESL) (2.7%), exchange student program (domestic) (1%), honors program (6.1%), independent study (22.1%), internships (59.5%), student-designed major (4%), study abroad (54.1%), teacher certificate program (6.4%). **Teacher certification offered in:** early childhood, elementary, middle/junior high, secondary, bilingual/bicultural. **Cooperative education programs:** engineering, other. **Reserve Officers Training Corps (ROTC):** Air Force ROTC: Offered at cooperating institution (University of Portland). **Faculty and instruction (2009-2010):** Total instructional faculty: 165 full-time, 199 part-time (55% men; 45% women; 5% minorities). Full-time faculty with Ph.D. or other terminal degree: 67%. Student/faculty ratio: 11/1. Classes of fewer than 20 students: 59%; of 20 to 49 students: 40%; of 50 or more students: 1%. **Advanced Placement and International Baccalaureate credit:** AP tests may be used for: Credit only. Scores accepted: 3, 4, 5. International Baccalaureate exams may be used for: Credit only. **Freshmen returning for sophomore year:** 78%. **Graduation rates:** Four-year: 54%; five-year: 61%; six-year: 64%. **Graduate study:** Fields in which graduates pursue further study: engineering, 11%; theology (or the seminary), 5%; education, 47%; arts and sciences, 32%; veterinary medicine, 5%.

COSTS AND FINANCIAL AID

Financial aid office: (503) 554-2290. **Expenses (2010-2011):** Tuition and fees 2010-2011: $27,970; room/board: $8,630. Estimated books and supplies: $950; transportation: $800; personal expenses: $1,300. **Financial aid:** Priority filing date for institution's financial aid form: February 1. In 2009-2010, 82% of undergraduates applied for financial aid. Of those, 75% were determined to have financial need; 43% had their need fully met. Average financial aid package (proportion receiving): $23,840 (74%). Average amount of gift aid, such as scholarships or grants (proportion receiving): $9,057 (68%). Average amount of self-help aid, such as work study or loans (proportion receiving): $5,355 (74%). Average need-based loan (excluding PLUS or other private loans): $3,633. Among students who received need-based aid, the average percentage of need met: 89%. Among students who received aid based on merit, the average award (and the proportion receiving): $7,163 (6%). The average athletic scholarship (and the proportion receiving): $0 (0%). Average amount of debt of borrowers graduating in 2009: $24,624. Proportion who borrowed: 83%.

CAMPUS LIFE AND EXTRACURRICULAR ACTIVITIES

Campus housing available (% using): women's dorms (38%), men's dorms (22%), apartment for single students (27%), special housing for disabled students (1%), other housing options (12%). Students who live in college-owned, operated, or affiliated housing: 67%. **Student employment:** During the 2009-2010 academic year, 48% of undergraduates worked on campus. Average per-year earnings: $3,715. **Clubs and organizations:** Number of student organizations: 20. Activities include: campus ministries, choral groups, concert band, dance, drama/theater, international student organization, jazz band, literary magazine, music ensembles, musical theater, pep band, radio station, student government, student newspaper, symphony orchestra, yearbook. Number of fraternities: 0; sororities: 0. Average proportion of students who stay on campus on weekends: 60%. **Sports program (2009-2010):** Member of NCAA III. *Men's intercollegiate varsity sports:* baseball, basketball, cross country, golf, soccer, tennis, track and field (outdoor). *Women's intercollegiate varsity sports:* basketball, cross country, golf, soccer, softball, tennis, track and field (outdoor), volleyball.

SERVICES AND FACILITIES

Basic services: nonremedial tutoring, health service, health insurance. **Remedial assistance:** reading, math, writing, study skills. **Counseling services:** minority student, career, personal, academic, psychological, birth control, religious. **For learning-disabled students:** School does not offer a structured program with separate admission and additional fees. Total undergraduates in learning-disabled program or receiving services: 28. Services include: remedial English, remedial reading, tape recorders, untimed tests, note-taking services, oral tests, learning center, readers, extended time for tests, tutors, priority seating, texts on tape, other testing accommodations. **Library:** Number of titles: 218,240; number of current serial subscriptions: 5,374. **Information technology resources:** Students are not required to lease or own a computer. Number of campus computers available to all students: 139. School has a wireless network. Approximate number of users that can be accommodated: 2,240. Proportion of college-owned housing units wired for high-speed internet access: 100%. **Campus safety:** Security services offered: 24-hour foot-and-vehicle patrols, late-night transport/escort service, 24-hour emergency telephones, lighted pathways/sidewalks, student patrols, controlled dormitory access (key, security card, etc).

TRANSFER AND INTERNATIONAL STUDENTS

Transfer students: May apply for admission for the following academic terms: Fall, Spring. Applicants need a minimum number of credits to apply. For fall 2009: Transfer applications received: 241. Transfer applicants offered admission: 151. Transfer applicants enrolled: 87. **International students:** Number of foreign undergraduates: 96 (5% of student body). Number of countries represented: 7. Minimum TOEFL score required: 550 (paper); 80 (computer).

Lewis & Clark College

- **Address:** 0615 S.W. Palatine Hill Road, Portland, OR 97219-7899
- **Website:** http://www.lclark.edu
- **Private**
- **Enrollment:** 1,956 full-time; 21 part-time

KEY STATS

✔ **U.S News College Ranking:** 75, National Liberal Arts Colleges
✔ **SAT Score (25th/75th percentile):** 1220-1390
✔ **Tuition:** 2010-2011: $36,632

Selectivity: More selective	**Room/board:** $9,648
Acceptance rate: 65%	**Average debt:** $17,084
Student/faculty ratio: 12/1	**Proportion who borrowed:** 58%

UNDERGRADUATE STUDENT BODY STATS

2009-2010 enrollment: 1,956 full-time; 21 part-time. Men: 40%; women: 60%. **Ethnic makeup:** African American: 2%; American-Indian: 1%; Asian American: 7%; Hispanic: 5%; White: 78%; International: 6%. **Religious preference:** Roman Catholic: 5%; Protestant: 13%; Jewish: 7%; Muslim: 1%; Hindu: 1%; Buddhist: 3%; No preference: 55%; Unknown: 11%.

ADMISSIONS FACTS AND FIGURES

Phone: (800) 444-4111. **Email:** admissions@lclark.edu. **Website:** http://www.lclark.edu. **Application deadlines for fall 2011:** Regular decision: February 1; decision sent by April 1. Early decision: Not offered. Early action: Send application by: November 1; Decision sent by: January 15. Admission can be deferred. **Application fee:** $50. **To apply online, go to:** http://www.lclark.edu/college/offices/admissions/apply/common_application/. **Admissions requirements/recommendations:** High school units required (recommended): English: (4); Mathematics: (4); Science: (3); Foreign language: (3); Social studies: (4). **Tests:** The college uses SAT or ACT scores in admissions decisions. Neither SAT nor ACT required. For admission to the fall 2011 entering class, the school will accept: ACT with or without writing accepted. Campus visit: Recommended. Admissions interview: Neither required nor recommended. Off-campus interview: May be arranged. **Factors that count in admissions decisions:** *Academic:* Secondary school record: Very Important. Class rank: Important. Letters of recommendation: Important. Standardized test scores: Important. Essay: Important. *Nonacademic:* Interview: Considered. Extracurricular activities: Important. Talent/ability: Important. Character/personal qualities: Important. Alumni/ae relationship: Important. Geographical residence: Considered. State residency: Considered. Religious affiliation/commitment: Not Considered. Minority status: Very Important. Volunteer work: Important. Work experience: Considered. **Other schools with the greatest overlap in applicants:** Reed College; University of Oregon; University of Puget Sound; Whitman College; Willamette University. **Admissions statistics for the fall 2009 entering class:** Total applicants: 5,343. Total accepted: 3,448. Freshmen enrolled: 498; 91% were from out of state. Accepted through early-decision or early-action plans: 35%. Overall acceptance rate: 65%. Non-early acceptance rate: 62%. **Size of waiting list:** 742 applicants; enrolled from waiting list: 44. **Credentials of fall 2009 freshmen:** 46% ranked in the top 10 percent of their high school class; 81% were in the top 25 percent; 98% were in the top half. (Proportion submitting class standing: 63%.) **Average high school grade point average:** 3.7. **First-year students who submitted SAT scores:** 63%. Scores (25/75 percentile): Critical Reading: 610-710; Math: 610-680, Combined: 1220-1390. **First-year students submitting ACT scores:** 40%. Scores (25/75 percentile): English: 25-27, Math: 26-30, Composite: 27-30.

ACADEMICS

Year founded: 1867. **Academic calendar:** Semester. **Degrees offered:** bachelor's, master's, post-master's certificate, doctorate. **Most popular majors:** 26% social sciences, 15% psychology, 11% visual and performing arts, 10% foreign languages, literatures, and linguistics, 9% biological and biomedical sciences. **Major fields of study:** area, ethnic, cultural, and gender studies; biological and biomedical sciences; communication, journalism, and related programs; computer and information sciences and support services; English language and literature/letters; foreign languages, literatures, and linguistics; history; liberal arts and sciences studies, and humanities; mathematics and statistics; natural resources and conservation; philosophy and religious studies; physical sciences; psychology; social sciences; visual and performing arts. **Areas of required coursework:** arts/fine arts, humanities, mathematics, foreign languages, sciences (biological or physical), other. **Pre-professional programs:** pre-law, pre-dentistry, pre-medicine, pre-veterinary science, pre-optometry, pre-pharmacy. **Special academic programs (% participation):** accelerated program (1%), cross-registration (0%), double major (11%), dual enrollment, English as a Second Language (ESL) (1%), honors program (20%), independent study (15%), internships (32%), student-designed major (0%), study abroad (66.7%). **Faculty and instruction (2009-2010):** Total instructional faculty: 231 full-time, 149 part-time (50% men; 50% women; 9% minorities). Full-time faculty with Ph.D. or other terminal degree: 94%. Student/faculty ratio: 12/1. Classes of fewer than 20 students: 66%; of 20 to 49 students: 33%; of 50 or more students: 1%. **Advanced Placement and International Baccalaureate credit:** AP tests may be used for: Placement only. Scores accepted: 4, 5. International Baccalaureate exams may be used for: Placement only. **Freshmen returning for sophomore year:** 85%. **Graduation rates:** Four-year: 69%; five-year: 76%; six-year: 76%. **Graduate study:** 26% of students pursue further study immediately upon graduation; 26% within one year; 64% within five years. Fields in which graduates pursue further study: Master of Business Administration (MBA), 8%; law, 15%; medicine, 5%; dentistry, 1%; engineering, 1%; theology (or the seminary), 1%; education, 28%; arts and sciences, 40%; veterinary medicine, 1%.

COSTS AND FINANCIAL AID

Financial aid office: (503) 768-7090. **Expenses (2010-2011):** Tuition and fees 2010-2011: $36,632; room/board: $9,648. Estimated books and supplies: $1,050; transportation: $990; personal expenses: $990. **Financial aid:** Priority filing date for institution's financial aid form: February 15. In 2009-2010, 69% of undergraduates applied for financial aid. Of those, 55% were determined to have financial need; 35% had their need fully met. Average financial aid package (proportion receiving): $27,618 (55%). Average amount of gift aid, such as scholarships or grants (proportion receiving): $20,201 (54%). Average amount of self-help aid, such as work study or loans (proportion receiving): $6,018 (41%). Average need-based loan (excluding PLUS or other private loans): $4,408. Among students who received need-based aid, the average percentage of need met: 85%. Among students who received aid based on merit, the average award (and the proportion receiving): $10,371 (13%). Average amount of debt of borrowers graduating in 2009: $17,084. Proportion who borrowed: 58%.

CAMPUS LIFE AND EXTRACURRICULAR ACTIVITIES

Campus housing available (% using): coed dorms (63%), women's dorms (2%), apartment for single students (13%), other housing options. Students who live in college-owned, operated, or affiliated housing: 67%. **Student employment:** During the 2009-2010 academic year, 26% of undergraduates worked on campus. Average per-year earnings: $969. **Clubs and organizations:** Number of student organizations: 70. Activities include: campus ministries, choral groups, concert band, dance, drama/theater, international student organization, jazz band, literary magazine, model UN, music ensembles, musical theater, radio station, student government, student newspaper, symphony orchestra, television station, yearbook. Number of fraternities: 0; sororities: 0. Average proportion of students who stay on campus on weekends: 97%. **Sports program (2009-2010):** Member of NCAA III. *Men's intercollegiate varsity sports:* baseball, basketball, cross country, football, golf, swimming, tennis, track and field (indoor), track and field (outdoor). *Women's intercollegiate varsity sports:* basketball, cross country, golf, crew (lightweight), soccer, softball, swimming, tennis, track and field (indoor), track and field (outdoor), volleyball.

SERVICES AND FACILITIES

Basic services: nonremedial tutoring, women's center, placement service, health service, health insurance. **Remedial assistance:** math, writing, study skills, other. **Counseling services:** minority student, career, personal, academic, older student, psychological, birth control, religious. **For learning-disabled students:** School does not offer a structured program with separate admission and additional fees. Services include: tape recorders, diagnostic testing service, note-taking services, learning center, readers, extended time for tests, tutors, texts on tape, exams on tape or computer, other testing accommodations, other. **Library:** Number of titles: 310,810; number of current serial subscriptions: 3,513. **Information technology resources:** Students are not required to lease or own a computer. Number of campus computers available to all students: 200. School has a wireless network. Approximate number of users that can be accommodated: 3,500. Proportion of college-owned housing units wired for high-speed internet access: 100%. **Campus safety:** Security services offered: 24-hour foot-and-vehicle patrols, late-night transport/escort service, 24-hour emergency telephones, lighted pathways/sidewalks, student patrols, controlled dormitory access (key, security card, etc).

TRANSFER AND INTERNATIONAL STUDENTS

Transfer students: May apply for admission for the following academic terms: Fall, Spring, Summer. Applicants need a minimum number of credits to apply. For fall 2009: Transfer applications received: 306. Transfer applicants offered admission: 143. Transfer applicants enrolled: 54. **International students:** Number of foreign undergraduates: 118 (6% of student body). Number of countries represented: 38. Minimum TOEFL score required: 575 (paper); 232 (computer). Average TOEFL score: 610 (paper).

Linfield College

- **Address:** 900 S.E. Baker Street, McMinnville, OR 97128-6894
- **Website:** http://www.linfield.edu
- **Private; Religious affiliation:** American Baptist
- **Enrollment:** 1,627 full-time; 50 part-time

KEY STATS

✔ **U.S News College Ranking:** 105, National Liberal Arts Colleges
✔ **SAT Score (25th/75th percentile):** 970-1200
✔ **Tuition:** 2010-2011: $30,604

Selectivity: Selective	**Room/board:** $8,560
Acceptance rate: 82%	**Average debt:** $27,271
Student/faculty ratio: 12/1	**Proportion who borrowed:** 71%

UNDERGRADUATE STUDENT BODY STATS

2009-2010 enrollment: 1,627 full-time; 50 part-time. Men: 43%; women: 57%. **Ethnic makeup:** African American: 2%; American-Indian: 2%; Asian American: 9%; Hispanic: 5%; White: 77%; International: 5%.

ADMISSIONS FACTS AND FIGURES

Phone: (800) 640-2287. **Email:** admission@linfield.edu. **Website:** http://www.linfield.edu. **Application deadlines for fall 2011:** Regular decision: Rolling; decision sent by April 1. Early decision: Not offered. Early action: Send application by: November 15; Decision sent by: January 15. Admission can be deferred. **To apply online, go to:** http://www.linfield.edu/admission/apply.php. **Admissions requirements/recommendations:** High school units required (recommended): English: (4); Mathematics: (4); Science: (3); Foreign language: (2); Social studies: (4); Total units: (17). Tests: The college uses SAT or ACT scores in admissions decisions. Either SAT or ACT required. For admission to the fall 2011 entering class, the school will accept: ACT with or without writing accepted. Campus visit: Recommended. Admissions interview: Recommended. Off-campus interview: May be arranged. **Factors that count in admissions decisions:** *Academic:* Secondary school record: Very Important. Class rank: Important. Letters of recommendation: Important. Standardized test scores: Very Important. Essay: Important. *Nonacademic:* Interview: Not Considered. Extracurricular activities: Considered. Talent/ability: Considered. Character/personal qualities: Considered. Alumni/ae relationship: Considered. Geographical residence: Considered. State residency: Not Considered. Religious affiliation/commitment: Not Considered. Minority status: Considered. Volunteer work: Considered. Work experience: Considered. **Other schools with the greatest overlap in applicants:** Oregon State University; University of Oregon; University of Portland; University of Puget Sound; Willamette University. **Admissions statistics for the fall 2009 entering class:** Total applicants: 1,692. Total accepted: 1,381. Freshmen enrolled: 423; 49% were from out of state. Accepted through early-decision or early-action plans: 32%. Overall acceptance rate: 82%. Non-early acceptance rate: 77%. **Size of waiting list:** 0 applicants; enrolled from waiting list: 0. **Credentials of fall 2009 freshmen:** 30% ranked in the top 10 percent of their high school class; 69% were in the top 25 percent; 92% were in the top half. (Proportion submitting class standing: 60%.) **Average high school grade point average:** 3.6. **First-year students who submitted SAT scores:** 88%. Scores (25/75 percentile): Critical Reading: 480-600, Math: 490-600, Combined: 970-1200. **First-year students submitting ACT scores:** 37%. Scores (25/75 percentile): English: 20-27, Math: 20-26, Composite: 21-27.

ACADEMICS

Year founded: 1858. **Academic calendar:** 4-1-4. **Degrees offered:** bachelor's, post-bachelor's certificate. **Most popular majors:** 24% business, management, marketing, and related support services, 10% social sciences, 9% education, 8% history, 7% psychology. **Major fields of study:** area, ethnic, cultural, and gender studies; biological and biomedical sciences; business, management, marketing, and related support services; communication, journalism, and related programs; computer and information sciences and support services; education; English language and literature/letters; foreign languages, literatures, and linguistics; health professions and related clinical sciences; history; mathematics and statistics; natural resources and conservation; parks, recreation, leisure, and fitness studies; philosophy and religious studies; physical sciences; psychology; social sciences; visual and performing arts. **Areas of required coursework:** arts/fine arts, humanities, mathematics, English (including composition), philosophy, sciences (biological or physical), history, social science, other. **Pre-professional programs:** pre-law, pre-dentistry, pre-medicine, pre-veterinary science, pre-optometry, pre-pharmacy. **Special academic programs (% participation):** cross-registration (1%), distance learning (20%), double major (15%), English as a Second Language (ESL) (1%), external degree program, independent study (20%), internships (30%), liberal arts/career combination (3%), student-designed major (1%), study abroad (49%), teacher certificate program (10%). **Teacher certification offered in:** early childhood, elementary, middle/junior high, secondary. **Reserve Officers Training Corps (ROTC):** Air Force ROTC: Offered at cooperating institution (University of Portland). **Faculty and instruction (2009-2010):** Total instructional faculty: 108 full-time, 74 part-time (53% men; 47% women; 3% minorities). Full-time faculty with Ph.D. or other terminal degree: 96%. Student/faculty ratio: 12/1. Classes of fewer than 20 students: 68%; of 20 to 49 students: 31%; of 50 or more students: 1%. **Advanced Placement and International Baccalaureate credit:** AP tests may be used for: Credit and/or placement. Scores accepted: 4, 5. International Baccalaureate exams may be used for: Credit only. **Freshmen returning for sophomore year:** 82%. **Graduation rates:** Four-year: 64%; five-year: 72%; six-year: 74%. **Graduate study:** 13% of students pursue further study immediately upon graduation; 20% within one year; 30% within five years. Fields in which graduates pursue further study: Master of Business Administration (MBA), 15%; law, 5%; medicine, 5%; dentistry, 2%; education, 20%; arts and sciences, 52%; veterinary medicine, 1%.

COSTS AND FINANCIAL AID

Financial aid office: (503) 883-2225. **Expenses (2010-2011):** Tuition and fees 2010-2011: $30,604; room/board: $8,560. Estimated books and supplies: $750; transportation: $200; personal expenses: $1,100. **Financial aid:** Priority filing date for institution's financial aid form: February 1; deadline: February 1. In 2009-2010, 69% of undergraduates applied for financial aid. Of those, 69% were determined to have financial need; 26% had their need fully met. Average financial aid package (proportion receiving): $19,168 (69%). Average amount of gift aid, such as scholarships or grants (proportion receiving): $9,252 (60%). Average amount of self-help aid, such as work study or loans (proportion receiving): $6,108 (58%). Average need-based loan (excluding PLUS or other private loans): $4,280. Among students who received need-based aid, the average percentage of need met: 85%. Among students who received aid based on merit, the average award (and the proportion receiving): $11,388 (31%). The average athletic scholarship (and the proportion receiving): $0 (0%). Average amount of debt of borrowers graduating in 2009: $27,271. Proportion who borrowed: 71%.

CAMPUS LIFE AND EXTRACURRICULAR ACTIVITIES

Campus housing available (% using): coed dorms (53%), women's dorms (7%), men's dorms (2%), fraternity housing (3%), apartment for single students (29%), special housing for disabled students, other housing options. Students who live in college-owned, operated, or affiliated housing: 74%. **Student employment:** During the 2009-2010 academic year, 22% of undergraduates worked on campus. Average per-year earnings: $2,100. **Clubs and organizations:** Number of student organizations: 90. Activities include: campus ministries, choral groups, concert band, dance, drama/theater, international student organization, jazz band, literary magazine, model UN, music ensembles, musical theater, opera, pep band, radio station, student government, student newspaper, symphony orchestra. Number of fraternities: 4; sororities: 4. Proportion of men in fraternities: 22%; of women in sororities: 27%. Average proportion of students who stay on campus on weekends: 80%. **Sports program (2009-2010):** Member of NCAA III. *Men's intercollegiate varsity sports:* baseball, basketball, cross country, football, golf, soccer, swimming, tennis, track and field (indoor), track and field (outdoor). *Women's intercollegiate varsity sports:* basketball, cross country, golf, lacrosse, soccer, softball, swimming, tennis, track and field (indoor), track and field (outdoor), volleyball.

SERVICES AND FACILITIES

Basic services: nonremedial tutoring, women's center, health service, health insurance. **Counseling services:** minority student, career, personal, academic, psychological, birth control, religious. **For learning-disabled students:** School does not offer a structured program with separate admission and additional fees. Total undergraduates in learning-disabled program or receiving services: 400. Services include: reading machines, tape recorders, other special classes, note-taking services, oral tests, learning center, readers, extended time for tests, tutors, priority registration, priority seating, texts on tape, exams on tape or computer, other testing accommodations, other. **Library:** Number of titles: 185,842; number of current serial subscriptions: 970. **Information technology resources:** Students are not required to lease or own a computer. Number of campus computers available to all students: 266. School has a wireless network. Approximate number of users that can be accommodated: 17,000. Proportion of college-owned housing

units wired for high-speed internet access: 100%. **Campus safety:** Security services offered: 24-hour foot-and-vehicle patrols, late-night transport/escort service, 24-hour emergency telephones, lighted pathways/sidewalks, controlled dormitory access (key, security card, etc).

TRANSFER AND INTERNATIONAL STUDENTS

Transfer students: May apply for admission for the following academic terms: Fall, Spring. Applicants need a minimum number of credits to apply. For fall 2009: Transfer applications received: 133. Transfer applicants offered admission: 97. Transfer applicants enrolled: 61. **International students:** Number of foreign undergraduates: 77 (5% of student body). Number of countries represented: 25. Minimum TOEFL score required: 550 (paper); 213 (computer). Average TOEFL score: 546 (paper).

Marylhurst University

- ■ **Address:** PO Box 261, Marylhurst, OR 97036-0261
- ■ **Website:** http://www.marylhurst.edu
- ■ **Private; Religious affiliation:** Roman Catholic
- ■ **Enrollment:** 277 full-time; 692 part-time

KEY STATS

✔ **U.S News College Ranking:** Unranked, Regional Universities (West)
✔ **SAT or ACT Score (25th/75th percentile):** N/A
✔ **Tuition:** 2010-2011: $17,730

Selectivity: N/A	**Room/board:** $0
Acceptance rate: 70%	**Average debt:** $27,846
Student/faculty ratio: 6/1	**Proportion who borrowed:** 71%

UNDERGRADUATE STUDENT BODY STATS

2009-2010 enrollment: 277 full-time; 692 part-time. Men: 30%; women: 70%. **Ethnic makeup:** African American: 5%; Asian American: 1%; Hispanic: 3%; White: 89%; International: 1%.

ADMISSIONS FACTS AND FIGURES

Phone: (503) 699-6268. **Email:** admissions@marylhurst.edu. **Website:** http://www.marylhurst.edu. **Application deadlines for fall 2011:** Regular decision: Rolling. Early decision: Not offered. Early action: Not offered. Admission can be deferred. **Application fee:** $20. **To apply online, go to:** https://my.marylhurst.edu/ics/Admissions/Apply_Now.jnz. **Admissions requirements/recommendations:** High school units required (recommended): English: (4); Mathematics: (3); Science: (3); Foreign language: (2); Social studies: (2); History: (2); Academic electives: (4). Tests: The college does not use SAT or ACT scores in admissions decisions. Neither SAT nor ACT required. Campus visit: Recommended. Admissions interview: Required. Off-campus interview: May be arranged. **Factors that count in admissions decisions:** *Academic:* Secondary school record: Considered. Class rank: Not Considered. Letters of recommendation: Considered. Standardized test scores: Not Considered. Essay: Considered. *Nonacademic:* Interview: Important. Extracurricular activities: Not Considered. Talent/ability: Not Considered. Character/personal qualities: Not Considered. Alumni/ae relationship: Not Considered. Geographical residence: Considered. State residency: Not Considered. Religious affiliation/commitment: Not Considered. Minority status: Not Considered. Volunteer work: Not Considered. Work experience: Not Considered. **Admissions statistics for the fall 2009 entering class:** Total applicants: 44. Total accepted: 31. Freshmen enrolled: 23; 18% were from out of state. Overall acceptance rate: 70%.

ACADEMICS

Year founded: 1893. **Academic calendar:** Quarter. **Degrees offered:** certificate, bachelor's, post-bachelor's certificate, master's, post-master's certificate. **Most popular majors:** 34% business administration and management, 13% multi/interdisciplinary studies, 11% interior design, 8% communication studies/speech communication and rhetoric, 6% English language and literature. **Major fields of study:** business, management, marketing, and related support services; communication, journalism, and related programs; English language and literature/letters; health professions and related clinical sciences; liberal arts and sciences studies, and humanities; multi/interdisciplinary studies; natural resources and conservation; philosophy and religious studies; psychology; social sciences; visual and performing arts. **Areas of required coursework:** arts/fine arts, humanities, computer literacy, mathematics, English (including composition), philosophy, sciences (biological or physical), social science, other. **Special academic programs:**

accelerated program, cooperative (work-study plan) program, cross-registration, distance learning, double major, dual enrollment, English as a Second Language (ESL), independent study, internships, student-designed major, study abroad, teacher certificate program, weekend college. **Teacher certification offered in:** elementary, secondary. **Cooperative education programs:** education, other. **Faculty and instruction (2009-2010):** Total instructional faculty: 52 full-time, 201 part-time (45% men; 55% women; 8% minorities). Full-time faculty with Ph.D. or other terminal degree: 62%. Student/faculty ratio: 6/1. Classes of fewer than 20 students: 93%; of 20 to 49 students: 7%; of 50 or more students: 0%. **Advanced Placement and International Baccalaureate credit:** AP tests may be used for: Credit only. Scores accepted: 4, 5. International Baccalaureate exams may be used for: Credit only. **Freshmen returning for sophomore year:** 56%. **Graduation rates:** Four-year: 13%; five-year: 13%; six-year: 30%.

COSTS AND FINANCIAL AID

Financial aid office: (503) 699-6253. **Expenses (2010-2011):** Tuition and fees 2010-2011: $17,730; room/board: $0. **Financial aid:** Priority filing date for institution's financial aid form: March 1. In 2009-2010, 52% of undergraduates applied for financial aid. Of those, 50% were determined to have financial need; 4% had their need fully met. Average financial aid package (proportion receiving): $11,390 (49%). Average amount of gift aid, such as scholarships or grants (proportion receiving): $8,638 (40%). Average amount of self-help aid, such as work study or loans (proportion receiving): $4,778 (44%). Average need-based loan (excluding PLUS or other private loans): $4,450. Among students who received need-based aid, the average percentage of need met: 49%. Among students who received aid based on merit, the average award (and the proportion receiving): $4,737 (4%). The average athletic scholarship (and the proportion receiving): $0 (0%). Average amount of debt of borrowers graduating in 2009: $27,846. Proportion who borrowed: 71%.

CAMPUS LIFE AND EXTRACURRICULAR ACTIVITIES

Clubs and organizations: Number of student organizations: 8. Activities include: campus ministries, choral groups, literary magazine, music ensembles, student newspaper, symphony orchestra. Number of fraternities: 0; sororities: 0.

SERVICES AND FACILITIES

Basic services: health insurance, other. **Remedial assistance:** other. **Counseling services:** career, personal, academic, older student, religious, other. **For learning-disabled students:** School does not offer a structured program with separate admission and additional fees. Services include: tape recorders, untimed tests, note-taking services, oral tests, readers, extended time for tests, priority registration, priority seating, texts on tape, other testing accommodations, other. **Library:** Number of titles: 109,963; number of current serial subscriptions: 23,286. **Information technology resources:** Students are not required to lease or own a computer. Number of campus computers available to all students: 50. School has a wireless network. Approximate number of users that can be accommodated: 1,000. **Campus safety:** Security services offered: late-night transport/escort service, lighted pathways/sidewalks.

TRANSFER AND INTERNATIONAL STUDENTS

Transfer students: May apply for admission for the following academic terms: Fall, Winter, Spring, Summer. Applicants need a minimum number of credits to apply. For fall 2009: Transfer applications received: 347. Transfer applicants offered admission: 262. Transfer applicants enrolled: 171. **International students:** Number of foreign undergraduates: 12 (1% of student body). Number of countries represented: 13. Minimum TOEFL score required: 550 (paper); 213 (computer).

Northwest Christian University

- **Address:** 828 E. 11th Avenue, Eugene, OR 97401
- **Website:** http://www.northwestchristian.edu
- **Private; Religious affiliation:** Christian Church (Disciples of Christ)
- **Enrollment:** 366 full-time; 79 part-time

KEY STATS

✔ **U.S News College Ranking:** 21, Regional Colleges (West)
✔ **SAT Score (25th/75th percentile):** 900-1110
✔ **Tuition:** 2010-2011: $22,900

Selectivity: Selective	**Room/board:** $7,100
Acceptance rate: 95%	**Average debt:** $21,633
Student/faculty ratio: 22/1	**Proportion who borrowed:** 85%

UNDERGRADUATE STUDENT BODY STATS

2009-2010 enrollment: 366 full-time; 79 part-time. Men: 41%; women: 59%. **Ethnic makeup:** African American: 2%; American-Indian: 2%; Asian American: 3%; Hispanic: 5%; White: 89%. **Religious preference:** Roman Catholic: 5%; No preference: 2%; Unknown: 33%; Christian Church (Disciples of Christ): 8%; Non-denominational Christian: 20%; Other: 32%.

ADMISSIONS FACTS AND FIGURES

Phone: (541) 684-7201. **Email:** admissions@northwestchristian.edu. **Website:** http://www.northwestchristian.edu. **Application deadlines for fall 2011:** Regular decision: Rolling. Early decision: Not offered. Early action: Not offered. Admission can be deferred. **To apply online, go to:** http://www.northwestchristian.edu/undergrad/apply-now.aspx. **Admissions requirements/recommendations:** High school units required (recommended): English: (4); Mathematics: (3); Science: (2); Foreign language: (2); Social studies: (3); Total units: (14). Tests: The college uses SAT or ACT scores in admissions decisions. Either SAT or ACT required. For admission to the fall 2011 entering class, the school will accept: ACT with writing recommended. Campus visit: Recommended. Admissions interview: Recommended. Off-campus interview: May be arranged. **Factors that count in admissions decisions:** *Academic:* Secondary school record: Important. Class rank: Considered. Letters of recommendation: Considered. Standardized test scores: Very Important. Essay: Important. *Nonacademic:* Interview: Considered. Extracurricular activities: Important. Talent/ability: Not Considered. Character/personal qualities: Considered. Alumni/ae relationship: Not Considered. Geographical residence: Not Considered. State residency: Not Considered. Religious affiliation/commitment: Not Considered. Minority status: Not Considered. Volunteer work: Important. Work experience: Considered. **Other schools with the greatest overlap in applicants:** Concordia College; Corban University; George Fox University; Linfield College; Warner Pacific College. **Admissions statistics for the fall 2009 entering class:** Total applicants: 596. Total accepted: 568. Freshmen enrolled: 78; 17% were from out of state. Overall acceptance rate: 95%. **Credentials of fall 2009 freshmen:** 21% ranked in the top 10 percent of their high school class; 45% were in the top 25 percent; 74% were in the top half. (Proportion submitting class standing: 68%.) **Average high school grade point average:** 3.4. **First-year students who submitted SAT scores:** 88%. Scores (25/75 percentile): Critical Reading: 450-560, Math: 450-550, Combined: 900-1110. **First-year students submitting ACT scores:** 29%. Scores (25/75 percentile): English: 17-23, Math: 17-22, Composite: 20-23.

ACADEMICS

Year founded: 1895. **Academic calendar:** Semester. **Degrees offered:** certificate, associate, bachelor's, post-bachelor's certificate, master's. **Most popular majors:** 15% business administration, management, and operations, 10% elementary education and teaching, 5% accounting, 5% human services, 4% business administration and management. **Major fields of study:** area, ethnic, cultural, and gender studies; biological and biomedical sciences; business, management, marketing, and related support services; communication, journalism, and related programs; computer and information sciences and support services; education; health professions and related clinical sciences; liberal arts and sciences studies, and humanities; multi/interdisciplinary studies; psychology; public administration and social service professions; social sciences; theology and religious vocations; visual and performing arts. **Areas of required coursework:** humanities, computer literacy, mathematics, English (including composition), sciences (biological or physical), history, social science, other. **Pre-professional programs:** other. **Special academic programs:** accelerated program, distance learning, double major, independent study, internships, liberal arts/career combination, student-designed major, study abroad, teacher certificate program. **Teacher certification offered in:** early childhood, elementary, middle/junior high, secondary. **Reserve Officers Training Corps (ROTC):** Army ROTC: Offered on campus. **Faculty and instruction (2009-2010):** Total instructional faculty: 21 full-time, 4 part-time (56% men; 44% women). Full-time faculty with Ph.D. or other terminal degree: 67%. Student/faculty ratio: 22/1. Classes of fewer than 20 students: 73%; of 20 to 49 students: 27%; of 50 or more students: 0%. **Advanced Placement and International Baccalaureate credit:** AP tests may be used for: Credit only. Scores accepted: 3, 4, 5. International Baccalaureate exams may be used for: Credit only. **Freshmen returning for sophomore year:** 62%. **Graduation rates:** Four-year: 32%; five-year: 38%; six-year: 36%.

COSTS AND FINANCIAL AID

Financial aid office: (541) 684-7203. **Expenses (2010-2011):** Tuition and fees 2010-2011: $22,900; room/board: $7,100. Estimated books and supplies: $900; transportation: $1,170; personal expenses: $1,170. **Financial aid:** Priority filing date for institution's financial aid form: March 1. In 2009-2010, 80% of undergraduates applied for financial aid. Of those, 74% were determined to have financial need; 19% had their need fully met. Average financial aid package (proportion receiving): $19,146 (74%). Average amount of gift aid, such as scholarships or grants (proportion receiving): $14,903 (74%). Average amount of self-help aid, such as work study or loans (proportion receiving): $5,231 (60%). Average need-based loan (excluding PLUS or other private loans): $4,290. Among students who received need-based aid, the average percentage of need met: 79%. Among students who received aid based on merit, the average award (and the proportion receiving): $6,099 (10%). The average athletic scholarship (and the proportion receiving): $4,446 (7%). Average amount of debt of borrowers graduating in 2009: $21,633. Proportion who borrowed: 85%.

CAMPUS LIFE AND EXTRACURRICULAR ACTIVITIES

Campus housing available: coed dorms, apartment for single students. Activities include: campus ministries, choral groups, concert band, drama/theater, literary magazine, music ensembles, pep band, student government, student newspaper, yearbook. Number of fraternities: 0; sororities: 0. **Sports program (2009-2010):** Member of NAIA. *Men's intercollegiate varsity sports:* basketball, cross country, golf, soccer, track and field (outdoor). *Women's intercollegiate varsity sports:* cross country, golf, soccer, softball, track and field (outdoor), volleyball.

SERVICES AND FACILITIES

Basic services: nonremedial tutoring, placement service, health service, health insurance. **Remedial assistance:** reading, math, writing, study skills. **Counseling services:** career, personal, academic, psychological, religious. **For learning-disabled students:** School does not offer a structured program with separate admission and additional fees. Services include: remedial math, remedial English, remedial reading, tape recorders, videotaped classes, oral tests, extended time for tests, tutors. **Library:** Number of titles: 62,681; number of current serial subscriptions: 266. **Information technology resources:** Students are not required to lease or own a computer. Number of campus computers available to all students: 46. School has a wireless network. Proportion of college-owned housing units wired for high-speed internet access: 100%. **Campus safety:** Security services offered: 24-hour foot-and-vehicle patrols, late-night transport/escort service, 24-hour emergency telephones, lighted pathways/sidewalks, controlled dormitory access (key, security card, etc).

TRANSFER AND INTERNATIONAL STUDENTS

Transfer students: May apply for admission for the following academic terms: Fall, Spring, Summer. Applicants need a minimum number of credits to apply. For fall 2009: Transfer applications received: 132. Transfer applicants offered admission: 128. Transfer applicants enrolled: 49. **International students:** Number of foreign undergraduates: 0.

Oregon Institute of Technology

■ **Address:** 3201 Campus Drive, Klamath Falls, OR 97601
■ **Website:** http://www.oit.edu
■ **Public**
■ **Enrollment:** 2,078 full-time; 1,817 part-time

KEY STATS

✔ **U.S News College Ranking:** 7, Regional Colleges (West)
✔ **SAT Score (25th/75th percentile):** 910-1150
✔ **Tuition:** 2010-2011: $7,335 in state, $20,037 out of state

Selectivity: Selective	**Room/board:** $8,600
Acceptance rate: 93%	**Average debt:** $27,266
Student/faculty ratio: 20/1	**Proportion who borrowed:** 64%

UNDERGRADUATE STUDENT BODY STATS

2009-2010 enrollment: 2,078 full-time; 1,817 part-time. Men: 51%; women: 49%. **Ethnic makeup:** African American: 1%; American-Indian: 2%; Asian American: 6%; Hispanic: 5%; White: 84%; International: 1%.

ADMISSIONS FACTS AND FIGURES

Phone: (541) 885-1155. **Email:** oit@oit.edu. **Website:** http://www.oit.edu. **Application deadlines for fall 2011:** Regular decision: October 1. Early decision: Not offered. Early action: Not offered. Admission can be deferred. **Application fee:** $50. **To apply online, go to:** http://www.oit.edu/admissions/applications. **Admissions requirements/recommendations:** High school units required (recommended): English: 4; Mathematics: 3; Science: 2; Foreign language: 2; Social studies: 3; Total units: 14. Tests: The college uses SAT or ACT scores in admissions decisions. Either SAT or ACT required. For admission to the fall 2011 entering class, the school will accept: ACT with writing required. Campus visit: Recommended. Admissions interview: Recommended. Off-campus interview: Not available. **Factors that count in admissions decisions:** *Academic:* Secondary school record: Very Important. Class rank: Considered. Letters of recommendation: Considered. Standardized test scores: Very Important. Essay: Not Considered. *Nonacademic:* Interview: Not Considered. Extracurricular activities: Not Considered. Talent/ability: Not Considered. Character/personal qualities: Considered. Alumni/ae relationship: Not Considered. Geographical residence: Not Considered. State residency: Not Considered. Religious affiliation/commitment: Not Considered. Minority status: Not Considered. Volunteer work: Not Considered. Work experience: Not Considered. **Other schools with the greatest overlap in applicants:** Oregon State University; Southern Oregon University. **Admissions statistics for the fall 2009 entering class:** Total applicants: 775. Total accepted: 719. Freshmen enrolled: 368; 15% were from out of state. Overall acceptance rate: 93%. **Credentials of fall 2009 freshmen:** 18% ranked in the top 10 percent of their high school class; 52% were in the top 25 percent; 87% were in the top half. (Proportion submitting class standing: 74%.) **Average high school grade point average:** 3.4. **First-year students who submitted SAT scores:** 82%. Scores (25/75 percentile): Critical Reading: 440-560, Math: 470-590, Combined: 910-1150. **First-year students submitting ACT scores:** 23%. Scores (25/75 percentile): English: N/A, Math: N/A, Composite: 21-27.

ACADEMICS

Year founded: 1947. **Academic calendar:** Quarter. **Degrees offered:** certificate, associate, bachelor's, master's. **Most popular majors:** 0% dental hygiene/hygienist, 0% diagnostic medical sonography/sonographer and ultrasound technician, 0% mechanical engineering/mechanical technology/technician, 0% psychology, 0% radiologic technology/science ? radiographer. **Major fields of study:** business, management, marketing, and related support services; communication, journalism, and related programs; computer and information sciences and support services; engineering; engineering technologies/technicians; health professions and related clinical sciences; history; liberal arts and sciences studies, and humanities; multi/interdisciplinary studies; natural resources and conservation; psychology. **Areas of required coursework:** humanities, mathematics, English (including composition), sciences (biological or physical), social science. **Pre-professional programs:** pre-dentistry, pre-medicine, pre-veterinary science, pre-pharmacy. **Special academic programs (% participation):** cooperative (work-study plan) program (1%), cross-registration, distance learning (43%), double major (4%), dual enrollment (7%), external degree program, internships (23%), study abroad. **Cooperative education programs:** business, computer science, engineering, health professions, natural science, social/behavioral science, technologies, vocational arts. **Reserve Officers Training Corps**

(ROTC): Army ROTC: Offered at cooperating institution (Southern Oregon University). **Faculty and instruction (2009-2010):** Total instructional faculty: 134 full-time, 113 part-time (63% men; 37% women; 8% minorities). Full-time faculty with Ph.D. or other terminal degree: 45%. Student/faculty ratio: 20/1. Classes of fewer than 20 students: 53%; of 20 to 49 students: 43%; of 50 or more students: 4%. **Advanced Placement and International Baccalaureate credit:** AP tests may be used for: Credit only. Scores accepted: 3, 4, 5. International Baccalaureate exams may be used for: Placement only. **Freshmen returning for sophomore year:** 71%. **Graduation rates:** Four-year: 20%; five-year: 34%; six-year: 39%.

COSTS AND FINANCIAL AID

Financial aid office: (541) 885-1280. **Expenses (2010-2011):** Tuition and fees 2010-2011: $7,335 in state, $20,037 out of state; room/board: $8,600. Estimated books and supplies: $1,100; transportation: $1,500; personal expenses: $1,000. **Financial aid:** Priority filing date for institution's financial aid form: February 1. In 2009-2010, 92% of undergraduates applied for financial aid. Of those, 85% were determined to have financial need; 24% had their need fully met. Average financial aid package (proportion receiving): $5,554 (84%). Average amount of gift aid, such as scholarships or grants (proportion receiving): N/A (41%). Average amount of self-help aid, such as work study or loans (proportion receiving): N/A (60%). Among students who received need-based aid, the average percentage of need met: 19%. Among students who received aid based on merit, the average award (and the proportion receiving): $6,617 (0%). The average athletic scholarship (and the proportion receiving): $1,950 (0%). Average amount of debt of borrowers graduating in 2009: $27,266. Proportion who borrowed: 64%.

CAMPUS LIFE AND EXTRACURRICULAR ACTIVITIES

Campus housing available (% using): coed dorms (100%). Students who live in college-owned, operated, or affiliated housing: 13%. **Student employment:** During the 2009-2010 academic year, 13% of undergraduates worked on campus. **Clubs and organizations:** Number of student organizations: 52. Activities include: choral groups, pep band, radio station, student government, student newspaper, symphony orchestra, television station. Number of fraternities: 1; sororities: 0. Average proportion of students who stay on campus on weekends: 75%. **Sports program (2009-2010):** Member of NAIA. **Men's intercollegiate varsity sports:** baseball, basketball, cross country, soccer, track and field (outdoor). **Women's intercollegiate varsity sports:** basketball, cross country, soccer, softball, track and field (outdoor).

SERVICES AND FACILITIES

Basic services: nonremedial tutoring, placement service, health service, health insurance. **Remedial assistance:** reading, math, writing, study skills. **Counseling services:** minority student, career, personal, veteran student, academic, older student, psychological, birth control. **For learning-disabled students:** School does not offer a structured program with separate admission and additional fees. Services include: remedial math, reading machines, remedial reading, tape recorders, note-taking services, oral tests, learning center, readers, extended time for tests, tutors. **Library:** Number of titles: 260,884; number of current serial subscriptions: 2,451. **Information technology resources:** Students are not required to lease or own a computer. Number of campus computers available to all students: 694. School has a wireless network. Proportion of college-owned housing units wired for high-speed internet access: 100%. **Campus safety:** Security services offered: 24-hour foot-and-vehicle patrols, late-night transport/escort service, 24-hour emergency telephones, lighted pathways/sidewalks, student patrols, controlled dormitory access (key, security card, etc).

TRANSFER AND INTERNATIONAL STUDENTS

Transfer students: May apply for admission for the following academic terms: Fall, Winter, Spring, Summer. Applicants need a minimum number of credits to apply. For fall 2009: Transfer applications received: 704. Transfer applicants offered admission: 687. Transfer applicants enrolled: 493. **International students:** Number of foreign undergraduates: 23 (1% of student body). Minimum TOEFL score required: 520 (paper); 190 (computer).

Oregon State University

- **Address:** 104 Kerr Administration Building, Corvallis, OR 97331
- **Website:** http://oregonstate.edu
- **Public**
- **Enrollment:** 15,213 full-time; 2,854 part-time

KEY STATS

✔ **U.S News College Ranking:** 139, National Universities
✔ **SAT Score (25th/75th percentile):** 940-1190
✔ **Tuition:** 2009-2010: $6,727 in state, $19,651 out of state

Selectivity: Selective	**Room/board:** $8,352
Acceptance rate: 83%	**Average debt:** N/A
Student/faculty ratio: 22/1	**Proportion who borrowed:** N/A

UNDERGRADUATE STUDENT BODY STATS

2009-2010 enrollment: 15,213 full-time; 2,854 part-time. Men: 53%; women: 47%. **Ethnic makeup:** African American: 1%; American-Indian: 1%; Asian American: 9%; Hispanic: 5%; White: 81%; International: 2%.

ADMISSIONS FACTS AND FIGURES

Phone: (541) 737-4411. **Email:** osuadmit@oregonstate.edu. **Website:** http://oregonstate.edu. **Application deadlines for fall 2011:** Regular decision: September 1. Early decision: Not offered. Early action: Send application by: February 1; Decision sent by: March 15. Admission can be deferred. **Application fee:** $50. **To apply online, go to:** http://oregonstate.edu/admissions. **Admissions requirements/recommendations:** High school units required (recommended): English: 4; Mathematics: 3; Science: 2; Foreign language: 2; Social studies: 3; Total units: 14 (0). Tests: The college uses SAT or ACT scores in admissions decisions. Either SAT or ACT required. For admission to the fall 2011 entering class, the school will accept: ACT with writing required. Campus visit: Recommended. Admissions interview: Neither required nor recommended. Off-campus interview: May be arranged. **Factors that count in admissions decisions:** *Academic:* Secondary school record: Very Important. Class rank: Important. Letters of recommendation: Considered. Standardized test scores: Considered. Essay: Very Important. *Nonacademic:* Interview: Considered. Extracurricular activities: Considered. Talent/ability: Important. Character/personal qualities: Important. Alumni/ae relationship: Not Considered. Geographical residence: Not Considered. State residency: Not Considered. Religious affiliation/commitment: Not Considered. Minority status: Not Considered. Volunteer work: Important. Work experience: Considered. **Other schools with the greatest overlap in applicants:** Portland State University; University of California–Davis; University of Oregon; University of Washington; Washington State University. **Admissions statistics for the fall 2009 entering class:** Total applicants: 10,048. Total accepted: 8,303. Freshmen enrolled: 3,436; 19% were from out of state. Overall acceptance rate: 83%. Non-early acceptance rate: 83%. **Credentials of fall 2009 freshmen:** 24% ranked in the top 10 percent of their high school class; 52% were in the top 25 percent; 84% were in the top half. (Proportion submitting class standing: 45%.) **Average high school grade point average:** 3.5. **First-year students who submitted SAT scores:** 75%. Scores (25/75 percentile): Critical Reading: 460-580, Math: 480-610, Combined: 940-1190. **First-year students submitting ACT scores:** 32%. Scores (25/75 percentile): English: 19-25, Math: 20-27, Composite: 20-26.

ACADEMICS

Year founded: 1858. **Academic calendar:** Quarter. **Degrees offered:** certificate, bachelor's, post-bachelor's certificate, master's, post-master's certificate, doctorate. **Most popular majors:** 14% business administration and management, 5% health and physical education, 5% human development and family studies, 5% liberal arts and sciences/liberal studies, 4% biology/biological sciences. **Major fields of study:** agriculture, agriculture operations, and related sciences; area, ethnic, cultural, and gender studies; biological and biomedical sciences; business, management, marketing, and related support services; communication, journalism, and related programs; computer and information sciences and support services; education; engineering; English language and literature/letters; family and consumer sciences/human sciences; foreign languages, literatures, and linguistics; health professions and related clinical sciences; history; liberal arts and sciences studies, and humanities; mathematics and statistics; multi/interdisciplinary studies; natural resources and conservation; parks, recreation, leisure, and fitness studies; philosophy and religious studies; physical sciences; psychology; social sciences; visual and performing arts. **Areas of required**

coursework: humanities, mathematics, English (including composition), sciences (biological or physical), social science, other. **Pre-professional programs:** pre-dentistry, pre-medicine, pre-veterinary science, pre-optometry, pre-pharmacy, other. **Special academic programs (% participation):** accelerated program (30%), cooperative (work-study plan) program, cross-registration (24%), distance learning (59%), double major (18%), dual enrollment (22%), English as a Second Language (ESL) (2%), exchange student program (domestic) (1%), honors program (4%), independent study (4%), internships (26%), liberal arts/career combination, student-designed major (6%), study abroad (10%), teacher certificate program (5%). **Teacher certification offered in:** early childhood, elementary, vo-tech, middle/junior high, adult education, secondary, bilingual/bicultural. **Cooperative education programs:** agriculture, engineering, other. **Reserve Officers Training Corps (ROTC):** Army ROTC: Offered on campus; Navy ROTC: Offered on campus; Air Force ROTC: Offered on campus. **Faculty and instruction (2009-2010):** Total instructional faculty: 703 full-time, 492 part-time (59% men; 41% women; 12% minorities). Full-time faculty with Ph.D. or other terminal degree: 85%. Student/faculty ratio: 22/1. Classes of fewer than 20 students: 37%; of 20 to 49 students: 42%; of 50 or more students: 21%. **Advanced Placement and International Baccalaureate credit:** AP tests may be used for: Placement only. Scores accepted: 3, 4, 5. International Baccalaureate exams may be used for: Placement only. **Freshmen returning for sophomore year:** 82%. **Graduation rates:** Four-year: 27%; five-year: 52%; six-year: 60%. **Graduate study:** 27% of students pursue further study within one year.

COSTS AND FINANCIAL AID

Financial aid office: (541) 737-2241. **Expenses (2009-2010):** Tuition and fees 2009-2010: $6,727 in state, $19,651 out of state; room/board: $8,352. Estimated books and supplies: $1,603 personal expenses: $2,451. **Financial aid:** Priority filing date for institution's financial aid form: February 28. In 2009-2010, 71% of undergraduates applied for financial aid. Of those, 55% were determined to have financial need; 15% had their need fully met. Average financial aid package (proportion receiving): $9,856 (53%). Average amount of gift aid, such as scholarships or grants (proportion receiving): $2,957 (41%). Average amount of self-help aid, such as work study or loans (proportion receiving): $3,119 (47%). Average need-based loan (excluding PLUS or other private loans): $3,936. Among students who received need-based aid, the average percentage of need met: 62%. Among students who received aid based on merit, the average award (and the proportion receiving): $3,994 (0%). The average athletic scholarship (and the proportion receiving): $12,285 (3%).

CAMPUS LIFE AND EXTRACURRICULAR ACTIVITIES

Campus housing available (% using): coed dorms (71%), sorority housing, fraternity housing, apartments for married students, apartment for single students, special housing for disabled students, special housing for international students (3%), cooperative housing (6%), other housing options. Students who live in college-owned, operated, or affiliated housing: 21%. **Student employment:** During the 2009-2010 academic year, 23% of undergraduates worked on campus. Average per-year earnings: $3,400. **Clubs and organizations:** Number of student organizations: 300. Activities include: choral groups, concert band, dance, drama/theater, jazz band, literary magazine, marching band, music ensembles, musical theater, opera, pep band, radio station, student government, student newspaper, student film society, symphony orchestra, television station, yearbook. Number of fraternities: 21; sororities: 14. Proportion of men in fraternities: 9%; of women in sororities: 9%. Average proportion of students who stay on campus on weekends: 65%. **Sports program (2009-2010):** Member of NCAA I. *Men's intercollegiate varsity sports:* baseball, basketball, football, golf, soccer, wrestling. *Women's intercollegiate varsity sports:* basketball, crew (heavyweight), cross country, golf, gymnastics, crew (lightweight), soccer, softball, swimming, track and field (outdoor), volleyball.

SERVICES AND FACILITIES

Basic services: nonremedial tutoring, women's center, placement service, day care, health service, health insurance, other. **Remedial assistance:** math, writing, study skills, other. **Counseling services:** minority student, career, military, personal, veteran student, academic, older student, psychological, birth control. **For learning-disabled students:** School does not offer a structured program with separate admission and additional fees. Total undergraduates in learning-disabled program or receiving services: 113. Services include: remedial math, remedial English, remedial reading, tape recorders, other special classes, note-taking services, oral tests, learning center, readers, extended time for tests, priority registration, texts on tape, typist/scribe, other testing accommodations. **Library:** Number of titles: 1,614,197; number of current serial subscriptions: 53,303. **Information technology**

resources: Students are not required to lease or own a computer. Number of campus computers available to all students: 1,300. School has a wireless network. Approximate number of users that can be accommodated: 10,000. Proportion of college-owned housing units wired for high-speed internet access: 95%. **Campus safety:** Security services offered: 24-hour foot-and-vehicle patrols, late-night transport/escort service, 24-hour emergency telephones, lighted pathways/sidewalks, student patrols, controlled dormitory access (key, security card, etc).

TRANSFER AND INTERNATIONAL STUDENTS

Transfer students: May apply for admission for the following academic terms: Fall, Winter, Spring, Summer. Applicants need a minimum number of credits to apply. For fall 2009: Transfer applications received: 1,860. Transfer applicants offered admission: 1,543. Transfer applicants enrolled: 1,238. **International students:** Number of foreign undergraduates: 334 (2% of student body). Number of countries represented: 88. Minimum TOEFL score required: 550 (paper); 213 (computer).

Pacific Northwest College of Art

- ■ **Address:** 1241 N.W. Johnson, Portland, OR 97209
- ■ **Website:** http://www.pnca.edu
- ■ **Private**
- ■ **Enrollment:** N/A

KEY STATS

✔ **U.S News College Ranking:** Unranked Specialty School–Fine Arts
✔ **SAT or ACT Score (25th/75th percentile):** N/A
✔ **Tuition:** 2009-2010: $24,268

Selectivity: N/A	**Room/board:** $8,004
Acceptance rate: 51%	**Average debt:** N/A
Student/faculty ratio: N/A	**Proportion who borrowed:** N/A

Pacific University

- ■ **Address:** 2043 College Way, Forest Grove, OR 97116
- ■ **Website:** http://www.pacificu.edu
- ■ **Private**
- ■ **Enrollment:** 1,390 full-time; 84 part-time

KEY STATS

✔ **U.S News College Ranking:** 156, National Universities
✔ **SAT Score (25th/75th percentile):** 1010-1220
✔ **Tuition:** 2010-2011: $31,704

Selectivity: Selective	**Room/board:** $8,524
Acceptance rate: 78%	**Average debt:** $27,770
Student/faculty ratio: 11/1	**Proportion who borrowed:** 85%

UNDERGRADUATE STUDENT BODY STATS

2009-2010 enrollment: 1,390 full-time; 84 part-time. Men: 35%; women: 65%. **Ethnic makeup:** African American: 1%; American-Indian: 1%; Asian American: 23%; Hispanic: 5%; White: 68%; International: 2%.

ADMISSIONS FACTS AND FIGURES

Phone: (800) 677-6712. **Email:** admissions@pacificu.edu. **Website:** http://www.pacificu.edu. **Application deadlines for fall 2011:** Regular decision: August 15. Early decision: Not offered. Early action: Not offered. Admission can be deferred. **Application fee:** $40. **To apply online, go to:** http://www.pacificu.edu/admissions. **Admissions requirements/recommendations:** High school units required (recommended): English: (4); Mathematics: (3); Science: (3); Foreign language: (2); Social studies: (3); History: (1); Academic electives: (4); Total units: (21). Tests: The college uses SAT or ACT scores in admissions decisions. Either SAT or ACT required. For admission to the fall 2011 entering class, the school will accept: ACT with or without writing accepted. Campus visit: Recommended. Admissions interview: Recommended. Off-campus interview: May be arranged. **Factors that count in admissions decisions:** *Academic:* Secondary school record: Very Important. Class rank: Important. Letters of recommendation: Very Important. Standardized test scores: Very Important. Essay: Important. *Nonacademic:* Interview: Not Considered. Extracurricular activities: Very

Important. Talent/ability: Important. Character/personal qualities: Very Important. Alumni/ae relationship: Considered. Geographical residence: Not Considered. State residency: Not Considered. Religious affiliation/commitment: Not Considered. Minority status: Not Considered. Volunteer work: Very Important. Work experience: Considered. **Admissions statistics for the fall 2009 entering class:** Total applicants: 1,627. Total accepted: 1,275. Freshmen enrolled: 349; 51% were from out of state. Overall acceptance rate: 78%. **Credentials of fall 2009 freshmen:** 39% ranked in the top 10 percent of their high school class; 69% were in the top 25 percent; 95% were in the top half. (Proportion submitting class standing: 65%.) **Average high school grade point average:** 3.7. **First-year students who submitted SAT scores:** 85%. Scores (25/75 percentile): Critical Reading: 500-600, Math: 510-620, Combined: 1010-1220. **First-year students submitting ACT scores:** 47%. Scores (25/75 percentile): English: 20-27, Math: 21-27, Composite: 21-27.

ACADEMICS

Year founded: 1849. **Academic calendar:** Semester. **Degrees offered:** bachelor's, master's, doctorate. **Most popular majors:** 13% health professions and related clinical sciences, 10% parks, recreation, leisure, and fitness studies, 9% social sciences, 8% business, management, marketing, and related support services, 8% communication, journalism, and related programs. **Major fields of study:** biological and biomedical sciences; business, management, marketing, and related support services; communication, journalism, and related programs; computer and information sciences and support services; education; English language and literature/letters; foreign languages, literatures, and linguistics; health professions and related clinical sciences; history; liberal arts and sciences studies, and humanities; mathematics and statistics; multi/interdisciplinary studies; natural resources and conservation; parks, recreation, leisure, and fitness studies; philosophy and religious studies; physical sciences; psychology; public administration and social service professions; social sciences; visual and performing arts. **Areas of required coursework:** arts/fine arts, humanities, mathematics, English (including composition), foreign languages, sciences (biological or physical), social science, other. **Pre-professional programs:** pre-medicine, pre-optometry. **Special academic programs (% participation):** cross-registration (0%), double major (14%), English as a Second Language (ESL) (0%), independent study (44%), internships (32%), liberal arts/career combination (0%), study abroad (16%), teacher certificate program (7%). **Teacher certification offered in:** early childhood, elementary, middle/junior high, secondary. **Cooperative education programs:** engineering, health professions, natural science. **Reserve Officers Training Corps (ROTC):** Army ROTC: Offered at cooperating institution (Portland State University); Air Force ROTC: Offered at cooperating institution (University of Portland). **Faculty and instruction (2009-2010):** Total instructional faculty: 205 full-time, 148 part-time (47% men; 53% women; 13% minorities). Full-time faculty with Ph.D. or other terminal degree: 83%. Student/faculty ratio: 11/1. Classes of fewer than 20 students: 65%; of 20 to 49 students: 32%; of 50 or more students: 3%. **Advanced Placement and International Baccalaureate credit:** AP tests may be used for: Placement only. Scores accepted: 4. International Baccalaureate exams may be used for: Placement only. **Freshmen returning for sophomore year:** 79%. **Graduation rates:** Four-year: 52%; five-year: 58%; six-year: 60%. **Graduate study:** 30% of students pursue further study immediately upon graduation; 40% within one year; 45% within five years. Fields in which graduates pursue further study: Master of Business Administration (MBA), 1%; law, 2%; medicine, 2%; dentistry, 1%; engineering, 1%; theology (or the seminary), 1%; education, 6%; arts and sciences, 6%; veterinary medicine, 1%.

COSTS AND FINANCIAL AID

Financial aid office: (503) 352-2222. **Expenses (2010-2011):** Tuition and fees 2010-2011: $31,704; room/board: $8,524. Estimated books and supplies: $1,000; transportation: $690; personal expenses: $900. **Financial aid:** Priority filing date for institution's financial aid form: March 1. In 2009-2010, 90% of undergraduates applied for financial aid. Of those, 80% were determined to have financial need; 24% had their need fully met. Average financial aid package (proportion receiving): $23,485 (80%). Average amount of gift aid, such as scholarships or grants (proportion receiving): $14,309 (74%). Average amount of self-help aid, such as work study or loans (proportion receiving): $5,893 (73%). Average need-based loan (excluding PLUS or other private loans): $4,448. Among students who received need-based aid, the average percentage of need met: 83%. Among students who received aid based on merit, the average award (and the proportion receiving): $10,908 (19%). The average athletic scholarship (and the proportion receiving): $0 (0%). Average amount of debt of borrowers graduating in 2009: $27,770. Proportion who borrowed: 85%.

CAMPUS LIFE AND EXTRACURRICULAR ACTIVITIES

Campus housing available (% using): coed dorms (100%), apartment for single students, special housing for disabled students, other housing options. Students who live in college-owned, operated, or affiliated housing: 58%. **Clubs and organizations:** Number of student organizations: 59. Activities include: campus ministries, choral groups, concert band, dance, drama/theater, international student organization, jazz band, literary magazine, music ensembles, musical theater, pep band, radio station, student government, student newspaper, student film society, symphony orchestra. Number of fraternities: 3; sororities: 4. Proportion of men in fraternities: 8%; of women in sororities: 10%. Average proportion of students who stay on campus on weekends: 60%. **Sports program (2009-2010):** Member of NCAA III. *Men's intercollegiate varsity sports:* baseball, basketball, cross country, golf, soccer, swimming, tennis, track and field (outdoor), wrestling. *Women's intercollegiate varsity sports:* basketball, cross country, golf, lacrosse, soccer, softball, swimming, tennis, track and field (outdoor), volleyball.

SERVICES AND FACILITIES

Basic services: nonremedial tutoring, women's center, placement service, health service, health insurance. **Remedial assistance:** math, writing. **Counseling services:** minority student, career, personal, veteran student, academic, older student, psychological, birth control. **For learning-disabled students:** School does not offer a structured program with separate admission and additional fees. Services include: other special classes, untimed tests, note-taking services, oral tests, readers, extended time for tests, tutors, priority seating, texts on tape, other testing accommodations. **Library:** Number of titles: 211,912; number of current serial subscriptions: 1,209. **Information technology resources:** Students are not required to lease or own a computer. Number of campus computers available to all students: 315. School has a wireless network. Approximate number of users that can be accommodated: 11,000. Proportion of college-owned housing units wired for high-speed internet access: 100%. **Campus safety:** Security services offered: 24-hour foot-and-vehicle patrols, late-night transport/escort service, 24-hour emergency telephones, lighted pathways/sidewalks, controlled dormitory access (key, security card, etc).

TRANSFER AND INTERNATIONAL STUDENTS

Transfer students: May apply for admission for the following academic terms: Fall, Spring. Applicants need a minimum number of credits to apply. For fall 2009: Transfer applications received: 254. Transfer applicants offered admission: 180. Transfer applicants enrolled: 84. **International students:** Number of foreign undergraduates: 32 (2% of student body). Number of countries represented: 15. Minimum TOEFL score required: 550 (paper); 213 (computer). Average TOEFL score: 560 (paper).

Portland State University

- **Address:** PO Box 751, Portland, OR 97207-0751
- **Website:** http://www.pdx.edu
- **Public**
- **Enrollment:** 14,018 full-time; 7,600 part-time

KEY STATS

✔ **U.S News College Ranking:** second tier, National Universities
✔ **SAT Score (25th/75th percentile):** 920-1160
✔ **Tuition:** 2009-2010: $6,765 in state, $21,198 out of state

Selectivity: Selective	**Room/board:** $9,135
Acceptance rate: 79%	**Average debt:** $22,440
Student/faculty ratio: 20/1	**Proportion who borrowed:** 58%

UNDERGRADUATE STUDENT BODY STATS

2009-2010 enrollment: 14,018 full-time; 7,600 part-time. Men: 47%; women: 53%. **Ethnic makeup:** African American: 3%; American-Indian: 1%; Asian American: 9%; Hispanic: 5%; White: 76%; International: 4%.

ADMISSIONS FACTS AND FIGURES

Phone: (503) 725-3511. **Email:** admissions@pdx.edu. **Website:** http://www.pdx.edu. **Application deadlines for fall 2011:** Regular decision: Rolling. Early decision: Not offered. Early action: Not offered. Admission can be deferred. **Application fee:** $50. **To apply online, go to:** http://www.pdx.edu/admissions/apply.html/. **Admissions requirements/recommendations:** High school units required (recommended): English: 4; Mathematics: 3; Science: 2; Foreign language: 2; Social studies: 2; History: 1; Academic electives: 0;

Total units: 14 (1). Tests: The college uses SAT or ACT scores in admissions decisions. Either SAT or ACT required. For admission to the fall 2011 entering class, the school will accept: ACT with writing required. Campus visit: Recommended. Admissions interview: Neither required nor recommended. Off-campus interview: May be arranged. **Factors that count in admissions decisions:** *Academic:* Secondary school record: Very Important. Class rank: Not Considered. Letters of recommendation: Not Considered. Standardized test scores: Considered. Essay: Not Considered. *Nonacademic:* Interview: Not Considered. Extracurricular activities: Not Considered. Talent/ability: Not Considered. Character/personal qualities: Not Considered. Alumni/ae relationship: Not Considered. Geographical residence: Not Considered. State residency: Not Considered. Religious affiliation/commitment: Not Considered. Minority status: Not Considered. Volunteer work: Not Considered. Work experience: Not Considered. **Other schools with the greatest overlap in applicants:** Oregon State University; University of Oregon; University of Portland; University of Washington; Washington State University. **Admissions statistics for the fall 2009 entering class:** Total applicants: 5,088. Total accepted: 4,001. Freshmen enrolled: 1,675; Overall acceptance rate: 79%. **Average high school grade point average:** 3.3. **First-year students who submitted SAT scores:** 71%. Scores (25/75 percentile): Critical Reading: 460-590, Math: 460-570, Combined: 920-1160. **First-year students submitting ACT scores:** 31%. Scores (25/75 percentile): English: 18-25, Math: 18-24, Composite: 18-24.

ACADEMICS

Year founded: 1946. **Academic calendar:** Quarter. **Degrees offered:** certificate, bachelor's, post-bachelor's certificate, master's, doctorate. **Most popular majors:** 10% liberal arts and sciences studies, and humanities, 9% business administration, management, and operations, 8% social sciences, 7% psychology, 5% marketing. **Major fields of study:** architecture and related services; area, ethnic, cultural, and gender studies; biological and biomedical sciences; business, management, marketing, and related support services; communication, journalism, and related programs; computer and information sciences and support services; engineering; engineering technologies/technicians; English language and literature/letters; family and consumer sciences/human sciences; foreign languages, literatures, and linguistics; health professions and related clinical sciences; liberal arts and sciences studies, and humanities; mathematics and statistics; natural resources and conservation; parks, recreation, leisure, and fitness studies; philosophy and religious studies; physical sciences; psychology; public administration and social service professions; social sciences; visual and performing arts. **Areas of required coursework:** humanities, computer literacy, mathematics, English (including composition), philosophy, sciences (biological or physical), history, social science, other. **Pre-professional programs:** pre-law, pre-dentistry, pre-medicine, pre-veterinary science, pre-optometry, pre-pharmacy, other. **Special academic programs (% participation):** distance learning (50%), double major (10.8%), dual enrollment, English as a Second Language (ESL) (1.5%), exchange student program (domestic), honors program (.6%), independent study (24.2%), internships (14.8%), study abroad (6.2%), teacher certificate program. **Teacher certification offered in:** early childhood, special education, elementary, middle/junior high, adult education, secondary, bilingual/bicultural. **Cooperative education programs:** art, business, computer science, education, engineering, health professions, humanities, natural science, social/behavioral science, technologies. **Reserve Officers Training Corps (ROTC):** Army ROTC: Offered on campus; Air Force ROTC: Offered at cooperating institution (University of Portland). **Faculty and instruction (2009-2010):** Total instructional faculty: 837 full-time, 620 part-time (52% men; 48% women; 11% minorities). Full-time faculty with Ph.D. or other terminal degree: 76%. Student/faculty ratio: 20/1. Classes of fewer than 20 students: 31%; of 20 to 49 students: 54%; of 50 or more students: 15%. **Advanced Placement and International Baccalaureate credit:** AP tests may be used for: Placement only. International Baccalaureate exams may be used for: Placement only. **Freshmen returning for sophomore year:** 68%. **Graduation rates:** Four-year: 8%; five-year: 22%; six-year: 31%.

COSTS AND FINANCIAL AID

Financial aid office: (503) 725-3461. **Expenses (2009-2010):** Tuition and fees 2009-2010: $6,765 in state, $21,198 out of state; room/board: $9,135. Estimated books and supplies: $1,911; transportation: $900; personal expenses: $2,061. **Financial aid:** Priority filing date for institution's financial aid form: February 28. In 2009-2010, 71% of undergraduates applied for financial aid. Of those, 61% were determined to have financial need; 8% had their need fully met. Average financial aid package (proportion receiving): $9,343 (61%). Average amount of gift aid, such as scholarships or grants (proportion receiving): $6,302 (44%). Average amount of self-help aid, such as work study or loans (proportion receiving): $4,752 (57%).

Average need-based loan (excluding PLUS or other private loans): $4,536. Among students who received need-based aid, the average percentage of need met: 61%. Among students who received aid based on merit, the average award (and the proportion receiving): $1,988 (1%). The average athletic scholarship (and the proportion receiving): $14,934 (1%). Average amount of debt of borrowers graduating in 2009: $22,440. Proportion who borrowed: 58%.

CAMPUS LIFE AND EXTRACURRICULAR ACTIVITIES

Campus housing available: coed dorms, sorority housing, fraternity housing, apartments for married students, apartment for single students, special housing for disabled students, special housing for international students, other housing options. **Clubs and organizations:** Number of student organizations: 200. Activities include: campus ministries, choral groups, concert band, dance, drama/theater, international student organization, jazz band, literary magazine, model UN, music ensembles, musical theater, opera, pep band, radio station, student government, student newspaper, student film society, symphony orchestra. Number of fraternities: 4; sororities: 4. Average proportion of students who stay on campus on weekends: 10%. **Sports program (2009-2010):** Member of NCAA I.

SERVICES AND FACILITIES

Basic services: nonremedial tutoring, women's center, day care, health service, health insurance. **Remedial assistance:** math, writing, study skills. **Counseling services:** minority student, career, military, personal, veteran student, academic, older student, psychological, birth control, religious, other. **For learning-disabled students:** School does not offer a structured program with separate admission and additional fees. Services include: remedial math, remedial English, remedial reading, note-taking services, learning center, extended time for tests, tutors. **Library:** Number of titles: 1,365,233; number of current serial subscriptions: 4,643. **Information technology resources:** Students are not required to lease or own a computer. Number of campus computers available to all students: 875. School has a wireless network. Proportion of college-owned housing units wired for high-speed internet access: 100%. **Campus safety:** Security services offered: 24-hour foot-and-vehicle patrols, late-night transport/escort service, 24-hour emergency telephones, lighted pathways/sidewalks, controlled dormitory access (key, security card, etc).

TRANSFER AND INTERNATIONAL STUDENTS

Transfer students: May apply for admission for the following academic terms: Fall, Winter, Spring, Summer. Applicants need a minimum number of credits to apply. For fall 2009: Transfer applications received: 4,775. Transfer applicants offered admission: 3,930. Transfer applicants enrolled: 3,486. **International students:** Number of foreign undergraduates: 818 (4% of student body). Number of countries represented: 84. Minimum TOEFL score required: 525 (paper); 197 (computer).

Reed College

- **Address:** 3203 S.E. Woodstock Boulevard, Portland, OR 97202
- **Website:** http://www.reed.edu/
- Private
- **Enrollment:** 1,406 full-time; 46 part-time

KEY STATS

✔ **U.S News College Ranking:** 54, National Liberal Arts Colleges
✔ **SAT Score (25th/75th percentile):** 1280-1470
✔ **Tuition:** 2010-2011: $39,700
  Selectivity: More selective   **Room/board:** $10,250
  Acceptance rate: 41%   **Average debt:** $20,750
  Student/faculty ratio: 10/1   **Proportion who borrowed:** 53%

UNDERGRADUATE STUDENT BODY STATS

2009-2010 enrollment: 1,406 full-time; 46 part-time. Men: 45%; women: 55%. **Ethnic makeup:** African American: 3%; American-Indian: 1%; Asian American: 9%; Hispanic: 7%; White: 73%; International: 6%.

ADMISSIONS FACTS AND FIGURES

Phone: (503) 777-7511. **Email:** admission@reed.edu. **Website:** http://www.reed.edu/. **Application deadlines for fall 2011:** Regular decision: January 15; decision sent by April 1. Early decision: Send application by: November 15; Decision sent by: December 15. Early action: Not offered. Admission can be deferred. **Application fee:** $50. **To apply online, go to:** http://web.reed. edu/apply/application.html. **Admissions requirements/recommendations:** High school units required (recommended): English: (4); Mathematics: (4); Science: (3); Foreign language: (3); Social studies: (3); History: (3). Tests: The college uses SAT or ACT scores in admissions decisions. Either SAT or ACT required. For admission to the fall 2011 entering class, the school will accept: ACT with or without writing accepted. **Factors that count in admissions decisions:** *Academic:* Secondary school record: Very Important. Class rank: Important. Letters of recommendation: Important. Standardized test scores: Important. Essay: Very Important. *Nonacademic:* Interview: Important. Extracurricular activities: Considered. Talent/ability: Considered. Character/personal qualities: Considered. Alumni/ae relationship: Considered. Geographical residence: Considered. State residency: Not Considered. Religious affiliation/commitment: Not Considered. Minority status: Considered. Volunteer work: Considered. Work experience: Considered. **Admissions statistics for the fall 2009 entering class:** Total applicants: 3,161. Total accepted: 1,281. Freshmen enrolled: 368; 92% were from out of state. Overall acceptance rate: 41%. Early-decision acceptance rate: 51%. Non-early acceptance rate: 40%. **Size of waiting list:** 838 applicants; enrolled from waiting list: 30. **Credentials of fall 2009 freshmen:** 59% ranked in the top 10 percent of their high school class; 86% were in the top 25 percent; 99% were in the top half. (Proportion submitting class standing: 31%.) **Average high school grade point average:** 3.9. **First-year students who submitted SAT scores:** 93%. Scores (25/75 percentile): Critical Reading: 660-760, Math: 620-710, Combined: 1280-1470. **First-year students submitting ACT scores:** 34%. Scores (25/75 percentile): English: 27-32, Math: 30-35, Composite: 29-33.

ACADEMICS

Year founded: 1911. **Academic calendar:** Semester. **Degrees offered:** bachelor's, master's. **Most popular majors:** 18% social sciences, 13% English language and literature/letters, 13% foreign languages, literatures, and linguistics, 11% biological and biomedical sciences, 8% psychology. **Major fields of study:** area, ethnic, cultural, and gender studies; biological and biomedical sciences; English language and literature/letters; foreign languages, literatures, and linguistics; history; mathematics and statistics; multi/interdisciplinary studies; philosophy and religious studies; physical sciences; psychology; social sciences; visual and performing arts. **Areas of required coursework:** arts/fine arts, humanities, English (including composition), philosophy, foreign languages, sciences (biological or physical), social science, other. **Special academic programs:** cross-registration, double major, dual enrollment, exchange student program (domestic), independent study, internships, liberal arts/career combination, study abroad, other. **Faculty and instruction (2009-2010):** Total instructional faculty: 121 full-time, 12 part-time (62% men; 38% women; 11% minorities). Full-time faculty with Ph.D. or other terminal degree: 91%. Student/faculty ratio: 10/1. Classes of fewer than 20 students: 72%; of 20 to 49 students: 24%; of 50 or more students: 4%. **Freshmen returning for sophomore year:** 89%. **Graduation rates:** Four-year: 57%; five-year: 76%; six-year: 78%.

COSTS AND FINANCIAL AID

Financial aid office: (503) 777-7223. **Expenses (2010-2011):** Tuition and fees 2010-2011: $39,700; room/board: $10,250. Estimated books and supplies: $950 personal expenses: $900. **Financial aid:** Priority filing date for institution's financial aid form: January 15; deadline: January 15. In 2009-2010, 60% of undergraduates applied for financial aid. Of those, 52% were determined to have financial need; 98% had their need fully met. Average financial aid package (proportion receiving): $33,090 (52%). Average amount of gift aid, such as scholarships or grants (proportion receiving): $30,710 (48%). Average amount of self-help aid, such as work study or loans (proportion receiving): $4,965 (48%). Average need-based loan (excluding PLUS or other private loans): $4,234. Among students who received need-based aid, the average percentage of need met: 100%. Among students who received aid based on merit, the average award (and the proportion receiving): $0 (0%). The average athletic scholarship (and the proportion receiving): $0 (0%). Average amount of debt of borrowers graduating in 2009: $20,750. Proportion who borrowed: 53%.

CAMPUS LIFE AND EXTRACURRICULAR ACTIVITIES

Campus housing available: coed dorms, women's dorms, apartment for single students, special housing for disabled students, cooperative housing, other housing options. Students who live in college-owned, operated, or affiliated housing: 67%. Activities include: campus ministries, choral groups, dance, drama/theater, international student organization, literary magazine, model UN, music ensembles, radio station, student government, student newspaper, student film society, symphony orchestra.

SERVICES AND FACILITIES

Library: Number of titles: 528,090; number of current serial subscriptions: 10,232.

TRANSFER AND INTERNATIONAL STUDENTS

Transfer students: May apply for admission for the following academic terms: Fall, Winter, Spring. Applicants need a minimum number of credits to apply. For fall 2009: Transfer applications received: 252. Transfer applicants offered admission: 82. Transfer applicants enrolled: 41. **International students:** Number of foreign undergraduates: 90 (6% of student body).

Southern Oregon University

- **Address:** 1250 Siskiyou Boulevard, Ashland, OR 97520
- **Website:** http://www.sou.edu
- **Public**
- **Enrollment:** 3,365 full-time; 1,061 part-time

KEY STATS

✔ **U.S News College Ranking:** 80, Regional Universities (West)
✔ **SAT Score (25th/75th percentile):** 890-1040
✔ **Tuition:** 2009-2010: $6,252 in state, $19,914 out of state

Selectivity: Less selective	**Room/board:** $8,454
Acceptance rate: 89%	**Average debt:** N/A
Student/faculty ratio: N/A	**Proportion who borrowed:** N/A

UNDERGRADUATE STUDENT BODY STATS

2009-2010 enrollment: 3,365 full-time; 1,061 part-time. Men: 43%; women: 57%. **Ethnic makeup:** African American: 2%; American-Indian: 2%; Asian American: 5%; Hispanic: 5%; White: 84%; International: 2%.

ADMISSIONS FACTS AND FIGURES

Phone: (541) 552-6411. **Email:** admissions@sou.edu. **Website:** http://www. sou.edu. **Application deadlines for fall 2011:** Regular decision: Rolling. Early decision: Not offered. Early action: Not offered. Admission can be deferred. **Application fee:** $50. **To apply online, go to:** http://www.sou.edu/admissions/. **Admissions requirements/recommendations:** High school units required (recommended): English: 4; Mathematics: 3; Science: 2; Foreign language: 2; Social studies: 3; Total units: 14. Tests: The college uses SAT or ACT scores in admissions decisions. Either SAT or ACT required. For admission to the fall 2011 entering class, the school will accept: ACT with writing required. Campus visit: Recommended. Admissions interview: Neither required nor recommended. Off-campus interview: Not available. **Factors that count in admissions decisions:** *Academic:* Secondary school record: Very Important. Class rank: Not Considered. Letters of recommendation: Considered. Standardized test scores: Very Important. Essay: Considered. *Nonacademic:* Interview: Not Considered. Extracurricular activities: Considered. Talent/ability: Considered. Character/personal qualities: Considered. Alumni/ae relationship: Not Considered. Geographical residence: Not Considered. State residency: Not Considered. Religious affiliation/commitment: Not Considered. Minority status: Not Considered. Volunteer work: Considered. Work experience: Considered. **Other schools with the greatest overlap in applicants:** Eastern Oregon University; Oregon State University; Portland State University; University of Oregon; Western Oregon University. **Admissions statistics for the fall 2009 entering class:** Total applicants: 1,610. Total accepted: 1,429. Freshmen enrolled: 706; Overall acceptance rate: 89%. **First-year students who submitted SAT scores:** 78%. Scores (25/75 percentile): Critical Reading: 450-480, Math: 440-560, Combined: 890-1040. **First-year students submitting ACT scores:** 22%. Scores (25/75 percentile): English: N/A, Math: N/A, Composite: 18-24.

ACADEMICS

Year founded: 1926. **Academic calendar:** Quarter. **Degrees offered:** bachelor's, post-bachelor's certificate, master's. **Major fields of study:** biological and biomedical sciences; business, management, marketing, and related support services; communication, journalism, and related programs; communications technologies/technicians and support services; computer and information sciences and support services; education; English language and literature/letters; foreign languages, literatures, and linguistics; history; multi/interdisciplinary studies; natural resources and conservation; physical sciences; psychology; security and protective services; social sciences; visual and performing arts. **Areas of required coursework:** arts/fine arts, humanities, computer literacy, mathematics, English (including composition), sciences (biological or physical), social science. **Pre-professional programs:** pre-law, pre-dentistry, pre-medicine, pre-theology, pre-veterinary science, pre-optometry, pre-pharmacy, other. **Special academic programs:** accelerated program, cooperative (work-study plan) program, cross-registration, distance learning, double major, dual enrollment, English as a Second Language (ESL), exchange student program (domestic), external degree program, honors program, independent study, internships, liberal arts/career combination, student-designed major, study abroad, teacher certificate program. **Teacher certification offered in:** early childhood, special education, elementary, middle/junior high, secondary, bilingual/bicultural. **Cooperative education programs:** other. **Reserve Officers Training Corps (ROTC):** Army ROTC: Offered on campus. **Advanced Placement and International Baccalaureate credit:** AP tests may be used for: Placement only. Scores accepted: 3, 4, 5. International Baccalaureate exams may be used for: Placement only. **Freshmen returning for sophomore year:** 66%. **Graduation rates:** Six-year: 36%.

COSTS AND FINANCIAL AID

Financial aid office: (541) 552-6754. **Expenses (2009-2010):** Tuition and fees 2009-2010: $6,252 in state, $19,914 out of state; room/board: $8,454. Estimated books and supplies: $1,350. **Financial aid:** Priority filing date for institution's financial aid form: March 1.

CAMPUS LIFE AND EXTRACURRICULAR ACTIVITIES

Campus housing available: coed dorms, apartments for married students, apartment for single students, special housing for disabled students, special housing for international students, other housing options. **Clubs and organizations:** Number of student organizations: 70. Activities include: choral groups, concert band, dance, drama/theater, jazz band, literary magazine, music ensembles, musical theater, opera, pep band, radio station, student government, student newspaper, symphony orchestra, television station. Number of fraternities: 0; sororities: 0. **Sports program (2009-2010):** Member of NAIA.

SERVICES AND FACILITIES

Basic services: nonremedial tutoring, women's center, placement service, day care, health service, health insurance. **Remedial assistance:** math. **Counseling services:** minority student, career, military, personal, veteran student, academic, older student, psychological, birth control. **For learning-disabled students:** School offers a structured program with separate admission and additional fees. Services include: remedial math, reading machines, tape recorders, other special classes, note-taking services, oral tests, learning center, readers, extended time for tests, tutors, priority registration, texts on tape, other testing accommodations. **Information technology resources:** Students are not required to lease or own a computer. Number of campus computers available to all students: 1,000. School has a wireless network. Proportion of college-owned housing units wired for high-speed internet access: 95%. **Campus safety:** Security services offered: 24-hour foot-and-vehicle patrols, late-night transport/escort service, 24-hour emergency telephones, lighted pathways/sidewalks, controlled dormitory access (key, security card, etc).

TRANSFER AND INTERNATIONAL STUDENTS

Transfer students: May apply for admission for the following academic terms: Fall, Winter, Spring, Summer. Applicants need a minimum number of credits to apply. **International students:** Number of foreign undergraduates: 72 (2% of student body). Minimum TOEFL score required: 520 (paper).

University of Oregon

- **Address:** 1226 University of Oregon, Eugene, OR 97403-1226
- **Website:** http://www.uoregon.edu
- **Public**
- **Enrollment:** 16,971 full-time; 1,538 part-time

KEY STATS

✔ **U.S News College Ranking:** 111, National Universities
✔ **SAT Score (25th/75th percentile):** 990-1225
✔ **Tuition:** 2009-2010: $7,430 in state, $23,720 out of state
Selectivity: Selective   **Room/board:** $8,939
Acceptance rate: 80%   **Average debt:** $19,336
Student/faculty ratio: 20/1   **Proportion who borrowed:** 55%

UNDERGRADUATE STUDENT BODY STATS

2009-2010 enrollment: 16,971 full-time; 1,538 part-time. Men: 50%; women: 50%. **Ethnic makeup:** African American: 2%; American-Indian: 1%; Asian American: 6%; Hispanic: 4%; White: 81%; International: 6%.

ADMISSIONS FACTS AND FIGURES

Phone: (800) 232-3825. **Email:** uoadmit@uoregon.edu. **Website:** http://www.uoregon.edu. **Application deadlines for fall 2011:** Regular decision: January 15. Early decision: Not offered. Early action: Send application by: November 1; Decision sent by: December 15. Admission cannot be deferred. **Application fee:** $50. **To apply online, go to:** http://admissions.uoregon.edu/apply. **Admissions requirements/recommendations:** High school units required (recommended): English: 4; Mathematics: 3; Science: 2; Foreign language: 2; Social studies: 3; Total units: 14 (16). Tests: The college uses SAT or ACT scores in admissions decisions. Either SAT or ACT required. For admission to the fall 2011 entering class, the school will accept: ACT with writing required. Campus visit: Neither required nor recommended. Admissions interview: Neither required nor recommended. Off-campus interview: Not available. **Factors that count in admissions decisions:** *Academic:* Secondary school record: Very Important. Class rank: Considered. Letters of recommendation: Considered. Standardized test scores: Considered. Essay: Considered. *Nonacademic:* Interview: Not Considered. Extracurricular activities: Considered. Talent/ability: Considered. Character/personal qualities: Not Considered. Alumni/ae relationship: Not Considered. Geographical residence: Considered. State residency: Considered. Religious affiliation/commitment: Not Considered. Minority status: Considered. Volunteer work: Considered. Work experience: Considered. **Other schools with the greatest overlap in applicants:** Oregon State University; University of California–Davis; University of California–Santa Barbara; University of Colorado–Boulder; University of Washington. **Admissions statistics for the fall 2009 entering class:** Total applicants: 16,780. Total accepted: 13,367. Freshmen enrolled: 3,839; 39% were from out of state. Overall acceptance rate: 80%. Non-early acceptance rate: 80%. **Credentials of fall 2009 freshmen:** 28% ranked in the top 10 percent of their high school class; 62% were in the top 25 percent; 93% were in the top half. (Proportion submitting class standing: 43%.) **Average high school grade point average:** 3.5. **First-year students who submitted SAT scores:** 83%. Scores (25/75 percentile): Critical Reading: 492-611, Math: 498-614, Combined: 990-1225.

ACADEMICS

Year founded: 1876. **Academic calendar:** Quarter. **Degrees offered:** bachelor's, post-bachelor's certificate, master's, post-master's certificate, doctorate. **Most popular majors:** 10% business/commerce, 9% journalism, 8% psychology, 7% political science and government, 6% sociology. **Major fields of study:** architecture and related services; area, ethnic, cultural, and gender studies; biological and biomedical sciences; business, management, marketing, and related support services; communication, journalism, and related programs; computer and information sciences and support services; education; English language and literature/letters; foreign languages, literatures, and linguistics; health professions and related clinical sciences; history; liberal arts and sciences studies, and humanities; mathematics and statistics; multi/interdisciplinary studies; natural resources and conservation; philosophy and religious studies; physical sciences; psychology; public administration and social service professions; social sciences; visual and performing arts. **Areas of required coursework:** humanities, English (including composition), sciences (biological or physical), social science, other. **Pre-professional programs:** pre-law, pre-dentistry, pre-medicine, pre-veterinary science, pre-optometry, pre-pharmacy, other. **Special academic programs:**

cross-registration, distance learning, double major, dual enrollment, English as a Second Language (ESL), exchange student program (domestic), honors program, independent study, internships, liberal arts/career combination, student-designed major, study abroad, teacher certificate program, other. **Teacher certification offered in:** early childhood, special education, elementary, middle/junior high, secondary, bilingual/bicultural. **Reserve Officers Training Corps (ROTC):** Army ROTC: Offered on campus; Air Force ROTC: Offered at cooperating institution (Oregon State University). **Faculty and instruction (2009-2010):** Total instructional faculty: 892 full-time, 382 part-time (56% men; 44% women; 14% minorities). Full-time faculty with Ph.D. or other terminal degree: 96%. Student/faculty ratio: 20/1. Classes of fewer than 20 students: 37%; of 20 to 49 students: 46%; of 50 or more students: 17%. **Advanced Placement and International Baccalaureate credit:** AP tests may be used for: Credit and/or placement. Scores accepted: 3, 4, 5. International Baccalaureate exams may be used for: Credit and/or placement. **Freshmen returning for sophomore year:** 83%. **Graduation rates:** Four-year: 46%; five-year: 66%; six-year: 70%. **Graduate study:** 28% of students pursue further study within one year.

COSTS AND FINANCIAL AID

Financial aid office: (541) 346-3221. **Expenses (2009-2010):** Tuition and fees 2009-2010: $7,430 in state, $23,720 out of state; room/board: $8,939. Estimated books and supplies: $1,050 personal expenses: $2,412. **Financial aid:** Priority filing date for institution's financial aid form: March 1. In 2009-2010, 59% of undergraduates applied for financial aid. Of those, 43% were determined to have financial need; 13% had their need fully met. Average financial aid package (proportion receiving): $9,168 (41%). Average amount of gift aid, such as scholarships or grants (proportion receiving): $6,321 (23%). Average amount of self-help aid, such as work study or loans (proportion receiving): $4,679 (35%). Average need-based loan (excluding PLUS or other private loans): $4,471. Among students who received need-based aid, the average percentage of need met: 63%. Among students who received aid based on merit, the average award (and the proportion receiving): $2,544 (6%). The average athletic scholarship (and the proportion receiving): $22,219 (2%). Average amount of debt of borrowers graduating in 2009: $19,336. Proportion who borrowed: 55%.

CAMPUS LIFE AND EXTRACURRICULAR ACTIVITIES

Campus housing available: coed dorms, sorority housing, fraternity housing, apartments for married students, apartment for single students, cooperative housing, other housing options. Students who live in college-owned, operated, or affiliated housing: 20%. **Student employment:** During the 2009-2010 academic year, 13% of undergraduates worked on campus. Average per-year earnings: $4,502. **Clubs and organizations:** Number of student organizations: 250. Activities include: campus ministries, choral groups, concert band, dance, drama/theater, international student organization, jazz band, literary magazine, marching band, music ensembles, musical theater, opera, pep band, radio station, student government, student newspaper, student film society, symphony orchestra. Number of fraternities: 12; sororities: 10. Proportion of men in fraternities: 9%; of women in sororities: 13%. Average proportion of students who stay on campus on weekends: 80%. **Sports program (2009-2010):** Member of NCAA I. ***Men's intercollegiate varsity sports:*** baseball, basketball, cross country, football, golf, tennis, track and field (indoor), track and field (outdoor). ***Women's intercollegiate varsity sports:*** basketball, cross country, golf, gymnastics, lacrosse, soccer, softball, tennis, track and field (indoor), track and field (outdoor), volleyball.

SERVICES AND FACILITIES

Basic services: nonremedial tutoring, women's center, placement service, day care, health service, health insurance. **Counseling services:** minority student, career, military, personal, veteran student, academic, older student, psychological, birth control. **For learning-disabled students:** School does not offer a structured program with separate admission and additional fees. Total undergraduates in learning-disabled program or receiving services: 250. Services include: reading machines, tape recorders, untimed tests, note-taking services, oral tests, learning center, readers, extended time for tests, tutors, priority seating, texts on tape, other testing accommodations, other. **Library:** Number of titles: 3,083,407; number of current serial subscriptions: 46,879. **Information technology resources:** Students are not required to lease or own a computer. Number of campus computers available to all students: 1,800. School has a wireless network. Approximate number of users that can be accommodated: 10,000. Proportion of college-owned housing units wired for high-speed internet access: 90%. **Campus safety:** Security services offered: 24-hour foot-and-vehicle patrols, late-night transport/escort service, 24-hour emergency telephones, lighted pathways/ sidewalks, student patrols, controlled dormitory access (key, security card, etc).

TRANSFER AND INTERNATIONAL STUDENTS

Transfer students: May apply for admission for the following academic terms: Fall, Winter, Spring, Summer. Applicants need a minimum number of credits to apply. For fall 2009: Transfer applications received: 3,334. Transfer applicants offered admission: 2,123. Transfer applicants enrolled: 1,360. **International students:** Number of foreign undergraduates: 1019 (6% of student body). Number of countries represented: 65. Minimum TOEFL score required: 500 (paper); 88 (computer). Average TOEFL score: 515 (paper).

University of Portland

- **Address:** 5000 N. Willamette Boulevard, Portland, OR 97203
- **Website:** http://www.up.edu
- **Private; Religious affiliation:** Roman Catholic
- **Enrollment:** 3,038 full-time; 68 part-time

KEY STATS
✔ **U.S News College Ranking:** 9, Regional Universities (West)
✔ **SAT Score (25th/75th percentile):** 1080-1290
✔ **Tuition:** 2010-2011: $32,450

Selectivity: More selective **Room/board:** $9,540
Acceptance rate: 56% **Average debt:** N/A
Student/faculty ratio: 13/1 **Proportion who borrowed:** N/A

UNDERGRADUATE STUDENT BODY STATS

2009-2010 enrollment: 3,038 full-time; 68 part-time. Men: 39%; women: 61%. **Ethnic makeup:** African American: 1%; American-Indian: 1%; Asian American: 12%; Hispanic: 5%; White: 78%; International: 2%. **Religious preference:** Protestant: 27%; Buddhist: 1%; No preference: 11%; Unknown: 11%; Roman Catholic: 45%; Other: 5%.

ADMISSIONS FACTS AND FIGURES

Phone: (888) 627-5601. **Email:** admissio@up.edu. **Website:** http://www. up.edu. **Application deadlines for fall 2011:** Regular decision: February 1. Early decision: Not offered. Early action: Not offered. Admission can be deferred. **Application fee:** $50. **To apply online, go to:** http://www.up.edu/ admissions/default.aspx?cid=8211&pid=3180. **Admissions requirements/recommendations:** High school units required (recommended): English: 3 (4); Mathematics: 2 (3); Science: 2 (2); Social studies: 2 (2); History: 2 (2); Academic electives: 7 (7). Tests: The college uses SAT or ACT scores in admissions decisions. Either SAT or ACT required. For admission to the fall 2011 entering class, the school will accept: ACT with or without writing accepted. Campus visit: Recommended. Admissions interview: Neither required nor recommended. Off-campus interview: May be arranged. **Factors that count in admissions decisions: *Academic:*** Secondary school record: Very Important. Class rank: Important. Letters of recommendation: Important. Standardized test scores: Very Important. Essay: Important. ***Nonacademic:*** Interview: Considered. Extracurricular activities: Important. Talent/ability: Important. Character/personal qualities: Considered. Alumni/ae relationship: Considered. Geographical residence: Considered. State residency: Not Considered. Religious affiliation/commitment: Considered. Minority status: Considered. Volunteer work: Important. Work experience: Considered. **Other schools with the greatest overlap in applicants:** Gonzaga University; Santa Clara University; Seattle University; University of Oregon; University of Washington. **Admissions statistics for the fall 2009 entering class:** Total applicants: 9,382. Total accepted: 5,220. Freshmen enrolled: 816; 66% were from out of state. Overall acceptance rate: 56%. **Size of waiting list:** 1017 applicants; enrolled from waiting list: 100. **Credentials of fall 2009 freshmen:** 43% ranked in the top 10 percent of their high school class; 76% were in the top 25 percent; 94% were in the top half. (Proportion submitting class standing: 50%.) **Average high school grade point average:** 3.6. **First-year students who submitted SAT scores:** 99%. Scores (25/75 percentile): Critical Reading: 530-640, Math: 550-650, Combined: 1080-1290.

ACADEMICS

Year founded: 1901. **Academic calendar:** Semester. **Degrees offered:** bachelor's, master's, post-master's certificate. **Most popular majors:** 24% health professions and related clinical sciences, 16% business, management, marketing, and related support services, 10% biological and biomedical sciences, 8% engineering, 8% foreign languages, literatures, and linguistics. **Major fields of study:** area, ethnic, cultural, and gender studies; biological and biomedical sciences; business, management, marketing, and related support services; communication, journalism, and related programs; computer and information sciences and support services; education; engineering; English language and literature/letters; foreign languages, literatures, and linguistics; health professions and related clinical sciences; history; mathematics and statistics; multi/interdisciplinary studies; natural resources and conservation; philosophy and religious studies; physical sciences; psychology; public administration and social service professions; social sciences; theology and religious vocations; visual and performing arts. **Areas of required coursework:** arts/fine arts, mathematics, English (including composition), philosophy, sciences (biological or physical), history, social science, other. **Pre-professional programs:** pre-law, pre-dentistry, pre-medicine, pre-veterinary science, pre-optometry, pre-pharmacy. **Special academic programs (% participation):** cross-registration, double major (15%), honors program (4%), independent study (90%), internships (45%), liberal arts/career combination (58%), study abroad (38%), teacher certificate program (6%). **Teacher certification offered in:** early childhood, elementary, middle/junior high, secondary. **Reserve Officers Training Corps (ROTC):** Army ROTC: Offered on campus; Air Force ROTC: Offered on campus. **Faculty and instruction (2009-2010):** Total instructional faculty: 207 full-time, 108 part-time (55% men; 45% women; 3% minorities). Full-time faculty with Ph.D. or other terminal degree: 90%. Student/faculty ratio: 13/1. Classes of fewer than 20 students: 36%; of 20 to 49 students: 61%; of 50 or more students: 3%. **Advanced Placement and International Baccalaureate credit:** International Baccalaureate exams may be used for: Placement only. **Freshmen returning for sophomore year:** 86%. **Graduation rates:** Four-year: 68%; five-year: 75%; six-year: 72%. **Graduate study:** 25% of students pursue further study immediately upon graduation; 45% within five years.

COSTS AND FINANCIAL AID

Financial aid office: (503) 943-7311. **Expenses (2010-2011):** Tuition and fees 2010-2011: $32,450; room/board: $9,540. Estimated books and supplies: $1,300; transportation: $1,000; personal expenses: $1,000. **Financial aid:** Priority filing date for institution's financial aid form: March 1. In 2009-2010, 75% of undergraduates applied for financial aid. Of those, 64% were determined to have financial need; 9% had their need fully met. Average financial aid package (proportion receiving): $25,029 (64%). Average amount of gift aid, such as scholarships or grants (proportion receiving): $16,705 (49%). Average amount of self-help aid, such as work study or loans (proportion receiving): $6,290 (51%). Average need-based loan (excluding PLUS or other private loans): $4,824. Among students who received need-based aid, the average percentage of need met: 83%. Among students who received aid based on merit, the average award (and the proportion receiving): $11,193 (26%). The average athletic scholarship (and the proportion receiving): $27,937 (4%).

CAMPUS LIFE AND EXTRACURRICULAR ACTIVITIES

Campus housing available (% using): coed dorms (53%), women's dorms (23%), men's dorms (17%), other housing options (7%). Students who live in college-owned, operated, or affiliated housing: 54%. **Student employment:** During the 2009-2010 academic year, 51% of undergraduates worked on campus. Average per-year earnings: $1,665. **Clubs and organizations:** Number of student organizations: 60. Activities include: campus ministries, choral groups, concert band, dance, drama/theater, international student organization, jazz band, literary magazine, music ensembles, musical theater, pep band, radio station, student government, student newspaper, student film society, symphony orchestra, yearbook. Number of fraternities: 0; sororities: 0. **Sports program (2009-2010):** Member of NCAA I. *Men's intercollegiate varsity sports:* baseball, basketball, cross country, golf, soccer, tennis, track and field (indoor), track and field (outdoor). *Women's intercollegiate varsity sports:* basketball, cross country, golf, soccer, tennis, track and field (indoor), track and field (outdoor), volleyball.

SERVICES AND FACILITIES

Basic services: nonremedial tutoring, placement service, health service, health insurance. **Remedial assistance:** math, writing. **Counseling services:** career, personal, academic, psychological, religious. **For learning-disabled students:** School does not offer a structured program with separate admission and additional fees. Services include: reading machines, note-taking services, readers, extended time for tests, other. **Library:** Number of titles: 250,717; number of current serial subscriptions: 40,563. **Information technology resources:** Students are not required to lease or own a computer. Number of campus computers available to all students: 350. School has a

wireless network. Approximate number of users that can be accommodated: 4,000. Proportion of college-owned housing units wired for high-speed internet access: 100%. **Campus safety:** Security services offered: 24-hour foot-and-vehicle patrols, late-night transport/escort service, 24-hour emergency telephones, lighted pathways/sidewalks, controlled dormitory access (key, security card, etc).

TRANSFER AND INTERNATIONAL STUDENTS

Transfer students: May apply for admission for the following academic terms: Fall, Spring, Summer. Applicants do not need a minimum number of credits to apply. For fall 2009: Transfer applications received: 244. Transfer applicants offered admission: 202. Transfer applicants enrolled: 82. **International students:** Number of foreign undergraduates: 74 (2% of student body). Number of countries represented: 32. Minimum TOEFL score required: 71 (computer).

Warner Pacific College

- **Address:** 2219 S.E. 68th Avenue, Portland, OR 97215
- **Website:** http://www.warnerpacific.edu
- **Private; Religious affiliation:** Church of God
- **Enrollment:** 1,167 full-time; 13 part-time

KEY STATS

✔ **U.S News College Ranking:** 17, Regional Colleges (West)
✔ **SAT Score (25th/75th percentile):** 870-1150
✔ **Tuition:** 2010-2011: $17,604

Selectivity: Less selective	**Room/board:** $6,980
Acceptance rate: 61%	**Average debt:** $22,433
Student/faculty ratio: 18/1	**Proportion who borrowed:** 93%

UNDERGRADUATE STUDENT BODY STATS

2009-2010 enrollment: 1,167 full-time; 13 part-time. Men: 38%; women: 62%. **Ethnic makeup:** African American: 4%; Asian American: 3%; Hispanic: 4%; White: 89%. **Religious preference:** Roman Catholic: 2%; Protestant: 25%; No preference: 6%; Unknown: 25%; Church of God: 13%; Other: 29%.

ADMISSIONS FACTS AND FIGURES

Phone: (503) 517-1020. **Email:** admissions@warnerpacific.edu. **Website:** http://www.warnerpacific.edu. **Application deadlines for fall 2011:** Regular decision: May 30. Early decision: Not offered. Early action: Not offered. Admission can be deferred. **Application fee:** $50. **To apply online, go to:** https://www.applyweb.com/apply/wpcapp/. **Admissions requirements/recommendations:** High school units required (recommended): English: (4); Mathematics: (2); Science: (2); Social studies: (3). Tests: The college uses SAT or ACT scores in admissions decisions. Neither SAT nor ACT required. For admission to the fall 2011 entering class, the school will accept: ACT with or without writing accepted. Campus visit: Recommended. Admissions interview: Recommended. Off-campus interview: Not available. **Factors that count in admissions decisions:** *Academic:* Secondary school record: Very Important. Class rank: Considered. Letters of recommendation: Not Considered. Standardized test scores: Very Important. Essay: Very Important. *Nonacademic:* Interview: Not Considered. Extracurricular activities: Not Considered. Talent/ability: Not Considered. Character/personal qualities: Considered. Alumni/ae relationship: Not Considered. Geographical residence: Not Considered. State residency: Not Considered. Religious affiliation/commitment: Not Considered. Minority status: Not Considered. Volunteer work: Not Considered. Work experience: Not Considered. **Other schools with the greatest overlap in applicants:** Concordia University; Corban University; George Fox University; Seattle Pacific University; Whitworth University. **Admissions statistics for the fall 2009 entering class:** Total applicants: 514. Total accepted: 311. Freshmen enrolled: 101; 27% were from out of state. Overall acceptance rate: 61%. **Average high school grade point average:** 3.2. **First-year students who submitted SAT scores:** 70%. Scores (25/75 percentile): Critical Reading: 440-580, Math: 430-570, Combined: 870-1150. **First-year students submitting ACT scores:** 45%. Scores (25/75 percentile): English: 16-21, Math: 16-21, Composite: 17-25.

ACADEMICS

Year founded: 1937. **Academic calendar:** Semester. **Degrees offered:** associate, bachelor's, post-bachelor's certificate, master's. **Most popular majors:**

32% business administration and management, 26% human development and family studies, 6% education, 3% social sciences. **Major fields of study:** biological and biomedical sciences; business, management, marketing, and related support services; education; English language and literature/letters; family and consumer sciences/human sciences; history; liberal arts and sciences studies, and humanities; multi/interdisciplinary studies; parks, recreation, leisure, and fitness studies; philosophy and religious studies; physical sciences; psychology; public administration and social service professions; social sciences; theology and religious vocations; visual and performing arts. **Areas of required coursework:** arts/fine arts, humanities, mathematics, English (including composition), philosophy, sciences (biological or physical), history, social science, other. **Pre-professional programs:** pre-dentistry, pre-medicine, pre-theology, other. **Special academic programs (% participation):** accelerated program (67%), cross-registration (5.7%), double major (5.2%), independent study (13.1%), internships (40%), student-designed major (1.2%), study abroad (2.9%), teacher certificate program (12.1%). **Teacher certification offered in:** early childhood, elementary, middle/junior high, secondary. **Cooperative education programs:** health professions. **Reserve Officers Training Corps (ROTC):** Air Force ROTC: Offered at cooperating institution (University of Portland). **Faculty and instruction (2009-2010):** Total instructional faculty: 24 full-time, 65 part-time (55% men; 45% women; 8% minorities). Full-time faculty with Ph.D. or other terminal degree: 58%. Student/faculty ratio: 18/1. Classes of fewer than 20 students: 83%; of 20 to 49 students: 17%. **Advanced Placement and International Baccalaureate credit:** AP tests may be used for: Credit and/or placement. Scores accepted: 3, 4, 5. International Baccalaureate exams may be used for: Credit and/or placement. **Freshmen returning for sophomore year:** 66%. **Graduation rates:** Four-year: 36%; five-year: 51%; six-year: 43%. **Graduate study:** 18% of students pursue further study immediately upon graduation; 12% within one year; 5% within five years. Fields in which graduates pursue further study: Master of Business Administration (MBA), 25%; law, 4%; medicine, 4%; theology (or the seminary), 15%; education, 30%; arts and sciences, 19%.

COSTS AND FINANCIAL AID

Financial aid office: (503) 517-1017. **Expenses (2010-2011):** Tuition and fees 2010-2011: $17,604; room/board: $6,980. Estimated books and supplies: $1,100; transportation: $1,010; personal expenses: $1,646. **Financial aid:** Priority filing date for institution's financial aid form: March 1. In 2009-2010, 97% of undergraduates applied for financial aid. Of those, 90% were determined to have financial need; 16% had their need fully met. Average financial aid package (proportion receiving): $15,928 (90%). Average amount of gift aid, such as scholarships or grants (proportion receiving): $5,436 (79%). Average amount of self-help aid, such as work study or loans (proportion receiving): $5,743 (82%). Average need-based loan (excluding PLUS or other private loans): $4,423. Among students who received need-based aid, the average percentage of need met: 72%. Among students who received aid based on merit, the average award (and the proportion receiving): $3,346 (9%). The average athletic scholarship (and the proportion receiving): $6,051 (3%). Average amount of debt of borrowers graduating in 2009: $22,433. Proportion who borrowed: 93%.

CAMPUS LIFE AND EXTRACURRICULAR ACTIVITIES

Campus housing available (% using): women's dorms (28%), men's dorms (17%), apartments for married students (3%), apartment for single students (42%), other housing options (10%). Students who live in college-owned, operated, or affiliated housing: 10%. **Student employment:** During the 2009-2010 academic year, 13% of undergraduates worked on campus. Average per-year earnings: $1,130. **Clubs and organizations:** Number of student organizations: 2. Activities include: campus ministries, choral groups, concert band, drama/theater, jazz band, literary magazine, music ensembles, musical theater, student government, student newspaper, yearbook. Number of fraternities: 0; sororities: 0. Average proportion of students who stay on campus on weekends: 60%. **Sports program (2009-2010):** Member of NAIA. *Men's intercollegiate varsity sports:* basketball, cross country, golf, soccer, track and field (outdoor). *Women's intercollegiate varsity sports:* basketball, cross country, golf, soccer, track and field (outdoor), volleyball.

SERVICES AND FACILITIES

Basic services: nonremedial tutoring, health service, health insurance, other. **Remedial assistance:** reading, math, writing, study skills. **Counseling services:** minority student, career, personal, veteran student, academic, psychological, birth control, religious, other. **For learning-disabled students:** School does not offer a structured program with separate admission and additional fees. Services include: remedial math, remedial English, other special classes, untimed tests, learning center, readers, extended time

for tests, tutors, priority seating, other testing accommodations. **Library:** Number of titles: 64,448; number of current serial subscriptions: 27,038. **Information technology resources:** Students are not required to lease or own a computer. Number of campus computers available to all students: 101. School has a wireless network. Approximate number of users that can be accommodated: 925. Proportion of college-owned housing units wired for high-speed internet access: 100%. **Campus safety:** Security services offered: 24-hour foot-and-vehicle patrols, late-night transport/escort service, 24-hour emergency telephones, lighted pathways/sidewalks, student patrols, controlled dormitory access (key, security card, etc).

TRANSFER AND INTERNATIONAL STUDENTS

Transfer students: May apply for admission for the following academic terms: Fall, Spring, Summer. Applicants need a minimum number of credits to apply. For fall 2009: Transfer applications received: 276. Transfer applicants offered admission: 191. Transfer applicants enrolled: 116. **International students:** Number of foreign undergraduates: 2. Number of countries represented: 9. Minimum TOEFL score required: 525 (paper); 195 (computer). Average TOEFL score: 525 (paper).

Western Oregon University

- **Address:** 345 N. Monmouth Avenue, Monmouth, OR 97361-1394
- **Website:** http://www.wou.edu
- **Public**
- **Enrollment:** 4,274 full-time; 601 part-time

KEY STATS
- ✔ **U.S News College Ranking:** 84, Regional Universities (West)
- ✔ **SAT Score (25th/75th percentile):** 770-1150
- ✔ **Tuition:** 2010-2011: $6,855 in state, $18,951 out of state
  - **Selectivity:** Less selective   **Room/board:** $8,439
  - **Acceptance rate:** 89%   **Average debt:** $25,063
  - **Student/faculty ratio:** 17/1   **Proportion who borrowed:** 61%

UNDERGRADUATE STUDENT BODY STATS

2009-2010 enrollment: 4,274 full-time; 601 part-time. Men: 43%; women: 57%. **Ethnic makeup:** African American: 3%; American-Indian: 2%; Asian American: 4%; Hispanic: 9%; White: 78%; International: 5%.

ADMISSIONS FACTS AND FIGURES

Phone: (503) 838-8211. **Email:** wolfgram@wou.edu. **Website:** http://www.wou.edu. **Application deadlines for fall 2011:** Regular decision: Rolling. Early decision: Not offered. Early action: Not offered. Admission can be deferred. **Application fee:** $50. **To apply online, go to:** http://www.wou.edu/studentaffairs/admissions/apply/. **Admissions requirements/recommendations:** High school units required (recommended): English: 4; Mathematics: 3; Science: 2; Foreign language: 2; Social studies: 2; History: 1; Total units: 14. Tests: The college uses SAT or ACT scores in admissions decisions. Either SAT or ACT required. For admission to the fall 2011 entering class, the school will accept: ACT with writing required. Campus visit: Recommended. Admissions interview: Neither required nor recommended. Off-campus interview: Not available. **Factors that count in admissions decisions:** *Academic:* Secondary school record: Very Important. Class rank: Important. Letters of recommendation: Considered. Standardized test scores: Very Important. Essay: Not Considered. *Nonacademic:* Interview: Not Considered. Extracurricular activities: Not Considered. Talent/ability: Considered. Character/personal qualities: Not Considered. Alumni/ae relationship: Considered. Geographical residence: Not Considered. State residency: Not Considered. Religious affiliation/commitment: Not Considered. Minority status: Not Considered. Volunteer work: Not Considered. Work experience: Not Considered. **Other schools with the greatest overlap in applicants:** George Fox University; Oregon State University; Portland State University; Southern Oregon University; University of Oregon. **Admissions statistics for the fall 2009 entering class:** Total applicants: 2,326. Total accepted: 2,062. Freshmen enrolled: 1,013; 27% were from out of state. Overall acceptance rate: 89%. **Credentials of fall 2009 freshmen:** 12% ranked in the top 10 percent of their high school class; 37% were in the top 25 percent; 77% were in the top half. (Proportion submitting class standing: 80%.) **Average high school grade point average:** 3.2. **First-year students who submitted SAT scores:** 51%. Scores (25/75 percentile): Critical Reading: 420-540, Math: 350-610, Combined: 770-1150. **First-year students submit-**

ting ACT scores: 11%. Scores (25/75 percentile): English: 15-21, Math: 16-22, Composite: 17-22.

ACADEMICS

Year founded: 1856. **Academic calendar:** Quarter. **Degrees offered:** associate, bachelor's, post-bachelor's certificate, master's. **Major fields of study:** biological and biomedical sciences; business, management, marketing, and related support services; computer and information sciences and support services; education; English language and literature/letters; foreign languages, literatures, and linguistics; health professions and related clinical sciences; history; liberal arts and sciences studies, and humanities; mathematics and statistics; multi/interdisciplinary studies; philosophy and religious studies; physical sciences; psychology; public administration and social service professions; security and protective services; social sciences; visual and performing arts. **Areas of required coursework:** arts/fine arts, humanities, computer literacy, mathematics, English (including composition), philosophy, foreign languages, sciences (biological or physical), social science. **Pre-professional programs:** pre-law, pre-dentistry, pre-medicine, pre-veterinary science, pre-optometry, pre-pharmacy, other. **Special academic programs (% participation):** distance learning (4%), double major (1%), dual enrollment (1%), English as a Second Language (ESL), honors program (3%), independent study (1%), internships (3%), student-designed major, study abroad (3%), teacher certificate program (25%). **Teacher certification offered in:** early childhood, special education, elementary, middle/junior high, secondary, bilingual/bicultural. **Reserve Officers Training Corps (ROTC):** Army ROTC: Offered on campus; Navy ROTC: Offered at cooperating institution (Oregon State University); Air Force ROTC: Offered at cooperating institution (Oregon State University). **Faculty and instruction (2009-2010):** Total instructional faculty: 209 full-time, 150 part-time (52% men; 48% women; 8% minorities). Full-time faculty with Ph.D. or other terminal degree: 72%. Student/faculty ratio: 17/1. Classes of fewer than 20 students: 51%; of 20 to 49 students: 44%; of 50 or more students: 4%. **Advanced Placement and International Baccalaureate credit:** AP tests may be used for: Credit only. Scores accepted: 3, 4, 5. International Baccalaureate exams may be used for: Credit only. **Freshmen returning for sophomore year:** 67%. **Graduation rates:** Six-year: 43%. **Graduate study:** 30% of students pursue further study within one year. Fields in which graduates pursue further study: Master of Business Administration (MBA), 6%; education, 15%.

COSTS AND FINANCIAL AID

Financial aid office: (503) 838-8475. **Expenses (2010-2011):** Tuition and fees 2010-2011: $6,855 in state, $18,951 out of state; room/board: $8,439. Estimated books and supplies: $1,200; transportation: $945; personal expenses: $1,890. **Financial aid:** Priority filing date for institution's financial aid form: March 1. In 2009-2010, 93% of undergraduates applied for financial aid. Of those, 75% were determined to have financial need; 17% had their need fully met. Average financial aid package (proportion receiving): $8,626 (75%). Average amount of gift aid, such as scholarships or grants (proportion receiving): $6,271 (58%). Average amount of self-help aid, such as work study or loans (proportion receiving): $4,234 (67%). Average need-based loan (excluding PLUS or other private loans): $3,969. Among students who received need-based aid, the average percentage of need met: 67%. Among students who received aid based on merit, the average award (and the proportion receiving): $2,159 (7%). The average athletic scholarship (and the proportion receiving): $2,433 (3%). Average amount of debt of borrowers graduating in 2009: $25,063. Proportion who borrowed: 61%.

CAMPUS LIFE AND EXTRACURRICULAR ACTIVITIES

Campus housing available (% using): coed dorms (79%), apartments for married students (2%), apartment for single students (16%), special housing for disabled students (3%). Students who live in college-owned, operated, or affiliated housing: 32%. **Student employment:** During the 2009-2010 academic year, 30% of undergraduates worked on campus. Average per-year earnings: $1,656. **Clubs and organizations:** Number of student organizations: 64. Activities include: campus ministries, choral groups, concert band, dance, drama/theater, jazz band, literary magazine, model UN, music ensembles, musical theater, pep band, student government, student newspaper, symphony orchestra, television station. Number of fraternities: 0; sororities: 0. Average proportion of students who stay on campus on weekends: 50%. **Sports program (2009-2010):** Member of NCAA II. *Men's intercollegiate varsity sports:* baseball, basketball, cross country, football, skiing (alpine), track and field (indoor). *Women's intercollegiate varsity sports:* basketball, cross country, skiing (alpine), soccer, track and field (indoor), volleyball.

SERVICES AND FACILITIES

Basic services: nonremedial tutoring, women's center, placement service, day care, health service, health insurance. **Remedial assistance:** reading, math, writing, study skills. **Counseling services:** minority student, career, personal, veteran student, academic, older student, psychological, birth control. **For learning-disabled students:** School does not offer a structured program with separate admission and additional fees. Services include: remedial math, remedial English, reading machines, tape recorders, diagnostic testing service, note-taking services, oral tests, learning center, extended time for tests, tutors, priority registration, priority seating, texts on tape, other testing accommodations, other. **Library:** Number of titles: 250,000; number of current serial subscriptions: 4,600. **Information technology resources:** Students are not required to lease or own a computer. Number of campus computers available to all students: 700. School has a wireless network. Approximate number of users that can be accommodated: 4,000. Proportion of college-owned housing units wired for high-speed internet access: 100%. **Campus safety:** Security services offered: 24-hour foot-and-vehicle patrols, late-night transport/escort service, 24-hour emergency telephones, lighted pathways/sidewalks, controlled dormitory access (key, security card, etc).

TRANSFER AND INTERNATIONAL STUDENTS

Transfer students: May apply for admission for the following academic terms: Fall, Winter, Spring, Summer. Applicants need a minimum number of credits to apply. **International students:** Number of foreign undergraduates: 256 (5% of student body). Number of countries represented: 24. Minimum TOEFL score required: 500 (paper); 173 (computer). Average TOEFL score: 520 (paper).

Willamette University

- **Address:** 900 State Street, Salem, OR 97301
- **Website:** http://www.willamette.edu
- **Private; Religious affiliation:** United Methodist
- **Enrollment:** 1,856 full-time; 141 part-time

KEY STATS

✔ **U.S News College Ranking:** 59, National Liberal Arts Colleges
✔ **SAT Score (25th/75th percentile):** 1120-1320
✔ **Tuition:** 2010-2011: $37,362

Selectivity: More selective	**Room/board:** $8,900
Acceptance rate: 60%	**Average debt:** $23,643
Student/faculty ratio: 10/1	**Proportion who borrowed:** 63%

UNDERGRADUATE STUDENT BODY STATS

2009-2010 enrollment: 1,856 full-time; 141 part-time. Men: 44%; women: 56%. **Ethnic makeup:** African American: 2%; American-Indian: 1%; Asian American: 7%; Hispanic: 6%; White: 83%; International: 1%. **Religious preference:** Roman Catholic: 9%; Protestant: 26%; Jewish: 5%; Muslim: 1%; Hindu: 1%; Buddhist: 2%; No preference: 45%; United Methodist: 4%; Agnostic: N/A; Other: 7%.

ADMISSIONS FACTS AND FIGURES

Phone: (503) 370-6303. **Email:** LIBARTS@willamette.edu. **Website:** http://www.willamette.edu. **Application deadlines for fall 2011:** Regular decision: February 1. Early decision: Not offered. Early action: Send application by: December 1; Decision sent by: January 15. Admission can be deferred. **Application fee:** $50. **To apply online, go to:** http://www.willamette.edu/admission/application/. **Admissions requirements/recommendations:** High school units required (recommended): English: 4 (4); Mathematics: 4 (4); Science: 3 (3); Foreign language: 3 (4); Social studies: 1 (1); History: 2 (2); Academic electives: (2); Total units: 17 (20). Tests: The college uses SAT or ACT scores in admissions decisions. Either SAT or ACT required. For admission to the fall 2011 entering class, the school will accept: ACT with writing required. Campus visit: Recommended. Admissions interview: Recommended. Off-campus interview: May be arranged. **Factors that count in admissions decisions:** *Academic:* Secondary school record: Very Important. Class rank: Very Important. Letters of recommendation: Important. Standardized test scores: Very Important. Essay: Very Important. *Nonacademic:* Interview: Important. Extracurricular activities: Considered. Talent/ability: Considered. Character/personal qualities: Considered. Alumni/ae relationship: Considered. Geographical residence: Considered. State residency: Not Considered. Religious affiliation/commitment: Not

Considered. Minority status: Considered. Volunteer work: Not Considered. Work experience: Not Considered. **Other schools with the greatest overlap in applicants:** Lewis & Clark College; Linfield College; University of Oregon; University of Puget Sound; Whitman College. **Admissions statistics for the fall 2009 entering class:** Total applicants: 5,739. Total accepted: 3,416. Freshmen enrolled: 541; 71% were from out of state. Accepted through early-decision or early-action plans: 8%. Overall acceptance rate: 60%. Non-early acceptance rate: 58%. **Size of waiting list:** 97 applicants; enrolled from waiting list: 11. **Credentials of fall 2009 freshmen:** 49% ranked in the top 10 percent of their high school class; 80% were in the top 25 percent; 100% were in the top half. (Proportion submitting class standing: 72%.) **Average high school grade point average:** 3.7. **First-year students who submitted SAT scores:** 89%. Scores (25/75 percentile): Critical Reading: 560-670, Math: 560-650, Combined: 1120-1320. **First-year students submitting ACT scores:** 39%. Scores (25/75 percentile): English: N/A, Math: N/A, Composite: 25-30.

ACADEMICS

Year founded: 1842. **Academic calendar:** Semester. **Degrees offered:** bachelor's, master's. **Most popular majors:** 26% social sciences, 11% English language and literature/letters, 9% foreign languages, literatures, and linguistics, 9% psychology, 7% multi/interdisciplinary studies. **Major fields of study:** area, ethnic, cultural, and gender studies; biological and biomedical sciences; computer and information sciences and support services; English language and literature/letters; foreign languages, literatures, and linguistics; history; liberal arts and sciences studies, and humanities; mathematics and statistics; multi/interdisciplinary studies; natural resources and conservation; parks, recreation, leisure, and fitness studies; philosophy and religious studies; physical sciences; psychology; social sciences; visual and performing arts. **Areas of required coursework:** arts/fine arts, humanities, mathematics, English (including composition), foreign languages, sciences (biological or physical), history, social science. **Pre-professional programs:** pre-law, pre-dentistry, pre-medicine, pre-veterinary science. **Special academic programs (% participation):** accelerated program (2%), cross-registration (.1%), double major (17%), dual enrollment (.2%), exchange student program (domestic) (3%), independent study (20%), internships (68%), student-designed major (1%), study abroad (45%), teacher certificate program. **Reserve Officers Training Corps (ROTC):** Army ROTC: Offered at cooperating institution (Oregon State University); Air Force ROTC: Offered at cooperating institution (University of Portland). **Faculty and instruction (2009-2010):** Total instructional faculty: 213 full-time, 83 part-time (57% men; 43% women; 14% minorities). Full-time faculty with Ph.D. or other terminal degree: 96%. Student/faculty ratio: 10/1. Classes of fewer than 20 students: 69%; of 20 to 49 students: 31%. **Advanced Placement and International Baccalaureate credit:** AP tests may be used for: Credit and/or placement. Scores accepted: 4, 5. International Baccalaureate exams may be used for: Credit only. **Freshmen returning for sophomore year:** 87%. **Graduation rates:** Four-year: 71%; five-year: 78%; six-year: 79%. **Graduate study:** 26% of students pursue further study immediately upon graduation; 42% within one year; 68% within five years. Fields in which graduates pursue further study: Master of Business Administration (MBA), 15%; law, 10%; medicine, 10%; engineering, 5%; education, 19%; arts and sciences, 40%; veterinary medicine, 1%.

COSTS AND FINANCIAL AID

Financial aid office: (503) 370-6273. **Expenses (2010-2011):** Tuition and fees 2010-2011: $37,362; room/board: $8,900. Estimated books and supplies: $920 personal expenses: $1,100. **Financial aid:** Priority filing date for institution's financial aid form: February 1. In 2009-2010, 73% of undergraduates applied for financial aid. Of those, 63% were determined to have financial need; 17% had their need fully met. Average financial aid package (proportion receiving): $29,387 (63%). Average amount of gift aid, such as scholarships or grants (proportion receiving): $23,226 (62%). Average amount of self-help aid, such as work study or loans (proportion receiving): $5,932 (59%). Average need-based loan (excluding PLUS or other private loans): $4,334. Among students who received need-based aid, the average percentage of need met: 89%. Among students who received aid based on merit, the average award (and the proportion receiving): $11,727 (32%). The average athletic scholarship (and the proportion receiving): $0 (0%). Average amount of debt of borrowers graduating in 2009: $23,643. Proportion who borrowed: 63%.

CAMPUS LIFE AND EXTRACURRICULAR ACTIVITIES

Campus housing available (% using): coed dorms (51%), sorority housing (9%), fraternity housing (8%), apartment for single students (8%), other housing options (24%). Students who live in college-owned, operated, or affiliated housing: 71%. **Student employment:** During the 2009-2010 academic year, 70% of undergraduates worked on campus. Average per-year earnings: $1,770. **Clubs and organizations:** Number of student organizations: 110. Activities include: campus ministries, choral groups, concert band, dance, drama/theater, international student organization, jazz band, literary magazine, model UN, music ensembles, musical theater, opera, radio station, student government, student newspaper, student film society, symphony orchestra, yearbook. Number of fraternities: 4; sororities: 3. Proportion of men in fraternities: 19%; of women in sororities: 17%. Average proportion of students who stay on campus on weekends: 60%. **Sports program (2009-2010):** Member of NCAA III. *Men's intercollegiate varsity sports:* baseball, basketball, cross country, football, golf, soccer, swimming, tennis, track and field (indoor), track and field (outdoor). *Women's intercollegiate varsity sports:* basketball, crew (heavyweight), cross country, golf, crew (lightweight), soccer, softball, swimming, tennis, track and field (indoor), track and field (outdoor), volleyball.

SERVICES AND FACILITIES

Basic services: nonremedial tutoring, women's center, health service, health insurance. **Counseling services:** minority student, career, military, personal, veteran student, academic, older student, psychological, birth control, religious, other. **For learning-disabled students:** School does not offer a structured program with separate admission and additional fees. Services include: remedial English, tape recorders, note-taking services, oral tests, readers, extended time for tests, tutors, priority registration, priority seating, texts on tape, typist/scribe, exams on tape or computer, other testing accommodations, other. **Library:** Number of titles: 397,224; number of current serial subscriptions: 13,913. **Information technology resources:** Students are not required to lease or own a computer. Number of campus computers available to all students: 450. School has a wireless network. Approximate number of users that can be accommodated: 1,500. Proportion of college-owned housing units wired for high-speed internet access: 100%. **Campus safety:** Security services offered: 24-hour foot-and-vehicle patrols, late-night transport/escort service, 24-hour emergency telephones, lighted pathways/sidewalks, student patrols, controlled dormitory access (key, security card, etc).

TRANSFER AND INTERNATIONAL STUDENTS

Transfer students: May apply for admission for the following academic terms: Fall, Spring. Applicants do not need a minimum number of credits to apply. For fall 2009: Transfer applications received: 285. Transfer applicants offered admission: 122. Transfer applicants enrolled: 72. **International students:** Number of foreign undergraduates: 14 (1% of student body). Number of countries represented: 20. Minimum TOEFL score required: 560 (paper); 83 (computer). Average TOEFL score: 610 (paper).

Pennsylvania

Albright College

- **Address:** PO Box 15234, 13th and Bern Streets, Reading, PA 19612-5234
- **Website:** http://www.albright.edu
- **Private; Religious affiliation:** United Methodist
- **Enrollment:** 2,253 full-time; 29 part-time

KEY STATS

✔ **U.S News College Ranking:** 166, National Liberal Arts Colleges
✔ **SAT Score (25th/75th percentile):** 960-1140
✔ **Tuition:** 2010-2011: $32,740

Selectivity: Selective	**Room/board:** $8,858
Acceptance rate: 56%	**Average debt:** $31,845
Student/faculty ratio: 13/1	**Proportion who borrowed:** 83%

UNDERGRADUATE STUDENT BODY STATS

2009-2010 enrollment: 2,253 full-time; 29 part-time. Men: 41%; women: 59%. **Ethnic makeup:** African American: 11%; Asian American: 1%; Hispanic: 6%; White: 76%; International: 6%. **Religious preference:** Roman Catholic: 20%; Protestant: 3%; Jewish: 1%; No preference: 56%; United Methodist: 13%; Other: 7%.

ADMISSIONS FACTS AND FIGURES

Phone: (800) 252-1856. **Email:** admission@alb.edu. **Website:** http://www.albright.edu. **Application deadlines for fall 2011:** Regular decision: Rolling. Early decision: Not offered. Early action: Not offered. Admission can be deferred. **Application fee:** $25. **To apply online, go to:** http://www.albright.edu/admission/application.html. **Admissions requirements/recommendations:** High school units required (recommended): English: 4 (4); Mathematics: 2 (3); Science: 3 (4); Foreign language: 2 (3); Social studies: 2 (2); History: 1 (2); Academic electives: 2 (2); Total units: 16 (20). Tests: The college uses SAT or ACT scores in admissions decisions. Neither SAT nor ACT required. For admission to the fall 2011 entering class, the school will accept: ACT with or without writing accepted. Campus visit: Recommended. Admissions interview: Recommended. Off-campus interview: Not available. **Factors that count in admissions decisions: Academic:** Secondary school record: Very Important. Class rank: Important. Letters of recommendation: Important. Standardized test scores: Considered. Essay: Important. **Nonacademic:** Interview: Considered. Extracurricular activities: Considered. Talent/ability: Considered. Character/personal qualities: Not Considered. Alumni/ae relationship: Considered. Geographical residence: Not Considered. State residency: Not Considered. Religious affiliation/commitment: Not Considered. Minority status: Not Considered. Volunteer work: Considered. Work experience: Considered. **Other schools with the greatest overlap in applicants:** Elizabethtown College; Moravian College; Muhlenberg College; Susquehanna University; Ursinus College. **Admissions statistics for the fall 2009 entering class:** Total applicants: 5,565. Total accepted: 3,113. Freshmen enrolled: 541; 42% were from out of state. Overall acceptance rate: 56%. **Credentials of fall 2009 freshmen:** 23% ranked in the top 10 percent of their high school class; 48% were in the top 25 percent; 76% were in the top half. (Proportion submitting class standing: 71%.) **Average high school grade point average:** 3.3. **First-year students who submitted SAT scores:** 66%. Scores (25/75 percentile): Critical Reading: 480-570; Math: 480-570, Combined: 960-1140. **First-year students submitting ACT scores:** 9%. Scores (25/75 percentile): English: N/A, Math: N/A, Composite: 20-25.

ACADEMICS

Year founded: 1856. **Academic calendar:** 4-1-4. **Degrees offered:** certificate, bachelor's, master's. **Most popular majors:** 30% business, management, marketing, and related support services, 16% psychology, 10% social sciences, 10% visual and performing arts, 6% biological and biomedical sciences. **Major fields of study:** area, ethnic, cultural, and gender studies; biological and biomedical sciences; business, management, marketing, and related support services; communication, journalism, and related programs; computer and information sciences and support services; education; English language and literature/letters; foreign languages, literatures, and linguistics; history; mathematics and statistics; multi/interdisciplinary studies; natural resources and conservation; philosophy and religious studies; physical sciences; psychology; social sciences; visual and performing arts. **Areas of required coursework:** arts/fine arts, humanities, computer literacy, mathematics, English (including composition), philosophy, foreign languages, sciences (biological or physical), history, social science, other. **Pre-professional programs:** pre-law, pre-dentistry, pre-medicine, pre-theology, pre-veterinary science, pre-optometry. **Special academic programs (% participation):** accelerated program (1%), cross-registration (1%), double major (41%), dual enrollment (0%), English as a Second Language (ESL) (1%), exchange student program (domestic) (1%), honors program (14%), independent study (16%), internships (29%), liberal arts/career combination (24%), student-designed major (1%), study abroad (5%), teacher certificate program (37%), other. **Teacher certification offered in:** early childhood, special education, elementary, secondary. **Faculty and instruction (2009-2010):** Total instructional faculty: 114 full-time, 47 part-time (48% men; 52% women; 10% minorities). Full-time faculty with Ph.D. or other terminal degree: 84%. Student/faculty ratio: 13/1. Classes of fewer than 20 students: 66%; of 20 to 49 students: 34%; of 50 or more students: 1%. **Advanced Placement and International Baccalaureate credit:** AP tests may be used for: Credit and/or placement. Scores accepted: 3, 4, 5. International Baccalaureate exams may be used for: Placement only. **Freshmen returning for sophomore year:** 74%. **Graduation rates:** Four-year: 55%; five-year: 60%; six-year: 62%. **Graduate study:** 26% of students pursue further study immediately upon graduation. Fields in which graduates pursue further study: Master of Business Administration (MBA), 4%; law, 7%; medicine, 9%; dentistry, 1%; theology (or the seminary), 3%; education, 24%; arts and sciences, 51%; veterinary medicine, 1%.

COSTS AND FINANCIAL AID

Financial aid office: (610) 921-7515. **Expenses (2010-2011):** Tuition and fees 2010-2011: $32,740; room/board: $8,858. Estimated books and supplies: $1,000; transportation: $400; personal expenses: $1,100. **Financial aid:** Priority filing date for institution's financial aid form: March 1. In 2009-2010, 91% of undergraduates applied for financial aid. Of those, 83% were determined to have financial need; 17% had their need fully met. Average financial aid package (proportion receiving): $25,053 (82%). Average amount of gift aid, such as scholarships or grants (proportion receiving): $19,406 (82%). Average amount of self-help aid, such as work study or loans (proportion receiving): $6,464 (72%). Average need-based loan (excluding PLUS or other private loans): $4,935. Among students who received need-based aid, the average percentage of need met: 78%. Among students who received aid based on merit, the average award (and the proportion receiving): $12,235 (12%). Average amount of debt of borrowers graduating in 2009: $31,845. Proportion who borrowed: 83%.

CAMPUS LIFE AND EXTRACURRICULAR ACTIVITIES

Campus housing available (% using): coed dorms (77%), apartment for single students (13%), special housing for international students (2%), other housing options (8%). Students who live in college-owned, operated, or affiliated housing: 69%. **Student employment:** During the 2009-2010 academic year, 17% of undergraduates worked on campus. Average per-year earnings: $1,800. **Clubs and organizations:** Number of student organizations: 75. Activities include: campus ministries, choral groups, concert band, dance, drama/theater, international student organization, jazz band, literary magazine, music ensembles, musical theater, pep band, radio station, student government, student newspaper, television station, yearbook. Number of fraternities: 3; sororities: 3. Proportion of men in fraternities: 13%; of women in sororities: 19%. Average proportion of students who stay on campus on weekends: 80%. **Sports program (2009-2010):** Member of NCAA III. **Men's intercollegiate varsity sports:** baseball, basketball, cross country, football, golf, soccer, swimming, tennis, track and field (indoor), track and field (outdoor). **Women's intercollegiate varsity sports:** basketball, cross country, field hockey, soccer, softball, swimming, tennis, track and field (indoor), track and field (outdoor), volleyball.

SERVICES AND FACILITIES

Basic services: nonremedial tutoring, women's center, health service. **Counseling services:** minority student, career, personal, veteran student, academic, older student, psychological, religious. **For learning-disabled students:** School does not offer a structured program with separate admission and additional fees. Total undergraduates in learning-disabled program or receiving services: 70. Services include: tape recorders, note-taking services, learning center, readers, extended time for tests, tutors, priority seating, texts on tape, exams on tape or computer, other testing accommodations, other. **Library:** Number of titles: 229,687; number of current serial subscriptions: 6,068. **Information technology resources:** Students are not required to lease or own a computer. Number of campus computers available to all students: 350. School has a wireless network. Approximate number of users that can be accommodated: 1,700. Proportion of college-owned housing units wired for high-speed internet access: 100%. **Campus safety:** Security services offered: 24-hour foot-and-vehicle patrols, late-night transport/escort service, 24-hour emergency telephones, lighted pathways/sidewalks, student patrols, controlled dormitory access (key, security card, etc).

TRANSFER AND INTERNATIONAL STUDENTS

Transfer students: May apply for admission for the following academic terms: Fall, Spring, Summer. Applicants do not need a minimum number of credits to apply. For fall 2009: Transfer applications received: 243. Transfer applicants offered admission: 78. Transfer applicants enrolled: 48. **International students:** Number of foreign undergraduates: 125 (6% of student body). Number of countries represented: 21. Minimum TOEFL score required: 525 (paper); 542 (computer). Average TOEFL score: 548 (paper).

Allegheny College

- **Address:** 520 N. Main Street, Meadville, PA 16335
- **Website:** http://www.allegheny.edu
- **Private; Religious affiliation:** United Methodist
- **Enrollment:** 2,094 full-time; 38 part-time

KEY STATS

✔ **U.S News College Ranking:** 93, National Liberal Arts Colleges
✔ **SAT Score (25th/75th percentile):** 1110-1310
✔ **Tuition:** 2010-2011: $34,810

Selectivity: More selective	**Room/board:** $8,790
Acceptance rate: 66%	**Average debt:** N/A
Student/faculty ratio: 13/1	**Proportion who borrowed:** N/A

UNDERGRADUATE STUDENT BODY STATS

2009-2010 enrollment: 2,094 full-time; 38 part-time. Men: 45%; women: 55%. **Ethnic makeup:** African American: 4%; Asian American: 3%; Hispanic: 3%; White: 89%; International: 1%. **Religious preference:** Roman Catholic: 35%; Protestant: 20%; Jewish: 4%; Muslim: 1%; No preference: 15%; Unknown: 10%; United Methodist: 7%; Non Christian: 2%; Other: 6%.

ADMISSIONS FACTS AND FIGURES

Phone: (800) 521-5293. **Email:** admissions@allegheny.edu. **Website:** http://www.allegheny.edu. **Application deadlines for fall 2011:** Regular decision: February 15; decision sent by April 1. Early decision: Send application by: November 15; Decision sent by: December 15. Early action: Not offered. Admission can be deferred. **Application fee:** $35. **To apply online, go to:** http://www.allegheny.edu/admissions/apply. **Admissions requirements/recommendations:** High school units required (recommended): English: 4; Mathematics: 3; Science: 3; Foreign language: 2; Social studies: 3; History: 0; Academic electives: 1; Total units: 16. Tests: The college uses SAT or ACT scores in admissions decisions. Either SAT or ACT required. For admission to the fall 2011 entering class, the school will accept: ACT with writing recommended. Campus visit: Recommended. Admissions interview: Recommended. Off-campus interview: May be arranged. **Factors that count in admissions decisions:** *Academic:* Secondary school record: Very Important. Class rank: Very Important. Letters of recommendation: Important. Standardized test scores: Important. Essay: Considered. *Nonacademic:* Interview: Important. Extracurricular activities: Important. Talent/ability: Considered. Character/personal qualities: Important. Alumni/ae relationship: Considered. Geographical residence: Considered. State residency: Not Considered. Religious affiliation/commitment: Not Considered. Minority status: Considered. Volunteer work: Considered.

Work experience: Considered. **Other schools with the greatest overlap in applicants:** College of Wooster; Pennsylvania State University–University Park; University of Pittsburgh; Washington and Jefferson College; Westminster College. **Admissions statistics for the fall 2009 entering class:** Total applicants: 3,916. Total accepted: 2,594. Freshmen enrolled: 583; 46% were from out of state. Accepted through early-decision or early-action plans: 9%. Overall acceptance rate: 66%. Early-decision acceptance rate: 66%. Non-early acceptance rate: 66%. **Size of waiting list:** 327 applicants; enrolled from waiting list: 6. **Credentials of fall 2009 freshmen:** 45% ranked in the top 10 percent of their high school class; 76% were in the top 25 percent; 97% were in the top half. (Proportion submitting class standing: 64%.) **Average high school grade point average:** 3.8. **First-year students who submitted SAT scores:** 72%. Scores (25/75 percentile): Critical Reading: 550-660, Math: 560-650, Combined: 1110-1310. **First-year students submitting ACT scores:** 41%. Scores (25/75 percentile): English: 23-31, Math: 23-29, Composite: 23-29.

ACADEMICS

Year founded: 1815. **Academic calendar:** Semester. **Degrees offered:** bachelor's. **Most popular majors:** 17% psychology, 11% biology/biological sciences, 9% political science and government, 8% economics, 7% English language and literature. **Major fields of study:** area, ethnic, cultural, and gender studies; biological and biomedical sciences; business, management, marketing, and related support services; communication, journalism, and related programs; computer and information sciences and support services; education; engineering; English language and literature/letters; foreign languages, literatures, and linguistics; health professions and related clinical sciences; history; legal professions and studies; mathematics and statistics; multi/interdisciplinary studies; natural resources and conservation; philosophy and religious studies; physical sciences; psychology; social sciences; visual and performing arts. **Areas of required coursework:** humanities, sciences (biological or physical), social science. **Pre-professional programs:** pre-law, pre-dentistry, pre-medicine, pre-veterinary science, pre-pharmacy, other. **Special academic programs (% participation):** double major (14%), dual enrollment (0%), English as a Second Language (ESL) (1%), exchange student program (domestic) (2%), independent study (100%), internships (27%), student-designed major (1%), study abroad (32%), other (1%). **Cooperative education programs:** business, education, engineering, health professions, other. **Faculty and instruction (2009-2010):** Total instructional faculty: 152 full-time, 33 part-time (55% men; 45% women; 12% minorities). Full-time faculty with Ph.D. or other terminal degree: 95%. Student/faculty ratio: 13/1. Classes of fewer than 20 students: 59%; of 20 to 49 students: 39%; of 50 or more students: 1%. **Advanced Placement and International Baccalaureate credit:** AP tests may be used for: Credit and/or placement. Scores accepted: 4, 5. International Baccalaureate exams may be used for: Credit only. **Freshmen returning for sophomore year:** 88%. **Graduation rates:** Four-year: 66%; five-year: 74%; six-year: 74%. **Graduate study:** 43% of students pursue further study immediately upon graduation. Fields in which graduates pursue further study: Master of Business Administration (MBA), 4%; law, 5%; medicine, 11%; education, 7%; arts and sciences, 8%; veterinary medicine, 1%.

COSTS AND FINANCIAL AID

Financial aid office: (800) 835-7780. **Expenses (2010-2011):** Tuition and fees 2010-2011: $34,810; room/board: $8,790. Estimated books and supplies: $1,000; transportation: $900; personal expenses: $900. **Financial aid:** Priority filing date for institution's financial aid form: February 15. In 2009-2010, 79% of undergraduates applied for financial aid. Of those, 69% were determined to have financial need; 33% had their need fully met. Average financial aid package (proportion receiving): $27,087 (69%). Average amount of gift aid, such as scholarships or grants (proportion receiving): $20,179 (69%). Average amount of self-help aid, such as work study or loans (proportion receiving): $6,638 (61%). Average need-based loan (excluding PLUS or other private loans): $5,023. Among students who received need-based aid, the average percentage of need met: 89%. Among students who received aid based on merit, the average award (and the proportion receiving): $11,621 (28%).

CAMPUS LIFE AND EXTRACURRICULAR ACTIVITIES

Campus housing available (% using): coed dorms (61%), women's dorms (10%), men's dorms (4%), fraternity housing (3%), apartment for single students (16%), special housing for disabled students. Students who live in college-owned, operated, or affiliated housing: 78%. **Student employment:** During the 2009-2010 academic year, 22% of undergraduates worked on campus. Average per-year earnings: $1,543. **Clubs and organizations:** Number of student organizations: 113. Activities include: campus ministries, choral groups, concert band, dance, drama/theater, international student organization, jazz band, literary magazine, model UN, music ensembles, musical theater, radio station, student government, student newspaper, symphony orchestra, television station, yearbook. Number of fraternities: 5; sororities: 5. Proportion of men in fraternities: 22%; of women in sororities: 33%. Average proportion of students who stay on campus on weekends: 80%. **Sports program (2009-2010):** Member of NCAA III. *Men's intercollegiate varsity sports:* baseball, basketball, cross country, football, golf, soccer, swimming, tennis, track and field (indoor), track and field (outdoor). *Women's intercollegiate varsity sports:* basketball, cross country, golf, lacrosse, soccer, softball, swimming, tennis, track and field (indoor), track and field (outdoor), volleyball.

SERVICES AND FACILITIES

Basic services: nonremedial tutoring, placement service, health service, health insurance, other. **Counseling services:** minority student, career, personal, academic, older student, psychological, birth control, religious, other. **For learning-disabled students:** School does not offer a structured program with separate admission and additional fees. Services include: tape recorders, note-taking services, oral tests, learning center, extended time for tests, tutors, priority registration, priority seating, texts on tape, exams on tape or computer, other. **Library:** Number of titles: 305,767; number of current serial subscriptions: 21,752. **Information technology resources:** Students are not required to lease or own a computer. Number of campus computers available to all students: 185. School has a wireless network. Approximate number of users that can be accommodated: 500. Proportion of college-owned housing units wired for high-speed internet access: 100%. **Campus safety:** Security services offered: 24-hour foot-and-vehicle patrols, late-night transport/escort service, 24-hour emergency telephones, lighted pathways/sidewalks, student patrols, controlled dormitory access (key, security card, etc).

TRANSFER AND INTERNATIONAL STUDENTS

Transfer students: May apply for admission for the following academic terms: Fall, Spring. Applicants do not need a minimum number of credits to apply. For fall 2009: Transfer applications received: 116. Transfer applicants offered admission: 58. Transfer applicants enrolled: 26. **International students:** Number of foreign undergraduates: 29 (1% of student body). Number of countries represented: 17. Minimum TOEFL score required: 550 (paper); 80 (computer).

Alvernia University

- **Address:** 400 St. Bernardine Street, Reading, PA 19607-1799
- **Website:** http://www.alvernia.edu
- **Private; Religious affiliation:** Roman Catholic
- **Enrollment:** 1,612 full-time; 464 part-time

KEY STATS

✔ **U.S News College Ranking:** 121, Regional Universities (North)
✔ **SAT Score (25th/75th percentile):** 878-1090
✔ **Tuition:** 2010-2011: $25,480

Selectivity: Less selective	**Room/board:** $9,300
Acceptance rate: 78%	**Average debt:** $34,062
Student/faculty ratio: 14/1	**Proportion who borrowed:** 94%

UNDERGRADUATE STUDENT BODY STATS

2009-2010 enrollment: 1,612 full-time; 464 part-time. Men: 32%; women: 68%. **Ethnic makeup:** African American: 11%; American-Indian: 1%; Asian American: 2%; Hispanic: 6%; White: 80%; International: 1%. **Religious preference:** Protestant: 12%; No preference: 3%; Unknown: 7%; Roman Catholic: 46%; Other: 24%.

ADMISSIONS FACTS AND FIGURES

Phone: (610) 796-8220. **Email:** admissions@alvernia.edu. **Website:** http://www.alvernia.edu. **Application deadlines for fall 2011:** Regular decision: Rolling. Early decision: Not offered. Early action: Not offered. Admission can be deferred. **Application fee:** $25. **To apply online, go to:** https://www.applyweb.com/apply/alveru/. **Admissions requirements/recommendations:** High school units required (recommended): English: (4); Mathematics: (4); Science: (2); Foreign language: (2); Social studies: (3); History: (0); Academic electives: (1); Total units: (16). Tests: The college uses SAT or ACT scores in admissions decisions. Either SAT or ACT required. For

admission to the fall 2011 entering class, the school will accept: ACT with or without writing accepted. Campus visit: Recommended. Admissions interview: Neither required nor recommended. Off-campus interview: May be arranged. **Factors that count in admissions decisions:** *Academic:* Secondary school record: Important. Class rank: Important. Letters of recommendation: Considered. Standardized test scores: Very Important. Essay: Important. *Nonacademic:* Interview: Considered. Extracurricular activities: Important. Talent/ability: Considered. Character/personal qualities: Important. Alumni/ae relationship: Important. Geographical residence: Not Considered. State residency: Not Considered. Religious affiliation/commitment: Not Considered. Minority status: Not Considered. Volunteer work: Important. Work experience: Important. **Other schools with the greatest overlap in applicants:** Cabrini College; Kutztown University of Pennsylvania; Pennsylvania State University–University Park; West Chester University of Pennsylvania; York College of Pennsylvania. **Admissions statistics for the fall 2009 entering class:** Total applicants: 1,605. Total accepted: 1,252. Freshmen enrolled: 328; 27% were from out of state. Overall acceptance rate: 78%. **Credentials of fall 2009 freshmen:** 6% ranked in the top 10 percent of their high school class; 25% were in the top 25 percent; 59% were in the top half. (Proportion submitting class standing: 43%.) **Average high school grade point average:** 3.1. **First-year students who submitted SAT scores:** 98%. Scores (25/75 percentile): Critical Reading: 438-540, Math: 440-550, Combined: 878-1090. **First-year students submitting ACT scores:** 17%. Scores (25/75 percentile): English: N/A, Math: N/A, Composite: 17-21.

ACADEMICS

Year founded: 1958. **Academic calendar:** Semester. **Degrees offered:** associate, bachelor's, master's, doctorate. **Most popular majors:** 30% health professions and related clinical sciences, 18% business, management, marketing, and related support services, 14% security and protective services, 11% education, 5% psychology. **Major fields of study:** biological and biomedical sciences; business, management, marketing, and related support services; communication, journalism, and related programs; computer and information sciences and support services; education; English language and literature/letters; health professions and related clinical sciences; history; liberal arts and sciences studies, and humanities; mathematics and statistics; parks, recreation, leisure, and fitness studies; philosophy and religious studies; physical sciences; psychology; public administration and social service professions; security and protective services; social sciences; theology and religious vocations. **Areas of required coursework:** arts/fine arts, humanities, mathematics, English (including composition), philosophy, foreign languages, sciences (biological or physical), history, social science, other. **Pre-professional programs:** pre-law, pre-dentistry, pre-medicine, pre-theology. **Special academic programs:** accelerated program, cross-registration, distance learning, double major, dual enrollment, English as a Second Language (ESL), honors program, independent study, internships, student-designed major, study abroad, teacher certificate program. **Teacher certification offered in:** early childhood, special education, elementary, middle/junior high, secondary. **Reserve Officers Training Corps (ROTC):** Army ROTC: Offered at cooperating institution (Lehigh University). **Faculty and instruction (2009-2010):** Total instructional faculty: 85 full-time, 212 part-time (49% men; 51% women; 21% minorities). Full-time faculty with Ph.D. or other terminal degree: 60%. Student/faculty ratio: 14/1. Classes of fewer than 20 students: 54%; of 20 to 49 students: 46%; of 50 or more students: 0%. **Advanced Placement and International Baccalaureate credit:** AP tests may be used for: Credit only. Scores accepted: 3, 4, 5. International Baccalaureate exams may be used for: Placement only. **Freshmen returning for sophomore year:** 71%. **Graduation rates:** Four-year: 36%; five-year: 53%; six-year: 54%.

COSTS AND FINANCIAL AID

Financial aid office: (610) 796-8356. **Expenses (2010-2011):** Tuition and fees 2010-2011: $25,480; room/board: $9,300. Estimated books and supplies: $1,500; transportation: $2,202; personal expenses: $0. **Financial aid:** Priority filing date for institution's financial aid form: May 1. In 2009-2010, 95% of undergraduates applied for financial aid. Of those, 89% were determined to have financial need; 11% had their need fully met. Average financial aid package (proportion receiving): $16,156 (88%). Average amount of gift aid, such as scholarships or grants (proportion receiving): $10,774 (85%). Average amount of self-help aid, such as work study or loans (proportion receiving): $6,336 (80%). Average need-based loan (excluding PLUS or other private loans): $5,593. Among students who received need-based aid, the average percentage of need met: 66%. Among students who received aid based on merit, the average award (and the proportion receiving): $6,749 (8%). The average athletic scholarship (and the proportion receiving): $0 (0%). Average amount of debt of borrowers graduating in 2009: $34,062. Proportion who borrowed: 94%.

CAMPUS LIFE AND EXTRACURRICULAR ACTIVITIES
Campus housing available (% using): coed dorms (84%), special housing for disabled students (1%), other housing options (15%). Students who live in college-owned, operated, or affiliated housing: 49%. Activities include: campus ministries, choral groups, dance, drama/theater, literary magazine, student government, student newspaper. Number of fraternities: 0; sororities: 0. Average proportion of students who stay on campus on weekends: 40%. **Sports program (2009-2010):** Member of NCAA III. *Men's intercollegiate varsity sports:* baseball, basketball, cross country, golf, lacrosse, soccer, tennis, track and field (outdoor). *Women's intercollegiate varsity sports:* basketball, cross country, field hockey, golf, lacrosse, soccer, softball, tennis, track and field (outdoor), volleyball.

SERVICES AND FACILITIES
Basic services: health service, health insurance. **Remedial assistance:** reading, math, writing, study skills. **Counseling services:** minority student, career, personal, academic, psychological, religious. **For learning-disabled students:** School does not offer a structured program with separate admission and additional fees. Total undergraduates in learning-disabled program or receiving services: 29. Services include: remedial math, remedial English, remedial reading, tape recorders, note-taking services, oral tests, learning center, extended time for tests, tutors, priority registration, priority seating, texts on tape, other testing accommodations. **Library:** Number of titles: 86,823; number of current serial subscriptions: 362. **Information technology resources:** Students are not required to lease or own a computer. Number of campus computers available to all students: 360. School has a wireless network. Approximate number of users that can be accommodated: 700. Proportion of college-owned housing units wired for high-speed internet access: 100%. **Campus safety:** Security services offered: 24-hour foot-and-vehicle patrols, late-night transport/escort service, 24-hour emergency telephones, lighted pathways/sidewalks, controlled dormitory access (key, security card, etc).

TRANSFER AND INTERNATIONAL STUDENTS
Transfer students: May apply for admission for the following academic terms: Fall, Spring, Summer. Applicants do not need a minimum number of credits to apply. For fall 2009: Transfer applications received: 457. Transfer applicants offered admission: 128. Transfer applicants enrolled: 127. **International students:** Number of foreign undergraduates: 11 (1% of student body). Number of countries represented: 10. Minimum TOEFL score required: 550 (paper); 75 (computer).

Arcadia University

- **Address:** 450 S. Easton Road, Glenside, PA 19038-3295
- **Website:** http://www.arcadia.edu
- **Private; Religious affiliation:** Presbyterian Church, USA
- **Enrollment:** 2,022 full-time; 231 part-time

KEY STATS
✔ **U.S News College Ranking:** 29, Regional Universities (North)
✔ **SAT Score (25th/75th percentile):** 1010-1210
✔ **Tuition:** 2010-2011: $32,720

Selectivity: Selective	**Room/board:** $11,150
Acceptance rate: 61%	**Average debt:** $35,975
Student/faculty ratio: 14/1	**Proportion who borrowed:** 88%

UNDERGRADUATE STUDENT BODY STATS
2009-2010 enrollment: 2,022 full-time; 231 part-time. Men: 27%; women: 73%. **Ethnic makeup:** African American: 8%; Asian American: 3%; Hispanic: 4%; White: 83%; International: 1%.

ADMISSIONS FACTS AND FIGURES
Phone: (215) 572-2910. **Email:** admiss@arcadia.edu. **Website:** http://www.arcadia.edu. **Application deadlines for fall 2011:** Regular decision: Rolling. Early decision: Not offered. Early action: Not offered. Admission can be deferred. **Application fee:** $30. **To apply online, go to:** http://www.arcadia.edu/prospective/default.aspx?id=1445. **Admissions requirements/recommendations:** High school units required (recommended): English: 4; Mathematics: 3; Science: 3; Foreign language: 2; Social studies: 4; Academic

electives: 3; Total units: 19. Tests: The college uses SAT or ACT scores in admissions decisions. Either SAT or ACT required. For admission to the fall 2011 entering class, the school will accept: ACT with writing required. Campus visit: Recommended. Admissions interview: Neither required nor recommended. Off-campus interview: May be arranged. **Factors that count in admissions decisions:** *Academic:* Secondary school record: Very Important. Class rank: Very Important. Letters of recommendation: Very Important. Standardized test scores: Very Important. Essay: Important. *Nonacademic:* Interview: Considered. Extracurricular activities: Important. Talent/ability: Considered. Character/personal qualities: Considered. Alumni/ae relationship: Important. Geographical residence: Not Considered. State residency: Not Considered. Religious affiliation/commitment: Not Considered. Minority status: Not Considered. Volunteer work: Considered. Work experience: Considered. **Other schools with the greatest overlap in applicants:** Drexel University; La Salle University; Pennsylvania State University–University Park; St. Joseph's University; Temple University. **Admissions statistics for the fall 2009 entering class:** Total applicants: 5,175. Total accepted: 3,151. Freshmen enrolled: 534; 44% were from out of state. Overall acceptance rate: 61%. **Size of waiting list:** 0 applicants; enrolled from waiting list: 0. **Credentials of fall 2009 freshmen:** 23% ranked in the top 10 percent of their high school class; 58% were in the top 25 percent; 87% were in the top half. (Proportion submitting class standing: 71%.) **Average high school grade point average:** 3.6. **First-year students who submitted SAT scores:** 94%. Scores (25/75 percentile): Critical Reading: 510-610, Math: 500-600, Combined: 1010-1210. **First-year students submitting ACT scores:** 14%. Scores (25/75 percentile): English: N/A, Math: N/A, Composite: 21-27.

ACADEMICS
Year founded: 1853. **Academic calendar:** Semester. **Degrees offered:** certificate, bachelor's, post-bachelor's certificate, master's, post-master's certificate, doctorate. **Most popular majors:** 10% biology/biological sciences, 10% elementary education and teaching, 10% psychology, 5% drama and dramatics/theater arts, 5% history. **Major fields of study:** biological and biomedical sciences; business, management, marketing, and related support services; communication, journalism, and related programs; computer and information sciences and support services; education; engineering; English language and literature/letters; foreign languages, literatures, and linguistics; health professions and related clinical sciences; history; legal professions and studies; liberal arts and sciences studies, and humanities; mathematics and statistics; philosophy and religious studies; physical sciences; psychology; social sciences; visual and performing arts. **Areas of required coursework:** arts/fine arts, humanities, mathematics, English (including composition), foreign languages, sciences (biological or physical), social science, other. **Pre-professional programs:** pre-law, pre-dentistry, pre-medicine, pre-veterinary science, pre-optometry, pre-pharmacy, other. **Special academic programs (% participation):** cooperative (work-study plan) program (1%), cross-registration (1%), distance learning (49%), double major (7%), exchange student program (domestic) (0%), external degree program (1%), honors program (6%), independent study (11%), internships (38%), student-designed major (4%), study abroad (50%), teacher certificate program (17%). **Teacher certification offered in:** early childhood, special education, elementary, middle/junior high, secondary. **Cooperative education programs:** business, computer science, natural science. **Faculty and instruction (2009-2010):** Total instructional faculty: 125 full-time, 303 part-time (35% men; 65% women; 12% minorities). Full-time faculty with Ph.D. or other terminal degree: 86%. Student/faculty ratio: 14/1. Classes of fewer than 20 students: 73%; of 20 to 49 students: 26%; of 50 or more students: 1%. **Advanced Placement and International Baccalaureate credit:** AP tests may be used for: Credit and/or placement. Scores accepted: 3, 4, 5. International Baccalaureate exams may be used for: Credit and/or placement. **Freshmen returning for sophomore year:** 78%. **Graduation rates:** Four-year: 53%; five-year: 59%; six-year: 62%. **Graduate study:** 33% of students pursue further study immediately upon graduation; 39% within one year; 40% within five years. Fields in which graduates pursue further study: Master of Business Administration (MBA), 9%; law, 5%; medicine, 5%; dentistry, 3%; engineering, 3%; theology (or the seminary), 1%; education, 34%; arts and sciences, 41%; veterinary medicine, 2%.

COSTS AND FINANCIAL AID
Financial aid office: (215) 572-2980. **Expenses (2010-2011):** Tuition and fees 2010-2011: $32,720; room/board: $11,150. Estimated books and supplies: $1,100; transportation: $250; personal expenses: $850. **Financial aid:** Priority filing date for institution's financial aid form: March 1. In 2009-2010, 96% of undergraduates applied for financial aid. Of those, 90% were determined to have financial need; 22% had their need fully met. Average financial

aid package (proportion receiving): $21,411 (88%). Average amount of gift aid, such as scholarships or grants (proportion receiving): $17,923 (86%). Average amount of self-help aid, such as work study or loans (proportion receiving): $5,527 (68%). Average need-based loan (excluding PLUS or other private loans): $4,409. Among students who received need-based aid, the average percentage of need met: 74%. Among students who received aid based on merit, the average award (and the proportion receiving): $12,735 (7%). The average athletic scholarship (and the proportion receiving): $0 (0%). Average amount of debt of borrowers graduating in 2009: $35,975. Proportion who borrowed: 88%.

CAMPUS LIFE AND EXTRACURRICULAR ACTIVITIES

Campus housing available (% using): coed dorms (45%), women's dorms (5%), apartment for single students (47%), special housing for disabled students (3%). Students who live in college-owned, operated, or affiliated housing: 65%. **Student employment:** During the 2009-2010 academic year, 48% of undergraduates worked on campus. Average per-year earnings: $1,449. **Clubs and organizations:** Number of student organizations: 90. Activities include: choral groups, dance, drama/theater, international student organization, literary magazine, model UN, music ensembles, radio station, student government, student newspaper, television station, yearbook. Number of fraternities: 0; sororities: 0. Average proportion of students who stay on campus on weekends: 65%. **Sports program (2009-2010):** Member of NCAA III. *Men's intercollegiate varsity sports:* baseball, basketball, golf, soccer, swimming, tennis. *Women's intercollegiate varsity sports:* basketball, field hockey, lacrosse, soccer, softball, swimming, tennis, volleyball.

SERVICES AND FACILITIES

Basic services: nonremedial tutoring, health service, health insurance, other. **Remedial assistance:** math, writing, study skills. **Counseling services:** minority student, career, personal, academic, psychological, birth control, other. **For learning-disabled students:** School does not offer a structured program with separate admission and additional fees. Total undergraduates in learning-disabled program or receiving services: 78. Services include: remedial math, remedial English, reading machines, note-taking services, learning center, extended time for tests, tutors, priority seating, texts on tape, other testing accommodations, other. **Library:** Number of titles: 125,015; number of current serial subscriptions: 14,571. **Information technology resources:** Students are not required to lease or own a computer. Number of campus computers available to all students: 375. School has a wireless network. Approximate number of users that can be accommodated: 5,000. Proportion of college-owned housing units wired for high-speed internet access: 100%. **Campus safety:** Security services offered: 24-hour foot-and-vehicle patrols, late-night transport/escort service, 24-hour emergency telephones, lighted pathways/sidewalks, student patrols, controlled dormitory access (key, security card, etc).

TRANSFER AND INTERNATIONAL STUDENTS

Transfer students: May apply for admission for the following academic terms: Fall, Spring, Summer. Applicants do not need a minimum number of credits to apply. For fall 2009: Transfer applications received: 763. Transfer applicants offered admission: 363. Transfer applicants enrolled: 135. **International students:** Number of foreign undergraduates: 30 (1% of student body). Number of countries represented: 26. Minimum TOEFL score required: 530 (paper); 73 (computer). Average TOEFL score: 607 (paper).

Baptist Bible College and Seminary

■ **Address:** 538 Venard Road, Clarks Summit, PA 18411
■ **Website:** http://www.bbc.edu
■ **Private; Religious affiliation:** Baptist
■ **Enrollment:** N/A

KEY STATS

✔ **U.S News College Ranking:** 48, Regional Colleges (North)
✔ **SAT Score (25th/75th percentile):** 890-1130
✔ **Tuition:** 2010-2011: $17,340

Selectivity: Less selective	**Room/board:** $6,350
Acceptance rate: 70%	**Average debt:** N/A
Student/faculty ratio: N/A	**Proportion who borrowed:** N/A

Bloomsburg University of Pennsylvania

■ **Address:** 400 E. Second Street, Bloomsburg, PA 17815
■ **Website:** http://www.bloomu.edu
■ **Public**
■ **Enrollment:** 8,105 full-time; 500 part-time

KEY STATS

✔ **U.S News College Ranking:** 88, Regional Universities (North)
✔ **SAT Score (25th/75th percentile):** 910-1100
✔ **Tuition:** 2009-2010: $7,110 in state, $15,546 out of state

Selectivity: Selective	**Room/board:** $6,488
Acceptance rate: 64%	**Average debt:** $21,322
Student/faculty ratio: 21/1	**Proportion who borrowed:** 71%

UNDERGRADUATE STUDENT BODY STATS

2009-2010 enrollment: 8,105 full-time; 500 part-time. Men: 42%; women: 58%. **Ethnic makeup:** African American: 7%; Asian American: 1%; Hispanic: 3%; White: 88%; International: 1%.

ADMISSIONS FACTS AND FIGURES

Phone: (570) 389-4316. **Email:** buadmiss@bloomu.edu. **Website:** http://www.bloomu.edu. **Application deadlines for fall 2011:** Regular decision: Rolling. Early decision: Not offered. Early action: Send application by: N/A; Decision sent by: N/A. Admission can be deferred. **Application fee:** $30. **To apply online, go to:** http://www.bloomu.edu/admissions. **Admissions requirements/recommendations:** High school units required (recommended): English: 4 (4); Mathematics: 3 (4); Science: 3 (4); Foreign language: 0 (2); Social studies: 2 (2); History: 2 (2); Academic electives: 2 (0); Total units: 16 (19). Tests: The college uses SAT or ACT scores in admissions decisions. Either SAT or ACT required. For admission to the fall 2011 entering class, the school will accept: ACT with or without writing accepted. Campus visit: Recommended. Admissions interview: Neither required nor recommended. Off-campus interview: May be arranged. **Factors that count in admissions decisions:** *Academic:* Secondary school record: Very Important. Class rank: Very Important. Letters of recommendation: Considered. Standardized test scores: Very Important. Essay: Considered. *Nonacademic:* Interview: Considered. Extracurricular activities: Considered. Talent/ability: Considered. Character/personal qualities: Considered. Alumni/ae relationship: Not Considered. Geographical residence: Considered. State residency: Considered. Religious affiliation/commitment: Not Considered. Minority status: Not Considered. Volunteer work: Considered. Work experience: Considered. **Other schools with the greatest overlap in applicants:** Kutztown University of Pennsylvania; Lock Haven University of Pennsylvania; Millersville University of Pennsylvania; Pennsylvania State University–University Park; Shippensburg University of Pennsylvania. **Admissions statistics for the fall 2009 entering class:** Total applicants: 11,749. Total accepted: 7,473. Freshmen enrolled: 2,040; 13% were from out of state. Overall acceptance rate: 64%. Non-early acceptance rate: 64%. **Size of waiting list:** 215 applicants; enrolled from waiting list: 23. **Credentials of fall 2009 freshmen:** 12% ranked in the top 10 percent of their high school class; 36% were in the top 25 percent; 76% were in the top half. (Proportion submitting class standing: 81%.) **Average high school grade point average:** 3.4. **First-year students who submitted SAT scores:** 99%. Scores (25/75 percentile): Critical Reading: 450-540, Math: 460-560, Combined: 910-1100.

ACADEMICS

Year founded: 1839. **Academic calendar:** Semester. **Degrees offered:** certificate, bachelor's, post-bachelor's certificate, master's, post-master's certificate. **Most popular majors:** 17% business administration and management, 10% elementary education and teaching, 6% special education and teaching, 5% audiology/audiologist and speech-language pathology/pathologist, 5% speech and rhetorical studies. **Major fields of study:** biological and biomedical sciences; business, management, marketing, and related support services; communication, journalism, and related programs; computer and information sciences and support services; education; engineering; English language and literature/letters; foreign languages, literatures, and linguistics; health professions and related clinical sciences; history; mathematics and statistics; parks, recreation, leisure, and fitness studies; philosophy and religious studies; physical sciences; psychology; public administration and social service professions; security and protective services; social sciences; visual and performing arts. **Areas of required coursework:** arts/fine arts, humanities, mathematics, English (including composition), philosophy, sciences (biological or physical), history, social science, other. **Pre-professional programs:** pre-law, pre-medicine, pre-pharmacy, other. **Special academic programs (% participation):** cooperative (work-study plan) program, cross-registration, distance learning (7%), double major (7%), dual enrollment, English as a Second Language (ESL), exchange student program (domestic), honors program (1%), independent study (6%), internships (32%), liberal arts/career combination, study abroad (1%), teacher certificate program (21%). **Teacher certification offered in:** early childhood, special education, middle/junior high, secondary. **Reserve Officers Training Corps (ROTC):** Army ROTC: Offered on campus; Air Force ROTC: Offered at cooperating institution (Wilkes University). **Faculty and instruction (2009-2010):** Total instructional faculty: 397 full-time, 82 part-time (55% men; 45% women; 11% minorities). Full-time faculty with Ph.D. or other terminal degree: 85%. Student/faculty ratio: 21/1. Classes of fewer than 20 students: 21%; of 20 to 49 students: 72%; of 50 or more students: 7%. **Advanced Placement and International Baccalaureate credit:** AP tests may be used for: Placement only. Scores accepted: 3, 4, 5. **Freshmen returning for sophomore year:** 80%. **Graduation rates:** Four-year: 41%; five-year: 61%; six-year: 64%. **Graduate study:** 26% of students pursue further study within one year.

COSTS AND FINANCIAL AID
Financial aid office: (570) 389-4297. **Expenses (2009-2010):** Tuition and fees 2009-2010: $7,110 in state, $15,546 out of state; room/board: $6,488. Estimated books and supplies: $1,200; transportation: $1,662; personal expenses: $3,202. **Financial aid:** Priority filing date for institution's financial aid form: March 15. In 2009-2010, 87% of undergraduates applied for financial aid. Of those, 83% were determined to have financial need; 87% had their need fully met. Average financial aid package (proportion receiving): $11,899 (80%). Average amount of gift aid, such as scholarships or grants (proportion receiving): $5,822 (40%). Average amount of self-help aid, such as work study or loans (proportion receiving): $4,815 (51%). Average need-based loan (excluding PLUS or other private loans): $4,162. Among students who received need-based aid, the average percentage of need met: 72%. Among students who received aid based on merit, the average award (and the proportion receiving): $1,971 (2%). The average athletic scholarship (and the proportion receiving): $2,581 (3%). Average amount of debt of borrowers graduating in 2009: $21,322. Proportion who borrowed: 71%.

CAMPUS LIFE AND EXTRACURRICULAR ACTIVITIES
Campus housing available (% using): coed dorms (61%), apartment for single students (30%), other housing options (9%). Students who live in college-owned, operated, or affiliated housing: 49%. **Student employment:** During the 2009-2010 academic year, 9% of undergraduates worked on campus. Average per-year earnings: $2,054. **Clubs and organizations:** Number of student organizations: 200. Activities include: campus ministries, choral groups, concert band, dance, drama/theater, international student organization, jazz band, literary magazine, marching band, model UN, music ensembles, pep band, radio station, student government, student newspaper, symphony orchestra, television station, yearbook. Number of fraternities: 15; sororities: 13. Proportion of men in fraternities: 7%; of women in sororities: 9%. **Sports program (2009-2010):** Member of NCAA II. *Men's intercollegiate varsity sports:* baseball, basketball, cross country, football, soccer, swimming, tennis, track and field (indoor), track and field (outdoor), wrestling. *Women's intercollegiate varsity sports:* basketball, cross country, field hockey, lacrosse, soccer, softball, swimming, tennis, track and field (indoor), track and field (outdoor).

SERVICES AND FACILITIES
Basic services: nonremedial tutoring, women's center, placement service, day care, health service, health insurance. **Remedial assistance:** reading, math, writing, study skills. **Counseling services:** career, personal, academic, psychological. **For learning-disabled students:** School does not offer a structured program with separate admission and additional fees. Total undergraduates in learning-disabled program or receiving services: 174. Services include: remedial math, remedial English, reading machines, remedial reading, tape recorders, other special classes, note-taking services, oral tests, readers, extended time for tests, tutors, priority registration, priority seating, texts on tape, typist/scribe, exams on tape or computer, other. **Library:** Number of titles: 547,535; number of current serial subscriptions: 51,213. **Information technology resources:** Students are not required to lease or own a computer. Number of campus computers available to all students: 1,469. School has a wireless network. Approximate number of users that can be accommodated: 5,000. Proportion of college-owned housing units wired for high-speed internet access: 100%. **Campus safety:** Security services offered: 24-hour foot-and-vehicle patrols, late-night transport/escort service, 24-hour

emergency telephones, lighted pathways/sidewalks, controlled dormitory access (key, security card, etc).

TRANSFER AND INTERNATIONAL STUDENTS
Transfer students: May apply for admission for the following academic terms: Fall, Spring, Summer. Applicants need a minimum number of credits to apply. For fall 2009: Transfer applications received: 1,406. Transfer applicants offered admission: 867. Transfer applicants enrolled: 473. **International students:** Number of foreign undergraduates: 71 (1% of student body). Number of countries represented: 20. Minimum TOEFL score required: 500 (paper); 173 (computer). Average TOEFL score: 550 (paper).

Bryn Athyn College of the New Church

- **Address:** 2965 College Drive, PO Box 717, Bryn Athyn, PA 19009
- **Website:** http://www.brynathyn.edu
- **Private; Religious affiliation:** General Church of the New Jerusalem
- **Enrollment:** 181 full-time; 7 part-time

KEY STATS
✔ **U.S News College Ranking:** Unranked, National Liberal Arts Colleges
✔ **SAT Score (25th/75th percentile):** 960-1230
✔ **Tuition:** 2010-2011: $15,540

Selectivity: N/A	Room/board: $8,540
Acceptance rate: 92%	Average debt: $12,729
Student/faculty ratio: 6/1	Proportion who borrowed: 57%

UNDERGRADUATE STUDENT BODY STATS
2009-2010 enrollment: 181 full-time; 7 part-time. Men: 50%; women: 50%. **Ethnic makeup:** African American: 7%; Asian American: 2%; White: 70%; International: 21%.

ADMISSIONS FACTS AND FIGURES
Phone: (267) 502-6000. **Email:** admissions@brynathyn.edu. **Website:** http://www.brynathyn.edu. **Application deadlines for fall 2011:** Regular decision: July 1. Early decision: Not offered. Early action: Not offered. Admission can be deferred. **To apply online, go to:** http://www.brynathyn.edu/admissions/info/apply.html. **Admissions requirements/recommendations:** High school units required (recommended): English: 4; Mathematics: 3; Science: 3; Foreign language: 2; Total units: 15. Tests: The college uses SAT or ACT scores in admissions decisions. Either SAT or ACT required. For admission to the fall 2011 entering class, the school will accept: ACT with writing recommended. Campus visit: Recommended. Admissions interview: Recommended. Off-campus interview: May be arranged. **Factors that count in admissions decisions:** *Academic:* Secondary school record: Very Important. Class rank: Considered. Letters of recommendation: Very Important. Standardized test scores: Very Important. Essay: Very Important. *Nonacademic:* Interview: Considered. Extracurricular activities: Considered. Talent/ability: Important. Character/personal qualities: Important. Alumni/ae relationship: Considered. Geographical residence: Not Considered. State residency: Not Considered. Religious affiliation/commitment: Important. Minority status: Not Considered. Volunteer work: Considered. Work experience: Considered. **Admissions statistics for the fall 2009 entering class:** Total applicants: 227. Total accepted: 208. Freshmen enrolled: 70; 35% were from out of state. Overall acceptance rate: 92%. **Average high school grade point average:** 3.4. **First-year students who submitted SAT scores:** 92%. Scores (25/75 percentile): Critical Reading: 490-630, Math: 470-600, Combined: 960-1230. **First-year students submitting ACT scores:** 22%. Scores (25/75 percentile): English: 17-24, Math: 17-23, Composite: 20-23.

ACADEMICS
Year founded: 1877. **Academic calendar:** Trimester. **Degrees offered:** associate, bachelor's, master's. **Most popular majors:** 59% multi/interdisciplinary studies, 20% history, 7% English language and literature, 7% education, 7% religion/religious studies. **Major fields of study:** biological and biomedical sciences; education; English language and literature/letters; history; multi/interdisciplinary studies; philosophy and religious studies. **Areas of required coursework:** humanities, mathematics, English (including composition), philosophy, foreign languages, sciences (biological or physical), history, social science, other. **Special academic programs (% participation):** cooperative (work-study plan) program (27.2%), cross-registration (0%), English as a Second Language (ESL) (9.09%), independent study (81.8%), internships (54.5%), student-designed major (27.2%), study abroad (0%), teacher

certificate program (0%). **Teacher certification offered in:** early childhood, elementary, secondary. **Cooperative education programs:** other. **Reserve Officers Training Corps (ROTC):** Army ROTC: Offered at cooperating institution (Temple University); Air Force ROTC: Offered at cooperating institution (St. Joseph's University). **Faculty and instruction (2009-2010):** Total instructional faculty: 24 full-time, 26 part-time (52% men; 48% women; 0% minorities). Full-time faculty with Ph.D. or other terminal degree: 58%. Student/faculty ratio: 6/1. Classes of fewer than 20 students: 89%; of 20 to 49 students: 11%; of 50 or more students: 0%. **Advanced Placement and International Baccalaureate credit:** AP tests may be used for: Credit and/or placement. International Baccalaureate exams may be used for: Credit and/or placement. **Freshmen returning for sophomore year:** 72%. **Graduation rates:** Four-year: 22%; five-year: 31%; six-year: 25%.

COSTS AND FINANCIAL AID

Financial aid office: (267) 502-2630. **Expenses (2010-2011):** Tuition and fees 2010-2011: $15,540; room/board: $8,540. Estimated books and supplies: $950 personal expenses: $700. **Financial aid:** In 2009-2010, 72% of undergraduates applied for financial aid. Of those, 62% were determined to have financial need; 36% had their need fully met. Average financial aid package (proportion receiving): $14,592 (62%). Average amount of gift aid, such as scholarships or grants (proportion receiving): $10,548 (57%). Average amount of self-help aid, such as work study or loans (proportion receiving): $2,977 (23%). Average need-based loan (excluding PLUS or other private loans): $2,977. Among students who received need-based aid, the average percentage of need met: 92%. Among students who received aid based on merit, the average award (and the proportion receiving): $3,531 (8%). The average athletic scholarship (and the proportion receiving): $0 (0%). Average amount of debt of borrowers graduating in 2009: $12,729. Proportion who borrowed: 57%.

CAMPUS LIFE AND EXTRACURRICULAR ACTIVITIES

Campus housing available (% using): women's dorms (34%), men's dorms (37%), other housing options (27%). Students who live in college-owned, operated, or affiliated housing: 68%. **Student employment:** During the 2009-2010 academic year, 44% of undergraduates worked on campus. Average per-year earnings: $2,500. **Clubs and organizations:** Number of student organizations: 15. Activities include: choral groups, dance, drama/theater, international student organization, music ensembles, student government, student newspaper. Number of fraternities: 0; sororities: 0.

SERVICES AND FACILITIES

Basic services: nonremedial tutoring, health service. **Remedial assistance:** math, writing, other. **Counseling services:** career, personal, academic, psychological, religious. **For learning-disabled students:** School does not offer a structured program with separate admission and additional fees. Services include: remedial English, tape recorders, untimed tests, oral tests, extended time for tests, tutors, other. **Library:** Number of titles: 119,009; number of current serial subscriptions: 527. **Information technology resources:** Students are not required to lease or own a computer. Number of campus computers available to all students: 55. School has a wireless network. Approximate number of users that can be accommodated: 550. Proportion of college-owned housing units wired for high-speed internet access: 100%. **Campus safety:** Security services offered: 24-hour foot-and-vehicle patrols, 24-hour emergency telephones, lighted pathways/sidewalks, controlled dormitory access (key, security card, etc).

TRANSFER AND INTERNATIONAL STUDENTS

Transfer students: May apply for admission for the following academic terms: Fall, Winter, Spring. Applicants need a minimum number of credits to apply. For fall 2009: Transfer applications received: 5. Transfer applicants offered admission: 5. Transfer applicants enrolled: 4. **International students:** Number of foreign undergraduates: 40 (21% of student body). Number of countries represented: 15. Minimum TOEFL score required: 520 (paper); 190 (computer).

Bryn Mawr College

- **Address:** 101 N. Merion Avenue, Bryn Mawr, PA 19010
- **Website:** http://www.brynmawr.edu
- **Private**
- **Enrollment:** 1,283 full-time; 24 part-time

KEY STATS

✔ **U.S News College Ranking:** 30, National Liberal Arts Colleges
✔ **SAT Score (25th/75th percentile):** 1180-1380
✔ **Tuition:** 2010-2011: $39,360

Selectivity: More selective	**Room/board:** $12,420
Acceptance rate: 49%	**Average debt:** $20,156
Student/faculty ratio: 8/1	**Proportion who borrowed:** 52%

UNDERGRADUATE STUDENT BODY STATS

2009-2010 enrollment: 1,283 full-time; 24 part-time. Men: 0%; women: 100%. **Ethnic makeup:** African American: 6%; Asian American: 12%; Hispanic: 5%; White: 66%; International: 10%.

ADMISSIONS FACTS AND FIGURES

Phone: (610) 526-5152. **Email:** admissions@brynmawr.edu. **Website:** http://www.brynmawr.edu. **Application deadlines for fall 2011:** Regular decision: January 15; decision sent by April 1. Early decision: Send application by: November 15; Decision sent by: December 15. Early action: Not offered. Admission can be deferred. **Application fee:** $50. **To apply online, go to:** http://www.brynmawr.edu/admissions/applicationoptions.shtml. **Admissions requirements/recommendations:** High school units required (recommended): English: (4); Mathematics: (3); Science: (2); Foreign language: (3); Social studies: (2); History: (2); Academic electives: (2); Total units: (16). Tests: The college uses SAT or ACT scores in admissions decisions. Either SAT or ACT required. For admission to the fall 2011 entering class, the school will accept: ACT with or without writing accepted. Campus visit: Recommended. Admissions interview: Recommended. Off-campus interview: May be arranged. **Factors that count in admissions decisions:** *Academic:* Secondary school record: Very Important. Class rank: Considered. Letters of recommendation: Very Important. Standardized test scores: Considered. Essay: Important. *Nonacademic:* Interview: Considered. Extracurricular activities: Important. Talent/ability: Considered. Character/personal qualities: Important. Alumni/ae relationship: Considered. Geographical residence: Considered. State residency: Not Considered. Religious affiliation/commitment: Not Considered. Minority status: Considered. Volunteer work: Considered. Work experience: Considered. **Other schools with the greatest overlap in applicants:** Haverford College; Mount Holyoke College; Smith College; Swarthmore College; Wellesley College. **Admissions statistics for the fall 2009 entering class:** Total applicants: 2,276. Total accepted: 1,107. Freshmen enrolled: 362; 89% were from out of state. Overall acceptance rate: 49%. Non-early acceptance rate: 49%. Size of waiting list: 394 applicants; enrolled from waiting list: 39. **Credentials of fall 2009 freshmen:** 61% ranked in the top 10 percent of their high school class; 87% were in the top 25 percent; 99% were in the top half. (Proportion submitting class standing: 39%.) **First-year students who submitted SAT scores:** 90%. Scores (25/75 percentile): Critical Reading: 600-700, Math: 580-680, Combined: 1180-1380. **First-year students submitting ACT scores:** 33%. Scores (25/75 percentile): English: 28-33, Math: 25-30, Composite: 26-30.

ACADEMICS

Year founded: 1885. **Academic calendar:** Semester. **Degrees offered:** bachelor's, post-bachelor's certificate, master's, doctorate. **Most popular majors:** 12% English language and literature, 12% psychology, 9% biology/biological sciences, 8% political science and government, 7% anthropology. **Major fields of study:** area, ethnic, cultural, and gender studies; biological and biomedical sciences; computer and information sciences and support services; English language and literature/letters; foreign languages, literatures, and linguistics; history; mathematics and statistics; multi/interdisciplinary studies; philosophy and religious studies; physical sciences; psychology; social sciences; visual and performing arts. **Areas of required coursework:** humanities, mathematics, English (including composition), foreign languages, sciences (biological or physical), social science, other. **Pre-professional programs:** pre-law, pre-medicine. **Special academic programs (% participation):** cross-registration (93%), double major (13%), exchange student program (domestic) (0%), independent study (30%), internships, liberal arts/career combination, student-designed major (2%), study abroad (37%), teacher certificate program (1%). **Teacher certification offered in:** elementary, middle/junior high, secondary. **Cooperative education programs:** engineering, other. **Reserve Officers Training Corps (ROTC):** Air Force ROTC: Offered at cooperating institution (St. Joseph's University). **Faculty and instruction (2009-2010):** Total instructional faculty: 158 full-time, 53 part-time (43% men; 57% women; 15% minorities). Full-time faculty with Ph.D. or other terminal degree: 97%. Student/faculty ratio: 8/1. Classes of fewer than 20 students: 72%; of 20 to 49 students: 24%; of 50 or more students: 4%. **Advanced Placement and International Baccalaureate credit:** AP tests may be used for: Placement only. Scores accepted: 4, 5. International Baccalaureate exams may be used for: Credit and/or placement. **Freshmen returning for sophomore year:** 93%. **Graduation rates:** Four-year: 74%; five-year: 79%; six-year: 80%. **Graduate study:** 26% of students pursue further study immediately upon graduation; 27% within one year; 70% within five years. Fields in which graduates pursue further study: Master of Business Administration (MBA), 8%; law, 20%; medicine, 19%; education, 4%; arts and sciences, 41%.

COSTS AND FINANCIAL AID

Financial aid office: (610) 526-5245. **Expenses (2010-2011):** Tuition and fees 2010-2011: $39,360; room/board: $12,420. **Financial aid:** Priority filing date for institution's financial aid form: February 5; deadline: March 1. In 2009-2010, 63% of undergraduates applied for financial aid. Of those, 57% were determined to have financial need; 100% had their need fully met. Average financial aid package (proportion receiving): $35,351 (57%). Average amount of gift aid, such as scholarships or grants (proportion receiving): $29,927 (57%). Average amount of self-help aid, such as work study or loans (proportion receiving): $5,895 (51%). Average need-based loan (excluding PLUS or other private loans): $5,018. Among students who received need-based aid, the average percentage of need met: 100%. Among students who received aid based on merit, the average award (and the proportion receiving): $15,438 (2%). The average athletic scholarship (and the proportion receiving): $0 (0%). Average amount of debt of borrowers graduating in 2009: $20,156. Proportion who borrowed: 52%.

CAMPUS LIFE AND EXTRACURRICULAR ACTIVITIES

Campus housing available (% using): women's dorms (100%), apartment for single students, cooperative housing (0%), other housing options. Students who live in college-owned, operated, or affiliated housing: 95%. **Student employment:** During the 2009-2010 academic year, 66% of undergraduates worked on campus. Average per-year earnings: $2,000. **Clubs and organizations:** Number of student organizations: 100. Activities include: choral groups, dance, drama/theater, jazz band, literary magazine, marching band, music ensembles, musical theater, radio station, student government, student newspaper, student film society, yearbook. Number of fraternities: 0; sororities: 0. Average proportion of students who stay on campus on weekends: 97%. **Sports program (2009-2010):** Member of NCAA III. *Women's intercollegiate varsity sports:* badminton, basketball, crew (heavyweight), cross country, field hockey, lacrosse, soccer, swimming, tennis, track and field (indoor), track and field (outdoor), volleyball.

SERVICES AND FACILITIES

Basic services: nonremedial tutoring, women's center, health service, health insurance. **Remedial assistance:** other. **Counseling services:** minority student, career, personal, academic, older student, psychological, birth control, religious. **For learning-disabled students:** School does not offer a structured program with separate admission and additional fees. **Library:** Number of titles: 952,890; number of current serial subscriptions: 32,914. **Information technology resources:** Students are not required to lease or own a computer. Number of campus computers available to all students: 200. School has a wireless network. Approximate number of users that can be accommodated: 600. Proportion of college-owned housing units wired for high-speed internet access: 100%. **Campus safety:** Security services offered: 24-hour foot-and-vehicle patrols, 24-hour emergency telephones, lighted pathways/sidewalks, controlled dormitory access (key, security card, etc).

TRANSFER AND INTERNATIONAL STUDENTS

Transfer students: May apply for admission for the following academic terms: Fall, Spring. Applicants do not need a minimum number of credits to apply. For fall 2009: Transfer applications received: 155. Transfer applicants offered admission: 28. Transfer applicants enrolled: 10. **International students:** Number of foreign undergraduates: 128 (10% of student body). Number of countries represented: 44. Minimum TOEFL score required: 600 (paper); 250 (computer). Average TOEFL score: 617 (paper).

Bucknell University

- **Address:** Lewisburg, PA 17837
- **Website:** http://www.bucknell.edu
- **Private**
- **Enrollment:** 3,523 full-time; 20 part-time

KEY STATS

✔ **U.S News College Ranking:** 30, National Liberal Arts Colleges
✔ **SAT Score (25th/75th percentile):** 1230-1400
✔ **Tuition:** 2010-2011: $42,342

Selectivity: More selective	**Room/board:** $9,938
Acceptance rate: 30%	**Average debt:** $18,800
Student/faculty ratio: 10/1	**Proportion who borrowed:** 61%

UNDERGRADUATE STUDENT BODY STATS

2009-2010 enrollment: 3,523 full-time; 20 part-time. Men: 49%; women: 51%. **Ethnic makeup:** African American: 3%; Asian American: 4%; Hispanic: 3%; White: 87%; International: 3%. **Religious preference:** Roman Catholic: 27%; Protestant: 25%; Jewish: 9%; No preference: 36%; Other: 3%.

ADMISSIONS FACTS AND FIGURES

Phone: (570) 577-1101. **Email:** admissions@bucknell.edu. **Website:** http://www.bucknell.edu. **Application deadlines for fall 2011:** Regular decision: January 15; decision sent by April 1. Early decision: Send application by: November 15; Decision sent by: December 15. Early action: Not offered. Admission can be deferred. **Application fee:** $60. **To apply online, go to:** http://www.bucknell.edu/x14032.xml. **Admissions requirements/recommendations:** High school units required (recommended): English: 4 (4); Mathematics: 3 (4); Science: 2 (3); Foreign language: 2 (4); Social studies: 2 (2); History: 2 (2); Academic electives: 1 (1); Total units: 16 (20). Tests: The college uses SAT or ACT scores in admissions decisions. Either SAT or ACT required. For admission to the fall 2011 entering class, the school will accept: ACT with writing required. Campus visit: Recommended. Admissions interview: Neither required nor recommended. Off-campus interview: Not available. **Factors that count in admissions decisions:** *Academic:* Secondary school record: Very Important. Class rank: Very Important. Letters of recommendation: Important. Standardized test scores: Very Important. Essay: Very Important. *Nonacademic:* Interview: Not Considered. Extracurricular activities: Important. Talent/ability: Very Important. Character/personal qualities: Very Important. Alumni/ae relationship: Considered. Geographical residence: Considered. State residency: Not Considered. Religious affiliation/commitment: Considered. Minority status: Considered. Volunteer work: Important. Work experience: Important. **Other schools with the greatest overlap in applicants:** Colgate University; Cornell University; Lehigh University; Pennsylvania State University–University Park; Villanova University. **Admissions statistics for the fall 2009 entering class:** Total applicants: 7,572. Total accepted: 2,263. Freshmen enrolled: 920; 77% were from out of state. Accepted through early-decision or early-action plans: 44%. Overall acceptance rate: 30%. Early-decision acceptance rate: 62%. Non-early acceptance rate: 27%. **Size of waiting list:** 2073 applicants; enrolled from waiting list: 23. **Credentials of fall 2009 freshmen:** 59% ranked in the top 10 percent of their high school class; 88% were in the top 25 percent; 99% were in the top half. (Proportion submitting class standing: 32%.) **Average high school grade point average:** 3.5. **First-year students who submitted SAT scores:** 75%. Scores (25/75 percentile): Critical Reading: 600-680, Math: 630-720, Combined: 1230-1400. **First-year students submitting ACT scores:** 36%. Scores (25/75 percentile): English: N/A, Math: N/A, Composite: 27-31.

ACADEMICS

Year founded: 1846. **Academic calendar:** Semester. **Degrees offered:** bachelor's, master's. **Most popular majors:** 13% economics, 9% business administration and management, 7% psychology, 6% English language and literature, 5% biology/biological sciences. **Major fields of study:** area, ethnic, cultural, and gender studies; biological and biomedical sciences; business, management, marketing, and related support services; computer and information sciences and support services; education; engineering; English language and literature/letters; foreign languages, literatures, and linguistics; history; liberal arts and sciences studies, and humanities; mathematics and statistics; multi/interdisciplinary studies; natural resources and conservation; philosophy and religious studies; physical sciences; psychology; social sciences; visual and performing arts. **Areas of required coursework:** humanities, mathematics, English (including composition), sciences (biological or physical), social science. **Special academic programs (% participation):** double major (28%), dual enrollment, honors program (5%), independent study (25%), internships (5%), liberal arts/career combination (3%), student-designed major (1%), study abroad (45%), teacher certificate program (5%). **Teacher certification offered in:** early childhood, elementary, secondary. **Reserve Officers Training Corps (ROTC):** Army ROTC: Offered on campus. **Faculty and instruction (2009-2010):** Total instructional faculty: 345 full-time, 22 part-time (61% men; 39% women; 13% minorities). Full-time faculty with Ph.D. or other terminal degree: 97%. Student/faculty ratio: 10/1. Classes of fewer than 20 students: 56%; of 20 to 49 students: 42%; of 50 or more students: 2%. **Advanced Placement and International Baccalaureate credit:** AP tests may be used for: Credit and/or placement. Scores accepted: 4, 5. International Baccalaureate exams may be used for: Placement only. **Freshmen returning for sophomore year:** 95%. **Graduation rates:** Four-year: 88%; five-year: 90%; six-year: 90%. **Graduate study:** 27% of students pursue further study immediately upon graduation. Fields in which graduates pursue further study: Master of Business Administration (MBA), 2%; law, 18%; medicine, 18%; engineering, 15%; education, 7%; arts and sciences, 29%.

COSTS AND FINANCIAL AID

Financial aid office: (570) 577-1331. **Expenses (2010-2011):** Tuition and fees 2010-2011: $42,342; room/board: $9,938. Estimated books and supplies: $900; transportation: $400; personal expenses: $2,000. **Financial aid:** In 2009-2010, 53% of undergraduates applied for financial aid. Of those, 46% were determined to have financial need; 95% had their need fully met. Average financial aid package (proportion receiving): $25,500 (46%). Average amount of gift aid, such as scholarships or grants (proportion receiving): $21,300 (42%). Average amount of self-help aid, such as work study or loans (proportion receiving): $2,400 (46%). Average need-based loan (excluding PLUS or other private loans): $5,400. Among students who received need-based aid, the average percentage of need met: 95%. Among students who received aid based on merit, the average award (and the proportion receiving): $11,907 (4%). The average athletic scholarship (and the proportion receiving): $9,304 (1%). Average amount of debt of borrowers graduating in 2009: $18,800. Proportion who borrowed: 61%.

CAMPUS LIFE AND EXTRACURRICULAR ACTIVITIES

Campus housing available (% using): coed dorms (57%), men's dorms (1%), sorority housing (4%), fraternity housing (10%), apartment for single students (17%), special housing for disabled students (0%), special housing for international students (0%), cooperative housing (0%), other housing options (4%). Students who live in college-owned, operated, or affiliated housing: 87%. **Student employment:** During the 2009-2010 academic year, 28% of undergraduates worked on campus. Average per-year earnings: $1,500. **Clubs and organizations:** Number of student organizations: 150. Activities include: campus ministries, choral groups, concert band, dance, drama/theater, international student organization, jazz band, literary magazine, model UN, music ensembles, musical theater, opera, pep band, radio station, student government, student newspaper, student film society, symphony orchestra, yearbook. Number of fraternities: 12; sororities: 8. Proportion of men in fraternities: 42%; of women in sororities: 47%. Average proportion of students who stay on campus on weekends: 85%. **Sports program (2009-2010):** Member of NCAA I. *Men's intercollegiate varsity sports:* baseball, basketball, cross country, football, golf, lacrosse, soccer, swimming, tennis, track and field (indoor), track and field (outdoor), water polo, wrestling. *Women's intercollegiate varsity sports:* basketball, crew (heavyweight), cross country, field hockey, golf, lacrosse, soccer, softball, swimming, tennis, track and field (indoor), track and field (outdoor), volleyball, water polo.

SERVICES AND FACILITIES

Basic services: nonremedial tutoring, women's center, placement service, health service, health insurance. **Counseling services:** minority student, career, military, personal, academic, psychological, birth control, religious. **For learning-disabled students:** School does not offer a structured program with separate admission and additional fees. Total undergraduates in learning-disabled program or receiving services: 88. Services include: reading machines, tape recorders, oral tests, extended time for tests, tutors, other testing accommodations, other. **Library:** Number of titles: 818,837; number of current serial subscriptions: 36,242. **Information technology resources:** Students are not required to lease or own a computer. Number of campus computers available to all students: 970. School has a wireless network. Approximate number of users that can be accommodated: 5,000. Proportion of college-owned housing units wired for high-speed internet access: 100%. **Campus safety:** Security services offered: 24-hour foot-and-vehicle patrols, late-night transport/escort service, 24-hour emergency telephones, lighted pathways/sidewalks, student patrols, controlled dormitory access (key, security card, etc).

TRANSFER AND INTERNATIONAL STUDENTS

Transfer students: May apply for admission for the following academic terms: Fall, Spring. Applicants need a minimum number of credits to apply. For fall 2009: Transfer applications received: 198. Transfer applicants offered admission: 41. Transfer applicants enrolled: 24. **International students:** Number of foreign undergraduates: 115 (3% of student body). Number of countries represented: 52. Minimum TOEFL score required: 550 (paper); 213 (computer). Average TOEFL score: 607 (paper).

Cabrini College

- **Address:** 610 King of Prussia Road, Radnor, PA 19087-3698
- **Website:** http://www.cabrini.edu
- **Private; Religious affiliation:** Roman Catholic
- **Enrollment:** 1,452 full-time; 102 part-time

KEY STATS

✔ **U.S News College Ranking:** 114, Regional Universities (North)
✔ **SAT Score (25th/75th percentile):** 860-1030
✔ **Tuition:** 2009-2010: $31,028

Selectivity: Less selective	**Room/board:** $11,340
Acceptance rate: 75%	**Average debt:** $30,633
Student/faculty ratio: 14/1	**Proportion who borrowed:** 81%

UNDERGRADUATE STUDENT BODY STATS

2009-2010 enrollment: 1,452 full-time; 102 part-time. Men: 36%; women: 64%. **Ethnic makeup:** African American: 6%; Asian American: 1%; Hispanic: 1%; White: 91%. **Religious preference:** Protestant: 14%; Jewish: 1%; No preference: 7%; Roman Catholic: 60%.

ADMISSIONS FACTS AND FIGURES

Phone: (610) 902-8552. **Email:** admit@cabrini.edu. **Website:** http://www.cabrini.edu. **Application deadlines for fall 2011:** Regular decision: Rolling. Early decision: Not offered. Early action: Not offered. Admission can be deferred. **Application fee:** $35. **To apply online, go to:** http://www.cabrini.edu/application. **Admissions requirements/recommendations:** High school units required (recommended): English: 4 (4); Mathematics: 3 (4); Science: 3 (3); Foreign language: 2 (2); Social studies: 3 (3); Academic electives: (2); Total units: 17 (21). Tests: The college uses SAT or ACT scores in admissions decisions. Either SAT or ACT required. For admission to the fall 2011 entering class, the school will accept: ACT with or without writing accepted. Campus visit: Recommended. Admissions interview: Recommended. Off-campus interview: May be arranged. **Factors that count in admissions decisions:** *Academic:* Secondary school record: Considered. Class rank: Considered. Letters of recommendation: Considered. Standardized test scores: Very Important. Essay: Considered. *Nonacademic:* Interview: Considered. Extracurricular activities: Considered. Talent/ability: Considered. Character/personal qualities: Considered. Alumni/ae relationship: Considered. Geographical residence: Not Considered. State residency: Not Considered. Religious affiliation/commitment: Not Considered. Minority status: Not Considered. Volunteer work: Considered. Work experience: Considered. **Other schools with the greatest overlap in applicants:** La Salle University; Neumann University; St. Joseph's University; Temple University; West Chester University of Pennsylvania. **Admissions statistics for the fall 2009 entering class:** Total applicants: 2,666. Total accepted: 1,988. Freshmen enrolled: 359; 49% were from out of state. Overall acceptance rate: 75%. **Credentials of fall 2009 freshmen:** 4% ranked in the top 10 percent of their high school class; 20% were in the top 25 percent; 50% were in the top half. (Proportion submitting class standing: 58%.) **Average high school grade point average:** 3.1. **First-year students who submitted SAT scores:** 99%. Scores (25/75 percentile): Critical Reading: 430-520, Math: 430-510, Combined: 860-1030.

ACADEMICS

Year founded: 1957. **Academic calendar:** Semester. **Degrees offered:** certificate, bachelor's, post-bachelor's certificate, master's. **Most popular majors:** 24% business, management, marketing, and related support services, 18% education, 14% communication studies/speech communication and rhetoric, 6% biology/biological sciences, 6% kinesiology and exercise science.

Major fields of study: area, ethnic, cultural, and gender studies; biological and biomedical sciences; business, management, marketing, and related support services; communication, journalism, and related programs; computer and information sciences and support services; education; English language and literature/letters; foreign languages, literatures, and linguistics; health professions and related clinical sciences; history; liberal arts and sciences studies, and humanities; mathematics and statistics; parks, recreation, leisure, and fitness studies; philosophy and religious studies; physical sciences; psychology; public administration and social service professions; social sciences; visual and performing arts. **Areas of required coursework:** arts/fine arts, humanities, computer literacy, mathematics, English (including composition), philosophy, foreign languages, sciences (biological or physical), history, social science, other. **Pre-professional programs:** pre-law, pre-medicine, pre-pharmacy. **Special academic programs:** cooperative (work-study plan) program, cross-registration, double major, honors program, independent study, internships, liberal arts/career combination, student-designed major, study abroad, teacher certificate program. **Teacher certification offered in:** early childhood, special education, elementary, middle/junior high, secondary. **Cooperative education programs:** business, humanities. **Reserve Officers Training Corps (ROTC):** Army ROTC: Offered at cooperating institution; Air Force ROTC: Offered at cooperating institution (St. Joseph's University). **Faculty and instruction (2009-2010):** Total instructional faculty: 70 full-time, 254 part-time (42% men; 58% women; 9% minorities). Full-time faculty with Ph.D. or other terminal degree: 83%. Student/faculty ratio: 14/1. Classes of fewer than 20 students: 59%; of 20 to 49 students: 41%; of 50 or more students: 0%. **Advanced Placement and International Baccalaureate credit:** AP tests may be used for: Credit and/or placement. Scores accepted: 3, 4, 5. **Freshmen returning for sophomore year:** 68%. **Graduation rates:** Four-year: 47%; five-year: 51%; six-year: 54%. **Graduate study:** 22% of students pursue further study within one year. Fields in which graduates pursue further study: Master of Business Administration (MBA), 4%; law, 2%; medicine, 2%; education, 49%; arts and sciences, 35%.

COSTS AND FINANCIAL AID
Financial aid office: (610) 902-8420. **Expenses (2009-2010):** Tuition and fees 2009-2010: $31,028; room/board: $11,340. Estimated books and supplies: $1,050; transportation: $95; personal expenses: $2,702. **Financial aid:** In 2009-2010, 80% of undergraduates applied for financial aid. Of those, 73% were determined to have financial need; 16% had their need fully met. Average financial aid package (proportion receiving): $21,251 (73%). Average amount of gift aid, such as scholarships or grants (proportion receiving): $8,116 (60%). Average amount of self-help aid, such as work study or loans (proportion receiving): $5,117 (70%). Average need-based loan (excluding PLUS or other private loans): $4,657. Among students who received need-based aid, the average percentage of need met: 71%. Among students who received aid based on merit, the average award (and the proportion receiving): $10,454 (24%). The average athletic scholarship (and the proportion receiving): $0 (0%). Average amount of debt of borrowers graduating in 2009: $30,633. Proportion who borrowed: 81%.

CAMPUS LIFE AND EXTRACURRICULAR ACTIVITIES
Campus housing available (% using): coed dorms (66%), women's dorms (20%), apartment for single students (12%), special housing for disabled students, other housing options. Students who live in college-owned, operated, or affiliated housing: 52%. **Student employment:** During the 2009-2010 academic year, 6% of undergraduates worked on campus. Average per-year earnings: $1,200. **Clubs and organizations:** Number of student organizations: 54. Activities include: campus ministries, choral groups, dance, drama/theater, international student organization, literary magazine, music ensembles, musical theater, radio station, student government, student newspaper, student film society, television station, yearbook. Number of fraternities: 0; sororities: 0. Average proportion of students who stay on campus on weekends: 50%. **Sports program (2009-2010):** Member of NCAA III. *Men's intercollegiate varsity sports:* basketball, cross country, golf, lacrosse, soccer, swimming, tennis, track and field (outdoor). *Women's intercollegiate varsity sports:* basketball, cross country, field hockey, lacrosse, soccer, softball, swimming, tennis, track and field (outdoor), volleyball.

SERVICES AND FACILITIES
Basic services: nonremedial tutoring, health service, health insurance. **Remedial assistance:** reading, math, writing, study skills. **Counseling services:** minority student, career, personal, academic, psychological, religious. **For learning-disabled students:** School does not offer a structured program with separate admission and additional fees. Total undergraduates in learning-disabled program or receiving services: 112. Services include:

remedial math, tape recorders, note-taking services, oral tests, learning center, extended time for tests, tutors, priority seating, texts on tape, typist/scribe, exams on tape or computer, other testing accommodations, other. **Library:** Number of titles: 112,749; number of current serial subscriptions: 43,038. **Information technology resources:** Students are not required to lease or own a computer. Number of campus computers available to all students: 469. School has a wireless network. Proportion of college-owned housing units wired for high-speed internet access: 100%. **Campus safety:** Security services offered: 24-hour foot-and-vehicle patrols, late-night transport/escort service, 24-hour emergency telephones, lighted pathways/sidewalks, student patrols, controlled dormitory access (key, security card, etc.).

TRANSFER AND INTERNATIONAL STUDENTS
Transfer students: May apply for admission for the following academic terms: Fall, Spring, Summer. Applicants need a minimum number of credits to apply. For fall 2009: Transfer applications received: 267. Transfer applicants offered admission: 139. Transfer applicants enrolled: 57. **International students:** Number of foreign undergraduates: 7. Number of countries represented: 11. Minimum TOEFL score required: 500 (paper); 300 (computer). Average TOEFL score: 500 (paper).

California University of Pennsylvania

- **Address:** 250 University Avenue, Box 94, California, PA 15419
- **Website:** http://www.cup.edu
- **Public**
- **Enrollment:** 6,499 full-time; 707 part-time

KEY STATS
✔ **U.S News College Ranking:** second tier, Regional Universities (North)
✔ **SAT Score (25th/75th percentile):** 940-1110
✔ **Tuition:** 2009-2010: $7,765 in state, $11,099 out of state

Selectivity: Selective	**Room/board:** $9,320
Acceptance rate: 55%	**Average debt:** $23,824
Student/faculty ratio: 20/1	**Proportion who borrowed:** 80%

UNDERGRADUATE STUDENT BODY STATS
2009-2010 enrollment: 6,499 full-time; 707 part-time. Men: 48%; women: 52%. **Ethnic makeup:** African American: 7%; Hispanic: 2%; White: 90%; International: 1%.

ADMISSIONS FACTS AND FIGURES
Phone: (724) 938-4404. **Email:** inquiry@cup.edu. **Website:** http://www.cup.edu. **Application deadlines for fall 2011:** Regular decision: Rolling. Early decision: Not offered. Early action: Not offered. Admission can be deferred. **Application fee:** $25. **To apply online, go to:** http://www.cup.edu/prospective/index.jsp?pageId=1580830010421122045539486. **Admissions requirements/recommendations:** High school units required (recommended): English: 4 (4); Mathematics: 3 (3); Science: 1 (1); Foreign language: (2); Social studies: 2 (2); History: 2 (2); Academic electives: 6 (6); Total units: 19 (21). Tests: The college uses SAT or ACT scores in admissions decisions. Either SAT or ACT required. For admission to the fall 2011 entering class, the school will accept: ACT with writing recommended. Campus visit: Recommended. Admissions interview: Recommended. Off-campus interview: May be arranged. **Factors that count in admissions decisions:** *Academic:* Secondary school record: Very Important. Class rank: Very Important. Letters of recommendation: Considered. Standardized test scores: Very Important. Essay: Considered. *Nonacademic:* Interview: Considered. Extracurricular activities: Considered. Talent/ability: Important. Character/personal qualities: Important. Alumni/ae relationship: Not Considered. Geographical residence: Not Considered. State residency: Not Considered. Religious affiliation/commitment: Not Considered. Minority status: Not Considered. Volunteer work: Considered. Work experience: Considered. **Other schools with the greatest overlap in applicants:** Clarion University of Pennsylvania; Edinboro University of Pennsylvania; Indiana University of Pennsylvania; Pennsylvania State University–University Park; Slippery Rock University of Pennsylvania. **Admissions statistics for the fall 2009 entering class:** Total applicants: 5,855. Total accepted: 3,238. Freshmen enrolled: 951; 5% were from out of state. Overall acceptance rate: 55%. **Size of waiting list:** 0 applicants; enrolled from waiting list: 0. **Credentials of fall 2009 freshmen:** 7% ranked in the top 10 percent of their high school class; 24% were in the top 25 percent; 58% were in the top half. (Proportion submitting class standing: 83%.) **Average high school grade point average:** 3.1.

First-year students who submitted SAT scores: 89%. Scores (25/75 percentile): Critical Reading: 470-550, Math: 470-560, Combined: 940-1110.

ACADEMICS
Year founded: 1852. **Academic calendar:** Semester. **Degrees offered:** certificate, associate, terminal-associate, bachelor's, post-bachelor's certificate, master's, post-master's certificate. **Most popular majors:** 21% elementary education and teaching, 11% business administration and management, 10% criminal justice/safety studies, 6% education, 6% psychology. **Major fields of study:** biological and biomedical sciences; business, management, marketing, and related support services; communication, journalism, and related programs; computer and information sciences and support services; education; engineering technologies/technicians; English language and literature/letters; foreign languages, literatures, and linguistics; health professions and related clinical sciences; history; liberal arts and sciences studies, and humanities; mathematics and statistics; multi/interdisciplinary studies; natural resources and conservation; parks, recreation, leisure, and fitness studies; philosophy and religious studies; physical sciences; psychology; public administration and social service professions; security and protective services; social sciences; visual and performing arts. **Areas of required coursework:** arts/fine arts, humanities, computer literacy, mathematics, English (including composition), sciences (biological or physical), history, social science, other. **Pre-professional programs:** pre-law, pre-dentistry, pre-medicine, pre-veterinary science, pre-optometry, pre-pharmacy, other. **Special academic programs (% participation):** accelerated program (4%), cooperative (work-study plan) program (6%), cross-registration (2%), distance learning (6%), double major (1%), dual enrollment (2%), exchange student program (domestic) (1%), external degree program (0%), honors program (2%), independent study (10%), internships (68.5%), student-designed major (2%), study abroad (.5%), teacher certificate program (15%), weekend college (1%). **Teacher certification offered in:** early childhood, special education, elementary, vo-tech, middle/junior high, adult education, secondary. **Cooperative education programs:** agriculture, art, business, computer science, education, engineering, health professions, humanities, natural science, social/behavioral science, technologies, vocational arts. **Reserve Officers Training Corps (ROTC):** Army ROTC: Offered on campus; Air Force ROTC: Offered at cooperating institution (University of Pittsburgh). **Faculty and instruction (2009-2010):** Total instructional faculty: 305 full-time, 88 part-time (54% men; 46% women; 11% minorities). Full-time faculty with Ph.D. or other terminal degree: 72%. Student/faculty ratio: 20/1. Classes of fewer than 20 students: 14%; of 20 to 49 students: 67%; of 50 or more students: 19%. **Advanced Placement and International Baccalaureate credit:** AP tests may be used for: Credit only. Scores accepted: 3, 4, 5. International Baccalaureate exams may be used for: Placement only. **Freshmen returning for sophomore year:** 78%. **Graduation rates:** Four-year: 30%; five-year: 48%; six-year: 51%. **Graduate study:** 20% of students pursue further study immediately upon graduation; 17% within one year. Fields in which graduates pursue further study: Master of Business Administration (MBA), 5%; law, 2%; medicine, 1%; dentistry, 1%; engineering, 1%; education, 8%; arts and sciences, 1%.

COSTS AND FINANCIAL AID
Financial aid office: (724) 938-4415. **Expenses (2009-2010):** Tuition and fees 2009-2010: $7,765 in state, $11,099 out of state; room/board: $9,320. Estimated books and supplies: $1,000; transportation: $875; personal expenses: $1,626. **Financial aid:** Priority filing date for institution's financial aid form: May 1. In 2009-2010, 86% of undergraduates applied for financial aid. Of those, 71% were determined to have financial need; 2% had their need fully met. Average financial aid package (proportion receiving): $9,093 (70%). Average amount of gift aid, such as scholarships or grants (proportion receiving): $5,070 (50%). Average amount of self-help aid, such as work study or loans (proportion receiving): $3,572 (62%). Average need-based loan (excluding PLUS or other private loans): $3,860. Among students who received need-based aid, the average percentage of need met: 92%. Among students who received aid based on merit, the average award (and the proportion receiving): $2,747 (13%). The average athletic scholarship (and the proportion receiving): $7,274 (4%). Average amount of debt of borrowers graduating in 2009: $23,824. Proportion who borrowed: 80%.

CAMPUS LIFE AND EXTRACURRICULAR ACTIVITIES
Campus housing available (% using): coed dorms (98%), special housing for disabled students (2%), other housing options. Students who live in college-owned, operated, or affiliated housing: 30%. Average per-year earnings: $1,600. **Clubs and organizations:** Number of student organizations: 176. Activities include: campus ministries, choral groups, concert band, dance, drama/theater, international student organization, jazz band, literary maga-

zine, marching band, music ensembles, musical theater, opera, pep band, radio station, student government, student newspaper, student film society, symphony orchestra, television station, yearbook. Number of fraternities: 7; sororities: 7. Proportion of men in fraternities: 5%; of women in sororities: 5%. Average proportion of students who stay on campus on weekends: 35%. **Sports program (2009-2010):** Member of NCAA II. *Men's intercollegiate varsity sports:* baseball, basketball, cross country, football, golf, soccer, track and field (indoor), track and field (outdoor). *Women's intercollegiate varsity sports:* basketball, cross country, golf, soccer, softball, swimming, tennis, track and field (indoor), track and field (outdoor), volleyball.

SERVICES AND FACILITIES
Basic services: nonremedial tutoring, women's center, placement service, day care, health service, health insurance, other. **Remedial assistance:** reading, math, writing, study skills, other. **Counseling services:** minority student, career, military, personal, veteran student, academic, older student, psychological, birth control, religious, other. **For learning-disabled students:** School does not offer a structured program with separate admission and additional fees. **Library:** Number of titles: 456,718; number of current serial subscriptions: 373. **Information technology resources:** Students are not required to lease or own a computer. Number of campus computers available to all students: 3,272. School has a wireless network. Approximate number of users that can be accommodated: 10,000. Proportion of college-owned housing units wired for high-speed internet access: 100%. **Campus safety:** Security services offered: 24-hour foot-and-vehicle patrols, late-night transport/escort service, 24-hour emergency telephones, lighted pathways/sidewalks, controlled dormitory access (key, security card, etc).

TRANSFER AND INTERNATIONAL STUDENTS
Transfer students: May apply for admission for the following academic terms: Fall, Spring, Summer. Applicants do not need a minimum number of credits to apply. For fall 2009: Transfer applications received: 2,336. Transfer applicants offered admission: 1,592. Transfer applicants enrolled: 750. **International students:** Number of foreign undergraduates: 94 (1% of student body). Number of countries represented: 58. Minimum TOEFL score required: 450 (paper); 133 (computer). Average TOEFL score: 510 (paper).

Carlow University

- **Address:** 3333 Fifth Avenue, Pittsburgh, PA 15213-3165
- **Website:** http://www.carlow.edu
- **Private; Religious affiliation:** Roman Catholic
- **Enrollment:** N/A

KEY STATS
✔ **U.S News College Ranking:** second tier, Regional Universities (North)
✔ **SAT or ACT Score (25th/75th percentile):** N/A
✔ **Tuition:** 2009-2010: $21,720

Selectivity: Less selective	**Room/board:** $8,552
Acceptance rate: N/A	**Average debt:** N/A
Student/faculty ratio: N/A	**Proportion who borrowed:** N/A

Carnegie Mellon University

- **Address:** 5000 Forbes Avenue, Pittsburgh, PA 15213
- **Website:** http://www.cmu.edu
- **Private**
- **Enrollment:** 5,862 full-time; 161 part-time

KEY STATS
✔ **U.S News College Ranking:** 23, National Universities
✔ **SAT Score (25th/75th percentile):** 1290-1500
✔ **Tuition:** 2010-2011: $41,940

Selectivity: Most selective	**Room/board:** $10,440
Acceptance rate: 36%	**Average debt:** $29,456
Student/faculty ratio: 12/1	**Proportion who borrowed:** 50%

UNDERGRADUATE STUDENT BODY STATS

2009-2010 enrollment: 5,862 full-time; 161 part-time. Men: 58%; women: 42%. **Ethnic makeup:** African American: 5%; American-Indian: 1%; Asian American: 24%; Hispanic: 5%; White: 49%; International: 15%. **Religious preference:** Roman Catholic: 19%; Protestant: 27%; Jewish: 6%; Muslim: 2%; Hindu: 5%; Buddhist: 3%; No preference: 34%.

ADMISSIONS FACTS AND FIGURES

Phone: (412) 268-2082. **Email:** undergraduate-admissions@andrew. cmu.edu. **Website:** http://www.cmu.edu. **Application deadlines for fall 2011:** Regular decision: January 1; decision sent by April 15. Early decision: Send application by: November 1; Decision sent by: December 15. Early action: Not offered. Admission can be deferred. **Application fee:** $70. **To apply online, go to:** http://www.cmu.edu/enrollment/admission. **Admissions requirements/recommendations:** High school units required (recommended): English: 4 (4); Mathematics: 4 (4); Science: 3 (3); Foreign language: 2 (2); Social studies: 0 (0); History: 0 (0); Academic electives: 3 (4). Tests: The college uses SAT or ACT scores in admissions decisions. Either SAT or ACT required. For admission to the fall 2011 entering class, the school will accept: ACT with writing required. Campus visit: Recommended. Admissions interview: Recommended. Off-campus interview: May be arranged. **Factors that count in admissions decisions:** *Academic:* Secondary school record: Very Important. Class rank: Very Important. Letters of recommendation: Important. Standardized test scores: Very Important. Essay: Important. *Nonacademic:* Interview: Important. Extracurricular activities: Important. Talent/ability: Important. Character/personal qualities: Important. Alumni/ae relationship: Important. Geographical residence: Not Considered. State residency: Not Considered. Religious affiliation/commitment: Not Considered. Minority status: Important. Volunteer work: Important. Work experience: Important. **Other schools with the greatest overlap in applicants:** Cornell University; Massachusetts Institute of Technology; Princeton University; Stanford University; University of Pennsylvania. **Admissions statistics for the fall 2009 entering class:** Total applicants: 14,153. Total accepted: 5,132. Freshmen enrolled: 1,423; 83% were from out of state. Accepted through early-decision or early-action plans: 19%. Overall acceptance rate: 36%. Early-decision acceptance rate: 24%. Non-early acceptance rate: 37%. **Size of waiting list:** 3938 applicants; enrolled from waiting list: 108. **Credentials of fall 2009 freshmen:** 75% ranked in the top 10 percent of their high school class; 93% were in the top 25 percent; 99% were in the top half. (Proportion submitting class standing: 38%.) **Average high school grade point average:** 3.6. **First-year students who submitted SAT scores:** 97%. Scores (25/75 percentile): Critical Reading: 620-720, Math: 670-780, Combined: 1290-1500. **First-year students submitting ACT scores:** 24%. Scores (25/75 percentile): English: 28-34, Math: 29-34, Composite: 29-33.

ACADEMICS

Year founded: 1900. **Academic calendar:** Semester. **Degrees offered:** bachelor's, master's, post-master's certificate, doctorate. **Most popular majors:** 11% computer science, 9% electrical, electronics, and communications engineering, 7% mechanical engineering, 5% biology/biological sciences, 5% business administration and management. **Major fields of study:** architecture and related services; area, ethnic, cultural, and gender studies; biological and biomedical sciences; business, management, marketing, and related support services; communication, journalism, and related programs; computer and information sciences and support services; education; engineering; English language and literature/letters; foreign languages, literatures, and linguistics; history; liberal arts and sciences studies, and humanities; mathematics and statistics; multi/interdisciplinary studies; natural resources and conservation; philosophy and religious studies; physical sciences; psychology; public administration and social service professions; social sciences; visual and performing arts. **Areas of required coursework:** humanities, computer literacy, mathematics, English (including composition), history, social science. **Special academic programs:** cooperative (work-study plan) program, cross-registration, distance learning, double major, dual enrollment, exchange student program (domestic), independent study, internships, liberal arts/career combination, student-designed major, study abroad, teacher certificate program. **Cooperative education programs:** computer science, engineering. **Reserve Officers Training Corps (ROTC):** Army ROTC: Offered at cooperating institution (University of Pittsburgh); Navy ROTC: Offered on campus; Air Force ROTC: Offered at cooperating institution (University of Pittsburgh). **Faculty and instruction (2009-2010):** Total instructional faculty: 883 full-time, 80 part-time (72% men; 28% women; 16% minorities). Full-time faculty with Ph.D. or other terminal degree: 98%. Student/faculty ratio: 12/1. Classes of fewer than 20 students: 62%; of 20 to 49 students: 28%; of 50 or more students: 11%. **Advanced Placement and International Baccalaureate credit:** AP tests may be used for: Credit and/or placement. Scores accepted: 4, 5. International Baccalaureate exams may be used for: Credit and/or placement. **Freshmen returning for sophomore year:** 95%. **Graduation rates:** Four-year: 67%; five-year: 82%; six-year: 84%. **Graduate study:** 33% of students pursue further study immediately upon graduation; 33% within one year; 60% within five years. Fields in which graduates pursue further study: Master of Business Administration (MBA), 7%; law, 3%; medicine, 7%; dentistry, 1%; engineering, 20%; education, 6%; arts and sciences, 33%.

COSTS AND FINANCIAL AID

Financial aid office: (412) 268-8186. **Expenses (2010-2011):** Tuition and fees 2010-2011: $41,940; room/board: $10,440. Estimated books and supplies: $1,000 personal expenses: $1,400. **Financial aid:** Priority filing date for institution's financial aid form: February 15; deadline: May 1. In 2009-2010, 59% of undergraduates applied for financial aid. Of those, 50% were determined to have financial need; 30% had their need fully met. Average financial aid package (proportion receiving): $28,013 (49%). Average amount of gift aid, such as scholarships or grants (proportion receiving): $22,789 (47%). Average amount of self-help aid, such as work study or loans (proportion receiving): $6,665 (46%). Average need-based loan (excluding PLUS or other private loans): $4,661. Among students who received need-based aid, the average percentage of need met: 80%. Among students who received aid based on merit, the average award (and the proportion receiving): $12,083 (8%). The average athletic scholarship (and the proportion receiving): $0 (0%). Average amount of debt of borrowers graduating in 2009: $29,456. Proportion who borrowed: 50%.

CAMPUS LIFE AND EXTRACURRICULAR ACTIVITIES

Campus housing available (% using): coed dorms (45%), women's dorms (2%), men's dorms (6%), sorority housing (4%), fraternity housing (7%), apartment for single students (29%), special housing for disabled students (1%). Students who live in college-owned, operated, or affiliated housing: 64%. **Student employment:** During the 2009-2010 academic year, 28% of undergraduates worked on campus. Average per-year earnings: $1,680. **Clubs and organizations:** Number of student organizations: 239. Activities include: campus ministries, choral groups, concert band, dance, drama/theater, international student organization, literary magazine, marching band, model UN, music ensembles, musical theater, pep band, radio station, student government, student newspaper, student film society, symphony orchestra, television station, yearbook. Number of fraternities: 18; sororities: 8. Proportion of men in fraternities: 15%; of women in sororities: 10%. **Sports program (2009-2010):** Member of NCAA III. ***Men's intercollegiate varsity sports:*** basketball, cross country, football, golf, soccer, swimming, tennis, track and field (indoor), track and field (outdoor). ***Women's intercollegiate varsity sports:*** basketball, cross country, soccer, swimming, tennis, track and field (indoor), track and field (outdoor), volleyball.

SERVICES AND FACILITIES

Basic services: nonremedial tutoring, women's center, placement service, day care, health service, health insurance, other. **Counseling services:** minority student, career, military, personal, veteran student, academic, psychological, birth control, religious. **For learning-disabled students:** School does not offer a structured program with separate admission and additional fees. Total undergraduates in learning-disabled program or receiving services: 200. Services include: tape recorders, note-taking services, oral tests, learning center, extended time for tests, tutors, priority seating, texts on tape, exams on tape or computer, other. **Library:** Number of titles: 1,374,525; number of current serial subscriptions: 75,321. **Information technology resources:** Students are not required to lease or own a computer. Number of campus computers available to all students: 384. School has a wireless network. Approximate number of users that can be accommodated: 8,192. Proportion of college-owned housing units wired for high-speed internet access: 100%. **Campus safety:** Security services offered: 24-hour foot-and-vehicle patrols, late-night transport/escort service, 24-hour emergency telephones, lighted pathways/sidewalks, controlled dormitory access (key, security card, etc).

TRANSFER AND INTERNATIONAL STUDENTS

Transfer students: May apply for admission for the following academic terms: Fall, Spring. Applicants do not need a minimum number of credits to apply. For fall 2009: Transfer applications received: 550. Transfer applicants offered admission: 84. Transfer applicants enrolled: 47. **International students:** Number of foreign undergraduates: 911 (15% of student body). Number of countries represented: 39.

Cedar Crest College

- Address: 100 College Drive, Allentown, PA 18104-6196
- Website: http://www.cedarcrest.edu
- Private
- Enrollment: 967 full-time; 718 part-time

KEY STATS

✔ U.S News College Ranking: second tier, National Liberal Arts Colleges
✔ SAT Score (25th/75th percentile): 970-1180
✔ Tuition: 2010-2011: $28,967

Selectivity: Selective	Room/board: $9,540
Acceptance rate: 63%	Average debt: $24,641
Student/faculty ratio: 10/1	Proportion who borrowed: 92%

UNDERGRADUATE STUDENT BODY STATS

2009-2010 enrollment: 967 full-time; 718 part-time. Men: 5%; women: 95%. **Ethnic makeup:** African American: 8%; Asian American: 3%; Hispanic: 7%; White: 81%; International: 1%. **Religious preference:** Roman Catholic: 19%; Protestant: 20%; Jewish: 1%; Muslim: 1%; Hindu: 1%; Buddhist: 1%; No preference: 55%; Other: 2%.

ADMISSIONS FACTS AND FIGURES

Phone: (800) 360-1222. **Email:** cccadmis@cedarcrest.edu. **Website:** http://www.cedarcrest.edu. **Application deadlines for fall 2011:** Regular decision: Rolling. Early decision: Not offered. Early action: Not offered. Admission can be deferred. **Application fee:** $30. **To apply online, go to:** http://cedarcrest.edu/ca/applyframe.shtm. **Admissions requirements/recommendations:** High school units required (recommended): English: 4; Mathematics: 3; Science: 2; Foreign language: 2; Social studies: 3; History: 0; Academic electives: (3); Total units: 16. Tests: The college uses SAT or ACT scores in admissions decisions. Either SAT or ACT required. For admission to the fall 2011 entering class, the school will accept: ACT with or without writing accepted. Campus visit: Recommended. Admissions interview: Recommended. Off-campus interview: May be arranged. **Factors that count in admissions decisions:** *Academic:* Secondary school record: Very Important. Class rank: Very Important. Letters of recommendation: Very Important. Standardized test scores: Very Important. Essay: Very Important. *Nonacademic:* Interview: Considered. Extracurricular activities: Considered. Talent/ability: Not Considered. Character/personal qualities: Not Considered. Alumni/ae relationship: Considered. Geographical residence: Not Considered. State residency: Not Considered. Religious affiliation/commitment: Not Considered. Minority status: Not Considered. Volunteer work: Considered. Work experience: Considered. **Other schools with the greatest overlap in applicants:** DeSales University; Moravian College; Muhlenberg College; Pennsylvania State University–University Park; Temple University. **Admissions statistics for the fall 2009 entering class:** Total applicants: 1,583. Total accepted: 1,003. Freshmen enrolled: 196; 49% were from out of state. Overall acceptance rate: 63%. **Credentials of fall 2009 freshmen:** 26% ranked in the top 10 percent of their high school class; 56% were in the top 25 percent; 89% were in the top half. (Proportion submitting class standing: 71%.) **Average high school grade point average:** 3.2. **First-year students who submitted SAT scores:** 94%. Scores (25/75 percentile): Critical Reading: 490-590, Math: 480-590, Combined: 970-1180. **First-year students submitting ACT scores:** 24%. Scores (25/75 percentile): English: 20-27, Math: 20-26, Composite: 20-26.

ACADEMICS

Year founded: 1867. **Academic calendar:** Semester. **Degrees offered:** certificate, bachelor's, master's. **Most popular majors:** 30% health professions and related clinical sciences, 12% biological and biomedical sciences, 12% business, management, marketing, and related support services, 12% psychology, 6% physical sciences. **Major fields of study:** biological and biomedical sciences; business, management, marketing, and related support services; communication, journalism, and related programs; computer and information sciences and support services; education; engineering; English language and literature/letters; family and consumer sciences/human sciences; foreign languages, literatures, and linguistics; health professions and related clinical sciences; history; liberal arts and sciences studies, and humanities; mathematics and statistics; physical sciences; psychology; public administration and social service professions; security and protective services; social sciences; visual and performing arts. **Areas of required coursework:** arts/fine arts, humanities, mathematics, English (including composition), sciences (biological or physical), social science, other. **Pre-professional programs:** pre-

law, pre-dentistry, pre-medicine, pre-veterinary science. **Special academic programs (% participation):** cross-registration (11%), double major (6%), honors program (4.2%), independent study (10%), internships (12%), liberal arts/career combination (1%), student-designed major (0%), study abroad (1%), teacher certificate program (5%), weekend college (0%). **Teacher certification offered in:** early childhood, special education, elementary, middle/junior high, secondary. **Reserve Officers Training Corps (ROTC):** Army ROTC: Offered at cooperating institution. **Faculty and instruction (2009-2010):** Total instructional faculty: 90 full-time, 101 part-time (31% men; 69% women; 4% minorities). Full-time faculty with Ph.D. or other terminal degree: 72%. Student/faculty ratio: 10/1. Classes of fewer than 20 students: 68%; of 20 to 49 students: 29%; of 50 or more students: 3%. **Advanced Placement and International Baccalaureate credit:** AP tests may be used for: Placement only. Scores accepted: 3, 4, 5. International Baccalaureate exams may be used for: Placement only. **Freshmen returning for sophomore year:** 79%. **Graduation rates:** Four-year: 45%; five-year: 52%; six-year: 55%. **Graduate study:** 15% of students pursue further study immediately upon graduation; 36% within one year; 39% within five years. Fields in which graduates pursue further study: Master of Business Administration (MBA), 7%; law, 1%; medicine, 10%; education, 7%; arts and sciences, 11%.

COSTS AND FINANCIAL AID

Financial aid office: (610) 740-3785. **Expenses (2010-2011):** Tuition and fees 2010-2011: $28,967; room/board: $9,540. Estimated books and supplies: $1,000; transportation: $0; personal expenses: $500. **Financial aid:** Priority filing date for institution's financial aid form: May 1. In 2009-2010, 97% of undergraduates applied for financial aid. Of those, 90% were determined to have financial need; 12% had their need fully met. Average financial aid package (proportion receiving): $21,570 (90%). Average amount of gift aid, such as scholarships or grants (proportion receiving): $16,975 (90%). Average amount of self-help aid, such as work study or loans (proportion receiving): $5,147 (80%). Average need-based loan (excluding PLUS or other private loans): $4,628. Among students who received need-based aid, the average percentage of need met: 76%. Among students who received aid based on merit, the average award (and the proportion receiving): $8,626 (10%). The average athletic scholarship (and the proportion receiving): $0 (0%). Average amount of debt of borrowers graduating in 2009: $24,641. Proportion who borrowed: 92%.

CAMPUS LIFE AND EXTRACURRICULAR ACTIVITIES

Campus housing available (% using): women's dorms (97%). Students who live in college-owned, operated, or affiliated housing: 55%. **Student employment:** During the 2009-2010 academic year, 43% of undergraduates worked on campus. Average per-year earnings: $1,800. **Clubs and organizations:** Number of student organizations: 52. Activities include: campus ministries, choral groups, dance, drama/theater, international student organization, literary magazine, music ensembles, musical theater, radio station, student government, student newspaper, yearbook. Number of fraternities: 0; sororities: 0. Average proportion of students who stay on campus on weekends: 65%. **Sports program (2009-2010):** Member of NCAA III. *Women's intercollegiate varsity sports:* basketball, cross country, field hockey, lacrosse, soccer, softball, tennis, volleyball.

SERVICES AND FACILITIES

Basic services: nonremedial tutoring. **Remedial assistance:** writing, study skills. **Counseling services:** career, personal, academic, older student, psychological. **For learning-disabled students:** School does not offer a structured program with separate admission and additional fees. Total undergraduates in learning-disabled program or receiving services: 49. Services include: remedial English, tape recorders, other special classes, note-taking services, learning center, extended time for tests, tutors, priority registration, priority seating, texts on tape, exams on tape or computer, other testing accommodations, other. **Library:** Number of titles: 145,154; number of current serial subscriptions: 25,552. **Information technology resources:** Students are not required to lease or own a computer. Number of campus computers available to all students: 287. School has a wireless network. Approximate number of users that can be accommodated: 820. Proportion of college-owned housing units wired for high-speed internet access: 100%. **Campus safety:** Security services offered: 24-hour foot-and-vehicle patrols, late-night transport/escort service, 24-hour emergency telephones, lighted pathways/sidewalks, controlled dormitory access (key, security card, etc).

TRANSFER AND INTERNATIONAL STUDENTS

Transfer students: May apply for admission for the following academic terms: Fall, Spring. Applicants need a minimum number of credits to apply. For fall 2009: Transfer applications received: 219. Transfer applicants offered admission: 107. Transfer applicants enrolled: 44. **International students:** Number of foreign undergraduates: 10 (1% of student body). Number of countries represented: 7. Minimum TOEFL score required: 500 (paper); 222 (computer). Average TOEFL score: 520 (paper).

Chatham University

- **Address:** Woodland Road, Pittsburgh, PA 15232
- **Website:** http://www.chatham.edu
- **Private**
- **Enrollment:** 683 full-time; 393 part-time

KEY STATS
- ✔ **U.S News College Ranking:** 67, Regional Universities (North)
- ✔ **SAT Score (25th/75th percentile):** 936-1183
- ✔ **Tuition:** 2009-2010: $28,026

Selectivity: Selective	**Room/board:** $8,700
Acceptance rate: 68%	**Average debt:** N/A
Student/faculty ratio: 10/1	**Proportion who borrowed:** N/A

UNDERGRADUATE STUDENT BODY STATS

2009-2010 enrollment: 683 full-time; 393 part-time. Men: 6%; women: 94%. **Ethnic makeup:** African American: 12%; Asian American: 2%; Hispanic: 2%; White: 79%; International: 6%.

ADMISSIONS FACTS AND FIGURES

Phone: (800) 837-1290. **Email:** admissions@chatham.edu. **Website:** http://www.chatham.edu. **Application deadlines for fall 2011:** Regular decision: August 1. Early decision: Not offered. Early action: Not offered. Admission can be deferred. **Application fee:** $35. **To apply online, go to:** http://www.chatham.edu. **Admissions requirements/recommendations:** High school units required (recommended): English: 4 (4); Mathematics: 2 (3); Science: 2 (3); Foreign language: 0 (2); Total units: 11 (15). Tests: The college uses SAT or ACT scores in admissions decisions. Neither SAT nor ACT required. For admission to the fall 2011 entering class, the school will accept: ACT with or without writing accepted. Campus visit: Recommended. Admissions interview: Recommended. Off-campus interview: May be arranged. **Factors that count in admissions decisions:** *Academic:* Secondary school record: Very Important. Class rank: Considered. Letters of recommendation: Considered. Standardized test scores: Considered. Essay: Important. *Nonacademic:* Interview: Considered. Extracurricular activities: Considered. Talent/ability: Considered. Character/personal qualities: Considered. Alumni/ae relationship: Considered. Geographical residence: Not Considered. State residency: Not Considered. Religious affiliation/commitment: Not Considered. Minority status: Not Considered. Volunteer work: Considered. Work experience: Considered. **Other schools with the greatest overlap in applicants:** Carlow University; Duquesne University; Point Park University; Robert Morris University; University of Pittsburgh. **Admissions statistics for the fall 2009 entering class:** Total applicants: 641. Total accepted: 433. Freshmen enrolled: 131; 28% were from out of state. Overall acceptance rate: 68%. **Credentials of fall 2009 freshmen:** 15% ranked in the top 10 percent of their high school class; 35% were in the top 25 percent; 73% were in the top half. (Proportion submitting class standing: 63%.) **Average high school grade point average:** 3.4. **First-year students who submitted SAT scores:** 75%. Scores (25/75 percentile): Critical Reading: 478-600, Math: 458-583, Combined: 936-1183. **First-year students submitting ACT scores:** 18%. Scores (25/75 percentile): English: N/A, Math: N/A, Composite: 22-25.

ACADEMICS

Year founded: 1869. **Academic calendar:** Other. **Degrees offered:** bachelor's, post-bachelor's certificate, master's, post-master's certificate. **Most popular majors:** 14% biological and biomedical sciences, 13% health professions and related clinical sciences, 13% psychology, 11% visual and performing arts, 6% social sciences. **Major fields of study:** architecture and related services; area, ethnic, cultural, and gender studies; biological and biomedical sciences; business, management, marketing, and related support services; communication, journalism, and related programs; education; English language and literature/letters; foreign languages, literatures, and linguistics; health professions and related clinical sciences; history; mathematics and statistics; natural resources and conservation; parks, recreation, leisure, and fitness studies; physical sciences; psychology; public administration and social service professions; security and protective services; social sciences; visual and performing arts. **Areas of required coursework:** arts/fine arts,

mathematics, English (including composition), sciences (biological or physical), other. **Pre-professional programs:** pre-law, pre-dentistry, pre-medicine, pre-veterinary science. **Special academic programs (% participation):** accelerated program, cooperative (work-study plan) program, cross-registration (10%), distance learning, double major (10%), dual enrollment (1%), English as a Second Language (ESL) (5%), exchange student program (domestic), honors program, independent study (36%), internships (39%), liberal arts/career combination, student-designed major (1%), study abroad (42%), teacher certificate program (5%). **Teacher certification offered in:** early childhood, special education, elementary, middle/junior high, secondary. **Cooperative education programs:** art, business, education, natural science, social/behavioral science. **Reserve Officers Training Corps (ROTC):** Army ROTC: Offered at cooperating institution (University of Pittsburgh); Navy ROTC: Offered at cooperating institution (Carnegie Mellon University); Air Force ROTC: Offered at cooperating institution (University of Pittsburgh). **Faculty and instruction (2009-2010):** Total instructional faculty: 88 full-time, 180 part-time (33% men; 67% women; 10% minorities). Full-time faculty with Ph.D. or other terminal degree: 97%. Student/faculty ratio: 10/1. Classes of fewer than 20 students: 69%; of 20 to 49 students: 30%; of 50 or more students: 1%. **Advanced Placement and International Baccalaureate credit:** AP tests may be used for: Credit and/or placement. Scores accepted: 3, 4, 5. International Baccalaureate exams may be used for: Credit and/or placement. **Freshmen returning for sophomore year:** 70%. **Graduation rates:** Four-year: 51%; five-year: 57%; six-year: 51%. **Graduate study:** 31% of students pursue further study within one year. Fields in which graduates pursue further study: Master of Business Administration (MBA), 11%; medicine, 6%; theology (or the seminary), 2%; education, 3%; arts and sciences, 11%.

COSTS AND FINANCIAL AID

Financial aid office: (412) 365-1777. **Expenses (2009-2010):** Tuition and fees 2009-2010: $28,026; room/board: $8,700. Estimated books and supplies: $860 personal expenses: $2,862. **Financial aid:** Priority filing date for institution's financial aid form: May 1. In 2009-2010, 77% of undergraduates applied for financial aid. Of those, 76% were determined to have financial need; 15% had their need fully met. Average financial aid package (proportion receiving): $15,515 (76%). Average amount of gift aid, such as scholarships or grants (proportion receiving): $8,645 (64%). Average amount of self-help aid, such as work study or loans (proportion receiving): $10,516 (73%). Average need-based loan (excluding PLUS or other private loans): $9,265. Among students who received need-based aid, the average percentage of need met: 66%. Among students who received aid based on merit, the average award (and the proportion receiving): $13,107 (4%). The average athletic scholarship (and the proportion receiving): $0 (0%).

CAMPUS LIFE AND EXTRACURRICULAR ACTIVITIES

Campus housing available (% using): women's dorms (75%), apartments for married students (2%), apartment for single students (23%), other housing options. Students who live in college-owned, operated, or affiliated housing: 54%. **Student employment:** During the 2009-2010 academic year, 50% of undergraduates worked on campus. **Clubs and organizations:** Number of student organizations: 27. Activities include: choral groups, dance, drama/theater, international student organization, literary magazine, music ensembles, musical theater, student government, student newspaper, yearbook. Number of fraternities: 0; sororities: 0. Average proportion of students who stay on campus on weekends: 70%. **Sports program (2009-2010):** Member of NCAA III. *Women's intercollegiate varsity sports:* basketball, cross country, ice hockey, soccer, softball, swimming, tennis, volleyball, water polo.

SERVICES AND FACILITIES

Basic services: nonremedial tutoring, placement service, health service, health insurance. **Remedial assistance:** reading, math, writing, study skills, other. **Counseling services:** minority student, career, military, personal, veteran student, academic, older student, psychological, birth control. **For learning-disabled students:** School does not offer a structured program with separate admission and additional fees. Services include: reading machines, tape recorders, note-taking services, oral tests, learning center, readers, extended time for tests, tutors, priority seating, texts on tape, other testing accommodations, other. **Library:** Number of titles: 91,356; number of current serial subscriptions: 366. **Information technology resources:** Students are required to lease or own a computer. Number of campus computers available to all students: 300. School has a wireless network. Proportion of college-owned housing units wired for high-speed internet access: 100%. **Campus safety:** Security services offered: 24-hour foot-and-vehicle patrols, late-night transport/escort service, 24-hour emergency telephones, lighted pathways/sidewalks, controlled dormitory access (key, security card, etc).

TRANSFER AND INTERNATIONAL STUDENTS

Transfer students: May apply for admission for the following academic terms: Fall, Spring. Applicants need a minimum number of credits to apply. For fall 2009: Transfer applications received: 171. Transfer applicants offered admission: 133. Transfer applicants enrolled: 87. **International students:** Number of foreign undergraduates: 43 (6% of student body). Number of countries represented: 18. Minimum TOEFL score required: 550 (paper); 213 (computer).

Chestnut Hill College

- **Address:** 9601 Germantown Avenue, Philadelphia, PA 19118-2693
- **Website:** http://www.chc.edu
- **Private; Religious affiliation:** Roman Catholic
- **Enrollment:** 1,149 full-time; 331 part-time

KEY STATS

✔ **U.S News College Ranking:** 110, Regional Universities (North)
✔ **SAT Score (25th/75th percentile):** 900-1090
✔ **Tuition:** 2010-2011: $28,100

Selectivity: Less selective	**Room/board:** $9,065
Acceptance rate: 91%	**Average debt:** N/A
Student/faculty ratio: 12/1	**Proportion who borrowed:** N/A

UNDERGRADUATE STUDENT BODY STATS

2009-2010 enrollment: 1,149 full-time; 331 part-time. Men: 31%; women: 69%. **Ethnic makeup:** African American: 38%; Asian American: 2%; Hispanic: 4%; White: 56%; International: 1%. **Religious preference:** Protestant: 10%; Jewish: 1%; Muslim: 1%; Buddhist: 1%; No preference: 1%; Unknown: 37%; Roman Catholic: 42%; Other: 6%.

ADMISSIONS FACTS AND FIGURES

Phone: (215) 248-7001. **Email:** chcapply@chc.edu. **Website:** http://www.chc.edu. **Application deadlines for fall 2011:** Regular decision: Rolling. Early decision: Not offered. Early action: Not offered. Admission can be deferred. **Application fee:** $35. **To apply online, go to:** https://www.applyweb.com/apply/chillc/index.html. **Admissions requirements/recommendations:** High school units required (recommended): English: (4); Mathematics: (3); Science or (3); Foreign language: (2); Total units: (16). Tests: The college uses SAT or ACT scores in admissions decisions. Either SAT or ACT required. For admission to the fall 2011 entering class, the school will accept: ACT with or without writing accepted. Campus visit: Recommended. Admissions interview: Recommended. Off-campus interview: May be arranged. **Factors that count in admissions decisions:** *Academic:* Secondary school record: Very Important. Class rank: Important. Letters of recommendation: Important. Standardized test scores: Important. Essay: Very Important. *Nonacademic:* Interview: Important. Extracurricular activities: Important. Talent/ability: Considered. Character/personal qualities: Important. Alumni/ae relationship: Considered. Geographical residence: Not Considered. State residency: Not Considered. Religious affiliation/commitment: Not Considered. Minority status: Not Considered. Volunteer work: Considered. Work experience: Considered. **Other schools with the greatest overlap in applicants:** Drexel University; La Salle University; Pennsylvania State University–University Park; Temple University; West Chester University of Pennsylvania. **Admissions statistics for the fall 2009 entering class:** Total applicants: 2,039. Total accepted: 1,846. Freshmen enrolled: 273; 42% were from out of state. Overall acceptance rate: 91%. **Credentials of fall 2009 freshmen:** 7% ranked in the top 10 percent of their high school class; 23% were in the top 25 percent; 61% were in the top half. (Proportion submitting class standing: 63%.) **Average high school grade point average:** 3.1. **First-year students who submitted SAT scores:** 97%. Scores (25/75 percentile): Critical Reading: 450-550, Math: 450-540, Combined: 900-1090. **First-year students submitting ACT scores:** 12%. Scores (25/75 percentile): English: N/A, Math: N/A, Composite: 17-22.

ACADEMICS

Year founded: 1924. **Academic calendar:** Semester. **Degrees offered:** certificate, associate, transfer-associate, bachelor's, post-bachelor's certificate, master's, post-master's certificate. **Most popular majors:** 22% public administration and social service professions, 18% business, management, marketing, and related support services, 16% security and protective services, 14% physical sciences, 12% education. **Major fields of study:** biological and biomedical sciences; business, management, marketing, and related

support services; communication, journalism, and related programs; communications technologies/technicians and support services; computer and information sciences and support services; education; English language and literature/letters; family and consumer sciences/human sciences; foreign languages, literatures, and linguistics; health professions and related clinical sciences; history; liberal arts and sciences studies, and humanities; mathematics and statistics; multi/interdisciplinary studies; natural resources and conservation; physical sciences; psychology; public administration and social service professions; security and protective services; social sciences; visual and performing arts. **Areas of required coursework:** arts/fine arts, humanities, mathematics, English (including composition), foreign languages, sciences (biological or physical), history, social science, other. **Pre-professional programs:** pre-law, pre-medicine, pre-veterinary science. **Special academic programs:** cross-registration, double major, dual enrollment, English as a Second Language (ESL), exchange student program (domestic), honors program, independent study, internships, student-designed major, study abroad, teacher certificate program. **Teacher certification offered in:** early childhood, special education, elementary, middle/junior high, secondary. **Faculty and instruction (2009-2010):** Total instructional faculty: 76 full-time, 266 part-time (50% men; 50% women; 10% minorities). Full-time faculty with Ph.D. or other terminal degree: 82%. Student/faculty ratio: 12/1. Classes of fewer than 20 students: 86%; of 20 to 49 students: 14%; of 50 or more students: 0%. **Advanced Placement and International Baccalaureate credit:** AP tests may be used for: Placement only. Scores accepted: 3, 4, 5. International Baccalaureate exams may be used for: Placement only. **Freshmen returning for sophomore year:** 67%. **Graduation rates:** Four-year: 35%; five-year: 43%; six-year: 48%. **Graduate study:** 40% of students pursue further study immediately upon graduation. Fields in which graduates pursue further study: Master of Business Administration (MBA), 29%; medicine, 11%; theology (or the seminary), 4%; education, 30%; arts and sciences, 26%.

COSTS AND FINANCIAL AID

Financial aid office: (215) 248-7182. **Expenses (2010-2011):** Tuition and fees 2010-2011: $28,100; room/board: $9,065. Estimated books and supplies: $1,000; transportation: $700; personal expenses: $1,400. **Financial aid:** Priority filing date for institution's financial aid form: April 16. In 2009-2010, 85% of undergraduates applied for financial aid. Of those, 77% were determined to have financial need; 17% had their need fully met. Average financial aid package (proportion receiving): $17,839 (77%). Average amount of gift aid, such as scholarships or grants (proportion receiving): $13,510 (77%). Average amount of self-help aid, such as work study or loans (proportion receiving): $4,939 (67%). Average need-based loan (excluding PLUS or other private loans): $5. Among students who received need-based aid, the average percentage of need met: 71%. Among students who received aid based on merit, the average award (and the proportion receiving): $5,837 (1%). The average athletic scholarship (and the proportion receiving): $4,465 (5%).

CAMPUS LIFE AND EXTRACURRICULAR ACTIVITIES

Campus housing available (% using): coed dorms (100%), other housing options. Students who live in college-owned, operated, or affiliated housing: 35%. **Student employment:** During the 2009-2010 academic year, 15% of undergraduates worked on campus. Average per-year earnings: $1,000. **Clubs and organizations:** Number of student organizations: 29. Activities include: campus ministries, choral groups, concert band, dance, drama/theater, jazz band, literary magazine, music ensembles, musical theater, student government, student newspaper, symphony orchestra, television station, yearbook. Number of fraternities: 0; sororities: 0. Average proportion of students who stay on campus on weekends: 35%. **Sports program (2009-2010):** Member of NCAA II. *Men's intercollegiate varsity sports:* baseball, basketball, cross country, golf, lacrosse, soccer, tennis. *Women's intercollegiate varsity sports:* basketball, cross country, lacrosse, soccer, softball, tennis, volleyball.

SERVICES AND FACILITIES

Basic services: placement service, health service, health insurance. **Remedial assistance:** reading, math, writing, study skills, other. **Counseling services:** career, personal, academic, psychological, religious. **For learning-disabled students:** School does not offer a structured program with separate admission and additional fees. Total undergraduates in learning-disabled program or receiving services: 12. Services include: remedial math, remedial English, remedial reading, tape recorders, other special classes, videotaped classes, untimed tests, note-taking services, oral tests, learning center, readers, extended time for tests, tutors, early syllabus, priority seating, proofreading services, texts on tape, typist/scribe, exams on tape or computer, other testing accommodations. **Library:** Number of titles: 132,434; number of current serial subscriptions: 1,296. **Information technology resources:** Students are required to lease or own a computer. Number of campus computers available to all students: 65. School has a wireless network. Proportion of college-owned housing units wired for high-speed internet access: 25%. **Campus safety:** Security services offered: 24-hour foot-and-vehicle patrols, late-night transport/escort service, 24-hour emergency telephones, lighted pathways/sidewalks, controlled dormitory access (key, security card, etc).

TRANSFER AND INTERNATIONAL STUDENTS

Transfer students: May apply for admission for the following academic terms: Fall, Spring, Summer. Applicants do not need a minimum number of credits to apply. For fall 2009: Transfer applications received: 246. Transfer applicants offered admission: 236. Transfer applicants enrolled: 76. **International students:** Number of foreign undergraduates: 9 (1% of student body). Number of countries represented: 4. Minimum TOEFL score required: 500 (paper); 213 (computer). Average TOEFL score: 520 (paper).

Cheyney University of Pennsylvania

- **Address:** 1837 University Circle, PO Box 200, Cheyney, PA 19319
- **Website:** http://www.cheyney.edu
- **Public**
- **Enrollment:** 1,262 full-time; 140 part-time

KEY STATS

✔ **U.S News College Ranking:** second tier, Regional Universities (North)
✔ **SAT Score (25th/75th percentile):** 650-830
✔ **Tuition:** 2009-2010: $7,360 in state, $15,692 out of state

Selectivity: Least selective	Room/board: $8,038
Acceptance rate: 50%	Average debt: N/A
Student/faculty ratio: 15/1	Proportion who borrowed: N/A

UNDERGRADUATE STUDENT BODY STATS

2009-2010 enrollment: 1,262 full-time; 140 part-time. Men: 46%; women: 54%. **Ethnic makeup:** African American: 92%; Hispanic: 1%; White: 6%.

ADMISSIONS FACTS AND FIGURES

Phone: (610) 399-2275. **Email:** abrown@cheyney.edu. **Website:** http://www.cheyney.edu. **Application deadlines for fall 2011:** Regular decision: March 31. Early decision: Not offered. Early action: Not offered. Admission can be deferred. **Application fee:** $20. **To apply online, go to:** http://www.cheyney.edu/pages/index.asp?p=329. **Admissions requirements/recommendations:** High school units required (recommended): English: 4; Mathematics: 3; Science: 2; Foreign language: 2; History: 2; Total units: 13. Tests: The college uses SAT or ACT scores in admissions decisions. SAT required. Campus visit: Neither required nor recommended. Admissions interview: Neither required nor recommended. Off-campus interview: Not available. **Factors that count in admissions decisions:** *Academic:* Secondary school record: Very Important. Class rank: Important. Letters of recommendation: Very Important. Standardized test scores: Important. Essay: Important. *Nonacademic:* Interview: Important. Extracurricular activities: Important. Talent/ability: Considered. Character/personal qualities: Not Considered. Alumni/ae relationship: Not Considered. Geographical residence: Not Considered. State residency: Important. Religious affiliation/commitment: Not Considered. Minority status: Considered. Volunteer work: Not Considered. Work experience: Not Considered. **Other schools with the greatest overlap in applicants:** Drexel University; Lincoln University; Pennsylvania State University–University Park; Temple University; West Chester University of Pennsylvania. **Admissions statistics for the fall 2009 entering class:** Total applicants: 3,298. Total accepted: 1,637. Freshmen enrolled: 607; 33% were from out of state. Overall acceptance rate: 50%. **Credentials of fall 2009 freshmen:** 6% ranked in the top 10 percent of their high school class; 15% were in the top 25 percent; 46% were in the top half. (Proportion submitting class standing: 19%.) **Average high school grade point average:** 2.4. **First-year students who submitted SAT scores:** 56%. Scores (25/75 percentile): Critical Reading: 330-420, Math: 320-410, Combined: 650-830. **First-year students submitting ACT scores:** 2%. Scores (25/75 percentile): English: N/A, Math: N/A, Composite: 14-21.

ACADEMICS

Year founded: 1837. **Academic calendar:** Semester. **Degrees offered:** associate, bachelor's, post-bachelor's certificate, master's. **Most popular majors:**

26% social sciences, 25% business, management, marketing, and related support services, 12% psychology, 7% communication, journalism, and related programs, 7% parks, recreation, leisure, and fitness studies. **Major fields of study:** biological and biomedical sciences; business, management, marketing, and related support services; communication, journalism, and related programs; communications technologies/technicians and support services; computer and information sciences and support services; education; English language and literature/letters; family and consumer sciences/human sciences; foreign languages, literatures, and linguistics; health professions and related clinical sciences; mathematics and statistics; parks, recreation, leisure, and fitness studies; physical sciences; psychology; social sciences; visual and performing arts. **Areas of required coursework:** arts/fine arts, humanities, computer literacy, mathematics, English (including composition), foreign languages, sciences (biological or physical), social science. **Special academic programs:** cooperative (work-study plan) program, cross-registration, distance learning, double major, honors program, independent study, internships, study abroad, teacher certificate program. **Teacher certification offered in:** early childhood, special education, elementary, secondary. **Cooperative education programs:** business, computer science, natural science, social/behavioral science. **Reserve Officers Training Corps (ROTC):** Army ROTC: Offered at cooperating institution (Widener University). **Faculty and instruction (2009-2010):** Total instructional faculty: 75 full-time, 24 part-time (51% men; 49% women; 79% minorities). Full-time faculty with Ph.D. or other terminal degree: 69%. Student/faculty ratio: 15/1. Classes of fewer than 20 students: 50%; of 20 to 49 students: 48%; of 50 or more students: 3%. **Advanced Placement and International Baccalaureate credit:** AP tests may be used for: Credit and/or placement. International Baccalaureate exams may be used for: Placement only. **Freshmen returning for sophomore year:** 59%. **Graduation rates:** Six-year: 27%.

COSTS AND FINANCIAL AID

Financial aid office: (610) 399-2302. **Expenses (2009-2010):** Tuition and fees 2009-2010: $7,360 in state, $15,692 out of state; room/board: $8,038. Estimated books and supplies: $1,300; transportation: $2,655. **Financial aid:** Priority filing date for institution's financial aid form: April 1.

CAMPUS LIFE AND EXTRACURRICULAR ACTIVITIES

Campus housing available: coed dorms, women's dorms, men's dorms, other housing options. Students who live in college-owned, operated, or affiliated housing: 74%. Activities include: choral groups, drama/theater, jazz band, marching band, music ensembles, radio station, student government, student newspaper, student film society, television station, yearbook. Number of fraternities: 5; sororities: 4. Proportion of men in fraternities: 5%; of women in sororities: 8%. **Sports program (2009-2010):** Member of NCAA II.

SERVICES AND FACILITIES

Basic services: nonremedial tutoring, placement service, health service. **Remedial assistance:** reading, math, study skills. **Counseling services:** career, academic. **Information technology resources:** Students are not required to lease or own a computer. School has a wireless network. Proportion of college-owned housing units wired for high-speed internet access: 100%. **Campus safety:** Security services offered: 24-hour emergency telephones, lighted pathways/sidewalks.

TRANSFER AND INTERNATIONAL STUDENTS

Transfer students: May apply for admission for the following academic terms: Fall, Spring. Applicants do not need a minimum number of credits to apply. For fall 2009: Transfer applications received: 223. Transfer applicants offered admission: 161. Transfer applicants enrolled: 88. **International students:** Number of foreign undergraduates: 2. Number of countries represented: 5. Minimum TOEFL score required: 500 (paper).

Clarion University of Pennsylvania

- **Address:** 840 Wood Street, Clarion, PA 16214
- **Website:** http://www.clarion.edu
- **Public**
- **Enrollment:** 5,258 full-time; 965 part-time

UNDERGRADUATE STUDENT BODY STATS

2009-2010 enrollment: 5,258 full-time; 965 part-time. Men: 39%; women: 61%. **Ethnic makeup:** African American: 6%; Asian American: 1%; Hispanic: 1%; White: 91%; International: 1%.

ADMISSIONS FACTS AND FIGURES

Phone: (814) 393-2306. **Email:** admissions@clarion.edu. **Website:** http://www.clarion.edu. **Application deadlines for fall 2011:** Regular decision: Rolling. Early decision: Not offered. Early action: Not offered. Admission can be deferred. **Application fee:** $30. **To apply online, go to:** http://www.applyweb.com/aw?clarion. **Admissions requirements/recommendations:** High school units required (recommended): English: 4 (4); Mathematics: 3 (4); Science: 3 (4); Foreign language: 0 (2); Social studies: 3 (4); History: 0 (0); Academic electives: 0 (0); Total units: 13 (19). Tests: The college uses SAT or ACT scores in admissions decisions. Either SAT or ACT required. For admission to the fall 2011 entering class, the school will accept: ACT with or without writing accepted. Campus visit: Recommended. Admissions interview: Recommended. Off-campus interview: Not available. **Factors that count in admissions decisions: Academic:** Secondary school record: Very Important. Class rank: Very Important. Letters of recommendation: Important. Standardized test scores: Very Important. Essay: Important. **Nonacademic:** Interview: Considered. Extracurricular activities: Considered. Talent/ability: Considered. Character/personal qualities: Considered. Alumni/ae relationship: Not Considered. Geographical residence: Not Considered. State residency: Not Considered. Religious affiliation/commitment: Not Considered. Minority status: Considered. Volunteer work: Considered. Work experience: Considered. **Other schools with the greatest overlap in applicants:** California University of Pennsylvania; Edinboro University of Pennsylvania; Indiana University of Pennsylvania; Shippensburg University of Pennsylvania; Slippery Rock University of Pennsylvania. **Admissions statistics for the fall 2009 entering class:** Total applicants: 4,777. Total accepted: 3,271. Freshmen enrolled: 1,449; 5% were from out of state. Overall acceptance rate: 68%. **Credentials of fall 2009 freshmen:** 6% ranked in the top 10 percent of their high school class; 22% were in the top 25 percent; 52% were in the top half. (Proportion submitting class standing: 87%.) **Average high school grade point average:** 3.2. **First-year students who submitted SAT scores:** 90%. Scores (25/75 percentile): Critical Reading: 410-520, Math: 420-530, Combined: 830-1050. **First-year students submitting ACT scores:** 16%. Scores (25/75 percentile): English: N/A, Math: N/A, Composite: 17-21.

ACADEMICS

Year founded: 1867. **Academic calendar:** Semester. **Degrees offered:** certificate, associate, bachelor's, master's, post-master's certificate. **Most popular majors:** 19% business, management, marketing, and related support services, 17% education, 12% health professions and related clinical sciences, 10% communication, journalism, and related programs, 8% liberal arts and sciences studies, and humanities. **Major fields of study:** biological and biomedical sciences; business, management, marketing, and related support services; communication, journalism, and related programs; computer and information sciences and support services; education; engineering technologies/technicians; English language and literature/letters; foreign languages, literatures, and linguistics; health professions and related clinical sciences; history; legal professions and studies; liberal arts and sciences studies, and humanities; library science; mathematics and statistics; multi/interdisciplinary studies; natural resources and conservation; philosophy and religious studies; physical sciences; psychology; security and protective services; social sciences; visual and performing arts. **Areas of required coursework:** arts/fine arts, humanities, mathematics, English (including composition),

sciences (biological or physical), social science, other. **Pre-professional programs:** pre-law, pre-dentistry, pre-medicine, pre-theology, pre-veterinary science, pre-optometry, pre-pharmacy, other. **Special academic programs:** accelerated program, cooperative (work-study plan) program, distance learning, double major, dual enrollment, honors program, independent study, internships, liberal arts/career combination, student-designed major, study abroad, teacher certificate program, weekend college. **Teacher certification offered in:** early childhood, special education, elementary, middle/junior high, secondary. **Cooperative education programs:** engineering, health professions, social/behavioral science. **Reserve Officers Training Corps (ROTC):** Army ROTC: Offered on campus. **Faculty and instruction (2009-2010):** Total instructional faculty: 256 full-time, 120 part-time (50% men; 50% women; 8% minorities). Full-time faculty with Ph.D. or other terminal degree: 82%. Student/faculty ratio: 19/1. Classes of fewer than 20 students: 25%; of 20 to 49 students: 67%; of 50 or more students: 8%. **Advanced Placement and International Baccalaureate credit:** AP tests may be used for: Credit only. Scores accepted: 3, 4, 5. **Freshmen returning for sophomore year:** 73%. **Graduation rates:** Four-year: 40%; five-year: 51%; six-year: 52%.

COSTS AND FINANCIAL AID

Financial aid office: (814) 393-2315. **Expenses (2009-2010):** Tuition and fees 2009-2010: $7,380 in state, $12,934 out of state; room/board: $6,390. Estimated books and supplies: $900; transportation: $750; personal expenses: $2,500. **Financial aid:** Priority filing date for institution's financial aid form: April 15; deadline: April 15. In 2009-2010, 87% of undergraduates applied for financial aid. Of those, 74% were determined to have financial need; 12% had their need fully met. Average financial aid package (proportion receiving): $8,210 (71%). Average amount of gift aid, such as scholarships or grants (proportion receiving): $5,943 (53%). Average amount of self-help aid, such as work study or loans (proportion receiving): $4,584 (61%). Average need-based loan (excluding PLUS or other private loans): $4,003. Among students who received need-based aid, the average percentage of need met: 72%. Among students who received aid based on merit, the average award (and the proportion receiving): $2,666 (5%). The average athletic scholarship (and the proportion receiving): $2,745 (4%).

CAMPUS LIFE AND EXTRACURRICULAR ACTIVITIES

Campus housing available: coed dorms, women's dorms, men's dorms, sorority housing, fraternity housing, apartment for single students, other housing options. Students who live in college-owned, operated, or affiliated housing: 33%. **Clubs and organizations:** Number of student organizations: 150. Activities include: choral groups, concert band, dance, drama/theater, international student organization, jazz band, marching band, music ensembles, musical theater, pep band, radio station, student government, student newspaper, television station. Number of fraternities: 7; sororities: 7. **Sports program (2009-2010):** Member of NCAA II. **Men's intercollegiate varsity sports:** baseball, basketball, football, golf, swimming, wrestling. **Women's intercollegiate varsity sports:** basketball, cross country, golf, soccer, softball, swimming, tennis, track and field (indoor), track and field (outdoor), volleyball.

SERVICES AND FACILITIES

Basic services: nonremedial tutoring, women's center, placement service, health service, health insurance. **Remedial assistance:** reading, math, writing, study skills. **Counseling services:** minority student, career, military, personal, veteran student, academic, older student, psychological, birth control, religious. **For learning-disabled students:** School does not offer a structured program with separate admission and additional fees. Services include: remedial math, remedial English, reading machines, remedial reading, tape recorders, note-taking services, oral tests, learning center, readers, extended time for tests, tutors, priority seating, texts on tape, other testing accommodations, other. **Library:** Number of titles: 454,580; number of current serial subscriptions: 24,455. **Information technology resources:** Students are not required to lease or own a computer. Number of campus computers available to all students: 1,200. School has a wireless network. Approximate number of users that can be accommodated: 300. Proportion of college-owned housing units wired for high-speed internet access: 100%. **Campus safety:** Security services offered: 24-hour foot-and-vehicle patrols, late-night transport/escort service, 24-hour emergency telephones, lighted pathways/sidewalks, student patrols, controlled dormitory access (key, security card, etc).

TRANSFER AND INTERNATIONAL STUDENTS

Transfer students: May apply for admission for the following academic terms: Fall, Winter, Spring, Summer. Applicants need a minimum number of credits to apply. For fall 2009: Transfer applications received: 1,131.

Transfer applicants offered admission: 800. Transfer applicants enrolled: 379. **International students:** Number of foreign undergraduates: 53 (1% of student body). Number of countries represented: 27. Minimum TOEFL score required: 500 (paper); 173 (computer).

Curtis Institute of Music

- ■ **Address:** 1726 Locust Street, Philadelphia, PA 19103
- ■ **Website:** http://www.curtis.edu
- ■ **Private**
- ■ **Enrollment:** 127 full-time

KEY STATS

- ✔ **U.S News College Ranking:** Unranked Specialty School–Fine Arts
- ✔ **SAT or ACT Score (25th/75th percentile):** N/A
- ✔ **Tuition:** 2010-2011: $2,290

Selectivity: N/A	Room/board: $14,940
Acceptance rate: 5%	Average debt: $14,057
Student/faculty ratio: N/A	Proportion who borrowed: 75%

UNDERGRADUATE STUDENT BODY STATS

2009-2010 enrollment: 127 full-time. Men: 50%; women: 50%. **Ethnic makeup:** African American: 3%; Asian American: 13%; Hispanic: 2%; White: 42%; International: 39%.

ADMISSIONS FACTS AND FIGURES

Phone: (215) 893-5262. **Email:** admissions@curtis.edu. **Website:** http://www.curtis.edu. **Application deadlines for fall 2011:** Regular decision: December 15; decision sent by April 1. Early decision: Not offered. Early action: Not offered. Admission cannot be deferred. **Application fee:** $150. **Admissions requirements/recommendations:** Tests: The college uses SAT or ACT scores in admissions decisions. SAT required. For admission to the fall 2011 entering class, the school will accept: ACT with or without writing accepted. Campus visit: Neither required nor recommended. Admissions interview: Neither required nor recommended. Off-campus interview: Not available. **Factors that count in admissions decisions:** *Academic:* Secondary school record: Considered. Class rank: Not Considered. Letters of recommendation: Important. Standardized test scores: Considered. Essay: Considered. *Nonacademic:* Interview: Not Considered. Extracurricular activities: Not Considered. Talent/ability: Very Important. Character/personal qualities: Not Considered. Alumni/ae relationship: Not Considered. Geographical residence: Not Considered. State residency: Not Considered. Religious affiliation/commitment: Not Considered. Minority status: Not Considered. Volunteer work: Not Considered. Work experience: Not Considered. **Other schools with the greatest overlap in applicants:** Cleveland Institute of Music; Juilliard School; New England Conservatory of Music; Oberlin College. **Admissions statistics for the fall 2009 entering class:** Total applicants: 255. Total accepted: 13. Freshmen enrolled: 13; 96% were from out of state. Overall acceptance rate: 5%. **Size of waiting list:** 4 applicants; enrolled from waiting list: 1. **First-year students who submitted SAT scores:** 100%.

ACADEMICS

Year founded: 1924. **Academic calendar:** Semester. **Degrees offered:** certificate, diploma, bachelor's, master's. **Most popular majors:** 100% music performance. **Major fields of study:** visual and performing arts. **Special academic programs (% participation):** cross-registration (5%); double major (0%); English as a Second Language (ESL) (15%); liberal arts/career combination (59%). **Faculty and instruction (2009-2010):** Total instructional faculty: 1 full-time, 86 part-time (69% men; 31% women; 13% minorities). **Advanced Placement and International Baccalaureate credit:** AP tests may be used for: Credit and/or placement. Scores accepted: 4, 5. **Freshmen returning for sophomore year:** 100%. **Graduation rates:** Six-year: 88%. **Graduate study:** 47% of students pursue further study immediately upon graduation.

COSTS AND FINANCIAL AID

Financial aid office: (215) 717-3165. **Expenses (2010-2011):** Tuition and fees 2010-2011: $2,290; room/board: $14,940. Estimated books and supplies: $1,575; transportation: $0; personal expenses: $1,620. **Financial aid:** Priority filing date for institution's financial aid form: March 1. In 2009-2010, 70% of undergraduates applied for financial aid. Of those, 58% were determined to have financial need; 36% had their need fully met. Average financial aid package (proportion receiving): $14,821 (58%). Average amount of gift aid, such as scholarships or grants (proportion receiving): $8,467 (54%).

Average amount of self-help aid, such as work study or loans (proportion receiving): $6,432 (57%). Average need-based loan (excluding PLUS or other private loans): $4,499. Among students who received need-based aid, the average percentage of need met: 88%. Among students who received aid based on merit, the average award (and the proportion receiving): $0 (0%). The average athletic scholarship (and the proportion receiving): $0 (0%). Average amount of debt of borrowers graduating in 2009: $14,057. Proportion who borrowed: 75%.

CAMPUS LIFE AND EXTRACURRICULAR ACTIVITIES

Student employment: During the 2009-2010 academic year, 0% of undergraduates worked on campus. Activities include: music ensembles, opera, student government, symphony orchestra. Number of fraternities: 0; sororities: 0.

SERVICES AND FACILITIES

Basic services: nonremedial tutoring, placement service, health service, health insurance. **Counseling services:** career, personal, veteran student, academic, psychological, birth control. **For learning-disabled students:** School does not offer a structured program with separate admission and additional fees. Services include: other special classes, diagnostic testing service, oral tests, extended time for tests, tutors, priority seating, other testing accommodations. **Library:** Number of titles: 62,215; number of current serial subscriptions: 75. **Information technology resources:** Students are not required to lease or own a computer. Number of campus computers available to all students: 16. School has a wireless network. Approximate number of users that can be accommodated: 75. Proportion of college-owned housing units wired for high-speed internet access: 0%. **Campus safety:** Security services offered: late-night transport/escort service.

TRANSFER AND INTERNATIONAL STUDENTS

Transfer students: May apply for admission for the following academic terms: Fall. Applicants do not need a minimum number of credits to apply. For fall 2009: Transfer applications received: 396. Transfer applicants offered admission: 21. Transfer applicants enrolled: 21. **International students:** Number of foreign undergraduates: 50 (39% of student body). Number of countries represented: 9. Minimum TOEFL score required: 550 (paper); 213 (computer).

Delaware Valley College

- ■ **Address:** 700 E. Butler Avenue, Doylestown, PA 18901
- ■ **Website:** http://www.delval.edu
- ■ **Private**
- ■ **Enrollment:** 1,660 full-time; 328 part-time

KEY STATS

- ✔ **U.S News College Ranking:** 24, Regional Colleges (North)
- ✔ **SAT Score (25th/75th percentile):** 910-1110
- ✔ **Tuition:** 2010-2011: $29,284

Selectivity: Selective	Room/board: $10,326
Acceptance rate: 68%	Average debt: $26,350
Student/faculty ratio: 15/1	Proportion who borrowed: 63%

UNDERGRADUATE STUDENT BODY STATS

2009-2010 enrollment: 1,660 full-time; 328 part-time. Men: 43%; women: 57%. **Ethnic makeup:** African American: 4%; Asian American: 1%; Hispanic: 2%; White: 93%. **Religious preference:** Roman Catholic: 35%; Protestant: 39%; Jewish: 1%; Muslim: 1%; Hindu: 1%; Buddhist: 1%; No preference: 20%.

ADMISSIONS FACTS AND FIGURES

Phone: (215) 489-2211. **Email:** admitme@delval.edu. **Website:** http://www.delval.edu. **Application deadlines for fall 2011:** Regular decision: Rolling. Early decision: Not offered. Early action: Not offered. Admission can be deferred. **Application fee:** $50. **To apply online, go to:** http://www.pennsylvaniamentor.org/Applications/Delaware_Valley_College/apply.html?. **Admissions requirements/recommendations:** High school units required (recommended): English: 3; Mathematics: 2; Science: 2; Social studies: 2; Academic electives: 6; Total units: 15. Tests: The college uses SAT or ACT scores in admissions decisions. Either SAT or ACT required. For admission to the fall 2011 entering class, the school will accept: ACT with writing recommended. Campus visit: Recommended. Admissions interview: Recommended. Off-campus interview: May be arranged. **Factors that count in admissions decisions:** *Academic:* Secondary school record: Important. Class rank: Important. Letters of recommendation: Considered. Standardized test scores: Very Important. Essay: Considered. *Nonacademic:* Interview: Important. Extracurricular activities: Considered. Talent/ability: Considered. Character/personal qualities: Considered. Alumni/ae relationship: Considered. Geographical residence: Not Considered. State residency: Not Considered. Religious affiliation/commitment: Not Considered. Minority status: Not Considered. Volunteer work: Considered. Work experience: Considered. **Other schools with the greatest overlap in applicants:** Cornell University; Pennsylvania State University–University Park; Rutgers, the State University of New Jersey–New Brunswick; Temple University; West Chester University of Pennsylvania. **Admissions statistics for the fall 2009 entering class:** Total applicants: 1,769. Total accepted: 1,207. Freshmen enrolled: 452; 48% were from out of state. Overall acceptance rate: 68%. **Credentials of fall 2009 freshmen:** 13% ranked in the top 10 percent of their high school class; 37% were in the top 25 percent; 73% were in the top half. (Proportion submitting class standing: 74%.) **Average high school grade point average:** 3.5. **First-year students who submitted SAT scores:** 88%. Scores (25/75 percentile): Critical Reading: 450-550, Math: 460-560, Combined: 910-1110. **First-year students submitting ACT scores:** 12%. Scores (25/75 percentile): English: 20-24, Math: 19-24, Composite: 20-25.

ACADEMICS

Year founded: 1896. **Academic calendar:** Semester. **Degrees offered:** certificate, associate, transfer-associate, terminal-associate, bachelor's, master's. **Most popular majors:** 46% agriculture, agriculture operations, and related sciences, 18% business, management, marketing, and related support services, 12% biological and biomedical sciences, 8% natural resources and conservation, 6% education. **Major fields of study:** agriculture, agriculture operations, and related sciences; biological and biomedical sciences; business, management, marketing, and related support services; computer and information sciences and support services; education; English language and literature/letters; mathematics and statistics; natural resources and conservation; physical sciences; security and protective services. **Areas of required coursework:** arts/fine arts, humanities, computer literacy, mathematics, English (including composition), philosophy, sciences (biological or physical), history, social science, other. **Pre-professional programs:** pre-law, pre-dentistry, pre-medicine, pre-veterinary science, pre-optometry, pre-pharmacy. **Special academic programs (% participation):** accelerated program, cooperative (work-study plan) program (100%), cross-registration (17%), distance learning (15%), double major (18%), honors program (19%), independent study (36%), internships (100%), study abroad (9%), teacher certificate program (14%), weekend college (2%). **Teacher certification offered in:** vo-tech, middle/junior high, secondary. **Cooperative education programs:** agriculture, business, computer science, social/behavioral science. **Faculty and instruction (2009-2010):** Total instructional faculty: 82 full-time, 118 part-time (64% men; 37% women; 6% minorities). Full-time faculty with Ph.D. or other terminal degree: 60%. Student/faculty ratio: 15/1. Classes of fewer than 20 students: 55%; of 20 to 49 students: 42%; of 50 or more students: 3%. **Advanced Placement and International Baccalaureate credit:** AP tests may be used for: Placement only. Scores accepted: 2, 3. International Baccalaureate exams may be used for: Placement only. **Freshmen returning for sophomore year:** 75%. **Graduation rates:** Four-year: 37%; five-year: 47%; six-year: 51%. **Graduate study:** 22% of students pursue further study immediately upon graduation; 23% within one year. Fields in which graduates pursue further study: Master of Business Administration (MBA), 9%; education, 9%; arts and sciences, 28%; veterinary medicine, 11%.

COSTS AND FINANCIAL AID

Financial aid office: (215) 489-2272. **Expenses (2010-2011):** Tuition and fees 2010-2011: $29,284; room/board: $10,326. Estimated books and supplies: $1,000; transportation: $500; personal expenses: $1,100. **Financial aid:** Priority filing date for institution's financial aid form: April 1; deadline: April 1. In 2009-2010, 86% of undergraduates applied for financial aid. Of those, 79% were determined to have financial need; 11% had their need fully met. Average financial aid package (proportion receiving): $19,249 (79%). Average amount of gift aid, such as scholarships or grants (proportion receiving): $14,435 (78%). Average amount of self-help aid, such as work study or loans (proportion receiving): $4,642 (66%). Average need-based loan (excluding PLUS or other private loans): $4,371. Among students who received need-based aid, the average percentage of need met: 68%. Among students who received aid based on merit, the average award (and the proportion receiving): $10,096 (20%). The average athletic scholarship (and the proportion receiving): $0 (0%). Average amount of debt of borrowers graduating in 2009: $26,350. Proportion who borrowed: 63%.

CAMPUS LIFE AND EXTRACURRICULAR ACTIVITIES

Campus housing available (% using): coed dorms (88%), women's dorms (11%). Students who live in college-owned, operated, or affiliated housing: 67%. **Student employment:** During the 2009-2010 academic year, 13% of undergraduates worked on campus. Average per-year earnings: $1,732. **Clubs and organizations:** Number of student organizations: 61. Activities include: choral groups, concert band, drama/theater, literary magazine, music ensembles, radio station, student government, student newspaper, yearbook. Number of fraternities: 3; sororities: 3. Proportion of men in fraternities: 4%; of women in sororities: 5%. Average proportion of students who stay on campus on weekends: 55%. **Sports program (2009-2010):** Member of NCAA III. **Men's intercollegiate varsity sports:** baseball, basketball, cross country, football, golf, soccer, track and field (indoor), track and field (outdoor), wrestling. **Women's intercollegiate varsity sports:** basketball, cross country, field hockey, soccer, softball, track and field (indoor), track and field (outdoor), volleyball.

SERVICES AND FACILITIES

Basic services: nonremedial tutoring, placement service, health service, health insurance. **Remedial assistance:** reading, math, writing, study skills. **Counseling services:** career, personal, veteran student, academic, older student, psychological. **For learning-disabled students:** School does not offer a structured program with separate admission and additional fees. Services include: reading machines, note-taking services, extended time for tests. **Library:** Number of titles: 59,920; number of current serial subscriptions: 19,362. **Information technology resources:** Students are not required to lease or own a computer. Number of campus computers available to all students: 150. School has a wireless network. Approximate number of users that can be accommodated: 500. Proportion of college-owned housing units wired for high-speed internet access: 100%. **Campus safety:** Security services offered: 24-hour foot-and-vehicle patrols, late-night transport/escort service, lighted pathways/sidewalks, controlled dormitory access (key, security card, etc).

TRANSFER AND INTERNATIONAL STUDENTS

Transfer students: May apply for admission for the following academic terms: Fall, Spring. Applicants need a minimum number of credits to apply. For fall 2009: Transfer applications received: 301. Transfer applicants offered admission: 203. Transfer applicants enrolled: 101. **International students:** Number of foreign undergraduates: 5. Minimum TOEFL score required: 500 (paper); 173 (computer).

DeSales University

- ■ **Address:** 2755 Station Avenue, Center Valley, PA 18034-9568
- ■ **Website:** http://www.desales.edu
- ■ **Private; Religious affiliation:** Roman Catholic
- ■ **Enrollment:** 1,729 full-time; 604 part-time

KEY STATS

✔ **U.S News College Ranking:** 67, Regional Universities (North)
✔ **SAT Score (25th/75th percentile):** 970-1190
✔ **Tuition:** 2010-2011: $28,000

Selectivity: Selective	**Room/board:** $10,140
Acceptance rate: 73%	**Average debt:** $31,077
Student/faculty ratio: 12/1	**Proportion who borrowed:** 76%

UNDERGRADUATE STUDENT BODY STATS

2009-2010 enrollment: 1,729 full-time; 604 part-time. Men: 41%; women: 59%. **Ethnic makeup:** African American: 2%; Asian American: 2%; Hispanic: 4%; White: 92%. **Religious preference:** Roman Catholic: 69%; Protestant: 20%; Muslim: 1%; No preference: 7%; Other: 2%.

ADMISSIONS FACTS AND FIGURES

Phone: (610) 282-4443. **Email:** admiss@desales.edu. **Website:** http://www.desales.edu. **Application deadlines for fall 2011:** Regular decision: August 1. Early decision: Not offered. Early action: Not offered. Admission can be deferred. **Application fee:** $30. **To apply online, go to:** https://www7.desales.edu/secforms/admiss/Application07.html. **Admissions requirements/recommendations:** High school units required (recommended):

English: 4 (4); Mathematics: 3 (4); Science: 2 (2); Foreign language: 2 (2); Social studies: 3 (4); Total units: 16 (18). Tests: The college uses SAT or ACT scores in admissions decisions. Either SAT or ACT required. Campus visit: Recommended. Admissions interview: Recommended. Off-campus interview: May be arranged. **Factors that count in admissions decisions:** *Academic:* Secondary school record: Very Important. Class rank: Very Important. Letters of recommendation: Very Important. Standardized test scores: Important. Essay: Considered. *Nonacademic:* Interview: Important. Extracurricular activities: Important. Talent/ability: Important. Character/personal qualities: Considered. Alumni/ae relationship: Considered. Geographical residence: Considered. State residency: Considered. Religious affiliation/commitment: Considered. Minority status: Considered. Volunteer work: Considered. Work experience: Considered. **Other schools with the greatest overlap in applicants:** King's College; Moravian College; Pennsylvania State University–University Park; St. Joseph's University; University of Scranton. **Admissions statistics for the fall 2009 entering class:** Total applicants: 1,998. Total accepted: 1,465. Freshmen enrolled: 378; 24% were from out of state. Overall acceptance rate: 73%. **Credentials of fall 2009 freshmen:** 22% ranked in the top 10 percent of their high school class; 49% were in the top 25 percent; 82% were in the top half. (Proportion submitting class standing: 58%.) **First-year students who submitted SAT scores:** 91%. Scores (25/75 percentile): Critical Reading: 490-600, Math: 480-590, Combined: 970-1190. **First-year students submitting ACT scores:** 10%. Scores (25/75 percentile): English: 20-29, Math: 18-27, Composite: 19-25.

ACADEMICS

Year founded: 1964. **Academic calendar:** Semester. **Degrees offered:** certificate, bachelor's, post-bachelor's certificate, master's, post-master's certificate. **Most popular majors:** 23% business, management, marketing, and related support services, 19% health professions and related clinical sciences, 9% visual and performing arts, 8% education, 8% security and protective services. **Major fields of study:** biological and biomedical sciences; business, management, marketing, and related support services; communication, journalism, and related programs; computer and information sciences and support services; education; English language and literature/letters; family and consumer sciences/human sciences; foreign languages, literatures, and linguistics; health professions and related clinical sciences; history; legal professions and studies; liberal arts and sciences studies, and humanities; mathematics and statistics; parks, recreation, leisure, and fitness studies; philosophy and religious studies; physical sciences; psychology; security and protective services; social sciences; theology and religious vocations; visual and performing arts. **Areas of required coursework:** arts/fine arts, humanities, computer literacy, mathematics, English (including composition), philosophy, foreign languages, sciences (biological or physical), history, social science, other. **Pre-professional programs:** pre-law, pre-dentistry, pre-medicine, pre-theology, pre-veterinary science, pre-optometry, pre-pharmacy. **Special academic programs:** accelerated program, cross-registration, distance learning, double major, dual enrollment, honors program, independent study, internships, liberal arts/career combination, study abroad, teacher certificate program, weekend college. **Teacher certification offered in:** special education, elementary, middle/junior high, secondary. **Reserve Officers Training Corps (ROTC):** Army ROTC: Offered at cooperating institution. **Faculty and instruction (2009-2010):** Total instructional faculty: 104 full-time, 184 part-time (48% men; 52% women). Full-time faculty with Ph.D. or other terminal degree: 69%. Student/faculty ratio: 12/1. Classes of fewer than 20 students: 40%; of 20 to 49 students: 58%; of 50 or more students: 2%. **Advanced Placement and International Baccalaureate credit:** AP tests may be used for: Placement only. Scores accepted: 3, 4, 5. **Freshmen returning for sophomore year:** 82%. **Graduation rates:** Four-year: 63%; five-year: 68%; six-year: 69%. **Graduate study:** 25% of students pursue further study immediately upon graduation; 20% within one year. Fields in which graduates pursue further study: Master of Business Administration (MBA), 3%; medicine, 1%; education, 1%; arts and sciences, 20%.

COSTS AND FINANCIAL AID

Financial aid office: (610) 282-1100. **Expenses (2010-2011):** Tuition and fees 2010-2011: $28,000; room/board: $10,140. Estimated books and supplies: $1,200 personal expenses: $4,114. **Financial aid:** Priority filing date for institution's financial aid form: February 1; deadline: May 1. In 2009-2010, 85% of undergraduates applied for financial aid. Of those, 75% were determined to have financial need; 15% had their need fully met. Average financial aid package (proportion receiving): $17,336 (74%). Average amount of gift aid, such as scholarships or grants (proportion receiving): $13,352 (68%). Average amount of self-help aid, such as work study or loans (proportion receiving): $5,542 (63%). Average need-based loan (excluding PLUS or other private loans): $4,287. Among students who received need-based aid, the average percentage of need met: 68%. Among students who received aid based on merit, the average award (and the proportion receiving): $8,494 (15%). The average athletic scholarship (and the proportion receiving): $0 (0%). Average amount of debt of borrowers graduating in 2009: $31,077. Proportion who borrowed: 76%.

CAMPUS LIFE AND EXTRACURRICULAR ACTIVITIES

Campus housing available (% using): women's dorms (20%), men's dorms (15%), apartment for single students (13%), other housing options (42%). Students who live in college-owned, operated, or affiliated housing: 65%. **Student employment:** During the 2009-2010 academic year, 45% of undergraduates worked on campus. Average per-year earnings: $725. **Clubs and organizations:** Number of student organizations: 42. Activities include: campus ministries, choral groups, dance, drama/theater, international student organization, literary magazine, marching band, model UN, musical theater, pep band, radio station, student government, student newspaper, student film society, television station, yearbook. Number of fraternities: 0; sororities: 0. Average proportion of students who stay on campus on weekends: 75%. **Sports program (2009-2010):** Member of NCAA III. *Men's intercollegiate varsity sports:* baseball, basketball, cross country, lacrosse, soccer, tennis, track and field (indoor), track and field (outdoor). *Women's intercollegiate varsity sports:* basketball, cross country, field hockey, lacrosse, soccer, softball, tennis, track and field (indoor), track and field (outdoor), volleyball.

SERVICES AND FACILITIES

Basic services: nonremedial tutoring, placement service, health service, health insurance. **Remedial assistance:** reading, math, writing, study skills. **Counseling services:** career, personal, academic, older student, religious. **For learning-disabled students:** School does not offer a structured program with separate admission and additional fees. Total undergraduates in learning-disabled program or receiving services: 39. Services include: remedial math, remedial English, reading machines, remedial reading, tape recorders, untimed tests, note-taking services, oral tests, learning center, readers, extended time for tests, tutors, priority seating, texts on tape, typist/scribe, exams on tape or computer, other testing accommodations, other. **Library:** Number of titles: 154,960; number of current serial subscriptions: 8,527. **Information technology resources:** Students are not required to lease or own a computer. Number of campus computers available to all students: 250. School has a wireless network. Approximate number of users that can be accommodated: 500. Proportion of college-owned housing units wired for high-speed internet access: 100%. **Campus safety:** Security services offered: 24-hour foot-and-vehicle patrols, late-night transport/escort service, 24-hour emergency telephones, lighted pathways/sidewalks, controlled dormitory access (key, security card, etc).

TRANSFER AND INTERNATIONAL STUDENTS

Transfer students: May apply for admission for the following academic terms: Fall, Spring. Applicants need a minimum number of credits to apply. For fall 2009: Transfer applications received: 351. Transfer applicants offered admission: 130. Transfer applicants enrolled: 62. **International students:** Number of foreign undergraduates: 0. Number of countries represented: 3. Minimum TOEFL score required: 550 (paper); 213 (computer). Average TOEFL score: 550 (paper).

Dickinson College

- **Address:** PO Box 1773, Carlisle, PA 17013-2896
- **Website:** http://www.dickinson.edu
- **Private; Religious affiliation:** No Religious Affiliation
- **Enrollment:** 2,340 full-time; 36 part-time

KEY STATS

✔ **U.S News College Ranking:** 47, National Liberal Arts Colleges
✔ **SAT Score (25th/75th percentile):** 1190-1370
✔ **Tuition:** 2010-2011: $41,520

Selectivity: More selective	**Room/board:** $10,430
Acceptance rate: 49%	**Average debt:** $23,224
Student/faculty ratio: 10/1	**Proportion who borrowed:** 55%

UNDERGRADUATE STUDENT BODY STATS

2009-2010 enrollment: 2,340 full-time; 36 part-time. Men: 44%; women: 56%. **Ethnic makeup:** African American: 4%; Asian American: 4%; Hispanic: 5%; White: 80%; International: 6%. **Religious preference:** Roman

Catholic: 20%; Protestant: 28%; Jewish: 10%; Hindu: 1%; Buddhist: 2%; No preference: 36%.

ADMISSIONS FACTS AND FIGURES

Phone: (800) 644-1773. **Email:** admit@dickinson.edu. **Website:** http://www.dickinson.edu. **Application deadlines for fall 2011:** Regular decision: February 1; decision sent by March 31. Early decision: Send application by: November 15; Decision sent by: December 15. Early action: Send application by: December 1; Decision sent by: February 1. Admission can be deferred. **Application fee:** $65. **To apply online, go to:** http://www.dickinson.edu/admit. **Admissions requirements/recommendations:** High school units required (recommended): English: 4; Mathematics: 3; Science: 3; Foreign language: 2 (3); Social studies: 2; Academic electives: 2; Total units: 16. Tests: The college uses SAT or ACT scores in admissions decisions. Neither SAT nor ACT required. For admission to the fall 2011 entering class, the school will accept: ACT with or without writing accepted. Campus visit: Recommended. Admissions interview: Recommended. Off-campus interview: May be arranged. **Factors that count in admissions decisions:** *Academic:* Secondary school record: Very Important. Class rank: Important. Letters of recommendation: Important. Standardized test scores: Important. Essay: Considered. *Nonacademic:* Interview: Considered. Extracurricular activities: Very Important. Talent/ability: Very Important. Character/personal qualities: Considered. Alumni/ae relationship: Important. Geographical residence: Considered. State residency: Considered. Religious affiliation/commitment: Not Considered. Minority status: Considered. Volunteer work: Very Important. Work experience: Important. **Other schools with the greatest overlap in applicants:** Bucknell University; Franklin and Marshall College; Gettysburg College; Hamilton College; Kenyon College. **Admissions statistics for the fall 2009 entering class:** Total applicants: 5,026. Total accepted: 2,459. Freshmen enrolled: 581; 77% were from out of state. Accepted through early-decision or early-action plans: 71%. Overall acceptance rate: 49%. Early-decision acceptance rate: 76%. Non-early acceptance rate: 33%. **Size of waiting list:** 297 applicants; enrolled from waiting list: 65. **Credentials of fall 2009 freshmen:** 37% ranked in the top 10 percent of their high school class; 71% were in the top 25 percent; 95% were in the top half. (Proportion submitting class standing: 33%.) **First-year students who submitted SAT scores:** 58%. Scores (25/75 percentile): Critical Reading: 600-690, Math: 590-680, Combined: 1190-1370. **First-year students submitting ACT scores:** 22%. Scores (25/75 percentile): English: N/A, Math: N/A, Composite: 26-30.

ACADEMICS

Year founded: 1783. **Academic calendar:** Semester. **Degrees offered:** bachelor's. **Most popular majors:** 12% international business/trade/commerce, 10% political science and government, 6% English language and literature, 6% psychology, 5% biology/biological sciences. **Major fields of study:** area, ethnic, cultural, and gender studies; biological and biomedical sciences; business, management, marketing, and related support services; computer and information sciences and support services; engineering; English language and literature/letters; foreign languages, literatures, and linguistics; history; legal professions and studies; mathematics and statistics; multi/interdisciplinary studies; natural resources and conservation; philosophy and religious studies; physical sciences; psychology; public administration and social service professions; social sciences; visual and performing arts. **Areas of required coursework:** humanities, foreign languages, sciences (biological or physical), social science, other. **Pre-professional programs:** pre-law, pre-dentistry, pre-medicine, pre-theology, pre-veterinary science, pre-optometry, pre-pharmacy. **Special academic programs (% participation):** accelerated program, cross-registration, double major (18%), English as a Second Language (ESL), exchange student program (domestic) (6%), independent study, internships (58%), liberal arts/career combination, student-designed major, study abroad (59%), teacher certificate program. **Teacher certification offered in:** secondary. **Reserve Officers Training Corps (ROTC):** Army ROTC: Offered on campus. **Faculty and instruction (2009-2010):** Total instructional faculty: 193 full-time, 44 part-time (54% men; 46% women; 9% minorities). Full-time faculty with Ph.D. or other terminal degree: 93%. Student/faculty ratio: 10/1. Classes of fewer than 20 students: 71%; of 20 to 49 students: 29%; of 50 or more students: 0%. **Advanced Placement and International Baccalaureate credit:** AP tests may be used for: Credit and/or placement. Scores accepted: 4, 5. International Baccalaureate exams may be used for: Credit and/or placement. **Freshmen returning for sophomore year:** 92%. **Graduation rates:** Four-year: 81%; five-year: 84%; six-year: 84%. **Graduate study:** 35% of students pursue further study within one year; 59% within five years. Fields in which graduates pursue further study: Master of Business Administration (MBA), 9%; law, 17%; medicine, 5%; education, 21%; arts and sciences, 46%; veterinary medicine, 2%.

COSTS AND FINANCIAL AID

Financial aid office: (717) 245-1308. **Expenses (2010-2011):** Tuition and fees 2010-2011: $41,520; room/board: $10,430. Estimated books and supplies: $1,000; transportation: $300; personal expenses: $1,200. **Financial aid:** Priority filing date for institution's financial aid form: November 15; deadline: February 1. In 2009-2010, 59% of undergraduates applied for financial aid. Of those, 52% were determined to have financial need; 66% had their need fully met. Average financial aid package (proportion receiving): $33,332 (52%). Average amount of gift aid, such as scholarships or grants (proportion receiving): $27,318 (50%). Average amount of self-help aid, such as work study or loans (proportion receiving): $6,395 (47%). Average need-based loan (excluding PLUS or other private loans): $4,716. Among students who received need-based aid, the average percentage of need met: 94%. Among students who received aid based on merit, the average award (and the proportion receiving): $11,709 (8%). The average athletic scholarship (and the proportion receiving): $0 (0%). Average amount of debt of borrowers graduating in 2009: $23,224. Proportion who borrowed: 55%.

CAMPUS LIFE AND EXTRACURRICULAR ACTIVITIES

Campus housing available: coed dorms, sorority housing, fraternity housing, apartment for single students, special housing for disabled students, other housing options. Students who live in college-owned, operated, or affiliated housing: 94%. **Student employment:** During the 2009-2010 academic year, 23% of undergraduates worked on campus. Average per-year earnings: $712. **Clubs and organizations:** Number of student organizations: 112. Activities include: choral groups, concert band, dance, drama/theater, international student organization, jazz band, literary magazine, model UN, music ensembles, musical theater, radio station, student government, student newspaper, student film society, symphony orchestra, yearbook. Number of fraternities: 6; sororities: 6. Proportion of men in fraternities: 13%; of women in sororities: 18%. Average proportion of students who stay on campus on weekends: 85%. **Sports program (2009-2010):** Member of NCAA III. *Men's intercollegiate varsity sports:* baseball, basketball, cross country, football, golf, lacrosse, soccer, swimming, tennis, track and field (indoor), track and field (outdoor). *Women's intercollegiate varsity sports:* basketball, cross country, field hockey, golf, lacrosse, soccer, softball, swimming, tennis, track and field (indoor), track and field (outdoor), volleyball.

SERVICES AND FACILITIES

Basic services: nonremedial tutoring, women's center, placement service, day care, health service, health insurance, other. **Counseling services:** minority student, career, personal, veteran student, academic, older student, psychological, birth control, religious. **For learning-disabled students:** School does not offer a structured program with separate admission and additional fees. Total undergraduates in learning-disabled program or receiving services: 154. Services include: tape recorders, untimed tests, note-taking services, oral tests, readers, tutors, other. **Library:** Number of titles: 501,043; number of current serial subscriptions: 2,451. **Information technology resources:** Students are not required to lease or own a computer. Number of campus computers available to all students: 661. School has a wireless network. Approximate number of users that can be accommodated: 2,048. Proportion of college-owned housing units wired for high-speed internet access: 100%. **Campus safety:** Security services offered: 24-hour foot-and-vehicle patrols, late-night transport/escort service, 24-hour emergency telephones, lighted pathways/sidewalks, student patrols, controlled dormitory access (key, security card, etc).

TRANSFER AND INTERNATIONAL STUDENTS

Transfer students: May apply for admission for the following academic terms: Fall, Spring. Applicants need a minimum number of credits to apply. For fall 2009: Transfer applications received: 123. Transfer applicants offered admission: 39. Transfer applicants enrolled: 29. **International students:** Number of foreign undergraduates: 145 (6% of student body). Number of countries represented: 41. Minimum TOEFL score required: 600 (paper); 250 (computer).

Drexel University

- **Address:** 3141 Chestnut Street, Philadelphia, PA 19104-2875
- **Website:** http://www.drexel.edu
- **Private**
- **Enrollment:** 8,846 full-time; 2,017 part-time

KEY STATS

✔ **U.S News College Ranking:** 86, National Universities
✔ **SAT Score (25th/75th percentile):** 1110-1300
✔ **Tuition:** 2010-2011: $33,005

Selectivity: More selective	**Room/board:** $13,125
Acceptance rate: 55%	**Average debt:** N/A
Student/faculty ratio: 9/1	**Proportion who borrowed:** N/A

UNDERGRADUATE STUDENT BODY STATS

2009-2010 enrollment: 8,846 full-time; 2,017 part-time. Men: 57%; women: 43%. **Ethnic makeup:** African American: 9%; Asian American: 12%; Hispanic: 3%; White: 68%; International: 7%.

ADMISSIONS FACTS AND FIGURES

Phone: (800) 237-3935. **Email:** enroll@drexel.edu. **Website:** http://www.drexel.edu. **Application deadlines for fall 2011:** Regular decision: March 1. Early decision: Not offered. Early action: Not offered. Admission can be deferred. **Application fee:** $75. **To apply online, go to:** http://www.drexel.edu/em/apply/. **Admissions requirements/recommendations:** High school units required (recommended): Mathematics: 3; Science: 1; Foreign language: (1). Tests: The college uses SAT or ACT scores in admissions decisions. Either SAT or ACT required. For admission to the fall 2011 entering class, the school will accept: ACT with or without writing accepted. Campus visit: Recommended. Admissions interview: Recommended. Off-campus interview: May be arranged. **Factors that count in admissions decisions:** *Academic:* Secondary school record: Very Important. Class rank: Very Important. Letters of recommendation: Important. Standardized test scores: Very Important. Essay: Important. *Nonacademic:* Interview: Considered. Extracurricular activities: Considered. Talent/ability: Considered. Character/personal qualities: Important. Alumni/ae relationship: Considered. Geographical residence: Not Considered. State residency: Not Considered. Religious affiliation/commitment: Not Considered. Minority status: Not Considered. Volunteer work: Considered. Work experience: Considered. **Other schools with the greatest overlap in applicants:** New York University; Northeastern University; Pennsylvania State University–University Park; Rutgers, the State University of New Jersey–New Brunswick; University of Pennsylvania. **Admissions statistics for the fall 2009 entering class:** Total applicants: 39,827. Total accepted: 21,729. Freshmen enrolled: 2,346; 49% were from out of state. Overall acceptance rate: 55%. **Size of waiting list:** 3849 applicants; enrolled from waiting list: 924. **Credentials of fall 2009 freshmen:** 30% ranked in the top 10 percent of their high school class; 63% were in the top 25 percent; 91% were in the top half. (Proportion submitting class standing: 49%.) **First-year students who submitted SAT scores:** 94%. Scores (25/75 percentile): Critical Reading: 540-630, Math: 570-670, Combined: 1110-1300. **First-year students submitting ACT scores:** 17%. Scores (25/75 percentile): English: N/A, Math: N/A, Composite: 23-28.

ACADEMICS

Year founded: 1891. **Academic calendar:** Quarter. **Degrees offered:** certificate, associate, bachelor's, post-bachelor's certificate, master's, post-master's certificate, doctorate. **Most popular majors:** 24% business, management, marketing, and related support services, 21% engineering, 19% health professions and related clinical sciences, 10% visual and performing arts, 6% computer and information sciences and support services. **Major fields of study:** architecture and related services; area, ethnic, cultural, and gender studies; biological and biomedical sciences; business, management, marketing, and related support services; computer and information sciences and support services; construction trades; education; engineering; English language and literature/letters; health professions and related clinical sciences; history; liberal arts and sciences studies, and humanities; mathematics and statistics; multi/interdisciplinary studies; natural resources and conservation; parks, recreation, leisure, and fitness studies; personal and culinary services; physical sciences; psychology; security and protective services; social sciences; visual and performing arts. **Areas of required coursework:** humanities, computer literacy, mathematics, English (including composition), sciences (biological or physical), history. **Pre-professional programs:** pre-medicine, other. **Special academic programs (% participa-**

tion): accelerated program (2%), cooperative (work-study plan) program (95%), distance learning, double major (1%), dual enrollment, English as a Second Language (ESL) (6%), honors program (12%), independent study, student-designed major, study abroad, teacher certificate program (2%), weekend college. **Teacher certification offered in:** elementary, middle/junior high, secondary. **Cooperative education programs:** art, business, computer science, education, engineering, health professions, humanities, natural science, social/behavioral science, technologies, other. **Reserve Officers Training Corps (ROTC):** Army ROTC: Offered on campus; Navy ROTC: Offered at cooperating institution (University of Pennsylvania); Air Force ROTC: Offered at cooperating institution (St. Joseph's University). **Faculty and instruction (2009-2010):** Total instructional faculty: 928 full-time, 571 part-time (57% men; 43% women; 15% minorities). Full-time faculty with Ph.D. or other terminal degree: 81%. Student/faculty ratio: 9/1. Classes of fewer than 20 students: 65%; of 20 to 49 students: 31%; of 50 or more students: 4%. **Advanced Placement and International Baccalaureate credit:** AP tests may be used for: Credit and/or placement. Scores accepted: 4, 5. International Baccalaureate exams may be used for: Placement only. **Freshmen returning for sophomore year:** 84%. **Graduation rates:** Four-year: 25%; five-year: 66%; six-year: 66%. **Graduate study:** 13% of students pursue further study within one year; 45% within five years. Fields in which graduates pursue further study: Master of Business Administration (MBA), 25%; law, 2%; medicine, 5%; engineering, 35%; education, 5%; arts and sciences, 20%; veterinary medicine, 2%.

COSTS AND FINANCIAL AID

Financial aid office: (215) 895-2537. **Expenses (2010-2011):** Tuition and fees 2010-2011: $33,005; room/board: $13,125. Estimated books and supplies: $1,950; transportation: $850; personal expenses: $3,000. **Financial aid:** Priority filing date for institution's financial aid form: March 1; deadline: March 1.

CAMPUS LIFE AND EXTRACURRICULAR ACTIVITIES

Campus housing available (% using): coed dorms (95%), sorority housing (3%), fraternity housing (1%), special housing for disabled students (0%), special housing for international students (1%). Students who live in college-owned, operated, or affiliated housing: 34%. **Student employment:** During the 2009-2010 academic year, 8% of undergraduates worked on campus. **Clubs and organizations:** Number of student organizations: 180. Activities include: campus ministries, choral groups, concert band, dance, drama/theater, jazz band, literary magazine, music ensembles, musical theater, pep band, radio station, student government, student newspaper, student film society, television station, yearbook. Number of fraternities: 15; sororities: 10. Proportion of men in fraternities: 9%; of women in sororities: 8%. Average proportion of students who stay on campus on weekends: 50%. **Sports program (2009-2010):** Member of NCAA I. *Men's intercollegiate varsity sports:* basketball, golf, lacrosse, soccer, swimming, tennis, wrestling. *Women's intercollegiate varsity sports:* basketball, crew (heavyweight), field hockey, lacrosse, crew (lightweight), soccer, softball, swimming, tennis.

SERVICES AND FACILITIES

Basic services: nonremedial tutoring, women's center, placement service, health service, health insurance. **Remedial assistance:** reading, math, writing, study skills. **Counseling services:** minority student, career, personal, academic, older student, psychological, other. **For learning-disabled students:** School does not offer a structured program with separate admission and additional fees. Total undergraduates in learning-disabled program or receiving services: 106. Services include: reading machines, tape recorders, diagnostic testing service, note-taking services, oral tests, learning center, readers, extended time for tests, tutors, priority registration, priority seating, texts on tape, exams on tape or computer, other testing accommodations. **Library:** Number of titles: 643,869; number of current serial subscriptions: 27,399. **Information technology resources:** Students are required to lease or own a computer. Number of campus computers available to all students: 3,000. School has a wireless network. Approximate number of users that can be accommodated: 24,000. Proportion of college-owned housing units wired for high-speed internet access: 100%. **Campus safety:** Security services offered: 24-hour foot-and-vehicle patrols, late-night transport/escort service, 24-hour emergency telephones, lighted pathways/sidewalks, controlled dormitory access (key, security card, etc).

TRANSFER AND INTERNATIONAL STUDENTS

Transfer students: May apply for admission for the following academic terms: Fall, Winter, Spring, Summer. Applicants need a minimum number of credits to apply. For fall 2009: Transfer applications received: 4,585.

Transfer applicants offered admission: 3,334. Transfer applicants enrolled: 1,368. **International students:** Number of foreign undergraduates: 756 (7% of student body). Number of countries represented: 118. Minimum TOEFL score required: 550 (paper); 79 (computer). Average TOEFL score: 570 (paper).

Duquesne University

- ■ **Address:** 600 Forbes Avenue, Pittsburgh, PA 15282
- ■ **Website:** http://www.duq.edu
- ■ **Private; Religious affiliation:** Roman Catholic
- ■ **Enrollment:** 5,545 full-time; 246 part-time

KEY STATS
- ✔ **U.S News College Ranking:** 120, National Universities
- ✔ **SAT Score (25th/75th percentile):** 1030-1210
- ✔ **Tuition:** 2010-2011: $27,502

Selectivity: Selective	**Room/board:** $9,476
Acceptance rate: 76%	**Average debt:** N/A
Student/faculty ratio: 14/1	**Proportion who borrowed:** N/A

UNDERGRADUATE STUDENT BODY STATS
2009-2010 enrollment: 5,545 full-time; 246 part-time. Men: 44%; women: 56%. **Ethnic makeup:** African American: 4%; Asian American: 2%; Hispanic: 2%; White: 90%; International: 2%. **Religious preference:** Protestant: 3%; Jewish: 1%; Unknown: 29%; Roman Catholic: 51%; Other: 16%.

ADMISSIONS FACTS AND FIGURES
Phone: (412) 396-6222. **Email:** admissions@duq.edu. **Website:** http://www.duq.edu. **Application deadlines for fall 2011:** Regular decision: July 1. Early decision: Send application by: November 1; Decision sent by: December 15. Early action: Send application by: December 1; Decision sent by: January 15. Admission can be deferred. **Application fee:** $50. **To apply online, go to:** http://www.admissions.duq.edu/apply.html. **Admissions requirements/ recommendations:** High school units required (recommended): English: (4); Mathematics: (2); Science: (2); Foreign language: (2); Social studies: (2); Academic electives: (4); Total units: (16). Tests: The college uses SAT or ACT scores in admissions decisions. Either SAT or ACT required. For admission to the fall 2011 entering class, the school will accept: ACT with writing required. Campus visit: Recommended. Admissions interview: Recommended. Off-campus interview: May be arranged. **Factors that count in admissions decisions:** *Academic:* Secondary school record: Very Important. Class rank: Important. Letters of recommendation: Very Important. Standardized test scores: Very Important. Essay: Very Important. *Nonacademic:* Interview: Important. Extracurricular activities: Important. Talent/ability: Important. Character/personal qualities: Important. Alumni/ ae relationship: Considered. Geographical residence: Not Considered. State residency: Not Considered. Religious affiliation/commitment: Not Considered. Minority status: Considered. Volunteer work: Important. Work experience: Considered. **Other schools with the greatest overlap in applicants:** Pennsylvania State University–University Park; University of Pittsburgh; Washington and Jefferson College. **Admissions statistics for the fall 2009 entering class:** Total applicants: 6,626. Total accepted: 5,054. Freshmen enrolled: 1,432; 26% were from out of state. Accepted through early-decision or early-action plans: 28%. Overall acceptance rate: 76%. Early-decision acceptance rate: 57%. Non-early acceptance rate: 83%. **Credentials of fall 2009 freshmen:** 24% ranked in the top 10 percent of their high school class; 55% were in the top 25 percent; 87% were in the top half. (Proportion submitting class standing: 67%.) **Average high school grade point average:** 3.6. **First-year students who submitted SAT scores:** 94%. Scores (25/75 percentile): Critical Reading: 510-600, Math: 520-610, Combined: 1030-1210. **First-year students submitting ACT scores:** 40%. Scores (25/75 percentile): English: 22-27, Math: 23-28, Composite: 23-28.

ACADEMICS
Year founded: 1878. **Academic calendar:** Semester. **Degrees offered:** bachelor's, post-bachelor's certificate, master's, post-master's certificate, doctorate. **Most popular majors:** 25% business, management, marketing, and related support services, 22% health professions and related clinical sciences, 9% education, 5% biological and biomedical sciences, 5% social sciences. **Major fields of study:** biological and biomedical sciences; business, management, marketing, and related support services; communication, journalism, and

related programs; computer and information sciences and support services; education; English language and literature/letters; foreign languages, literatures, and linguistics; health professions and related clinical sciences; history; liberal arts and sciences studies, and humanities; mathematics and statistics; natural resources and conservation; philosophy and religious studies; physical sciences; psychology; social sciences; theology and religious vocations; visual and performing arts. **Areas of required coursework:** arts/ fine arts, humanities, computer literacy, mathematics, English (including composition), philosophy, foreign languages, sciences (biological or physical), history, social science, other. **Pre-professional programs:** pre-law, pre-dentistry, pre-medicine, pre-veterinary science, pre-optometry, pre-pharmacy, other. **Special academic programs (% participation):** accelerated program, cross-registration, distance learning (7%), double major (20%), dual enrollment, English as a Second Language (ESL) (3%), external degree program, honors program, independent study, internships, liberal arts/career combination (2%), student-designed major (6%), study abroad, teacher certificate program (8%), weekend college. **Teacher certification offered in:** early childhood, special education, elementary, middle/junior high, secondary. **Reserve Officers Training Corps (ROTC):** Army ROTC: Offered on campus; Navy ROTC: Offered at cooperating institution (Carnegie Mellon University); Air Force ROTC: Offered at cooperating institution (University of Pittsburgh). **Faculty and instruction (2009-2010):** Total instructional faculty: 472 full-time, 511 part-time (55% men; 45% women; 6% minorities). Full-time faculty with Ph.D. or other terminal degree: 87%. Student/faculty ratio: 14/1. Classes of fewer than 20 students: 48%; of 20 to 49 students: 48%; of 50 or more students: 5%. **Advanced Placement and International Baccalaureate credit:** AP tests may be used for: Credit only. Scores accepted: 3, 4, 5. International Baccalaureate exams may be used for: Credit only. **Freshmen returning for sophomore year:** 87%. **Graduation rates:** Four-year: 61%; five-year: 72%; six-year: 74%. **Graduate study:** 35% of students pursue further study immediately upon graduation; 35% within one year; 35% within five years. Fields in which graduates pursue further study: Master of Business Administration (MBA), 17%; law, 17%; arts and sciences, 67%.

COSTS AND FINANCIAL AID
Financial aid office: (412) 396-6607. **Expenses (2010-2011):** Tuition and fees 2010-2011: $27,502; room/board: $9,476. Estimated books and supplies: $1,000; transportation: $550; personal expenses: $600. **Financial aid:** In 2009-2010, 83% of undergraduates applied for financial aid. Of those, 70% were determined to have financial need; 27% had their need fully met. Average financial aid package (proportion receiving): $20,623 (70%). Average amount of gift aid, such as scholarships or grants (proportion receiving): $12,312 (68%). Average amount of self-help aid, such as work study or loans (proportion receiving): $6,860 (59%). Average need-based loan (excluding PLUS or other private loans): $4,400. Among students who received need-based aid, the average percentage of need met: 80%. Among students who received aid based on merit, the average award (and the proportion receiving): $7,759 (25%). The average athletic scholarship (and the proportion receiving): $18,425 (2%).

CAMPUS LIFE AND EXTRACURRICULAR ACTIVITIES
Campus housing available (% using): coed dorms (75%), sorority housing (6%), fraternity housing (3%), apartments for married students (0%), apartment for single students (15%), special housing for disabled students (1%). Students who live in college-owned, operated, or affiliated housing: 58%. **Clubs and organizations:** Number of student organizations: 160. Activities include: campus ministries, choral groups, concert band, dance, drama/ theater, international student organization, jazz band, literary magazine, marching band, model UN, music ensembles, musical theater, opera, pep band, radio station, student government, student newspaper, student film society, symphony orchestra, television station, yearbook. Number of fraternities: 10; sororities: 7. Proportion of men in fraternities: 12%; of women in sororities: 14%. Average proportion of students who stay on campus on weekends: 70%. **Sports program (2009-2010):** Member of NCAA I. *Men's intercollegiate varsity sports:* basketball, cross country, football, soccer, tennis, track and field (outdoor). *Women's intercollegiate varsity sports:* basketball, crew (heavyweight), cross country, lacrosse, crew (lightweight), soccer, swimming, tennis, track and field (indoor), track and field (outdoor), volleyball.

SERVICES AND FACILITIES
Basic services: nonremedial tutoring, placement service, day care, health service, health insurance, other. **Remedial assistance:** reading, math, writing, study skills, other. **Counseling services:** minority student, career, personal, veteran student, academic, older student, psychological, religious. **For learning-disabled students:** School does not offer a structured program with

separate admission and additional fees. Total undergraduates in learning-disabled program or receiving services: 46. Services include: tape recorders, note-taking services, oral tests, learning center, readers, extended time for tests, tutors, priority registration, priority seating, typist/scribe, exams on tape or computer, other testing accommodations, other. **Library:** Number of titles: 715,518; number of current serial subscriptions: 31,060. **Information technology resources:** Students are not required to lease or own a computer. Number of campus computers available to all students: 850. School has a wireless network. Approximate number of users that can be accommodated: 500. Proportion of college-owned housing units wired for high-speed internet access: 100%. **Campus safety:** Security services offered: 24-hour foot-and-vehicle patrols, late-night transport/escort service, 24-hour emergency telephones, lighted pathways/sidewalks, controlled dormitory access (key, security card, etc).

TRANSFER AND INTERNATIONAL STUDENTS

Transfer students: May apply for admission for the following academic terms: Fall, Spring. Applicants need a minimum number of credits to apply. For fall 2009: Transfer applications received: 422. Transfer applicants offered admission: 331. Transfer applicants enrolled: 179. **International students:** Number of foreign undergraduates: 126 (2% of student body). Number of countries represented: 45. Minimum TOEFL score required: 575 (paper).

Eastern University

- **Address:** 1300 Eagle Road, St. Davids, PA 19087-3696
- **Website:** http://www.eastern.edu
- **Private; Religious affiliation:** American Baptist
- **Enrollment:** 2,198 full-time; 515 part-time

KEY STATS
✔ **U.S News College Ranking:** 84, Regional Universities (North)
✔ **SAT Score (25th/75th percentile):** 960-1190
✔ **Tuition:** 2010-2011: $24,600

Selectivity: Selective	**Room/board:** $9,090
Acceptance rate: 71%	**Average debt:** N/A
Student/faculty ratio: N/A	**Proportion who borrowed:** N/A

UNDERGRADUATE STUDENT BODY STATS

2009-2010 enrollment: 2,198 full-time; 515 part-time. Men: 31%; women: 69%. **Ethnic makeup:** African American: 21%; Asian American: 2%; Hispanic: 11%; White: 64%; International: 1%. **Religious preference:** Roman Catholic: 5%; Protestant: 21%; No preference: 10%; Unknown: 1%; American Baptist: 2%; All Other Baptist: 10%; Other: 51%.

ADMISSIONS FACTS AND FIGURES

Phone: (610) 341-5967. **Email:** ugadm@eastern.edu. **Website:** http://www.eastern.edu. **Application deadlines for fall 2011:** Regular decision: Rolling. Early decision: Not offered. Early action: Not offered. Admission can be deferred. **Application fee:** $25. **To apply online, go to:** https://mail.eastern.edu/application/. **Admissions requirements/recommendations:** High school units required (recommended): English: 4 (4); Mathematics: 3 (3); Science: 3 (3); Foreign language: 3 (3); Social studies: 3 (3); History: 3 (3); Academic electives: 0 (0); Total units: 22 (22). Tests: The college uses SAT or ACT scores in admissions decisions. Either SAT or ACT required. For admission to the fall 2011 entering class, the school will accept: ACT with writing recommended. Campus visit: Recommended. Admissions interview: Recommended. Off-campus interview: May be arranged. **Factors that count in admissions decisions:** *Academic:* Secondary school record: Very Important. Class rank: Very Important. Letters of recommendation: Considered. Standardized test scores: Important. Essay: Considered. *Nonacademic:* Interview: Considered. Extracurricular activities: Considered. Talent/ability: Considered. Character/personal qualities: Considered. Alumni/ae relationship: Considered. Geographical residence: Not Considered. State residency: Not Considered. Religious affiliation/commitment: Considered. Minority status: Not Considered. Volunteer work: Considered. Work experience: Considered. **Other schools with the greatest overlap in applicants:** Liberty University; Messiah College. **Admissions statistics for the fall 2009 entering class:** Total applicants: 1,416. Total accepted: 1,002. Freshmen enrolled: 408; 43% were from out of state. Overall acceptance rate: 71%. **Size of waiting list:** 0 applicants; enrolled from waiting list: 0. **Credentials of fall 2009 freshmen:** 21% ranked in the top 10 percent of their high school class; 53% were in the top 25 percent; 76% were in the top half. (Proportion submitting class standing: 56%.) **Average high school grade point average:** 3.4. **First-year students who submitted SAT scores:** 89%. Scores (25/75 percentile): Critical Reading: 480-600, Math: 480-590, Combined: 960-1190. **First-year students submitting ACT scores:** 10%. Scores (25/75 percentile): English: 17-21, Math: 19-25, Composite: 19-23.

ACADEMICS

Year founded: 1952. **Academic calendar:** Semester. **Degrees offered:** transfer-associate, bachelor's, master's, doctorate. **Most popular majors:** 20% elementary education and teaching, 7% psychology, 6% business administration and management, 5% kinesiology and exercise science, 5% youth ministry. **Major fields of study:** biological and biomedical sciences; business, management, marketing, and related support services; communication, journalism, and related programs; education; English language and literature/letters; foreign languages, literatures, and linguistics; health professions and related clinical sciences; history; mathematics and statistics; natural resources and conservation; parks, recreation, leisure, and fitness studies; physical sciences; psychology; public administration and social service professions; social sciences; theology and religious vocations; visual and performing arts. **Areas of required coursework:** arts/fine arts, humanities, English (including composition), philosophy, foreign languages, sciences (biological or physical), history, social science. **Special academic programs (% participation):** accelerated program, cross-registration (2%), double major (10%), honors program (9%), independent study (10%), internships, student-designed major (2%), study abroad (20%), teacher certificate program (20%). **Teacher certification offered in:** early childhood, special education, elementary, secondary. **Reserve Officers Training Corps (ROTC):** Army ROTC: Offered at cooperating institution; Air Force ROTC: Offered at cooperating institution (St. Joseph's University). **Advanced Placement and International Baccalaureate credit:** AP tests may be used for: Credit and/or placement. Scores accepted: 3, 4, 5. International Baccalaureate exams may be used for: Credit and/or placement. **Freshmen returning for sophomore year:** 76%. **Graduation rates:** Four-year: 58%; five-year: 64%; six-year: 62%. **Graduate study:** 20% of students pursue further study immediately upon graduation. Fields in which graduates pursue further study: Master of Business Administration (MBA), 1%; law, 1%; medicine, 2%; dentistry, 1%; theology (or the seminary), 1%; education, 28%; arts and sciences, 46%.

COSTS AND FINANCIAL AID

Financial aid office: (610) 341-5842. **Expenses (2010-2011):** Tuition and fees 2010-2011: $24,600; room/board: $9,090. Estimated books and supplies: $1,200; transportation: $1,100; personal expenses: $2,500. **Financial aid:** Priority filing date for institution's financial aid form: April 1.

CAMPUS LIFE AND EXTRACURRICULAR ACTIVITIES

Campus housing available (% using): coed dorms (97%), apartment for single students (3%). Students who live in college-owned, operated, or affiliated housing: 72%. **Student employment:** During the 2009-2010 academic year, 25% of undergraduates worked on campus. Average per-year earnings: $1,400. **Clubs and organizations:** Number of student organizations: 81. Activities include: choral groups, concert band, dance, drama/theater, international student organization, jazz band, literary magazine, music ensembles, musical theater, pep band, student government, student newspaper, yearbook. Number of fraternities: 0; sororities: 0. Average proportion of students who stay on campus on weekends: 70%. **Sports program (2009-2010):** Member of NCAA III. *Men's intercollegiate varsity sports:* baseball, basketball, cross country, golf, lacrosse, soccer, tennis. *Women's intercollegiate varsity sports:* basketball, cross country, field hockey, golf, lacrosse, soccer, softball, tennis, volleyball.

SERVICES AND FACILITIES

Basic services: nonremedial tutoring, women's center, health service, health insurance. **Remedial assistance:** reading, writing. **Counseling services:** minority student, career, military, personal, academic, psychological, birth control, religious. **For learning-disabled students:** Services include: learning center, tutors, other. **Library:** Number of titles: 295,375; number of current serial subscriptions: 525. **Information technology resources:** Students are not required to lease or own a computer. Number of campus computers available to all students: 125. School has a wireless network. Approximate number of users that can be accommodated: 300. Proportion of college-owned housing units wired for high-speed internet access: 100%. **Campus safety:** Security services offered: 24-hour foot-and-vehicle patrols, late-night transport/escort service, 24-hour emergency telephones, lighted pathways/sidewalks, controlled dormitory access (key, security card, etc).

TRANSFER AND INTERNATIONAL STUDENTS

Transfer students: May apply for admission for the following academic terms: Fall, Spring, Summer. Applicants do not need a minimum number of credits to apply. For fall 2009: Transfer applications received: 336. Transfer applicants offered admission: 225. Transfer applicants enrolled: 105. **International students:** Number of foreign undergraduates: 38 (1% of student body). Number of countries represented: 12. Minimum TOEFL score required: 550 (paper); 213 (computer). Average TOEFL score: 579 (paper).

East Stroudsburg Univ. of Pennsylvania

- **Address:** 200 Prospect Street, East Stroudsburg, PA 18301-2999
- **Website:** http://www.esu.edu
- **Public**
- **Enrollment:** 5,837 full-time; 554 part-time

KEY STATS

✔ **U.S News College Ranking:** 114, Regional Universities (North)
✔ **SAT Score (25th/75th percentile):** 890-1060
✔ **Tuition:** 2009-2010: $7,394 in state, $15,726 out of state

Selectivity: Less selective	**Room/board:** $6,418
Acceptance rate: 69%	**Average debt:** $25,887
Student/faculty ratio: 18/1	**Proportion who borrowed:** 73%

UNDERGRADUATE STUDENT BODY STATS

2009-2010 enrollment: 5,837 full-time; 554 part-time. Men: 46%; women: 54%. **Ethnic makeup:** African American: 6%; Asian American: 2%; Hispanic: 6%; White: 86%; International: 1%.

ADMISSIONS FACTS AND FIGURES

Phone: (570) 422-3542. **Email:** undergrads@po-box.esu.edu. **Website:** http://www.esu.edu. **Application deadlines for fall 2011:** Regular decision: April 1. Early decision: Not offered. Early action: Not offered. Admission cannot be deferred. **Application fee:** $35. **To apply online, go to:** https://www.applyweb.com/public/account?paeast. **Admissions requirements/recommendations:** High school units required (recommended): English: 4 (4); Mathematics: 3 (3); Science: 3 (3); Foreign language: 3 (3); Social studies: 3 (3); History: 3 (3); Total units: 19 (19). Tests: The college uses SAT or ACT scores in admissions decisions. Either SAT or ACT required. For admission to the fall 2011 entering class, the school will accept: ACT with or without writing accepted. Campus visit: Recommended. Admissions interview: Neither required nor recommended. Off-campus interview: Not available. **Factors that count in admissions decisions:** *Academic:* Secondary school record: Very Important. Class rank: Very Important. Letters of recommendation: Not Considered. Standardized test scores: Very Important. Essay: Not Considered. *Nonacademic:* Interview: Not Considered. Extracurricular activities: Not Considered. Talent/ability: Not Considered. Character/personal qualities: Not Considered. Alumni/ae relationship: Not Considered. Geographical residence: Not Considered. State residency: Not Considered. Religious affiliation/commitment: Not Considered. Minority status: Not Considered. Volunteer work: Not Considered. Work experience: Not Considered. **Admissions statistics for the fall 2009 entering class:** Total applicants: 6,960. Total accepted: 4,815. Freshmen enrolled: 1,358; Overall acceptance rate: 69%. **Size of waiting list:** 64 applicants; enrolled from waiting list: 13. **Credentials of fall 2009 freshmen:** 6% ranked in the top 10 percent of their high school class; 27% were in the top 25 percent; 67% were in the top half. (Proportion submitting class standing: 79%.) **First-year students who submitted SAT scores:** 99%. Scores (25/75 percentile): Critical Reading: 440-520, Math: 450-540, Combined: 890-1060.

ACADEMICS

Year founded: 1893. **Academic calendar:** Semester. **Degrees offered:** associate, bachelor's, master's. **Most popular majors:** 21% education, 14% business, management, marketing, and related support services; 10% social sciences, 9% health professions and related clinical sciences, 9% parks, recreation, leisure, and fitness studies. **Major fields of study:** biological and biomedical sciences; business, management, marketing, and related support services; communication, journalism, and related programs; communications technologies/technicians and support services; computer and information sciences and support services; education; English language and literature/letters; foreign languages, literatures, and linguistics; health professions and related clinical sciences; history; liberal arts and sciences

studies, and humanities; mathematics and statistics; multi/interdisciplinary studies; parks, recreation, leisure, and fitness studies; philosophy and religious studies; physical sciences; psychology; social sciences; visual and performing arts. **Areas of required coursework:** arts/fine arts, humanities, English (including composition), sciences (biological or physical), social science. **Pre-professional programs:** pre-law, pre-dentistry, pre-medicine, pre-pharmacy. **Special academic programs (% participation):** accelerated program (1%), cross-registration, distance learning, double major (3%), dual enrollment, exchange student program (domestic) (1%), honors program (2%), independent study (10%), internships (20%), student-designed major (1%), study abroad (1%), teacher certificate program (25%). **Teacher certification offered in:** early childhood, special education, elementary, middle/junior high, secondary. **Reserve Officers Training Corps (ROTC):** Army ROTC: Offered on campus; Air Force ROTC: Offered at cooperating institution (Wilkes University). **Faculty and instruction (2009-2010):** Total instructional faculty: 311 full-time, 55 part-time (50% men; 50% women; 13% minorities). Full-time faculty with Ph.D. or other terminal degree: 77%. Student/faculty ratio: 18/1. Classes of fewer than 20 students: 25%; of 20 to 49 students: 73%; of 50 or more students: 3%. **Advanced Placement and International Baccalaureate credit:** AP tests may be used for: Credit only. Scores accepted: 3, 4, 5. International Baccalaureate exams may be used for: Credit only. **Freshmen returning for sophomore year:** 78%. **Graduation rates:** Four-year: 36%; five-year: 54%; six-year: 54%. **Graduate study:** 10% of students pursue further study immediately upon graduation; 15% within one year; 35% within five years.

COSTS AND FINANCIAL AID

Financial aid office: (570) 422-2800. **Expenses (2009-2010):** Tuition and fees 2009-2010: $7,394 in state, $15,726 out of state; room/board: $6,418. Estimated books and supplies: $1,000; transportation: $1,350; personal expenses: $2,306. **Financial aid:** Priority filing date for institution's financial aid form: March 1; deadline: March 1. In 2009-2010, 71% of undergraduates applied for financial aid. Of those, 52% were determined to have financial need; 59% had their need fully met. Average financial aid package (proportion receiving): $5,933 (43%). Average amount of gift aid, such as scholarships or grants (proportion receiving): $4,312 (27%). Average amount of self-help aid, such as work study or loans (proportion receiving): $7,073 (37%). Average need-based loan (excluding PLUS or other private loans): $4,106. Among students who received need-based aid, the average percentage of need met: 83%. Among students who received aid based on merit, the average award (and the proportion receiving): $10,063 (18%). The average athletic scholarship (and the proportion receiving): $2,455 (4%). Average amount of debt of borrowers graduating in 2009: $25,887. Proportion who borrowed: 73%.

CAMPUS LIFE AND EXTRACURRICULAR ACTIVITIES

Campus housing available (% using): coed dorms (90%), special housing for disabled students, special housing for international students. Students who live in college-owned, operated, or affiliated housing: 43%. **Student employment:** During the 2009-2010 academic year, 17% of undergraduates worked on campus. Average per-year earnings: $2,145. **Clubs and organizations:** Number of student organizations: 100. Activities include: campus ministries, choral groups, concert band, dance, drama/theater, international student organization, jazz band, literary magazine, marching band, music ensembles, musical theater, pep band, radio station, student government, student newspaper, symphony orchestra. Number of fraternities: 4; sororities: 4. Proportion of men in fraternities: 4%; of women in sororities: 5%. Average proportion of students who stay on campus on weekends: 45%. **Sports program (2009-2010):** Member of NCAA II. *Men's intercollegiate varsity sports:* baseball, basketball, cross country, football, soccer, tennis, track and field (indoor), track and field (outdoor), volleyball, wrestling. *Women's intercollegiate varsity sports:* basketball, cross country, field hockey, golf, lacrosse, soccer, softball, swimming, tennis, track and field (indoor), track and field (outdoor), volleyball.

SERVICES AND FACILITIES

Basic services: nonremedial tutoring, women's center, placement service, day care, health service. **Remedial assistance:** reading, math, writing, study skills. **Counseling services:** minority student, career, personal, veteran student, academic, older student, psychological. **For learning-disabled students:** School does not offer a structured program with separate admission and additional fees. Services include: remedial math, remedial English, reading machines, tape recorders, note-taking services, oral tests, learning center, readers, extended time for tests, tutors, priority registration, texts on tape, exams on tape or computer, other. **Library:** Number of titles: 559,231; number of current serial subscriptions: 28,670. **Information technology**

resources: Students are not required to lease or own a computer. Number of campus computers available to all students: 500. School has a wireless network. Approximate number of users that can be accommodated: 220. Proportion of college-owned housing units wired for high-speed internet access: 100%. **Campus safety:** Security services offered: 24-hour foot-and-vehicle patrols, late-night transport/escort service, 24-hour emergency telephones, lighted pathways/sidewalks, student patrols, controlled dormitory access (key, security card, etc).

TRANSFER AND INTERNATIONAL STUDENTS

Transfer students: May apply for admission for the following academic terms: Fall, Spring. Applicants need a minimum number of credits to apply. For fall 2009: Transfer applicants enrolled: 578. **International students:** Number of foreign undergraduates: 47 (1% of student body). Number of countries represented: 9. Minimum TOEFL score required: 560 (paper); 220 (computer).

Edinboro University of Pennsylvania

- **Address:** 219 Meadville Street, Edinboro, PA 16444
- **Website:** http://www.edinboro.edu
- **Public**
- **Enrollment:** 5,731 full-time; 740 part-time

KEY STATS

✔ **U.S News College Ranking:** 121, Regional Universities (North)
✔ **SAT Score (25th/75th percentile):** 825-1040
✔ **Tuition:** 2009-2010: $7,316 in state, $10,094 out of state
   Selectivity: Less selective   **Room/board:** $7,130
   Acceptance rate: 73%   **Average debt:** $21,518
   Student/faculty ratio: 19/1   **Proportion who borrowed:** 46%

UNDERGRADUATE STUDENT BODY STATS

2009-2010 enrollment: 5,731 full-time; 740 part-time. Men: 44%; women: 56%. **Ethnic makeup:** African American: 9%; Asian American: 1%; Hispanic: 2%; White: 88%; International: 1%.

ADMISSIONS FACTS AND FIGURES

Phone: (888) 846-2676. **Email:** eup_admissions@edinboro.edu. **Website:** http://www.edinboro.edu. **Application deadlines for fall 2011:** Regular decision: Rolling. Early decision: Not offered. Early action: Not offered. Admission can be deferred. **Application fee:** $30. **To apply online, go to:** http://www.edinboro.edu/departments/admissions/apply.dot. **Admissions requirements/recommendations:** High school units required (recommended): English: (4); Mathematics: (3); Science: (3); Foreign language: (2); Social studies: (4); History: (0); Academic electives: (0); Total units: 0 (17). Tests: The college uses SAT or ACT scores in admissions decisions. Neither SAT nor ACT required. For admission to the fall 2011 entering class, the school will accept: ACT with writing recommended. Campus visit: Recommended. Admissions interview: Recommended. Off-campus interview: May be arranged. **Factors that count in admissions decisions:** *Academic:* Secondary school record: Very Important. Class rank: Very Important. Letters of recommendation: Considered. Standardized test scores: Very Important. Essay: Considered. *Nonacademic:* Interview: Considered. Extracurricular activities: Considered. Talent/ability: Considered. Character/personal qualities: Considered. Alumni/ae relationship: Not Considered. Geographical residence: Not Considered. State residency: Not Considered. Religious affiliation/commitment: Not Considered. Minority status: Not Considered. Volunteer work: Considered. Work experience: Considered. **Other schools with the greatest overlap in applicants:** Clarion University of Pennsylvania; Gannon University; Mercyhurst College; Pennsylvania State University–Erie, The Behrend College; Slippery Rock University of Pennsylvania. **Admissions statistics for the fall 2009 entering class:** Total applicants: 4,411. Total accepted: 3,238. Freshmen enrolled: 1,440; 16% were from out of state. Overall acceptance rate: 73%. **Credentials of fall 2009 freshmen:** 5% ranked in the top 10 percent of their high school class; 20% were in the top 25 percent; 51% were in the top half. (Proportion submitting class standing: 88%.) **Average high school grade point average:** 3.2. **First-year students who submitted SAT scores:** 83%. Scores (25/75 percentile): Critical Reading: 415-520, Math: 410-520, Combined: 825-1040. **First-year students submitting ACT scores:** 23%. Scores (25/75 percentile): English: N/A, Math: N/A, Composite: 17-22.

ACADEMICS

Year founded: 1857. **Academic calendar:** Semester. **Degrees offered:** associate, bachelor's, post-bachelor's certificate, master's, post-master's certificate. **Most popular majors:** 15% visual and performing arts, 11% education, 10% health professions and related clinical sciences, 9% business, management, marketing, and related support services, 8% communication, journalism, and related programs. **Major fields of study:** biological and biomedical sciences; business, management, marketing, and related support services; communication, journalism, and related programs; computer and information sciences and support services; education; English language and literature/letters; foreign languages, literatures, and linguistics; health professions and related clinical sciences; history; liberal arts and sciences studies, and humanities; mathematics and statistics; multi/interdisciplinary studies; natural resources and conservation; parks, recreation, leisure, and fitness studies; philosophy and religious studies; physical sciences; psychology; public administration and social service professions; security and protective services; social sciences; visual and performing arts. **Areas of required coursework:** arts/fine arts, computer literacy, mathematics, English (including composition), sciences (biological or physical), history, social science, other. **Pre-professional programs:** pre-law, pre-dentistry, pre-medicine, pre-veterinary science, pre-pharmacy. **Special academic programs (% participation):** cooperative (work-study plan) program, cross-registration, distance learning (23.1%), double major (4.28%), dual enrollment (.559%), honors program (2.6%), independent study (3.44%), internships (28.1%), liberal arts/career combination, student-designed major, study abroad (.559%), teacher certificate program. **Teacher certification offered in:** early childhood, special education, elementary, middle/junior high, secondary. **Cooperative education programs:** education, engineering, health professions, natural science, other. **Reserve Officers Training Corps (ROTC):** Army ROTC: Offered on campus. **Faculty and instruction (2009-2010):** Total instructional faculty: 336 full-time, 58 part-time (51% men; 49% women; 7% minorities). Full-time faculty with Ph.D. or other terminal degree: 79%. Student/faculty ratio: 19/1. Classes of fewer than 20 students: 29%; of 20 to 49 students: 64%; of 50 or more students: 7%. **Advanced Placement and International Baccalaureate credit:** AP tests may be used for: Credit and/or placement. Scores accepted: 3, 4, 5. International Baccalaureate exams may be used for: Credit only. **Freshmen returning for sophomore year:** 72%. **Graduation rates:** Four-year: 24%; five-year: 42%; six-year: 47%. **Graduate study:** 17% of students pursue further study immediately upon graduation.

COSTS AND FINANCIAL AID

Financial aid office: (814) 732-5555. **Expenses (2009-2010):** Tuition and fees 2009-2010: $7,316 in state, $10,094 out of state; room/board: $7,130. Estimated books and supplies: $900; transportation: $800; personal expenses: $1,300. **Financial aid:** Priority filing date for institution's financial aid form: March 15; deadline: May 1. In 2009-2010, 92% of undergraduates applied for financial aid. Of those, 77% were determined to have financial need; 8% had their need fully met. Average financial aid package (proportion receiving): $7,473 (75%). Average amount of gift aid, such as scholarships or grants (proportion receiving): $3,080 (70%). Average amount of self-help aid, such as work study or loans (proportion receiving): $3,419 (66%). Average need-based loan (excluding PLUS or other private loans): $3,622. Among students who received need-based aid, the average percentage of need met: 63%. Among students who received aid based on merit, the average award (and the proportion receiving): $2,100 (6%). The average athletic scholarship (and the proportion receiving): $2,700 (2%). Average amount of debt of borrowers graduating in 2009: $21,518. Proportion who borrowed: 46%.

CAMPUS LIFE AND EXTRACURRICULAR ACTIVITIES

Campus housing available (% using): coed dorms (54%), special housing for disabled students (2%), other housing options (44%). Students who live in college-owned, operated, or affiliated housing: 29%. **Student employment:** During the 2009-2010 academic year, 9% of undergraduates worked on campus. Average per-year earnings: $3,263. **Clubs and organizations:** Number of student organizations: 200. Activities include: campus ministries, choral groups, concert band, dance, drama/theater, international student organization, jazz band, literary magazine, marching band, model UN, music ensembles, opera, radio station, student government, student newspaper, student film society, television station. Number of fraternities: 12; sororities: 7. Proportion of men in fraternities: 3%; of women in sororities: 3%. **Sports program (2009-2010):** Member of NCAA II. *Men's intercollegiate varsity sports:* basketball, cross country, football, swimming, track and field (outdoor), wrestling. *Women's intercollegiate varsity sports:* basketball, cross country, lacrosse, soccer, softball, swimming, track and field (indoor), track and field (outdoor), volleyball.

SERVICES AND FACILITIES

Basic services: nonremedial tutoring, women's center, day care, health service, health insurance, other. **Remedial assistance:** reading, math, writing, study skills, other. **Counseling services:** minority student, career, military, personal, veteran student, academic, older student, psychological, birth control, religious. **For learning-disabled students:** School does not offer a structured program with separate admission and additional fees. Services include: remedial math, remedial English, tape recorders, readers, extended time for tests, tutors, priority registration, texts on tape, other. **Library:** Number of titles: 496,628; number of current serial subscriptions: 33,178. **Information technology resources:** Students are not required to lease or own a computer. Number of campus computers available to all students: 1,010. School has a wireless network. Approximate number of users that can be accommodated: 2,000. Proportion of college-owned housing units wired for high-speed internet access: 100%. **Campus safety:** Security services offered: 24-hour foot-and-vehicle patrols, late-night transport/escort service, 24-hour emergency telephones, lighted pathways/sidewalks, student patrols, controlled dormitory access (key, security card, etc).

TRANSFER AND INTERNATIONAL STUDENTS

Transfer students: May apply for admission for the following academic terms: Fall, Spring, Summer. Applicants do not need a minimum number of credits to apply. For fall 2009: Transfer applications received: 1,214. Transfer applicants offered admission: 705. Transfer applicants enrolled: 464. **International students:** Number of foreign undergraduates: 47 (1% of student body). Number of countries represented: 27. Minimum TOEFL score required: 500 (paper); 173 (computer). Average TOEFL score: 532 (paper).

Elizabethtown College

- **Address:** 1 Alpha Drive, Elizabethtown, PA 17022-2298
- **Website:** http://www.etown.edu
- **Private; Religious affiliation:** Church of the Brethren
- **Enrollment:** 1,886 full-time; 436 part-time

KEY STATS

✔ **U.S News College Ranking:** 5, Regional Colleges (North)
✔ **SAT Score (25th/75th percentile):** 1010-1230
✔ **Tuition:** 2010-2011: $33,250

Selectivity: Selective	**Room/board:** $8,500
Acceptance rate: 75%	**Average debt:** $29,178
Student/faculty ratio: 12/1	**Proportion who borrowed:** 85%

UNDERGRADUATE STUDENT BODY STATS

2009-2010 enrollment: 1,886 full-time; 436 part-time. Men: 36%; women: 64%. **Ethnic makeup:** African American: 3%; Asian American: 2%; Hispanic: 2%; White: 90%; International: 1%. **Religious preference:** Roman Catholic: 26%; Protestant: 32%; Jewish: 1%; No preference: 7%; Unknown: 29%; Church of the Brethren: 2%.

ADMISSIONS FACTS AND FIGURES

Phone: (717) 361-1400. **Email:** admissions@etown.edu. **Website:** http://www.etown.edu. **Application deadlines for fall 2011:** Regular decision: Rolling; decision sent by April 1. Early decision: Not offered. Early action: Not offered. Admission can be deferred. **Application fee:** $30. **To apply online, go to:** http://www.etown.edu/admissions_services.aspx. **Admissions requirements/recommendations:** High school units required (recommended): English: 4 (4); Mathematics: 3 (4); Science: 2 (4); Foreign language: 2 (2); Social studies: 2 (2); History: 2 (2); Academic electives: 0 (2); Total units: 15 (20). Tests: The college uses SAT or ACT scores in admissions decisions. Either SAT or ACT required. For admission to the fall 2011 entering class, the school will accept: ACT with or without writing accepted. Campus visit: Recommended. Admissions interview: Recommended. Off-campus interview: May be arranged. **Factors that count in admissions decisions:** *Academic:* Secondary school record: Very Important. Class rank: Important. Letters of recommendation: Important. Standardized test scores: Important. Essay: Considered. *Nonacademic:* Interview: Important. Extracurricular activities: Considered. Talent/ability: Considered. Character/personal qualities: Considered. Alumni/ae relationship: Considered. Geographical residence: Considered. State residency: Considered. Religious affiliation/commitment: Considered. Minority status: Considered. Volunteer work: Considered. Work experience: Considered. **Other schools with the greatest overlap in applicants:** Albright College; Gettysburg College; Juniata College; Lebanon Valley College; Susquehanna University. **Admissions statistics for the fall 2009 entering class:** Total applicants: 3,322. Total accepted: 2,487. Freshmen enrolled: 568; 36% were from out of state. Overall acceptance rate: 75%. **Size of waiting list:** 80 applicants; enrolled from waiting list: 0. **Credentials of fall 2009 freshmen:** 30% ranked in the top 10 percent of their high school class; 62% were in the top 25 percent; 92% were in the top half. (Proportion submitting class standing: 77%.) **Average high school grade point average:** 3.7. **First-year students who submitted SAT scores:** 95%. Scores (25/75 percentile): Critical Reading: 500-600, Math: 510-630, Combined: 1010-1230. **First-year students submitting ACT scores:** 16%. Scores (25/75 percentile): English: 20-27, Math: 20-27, Composite: 20-27.

ACADEMICS

Year founded: 1899. **Academic calendar:** Semester. **Degrees offered:** certificate, diploma, associate, bachelor's, post-bachelor's certificate, master's. **Most popular majors:** 27% business, management, marketing, and related support services, 11% education, 10% communication, journalism, and related programs, 9% social sciences, 8% biological and biomedical sciences. **Major fields of study:** biological and biomedical sciences; business, management, marketing, and related support services; communication, journalism, and related programs; computer and information sciences and support services; education; engineering; English language and literature/letters; foreign languages, literatures, and linguistics; health professions and related clinical sciences; history; legal professions and studies; mathematics and statistics; natural resources and conservation; philosophy and religious studies; physical sciences; psychology; public administration and social service professions; social sciences; visual and performing arts. **Areas of required coursework:** arts/fine arts, humanities, mathematics, English (including composition), foreign languages, sciences (biological or physical), social science, other. **Pre-professional programs:** pre-law, pre-dentistry, pre-medicine, pre-veterinary science. **Special academic programs:** accelerated program, distance learning, double major, dual enrollment, English as a Second Language (ESL), exchange student program (domestic), external degree program, honors program, independent study, internships, study abroad, teacher certificate program. **Teacher certification offered in:** early childhood, special education, elementary, middle/junior high, secondary. **Cooperative education programs:** engineering, health professions, natural science, other. **Faculty and instruction (2009-2010):** Total instructional faculty: 125 full-time, 149 part-time (51% men; 49% women; 9% minorities). Full-time faculty with Ph.D. or other terminal degree: 87%. Student/faculty ratio: 12/1. Classes of fewer than 20 students: 67%; of 20 to 49 students: 32%; of 50 or more students: 1%. **Advanced Placement and International Baccalaureate credit:** AP tests may be used for: Credit only. Scores accepted: 4, 5. International Baccalaureate exams may be used for: Credit only. **Freshmen returning for sophomore year:** 86%. **Graduation rates:** Four-year: 66%; five-year: 72%; six-year: 71%. **Graduate study:** 23% of students pursue further study immediately upon graduation; 27% within one year. Fields in which graduates pursue further study: Master of Business Administration (MBA), 1%; law, 7%; medicine, 53%; engineering, 1%; theology (or the seminary), 4%; education, 5%; arts and sciences, 27%; veterinary medicine, 2%.

COSTS AND FINANCIAL AID

Financial aid office: (717) 361-1404. **Expenses (2010-2011):** Tuition and fees 2010-2011: $33,250; room/board: $8,500. Estimated books and supplies: $1,000; transportation: $150; personal expenses: $800. **Financial aid:** Priority filing date for institution's financial aid form: March 15. In 2009-2010, 83% of undergraduates applied for financial aid. Of those, 73% were determined to have financial need; 19% had their need fully met. Average financial aid package (proportion receiving): $22,582 (73%). Average amount of gift aid, such as scholarships or grants (proportion receiving): $17,947 (72%). Average amount of self-help aid, such as work study or loans (proportion receiving): $5,528 (63%). Average need-based loan (excluding PLUS or other private loans): $4,438. Among students who received need-based aid, the average percentage of need met: 82%. Among students who received aid based on merit, the average award (and the proportion receiving): $11,974 (21%). The average athletic scholarship (and the proportion receiving): $0 (0%). Average amount of debt of borrowers graduating in 2009: $29,178. Proportion who borrowed: 85%.

CAMPUS LIFE AND EXTRACURRICULAR ACTIVITIES

Campus housing available (% using): coed dorms (54%), women's dorms (23%), apartment for single students (19%), special housing for disabled students (1%), cooperative housing (3%). Students who live in college-owned, operated, or affiliated housing: 83%. **Student employment:** During the 2009-2010 academic year, 56% of undergraduates worked on campus.

Average per-year earnings: $817. **Clubs and organizations:** Number of student organizations: 83. Activities include: campus ministries, choral groups, concert band, dance, drama/theater, international student organization, jazz band, literary magazine, music ensembles, musical theater, radio station, student government, student newspaper, symphony orchestra, television station, yearbook. Number of fraternities: 0; sororities: 0. Average proportion of students who stay on campus on weekends: 65%. **Sports program (2009-2010):** Member of NCAA III. *Men's intercollegiate varsity sports:* baseball, basketball, cross country, golf, lacrosse, soccer, swimming, tennis, track and field (indoor), track and field (outdoor), wrestling. *Women's intercollegiate varsity sports:* basketball, cross country, field hockey, lacrosse, soccer, softball, swimming, tennis, track and field (indoor), track and field (outdoor), volleyball.

SERVICES AND FACILITIES

Basic services: nonremedial tutoring, health service, health insurance. **Remedial assistance:** reading, math, writing, study skills, other. **Counseling services:** minority student, career, personal, academic, psychological, birth control, religious. **For learning-disabled students:** School does not offer a structured program with separate admission and additional fees. Total undergraduates in learning-disabled program or receiving services: 107. Services include: reading machines, tape recorders, note-taking services, oral tests, learning center, readers, extended time for tests, tutors, early syllabus, priority registration, priority seating, substitution of courses, texts on tape, exams on tape or computer, other. **Library:** Number of titles: 255,497; number of current serial subscriptions: 35,971. **Information technology resources:** Students are not required to lease or own a computer. Number of campus computers available to all students: 200. School has a wireless network. Approximate number of users that can be accommodated: 10,000. Proportion of college-owned housing units wired for high-speed internet access: 100%. **Campus safety:** Security services offered: 24-hour foot-and-vehicle patrols, late-night transport/escort service, 24-hour emergency telephones, lighted pathways/sidewalks, student patrols, controlled dormitory access (key, security card, etc).

TRANSFER AND INTERNATIONAL STUDENTS

Transfer students: May apply for admission for the following academic terms: Fall, Spring. Applicants do not need a minimum number of credits to apply. For fall 2009: Transfer applications received: 111. Transfer applicants offered admission: 50. Transfer applicants enrolled: 24. **International students:** Number of foreign undergraduates: 32 (1% of student body). Number of countries represented: 40. Minimum TOEFL score required: 525 (paper); 200 (computer). Average TOEFL score: 565 (paper).

Franklin and Marshall College

- **Address:** PO Box 3003, Lancaster, PA 17604
- **Website:** http://www.fandm.edu
- **Private**
- **Enrollment:** 2,132 full-time; 47 part-time

KEY STATS

✔ **U.S News College Ranking:** 41, National Liberal Arts Colleges
✔ **SAT Score (25th/75th percentile):** 1230-1370
✔ **Tuition:** 2010-2011: $41,190

Selectivity: More selective	**Room/board:** $10,920
Acceptance rate: 48%	**Average debt:** $27,162
Student/faculty ratio: 10/1	**Proportion who borrowed:** 52%

UNDERGRADUATE STUDENT BODY STATS

2009-2010 enrollment: 2,132 full-time; 47 part-time. Men: 48%; women: 52%. **Ethnic makeup:** African American: 4%; American-Indian: 1%; Asian American: 4%; Hispanic: 5%; White: 78%; International: 8%.

ADMISSIONS FACTS AND FIGURES

Phone: (717) 291-3953. **Email:** admission@fandm.edu. **Website:** http://www.fandm.edu. **Application deadlines for fall 2011:** Regular decision: February 1; decision sent by April 1. Early decision: Send application by: November 15; Decision sent by: December 15. Early action: Not offered. Admission can be deferred. **Application fee:** $60. **To apply online, go to:** http://admission.fandm.edu/admission/process.asp. **Admissions requirements/recommendations:** High school units required (recommended): English: 4; Mathematics: 3 (4); Science: 2 (3); Foreign language: 2 (4); Social studies: 1 (3); History:

2 (3). Tests: The college uses SAT or ACT scores in admissions decisions. Neither SAT nor ACT required. For admission to the fall 2011 entering class, the school will accept: ACT with or without writing accepted. Campus visit: Recommended. Admissions interview: Recommended. Off-campus interview: May be arranged. **Factors that count in admissions decisions:** *Academic:* Secondary school record: Very Important. Class rank: Very Important. Letters of recommendation: Important. Standardized test scores: Important. Essay: Important. *Nonacademic:* Interview: Important. Extracurricular activities: Important. Talent/ability: Important. Character/personal qualities: Very Important. Alumni/ae relationship: Considered. Geographical residence: Considered. State residency: Not Considered. Religious affiliation/commitment: Not Considered. Minority status: Considered. Volunteer work: Important. Work experience: Considered. **Other schools with the greatest overlap in applicants:** Bucknell University; Dickinson College; Gettysburg College; Lafayette College; Pennsylvania State University–University Park. **Admissions statistics for the fall 2009 entering class:** Total applicants: 5,256. Total accepted: 2,548. Freshmen enrolled: 629; 70% were from out of state. Overall acceptance rate: 48%. Non-early acceptance rate: 48%. **Size of waiting list:** 1630 applicants; enrolled from waiting list: 13. **Credentials of fall 2009 freshmen:** 63% ranked in the top 10 percent of their high school class; 86% were in the top 25 percent; 99% were in the top half. (Proportion submitting class standing: 33%.) **First-year students who submitted SAT scores:** 58%. Scores (25/75 percentile): Critical Reading: 600-670, Math: 630-700, Combined: 1230-1370. **First-year students submitting ACT scores:** 11%. Scores (25/75 percentile): English: N/A, Math: N/A, Composite: 28-31.

ACADEMICS

Year founded: 1787. **Academic calendar:** Semester. **Degrees offered:** bachelor's. **Most popular majors:** 15% business administration and management, 15% political science and government, 7% economics, 6% history, 5% psychology. **Major fields of study:** area, ethnic, cultural, and gender studies; biological and biomedical sciences; business, management, marketing, and related support services; English language and literature/letters; foreign languages, literatures, and linguistics; history; mathematics and statistics; multi/interdisciplinary studies; natural resources and conservation; philosophy and religious studies; physical sciences; psychology; public administration and social service professions; social sciences; visual and performing arts. **Areas of required coursework:** arts/fine arts, humanities, foreign languages, sciences (biological or physical), social science, other. **Pre-professional programs:** pre-law, pre-dentistry, pre-medicine, pre-veterinary science, pre-optometry. **Special academic programs (% participation):** accelerated program, cross-registration, double major (17%), dual enrollment, exchange student program (domestic), honors program (10%), independent study (40%), internships (20%), liberal arts/career combination, student-designed major (5%), study abroad (38%), teacher certificate program. **Teacher certification offered in:** secondary. **Cooperative education programs:** engineering. **Reserve Officers Training Corps (ROTC):** Army ROTC: Offered at cooperating institution (Millersville University of Pennsylvania). **Faculty and instruction (2009-2010):** Total instructional faculty: 201 full-time, 49 part-time (60% men; 40% women; 10% minorities). Full-time faculty with Ph.D. or other terminal degree: 94%. Student/faculty ratio: 10/1. Classes of fewer than 20 students: 57%; of 20 to 49 students: 43%; of 50 or more students: 1%. **Advanced Placement and International Baccalaureate credit:** AP tests may be used for: Credit and/or placement. Scores accepted: 4, 5. International Baccalaureate exams may be used for: Credit and/or placement. **Freshmen returning for sophomore year:** 92%. **Graduation rates:** Four-year: 79%; five-year: 84%; six-year: 85%. **Graduate study:** 25% of students pursue further study immediately upon graduation. Fields in which graduates pursue further study: Master of Business Administration (MBA), 35%; law, 18%; medicine, 11%; dentistry, 2%; education, 4%; arts and sciences, 28%; veterinary medicine, 2%.

COSTS AND FINANCIAL AID

Financial aid office: (717) 291-3991. **Expenses (2010-2011):** Tuition and fees 2010-2011: $41,190; room/board: $10,920. Estimated books and supplies: $1,150; transportation: $100; personal expenses: $1,300. **Financial aid:** Priority filing date for institution's financial aid form: February 15; deadline: March 15. In 2009-2010, 54% of undergraduates applied for financial aid. Of those, 44% were determined to have financial need; 48% had their need fully met. Average financial aid package (proportion receiving): $29,613 (44%). Average amount of gift aid, such as scholarships or grants (proportion receiving): $25,470 (41%). Average amount of self-help aid, such as work study or loans (proportion receiving): $6,321 (41%). Average need-based loan (excluding PLUS or other private loans): $4,569. Among students who received need-based aid, the average percentage of need met:

93%. Among students who received aid based on merit, the average award (and the proportion receiving): $10,748 (12%). The average athletic scholarship (and the proportion receiving): $0 (0%). Average amount of debt of borrowers graduating in 2009: $27,162. Proportion who borrowed: 52%.

CAMPUS LIFE AND EXTRACURRICULAR ACTIVITIES

Campus housing available (% using): coed dorms (58%), women's dorms (1%), men's dorms (1%), sorority housing (2%), fraternity housing (2%), apartment for single students (32%), special housing for disabled students (0%), special housing for international students, other housing options (1%). Students who live in college-owned, operated, or affiliated housing: 96%. Average per-year earnings: $2,175. **Clubs and organizations:** Number of student organizations: 125. Activities include: campus ministries, choral groups, concert band, dance, drama/theater, international student organization, jazz band, literary magazine, music ensembles, musical theater, radio station, student government, student newspaper, student film society, symphony orchestra, television station, yearbook. Number of fraternities: 7; sororities: 3. Proportion of men in fraternities: 28%; of women in sororities: 23%. **Sports program (2009-2010):** Member of NCAA III. *Men's intercollegiate varsity sports:* baseball, basketball, cross country, football, golf, lacrosse, soccer, swimming, tennis, track and field (indoor), track and field (outdoor), wrestling. *Women's intercollegiate varsity sports:* basketball, crew (heavyweight), cross country, field hockey, golf, lacrosse, crew (lightweight), softball, squash, swimming, tennis, track and field (indoor), track and field (outdoor), volleyball.

SERVICES AND FACILITIES

Basic services: nonremedial tutoring, women's center, placement service, day care, health service, health insurance, other. **Counseling services:** minority student, career, personal, academic, psychological, birth control, religious. **For learning-disabled students:** School does not offer a structured program with separate admission and additional fees. Services include: note-taking services, readers, extended time for tests, typist/scribe, exams on tape or computer, other testing accommodations. **Library:** Number of titles: 523,323; number of current serial subscriptions: 29,096. **Information technology resources:** Students are not required to lease or own a computer. Number of campus computers available to all students: 272. School has a wireless network. Proportion of college-owned housing units wired for high-speed internet access: 100%. **Campus safety:** Security services offered: 24-hour foot-and-vehicle patrols, late-night transport/escort service, 24-hour emergency telephones, lighted pathways/sidewalks, controlled dormitory access (key, security card, etc).

TRANSFER AND INTERNATIONAL STUDENTS

Transfer students: May apply for admission for the following academic terms: Fall, Spring. Applicants need a minimum number of credits to apply. For fall 2009: Transfer applications received: 103. Transfer applicants offered admission: 35. Transfer applicants enrolled: 11. **International students:** Number of foreign undergraduates: 170 (8% of student body). Number of countries represented: 42. Minimum TOEFL score required: 600 (paper); 250 (computer).

Gannon University

- **Address:** 109 University Square, Erie, PA 16541
- **Website:** http://www.gannon.edu
- **Private; Religious affiliation:** Roman Catholic
- **Enrollment:** 2,444 full-time; 534 part-time

KEY STATS

✔ **U.S News College Ranking:** 46, Regional Universities (North)
✔ **SAT Score (25th/75th percentile):** 890-1150
✔ **Tuition:** 2010-2011: $24,582

Selectivity: Selective	**Room/board:** $9,720
Acceptance rate: 84%	**Average debt:** $31,234
Student/faculty ratio: 13/1	**Proportion who borrowed:** 86%

UNDERGRADUATE STUDENT BODY STATS

2009-2010 enrollment: 2,444 full-time; 534 part-time. Men: 41%; women: 59%. **Ethnic makeup:** African American: 6%; Asian American: 2%; Hispanic: 2%; White: 88%; International: 2%. **Religious preference:** Protestant: 19%; Unknown: 27%; Roman Catholic: 46%; Other: 8%.

ADMISSIONS FACTS AND FIGURES

Phone: (814) 871-7240. **Email:** admissions@gannon.edu. **Website:** http://www.gannon.edu. **Application deadlines for fall 2011:** Regular decision: Rolling. Early decision: Not offered. Early action: Not offered. Admission can be deferred. **Application fee:** $25. **To apply online, go to:** http://www.gannon.edu/admiss/undergrad/apply/default.asp. **Admissions requirements/recommendations:** High school units required (recommended): English: 4 (4); Mathematics: 2 (4); Science: 2 (4); Foreign language: 0 (2); Social studies: 2 (2); History: 1 (1); Academic electives: 3 (3); Total units: 16 (25). Tests: The college uses SAT or ACT scores in admissions decisions. Either SAT or ACT required. For admission to the fall 2011 entering class, the school will accept: ACT with or without writing accepted. Campus visit: Recommended. Admissions interview: Recommended. Off-campus interview: May be arranged. **Factors that count in admissions decisions:** *Academic:* Secondary school record: Very Important. Class rank: Very Important. Letters of recommendation: Important. Standardized test scores: Very Important. Essay: Considered. *Nonacademic:* Interview: Considered. Extracurricular activities: Considered. Talent/ability: Considered. Character/personal qualities: Not Considered. Alumni/ae relationship: Not Considered. Geographical residence: Not Considered. State residency: Not Considered. Religious affiliation/commitment: Not Considered. Minority status: Not Considered. Volunteer work: Considered. Work experience: Not Considered. **Other schools with the greatest overlap in applicants:** Duquesne University; Mercyhurst College; Pennsylvania State University–Erie, The Behrend College; Pennsylvania State University–University Park; University of Pittsburgh. **Admissions statistics for the fall 2009 entering class:** Total applicants: 3,019. Total accepted: 2,527. Freshmen enrolled: 660; 28% were from out of state. Overall acceptance rate: 84%. **Size of waiting list:** 25 applicants; enrolled from waiting list: 25. **Credentials of fall 2009 freshmen:** 28% ranked in the top 10 percent of their high school class; 50% were in the top 25 percent; 78% were in the top half. (Proportion submitting class standing: 89%.) **Average high school grade point average:** 3.4. **First-year students who submitted SAT scores:** 80%. Scores (25/75 percentile): Critical Reading: 440-560, Math: 450-590, Combined: 890-1150. **First-year students submitting ACT scores:** 40%. Scores (25/75 percentile): English: 18-26, Math: 18-26, Composite: 19-26.

ACADEMICS

Year founded: 1925. **Academic calendar:** Semester. **Degrees offered:** certificate, associate, bachelor's, post-bachelor's certificate, master's, post-master's certificate, doctorate. **Most popular majors:** 27% health professions and related clinical sciences, 16% business, management, marketing, and related support services, 11% biological and biomedical sciences, 6% education, 5% parks, recreation, leisure, and fitness studies. **Major fields of study:** area, ethnic, cultural, and gender studies; biological and biomedical sciences; business, management, marketing, and related support services; communication, journalism, and related programs; communications technologies/technicians and support services; computer and information sciences and support services; education; engineering; English language and literature/letters; foreign languages, literatures, and linguistics; health professions and related clinical sciences; history; legal professions and studies; liberal arts and sciences studies, and humanities; mathematics and statistics; multi/interdisciplinary studies; natural resources and conservation; parks, recreation, leisure, and fitness studies; personal and culinary services; philosophy and religious studies; physical sciences; psychology; public administration and social service professions; science technologies/technicians; security and protective services; social sciences; theology and religious vocations; visual and performing arts. **Areas of required coursework:** arts/fine arts, mathematics, English (including composition), philosophy, foreign languages, sciences (biological or physical), history, social science, other. **Pre-professional programs:** pre-law, pre-dentistry, pre-medicine, pre-veterinary science, pre-optometry, pre-pharmacy, other. **Special academic programs:** accelerated program, distance learning, double major, dual enrollment, English as a Second Language (ESL), honors program, independent study, internships, liberal arts/career combination, study abroad, teacher certificate program. **Teacher certification offered in:** early childhood, special education, elementary, secondary. **Cooperative education programs:** engineering. **Reserve Officers Training Corps (ROTC):** Army ROTC: Offered on campus. **Faculty and instruction (2009-2010):** Total instructional faculty: 200 full-time, 155 part-time (54% men; 46% women; 8% minorities). Full-time faculty with Ph.D. or other terminal degree: 72%. Student/faculty ratio: 13/1. Classes of fewer than 20 students: 52%; of 20 to 49 students: 47%; of 50 or more students: 0%. **Advanced Placement and International Baccalaureate credit:** AP tests may be used for: Credit and/or placement. Scores accepted: 3, 4, 5. International Baccalaureate exams may be used for: Credit and/or placement. **Freshmen returning for sopho-**

more year: 81%. **Graduation rates:** Four-year: 46%; five-year: 60%; six-year: 64%. **Graduate study:** 42% of students pursue further study immediately upon graduation. Fields in which graduates pursue further study: Master of Business Administration (MBA), 3%; law, 4%; medicine, 10%; dentistry, 1%; engineering, 3%; theology (or the seminary), 1%; education, 7%; arts and sciences, 70%; veterinary medicine, 1%.

COSTS AND FINANCIAL AID
Financial aid office: (814) 871-7337. **Expenses (2010-2011):** Tuition and fees 2010-2011: $24,582; room/board: $9,720. Estimated books and supplies: $1,230; transportation: $1,132; personal expenses: $1,400. **Financial aid:** Priority filing date for institution's financial aid form: March 15. In 2009-2010, 93% of undergraduates applied for financial aid. Of those, 86% were determined to have financial need; 24% had their need fully met. Average financial aid package (proportion receiving): $19,802 (85%). Average amount of gift aid, such as scholarships or grants (proportion receiving): $15,398 (84%). Average amount of self-help aid, such as work study or loans (proportion receiving): $4,991 (81%). Average need-based loan (excluding PLUS or other private loans): $4,180. Among students who received need-based aid, the average percentage of need met: 79%. Among students who received aid based on merit, the average award (and the proportion receiving): $8,170 (9%). The average athletic scholarship (and the proportion receiving): $19,075 (3%). Average amount of debt of borrowers graduating in 2009: $31,234. Proportion who borrowed: 86%.

CAMPUS LIFE AND EXTRACURRICULAR ACTIVITIES
Campus housing available (% using): coed dorms (31%), apartment for single students (69%), special housing for disabled students. Students who live in college-owned, operated, or affiliated housing: 46%. **Student employment:** During the 2009-2010 academic year, 7% of undergraduates worked on campus. Average per-year earnings: $2,300. **Clubs and organizations:** Number of student organizations: 75. Activities include: campus ministries, choral groups, concert band, dance, drama/theater, international student organization, literary magazine, model UN, music ensembles, musical theater, pep band, radio station, student government, student newspaper, yearbook. Number of fraternities: 6; sororities: 5. Proportion of men in fraternities: 13%; of women in sororities: 11%. Average proportion of students who stay on campus on weekends: 60%. **Sports program (2009-2010):** Member of NCAA II. *Men's intercollegiate varsity sports:* baseball, basketball, cross country, football, golf, soccer, swimming, water polo, wrestling. *Women's intercollegiate varsity sports:* basketball, cross country, golf, lacrosse, soccer, softball, swimming, volleyball, water polo.

SERVICES AND FACILITIES
Basic services: nonremedial tutoring, placement service, health service, health insurance. **Remedial assistance:** math, writing, study skills, other. **Counseling services:** career, personal, academic, older student, psychological, religious. **For learning-disabled students:** School does not offer a structured program with separate admission and additional fees. Total undergraduates in learning-disabled program or receiving services: 50. Services include: reading machines, tape recorders, other special classes, note-taking services, oral tests, learning center, readers, extended time for tests, tutors, priority registration, texts on tape, typist/scribe, exams on tape or computer, other. **Library:** Number of titles: 263,600; number of current serial subscriptions: 39,737. **Information technology resources:** Students are not required to lease or own a computer. Number of campus computers available to all students: 380. School has a wireless network. Approximate number of users that can be accommodated: 1,500. Proportion of college-owned housing units wired for high-speed internet access: 100%. **Campus safety:** Security services offered: 24-hour foot-and-vehicle patrols, late-night transport/escort service, 24-hour emergency telephones, lighted pathways/sidewalks, controlled dormitory access (key, security card, etc).

TRANSFER AND INTERNATIONAL STUDENTS
Transfer students: May apply for admission for the following academic terms: Fall, Spring, Summer. Applicants need a minimum number of credits to apply. For fall 2009: Transfer applications received: 362. Transfer applicants offered admission: 241. Transfer applicants enrolled: 102. **International students:** Number of foreign undergraduates: 57 (2% of student body). Number of countries represented: 9. Minimum TOEFL score required: 550 (paper); 79 (computer).

Geneva College

- **Address:** 3200 College Avenue, Beaver Falls, PA 15010
- **Website:** http://www.geneva.edu
- **Private; Religious affiliation:** Reformed Presbyterian of N.A.
- **Enrollment:** N/A

KEY STATS
✔ **U.S News College Ranking:** 36, Regional Colleges (North)
✔ **SAT or ACT Score (25th/75th percentile):** N/A
✔ **Tuition:** 2009-2010: $21,400
   Selectivity: Less selective   **Room/board:** $7,770
   Acceptance rate: N/A   **Average debt:** N/A
   Student/faculty ratio: N/A   **Proportion who borrowed:** N/A

Gettysburg College

- **Address:** 300 N. Washington Street, Gettysburg, PA 17325
- **Website:** http://www.gettysburg.edu
- **Private; Religious affiliation:** Lutheran
- **Enrollment:** 2,498 full-time; 18 part-time

KEY STATS
✔ **U.S News College Ranking:** 47, National Liberal Arts Colleges
✔ **SAT Score (25th/75th percentile):** 1220-1380
✔ **Tuition:** 2010-2011: $41,070
   Selectivity: More selective   **Room/board:** $9,810
   Acceptance rate: 40%   **Average debt:** $23,258
   Student/faculty ratio: 11/1   **Proportion who borrowed:** 61%

UNDERGRADUATE STUDENT BODY STATS
2009-2010 enrollment: 2,498 full-time; 18 part-time. Men: 49%; women: 51%. **Ethnic makeup:** African American: 5%; Asian American: 2%; Hispanic: 3%; White: 88%; International: 2%. **Religious preference:** Roman Catholic: 30%; Protestant: 30%; Jewish: 4%; No preference: 4%; Unknown: 13%; Lutheran: 5%; Other: 14%.

ADMISSIONS FACTS AND FIGURES
Phone: (800) 431-0803. **Email:** admiss@gettysburg.edu. **Website:** http://www.gettysburg.edu. **Application deadlines for fall 2011:** Regular decision: February 1; decision sent by April 1. Early decision: Send application by: November 15; Decision sent by: December 15. Early action: Not offered. Admission can be deferred. **Application fee:** $55. **To apply online, go to:** http://www.gettysburg.edu/admissions/application_process/. **Admissions requirements/recommendations:** High school units required (recommended): English: 3 (4); Mathematics: 3 (4); Science: 3 (4); Foreign language: 3 (4); Social studies: 3 (4); History: 3 (4); Academic electives: 4 (4); Total units: 4 (4). Tests: The college uses SAT or ACT scores in admissions decisions. Neither SAT nor ACT required. For admission to the fall 2011 entering class, the school will accept: ACT with or without writing accepted. Campus visit: Recommended. Admissions interview: Recommended. **Factors that count in admissions decisions:** *Academic:* Secondary school record: Very Important. Class rank: Very Important. Letters of recommendation: Very Important. Standardized test scores: Important. Essay: Important. *Nonacademic:* Interview: Important. Extracurricular activities: Important. Talent/ability: Important. Character/personal qualities: Important. Alumni/ae relationship: Considered. Geographical residence: Considered. State residency: Not Considered. Religious affiliation/commitment: Not Considered. Minority status: Considered. Volunteer work: Important. Work experience: Considered. **Other schools with the greatest overlap in applicants:** Bucknell University; Dickinson College; Franklin and Marshall College; Lafayette College; University of Richmond. **Admissions statistics for the fall 2009 entering class:** Total applicants: 5,448. Total accepted: 2,201. Freshmen enrolled: 739; 78% were from out of state. Accepted through early-decision or early-action plans: 43%. Overall acceptance rate: 40%. Early-decision acceptance rate: 71%. Non-early acceptance rate: 37%. **Credentials of fall 2009 freshmen:** 68% ranked in the top 10 percent of their high school class; 86% were in the top 25 percent; 99% were in the top half. (Proportion submitting class standing: 50%.) **First-year students who submitted SAT scores:** 83%. Scores (25/75 percentile): Critical Reading: 610-690, Math: 610-690, Combined: 1220-1380. **First-year stu-**

dents submitting ACT scores: 8%. Scores (25/75 percentile): English: N/A, Math: N/A, Composite: 27-30.

ACADEMICS

Year founded: 1832. **Academic calendar:** Semester. **Degrees offered:** bachelor's. **Most popular majors:** 20% social sciences, 13% biology/biological sciences, 12% business administration and management, 8% history, 8% psychology. **Major fields of study:** agriculture, agriculture operations, and related sciences; area, ethnic, cultural, and gender studies; biological and biomedical sciences; business, management, marketing, and related support services; computer and information sciences and support services; education; English language and literature/letters; foreign languages, literatures, and linguistics; history; mathematics and statistics; multi/interdisciplinary studies; natural resources and conservation; philosophy and religious studies; physical sciences; psychology; social sciences; visual and performing arts. **Areas of required coursework:** arts/fine arts, humanities, computer literacy, English (including composition), foreign languages, sciences (biological or physical), social science, other. **Pre-professional programs:** pre-law, pre-dentistry, pre-medicine, pre-theology, pre-veterinary science, pre-optometry, pre-pharmacy. **Special academic programs (% participation):** double major (15%), independent study (36%), internships (20%), student-designed major (3%), study abroad (50%), teacher certificate program (4%). **Teacher certification offered in:** elementary, middle/junior high, secondary. **Reserve Officers Training Corps (ROTC):** Army ROTC: Offered at cooperating institution (Dickinson College). **Faculty and instruction (2009-2010):** Total instructional faculty: 209 full-time, 77 part-time (57% men; 43% women; 13% minorities). Full-time faculty with Ph.D. or other terminal degree: 92%. Student/faculty ratio: 11/1. Classes of fewer than 20 students: 69%; of 20 to 49 students: 31%; of 50 or more students: 0%. **Advanced Placement and International Baccalaureate credit:** AP tests may be used for: Credit only. Scores accepted: 4, 5. International Baccalaureate exams may be used for: Placement only. **Freshmen returning for sophomore year:** 91%. **Graduation rates:** Four-year: 78%; five-year: 82%; six-year: 83%. **Graduate study:** 34% of students pursue further study immediately upon graduation; 36% within one year; 48% within five years. Fields in which graduates pursue further study: Master of Business Administration (MBA), 24%; law, 12%; medicine, 8%; engineering, 1%; theology (or the seminary), 2%; education, 13%.

COSTS AND FINANCIAL AID

Financial aid office: (717) 337-6611. **Expenses (2010-2011):** Tuition and fees 2010-2011: $41,070; room/board: $9,810. Estimated books and supplies: $1,000; transportation: $1,209; personal expenses: $1,209. **Financial aid:** In 2009-2010, 66% of undergraduates applied for financial aid. Of those, 54% were determined to have financial need; 96% had their need fully met. Average financial aid package (proportion receiving): $31,030 (53%). Average amount of gift aid, such as scholarships or grants (proportion receiving): $23,781 (52%). Average amount of self-help aid, such as work study or loans (proportion receiving): $5,851 (47%). Average need-based loan (excluding PLUS or other private loans): $5,851. Among students who received need-based aid, the average percentage of need met: 100%. Among students who received aid based on merit, the average award (and the proportion receiving): $10,713 (14%). The average athletic scholarship (and the proportion receiving): $0 (0%). Average amount of debt of borrowers graduating in 2009: $23,258. Proportion who borrowed: 61%.

CAMPUS LIFE AND EXTRACURRICULAR ACTIVITIES

Campus housing available: coed dorms, women's dorms, men's dorms, fraternity housing, apartment for single students, cooperative housing. Students who live in college-owned, operated, or affiliated housing: 94%. **Student employment:** During the 2009-2010 academic year, 30% of undergraduates worked on campus. Average per-year earnings: $1,600. **Clubs and organizations:** Number of student organizations: 123. Activities include: campus ministries, choral groups, concert band, dance, drama/theater, international student organization, jazz band, literary magazine, marching band, model UN, music ensembles, radio station, student government, student newspaper, symphony orchestra, television station, yearbook. Number of fraternities: 11; sororities: 6. Proportion of men in fraternities: 38%; of women in sororities: 26%. Average proportion of students who stay on campus on weekends: 90%. **Sports program (2009-2010):** Member of NCAA III. *Men's intercollegiate varsity sports:* baseball, basketball, cross country, football, golf, lacrosse, soccer, swimming, tennis, track and field (indoor), wrestling. *Women's intercollegiate varsity sports:* basketball, cross country, field hockey, golf, lacrosse, soccer, softball, swimming, tennis, track and field (indoor), volleyball.

SERVICES AND FACILITIES

Basic services: nonremedial tutoring, women's center, placement service, health service. **Remedial assistance:** math, writing. **Counseling services:** minority student, career, personal, academic, psychological, birth control, religious, other. **For learning-disabled students:** School does not offer a structured program with separate admission and additional fees. Services include: tape recorders, extended time for tests, tutors. **Library:** Number of titles: 416,595; number of current serial subscriptions: 9,275. **Information technology resources:** Students are not required to lease or own a computer. Number of campus computers available to all students: 228. School has a wireless network. Approximate number of users that can be accommodated: 3,000. Proportion of college-owned housing units wired for high-speed internet access: 100%. **Campus safety:** Security services offered: 24-hour foot-and-vehicle patrols, late-night transport/escort service, 24-hour emergency telephones, lighted pathways/sidewalks, controlled dormitory access (key, security card, etc).

TRANSFER AND INTERNATIONAL STUDENTS

Transfer students: May apply for admission for the following academic terms: Fall, Spring. Applicants do not need a minimum number of credits to apply. For fall 2009: Transfer applications received: 144. Transfer applicants offered admission: 36. Transfer applicants enrolled: 10. **International students:** Number of foreign undergraduates: 57 (2% of student body). Number of countries represented: 31. Minimum TOEFL score required: 550 (paper).

Gratz College

- **Address:** 7605 Old York Road, Melrose Park, PA 19027
- **Website:** http://www.gratzcollege.edu
- **Private; Religious affiliation:** Jewish
- **Enrollment:** N/A

KEY STATS
✔ **U.S News College Ranking:** Unranked, Regional Universities (North)
✔ **SAT or ACT Score (25th/75th percentile):** N/A
✔ **Tuition:** 2009-2010: $12,300

Selectivity: N/A	**Room/board:** $10,750
Acceptance rate: N/A	**Average debt:** N/A
Student/faculty ratio: N/A	**Proportion who borrowed:** N/A

Grove City College

- **Address:** 100 Campus Drive, Grove City, PA 16127
- **Website:** http://www.gcc.edu
- **Private; Religious affiliation:** Presbyterian
- **Enrollment:** 2,499 full-time; 31 part-time

KEY STATS
✔ **U.S News College Ranking:** 127, National Liberal Arts Colleges
✔ **SAT Score (25th/75th percentile):** 1131-1367
✔ **Tuition:** 2010-2011: $13,088

Selectivity: More selective	**Room/board:** $7,123
Acceptance rate: 64%	**Average debt:** $24,895
Student/faculty ratio: 16/1	**Proportion who borrowed:** 45%

UNDERGRADUATE STUDENT BODY STATS

2009-2010 enrollment: 2,499 full-time; 31 part-time. Men: 50%; women: 50%. **Ethnic makeup:** African American: 1%; Asian American: 2%; Hispanic: 2%; White: 95%. **Religious preference:** Roman Catholic: 6%; Protestant: 51%; No preference: 26%; Presbyterian: 17%.

ADMISSIONS FACTS AND FIGURES

Phone: (724) 458-2100. **Email:** admissions@gcc.edu. **Website:** http://www.gcc.edu. **Application deadlines for fall 2011:** Regular decision: February 1. Early decision: Send application by: November 15; Decision sent by: December 15. Early action: Not offered. Admission can be deferred. **Application fee:** $50. **To apply online, go to:** https://my.gcc.edu/gcc_misc/admissionsapp.aspx. **Admissions requirements/recommendations:** High school units required (recommended): English: 4 (4); Mathematics: 3

(3); Science: 3 (3); Foreign language: 3 (3); Social studies: 2 (2); History: 2 (2); Total units: 17 (17). **Tests:** The college uses SAT or ACT scores in admissions decisions. Either SAT or ACT required. For admission to the fall 2011 entering class, the school will accept: ACT with or without writing accepted. **Campus visit:** Recommended. Admissions interview: Recommended. Off-campus interview: May be arranged. **Factors that count in admissions decisions:** *Academic:* Secondary school record: Very Important. Class rank: Considered. Letters of recommendation: Important. Standardized test scores: Very Important. Essay: Important. *Nonacademic:* Interview: Very Important. Extracurricular activities: Important. Talent/ability: Important. Character/personal qualities: Very Important. Alumni/ae relationship: Considered. Geographical residence: Important. State residency: Considered. Religious affiliation/commitment: Very Important. Minority status: Considered. Volunteer work: Considered. Work experience: Considered. **Other schools with the greatest overlap in applicants:** Hillsdale College; Messiah College; Pennsylvania State University–University Park; University of Pittsburgh; Wheaton College. **Admissions statistics for the fall 2009 entering class:** Total applicants: 1,761. Total accepted: 1,123. Freshmen enrolled: 633; 53% were from out of state. Accepted through early-decision or early-action plans: 51%. Overall acceptance rate: 64%. Early-decision acceptance rate: 60%. Non-early acceptance rate: 65%. **Size of waiting list:** 552 applicants; enrolled from waiting list: 61. **Credentials of fall 2009 freshmen:** 51% ranked in the top 10 percent of their high school class; 85% were in the top 25 percent; 97% were in the top half. (Proportion submitting class standing: 69%.) **Average high school grade point average:** 3.8. **First-year students who submitted SAT scores:** 88%. Scores (25/75 percentile): Critical Reading: 563-685, Math: 568-682, Combined: 1131-1367. **First-year students submitting ACT scores:** 42%. Scores (25/75 percentile): English: 25-30, Math: 25-31, Composite: 25-30.

ACADEMICS

Year founded: 1876. **Academic calendar:** Semester. **Degrees offered:** bachelor's. **Most popular majors:** 18% business, management, marketing, and related support services, 11% education, 9% biological and biomedical sciences, 9% engineering, 8% social sciences. **Major fields of study:** biological and biomedical sciences; business, management, marketing, and related support services; communication, journalism, and related programs; computer and information sciences and support services; education; engineering; English language and literature/letters; history; mathematics and statistics; philosophy and religious studies; physical sciences; psychology; social sciences; theology and religious vocations; visual and performing arts. **Areas of required coursework:** arts/fine arts, humanities, mathematics, philosophy, foreign languages, sciences (biological or physical), history, social science, other. **Pre-professional programs:** pre-law, pre-dentistry, pre-medicine, pre-theology, pre-veterinary science. **Special academic programs:** accelerated program, cross-registration, double major, independent study, internships, student-designed major, study abroad, teacher certificate program. **Teacher certification offered in:** early childhood, elementary, middle/junior high, secondary. **Reserve Officers Training Corps (ROTC):** Army ROTC: Offered at cooperating institution (Slippery Rock University of Pennsylvania). **Faculty and instruction (2009-2010):** Total instructional faculty: 128 full-time, 86 part-time (67% men; 33% women; 3% minorities). Full-time faculty with Ph.D. or other terminal degree: 92%. Student/faculty ratio: 16/1. Classes of fewer than 20 students: 42%; of 20 to 49 students: 52%; of 50 or more students: 7%. **Advanced Placement and International Baccalaureate credit:** AP tests may be used for: Credit only. Scores accepted: 3, 4, 5. International Baccalaureate exams may be used for: Credit only. **Freshmen returning for sophomore year:** 92%. **Graduation rates:** Four-year: 78%; five-year: 83%; six-year: 83%. **Graduate study:** 24% of students pursue further study immediately upon graduation; 50% within five years. Fields in which graduates pursue further study: Master of Business Administration (MBA), 1%; law, 1%; medicine, 2%; engineering, 1%; education, 2%; arts and sciences, 17%.

COSTS AND FINANCIAL AID

Financial aid office: (724) 458-3300. **Expenses (2010-2011):** Tuition and fees 2010-2011: $13,088; room/board: $7,123. Estimated books and supplies: $1,000; transportation: $500; personal expenses: $350. **Financial aid:** Priority filing date for institution's financial aid form: April 15; deadline: April 15. In 2009-2010, 46% of undergraduates applied for financial aid. Of those, 38% were determined to have financial need; 9% had their need fully met. Average financial aid package (proportion receiving): $5,942 (38%). Average amount of gift aid, such as scholarships or grants (proportion receiving): $5,726 (36%). Average amount of self-help aid, such as work study or loans (proportion receiving): $0 (22%). Average need-based loan (excluding PLUS or other private loans): $0. Among students who received

need-based aid, the average percentage of need met: 50%. Among students who received aid based on merit, the average award (and the proportion receiving): $2,369 (13%). The average athletic scholarship (and the proportion receiving): $0 (0%). Average amount of debt of borrowers graduating in 2009: $24,895. Proportion who borrowed: 45%.

CAMPUS LIFE AND EXTRACURRICULAR ACTIVITIES

Campus housing available (% using): women's dorms (46%), men's dorms (46%), apartment for single students (8%). Students who live in college-owned, operated, or affiliated housing: 93%. **Student employment:** During the 2009-2010 academic year, 40% of undergraduates worked on campus. Average per-year earnings: $1,000. **Clubs and organizations:** Number of student organizations: 130. Activities include: campus ministries, choral groups, concert band, dance, drama/theater, international student organization, jazz band, literary magazine, marching band, music ensembles, musical theater, opera, pep band, radio station, student government, student newspaper, symphony orchestra, television station, yearbook. Number of fraternities: 8; sororities: 9. Proportion of men in fraternities: 15%; of women in sororities: 24%. Average proportion of students who stay on campus on weekends: 80%. **Sports program (2009-2010):** Member of NCAA III. **Men's intercollegiate varsity sports:** baseball, basketball, cross country, football, golf, soccer, swimming, tennis, track and field (outdoor). **Women's intercollegiate varsity sports:** basketball, cross country, golf, soccer, softball, swimming, tennis, track and field (outdoor), volleyball, water polo.

SERVICES AND FACILITIES

Basic services: nonremedial tutoring, placement service, health service, health insurance. **Counseling services:** minority student, career, personal, academic, psychological, birth control, religious. **For learning-disabled students:** School does not offer a structured program with separate admission and additional fees. Services include: tape recorders, oral tests, extended time for tests, tutors. **Library:** Number of titles: 135,100; number of current serial subscriptions: 16,811. **Information technology resources:** Students are required to lease or own a computer. Number of campus computers available to all students: 2,491. School has a wireless network. Approximate number of users that can be accommodated: 3,000. Proportion of college-owned housing units wired for high-speed internet access: 100%. **Campus safety:** Security services offered: 24-hour foot-and-vehicle patrols, late-night transport/escort service, 24-hour emergency telephones, lighted pathways/sidewalks, student patrols, controlled dormitory access (key, security card, etc).

TRANSFER AND INTERNATIONAL STUDENTS

Transfer students: May apply for admission for the following academic terms: Fall, Spring. Applicants do not need a minimum number of credits to apply. For fall 2009: Transfer applications received: 106. Transfer applicants offered admission: 45. Transfer applicants enrolled: 34. **International students:** Number of foreign undergraduates: 9. Minimum TOEFL score required: 550 (paper); 79 (computer). Average TOEFL score: 650 (paper).

Gwynedd-Mercy College

- **Address:** 1325 Sumneytown Pike, PO Box 901, Gwynedd Valley, PA 19437-0901
- **Website:** http://www.gmc.edu
- **Private; Religious affiliation:** Roman Catholic
- **Enrollment:** 1,493 full-time; 703 part-time

KEY STATS
✔ **U.S News College Ranking:** 93, Regional Universities (North)
✔ **SAT Score (25th/75th percentile):** 870-1060
✔ **Tuition:** 2010-2011: $25,610

Selectivity: Less selective	**Room/board:** $9,760
Acceptance rate: 67%	**Average debt:** $36,255
Student/faculty ratio: 13/1	**Proportion who borrowed:** 90%

UNDERGRADUATE STUDENT BODY STATS
2009-2010 enrollment: 1,493 full-time; 703 part-time. Men: 26%; women: 74%. **Ethnic makeup:** African American: 21%; Asian American: 2%; Hispanic: 1%; White: 75%.

ADMISSIONS FACTS AND FIGURES

Phone: (215) 681-5510. **Email:** admissions@gmc.edu. **Website:** http://www.gmc.edu. **Application deadlines for fall 2011:** Regular decision: August 20. Early decision: Not offered. Early action: Not offered. Admission can be deferred. **Application fee:** $25. **To apply online, go to:** http://www.gmc.edu/admissions/apply.html. **Admissions requirements/recommendations:** High school units required (recommended): English: 4; Mathematics: 3; Science: 3; History: 1; Academic electives: 3; Total units: 16. Tests: The college uses SAT or ACT scores in admissions decisions. Either SAT or ACT required. Campus visit: Recommended. Admissions interview: Recommended. Off-campus interview: May be arranged. **Factors that count in admissions decisions:** *Academic:* Secondary school record: Very Important. Class rank: Important. Letters of recommendation: Important. Standardized test scores: Important. Essay: Considered. *Nonacademic:* Interview: Considered. Extracurricular activities: Important. Talent/ability: Not Considered. Character/personal qualities: Considered. Alumni/ae relationship: Considered. Geographical residence: Not Considered. State residency: Not Considered. Religious affiliation/commitment: Not Considered. Minority status: Not Considered. Volunteer work: Considered. Work experience: Considered. **Admissions statistics for the fall 2009 entering class:** Total applicants: 1,844. Total accepted: 1,237. Freshmen enrolled: 315; 15% were from out of state. Overall acceptance rate: 67%. Size of waiting list: 0 applicants; enrolled from waiting list: 0. **Credentials of fall 2009 freshmen:** 8% ranked in the top 10 percent of their high school class; 26% were in the top 25 percent; 57% were in the top half. (Proportion submitting class standing: 68%.) **First-year students who submitted SAT scores:** 97%. Scores (25/75 percentile): Critical Reading: 440-530, Math: 430-530, Combined: 870-1060.

ACADEMICS

Year founded: 1948. **Academic calendar:** Semester. **Degrees offered:** certificate, associate, bachelor's, post-bachelor's certificate, master's, post-master's certificate. **Most popular majors:** 48% health professions and related clinical sciences, 30% business, management, marketing, and related support services, 10% education, 4% psychology, 2% English language and literature/letters. **Major fields of study:** biological and biomedical sciences; business, management, marketing, and related support services; communication, journalism, and related programs; computer and information sciences and support services; education; English language and literature/letters; health professions and related clinical sciences; history; mathematics and statistics; psychology; public administration and social service professions; security and protective services; social sciences. **Areas of required coursework:** arts/fine arts, humanities, English (including composition), philosophy, history, social science, other. **Pre-professional programs:** pre-law. **Special academic programs (% participation):** accelerated program (12%), cross-registration, double major (1%), honors program (2%), independent study, internships, liberal arts/career combination (50%), study abroad, teacher certificate program (10%), weekend college. **Teacher certification offered in:** early childhood, special education, elementary, secondary. **Faculty and instruction (2009-2010):** Total instructional faculty: 75 full-time, 206 part-time (42% men; 58% women; 5% minorities). Full-time faculty with Ph.D. or other terminal degree: 63%. Student/faculty ratio: 13/1. Classes of fewer than 20 students: 65%; of 20 to 49 students: 31%; of 50 or more students: 4%. **Advanced Placement and International Baccalaureate credit:** AP tests may be used for: Credit only. Scores accepted: 3, 4, 5. **Freshmen returning for sophomore year:** 78%. **Graduation rates:** Four-year: 50%; five-year: 67%; six-year: 72%.

COSTS AND FINANCIAL AID

Financial aid office: (215) 641-5570. **Expenses (2010-2011):** Tuition and fees 2010-2011: $25,610; room/board: $9,760. Estimated books and supplies: $1,000; transportation: $500; personal expenses: $1,000. **Financial aid:** Priority filing date for institution's financial aid form: March 1; deadline: July 15. In 2009-2010, 88% of undergraduates applied for financial aid. Of those, 74% were determined to have financial need; 18% had their need fully met. Average financial aid package (proportion receiving): $14,187 (74%). Average amount of gift aid, such as scholarships or grants (proportion receiving): $11,605 (72%). Average amount of self-help aid, such as work study or loans (proportion receiving): $6,788 (61%). Average need-based loan (excluding PLUS or other private loans): $6,441. Among students who received need-based aid, the average percentage of need met: 72%. Among students who received aid based on merit, the average award (and the proportion receiving): $15,592 (20%). Average amount of debt of borrowers graduating in 2009: $36,255. Proportion who borrowed: 90%.

CAMPUS LIFE AND EXTRACURRICULAR ACTIVITIES

Campus housing available (% using): coed dorms (100%), special housing for disabled students (0%). Students who live in college-owned, operated, or affiliated housing: 29%. **Clubs and organizations:** Number of student organizations: 30. Activities include: campus ministries, choral groups, dance, drama/theater, literary magazine, student government, student newspaper, yearbook. Number of fraternities: 0; sororities: 0. Average proportion of students who stay on campus on weekends: 41%. **Sports program (2009-2010):** Member of NCAA III. *Men's intercollegiate varsity sports:* baseball, basketball, cross country, golf, soccer, tennis, track and field (indoor), track and field (outdoor), volleyball. *Women's intercollegiate varsity sports:* basketball, cross country, field hockey, lacrosse, soccer, softball, tennis, track and field (indoor), track and field (outdoor).

SERVICES AND FACILITIES

Basic services: nonremedial tutoring, health service, health insurance. **Remedial assistance:** math, writing, study skills. **Counseling services:** career, personal, academic, psychological, religious. **For learning-disabled students:** School does not offer a structured program with separate admission and additional fees. Services include: remedial math, remedial English, reading machines, tape recorders, untimed tests, oral tests, learning center, readers, extended time for tests, tutors, texts on tape, other. **Library:** Number of titles: 104,899; number of current serial subscriptions: 490. **Information technology resources:** Students are not required to lease or own a computer. Number of campus computers available to all students: 265. School has a wireless network. **Campus safety:** Security services offered: 24-hour foot-and-vehicle patrols, late-night transport/escort service, 24-hour emergency telephones, lighted pathways/sidewalks, controlled dormitory access (key, security card, etc).

TRANSFER AND INTERNATIONAL STUDENTS

Transfer students: May apply for admission for the following academic terms: Fall. Applicants do not need a minimum number of credits to apply. For fall 2009: Transfer applications received: 1,492. Transfer applicants offered admission: 287. Transfer applicants enrolled: 162. **International students:** Number of foreign undergraduates: 7. Number of countries represented: 51. Minimum TOEFL score required: 525 (paper); 195 (computer).

Haverford College

- **Address:** 370 Lancaster Avenue, Haverford, PA 19041-1392
- **Website:** http://www.haverford.edu
- **Private**
- **Enrollment:** 1,190 full-time

KEY STATS

✔ **U.S News College Ranking:** 9, National Liberal Arts Colleges
✔ **SAT Score (25th/75th percentile):** 1300-1480
✔ **Tuition:** 2010-2011: $40,624

Selectivity: Most selective	**Room/board:** $12,346
Acceptance rate: 25%	**Average debt:** $16,500
Student/faculty ratio: 8/1	**Proportion who borrowed:** 38%

UNDERGRADUATE STUDENT BODY STATS

2009-2010 enrollment: 1,190 full-time. Men: 45%; women: 55%. **Ethnic makeup:** African American: 8%; Asian American: 9%; Hispanic: 8%; White: 73%; International: 3%.

ADMISSIONS FACTS AND FIGURES

Phone: (610) 896-1350. **Email:** admission@haverford.edu. **Website:** http://www.haverford.edu. **Application deadlines for fall 2011:** Regular decision: January 15; decision sent by April 1. Early decision: Send application by: November 15; Decision sent by: December 15. Early action: Not offered. Admission can be deferred. **Application fee:** $60. **To apply online, go to:** http://www.haverford.edu/admission/applying/. **Admissions requirements/recommendations:** High school units required (recommended): English: (4); Mathematics: (3); Science: (3); Foreign language: (2); Social studies: (2); History: (3). Tests: The college uses SAT or ACT scores in admissions decisions. Either SAT or ACT required. For admission to the fall 2011 entering class, the school will accept: ACT with writing required. Campus visit: Recommended. Admissions interview: Recommended. Off-campus interview: May be arranged. **Factors that count in admissions decisions:** *Academic:* Secondary school record: Very Important. Class rank:

Important. Letters of recommendation: Very Important. Standardized test scores: Important. Essay: Very Important. *Nonacademic:* Interview: Considered. Extracurricular activities: Very Important. Talent/ability: Important. Character/personal qualities: Very Important. Alumni/ae relationship: Considered. Geographical residence: Considered. State residency: Not Considered. Religious affiliation/commitment: Not Considered. Minority status: Considered. Volunteer work: Important. Work experience: Important. **Other schools with the greatest overlap in applicants:** Amherst College; Brown University; Swarthmore College; Tufts University; University of Pennsylvania. **Admissions statistics for the fall 2009 entering class:** Total applicants: 3,403. Total accepted: 862. Freshmen enrolled: 323; 87% were from out of state. Accepted through early-decision or early-action plans: 37%. Overall acceptance rate: 25%. Early-decision acceptance rate: 49%. Non-early acceptance rate: 24%. **Size of waiting list:** 725 applicants; enrolled from waiting list: 13. **Credentials of fall 2009 freshmen:** 94% ranked in the top 10 percent of their high school class; 99% were in the top 25 percent; 100% were in the top half. (Proportion submitting class standing: 44%.) **First-year students who submitted SAT scores:** 95%. Scores (25/75 percentile): Critical Reading: 660-740, Math: 640-740, Combined: 1300-1480.

ACADEMICS

Year founded: 1833. **Academic calendar:** Semester. **Degrees offered:** bachelor's. **Most popular majors:** 13% biology/biological sciences, 12% political science and government, 11% economics, 9% English language and literature, 9% psychology. **Major fields of study:** area, ethnic, cultural, and gender studies; biological and biomedical sciences; computer and information sciences and support services; English language and literature/letters; foreign languages, literatures, and linguistics; history; liberal arts and sciences studies, and humanities; mathematics and statistics; multi/interdisciplinary studies; philosophy and religious studies; physical sciences; psychology; social sciences; visual and performing arts. **Areas of required coursework:** humanities, mathematics, English (including composition), foreign languages, sciences (biological or physical), social science. **Pre-professional programs:** pre-law, pre-medicine, other. **Special academic programs (% participation):** cross-registration (65%), double major (5%), exchange student program (domestic) (1%), independent study (4%), student-designed major (1%), study abroad (40%), teacher certificate program (1%). **Teacher certification offered in:** elementary, middle/junior high, secondary. **Faculty and instruction (2009-2010):** Total instructional faculty: 121 full-time, 17 part-time (53% men; 47% women; 25% minorities). Full-time faculty with Ph.D. or other terminal degree: 97%. Student/faculty ratio: 8/1. Classes of fewer than 20 students: 76%; of 20 to 49 students: 22%; of 50 or more students: 2%. **Advanced Placement and International Baccalaureate credit:** AP tests may be used for: Credit and/or placement. Scores accepted: 4, 5. International Baccalaureate exams may be used for: Credit only. **Freshmen returning for sophomore year:** 96%. **Graduation rates:** Four-year: 88%; five-year: 92%; six-year: 92%. **Graduate study:** 17% of students pursue further study immediately upon graduation; 72% within five years. Fields in which graduates pursue further study: law, 3%; medicine, 3%; education, 1%; arts and sciences, 9%.

COSTS AND FINANCIAL AID

Financial aid office: (610) 896-1350. **Expenses (2010-2011):** Tuition and fees 2010-2011: $40,624; room/board: $12,346. Estimated books and supplies: $1,194; transportation: $173; personal expenses: $1,468. **Financial aid:** In 2009-2010, 56% of undergraduates applied for financial aid. Of those, 48% were determined to have financial need; 100% had their need fully met. Average financial aid package (proportion receiving): $34,629 (48%). Average amount of gift aid, such as scholarships or grants (proportion receiving): $33,093 (46%). Average amount of self-help aid, such as work study or loans (proportion receiving): $3,783 (44%). Average need-based loan (excluding PLUS or other private loans): $17,534. Among students who received need-based aid, the average percentage of need met: 100%. Average amount of debt of borrowers graduating in 2009: $16,500. Proportion who borrowed: 38%.

CAMPUS LIFE AND EXTRACURRICULAR ACTIVITIES

Campus housing available (% using): coed dorms (100%), other housing options. Students who live in college-owned, operated, or affiliated housing: 99%. **Student employment:** During the 2009-2010 academic year, 20% of undergraduates worked on campus. **Clubs and organizations:** Number of student organizations: 144. Activities include: choral groups, dance, drama/theater, literary magazine, music ensembles, musical theater, radio station, student government, student newspaper, yearbook. Number of fraternities: 0; sororities: 0. Average proportion of students who stay on campus on weekends: 85%. **Sports program (2009-2010):** Member of NCAA III. *Men's intercollegiate varsity sports:* baseball, basketball, cross country, fencing, lacrosse, soccer, tennis, track and field (indoor), track and field (outdoor). *Women's intercollegiate varsity sports:* basketball, cross country, fencing, field hockey, lacrosse, soccer, softball, squash, tennis, track and field (indoor), track and field (outdoor), volleyball.

SERVICES AND FACILITIES

Basic services: nonremedial tutoring, women's center, placement service, health service, health insurance. **Counseling services:** minority student, career, personal, academic, psychological, birth control, religious. **For learning-disabled students:** School does not offer a structured program with separate admission and additional fees. Total undergraduates in learning-disabled program or receiving services: 68. Services include: reading machines, note-taking services, extended time for tests, priority registration, priority seating, substitution of courses, texts on tape, other. **Library:** Number of titles: 595,522; number of current serial subscriptions: 21,641. **Information technology resources:** Students are not required to lease or own a computer. Number of campus computers available to all students: 300. School has a wireless network. Proportion of college-owned housing units wired for high-speed internet access: 100%. **Campus safety:** Security services offered: 24-hour foot-and-vehicle patrols, late-night transport/escort service, 24-hour emergency telephones, lighted pathways/sidewalks, controlled dormitory access (key, security card, etc).

TRANSFER AND INTERNATIONAL STUDENTS

Transfer students: May apply for admission for the following academic terms: Fall. Applicants need a minimum number of credits to apply. For fall 2009: Transfer applications received: 129. Transfer applicants offered admission: 20. Transfer applicants enrolled: 7. **International students:** Number of foreign undergraduates: 33 (3% of student body). Minimum TOEFL score required: 600 (paper); 250 (computer).

Holy Family University

- **Address:** 9801 Frankford Avenue, Philadelphia, PA 19114-2009
- **Website:** http://www.holyfamily.edu
- **Private; Religious affiliation:** Roman Catholic
- **Enrollment:** 1,556 full-time; 701 part-time

KEY STATS

✔ **U.S News College Ranking:** 99, Regional Universities (North)
✔ **SAT Score (25th/75th percentile):** 840-1020
✔ **Tuition:** 2010-2011: $23,520

Selectivity: Less selective	**Room/board:** $10,390
Acceptance rate: 74%	**Average debt:** $31,855
Student/faculty ratio: 12/1	**Proportion who borrowed:** 82%

UNDERGRADUATE STUDENT BODY STATS

2009-2010 enrollment: 1,556 full-time; 701 part-time. Men: 28%; women: 72%. **Ethnic makeup:** African American: 7%; American-Indian: 1%; Asian American: 5%; Hispanic: 5%; White: 83%; International: 1%. **Religious preference:** Protestant: 12%; Jewish: 2%; No preference: 1%; Unknown: 22%; Roman Catholic: 59%; Other: 4%.

ADMISSIONS FACTS AND FIGURES

Phone: (215) 637-3050. **Email:** admissions@holyfamily.edu. **Website:** http://www.holyfamily.edu. **Application deadlines for fall 2011:** Regular decision: Rolling. Early decision: Not offered. Early action: Not offered. Admission can be deferred. **Application fee:** $25. **To apply online, go to:** http://my.holyfamily.edu/apply. **Admissions requirements/recommendations:** High school units required (recommended): English: 4 (4); Mathematics: 3 (3); Science: 2 (2); Foreign language: (2); Social studies: (0); History: 2 (2); Academic electives: 3 (3); Total units: 14 (16). Tests: The college uses SAT or ACT scores in admissions decisions. Either SAT or ACT required. For admission to the fall 2011 entering class, the school will accept: ACT with writing required. Campus visit: Recommended. Admissions interview: Recommended. Off-campus interview: May be arranged. **Factors that count in admissions decisions:** *Academic:* Secondary school record: Important. Class rank: Important. Letters of recommendation: Considered. Standardized test scores: Important. Essay: Considered. *Nonacademic:* Interview: Considered. Extracurricular activities: Important. Talent/ability: Considered. Character/personal qualities: Considered. Alumni/

ae relationship: Considered. Geographical residence: Not Considered. State residency: Not Considered. Religious affiliation/commitment: Not Considered. Minority status: Not Considered. Volunteer work: Considered. Work experience: Considered. **Other schools with the greatest overlap in applicants:** Arcadia University; Gwynedd-Mercy College; La Salle University; Pennsylvania State University–University Park; Temple University. **Admissions statistics for the fall 2009 entering class:** Total applicants: 1,241. Total accepted: 913. Freshmen enrolled: 382; 15% were from out of state. Overall acceptance rate: 74%. **Size of waiting list:** 0 applicants; enrolled from waiting list: 0. **Credentials of fall 2009 freshmen:** 8% ranked in the top 10 percent of their high school class; 38% were in the top 25 percent. **Average high school grade point average:** 3.1. **First-year students who submitted SAT scores:** 98%. Scores (25/75 percentile): Critical Reading: 420-510, Math: 420-510, Combined: 840-1020. **First-year students submitting ACT scores:** 2%. Scores (25/75 percentile): English: N/A, Math: N/A, Composite: 19-21.

ACADEMICS

Year founded: 1954. **Academic calendar:** Semester. **Degrees offered:** associate, bachelor's, master's. **Most popular majors:** 38% health professions and related clinical sciences, 20% education, 17% business, management, marketing, and related support services, 8% psychology, 5% security and protective services. **Major fields of study:** biological and biomedical sciences; business, management, marketing, and related support services; communication, journalism, and related programs; education; English language and literature/letters; foreign languages, literatures, and linguistics; health professions and related clinical sciences; history; liberal arts and sciences studies, and humanities; mathematics and statistics; parks, recreation, leisure, and fitness studies; philosophy and religious studies; physical sciences; psychology; public administration and social service professions; security and protective services; social sciences; visual and performing arts. **Areas of required coursework:** humanities, computer literacy, English (including composition), philosophy, foreign languages, sciences (biological or physical), social science. **Pre-professional programs:** pre-law, pre-dentistry, pre-medicine, pre-optometry, pre-pharmacy. **Special academic programs (% participation):** accelerated program (7%), cooperative (work-study plan) program (2%), honors program (3%), independent study (2%), internships (8%), study abroad (1%), teacher certificate program (15%). **Teacher certification offered in:** early childhood, special education, elementary, secondary. **Cooperative education programs:** art, business, computer science, humanities, natural science, social/behavioral science, technologies. **Faculty and instruction (2009-2010):** Total instructional faculty: 94 full-time, 259 part-time (48% men; 52% women; 6% minorities). Full-time faculty with Ph.D. or other terminal degree: 76%. Student/faculty ratio: 12/1. Classes of fewer than 20 students: 67%; of 20 to 49 students: 33%; of 50 or more students: 0%. **Advanced Placement and International Baccalaureate credit:** AP tests may be used for: Placement only. Scores accepted: 3, 4, 5. International Baccalaureate exams may be used for: Placement only. **Freshmen returning for sophomore year:** 79%. **Graduation rates:** Four-year: 48%; five-year: 62%; six-year: 60%. **Graduate study:** 12% of students pursue further study immediately upon graduation; 3% within one year. Fields in which graduates pursue further study: law, 1%; medicine, 1%; education, 50%; arts and sciences, 48%.

COSTS AND FINANCIAL AID

Financial aid office: (215) 637-5538. **Expenses (2010-2011):** Tuition and fees 2010-2011: $23,520; room/board: $10,390. Estimated books and supplies: $1,010; transportation: $848. **Financial aid:** Priority filing date for institution's financial aid form: March 1. In 2009-2010, 93% of undergraduates applied for financial aid. Of those, 83% were determined to have financial need; 17% had their need fully met. Average financial aid package (proportion receiving): $16,005 (82%). Average amount of gift aid, such as scholarships or grants (proportion receiving): $11,705 (79%). Average amount of self-help aid, such as work study or loans (proportion receiving): $4,994 (71%). Average need-based loan (excluding PLUS or other private loans): $4,351. Among students who received need-based aid, the average percentage of need met: 71%. Among students who received aid based on merit, the average award (and the proportion receiving): $8,093 (8%). The average athletic scholarship (and the proportion receiving): $8,508 (2%). Average amount of debt of borrowers graduating in 2009: $31,855. Proportion who borrowed: 82%.

CAMPUS LIFE AND EXTRACURRICULAR ACTIVITIES

Campus housing available (% using): coed dorms (53%), other housing options (47%). Students who live in college-owned, operated, or affiliated housing: 17%. **Student employment:** During the 2009-2010 academic year, 3% of undergraduates worked on campus. Average per-year earnings:

$1,200. **Clubs and organizations:** Number of student organizations: 24. Activities include: campus ministries, choral groups, literary magazine, radio station, student government, student newspaper, television station, yearbook. Number of fraternities: 0; sororities: 0. Average proportion of students who stay on campus on weekends: 20%. **Sports program (2009-2010):** Member of NCAA II. *Men's intercollegiate varsity sports:* basketball, cross country, golf, soccer, track and field (outdoor). *Women's intercollegiate varsity sports:* basketball, cross country, soccer, softball, track and field (outdoor), volleyball.

SERVICES AND FACILITIES

Basic services: placement service. **Remedial assistance:** reading, math, writing, study skills. **Counseling services:** minority student, career, academic, psychological, religious. **For learning-disabled students:** School does not offer a structured program with separate admission and additional fees. Total undergraduates in learning-disabled program or receiving services: 254. Services include: remedial math, remedial English, reading machines, remedial reading, tape recorders, other special classes, note-taking services, oral tests, learning center, readers, extended time for tests, tutors, priority seating, texts on tape, other testing accommodations, other. **Library:** Number of titles: 142,800; number of current serial subscriptions: 12,490. **Information technology resources:** Students are not required to lease or own a computer. Number of campus computers available to all students: 1,000. School has a wireless network. Approximate number of users that can be accommodated: 500. Proportion of college-owned housing units wired for high-speed internet access: 100%. **Campus safety:** Security services offered: 24-hour foot-and-vehicle patrols, late-night transport/escort service, 24-hour emergency telephones, lighted pathways/sidewalks, controlled dormitory access (key, security card, etc).

TRANSFER AND INTERNATIONAL STUDENTS

Transfer students: May apply for admission for the following academic terms: Fall, Spring, Summer. Applicants do not need a minimum number of credits to apply. **International students:** Number of foreign undergraduates: 12 (1% of student body). Number of countries represented: 10. Minimum TOEFL score required: 550 (paper); 213 (computer).

Immaculata University

- **Address:** 1145 King Road, Immaculata, PA 19345-0702
- **Website:** http://www.immaculata.edu
- **Private; Religious affiliation:** Roman Catholic
- **Enrollment:** 1,062 full-time; 2,009 part-time

KEY STATS

✔ **U.S News College Ranking:** 176, National Universities
✔ **SAT Score (25th/75th percentile):** 830-1020
✔ **Tuition:** 2010-2011: $27,870

Selectivity: Less selective	**Room/board:** $11,460
Acceptance rate: 80%	**Average debt:** N/A
Student/faculty ratio: 11/1	**Proportion who borrowed:** N/A

UNDERGRADUATE STUDENT BODY STATS

2009-2010 enrollment: 1,062 full-time; 2,009 part-time. Men: 22%; women: 78%. **Ethnic makeup:** African American: 13%; American-Indian: 1%; Asian American: 2%; Hispanic: 2%; White: 82%; International: 1%. **Religious preference:** Roman Catholic: 60%; Other: 40%.

ADMISSIONS FACTS AND FIGURES

Phone: (877) 428-6329. **Email:** admiss@immaculata.edu. **Website:** http://www.immaculata.edu. **Application deadlines for fall 2011:** Regular decision: Rolling. Early decision: Not offered. Early action: Not offered. Admission can be deferred. **Application fee:** $35. **To apply online, go to:** https://charity.immaculata.edu/pls/PROD/bwskalog.P_DispLoginNew. **Admissions requirements/recommendations:** High school units required (recommended): English: 4; Mathematics: 2; Science: 2; Foreign language: 2; Social studies: 2; Total units: 16. Tests: The college uses SAT or ACT scores in admissions decisions. Either SAT or ACT required. For admission to the fall 2011 entering class, the school will accept: ACT with writing recommended. Campus visit: Recommended. Admissions interview: Recommended. Off-campus interview: Not available. **Factors that count in admissions decisions:** *Academic:* Secondary school record: Very Important. Class rank: Important. Letters of recommendation: Important.

Standardized test scores: Important. Essay: Important. **Nonacademic:** Interview: Considered. Extracurricular activities: Considered. Talent/ability: Considered. Character/personal qualities: Considered. Alumni/ae relationship: Considered. Geographical residence: Considered. State residency: Not Considered. Religious affiliation/commitment: Considered. Minority status: Not Considered. Volunteer work: Considered. Work experience: Considered. **Other schools with the greatest overlap in applicants:** Cabrini College; Marywood University; Millersville University of Pennsylvania; Shippensburg University of Pennsylvania; West Chester University of Pennsylvania. **Admissions statistics for the fall 2009 entering class:** Total applicants: 1,216. Total accepted: 975. Freshmen enrolled: 196; 39% were from out of state. Overall acceptance rate: 80%. **First-year students who submitted SAT scores:** 97%. Scores (25/75 percentile): Critical Reading: 420-510, Math: 410-510, Combined: 830-1020. **First-year students submitting ACT scores:** 19%. Scores (25/75 percentile): English: N/A, Math: N/A, Composite: 17-21.

ACADEMICS

Year founded: 1920. **Academic calendar:** Semester. **Degrees offered:** certificate, associate, bachelor's, master's, doctorate. **Most popular majors:** 40% health professions and related clinical sciences, 30% business, management, marketing, and related support services, 6% psychology, 3% English language and literature/letters, 3% parks, recreation, leisure, and fitness studies. **Major fields of study:** biological and biomedical sciences; business, management, marketing, and related support services; communication, journalism, and related programs; computer and information sciences and support services; education; English language and literature/letters; foreign languages, literatures, and linguistics; health professions and related clinical sciences; history; mathematics and statistics; multi/interdisciplinary studies; natural resources and conservation; parks, recreation, leisure, and fitness studies; physical sciences; psychology; public administration and social service professions; security and protective services; social sciences; theology and religious vocations; visual and performing arts. **Areas of required coursework:** arts/fine arts, humanities, computer literacy, mathematics, English (including composition), philosophy, foreign languages, sciences (biological or physical), history, social science, other. **Pre-professional programs:** pre-law, pre-dentistry, pre-medicine, pre-theology, pre-veterinary science, pre-optometry, pre-pharmacy, other. **Special academic programs (% participation):** accelerated program (75%), cross-registration (1%), distance learning, double major (20%), dual enrollment, honors program (11%), independent study (10%), internships (30%), liberal arts/career combination (85%), study abroad (1%), teacher certificate program (35%). **Teacher certification offered in:** early childhood, special education, elementary, middle/junior high, secondary. **Reserve Officers Training Corps (ROTC):** Army ROTC: Offered at cooperating institution (West Chester University of Pennsylvania). **Faculty and instruction (2009-2010):** Total instructional faculty: 103 full-time, 308 part-time (38% men; 62% women; 2% minorities). Full-time faculty with Ph.D. or other terminal degree: 79%. Student/faculty ratio: 11/1. Classes of fewer than 20 students: 80%; of 20 to 49 students: 20%; of 50 or more students: 0%. **Advanced Placement and International Baccalaureate credit:** AP tests may be used for: Placement only. Scores accepted: 3, 4, 5. **Freshmen returning for sophomore year:** 69%. **Graduation rates:** Four-year: 57%; five-year: 62%; six-year: 62%. **Graduate study:** 24% of students pursue further study immediately upon graduation.

COSTS AND FINANCIAL AID

Financial aid office: (610) 647-4400. **Expenses (2010-2011):** Tuition and fees 2010-2011: $27,870; room/board: $11,460. Estimated books and supplies: $1,695; transportation: $1,010; personal expenses: $3,580. **Financial aid:** Priority filing date for institution's financial aid form: February 15; deadline: April 15. In 2009-2010, 82% of undergraduates applied for financial aid. Of those, 70% were determined to have financial need; 2% had their need fully met. Average financial aid package (proportion receiving): $16,583 (70%). Average amount of gift aid, such as scholarships or grants (proportion receiving): $2,749 (46%). Average amount of self-help aid, such as work study or loans (proportion receiving): $3,627 (62%). Average need-based loan (excluding PLUS or other private loans): $4,093. Among students who received need-based aid, the average percentage of need met: 25%. Among students who received aid based on merit, the average award (and the proportion receiving): $7,713 (18%).

CAMPUS LIFE AND EXTRACURRICULAR ACTIVITIES

Campus housing available (% using): coed dorms (34%), women's dorms (55%), men's dorms, apartment for single students (10%), special housing for disabled students (1%). Students who live in college-owned, operated, or affiliated housing: 58%. **Student employment:** During the 2009-2010 aca-

demic year, 40% of undergraduates worked on campus. Average per-year earnings: $1,000. **Clubs and organizations:** Number of student organizations: 46. Activities include: campus ministries, choral groups, concert band, dance, drama/theater, international student organization, jazz band, literary magazine, music ensembles, musical theater, student government, student newspaper, symphony orchestra, yearbook. Number of fraternities: 1; sororities: 4. Proportion of men in fraternities: 6%; of women in sororities: 7%. Average proportion of students who stay on campus on weekends: 45%. **Sports program (2009-2010):** Member of NCAA III.

SERVICES AND FACILITIES

Basic services: nonremedial tutoring, placement service, health service, health insurance, other. **Remedial assistance:** math, writing, study skills. **Counseling services:** minority student, career, personal, academic, older student, psychological, religious. **For learning-disabled students:** School does not offer a structured program with separate admission and additional fees. Services include: tape recorders, untimed tests, note-taking services, oral tests, learning center, extended time for tests, tutors, priority registration, priority seating, other testing accommodations. **Library:** Number of titles: 158,030; number of current serial subscriptions: 570. **Information technology resources:** Students are not required to lease or own a computer. Number of campus computers available to all students: 254. School has a wireless network. Proportion of college-owned housing units wired for high-speed internet access: 100%. **Campus safety:** Security services offered: 24-hour foot-and-vehicle patrols, late-night transport/escort service, 24-hour emergency telephones, lighted pathways/sidewalks, student patrols, controlled dormitory access (key, security card, etc).

TRANSFER AND INTERNATIONAL STUDENTS

Transfer students: May apply for admission for the following academic terms: Fall, Spring. Applicants do not need a minimum number of credits to apply. For fall 2009: Transfer applications received: 243. Transfer applicants offered admission: 157. Transfer applicants enrolled: 77. **International students:** Number of foreign undergraduates: 18 (1% of student body). Number of countries represented: 9. Minimum TOEFL score required: 550 (paper). Average TOEFL score: 590 (paper).

Indiana University of Pennsylvania

- **Address:** 1011 South Drive, Indiana, PA 15705
- **Website:** http://www.iup.edu
- **Public**
- **Enrollment:** 11,361 full-time; 930 part-time

KEY STATS
✔ **U.S News College Ranking:** second tier, National Universities
✔ **SAT Score (25th/75th percentile):** 900-1070
✔ **Tuition:** 2009-2010: $7,225 in state, $15,557 out of state
  Selectivity: Selective   **Room/board:** $6,296
  Acceptance rate: 60%   **Average debt:** N/A
  Student/faculty ratio: 18/1   **Proportion who borrowed:** N/A

UNDERGRADUATE STUDENT BODY STATS

2009-2010 enrollment: 11,361 full-time; 930 part-time. Men: 44%; women: 56%. **Ethnic makeup:** African American: 11%; Asian American: 1%; Hispanic: 2%; White: 84%; International: 1%.

ADMISSIONS FACTS AND FIGURES

Phone: (800) 442-6830. **Email:** admissions-inquiry@iup.edu. **Website:** http://www.iup.edu. **Application deadlines for fall 2011:** Regular decision: Rolling. Early decision: Not offered. Early action: Not offered. Admission can be deferred. **Application fee:** $35. **To apply online, go to:** http://www.iup.edu/admissions. **Admissions requirements/recommendations:** High school units required (recommended): English: (4); Mathematics: (3); Science: (3); Foreign language: (2); Social studies: (3); History: (0); Academic electives: (0); Total units: (15). Tests: The college uses SAT or ACT scores in admissions decisions. Either SAT or ACT required. For admission to the fall 2011 entering class, the school will accept: ACT with or without writing accepted. **Campus visit:** Recommended. **Admissions interview:** Neither required nor recommended. Off-campus interview: May be arranged. **Factors that count in admissions decisions: Academic:** Secondary school record: Important. Class rank: Considered. Letters of recommendation: Considered. Standardized test scores: Very Important. Essay: Considered. **Nonacademic:**

Interview: Not Considered. Extracurricular activities: Considered. Talent/ability: Considered. Character/personal qualities: Not Considered. Alumni/ae relationship: Not Considered. Geographical residence: Not Considered. State residency: Not Considered. Religious affiliation/commitment: Not Considered. Minority status: Not Considered. Volunteer work: Not Considered. Work experience: Not Considered. **Other schools with the greatest overlap in applicants:** Pennsylvania State University–University Park; Slippery Rock University of Pennsylvania; University of Pittsburgh. **Admissions statistics for the fall 2009 entering class:** Total applicants: 11,669. Total accepted: 7,041. Freshmen enrolled: 3,008; 7% were from out of state. Overall acceptance rate: 60%. **Credentials of fall 2009 freshmen:** 7% ranked in the top 10 percent of their high school class; 26% were in the top 25 percent; 61% were in the top half. (Proportion submitting class standing: 83%.) **First-year students who submitted SAT scores:** 83%. Scores (25/75 percentile): Critical Reading: 450-530, Math: 450-540, Combined: 900-1070.

ACADEMICS

Year founded: 1875. **Academic calendar:** Semester. **Degrees offered:** certificate, associate, bachelor's, post-bachelor's certificate, master's, post-master's certificate, doctorate. **Most popular majors:** 24% business, management, marketing, and related support services, 16% social sciences, 8% education, 8% visual and performing arts, 7% communication, journalism, and related programs. **Major fields of study:** architecture and related services; biological and biomedical sciences; business, management, marketing, and related support services; communication, journalism, and related programs; computer and information sciences and support services; education; engineering technologies/technicians; English language and literature/letters; family and consumer sciences/human sciences; foreign languages, literatures, and linguistics; health professions and related clinical sciences; history; liberal arts and sciences studies, and humanities; mathematics and statistics; multi/interdisciplinary studies; parks, recreation, leisure, and fitness studies; philosophy and religious studies; physical sciences; psychology; social sciences; visual and performing arts. **Areas of required coursework:** arts/fine arts, humanities, computer literacy, mathematics, English (including composition), philosophy, sciences (biological or physical), history, social science. **Pre-professional programs:** pre-law, pre-dentistry, pre-medicine, pre-veterinary science, pre-optometry, pre-pharmacy, other. **Special academic programs:** accelerated program, cooperative (work-study plan) program, cross-registration, distance learning, double major, dual enrollment, English as a Second Language (ESL), exchange student program (domestic), external degree program, honors program, independent study, internships, liberal arts/career combination, study abroad, teacher certificate program, weekend college. **Teacher certification offered in:** early childhood, special education, elementary, vo-tech, secondary. **Cooperative education programs:** health professions, natural science, other. **Reserve Officers Training Corps (ROTC):** Army ROTC: Offered on campus. **Faculty and instruction (2009-2010):** Total instructional faculty: 611 full-time, 62 part-time (50% men; 50% women; 12% minorities). Student/faculty ratio: 18/1. Classes of fewer than 20 students: 33%; of 20 to 49 students: 54%; of 50 or more students: 13%. **Advanced Placement and International Baccalaureate credit:** AP tests may be used for: Placement only. Scores accepted: 3, 4, 5. **Freshmen returning for sophomore year:** 75%. **Graduation rates:** Four-year: 33%; five-year: 51%; six-year: 54%.

COSTS AND FINANCIAL AID

Financial aid office: (724) 357-2218. **Expenses (2009-2010):** Tuition and fees 2009-2010: $7,225 in state, $15,557 out of state; room/board: $6,296. Estimated books and supplies: $1,100; transportation: $300; personal expenses: $2,828. **Financial aid:** Priority filing date for institution's financial aid form: April 15. In 2009-2010, 85% of undergraduates applied for financial aid. Of those, 67% were determined to have financial need; 10% had their need fully met. Average financial aid package (proportion receiving): $8,991 (66%). Average amount of gift aid, such as scholarships or grants (proportion receiving): $5,035 (46%). Average amount of self-help aid, such as work study or loans (proportion receiving): $4,988 (61%). Average need-based loan (excluding PLUS or other private loans): $4,093. Among students who received need-based aid, the average percentage of need met: 70%. Among students who received aid based on merit, the average award (and the proportion receiving): $2,705 (3%). The average athletic scholarship (and the proportion receiving): $3,474 (2%).

CAMPUS LIFE AND EXTRACURRICULAR ACTIVITIES

Campus housing available (% using): coed dorms (46%), apartment for single students (1%), special housing for disabled students (1%), special housing for international students (5%), other housing options (47%). Students who live in college-owned, operated, or affiliated housing: 33%. **Student**

employment: During the 2009-2010 academic year, 12% of undergraduates worked on campus. Average per-year earnings: $8,186. **Clubs and organizations:** Number of student organizations: 210. Activities include: campus ministries, choral groups, concert band, dance, drama/theater, international student organization, jazz band, marching band, music ensembles, musical theater, radio station, student government, student newspaper, symphony orchestra, television station. Number of fraternities: 18; sororities: 14. Proportion of men in fraternities: 9%; of women in sororities: 8%. **Sports program (2009-2010):** Member of NCAA II. **Men's intercollegiate varsity sports:** baseball, basketball, cross country, football, golf, swimming, track and field (indoor), track and field (outdoor). **Women's intercollegiate varsity sports:** basketball, cross country, field hockey, lacrosse, soccer, softball, swimming, tennis, track and field (indoor), track and field (outdoor), volleyball.

SERVICES AND FACILITIES

Basic services: day care, health service. **Remedial assistance:** reading, math, writing, study skills. **Counseling services:** minority student, career, military, personal, veteran student, academic, older student, psychological, birth control. **For learning-disabled students:** School does not offer a structured program with separate admission and additional fees. Services include: remedial math, reading machines, remedial reading, tape recorders, note-taking services, oral tests, learning center, readers, extended time for tests, priority seating, texts on tape, other testing accommodations. **Library:** Number of titles: 875,888; number of current serial subscriptions: 23,425. **Information technology resources:** Students are not required to lease or own a computer. Number of campus computers available to all students: 2,031. School has a wireless network. Approximate number of users that can be accommodated: 16,000. Proportion of college-owned housing units wired for high-speed internet access: 100%. **Campus safety:** Security services offered: 24-hour foot-and-vehicle patrols, late-night transport/escort service, 24-hour emergency telephones, lighted pathways/sidewalks, student patrols, controlled dormitory access (key, security card, etc).

TRANSFER AND INTERNATIONAL STUDENTS

Transfer students: May apply for admission for the following academic terms: Fall, Spring. Applicants need a minimum number of credits to apply. For fall 2009: Transfer applications received: 1,432. Transfer applicants offered admission: 999. Transfer applicants enrolled: 596. **International students:** Number of foreign undergraduates: 145 (1% of student body). Number of countries represented: 57. Minimum TOEFL score required: 500 (paper); 173 (computer).

Juniata College

- **Address:** 1700 Moore Street, Huntingdon, PA 16652
- **Website:** http://www.juniata.edu
- **Private**
- **Enrollment:** 1,399 full-time; 69 part-time

KEY STATS

✔ **U.S News College Ranking:** 81, National Liberal Arts Colleges
✔ **SAT Score (25th/75th percentile):** 1100-1310
✔ **Tuition:** 2010-2011: $32,820

Selectivity: More selective	**Room/board:** $8,980
Acceptance rate: 72%	**Average debt:** $23,618
Student/faculty ratio: 13/1	**Proportion who borrowed:** 89%

UNDERGRADUATE STUDENT BODY STATS

2009-2010 enrollment: 1,399 full-time; 69 part-time. Men: 44%; women: 56%. **Ethnic makeup:** African American: 2%; Asian American: 2%; Hispanic: 2%; White: 88%; International: 7%. **Religious preference:** Roman Catholic: 29%; Protestant: 60%; Jewish: 3%; Buddhist: 1%; No preference: 3%; Wicca, Pagan, Bahai, Latter Day Saints, Other : 4%.

ADMISSIONS FACTS AND FIGURES

Phone: (877) 586-4282. **Email:** admissions@juniata.edu. **Website:** http://www.juniata.edu. **Application deadlines for fall 2011:** Regular decision: March 15. Early decision: Send application by: December 1; Decision sent by: December 31. Early action: Send application by: January 1; Decision sent by: January 30. Admission can be deferred. **Application fee:** $30. **To apply online, go to:** https://www.juniata.edu/admission/apply.html. **Admissions requirements/recommendations:** High school units required (recommended): English: 4 (4); Mathematics: 3 (4); Science: 3 (4); Foreign language: 2 (2); Social studies: 1 (1); History: 3 (3); Total units: 16 (18). Tests: The college uses SAT or ACT scores in admissions decisions. Neither SAT nor ACT required. For admission to the fall 2011 entering class, the school will accept: ACT with or without writing accepted. Campus visit: Recommended. Admissions interview: Recommended. Off-campus interview: May be arranged. **Factors that count in admissions decisions:** *Academic:* Secondary school record: Very Important. Class rank: Not Considered. Letters of recommendation: Very Important. Standardized test scores: Very Important. Essay: Very Important. *Nonacademic:* Interview: Important. Extracurricular activities: Important. Talent/ability: Important. Character/personal qualities: Very Important. Alumni/ae relationship: Considered. Geographical residence: Considered. State residency: Considered. Religious affiliation/commitment: Not Considered. Minority status: Considered. Volunteer work: Important. Work experience: Not Considered. **Other schools with the greatest overlap in applicants:** Allegheny College; Gettysburg College; Pennsylvania State University–University Park; University of Pittsburgh; Ursinus College. **Admissions statistics for the fall 2009 entering class:** Total applicants: 1,964. Total accepted: 1,410. Freshmen enrolled: 366; 32% were from out of state. Accepted through early-decision or early-action plans: 71%. Overall acceptance rate: 72%. Early-decision acceptance rate: 86%. Non-early acceptance rate: 56%. **Size of waiting list:** 83 applicants; enrolled from waiting list: N/A. **Credentials of fall 2009 freshmen:** 41% ranked in the top 10 percent of their high school class; 74% were in the top 25 percent; 96% were in the top half. (Proportion submitting class standing: 75%.) **Average high school grade point average:** 3.8. **First-year students who submitted SAT scores:** 96%. Scores (25/75 percentile): Critical Reading: 550-650, Math: 550-660, Combined: 1100-1310. **First-year students submitting ACT scores:** 7%. Scores (25/75 percentile): English: N/A, Math: N/A, Composite: N/A.

ACADEMICS
Year founded: 1876. **Academic calendar:** Semester. **Degrees offered:** bachelor's. **Most popular majors:** 18% biological and biomedical sciences, 15% business, management, marketing, and related support services, 8% psychology, 8% social sciences, 7% communication, journalism, and related programs. **Major fields of study:** biological and biomedical sciences; business, management, marketing, and related support services; communication, journalism, and related programs; computer and information sciences and support services; education; engineering; English language and literature/letters; foreign languages, literatures, and linguistics; health professions and related clinical sciences; history; legal professions and studies; liberal arts and sciences studies, and humanities; mathematics and statistics; multi/interdisciplinary studies; natural resources and conservation; philosophy and religious studies; physical sciences; psychology; public administration and social service professions; social sciences; theology and religious vocations; visual and performing arts. **Areas of required coursework:** arts/fine arts, humanities, computer literacy, mathematics, English (including composition), sciences (biological or physical), social science, other. **Pre-professional programs:** pre-law, pre-dentistry, pre-medicine, pre-veterinary science, pre-optometry, pre-pharmacy, other. **Special academic programs (% participation):** double major, dual enrollment (3%), English as a Second Language (ESL) (.3%), exchange student program (domestic), honors program (100%), independent study (41%), internships (78%), student-designed major (42%), study abroad (43%), teacher certificate program (8%), other (0%). **Teacher certification offered in:** early childhood, special education, elementary, secondary. **Cooperative education programs:** engineering, health professions, other. **Faculty and instruction (2009-2010):** Total instructional faculty: 100 full-time, 40 part-time (53% men; 47% women; 6% minorities). Full-time faculty with Ph.D. or other terminal degree: 94%. Student/faculty ratio: 13/1. Classes of fewer than 20 students: 76%; of 20 to 49 students: 23%; of 50 or more students: 1%. **Advanced Placement and International Baccalaureate credit:** AP tests may be used for: Placement only. Scores accepted: 4, 5. International Baccalaureate exams may be used for: Placement only. **Freshmen returning for sophomore year:** 85%. **Graduation rates:** Four-year: 75%; five-year: 78%; six-year: 79%. **Graduate study:** 37% of students pursue further study immediately upon graduation; 31% within one year. Fields in which graduates pursue further study: Master of Business Administration (MBA), 1%; law, 1%; medicine, 6%; dentistry, 2%; education, 3%; arts and sciences, 19%; veterinary medicine, 2%.

COSTS AND FINANCIAL AID
Financial aid office: (814) 641-3142. **Expenses (2010-2011):** Tuition and fees 2010-2011: $32,820; room/board: $8,980. Estimated books and supplies: $600; transportation: $250; personal expenses: $1,000. **Financial aid:**

Priority filing date for institution's financial aid form: March 1. In 2009-2010, 80% of undergraduates applied for financial aid. Of those, 71% were determined to have financial need; 23% had their need fully met. Average financial aid package (proportion receiving): $24,152 (71%). Average amount of gift aid, such as scholarships or grants (proportion receiving): $18,970 (71%). Average amount of self-help aid, such as work study or loans (proportion receiving): $6,184 (60%). Average need-based loan (excluding PLUS or other private loans): $4,865. Among students who received need-based aid, the average percentage of need met: 83%. Among students who received aid based on merit, the average award (and the proportion receiving): $13,879 (28%). The average athletic scholarship (and the proportion receiving): $0 (0%). Average amount of debt of borrowers graduating in 2009: $23,618. Proportion who borrowed: 89%.

CAMPUS LIFE AND EXTRACURRICULAR ACTIVITIES
Campus housing available (% using): coed dorms (60%), women's dorms (12%), apartment for single students (26%), special housing for international students, other housing options (2%). Students who live in college-owned, operated, or affiliated housing: 82%. **Student employment:** During the 2009-2010 academic year, 46% of undergraduates worked on campus. Average per-year earnings: $719. **Clubs and organizations:** Number of student organizations: 80. Activities include: campus ministries, choral groups, concert band, dance, drama/theater, international student organization, jazz band, literary magazine, model UN, music ensembles, musical theater, radio station, student government, student newspaper, symphony orchestra, television station. Number of fraternities: 0; sororities: 0. Average proportion of students who stay on campus on weekends: 75%. **Sports program (2009-2010):** Member of NCAA III. *Men's intercollegiate varsity sports:* baseball, basketball, cross country, football, soccer, tennis, track and field (indoor), track and field (outdoor), volleyball. *Women's intercollegiate varsity sports:* basketball, cross country, field hockey, soccer, softball, swimming, tennis, track and field (indoor), track and field (outdoor), volleyball.

SERVICES AND FACILITIES
Basic services: nonremedial tutoring, placement service, health service, health insurance, other. **Remedial assistance:** study skills. **Counseling services:** minority student, career, personal, academic, older student, psychological, birth control, religious, other. **For learning-disabled students:** School does not offer a structured program with separate admission and additional fees. Services include: untimed tests, extended time for tests, tutors, other. **Library:** Number of titles: 350,000; number of current serial subscriptions: 1,000. **Information technology resources:** Students are required to lease or own a computer. Number of campus computers available to all students: 340. School has a wireless network. Approximate number of users that can be accommodated: 400. Proportion of college-owned housing units wired for high-speed internet access: 100%. **Campus safety:** Security services offered: 24-hour foot-and-vehicle patrols, late-night transport/escort service, 24-hour emergency telephones, lighted pathways/sidewalks, student patrols, controlled dormitory access (key, security card, etc).

TRANSFER AND INTERNATIONAL STUDENTS
Transfer students: May apply for admission for the following academic terms: Fall, Spring. Applicants need a minimum number of credits to apply. For fall 2009: Transfer applications received: 74. Transfer applicants offered admission: 36. Transfer applicants enrolled: 20. **International students:** Number of foreign undergraduates: 98 (7% of student body). Number of countries represented: 32. Minimum TOEFL score required: 550 (paper); 79 (computer). Average TOEFL score: 562 (paper).

Keystone College

- **Address:** 1 College Green, La Plume, PA 18440
- **Website:** http://www.keystone.edu
- **Private**
- **Enrollment:** 1,278 full-time; 363 part-time

KEY STATS

✔ **U.S News College Ranking:** 44, Regional Colleges (North)
✔ **SAT Score (25th/75th percentile):** 770-960
✔ **Tuition:** 2010-2011: $19,020

Selectivity: Least selective	**Room/board:** $8,950
Acceptance rate: 95%	**Average debt:** $24,750
Student/faculty ratio: 10/1	**Proportion who borrowed:** 89%

UNDERGRADUATE STUDENT BODY STATS

2009-2010 enrollment: 1,278 full-time; 363 part-time. Men: 40%; women: 60%. **Ethnic makeup:** African American: 2%; Asian American: 1%; Hispanic: 2%; White: 94%; International: 1%.

ADMISSIONS FACTS AND FIGURES

Phone: (570) 945-8000. **Email:** admissions@keystone.edu. **Website:** http://www.keystone.edu. **Application deadlines for fall 2011:** Regular decision: July 15. Early decision: Not offered. Early action: Not offered. Admission can be deferred. **Application fee:** $30. **To apply online, go to:** http://www.keystone.edu/admissions/applying/. **Admissions requirements/recommendations:** High school units required (recommended): English: 4; Mathematics: 3; Science: 2 (3); Foreign language: 0 (2); Social studies: 2 (2); History: 1 (1); Academic electives: 4 (3). Tests: The college uses SAT or ACT scores in admissions decisions. Either SAT or ACT required. For admission to the fall 2011 entering class, the school will accept: ACT with writing recommended. Campus visit: Recommended. Admissions interview: Recommended. Off-campus interview: Not available. **Factors that count in admissions decisions:** *Academic:* Secondary school record: Very Important. Class rank: Considered. Letters of recommendation: Considered. Standardized test scores: Important. Essay: Considered. *Nonacademic:* Interview: Very Important. Extracurricular activities: Important. Talent/ability: Very Important. Character/personal qualities: Important. Alumni/ae relationship: Considered. Geographical residence: Not Considered. State residency: Not Considered. Religious affiliation/commitment: Not Considered. Minority status: Not Considered. Volunteer work: Important. Work experience: Important. **Other schools with the greatest overlap in applicants:** East Stroudsburg University of Pennsylvania; Marywood University; Pennsylvania State University–University Park; University of Scranton; Wilkes University. **Admissions statistics for the fall 2009 entering class:** Total applicants: 778. Total accepted: 739. Freshmen enrolled: 336; 16% were from out of state. Overall acceptance rate: 95%. **Credentials of fall 2009 freshmen:** 3% ranked in the top 10 percent of their high school class; 11% were in the top 25 percent; 45% were in the top half. (Proportion submitting class standing: 91%.) **Average high school grade point average:** 2.9. **First-year students who submitted SAT scores:** 89%. Scores (25/75 percentile): Critical Reading: 390-480, Math: 380-480, Combined: 770-960. **First-year students submitting ACT scores:** 4%. Scores (25/75 percentile): English: 15-17, Math: 14-19, Composite: 16-18.

ACADEMICS

Year founded: 1868. **Academic calendar:** Semester. **Degrees offered:** certificate, associate, bachelor's, post-bachelor's certificate. **Most popular majors:** 25% business, management, marketing, and related support services; 18% education, 17% security and protective services, 9% communication, journalism, and related programs, 9% parks, recreation, leisure, and fitness studies. **Areas of required coursework:** humanities, computer literacy, mathematics, English (including composition), sciences (biological or physical), social science, other. **Pre-professional programs:** pre-law, pre-dentistry, pre-medicine, pre-veterinary science, pre-pharmacy, other. **Special academic programs:** cooperative (work-study plan) program, cross-registration, distance learning, double major, dual enrollment, English as a Second Language (ESL), honors program, independent study, internships, study abroad, teacher certificate program, weekend college. **Teacher certification offered in:** early childhood, special education, elementary, secondary. **Reserve Officers Training Corps (ROTC):** Army ROTC: Offered at cooperating institution (University of Scranton); Air Force ROTC: Offered at cooperating institution (Wilkes University). **Faculty and instruction (2009-2010):** Total instructional faculty: 71 full-time, 206 part-time (44% men; 56% women; 2% minorities).

Full-time faculty with Ph.D. or other terminal degree: 41%. Student/faculty ratio: 10/1. Classes of fewer than 20 students: 80%; of 20 to 49 students: 20%; of 50 or more students: 0%. **Advanced Placement and International Baccalaureate credit:** AP tests may be used for: Credit and/or placement. Scores accepted: 3. International Baccalaureate exams may be used for: Credit only. **Freshmen returning for sophomore year:** 64%. **Graduation rates:** Six-year: 39%. **Graduate study:** 9% of students pursue further study immediately upon graduation. Fields in which graduates pursue further study: Master of Business Administration (MBA), 20%; medicine, 10%; education, 30%; arts and sciences, 40%.

COSTS AND FINANCIAL AID

Financial aid office: (877) 426-5534. **Expenses (2010-2011):** Tuition and fees 2010-2011: $19,020; room/board: $8,950. Estimated books and supplies: $1,700; transportation: $500; personal expenses: $1,500. **Financial aid:** Priority filing date for institution's financial aid form: May 1; deadline: May 1. In 2009-2010, 93% of undergraduates applied for financial aid. Of those, 86% were determined to have financial need; 35% had their need fully met. Average financial aid package (proportion receiving): $22,554 (93%). Average amount of gift aid, such as scholarships or grants (proportion receiving): $20,719 (86%). Average amount of self-help aid, such as work study or loans (proportion receiving): $3,538 (86%). Average need-based loan (excluding PLUS or other private loans): $6,500. Among students who received need-based aid, the average percentage of need met: 77%. Among students who received aid based on merit, the average award (and the proportion receiving): $11,868 (3%). The average athletic scholarship (and the proportion receiving): $0 (0%). Average amount of debt of borrowers graduating in 2009: $24,750. Proportion who borrowed: 89%.

CAMPUS LIFE AND EXTRACURRICULAR ACTIVITIES

Campus housing available: coed dorms, women's dorms, special housing for disabled students. Students who live in college-owned, operated, or affiliated housing: 23%. **Clubs and organizations:** Number of student organizations: 26. Activities include: campus ministries, choral groups, drama/theater, international student organization, literary magazine, musical theater, radio station, student government, student newspaper, yearbook. Number of fraternities: 0; sororities: 0. Average proportion of students who stay on campus on weekends: 40%. **Sports program (2009-2010):** Member of NCAA III. *Men's intercollegiate varsity sports:* baseball, basketball, cross country, golf, soccer, tennis, track and field (indoor), track and field (outdoor). *Women's intercollegiate varsity sports:* basketball, cross country, field hockey, soccer, softball, tennis, track and field (indoor), track and field (outdoor), volleyball.

SERVICES AND FACILITIES

Basic services: nonremedial tutoring, day care, health service, health insurance. **Remedial assistance:** reading, study skills. **Counseling services:** minority student, career, military, personal, veteran student, academic, older student, psychological, birth control. **For learning-disabled students:** School does not offer a structured program with separate admission and additional fees. Services include: remedial reading, learning center, extended time for tests, tutors, priority seating, other testing accommodations. **Library:** Number of titles: 42,473; number of current serial subscriptions: 168. **Information technology resources:** Students are not required to lease or own a computer. Number of campus computers available to all students: 230. School has a wireless network. Approximate number of users that can be accommodated: 2,000. Proportion of college-owned housing units wired for high-speed internet access: 100%. **Campus safety:** Security services offered: 24-hour foot-and-vehicle patrols, late-night transport/escort service, 24-hour emergency telephones, lighted pathways/sidewalks, controlled dormitory access (key, security card, etc).

TRANSFER AND INTERNATIONAL STUDENTS

Transfer students: May apply for admission for the following academic terms: Fall, Spring, Summer. Applicants need a minimum number of credits to apply. For fall 2009: Transfer applications received: 254. Transfer applicants offered admission: 246. Transfer applicants enrolled: 173. **International students:** Number of foreign undergraduates: 8 (1% of student body). Number of countries represented: 11. Minimum TOEFL score required: 550 (paper); 213 (computer).

King's College

- **Address:** 133 N. River Street, Wilkes-Barre, PA 18711
- **Website:** http://www.kings.edu
- **Private; Religious affiliation:** Catholic
- **Enrollment:** 1,966 full-time; 330 part-time

KEY STATS

✔ **U.S News College Ranking:** 40, Regional Universities (North)
✔ **SAT Score (25th/75th percentile):** 930-1110
✔ **Tuition:** 2010-2011: $26,644

Selectivity: Selective	**Room/board:** $10,068
Acceptance rate: 75%	**Average debt:** $30,843
Student/faculty ratio: 14/1	**Proportion who borrowed:** 84%

UNDERGRADUATE STUDENT BODY STATS

2009-2010 enrollment: 1,966 full-time; 330 part-time. Men: 50%; women: 50%. **Ethnic makeup:** African American: 2%; Asian American: 1%; Hispanic: 4%; White: 92%. **Religious preference:** Protestant: 10%; Unknown: 29%; Catholic: 58%; Other: 3%.

ADMISSIONS FACTS AND FIGURES

Phone: (888) 546-4772. **Email:** admissions@kings.edu. **Website:** http://www.kings.edu. **Application deadlines for fall 2011:** Regular decision: Rolling. Early decision: Not offered. Early action: Not offered. Admission can be deferred. **Application fee:** $30. **To apply online, go to:** http://www.kings.edu/Admissions/applyonline.htm. **Admissions requirements/recommendations:** High school units required (recommended): English: 4 (4); Mathematics: 3 (4); Science: 3 (4); Foreign language: 2 (3); Social studies: 3 (3); History: 1 (1); Academic electives: (1); Total units: 16 (24). Tests: The college uses SAT or ACT scores in admissions decisions. Neither SAT nor ACT required. For admission to the fall 2011 entering class, the school will accept: ACT with writing recommended. Campus visit: Recommended. Admissions interview: Recommended. Off-campus interview: May be arranged. **Factors that count in admissions decisions:** *Academic:* Secondary school record: Very Important. Class rank: Very Important. Letters of recommendation: Considered. Standardized test scores: Important. Essay: Important. *Nonacademic:* Interview: Considered. Extracurricular activities: Considered. Talent/ability: Not Considered. Character/personal qualities: Important. Alumni/ae relationship: Considered. Geographical residence: Not Considered. State residency: Not Considered. Religious affiliation/commitment: Not Considered. Minority status: Not Considered. Volunteer work: Considered. Work experience: Considered. **Other schools with the greatest overlap in applicants:** Bloomsburg University of Pennsylvania; Misericordia University; Pennsylvania State University–University Park; University of Scranton; Wilkes University. **Admissions statistics for the fall 2009 entering class:** Total applicants: 2,172. Total accepted: 1,633. Freshmen enrolled: 496; 34% were from out of state. Overall acceptance rate: 75%. **Credentials of fall 2009 freshmen:** 15% ranked in the top 10 percent of their high school class; 40% were in the top 25 percent; 75% were in the top half. (Proportion submitting class standing: 78%.) **Average high school grade point average:** 3.3. **First-year students who submitted SAT scores:** 84%. Scores (25/75 percentile): Critical Reading: 460-550, Math: 470-560, Combined: 930-1110.

ACADEMICS

Year founded: 1946. **Academic calendar:** Semester. **Degrees offered:** certificate, associate, bachelor's, post-bachelor's certificate, master's. **Most popular majors:** 13% business administration and management, 11% accounting, 11% elementary education and teaching, 6% communication and media studies, 6% criminal justice/safety studies. **Major fields of study:** biological and biomedical sciences; business, management, marketing, and related support services; communication, journalism, and related programs; computer and information sciences and support services; education; English language and literature/letters; foreign languages, literatures, and linguistics; health professions and related clinical sciences; history; mathematics and statistics; multi/interdisciplinary studies; natural resources and conservation; philosophy and religious studies; physical sciences; psychology; security and protective services; social sciences; theology and religious vocations; visual and performing arts. **Areas of required coursework:** arts/fine arts, humanities, computer literacy, mathematics, English (including composition), philosophy, foreign languages, sciences (biological or physical), history, social science, other. **Pre-professional programs:** pre-law, pre-dentistry, pre-medicine, pre-theology, pre-veterinary science, pre-optometry, pre-pharmacy. **Special academic programs:** accelerated program, cross-

registration, distance learning, double major, dual enrollment, English as a Second Language (ESL), exchange student program (domestic), honors program, independent study, internships, student-designed major, study abroad, teacher certificate program, weekend college. **Teacher certification offered in:** early childhood, special education, elementary, middle/junior high, secondary. **Reserve Officers Training Corps (ROTC):** Army ROTC: Offered on campus; Air Force ROTC: Offered at cooperating institution (Wilkes University). **Faculty and instruction (2009-2010):** Total instructional faculty: 124 full-time, 87 part-time (56% men; 44% women; 3% minorities). Full-time faculty with Ph.D. or other terminal degree: 85%. Student/faculty ratio: 14/1. Classes of fewer than 20 students: 53%; of 20 to 49 students: 46%; of 50 or more students: 0%. **Advanced Placement and International Baccalaureate credit:** AP tests may be used for: Placement only. Scores accepted: 3, 4, 5. **Freshmen returning for sophomore year:** 78%. **Graduation rates:** Four-year: 63%; five-year: 68%; six-year: 70%. **Graduate study:** 28% of students pursue further study within one year. Fields in which graduates pursue further study: Master of Business Administration (MBA), 2%; law, 11%; medicine, 9%; dentistry, 1%; education, 1%; arts and sciences, 75%; veterinary medicine, 1%.

COSTS AND FINANCIAL AID

Financial aid office: (570) 208-5868. **Expenses (2010-2011):** Tuition and fees 2010-2011: $26,644; room/board: $10,068. Estimated books and supplies: $1,250; transportation: $900; personal expenses: $1,300. **Financial aid:** Priority filing date for institution's financial aid form: February 15. In 2009-2010, 90% of undergraduates applied for financial aid. Of those, 81% were determined to have financial need; 16% had their need fully met. Average financial aid package (proportion receiving): $18,300 (80%). Average amount of gift aid, such as scholarships or grants (proportion receiving): $14,278 (80%). Average amount of self-help aid, such as work study or loans (proportion receiving): $5,097 (70%). Average need-based loan (excluding PLUS or other private loans): $4,830. Among students who received need-based aid, the average percentage of need met: 69%. Among students who received aid based on merit, the average award (and the proportion receiving): $11,244 (18%). The average athletic scholarship (and the proportion receiving): $0 (0%). Average amount of debt of borrowers graduating in 2009: $30,843. Proportion who borrowed: 84%.

CAMPUS LIFE AND EXTRACURRICULAR ACTIVITIES

Campus housing available (% using): women's dorms (25%), men's dorms (33%), apartment for single students (41%), special housing for disabled students (1%). Students who live in college-owned, operated, or affiliated housing: 52%. **Student employment:** During the 2009-2010 academic year, 20% of undergraduates worked on campus. Average per-year earnings: $1,200. **Clubs and organizations:** Number of student organizations: 50. Activities include: campus ministries, choral groups, dance, drama/theater, literary magazine, music ensembles, musical theater, pep band, radio station, student government, student newspaper, student film society, yearbook. Average proportion of students who stay on campus on weekends: 75%. **Sports program (2009-2010):** Member of NCAA III. *Men's intercollegiate varsity sports:* baseball, basketball, cross country, football, golf, lacrosse, soccer, swimming, tennis, wrestling. *Women's intercollegiate varsity sports:* basketball, cross country, field hockey, lacrosse, soccer, softball, swimming, tennis, volleyball.

SERVICES AND FACILITIES

Basic services: nonremedial tutoring, women's center, placement service, day care, health service, health insurance. **Remedial assistance:** reading, math, writing, study skills. **Counseling services:** minority student, career, military, personal, academic, older student, psychological, religious. **For learning-disabled students:** School does not offer a structured program with separate admission and additional fees. Total undergraduates in learning-disabled program or receiving services: 133. Services include: remedial math, remedial English, reading machines, tape recorders, untimed tests, note-taking services, oral tests, learning center, extended time for tests, tutors, priority registration, priority seating, exams on tape or computer, other testing accommodations. **Library:** Number of titles: 180,042; number of current serial subscriptions: 490. **Information technology resources:** Students are not required to lease or own a computer. Number of campus computers available to all students: 470. School has a wireless network. Proportion of college-owned housing units wired for high-speed internet access: 100%. **Campus safety:** Security services offered: 24-hour foot-and-vehicle patrols, late-night transport/escort service, 24-hour emergency telephones, lighted pathways/sidewalks, controlled dormitory access (key, security card, etc).

TRANSFER AND INTERNATIONAL STUDENTS

Transfer students: May apply for admission for the following academic terms: Fall, Spring, Summer. Applicants need a minimum number of credits to apply. For fall 2009: Transfer applications received: 255. Transfer applicants offered admission: 147. Transfer applicants enrolled: 86. **International students:** Number of foreign undergraduates: 6. Number of countries represented: 6. Minimum TOEFL score required: 530 (paper); 197 (computer). Average TOEFL score: 550 (paper).

Kutztown University of Pennsylvania

- **Address:** 15200 Kutztown Road, Kutztown, PA 19530-0730
- **Website:** http://www.kutztown.edu
- **Public**
- **Enrollment:** 8,734 full-time; 880 part-time

KEY STATS
✔ **U.S News College Ranking:** 117, Regional Universities (North)
✔ **SAT Score (25th/75th percentile):** 870-1060
✔ **Tuition:** 2009-2010: $7,397 in state, $15,729 out of state

Selectivity: Less selective	**Room/board:** $7,698
Acceptance rate: 66%	**Average debt:** $20,707
Student/faculty ratio: 19/1	**Proportion who borrowed:** 86%

UNDERGRADUATE STUDENT BODY STATS

2009-2010 enrollment: 8,734 full-time; 880 part-time. Men: 42%; women: 58%. **Ethnic makeup:** African American: 6%; Asian American: 1%; Hispanic: 5%; White: 87%; International: 1%.

ADMISSIONS FACTS AND FIGURES

Phone: (610) 683-4060. **Email:** admission@kutztown.edu. **Website:** http://www.kutztown.edu. **Application deadlines for fall 2011:** Regular decision: Rolling. Early decision: Not offered. Early action: Not offered. Admission can be deferred. **Application fee:** $35. **To apply online, go to:** http://www.kutztown.edu/admissions/apply_online.shtml. **Admissions requirements/recommendations:** High school units required (recommended): English: (4); Mathematics: (4); Science: (4); Foreign language: (2); Social studies: (4); Total units: (18). Tests: The college uses SAT or ACT scores in admissions decisions. Either SAT or ACT required. For admission to the fall 2011 entering class, the school will accept: ACT with or without writing accepted. Campus visit: Recommended. Admissions interview: Recommended. Off-campus interview: Not available. **Factors that count in admissions decisions:** *Academic:* Secondary school record: Very Important. Class rank: Very Important. Letters of recommendation: Considered. Standardized test scores: Very Important. Essay: Not Considered. *Nonacademic:* Interview: Considered. Extracurricular activities: Considered. Talent/ability: Considered. Character/personal qualities: Considered. Alumni/ae relationship: Not Considered. Geographical residence: Considered. State residency: Considered. Religious affiliation/commitment: Not Considered. Minority status: Considered. Volunteer work: Considered. Work experience: Considered. **Other schools with the greatest overlap in applicants:** Bloomsburg University of Pennsylvania; East Stroudsburg University of Pennsylvania; Millersville University of Pennsylvania; Pennsylvania State University–University Park. **Admissions statistics for the fall 2009 entering class:** Total applicants: 9,540. Total accepted: 6,301. Freshmen enrolled: 1,989; 14% were from out of state. Overall acceptance rate: 66%. **Size of waiting list:** 0 applicants; enrolled from waiting list: 0. **Credentials of fall 2009 freshmen:** 6% ranked in the top 10 percent of their high school class; 22% were in the top 25 percent; 63% were in the top half. (Proportion submitting class standing: 76%.) **Average high school grade point average:** 3.0. **First-year students who submitted SAT scores:** 98%. Scores (25/75 percentile): Critical Reading: 440-530, Math: 430-530, Combined: 870-1060. **First-year students submitting ACT scores:** 9%. Scores (25/75 percentile): English: 16-22, Math: 17-22, Composite: 17-22.

ACADEMICS

Year founded: 1866. **Academic calendar:** Semester. **Degrees offered:** bachelor's, post-bachelor's certificate, master's. **Most popular majors:** 10% psychology, 7% elementary education and teaching, 7% human resources management/personnel administration, 6% marketing/marketing management, 5% criminal justice/safety studies. **Major fields of study:** biological and biomedical sciences; business, management, marketing, and related support services; communication, journalism, and related programs; com-

puter and information sciences and support services; education; English language and literature/letters; foreign languages, literatures, and linguistics; health professions and related clinical sciences; history; liberal arts and sciences studies, and humanities; library science; mathematics and statistics; multi/interdisciplinary studies; natural resources and conservation; parks, recreation, leisure, and fitness studies; philosophy and religious studies; physical sciences; psychology; public administration and social service professions; security and protective services; social sciences; visual and performing arts. **Areas of required coursework:** humanities, mathematics, English (including composition), sciences (biological or physical), social science, other. **Pre-professional programs:** pre-law, pre-dentistry, pre-medicine, pre-veterinary science, pre-optometry. **Special academic programs:** cross-registration, distance learning, double major, dual enrollment, honors program, independent study, internships, liberal arts/career combination, student-designed major, study abroad, teacher certificate program. **Teacher certification offered in:** early childhood, special education, elementary, middle/junior high, secondary. **Reserve Officers Training Corps (ROTC):** Army ROTC: Offered at cooperating institution (Lehigh University). **Faculty and instruction (2009-2010):** Total instructional faculty: 461 full-time, 43 part-time (54% men; 46% women; 14% minorities). Full-time faculty with Ph.D. or other terminal degree: 77%. Student/faculty ratio: 19/1. Classes of fewer than 20 students: 27%; of 20 to 49 students: 61%; of 50 or more students: 11%. **Advanced Placement and International Baccalaureate credit:** AP tests may be used for: Credit only. Scores accepted: 3, 4, 5. **Freshmen returning for sophomore year:** 78%. **Graduation rates:** Four-year: 30%; five-year: 48%; six-year: 53%. **Graduate study:** Fields in which graduates pursue further study: Master of Business Administration (MBA), 6%; law, 2%; medicine, 2%; education, 54%; arts and sciences, 14%.

COSTS AND FINANCIAL AID

Financial aid office: (610) 683-4077. **Expenses (2009-2010):** Tuition and fees 2009-2010: $7,397 in state, $15,729 out of state; room/board: $7,698. Estimated books and supplies: $1,100 personal expenses: $2,600. **Financial aid:** Priority filing date for institution's financial aid form: March 1. In 2009-2010, 83% of undergraduates applied for financial aid. Of those, 59% were determined to have financial need; 83% had their need fully met. Average financial aid package (proportion receiving): $7,379 (57%). Average amount of gift aid, such as scholarships or grants (proportion receiving): $4,698 (39%). Average amount of self-help aid, such as work study or loans (proportion receiving): $4,097 (50%). Average need-based loan (excluding PLUS or other private loans): $4,048. Among students who received need-based aid, the average percentage of need met: 58%. Among students who received aid based on merit, the average award (and the proportion receiving): $2,071 (4%). The average athletic scholarship (and the proportion receiving): $1,840 (2%). Average amount of debt of borrowers graduating in 2009: $20,707. Proportion who borrowed: 86%.

CAMPUS LIFE AND EXTRACURRICULAR ACTIVITIES

Campus housing available: coed dorms, women's dorms, apartment for single students, cooperative housing, other housing options. Students who live in college-owned, operated, or affiliated housing: 48%. **Student employment:** During the 2009-2010 academic year, 15% of undergraduates worked on campus. Average per-year earnings: $1,700. **Clubs and organizations:** Number of student organizations: 242. Activities include: campus ministries, choral groups, concert band, dance, drama/theater, international student organization, jazz band, literary magazine, marching band, model UN, music ensembles, musical theater, radio station, student government, student newspaper, student film society, symphony orchestra, television station, yearbook. Number of fraternities: 9; sororities: 8. Proportion of men in fraternities: 1%; of women in sororities: 2%. Average proportion of students who stay on campus on weekends: 60%. **Sports program (2009-2010):** Member of NCAA II. *Men's intercollegiate varsity sports:* baseball, basketball, cross country, football, tennis, track and field (indoor), track and field (outdoor), wrestling. *Women's intercollegiate varsity sports:* basketball, bowling, cross country, field hockey, golf, lacrosse, soccer, softball, swimming, tennis, track and field (indoor), track and field (outdoor), volleyball.

SERVICES AND FACILITIES

Basic services: nonremedial tutoring, women's center, placement service, day care, health service, health insurance. **Remedial assistance:** reading, math, writing, study skills. **Counseling services:** minority student, career, personal, veteran student, academic, older student, psychological, birth control, religious, other. **For learning-disabled students:** School does not offer a structured program with separate admission and additional fees. Total undergraduates in learning-disabled program or receiving services: 350. Services include: reading machines, tape recorders, note-taking services, oral tests, learning center, readers, extended time for tests, tutors, priority registration, priority seating, substitution of courses, texts on tape, typist/scribe, exams on tape or computer, other testing accommodations. **Library:** Number of titles: 542,386; number of current serial subscriptions: 47,361. **Information technology resources:** Students are not required to lease or own a computer. Number of campus computers available to all students: 1,400. School has a wireless network. Proportion of college-owned housing units wired for high-speed internet access: 100%. **Campus safety:** Security services offered: 24-hour foot-and-vehicle patrols, late-night transport/escort service, 24-hour emergency telephones, lighted pathways/sidewalks, controlled dormitory access (key, security card, etc).

TRANSFER AND INTERNATIONAL STUDENTS

Transfer students: May apply for admission for the following academic terms: Fall, Spring, Summer. Applicants need a minimum number of credits to apply. For fall 2009: Transfer applications received: 1,704. Transfer applicants offered admission: 1,122. Transfer applicants enrolled: 785. **International students:** Number of foreign undergraduates: 62 (1% of student body). Number of countries represented: 25. Minimum TOEFL score required: 550 (paper); 79 (computer).

Lafayette College

■ **Address:** 118 Markle Hall, Easton, PA 18042
■ **Website:** http://www.lafayette.edu
■ **Private; Religious affiliation:** Presbyterian
■ **Enrollment:** 2,365 full-time; 41 part-time

KEY STATS

✔ **U.S News College Ranking:** 38, National Liberal Arts Colleges
✔ **SAT Score (25th/75th percentile):** 1170-1380
✔ **Tuition:** 2009-2010: $38,490
   Selectivity: More selective **Room/board:** $11,799
   Acceptance rate: 42% **Average debt:** $20,745
   Student/faculty ratio: 11/1 **Proportion who borrowed:** 47%

UNDERGRADUATE STUDENT BODY STATS

2009-2010 enrollment: 2,365 full-time; 41 part-time. Men: 53%; women: 47%. **Ethnic makeup:** African American: 5%; Asian American: 4%; Hispanic: 5%; White: 78%; International: 7%.

ADMISSIONS FACTS AND FIGURES

Phone: (610) 330-5100. **Email:** admissions@lafayette.edu. **Website:** http://www.lafayette.edu. **Application deadlines for fall 2011:** Regular decision: January 1; decision sent by April 1. Early decision: Send application by: February 15; Decision sent by: N/A. Early action: Not offered. Admission can be deferred. **Application fee:** $60. **To apply online, go to:** http://www.lafayette.edu/admissions/application/download.html. **Admissions requirements/recommendations:** High school units required (recommended): English: (4); Mathematics: (3); Science: (2); Foreign language: (2); Academic electives: (5); Total units: (18). Tests: The college uses SAT or ACT scores in admissions decisions. Either SAT or ACT required. For admission to the fall 2011 entering class, the school will accept: ACT with writing required. Campus visit: Recommended. Admissions interview: Recommended. Off-campus interview: May be arranged. **Factors that count in admissions decisions:** *Academic:* Secondary school record: Very Important. Class rank: Important. Letters of recommendation: Important. Standardized test scores: Important. Essay: Important. *Nonacademic:* Interview: Considered. Extracurricular activities: Important. Talent/ability: Important. Character/personal qualities: Important. Alumni/ae relationship: Considered. Geographical residence: Considered. State residency: Not Considered. Religious affiliation/commitment: Not Considered. Minority status: Considered. Volunteer work: Considered. Work experience: Considered. **Other schools with the greatest overlap in applicants:** Bucknell University; Colgate University; Lehigh University; University of Pennsylvania; Villanova University. **Admissions statistics for the fall 2009 entering class:** Total applicants: 5,635. Total accepted: 2,387. Freshmen enrolled: 616; 79% were from out of state. Accepted through early-decision or early-action plans: 45%. Overall acceptance rate: 42%. Early-decision acceptance rate: 62%. Non-early acceptance rate: 41%. **Size of waiting list:** 1449 applicants; enrolled from waiting list: 79. **Credentials of fall 2009 freshmen:** 59% ranked in the top 10 percent of their high school class; 87% were in the top 25 percent; 99% were in the top half. (Proportion submitting class standing:

50%.) **Average high school grade point average:** 3.5. **First-year students who submitted SAT scores:** 90%. Scores (25/75 percentile): Critical Reading: 570-670, Math: 600-710, Combined: 1170-1380. **First-year students submitting ACT scores:** 33%. Scores (25/75 percentile): English: N/A, Math: N/A, Composite: 26-30.

ACADEMICS

Year founded: 1826. **Academic calendar:** Semester. **Degrees offered:** bachelor's. **Most popular majors:** 35% social sciences, 16% engineering, 9% psychology, 7% English language and literature/letters, 6% biological and biomedical sciences. **Major fields of study:** area, ethnic, cultural, and gender studies; biological and biomedical sciences; computer and information sciences and support services; engineering; English language and literature/letters; foreign languages, literatures, and linguistics; history; mathematics and statistics; multi/interdisciplinary studies; philosophy and religious studies; physical sciences; psychology; social sciences; visual and performing arts. **Areas of required coursework:** humanities, mathematics, English (including composition), sciences (biological or physical), social science. **Pre-professional programs:** pre-law, pre-dentistry, pre-medicine, pre-veterinary science, pre-optometry, pre-pharmacy. **Special academic programs:** cross-registration, double major, dual enrollment, exchange student program (domestic), honors program, independent study, internships, student-designed major, study abroad, other. **Cooperative education programs:** health professions. **Reserve Officers Training Corps (ROTC):** Army ROTC: Offered at cooperating institution (Lehigh University). **Faculty and instruction (2009-2010):** Total instructional faculty: 208 full-time, 48 part-time (65% men; 35% women; 12% minorities). Full-time faculty with Ph.D. or other terminal degree: 100%. Student/faculty ratio: 11/1. Classes of fewer than 20 students: 57%; of 20 to 49 students: 40%; of 50 or more students: 3%. **Freshmen returning for sophomore year:** 94%. **Graduation rates:** Four-year: 86%; five-year: 89%; six-year: 90%. **Graduate study:** 27% of students pursue further study immediately upon graduation. Fields in which graduates pursue further study: Master of Business Administration (MBA), 4%; law, 20%; medicine, 9%; dentistry, 2%; engineering, 11%; education, 9%; arts and sciences, 35%; veterinary medicine, 1%.

COSTS AND FINANCIAL AID

Financial aid office: (610) 330-5055. **Expenses (2009-2010):** Tuition and fees 2009-2010: $38,490; room/board: $11,799. Estimated books and supplies: $1,000; transportation: $100; personal expenses: $900. **Financial aid:** Priority filing date for institution's financial aid form: February 1; deadline: March 15. In 2009-2010, 60% of undergraduates applied for financial aid. Of those, 46% were determined to have financial need; 83% had their need fully met. Average financial aid package (proportion receiving): $34,061 (46%). Average amount of gift aid, such as scholarships or grants (proportion receiving): $28,697 (45%). Average amount of self-help aid, such as work study or loans (proportion receiving): $4,872 (38%). Average need-based loan (excluding PLUS or other private loans): $4,090. Among students who received need-based aid, the average percentage of need met: 98%. Among students who received aid based on merit, the average award (and the proportion receiving): $17,090 (7%). The average athletic scholarship (and the proportion receiving): $34,957 (2%). Average amount of debt of borrowers graduating in 2009: $20,745. Proportion who borrowed: 47%.

CAMPUS LIFE AND EXTRACURRICULAR ACTIVITIES

Campus housing available: coed dorms, women's dorms, men's dorms, sorority housing, fraternity housing, apartment for single students, special housing for disabled students. Students who live in college-owned, operated, or affiliated housing: 94%. **Student employment:** During the 2009-2010 academic year, 8% of undergraduates worked on campus. **Clubs and organizations:** Number of student organizations: 175. Activities include: choral groups, concert band, dance, drama/theater, international student organization, jazz band, literary magazine, music ensembles, musical theater, pep band, radio station, student government, student newspaper, student film society, symphony orchestra, yearbook. Number of fraternities: 5; sororities: 6. Proportion of men in fraternities: 11%; of women in sororities: 18%. **Sports program (2009-2010):** Member of NCAA I. *Men's intercollegiate varsity sports:* baseball, basketball, cross country, fencing, football, golf, lacrosse, soccer, swimming, tennis, track and field (indoor), track and field (outdoor). *Women's intercollegiate varsity sports:* basketball, cross country, fencing, field hockey, lacrosse, soccer, softball, swimming, tennis, track and field (indoor), track and field (outdoor), volleyball.

SERVICES AND FACILITIES

For learning-disabled students: School does not offer a structured program with separate admission and additional fees. Total undergraduates in learning-disabled program or receiving services: 116. Services include: reading machines, tape recorders, note-taking services, oral tests, learning center, readers, extended time for tests, tutors, priority registration, priority seating, proofreading services, texts on tape, typist/scribe, exams on tape or computer, other testing accommodations. **Information technology resources:** Students are not required to lease or own a computer. Number of campus computers available to all students: 600. School has a wireless network. Proportion of college-owned housing units wired for high-speed internet access: 100%.

TRANSFER AND INTERNATIONAL STUDENTS

Transfer students: May apply for admission for the following academic terms: Fall, Spring. Applicants need a minimum number of credits to apply. For fall 2009: Transfer applications received: 125. Transfer applicants offered admission: 43. Transfer applicants enrolled: 21. **International students:** Number of foreign undergraduates: 159 (7% of student body). Minimum TOEFL score required: 550 (paper); 80 (computer).

La Roche College

- **Address:** 9000 Babcock Boulevard, Pittsburgh, PA 15237
- **Website:** http://www.laroche.edu
- **Private; Religious affiliation:** Roman Catholic
- **Enrollment:** 984 full-time; 246 part-time

KEY STATS

✔ **U.S News College Ranking:** second tier, Regional Universities (North)
✔ **SAT Score (25th/75th percentile):** 770-1000
✔ **Tuition:** 2010-2011: $22,270

Selectivity: Less selective	**Room/board:** $8,916
Acceptance rate: 68%	**Average debt:** $69,494
Student/faculty ratio: 12/1	**Proportion who borrowed:** 78%

UNDERGRADUATE STUDENT BODY STATS

2009-2010 enrollment: 984 full-time; 246 part-time. Men: 36%; women: 64%. **Ethnic makeup:** African American: 6%; Asian American: 1%; Hispanic: 1%; White: 82%; International: 11%. **Religious preference:** Protestant: 17%; Jewish: 1%; Muslim: 1%; Hindu: 1%; Buddhist: 1%; Unknown: 48%; Roman Catholic: 30%; Other: 1%.

ADMISSIONS FACTS AND FIGURES

Phone: (800) 838-4572. **Email:** admissions@laroche.edu. **Website:** http://www.laroche.edu. **Application deadlines for fall 2011:** Regular decision: Rolling. Early decision: Not offered. Early action: Not offered. Admission can be deferred. **Application fee:** $50. **To apply online, go to:** http://apply.laroche.edu/. **Admissions requirements/recommendations:** High school units required (recommended): English: 4 (4); Mathematics: 3 (3); Science: 3 (3); Foreign language: 0 (2); Social studies: 3 (3); History: 3 (3); Total units: 16 (18). Tests: The college uses SAT or ACT scores in admissions decisions. Either SAT or ACT required. For admission to the fall 2011 entering class, the school will accept: ACT with or without writing accepted. Campus visit: Recommended. Admissions interview: Recommended. Off-campus interview: May be arranged. **Factors that count in admissions decisions:** *Academic:* Secondary school record: Very Important. Class rank: Considered. Letters of recommendation: Important. Standardized test scores: Very Important. Essay: Important. *Nonacademic:* Interview: Considered. Extracurricular activities: Considered. Talent/ability: Important. Character/personal qualities: Considered. Alumni/ae relationship: Considered. Geographical residence: Considered. State residency: Not Considered. Religious affiliation/commitment: Not Considered. Minority status: Not Considered. Volunteer work: Considered. Work experience: Considered. **Other schools with the greatest overlap in applicants:** Duquesne University; Indiana University of Pennsylvania; Robert Morris University; Slippery Rock University of Pennsylvania; University of Pittsburgh. **Admissions statistics for the fall 2009 entering class:** Total applicants: 859. Total accepted: 580. Freshmen enrolled: 193; 11% were from out of state. Overall acceptance rate: 68%. **Credentials of fall 2009 freshmen:** 3% ranked in the top 10 percent of their high school class; 21% were in the top 25 percent; 53% were in the top half. (Proportion submitting class standing: 50%.) **Average high school grade point average:** 3.0. **First-year students who submitted SAT scores:** 71%. Scores (25/75 percentile): Critical Reading: 380-500, Math: 390-500, Combined: 770-1000. **First-year students submitting**

ACT scores: 14%. Scores (25/75 percentile): English: 16-22, Math: 14-23, Composite: 17-22.

ACADEMICS

Year founded: 1963. **Academic calendar:** Semester. **Degrees offered:** certificate, associate, terminal-associate, bachelor's, post-bachelor's certificate, master's. **Most popular majors:** 10% interior architecture, 9% management science, 9% psychology, 8% design and visual communications, 7% marketing/marketing management. **Major fields of study:** architecture and related services; biological and biomedical sciences; business, management, marketing, and related support services; communication, journalism, and related programs; computer and information sciences and support services; education; English language and literature/letters; health professions and related clinical sciences; history; liberal arts and sciences studies, and humanities; mathematics and statistics; philosophy and religious studies; physical sciences; psychology; public administration and social service professions; security and protective services; social sciences; theology and religious vocations; visual and performing arts. **Areas of required coursework:** arts/fine arts, humanities, computer literacy, mathematics, English (including composition), philosophy, foreign languages, sciences (biological or physical), history, social science. **Special academic programs (% participation):** accelerated program (8%), cross-registration (2%), distance learning (60%), double major (17%), English as a Second Language (ESL) (4%), honors program (0%), independent study (33%), internships (31%), student-designed major (0%), study abroad (3%). **Teacher certification offered in:** special education, elementary, secondary. **Reserve Officers Training Corps (ROTC):** Army ROTC: Offered at cooperating institution (University of Pittsburgh); Air Force ROTC: Offered at cooperating institution (Duquesne University). **Faculty and instruction (2009-2010):** Total instructional faculty: 63 full-time, 110 part-time (47% men; 53% women; 3% minorities). Full-time faculty with Ph.D. or other terminal degree: 75%. Student/faculty ratio: 12/1. Classes of fewer than 20 students: 75%; of 20 to 49 students: 25%; of 50 or more students: 0%. **Advanced Placement and International Baccalaureate credit:** AP tests may be used for: Credit only. Scores accepted: 4. International Baccalaureate exams may be used for: Credit only. **Freshmen returning for sophomore year:** 65%. **Graduation rates:** Four-year: 34%; five-year: 57%; six-year: 63%. **Graduate study:** 6% of students pursue further study within one year.

COSTS AND FINANCIAL AID

Financial aid office: (412) 536-1120. **Expenses (2010-2011):** Tuition and fees 2010-2011: $22,270; room/board: $8,916. Estimated books and supplies: $1,200; transportation: $600; personal expenses: $1,512. **Financial aid:** Priority filing date for institution's financial aid form: May 1. In 2009-2010, 83% of undergraduates applied for financial aid. Of those, 75% were determined to have financial need; 49% had their need fully met. Average financial aid package (proportion receiving): $21,212 (74%). Average amount of gift aid, such as scholarships or grants (proportion receiving): $2,292 (55%). Average amount of self-help aid, such as work study or loans (proportion receiving): $2,382 (65%). Average need-based loan (excluding PLUS or other private loans): $2,596. Among students who received need-based aid, the average percentage of need met: 90%. Among students who received aid based on merit, the average award (and the proportion receiving): $4,803 (7%). The average athletic scholarship (and the proportion receiving): $0 (0%). Average amount of debt of borrowers graduating in 2009: $69,494. Proportion who borrowed: 78%.

CAMPUS LIFE AND EXTRACURRICULAR ACTIVITIES

Campus housing available (% using): coed dorms (100%). Students who live in college-owned, operated, or affiliated housing: 37%. **Clubs and organizations:** Number of student organizations: 47. Activities include: campus ministries, choral groups, dance, drama/theater, international student organization, literary magazine, musical theater, radio station, student government, student newspaper. Number of fraternities: 0; sororities: 0. Average proportion of students who stay on campus on weekends: 35%. **Sports program (2009-2010):** Member of NCAA III. *Men's intercollegiate varsity sports:* baseball, basketball, cross country, golf, lacrosse, soccer. *Women's intercollegiate varsity sports:* basketball, cross country, soccer, softball, tennis, volleyball.

SERVICES AND FACILITIES

Basic services: nonremedial tutoring, placement service, health service, health insurance. **Remedial assistance:** reading, math, writing, study skills. **Counseling services:** minority student, career, military, personal, veteran student, academic, psychological, religious. **For learning-disabled students:** School does not offer a structured program with separate admission and additional fees. Services include: remedial math, remedial English, remedial reading, tape recorders, videotaped classes, untimed tests, note-taking services, oral tests, learning center, readers, extended time for tests, tutors, priority registration, other testing accommodations. **Library:** Number of titles: 127,509; number of current serial subscriptions: 582. **Information technology resources:** Students are not required to lease or own a computer. Number of campus computers available to all students: 165. School has a wireless network. Approximate number of users that can be accommodated: 200. Proportion of college-owned housing units wired for high-speed internet access: 100%. **Campus safety:** Security services offered: 24-hour foot-and-vehicle patrols, late-night transport/escort service, 24-hour emergency telephones, lighted pathways/sidewalks, student patrols, controlled dormitory access (key, security card, etc.).

TRANSFER AND INTERNATIONAL STUDENTS

Transfer students: May apply for admission for the following academic terms: Fall, Spring, Summer. Applicants need a minimum number of credits to apply. For fall 2009: Transfer applications received: 395. Transfer applicants offered admission: 301. Transfer applicants enrolled: 171. **International students:** Number of foreign undergraduates: 126 (11% of student body). Number of countries represented: 29. Minimum TOEFL score required: 550 (paper); 80 (computer).

La Salle University

- **Address:** 1900 W. Olney Avenue, Philadelphia, PA 19141-1199
- **Website:** http://www.lasalle.edu
- **Private; Religious affiliation:** Roman Catholic
- **Enrollment:** 3,320 full-time; 1,127 part-time

KEY STATS

✔ **U.S News College Ranking:** 19, Regional Universities (North)
✔ **SAT Score (25th/75th percentile):** 920-1140
✔ **Tuition:** 2010-2011: $33,700

Selectivity: Selective	**Room/board:** $11,540
Acceptance rate: 66%	**Average debt:** $44,645
Student/faculty ratio: 14/1	**Proportion who borrowed:** 84%

UNDERGRADUATE STUDENT BODY STATS

2009-2010 enrollment: 3,320 full-time; 1,127 part-time. Men: 36%; women: 64%. **Ethnic makeup:** African American: 17%; Asian American: 4%; Hispanic: 9%; White: 68%; International: 1%. **Religious preference:** Protestant: 1%; Jewish: 1%; Muslim: 1%; Hindu: 1%; Buddhist: 1%; Roman Catholic: 78%; Christian: 14%; Other: 3%.

ADMISSIONS FACTS AND FIGURES

Phone: (215) 951-1500. **Email:** admiss@lasalle.edu. **Website:** http://www.lasalle.edu. **Application deadlines for fall 2011:** Regular decision: Rolling. Early decision: Not offered. Early action: Send application by: November 15; Decision sent by: December 15. Admission can be deferred. **Application fee:** $35. **To apply online, go to:** http://www.lasalle.edu/admission/#/applynow/. **Admissions requirements/recommendations:** High school units required (recommended): English: 4; Mathematics: 3; Science: 1 (2); Foreign language: 2; Social studies: 0; History: 1 (3); Academic electives: 5; Total units: 16 (5). Tests: The college uses SAT or ACT scores in admissions decisions. Either SAT or ACT required. For admission to the fall 2011 entering class, the school will accept: ACT with or without writing accepted. Campus visit: Recommended. Admissions interview: Recommended. Off-campus interview: Not available. **Factors that count in admissions decisions:** *Academic:* Secondary school record: Important. Class rank: Considered. Letters of recommendation: Important. Standardized test scores: Very Important. Essay: Important. *Nonacademic:* Interview: Considered. Extracurricular activities: Important. Talent/ability: Important. Character/personal qualities: Important. Alumni/ae relationship: Important. Geographical residence: Not Considered. State residency: Not Considered. Religious affiliation/commitment: Not Considered. Minority status: Considered. Volunteer work: Considered. Work experience: Considered. **Other schools with the greatest overlap in applicants:** Drexel University; Pennsylvania State University–University Park; St. Joseph's University; Temple University; Villanova University. **Admissions statistics for the fall 2009 entering class:** Total applicants: 5,596. Total accepted: 3,693. Freshmen enrolled: 1,009; 38% were from out of state. Accepted through early-decision or early-action plans: 38%. Overall acceptance rate: 66%. Non-early acceptance rate: 56%.

Size of waiting list: 0 applicants; enrolled from waiting list: 0. **Credentials of fall 2009 freshmen:** 16% ranked in the top 10 percent of their high school class; 43% were in the top 25 percent; 77% were in the top half. (Proportion submitting class standing: 63%.) **Average high school grade point average:** 3.3. **First-year students who submitted SAT scores:** 88%. Scores (25/75 percentile): Critical Reading: 460-570, Math: 460-570, Combined: 920-1140. **First-year students submitting ACT scores:** 14%. Scores (25/75 percentile): English: N/A, Math: N/A, Composite: 22-26.

ACADEMICS

Year founded: 1863. **Academic calendar:** Semester. **Degrees offered:** certificate, associate, bachelor's, post-bachelor's certificate, master's, post-master's certificate, doctorate. **Most popular majors:** 27% nursing, 9% communication studies/speech communication and rhetoric, 7% marketing, 7% psychology, 6% accounting. **Major fields of study:** area, ethnic, cultural, and gender studies; biological and biomedical sciences; business, management, marketing, and related support services; communication, journalism, and related programs; computer and information sciences and support services; education; English language and literature/letters; foreign languages, literatures, and linguistics; health professions and related clinical sciences; history; mathematics and statistics; multi/interdisciplinary studies; natural resources and conservation; philosophy and religious studies; physical sciences; psychology; public administration and social service professions; security and protective services; social sciences; visual and performing arts. **Areas of required coursework:** arts/fine arts, computer literacy, mathematics, English (including composition), philosophy, foreign languages, sciences (biological or physical), history, social science, other. **Pre-professional programs:** pre-law, pre-dentistry, pre-medicine, pre-veterinary science. **Special academic programs (% participation):** accelerated program (5%), cooperative (work-study plan) program (4%), double major (24%), dual enrollment (1%), English as a Second Language (ESL) (.5%), honors program (8%), independent study (15%), internships (31%), study abroad (6%), teacher certificate program (7%). **Teacher certification offered in:** special education, elementary, secondary. **Cooperative education programs:** business, computer science, education, health professions, social/behavioral science. **Reserve Officers Training Corps (ROTC):** Army ROTC: Offered at cooperating institution (Drexel University); Air Force ROTC: Offered at cooperating institution (St. Joseph's University). **Faculty and instruction (2009-2010):** Total instructional faculty: 231 full-time, 111 part-time (49% men; 51% women; 9% minorities). Full-time faculty with Ph.D. or other terminal degree: 79%. Student/faculty ratio: 14/1. Classes of fewer than 20 students: 47%; of 20 to 49 students: 53%; of 50 or more students: 0%. **Advanced Placement and International Baccalaureate credit:** AP tests may be used for: Placement only. Scores accepted: 3, 4, 5. International Baccalaureate exams may be used for: Credit only. Freshmen returning for sophomore year: 83%. **Graduation rates:** Four-year: 61%; five-year: 72%; six-year: 72%. **Graduate study:** 13% of students pursue further study within one year. Fields in which graduates pursue further study: Master of Business Administration (MBA), 10%; law, 15%; medicine, 11%; dentistry, 1%; theology (or the seminary), 1%; education, 9%; arts and sciences, 41%.

COSTS AND FINANCIAL AID

Financial aid office: (215) 951-1070. **Expenses (2010-2011):** Tuition and fees 2010-2011: $33,700; room/board: $11,540. Estimated books and supplies: $500 personal expenses: $1,119. **Financial aid:** Priority filing date for institution's financial aid form: February 15; deadline: March 15. In 2009-2010, 87% of undergraduates applied for financial aid. Of those, 79% were determined to have financial need; 18% had their need fully met. Average financial aid package (proportion receiving): $22,923 (78%). Average amount of gift aid, such as scholarships or grants (proportion receiving): $18,743 (77%). Average amount of self-help aid, such as work study or loans (proportion receiving): $4,919 (63%). Average need-based loan (excluding PLUS or other private loans): $4,577. Among students who received need-based aid, the average percentage of need met: 76%. Among students who received aid based on merit, the average award (and the proportion receiving): $12,962 (17%). The average athletic scholarship (and the proportion receiving): $16,432 (3%). Average amount of debt of borrowers graduating in 2009: $44,645. Proportion who borrowed: 84%.

CAMPUS LIFE AND EXTRACURRICULAR ACTIVITIES

Campus housing available (% using): coed dorms (96%), special housing for disabled students (1%), other housing options (3%). Students who live in college-owned, operated, or affiliated housing: 59%. **Student employment:** During the 2009-2010 academic year, 13% of undergraduates worked on campus. Average per-year earnings: $2,781. **Clubs and organizations:** Number of student organizations: 121. Activities include: campus ministries, choral groups, dance, drama/theater, jazz band, literary magazine, music ensembles, musical theater, pep band, radio station, student government, student newspaper, student film society, television station, yearbook. Number of fraternities: 7; sororities: 6. Proportion of men in fraternities: 7%; of women in sororities: 10%. Average proportion of students who stay on campus on weekends: 80%. **Sports program (2009-2010):** Member of NCAA I. *Men's intercollegiate varsity sports:* baseball, basketball, cross country, golf, soccer, swimming, tennis, track and field (indoor), track and field (outdoor). *Women's intercollegiate varsity sports:* basketball, crew (heavyweight), cross country, field hockey, lacrosse, crew (lightweight), soccer, softball, swimming, tennis, track and field (indoor), track and field (outdoor), volleyball.

SERVICES AND FACILITIES

Basic services: nonremedial tutoring, women's center, placement service, health service, health insurance. **Remedial assistance:** writing, study skills. **Counseling services:** minority student, career, military, personal, veteran student, academic, older student, psychological, religious, other. **For learning-disabled students:** School does not offer a structured program with separate admission and additional fees. Services include: tape recorders, untimed tests, note-taking services, extended time for tests, tutors. **Library:** Number of titles: 405,000; number of current serial subscriptions: 1,450. **Information technology resources:** Students are required to lease or own a computer. Number of campus computers available to all students: 750. School has a wireless network. Approximate number of users that can be accommodated: 500. Proportion of college-owned housing units wired for high-speed internet access: 100%. **Campus safety:** Security services offered: 24-hour foot-and-vehicle patrols, late-night transport/escort service, 24-hour emergency telephones, lighted pathways/sidewalks, controlled dormitory access (key, security card, etc).

TRANSFER AND INTERNATIONAL STUDENTS

Transfer students: May apply for admission for the following academic terms: Fall, Spring. Applicants do not need a minimum number of credits to apply. For fall 2009: Transfer applications received: 976. Transfer applicants offered admission: 331. Transfer applicants enrolled: 113. **International students:** Number of foreign undergraduates: 32 (1% of student body). Number of countries represented: 14. Minimum TOEFL score required: 500 (paper); 175 (computer). Average TOEFL score: 540 (paper).

Lebanon Valley College

- **Address:** 101 N. College Avenue, Annville, PA 17003
- **Website:** http://www.lvc.edu
- **Private; Religious affiliation:** Methodist
- **Enrollment:** 1,582 full-time; 165 part-time

KEY STATS

✔ **U.S News College Ranking:** 7, Regional Colleges (North)
✔ **SAT Score (25th/75th percentile):** 980-1210
✔ **Tuition:** 2010-2011: $31,620

Selectivity: Selective	**Room/board:** $8,365
Acceptance rate: 81%	**Average debt:** $33,348
Student/faculty ratio: 13/1	**Proportion who borrowed:** 82%

UNDERGRADUATE STUDENT BODY STATS

2009-2010 enrollment: 1,582 full-time; 165 part-time. Men: 44%; women: 56%. **Ethnic makeup:** African American: 2%; Asian American: 2%; Hispanic: 2%; White: 94%.

ADMISSIONS FACTS AND FIGURES

Phone: (717) 867-6181. **Email:** admission@lvc.edu. **Website:** http://www. lvc.edu. **Application deadlines for fall 2011:** Regular decision: Rolling. Early decision: Not offered. Early action: Not offered. Admission cannot be deferred. **Application fee:** $30. **To apply online, go to:** http://www.lvc.edu/ admission/full-time.aspx. **Admissions requirements/recommendations:** High school units required (recommended): English: 4 (4); Mathematics: 3 (3); Science: 2 (3); Foreign language: 2 (3); Social studies: 1; History: (2); Total units: 16. Tests: The college uses SAT or ACT scores in admissions decisions. Neither SAT nor ACT required. For admission to the fall 2011 entering class, the school will accept: ACT with or without writing accepted. Campus visit: Recommended. Admissions interview: Recommended. Off-campus interview: May be arranged. **Factors that count in admissions**

decisions: *Academic:* Secondary school record: Very Important. Class rank: Very Important. Letters of recommendation: Considered. Standardized test scores: Considered. Essay: Considered. *Nonacademic:* Interview: Important. Extracurricular activities: Important. Talent/ability: Important. Character/ personal qualities: Important. Alumni/ae relationship: Considered. Geographical residence: Considered. State residency: Considered. Religious affiliation/commitment: Not Considered. Minority status: Considered. Volunteer work: Considered. Work experience: Considered. **Other schools with the greatest overlap in applicants:** Elizabethtown College; Millersville University of Pennsylvania; Pennsylvania State University–University Park; Shippensburg University of Pennsylvania; Susquehanna University. **Admissions statistics for the fall 2009 entering class:** Total applicants: 1,698. Total accepted: 1,368. Freshmen enrolled: 378; 20% were from out of state. Overall acceptance rate: 81%. **Credentials of fall 2009 freshmen:** 34% ranked in the top 10 percent of their high school class; 71% were in the top 25 percent; 93% were in the top half. (Proportion submitting class standing: 87%.) **First-year students who submitted SAT scores:** 88%. Scores (25/75 percentile): Critical Reading: 480-590, Math: 500-620, Combined: 980-1210. **First-year students submitting ACT scores:** 13%. Scores (25/75 percentile): English: 19-25, Math: 19-25, Composite: 19-25.

ACADEMICS

Year founded: 1866. **Academic calendar:** Semester. **Degrees offered:** certificate, associate, terminal-associate, bachelor's, post-bachelor's certificate, master's. **Most popular majors:** 17% education, 14% business, management, marketing, and related support services, 11% social sciences, 11% visual and performing arts, 8% health professions and related clinical sciences. **Major fields of study:** area, ethnic, cultural, and gender studies; biological and biomedical sciences; business, management, marketing, and related support services; communication, journalism, and related programs; communications technologies/technicians and support services; computer and information sciences and support services; education; English language and literature/letters; foreign languages, literatures, and linguistics; health professions and related clinical sciences; history; mathematics and statistics; multi/interdisciplinary studies; philosophy and religious studies; physical sciences; psychology; social sciences; visual and performing arts. **Areas of required coursework:** arts/fine arts, humanities, mathematics, English (including composition), philosophy, foreign languages, sciences (biological or physical), history, social science, other. **Pre-professional programs:** pre-law, pre-dentistry, pre-medicine, pre-veterinary science, pre-optometry, pre-pharmacy. **Special academic programs (% participation):** double major (15%), dual enrollment (0%), independent study (13%), internships (31%), liberal arts/career combination, student-designed major (1%), study abroad (18%), teacher certificate program (25%). **Teacher certification offered in:** early childhood, special education, elementary, secondary. **Cooperative education programs:** engineering, health professions, other. **Reserve Officers Training Corps (ROTC):** Army ROTC: Offered at cooperating institution (Millersville University of Pennsylvania). **Faculty and instruction (2009-2010):** Total instructional faculty: 100 full-time, 98 part-time (61% men; 39% women; 4% minorities). Full-time faculty with Ph.D. or other terminal degree: 88%. Student/faculty ratio: 13/1. Classes of fewer than 20 students: 55%; of 20 to 49 students: 43%; of 50 or more students: 2%. **Advanced Placement and International Baccalaureate credit:** AP tests may be used for: Credit only. Scores accepted: 4, 5. International Baccalaureate exams may be used for: Credit only. **Freshmen returning for sophomore year:** 83%. **Graduation rates:** Four-year: 68%; five-year: 75%; six-year: 71%. **Graduate study:** 26% of students pursue further study within one year. Fields in which graduates pursue further study: Master of Business Administration (MBA), 6%; law, 3%; medicine, 1%; engineering, 1%; education, 3%; arts and sciences, 85%.

COSTS AND FINANCIAL AID

Financial aid office: (717) 867-6126. **Expenses (2010-2011):** Tuition and fees 2010-2011: $31,620; room/board: $8,365. Estimated books and supplies: $1,000; transportation: $700; personal expenses: $1,200. **Financial aid:** Priority filing date for institution's financial aid form: March 1. In 2009-2010, 89% of undergraduates applied for financial aid. Of those, 81% were determined to have financial need; 25% had their need fully met. Average financial aid package (proportion receiving): $22,686 (81%). Average amount of gift aid, such as scholarships or grants (proportion receiving): $18,957 (80%). Average amount of self-help aid, such as work study or loans (proportion receiving): $5,915 (69%). Average need-based loan (excluding PLUS or other private loans): $4,705. Among students who received need-based aid, the average percentage of need met: 82%. Among students who received aid based on merit, the average award (and the proportion receiving): $12,717 (15%). The average athletic scholarship (and the proportion receiving): $0 (0%). Average amount of debt of borrowers graduating in 2009: $33,348. Proportion who borrowed: 82%.

CAMPUS LIFE AND EXTRACURRICULAR ACTIVITIES

Campus housing available (% using): coed dorms (67%), women's dorms (6%), apartment for single students (8%), special housing for disabled students (1%), other housing options (18%). Students who live in college-owned, operated, or affiliated housing: 74%. **Student employment:** During the 2009-2010 academic year, 51% of undergraduates worked on campus. Average per-year earnings: $937. **Clubs and organizations:** Number of student organizations: 85. Activities include: campus ministries, choral groups, drama/theater, international student organization, jazz band, literary magazine, marching band, music ensembles, musical theater, radio station, student government, student newspaper, symphony orchestra, yearbook. Number of fraternities: 4; sororities: 4. Proportion of men in fraternities: 9%; of women in sororities: 9%. Average proportion of students who stay on campus on weekends: 60%. **Sports program (2009-2010):** Member of NCAA III. *Men's intercollegiate varsity sports:* baseball, basketball, cross country, football, golf, lacrosse, soccer, swimming, tennis, track and field (indoor), track and field (outdoor). *Women's intercollegiate varsity sports:* basketball, cross country, field hockey, lacrosse, soccer, softball, swimming, tennis, track and field (indoor), track and field (outdoor), volleyball.

SERVICES AND FACILITIES

Basic services: nonremedial tutoring, placement service, health service, health insurance. **Counseling services:** minority student, career, personal, academic, older student, psychological, birth control, religious, other. **For learning-disabled students:** School does not offer a structured program with separate admission and additional fees. Total undergraduates in learning-disabled program or receiving services: 129. Services include: reading machines, tape recorders, videotaped classes, diagnostic testing service, untimed tests, note-taking services, oral tests, learning center, readers, extended time for tests, tutors, early syllabus, priority registration, priority seating, substitution of courses, texts on tape, typist/scribe, exams on tape or computer, other testing accommodations. **Library:** Number of titles: 196,912; number of current serial subscriptions: 26,980. **Information technology resources:** Students are not required to lease or own a computer. Number of campus computers available to all students: 181. School has a wireless network. Approximate number of users that can be accommodated: 2,500. Proportion of college-owned housing units wired for high-speed internet access: 100%. **Campus safety:** Security services offered: 24-hour foot-and-vehicle patrols, late-night transport/escort service, 24-hour emergency telephones, lighted pathways/sidewalks, student patrols, controlled dormitory access (key, security card, etc).

TRANSFER AND INTERNATIONAL STUDENTS

Transfer students: May apply for admission for the following academic terms: Fall, Spring. Applicants need a minimum number of credits to apply. For fall 2009: Transfer applications received: 205. Transfer applicants offered admission: 130. Transfer applicants enrolled: 69. **International students:** Number of foreign undergraduates: 6. Number of countries represented: 2. Minimum TOEFL score required: 550 (paper); 80 (computer).

Lehigh University

- **Address:** 27 Memorial Drive W, Bethlehem, PA 18015
- **Website:** http://www.lehigh.edu
- **Private**
- **Enrollment:** 4,755 full-time; 54 part-time

KEY STATS

✔ **U.S News College Ranking:** 37, National Universities
✔ **SAT Score (25th/75th percentile):** 1220-1340
✔ **Tuition:** 2010-2011: $39,780

Selectivity: Most selective	**Room/board:** $10,520
Acceptance rate: 33%	**Average debt:** $31,123
Student/faculty ratio: 10/1	**Proportion who borrowed:** 54%

UNDERGRADUATE STUDENT BODY STATS

2009-2010 enrollment: 4,755 full-time; 54 part-time. Men: 59%; women: 41%. **Ethnic makeup:** African American: 4%; Asian American: 6%; Hispanic: 6%; White: 80%; International: 4%.

ADMISSIONS FACTS AND FIGURES

Phone: (610) 758-3100. **Email:** admissions@lehigh.edu. **Website:** http://www.lehigh.edu. **Application deadlines for fall 2011:** Regular decision: January 1; decision sent by April 1. Early decision: Send application by: November 15; Decision sent by: December 15. Early action: Not offered. Admission can be deferred. **Application fee:** $70. **To apply online, go to:** http://www4.lehigh.edu/admissions/undergrad/apply. **Admissions requirements/recommendations:** High school units required (recommended): English: 4 (4); Mathematics: 3 (3); Science: 2 (2); Foreign language: 2 (2); Social studies: 2 (2); Academic electives: 3 (3); Total units: 16 (16). Tests: The college uses SAT or ACT scores in admissions decisions. Either SAT or ACT required. For admission to the fall 2011 entering class, the school will accept: ACT with writing required. Campus visit: Recommended. Admissions interview: Neither required nor recommended. Off-campus interview: May be arranged. **Factors that count in admissions decisions:** *Academic:* Secondary school record: Very Important. Class rank: Considered. Letters of recommendation: Very Important. Standardized test scores: Important. Essay: Important. *Nonacademic:* Interview: Not Considered. Extracurricular activities: Important. Talent/ability: Important. Character/personal qualities: Important. Alumni/ae relationship: Considered. Geographical residence: Considered. State residency: Not Considered. Religious affiliation/commitment: Not Considered. Minority status: Considered. Volunteer work: Important. Work experience: Considered. **Other schools with the greatest overlap in applicants:** Boston College; Carnegie Mellon University; Cornell University; Johns Hopkins University; University of Pennsylvania. **Admissions statistics for the fall 2009 entering class:** Total applicants: 11,170. Total accepted: 3,662. Freshmen enrolled: 1,193; 78% were from out of state. Accepted through early-decision or early-action plans: 46%. Overall acceptance rate: 33%. Early-decision acceptance rate: 65%. Non-early acceptance rate: 30%. **Size of waiting list:** 3226 applicants; enrolled from waiting list: 43. **Credentials of fall 2009 freshmen:** 93% ranked in the top 10 percent of their high school class; 99% were in the top 25 percent; 100% were in the top half. (Proportion submitting class standing: 33%.) **First-year students who submitted SAT scores:** 90%. Scores (25/75 percentile): Critical Reading: 590-630, Math: 630-710, Combined: 1220-1340.

ACADEMICS

Year founded: 1865. **Academic calendar:** Semester. **Degrees offered:** bachelor's, post-bachelor's certificate, master's, post-master's certificate, doctorate. **Most popular majors:** 13% finance, 9% accounting, 6% marketing/marketing management, 6% mechanical engineering, 6% psychology. **Major fields of study:** architecture and related services; area, ethnic, cultural, and gender studies; biological and biomedical sciences; business, management, marketing, and related support services; communication, journalism, and related programs; computer and information sciences and support services; engineering; English language and literature/letters; foreign languages, literatures, and linguistics; health professions and related clinical sciences; history; mathematics and statistics; multi/interdisciplinary studies; natural resources and conservation; philosophy and religious studies; physical sciences; psychology; social sciences; visual and performing arts. **Areas of required coursework:** humanities, computer literacy, mathematics, English (including composition), sciences (biological or physical), social science. **Pre-professional programs:** pre-law, pre-dentistry, pre-medicine, pre-optometry. **Special academic programs (% participation):** accelerated program (2.3%), cooperative (work-study plan) program (18%), cross-registration (1%), distance learning (13.4%), double major (12.2%), English as a Second Language (ESL) (2.9%), exchange student program (domestic) (1.3%), honors program (14.3%), independent study (29.1%), internships (12.8%), liberal arts/career combination (1.1%), study abroad (32%). **Cooperative education programs:** education, engineering. **Reserve Officers Training Corps (ROTC):** Army ROTC: Offered on campus. **Faculty and instruction (2009-2010):** Total instructional faculty: 464 full-time, 208 part-time (67% men; 33% women; 13% minorities). Full-time faculty with Ph.D. or other terminal degree: 99%. Student/faculty ratio: 10/1. Classes of fewer than 20 students: 49%; of 20 to 49 students: 41%; of 50 or more students: 10%. **Advanced Placement and International Baccalaureate credit:** AP tests may be used for: Credit and/or placement. Scores accepted: 4, 5. International Baccalaureate exams may be used for: Credit and/or placement. **Freshmen returning for sophomore year:** 94%. **Graduation rates:** Four-year: 76%; five-year: 85%; six-year: 86%. **Graduate study:** 33% of students pursue further study immediately upon graduation. Fields in which graduates pursue further study: Master of Business Administration (MBA), 9%; law, 7%; medicine, 15%; engineering, 28%; education, 8%; arts and sciences, 33%.

COSTS AND FINANCIAL AID

Financial aid office: (610) 758-3181. **Expenses (2010-2011):** Tuition and fees 2010-2011: $39,780; room/board: $10,520. Estimated books and supplies: $1,000; transportation: $0; personal expenses: $1,220. **Financial aid:** In 2009-2010, 59% of undergraduates applied for financial aid. Of those, 45% were determined to have financial need; 69% had their need fully met. Average financial aid package (proportion receiving): $33,008 (45%). Average amount of gift aid, such as scholarships or grants (proportion receiving): $27,718 (44%). Average amount of self-help aid, such as work study or loans (proportion receiving): $5,579 (43%). Average need-based loan (excluding PLUS or other private loans): $4,581. Among students who received need-based aid, the average percentage of need met: 96%. Among students who received aid based on merit, the average award (and the proportion receiving): $10,524 (7%). The average athletic scholarship (and the proportion receiving): $33,861 (1%). Average amount of debt of borrowers graduating in 2009: $31,123. Proportion who borrowed: 54%.

CAMPUS LIFE AND EXTRACURRICULAR ACTIVITIES

Campus housing available (% using): coed dorms (46%), sorority housing (11%), fraternity housing (15%), apartment for single students (24%), special housing for disabled students (1%). Students who live in college-owned, operated, or affiliated housing: 68%. **Student employment:** During the 2009-2010 academic year, 30% of undergraduates worked on campus. Average per-year earnings: $1,230. **Clubs and organizations:** Number of student organizations: 150. Activities include: campus ministries, choral groups, concert band, dance, drama/theater, international student organization, jazz band, literary magazine, marching band, model UN, music ensembles, musical theater, pep band, radio station, student government, student newspaper, student film society, symphony orchestra, yearbook. Number of fraternities: 21; sororities: 9. Proportion of men in fraternities: 38%; of women in sororities: 39%. Average proportion of students who stay on campus on weekends: 85%. **Sports program (2009-2010):** Member of NCAA I. *Men's intercollegiate varsity sports:* baseball, basketball, cross country, football, golf, lacrosse, soccer, swimming, tennis, track and field (indoor), track and field (outdoor), wrestling. *Women's intercollegiate varsity sports:* basketball, crew (heavyweight), cross country, field hockey, golf, lacrosse, crew (lightweight), soccer, softball, swimming, tennis, track and field (indoor), track and field (outdoor), volleyball.

SERVICES AND FACILITIES

Basic services: nonremedial tutoring, women's center, placement service, day care, health service, health insurance, other. **Remedial assistance:** reading, math, writing, study skills. **Counseling services:** minority student, career, military, personal, academic, older student, psychological, birth control, religious. **For learning-disabled students:** School does not offer a structured program with separate admission and additional fees. Total undergraduates in learning-disabled program or receiving services: 165. Services include: reading machines, learning center, extended time for tests, tutors. **Library:** Number of titles: 1,182,975; number of current serial subscriptions: 51,230. **Information technology resources:** Students are not required to lease or own a computer. Number of campus computers available to all students: 588. School has a wireless network. Approximate number of users that can be accommodated: 6,300. Proportion of college-owned housing units wired for high-speed internet access: 100%. **Campus safety:** Security services offered: 24-hour foot-and-vehicle patrols, late-night transport/escort service, 24-hour emergency telephones, lighted pathways/sidewalks, controlled dormitory access (key, security card, etc).

TRANSFER AND INTERNATIONAL STUDENTS

Transfer students: May apply for admission for the following academic terms: Fall, Spring. Applicants need a minimum number of credits to apply. For fall 2009: Transfer applications received: 337. Transfer applicants offered admission: 130. Transfer applicants enrolled: 49. **International students:** Number of foreign undergraduates: 182 (4% of student body). Number of countries represented: 51. Minimum TOEFL score required: 570 (paper); 230 (computer).

Lincoln University

- **Address:** PO Box 179, Lincoln University, PA 19352
- **Website:** http://www.lincoln.edu
- **Public**
- **Enrollment:** 2,001 full-time; 34 part-time

KEY STATS

✔ **U.S News College Ranking:** second tier, Regional Universities (North)
✔ **SAT Score (25th/75th percentile):** 730-890
✔ **Tuition:** 2009-2010: $8,390 in state, $12,390 out of state

Selectivity: Less selective	**Room/board:** $7,900
Acceptance rate: 31%	**Average debt:** $30,818
Student/faculty ratio: 19/1	**Proportion who borrowed:** 89%

UNDERGRADUATE STUDENT BODY STATS

2009-2010 enrollment: 2,001 full-time; 34 part-time. Men: 42%; women: 58%. **Ethnic makeup:** African American: 79%; White: 18%; International: 2%.

ADMISSIONS FACTS AND FIGURES

Phone: (800) 790-0191. **Email:** admiss@lu.lincoln.edu. **Website:** http://www.lincoln.edu. **Application deadlines for fall 2011:** Regular decision: July 1. Early decision: Not offered. Early action: Not offered. Admission can be deferred. **Application fee:** $20. **To apply online, go to:** http://www.lincoln.edu/admissions/application.html#app. **Admissions requirements/recommendations:** High school units required (recommended): English: 4; Mathematics: 3; Science: 3; Social studies: 3; Academic electives: 5; Total units: 21. Tests: The college uses SAT or ACT scores in admissions decisions. Either SAT or ACT required. For admission to the fall 2011 entering class, the school will accept: ACT with or without writing accepted. Campus visit: Recommended. Admissions interview: Recommended. Off-campus interview: Not available. **Factors that count in admissions decisions:** *Academic:* Secondary school record: Very Important. Class rank: Very Important. Letters of recommendation: Important. Standardized test scores: Important. Essay: Considered. *Nonacademic:* Interview: Considered. Extracurricular activities: Considered. Talent/ability: Important. Character/personal qualities: Considered. Alumni/ae relationship: Considered. Geographical residence: Considered. State residency: Considered. Religious affiliation/commitment: Considered. Minority status: Not Considered. Volunteer work: Considered. Work experience: Considered. **Admissions statistics for the fall 2009 entering class:** Total applicants: 7,440. Total accepted: 2,303. Freshmen enrolled: 579; 52% were from out of state. Overall acceptance rate: 31%. **Credentials of fall 2009 freshmen:** 6% ranked in the top 10 percent of their high school class; 19% were in the top 25 percent; 48% were in the top half. (Proportion submitting class standing: 61%.) **Average high school grade point average:** 2.6. **First-year students who submitted SAT scores:** 97%. Scores (25/75 percentile): Critical Reading: 370-450, Math: 360-440, Combined: 730-890. **First-year students submitting ACT scores:** 11%. Scores (25/75 percentile): English: 13-20, Math: 15-19, Composite: 14-20.

ACADEMICS

Year founded: 1854. **Academic calendar:** Semester. **Degrees offered:** bachelor's, master's. **Most popular majors:** 19% business, management, marketing, and related support services, 12% communication, journalism, and related programs, 11% social sciences, 8% psychology, 8% security and protective services. **Major fields of study:** area, ethnic, cultural, and gender studies; biological and biomedical sciences; business, management, marketing, and related support services; communication, journalism, and related programs; computer and information sciences and support services; education; engineering; English language and literature/letters; foreign languages, literatures, and linguistics; health professions and related clinical sciences; history; mathematics and statistics; natural resources and conservation; parks, recreation, leisure, and fitness studies; philosophy and religious studies; physical sciences; psychology; public administration and social service professions; security and protective services; social sciences; visual and performing arts. **Areas of required coursework:** arts/fine arts, humanities, computer literacy, mathematics, English (including composition), philosophy, foreign languages, sciences (biological or physical), history, social science. **Pre-professional programs:** pre-law, pre-medicine, other. **Special academic programs:** double major, exchange student program (domestic), honors program, independent study, internships, study abroad, teacher certificate program. **Teacher certification offered in:** early childhood, special education, elementary, secondary. **Reserve Officers Training Corps (ROTC):** Army ROTC: Offered at cooperating institution (University of Delaware). **Faculty and instruction (2009-2010):** Total instructional faculty: 100 full-time, 93 part-time (; 45% women; 69% minorities). Full-time faculty with Ph.D. or other terminal degree: 77%. Student/faculty ratio: 19/1. Classes of fewer than 20 students: 44%; of 20 to 49 students: 56%; of 50 or more students: 0%. **Advanced Placement and International Baccalaureate credit:** AP tests may be used for: Credit only. **Freshmen returning for sophomore year:** 70%. **Graduation rates:** Four-year: 10%; five-year: 23%; six-year: 38%. **Graduate study:** 14% of students pursue further study immediately upon graduation.

COSTS AND FINANCIAL AID

Financial aid office: (800) 561-2606. **Expenses (2009-2010):** Tuition and fees 2009-2010: $8,390 in state, $12,390 out of state; room/board: $7,900. Estimated books and supplies: $1,430; transportation: $850; personal expenses: $1,240. **Financial aid:** Priority filing date for institution's financial aid form: May 1; deadline: May 1. In 2009-2010, 96% of undergraduates applied for financial aid. Of those, 90% were determined to have financial need; 3% had their need fully met. Average financial aid package (proportion receiving): $10,678 (87%). Average amount of gift aid, such as scholarships or grants (proportion receiving): $5,249 (67%). Average amount of self-help aid, such as work study or loans (proportion receiving): $3,892 (83%). Average need-based loan (excluding PLUS or other private loans): $3,791. Among students who received need-based aid, the average percentage of need met: 49%. Among students who received aid based on merit, the average award (and the proportion receiving): $2,793 (2%). The average athletic scholarship (and the proportion receiving): $3,893 (6%). Average amount of debt of borrowers graduating in 2009: $30,818. Proportion who borrowed: 89%.

CAMPUS LIFE AND EXTRACURRICULAR ACTIVITIES

Campus housing available (% using): coed dorms (24%), women's dorms (49%), men's dorms (27%). Students who live in college-owned, operated, or affiliated housing: 97%. **Student employment:** During the 2009-2010 academic year, 36% of undergraduates worked on campus. Average per-year earnings: $700. **Clubs and organizations:** Number of student organizations: 65. Activities include: choral groups, dance, drama/theater, jazz band, music ensembles, radio station, student government, student newspaper, television station, yearbook. Number of fraternities: 5; sororities: 4. Proportion of men in fraternities: 1%; of women in sororities: 2%. Average proportion of students who stay on campus on weekends: 90%. **Sports program (2009-2010):** Member of NCAA III. *Men's intercollegiate varsity sports:* baseball, basketball, cross country, soccer, tennis, track and field (indoor), track and field (outdoor), volleyball. *Women's intercollegiate varsity sports:* basketball, cross country, soccer, softball, tennis, track and field (indoor), track and field (outdoor), volleyball.

SERVICES AND FACILITIES

Basic services: nonremedial tutoring, women's center, placement service, health service, health insurance. **Remedial assistance:** reading, math, writing, study skills. **Counseling services:** career, personal, academic. **For learning-disabled students:** School does not offer a structured program with separate admission and additional fees. Services include: remedial math, remedial English, remedial reading, tape recorders, videotaped classes, untimed tests, oral tests, learning center, readers, extended time for tests, tutors. **Library:** Number of titles: 183,306; number of current serial subscriptions: 540. **Information technology resources:** Students are not required to lease or own a computer. Number of campus computers available to all students: 537. School has a wireless network. Approximate number of users that can be accommodated: 2,500. Proportion of college-owned housing units wired for high-speed internet access: 30%. **Campus safety:** Security services offered: 24-hour foot-and-vehicle patrols, late-night transport/escort service, 24-hour emergency telephones, lighted pathways/sidewalks, controlled dormitory access (key, security card, etc).

TRANSFER AND INTERNATIONAL STUDENTS

Transfer students: May apply for admission for the following academic terms: Fall, Spring, Summer. Applicants need a minimum number of credits to apply. For fall 2009: Transfer applications received: 362. Transfer applicants offered admission: 76. Transfer applicants enrolled: 45. **International students:** Number of foreign undergraduates: 43 (2% of student body). Number of countries represented: 33. Minimum TOEFL score required: 500 (paper); 90 (computer). Average TOEFL score: 567 (paper).

Lock Haven University of Pennsylvania

- **Address:** 401 N. Fairview Street, Lock Haven, PA 17745
- **Website:** http://www.lhup.edu
- **Public**
- **Enrollment:** 4,669 full-time; 375 part-time

KEY STATS

✔ **U.S News College Ranking:** second tier, Regional Universities (North)
✔ **SAT Score (25th/75th percentile):** 830-1030
✔ **Tuition:** 2010-2011: $7,305 in state, $13,637 out of state
  Selectivity: Less selective   **Room/board:** $6,736
  Acceptance rate: 76%   **Average debt:** $22,585
  Student/faculty ratio: 21/1   **Proportion who borrowed:** 85%

UNDERGRADUATE STUDENT BODY STATS

2009-2010 enrollment: 4,669 full-time; 375 part-time. Men: 43%; women: 57%. **Ethnic makeup:** African American: 7%; Asian American: 1%; Hispanic: 2%; White: 89%; International: 1%.

ADMISSIONS FACTS AND FIGURES

Phone: (570) 893-2027. **Email:** admissions@lhup.edu. **Website:** http://www.lhup.edu. **Application deadlines for fall 2011:** Regular decision: Rolling. Early decision: Not offered. Early action: Not offered. Admission can be deferred. **Application fee:** $25. **To apply online, go to:** http://www.lhup.edu/admissions/application_form.html. **Admissions requirements/recommendations:** High school units required (recommended): English: 4 (4); Mathematics: 3 (4); Science: 3 (4); Foreign language: 0 (2); Social studies: 2 (2); History: 2 (2); Total units: 16 (21). Tests: The college uses SAT or ACT scores in admissions decisions. Either SAT or ACT required. For admission to the fall 2011 entering class, the school will accept: ACT with or without writing accepted. Campus visit: Recommended. Admissions interview: Recommended. Off-campus interview: May be arranged. **Factors that count in admissions decisions:** *Academic:* Secondary school record: Very Important. Class rank: Very Important. Letters of recommendation: Considered. Standardized test scores: Important. Essay: Considered. *Nonacademic:* Interview: Considered. Extracurricular activities: Considered. Talent/ability: Very Important. Character/personal qualities: Very Important. Alumni/ae relationship: Not Considered. Geographical residence: Not Considered. State residency: Not Considered. Religious affiliation/commitment: Not Considered. Minority status: Important. Volunteer work: Considered. Work experience: Considered. **Other schools with the greatest overlap in applicants:** Clarion University of Pennsylvania; Kutztown University of Pennsylvania; Mansfield University of Pennsylvania; Millersville University of Pennsylvania; West Chester University of Pennsylvania. **Admissions statistics for the fall 2009 entering class:** Total applicants: 4,499. Total accepted: 3,438. Freshmen enrolled: 1,202; 9% were from out of state. Overall acceptance rate: 76%. **Credentials of fall 2009 freshmen:** 7% ranked in the top 10 percent of their high school class; 25% were in the top 25 percent; 62% were in the top half. (Proportion submitting class standing: 85%.) **Average high school grade point average:** 3.2. **First-year students who submitted SAT scores:** 95%. Scores (25/75 percentile): Critical Reading: 410-510, Math: 420-520, Combined: 830-1030. **First-year students submitting ACT scores:** 11%. Scores (25/75 percentile): English: N/A, Math: N/A, Composite: 17-21.

ACADEMICS

Year founded: 1870. **Academic calendar:** Semester. **Degrees offered:** associate, bachelor's, master's. **Most popular majors:** 9% criminal justice/law enforcement administration, 9% elementary education and teaching, 9% business administration and management, 8% health and physical education/fitness, 8% sport and fitness administration/management. **Major fields of study:** biological and biomedical sciences; business, management, marketing, and related support services; communication, journalism, and related programs; computer and information sciences and support services; education; English language and literature/letters; foreign languages, literatures, and linguistics; health professions and related clinical sciences; history; legal professions and studies; liberal arts and sciences studies, and humanities; mathematics and statistics; multi/interdisciplinary studies; parks, recreation, leisure, and fitness studies; philosophy and religious studies; physical sciences; psychology; public administration and social service professions; security and protective services; social sciences; visual and performing arts. **Areas of required coursework:** arts/fine arts, humanities, computer literacy, mathematics, English (including composition), philosophy, sciences (biological or physical), history, social science. **Pre-professional programs:** pre-law, pre-dentistry, pre-medicine, pre-veterinary science, pre-pharmacy, other. **Special academic programs:** cooperative (work-study plan) program, cross-registration, distance learning, double major, dual enrollment, honors program, independent study, internships, student-designed major, study abroad, teacher certificate program. **Teacher certification offered in:** early childhood, special education, elementary, middle/junior high, secondary. **Cooperative education programs:** engineering, other. **Reserve Officers Training Corps (ROTC):** Army ROTC: Offered on campus. **Faculty and instruction (2009-2010):** Total instructional faculty: 236 full-time, 12 part-time (54% men; 46% women; 13% minorities). Full-time faculty with Ph.D. or other terminal degree: 74%. Student/faculty ratio: 21/1. Classes of fewer than 20 students: 28%; of 20 to 49 students: 62%; of 50 or more students: 10%. **Advanced Placement and International Baccalaureate credit:** AP tests may be used for: Placement only. Scores accepted: 3, 4, 5. International Baccalaureate exams may be used for: Credit only. **Freshmen returning for sophomore year:** 69%. **Graduation rates:** Four-year: 29%; five-year: 49%; six-year: 53%. **Graduate study:** 12% of students pursue further study within one year. Fields in which graduates pursue further study: Master of Business Administration (MBA), 13%; law, 2%; medicine, 41%; theology (or the seminary), 2%; education, 11%; arts and sciences, 28%.

COSTS AND FINANCIAL AID

Financial aid office: (570) 893-2344. **Expenses (2010-2011):** Tuition and fees 2010-2011: $7,305 in state, $13,637 out of state; room/board: $6,736. Estimated books and supplies: $1,139; transportation: $400; personal expenses: $0. **Financial aid:** Priority filing date for institution's financial aid form: March 15; deadline: March 15. In 2009-2010, 94% of undergraduates applied for financial aid. Of those, 72% were determined to have financial need; 55% had their need fully met. Average financial aid package (proportion receiving): $8,394 (72%). Average amount of gift aid, such as scholarships or grants (proportion receiving): $6,304 (48%). Average amount of self-help aid, such as work study or loans (proportion receiving): $5,461 (56%). Average need-based loan (excluding PLUS or other private loans): $4,172. Among students who received need-based aid, the average percentage of need met: 75%. Among students who received aid based on merit, the average award (and the proportion receiving): $1,076 (5%). The average athletic scholarship (and the proportion receiving): $3,032 (5%). Average amount of debt of borrowers graduating in 2009: $22,585. Proportion who borrowed: 85%.

CAMPUS LIFE AND EXTRACURRICULAR ACTIVITIES

Campus housing available: coed dorms, apartment for single students. Students who live in college-owned, operated, or affiliated housing: 42%. **Student employment:** During the 2009-2010 academic year, 16% of undergraduates worked on campus. Average per-year earnings: $2,318. **Clubs and organizations:** Number of student organizations: 140. Activities include: campus ministries, choral groups, concert band, dance, drama/theater, international student organization, jazz band, literary magazine, marching band, music ensembles, pep band, radio station, student government, student newspaper, television station, yearbook. Number of fraternities: 6; sororities: 4. Proportion of men in fraternities: 3%; of women in sororities: 4%. Average proportion of students who stay on campus on weekends: 50%. **Sports program (2009-2010):** Member of NCAA II.

SERVICES AND FACILITIES

Basic services: nonremedial tutoring, women's center, placement service, health service. **Remedial assistance:** reading, math, writing, study skills. **Counseling services:** minority student, career, military, personal, veteran student, academic, older student, psychological, birth control, religious. **For learning-disabled students:** School does not offer a structured program with separate admission and additional fees. Services include: reading machines, tape recorders, note-taking services, learning center, readers, extended time for tests, tutors, early syllabus, priority registration, priority seating, proofreading services, substitution of courses, texts on tape, typist/scribe, other testing accommodations. **Library:** Number of titles: 411,781; number of current serial subscriptions: 20,525. **Information technology resources:** Students are required to lease or own a computer. Number of campus computers available to all students: 300. School has a wireless network. Approximate number of users that can be accommodated: 700. Proportion of college-owned housing units wired for high-speed internet access: 100%. **Campus safety:** Security services offered: 24-hour foot-and-vehicle patrols, late-night transport/escort service, 24-hour emergency telephones, lighted pathways/sidewalks, controlled dormitory access (key, security card, etc).

TRANSFER AND INTERNATIONAL STUDENTS

Transfer students: May apply for admission for the following academic terms: Fall, Spring, Summer. Applicants do not need a minimum number of credits to apply. For fall 2009: Transfer applications received: 548. Transfer applicants offered admission: 353. Transfer applicants enrolled: 205. **International students:** Number of foreign undergraduates: 52 (1% of student body). Number of countries represented: 32. Minimum TOEFL score required: 550 (paper); 213 (computer).

Lycoming College

- **Address:** 700 College Place, Williamsport, PA 17701
- **Website:** http://www.lycoming.edu
- **Private; Religious affiliation:** Methodist
- **Enrollment:** 1,347 full-time; 26 part-time

KEY STATS

✔ **U.S News College Ranking:** 144, National Liberal Arts Colleges
✔ **SAT Score (25th/75th percentile):** 940-1160
✔ **Tuition:** 2010-2011: $30,800

Selectivity: Selective	**Room/board:** $8,542
Acceptance rate: 68%	**Average debt:** $29,478
Student/faculty ratio: 13/1	**Proportion who borrowed:** 85%

UNDERGRADUATE STUDENT BODY STATS

2009-2010 enrollment: 1,347 full-time; 26 part-time. Men: 47%; women: 53%. **Ethnic makeup:** African American: 3%; American-Indian: 1%; Asian American: 1%; Hispanic: 2%; White: 92%; International: 1%. **Religious preference:** Roman Catholic: 25%; Protestant: 2%; Jewish: 1%; No preference: 32%; Unknown: 12%; Methodist: 9%; Lutheran: 5%; Other: 14%.

ADMISSIONS FACTS AND FIGURES

Phone: (800) 345-3920. **Email:** admissions@lycoming.edu. **Website:** http://www.lycoming.edu. **Application deadlines for fall 2011:** Regular decision: June 1. Early decision: Not offered. Early action: Not offered. Admission can be deferred. **Application fee:** $35. **To apply online, go to:** http://www.lycoming.edu/admissions/Forms/OnlineApplication.html. **Admissions requirements/recommendations:** High school units required (recommended): English: 4 (4); Mathematics: 3 (4); Science: 2 (3); Foreign language: 2 (3); Social studies: 3 (4); Academic electives: 2 (2); Total units: 16 (21). Tests: The college uses SAT or ACT scores in admissions decisions. Either SAT or ACT required. Campus visit: Recommended. Admissions interview: Recommended. Off-campus interview: May be arranged. **Factors that count in admissions decisions:** *Academic:* Secondary school record: Very Important. Class rank: Very Important. Letters of recommendation: Important. Standardized test scores: Important. Essay: Important. *Nonacademic:* Interview: Important. Extracurricular activities: Important. Talent/ability: Important. Character/personal qualities: Important. Alumni/ae relationship: Important. Geographical residence: Important. State residency: Considered. Religious affiliation/commitment: Considered. Minority status: Important. Volunteer work: Considered. Work experience: Considered. **Other schools with the greatest overlap in applicants:** Bucknell University; Juniata College; Lock Haven University of Pennsylvania; Pennsylvania State University–University Park; Susquehanna University. **Admissions statistics for the fall 2009 entering class:** Total applicants: 1,913. Total accepted: 1,297. Freshmen enrolled: 386; 37% were from out of state. Overall acceptance rate: 68%. **Credentials of fall 2009 freshmen:** 19% ranked in the top 10 percent of their high school class; 43% were in the top 25 percent; 80% were in the top half. (Proportion submitting class standing: 79%.) **First-year students who submitted SAT scores:** 94%. Scores (25/75 percentile): Critical Reading: 470-580, Math: 470-580, Combined: 940-1160. **First-year students submitting ACT scores:** 20%. Scores (25/75 percentile): English: N/A, Math: N/A, Composite: 20-27.

ACADEMICS

Year founded: 1812. **Academic calendar:** Semester. **Degrees offered:** bachelor's. **Most popular majors:** 18% business administration and management, 14% social sciences, 10% psychology, 8% biology/biological sciences, 7% communications technologies/technicians and support services. **Major fields of study:** area, ethnic, cultural, and gender studies; biological and biomedical sciences; business, management, marketing, and related support services; communication, journalism, and related programs; computer and information sciences and support services; English language and literature/

letters; foreign languages, literatures, and linguistics; history; mathematics and statistics; multi/interdisciplinary studies; philosophy and religious studies; physical sciences; psychology; security and protective services; social sciences; visual and performing arts. **Areas of required coursework:** arts/fine arts, humanities, mathematics, English (including composition), foreign languages, sciences (biological or physical), social science. **Pre-professional programs:** pre-law, pre-dentistry, pre-medicine, pre-theology, pre-veterinary science, pre-optometry, pre-pharmacy. **Special academic programs (% participation):** cross-registration (1%), double major (19%), honors program (19%), independent study (14%), internships (20%), student-designed major (1%), study abroad (5%), teacher certificate program (15%). **Teacher certification offered in:** special education, elementary, secondary. **Reserve Officers Training Corps (ROTC):** Army ROTC: Offered at cooperating institution (Bucknell University). **Faculty and instruction (2009-2010):** Total instructional faculty: 89 full-time, 37 part-time (61% men; 39% women; 5% minorities). Full-time faculty with Ph.D. or other terminal degree: 97%. Student/faculty ratio: 13/1. Classes of fewer than 20 students: 65%; of 20 to 49 students: 34%; of 50 or more students: 1%. **Advanced Placement and International Baccalaureate credit:** AP tests may be used for: Credit only. Scores accepted: 4, 5. International Baccalaureate exams may be used for: Credit only. **Freshmen returning for sophomore year:** 79%. **Graduation rates:** Four-year: 67%; five-year: 71%; six-year: 74%. **Graduate study:** 20% of students pursue further study immediately upon graduation; 35% within five years. Fields in which graduates pursue further study: Master of Business Administration (MBA), 5%; law, 18%; medicine, 7%; theology (or the seminary), 2%; education, 10%; arts and sciences, 37%.

COSTS AND FINANCIAL AID

Financial aid office: (570) 321-4040. **Expenses (2010-2011):** Tuition and fees 2010-2011: $30,800; room/board: $8,542. Estimated books and supplies: $1,000; transportation: $900; personal expenses: $1,200. **Financial aid:** Priority filing date for institution's financial aid form: March 1. In 2009-2010, 91% of undergraduates applied for financial aid. Of those, 85% were determined to have financial need; 15% had their need fully met. Average financial aid package (proportion receiving): $23,264 (85%). Average amount of gift aid, such as scholarships or grants (proportion receiving): $18,340 (85%). Average amount of self-help aid, such as work study or loans (proportion receiving): $5,078 (73%). Average need-based loan (excluding PLUS or other private loans): $4,760. Among students who received need-based aid, the average percentage of need met: 78%. Among students who received aid based on merit, the average award (and the proportion receiving): $10,852 (12%). The average athletic scholarship (and the proportion receiving): $0 (0%). Average amount of debt of borrowers graduating in 2009: $29,478. Proportion who borrowed: 85%.

CAMPUS LIFE AND EXTRACURRICULAR ACTIVITIES

Campus housing available (% using): coed dorms (70%), women's dorms (10%), sorority housing (6%), fraternity housing (4%), apartment for single students (9%), special housing for disabled students (1%). Students who live in college-owned, operated, or affiliated housing: 85%. **Student employment:** During the 2009-2010 academic year, 40% of undergraduates worked on campus. Average per-year earnings: $1,281. **Clubs and organizations:** Number of student organizations: 85. Activities include: campus ministries, choral groups, concert band, dance, drama/theater, international student organization, jazz band, literary magazine, music ensembles, musical theater, pep band, radio station, student government, student newspaper, student film society, television station, yearbook. Number of fraternities: 5; sororities: 5. Proportion of men in fraternities: 8%; of women in sororities: 12%. Average proportion of students who stay on campus on weekends: 75%. **Sports program (2009-2010):** Member of NCAA III. *Men's intercollegiate varsity sports:* basketball, cross country, football, golf, lacrosse, soccer, swimming, tennis, wrestling. *Women's intercollegiate varsity sports:* basketball, cross country, golf, lacrosse, soccer, softball, swimming, tennis, volleyball.

SERVICES AND FACILITIES

Basic services: nonremedial tutoring, women's center, placement service, health service, health insurance. **Remedial assistance:** math, writing, study skills, other. **Counseling services:** minority student, career, personal, academic, older student, psychological, religious. **For learning-disabled students:** School does not offer a structured program with separate admission and additional fees. Services include: remedial math, reading machines, tape recorders, other special classes, videotaped classes, untimed tests, note-taking services, oral tests, learning center, readers, extended time for tests, tutors. **Library:** Number of titles: 207,644; number of current serial subscriptions: 4,347. **Information technology resources:** Students are not required to lease or own a computer. Number of campus computers available to all students: 125. School has a wireless network. Approximate number of users that can be accommodated: 3,825. Proportion of college-owned housing units wired for high-speed internet access: 100%. **Campus safety:** Security services offered: 24-hour foot-and-vehicle patrols, late-night transport/escort service, 24-hour emergency telephones, lighted pathways/sidewalks, student patrols, controlled dormitory access (key, security card, etc).

TRANSFER AND INTERNATIONAL STUDENTS

Transfer students: May apply for admission for the following academic terms: Fall, Spring. Applicants do not need a minimum number of credits to apply. For fall 2009: Transfer applications received: 145. Transfer applicants offered admission: 72. Transfer applicants enrolled: 43. **International students:** Number of foreign undergraduates: 18 (1% of student body). Number of countries represented: 7. Minimum TOEFL score required: 500 (paper); 500 (computer). Average TOEFL score: 560 (paper).

Mansfield University of Pennsylvania

- **Address:** Alumni Hall, Mansfield, PA 16933
- **Website:** http://www.mansfield.edu
- **Public**
- **Enrollment:** 2,838 full-time; 230 part-time

KEY STATS

✔ **U.S News College Ranking:** 126, Regional Universities (North)
✔ **SAT Score (25th/75th percentile):** 850-1070
✔ **Tuition:** 2009-2010: $7,756 in state, $16,088 out of state
Selectivity: Less selective   **Room/board:** $7,016
Acceptance rate: 75%   **Average debt:** $28,937
Student/faculty ratio: 16/1   **Proportion who borrowed:** 81%

UNDERGRADUATE STUDENT BODY STATS

2009-2010 enrollment: 2,838 full-time; 230 part-time. Men: 40%; women: 60%. **Ethnic makeup:** African American: 7%; American-Indian: 1%; Asian American: 1%; Hispanic: 2%; White: 89%; International: 1%.

ADMISSIONS FACTS AND FIGURES

Phone: (800) 577-6826. **Email:** admissns@mansfield.edu. **Website:** http://www.mansfield.edu. **Application deadlines for fall 2011:** Regular decision: July 6. Early decision: Not offered. Early action: Not offered. Admission can be deferred. **Application fee:** $25. **To apply online, go to:** http://admissions.mansfield.edu/apply-now/. **Admissions requirements/recommendations:** High school units required (recommended): English: 4 (4); Mathematics: 3 (4); Science: 2 (3); Foreign language: 2 (4); Social studies: 4; History: 4; Academic electives: 6 (3); Total units: 21 (25). Tests: The college uses SAT or ACT scores in admissions decisions. Either SAT or ACT required. For admission to the fall 2011 entering class, the school will accept: ACT with or without writing accepted. Campus visit: Recommended. Admissions interview: Recommended. Off-campus interview: Not available. **Factors that count in admissions decisions:** *Academic:* Secondary school record: Very Important. Class rank: Very Important. Letters of recommendation: Considered. Standardized test scores: Very Important. Essay: Considered. *Nonacademic:* Interview: Considered. Extracurricular activities: Considered. Talent/ability: Considered. Character/personal qualities: Important. Alumni/ae relationship: Considered. Geographical residence: Considered. State residency: Not Considered. Religious affiliation/commitment: Not Considered. Minority status: Not Considered. Volunteer work: Important. Work experience: Considered. **Other schools with the greatest overlap in applicants:** Bloomsburg University of Pennsylvania; Clarion University of Pennsylvania; Lock Haven University of Pennsylvania; Lycoming College; Pennsylvania State University–University Park. **Admissions statistics for the fall 2009 entering class:** Total applicants: 2,800. Total accepted: 2,108. Freshmen enrolled: 717; 16% were from out of state. Overall acceptance rate: 75%. **Credentials of fall 2009 freshmen:** 9% ranked in the top 10 percent of their high school class; 32% were in the top 25 percent; 65% were in the top half. (Proportion submitting class standing: 88%.) **Average high school grade point average:** 3.3. **First-year students who submitted SAT scores:** 96%. Scores (25/75 percentile): Critical Reading: 420-530, Math: 430-540, Combined: 850-1070. **First-year students submitting ACT scores:** 10%. Scores (25/75 percentile): English: N/A, Math: N/A, Composite: 18-23.

ACADEMICS

Year founded: 1857. **Academic calendar:** Semester. **Degrees offered:** certificate, associate, bachelor's, master's. **Most popular majors:** 13% education, 11% security and protective services, 11% visual and performing arts, 9% business, management, marketing, and related support services, 9% health professions and related clinical sciences. **Major fields of study:** biological and biomedical sciences; business, management, marketing, and related support services; communication, journalism, and related programs; computer and information sciences and support services; education; English language and literature/letters; family and consumer sciences/human sciences; foreign languages, literatures, and linguistics; health professions and related clinical sciences; history; legal professions and studies; liberal arts and sciences studies, and humanities; mathematics and statistics; natural resources and conservation; philosophy and religious studies; physical sciences; psychology; public administration and social service professions; science technologies/technicians; security and protective services; social sciences; visual and performing arts. **Areas of required coursework:** arts/fine arts, humanities, computer literacy, mathematics, English (including composition), philosophy, foreign languages, sciences (biological or physical), history, social science. **Pre-professional programs:** pre-law, pre-dentistry, pre-medicine, pre-veterinary science, pre-pharmacy. **Special academic programs:** cooperative (work-study plan) program, cross-registration, distance learning, double major, dual enrollment, exchange student program (domestic), honors program, independent study, internships, liberal arts/career combination, student-designed major, study abroad, teacher certificate program. **Teacher certification offered in:** early childhood, special education, elementary, middle/junior high, secondary. **Cooperative education programs:** education, health professions. **Reserve Officers Training Corps (ROTC):** Army ROTC: Offered at cooperating institution (Lock Haven University of Pennsylvania). **Faculty and instruction (2009-2010):** Total instructional faculty: 156 full-time, 67 part-time (49% men; 51% women; 9% minorities). Full-time faculty with Ph.D. or other terminal degree: 72%. Student/faculty ratio: 16/1. Classes of fewer than 20 students: 32%; of 20 to 49 students: 61%; of 50 or more students: 8%. **Advanced Placement and International Baccalaureate credit:** AP tests may be used for: Credit only. Scores accepted: 3, 4, 5. International Baccalaureate exams may be used for: Placement only. **Freshmen returning for sophomore year:** 71%. **Graduation rates:** Four-year: 28%; five-year: 41%; six-year: 47%. **Graduate study:** 15% of students pursue further study immediately upon graduation. Fields in which graduates pursue further study: Master of Business Administration (MBA), 1%; law, 1%; medicine, 1%; engineering, 1%; education, 95%; arts and sciences, 1%.

COSTS AND FINANCIAL AID

Financial aid office: (570) 662-4878. **Expenses (2009-2010):** Tuition and fees 2009-2010: $7,756 in state, $16,088 out of state; room/board: $7,016. **Financial aid:** Priority filing date for institution's financial aid form: March 15; deadline: April 30. Of those, 100% were determined to have financial need; 28% had their need fully met. Average financial aid package (proportion receiving): $2,694 (85%). Average amount of gift aid, such as scholarships or grants (proportion receiving): $2,404 (66%). Average amount of self-help aid, such as work study or loans (proportion receiving): $4,365 (75%). Average need-based loan (excluding PLUS or other private loans): $3,309. Among students who received need-based aid, the average percentage of need met: 81%. Among students who received aid based on merit, the average award (and the proportion receiving): $594 (0%). The average athletic scholarship (and the proportion receiving): $1,115 (1%). Average amount of debt of borrowers graduating in 2009: $28,937. Proportion who borrowed: 81%.

CAMPUS LIFE AND EXTRACURRICULAR ACTIVITIES

Campus housing available (% using): coed dorms (94%), women's dorms (0%), sorority housing (1%), fraternity housing (5%). Students who live in college-owned, operated, or affiliated housing: 50%. **Student employment:** During the 2009-2010 academic year, 15% of undergraduates worked on campus. Average per-year earnings: $1,300. **Clubs and organizations:** Number of student organizations: 120. Activities include: campus ministries, choral groups, concert band, dance, drama/theater, international student organization, jazz band, literary magazine, marching band, model UN, music ensembles, musical theater, pep band, radio station, student government, student newspaper, symphony orchestra, television station. Number of fraternities: 6; sororities: 4. Proportion of men in fraternities: 7%; of women in sororities: 6%. Average proportion of students who stay on campus on weekends: 50%. **Sports program (2009-2010):** Member of NCAA II. **Men's intercollegiate varsity sports:** baseball, basketball, cross country, track and field (indoor), track and field (outdoor). **Women's intercollegiate varsity**

sports: basketball, cross country, field hockey, soccer, softball, swimming, track and field (indoor), track and field (outdoor).

SERVICES AND FACILITIES

Basic services: nonremedial tutoring, women's center, placement service, day care, health service, health insurance. **Remedial assistance:** reading, math, writing, study skills. **Counseling services:** minority student, career, military, personal, veteran student, academic, older student, psychological, birth control, religious. **For learning-disabled students:** School does not offer a structured program with separate admission and additional fees. Services include: remedial math, remedial English, tape recorders, diagnostic testing service, note-taking services, learning center, extended time for tests, tutors, priority registration, other testing accommodations. **Library:** Number of titles: 1,786,670; number of current serial subscriptions: 1,386. **Information technology resources:** Students are not required to lease or own a computer. Number of campus computers available to all students: 661. School has a wireless network. Approximate number of users that can be accommodated: 4,000. Proportion of college-owned housing units wired for high-speed internet access: 100%. **Campus safety:** Security services offered: 24-hour foot-and-vehicle patrols, late-night transport/escort service, 24-hour emergency telephones, lighted pathways/sidewalks, student patrols, controlled dormitory access (key, security card, etc.).

TRANSFER AND INTERNATIONAL STUDENTS

Transfer students: May apply for admission for the following academic terms: Fall, Spring, Summer. Applicants do not need a minimum number of credits to apply. For fall 2009: Transfer applications received: 785. Transfer applicants offered admission: 498. Transfer applicants enrolled: 263. **International students:** Number of foreign undergraduates: 27 (1% of student body). Number of countries represented: 16. Minimum TOEFL score required: 550 (paper); 213 (computer).

Marywood University

- **Address:** 2300 Adams Avenue, Scranton, PA 18509-1598
- **Website:** http://www.marywood.edu
- **Private; Religious affiliation:** Roman Catholic
- **Enrollment:** 2,053 full-time; 131 part-time

KEY STATS

✔ **U.S News College Ranking:** 51, Regional Universities (North)
✔ **SAT Score (25th/75th percentile):** 960-1140
✔ **Tuition:** 2010-2011: $27,150

Selectivity: Selective	**Room/board:** $12,172
Acceptance rate: 72%	**Average debt:** $31,471
Student/faculty ratio: 13/1	**Proportion who borrowed:** 94%

UNDERGRADUATE STUDENT BODY STATS

2009-2010 enrollment: 2,053 full-time; 131 part-time. Men: 30%; women: 70%. **Ethnic makeup:** African American: 1%; Asian American: 2%; Hispanic: 3%; White: 93%; International: 1%. **Religious preference:** Roman Catholic: 61%; Protestant: 23%; Muslim: 1%; Hindu: 1%; No preference: 10%.

ADMISSIONS FACTS AND FIGURES

Phone: (570) 348-6234. **Email:** YourFuture@marywood.edu. **Website:** http://www.marywood.edu. **Application deadlines for fall 2011:** Regular decision: Rolling. Early decision: Not offered. Early action: Not offered. Admission can be deferred. **Application fee:** $35. **To apply online, go to:** http://mymarywood.com/home/apply.html. **Admissions requirements/recommendations:** High school units required (recommended): English: 4; Mathematics: 2; Science: 1; Social studies: 3; Academic electives: 6. Tests: The college uses SAT or ACT scores in admissions decisions. Either SAT or ACT required. For admission to the fall 2011 entering class, the school will accept: ACT with or without writing accepted. Campus visit: Recommended. Admissions interview: Recommended. Off-campus interview: May be arranged. **Factors that count in admissions decisions:** *Academic:* Secondary school record: Very Important. Class rank: Very Important. Letters of recommendation: Important. Standardized test scores: Very Important. Essay: Important. *Nonacademic:* Interview: Important. Extracurricular activities: Considered. Talent/ability: Important. Character/personal qualities: Very Important. Alumni/ae relationship: Not Considered. Geographical residence: Not Considered. State residency: Not Considered. Religious affiliation/commitment: Not Considered. Minority status: Not Considered. Volunteer work: Considered. Work experience: Not Considered. **Other schools with the greatest overlap in applicants:** King's College; Misericordia University; University of Scranton; Wilkes University. **Admissions statistics for the fall 2009 entering class:** Total applicants: 1,923. Total accepted: 1,392. Freshmen enrolled: 473; 31% were from out of state. Overall acceptance rate: 72%. **Credentials of fall 2009 freshmen:** 22% ranked in the top 10 percent of their high school class; 56% were in the top 25 percent; 84% were in the top half. (Proportion submitting class standing: 82%.) **Average high school grade point average:** 3.2. **First-year students who submitted SAT scores:** 93%. Scores (25/75 percentile): Critical Reading: 480-570, Math: 480-570, Combined: 960-1140. **First-year students submitting ACT scores:** 10%. Scores (25/75 percentile): English: N/A, Math: N/A, Composite: 20-23.

ACADEMICS

Year founded: 1915. **Academic calendar:** Semester. **Degrees offered:** bachelor's, post-bachelor's certificate, master's, post-master's certificate. **Most popular majors:** 22% health professions and related clinical sciences, 18% education, 17% visual and performing arts, 11% business, management, marketing, and related support services, 7% psychology. **Major fields of study:** biological and biomedical sciences; business, management, marketing, and related support services; communication, journalism, and related programs; computer and information sciences and support services; education; English language and literature/letters; foreign languages, literatures, and linguistics; health professions and related clinical sciences; history; mathematics and statistics; natural resources and conservation; parks, recreation, leisure, and fitness studies; philosophy and religious studies; psychology; public administration and social service professions; security and protective services; social sciences; transportation and materials moving; visual and performing arts. **Areas of required coursework:** arts/fine arts, humanities, mathematics, English (including composition), philosophy, foreign languages, sciences (biological or physical), history, social science, other. **Pre-professional programs:** pre-law, pre-medicine, other. **Special academic programs:** cross-registration, double major, dual enrollment, English as a Second Language (ESL), honors program, independent study, internships, student-designed major, study abroad, teacher certificate program. **Teacher certification offered in:** early childhood, special education, elementary, adult education, secondary, bilingual/bicultural. **Reserve Officers Training Corps (ROTC):** Army ROTC: Offered at cooperating institution (University of Scranton); Air Force ROTC: Offered at cooperating institution (Wilkes University). **Faculty and instruction (2009-2010):** Total instructional faculty: 142 full-time, 240 part-time (45% men; 55% women; 7% minorities). Full-time faculty with Ph.D. or other terminal degree: 85%. Student/faculty ratio: 13/1. Classes of fewer than 20 students: 52%; of 20 to 49 students: 46%; of 50 or more students: 1%. **Advanced Placement and International Baccalaureate credit:** AP tests may be used for: Credit and/or placement. Scores accepted: 3, 4, 5. International Baccalaureate exams may be used for: Placement only. **Freshmen returning for sophomore year:** 80%. **Graduation rates:** Four-year: 55%; five-year: 68%; six-year: 65%. **Graduate study:** 30% of students pursue further study within one year. Fields in which graduates pursue further study: Master of Business Administration (MBA), 8%; law, 2%; medicine, 6%; education, 23%; arts and sciences, 61%.

COSTS AND FINANCIAL AID

Financial aid office: (570) 348-6225. **Expenses (2010-2011):** Tuition and fees 2010-2011: $27,150; room/board: $12,172. Estimated books and supplies: $1,000; transportation: $600; personal expenses: $700. **Financial aid:** Priority filing date for institution's financial aid form: February 15. In 2009-2010, 92% of undergraduates applied for financial aid. Of those, 85% were determined to have financial need; 26% had their need fully met. Average financial aid package (proportion receiving): $22,222 (85%). Average amount of gift aid, such as scholarships or grants (proportion receiving): $7,524 (72%). Average amount of self-help aid, such as work study or loans (proportion receiving): $6,094 (70%). Average need-based loan (excluding PLUS or other private loans): $5,211. Among students who received need-based aid, the average percentage of need met: 81%. Among students who received aid based on merit, the average award (and the proportion receiving): $10,678 (14%). Average amount of debt of borrowers graduating in 2009: $31,471. Proportion who borrowed: 94%.

CAMPUS LIFE AND EXTRACURRICULAR ACTIVITIES

Campus housing available (% using): coed dorms (79%), women's dorms (3%), men's dorms (2%), apartment for single students (12%), special housing for disabled students (4%), other housing options (0%). Students who live in college-owned, operated, or affiliated housing: 45%. **Clubs and orga-**

nizations: Number of student organizations: 55. Activities include: campus ministries, choral groups, concert band, dance, drama/theater, international student organization, jazz band, literary magazine, music ensembles, musical theater, radio station, student government, student newspaper, television station. Number of fraternities: 0; sororities: 1. of women in sororities: 4%. Average proportion of students who stay on campus on weekends: 50%. **Sports program (2009-2010):** Member of NCAA III. **Men's intercollegiate varsity sports:** baseball, basketball, cross country, lacrosse, soccer, swimming, tennis. **Women's intercollegiate varsity sports:** basketball, cross country, field hockey, lacrosse, soccer, softball, swimming, tennis, volleyball.

SERVICES AND FACILITIES

Basic services: nonremedial tutoring, day care, health service, other. **Remedial assistance:** reading, math, writing, study skills. **Counseling services:** minority student, career, personal, academic, older student, psychological, religious. **For learning-disabled students:** School does not offer a structured program with separate admission and additional fees. Services include: reading machines, tape recorders, diagnostic testing service, note-taking services, oral tests, learning center, readers, extended time for tests, tutors, priority registration, priority seating, substitution of courses, texts on tape, typist/scribe, exams on tape or computer, other testing accommodations, other. **Library:** Number of titles: 220,998; number of current serial subscriptions: 17,923. **Information technology resources:** Students are not required to lease or own a computer. Number of campus computers available to all students: 350. School has a wireless network. Approximate number of users that can be accommodated: 300. Proportion of college-owned housing units wired for high-speed internet access: 100%. **Campus safety:** Security services offered: 24-hour foot-and-vehicle patrols, late-night transport/escort service, 24-hour emergency telephones, lighted pathways/sidewalks, controlled dormitory access (key, security card, etc).

TRANSFER AND INTERNATIONAL STUDENTS

Transfer students: May apply for admission for the following academic terms: Fall, Spring. Applicants need a minimum number of credits to apply. For fall 2009: Transfer applications received: 489. Transfer applicants offered admission: 275. Transfer applicants enrolled: 172. **International students:** Number of foreign undergraduates: 17 (1% of student body). Number of countries represented: 20. Minimum TOEFL score required: 530 (paper); 71 (computer). Average TOEFL score: 567 (paper).

Mercyhurst College

- **Address:** 501 E. 38th Street, Erie, PA 16546
- **Website:** http://www.mercyhurst.edu
- **Private; Religious affiliation:** Roman Catholic
- **Enrollment:** 2,650 full-time; 214 part-time

KEY STATS

✔ **U.S News College Ranking:** 67, Regional Universities (North)
✔ **SAT Score (25th/75th percentile):** 940-1150
✔ **Tuition:** 2010-2011: $26,346

Selectivity: Selective	**Room/board:** $9,195
Acceptance rate: 74%	**Average debt:** $22,630
Student/faculty ratio: 15/1	**Proportion who borrowed:** 76%

UNDERGRADUATE STUDENT BODY STATS

2009-2010 enrollment: 2,650 full-time; 214 part-time. Men: 42%; women: 58%. **Ethnic makeup:** African American: 4%; Asian American: 1%; Hispanic: 2%; White: 86%; International: 6%. **Religious preference:** Protestant: 18%; Muslim: 1%; No preference: 27%; Roman Catholic: 50%; Other: 4%.

ADMISSIONS FACTS AND FIGURES

Phone: (814) 824-2202. **Email:** ccoons@mercyhurst.edu. **Website:** http://www.mercyhurst.edu. **Application deadlines for fall 2011:** Regular decision: Rolling. Early decision: Not offered. Early action: Not offered. Admission can be deferred. **Application fee:** $30. **To apply online, go to:** http://apply.mercyhurst.edu. **Admissions requirements/recommendations:** High school units required (recommended): English: 4 (4); Mathematics: 3 (3); Science: 2 (3); Foreign language: 2 (2); Social studies: 4 (4); Total units: 16 (17). Tests: The college uses SAT or ACT scores in admissions decisions. Either SAT or ACT required. For admission to the fall 2011 entering class, the school will accept: ACT with or without writing accepted.

Campus visit: Recommended. Admissions interview: Recommended. Off-campus interview: May be arranged. **Factors that count in admissions decisions:** *Academic:* Secondary school record: Very Important. Class rank: Important. Letters of recommendation: Important. Standardized test scores: Very Important. Essay: Important. *Nonacademic:* Interview: Considered. Extracurricular activities: Considered. Talent/ability: Important. Character/personal qualities: Important. Alumni/ae relationship: Considered. Geographical residence: Considered. State residency: Considered. Religious affiliation/commitment: Considered. Minority status: Not Considered. Volunteer work: Considered. Work experience: Considered. **Other schools with the greatest overlap in applicants:** Allegheny College; Canisius College; Duquesne University; Gannon University; John Carroll University. **Admissions statistics for the fall 2009 entering class:** Total applicants: 2,991. Total accepted: 2,210. Freshmen enrolled: 669; 47% were from out of state. Overall acceptance rate: 74%. **Credentials of fall 2009 freshmen:** 19% ranked in the top 10 percent of their high school class; 44% were in the top 25 percent; 76% were in the top half. (Proportion submitting class standing: 67%.) **Average high school grade point average:** 3.4. **First-year students who submitted SAT scores:** 79%. Scores (25/75 percentile): Critical Reading: 470-570, Math: 470-580, Combined: 940-1150. **First-year students submitting ACT scores:** 36%. Scores (25/75 percentile): English: N/A, Math: N/A, Composite: 21-25.

ACADEMICS

Year founded: 1926. **Academic calendar:** Trimester. **Degrees offered:** bachelor's, post-bachelor's certificate, master's. **Most popular majors:** 23% business, management, marketing, and related support services, 13% multi/interdisciplinary studies, 12% education, 11% security and protective services, 6% visual and performing arts. **Major fields of study:** biological and biomedical sciences; business, management, marketing, and related support services; communication, journalism, and related programs; computer and information sciences and support services; education; English language and literature/letters; family and consumer sciences/human sciences; foreign languages, literatures, and linguistics; health professions and related clinical sciences; history; liberal arts and sciences studies, and humanities; mathematics and statistics; multi/interdisciplinary studies; philosophy and religious studies; physical sciences; psychology; public administration and social service professions; security and protective services; social sciences; theology and religious vocations; visual and performing arts. **Areas of required coursework:** arts/fine arts, humanities, mathematics, English (including composition), philosophy, foreign languages, sciences (biological or physical), history, social science. **Pre-professional programs:** pre-law, pre-dentistry, pre-medicine, pre-veterinary science, pre-pharmacy. **Special academic programs (% participation):** cooperative (work-study plan) program (3%), cross-registration (1%), distance learning (1%), double major (3%), honors program (8%), independent study (1%), internships (56%), liberal arts/career combination (2%), student-designed major (1%), study abroad (2%), teacher certificate program (12%). **Teacher certification offered in:** early childhood, special education, elementary, middle/junior high, secondary. **Cooperative education programs:** art, business, computer science, natural science, social/behavioral science. **Reserve Officers Training Corps (ROTC):** Army ROTC: Offered at cooperating institution (Gannon University). **Faculty and instruction (2009-2010):** Total instructional faculty: 145 full-time, 94 part-time (56% men; 44% women; 3% minorities). Full-time faculty with Ph.D. or other terminal degree: 59%. Student/faculty ratio: 15/1. Classes of fewer than 20 students: 54%; of 20 to 49 students: 46%; of 50 or more students: 0%. **Advanced Placement and International Baccalaureate credit:** AP tests may be used for: Credit and/or placement. Scores accepted: 4, 5. International Baccalaureate exams may be used for: Credit only. **Freshmen returning for sophomore year:** 79%. **Graduation rates:** Four-year: 57%; five-year: 67%; six-year: 66%. **Graduate study:** 30% of students pursue further study immediately upon graduation; 35% within one year; 60% within five years. Fields in which graduates pursue further study: Master of Business Administration (MBA), 5%; law, 8%; medicine, 13%; education, 13%; arts and sciences, 61%.

COSTS AND FINANCIAL AID

Financial aid office: (814) 824-2288. **Expenses (2010-2011):** Tuition and fees 2010-2011: $26,346; room/board: $9,195. Estimated books and supplies: $1,000; transportation: $1,000; personal expenses: $750. **Financial aid:** Priority filing date for institution's financial aid form: March 15. In 2009-2010, 84% of undergraduates applied for financial aid. Of those, 71% were determined to have financial need; 31% had their need fully met. Average financial aid package (proportion receiving): $19,803 (71%). Average amount of gift aid, such as scholarships or grants (proportion receiving): $10,956 (69%). Average amount of self-help aid, such as work study or loans (proportion receiving): $6,599 (69%). Average need-based loan (excluding PLUS or other private loans): $5,913. Among students who received need-based aid, the average percentage of need met: 62%. Among students who received aid based on merit, the average award (and the proportion receiving): $10,475 (22%). The average athletic scholarship (and the proportion receiving): $19,790 (6%). Average amount of debt of borrowers graduating in 2009: $22,630. Proportion who borrowed: 76%.

CAMPUS LIFE AND EXTRACURRICULAR ACTIVITIES

Campus housing available (% using): coed dorms (17%), women's dorms (9%), men's dorms (8%), apartment for single students (56%), special housing for disabled students (1%), other housing options (9%). Students who live in college-owned, operated, or affiliated housing: 64%. **Student employment:** During the 2009-2010 academic year, 38% of undergraduates worked on campus. Average per-year earnings: $1,200. **Clubs and organizations:** Number of student organizations: 82. Activities include: campus ministries, choral groups, concert band, dance, drama/theater, international student organization, jazz band, literary magazine, music ensembles, musical theater, opera, pep band, radio station, student government, student newspaper, symphony orchestra, television station, yearbook. Number of fraternities: 0; sororities: 0. Average proportion of students who stay on campus on weekends: 80%. **Sports program (2009-2010):** Member of NCAA II. *Men's intercollegiate varsity sports:* baseball, basketball, cross country, football, golf, ice hockey, lacrosse, soccer, tennis, water polo, wrestling. *Women's intercollegiate varsity sports:* basketball, crew (heavyweight), cross country, field hockey, golf, ice hockey, lacrosse, crew (lightweight), soccer, softball, tennis, volleyball, water polo.

SERVICES AND FACILITIES

Basic services: nonremedial tutoring, placement service, health service, health insurance. **Remedial assistance:** reading, math, writing, study skills. **Counseling services:** minority student, career, personal, veteran student, academic, psychological, religious. **For learning-disabled students:** School does not offer a structured program with separate admission and additional fees. Total undergraduates in learning-disabled program or receiving services: 131. Services include: remedial math, remedial English, reading machines, remedial reading, tape recorders, untimed tests, note-taking services, learning center, readers, extended time for tests, tutors, priority registration, proofreading services, texts on tape, typist/scribe, exams on tape or computer, other testing accommodations, waiver of foreign language degree requirement. **Library:** Number of titles: 140,000; number of current serial subscriptions: 275. **Information technology resources:** Students are not required to lease or own a computer. Number of campus computers available to all students: 400. School has a wireless network. Approximate number of users that can be accommodated: 5,000. Proportion of college-owned housing units wired for high-speed internet access: 100%. **Campus safety:** Security services offered: 24-hour foot-and-vehicle patrols, 24-hour emergency telephones, lighted pathways/sidewalks, controlled dormitory access (key, security card, etc).

TRANSFER AND INTERNATIONAL STUDENTS

Transfer students: May apply for admission for the following academic terms: Fall, Winter, Spring, Summer. Applicants do not need a minimum number of credits to apply. For fall 2009: Transfer applications received: 288. Transfer applicants offered admission: 140. Transfer applicants enrolled: 72. **International students:** Number of foreign undergraduates: 171 (6% of student body). Number of countries represented: 31. Minimum TOEFL score required: 550 (paper); 80 (computer). Average TOEFL score: 587 (paper).

Messiah College

- **Address:** 1 College Avenue, Grantham, PA 17027-0800
- **Website:** http://www.messiah.edu
- **Private; Religious affiliation:** Christian interdenominational
- **Enrollment:** 2,712 full-time; 54 part-time

KEY STATS

✔ **U.S News College Ranking:** 4, Regional Colleges (North)
✔ **SAT Score (25th/75th percentile):** 1020-1260
✔ **Tuition:** 2010-2011: $27,480

Selectivity: More selective	**Room/board:** $8,160
Acceptance rate: 69%	**Average debt:** $33,867
Student/faculty ratio: 13/1	**Proportion who borrowed:** 76%

UNDERGRADUATE STUDENT BODY STATS

2009-2010 enrollment: 2,712 full-time; 54 part-time. Men: 37%; women: 63%. **Ethnic makeup:** African American: 2%; Asian American: 2%; Hispanic: 2%; White: 92%; International: 2%. **Religious preference:** Roman Catholic: 6%; Protestant: 55%; Unknown: 24%; Christian interdenominational: 10%; Brethren in Christ: 5%.

ADMISSIONS FACTS AND FIGURES

Phone: (717) 691-6000. **Email:** admiss@messiah.edu. **Website:** http://www.messiah.edu. **Application deadlines for fall 2011:** Regular decision: Rolling. Early decision: Not offered. Early action: Not offered. Admission can be deferred. **Application fee:** $30. **To apply online, go to:** http://www.messiah.edu/admissions. **Admissions requirements/recommendations:** High school units required (recommended): English: 4 (4); Mathematics: 2 (3); Science: 2 (3); Foreign language: 2 (2); Social studies: 2 (2); History: 0 (2); Academic electives: 4 (4); Total units: 16 (20). Tests: The college uses SAT or ACT scores in admissions decisions. Neither SAT nor ACT required. For admission to the fall 2011 entering class, the school will accept: ACT with or without writing accepted. Campus visit: Recommended. Admissions interview: Recommended. Off-campus interview: Not available. **Factors that count in admissions decisions: Academic:** Secondary school record: Very Important. Class rank: Very Important. Letters of recommendation: Very Important. Standardized test scores: Very Important. Essay: Important. *Nonacademic:* Interview: Considered. Extracurricular activities: Very Important. Talent/ability: Very Important. Character/personal qualities: Very Important. Alumni/ae relationship: Considered. Geographical residence: Not Considered. State residency: Not Considered. Religious affiliation/commitment: Very Important. Minority status: Considered. Volunteer work: Important. Work experience: Considered. **Other schools with the greatest overlap in applicants:** Cedarville University; Eastern University; Elizabethtown College; Gordon College; Grove City College. **Admissions statistics for the fall 2009 entering class:** Total applicants: 3,014. Total accepted: 2,072. Freshmen enrolled: 698; 44% were from out of state. Overall acceptance rate: 69%. **Size of waiting list:** 2 applicants; enrolled from waiting list: 2. **Credentials of fall 2009 freshmen:** 35% ranked in the top 10 percent of their high school class; 67% were in the top 25 percent; 94% were in the top half. (Proportion submitting class standing: 73%.) **Average high school grade point average:** 3.7. **First-year students who submitted SAT scores:** 96%. Scores (25/75 percentile): Critical Reading: 510-620, Math: 510-640, Combined: 1020-1260. **First-year students submitting ACT scores:** 21%. Scores (25/75 percentile): English: 23-29, Math: 22-28, Composite: 23-28.

ACADEMICS

Year founded: 1909. **Academic calendar:** Semester. **Degrees offered:** bachelor's, master's, post-master's certificate. **Most popular majors:** 8% nursing/registered nurse training (R.N., A.S.N., B.S.N., M.S.N.), 7% psychology, 6% communication studies/speech communication and rhetoric, 6% elementary education and teaching, 5% English language and literature. **Major fields of study:** biological and biomedical sciences; business, management, marketing, and related support services; communication, journalism, and related programs; computer and information sciences and support services; education; engineering; English language and literature/letters; family and consumer sciences/human sciences; foreign languages, literatures, and linguistics; health professions and related clinical sciences; history; liberal arts and sciences studies, and humanities; mathematics and statistics; multi/interdisciplinary studies; natural resources and conservation; parks, recreation, leisure, and fitness studies; philosophy and religious studies; physical sciences; psychology; public administration and social service professions; security and protective services; social sciences; theology and religious voca-

tions; visual and performing arts. **Areas of required coursework:** arts/fine arts, humanities, computer literacy, mathematics, English (including composition), philosophy, foreign languages, sciences (biological or physical), history, social science, other. **Pre-professional programs:** pre-law, pre-dentistry, pre-medicine, pre-veterinary science, other. **Special academic programs (% participation):** accelerated program (1%), cross-registration (16%), distance learning (1%), double major (2%), dual enrollment (1%), English as a Second Language (ESL) (1%), exchange student program (domestic) (8%), honors program (9%), independent study (22%), internships (23%), student-designed major (1%), study abroad (47%), teacher certificate program (14%). **Teacher certification offered in:** early childhood, special education, elementary, middle/junior high, secondary, bilingual/bicultural. **Faculty and instruction (2009-2010):** Total instructional faculty: 170 full-time, 109 part-time (56% men; 44% women; 8% minorities). Full-time faculty with Ph.D. or other terminal degree: 81%. Student/faculty ratio: 13/1. Classes of fewer than 20 students: 45%; of 20 to 49 students: 51%; of 50 or more students: 4%. **Advanced Placement and International Baccalaureate credit:** AP tests may be used for: Credit and/or placement. Scores accepted: 2, 3, 4, 5. International Baccalaureate exams may be used for: Credit and/or placement. **Freshmen returning for sophomore year:** 85%. **Graduation rates:** Four-year: 71%; five-year: 78%; six-year: 77%. **Graduate study:** 19% of students pursue further study immediately upon graduation. Fields in which graduates pursue further study: Master of Business Administration (MBA), 5%; law, 6%; medicine, 17%; dentistry, 1%; theology (or the seminary), 9%; education, 11%; arts and sciences, 51%.

COSTS AND FINANCIAL AID

Financial aid office: (717) 691-6007. **Expenses (2010-2011):** Tuition and fees 2010-2011: $27,480; room/board: $8,160. Estimated books and supplies: $1,100; transportation: $720; personal expenses: $1,250. **Financial aid:** Priority filing date for institution's financial aid form: April 1. In 2009-2010, 81% of undergraduates applied for financial aid. Of those, 72% were determined to have financial need; 18% had their need fully met. Average financial aid package (proportion receiving): $18,236 (72%). Average amount of gift aid, such as scholarships or grants (proportion receiving): $12,640 (71%). Average amount of self-help aid, such as work study or loans (proportion receiving): $5,670 (60%). Average need-based loan (excluding PLUS or other private loans): $4,803. Among students who received need-based aid, the average percentage of need met: 69%. Among students who received aid based on merit, the average award (and the proportion receiving): $9,283 (26%). The average athletic scholarship (and the proportion receiving): $0 (0%). Average amount of debt of borrowers graduating in 2009: $33,867. Proportion who borrowed: 76%.

CAMPUS LIFE AND EXTRACURRICULAR ACTIVITIES

Campus housing available (% using): coed dorms (45%), women's dorms (16%), men's dorms (5%), fraternity housing (0%), apartments for married students (0%), apartment for single students (30%), special housing for disabled students (0%), special housing for international students (0%), cooperative housing (2%), other housing options (2%). Students who live in college-owned, operated, or affiliated housing: 87%. **Student employment:** During the 2009-2010 academic year, 26% of undergraduates worked on campus. Average per-year earnings: $1,606. **Clubs and organizations:** Number of student organizations: 81. Activities include: campus ministries, choral groups, concert band, dance, drama/theater, international student organization, jazz band, literary magazine, music ensembles, musical theater, pep band, radio station, student government, student newspaper, student film society, symphony orchestra, yearbook. Number of fraternities: 0; sororities: 0. Average proportion of students who stay on campus on weekends: 70%. **Sports program (2009-2010):** Member of NCAA III. *Men's intercollegiate varsity sports:* baseball, basketball, cross country, golf, lacrosse, soccer, swimming, tennis, track and field (indoor), track and field (outdoor), wrestling. *Women's intercollegiate varsity sports:* basketball, cross country, field hockey, lacrosse, soccer, softball, swimming, tennis, track and field (indoor), track and field (outdoor), volleyball.

SERVICES AND FACILITIES

Basic services: nonremedial tutoring, day care, health service. **Remedial assistance:** reading, math, writing, study skills. **Counseling services:** minority student, career, personal, academic, psychological, religious. **For learning-disabled students:** School does not offer a structured program with separate admission and additional fees. Total undergraduates in learning-disabled program or receiving services: 34. Services include: reading machines, tape recorders, other special classes, untimed tests, note-taking services, oral tests, learning center, readers, extended time for tests, tutors, priority registration, other testing accommodations, other. **Library:**

Number of titles: 274,259; number of current serial subscriptions: 48,840. **Information technology resources:** Students are not required to lease or own a computer. Number of campus computers available to all students: 571. School has a wireless network. Approximate number of users that can be accommodated: 3,500. Proportion of college-owned housing units wired for high-speed internet access: 100%. **Campus safety:** Security services offered: 24-hour foot-and-vehicle patrols, late-night transport/escort service, 24-hour emergency telephones, lighted pathways/sidewalks, student patrols, controlled dormitory access (key, security card, etc).

TRANSFER AND INTERNATIONAL STUDENTS

Transfer students: May apply for admission for the following academic terms: Fall, Spring. Applicants need a minimum number of credits to apply. For fall 2009: Transfer applications received: 211. Transfer applicants offered admission: 125. Transfer applicants enrolled: 63. **International students:** Number of foreign undergraduates: 67 (2% of student body). Number of countries represented: 30. Minimum TOEFL score required: 550 (paper); 213 (computer). Average TOEFL score: 570 (paper).

Millersville University of Pennsylvania

- **Address:** PO Box 1002, Millersville, PA 17551-0302
- **Website:** http://www.millersville.edu
- **Public**
- **Enrollment:** 6,689 full-time; 670 part-time

KEY STATS

✔ **U.S News College Ranking:** 67, Regional Universities (North)
✔ **SAT Score (25th/75th percentile):** 970-1160
✔ **Tuition:** 2010-2011: $7,644 in state, $16,308 out of state
   Selectivity: Selective **Room/board:** $8,298
   Acceptance rate: 53% **Average debt:** $22,479
   Student/faculty ratio: 21/1 **Proportion who borrowed:** 72%

UNDERGRADUATE STUDENT BODY STATS

2009-2010 enrollment: 6,689 full-time; 670 part-time. Men: 44%; women: 56%. **Ethnic makeup:** African American: 7%; Asian American: 1%; Hispanic: 4%; White: 87%.

ADMISSIONS FACTS AND FIGURES

Phone: (717) 872-3371. **Email:** Admissions@millersville.edu. **Website:** http://www.millersville.edu. **Application deadlines for fall 2011:** Regular decision: Rolling. Early decision: Not offered. Early action: Not offered. Admission can be deferred. **Application fee:** $50. **To apply online, go to:** http://www.millersville.edu/~admit/. **Admissions requirements/recommendations:** High school units required (recommended): English: 4 (0); Mathematics: 3 (0); Science: 3 (0); Foreign language: 0 (2); Social studies: 3 (0); History: 2 (0); Academic electives: 0 (4); Total units: 15 (21). Tests: The college uses SAT or ACT scores in admissions decisions. Either SAT or ACT required. For admission to the fall 2011 entering class, the school will accept: ACT with writing recommended. Campus visit: Recommended. Admissions interview: Neither required nor recommended. Off-campus interview: Not available. **Factors that count in admissions decisions:** *Academic:* Secondary school record: Very Important. Class rank: Very Important. Letters of recommendation: Considered. Standardized test scores: Very Important. Essay: Considered. *Nonacademic:* Interview: Considered. Extracurricular activities: Important. Talent/ability: Important. Character/personal qualities: Important. Alumni/ae relationship: Considered. Geographical residence: Considered. State residency: Considered. Religious affiliation/commitment: Not Considered. Minority status: Considered. Volunteer work: Important. Work experience: Important. **Other schools with the greatest overlap in applicants:** Bloomsburg University of Pennsylvania; Pennsylvania State University–University Park; Shippensburg University of Pennsylvania; Temple University; West Chester University of Pennsylvania. **Admissions statistics for the fall 2009 entering class:** Total applicants: 7,241. Total accepted: 3,849. Freshmen enrolled: 1,333; 6% were from out of state. Overall acceptance rate: 53%. **Size of waiting list:** 862 applicants; enrolled from waiting list: 65. **Credentials of fall 2009 freshmen:** 16% ranked in the top 10 percent of their high school class; 45% were in the top 25 percent; 81% were in the top half. (Proportion submitting class standing: 80%.) **First-year students who submitted SAT scores:** 95%. Scores (25/75 percentile): Critical Reading: 480-570, Math: 490-590, Combined: 970-1160.

First-year students submitting ACT scores: 12%. Scores (25/75 percentile): English: N/A, Math: N/A, Composite: 20-24.

ACADEMICS

Year founded: 1855. **Academic calendar:** 4-1-4. **Degrees offered:** associate, bachelor's, post-bachelor's certificate, master's, post-master's certificate. **Most popular majors:** 17% education, 14% business, management, marketing, and related support services, 9% psychology, 6% biological and biomedical sciences, 6% communication, journalism, and related programs. **Major fields of study:** area, ethnic, cultural, and gender studies; biological and biomedical sciences; business, management, marketing, and related support services; communication, journalism, and related programs; computer and information sciences and support services; education; engineering technologies/technicians; English language and literature/letters; foreign languages, literatures, and linguistics; health professions and related clinical sciences; history; mathematics and statistics; philosophy and religious studies; physical sciences; psychology; public administration and social service professions; social sciences; visual and performing arts. **Areas of required coursework:** humanities, mathematics, English (including composition), sciences (biological or physical), social science, other. **Pre-professional programs:** pre-optometry, pre-pharmacy, other. **Special academic programs:** accelerated program, cooperative (work-study plan) program, cross-registration, distance learning, double major, dual enrollment, honors program, independent study, internships, study abroad, teacher certificate program, other. **Teacher certification offered in:** early childhood, special education, elementary, vo-tech, middle/junior high, secondary, bilingual/bicultural. **Cooperative education programs:** art, business, computer science, education, engineering, health professions, humanities, natural science, social/behavioral science, technologies. **Reserve Officers Training Corps (ROTC):** Army ROTC: Offered on campus. **Faculty and instruction (2009-2010):** Total instructional faculty: 304 full-time, 133 part-time (51% men; 49% women; 13% minorities). Full-time faculty with Ph.D. or other terminal degree: 97%. Student/faculty ratio: 21/1. Classes of fewer than 20 students: 17%; of 20 to 49 students: 77%; of 50 or more students: 6%. **Advanced Placement and International Baccalaureate credit:** AP tests may be used for: Credit and/or placement. Scores accepted: 3, 4, 5. **Freshmen returning for sophomore year:** 82%. **Graduation rates:** Four-year: 36%; five-year: 57%; six-year: 64%. **Graduate study:** Fields in which graduates pursue further study: Master of Business Administration (MBA), 1%; law, 1%; medicine, 1%; dentistry, 1%; engineering, 2%; theology (or the seminary), 1%; education, 5%; arts and sciences, 4%; veterinary medicine, 1%.

COSTS AND FINANCIAL AID

Financial aid office: (717) 872-3026. **Expenses (2010-2011):** Tuition and fees 2010-2011: $7,644 in state, $16,308 out of state; room/board: $8,298. Estimated books and supplies: $1,000; transportation: $800; personal expenses: $1,750. **Financial aid:** Priority filing date for institution's financial aid form: March 15. In 2009-2010, 79% of undergraduates applied for financial aid. Of those, 59% were determined to have financial need; 12% had their need fully met. Average financial aid package (proportion receiving): $8,124 (57%). Average amount of gift aid, such as scholarships or grants (proportion receiving): $5,447 (40%). Average amount of self-help aid, such as work study or loans (proportion receiving): $4,209 (53%). Average need-based loan (excluding PLUS or other private loans): $4,099. Among students who received need-based aid, the average percentage of need met: 77%. Among students who received aid based on merit, the average award (and the proportion receiving): $3,002 (2%). The average athletic scholarship (and the proportion receiving): $1,797 (1%). Average amount of debt of borrowers graduating in 2009: $22,479. Proportion who borrowed: 72%.

CAMPUS LIFE AND EXTRACURRICULAR ACTIVITIES

Campus housing available (% using): coed dorms (100%), other housing options. Students who live in college-owned, operated, or affiliated housing: 31%. **Student employment:** During the 2009-2010 academic year, 26% of undergraduates worked on campus. Average per-year earnings: $1,496. **Clubs and organizations:** Number of student organizations: 126. Activities include: campus ministries, choral groups, concert band, dance, drama/theater, jazz band, literary magazine, marching band, music ensembles, musical theater, pep band, radio station, student government, student newspaper, symphony orchestra, television station, yearbook. Number of fraternities: 9; sororities: 10. Proportion of men in fraternities: 4%; of women in sororities: 5%. **Sports program (2009-2010):** Member of NCAA II. *Men's intercollegiate varsity sports:* baseball, basketball, cross country, football, golf, soccer, tennis, track and field (indoor), track and field (outdoor), wrestling. *Women's intercollegiate varsity sports:* basketball, cross country, field hockey, lacrosse, soccer, softball, swimming, tennis, track and field (indoor), track and field (outdoor), volleyball.

SERVICES AND FACILITIES

Basic services: nonremedial tutoring, women's center, placement service, health service, health insurance, other. **Remedial assistance:** math, writing, other. **Counseling services:** minority student, career, personal, veteran student, academic, older student, psychological. **For learning-disabled students:** School does not offer a structured program with separate admission and additional fees. Total undergraduates in learning-disabled program or receiving services: 190. Services include: remedial math, remedial English, reading machines, tape recorders, diagnostic testing service, untimed tests, note-taking services, oral tests, learning center, readers, extended time for tests, tutors, typist/scribe, exams on tape or computer, other testing accommodations, other. **Library:** Number of titles: 603,224; number of current serial subscriptions: 16,712. **Information technology resources:** Students are not required to lease or own a computer. Number of campus computers available to all students: 712. School has a wireless network. Approximate number of users that can be accommodated: 8,000. Proportion of college-owned housing units wired for high-speed internet access: 100%. **Campus safety:** Security services offered: 24-hour foot-and-vehicle patrols, late-night transport/escort service, 24-hour emergency telephones, lighted pathways/sidewalks, student patrols, controlled dormitory access (key, security card, etc).

TRANSFER AND INTERNATIONAL STUDENTS

Transfer students: May apply for admission for the following academic terms: Fall, Winter, Spring, Summer. Applicants need a minimum number of credits to apply. For fall 2009: Transfer applications received: 1,262. Transfer applicants offered admission: 871. Transfer applicants enrolled: 542. **International students:** Number of foreign undergraduates: 26. Number of countries represented: 53. Minimum TOEFL score required: 500 (paper); 65 (computer).

Misericordia University

- **Address:** 301 Lake Street, Dallas, PA 18612-1098
- **Website:** http://www.misericordia.edu/
- **Private; Religious affiliation:** Roman Catholic
- **Enrollment:** 1,665 full-time; 703 part-time

KEY STATS

✔ **U.S News College Ranking:** 51, Regional Universities (North)
✔ **SAT Score (25th/75th percentile):** 950-1120
✔ **Tuition:** 2010-2011: $24,990

Selectivity: Selective	**Room/board:** $10,410
Acceptance rate: 69%	**Average debt:** $33,641
Student/faculty ratio: 13/1	**Proportion who borrowed:** 78%

UNDERGRADUATE STUDENT BODY STATS

2009-2010 enrollment: 1,665 full-time; 703 part-time. Men: 29%; women: 71%. **Ethnic makeup:** African American: 1%; Asian American: 1%; Hispanic: 2%; White: 96%. **Religious preference:** Protestant: 26%; No preference: 6%; Roman Catholic: 59%; Other: 9%.

ADMISSIONS FACTS AND FIGURES

Phone: (570) 674-6264. **Email:** admiss@misericordia.edu. **Website:** http://www.misericordia.edu/. **Application deadlines for fall 2011:** Regular decision: Rolling. Early decision: Not offered. Early action: Not offered. Admission can be deferred. **Application fee:** $25. **To apply online, go to:** https://www.misericordia.edu/apply/. **Admissions requirements/recommendations:** High school units required (recommended): English: 4; Mathematics: 4; Science: 4; Social studies: 4; Total units: 16. Tests: The college uses SAT or ACT scores in admissions decisions. Either SAT or ACT required. For admission to the fall 2011 entering class, the school will accept: ACT with or without writing accepted. Campus visit: Recommended. Admissions interview: Recommended. Off-campus interview: May be arranged. **Factors that count in admissions decisions:** *Academic:* Secondary school record: Very Important. Class rank: Important. Letters of recommendation: Considered. Standardized test scores: Important. Essay: Considered. *Nonacademic:* Interview: Considered. Extracurricular activities: Considered. Talent/ability: Not Considered. Character/personal qualities: Considered. Alumni/ae relationship: Not

Considered. Geographical residence: Not Considered. State residency: Not Considered. Religious affiliation/commitment: Not Considered. Minority status: Considered. Volunteer work: Considered. Work experience: Considered. **Other schools with the greatest overlap in applicants:** Bloomsburg University of Pennsylvania; Elizabethtown College; King's College; University of Scranton; Wilkes University. **Admissions statistics for the fall 2009 entering class:** Total applicants: 1,533. Total accepted: 1,060. Freshmen enrolled: 381; 25% were from out of state. Overall acceptance rate: 69%. **Size of waiting list:** 50 applicants; enrolled from waiting list: 10. **Credentials of fall 2009 freshmen:** 15% ranked in the top 10 percent of their high school class; 49% were in the top 25 percent; 79% were in the top half. (Proportion submitting class standing: 84%.) **Average high school grade point average:** 3.2. **First-year students who submitted SAT scores:** 87%. Scores (25/75 percentile): Critical Reading: 470-550, Math: 480-570, Combined: 950-1120. **First-year students submitting ACT scores:** 8%. Scores (25/75 percentile): English: 20-24, Math: 18-24, Composite: 20-25.

ACADEMICS

Year founded: 1924. **Academic calendar:** Semester. **Degrees offered:** certificate, bachelor's, post-bachelor's certificate, master's, post-master's certificate. **Most popular majors:** 21% nursing, 16% health professions and related clinical sciences, 14% business administration and management, 8% elementary education and teaching, 6% medical radiologic technology/science-radiation therapist. **Major fields of study:** biological and biomedical sciences; business, management, marketing, and related support services; communication, journalism, and related programs; computer and information sciences and support services; education; English language and literature/letters; health professions and related clinical sciences; history; liberal arts and sciences studies, and humanities; mathematics and statistics; multi/interdisciplinary studies; parks, recreation, leisure, and fitness studies; philosophy and religious studies; physical sciences; psychology; public administration and social service professions. **Areas of required coursework:** arts/fine arts, humanities, computer literacy, mathematics, English (including composition), philosophy, sciences (biological or physical), history, social science, other. **Pre-professional programs:** pre-law, pre-dentistry, pre-medicine, pre-veterinary science, pre-optometry. **Special academic programs:** accelerated program, cross-registration, distance learning, double major, dual enrollment, honors program, independent study, internships, student-designed major, study abroad, teacher certificate program, weekend college. **Teacher certification offered in:** early childhood, special education, elementary, secondary. **Reserve Officers Training Corps (ROTC):** Army ROTC: Offered at cooperating institution; Air Force ROTC: Offered at cooperating institution. **Faculty and instruction (2009-2010):** Total instructional faculty: 96 full-time, 179 part-time (47% men; 53% women; 4% minorities). Full-time faculty with Ph.D. or other terminal degree: 79%. Student/faculty ratio: 13/1. Classes of fewer than 20 students: 54%; of 20 to 49 students: 46%; of 50 or more students: 0%. **Advanced Placement and International Baccalaureate credit:** AP tests may be used for: Credit only. Scores accepted: 3, 4, 5. International Baccalaureate exams may be used for: Credit only. **Freshmen returning for sophomore year:** 82%. **Graduation rates:** Four-year: 66%; five-year: 72%; six-year: 69%. **Graduate study:** 20% of students pursue further study within one year. Fields in which graduates pursue further study: Master of Business Administration (MBA), 35%; law, 2%; medicine, 4%; education, 16%; arts and sciences, 23%.

COSTS AND FINANCIAL AID

Financial aid office: (570) 674-6280. **Expenses (2010-2011):** Tuition and fees 2010-2011: $24,990; room/board: $10,410. Estimated books and supplies: $900; transportation: $400; personal expenses: $500. **Financial aid:** Priority filing date for institution's financial aid form: March 1; deadline: May 1. In 2009-2010, 93% of undergraduates applied for financial aid. Of those, 83% were determined to have financial need; 13% had their need fully met. Average financial aid package (proportion receiving): $16,738 (83%). Average amount of gift aid, such as scholarships or grants (proportion receiving): $12,018 (82%). Average amount of self-help aid, such as work study or loans (proportion receiving): $1,600 (70%). Average need-based loan (excluding PLUS or other private loans): $8,612. Among students who received need-based aid, the average percentage of need met: 71%. Among students who received aid based on merit, the average award (and the proportion receiving): $6,835 (9%). The average athletic scholarship (and the proportion receiving): $0 (0%). Average amount of debt of borrowers graduating in 2009: $33,641. Proportion who borrowed: 78%.

CAMPUS LIFE AND EXTRACURRICULAR ACTIVITIES

Campus housing available (% using): coed dorms (98%), other housing options (2%). Students who live in college-owned, operated, or affiliated housing: 37%. **Student employment:** During the 2009-2010 academic year, 5% of undergraduates worked on campus. Average per-year earnings: $500. **Clubs and organizations:** Number of student organizations: 37. Activities include: campus ministries, choral groups, dance, drama/theater, jazz band, literary magazine, music ensembles, radio station, student government, student newspaper, television station. Number of fraternities: 0; sororities: 0. Average proportion of students who stay on campus on weekends: 50%. **Sports program (2009-2010):** Member of NCAA III. **Men's intercollegiate varsity sports:** baseball, basketball, cross country, golf, lacrosse, soccer, swimming, tennis, track and field (outdoor). **Women's intercollegiate varsity sports:** basketball, cross country, field hockey, lacrosse, soccer, softball, swimming, tennis, track and field (outdoor), volleyball.

SERVICES AND FACILITIES

Basic services: nonremedial tutoring, placement service, health service, health insurance. **Remedial assistance:** study skills. **Counseling services:** minority student, career, personal, veteran student, academic, older student, psychological, religious. **For learning-disabled students:** School does not offer a structured program with separate admission and additional fees. Total undergraduates in learning-disabled program or receiving services: 77. Services include: reading machines, tape recorders, diagnostic testing service, note-taking services, oral tests, learning center, readers, extended time for tests, tutors, priority seating, proofreading services, texts on tape, typist/scribe, other testing accommodations, other. **Library:** Number of titles: 79,612; number of current serial subscriptions: 373. **Information technology resources:** Students are not required to lease or own a computer. Number of campus computers available to all students: 100. School has a wireless network. Approximate number of users that can be accommodated: 100. Proportion of college-owned housing units wired for high-speed internet access: 100%. **Campus safety:** Security services offered: 24-hour foot-and-vehicle patrols, late-night transport/escort service, 24-hour emergency telephones, lighted pathways/sidewalks, controlled dormitory access (key, security card, etc).

TRANSFER AND INTERNATIONAL STUDENTS

Transfer students: May apply for admission for the following academic terms: Fall, Spring, Summer. Applicants need a minimum number of credits to apply. For fall 2009: Transfer applications received: 514. Transfer applicants offered admission: 249. Transfer applicants enrolled: 153. **International students:** Number of foreign undergraduates: 2. Number of countries represented: 1. Minimum TOEFL score required: 550 (paper); 120 (computer).

Moore College of Art and Design

■ **Address:** 20th and the Parkway, Philadelphia, PA 19103
■ **Website:** http://www.moore.edu
■ **Private**
■ **Enrollment:** N/A

KEY STATS

✔ **U.S News College Ranking:** Unranked Specialty School–Fine Arts
✔ **SAT or ACT Score (25th/75th percentile):** N/A
✔ **Tuition:** 2009-2010: $29,104

Selectivity: N/A	**Room/board:** $10,930
Acceptance rate: N/A	**Average debt:** N/A
Student/faculty ratio: N/A	**Proportion who borrowed:** N/A

Moravian College

■ **Address:** 1200 Main Street, Bethlehem, PA 18018
■ **Website:** http://www.moravian.edu
■ **Private; Religious affiliation:** Moravian Church in America
■ **Enrollment:** 1,558 full-time; 237 part-time

KEY STATS

✔ **U.S News College Ranking:** 131, National Liberal Arts Colleges
✔ **SAT Score (25th/75th percentile):** 980-1190
✔ **Tuition:** 2010-2011: $32,177

Selectivity: Selective	**Room/board:** $9,164
Acceptance rate: 75%	**Average debt:** N/A
Student/faculty ratio: 10/1	**Proportion who borrowed:** N/A

UNDERGRADUATE STUDENT BODY STATS

2009-2010 enrollment: 1,558 full-time; 237 part-time. Men: 40%; women: 60%. **Ethnic makeup:** African American: 3%; Asian American: 2%; Hispanic: 6%; White: 88%; International: 1%.

ADMISSIONS FACTS AND FIGURES

Phone: (610) 861-1320. **Email:** admissions@moravian.edu. **Website:** http://www.moravian.edu. **Application deadlines for fall 2011:** Regular decision: March 1; decision sent by March 15. Early decision: Send application by: February 1; Decision sent by: December 15. Early action: Not offered. Admission can be deferred. **Application fee:** $40. **To apply online, go to:** http://www.moravian.edu/admission/applying.htm. **Admissions requirements/recommendations:** High school units required (recommended): English: 4; Mathematics: 3 (4); Science: 3; Foreign language: 2 (3); Social studies: 4; Total units: 16 (18). Tests: The college uses SAT or ACT scores in admissions decisions. Either SAT or ACT required. For admission to the fall 2011 entering class, the school will accept: ACT with writing required. Campus visit: Recommended. Admissions interview: Recommended. Off-campus interview: May be arranged. **Factors that count in admissions decisions: Academic:** Secondary school record: Very Important. Class rank: Very Important. Letters of recommendation: Important. Standardized test scores: Important. Essay: Important. **Nonacademic:** Interview: Considered. Extracurricular activities: Important. Talent/ability: Important. Character/personal qualities: Very Important. Alumni/ae relationship: Very Important. Geographical residence: Considered. State residency: Not Considered. Religious affiliation/commitment: Not Considered. Minority status: Important. Volunteer work: Important. Work experience: Important. **Other schools with the greatest overlap in applicants:** Gettysburg College; Lehigh University; Muhlenberg College; Susquehanna University; University of Scranton. **Admissions statistics for the fall 2009 entering class:** Total applicants: 2,021. Total accepted: 1,521. Freshmen enrolled: 380; 42% were from out of state. Overall acceptance rate: 75%. Early-decision acceptance rate: 79%. Non-early acceptance rate: 75%. **Size of waiting list:** 114 applicants; enrolled from waiting list: 27. **Credentials of fall 2009 freshmen:** 28% ranked in the top 10 percent of their high school class; 51% were in the top 25 percent; 82% were in the top half. (Proportion submitting class standing: 77%.) **First-year students who submitted SAT scores:** 81%. Scores (25/75 percentile): Critical Reading: 490-590, Math: 490-600, Combined: 980-1190. **First-year students submitting ACT scores:** 12%. Scores (25/75 percentile): English: N/A, Math: N/A, Composite: 20-22.

ACADEMICS

Year founded: 1742. **Academic calendar:** Semester. **Degrees offered:** bachelor's, post-bachelor's certificate, master's. **Most popular majors:** 18% business, management, marketing, and related support services, 17% social sciences, 11% English language and literature/letters, 11% visual and performing arts, 10% psychology. **Major fields of study:** biological and biomedical sciences; business, management, marketing, and related support services; computer and information sciences and support services; education; engineering; English language and literature/letters; foreign languages, literatures, and linguistics; health professions and related clinical sciences; history; mathematics and statistics; multi/interdisciplinary studies; natural resources and conservation; philosophy and religious studies; physical sciences; psychology; social sciences; visual and performing arts. **Areas of required coursework:** arts/fine arts, humanities, mathematics, English (including composition), philosophy, foreign languages, sciences (biological or physical), history, social science. **Pre-professional programs:** pre-law, pre-dentistry, pre-medicine, pre-theology, pre-veterinary science, other. **Special academic programs:** cross-registration, double major, honors program, independent study, internships, student-designed major, study abroad, teacher certificate program. **Teacher certification offered in:** elementary, secondary. **Cooperative education programs:** engineering, health professions. **Reserve Officers Training Corps (ROTC):** Army ROTC: Offered at cooperating institution (Lehigh University). **Faculty and instruction (2009-2010):** Total instructional faculty: 121 full-time, 79 part-time (48% men; 52% women; 5% minorities). Student/faculty ratio: 10/1. Classes of fewer than 20 students: 62%; of 20 to 49 students: 38%; of 50 or more students: 0%. **Advanced Placement and International Baccalaureate credit:** AP tests may be used for: Placement only. Scores accepted: 4, 5. International Baccalaureate exams may be used for: Placement only. **Freshmen returning for sophomore year:** 83%. **Graduation rates:** Four-year: 71%; five-year: 74%; six-year: 75%. **Graduate study:** 18% of students pursue further study within one year.

COSTS AND FINANCIAL AID

Financial aid office: (610) 861-1330. **Expenses (2010-2011):** Tuition and fees 2010-2011: $32,177; room/board: $9,164. Estimated books and supplies: $1,000; transportation: $466; personal expenses: $1,406. **Financial aid:** Priority filing date for institution's financial aid form: February 14; deadline: April 15. In 2009-2010, 87% of undergraduates applied for financial aid. Of those, 79% were determined to have financial need; 13% had their need fully met. Average financial aid package (proportion receiving): $23,421 (79%). Average amount of gift aid, such as scholarships or grants (proportion receiving): $17,584 (78%). Average amount of self-help aid, such as work study or loans (proportion receiving): $6,495 (73%). Average need-based loan (excluding PLUS or other private loans): $4,706. Among students who received need-based aid, the average percentage of need met: 79%. Among students who received aid based on merit, the average award (and the proportion receiving): $9,240 (14%). The average athletic scholarship (and the proportion receiving): $0 (0%).

CAMPUS LIFE AND EXTRACURRICULAR ACTIVITIES

Campus housing available (% using): coed dorms (36%), women's dorms (12%), men's dorms (2%), sorority housing (2%), fraternity housing (3%), apartment for single students (45%). Students who live in college-owned, operated, or affiliated housing: 71%. **Clubs and organizations:** Number of student organizations: 85. Activities include: campus ministries, choral groups, concert band, dance, drama/theater, international student organization, jazz band, literary magazine, marching band, model UN, music ensembles, opera, pep band, radio station, student government, student newspaper, symphony orchestra, yearbook. Number of fraternities: 3; sororities: 4. Proportion of men in fraternities: 12%; of women in sororities: 18%. Average proportion of students who stay on campus on weekends: 75%. **Sports program (2009-2010):** Member of NCAA III. *Men's intercollegiate varsity sports:* baseball, basketball, cross country, football, golf, soccer, tennis, track and field (indoor), track and field (outdoor). *Women's intercollegiate varsity sports:* basketball, cross country, field hockey, soccer, softball, tennis, track and field (indoor), track and field (outdoor), volleyball.

SERVICES AND FACILITIES

Basic services: nonremedial tutoring, placement service, health service, health insurance. **Counseling services:** minority student, career, personal, academic, older student, psychological, birth control, religious. **For learning-disabled students:** School does not offer a structured program with separate admission and additional fees. Total undergraduates in learning-disabled program or receiving services: 27. Services include: reading machines, tape recorders, note-taking services, oral tests, learning center, readers, extended time for tests, tutors, priority seating, substitution of courses, texts on tape, typist/scribe, exams on tape or computer, other testing accommodations, other. **Library:** Number of titles: 249,308; number of current serial subscriptions: 27,167. **Information technology resources:** Students are not required to lease or own a computer. Number of campus computers available to all students: 250. School has a wireless network. Approximate number of users that can be accommodated: 1,024. Proportion of college-owned housing units wired for high-speed internet access: 100%. **Campus safety:** Security services offered: 24-hour foot-and-vehicle patrols, late-night transport/escort service, 24-hour emergency telephones, lighted pathways/sidewalks, controlled dormitory access (key, security card, etc).

TRANSFER AND INTERNATIONAL STUDENTS

Transfer students: May apply for admission for the following academic terms: Fall, Spring. Applicants need a minimum number of credits to apply. For fall 2009: Transfer applications received: 270. Transfer applicants offered admission: 107. Transfer applicants enrolled: 85. **International students:** Number of foreign undergraduates: 13 (1% of student body).

Number of countries represented: 18. Minimum TOEFL score required: 550 (paper); 213 (computer). Average TOEFL score: 553 (paper).

Mount Aloysius College

- **Address:** 7373 Admiral Peary Highway, Cresson, PA 16630
- **Website:** http://www.mtaloy.edu
- **Private; Religious affiliation:** Roman Catholic (Sisters of Mercy)
- **Enrollment:** 1,165 full-time; 412 part-time

KEY STATS
- ✔ **U.S News College Ranking:** 44, Regional Colleges (North)
- ✔ **SAT Score (25th/75th percentile):** 840-1020
- ✔ **Tuition:** 2010-2011: $18,000

Selectivity: Less selective	**Room/board:** $7,660
Acceptance rate: 80%	**Average debt:** $29,802
Student/faculty ratio: 14/1	**Proportion who borrowed:** 80%

UNDERGRADUATE STUDENT BODY STATS
2009-2010 enrollment: 1,165 full-time; 412 part-time. Men: 27%; women: 73%. **Ethnic makeup:** African American: 3%; Hispanic: 1%; White: 96%; International: 1%. **Religious preference:** Roman Catholic: 40%; Protestant: 14%; No preference: 2%; Other: 44%.

ADMISSIONS FACTS AND FIGURES
Phone: (814) 886-6383. **Email:** admissions@mtaloy.edu. **Website:** http://www.mtaloy.edu. **Application deadlines for fall 2011:** Regular decision: Rolling. Early decision: Not offered. Early action: Not offered. Admission can be deferred. **Application fee:** $30. **To apply online, go to:** http://www.applyweb.com/aw?mta. **Admissions requirements/recommendations:** High school units required (recommended): English: 4; Mathematics: 3; Science: 3; Foreign language: (2); Social studies: 3; History: (3); Academic electives: 3; Total units: 16 (5). Tests: The college uses SAT or ACT scores in admissions decisions. Either SAT or ACT required. For admission to the fall 2011 entering class, the school will accept: ACT with or without writing accepted. Campus visit: Recommended. Admissions interview: Neither required nor recommended. Off-campus interview: Not available. **Factors that count in admissions decisions: *Academic:*** Secondary school record: Very Important. Class rank: Important. Letters of recommendation: Important. Standardized test scores: Important. Essay: Considered. ***Nonacademic:*** Interview: Very Important. Extracurricular activities: Very Important. Talent/ability: Very Important. Character/personal qualities: Very Important. Alumni/ae relationship: Not Considered. Geographical residence: Not Considered. State residency: Not Considered. Religious affiliation/commitment: Not Considered. Minority status: Not Considered. Volunteer work: Very Important. Work experience: Not Considered. **Admissions statistics for the fall 2009 entering class:** Total applicants: 1,219. Total accepted: 972. Freshmen enrolled: 360; 7% were from out of state. Overall acceptance rate: 80%. **Average high school grade point average:** 3.2. **First-year students who submitted SAT scores:** 79%. Scores (25/75 percentile): Critical Reading: 420-510, Math: 420-510, Combined: 840-1020. **First-year students submitting ACT scores:** 22%. Scores (25/75 percentile): English: 16-20, Math: 15-20, Composite: 17-21.

ACADEMICS
Year founded: 1853. **Academic calendar:** Semester. **Degrees offered:** certificate, associate, bachelor's, master's. **Major fields of study:** biological and biomedical sciences; business, management, marketing, and related support services; computer and information sciences and support services; education; English language and literature/letters; foreign languages, literatures, and linguistics; health professions and related clinical sciences; liberal arts and sciences studies, and humanities; psychology; security and protective services; social sciences. **Areas of required coursework:** arts/fine arts, humanities, computer literacy, mathematics, English (including composition), philosophy, sciences (biological or physical), history, social science. **Pre-professional programs:** pre-law. **Special academic programs:** accelerated program, distance learning, honors program, independent study, internships, student-designed major, teacher certificate program. **Teacher certification offered in:** early childhood, elementary. **Cooperative education programs:** art, business, computer science, education, health professions, humanities, natural science, social/behavioral science. **Faculty and instruction (2009-2010):** Total instructional faculty: 62 full-time, 103 part-time (37% men; 63% women; 1% minorities). Full-time faculty with Ph.D.

or other terminal degree: 35%. Student/faculty ratio: 14/1. Classes of fewer than 20 students: 63%; of 20 to 49 students: 37%; of 50 or more students: 0%. **Advanced Placement and International Baccalaureate credit:** AP tests may be used for: Credit and/or placement. Scores accepted: 5. International Baccalaureate exams may be used for: Credit only. **Freshmen returning for sophomore year:** 64%. **Graduation rates:** Four-year: 22%; five-year: 30%; six-year: 37%.

COSTS AND FINANCIAL AID

Financial aid office: (814) 886-6357. **Expenses (2010-2011):** Tuition and fees 2010-2011: $18,000; room/board: $7,660. Estimated books and supplies: $2,000 personal expenses: $3,000. **Financial aid:** Priority filing date for institution's financial aid form: April 1. In 2009-2010, 100% of undergraduates applied for financial aid. Of those, 97% were determined to have financial need; Average financial aid package (proportion receiving): $11,300 (97%). Average amount of gift aid, such as scholarships or grants (proportion receiving): $2,000 (97%). Average amount of self-help aid, such as work study or loans (proportion receiving): $3,500 (97%). Average need-based loan (excluding PLUS or other private loans): $3,400. Among students who received need-based aid, the average percentage of need met: 35%. Among students who received aid based on merit, the average award (and the proportion receiving): $3,500 (3%). The average athletic scholarship (and the proportion receiving): $0 (0%). Average amount of debt of borrowers graduating in 2009: $29,802. Proportion who borrowed: 80%.

CAMPUS LIFE AND EXTRACURRICULAR ACTIVITIES

Campus housing available: coed dorms. Students who live in college-owned, operated, or affiliated housing: 26%. **Clubs and organizations:** Number of student organizations: 60. Activities include: choral groups, drama/theater, student government, student newspaper. Average proportion of students who stay on campus on weekends: 50%. **Sports program (2009-2010):** Member of NCAA III. *Men's intercollegiate varsity sports:* baseball, basketball, cross country, golf, soccer. *Women's intercollegiate varsity sports:* basketball, cross country, golf, soccer, volleyball.

SERVICES AND FACILITIES

Basic services: nonremedial tutoring, placement service, day care, health service. **Remedial assistance:** reading, math, writing. **Counseling services:** military, personal, veteran student, academic, psychological, religious. **For learning-disabled students:** Services include: remedial math, remedial English, remedial reading, tape recorders, note-taking services, special bookstore section, oral tests, learning center, readers, extended time for tests, tutors. **Library:** Number of titles: 81,059; number of current serial subscriptions: 275. **Information technology resources:** Students are not required to lease or own a computer. Number of campus computers available to all students: 125. School has a wireless network. Proportion of college-owned housing units wired for high-speed internet access: 100%. **Campus safety:** Security services offered: 24-hour foot-and-vehicle patrols, late-night transport/escort service, 24-hour emergency telephones, lighted pathways/sidewalks, controlled dormitory access (key, security card, etc).

TRANSFER AND INTERNATIONAL STUDENTS

Transfer students: May apply for admission for the following academic terms: Fall, Winter, Spring, Summer. Applicants need a minimum number of credits to apply. For fall 2009: Transfer applicants enrolled: 139. **International students:** Number of foreign undergraduates: 8 (1% of student body). Minimum TOEFL score required: 500 (paper); 173 (computer).

Muhlenberg College

- **Address:** 2400 W. Chew Street, Allentown, PA 18104
- **Website:** http://www.muhlenberg.edu
- **Private; Religious affiliation:** Lutheran
- **Enrollment:** 2,352 full-time; 165 part-time

KEY STATS

✔ **U.S News College Ranking:** 75, National Liberal Arts Colleges
✔ **SAT Score (25th/75th percentile):** 1120-1320
✔ **Tuition:** 2010-2011: $38,380

Selectivity: More selective	**Room/board:** $8,735
Acceptance rate: 45%	**Average debt:** $20,602
Student/faculty ratio: 12/1	**Proportion who borrowed:** 83%

UNDERGRADUATE STUDENT BODY STATS

2009-2010 enrollment: 2,352 full-time; 165 part-time. Men: 43%; women: 57%. **Ethnic makeup:** African American: 2%; Asian American: 2%; Hispanic: 3%; White: 91%. **Religious preference:** Roman Catholic: 30%; Protestant: 15%; Jewish: 29%; No preference: 14%; Unknown: 1%; Lutheran: 6%; Eastern Orthodox: 0%; Other: 5%.

ADMISSIONS FACTS AND FIGURES

Phone: (484) 664-3200. **Email:** admissions@muhlenberg.edu. **Website:** http://www.muhlenberg.edu. **Application deadlines for fall 2011:** Regular decision: February 15. Early decision: Send application by: February 1; Decision sent by: December 1. Early action: Not offered. Admission can be deferred. **Application fee:** $50. **To apply online, go to:** https://www.commonapp.org/CommonApp/default.aspx. **Admissions requirements/recommendations:** High school units required (recommended): English: 4 (4); Mathematics: 3 (4); Science: 2 (3); Foreign language: 2 (4); Social studies: 0 (2); History: 2 (3); Total units: 16 (20). Tests: The college uses SAT or ACT scores in admissions decisions. Neither SAT nor ACT required. For admission to the fall 2011 entering class, the school will accept: ACT with writing required. Campus visit: Recommended. Admissions interview: Recommended. Off-campus interview: May be arranged. **Factors that count in admissions decisions:** *Academic:* Secondary school record: Very Important. Class rank: Considered. Letters of recommendation: Important. Standardized test scores: Important. Essay: Important. *Nonacademic:* Interview: Important. Extracurricular activities: Important. Talent/ability: Important. Character/personal qualities: Important. Alumni/ae relationship: Considered. Geographical residence: Not Considered. State residency: Not Considered. Religious affiliation/commitment: Not Considered. Minority status: Considered. Volunteer work: Considered. Work experience: Considered. **Other schools with the greatest overlap in applicants:** Binghamton University–SUNY; Franklin and Marshall College; Ithaca College; Lehigh University; Ursinus College. **Admissions statistics for the fall 2009 entering class:** Total applicants: 4,410. Total accepted: 2,002. Freshmen enrolled: 577; 72% were from out of state. Overall acceptance rate: 45%. Non-early acceptance rate: 45%. **Size of waiting list:** 1465 applicants; enrolled from waiting list: 21. **Credentials of fall 2009 freshmen:** 41% ranked in the top 10 percent of their high school class; 84% were in the top 25 percent; 96% were in the top half. (Proportion submitting class standing: 32%.) **Average high school grade point average:** 3.3. First-year students who submitted SAT scores: 75%. Scores (25/75 percentile): Critical Reading: 560-660, Math: 560-660, Combined: 1120-1320. **First-year students submitting ACT scores:** 19%. Scores (25/75 percentile): English: N/A, Math: N/A, Composite: 25-31.

ACADEMICS

Year founded: 1848. **Academic calendar:** Semester. **Degrees offered:** certificate, associate, terminal-associate, bachelor's. **Most popular majors:** 11% business, management, marketing, and related support services, 10% psychology, 9% communication studies/speech communication and rhetoric, 8% drama and dramatics/theater arts, 7% finance. **Major fields of study:** area, ethnic, cultural, and gender studies; biological and biomedical sciences; business, management, marketing, and related support services; communication, journalism, and related programs; computer and information sciences and support services; English language and literature/letters; foreign languages, literatures, and linguistics; history; mathematics and statistics; multi/interdisciplinary studies; natural resources and conservation; philosophy and religious studies; physical sciences; psychology; social sciences; visual and performing arts. **Areas of required coursework:** arts/fine arts, mathematics, English (including composition), philosophy, foreign languages, sciences (biological or physical), history, social science, other. **Pre-professional programs:** pre-law, pre-dentistry, pre-medicine, pre-theology, pre-veterinary science, pre-optometry, other. **Special academic programs (% participation):** accelerated program (4%), cross-registration (2%), double major (34%), exchange student program (domestic) (1%), honors program (1%), independent study (19%), internships (18%), student-designed major (1%), study abroad (24%), teacher certificate program (5%). **Teacher certification offered in:** elementary, secondary. **Reserve Officers Training Corps (ROTC):** Army ROTC: Offered at cooperating institution (Lehigh University). **Faculty and instruction (2009-2010):** Total instructional faculty: 166 full-time, 94 part-time (53% men; 47% women; 7% minorities). Full-time faculty with Ph.D. or other terminal degree: 87%. Student/faculty ratio: 12/1. Classes of fewer than 20 students: 64%; of 20 to 49 students: 35%; of 50 or more students: 1%. **Advanced Placement and International Baccalaureate credit:** AP tests may be used for: Placement only. Scores accepted: 3, 4, 5. International Baccalaureate exams may be used for: Placement only. **Freshmen returning for sophomore year:** 93%. **Graduation**

rates: Four-year: 79%; five-year: 85%; six-year: 85%. **Graduate study:** 20% of students pursue further study immediately upon graduation; 25% within one year; 50% within five years. Fields in which graduates pursue further study: Master of Business Administration (MBA), 5%; law, 10%; medicine, 12%; dentistry, 5%; engineering, 1%; theology (or the seminary), 2%; education, 16%; arts and sciences, 47%; veterinary medicine, 2%.

COSTS AND FINANCIAL AID

Financial aid office: (484) 664-3174. **Expenses (2010-2011):** Tuition and fees 2010-2011: $38,380; room/board: $8,735. Estimated books and supplies: $1,440; transportation: $515; personal expenses: $1,400. **Financial aid:** Priority filing date for institution's financial aid form: February 15; deadline: February 15. In 2009-2010, 65% of undergraduates applied for financial aid. Of those, 52% were determined to have financial need; 84% had their need fully met. Average financial aid package (proportion receiving): $23,370 (51%). Average amount of gift aid, such as scholarships or grants (proportion receiving): $20,674 (48%). Average amount of self-help aid, such as work study or loans (proportion receiving): $5,115 (38%). Average need-based loan (excluding PLUS or other private loans): $4,388. Among students who received need-based aid, the average percentage of need met: 93%. Among students who received aid based on merit, the average award (and the proportion receiving): $9,228 (26%). The average athletic scholarship (and the proportion receiving): $0 (0%). Average amount of debt of borrowers graduating in 2009: $20,602. Proportion who borrowed: 83%.

CAMPUS LIFE AND EXTRACURRICULAR ACTIVITIES

Campus housing available (% using): coed dorms (65%), women's dorms (9%), sorority housing (3%), fraternity housing (2%), special housing for disabled students (0%), special housing for international students (0%), other housing options (0%). Students who live in college-owned, operated, or affiliated housing: 92%. **Student employment:** During the 2009-2010 academic year, 20% of undergraduates worked on campus. Average per-year earnings: $1,800. **Clubs and organizations:** Number of student organizations: 128. Activities include: concert band, dance, drama/theater, jazz band, literary magazine, music ensembles, musical theater, pep band, radio station, student government, student newspaper, student film society, yearbook. Number of fraternities: 4; sororities: 4. Proportion of men in fraternities: 15%; of women in sororities: 18%. Average proportion of students who stay on campus on weekends: 75%. **Sports program (2009-2010):** Member of NCAA III. *Men's intercollegiate varsity sports:* baseball, basketball, cross country, football, golf, lacrosse, soccer, tennis, track and field (indoor), track and field (outdoor), wrestling. *Women's intercollegiate varsity sports:* basketball, cross country, field hockey, golf, lacrosse, soccer, softball, tennis, track and field (indoor), track and field (outdoor), volleyball.

SERVICES AND FACILITIES

Basic services: nonremedial tutoring, placement service, health service. **Counseling services:** minority student, career, personal, academic, older student, psychological, birth control, religious. **For learning-disabled students:** School does not offer a structured program with separate admission and additional fees. Services include: reading machines, tape recorders, note-taking services, oral tests, learning center, readers, extended time for tests, tutors, priority registration, priority seating, texts on tape. **Library:** Number of titles: 295,629; number of current serial subscriptions: 11,157. **Information technology resources:** Students are not required to lease or own a computer. Number of campus computers available to all students: 265. School has a wireless network. Approximate number of users that can be accommodated: 1,400. Proportion of college-owned housing units wired for high-speed internet access: 100%. **Campus safety:** Security services offered: 24-hour foot-and-vehicle patrols, late-night transport/escort service, 24-hour emergency telephones, lighted pathways/sidewalks, controlled dormitory access (key, security card, etc).

TRANSFER AND INTERNATIONAL STUDENTS

Transfer students: May apply for admission for the following academic terms: Fall, Spring. Applicants do not need a minimum number of credits to apply. For fall 2009: Transfer applications received: 103. Transfer applicants offered admission: 27. Transfer applicants enrolled: 15. **International students:** Number of foreign undergraduates: 5. Number of countries represented: 5. Minimum TOEFL score required: 550 (paper); 213 (computer). Average TOEFL score: 585 (paper).

Neumann University

■ **Address:** 1 Neumann Drive, Aston, PA 19014-1298
■ **Website:** http://www.neumann.edu
■ **Private; Religious affiliation:** Roman Catholic
■ **Enrollment:** 2,012 full-time; 489 part-time

KEY STATS

✔ **U.S News College Ranking:** second tier, Regional Universities (North)
✔ **SAT Score (25th/75th percentile):** 810-980
✔ **Tuition:** 2010-2011: $22,256

Selectivity: Less selective   **Room/board:** $10,162
Acceptance rate: 94%   **Average debt:** $40,000
Student/faculty ratio: 14/1   **Proportion who borrowed:** 80%

UNDERGRADUATE STUDENT BODY STATS

2009-2010 enrollment: 2,012 full-time; 489 part-time. Men: 35%; women: 65%. **Ethnic makeup:** African American: 13%; Asian American: 1%; Hispanic: 3%; White: 80%; International: 2%. **Religious preference:** Roman Catholic: 4%; Protestant: 24%; Jewish: 1%; Muslim: 1%; No preference: 11%; Roman Catholic: 56%; Other: 3%.

ADMISSIONS FACTS AND FIGURES

Phone: (800) 963-8626. **Email:** neumann@neumann.edu. **Website:** http://www.neumann.edu. **Application deadlines for fall 2011:** Regular decision: August 1. Early decision: Not offered. Early action: Not offered. Admission can be deferred. **Application fee:** $35. **To apply online, go to:** http://www.neumann.edu/i2e/app/app_int.asp. **Admissions requirements/recommendations:** High school units required (recommended): English: 4; Mathematics: 2; Science: 2 (3); Foreign language: 2; Social studies: 2; Academic electives: 4; Total units: 16 (17). Tests: The college uses SAT or ACT scores in admissions decisions. Either SAT or ACT required. For admission to the fall 2011 entering class, the school will accept: ACT with or without writing accepted. Campus visit: Recommended. Admissions interview: Recommended. Off-campus interview: May be arranged. **Factors that count in admissions decisions:** *Academic:* Secondary school record: Very Important. Class rank: Very Important. Letters of recommendation: Important. Standardized test scores: Very Important. Essay: Important. *Nonacademic:* Interview: Considered. Extracurricular activities: Considered. Talent/ability: Considered. Character/personal qualities: Very Important. Alumni/ae relationship: Important. Geographical residence: Considered. State residency: Considered. Religious affiliation/commitment: Important. Minority status: Considered. Volunteer work: Important. Work experience: Not Considered. **Other schools with the greatest overlap in applicants:** Cabrini College; Rowan University; Temple University; Villanova University; West Chester University of Pennsylvania. **Admissions statistics for the fall 2009 entering class:** Total applicants: 2,358. Total accepted: 2,213. Freshmen enrolled: 520; 32% were from out of state. Overall acceptance rate: 94%. **Credentials of fall 2009 freshmen:** 30% ranked in the top 10 percent of their high school class; 50% were in the top 25 percent; 95% were in the top half. (Proportion submitting class standing: 99%.) **Average high school grade point average:** 3.3. **First-year students who submitted SAT scores:** 98%. Scores (25/75 percentile): Critical Reading: 410-490, Math: 400-490, Combined: 810-980.

ACADEMICS

Year founded: 1965. **Academic calendar:** Semester. **Degrees offered:** associate, bachelor's, post-bachelor's certificate, master's. **Major fields of study:** agriculture, agriculture operations, and related sciences; biological and biomedical sciences; business, management, marketing, and related support services; communication, journalism, and related programs; computer and information sciences and support services; education; English language and literature/letters; health professions and related clinical sciences; liberal arts and sciences studies, and humanities; natural resources and conservation; parks, recreation, leisure, and fitness studies; psychology; security and protective services; social sciences. **Areas of required coursework:** arts/fine arts, humanities, computer literacy, mathematics, English (including composition), philosophy, foreign languages, sciences (biological or physical), history, social science, other. **Pre-professional programs:** pre-law, pre-medicine, pre-pharmacy. **Special academic programs (% participation):** accelerated program (20%), cooperative (work-study plan) program (50%), distance learning (10%), double major (5%), honors program (5%), independent study (30%), internships (50%), liberal arts/career combination (20%), study abroad (5%), teacher certificate program (20%), weekend college (20%). **Teacher certification offered in:** early childhood, special education, elementary, middle/junior high, secondary. **Cooperative education programs:** business, computer science, education, health professions, social/behavioral science. **Reserve Officers Training Corps (ROTC):** Army ROTC: Offered at cooperating institution (Widener University). **Faculty and instruction (2009-2010):** Total instructional faculty: 91 full-time, 195 part-time (34% men; 66% women; 5% minorities). Full-time faculty with Ph.D. or other terminal degree: 77%. Student/faculty ratio: 14/1. Classes of fewer than 20 students: 44%; of 20 to 49 students: 54%; of 50 or more students: 1%. **Advanced Placement and International Baccalaureate credit:** AP tests may be used for: Credit only. Scores accepted: 2, 3, 4, 5. International Baccalaureate exams may be used for: Credit only. **Freshmen returning for sophomore year:** 73%. **Graduation rates:** Five-year: 41%; six-year: 51%. **Graduate study:** 20% of students pursue further study immediately upon graduation; 20% within one year; 20% within five years. Fields in which graduates pursue further study: Master of Business Administration (MBA), 30%; law, 1%; medicine, 1%; theology (or the seminary), 1%; education, 50%; arts and sciences, 17%.

COSTS AND FINANCIAL AID
Financial aid office: (610) 558-5521. **Expenses (2010-2011):** Tuition and fees 2010-2011: $22,256; room/board: $10,162. Estimated books and supplies: $1,200; transportation: $1,500; personal expenses: $1,500. **Financial aid:** Priority filing date for institution's financial aid form: March 15; deadline: May 15. In 2009-2010, 90% of undergraduates applied for financial aid. Of those, 90% were determined to have financial need; 60% had their need fully met. Average financial aid package (proportion receiving): $19,000 (90%). Average amount of gift aid, such as scholarships or grants (proportion receiving): $15,000 (82%). Average amount of self-help aid, such as work study or loans (proportion receiving): $2,000 (15%). Average need-based loan (excluding PLUS or other private loans): $5,000. Among students who received need-based aid, the average percentage of need met: 65%. Average amount of debt of borrowers graduating in 2009: $40,000. Proportion who borrowed: 80%.

CAMPUS LIFE AND EXTRACURRICULAR ACTIVITIES
Campus housing available (% using): coed dorms (90%), other housing options (10%). Students who live in college-owned, operated, or affiliated housing: 40%. **Student employment:** During the 2009-2010 academic year, 20% of undergraduates worked on campus. Average per-year earnings: $2,000. **Clubs and organizations:** Number of student organizations: 30. Activities include: campus ministries, choral groups, concert band, dance, drama/theater, jazz band, literary magazine, marching band, model UN, music ensembles, musical theater, radio station, student government, student newspaper, symphony orchestra, television station, yearbook. Number of fraternities: 0; sororities: 0. Average proportion of students who stay on campus on weekends: 30%. **Sports program (2009-2010):** Member of NCAA III. *Men's intercollegiate varsity sports:* baseball, basketball, golf, ice hockey, lacrosse, soccer, tennis. *Women's intercollegiate varsity sports:* basketball, field hockey, ice hockey, lacrosse, soccer, softball, tennis, volleyball.

SERVICES AND FACILITIES
Basic services: nonremedial tutoring, placement service, day care, health service, health insurance. **Remedial assistance:** reading, math, writing, study skills. **Counseling services:** career, personal, academic, psychological, religious. **For learning-disabled students:** School does not offer a structured program with separate admission and additional fees. Total undergraduates in learning-disabled program or receiving services: 165. Services include: remedial math, remedial English, remedial reading, tape recorders, note-taking services, oral tests, learning center, readers, extended time for tests, tutors. **Library:** Number of titles: 80,000; number of current serial subscriptions: 400. **Information technology resources:** Students are not required to lease or own a computer. Number of campus computers available to all students: 800. School has a wireless network. Approximate number of users that can be accommodated: 400. Proportion of college-owned housing units wired for high-speed internet access: 100%. **Campus safety:** Security services offered: 24-hour foot-and-vehicle patrols, 24-hour emergency telephones, lighted pathways/sidewalks, controlled dormitory access (key, security card, etc).

TRANSFER AND INTERNATIONAL STUDENTS
Transfer students: May apply for admission for the following academic terms: Fall, Spring. Applicants need a minimum number of credits to apply. For fall 2009: Transfer applications received: 213. Transfer applicants offered admission: 203. Transfer applicants enrolled: 83. **International students:** Number of foreign undergraduates: 55 (2% of student body). Number of countries represented: 10. Minimum TOEFL score required: 550 (paper); 213 (computer). Average TOEFL score: 550 (paper).

Peirce College

- **Address:** 1420 Pine Street, Philadelphia, PA 19102
- **Website:** http://www.peirce.edu
- **Private**
- **Enrollment:** 831 full-time; 1,252 part-time

KEY STATS
✔ **U.S News College Ranking:** Unranked, Regional Colleges (North)
✔ **SAT or ACT Score (25th/75th percentile):** N/A
✔ **Tuition:** 2010-2011: $15,300

Selectivity: N/A	**Room/board:** N/A
Acceptance rate: N/A	**Average debt:** $19,748
Student/faculty ratio: 17/1	**Proportion who borrowed:** 87%

UNDERGRADUATE STUDENT BODY STATS
2009-2010 enrollment: 831 full-time; 1,252 part-time. Men: 28%; women: 72%. **Ethnic makeup:** African American: 60%; Asian American: 1%; Hispanic: 5%; White: 32%; International: 2%.

ADMISSIONS FACTS AND FIGURES
Phone: (888) 467-3472. **Email:** info@peirce.edu. **Website:** http://www.peirce.edu. **Application deadlines for fall 2011:** Regular decision: Rolling. Early decision: Not offered. Early action: Not offered. Admission can be deferred. **Application fee:** $50. **To apply online, go to:** http://www.peirce.edu/apply. **Admissions requirements/recommendations:** Tests: The college does not use SAT or ACT scores in admissions decisions. Neither SAT nor ACT required. Campus visit: Neither required nor recommended. Admissions interview: Neither required nor recommended. Off-campus interview: May be arranged. **Factors that count in admissions decisions:** *Academic:* Secondary school record: Not Considered. Class rank: Not Considered. Letters of recommendation: Not Considered. Standardized test scores: Not Considered. Essay: Not Considered. *Nonacademic:* Interview: Not Considered. Extracurricular activities: Not Considered. Talent/ability: Not Considered. Character/personal qualities: Not Considered. Alumni/ae relationship: Not Considered. Geographical residence: Not Considered. State residency: Not Considered. Religious affiliation/commitment: Not Considered. Minority status: Not Considered. Volunteer work: Not Considered. Work experience: Not Considered. **Admissions statistics for the fall 2009 entering class:** 9% were from out of state.

ACADEMICS
Year founded: 1865. **Academic calendar:** Semester. **Degrees offered:** certificate, associate, bachelor's. **Most popular majors:** 59% business administration and management, 23% information science/studies, 16% legal assistant/paralegal. **Major fields of study:** business, management, marketing, and related support services; computer and information sciences and support services; legal professions and studies. **Areas of required coursework:** humanities, computer literacy, mathematics, English (including composition), sciences (biological or physical), history, social science. **Special academic programs (% participation):** accelerated program (100%), cooperative (work-study plan) program (8%), distance learning (100%). **Cooperative education programs:** business, computer science, other. **Faculty and instruction (2009-2010):** Total instructional faculty: 30 full-time, 129 part-time (56% men; 44% women; 31% minorities). Full-time faculty with Ph.D. or other terminal degree: 63%. Student/faculty ratio: 17/1. Classes of fewer than 20 students: 81%; of 20 to 49 students: 19%. **Advanced Placement and International Baccalaureate credit:** AP tests may be used for: Credit only. Scores accepted: 3. **Freshmen returning for sophomore year:** 64%. **Graduation rates:** Four-year: 7%; five-year: 7%; six-year: 56%. **Graduate study:** 17% of students pursue further study within one year.

COSTS AND FINANCIAL AID
Financial aid office: (215) 670-9370. **Expenses (2010-2011):** Tuition and fees 2010-2011: $15,300. Average amount of debt of borrowers graduating in 2009: $19,748. Proportion who borrowed: 87%.

CAMPUS LIFE AND EXTRACURRICULAR ACTIVITIES
Students who live in college-owned, operated, or affiliated housing: 0%. Number of fraternities: 0; sororities: 0.

SERVICES AND FACILITIES
Basic services: nonremedial tutoring, health service. **Remedial assistance:** other. **Counseling services:** career, academic. **For learning-disabled stu-**

dents: School does not offer a structured program with separate admission and additional fees. Total undergraduates in learning-disabled program or receiving services: 18. Services include: tape recorders, diagnostic testing service, untimed tests, note-taking services, oral tests, learning center, readers, extended time for tests, tutors, early syllabus, texts on tape, other testing accommodations, other. **Library:** Number of titles: 22,556; number of current serial subscriptions: 68. **Information technology resources:** Students are required to lease or own a computer. Number of campus computers available to all students: 229. School has a wireless network. Approximate number of users that can be accommodated: 250. Proportion of college-owned housing units wired for high-speed internet access: 0%. **Campus safety:** Security services offered: 24-hour foot-and-vehicle patrols, late-night transport/escort service, 24-hour emergency telephones, lighted pathways/sidewalks.

TRANSFER AND INTERNATIONAL STUDENTS

Transfer students: May apply for admission for the following academic terms: Fall, Winter, Spring, Summer. Applicants do not need a minimum number of credits to apply. **International students:** Number of foreign undergraduates: 44 (2% of student body). Number of countries represented: 29.

Pennsylvania College of Technology

- ■ **Address:** 1 College Avenue, Williamsport, PA 17701
- ■ **Website:** http://www.pct.edu
- ■ **Public**
- ■ **Enrollment:** 5,469 full-time; 940 part-time

KEY STATS
✔ **U.S News College Ranking:** 31, Regional Colleges (North)
✔ **SAT or ACT Score (25th/75th percentile):** N/A
✔ **Tuition:** 2009-2010: $12,480 in state, $15,630 out of state
Selectivity: Less selective	**Room/board:** $8,350
Acceptance rate: 88%	**Average debt:** N/A
Student/faculty ratio: 18/1	**Proportion who borrowed:** N/A

UNDERGRADUATE STUDENT BODY STATS
2009-2010 enrollment: 5,469 full-time; 940 part-time. Men: 65%; women: 35%. **Ethnic makeup:** African American: 3%; Asian American: 1%; Hispanic: 2%; White: 93%. **Religious preference:** Roman Catholic: 21%; Protestant: 56%; Jewish: 1%; No preference: 20%; Islamic, Buddhist, Other: 2%.

ADMISSIONS FACTS AND FIGURES
Phone: (570) 327-4761. **Email:** admissions@pct.edu. **Website:** http://www.pct.edu. **Application deadlines for fall 2011:** Regular decision: July 1. Early decision: Not offered. Early action: Not offered. Admission can be deferred. **Application fee:** $50. **To apply online, go to:** https://as400sec.pct.edu/Apply/. **Admissions requirements/recommendations:** Tests: The college uses SAT or ACT scores in admissions decisions. Neither SAT nor ACT required. For admission to the fall 2011 entering class, the school will accept: ACT with or without writing accepted. Campus visit: Neither required nor recommended. Admissions interview: Neither required nor recommended. Off-campus interview: Not available. **Factors that count in admissions decisions:** *Academic:* Secondary school record: Not Considered. Class rank: Not Considered. Letters of recommendation: Not Considered. Standardized test scores: Considered. Essay: Not Considered. *Nonacademic:* Interview: Not Considered. Extracurricular activities: Not Considered. Talent/ability: Not Considered. Character/personal qualities: Not Considered. Alumni/ae relationship: Not Considered. Geographical residence: Not Considered. State residency: Not Considered. Religious affiliation/commitment: Not Considered. Minority status: Not Considered. Volunteer work: Not Considered. Work experience: Not Considered. **Admissions statistics for the fall 2009 entering class:** Total applicants: 4,061. Total accepted: 3,567. Freshmen enrolled: 2,347; Overall acceptance rate: 88%. **Size of waiting list:** 49 applicants; enrolled from waiting list: 46. **Credentials of fall 2009 freshmen:** (Proportion submitting class standing: 84%.) **First-year students who submitted SAT scores:** 69%.

ACADEMICS
Year founded: 1941. **Academic calendar:** Semester. **Degrees offered:** certificate, associate, bachelor's. **Most popular majors:** 4% automotive engineering technology/technician, 4% construction engineering technology/technician,

4% nursing/registered nurse training (R.N., A.S.N., B.S.N., M.S.N.), 2% civil engineering technology/technician, 2% computer systems networking and telecommunications. **Major fields of study:** business, management, marketing, and related support services; communications technologies/technicians and support services; computer and information sciences and support services; engineering technologies/technicians; health professions and related clinical sciences; legal professions and studies; mechanic and repair technologies/technicians; natural resources and conservation; personal and culinary services; visual and performing arts. **Areas of required coursework:** humanities, computer literacy, mathematics, English (including composition), foreign languages, sciences (biological or physical), social science, other. **Special academic programs:** cooperative (work-study plan) program, cross-registration, distance learning, internships, study abroad, weekend college. **Cooperative education programs:** health professions, technologies, vocational arts. **Reserve Officers Training Corps (ROTC):** Army ROTC: Offered at cooperating institution (Bucknell University). **Faculty and instruction (2009-2010):** Total instructional faculty: 296 full-time, 188 part-time (62% men; 38% women; 3% minorities). Student/faculty ratio: 18/1. Classes of fewer than 20 students: 59%; of 20 to 49 students: 41%. **Freshmen returning for sophomore year:** 69%. **Graduation rates:** Four-year: 40%; five-year: 49%; six-year: 48%. **Graduate study:** 22% of students pursue further study within one year.

COSTS AND FINANCIAL AID
Financial aid office: (570) 327-4766. **Expenses (2009-2010):** Tuition and fees 2009-2010: $12,480 in state, $15,630 out of state; room/board: $8,350. Estimated books and supplies: $1,000. **Financial aid:** Priority filing date for institution's financial aid form: April 1. In 2009-2010, 100% of undergraduates applied for financial aid. Of those, 100% were determined to have financial need; Average financial aid package (proportion receiving): N/A (100%). Average amount of gift aid, such as scholarships or grants (proportion receiving): $6,762 (77%). Average amount of self-help aid, such as work study or loans (proportion receiving): N/A (90%).

CAMPUS LIFE AND EXTRACURRICULAR ACTIVITIES
Campus housing available (% using): other housing options (100%). Students who live in college-owned, operated, or affiliated housing: 23%. **Clubs and organizations:** Number of student organizations: 48. Activities include: campus ministries, dance, drama/theater, international student organization, radio station, student government. Number of fraternities: 4; sororities: 2. Proportion of men in fraternities: 1%; of women in sororities: 1%.

SERVICES AND FACILITIES
Basic services: nonremedial tutoring, placement service, day care, health service. **Remedial assistance:** reading, math, writing, study skills. **Counseling services:** career, personal, academic, other. **For learning-disabled students:** Total undergraduates in learning-disabled program or receiving services: 418. Services include: remedial math, remedial English, remedial reading, tape recorders, other special classes, note-taking services, oral tests, learning center, readers, extended time for tests, tutors, priority registration, priority seating, other testing accommodations. **Library:** Number of titles: 110,501; number of current serial subscriptions: 1,537. **Information technology resources:** Students are not required to lease or own a computer. Number of campus computers available to all students: 2,400. School has a wireless network. Proportion of college-owned housing units wired for high-speed internet access: 100%. **Campus safety:** Security services offered: 24-hour foot-and-vehicle patrols, late-night transport/escort service, 24-hour emergency telephones, lighted pathways/sidewalks, controlled dormitory access (key, security card, etc).

TRANSFER AND INTERNATIONAL STUDENTS
Transfer students: May apply for admission for the following academic terms: Fall, Spring, Summer. Applicants do not need a minimum number of credits to apply. For fall 2009: Transfer applications received: 1,191. Transfer applicants offered admission: 1,102. Transfer applicants enrolled: 626. **International students:** Number of foreign undergraduates: 18. Number of countries represented: 11. Minimum TOEFL score required: 520 (paper); 68 (computer).

Pennsylvania State Univ.—University Park

- ■ **Address:** 201 Old Main, University Park, PA 16802
- ■ **Website:** http://www.psu.edu
- ■ **Public**
- ■ **Enrollment:** 37,485 full-time; 1,145 part-time

KEY STATS

- ✔ **U.S News College Ranking:** 47, National Universities
- ✔ **SAT Score (25th/75th percentile):** 1090-1300
- ✔ **Tuition:** 2009-2010: $14,416 in state, $25,946 out of state

Selectivity: More selective	**Room/board:** $8,790
Acceptance rate: 52%	**Average debt:** $28,680
Student/faculty ratio: 17/1	**Proportion who borrowed:** 68%

UNDERGRADUATE STUDENT BODY STATS

2009-2010 enrollment: 37,485 full-time; 1,145 part-time. Men: 55%; women: 45%.

ADMISSIONS FACTS AND FIGURES

Phone: (814) 865-5471. **Email:** admissions@psu.edu. **Website:** http://www.psu.edu. **Application deadlines for fall 2011:** Regular decision: Rolling. Early decision: Not offered. Early action: Not offered. Admission can be deferred. **Application fee:** $50. **To apply online, go to:** http://admissions.psu.edu/apply/. **Admissions requirements/recommendations:** High school units required (recommended): English: 4 (0); Mathematics: 3 (0); Science: 3 (0); Foreign language: 2 (0); Social studies: 3 (0); History: 0 (0); Academic electives: 0 (0); Total units: 15 (0). Tests: The college uses SAT or ACT scores in admissions decisions. Either SAT or ACT required. For admission to the fall 2011 entering class, the school will accept: ACT with writing required. Campus visit: Recommended. Admissions interview: Neither required nor recommended. Off-campus interview: Not available. **Factors that count in admissions decisions:** *Academic:* Secondary school record: Important. Class rank: Considered. Letters of recommendation: Considered. Standardized test scores: Very Important. Essay: Considered. *Nonacademic:* Interview: Not Considered. Extracurricular activities: Considered. Talent/ability: Considered. Character/personal qualities: Considered. Alumni/ae relationship: Considered. Geographical residence: Not Considered. State residency: Not Considered. Religious affiliation/commitment: Not Considered. Minority status: Not Considered. Volunteer work: Considered. Work experience: Considered. **Other schools with the greatest overlap in applicants:** Rutgers, the State University of New Jersey–New Brunswick; Temple University; University of Delaware; University of Maryland–College Park; University of Pittsburgh. **Admissions statistics for the fall 2009 entering class:** Total applicants: 40,714. Total accepted: 21,017. Freshmen enrolled: 6,560; 34% were from out of state. Overall acceptance rate: 52%. **Size of waiting list:** 1494 applicants; enrolled from waiting list: 1455. **Credentials of fall 2009 freshmen:** 50% ranked in the top 10 percent of their high school class; 86% were in the top 25 percent; 98% were in the top half. (Proportion submitting class standing: 65%.) **Average high school grade point average:** 3.6. **First-year students who submitted SAT scores:** 82%. Scores (25/75 percentile): Critical Reading: 530-630, Math: 560-670, Combined: 1090-1300. **First-year students submitting ACT scores:** 11%. Scores (25/75 percentile): English: N/A, Math: N/A, Composite: N/A.

ACADEMICS

Year founded: 1855. **Academic calendar:** Semester. **Degrees offered:** certificate, associate, transfer-associate, terminal-associate, bachelor's, master's, post-master's certificate, doctorate. **Most popular majors:** 18% business, management, marketing, and related support services, 13% engineering, 9% communication, journalism, and related programs, 7% computer and information sciences and support services, 7% social sciences. **Major fields of study:** agriculture, agriculture operations, and related sciences; architecture and related services; area, ethnic, cultural, and gender studies; biological and biomedical sciences; business, management, marketing, and related support services; communication, journalism, and related programs; computer and information sciences and support services; education; engineering; English language and literature/letters; family and consumer sciences/human sciences; foreign languages, literatures, and linguistics; health professions and related clinical sciences; history; liberal arts and sciences studies, and humanities; mathematics and statistics; multi/interdisciplinary studies; natural resources and conservation; parks, recreation, leisure, and fitness studies; philosophy and religious studies; physical sciences; psychology; science technologies/technicians; security and protective services; social

sciences; visual and performing arts. **Areas of required coursework:** arts/fine arts, humanities, computer literacy, mathematics, English (including composition), foreign languages, sciences (biological or physical), social science, other. **Pre-professional programs:** pre-law, pre-dentistry, pre-medicine, pre-veterinary science, pre-optometry, other. **Special academic programs:** accelerated program, cooperative (work-study plan) program, cross-registration, distance learning, double major, dual enrollment, English as a Second Language (ESL), exchange student program (domestic), external degree program, honors program, independent study, internships, liberal arts/career combination, student-designed major, study abroad, teacher certificate program, weekend college. **Teacher certification offered in:** early childhood, special education, elementary, vo-tech, secondary, bilingual/bicultural. **Cooperative education programs:** business, engineering, other. **Reserve Officers Training Corps (ROTC):** Army ROTC: Offered on campus; Navy ROTC: Offered on campus; Air Force ROTC: Offered on campus. **Faculty and instruction (2009-2010):** Total instructional faculty: 2,432 full-time, 365 part-time (61% men; 39% women; 18% minorities). Full-time faculty with Ph.D. or other terminal degree: 78%. Student/faculty ratio: 17/1. Classes of fewer than 20 students: 30%; of 20 to 49 students: 51%; of 50 or more students: 19%. **Advanced Placement and International Baccalaureate credit:** AP tests may be used for: Credit only. Scores accepted: 3, 4, 5. International Baccalaureate exams may be used for: Credit and/or placement. **Freshmen returning for sophomore year:** 93%. **Graduation rates:** Four-year: 62%; five-year: 82%; six-year: 85%. **Graduate study:** 22% of students pursue further study within one year.

COSTS AND FINANCIAL AID

Financial aid office: (814) 865-6301. **Expenses (2009-2010):** Tuition and fees 2009-2010: $14,416 in state, $25,946 out of state; room/board: $8,790. Estimated books and supplies: $1,360; transportation: $702; personal expenses: $3,222. **Financial aid:** Priority filing date for institution's financial aid form: February 15. In 2009-2010, 68% of undergraduates applied for financial aid. Of those, 53% were determined to have financial need; 6% had their need fully met. Average financial aid package (proportion receiving): $10,179 (51%). Average amount of gift aid, such as scholarships or grants (proportion receiving): $6,498 (29%). Average amount of self-help aid, such as work study or loans (proportion receiving): $4,800 (45%). Average need-based loan (excluding PLUS or other private loans): $4,638. Among students who received need-based aid, the average percentage of need met: 57%. Among students who received aid based on merit, the average award (and the proportion receiving): $3,262 (6%). The average athletic scholarship (and the proportion receiving): $19,923 (1%). Average amount of debt of borrowers graduating in 2009: $28,680. Proportion who borrowed: 68%.

CAMPUS LIFE AND EXTRACURRICULAR ACTIVITIES

Campus housing available: coed dorms, women's dorms, men's dorms, sorority housing, apartments for married students, apartment for single students, special housing for disabled students, special housing for international students, other housing options. Students who live in college-owned, operated, or affiliated housing: 36%. **Clubs and organizations:** Number of student organizations: 700. Activities include: campus ministries, choral groups, concert band, dance, drama/theater, international student organization, jazz band, literary magazine, marching band, model UN, music ensembles, musical theater, opera, pep band, radio station, student government, student newspaper, student film society, symphony orchestra, television station, yearbook. Number of fraternities: 56; sororities: 31. Proportion of men in fraternities: 13%; of women in sororities: 11%. Average proportion of students who stay on campus on weekends: 90%. **Sports program (2009-2010):** Member of NCAA I. **Men's intercollegiate varsity sports:** baseball, basketball, cross country, fencing, football, golf, gymnastics, lacrosse, soccer, swimming, tennis, track and field (indoor), track and field (outdoor), volleyball, wrestling. **Women's intercollegiate varsity sports:** basketball, cross country, fencing, field hockey, golf, gymnastics, lacrosse, soccer, softball, swimming, tennis, track and field (indoor), track and field (outdoor), volleyball.

SERVICES AND FACILITIES

Basic services: nonremedial tutoring, women's center, placement service, day care, health service, health insurance. **Remedial assistance:** reading, math, writing, study skills, other. **Counseling services:** minority student, career, military, personal, veteran student, academic, older student, psychological, birth control, religious, other. **For learning-disabled students:** School does not offer a structured program with separate admission and additional fees. Services include: remedial math, remedial English, reading machines, remedial reading, tape recorders, note-taking services, learning center, readers, extended time for tests, tutors, priority registration, priority seating, texts on tape, other testing accommodations. **Library:** Number of titles: 5,365,489; number of current serial subscriptions: 99,091. **Information technology resources:** Students are not required to lease or own a computer. Number of campus computers available to all students: 4,727. School has a wireless network. Approximate number of users that can be accommodated: 10,000. Proportion of college-owned housing units wired for high-speed internet access: 100%. **Campus safety:** Security services offered: 24-hour foot-and-vehicle patrols, late-night transport/escort service, 24-hour emergency telephones, lighted pathways/sidewalks, student patrols, controlled dormitory access (key, security card, etc).

TRANSFER AND INTERNATIONAL STUDENTS

Transfer students: May apply for admission for the following academic terms: Fall, Spring, Summer. Applicants need a minimum number of credits to apply. For fall 2009: Transfer applications received: 1,650. Transfer applicants offered admission: 732. Transfer applicants enrolled: 398. **International students:** Number of countries represented: 86. Minimum TOEFL score required: 550 (paper); 213 (computer).

Philadelphia Biblical University

- **Address:** 200 Manor Avenue, Langhorne, PA 19047-2990
- **Website:** http://www.pbu.edu
- **Private; Religious affiliation:** Evangelical
- **Enrollment:** 977 full-time; 78 part-time

KEY STATS

✔ **U.S News College Ranking:** 126, Regional Universities (North)
✔ **SAT Score (25th/75th percentile):** 932-1140
✔ **Tuition:** 2010-2011: $19,997

Selectivity: Selective	**Room/board:** $8,050
Acceptance rate: 77%	**Average debt:** $28,214
Student/faculty ratio: 16/1	**Proportion who borrowed:** 97%

UNDERGRADUATE STUDENT BODY STATS

2009-2010 enrollment: 977 full-time; 78 part-time. Men: 46%; women: 54%. **Ethnic makeup:** African American: 13%; Asian American: 4%; Hispanic: 4%; White: 78%; International: 1%. **Religious preference:** Protestant: 100%.

ADMISSIONS FACTS AND FIGURES

Phone: (215) 702-4235. **Email:** admissions@pbu.edu. **Website:** http://www.pbu.edu. **Application deadlines for fall 2011:** Regular decision: Rolling. Early decision: Not offered. Early action: Not offered. Admission can be deferred. **Application fee:** $25. **To apply online, go to:** http://www.pbu.edu/admissions/undergrad/onlineapp.htm. **Admissions requirements/recommendations:** High school units required (recommended): English: (4); Mathematics: (1); Science: (2); Foreign language: (2); Social studies: (3); Total units: (15). Tests: The college uses SAT or ACT scores in admissions decisions. Either SAT or ACT required. For admission to the fall 2011 entering class, the school will accept: ACT with or without writing accepted. Admissions interview: Recommended. Off-campus interview: May not be arranged. **Factors that count in admissions decisions:** *Academic:* Secondary school record: Important. Class rank: Considered. Letters of recommendation: Considered. Standardized test scores: Very Important. Essay: Important. *Nonacademic:* Interview: Important. Extracurricular activities: Considered. Talent/ability: Not Considered. Character/personal qualities: Important. Alumni/ae relationship: Not Considered. Geographical residence: Not Considered. State residency: Not Considered. Religious affiliation/commitment: Very Important. Minority status: Not Considered. Volunteer work: Not Considered. Work experience: Not Considered. **Other schools with the greatest overlap in applicants:** Eastern University; Lancaster Bible College; Liberty University; Messiah College; Moody Bible Institute. **Admissions statistics for the fall 2009 entering class:** Total applicants: 465. Total accepted: 356. Freshmen enrolled: 195; 54% were from out of state. Overall acceptance rate: 77%. **Credentials of fall 2009 freshmen:** 18% ranked in the top 10 percent of their high school class; 35% were in the top 25 percent; 64% were in the top half. (Proportion submitting class standing: 59%.) **Average high school grade point average:** 3.3. **First-year students who submitted SAT scores:** 74%. Scores (25/75 percentile): Critical Reading: 480-570, Math: 452-570, Combined: 932-1140. **First-year students submitting ACT scores:** 14%. Scores (25/75 percentile): English: 17-26, Math: 18-25, Composite: 19-26.

ACADEMICS

Year founded: 1913. **Academic calendar:** Semester. **Degrees offered:** certificate, bachelor's, master's. **Most popular majors:** 70% philosophy and religious studies, 12% education, 9% public administration and social service professions, 7% business, management, marketing, and related support services, 2% visual and performing arts. **Major fields of study:** philosophy and religious studies. **Areas of required coursework:** arts/fine arts, humanities, mathematics, English (including composition), philosophy, sciences (biological or physical), history, social science, other. **Pre-professional programs:** pre-theology. **Special academic programs:** accelerated program, double major, honors program, internships, study abroad, teacher certificate program. **Teacher certification offered in:** early childhood, elementary, secondary. **Reserve Officers Training Corps (ROTC):** Air Force ROTC: Offered at cooperating institution (St. Joseph's University). **Faculty and instruction (2009-2010):** Total instructional faculty: 52 full-time, 57 part-time (68% men; 32% women; 11% minorities). Full-time faculty with Ph.D. or other terminal degree: 65%. Student/faculty ratio: 16/1. Classes of fewer than 20 students: 61%; of 20 to 49 students: 36%; of 50 or more students: 3%. **Advanced Placement and International Baccalaureate credit:** AP tests may be used for: Credit and/or placement. Scores accepted: 3, 4, 5. International Baccalaureate exams may be used for: Credit and/or placement. **Freshmen returning for sophomore year:** 81%. **Graduation rates:** Four-year: 19%; five-year: 49%; six-year: 58%.

COSTS AND FINANCIAL AID

Financial aid office: (215) 702-4246. **Expenses (2010-2011):** Tuition and fees 2010-2011: $19,997; room/board: $8,050. Estimated books and supplies: $1,000; transportation: $1,400; personal expenses: $1,600. **Financial aid:** In 2009-2010, 90% of undergraduates applied for financial aid. Of those, 84% were determined to have financial need; 9% had their need fully met. Average financial aid package (proportion receiving): $14,138 (84%). Average amount of gift aid, such as scholarships or grants (proportion receiving): $10,131 (79%). Average amount of self-help aid, such as work study or loans (proportion receiving): $5,115 (74%). Average need-based loan (excluding PLUS or other private loans): $4,955. Among students who received need-based aid, the average percentage of need met: 66%. Among students who received aid based on merit, the average award (and the proportion receiving): $6,421 (5%). The average athletic scholarship (and the proportion receiving): $0 (0%). Average amount of debt of borrowers graduating in 2009: $28,214. Proportion who borrowed: 97%.

CAMPUS LIFE AND EXTRACURRICULAR ACTIVITIES

Campus housing available (% using): women's dorms (57%), men's dorms (41%), apartments for married students (1%), apartment for single students, special housing for disabled students (1%), special housing for international students (0%). Students who live in college-owned, operated, or affiliated housing: 64%. **Student employment:** During the 2009-2010 academic year, 25% of undergraduates worked on campus. Average per-year earnings: $1,750. **Clubs and organizations:** Number of student organizations: 25. Activities include: campus ministries, choral groups, concert band, drama/theater, international student organization, music ensembles, musical theater, opera, student government, student newspaper, symphony orchestra, yearbook. Number of fraternities: 0; sororities: 0. **Sports program (2009-2010):** Member of NCAA III. *Men's intercollegiate varsity sports:* baseball, basketball, golf, soccer, tennis, volleyball. *Women's intercollegiate varsity sports:* basketball, field hockey, soccer, softball, tennis, volleyball.

SERVICES AND FACILITIES

Remedial assistance: writing. **Counseling services:** personal, academic, religious. **For learning-disabled students:** School does not offer a structured program with separate admission and additional fees. Total undergraduates in learning-disabled program or receiving services: 30. Services include: remedial English, reading machines, tape recorders, untimed tests, note-taking services, oral tests, learning center, readers, tutors, other testing accommodations, other. **Library:** Number of titles: 97,448; number of current serial subscriptions: 15,375. **Information technology resources:** Students are not required to lease or own a computer. Number of campus computers available to all students: 79. School has a wireless network. Approximate number of users that can be accommodated: 800. Proportion of college-owned housing units wired for high-speed internet access: 100%. **Campus safety:** Security services offered: late-night transport/escort service, 24-hour emergency telephones, lighted pathways/sidewalks, controlled dormitory access (key, security card, etc).

TRANSFER AND INTERNATIONAL STUDENTS

Transfer students: May apply for admission for the following academic terms: Fall, Winter, Spring, Summer. Applicants do not need a minimum number of credits to apply. For fall 2009: Transfer applications received: 388. Transfer applicants offered admission: 235. Transfer applicants enrolled: 90. **International students:** Number of foreign undergraduates: 11 (1% of student body). Number of countries represented: 13. Minimum TOEFL score required: 190 (computer). Average TOEFL score: 520 (paper).

Philadelphia University

- ■ **Address:** School House Lane and Henry Avenue, Philadelphia, PA 19144
- ■ **Website:** http://www.philau.edu
- ■ **Private**
- ■ **Enrollment:** 2,675 full-time; 217 part-time

KEY STATS

- ✔ **U.S News College Ranking:** 61, Regional Universities (North)
- ✔ **SAT Score (25th/75th percentile):** 980-1170
- ✔ **Tuition:** 2010-2011: $28,800

Selectivity: Selective	**Room/board:** $9,502
Acceptance rate: 71%	**Average debt:** $32,037
Student/faculty ratio: 15/1	**Proportion who borrowed:** 81%

UNDERGRADUATE STUDENT BODY STATS

2009-2010 enrollment: 2,675 full-time; 217 part-time. Men: 33%; women: 67%.

ADMISSIONS FACTS AND FIGURES

Phone: (215) 951-2800. **Email:** admissions@philau.edu. **Website:** http://www.philau.edu. **Application deadlines for fall 2011:** Regular decision: Rolling. Early decision: Not offered. Early action: Not offered. Admission can be deferred. **Application fee:** $35. **To apply online, go to:** http://www.philau.edu/admissions/apply.html. **Admissions requirements/recommendations:** High school units required (recommended): English: 4 (4); Mathematics: 3 (4); Science: 3 (4); Foreign language: (2); Social studies: 2 (3); History: 1 (2); Academic electives: 2. Tests: The college uses SAT or ACT scores in admissions decisions. Either SAT or ACT required. For admission to the fall 2011 entering class, the school will accept: ACT with writing recommended. Campus visit: Recommended. Admissions interview: Recommended. Off-campus interview: Not available. **Factors that count in admissions decisions:** *Academic:* Secondary school record: Very Important. Class rank: Important. Letters of recommendation: Important. Standardized test scores: Very Important. Essay: Considered. ***Nonacademic:*** Interview: Important. Extracurricular activities: Important. Alumni/ae relationship: Not Considered. Volunteer work: Not Considered. Work experience: Not Considered. **Admissions statistics for the fall 2009 entering class:** Total applicants: 3,800. Total accepted: 2,707. Freshmen enrolled: 720; 54% were from out of state. Overall acceptance rate: 71%. **Credentials of fall 2009 freshmen:** 18% ranked in the top 10 percent of their high school class; 45% were in the top 25 percent; 81% were in the top half. (Proportion submitting class standing: 61%.) **Average high school grade point average:** 3.4. **First-year students who submitted SAT scores:** 91%. Scores (25/75 percentile): Critical Reading: 490-570, Math: 490-600, Combined: 980-1170. **First-year students submitting ACT scores:** 8%. Scores (25/75 percentile): English: N/A, Math: N/A, Composite: 21-26.

ACADEMICS

Year founded: 1884. **Academic calendar:** Semester. **Degrees offered:** certificate, bachelor's, post-bachelor's certificate, master's, post-master's certificate, doctorate. **Most popular majors:** 15% fashion merchandising, 10% fashion/apparel design, 8% architecture (B.Arch., B.A./B.S., M.Arch., M.A./M.S., Ph.D.), 6% graphic design, 6% interior architecture. **Major fields of study:** architecture and related services; biological and biomedical sciences; business, management, marketing, and related support services; communication, journalism, and related programs; communications technologies/technicians and support services; computer and information sciences and support services; engineering; health professions and related clinical sciences; legal professions and studies; multi/interdisciplinary studies; natural resources and conservation; physical sciences; psychology; visual and performing arts. **Areas of required coursework:** arts/fine arts, humanities, computer literacy, mathematics, English (including composition), sciences

(biological or physical), history, social science. **Pre-professional programs:** pre-law, pre-dentistry, pre-medicine, pre-veterinary science, pre-optometry, pre-pharmacy. **Special academic programs (% participation):** accelerated program, distance learning (5%), double major (1%), honors program (6%), independent study (15%), internships (15%), liberal arts/career combination (100%), study abroad (30%). **Cooperative education programs:** business, health professions, social/behavioral science. **Faculty and instruction (2009-2010):** Total instructional faculty: 110 full-time, 328 part-time (58% men; 42% women; 11% minorities). Full-time faculty with Ph.D. or other terminal degree: 75%. Student/faculty ratio: 15/1. Classes of fewer than 20 students: 64%; of 20 to 49 students: 35%; of 50 or more students: 1%. **Advanced Placement and International Baccalaureate credit:** AP tests may be used for: Credit only. Scores accepted: 3, 4, 5. **Freshmen returning for sophomore year:** 76%. **Graduation rates:** Four-year: 43%; five-year: 58%; six-year: 56%. **Graduate study:** 20% of students pursue further study within one year. Fields in which graduates pursue further study: Master of Business Administration (MBA), 50%; medicine, 10%; arts and sciences, 40%.

COSTS AND FINANCIAL AID

Financial aid office: (215) 951-2940. **Expenses (2010-2011):** Tuition and fees 2010-2011: $28,800; room/board: $9,502. **Financial aid:** Priority filing date for institution's financial aid form: April 15; deadline: April 15. In 2009-2010, 83% of undergraduates applied for financial aid. Of those, 73% were determined to have financial need; 9% had their need fully met. Average financial aid package (proportion receiving): $21,048 (73%). Average amount of gift aid, such as scholarships or grants (proportion receiving): $13,751 (71%). Average amount of self-help aid, such as work study or loans (proportion receiving): $6,613 (67%). Average need-based loan (excluding PLUS or other private loans): $5,277. Among students who received need-based aid, the average percentage of need met: 72%. Among students who received aid based on merit, the average award (and the proportion receiving): $5,137 (27%). The average athletic scholarship (and the proportion receiving): $12,278 (3%). Average amount of debt of borrowers graduating in 2009: $32,037. Proportion who borrowed: 81%.

CAMPUS LIFE AND EXTRACURRICULAR ACTIVITIES

Campus housing available (% using): coed dorms (55%), women's dorms (15%), apartment for single students (30%). Students who live in college-owned, operated, or affiliated housing: 49%. **Student employment:** During the 2009-2010 academic year, 10% of undergraduates worked on campus. Average per-year earnings: $2,000. **Clubs and organizations:** Number of student organizations: 35. Activities include: campus ministries, choral groups, dance, drama/theater, international student organization, student government, student newspaper, yearbook. Number of fraternities: 1; sororities: 1. Proportion of men in fraternities: 1%; of women in sororities: 1%. Average proportion of students who stay on campus on weekends: 60%. **Sports program (2009-2010):** Member of NCAA II. *Men's intercollegiate varsity sports:* baseball, basketball, cross country, golf, soccer, tennis. *Women's intercollegiate varsity sports:* basketball, cross country, field hockey, lacrosse, crew (lightweight), soccer, softball, tennis, volleyball.

SERVICES AND FACILITIES

Basic services: nonremedial tutoring, placement service, health service. **Remedial assistance:** reading, math, writing, study skills. **Counseling services:** career, personal, academic, psychological. **For learning-disabled students:** School does not offer a structured program with separate admission and additional fees. Services include: remedial math, remedial English, reading machines, remedial reading, tape recorders, videotaped classes, note-taking services, oral tests, learning center, readers, extended time for tests, tutors, priority registration, texts on tape, other testing accommodations. **Library:** Number of titles: 112,955; number of current serial subscriptions: 923. **Information technology resources:** Students are required to lease or own a computer. Number of campus computers available to all students: 700. School has a wireless network. Approximate number of users that can be accommodated: 500. Proportion of college-owned housing units wired for high-speed internet access: 100%. **Campus safety:** Security services offered: 24-hour foot-and-vehicle patrols, late-night transport/escort service, 24-hour emergency telephones, lighted pathways/sidewalks, controlled dormitory access (key, security card, etc).

TRANSFER AND INTERNATIONAL STUDENTS

Transfer students: May apply for admission for the following academic terms: Fall, Spring, Summer. Applicants need a minimum number of credits to apply. For fall 2009: Transfer applications received: 517. Transfer applicants offered admission: 268. Transfer applicants enrolled: 95. **International students:** Number of foreign undergraduates: 14. Number of countries represented: 31. Minimum TOEFL score required: 500 (paper); 170 (computer).

Point Park University

- **Address:** 201 Wood Street, Pittsburgh, PA 15222
- **Website:** http://www.pointpark.edu
- **Private**
- **Enrollment:** 2,602 full-time; 805 part-time

KEY STATS
- ✔ **U.S News College Ranking:** 117, Regional Universities (North)
- ✔ **SAT Score (25th/75th percentile):** 920-1130
- ✔ **Tuition:** 2010-2011: $22,500
  - **Selectivity:** Selective
  - **Acceptance rate:** 72%
  - **Student/faculty ratio:** 14/1
  - **Room/board:** $9,480
  - **Average debt:** $31,656
  - **Proportion who borrowed:** 83%

UNDERGRADUATE STUDENT BODY STATS
2009-2010 enrollment: 2,602 full-time; 805 part-time. Men: 40%; women: 60%. **Ethnic makeup:** African American: 19%; Asian American: 1%; Hispanic: 2%; White: 77%; International: 1%.

ADMISSIONS FACTS AND FIGURES
Phone: (800) 321-0129. **Email:** enroll@pointpark.edu. **Website:** http://www.pointpark.edu. **Application deadlines for fall 2011:** Regular decision: Rolling. Early decision: Not offered. Early action: Not offered. Admission can be deferred. **Application fee:** $40. **To apply online, go to:** http://www.pointpark.edu/default.aspx?id=551. **Admissions requirements/recommendations:** High school units required (recommended): English: (4); Mathematics: (4); Science: (4); Foreign language: (2); Social studies: (4); History: (4). Tests: The college uses SAT or ACT scores in admissions decisions. Either SAT or ACT required. For admission to the fall 2011 entering class, the school will accept: ACT with or without writing accepted. Campus visit: Neither required nor recommended. Admissions interview: Neither required nor recommended. Off-campus interview: Not available. **Factors that count in admissions decisions:** *Academic:* Secondary school record: Considered. Class rank: Considered. Letters of recommendation: Not Considered. Standardized test scores: Considered. Essay: Not Considered. *Nonacademic:* Interview: Not Considered. Extracurricular activities: Not Considered. Talent/ability: Not Considered. Character/personal qualities: Not Considered. Alumni/ae relationship: Not Considered. Geographical residence: Not Considered. State residency: Not Considered. Religious affiliation/commitment: Not Considered. Minority status: Not Considered. Volunteer work: Not Considered. Work experience: Not Considered. **Other schools with the greatest overlap in applicants:** Duquesne University; New York University; Pennsylvania State University–University Park; Slippery Rock University of Pennsylvania; University of Pittsburgh. **Admissions statistics for the fall 2009 entering class:** Total applicants: 3,089. Total accepted: 2,235. Freshmen enrolled: 530; 32% were from out of state. Overall acceptance rate: 72%. **Credentials of fall 2009 freshmen:** 16% ranked in the top 10 percent of their high school class; 41% were in the top 25 percent; 77% were in the top half. (Proportion submitting class standing: 71%.) **Average high school grade point average:** 3.2. **First-year students who submitted SAT scores:** 84%. Scores (25/75 percentile): Critical Reading: 470-570, Math: 450-560, Combined: 920-1130. **First-year students submitting ACT scores:** 32%. Scores (25/75 percentile): English: 18-24, Math: 20-25, Composite: 19-24.

ACADEMICS
Year founded: 1960. **Academic calendar:** Semester. **Degrees offered:** certificate, associate, bachelor's, master's. **Most popular majors:** 12% criminal justice/safety studies, 11% drama and dramatics/theater arts, 10% business administration and management, 7% dance, 6% computer/information technology services administration and management. **Major fields of study:** area, ethnic, cultural, and gender studies; biological and biomedical sciences; business, management, marketing, and related support services; communication, journalism, and related programs; computer and information sciences and support services; education; engineering technologies/technicians; English language and literature/letters; health professions and related clinical sciences; history; legal professions and studies; liberal arts and sciences studies, and humanities; multi/interdisciplinary studies; natural resources and conservation; personal and culinary services; psychology;

public administration and social service professions; security and protective services; social sciences; visual and performing arts. **Special academic programs:** accelerated program, cross-registration, distance learning, double major, dual enrollment, English as a Second Language (ESL), honors program, independent study, internships, liberal arts/career combination, student-designed major, study abroad, teacher certificate program, weekend college. **Teacher certification offered in:** early childhood, elementary, secondary. **Cooperative education programs:** education. **Reserve Officers Training Corps (ROTC):** Army ROTC: Offered at cooperating institution (Duquesne University); Air Force ROTC: Offered at cooperating institution (University of Pittsburgh). **Faculty and instruction (2009-2010):** Total instructional faculty: 121 full-time, 327 part-time. Full-time faculty with Ph.D. or other terminal degree: 64%. Student/faculty ratio: 14/1. Classes of fewer than 20 students: 74%; of 20 to 49 students: 26%; of 50 or more students: 1%. **Advanced Placement and International Baccalaureate credit:** AP tests may be used for: Credit only. Scores accepted: 3, 4, 5. International Baccalaureate exams may be used for: Credit only. **Freshmen returning for sophomore year:** 73%. **Graduation rates:** Four-year: 41%; five-year: 52%; six-year: 48%.

COSTS AND FINANCIAL AID
Financial aid office: (412) 392-3930. **Expenses (2010-2011):** Tuition and fees 2010-2011: $22,500; room/board: $9,480. Estimated books and supplies: $1,000; transportation: $1,200; personal expenses: $900. **Financial aid:** Priority filing date for institution's financial aid form: April 15. In 2009-2010, 90% of undergraduates applied for financial aid. Of those, 81% were determined to have financial need; 12% had their need fully met. Average financial aid package (proportion receiving): $15,767 (81%). Average amount of gift aid, such as scholarships or grants (proportion receiving): $10,080 (79%). Average amount of self-help aid, such as work study or loans (proportion receiving): $6,527 (74%). Average need-based loan (excluding PLUS or other private loans): $5,159. Among students who received need-based aid, the average percentage of need met: 65%. Among students who received aid based on merit, the average award (and the proportion receiving): $6,170 (15%). The average athletic scholarship (and the proportion receiving): $8,853 (2%). Average amount of debt of borrowers graduating in 2009: $31,656. Proportion who borrowed: 83%.

CAMPUS LIFE AND EXTRACURRICULAR ACTIVITIES
Campus housing available (% using): coed dorms (98%), women's dorms (2%), men's dorms (0%), apartment for single students (0%). Students who live in college-owned, operated, or affiliated housing: 25%. **Student employment:** During the 2009-2010 academic year, 0% of undergraduates worked on campus. Average per-year earnings: $0. **Clubs and organizations:** Number of student organizations: 38. Activities include: choral groups, dance, drama/theater, international student organization, literary magazine, musical theater, radio station, student government, student newspaper, student film society, television station. Number of fraternities: 0; sororities: 0. **Sports program (2009-2010):** Member of NAIA.

SERVICES AND FACILITIES
Basic services: nonremedial tutoring, day care, health service, health insurance. **Remedial assistance:** reading, math, writing, study skills. **Counseling services:** career, personal, academic, psychological. **For learning-disabled students:** School does not offer a structured program with separate admission and additional fees. Total undergraduates in learning-disabled program or receiving services: 27. Services include: tape recorders, note-taking services, oral tests, readers, extended time for tests, tutors, priority registration, priority seating, substitution of courses, exams on tape or computer, other testing accommodations, waiver of foreign language degree requirement, other. **Library:** Number of titles: 99,190; number of current serial subscriptions: 224. **Information technology resources:** Students are not required to lease or own a computer. Number of campus computers available to all students: 300. School has a wireless network. Approximate number of users that can be accommodated: 500. Proportion of college-owned housing units wired for high-speed internet access: 100%. **Campus safety:** Security services offered: 24-hour emergency telephones, lighted pathways/sidewalks, controlled dormitory access (key, security card, etc).

TRANSFER AND INTERNATIONAL STUDENTS
Transfer students: May apply for admission for the following academic terms: Fall, Spring, Summer. Applicants need a minimum number of credits to apply. For fall 2009: Transfer applications received: 1,511. Transfer applicants offered admission: 972. Transfer applicants enrolled: 553. **International students:** Number of foreign undergraduates: 23 (1% of student body). Number of countries represented: 28. Minimum TOEFL score required: 500 (paper); 173 (computer). Average TOEFL score: 520 (paper).

Robert Morris University

- **Address:** 6001 University Boulevard, Moon Township, PA 15108-1189
- **Website:** http://www.rmu.edu
- **Private**
- **Enrollment:** 3,106 full-time; 551 part-time

KEY STATS
✔ **U.S News College Ranking:** 93, Regional Universities (North)
✔ **SAT Score (25th/75th percentile):** 910-1120
✔ **Tuition:** 2010-2011: $21,550

Selectivity: Selective	Room/board: $10,660
Acceptance rate: 92%	Average debt: $35,055
Student/faculty ratio: 15/1	Proportion who borrowed: 84%

UNDERGRADUATE STUDENT BODY STATS
2009-2010 enrollment: 3,106 full-time; 551 part-time. Men: 55%; women: 45%. **Ethnic makeup:** African American: 9%; Asian American: 1%; Hispanic: 1%; White: 86%; International: 3%. **Religious preference:** Roman Catholic: 48%; Protestant: 47%; Jewish: 1%; Muslim: 1%; No preference: 3%.

ADMISSIONS FACTS AND FIGURES
Phone: (412) 397-5200. **Email:** admissions@rmu.edu. **Website:** http://www.rmu.edu. **Application deadlines for fall 2011:** Regular decision: July 1. Early decision: Not offered. Early action: Not offered. Admission can be deferred. **Application fee:** $30. **To apply online, go to:** http://undergraduate.rmu.edu/admapplytormu.aspx. **Admissions requirements/recommendations:** High school units required (recommended): English: 4; Mathematics: 3; Science: 2; Foreign language: (2); Social studies: 4; Academic electives: 3; Total units: 16 (18). Tests: The college uses SAT or ACT scores in admissions decisions. Either SAT or ACT required. For admission to the fall 2011 entering class, the school will accept: ACT with or without writing accepted. Campus visit: Recommended. Admissions interview: Recommended. Off-campus interview: May be arranged. **Factors that count in admissions decisions:** *Academic:* Secondary school record: Important. Class rank: Important. Letters of recommendation: Considered. Standardized test scores: Very Important. Essay: Considered. *Nonacademic:* Interview: Important. Extracurricular activities: Important. Talent/ability: Considered. Character/personal qualities: Important. Alumni/ae relationship: Considered. Geographical residence: Not Considered. State residency: Not Considered. Religious affiliation/commitment: Not Considered. Minority status: Not Considered. Volunteer work: Considered. Work experience: Considered. **Other schools with the greatest overlap in applicants:** Clarion University of Pennsylvania; Duquesne University; Indiana University of Pennsylvania; Pennsylvania State University–University Park; University of Pittsburgh. **Admissions statistics for the fall 2009 entering class:** Total applicants: 3,775. Total accepted: 3,460. Freshmen enrolled: 726; 22% were from out of state. Overall acceptance rate: 92%. **Credentials of fall 2009 freshmen:** 9% ranked in the top 10 percent of their high school class; 33% were in the top 25 percent; 69% were in the top half. (Proportion submitting class standing: 69%.) **Average high school grade point average:** 3.3. **First-year students who submitted SAT scores:** 86%. Scores (25/75 percentile): Critical Reading: 450-540, Math: 460-580, Combined: 910-1120. **First-year students submitting ACT scores:** 13%. Scores (25/75 percentile): English: 18-23, Math: 18-24, Composite: 20-24.

ACADEMICS
Year founded: 1921. **Academic calendar:** Semester. **Degrees offered:** certificate, bachelor's, post-bachelor's certificate, master's. **Most popular majors:** 13% business administration and management, 11% accounting, 10% marketing/marketing management, 8% communication studies/speech communication and rhetoric, 6% sport and fitness administration/management. **Major fields of study:** business, management, marketing, and related support services; communication, journalism, and related programs; computer and information sciences and support services; education; engineering; English language and literature/letters; health professions and related clinical sciences; mathematics and statistics; multi/interdisciplinary studies; natural resources and conservation; parks, recreation, leisure, and fitness studies; psychology; social sciences; transportation and materials moving; visual and performing arts. **Areas of required coursework:** humanities, computer literacy, mathematics, English (including composition), sciences (biological or physical), history, social science. **Pre-professional programs:** pre-law, pre-medicine. **Special academic programs:** cooperative (work-study plan) program, cross-registration, distance learning, double major, honors program, independent study, internships, study abroad, teacher certificate program, weekend college. **Teacher certification offered in:** early childhood, special education, elementary, middle/junior high, secondary. **Cooperative education programs:** business, computer science, education, engineering, health professions. **Reserve Officers Training Corps (ROTC):** Army ROTC: Offered on campus; Air Force ROTC: Offered at cooperating institution (University of Pittsburgh). **Faculty and instruction (2009-2010):** Total instructional faculty: 177 full-time, 202 part-time (55% men; 45% women; 8% minorities). Full-time faculty with Ph.D. or other terminal degree: 81%. Student/faculty ratio: 15/1. Classes of fewer than 20 students: 42%; of 20 to 49 students: 57%; of 50 or more students: 1%. **Advanced Placement and International Baccalaureate credit:** AP tests may be used for: Credit only. Scores accepted: 3. International Baccalaureate exams may be used for: Credit only. **Freshmen returning for sophomore year:** 75%. **Graduation rates:** Four-year: 34%; five-year: 53%; six-year: 55%. **Graduate study:** 8% of students pursue further study immediately upon graduation; 8% within one year; 15% within five years.

COSTS AND FINANCIAL AID
Financial aid office: (412) 262-8545. **Expenses (2010-2011):** Tuition and fees 2010-2011: $21,550; room/board: $10,660. Estimated books and supplies: $1,200; transportation: $1,000; personal expenses: $1,648. **Financial aid:** In 2009-2010, 86% of undergraduates applied for financial aid. Of those, 77% were determined to have financial need; 15% had their need fully met. Average financial aid package (proportion receiving): $16,548 (77%). Average amount of gift aid, such as scholarships or grants (proportion receiving): $10,397 (73%). Average amount of self-help aid, such as work study or loans (proportion receiving): $7,505 (70%). Average need-based loan (excluding PLUS or other private loans): $5,774. Among students who received need-based aid, the average percentage of need met: 71%. Among students who received aid based on merit, the average award (and the proportion receiving): $7,763 (15%). The average athletic scholarship (and the proportion receiving): $13,427 (3%). Average amount of debt of borrowers graduating in 2009: $35,055. Proportion who borrowed: 84%.

CAMPUS LIFE AND EXTRACURRICULAR ACTIVITIES
Campus housing available (% using): coed dorms (66%), women's dorms (6%), men's dorms (5%), apartment for single students (23%). Students who live in college-owned, operated, or affiliated housing: 33%. **Student employment:** During the 2009-2010 academic year, 5% of undergraduates worked on campus. **Clubs and organizations:** Number of student organizations: 92. Activities include: campus ministries, choral groups, drama/theater, international student organization, literary magazine, marching band, musical theater, pep band, radio station, student government, student newspaper, television station. Number of fraternities: 6; sororities: 3. Proportion of men in fraternities: 3%; of women in sororities: 4%. Average proportion of students who stay on campus on weekends: 40%. **Sports program (2009-2010):** Member of NCAA I. *Men's intercollegiate varsity sports:* basketball, football, golf, ice hockey, lacrosse, soccer, tennis, track and field (indoor), track and field (outdoor). *Women's intercollegiate varsity sports:* basketball, crew (heavyweight), field hockey, golf, ice hockey, lacrosse, crew (lightweight), soccer, softball, tennis, track and field (indoor), track and field (outdoor), volleyball.

SERVICES AND FACILITIES
Basic services: nonremedial tutoring, placement service, health service. **Remedial assistance:** reading, math, writing, study skills. **Counseling services:** minority student, career, military, personal, veteran student, psychological, religious. **For learning-disabled students:** School does not offer a structured program with separate admission and additional fees. Total undergraduates in learning-disabled program or receiving services: 108. Services include: remedial math, remedial English, reading machines, remedial reading, tape recorders, note-taking services, oral tests, learning center, readers, extended time for tests, tutors, priority registration, priority seating, texts on tape, other testing accommodations. **Library:** Number of titles: 125,121; number of current serial subscriptions: 766. **Information technology resources:** Students are not required to lease or own a computer. Number of campus computers available to all students: 360. School has a wireless network. Approximate number of users that can be accommodated: 100. Proportion of college-owned housing units wired for high-speed internet access: 100%. **Campus safety:** Security services offered: 24-hour foot-and-vehicle patrols, late-night transport/escort service, 24-hour emergency telephones, lighted pathways/sidewalks, controlled dormitory access (key, security card, etc).

TRANSFER AND INTERNATIONAL STUDENTS

Transfer students: May apply for admission for the following academic terms: Fall, Spring, Summer. Applicants do not need a minimum number of credits to apply. For fall 2009: Transfer applications received: 713. Transfer applicants offered admission: 658. Transfer applicants enrolled: 384. **International students:** Number of foreign undergraduates: 97 (3% of student body). Number of countries represented: 37. Minimum TOEFL score required: 500 (paper); 173 (computer).

Rosemont College

- ■ **Address:** 1400 Montgomery Avenue, Rosemont, PA 19010-1699
- ■ **Website:** http://www.rosemont.edu
- ■ **Private; Religious affiliation:** Roman Catholic
- ■ **Enrollment:** 434 full-time; 122 part-time

KEY STATS

✔ **U.S News College Ranking:** 77, Regional Universities (North)

✔ **SAT Score (25th/75th percentile):** 835-1060

✔ **Tuition:** 2010-2011: $27,450

Selectivity: Selective	**Room/board:** $11,000
Acceptance rate: 54%	**Average debt:** $21,338
Student/faculty ratio: 10/1	**Proportion who borrowed:** 87%

UNDERGRADUATE STUDENT BODY STATS

2009-2010 enrollment: 434 full-time; 122 part-time. Men: 20%; women: 80%. **Ethnic makeup:** African American: 46%; Asian American: 4%; Hispanic: 7%; White: 42%; International: 1%. **Religious preference:** Roman Catholic: 65%; Other: 35%.

ADMISSIONS FACTS AND FIGURES

Phone: (800) 331-0708. **Email:** admissions@rosemont.edu. **Website:** http://www.rosemont.edu. **Application deadlines for fall 2011:** Regular decision: July 15. Early decision: Not offered. Early action: Not offered. Admission can be deferred. **Application fee:** $35. **To apply online, go to:** http://www.rosemont.edu/uwc/admissions/apply.php. **Admissions requirements/recommendations:** High school units required (recommended): English: 4 (4); Mathematics: 2 (2); Science: 2 (2); Foreign language: 2 (2); Social studies: 2 (2); History: 2 (2); Academic electives: 2 (2); Total units: 18 (18). **Tests:** The college uses SAT or ACT scores in admissions decisions. Either SAT or ACT required. For admission to the fall 2011 entering class, the school will accept: ACT with or without writing accepted. Campus visit: Recommended. Admissions interview: Recommended. Off-campus interview: May be arranged. **Factors that count in admissions decisions:** *Academic:* Secondary school record: Very Important. Class rank: Important. Letters of recommendation: Very Important. Standardized test scores: Important. Essay: Very Important. *Nonacademic:* Interview: Very Important. Extracurricular activities: Important. Talent/ability: Important. Character/personal qualities: Very Important. Alumni/ae relationship: Considered. Geographical residence: Not Considered. State residency: Not Considered. Religious affiliation/commitment: Not Considered. Minority status: Not Considered. Volunteer work: Very Important. Work experience: Considered. **Other schools with the greatest overlap in applicants:** Drexel University; Rutgers, the State University of New Jersey–New Brunswick; St. Joseph's University; Temple University; Villanova University. **Admissions statistics for the fall 2009 entering class:** Total applicants: 1,104. Total accepted: 595. Freshmen enrolled: 177; 30% were from out of state. Overall acceptance rate: 54%. **Credentials of fall 2009 freshmen:** 23% ranked in the top 10 percent of their high school class; 48% were in the top 25 percent; 68% were in the top half. (Proportion submitting class standing: 21%.) **Average high school grade point average:** 3.2. **First-year students who submitted SAT scores:** 100%. Scores (25/75 percentile): Critical Reading: 425-570, Math: 410-490, Combined: 835-1060. **First-year students submitting ACT scores:** 1%. Scores (25/75 percentile): English: 17-24, Math: 17-24, Composite: 19-24.

ACADEMICS

Year founded: 1921. **Academic calendar:** Semester. **Degrees offered:** certificate, bachelor's, post-bachelor's certificate, master's. **Most popular majors:** 37% business/commerce, 15% social sciences, 11% fine/studio arts, 7% psychology, 6% biology/biological sciences. **Major fields of study:** area, ethnic, cultural, and gender studies; biological and biomedical sciences; business, management, marketing, and related support services; communication, journalism, and related programs; English language and literature/

letters; foreign languages, literatures, and linguistics; history; liberal arts and sciences studies, and humanities; mathematics and statistics; multi/interdisciplinary studies; natural resources and conservation; philosophy and religious studies; physical sciences; psychology; social sciences; visual and performing arts. **Areas of required coursework:** arts/fine arts, humanities, computer literacy, mathematics, English (including composition), philosophy, foreign languages, sciences (biological or physical), history, social science. **Pre-professional programs:** pre-law, pre-dentistry, pre-medicine, pre-veterinary science. **Special academic programs (% participation):** accelerated program (20%), cross-registration (47%), distance learning (10%), double major (16%), dual enrollment (2%), honors program (12%), independent study (20%), internships (96%), student-designed major (2%), study abroad (56%), teacher certificate program (6%). **Teacher certification offered in:** early childhood, special education, elementary, secondary. **Cooperative education programs:** art, engineering, health professions. **Faculty and instruction (2009-2010):** Total instructional faculty: 29 full-time, 108 part-time (36% men; 64% women; 12% minorities). Full-time faculty with Ph.D. or other terminal degree: 93%. Student/faculty ratio: 10/1. Classes of fewer than 20 students: 82%; of 20 to 49 students: 18%; of 50 or more students: 0%. **Advanced Placement and International Baccalaureate credit:** AP tests may be used for: Placement only. Scores accepted: 3, 4, 5. International Baccalaureate exams may be used for: Placement only. **Freshmen returning for sophomore year:** 72%. **Graduation rates:** Four-year: 44%; five-year: 61%; six-year: 62%. **Graduate study:** 15% of students pursue further study immediately upon graduation; 20% within one year; 30% within five years. Fields in which graduates pursue further study: Master of Business Administration (MBA), 15%; law, 3%; medicine, 5%; education, 30%; arts and sciences, 35%.

COSTS AND FINANCIAL AID

Financial aid office: (610) 527-0200. **Expenses (2010-2011):** Tuition and fees 2010-2011: $27,450; room/board: $11,000. Estimated books and supplies: $1,500; transportation: $200; personal expenses: $1,000. **Financial aid:** Priority filing date for institution's financial aid form: February 15. In 2009-2010, 96% of undergraduates applied for financial aid. Of those, 93% were determined to have financial need; 10% had their need fully met. Average financial aid package (proportion receiving): $22,951 (93%). Average amount of gift aid, such as scholarships or grants (proportion receiving): $19,749 (93%). Average amount of self-help aid, such as work study or loans (proportion receiving): $3,678 (81%). Average need-based loan (excluding PLUS or other private loans): $3,342. Among students who received need-based aid, the average percentage of need met: 71%. Among students who received aid based on merit, the average award (and the proportion receiving): $10,490 (6%). The average athletic scholarship (and the proportion receiving): $0 (0%). Average amount of debt of borrowers graduating in 2009: $21,338. Proportion who borrowed: 87%.

CAMPUS LIFE AND EXTRACURRICULAR ACTIVITIES

Campus housing available (% using): coed dorms (100%), special housing for disabled students. Students who live in college-owned, operated, or affiliated housing: 70%. **Student employment:** During the 2009-2010 academic year, 35% of undergraduates worked on campus. Average per-year earnings: $2,000. **Clubs and organizations:** Number of student organizations: 23. Activities include: campus ministries, choral groups, dance, drama/theater, international student organization, jazz band, literary magazine, model UN, music ensembles, radio station, student government, student newspaper, yearbook. Number of fraternities: 0; sororities: 0. Average proportion of students who stay on campus on weekends: 70%. **Sports program (2009-2010):** Member of NCAA III. *Men's intercollegiate varsity sports:* basketball, cross country, golf, lacrosse, soccer, tennis. *Women's intercollegiate varsity sports:* basketball, cross country, field hockey, lacrosse, softball, tennis, volleyball.

SERVICES AND FACILITIES

Basic services: nonremedial tutoring, women's center, placement service, health service, health insurance. **Remedial assistance:** reading, math, writing, study skills. **Counseling services:** minority student, career, personal, academic, older student, psychological, religious. **For learning-disabled students:** School does not offer a structured program with separate admission and additional fees. Services include: remedial math, remedial English, tape recorders, diagnostic testing service, untimed tests, note-taking services, oral tests, learning center, readers, extended time for tests, tutors. **Library:** Number of titles: 165,000; number of current serial subscriptions: 1,660. **Information technology resources:** Students are not required to lease or own a computer. Number of campus computers available to all students: 100. School has a wireless network. Approximate number of users that can be accommodated: 300. Proportion of college-owned housing units wired for high-speed internet access: 100%. **Campus safety:** Security services offered: 24-hour foot-and-vehicle patrols, late-night transport/escort service, 24-hour emergency telephones, lighted pathways/sidewalks, controlled dormitory access (key, security card, etc).

TRANSFER AND INTERNATIONAL STUDENTS

Transfer students: May apply for admission for the following academic terms: Fall, Spring. Applicants do not need a minimum number of credits to apply. For fall 2009: Transfer applications received: 147. Transfer applicants offered admission: 73. Transfer applicants enrolled: 44. **International students:** Number of foreign undergraduates: 3 (1% of student body). Number of countries represented: 10. Minimum TOEFL score required: 500 (paper); 61 (computer). Average TOEFL score: 550 (paper).

Seton Hill University

- ■ **Address:** Seton Hill Drive, Greensburg, PA 15601
- ■ **Website:** http://www.setonhill.edu
- ■ **Private; Religious affiliation:** Roman Catholic
- ■ **Enrollment:** 1,376 full-time; 356 part-time

KEY STATS

✔ **U.S News College Ranking:** 12, Regional Colleges (North)
✔ **SAT Score (25th/75th percentile):** 880-1130
✔ **Tuition:** 2010-2011: $27,548

Selectivity: Selective	**Room/board:** $9,076
Acceptance rate: 66%	**Average debt:** $25,807
Student/faculty ratio: 15/1	**Proportion who borrowed:** 91%

UNDERGRADUATE STUDENT BODY STATS

2009-2010 enrollment: 1,376 full-time; 356 part-time. Men: 37%; women: 63%. **Ethnic makeup:** African American: 9%; Asian American: 1%; Hispanic: 1%; White: 87%; International: 2%.

ADMISSIONS FACTS AND FIGURES

Phone: (724) 838-4255. **Email:** admit@setonhill.edu. **Website:** http://www.setonhill.edu. **Application deadlines for fall 2011:** Regular decision: August 15. Early decision: Not offered. Early action: Not offered. Admission can be deferred. **Application fee:** $35. **To apply online, go to:** http://apply.setonhill.edu/. **Admissions requirements/recommendations:** High school units required (recommended): English: 4; Mathematics: 2; Science: 1; Foreign language: (2); Social studies: 2; Academic electives: 4; Total units: 15. Tests: The college uses SAT or ACT scores in admissions decisions. Neither SAT nor ACT required. For admission to the fall 2011 entering class, the school will accept: ACT with writing recommended. Campus visit: Recommended. Admissions interview: Recommended. Off-campus interview: May be arranged. **Factors that count in admissions decisions:** *Academic:* Secondary school record: Very Important. Class rank: Important. Letters of recommendation: Considered. Standardized test scores: Important. Essay: Considered. *Nonacademic:* Interview: Very Important. Extracurricular activities: Important. Talent/ability: Important. Character/personal qualities: Important. Alumni/ae relationship: Considered. Geographical residence: Not Considered. State residency: Not Considered. Religious affiliation/commitment: Not Considered. Minority status: Not Considered. Volunteer work: Considered. Work experience: Considered. **Other schools with the greatest overlap in applicants:** Indiana University of Pennsylvania; Pennsylvania State University–University Park; Slippery Rock University of Pennsylvania; St. Vincent College; Washington and Jefferson College. **Admissions statistics for the fall 2009 entering class:** Total applicants: 1,729. Total accepted: 1,143. Freshmen enrolled: 299; 25% were from out of state. Overall acceptance rate: 66%. **Credentials of fall 2009 freshmen:** 18% ranked in the top 10 percent of their high school class; 44% were in the top 25 percent; 71% were in the top half. (Proportion submitting class standing: 82%.) **Average high school grade point average:** 3.2. **First-year students who submitted SAT scores:** 94%. **First-year students submitting ACT scores:** 27%. Scores (25/75 percentile): English: N/A, Math: N/A, Composite: N/A.

ACADEMICS

Year founded: 1883. **Academic calendar:** Semester. **Degrees offered:** certificate, bachelor's, post-bachelor's certificate, master's, post-master's certificate. **Most popular majors:** 31% business, management, marketing, and related support services, 11% visual and performing arts, 8% public administration and social service professions, 7% health professions and related

clinical sciences, 7% social sciences. **Major fields of study:** biological and biomedical sciences; business, management, marketing, and related support services; communication, journalism, and related programs; computer and information sciences and support services; education; English language and literature/letters; family and consumer sciences/human sciences; foreign languages, literatures, and linguistics; health professions and related clinical sciences; history; liberal arts and sciences studies, and humanities; mathematics and statistics; philosophy and religious studies; physical sciences; psychology; public administration and social service professions; security and protective services; social sciences; theology and religious vocations; visual and performing arts. **Areas of required coursework:** arts/fine arts, humanities, mathematics, English (including composition), philosophy, foreign languages, sciences (biological or physical), history, other. **Pre-professional programs:** pre-law, pre-dentistry, pre-medicine, pre-veterinary science, pre-optometry, pre-pharmacy. **Special academic programs:** accelerated program, cross-registration, distance learning, double major, English as a Second Language (ESL), exchange student program (domestic), honors program, independent study, internships, liberal arts/career combination, student-designed major, study abroad, teacher certificate program, weekend college. **Teacher certification offered in:** early childhood, special education, elementary, middle/junior high, secondary. **Cooperative education programs:** engineering, health professions. **Reserve Officers Training Corps (ROTC):** Army ROTC: Offered on campus; Air Force ROTC: Offered at cooperating institution. **Faculty and instruction (2009-2010):** Total instructional faculty: 78 full-time, 107 part-time (52% men; 48% women; 3% minorities). Full-time faculty with Ph.D. or other terminal degree: 85%. Student/faculty ratio: 15/1. Classes of fewer than 20 students: 54%; of 20 to 49 students: 45%; of 50 or more students: 0%. **Advanced Placement and International Baccalaureate credit:** AP tests may be used for: Credit only. Scores accepted: 3, 4, 5. International Baccalaureate exams may be used for: Credit only. **Freshmen returning for sophomore year:** 74%. **Graduation rates:** Four-year: 46%; five-year: 59%; six-year: 56%. **Graduate study:** 21% of students pursue further study immediately upon graduation. Fields in which graduates pursue further study: Master of Business Administration (MBA), 24%; law, 7%; engineering, 3%; education, 31%; arts and sciences, 38%.

COSTS AND FINANCIAL AID

Financial aid office: (724) 838-4293. **Expenses (2010-2011):** Tuition and fees 2010-2011: $27,548; room/board: $9,076. Estimated books and supplies: $1,000; transportation: $500; personal expenses: $2,000. **Financial aid:** Priority filing date for institution's financial aid form: May 1. In 2009-2010, 92% of undergraduates applied for financial aid. Of those, 86% were determined to have financial need; 16% had their need fully met. Average financial aid package (proportion receiving): $21,411 (83%). Average amount of gift aid, such as scholarships or grants (proportion receiving): $16,733 (83%). Average amount of self-help aid, such as work study or loans (proportion receiving): $5,856 (68%). Average need-based loan (excluding PLUS or other private loans): $5,108. Among students who received need-based aid, the average percentage of need met: 75%. Among students who received aid based on merit, the average award (and the proportion receiving): $11,798 (10%). The average athletic scholarship (and the proportion receiving): $10,847 (8%). Average amount of debt of borrowers graduating in 2009: $25,807. Proportion who borrowed: 91%.

CAMPUS LIFE AND EXTRACURRICULAR ACTIVITIES

Campus housing available: coed dorms, women's dorms, men's dorms. Students who live in college-owned, operated, or affiliated housing: 56%. **Student employment:** During the 2009-2010 academic year, 35% of undergraduates worked on campus. Average per-year earnings: $1,288. **Clubs and organizations:** Number of student organizations: 56. Activities include: campus ministries, choral groups, concert band, dance, drama/theater, international student organization, jazz band, literary magazine, marching band, music ensembles, musical theater, pep band, student government, student newspaper, symphony orchestra. Number of fraternities: 0; sororities: 0. **Sports program (2009-2010):** Member of NCAA II. *Men's intercollegiate varsity sports:* baseball, basketball, cross country, football, lacrosse, soccer, track and field (outdoor), wrestling. *Women's intercollegiate varsity sports:* basketball, cross country, equestrian, field hockey, golf, lacrosse, soccer, softball, tennis, track and field (indoor), track and field (outdoor), volleyball.

SERVICES AND FACILITIES

Basic services: nonremedial tutoring, placement service, health service. **Remedial assistance:** math, writing, study skills. **Counseling services:** minority student, career, personal, veteran student, academic, older student, psychological, religious. **For learning-disabled students:** School does not offer a structured program with separate admission and additional fees. Services include: reading machines, tape recorders, videotaped classes, untimed tests, note-taking services, oral tests, readers, extended time for tests, tutors, priority seating, texts on tape, other testing accommodations. **Library:** Number of titles: 124,120; number of current serial subscriptions: 252. **Information technology resources:** Students are not required to lease or own a computer. Number of campus computers available to all students: 362. School has a wireless network. Approximate number of users that can be accommodated: 500. Proportion of college-owned housing units wired for high-speed internet access: 100%. **Campus safety:** Security services offered: 24-hour foot-and-vehicle patrols, late-night transport/escort service, 24-hour emergency telephones, lighted pathways/sidewalks, controlled dormitory access (key, security card, etc).

TRANSFER AND INTERNATIONAL STUDENTS
Transfer students: May apply for admission for the following academic terms: Fall, Spring, Summer. Applicants do not need a minimum number of credits to apply. For fall 2009: Transfer applications received: 307. Transfer applicants offered admission: 153. Transfer applicants enrolled: 90. **International students:** Number of foreign undergraduates: 31 (2% of student body). Number of countries represented: 24. Minimum TOEFL score required: 550 (paper); 213 (computer).

Shippensburg University of Pennsylvania

- **Address:** 1871 Old Main Drive, Shippensburg, PA 17257-2299
- **Website:** http://www.ship.edu
- **Public**
- **Enrollment:** 6,636 full-time; 306 part-time

KEY STATS
✔ **U.S News College Ranking:** 77, Regional Universities (North)
✔ **SAT Score (25th/75th percentile):** 910-1100
✔ **Tuition:** 2009-2010: $7,444 in state, $15,776 out of state

Selectivity: Selective	**Room/board:** $7,086
Acceptance rate: 72%	**Average debt:** $21,163
Student/faculty ratio: 20/1	**Proportion who borrowed:** 74%

UNDERGRADUATE STUDENT BODY STATS
2009-2010 enrollment: 6,636 full-time; 306 part-time. Men: 47%; women: 53%. **Ethnic makeup:** African American: 7%; Asian American: 1%; Hispanic: 2%; White: 90%.

ADMISSIONS FACTS AND FIGURES
Phone: (717) 477-1231. **Email:** admiss@ship.edu. **Website:** http://www.ship.edu. **Application deadlines for fall 2011:** Regular decision: Rolling. Early decision: Not offered. Early action: Send application by: N/A; Decision sent by: N/A. Admission can be deferred. **Application fee:** $30. **To apply online, go to:** https://www.applyweb.com/apply/ship/. **Admissions requirements/recommendations:** High school units required (recommended): English: 4 (4); Mathematics: 3 (3); Science: 3 (3); Foreign language: 3 (3); Social studies: 3 (3); History: 0; Academic electives: 0; Total units: 16 (16). Tests: The college uses SAT or ACT scores in admissions decisions. Either SAT or ACT required. For admission to the fall 2011 entering class, the school will accept: ACT with or without writing accepted. Campus visit: Recommended. Admissions interview: Neither required nor recommended. Off-campus interview: Not available. **Factors that count in admissions decisions:** *Academic:* Secondary school record: Very Important. Class rank: Very Important. Letters of recommendation: Considered. Standardized test scores: Very Important. Essay: Considered. *Nonacademic:* Interview: Considered. Extracurricular activities: Considered. Talent/ability: Considered. Character/personal qualities: Considered. Alumni/ae relationship: Not Considered. Geographical residence: Not Considered. State residency: Not Considered. Religious affiliation/commitment: Not Considered. Minority status: Not Considered. Volunteer work: Considered. Work experience: Considered. **Other schools with the greatest overlap in applicants:** Bloomsburg University of Pennsylvania; Indiana University of Pennsylvania; Millersville University of Pennsylvania; Pennsylvania State University–University Park; West Chester University of Pennsylvania. **Admissions statistics for the fall 2009 entering class:** Total applicants: 7,001. Total accepted: 5,008. Freshmen enrolled: 1,679; 7% were from out of state. Overall acceptance rate: 72%. Non-early acceptance rate: 72%. **Credentials of fall 2009 freshmen:** 9% ranked in the top 10 percent of their high school class; 32% were in the top 25 percent; 69% were in the top half. (Proportion

submitting class standing: 84%.) **Average high school grade point average:** 3.2. **First-year students who submitted SAT scores:** 99%. Scores (25/75 percentile): Critical Reading: 450-540, Math: 460-560, Combined: 910-1100. **First-year students submitting ACT scores:** 10%. Scores (25/75 percentile): English: N/A, Math: N/A, Composite: N/A.

ACADEMICS
Year founded: 1871. **Academic calendar:** Semester. **Degrees offered:** certificate, bachelor's, post-bachelor's certificate, master's, post-master's certificate. **Most popular majors:** 14% elementary education and teaching, 8% marketing/marketing management, 8% psychology, 7% criminal justice/safety studies, 6% journalism. **Major fields of study:** agriculture, agriculture operations, and related sciences; biological and biomedical sciences; business, management, marketing, and related support services; communication, journalism, and related programs; computer and information sciences and support services; education; English language and literature/letters; foreign languages, literatures, and linguistics; health professions and related clinical sciences; history; mathematics and statistics; multi/interdisciplinary studies; natural resources and conservation; parks, recreation, leisure, and fitness studies; physical sciences; psychology; public administration and social service professions; security and protective services; social sciences; visual and performing arts. **Areas of required coursework:** humanities, mathematics, English (including composition), sciences (biological or physical), history, social science, other. **Pre-professional programs:** pre-law, pre-dentistry, pre-medicine, pre-veterinary science, pre-optometry, pre-pharmacy, other. **Special academic programs:** accelerated program, cooperative (work-study plan) program, cross-registration, distance learning, double major, dual enrollment, exchange student program (domestic), honors program, independent study, internships, study abroad, teacher certificate program, other. **Teacher certification offered in:** early childhood, special education, elementary, middle/junior high, secondary. **Cooperative education programs:** art, engineering, health professions. **Reserve Officers Training Corps (ROTC):** Army ROTC: Offered on campus. **Faculty and instruction (2009-2010):** Total instructional faculty: 329 full-time, 73 part-time (55% men; 45% women; 12% minorities). Full-time faculty with Ph.D. or other terminal degree: 93%. Student/faculty ratio: 20/1. Classes of fewer than 20 students: 22%; of 20 to 49 students: 75%; of 50 or more students: 3%. **Advanced Placement and International Baccalaureate credit:** AP tests may be used for: Credit and/or placement. Scores accepted: 3, 4, 5. **Freshmen returning for sophomore year:** 74%. **Graduation rates:** Four-year: 45%; five-year: 60%; six-year: 64%.

COSTS AND FINANCIAL AID
Financial aid office: (717) 477-1131. **Expenses (2009-2010):** Tuition and fees 2009-2010: $7,444 in state, $15,776 out of state; room/board: $7,086. Estimated books and supplies: $1,100; transportation: $1,600; personal expenses: $414. **Financial aid:** Priority filing date for institution's financial aid form: March 15. In 2009-2010, 80% of undergraduates applied for financial aid. Of those, 58% were determined to have financial need; 17% had their need fully met. Average financial aid package (proportion receiving): $7,738 (55%). Average amount of gift aid, such as scholarships or grants (proportion receiving): $5,705 (39%). Average amount of self-help aid, such as work study or loans (proportion receiving): $3,972 (50%). Average need-based loan (excluding PLUS or other private loans): $3,844. Among students who received need-based aid, the average percentage of need met: 69%. Among students who received aid based on merit, the average award (and the proportion receiving): $3,969 (8%). The average athletic scholarship (and the proportion receiving): $2,352 (4%). Average amount of debt of borrowers graduating in 2009: $21,163. Proportion who borrowed: 74%.

CAMPUS LIFE AND EXTRACURRICULAR ACTIVITIES
Campus housing available (% using): coed dorms (77%), apartment for single students (23%). Students who live in college-owned, operated, or affiliated housing: 37%. **Clubs and organizations:** Number of student organizations: 252. Activities include: campus ministries, choral groups, concert band, dance, drama/theater, international student organization, jazz band, literary magazine, marching band, music ensembles, musical theater, radio station, student government, student newspaper, television station, yearbook. Number of fraternities: 10; sororities: 12. Proportion of men in fraternities: 6%; of women in sororities: 8%. Average proportion of students who stay on campus on weekends: 50%. **Sports program (2009-2010):** Member of NCAA II. *Men's intercollegiate varsity sports:* baseball, basketball, cross country, football, soccer, swimming, track and field (indoor), track and field (outdoor), wrestling. *Women's intercollegiate varsity sports:* basketball, cross

country, field hockey, lacrosse, soccer, softball, swimming, tennis, track and field (indoor), track and field (outdoor), volleyball.

SERVICES AND FACILITIES

Basic services: nonremedial tutoring, women's center, placement service, day care, health service, health insurance. **Remedial assistance:** reading, math, writing, study skills. **Counseling services:** minority student, career, military, personal, veteran student, academic, older student, psychological, other. **For learning-disabled students:** School does not offer a structured program with separate admission and additional fees. Total undergraduates in learning-disabled program or receiving services: 511. Services include: reading machines, tape recorders, note-taking services, oral tests, learning center, readers, extended time for tests, tutors, priority registration, priority seating, texts on tape, other testing accommodations, other. **Library:** Number of titles: 377,846; number of current serial subscriptions: 996. **Information technology resources:** Students are not required to lease or own a computer. Number of campus computers available to all students: 996. School has a wireless network. Approximate number of users that can be accommodated: 4,000. Proportion of college-owned housing units wired for high-speed internet access: 100%. **Campus safety:** Security services offered: 24-hour foot-and-vehicle patrols, late-night transport/escort service, 24-hour emergency telephones, lighted pathways/sidewalks, student patrols, controlled dormitory access (key, security card, etc.).

TRANSFER AND INTERNATIONAL STUDENTS

Transfer students: May apply for admission for the following academic terms: Fall, Winter, Spring, Summer. Applicants do not need a minimum number of credits to apply. For fall 2009: Transfer applications received: 1,049. Transfer applicants offered admission: 752. Transfer applicants enrolled: 458. **International students:** Number of foreign undergraduates: 15. Number of countries represented: 9. Minimum TOEFL score required: 560 (paper); 62 (computer).

Slippery Rock University of Pennsylvania

- **Address:** 1 Morrow Way, Slippery Rock, PA 16057-1383
- **Website:** http://www.sru.edu
- **Public**
- **Enrollment:** 7,250 full-time; 575 part-time

KEY STATS

✔ **U.S News College Ranking:** 93, Regional Universities (North)
✔ **SAT Score (25th/75th percentile):** 930-1110
✔ **Tuition:** 2009-2010: $7,235 in state, $10,012 out of state

Selectivity: Selective	**Room/board:** $8,322
Acceptance rate: 63%	**Average debt:** $23,879
Student/faculty ratio: 20/1	**Proportion who borrowed:** 81%

UNDERGRADUATE STUDENT BODY STATS

2009-2010 enrollment: 7,250 full-time; 575 part-time. Men: 44%; women: 56%. **Ethnic makeup:** African American: 5%; Asian American: 1%; Hispanic: 1%; White: 91%; International: 1%.

ADMISSIONS FACTS AND FIGURES

Phone: (800) 929-4778. **Email:** asktherock@sru.edu. **Website:** http://www.sru.edu. **Application deadlines for fall 2011:** Regular decision: Rolling. Early decision: Not offered. Early action: Not offered. Admission can be deferred. **Application fee:** $30. **To apply online, go to:** https://www.apply-web.com/apply/paslip. **Admissions requirements/recommendations:** High school units required (recommended): English: 0 (4); Mathematics: 0 (3); Science: 0 (3); Foreign language: 0 (2); Social studies: 0 (3); History: 0 (3); Academic electives: 0 (0); Total units: 0 (16). Tests: The college uses SAT or ACT scores in admissions decisions. Either SAT or ACT required. For admission to the fall 2011 entering class, the school will accept: ACT with or without writing accepted. Campus visit: Recommended. Admissions interview: Neither required nor recommended. Off-campus interview: Not available. **Factors that count in admissions decisions:** *Academic:* Secondary school record: Important. Class rank: Important. Letters of recommendation: Considered. Standardized test scores: Important. Essay: Considered. *Nonacademic:* Interview: Not Considered. Extracurricular activities: Not Considered. Talent/ability: Considered. Character/personal qualities: Not Considered. Alumni/ae relationship: Not Considered. Geographical residence: Not Considered. State residency: Not Considered. Religious

affiliation/commitment: Not Considered. Minority status: Not Considered. Volunteer work: Not Considered. Work experience: Not Considered. **Other schools with the greatest overlap in applicants:** California University of Pennsylvania; Clarion University of Pennsylvania; Edinboro University of Pennsylvania; Indiana University of Pennsylvania; University of Pittsburgh. **Admissions statistics for the fall 2009 entering class:** Total applicants: 5,928. Total accepted: 3,718. Freshmen enrolled: 1,545; 11% were from out of state. Overall acceptance rate: 63%. **Size of waiting list:** 2278 applicants; enrolled from waiting list: 459. **Credentials of fall 2009 freshmen:** 12% ranked in the top 10 percent of their high school class; 42% were in the top 25 percent; 84% were in the top half. (Proportion submitting class standing: 84%.) **Average high school grade point average:** 3.4. **First-year students who submitted SAT scores:** 87%. Scores (25/75 percentile): Critical Reading: 460-550, Math: 470-560, Combined: 930-1110. **First-year students submitting ACT scores:** 24%. Scores (25/75 percentile): English: 18-24, Math: 18-23, Composite: 19-24.

ACADEMICS

Year founded: 1889. **Academic calendar:** Semester. **Degrees offered:** certificate, bachelor's, post-bachelor's certificate, master's. **Most popular majors:** 23% education, 16% business, management, marketing, and related support services, 15% health professions and related clinical sciences, 10% parks, recreation, leisure, and fitness studies, 5% social sciences. **Major fields of study:** biological and biomedical sciences; business, management, marketing, and related support services; communication, journalism, and related programs; computer and information sciences and support services; education; engineering technologies/technicians; English language and literature/letters; foreign languages, literatures, and linguistics; health professions and related clinical sciences; history; mathematics and statistics; multi/interdisciplinary studies; natural resources and conservation; parks, recreation, leisure, and fitness studies; philosophy and religious studies; physical sciences; psychology; public administration and social service professions; social sciences; visual and performing arts. **Areas of required coursework:** arts/fine arts, humanities, computer literacy, mathematics, English (including composition), sciences (biological or physical), history, social science. **Pre-professional programs:** pre-law, pre-dentistry, pre-medicine, pre-veterinary science, pre-optometry, pre-pharmacy, other. **Special academic programs:** distance learning, double major, dual enrollment, exchange student program (domestic), honors program, independent study, internships, liberal arts/career combination, student-designed major, study abroad, teacher certificate program. **Teacher certification offered in:** early childhood, special education, elementary, middle/junior high, secondary, bilingual/bicultural. **Cooperative education programs:** art. **Reserve Officers Training Corps (ROTC):** Army ROTC: Offered on campus. **Faculty and instruction (2009-2010):** Total instructional faculty: 348 full-time, 61 part-time (51% men; 49% women; 16% minorities). Full-time faculty with Ph.D. or other terminal degree: 89%. Student/faculty ratio: 20/1. Classes of fewer than 20 students: 16%; of 20 to 49 students: 76%; of 50 or more students: 8%. **Advanced Placement and International Baccalaureate credit:** AP tests may be used for: Credit only. Scores accepted: 3, 4, 5. **Freshmen returning for sophomore year:** 79%. **Graduation rates:** Four-year: 31%; five-year: 53%; six-year: 56%. **Graduate study:** 28% of students pursue further study immediately upon graduation; 35% within one year; 50% within five years. Fields in which graduates pursue further study: Master of Business Administration (MBA), 10%; law, 3%; medicine, 1%; dentistry, 1%; theology (or the seminary), 1%; education, 38%; arts and sciences, 45%; veterinary medicine, 1%.

COSTS AND FINANCIAL AID

Financial aid office: (724) 738-2044. **Expenses (2009-2010):** Tuition and fees 2009-2010: $7,235 in state, $10,012 out of state; room/board: $8,322. Estimated books and supplies: $1,400; transportation: $1,282; personal expenses: $659. **Financial aid:** Priority filing date for institution's financial aid form: May 1. In 2009-2010, 90% of undergraduates applied for financial aid. Of those, 68% were determined to have financial need; 38% had their need fully met. Average financial aid package (proportion receiving): $8,260 (67%). Average amount of gift aid, such as scholarships or grants (proportion receiving): $3,563 (45%). Average amount of self-help aid, such as work study or loans (proportion receiving): $3,898 (61%). Average need-based loan (excluding PLUS or other private loans): $3,863. Among students who received need-based aid, the average percentage of need met: 67%. Among students who received aid based on merit, the average award (and the proportion receiving): $7,241 (18%). The average athletic scholarship (and the proportion receiving): $3,611 (3%). Average amount of debt of borrowers graduating in 2009: $23,879. Proportion who borrowed: 81%.

CAMPUS LIFE AND EXTRACURRICULAR ACTIVITIES

Campus housing available (% using): coed dorms (91%), apartment for single students (7%), special housing for disabled students (2%). Students who live in college-owned, operated, or affiliated housing: 36%. **Student employment:** During the 2009-2010 academic year, 16% of undergraduates worked on campus. Average per-year earnings: $3,572. **Clubs and organizations:** Number of student organizations: 145. Activities include: campus ministries, choral groups, concert band, dance, drama/theater, international student organization, jazz band, literary magazine, marching band, model UN, music ensembles, musical theater, radio station, student government, student newspaper, student film society, symphony orchestra, television station, yearbook. Number of fraternities: 9; sororities: 8. Proportion of men in fraternities: 5%; of women in sororities: 5%. Average proportion of students who stay on campus on weekends: 50%. **Sports program (2009-2010):** Member of NCAA II. *Men's intercollegiate varsity sports:* baseball, basketball, cross country, football, soccer, track and field (indoor), track and field (outdoor). *Women's intercollegiate varsity sports:* basketball, cross country, field hockey, lacrosse, soccer, softball, tennis, track and field (indoor), track and field (outdoor), volleyball.

SERVICES AND FACILITIES

Basic services: nonremedial tutoring, women's center, placement service, day care, health service, health insurance, other. **Remedial assistance:** reading, math, writing, study skills, other. **Counseling services:** minority student, career, military, personal, veteran student, academic, older student, psychological, birth control, religious. **For learning-disabled students:** School does not offer a structured program with separate admission and additional fees. Services include: reading machines, tape recorders, untimed tests, note-taking services, oral tests, readers, extended time for tests, tutors, priority registration, priority seating, texts on tape, exams on tape or computer, other testing accommodations, other. **Library:** Number of titles: 515,095; number of current serial subscriptions: 436. **Information technology resources:** Students are not required to lease or own a computer. Number of campus computers available to all students: 1,323. School has a wireless network. Approximate number of users that can be accommodated: 750. Proportion of college-owned housing units wired for high-speed internet access: 100%. **Campus safety:** Security services offered: 24-hour foot-and-vehicle patrols, late-night transport/escort service, 24-hour emergency telephones, lighted pathways/sidewalks, student patrols, controlled dormitory access (key, security card, etc).

TRANSFER AND INTERNATIONAL STUDENTS

Transfer students: May apply for admission for the following academic terms: Fall, Spring, Summer. Applicants do not need a minimum number of credits to apply. For fall 2009: Transfer applications received: 1,193. Transfer applicants offered admission: 933. Transfer applicants enrolled: 689. **International students:** Number of foreign undergraduates: 82 (1% of student body). Number of countries represented: 37. Minimum TOEFL score required: 500 (paper); 173 (computer). Average TOEFL score: 550 (paper).

St. Francis University

- **Address:** PO Box 600, Loretto, PA 15940
- **Website:** http://www.francis.edu/
- **Private; Religious affiliation:** Roman Catholic
- **Enrollment:** 1,566 full-time; 113 part-time

KEY STATS

✔ **U.S News College Ranking:** 51, Regional Universities (North)
✔ **SAT Score (25th/75th percentile):** 920-1140
✔ **Tuition:** 2010-2011: $26,534

Selectivity: Selective	**Room/board:** $9,066
Acceptance rate: 77%	**Average debt:** $22,500
Student/faculty ratio: 14/1	**Proportion who borrowed:** 85%

UNDERGRADUATE STUDENT BODY STATS

2009-2010 enrollment: 1,566 full-time; 113 part-time. Men: 40%; women: 60%. **Ethnic makeup:** African American: 5%; Asian American: 1%; Hispanic: 1%; White: 91%; International: 1%. **Religious preference:** Roman Catholic: 55%; Protestant: 45%.

ADMISSIONS FACTS AND FIGURES

Phone: (814) 472-3100. **Email:** admissions@francis.edu. **Website:** http://www.francis.edu/. **Application deadlines for fall 2011:** Regular decision: July 30. Early decision: Not offered. Early action: Not offered. Admission can be deferred. **Application fee:** $30. **To apply online, go to:** https://francis.gotoextinguisher.com/application/login/. **Admissions requirements/recommendations:** High school units required (recommended): English: 4 (4); Mathematics: 2 (2); Science: 1 (2); Foreign language: (2); Social studies: 2 (2); Academic electives: 7 (6); Total units: 16 (19). Tests: The college uses SAT or ACT scores in admissions decisions. Either SAT or ACT required. For admission to the fall 2011 entering class, the school will accept: ACT with writing recommended. Campus visit: Recommended. Admissions interview: Recommended. Off-campus interview: May be arranged. **Factors that count in admissions decisions:** *Academic:* Secondary school record: Very Important. Class rank: Important. Letters of recommendation: Important. Standardized test scores: Important. Essay: Important. *Nonacademic:* Interview: Important. Extracurricular activities: Very Important. Talent/ability: Important. Character/personal qualities: Considered. Alumni/ae relationship: Considered. Geographical residence: Considered. State residency: Considered. Religious affiliation/commitment: Not Considered. Minority status: Not Considered. Volunteer work: Important. Work experience: Important. **Other schools with the greatest overlap in applicants:** Duquesne University; Gannon University; Pennsylvania State University–University Park; St. Vincent College; University of Pittsburgh–Johnstown. **Admissions statistics for the fall 2009 entering class:** Total applicants: 1,501. Total accepted: 1,161. Freshmen enrolled: 433; 28% were from out of state. Overall acceptance rate: 77%. **Credentials of fall 2009 freshmen:** 26% ranked in the top 10 percent of their high school class; 56% were in the top 25 percent; 84% were in the top half. (Proportion submitting class standing: 71%.) **First-year students who submitted SAT scores:** 80%. Scores (25/75 percentile): Critical Reading: 450-560, Math: 470-580, Combined: 920-1140. **First-year students submitting ACT scores:** 45%. Scores (25/75 percentile): English: N/A, Math: N/A, Composite: 19-25.

ACADEMICS

Year founded: 1847. **Academic calendar:** Semester. **Degrees offered:** certificate, associate, bachelor's, master's, doctorate. **Most popular majors:** 33% health professions and related clinical sciences, 25% business administration and management, 11% education, 7% biological and biomedical sciences, 7% psychology. **Major fields of study:** biological and biomedical sciences; business, management, marketing, and related support services; communication, journalism, and related programs; computer and information sciences and support services; education; engineering; English language and literature/letters; foreign languages, literatures, and linguistics; health professions and related clinical sciences; history; legal professions and studies; mathematics and statistics; natural resources and conservation; philosophy and religious studies; physical sciences; psychology; public administration and social service professions; security and protective services; social sciences. **Areas of required coursework:** arts/fine arts, humanities, computer literacy, mathematics, English (including composition), philosophy, foreign languages, sciences (biological or physical), history, social science. **Pre-professional programs:** pre-law, pre-dentistry, pre-medicine, pre-veterinary science, pre-optometry, pre-pharmacy. **Special academic programs (% participation):** cooperative (work-study plan) program, distance learning, double major, honors program, independent study, internships, liberal arts/career combination, student-designed major, study abroad, teacher certificate program, weekend college (10%). **Teacher certification offered in:** special education, elementary, secondary. **Cooperative education programs:** engineering, health professions. **Reserve Officers Training Corps (ROTC):** Army ROTC: Offered on campus. **Faculty and instruction (2009-2010):** Total instructional faculty: 108 full-time, 82 part-time (56% men; 44% women; 4% minorities). Full-time faculty with Ph.D. or other terminal degree: 64%. Student/faculty ratio: 14/1. Classes of fewer than 20 students: 48%; of 20 to 49 students: 49%; of 50 or more students: 3%. **Advanced Placement and International Baccalaureate credit:** AP tests may be used for: Credit and/or placement. Scores accepted: 3, 4, 5. International Baccalaureate exams may be used for: Credit and/or placement. **Freshmen returning for sophomore year:** 84%. **Graduation rates:** Four-year: 57%; five-year: 70%; six-year: 61%. **Graduate study:** 24% of students pursue further study immediately upon graduation. Fields in which graduates pursue further study: Master of Business Administration (MBA), 7%; law, 6%; medicine, 6%; dentistry, 1%; engineering, 1%; theology (or the seminary), 1%; education, 4%; arts and sciences, 71%; veterinary medicine, 3%.

COSTS AND FINANCIAL AID

Financial aid office: (814) 472-3010. **Expenses (2010-2011):** Tuition and fees 2010-2011: $26,534; room/board: $9,066. Estimated books and supplies: $1,500; transportation: $0; personal expenses: $2,000. **Financial aid:** Priority filing date for institution's financial aid form: May 1. In 2009-2010, 98% of undergraduates applied for financial aid. Of those, 92% were determined to have financial need; 30% had their need fully met. Average financial aid package (proportion receiving): $19,405 (93%). Average amount of gift aid, such as scholarships or grants (proportion receiving): $16,230 (75%). Average amount of self-help aid, such as work study or loans (proportion receiving): $4,646 (74%). Average need-based loan (excluding PLUS or other private loans): $4,203. Among students who received need-based aid, the average percentage of need met: 78%. Among students who received aid based on merit, the average award (and the proportion receiving): $19,763 (38%). The average athletic scholarship (and the proportion receiving): $8,787 (74%). Average amount of debt of borrowers graduating in 2009: $22,500. Proportion who borrowed: 85%.

CAMPUS LIFE AND EXTRACURRICULAR ACTIVITIES

Campus housing available (% using): women's dorms (60%), men's dorms (30%), apartment for single students (5%), special housing for disabled students. Students who live in college-owned, operated, or affiliated housing: 90%. **Student employment:** During the 2009-2010 academic year, 10% of undergraduates worked on campus. Average per-year earnings: $800. **Clubs and organizations:** Number of student organizations: 63. Activities include: campus ministries, choral groups, dance, drama/theater, literary magazine, music ensembles, pep band, radio station, student government, student newspaper, television station, yearbook. Number of fraternities: 5; sororities: 5. Proportion of men in fraternities: 40%; of women in sororities: 30%. Average proportion of students who stay on campus on weekends: 60%. **Sports program (2009-2010):** Member of NCAA I. *Men's intercollegiate varsity sports:* basketball, cross country, football, golf, soccer, swimming, tennis, track and field (indoor), track and field (outdoor), volleyball. *Women's intercollegiate varsity sports:* basketball, cross country, field hockey, golf, lacrosse, softball, swimming, tennis, track and field (indoor), track and field (outdoor), volleyball.

SERVICES AND FACILITIES

Basic services: health service. **Remedial assistance:** writing, study skills. **Counseling services:** psychological, religious. **For learning-disabled students:** School does not offer a structured program with separate admission and additional fees. Services include: remedial math, remedial English, reading machines, tape recorders, untimed tests, note-taking services, oral tests, learning center, readers, extended time for tests, tutors, priority registration, priority seating, texts on tape. **Library:** Number of titles: 126,167; number of current serial subscriptions: 23,038. **Information technology resources:** Students are required to lease or own a computer. Number of campus computers available to all students: 1,800. School has a wireless network. Approximate number of users that can be accommodated: 1,800. Proportion of college-owned housing units wired for high-speed internet access: 100%. **Campus safety:** Security services offered: 24-hour foot-and-vehicle patrols, late-night transport/escort service, 24-hour emergency telephones, lighted pathways/sidewalks, controlled dormitory access (key, security card, etc).

TRANSFER AND INTERNATIONAL STUDENTS

Transfer students: May apply for admission for the following academic terms: Fall, Spring, Summer. Applicants need a minimum number of credits to apply. For fall 2009: Transfer applications received: 117. Transfer applicants offered admission: 76. Transfer applicants enrolled: 42. **International students:** Number of foreign undergraduates: 18 (1% of student body). Number of countries represented: 2. Minimum TOEFL score required: 550 (paper); 213 (computer). Average TOEFL score: 627 (paper).

St. Joseph's University

- **Address:** 5600 City Avenue, Philadelphia, PA 19131
- **Website:** http://www.sju.edu
- **Private; Religious affiliation:** Roman Catholic (Jesuit)
- **Enrollment:** 4,526 full-time; 877 part-time

KEY STATS

✔ **U.S News College Ranking:** 13, Regional Universities (North)
✔ **SAT Score (25th/75th percentile):** 1020-1220
✔ **Tuition:** 2010-2011: $35,230

Selectivity: Selective	**Room/board:** $11,925
Acceptance rate: 82%	**Average debt:** $40,933
Student/faculty ratio: 16/1	**Proportion who borrowed:** 59%

UNDERGRADUATE STUDENT BODY STATS

2009-2010 enrollment: 4,526 full-time; 877 part-time. Men: 48%; women: 52%. **Ethnic makeup:** African American: 7%; Asian American: 2%; Hispanic: 4%; White: 85%; International: 1%. **Religious preference:** Roman Catholic: 72%; Jewish: 1%; Unknown: 10%; Christian/Non-catholic: 13%; Other: 4%.

ADMISSIONS FACTS AND FIGURES

Phone: (610) 660-1300. **Email:** admit@sju.edu. **Website:** http://www.sju.edu. **Application deadlines for fall 2011:** Regular decision: February 1; decision sent by March 15. Early decision: Not offered. Early action: Send application by: November 15; Decision sent by: December 25. Admission can be deferred. **Application fee:** $60. **To apply online, go to:** http://www.sju.edu/admissions/content.php?page=33. **Admissions requirements/recommendations:** High school units required (recommended): English: 4 (4); Mathematics: 3 (3); Science: 2 (2); Foreign language: 2 (2); Social studies: 0 (0); History: 1 (1); Academic electives: 0 (0); Total units: 12 (12). Tests: The college uses SAT or ACT scores in admissions decisions. Either SAT or ACT required. For admission to the fall 2011 entering class, the school will accept: ACT with or without writing accepted. Campus visit: Recommended. Admissions interview: Neither required nor recommended. Off-campus interview: Not available. **Factors that count in admissions decisions:** *Academic:* Secondary school record: Very Important. Class rank: Considered. Letters of recommendation: Important. Standardized test scores: Considered. Essay: Important. *Nonacademic:* Interview: Not Considered. Extracurricular activities: Considered. Talent/ability: Considered. Character/personal qualities: Important. Alumni/ae relationship: Considered. Geographical residence: Not Considered. State residency: Not Considered. Religious affiliation/commitment: Not Considered. Minority status: Not Considered. Volunteer work: Considered. Work experience: Considered. **Other schools with the greatest overlap in applicants:** Loyola University Maryland; Pennsylvania State University–University Park; Temple University; University of Delaware; Villanova University. **Admissions statistics for the fall 2009 entering class:** Total applicants: 6,520. Total accepted: 5,370. Freshmen enrolled: 1,192; 61% were from out of state. Accepted through early-decision or early-action plans: 65%. Overall acceptance rate: 82%. Non-early acceptance rate: 69%. **Size of waiting list:** 641 applicants; enrolled from waiting list: 114. **Credentials of fall 2009 freshmen:** 23% ranked in the top 10 percent of their high school class; 55% were in the top 25 percent; 86% were in the top half. (Proportion submitting class standing: 39%.) **Average high school grade point average:** 3.4. **First-year students who submitted SAT scores:** 96%. Scores (25/75 percentile): Critical Reading: 510-600, Math: 510-620, Combined: 1020-1220. **First-year students submitting ACT scores:** 17%. Scores (25/75 percentile): English: 21-26, Math: 21-26, Composite: 21-26.

ACADEMICS

Year founded: 1851. **Academic calendar:** Semester. **Degrees offered:** certificate, associate, transfer-associate, bachelor's, post-bachelor's certificate, master's, post-master's certificate, doctorate. **Most popular majors:** 14% marketing/marketing management, 10% finance, 7% accounting, 6% English language and literature, 6% business administration and management. **Major fields of study:** area, ethnic, cultural, and gender studies; biological and biomedical sciences; business, management, marketing, and related support services; communication, journalism, and related programs; computer and information sciences and support services; education; English language and literature/letters; foreign languages, literatures, and linguistics; health professions and related clinical sciences; history; legal professions and studies; liberal arts and sciences studies, and humanities;

mathematics and statistics; natural resources and conservation; philosophy and religious studies; physical sciences; psychology; public administration and social service professions; social sciences; visual and performing arts. **Areas of required coursework:** arts/fine arts, humanities, mathematics, English (including composition), philosophy, foreign languages, sciences (biological or physical), history, social science, other. **Special academic programs (% participation):** accelerated program (2%), cooperative (work-study plan) program (1%), double major (7%), dual enrollment (1%), English as a Second Language (ESL) (0%), honors program (9%), independent study (29%), internships (18%), student-designed major (0%), study abroad (15%), teacher certificate program (8%). **Teacher certification offered in:** special education, elementary, secondary. **Cooperative education programs:** business. **Reserve Officers Training Corps (ROTC):** Army ROTC: Offered at cooperating institution (University of Pennsylvania); Navy ROTC: Offered at cooperating institution (Villanova University); Air Force ROTC: Offered on campus. **Faculty and instruction (2009-2010):** Total instructional faculty: 238 full-time, 372 part-time (59% men; 41% women; 11% minorities). Full-time faculty with Ph.D. or other terminal degree: 98%. Student/faculty ratio: 16/1. Classes of fewer than 20 students: 35%; of 20 to 49 students: 63%; of 50 or more students: 1%. **Advanced Placement and International Baccalaureate credit:** AP tests may be used for: Credit and/or placement. Scores accepted: 4, 5. International Baccalaureate exams may be used for: Credit only. **Freshmen returning for sophomore year:** 87%. **Graduation rates:** Four-year: 71%; five-year: 76%; six-year: 77%. **Graduate study:** 28% of students pursue further study immediately upon graduation; 62% within one year; 78% within five years. Fields in which graduates pursue further study: Master of Business Administration (MBA), 15%; law, 10%; medicine, 26%; education, 23%; arts and sciences, 26%.

COSTS AND FINANCIAL AID
Financial aid office: (610) 660-1556. **Expenses (2010-2011):** Tuition and fees 2010-2011: $35,230; room/board: $11,925. Estimated books and supplies: $1,500; transportation: $0; personal expenses: $2,500. **Financial aid:** Priority filing date for institution's financial aid form: February 15. In 2009-2010, 62% of undergraduates applied for financial aid. Of those, 50% were determined to have financial need; 23% had their need fully met. Average financial aid package (proportion receiving): $19,271 (50%). Average amount of gift aid, such as scholarships or grants (proportion receiving): $14,947 (48%). Average amount of self-help aid, such as work study or loans (proportion receiving): $7,500 (37%). Average need-based loan (excluding PLUS or other private loans): $5,179. Among students who received need-based aid, the average percentage of need met: 76%. Among students who received aid based on merit, the average award (and the proportion receiving): $10,206 (40%). The average athletic scholarship (and the proportion receiving): $16,949 (3%). Average amount of debt of borrowers graduating in 2009: $40,933. Proportion who borrowed: 59%.

CAMPUS LIFE AND EXTRACURRICULAR ACTIVITIES
Campus housing available (% using): coed dorms (91%), women's dorms (4%), men's dorms (5%), apartment for single students, other housing options. Students who live in college-owned, operated, or affiliated housing: 59%. **Student employment:** During the 2009-2010 academic year, 30% of undergraduates worked on campus. Average per-year earnings: $1,500. **Clubs and organizations:** Number of student organizations: 100. Activities include: campus ministries, choral groups, concert band, dance, drama/theater, international student organization, jazz band, literary magazine, music ensembles, musical theater, pep band, radio station, student government, student newspaper, yearbook. Number of fraternities: 4; sororities: 4. Proportion of men in fraternities: 8%; of women in sororities: 11%. **Sports program (2009-2010):** Member of NCAA I. *Men's intercollegiate varsity sports:* baseball, basketball, cross country, golf, lacrosse, soccer, tennis, track and field (indoor), track and field (outdoor). *Women's intercollegiate varsity sports:* basketball, crew (heavyweight), cross country, field hockey, lacrosse, crew (lightweight), soccer, softball, tennis, track and field (indoor), track and field (outdoor).

SERVICES AND FACILITIES
Basic services: nonremedial tutoring, health service, health insurance, other. **Counseling services:** minority student, career, personal, academic, older student, psychological, religious. **For learning-disabled students:** School does not offer a structured program with separate admission and additional fees. Total undergraduates in learning-disabled program or receiving services: 267. Services include: reading machines, tape recorders, note-taking services, oral tests, learning center, readers, extended time for tests, tutors, priority seating, texts on tape, other testing accommodations, other. **Library:** Number of titles: 355,000; number of current serial subscriptions: 28,750.

Information technology resources: Students are not required to lease or own a computer. Number of campus computers available to all students: 723. School has a wireless network. Approximate number of users that can be accommodated: 3,000. Proportion of college-owned housing units wired for high-speed internet access: 100%. **Campus safety:** Security services offered: 24-hour foot-and-vehicle patrols, late-night transport/escort service, 24-hour emergency telephones, lighted pathways/sidewalks, controlled dormitory access (key, security card, etc).

TRANSFER AND INTERNATIONAL STUDENTS
Transfer students: May apply for admission for the following academic terms: Fall, Spring. Applicants need a minimum number of credits to apply. For fall 2009: Transfer applications received: 243. Transfer applicants offered admission: 164. Transfer applicants enrolled: 67. **International students:** Number of foreign undergraduates: 75 (1% of student body). Number of countries represented: 33. Minimum TOEFL score required: 550 (paper); 79 (computer).

St. Vincent College

- **Address:** 300 Fraser Purchase Road, Latrobe, PA 15650-2690
- **Website:** http://www.stvincent.edu
- **Private; Religious affiliation:** Roman Catholic
- **Enrollment:** 1,645 full-time; 96 part-time

KEY STATS
✔ **U.S News College Ranking:** 152, National Liberal Arts Colleges
✔ **SAT Score (25th/75th percentile):** 970-1190
✔ **Tuition:** 2010-2011: $27,090

Selectivity: Selective	**Room/board:** $8,508
Acceptance rate: 67%	**Average debt:** N/A
Student/faculty ratio: 13/1	**Proportion who borrowed:** N/A

UNDERGRADUATE STUDENT BODY STATS
2009-2010 enrollment: 1,645 full-time; 96 part-time. Men: 53%; women: 47%. **Ethnic makeup:** African American: 6%; Asian American: 1%; Hispanic: 2%; White: 90%; International: 1%. **Religious preference:** Protestant: 2%; No preference: 2%; Unknown: 12%; Roman Catholic: 65%; Christian: 4%; Other: 15%.

ADMISSIONS FACTS AND FIGURES
Phone: (800) 782-5549. **Email:** admission@stvincent.edu. **Website:** http://www.stvincent.edu. **Application deadlines for fall 2011:** Regular decision: April 1. Early decision: Not offered. Early action: Not offered. Admission can be deferred. **Application fee:** $25. **To apply online, go to:** https://secure.stvincent.edu/. **Admissions requirements/recommendations:** High school units required (recommended): English: 4 (4); Mathematics: 3 (3); Science: 1 (3); Foreign language: 0 (2); Social studies: 3 (3); History: 0 (0); Academic electives: 5 (5); Total units: 16 (20). Tests: The college uses SAT or ACT scores in admissions decisions. Either SAT or ACT required. For admission to the fall 2011 entering class, the school will accept: ACT with or without writing accepted. Campus visit: Recommended. Admissions interview: Recommended. Off-campus interview: May be arranged. **Factors that count in admissions decisions:** *Academic:* Secondary school record: Very Important. Class rank: Important. Letters of recommendation: Considered. Standardized test scores: Important. Essay: Important. *Nonacademic:* Interview: Considered. Extracurricular activities: Considered. Talent/ability: Considered. Character/personal qualities: Important. Alumni/ae relationship: Not Considered. Geographical residence: Not Considered. State residency: Not Considered. Religious affiliation/commitment: Not Considered. Minority status: Not Considered. Volunteer work: Not Considered. Work experience: Not Considered. **Admissions statistics for the fall 2009 entering class:** Total applicants: 1,765. Total accepted: 1,191. Freshmen enrolled: 448; 23% were from out of state. Overall acceptance rate: 67%. **Size of waiting list:** 189 applicants; enrolled from waiting list: 28. **Credentials of fall 2009 freshmen:** 24% ranked in the top 10 percent of their high school class; 51% were in the top 25 percent; 82% were in the top half. (Proportion submitting class standing: 72%.) **Average high school grade point average:** 3.5. **First-year students who submitted SAT scores:** 96%. Scores (25/75 percentile): Critical Reading: 480-590, Math: 490-600, Combined: 970-1190. **First-year students submitting ACT scores:** 28%. Scores (25/75 percentile): English: 20-26, Math: 20-26, Composite: 20-26.

ACADEMICS

Year founded: 1846. **Academic calendar:** Semester. **Degrees offered:** certificate, bachelor's, post-bachelor's certificate, master's. **Most popular majors:** 29% business, management, marketing, and related support services, 10% biological and biomedical sciences, 9% psychology, 8% social sciences, 6% communication, journalism, and related programs. **Major fields of study:** biological and biomedical sciences; business, management, marketing, and related support services; communication, journalism, and related programs; computer and information sciences and support services; education; engineering; English language and literature/letters; foreign languages, literatures, and linguistics; health professions and related clinical sciences; history; liberal arts and sciences studies, and humanities; mathematics and statistics; natural resources and conservation; philosophy and religious studies; physical sciences; psychology; public administration and social service professions; social sciences; theology and religious vocations; visual and performing arts. **Areas of required coursework:** arts/fine arts, mathematics, English (including composition), philosophy, foreign languages, sciences (biological or physical), history, social science, other. **Pre-professional programs:** pre-law, pre-dentistry, pre-medicine, pre-theology, pre-veterinary science, pre-optometry, pre-pharmacy, other. **Special academic programs:** accelerated program, cooperative (work-study plan) program, cross-registration, distance learning, double major, dual enrollment, external degree program, honors program, independent study, internships, liberal arts/career combination, study abroad, teacher certificate program. **Teacher certification offered in:** early childhood, elementary, middle/junior high, secondary. **Cooperative education programs:** art, business, computer science, education, engineering, health professions, humanities, natural science, social/behavioral science, technologies, other. **Reserve Officers Training Corps (ROTC):** Army ROTC: Offered at cooperating institution (University of Pittsburgh); Air Force ROTC: Offered at cooperating institution (University of Pittsburgh). **Faculty and instruction (2009-2010):** Total instructional faculty: 104 full-time, 83 part-time (66% men; 34% women; 1% minorities). Full-time faculty with Ph.D. or other terminal degree: 88%. Student/faculty ratio: 13/1. Classes of fewer than 20 students: 47%; of 20 to 49 students: 53%; of 50 or more students: 0%. **Advanced Placement and International Baccalaureate credit:** AP tests may be used for: Placement only. Scores accepted: 3, 4, 5. International Baccalaureate exams may be used for: Placement only. **Freshmen returning for sophomore year:** 85%. **Graduation rates:** Four-year: 61%; five-year: 73%; six-year: 73%. **Graduate study:** 22% of students pursue further study immediately upon graduation.

COSTS AND FINANCIAL AID

Financial aid office: (724) 537-4540. **Expenses (2010-2011):** Tuition and fees 2010-2011: $27,090; room/board: $8,508. Estimated books and supplies: $1,200; transportation: $0; personal expenses: $1,600. **Financial aid:** Priority filing date for institution's financial aid form: March 1; deadline: May 1. In 2009-2010, 89% of undergraduates applied for financial aid. Of those, 77% were determined to have financial need; 25% had their need fully met. Average financial aid package (proportion receiving): $21,705 (77%). Average amount of gift aid, such as scholarships or grants (proportion receiving): $16,506 (77%). Average amount of self-help aid, such as work study or loans (proportion receiving): $4,597 (77%). Average need-based loan (excluding PLUS or other private loans): $4,662. Among students who received need-based aid, the average percentage of need met: 81%. Among students who received aid based on merit, the average award (and the proportion receiving): $12,349 (23%). The average athletic scholarship (and the proportion receiving): $0 (0%).

CAMPUS LIFE AND EXTRACURRICULAR ACTIVITIES

Campus housing available (% using): coed dorms (92%), apartment for single students (8%). Students who live in college-owned, operated, or affiliated housing: 70%. **Student employment:** During the 2009-2010 academic year, 46% of undergraduates worked on campus. Average per-year earnings: $3,400. **Clubs and organizations:** Number of student organizations: 67. Activities include: campus ministries, choral groups, dance, drama/theater, international student organization, literary magazine, music ensembles, musical theater, pep band, radio station, student government, student newspaper, television station. Number of fraternities: 0; sororities: 0. Average proportion of students who stay on campus on weekends: 60%. **Sports program (2009-2010):** Member of NCAA III. *Men's intercollegiate varsity sports:* baseball, basketball, cross country, football, golf, lacrosse, soccer, swimming, tennis, track and field (outdoor). *Women's intercollegiate varsity sports:* basketball, cross country, field hockey, golf, lacrosse, soccer, softball, swimming, tennis, volleyball.

SERVICES AND FACILITIES

Basic services: nonremedial tutoring, placement service, health service, health insurance. **Counseling services:** career, personal, academic, psychological, religious. **For learning-disabled students:** School does not offer a structured program with separate admission and additional fees. Total undergraduates in learning-disabled program or receiving services: 23. Services include: reading machines, tape recorders, note-taking services, oral tests, learning center, readers, extended time for tests, tutors, priority registration, priority seating, texts on tape, typist/scribe, exams on tape or computer, other testing accommodations. **Library:** Number of titles: 382,031; number of current serial subscriptions: 421. **Information technology resources:** Students are not required to lease or own a computer. Number of campus computers available to all students: 256. School has a wireless network. Approximate number of users that can be accommodated: 500. Proportion of college-owned housing units wired for high-speed internet access: 100%. **Campus safety:** Security services offered: late-night transport/escort service, 24-hour emergency telephones, lighted pathways/sidewalks, controlled dormitory access (key, security card, etc).

TRANSFER AND INTERNATIONAL STUDENTS

Transfer students: May apply for admission for the following academic terms: Fall, Spring. Applicants do not need a minimum number of credits to apply. For fall 2009: Transfer applications received: 147. Transfer applicants offered admission: 87. Transfer applicants enrolled: 56. **International students:** Number of foreign undergraduates: 15 (1% of student body). Number of countries represented: 11. Minimum TOEFL score required: 550 (paper); 213 (computer).

Susquehanna University

- **Address:** 514 University Avenue, Selinsgrove, PA 17870
- **Website:** http://www.susqu.edu
- **Private; Religious affiliation:** Lutheran
- **Enrollment:** 2,187 full-time; 44 part-time

KEY STATS

✔ **U.S News College Ranking:** 114, National Liberal Arts Colleges
✔ **SAT Score (25th/75th percentile):** 1010-1210
✔ **Tuition:** 2010-2011: $34,070

Selectivity: Selective	Room/board: $9,230
Acceptance rate: 75%	Average debt: N/A
Student/faculty ratio: 13/1	Proportion who borrowed: N/A

UNDERGRADUATE STUDENT BODY STATS

2009-2010 enrollment: 2,187 full-time; 44 part-time. Men: 47%; women: 53%. **Ethnic makeup:** African American: 3%; Asian American: 2%; Hispanic: 3%; White: 92%; International: 1%. **Religious preference:** Roman Catholic: 36%; Protestant: 28%; Jewish: 2%; Buddhist: 1%; No preference: 14%; Unknown: 3%; Lutheran: 11%; Other: 5%.

ADMISSIONS FACTS AND FIGURES

Phone: (800) 326-9672. **Email:** suadmiss@susqu.edu. **Website:** http://www.susqu.edu. **Application deadlines for fall 2011:** Regular decision: March 1. Early decision: Send application by: November 15; Decision sent by: December 1. Early action: Not offered. Admission can be deferred. **Application fee:** $35. **To apply online, go to:** http://www.susqu.edu/admissions/. **Admissions requirements/recommendations:** High school units required (recommended): English: 4 (4); Mathematics: 3 (4); Science: 2 (3); Foreign language: 2 (4); Social studies: 2 (4); History: 2 (2); Academic electives: 2 (3); Total units: 18 (25). Tests: The college uses SAT or ACT scores in admissions decisions. Neither SAT nor ACT required. For admission to the fall 2011 entering class, the school will accept: ACT with or without writing accepted. Campus visit: Recommended. Admissions interview: Recommended. Off-campus interview: May be arranged. **Factors that count in admissions decisions:** *Academic:* Secondary school record: Very Important. Class rank: Important. Letters of recommendation: Important. Standardized test scores: Important. Essay: Important. *Nonacademic:* Interview: Important. Extracurricular activities: Important. Talent/ability: Important. Character/personal qualities: Important. Alumni/ae relationship: Important. Geographical residence: Considered. State residency: Considered. Religious affiliation/commitment: Considered. Minority status: Important. Volunteer work: Important. Work experience: Important. **Other schools with the greatest overlap in applicants:** Bucknell University;

Dickinson College; Gettysburg College; Muhlenberg College; Pennsylvania State University–University Park. **Admissions statistics for the fall 2009 entering class:** Total applicants: 2,954. Total accepted: 2,212. Freshmen enrolled: 624; 49% were from out of state. Overall acceptance rate: 75%. Non-early acceptance rate: 75%. **Size of waiting list:** 97 applicants; enrolled from waiting list: 5. **Credentials of fall 2009 freshmen:** 23% ranked in the top 10 percent of their high school class; 51% were in the top 25 percent; 86% were in the top half. (Proportion submitting class standing: 63%.) **Average high school grade point average:** 3.2. **First-year students who submitted SAT scores:** 85%. Scores (25/75 percentile): Critical Reading: 500-600, Math: 510-610, Combined: 1010-1210. **First-year students submitting ACT scores:** 10%. Scores (25/75 percentile): English: 21-27, Math: 21-28, Composite: 23-27.

ACADEMICS

Year founded: 1858. **Academic calendar:** Semester. **Degrees offered:** bachelor's. **Most popular majors:** 28% business administration and management, 12% communication studies/speech communication and rhetoric, 10% English language and literature, 9% social sciences, 9% visual and performing arts. **Major fields of study:** biological and biomedical sciences; business, management, marketing, and related support services; communication, journalism, and related programs; computer and information sciences and support services; education; English language and literature/letters; foreign languages, literatures, and linguistics; history; mathematics and statistics; philosophy and religious studies; physical sciences; psychology; social sciences; theology and religious vocations; visual and performing arts. **Areas of required coursework:** arts/fine arts, humanities, mathematics, English (including composition), foreign languages, sciences (biological or physical), history, social science, other. **Pre-professional programs:** pre-law, pre-dentistry, pre-medicine, pre-theology, pre-veterinary science, pre-optometry. **Special academic programs (% participation):** accelerated program (2.3%), cross-registration (0%), distance learning (13%), double major (10.1%), dual enrollment (0%), exchange student program (domestic) (2.5%), honors program (13.5%), independent study (51.7%), internships (38.4%), student-designed major (.2%), study abroad (37.1%), teacher certificate program (12.6%). **Teacher certification offered in:** early childhood, elementary, middle/junior high, secondary. **Reserve Officers Training Corps (ROTC):** Army ROTC: Offered at cooperating institution (Bucknell University). **Faculty and instruction (2009-2010):** Total instructional faculty: 133 full-time, 104 part-time (54% men; 46% women; 11% minorities). Full-time faculty with Ph.D. or other terminal degree: 93%. Student/faculty ratio: 13/1. Classes of fewer than 20 students: 51%; of 20 to 49 students: 49%; of 50 or more students: 0%. **Advanced Placement and International Baccalaureate credit:** AP tests may be used for: Placement only. Scores accepted: 4, 5. International Baccalaureate exams may be used for: Placement only. **Freshmen returning for sophomore year:** 86%. **Graduation rates:** Four-year: 80%; five-year: 81%; six-year: 81%. **Graduate study:** 27% of students pursue further study immediately upon graduation. Fields in which graduates pursue further study: Master of Business Administration (MBA), 6%; law, 14%; medicine, 10%; dentistry, 2%; theology (or the seminary), 6%; education, 2%; arts and sciences, 60%.

COSTS AND FINANCIAL AID

Financial aid office: (570) 372-4450. **Expenses (2010-2011):** Tuition and fees 2010-2011: $34,070; room/board: $9,230. Estimated books and supplies: $850; transportation: $350; personal expenses: $750. **Financial aid:** Priority filing date for institution's financial aid form: March 1; deadline: May 1. In 2009-2010, 78% of undergraduates applied for financial aid. Of those, 68% were determined to have financial need; 17% had their need fully met. Average financial aid package (proportion receiving): $23,880 (68%). Average amount of gift aid, such as scholarships or grants (proportion receiving): $19,015 (67%). Average amount of self-help aid, such as work study or loans (proportion receiving): $5,812 (59%). Average need-based loan (excluding PLUS or other private loans): $4,390. Among students who received need-based aid, the average percentage of need met: 79%. Among students who received aid based on merit, the average award (and the proportion receiving): $10,081 (24%). The average athletic scholarship (and the proportion receiving): $0 (0%).

CAMPUS LIFE AND EXTRACURRICULAR ACTIVITIES

Campus housing available (% using): coed dorms (58%), sorority housing (3%), fraternity housing (3%), apartment for single students (32%), special housing for disabled students (1%), special housing for international students (1%), other housing options (1%). Students who live in college-owned, operated, or affiliated housing: 77%. **Student employment:** During the 2009-2010 academic year, 44% of undergraduates worked on campus.

Average per-year earnings: $800. **Clubs and organizations:** Number of student organizations: 116. Activities include: campus ministries, choral groups, concert band, dance, drama/theater, international student organization, jazz band, literary magazine, music ensembles, musical theater, opera, pep band, radio station, student government, student newspaper, student film society, symphony orchestra, television station, yearbook. Number of fraternities: 5; sororities: 6. Proportion of men in fraternities: 5%; of women in sororities: 5%. Average proportion of students who stay on campus on weekends: 85%. **Sports program (2009-2010):** Member of NCAA III. *Men's intercollegiate varsity sports:* baseball, basketball, cross country, football, golf, lacrosse, soccer, swimming, tennis, track and field (indoor), track and field (outdoor). *Women's intercollegiate varsity sports:* basketball, cross country, field hockey, golf, lacrosse, soccer, softball, swimming, tennis, track and field (indoor), track and field (outdoor), volleyball.

SERVICES AND FACILITIES

Basic services: nonremedial tutoring, placement service, day care, health service, health insurance. **Counseling services:** minority student, career, personal, academic, older student, psychological, birth control, religious, other. **For learning-disabled students:** School does not offer a structured program with separate admission and additional fees. Total undergraduates in learning-disabled program or receiving services: 105. Services include: tape recorders, diagnostic testing service, untimed tests, note-taking services, oral tests, learning center, readers, extended time for tests, early syllabus, priority registration, priority seating, substitution of courses, texts on tape, typist/scribe, exams on tape or computer, other testing accommodations. **Library:** Number of titles: 258,263; number of current serial subscriptions: 50,390. **Information technology resources:** Students are not required to lease or own a computer. Number of campus computers available to all students: 292. School has a wireless network. Approximate number of users that can be accommodated: 2,300. Proportion of college-owned housing units wired for high-speed internet access: 100%. **Campus safety:** Security services offered: 24-hour foot-and-vehicle patrols, late-night transport/escort service, 24-hour emergency telephones, lighted pathways/sidewalks, controlled dormitory access (key, security card, etc).

TRANSFER AND INTERNATIONAL STUDENTS

Transfer students: May apply for admission for the following academic terms: Fall, Spring. Applicants do not need a minimum number of credits to apply. For fall 2009: Transfer applications received: 75. Transfer applicants offered admission: 62. Transfer applicants enrolled: 40. **International students:** Number of foreign undergraduates: 17 (1% of student body). Number of countries represented: 12. Minimum TOEFL score required: 550 (paper); 213 (computer).

Swarthmore College

- **Address:** 500 College Avenue, Swarthmore, PA 19081
- **Website:** http://www.swarthmore.edu
- **Private**
- **Enrollment:** 1,510 full-time; 15 part-time

KEY STATS

✔ **U.S News College Ranking:** 3, National Liberal Arts Colleges
✔ **SAT Score (25th/75th percentile):** 1340-1530
✔ **Tuition:** 2010-2011: $39,600

Selectivity: Most selective	**Room/board:** $11,900
Acceptance rate: 17%	**Average debt:** $15,737
Student/faculty ratio: 8/1	**Proportion who borrowed:** 45%

UNDERGRADUATE STUDENT BODY STATS

2009-2010 enrollment: 1,510 full-time; 15 part-time. Men: 48%; women: 52%. **Ethnic makeup:** African American: 10%; American-Indian: 1%; Asian American: 16%; Hispanic: 11%; White: 56%; International: 7%. **Religious preference:** Roman Catholic: 9%; Protestant: 13%; Jewish: 12%; Hindu: 3%; Buddhist: 4%; No preference: 51%; Quaker (not counted elsewhere): 2%; Other: 6%.

ADMISSIONS FACTS AND FIGURES

Phone: (610) 328-8300. **Email:** admissions@swarthmore.edu. **Website:** http://www.swarthmore.edu. **Application deadlines for fall 2011:** Regular decision: January 2; decision sent by April 1. Early decision: Send application by: November 15; Decision sent by: December 15. Early action: Not offered. Admission can be deferred. **Application fee:** $60. **To apply online, go to:** http://www.commonapp.org. **Admissions requirements/recommendations:** High school units required (recommended): English: (4); Mathematics: (3); Science: (3). Tests: The college uses SAT or ACT scores in admissions decisions. Either SAT or ACT required. For admission to the fall 2011 entering class, the school will accept: ACT with writing required. Campus visit: Recommended. Admissions interview: Recommended. Off-campus interview: May be arranged. **Factors that count in admissions decisions:** *Academic:* Secondary school record: Very Important. Class rank: Very Important. Letters of recommendation: Very Important. Standardized test scores: Important. Essay: Very Important. *Nonacademic:* Interview: Considered. Extracurricular activities: Important. Talent/ability: Considered. Character/personal qualities: Very Important. Alumni/ae relationship: Considered. Geographical residence: Considered. State residency: Not Considered. Religious affiliation/commitment: Not Considered. Minority status: Considered. Volunteer work: Considered. Work experience: Considered. **Other schools with the greatest overlap in applicants:** Brown University; Harvard University; Princeton University; Stanford University; Yale University. **Admissions statistics for the fall 2009 entering class:** Total applicants: 5,575. Total accepted: 969. Freshmen enrolled: 394; 89% were from out of state. Accepted through early-decision or early-action plans: 42%. Overall acceptance rate: 17%. Early-decision acceptance rate: 33%. Non-early acceptance rate: 16%. **Size of waiting list:** N/A applicants; enrolled from waiting list: 12. **Credentials of fall 2009 freshmen:** 87% ranked in the top 10 percent of their high school class; 99% were in the top 25 percent; 100% were in the top half. (Proportion submitting class standing: 50%.) **First-year students who submitted SAT scores:** 91%. Scores (25/75 percentile): Critical Reading: 670-760, Math: 670-770, Combined: 1340-1530. **First-year students submitting ACT scores:** 32%. Scores (25/75 percentile): English: N/A, Math: N/A, Composite: 29-33.

ACADEMICS

Year founded: 1864. **Academic calendar:** Semester. **Degrees offered:** bachelor's. **Most popular majors:** 25% social sciences, 9% biological and biomedical sciences, 9% visual and performing arts, 8% foreign languages, literatures, and linguistics, 8% psychology. **Major fields of study:** area, ethnic, cultural, and gender studies; biological and biomedical sciences; computer and information sciences and support services; education; engineering; English language and literature/letters; foreign languages, literatures, and linguistics; history; mathematics and statistics; multi/interdisciplinary studies; philosophy and religious studies; physical sciences; psychology; social sciences; visual and performing arts. **Areas of required coursework:** humanities, foreign languages, sciences (biological or physical), social science. **Special academic programs (% participation):** accelerated program (.8%), cross-registration (23.7%), double major (23%), exchange student program (domestic) (.5%), honors program (29%), independent study (75%), internships (1%), student-designed major (10.7%), study abroad (37%), teacher certificate program (3.9%), other. **Teacher certification offered in:** secondary. **Reserve Officers Training Corps (ROTC):** Army ROTC: Offered at cooperating institution (Widener University); Navy ROTC: Offered at cooperating institution (University of Pennsylvania); Air Force ROTC: Offered at cooperating institution (St. Joseph's University). **Faculty and instruction (2009-2010):** Total instructional faculty: 171 full-time, 40 part-time (57% men; 43% women; 16% minorities). Full-time faculty with Ph.D. or other terminal degree: 100%. Student/faculty ratio: 8/1. Classes of fewer than 20 students: 78%; of 20 to 49 students: 20%; of 50 or more students: 2%. **Advanced Placement and International Baccalaureate credit:** AP tests may be used for: Credit and/or placement. Scores accepted: 4, 5. International Baccalaureate exams may be used for: Credit and/or placement. **Freshmen returning for sophomore year:** 97%. **Graduation rates:** Four-year: 86%; five-year: 92%; six-year: 93%. **Graduate study:** 23% of students pursue further study immediately upon graduation; 36% within one year; 71% within five years. Fields in which graduates pursue further study: Master of Business Administration (MBA), 8%; law, 12%; medicine, 13%; engineering, 2%; arts and sciences, 65%.

COSTS AND FINANCIAL AID

Financial aid office: (610) 328-8358. **Expenses (2010-2011):** Tuition and fees 2010-2011: $39,600; room/board: $11,900. Estimated books and supplies: $1,150; transportation: $400; personal expenses: $1,120. **Financial aid:** Priority filing date for institution's financial aid form: February 15; deadline: February 15. In 2009-2010, 54% of undergraduates applied for financial aid. Of those, 49% were determined to have financial need; 100% had their need fully met. Average financial aid package (proportion receiving): $35,342 (49%). Average amount of gift aid, such as scholarships or grants (proportion receiving): $33,859 (49%). Average amount of self-help aid,

such as work study or loans (proportion receiving): $1,483 (48%). Average need-based loan (excluding PLUS or other private loans): $0. Among students who received need-based aid, the average percentage of need met: 100%. Among students who received aid based on merit, the average award (and the proportion receiving): $37,510 (1%). The average athletic scholarship (and the proportion receiving): $0 (0%). Average amount of debt of borrowers graduating in 2009: $15,737. Proportion who borrowed: 45%.

CAMPUS LIFE AND EXTRACURRICULAR ACTIVITIES

Campus housing available (% using): coed dorms (88%), women's dorms (8%), men's dorms (4%), special housing for disabled students (0%), other housing options. Students who live in college-owned, operated, or affiliated housing: 95%. **Student employment:** During the 2009-2010 academic year, 80% of undergraduates worked on campus. Average per-year earnings: $1,780. **Clubs and organizations:** Number of student organizations: 100. Activities include: campus ministries, choral groups, dance, drama/theater, international student organization, jazz band, literary magazine, music ensembles, opera, radio station, student government, student newspaper, student film society, symphony orchestra, yearbook. Number of fraternities: 2; sororities: 0. Proportion of men in fraternities: 12%; Average proportion of students who stay on campus on weekends: 90%. **Sports program (2009-2010):** Member of NCAA III. *Men's intercollegiate varsity sports:* baseball, basketball, cross country, golf, lacrosse, soccer, swimming, tennis, track and field (indoor), track and field (outdoor). *Women's intercollegiate varsity sports:* badminton, basketball, cross country, field hockey, lacrosse, soccer, softball, swimming, tennis, track and field (indoor), track and field (outdoor), volleyball.

SERVICES AND FACILITIES

Basic services: nonremedial tutoring, women's center, placement service, health service, health insurance, other. **Counseling services:** minority student, career, personal, academic, psychological, birth control, religious, other. **For learning-disabled students:** School does not offer a structured program with separate admission and additional fees. Total undergraduates in learning-disabled program or receiving services: 39. Services include: reading machines, tape recorders, videotaped classes, diagnostic testing service, note-taking services, oral tests, readers, extended time for tests, tutors, priority registration, priority seating, texts on tape, typist/scribe, other testing accommodations. **Library:** Number of titles: 842,722; number of current serial subscriptions: 17,786. **Information technology resources:** Students are not required to lease or own a computer. Number of campus computers available to all students: 315. School has a wireless network. Approximate number of users that can be accommodated: 3,500. Proportion of college-owned housing units wired for high-speed internet access: 100%. **Campus safety:** Security services offered: 24-hour foot-and-vehicle patrols, late-night transport/escort service, 24-hour emergency telephones, lighted pathways/sidewalks, controlled dormitory access (key, security card, etc.).

TRANSFER AND INTERNATIONAL STUDENTS

Transfer students: May apply for admission for the following academic terms: Fall. Applicants need a minimum number of credits to apply. For fall 2009: Transfer applications received: 192. Transfer applicants offered admission: 46. Transfer applicants enrolled: 25. **International students:** Number of foreign undergraduates: 98 (7% of student body). Number of countries represented: 32. Average TOEFL score: 611 (paper).

Temple University

- **Address:** 1801 N. Broad Street, Philadelphia, PA 19122-6096
- **Website:** http://www.temple.edu
- **Public**
- **Enrollment:** 24,114 full-time; 2,933 part-time

KEY STATS

✔ **U.S News College Ranking:** 132, National Universities
✔ **SAT Score (25th/75th percentile):** 1000-1210
✔ **Tuition:** 2009-2010: $11,764 in state, $21,044 out of state

Selectivity: Selective	**Room/board:** $9,234
Acceptance rate: 61%	**Average debt:** $29,886
Student/faculty ratio: 16/1	**Proportion who borrowed:** 75%

UNDERGRADUATE STUDENT BODY STATS

2009-2010 enrollment: 24,114 full-time; 2,933 part-time. Men: 47%; women: 53%. **Ethnic makeup:** African American: 16%; Asian American: 10%; Hispanic: 4%; White: 67%; International: 3%.

ADMISSIONS FACTS AND FIGURES

Phone: (215) 204-7200. **Email:** tuadm@temple.edu. **Website:** http://www.temple.edu. **Application deadlines for fall 2011:** Regular decision: March 1; decision sent by October 15. Early decision: Not offered. Early action: Not offered. Admission can be deferred. **Application fee:** $50. **To apply online, go to:** http://www.temple.edu/undergrad/applying/index.htm. **Admissions requirements/recommendations:** High school units required (recommended): English: 4 (4); Mathematics: 3 (4); Science: 2 (3); Foreign language: 2 (2); Social studies: 2 (2); History: 1 (2); Academic electives: 1 (3); Total units: 16 (22). Tests: The college uses SAT or ACT scores in admissions decisions. Either SAT or ACT required. For admission to the fall 2011 entering class, the school will accept: ACT with writing required. Campus visit: Recommended. Admissions interview: Neither required nor recommended. Off-campus interview: Not available. **Factors that count in admissions decisions:** *Academic:* Secondary school record: Very Important. Class rank: Important. Letters of recommendation: Considered. Standardized test scores: Important. Essay: Considered. *Nonacademic:* Interview: Not Considered. Extracurricular activities: Considered. Talent/ability: Considered. Character/personal qualities: Considered. Alumni/ae relationship: Considered. Geographical residence: Not Considered. State residency: Not Considered. Religious affiliation/commitment: Not Considered. Minority status: Not Considered. Volunteer work: Considered. Work experience: Considered. **Other schools with the greatest overlap in applicants:** Howard University; Pennsylvania State University–University Park; Rutgers, the State University of New Jersey–New Brunswick; University of Pittsburgh; West Chester University of Pennsylvania. **Admissions statistics for the fall 2009 entering class:** Total applicants: 18,574. Total accepted: 11,265. Freshmen enrolled: 4,203; 25% were from out of state. Overall acceptance rate: 61%. **Size of waiting list:** 1200 applicants; enrolled from waiting list: 288. **Credentials of fall 2009 freshmen:** 21% ranked in the top 10 percent of their high school class; 57% were in the top 25 percent; 94% were in the top half. (Proportion submitting class standing: 66%.) **Average high school grade point average:** 3.4. **First-year students who submitted SAT scores:** 97%. Scores (25/75 percentile): Critical Reading: 490-600, Math: 510-610, Combined: 1000-1210. **First-year students submitting ACT scores:** 15%. Scores (25/75 percentile): English: N/A, Math: N/A, Composite: 21-26.

ACADEMICS

Year founded: 1888. **Academic calendar:** Semester. **Degrees offered:** certificate, diploma, associate, transfer-associate, terminal-associate, bachelor's, post-bachelor's certificate, master's, post-master's certificate, doctorate. **Most popular majors:** 22% marketing, 11% communication, journalism, and related programs, 11% visual and performing arts, 8% education, 6% psychology. **Major fields of study:** agriculture, agriculture operations, and related sciences; architecture and related services; area, ethnic, cultural, and gender studies; biological and biomedical sciences; business, management, marketing, and related support services; communication, journalism, and related programs; computer and information sciences and support services; education; engineering; English language and literature/letters; foreign languages, literatures, and linguistics; health professions and related clinical sciences; history; legal professions and studies; liberal arts and sciences studies, and humanities; mathematics and statistics; multi/interdisciplinary studies; natural resources and conservation; parks, recreation, leisure, and fitness studies; philosophy and religious studies; physical sciences; psychology; public administration and social service professions; security and protective services; social sciences; visual and performing arts. **Areas of required coursework:** arts/fine arts, humanities, mathematics, English (including composition), sciences (biological or physical), history, social science, other. **Pre-professional programs:** pre-law, pre-dentistry, pre-medicine, pre-veterinary science, pre-optometry, pre-pharmacy, other. **Special academic programs:** cooperative (work-study plan) program, cross-registration, distance learning, double major, dual enrollment, English as a Second Language (ESL), exchange student program (domestic), external degree program, honors program, independent study, internships, liberal arts/career combination, study abroad, teacher certificate program, other. **Teacher certification offered in:** early childhood, special education, elementary, vo-tech, middle/junior high, secondary, bilingual/bicultural. **Cooperative education programs:** business, computer science, education, engineering. **Reserve Officers Training Corps (ROTC):** Army ROTC: Offered on campus; Navy ROTC: Offered at cooperating institution (University of Pennsylvania); Air Force ROTC: Offered at cooperating institution (St.

Joseph's University). **Faculty and instruction (2009-2010):** Total instructional faculty: 1,427 full-time, 1,509 part-time (59% men; 41% women; 15% minorities). Full-time faculty with Ph.D. or other terminal degree: 74%. Student/faculty ratio: 16/1. Classes of fewer than 20 students: 34%; of 20 to 49 students: 57%; of 50 or more students: 9%. **Advanced Placement and International Baccalaureate credit:** AP tests may be used for: Credit only. Scores accepted: 3. International Baccalaureate exams may be used for: Credit only. **Freshmen returning for sophomore year:** 87%. **Graduation rates:** Four-year: 40%; five-year: 62%; six-year: 67%.

COSTS AND FINANCIAL AID

Financial aid office: (215) 204-8760. **Expenses (2009-2010):** Tuition and fees 2009-2010: $11,764 in state, $21,044 out of state; room/board: $9,234. Estimated books and supplies: $1,000 personal expenses: $4,436. **Financial aid:** Priority filing date for institution's financial aid form: March 1. In 2009-2010, 90% of undergraduates applied for financial aid. Of those, 71% were determined to have financial need; 29% had their need fully met. Average financial aid package (proportion receiving): $15,577 (67%). Average amount of gift aid, such as scholarships or grants (proportion receiving): $5,972 (67%). Average amount of self-help aid, such as work study or loans (proportion receiving): $4,175 (60%). Average need-based loan (excluding PLUS or other private loans): $4,184. Among students who received need-based aid, the average percentage of need met: 84%. Among students who received aid based on merit, the average award (and the proportion receiving): $8,528 (12%). The average athletic scholarship (and the proportion receiving): $19,494 (1%). Average amount of debt of borrowers graduating in 2009: $29,886. Proportion who borrowed: 75%.

CAMPUS LIFE AND EXTRACURRICULAR ACTIVITIES

Campus housing available (% using): coed dorms (100%), apartment for single students, special housing for disabled students, other housing options. Students who live in college-owned, operated, or affiliated housing: 19%. **Clubs and organizations:** Number of student organizations: 270. Activities include: campus ministries, choral groups, concert band, dance, drama/theater, international student organization, jazz band, literary magazine, marching band, model UN, music ensembles, musical theater, opera, pep band, radio station, student government, student newspaper, student film society, symphony orchestra, yearbook. Number of fraternities: 17; sororities: 11. Proportion of men in fraternities: 1%; of women in sororities: 1%. **Sports program (2009-2010):** Member of NCAA I. *Men's intercollegiate varsity sports:* baseball, basketball, cross country, football, golf, gymnastics, soccer, tennis, track and field (indoor), track and field (outdoor). *Women's intercollegiate varsity sports:* basketball, crew (heavyweight), cross country, fencing, field hockey, gymnastics, lacrosse, soccer, softball, tennis, track and field (indoor), track and field (outdoor), volleyball.

SERVICES AND FACILITIES

Basic services: nonremedial tutoring, placement service, health service, health insurance. **Remedial assistance:** reading, math, writing, study skills. **Counseling services:** career, personal, veteran student, academic, older student, psychological, birth control. **For learning-disabled students:** School does not offer a structured program with separate admission and additional fees. Total undergraduates in learning-disabled program or receiving services: 295. Services include: reading machines, tape recorders, videotaped classes, note-taking services, extended time for tests, texts on tape, typist/scribe, other testing accommodations, other. **Library:** Number of titles: 3,265,341; number of current serial subscriptions: 62,173. **Information technology resources:** Students are not required to lease or own a computer. Number of campus computers available to all students: 3,670. School has a wireless network. Approximate number of users that can be accommodated: 7,056. Proportion of college-owned housing units wired for high-speed internet access: 100%. **Campus safety:** Security services offered: 24-hour foot-and-vehicle patrols, late-night transport/escort service, 24-hour emergency telephones, lighted pathways/sidewalks, controlled dormitory access (key, security card, etc).

TRANSFER AND INTERNATIONAL STUDENTS

Transfer students: May apply for admission for the following academic terms: Fall, Spring. Applicants need a minimum number of credits to apply. For fall 2009: Transfer applications received: 6,981. Transfer applicants offered admission: 4,362. Transfer applicants enrolled: 2,900. **International students:** Number of foreign undergraduates: 684 (3% of student body). Number of countries represented: 117. Minimum TOEFL score required: 550 (paper); 213 (computer). Average TOEFL score: 555 (paper).

Thiel College

- **Address:** 75 College Avenue, Greenville, PA 16125
- **Website:** http://www.thiel.edu
- **Private; Religious affiliation:** Lutheran
- **Enrollment:** 942 full-time; 57 part-time

KEY STATS

✔ **U.S News College Ranking:** second tier, National Liberal Arts Colleges
✔ **SAT Score (25th/75th percentile):** 830-1025
✔ **Tuition:** 2010-2011: $23,728

Selectivity: Less selective	**Room/board:** $9,200
Acceptance rate: 72%	**Average debt:** $37,783
Student/faculty ratio: 13/1	**Proportion who borrowed:** 92%

UNDERGRADUATE STUDENT BODY STATS

2009-2010 enrollment: 942 full-time; 57 part-time. Men: 53%; women: 47%. **Ethnic makeup:** African American: 4%; Hispanic: 1%; White: 88%; International: 5%. **Religious preference:** Roman Catholic: 19%; Protestant: 24%; Jewish: 1%; Muslim: 1%; Hindu: 1%; No preference: 41%; Lutheran: 13%.

ADMISSIONS FACTS AND FIGURES

Phone: (800) 248-4435. **Email:** admission@thiel.edu. **Website:** http://www.thiel.edu. **Application deadlines for fall 2011:** Regular decision: Rolling. Early decision: Not offered. Early action: Not offered. Admission can be deferred. **To apply online, go to:** http://www.thiel.edu/admissions/applynow.htm. **Admissions requirements/recommendations:** High school units required (recommended): English: 4 (4); Mathematics: 2 (2); Science: 2 (2); Foreign language: 2 (2); Social studies: 3 (3); Academic electives: (3); Total units: 16 (16). Tests: The college uses SAT or ACT scores in admissions decisions. Either SAT or ACT required. For admission to the fall 2011 entering class, the school will accept: ACT with or without writing accepted. Campus visit: Recommended. Admissions interview: Recommended. Off-campus interview: May be arranged. **Factors that count in admissions decisions:** *Academic:* Secondary school record: Very Important. Class rank: Important. Letters of recommendation: Very Important. Standardized test scores: Very Important. Essay: Very Important. *Nonacademic:* Interview: Considered. Extracurricular activities: Considered. Talent/ability: Considered. Character/personal qualities: Important. Alumni/ae relationship: Not Considered. Geographical residence: Not Considered. State residency: Not Considered. Religious affiliation/commitment: Not Considered. Minority status: Not Considered. Volunteer work: Considered. Work experience: Considered. **Other schools with the greatest overlap in applicants:** Clarion University of Pennsylvania; Edinboro University of Pennsylvania; Gannon University; Geneva College; Slippery Rock University of Pennsylvania. **Admissions statistics for the fall 2009 entering class:** Total applicants: 1,265. Total accepted: 907. Freshmen enrolled: 272; 39% were from out of state. Overall acceptance rate: 72%. **Credentials of fall 2009 freshmen:** 10% ranked in the top 10 percent of their high school class; 31% were in the top 25 percent; 63% were in the top half. (Proportion submitting class standing: 78%.) **Average high school grade point average:** 3.0. **First-year students who submitted SAT scores:** 65%. Scores (25/75 percentile): Critical Reading: 420-505, Math: 410-520, Combined: 830-1025. **First-year students submitting ACT scores:** 45%. Scores (25/75 percentile): English: 15-23, Math: 16-23, Composite: 17-23.

ACADEMICS

Year founded: 1866. **Academic calendar:** Semester. **Degrees offered:** associate, bachelor's. **Most popular majors:** 35% business, management, marketing, and related support services, 12% psychology, 7% security and protective services, 6% education, 6% social sciences. **Major fields of study:** biological and biomedical sciences; business, management, marketing, and related support services; communication, journalism, and related programs; computer and information sciences and support services; education; engineering; English language and literature/letters; health professions and related clinical sciences; history; legal professions and studies; mathematics and statistics; natural resources and conservation; personal and culinary services; philosophy and religious studies; physical sciences; psychology; social sciences. **Areas of required coursework:** arts/fine arts, humanities, mathematics, English (including composition), foreign languages, sciences (biological or physical), history, social science. **Pre-professional programs:** pre-law, pre-dentistry, pre-medicine, pre-theology, pre-veterinary science, pre-pharmacy. **Special academic programs (% participation):** distance learning (1%), double major (34%), dual enrollment (1%), English as a Second Language (ESL) (1%), honors program (8%), internships (24%), liberal arts/career combination (92%), study abroad (2%), teacher certificate program (12%). **Teacher certification offered in:** elementary, secondary. **Cooperative education programs:** art, business, computer science, engineering, humanities, natural science, social/behavioral science, technologies. **Faculty and instruction (2009-2010):** Total instructional faculty: 61 full-time, 50 part-time (52% men; 48% women; 6% minorities). Full-time faculty with Ph.D. or other terminal degree: 72%. Student/faculty ratio: 13/1. Classes of fewer than 20 students: 65%; of 20 to 49 students: 34%; of 50 or more students: 1%. **Advanced Placement and International Baccalaureate credit:** AP tests may be used for: Credit and/or placement. Scores accepted: 5. **Freshmen returning for sophomore year:** 60%. **Graduation rates:** Four-year: 31%; five-year: 40%; six-year: 40%. **Graduate study:** 16% of students pursue further study immediately upon graduation. Fields in which graduates pursue further study: Master of Business Administration (MBA), 3%; law, 6%; medicine, 5%; dentistry, 1%; engineering, 3%; theology (or the seminary), 5%; education, 6%; arts and sciences, 70%.

COSTS AND FINANCIAL AID

Financial aid office: (724) 589-2178. **Expenses (2010-2011):** Tuition and fees 2010-2011: $23,728; room/board: $9,200. Estimated books and supplies: $1,000 personal expenses: $3,000. **Financial aid:** Priority filing date for institution's financial aid form: March 15. In 2009-2010, 83% of undergraduates applied for financial aid. Of those, 80% were determined to have financial need; 11% had their need fully met. Average financial aid package (proportion receiving): $19,313 (80%). Average amount of gift aid, such as scholarships or grants (proportion receiving): $15,071 (80%). Average amount of self-help aid, such as work study or loans (proportion receiving): $4,745 (72%). Average need-based loan (excluding PLUS or other private loans): $4,548. Among students who received need-based aid, the average percentage of need met: 71%. Among students who received aid based on merit, the average award (and the proportion receiving): $7,810 (11%). The average athletic scholarship (and the proportion receiving): $0 (0%). Average amount of debt of borrowers graduating in 2009: $37,783. Proportion who borrowed: 92%.

CAMPUS LIFE AND EXTRACURRICULAR ACTIVITIES

Campus housing available (% using): coed dorms (54%), sorority housing (3%), fraternity housing (3%), apartment for single students (10%), other housing options (30%). Students who live in college-owned, operated, or affiliated housing: 80%. **Student employment:** During the 2009-2010 academic year, 4% of undergraduates worked on campus. Average per-year earnings: $1,225. **Clubs and organizations:** Number of student organizations: 35. Activities include: campus ministries, choral groups, concert band, dance, drama/theater, international student organization, literary magazine, marching band, musical theater, pep band, radio station, student government, student newspaper, symphony orchestra, television station, yearbook. Number of fraternities: 3; sororities: 4. Proportion of men in fraternities: 18%; of women in sororities: 26%. Average proportion of students who stay on campus on weekends: 85%. **Sports program (2009-2010):** Member of NCAA III. **Men's intercollegiate varsity sports:** baseball, basketball, cross country, football, golf, lacrosse, soccer, track and field (indoor), track and field (outdoor), volleyball, wrestling. **Women's intercollegiate varsity sports:** basketball, cross country, golf, lacrosse, soccer, softball, track and field (indoor), track and field (outdoor), volleyball.

SERVICES AND FACILITIES

Basic services: nonremedial tutoring, health service. **Remedial assistance:** reading, math, writing, study skills. **Counseling services:** minority student, career, academic, psychological, religious. **For learning-disabled students:** School does not offer a structured program with separate admission and additional fees. Services include: remedial math, remedial English, remedial reading, tape recorders, videotaped classes, untimed tests, note-taking services, oral tests, learning center, readers, extended time for tests, tutors, priority seating. **Library:** Number of titles: 187,476; number of current serial subscriptions: 399. **Information technology resources:** Students are required to lease or own a computer. Number of campus computers available to all students: 220. School has a wireless network. Approximate number of users that can be accommodated: 2,000. Proportion of college-owned housing units wired for high-speed internet access: 100%. **Campus safety:** Security services offered: 24-hour foot-and-vehicle patrols, late-night transport/escort service, 24-hour emergency telephones, lighted pathways/sidewalks, controlled dormitory access (key, security card, etc).

TRANSFER AND INTERNATIONAL STUDENTS

Transfer students: May apply for admission for the following academic terms: Fall, Spring, Summer. Applicants do not need a minimum number of credits to apply. For fall 2009: Transfer applications received: 138. Transfer applicants offered admission: 76. Transfer applicants enrolled: 52. **International students:** Number of foreign undergraduates: 51 (5% of student body). Number of countries represented: 15. Minimum TOEFL score required: 450 (paper); 173 (computer). Average TOEFL score: 485 (paper).

University of Pennsylvania

- **Address:** 3451 Walnut Street, Philadelphia, PA 19104
- **Website:** http://www.upenn.edu
- **Private**
- **Enrollment:** 9,490 full-time; 278 part-time

KEY STATS

✔ **U.S News College Ranking:** 5, National Universities
✔ **SAT Score (25th/75th percentile):** 1350-1530
✔ **Tuition:** 2010-2011: $40,514

Selectivity: Most selective	**Room/board:** $11,430
Acceptance rate: 18%	**Average debt:** $17,787
Student/faculty ratio: 6/1	**Proportion who borrowed:** 41%

UNDERGRADUATE STUDENT BODY STATS

2009-2010 enrollment: 9,490 full-time; 278 part-time. Men: 49%; women: 51%. **Ethnic makeup:** African American: 8%; Asian American: 19%; Hispanic: 6%; White: 56%; International: 10%. **Religious preference:** Roman Catholic: 18%; Protestant: 21%; Jewish: 17%; Muslim: 2%; Hindu: 5%; Buddhist: 2%; No preference: 32%; Other: 3%.

ADMISSIONS FACTS AND FIGURES

Phone: (215) 898-7507. **Email:** info@admissions.ugao.upenn.edu. **Website:** http://www.upenn.edu. **Application deadlines for fall 2011:** Regular decision: January 1; decision sent by April 1. Early decision: Send application by: November 1; Decision sent by: December 15. Early action: Not offered. Admission can be deferred. **Application fee:** $75. **To apply online, go to:** http://www.admissionsug.upenn.edu/applying/. **Admissions requirements/recommendations:** High school units required (recommended): English: (4); Mathematics: (4); Science: (3); Foreign language: (4); Social studies: (2); History: (3); Total units: (20). Tests: The college uses SAT or ACT scores in admissions decisions. Either SAT or ACT required. For admission to the fall 2011 entering class, the school will accept: ACT with writing required. Campus visit: Recommended. Admissions interview: Recommended. Off-campus interview: May not be arranged. **Factors that count in admissions decisions:** *Academic:* Secondary school record: Very Important. Class rank: Considered. Letters of recommendation: Very Important. Standardized test scores: Considered. Essay: Very Important. *Nonacademic:* Interview: Considered. Extracurricular activities: Important. Talent/ability: Considered. Character/personal qualities: Very Important. Alumni/ae relationship: Considered. Geographical residence: Considered. State residency: Not Considered. Religious affiliation/commitment: Not Considered. Minority status: Considered. Volunteer work: Considered. Work experience: Important. **Other schools with the greatest overlap in applicants:** Columbia University; Cornell University; Harvard University; Stanford University; Yale University. **Admissions statistics for the fall 2009 entering class:** Total applicants: 22,808. Total accepted: 4,040. Freshmen enrolled: 2,475; 83% were from out of state. Accepted through early-decision or early-action plans: 45%. Overall acceptance rate: 18%. Early-decision acceptance rate: 31%. Non-early acceptance rate: 15%. **Size of waiting list:** 2938 applicants; enrolled from waiting list: 96. **Credentials of fall 2009 freshmen:** 96% ranked in the top 10 percent of their high school class; 99% were in the top 25 percent; 100% were in the top half. (Proportion submitting class standing: 100%.) **Average high school grade point average:** 3.8. **First-year students who submitted SAT scores:** 89%. Scores (25/75 percentile): Critical Reading: 660-750, Math: 690-780, Combined: 1350-1530. **First-year students submitting ACT scores:** 36%. Scores (25/75 percentile): English: 30-35, Math: 30-35, Composite: 30-34.

ACADEMICS

Year founded: 1740. **Academic calendar:** Semester. **Degrees offered:** associate, terminal-associate, bachelor's, post-bachelor's certificate, master's, post-master's certificate, doctorate. **Most popular majors:** 14% finance,

7% economics, 5% history, 5% nursing/registered nurse training (R.N., A.S.N., B.S.N., M.S.N.), 5% political science and government. **Major fields of study:** architecture and related services; area, ethnic, cultural, and gender studies; biological and biomedical sciences; business, management, marketing, and related support services; communication, journalism, and related programs; computer and information sciences and support services; education; engineering; English language and literature/letters; foreign languages, literatures, and linguistics; health professions and related clinical sciences; history; legal professions and studies; liberal arts and sciences studies, and humanities; mathematics and statistics; multi/interdisciplinary studies; natural resources and conservation; philosophy and religious studies; physical sciences; psychology; public administration and social service professions; social sciences; visual and performing arts. **Areas of required coursework:** humanities, mathematics, English (including composition), foreign languages, sciences (biological or physical), history, social science. **Pre-professional programs:** pre-law, pre-dentistry, pre-medicine, pre-theology, pre-veterinary science. **Special academic programs (% participation):** accelerated program (3%), cross-registration, double major (24%), dual enrollment (3%), English as a Second Language (ESL) (1%), exchange student program (domestic), honors program (23%), independent study (33%), internships (90%), liberal arts/career combination, student-designed major (1%), study abroad (26%), teacher certificate program, other. **Teacher certification offered in:** elementary, secondary. **Reserve Officers Training Corps (ROTC):** Army ROTC: Offered at cooperating institution (Drexel University); Navy ROTC: Offered on campus; Air Force ROTC: Offered at cooperating institution (St. Joseph's University). **Faculty and instruction (2009-2010):** Total instructional faculty: 1,411 full-time, 789 part-time (62% men; 38% women; 16% minorities). Full-time faculty with Ph.D. or other terminal degree: 100%. Student/faculty ratio: 6/1. Classes of fewer than 20 students: 72%; of 20 to 49 students: 21%; of 50 or more students: 7%. **Advanced Placement and International Baccalaureate credit:** AP tests may be used for: Credit and/or placement. Scores accepted: 5. International Baccalaureate exams may be used for: Credit and/or placement. **Freshmen returning for sophomore year:** 98%. **Graduation rates:** Four-year: 88%; five-year: 94%; six-year: 95%. **Graduate study:** 20% of students pursue further study immediately upon graduation; 30% within one year; 65% within five years. Fields in which graduates pursue further study: Master of Business Administration (MBA), 21%; law, 24%; medicine, 16%; dentistry, 1%; engineering, 5%; theology (or the seminary), 1%; education, 4%; arts and sciences, 14%; veterinary medicine, 1%.

COSTS AND FINANCIAL AID

Financial aid office: (215) 898-1988. **Expenses (2010-2011):** Tuition and fees 2010-2011: $40,514; room/board: $11,430. Estimated books and supplies: $1,120; transportation: $550; personal expenses: $2,186. **Financial aid:** Priority filing date for institution's financial aid form: February 15. In 2009-2010, 49% of undergraduates applied for financial aid. Of those, 43% were determined to have financial need; 100% had their need fully met. Average financial aid package (proportion receiving): $33,060 (43%). Average amount of gift aid, such as scholarships or grants (proportion receiving): $30,043 (40%). Average amount of self-help aid, such as work study or loans (proportion receiving): $3,430 (43%). Average need-based loan (excluding PLUS or other private loans): $1,491. Among students who received need-based aid, the average percentage of need met: 100%. Average amount of debt of borrowers graduating in 2009: $17,787. Proportion who borrowed: 41%.

CAMPUS LIFE AND EXTRACURRICULAR ACTIVITIES

Campus housing available: coed dorms, sorority housing, fraternity housing, apartments for married students, apartment for single students, special housing for disabled students. Students who live in college-owned, operated, or affiliated housing: 58%. **Student employment:** During the 2009-2010 academic year, 39% of undergraduates worked on campus. Average per-year earnings: $1,744. **Clubs and organizations:** Number of student organizations: 350. Activities include: campus ministries, choral groups, concert band, dance, drama/theater, international student organization, jazz band, literary magazine, marching band, model UN, music ensembles, musical theater, opera, pep band, radio station, student government, student newspaper, student film society, symphony orchestra, television station, yearbook. Number of fraternities: 38; sororities: 13. Proportion of men in fraternities: 30%; of women in sororities: 27%. Average proportion of students who stay on campus on weekends: 95%. **Sports program (2009-2010):** Member of NCAA I. *Men's intercollegiate varsity sports:* baseball, basketball, cross country, fencing, football, golf, lacrosse, soccer, swimming, tennis, track and field (indoor), track and field (outdoor), wrestling. *Women's intercollegiate varsity sports:* basketball, cross country, fencing, field hockey, golf, gymnastics, lacrosse, soccer, softball, squash, swimming, tennis, track and field (indoor), track and field (outdoor), volleyball.

SERVICES AND FACILITIES

Basic services: nonremedial tutoring, women's center, placement service, day care, health service, health insurance, other. **Remedial assistance:** reading, writing, study skills. **Counseling services:** minority student, career, military, personal, veteran student, academic, older student, psychological, birth control, religious, other. **For learning-disabled students:** School does not offer a structured program with separate admission and additional fees. Total undergraduates in learning-disabled program or receiving services: 222. Services include: reading machines, tape recorders, note-taking services, learning center, readers, extended time for tests, texts on tape, other testing accommodations, other. **Library:** Number of titles: 5,842,099; number of current serial subscriptions: 72,688. **Information technology resources:** Students are not required to lease or own a computer. Number of campus computers available to all students: 1,800. School has a wireless network. Approximate number of users that can be accommodated: 30,000. Proportion of college-owned housing units wired for high-speed internet access: 100%. **Campus safety:** Security services offered: 24-hour foot-and-vehicle patrols, late-night transport/escort service, 24-hour emergency telephones, lighted pathways/sidewalks, controlled dormitory access (key, security card, etc).

TRANSFER AND INTERNATIONAL STUDENTS

Transfer students: May apply for admission for the following academic terms: Fall. Applicants need a minimum number of credits to apply. For fall 2009: Transfer applications received: 1,878. Transfer applicants offered admission: 366. Transfer applicants enrolled: 247. **International students:** Number of foreign undergraduates: 1008 (10% of student body). Number of countries represented: 99. Minimum TOEFL score required: 600 (paper); 110 (computer).

University of Pittsburgh

- ■ **Address:** 4200 Fifth Avenue, Pittsburgh, PA 15260
- ■ **Website:** http://www.oafa.pitt.edu/
- ■ **Public**
- ■ **Enrollment:** 16,719 full-time; 1,312 part-time

KEY STATS

✔ **U.S News College Ranking:** 64, National Universities
✔ **SAT Score (25th/75th percentile):** 1160-1360
✔ **Tuition:** 2009-2010: $14,154 in state, $23,852 out of state

Selectivity: More selective	**Room/board:** $8,900
Acceptance rate: 59%	**Average debt:** N/A
Student/faculty ratio: 15/1	**Proportion who borrowed:** N/A

UNDERGRADUATE STUDENT BODY STATS

2009-2010 enrollment: 16,719 full-time; 1,312 part-time. Men: 49%; women: 51%. **Ethnic makeup:** African American: 8%; Asian American: 5%; Hispanic: 1%; White: 84%; International: 1%.

ADMISSIONS FACTS AND FIGURES

Phone: (412) 624-7488. **Email:** oafa@pitt.edu. **Website:** http://www.oafa.pitt.edu/. **Application deadlines for fall 2011:** Regular decision: Rolling. Early decision: Not offered. Early action: Not offered. Admission cannot be deferred. **Application fee:** $45. **To apply online, go to:** https://www.admissions.pitt.edu/freshapp/freshman.asp. **Admissions requirements/recommendations:** High school units required (recommended): English: 4 (4); Mathematics: 3 (4); Science: 3 (4); Foreign language: 2 (3); Social studies: 2 (3); Academic electives: 3 (5); Total units: 17 (23). Tests: The college uses SAT or ACT scores in admissions decisions. Either SAT or ACT required. For admission to the fall 2011 entering class, the school will accept: ACT with or without writing accepted. Campus visit: Recommended. Admissions interview: Neither required nor recommended. Off-campus interview: Not available. **Factors that count in admissions decisions:** *Academic:* Secondary school record: Very Important. Class rank: Considered. Letters of recommendation: Considered. Standardized test scores: Important. Essay: Considered. *Nonacademic:* Interview: Considered. Extracurricular activities: Considered. Talent/ability: Considered. Character/personal qualities: Considered. Alumni/ae relationship: Not Considered. Geographical residence: Considered. State residency: Not Considered. Religious affiliation/

commitment: Not Considered. Minority status: Considered. Volunteer work: Considered. Work experience: Considered. **Other schools with the greatest overlap in applicants:** Boston University; Carnegie Mellon University; Pennsylvania State University–University Park; University of Maryland–College Park; University of Pennsylvania. **Admissions statistics for the fall 2009 entering class:** Total applicants: 21,737. Total accepted: 12,722. Freshmen enrolled: 3,642; 29% were from out of state. Overall acceptance rate: 59%. **Size of waiting list:** 911 applicants; enrolled from waiting list: 22. **Credentials of fall 2009 freshmen:** 49% ranked in the top 10 percent of their high school class; 86% were in the top 25 percent; 99% were in the top half. (Proportion submitting class standing: 65%.) **Average high school grade point average:** 3.9. **First-year students who submitted SAT scores:** 98%. Scores (25/75 percentile): Critical Reading: 570-680, Math: 590-680, Combined: 1160-1360. **First-year students submitting ACT scores:** 35%. Scores (25/75 percentile): English: 25-31, Math: 25-30, Composite: 25-30.

ACADEMICS

Year founded: 1787. **Academic calendar:** Semester. **Degrees offered:** certificate, bachelor's, post-bachelor's certificate, master's, post-master's certificate, doctorate. **Most popular majors:** 14% business, management, marketing, and related support services, 14% social sciences, 11% English language and literature/letters, 9% engineering, 9% psychology. **Major fields of study:** area, ethnic, cultural, and gender studies; biological and biomedical sciences; business, management, marketing, and related support services; communication, journalism, and related programs; computer and information sciences and support services; education; engineering; English language and literature/letters; foreign languages, literatures, and linguistics; health professions and related clinical sciences; history; legal professions and studies; liberal arts and sciences studies, and humanities; mathematics and statistics; multi/interdisciplinary studies; philosophy and religious studies; physical sciences; psychology; public administration and social service professions; security and protective services; social sciences; visual and performing arts. **Areas of required coursework:** arts/fine arts, humanities, mathematics, English (including composition), philosophy, foreign languages, sciences (biological or physical), history, social science. **Pre-professional programs:** pre-law, pre-dentistry, pre-medicine, pre-pharmacy, other. **Special academic programs (% participation):** accelerated program (5%), cooperative (work-study plan) program (5%), cross-registration (2%), distance learning, double major (17%), dual enrollment, English as a Second Language (ESL), exchange student program (domestic), external degree program, honors program, independent study, internships (72%), liberal arts/career combination, student-designed major, study abroad, teacher certificate program. **Teacher certification offered in:** early childhood, special education, elementary, secondary. **Cooperative education programs:** engineering. **Reserve Officers Training Corps (ROTC):** Army ROTC: Offered on campus; Navy ROTC: Offered at cooperating institution (Carnegie Mellon University); Air Force ROTC: Offered on campus. **Faculty and instruction (2009-2010):** Total instructional faculty: 1,642 full-time, 623 part-time (57% men; 43% women; 17% minorities). Full-time faculty with Ph.D. or other terminal degree: 93%. Student/faculty ratio: 15/1. Classes of fewer than 20 students: 40%; of 20 to 49 students: 42%; of 50 or more students: 18%. **Advanced Placement and International Baccalaureate credit:** AP tests may be used for: Credit and/or placement. Scores accepted: 3, 4, 5. International Baccalaureate exams may be used for: Credit only. **Freshmen returning for sophomore year:** 91%. **Graduation rates:** Four-year: 57%; five-year: 75%; six-year: 78%. **Graduate study:** 39% of students pursue further study within one year; 36% within five years. Fields in which graduates pursue further study: Master of Business Administration (MBA), 21%; law, 10%; medicine, 8%; dentistry, 1%; engineering, 4%; education, 12%; arts and sciences, 16%.

COSTS AND FINANCIAL AID

Financial aid office: (412) 624-7488. **Expenses (2009-2010):** Tuition and fees 2009-2010: $14,154 in state, $23,852 out of state; room/board: $8,900. Estimated books and supplies: $1,050; transportation: $1,326; personal expenses: $1,570. **Financial aid:** Priority filing date for institution's financial aid form: March 1. In 2009-2010, 72% of undergraduates applied for financial aid. Of those, 56% were determined to have financial need; 35% had their need fully met. Average financial aid package (proportion receiving): $10,132 (55%). Average amount of gift aid, such as scholarships or grants (proportion receiving): $8,321 (38%). Average amount of self-help aid, such as work study or loans (proportion receiving): $5,188 (45%). Average need-based loan (excluding PLUS or other private loans): $4,894. Among students who received need-based aid, the average percentage of need met: 79%. Among students who received aid based on merit, the average award (and the proportion receiving): $15,282 (7%). The average athletic scholarship (and the proportion receiving): $21,314 (1%).

CAMPUS LIFE AND EXTRACURRICULAR ACTIVITIES

Campus housing available (% using): coed dorms (69%), women's dorms (8%), men's dorms (1%), sorority housing (2%), fraternity housing (2%), apartment for single students (18%), other housing options. Students who live in college-owned, operated, or affiliated housing: 45%. **Clubs and organizations:** Number of student organizations: 395. Activities include: campus ministries, choral groups, concert band, dance, drama/theater, international student organization, jazz band, literary magazine, marching band, model UN, music ensembles, pep band, radio station, student government, student newspaper, student film society, television station, yearbook. Number of fraternities: 21; sororities: 16. Proportion of men in fraternities: 10%; of women in sororities: 9%. **Sports program (2009-2010)** Member of NCAA I. *Men's intercollegiate varsity sports:* baseball, basketball, cross country, football, soccer, swimming, track and field (indoor), track and field (outdoor), wrestling. *Women's intercollegiate varsity sports:* basketball, cross country, gymnastics, soccer, softball, swimming, tennis, track and field (indoor), track and field (outdoor), volleyball.

SERVICES AND FACILITIES

Basic services: nonremedial tutoring, placement service, health service. **Remedial assistance:** math, writing, study skills. **Counseling services:** minority student, career, personal, academic, older student, psychological, birth control. **For learning-disabled students:** School does not offer a structured program with separate admission and additional fees. Total undergraduates in learning-disabled program or receiving services: 200. Services include: reading machines, extended time for tests, texts on tape, typist/scribe, exams on tape or computer, other testing accommodations. **Library:** Number of titles: 5,897,931; number of current serial subscriptions: 87,637. **Information technology resources:** Students are not required to lease or own a computer. Number of campus computers available to all students: 1,000. School has a wireless network. Approximate number of users that can be accommodated: 42,000. Proportion of college-owned housing units wired for high-speed internet access: 100%. **Campus safety:** Security services offered: 24-hour foot-and-vehicle patrols, late-night transport/escort service, 24-hour emergency telephones, lighted pathways/sidewalks, controlled dormitory access (key, security card, etc).

TRANSFER AND INTERNATIONAL STUDENTS

Transfer students: May apply for admission for the following academic terms: Fall, Winter, Spring, Summer. Applicants need a minimum number of credits to apply. For fall 2009: Transfer applications received: 2,552. Transfer applicants offered admission: 1,359. Transfer applicants enrolled: 970. **International students:** Number of foreign undergraduates: 264 (1% of student body). Number of countries represented: 35. Minimum TOEFL score required: 550 (paper); 213 (computer).

University of Pittsburgh–Bradford

- **Address:** 300 Campus Drive, Bradford, PA 16701
- **Website:** http://www.upb.pitt.edu
- **Public**
- **Enrollment:** 1,453 full-time; 199 part-time

KEY STATS

✔ **U.S News College Ranking:** 31, Regional Colleges (North)
✔ **SAT Score (25th/75th percentile):** 890-1070
✔ **Tuition:** 2009-2010: $11,722 in state, $21,282 out of state

Selectivity: Less selective	**Room/board:** $7,480
Acceptance rate: 83%	**Average debt:** $21,683
Student/faculty ratio: 18/1	**Proportion who borrowed:** 82%

UNDERGRADUATE STUDENT BODY STATS

2009-2010 enrollment: 1,453 full-time; 199 part-time. Men: 45%; women: 55%. **Ethnic makeup:** African American: 6%; American-Indian: 1%; Asian American: 2%; Hispanic: 1%; White: 90%. **Religious preference:** Roman Catholic: 31%; Protestant: 39%; Jewish: 1%; No preference: 26%; Other: 1%.

ADMISSIONS FACTS AND FIGURES

Phone: (814) 362-7555. **Email:** admissions@upb.pitt.edu. **Website:** http://www.upb.pitt.edu. **Application deadlines for fall 2011:** Regular decision:

Rolling. Early decision: Not offered. Early action: Not offered. Admission can be deferred. **Application fee:** $45. **To apply online, go to:** https://app.applyyourself.com/?id=up-upb. **Admissions requirements/recommendations:** High school units required (recommended): English: 4 (4); Mathematics: 2 (3); Science: 1 (2); Foreign language: 2 (2); Social studies: 0 (0); History: 1 (1); Academic electives: 5 (5); Total units: 15 (15). Tests: The college uses SAT or ACT scores in admissions decisions. Either SAT or ACT required. For admission to the fall 2011 entering class, the school will accept: ACT with or without writing accepted. Campus visit: Recommended. Admissions interview: Recommended. Off-campus interview: May be arranged. **Factors that count in admissions decisions:** *Academic:* Secondary school record: Important. Class rank: Considered. Letters of recommendation: Considered. Standardized test scores: Important. Essay: Considered. *Nonacademic:* Interview: Important. Extracurricular activities: Considered. Talent/ability: Considered. Character/personal qualities: Considered. Alumni/ae relationship: Not Considered. Geographical residence: Not Considered. State residency: Not Considered. Religious affiliation/commitment: Not Considered. Minority status: Not Considered. Volunteer work: Considered. Work experience: Considered. **Other schools with the greatest overlap in applicants:** Clarion University of Pennsylvania; Edinboro University of Pennsylvania; Mansfield University of Pennsylvania; Pennsylvania State University–Erie, The Behrend College; University of Pittsburgh–Greensburg. **Admissions statistics for the fall 2009 entering class:** Total applicants: 987. Total accepted: 816. Freshmen enrolled: 420; 17% were from out of state. Overall acceptance rate: 83%. **Size of waiting list:** 10 applicants; enrolled from waiting list: 10. **Credentials of fall 2009 freshmen:** 8% ranked in the top 10 percent of their high school class; 6% were in the top 25 percent; 42% were in the top half. (Proportion submitting class standing: 81%.) **Average high school grade point average:** 3.1. **First-year students who submitted SAT scores:** 90%. Scores (25/75 percentile): Critical Reading: 440-520, Math: 450-550, Combined: 890-1070. **First-year students submitting ACT scores:** 15%. Scores (25/75 percentile): English: 19-23, Math: 19-24, Composite: 19-23.

ACADEMICS

Year founded: 1963. **Academic calendar:** Semester. **Degrees offered:** associate, transfer-associate, terminal-associate, bachelor's. **Most popular majors:** 18% nursing/registered nurse training (R.N., A.S.N., B.S.N., M.S.N.), 10% business/commerce, 10% social sciences, 7% adult and continuing education and teaching, 6% criminal justice/law enforcement administration. **Major fields of study:** agriculture, agriculture operations, and related sciences; biological and biomedical sciences; business, management, marketing, and related support services; communication, journalism, and related programs; computer and information sciences and support services; education; engineering; engineering technologies/technicians; English language and literature/letters; health professions and related clinical sciences; mathematics and statistics; parks, recreation, leisure, and fitness studies; physical sciences; psychology; security and protective services; social sciences; visual and performing arts. **Areas of required coursework:** arts/fine arts, humanities, computer literacy, mathematics, English (including composition), philosophy, sciences (biological or physical), history, social science. **Pre-professional programs:** pre-law, pre-dentistry, pre-medicine, pre-veterinary science, pre-optometry, pre-pharmacy, other. **Special academic programs (% participation):** cooperative (work-study plan) program (1%), cross-registration (12%), distance learning (63%), double major (17%), dual enrollment (1%), exchange student program (domestic) (1%), external degree program (0%), honors program (4%), independent study (39%), internships (31%), study abroad (2%), teacher certificate program (21%), weekend college (0%). **Teacher certification offered in:** elementary, middle/junior high, secondary. **Cooperative education programs:** business, other. **Reserve Officers Training Corps (ROTC):** Army ROTC: Offered at cooperating institution (St. Bonaventure University). **Faculty and instruction (2009-2010):** Total instructional faculty: 72 full-time, 76 part-time (55% men; 45% women; 9% minorities). Full-time faculty with Ph.D. or other terminal degree: 63%. Student/faculty ratio: 18/1. Classes of fewer than 20 students: 48%; of 20 to 49 students: 49%; of 50 or more students: 4%. **Advanced Placement and International Baccalaureate credit:** AP tests may be used for: Credit only. Scores accepted: 3, 4, 5. International Baccalaureate exams may be used for: Credit only. **Freshmen returning for sophomore year:** 71%. **Graduation rates:** Four-year: 28%; five-year: 42%; six-year: 45%. **Graduate study:** 24% of students pursue further study within one year. Fields in which graduates pursue further study: Master of Business Administration (MBA), 3%; law, 2%; medicine, 3%; arts and sciences, 14%.

COSTS AND FINANCIAL AID

Financial aid office: (814) 362-7550. **Expenses (2009-2010):** Tuition and fees 2009-2010: $11,722 in state, $21,282 out of state; room/board: $7,480. Estimated books and supplies: $1,050; transportation: $1,326; personal expenses: $1,570. **Financial aid:** Priority filing date for institution's financial aid form: March 1. In 2009-2010, 100% of undergraduates applied for financial aid. Of those, 91% were determined to have financial need; 59% had their need fully met. Average financial aid package (proportion receiving): $12,600 (89%). Average amount of gift aid, such as scholarships or grants (proportion receiving): $5,520 (36%). Average amount of self-help aid, such as work study or loans (proportion receiving): $5,438 (57%). Average need-based loan (excluding PLUS or other private loans): $4,327. Among students who received need-based aid, the average percentage of need met: 90%. Among students who received aid based on merit, the average award (and the proportion receiving): $5,589 (18%). Average amount of debt of borrowers graduating in 2009: $21,683. Proportion who borrowed: 82%.

CAMPUS LIFE AND EXTRACURRICULAR ACTIVITIES

Campus housing available (% using): apartments for married students (0%), apartment for single students (97%), special housing for disabled students (3%). Students who live in college-owned, operated, or affiliated housing: 55%. **Student employment:** During the 2009-2010 academic year, 12% of undergraduates worked on campus. Average per-year earnings: $1,740. **Clubs and organizations:** Number of student organizations: 54. Activities include: choral groups, dance, drama/theater, international student organization, literary magazine, radio station, student government, student newspaper. Number of fraternities: 3; sororities: 3. Proportion of men in fraternities: 2%; of women in sororities: 4%. Average proportion of students who stay on campus on weekends: 31%. **Sports program (2009-2010):** Member of NCAA III. *Men's intercollegiate varsity sports:* baseball, basketball, cross country, golf, soccer, swimming. *Women's intercollegiate varsity sports:* basketball, cross country, golf, soccer, softball, swimming, volleyball.

SERVICES AND FACILITIES

Basic services: nonremedial tutoring, placement service, health service. **Remedial assistance:** reading, math, writing, study skills. **Counseling services:** career, military, personal, veteran student, academic, older student, psychological. **For learning-disabled students:** School does not offer a structured program with separate admission and additional fees. Total undergraduates in learning-disabled program or receiving services: 18. Services include: remedial math, remedial English, reading machines, remedial reading, tape recorders, other special classes, untimed tests, note-taking services, oral tests, learning center, extended time for tests, tutors, priority seating, texts on tape, other testing accommodations. **Library:** Number of titles: 97,963; number of current serial subscriptions: 245. **Information technology resources:** Students are not required to lease or own a computer. Number of campus computers available to all students: 120. School has a wireless network. Approximate number of users that can be accommodated: 200. Proportion of college-owned housing units wired for high-speed internet access: 100%. **Campus safety:** Security services offered: 24-hour foot-and-vehicle patrols, late-night transport/escort service, 24-hour emergency telephones, lighted pathways/sidewalks, controlled dormitory access (key, security card, etc).

TRANSFER AND INTERNATIONAL STUDENTS

Transfer students: May apply for admission for the following academic terms: Fall, Spring, Summer. Applicants do not need a minimum number of credits to apply. For fall 2009: Transfer applications received: 256. Transfer applicants offered admission: 195. Transfer applicants enrolled: 117. **International students:** Number of foreign undergraduates: 7. Number of countries represented: 7. Minimum TOEFL score required: 550 (paper); 213 (computer). Average TOEFL score: 575 (paper).

University of Pittsburgh–Johnstown

- **Address:** 450 Schoolhouse Road, Johnstown, PA 15904
- **Website:** http://www.upj.pitt.edu
- **Public**
- **Enrollment:** 2,925 full-time; 132 part-time

KEY STATS

✔ **U.S News College Ranking:** 21, Regional Colleges (North)
✔ **SAT Score (25th/75th percentile):** 910-1110
✔ **Tuition:** 2009-2010: $11,754 in state, $21,314 out of state
  Selectivity: Selective   **Room/board:** $7,370
  Acceptance rate: 87%   **Average debt:** $23,243
  Student/faculty ratio: 19/1   **Proportion who borrowed:** 85%

UNDERGRADUATE STUDENT BODY STATS

2009-2010 enrollment: 2,925 full-time; 132 part-time. Men: 54%; women: 46%. **Ethnic makeup:** African American: 2%; Asian American: 2%; Hispanic: 1%; White: 94%; International: 1%.

ADMISSIONS FACTS AND FIGURES

Phone: (800) 765-4875. **Email:** upjadmit@pitt.edu. **Website:** http://www.upj.pitt.edu. **Application deadlines for fall 2011:** Regular decision: Rolling. Early decision: Not offered. Early action: Not offered. Admission can be deferred. **Application fee:** $45. **To apply online, go to:** https://app.applyyourself.com/?id=up-upj. **Admissions requirements/recommendations:** High school units required (recommended): English: 4; Mathematics: 2 (3); Science: 2; Foreign language: 2; Social studies: 4; Total units: 15. Tests: The college uses SAT or ACT scores in admissions decisions. Either SAT or ACT required. For admission to the fall 2011 entering class, the school will accept: ACT with writing recommended. Campus visit: Recommended. Admissions interview: Recommended. Off-campus interview: Not available. **Factors that count in admissions decisions:** *Academic:* Secondary school record: Very Important. Class rank: Very Important. Letters of recommendation: Important. Standardized test scores: Important. Essay: Important. *Nonacademic:* Interview: Important. Extracurricular activities: Important. Talent/ability: Important. Character/personal qualities: Considered. Alumni/ae relationship: Not Considered. Geographical residence: Not Considered. State residency: Not Considered. Religious affiliation/commitment: Not Considered. Minority status: Considered. Volunteer work: Important. Work experience: Important. **Other schools with the greatest overlap in applicants:** Clarion University of Pennsylvania; Duquesne University; Indiana University of Pennsylvania; Pennsylvania State University–University Park; Slippery Rock University of Pennsylvania. **Admissions statistics for the fall 2009 entering class:** Total applicants: 1,652. Total accepted: 1,431. Freshmen enrolled: 822; 1% were from out of state. Overall acceptance rate: 87%. **Credentials of fall 2009 freshmen:** 10% ranked in the top 10 percent of their high school class; 35% were in the top 25 percent; 73% were in the top half. (Proportion submitting class standing: 78%.) **Average high school grade point average:** 3.4. **First-year students who submitted SAT scores:** 98%. Scores (25/75 percentile): Critical Reading: 450-540, Math: 460-570, Combined: 910-1110. **First-year students submitting ACT scores:** 15%. Scores (25/75 percentile): English: 16-23, Math: 17-25, Composite: 18-23.

ACADEMICS

Year founded: 1927. **Academic calendar:** Semester. **Degrees offered:** certificate, associate, bachelor's. **Most popular majors:** 27% business, management, marketing, and related support services, 16% education, 10% communication, journalism, and related programs, 10% engineering technologies/technicians, 8% biological and biomedical sciences. **Major fields of study:** area, ethnic, cultural, and gender studies; biological and biomedical sciences; business, management, marketing, and related support services; communication, journalism, and related programs; computer and information sciences and support services; education; engineering technologies/technicians; English language and literature/letters; health professions and related clinical sciences; history; legal professions and studies; liberal arts and sciences studies, and humanities; mathematics and statistics; natural resources and conservation; physical sciences; psychology; social sciences; visual and performing arts. **Areas of required coursework:** humanities, mathematics, English (including composition), sciences (biological or physical), history, social science. **Pre-professional programs:** pre-law, pre-dentistry, pre-medicine, pre-theology, pre-veterinary science, pre-optometry, pre-pharmacy, other. **Special academic programs:** accelerated program, cooperative (work-study plan) program, cross-registration, distance learning, double major, dual enrollment, independent study, internships, liberal arts/career combination, student-designed major, study abroad, teacher certificate program. **Teacher certification offered in:** elementary, middle/junior high, secondary. **Cooperative education programs:** engineering. **Faculty and instruction (2009-2010):** Total instructional faculty: 147 full-time, 20 part-time (56% men; 44% women; 7% minorities). Full-time faculty with Ph.D. or other terminal degree: 66%. Student/faculty ratio: 19/1. Classes of fewer than 20 students: 22%; of 20 to 49 students: 74%; of 50 or more students: 4%. **Advanced Placement and International Baccalaureate credit:** AP tests may be used for: Placement only. Scores accepted: 3, 4, 5. International Baccalaureate exams may be used for: Placement only. **Freshmen returning for sophomore year:** 74%. **Graduation rates:** Four-year: 42%; five-year: 60%; six-year: 61%. **Graduate study:** 11% of students pursue further study within one year. Fields in which graduates pursue further study: Master of Business Administration (MBA), 9%; law, 11%; medicine, 4%; dentistry, 2%; engineering, 5%; theology (or the seminary), 4%; education, 9%; arts and sciences, 29%.

COSTS AND FINANCIAL AID

Financial aid office: (814) 269-7045. **Expenses (2009-2010):** Tuition and fees 2009-2010: $11,754 in state, $21,314 out of state; room/board: $7,370. Estimated books and supplies: $1,050; transportation: $1,326; personal expenses: $1,570. **Financial aid:** Priority filing date for institution's financial aid form: April 1. In 2009-2010, 88% of undergraduates applied for financial aid. Of those, 75% were determined to have financial need; 9% had their need fully met. Average financial aid package (proportion receiving): $10,226 (73%). Average amount of gift aid, such as scholarships or grants (proportion receiving): $5,373 (52%). Average amount of self-help aid, such as work study or loans (proportion receiving): $5,057 (65%). Average need-based loan (excluding PLUS or other private loans): $4,297. Among students who received need-based aid, the average percentage of need met: 57%. Among students who received aid based on merit, the average award (and the proportion receiving): $2,869 (1%). The average athletic scholarship (and the proportion receiving): $4,065 (5%). Average amount of debt of borrowers graduating in 2009: $23,243. Proportion who borrowed: 85%.

CAMPUS LIFE AND EXTRACURRICULAR ACTIVITIES

Campus housing available (% using): coed dorms (58%), sorority housing (3%), fraternity housing (4%), apartment for single students (25%), special housing for disabled students, other housing options (10%). Students who live in college-owned, operated, or affiliated housing: 56%. **Student employment:** During the 2009-2010 academic year, 10% of undergraduates worked on campus. Average per-year earnings: $2,663. **Clubs and organizations:** Number of student organizations: 73. Activities include: campus ministries, choral groups, concert band, dance, drama/theater, literary magazine, model UN, music ensembles, musical theater, pep band, radio station, student government, student newspaper, television station, yearbook. Number of fraternities: 5; sororities: 4. Proportion of men in fraternities: 7%; of women in sororities: 7%. Average proportion of students who stay on campus on weekends: 55%. **Sports program (2009-2010):** Member of NCAA II. **Men's intercollegiate varsity sports:** baseball, basketball, golf, soccer, wrestling. **Women's intercollegiate varsity sports:** basketball, cross country, golf, soccer, track and field (indoor), track and field (outdoor), volleyball.

SERVICES AND FACILITIES

Basic services: nonremedial tutoring, health service. **Remedial assistance:** math, study skills. **Counseling services:** minority student, personal, academic, psychological, religious. **For learning-disabled students:** School does not offer a structured program with separate admission and additional fees. Services include: remedial math, reading machines, tape recorders, note-taking services, oral tests, learning center, readers, extended time for tests, tutors, priority registration, priority seating, texts on tape, other testing accommodations, other. **Library:** Number of titles: 5,116,305; number of current serial subscriptions: 48,637. **Information technology resources:** Students are not required to lease or own a computer. Number of campus computers available to all students: 200. School has a wireless network. Approximate number of users that can be accommodated: 700. Proportion of college-owned housing units wired for high-speed internet access: 100%. **Campus safety:** Security services offered: 24-hour foot-and-vehicle patrols, late-night transport/escort service, 24-hour emergency telephones, lighted pathways/sidewalks, controlled dormitory access (key, security card, etc).

TRANSFER AND INTERNATIONAL STUDENTS

Transfer students: May apply for admission for the following academic terms: Fall, Spring, Summer. Applicants do not need a minimum number of credits to apply. For fall 2009: Transfer applications received: 290. Transfer applicants offered admission: 215. Transfer applicants enrolled: 84. **International students:** Number of foreign undergraduates: 21 (1% of student body). Minimum TOEFL score required: 550 (paper); 213 (computer).

University of Scranton

- **Address:** 800 Linden Street, Scranton, PA 18510-4694
- **Website:** http://www.scranton.edu
- **Private; Religious affiliation:** Roman Catholic (Jesuit)
- **Enrollment:** 3,952 full-time; 202 part-time

KEY STATS

✔ **U.S News College Ranking:** 10, Regional Universities (North)
✔ **SAT Score (25th/75th percentile):** 1030-1220
✔ **Tuition:** 2010-2011: $34,536

Selectivity: Selective	**Room/board:** $11,862
Acceptance rate: 71%	**Average debt:** $30,920
Student/faculty ratio: 12/1	**Proportion who borrowed:** 75%

UNDERGRADUATE STUDENT BODY STATS

2009-2010 enrollment: 3,952 full-time; 202 part-time. Men: 44%; women: 56%. **Ethnic makeup:** African American: 1%; Asian American: 3%; Hispanic: 4%; White: 91%; International: 1%. **Religious preference:** Roman Catholic: 69%; Protestant: 2%; Unknown: 29%.

ADMISSIONS FACTS AND FIGURES

Phone: (570) 941-7540. **Email:** admissions@scranton.edu. **Website:** http://www.scranton.edu. **Application deadlines for fall 2011:** Regular decision: March 1. Early decision: Not offered. Early action: Send application by: November 15; Decision sent by: December 15. Admission can be deferred. **To apply online, go to:** http://www.scranton.edu/apply. **Admissions requirements/recommendations:** High school units required (recommended): English: 4 (4); Mathematics: 3 (4); Science: 3 (3); Foreign language: 2 (2); Social studies: 2 (3); Academic electives: 4 (4); Total units: 16 (16). Tests: The college uses SAT or ACT scores in admissions decisions. Either SAT or ACT required. For admission to the fall 2011 entering class, the school will accept: ACT with or without writing accepted. Campus visit: Recommended. Admissions interview: Recommended. Off-campus interview: May be arranged. **Factors that count in admissions decisions:** *Academic:* Secondary school record: Very Important. Class rank: Very Important. Letters of recommendation: Considered. Standardized test scores: Very Important. Essay: Considered. *Nonacademic:* Interview: Considered. Extracurricular activities: Important. Talent/ability: Considered. Character/personal qualities: Considered. Alumni/ae relationship: Considered. Geographical residence: Not Considered. State residency: Not Considered. Religious affiliation/commitment: Not Considered. Minority status: Not Considered. Volunteer work: Considered. Work experience: Considered. **Other schools with the greatest overlap in applicants:** Loyola University Maryland; Pennsylvania State University–University Park; St. Joseph's University; University of Delaware; Villanova University. **Admissions statistics for the fall 2009 entering class:** Total applicants: 8,054. Total accepted: 5,749. Freshmen enrolled: 1,038; 59% were from out of state. Overall acceptance rate: 71%. Non-early acceptance rate: 71%. **Size of waiting list:** 1505 applicants; enrolled from waiting list: 38. **Credentials of fall 2009 freshmen:** 27% ranked in the top 10 percent of their high school class; 62% were in the top 25 percent; 90% were in the top half. (Proportion submitting class standing: 49%.) **Average high school grade point average:** 3.4. **First-year students who submitted SAT scores:** 87%. Scores (25/75 percentile): Critical Reading: 510-600, Math: 520-620, Combined: 1030-1220.

ACADEMICS

Year founded: 1888. **Academic calendar:** Semester. **Degrees offered:** certificate, associate, bachelor's, post-bachelor's certificate, master's, post-master's certificate, doctorate. **Major fields of study:** biological and biomedical sciences; business, management, marketing, and related support services; communication, journalism, and related programs; computer and information sciences and support services; education; engineering; engineering technologies/technicians; family and consumer sciences/human sciences; foreign languages, literatures, and linguistics; health professions and related clinical sciences; history; liberal arts and sciences studies, and humanities; mathematics and statistics; multi/interdisciplinary studies; parks, recreation, leisure, and fitness studies; philosophy and religious studies; physical sciences; psychology; security and protective services; social sciences; visual and performing arts. **Areas of required coursework:** humanities, computer literacy, mathematics, English (including composition), philosophy, sciences (biological or physical), social science, other. **Pre-professional programs:** pre-law, pre-dentistry, pre-medicine, pre-veterinary science, pre-optometry, other. **Special academic programs (% participation):** accelerated program, cross-registration (1%), distance learning (33%), double major (12%), dual enrollment (.1%), exchange student program (domestic) (0%), honors program (10%), independent study (11%), internships (24%), study abroad (14%), teacher certificate program (11%), other (1%). **Teacher certification offered in:** early childhood, special education, elementary, middle/junior high, secondary. **Reserve Officers Training Corps (ROTC):** Army ROTC: Offered on campus; Air Force ROTC: Offered at cooperating institution. **Faculty and instruction (2009-2010):** Total instructional faculty: 267 full-time, 235 part-time (55% men; 45% women; 7% minorities). Full-time faculty with Ph.D. or other terminal degree: 81%. Student/faculty ratio: 12/1. Classes of fewer than 20 students: 45%; of 20 to 49 students: 55%; of 50 or more students: 0%. **Advanced Placement and International Baccalaureate credit:** AP tests may be used for: Credit only. Scores accepted: 3, 4, 5. International Baccalaureate exams may be used for: Credit only. **Freshmen returning for sophomore year:** 90%. **Graduation rates:** Four-year: 73%; five-year: 76%; six-year: 80%. **Graduate study:** 36% of students pursue further study within one year. Fields in which graduates pursue further study: Master of Business Administration (MBA), 6%; law, 5%; medicine, 20%; dentistry, 1%; education, 16%; arts and sciences, 53%.

COSTS AND FINANCIAL AID

Financial aid office: (570) 941-7700. **Expenses (2010-2011):** Tuition and fees 2010-2011: $34,536; room/board: $11,862. Estimated books and supplies: $1,150; transportation: $700; personal expenses: $1,100. **Financial aid:** Priority filing date for institution's financial aid form: February 15. In 2009-2010, 80% of undergraduates applied for financial aid. Of those, 69% were determined to have financial need; 11% had their need fully met. Average financial aid package (proportion receiving): $22,585 (68%). Average amount of gift aid, such as scholarships or grants (proportion receiving): $16,794 (66%). Average amount of self-help aid, such as work study or loans (proportion receiving): $5,579 (58%). Average need-based loan (excluding PLUS or other private loans): $4,590. Among students who received need-based aid, the average percentage of need met: 74%. Among students who received aid based on merit, the average award (and the proportion receiving): $9,932 (16%). The average athletic scholarship (and the proportion receiving): $0 (0%). Average amount of debt of borrowers graduating in 2009: $30,920. Proportion who borrowed: 75%.

CAMPUS LIFE AND EXTRACURRICULAR ACTIVITIES

Campus housing available (% using): coed dorms (58%), women's dorms (12%), men's dorms (8%), apartment for single students (16%), special housing for disabled students, special housing for international students. Students who live in college-owned, operated, or affiliated housing: 53%. **Student employment:** During the 2009-2010 academic year, 22% of undergraduates worked on campus. Average per-year earnings: $1,500. **Clubs and organizations:** Number of student organizations: 75. Activities include: campus ministries, choral groups, concert band, dance, drama/theater, international student organization, jazz band, literary magazine, music ensembles, musical theater, radio station, student government, student newspaper, symphony orchestra, television station, yearbook. Number of fraternities: 0; sororities: 0. Average proportion of students who stay on campus on weekends: 80%. **Sports program (2009-2010):** Member of NCAA III. **Men's intercollegiate varsity sports:** baseball, basketball, cross country, golf, lacrosse, swimming, tennis, wrestling. **Women's intercollegiate varsity sports:** basketball, cross country, field hockey, lacrosse, softball, swimming, tennis, volleyball.

SERVICES AND FACILITIES

Basic services: nonremedial tutoring, women's center, placement service, health service, health insurance, other. **Remedial assistance:** writing, other. **Counseling services:** minority student, career, personal, academic, older student, psychological, religious, other. **For learning-disabled students:** School does not offer a structured program with separate admission and additional fees. Total undergraduates in learning-disabled program or receiving services: 140. Services include: reading machines, tape recorders, diagnostic testing service, oral tests, learning center, extended time for tests, tutors, priority registration, priority seating, texts on tape, other testing accommodations, other. **Library:** Number of titles: 377,810; number of current serial subscriptions: 33,804. **Information technology resources:** Students are not required to lease or own a computer. Number of campus computers available to all students: 910. School has a wireless network. Approximate number of users that can be accommodated: 6,250. Proportion of college-owned housing units wired for high-speed internet access: 100%. **Campus safety:** Security services offered: 24-hour foot-and-vehicle patrols, late-night transport/escort service, 24-hour emergency telephones, lighted pathways/sidewalks, student patrols, controlled dormitory access (key, security card, etc).

TRANSFER AND INTERNATIONAL STUDENTS

Transfer students: May apply for admission for the following academic terms: Fall, Winter, Spring, Summer. Applicants do not need a minimum number of credits to apply. For fall 2009: Transfer applications received: 363. Transfer applicants offered admission: 163. Transfer applicants enrolled: 80. **International students:** Number of foreign undergraduates: 25 (1% of student body). Number of countries represented: 6. Minimum TOEFL score required: 500 (paper); 170 (computer). Average TOEFL score: 618 (paper).

University of the Arts

- **Address:** 320 S. Broad Street, Philadelphia, PA 19102
- **Website:** http://www.uarts.edu
- **Private**
- **Enrollment:** 2,115 full-time; 49 part-time

KEY STATS

✔ **U.S News College Ranking:** Unranked Specialty School–Fine Arts
✔ **SAT Score (25th/75th percentile):** 890-1140
✔ **Tuition:** 2010-2011: $32,200

Selectivity: N/A	**Room/board:** $7,800
Acceptance rate: 50%	**Average debt:** N/A
Student/faculty ratio: 10/1	**Proportion who borrowed:** N/A

UNDERGRADUATE STUDENT BODY STATS

2009-2010 enrollment: 2,115 full-time; 49 part-time. Men: 43%; women: 57%. **Ethnic makeup:** African American: 11%; American-Indian: 1%; Asian American: 3%; Hispanic: 5%; White: 76%; International: 4%.

ADMISSIONS FACTS AND FIGURES

Phone: (215) 717-6049. **Email:** admissions@uarts.edu. **Website:** http://www.uarts.edu. **Application deadlines for fall 2011:** Regular decision: Rolling. Early decision: Not offered. Early action: Not offered. Admission can be deferred. **Application fee:** $60. **To apply online, go to:** http://www.uarts.edu/applynow. **Admissions requirements/recommendations:** High school units required (recommended): English: 4; Mathematics: (3); Science: (2); Foreign language: (2); Social studies: (2); History: (2); Total units: 4 (13). Tests: The college uses SAT or ACT scores in admissions decisions. Either SAT or ACT required. For admission to the fall 2011 entering class, the school will accept: ACT with or without writing accepted. Campus visit: Recommended. Admissions interview: Recommended. Off-campus interview: May be arranged. **Factors that count in admissions decisions:** *Academic:* Secondary school record: Very Important. Class rank: Important. Letters of recommendation: Considered. Standardized test scores: Important. Essay: Important. *Nonacademic:* Interview: Very Important. Extracurricular activities: Important. Talent/ability: Very Important. Character/personal qualities: Important. Alumni/ae relationship: Considered. Geographical residence: Considered. State residency: Not Considered. Religious affiliation/commitment: Not Considered. Minority status: Considered. Volunteer work: Considered. Work experience: Considered. **Other schools with the greatest overlap in applicants:** Maryland Institute College of Art; New School; Pratt Institute; Savannah College of Art and Design; Temple University. **Admissions statistics for the fall 2009 entering class:** Total applicants: 2,449. Total accepted: 1,215. Freshmen enrolled: 473; 64% were from out of state. Overall acceptance rate: 50%. **Size of waiting list:** 62 applicants; enrolled from waiting list: N/A. **First-year students who submitted SAT scores:** 89%. Scores (25/75 percentile): Critical Reading: 460-590, Math: 430-550, Combined: 890-1140. **First-year students submitting ACT scores:** 18%. Scores (25/75 percentile): English: 18-27, Math: N/A, Composite: 18-25.

ACADEMICS

Year founded: 1876. **Academic calendar:** Semester. **Degrees offered:** certificate, diploma, bachelor's, post-bachelor's certificate, master's. **Most popular majors:** 12% dance, 12% technical theater/theater design and technology, 11% illustration, 8% graphic design, 8% photography. **Major fields of study:**

communication, journalism, and related programs; education; multi/inter-disciplinary studies; visual and performing arts. **Areas of required course-work:** arts/fine arts, humanities, computer literacy, mathematics, English (including composition), sciences (biological or physical), history, social science. **Special academic programs (% participation):** accelerated program, cross-registration, double major (1%), dual enrollment (1%), exchange student program (domestic) (1%), independent study (10%), internships (5%), study abroad (1%), teacher certificate program (10%). **Faculty and instruction (2009-2010):** Total instructional faculty: 118 full-time, 355 part-time (58% men; 42% women; 8% minorities). Full-time faculty with Ph.D. or other terminal degree: 74%. Student/faculty ratio: 10/1. Classes of fewer than 20 students: 79%; of 20 to 49 students: 21%; of 50 or more students: 0%. **Advanced Placement and International Baccalaureate credit:** AP tests may be used for: Credit only. Scores accepted: 4, 5. **Freshmen returning for sophomore year:** 78%. **Graduation rates:** Four-year: 59%; five-year: 64%; six-year: 65%.

COSTS AND FINANCIAL AID
Financial aid office: (215) 717-6170. **Expenses (2010-2011):** Tuition and fees 2010-2011: $32,200; room/board: $7,800. Estimated books and supplies: $2,100; transportation: $1,053; personal expenses: $1,665. **Financial aid:** Priority filing date for institution's financial aid form: March 1; deadline: March 1.

CAMPUS LIFE AND EXTRACURRICULAR ACTIVITIES
Campus housing available (% using): coed dorms (100%). Students who live in college-owned, operated, or affiliated housing: 20%. **Student employment:** During the 2009-2010 academic year, 0% of undergraduates worked on campus. **Clubs and organizations:** Number of student organizations: 17. Activities include: choral groups, concert band, dance, drama/theater, international student organization, jazz band, music ensembles, musical theater, radio station, student government. Number of fraternities: 0; sororities: 0. Average proportion of students who stay on campus on weekends: 60%.

SERVICES AND FACILITIES
Basic services: nonremedial tutoring, health service, health insurance. **Remedial assistance:** writing, study skills. **Counseling services:** minority student, career, personal, academic, psychological, birth control. **For learning-disabled students:** School does not offer a structured program with separate admission and additional fees. Services include: remedial math, remedial English, tape recorders, note-taking services, oral tests, readers, extended time for tests, tutors, priority seating, texts on tape, other testing accommodations, other. **Information technology resources:** Students are required to lease or own a computer. School has a wireless network. Approximate number of users that can be accommodated: 3,000. Proportion of college-owned housing units wired for high-speed internet access: 100%. **Campus safety:** Security services offered: 24-hour foot-and-vehicle patrols, late-night transport/escort service, lighted pathways/sidewalks, controlled dormitory access (key, security card, etc).

TRANSFER AND INTERNATIONAL STUDENTS
Transfer students: May apply for admission for the following academic terms: Fall, Spring. Applicants do not need a minimum number of credits to apply. For fall 2009: Transfer applicants enrolled: 118. **International students:** Number of foreign undergraduates: 96 (4% of student body). Number of countries represented: 19. Minimum TOEFL score required: 550 (paper); 213 (computer).

Ursinus College

■ **Address:** Box 1000, Collegeville, PA 19426
■ **Website:** http://www.ursinus.edu
■ **Private**
■ **Enrollment:** 1,718 full-time; 24 part-time

KEY STATS
✔ **U.S News College Ranking:** 71, National Liberal Arts Colleges
✔ **SAT Score (25th/75th percentile):** 1140-1350
✔ **Tuition:** 2010-2011: $40,120
Selectivity: More selective   **Room/board:** $9,750
Acceptance rate: 57%   **Average debt:** $25,875
Student/faculty ratio: 12/1   **Proportion who borrowed:** 80%

UNDERGRADUATE STUDENT BODY STATS
2009-2010 enrollment: 1,718 full-time; 24 part-time. Men: 46%; women: 54%. **Ethnic makeup:** African American: 6%; Asian American: 4%; Hispanic: 3%; White: 87%; International: 1%.

ADMISSIONS FACTS AND FIGURES
Phone: (610) 409-3200. **Email:** Admissions@Ursinus.edu. **Website:** http://www.ursinus.edu. **Application deadlines for fall 2011:** Regular decision: February 15; decision sent by April 1. Early decision: Send application by: January 15; Decision sent by: February 1. Early action: Send application by: December 1; Decision sent by: January 15. Admission can be deferred. **Application fee:** $50. **To apply online, go to:** http://www.ursinus.edu/apply. **Admissions requirements/recommendations:** High school units required (recommended): English: 4 (4); Mathematics: 3 (4); Science: 1 (4); Foreign language: 2 (4); Social studies: 1 (4); History: 0 (0); Academic electives: 3; Total units: 16 (20). Tests: The college uses SAT or ACT scores in admissions decisions. Neither SAT nor ACT required. For admission to the fall 2011 entering class, the school will accept ACT with or without writing accepted. Campus visit: Recommended. Admissions interview: Recommended. Off-campus interview: May be arranged. **Factors that count in admissions decisions:** *Academic:* Secondary school record: Very Important. Class rank: Important. Letters of recommendation: Important. Standardized test scores: Important. Essay: Important. *Nonacademic:* Interview: Considered. Extracurricular activities: Important. Talent/ability: Considered. Character/personal qualities: Important. Alumni/ae relationship: Considered. Geographical residence: Considered. State residency: Not Considered. Religious affiliation/commitment: Not Considered. Minority status: Considered. Volunteer work: Considered. Work experience: Considered. **Other schools with the greatest overlap in applicants:** Dickinson College; Franklin and Marshall College; Gettysburg College; Haverford College; Lafayette College. **Admissions statistics for the fall 2009 entering class:** Total applicants: 6,125. Total accepted: 3,471. Freshmen enrolled: 513; 58% were from out of state. Accepted through early-decision or early-action plans: 88%. Overall acceptance rate: 57%. Early-decision acceptance rate: 48%. Non-early acceptance rate: 34%. **Size of waiting list:** 515 applicants; enrolled from waiting list: 72. **Credentials of fall 2009 freshmen:** 47% ranked in the top 10 percent of their high school class; 77% were in the top 25 percent; 96% were in the top half. (Proportion submitting class standing: 55%.) **Average high school grade point average:** 3.6. **First-year students who submitted SAT scores:** 75%. Scores (25/75 percentile): Critical Reading: 570-680, Math: 570-670, Combined: 1140-1350. **First-year students submitting ACT scores:** 10%. Scores (25/75 percentile): English: N/A, Math: N/A, Composite: 25-29.

ACADEMICS
Year founded: 1869. **Academic calendar:** Semester. **Degrees offered:** certificate, bachelor's. **Most popular majors:** 23% social sciences, 16% biological and biomedical sciences, 10% parks, recreation, leisure, and fitness studies, 8% multi/interdisciplinary studies, 8% psychology. **Major fields of study:** area, ethnic, cultural, and gender studies; biological and biomedical sciences; communication, journalism, and related programs; computer and information sciences and support services; engineering; English language and literature/letters; foreign languages, literatures, and linguistics; history; mathematics and statistics; multi/interdisciplinary studies; natural resources and conservation; parks, recreation, leisure, and fitness studies; philosophy and religious studies; physical sciences; psychology; social sciences; visual and performing arts. **Areas of required coursework:** arts/fine arts, humanities, mathematics, foreign languages, sciences (biological or physical), social science, other. **Pre-professional programs:** pre-law, pre-dentistry, pre-medicine, pre-veterinary science, other. **Special academic programs (% participation):** double major (19%), dual enrollment, exchange student program (domestic) (1%), honors program (14%), independent study (68%), internships (44%), student-designed major (1%), study abroad (33%), teacher certificate program (6%). **Teacher certification offered in:** middle/junior high, secondary. **Faculty and instruction (2009-2010):** Total instructional faculty: 125 full-time, 69 part-time (48% men; 52% women; 13% minorities). Full-time faculty with Ph.D. or other terminal degree: 90%. Student/faculty ratio: 12/1. Classes of fewer than 20 students: 75%; of 20 to 49 students: 24%; of 50 or more students: 1%. **Advanced Placement and International Baccalaureate credit:** AP tests may be used for: Credit and/or placement. Scores accepted: 4, 5. International Baccalaureate exams may be used for: Credit and/or placement. **Freshmen returning for sophomore year:** 89%. **Graduation rates:** Four-year: 79%; five-year: 83%; six-year: 83%. **Graduate study:** 25% of students pursue further study immediately upon graduation; 33% within one year; 65% within five years. Fields in which graduates pursue further study: Master of Business Administration (MBA),

4%; law, 11%; medicine, 10%; dentistry, 3%; engineering, 1%; theology (or the seminary), 1%; education, 5%; arts and sciences, 61%; veterinary medicine, 4%.

COSTS AND FINANCIAL AID
Financial aid office: (610) 409-3600. **Expenses (2010-2011):** Tuition and fees 2010-2011: $40,120; room/board: $9,750. Estimated books and supplies: $1,000; transportation: $250; personal expenses: $1,450. **Financial aid:** Priority filing date for institution's financial aid form: February 15; deadline: February 15. In 2009-2010, 83% of undergraduates applied for financial aid. Of those, 70% were determined to have financial need; 21% had their need fully met. Average financial aid package (proportion receiving): $27,627 (69%). Average amount of gift aid, such as scholarships or grants (proportion receiving): $23,120 (69%). Average amount of self-help aid, such as work study or loans (proportion receiving): $5,459 (57%). Average need-based loan (excluding PLUS or other private loans): $4,377. Among students who received need-based aid, the average percentage of need met: 80%. Among students who received aid based on merit, the average award (and the proportion receiving): $13,682 (24%). Average amount of debt of borrowers graduating in 2009: $25,875. Proportion who borrowed: 80%.

CAMPUS LIFE AND EXTRACURRICULAR ACTIVITIES
Campus housing available (% using): coed dorms (65%), women's dorms (10%), men's dorms (10%), special housing for international students (5%), other housing options (10%). Students who live in college-owned, operated, or affiliated housing: 95%. **Student employment:** During the 2009-2010 academic year, 43% of undergraduates worked on campus. Average per-year earnings: $1,800. **Clubs and organizations:** Number of student organizations: 86. Activities include: campus ministries, choral groups, concert band, dance, drama/theater, jazz band, literary magazine, model UN, music ensembles, pep band, radio station, student government, student newspaper, student film society, television station, yearbook. Number of fraternities: 7; sororities: 5. Proportion of men in fraternities: 10%; of women in sororities: 13%. Average proportion of students who stay on campus on weekends: 80%. **Sports program (2009-2010):** Member of NCAA III. *Men's intercollegiate varsity sports:* baseball, basketball, cross country, football, golf, lacrosse, soccer, swimming, tennis, track and field (indoor), track and field (outdoor), wrestling. *Women's intercollegiate varsity sports:* basketball, cross country, field hockey, gymnastics, lacrosse, soccer, softball, swimming, tennis, track and field (indoor), track and field (outdoor), volleyball.

SERVICES AND FACILITIES
Basic services: nonremedial tutoring, placement service, health service, health insurance, other. **Counseling services:** minority student, career, personal, academic, psychological, birth control, religious. **For learning-disabled students:** School does not offer a structured program with separate admission and additional fees. Total undergraduates in learning-disabled program or receiving services: 55. Services include: tape recorders, note-taking services, readers, extended time for tests, tutors, priority seating. **Library:** Number of titles: 420,000; number of current serial subscriptions: 25,900. **Information technology resources:** Students are required to lease or own a computer. Number of campus computers available to all students: 1,875. School has a wireless network. Approximate number of users that can be accommodated: 2,376. Proportion of college-owned housing units wired for high-speed internet access: 100%. **Campus safety:** Security services offered: 24-hour foot-and-vehicle patrols, late-night transport/escort service, 24-hour emergency telephones, lighted pathways/sidewalks, controlled dormitory access (key, security card, etc).

TRANSFER AND INTERNATIONAL STUDENTS
Transfer students: May apply for admission for the following academic terms: Fall, Spring. Applicants do not need a minimum number of credits to apply. For fall 2009: Transfer applications received: 95. Transfer applicants offered admission: 20. Transfer applicants enrolled: 9. **International students:** Number of foreign undergraduates: 10 (1% of student body). Number of countries represented: 14. Minimum TOEFL score required: 500 (paper); 173 (computer). Average TOEFL score: 580 (paper).

Valley Forge Christian College

- ■ **Address:** 1401 Charlestown Road, Phoenixville, PA 19460
- ■ **Website:** http://www.vfcc.edu
- ■ **Private; Religious affiliation:** Assemblies of God
- ■ **Enrollment:** 896 full-time; 293 part-time

KEY STATS
✔ **U.S News College Ranking:** second tier, Regional Colleges (North)
✔ **ACT Score (25th/75th percentile):** 17-23
✔ **Tuition:** 2010-2011: $16,282

Selectivity: Less selective	**Room/board:** $7,556
Acceptance rate: 81%	**Average debt:** $42,894
Student/faculty ratio: N/A	**Proportion who borrowed:** 96%

UNDERGRADUATE STUDENT BODY STATS
2009-2010 enrollment: 896 full-time; 293 part-time. Men: 48%; women: 52%. **Ethnic makeup:** African American: 10%; Asian American: 2%; Hispanic: 10%; White: 77%. **Religious preference:** Roman Catholic: 1%; Unknown: 7%; Assemblies of God: 64%; Protestant/non-AOG: 26%; Other: 2%.

ADMISSIONS FACTS AND FIGURES
Phone: (800) 432-8322. **Email:** admissions@vfcc.edu. **Website:** http://www.vfcc.edu. **Application deadlines for fall 2011:** Regular decision: Rolling. Early decision: Not offered. Early action: Not offered. Admission can be deferred. **Application fee:** $25. **To apply online, go to:** http://www.vfcc.edu/admissions/apply. **Admissions requirements/recommendations:** High school units required (recommended): English: 4 (4); Mathematics: 3 (3); Science: 2 (2); Social studies: 3 (3); Total units: 12 (12). Tests: The college uses SAT or ACT scores in admissions decisions. Either SAT or ACT required. For admission to the fall 2011 entering class, the school will accept: ACT with writing required. Campus visit: Recommended. Admissions interview: Neither required nor recommended. Off-campus interview: Not available. **Factors that count in admissions decisions:** *Academic:* Secondary school record: Considered. Class rank: Considered. Letters of recommendation: Very Important. Standardized test scores: Important. Essay: Very Important. *Nonacademic:* Interview: Not Considered. Extracurricular activities: Considered. Talent/ability: Considered. Character/personal qualities: Very Important. Alumni/ae relationship: Not Considered. Geographical residence: Not Considered. State residency: Not Considered. Religious affiliation/commitment: Very Important. Minority status: Not Considered. Volunteer work: Considered. Work experience: Considered. **Admissions statistics for the fall 2009 entering class:** Overall acceptance rate: 81%.

ACADEMICS
Year founded: 1939. **Academic calendar:** Semester. **Degrees offered:** certificate, associate, bachelor's, master's. **Areas of required coursework:** arts/fine arts, humanities, computer literacy, mathematics, English (including composition), philosophy, sciences (biological or physical), history, social science, other. **Pre-professional programs:** pre-theology. **Special academic programs (% participation):** distance learning, double major (1%), dual enrollment, English as a Second Language (ESL) (0%), exchange student program (domestic), honors program, independent study, internships (100%), study abroad (2%), teacher certificate program (20%). **Teacher certification offered in:** early childhood, elementary. **Faculty and instruction (2009-2010):** Total instructional faculty: N/A. Classes of fewer than 20 students: 64%; of 20 to 49 students: 28%; of 50 or more students: 8%. **Advanced Placement and International Baccalaureate credit:** AP tests may be used for: Credit and/or placement. Scores accepted: 3. International Baccalaureate exams may be used for: Credit and/or placement. **Freshmen returning for sophomore year:** 70%. **Graduation rates:** Four-year: 45%; five-year: 49%; six-year: 48%.

COSTS AND FINANCIAL AID
Financial aid office: (610) 917-1498. **Expenses (2010-2011):** Tuition and fees 2010-2011: $16,282; room/board: $7,556. Estimated books and supplies: $818; transportation: $1,418; personal expenses: $1,816. **Financial aid:** Priority filing date for institution's financial aid form: May 1. In 2009-2010, 85% of undergraduates applied for financial aid. Of those, 77% were determined to have financial need; 8% had their need fully met. Average financial aid package (proportion receiving): $8,841 (73%). Average amount of gift aid, such as scholarships or grants (proportion receiving): $6,048 (66%). Average amount of self-help aid, such as work study or loans

(proportion receiving): $4,180 (58%). Average need-based loan (excluding PLUS or other private loans): $3,980. Among students who received need-based aid, the average percentage of need met: 44%. Among students who received aid based on merit, the average award (and the proportion receiving): $2,283 (20%). The average athletic scholarship (and the proportion receiving): $0 (0%). Average amount of debt of borrowers graduating in 2009: $42,894. Proportion who borrowed: 96%.

CAMPUS LIFE AND EXTRACURRICULAR ACTIVITIES

Campus housing available (% using): women's dorms (38%), men's dorms (37%), apartments for married students (5%), apartment for single students (20%). **Student employment:** During the 2009-2010 academic year, 5% of undergraduates worked on campus. Average per-year earnings: $2,240. Activities include: choral groups, concert band, drama/theater, jazz band, music ensembles, student government, student newspaper, yearbook. Number of fraternities: 0; sororities: 0. Average proportion of students who stay on campus on weekends: 50%. **Sports program (2009-2010):** *Men's intercollegiate varsity sports:* baseball, basketball, soccer. *Women's intercollegiate varsity sports:* basketball, soccer, softball, volleyball.

SERVICES AND FACILITIES

Remedial assistance: reading, math, writing, study skills. **Counseling services:** career, personal, academic, religious. **For learning-disabled students:** School does not offer a structured program with separate admission and additional fees. Services include: remedial math, remedial English, reading machines, tape recorders, diagnostic testing service, untimed tests, oral tests, learning center, extended time for tests, tutors, priority seating. **Library:** Number of titles: 71,902; number of current serial subscriptions: 175. **Information technology resources:** Students are required to lease or own a computer. School has a wireless network. Approximate number of users that can be accommodated: 20,000. Proportion of college-owned housing units wired for high-speed internet access: 100%. **Campus safety:** Security services offered: 24-hour foot-and-vehicle patrols, late-night transport/escort service, 24-hour emergency telephones, lighted pathways/sidewalks, student patrols, controlled dormitory access (key, security card, etc).

TRANSFER AND INTERNATIONAL STUDENTS

Transfer students: May apply for admission for the following academic terms: Fall, Spring. Applicants need a minimum number of credits to apply. **International students:** Number of foreign undergraduates: 2. Number of countries represented: 2. Minimum TOEFL score required: 500 (paper); 173 (computer).

Villanova University

- **Address:** 800 Lancaster Avenue, Villanova, PA 19085
- **Website:** http://www.villanova.edu
- **Private; Religious affiliation:** Roman Catholic
- **Enrollment:** 6,604 full-time; 597 part-time

KEY STATS

✔ **U.S News College Ranking:** 1, Regional Universities (North)
✔ **SAT Score (25th/75th percentile):** 1200-1390
✔ **Tuition:** 2010-2011: $39,665

Selectivity: More selective	**Room/board:** $10,620
Acceptance rate: 46%	**Average debt:** $31,048
Student/faculty ratio: 11/1	**Proportion who borrowed:** 55%

UNDERGRADUATE STUDENT BODY STATS

2009-2010 enrollment: 6,604 full-time; 597 part-time. Men: 50%; women: 50%. **Ethnic makeup:** African American: 5%; Asian American: 7%; Hispanic: 7%; White: 78%; International: 3%. **Religious preference:** Protestant: 14%; Jewish: 1%; Muslim: 1%; Hindu: 1%; Buddhist: 1%; No preference: 6%; Roman Catholic: 72%.

ADMISSIONS FACTS AND FIGURES

Phone: (610) 519-4000. **Email:** gotovu@villanova.edu. **Website:** http://www.villanova.edu. **Application deadlines for fall 2011:** Regular decision: January 7; decision sent by April 1. Early decision: Not offered. Early action: Send application by: November 1; Decision sent by: December 20. Admission can be deferred. **Application fee:** $75. **To apply online, go to:** http://www.villanova.edu/enroll/admission. **Admissions requirements/recommendations:** High school units required (recommended): English: 4 (4); Mathematics:

4 (4); Science: 4 (4); Foreign language: 2 (4); Academic electives: 2 (2); Total units: 22 (25). **Tests:** The college uses SAT or ACT scores in admissions decisions. Either SAT or ACT required. For admission to the fall 2011 entering class, the school will accept: ACT with writing required. Campus visit: Recommended. Admissions interview: Neither required nor recommended. Off-campus interview: May be arranged. **Factors that count in admissions decisions:** *Academic:* Secondary school record: Very Important. Class rank: Very Important. Letters of recommendation: Important. Standardized test scores: Very Important. Essay: Important. *Nonacademic:* Interview: Not Considered. Extracurricular activities: Important. Talent/ability: Important. Character/personal qualities: Important. Alumni/ae relationship: Considered. Geographical residence: Considered. State residency: Considered. Religious affiliation/commitment: Not Considered. Minority status: Considered. Volunteer work: Important. Work experience: Important. **Other schools with the greatest overlap in applicants:** Boston College; Georgetown University; Lehigh University; University of Notre Dame; University of Pennsylvania. **Admissions statistics for the fall 2009 entering class:** Total applicants: 13,098. Total accepted: 6,079. Freshmen enrolled: 1,643; 79% were from out of state. Accepted through early-decision or early-action plans: 31%. Overall acceptance rate: 46%. Non-early acceptance rate: 47%. **Size of waiting list:** 3557 applicants; enrolled from waiting list: 82. **Credentials of fall 2009 freshmen:** 58% ranked in the top 10 percent of their high school class; 88% were in the top 25 percent; 98% were in the top half. (Proportion submitting class standing: 36%.) **Average high school grade point average:** 3.8. **First-year students who submitted SAT scores:** 76%. Scores (25/75 percentile): Critical Reading: 580-680, Math: 620-710, Combined: 1200-1390. **First-year students submitting ACT scores:** 24%. Scores (25/75 percentile): English: N/A, Math: N/A, Composite: 28-31.

ACADEMICS

Year founded: 1842. **Academic calendar:** Semester. **Degrees offered:** certificate, associate, bachelor's, post-bachelor's certificate, master's, post-master's certificate, doctorate. **Most popular majors:** 31% business, management, marketing, and related support services, 11% engineering, 11% health professions and related clinical sciences, 10% social sciences, 8% communication, journalism, and related programs. **Major fields of study:** biological and biomedical sciences; business, management, marketing, and related support services; communication, journalism, and related programs; computer and information sciences and support services; education; engineering; English language and literature/letters; foreign languages, literatures, and linguistics; health professions and related clinical sciences; history; liberal arts and sciences studies, and humanities; mathematics and statistics; philosophy and religious studies; physical sciences; psychology; public administration and social service professions; security and protective services; social sciences; visual and performing arts. **Areas of required coursework:** humanities, mathematics, English (including composition), philosophy, sciences (biological or physical), history, social science, other. **Special academic programs (% participation):** accelerated program (3%), cooperative (work-study plan) program (1%), cross-registration (1%), distance learning (25%), double major (19%), dual enrollment (.1%), English as a Second Language (ESL) (0%), honors program (8%), independent study (17%), internships (22%), study abroad (36%), teacher certificate program (1%). **Teacher certification offered in:** elementary, secondary. **Reserve Officers Training Corps (ROTC):** Army ROTC: Offered on campus; Navy ROTC: Offered on campus; Air Force ROTC: Offered at cooperating institution (St. Joseph's University). **Faculty and instruction (2009-2010):** Total instructional faculty: 614 full-time, 404 part-time (57% men; 43% women; 11% minorities). Full-time faculty with Ph.D. or other terminal degree: 87%. Student/faculty ratio: 11/1. Classes of fewer than 20 students: 43%; of 20 to 49 students: 54%; of 50 or more students: 2%. **Advanced Placement and International Baccalaureate credit:** AP tests may be used for: Credit and/or placement. Scores accepted: 4, 5. International Baccalaureate exams may be used for: Credit and/or placement. **Freshmen returning for sophomore year:** 95%. **Graduation rates:** Four-year: 82%; five-year: 86%; six-year: 88%. **Graduate study:** 17% of students pursue further study immediately upon graduation; 25% within one year. Fields in which graduates pursue further study: Master of Business Administration (MBA), 6%; law, 23%; medicine, 16%; dentistry, 3%; engineering, 11%; education, 11%; arts and sciences, 31%; veterinary medicine, 1%.

COSTS AND FINANCIAL AID

Financial aid office: (610) 519-4010. **Expenses (2010-2011):** Tuition and fees 2010-2011: $39,665; room/board: $10,620. Estimated books and supplies: $950; transportation: $600; personal expenses: $900. **Financial aid:** In 2009-2010, 60% of undergraduates applied for financial aid. Of those, 49% were determined to have financial need; 19% had their need fully met. Average financial aid package (proportion receiving): $26,967 (48%). Average amount of gift aid, such as scholarships or grants (proportion receiving): $22,101 (42%). Average amount of self-help aid, such as work study or loans (proportion receiving): $7,247 (45%). Average need-based loan (excluding PLUS or other private loans): $4,643. Among students who received need-based aid, the average percentage of need met: 80%. Among students who received aid based on merit, the average award (and the proportion receiving): $11,337 (7%). The average athletic scholarship (and the proportion receiving): $41,493 (2%). Average amount of debt of borrowers graduating in 2009: $31,048. Proportion who borrowed: 55%.

CAMPUS LIFE AND EXTRACURRICULAR ACTIVITIES

Campus housing available (% using): coed dorms (98%), women's dorms (1%), men's dorms (1%), special housing for disabled students. Students who live in college-owned, operated, or affiliated housing: 70%. **Student employment:** During the 2009-2010 academic year, 34% of undergraduates worked on campus. Average per-year earnings: $1,622. **Clubs and organizations:** Number of student organizations: 165. Activities include: campus ministries, choral groups, concert band, dance, drama/theater, international student organization, jazz band, literary magazine, marching band, model UN, music ensembles, musical theater, opera, pep band, radio station, student government, student newspaper, student film society, television station, yearbook. Number of fraternities: 10; sororities: 12. Proportion of men in fraternities: 16%; of women in sororities: 31%. Average proportion of students who stay on campus on weekends: 85%. **Sports program (2009-2010):** Member of NCAA I. *Men's intercollegiate varsity sports:* baseball, basketball, cross country, football, golf, lacrosse, soccer, swimming, tennis, track and field (indoor), track and field (outdoor). *Women's intercollegiate varsity sports:* basketball, crew (heavyweight), crew (lightweight), cross country, field hockey, lacrosse, soccer, softball, swimming, tennis, track and field (indoor), track and field (outdoor), volleyball, water polo.

SERVICES AND FACILITIES

Basic services: health service, health insurance, other. **Remedial assistance:** math, writing, study skills, other. **Counseling services:** minority student, career, military, personal, veteran student, academic, older student, psychological, religious. **For learning-disabled students:** School does not offer a structured program with separate admission and additional fees. Total undergraduates in learning-disabled program or receiving services: 240. Services include: reading machines, tape recorders, untimed tests, note-taking services, learning center, readers, extended time for tests, tutors, priority seating, texts on tape, typist/scribe, exams on tape or computer, other testing accommodations, other. **Library:** Number of titles: 785,000; number of current serial subscriptions: 11,000. **Information technology resources:** Students are required to lease or own a computer. Number of campus computers available to all students: 1,400. School has a wireless network. Approximate number of users that can be accommodated: 25,000. Proportion of college-owned housing units wired for high-speed internet access: 100%. **Campus safety:** Security services offered: 24-hour foot-and-vehicle patrols, late-night transport/escort service, 24-hour emergency telephones, lighted pathways/sidewalks, student patrols, controlled dormitory access (key, security card, etc).

TRANSFER AND INTERNATIONAL STUDENTS

Transfer students: May apply for admission for the following academic terms: Fall, Spring. Applicants do not need a minimum number of credits to apply. For fall 2009: Transfer applications received: 647. Transfer applicants offered admission: 243. Transfer applicants enrolled: 127. **International students:** Number of foreign undergraduates: 204 (3% of student body). Number of countries represented: 53. Minimum TOEFL score required: 550 (paper); 213 (computer). Average TOEFL score: 606 (paper).

Washington and Jefferson College

- **Address:** 60 S. Lincoln Street, Washington, PA 15301
- **Website:** http://www.washjeff.edu
- **Private**
- **Enrollment:** 1,496 full-time; 18 part-time

....

KEY STATS

✔ **U.S News College Ranking:** 101, National Liberal Arts Colleges

✔ **SAT Score (25th/75th percentile):** 1030-1230

✔ **Tuition:** 2010-2011: $34,610

Selectivity: More selective	**Room/board:** $9,280
Acceptance rate: 42%	**Average debt:** $23,000
Student/faculty ratio: 12/1	**Proportion who borrowed:** 75%

UNDERGRADUATE STUDENT BODY STATS

2009-2010 enrollment: 1,496 full-time; 18 part-time. Men: 52%; women: 48%. **Ethnic makeup:** African American: 3%; Asian American: 1%; Hispanic: 1%; White: 94%.

ADMISSIONS FACTS AND FIGURES

Phone: (724) 223-6025. **Email:** admission@washjeff.edu. **Website:** http://www.washjeff.edu. **Application deadlines for fall 2011:** Regular decision: March 1. Early decision: Send application by: December 1; Decision sent by: December 15. Early action: Send application by: January 15; Decision sent by: February 15. Admission can be deferred. **Application fee:** $25. **To apply online, go to:** http://www.washjeff.edu/content.aspx?section=1850&menu_id=472&crumb=380&id=1629. **Admissions requirements/recommendations:** High school units required (recommended): English: 3; Mathematics: 3; Foreign language: 2; History: 1; Total units: 15. Tests: The college uses SAT or ACT scores in admissions decisions. Neither SAT nor ACT required. For admission to the fall 2011 entering class, the school will accept: ACT with or without writing accepted. Campus visit: Recommended. Admissions interview: Recommended. Off-campus interview: May be arranged. **Factors that count in admissions decisions: *Academic:*** Secondary school record: Very Important. Class rank: Very Important. Letters of recommendation: Very Important. Standardized test scores: Important. Essay: Very Important. ***Nonacademic:*** Interview: Very Important. Extracurricular activities: Important. Talent/ability: Considered. Character/personal qualities: Very Important. Alumni/ae relationship: Considered. Geographical residence: Considered. State residency: Considered. Religious affiliation/commitment: Not Considered. Minority status: Considered. Volunteer work: Considered. Work experience: Considered. **Other schools with the greatest overlap in applicants:** Allegheny College; College of Wooster; Pennsylvania State University–University Park; University of Pittsburgh; Westminster College. **Admissions statistics for the fall 2009 entering class:** Total applicants: 6,658. Total accepted: 2,777. Freshmen enrolled: 393; 31% were from out of state. Accepted through early-decision or early-action plans: 97%. Overall acceptance rate: 42%. Non-early acceptance rate: 23%. **Size of waiting list:** 52 applicants; enrolled from waiting list: 4. **Credentials of fall 2009 freshmen:** 38% ranked in the top 10 percent of their high school class; 71% were in the top 25 percent; 94% were in the top half. (Proportion submitting class standing: 66%.) **Average high school grade point average:** 3.3. **First-year students who submitted SAT scores:** 85%. Scores (25/75 percentile): Critical Reading: 510-610, Math: 520-620, Combined: 1030-1230. **First-year students submitting ACT scores:** 30%. Scores (25/75 percentile): English: 21-28, Math: 21-27, Composite: 22-28.

ACADEMICS

Year founded: 1781. **Academic calendar:** 4-1-4. **Degrees offered:** bachelor's. **Most popular majors:** 14% business/commerce, 12% psychology, 10% accounting, 8% English language and literature, 7% political science and government. **Major fields of study:** biological and biomedical sciences; business, management, marketing, and related support services; computer and information sciences and support services; education; English language and literature/letters; foreign languages, literatures, and linguistics; history; mathematics and statistics; multi/interdisciplinary studies; natural resources and conservation; philosophy and religious studies; physical sciences; psychology; social sciences; visual and performing arts. **Areas of required coursework:** arts/fine arts, humanities, computer literacy, mathematics, English (including composition), foreign languages, sciences (biological or physical), social science. **Pre-professional programs:** pre-law, pre-dentistry, pre-medicine, pre-veterinary science, pre-optometry, other. **Special academic programs (% participation):** accelerated program (1%), double major (17%), dual enrollment (1%), honors program (3%), independent study (15%), internships (16%), student-designed major (0%), study abroad (33%), teacher certificate program (10%), other (8%). **Teacher certification offered in:** early childhood, elementary, middle/junior high, secondary. **Reserve Officers Training Corps (ROTC):** Army ROTC: Offered at cooperating institution (University of Pittsburgh); Air Force ROTC: Offered at cooperating institution (University of Pittsburgh). **Faculty and instruction (2009-2010):** Total instructional faculty: 116 full-time, 43 part-time (60% men; 40% women; 13% minorities). Full-time faculty with Ph.D. or other terminal degree: 91%. Student/faculty ratio: 12/1. Classes of fewer than 20 students: 70%; of 20 to 49 students: 30%; of 50 or more students: 0%. **Advanced Placement and International Baccalaureate credit:** AP tests may be used for: Credit and/or placement. Scores accepted: 4, 5. International Baccalaureate exams may be used for: Credit only. **Freshmen returning for sophomore year:** 86%. **Graduation rates:** Four-year: 69%; five-year: 72%; six-year: 73%. **Graduate study:** 34% of students pursue further study immediately upon graduation. Fields in which graduates pursue further study: Master of Business Administration (MBA), 1%; law, 24%; medicine, 21%; dentistry, 1%; theology (or the seminary), 1%; education, 8%; arts and sciences, 43%.

COSTS AND FINANCIAL AID

Financial aid office: (724) 223-6019. **Expenses (2010-2011):** Tuition and fees 2010-2011: $34,610; room/board: $9,280. Estimated books and supplies: $800; transportation: $200; personal expenses: $700. **Financial aid:** Priority filing date for institution's financial aid form: February 15. In 2009-2010, 86% of undergraduates applied for financial aid. Of those, 77% were determined to have financial need; 18% had their need fully met. Average financial aid package (proportion receiving): $24,008 (77%). Average amount of gift aid, such as scholarships or grants (proportion receiving): $9,786 (65%). Average amount of self-help aid, such as work study or loans (proportion receiving): $5,996 (68%). Average need-based loan (excluding PLUS or other private loans): $4,809. Among students who received need-based aid, the average percentage of need met: 79%. Among students who received aid based on merit, the average award (and the proportion receiving): $10,736 (19%). The average athletic scholarship (and the proportion receiving): $0 (0%). Average amount of debt of borrowers graduating in 2009: $23,000. Proportion who borrowed: 75%.

CAMPUS LIFE AND EXTRACURRICULAR ACTIVITIES

Campus housing available (% using): coed dorms (33%), women's dorms (15%), men's dorms (15%), sorority housing (13%), fraternity housing (19%), apartment for single students (0%), special housing for disabled students (1%), other housing options (0%). Students who live in college-owned, operated, or affiliated housing: 92%. **Student employment:** During the 2009-2010 academic year, 43% of undergraduates worked on campus. Average per-year earnings: $1,100. **Clubs and organizations:** Number of student organizations: 70. Activities include: campus ministries, choral groups, concert band, dance, drama/theater, international student organization, jazz band, literary magazine, model UN, music ensembles, musical theater, pep band, radio station, student government, student newspaper, student film society, symphony orchestra, yearbook. Number of fraternities: 6; sororities: 4. Proportion of men in fraternities: 29%; of women in sororities: 35%. Average proportion of students who stay on campus on weekends: 80%. **Sports program (2009-2010):** Member of NCAA III. *Men's intercollegiate varsity sports:* baseball, basketball, cross country, football, golf, lacrosse, soccer, swimming, tennis, track and field (indoor), track and field (outdoor), water polo, wrestling. *Women's intercollegiate varsity sports:* basketball, cross country, field hockey, golf, lacrosse, soccer, softball, swimming, tennis, track and field (indoor), track and field (outdoor), volleyball, water polo.

SERVICES AND FACILITIES

Basic services: nonremedial tutoring, women's center, placement service, health service, health insurance. **Remedial assistance:** reading, study skills. **Counseling services:** minority student, career, personal, academic, psychological, birth control, religious. **For learning-disabled students:** School does not offer a structured program with separate admission and additional fees. Total undergraduates in learning-disabled program or receiving services: 21. Services include: oral tests, learning center, extended time for tests, tutors, priority seating, texts on tape, exams on tape or computer, other testing accommodations, waiver of foreign language degree requirement. **Library:** Number of titles: 163,148; number of current serial subscriptions: 32,698. **Information technology resources:** Students are not required to lease or own a computer. Number of campus computers available to all students: 450. School has a wireless network. Approximate number of users that can be accommodated: 1,000. Proportion of college-owned housing units wired for

high-speed internet access: 100%. **Campus safety:** Security services offered: 24-hour foot-and-vehicle patrols, late-night transport/escort service, 24-hour emergency telephones, lighted pathways/sidewalks, controlled dormitory access (key, security card, etc).

TRANSFER AND INTERNATIONAL STUDENTS

Transfer students: May apply for admission for the following academic terms: Fall, Winter, Spring. Applicants do not need a minimum number of credits to apply. For fall 2009: Transfer applications received: 37. Transfer applicants offered admission: 21. Transfer applicants enrolled: 9. **International students:** Number of foreign undergraduates: 2. Number of countries represented: 2. Minimum TOEFL score required: 567 (paper); 86 (computer). Average TOEFL score: 592 (paper).

Waynesburg University

- **Address:** 51 W. College Street, Waynesburg, PA 15370
- **Website:** http://www.waynesburg.edu/
- **Private; Religious affiliation:** Presbyterian
- **Enrollment:** 1,547 full-time; 165 part-time

KEY STATS

✔ **U.S News College Ranking:** 105, Regional Universities (North)
✔ **SAT Score (25th/75th percentile):** 900-1100
✔ **Tuition:** 2010-2011: $18,410

Selectivity: Selective	**Room/board:** $7,580
Acceptance rate: 71%	**Average debt:** $22,000
Student/faculty ratio: 15/1	**Proportion who borrowed:** 87%

UNDERGRADUATE STUDENT BODY STATS

2009-2010 enrollment: 1,547 full-time; 165 part-time. Men: 38%; women: 62%. **Ethnic makeup:** African American: 3%; Hispanic: 1%; White: 96%. **Religious preference:** Roman Catholic: 22%; Protestant: 35%; No preference: 3%; Unknown: 23%; Presbyterian: 12%.

ADMISSIONS FACTS AND FIGURES

Phone: (800) 225-7393. **Email:** admissions@waynesburg.edu. **Website:** http://www.waynesburg.edu/. **Application deadlines for fall 2011:** Regular decision: Rolling. Early decision: Not offered. Early action: Not offered. Admission cannot be deferred. **Application fee:** $20. **To apply online, go to:** http://www.waynesburg.edu/apply.htm. **Admissions requirements/recommendations:** High school units required (recommended): English: 4; Mathematics: 3; Science: 2 (3); Foreign language: (2); Social studies: 2; Academic electives: 5; Total units: 16. Tests: The college uses SAT or ACT scores in admissions decisions. SAT required. For admission to the fall 2011 entering class, the school will accept: ACT with writing required. Campus visit: Recommended. Admissions interview: Recommended. Off-campus interview: May be arranged. **Factors that count in admissions decisions:** *Academic:* Secondary school record: Very Important. Class rank: Very Important. Letters of recommendation: Considered. Standardized test scores: Very Important. Essay: Considered. *Nonacademic:* Interview: Very Important. Extracurricular activities: Important. Talent/ability: Not Considered. Character/personal qualities: Considered. Alumni/ae relationship: Considered. Geographical residence: Not Considered. State residency: Not Considered. Religious affiliation/commitment: Not Considered. Minority status: Not Considered. Volunteer work: Considered. Work experience: Considered. **Other schools with the greatest overlap in applicants:** California University of Pennsylvania; Geneva College; Washington and Jefferson College; West Virginia University; Westminster College. **Admissions statistics for the fall 2009 entering class:** Total applicants: 1,875. Total accepted: 1,339. Freshmen enrolled: 386; 19% were from out of state. Overall acceptance rate: 71%. **Credentials of fall 2009 freshmen:** 15% ranked in the top 10 percent of their high school class; 43% were in the top 25 percent; 77% were in the top half. (Proportion submitting class standing: 88%.) **Average high school grade point average:** 3.4. **First-year students who submitted SAT scores:** 82%. Scores (25/75 percentile): Critical Reading: 450-540, Math: 450-560, Combined: 900-1100. **First-year students submitting ACT scores:** 29%. Scores (25/75 percentile): English: N/A, Math: N/A, Composite: N/A.

ACADEMICS

Year founded: 1849. **Academic calendar:** Semester. **Degrees offered:** associate, bachelor's, master's, doctorate. **Most popular majors:** 34% nursing,

19% business, management, marketing, and related support services, 9% public administration and social service professions, 7% communication and media studies. **Major fields of study:** biological and biomedical sciences; business, management, marketing, and related support services; communication, journalism, and related programs; computer and information sciences and support services; education; English language and literature/letters; health professions and related clinical sciences; history; mathematics and statistics; multi/interdisciplinary studies; physical sciences; psychology; public administration and social service professions; security and protective services; social sciences; visual and performing arts. **Areas of required coursework:** arts/fine arts, computer literacy, mathematics, English (including composition), philosophy, sciences (biological or physical), history, social science, other. **Pre-professional programs:** pre-law, pre-dentistry, pre-medicine, pre-veterinary science, other. **Special academic programs (% participation):** accelerated program (36%), distance learning (0%), double major (4%), dual enrollment (1%), honors program (6%), independent study (8%), internships (30%), liberal arts/career combination (1%), student-designed major (0%), study abroad (1%), teacher certificate program (9%). **Teacher certification offered in:** special education, elementary, secondary. **Reserve Officers Training Corps (ROTC):** Army ROTC: Offered at cooperating institution. **Faculty and instruction (2009-2010):** Total instructional faculty: 72 full-time, 190 part-time (46% men; 54% women). Full-time faculty with Ph.D. or other terminal degree: 68%. Student/faculty ratio: 15/1. Classes of fewer than 20 students: 68%; of 20 to 49 students: 31%; of 50 or more students: 1%. **Advanced Placement and International Baccalaureate credit:** AP tests may be used for: Credit and/or placement. Scores accepted: 3, 4, 5. International Baccalaureate exams may be used for: Credit and/or placement. **Freshmen returning for sophomore year:** 75%. **Graduation rates:** Four-year: 48%; five-year: 59%; six-year: 56%. **Graduate study:** 10% of students pursue further study immediately upon graduation; 16% within one year; 17% within five years. Fields in which graduates pursue further study: Master of Business Administration (MBA), 55%; law, 5%; medicine, 5%; dentistry, 2%; engineering, 2%; theology (or the seminary), 2%; education, 18%; arts and sciences, 10%; veterinary medicine, 1%.

COSTS AND FINANCIAL AID

Financial aid office: (724) 852-3208. **Expenses (2010-2011):** Tuition and fees 2010-2011: $18,410; room/board: $7,580. Estimated books and supplies: $1,300; transportation: $500; personal expenses: $210. **Financial aid:** Priority filing date for institution's financial aid form: March 15. In 2009-2010, 80% of undergraduates applied for financial aid. Of those, 70% were determined to have financial need; 20% had their need fully met. Average financial aid package (proportion receiving): $12,864 (69%). Average amount of gift aid, such as scholarships or grants (proportion receiving): $10,051 (64%). Average amount of self-help aid, such as work study or loans (proportion receiving): $4,212 (59%). Average need-based loan (excluding PLUS or other private loans): $3,877. Among students who received need-based aid, the average percentage of need met: 76%. Among students who received aid based on merit, the average award (and the proportion receiving): $7,094 (7%). The average athletic scholarship (and the proportion receiving): $0 (0%). Average amount of debt of borrowers graduating in 2009: $22,000. Proportion who borrowed: 87%.

CAMPUS LIFE AND EXTRACURRICULAR ACTIVITIES

Campus housing available (% using): coed dorms (0%), women's dorms (50%), men's dorms (30%), other housing options (15%). Students who live in college-owned, operated, or affiliated housing: 56%. **Student employment:** During the 2009-2010 academic year, 30% of undergraduates worked on campus. Average per-year earnings: $1,750. **Clubs and organizations:** Number of student organizations: 53. Activities include: choral groups, concert band, dance, drama/theater, jazz band, literary magazine, marching band, music ensembles, musical theater, pep band, radio station, student government, student newspaper, television station, yearbook. Number of fraternities: 0; sororities: 0. Average proportion of students who stay on campus on weekends: 40%. **Sports program (2009-2010):** Member of NCAA III. *Men's intercollegiate varsity sports:* baseball, basketball, cross country, football, golf, soccer, tennis, track and field (outdoor), wrestling. *Women's intercollegiate varsity sports:* basketball, cross country, golf, lacrosse, soccer, softball, tennis, track and field (outdoor), volleyball.

SERVICES AND FACILITIES

Basic services: nonremedial tutoring, placement service, health service. **Remedial assistance:** math, writing, study skills. **Counseling services:** minority student, career, personal, academic, older student, psychological, religious, other. **For learning-disabled students:** School does not offer a structured program with separate admission and additional fees. Total undergraduates in learning-disabled program or receiving services: 47. Services include: remedial math, remedial English, reading machines, tape recorders, note-taking services, oral tests, learning center, readers, extended time for tests, tutors, priority seating. **Library:** Number of titles: 89,687; number of current serial subscriptions: 379. **Information technology resources:** Students are not required to lease or own a computer. Number of campus computers available to all students: 160. School has a wireless network. Proportion of college-owned housing units wired for high-speed internet access: 100%. **Campus safety:** Security services offered: 24-hour foot-and-vehicle patrols, late-night transport/escort service, 24-hour emergency telephones, lighted pathways/sidewalks, controlled dormitory access (key, security card, etc).

TRANSFER AND INTERNATIONAL STUDENTS

Transfer students: May apply for admission for the following academic terms: Fall, Spring, Summer. Applicants do not need a minimum number of credits to apply. For fall 2009: Transfer applications received: 112. Transfer applicants offered admission: 102. Transfer applicants enrolled: 59. **International students:** Number of foreign undergraduates: 0. Number of countries represented: 3. Minimum TOEFL score required: 550 (paper); 213 (computer). Average TOEFL score: 550 (paper).

West Chester University of Pennsylvania

- **Address:** West Chester, PA 19383
- **Website:** http://www.wcupa.edu/
- **Public**
- **Enrollment:** 10,844 full-time; 1,076 part-time

KEY STATS
- ✔ U.S News College Ranking: 84, Regional Universities (North)
- ✔ SAT Score (25th/75th percentile): 970-1140
- ✔ Tuition: 2009-2010: $7,211 in state, $15,543 out of state

Selectivity: Selective	**Room/board:** $7,214
Acceptance rate: 49%	**Average debt:** $24,471
Student/faculty ratio: 19/1	**Proportion who borrowed:** 70%

UNDERGRADUATE STUDENT BODY STATS
2009-2010 enrollment: 10,844 full-time; 1,076 part-time. Men: 40%; women: 60%. **Ethnic makeup:** African American: 9%; Asian American: 2%; Hispanic: 3%; White: 86%.

ADMISSIONS FACTS AND FIGURES
Phone: (610) 436-3414. **Email:** ugadmiss@wcupa.edu. **Website:** http://www.wcupa.edu/. **Application deadlines for fall 2011:** Regular decision: Rolling. Early decision: Not offered. Early action: Not offered. Admission can be deferred. **Application fee:** $35. **To apply online, go to:** https://www.applyweb.com/apply/pawest/menu.html. **Admissions requirements/recommendations:** High school units required (recommended): English: 4 (4); Mathematics: 3 (4); Science: 2 (3); Foreign language: 0 (2); Social studies: 2 (2); History: 2 (2); Academic electives: 1 (2); Total units: 16 (25). Tests: The college uses SAT or ACT scores in admissions decisions. Either SAT or ACT required. For admission to the fall 2011 entering class, the school will accept: ACT with writing required. Campus visit: Recommended. Admissions interview: Neither required nor recommended. Off-campus interview: Not available. **Factors that count in admissions decisions:** *Academic:* Secondary school record: Very Important. Class rank: Very Important. Letters of recommendation: Not Considered. Standardized test scores: Important. Essay: Considered. *Nonacademic:* Interview: Not Considered. Extracurricular activities: Considered. Talent/ability: Considered. Character/personal qualities: Considered. Alumni/ae relationship: Not Considered. Geographical residence: Not Considered. State residency: Not Considered. Religious affiliation/commitment: Not Considered. Minority status: Considered. Volunteer work: Considered. Work experience: Considered. **Other schools with the greatest overlap in applicants:** Bloomsburg University of Pennsylvania; Kutztown University of Pennsylvania; Pennsylvania State University–University Park; Temple University; University of Delaware. **Admissions statistics for the fall 2009 entering class:** Total applicants: 13,619. Total accepted: 6,667. Freshmen enrolled: 2,248; 15% were from out of state. Overall acceptance rate: 49%. **Size of waiting list:** 1205 applicants; enrolled from waiting list: 0. **Credentials of fall 2009 freshmen:** 9% ranked in the top 10 percent of their high school class; 33% were in the top 25 percent; 76% were in the top half. (Proportion submitting class standing: 78%.) **Average**

high school grade point average: 3.3. **First-year students who submitted SAT scores:** 100%. Scores (25/75 percentile): Critical Reading: 480-560, Math: 490-580, Combined: 970-1140.

ACADEMICS

Year founded: 1871. **Academic calendar:** Semester. **Degrees offered:** bachelor's, post-bachelor's certificate, master's, post-master's certificate. **Most popular majors:** 17% education, 16% business, management, marketing, and related support services, 11% health professions and related clinical sciences, 10% liberal arts and sciences studies, and humanities, 8% English language and literature/letters. **Major fields of study:** area, ethnic, cultural, and gender studies; biological and biomedical sciences; business, management, marketing, and related support services; communication, journalism, and related programs; computer and information sciences and support services; education; English language and literature/letters; foreign languages, literatures, and linguistics; health professions and related clinical sciences; history; liberal arts and sciences studies, and humanities; mathematics and statistics; parks, recreation, leisure, and fitness studies; philosophy and religious studies; physical sciences; psychology; public administration and social service professions; security and protective services; social sciences; visual and performing arts. **Areas of required coursework:** arts/fine arts, humanities, computer literacy, mathematics, English (including composition), foreign languages, sciences (biological or physical), history, social science, other. **Pre-professional programs:** pre-law, pre-medicine, pre-theology. **Special academic programs:** cross-registration, distance learning, double major, dual enrollment, English as a Second Language (ESL), exchange student program (domestic), honors program, independent study, internships, liberal arts/career combination, student-designed major, study abroad, teacher certificate program. **Teacher certification offered in:** early childhood, special education, elementary, middle/junior high, secondary. **Cooperative education programs:** art, business, computer science, education, health professions, humanities, natural science, social/behavioral science. **Reserve Officers Training Corps (ROTC):** Army ROTC: Offered at cooperating institution (Widener University); Air Force ROTC: Offered at cooperating institution (St. Joseph's University). **Faculty and instruction (2009-2010):** Total instructional faculty: 516 full-time, 264 part-time (48% men; 52% women; 11% minorities). Full-time faculty with Ph.D. or other terminal degree: 83%. Student/faculty ratio: 19/1. Classes of fewer than 20 students: 25%; of 20 to 49 students: 70%; of 50 or more students: 5%. **Advanced Placement and International Baccalaureate credit:** AP tests may be used for: Credit and/or placement. Scores accepted: 3, 4, 5. International Baccalaureate exams may be used for: Credit only. **Freshmen returning for sophomore year:** 85%. **Graduation rates:** Four-year: 40%; five-year: 61%; six-year: 63%.

COSTS AND FINANCIAL AID

Financial aid office: (610) 436-2627. **Expenses (2009-2010):** Tuition and fees 2009-2010: $7,211 in state, $15,543 out of state; room/board: $7,214. Estimated books and supplies: $1,320; transportation: $1,504; personal expenses: $2,072. **Financial aid:** Priority filing date for institution's financial aid form: March 1. In 2009-2010, 74% of undergraduates applied for financial aid. Of those, 53% were determined to have financial need; 35% had their need fully met. Average financial aid package (proportion receiving): $7,648 (53%). Average amount of gift aid, such as scholarships or grants (proportion receiving): $5,289 (34%). Average amount of self-help aid, such as work study or loans (proportion receiving): $4,437 (49%). Average need-based loan (excluding PLUS or other private loans): $4,203. Among students who received need-based aid, the average percentage of need met: 71%. Among students who received aid based on merit, the average award (and the proportion receiving): $3,601 (2%). The average athletic scholarship (and the proportion receiving): $3,093 (1%). Average amount of debt of borrowers graduating in 2009: $24,471. Proportion who borrowed: 70%.

CAMPUS LIFE AND EXTRACURRICULAR ACTIVITIES

Campus housing available (% using): coed dorms (75%), women's dorms (0%), apartment for single students (23%), special housing for disabled students (1%), special housing for international students (1%). Students who live in college-owned, operated, or affiliated housing: 38%. **Student employment:** During the 2009-2010 academic year, 11% of undergraduates worked on campus. Average per-year earnings: $2,403. **Clubs and organizations:** Number of student organizations: 231. Activities include: campus ministries, choral groups, concert band, dance, drama/theater, jazz band, literary magazine, marching band, music ensembles, musical theater, opera, pep band, radio station, student government, student newspaper, symphony orchestra, television station, yearbook. Number of fraternities: 12; sororities: 13. Proportion of men in fraternities: 8%; of women in sororities: 8%. Average proportion of students who stay on campus on weekends: 50%.

Sports program (2009-2010): Member of NCAA II. *Men's intercollegiate varsity sports:* baseball, basketball, cross country, football, golf, soccer, swimming, tennis, track and field (indoor), track and field (outdoor). *Women's intercollegiate varsity sports:* basketball, cross country, field hockey, golf, gymnastics, lacrosse, rugby, soccer, softball, swimming, tennis, track and field (indoor), track and field (outdoor), volleyball.

SERVICES AND FACILITIES

Basic services: nonremedial tutoring, women's center, placement service, day care, health service, health insurance, other. **Remedial assistance:** reading, math, writing, study skills. **Counseling services:** minority student, career, personal, veteran student, academic, psychological, birth control, religious. **For learning-disabled students:** School does not offer a structured program with separate admission and additional fees. Total undergraduates in learning-disabled program or receiving services: 650. Services include: remedial math, remedial English, reading machines, tape recorders, note-taking services, learning center, readers, extended time for tests, tutors, priority registration, priority seating, typist/scribe, exams on tape or computer, other testing accommodations, other. **Library:** Number of titles: 1,337,040; number of current serial subscriptions: 9,661. **Information technology resources:** Students are not required to lease or own a computer. Number of campus computers available to all students: 1,200. School has a wireless network. Approximate number of users that can be accommodated: 4,400. Proportion of college-owned housing units wired for high-speed internet access: 100%. **Campus safety:** Security services offered: 24-hour foot-and-vehicle patrols, late-night transport/escort service, 24-hour emergency telephones, lighted pathways/sidewalks, controlled dormitory access (key, security card, etc).

TRANSFER AND INTERNATIONAL STUDENTS

Transfer students: May apply for admission for the following academic terms: Fall, Spring. Applicants do not need a minimum number of credits to apply. For fall 2009: Transfer applications received: 3,639. Transfer applicants offered admission: 1,821. Transfer applicants enrolled: 1,179. **International students:** Number of foreign undergraduates: 22. Number of countries represented: 57. Minimum TOEFL score required: 550 (paper); 213 (computer).

Westminster College

- **Address:** 319 S. Market Street, New Wilmington, PA 16172
- **Website:** http://www.westminster.edu
- **Private; Religious affiliation:** Presbyterian Church (USA)
- **Enrollment:** 1,437 full-time; 34 part-time

KEY STATS

- ✔ **U.S News College Ranking:** 119, National Liberal Arts Colleges
- ✔ **SAT Score (25th/75th percentile):** 970-1170
- ✔ **Tuition:** 2010-2011: $29,150

Selectivity: Selective	**Room/board:** $8,840
Acceptance rate: 61%	**Average debt:** $28,262
Student/faculty ratio: 12/1	**Proportion who borrowed:** 80%

UNDERGRADUATE STUDENT BODY STATS

2009-2010 enrollment: 1,437 full-time; 34 part-time. Men: 41%; women: 59%. **Ethnic makeup:** African American: 1%; Asian American: 1%; White: 97%. **Religious preference:** Roman Catholic: 29%; Protestant: 40%; Jewish: 1%; Muslim: 1%; Hindu: 1%; Buddhist: 1%; No preference: 20%.

ADMISSIONS FACTS AND FIGURES

Phone: (800) 942-8033. **Email:** admis@westminster.edu. **Website:** http://www.westminster.edu. **Application deadlines for fall 2011:** Regular decision: January 5. Early decision: Not offered. Early action: Send application by: November 15; Decision sent by: December 1. Admission can be deferred. **Application fee:** $35. **To apply online, go to:** http://www.commonapp.org. **Admissions requirements/recommendations:** High school units required (recommended): English: 4; Mathematics: 3; Science: 2; Foreign language: 2; Social studies: 2; History: 1; Academic electives: 3; Total units: 16. Tests: The college uses SAT or ACT scores in admissions decisions. Either SAT or ACT required. Campus visit: Recommended. Admissions interview: Recommended. Off-campus interview: May be arranged. **Factors that count in admissions decisions:** *Academic:* Secondary school record: Very Important. Class rank: Very Important. Letters of recommendation: Important. Standardized test scores: Very Important. Essay: Important. **Nonacademic:** Interview: Very Important. Extracurricular activities: Considered. Talent/ability: Considered. Character/personal qualities: Important. Alumni/ae relationship: Considered. Geographical residence: Not Considered. State residency: Not Considered. Religious affiliation/commitment: Considered. Minority status: Considered. Volunteer work: Considered. Work experience: Considered. **Other schools with the greatest overlap in applicants:** Allegheny College; Geneva College; Grove City College; Thiel College; Washington and Jefferson College. **Admissions statistics for the fall 2009 entering class:** Total applicants: 3,908. Total accepted: 2,394. Freshmen enrolled: 451; Overall acceptance rate: 61%. Non-early acceptance rate: 61%. **Credentials of fall 2009 freshmen:** 28% ranked in the top 10 percent of their high school class; 62% were in the top 25 percent; 93% were in the top half. (Proportion submitting class standing: 83%.) **Average high school grade point average:** 3.5. **First-year students who submitted SAT scores:** 82%. Scores (25/75 percentile): Critical Reading: 480-570, Math: 490-600, Combined: 970-1170. **First-year students submitting ACT scores:** 46%. Scores (25/75 percentile): English: 19-26, Math: 19-25, Composite: 20-26.

ACADEMICS

Year founded: 1852. **Academic calendar:** Semester. **Degrees offered:** bachelor's, master's. **Most popular majors:** 14% elementary education and teaching, 13% business administration and management, 6% English language and literature, 6% biology/biological sciences, 6% history. **Major fields of study:** biological and biomedical sciences; business, management, marketing, and related support services; communication, journalism, and related programs; computer and information sciences and support services; education; English language and literature/letters; foreign languages, literatures, and linguistics; history; mathematics and statistics; multi/interdisciplinary studies; natural resources and conservation; philosophy and religious studies; physical sciences; psychology; social sciences; theology and religious vocations; visual and performing arts. **Areas of required coursework:** arts/fine arts, humanities, mathematics, English (including composition), philosophy, foreign languages, sciences (biological or physical), history, social science, other. **Pre-professional programs:** pre-law, pre-dentistry, pre-medicine, pre-theology, pre-veterinary science, pre-optometry, pre-pharmacy. **Special academic programs (% participation):** accelerated program (2%), cross-registration (1%), double major (2%), exchange student program (domestic) (1%), honors program (1%), independent study (2%), internships (70%), liberal arts/career combination (100%), student-designed major (1%), study abroad (6%), teacher certificate program. **Teacher certification offered in:** special education, elementary, middle/junior high, secondary. **Reserve Officers Training Corps (ROTC):** Army ROTC: Offered at cooperating institution. **Faculty and instruction (2009-2010):** Total instructional faculty: 105 full-time, 57 part-time (52% men; 48% women). Full-time faculty with Ph.D. or other terminal degree: 92%. Student/faculty ratio: 12/1. **Advanced Placement and International Baccalaureate credit:** AP tests may be used for: Placement only. Scores accepted: 3, 5. International Baccalaureate exams may be used for: Placement only. **Freshmen returning for sophomore year:** 87%. **Graduation rates:** Four-year: 59%; five-year: 74%; six-year: 77%. **Graduate study:** 35% of students pursue further study within one year. Fields in which graduates pursue further study: Master of Business Administration (MBA), 1%; law, 6%; medicine, 7%; theology (or the seminary), 2%; education, 10%; arts and sciences, 10%; veterinary medicine, 2%.

COSTS AND FINANCIAL AID

Financial aid office: (724) 946-7102. **Expenses (2010-2011):** Tuition and fees 2010-2011: $29,150; room/board: $8,840. Estimated books and supplies: $1,000 personal expenses: $1,250. **Financial aid:** Priority filing date for institution's financial aid form: May 1. In 2009-2010, 92% of undergraduates applied for financial aid. Of those, 84% were determined to have financial need; 28% had their need fully met. Average financial aid package (proportion receiving): $23,163 (83%). Average amount of gift aid, such as scholarships or grants (proportion receiving): $18,663 (83%). Average amount of self-help aid, such as work study or loans (proportion receiving): $4,979 (67%). Average need-based loan (excluding PLUS or other private loans): $4,312. Among students who received need-based aid, the average percentage of need met: 83%. Among students who received aid based on merit, the average award (and the proportion receiving): $12,701 (16%). The average athletic scholarship (and the proportion receiving): $0 (0%). Average amount of debt of borrowers graduating in 2009: $28,262. Proportion who borrowed: 80%.

CAMPUS LIFE AND EXTRACURRICULAR ACTIVITIES

Campus housing available (% using): women's dorms (40%), men's dorms (31%), fraternity housing (18%), other housing options (10%). **Student employment:** During the 2009-2010 academic year, 21% of undergraduates worked on campus. **Clubs and organizations:** Number of student organizations: 69. Activities include: choral groups, concert band, dance, drama/theater, jazz band, literary magazine, marching band, music ensembles, musical theater, opera, pep band, radio station, student government, student newspaper, student film society, symphony orchestra, television station, yearbook. Number of fraternities: 5; sororities: 5. Average proportion of students who stay on campus on weekends: 75%. **Sports program (2009-2010):** Member of NCAA III.

SERVICES AND FACILITIES

Basic services: nonremedial tutoring, placement service, health service, health insurance. **Remedial assistance:** reading, study skills. **Counseling services:** minority student, career, personal, academic, older student, psychological, religious. **For learning-disabled students:** School does not offer a structured program with separate admission and additional fees. Services include: reading machines, remedial reading, tape recorders, videotaped classes, untimed tests, note-taking services, oral tests, learning center, readers, extended time for tests, tutors, priority seating, other. **Library:** Number of titles: 283,070; number of current serial subscriptions: 848. **Information technology resources:** Students are not required to lease or own a computer. Number of campus computers available to all students: 120. School has a wireless network. Approximate number of users that can be accommodated: 1,200. Proportion of college-owned housing units wired for high-speed internet access: 100%. **Campus safety:** Security services offered: 24-hour foot-and-vehicle patrols, late-night transport/escort service, 24-hour emergency telephones, lighted pathways/sidewalks, controlled dormitory access (key, security card, etc).

TRANSFER AND INTERNATIONAL STUDENTS

Transfer students: May apply for admission for the following academic terms: Fall, Spring. Applicants do not need a minimum number of credits to apply. For fall 2009: Transfer applications received: 45. Transfer applicants offered admission: 19. Transfer applicants enrolled: 10. **International students:** Number of foreign undergraduates: 0. Minimum TOEFL score required: 500 (paper); 173 (computer).

Widener University

- **Address:** 1 University Place, Chester, PA 19013
- **Website:** http://www.widener.edu
- **Private**
- **Enrollment:** 2,717 full-time; 695 part-time

KEY STATS

✔ **U.S News College Ranking:** 159, National Universities
✔ **SAT Score (25th/75th percentile):** 900-1100
✔ **Tuition:** 2010-2011: $33,270

Selectivity: Selective	**Room/board:** $11,720
Acceptance rate: 70%	**Average debt:** $38,372
Student/faculty ratio: 12/1	**Proportion who borrowed:** 87%

UNDERGRADUATE STUDENT BODY STATS

2009-2010 enrollment: 2,717 full-time; 695 part-time. Men: 44%; women: 56%. **Ethnic makeup:** African American: 14%; Asian American: 3%; Hispanic: 3%; White: 77%; International: 2%.

ADMISSIONS FACTS AND FIGURES

Phone: (610) 499-4126. **Email:** admissions.office@widener.edu. **Website:** http://www.widener.edu. **Application deadlines for fall 2011:** Regular decision: Rolling. Early decision: Not offered. Early action: Not offered. Admission can be deferred. **Application fee:** $35. **To apply online, go to:** https://www.applyweb.com/apply/wideneru/. **Admissions requirements/recommendations:** High school units required (recommended): English: 4 (4); Mathematics: 3 (4); Science: 3 (4); Foreign language: 2 (2); Social studies: 3 (4); History: 0 (0); Academic electives: 3 (3); Total units: 18 (23). Tests: The college uses SAT or ACT scores in admissions decisions. Either SAT or ACT required. For admission to the fall 2011 entering class, the school will accept: ACT with or without writing accepted. Campus visit: Recommended. Admissions interview: Recommended. Off-campus interview: May be arranged. **Factors that count in admissions decisions:** *Academic:* Secondary school record: Very Important. Class rank: Very Important. Letters of recommendation: Considered. Standardized test scores: Very Important. Essay: Considered. *Nonacademic:* Interview: Considered. Extracurricular activities: Considered. Talent/ability: Considered. Character/personal qualities: Considered. Alumni/ae relationship: Considered. Geographical residence: Not Considered. State residency: Not Considered. Religious affiliation/commitment: Not Considered. Minority status: Not Considered. Volunteer work: Considered. Work experience: Not Considered. **Other schools with the greatest overlap in applicants:** Drexel University; La Salle University; St. Joseph's University; Temple University; West Chester University of Pennsylvania. **Admissions statistics for the fall 2009 entering class:** Total applicants: 4,636. Total accepted: 3,251. Freshmen enrolled: 720; 44% were from out of state. Overall acceptance rate: 70%. **Size of waiting list:** 54 applicants; enrolled from waiting list: 14. **Credentials of fall 2009 freshmen:** 13% ranked in the top 10 percent of their high school class; 39% were in the top 25 percent; 73% were in the top half. (Proportion submitting class standing: 75%.) **Average high school grade point average:** 3.3. **First-year students who submitted SAT scores:** 99%. Scores (25/75 percentile): Critical Reading: 440-540, Math: 460-560, Combined: 900-1100.

ACADEMICS

Year founded: 1821. **Academic calendar:** Semester. **Degrees offered:** certificate, associate, bachelor's, master's, doctorate. **Most popular majors:** 27% business, management, marketing, and related support services, 24% health professions and related clinical sciences, 10% psychology, 9% engineering, 5% education. **Major fields of study:** biological and biomedical sciences; business, management, marketing, and related support services; communication, journalism, and related programs; computer and information sciences and support services; education; engineering; English language and literature/letters; foreign languages, literatures, and linguistics; health professions and related clinical sciences; history; legal professions and studies; liberal arts and sciences studies, and humanities; mathematics and statistics; multi/interdisciplinary studies; psychology; public administration and social service professions; security and protective services; social sciences. **Areas of required coursework:** humanities, computer literacy, mathematics, English (including composition), sciences (biological or physical), social science. **Pre-professional programs:** pre-law, pre-dentistry, pre-medicine, pre-veterinary science, pre-optometry, pre-pharmacy, other. **Special academic programs:** accelerated program, cooperative (work-study plan) program, distance learning, double major, English as a Second Language (ESL), honors program, independent study, internships, liberal arts/career combination, student-designed major, study abroad, teacher certificate program, weekend college. **Teacher certification offered in:** early childhood, special education, elementary, secondary, bilingual/bicultural. **Cooperative education programs:** business, computer science, engineering, other. **Reserve Officers Training Corps (ROTC):** Army ROTC: Offered on campus; Navy ROTC: Offered at cooperating institution (Villanova University); Air Force ROTC: Offered at cooperating institution (St. Joseph's University). **Faculty and instruction (2009-2010):** Total instructional faculty: 310 full-time, 353 part-time (52% men; 48% women; 12% minorities). Full-time faculty with Ph.D. or other terminal degree: 89%. Student/faculty ratio: 12/1. Classes of fewer than 20 students: 60%; of 20 to 49 students: 39%; of 50 or more students: 1%. **Advanced Placement and International Baccalaureate credit:** AP tests may be used for: Placement only. Scores accepted: 3, 4, 5. International Baccalaureate exams may be used for: Credit only. **Freshmen returning for sophomore year:** 73%. **Graduation rates:** Four-year: 41%; five-year: 54%; six-year: 57%. **Graduate study:** 24% of students pursue further study immediately upon graduation.

COSTS AND FINANCIAL AID

Financial aid office: (610) 499-4174. **Expenses (2010-2011):** Tuition and fees 2010-2011: $33,270; room/board: $11,720. Estimated books and supplies: $1,200; transportation: $495; personal expenses: $1,170. **Financial aid:** Priority filing date for institution's financial aid form: February 15. In 2009-2010, 88% of undergraduates applied for financial aid. Of those, 81% were determined to have financial need; 15% had their need fully met. Average financial aid package (proportion receiving): $23,048 (80%). Average amount of gift aid, such as scholarships or grants (proportion receiving): $8,804 (64%). Average amount of self-help aid, such as work study or loans (proportion receiving): $6,074 (70%). Average need-based loan (excluding PLUS or other private loans): $4,794. Among students who received need-based aid, the average percentage of need met: 72%. Among students who received aid based on merit, the average award (and the proportion receiving): $11,490 (12%). The average athletic scholarship (and the proportion

receiving): $0 (0%). Average amount of debt of borrowers graduating in 2009: $38,372. Proportion who borrowed: 87%.

CAMPUS LIFE AND EXTRACURRICULAR ACTIVITIES

Campus housing available: coed dorms, women's dorms, men's dorms, sorority housing, fraternity housing, apartment for single students, cooperative housing, other housing options. Students who live in college-owned, operated, or affiliated housing: 47%. **Student employment:** During the 2009-2010 academic year, 45% of undergraduates worked on campus. Average per-year earnings: $2,500. **Clubs and organizations:** Number of student organizations: 99. Activities include: campus ministries, choral groups, concert band, dance, drama/theater, international student organization, jazz band, literary magazine, music ensembles, pep band, radio station, student government, student newspaper, student film society, television station, yearbook. Number of fraternities: 6; sororities: 3. Proportion of men in fraternities: 10%; of women in sororities: 9%. Average proportion of students who stay on campus on weekends: 65%. **Sports program (2009-2010):** Member of NCAA III. *Men's intercollegiate varsity sports:* baseball, basketball, cross country, football, golf, lacrosse, soccer, swimming, tennis, track and field (indoor), track and field (outdoor). *Women's intercollegiate varsity sports:* basketball, cross country, field hockey, lacrosse, soccer, softball, swimming, tennis, track and field (indoor), track and field (outdoor), volleyball.

SERVICES AND FACILITIES

Basic services: nonremedial tutoring, placement service, day care, health service, health insurance. **Remedial assistance:** reading, math, writing, study skills. **Counseling services:** minority student, career, military, personal, veteran student, academic, older student, psychological, birth control, religious. **For learning-disabled students:** School does not offer a structured program with separate admission and additional fees. Services include: remedial math, remedial English, reading machines, remedial reading, tape recorders, diagnostic testing service, untimed tests, note-taking services, oral tests, learning center, readers, extended time for tests, tutors, texts on tape. **Library:** Number of titles: 217,995; number of current serial subscriptions: 2,566. **Information technology resources:** Students are not required to lease or own a computer. Number of campus computers available to all students: 720. School has a wireless network. Proportion of college-owned housing units wired for high-speed internet access: 100%. **Campus safety:** Security services offered: 24-hour foot-and-vehicle patrols, late-night transport/escort service, 24-hour emergency telephones, lighted pathways/sidewalks, controlled dormitory access (key, security card, etc).

TRANSFER AND INTERNATIONAL STUDENTS

Transfer students: May apply for admission for the following academic terms: Fall, Spring, Summer. Applicants need a minimum number of credits to apply. For fall 2009: Transfer applications received: 1,037. Transfer applicants offered admission: 429. Transfer applicants enrolled: 160. **International students:** Number of foreign undergraduates: 74 (2% of student body). Number of countries represented: 38. Minimum TOEFL score required: 500 (paper); 173 (computer). Average TOEFL score: 550 (paper).

Wilkes University

- **Address:** 84 W. South Street, Wilkes-Barre, PA 18766
- **Website:** http://www.wilkes.edu
- Private
- **Enrollment:** 2,011 full-time; 229 part-time

KEY STATS

✔ **U.S News College Ranking:** 67, Regional Universities (North)
✔ **SAT Score (25th/75th percentile):** 940-1180
✔ **Tuition:** 2010-2011: $27,178

Selectivity: Selective	**Room/board:** $11,470
Acceptance rate: 76%	**Average debt:** $34,775
Student/faculty ratio: 15/1	**Proportion who borrowed:** 87%

UNDERGRADUATE STUDENT BODY STATS

2009-2010 enrollment: 2,011 full-time; 229 part-time. Men: 51%; women: 49%. **Ethnic makeup:** African American: 3%; Asian American: 2%; Hispanic: 2%; White: 90%; International: 2%.

ADMISSIONS FACTS AND FIGURES

Phone: (570) 408-4400. **Email:** admissions@wilkes.edu. **Website:** http://www.wilkes.edu. **Application deadlines for fall 2011:** Regular decision: Rolling. Early decision: Not offered. Early action: Not offered. Admission can be deferred. **Application fee:** $40. **To apply online, go to:** https://inter-act.csc.wilkes.edu:4443/WILK/bwskalog.P_DispLoginNew. **Admissions requirements/recommendations:** High school units required (recommended): English: (4); Mathematics: (3); Science: (2); Social studies: (3). Tests: The college uses SAT or ACT scores in admissions decisions. Either SAT or ACT required. Campus visit: Recommended. Admissions interview: Recommended. Off-campus interview: May be arranged. **Factors that count in admissions decisions:** *Academic:* Secondary school record: Very Important. Class rank: Very Important. Letters of recommendation: Considered. Standardized test scores: Important. Essay: Not Considered. *Nonacademic:* Interview: Considered. Extracurricular activities: Important. Talent/ability: Considered. Character/personal qualities: Important. Alumni/ae relationship: Considered. Geographical residence: Not Considered. State residency: Not Considered. Religious affiliation/commitment: Not Considered. Minority status: Not Considered. Volunteer work: Considered. Work experience: Considered. **Other schools with the greatest overlap in applicants:** King's College; Pennsylvania State University–University Park; Temple University; University of Scranton; University of the Sciences in Philadelphia. **Admissions statistics for the fall 2009 entering class:** Total applicants: 2,641. Total accepted: 1,995. Freshmen enrolled: 532; 20% were from out of state. Overall acceptance rate: 76%. **Credentials of fall 2009 freshmen:** 25% ranked in the top 10 percent of their high school class; 53% were in the top 25 percent; 86% were in the top half. (Proportion submitting class standing: 82%.) **First-year students who submitted SAT scores:** 99%. Scores (25/75 percentile): Critical Reading: 460-580, Math: 480-600, Combined: 940-1180.

ACADEMICS

Year founded: 1933. **Academic calendar:** Semester. **Degrees offered:** bachelor's, master's, doctorate. **Most popular majors:** 15% business, management, marketing, and related support services, 11% health professions and related clinical sciences, 10% biological and biomedical sciences, 10% engineering, 9% psychology. **Major fields of study:** biological and biomedical sciences; business, management, marketing, and related support services; communication, journalism, and related programs; computer and information sciences and support services; education; engineering; engineering technologies/technicians; English language and literature/letters; foreign languages, literatures, and linguistics; health professions and related clinical sciences; history; liberal arts and sciences studies, and humanities; mathematics and statistics; multi/interdisciplinary studies; philosophy and religious studies; physical sciences; psychology; security and protective services; social sciences; visual and performing arts. **Areas of required coursework:** arts/fine arts, humanities, computer literacy, mathematics, English (including composition), sciences (biological or physical), social science. **Pre-professional programs:** pre-law, pre-dentistry, pre-medicine, pre-veterinary science, pre-optometry, pre-pharmacy. **Special academic programs:** cooperative (work-study plan) program, cross-registration, distance learning, double major, dual enrollment, English as a Second Language (ESL), external degree program, honors program, independent study, internships, student-designed major, study abroad, teacher certificate program, weekend college. **Teacher certification offered in:** early childhood, special education, elementary, middle/junior high, secondary, bilingual/bicultural. **Reserve Officers Training Corps (ROTC):** Army ROTC: Offered at cooperating institution (King's College); Air Force ROTC: Offered on campus. **Faculty and instruction (2009-2010):** Total instructional faculty: 149 full-time, 305 part-time (53% men; 47% women; 5% minorities). Full-time faculty with Ph.D. or other terminal degree: 89%. Student/faculty ratio: 15/1. Classes of fewer than 20 students: 52%; of 20 to 49 students: 43%; of 50 or more students: 5%. **Advanced Placement and International Baccalaureate credit:** AP tests may be used for: Credit and/or placement. Scores accepted: 3, 4, 5. International Baccalaureate exams may be used for: Placement only. **Freshmen returning for sophomore year:** 78%. **Graduation rates:** Four-year: 50%; five-year: 61%; six-year: 60%.

COSTS AND FINANCIAL AID

Financial aid office: (570) 408-4346. **Expenses (2010-2011):** Tuition and fees 2010-2011: $27,178; room/board: $11,470. Estimated books and supplies: $1,500; transportation: $1,000; personal expenses: $1,500. **Financial aid:** Priority filing date for institution's financial aid form: March 1. In 2009-2010, 90% of undergraduates applied for financial aid. Of those, 83% were determined to have financial need; 14% had their need fully met. Average financial aid package (proportion receiving): $20,291 (83%).

Average amount of gift aid, such as scholarships or grants (proportion receiving): $14,948 (80%). Average amount of self-help aid, such as work study or loans (proportion receiving): $5,739 (74%). Average need-based loan (excluding PLUS or other private loans): $4,433. Among students who received need-based aid, the average percentage of need met: 73%. Among students who received aid based on merit, the average award (and the proportion receiving): $9,743 (12%). The average athletic scholarship (and the proportion receiving): $0 (0%). Average amount of debt of borrowers graduating in 2009: $34,775. Proportion who borrowed: 87%.

CAMPUS LIFE AND EXTRACURRICULAR ACTIVITIES

Campus housing available: coed dorms, women's dorms, men's dorms, apartment for single students. Students who live in college-owned, operated, or affiliated housing: 40%. **Clubs and organizations:** Number of student organizations: 60. Activities include: campus ministries, choral groups, dance, drama/theater, international student organization, jazz band, literary magazine, music ensembles, musical theater, pep band, radio station, student government, student newspaper, television station, yearbook. Number of fraternities: 0; sororities: 0. Average proportion of students who stay on campus on weekends: 85%. **Sports program (2009-2010):** Member of NCAA III. **Men's intercollegiate varsity sports:** baseball, basketball, cross country, football, golf, soccer, tennis, wrestling. **Women's intercollegiate varsity sports:** basketball, cross country, field hockey, lacrosse, soccer, softball, tennis, volleyball.

SERVICES AND FACILITIES

Basic services: nonremedial tutoring, placement service, health service. **Remedial assistance:** reading, math, writing, study skills. **Counseling services:** minority student, career, military, personal, veteran student, academic, older student, psychological. **For learning-disabled students:** School does not offer a structured program with separate admission and additional fees. Services include: remedial math, remedial English, reading machines, remedial reading, tape recorders, diagnostic testing service, note-taking services, oral tests, learning center, readers, extended time for tests, tutors, priority registration, priority seating, texts on tape, other testing accommodations. **Library:** Number of titles: 178,863; number of current serial subscriptions: 474. **Information technology resources:** Students are not required to lease or own a computer. Number of campus computers available to all students: 600. School has a wireless network. Approximate number of users that can be accommodated: 6,500. Proportion of college-owned housing units wired for high-speed internet access: 100%. **Campus safety:** Security services offered: 24-hour foot-and-vehicle patrols, late-night transport/escort service, 24-hour emergency telephones, lighted pathways/sidewalks, controlled dormitory access (key, security card, etc.).

TRANSFER AND INTERNATIONAL STUDENTS

Transfer students: May apply for admission for the following academic terms: Fall, Spring, Summer. Applicants need a minimum number of credits to apply. For fall 2009: Transfer applications received: 397. Transfer applicants offered admission: 264. Transfer applicants enrolled: 122. **International students:** Number of foreign undergraduates: 50 (2% of student body). Minimum TOEFL score required: 500 (paper); 173 (computer).

Wilson College

- **Address:** 1015 Philadelphia Avenue, Chambersburg, PA 17201
- **Website:** http://www.wilson.edu
- **Private; Religious affiliation:** Presbyterian Church (USA)
- **Enrollment:** 375 full-time; 432 part-time

KEY STATS

✔ **U.S News College Ranking:** 15, Regional Colleges (North)
✔ **SAT Score (25th/75th percentile):** 860-1110
✔ **Tuition:** 2010-2011: $28,220

Selectivity: Selective	**Room/board:** $9,434
Acceptance rate: 70%	**Average debt:** $33,673
Student/faculty ratio: 10/1	**Proportion who borrowed:** 87%

UNDERGRADUATE STUDENT BODY STATS

2009-2010 enrollment: 375 full-time; 432 part-time. Men: 16%; women: 84%. **Ethnic makeup:** African American: 2%; American-Indian: 1%; Hispanic: 2%; White: 92%; International: 4%. **Religious preference:** Roman

Catholic: 2%; Protestant: 7%; Jewish: 1%; Muslim: 1%; No preference: 88%; Presbyterian Church (USA): 1%.

ADMISSIONS FACTS AND FIGURES

Phone: (800) 421-8402. **Email:** admissions@wilson.edu. **Website:** http://www.wilson.edu. **Application deadlines for fall 2011:** Regular decision: Rolling. Early decision: Not offered. Early action: Not offered. Admission can be deferred. **Application fee:** $35. **To apply online, go to:** http://www.wilson.edu/apply. **Admissions requirements/recommendations:** High school units required (recommended): English: 4 (4); Mathematics: 3 (3); Science: 3 (2); Foreign language: 2 (2); Social studies: (0); History: 3 (4); Total units: 15 (15). Tests: The college uses SAT or ACT scores in admissions decisions. Neither SAT nor ACT required. For admission to the fall 2011 entering class, the school will accept: ACT with or without writing accepted. Campus visit: Recommended. Admissions interview: Recommended. Off-campus interview: May be arranged. **Factors that count in admissions decisions:** *Academic:* Secondary school record: Very Important. Class rank: Important. Letters of recommendation: Very Important. Standardized test scores: Considered. Essay: Very Important. *Nonacademic:* Interview: Important. Extracurricular activities: Important. Talent/ability: Considered. Character/personal qualities: Important. Alumni/ae relationship: Considered. Geographical residence: Not Considered. State residency: Not Considered. Religious affiliation/commitment: Not Considered. Minority status: Not Considered. Volunteer work: Considered. Work experience: Not Considered. **Other schools with the greatest overlap in applicants:** Delaware Valley College; Lebanon Valley College; Pennsylvania State University–University Park; Shippensburg University of Pennsylvania. **Admissions statistics for the fall 2009 entering class:** Total applicants: 566. Total accepted: 394. Freshmen enrolled: 103; 47% were from out of state. Overall acceptance rate: 70%. **Credentials of fall 2009 freshmen:** 8% ranked in the top 10 percent of their high school class; 40% were in the top 25 percent; 73% were in the top half. (Proportion submitting class standing: 72%.) **Average high school grade point average:** 3.2. **First-year students who submitted SAT scores:** 79%. Scores (25/75 percentile): Critical Reading: 440-550, Math: 420-560, Combined: 860-1110. **First-year students submitting ACT scores:** 21%. Scores (25/75 percentile): English: N/A, Math: N/A, Composite: 16-21.

ACADEMICS

Year founded: 1869. **Academic calendar:** 4-1-4. **Degrees offered:** certificate, associate, bachelor's, master's. **Most popular majors:** 28% veterinary/animal health technology/technician and veterinary assistant, 18% elementary education and teaching, 13% equestrian/equine studies, 12% business administration and management, 10% social sciences. **Major fields of study:** agriculture, agriculture operations, and related sciences; biological and biomedical sciences; business, management, marketing, and related support services; communication, journalism, and related programs; education; English language and literature/letters; foreign languages, literatures, and linguistics; health professions and related clinical sciences; mathematics and statistics; multi/interdisciplinary studies; natural resources and conservation; parks, recreation, leisure, and fitness studies; philosophy and religious studies; physical sciences; psychology; social sciences; visual and performing arts. **Areas of required coursework:** arts/fine arts, humanities, computer literacy, mathematics, English (including composition), foreign languages, sciences (biological or physical), history, social science, other. **Pre-professional programs:** pre-law, pre-dentistry, pre-medicine, pre-veterinary science, pre-optometry, pre-pharmacy. **Special academic programs (% participation):** double major (13%), English as a Second Language (ESL) (2%), exchange student program (domestic) (6%), honors program (6%), independent study (16%), internships (20%), liberal arts/career combination (59%), student-designed major (8%), study abroad (0%), teacher certificate program (20%). **Teacher certification offered in:** elementary, secondary. **Reserve Officers Training Corps (ROTC):** Army ROTC: Offered at cooperating institution (Shippensburg University of Pennsylvania). **Faculty and instruction (2009-2010):** Total instructional faculty: 45 full-time, 35 part-time (40% men; 60% women; 5% minorities). Full-time faculty with Ph.D. or other terminal degree: 84%. Student/faculty ratio: 10/1. Classes of fewer than 20 students: 82%; of 20 to 49 students: 18%. **Advanced Placement and International Baccalaureate credit:** AP tests may be used for: Credit only. Scores accepted: 4, 5. International Baccalaureate exams may be used for: Credit and/or placement. **Freshmen returning for sophomore year:** 69%. **Graduation rates:** Four-year: 34%; five-year: 40%; six-year: 55%. **Graduate study:** 33% of students pursue further study immediately upon graduation. Fields in which graduates pursue further study: Master of Business Administration (MBA), 13%; law, 2%; medicine, 2%; theology (or the seminary), 2%; education, 13%; arts and sciences, 46%; veterinary medicine, 20%.

COSTS AND FINANCIAL AID

Financial aid office: (717) 262-2016. **Expenses (2010-2011):** Tuition and fees 2010-2011: $28,220; room/board: $9,434. Estimated books and supplies: $1,000; transportation: $400; personal expenses: $800. **Financial aid:** Priority filing date for institution's financial aid form: April 30. In 2009-2010, 91% of undergraduates applied for financial aid. Of those, 84% were determined to have financial need; 18% had their need fully met. Average financial aid package (proportion receiving): $22,148 (84%). Average amount of gift aid, such as scholarships or grants (proportion receiving): $18,314 (83%). Average amount of self-help aid, such as work study or loans (proportion receiving): $4,861 (69%). Average need-based loan (excluding PLUS or other private loans): $4,344. Among students who received need-based aid, the average percentage of need met: 78%. Among students who received aid based on merit, the average award (and the proportion receiving): $12,357 (14%). The average athletic scholarship (and the proportion receiving): $0 (0%). Average amount of debt of borrowers graduating in 2009: $33,673. Proportion who borrowed: 87%.

CAMPUS LIFE AND EXTRACURRICULAR ACTIVITIES

Campus housing available (% using): women's dorms (78%), other housing options (12%). Students who live in college-owned, operated, or affiliated housing: 48%. **Student employment:** During the 2009-2010 academic year, 5% of undergraduates worked on campus. Average per-year earnings: $2,250. **Clubs and organizations:** Number of student organizations: 47. Activities include: choral groups, dance, drama/theater, international student organization, literary magazine, model UN, music ensembles, student government, student newspaper, yearbook. Number of fraternities: 0; sororities: 0. Average proportion of students who stay on campus on weekends: 30%. **Sports program (2009-2010):** Member of NCAA III. *Women's intercollegiate varsity sports:* basketball, field hockey, gymnastics, lacrosse, soccer, softball, tennis.

SERVICES AND FACILITIES

Basic services: nonremedial tutoring, women's center, placement service, day care, health service, health insurance, other. **Remedial assistance:** math, writing, study skills. **Counseling services:** minority student, career, personal, veteran student, academic, older student, psychological, birth control, religious. **For learning-disabled students:** School does not offer a structured program with separate admission and additional fees. Total undergraduates in learning-disabled program or receiving services: 12. Services include: remedial math, reading machines, tape recorders, untimed tests, note-taking services, oral tests, learning center, readers, extended time for tests, tutors, priority seating, substitution of courses, texts on tape, typist/scribe, exams on tape or computer, other testing accommodations, waiver of foreign language degree requirement. **Library:** Number of titles: 184,964; number of current serial subscriptions: 3,739. **Information technology resources:** Students are not required to lease or own a computer. Number of campus computers available to all students: 112. School has a wireless network. Approximate number of users that can be accommodated: 200. Proportion of college-owned housing units wired for high-speed internet access: 100%. **Campus safety:** Security services offered: 24-hour foot-and-vehicle patrols, late-night transport/escort service, 24-hour emergency telephones, lighted pathways/sidewalks, controlled dormitory access (key, security card, etc).

TRANSFER AND INTERNATIONAL STUDENTS

Transfer students: May apply for admission for the following academic terms: Fall, Spring. Applicants do not need a minimum number of credits to apply. For fall 2009: Transfer applications received: 74. Transfer applicants offered admission: 31. Transfer applicants enrolled: 25. **International students:** Number of foreign undergraduates: 22 (4% of student body). Number of countries represented: 21. Minimum TOEFL score required: 500 (paper); 173 (computer). Average TOEFL score: 551 (paper).

York College of Pennsylvania

- **Address:** Country Club Road, York, PA 17405-7199
- **Website:** http://www.ycp.edu
- **Private**
- **Enrollment:** 4,596 full-time; 685 part-time

KEY STATS

✔ **U.S News College Ranking:** 13, Regional Colleges (North)

✔ **SAT Score (25th/75th percentile):** 1000-1170

✔ **Tuition:** 2010-2011: $15,140

Selectivity: Selective	**Room/board:** $8,530
Acceptance rate: 56%	**Average debt:** $27,583
Student/faculty ratio: 17/1	**Proportion who borrowed:** 75%

UNDERGRADUATE STUDENT BODY STATS

2009-2010 enrollment: 4,596 full-time; 685 part-time. Men: 45%; women: 55%. **Ethnic makeup:** African American: 3%; Asian American: 1%; Hispanic: 1%; White: 93%. **Religious preference:** Roman Catholic: 21%; Protestant: 23%; Jewish: 1%; Unknown: 42%; Other: 13%.

ADMISSIONS FACTS AND FIGURES

Phone: (717) 849-1600. **Email:** admissions@ycp.edu. **Website:** http://www.ycp.edu. **Application deadlines for fall 2011:** Regular decision: Rolling. Early decision: Not offered. Early action: Not offered. Admission can be deferred. **Application fee:** $30. **To apply online, go to:** http://www.ycp.edu/admissions/370.htm. **Admissions requirements/recommendations:** High school units required (recommended): English: 4; Mathematics: 3 (4); Science: 3; Foreign language: 2; Social studies: 3; Total units: 15. Tests: The college uses SAT or ACT scores in admissions decisions. Either SAT or ACT required. For admission to the fall 2011 entering class, the school will accept: ACT with writing required. Campus visit: Recommended. Admissions interview: Recommended. Off-campus interview: May be arranged. **Factors that count in admissions decisions:** *Academic:* Secondary school record: Very Important. Class rank: Important. Letters of recommendation: Considered. Standardized test scores: Important. Essay: Considered. *Nonacademic:* Interview: Considered. Extracurricular activities: Considered. Talent/ability: Considered. Character/personal qualities: Important. Alumni/ae relationship: Considered. Geographical residence: Not Considered. State residency: Not Considered. Religious affiliation/commitment: Not Considered. Minority status: Not Considered. Volunteer work: Considered. Work experience: Considered. **Other schools with the greatest overlap in applicants:** Millersville University of Pennsylvania; Pennsylvania State University–University Park; Towson University; University of Delaware; West Chester University of Pennsylvania. **Admissions statistics for the fall 2009 entering class:** Total applicants: 11,048. Total accepted: 6,197. Freshmen enrolled: 1,102; 45% were from out of state. Overall acceptance rate: 56%. **Credentials of fall 2009 freshmen:** 13% ranked in the top 10 percent of their high school class; 41% were in the top 25 percent; 77% were in the top half. (Proportion submitting class standing: 74%.) **Average high school grade point average:** 3.5. **First-year students who submitted SAT scores:** 78%. Scores (25/75 percentile): Critical Reading: 510-600, Math: 490-570, Combined: 1000-1170. **First-year students submitting ACT scores:** 17%. Scores (25/75 percentile): English: 19-24, Math: 18-25, Composite: 20-24.

ACADEMICS

Year founded: 1787. **Academic calendar:** Semester. **Degrees offered:** associate, bachelor's, master's. **Most popular majors:** 20% business, management, marketing, and related support services, 13% health professions and related clinical sciences, 12% education, 9% security and protective services, 7% communication, journalism, and related programs. **Major fields of study:** biological and biomedical sciences; business, management, marketing, and related support services; communication, journalism, and related programs; communications technologies/technicians and support services; computer and information sciences and support services; education; engineering; engineering technologies/technicians; English language and literature/letters; foreign languages, literatures, and linguistics; health professions and related clinical sciences; history; legal professions and studies; liberal arts and sciences studies, and humanities; mathematics and statistics; multi/interdisciplinary studies; parks, recreation, leisure, and fitness studies; physical sciences; psychology; public administration and social service professions; security and protective services; social sciences; visual and performing arts. **Areas of required coursework:** arts/fine arts, humanities, computer literacy, mathematics, English (including composition), sciences (biological or physical), history, social science. **Pre-professional programs:** pre-law, pre-medicine. **Special academic programs:** cooperative (work-study plan) program, double major, dual enrollment, honors program, independent study, internships, liberal arts/career combination, student-designed major, study abroad, teacher certificate program. **Teacher certification offered in:** early childhood, special education, elementary, middle/junior high, secondary. **Cooperative education programs:** education, engineering, health professions. **Reserve Officers Training Corps (ROTC):** Army ROTC: Offered at cooperating institution (Dickinson College). **Faculty and instruction (2009-2010):** Total instructional faculty: 156 full-time, 400 part-time (49% men; 51% women; 0% minorities). Full-time faculty with Ph.D. or other terminal degree: 87%. Student/faculty ratio: 17/1. Classes of fewer than 20 students: 47%; of 20 to 49 students: 52%; of 50 or more students: 1%. **Advanced Placement and International Baccalaureate credit:** AP tests may be used for: Credit only. Scores accepted: 3, 4, 5. International Baccalaureate exams may be used for: Credit only. **Freshmen returning for sophomore year:** 78%. **Graduation rates:** Four-year: 42%; five-year: 61%; six-year: 59%.

COSTS AND FINANCIAL AID

Financial aid office: (717) 849-1682. **Expenses (2010-2011):** Tuition and fees 2010-2011: $15,140; room/board: $8,530. Estimated books and supplies: $1,200; transportation: $800; personal expenses: $1,000. **Financial aid:** In 2009-2010, 82% of undergraduates applied for financial aid. Of those, 61% were determined to have financial need; 25% had their need fully met. Average financial aid package (proportion receiving): $10,915 (61%). Average amount of gift aid, such as scholarships or grants (proportion receiving): $5,383 (44%). Average amount of self-help aid, such as work study or loans (proportion receiving): $6,192 (57%). Average need-based loan (excluding PLUS or other private loans): $5,961. Among students who received need-based aid, the average percentage of need met: 70%. Among students who received aid based on merit, the average award (and the proportion receiving): $3,717 (11%). The average athletic scholarship (and the proportion receiving): $0 (0%). Average amount of debt of borrowers graduating in 2009: $27,583. Proportion who borrowed: 75%.

CAMPUS LIFE AND EXTRACURRICULAR ACTIVITIES

Campus housing available (% using): coed dorms (42%), women's dorms (2%), sorority housing (2%), apartment for single students (54%). Students who live in college-owned, operated, or affiliated housing: 45%. **Student employment:** During the 2009-2010 academic year, 27% of undergraduates worked on campus. Average per-year earnings: $3,262. **Clubs and organizations:** Number of student organizations: 85. Activities include: campus ministries, choral groups, concert band, dance, drama/theater, international student organization, jazz band, literary magazine, model UN, music ensembles, musical theater, radio station, student government, student newspaper, symphony orchestra, television station. Number of fraternities: 8; sororities: 6. Proportion of men in fraternities: 7%; of women in sororities: 7%. Average proportion of students who stay on campus on weekends: 70%. **Sports program (2009-2010):** Member of NCAA III. *Men's intercollegiate varsity sports:* baseball, basketball, cross country, golf, lacrosse, soccer, swimming, tennis, track and field (outdoor), wrestling. *Women's intercollegiate varsity sports:* basketball, cross country, field hockey, lacrosse, soccer, softball, swimming, tennis, track and field (outdoor), volleyball.

SERVICES AND FACILITIES

Basic services: nonremedial tutoring, placement service, health service, health insurance. **Counseling services:** minority student, career, personal, veteran student, academic, older student, psychological, birth control, religious. **For learning-disabled students:** School does not offer a structured program with separate admission and additional fees. Total undergraduates in learning-disabled program or receiving services: 40. Services include: remedial math, remedial English, reading machines, remedial reading, other special classes, untimed tests, oral tests, learning center, readers, extended time for tests, tutors, priority registration, priority seating, proofreading services, texts on tape, typist/scribe, exams on tape or computer, other testing accommodations, waiver of foreign language degree requirement. **Library:** Number of titles: 250,642; number of current serial subscriptions: 31,713. **Information technology resources:** Students are not required to lease or own a computer. Number of campus computers available to all students: 650. School has a wireless network. Approximate number of users that can be accommodated: 3,750. Proportion of college-owned housing units wired for high-speed internet access: 100%. **Campus safety:** Security services offered: 24-hour foot-and-vehicle patrols, late-night transport/escort service, 24-hour emergency telephones, lighted pathways/sidewalks, student patrols, controlled dormitory access (key, security card, etc).

TRANSFER AND INTERNATIONAL STUDENTS

Transfer students: May apply for admission for the following academic terms: Fall, Spring. Applicants do not need a minimum number of credits to apply. For fall 2009: Transfer applications received: 924. Transfer applicants offered admission: 500. Transfer applicants enrolled: 282.

International students: Number of foreign undergraduates: 20. Number of countries represented: 17. Minimum TOEFL score required: 530 (paper); 200 (computer). Average TOEFL score: 600 (paper).

Rhode Island

Brown University

- **Address:** Box 1920, Providence, RI 02912
- **Website:** http://www.brown.edu
- **Private**
- **Enrollment:** 6,002 full-time; 242 part-time

KEY STATS

✔ **U.S News College Ranking:** 15, National Universities
✔ **SAT Score (25th/75th percentile):** 1320-1530
✔ **Tuition:** 2010-2011: $40,820

Selectivity: Most selective   **Room/board:** $10,540
Acceptance rate: 11%   **Average debt:** $21,858
Student/faculty ratio: 9/1   **Proportion who borrowed:** 41%

UNDERGRADUATE STUDENT BODY STATS

2009-2010 enrollment: 6,002 full-time; 242 part-time. Men: 47%; women: 53%. **Ethnic makeup:** African American: 7%; American-Indian: 1%; Asian American: 16%; Hispanic: 9%; White: 59%; International: 9%. **Religious preference:** Roman Catholic: 16%; Protestant: 21%; Jewish: 14%; Muslim: 1%; Hindu: 2%; Buddhist: 1%; No preference: 17%; Unknown: 26%; Orthodox: 1%; Other: 1%.

ADMISSIONS FACTS AND FIGURES

Phone: (401) 863-2378. **Email:** admission_undergraduate@brown.edu. **Website:** http://www.brown.edu. **Application deadlines for fall 2011:** Regular decision: January 1; decision sent by April 1. Early decision: Send application by: November 1; Decision sent by: December 15. Early action: Not offered. Admission can be deferred. **Application fee:** $75. **To apply online, go to:** http://www.brown.edu/Admission. **Admissions requirements/recommendations:** High school units required (recommended): English: 4 (4); Mathematics: 3 (4); Science: 3 (4); Foreign language: 3 (4); History: 2 (2); Academic electives: 1 (1); Total units: 16 (20). Tests: The college uses SAT or ACT scores in admissions decisions. Either SAT or ACT required. For admission to the fall 2011 entering class, the school will accept: ACT with writing required. Campus visit: Recommended. Admissions interview: Neither required nor recommended. Off-campus interview: May be arranged. **Factors that count in admissions decisions:** *Academic:* Secondary school record: Very Important. Class rank: Important. Letters of recommendation: Important. Standardized test scores: Important. Essay: Important. *Nonacademic:* Interview: Considered. Extracurricular activities: Important. Talent/ability: Very Important. Character/personal qualities: Very Important. Alumni/ae relationship: Considered. Geographical residence: Considered. State residency: Considered. Religious affiliation/commitment: Not Considered. Minority status: Considered. Volunteer work: Considered. Work experience: Considered. **Other schools with the greatest overlap in applicants:** Cornell University; Harvard University; Princeton University; Stanford University; Yale University. **Admissions statistics for the fall 2009 entering class:** Total applicants: 24,988. Total accepted: 2,790. Freshmen enrolled: 1,494; 95% were from out of state. Overall acceptance rate: 11%. Early-decision acceptance rate: 24%. Non-early acceptance rate: 10%. **Size of waiting list:** 1500 applicants; enrolled from waiting list: 82. **Credentials of fall 2009 freshmen:** 92% ranked in the top 10 percent of their high school class; 99% were in the top 25 percent; 100% were in the top half. (Proportion submitting class standing: 36%.) **First-year students who submitted SAT scores:** 89%. Scores (25/75 percentile): Critical Reading: 650-760, Math: 670-770, Combined: 1320-1530. **First-year students submitting ACT scores:** 33%. Scores (25/75 percentile): English: 29-35, Math: 28-34, Composite: 29-34.

ACADEMICS

Year founded: 1764. **Academic calendar:** Semester. **Degrees offered:** bachelor's, master's, doctorate. **Most popular majors:** 9% biology, 9% economics, 6% international relations and affairs, 5% entrepreneurial and small business operations, 5% history. **Major fields of study:** architecture and related services; area, ethnic, cultural, and gender studies; biological and biomedical sciences; business, management, marketing, and related support services; communication, journalism, and related programs; computer and information sciences and support services; education; engineering; English language and literature/letters; foreign languages, literatures, and linguistics; health professions and related clinical sciences; history; mathematics and statistics; multi/interdisciplinary studies; natural resources and conservation; philosophy and religious studies; physical sciences; psychology; public administration and social service professions; social sciences; visual and performing arts. **Areas of required coursework:** English (including composition). **Pre-professional programs:** pre-medicine. **Special academic programs (% participation):** cross-registration (9%), double major (21%), exchange student program (domestic) (1%), honors program (30%), independent study (56%), internships, student-designed major (.4%), study abroad (36%), teacher certificate program (.1%). **Teacher certification offered in:** elementary, middle/junior high, secondary. **Reserve Officers Training Corps (ROTC):** Army ROTC: Offered at cooperating institution (Providence College). **Faculty and instruction (2009-2010):** Total instructional faculty: 792 full-time, 184 part-time (63% men; 37% women; 16% minorities). Full-time faculty with Ph.D. or other terminal degree: 94%. Student/faculty ratio: 9/1. Classes of fewer than 20 students: 70%; of 20 to 49 students: 20%; of 50 or more students: 10%. **Advanced Placement and International Baccalaureate credit:** AP tests may be used for: Credit and/or placement. Scores accepted: 4, 5. International Baccalaureate exams may be used for: Placement only. **Freshmen returning for sophomore year:** 97%. **Graduation rates:** Four-year: 86%; five-year: 94%; six-year: 95%. **Graduate study:** 30% of students pursue further study immediately upon graduation.

COSTS AND FINANCIAL AID

Financial aid office: (401) 863-2721. **Expenses (2010-2011):** Tuition and fees 2010-2011: $40,820; room/board: $10,540. Estimated books and supplies: $1,310; transportation: $440; personal expenses: $1,700. **Financial aid:** Priority filing date for institution's financial aid form: February 1; deadline: February 1. In 2009-2010, 52% of undergraduates applied for financial aid. Of those, 44% were determined to have financial need; 100% had their need fully met. Average financial aid package (proportion receiving): $34,586 (44%). Average amount of gift aid, such as scholarships or grants (proportion receiving): $31,474 (39%). Average amount of self-help aid, such as work study or loans (proportion receiving): $4,735 (39%). Average need-based loan (excluding PLUS or other private loans): $5,208. Among students who received need-based aid, the average percentage of need met: 100%. Among students who received aid based on merit, the average award (and the proportion receiving): $14,000 (0%). The average athletic scholarship (and the proportion receiving): $0 (0%). Average amount of debt of borrowers graduating in 2009: $21,858. Proportion who borrowed: 41%.

CAMPUS LIFE AND EXTRACURRICULAR ACTIVITIES

Campus housing available (% using): coed dorms (84%), sorority housing (1%), fraternity housing (5%), apartment for single students (9%), special housing for disabled students (1%), cooperative housing. Students who live in college-owned, operated, or affiliated housing: 79%. **Student employment:** During the 2009-2010 academic year, 14% of undergraduates worked on campus. Average per-year earnings: $1,049. **Clubs and organizations:** Number of student organizations: 400. Activities include: campus ministries, choral groups, concert band, dance, drama/theater, international student organization, jazz band, literary magazine, marching band, model UN, music ensembles, musical theater, opera, pep band, radio station, student government, student newspaper, student film society, symphony orchestra, television station, yearbook. Number of fraternities: 10; sororities: 5. Proportion of men in fraternities: 12%; of women in sororities: 4%. Average proportion of students who stay on campus on weekends: 85%. **Sports program (2009-2010):** Member of NCAA I. *Men's intercollegiate varsity sports:* baseball, basketball, cross country, fencing, football, golf, ice hockey, lacrosse, soccer, swimming, tennis, track and field (indoor), track and field (outdoor), water polo, wrestling. *Women's intercollegiate varsity sports:* basketball, crew (heavyweight), cross country, equestrian, fencing, field hockey, golf, gymnastics, ice hockey, lacrosse, skiing (alpine), soccer, softball, squash, swimming, tennis, track and field (indoor), track and field (outdoor), volleyball, water polo.

SERVICES AND FACILITIES

Basic services: nonremedial tutoring, women's center, placement service, health service, health insurance. **Remedial assistance:** math, writing, study skills. **Counseling services:** minority student, career, personal, academic, older student, psychological, birth control, religious. **For learning-disabled students:** School does not offer a structured program with separate admission and additional fees. Services include: reading machines, tape recorders, note-taking services, learning center, readers, extended time for tests, tutors, priority seating, texts on tape, exams on tape or computer, other testing accommodations, other. **Library:** Number of titles: 3,936,274; number of current serial subscriptions: 65,908. **Information technology resources:** Students are not required to lease or own a computer. Number of campus computers available to all students: 350. School has a wireless network. Approximate number of users that can be accommodated: 14,000. Proportion of college-owned housing units wired for high-speed internet access: 100%. **Campus safety:** Security services offered: 24-hour foot-and-vehicle patrols, late-night transport/escort service, 24-hour emergency telephones, lighted pathways/sidewalks, student patrols, controlled dormitory access (key, security card, etc.).

TRANSFER AND INTERNATIONAL STUDENTS

Transfer students: May apply for admission for the following academic terms: Fall, Spring. Applicants need a minimum number of credits to apply. For fall 2009: Transfer applications received: 1,468. Transfer applicants offered admission: 121. Transfer applicants enrolled: 87. **International students:** Number of foreign undergraduates: 536 (9% of student body). Number of countries represented: 72. Minimum TOEFL score required: 600 (paper); 250 (computer).

Bryant University

- **Address:** 1150 Douglas Pike, Smithfield, RI 02917
- **Website:** http://www.bryant.edu
- **Private**
- **Enrollment:** 3,254 full-time; 132 part-time

KEY STATS

✔ **U.S News College Ranking:** 16, Regional Universities (North)
✔ **SAT Score (25th/75th percentile):** 1060-1220
✔ **Tuition:** 2010-2011: $33,357

Selectivity: Selective	**Room/board:** $12,215
Acceptance rate: 53%	**Average debt:** $38,270
Student/faculty ratio: 18/1	**Proportion who borrowed:** 75%

UNDERGRADUATE STUDENT BODY STATS

2009-2010 enrollment: 3,254 full-time; 132 part-time. Men: 57%; women: 43%. **Ethnic makeup:** African American: 4%; Asian American: 3%; Hispanic: 4%; White: 84%; International: 5%.

ADMISSIONS FACTS AND FIGURES

Phone: (800) 622-7001. **Email:** admission@bryant.edu. **Website:** http://www.bryant.edu. **Application deadlines for fall 2011:** Regular decision: February 1; decision sent by March 21. Early decision: Send application by: November 16; Decision sent by: December 16. Early action: Send application by: December 1; Decision sent by: January 15. Admission can be deferred. **Application fee:** $50. **To apply online, go to:** http://admission.bryant.edu/admissions/application/apply.asp. **Admissions requirements/recommendations:** High school units required (recommended): English: 4 (4); Mathematics: 4 (4); Science: 2 (3); Foreign language: 2 (2); History: 2 (3); Total units: 16 (18). Tests: The college uses SAT or ACT scores in admissions decisions. Either SAT or ACT required. For admission to the fall 2011 entering class, the school will accept: ACT with or without writing accepted. Campus visit: Recommended. Admissions interview: Neither required nor recommended. Off-campus interview: May be arranged. **Factors that count in admissions decisions:** *Academic:* Secondary school record: Very Important. Class rank: Important. Letters of recommendation: Important. Standardized test scores: Important. Essay: Important. *Nonacademic:* Interview: Considered. Extracurricular activities: Considered. Talent/ability: Considered. Character/personal qualities: Considered. Alumni/ae relationship: Considered. Geographical residence: Considered. State residency: Considered. Religious affiliation/commitment: Not Considered. Minority status: Considered. Volunteer work: Considered. Work experience: Considered. **Other schools with the greatest overlap in applicants:** Bentley University; Northeastern University; Providence College; Quinnipiac University; University of Connecticut. **Admissions statistics for the fall 2009 entering class:** Total applicants: 5,393. Total accepted: 2,870. Freshmen enrolled: 751; 87% were from out of state. Accepted through early-decision or early-action plans: 25%. Overall acceptance rate: 53%. Early-decision acceptance rate: 71%. Non-early acceptance rate: 52%. **Size of waiting list:** 1189 applicants; enrolled from waiting list: 125. **Credentials of fall 2009 freshmen:** 25% ranked in the top 10 percent of their high school class; 58% were in the top 25 percent; 93% were in the top half. (Proportion submitting class standing: 53%.) **Average high school grade point average:** 3.4. **First-year students who submitted SAT scores:** 99%. Scores (25/75 percentile): Critical Reading: 510-590, Math: 550-630, Combined: 1060-1220. **First-year students submitting ACT scores:** 22%. Scores (25/75 percentile): English: N/A, Math: N/A, Composite: 23-27.

ACADEMICS

Year founded: 1863. **Academic calendar:** Semester. **Degrees offered:** bachelor's, master's. **Most popular majors:** 84% business, management, marketing, and related support services, 5% communication, journalism, and related programs, 4% mathematics and statistics, 2% computer and information sciences and support services, 2% psychology. **Major fields of study:** business, management, marketing, and related support services; communication, journalism, and related programs; computer and information sciences and support services; English language and literature/letters; history; liberal arts and sciences studies, and humanities; mathematics and statistics; multi/interdisciplinary studies; psychology; social sciences. **Areas of required coursework:** humanities, computer literacy, mathematics, English (including composition), sciences (biological or physical), history, social science, other. **Pre-professional programs:** pre-law, other. **Special academic programs:** double major, English as a Second Language (ESL), honors program, independent study, internships, study abroad. **Reserve Officers Training Corps (ROTC):** Army ROTC: Offered on campus. **Faculty and instruction (2009-2010):** Total instructional faculty: 158 full-time, 98 part-time (60% men; 40% women; 11% minorities). Full-time faculty with Ph.D. or other terminal degree: 85%. Student/faculty ratio: 18/1. Classes of fewer than 20 students: 25%; of 20 to 49 students: 75%. **Advanced Placement and International Baccalaureate credit:** AP tests may be used for: Credit and/or placement. Scores accepted: 3, 4, 5. International Baccalaureate exams may be used for: Placement only. **Freshmen returning for sophomore year:** 88%. **Graduation rates:** Four-year: 62%; five-year: 68%; six-year: 70%. **Graduate study:** 5% of students pursue further study immediately upon graduation. Fields in which graduates pursue further study: Master of Business Administration (MBA), 62%; law, 14%; education, 6%; arts and sciences, 18%.

COSTS AND FINANCIAL AID

Financial aid office: (401) 232-6020. **Expenses (2010-2011):** Tuition and fees 2010-2011: $33,357; room/board: $12,215. Estimated books and supplies: $1,300; transportation: $400; personal expenses: $1,000. **Financial aid:** Priority filing date for institution's financial aid form: February 15; deadline: February 15. In 2009-2010, 76% of undergraduates applied for financial aid. Of those, 67% were determined to have financial need; 66% had their need fully met. Average financial aid package (proportion receiving): $20,116 (67%). Average amount of gift aid, such as scholarships or grants (proportion receiving): $12,555 (57%). Average amount of self-help aid, such as work study or loans (proportion receiving): $5,645 (60%). Average need-based loan (excluding PLUS or other private loans): $4,521. Among students who received need-based aid, the average percentage of need met: 66%. Among students who received aid based on merit, the average award (and the proportion receiving): $12,455 (12%). The average athletic scholarship (and the proportion receiving): $12,023 (5%). Average amount of debt of borrowers graduating in 2009: $38,270. Proportion who borrowed: 75%.

CAMPUS LIFE AND EXTRACURRICULAR ACTIVITIES

Campus housing available (% using): coed dorms (78%), women's dorms (3%), apartment for single students (19%), special housing for disabled students (0%), other housing options. Students who live in college-owned, operated, or affiliated housing: 83%. **Clubs and organizations:** Number of student organizations: 88. Activities include: campus ministries, choral groups, dance, drama/theater, international student organization, jazz band, literary magazine, music ensembles, musical theater, pep band, radio station, student government, student newspaper, television station, yearbook. Number of fraternities: 6; sororities: 3. Proportion of men in fraternities: 5%; of women in sororities: 6%. Average proportion of students who stay on campus on weekends: 80%. **Sports program (2009-2010):** Member of NCAA II. *Men's intercollegiate varsity sports:* baseball, basketball, cross country, football, golf, lacrosse, soccer, swimming, tennis, track and field (indoor), track and field (outdoor). *Women's intercollegiate varsity sports:* basketball, cross country, field hockey, lacrosse, soccer, softball, swimming, tennis, track and field (indoor), track and field (outdoor), volleyball.

SERVICES AND FACILITIES
Basic services: nonremedial tutoring, women's center, placement service, health service, health insurance. **Counseling services:** minority student, career, personal, academic, older student, psychological, birth control, religious. **For learning-disabled students:** School does not offer a structured program with separate admission and additional fees. Services include: reading machines, learning center, extended time for tests. **Library:** Number of titles: 145,199; number of current serial subscriptions: 1,184. **Information technology resources:** Students are required to lease or own a computer. Number of campus computers available to all students: 478. School has a wireless network. Approximate number of users that can be accommodated: 12,500. Proportion of college-owned housing units wired for high-speed internet access: 100%. **Campus safety:** Security services offered: 24-hour foot-and-vehicle patrols, late-night transport/escort service, 24-hour emergency telephones, lighted pathways/sidewalks, controlled dormitory access (key, security card, etc).

TRANSFER AND INTERNATIONAL STUDENTS
Transfer students: May apply for admission for the following academic terms: Fall, Spring. Applicants need a minimum number of credits to apply. For fall 2009: Transfer applications received: 323. Transfer applicants offered admission: 230. Transfer applicants enrolled: 113. **International students:** Number of foreign undergraduates: 165 (5% of student body). Number of countries represented: 45. Minimum TOEFL score required: 550 (paper); 80 (computer). Average TOEFL score: 584 (paper).

Johnson and Wales University

- **Address:** 8 Abbott Park Place, Providence, RI 02903-3703
- **Website:** http://www.jwu.edu
- **Private**
- **Enrollment:** 8,707 full-time; 788 part-time

KEY STATS
✔ **U.S News College Ranking:** 84, Regional Universities (North)
✔ **SAT Score (25th/75th percentile):** 840-1060
✔ **Tuition:** 2010-2011: $24,141

Selectivity: Less selective	**Room/board:** $8,904
Acceptance rate: 72%	**Average debt:** N/A
Student/faculty ratio: 31/1	**Proportion who borrowed:** 83%

UNDERGRADUATE STUDENT BODY STATS
2009-2010 enrollment: 8,707 full-time; 788 part-time. Men: 46%; women: 54%. **Ethnic makeup:** African American: 7%; Asian American: 2%; Hispanic: 6%; White: 76%; International: 8%.

ADMISSIONS FACTS AND FIGURES
Phone: (800) 342-5598. **Email:** admissions.pvd@jwu.edu. **Website:** http://www.jwu.edu. **Application deadlines for fall 2011:** Regular decision: Rolling. Early decision: Not offered. Early action: Not offered. Admission can be deferred. **Application fee:** None. **To apply online, go to:** http://www.jwu.edu/apply/. **Admissions requirements/recommendations:** High school units required (recommended): English: 4; Mathematics: 3; Science: 3; Social studies: 2. **Tests:** The college uses SAT or ACT scores in admissions decisions. Neither SAT nor ACT required. For admission to the fall 2011 entering class, the school will accept: ACT with or without writing accepted. Campus visit: Recommended. Admissions interview: Recommended. Off-campus interview: May be arranged. **Factors that count in admissions decisions:** *Academic:* Secondary school record: Very Important. Class rank: Very Important. Letters of recommendation: Considered. Standardized test scores: Considered. Essay: Important. *Nonacademic:* Interview: Important. Extracurricular activities: Important. Talent/ability: Not Considered. Character/personal qualities: Not Considered. Alumni/ae relationship: Considered. Geographical residence: Not Considered. State residency: Not Considered. Religious affiliation/commitment: Not Considered. Minority status: Not Considered. Volunteer work: Considered. Work experience: Important. **Admissions statistics for the fall 2009 entering class:** Total applicants: 14,072. Total accepted: 10,076. Freshmen enrolled: 2,299; 89%

were from out of state. Overall acceptance rate: 72%. **Credentials of fall 2009 freshmen:** 3% ranked in the top 10 percent of their high school class; 26% were in the top 25 percent. **First-year students who submitted SAT scores:** 40%. Scores (25/75 percentile): Critical Reading: 420-520, Math: 420-540, Combined: 840-1060.

ACADEMICS
Year founded: 1914. **Academic calendar:** Quarter. **Degrees offered:** certificate, associate, bachelor's, master's, post-master's certificate. **Major fields of study:** agriculture, agriculture operations, and related sciences; business, management, marketing, and related support services; communication, journalism, and related programs; computer and information sciences and support services; education; engineering; engineering technologies/technicians; family and consumer sciences/human sciences; health professions and related clinical sciences; legal professions and studies; parks, recreation, leisure, and fitness studies; personal and culinary services; security and protective services. **Areas of required coursework:** computer literacy, mathematics, English (including composition), philosophy, sciences (biological or physical), history, social science. **Pre-professional programs:** other. **Special academic programs:** accelerated program, cooperative (work-study plan) program, dual enrollment, English as a Second Language (ESL), exchange student program (domestic), honors program, independent study, internships, study abroad. **Cooperative education programs:** business, computer science, technologies, other. **Reserve Officers Training Corps (ROTC):** Army ROTC: Offered on campus. **Faculty and instruction (2009-2010):** Total instructional faculty: 292 full-time, 182 part-time (57% men; 43% women). Student/faculty ratio: 31/1. Classes of fewer than 20 students: 45%; of 20 to 49 students: 55%; of 50 or more students: 0%. **Advanced Placement and International Baccalaureate credit:** AP tests may be used for: Credit only. Scores accepted: 3, 4, 5. International Baccalaureate exams may be used for: Credit only. **Freshmen returning for sophomore year:** 71%. **Graduation rates:** Four-year: 43%; five-year: 52%; six-year: 54%.

COSTS AND FINANCIAL AID
Financial aid office: (401) 598-1468. **Expenses (2010-2011):** Tuition and fees 2010-2011: $24,141; room/board: $8,904. Estimated books and supplies: $1,500; transportation: $750. **Financial aid:** Priority filing date for institution's financial aid form: March 1. In 2009-2010, 77% of undergraduates applied for financial aid. Of those, 68% were determined to have financial need; 12% had their need fully met. Average financial aid package (proportion receiving): $15,772 (68%). Average amount of gift aid, such as scholarships or grants (proportion receiving): $7,226 (58%). Average amount of self-help aid, such as work study or loans (proportion receiving): $6,093 (62%). Average need-based loan (excluding PLUS or other private loans): $5,297. Among students who received need-based aid, the average percentage of need met: 68%. Among students who received aid based on merit, the average award (and the proportion receiving): $4,618 (17%). The average athletic scholarship (and the proportion receiving): $0 (0%). Proportion who borrowed: 83%.

CAMPUS LIFE AND EXTRACURRICULAR ACTIVITIES
Campus housing available: coed dorms, special housing for international students. Students who live in college-owned, operated, or affiliated housing: 40%. **Student employment:** During the 2009-2010 academic year, 10% of undergraduates worked on campus. Average per-year earnings: $5,000. **Clubs and organizations:** Number of student organizations: 70. Activities include: campus ministries, international student organization, student government, student newspaper, yearbook. Number of fraternities: 7; sororities: 7. **Sports program (2009-2010):** Member of NCAA III. *Men's intercollegiate varsity sports:* baseball, basketball, cross country, golf, ice hockey, soccer, tennis, volleyball, wrestling. *Women's intercollegiate varsity sports:* basketball, cross country, equestrian, soccer, softball, tennis, volleyball.

SERVICES AND FACILITIES
Basic services: nonremedial tutoring, women's center, placement service, health service, health insurance. **Remedial assistance:** reading, math, writing, study skills. **Counseling services:** minority student, career, personal, academic, psychological. **For learning-disabled students:** School does not offer a structured program with separate admission and additional fees. Total undergraduates in learning-disabled program or receiving services: 675. Services include: remedial math, reading machines, tape recorders, untimed tests, note-taking services, oral tests, learning center, readers, extended time for tests, tutors, early syllabus, priority registration, pri[...] seating, proofreading services, texts on tape, exams on tape or com[...] other testing accommodations. **Library:** Number of titles: 115,97[...] current serial subscriptions: 555. **Information technology reso[...]

are not required to lease or own a computer. Number of campus computers available to all students: 600. School has a wireless network. **Campus safety:** Security services offered: 24-hour foot-and-vehicle patrols, late-night transport/escort service, 24-hour emergency telephones, lighted pathways/sidewalks, controlled dormitory access (key, security card, etc).

TRANSFER AND INTERNATIONAL STUDENTS

Transfer students: May apply for admission for the following academic terms: Fall, Winter, Spring, Summer. Applicants do not need a minimum number of credits to apply. For fall 2009: Transfer applications received: 1,717. Transfer applicants offered admission: 1,362. Transfer applicants enrolled: 613. **International students:** Number of foreign undergraduates: 764 (8% of student body). Number of countries represented: 98. Minimum TOEFL score required: 550 (paper); 210 (computer).

Providence College

- **Address:** 1 Cunningham Square, Providence, RI 02918
- **Website:** http://www.providence.edu
- **Private; Religious affiliation:** Roman Catholic
- **Enrollment:** 3,831 full-time; 473 part-time

KEY STATS

✔ **U.S News College Ranking:** 2, Regional Universities (North)
✔ **SAT Score (25th/75th percentile):** 1060-1270
✔ **Tuition:** 2010-2011: $34,435

Selectivity: More selective	**Room/board:** $11,690
Acceptance rate: 60%	**Average debt:** $34,927
Student/faculty ratio: 12/1	**Proportion who borrowed:** 63%

UNDERGRADUATE STUDENT BODY STATS

2009-2010 enrollment: 3,831 full-time; 473 part-time. Men: 44%; women: 56%. **Ethnic makeup:** African American: 3%; Asian American: 2%; Hispanic: 4%; White: 90%; International: 1%. **Religious preference:** Protestant: 5%; Jewish: 1%; No preference: 5%; Roman Catholic: 78%; Greek Orthodox: 1%; Other: 10%.

ADMISSIONS FACTS AND FIGURES

Phone: (401) 865-2535. **Email:** pcadmiss@providence.edu. **Website:** http://www.providence.edu. **Application deadlines for fall 2011:** Regular decision: January 15; decision sent by April 1. Early decision: Not offered. Early action: Send application by: November 1; Decision sent by: January 1. Admission can be deferred. **Application fee:** $55. **To apply online, go to:** http://www.commonapp.org. **Admissions requirements/recommendations:** High school units required (recommended): English: 4 (4); Mathematics: 4 (4); Science: 3 (4); Foreign language: 3 (3); Social studies: 2 (2); History: 2 (2); Total units: 16 (18). Tests: The college uses SAT or ACT scores in admissions decisions. Neither SAT nor ACT required. For admission to the fall 2011 entering class, the school will accept: ACT with or without writing accepted. Campus visit: Recommended. Admissions interview: Neither required nor recommended. Off-campus interview: Not available. **Factors that count in admissions decisions:** *Academic:* Secondary school record: Very Important. Class rank: Considered. Letters of recommendation: Important. Standardized test scores: Considered. Essay: Very Important. *Nonacademic:* Interview: Not Considered. Extracurricular activities: Important. Talent/ability: Considered. Character/personal qualities: Important. Alumni/ae relationship: Considered. Geographical residence: Considered. State residency: Not Considered. Religious affiliation/commitment: Not Considered. Minority status: Considered. Volunteer work: Considered. Work experience: Considered. **Other schools with the greatest overlap in applicants:** Boston College; College of the Holy Cross; Fairfield University; Loyola University Maryland; Villanova University. **Admissions statistics for the fall 2009 entering class:** Total applicants: 8,376. Total accepted: 5,008. Freshmen enrolled: 955; 88% were from out of state. Overall acceptance rate: 60%. Non-early acceptance rate: 60%. **Size of waiting list:** 2166 applicants; enrolled from list: 682. **Credentials of fall 2009 freshmen:** 37% ranked in the top ⅒ their high school class; 72% were in the top 25 percent; 96% ____ half. (Proportion submitting class standing: 48%.) **Average ____ int average:** 3.4. **First-year students who submitted SAT ____ 75 percentile):** Critical Reading: 530-630, Math: ____0-1270. **First-year students submitting ACT scores:** ____tile): English: N/A, Math: N/A, Composite: 23-28.

ACADEMICS

Year founded: 1917. **Academic calendar:** Semester. **Degrees offered:** certificate, associate, terminal-associate, bachelor's, master's. **Most popular majors:** 10% marketing/marketing management, 8% business administration and management, 7% English language and literature, 7% biology/biological sciences, 7% finance. **Major fields of study:** area, ethnic, cultural, and gender studies; biological and biomedical sciences; business, management, marketing, and related support services; computer and information sciences and support services; education; engineering; English language and literature/letters; foreign languages, literatures, and linguistics; health professions and related clinical sciences; history; liberal arts and sciences studies, and humanities; mathematics and statistics; multi/interdisciplinary studies; philosophy and religious studies; physical sciences; psychology; public administration and social service professions; security and protective services; social sciences; theology and religious vocations; visual and performing arts. **Areas of required coursework:** arts/fine arts, mathematics, English (including composition), philosophy, sciences (biological or physical), social science, other. **Pre-professional programs:** pre-law, pre-dentistry, pre-medicine, pre-veterinary science, pre-optometry, other. **Special academic programs (% participation):** cross-registration, double major (9.2%), exchange student program (domestic) (.4%), honors program (10%), independent study (13.9%), internships (23.2%), student-designed major (.2%), study abroad (15.5%), teacher certificate program, other (1.4%). **Teacher certification offered in:** special education, elementary, secondary. **Reserve Officers Training Corps (ROTC):** Army ROTC: Offered on campus. **Faculty and instruction (2009-2010):** Total instructional faculty: 297 full-time, 103 part-time (64% men; 36% women; 9% minorities). Full-time faculty with Ph.D. or other terminal degree: 93%. Student/faculty ratio: 12/1. Classes of fewer than 20 students: 48%; of 20 to 49 students: 49%; of 50 or more students: 3%. **Advanced Placement and International Baccalaureate credit:** AP tests may be used for: Credit only. Scores accepted: 4, 5. International Baccalaureate exams may be used for: Credit and/or placement. **Freshmen returning for sophomore year:** 92%. **Graduation rates:** Four-year: 84%; five-year: 87%; six-year: 87%. **Graduate study:** Fields in which graduates pursue further study: Master of Business Administration (MBA), 14%; law, 14%; medicine, 14%; education, 18%; arts and sciences, 13%.

COSTS AND FINANCIAL AID

Financial aid office: (401) 865-2286. **Expenses (2010-2011):** Tuition and fees 2010-2011: $34,435; room/board: $11,690. Estimated books and supplies: $900; transportation: $0; personal expenses: $800. **Financial aid:** Priority filing date for institution's financial aid form: February 1; deadline: February 1. In 2009-2010, 68% of undergraduates applied for financial aid. Of those, 55% were determined to have financial need; 32% had their need fully met. Average financial aid package (proportion receiving): $20,770 (55%). Average amount of gift aid, such as scholarships or grants (proportion receiving): $17,013 (49%). Average amount of self-help aid, such as work study or loans (proportion receiving): $5,642 (48%). Average need-based loan (excluding PLUS or other private loans): $4,745. Among students who received need-based aid, the average percentage of need met: 78%. Among students who received aid based on merit, the average award (and the proportion receiving): $26,886 (6%). The average athletic scholarship (and the proportion receiving): $29,202 (4%). Average amount of debt of borrowers graduating in 2009: $34,927. Proportion who borrowed: 63%.

CAMPUS LIFE AND EXTRACURRICULAR ACTIVITIES

Campus housing available (% using): coed dorms (11%), women's dorms (27%), men's dorms (21%), apartment for single students (29%), special housing for disabled students, other housing options (12%). Students who live in college-owned, operated, or affiliated housing: 78%. **Student employment:** During the 2009-2010 academic year, 23% of undergraduates worked on campus. Average per-year earnings: $1,387. **Clubs and organizations:** Number of student organizations: 116. Activities include: campus ministries, choral groups, concert band, dance, drama/theater, jazz band, literary magazine, music ensembles, musical theater, pep band, radio station, student government, student newspaper, television station, yearbook. Number of fraternities: 0; sororities: 0. Average proportion of students who stay on campus on weekends: 85%. **Sports program (2009-2010):** Member of NCAA I. *Men's intercollegiate varsity sports:* basketball, cross country, ice hockey, lacrosse, soccer, swimming, track and field (indoor), track and field (outdoor). *Women's intercollegiate varsity sports:* basketball, cross country, field hockey, ice hockey, soccer, softball, swimming, tennis, track and field (indoor), track and field (outdoor), volleyball.

SERVICES AND FACILITIES

Basic services: nonremedial tutoring, placement service, health service, other. **Counseling services:** minority student, career, military, personal, academic, psychological, religious, other. **For learning-disabled students:** School does not offer a structured program with separate admission and additional fees. Total undergraduates in learning-disabled program or receiving services: 146. Services include: reading machines, tape recorders, note-taking services, oral tests, learning center, readers, extended time for tests, tutors, priority registration, priority seating, texts on tape, other testing accommodations, other. **Library:** Number of titles: 636,909; number of current serial subscriptions: 44,833. **Information technology resources:** Students are not required to lease or own a computer. Number of campus computers available to all students: 282. School has a wireless network. Approximate number of users that can be accommodated: 6,000. Proportion of college-owned housing units wired for high-speed internet access: 100%. **Campus safety:** Security services offered: 24-hour foot-and-vehicle patrols, late-night transport/escort service, 24-hour emergency telephones, lighted pathways/sidewalks, student patrols, controlled dormitory access (key, security card, etc).

TRANSFER AND INTERNATIONAL STUDENTS

Transfer students: May apply for admission for the following academic terms: Fall, Spring. Applicants need a minimum number of credits to apply. For fall 2009: Transfer applications received: 223. Transfer applicants offered admission: 109. Transfer applicants enrolled: 63. **International students:** Number of foreign undergraduates: 52 (1% of student body). Number of countries represented: 18. Minimum TOEFL score required: 550 (paper); 80 (computer). Average TOEFL score: 600 (paper).

Rhode Island College

- **Address:** 600 Mount Pleasant Avenue, Providence, RI 02908
- **Website:** http://www.ric.edu
- **Public**
- **Enrollment:** 5,842 full-time; 2,041 part-time

KEY STATS

✔ **U.S News College Ranking:** 105, Regional Universities (North)
✔ **SAT Score (25th/75th percentile):** 840-1040
✔ **Tuition:** 2010-2011: $6,986 in state, $16,878 out of state

Selectivity: Less selective	**Room/board:** $9,270
Acceptance rate: 77%	**Average debt:** $18,352
Student/faculty ratio: 16/1	**Proportion who borrowed:** 71%

UNDERGRADUATE STUDENT BODY STATS

2009-2010 enrollment: 5,842 full-time; 2,041 part-time. Men: 33%; women: 67%. **Ethnic makeup:** African American: 4%; Asian American: 2%; Hispanic: 5%; White: 88%.

ADMISSIONS FACTS AND FIGURES

Phone: (800) 669-5760. **Email:** admissions@ric.edu. **Website:** http://www.ric.edu. **Application deadlines for fall 2011:** Regular decision: March 15. Early decision: Not offered. Early action: Not offered. Admission cannot be deferred. **Application fee:** $50. **To apply online, go to:** http://www.ric.edu/admissions/apply.php. **Admissions requirements/recommendations:** High school units required (recommended): English: 4; Mathematics: 3; Science: 2; Foreign language: 2; Social studies: 2; Academic electives: 5; Total units: 18. Tests: The college uses SAT or ACT scores in admissions decisions. Either SAT or ACT required. For admission to the fall 2011 entering class, the school will accept: ACT with writing required. Campus visit: Recommended. Admissions interview: Recommended. Off-campus interview: Not available. **Factors that count in admissions decisions:** *Academic:* Secondary school record: Very Important. Class rank: Very Important. Letters of recommendation: Important. Standardized test scores: Important. Essay: Important. *Nonacademic:* Interview: Considered. Extracurricular activities: Considered. Talent/ability: Considered. Character/personal qualities: Not Considered. Alumni/ae relationship: Considered. Geographical residence: Not Considered. State residency: Not Considered. Religious affiliation/commitment: Not Considered. Minority status: Not Considered. Volunteer work: Considered. Work experience: Considered. **Other schools with the greatest overlap in applicants:** Eastern Connecticut State University; Roger Williams University; University of Massachusetts–Dartmouth; University of Rhode Island. **Admissions statistics for the fall 2009 entering class:** Total applicants: 3,938. Total accepted: 3,027. Freshmen enrolled: 1,253; 20% were from out of state. Overall acceptance rate: 77%. **Credentials of fall 2009 freshmen:** 11% ranked in the top 10 percent of their high school class; 33% were in the top 25 percent; 77% were in the top half. (Proportion submitting class standing: 77%.) **First-year students who submitted SAT scores:** 93%. Scores (25/75 percentile): Critical Reading: 420-520, Math: 420-520, Combined: 840-1040. **First-year students submitting ACT scores:** 6%. Scores (25/75 percentile): English: 16-21, Math: 16-20, Composite: 16-21.

ACADEMICS

Year founded: 1854. **Academic calendar:** Semester. **Degrees offered:** certificate, bachelor's, post-bachelor's certificate, master's, post-master's certificate, doctorate. **Most popular majors:** 22% education, 12% business, management, marketing, and related support services, 12% psychology, 10% nursing/registered nurse training (R.N., A.S.N., B.S.N., M.S.N.), 8% communication studies/speech communication and rhetoric. **Major fields of study:** area, ethnic, cultural, and gender studies; biological and biomedical sciences; business, management, marketing, and related support services; communication, journalism, and related programs; computer and information sciences and support services; education; English language and literature/letters; foreign languages, literatures, and linguistics; health professions and related clinical sciences; history; liberal arts and sciences studies, and humanities; mathematics and statistics; multi/interdisciplinary studies; philosophy and religious studies; physical sciences; psychology; public administration and social service professions; security and protective services; social sciences; visual and performing arts. **Areas of required coursework:** arts/fine arts, mathematics, English (including composition), sciences (biological or physical), history, social science. **Pre-professional programs:** pre-law, pre-dentistry, pre-medicine, pre-veterinary science, pre-optometry, other. **Special academic programs (% participation):** double major (5.62%), dual enrollment, English as a Second Language (ESL), exchange student program (domestic), honors program (2.61%), independent study (8.71%), internships, student-designed major, study abroad, teacher certificate program (22.1%). **Teacher certification offered in:** early childhood, special education, elementary, middle/junior high, secondary. **Reserve Officers Training Corps (ROTC):** Army ROTC: Offered at cooperating institution (Providence College). **Faculty and instruction (2009-2010):** Total instructional faculty: 311 full-time, 450 part-time (43% men; 57% women; 4% minorities). Full-time faculty with Ph.D. or other terminal degree: 91%. Student/faculty ratio: 16/1. Classes of fewer than 20 students: 40%; of 20 to 49 students: 59%; of 50 or more students: 1%. **Advanced Placement and International Baccalaureate credit:** AP tests may be used for: Credit only. Scores accepted: 3. **Freshmen returning for sophomore year:** 76%. **Graduation rates:** Four-year: 15%; five-year: 36%; six-year: 45%.

COSTS AND FINANCIAL AID

Financial aid office: (401) 456-8033. **Expenses (2010-2011):** Tuition and fees 2010-2011: $6,986 in state, $16,878 out of state; room/board: $9,270. Estimated books and supplies: $1,000; transportation: $440; personal expenses: $1,000. **Financial aid:** Priority filing date for institution's financial aid form: March 1. In 2009-2010, 77% of undergraduates applied for financial aid. Of those, 59% were determined to have financial need; 31% had their need fully met. Average financial aid package (proportion receiving): $8,365 (56%). Average amount of gift aid, such as scholarships or grants (proportion receiving): $5,360 (47%). Average amount of self-help aid, such as work study or loans (proportion receiving): $4,147 (51%). Average need-based loan (excluding PLUS or other private loans): $3,759. Among students who received need-based aid, the average percentage of need met: 75%. Among students who received aid based on merit, the average award (and the proportion receiving): $1,819 (2%). The average athletic scholarship (and the proportion receiving): $0 (0%). Average amount of debt of borrowers graduating in 2009: $18,352. Proportion who borrowed: 71%.

CAMPUS LIFE AND EXTRACURRICULAR ACTIVITIES

Campus housing available (% using): coed dorms (88%), women's dorms (12%), special housing for disabled students. Students who live in college-owned, operated, or affiliated housing: 16%. **Student employment:** During the 2009-2010 academic year, 8% of undergraduates worked on campus. **Clubs and organizations:** Number of student organizations: 78. Activities include: campus ministries, choral groups, concert band, dance, drama/theater, international student organization, jazz band, literary magazine, music ensembles, musical theater, radio station, student government, student newspaper, student film society, symphony orchestra, television station. Number of fraternities: 1; sororities: 2. **Sports program (2009-2010):** Member of NCAA III. *Men's intercollegiate varsity sports:* baseball, basketball, cross country, golf, soccer, tennis, track and field (indoor), track and field (outdoor), wrestling. *Women's intercollegiate varsity sports:* basketball, cross country, gymnastics, lacrosse, soccer, softball, tennis, track and field (indoor), track and field (outdoor), volleyball.

SERVICES AND FACILITIES
Basic services: women's center, placement service, day care, health service, health insurance. **Remedial assistance:** reading, math, writing, study skills. **Counseling services:** minority student, career, personal, academic, older student, psychological, birth control, religious. **For learning-disabled students:** School does not offer a structured program with separate admission and additional fees. Total undergraduates in learning-disabled program or receiving services: 172. Services include: remedial math, remedial English, reading machines, remedial reading, tape recorders, note-taking services, oral tests, learning center, readers, extended time for tests, tutors, priority registration, priority seating, texts on tape, typist/scribe, exams on tape or computer, other testing accommodations. **Library:** Number of titles: 694,541; number of current serial subscriptions: 1,326,100. **Information technology resources:** Students are not required to lease or own a computer. Number of campus computers available to all students: 690. School has a wireless network. Approximate number of users that can be accommodated: 1,024. Proportion of college-owned housing units wired for high-speed internet access: 100%. **Campus safety:** Security services offered: 24-hour foot-and-vehicle patrols, late-night transport/escort service, 24-hour emergency telephones, lighted pathways/sidewalks, controlled dormitory access (key, security card, etc).

TRANSFER AND INTERNATIONAL STUDENTS
Transfer students: May apply for admission for the following academic terms: Fall, Spring. Applicants need a minimum number of credits to apply. For fall 2009: Transfer applications received: 1,319. Transfer applicants offered admission: 1,097. Transfer applicants enrolled: 709. **International students:** Number of foreign undergraduates: 19. Number of countries represented: 7. Minimum TOEFL score required: 550 (paper); 213 (computer).

Rhode Island School of Design

- **Address:** 2 College Street, Providence, RI 02903
- **Website:** http://www.risd.edu
- **Private**
- **Enrollment:** 1,940 full-time

KEY STATS
- ✔ **U.S News College Ranking:** Unranked Specialty School–Fine Arts
- ✔ **SAT Score (25th/75th percentile):** 1130-1370
- ✔ **Tuition:** 2010-2011: $38,295

Selectivity: N/A	Room/board: $11,310
Acceptance rate: 35%	Average debt: $26,300
Student/faculty ratio: 9/1	Proportion who borrowed: 59%

UNDERGRADUATE STUDENT BODY STATS
2009-2010 enrollment: 1,940 full-time. Men: 31%; women: 69%. **Ethnic makeup:** African American: 2%; Asian American: 14%; Hispanic: 5%; White: 64%; International: 15%.

ADMISSIONS FACTS AND FIGURES
Phone: (401) 454-6300. **Email:** admissions@risd.edu. **Website:** http://www.risd.edu. **Application deadlines for fall 2011:** Regular decision: February 15; decision sent by April 1. Early decision: Not offered. Early action: Send application by: December 15; Decision sent by: January 31. Admission can be deferred. **Application fee:** $60. **To apply online, go to:** http://www.risd.edu/apply_applic.cfm. **Admissions requirements/recommendations:** Tests: The college uses SAT or ACT scores in admissions decisions. Either SAT or ACT required. For admission to the fall 2011 entering class, the school will accept: ACT with writing required. Campus visit: Recommended. Admissions interview: Neither required nor recommended. Off-campus interview: Not available. **Factors that count in admissions decisions:** *Academic:* Secondary school record: Very Important. Class rank: Considered. Letters of recommendation: Considered. Standardized test scores: Considered. Essay: Important. *Nonacademic:* Interview: Not Considered. Extracurricular activities: Important. Talent/ability: Very Important. Character/personal qualities: Important. Alumni/ae relation-

ship: Considered. Geographical residence: Considered. State residency: Considered. Religious affiliation/commitment: Not Considered. Minority status: Considered. Volunteer work: Considered. Work experience: Considered. **Other schools with the greatest overlap in applicants:** Maryland Institute College of Art; Parsons the New School for Design; Pratt Institute; Savannah College of Art and Design; School of the Art Institute of Chicago. **Admissions statistics for the fall 2009 entering class:** Total applicants: 2,819. Total accepted: 973. Freshmen enrolled: 460; 96% were from out of state. Overall acceptance rate: 35%. Non-early acceptance rate: 35%. **Size of waiting list:** 300 applicants; enrolled from waiting list: 43. **Credentials of fall 2009 freshmen:** 35% ranked in the top 10 percent of their high school class; 57% were in the top 25 percent; 91% were in the top half. (Proportion submitting class standing: 13%.) **Average high school grade point average:** 3.4. **First-year students who submitted SAT scores:** 92%. Scores (25/75 percentile): Critical Reading: 540-680, Math: 590-690, Combined: 1130-1370. **First-year students submitting ACT scores:** 7%. Scores (25/75 percentile): English: 25-30, Math: 24-33, Composite: 23-30.

ACADEMICS
Year founded: 1877. **Academic calendar:** 4-1-4. **Degrees offered:** bachelor's, master's. **Most popular majors:** 43% fine and studio art, 14% industrial design, 11% graphic design, 6% architecture (B.Arch., B.A./B.S., M.Arch., M.A./M.S., Ph.D.). **Major fields of study:** visual and performing arts. **Areas of required coursework:** arts/fine arts, humanities, English (including composition), philosophy, history, social science. **Special academic programs (% participation):** cross-registration (10%), double major (5%), English as a Second Language (ESL) (10%), exchange student program (domestic), honors program (2%), independent study (20%), internships (20%), study abroad (20%). **Faculty and instruction (2009-2010):** Total instructional faculty: 135 full-time, 375 part-time. Full-time faculty with Ph.D. or other terminal degree: 79%. Student/faculty ratio: 9/1. Classes of fewer than 20 students: 75%; of 20 to 49 students: 24%; of 50 or more students: 1%. **Advanced Placement and International Baccalaureate credit:** AP tests may be used for: Credit only. Scores accepted: 4, 5. International Baccalaureate exams may be used for: Credit only. **Freshmen returning for sophomore year:** 95%. **Graduation rates:** Four-year: 71%; five-year: 89%; six-year: 89%. **Graduate study:** 2% of students pursue further study immediately upon graduation; 6% within one year. Fields in which graduates pursue further study: Master of Business Administration (MBA), 1%; law, 1%; medicine, 1%; dentistry, 1%; engineering, 1%; theology (or the seminary), 1%; education, 5%; arts and sciences, 2%.

COSTS AND FINANCIAL AID
Financial aid office: (401) 454-6636. **Expenses (2010-2011):** Tuition and fees 2010-2011: $38,295; room/board: $11,310. Estimated books and supplies: $2,700; transportation: $1,000; personal expenses: $2,500. **Financial aid:** Priority filing date for institution's financial aid form: February 15; deadline: February 15. In 2009-2010, 59% of undergraduates applied for financial aid. Of those, 53% were determined to have financial need; Average financial aid package (proportion receiving): $19,007 (53%). Average amount of gift aid, such as scholarships or grants (proportion receiving): $11,556 (40%). Average amount of self-help aid, such as work study or loans (proportion receiving): $6,447 (40%). Average need-based loan (excluding PLUS or other private loans): $5,723. Among students who received need-based aid, the average percentage of need met: 68%. Among students who received aid based on merit, the average award (and the proportion receiving): $10,000 (2%). The average athletic scholarship (and the proportion receiving): $0 (0%). Average amount of debt of borrowers graduating in 2009: $26,300. Proportion who borrowed: 59%.

CAMPUS LIFE AND EXTRACURRICULAR ACTIVITIES
Campus housing available (% using): coed dorms (59%), apartment for single students (37%), special housing for disabled students. Students who live in college-owned, operated, or affiliated housing: 68%. **Student employment:** During the 2009-2010 academic year, 38% of undergraduates worked on campus. Average per-year earnings: $1,025. **Clubs and organizations:** Number of student organizations: 31. Activities include: dance, drama/theater, international student organization, literary magazine, student government, student newspaper, student film society, yearbook. Number of fraternities: 0; sororities: 0. Average proportion of students who stay on campus on weekends: 90%.

SERVICES AND FACILITIES
Basic services: placement service, health service, health insurance, other. **Remedial assistance:** writing. **Counseling services:** minority student, career, personal, academic, psychological, birth control, other. **For learning-dis-**

abled students: School does not offer a structured program with separate admission and additional fees. Total undergraduates in learning-disabled program or receiving services: 153. Services include: reading machines, untimed tests, note-taking services, oral tests, extended time for tests, priority seating, other. **Library:** Number of titles: 148,829; number of current serial subscriptions: 380. **Information technology resources:** Students are not required to lease or own a computer. Number of campus computers available to all students: 400. School has a wireless network. Approximate number of users that can be accommodated: 3,000. Proportion of college-owned housing units wired for high-speed internet access: 100%. **Campus safety:** Security services offered: 24-hour foot-and-vehicle patrols, late-night transport/escort service, 24-hour emergency telephones, lighted pathways/sidewalks, controlled dormitory access (key, security card, etc).

TRANSFER AND INTERNATIONAL STUDENTS

Transfer students: May apply for admission for the following academic terms: Fall, Winter, Spring. Applicants need a minimum number of credits to apply. For fall 2009: Transfer applications received: 434. Transfer applicants offered admission: 137. Transfer applicants enrolled: 93. **International students:** Number of foreign undergraduates: 212 (15% of student body). Number of countries represented: 49. Minimum TOEFL score required: 580 (paper); 237 (computer).

Roger Williams University

- ■ **Address:** 1 Old Ferry Road, Bristol, RI 02809
- ■ **Website:** http://www.rwu.edu
- ■ **Private**
- ■ **Enrollment:** 3,662 full-time; 607 part-time

KEY STATS

✔ **U.S News College Ranking:** 8, Regional Colleges (North)
✔ **SAT Score (25th/75th percentile):** 1005-1180
✔ **Tuition:** 2010-2011: $29,718

Selectivity: Selective	**Room/board:** $12,710
Acceptance rate: 78%	**Average debt:** $32,586
Student/faculty ratio: 12/1	**Proportion who borrowed:** 79%

UNDERGRADUATE STUDENT BODY STATS

2009-2010 enrollment: 3,662 full-time; 607 part-time. Men: 51%; women: 49%. **Ethnic makeup:** African American: 1%; Asian American: 1%; Hispanic: 3%; White: 91%; International: 3%.

ADMISSIONS FACTS AND FIGURES

Phone: (401) 254-3500. **Email:** admit@rwu.edu. **Website:** http://www.rwu.edu. **Application deadlines for fall 2011:** Regular decision: February 1; decision sent by March 15. Early decision: Not offered. Early action: Send application by: November 1; Decision sent by: December 15. Admission can be deferred. **Application fee:** $50. **To apply online, go to:** http://www.rwu.edu/admission/apply/. **Admissions requirements/recommendations:** High school units required (recommended): English: 4 (4); Mathematics: 3 (4); Science: 2 (4); Foreign language: 0 (2); Social studies: 2 (3); History: 2 (3); Academic electives: 2 (3); Total units: 22 (26). Tests: The college uses SAT or ACT scores in admissions decisions. Either SAT or ACT required. For admission to the fall 2011 entering class, the school will accept: ACT with writing recommended. Campus visit: Recommended. Admissions interview: Recommended. Off-campus interview: May be arranged. **Factors that count in admissions decisions: Academic:** Secondary school record: Very Important. Class rank: Important. Letters of recommendation: Very Important. Standardized test scores: Very Important. Essay: Very Important. **Nonacademic:** Interview: Considered. Extracurricular activities: Important. Talent/ability: Considered. Character/personal qualities: Not Considered. Alumni/ae relationship: Considered. Geographical residence: Not Considered. State residency: Not Considered. Religious affiliation/commitment: Not Considered. Minority status: Not Considered. Volunteer work: Considered. Work experience: Considered. **Other schools with the greatest overlap in applicants:** Bryant University; Quinnipiac University; University of Massachusetts–Amherst; University of New Hampshire; University of Rhode Island. **Admissions statistics for the fall 2009 entering class:** Total applicants: 7,914. Total accepted: 6,184. Freshmen enrolled: 1,026; 93% were from out of state. Overall acceptance rate: 78%. Non-early acceptance rate: 78%. **Size of waiting list:** N/A applicants; enrolled from waiting list: 0. **Credentials of fall 2009 freshmen:** 15% ranked in the top 10 percent of

their high school class; 39% were in the top 25 percent; 76% were in the top half. (Proportion submitting class standing: 51%.) **Average high school grade point average:** 3.2. **First-year students who submitted SAT scores:** 99%. Scores (25/75 percentile): Critical Reading: 495-580, Math: 510-600, Combined: 1005-1180. **First-year students submitting ACT scores:** 20%. Scores (25/75 percentile): English: N/A, Math: N/A, Composite: 21-25.

ACADEMICS

Year founded: 1956. **Academic calendar:** Semester. **Degrees offered:** certificate, associate, terminal-associate, bachelor's, post-bachelor's certificate, master's. **Most popular majors:** 19% business, management, marketing, and related support services; 15% security and protective services; 11% psychology, 10% communication, journalism, and related programs, 6% education. **Major fields of study:** architecture and related services; biological and biomedical sciences; business, management, marketing, and related support services; communication, journalism, and related programs; computer and information sciences and support services; construction trades; education; engineering; English language and literature/letters; foreign languages, literatures, and linguistics; health professions and related clinical sciences; history; legal professions and studies; liberal arts and sciences studies, and humanities; mathematics and statistics; multi/interdisciplinary studies; philosophy and religious studies; physical sciences; psychology; security and protective services; social sciences; visual and performing arts. **Areas of required coursework:** arts/fine arts, humanities, mathematics, English (including composition), philosophy, sciences (biological or physical), history, social science. **Pre-professional programs:** pre-law, pre-medicine, pre-veterinary science. **Special academic programs:** cooperative (work-study plan) program, distance learning, double major, dual enrollment, English as a Second Language (ESL), exchange student program (domestic), external degree program, honors program, independent study, internships, liberal arts/career combination, student-designed major, study abroad, teacher certificate program, weekend college. **Teacher certification offered in:** elementary, secondary. **Cooperative education programs:** business, humanities, social/behavioral science. **Reserve Officers Training Corps (ROTC):** Army ROTC: Offered at cooperating institution (University of Rhode Island). **Faculty and instruction (2009-2010):** Total instructional faculty: 203 full-time, 331 part-time (60% men; 40% women; 8% minorities). Full-time faculty with Ph.D. or other terminal degree: 91%. Student/faculty ratio: 12/1. Classes of fewer than 20 students: 47%; of 20 to 49 students: 53%; of 50 or more students: 0%. **Advanced Placement and International Baccalaureate credit:** AP tests may be used for: Placement only. Scores accepted: 3, 4, 5. International Baccalaureate exams may be used for: Placement only. **Freshmen returning for sophomore year:** 80%. **Graduation rates:** Four-year: 51%; five-year: 57%; six-year: 59%. **Graduate study:** 25% of students pursue further study within five years.

COSTS AND FINANCIAL AID

Financial aid office: (401) 254-3100. **Expenses (2010-2011):** Tuition and fees 2010-2011: $29,718; room/board: $12,710. Estimated books and supplies: $900; transportation: $821; personal expenses: $822. **Financial aid:** Priority filing date for institution's financial aid form: January 1; deadline: February 1. In 2009-2010, 73% of undergraduates applied for financial aid. Of those, 66% were determined to have financial need; 5% had their need fully met. Average financial aid package (proportion receiving): $22,835 (58%). Average amount of gift aid, such as scholarships or grants (proportion receiving): $12,815 (52%). Average amount of self-help aid, such as work study or loans (proportion receiving): $10,020 (53%). Average need-based loan (excluding PLUS or other private loans): $7,542. Among students who received need-based aid, the average percentage of need met: 86%. Among students who received aid based on merit, the average award (and the proportion receiving): $7,841 (11%). The average athletic scholarship (and the proportion receiving): $0 (0%). Average amount of debt of borrowers graduating in 2009: $32,586. Proportion who borrowed: 79%.

CAMPUS LIFE AND EXTRACURRICULAR ACTIVITIES

Campus housing available (% using): coed dorms (66%), apartment for single students (34%), special housing for disabled students. Students who live in college-owned, operated, or affiliated housing: 66%. **Student employment:** During the 2009-2010 academic year, 5% of undergraduates worked on campus. Average per-year earnings: $3,300. **Clubs and organizations:** Number of student organizations: 92. Activities include: choral groups, dance, drama/theater, international student organization, literary magazine, model UN, musical theater, radio station, student government, student newspaper, student film society, yearbook. Number of fraternities: 0; sororities: 0. Average proportion of students who stay on campus on weekends: 70%. **Sports program (2009-2010):** Member of NCAA III. *Men's intercol-*

legiate varsity sports: baseball, basketball, cross country, lacrosse, soccer, swimming, tennis, wrestling. *Women's intercollegiate varsity sports:* basketball, cross country, lacrosse, soccer, softball, swimming, tennis, volleyball.

SERVICES AND FACILITIES

Basic services: nonremedial tutoring, women's center, placement service, health service, health insurance. **Remedial assistance:** reading, math, writing, study skills. **Counseling services:** minority student, career, military, personal, veteran student, academic, older student, psychological, birth control. **For learning-disabled students:** School does not offer a structured program with separate admission and additional fees. Services include: note-taking services, learning center, readers, extended time for tests, tutors. **Library:** Number of titles: 233,868; number of current serial subscriptions: 47,805. **Information technology resources:** Students are not required to lease or own a computer. Number of campus computers available to all students: 500. School has a wireless network. Approximate number of users that can be accommodated: 1,500. Proportion of college-owned housing units wired for high-speed internet access: 100%. **Campus safety:** Security services offered: 24-hour foot-and-vehicle patrols, late-night transport/escort service, 24-hour emergency telephones, lighted pathways/sidewalks, controlled dormitory access (key, security card, etc).

TRANSFER AND INTERNATIONAL STUDENTS

Transfer students: May apply for admission for the following academic terms: Fall, Spring. Applicants do not need a minimum number of credits to apply. For fall 2009: Transfer applications received: 308. Transfer applicants offered admission: 205. Transfer applicants enrolled: 77. **International students:** Number of foreign undergraduates: 114 (3% of student body). Number of countries represented: 47.

Salve Regina University

- **Address:** 100 Ochre Point Avenue, Newport, RI 02840-4192
- **Website:** http://www.salve.edu
- **Private; Religious affiliation:** Roman Catholic
- **Enrollment:** 1,889 full-time; 95 part-time

KEY STATS
- ✔ **U.S News College Ranking:** 40, Regional Universities (North)
- ✔ **SAT Score (25th/75th percentile):** 1000-1175
- ✔ **Tuition:** 2010-2011: $31,450

Selectivity: Selective	**Room/board:** $11,300
Acceptance rate: 64%	**Average debt:** $35,394
Student/faculty ratio: 14/1	**Proportion who borrowed:** 81%

UNDERGRADUATE STUDENT BODY STATS

2009-2010 enrollment: 1,889 full-time; 95 part-time. Men: 31%; women: 69%. **Ethnic makeup:** African American: 2%; American-Indian: 1%; Asian American: 1%; Hispanic: 3%; White: 92%; International: 1%.

ADMISSIONS FACTS AND FIGURES

Phone: (888) 467-2583. **Email:** sruadmis@salve.edu. **Website:** http://www.salve.edu. **Application deadlines for fall 2011:** Regular decision: February 1; decision sent by April 1. Early decision: Not offered. Early action: Send application by: November 1; Decision sent by: December 25. Admission can be deferred. **Application fee:** $50. **To apply online, go to:** http://www.salve.edu/explore. **Admissions requirements/recommendations:** High school units required (recommended): English: 4; Mathematics: 3; Science: 2; Foreign language: 2; Social studies: 1; Academic electives: 4; Total units: 16. Tests: The college uses SAT or ACT scores in admissions decisions. Either SAT or ACT required. For admission to the fall 2011 entering class, the school will accept: ACT with or without writing accepted. Campus visit: Recommended. Admissions interview: Neither required nor recommended. Off-campus interview: May be arranged. **Factors that count in admissions decisions: *Academic:*** Secondary school record: Very Important. Class rank: Very Important. Letters of recommendation: Important. Standardized test scores: Important. Essay: Important. *Nonacademic:* Interview: Not Considered. Extracurricular activities: Considered. Talent/ability: Considered. Character/personal qualities: Considered. Alumni/ae relationship: Considered. Geographical residence: Not Considered. State residency: Not Considered. Religious affiliation/commitment: Not Considered. Minority status: Considered. Volunteer work: Considered. Work experience: Considered. **Other schools with the greatest overlap in applicants:** College of

the Holy Cross; Fairfield University; Providence College; Stonehill College; University of Rhode Island. **Admissions statistics for the fall 2009 entering class:** Total applicants: 5,256. Total accepted: 3,385. Freshmen enrolled: 505; 88% were from out of state. Accepted through early-decision or early-action plans: 41%. Overall acceptance rate: 64%. Non-early acceptance rate: 63%. **Size of waiting list:** 614 applicants; enrolled from waiting list: 35. **Credentials of fall 2009 freshmen:** 21% ranked in the top 10 percent of their high school class; 57% were in the top 25 percent; 88% were in the top half. (Proportion submitting class standing: 51%.) **Average high school grade point average:** 3.3. **First-year students who submitted SAT scores:** 86%. Scores (25/75 percentile): Critical Reading: 500-585, Math: 500-590, Combined: 1000-1175. **First-year students submitting ACT scores:** 16%. Scores (25/75 percentile): English: 22-27, Math: 21-25, Composite: 22-26.

ACADEMICS

Year founded: 1934. **Academic calendar:** Semester. **Degrees offered:** certificate, associate, bachelor's, post-bachelor's certificate, master's, post-master's certificate, doctorate. **Most popular majors:** 11% nursing/registered nurse training (R.N., A.S.N., B.S.N., M.S.N.), 8% criminal justice/law enforcement administration, 8% special education and teaching, 7% marketing/marketing management, 6% business administration and management. **Major fields of study:** area, ethnic, cultural, and gender studies; biological and biomedical sciences; business, management, marketing, and related support services; communication, journalism, and related programs; computer and information sciences and support services; education; English language and literature/letters; foreign languages, literatures, and linguistics; health professions and related clinical sciences; history; liberal arts and sciences studies, and humanities; mathematics and statistics; multi/interdisciplinary studies; philosophy and religious studies; physical sciences; psychology; public administration and social service professions; security and protective services; social sciences; visual and performing arts. **Areas of required coursework:** arts/fine arts, humanities, mathematics, English (including composition), philosophy, foreign languages, sciences (biological or physical), history, social science, other. **Pre-professional programs:** prelaw, pre-dentistry, pre-medicine, pre-veterinary science. **Special academic programs (% participation):** accelerated program (3%), distance learning (1%), double major (13%), English as a Second Language (ESL) (0%), honors program (4%), independent study (20%), internships (41%), liberal arts/career combination, study abroad (12%). **Teacher certification offered in:** early childhood, special education, elementary, middle/junior high, secondary. **Reserve Officers Training Corps (ROTC):** Army ROTC: Offered at cooperating institution (University of Rhode Island). **Faculty and instruction (2009-2010):** Total instructional faculty: 117 full-time, 131 part-time (48% men; 52% women; 7% minorities). Full-time faculty with Ph.D. or other terminal degree: 79%. Student/faculty ratio: 14/1. Classes of fewer than 20 students: 50%; of 20 to 49 students: 50%; of 50 or more students: 0%. **Advanced Placement and International Baccalaureate credit:** AP tests may be used for: Credit and/or placement. Scores accepted: 3, 4, 5. International Baccalaureate exams may be used for: Credit and/or placement. **Freshmen returning for sophomore year:** 78%. **Graduation rates:** Four-year: 63%; five-year: 68%; six-year: 66%. **Graduate study:** 20% of students pursue further study immediately upon graduation; 32% within one year; 39% within five years. Fields in which graduates pursue further study: Master of Business Administration (MBA), 12%; law, 12%; education, 28%; arts and sciences, 48%.

COSTS AND FINANCIAL AID

Financial aid office: (401) 341-2901. **Expenses (2010-2011):** Tuition and fees 2010-2011: $31,450; room/board: $11,300. Estimated books and supplies: $900; transportation: $800; personal expenses: $1,000. **Financial aid:** Priority filing date for institution's financial aid form: March 1; deadline: May 15. In 2009-2010, 84% of undergraduates applied for financial aid. Of those, 75% were determined to have financial need; 6% had their need fully met. Average financial aid package (proportion receiving): $21,024 (72%). Average amount of gift aid, such as scholarships or grants (proportion receiving): $16,603 (68%). Average amount of self-help aid, such as work study or loans (proportion receiving): $5,633 (68%). Average need-based loan (excluding PLUS or other private loans): $4,559. Among students who received need-based aid, the average percentage of need met: 66%. Among students who received aid based on merit, the average award (and the proportion receiving): $6,462 (11%). The average athletic scholarship (and the proportion receiving): $0 (0%). Average amount of debt of borrowers graduating in 2009: $35,394. Proportion who borrowed: 81%.

CAMPUS LIFE AND EXTRACURRICULAR ACTIVITIES

Campus housing available (% using): coed dorms (86%), women's dorms (12%), men's dorms (1%), apartment for single students (0%), special housing for disabled students (0%), other housing options (1%). Students who live in college-owned, operated, or affiliated housing: 60%. **Student employment:** During the 2009-2010 academic year, 29% of undergraduates worked on campus. Average per-year earnings: $2,000. **Clubs and organizations:** Number of student organizations: 43. Activities include: campus ministries, choral groups, concert band, dance, drama/theater, international student organization, jazz band, literary magazine, model UN, music ensembles, pep band, radio station, student government, student newspaper, student film society, yearbook. Number of fraternities: 0; sororities: 0. Average proportion of students who stay on campus on weekends: 70%. **Sports program (2009-2010):** Member of NCAA III. *Men's intercollegiate varsity sports:* baseball, basketball, cross country, football, ice hockey, lacrosse, soccer, tennis. *Women's intercollegiate varsity sports:* basketball, cross country, field hockey, ice hockey, lacrosse, soccer, softball, tennis, track and field (outdoor), volleyball.

SERVICES AND FACILITIES

Basic services: nonremedial tutoring, health service, health insurance, other. **Counseling services:** minority student, career, military, personal, academic, psychological, religious. **For learning-disabled students:** School does not offer a structured program with separate admission and additional fees. Services include: reading machines, tape recorders, videotaped classes, untimed tests, note-taking services, oral tests, learning center, readers, extended time for tests, tutors, other testing accommodations. **Library:** Number of titles: 139,441; number of current serial subscriptions: 1,221. **Information technology resources:** Students are not required to lease or own a computer. Number of campus computers available to all students: 215. School has a wireless network. Approximate number of users that can be accommodated: 1,675. Proportion of college-owned housing units wired for high-speed internet access: 100%. **Campus safety:** Security services offered: 24-hour foot-and-vehicle patrols, late-night transport/escort service, 24-hour emergency telephones, lighted pathways/sidewalks, controlled dormitory access (key, security card, etc).

TRANSFER AND INTERNATIONAL STUDENTS

Transfer students: May apply for admission for the following academic terms: Fall, Spring. Applicants need a minimum number of credits to apply. For fall 2009: Transfer applications received: 183. Transfer applicants offered admission: 109. Transfer applicants enrolled: 42. **International students:** Number of foreign undergraduates: 29 (1% of student body). Number of countries represented: 8. Minimum TOEFL score required: 500 (paper); 173 (computer). Average TOEFL score: 520 (paper).

University of Rhode Island

- **Address:** Kingston, RI 02881-0806
- **Website:** http://www.uri.edu
- **Public**
- **Enrollment:** 11,776 full-time; 1,458 part-time

KEY STATS

✔ **U.S News College Ranking:** 167, National Universities
✔ **SAT Score (25th/75th percentile):** 970-1180
✔ **Tuition:** 2010-2011: $10,476 in state, $27,182 out of state

Selectivity: Selective	**Room/board:** $10,854
Acceptance rate: 84%	**Average debt:** $22,500
Student/faculty ratio: 15/1	**Proportion who borrowed:** 72%

UNDERGRADUATE STUDENT BODY STATS

2009-2010 enrollment: 11,776 full-time; 1,458 part-time. Men: 45%; women: 55%. **Ethnic makeup:** African American: 5%; Asian American: 3%; Hispanic: 6%; White: 86%.

ADMISSIONS FACTS AND FIGURES

Phone: (401) 874-7100. **Email:** admission@uri.edu. **Website:** http://www.uri.edu. **Application deadlines for fall 2011:** Regular decision: February 1. Early decision: Not offered. Early action: Send application by: December 1; Decision sent by: January 31. Admission can be deferred. **Application fee:** $65. **To apply online, go to:** http://www.uri.edu/admission. **Admissions requirements/recommendations:** High school units required (recom-

mended): English: 4; Mathematics: 3; Science: 2; Foreign language: 2; Social studies: 2; History: 0; Academic electives: 5; Total units: 18. Tests: The college uses SAT or ACT scores in admissions decisions. Either SAT or ACT required. For admission to the fall 2011 entering class, the school will accept: ACT with writing recommended. Campus visit: Recommended. Admissions interview: Neither required nor recommended. Off-campus interview: Not available. **Factors that count in admissions decisions:** *Academic:* Secondary school record: Very Important. Class rank: Important. Letters of recommendation: Considered. Standardized test scores: Important. Essay: Important. *Nonacademic:* Interview: Not Considered. Extracurricular activities: Considered. Talent/ability: Considered. Character/personal qualities: Considered. Alumni/ae relationship: Considered. Geographical residence: Considered. State residency: Considered. Religious affiliation/commitment: Not Considered. Minority status: Considered. Volunteer work: Considered. Work experience: Considered. **Admissions statistics for the fall 2009 entering class:** Total applicants: 16,126. Total accepted: 13,484. Freshmen enrolled: 3,055; 52% were from out of state. Accepted through early-decision or early-action plans: 68%. Overall acceptance rate: 84%. Non-early acceptance rate: 71%. **Credentials of fall 2009 freshmen:** 17% ranked in the top 10 percent of their high school class; 45% were in the top 25 percent; 82% were in the top half. (Proportion submitting class standing: 62%.) **Average high school grade point average:** 3.2. **First-year students who submitted SAT scores:** 96%. Scores (25/75 percentile): Critical Reading: 480-580, Math: 490-600, Combined: 970-1180. **First-year students submitting ACT scores:** 17%. Scores (25/75 percentile): English: N/A, Math: N/A, Composite: 21-26.

ACADEMICS

Year founded: 1892. **Academic calendar:** Semester. **Degrees offered:** bachelor's, post-bachelor's certificate, master's, doctorate. **Most popular majors:** 8% communication studies/speech communication and rhetoric, 7% nursing/registered nurse training (R.N., A.S.N., B.S.N., M.S.N.), 7% psychology, 5% kinesiology and exercise science, 4% human development and family studies. **Major fields of study:** agriculture, agriculture operations, and related sciences; architecture and related services; area, ethnic, cultural, and gender studies; biological and biomedical sciences; business, management, marketing, and related support services; communication, journalism, and related programs; computer and information sciences and support services; education; engineering; English language and literature/letters; family and consumer sciences/human sciences; foreign languages, literatures, and linguistics; health professions and related clinical sciences; history; liberal arts and sciences studies, and humanities; mathematics and statistics; natural resources and conservation; philosophy and religious studies; physical sciences; psychology; public administration and social service professions; social sciences; visual and performing arts. **Areas of required coursework:** arts/fine arts, humanities, mathematics, English (including composition), foreign languages, sciences (biological or physical), social science, other. **Pre-professional programs:** pre-law, pre-medicine, pre-veterinary science, pre-pharmacy. **Special academic programs:** cooperative (work-study plan) program, distance learning, double major, dual enrollment, exchange student program (domestic), honors program, independent study, internships, study abroad, teacher certificate program, weekend college. **Teacher certification offered in:** early childhood, special education, elementary, middle/junior high, adult education, secondary, bilingual/bicultural. **Cooperative education programs:** agriculture, art, business, computer science, education, engineering, health professions, other. **Reserve Officers Training Corps (ROTC):** Army ROTC: Offered on campus. **Faculty and instruction (2009-2010):** Total instructional faculty: 662 full-time, 600 part-time (52% men; 48% women; 7% minorities). Full-time faculty with Ph.D. or other terminal degree: 84%. Student/faculty ratio: 15/1. Classes of fewer than 20 students: 35%; of 20 to 49 students: 57%; of 50 or more students: 8%. **Advanced Placement and International Baccalaureate credit:** AP tests may be used for: Credit and/or placement. Scores accepted: 3, 4, 5. International Baccalaureate exams may be used for: Credit and/or placement. **Freshmen returning for sophomore year:** 80%. **Graduation rates:** Four-year: 39%; five-year: 56%; six-year: 60%.

COSTS AND FINANCIAL AID

Financial aid office: (401) 874-9500. **Expenses (2010-2011):** Tuition and fees 2010-2011: $10,476 in state, $27,182 out of state; room/board: $10,854. **Financial aid:** Priority filing date for institution's financial aid form: March 1. In 2009-2010, 90% of undergraduates applied for financial aid. Of those, 76% were determined to have financial need; 68% had their need fully met. Average financial aid package (proportion receiving): $12,794 (60%). Average amount of gift aid, such as scholarships or grants (proportion receiving): $7,540 (60%). Average amount of self-help aid, such as work study or loans (proportion receiving): $5,353 (59%). Average need-based loan (excluding PLUS or other private loans): $5,499. Among students who received need-based aid, the average percentage of need met: 57%. Among students who received aid based on merit, the average award (and the proportion receiving): $5,057 (3%). The average athletic scholarship (and the proportion receiving): $2,745 (0%). Average amount of debt of borrowers graduating in 2009: $22,500. Proportion who borrowed: 72%.

CAMPUS LIFE AND EXTRACURRICULAR ACTIVITIES

Campus housing available (% using): coed dorms (74%), women's dorms (1%), sorority housing (6%), fraternity housing (5%), apartments for married students (0%), apartment for single students (9%), special housing for disabled students (2%), special housing for international students (1%), other housing options (0%). Students who live in college-owned, operated, or affiliated housing: 45%. **Clubs and organizations:** Number of student organizations: 100. Activities include: campus ministries, choral groups, concert band, dance, drama/theater, international student organization, jazz band, literary magazine, marching band, music ensembles, musical theater, pep band, radio station, student government, student newspaper, student film society, symphony orchestra, television station, yearbook. Number of fraternities: 12; sororities: 10. Proportion of men in fraternities: 12%; of women in sororities: 15%. Average proportion of students who stay on campus on weekends: 62%. **Sports program (2009-2010):** Member of NCAA I. *Men's intercollegiate varsity sports:* baseball, basketball, cross country, football, golf, soccer, track and field (indoor), track and field (outdoor). *Women's intercollegiate varsity sports:* basketball, crew (heavyweight), cross country, crew (lightweight), soccer, softball, swimming, tennis, track and field (indoor), track and field (outdoor), volleyball.

SERVICES AND FACILITIES

Basic services: nonremedial tutoring, women's center, placement service, day care, health service, health insurance, other. **Remedial assistance:** reading, math, writing, study skills, other. **Counseling services:** minority student, career, military, personal, veteran student, academic, older student, psychological, birth control, religious, other. **For learning-disabled students:** School does not offer a structured program with separate admission and additional fees. Total undergraduates in learning-disabled program or receiving services: 450. Services include: reading machines, tape recorders, note-taking services, special bookstore section, learning center, readers, extended time for tests, early syllabus, priority registration, priority seating, texts on tape, exams on tape or computer, other testing accommodations, waiver of foreign language degree requirement, other. **Library:** Number of titles: 1,396,958; number of current serial subscriptions: 18,742. **Information technology resources:** Students are not required to lease or own a computer. Number of campus computers available to all students: 2,500. School has a wireless network. Approximate number of users that can be accommodated: 5,000. Proportion of college-owned housing units wired for high-speed internet access: 98%. **Campus safety:** Security services offered: 24-hour foot-and-vehicle patrols, late-night transport/escort service, 24-hour emergency telephones, lighted pathways/sidewalks, controlled dormitory access (key, security card, etc.).

TRANSFER AND INTERNATIONAL STUDENTS

Transfer students: May apply for admission for the following academic terms: Fall, Spring. Applicants need a minimum number of credits to apply. For fall 2009: Transfer applications received: 1,329. Transfer applicants offered admission: 941. Transfer applicants enrolled: 776. **International students:** Number of foreign undergraduates: 31. Minimum TOEFL score required: 550 (paper); 79 (computer).

South Carolina

Allen University

- **Address:** 1530 Harden Street, Columbia, SC 29204
- **Website:** http://www.allenuniversity.edu
- **Private; Religious affiliation:** African Methodist Episcopal
- **Enrollment:** 804 full-time; 23 part-time

KEY STATS
- ✔ **U.S News College Ranking:** second tier, National Liberal Arts Colleges
- ✔ **SAT or ACT Score (25th/75th percentile):** N/A
- ✔ **Tuition:** 2010-2011: $11,334
  - **Selectivity:** Least selective
  - **Acceptance rate:** 72%
  - **Student/faculty ratio:** 25/1
  - **Room/board:** $5,240
  - **Average debt:** $21,970
  - **Proportion who borrowed:** 85%

UNDERGRADUATE STUDENT BODY STATS
2009-2010 enrollment: 804 full-time; 23 part-time. Men: 44%; women: 56%. **Ethnic makeup:** African American: 99%.

ADMISSIONS FACTS AND FIGURES
Phone: (803) 376-5735. **Email:** admissions@allenuniversity.edu. **Website:** http://www.allenuniversity.edu. **Application deadlines for fall 2011:** Regular decision: Rolling. Early decision: Not offered. Early action: Not offered. Admission can be deferred. **Application fee:** None. **Admissions requirements/recommendations:** High school units required (recommended): English: 4 (4); Mathematics: 3 (3); Science: 3 (3); Foreign language: 2 (2); Social studies: 3 (3); History: 3 (3); Academic electives: 5 (5); Total units: 24 (24). Tests: The college uses SAT or ACT scores in admissions decisions. Neither SAT nor ACT required. For admission to the fall 2011 entering class, the school will accept: ACT with or without writing accepted. Campus visit: Recommended. Admissions interview: Neither required nor recommended. Off-campus interview: Not available. **Factors that count in admissions decisions:** *Academic:* Secondary school record: Very Important. Class rank: Important. Letters of recommendation: Considered. Standardized test scores: Considered. Essay: Considered. *Nonacademic:* Interview: Important. Extracurricular activities: Important. Talent/ability: Important. Character/personal qualities: Important. Alumni/ae relationship: Important. Geographical residence: Important. State residency: Not Considered. Religious affiliation/commitment: Very Important. Minority status: Not Considered. Volunteer work: Important. Work experience: Considered. **Other schools with the greatest overlap in applicants:** Benedict College; Claflin University; Morris College; South Carolina State University; Voorhees College. **Admissions statistics for the fall 2009 entering class:** Total applicants: 1,937. Total accepted: 1,395. Freshmen enrolled: 242; 0% were from out of state. Overall acceptance rate: 72%. **Credentials of fall 2009 freshmen:** 9% ranked in the top 10 percent of their high school class; 8% were in the top 25 percent; 48% were in the top half. (Proportion submitting class standing: 100%.) **First-year students who submitted SAT scores:** 21%. **First-year students submitting ACT scores:** 8%. Scores (25/75 percentile): English: N/A, Math: N/A, Composite: N/A.

ACADEMICS
Year founded: 1870. **Academic calendar:** Semester. **Degrees offered:** bachelor's. **Most popular majors:** 17% business administration and management, 16% social sciences, 6% religion/religious studies, 5% biology/biological sciences, 2% mathematics. **Major fields of study:** biological and biomedical sciences; business, management, marketing, and related support services; education; English language and literature/letters; liberal arts and sciences studies, and humanities; mathematics and statistics; philosophy and religious studies; physical sciences; social sciences; visual and performing arts. **Areas of required coursework:** arts/fine arts, humanities, computer literacy, mathematics, English (including composition), foreign languages, sciences (biological or physical), history, social science. **Special academic programs:** honors program, independent study, internships, weekend college, other. **Cooperative education programs:** business, social/behavioral science. **Reserve Officers Training Corps (ROTC):** Army ROTC: Offered at cooper-

ating institution (Benedict College); Navy ROTC: Offered at cooperating institution; Air Force ROTC: Offered at cooperating institution (University of South Carolina). **Faculty and instruction (2009-2010):** Total instructional faculty: 29 full-time, 12 part-time (51% men; 49% women; 66% minorities). Full-time faculty with Ph.D. or other terminal degree: 45%. Student/faculty ratio: 25/1. Classes of fewer than 20 students: 43%; of 20 to 49 students: 47%; of 50 or more students: 10%. **Advanced Placement and International Baccalaureate credit:** International Baccalaureate exams may be used for: Credit only. **Freshmen returning for sophomore year:** 48%. **Graduation rates:** Four-year: 9%; five-year: 17%; six-year: 19%. **Graduate study:** 13% of students pursue further study immediately upon graduation; 8% within one year. Fields in which graduates pursue further study: Master of Business Administration (MBA), 5%; medicine, 3%; theology (or the seminary), 8%.

COSTS AND FINANCIAL AID
Financial aid office: (803) 376-5736. **Expenses (2010-2011):** Tuition and fees 2010-2011: $11,334; room/board: $5,240. Estimated books and supplies: $1,800; transportation: $1,000; personal expenses: $800. **Financial aid:** Priority filing date for institution's financial aid form: April 15. In 2009-2010, 100% of undergraduates applied for financial aid. Of those, 99% were determined to have financial need; 5% had their need fully met. Average financial aid package (proportion receiving): $10,149 (98%). Average amount of gift aid, such as scholarships or grants (proportion receiving): $7,104 (95%). Average amount of self-help aid, such as work study or loans (proportion receiving): $3,505 (91%). Average need-based loan (excluding PLUS or other private loans): $3,342. Among students who received need-based aid, the average percentage of need met: 59%. Among students who received aid based on merit, the average award (and the proportion receiving): $2,000 (0%). The average athletic scholarship (and the proportion receiving): $0 (0%). Average amount of debt of borrowers graduating in 2009: $21,970. Proportion who borrowed: 85%.

CAMPUS LIFE AND EXTRACURRICULAR ACTIVITIES
Campus housing available: women's dorms, men's dorms, apartment for single students. Students who live in college-owned, operated, or affiliated housing: 77%. **Student employment:** During the 2009-2010 academic year, 0% of undergraduates worked on campus. Average per-year earnings: $0. **Clubs and organizations:** Number of student organizations: 12. Activities include: campus ministries, choral groups, dance, jazz band, music ensembles, pep band, student government. Number of fraternities: 4; sororities: 3. Proportion of men in fraternities: 72%; of women in sororities: 28%. Average proportion of students who stay on campus on weekends: 80%. **Sports program (2009-2010):** Member of NAIA. *Men's intercollegiate varsity sports:* basketball, cross country, golf, track and field (indoor), track and field (outdoor). *Women's intercollegiate varsity sports:* basketball, bowling, cross country, golf, track and field (indoor), track and field (outdoor), volleyball.

SERVICES AND FACILITIES
Basic services: nonremedial tutoring, placement service, health service, health insurance. **Remedial assistance:** reading, math, writing, study skills. **Counseling services:** minority student, career, military, personal, veteran student, academic, older student, psychological, birth control, religious. **For learning-disabled students:** Total undergraduates in learning-disabled program or receiving services: 0. Services include: untimed tests, learning center, extended time for tests, tutors, priority seating, exams on tape or computer, take home exams. **Library:** Number of titles: 52,210; number of current serial subscriptions: 45. **Information technology resources:** Students are not required to lease or own a computer. Number of campus computers available to all students: 338. School has a wireless network. Approximate number of users that can be accommodated: 827. Proportion of college-owned housing units wired for high-speed internet access: 10%. **Campus safety:** Security services offered: 24-hour foot-and-vehicle patrols, 24-hour emergency telephones, lighted pathways/sidewalks, controlled dormitory access (key, security card, etc).

TRANSFER AND INTERNATIONAL STUDENTS
Transfer students: May apply for admission for the following academic terms: Fall, Spring. Applicants do not need a minimum number of credits

to apply. For fall 2009: Transfer applicants enrolled: 54. **International students:** Number of foreign undergraduates: 0.

Anderson University

- **Address:** 316 Boulevard, Anderson, SC 29621
- **Website:** http://www.andersonuniversity.edu
- **Private; Religious affiliation:** South Carolina Baptist Convention
- **Enrollment:** 1,689 full-time; 442 part-time

KEY STATS
✔ **U.S News College Ranking:** 21, Regional Colleges (South)
✔ **SAT Score (25th/75th percentile):** 890-1160
✔ **Tuition:** 2010-2011: $19,950

Selectivity: Selective	**Room/board:** $7,550
Acceptance rate: 68%	**Average debt:** $16,488
Student/faculty ratio: 18/1	**Proportion who borrowed:** 82%

UNDERGRADUATE STUDENT BODY STATS
2009-2010 enrollment: 1,689 full-time; 442 part-time. Men: 33%; women: 67%. **Ethnic makeup:** African American: 12%; Asian American: 1%; Hispanic: 2%; White: 82%; International: 2%. **Religious preference:** Roman Catholic: 3%; Protestant: 24%; No preference: 5%; Unknown: 15%; South Carolina Baptist Convention: 52%.

ADMISSIONS FACTS AND FIGURES
Phone: (864) 231-5607. **Email:** admissions@ac.edu. **Website:** http://www.andersonuniversity.edu. **Application deadlines for fall 2011:** Regular decision: Rolling. Early decision: Not offered. Early action: Not offered. Admission can be deferred. **Application fee:** $25. **To apply online, go to:** http://www.andersonuniversity.edu/admissions.aspx?id=2135. **Admissions requirements/recommendations:** High school units required (recommended): English: 4 (4); Mathematics: 3 (4); Science: 3 (4); Foreign language: 2 (2); Social studies: 2 (3); History: 2 (2); Academic electives: 4 (4); Total units: 20 (22). Tests: The college uses SAT or ACT scores in admissions decisions. Either SAT or ACT required. For admission to the fall 2011 entering class, the school will accept: ACT with writing recommended. Campus visit: Neither required nor recommended. Admissions interview: Recommended. Off-campus interview: May be arranged. **Factors that count in admissions decisions:** *Academic:* Secondary school record: Very Important. Class rank: Important. Letters of recommendation: Considered. Standardized test scores: Very Important. Essay: Considered. *Nonacademic:* Interview: Considered. Extracurricular activities: Not Considered. Talent/ability: Considered. Character/personal qualities: Important. Alumni/ae relationship: Considered. Geographical residence: Not Considered. State residency: Not Considered. Religious affiliation/commitment: Considered. Minority status: Considered. Volunteer work: Considered. Work experience: Not Considered. **Other schools with the greatest overlap in applicants:** Clemson University; College of Charleston; Lander University; University of South Carolina; Winthrop University. **Admissions statistics for the fall 2009 entering class:** Total applicants: 1,926. Total accepted: 1,319. Freshmen enrolled: 495; 5% were from out of state. Overall acceptance rate: 68%. **Credentials of fall 2009 freshmen:** 33% ranked in the top 10 percent of their high school class; 52% were in the top 25 percent; 80% were in the top half. (Proportion submitting class standing: 94%.) **Average high school grade point average:** 3.3. **First-year students who submitted SAT scores:** 85%. Scores (25/75 percentile): Critical Reading: 440-580, Math: 450-580, Combined: 890-1160. **First-year students submitting ACT scores:** 58%. Scores (25/75 percentile): English: 17-25, Math: 17-24, Composite: 18-24.

ACADEMICS
Year founded: 1911. **Academic calendar:** Semester. **Degrees offered:** bachelor's, master's. **Most popular majors:** 33% education, 32% business, management, marketing, and related support services, 10% visual and performing arts, 5% philosophy and religious studies, 5% psychology. **Major fields of study:** biological and biomedical sciences; business, management, marketing, and related support services; communication, journalism, and related programs; education; English language and literature/letters; foreign languages, literatures, and linguistics; health professions and related clinical sciences; history; mathematics and statistics; parks, recreation, leisure, and fitness studies; philosophy and religious studies; psychology; security and protective services; theology and religious vocations; visual and performing arts. **Areas of required coursework:** arts/fine arts, humanities, mathematics,

English (including composition), foreign languages, sciences (biological or physical), history, social science, other. **Pre-professional programs:** pre-law, pre-dentistry, pre-medicine, pre-theology, pre-veterinary science, pre-pharmacy, other. **Special academic programs:** accelerated program, distance learning, double major, dual enrollment, honors program, independent study, internships, liberal arts/career combination, study abroad, teacher certificate program. **Teacher certification offered in:** early childhood, special education, elementary, middle/junior high, secondary. **Reserve Officers Training Corps (ROTC):** Army ROTC: Offered at cooperating institution; Air Force ROTC: Offered at cooperating institution (Clemson University). **Faculty and instruction (2009-2010):** Total instructional faculty: 76 full-time, 106 part-time (51% men; 49% women; 5% minorities). Full-time faculty with Ph.D. or other terminal degree: 71%. Student/faculty ratio: 18/1. Classes of fewer than 20 students: 48%; of 20 to 49 students: 50%; of 50 or more students: 2%. **Advanced Placement and International Baccalaureate credit:** AP tests may be used for: Credit only. Scores accepted: 3, 4, 5. International Baccalaureate exams may be used for: Credit only. **Freshmen returning for sophomore year:** 67%. **Graduation rates:** Four-year: 46%; five-year: 52%; six-year: 46%. **Graduate study:** 17% of students pursue further study immediately upon graduation. Fields in which graduates pursue further study: Master of Business Administration (MBA), 29%; law, 3%; medicine, 5%; dentistry, 1%; theology (or the seminary), 7%; education, 12%; arts and sciences, 23%.

COSTS AND FINANCIAL AID
Financial aid office: (864) 231-2070. **Expenses (2010-2011):** Tuition and fees 2010-2011: $19,950; room/board: $7,550. Estimated books and supplies: $1,600; transportation: $2,250; personal expenses: $1,625. **Financial aid:** Priority filing date for institution's financial aid form: March 1; deadline: June 30. In 2009-2010, 92% of undergraduates applied for financial aid. Of those, 81% were determined to have financial need; 26% had their need fully met. Average financial aid package (proportion receiving): $15,340 (81%). Average amount of gift aid, such as scholarships or grants (proportion receiving): $12,216 (80%). Average amount of self-help aid, such as work study or loans (proportion receiving): $4,671 (58%). Average need-based loan (excluding PLUS or other private loans): $4,339. Among students who received need-based aid, the average percentage of need met: 72%. Among students who received aid based on merit, the average award (and the proportion receiving): $8,064 (17%). The average athletic scholarship (and the proportion receiving): $5,949 (7%). Average amount of debt of borrowers graduating in 2009: $16,488. Proportion who borrowed: 82%.

CAMPUS LIFE AND EXTRACURRICULAR ACTIVITIES
Campus housing available (% using): women's dorms (62%), men's dorms (36%), other housing options (2%). Students who live in college-owned, operated, or affiliated housing: 56%. **Student employment:** During the 2009-2010 academic year, 19% of undergraduates worked on campus. Average per-year earnings: $1,780. **Clubs and organizations:** Number of student organizations: 33. Activities include: campus ministries, choral groups, concert band, dance, drama/theater, jazz band, literary magazine, music ensembles, musical theater, student government, student newspaper, symphony orchestra. Number of fraternities: 0; sororities: 0. Average proportion of students who stay on campus on weekends: 30%. **Sports program (2009-2010):** Member of NCAA II. *Men's intercollegiate varsity sports:* baseball, basketball, cross country, golf, soccer, tennis, track and field (indoor), wrestling. *Women's intercollegiate varsity sports:* basketball, cross country, golf, soccer, softball, tennis, track and field (indoor), volleyball.

SERVICES AND FACILITIES
Basic services: nonremedial tutoring, placement service, health service. **Counseling services:** career, personal, academic, psychological, religious. **For learning-disabled students:** School does not offer a structured program with separate admission and additional fees. Services include: tape recorders, note-taking services, oral tests, readers, extended time for tests, priority registration, priority seating, typist/scribe, other testing accommodations. **Library:** Number of titles: 80,212; number of current serial subscriptions: 297. **Information technology resources:** Students are not required to lease or own a computer. Number of campus computers available to all students: 235. School has a wireless network. Approximate number of users that can be accommodated: 900. Proportion of college-owned housing units wired for high-speed internet access: 100%. **Campus safety:** Security services offered: 24-hour foot-and-vehicle patrols, late-night transport/escort service, 24-hour emergency telephones, lighted pathways/sidewalks, student patrols, controlled dormitory access (key, security card, etc).

TRANSFER AND INTERNATIONAL STUDENTS

Transfer students: May apply for admission for the following academic terms: Fall, Spring, Summer. Applicants do not need a minimum number of credits to apply. For fall 2009: Transfer applications received: 383. Transfer applicants offered admission: 202. Transfer applicants enrolled: 105. **International students:** Number of foreign undergraduates: 38 (2% of student body). Number of countries represented: 15. Minimum TOEFL score required: 550 (paper); 75 (computer).

Benedict College

- **Address:** 1600 Harden Street, Columbia, SC 29204
- **Website:** http://www.benedict.edu
- **Private; Religious affiliation:** Baptist
- **Enrollment:** N/A

KEY STATS

✔ **U.S News College Ranking:** 71, Regional Colleges (South)
✔ **ACT Score (25th/75th percentile):** 13-17
✔ **Tuition:** 2009-2010: $15,590

Selectivity: Least selective	**Room/board:** $7,172
Acceptance rate: 70%	**Average debt:** N/A
Student/faculty ratio: N/A	**Proportion who borrowed:** N/A

Charleston Southern University

- **Address:** PO Box 118087, 9200 University Boulevard, Charleston, SC 29423
- **Website:** http://www.csuniv.edu
- **Private; Religious affiliation:** Baptist
- **Enrollment:** 2,364 full-time; 407 part-time

KEY STATS

✔ **U.S News College Ranking:** 87, Regional Universities (South)
✔ **SAT Score (25th/75th percentile):** 1000-1170
✔ **Tuition:** 2010-2011: $19,854

Selectivity: Selective	**Room/board:** $7,616
Acceptance rate: 64%	**Average debt:** N/A
Student/faculty ratio: 16/1	**Proportion who borrowed:** N/A

UNDERGRADUATE STUDENT BODY STATS

2009-2010 enrollment: 2,364 full-time; 407 part-time. Men: 38%; women: 62%. **Ethnic makeup:** African American: 29%; Asian American: 1%; Hispanic: 3%; White: 66%; International: 1%. **Religious preference:** Roman Catholic: 8%; Protestant: 14%; Unknown: 32%; Baptist: 35%; Methodist: 7%; Other: 4%.

ADMISSIONS FACTS AND FIGURES

Phone: (843) 863-7050. **Email:** enroll@csuniv.edu. **Website:** http://www.csuniv.edu. **Application deadlines for fall 2011:** Regular decision: Rolling. Early decision: Not offered. Early action: Not offered. Admission cannot be deferred. **Application fee:** $40. **To apply online, go to:** https://www.applyweb.com/apply/chsu/menu.html. **Admissions requirements/recommendations:** High school units required (recommended): English: 4; Mathematics: 3 (4); Science: 3; Foreign language: 0 (2); Social studies: 2; History: (2); Total units: 12 (8). Tests: The college uses SAT or ACT scores in admissions decisions. Either SAT or ACT required. For admission to the fall 2011 entering class, the school will accept: ACT with writing required. Campus visit: Recommended. Admissions interview: Required. Off-campus interview: Not available. **Factors that count in admissions decisions:** *Academic:* Secondary school record: Important. Class rank: Important. Letters of recommendation: Considered. Standardized test scores: Very Important. Essay: Considered. *Nonacademic:* Interview: Considered. Extracurricular activities: Considered. Talent/ability: Considered. Character/personal qualities: Considered. Alumni/ae relationship: Considered. Geographical residence: Not Considered. State residency: Not Considered. Religious affiliation/commitment: Not Considered. Minority status: Not Considered. Volunteer work: Not Considered. Work experience: Considered. **Other schools with the greatest overlap in applicants:** Anderson University; College of Charleston; Furman University; North Greenville University; University of South

Carolina. **Admissions statistics for the fall 2009 entering class:** Total applicants: 3,431. Total accepted: 2,190. Freshmen enrolled: 658; Overall acceptance rate: 64%. **First-year students who submitted SAT scores:** 81%. Scores (25/75 percentile): Critical Reading: 500-570, Math: 500-600, Combined: 1000-1170. **First-year students submitting ACT scores:** 41%. Scores (25/75 percentile): English: 21-28, Math: 20-26, Composite: 21-27.

ACADEMICS

Year founded: 1964. **Academic calendar:** Other. **Degrees offered:** bachelor's, master's. **Most popular majors:** 14% business administration, management, and operations, 8% biology/biological sciences, 6% psychology, 4% business administration and management, 4% nursing/registered nurse training (R.N., A.S.N., B.S.N., M.S.N.). **Major fields of study:** biological and biomedical sciences; business, management, marketing, and related support services; computer and information sciences and support services; education; engineering; English language and literature/letters; foreign languages, literatures, and linguistics; health professions and related clinical sciences; legal professions and studies; liberal arts and sciences studies, and humanities; mathematics and statistics; multi/interdisciplinary studies; natural resources and conservation; parks, recreation, leisure, and fitness studies; philosophy and religious studies; physical sciences; psychology; science technologies/technicians; security and protective services; social sciences; theology and religious vocations; visual and performing arts. **Areas of required coursework:** arts/fine arts, humanities, computer literacy, mathematics, English (including composition), foreign languages, sciences (biological or physical), history, social science, other. **Pre-professional programs:** pre-law, pre-dentistry, pre-medicine, pre-theology, pre-pharmacy, other. **Special academic programs (% participation):** double major (4.3%), honors program (5.7%), internships (25%), teacher certificate program (7.6%). **Teacher certification offered in:** early childhood, elementary, middle/junior high, secondary, bilingual/bicultural. **Cooperative education programs:** computer science, engineering, technologies. **Reserve Officers Training Corps (ROTC):** Army ROTC: Offered on campus; Air Force ROTC: Offered on campus. **Faculty and instruction (2009-2010):** Total instructional faculty: 132 full-time, 92 part-time (52% men; 48% women; 7% minorities). Full-time faculty with Ph.D. or other terminal degree: 68%. Student/faculty ratio: 16/1. Classes of fewer than 20 students: 45%; of 20 to 49 students: 49%; of 50 or more students: 5%. **Advanced Placement and International Baccalaureate credit:** AP tests may be used for: Credit only. Scores accepted: 3, 4, 5. **Freshmen returning for sophomore year:** 61%. **Graduation rates:** Four-year: 19%; five-year: 31%; six-year: 38%. **Graduate study:** 15% of students pursue further study immediately upon graduation; 20% within one year. Fields in which graduates pursue further study: Master of Business Administration (MBA), 5%; law, 2%; medicine, 3%; dentistry, 1%; theology (or the seminary), 1%; education, 2%.

COSTS AND FINANCIAL AID

Financial aid office: (843) 863-7050. **Expenses (2010-2011):** Tuition and fees 2010-2011: $19,854; room/board: $7,616. **Financial aid:** Priority filing date for institution's financial aid form: April 15.

CAMPUS LIFE AND EXTRACURRICULAR ACTIVITIES

Campus housing available (% using): women's dorms (65%), men's dorms (34%), apartments for married students (1%). **Student employment:** During the 2009-2010 academic year, 42% of undergraduates worked on campus. Average per-year earnings: $2,000. **Clubs and organizations:** Number of student organizations: 152. Activities include: choral groups, concert band, dance, drama/theater, jazz band, literary magazine, music ensembles, radio station, student government, student newspaper, student film society, symphony orchestra. Number of fraternities: 0; sororities: 0. Average proportion of students who stay on campus on weekends: 65%. **Sports program (2009-2010):** Member of NCAA II. *Men's intercollegiate varsity sports:* baseball, basketball, cross country, football, golf, tennis, track and field (outdoor), volleyball. *Women's intercollegiate varsity sports:* basketball, cross country, golf, soccer, softball, tennis, track and field (outdoor), volleyball.

SERVICES AND FACILITIES

Basic services: nonremedial tutoring, placement service. **Remedial assistance:** math, writing, study skills. **Counseling services:** personal, veteran student, academic, psychological, religious. **For learning-disabled students:** School does not offer a structured program with separate admission and additional fees. Services include: remedial math, remedial English, tape recorders, note-taking services, oral tests, learning center, readers, extended time for tests, tutors. **Library:** Number of titles: 169,975; number of current serial subscriptions: 1,037. **Information technology resources:** Students are not required to lease or own a computer. Number of campus computers available to all students: 255. School has a wireless network. Proportion of college-owned housing units wired for high-speed internet access: 100%. **Campus safety:** Security services offered: 24-hour foot-and-vehicle patrols, late-night transport/escort service, 24-hour emergency telephones, lighted pathways/sidewalks, controlled dormitory access (key, security card, etc).

TRANSFER AND INTERNATIONAL STUDENTS

Transfer students: May apply for admission for the following academic terms: Fall, Spring, Summer. Applicants need a minimum number of credits to apply. **International students:** Number of foreign undergraduates: 27 (1% of student body). Minimum TOEFL score required: 550 (paper); 213 (computer).

The Citadel

- **Address:** 171 Moultrie Street, Charleston, SC 29409
- **Website:** http://www.citadel.edu
- **Public**
- **Enrollment:** 2,238 full-time; 128 part-time

KEY STATS

✔ **U.S News College Ranking:** 6, Regional Universities (South)
✔ **SAT Score (25th/75th percentile):** 990-1180
✔ **Tuition:** 2009-2010: $9,993 in state, $23,227 out of state
Selectivity: Selective   **Room/board:** $6,038
Acceptance rate: 79%   **Average debt:** $11,927
Student/faculty ratio: 16/1   **Proportion who borrowed:** 43%

UNDERGRADUATE STUDENT BODY STATS

2009-2010 enrollment: 2,238 full-time; 128 part-time. Men: 92%; women: 8%. **Ethnic makeup:** African American: 7%; Asian American: 3%; Hispanic: 5%; White: 83%; International: 1%.

ADMISSIONS FACTS AND FIGURES

Phone: (843) 953-5230. **Email:** admissions@citadel.edu. **Website:** http://www.citadel.edu. **Application deadlines for fall 2011:** Regular decision: Rolling. Early decision: Not offered. Early action: Not offered. Admission cannot be deferred. **Application fee:** $40. **To apply online, go to:** http://www.applyweb.com/apply/citadel/. **Admissions requirements/recommendations:** High school units required (recommended): English: 4; Mathematics: 3 (4); Science: 3; Foreign language: 2; Social studies: 2; History: 1; Academic electives: 4; Total units: 20. Tests: The college uses SAT or ACT scores in admissions decisions. Either SAT or ACT required. For admission to the fall 2011 entering class, the school will accept: ACT with writing required. Campus visit: Recommended. Admissions interview: Recommended. Off-campus interview: May be arranged. **Factors that count in admissions decisions:** *Academic:* Secondary school record: Important. Class rank: Considered. Letters of recommendation: Considered. Standardized test scores: Very Important. Essay: Not Considered. *Nonacademic:* Interview: Considered. Extracurricular activities: Important. Talent/ability: Important. Character/personal qualities: Important. Alumni/ae relationship: Considered. Geographical residence: Considered. State residency: Important. Religious affiliation/commitment: Not Considered. Minority status: Not Considered. Volunteer work: Considered. Work experience: Not Considered. **Other schools with the greatest overlap in applicants:** Clemson University; Norwich University; United States Military Academy; University of South Carolina; Virginia Military Institute. **Admissions statistics for the fall 2009 entering class:** Total applicants: 2,165. Total accepted: 1,717. Freshmen enrolled: 591; 54% were from out of state. Overall acceptance rate: 79%. **Credentials of fall 2009 freshmen:** 12% ranked in the top 10 percent of their high school class; 33% were in the top 25 percent; 70% were in the top half. (Proportion submitting class standing: 77%.) **Average high school grade point average:** 3.4. **First-year students who submitted SAT scores:** 72%. Scores (25/75 percentile): Critical Reading: 480-580, Math: 510-600, Combined: 990-1180. **First-year students submitting ACT scores:** 27%. Scores (25/75 percentile): English: N/A, Math: N/A, Composite: 19-23.

ACADEMICS

Year founded: 1842. **Academic calendar:** Semester. **Degrees offered:** bachelor's, master's, post-master's certificate. **Most popular majors:** 34% business administration and management, 14% criminal justice/law enforcement administration, 10% political science and government, 7% history, 7% physical education teaching and coaching. **Major fields of study:** biological and biomedical sciences; business, management, marketing, and related support services; computer and information sciences and support services; education; engineering; English language and literature/letters; foreign languages, literatures, and linguistics; history; mathematics and statistics; physical sciences; psychology; security and protective services; social sciences. **Areas of required coursework:** computer literacy, mathematics, English (including composition), foreign languages, sciences (biological or physical), history, social science, other. **Special academic programs:** cooperative (work-study plan) program, distance learning, double major, English as a Second Language (ESL), honors program, independent study, internships, study abroad, teacher certificate program. **Teacher certification offered in:** secondary. **Reserve Officers Training Corps (ROTC):** Army ROTC: Offered on campus; Navy ROTC: Offered on campus; Air Force ROTC: Offered on campus. **Faculty and instruction (2009-2010):** Total instructional faculty: 172 full-time, 66 part-time (64% men; 36% women; 11% minorities). Full-time faculty with Ph.D. or other terminal degree: 95%. Student/faculty ratio: 16/1. Classes of fewer than 20 students: 42%; of 20 to 49 students: 55%; of 50 or more students: 3%. **Advanced Placement and International Baccalaureate credit:** AP tests may be used for: Credit only. Scores accepted: 3, 4, 5. International Baccalaureate exams may be used for: Credit only. **Freshmen returning for sophomore year:** 83%. **Graduation rates:** Four-year: 67%; five-year: 74%; six-year: 70%. **Graduate study:** 14% of students pursue further study immediately upon graduation; 17% within one year; 23% within five years. Fields in which graduates pursue further study: Master of Business Administration (MBA), 35%; law, 15%; medicine, 10%; dentistry, 3%; engineering, 10%; theology (or the seminary), 2%; education, 10%; arts and sciences, 15%.

COSTS AND FINANCIAL AID

Financial aid office: (843) 953-5187. **Expenses (2009-2010):** Tuition and fees 2009-2010: $9,993 in state, $23,227 out of state; room/board: $6,038. Estimated books and supplies: $5,940; transportation: $1,694; personal expenses: $1,618. **Financial aid:** Priority filing date for institution's financial aid form: March 1. In 2009-2010, 71% of undergraduates applied for financial aid. Of those, 53% were determined to have financial need; 34% had their need fully met. Average financial aid package (proportion receiving): $15,434 (52%). Average amount of gift aid, such as scholarships or grants (proportion receiving): $14,670 (41%). Average amount of self-help aid, such as work study or loans (proportion receiving): $4,362 (35%). Average need-based loan (excluding PLUS or other private loans): $4,171. Among students who received need-based aid, the average percentage of need met: 71%. Among students who received aid based on merit, the average award (and the proportion receiving): $15,830 (7%). The average athletic scholarship (and the proportion receiving): $21,419 (5%). Average amount of debt of borrowers graduating in 2009: $11,927. Proportion who borrowed: 43%.

CAMPUS LIFE AND EXTRACURRICULAR ACTIVITIES

Campus housing available (% using): coed dorms (100%). Students who live in college-owned, operated, or affiliated housing: 100%. **Clubs and organizations:** Number of student organizations: 10. Activities include: campus ministries, choral groups, concert band, jazz band, literary magazine, marching band, pep band, student government, student newspaper, yearbook. Number of fraternities: 0; sororities: 0. **Sports program (2009-2010):** Member of NCAA I. *Men's intercollegiate varsity sports:* baseball, basketball, cross country, football, rifle, tennis, track and field (indoor), track and field (outdoor), wrestling. *Women's intercollegiate varsity sports:* cross country, golf, rifle, soccer, track and field (indoor), track and field (outdoor), volleyball.

SERVICES AND FACILITIES

Basic services: nonremedial tutoring, health service, health insurance. **Remedial assistance:** reading, math, writing, study skills. **Counseling services:** minority student, career, personal, academic, psychological, religious. **For learning-disabled students:** School does not offer a structured program with separate admission and additional fees. Total undergraduates in learning-disabled program or receiving services: 100. Services include: untimed tests, note-taking services, learning center, readers, extended time for tests, tutors, priority registration, substitution of courses, texts on tape, exams on tape or computer, other. **Library:** Number of titles: 207,950; number of current serial subscriptions: 367. **Information technology resources:** Students are not required to lease or own a computer. Number of campus computers available to all students: 391. School has a wireless network. Approximate number of users that can be accommodated: 5,000. Proportion of college-owned housing units wired for high-speed internet access: 100%. **Campus safety:** Security services offered: 24-hour foot-and-vehicle patrols, 24-hour

emergency telephones, lighted pathways/sidewalks, controlled dormitory access (key, security card, etc).

TRANSFER AND INTERNATIONAL STUDENTS

Transfer students: May apply for admission for the following academic terms: Fall. Applicants need a minimum number of credits to apply. For fall 2009: Transfer applications received: 201. Transfer applicants offered admission: 111. Transfer applicants enrolled: 77. **International students:** Number of foreign undergraduates: 33 (1% of student body). Number of countries represented: 19. Minimum TOEFL score required: 550 (paper); 79 (computer).

Claflin University

- ■ **Address:** 400 Magnolia Street, Orangeburg, SC 29115
- ■ **Website:** http://www.claflin.edu
- ■ **Private; Religious affiliation:** United Methodist
- ■ **Enrollment:** 1,710 full-time; 69 part-time

KEY STATS

✔ **U.S News College Ranking:** 14, Regional Colleges (South)
✔ **SAT Score (25th/75th percentile):** 800-990
✔ **Tuition:** 2010-2011: $13,332

Selectivity: Less selective	**Room/board:** $8,932
Acceptance rate: 35%	**Average debt:** $33,816
Student/faculty ratio: 14/1	**Proportion who borrowed:** 81%

UNDERGRADUATE STUDENT BODY STATS

2009-2010 enrollment: 1,710 full-time; 69 part-time. Men: 34%; women: 66%. **Ethnic makeup:** African American: 95%; White: 2%; International: 2%. **Religious preference:** Roman Catholic: 1%; Protestant: 49%; Muslim: 1%; No preference: 7%; Unknown: 30%; United Methodist: 7%.

ADMISSIONS FACTS AND FIGURES

Phone: (803) 535-5340. **Email:** mike.zeigler@claflin.edu. **Website:** http://www.claflin.edu. **Application deadlines for fall 2011:** Regular decision: Rolling. Early decision: Not offered. Early action: Not offered. Admission can be deferred. **Application fee:** $20. **To apply online, go to:** https://my.claflin.edu/ics/Admissions/. **Admissions requirements/recommendations:** High school units required (recommended): English: 4 (4); Mathematics: 3 (3); Science: 2 (2); Social studies: 2 (2); History: 1 (1); Academic electives: 7 (7); Total units: 20 (20). Tests: The college uses SAT or ACT scores in admissions decisions. Either SAT or ACT required. For admission to the fall 2011 entering class, the school will accept: ACT with or without writing accepted. Campus visit: Recommended. Admissions interview: Neither required nor recommended. Off-campus interview: Not available. **Factors that count in admissions decisions:** *Academic:* Secondary school record: Very Important. Class rank: Very Important. Letters of recommendation: Considered. Standardized test scores: Very Important. Essay: Important. *Nonacademic:* Interview: Not Considered. Extracurricular activities: Important. Talent/ability: Important. Character/personal qualities: Very Important. Alumni/ae relationship: Important. Geographical residence: Not Considered. State residency: Considered. Religious affiliation/commitment: Not Considered. Minority status: Not Considered. Volunteer work: Considered. Work experience: Considered. **Other schools with the greatest overlap in applicants:** Benedict College; Columbia College; South Carolina State University; University of South Carolina; Voorhees College. **Admissions statistics for the fall 2009 entering class:** Total applicants: 4,092. Total accepted: 1,423. Freshmen enrolled: 468; 24% were from out of state. Overall acceptance rate: 35%. **Credentials of fall 2009 freshmen:** 9% ranked in the top 10 percent of their high school class; 45% were in the top 25 percent; 59% were in the top half. (Proportion submitting class standing: 87%.) **Average high school grade point average:** 3.0. **First-year students who submitted SAT scores:** 70%. Scores (25/75 percentile): Critical Reading: 410-500, Math: 390-490, Combined: 800-990. **First-year students submitting ACT scores:** 68%. Scores (25/75 percentile): English: N/A, Math: N/A, Composite: N/A.

ACADEMICS

Year founded: 1869. **Academic calendar:** Semester. **Degrees offered:** bachelor's, master's. **Most popular majors:** 21% sociology, 12% criminal justice/safety studies, 10% organizational behavior studies, 8% mass communication/media studies, 7% business administration and management. **Major**

fields of study: area, ethnic, cultural, and gender studies; biological and biomedical sciences; business, management, marketing, and related support services; communication, journalism, and related programs; computer and information sciences and support services; education; engineering; English language and literature/letters; history; mathematics and statistics; natural resources and conservation; parks, recreation, leisure, and fitness studies; philosophy and religious studies; physical sciences; security, and protective services; social sciences; visual and performing arts. **Areas of required coursework:** arts/fine arts, humanities, computer literacy, mathematics, English (including composition), philosophy, foreign languages, sciences (biological or physical), history, social science, other. **Special academic programs (% participation):** cooperative (work-study plan) program, cross-registration, distance learning, double major, honors program (16%), independent study, internships, study abroad, teacher certificate program (4%), weekend college, other. **Teacher certification offered in:** early childhood, elementary, middle/junior high, secondary. **Cooperative education programs:** engineering, natural science. **Reserve Officers Training Corps (ROTC):** Army ROTC: Offered at cooperating institution (South Carolina State University); Air Force ROTC: Offered at cooperating institution (University of South Carolina). **Faculty and instruction (2009-2010):** Total instructional faculty: 109 full-time, 26 part-time (56% men; 44% women; 72% minorities). Full-time faculty with Ph.D. or other terminal degree: 77%. Student/faculty ratio: 14/1. Classes of fewer than 20 students: 51%; of 20 to 49 students: 49%; of 50 or more students: 0%. **Advanced Placement and International Baccalaureate credit:** AP tests may be used for: Placement only. International Baccalaureate exams may be used for: Placement only. **Freshmen returning for sophomore year:** 71%. **Graduation rates:** Four-year: 29%; five-year: 44%; six-year: 53%. **Graduate study:** 20% of students pursue further study immediately upon graduation.

COSTS AND FINANCIAL AID

Financial aid office: (803) 535-5334. **Expenses (2010-2011):** Tuition and fees 2010-2011: $13,332; room/board: $8,932. Estimated books and supplies: $750; transportation: $1,800; personal expenses: $3,600. **Financial aid:** Priority filing date for institution's financial aid form: April 15; deadline: July 15. In 2009-2010, 99% of undergraduates applied for financial aid. Of those, 98% were determined to have financial need; 22% had their need fully met. Average financial aid package (proportion receiving): $17,933 (98%). Average amount of gift aid, such as scholarships or grants (proportion receiving): $15,698 (94%). Average amount of self-help aid, such as work study or loans (proportion receiving): $6,099 (88%). Average need-based loan (excluding PLUS or other private loans): $6,223. Among students who received need-based aid, the average percentage of need met: 84%. Among students who received aid based on merit, the average award (and the proportion receiving): $0 (0%). The average athletic scholarship (and the proportion receiving): $0 (0%). Average amount of debt of borrowers graduating in 2009: $33,816. Proportion who borrowed: 81%.

CAMPUS LIFE AND EXTRACURRICULAR ACTIVITIES

Campus housing available (% using): women's dorms (67%), men's dorms (33%). Students who live in college-owned, operated, or affiliated housing: 62%. **Student employment:** During the 2009-2010 academic year, 10% of undergraduates worked on campus. Average per-year earnings: $1,500. **Clubs and organizations:** Number of student organizations: 58. Activities include: choral groups, concert band, drama/theater, international student organization, jazz band, literary magazine, music ensembles, radio station, student government, student newspaper, student film society, television station, yearbook. Number of fraternities: 4; sororities: 4. Proportion of men in fraternities: 2%; of women in sororities: 5%. Average proportion of students who stay on campus on weekends: 70%. **Sports program (2009-2010):** Member of NCAA II. *Men's intercollegiate varsity sports:* baseball, basketball, cross country, track and field (indoor), track and field (outdoor). *Women's intercollegiate varsity sports:* basketball, cross country, softball, track and field (indoor), track and field (outdoor), volleyball.

SERVICES AND FACILITIES

Basic services: nonremedial tutoring, placement service, health service, health insurance. **Remedial assistance:** reading, math, writing, study skills. **Counseling services:** minority student, career, personal, veteran student, academic, older student, psychological, religious. **For learning-disabled students:** School does not offer a structured program with separate admission and additional fees. Total undergraduates in learning-disabled program or receiving services: 18. Services include: remedial math, remedial English, reading machines, tape recorders, other special classes, diagnostic testing service, untimed tests, note-taking services, special bookstore section, extended time for tests, tutors, early syllabus, other testing accommodations. **Library:** Number of titles: 162,248; number of current serial subscriptions: 445. **Information technology resources:** Students are not required to lease or own a computer. Number of campus computers available to all students: 500. School has a wireless network. Approximate number of users that can be accommodated: 400. Proportion of college-owned housing units wired for high-speed internet access: 100%. **Campus safety:** Security services offered: 24-hour foot-and-vehicle patrols, late-night transport/escort service, 24-hour emergency telephones, lighted pathways/sidewalks, controlled dormitory access (key, security card, etc).

TRANSFER AND INTERNATIONAL STUDENTS

Transfer students: May apply for admission for the following academic terms: Fall, Spring, Summer. Applicants need a minimum number of credits to apply. For fall 2009: Transfer applications received: 265. Transfer applicants offered admission: 51. Transfer applicants enrolled: 45. **International students:** Number of foreign undergraduates: 36 (2% of student body). Number of countries represented: 11. Minimum TOEFL score required: 500 (paper); 213 (computer).

Clemson University

- **Address:** 105 Sikes Hall, Clemson, SC 29634
- **Website:** http://www.clemson.edu
- **Public**
- **Enrollment:** 14,371 full-time; 975 part-time

KEY STATS

✔ **U.S News College Ranking:** 64, National Universities
✔ **SAT Score (25th/75th percentile):** 1130-1310
✔ **Tuition:** 2010-2011: $11,958 in state, $27,470 out of state
  Selectivity: More selective   **Room/board:** $7,034
  Acceptance rate: 63%   **Average debt:** $18,463
  Student/faculty ratio: 16/1   **Proportion who borrowed:** 49%

UNDERGRADUATE STUDENT BODY STATS

2009-2010 enrollment: 14,371 full-time; 975 part-time. Men: 54%; women: 46%. **Ethnic makeup:** African American: 7%; Asian American: 2%; Hispanic: 1%; White: 89%; International: 1%.

ADMISSIONS FACTS AND FIGURES

Phone: (864) 656-2287. **Email:** cuadmissions@clemson.edu. **Website:** http://www.clemson.edu. **Application deadlines for fall 2011:** Regular decision: May 1. Early decision: Not offered. Early action: Not offered. Admission can be deferred. **Application fee:** $60. **To apply online, go to:** http://www.clemson.edu/attend/undrgrd/undergrad.htm. **Admissions requirements/recommendations:** High school units required (recommended): English: 4; Mathematics: 3 (4); Science: 3 (4); Foreign language: 3 (4); Social studies: 3 (4); History: 1 (2); Academic electives: 2 (2); Total units: 19 (23). Tests: The college uses SAT or ACT scores in admissions decisions. Either SAT or ACT required. For admission to the fall 2011 entering class, the school will accept: ACT with writing required. Campus visit: Recommended. Admissions interview: Neither required nor recommended. Off-campus interview: Not available. **Factors that count in admissions decisions:** *Academic:* Secondary school record: Very Important. Class rank: Very Important. Letters of recommendation: Considered. Standardized test scores: Very Important. Essay: Considered. *Nonacademic:* Interview: Not Considered. Extracurricular activities: Considered. Talent/ability: Considered. Character/personal qualities: Not Considered. Alumni/ae relationship: Important. Geographical residence: Considered. State residency: Very Important. Religious affiliation/commitment: Not Considered. Minority status: Not Considered. Volunteer work: Considered. Work experience: Considered. **Other schools with the greatest overlap in applicants:** College of Charleston; Georgia Institute of Technology; University of Georgia; University of North Carolina–Chapel Hill; University of South Carolina. **Admissions statistics for the fall 2009 entering class:** Total applicants: 16,282. Total accepted: 10,224. Freshmen enrolled: 3,339; Overall acceptance rate: 63%. **Size of waiting list:** 1577 applicants; enrolled from waiting list: 832. **Credentials of fall 2009 freshmen:** 45% ranked in the top 10 percent of their high school class; 78% were in the top 25 percent; 97% were in the top half. (Proportion submitting class standing: 100%.) **Average high school grade point average:** 3.8. **First-year students who submitted SAT scores:** 79%. Scores (25/75 percentile): Critical Reading: 550-640, Math:

580-670, Combined: 1130-1310. **First-year students submitting ACT scores:** 21%. Scores (25/75 percentile): English: N/A, Math: N/A, Composite: 25-30.

ACADEMICS

Year founded: 1889. **Academic calendar:** Semester. **Degrees offered:** certificate, bachelor's, master's, post-master's certificate, doctorate. **Most popular majors:** 22% business, management, marketing, and related support services, 14% engineering, 8% health professions and related clinical sciences, 7% social sciences, 6% biological and biomedical sciences. **Major fields of study:** agriculture, agriculture operations, and related sciences; architecture and related services; biological and biomedical sciences; business, management, marketing, and related support services; communication, journalism, and related programs; communications technologies/technicians and support services; computer and information sciences and support services; education; engineering; engineering technologies/technicians; English language and literature/letters; family and consumer sciences/human sciences; health professions and related clinical sciences; history; mathematics and statistics; natural resources and conservation; philosophy and religious studies; physical sciences; psychology; social sciences; visual and performing arts. **Areas of required coursework:** arts/fine arts, humanities, computer literacy, mathematics, English (including composition), foreign languages, sciences (biological or physical), social science, other. **Pre-professional programs:** pre-law, pre-dentistry, pre-medicine, pre-veterinary science, pre-optometry, pre-pharmacy, other. **Special academic programs (% participation):** accelerated program (4%), cooperative (work-study plan) program (12%), distance learning (46%), double major (3%), dual enrollment (0%), honors program (11%), independent study (26%), internships (13%), study abroad (12%), teacher certificate program (8%). **Teacher certification offered in:** early childhood, special education, elementary, secondary. **Cooperative education programs:** agriculture, art, business, computer science, education, engineering, health professions, home economics, humanities, natural science, social/behavioral science, technologies, vocational arts. **Reserve Officers Training Corps (ROTC):** Army ROTC: Offered on campus; Air Force ROTC: Offered on campus. **Faculty and instruction (2009-2010):** Total instructional faculty: 1,052 full-time, 130 part-time (66% men; 34% women; 14% minorities). Full-time faculty with Ph.D. or other terminal degree: 88%. Student/faculty ratio: 16/1. Classes of fewer than 20 students: 43%; of 20 to 49 students: 44%; of 50 or more students: 13%. **Advanced Placement and International Baccalaureate credit:** AP tests may be used for: Credit and/or placement. Scores accepted: 3, 4, 5. International Baccalaureate exams may be used for: Credit and/or placement. **Freshmen returning for sophomore year:** 91%. **Graduation rates:** Four-year: 50%; five-year: 75%; six-year: 77%. **Graduate study:** 41% of students pursue further study within five years. Fields in which graduates pursue further study: Master of Business Administration (MBA), 21%; law, 5%; medicine, 8%; arts and sciences, 25%.

COSTS AND FINANCIAL AID

Financial aid office: (864) 656-2280. **Expenses (2010-2011):** Tuition and fees 2010-2011: $11,958 in state, $27,470 out of state; room/board: $7,034. Estimated books and supplies: $940; transportation: $3,172; personal expenses: $2,006. **Financial aid:** Priority filing date for institution's financial aid form: April 1. In 2009-2010, 61% of undergraduates applied for financial aid. Of those, 45% were determined to have financial need; 23% had their need fully met. Average financial aid package (proportion receiving): $10,911 (43%). Average amount of gift aid, such as scholarships or grants (proportion receiving): $4,714 (19%). Average amount of self-help aid, such as work study or loans (proportion receiving): $4,495 (32%). Average need-based loan (excluding PLUS or other private loans): $4,196. Among students who received need-based aid, the average percentage of need met: 61%. Among students who received aid based on merit, the average award (and the proportion receiving): $2,489 (18%). The average athletic scholarship (and the proportion receiving): $13,516 (2%). Average amount of debt of borrowers graduating in 2009: $18,463. Proportion who borrowed: 49%.

CAMPUS LIFE AND EXTRACURRICULAR ACTIVITIES

Campus housing available (% using): coed dorms (27%), women's dorms (19%), men's dorms (20%), sorority housing (3%), fraternity housing (2%), apartment for single students (1%), special housing for disabled students (0%), special housing for international students (0%), other housing options (28%). Students who live in college-owned, operated, or affiliated housing: 67%. **Student employment:** During the 2009-2010 academic year, 30% of undergraduates worked on campus. Average per-year earnings: $4,200. **Clubs and organizations:** Number of student organizations: 301. Activities include: campus ministries, choral groups, concert band, dance, drama/theater, international student organization, jazz band, literary magazine, marching band, music ensembles, pep band, radio station, student government, student newspaper, symphony orchestra, television station, yearbook. Number of fraternities: 19; sororities: 10. Proportion of men in fraternities: 19%; of women in sororities: 24%. Average proportion of students who stay on campus on weekends: 70%. **Sports program (2009-2010):** Member of NCAA I. *Men's intercollegiate varsity sports:* baseball, basketball, cross country, football, golf, soccer, swimming, tennis, track and field (indoor), track and field (outdoor). *Women's intercollegiate varsity sports:* basketball, crew (heavyweight), cross country, soccer, swimming, tennis, track and field (indoor), track and field (outdoor), volleyball.

SERVICES AND FACILITIES
Basic services: nonremedial tutoring, placement service, health service, health insurance. **Counseling services:** minority student, career, military, personal, veteran student, academic, older student, psychological, birth control. **For learning-disabled students:** School does not offer a structured program with separate admission and additional fees. Services include: tape recorders, diagnostic testing service, note-taking services, oral tests, readers, extended time for tests, tutors, priority registration, substitution of courses, texts on tape, exams on tape or computer, other testing accommodations, other. **Library:** Number of titles: 1,307,448; number of current serial subscriptions: 19,900. **Information technology resources:** Students are required to lease or own a computer. Number of campus computers available to all students: 7,500. School has a wireless network. Approximate number of users that can be accommodated: 30,000. Proportion of college-owned housing units wired for high-speed internet access: 100%. **Campus safety:** Security services offered: 24-hour foot-and-vehicle patrols, late-night transport/escort service, 24-hour emergency telephones, lighted pathways/sidewalks, student patrols, controlled dormitory access (key, security card, etc).

TRANSFER AND INTERNATIONAL STUDENTS
Transfer students: May apply for admission for the following academic terms: Fall, Spring, Summer. Applicants need a minimum number of credits to apply. For fall 2009: Transfer applications received: 2,014. Transfer applicants offered admission: 1,392. Transfer applicants enrolled: 980. **International students:** Number of foreign undergraduates: 115 (1% of student body). Number of countries represented: 84. Minimum TOEFL score required: 550 (paper); 213 (computer).

Coastal Carolina University

- **Address:** PO Box 261954, Conway, SC 29528-6054
- **Website:** http://www.coastal.edu
- **Public**
- **Enrollment:** 7,138 full-time; 782 part-time

KEY STATS
- ✔ **U.S News College Ranking:** second tier, National Liberal Arts Colleges
- ✔ **SAT Score (25th/75th percentile):** 930-1120
- ✔ **Tuition:** 2009-2010: $8,950 in state, $18,770 out of state

Selectivity: Selective	**Room/board:** $7,200
Acceptance rate: 74%	**Average debt:** $31,472
Student/faculty ratio: 18/1	**Proportion who borrowed:** 77%

UNDERGRADUATE STUDENT BODY STATS
2009-2010 enrollment: 7,138 full-time; 782 part-time. Men: 47%; women: 53%. **Ethnic makeup:** African American: 15%; Asian American: 1%; Hispanic: 3%; White: 80%; International: 1%.

ADMISSIONS FACTS AND FIGURES
Phone: (843) 349-2026. **Email:** admissions@coastal.edu. **Website:** http://www.coastal.edu. **Application deadlines for fall 2011:** Regular decision: August 15. Early decision: Not offered. Early action: Not offered. Admission can be deferred. **Application fee:** $45. **To apply online, go to:** http://www.coastal.edu/admissions/applications.html. **Admissions requirements/recommendations:** High school units required (recommended): English: 4; Mathematics: 3; Science: 3; Foreign language: 2; Social studies: 2; History: 1; Academic electives: 4; Total units: 20. Tests: The college uses SAT or ACT scores in admissions decisions. Either SAT or ACT required. For admission to the fall 2011 entering class, the school will accept: ACT with or without writing accepted. Campus visit: Recommended. Admissions interview: Recommended. Off-campus interview: May be arranged. **Factors that count in admissions decisions:** *Academic:* Secondary school record: Very Important. Class rank: Important. Letters of recommendation: Considered.

Standardized test scores: Very Important. Essay: Considered. *Nonacademic:* Interview: Considered. Extracurricular activities: Considered. Talent/ability: Considered. Character/personal qualities: Considered. Alumni/ae relationship: Not Considered. Geographical residence: Considered. State residency: Considered. Religious affiliation/commitment: Not Considered. Minority status: Not Considered. Volunteer work: Not Considered. Work experience: Considered. **Other schools with the greatest overlap in applicants:** Clemson University; College of Charleston; Francis Marion University; University of South Carolina; Winthrop University. **Admissions statistics for the fall 2009 entering class:** Total applicants: 8,706. Total accepted: 6,438. Freshmen enrolled: 1,775; 55% were from out of state. Overall acceptance rate: 74%. **Credentials of fall 2009 freshmen:** 9% ranked in the top 10 percent of their high school class; 32% were in the top 25 percent; 71% were in the top half. (Proportion submitting class standing: 81%.) **Average high school grade point average:** 3.3. **First-year students who submitted SAT scores:** 69%. Scores (25/75 percentile): Critical Reading: 460-550, Math: 470-570, Combined: 930-1120. **First-year students submitting ACT scores:** 31%. Scores (25/75 percentile): English: N/A, Math: N/A, Composite: 19-22.

ACADEMICS
Year founded: 1954. **Academic calendar:** Semester. **Degrees offered:** certificate, bachelor's, master's. **Most popular majors:** 11% business administration and management, 10% marketing/marketing management, 7% psychology, 7% public health education and promotion, 6% communication studies/speech communication and rhetoric. **Major fields of study:** biological and biomedical sciences; business, management, marketing, and related support services; communication, journalism, and related programs; computer and information sciences and support services; education; English language and literature/letters; foreign languages, literatures, and linguistics; health professions and related clinical sciences; history; liberal arts and sciences studies, and humanities; mathematics and statistics; parks, recreation, leisure, and fitness studies; philosophy and religious studies; physical sciences; psychology; social sciences; visual and performing arts. **Areas of required coursework:** humanities, computer literacy, mathematics, English (including composition), philosophy, foreign languages, sciences (biological or physical), history, social science. **Pre-professional programs:** pre-law, predentistry, pre-medicine, pre-theology, pre-veterinary science, pre-pharmacy. **Special academic programs (% participation):** accelerated program (1%), cooperative (work-study plan) program (19%), distance learning (5%), double major (9%), dual enrollment (2%), honors program (3%), independent study (25%), internships (43%), student-designed major (6%), study abroad (2%), teacher certificate program (18%). **Teacher certification offered in:** early childhood, special education, elementary, middle/junior high, secondary. **Cooperative education programs:** business, computer science, education, humanities, natural science, social/behavioral science, technologies. **Reserve Officers Training Corps (ROTC):** Army ROTC: Offered on campus. **Faculty and instruction (2009-2010):** Total instructional faculty: 315 full-time, 242 part-time (52% men; 48% women; 9% minorities). Full-time faculty with Ph.D. or other terminal degree: 82%. Student/faculty ratio: 18/1. Classes of fewer than 20 students: 36%; of 20 to 49 students: 59%; of 50 or more students: 5%. **Advanced Placement and International Baccalaureate credit:** AP tests may be used for: Placement only. Scores accepted: 3, 4, 5. International Baccalaureate exams may be used for: Placement only. **Freshmen returning for sophomore year:** 69%. **Graduation rates:** Four-year: 22%; five-year: 41%; six-year: 46%. **Graduate study:** 18% of students pursue further study immediately upon graduation; 31% within five years. Fields in which graduates pursue further study: Master of Business Administration (MBA), 14%; law, 4%; medicine, 3%; dentistry, 1%; education, 18%; arts and sciences, 56%; veterinary medicine, 1%.

COSTS AND FINANCIAL AID
Financial aid office: (843) 349-2313. **Expenses (2009-2010):** Tuition and fees 2009-2010: $8,950 in state, $18,770 out of state; room/board: $7,200. Estimated books and supplies: $1,071; transportation: $2,588; personal expenses: $1,877. **Financial aid:** Priority filing date for institution's financial aid form: March 1. In 2009-2010, 82% of undergraduates applied for financial aid. Of those, 66% were determined to have financial need; 11% had their need fully met. Average financial aid package (proportion receiving): $8,878 (64%). Average amount of gift aid, such as scholarships or grants (proportion receiving): $5,106 (32%). Average amount of self-help aid, such as work study or loans (proportion receiving): $8,102 (58%). Average need-based loan (excluding PLUS or other private loans): $8,033. Among students who received need-based aid, the average percentage of need met: 51%. Among students who received aid based on merit, the average award (and the proportion receiving): $10,946 (17%). The average athletic scholar-

ship (and the proportion receiving): $8,212 (5%). Average amount of debt of borrowers graduating in 2009: $31,472. Proportion who borrowed: 77%.

CAMPUS LIFE AND EXTRACURRICULAR ACTIVITIES

Campus housing available (% using): coed dorms (22%), apartment for single students (72%), special housing for disabled students (1%). Students who live in college-owned, operated, or affiliated housing: 28%. **Student employment:** During the 2009-2010 academic year, 14% of undergraduates worked on campus. Average per-year earnings: $2,000. **Clubs and organizations:** Number of student organizations: 91. Activities include: campus ministries, choral groups, concert band, dance, drama/theater, international student organization, jazz band, literary magazine, marching band, music ensembles, musical theater, pep band, radio station, student government, student newspaper, student film society. Number of fraternities: 9; sororities: 7. Proportion of men in fraternities: 7%; of women in sororities: 9%. Average proportion of students who stay on campus on weekends: 50%. **Sports program (2009-2010):** Member of NCAA I. *Men's intercollegiate varsity sports:* baseball, basketball, cross country, football, golf, soccer, tennis, track and field (indoor), track and field (outdoor). *Women's intercollegiate varsity sports:* basketball, cross country, golf, soccer, softball, tennis, track and field (indoor), track and field (outdoor), volleyball.

SERVICES AND FACILITIES

Basic services: nonremedial tutoring, women's center, placement service, health service, health insurance. **Counseling services:** minority student, career, personal, veteran student, academic, older student, psychological, birth control. **For learning-disabled students:** School does not offer a structured program with separate admission and additional fees. Services include: remedial math, reading machines, tape recorders, other special classes, videotaped classes, untimed tests, note-taking services, oral tests, learning center, readers, extended time for tests, tutors, priority registration, priority seating, substitution of courses, texts on tape, exams on tape or computer, other testing accommodations. **Library:** Number of titles: 190,564; number of current serial subscriptions: 17,962. **Information technology resources:** Students are not required to lease or own a computer. Number of campus computers available to all students: 600. School has a wireless network. Approximate number of users that can be accommodated: 1,500. Proportion of college-owned housing units wired for high-speed internet access: 100%. **Campus safety:** Security services offered: 24-hour foot-and-vehicle patrols, late-night transport/escort service, 24-hour emergency telephones, lighted pathways/sidewalks, controlled dormitory access (key, security card, etc).

TRANSFER AND INTERNATIONAL STUDENTS

Transfer students: May apply for admission for the following academic terms: Fall, Spring, Summer. Applicants do not need a minimum number of credits to apply. For fall 2009: Transfer applications received: 1,748. Transfer applicants offered admission: 1,208. Transfer applicants enrolled: 754. **International students:** Number of foreign undergraduates: 73 (1% of student body). Number of countries represented: 33. Minimum TOEFL score required: 550 (paper); 213 (computer). Average TOEFL score: 556 (paper).

Coker College

- Address: 300 E. College Avenue, Hartsville, SC 29550
- Website: http://www.coker.edu
- Private
- Enrollment: 645 full-time; 13 part-time

KEY STATS

✔ **U.S News College Ranking:** 17, Regional Colleges (South)
✔ **SAT Score (25th/75th percentile):** 870-1090
✔ **Tuition:** 2010-2011: $20,818

Selectivity: Selective	Room/board: $6,590
Acceptance rate: 56%	Average debt: $24,601
Student/faculty ratio: 10/1	Proportion who borrowed: 81%

UNDERGRADUATE STUDENT BODY STATS

2009-2010 enrollment: 645 full-time; 13 part-time. Men: 38%; women: 62%. **Ethnic makeup:** African American: 25%; American-Indian: 1%; Hispanic: 2%; White: 69%; International: 3%.

ADMISSIONS FACTS AND FIGURES

Phone: (843) 383-8050. **Email:** admissions@coker.edu. **Website:** http://www.coker.edu. **Application deadlines for fall 2011:** Regular decision: August 1. Early decision: Not offered. Early action: Not offered. Admission can be deferred. **Application fee:** $15. **To apply online, go to:** http://students.coker.edu/apply/. **Admissions requirements/recommendations:** High school units required (recommended): English: 4; Mathematics: 3; Science: 3; Foreign language: 2; Social studies: 3; Total units: 15. Tests: The college uses SAT or ACT scores in admissions decisions. Either SAT or ACT required. For admission to the fall 2011 entering class, the school will accept: ACT with or without writing accepted. Campus visit: Recommended. Admissions interview: Recommended. Off-campus interview: May be arranged. **Factors that count in admissions decisions:** *Academic:* Secondary school record: Important. Class rank: Important. Letters of recommendation: Considered. Standardized test scores: Very Important. Essay: Considered. *Nonacademic:* Interview: Considered. Extracurricular activities: Considered. Talent/ability: Considered. Character/personal qualities: Considered. Alumni/ae relationship: Considered. Geographical residence: Not Considered. State residency: Not Considered. Religious affiliation/commitment: Not Considered. Minority status: Not Considered. Volunteer work: Considered. Work experience: Considered. **Admissions statistics for the fall 2009 entering class:** Total applicants: 1,112. Total accepted: 624. Freshmen enrolled: 192; 20% were from out of state. Overall acceptance rate: 56%. **Credentials of fall 2009 freshmen:** 17% ranked in the top 10 percent of their high school class; 39% were in the top 25 percent; 77% were in the top half. (Proportion submitting class standing: 88%.) **Average high school grade point average:** 3.3. **First-year students who submitted SAT scores:** 58%. Scores (25/75 percentile): Critical Reading: 440-540, Math: 430-550, Combined: 870-1090. **First-year students submitting ACT scores:** 44%. Scores (25/75 percentile): English: N/A, Math: N/A, Composite: 18-23.

ACADEMICS

Year founded: 1908. **Academic calendar:** Semester. **Degrees offered:** bachelor's. **Most popular majors:** 24% business administration and management, 11% communication studies/speech communication and rhetoric, 7% counseling psychology, 6% history, 5% sport and fitness administration/management. **Major fields of study:** biological and biomedical sciences; business, management, marketing, and related support services; communication, journalism, and related programs; computer and information sciences and support services; education; English language and literature/letters; foreign languages, literatures, and linguistics; health professions and related clinical sciences; history; mathematics and statistics; parks, recreation, leisure, and fitness studies; physical sciences; psychology; public administration and social service professions; security and protective services; social sciences; visual and performing arts. **Areas of required coursework:** arts/fine arts, humanities, mathematics, English (including composition), foreign languages, sciences (biological or physical), social science, other. **Pre-professional programs:** pre-law, pre-medicine. **Special academic programs:** double major, dual enrollment, honors program, independent study, internships, student-designed major, study abroad, teacher certificate program. **Teacher certification offered in:** early childhood, elementary, secondary. **Faculty and instruction (2009-2010):** Total instructional faculty: 60 full-time, 4 part-time (55% men; 45% women; 13% minorities). Full-time faculty with Ph.D. or other terminal degree: 83%. Student/faculty ratio: 10/1. Classes of fewer than 20 students: 71%; of 20 to 49 students: 29%; of 50 or more students: 0%. **Advanced Placement and International Baccalaureate credit:** AP tests may be used for: Placement only. Scores accepted: 3, 4, 5. International Baccalaureate exams may be used for: Credit only. **Freshmen returning for sophomore year:** 68%. **Graduation rates:** Four-year: 35%; five-year: 42%; six-year: 47%.

COSTS AND FINANCIAL AID

Financial aid office: (843) 383-8055. **Expenses (2010-2011):** Tuition and fees 2010-2011: $20,818; room/board: $6,590. Estimated books and supplies: $1,200 personal expenses: $1,311. **Financial aid:** Priority filing date for institution's financial aid form: April 1; deadline: June 1. In 2009-2010, 93% of undergraduates applied for financial aid. Of those, 86% were determined to have financial need; 39% had their need fully met. Average financial aid package (proportion receiving): $19,956 (86%). Average amount of gift aid, such as scholarships or grants (proportion receiving): $7,208 (81%). Average amount of self-help aid, such as work study or loans (proportion receiving): $4,503 (76%). Average need-based loan (excluding PLUS or other private loans): $4,258. Among students who received need-based aid, the average percentage of need met: 89%. Among students who received aid based on merit, the average award (and the proportion receiving): $7,228 (13%). The average athletic scholarship (and the proportion receiving): $6,807 (7%). Average amount of debt of borrowers graduating in 2009: $24,601. Proportion who borrowed: 81%.

CAMPUS LIFE AND EXTRACURRICULAR ACTIVITIES

Campus housing available (% using): coed dorms (100%), special housing for disabled students, other housing options. Students who live in college-owned, operated, or affiliated housing: 72%. **Student employment:** During the 2009-2010 academic year, 1% of undergraduates worked on campus. Average per-year earnings: $800. **Clubs and organizations:** Number of student organizations: 22. Activities include: campus ministries, choral groups, dance, drama/theater, literary magazine, marching band, music ensembles, musical theater, student government. Number of fraternities: 0; sororities: 0. Average proportion of students who stay on campus on weekends: 75%. **Sports program (2009-2010):** Member of NCAA II. *Men's intercollegiate varsity sports:* baseball, basketball, cross country, golf, soccer, tennis. *Women's intercollegiate varsity sports:* basketball, cross country, soccer, softball, tennis, volleyball.

SERVICES AND FACILITIES

Basic services: nonremedial tutoring, placement service, health service, health insurance. **Remedial assistance:** math, writing, study skills. **Counseling services:** minority student, career, personal, veteran student, academic, older student, psychological, birth control, other. **For learning-disabled students:** School does not offer a structured program with separate admission and additional fees. Total undergraduates in learning-disabled program or receiving services: 23. Services include: remedial math, remedial English, untimed tests, note-taking services, oral tests, extended time for tests, tutors, priority seating, texts on tape, typist/scribe, other. **Library:** Number of titles: 71,429; number of current serial subscriptions: 119. **Information technology resources:** Students are not required to lease or own a computer. Number of campus computers available to all students: 116. School has a wireless network. Approximate number of users that can be accommodated: 600. Proportion of college-owned housing units wired for high-speed internet access: 100%. **Campus safety:** Security services offered: 24-hour foot-and-vehicle patrols, lighted pathways/sidewalks, controlled dormitory access (key, security card, etc).

TRANSFER AND INTERNATIONAL STUDENTS

Transfer students: May apply for admission for the following academic terms: Fall, Spring, Summer. Applicants need a minimum number of credits to apply. For fall 2009: Transfer applications received: 185. Transfer applicants offered admission: 59. Transfer applicants enrolled: 39. **International students:** Number of foreign undergraduates: 17 (3% of student body). Number of countries represented: 12. Minimum TOEFL score required: 500 (paper); 173 (computer).

College of Charleston

- **Address:** 66 George Street, Charleston, SC 29424-0001
- **Website:** http://www.cofc.edu
- **Public**
- **Enrollment:** 9,334 full-time; 813 part-time

KEY STATS

✔ **U.S News College Ranking:** 11, Regional Universities (South)
✔ **SAT Score (25th/75th percentile):** 1120-1290
✔ **Tuition:** 2009-2010: $8,988 in state, $21,846 out of state

Selectivity: More selective	**Room/board:** $9,411
Acceptance rate: 70%	**Average debt:** $19,875
Student/faculty ratio: 16/1	**Proportion who borrowed:** 46%

UNDERGRADUATE STUDENT BODY STATS

2009-2010 enrollment: 9,334 full-time; 813 part-time. Men: 36%; women: 64%. **Ethnic makeup:** African American: 5%; Asian American: 2%; Hispanic: 2%; White: 89%; International: 1%.

ADMISSIONS FACTS AND FIGURES

Phone: (843) 953-5670. **Email:** admissions@cofc.edu. **Website:** http://www.cofc.edu. **Application deadlines for fall 2011:** Regular decision: February 1. Early decision: Not offered. Early action: Send application by: November 1; Decision sent by: December 15. Admission can be deferred. **Application fee:** $50. **To apply online, go to:** https://www.applyweb.com/apply/charles/index_f.html. **Admissions requirements/recommendations:** High school

units required (recommended): English: 4 (4); Mathematics: 3 (4); Science: 3; Foreign language: 3; Social studies: 3; History: (2); Academic electives: 4; Total units: 20. Tests: The college uses SAT or ACT scores in admissions decisions. Either SAT or ACT required. For admission to the fall 2011 entering class, the school will accept: ACT with or without writing accepted. Campus visit: Recommended. Admissions interview: Neither required nor recommended. Off-campus interview: Not available. **Factors that count in admissions decisions:** *Academic:* Secondary school record: Very Important. Class rank: Important. Letters of recommendation: Considered. Standardized test scores: Very Important. Essay: Considered. ***Nonacademic:*** Interview: Not Considered. Extracurricular activities: Considered. Talent/ability: Important. Character/personal qualities: Important. Alumni/ae relationship: Not Considered. Geographical residence: Not Considered. State residency: Very Important. Religious affiliation/commitment: Not Considered. Minority status: Considered. Volunteer work: Considered. Work experience: Considered. **Other schools with the greatest overlap in applicants:** Clemson University; Elon University; University of Georgia; University of North Carolina–Chapel Hill; University of South Carolina. **Admissions statistics for the fall 2009 entering class:** Total applicants: 11,083. Total accepted: 7,703. Freshmen enrolled: 2,143; 57% were from out of state. Accepted through early-decision or early-action plans: 56%. Overall acceptance rate: 70%. Non-early acceptance rate: 69%. **Size of waiting list:** 309 applicants; enrolled from waiting list: 27. **Credentials of fall 2009 freshmen:** 31% ranked in the top 10 percent of their high school class; 68% were in the top 25 percent; 94% were in the top half. (Proportion submitting class standing: 66%.) **Average high school grade point average:** 3.9. **First-year students who submitted SAT scores:** 60%. Scores (25/75 percentile): Critical Reading: 560-650, Math: 560-640, Combined: 1120-1290. **First-year students submitting ACT scores:** 40%. Scores (25/75 percentile): English: 23-28, Math: 21-26, Composite: 23-27.

ACADEMICS

Year founded: 1770. **Academic calendar:** Semester. **Degrees offered:** bachelor's, post-bachelor's certificate, master's. **Most popular majors:** 24% business/commerce, 13% communication studies/speech communication and rhetoric, 11% social sciences, 10% biology/biological sciences, 9% visual and performing arts. **Major fields of study:** area, ethnic, cultural, and gender studies; biological and biomedical sciences; business, management, marketing, and related support services; communication, journalism, and related programs; computer and information sciences and support services; education; English language and literature/letters; foreign languages, literatures, and linguistics; health professions and related clinical sciences; history; mathematics and statistics; multi/interdisciplinary studies; philosophy and religious studies; physical sciences; psychology; social sciences; visual and performing arts. **Areas of required coursework:** humanities, mathematics, English (including composition), foreign languages, sciences (biological or physical), history, social science. **Special academic programs:** accelerated program, cooperative (work-study plan) program, cross-registration, distance learning, double major, dual enrollment, English as a Second Language (ESL), exchange student program (domestic), honors program, independent study, internships, liberal arts/career combination, study abroad, teacher certificate program, other. **Teacher certification offered in:** early childhood, special education, elementary, middle/junior high, secondary. **Reserve Officers Training Corps (ROTC):** Air Force ROTC: Offered at cooperating institution (Charleston Southern University). **Faculty and instruction (2009-2010):** Total instructional faculty: 523 full-time, 370 part-time (52% men; 48% women; 9% minorities). Full-time faculty with Ph.D. or other terminal degree: 87%. Student/faculty ratio: 16/1. Classes of fewer than 20 students: 27%; of 20 to 49 students: 68%; of 50 or more students: 5%. **Advanced Placement and International Baccalaureate credit:** AP tests may be used for: Placement only. Scores accepted: 3, 4, 5. International Baccalaureate exams may be used for: Placement only. **Freshmen returning for sophomore year:** 82%. **Graduation rates:** Four-year: 48%; five-year: 61%; six-year: 62%. **Graduate study:** 40% of students pursue further study within one year; 53% within five years. Fields in which graduates pursue further study: Master of Business Administration (MBA), 15%; law, 14%; medicine, 8%; dentistry, 1%; theology (or the seminary), 1%; education, 9%; arts and sciences, 10%.

COSTS AND FINANCIAL AID

Financial aid office: (843) 953-5540. **Expenses (2009-2010):** Tuition and fees 2009-2010: $8,988 in state, $21,846 out of state; room/board: $9,411. Estimated books and supplies: $1,170; transportation: $1,331; personal expenses: $1,639. **Financial aid:** Priority filing date for institution's financial aid form: March 15. In 2009-2010, 58% of undergraduates applied for financial aid. Of those, 44% were determined to have financial need; 27% had their need fully met. Average financial aid package (proportion receiving): $12,882 (42%). Average amount of gift aid, such as scholarships or grants (proportion receiving): $3,173 (28%). Average amount of self-help aid, such as work study or loans (proportion receiving): $3,980 (35%). Average need-based loan (excluding PLUS or other private loans): $4,008. Among students who received need-based aid, the average percentage of need met: 63%. Among students who received aid based on merit, the average award (and the proportion receiving): $11,423 (12%). The average athletic scholarship (and the proportion receiving): $18,939 (2%). Average amount of debt of borrowers graduating in 2009: $19,875. Proportion who borrowed: 46%.

CAMPUS LIFE AND EXTRACURRICULAR ACTIVITIES

Campus housing available (% using): coed dorms (43%), women's dorms (19%), men's dorms (4%), sorority housing (2%), fraternity housing (1%), apartment for single students (25%), other housing options (5%). Students who live in college-owned, operated, or affiliated housing: 34%. **Student employment:** During the 2009-2010 academic year, 15% of undergraduates worked on campus. Average per-year earnings: $4,500. **Clubs and organizations:** Number of student organizations: 150. Activities include: campus ministries, choral groups, dance, drama/theater, international student organization, jazz band, literary magazine, music ensembles, musical theater, pep band, radio station, student government, student newspaper, symphony orchestra, yearbook. Number of fraternities: 13; sororities: 12. Proportion of men in fraternities: 15%; of women in sororities: 20%. Average proportion of students who stay on campus on weekends: 50%. **Sports program (2009-2010):** Member of NCAA I. *Men's intercollegiate varsity sports:* baseball, basketball, cross country, golf, soccer, swimming, tennis. *Women's intercollegiate varsity sports:* basketball, cross country, equestrian, golf, soccer, softball, swimming, tennis, volleyball.

SERVICES AND FACILITIES

Basic services: nonremedial tutoring, placement service, health service, health insurance. **Remedial assistance:** reading, math, writing, study skills. **Counseling services:** minority student, career, military, personal, veteran student, academic, older student, psychological, birth control, religious. **For learning-disabled students:** School does not offer a structured program with separate admission and additional fees. Total undergraduates in learning-disabled program or receiving services: 752. Services include: reading machines, tape recorders, other special classes, diagnostic testing service, untimed tests, note-taking services, learning center, readers, extended time for tests, tutors, priority registration, substitution of courses, texts on tape, typist/scribe, exams on tape or computer, other testing accommodations, waiver of foreign language degree requirement, other. **Library:** Number of titles: 660,560; number of current serial subscriptions: 46,730. **Information technology resources:** Students are not required to lease or own a computer. Number of campus computers available to all students: 900. School has a wireless network. Approximate number of users that can be accommodated: 7,950. Proportion of college-owned housing units wired for high-speed internet access: 100%. **Campus safety:** Security services offered: 24-hour foot-and-vehicle patrols, late-night transport/escort service, 24-hour emergency telephones, lighted pathways/sidewalks, student patrols, controlled dormitory access (key, security card, etc).

TRANSFER AND INTERNATIONAL STUDENTS

Transfer students: May apply for admission for the following academic terms: Fall, Spring. Applicants need a minimum number of credits to apply. For fall 2009: Transfer applications received: 1,922. Transfer applicants offered admission: 1,260. Transfer applicants enrolled: 724. **International students:** Number of foreign undergraduates: 63 (1% of student body). Number of countries represented: 66. Minimum TOEFL score required: 550 (paper); 213 (computer).

Columbia College

- **Address:** 1301 Columbia College Drive, Columbia, SC 29203
- **Website:** http://www.columbiacollegesc.edu
- **Private; Religious affiliation:** United Methodist
- **Enrollment:** 964 full-time; 225 part-time

KEY STATS

✔ **U.S News College Ranking:** 56, Regional Universities (South)
✔ **SAT Score (25th/75th percentile):** 880-1110
✔ **Tuition:** 2009-2010: $23,480

Selectivity: Selective	Room/board: $6,450
Acceptance rate: 74%	Average debt: N/A
Student/faculty ratio: 12/1	Proportion who borrowed: N/A

UNDERGRADUATE STUDENT BODY STATS

2009-2010 enrollment: 964 full-time; 225 part-time. Men: 2%; women: 98%. **Ethnic makeup:** African American: 42%; American-Indian: 1%; Asian American: 2%; Hispanic: 2%; White: 52%; International: 1%. **Religious preference:** Roman Catholic: 5%; Protestant: 58%; Muslim: 1%; No preference: 3%; Unknown: 14%; United Methodist: 9%; Pentecostal Holiness: 3%; Other: 7%.

ADMISSIONS FACTS AND FIGURES

Phone: (800) 277-1301. **Email:** admissions@colacoll.edu. **Website:** http://www.columbiacollegesc.edu. **Application deadlines for fall 2011:** Regular decision: August 1. Early decision: Not offered. Early action: Not offered. Admission can be deferred. **Application fee:** $25. **To apply online, go to:** https://kc.columbiasc.edu/ics/Admissions/Apply_For_Admission.jnz. **Admissions requirements/recommendations:** High school units required (recommended): English: (4); Mathematics: (3); Science: (2); Foreign language: (2); Social studies: (2); History: (1); Academic electives: (2); Total units: (16). Tests: The college uses SAT or ACT scores in admissions decisions. Either SAT or ACT required. For admission to the fall 2011 entering class, the school will accept: ACT with writing recommended. Campus visit: Recommended. Admissions interview: Neither required nor recommended. Off-campus interview: May be arranged. **Factors that count in admissions decisions:** *Academic:* Secondary school record: Very Important. Class rank: Very Important. Letters of recommendation: Very Important. Standardized test scores: Very Important. Essay: Considered. *Nonacademic:* Interview: Not Considered. Extracurricular activities: Not Considered. Talent/ability: Not Considered. Character/personal qualities: Not Considered. Alumni/ae relationship: Not Considered. Geographical residence: Not Considered. State residency: Not Considered. Religious affiliation/commitment: Not Considered. Minority status: Not Considered. Volunteer work: Not Considered. Work experience: Not Considered. **Other schools with the greatest overlap in applicants:** Clemson University; College of Charleston; Furman University; University of South Carolina; Winthrop University. **Admissions statistics for the fall 2009 entering class:** Total applicants: 1,019. Total accepted: 750. Freshmen enrolled: 219; Overall acceptance rate: 74%. **Size of waiting list:** 0 applicants; enrolled from waiting list: 0. **Credentials of fall 2009 freshmen:** 16% ranked in the top 10 percent of their high school class; 41% were in the top 25 percent; 77% were in the top half. (Proportion submitting class standing: 92%.) **Average high school grade point average:** 3.5. **First-year students who submitted SAT scores:** 87%. Scores (25/75 percentile): Critical Reading: 440-570, Math: 440-540, Combined: 880-1110. **First-year students submitting ACT scores:** 60%. Scores (25/75 percentile): English: 18-23, Math: 17-24, Composite: 18-23.

ACADEMICS

Year founded: 1854. **Academic calendar:** Semester. **Degrees offered:** bachelor's, post-bachelor's certificate, master's. **Most popular majors:** 13% business administration and management, 10% accounting, 7% psychology, 6% behavioral sciences, 6% biology/biological sciences. **Major fields of study:** biological and biomedical sciences; business, management, marketing, and related support services; communication, journalism, and related programs; computer and information sciences and support services; education; English language and literature/letters; family and consumer sciences/human sciences; foreign languages, literatures, and linguistics; health professions and related clinical sciences; history; liberal arts and sciences studies, and humanities; mathematics and statistics; multi/interdisciplinary studies; philosophy and religious studies; physical sciences; psychology; public administration and social service professions; social sciences; theology and religious vocations; visual and performing arts. **Areas of required**

coursework: arts/fine arts, humanities, computer literacy, mathematics, English (including composition), foreign languages, sciences (biological or physical), history, social science, other. **Pre-professional programs:** pre-medicine, pre-pharmacy. **Special academic programs (% participation):** cross-registration (25%), distance learning (8%), double major (7%), dual enrollment (9%), honors program (16%), independent study (15%), internships (50%), student-designed major (0%), study abroad (16%), teacher certificate program (23%). **Teacher certification offered in:** early childhood, special education, elementary, middle/junior high, secondary. **Reserve Officers Training Corps (ROTC):** Army ROTC: Offered at cooperating institution. **Faculty and instruction (2009-2010):** Total instructional faculty: 78 full-time, 65 part-time (32% men; 68% women; 12% minorities). Full-time faculty with Ph.D. or other terminal degree: 79%. Student/faculty ratio: 12/1. Classes of fewer than 20 students: 58%; of 20 to 49 students: 42%; of 50 or more students: 0%. **Advanced Placement and International Baccalaureate credit:** AP tests may be used for: Credit only. Scores accepted: 4, 5. International Baccalaureate exams may be used for: Credit only. **Freshmen returning for sophomore year:** 66%. **Graduation rates:** Four-year: 33%; five-year: 41%; six-year: 45%. **Graduate study:** 50% of students pursue further study immediately upon graduation; 1% within one year; 48% within five years. Fields in which graduates pursue further study: Master of Business Administration (MBA), 4%; law, 1%; medicine, 3%; dentistry, 1%; theology (or the seminary), 1%; education, 6%; arts and sciences, 23%.

COSTS AND FINANCIAL AID
Financial aid office: (803) 786-3612. **Expenses (2009-2010):** Tuition and fees 2009-2010: $23,480; room/board: $6,450. Estimated books and supplies: $1,100. **Financial aid:** Priority filing date for institution's financial aid form: March 15.

CAMPUS LIFE AND EXTRACURRICULAR ACTIVITIES
Campus housing available (% using): women's dorms (100%). **Student employment:** During the 2009-2010 academic year, 18% of undergraduates worked on campus. Average per-year earnings: $1,000. **Clubs and organizations:** Number of student organizations: 55. Activities include: choral groups, concert band, dance, drama/theater, international student organization, model UN, music ensembles, musical theater, opera, student government, student newspaper, symphony orchestra, yearbook. Number of fraternities: 0; sororities: 0. Average proportion of students who stay on campus on weekends: 60%. **Sports program (2009-2010):** Member of NAIA. **Women's intercollegiate varsity sports:** basketball, soccer, softball, tennis, volleyball.

SERVICES AND FACILITIES
Basic services: nonremedial tutoring, health service, health insurance, other. **Remedial assistance:** reading, math, writing, study skills, other. **Counseling services:** career, personal, academic, psychological, birth control, religious, other. **For learning-disabled students:** School does not offer a structured program with separate admission and additional fees. **Library:** Number of titles: 127,874; number of current serial subscriptions: 235. **Information technology resources:** Students are not required to lease or own a computer. Number of campus computers available to all students: 120. School has a wireless network. Approximate number of users that can be accommodated: 600. Proportion of college-owned housing units wired for high-speed internet access: 100%. **Campus safety:** Security services offered: 24-hour foot-and-vehicle patrols, late-night transport/escort service, 24-hour emergency telephones, lighted pathways/sidewalks, controlled dormitory access (key, security card, etc).

TRANSFER AND INTERNATIONAL STUDENTS
Transfer students: May apply for admission for the following academic terms: Fall, Spring, Summer. Applicants need a minimum number of credits to apply. For fall 2009: Transfer applications received: 138. Transfer applicants offered admission: 125. Transfer applicants enrolled: 94. **International students:** Number of foreign undergraduates: 15 (1% of student body). Number of countries represented: 14. Minimum TOEFL score required: 550 (paper); 213 (computer).

Converse College

- **Address:** 580 E. Main Street, Spartanburg, SC 29302
- **Website:** http://www.converse.edu
- **Private**
- **Enrollment:** 621 full-time; 108 part-time

KEY STATS
✔ **U.S News College Ranking:** 15, Regional Universities (South)
✔ **SAT Score (25th/75th percentile):** 960-1170
✔ **Tuition:** 2010-2011: $26,138

Selectivity: Selective	Room/board: $8,032
Acceptance rate: 68%	Average debt: $20,739
Student/faculty ratio: 10/1	Proportion who borrowed: 61%

UNDERGRADUATE STUDENT BODY STATS
2009-2010 enrollment: 621 full-time; 108 part-time. Men: 0%; women: 100%. **Ethnic makeup:** African American: 15%; American-Indian: 1%; Asian American: 1%; Hispanic: 3%; White: 79%; International: 2%.

ADMISSIONS FACTS AND FIGURES
Phone: (864) 596-9040. **Email:** info@converse.edu. **Website:** http://www.converse.edu. **Application deadlines for fall 2011:** Regular decision: Rolling. Early decision: Not offered. Early action: Not offered. Admission can be deferred. **To apply online, go to:** http://www.converse.edu/Admissions/apply.htm. **Admissions requirements/recommendations:** High school units required (recommended): English: (4); Mathematics: (3); Science: (3); Foreign language: (2); Social studies: (2); History: (2); Academic electives: (8); Total units: (24). Tests: The college uses SAT or ACT scores in admissions decisions. Either SAT or ACT required. For admission to the fall 2011 entering class, the school will accept: ACT with or without writing accepted. Campus visit: Recommended. Admissions interview: Recommended. Off-campus interview: May be arranged. **Factors that count in admissions decisions: Academic:** Secondary school record: Important. Class rank: Important. Letters of recommendation: Important. Standardized test scores: Important. Essay: Important. **Nonacademic:** Interview: Considered. Extracurricular activities: Considered. Talent/ability: Considered. Character/personal qualities: Considered. Alumni/ae relationship: Considered. Geographical residence: Not Considered. State residency: Not Considered. Religious affiliation/commitment: Not Considered. Minority status: Not Considered. Volunteer work: Considered. Work experience: Considered. **Other schools with the greatest overlap in applicants:** Clemson University; College of Charleston; College of Charleston; University of South Carolina; University of South Carolina; Winthrop University; Winthrop University; Wofford College; Wofford College. **Admissions statistics for the fall 2009 entering class:** Total applicants: 602. Total accepted: 409. Freshmen enrolled: 157; 25% were from out of state. Overall acceptance rate: 68%. **Size of waiting list:** 0 applicants; enrolled from waiting list: 0. **Credentials of fall 2009 freshmen:** 33% ranked in the top 10 percent of their high school class; 64% were in the top 25 percent; 91% were in the top half. (Proportion submitting class standing: 87%.) **Average high school grade point average:** 3.9. **First-year students who submitted SAT scores:** 88%. Scores (25/75 percentile): Critical Reading: 480-590, Math: 480-580, Combined: 960-1170. **First-year students submitting ACT scores:** 61%. Scores (25/75 percentile): English: 20-25, Math: 18-24, Composite: 20-25.

ACADEMICS
Year founded: 1889. **Academic calendar:** 4-1-4. **Degrees offered:** bachelor's, master's, post-master's certificate. **Most popular majors:** 22% education, 22% visual and performing arts, 13% psychology, 9% English language and literature/letters, 5% foreign languages, literatures, and linguistics. **Major fields of study:** biological and biomedical sciences; business, management, marketing, and related support services; computer and information sciences and support services; education; English language and literature/letters; foreign languages, literatures, and linguistics; history; mathematics and statistics; philosophy and religious studies; physical sciences; psychology; social sciences; visual and performing arts. **Areas of required coursework:** arts/fine arts, humanities, computer literacy, mathematics, English (including composition), philosophy, foreign languages, sciences (biological or physical), history, social science, other. **Pre-professional programs:** pre-law, pre-dentistry, pre-medicine, pre-theology, pre-veterinary science, pre-pharmacy. **Special academic programs (% participation):** cross-registration (5%), double major (15%), dual enrollment (1%), English as a Second Language (ESL), honors program (15%), independent study (10%), internships (20%), liberal

arts/career combination, student-designed major (1%), study abroad (20%), teacher certificate program (20%), other. **Teacher certification offered in:** early childhood, special education, elementary, middle/junior high, secondary. **Reserve Officers Training Corps (ROTC):** Army ROTC: Offered at cooperating institution (Wofford College). **Faculty and instruction (2009-2010):** Total instructional faculty: 80 full-time, 8 part-time (43% men; 57% women; 8% minorities). Full-time faculty with Ph.D. or other terminal degree: 94%. Student/faculty ratio: 10/1. Classes of fewer than 20 students: 81%; of 20 to 49 students: 19%; of 50 or more students: 0%. **Advanced Placement and International Baccalaureate credit:** AP tests may be used for: Credit and/or placement. Scores accepted: 3, 4, 5. International Baccalaureate exams may be used for: Credit and/or placement. **Freshmen returning for sophomore year:** 73%. **Graduation rates:** Four-year: 64%; five-year: 64%; six-year: 62%. **Graduate study:** 27% of students pursue further study immediately upon graduation; 40% within one year. Fields in which graduates pursue further study: Master of Business Administration (MBA), 7%; law, 1%; medicine, 2%; education, 50%; arts and sciences, 40%.

COSTS AND FINANCIAL AID

Financial aid office: (864) 596-9019. **Expenses (2010-2011):** Tuition and fees 2010-2011: $26,138; room/board: $8,032. Estimated books and supplies: $1,000; transportation: $900; personal expenses: $1,750. **Financial aid:** Priority filing date for institution's financial aid form: March 15. In 2009-2010, 90% of undergraduates applied for financial aid. Of those, 83% were determined to have financial need; 29% had their need fully met. Average financial aid package (proportion receiving): $22,193 (83%). Average amount of gift aid, such as scholarships or grants (proportion receiving): $18,754 (82%). Average amount of self-help aid, such as work study or loans (proportion receiving): $5,294 (59%). Average need-based loan (excluding PLUS or other private loans): $4,989. Among students who received need-based aid, the average percentage of need met: 82%. Among students who received aid based on merit, the average award (and the proportion receiving): $13,251 (16%). The average athletic scholarship (and the proportion receiving): $6,551 (6%). Average amount of debt of borrowers graduating in 2009: $20,739. Proportion who borrowed: 61%.

CAMPUS LIFE AND EXTRACURRICULAR ACTIVITIES

Campus housing available (% using): women's dorms (100%). Students who live in college-owned, operated, or affiliated housing: 80%. **Student employment:** During the 2009-2010 academic year, 20% of undergraduates worked on campus. **Clubs and organizations:** Number of student organizations: 60. Activities include: campus ministries, choral groups, concert band, dance, drama/theater, literary magazine, model UN, music ensembles, musical theater, opera, student government, student newspaper, symphony orchestra, yearbook. Number of fraternities: 0; sororities: 0. Average proportion of students who stay on campus on weekends: 50%. **Sports program (2009-2010):** Member of NCAA II. *Women's intercollegiate varsity sports:* basketball, cross country, lacrosse, soccer, swimming, tennis, volleyball.

SERVICES AND FACILITIES

Basic services: nonremedial tutoring, placement service, health service, health insurance. **Remedial assistance:** reading, math, writing, study skills. **Counseling services:** career, personal, academic, psychological, birth control, religious. **For learning-disabled students:** School does not offer a structured program with separate admission and additional fees. Services include: remedial math, remedial English. **Library:** Number of titles: 155,731; number of current serial subscriptions: 500. **Information technology resources:** Students are not required to lease or own a computer. Number of campus computers available to all students: 85. School has a wireless network. Approximate number of users that can be accommodated: 253. Proportion of college-owned housing units wired for high-speed internet access: 100%. **Campus safety:** Security services offered: 24-hour foot-and-vehicle patrols, late-night transport/escort service, 24-hour emergency telephones, lighted pathways/sidewalks, controlled dormitory access (key, security card, etc).

TRANSFER AND INTERNATIONAL STUDENTS

Transfer students: May apply for admission for the following academic terms: Fall, Winter, Spring, Summer. Applicants need a minimum number of credits to apply. For fall 2009: Transfer applications received: 67. Transfer applicants offered admission: 53. Transfer applicants enrolled: 30. **International students:** Number of foreign undergraduates: 13 (2% of student body). Number of countries represented: 10. Minimum TOEFL score required: 550 (paper); 213 (computer).

Erskine College

- **Address:** PO Box 338, Due West, SC 29639
- **Website:** http://www.erskine.edu
- **Private; Religious affiliation:** Associate Reformed Presbyterian
- **Enrollment:** 567 full-time; 15 part-time

KEY STATS

✔ **U.S News College Ranking:** 4, Regional Colleges (South)
✔ **SAT Score (25th/75th percentile):** 960-1190
✔ **Tuition:** 2010-2011: $26,475

Selectivity: Selective	**Room/board:** $8,775
Acceptance rate: 70%	**Average debt:** $24,058
Student/faculty ratio: 11/1	**Proportion who borrowed:** 66%

UNDERGRADUATE STUDENT BODY STATS

2009-2010 enrollment: 567 full-time; 15 part-time. Men: 45%; women: 55%. **Ethnic makeup:** African American: 7%; Asian American: 1%; Hispanic: 1%; White: 88%; International: 3%.

ADMISSIONS FACTS AND FIGURES

Phone: (864) 379-8838. **Email:** admissions@erskine.edu. **Website:** http://www.erskine.edu. **Application deadlines for fall 2011:** Regular decision: Rolling. Early decision: Not offered. Early action: Send application by: November 1; Decision sent by: November 15. Admission can be deferred. **Application fee:** $25. **To apply online, go to:** http://www.erskine.edu/admissions/application.shtml. **Admissions requirements/recommendations:** High school units required (recommended): English: 4; Mathematics: 2 (4); Science: 2 (3); Foreign language: (2); Social studies: (2); Total units: 14. Tests: The college uses SAT or ACT scores in admissions decisions. Either SAT or ACT required. For admission to the fall 2011 entering class, the school will accept: ACT with or without writing accepted. Campus visit: Recommended. Admissions interview: Recommended. Off-campus interview: Not available. **Factors that count in admissions decisions:** *Academic:* Secondary school record: Very Important. Class rank: Considered. Letters of recommendation: Very Important. Standardized test scores: Very Important. Essay: Very Important. *Nonacademic:* Interview: Considered. Extracurricular activities: Important. Talent/ability: Important. Character/personal qualities: Important. Alumni/ae relationship: Very Important. Geographical residence: Considered. State residency: Considered. Religious affiliation/commitment: Considered. Minority status: Considered. Volunteer work: Considered. Work experience: Considered. **Other schools with the greatest overlap in applicants:** Clemson University; College of Charleston; Furman University; Presbyterian College; Winthrop University. **Admissions statistics for the fall 2009 entering class:** Total applicants: 589. Total accepted: 415. Freshmen enrolled: 182; 24% were from out of state. Overall acceptance rate: 70%. Non-early acceptance rate: 70%. **Credentials of fall 2009 freshmen:** 31% ranked in the top 10 percent of their high school class; 67% were in the top 25 percent; 88% were in the top half. (Proportion submitting class standing: 89%.) **Average high school grade point average:** 3.8. **First-year students who submitted SAT scores:** 80%. Scores (25/75 percentile): Critical Reading: 470-580, Math: 490-610, Combined: 960-1190. **First-year students submitting ACT scores:** 20%. Scores (25/75 percentile): English: N/A, Math: N/A, Composite: 23-27.

ACADEMICS

Year founded: 1839. **Academic calendar:** 4-1-4. **Degrees offered:** certificate, bachelor's, master's, doctorate. **Most popular majors:** 20% biological and biomedical sciences, 16% business, management, marketing, and related support services, 12% education, 11% psychology, 9% philosophy and religious studies. **Major fields of study:** area, ethnic, cultural, and gender studies; biological and biomedical sciences; business, management, marketing, and related support services; education; English language and literature/letters; foreign languages, literatures, and linguistics; health professions and related clinical sciences; history; mathematics and statistics; parks, recreation, leisure, and fitness studies; philosophy and religious studies; physical sciences; psychology; theology and religious vocations; visual and performing arts. **Areas of required coursework:** arts/fine arts, humanities, computer literacy, mathematics, English (including composition), foreign languages, sciences (biological or physical), history. **Pre-professional programs:** pre-law, pre-dentistry, pre-medicine, pre-theology, pre-veterinary science, pre-pharmacy. **Special academic programs:** double major, independent study, internships, study abroad, teacher certificate program. **Teacher certification offered in:** early childhood, special education, elementary, secondary. **Faculty**

and instruction (2009-2010): Total instructional faculty: 42 full-time, 25 part-time (64% men; 36% women; 6% minorities). Full-time faculty with Ph.D. or other terminal degree: 86%. Student/faculty ratio: 11/1. Classes of fewer than 20 students: 73%; of 20 to 49 students: 27%; of 50 or more students: 0%. **Advanced Placement and International Baccalaureate credit:** AP tests may be used for: Credit only. Scores accepted: 4. International Baccalaureate exams may be used for: Credit only. **Freshmen returning for sophomore year:** 73%. **Graduation rates:** Four-year: 63%; five-year: 69%; six-year: 65%. **Graduate study:** 42% of students pursue further study within one year.

COSTS AND FINANCIAL AID
Financial aid office: (864) 379-8832. **Expenses (2010-2011):** Tuition and fees 2010-2011: $26,475; room/board: $8,775. Estimated books and supplies: $2,000; transportation: $2,250; personal expenses: $1,250. **Financial aid:** Priority filing date for institution's financial aid form: April 1. In 2009-2010, 87% of undergraduates applied for financial aid. Of those, 69% were determined to have financial need; 38% had their need fully met. Average financial aid package (proportion receiving): $20,694 (69%). Average amount of gift aid, such as scholarships or grants (proportion receiving): $16,158 (69%). Average amount of self-help aid, such as work study or loans (proportion receiving): $4,200 (66%). Average need-based loan (excluding PLUS or other private loans): $4,750. Among students who received need-based aid, the average percentage of need met: 83%. Among students who received aid based on merit, the average award (and the proportion receiving): $10,645 (20%). The average athletic scholarship (and the proportion receiving): $15,020 (38%). Average amount of debt of borrowers graduating in 2009: $24,058. Proportion who borrowed: 66%.

CAMPUS LIFE AND EXTRACURRICULAR ACTIVITIES
Campus housing available (% using): women's dorms (57%), men's dorms (43%). Students who live in college-owned, operated, or affiliated housing: 90%. **Student employment:** During the 2009-2010 academic year, 3% of undergraduates worked on campus. Average per-year earnings: $1,200. **Clubs and organizations:** Number of student organizations: 51. Activities include: campus ministries, choral groups, concert band, dance, drama/theater, jazz band, literary magazine, music ensembles, musical theater, radio station, student government, student newspaper, yearbook. Average proportion of students who stay on campus on weekends: 25%. **Sports program (2009-2010):** Member of NCAA II. *Men's intercollegiate varsity sports:* baseball, basketball, cross country, golf, soccer, tennis. *Women's intercollegiate varsity sports:* basketball, cross country, golf, lacrosse, soccer, softball, tennis, volleyball.

SERVICES AND FACILITIES
Basic services: nonremedial tutoring, placement service, health service. **Remedial assistance:** math, writing. **Counseling services:** career, personal, academic, psychological, religious. **For learning-disabled students:** School does not offer a structured program with separate admission and additional fees. Services include: tape recorders, untimed tests, extended time for tests, tutors. **Library:** Number of titles: 199,961; number of current serial subscriptions: 1,550. **Information technology resources:** Students are not required to lease or own a computer. School has a wireless network. Proportion of college-owned housing units wired for high-speed internet access: 100%. **Campus safety:** Security services offered: late-night transport/escort service, lighted pathways/sidewalks, controlled dormitory access (key, security card, etc).

TRANSFER AND INTERNATIONAL STUDENTS
Transfer students: May apply for admission for the following academic terms: Fall, Winter, Spring, Summer. Applicants do not need a minimum number of credits to apply. For fall 2009: Transfer applications received: 53. Transfer applicants offered admission: 33. Transfer applicants enrolled: 25. **International students:** Number of foreign undergraduates: 19 (3% of student body). Number of countries represented: 10. Minimum TOEFL score required: 550 (paper).

Francis Marion University

■ **Address:** PO Box 100547, Florence, SC 29502-0547
■ **Website:** http://www.fmarion.edu
■ **Public**
■ **Enrollment:** 3,302 full-time; 327 part-time

KEY STATS
✔ **U.S News College Ranking:** 69, Regional Universities (South)
✔ **SAT Score (25th/75th percentile):** 860-1060
✔ **Tuition:** 2010-2011: $8,480 in state, $16,625 out of state
Selectivity: Selective **Room/board:** $6,380
Acceptance rate: 56% **Average debt:** $26,356
Student/faculty ratio: 15/1 **Proportion who borrowed:** 76%

UNDERGRADUATE STUDENT BODY STATS
2009-2010 enrollment: 3,302 full-time; 327 part-time. Men: 32%; women: 68%. **Ethnic makeup:** African American: 48%; American-Indian: 1%; Asian American: 1%; Hispanic: 1%; White: 49%; International: 1%.

ADMISSIONS FACTS AND FIGURES
Phone: (843) 661-1231. **Email:** admission@fmarion.edu. **Website:** http://www.fmarion.edu. **Application deadlines for fall 2011:** Regular decision: August 17. Early decision: Not offered. Early action: Not offered. Admission can be deferred. **Application fee:** $30. **To apply online, go to:** http://admissions.fmarion.edu/ApplyNow/tabid/893/Default.aspx. **Admissions requirements/recommendations:** High school units required (recommended): English: 4; Mathematics: 3 (4); Science: 3 (3); Foreign language: 2; Social studies: 2; History: 1; Academic electives: 4; Total units: 20. Tests: The college uses SAT or ACT scores in admissions decisions. Either SAT or ACT required. For admission to the fall 2011 entering class, the school will accept: ACT with writing recommended. Campus visit: Recommended. Admissions interview: Neither required nor recommended. Off-campus interview: May be arranged. **Factors that count in admissions decisions:** *Academic:* Secondary school record: Very Important. Class rank: Not Considered. Letters of recommendation: Considered. Standardized test scores: Very Important. Essay: Not Considered. *Nonacademic:* Interview: Not Considered. Extracurricular activities: Not Considered. Talent/ability: Not Considered. Character/personal qualities: Not Considered. Alumni/ae relationship: Not Considered. Geographical residence: Not Considered. State residency: Not Considered. Religious affiliation/commitment: Not Considered. Minority status: Not Considered. Volunteer work: Not Considered. Work experience: Not Considered. **Other schools with the greatest overlap in applicants:** Clemson University; Coastal Carolina University; College of Charleston; University of South Carolina; Winthrop University. **Admissions statistics for the fall 2009 entering class:** Total applicants: 3,432. Total accepted: 1,930. Freshmen enrolled: 794; 1% were from out of state. Overall acceptance rate: 56%. **Credentials of fall 2009 freshmen:** 16% ranked in the top 10 percent of their high school class; 47% were in the top 25 percent; 82% were in the top half. (Proportion submitting class standing: 95%.) **Average high school grade point average:** 3.6. **First-year students who submitted SAT scores:** 65%. Scores (25/75 percentile): Critical Reading: 430-530, Math: 430-530, Combined: 860-1060. **First-year students submitting ACT scores:** 33%. Scores (25/75 percentile): English: 16-22, Math: 16-21, Composite: 18-22.

ACADEMICS
Year founded: 1970. **Academic calendar:** Semester. **Degrees offered:** bachelor's, master's. **Most popular majors:** 26% business, management, marketing, and related support services, 17% biological and biomedical sciences, 13% social sciences, 9% education, 9% psychology. **Major fields of study:** agriculture, agriculture operations, and related sciences; biological and biomedical sciences; business, management, marketing, and related support services; communication, journalism, and related programs; computer and information sciences and support services; education; English language and literature/letters; foreign languages, literatures, and linguistics; health professions and related clinical sciences; history; liberal arts and sciences studies, and humanities; mathematics and statistics; physical sciences; psychology; social sciences; visual and performing arts. **Areas of required coursework:** arts/fine arts, humanities, computer literacy, mathematics, English (including composition), philosophy, foreign languages, sciences (biological or physical), history, social science. **Pre-professional programs:** pre-law, pre-dentistry, pre-medicine, pre-veterinary science, pre-pharmacy. **Special academic programs (% participation):** double major (2%), dual

enrollment (6%), honors program (5%), independent study (1%), internships (1%), study abroad (.1%), teacher certificate program (13%). **Teacher certification offered in:** early childhood, elementary, middle/junior high, secondary. **Cooperative education programs:** engineering, natural science, other. **Reserve Officers Training Corps (ROTC):** Army ROTC: Offered on campus. **Faculty and instruction (2009-2010):** Total instructional faculty: 200 full-time, 54 part-time (52% men; 48% women; 9% minorities). Full-time faculty with Ph.D. or other terminal degree: 81%. Student/faculty ratio: 15/1. Classes of fewer than 20 students: 46%; of 20 to 49 students: 49%; of 50 or more students: 5%. **Advanced Placement and International Baccalaureate credit:** AP tests may be used for: Credit only. Scores accepted: 3, 4, 5. International Baccalaureate exams may be used for: Credit only. **Freshmen returning for sophomore year:** 68%. **Graduation rates:** Four-year: 20%; five-year: 35%; six-year: 40%.

COSTS AND FINANCIAL AID

Financial aid office: (843) 661-1190. **Expenses (2010-2011):** Tuition and fees 2010-2011: $8,480 in state, $16,625 out of state; room/board: $6,380. **Financial aid:** Priority filing date for institution's financial aid form: March 1; deadline: June 30. In 2009-2010, 81% of undergraduates applied for financial aid. Of those, 75% were determined to have financial need; Average financial aid package (proportion receiving): N/A (75%). Average amount of gift aid, such as scholarships or grants (proportion receiving): $4,873 (58%). Average amount of self-help aid, such as work study or loans (proportion receiving): $4,349 (62%). Average need-based loan (excluding PLUS or other private loans): $4,349. Among students who received aid based on merit, the average award (and the proportion receiving): $3,134 (1%). The average athletic scholarship (and the proportion receiving): $4,667 (2%). Average amount of debt of borrowers graduating in 2009: $26,356. Proportion who borrowed: 76%.

CAMPUS LIFE AND EXTRACURRICULAR ACTIVITIES

Campus housing available: women's dorms, men's dorms, apartment for single students, special housing for disabled students. Students who live in college-owned, operated, or affiliated housing: 41%. **Student employment:** During the 2009-2010 academic year, 15% of undergraduates worked on campus. Average per-year earnings: $7,500. **Clubs and organizations:** Number of student organizations: 60. Activities include: choral groups, drama/theater, jazz band, literary magazine, music ensembles, student government, student newspaper, television station. Number of fraternities: 7; sororities: 7. Proportion of men in fraternities: 6%; of women in sororities: 10%. Average proportion of students who stay on campus on weekends: 35%. **Sports program (2009-2010):** Member of NCAA II. *Men's intercollegiate varsity sports:* baseball, basketball, cross country, golf, soccer, tennis, track and field (outdoor). *Women's intercollegiate varsity sports:* basketball, cross country, soccer, softball, tennis, track and field (outdoor), volleyball.

SERVICES AND FACILITIES

Basic services: health service, health insurance. **Remedial assistance:** study skills. **Counseling services:** career, personal, academic, psychological, birth control. **For learning-disabled students:** School does not offer a structured program with separate admission and additional fees. Services include: tape recorders, note-taking services, oral tests, readers, extended time for tests. **Library:** Number of titles: 343,220; number of current serial subscriptions: 1,338. **Information technology resources:** Students are not required to lease or own a computer. Number of campus computers available to all students: 551. School has a wireless network. Approximate number of users that can be accommodated: 250. Proportion of college-owned housing units wired for high-speed internet access: 100%. **Campus safety:** Security services offered: 24-hour foot-and-vehicle patrols, late-night transport/escort service, 24-hour emergency telephones, lighted pathways/sidewalks, controlled dormitory access (key, security card, etc).

TRANSFER AND INTERNATIONAL STUDENTS

Transfer students: May apply for admission for the following academic terms: Fall, Spring, Summer. Applicants need a minimum number of credits to apply. For fall 2009: Transfer applications received: 555. Transfer applicants offered admission: 405. Transfer applicants enrolled: 283. **International students:** Number of foreign undergraduates: 33 (1% of student body). Number of countries represented: 24. Minimum TOEFL score required: 500 (paper); 173 (computer). Average TOEFL score: 500 (paper).

Furman University

■ **Address:** 3300 Poinsett Highway, Greenville, SC 29613
■ **Website:** http://www.furman.edu/
■ **Private**
■ **Enrollment:** 2,622 full-time; 132 part-time

KEY STATS

✔ **U.S News College Ranking:** 41, National Liberal Arts Colleges
✔ **SAT Score (25th/75th percentile):** 1180-1370
✔ **Tuition:** 2010-2011: $38,088
  Selectivity: More selective   **Room/board:** $9,572
  Acceptance rate: 68%   **Average debt:** $27,373
  Student/faculty ratio: 11/1   **Proportion who borrowed:** 40%

UNDERGRADUATE STUDENT BODY STATS

2009-2010 enrollment: 2,622 full-time; 132 part-time. Men: 43%; women: 57%. **Ethnic makeup:** African American: 7%; Asian American: 2%; Hispanic: 2%; White: 87%; International: 1%. **Religious preference:** Roman Catholic: 15%; Protestant: 73%; No preference: 8%; Other: 4%.

ADMISSIONS FACTS AND FIGURES

Phone: (864) 294-2034. **Email:** admissions@furman.edu. **Website:** http://www.furman.edu/. **Application deadlines for fall 2011:** Regular decision: January 15; decision sent by March 15. Early decision: Send application by: November 15; Decision sent by: December 15. Early action: Not offered. Admission cannot be deferred. **To apply online, go to:** http://www.engagefurman.com/index.asp?id=259. **Admissions requirements/recommendations:** High school units required (recommended): English: 4 (4); Mathematics: 3 (4); Science: 2 (3); Foreign language: 2 (3); Social studies: 3 (4); Total units: 14 (18). Tests: The college uses SAT or ACT scores in admissions decisions. Neither SAT nor ACT required. For admission to the fall 2011 entering class, the school will accept: ACT with writing recommended. Campus visit: Recommended. Admissions interview: Neither required nor recommended. Off-campus interview: May be arranged. **Factors that count in admissions decisions:** *Academic:* Secondary school record: Very Important. Class rank: Important. Letters of recommendation: Considered. Standardized test scores: Important. Essay: Important. *Nonacademic:* Interview: Not Considered. Extracurricular activities: Important. Talent/ability: Considered. Character/personal qualities: Important. Alumni/ae relationship: Considered. Geographical residence: Not Considered. State residency: Not Considered. Religious affiliation/commitment: Not Considered. Minority status: Considered. Volunteer work: Considered. Work experience: Considered. **Other schools with the greatest overlap in applicants:** Davidson College; Duke University; University of North Carolina–Chapel Hill; Vanderbilt University; Wake Forest University. **Admissions statistics for the fall 2009 entering class:** Total applicants: 4,538. Total accepted: 3,080. Freshmen enrolled: 656; 70% were from out of state. Accepted through early-decision or early-action plans: 34%. Overall acceptance rate: 68%. Early-decision acceptance rate: 71%. Non-early acceptance rate: 67%. **Size of waiting list:** 212 applicants; enrolled from waiting list: 38. **Credentials of fall 2009 freshmen:** 61% ranked in the top 10 percent of their high school class; 86% were in the top 25 percent; 98% were in the top half. (Proportion submitting class standing: 71%.) **Average high school grade point average:** 3.8. **First-year students who submitted SAT scores:** 89%. Scores (25/75 percentile): Critical Reading: 580-690, Math: 600-680, Combined: 1180-1370. **First-year students submitting ACT scores:** 63%. Scores (25/75 percentile): English: 26-33, Math: 25-30, Composite: 25-30.

ACADEMICS

Year founded: 1826. **Academic calendar:** Semester. **Degrees offered:** bachelor's, post-bachelor's certificate, master's. **Most popular majors:** 11% political science and government, 10% business administration, management, and operations, 9% history, 7% communication and media studies, 6% biology. **Major fields of study:** area, ethnic, cultural, and gender studies; biological and biomedical sciences; business, management, marketing, and related support services; communication, journalism, and related programs; computer and information sciences and support services; education; English language and literature/letters; foreign languages, literatures, and linguistics; health professions and related clinical sciences; history; mathematics and statistics; multi/interdisciplinary studies; parks, recreation, leisure, and fitness studies; philosophy and religious studies; physical sciences; psychology; social sciences; theology and religious vocations; visual and performing arts. **Areas of required coursework:** arts/fine arts, humanities, mathematics,

English (including composition), philosophy, foreign languages, sciences (biological or physical), history, social science, other. **Pre-professional programs:** pre-law, pre-dentistry, pre-medicine, pre-theology, pre-veterinary science, pre-optometry, pre-pharmacy, other. **Special academic programs (% participation):** double major (15%), independent study (33%), internships (50%), student-designed major (1%), study abroad (42%), teacher certificate program (4%). **Teacher certification offered in:** early childhood, special education, elementary, middle/junior high, secondary. **Reserve Officers Training Corps (ROTC):** Army ROTC: Offered on campus. **Faculty and instruction (2009-2010):** Total instructional faculty: 234 full-time, 36 part-time (64% men; 36% women; 11% minorities). Full-time faculty with Ph.D. or other terminal degree: 96%. Student/faculty ratio: 11/1. Classes of fewer than 20 students: 57%; of 20 to 49 students: 43%; of 50 or more students: 0%. **Advanced Placement and International Baccalaureate credit:** AP tests may be used for: Credit and/or placement. Scores accepted: 4, 5. International Baccalaureate exams may be used for: Credit and/or placement. **Freshmen returning for sophomore year:** 92%. **Graduation rates:** Four-year: 81%; five-year: 85%; six-year: 86%. **Graduate study:** 41% of students pursue further study immediately upon graduation; 45% within one year. Fields in which graduates pursue further study: Master of Business Administration (MBA), 4%; law, 16%; medicine, 16%; dentistry, 2%; engineering, 2%; theology (or the seminary), 4%; education, 12%; arts and sciences, 43%; veterinary medicine, 1%.

COSTS AND FINANCIAL AID

Financial aid office: (864) 294-2204. **Expenses (2010-2011):** Tuition and fees 2010-2011: $38,088; room/board: $9,572. Estimated books and supplies: $1,150; transportation: $1,126; personal expenses: $1,000. **Financial aid:** In 2009-2010, 56% of undergraduates applied for financial aid. Of those, 47% were determined to have financial need; 36% had their need fully met. Average financial aid package (proportion receiving): $28,079 (47%). Average amount of gift aid, such as scholarships or grants (proportion receiving): $24,782 (47%). Average amount of self-help aid, such as work study or loans (proportion receiving): $5,617 (35%). Average need-based loan (excluding PLUS or other private loans): $4,935. Among students who received need-based aid, the average percentage of need met: 81%. Among students who received aid based on merit, the average award (and the proportion receiving): $16,007 (27%). The average athletic scholarship (and the proportion receiving): $32,431 (9%). Average amount of debt of borrowers graduating in 2009: $27,373. Proportion who borrowed: 40%.

CAMPUS LIFE AND EXTRACURRICULAR ACTIVITIES

Campus housing available (% using): coed dorms (50%), women's dorms (7%), apartment for single students (42%), special housing for disabled students (1%), other housing options (0%). Students who live in college-owned, operated, or affiliated housing: 96%. **Student employment:** During the 2009-2010 academic year, 4% of undergraduates worked on campus. Average per-year earnings: $1,250. **Clubs and organizations:** Number of student organizations: 137. Activities include: campus ministries, choral groups, concert band, dance, drama/theater, international student organization, jazz band, literary magazine, marching band, music ensembles, musical theater, opera, pep band, radio station, student government, student newspaper, student film society, symphony orchestra, television station, yearbook. Number of fraternities: 7; sororities: 7. Proportion of men in fraternities: 40%; of women in sororities: 47%. Average proportion of students who stay on campus on weekends: 80%. **Sports program (2009-2010):** Member of NCAA I. *Men's intercollegiate varsity sports:* baseball, basketball, cross country, football, golf, soccer, tennis, track and field (outdoor). *Women's intercollegiate varsity sports:* basketball, cross country, golf, soccer, softball, tennis, track and field (indoor), track and field (outdoor), volleyball.

SERVICES AND FACILITIES

Basic services: nonremedial tutoring, women's center, placement service, health service, health insurance. **Remedial assistance:** study skills. **Counseling services:** minority student, career, personal, veteran student, academic, psychological, birth control, religious. **For learning-disabled students:** School does not offer a structured program with separate admission and additional fees. Services include: tape recorders, note-taking services, oral tests, readers, extended time for tests, tutors, other. **Library:** Number of titles: 507,213; number of current serial subscriptions: 13,000. **Information technology resources:** Students are not required to lease or own a computer. Number of campus computers available to all students: 425. School has a wireless network. Approximate number of users that can be accommodated: 1,900. Proportion of college-owned housing units wired for high-speed internet access: 100%. **Campus safety:** Security services offered: 24-hour foot-and-vehicle patrols, late-night transport/escort service, 24-hour emer-

gency telephones, lighted pathways/sidewalks, controlled dormitory access (key, security card, etc).

TRANSFER AND INTERNATIONAL STUDENTS

Transfer students: May apply for admission for the following academic terms: Fall, Spring, Summer. Applicants need a minimum number of credits to apply. For fall 2009: Transfer applications received: 141. Transfer applicants offered admission: 50. Transfer applicants enrolled: 27. **International students:** Number of foreign undergraduates: 38 (1% of student body). Number of countries represented: 46. Minimum TOEFL score required: 570 (paper); 230 (computer). Average TOEFL score: 630 (paper).

Lander University

- ■ **Address:** 320 Stanley Avenue, Greenwood, SC 29649-2099
- ■ **Website:** http://www.lander.edu
- ■ **Public**
- ■ **Enrollment:** N/A

....

KEY STATS

✔ **U.S News College Ranking:** 31, Regional Colleges (South)
✔ **ACT Score (25th/75th percentile):** 18-22
✔ **Tuition:** 2009-2010: $8,770 in state, $16,570 out of state

Selectivity: Selective	**Room/board:** $6,186
Acceptance rate: 47%	**Average debt:** N/A
Student/faculty ratio: N/A	**Proportion who borrowed:** N/A

Limestone College

- ■ **Address:** 1115 College Drive, Gaffney, SC 29340-3799
- ■ **Website:** http://www.limestone.edu
- ■ **Private; Religious affiliation:** Christian nondenominational
- ■ **Enrollment:** 795 full-time; 13 part-time

....

KEY STATS

✔ **U.S News College Ranking:** 59, Regional Colleges (South)
✔ **SAT Score (25th/75th percentile):** 840-1030
✔ **Tuition:** 2010-2011: $19,200

Selectivity: Less selective	**Room/board:** $7,000
Acceptance rate: 71%	**Average debt:** $20,701
Student/faculty ratio: 12/1	**Proportion who borrowed:** 89%

UNDERGRADUATE STUDENT BODY STATS

2009-2010 enrollment: 795 full-time; 13 part-time. Men: 58%; women: 42%. **Ethnic makeup:** African American: 20%; Hispanic: 3%; White: 76%. **Religious preference:** Roman Catholic: 14%; Protestant: 73%; Jewish: 1%; No preference: 11%; Other: 1%.

ADMISSIONS FACTS AND FIGURES

Phone: (864) 488-4554. **Email:** admiss@limestone.edu. **Website:** http://www.limestone.edu. **Application deadlines for fall 2011:** Regular decision: August 26. Early decision: Not offered. Early action: Not offered. Admission can be deferred. **Application fee:** $25. **To apply online, go to:** http://www.limestone.edu/applyonline.htm. **Admissions requirements/recommendations:** High school units required (recommended): English: 4; Mathematics: 3; Science: 2; Social studies: 3; Total units: 12. Tests: The college uses SAT or ACT scores in admissions decisions. Either SAT or ACT required. For admission to the fall 2011 entering class, the school will accept: ACT with or without writing accepted. Campus visit: Recommended. Admissions interview: Neither required nor recommended. Off-campus interview: May be arranged. **Factors that count in admissions decisions:** *Academic:* Secondary school record: Very Important. Class rank: Important. Letters of recommendation: Considered. Standardized test scores: Very Important. Essay: Not Considered. *Nonacademic:* Interview: Considered. Extracurricular activities: Not Considered. Talent/ability: Not Considered. Character/personal qualities: Not Considered. Alumni/ae relationship: Not Considered. Geographical residence: Not Considered. State residency: Not Considered. Religious affiliation/commitment: Not Considered. Minority status: Not Considered. Volunteer work: Not Considered. Work experience: Not Considered. **Other schools with the greatest overlap in applicants:** Anderson

University; Gardner-Webb University; Lees-McRae College; Newberry College; University of South Carolina–Upstate. **Admissions statistics for the fall 2009 entering class:** Total applicants: 1,236. Total accepted: 874. Freshmen enrolled: 257; 41% were from out of state. Overall acceptance rate: 71%. **Credentials of fall 2009 freshmen:** 3% ranked in the top 10 percent of their high school class; 12% were in the top 25 percent; 43% were in the top half. (Proportion submitting class standing: 73%.) **Average high school grade point average:** 3.1. **First-year students who submitted SAT scores:** 68%. Scores (25/75 percentile): Critical Reading: 410-490, Math: 430-540, Combined: 840-1030. **First-year students submitting ACT scores:** 32%. Scores (25/75 percentile): English: 15-26, Math: 11-26, Composite: 15-26.

ACADEMICS

Year founded: 1845. **Academic calendar:** Semester. **Degrees offered:** associate, bachelor's. **Most popular majors:** 26% education, 20% business, management, marketing, and related support services, 13% parks, recreation, leisure, and fitness studies, 6% history, 6% psychology. **Major fields of study:** biological and biomedical sciences; business, management, marketing, and related support services; computer and information sciences and support services; education; English language and literature/letters; health professions and related clinical sciences; history; legal professions and studies; liberal arts and sciences studies, and humanities; mathematics and statistics; parks, recreation, leisure, and fitness studies; physical sciences; psychology; public administration and social service professions; security and protective services; social sciences; visual and performing arts. **Areas of required coursework:** arts/fine arts, humanities, computer literacy, mathematics, English (including composition), sciences (biological or physical), history, social science, other. **Pre-professional programs:** pre-law, pre-dentistry, pre-medicine, pre-veterinary science, pre-pharmacy, other. **Special academic programs (% participation):** accelerated program (79%), distance learning (76%), double major (16%), honors program (28%), independent study (30%), internships (30%), teacher certificate program (22%). **Teacher certification offered in:** elementary, secondary. **Reserve Officers Training Corps (ROTC):** Army ROTC: Offered on campus. **Faculty and instruction (2009-2010):** Total instructional faculty: 63 full-time, 16 part-time (51% men; 49% women; 6% minorities). Full-time faculty with Ph.D. or other terminal degree: 81%. Student/faculty ratio: 12/1. Classes of fewer than 20 students: 61%; of 20 to 49 students: 39%; of 50 or more students: 0%. **Advanced Placement and International Baccalaureate credit:** AP tests may be used for: Credit only. Scores accepted: 3, 4, 5. International Baccalaureate exams may be used for: Credit only. **Freshmen returning for sophomore year:** 67%. **Graduation rates:** Four-year: 21%; five-year: 35%; six-year: 37%.

COSTS AND FINANCIAL AID

Financial aid office: (864) 488-8231. **Expenses (2010-2011):** Tuition and fees 2010-2011: $19,200; room/board: $7,000. Estimated books and supplies: $2,304; transportation: $2,592; personal expenses: $1,640. **Financial aid:** Priority filing date for institution's financial aid form: February 1. In 2009-2010, 93% of undergraduates applied for financial aid. Of those, 81% were determined to have financial need; 32% had their need fully met. Average financial aid package (proportion receiving): $13,802 (81%). Average amount of gift aid, such as scholarships or grants (proportion receiving): $11,174 (81%). Average amount of self-help aid, such as work study or loans (proportion receiving): $4,049 (63%). Average need-based loan (excluding PLUS or other private loans): $3,755. Among students who received need-based aid, the average percentage of need met: 45%. Among students who received aid based on merit, the average award (and the proportion receiving): $4,807 (9%). The average athletic scholarship (and the proportion receiving): $6,283 (8%). Average amount of debt of borrowers graduating in 2009: $20,701. Proportion who borrowed: 89%.

CAMPUS LIFE AND EXTRACURRICULAR ACTIVITIES

Campus housing available (% using): women's dorms (41%), men's dorms (52%), apartment for single students (5%), other housing options (2%). Students who live in college-owned, operated, or affiliated housing: 43%. **Student employment:** During the 2009-2010 academic year, 25% of undergraduates worked on campus. Average per-year earnings: $1,496. **Clubs and organizations:** Number of student organizations: 14. Activities include: campus ministries, choral groups, concert band, drama/theater, international student organization, jazz band, literary magazine, music ensembles, musical theater, pep band, student government, yearbook. Number of fraternities: 0; sororities: 0. Average proportion of students who stay on campus on weekends: 65%. **Sports program (2009-2010):** Member of NCAA II. *Men's intercollegiate varsity sports:* baseball, basketball, cross country, golf, lacrosse, soccer, swimming, tennis, track and field (outdoor), volleyball,

wrestling. *Women's intercollegiate varsity sports:* basketball, cross country, field hockey, golf, lacrosse, soccer, softball, swimming, tennis, track and field (outdoor), volleyball.

SERVICES AND FACILITIES

Basic services: nonremedial tutoring, placement service, health service, health insurance. **Remedial assistance:** math, writing, study skills, other. **Counseling services:** minority student, career, military, personal, veteran student, academic, older student, psychological, birth control, religious, other. **For learning-disabled students:** School does not offer a structured program with separate admission and additional fees. Total undergraduates in learning-disabled program or receiving services: 65. Services include: remedial math, remedial English, reading machines, remedial reading, tape recorders, other special classes, diagnostic testing service, untimed tests, note-taking services, oral tests, learning center, readers, extended time for tests, tutors, priority seating, texts on tape, other testing accommodations, other. **Library:** Number of titles: 132,203; number of current serial subscriptions: 36,572. **Information technology resources:** Students are not required to lease or own a computer. Number of campus computers available to all students: 139. School has a wireless network. Approximate number of users that can be accommodated: 300. Proportion of college-owned housing units wired for high-speed internet access: 100%. **Campus safety:** Security services offered: 24-hour foot-and-vehicle patrols, late-night transport/escort service, lighted pathways/sidewalks, controlled dormitory access (key, security card, etc).

TRANSFER AND INTERNATIONAL STUDENTS

Transfer students: May apply for admission for the following academic terms: Fall, Spring, Summer. Applicants need a minimum number of credits to apply. For fall 2009: Transfer applications received: 243. Transfer applicants offered admission: 120. Transfer applicants enrolled: 64. **International students:** Number of foreign undergraduates: 1. Number of countries represented: 19. Minimum TOEFL score required: 500 (paper); 173 (computer).

Morris College

- **Address:** 100 W. College Street, Sumter, SC 29150
- **Website:** http://www.morris.edu
- **Private; Religious affiliation:** Baptist
- **Enrollment:** N/A

KEY STATS

✔ **U.S News College Ranking:** Unranked, Regional Colleges (South)
✔ **SAT or ACT Score (25th/75th percentile):** N/A
✔ **Tuition:** 2009-2010: $9,901

Selectivity: N/A	**Room/board:** $4,386
Acceptance rate: N/A	**Average debt:** N/A
Student/faculty ratio: N/A	**Proportion who borrowed:** N/A

Newberry College

- **Address:** 2100 College Street, Newberry, SC 29108
- **Website:** http://www.newberry.edu/
- **Private; Religious affiliation:** Evangelical Lutheran Church of America
- **Enrollment:** 1,083 full-time; 20 part-time

KEY STATS

✔ **U.S News College Ranking:** 35, Regional Colleges (South)
✔ **SAT Score (25th/75th percentile):** 840-1080
✔ **Tuition:** 2010-2011: $22,518

Selectivity: Less selective	**Room/board:** $8,150
Acceptance rate: 69%	**Average debt:** $30,693
Student/faculty ratio: 17/1	**Proportion who borrowed:** 86%

UNDERGRADUATE STUDENT BODY STATS

2009-2010 enrollment: 1,083 full-time; 20 part-time. Men: 55%; women: 45%. **Ethnic makeup:** African American: 27%; Asian American: 1%; Hispanic: 2%; White: 67%; International: 3%. **Religious preference:** Roman

Catholic: 7%; Protestant: 31%; Unknown: 21%; Evangelical Lutheran Church of America: 11%; Partners with the ELCA: 16%; Other: 14%.

ADMISSIONS FACTS AND FIGURES

Phone: (800) 845-4955. **Email:** admissions@newberry.edu. **Website:** http://www.newberry.edu/. **Application deadlines for fall 2011:** Regular decision: Rolling. Early decision: Not offered. Early action: Not offered. Admission can be deferred. **Application fee:** $30. **To apply online, go to:** https://secure.newberry.edu/application_center/. **Admissions requirements/recommendations:** High school units required (recommended): English: 4 (4); Mathematics: 3 (3); Science: 2 (2); Foreign language: 2 (2); Social studies: 2 (2); History: 1 (1); Academic electives: 1 (1); Total units: 15 (15). Tests: The college uses SAT or ACT scores in admissions decisions. Either SAT or ACT required. For admission to the fall 2011 entering class, the school will accept: ACT with or without writing accepted. Campus visit: Recommended. Admissions interview: Recommended. Off-campus interview: May be arranged. **Factors that count in admissions decisions:** *Academic:* Secondary school record: Important. Class rank: Considered. Letters of recommendation: Considered. Standardized test scores: Very Important. Essay: Considered. *Nonacademic:* Interview: Considered. Extracurricular activities: Considered. Talent/ability: Considered. Character/personal qualities: Considered. Alumni/ae relationship: Considered. Geographical residence: Considered. State residency: Considered. Religious affiliation/commitment: Considered. Minority status: Considered. Volunteer work: Considered. Work experience: Considered. **Other schools with the greatest overlap in applicants:** Clemson University; Furman University; Lander University; University of South Carolina; Winthrop University. **Admissions statistics for the fall 2009 entering class:** Total applicants: 1,516. Total accepted: 1,045. Freshmen enrolled: 345; 20% were from out of state. Overall acceptance rate: 69%. **Size of waiting list:** 0 applicants; enrolled from waiting list: 0. **Credentials of fall 2009 freshmen:** 12% ranked in the top 10 percent of their high school class; 30% were in the top 25 percent; 63% were in the top half. (Proportion submitting class standing: 100%.) **First-year students who submitted SAT scores:** 78%. Scores (25/75 percentile): Critical Reading: 410-520, Math: 430-560, Combined: 840-1080. **First-year students submitting ACT scores:** 66%. Scores (25/75 percentile): English: N/A, Math: N/A, Composite: 17-23.

ACADEMICS

Year founded: 1856. **Academic calendar:** Semester. **Degrees offered:** bachelor's. **Most popular majors:** 27% business administration and management, 12% sport and fitness administration/management, 8% biology/biological sciences, 8% communication, journalism, and related programs, 8% history. **Major fields of study:** biological and biomedical sciences; business, management, marketing, and related support services; communication, journalism, and related programs; education; English language and literature/letters; foreign languages, literatures, and linguistics; health professions and related clinical sciences; history; mathematics and statistics; multi/interdisciplinary studies; parks, recreation, leisure, and fitness studies; philosophy and religious studies; physical sciences; psychology; social sciences; theology and religious vocations; visual and performing arts. **Areas of required coursework:** arts/fine arts, humanities, computer literacy, mathematics, English (including composition), sciences (biological or physical), history, social science, other. **Pre-professional programs:** pre-law, pre-medicine, pre-theology. **Special academic programs (% participation):** cooperative (work-study plan) program (0%), double major (4%), dual enrollment (0%), honors program (3%), independent study (3%), internships (3%), liberal arts/career combination, student-designed major (0%), study abroad (0%), teacher certificate program (11%). **Teacher certification offered in:** early childhood, elementary, secondary. **Cooperative education programs:** health professions, other. **Reserve Officers Training Corps (ROTC):** Army ROTC: Offered at cooperating institution. **Faculty and instruction (2009-2010):** Total instructional faculty: 52 full-time, 33 part-time (46% men; 54% women; 6% minorities). Full-time faculty with Ph.D. or other terminal degree: 71%. Student/faculty ratio: 17/1. Classes of fewer than 20 students: 61%; of 20 to 49 students: 38%; of 50 or more students: 1%. **Advanced Placement and International Baccalaureate credit:** AP tests may be used for: Placement only. Scores accepted: 3, 4, 5. International Baccalaureate exams may be used for: Placement only. **Freshmen returning for sophomore year:** 60%. **Graduation rates:** Four-year: 31%; five-year: 40%; six-year: 44%. **Graduate study:** 21% of students pursue further study immediately upon graduation; 11% within one year. Fields in which graduates pursue further study: law, 7%; medicine, 1%; theology (or the seminary), 4%; education, 7%; arts and sciences, 6%.

COSTS AND FINANCIAL AID

Financial aid office: (803) 321-5120. **Expenses (2010-2011):** Tuition and fees 2010-2011: $22,518; room/board: $8,150. Estimated books and supplies: $1,600; transportation: $1,495; personal expenses: $2,450. **Financial aid:** Priority filing date for institution's financial aid form: March 15. 24% had their need fully met. Average financial aid package (proportion receiving): $20,440 (N/A). Average amount of gift aid, such as scholarships or grants (proportion receiving): $16,969 (N/A). Average amount of self-help aid, such as work study or loans (proportion receiving): $4,603 (N/A). Average need-based loan (excluding PLUS or other private loans): $4,474. Among students who received need-based aid, the average percentage of need met: 76%. Among students who received aid based on merit, the average award (and the proportion receiving): $11,552 (N/A). The average athletic scholarship (and the proportion receiving): $7,707 (N/A). Average amount of debt of borrowers graduating in 2009: $30,693. Proportion who borrowed: 86%.

CAMPUS LIFE AND EXTRACURRICULAR ACTIVITIES

Campus housing available (% using): coed dorms (19%), women's dorms (32%), men's dorms (49%), special housing for disabled students. Students who live in college-owned, operated, or affiliated housing: 74%. **Student employment:** During the 2009-2010 academic year, 8% of undergraduates worked on campus. Average per-year earnings: $500. **Clubs and organizations:** Number of student organizations: 50. Activities include: campus ministries, choral groups, concert band, drama/theater, international student organization, jazz band, literary magazine, marching band, music ensembles, musical theater, radio station, student government, student newspaper, television station. Number of fraternities: 5; sororities: 4. Proportion of men in fraternities: 16%; of women in sororities: 31%. Average proportion of students who stay on campus on weekends: 60%. **Sports program (2009-2010):** Member of NCAA II. *Men's intercollegiate varsity sports:* baseball, basketball, cross country, football, golf, soccer, tennis, wrestling. *Women's intercollegiate varsity sports:* basketball, cross country, golf, soccer, softball, tennis, volleyball.

SERVICES AND FACILITIES

Basic services: nonremedial tutoring, placement service, health service, health insurance. **Remedial assistance:** reading, math, writing, study skills. **Counseling services:** career, military, personal, academic, psychological, religious. **For learning-disabled students:** School does not offer a structured program with separate admission and additional fees. Services include: remedial math, remedial English, reading machines, tape recorders, untimed tests, note-taking services, oral tests, learning center, extended time for tests, tutors, priority seating. **Library:** Number of titles: 84,899; number of current serial subscriptions: 136. **Information technology resources:** Students are required to lease or own a computer. Number of campus computers available to all students: 12. School has a wireless network. Approximate number of users that can be accommodated: 600. Proportion of college-owned housing units wired for high-speed internet access: 100%. **Campus safety:** Security services offered: 24-hour foot-and-vehicle patrols, late-night transport/escort service, 24-hour emergency telephones, lighted pathways/sidewalks, controlled dormitory access (key, security card, etc).

TRANSFER AND INTERNATIONAL STUDENTS

Transfer students: May apply for admission for the following academic terms: Fall, Spring, Summer. Applicants need a minimum number of credits to apply. **International students:** Number of foreign undergraduates: 34 (3% of student body). Number of countries represented: 24. Minimum TOEFL score required: 525 (paper); 71 (computer).

North Greenville University

■ **Address:** PO Box 1892, Tigerville, SC 29688
■ **Website:** http://www.ngu.edu
■ **Private; Religious affiliation:** Southern Baptist Convention
■ **Enrollment:** 1,894 full-time; 237 part-time

KEY STATS

✔ **U.S News College Ranking:** second tier, National Liberal Arts Colleges
✔ **SAT Score (25th/75th percentile):** 910-1290
✔ **Tuition:** 2010-2011: $12,820

Selectivity: Selective	**Room/board:** $7,510
Acceptance rate: 55%	**Average debt:** $18,100
Student/faculty ratio: 14/1	**Proportion who borrowed:** 61%

UNDERGRADUATE STUDENT BODY STATS

2009-2010 enrollment: 1,894 full-time; 237 part-time. Men: 49%; women: 51%. **Ethnic makeup:** African American: 8%; Hispanic: 1%; White: 90%; International: 1%. **Religious preference:** Roman Catholic: 1%; Protestant: 21%; Unknown: 11%; Southern Baptist Convention: 55%; Other Baptist: 12%.

ADMISSIONS FACTS AND FIGURES

Phone: (864) 977-7001. **Email:** admissions@ngu.edu. **Website:** http://www.ngu.edu. **Application deadlines for fall 2011:** Regular decision: Rolling. Early decision: Not offered. Early action: Not offered. Admission can be deferred. **Application fee:** $25. **To apply online, go to:** http://www.ngu.edu/admissions/NGU%20application.pdf. **Admissions requirements/recommendations:** High school units required (recommended): English: 4 (4); Mathematics: 2 (4); Science: 2 (2); Foreign language: 2 (2); Social studies: 1 (2); History: 1 (2); Academic electives: 2 (4); Total units: 14 (20). Tests: The college uses SAT or ACT scores in admissions decisions. Either SAT or ACT required. For admission to the fall 2011 entering class, the school will accept: ACT with or without writing accepted. Campus visit: Recommended. Admissions interview: Recommended. Off-campus interview: May be arranged. **Factors that count in admissions decisions:** *Academic:* Secondary school record: Very Important. Class rank: Very Important. Letters of recommendation: Considered. Standardized test scores: Very Important. Essay: Considered. *Nonacademic:* Interview: Considered. Extracurricular activities: Important. Talent/ability: Important. Character/personal qualities: Very Important. Alumni/ae relationship: Considered. Geographical residence: Not Considered. State residency: Not Considered. Religious affiliation/commitment: Considered. Minority status: Not Considered. Volunteer work: Considered. Work experience: Considered. **Other schools with the greatest overlap in applicants:** Anderson University; Clemson University; Lander University; Liberty University; University of South Carolina–Upstate. **Admissions statistics for the fall 2009 entering class:** Total applicants: 1,618. Total accepted: 893. Freshmen enrolled: 494; 21% were from out of state. Overall acceptance rate: 55%. **Credentials of fall 2009 freshmen:** 20% ranked in the top 10 percent of their high school class; 45% were in the top 25 percent; 75% were in the top half. (Proportion submitting class standing: 91%.) **First-year students who submitted SAT scores:** 89%. Scores (25/75 percentile): Critical Reading: 440-660, Math: 470-630, Combined: 910-1290. **First-year students submitting ACT scores:** 59%. Scores (25/75 percentile): English: N/A, Math: N/A, Composite: 21-29.

ACADEMICS

Year founded: 1892. **Academic calendar:** Semester. **Degrees offered:** bachelor's, master's. **Most popular majors:** 21% business, management, marketing, and related support services, 17% theology and religious vocations, 14% education, 13% liberal arts and sciences studies, and humanities, 9% communication, journalism, and related programs. **Major fields of study:** biological and biomedical sciences; business, management, marketing, and related support services; communication, journalism, and related programs; education; English language and literature/letters; health professions and related clinical sciences; history; mathematics and statistics; multi/interdisciplinary studies; parks, recreation, leisure, and fitness studies; philosophy and religious studies; psychology; theology and religious vocations; visual and performing arts. **Areas of required coursework:** arts/fine arts, humanities, computer literacy, mathematics, English (including composition), foreign languages, sciences (biological or physical), history, social science, other. **Pre-professional programs:** pre-law, pre-dentistry, pre-medicine, pre-theology, pre-veterinary science, pre-optometry, pre-pharmacy. **Special academic programs (% participation):** cooperative (work-study plan) program,

double major, dual enrollment (1%), English as a Second Language (ESL), honors program (3%), independent study (10%), internships (26%), study abroad (1%), teacher certificate program (22%). **Teacher certification offered in:** early childhood, elementary, middle/junior high, secondary. **Reserve Officers Training Corps (ROTC):** Army ROTC: Offered at cooperating institution (Furman University). **Faculty and instruction (2009-2010):** Total instructional faculty: 124 full-time, 43 part-time (57% men; 43% women; 10% minorities). Full-time faculty with Ph.D. or other terminal degree: 67%. Student/faculty ratio: 14/1. Classes of fewer than 20 students: 61%; of 20 to 49 students: 39%; of 50 or more students: 0%. **Advanced Placement and International Baccalaureate credit:** AP tests may be used for: Credit and/or placement. Scores accepted: 3, 4, 5. International Baccalaureate exams may be used for: Credit and/or placement. **Freshmen returning for sophomore year:** 69%. **Graduation rates:** Four-year: 35%; five-year: 49%; six-year: 52%.

COSTS AND FINANCIAL AID

Financial aid office: (864) 977-7058. **Expenses (2010-2011):** Tuition and fees 2010-2011: $12,820; room/board: $7,510. Estimated books and supplies: $1,800; transportation: $2,675; personal expenses: $3,525. **Financial aid:** In 2009-2010, 95% of undergraduates applied for financial aid. Of those, 94% were determined to have financial need; 90% had their need fully met. Average financial aid package (proportion receiving): N/A (94%). Average amount of gift aid, such as scholarships or grants (proportion receiving): N/A (57%). Average amount of self-help aid, such as work study or loans (proportion receiving): N/A (57%). Among students who received need-based aid, the average percentage of need met: 95%. Average amount of debt of borrowers graduating in 2009: $18,100. Proportion who borrowed: 61%.

CAMPUS LIFE AND EXTRACURRICULAR ACTIVITIES

Campus housing available (% using): women's dorms (53%), men's dorms (47%), special housing for disabled students (0%). Students who live in college-owned, operated, or affiliated housing: 70%. **Student employment:** During the 2009-2010 academic year, 10% of undergraduates worked on campus. Average per-year earnings: $1,000. **Clubs and organizations:** Number of student organizations: 14. Activities include: campus ministries, choral groups, concert band, drama/theater, jazz band, literary magazine, marching band, music ensembles, pep band, radio station, student government, student newspaper, television station, yearbook. Number of fraternities: 0; sororities: 0. Average proportion of students who stay on campus on weekends: 30%. **Sports program (2009-2010):** Member of NCAA II. *Men's intercollegiate varsity sports:* baseball, basketball, cross country, football, golf, soccer, tennis. *Women's intercollegiate varsity sports:* basketball, cross country, golf, soccer, softball, tennis, volleyball.

SERVICES AND FACILITIES

Basic services: nonremedial tutoring, placement service, health service, health insurance. **Remedial assistance:** reading, math, writing, study skills. **Counseling services:** career, military, personal, veteran student, academic, psychological, religious. **For learning-disabled students:** School does not offer a structured program with separate admission and additional fees. Services include: remedial math, remedial English, remedial reading, tape recorders, untimed tests, note-taking services, oral tests, extended time for tests, tutors, priority registration. **Library:** Number of titles: 50,830; number of current serial subscriptions: 324. **Information technology resources:** Students are not required to lease or own a computer. Number of campus computers available to all students: 78. School has a wireless network. Approximate number of users that can be accommodated: 150. Proportion of college-owned housing units wired for high-speed internet access: 100%. **Campus safety:** Security services offered: 24-hour foot-and-vehicle patrols, late-night transport/escort service, 24-hour emergency telephones, lighted pathways/sidewalks, controlled dormitory access (key, security card, etc).

TRANSFER AND INTERNATIONAL STUDENTS

Transfer students: May apply for admission for the following academic terms: Fall, Spring, Summer. Applicants need a minimum number of credits to apply. For fall 2009: Transfer applicants enrolled: 116. **International students:** Number of foreign undergraduates: 24 (1% of student body). Minimum TOEFL score required: 500 (paper); 174 (computer). Average TOEFL score: 500 (paper).

Presbyterian College

- **Address:** 503 S. Broad Street, Clinton, SC 29325
- **Website:** http://www.presby.edu
- **Private; Religious affiliation:** Presbyterian Church (USA)
- **Enrollment:** 1,198 full-time; 23 part-time

KEY STATS

✔ **U.S News College Ranking:** 119, National Liberal Arts Colleges
✔ **SAT Score (25th/75th percentile):** 1000-1250
✔ **Tuition:** 2010-2011: $30,180

Selectivity: More selective	**Room/board:** $8,670
Acceptance rate: 70%	**Average debt:** $23,391
Student/faculty ratio: 11/1	**Proportion who borrowed:** 56%

UNDERGRADUATE STUDENT BODY STATS

2009-2010 enrollment: 1,198 full-time; 23 part-time. Men: 49%; women: 51%. **Ethnic makeup:** African American: 8%; Asian American: 1%; Hispanic: 1%; White: 89%. **Religious preference:** Roman Catholic: 10%; Protestant: 53%; No preference: 3%; Unknown: 10%; Presbyterian Church (USA): 24%.

ADMISSIONS FACTS AND FIGURES

Phone: (864) 833-8230. **Email:** admissions@presby.edu. **Website:** http://www.presby.edu. **Application deadlines for fall 2011:** Regular decision: June 30; decision sent by March 15. Early decision: Send application by: November 1; Decision sent by: December 1. Early action: Send application by: November 15; Decision sent by: December 15. Admission can be deferred. **Application fee:** $40. **To apply online, go to:** http://applyweb.com/apply/pc/indexa.html. **Admissions requirements/recommendations:** High school units required (recommended): English: 4; Mathematics: 4; Science: 2 (4); Foreign language: 2 (3); Social studies: 2; History: 2; Academic electives: 2; Total units: 18. Tests: The college uses SAT or ACT scores in admissions decisions. Either SAT or ACT required. For admission to the fall 2011 entering class, the school will accept: ACT with or without writing accepted. Campus visit: Recommended. Admissions interview: Recommended. Off-campus interview: Not available. **Factors that count in admissions decisions:** *Academic:* Secondary school record: Very Important. Class rank: Very Important. Letters of recommendation: Important. Standardized test scores: Very Important. Essay: Very Important. *Nonacademic:* Interview: Considered. Extracurricular activities: Important. Talent/ability: Considered. Character/personal qualities: Important. Alumni/ae relationship: Considered. Geographical residence: Not Considered. State residency: Not Considered. Religious affiliation/commitment: Not Considered. Minority status: Not Considered. Volunteer work: Considered. Work experience: Considered. **Other schools with the greatest overlap in applicants:** Clemson University; Davidson College; Furman University; University of South Carolina; Wofford College. **Admissions statistics for the fall 2009 entering class:** Total applicants: 1,455. Total accepted: 1,017. Freshmen enrolled: 364; 36% were from out of state. Accepted through early-decision or early-action plans: 71%. Overall acceptance rate: 70%. Early-decision acceptance rate: 78%. Non-early acceptance rate: 48%. **Size of waiting list:** 13 applicants; enrolled from waiting list: 3. **Credentials of fall 2009 freshmen:** 35% ranked in the top 10 percent of their high school class; 69% were in the top 25 percent; 92% were in the top half. (Proportion submitting class standing: 85%.) **Average high school grade point average:** 3.4. **First-year students who submitted SAT scores:** 91%. Scores (25/75 percentile): Critical Reading: 490-620, Math: 510-630, Combined: 1000-1250. **First-year students submitting ACT scores:** 60%. Scores (25/75 percentile): English: N/A, Math: N/A, Composite: 21-27.

ACADEMICS

Year founded: 1880. **Academic calendar:** Semester. **Degrees offered:** bachelor's. **Most popular majors:** 26% business, management, marketing, and related support services, 11% social sciences, 10% philosophy and religious studies, 9% biological and biomedical sciences, 6% history. **Major fields of study:** biological and biomedical sciences; business, management, marketing, and related support services; computer and information sciences and support services; education; English language and literature/letters; foreign languages, literatures, and linguistics; history; mathematics and statistics; philosophy and religious studies; physical sciences; psychology; social sciences; theology and religious vocations; visual and performing arts. **Areas of required coursework:** arts/fine arts, humanities, mathematics, English (including composition), philosophy, foreign languages, sciences (biological or physical), history, social science, other. **Pre-professional pro-**

grams: pre-law, pre-dentistry, pre-medicine, pre-theology, pre-veterinary science, pre-pharmacy, other. **Special academic programs:** double major, dual enrollment, exchange student program (domestic), honors program, independent study, internships, study abroad, teacher certificate program. **Teacher certification offered in:** early childhood, elementary, middle/junior high, secondary. **Reserve Officers Training Corps (ROTC):** Army ROTC: Offered on campus. **Faculty and instruction (2009-2010):** Total instructional faculty: 87 full-time, 61 part-time (65% men; 35% women; 7% minorities). Full-time faculty with Ph.D. or other terminal degree: 92%. Student/faculty ratio: 11/1. Classes of fewer than 20 students: 59%; of 20 to 49 students: 41%; of 50 or more students: 0%. **Advanced Placement and International Baccalaureate credit:** AP tests may be used for: Credit only. Scores accepted: 3, 4, 5. International Baccalaureate exams may be used for: Credit only. **Freshmen returning for sophomore year:** 84%. **Graduation rates:** Four-year: 63%; five-year: 67%; six-year: 68%. **Graduate study:** 31% of students pursue further study immediately upon graduation. Fields in which graduates pursue further study: Master of Business Administration (MBA), 14%; law, 12%; medicine, 14%; theology (or the seminary), 6%; education, 8%; arts and sciences, 46%.

COSTS AND FINANCIAL AID

Financial aid office: (864) 833-8289. **Expenses (2010-2011):** Tuition and fees 2010-2011: $30,180; room/board: $8,670. Estimated books and supplies: $1,200; transportation: $1,848; personal expenses: $2,502. **Financial aid:** Priority filing date for institution's financial aid form: March 15; deadline: June 30. In 2009-2010, 78% of undergraduates applied for financial aid. Of those, 68% were determined to have financial need; 50% had their need fully met. Average financial aid package (proportion receiving): $29,765 (68%). Average amount of gift aid, such as scholarships or grants (proportion receiving): $27,536 (68%). Average amount of self-help aid, such as work study or loans (proportion receiving): $4,618 (32%). Average need-based loan (excluding PLUS or other private loans): $4,111. Among students who received need-based aid, the average percentage of need met: 88%. Among students who received aid based on merit, the average award (and the proportion receiving): $13,050 (28%). The average athletic scholarship (and the proportion receiving): $17,319 (13%). Average amount of debt of borrowers graduating in 2009: $23,391. Proportion who borrowed: 56%.

CAMPUS LIFE AND EXTRACURRICULAR ACTIVITIES

Campus housing available (% using): coed dorms (9%), women's dorms (41%), men's dorms (39%), fraternity housing (2%), apartment for single students (6%), special housing for international students (3%). Students who live in college-owned, operated, or affiliated housing: 96%. **Clubs and organizations:** Number of student organizations: 85. Activities include: campus ministries, choral groups, concert band, dance, drama/theater, jazz band, literary magazine, music ensembles, musical theater, opera, pep band, radio station, student government, student newspaper, symphony orchestra, yearbook. Number of fraternities: 6; sororities: 3. Proportion of men in fraternities: 42%; of women in sororities: 43%. Average proportion of students who stay on campus on weekends: 75%. **Sports program (2009-2010):** Member of NCAA I. *Men's intercollegiate varsity sports:* baseball, basketball, cross country, football, golf, lacrosse, soccer, tennis. *Women's intercollegiate varsity sports:* basketball, cross country, golf, lacrosse, soccer, softball, tennis, volleyball.

SERVICES AND FACILITIES

Basic services: nonremedial tutoring, placement service, health service, other. **Counseling services:** minority student, career, military, personal, veteran student, academic, psychological, birth control, religious. **For learning-disabled students:** School does not offer a structured program with separate admission and additional fees. Total undergraduates in learning-disabled program or receiving services: 85. Services include: tape recorders, oral tests, extended time for tests, tutors, other testing accommodations, other. **Library:** Number of titles: 140,467; number of current serial subscriptions: 8,094. **Information technology resources:** Students are not required to lease or own a computer. Number of campus computers available to all students: 100. School has a wireless network. Approximate number of users that can be accommodated: 500. Proportion of college-owned housing units wired for high-speed internet access: 100%. **Campus safety:** Security services offered: 24-hour foot-and-vehicle patrols, 24-hour emergency telephones, lighted pathways/sidewalks, controlled dormitory access (key, security card, etc).

TRANSFER AND INTERNATIONAL STUDENTS

Transfer students: May apply for admission for the following academic terms: Fall, Spring, Summer. Applicants need a minimum number of cred-

its to apply. For fall 2009: Transfer applicants enrolled: 16. **International students:** Number of foreign undergraduates: 5. Number of countries represented: 9. Minimum TOEFL score required: 550 (paper); 93 (computer). Average TOEFL score: 580 (paper).

South Carolina State University

- **Address:** 300 College Street NE, Orangeburg, SC 29117
- **Website:** http://www.scsu.edu
- **Public**
- **Enrollment:** 3,567 full-time; 307 part-time

KEY STATS

✔ **U.S News College Ranking:** 170, National Universities
✔ **SAT Score (25th/75th percentile):** 763-948
✔ **Tuition:** 2009-2010: $8,462 in state, $16,626 out of state
  Selectivity: Less selective **Room/board:** $8,262
  Acceptance rate: 73% **Average debt:** N/A
  Student/faculty ratio: 16/1 **Proportion who borrowed:** N/A

UNDERGRADUATE STUDENT BODY STATS

2009-2010 enrollment: 3,567 full-time; 307 part-time. Men: 46%; women: 54%. **Ethnic makeup:** African American: 96%; Hispanic: 1%; White: 3%.

ADMISSIONS FACTS AND FIGURES

Phone: (803) 536-7185. **Email:** admissions@scsu.edu. **Website:** http://www.scsu.edu. **Application deadlines for fall 2011:** Regular decision: May 31; decision sent by September 30. Early decision: Not offered. Early action: Not offered. Admission can be deferred. **Application fee:** $25. **To apply online, go to:** http://www.applyweb.com/aw?scsu. **Admissions requirements/recommendations:** High school units required (recommended): English: 4; Mathematics: 3; Science: 3; Foreign language: 2; Social studies: 3; Academic electives: 4; Total units: 20. Tests: The college uses SAT or ACT scores in admissions decisions. Either SAT or ACT required. For admission to the fall 2011 entering class, the school will accept: ACT with or without writing accepted. Campus visit: Recommended. Admissions interview: Recommended. Off-campus interview: May be arranged. **Factors that count in admissions decisions:** *Academic:* Secondary school record: Very Important. Class rank: Very Important, Letters of recommendation: Considered. Standardized test scores: Very Important. Essay: Considered. *Nonacademic:* Interview: Considered. Extracurricular activities: Considered. Talent/ability: Considered. Character/personal qualities: Considered. Alumni/ae relationship: Considered. Geographical residence: Considered. State residency: Considered. Religious affiliation/commitment: Not Considered. Minority status: Not Considered. Volunteer work: Considered. Work experience: Considered. **Admissions statistics for the fall 2009 entering class:** Total applicants: 3,715. Total accepted: 2,726. Freshmen enrolled: 723; 28% were from out of state. Overall acceptance rate: 73%. **Credentials of fall 2009 freshmen:** 6% ranked in the top 10 percent of their high school class; 17% were in the top 25 percent; 57% were in the top half. (Proportion submitting class standing: 73%.) **Average high school grade point average:** 2.8. **First-year students who submitted SAT scores:** 53%. Scores (25/75 percentile): Critical Reading: 380-470, Math: 383-478, Combined: 763-948. **First-year students submitting ACT scores:** 47%. Scores (25/75 percentile): English: N/A, Math: N/A, Composite: 15-18.

ACADEMICS

Year founded: 1896. **Academic calendar:** Semester. **Degrees offered:** bachelor's, post-bachelor's certificate, master's, post-master's certificate, doctorate. **Most popular majors:** 9% biology/biological sciences, 9% business/commerce, 8% family and consumer sciences/human sciences, 7% psychology, 5% social work. **Major fields of study:** agriculture, agriculture operations, and related sciences; biological and biomedical sciences; business, management, marketing, and related support services; computer and information sciences and support services; education; engineering; engineering technologies/technicians; English language and literature/letters; family and consumer sciences/human sciences; foreign languages, literatures, and linguistics; health professions and related clinical sciences; history; mathematics and statistics; parks, recreation, leisure, and fitness studies; physical sciences; psychology; public administration and social service professions; security and protective services; social sciences; visual and performing arts. **Areas of required coursework:** arts/fine arts, humanities, computer literacy, mathematics, English (including composition), philosophy, foreign languages, sciences (biological or physical), history, social science. **Pre-professional programs:** pre-law, pre-dentistry, pre-medicine, pre-veterinary science, pre-optometry, other. **Special academic programs (% participation):** accelerated program, cooperative (work-study plan) program (20%), cross-registration (2%), distance learning (8%), double major (1%), dual enrollment, honors program (2%), independent study (8%), internships (2%), study abroad (2%), teacher certificate program (8%). **Teacher certification offered in:** early childhood, special education, elementary, secondary. **Cooperative education programs:** agriculture, art, business, computer science, education, engineering, health professions, home economics, humanities, natural science, social/behavioral science, technologies, vocational arts. **Reserve Officers Training Corps (ROTC):** Army ROTC: Offered on campus. **Faculty and instruction (2009-2010):** Total instructional faculty: 229 full-time, 64 part-time (55% men; 45% women; 76% minorities). Full-time faculty with Ph.D. or other terminal degree: 85%. Student/faculty ratio: 16/1. Classes of fewer than 20 students: 48%; of 20 to 49 students: 50%; of 50 or more students: 2%. **Advanced Placement and International Baccalaureate credit:** AP tests may be used for: Credit and/or placement. Scores accepted: 3, 4, 5. International Baccalaureate exams may be used for: Placement only. **Freshmen returning for sophomore year:** 65%. **Graduation rates:** Four-year: 13%; five-year: 31%; six-year: 36%. **Graduate study:** 15% of students pursue further study immediately upon graduation; 70% within one year; 15% within five years. Fields in which graduates pursue further study: Master of Business Administration (MBA), 15%; law, 10%; medicine, 10%; dentistry, 5%; engineering, 10%; education, 30%; arts and sciences, 20%.

COSTS AND FINANCIAL AID

Financial aid office: (803) 536-7067. **Expenses (2009-2010):** Tuition and fees 2009-2010: $8,462 in state, $16,626 out of state; room/board: $8,262. **Financial aid:** Priority filing date for institution's financial aid form: May 1.

CAMPUS LIFE AND EXTRACURRICULAR ACTIVITIES

Campus housing available (% using): coed dorms (54%), women's dorms (26%), men's dorms (19%), apartments for married students (1%), special housing for disabled students (0%), other housing options (0%). Students who live in college-owned, operated, or affiliated housing: 45%. **Student employment:** During the 2009-2010 academic year, 13% of undergraduates worked on campus. Average per-year earnings: $1,800. **Clubs and organizations:** Number of student organizations: 77. Activities include: campus ministries, choral groups, concert band, dance, drama/theater, international student organization, jazz band, literary magazine, marching band, music ensembles, pep band, radio station, student government, student newspaper, yearbook. Number of fraternities: 3; sororities: 3. Proportion of men in fraternities: 20%; of women in sororities: 20%. Average proportion of students who stay on campus on weekends: 30%. **Sports program (2009-2010):** Member of NCAA I. *Men's intercollegiate varsity sports:* basketball, cross country, football, golf, tennis, track and field (indoor), track and field (outdoor). *Women's intercollegiate varsity sports:* basketball, bowling, cross country, golf, soccer, softball, tennis, track and field (indoor), track and field (outdoor), volleyball.

SERVICES AND FACILITIES

Basic services: nonremedial tutoring, placement service, health service, health insurance. **Remedial assistance:** study skills. **Counseling services:** minority student, personal, psychological. **For learning-disabled students:** School does not offer a structured program with separate admission and additional fees. Total undergraduates in learning-disabled program or receiving services: 6. Services include: tape recorders, diagnostic testing service, note-taking services, oral tests, learning center, extended time for tests, tutors, other testing accommodations. **Library:** Number of titles: 313,329; number of current serial subscriptions: 3,031. **Information technology resources:** Students are not required to lease or own a computer. Number of campus computers available to all students: 600. School has a wireless network. Approximate number of users that can be accommodated: 1,000. Proportion of college-owned housing units wired for high-speed internet access: 100%. **Campus safety:** Security services offered: 24-hour foot-and-vehicle patrols, 24-hour emergency telephones, lighted pathways/sidewalks, controlled dormitory access (key, security card, etc.).

TRANSFER AND INTERNATIONAL STUDENTS

Transfer students: May apply for admission for the following academic terms: Fall, Spring, Summer. Applicants need a minimum number of credits to apply. For fall 2009: Transfer applications received: 647. Transfer applicants offered admission: 320. Transfer applicants enrolled: 218. **International students:** Number of foreign undergraduates: 5. Number of countries represented: 27. Minimum TOEFL score required: 500 (paper); 173 (computer). Average TOEFL score: 500 (paper).

Southern Wesleyan University

- **Address:** PO Box 1020, Wesleyan Drive, Central, SC 29630
- **Website:** http://www.swu.edu
- **Private; Religious affiliation:** Wesleyan Church
- **Enrollment:** 1,677 full-time; 28 part-time

KEY STATS

✔ **U.S News College Ranking:** 87, Regional Universities (South)
✔ **SAT Score (25th/75th percentile):** 878-1090
✔ **Tuition:** 2010-2011: $19,500

Selectivity: Less selective	**Room/board:** $8,150
Acceptance rate: 95%	**Average debt:** $26,923
Student/faculty ratio: 23/1	**Proportion who borrowed:** 85%

UNDERGRADUATE STUDENT BODY STATS

2009-2010 enrollment: 1,677 full-time; 28 part-time. Men: 37%; women: 63%. **Ethnic makeup:** African American: 29%; American-Indian: 1%; Hispanic: 2%; White: 67%; International: 1%. **Religious preference:** Roman Catholic: 3%; Protestant: 56%; Wesleyan Church: 26%; None Indicated: N/A; Other: 15%.

ADMISSIONS FACTS AND FIGURES

Phone: (864) 644-5550. **Email:** admissions@swu.edu. **Website:** http://www.swu.edu. **Application deadlines for fall 2011:** Regular decision: August 1. Early decision: Not offered. Early action: Not offered. Admission can be deferred. **Application fee:** $25. **To apply online, go to:** https://www.applyweb.com/apply/swuu/menu.html. **Admissions requirements/recommendations:** High school units required (recommended): English: 4; Mathematics: 2; Science: 2; Social studies: 2; Total units: 10. Tests: The college uses SAT or ACT scores in admissions decisions. Either SAT or ACT required. For admission to the fall 2011 entering class, the school will accept: ACT with or without writing accepted. Campus visit: Recommended. Admissions interview: Neither required nor recommended. Off-campus interview: Not available. **Factors that count in admissions decisions:** *Academic:* Secondary school record: Important. Class rank: Considered. Letters of recommendation: Not Considered. Standardized test scores: Very Important. Essay: Not Considered. *Nonacademic:* Interview: Not Considered. Extracurricular activities: Considered. Talent/ability: Not Considered. Character/personal qualities: Considered. Alumni/ae relationship: Not Considered. Geographical residence: Not Considered. State residency: Not Considered. Religious affiliation/commitment: Very Important. Minority status: Not Considered. Volunteer work: Considered. Work experience: Considered. **Other schools with the greatest overlap in applicants:** Anderson University; Charleston Southern University; Clemson University; North Greenville University; University of South Carolina. **Admissions statistics for the fall 2009 entering class:** Total applicants: 596. Total accepted: 566. Freshmen enrolled: 221; 21% were from out of state. Overall acceptance rate: 95%. **Credentials of fall 2009 freshmen:** 13% ranked in the top 10 percent of their high school class; 36% were in the top 25 percent; 75% were in the top half. (Proportion submitting class standing: 88%.) **Average high school grade point average:** 3.6. **First-year students who submitted SAT scores:** 73%. Scores (25/75 percentile): Critical Reading: 438-540, Math: 440-550, Combined: 878-1090. **First-year students submitting ACT scores:** 36%. Scores (25/75 percentile): English: 17-22, Math: 17-22, Composite: 18-22.

ACADEMICS

Year founded: 1906. **Academic calendar:** Semester. **Degrees offered:** associate, bachelor's, master's. **Most popular majors:** 69% business administration and management, 8% elementary education and teaching, 4% psychology, 4% parks, recreation, leisure, and fitness studies, 3% religion/religious studies. **Major fields of study:** biological and biomedical sciences; business, management, marketing, and related support services; communication, journalism, and related programs; education; English language and literature/letters; health professions and related clinical sciences; history; mathematics and statistics; parks, recreation, leisure, and fitness studies; philosophy and religious studies; physical sciences; psychology; public administration and social service professions; security and protective services; social sciences; visual and performing arts. **Areas of required coursework:** arts/fine arts, humanities, computer literacy, mathematics,

English (including composition), philosophy, sciences (biological or physical), history, social science, other. **Pre-professional programs:** pre-dentistry, pre-medicine, pre-theology. **Special academic programs:** cross-registration, distance learning, double major, dual enrollment, honors program, independent study, internships, student-designed major, study abroad, teacher certificate program, other. **Teacher certification offered in:** early childhood, special education, elementary, secondary. **Cooperative education programs:** health professions. **Reserve Officers Training Corps (ROTC):** Army ROTC: Offered at cooperating institution; Air Force ROTC: Offered at cooperating institution. **Faculty and instruction (2009-2010):** Total instructional faculty: 50 full-time, 169 part-time (61% men; 39% women; 26% minorities). Full-time faculty with Ph.D. or other terminal degree: 76%. Student/faculty ratio: 23/1. Classes of fewer than 20 students: 79%; of 20 to 49 students: 21%; of 50 or more students: 0%. **Freshmen returning for sophomore year:** 68%. **Graduation rates:** Four-year: 33%; five-year: 42%; six-year: 47%.

COSTS AND FINANCIAL AID

Financial aid office: (864) 644-5500. **Expenses (2010-2011):** Tuition and fees 2010-2011: $19,500; room/board: $8,150. Estimated books and supplies: $950; transportation: $900; personal expenses: $1,000. **Financial aid:** Priority filing date for institution's financial aid form: March 31; deadline: June 30. In 2009-2010, 86% of undergraduates applied for financial aid. Of those, 46% were determined to have financial need; 14% had their need fully met. Average financial aid package (proportion receiving): $11,837 (46%). Average amount of gift aid, such as scholarships or grants (proportion receiving): $9,305 (43%). Average amount of self-help aid, such as work study or loans (proportion receiving): $4,118 (34%). Average need-based loan (excluding PLUS or other private loans): $3,772. Among students who received need-based aid, the average percentage of need met: 69%. Among students who received aid based on merit, the average award (and the proportion receiving): $7,453 (2%). The average athletic scholarship (and the proportion receiving): $4,605 (2%). Average amount of debt of borrowers graduating in 2009: $26,923. Proportion who borrowed: 85%.

CAMPUS LIFE AND EXTRACURRICULAR ACTIVITIES

Campus housing available (% using): coed dorms (68%), women's dorms (6%), apartment for single students (26%). Students who live in college-owned, operated, or affiliated housing: 24%. **Clubs and organizations:** Number of student organizations: 12. Activities include: campus ministries, choral groups, concert band, drama/theater, jazz band, literary magazine, music ensembles, musical theater, student government, yearbook. Number of fraternities: 0; sororities: 0. Average proportion of students who stay on campus on weekends: 50%. **Sports program (2009-2010):** Member of NAIA. *Men's intercollegiate varsity sports:* baseball, basketball, cross country, golf, soccer. *Women's intercollegiate varsity sports:* basketball, cross country, soccer, softball, volleyball.

SERVICES AND FACILITIES

Basic services: nonremedial tutoring, health service. **Remedial assistance:** reading, math, writing, study skills. **Counseling services:** minority student, career, personal, academic, older student, psychological, religious. **For learning-disabled students:** School does not offer a structured program with separate admission and additional fees. Total undergraduates in learning-disabled program or receiving services: 11. Services include: remedial math, remedial English, remedial reading, tape recorders, untimed tests, note-taking services, oral tests, learning center, readers, extended time for tests, tutors, priority registration, priority seating, other. **Library:** Number of titles: 116,200; number of current serial subscriptions: 510. **Information technology resources:** Students are not required to lease or own a computer. Number of campus computers available to all students: 256. School has a wireless network. Approximate number of users that can be accommodated: 525. Proportion of college-owned housing units wired for high-speed internet access: 100%. **Campus safety:** Security services offered: 24-hour foot-and-vehicle patrols, 24-hour emergency telephones, lighted pathways/sidewalks, controlled dormitory access (key, security card, etc).

TRANSFER AND INTERNATIONAL STUDENTS

Transfer students: May apply for admission for the following academic terms: Fall, Spring, Summer. Applicants need a minimum number of credits to apply. For fall 2009: Transfer applications received: 378. Transfer applicants offered admission: 366. Transfer applicants enrolled: 238. **International students:** Number of foreign undergraduates: 12 (1% of student body). Number of countries represented: 11. Minimum TOEFL score required: 500 (paper); 173 (computer).

University of South Carolina

- **Address:** Columbia, SC 29208
- **Website:** http://www.sc.edu
- **Public**
- **Enrollment:** 18,979 full-time; 1,515 part-time

KEY STATS

- ✔ **U.S News College Ranking:** 111, National Universities
- ✔ **SAT Score (25th/75th percentile):** 1090-1290
- ✔ **Tuition:** 2009-2010: $9,156 in state, $23,732 out of state
- **Selectivity:** More selective **Room/board:** $7,328
- **Acceptance rate:** 64% **Average debt:** $21,755
- **Student/faculty ratio:** 18/1 **Proportion who borrowed:** 46%

UNDERGRADUATE STUDENT BODY STATS

2009-2010 enrollment: 18,979 full-time; 1,515 part-time. Men: 46%; women: 54%. **Ethnic makeup:** African American: 11%; Asian American: 3%; Hispanic: 3%; White: 81%; International: 1%.

ADMISSIONS FACTS AND FIGURES

Phone: (803) 777-7700. **Email:** admissions-ugrad@sc.edu. **Website:** http://www.sc.edu. **Application deadlines for fall 2011:** Regular decision: December 1; decision sent by March 15. Early decision: Not offered. Early action: Send application by: October 15; Decision sent by: December 20. Admission cannot be deferred. **Application fee:** $50. **To apply online, go to:** http://www.sc.edu/admissions. **Admissions requirements/recommendations:** High school units required (recommended): English: 4; Mathematics: 4; Science: 3; Foreign language: 2; Social studies: 2; History: 1; Academic electives: 1; Total units: 19. Tests: The college uses SAT or ACT scores in admissions decisions. Either SAT or ACT required. For admission to the fall 2011 entering class, the school will accept: ACT with writing required. Campus visit: Recommended. Admissions interview: Neither required nor recommended. Off-campus interview: Not available. **Factors that count in admissions decisions:** *Academic:* Secondary school record: Very Important. Class rank: Important. Letters of recommendation: Considered. Standardized test scores: Very Important. Essay: Considered. *Nonacademic:* Interview: Not Considered. Extracurricular activities: Considered. Talent/ability: Considered. Character/personal qualities: Considered. Alumni/ae relationship: Considered. Geographical residence: Not Considered. State residency: Considered. Religious affiliation/commitment: Not Considered. Minority status: Considered. Volunteer work: Considered. Work experience: Considered. **Other schools with the greatest overlap in applicants:** Clemson University; College of Charleston; North Carolina State University–Raleigh; University of Georgia; University of North Carolina–Chapel Hill. **Admissions statistics for the fall 2009 entering class:** Total applicants: 17,694. Total accepted: 11,262. Freshmen enrolled: 3,917; 37% were from out of state. Accepted through early-decision or early-action plans: 49%. Overall acceptance rate: 64%. Non-early acceptance rate: 69%. **Size of waiting list:** 0 applicants; enrolled from waiting list: 0. **Credentials of fall 2009 freshmen:** 27% ranked in the top 10 percent of their high school class; 60% were in the top 25 percent; 91% were in the top half. (Proportion submitting class standing: 76%.) **Average high school grade point average:** 3.9. **First-year students who submitted SAT scores:** 71%. Scores (25/75 percentile): Critical Reading: 530-640, Math: 560-650, Combined: 1090-1290. **First-year students submitting ACT scores:** 28%. Scores (25/75 percentile): English: N/A, Math: N/A, Composite: 24-29.

ACADEMICS

Year founded: 1801. **Academic calendar:** Semester. **Degrees offered:** associate, bachelor's, post-bachelor's certificate, master's, post-master's certificate, doctorate. **Most popular majors:** 7% health and physical education/fitness, 6% nursing, 5% biology, 5% experimental psychology, 5% teacher education and professional development. **Major fields of study:** area, ethnic, cultural, and gender studies; biological and biomedical sciences; business, management, marketing, and related support services; communication, journalism, and related programs; computer and information sciences and support services; education; engineering; English language and literature/letters; foreign languages, literatures, and linguistics; health professions and related clinical sciences; history; liberal arts and sciences studies, and humanities; mathematics and statistics; parks, recreation, leisure, and fitness studies; philosophy and religious studies; physical sciences; psychology; security and protective services; social sciences; visual and performing arts. **Areas of required coursework:** arts/fine arts, humanities, computer

literacy, mathematics, English (including composition), philosophy, foreign languages, sciences (biological or physical), history, social science. **Pre-professional programs:** pre-law, pre-dentistry, pre-medicine, pre-theology, other. **Special academic programs (% participation):** accelerated program, cooperative (work-study plan) program, cross-registration, distance learning, double major, dual enrollment, English as a Second Language (ESL), exchange student program (domestic), honors program, independent study, internships, liberal arts/career combination, student-designed major, study abroad (4.6%), teacher certificate program, weekend college, other. **Teacher certification offered in:** early childhood, special education, elementary, middle/junior high, secondary, bilingual/bicultural. **Cooperative education programs:** art, business, computer science, education, engineering, health professions, humanities, natural science, social/behavioral science. **Reserve Officers Training Corps (ROTC):** Army ROTC: Offered on campus; Navy ROTC: Offered on campus; Air Force ROTC: Offered on campus. **Faculty and instruction (2009-2010):** Total instructional faculty: 1,142 full-time, 518 part-time (57% men; 43% women; 11% minorities). Full-time faculty with Ph.D. or other terminal degree: 84%. Student/faculty ratio: 18/1. Classes of fewer than 20 students: 40%; of 20 to 49 students: 49%; of 50 or more students: 11%. **Advanced Placement and International Baccalaureate credit:** AP tests may be used for: Credit only. Scores accepted: 3. International Baccalaureate exams may be used for: Credit only. **Freshmen returning for sophomore year:** 87%. **Graduation rates:** Four-year: 46%; five-year: 66%; six-year: 69%. **Graduate study:** 23% of students pursue further study immediately upon graduation.

COSTS AND FINANCIAL AID

Financial aid office: (803) 777-8134. **Expenses (2009-2010):** Tuition and fees 2009-2010: $9,156 in state, $23,732 out of state; room/board: $7,328. Estimated books and supplies: $936; transportation: $1,650; personal expenses: $2,420. **Financial aid:** Priority filing date for institution's financial aid form: April 1. In 2009-2010, 63% of undergraduates applied for financial aid. Of those, 45% were determined to have financial need; 26% had their need fully met. Average financial aid package (proportion receiving): $12,016 (45%). Average amount of gift aid, such as scholarships or grants (proportion receiving): $4,341 (22%). Average amount of self-help aid, such as work study or loans (proportion receiving): $4,058 (35%). Average need-based loan (excluding PLUS or other private loans): $3,922. Among students who received need-based aid, the average percentage of need met: 76%. Among students who received aid based on merit, the average award (and the proportion receiving): $6,688 (38%). The average athletic scholarship (and the proportion receiving): $9,425 (3%). Average amount of debt of borrowers graduating in 2009: $21,755. Proportion who borrowed: 46%.

CAMPUS LIFE AND EXTRACURRICULAR ACTIVITIES

Campus housing available (% using): coed dorms (30%), women's dorms (20%), men's dorms (3%), sorority housing (6%), fraternity housing (7%), apartments for married students (2%), apartment for single students (30%), special housing for disabled students (1%), special housing for international students (1%), other housing options (0%). Students who live in college-owned, operated, or affiliated housing: 33%. **Student employment:** During the 2009-2010 academic year, 13% of undergraduates worked on campus. Average per-year earnings: $2,203. **Clubs and organizations:** Number of student organizations: 340. Activities include: campus ministries, choral groups, concert band, dance, drama/theater, international student organization, jazz band, literary magazine, marching band, model UN, music ensembles, musical theater, opera, pep band, radio station, student government, student newspaper, student film society, symphony orchestra, television station, yearbook. Number of fraternities: 20; sororities: 14. Proportion of men in fraternities: 18%; of women in sororities: 18%. Average proportion of students who stay on campus on weekends: 70%. **Sports program (2009-2010):** Member of NCAA I. *Men's intercollegiate varsity sports:* baseball, basketball, football, golf, soccer, swimming, tennis, track and field (indoor), track and field (outdoor). *Women's intercollegiate varsity sports:* basketball, cross country, equestrian, golf, soccer, softball, swimming, tennis, track and field (indoor), track and field (outdoor), volleyball.

SERVICES AND FACILITIES

Basic services: nonremedial tutoring, women's center, placement service, health service, health insurance. **Remedial assistance:** reading, math, writing, study skills. **Counseling services:** minority student, career, military, personal, veteran student, academic, older student, psychological, birth control. **For learning-disabled students:** School does not offer a structured program with separate admission and additional fees. Total undergraduates in learning-disabled program or receiving services: 327. Services include: reading machines, tape recorders, untimed tests, note-taking services, readers, extended time for tests, priority registration, priority seating. **Library:** Number of titles: 4,338,655; number of current serial subscriptions: 66,309. **Information technology resources:** Students are not required to lease or own a computer. Number of campus computers available to all students: 2,800. School has a wireless network. Approximate number of users that can be accommodated: 49,000. Proportion of college-owned housing units wired for high-speed internet access: 100%. **Campus safety:** Security services offered: 24-hour foot-and-vehicle patrols, late-night transport/escort service, 24-hour emergency telephones, lighted pathways/sidewalks, student patrols, controlled dormitory access (key, security card, etc).

TRANSFER AND INTERNATIONAL STUDENTS

Transfer students: May apply for admission for the following academic terms: Fall, Spring, Summer. Applicants need a minimum number of credits to apply. For fall 2009: Transfer applications received: 4,074. Transfer applicants offered admission: 2,258. Transfer applicants enrolled: 1,602. **International students:** Number of foreign undergraduates: 282 (1% of student body). Number of countries represented: 75. Minimum TOEFL score required: 550 (paper); 77 (computer).

University of South Carolina–Aiken

- **Address:** 471 University Parkway, Aiken, SC 29801
- **Website:** http://www.usca.edu
- **Public**
- **Enrollment:** 2,459 full-time; 743 part-time

KEY STATS

✔ **U.S News College Ranking:** 20, Regional Colleges (South)
✔ **SAT Score (25th/75th percentile):** 880-1090
✔ **Tuition:** 2009-2010: $7,950 in state, $15,682 out of state

Selectivity: Selective	**Room/board:** $6,400
Acceptance rate: 38%	**Average debt:** $31,462
Student/faculty ratio: 15/1	**Proportion who borrowed:** 54%

UNDERGRADUATE STUDENT BODY STATS

2009-2010 enrollment: 2,459 full-time; 743 part-time. Men: 34%; women: 66%. **Ethnic makeup:** African American: 28%; Asian American: 1%; Hispanic: 3%; White: 66%; International: 1%. **Religious preference:** Roman Catholic: 7%; Protestant: 80%; Muslim: 1%; No preference: 9%; Other: 3%.

ADMISSIONS FACTS AND FIGURES

Phone: (803) 641-3366. **Email:** admit@sc.edu. **Website:** http://www.usca.edu. **Application deadlines for fall 2011:** Regular decision: August 1. Early decision: Not offered. Early action: Not offered. Admission cannot be deferred. **Application fee:** $45. **To apply online, go to:** http://web.csd.sc.edu/app/ugrad_aiken/. **Admissions requirements/recommendations:** High school units required (recommended): English: 4; Mathematics: 4; Science: 3; Foreign language: 2; Social studies: 2; History: 1; Academic electives: 4; Total units: 21. Tests: The college uses SAT or ACT scores in admissions decisions. Either SAT or ACT required. For admission to the fall 2011 entering class, the school will accept: ACT with writing recommended. Campus visit: Recommended. Admissions interview: Neither required nor recommended. Off-campus interview: Not available. **Factors that count in admissions decisions:** *Academic:* Secondary school record: Very Important. Class rank: Very Important. Letters of recommendation: Not Considered. Standardized test scores: Very Important. Essay: Not Considered. *Nonacademic:* Interview: Not Considered. Extracurricular activities: Not Considered. Talent/ability: Not Considered. Character/personal qualities: Not Considered. Alumni/ae relationship: Not Considered. Geographical residence: Not Considered. State residency: Not Considered. Religious affiliation/commitment: Not Considered. Minority status: Not Considered. Volunteer work: Not Considered. Work experience: Not Considered. **Other schools with the greatest overlap in applicants:** Clemson University; College of Charleston; Lander University; University of South Carolina; Winthrop University. **Admissions statistics for the fall 2009 entering class:** Total applicants: 2,712. Total accepted: 1,017. Freshmen enrolled: 689; 9% were from out of state. Overall acceptance rate: 38%. **Credentials of fall 2009 freshmen:** 15% ranked in the top 10 percent of their high school class; 43% were in the top 25 percent; 78% were in the top half. (Proportion submitting class standing: 93%.) **Average high school grade point average:** 3.6. **First-year students who submitted SAT scores:** 73%. Scores (25/75 percentile): Critical Reading: 430-540, Math: 450-550, Combined: 880-1090. **First-year students**

---

submitting ACT scores: 32%. Scores (25/75 percentile): English: 17-22, Math: 17-23, Composite: 18-23.

ACADEMICS

Year founded: 1961. **Academic calendar:** Semester. **Degrees offered:** bachelor's, master's. **Most popular majors:** 23% business, management, marketing, and related support services; 14% health professions and related clinical sciences; 12% education; 12% social sciences; 7% communication, journalism, and related programs. **Major fields of study:** biological and biomedical sciences; business, management, marketing, and related support services; communication, journalism, and related programs; education; English language and literature/letters; health professions and related clinical sciences; history; mathematics and statistics; multi/interdisciplinary studies; parks, recreation, leisure, and fitness studies; physical sciences; psychology; social sciences; visual and performing arts. **Areas of required coursework:** arts/fine arts, humanities, mathematics, English (including composition), foreign languages, sciences (biological or physical), history, social science, other. **Pre-professional programs:** pre-law, pre-dentistry, pre-medicine, pre-veterinary science, pre-pharmacy. **Special academic programs:** cooperative (work-study plan) program, distance learning, double major, dual enrollment, English as a Second Language (ESL), honors program, independent study, internships, student-designed major, study abroad, teacher certificate program. **Teacher certification offered in:** early childhood, special education, elementary, middle/junior high, secondary. **Cooperative education programs:** art, business, computer science, education, engineering, health professions, humanities, natural science, social/behavioral science, technologies. **Faculty and instruction (2009-2010):** Total instructional faculty: 150 full-time, 83 part-time (53% men; 47% women; 8% minorities). Full-time faculty with Ph.D. or other terminal degree: 73%. Student/faculty ratio: 15/1. Classes of fewer than 20 students: 54%; of 20 to 49 students: 45%; of 50 or more students: 0%. **Advanced Placement and International Baccalaureate credit:** AP tests may be used for: Credit and/or placement. Scores accepted: 3, 4, 5. International Baccalaureate exams may be used for: Placement only. **Freshmen returning for sophomore year:** 68%. **Graduation rates:** Four-year: 17%; five-year: 32%; six-year: 39%.

COSTS AND FINANCIAL AID

Financial aid office: (803) 641-3476. **Expenses (2009-2010):** Tuition and fees 2009-2010: $7,950 in state, $15,682 out of state; room/board: $6,400. Estimated books and supplies: $1,080; transportation: $1,020; personal expenses: $1,690. **Financial aid:** Priority filing date for institution's financial aid form: March 15. In 2009-2010, 91% of undergraduates applied for financial aid. Of those, 59% were determined to have financial need; 19% had their need fully met. Average financial aid package (proportion receiving): $9,108 (58%). Average amount of gift aid, such as scholarships or grants (proportion receiving): $6,552 (48%). Average amount of self-help aid, such as work study or loans (proportion receiving): $4,433 (46%). Average need-based loan (excluding PLUS or other private loans): $4,254. Among students who received need-based aid, the average percentage of need met: 69%. Among students who received aid based on merit, the average award (and the proportion receiving): $5,686 (22%). The average athletic scholarship (and the proportion receiving): $3,624 (5%). Average amount of debt of borrowers graduating in 2009: $31,462. Proportion who borrowed: 54%.

CAMPUS LIFE AND EXTRACURRICULAR ACTIVITIES

Campus housing available (% using): coed dorms (50%), apartment for single students (50%), special housing for disabled students. Students who live in college-owned, operated, or affiliated housing: 27%. **Student employment:** During the 2009-2010 academic year, 5% of undergraduates worked on campus. **Clubs and organizations:** Number of student organizations: 89. Activities include: concert band, dance, drama/theater, international student organization, literary magazine, music ensembles, musical theater, pep band, student government, student newspaper, symphony orchestra, yearbook. Number of fraternities: 5; sororities: 7. Proportion of men in fraternities: 7%; of women in sororities: 8%. Average proportion of students who stay on campus on weekends: 24%. **Sports program (2009-2010):** Member of NCAA II. *Men's intercollegiate varsity sports:* baseball, basketball, golf, soccer, tennis. *Women's intercollegiate varsity sports:* basketball, cross country, soccer, softball, tennis, volleyball.

SERVICES AND FACILITIES

Basic services: nonremedial tutoring, day care, health service. **Counseling services:** minority student, career, personal, academic, psychological. **For learning-disabled students:** School does not offer a structured program with separate admission and additional fees. Services include: reading

---

machines, tape recorders, videotaped classes, diagnostic testing service, note-taking services, oral tests, learning center, readers, extended time for tests, tutors, priority registration, priority seating, texts on tape, other testing accommodations. **Library:** Number of titles: 219,572; number of current serial subscriptions: 1,328. **Information technology resources:** Students are not required to lease or own a computer. Number of campus computers available to all students: 850. School has a wireless network. Approximate number of users that can be accommodated: 700. Proportion of college-owned housing units wired for high-speed internet access: 100%. **Campus safety:** Security services offered: 24-hour foot-and-vehicle patrols, late-night transport/escort service, 24-hour emergency telephones, lighted pathways/sidewalks, controlled dormitory access (key, security card, etc).

TRANSFER AND INTERNATIONAL STUDENTS
Transfer students: May apply for admission for the following academic terms: Fall, Spring, Summer. Applicants need a minimum number of credits to apply. For fall 2009: Transfer applications received: 889. Transfer applicants offered admission: 357. Transfer applicants enrolled: 247. **International students:** Number of foreign undergraduates: 43 (1% of student body). Number of countries represented: 19. Minimum TOEFL score required: 550 (paper); 213 (computer).

University of South Carolina–Upstate

- **Address:** 800 University Way, Spartanburg, SC 29303
- **Website:** http://www.uscupstate.edu/
- **Public**
- **Enrollment:** 4,157 full-time; 1,134 part-time

KEY STATS
✔ **U.S News College Ranking:** 28, Regional Colleges (South)
✔ **SAT Score (25th/75th percentile):** 870-1060
✔ **Tuition:** 2009-2010: $8,817 in state, $17,459 out of state

Selectivity: Less selective	**Room/board:** $6,580
Acceptance rate: 78%	**Average debt:** $21,099
Student/faculty ratio: 17/1	**Proportion who borrowed:** 67%

UNDERGRADUATE STUDENT BODY STATS
2009-2010 enrollment: 4,157 full-time; 1,134 part-time. Men: 36%; women: 64%. **Ethnic makeup:** African American: 27%; Asian American: 2%; Hispanic: 4%; White: 66%; International: 1%. **Religious preference:** Roman Catholic: 6%; Protestant: 80%; Hindu: 1%; Buddhist: 1%; No preference: 7%; Other: 5%.

ADMISSIONS FACTS AND FIGURES
Phone: (864) 503-5246. **Email:** admissions@uscupstate.edu. **Website:** http://www.uscupstate.edu/. **Application deadlines for fall 2011:** Regular decision: Rolling; decision sent by May 1. Early decision: Not offered. Early action: Not offered. Admission can be deferred. **Application fee:** $40. **To apply online, go to:** https://www.applyweb.com/apply/uscs/. **Admissions requirements/recommendations:** High school units required (recommended): English: 4; Mathematics: 3 (4); Science: 3; Foreign language: 2 (3); Social studies: 2; History: 1; Academic electives: 4; Total units: 20 (22). Tests: The college uses SAT or ACT scores in admissions decisions. Either SAT or ACT required. For admission to the fall 2011 entering class, the school will accept: ACT with or without writing accepted. Campus visit: Recommended. Admissions interview: Recommended. Off-campus interview: May be arranged. **Factors that count in admissions decisions:** *Academic:* Secondary school record: Very Important. Class rank: Very Important. Letters of recommendation: Considered. Standardized test scores: Very Important. Essay: Considered. *Nonacademic:* Interview: Considered. Extracurricular activities: Considered. Talent/ability: Not Considered. Character/personal qualities: Not Considered. Alumni/ae relationship: Not Considered. Geographical residence: Not Considered. State residency: Not Considered. Religious affiliation/commitment: Not Considered. Minority status: Not Considered. Volunteer work: Not Considered. Work experience: Not Considered. **Other schools with the greatest overlap in applicants:** Clemson University; Coastal Carolina University; College of Charleston; University of South Carolina; Winthrop University. **Admissions statistics for the fall 2009 entering class:** Total applicants: 2,822. Total accepted: 2,213. Freshmen enrolled: 875; 5% were from out of state. Overall acceptance rate: 78%. **Credentials of fall 2009 freshmen:** 11% ranked in the top 10 percent of their high school class; 36% were in the top 25 percent; 75% were in the top half. (Proportion submitting

class standing: 96%.) **Average high school grade point average:** 2.8. **First-year students who submitted SAT scores:** 78%. Scores (25/75 percentile): Critical Reading: 430-530, Math: 440-530, Combined: 870-1060. **First-year students submitting ACT scores:** 51%. Scores (25/75 percentile): English: 17-22, Math: 17-22, Composite: 18-22.

ACADEMICS
Year founded: 1967. **Academic calendar:** Semester. **Degrees offered:** bachelor's, post-bachelor's certificate, master's. **Most popular majors:** 27% nursing/registered nurse training (R.N., A.S.N., B.S.N., M.S.N.), 17% business administration and management, 16% education, 9% liberal arts and sciences/liberal studies, 6% psychology. **Major fields of study:** biological and biomedical sciences; business, management, marketing, and related support services; communication, journalism, and related programs; computer and information sciences and support services; education; engineering technologies/technicians; English language and literature/letters; foreign languages, literatures, and linguistics; health professions and related clinical sciences; history; liberal arts and sciences studies, and humanities; mathematics and statistics; multi/interdisciplinary studies; physical sciences; psychology; security and protective services; social sciences; visual and performing arts. **Areas of required coursework:** arts/fine arts, humanities, computer literacy, mathematics, English (including composition), foreign languages, sciences (biological or physical), history, social science, other. **Pre-professional programs:** pre-law, pre-dentistry, pre-medicine, pre-veterinary science, pre-optometry, pre-pharmacy, other. **Special academic programs:** accelerated program, cooperative (work-study plan) program, cross-registration, distance learning, double major, dual enrollment, English as a Second Language (ESL), honors program, independent study, internships, liberal arts/career combination, student-designed major, study abroad, teacher certificate program. **Teacher certification offered in:** early childhood, special education, elementary, middle/junior high, secondary. **Cooperative education programs:** business, engineering, health professions. **Reserve Officers Training Corps (ROTC):** Army ROTC: Offered at cooperating institution (Wofford College). **Faculty and instruction (2009-2010):** Total instructional faculty: 206 full-time, 176 part-time (47% men; 53% women; 9% minorities). Full-time faculty with Ph.D. or other terminal degree: 78%. Student/faculty ratio: 17/1. Classes of fewer than 20 students: 49%; of 20 to 49 students: 50%; of 50 or more students: 1%. **Advanced Placement and International Baccalaureate credit:** AP tests may be used for: Placement only. Scores accepted: 3, 4, 5. **Freshmen returning for sophomore year:** 64%. **Graduation rates:** Four-year: 20%; five-year: 35%; six-year: 38%. **Graduate study:** 5% of students pursue further study immediately upon graduation; 10% within one year; 15% within five years.

COSTS AND FINANCIAL AID
Financial aid office: (864) 503-5340. **Expenses (2009-2010):** Tuition and fees 2009-2010: $8,817 in state, $17,459 out of state; room/board: $6,580. Estimated books and supplies: $1,000. **Financial aid:** Priority filing date for institution's financial aid form: March 1. In 2009-2010, 85% of undergraduates applied for financial aid. Of those, 72% were determined to have financial need; 9% had their need fully met. Average financial aid package (proportion receiving): $9,335 (71%). Average amount of gift aid, such as scholarships or grants (proportion receiving): $4,872 (46%). Average amount of self-help aid, such as work study or loans (proportion receiving): $4,132 (56%). Average need-based loan (excluding PLUS or other private loans): $4,045. Among students who received need-based aid, the average percentage of need met: 57%. Among students who received aid based on merit, the average award (and the proportion receiving): $1,920 (2%). The average athletic scholarship (and the proportion receiving): $6,539 (12%). Average amount of debt of borrowers graduating in 2009: $21,099. Proportion who borrowed: 67%.

CAMPUS LIFE AND EXTRACURRICULAR ACTIVITIES
Campus housing available (% using): coed dorms (53%), apartment for single students (47%). Students who live in college-owned, operated, or affiliated housing: 18%. **Student employment:** During the 2009-2010 academic year, 15% of undergraduates worked on campus. Average per-year earnings: $4,300. **Clubs and organizations:** Number of student organizations: 85. Activities include: choral groups, dance, drama/theater, international student organization, jazz band, literary magazine, music ensembles, musical theater, pep band, student government, student newspaper. Number of fraternities: 6; sororities: 7. Proportion of men in fraternities: 2%; of women in sororities: 2%. Average proportion of students who stay on campus on weekends: 60%. **Sports program (2009-2010):** Member of NCAA II. *Men's intercollegiate varsity sports:* baseball, basketball, cross country, golf, soccer, tennis, track and field (outdoor). *Women's intercollegiate varsity sports:* bas-

ketball, cross country, golf, soccer, softball, tennis, track and field (outdoor), volleyball.

SERVICES AND FACILITIES

Basic services: nonremedial tutoring, women's center, placement service, day care, health service, health insurance. **Remedial assistance:** reading, math, writing, study skills. **Counseling services:** minority student, career, personal, veteran student, academic, older student, psychological. **For learning-disabled students:** School does not offer a structured program with separate admission and additional fees. Total undergraduates in learning-disabled program or receiving services: 29. Services include: reading machines, tape recorders, note-taking services, learning center, extended time for tests, tutors, priority registration, priority seating, texts on tape, other testing accommodations. **Library:** Number of titles: 237,052; number of current serial subscriptions: 28,000. **Information technology resources:** Students are not required to lease or own a computer. Number of campus computers available to all students: 850. School has a wireless network. Approximate number of users that can be accommodated: 500. Proportion of college-owned housing units wired for high-speed internet access: 100%. **Campus safety:** Security services offered: 24-hour foot-and-vehicle patrols, late-night transport/escort service, 24-hour emergency telephones, lighted pathways/sidewalks, controlled dormitory access (key, security card, etc).

TRANSFER AND INTERNATIONAL STUDENTS

Transfer students: May apply for admission for the following academic terms: Fall, Winter, Spring, Summer. Applicants need a minimum number of credits to apply. For fall 2009: Transfer applications received: 1,573. Transfer applicants offered admission: 1,055. Transfer applicants enrolled: 710. **International students:** Number of foreign undergraduates: 55 (1% of student body). Number of countries represented: 38. Minimum TOEFL score required: 500 (paper); 173 (computer). Average TOEFL score: 600 (paper).

Voorhees College

- **Address:** 1411 Voorhees Road, PO Box 678, Denmark, SC 29042
- **Website:** http://www.voorhees.edu
- **Private; Religious affiliation:** Episcopal
- **Enrollment:** N/A

KEY STATS

✔ **U.S News College Ranking:** second tier, Regional Colleges (South)
✔ **SAT or ACT Score (25th/75th percentile):** N/A
✔ **Tuition:** 2009-2010: $10,164

Selectivity: Less selective	**Room/board:** $6,314
Acceptance rate: N/A	**Average debt:** N/A
Student/faculty ratio: N/A	**Proportion who borrowed:** N/A

Winthrop University

- **Address:** 701 Oakland Avenue, Rock Hill, SC 29733
- **Website:** http://www.winthrop.edu
- **Public**
- **Enrollment:** 4,473 full-time; 624 part-time

KEY STATS

✔ **U.S News College Ranking:** 25, Regional Universities (South)
✔ **SAT Score (25th/75th percentile):** 950-1150
✔ **Tuition:** 2009-2010: $11,606 in state, $21,596 out of state

Selectivity: Selective	**Room/board:** $6,530
Acceptance rate: 65%	**Average debt:** $24,463
Student/faculty ratio: 15/1	**Proportion who borrowed:** 68%

UNDERGRADUATE STUDENT BODY STATS

2009-2010 enrollment: 4,473 full-time; 624 part-time. Men: 32%; women: 68%. **Ethnic makeup:** African American: 27%; Asian American: 2%; Hispanic: 2%; White: 66%; International: 2%. **Religious preference:** Roman Catholic: 7%; No preference: 2%; Unknown: 37%; Baptist : 20%; Other: 34%.

ADMISSIONS FACTS AND FIGURES

Phone: (803) 323-2191. **Email:** admissions@winthrop.edu. **Website:** http://www.winthrop.edu. **Application deadlines for fall 2011:** Regular decision: Rolling. Early decision: Not offered. Early action: Not offered. Admission can be deferred. **Application fee:** $40. **To apply online, go to:** https://www.applyweb.com/apply/winthrop/menu.html. **Admissions requirements/recommendations:** High school units required (recommended): English: 4 (4); Mathematics: 4 (4); Science: 3 (3); Foreign language: 2 (2); Social studies: 2 (2); History: 1 (1); Academic electives: 4 (4); Total units: 20 (21). Tests: The college uses SAT or ACT scores in admissions decisions. Either SAT or ACT required. For admission to the fall 2011 entering class, the school will accept: ACT with or without writing accepted. Campus visit: Recommended. Admissions interview: Neither required nor recommended. Off-campus interview: May be arranged. **Factors that count in admissions decisions:** *Academic:* Secondary school record: Very Important. Class rank: Important. Letters of recommendation: Considered. Standardized test scores: Important. Essay: Considered. *Nonacademic:* Interview: Considered. Extracurricular activities: Considered. Talent/ability: Considered. Character/personal qualities: Not Considered. Alumni/ae relationship: Not Considered. Geographical residence: Not Considered. State residency: Not Considered. Religious affiliation/commitment: Not Considered. Minority status: Not Considered. Volunteer work: Considered. Work experience: Not Considered. **Other schools with the greatest overlap in applicants:** Clemson University; Coastal Carolina University; College of Charleston; University of South Carolina; University of South Carolina–Upstate. **Admissions statistics for the fall 2009 entering class:** Total applicants: 4,511. Total accepted: 2,946. Freshmen enrolled: 1,060; 10% were from out of state. Overall acceptance rate: 65%. **Credentials of fall 2009 freshmen:** 22% ranked in the top 10 percent of their high school class; 55% were in the top 25 percent; 90% were in the top half. (Proportion submitting class standing: 93%.) **Average high school grade point average:** 3.7. **First-year students who submitted SAT scores:** 69%. Scores (25/75 percentile): Critical Reading: 470-580, Math: 480-570, Combined: 950-1150. **First-year students submitting ACT scores:** 31%. Scores (25/75 percentile): English: N/A, Math: N/A, Composite: 20-25.

ACADEMICS

Year founded: 1886. **Academic calendar:** Semester. **Degrees offered:** bachelor's, post-bachelor's certificate, master's, post-master's certificate. **Most popular majors:** 22% business administration and management, 17% education, 12% visual and performing arts, 8% psychology, 7% biology/biological sciences. **Major fields of study:** biological and biomedical sciences; business, management, marketing, and related support services; communication, journalism, and related programs; computer and information sciences and support services; education; English language and literature/letters; family and consumer sciences/human sciences; foreign languages, literatures, and linguistics; health professions and related clinical sciences; history; mathematics and statistics; natural resources and conservation; parks, recreation, leisure, and fitness studies; philosophy and religious studies; physical sciences; psychology; public administration and social service professions; social sciences; visual and performing arts. **Areas of required coursework:** arts/fine arts, humanities, computer literacy, mathematics, English (including composition), foreign languages, sciences (biological or physical), history, social science, other. **Pre-professional programs:** pre-law, pre-dentistry, pre-medicine, pre-veterinary science, pre-optometry, pre-pharmacy, other. **Special academic programs (% participation):** cross-registration (2%), distance learning (1%), double major (2%), dual enrollment (6%), exchange student program (domestic) (1%), honors program (2%), independent study (33%), internships (43%), study abroad (7%), teacher certificate program (16%). **Teacher certification offered in:** early childhood, special education, elementary, middle/junior high, secondary. **Reserve Officers Training Corps (ROTC):** Army ROTC: Offered at cooperating institution (University of North Carolina–Charlotte); Air Force ROTC: Offered at cooperating institution (University of North Carolina–Charlotte). **Faculty and instruction (2009-2010):** Total instructional faculty: 276 full-time, 276 part-time (42% men; 58% women; 11% minorities). Full-time faculty with Ph.D. or other terminal degree: 86%. Student/faculty ratio: 15/1. Classes of fewer than 20 students: 35%; of 20 to 49 students: 62%; of 50 or more students: 3%. **Advanced Placement and International Baccalaureate credit:** AP tests may be used for: Placement only. Scores accepted: 4, 5. International Baccalaureate exams may be used for: Placement only. **Freshmen returning for sophomore year:** 71%. **Graduation rates:** Four-year: 37%; five-year: 58%; six-year: 60%. **Graduate study:** 22% of students pursue further study immediately upon graduation; 32% within one year. Fields in which graduates pursue further study: Master of Business Administration (MBA), 6%; law, 2%; medicine, 1%; education, 27%; arts and sciences, 12%.

COSTS AND FINANCIAL AID

Financial aid office: (803) 323-2189. **Expenses (2009-2010):** Tuition and fees 2009-2010: $11,606 in state, $21,596 out of state; room/board: $6,530. Estimated books and supplies: $1,000; transportation: $1,450; personal expenses: $1,450. **Financial aid:** Priority filing date for institution's financial aid form: March 1. In 2009-2010, 81% of undergraduates applied for financial aid. Of those, 69% were determined to have financial need; 17% had their need fully met. Average financial aid package (proportion receiving): $10,109 (68%). Average amount of gift aid, such as scholarships or grants (proportion receiving): $7,768 (57%). Average amount of self-help aid, such as work study or loans (proportion receiving): $4,384 (55%). Average need-based loan (excluding PLUS or other private loans): $4,281. Among students who received need-based aid, the average percentage of need met: 59%. Among students who received aid based on merit, the average award (and the proportion receiving): $7,376 (13%). The average athletic scholarship (and the proportion receiving): $8,657 (4%). Average amount of debt of borrowers graduating in 2009: $24,463. Proportion who borrowed: 68%.

CAMPUS LIFE AND EXTRACURRICULAR ACTIVITIES

Campus housing available (% using): coed dorms (24%), women's dorms (40%), men's dorms (15%), apartments for married students (4%), apartment for single students (17%). Students who live in college-owned, operated, or affiliated housing: 44%. **Clubs and organizations:** Number of student organizations: 144. Activities include: campus ministries, choral groups, concert band, dance, drama/theater, international student organization, jazz band, literary magazine, model UN, music ensembles, musical theater, pep band, radio station, student government, student newspaper, television station. Number of fraternities: 7; sororities: 9. Proportion of men in fraternities: 1%; of women in sororities: 3%. Average proportion of students who stay on campus on weekends: 60%. **Sports program (2009-2010):** Member of NCAA I. *Men's intercollegiate varsity sports:* baseball, basketball, cross country, golf, soccer, tennis, track and field (indoor), track and field (outdoor). *Women's intercollegiate varsity sports:* basketball, cross country, golf, soccer, softball, tennis, track and field (indoor), track and field (outdoor), volleyball.

SERVICES AND FACILITIES

Basic services: nonremedial tutoring, placement service, health service, health insurance. **Counseling services:** minority student, career, personal, veteran student, academic, older student, psychological, birth control, religious. **For learning-disabled students:** School does not offer a structured program with separate admission and additional fees. Services include: tape recorders, note-taking services, oral tests, readers, extended time for tests, priority seating, other testing accommodations, other. **Library:** Number of titles: 434,732; number of current serial subscriptions: 36,684. **Information technology resources:** Students are not required to lease or own a computer. Number of campus computers available to all students: 821. School has a wireless network. Approximate number of users that can be accommodated: 1,310. Proportion of college-owned housing units wired for high-speed internet access: 100%. **Campus safety:** Security services offered: 24-hour foot-and-vehicle patrols, 24-hour emergency telephones, lighted pathways/sidewalks, controlled dormitory access (key, security card, etc).

TRANSFER AND INTERNATIONAL STUDENTS

Transfer students: May apply for admission for the following academic terms: Fall, Spring, Summer. Applicants do not need a minimum number of credits to apply. For fall 2009: Transfer applications received: 783. Transfer applicants offered admission: 557. Transfer applicants enrolled: 314. **International students:** Number of foreign undergraduates: 103 (2% of student body). Number of countries represented: 49. Minimum TOEFL score required: 520 (paper); 68 (computer).

Wofford College

- ■ **Address:** 429 N. Church Street, Spartanburg, SC 29303-3663
- ■ **Website:** http://www.wofford.edu
- ■ **Private; Religious affiliation:** United Methodist
- ■ **Enrollment:** 1,420 full-time; 19 part-time

KEY STATS

✔ **U.S News College Ranking:** 62, National Liberal Arts Colleges
✔ **SAT Score (25th/75th percentile):** 1140-1350
✔ **Tuition:** 2010-2011: $31,710
　Selectivity: More selective　**Room/board:** $8,870
　Acceptance rate: 58%　**Average debt:** $22,199
　Student/faculty ratio: 11/1　**Proportion who borrowed:** 45%

UNDERGRADUATE STUDENT BODY STATS

2009-2010 enrollment: 1,420 full-time; 19 part-time. Men: 50%; women: 50%. **Ethnic makeup:** African American: 7%; Asian American: 3%; Hispanic: 2%; White: 86%; International: 1%. **Religious preference:** Roman Catholic: 12%; Protestant: 53%; Jewish: 1%; Muslim: 1%; Hindu: 1%; No preference: 2%; Unknown: 11%; United Methodist: 17%; Other: 2%.

ADMISSIONS FACTS AND FIGURES

Phone: (864) 597-4130. **Email:** admissions@wofford.edu. **Website:** http://www.wofford.edu. **Application deadlines for fall 2011:** Regular decision: February 1; decision sent by March 15. Early decision: Send application by: November 15; Decision sent by: December 5. Early action: Not offered. Admission can be deferred. **Application fee:** $35. **To apply online, go to:** https://connect.wofford.edu/axiomweb/Login.aspx?SourceID=6. **Admissions requirements/recommendations:** High school units required (recommended): English: (4); Mathematics: (4); Science: (3); Foreign language: (3); Social studies: (3); History: (1); Academic electives: (2); Total units: (20). Tests: The college uses SAT or ACT scores in admissions decisions. Either SAT or ACT required. For admission to the fall 2011 entering class, the school will accept: ACT with writing required. Campus visit: Recommended. Admissions interview: Recommended. Off-campus interview: May be arranged. **Factors that count in admissions decisions: *Academic:*** Secondary school record: Very Important. Class rank: Important. Letters of recommendation: Considered. Standardized test scores: Important. Essay: Important. ***Nonacademic:*** Interview: Considered. Extracurricular activities: Important. Talent/ability: Important. Character/personal qualities: Important. Alumni/ae relationship: Considered. Geographical residence: Considered. State residency: Not Considered. Religious affiliation/commitment: Not Considered. Minority status: Considered. Volunteer work: Important. Work experience: Considered. **Other schools with the greatest overlap in applicants:** Clemson University; Davidson College; Furman University; Sewanee–University of the South; University of South Carolina. **Admissions statistics for the fall 2009 entering class:** Total applicants: 2,442. Total accepted: 1,415. Freshmen enrolled: 392; 39% were from out of state. Accepted through early-decision or early-action plans: 51%. Overall acceptance rate: 58%. Early-decision acceptance rate: 80%. Non-early acceptance rate: 51%. **Size of waiting list:** 130 applicants; enrolled from waiting list: 22. **Credentials of fall 2009 freshmen:** 57% ranked in the top 10 percent of their high school class; 87% were in the top 25 percent; 98% were in the top half. (Proportion submitting class standing: 69%.) **Average high school grade point average:** 3.5. **First-year students who submitted SAT scores:** 53%. Scores (25/75 percentile): Critical Reading: 560-670, Math: 580-680, Combined: 1140-1350. **First-year students submitting ACT scores:** 47%. Scores (25/75 percentile): English: 23-30, Math: 23-28, Composite: 22-29.

ACADEMICS

Year founded: 1854. **Academic calendar:** 4-1-4. **Degrees offered:** bachelor's. **Most popular majors:** 18% biology/biological sciences, 12% finance, 11% business/managerial economics, 7% English language and literature, 7% political science and government. **Major fields of study:** biological and biomedical sciences; business, management, marketing, and related support services; computer and information sciences and support services; English language and literature/letters; foreign languages, literatures, and linguistics; history; liberal arts and sciences studies, and humanities; mathematics and statistics; multi/interdisciplinary studies; philosophy and religious studies; physical sciences; psychology; social sciences; visual and performing arts. **Areas of required coursework:** arts/fine arts, humanities, computer literacy, mathematics, English (including composition), philosophy, foreign languages, sciences (biological or physical), history, social science. **Pre-professional programs:** pre-law, pre-dentistry, pre-medicine, pre-theology, pre-veterinary science, pre-pharmacy, other. **Special academic programs (% participation):** cross-registration (0%), double major (16%), dual enrollment, independent study (7%), internships (23%), student-designed major (0%), study abroad (57%), teacher certificate program (0%). **Teacher certification offered in:** middle/junior high, secondary. **Reserve Officers Training Corps (ROTC):** Army ROTC: Offered on campus. **Faculty and instruction (2009-2010):** Total instructional faculty: 117 full-time, 30 part-time (61% men; 39% women; 9% minorities). Full-time faculty with Ph.D. or other terminal degree: 93%. Student/faculty ratio: 11/1. Classes of fewer than 20 students: 62%; of 20 to 49 students: 37%; of 50 or more students: 1%. **Advanced Placement and International Baccalaureate credit:** AP tests may be used for: Placement only. Scores accepted: 4. International Baccalaureate exams may be used for: Credit only. **Freshmen returning for sophomore year:** 90%. **Graduation rates:** Four-year: 77%; five-year: 82%; six-year: 82%. **Graduate study:** 52% of students pursue further study immediately upon graduation. Fields in which graduates pursue further study: Master of Business Administration (MBA), 5%; law, 12%; medicine, 16%; dentistry, 3%; theology (or the seminary), 2%; education, 5%; arts and sciences, 8%; veterinary medicine, 1%.

COSTS AND FINANCIAL AID

Financial aid office: (864) 597-4160. **Expenses (2010-2011):** Tuition and fees 2010-2011: $31,710; room/board: $8,870. Estimated books and supplies: $1,076; transportation: $1,194; personal expenses: $1,260. **Financial aid:** Priority filing date for institution's financial aid form: March 15. In 2009-2010, 68% of undergraduates applied for financial aid. Of those, 56% were determined to have financial need; 51% had their need fully met. Average financial aid package (proportion receiving): $28,954 (56%). Average amount of gift aid, such as scholarships or grants (proportion receiving): $24,703 (52%). Average amount of self-help aid, such as work study or loans (proportion receiving): $4,873 (29%). Average need-based loan (excluding PLUS or other private loans): $4,364. Among students who received need-based aid, the average percentage of need met: 87%. Among students who received aid based on merit, the average award (and the proportion receiving): $13,278 (25%). The average athletic scholarship (and the proportion receiving): $13,884 (11%). Average amount of debt of borrowers graduating in 2009: $22,199. Proportion who borrowed: 45%.

CAMPUS LIFE AND EXTRACURRICULAR ACTIVITIES

Campus housing available (% using): coed dorms (76%), fraternity housing (0%), apartment for single students (24%), special housing for disabled students (0%). Students who live in college-owned, operated, or affiliated housing: 94%. **Student employment:** During the 2009-2010 academic year, 25% of undergraduates worked on campus. Average per-year earnings: $1,290. **Clubs and organizations:** Number of student organizations: 105. Activities include: campus ministries, choral groups, concert band, dance, drama/theater, jazz band, literary magazine, music ensembles, pep band, student government, student newspaper, yearbook. Number of fraternities: 8; sororities: 4. Proportion of men in fraternities: 46%; of women in sororities: 56%. Average proportion of students who stay on campus on weekends: 75%. **Sports program (2009-2010):** Member of NCAA I. *Men's intercollegiate varsity sports:* baseball, basketball, football, golf, rifle, soccer, tennis. *Women's intercollegiate varsity sports:* basketball, golf, rifle, soccer, tennis, volleyball.

SERVICES AND FACILITIES

Basic services: nonremedial tutoring, placement service, health service. **Remedial assistance:** reading, math, writing, study skills. **Counseling services:** minority student, career, personal, academic, psychological, birth control, religious. **For learning-disabled students:** School does not offer a structured program with separate admission and additional fees. Total undergraduates in learning-disabled program or receiving services: 93. Services include: tape recorders, oral tests, extended time for tests, tutors, priority seating, substitution of courses, texts on tape, exams on tape or computer, other testing accommodations, waiver of foreign language degree requirement. **Library:** Number of titles: 205,013; number of current serial subscriptions: 38,292. **Information technology resources:** Students are not required to lease or own a computer. Number of campus computers available to all students: 110. School has a wireless network. Approximate number of users that can be accommodated: 1,375. Proportion of college-owned housing units wired for high-speed internet access: 100%. **Campus safety:** Security services offered: 24-hour foot-and-vehicle patrols, late-night transport/escort service, 24-hour emergency telephones, lighted pathways/sidewalks, controlled dormitory access (key, security card, etc).

TRANSFER AND INTERNATIONAL STUDENTS

Transfer students: May apply for admission for the following academic terms: Fall, Winter, Spring, Summer. Applicants do not need a minimum number of credits to apply. For fall 2009: Transfer applications received: 101. Transfer applicants offered admission: 38. Transfer applicants enrolled: 18. **International students:** Number of foreign undergraduates: 17 (1% of student body). Number of countries represented: 10. Minimum TOEFL score required: 550 (paper); 80 (computer). Average TOEFL score: 596 (paper).

South Dakota

Augustana College

■ **Address:** 2001 S. Summit Avenue, Sioux Falls, SD 57197
■ **Website:** http://www.augie.edu
■ **Private; Religious affiliation:** ELCA Lutheran
■ **Enrollment:** 1,666 full-time; 105 part-time

KEY STATS

✔ **U.S News College Ranking:** 5, Regional Colleges (Midwest)
✔ **ACT Score (25th/75th percentile):** 22-28
✔ **Tuition:** 2010-2011: $25,104

Selectivity: More selective	**Room/board:** $6,486
Acceptance rate: 81%	**Average debt:** $29,531
Student/faculty ratio: 12/1	**Proportion who borrowed:** 76%

UNDERGRADUATE STUDENT BODY STATS

2009-2010 enrollment: 1,666 full-time; 105 part-time. Men: 37%; women: 63%. **Ethnic makeup:** African American: 1%; Asian American: 1%; White: 95%; International: 2%. **Religious preference:** Roman Catholic: 21%; Protestant: 16%; ELCA Lutheran: 38%.

ADMISSIONS FACTS AND FIGURES

Phone: (605) 274-5516. **Email:** admission@augie.edu. **Website:** http://www.augie.edu. **Application deadlines for fall 2011:** Regular decision: Rolling. Early decision: Not offered. Early action: Not offered. Admission can be deferred. **Application fee:** None. **To apply online, go to:** http://www.augie.edu/admission/apply.html. **Admissions requirements/recommendations:** High school units required (recommended): English: (4); Mathematics: (3); Science: (2); Foreign language: (2); Social studies: (3); History: (2); Academic electives: (0); Total units: (20). Tests: The college uses SAT or ACT scores in admissions decisions. Either SAT or ACT required. For admission to the fall 2011 entering class, the school will accept: ACT with or without writing accepted. Campus visit: Recommended. Admissions interview: Recommended. Off-campus interview: May be arranged. **Factors that count in admissions decisions: Academic:** Secondary school record: Important. Class rank: Important. Letters of recommendation: Important. Standardized test scores: Very Important. Essay: Important. *Nonacademic:* Interview: Considered. Extracurricular activities: Important. Talent/ability: Not Considered. Character/personal qualities: Not Considered. Alumni/ae relationship: Not Considered. Geographical residence: Not Considered. State residency: Not Considered. Religious affiliation/commitment: Not Considered. Minority status: Not Considered. Volunteer work: Considered. Work experience: Considered. **Other schools with the greatest overlap in applicants:** Concordia College–Moorhead; Gustavus Adolphus College; South Dakota State University; University of Sioux Falls; University of South Dakota. **Admissions statistics for the fall 2009 entering class:** Total applicants: 1,284. Total accepted: 1,036. Freshmen enrolled: 432; 60% were from out of state. Overall acceptance rate: 81%. **Credentials of fall 2009 freshmen:** 29% ranked in the top 10 percent of their high school class; 61% were in the top 25 percent; 89% were in the top half. (Proportion submitting class standing: 94%.) **Average high school grade point average:** 3.6. **First-year students who submitted SAT scores:** 2%. **First-year students submitting ACT scores:** 97%. Scores (25/75 percentile): English: 22-28, Math: 22-27, Composite: 22-28.

ACADEMICS

Year founded: 1860. **Academic calendar:** 4-1-4. **Degrees offered:** bachelor's, master's. **Most popular majors:** 19% education, 18% health professions and related clinical sciences, 14% social sciences, 11% business, management, marketing, and related support services, 7% biological and biomedical sciences. **Major fields of study:** biological and biomedical sciences; business, management, marketing, and related support services; communication, journalism, and related programs; computer and information sciences and support services; education; English language and literature/letters; foreign languages, literatures, and linguistics; health professions and related clinical sciences; history; liberal arts and sciences studies, and humanities;

mathematics and statistics; parks, recreation, leisure, and fitness studies; philosophy and religious studies; psychology; social sciences; visual and performing arts. **Areas of required coursework:** arts/fine arts, humanities, computer literacy, mathematics, English (including composition), foreign languages, sciences (biological or physical), history, social science, other. **Pre-professional programs:** pre-law, pre-dentistry, pre-medicine, pre-theology, pre-veterinary science, pre-optometry, pre-pharmacy, other. **Special academic programs (% participation):** cross-registration (7%), distance learning (16%), double major (28%), dual enrollment, exchange student program (domestic), honors program, independent study (35%), internships (40%), student-designed major (1%), study abroad (48%), teacher certificate program. **Teacher certification offered in:** special education, elementary, middle/junior high, secondary. **Reserve Officers Training Corps (ROTC):** Army ROTC: Offered at cooperating institution (South Dakota State University); Air Force ROTC: Offered at cooperating institution (South Dakota State University). **Faculty and instruction (2009-2010):** Total instructional faculty: 125 full-time, 56 part-time (48% men; 52% women; 2% minorities). Full-time faculty with Ph.D. or other terminal degree: 79%. Student/faculty ratio: 12/1. Classes of fewer than 20 students: 57%; of 20 to 49 students: 41%; of 50 or more students: 2%. **Advanced Placement and International Baccalaureate credit:** AP tests may be used for: Credit and/or placement. Scores accepted: 4, 5. International Baccalaureate exams may be used for: Credit and/or placement. **Freshmen returning for sophomore year:** 79%. **Graduation rates:** Four-year: 51%; five-year: 65%; six-year: 66%. **Graduate study:** 27% of students pursue further study immediately upon graduation. Fields in which graduates pursue further study: Master of Business Administration (MBA), 1%; law, 10%; medicine, 28%; theology (or the seminary), 5%; education, 4%; arts and sciences, 56%.

COSTS AND FINANCIAL AID

Financial aid office: (605) 274-5216. **Expenses (2010-2011):** Tuition and fees 2010-2011: $25,104; room/board: $6,486. Estimated books and supplies: $1,000; transportation: $600; personal expenses: $800. **Financial aid:** Priority filing date for institution's financial aid form: March 1. In 2009-2010, 82% of undergraduates applied for financial aid. Of those, 69% were determined to have financial need; 18% had their need fully met. Average financial aid package (proportion receiving): $19,740 (69%). Average amount of gift aid, such as scholarships or grants (proportion receiving): $14,921 (69%). Average amount of self-help aid, such as work study or loans (proportion receiving): $5,937 (56%). Average need-based loan (excluding PLUS or other private loans): $5,461. Among students who received need-based aid, the average percentage of need met: 89%. Among students who received aid based on merit, the average award (and the proportion receiving): $10,019 (29%). The average athletic scholarship (and the proportion receiving): $8,000 (9%). Average amount of debt of borrowers graduating in 2009: $29,531. Proportion who borrowed: 76%.

CAMPUS LIFE AND EXTRACURRICULAR ACTIVITIES

Campus housing available (% using): coed dorms (82%), apartments for married students (1%), apartment for single students (10%), special housing for disabled students, special housing for international students. Students who live in college-owned, operated, or affiliated housing: 74%. **Student employment:** During the 2009-2010 academic year, 3% of undergraduates worked on campus. Average per-year earnings: $2,000. **Clubs and organizations:** Number of student organizations: 92. Activities include: campus ministries, choral groups, concert band, dance, drama/theater, international student organization, jazz band, literary magazine, music ensembles, musical theater, opera, pep band, radio station, student government, student newspaper, symphony orchestra, yearbook. Number of fraternities: 0; sororities: 0. Average proportion of students who stay on campus on weekends: 60%. **Sports program (2009-2010):** Member of NCAA II. *Men's intercollegiate varsity sports:* baseball, basketball, cross country, football, golf, tennis, track and field (indoor), track and field (outdoor), wrestling. *Women's intercollegiate varsity sports:* basketball, cross country, golf, soccer, softball, tennis, track and field (indoor), track and field (outdoor), volleyball.

SERVICES AND FACILITIES

Basic services: nonremedial tutoring, placement service, day care, health service, health insurance. **Remedial assistance:** writing, study skills. **Counseling services:** minority student, career, military, personal, veteran student, academic, older student, psychological, birth control, religious. **For learning-disabled students:** School does not offer a structured program with separate admission and additional fees. Services include: tape recorders, note-taking services, oral tests, learning center, readers, extended time for tests, tutors, priority seating, texts on tape, typist/scribe, exams on tape or computer, other testing accommodations, other. **Library:** Number of titles: 213,308; number of current serial subscriptions: 6,333. **Information technology resources:** Students are not required to lease or own a computer. Number of campus computers available to all students: 238. School has a wireless network. Approximate number of users that can be accommodated: 1,000. Proportion of college-owned housing units wired for high-speed internet access: 100%. **Campus safety:** Security services offered: 24-hour foot-and-vehicle patrols, late-night transport/escort service, 24-hour emergency telephones, lighted pathways/sidewalks, controlled dormitory access (key, security card, etc).

TRANSFER AND INTERNATIONAL STUDENTS

Transfer students: May apply for admission for the following academic terms: Fall, Winter, Spring, Summer. Applicants do not need a minimum number of credits to apply. For fall 2009: Transfer applications received: 138. Transfer applicants enrolled: 69. **International students:** Number of foreign undergraduates: 40 (2% of student body). Number of countries represented: 14. Minimum TOEFL score required: 550 (paper); 80 (computer). Average TOEFL score: 550 (paper).

Black Hills State University

- **Address:** 1200 University Street, Unit 9500, Spearfish, SD 57799-9500
- **Website:** http://www.bhsu.edu
- **Public**
- **Enrollment:** 2,549 full-time; 1,220 part-time

KEY STATS

✔ **U.S News College Ranking:** second tier, Regional Colleges (Midwest)
✔ **ACT Score (25th/75th percentile):** 19-23
✔ **Tuition:** 2009-2010: $6,641 in state, $6,641 out of state

Selectivity: Selective	**Room/board:** $5,523
Acceptance rate: 93%	**Average debt:** N/A
Student/faculty ratio: 22/1	**Proportion who borrowed:** N/A

UNDERGRADUATE STUDENT BODY STATS

2009-2010 enrollment: 2,549 full-time; 1,220 part-time. Men: 38%; women: 62%. **Ethnic makeup:** African American: 1%; American-Indian: 4%; Asian American: 1%; Hispanic: 2%; White: 92%; International: 1%.

ADMISSIONS FACTS AND FIGURES

Phone: (800) 255-2478. **Email:** admissions@bhsu.edu. **Website:** http://www.bhsu.edu. **Application deadlines for fall 2011:** Regular decision: July 1. Early decision: Not offered. Early action: Not offered. Admission cannot be deferred. **Application fee:** $20. **Admissions requirements/recommendations:** High school units required (recommended): English: 4; Mathematics: 3; Science: 3; Foreign language: 0; Social studies: 3; History: 0; Academic electives: 0; Total units: 14. Tests: The college uses SAT or ACT scores in admissions decisions. Neither SAT nor ACT required. Campus visit: Recommended. Admissions interview: Neither required nor recommended. Off-campus interview: May be arranged. **Factors that count in admissions decisions:** *Academic:* Secondary school record: Important. Class rank: Important. Letters of recommendation: Not Considered. Standardized test scores: Important. Essay: Not Considered. *Nonacademic:* Interview: Not Considered. Extracurricular activities: Not Considered. Talent/ability: Not Considered. Character/personal qualities: Not Considered. Alumni/ae relationship: Not Considered. Geographical residence: Not Considered. State residency: Not Considered. Religious affiliation/commitment: Not Considered. Minority status: Not Considered. Volunteer work: Not Considered. Work experience: Not Considered. **Admissions statistics for the fall 2009 entering class:** Total applicants: 1,003. Total accepted: 932. Freshmen enrolled: 600; 23% were from out of state. Overall acceptance rate: 93%. **Credentials of fall 2009 freshmen:** 8% ranked in the top 10 percent of their high school class; 18% were in the top 25 percent; 60% were

in the top half. (Proportion submitting class standing: 96%.) **Average high school grade point average:** 3.1. **First-year students submitting ACT scores:** 88%. Scores (25/75 percentile): English: 17-23, Math: 17-23, Composite: 19-23.

ACADEMICS

Year founded: 1883. **Academic calendar:** Semester. **Degrees offered:** associate, bachelor's, post-bachelor's certificate, master's. **Most popular majors:** 19% business, management, marketing, and related support services, 18% education, 9% parks, recreation, leisure, and fitness studies, 6% communication, journalism, and related programs, 6% public administration and social service professions. **Major fields of study:** area, ethnic, cultural, and gender studies; biological and biomedical sciences; business, management, marketing, and related support services; communication, journalism, and related programs; education; engineering technologies/technicians; English language and literature/letters; foreign languages, literatures, and linguistics; health professions and related clinical sciences; history; mathematics and statistics; parks, recreation, leisure, and fitness studies; physical sciences; psychology; public administration and social service professions; social sciences; visual and performing arts. **Areas of required coursework:** humanities, mathematics, English (including composition), history, social science. **Pre-professional programs:** pre-law, pre-dentistry, pre-medicine, pre-veterinary science, pre-optometry, pre-pharmacy. **Special academic programs:** distance learning, double major, dual enrollment, honors program, independent study, internships, teacher certificate program. **Teacher certification offered in:** early childhood, special education, elementary, middle/junior high, secondary. **Reserve Officers Training Corps (ROTC):** Army ROTC: Offered on campus. **Faculty and instruction (2009-2010):** Total instructional faculty: 133 full-time, 63 part-time (54% men; 46% women; 7% minorities). Full-time faculty with Ph.D. or other terminal degree: 73%. Student/faculty ratio: 22/1. Classes of fewer than 20 students: 40%; of 20 to 49 students: 55%; of 50 or more students: 5%. **Advanced Placement and International Baccalaureate credit:** AP tests may be used for: Placement only. **Freshmen returning for sophomore year:** 57%. **Graduation rates:** Four-year: 9%; five-year: 23%; six-year: 26%. **Graduate study:** 12% of students pursue further study immediately upon graduation; 30% within five years. Fields in which graduates pursue further study: Master of Business Administration (MBA), 30%; law, 10%; medicine, 10%; education, 50%.

COSTS AND FINANCIAL AID

Financial aid office: (605) 642-6145. **Expenses (2009-2010):** Tuition and fees 2009-2010: $6,641 in state, $6,641 out of state; room/board: $5,523. Estimated books and supplies: $800.

CAMPUS LIFE AND EXTRACURRICULAR ACTIVITIES

Campus housing available: coed dorms, women's dorms, men's dorms, apartments for married students, apartment for single students. Students who live in college-owned, operated, or affiliated housing: 21%. Activities include: campus ministries, choral groups, concert band, dance, drama/theater, international student organization, jazz band, musical theater, pep band, radio station, student government, student newspaper. Number of fraternities: 0; sororities: 0. **Sports program (2009-2010):** Member of NAIA. *Men's intercollegiate varsity sports:* basketball, cross country, football, track and field (indoor), track and field (outdoor). *Women's intercollegiate varsity sports:* basketball, cross country, golf, track and field (indoor), track and field (outdoor), volleyball.

SERVICES AND FACILITIES

Basic services: nonremedial tutoring, placement service, day care, health service, health insurance. **Remedial assistance:** reading, math, writing, study skills. **Counseling services:** career, personal, veteran student, academic, psychological. **For learning-disabled students:** School does not offer a structured program with separate admission and additional fees. Total undergraduates in learning-disabled program or receiving services: 60. Services include: remedial math, remedial English, reading machines, remedial reading, tape recorders, untimed tests, note-taking services, oral tests, learning center, readers, extended time for tests, tutors, priority registration, priority seating, proofreading services, texts on tape, typist/scribe, exams on tape or computer, other testing accommodations, other. **Information technology resources:** Students are not required to lease or own a computer. Number of campus computers available to all students: 411. School has a wireless network. Approximate number of users that can be accommodated: 1,000. Proportion of college-owned housing units wired for high-speed internet access: 100%. **Campus safety:** Security services offered: 24-hour emergency telephones, lighted pathways/sidewalks, controlled dormitory access (key, security card, etc).

Transfer students: May apply for admission for the following academic terms: Fall, Spring, Summer. Applicants need a minimum number of credits to apply. For fall 2009: Transfer applications received: 716. Transfer applicants offered admission: 625. Transfer applicants enrolled: 320. **International students:** Number of foreign undergraduates: 47 (1% of student body). Number of countries represented: 13. Minimum TOEFL score required: 500 (paper); 171 (computer).

Dakota State University

- **Address:** 820 N. Washington Avenue, Madison, SD 57042
- **Website:** http://www.dsu.edu
- **Public**
- **Enrollment:** 1,143 full-time; 1,449 part-time

KEY STATS

✔ **U.S News College Ranking:** 41, Regional Colleges (Midwest)
✔ **ACT Score (25th/75th percentile):** 19-25
✔ **Tuition:** 2010-2011: $7,172 in state, $8,669 out of state

Selectivity: Selective	**Room/board:** $5,004
Acceptance rate: 94%	**Average debt:** $23,368
Student/faculty ratio: 17/1	**Proportion who borrowed:** 80%

UNDERGRADUATE STUDENT BODY STATS

2009-2010 enrollment: 1,143 full-time; 1,449 part-time. Men: 45%; women: 55%. **Ethnic makeup:** African American: 2%; American-Indian: 1%; Asian American: 2%; Hispanic: 1%; White: 92%; International: 2%.

ADMISSIONS FACTS AND FIGURES

Phone: (888) 378-9988. **Email:** dsuinfo@dsu.edu. **Website:** http://www.dsu.edu. **Application deadlines for fall 2011:** Regular decision: Rolling. Early decision: Not offered. Early action: Not offered. Admission cannot be deferred. **Application fee:** $20. **To apply online, go to:** http://www.dsu.edu/apply.aspx. **Admissions requirements/recommendations:** High school units required (recommended): English: (4); Mathematics: (3); Science: (3); Social studies: (3). Tests: The college uses SAT or ACT scores in admissions decisions. Either SAT or ACT required. For admission to the fall 2011 entering class, the school will accept: ACT with or without writing accepted. Campus visit: Recommended. Admissions interview: Neither required nor recommended. Off-campus interview: Not available. **Factors that count in admissions decisions:** *Academic:* Secondary school record: Important. Class rank: Important. Letters of recommendation: Not Considered. Standardized test scores: Important. Essay: Not Considered. *Nonacademic:* Interview: Not Considered. Extracurricular activities: Not Considered. Talent/ability: Not Considered. Character/personal qualities: Not Considered. Alumni/ae relationship: Not Considered. Geographical residence: Not Considered. State residency: Not Considered. Religious affiliation/commitment: Not Considered. Minority status: Not Considered. Volunteer work: Not Considered. Work experience: Not Considered. **Other schools with the greatest overlap in applicants:** Black Hills State University; Northern State University; South Dakota School of Mines and Technology; South Dakota State University; University of South Dakota. **Admissions statistics for the fall 2009 entering class:** Total applicants: 672. Total accepted: 630. Freshmen enrolled: 323; 26% were from out of state. Overall acceptance rate: 94%. **Credentials of fall 2009 freshmen:** 7% ranked in the top 10 percent of their high school class; 24% were in the top 25 percent; 55% were in the top half. (Proportion submitting class standing: 98%.) **Average high school grade point average:** 3.1. **First-year students submitting ACT scores:** 94%. Scores (25/75 percentile): English: 17-25, Math: 17-24, Composite: 19-25.

ACADEMICS

Year founded: 1881. **Academic calendar:** Semester. **Degrees offered:** certificate, associate, bachelor's, master's, doctorate. **Most popular majors:** 30% computer and information sciences and support services, 29% business, management, marketing, and related support services, 22% education, 7% parks, recreation, leisure, and fitness studies, 4% health professions and related clinical sciences. **Major fields of study:** biological and biomedical sciences; business, management, marketing, and related support services; computer and information sciences and support services; education; English language and literature/letters; health professions and related clinical sciences; mathematics and statistics; parks, recreation, leisure, and fitness studies; physical sciences; science technologies/technicians. **Areas of required coursework:** arts/fine arts, humanities, computer literacy, mathematics, English (including composition), sciences (biological or physical), social science. **Special academic programs:** cooperative (work-study plan) program, cross-registration, distance learning, double major, dual enrollment, English as a Second Language (ESL), honors program, independent study, internships, teacher certificate program. **Teacher certification offered in:** special education, elementary, middle/junior high, secondary. **Cooperative education programs:** education. **Reserve Officers Training Corps (ROTC):** Air Force ROTC: Offered at cooperating institution (South Dakota State University). **Faculty and instruction (2009-2010):** Total instructional faculty: 94 full-time, 28 part-time (61% men; 39% women; 7% minorities). Full-time faculty with Ph.D. or other terminal degree: 69%. Student/faculty ratio: 17/1. Classes of fewer than 20 students: 51%; of 20 to 49 students: 47%; of 50 or more students: 2%. **Advanced Placement and International Baccalaureate credit:** AP tests may be used for: Credit only. Scores accepted: 3, 4, 5. International Baccalaureate exams may be used for: Credit only. **Freshmen returning for sophomore year:** 70%. **Graduation rates:** Four-year: 18%; five-year: 36%; six-year: 48%. **Graduate study:** 12% of students pursue further study immediately upon graduation.

COSTS AND FINANCIAL AID

Financial aid office: (605) 256-5152. **Expenses (2010-2011):** Tuition and fees 2010-2011: $7,172 in state, $8,669 out of state; room/board: $5,004. Estimated books and supplies: $1,000; transportation: $1,000; personal expenses: $2,413. **Financial aid:** Priority filing date for institution's financial aid form: March 1. In 2009-2010, 87% of undergraduates applied for financial aid. Of those, 68% were determined to have financial need; 16% had their need fully met. Average financial aid package (proportion receiving): $7,897 (68%). Average amount of gift aid, such as scholarships or grants (proportion receiving): $4,756 (40%). Average amount of self-help aid, such as work study or loans (proportion receiving): $4,214 (64%). Average need-based loan (excluding PLUS or other private loans): $3,868. Among students who received need-based aid, the average percentage of need met: 84%. Among students who received aid based on merit, the average award (and the proportion receiving): $3,454 (9%). The average athletic scholarship (and the proportion receiving): $1,589 (12%). Average amount of debt of borrowers graduating in 2009: $23,368. Proportion who borrowed: 80%.

CAMPUS LIFE AND EXTRACURRICULAR ACTIVITIES

Campus housing available (% using): coed dorms (37%), women's dorms (27%), men's dorms (28%), apartment for single students (8%). Students who live in college-owned, operated, or affiliated housing: 37%. **Student employment:** During the 2009-2010 academic year, 1% of undergraduates worked on campus. Average per-year earnings: $1,500. **Clubs and organizations:** Number of student organizations: 35. Activities include: choral groups, dance, drama/theater, international student organization, literary magazine, music ensembles, musical theater, pep band, radio station, student government, student newspaper. Number of fraternities: 0; sororities: 0. Average proportion of students who stay on campus on weekends: 35%. **Sports program (2009-2010):** Member of NAIA. *Men's intercollegiate varsity sports:* baseball, basketball, cross country, football, track and field (indoor), track and field (outdoor). *Women's intercollegiate varsity sports:* basketball, cross country, softball, track and field (indoor), track and field (outdoor), volleyball.

SERVICES AND FACILITIES

Basic services: nonremedial tutoring, placement service, health service. **Remedial assistance:** reading, math, writing, study skills. **Counseling services:** minority student, career, personal, academic, older student, psychological, religious. **For learning-disabled students:** School does not offer a structured program with separate admission and additional fees. Services include: remedial math, remedial English, remedial reading, note-taking services, oral tests, learning center, readers, extended time for tests, tutors, texts on tape, other testing accommodations. **Library:** Number of titles: 92,362; number of current serial subscriptions: 26,227. **Information technology resources:** Students are required to lease or own a computer. Number of campus computers available to all students: 178. School has a wireless network. Approximate number of users that can be accommodated: 2,700. Proportion of college-owned housing units wired for high-speed internet access: 100%. **Campus safety:** Security services offered: lighted pathways/sidewalks, controlled dormitory access (key, security card, etc).

TRANSFER AND INTERNATIONAL STUDENTS

Transfer students: May apply for admission for the following academic terms: Fall, Spring, Summer. Applicants do not need a minimum number of credits to apply. For fall 2009: Transfer applications received: 430. Transfer applicants offered admission: 351. Transfer applicants enrolled: 180. **International students:** Number of foreign undergraduates: 26 (2% of student body). Number of countries represented: 7. Minimum TOEFL score required: 550 (paper); 78 (computer).

Dakota Wesleyan University

- **Address:** 1200 W. University Avenue, Mitchell, SD 57301
- **Website:** http://www.dwu.edu
- **Private; Religious affiliation:** United Methodist
- **Enrollment:** 677 full-time; 59 part-time

KEY STATS

✔ **U.S News College Ranking:** 56, Regional Colleges (Midwest)
✔ **ACT Score (25th/75th percentile):** 18-26
✔ **Tuition:** 2010-2011: $19,850

Selectivity: Less selective	**Room/board:** $6,900
Acceptance rate: 81%	**Average debt:** $30,000
Student/faculty ratio: 13/1	**Proportion who borrowed:** 67%

UNDERGRADUATE STUDENT BODY STATS

2009-2010 enrollment: 677 full-time; 59 part-time. Men: 41%; women: 59%. **Ethnic makeup:** African American: 2%; American-Indian: 2%; Asian American: 1%; Hispanic: 4%; White: 89%; International: 1%. **Religious preference:** Roman Catholic: 35%; Protestant: 45%; No preference: 12%; Unknown: 8%.

ADMISSIONS FACTS AND FIGURES

Phone: (800) 333-8506. **Email:** admissions@dwu.edu. **Website:** http://www.dwu.edu. **Application deadlines for fall 2011:** Regular decision: August 25. Early decision: Not offered. Early action: Not offered. Admission cannot be deferred. **Application fee:** $25. **To apply online, go to:** http://www.dwu.edu/apply/. **Admissions requirements/recommendations:** High school units required (recommended): English: 4 (4); Mathematics: 4 (4); Science: 3 (3); Foreign language: 2 (2); Social studies: 4 (4); History: 3 (3). Tests: The college uses SAT or ACT scores in admissions decisions. Either SAT or ACT required. For admission to the fall 2011 entering class, the school will accept: ACT with or without writing accepted. Campus visit: Recommended. Admissions interview: Neither required nor recommended. Off-campus interview: May be arranged. **Factors that count in admissions decisions: _Academic:_** Secondary school record: Very Important. Class rank: Very Important. Letters of recommendation: Considered. Standardized test scores: Very Important. Essay: Important. _**Nonacademic:**_ Interview: Not Considered. Extracurricular activities: Not Considered. Talent/ability: Not Considered. Character/personal qualities: Not Considered. Alumni/ae relationship: Not Considered. Geographical residence: Not Considered. State residency: Not Considered. Religious affiliation/commitment: Not Considered. Minority status: Not Considered. Volunteer work: Not Considered. Work experience: Not Considered. **Other schools with the greatest overlap in applicants:** Augustana College; Northern State University; South Dakota State University; University of Sioux Falls; University of South Dakota. **Admissions statistics for the fall 2009 entering class:** Total applicants: 538. Total accepted: 434. Freshmen enrolled: 168; Overall acceptance rate: 81%. **Credentials of fall 2009 freshmen:** 7% ranked in the top 10 percent of their high school class; 19% were in the top 25 percent; 56% were in the top half. (Proportion submitting class standing: 93%.) **First-year students who submitted SAT scores:** 8%. Scores (25/75 percentile): Critical Reading: 390-630, Math: 410-580, Combined: 800-1210. **First-year students submitting ACT scores:** 91%. Scores (25/75 percentile): English: N/A, Math: N/A, Composite: 18-26.

ACADEMICS

Year founded: 1885. **Academic calendar:** Semester. **Degrees offered:** associate, terminal-associate, bachelor's, master's. **Major fields of study:** biological and biomedical sciences; business, management, marketing, and related support services; communication, journalism, and related programs; computer and information sciences and support services; education; English language and literature/letters; foreign languages, literatures, and linguistics; health professions and related clinical sciences; history; liberal arts and sciences studies, and humanities; mathematics and statistics; multi/interdisciplinary studies; parks, recreation, leisure, and fitness studies; philosophy and religious studies; psychology; public administration and social service professions; security and protective services; social sciences; visual and performing arts. **Areas of required coursework:** arts/fine arts, humanities, computer literacy, mathematics, English (including composition), philosophy, sciences (biological or physical), history, social science, other. **Pre-professional programs:** pre-law, pre-dentistry, pre-medicine, pre-theology, pre-optometry, pre-pharmacy, other. **Special academic programs (% participation):** distance learning (1%), double major (16%), honors program (10%), independent study (15%), internships (70%), liberal arts/career combination (90%), student-designed major (1%), study abroad (1%), teacher certificate program (15%). **Teacher certification offered in:** special education, elementary, middle/junior high, secondary. **Reserve Officers Training Corps (ROTC):** Army ROTC: Offered on campus. **Faculty and instruction (2009-2010):** Total instructional faculty: 44 full-time, 32 part-time (46% men; 54% women; 1% minorities). Full-time faculty with Ph.D. or other terminal degree: 80%. Student/faculty ratio: 13/1. Classes of fewer than 20 students: 58%; of 20 to 49 students: 40%; of 50 or more students: 2%. **Advanced Placement and International Baccalaureate credit:** AP tests may be used for: Placement only. Scores accepted: 3, 4, 5. International Baccalaureate exams may be used for: Placement only. **Graduation rates:** Four-year: 31%; five-year: 37%; six-year: 41%. **Graduate study:** 10% of students pursue further study immediately upon graduation; 2% within one year; 1% within five years. Fields in which graduates pursue further study: Master of Business Administration (MBA), 2%; law, 1%; medicine, 9%; theology (or the seminary), 1%; education, 2%.

COSTS AND FINANCIAL AID

Financial aid office: (605) 995-2656. **Expenses (2010-2011):** Tuition and fees 2010-2011: $19,850; room/board: $6,900. Estimated books and supplies: $1,000; transportation: $800; personal expenses: $1,350. **Financial aid:** Priority filing date for institution's financial aid form: April 1. In 2009-2010, 93% of undergraduates applied for financial aid. Of those, 86% were determined to have financial need; 14% had their need fully met. Average financial aid package (proportion receiving): $19,000 (86%). Average amount of gift aid, such as scholarships or grants (proportion receiving): $9,800 (85%). Average amount of self-help aid, such as work study or loans (proportion receiving): $4,600 (75%). Average need-based loan (excluding PLUS or other private loans): $4,300. Among students who received need-based aid, the average percentage of need met: 70%. Among students who received aid based on merit, the average award (and the proportion receiving): $11,000 (7%). The average athletic scholarship (and the proportion receiving): $4,700 (5%). Average amount of debt of borrowers graduating in 2009: $30,000. Proportion who borrowed: 67%.

CAMPUS LIFE AND EXTRACURRICULAR ACTIVITIES

Campus housing available: coed dorms, women's dorms, men's dorms, apartments for married students, apartment for single students, special housing for disabled students. **Student employment:** During the 2009-2010 academic year, 0% of undergraduates worked on campus. **Clubs and organizations:** Number of student organizations: 26. Activities include: choral groups, concert band, dance, drama/theater, literary magazine, music ensembles, student government, student newspaper. Number of fraternities: 0; sororities: 0. Average proportion of students who stay on campus on weekends: 30%. **Sports program (2009-2010):** Member of NAIA. **_Men's intercollegiate varsity sports:_** baseball, basketball, cross country, football, golf, soccer, track and field (indoor), track and field (outdoor), wrestling. **_Women's intercollegiate varsity sports:_** basketball, cross country, golf, soccer, softball, track and field (indoor), track and field (outdoor), volleyball.

SERVICES AND FACILITIES

Basic services: nonremedial tutoring, women's center, placement service, day care, health service, health insurance. **Remedial assistance:** reading, math, writing, study skills. **Counseling services:** minority student, career, personal, academic, older student, psychological, religious, other. **For learning-disabled students:** School does not offer a structured program with separate admission and additional fees. Services include: remedial math, remedial English, reading machines, remedial reading, tape recorders, untimed tests, note-taking services, oral tests, learning center, readers, extended time for tests, tutors, priority seating, texts on tape, other testing accommodations. **Library:** Number of titles: 78,928; number of current serial subscriptions: 1,100. **Information technology resources:** Students are not required to lease or own a computer. Number of campus computers available to all students: 150. School has a wireless network. Approximate number of users that can be accommodated: 1,000. Proportion of college-owned housing units wired for high-speed internet access: 100%. **Campus safety:** Security services offered: late-night transport/escort service, 24-hour

emergency telephones, lighted pathways/sidewalks, controlled dormitory access (key, security card, etc).

TRANSFER AND INTERNATIONAL STUDENTS
Transfer students: May apply for admission for the following academic terms: Fall, Spring, Summer. Applicants do not need a minimum number of credits to apply. **International students:** Number of foreign undergraduates: 10 (1% of student body). Number of countries represented: 7. Minimum TOEFL score required: 500 (paper); 200 (computer). Average TOEFL score: 550 (paper).

Mount Marty College

- **Address:** 1105 W. Eighth Street, Yankton, SD 57078
- **Website:** http://www.mtmc.edu
- **Private; Religious affiliation:** Roman Catholic
- **Enrollment:** 588 full-time; 493 part-time

KEY STATS
✔ **U.S News College Ranking:** second tier, Regional Universities (Midwest)
✔ **ACT Score (25th/75th percentile):** 19-24
✔ **Tuition:** 2010-2011: $19,932

Selectivity: Selective	**Room/board:** $5,636
Acceptance rate: 78%	**Average debt:** $22,699
Student/faculty ratio: 13/1	**Proportion who borrowed:** 79%

UNDERGRADUATE STUDENT BODY STATS
2009-2010 enrollment: 588 full-time; 493 part-time. Men: 37%; women: 63%. **Ethnic makeup:** African American: 2%; American-Indian: 4%; Asian American: 1%; Hispanic: 4%; White: 89%. **Religious preference:** Roman Catholic: 50%; Protestant: 35%; No preference: 10%; Other: 5%.

ADMISSIONS FACTS AND FIGURES
Phone: (800) 658-4552. **Email:** mmcadmit@mtmc.edu. **Website:** http://www.mtmc.edu. **Application deadlines for fall 2011:** Regular decision: August 30. Early decision: Not offered. Early action: Not offered. Admission can be deferred. **Application fee:** $35. **To apply online, go to:** http://www.applyweb.com/aw?mtmc. **Admissions requirements/recommendations:** Tests: The college uses SAT or ACT scores in admissions decisions. Either SAT or ACT required. For admission to the fall 2011 entering class, the school will accept: ACT with or without writing accepted. Campus visit: Recommended. Admissions interview: Recommended. Off-campus interview: May be arranged. **Factors that count in admissions decisions:** *Academic:* Secondary school record: Very Important. Class rank: Important. Letters of recommendation: Considered. Standardized test scores: Very Important. Essay: Considered. *Nonacademic:* Interview: Considered. Extracurricular activities: Considered. Talent/ability: Considered. Character/personal qualities: Considered. Alumni/ae relationship: Considered. Geographical residence: Considered. State residency: Considered. Religious affiliation/commitment: Considered. Minority status: Considered. Volunteer work: Considered. Work experience: Considered. **Other schools with the greatest overlap in applicants:** Dakota Wesleyan University; South Dakota State University; University of South Dakota; Wayne State College. **Admissions statistics for the fall 2009 entering class:** Total applicants: 333. Total accepted: 259. Freshmen enrolled: 116; 40% were from out of state. Overall acceptance rate: 78%. **Size of waiting list:** 0 applicants; enrolled from waiting list: N/A. **First-year students submitting ACT scores:** 90%. Scores (25/75 percentile): English: 22-26, Math: 17-22, Composite: 19-24.

ACADEMICS
Year founded: 1936. **Academic calendar:** Semester. **Degrees offered:** certificate, associate, bachelor's, master's. **Most popular majors:** 15% business administration and management, 11% nursing/registered nurse training (R.N., A.S.N., B.S.N., M.S.N.), 9% elementary education and teaching, 5% accounting, 4% forensic science and technology. **Major fields of study:** biological and biomedical sciences; business, management, marketing, and related support services; communications technologies/technicians and support services; computer and information sciences and support services; education; English language and literature/letters; health professions and related clinical sciences; history; liberal arts and sciences studies, and humanities; mathematics and statistics; parks, recreation, leisure, and fitness studies; philosophy and religious studies; physical sciences; psychology; security and protective services; social sciences; visual and performing arts. **Areas of required coursework:** arts/fine arts, humanities, computer literacy, mathematics, English (including composition), philosophy, sciences (biological or physical), history, social science. **Pre-professional programs:** pre-law, pre-dentistry, pre-medicine, pre-theology, pre-veterinary science, pre-optometry, pre-pharmacy, other. **Special academic programs (% participation):** cooperative (work-study plan) program (85%), double major (10%), honors program (5%), independent study (10%), internships (35%), student-designed major (5%), teacher certificate program (15%), weekend college (1%). **Teacher certification offered in:** special education, elementary, middle/junior high, secondary. **Reserve Officers Training Corps (ROTC):** Army ROTC: Offered on campus. **Faculty and instruction (2009-2010):** Total instructional faculty: 43 full-time, 57 part-time (60% men; 40% women; 1% minorities). Full-time faculty with Ph.D. or other terminal degree: 70%. Student/faculty ratio: 13/1. **Advanced Placement and International Baccalaureate credit:** AP tests may be used for: Placement only. International Baccalaureate exams may be used for: Placement only. **Freshmen returning for sophomore year:** 76%. **Graduation rates:** Four-year: 21%; five-year: 41%; six-year: 47%. **Graduate study:** 20% of students pursue further study immediately upon graduation; 22% within one year; 27% within five years. Fields in which graduates pursue further study: law, 5%; medicine, 70%; theology (or the seminary), 5%; arts and sciences, 20%.

COSTS AND FINANCIAL AID
Financial aid office: (605) 668-1589. **Expenses (2010-2011):** Tuition and fees 2010-2011: $19,932; room/board: $5,636. **Financial aid:** Priority filing date for institution's financial aid form: March 1. In 2009-2010, 95% of undergraduates applied for financial aid. Of those, 90% were determined to have financial need; 52% had their need fully met. Average financial aid package (proportion receiving): $18,937 (90%). Average amount of gift aid, such as scholarships or grants (proportion receiving): $7,508 (90%). Average amount of self-help aid, such as work study or loans (proportion receiving): $1,397 (90%). Average need-based loan (excluding PLUS or other private loans): $5,168. Among students who received need-based aid, the average percentage of need met: 89%. Among students who received aid based on merit, the average award (and the proportion receiving): $14,147 (8%). The average athletic scholarship (and the proportion receiving): $3,736 (29%). Average amount of debt of borrowers graduating in 2009: $22,699. Proportion who borrowed: 79%.

CAMPUS LIFE AND EXTRACURRICULAR ACTIVITIES
Campus housing available (% using): women's dorms (74%), men's dorms (26%). Students who live in college-owned, operated, or affiliated housing: 40%. **Student employment:** During the 2009-2010 academic year, 0% of undergraduates worked on campus. Average per-year earnings: $0. **Clubs and organizations:** Number of student organizations: 40. Activities include: campus ministries, choral groups, concert band, drama/theater, jazz band, literary magazine, music ensembles, musical theater, pep band, student government, student newspaper. Number of fraternities: 0; sororities: 0. Average proportion of students who stay on campus on weekends: 35%. **Sports program (2009-2010):** Member of NAIA. *Men's intercollegiate varsity sports:* baseball, basketball, cross country, golf, soccer, track and field (indoor), track and field (outdoor). *Women's intercollegiate varsity sports:* basketball, cross country, golf, soccer, softball, track and field (indoor), track and field (outdoor), volleyball.

SERVICES AND FACILITIES
Basic services: nonremedial tutoring, placement service, day care, health service, health insurance. **Remedial assistance:** reading, math, writing, study skills. **Counseling services:** career, personal, academic, older student, psychological, religious. **For learning-disabled students:** School does not offer a structured program with separate admission and additional fees. Total undergraduates in learning-disabled program or receiving services: 40. Services include: remedial math, remedial English, remedial reading, tape recorders, untimed tests, note-taking services, oral tests, learning center, readers, extended time for tests, tutors, early syllabus. **Library:** Number of titles: 76,152; number of current serial subscriptions: 400. **Information technology resources:** Students are required to lease or own a computer. Number of campus computers available to all students: 30. School has a wireless network. Approximate number of users that can be accommodated: 700. Proportion of college-owned housing units wired for high-speed internet access: 100%. **Campus safety:** Security services offered: late-night transport/escort service, 24-hour emergency telephones, lighted pathways/sidewalks, controlled dormitory access (key, security card, etc).

TRANSFER AND INTERNATIONAL STUDENTS

Transfer students: May apply for admission for the following academic terms: Fall, Spring, Summer. Applicants do not need a minimum number of credits to apply. For fall 2009: Transfer applicants enrolled: 34. **International students:** Number of foreign undergraduates: 0. Minimum TOEFL score required: 500 (paper); 60 (computer).

Northern State University

- **Address:** 1200 S. Jay Street, Aberdeen, SD 57401-7198
- **Website:** http://www.northern.edu
- **Public**
- **Enrollment:** 1,539 full-time; 761 part-time

KEY STATS

✔ **U.S News College Ranking:** 48, Regional Colleges (Midwest)
✔ **ACT Score (25th/75th percentile):** 19-24
✔ **Tuition:** 2010-2011: $6,351 in state, $7,848 out of state

Selectivity: Selective	**Room/board:** $5,951
Acceptance rate: 94%	**Average debt:** N/A
Student/faculty ratio: 17/1	**Proportion who borrowed:** N/A

UNDERGRADUATE STUDENT BODY STATS

2009-2010 enrollment: 1,539 full-time; 761 part-time. Men: 39%; women: 61%. **Ethnic makeup:** African American: 2%; American-Indian: 3%; Asian American: 1%; Hispanic: 2%; White: 91%; International: 2%.

ADMISSIONS FACTS AND FIGURES

Phone: (800) 678-5330. **Email:** admissions@northern.edu. **Website:** http://www.northern.edu. **Application deadlines for fall 2011:** Early decision: Not offered. Early action: Not offered. Admission can be deferred. **Application fee:** $20. **To apply online, go to:** http://www.northern.edu/prospective/index.html. **Admissions requirements/recommendations:** High school units required (recommended): English: 4; Mathematics: 3; Science: 3; Social studies: 3; Total units: 13. Tests: The college uses SAT or ACT scores in admissions decisions. ACT required. For admission to the fall 2011 entering class, the school will accept: ACT with or without writing accepted. Campus visit: Recommended. Admissions interview: Recommended. Off-campus interview: May be arranged. **Factors that count in admissions decisions:** *Academic:* Secondary school record: Very Important. Class rank: Very Important. Letters of recommendation: Considered. Standardized test scores: Very Important. Essay: Not Considered. *Nonacademic:* Interview: Considered. Extracurricular activities: Considered. Talent/ability: Considered. Character/personal qualities: Considered. Alumni/ae relationship: Not Considered. Geographical residence: Not Considered. State residency: Not Considered. Religious affiliation/commitment: Not Considered. Minority status: Not Considered. Volunteer work: Not Considered. Work experience: Not Considered. **Other schools with the greatest overlap in applicants:** South Dakota State University; University of South Dakota. **Admissions statistics for the fall 2009 entering class:** Total applicants: 923. Total accepted: 863. Freshmen enrolled: 329; 25% were from out of state. Overall acceptance rate: 94%. **Credentials of fall 2009 freshmen:** 10% ranked in the top 10 percent of their high school class; 27% were in the top 25 percent; 59% were in the top half. (Proportion submitting class standing: 95%.) **First-year students who submitted SAT scores:** 4%. Scores (25/75 percentile): Critical Reading: 400-540, Math: 480-580, Combined: 880-1120. **First-year students submitting ACT scores:** 96%. Scores (25/75 percentile): English: 17-24, Math: 17-25, Composite: 19-24.

ACADEMICS

Year founded: 1901. **Academic calendar:** Semester. **Degrees offered:** certificate, associate, bachelor's, post-bachelor's certificate, master's. **Most popular majors:** 36% business, management, marketing, and related support services, 24% education, 10% social sciences, 7% biological and biomedical sciences, 5% visual and performing arts. **Major fields of study:** biological and biomedical sciences; business, management, marketing, and related support services; computer and information sciences and support services; education; English language and literature/letters; foreign languages, literatures, and linguistics; health professions and related clinical sciences; history; liberal arts and sciences studies, and humanities; mathematics and statistics; parks, recreation, leisure, and fitness studies; physical sciences; psychology; public administration and social service professions; social sciences; visual and performing arts. **Areas of required coursework:** arts/fine

arts, mathematics, English (including composition), sciences (biological or physical), history. **Pre-professional programs:** pre-law, pre-dentistry, pre-medicine, pre-veterinary science, other. **Special academic programs:** accelerated program, cooperative (work-study plan) program, cross-registration, distance learning, double major, dual enrollment, English as a Second Language (ESL), exchange student program (domestic), external degree program, honors program, independent study, internships, liberal arts/career combination, student-designed major, study abroad, teacher certificate program. **Teacher certification offered in:** early childhood, special education, elementary, middle/junior high, secondary. **Cooperative education programs:** business, education, health professions. **Faculty and instruction (2009-2010):** Total instructional faculty: 96 full-time, 41 part-time (58% men; 42% women; 4% minorities). Full-time faculty with Ph.D. or other terminal degree: 77%. Student/faculty ratio: 17/1. Classes of fewer than 20 students: 53%; of 20 to 49 students: 44%; of 50 or more students: 3%. **Advanced Placement and International Baccalaureate credit:** AP tests may be used for: Placement only. International Baccalaureate exams may be used for: Credit only. **Freshmen returning for sophomore year:** 68%. **Graduation rates:** Six-year: 45%. **Graduate study:** 13% of students pursue further study immediately upon graduation.

COSTS AND FINANCIAL AID

Financial aid office: (605) 626-2640. **Expenses (2010-2011):** Tuition and fees 2010-2011: $6,351 in state, $7,848 out of state; room/board: $5,951. Estimated books and supplies: $1,000; transportation: $1,600; personal expenses: $1,800. **Financial aid:** Priority filing date for institution's financial aid form: March 1. In 2009-2010, 82% of undergraduates applied for financial aid. Of those, 64% were determined to have financial need; 19% had their need fully met. Average financial aid package (proportion receiving): $7,047 (64%). Average amount of gift aid, such as scholarships or grants (proportion receiving): $3,574 (55%). Average amount of self-help aid, such as work study or loans (proportion receiving): $3,845 (57%). Average need-based loan (excluding PLUS or other private loans): $3,543. Among students who received need-based aid, the average percentage of need met: 69%. Among students who received aid based on merit, the average award (and the proportion receiving): $2,138 (8%). The average athletic scholarship (and the proportion receiving): $2,634 (18%).

CAMPUS LIFE AND EXTRACURRICULAR ACTIVITIES

Campus housing available: coed dorms, apartments for married students, apartment for single students, special housing for disabled students. Students who live in college-owned, operated, or affiliated housing: 70%. **Student employment:** During the 2009-2010 academic year, 10% of undergraduates worked on campus. Average per-year earnings: $2,000. **Clubs and organizations:** Number of student organizations: 100. Activities include: campus ministries, choral groups, concert band, dance, drama/theater, international student organization, jazz band, marching band, music ensembles, musical theater, pep band, student government, student newspaper, symphony orchestra, television station, yearbook. Average proportion of students who stay on campus on weekends: 35%. **Sports program (2009-2010):** Member of NCAA II. *Men's intercollegiate varsity sports:* baseball, basketball, cross country, football, golf, tennis, track and field (indoor), track and field (outdoor), wrestling. *Women's intercollegiate varsity sports:* basketball, cross country, golf, soccer, softball, swimming, tennis, track and field (indoor), track and field (outdoor), volleyball.

SERVICES AND FACILITIES

Basic services: nonremedial tutoring, placement service, day care, health service, health insurance. **Remedial assistance:** reading, math, writing, study skills. **Counseling services:** minority student, career, military, personal, veteran student, academic, older student, psychological, birth control, religious. **For learning-disabled students:** School does not offer a structured program with separate admission and additional fees. Total undergraduates in learning-disabled program or receiving services: 21. Services include: remedial math, remedial English, remedial reading, tape recorders, diagnostic testing service, note-taking services, learning center, readers, extended time for tests, tutors, early syllabus, priority registration, texts on tape, typist/scribe, exams on tape or computer, other testing accommodations. **Library:** Number of titles: 213,868; number of current serial subscriptions: 169. **Information technology resources:** Students are not required to lease or own a computer. Number of campus computers available to all students: 900. School has a wireless network. Approximate number of users that can be accommodated: 3,000. Proportion of college-owned housing units wired for high-speed internet access: 100%. **Campus safety:** Security services offered: 24-hour foot-and-vehicle patrols, late-night transport/escort service,

24-hour emergency telephones, lighted pathways/sidewalks, student patrols, controlled dormitory access (key, security card, etc).

TRANSFER AND INTERNATIONAL STUDENTS

Transfer students: May apply for admission for the following academic terms: Fall, Spring, Summer. Applicants do not need a minimum number of credits to apply. For fall 2009: Transfer applications received: 263. Transfer applicants offered admission: 207. Transfer applicants enrolled: 110. **International students:** Number of foreign undergraduates: 28 (2% of student body). Number of countries represented: 13. Minimum TOEFL score required: 500 (paper); 61 (computer).

South Dakota School of Mines and Tech.

- **Address:** 501 E. St. Joseph Street, Rapid City, SD 57701
- **Website:** http://www.sdsmt.edu
- **Public**
- **Enrollment:** 1,507 full-time; 406 part-time

KEY STATS
✔ **U.S News College Ranking:** Unranked Specialty School–Engineering
✔ **ACT Score (25th/75th percentile):** 24-28
✔ **Tuition:** 2010-2011: $7,120 in state, $8,620 out of state

Selectivity: More selective	**Room/board:** $5,610
Acceptance rate: 82%	**Average debt:** N/A
Student/faculty ratio: 14/1	**Proportion who borrowed:** N/A

UNDERGRADUATE STUDENT BODY STATS

2009-2010 enrollment: 1,507 full-time; 406 part-time. Men: 71%; women: 29%. **Ethnic makeup:** American-Indian: 3%; Asian American: 1%; Hispanic: 1%; White: 91%; International: 3%.

ADMISSIONS FACTS AND FIGURES

Phone: (605) 394-2414. **Email:** admissions@sdsmt.edu. **Website:** http://www.sdsmt.edu. **Application deadlines for fall 2011:** Regular decision: Rolling. Early decision: Not offered. Early action: Not offered. Admission can be deferred. **Application fee:** $20. **To apply online, go to:** http://www.applyweb.com. **Admissions requirements/recommendations:** High school units required (recommended): English: 4; Mathematics: 4; Science: 4; Foreign language: 2 (2); Social studies: 3; Total units: 18. Tests: The college uses SAT or ACT scores in admissions decisions. Either SAT or ACT required. For admission to the fall 2011 entering class, the school will accept: ACT with or without writing accepted. Campus visit: Recommended. Admissions interview: Neither required nor recommended. Off-campus interview: May be arranged. **Factors that count in admissions decisions:** *Academic:* Secondary school record: Very Important. Class rank: Very Important. Letters of recommendation: Not Considered. Standardized test scores: Very Important. Essay: Not Considered. *Nonacademic:* Interview: Not Considered. Extracurricular activities: Considered. Talent/ability: Considered. Character/personal qualities: Considered. Alumni/ae relationship: Not Considered. Geographical residence: Not Considered. State residency: Not Considered. Religious affiliation/commitment: Not Considered. Minority status: Not Considered. Volunteer work: Considered. Work experience: Considered. **Other schools with the greatest overlap in applicants:** Black Hills State University; Colorado School of Mines; South Dakota State University; University of South Dakota. **Admissions statistics for the fall 2009 entering class:** Total applicants: 975. Total accepted: 801. Freshmen enrolled: 362; 49% were from out of state. Overall acceptance rate: 82%. **Credentials of fall 2009 freshmen:** 22% ranked in the top 10 percent of their high school class; 55% were in the top 25 percent; 86% were in the top half. (Proportion submitting class standing: 90%.) **Average high school grade point average:** 3.5. **First-year students who submitted SAT scores:** 16%. Scores (25/75 percentile): Critical Reading: 500-630, Math: 550-670, Combined: 1050-1300. **First-year students submitting ACT scores:** 93%. Scores (25/75 percentile): English: 21-27, Math: 25-29, Composite: 24-28.

ACADEMICS

Year founded: 1885. **Academic calendar:** Semester. **Degrees offered:** associate, bachelor's, master's, doctorate. **Most popular majors:** 20% mechanical engineering, 14% civil engineering, 13% electrical, electronics, and communications engineering, 8% industrial engineering, 8% multi/interdisciplinary studies. **Major fields of study:** computer and information sciences and

support services; engineering; mathematics and statistics; multi/interdisciplinary studies; physical sciences. **Areas of required coursework:** arts/fine arts, humanities, mathematics, English (including composition), sciences (biological or physical), history, social science. **Pre-professional programs:** pre-law, pre-dentistry, pre-medicine, pre-veterinary science, pre-optometry, pre-pharmacy, other. **Special academic programs:** cooperative (work-study plan) program, cross-registration, distance learning, dual enrollment, independent study, internships, study abroad, other. **Cooperative education programs:** computer science, engineering, natural science, other. **Reserve Officers Training Corps (ROTC):** Army ROTC: Offered on campus. **Faculty and instruction (2009-2010):** Total instructional faculty: 121 full-time, 14 part-time (81% men; 19% women; 13% minorities). Full-time faculty with Ph.D. or other terminal degree: 83%. Student/faculty ratio: 14/1. Classes of fewer than 20 students: 38%; of 20 to 49 students: 54%; of 50 or more students: 8%. **Advanced Placement and International Baccalaureate credit:** AP tests may be used for: Credit only. Scores accepted: 3, 4, 5. International Baccalaureate exams may be used for: Credit only. **Freshmen returning for sophomore year:** 77%. **Graduation rates:** Four-year: 9%; five-year: 29%; six-year: 39%. **Graduate study:** 26% of students pursue further study within one year. Fields in which graduates pursue further study: Master of Business Administration (MBA), 1%; law, 1%; medicine, 1%; arts and sciences, 3%.

COSTS AND FINANCIAL AID

Financial aid office: (605) 394-2274. **Expenses (2010-2011):** Tuition and fees 2010-2011: $7,120 in state, $8,620 out of state; room/board: $5,610. Estimated books and supplies: $1,960; transportation: $2,200; personal expenses: $1,750. **Financial aid:** Priority filing date for institution's financial aid form: March 15. In 2009-2010, 91% of undergraduates applied for financial aid. Of those, 54% were determined to have financial need; 21% had their need fully met. Average financial aid package (proportion receiving): $8,764 (54%). Average amount of gift aid, such as scholarships or grants (proportion receiving): $4,176 (35%). Average amount of self-help aid, such as work study or loans (proportion receiving): $4,178 (47%). Average need-based loan (excluding PLUS or other private loans): $3,796. Among students who received need-based aid, the average percentage of need met: 66%. Among students who received aid based on merit, the average award (and the proportion receiving): $2,947 (23%). The average athletic scholarship (and the proportion receiving): $4,072 (4%).

CAMPUS LIFE AND EXTRACURRICULAR ACTIVITIES

Campus housing available (% using): coed dorms (78%), sorority housing (1%), fraternity housing (15%). Students who live in college-owned, operated, or affiliated housing: 33%. Average per-year earnings: $2,200. **Clubs and organizations:** Number of student organizations: 67. Activities include: campus ministries, choral groups, concert band, dance, drama/theater, international student organization, jazz band, music ensembles, pep band, radio station, student government, student newspaper. Number of fraternities: 4; sororities: 2. Proportion of men in fraternities: 18%; of women in sororities: 21%. **Sports program (2009-2010):** Member of NAIA. *Men's intercollegiate varsity sports:* basketball, cross country, football, golf, track and field (outdoor). *Women's intercollegiate varsity sports:* basketball, cross country, golf, track and field (outdoor), volleyball.

SERVICES AND FACILITIES

Basic services: nonremedial tutoring, placement service, day care, health service, health insurance, other. **Remedial assistance:** reading, math, writing. **Counseling services:** minority student, career, military, personal, veteran student, academic, older student, psychological, birth control, religious. **For learning-disabled students:** School does not offer a structured program with separate admission and additional fees. Total undergraduates in learning-disabled program or receiving services: 41. Services include: reading machines, tape recorders, note-taking services, oral tests, learning center, readers, extended time for tests, tutors, priority seating, texts on tape, other testing accommodations. **Library:** Number of titles: 252,260; number of current serial subscriptions: 15,149. **Information technology resources:** Students are required to lease or own a computer. Number of campus computers available to all students: 275. School has a wireless network. Approximate number of users that can be accommodated: 9,000. Proportion of college-owned housing units wired for high-speed internet access: 100%. **Campus safety:** Security services offered: late-night transport/escort service, 24-hour emergency telephones, lighted pathways/sidewalks, controlled dormitory access (key, security card, etc).

TRANSFER AND INTERNATIONAL STUDENTS

Transfer students: May apply for admission for the following academic terms: Fall, Spring, Summer. Applicants need a minimum number of credits to apply. For fall 2009: Transfer applications received: 241. Transfer applicants offered admission: 166. Transfer applicants enrolled: 93. **International students:** Number of foreign undergraduates: 50 (3% of student body). Number of countries represented: 14. Minimum TOEFL score required: 530 (paper); 71 (computer). Average TOEFL score: 576 (paper).

South Dakota State University

■ **Address:** Box 2201, Brookings, SD 57007
■ **Website:** http://www3.sdstate.edu
■ **Public**
■ **Enrollment:** 8,579 full-time; 2,215 part-time

KEY STATS

✔ **U.S News College Ranking:** second tier, National Universities
✔ **ACT Score (25th/75th percentile):** 20-26
✔ **Tuition:** 2010-2011: $6,444 in state, $7,941 out of state
  Selectivity: Selective   **Room/board:** $5,500
  Acceptance rate: 93%   **Average debt:** N/A
  Student/faculty ratio: N/A   **Proportion who borrowed:** 74%

UNDERGRADUATE STUDENT BODY STATS

2009-2010 enrollment: 8,579 full-time; 2,215 part-time. Men: 48%; women: 52%. Ethnic makeup: African American: 1%; American-Indian: 2%; Asian American: 1%; Hispanic: 1%; White: 94%; International: 1%.

ADMISSIONS FACTS AND FIGURES

Phone: (605) 688-4121. **Email:** SDSU_Admissions@sdstate.edu. **Website:** http://www3.sdstate.edu. **Application deadlines for fall 2011:** Regular decision: Rolling. Early decision: Not offered. Early action: Not offered. Admission can be deferred. **Application fee:** $20. **To apply online, go to:** http://www.applyweb.com/aw?sdksd/. **Admissions requirements/recommendations:** High school units required (recommended): English: 4; Mathematics: 3; Science: 3; Foreign language: 0; Social studies: 3; History: 0; Academic electives: 0; Total units: 14 (1). Tests: The college uses SAT or ACT scores in admissions decisions. Either SAT or ACT required. For admission to the fall 2011 entering class, the school will accept: ACT with or without writing accepted. Campus visit: Recommended. Admissions interview: Neither required nor recommended. Off-campus interview: Not available. **Factors that count in admissions decisions:** *Academic:* Secondary school record: Important. Class rank: Very Important. Letters of recommendation: Considered. Standardized test scores: Very Important. Essay: Not Considered. *Nonacademic:* Interview: Not Considered. Extracurricular activities: Not Considered. Talent/ability: Not Considered. Character/personal qualities: Not Considered. Alumni/ae relationship: Not Considered. Geographical residence: Not Considered. State residency: Not Considered. Religious affiliation/commitment: Not Considered. Minority status: Not Considered. Volunteer work: Not Considered. Work experience: Not Considered. **Other schools with the greatest overlap in applicants:** Iowa State University; North Dakota State University; University of Nebraska–Lincoln; University of South Dakota. **Admissions statistics for the fall 2009 entering class:** Total applicants: 4,191. Total accepted: 3,917. Freshmen enrolled: 2,135; 33% were from out of state. Overall acceptance rate: 93%. **Credentials of fall 2009 freshmen:** 15% ranked in the top 10 percent of their high school class; 37% were in the top 25 percent; 69% were in the top half. (Proportion submitting class standing: 95%.) **Average high school grade point average:** 3.3. **First-year students submitting ACT scores:** 97%. Scores (25/75 percentile): English: 19-25, Math: 19-26, Composite: 20-26.

ACADEMICS

Year founded: 1881. **Academic calendar:** Semester. **Degrees offered:** certificate, associate, bachelor's, post-bachelor's certificate, master's, post-master's certificate, doctorate. **Most popular majors:** 17% nursing/registered nurse training (R.N., A.S.N., B.S.N., M.S.N.), 12% economics, 11% agribusiness/ agricultural business operations, 6% biology/biological sciences, 5% pharmaceutics and drug design (M.S., Ph.D.). **Major fields of study:** agriculture, agriculture operations, and related sciences; biological and biomedical sciences; business, management, marketing, and related support services; communication, journalism, and related programs; computer and information sciences and support services; education; engineering; engineering

technologies/technicians; English language and literature/letters; family and consumer sciences/human sciences; foreign languages, literatures, and linguistics; health professions and related clinical sciences; history; liberal arts and sciences studies, and humanities; mathematics and statistics; multi/interdisciplinary studies; natural resources and conservation; parks, recreation, leisure, and fitness studies; physical sciences; psychology; social sciences; visual and performing arts. **Areas of required coursework:** arts/ fine arts, humanities, computer literacy, mathematics, English (including composition), sciences (biological or physical), social science, other. **Pre-professional programs:** pre-law, pre-dentistry, pre-medicine, pre-theology, pre-veterinary science, pre-optometry, pre-pharmacy, other. **Special academic programs:** accelerated program, cooperative (work-study plan) program, cross-registration, distance learning, double major, dual enrollment, exchange student program (domestic), honors program, independent study, internships, liberal arts/career combination, study abroad, teacher certificate program, other. **Teacher certification offered in:** early childhood, elementary, vo-tech, middle/junior high, secondary, bilingual/bicultural. **Cooperative education programs:** education, health professions, home economics. **Reserve Officers Training Corps (ROTC):** Army ROTC: Offered on campus; Air Force ROTC: Offered on campus. **Faculty and instruction (2009-2010):** Total instructional faculty: 476 full-time, 203 part-time (48% men; 52% women; 11% minorities). Full-time faculty with Ph.D. or other terminal degree: 72%. Classes of fewer than 20 students: 32%; of 20 to 49 students: 56%; of 50 or more students: 11%. **Advanced Placement and International Baccalaureate credit:** AP tests may be used for: Credit only. Scores accepted: 3, 4, 5. International Baccalaureate exams may be used for: Credit only. **Freshmen returning for sophomore year:** 77%. **Graduation rates:** Six-year: 54%.

COSTS AND FINANCIAL AID

Financial aid office: (605) 688-4695. **Expenses (2010-2011):** Tuition and fees 2010-2011: $6,444 in state, $7,941 out of state; room/board: $5,500. Estimated books and supplies: $1,100; transportation: $1,556; personal expenses: $2,116. **Financial aid:** Priority filing date for institution's financial aid form: March 15. In 2009-2010, 86% of undergraduates applied for financial aid. Of those, 76% were determined to have financial need; 76% had their need fully met. Average financial aid package (proportion receiving): $9,214 (76%). Average amount of gift aid, such as scholarships or grants (proportion receiving): $4,340 (45%). Average amount of self-help aid, such as work study or loans (proportion receiving): $5,314 (75%). Average need-based loan (excluding PLUS or other private loans): $5,010. Among students who received need-based aid, the average percentage of need met: 86%. Among students who received aid based on merit, the average award (and the proportion receiving): $1,422 (21%). The average athletic scholarship (and the proportion receiving): $6,361 (4%). Proportion who borrowed: 74%.

CAMPUS LIFE AND EXTRACURRICULAR ACTIVITIES

Campus housing available: coed dorms, sorority housing, fraternity housing, apartments for married students, apartment for single students, special housing for disabled students, other housing options. Students who live in college-owned, operated, or affiliated housing: 34%. **Student employment:** During the 2009-2010 academic year, 16% of undergraduates worked on campus. Average per-year earnings: $1,825. **Clubs and organizations:** Number of student organizations: 205. Activities include: campus ministries, choral groups, concert band, dance, drama/theater, international student organization, jazz band, literary magazine, marching band, music ensembles, musical theater, pep band, radio station, student government, student newspaper, symphony orchestra, yearbook. Number of fraternities: 6; sororities: 4. Average proportion of students who stay on campus on weekends: 68%. **Sports program (2009-2010):** Member of NCAA I. *Men's intercollegiate varsity sports:* baseball, basketball, cross country, football, golf, swimming, tennis, track and field (indoor), track and field (outdoor), wrestling. *Women's intercollegiate varsity sports:* basketball, cross country, equestrian, golf, soccer, softball, swimming, tennis, track and field (indoor), track and field (outdoor), volleyball.

SERVICES AND FACILITIES

Basic services: nonremedial tutoring, placement service, health service, health insurance, other. **Remedial assistance:** reading, math, writing, study skills. **Counseling services:** minority student, career, military, personal, veteran student, academic, older student, other. **For learning-disabled students:** School does not offer a structured program with separate admission and additional fees. Services include: remedial math, remedial English, reading machines, remedial reading, tape recorders, diagnostic testing service, note-taking services, learning center, readers, extended time for tests, tutors, priority seating, texts on tape, typist/scribe, other testing accommodations. **Library:** Number of titles: 926,000; number of current serial subscriptions: 44,579. **Information technology resources:** Students are not required to lease or own a computer. Number of campus computers available to all students: 692. School has a wireless network. Proportion of college-owned housing units wired for high-speed internet access: 100%. **Campus safety:** Security services offered: 24-hour foot-and-vehicle patrols, late-night transport/escort service, 24-hour emergency telephones, lighted pathways/sidewalks, student patrols, controlled dormitory access (key, security card, etc).

TRANSFER AND INTERNATIONAL STUDENTS

Transfer students: May apply for admission for the following academic terms: Fall, Spring, Summer. Applicants do not need a minimum number of credits to apply. For fall 2009: Transfer applications received: 1,594. Transfer applicants offered admission: 1,302. Transfer applicants enrolled: 787. **International students:** Number of foreign undergraduates: 114 (1% of student body). Number of countries represented: 22. Minimum TOEFL score required: 500 (paper); 173 (computer).

University of Sioux Falls

■ **Address:** 1101 W. 22nd Street, Sioux Falls, SD 57105
■ **Website:** http://www.usiouxfalls.edu
■ **Private; Religious affiliation:** American Baptist
■ **Enrollment:** 1,015 full-time; 228 part-time

KEY STATS
✔ **U.S News College Ranking:** 39, Regional Colleges (Midwest)
✔ **ACT Score (25th/75th percentile):** 20-26
✔ **Tuition:** 2010-2011: $21,895

Selectivity: Selective	**Room/board:** $6,330
Acceptance rate: 93%	**Average debt:** $21,332
Student/faculty ratio: 17/1	**Proportion who borrowed:** 78%

UNDERGRADUATE STUDENT BODY STATS

2009-2010 enrollment: 1,015 full-time; 228 part-time. Men: 47%; women: 53%. **Ethnic makeup:** African American: 2%; Hispanic: 1%; White: 95%. **Religious preference:** Roman Catholic: 15%; Protestant: 16%; Unknown: 25%; American Baptist: 16%; Lutheran: 18%; Other: 10%.

ADMISSIONS FACTS AND FIGURES

Phone: (605) 331-6600. **Email:** admissions@usiouxfalls.edu. **Website:** http://www.usiouxfalls.edu. **Application deadlines for fall 2011:** Regular decision: Rolling. Early decision: Not offered. Early action: Not offered. Admission can be deferred. **Application fee:** $25. **To apply online, go to:** https://www.usiouxfalls.edu/index.php?option=com_content&task=view&id=9&Itemid=160. **Admissions requirements/recommendations:** High school units required (recommended): English: (4); Mathematics: (3); Science: (2); Social studies: (3); History: (3); Total units: (16). Tests: The college uses SAT or ACT scores in admissions decisions. Either SAT or ACT required. For admission to the fall 2011 entering class, the school will accept: ACT with or without writing accepted. Campus visit: Recommended. Admissions interview: Neither required nor recommended. Off-campus interview: Not available. **Factors that count in admissions decisions:** *Academic:* Secondary school record: Very Important. Class rank: Very Important. Letters of recommendation: Considered. Standardized test scores: Very Important. Essay: Not Considered. *Nonacademic:* Interview: Considered. Extracurricular activities: Not Considered. Talent/ability: Not Considered. Character/personal qualities: Not Considered. Alumni/ae relationship: Not Considered. Geographical residence: Not Considered. State residency: Not Considered. Religious affiliation/commitment: Not Considered. Minority status: Not Considered. Volunteer work: Not Considered. Work experience: Not Considered. **Other schools with the greatest overlap in applicants:** Dordt College; Morningside College; Northwestern College; South Dakota State University; University of South Dakota. **Admissions statistics for the fall 2009 entering class:** Total applicants: 908. Total accepted: 843. Freshmen enrolled: 279; 46% were from out of state. Overall acceptance rate: 93%. **Credentials of fall 2009 freshmen:** 12% ranked in the top 10 percent of their high school class; 29% were in the top 25 percent; 78% were in the top half. (Proportion submitting class standing: 99%.) **Average high school grade point average:** 3.4. **First-year students who submitted SAT scores:** 3%. Scores (25/75 percentile): Critical Reading: 390-510, Math: 410-500, Combined: 800-1010. **First-year students submitting ACT scores:** 95%. Scores (25/75 percentile): English: 19-25, Math: 19-26, Composite: 20-26.

ACADEMICS

Year founded: 1883. **Academic calendar:** 4-1-4. **Degrees offered:** associate, bachelor's, master's, post-master's certificate. **Most popular majors:** 16% business administration and management, 16% organizational behavior studies, 10% elementary education and teaching, 6% criminal justice/safety studies, 5% kinesiology and exercise science. **Major fields of study:** biological and biomedical sciences; business, management, marketing, and related support services; communication, journalism, and related programs; computer and information sciences and support services; education; English language and literature/letters; foreign languages, literatures, and linguistics; health professions and related clinical sciences; history; liberal arts and sciences studies, and humanities; mathematics and statistics; parks, recreation, leisure, and fitness studies; philosophy and religious studies; physical sciences; psychology; public administration and social service professions; security and protective services; social sciences; theology and religious vocations; visual and performing arts. **Areas of required coursework:** arts/fine arts, humanities, computer literacy, mathematics, English (including composition), sciences (biological or physical), history, social science, other. **Pre-professional programs:** pre-law, pre-dentistry, pre-medicine, pre-theology, pre-veterinary science, other. **Special academic programs (% participation):** accelerated program (7%), cross-registration (2%), distance learning (3%), double major (10%), honors program (9%), independent study (20%), internships (15%), student-designed major (2%), study abroad (1%), teacher certificate program (2%). **Teacher certification offered in:** early childhood, elementary, middle/junior high, secondary. **Reserve Officers Training Corps (ROTC):** Air Force ROTC: Offered at cooperating institution (South Dakota State University). **Faculty and instruction (2009-2010):** Total instructional faculty: 60 full-time, 66 part-time (44% men; 56% women; 2% minorities). Full-time faculty with Ph.D. or other terminal degree: 75%. Student/faculty ratio: 17/1. Classes of fewer than 20 students: 62%; of 20 to 49 students: 36%; of 50 or more students: 2%. **Advanced Placement and International Baccalaureate credit:** AP tests may be used for: Credit only. Scores accepted: 4, 5. International Baccalaureate exams may be used for: Credit and/or placement. **Freshmen returning for sophomore year:** 68%. **Graduation rates:** Four-year: 28%; five-year: 48%; six-year: 48%. **Graduate study:** 9% of students pursue further study immediately upon graduation; 3% within one year. Fields in which graduates pursue further study: Master of Business Administration (MBA), 1%; law, 1%; medicine, 1%; theology (or the seminary), 2%; education, 8%; arts and sciences, 4%.

COSTS AND FINANCIAL AID

Financial aid office: (605) 331-6623. **Expenses (2010-2011):** Tuition and fees 2010-2011: $21,895; room/board: $6,330. Estimated books and supplies: $900; transportation: $1,235; personal expenses: $1,895. **Financial aid:** Priority filing date for institution's financial aid form: March 1. In 2009-2010, 100% of undergraduates applied for financial aid. Of those, 65% were determined to have financial need; Average financial aid package (proportion receiving): N/A (65%). Average amount of gift aid, such as scholarships or grants (proportion receiving): N/A (64%). Average amount of self-help aid, such as work study or loans (proportion receiving): $4,560 (52%). Average amount of debt of borrowers graduating in 2009: $21,332. Proportion who borrowed: 78%.

CAMPUS LIFE AND EXTRACURRICULAR ACTIVITIES

Campus housing available (% using): coed dorms (57%), women's dorms (18%), men's dorms (14%), apartments for married students (10%), apartment for single students (1%). Students who live in college-owned, operated, or affiliated housing: 58%. **Student employment:** During the 2009-2010 academic year, 10% of undergraduates worked on campus. Average per-year earnings: $1,200. **Clubs and organizations:** Number of student organizations: 31. Activities include: campus ministries, choral groups, concert band, drama/theater, jazz band, literary magazine, music ensembles, musical theater, pep band, radio station, student government, student newspaper, student film society, television station. Number of fraternities: 0; sororities: 0. Average proportion of students who stay on campus on weekends: 65%. **Sports program (2009-2010):** Member of NAIA. *Men's intercollegiate varsity sports:* baseball, basketball, cross country, football, golf, soccer, tennis, track and field (indoor), track and field (outdoor), wrestling. *Women's intercollegiate varsity sports:* basketball, cross country, golf, soccer, softball, tennis, track and field (indoor), track and field (outdoor), volleyball.

SERVICES AND FACILITIES

Basic services: nonremedial tutoring, placement service, health insurance. **Remedial assistance:** reading, math, writing, study skills. **Counseling services:** minority student, career, personal, veteran student, academic, older student, psychological, religious. **For learning-disabled students:** School does not offer a structured program with separate admission and additional fees. Total undergraduates in learning-disabled program or receiving services: 28. Services include: remedial math, tape recorders, untimed tests, note-taking services, oral tests, learning center, readers, extended time for tests, tutors, early syllabus, priority seating, texts on tape, typist/scribe, exams on tape or computer, other testing accommodations. **Library:** Number of titles: 84,296; number of current serial subscriptions: 277. **Information technology resources:** Students are not required to lease or own a computer. Number of campus computers available to all students: 155. School has a wireless network. Approximate number of users that can be accommodated: 160. Proportion of college-owned housing units wired for high-speed internet access: 100%. **Campus safety:** Security services offered: 24-hour foot-and-vehicle patrols, late-night transport/escort service, 24-hour emergency telephones, lighted pathways/sidewalks, student patrols, controlled dormitory access (key, security card, etc).

TRANSFER AND INTERNATIONAL STUDENTS

Transfer students: May apply for admission for the following academic terms: Fall, Spring, Summer. Applicants do not need a minimum number of credits to apply. For fall 2009: Transfer applications received: 179. Transfer applicants offered admission: 143. Transfer applicants enrolled: 73. **International students:** Number of foreign undergraduates: 4. Number of countries represented: 4. Minimum TOEFL score required: 500 (paper); 61 (computer). Average TOEFL score: 550 (paper).

University of South Dakota

- **Address:** 414 E. Clark Street, Vermillion, SD 57069
- **Website:** http://www.usd.edu
- **Public**
- **Enrollment:** 4,385 full-time; 2,713 part-time

KEY STATS

✔ **U.S News College Ranking:** second tier, National Universities
✔ **ACT Score (25th/75th percentile):** 20-26
✔ **Tuition:** 2010-2011: $6,762 in state, $8,259 out of state

Selectivity: Selective	**Room/board:** $6,123
Acceptance rate: 87%	**Average debt:** $23,676
Student/faculty ratio: 15/1	**Proportion who borrowed:** N/A

UNDERGRADUATE STUDENT BODY STATS

2009-2010 enrollment: 4,385 full-time; 2,713 part-time. Men: 38%; women: 62%. **Ethnic makeup:** African American: 2%; American-Indian: 2%; Asian American: 1%; Hispanic: 1%; White: 93%.

ADMISSIONS FACTS AND FIGURES

Phone: (605) 677-5434. **Email:** admiss@usd.edu. **Website:** http://www.usd.edu. **Application deadlines for fall 2011:** Regular decision: Rolling. Early decision: Not offered. Early action: Not offered. Admission can be deferred. **Application fee:** $20. **To apply online, go to:** http://www.usd.edu/admissions/applying/applications.cfm. **Admissions requirements/recommendations:** High school units required (recommended): English: 4 (4); Mathematics: 3 (4); Science: 3 (4); Foreign language: 0 (2); Social studies: 3 (3); History: 0 (0); Academic electives: 0 (0); Total units: 14 (18). Tests: The college uses SAT or ACT scores in admissions decisions. Either SAT or ACT required. For admission to the fall 2011 entering class, the school will accept: ACT with or without writing accepted. Campus visit: Recommended. Admissions interview: Recommended. Off-campus interview: May be arranged. **Factors that count in admissions decisions:** *Academic:* Secondary school record: Very Important. Class rank: Very Important. Letters of recommendation: Considered. Standardized test scores: Very Important. Essay: Considered. *Nonacademic:* Interview: Not Considered. Extracurricular activities: Considered. Talent/ability: Considered. Character/personal qualities: Considered. Alumni/ae relationship: Considered. Geographical residence: Considered. State residency: Considered. Religious affiliation/commitment: Not Considered. Minority status: Considered. Volunteer work: Considered. Work experience: Considered. **Other schools with the greatest overlap in applicants:** Augustana College; Dakota State University; Mount Marty

College; South Dakota State University; University of Nebraska–Lincoln. **Admissions statistics for the fall 2009 entering class:** Total applicants: 3,129. Total accepted: 2,721. Freshmen enrolled: 1,118; 29% were from out of state. Overall acceptance rate: 87%. **Credentials of fall 2009 freshmen:** 13% ranked in the top 10 percent of their high school class; 38% were in the top 25 percent; 71% were in the top half. (Proportion submitting class standing: 91%.) **Average high school grade point average:** 3.3. **First-year students who submitted SAT scores:** 3%. Scores (25/75 percentile): Critical Reading: 530-650, Math: 440-610, Combined: 970-1260. **First-year students submitting ACT scores:** 92%. Scores (25/75 percentile): English: 19-25, Math: 19-25, Composite: 20-26.

ACADEMICS

Year founded: 1862. **Academic calendar:** Semester. **Degrees offered:** certificate, associate, terminal-associate, bachelor's, post-bachelor's certificate, master's, post-master's certificate, doctorate. **Most popular majors:** 19% business, management, marketing, and related support services, 14% education, 14% health professions and related clinical sciences, 12% psychology, 9% social sciences. **Major fields of study:** agriculture, agriculture operations, and related sciences; area, ethnic, cultural, and gender studies; biological and biomedical sciences; business, management, marketing, and related support services; communication, journalism, and related programs; computer and information sciences and support services; education; English language and literature/letters; foreign languages, literatures, and linguistics; health professions and related clinical sciences; history; liberal arts and sciences studies, and humanities; mathematics and statistics; multi/interdisciplinary studies; parks, recreation, leisure, and fitness studies; philosophy and religious studies; physical sciences; psychology; security and protective services; social sciences; visual and performing arts. **Areas of required coursework:** arts/fine arts, humanities, computer literacy, mathematics, English (including composition), sciences (biological or physical), social science, other. **Pre-professional programs:** pre-law, pre-dentistry, pre-medicine, pre-veterinary science, pre-optometry, pre-pharmacy, other. **Special academic programs (% participation):** accelerated program (24%), cross-registration (40%), distance learning (69%), double major (11.2%), dual enrollment (6%), English as a Second Language (ESL) (.6%), exchange student program (domestic) (1.1%), external degree program (0%), honors program (9.6%), independent study (.2%), internships (51%), liberal arts/career combination (12.6%), student-designed major (.2%), study abroad (4.9%), teacher certificate program (14.4%). **Teacher certification offered in:** early childhood, special education, elementary, middle/junior high, adult education, secondary, bilingual/bicultural. **Reserve Officers Training Corps (ROTC):** Army ROTC: Offered on campus. **Faculty and instruction (2009-2010):** Total instructional faculty: 426 full-time, 63 part-time (46% men; 54% women; 12% minorities). Full-time faculty with Ph.D. or other terminal degree: 77%. Student/faculty ratio: 15/1. Classes of fewer than 20 students: 47%; of 20 to 49 students: 47%; of 50 or more students: 6%. **Advanced Placement and International Baccalaureate credit:** AP tests may be used for: Credit only. Scores accepted: 3, 4, 5. International Baccalaureate exams may be used for: Credit only. **Freshmen returning for sophomore year:** 73%. **Graduation rates:** Four-year: 22%; five-year: 42%; six-year: 46%. **Graduate study:** 32% of students pursue further study within one year. Fields in which graduates pursue further study: Master of Business Administration (MBA), 17%; law, 18%; medicine, 10%; theology (or the seminary), 3%; education, 3%; arts and sciences, 49%.

COSTS AND FINANCIAL AID

Financial aid office: (605) 677-5446. **Expenses (2010-2011):** Tuition and fees 2010-2011: $6,762 in state, $8,259 out of state; room/board: $6,123. Estimated books and supplies: $900; transportation: $1,000; personal expenses: $2,000. **Financial aid:** Priority filing date for institution's financial aid form: March 15. In 2009-2010, 76% of undergraduates applied for financial aid. Of those, 43% were determined to have financial need; 28% had their need fully met. Average financial aid package (proportion receiving): $6,471 (35%). Average amount of gift aid, such as scholarships or grants (proportion receiving): $3,846 (26%). Average amount of self-help aid, such as work study or loans (proportion receiving): $4,615 (34%). Average need-based loan (excluding PLUS or other private loans): $4,076. Among students who received need-based aid, the average percentage of need met: 78%. Among students who received aid based on merit, the average award (and the proportion receiving): $3,597 (22%). The average athletic scholarship (and the proportion receiving): $5,804 (5%). Average amount of debt of borrowers graduating in 2009: $23,676.

CAMPUS LIFE AND EXTRACURRICULAR ACTIVITIES

Campus housing available (% using): coed dorms (62%), sorority housing (12%), fraternity housing (15%), apartments for married students (2%), apartment for single students (6%), special housing for disabled students, other housing options. Students who live in college-owned, operated, or affiliated housing: 30%. **Student employment:** During the 2009-2010 academic year, 15% of undergraduates worked on campus. Average per-year earnings: $1,345. **Clubs and organizations:** Number of student organizations: 120. Activities include: campus ministries, choral groups, concert band, dance, drama/theater, jazz band, literary magazine, marching band, music ensembles, musical theater, opera, pep band, radio station, student government, student newspaper, symphony orchestra, television station. Number of fraternities: 8; sororities: 3. Proportion of men in fraternities: 15%; of women in sororities: 9%. Average proportion of students who stay on campus on weekends: 60%. **Sports program (2009-2010):** Member of NCAA I. *Men's intercollegiate varsity sports:* basketball, cross country, football, golf, swimming, track and field (indoor), track and field (outdoor). *Women's intercollegiate varsity sports:* basketball, cross country, golf, soccer, softball, swimming, tennis, track and field (indoor), track and field (outdoor), volleyball.

SERVICES AND FACILITIES

Basic services: nonremedial tutoring, placement service, day care, health service, health insurance, other. **Remedial assistance:** reading, math, writing, study skills. **Counseling services:** minority student, career, military, personal, veteran student, academic, psychological, birth control. **For learning-disabled students:** School does not offer a structured program with separate admission and additional fees. Services include: remedial math, remedial English, reading machines, tape recorders, note-taking services, oral tests, learning center, readers, extended time for tests, tutors, priority seating, texts on tape, typist/scribe, exams on tape or computer, other testing accommodations, other. **Library:** Number of titles: 943,242; number of current serial subscriptions: 2,232. **Information technology resources:** Students are not required to lease or own a computer. Number of campus computers available to all students: 917. School has a wireless network. Approximate number of users that can be accommodated: 1,950. Proportion of college-owned housing units wired for high-speed internet access: 100%. **Campus safety:** Security services offered: 24-hour foot-and-vehicle patrols, late-night transport/escort service, 24-hour emergency telephones, lighted pathways/sidewalks, controlled dormitory access (key, security card, etc).

TRANSFER AND INTERNATIONAL STUDENTS

Transfer students: May apply for admission for the following academic terms: Fall, Spring, Summer. Applicants do not need a minimum number of credits to apply. For fall 2009: Transfer applications received: 1,646. Transfer applicants offered admission: 1,207. Transfer applicants enrolled: 701. **International students:** Number of foreign undergraduates: 19. Number of countries represented: 28. Minimum TOEFL score required: 550 (paper); 79 (computer). Average TOEFL score: 550 (paper).

Tennessee

Aquinas College

- **Address:** 4210 Harding Road, Nashville, TN 37205
- **Website:** http://www.aquinascollege.edu
- **Private**
- **Enrollment:** N/A

....

KEY STATS

✔ **U.S News College Ranking:** second tier, Regional Colleges (South)
✔ **SAT or ACT Score (25th/75th percentile):** N/A
✔ **Tuition:** 2009-2010: $17,380
  - **Selectivity:** Less selective   **Room/board:** $12,442
  - **Acceptance rate:** N/A   **Average debt:** N/A
  - **Student/faculty ratio:** N/A   **Proportion who borrowed:** N/A

Austin Peay State University

- **Address:** PO Box 4675, Clarksville, TN 37044
- **Website:** http://www.apsu.edu
- **Public**
- **Enrollment:** 6,975 full-time; 2,321 part-time

....

KEY STATS

✔ **U.S News College Ranking:** 69, Regional Universities (South)
✔ **ACT Score (25th/75th percentile):** 19-23
✔ **Tuition:** 2009-2010: $5,808 in state, $17,736 out of state
  - **Selectivity:** Selective   **Room/board:** $6,120
  - **Acceptance rate:** 90%   **Average debt:** $20,158
  - **Student/faculty ratio:** 20/1   **Proportion who borrowed:** 56%

UNDERGRADUATE STUDENT BODY STATS

2009-2010 enrollment: 6,975 full-time; 2,321 part-time. Men: 39%; women: 61%.

ADMISSIONS FACTS AND FIGURES

Phone: (931) 221-7661. **Email:** admissions@apsu.edu. **Website:** http://www.apsu.edu. **Application deadlines for fall 2011:** Regular decision: July 23. Early decision: Not offered. Early action: Not offered. Admission can be deferred. **Application fee:** $15. **To apply online, go to:** http://www.apsu.edu/admissions. **Admissions requirements/recommendations:** High school units required (recommended): English: 4 (4); Mathematics: 3 (3); Science: 2 (2); Foreign language: 2 (2); Social studies: 1 (1); History: 1 (1); Total units: 14 (14). Tests: The college uses SAT or ACT scores in admissions decisions. Neither SAT nor ACT required. For admission to the fall 2011 entering class, the school will accept: ACT with or without writing accepted. Campus visit: Recommended. Admissions interview: Neither required nor recommended. Off-campus interview: Not available. **Factors that count in admissions decisions:** *Academic:* Secondary school record: Considered. Class rank: Not Considered. Letters of recommendation: Not Considered. Standardized test scores: Very Important. Essay: Not Considered. *Nonacademic:* Interview: Not Considered. Extracurricular activities: Not Considered. Talent/ability: Not Considered. Character/personal qualities: Not Considered. Alumni/ae relationship: Not Considered. Geographical residence: Not Considered. State residency: Not Considered. Religious affiliation/commitment: Not Considered. Minority status: Not Considered. Volunteer work: Not Considered. Work experience: Not Considered. **Admissions statistics for the fall 2009 entering class:** Total applicants: 3,111. Total accepted: 2,802. Freshmen enrolled: 1,645; 7% were from out of state. Overall acceptance rate: 90%. **Credentials of fall 2009 freshmen:** 14% ranked in the top 10 percent of their high school class; 39% were in the top 25 percent; 75% were in the top half. (Proportion submitting class standing: 70%.) **Average high school grade point average:** 3.1. **First-year students who submitted SAT scores:** 4%. Scores (25/75 percentile): Critical Reading: 443-550, Math: 450-538, Combined: 893-1088. **First-year students submitting ACT scores:** 79%. Scores (25/75 percentile): English: 19-24, Math: 17-23, Composite: 19-23.

ACADEMICS

Year founded: 1927. **Academic calendar:** Semester. **Degrees offered:** certificate, associate, transfer-associate, terminal-associate, bachelor's, post-bachelor's certificate, master's, post-master's certificate. **Most popular majors:** 18% business, management, marketing, and related support services, 12% health professions and related clinical sciences, 8% liberal arts and sciences studies, and humanities, 7% communication, journalism, and related programs, 7% multi/interdisciplinary studies. **Major fields of study:** agriculture, agriculture operations, and related sciences; biological and biomedical sciences; business, management, marketing, and related support services; communication, journalism, and related programs; computer and information sciences and support services; education; engineering technologies/technicians; English language and literature/letters; foreign languages, literatures, and linguistics; health professions and related clinical sciences; history; liberal arts and sciences studies, and humanities; mathematics and statistics; multi/interdisciplinary studies; parks, recreation, leisure, and fitness studies; philosophy and religious studies; physical sciences; psychology; public administration and social service professions; security and protective services; social sciences; visual and performing arts. **Areas of required coursework:** arts/fine arts, humanities, mathematics, English (including composition), foreign languages, sciences (biological or physical), history, social science. **Pre-professional programs:** pre-law, pre-dentistry, pre-medicine, pre-veterinary science, pre-optometry, pre-pharmacy, other. **Special academic programs:** accelerated program, cooperative (work-study plan) program, distance learning, double major, dual enrollment, English as a Second Language (ESL), honors program, independent study, internships, study abroad, teacher certificate program, other. **Teacher certification offered in:** special education, elementary, middle/junior high, secondary. **Cooperative education programs:** agriculture, art, business, computer science, education, engineering, health professions, humanities, natural science, social/behavioral science, technologies, vocational arts. **Reserve Officers Training Corps (ROTC):** Army ROTC: Offered on campus. **Faculty and instruction (2009-2010):** Total instructional faculty: 310 full-time, 240 part-time (49% men; 51% women; 10% minorities). Student/faculty ratio: 20/1. Classes of fewer than 20 students: 41%; of 20 to 49 students: 54%; of 50 or more students: 5%. **Advanced Placement and International Baccalaureate credit:** AP tests may be used for: Credit and/or placement. Scores accepted: 3, 4, 5. **Freshmen returning for sophomore year:** 67%. **Graduation rates:** Four-year: 13%; five-year: 27%; six-year: 31%.

COSTS AND FINANCIAL AID

Financial aid office: (931) 221-7907. **Expenses (2009-2010):** Tuition and fees 2009-2010: $5,808 in state, $17,736 out of state; room/board: $6,120. Estimated books and supplies: $1,550; transportation: $2,916; personal expenses: $2,000. **Financial aid:** Priority filing date for institution's financial aid form: April 1. In 2009-2010, 88% of undergraduates applied for financial aid. Of those, 73% were determined to have financial need; Average financial aid package (proportion receiving): $8,513 (72%). Average amount of gift aid, such as scholarships or grants (proportion receiving): $4,782 (41%). Average amount of self-help aid, such as work study or loans (proportion receiving): $4,494 (52%). Average need-based loan (excluding PLUS or other private loans): $4,422. Among students who received aid based on merit, the average award (and the proportion receiving): $4,655 (10%). The average athletic scholarship (and the proportion receiving): $8,180 (2%). Average amount of debt of borrowers graduating in 2009: $20,158. Proportion who borrowed: 56%.

CAMPUS LIFE AND EXTRACURRICULAR ACTIVITIES

Campus housing available (% using): coed dorms (64%), women's dorms (20%), men's dorms (8%), sorority housing (0%), apartments for married students (2%), apartment for single students (6%), special housing for disabled students (0%). Students who live in college-owned, operated, or affiliated housing: 14%. **Clubs and organizations:** Number of student organizations: 81. Activities include: campus ministries, choral groups, concert band, dance, drama/theater, international student organization, jazz band, literary magazine, marching band, music ensembles, musical theater, opera, pep band, radio station, student government, student newspaper, student film society, symphony orchestra, television station, yearbook. Number of fraternities: 8; sororities: 7. Proportion of men in fraternities: 7%; of women in sororities: 4%. **Sports program (2009-2010):** Member of NCAA I. **Men's intercollegiate varsity sports:** baseball, basketball, cross country, football, golf, tennis. **Women's intercollegiate varsity sports:** basketball, cross country, golf, soccer, softball, tennis, track and field (outdoor), volleyball.

SERVICES AND FACILITIES

Basic services: nonremedial tutoring, placement service, day care, health service, health insurance. **Remedial assistance:** reading, math, writing, study skills. **Counseling services:** minority student, career, military, personal, veteran student, academic, older student, psychological, birth control, religious, other. **For learning-disabled students:** School does not offer a structured program with separate admission and additional fees. Services include: remedial math, remedial English, reading machines, remedial reading, tape recorders, videotaped classes, note-taking services, oral tests, learning center, readers, extended time for tests, tutors, priority seating, texts on tape, exams on tape or computer, other testing accommodations. **Library:** Number of titles: 416,874; number of current serial subscriptions: 29,666. **Information technology resources:** Students are not required to lease or own a computer. Number of campus computers available to all students: 760. School has a wireless network. Approximate number of users that can be accommodated: 2,000. Proportion of college-owned housing units wired for high-speed internet access: 0%. **Campus safety:** Security services offered: 24-hour foot-and-vehicle patrols, late-night transport/escort service, 24-hour emergency telephones, lighted pathways/sidewalks, student patrols, controlled dormitory access (key, security card, etc).

TRANSFER AND INTERNATIONAL STUDENTS

Transfer students: May apply for admission for the following academic terms: Fall, Spring, Summer. Applicants need a minimum number of credits to apply. For fall 2009: Transfer applications received: 1,402. Transfer applicants offered admission: 1,336. Transfer applicants enrolled: 986. **International students:** Number of countries represented: 5. Minimum TOEFL score required: 500 (paper); 173 (computer).

Belmont University

- **Address:** 1900 Belmont Boulevard, Nashville, TN 37212
- **Website:** http://www.belmont.edu
- **Private; Religious affiliation:** Christian Ecumenical
- **Enrollment:** 4,035 full-time; 343 part-time

KEY STATS

✔ **U.S News College Ranking:** 5, Regional Universities (South)
✔ **ACT Score (25th/75th percentile):** 23-29
✔ **Tuition:** 2010-2011: $23,680

Selectivity: More selective	**Room/board:** $10,830
Acceptance rate: 77%	**Average debt:** $29,268
Student/faculty ratio: 12/1	**Proportion who borrowed:** 57%

UNDERGRADUATE STUDENT BODY STATS

2009-2010 enrollment: 4,035 full-time; 343 part-time. Men: 43%; women: 57%. **Ethnic makeup:** African American: 4%; Asian American: 3%; Hispanic: 2%; White: 90%; International: 1%. **Religious preference:** Roman Catholic: 8%; Protestant: 54%; Jewish: 1%; No preference: 34%.

ADMISSIONS FACTS AND FIGURES

Phone: (615) 460-6785. **Email:** buadmission@mail.belmont.edu. **Website:** http://www.belmont.edu. **Application deadlines for fall 2011:** Regular decision: August 1. Early decision: Not offered. Early action: Not offered. Admission can be deferred. **Application fee:** $50. **To apply online, go to:** http://www.xap.com/applications/Belmont_University/apply.html. **Admissions requirements/recommendations:** High school units required (recommended): English: 4 (4); Mathematics: 3 (4); Science: 3 (4); Foreign language: 2 (2); Social studies: 3 (3); Academic electives: 3 (3); Total units: 18 (18). Tests: The college uses SAT or ACT scores in admissions decisions. Either SAT or ACT required. For admission to the fall 2011 entering class, the school will accept: ACT with or without writing accepted. Campus visit: Neither required nor recommended. Admissions interview:

Neither required nor recommended. Off-campus interview: Not available. **Factors that count in admissions decisions:** *Academic:* Secondary school record: Very Important. Class rank: Very Important. Letters of recommendation: Important. Standardized test scores: Very Important. Essay: Important. *Nonacademic:* Interview: Not Considered. Extracurricular activities: Considered. Talent/ability: Considered. Character/personal qualities: Considered. Alumni/ae relationship: Considered. Geographical residence: Not Considered. State residency: Not Considered. Religious affiliation/commitment: Not Considered. Minority status: Considered. Volunteer work: Considered. Work experience: Considered. **Other schools with the greatest overlap in applicants:** Lipscomb University; Middle Tennessee State University; Samford University; University of Tennessee; Vanderbilt University. **Admissions statistics for the fall 2009 entering class:** Total applicants: 3,220. Total accepted: 2,466. Freshmen enrolled: 991; 64% were from out of state. Overall acceptance rate: 77%. **Size of waiting list:** 0 applicants; enrolled from waiting list: 0. **Credentials of fall 2009 freshmen:** 35% ranked in the top 10 percent of their high school class; 68% were in the top 25 percent; 95% were in the top half. (Proportion submitting class standing: 75%.) **Average high school grade point average:** 3.5. **First-year students who submitted SAT scores:** 47%. Scores (25/75 percentile): Critical Reading: 540-640, Math: 530-640, Combined: 1070-1280. **First-year students submitting ACT scores:** 75%. Scores (25/75 percentile): English: 22-27, Math: 24-30, Composite: 23-29.

ACADEMICS

Year founded: 1890. **Academic calendar:** Semester. **Degrees offered:** bachelor's, master's, post-master's certificate. **Most popular majors:** 34% music management and merchandising, 15% business administration, management, and operations, 10% nursing/registered nurse training (R.N., A.S.N., B.S.N., M.S.N.), 7% music, 4% public relations, advertising, and applied communication . **Major fields of study:** biological and biomedical sciences; business, management, marketing, and related support services; communication, journalism, and related programs; computer and information sciences and support services; education; engineering; English language and literature/letters; foreign languages, literatures, and linguistics; health professions and related clinical sciences; history; liberal arts and sciences studies, and humanities; mathematics and statistics; parks, recreation, leisure, and fitness studies; philosophy and religious studies; physical sciences; psychology; public administration and social service professions; social sciences; visual and performing arts. **Areas of required coursework:** arts/fine arts, humanities, computer literacy, mathematics, English (including composition), sciences (biological or physical), history, social science. **Pre-professional programs:** pre-law, pre-dentistry, pre-medicine, pre-theology, pre-veterinary science, pre-optometry, pre-pharmacy. **Special academic programs (% participation):** accelerated program (11%), cooperative (work-study plan) program (19%), cross-registration (.04%), distance learning (38%), double major (5%), dual enrollment (.01%), honors program (13%), independent study (8%), internships (44%), liberal arts/career combination (82%), student-designed major (3%), study abroad (40%), teacher certificate program (9%), weekend college (12%). **Teacher certification offered in:** early childhood, special education, elementary, middle/junior high, secondary. **Reserve Officers Training Corps (ROTC):** Army ROTC: Offered at cooperating institution (Vanderbilt University); Navy ROTC: Offered at cooperating institution (Vanderbilt University); Air Force ROTC: Offered at cooperating institution (Tennessee State University). **Faculty and instruction (2009-2010):** Total instructional faculty: 269 full-time, 336 part-time (46% men; 54% women; 8% minorities). Full-time faculty with Ph.D. or other terminal degree: 80%. Student/faculty ratio: 12/1. Classes of fewer than 20 students: 53%; of 20 to 49 students: 46%; of 50 or more students: 0%. **Advanced Placement and International Baccalaureate credit:** AP tests may be used for: Credit and/or placement. Scores accepted: 3, 4, 5. **Freshmen returning for sophomore year:** 80%. **Graduation rates:** Four-year: 52%; five-year: 67%; six-year: 65%. **Graduate study:** 10% of students pursue further study immediately upon graduation; 25% within one year. Fields in which graduates pursue further study: Master of Business Administration (MBA), 42%; law, 3%; medicine, 6%; dentistry, 4%; engineering, 1%; theology (or the seminary), 3%; education, 23%; arts and sciences, 19%; veterinary medicine, 1%.

COSTS AND FINANCIAL AID

Financial aid office: (615) 460-6403. **Expenses (2010-2011):** Tuition and fees 2010-2011: $23,680; room/board: $10,830. Estimated books and supplies: $1,350; transportation: $1,800; personal expenses: $2,150. **Financial aid:** Priority filing date for institution's financial aid form: March 1. In 2009-2010, 91% of undergraduates applied for financial aid. Of those, 54% were determined to have financial need; 21% had their need fully met. Average

financial aid package (proportion receiving): $11,966 (52%). Average amount of gift aid, such as scholarships or grants (proportion receiving): $5,881 (24%). Average amount of self-help aid, such as work study or loans (proportion receiving): $4,508 (40%). Average need-based loan (excluding PLUS or other private loans): $4,394. Among students who received need-based aid, the average percentage of need met: 80%. Among students who received aid based on merit, the average award (and the proportion receiving): $6,326 (13%). The average athletic scholarship (and the proportion receiving): $17,261 (5%). Average amount of debt of borrowers graduating in 2009: $29,268. Proportion who borrowed: 57%.

CAMPUS LIFE AND EXTRACURRICULAR ACTIVITIES
Campus housing available (% using): coed dorms (14%), women's dorms (28%), men's dorms (21%), apartment for single students (35%), special housing for disabled students (0%), other housing options (2%). Students who live in college-owned, operated, or affiliated housing: 27%. **Student employment:** During the 2009-2010 academic year, 17% of undergraduates worked on campus. Average per-year earnings: $2,100. **Clubs and organizations:** Number of student organizations: 97. Activities include: campus ministries, choral groups, concert band, dance, drama/theater, international student organization, jazz band, literary magazine, marching band, music ensembles, musical theater, opera, pep band, radio station, student government, student newspaper, symphony orchestra, television station. Number of fraternities: 4; sororities: 5. Proportion of men in fraternities: 3%; of women in sororities: 5%. Average proportion of students who stay on campus on weekends: 48%. **Sports program (2009-2010):** Member of NCAA I. *Men's intercollegiate varsity sports:* baseball, basketball, cross country, golf, soccer, tennis, track and field (indoor), track and field (outdoor). *Women's intercollegiate varsity sports:* basketball, cross country, golf, soccer, softball, tennis, track and field (indoor), track and field (outdoor), volleyball.

SERVICES AND FACILITIES
Basic services: placement service, health service. **Counseling services:** minority student, career, personal, veteran student, academic, older student, psychological, birth control, religious. **For learning-disabled students:** School does not offer a structured program with separate admission and additional fees. Total undergraduates in learning-disabled program or receiving services: 109. Services include: reading machines, tape recorders, note-taking services, oral tests, readers, extended time for tests, early syllabus, priority registration, priority seating, texts on tape, typist/scribe, exams on tape or computer, take home exams, other testing accommodations. **Library:** Number of titles: 220,637; number of current serial subscriptions: 1,072. **Information technology resources:** Students are not required to lease or own a computer. Number of campus computers available to all students: 550. School has a wireless network. Approximate number of users that can be accommodated: 800. Proportion of college-owned housing units wired for high-speed internet access: 100%. **Campus safety:** Security services offered: 24-hour foot-and-vehicle patrols, late-night transport/escort service, 24-hour emergency telephones, lighted pathways/sidewalks, controlled dormitory access (key, security card, etc).

TRANSFER AND INTERNATIONAL STUDENTS
Transfer students: May apply for admission for the following academic terms: Fall, Spring, Summer. Applicants need a minimum number of credits to apply. For fall 2009: Transfer applications received: 1,147. Transfer applicants offered admission: 600. Transfer applicants enrolled: 369. **International students:** Number of foreign undergraduates: 30 (1% of student body). Number of countries represented: 34. Minimum TOEFL score required: 550 (paper); 213 (computer). Average TOEFL score: 520 (paper).

Bethel College

- **Address:** 325 Cherry Avenue, McKenzie, TN 38201
- **Website:** http://www.bethel-college.edu
- **Private; Religious affiliation:** Cumberland Presbyterian
- **Enrollment:** 2,515 full-time; 35 part-time

KEY STATS
✔ **U.S News College Ranking:** second tier, Regional Universities (South)
✔ **ACT Score (25th/75th percentile):** 17-23
✔ **Tuition:** 2010-2011: $12,878

Selectivity: Selective	**Room/board:** $7,272
Acceptance rate: 54%	**Average debt:** N/A
Student/faculty ratio: 19/1	**Proportion who borrowed:** N/A

UNDERGRADUATE STUDENT BODY STATS
2009-2010 enrollment: 2,515 full-time; 35 part-time. Men: 41%; women: 59%. **Ethnic makeup:** African American: 37%; Hispanic: 1%; White: 59%; International: 2%.

ADMISSIONS FACTS AND FIGURES
Phone: (731) 352-4030. **Email:** admissions@bethel-college.edu. **Website:** http://www.bethel-college.edu. **Application deadlines for fall 2011:** Regular decision: August 4. Early decision: Not offered. Early action: Not offered. Admission can be deferred. **Application fee:** $30. **To apply online, go to:** https://secure.sitemason.com/site/deAwqQ/application. **Admissions requirements/recommendations:** High school units required (recommended): English: 4; Mathematics: 2; Science: 2. Tests: The college uses SAT or ACT scores in admissions decisions. Either SAT or ACT required. For admission to the fall 2011 entering class, the school will accept: ACT with or without writing accepted. Campus visit: Neither required nor recommended. Admissions interview: Recommended. Off-campus interview: May be arranged. **Factors that count in admissions decisions:** *Academic:* Secondary school record: Very Important. Class rank: Very Important. Letters of recommendation: Important. Standardized test scores: Very Important. Essay: Considered. *Nonacademic:* Interview: Important. Extracurricular activities: Considered. Talent/ability: Important. Character/personal qualities: Very Important. Alumni/ae relationship: Important. Geographical residence: Considered. State residency: Considered. Religious affiliation/commitment: Considered. Minority status: Considered. Volunteer work: Important. Work experience: Important. **Other schools with the greatest overlap in applicants:** Freed-Hardeman University; Lambuth University; Union University; University of Tennessee–Martin. **Admissions statistics for the fall 2009 entering class:** Total applicants: 1,057. Total accepted: 566. Freshmen enrolled: 1,623; Overall acceptance rate: 54%. **First-year students who submitted SAT scores:** 6%. Scores (25/75 percentile): Critical Reading: 420-530, Math: 470-570, Combined: 890-1100. **First-year students submitting ACT scores:** 89%. Scores (25/75 percentile): English: N/A, Math: N/A, Composite: 17-23.

ACADEMICS
Year founded: 1842. **Academic calendar:** Semester. **Degrees offered:** bachelor's, master's. **Major fields of study:** biological and biomedical sciences; business, management, marketing, and related support services; education; English language and literature/letters; history; liberal arts and sciences studies, and humanities; mathematics and statistics; psychology; public administration and social service professions. **Areas of required coursework:** arts/fine arts, humanities, computer literacy, mathematics, English (including composition), sciences (biological or physical), history, other. **Pre-professional programs:** pre-medicine, pre-pharmacy, other. **Special academic programs:** accelerated program, distance learning, double major, honors program, independent study, internships, student-designed major, study abroad, teacher certificate program, weekend college. **Teacher certification offered in:** early childhood, special education, elementary, middle/junior high, secondary. **Cooperative education programs:** health professions. **Faculty and instruction (2009-2010):** Total instructional faculty: 97 full-time, 194 part-time. Student/faculty ratio: 19/1. **Advanced Placement and International Baccalaureate credit:** AP tests may be used for: Placement only. **Freshmen returning for sophomore year:** 63%. **Graduation rates:** Six-year: 27%.

COSTS AND FINANCIAL AID
Financial aid office: (731) 352-4233. **Expenses (2010-2011):** Tuition and fees 2010-2011: $12,878; room/board: $7,272. Estimated books and supplies:

$1,000. **Financial aid:** Priority filing date for institution's financial aid form: February 15; deadline: March 1.

CAMPUS LIFE AND EXTRACURRICULAR ACTIVITIES
Campus housing available: women's dorms, men's dorms, apartment for single students, other housing options. **Student employment:** During the 2009-2010 academic year, 2% of undergraduates worked on campus. Average per-year earnings: $1,064. **Clubs and organizations:** Number of student organizations: 18. Activities include: campus ministries, choral groups, concert band, drama/theater, marching band, music ensembles, musical theater, student government, yearbook. Number of fraternities: 5; sororities: 5. Average proportion of students who stay on campus on weekends: 30%. **Sports program (2009-2010):** Member of NAIA. *Men's intercollegiate varsity sports:* baseball, basketball, cross country, football, golf, soccer, tennis, track and field (outdoor). *Women's intercollegiate varsity sports:* basketball, cross country, golf, soccer, softball, tennis, track and field (outdoor), volleyball.

SERVICES AND FACILITIES
Remedial assistance: math, writing, study skills. **Counseling services:** career, personal, veteran student, academic, psychological, religious. **For learning-disabled students:** School does not offer a structured program with separate admission and additional fees. Services include: remedial math, remedial English, tape recorders, untimed tests. **Information technology resources:** Students are required to lease or own a computer. School has a wireless network. Proportion of college-owned housing units wired for high-speed internet access: 100%. **Campus safety:** Security services offered: 24-hour foot-and-vehicle patrols, late-night transport/escort service, lighted pathways/sidewalks, controlled dormitory access (key, security card, etc).

TRANSFER AND INTERNATIONAL STUDENTS
Transfer students: May apply for admission for the following academic terms: Fall, Spring, Summer. Applicants need a minimum number of credits to apply. **International students:** Number of foreign undergraduates: 56 (2% of student body). Number of countries represented: 16. Minimum TOEFL score required: 513 (paper); 183 (computer).

Bryan College

- **Address:** PO Box 7000, Dayton, TN 37321-7000
- **Website:** http://www.bryan.edu
- **Private; Religious affiliation:** Christian nondenominational
- **Enrollment:** 974 full-time; 126 part-time

KEY STATS
✔ **U.S News College Ranking:** 16, Regional Colleges (South)
✔ **ACT Score (25th/75th percentile):** 20-28
✔ **Tuition:** 2010-2011: $18,740

Selectivity: Selective	**Room/board:** $5,454
Acceptance rate: 75%	**Average debt:** $14,976
Student/faculty ratio: 17/1	**Proportion who borrowed:** 74%

UNDERGRADUATE STUDENT BODY STATS
2009-2010 enrollment: 974 full-time; 126 part-time. Men: 46%; women: 54%. **Ethnic makeup:** African American: 5%; Asian American: 1%; Hispanic: 2%; White: 90%; International: 2%.

ADMISSIONS FACTS AND FIGURES
Phone: (800) 277-9522. **Email:** admissions@bryan.edu. **Website:** http://www.bryan.edu. **Application deadlines for fall 2011:** Regular decision: Rolling. Early decision: Not offered. Early action: Send application by: May 1; Decision sent by: N/A. Admission can be deferred. **Application fee:** $35. **To apply online, go to:** http://www.bryan.edu/apply. **Admissions requirements/recommendations:** High school units required (recommended): English: 4 (4); Mathematics: 3 (3); Science: 3 (3); Foreign language: 2 (2); Social studies: 3 (3); Total units: 18 (18). Tests: The college uses SAT or ACT scores in admissions decisions. Either SAT or ACT required. For admission to the fall 2011 entering class, the school will accept: ACT with writing recommended. Campus visit: Recommended. Admissions interview: Recommended. Off-campus interview: May be arranged. **Factors that count in admissions decisions:** *Academic:* Secondary school record: Very Important. Class rank: Considered. Letters of recommendation: Considered. Standardized test scores: Very Important. Essay: Very Important. *Nonacademic:* Interview: Considered. Extracurricular activi-

ties: Considered. Talent/ability: Considered. Character/personal qualities: Important. Alumni/ae relationship: Considered. Geographical residence: Not Considered. State residency: Not Considered. Religious affiliation/commitment: Important. Minority status: Not Considered. Volunteer work: Considered. Work experience: Not Considered. **Admissions statistics for the fall 2009 entering class:** Total applicants: 459. Total accepted: 344. Freshmen enrolled: 192; 52% were from out of state. Overall acceptance rate: 75%. Non-early acceptance rate: 75%. **Average high school grade point average:** 3.6. **First-year students who submitted SAT scores:** 39%. Scores (25/75 percentile): Critical Reading: 520-660, Math: 480-610, Combined: 1000-1270. **First-year students submitting ACT scores:** 77%. Scores (25/75 percentile): English: 21-30, Math: 19-26, Composite: 20-28.

ACADEMICS
Year founded: 1930. **Academic calendar:** Semester. **Degrees offered:** certificate, diploma, associate, bachelor's, master's. **Major fields of study:** communication, journalism, and related programs; computer and information sciences and support services; education; English language and literature/letters; foreign languages, literatures, and linguistics; history; liberal arts and sciences studies, and humanities; parks, recreation, leisure, and fitness studies; philosophy and religious studies; psychology; social sciences; theology and religious vocations; visual and performing arts. **Areas of required coursework:** arts/fine arts, humanities, mathematics, English (including composition), foreign languages, sciences (biological or physical), history, social science, other. **Special academic programs:** distance learning, double major, dual enrollment, honors program, independent study, internships, liberal arts/career combination, study abroad, teacher certificate program. **Teacher certification offered in:** elementary, secondary. **Faculty and instruction (2009-2010):** Total instructional faculty: 43 full-time, 23 part-time (82% men; 18% women; 2% minorities). Full-time faculty with Ph.D. or other terminal degree: 81%. Student/faculty ratio: 17/1. Classes of fewer than 20 students: 60%; of 20 to 49 students: 36%; of 50 or more students: 4%. **Advanced Placement and International Baccalaureate credit:** AP tests may be used for: Credit and/or placement. Scores accepted: 3, 4, 5. International Baccalaureate exams may be used for: Credit and/or placement. **Freshmen returning for sophomore year:** 76%. **Graduation rates:** Four-year: 45%; five-year: 52%; six-year: 57%.

COSTS AND FINANCIAL AID
Financial aid office: (423) 775-7339. **Expenses (2010-2011):** Tuition and fees 2010-2011: $18,740; room/board: $5,454. Estimated books and supplies: $1,400; transportation: $1,600; personal expenses: $1,500. **Financial aid:** Priority filing date for institution's financial aid form: February 15. In 2009-2010, 85% of undergraduates applied for financial aid. Of those, 75% were determined to have financial need; 51% had their need fully met. Average financial aid package (proportion receiving): $14,768 (75%). Average amount of gift aid, such as scholarships or grants (proportion receiving): $8,587 (66%). Average amount of self-help aid, such as work study or loans (proportion receiving): $4,270 (56%). Average need-based loan (excluding PLUS or other private loans): $3,678. Among students who received need-based aid, the average percentage of need met: 76%. Among students who received aid based on merit, the average award (and the proportion receiving): $4,703 (10%). The average athletic scholarship (and the proportion receiving): $5,911 (5%). Average amount of debt of borrowers graduating in 2009: $14,976. Proportion who borrowed: 74%.

CAMPUS LIFE AND EXTRACURRICULAR ACTIVITIES
Campus housing available (% using): women's dorms (53%), men's dorms (43%), apartments for married students (2%). Students who live in college-owned, operated, or affiliated housing: 58%. **Student employment:** During the 2009-2010 academic year, 2% of undergraduates worked on campus. Average per-year earnings: $1,000. Activities include: campus ministries, choral groups, drama/theater, music ensembles, student government, student newspaper, yearbook. Number of fraternities: 0; sororities: 0. Average proportion of students who stay on campus on weekends: 50%. **Sports program (2009-2010):** Member of NAIA. *Men's intercollegiate varsity sports:* baseball, basketball, cross country, soccer. *Women's intercollegiate varsity sports:* basketball, cross country, soccer, volleyball.

SERVICES AND FACILITIES
Basic services: nonremedial tutoring, placement service, health service, health insurance. **Remedial assistance:** reading, math, writing, study skills. **Counseling services:** minority student, career, personal, academic, psychological, religious. **For learning-disabled students:** School does not offer a structured program with separate admission and additional fees. Services include: remedial math, remedial English, remedial reading, tape

recorders, untimed tests, note-taking services, oral tests, learning center, readers, extended time for tests, tutors, texts on tape. **Library:** Number of titles: 154,375; number of current serial subscriptions: 10,000. **Information technology resources:** Students are not required to lease or own a computer. Number of campus computers available to all students: 203. School has a wireless network. Approximate number of users that can be accommodated: 858. Proportion of college-owned housing units wired for high-speed internet access: 100%. **Campus safety:** Security services offered: 24-hour emergency telephones, lighted pathways/sidewalks, controlled dormitory access (key, security card, etc).

TRANSFER AND INTERNATIONAL STUDENTS

Transfer students: May apply for admission for the following academic terms: Fall, Spring, Summer. Applicants need a minimum number of credits to apply. For fall 2009: Transfer applications received: 117. Transfer applicants offered admission: 77. Transfer applicants enrolled: 59. **International students:** Number of foreign undergraduates: 16 (2% of student body). Number of countries represented: 9. Minimum TOEFL score required: 533 (paper); 200 (computer).

Carson-Newman College

- **Address:** 1646 Russell Avenue, Jefferson City, TN 37760
- **Website:** http://www.cn.edu
- **Private; Religious affiliation:** Baptist
- **Enrollment:** 1,772 full-time; 128 part-time

....

KEY STATS

✔ **U.S News College Ranking:** 183, National Liberal Arts Colleges
✔ **ACT Score (25th/75th percentile):** 20-25
✔ **Tuition:** 2010-2011: $20,562

Selectivity: Selective	**Room/board:** $5,918
Acceptance rate: 74%	**Average debt:** $14,164
Student/faculty ratio: 11/1	**Proportion who borrowed:** 67%

UNDERGRADUATE STUDENT BODY STATS

2009-2010 enrollment: 1,772 full-time; 128 part-time. Men: 42%; women: 58%. **Ethnic makeup:** African American: 8%; Asian American: 1%; Hispanic: 1%; White: 87%; International: 2%. **Religious preference:** Roman Catholic: 3%; Protestant: 30%; No preference: 9%; Baptist: 56%.

ADMISSIONS FACTS AND FIGURES

Phone: (800) 678-9061. **Email:** thuebner@cn.edu. **Website:** http://www.cn.edu. **Application deadlines for fall 2011:** Regular decision: August 8. Early decision: Not offered. Early action: Not offered. Admission can be deferred. **Application fee:** $25. **To apply online, go to:** http://admissions.cn.edu/admissions/application/apply.asp. **Admissions requirements/recommendations:** High school units required (recommended): English: 4; Mathematics: 2 (3); Science: 2; Foreign language: (2); Social studies: 3; History: 2; Total units: 20. **Tests:** The college uses SAT or ACT scores in admissions decisions. Either SAT or ACT required. For admission to the fall 2011 entering class, the school will accept: ACT with or without writing accepted. Campus visit: Recommended. Admissions interview: Recommended. Off-campus interview: Not available. **Factors that count in admissions decisions: *Academic:*** Secondary school record: Very Important. Class rank: Considered. Letters of recommendation: Important. Standardized test scores: Important. Essay: Considered. ***Nonacademic:*** Interview: Considered. Extracurricular activities: Important. Talent/ability: Considered. Character/personal qualities: Important. Alumni/ae relationship: Considered. Geographical residence: Not Considered. State residency: Not Considered. Religious affiliation/commitment: Considered. Minority status: Considered. Volunteer work: Considered. Work experience: Considered. **Admissions statistics for the fall 2009 entering class:** Total applicants: 3,031. Total accepted: 2,236. Freshmen enrolled: 513; 32% were from out of state. Overall acceptance rate: 74%. **Credentials of fall 2009 freshmen:** 27% ranked in the top 10 percent of their high school class; 47% were in the top 25 percent; 73% were in the top half. (Proportion submitting class standing: 78%.) **Average high school grade point average:** 3.4. **First-year students who submitted SAT scores:** 20%. **First-year students submitting ACT scores:** 80%. Scores (25/75 percentile): English: N/A, Math: N/A, Composite: 20-25.

ACADEMICS

Year founded: 1851. **Academic calendar:** Semester. **Degrees offered:** bachelor's, master's. **Most popular majors:** 24% health professions and related clinical sciences, 15% education, 12% business, management, marketing, and related support services. **Major fields of study:** biological and biomedical sciences; business, management, marketing, and related support services; communication, journalism, and related programs; computer and information sciences and support services; education; English language and literature/letters; family and consumer sciences/human sciences; foreign languages, literatures, and linguistics; health professions and related clinical sciences; history; liberal arts and sciences studies, and humanities; mathematics and statistics; multi/interdisciplinary studies; parks, recreation, leisure, and fitness studies; philosophy and religious studies; physical sciences; psychology; social sciences; theology and religious vocations; visual and performing arts. **Areas of required coursework:** arts/fine arts, mathematics, English (including composition), foreign languages, sciences (biological or physical). **Special academic programs:** accelerated program, double major, dual enrollment, English as a Second Language (ESL), exchange student program (domestic), honors program, independent study, internships, liberal arts/career combination, student-designed major, study abroad, teacher certificate program, weekend college. **Teacher certification offered in:** early childhood, special education, elementary, middle/junior high, secondary. **Reserve Officers Training Corps (ROTC):** Army ROTC: Offered on campus; Air Force ROTC: Offered on campus. **Faculty and instruction (2009-2010):** Total instructional faculty: 130 full-time, 58 part-time. Full-time faculty with Ph.D. or other terminal degree: 73%. Student/faculty ratio: 11/1. Classes of fewer than 20 students: 63%; of 20 to 49 students: 37%; of 50 or more students: 0%. **Advanced Placement and International Baccalaureate credit:** AP tests may be used for: Placement only. Scores accepted: 4. International Baccalaureate exams may be used for: Credit only. **Freshmen returning for sophomore year:** 66%. **Graduation rates:** Four-year: 40%; five-year: 51%; six-year: 54%. **Graduate study:** 30% of students pursue further study immediately upon graduation; 41% within one year; 64% within five years.

COSTS AND FINANCIAL AID

Financial aid office: (865) 471-3247. **Expenses (2010-2011):** Tuition and fees 2010-2011: $20,562; room/board: $5,918. Estimated books and supplies: $1,088; transportation: $2,010; personal expenses: $1,921. **Financial aid:** In 2009-2010, 93% of undergraduates applied for financial aid. Of those, 79% were determined to have financial need; 25% had their need fully met. Average financial aid package (proportion receiving): $15,747 (79%). Average amount of gift aid, such as scholarships or grants (proportion receiving): $11,740 (78%). Average amount of self-help aid, such as work study or loans (proportion receiving): $3,671 (62%). Average need-based loan (excluding PLUS or other private loans): $3,517. Among students who received need-based aid, the average percentage of need met: 74%. Among students who received aid based on merit, the average award (and the proportion receiving): $6,853 (17%). The average athletic scholarship (and the proportion receiving): $9,593 (5%). Average amount of debt of borrowers graduating in 2009: $14,164. Proportion who borrowed: 67%.

CAMPUS LIFE AND EXTRACURRICULAR ACTIVITIES

Campus housing available: women's dorms, men's dorms, apartments for married students. Students who live in college-owned, operated, or affiliated housing: 55%. Activities include: choral groups, concert band, dance, drama/theater, jazz band, literary magazine, marching band, music ensembles, musical theater, pep band, radio station, student government, student newspaper, student film society, television station, yearbook. Average proportion of students who stay on campus on weekends: 25%. **Sports program (2009-2010):** Member of NCAA II.

SERVICES AND FACILITIES

For learning-disabled students: School does not offer a structured program with separate admission and additional fees. **Library:** Number of titles: 218,371; number of current serial subscriptions: 3,966. **Information technology resources:** Students are not required to lease or own a computer. Number of campus computers available to all students: 400. School has a wireless network. Approximate number of users that can be accommodated: 1,200. Proportion of college-owned housing units wired for high-speed internet access: 100%.

TRANSFER AND INTERNATIONAL STUDENTS

Transfer students: May apply for admission for the following academic terms: Fall, Spring, Summer. Applicants need a minimum number of credits to apply. For fall 2009: Transfer applications received: 445. Transfer applicants offered admission: 302. Transfer applicants enrolled: 114.

International students: Number of foreign undergraduates: 45 (2% of student body). Number of countries represented: 22. Minimum TOEFL score required: 550 (paper). Average TOEFL score: 570 (paper).

Christian Brothers University

- ■ **Address:** 650 East Parkway S, Memphis, TN 38104
- ■ **Website:** http://www.cbu.edu
- ■ **Private; Religious affiliation:** Roman Catholic
- ■ **Enrollment:** 1,257 full-time; 168 part-time

KEY STATS

- ✔ **U.S News College Ranking:** 21, Regional Universities (South)
- ✔ **ACT Score (25th/75th percentile):** 21-26
- ✔ **Tuition:** 2010-2011: $24,870

Selectivity: More selective	**Room/board:** $6,590
Acceptance rate: 49%	**Average debt:** $28,259
Student/faculty ratio: 13/1	**Proportion who borrowed:** 69%

UNDERGRADUATE STUDENT BODY STATS

2009-2010 enrollment: 1,257 full-time; 168 part-time. Men: 44%; women: 56%. **Ethnic makeup:** African American: 34%; Asian American: 5%; Hispanic: 2%; White: 57%; International: 2%. **Religious preference:** Protestant: 50%; Hindu: 1%; Buddhist: 1%; Unknown: 28%; Roman Catholic: 19%; Other: 1%.

ADMISSIONS FACTS AND FIGURES

Phone: (901) 321-3205. **Email:** admissions@cbu.edu. **Website:** http://www.cbu.edu. **Application deadlines for fall 2011:** Regular decision: Rolling. Early decision: Not offered. Early action: Send application by: N/A; Decision sent by: N/A. Admission can be deferred. **Application fee:** $25. **To apply online, go to:** http://www.cbu.edu/Admissions/apply.html. **Admissions requirements/recommendations:** High school units required (recommended): English: (4); Mathematics: (4); Science: (4). Tests: The college uses SAT or ACT scores in admissions decisions. Either SAT or ACT required. For admission to the fall 2011 entering class, the school will accept: ACT with or without writing accepted. Campus visit: Recommended. Admissions interview: Recommended. Off-campus interview: May be arranged. **Factors that count in admissions decisions:** *Academic:* Secondary school record: Very Important. Class rank: Important. Letters of recommendation: Important. Standardized test scores: Very Important. Essay: Important. *Nonacademic:* Interview: Important. Extracurricular activities: Important. Talent/ability: Important. Character/personal qualities: Important. Alumni/ae relationship: Important. Geographical residence: Not Considered. State residency: Not Considered. Religious affiliation/commitment: Not Considered. Minority status: Not Considered. Volunteer work: Important. Work experience: Important. **Other schools with the greatest overlap in applicants:** Middle Tennessee State University; Rhodes College; University of Memphis; University of Tennessee; University of Tennessee–Martin. **Admissions statistics for the fall 2009 entering class:** Total applicants: 1,912. Total accepted: 936. Freshmen enrolled: 301; 20% were from out of state. Overall acceptance rate: 49%. Non-early acceptance rate: 49%. **Credentials of fall 2009 freshmen:** 29% ranked in the top 10 percent of their high school class; 60% were in the top 25 percent; 90% were in the top half. (Proportion submitting class standing: 67%.) **Average high school grade point average:** 3.6. **First-year students who submitted SAT scores:** 18%. Scores (25/75 percentile): Critical Reading: 480-620, Math: 480-630, Combined: 960-1250. **First-year students submitting ACT scores:** 97%. Scores (25/75 percentile): English: 22-27, Math: 20-26, Composite: 21-26.

ACADEMICS

Year founded: 1871. **Academic calendar:** Semester. **Degrees offered:** bachelor's, post-bachelor's certificate, master's. **Most popular majors:** 34% business, management, marketing, and related support services, 24% psychology, 9% biological and biomedical sciences, 9% engineering, 7% physical sciences. **Major fields of study:** area, ethnic, cultural, and gender studies; biological and biomedical sciences; business, management, marketing, and related support services; communication, journalism, and related programs; computer and information sciences and support services; engineering; English language and literature/letters; history; liberal arts and sciences studies, and humanities; mathematics and statistics; multi/interdisciplinary studies; philosophy and religious studies; physical sciences; psychology. **Areas of required coursework:** mathematics, English (including

composition), sciences (biological or physical), history, social science. **Preprofessional programs:** pre-law, pre-dentistry, pre-medicine, pre-theology, pre-pharmacy. **Special academic programs (% participation):** accelerated program (35%), cross-registration (2%), distance learning (5%), double major (2%), honors program (10%), independent study (45%), internships (35%), study abroad (8%), teacher certificate program (15%). **Teacher certification offered in:** early childhood, special education, elementary, secondary. **Reserve Officers Training Corps (ROTC):** Army ROTC: Offered at cooperating institution (University of Memphis); Navy ROTC: Offered at cooperating institution (University of Memphis); Air Force ROTC: Offered at cooperating institution (University of Memphis). **Faculty and instruction (2009-2010):** Total instructional faculty: 98 full-time, 60 part-time (61% men; 39% women; 13% minorities). Full-time faculty with Ph.D. or other terminal degree: 87%. Student/faculty ratio: 13/1. Classes of fewer than 20 students: 66%; of 20 to 49 students: 34%; of 50 or more students: 0%. **Advanced Placement and International Baccalaureate credit:** AP tests may be used for: Credit only. **Freshmen returning for sophomore year:** 78%. **Graduation rates:** Four-year: 39%; five-year: 54%; six-year: 57%. **Graduate study:** 31% of students pursue further study immediately upon graduation; 60% within one year. Fields in which graduates pursue further study: Master of Business Administration (MBA), 30%; law, 10%; medicine, 25%; education, 3%.

COSTS AND FINANCIAL AID

Financial aid office: (901) 321-3305. **Expenses (2010-2011):** Tuition and fees 2010-2011: $24,870; room/board: $6,590. Estimated books and supplies: $1,500. **Financial aid:** Priority filing date for institution's financial aid form: February 15. In 2009-2010, 90% of undergraduates applied for financial aid. Of those, 75% were determined to have financial need; 27% had their need fully met. Average financial aid package (proportion receiving): $19,826 (75%). Average amount of gift aid, such as scholarships or grants (proportion receiving): $7,004 (44%). Average amount of self-help aid, such as work study or loans (proportion receiving): $4,537 (50%). Average need-based loan (excluding PLUS or other private loans): $4,404. Among students who received need-based aid, the average percentage of need met: 85%. Among students who received aid based on merit, the average award (and the proportion receiving): $10,240 (19%). The average athletic scholarship (and the proportion receiving): $8,315 (13%). Average amount of debt of borrowers graduating in 2009: $28,259. Proportion who borrowed: 69%.

CAMPUS LIFE AND EXTRACURRICULAR ACTIVITIES

Campus housing available (% using): coed dorms (15%), women's dorms (25%), men's dorms (30%), apartment for single students (30%). Students who live in college-owned, operated, or affiliated housing: 40%. **Clubs and organizations:** Number of student organizations: 37. Activities include: campus ministries, choral groups, drama/theater, literary magazine, radio station, student government, yearbook. Number of fraternities: 5; sororities: 6. Proportion of men in fraternities: 26%; of women in sororities: 21%. Average proportion of students who stay on campus on weekends: 40%. **Sports program (2009-2010):** Member of NCAA II. *Men's intercollegiate varsity sports:* baseball, basketball, cross country, golf, soccer, tennis. *Women's intercollegiate varsity sports:* basketball, cross country, golf, soccer, softball, tennis, volleyball.

SERVICES AND FACILITIES

Basic services: nonremedial tutoring, placement service, health service, health insurance. **Remedial assistance:** other. **Counseling services:** career, personal, academic, older student, psychological, religious. **For learning-disabled students:** School does not offer a structured program with separate admission and additional fees. Total undergraduates in learning-disabled program or receiving services: 24. Services include: tape recorders, untimed tests, note-taking services, oral tests, readers, extended time for tests, tutors, priority seating, texts on tape, other. **Library:** Number of titles: 165,204; number of current serial subscriptions: 1,818. **Information technology resources:** Students are not required to lease or own a computer. Number of campus computers available to all students: 310. School has a wireless network. Approximate number of users that can be accommodated: 500. Proportion of college-owned housing units wired for high-speed internet access: 100%. **Campus safety:** Security services offered: 24-hour foot-and-vehicle patrols, late-night transport/escort service, 24-hour emergency telephones, lighted pathways/sidewalks, controlled dormitory access (key, security card, etc).

TRANSFER AND INTERNATIONAL STUDENTS

Transfer students: May apply for admission for the following academic terms: Fall, Spring, Summer. Applicants do not need a minimum number of credits to apply. For fall 2009: Transfer applications received: 222.

Transfer applicants offered admission: 92. Transfer applicants enrolled: 43. **International students:** Number of foreign undergraduates: 30 (2% of student body). Number of countries represented: 17. Minimum TOEFL score required: 500 (paper); 173 (computer).

Cumberland University

- Address: 1 Cumberland Square, Lebanon, TN 37087-3408
- Website: http://www.cumberland.edu
- Private
- Enrollment: 903 full-time; 138 part-time

KEY STATS

✔ **U.S News College Ranking:** second tier, Regional Universities (South)
✔ **ACT Score (25th/75th percentile):** 20-24
✔ **Tuition:** 2010-2011: $18,256

Selectivity: Selective	**Room/board:** $6,760
Acceptance rate: 57%	**Average debt:** $20,973
Student/faculty ratio: 16/1	**Proportion who borrowed:** 69%

UNDERGRADUATE STUDENT BODY STATS

2009-2010 enrollment: 903 full-time; 138 part-time. Men: 45%; women: 55%. **Ethnic makeup:** African American: 11%; Asian American: 1%; Hispanic: 2%; White: 82%; International: 4%.

ADMISSIONS FACTS AND FIGURES

Phone: (615) 444-2562. **Email:** admissions@cumberland.edu. **Website:** http://www.cumberland.edu. **Application deadlines for fall 2011:** Regular decision: Rolling; decision sent by June 15. Early decision: Not offered. Early action: Not offered. Admission can be deferred. **Application fee:** $25. **To apply online, go to:** https://secure.collegefortn.org/logon.asp?nextpage=%2FAdmissionApp%2Fappmanager%2Easp. **Admissions requirements/recommendations:** High school units required (recommended): English: 4 (4); Mathematics: 3 (3); Science: 3 (3); Foreign language: 2 (2); Social studies: 2 (2); History: 1 (2); Academic electives: 12 (12); Total units: 27 (28). Tests: The college uses SAT or ACT scores in admissions decisions. ACT required. For admission to the fall 2011 entering class, the school will accept: ACT with writing recommended. Campus visit: Recommended. Admissions interview: Neither required nor recommended. Off-campus interview: May be arranged. **Factors that count in admissions decisions:** *Academic:* Secondary school record: Very Important. Class rank: Considered. Letters of recommendation: Considered. Standardized test scores: Very Important. Essay: Considered. *Nonacademic:* Interview: Considered. Extracurricular activities: Considered. Talent/ability: Considered. Character/personal qualities: Considered. Alumni/ae relationship: Important. Geographical residence: Not Considered. State residency: Not Considered. Religious affiliation/commitment: Not Considered. Minority status: Not Considered. Volunteer work: Not Considered. Work experience: Considered. **Other schools with the greatest overlap in applicants:** Belmont University; Freed-Hardeman University; Middle Tennessee State University; Trevecca Nazarene University; Union University. **Admissions statistics for the fall 2009 entering class:** Total applicants: 675. Total accepted: 384. Freshmen enrolled: 201; Overall acceptance rate: 57%. **Credentials of fall 2009 freshmen:** 19% ranked in the top 10 percent of their high school class; 38% were in the top 25 percent; 74% were in the top half. (Proportion submitting class standing: 66%.) **Average high school grade point average:** 3.3. **First-year students who submitted SAT scores:** 10%. Scores (25/75 percentile): Critical Reading: 410-510, Math: 450-560, Combined: 860-1070. **First-year students submitting ACT scores:** 90%. Scores (25/75 percentile): English: 20-25, Math: 17-24, Composite: 20-24.

ACADEMICS

Year founded: 1842. **Academic calendar:** Semester. **Degrees offered:** associate, bachelor's, master's. **Most popular majors:** 32% nursing/registered nurse training (R.N., A.S.N., B.S.N., M.S.N.), 19% elementary education and teaching, 16% business administration and management, 10% physical education teaching and coaching. **Major fields of study:** area, ethnic, cultural, and gender studies; biological and biomedical sciences; business, management, marketing, and related support services; computer and information sciences and support services; education; English language and literature/letters; health professions and related clinical sciences; history; liberal arts and sciences studies, and humanities; mathematics and statistics; parks, recreation, leisure, and fitness studies; psychology; security

and protective services; social sciences; visual and performing arts. **Areas of required coursework:** arts/fine arts, humanities, computer literacy, mathematics, English (including composition), philosophy, foreign languages, sciences (biological or physical), history, social science, other. **Pre-professional programs:** pre-law, pre-dentistry, pre-medicine, pre-veterinary science, pre-optometry, pre-pharmacy, other. **Special academic programs (% participation):** accelerated program (1%), double major (4%), dual enrollment (3%), independent study (3%), internships (2%), teacher certificate program (21%). **Teacher certification offered in:** early childhood, special education, elementary, middle/junior high, secondary. **Reserve Officers Training Corps (ROTC):** Army ROTC: Offered at cooperating institution (Middle Tennessee State University). **Faculty and instruction (2009-2010):** Total instructional faculty: 39 full-time, 71 part-time (50% men; 50% women; 7% minorities). Full-time faculty with Ph.D. or other terminal degree: 90%. Student/faculty ratio: 16/1. Classes of fewer than 20 students: 55%; of 20 to 49 students: 43%; of 50 or more students: 3%. **Advanced Placement and International Baccalaureate credit:** AP tests may be used for: Placement only. Scores accepted: 3, 4, 5. International Baccalaureate exams may be used for: Credit only. **Freshmen returning for sophomore year:** 57%. **Graduation rates:** Four-year: 16%; five-year: 31%; six-year: 35%. **Graduate study:** 20% of students pursue further study immediately upon graduation; 30% within one year; 10% within five years. Fields in which graduates pursue further study: Master of Business Administration (MBA), 10%; law, 1%; medicine, 1%; dentistry, 1%; education, 60%; arts and sciences, 3%; veterinary medicine, 1%.

COSTS AND FINANCIAL AID

Financial aid office: (615) 444-2562. **Expenses (2010-2011):** Tuition and fees 2010-2011: $18,256; room/board: $6,760. Estimated books and supplies: $1,400; transportation: $1,180; personal expenses: $2,516. **Financial aid:** Priority filing date for institution's financial aid form: February 15; deadline: May 1. In 2009-2010, 93% of undergraduates applied for financial aid. Of those, 81% were determined to have financial need; 17% had their need fully met. Average financial aid package (proportion receiving): $14,386 (81%). Average amount of gift aid, such as scholarships or grants (proportion receiving): $6,673 (39%). Average amount of self-help aid, such as work study or loans (proportion receiving): $4,088 (55%). Average need-based loan (excluding PLUS or other private loans): $4,068. Among students who received need-based aid, the average percentage of need met: 61%. Among students who received aid based on merit, the average award (and the proportion receiving): $4,636 (50%). The average athletic scholarship (and the proportion receiving): $7,975 (33%). Average amount of debt of borrowers graduating in 2009: $20,973. Proportion who borrowed: 69%.

CAMPUS LIFE AND EXTRACURRICULAR ACTIVITIES

Campus housing available (% using): women's dorms (45%), men's dorms (55%), special housing for disabled students. **Student employment:** During the 2009-2010 academic year, 2% of undergraduates worked on campus. Average per-year earnings: $1,500. **Clubs and organizations:** Number of student organizations: 38. Activities include: choral groups, concert band, dance, drama/theater, jazz band, marching band, music ensembles, musical theater, pep band, radio station, student government, student newspaper, yearbook. Number of fraternities: 3; sororities: 2. Average proportion of students who stay on campus on weekends: 30%. **Sports program (2009-2010):** Member of NAIA.

SERVICES AND FACILITIES

Basic services: placement service. **Remedial assistance:** reading, math, writing, study skills. **Counseling services:** minority student, career, personal, academic, psychological. **For learning-disabled students:** School does not offer a structured program with separate admission and additional fees. Services include: remedial math, remedial English, reading machines, remedial reading, tape recorders, other special classes, videotaped classes, untimed tests, note-taking services, oral tests, learning center, readers, extended time for tests, tutors, priority seating, texts on tape, other testing accommodations. **Library:** Number of titles: 75,000; number of current serial subscriptions: 335. **Information technology resources:** Students are not required to lease or own a computer. Number of campus computers available to all students: 150. School has a wireless network. Approximate number of users that can be accommodated: 10,752. Proportion of college-owned housing units wired for high-speed internet access: 100%. **Campus safety:** Security services offered: 24-hour foot-and-vehicle patrols, 24-hour emergency telephones, lighted pathways/sidewalks, controlled dormitory access (key, security card, etc.).

TRANSFER AND INTERNATIONAL STUDENTS

Transfer students: May apply for admission for the following academic terms: Fall, Spring, Summer. Applicants need a minimum number of credits to apply. For fall 2009: Transfer applications received: 464. Transfer applicants offered admission: 327. Transfer applicants enrolled: 181.
International students: Number of foreign undergraduates: 37 (4% of student body). Number of countries represented: 26. Minimum TOEFL score required: 500 (paper); 173 (computer). Average TOEFL score: 550 (paper).

East Tennessee State University

- **Address:** 807 University Parkway, Johnson City, TN 37614-0000
- **Website:** http://www.etsu.edu
- **Public**
- **Enrollment:** 9,855 full-time; 1,793 part-time

KEY STATS
✔ **U.S News College Ranking:** second tier, National Universities
✔ **ACT Score (25th/75th percentile):** 20-25
✔ **Tuition:** 2010-2011: $6,884 in state, $19,808 out of state
  Selectivity: Selective   **Room/board:** $7,568
  Acceptance rate: 85%   **Average debt:** N/A
  Student/faculty ratio: 19/1   **Proportion who borrowed:** N/A

UNDERGRADUATE STUDENT BODY STATS

2009-2010 enrollment: 9,855 full-time; 1,793 part-time. Men: 44%; women: 56%. **Ethnic makeup:** African American: 5%; American-Indian: 1%; Asian American: 2%; Hispanic: 1%; White: 90%; International: 1%.

ADMISSIONS FACTS AND FIGURES

Phone: (423) 439-4213. **Email:** go2etsu@etsu.edu. **Website:** http://www.etsu.edu. **Application deadlines for fall 2011:** Regular decision: Rolling. Early decision: Not offered. Early action: Not offered. Admission cannot be deferred. **Application fee:** $15. **To apply online, go to:** http://www.etsu.edu/admissions/apply.asp. **Admissions requirements/recommendations:** High school units required (recommended): English: 4; Mathematics: 3 (4); Science: 2 (3); Foreign language: 2; Social studies: 1; History: 1; Total units: 14 (16). Tests: The college uses SAT or ACT scores in admissions decisions. Either SAT or ACT required. For admission to the fall 2011 entering class, the school will accept: ACT with or without writing accepted. Campus visit: Recommended. Admissions interview: Recommended. Off-campus interview: May be arranged. **Factors that count in admissions decisions:** *Academic:* Secondary school record: Important. Class rank: Considered. Letters of recommendation: Not Considered. Standardized test scores: Very Important. Essay: Not Considered. *Nonacademic:* Interview: Not Considered. Extracurricular activities: Not Considered. Talent/ability: Not Considered. Character/personal qualities: Not Considered. Alumni/ae relationship: Not Considered. Geographical residence: Considered. State residency: Considered. Religious affiliation/commitment: Not Considered. Minority status: Not Considered. Volunteer work: Not Considered. Work experience: Not Considered. **Other schools with the greatest overlap in applicants:** Appalachian State University; University of Tennessee; University of Tennessee–Chattanooga; University of Virginia–Wise; Virginia Tech. **Admissions statistics for the fall 2009 entering class:** Total applicants: 4,721. Total accepted: 4,024. Freshmen enrolled: 2,099; 14% were from out of state. Overall acceptance rate: 85%. **Credentials of fall 2009 freshmen:** 19% ranked in the top 10 percent of their high school class; 44% were in the top 25 percent; 74% were in the top half. (Proportion submitting class standing: 69%.) **Average high school grade point average:** 3.2. **First-year students who submitted SAT scores:** 12%. Scores (25/75 percentile): Critical Reading: 420-550, Math: 430-560, Combined: 850-1110. **First-year students submitting ACT scores:** 92%. Scores (25/75 percentile): English: 19-25, Math: 18-24, Composite: 20-25.

ACADEMICS

Year founded: 1911. **Academic calendar:** Semester. **Degrees offered:** bachelor's, post-bachelor's certificate, master's, post-master's certificate, doctorate. **Most popular majors:** 23% health professions and related clinical sciences, 15% business, management, marketing, and related support services, 6% liberal arts and sciences studies, and humanities, 5% family and consumer sciences/human sciences, 5% multi/interdisciplinary studies. **Major fields of study:** biological and biomedical sciences; business, management, marketing, and related support services; communication, journalism, and related programs; communications technologies/technicians and support services; computer and information sciences and support services; education; engineering technologies/technicians; English language and literature/letters; family and consumer sciences/human sciences; foreign languages, literatures, and linguistics; health professions and related clinical sciences; history; liberal arts and sciences studies, and humanities; mathematics and statistics; multi/interdisciplinary studies; parks, recreation, leisure, and fitness studies; philosophy and religious studies; physical sciences; psychology; public administration and social service professions; security and protective services; social sciences; visual and performing arts. **Areas of required coursework:** arts/fine arts, humanities, computer literacy, mathematics, English (including composition), sciences (biological or physical), history, social science. **Pre-professional programs:** pre-law, pre-dentistry, pre-medicine, pre-veterinary science, pre-optometry, pre-pharmacy, other. **Special academic programs:** cooperative (work-study plan) program, distance learning, double major, dual enrollment, English as a Second Language (ESL), exchange student program (domestic), external degree program, honors program, independent study, internships, student-designed major, study abroad, teacher certificate program. **Teacher certification offered in:** early childhood, special education, elementary, middle/junior high, secondary. **Cooperative education programs:** art, business, computer science, education, health professions, home economics, humanities, natural science, social/behavioral science, technologies, other. **Reserve Officers Training Corps (ROTC):** Army ROTC: Offered on campus. **Faculty and instruction (2009-2010):** Total instructional faculty: 532 full-time, 309 part-time (55% men; 45% women; 7% minorities). Full-time faculty with Ph.D. or other terminal degree: 75%. Student/faculty ratio: 19/1. Classes of fewer than 20 students: 47%; of 20 to 49 students: 47%; of 50 or more students: 6%. **Advanced Placement and International Baccalaureate credit:** AP tests may be used for: Credit only. Scores accepted: 3, 4, 5. International Baccalaureate exams may be used for: Credit only. **Freshmen returning for sophomore year:** 69%. **Graduation rates:** Four-year: 19%; five-year: 36%; six-year: 43%.

COSTS AND FINANCIAL AID

Financial aid office: (423) 439-4300. **Expenses (2010-2011):** Tuition and fees 2010-2011: $6,884 in state, $19,808 out of state; room/board: $7,568. Estimated books and supplies: $1,090. **Financial aid:** Priority filing date for institution's financial aid form: April 15.

CAMPUS LIFE AND EXTRACURRICULAR ACTIVITIES

Campus housing available: coed dorms, women's dorms, men's dorms, fraternity housing, apartments for married students, apartment for single students, special housing for disabled students, special housing for international students. Students who live in college-owned, operated, or affiliated housing: 20%. **Clubs and organizations:** Number of student organizations: 200. Activities include: campus ministries, choral groups, concert band, drama/theater, international student organization, jazz band, literary magazine, music ensembles, pep band, radio station, student government, student newspaper, television station. Number of fraternities: 8; sororities: 8. Proportion of men in fraternities: 5%; of women in sororities: 5%. Average proportion of students who stay on campus on weekends: 10%. **Sports program (2009-2010):** Member of NCAA I. *Men's intercollegiate varsity sports:* baseball, basketball, cross country, golf, soccer, tennis, track and field (indoor), track and field (outdoor). *Women's intercollegiate varsity sports:* basketball, cross country, golf, soccer, softball, tennis, track and field (indoor), track and field (outdoor), volleyball.

SERVICES AND FACILITIES

Basic services: nonremedial tutoring, women's center, placement service, day care, health service, health insurance. **Counseling services:** minority student, career, military, personal, veteran student, academic, older student, psychological, birth control, religious. **For learning-disabled students:** School does not offer a structured program with separate admission and additional fees. Services include: untimed tests, note-taking services, oral tests, learning center, tutors. **Library:** Number of titles: 921,302; number of current serial subscriptions: 19,910. **Information technology resources:** Students are not required to lease or own a computer. Number of campus computers available to all students: 1,400. School has a wireless network. Approximate number of users that can be accommodated: 3,000. Proportion of college-owned housing units wired for high-speed internet access: 100%. **Campus safety:** Security services offered: 24-hour foot-and-vehicle patrols, late-night transport/escort service, 24-hour emergency telephones, lighted pathways/sidewalks, controlled dormitory access (key, security card, etc).

TRANSFER AND INTERNATIONAL STUDENTS
Transfer students: May apply for admission for the following academic terms: Fall, Spring, Summer. Applicants need a minimum number of credits to apply. For fall 2009: Transfer applications received: 2,184. Transfer applicants offered admission: 1,586. Transfer applicants enrolled: 1,173. **International students:** Number of foreign undergraduates: 136 (1% of student body). Number of countries represented: 60. Minimum TOEFL score required: 500 (paper); 173 (computer). Average TOEFL score: 545 (paper).

Fisk University

- **Address:** 1000 17th Avenue N, Nashville, TN 37208-3051
- **Website:** http://www.fisk.edu
- **Private**
- **Enrollment:** 558 full-time; 28 part-time

KEY STATS

✔ **U.S News College Ranking:** 122, National Liberal Arts Colleges
✔ **ACT Score (25th/75th percentile):** 18-22
✔ **Tuition:** 2010-2011: $18,358

Selectivity: Selective	**Room/board:** $8,586
Acceptance rate: 48%	**Average debt:** $27,345
Student/faculty ratio: 10/1	**Proportion who borrowed:** 77%

UNDERGRADUATE STUDENT BODY STATS

2009-2010 enrollment: 558 full-time; 28 part-time. Men: 34%; women: 66%. **Ethnic makeup:** African American: 85%; Asian American: 1%; White: 2%; International: 12%.

ADMISSIONS FACTS AND FIGURES

Phone: (888) 702-0022. **Email:** admissions@fisk.edu. **Website:** http://www.fisk.edu. **Application deadlines for fall 2011:** Regular decision: June 1. Early decision: Not offered. Early action: Not offered. Admission can be deferred. **Application fee:** $50. **To apply online, go to:** http://www.fisk.edu/admissions/apply.html. **Admissions requirements/recommendations:** High school units required (recommended): English: (4); Mathematics: (3); Science: (1); Foreign language: (1); Social studies: (3); History: (1); Academic electives: (6); Total units: (20). Tests: The college uses SAT or ACT scores in admissions decisions. Either SAT or ACT required. For admission to the fall 2011 entering class, the school will accept: ACT with or without writing accepted. Campus visit: Neither required nor recommended. Admissions interview: Recommended. Off-campus interview: May be arranged. **Factors that count in admissions decisions:** *Academic:* Secondary school record: Very Important. Class rank: Very Important. Letters of recommendation: Important. Standardized test scores: Important. Essay: Important. *Nonacademic:* Interview: Important. Talent/ability: Important. Character/personal qualities: Important. State residency: Not Considered. Religious affiliation/commitment: Not Considered. Minority status: Not Considered. **Other schools with the greatest overlap in applicants:** Clark Atlanta University; Hampton University; Howard University; Morehouse College; Spelman College. **Admissions statistics for the fall 2009 entering class:** Total applicants: 694. Total accepted: 336. Freshmen enrolled: 92; 72% were from out of state. Overall acceptance rate: 48%. **Credentials of fall 2009 freshmen:** 25% ranked in the top 10 percent of their high school class; 39% were in the top 25 percent; 70% were in the top half. (Proportion submitting class standing: 59%.) **Average high school grade point average:** 3.0. **First-year students who submitted SAT scores:** 34%. Scores (25/75 percentile): Critical Reading: 400-520, Math: 380-510, Combined: 780-1030. **First-year students submitting ACT scores:** 69%. Scores (25/75 percentile): English: 16-23, Math: 17-22, Composite: 18-22.

ACADEMICS

Year founded: 1866. **Academic calendar:** Semester. **Degrees offered:** bachelor's, master's. **Major fields of study:** biological and biomedical sciences; business, management, marketing, and related support services; computer and information sciences and support services; education; English language and literature/letters; foreign languages, literatures, and linguistics; history; philosophy and religious studies; physical sciences; psychology; social sciences; visual and performing arts. **Areas of required coursework:** arts/fine arts, humanities, computer literacy, mathematics, English (including composition), philosophy, foreign languages, sciences (biological or physical), history, social science. **Pre-professional programs:** pre-law, pre-dentistry, pre-medicine, pre-pharmacy. **Special academic programs (% par-**

ticipation):** cross-registration (2%), double major (10%), exchange student program (domestic) (3%), honors program (6%), independent study (1%), internships (7%), student-designed major (1%), study abroad (3%), teacher certificate program (4%). **Teacher certification offered in:** special education, elementary, secondary. **Cooperative education programs:** art, business, engineering, health professions, natural science. **Reserve Officers Training Corps (ROTC):** Army ROTC: Offered at cooperating institution (Vanderbilt University); Navy ROTC: Offered at cooperating institution (Vanderbilt University); Air Force ROTC: Offered at cooperating institution (Tennessee State University). **Faculty and instruction (2009-2010):** Total instructional faculty: 55 full-time, 17 part-time (51% men; 49% women; 71% minorities). Full-time faculty with Ph.D. or other terminal degree: 80%. Student/faculty ratio: 10/1. Classes of fewer than 20 students: 79%; of 20 to 49 students: 21%; of 50 or more students: 0%. **Advanced Placement and International Baccalaureate credit:** AP tests may be used for: Placement only. Scores accepted: 4, 5. **Freshmen returning for sophomore year:** 77%. **Graduation rates:** Four-year: 49%; five-year: 56%; six-year: 57%. **Graduate study:** 28% of students pursue further study immediately upon graduation; 40% within one year; 45% within five years. Fields in which graduates pursue further study: Master of Business Administration (MBA), 12%; law, 9%; medicine, 14%; dentistry, 3%; engineering, 2%; theology (or the seminary), 5%; education, 5%; arts and sciences, 50%.

COSTS AND FINANCIAL AID

Financial aid office: (615) 329-8585. **Expenses (2010-2011):** Tuition and fees 2010-2011: $18,358; room/board: $8,586. Estimated books and supplies: $2,000; transportation: $2,000; personal expenses: $2,000. **Financial aid:** Priority filing date for institution's financial aid form: March 1; deadline: June 1. In 2009-2010, 95% of undergraduates applied for financial aid. Of those, 95% were determined to have financial need; 27% had their need fully met. Average financial aid package (proportion receiving): $14,957 (95%). Average amount of gift aid, such as scholarships or grants (proportion receiving): $12,028 (88%). Average amount of self-help aid, such as work study or loans (proportion receiving): $4,953 (65%). Average need-based loan (excluding PLUS or other private loans): $4,387. Among students who received need-based aid, the average percentage of need met: 71%. Among students who received aid based on merit, the average award (and the proportion receiving): $0 (0%). The average athletic scholarship (and the proportion receiving): $0 (0%). Average amount of debt of borrowers graduating in 2009: $27,345. Proportion who borrowed: 77%.

CAMPUS LIFE AND EXTRACURRICULAR ACTIVITIES

Campus housing available (% using): coed dorms (24%), women's dorms (60%), men's dorms (16%). Students who live in college-owned, operated, or affiliated housing: 63%. **Student employment:** During the 2009-2010 academic year, 15% of undergraduates worked on campus. Average per-year earnings: $2,700. **Clubs and organizations:** Number of student organizations: 85. Activities include: choral groups, dance, drama/theater, jazz band, literary magazine, music ensembles, radio station, student government, yearbook. Number of fraternities: 4; sororities: 4. Proportion of men in fraternities: 5%; of women in sororities: 10%. Average proportion of students who stay on campus on weekends: 90%. **Sports program (2009-2010):** Member of NCAA III.

SERVICES AND FACILITIES

Basic services: nonremedial tutoring, health insurance. **Remedial assistance:** reading, math, writing, study skills. **Counseling services:** personal, academic, psychological, religious. **For learning-disabled students:** School does not offer a structured program with separate admission and additional fees. Services include: untimed tests, oral tests, learning center, readers, extended time for tests, tutors. **Library:** Number of titles: 214,674; number of current serial subscriptions: 30,000. **Information technology resources:** Students are not required to lease or own a computer. Number of campus computers available to all students: 165. School has a wireless network. Approximate number of users that can be accommodated: 400. Proportion of college-owned housing units wired for high-speed internet access: 100%. **Campus safety:** Security services offered: 24-hour foot-and-vehicle patrols, late-night transport/escort service, 24-hour emergency telephones, lighted pathways/sidewalks, controlled dormitory access (key, security card, etc).

TRANSFER AND INTERNATIONAL STUDENTS

Transfer students: May apply for admission for the following academic terms: Fall, Spring, Summer. Applicants do not need a minimum number of credits to apply. For fall 2009: Transfer applications received: 37. Transfer applicants offered admission: 24. Transfer applicants enrolled: 22. **International students:** Number of foreign undergraduates: 69 (12% of student body). Number of countries represented: 6. Minimum TOEFL score required: 225 (paper); 250 (computer).

Freed-Hardeman University

- **Address:** 158 E. Main Street, Henderson, TN 38340-2399
- **Website:** http://www.fhu.edu
- **Private; Religious affiliation:** Church of Christ
- **Enrollment:** 1,404 full-time; 92 part-time

KEY STATS

✔ **U.S News College Ranking:** 39, Regional Universities (South)
✔ **ACT Score (25th/75th percentile):** 20-26
✔ **Tuition:** 2010-2011: $15,922

Selectivity: Selective	**Room/board:** $7,216
Acceptance rate: 99%	**Average debt:** $33,659
Student/faculty ratio: 15/1	**Proportion who borrowed:** 67%

UNDERGRADUATE STUDENT BODY STATS

2009-2010 enrollment: 1,404 full-time; 92 part-time. Men: 44%; women: 56%. **Ethnic makeup:** African American: 5%; White: 90%; International: 3%. **Religious preference:** Roman Catholic: 1%; Protestant: 9%; No preference: 1%; Unknown: 2%; Church of Christ: 87%.

ADMISSIONS FACTS AND FIGURES

Phone: (800) 630-3480. **Email:** admissions@fhu.edu. **Website:** http://www.fhu.edu. **Application deadlines for fall 2011:** Regular decision: Rolling. Early decision: Not offered. Early action: Not offered. Admission can be deferred. **To apply online, go to:** http://www.fhu.edu/admissions/apply. **Admissions requirements/recommendations:** High school units required (recommended): English: (4); Mathematics: (2); Science: (2); Social studies: (2); Academic electives: (10); Total units: (20). Tests: The college uses SAT or ACT scores in admissions decisions. Either SAT or ACT required. For admission to the fall 2011 entering class, the school will accept: ACT with or without writing accepted. Campus visit: Recommended. Admissions interview: Neither required nor recommended. Off-campus interview: Not available. **Factors that count in admissions decisions:** *Academic:* Secondary school record: Very Important. Class rank: Not Considered. Letters of recommendation: Considered. Standardized test scores: Very Important. Essay: Not Considered. *Nonacademic:* Interview: Not Considered. Extracurricular activities: Considered. Talent/ability: Not Considered. Character/personal qualities: Considered. Alumni/ae relationship: Considered. Geographical residence: Not Considered. State residency: Not Considered. Religious affiliation/commitment: Considered. Minority status: Considered. Volunteer work: Considered. Work experience: Considered. **Other schools with the greatest overlap in applicants:** Harding University; Lipscomb University; Middle Tennessee State University; University of Tennessee–Martin. **Admissions statistics for the fall 2009 entering class:** Total applicants: 959. Total accepted: 954. Freshmen enrolled: 408; 43% were from out of state. Overall acceptance rate: 99%. **Credentials of fall 2009 freshmen:** 28% ranked in the top 10 percent of their high school class; 53% were in the top 25 percent; 78% were in the top half. (Proportion submitting class standing: 51%.) **Average high school grade point average:** 3.5. **First-year students who submitted SAT scores:** 10%. Scores (25/75 percentile): Critical Reading: 490-605, Math: 465-590, Combined: 955-1195. **First-year students submitting ACT scores:** 90%. Scores (25/75 percentile): English: 21-28, Math: 19-25, Composite: 20-26.

ACADEMICS

Year founded: 1869. **Academic calendar:** Semester. **Degrees offered:** associate, bachelor's, master's, post-master's certificate. **Most popular majors:** 14% education, 13% business, management, marketing, and related support services, 11% theology and religious vocations, 10% multi/interdisciplinary studies, 10% visual and performing arts. **Major fields of study:** biological and biomedical sciences; business, management, marketing, and related support services; communication, journalism, and related programs; computer and information sciences and support services; education; English language and literature/letters; family and consumer sciences/human sciences; health professions and related clinical sciences; history; mathematics and statistics; multi/interdisciplinary studies; parks, recreation, leisure, and fitness studies; philosophy and religious studies; physical sciences; psychology; public administration and social service professions; theology and religious vocations; visual and performing arts. **Areas of required coursework:**

arts/fine arts, humanities, computer literacy, mathematics, English (including composition), sciences (biological or physical), history, social science. **Special academic programs (% participation):** accelerated program, cross-registration, distance learning, double major (18%), dual enrollment (3%), honors program (8%), independent study, internships, liberal arts/career combination, student-designed major (2%), study abroad (2%), teacher certificate program (13%). **Teacher certification offered in:** early childhood, special education, elementary, middle/junior high, secondary. **Cooperative education programs:** engineering. **Faculty and instruction (2009-2010):** Total instructional faculty: 99 full-time, 47 part-time (68% men; 32% women; 6% minorities). Full-time faculty with Ph.D. or other terminal degree: 70%. Student/faculty ratio: 15/1. Classes of fewer than 20 students: 52%; of 20 to 49 students: 43%; of 50 or more students: 5%. **Advanced Placement and International Baccalaureate credit:** AP tests may be used for: Credit only. Scores accepted: 3, 4, 5. International Baccalaureate exams may be used for: Credit only. **Freshmen returning for sophomore year:** 73%. **Graduation rates:** Four-year: 41%; five-year: 57%; six-year: 55%. **Graduate study:** 27% of students pursue further study immediately upon graduation; 36% within one year; 46% within five years. Fields in which graduates pursue further study: Master of Business Administration (MBA), 10%; law, 3%; medicine, 5%; dentistry, 2%; theology (or the seminary), 30%; education, 30%; arts and sciences, 15%.

COSTS AND FINANCIAL AID

Financial aid office: (731) 989-6662. **Expenses (2010-2011):** Tuition and fees 2010-2011: $15,922; room/board: $7,216. Estimated books and supplies: $1,000; transportation: $1,700; personal expenses: $2,200. **Financial aid:** Priority filing date for institution's financial aid form: February 1. In 2009-2010, 94% of undergraduates applied for financial aid. Of those, 80% were determined to have financial need; 22% had their need fully met. Average financial aid package (proportion receiving): $13,942 (79%). Average amount of gift aid, such as scholarships or grants (proportion receiving): $10,139 (75%). Average amount of self-help aid, such as work study or loans (proportion receiving): $5,315 (63%). Average need-based loan (excluding PLUS or other private loans): $4,188. Among students who received need-based aid, the average percentage of need met: 66%. Among students who received aid based on merit, the average award (and the proportion receiving): $6,191 (17%). The average athletic scholarship (and the proportion receiving): $7,830 (5%). Average amount of debt of borrowers graduating in 2009: $33,659. Proportion who borrowed: 67%.

CAMPUS LIFE AND EXTRACURRICULAR ACTIVITIES

Campus housing available (% using): women's dorms (44%), men's dorms (39%), apartment for single students (16%), special housing for international students (1%). Students who live in college-owned, operated, or affiliated housing: 76%. **Student employment:** During the 2009-2010 academic year, 33% of undergraduates worked on campus. Average per-year earnings: $1,000. **Clubs and organizations:** Number of student organizations: 53. Activities include: campus ministries, choral groups, concert band, drama/theater, music ensembles, musical theater, pep band, radio station, student government, student newspaper, television station, yearbook. Number of fraternities: 6; sororities: 6. Average proportion of students who stay on campus on weekends: 66%. **Sports program (2009-2010):** Member of NAIA. **Men's intercollegiate varsity sports:** baseball, basketball, cross country, soccer. **Women's intercollegiate varsity sports:** basketball, cross country, soccer, softball, volleyball.

SERVICES AND FACILITIES

Basic services: placement service, day care, health service, health insurance. **Remedial assistance:** reading, math, writing, study skills. **Counseling services:** minority student, career, personal, academic, psychological, religious. **For learning-disabled students:** School does not offer a structured program with separate admission and additional fees. Services include: remedial math, remedial English, remedial reading, oral tests, extended time for tests, tutors, priority seating. **Library:** Number of titles: 147,821; number of current serial subscriptions: 33,319. **Information technology resources:** Students are not required to lease or own a computer. Number of campus computers available to all students: 240. School has a wireless network. Proportion of college-owned housing units wired for high-speed internet access: 100%. **Campus safety:** Security services offered: 24-hour foot-and-vehicle patrols, lighted pathways/sidewalks, controlled dormitory access (key, security card, etc).

TRANSFER AND INTERNATIONAL STUDENTS

Transfer students: May apply for admission for the following academic terms: Fall, Spring, Summer. Applicants need a minimum number of credits to apply. For fall 2009: Transfer applications received: 145. Transfer applicants offered admission: 142. Transfer applicants enrolled: 95. **International students:** Number of foreign undergraduates: 46 (3% of student body). Number of countries represented: 23. Minimum TOEFL score required: 500 (paper); 173 (computer).

Free Will Baptist Bible College

- **Address:** 3606 W. End Avenue, Nashville, TN 37205-2498
- **Website:** http://www.fwbbc.edu/
- **Private; Religious affiliation:** Free Will Baptist
- **Enrollment:** 229 full-time; 74 part-time

KEY STATS
✔ **U.S News College Ranking:** 54, Regional Colleges (South)
✔ **ACT Score (25th/75th percentile):** 17-27
✔ **Tuition:** 2010-2011: $14,306

Selectivity: Selective	**Room/board:** $6,042
Acceptance rate: 97%	**Average debt:** $18,911
Student/faculty ratio: 9/1	**Proportion who borrowed:** 78%

UNDERGRADUATE STUDENT BODY STATS
2009-2010 enrollment: 229 full-time; 74 part-time. Men: 55%; women: 45%. **Ethnic makeup:** African American: 9%; Hispanic: 1%; White: 87%; International: 2%. **Religious preference:** Protestant: 19%; Free Will Baptist: 81%.

ADMISSIONS FACTS AND FIGURES
Phone: (800) 763-9222. **Email:** Recruit@fwbbc.edu. **Website:** http://www.fwbbc.edu/. **Application deadlines for fall 2011:** Regular decision: Rolling. Early decision: Not offered. Early action: Not offered. Admission can be deferred. **Application fee:** $35. **To apply online, go to:** http://fwbbc.edu/application/index.cgi. **Admissions requirements/recommendations:** High school units required (recommended): English: (4); Mathematics: (4); Science: (4); Foreign language: (3); Social studies: (3); History: (2); Academic electives: (2); Total units: (22). Tests: The college uses SAT or ACT scores in admissions decisions. Either SAT or ACT required. For admission to the fall 2011 entering class, the school will accept: ACT with or without writing accepted. Campus visit: Recommended. Admissions interview: Neither required nor recommended. **Factors that count in admissions decisions:** *Academic:* Secondary school record: Considered. Class rank: Considered. Letters of recommendation: Considered. Standardized test scores: Considered. Essay: Considered. *Nonacademic:* Interview: Considered. Extracurricular activities: Considered. Talent/ability: Considered. Character/personal qualities: Considered. Alumni/ae relationship: Considered. Geographical residence: Not Considered. State residency: Not Considered. Religious affiliation/commitment: Considered. Minority status: Not Considered. Volunteer work: Considered. Work experience: Considered. **Other schools with the greatest overlap in applicants:** Lee University, Liberty University. **Admissions statistics for the fall 2009 entering class:** Total applicants: 208. Total accepted: 201. Freshmen enrolled: 61; 63% were from out of state. Overall acceptance rate: 97%. **Credentials of fall 2009 freshmen:** 24% ranked in the top 10 percent of their high school class; 35% were in the top 25 percent; 65% were in the top half. (Proportion submitting class standing: 41%.) **Average high school grade point average:** 3.2. **First-year students submitting ACT scores:** 67%. Scores (25/75 percentile): English: 16-27, Math: 17-24, Composite: 17-27.

ACADEMICS
Year founded: 1942. **Academic calendar:** Semester. **Degrees offered:** certificate, associate, bachelor's. **Most popular majors:** 19% Bible/biblical studies, 16% business administration and management, 9% English language and literature, 9% early childhood education and teaching, 9% elementary education and teaching. **Major fields of study:** business, management, marketing, and related support services; education; English language and literature/letters; history; parks, recreation, leisure, and fitness studies; psychology; theology and religious vocations; visual and performing arts. **Areas of required coursework:** arts/fine arts, humanities, computer literacy, mathematics, English (including composition), philosophy, foreign languages, sciences (biological or physical), history, social science, other. **Special academic programs (% participation):** distance learning (7%), double major (44%), independent study (22%), internships (9%), teacher certificate program (18%). **Teacher certification offered in:** early childhood, elementary, middle/

junior high, secondary. **Reserve Officers Training Corps (ROTC):** Army ROTC: Offered at cooperating institution (Vanderbilt University); Air Force ROTC: Offered at cooperating institution (Tennessee State University). **Faculty and instruction (2009-2010):** Total instructional faculty: 20 full-time, 28 part-time (73% men; 27% women; 4% minorities). Full-time faculty with Ph.D. or other terminal degree: 40%. Student/faculty ratio: 9/1. Classes of fewer than 20 students: 88%; of 20 to 49 students: 9%; of 50 or more students: 3%. **Advanced Placement and International Baccalaureate credit:** International Baccalaureate exams may be used for: Credit only. **Freshmen returning for sophomore year:** 65%. **Graduation rates:** Four-year: 29%; five-year: 44%; six-year: 49%. **Graduate study:** 10% of students pursue further study immediately upon graduation. Fields in which graduates pursue further study: theology (or the seminary), 50%; education, 50%.

COSTS AND FINANCIAL AID
Financial aid office: (615) 844-5250. **Expenses (2010-2011):** Tuition and fees 2010-2011: $14,306; room/board: $6,042. Estimated books and supplies: $800; transportation: $3,525; personal expenses: $1,300. **Financial aid:** Priority filing date for institution's financial aid form: April 15. In 2009-2010, 90% of undergraduates applied for financial aid. Of those, 40% were determined to have financial need; Average financial aid package (proportion receiving): $9,377 (39%). Average amount of gift aid, such as scholarships or grants (proportion receiving): $4,516 (12%). Average amount of self-help aid, such as work study or loans (proportion receiving): $4,729 (36%). Average need-based loan (excluding PLUS or other private loans): $4,467. Among students who received need-based aid, the average percentage of need met: 49%. Among students who received aid based on merit, the average award (and the proportion receiving): $3,263 (61%). The average athletic scholarship (and the proportion receiving): $0 (0%). Average amount of debt of borrowers graduating in 2009: $18,911. Proportion who borrowed: 78%.

CAMPUS LIFE AND EXTRACURRICULAR ACTIVITIES
Campus housing available (% using): women's dorms (50%), men's dorms (47%), apartments for married students (3%). Students who live in college-owned, operated, or affiliated housing: 60%. **Clubs and organizations:** Number of student organizations: 17. Activities include: campus ministries, choral groups, drama/theater, music ensembles, student government, yearbook. Number of fraternities: 4; sororities: 4. Proportion of men in fraternities: 97%; of women in sororities: 98%. Average proportion of students who stay on campus on weekends: 70%.

SERVICES AND FACILITIES
Basic services: nonremedial tutoring, health service, health insurance. **Remedial assistance:** math. **Counseling services:** career, personal, veteran student, academic, psychological, religious. **For learning-disabled students:** School does not offer a structured program with separate admission and additional fees. Services include: remedial math, untimed tests, note-taking services, oral tests, extended time for tests, tutors, priority seating, other testing accommodations. **Library:** Number of titles: 85,787; number of current serial subscriptions: 397. **Information technology resources:** Students are not required to lease or own a computer. Number of campus computers available to all students: 41. School has a wireless network. Approximate number of users that can be accommodated: 300. **Campus safety:** Security services offered: 24-hour emergency telephones, lighted pathways/sidewalks, student patrols, controlled dormitory access (key, security card, etc).

TRANSFER AND INTERNATIONAL STUDENTS
Transfer students: May apply for admission for the following academic terms: Fall, Spring, Summer. Applicants do not need a minimum number of credits to apply. For fall 2009: Transfer applications received: 47. Transfer applicants offered admission: 47. Transfer applicants enrolled: 21. **International students:** Number of foreign undergraduates: 6 (2% of student body). Minimum TOEFL score required: 550 (paper).

King College

- **Address:** 1350 King College Road, Bristol, TN 37620
- **Website:** http://www.king.edu
- **Private; Religious affiliation:** Presbyterian
- **Enrollment:** 1,342 full-time; 177 part-time

KEY STATS

✔ **U.S News College Ranking:** 19, Regional Colleges (South)
✔ **ACT Score (25th/75th percentile):** 20-25
✔ **Tuition:** 2010-2011: $22,908

Selectivity: Selective	**Room/board:** $7,790
Acceptance rate: 62%	**Average debt:** $15,756
Student/faculty ratio: 14/1	**Proportion who borrowed:** 96%

UNDERGRADUATE STUDENT BODY STATS

2009-2010 enrollment: 1,342 full-time; 177 part-time. Men: 36%; women: 64%. **Ethnic makeup:** African American: 3%; American-Indian: 1%; Hispanic: 2%; White: 92%; International: 2%. **Religious preference:** Roman Catholic: 3%; Protestant: 61%; Jewish: 1%; No preference: 2%; Presbyterian: 5%; Not specified: 27%; Other: 1%.

ADMISSIONS FACTS AND FIGURES

Phone: (423) 652-4861. **Email:** admissions@king.edu. **Website:** http://www.king.edu. **Application deadlines for fall 2011:** Regular decision: Rolling. Early decision: Not offered. Early action: Not offered. Admission can be deferred. **Application fee:** $20. **To apply online, go to:** http://apply.king.edu. **Admissions requirements/recommendations:** High school units required (recommended): English: 4 (4); Mathematics: 3 (4); Science: 1 (2); Foreign language: 2 (2); Social studies: 1 (1); History: 1 (1); Academic electives: 4 (4); Total units: 16 (25). Tests: The college uses SAT or ACT scores in admissions decisions. Either SAT or ACT required. For admission to the fall 2011 entering class, the school will accept: ACT with or without writing accepted. Campus visit: Recommended. Admissions interview: Recommended. Off-campus interview: May be arranged. **Factors that count in admissions decisions:** *Academic:* Secondary school record: Considered. Class rank: Considered. Letters of recommendation: Considered. Standardized test scores: Very Important. Essay: Important. *Nonacademic:* Interview: Considered. Extracurricular activities: Considered. Talent/ability: Not Considered. Character/personal qualities: Not Considered. Alumni/ae relationship: Not Considered. Geographical residence: Not Considered. State residency: Not Considered. Religious affiliation/commitment: Not Considered. Minority status: Not Considered. Volunteer work: Not Considered. Work experience: Not Considered. **Other schools with the greatest overlap in applicants:** Carson-Newman College; East Tennessee State University; Lee University; Milligan College; Tusculum College.
Admissions statistics for the fall 2009 entering class: Total applicants: 935. Total accepted: 576. Freshmen enrolled: 207; 41% were from out of state. Overall acceptance rate: 62%. **Size of waiting list:** 0 applicants; enrolled from waiting list: 0. **Credentials of fall 2009 freshmen:** 19% ranked in the top 10 percent of their high school class; 42% were in the top 25 percent; 78% were in the top half. (Proportion submitting class standing: 67%.) **Average high school grade point average:** 3.3. **First-year students who submitted SAT scores:** 40%. Scores (25/75 percentile): Critical Reading: 430-560, Math: 430-570, Combined: 860-1130. **First-year students submitting ACT scores:** 77%. Scores (25/75 percentile): English: 19-25, Math: 18-25, Composite: 20-25.

ACADEMICS

Year founded: 1867. **Academic calendar:** Semester. **Degrees offered:** bachelor's, post-bachelor's certificate, master's, post-master's certificate. **Most popular majors:** 45% nursing/registered nurse training (R.N., A.S.N., B.S.N., M.S.N.), 29% business administration and management, 3% biology/biological sciences, 3% elementary education and teaching, 2% psychology. **Major fields of study:** biological and biomedical sciences; business, management, marketing, and related support services; communication, journalism, and related programs; education; engineering; English language and literature/letters; foreign languages, literatures, and linguistics; health professions and related clinical sciences; history; mathematics and statistics; multi/interdisciplinary studies; physical sciences; psychology; security and protective services; social sciences; theology and religious vocations; visual and performing arts. **Areas of required coursework:** arts/fine arts, mathematics, English (including composition), foreign languages, sciences (biological or physical), history, social science. **Pre-professional programs:** pre-law, pre-

dentistry, pre-medicine, pre-theology, pre-veterinary science, pre-pharmacy, other. **Special academic programs (% participation):** accelerated program (2%), cross-registration (1.1%), double major (2.4%), dual enrollment (1.1%), exchange student program (domestic) (0%), honors program (3.1%), independent study (11.2%), internships (9.4%), student-designed major (.4%), study abroad (1%), teacher certificate program (2.6%). **Teacher certification offered in:** special education, elementary, middle/junior high, secondary. **Reserve Officers Training Corps (ROTC):** Army ROTC: Offered at cooperating institution (East Tennessee State University). **Faculty and instruction (2009-2010):** Total instructional faculty: 81 full-time, 71 part-time (44% men; 56% women; 3% minorities). Full-time faculty with Ph.D. or other terminal degree: 74%. Student/faculty ratio: 14/1. Classes of fewer than 20 students: 62%; of 20 to 49 students: 35%; of 50 or more students: 3%. **Advanced Placement and International Baccalaureate credit:** AP tests may be used for: Credit and/or placement. Scores accepted: 4, 5. International Baccalaureate exams may be used for: Credit only. **Freshmen returning for sophomore year:** 70%. **Graduation rates:** Four-year: 49%; five-year: 52%; six-year: 53%. **Graduate study:** 30% of students pursue further study immediately upon graduation. Fields in which graduates pursue further study: Master of Business Administration (MBA), 42%; law, 3%; medicine, 5%; theology (or the seminary), 5%; education, 5%; arts and sciences, 39%.

COSTS AND FINANCIAL AID

Financial aid office: (423) 652-4725. **Expenses (2010-2011):** Tuition and fees 2010-2011: $22,908; room/board: $7,790. Estimated books and supplies: $1,200; transportation: $1,030; personal expenses: $2,000. **Financial aid:** Priority filing date for institution's financial aid form: March 1. In 2009-2010, 86% of undergraduates applied for financial aid. Of those, 76% were determined to have financial need; 15% had their need fully met. Average financial aid package (proportion receiving): $16,736 (75%). Average amount of gift aid, such as scholarships or grants (proportion receiving): $14,125 (63%). Average amount of self-help aid, such as work study or loans (proportion receiving): $4,773 (58%). Average need-based loan (excluding PLUS or other private loans): $4,773. Among students who received need-based aid, the average percentage of need met: 69%. Among students who received aid based on merit, the average award (and the proportion receiving): $8,610 (7%). The average athletic scholarship (and the proportion receiving): $6,999 (7%). Average amount of debt of borrowers graduating in 2009: $15,756. Proportion who borrowed: 96%.

CAMPUS LIFE AND EXTRACURRICULAR ACTIVITIES

Campus housing available (% using): women's dorms (53%), men's dorms (47%). Students who live in college-owned, operated, or affiliated housing: 27%. **Student employment:** During the 2009-2010 academic year, 22% of undergraduates worked on campus. Average per-year earnings: $1,572. **Clubs and organizations:** Number of student organizations: 40. Activities include: campus ministries, choral groups, concert band, dance, drama/theater, international student organization, music ensembles, pep band, student government, student newspaper, symphony orchestra, yearbook. Number of fraternities: 0; sororities: 0. Average proportion of students who stay on campus on weekends: 60%. **Sports program (2009-2010):** Member of NCAA II. *Men's intercollegiate varsity sports:* baseball, basketball, cross country, golf, soccer, swimming, tennis, track and field (indoor), track and field (outdoor), volleyball, wrestling. *Women's intercollegiate varsity sports:* basketball, cross country, golf, soccer, softball, swimming, tennis, track and field (indoor), track and field (outdoor), volleyball.

SERVICES AND FACILITIES

Basic services: nonremedial tutoring, placement service, health insurance. **Remedial assistance:** reading, math, writing, study skills. **Counseling services:** minority student, career, personal, academic, older student, psychological, religious. **For learning-disabled students:** School does not offer a structured program with separate admission and additional fees. Total undergraduates in learning-disabled program or receiving services: 10. Services include: remedial math, remedial English, reading machines, remedial reading, tape recorders, other special classes, untimed tests, oral tests, learning center, extended time for tests, tutors, priority seating, other. **Library:** Number of titles: 117,607; number of current serial subscriptions: 477. **Information technology resources:** Students are required to lease or own a computer. Number of campus computers available to all students: 130. School has a wireless network. Approximate number of users that can be accommodated: 500. Proportion of college-owned housing units wired for high-speed internet access: 100%. **Campus safety:** Security services offered: 24-hour foot-and-vehicle patrols, late-night transport/escort service, 24-hour emergency telephones, lighted pathways/sidewalks, controlled dormitory access (key, security card, etc).

TRANSFER AND INTERNATIONAL STUDENTS

Transfer students: May apply for admission for the following academic terms: Fall, Spring, Summer. Applicants need a minimum number of credits to apply. For fall 2009: Transfer applications received: 319. Transfer applicants offered admission: 204. Transfer applicants enrolled: 93. **International students:** Number of foreign undergraduates: 33 (2% of student body). Number of countries represented: 42. Minimum TOEFL score required: 563 (paper); 223 (computer).

Lambuth University

- **Address:** 705 Lambuth Boulevard, Jackson, TN 38301
- **Website:** http://www.lambuth.edu
- **Private; Religious affiliation:** United Methodist
- **Enrollment:** N/A

KEY STATS

✔ **U.S News College Ranking:** second tier, National Liberal Arts Colleges
✔ **ACT Score (25th/75th percentile):** 20-25
✔ **Tuition:** 2009-2010: $18,570

Selectivity: Selective	**Room/board:** $8,015
Acceptance rate: 62%	**Average debt:** N/A
Student/faculty ratio: N/A	**Proportion who borrowed:** N/A

Lane College

- **Address:** 545 Lane Avenue, Jackson, TN 38301-4598
- **Website:** http://www.lanecollege.edu
- **Private; Religious affiliation:** Christian Methodist Episcopal
- **Enrollment:** 2,121 full-time; 25 part-time

KEY STATS

✔ **U.S News College Ranking:** second tier, National Liberal Arts Colleges
✔ **ACT Score (25th/75th percentile):** 16-19
✔ **Tuition:** 2010-2011: $8,000

Selectivity: Less selective	**Room/board:** $5,630
Acceptance rate: 37%	**Average debt:** $8,769
Student/faculty ratio: N/A	**Proportion who borrowed:** 88%

UNDERGRADUATE STUDENT BODY STATS

2009-2010 enrollment: 2,121 full-time; 25 part-time. Men: 47%; women: 53%. **Ethnic makeup:** African American: 100%. **Religious preference:** Roman Catholic: 3%; Protestant: 2%; Muslim: 2%; No preference: 1%; Unknown: 25%; Christian Methodist Episcopal: 28%; Other: 8%.

ADMISSIONS FACTS AND FIGURES

Phone: (731) 426-7533. **Email:** admissions@lanecollege.edu. **Website:** http://www.lanecollege.edu. **Application deadlines for fall 2011:** Regular decision: August 1. Early decision: Not offered. Early action: Not offered. Admission can be deferred. **Admissions requirements/recommendations:** High school units required (recommended): English: (4); Mathematics: (2); Science: (2); Foreign language: (2); Social studies: (2); Total units: (16). Tests: The college uses SAT or ACT scores in admissions decisions. Either SAT or ACT required. For admission to the fall 2011 entering class, the school will accept: ACT with or without writing accepted. Campus visit: Recommended. Admissions interview: Recommended. Off-campus interview: May be arranged. **Factors that count in admissions decisions:** *Academic:* Secondary school record: Very Important. Class rank: Not Considered. Letters of recommendation: Very Important. Standardized test scores: Important. Essay: Not Considered. *Nonacademic:* Interview: Considered. Extracurricular activities: Not Considered. Talent/ability: Considered. Character/personal qualities: Very Important. Alumni/ae relationship: Not Considered. Geographical residence: Not Considered. State residency: Not Considered. Religious affiliation/commitment: Not Considered. Minority status: Not Considered. Volunteer work: Not Considered. Work experience: Not Considered. **Admissions statistics for the fall 2009 entering class:** Total applicants: 5,619. Total accepted: 2,064. Freshmen enrolled: 692; 36% were from out of state. Overall acceptance rate: 37%. **Credentials of fall 2009 freshmen:** 4% ranked in the top 10 percent of their high school class; 16% were in the top 25 percent; 38% were in the top half. (Proportion submitting class standing: 52%.)

Average high school grade point average: 2.8. **First-year students submitting ACT scores:** 93%. Scores (25/75 percentile): English: 16-18, Math: 15-18, Composite: 16-19.

ACADEMICS

Year founded: 1882. **Academic calendar:** Semester. **Degrees offered:** bachelor's, post-bachelor's certificate. **Most popular majors:** 23% business, management, marketing, and related support services, 15% multi/interdisciplinary studies, 12% security and protective services, 11% biological and biomedical sciences, 9% social sciences. **Major fields of study:** biological and biomedical sciences; business, management, marketing, and related support services; communication, journalism, and related programs; computer and information sciences and support services; education; English language and literature/letters; foreign languages, literatures, and linguistics; history; mathematics and statistics; multi/interdisciplinary studies; philosophy and religious studies; physical sciences; security and protective services; social sciences; visual and performing arts. **Areas of required coursework:** arts/fine arts, humanities, computer literacy, mathematics, English (including composition), foreign languages, sciences (biological or physical), history, social science, other. **Pre-professional programs:** pre-law, pre-dentistry, pre-medicine, pre-theology, pre-veterinary science, pre-optometry, pre-pharmacy, other. **Special academic programs (% participation):** accelerated program (8%), internships (18%), study abroad (1%), teacher certificate program (7%). **Teacher certification offered in:** elementary, middle/junior high, secondary. **Faculty and instruction (2009-2010):** Total instructional faculty: 95 full-time, 4 part-time (72% men; 28% women; 64% minorities). Full-time faculty with Ph.D. or other terminal degree: 62%. Classes of fewer than 20 students: 30%; of 20 to 49 students: 69%; of 50 or more students: 0%. **Advanced Placement and International Baccalaureate credit:** AP tests may be used for: Placement only. International Baccalaureate exams may be used for: Placement only. **Freshmen returning for sophomore year:** 66%. **Graduation rates:** Four-year: 18%; five-year: 28%; six-year: 33%. **Graduate study:** 40% of students pursue further study immediately upon graduation; 52% within one year; 65% within five years. Fields in which graduates pursue further study: Master of Business Administration (MBA), 4%; law, 3%; medicine, 5%; education, 30%; arts and sciences, 41%.

COSTS AND FINANCIAL AID

Financial aid office: (731) 426-7535. **Expenses (2010-2011):** Tuition and fees 2010-2011: $8,000; room/board: $5,630. Estimated books and supplies: $1,100; transportation: $900; personal expenses: $650. **Financial aid:** Priority filing date for institution's financial aid form: April 1. In 2009-2010, 99% of undergraduates applied for financial aid. Of those, 95% were determined to have financial need; 45% had their need fully met. Average financial aid package (proportion receiving): $3,304 (95%). Average amount of gift aid, such as scholarships or grants (proportion receiving): $1,730 (16%). Average amount of self-help aid, such as work study or loans (proportion receiving): $1,852 (59%). Average need-based loan (excluding PLUS or other private loans): $1,968. Among students who received need-based aid, the average percentage of need met: 43%. Among students who received aid based on merit, the average award (and the proportion receiving): $2,713 (2%). The average athletic scholarship (and the proportion receiving): $2,713 (4%). Average amount of debt of borrowers graduating in 2009: $8,769. Proportion who borrowed: 88%.

CAMPUS LIFE AND EXTRACURRICULAR ACTIVITIES

Campus housing available (% using): women's dorms (49%), men's dorms (51%). Students who live in college-owned, operated, or affiliated housing: 61%. **Clubs and organizations:** Number of student organizations: 25. Activities include: campus ministries, choral groups, concert band, dance, drama/theater, marching band, music ensembles, student government, student newspaper, yearbook. Number of fraternities: 4; sororities: 4. Average proportion of students who stay on campus on weekends: 50%. **Sports program (2009-2010):** Member of NCAA II. *Men's intercollegiate varsity sports:* baseball, basketball, cross country, football, tennis. *Women's intercollegiate varsity sports:* basketball, cross country, softball.

SERVICES AND FACILITIES

Basic services: nonremedial tutoring, placement service, day care, health service, health insurance. **Remedial assistance:** reading, math, writing, study skills. **Counseling services:** minority student, career, personal, veteran student, academic, older student, psychological, birth control, religious, other. **Library:** Number of titles: 144,191; number of current serial subscriptions: 254. **Information technology resources:** Students are not required to lease or own a computer. Number of campus computers available to all students: 150. School has a wireless network. Approximate number of users that can be accommodated: 300. Proportion of college-owned housing units wired for high-speed internet access: 100%. **Campus safety:** Security services offered: 24-hour foot-and-vehicle patrols, late-night transport/escort service, lighted pathways/sidewalks.

TRANSFER AND INTERNATIONAL STUDENTS

Transfer students: May apply for admission for the following academic terms: Fall, Spring, Summer. Applicants need a minimum number of credits to apply. For fall 2009: Transfer applications received: 631. Transfer applicants offered admission: 127. Transfer applicants enrolled: 87. **International students:** Number of foreign undergraduates: 4. Number of countries represented: 4. Minimum TOEFL score required: 500 (paper). Average TOEFL score: 500 (paper).

Lee University

- **Address:** PO Box 3450, Cleveland, TN 37320
- **Website:** http://www.leeuniversity.edu
- **Private; Religious affiliation:** Pentecostal
- **Enrollment:** 3,431 full-time; 472 part-time

KEY STATS

✔ **U.S News College Ranking:** 54, Regional Universities (South)
✔ **ACT Score (25th/75th percentile):** 20-27
✔ **Tuition:** 2010-2011: $12,220

Selectivity: Selective	**Room/board:** $5,850
Acceptance rate: 65%	**Average debt:** $27,549
Student/faculty ratio: 18/1	**Proportion who borrowed:** 64%

UNDERGRADUATE STUDENT BODY STATS

2009-2010 enrollment: 3,431 full-time; 472 part-time. Men: 44%; women: 56%. **Ethnic makeup:** African American: 4%; Asian American: 1%; Hispanic: 3%; White: 85%; International: 5%.

ADMISSIONS FACTS AND FIGURES

Phone: (423) 614-8500. **Email:** admissions@leeuniversity.edu. **Website:** http://www.leeuniversity.edu. **Application deadlines for fall 2011:** Regular decision: September 1. Early decision: Not offered. Early action: Not offered. Admission can be deferred. **Application fee:** $25. **To apply online, go to:** https://secure.collegefortn.org/logon.asp?nextpage=/AdmissionApp/appmanager.asp. **Admissions requirements/recommendations:** High school units required (recommended): English: 4 (4); Mathematics: 3 (3); Science: 2 (2); Foreign language: 1 (1); Social studies: 2 (2); History: 1 (1); Academic electives: 0 (0); Total units: 13 (14). Tests: The college uses SAT or ACT scores in admissions decisions. Either SAT or ACT required. For admission to the fall 2011 entering class, the school will accept: ACT with or without writing accepted. Campus visit: Recommended. Admissions interview: Neither required nor recommended. Off-campus interview: May be arranged. **Factors that count in admissions decisions:** *Academic:* Secondary school record: Very Important. Class rank: Important. Letters of recommendation: Considered. Standardized test scores: Very Important. Essay: Not Considered. *Nonacademic:* Interview: Considered. Extracurricular activities: Considered. Talent/ability: Considered. Character/personal qualities: Important. Alumni/ae relationship: Considered. Geographical residence: Not Considered. State residency: Not Considered. Religious affiliation/commitment: Not Considered. Minority status: Not Considered. Volunteer work: Not Considered. Work experience: Not Considered. **Other schools with the greatest overlap in applicants:** Bryan College; Covenant College; University of Tennessee; University of Tennessee–Chattanooga. **Admissions statistics for the fall 2009 entering class:** Total applicants: 1,768. Total accepted: 1,142. Freshmen enrolled: 832; 53% were from out of state. Overall acceptance rate: 65%. **Credentials of fall 2009 freshmen:** 25% ranked in the top 10 percent of their high school class; 46% were in the top 25 percent; 72% were in the top half. (Proportion submitting class standing: 63%.) **Average high school grade point average:** 3.4. **First-year students who submitted SAT scores:** 38%. Scores (25/75 percentile): Critical Reading: 480-610, Math: 460-600, Combined: 940-1210. **First-year students submitting ACT scores:** 82%. Scores (25/75 percentile): English: 18-26, Math: 20-29, Composite: 20-27.

ACADEMICS

Year founded: 1918. **Academic calendar:** Semester. **Degrees offered:** bachelor's, master's, post-master's certificate. **Most popular majors:** 20% theol-

ogy and religious vocations, 18% education, 13% psychology, 12% business, management, marketing, and related support services, 9% communication, journalism, and related programs. **Major fields of study:** biological and biomedical sciences; business, management, marketing, and related support services; communication, journalism, and related programs; computer and information sciences and support services; education; English language and literature/letters; family and consumer sciences/human sciences; foreign languages, literatures, and linguistics; health professions and related clinical sciences; history; mathematics and statistics; multi/interdisciplinary studies; parks, recreation, leisure, and fitness studies; physical sciences; psychology; social sciences; theology and religious vocations; visual and performing arts. **Areas of required coursework:** arts/fine arts, humanities, computer literacy, mathematics, English (including composition), foreign languages, sciences (biological or physical), history, social science, other. **Pre-professional programs:** pre-law, pre-dentistry, pre-medicine, pre-theology, pre-veterinary science, pre-pharmacy. **Special academic programs (% participation):** distance learning (5%), double major (6%), dual enrollment (3%), English as a Second Language (ESL) (1%), external degree program (3%), honors program (4%), independent study (22%), internships (74%), study abroad (100%), teacher certificate program (.1%). **Teacher certification offered in:** early childhood, special education, elementary, vo-tech, middle/junior high, secondary, bilingual/bicultural. **Faculty and instruction (2009-2010):** Total instructional faculty: 149 full-time, 179 part-time (63% men; 38% women; 12% minorities). Full-time faculty with Ph.D. or other terminal degree: 76%. Student/faculty ratio: 18/1. Classes of fewer than 20 students: 46%; of 20 to 49 students: 48%; of 50 or more students: 6%. **Advanced Placement and International Baccalaureate credit:** AP tests may be used for: Credit and/or placement. Scores accepted: 3, 4, 5. International Baccalaureate exams may be used for: Credit and/or placement. **Freshmen returning for sophomore year:** 72%. **Graduation rates:** Four-year: 37%; five-year: 46%; six-year: 49%.

COSTS AND FINANCIAL AID

Financial aid office: (423) 614-8300. **Expenses (2010-2011):** Tuition and fees 2010-2011: $12,220; room/board: $5,850. Estimated books and supplies: $1,000; transportation: $1,700; personal expenses: $1,660. **Financial aid:** Priority filing date for institution's financial aid form: March 15. In 2009-2010, 80% of undergraduates applied for financial aid. Of those, 65% were determined to have financial need; 17% had their need fully met. Average financial aid package (proportion receiving): $10,108 (64%). Average amount of gift aid, such as scholarships or grants (proportion receiving): $7,803 (56%). Average amount of self-help aid, such as work study or loans (proportion receiving): $4,467 (48%). Average need-based loan (excluding PLUS or other private loans): $4,189. Among students who received need-based aid, the average percentage of need met: 58%. Among students who received aid based on merit, the average award (and the proportion receiving): $6,235 (17%). The average athletic scholarship (and the proportion receiving): $7,879 (4%). Average amount of debt of borrowers graduating in 2009: $27,549. Proportion who borrowed: 64%.

CAMPUS LIFE AND EXTRACURRICULAR ACTIVITIES

Campus housing available (% using): women's dorms (39%), men's dorms (25%), apartments for married students (2%), apartment for single students (34%), special housing for disabled students, other housing options. Students who live in college-owned, operated, or affiliated housing: 50%. **Student employment:** During the 2009-2010 academic year, 13% of undergraduates worked on campus. Average per-year earnings: $2,000. **Clubs and organizations:** Number of student organizations: 72. Activities include: campus ministries, choral groups, concert band, drama/theater, international student organization, jazz band, literary magazine, model UN, music ensembles, musical theater, opera, pep band, student government, student newspaper, symphony orchestra, yearbook. Number of fraternities: 5; sororities: 5. Proportion of men in fraternities: 10%; of women in sororities: 10%. Average proportion of students who stay on campus on weekends: 70%. **Sports program (2009-2010):** Member of NAIA. *Men's intercollegiate varsity sports:* baseball, basketball, cross country, golf, soccer, tennis. *Women's intercollegiate varsity sports:* basketball, cross country, soccer, softball, tennis, volleyball.

SERVICES AND FACILITIES

Basic services: nonremedial tutoring, placement service, health service. **Remedial assistance:** reading, math, writing, study skills. **Counseling services:** minority student, career, military, personal, veteran student, academic, older student, psychological, birth control, religious. **For learning-disabled students:** School does not offer a structured program with separate admission and additional fees. Total undergraduates in learning-disabled program or receiving services: 262. Services include: remedial math, remedial English, reading machines, remedial reading, tape recorders, videotaped classes, untimed tests, note-taking services, oral tests, learning center, readers, extended time for tests, tutors, texts on tape, other testing accommodations. **Library:** Number of titles: 156,812; number of current serial subscriptions: 34,881. **Information technology resources:** Students are not required to lease or own a computer. Number of campus computers available to all students: 500. School has a wireless network. Approximate number of users that can be accommodated: 1,950. Proportion of college-owned housing units wired for high-speed internet access: 80%. **Campus safety:** Security services offered: 24-hour foot-and-vehicle patrols, late-night transport/escort service, 24-hour emergency telephones, lighted pathways/sidewalks, student patrols, controlled dormitory access (key, security card, etc).

TRANSFER AND INTERNATIONAL STUDENTS

Transfer students: May apply for admission for the following academic terms: Fall, Spring, Summer. Applicants need a minimum number of credits to apply. For fall 2009: Transfer applications received: 511. Transfer applicants offered admission: 339. Transfer applicants enrolled: 265. **International students:** Number of foreign undergraduates: 195 (5% of student body). Number of countries represented: 51. Minimum TOEFL score required: 450 (paper); 45 (computer).

LeMoyne-Owen College

- **Address:** 807 Walker Avenue, Memphis, TN 38126
- **Website:** http://www.loc.edu/
- **Private; Religious affiliation:** United Church of Christ
- **Enrollment:** N/A

KEY STATS

✔ **U.S News College Ranking:** second tier, Regional Colleges (South)
✔ **ACT Score (25th/75th percentile):** 15-18
✔ **Tuition:** 2009-2010: $10,318

Selectivity: Less selective	Room/board: $4,850
Acceptance rate: 80%	Average debt: N/A
Student/faculty ratio: N/A	Proportion who borrowed: N/A

Lincoln Memorial University

- **Address:** Cumberland Gap Parkway, Harrogate, TN 37752-1901
- **Website:** http://www.lmunet.edu
- **Private**
- **Enrollment:** N/A

KEY STATS

✔ **U.S News College Ranking:** 78, Regional Universities (South)
✔ **ACT Score (25th/75th percentile):** 18-23
✔ **Tuition:** 2010-2011: $16,400

Selectivity: Selective	Room/board: $7,350
Acceptance rate: 78%	Average debt: $10,623
Student/faculty ratio: N/A	Proportion who borrowed: 60%

Lipscomb University

- **Address:** 1 University Park Drive, Nashville, TN 37204-3951
- **Website:** http://www.lipscomb.edu
- **Private; Religious affiliation:** Church of Christ
- **Enrollment:** 2,306 full-time; 207 part-time

KEY STATS

✔ **U.S News College Ranking:** 18, Regional Universities (South)
✔ **ACT Score (25th/75th percentile):** 21-27
✔ **Tuition:** 2010-2011: $21,790

Selectivity: More selective	Room/board: $8,360
Acceptance rate: 66%	Average debt: $19,523
Student/faculty ratio: 15/1	Proportion who borrowed: 64%

UNDERGRADUATE STUDENT BODY STATS

2009-2010 enrollment: 2,306 full-time; 207 part-time. Men: 42%; women: 58%. **Ethnic makeup:** African American: 6%; American-Indian: 1%; Asian American: 2%; Hispanic: 2%; White: 86%; International: 2%. **Religious preference:** Roman Catholic: 3%; Protestant: 18%; No preference: 1%; Unknown: 25%; Church of Christ: 50%; Other: 1%.

ADMISSIONS FACTS AND FIGURES

Phone: (615) 966-1776. **Email:** admissions@lipscomb.edu. **Website:** http://www.lipscomb.edu. **Application deadlines for fall 2011:** Regular decision: Rolling. Early decision: Not offered. Early action: Not offered. Admission can be deferred. **Application fee:** $25. **To apply online, go to:** http://admissions.lipscomb.edu/. **Admissions requirements/recommendations:** High school units required (recommended): English: 4; Mathematics: 2; Science: 2; Foreign language: 2; Social studies: 2; Academic electives: 2; Total units: 14. Tests: The college uses SAT or ACT scores in admissions decisions. Either SAT or ACT required. For admission to the fall 2011 entering class, the school will accept: ACT with writing recommended. Campus visit: Recommended. Admissions interview: Required. Off-campus interview: May be arranged. **Factors that count in admissions decisions:** *Academic:* Secondary school record: Important. Class rank: Very Important. Letters of recommendation: Important. Standardized test scores: Very Important. Essay: Not Considered. *Nonacademic:* Interview: Very Important. Extracurricular activities: Considered. Talent/ability: Considered. Character/personal qualities: Not Considered. Alumni/ae relationship: Not Considered. Geographical residence: Not Considered. State residency: Not Considered. Religious affiliation/commitment: Not Considered. Minority status: Not Considered. Volunteer work: Considered. Work experience: Considered. **Other schools with the greatest overlap in applicants:** Belmont University; Harding University; Middle Tennessee State University; University of Tennessee; Vanderbilt University. **Admissions statistics for the fall 2009 entering class:** Total applicants: 2,683. Total accepted: 1,783. Freshmen enrolled: 600; 35% were from out of state. Overall acceptance rate: 66%. **Credentials of fall 2009 freshmen:** 28% ranked in the top 10 percent of their high school class; 51% were in the top 25 percent; 77% were in the top half. (Proportion submitting class standing: 68%.) **Average high school grade point average:** 3.5. **First-year students who submitted SAT scores:** 27%. Scores (25/75 percentile): Critical Reading: 500-620, Math: 490-610, Combined: 990-1230. **First-year students submitting ACT scores:** 93%. Scores (25/75 percentile): English: 21-29, Math: 19-27, Composite: 21-27.

ACADEMICS

Year founded: 1891. **Academic calendar:** Semester. **Degrees offered:** bachelor's, post-bachelor's certificate, master's. **Most popular majors:** 10% elementary education and teaching, 8% biology/biological sciences, 7% nursing/registered nurse training (R.N., A.S.N., B.S.N., M.S.N.), 7% psychology, 6% business administration and management. **Major fields of study:** architecture and related services; area, ethnic, cultural, and gender studies; biological and biomedical sciences; business, management, marketing, and related support services; communication, journalism, and related programs; computer and information sciences and support services; education; engineering; English language and literature/letters; family and consumer sciences/human sciences; foreign languages, literatures, and linguistics; health professions and related clinical sciences; history; legal professions and studies; liberal arts and sciences studies, and humanities; mathematics and statistics; natural resources and conservation; parks, recreation, leisure, and fitness studies; philosophy and religious studies; physical sciences; psychology; public administration and social service professions; social sciences; theology and religious vocations; visual and performing arts. **Areas of required coursework:** arts/fine arts, humanities, computer literacy, mathematics, English (including composition), sciences (biological or physical), history, social science, other. **Pre-professional programs:** pre-law, pre-dentistry, pre-medicine, pre-theology, pre-veterinary science, pre-optometry, pre-pharmacy, other. **Special academic programs (% participation):** accelerated program, cross-registration, distance learning, double major (10%), dual enrollment, honors program (10%), independent study, internships, study abroad, teacher certificate program (12%), weekend college. **Teacher certification offered in:** early childhood, special education, elementary, middle/junior high, secondary. **Reserve Officers Training Corps (ROTC):** Army ROTC: Offered at cooperating institution (Vanderbilt University); Air Force ROTC: Offered at cooperating institution (Tennessee State University). **Faculty and instruction (2009-2010):** Total instructional faculty: 122 full-time, 205 part-time (62% men; 38% women; 6% minorities). Full-time faculty with Ph.D. or other terminal degree: 85%. Student/faculty ratio: 15/1. Classes of fewer than 20 students: 56%; of 20 to 49 students: 38%; of 50 or more students: 6%. **Advanced Placement and International Baccalaureate credit:** AP tests may be used for: Placement only. Scores accepted: 3, 4, 5. **Freshmen returning for sophomore year:** 77%. **Graduation rates:** Four-year: 35%; five-year: 56%; six-year: 58%. **Graduate study:** 9% of students pursue further study immediately upon graduation; 47% within one year; 36% within five years. Fields in which graduates pursue further study: Master of Business Administration (MBA), 11%; law, 8%; medicine, 11%; dentistry, 2%; engineering, 4%; theology (or the seminary), 10%; education, 23%; arts and sciences, 19%; veterinary medicine, 1%.

COSTS AND FINANCIAL AID

Financial aid office: (615) 269-1791. **Expenses (2010-2011):** Tuition and fees 2010-2011: $21,790; room/board: $8,360. Estimated books and supplies: $1,000; transportation: $1,250; personal expenses: $1,250. **Financial aid:** Priority filing date for institution's financial aid form: February 15. In 2009-2010, 92% of undergraduates applied for financial aid. Of those, 62% were determined to have financial need; 30% had their need fully met. Average financial aid package (proportion receiving): $16,409 (62%). Average amount of gift aid, such as scholarships or grants (proportion receiving): $6,819 (28%). Average amount of self-help aid, such as work study or loans (proportion receiving): $5,098 (51%). Average need-based loan (excluding PLUS or other private loans): $4,975. Among students who received need-based aid, the average percentage of need met: 62%. Among students who received aid based on merit, the average award (and the proportion receiving): $6,645 (17%). The average athletic scholarship (and the proportion receiving): $19,510 (3%). Average amount of debt of borrowers graduating in 2009: $19,523. Proportion who borrowed: 64%.

CAMPUS LIFE AND EXTRACURRICULAR ACTIVITIES

Campus housing available (% using): women's dorms (52%), men's dorms (37%), apartment for single students (11%). Students who live in college-owned, operated, or affiliated housing: 52%. **Student employment:** During the 2009-2010 academic year, 28% of undergraduates worked on campus. Average per-year earnings: $900. **Clubs and organizations:** Number of student organizations: 57. Activities include: campus ministries, choral groups, concert band, drama/theater, international student organization, jazz band, literary magazine, marching band, music ensembles, musical theater, pep band, radio station, student government, student newspaper, yearbook. Number of fraternities: 7; sororities: 7. Proportion of men in fraternities: 16%; of women in sororities: 19%. Average proportion of students who stay on campus on weekends: 40%. **Sports program (2009-2010):** Member of NCAA I. *Men's intercollegiate varsity sports:* baseball, basketball, cross country, golf, soccer, tennis, track and field (outdoor). *Women's intercollegiate varsity sports:* basketball, cross country, golf, soccer, softball, tennis, track and field (outdoor), volleyball.

SERVICES AND FACILITIES

Basic services: nonremedial tutoring, placement service, health service. **Remedial assistance:** reading, math, writing, study skills. **Counseling services:** minority student, career, personal, veteran student, academic, older student, psychological, religious. **For learning-disabled students:** School does not offer a structured program with separate admission and additional fees. Total undergraduates in learning-disabled program or receiving services: 25. Services include: remedial math, remedial English, reading machines, tape recorders, diagnostic testing service, untimed tests, note-taking services, oral tests, readers, extended time for tests, tutors, priority registration, priority seating, texts on tape, other testing accommodations. **Library:** Number of titles: 258,965; number of current serial subscriptions: 809. **Information technology resources:** Students are not required to lease or own a computer. Number of campus computers available to all students: 218. School has a wireless network. Approximate number of users that can be accommodated: 3,750. Proportion of college-owned housing units wired for high-speed internet access: 100%. **Campus safety:** Security services offered: 24-hour foot-and-vehicle patrols, late-night transport/escort service, 24-hour emergency telephones, lighted pathways/sidewalks, student patrols, controlled dormitory access (key, security card, etc).

TRANSFER AND INTERNATIONAL STUDENTS

Transfer students: May apply for admission for the following academic terms: Fall, Winter, Spring, Summer. Applicants do not need a minimum number of credits to apply. For fall 2009: Transfer applications received: 397. Transfer applicants offered admission: 249. Transfer applicants enrolled: 126. **International students:** Number of foreign undergraduates: 47 (2% of student body). Number of countries represented: 27. Minimum TOEFL score required: 550 (paper); 213 (computer). Average TOEFL score: 635 (paper).

Martin Methodist College

- **Address:** 433 W. Madison Street, Pulaski, TN 38478
- **Website:** http://www.martinmethodist.edu
- **Private; Religious affiliation:** Methodist
- **Enrollment:** N/A

KEY STATS
✔ **U.S News College Ranking:** second tier, Regional Colleges (South)
✔ **ACT Score (25th/75th percentile):** 16-23
✔ **Tuition:** 2009-2010: $18,638

Selectivity: Less selective	**Room/board:** $6,400
Acceptance rate: N/A	**Average debt:** N/A
Student/faculty ratio: N/A	**Proportion who borrowed:** N/A

Maryville College

- **Address:** 502 E. Lamar Alexander Parkway, Maryville, TN 37804-5907
- **Website:** http://www.maryvillecollege.edu
- **Private; Religious affiliation:** Presbyterian
- **Enrollment:** 1,092 full-time; 11 part-time

KEY STATS
✔ **U.S News College Ranking:** 174, National Liberal Arts Colleges
✔ **ACT Score (25th/75th percentile):** 21-27
✔ **Tuition:** 2010-2011: $29,473

Selectivity: Selective	**Room/board:** $9,032
Acceptance rate: 73%	**Average debt:** $22,268
Student/faculty ratio: 12/1	**Proportion who borrowed:** 66%

UNDERGRADUATE STUDENT BODY STATS

2009-2010 enrollment: 1,092 full-time; 11 part-time. Men: 45%; women: 55%. **Ethnic makeup:** African American: 6%; Asian American: 1%; Hispanic: 2%; White: 88%; International: 3%. **Religious preference:** Roman Catholic: 10%; Protestant: 50%; Unknown: 5%; Presbyterian: 11%.

ADMISSIONS FACTS AND FIGURES

Phone: (865) 981-8092. **Email:** admissions@maryvillecollege.edu. **Website:** http://www.maryvillecollege.edu. **Application deadlines for fall 2011:** Regular decision: March 1. Early decision: Send application by: November 15; Decision sent by: December 1. Early action: Send application by: October 1; Decision sent by: October 15. Admission can be deferred. **Application fee:** None. **To apply online, go to:** http://www.maryvillecollege.edu/admissions/application.asp. **Admissions requirements/recommendations:** High school units required (recommended): English: 4 (4); Mathematics: 3 (4); Science: 2 (4); Foreign language: 2 (4); Social studies: 2 (4); History: 1 (2); Academic electives: 1 (1); Total units: 15 (23). **Tests:** The college uses SAT or ACT scores in admissions decisions. Either SAT or ACT required. For admission to the fall 2011 entering class, the school will accept: ACT with or without writing accepted. Campus visit: Recommended. Admissions interview: Recommended. Off-campus interview: May be arranged. **Factors that count in admissions decisions:** *Academic:* Secondary school record: Very Important. Class rank: Very Important. Letters of recommendation: Important. Standardized test scores: Very Important. Essay: Important. *Nonacademic:* Interview: Important. Extracurricular activities: Important. Talent/ability: Important. Character/personal qualities: Important. Alumni/ae relationship: Not Considered. Geographical residence: Not Considered. State residency: Not Considered. Religious affiliation/commitment: Not Considered. Minority status: Not Considered. Volunteer work: Considered. Work experience: Not Considered. **Other schools with the greatest overlap in applicants:** Carson-Newman College; Centre College; Rhodes College; University of Tennessee. **Admissions statistics for the fall 2009 entering class:** Total applicants: 1,563. Total accepted: 1,143. Freshmen enrolled: 303; 15% were from out of state. Overall acceptance rate: 73%. Early-decision acceptance rate: 77%. Non-early acceptance rate: 73%. **Credentials of fall 2009 freshmen:** 25% ranked in the top 10 percent of their high school class; 52% were in the top 25 percent; 82% were in the top half. (Proportion submitting class standing: 43%.) **Average high school grade point average:** 3.5. **First-year students who submitted SAT scores:** 25%. Scores (25/75 percentile): Critical Reading: 470-590, Math: 470-580, Combined: 940-1170.

First-year students submitting ACT scores: 94%. Scores (25/75 percentile): English: 20-27, Math: 21-30, Composite: 21-27.

ACADEMICS

Year founded: 1819. **Academic calendar:** 4-1-4. **Degrees offered:** bachelor's. **Most popular majors:** 24% business, management, marketing, and related support services, 12% education, 12% psychology, 9% social sciences, 8% English language and literature/letters. **Major fields of study:** biological and biomedical sciences; business, management, marketing, and related support services; computer and information sciences and support services; education; engineering; English language and literature/letters; foreign languages, literatures, and linguistics; health professions and related clinical sciences; history; mathematics and statistics; multi/interdisciplinary studies; natural resources and conservation; parks, recreation, leisure, and fitness studies; philosophy and religious studies; physical sciences; psychology; social sciences; visual and performing arts. **Areas of required coursework:** arts/fine arts, humanities, computer literacy, mathematics, English (including composition), philosophy, foreign languages, sciences (biological or physical), history, social science, other. **Pre-professional programs:** pre-law, pre-dentistry, pre-medicine, pre-theology, pre-veterinary science, pre-pharmacy. **Special academic programs (% participation):** double major (8%), English as a Second Language (ESL) (2%), honors program (10%), independent study (100%), internships (16%), liberal arts/career combination (40%), student-designed major (1%), study abroad (10%), teacher certificate program (18%). **Teacher certification offered in:** elementary, middle/junior high, secondary. **Faculty and instruction (2009-2010):** Total instructional faculty: 75 full-time, 56 part-time (47% men; 53% women; 5% minorities). Full-time faculty with Ph.D. or other terminal degree: 91%. Student/faculty ratio: 12/1. Classes of fewer than 20 students: 56%; of 20 to 49 students: 44%; of 50 or more students: 0%. **Advanced Placement and International Baccalaureate credit:** AP tests may be used for: Credit only. Scores accepted: 4, 5. International Baccalaureate exams may be used for: Credit only. **Freshmen returning for sophomore year:** 72%. **Graduation rates:** Four-year: 45%; five-year: 55%; six-year: 57%. **Graduate study:** 20% of students pursue further study immediately upon graduation; 30% within one year; 35% within five years. Fields in which graduates pursue further study: Master of Business Administration (MBA), 5%; law, 6%; medicine, 5%; dentistry, 1%; engineering, 5%; theology (or the seminary), 3%; education, 8%; arts and sciences, 66%.

COSTS AND FINANCIAL AID

Financial aid office: (865) 981-8100. **Expenses (2010-2011):** Tuition and fees 2010-2011: $29,473; room/board: $9,032. Estimated books and supplies: $1,050; transportation: $1,050; personal expenses: $1,250. **Financial aid:** Priority filing date for institution's financial aid form: February 15. In 2009-2010, 100% of undergraduates applied for financial aid. Of those, 83% were determined to have financial need; 32% had their need fully met. Average financial aid package (proportion receiving): $26,285 (83%). Average amount of gift aid, such as scholarships or grants (proportion receiving): $21,732 (82%). Average amount of self-help aid, such as work study or loans (proportion receiving): $7,082 (72%). Average need-based loan (excluding PLUS or other private loans): $3,459. Among students who received need-based aid, the average percentage of need met: 87%. Among students who received aid based on merit, the average award (and the proportion receiving): $15,380 (12%). The average athletic scholarship (and the proportion receiving): $0 (0%). Average amount of debt of borrowers graduating in 2009: $22,268. Proportion who borrowed: 66%.

CAMPUS LIFE AND EXTRACURRICULAR ACTIVITIES

Campus housing available (% using): coed dorms (59%), women's dorms (14%), men's dorms (13%), apartment for single students (13%), special housing for disabled students (1%). Students who live in college-owned, operated, or affiliated housing: 71%. **Student employment:** During the 2009-2010 academic year, 15% of undergraduates worked on campus. Average per-year earnings: $1,200. **Clubs and organizations:** Number of student organizations: 62. Activities include: campus ministries, choral groups, concert band, dance, drama/theater, international student organization, jazz band, literary magazine, model UN, music ensembles, student government, student newspaper, symphony orchestra, yearbook. Number of fraternities: 0; sororities: 0. Average proportion of students who stay on campus on weekends: 50%. **Sports program (2009-2010):** Member of NCAA III. *Men's intercollegiate varsity sports:* baseball, basketball, cross country, football, golf, soccer, swimming, tennis. *Women's intercollegiate varsity sports:* basketball, cross country, golf, soccer, softball, swimming, tennis, volleyball.

SERVICES AND FACILITIES

Basic services: nonremedial tutoring, placement service, health service, health insurance. **Remedial assistance:** reading, math, writing, study skills, other. **Counseling services:** minority student, career, personal, academic, older student, psychological, religious. **For learning-disabled students:** School does not offer a structured program with separate admission and additional fees. Services include: remedial math, reading machines, tape recorders, note-taking services, oral tests, learning center, readers, extended time for tests, tutors, priority registration, priority seating, texts on tape, other testing accommodations. **Library:** Number of titles: 131,838; number of current serial subscriptions: 14,531. **Information technology resources:** Students are not required to lease or own a computer. Number of campus computers available to all students: 254. School has a wireless network. Approximate number of users that can be accommodated: 5,000. Proportion of college-owned housing units wired for high-speed internet access: 100%. **Campus safety:** Security services offered: 24-hour foot-and-vehicle patrols, 24-hour emergency telephones, lighted pathways/sidewalks, controlled dormitory access (key, security card, etc).

TRANSFER AND INTERNATIONAL STUDENTS

Transfer students: May apply for admission for the following academic terms: Fall, Winter, Spring, Summer. Applicants need a minimum number of credits to apply. For fall 2009: Transfer applications received: 233. Transfer applicants offered admission: 128. Transfer applicants enrolled: 56. **International students:** Number of foreign undergraduates: 36 (3% of student body). Number of countries represented: 25. Minimum TOEFL score required: 525 (paper); 200 (computer). Average TOEFL score: 550 (paper).

Memphis College of Art

- **Address:** Overton Park, 1930 Poplar Avenue, Memphis, TN 38104
- **Website:** http://www.mca.edu
- **Private**
- **Enrollment:** 338 full-time; 24 part-time

KEY STATS
✔ **U.S News College Ranking:** Unranked Specialty School–Fine Arts
✔ **ACT Score:** 22
✔ **Tuition:** 2010-2011: $23,950

Selectivity: N/A	Room/board: $8,000
Acceptance rate: 47%	Average debt: $35,000
Student/faculty ratio: 10/1	Proportion who borrowed: 98%

UNDERGRADUATE STUDENT BODY STATS

2009-2010 enrollment: 338 full-time; 24 part-time. Men: 40%; women: 60%. **Ethnic makeup:** African American: 18%; Asian American: 2%; Hispanic: 4%; White: 73%; International: 4%.

ADMISSIONS FACTS AND FIGURES

Phone: (800) 727-1088. **Email:** info@mca.edu. **Website:** http://www.mca.edu. **Application deadlines for fall 2011:** Regular decision: August 3. Early decision: Not offered. Early action: Not offered. Admission can be deferred. **Application fee:** $25. **To apply online, go to:** http://www.mca.edu/admissions/admission_form/admissions_form.htm. **Admissions requirements/recommendations:** Tests: The college uses SAT or ACT scores in admissions decisions. Either SAT or ACT required. For admission to the fall 2011 entering class, the school will accept: ACT with or without writing accepted. Campus visit: Recommended. Admissions interview: Recommended. Off-campus interview: May be arranged. **Factors that count in admissions decisions:** *Academic:* Secondary school record: Very Important. Class rank: Important. Letters of recommendation: Considered. Standardized test scores: Important. Essay: Considered. *Nonacademic:* Interview: Very Important. Extracurricular activities: Considered. Talent/ability: Very Important. Character/personal qualities: Considered. Alumni/ae relationship: Not Considered. Geographical residence: Not Considered. State residency: Not Considered. Religious affiliation/commitment: Not Considered. Minority status: Not Considered. Volunteer work: Considered. Work experience: Considered. **Other schools with the greatest overlap in applicants:** Kansas City Art Institute; Maryland Institute College of Art; Ringling College of Art and Design; Savannah College of Art and Design; University of Memphis. **Admissions statistics for the fall 2009 entering class:** Total applicants: 752. Total accepted: 351. Freshmen enrolled: 100; 45% were from out of state. Overall acceptance rate: 47%. **Average high school grade point**

average: 3.3. **First-year students who submitted SAT scores:** 10%. **First-year students submitting ACT scores:** 90%. Scores (25/75 percentile): English: N/A, Math: N/A, Composite: N/A.

ACADEMICS

Year founded: 1936. **Academic calendar:** Semester. **Degrees offered:** bachelor's, master's. **Major fields of study:** computer and information sciences and support services; visual and performing arts. **Areas of required coursework:** arts/fine arts, humanities, computer literacy, mathematics, English (including composition), sciences (biological or physical), social science. **Special academic programs (% participation):** cross-registration (3%), double major (2%), exchange student program (domestic) (5%), independent study (6%), internships (14%), study abroad (1%). **Teacher certification offered in:** elementary, middle/junior high, secondary. **Cooperative education programs:** art. **Faculty and instruction (2009-2010):** Total instructional faculty: 25 full-time, 41 part-time (48% men; 52% women; 6% minorities). Full-time faculty with Ph.D. or other terminal degree: 84%. Student/faculty ratio: 10/1. Classes of fewer than 20 students: 87%; of 20 to 49 students: 13%; of 50 or more students: 0%. **Advanced Placement and International Baccalaureate credit:** AP tests may be used for: Placement only. International Baccalaureate exams may be used for: Credit and/or placement. **Freshmen returning for sophomore year:** 62%. **Graduation rates:** Four-year: 20%; five-year: 37%; six-year: 41%. **Graduate study:** 6% of students pursue further study immediately upon graduation; 10% within one year; 15% within five years. Fields in which graduates pursue further study: education, 60%; arts and sciences, 40%.

COSTS AND FINANCIAL AID

Financial aid office: (901) 272-5136. **Expenses (2010-2011):** Tuition and fees 2010-2011: $23,950; room/board: $8,000. Estimated books and supplies: $1,650; transportation: $1,500; personal expenses: $1,500. **Financial aid:** Priority filing date for institution's financial aid form: February 12. In 2009-2010, 89% of undergraduates applied for financial aid. Of those, 82% were determined to have financial need; 23% had their need fully met. Average financial aid package (proportion receiving): $10,826 (82%). Average amount of gift aid, such as scholarships or grants (proportion receiving): $6,252 (52%). Average amount of self-help aid, such as work study or loans (proportion receiving): $5,500 (58%). Average need-based loan (excluding PLUS or other private loans): $5,500. Among students who received need-based aid, the average percentage of need met: 80%. Among students who received aid based on merit, the average award (and the proportion receiving): $9,000 (12%). The average athletic scholarship (and the proportion receiving): $0 (0%). Average amount of debt of borrowers graduating in 2009: $35,000. Proportion who borrowed: 98%.

CAMPUS LIFE AND EXTRACURRICULAR ACTIVITIES

Campus housing available (% using): apartment for single students (60%). Students who live in college-owned, operated, or affiliated housing: 46%. **Clubs and organizations:** Number of student organizations: 5. Activities include: student government, student newspaper, yearbook. Number of fraternities: 0; sororities: 0. Average proportion of students who stay on campus on weekends: 33%.

SERVICES AND FACILITIES

Basic services: nonremedial tutoring, placement service. **Remedial assistance:** writing, study skills. **Counseling services:** career, personal, academic, psychological. **For learning-disabled students:** School does not offer a structured program with separate admission and additional fees. Services include: remedial English, note-taking services, learning center, tutors, priority seating. **Library:** Number of titles: 14,500; number of current serial subscriptions: 108. **Information technology resources:** Students are not required to lease or own a computer. Number of campus computers available to all students: 80. School has a wireless network. Proportion of college-owned housing units wired for high-speed internet access: 100%. **Campus safety:** Security services offered: 24-hour foot-and-vehicle patrols, late-night transport/escort service, 24-hour emergency telephones, controlled dormitory access (key, security card, etc).

TRANSFER AND INTERNATIONAL STUDENTS

Transfer students: May apply for admission for the following academic terms: Fall, Spring. Applicants need a minimum number of credits to apply. For fall 2009: Transfer applications received: 135. Transfer applicants offered admission: 78. Transfer applicants enrolled: 44. **International students:** Number of foreign undergraduates: 13 (4% of student body). Number of countries represented: 6. Minimum TOEFL score required: 500 (paper); 197 (computer).

Middle Tennessee State University

■ **Address:** 1301 E. Main Street, CAB Room 205, Murfreesboro, TN 37132
■ **Website:** http://www.mtsu.edu
■ **Public**
■ **Enrollment:** 18,912 full-time; 3,387 part-time

KEY STATS

✔ **U.S News College Ranking:** 56, Regional Universities (South)
✔ **ACT Score (25th/75th percentile):** 20-25
✔ **Tuition:** 2009-2010: $5,988 in state, $17,916 out of state
  Selectivity: Selective   **Room/board:** $6,754
  Acceptance rate: 70%   **Average debt:** N/A
  Student/faculty ratio: 20/1 **Proportion who borrowed:** N/A

UNDERGRADUATE STUDENT BODY STATS

2009-2010 enrollment: 18,912 full-time; 3,387 part-time. **Men:** 48%; **women:** 52%. **Ethnic makeup:** African American: 16%; Asian American: 3%; Hispanic: 3%; White: 78%. **Religious preference:** Roman Catholic: 6%; Protestant: 42%; No preference: 1%; Unknown: 45%; Non-Denominational: 3%; Other: 3%.

ADMISSIONS FACTS AND FIGURES

Phone: (615) 898-2111. **Email:** admissions@mtsu.edu. **Website:** http://www.mtsu.edu. **Application deadlines for fall 2011:** Regular decision: Rolling. Early decision: Not offered. Early action: Not offered. Admission cannot be deferred. **Application fee:** $25. **Admissions requirements/recommendations:** High school units required (recommended): English: 4; Mathematics: 3; Science: 2; Foreign language: 2; Social studies: 1; History: 1; Total units: 14. Tests: The college uses SAT or ACT scores in admissions decisions. Either SAT or ACT required. For admission to the fall 2011 entering class, the school will accept: ACT with or without writing accepted. Campus visit: Recommended. Admissions interview: Neither required nor recommended. Off-campus interview: Not available. **Factors that count in admissions decisions:** *Academic:* Secondary school record: Considered. Class rank: Not Considered. Letters of recommendation: Considered. Standardized test scores: Very Important. Essay: Considered. *Nonacademic:* Interview: Not Considered. Extracurricular activities: Not Considered. Talent/ability: Not Considered. Character/personal qualities: Not Considered. Alumni/ae relationship: Not Considered. Geographical residence: Not Considered. State residency: Not Considered. Religious affiliation/commitment: Not Considered. Minority status: Not Considered. Volunteer work: Not Considered. Work experience: Not Considered. **Other schools with the greatest overlap in applicants:** University of Alabama–Huntsville; University of Memphis; University of Tennessee; University of Tennessee–Chattanooga; Western Kentucky University. **Admissions statistics for the fall 2009 entering class:** Total applicants: 9,431. Total accepted: 6,616. Freshmen enrolled: 3,596; Overall acceptance rate: 70%. **Credentials of fall 2009 freshmen:** 11% ranked in the top 10 percent of their high school class; 24% were in the top 25 percent; 44% were in the top half. (Proportion submitting class standing: 60%.) **First-year students who submitted SAT scores:** 4%. Scores (25/75 percentile): Critical Reading: 450-580, Math: 460-580, Combined: 910-1160. **First-year students submitting ACT scores:** 91%. Scores (25/75 percentile): English: 19-26, Math: 17-24, Composite: 20-25.

ACADEMICS

Year founded: 1911. **Academic calendar:** Semester. **Degrees offered:** bachelor's, post-bachelor's certificate, master's, post-master's certificate, doctorate. **Most popular majors:** 8% mass communication/media studies, 7% liberal arts and sciences/liberal studies, 6% multi/interdisciplinary studies, 6% music management and merchandising, 5% business administration and management. **Major fields of study:** agriculture, agriculture operations, and related sciences; biological and biomedical sciences; business, management, marketing, and related support services; communication, journalism, and related programs; computer and information sciences and support services; education; engineering technologies/technicians; English language and literature/letters; family and consumer sciences/human sciences; foreign languages, literatures, and linguistics; health professions and related clinical sciences; history; liberal arts and sciences studies, and humanities; mathematics and statistics; multi/interdisciplinary studies; parks, recreation, leisure, and fitness studies; philosophy and religious studies; physical sciences; psychology; public administration and social service professions; security and protective services; social sciences; transportation and materials moving; visual and performing arts. **Areas of required**

coursework: arts/fine arts, humanities, computer literacy, mathematics, English (including composition), sciences (biological or physical), history, social science. **Pre-professional programs:** pre-dentistry, pre-medicine, pre-pharmacy. **Special academic programs:** distance learning, double major, dual enrollment, honors program, independent study, internships, study abroad, teacher certificate program. **Teacher certification offered in:** early childhood, special education, elementary, vo-tech, middle/junior high, secondary. **Reserve Officers Training Corps (ROTC):** Army ROTC: Offered on campus; Air Force ROTC: Offered at cooperating institution. **Faculty and instruction (2009-2010):** Total instructional faculty: 934 full-time, 338 part-time (53% men; 47% women; 15% minorities). Student/faculty ratio: 20/1. Classes of fewer than 20 students: 32%; of 20 to 49 students: 60%; of 50 or more students: 7%. **Advanced Placement and International Baccalaureate credit:** AP tests may be used for: Credit and/or placement. Scores accepted: 3. **Freshmen returning for sophomore year:** 81%. **Graduation rates:** Six-year: 44%. **Graduate study:** 23% of students pursue further study immediately upon graduation.

COSTS AND FINANCIAL AID

Financial aid office: (615) 898-2830. **Expenses (2009-2010):** Tuition and fees 2009-2010: $5,988 in state, $17,916 out of state; room/board: $6,754. Estimated books and supplies: $1,000. **Financial aid:** Priority filing date for institution's financial aid form: May 1.

CAMPUS LIFE AND EXTRACURRICULAR ACTIVITIES

Campus housing available (% using): coed dorms (33%), women's dorms (15%), men's dorms (21%), fraternity housing (4%), apartments for married students (1%), apartment for single students (26%), special housing for disabled students. Students who live in college-owned, operated, or affiliated housing: 12%. **Student employment:** During the 2009-2010 academic year, 12% of undergraduates worked on campus. Average per-year earnings: $7,500. **Clubs and organizations:** Number of student organizations: 385. Activities include: campus ministries, choral groups, concert band, dance, drama/theater, international student organization, jazz band, literary magazine, marching band, model UN, music ensembles, musical theater, pep band, radio station, student government, student newspaper, student film society, symphony orchestra, television station. Number of fraternities: 16; sororities: 12. Proportion of men in fraternities: 5%; of women in sororities: 7%. Average proportion of students who stay on campus on weekends: 15%. **Sports program (2009-2010):** Member of NCAA I. *Men's intercollegiate varsity sports:* baseball, basketball, football, golf, tennis, track and field (indoor), track and field (outdoor). *Women's intercollegiate varsity sports:* basketball, golf, soccer, softball, tennis, track and field (indoor), track and field (outdoor), volleyball.

SERVICES AND FACILITIES

Basic services: nonremedial tutoring, women's center, placement service, day care, health service, health insurance. **Remedial assistance:** other. **Counseling services:** minority student, career, military, personal, veteran student, academic, older student, psychological. **For learning-disabled students:** School does not offer a structured program with separate admission and additional fees. Total undergraduates in learning-disabled program or receiving services: 412. Services include: remedial math, remedial English, remedial reading, note-taking services, oral tests, extended time for tests, priority registration, texts on tape, other testing accommodations. **Library:** Number of titles: 1,110,564; number of current serial subscriptions: 38,766. **Information technology resources:** Students are not required to lease or own a computer. Number of campus computers available to all students: 3,000. School has a wireless network. Approximate number of users that can be accommodated: 7,000. Proportion of college-owned housing units wired for high-speed internet access: 100%. **Campus safety:** Security services offered: 24-hour foot-and-vehicle patrols, late-night transport/escort service, 24-hour emergency telephones, lighted pathways/sidewalks, student patrols, controlled dormitory access (key, security card, etc.).

TRANSFER AND INTERNATIONAL STUDENTS

Transfer students: May apply for admission for the following academic terms: Fall, Spring, Summer. Applicants need a minimum number of credits to apply. For fall 2009: Transfer applications received: 4,273. Transfer applicants offered admission: 3,046. **International students:** Number of countries represented: 33. Minimum TOEFL score required: 500 (paper); 173 (computer).

Milligan College

- **Address:** PO Box 500, Milligan College, TN 37682
- **Website:** http://www.milligan.edu
- **Private; Religious affiliation:** Christian Churches/Churches of Christ
- **Enrollment:** 811 full-time; 92 part-time

KEY STATS

✔ **U.S News College Ranking:** 10, Regional Colleges (South)
✔ **ACT Score (25th/75th percentile):** 20-25
✔ **Tuition:** 2010-2011: $23,520

Selectivity: More selective	**Room/board:** $5,650
Acceptance rate: 68%	**Average debt:** $19,803
Student/faculty ratio: 13/1	**Proportion who borrowed:** 90%

UNDERGRADUATE STUDENT BODY STATS

2009-2010 enrollment: 811 full-time; 92 part-time. Men: 41%; women: 59%. **Ethnic makeup:** African American: 7%; Hispanic: 3%; White: 87%; International: 3%. **Religious preference:** Roman Catholic: 3%; Protestant: 40%; No preference: 6%; Unknown: 12%; Christian Churches/Churches of Christ: 38%; Other: 1%.

ADMISSIONS FACTS AND FIGURES

Phone: (423) 461-8730. **Email:** admissions@milligan.edu. **Website:** http://www.milligan.edu. **Application deadlines for fall 2011:** Regular decision: August 1. Early decision: Not offered. Early action: Not offered. Admission can be deferred. **Application fee:** $30. **To apply online, go to:** http://www.applyweb.com/aw?millgn. **Admissions requirements/recommendations:** High school units required (recommended): English: (4); Mathematics: (3); Science: (3); Foreign language: (2); Social studies: (2); History: (3); Total units: (17). Tests: The college uses SAT or ACT scores in admissions decisions. Either SAT or ACT required. For admission to the fall 2011 entering class, the school will accept: ACT with or without writing accepted. Campus visit: Recommended. Admissions interview: Neither required nor recommended. Off-campus interview: Not available. **Factors that count in admissions decisions:** *Academic:* Secondary school record: Very Important. Class rank: Considered. Letters of recommendation: Important. Standardized test scores: Very Important. Essay: Very Important. *Nonacademic:* Interview: Considered. Extracurricular activities: Important. Talent/ability: Considered. Character/personal qualities: Very Important. Alumni/ae relationship: Considered. Geographical residence: Not Considered. State residency: Not Considered. Religious affiliation/commitment: Very Important. Minority status: Considered. Volunteer work: Considered. Work experience: Considered. **Admissions statistics for the fall 2009 entering class:** Total applicants: 643. Total accepted: 438. Freshmen enrolled: 211; 37% were from out of state. Overall acceptance rate: 68%. **Credentials of fall 2009 freshmen:** 37% ranked in the top 10 percent of their high school class; 65% were in the top 25 percent; 89% were in the top half. (Proportion submitting class standing: 63%.) **Average high school grade point average:** 3.6. **First-year students who submitted SAT scores:** 42%. Scores (25/75 percentile): Critical Reading: 480-580, Math: 460-570, Combined: 940-1150. **First-year students submitting ACT scores:** 79%. Scores (25/75 percentile): English: 21-28, Math: 19-25, Composite: 20-25.

ACADEMICS

Year founded: 1866. **Academic calendar:** Semester. **Degrees offered:** bachelor's, master's. **Most popular majors:** 28% business, management, marketing, and related support services, 18% health professions and related clinical sciences, 11% education, 7% psychology, 6% visual and performing arts. **Major fields of study:** biological and biomedical sciences; business, management, marketing, and related support services; communication, journalism, and related programs; computer and information sciences and support services; education; English language and literature/letters; health professions and related clinical sciences; history; liberal arts and sciences studies, and humanities; mathematics and statistics; parks, recreation, leisure, and fitness studies; physical sciences; psychology; public administration and social service professions; social sciences; theology and religious vocations; visual and performing arts. **Areas of required coursework:** arts/fine arts, humanities, computer literacy, mathematics, English (including composition), philosophy, sciences (biological or physical), history, social science, other. **Pre-professional programs:** pre-law, pre-dentistry, pre-medicine, pre-theology, pre-veterinary science, pre-pharmacy. **Special academic programs (% participation):** double major (25%), independent study (15%), internships (50%), study abroad (2%), teacher certificate program (20%). **Teacher certi-**

fication offered in: early childhood, special education, elementary, middle/junior high, secondary. **Reserve Officers Training Corps (ROTC):** Army ROTC: Offered at cooperating institution (East Tennessee State University). **Faculty and instruction (2009-2010):** Total instructional faculty: 67 full-time, 50 part-time (51% men; 49% women; 3% minorities). Full-time faculty with Ph.D. or other terminal degree: 76%. Student/faculty ratio: 13/1. Classes of fewer than 20 students: 71%; of 20 to 49 students: 28%; of 50 or more students: 1%. **Advanced Placement and International Baccalaureate credit:** AP tests may be used for: Credit and/or placement. Scores accepted: 3, 4, 5. International Baccalaureate exams may be used for: Credit and/or placement. **Freshmen returning for sophomore year:** 73%. **Graduation rates:** Six-year: 59%.

COSTS AND FINANCIAL AID
Financial aid office: (423) 461-8949. **Expenses (2010-2011):** Tuition and fees 2010-2011: $23,520; room/board: $5,650. Estimated books and supplies: $900; transportation: $1,014; personal expenses: $1,236. **Financial aid:** Priority filing date for institution's financial aid form: March 1. In 2009-2010, 92% of undergraduates applied for financial aid. Of those, 79% were determined to have financial need; 29% had their need fully met. Average financial aid package (proportion receiving): $16,482 (79%). Average amount of gift aid, such as scholarships or grants (proportion receiving): $13,301 (77%). Average amount of self-help aid, such as work study or loans (proportion receiving): $4,950 (56%). Average need-based loan (excluding PLUS or other private loans): $4,445. Among students who received need-based aid, the average percentage of need met: 79%. Among students who received aid based on merit, the average award (and the proportion receiving): $7,283 (15%). The average athletic scholarship (and the proportion receiving): $7,952 (16%). Average amount of debt of borrowers graduating in 2009: $19,803. Proportion who borrowed: 90%.

CAMPUS LIFE AND EXTRACURRICULAR ACTIVITIES
Campus housing available (% using): women's dorms (54%), men's dorms (36%), apartments for married students (6%), apartment for single students (4%). Students who live in college-owned, operated, or affiliated housing: 74%. **Clubs and organizations:** Number of student organizations: 41. Activities include: choral groups, concert band, drama/theater, jazz band, literary magazine, music ensembles, musical theater, pep band, radio station, student government, student newspaper, student film society, symphony orchestra, yearbook. Number of fraternities: 0; sororities: 0. Average proportion of students who stay on campus on weekends: 65%. **Sports program (2009-2010):** Member of NAIA. *Men's intercollegiate varsity sports:* baseball, basketball, cross country, golf, soccer, swimming, tennis, track and field (indoor), track and field (outdoor). *Women's intercollegiate varsity sports:* basketball, cross country, soccer, softball, swimming, tennis, track and field (indoor), track and field (outdoor), volleyball.

SERVICES AND FACILITIES
Basic services: nonremedial tutoring, health service, health insurance. **Remedial assistance:** reading, math, writing, study skills. **Counseling services:** career, personal, academic, psychological. **For learning-disabled students:** School does not offer a structured program with separate admission and additional fees. Services include: remedial math, remedial English, remedial reading, untimed tests, note-taking services, special bookstore section, oral tests, learning center, extended time for tests, tutors, priority seating, texts on tape, other testing accommodations. **Library:** Number of titles: 81,114; number of current serial subscriptions: 11,097. **Information technology resources:** Students are not required to lease or own a computer. Number of campus computers available to all students: 123. School has a wireless network. Approximate number of users that can be accommodated: 1,170. Proportion of college-owned housing units wired for high-speed internet access: 100%. **Campus safety:** Security services offered: 24-hour emergency telephones, lighted pathways/sidewalks, controlled dormitory access (key, security card, etc).

TRANSFER AND INTERNATIONAL STUDENTS
Transfer students: May apply for admission for the following academic terms: Fall, Spring, Summer. Applicants need a minimum number of credits to apply. For fall 2009: Transfer applications received: 196. Transfer applicants offered admission: 148. Transfer applicants enrolled: 90. **International students:** Number of foreign undergraduates: 22 (3% of student body). Number of countries represented: 11. Minimum TOEFL score required: 550 (paper); 213 (computer). Average TOEFL score: 578 (paper).

Rhodes College

- **Address:** 2000 N. Parkway, Memphis, TN 38112
- **Website:** http://www.rhodes.edu
- **Private; Religious affiliation:** Presbyterian (USA)
- **Enrollment:** 1,661 full-time; 14 part-time

KEY STATS
✔ **U.S News College Ranking:** 47, National Liberal Arts Colleges
✔ **ACT Score (25th/75th percentile):** 26-30
✔ **Tuition:** 2009-2010: $32,446

Selectivity: More selective	**Room/board:** $7,842
Acceptance rate: 42%	**Average debt:** $26,071
Student/faculty ratio: 10/1	**Proportion who borrowed:** 47%

UNDERGRADUATE STUDENT BODY STATS
2009-2010 enrollment: 1,661 full-time; 14 part-time. Men: 43%; women: 57%. **Ethnic makeup:** African American: 7%; American-Indian: 1%; Asian American: 5%; Hispanic: 2%; White: 81%; International: 4%. **Religious preference:** Roman Catholic: 16%; Protestant: 35%; Jewish: 1%; Muslim: 2%; Hindu: 1%; Buddhist: 2%; No preference: 20%; Presbyterian (USA): 10%; Other: 13%.

ADMISSIONS FACTS AND FIGURES
Phone: (800) 844-5969. **Email:** adminfo@rhodes.edu. **Website:** http://www.rhodes.edu. **Application deadlines for fall 2011:** Regular decision: January 15; decision sent by April 1. Early decision: Send application by: November 1; Decision sent by: December 1. Early action: Send application by: November 15; Decision sent by: January 15. Admission can be deferred. **Application fee:** $45. **To apply online, go to:** https://apply.rhodes.edu/Default.asp. **Admissions requirements/recommendations:** High school units required (recommended): English: 4; Mathematics: 3; Science: 2; Foreign language: 2; Social studies: 2; Academic electives: 3; Total units: 16. Tests: The college uses SAT or ACT scores in admissions decisions. Either SAT or ACT required. For admission to the fall 2011 entering class, the school will accept: ACT with or without writing accepted. Campus visit: Recommended. Admissions interview: Recommended. Off-campus interview: May be arranged. **Factors that count in admissions decisions:** *Academic:* Secondary school record: Very Important. Class rank: Very Important. Letters of recommendation: Important. Standardized test scores: Important. Essay: Important. *Nonacademic:* Interview: Considered. Extracurricular activities: Considered. Talent/ability: Considered. Character/personal qualities: Important. Alumni/ae relationship: Important. Geographical residence: Considered. State residency: Considered. Religious affiliation/commitment: Not Considered. Minority status: Important. Volunteer work: Considered. Work experience: Considered. **Other schools with the greatest overlap in applicants:** Furman University; Hendrix College; Sewanee–University of the South; Tulane University; Vanderbilt University. **Admissions statistics for the fall 2009 entering class:** Total applicants: 5,039. Total accepted: 2,113. Freshmen enrolled: 432; 72% were from out of state. Accepted through early-decision or early-action plans: 20%. Overall acceptance rate: 42%. Early-decision acceptance rate: 31%. Non-early acceptance rate: 43%. **Size of waiting list:** 503 applicants; enrolled from waiting list: 48. **Credentials of fall 2009 freshmen:** 57% ranked in the top 10 percent of their high school class; 84% were in the top 25 percent; 96% were in the top half. (Proportion submitting class standing: 53%.) **Average high school grade point average:** 3.8. **First-year students who submitted SAT scores:** 68%. Scores (25/75 percentile): Critical Reading: 570-680, Math: 580-700, Combined: 1150-1380. **First-year students submitting ACT scores:** 73%. Scores (25/75 percentile): English: N/A, Math: N/A, Composite: 26-N/A.

ACADEMICS
Year founded: 1848. **Academic calendar:** Semester. **Degrees offered:** bachelor's, master's. **Most popular majors:** 21% social sciences, 12% biological and biomedical sciences, 11% history, 10% business, management, marketing, and related support services, 8% psychology. **Major fields of study:** area, ethnic, cultural, and gender studies; biological and biomedical sciences; business, management, marketing, and related support services; computer and information sciences and support services; English language and literature/letters; foreign languages, literatures, and linguistics; history; mathematics and statistics; multi/interdisciplinary studies; philosophy and religious studies; physical sciences; psychology; social sciences; visual and performing arts. **Areas of required coursework:** arts/fine arts, humanities, mathematics, English (including composition), philosophy, foreign

languages, sciences (biological or physical), history, social science, other. **Pre-professional programs:** pre-law, pre-medicine. **Special academic programs:** cooperative (work-study plan) program, cross-registration, double major, dual enrollment, exchange student program (domestic), honors program, independent study, internships, liberal arts/career combination, student-designed major, study abroad, other. **Cooperative education programs:** art, engineering, health professions. **Reserve Officers Training Corps (ROTC):** Army ROTC: Offered at cooperating institution (University of Memphis); Air Force ROTC: Offered at cooperating institution (University of Memphis). **Faculty and instruction (2009-2010):** Total instructional faculty: 161 full-time, 32 part-time (56% men; 44% women; 10% minorities). Full-time faculty with Ph.D. or other terminal degree: 98%. Student/faculty ratio: 10/1. Classes of fewer than 20 students: 75%; of 20 to 49 students: 23%; of 50 or more students: 1%. **Advanced Placement and International Baccalaureate credit:** AP tests may be used for: Credit and/or placement. Scores accepted: 4, 5. International Baccalaureate exams may be used for: Credit and/or placement. **Freshmen returning for sophomore year:** 88%. **Graduation rates:** Four-year: 75%; five-year: 82%; six-year: 82%. **Graduate study:** 40% of students pursue further study within one year. Fields in which graduates pursue further study: Master of Business Administration (MBA), 2%; law, 43%; medicine, 13%; dentistry, 2%; engineering, 1%; theology (or the seminary), 7%; education, 12%; arts and sciences, 20%.

COSTS AND FINANCIAL AID

Financial aid office: (901) 843-3810. **Expenses (2009-2010):** Tuition and fees 2009-2010: $32,446; room/board: $7,842. Estimated books and supplies: $1,020; transportation: $1,022; personal expenses: $1,350. **Financial aid:** Priority filing date for institution's financial aid form: March 1; deadline: March 1. Of those, 47% were determined to have financial need; 39% had their need fully met. Average financial aid package (proportion receiving): $31,373 (47%). Average amount of gift aid, such as scholarships or grants (proportion receiving): $20,727 (45%). Average amount of self-help aid, such as work study or loans (proportion receiving): $6,772 (32%). Average need-based loan (excluding PLUS or other private loans): $6,822. Among students who received need-based aid, the average percentage of need met: 80%. Among students who received aid based on merit, the average award (and the proportion receiving): $13,433 (36%). The average athletic scholarship (and the proportion receiving): $0 (0%). Average amount of debt of borrowers graduating in 2009: $26,071. Proportion who borrowed: 47%.

CAMPUS LIFE AND EXTRACURRICULAR ACTIVITIES

Campus housing available: coed dorms, women's dorms, men's dorms, apartment for single students, other housing options. Students who live in college-owned, operated, or affiliated housing: 76%. Average per-year earnings: $4,500. **Clubs and organizations:** Number of student organizations: 100. Activities include: campus ministries, choral groups, dance, drama/theater, international student organization, jazz band, literary magazine, model UN, music ensembles, musical theater, pep band, radio station, student government, student newspaper, student film society, symphony orchestra, television station, yearbook. Number of fraternities: 7; sororities: 6. Proportion of men in fraternities: 45%; of women in sororities: 53%. Average proportion of students who stay on campus on weekends: 90%. **Sports program (2009-2010):** Member of NCAA III.

SERVICES AND FACILITIES

Basic services: nonremedial tutoring, women's center, placement service, health service, health insurance. **Counseling services:** minority student, career, personal, academic, psychological, religious. **For learning-disabled students:** School does not offer a structured program with separate admission and additional fees. Services include: reading machines, tape recorders, note-taking services, readers, extended time for tests, tutors, priority seating, texts on tape. **Library:** Number of titles: 296,962; number of current serial subscriptions: 1,122. **Information technology resources:** Students are not required to lease or own a computer. Number of campus computers available to all students: 220. School has a wireless network. Proportion of college-owned housing units wired for high-speed internet access: 100%. **Campus safety:** Security services offered: 24-hour foot-and-vehicle patrols, late-night transport/escort service, 24-hour emergency telephones, lighted pathways/sidewalks, student patrols, controlled dormitory access (key, security card, etc).

TRANSFER AND INTERNATIONAL STUDENTS

Transfer students: May apply for admission for the following academic terms: Fall, Spring. Applicants need a minimum number of credits to apply. For fall 2009: Transfer applications received: 146. Transfer applicants offered admission: 31. Transfer applicants enrolled: 20. **International students:** Number of foreign undergraduates: 60 (4% of student body). Number of countries represented: 7. Minimum TOEFL score required: 550 (paper); 213 (computer).

Sewanee—University of the South

- **Address:** 735 University Avenue, Sewanee, TN 37383
- **Website:** http://www.sewanee.edu
- **Private; Religious affiliation:** Episcopal
- **Enrollment:** 1,455 full-time; 14 part-time

KEY STATS

✔ **U.S News College Ranking:** 32, National Liberal Arts Colleges
✔ **SAT Score (25th/75th percentile):** 1150-1360
✔ **Tuition:** 2010-2011: $35,862

Selectivity: More selective	**Room/board:** $10,250
Acceptance rate: 68%	**Average debt:** $18,717
Student/faculty ratio: 10/1	**Proportion who borrowed:** 38%

UNDERGRADUATE STUDENT BODY STATS

2009-2010 enrollment: 1,455 full-time; 14 part-time. Men: 49%; women: 51%. **Ethnic makeup:** African American: 5%; American-Indian: 1%; Asian American: 3%; Hispanic: 3%; White: 87%; International: 2%. **Religious preference:** Roman Catholic: 12%; Protestant: 30%; Jewish: 1%; Unknown: 24%; Episcopal: 33%.

ADMISSIONS FACTS AND FIGURES

Phone: (800) 522-2234. **Email:** admiss@sewanee.edu. **Website:** http://www.sewanee.edu. **Application deadlines for fall 2011:** Regular decision: February 1; decision sent by March 17. Early decision: Send application by: November 15; Decision sent by: December 17. Early action: Not offered. Admission can be deferred. **Application fee:** $45. **To apply online, go to:** http://admission.sewanee.edu/apply. **Admissions requirements/recommendations:** High school units required (recommended): English: 4 (4); Mathematics: 3 (4); Science: 2 (4); Foreign language: 2 (4); Social studies: 1 (2); History: 1 (2); Total units: 13 (20). Tests: The college uses SAT or ACT scores in admissions decisions. Neither SAT nor ACT required. For admission to the fall 2011 entering class, the school will accept: ACT with writing required. Campus visit: Recommended. Admissions interview: Recommended. Off-campus interview: May be arranged. **Factors that count in admissions decisions:** *Academic:* Secondary school record: Very Important. Class rank: Considered. Letters of recommendation: Very Important. Standardized test scores: Important. Essay: Important. *Nonacademic:* Interview: Considered. Extracurricular activities: Important. Talent/ability: Considered. Character/personal qualities: Important. Alumni/ae relationship: Considered. Geographical residence: Considered. State residency: Not Considered. Religious affiliation/commitment: Not Considered. Minority status: Considered. Volunteer work: Important. Work experience: Important. **Other schools with the greatest overlap in applicants:** Furman University; Rhodes College; University of Georgia; Vanderbilt University; Washington and Lee University. **Admissions statistics for the fall 2009 entering class:** Total applicants: 2,481. Total accepted: 1,688. Freshmen enrolled: 402; 75% were from out of state. Overall acceptance rate: 68%. Early-decision acceptance rate: 59%. Non-early acceptance rate: 69%. **Size of waiting list:** 317 applicants; enrolled from waiting list: 28. **Credentials of fall 2009 freshmen:** 43% ranked in the top 10 percent of their high school class; 67% were in the top 25 percent; 88% were in the top half. (Proportion submitting class standing: 37%.) **Average high school grade point average:** 3.6. **First-year students who submitted SAT scores:** 57%. Scores (25/75 percentile): Critical Reading: 570-690, Math: 580-670, Combined: 1150-1360. **First-year students submitting ACT scores:** 43%. Scores (25/75 percentile): English: 24-29, Math: 25-32, Composite: 26-30.

ACADEMICS

Year founded: 1857. **Academic calendar:** Semester. **Degrees offered:** bachelor's, master's. **Most popular majors:** 23% social sciences, 16% English language and literature/letters, 11% history, 8% biological and biomedical sciences, 7% psychology. **Major fields of study:** area, ethnic, cultural, and gender studies; biological and biomedical sciences; computer and information sciences and support services; English language and literature/letters; foreign languages, literatures, and linguistics; history; mathematics and statistics; natural resources and conservation; philosophy and religious studies; physical sciences; psychology; social sciences; visual and performing arts. **Areas of required coursework:** arts/fine arts, humanities, mathematics, English (including composition), philosophy, foreign languages, sciences (biological or physical), history, social science, other. **Pre-professional programs:** pre-law, pre-dentistry, pre-medicine, pre-veterinary science, other. **Special academic programs:** double major, independent study, internships, student-designed major, study abroad. **Faculty and instruction (2009-2010):** Total instructional faculty: 134 full-time, 38 part-time (65% men; 35% women; 8% minorities). Full-time faculty with Ph.D. or other terminal degree: 96%. Student/faculty ratio: 10/1. Classes of fewer than 20 students: 72%; of 20 to 49 students: 28%; of 50 or more students: 1%. **Advanced Placement and International Baccalaureate credit:** AP tests may be used for: Credit only. Scores accepted: 4, 5. International Baccalaureate exams may be used for: Credit only. **Freshmen returning for sophomore year:** 89%. **Graduation rates:** Four-year: 75%; five-year: 81%; six-year: 82%. **Graduate study:** 15% of students pursue further study immediately upon graduation; 19% within one year; 43% within five years. Fields in which graduates pursue further study: Master of Business Administration (MBA), 8%; law, 22%; medicine, 6%; dentistry, 1%; engineering, 1%; theology (or the seminary), 2%; education, 9%; arts and sciences, 38%; veterinary medicine, 1%.

COSTS AND FINANCIAL AID

Financial aid office: (931) 598-1312. **Expenses (2010-2011):** Tuition and fees 2010-2011: $35,862; room/board: $10,250. Estimated books and supplies: $800; transportation: $200; personal expenses: $900. **Financial aid:** Priority filing date for institution's financial aid form: March 1. In 2009-2010, 56% of undergraduates applied for financial aid. Of those, 54% were determined to have financial need; 78% had their need fully met. Average financial aid package (proportion receiving): $26,112 (54%). Average amount of gift aid, such as scholarships or grants (proportion receiving): $20,919 (53%). Average amount of self-help aid, such as work study or loans (proportion receiving): $3,998 (39%). Average need-based loan (excluding PLUS or other private loans): $4,234. Among students who received need-based aid, the average percentage of need met: 95%. Among students who received aid based on merit, the average award (and the proportion receiving): $14,376 (25%). The average athletic scholarship (and the proportion receiving): $0 (0%). Average amount of debt of borrowers graduating in 2009: $18,717. Proportion who borrowed: 38%.

CAMPUS LIFE AND EXTRACURRICULAR ACTIVITIES

Campus housing available (% using): coed dorms (68%), women's dorms (8%), men's dorms (14%), sorority housing (2%), fraternity housing (2%), apartments for married students (0%), special housing for disabled students, other housing options (1%). Students who live in college-owned, operated, or affiliated housing: 96%. **Student employment:** During the 2009-2010 academic year, 15% of undergraduates worked on campus. Average per-year earnings: $1,500. **Clubs and organizations:** Number of student organizations: 110. Activities include: campus ministries, choral groups, concert band, dance, drama/theater, international student organization, jazz band, literary magazine, model UN, music ensembles, musical theater, radio station, student government, student newspaper, student film society, symphony orchestra, yearbook. Number of fraternities: 12; sororities: 9. Proportion of men in fraternities: 70%; of women in sororities: 68%. Average proportion of students who stay on campus on weekends: 90%. **Sports program (2009-2010):** Member of NCAA III. **Men's intercollegiate varsity sports:** baseball, basketball, cross country, football, golf, lacrosse, soccer, swimming, tennis, track and field (indoor), track and field (outdoor). **Women's intercollegiate varsity sports:** basketball, cross country, equestrian, field hockey, golf, lacrosse, soccer, softball, swimming, tennis, track and field (indoor), track and field (outdoor), volleyball.

SERVICES AND FACILITIES

Basic services: nonremedial tutoring, women's center, day care, health service, health insurance, other. **Counseling services:** minority student, career, personal, academic, older student, psychological, birth control, religious. **For learning-disabled students:** School does not offer a structured program with separate admission and additional fees. Services include: untimed tests, note-taking services, extended time for tests, tutors, priority seating, other testing accommodations. **Library:** Number of titles: 743,062; number of current serial subscriptions: 7,920. **Information technology resources:** Students are not required to lease or own a computer. Number of campus computers available to all students: 170. School has a wireless network. Approximate number of users that can be accommodated: 650. Proportion of college-owned housing units wired for high-speed internet access: 100%. **Campus safety:** Security services offered: 24-hour foot-and-vehicle patrols, late-night transport/escort service, 24-hour emergency telephones, lighted pathways/sidewalks, controlled dormitory access (key, security card, etc).

TRANSFER AND INTERNATIONAL STUDENTS

Transfer students: May apply for admission for the following academic terms: Fall, Spring. Applicants do not need a minimum number of credits to apply. For fall 2009: Transfer applications received: 66. Transfer applicants offered admission: 34. Transfer applicants enrolled: 17. **International students:** Number of foreign undergraduates: 29 (2% of student body). Number of countries represented: 23. Minimum TOEFL score required: 550 (paper); 80 (computer).

Southern Adventist University

- **Address:** PO Box 370, Collegedale, TN 37315
- **Website:** http://www.southern.edu
- **Private; Religious affiliation:** Seventh-day Adventist
- **Enrollment:** 2,195 full-time; 452 part-time

KEY STATS

✔ **U.S News College Ranking:** 31, Regional Colleges (South)
✔ **ACT Score (25th/75th percentile):** 19-26
✔ **Tuition:** 2010-2011: $17,712

Selectivity: Selective	**Room/board:** $5,574
Acceptance rate: 71%	**Average debt:** $22,977
Student/faculty ratio: 16/1	**Proportion who borrowed:** 58%

UNDERGRADUATE STUDENT BODY STATS

2009-2010 enrollment: 2,195 full-time; 452 part-time. Men: 44%; women: 56%. **Ethnic makeup:** African American: 11%; Asian American: 6%; Hispanic: 17%; White: 60%; International: 6%. **Religious preference:** Protestant: 2%; No preference: 1%; Seventh-day Adventist: 95%; Unknown: 2%.

ADMISSIONS FACTS AND FIGURES

Phone: (423) 236-2844. **Email:** admissions@southern.edu. **Website:** http://www.southern.edu. **Application deadlines for fall 2011:** Regular decision: September 7. Early decision: Not offered. Early action: Not offered. Admission can be deferred. **Application fee:** $25. **To apply online, go to:** https://www.southern.edu/sites/enrollment/admission/Pages/applynowonline.aspx. **Admissions requirements/recommendations:** High school units required (recommended): English: 3 (4); Mathematics: 2 (3); Science: 2 (3); Foreign language: 0 (2); Social studies: 1 (1); History: 1 (2); Academic electives: 9 (7); Total units: 18 (24). Tests: The college uses SAT or ACT scores in admissions decisions. Either SAT or ACT required. For admission to the fall 2011 entering class, the school will accept: ACT with or without writing accepted. Campus visit: Recommended. Admissions interview: Recommended. Off-campus interview: May be arranged. **Factors that count in admissions decisions:** *Academic:* Secondary school record: Very Important. Class rank: Not Considered. Letters of recommendation: Not Considered. Standardized test scores: Very Important. Essay: Not Considered. *Nonacademic:* Interview: Not Considered. Extracurricular activities: Not Considered. Talent/ability: Not Considered. Character/personal qualities: Not Considered. Alumni/ae relationship: Not Considered. Geographical residence: Not Considered. State residency: Not Considered. Religious affiliation/commitment: Not Considered. Minority status: Not Considered. Volunteer work: Not Considered. Work experience: Not Considered. **Other schools with the greatest overlap in applicants:** Andrews University; Oakwood University; Washington Adventist University. **Admissions statistics for the fall 2009 entering class:** Total applicants: 1,513. Total accepted: 1,074. Freshmen enrolled: 603; 78% were from out of state. Overall acceptance rate: 71%. **Average high school grade point average:** 3.4. **First-year students who submitted SAT scores:** 47%. **First-year students submitting ACT scores:** 78%. Scores (25/75 percentile): English: 20-27, Math: 18-24, Composite: 19-26.

ACADEMICS

Year founded: 1892. **Academic calendar:** Semester. **Degrees offered:** certificate, associate, bachelor's, master's. **Most popular majors:** 21% health professions and related clinical sciences, 15% business, management, marketing, and related support services, 8% biological and biomedical sciences, 8% education. **Major fields of study:** area, ethnic, cultural, and gender studies; biological and biomedical sciences; business, management, marketing, and related support services; communication, journalism, and related programs; communications technologies/technicians and support services; computer and information sciences and support services; education; English language and literature/letters; family and consumer sciences/ human sciences; foreign languages, literatures, and linguistics; health professions and related clinical sciences; history; mathematics and statistics; multi/interdisciplinary studies; parks, recreation, leisure, and fitness studies; philosophy and religious studies; physical sciences; psychology; public administration and social service professions; social sciences; theology and religious vocations; visual and performing arts. **Areas of required coursework:** arts/fine arts, computer literacy, mathematics, English (including composition), philosophy, sciences (biological or physical), history, social science. **Pre-professional programs:** pre-law, pre-dentistry, pre-medicine, pre-theology, pre-optometry, pre-pharmacy. **Special academic programs:** double major, dual enrollment, English as a Second Language (ESL), honors program, independent study, internships, study abroad, teacher certificate program. **Teacher certification offered in:** elementary, secondary. **Faculty and instruction (2009-2010):** Total instructional faculty: 139 full-time, 118 part-time (61% men; 39% women; 11% minorities). Full-time faculty with Ph.D. or other terminal degree: 64%. Student/faculty ratio: 16/1. **Advanced Placement and International Baccalaureate credit:** AP tests may be used for: Credit only. Scores accepted: 3, 4, 5. International Baccalaureate exams may be used for: Placement only. **Freshmen returning for sophomore year:** 70%. **Graduation rates:** Four-year: 22%; five-year: 37%; six-year: 49%. **Graduate study:** 10% of students pursue further study immediately upon graduation. Fields in which graduates pursue further study: medicine, 33%; dentistry, 8%; theology (or the seminary), 21%; education, 4%; arts and sciences, 34%.

COSTS AND FINANCIAL AID

Financial aid office: (423) 236-2835. **Expenses (2010-2011):** Tuition and fees 2010-2011: $17,712; room/board: $5,574. Estimated books and supplies: $1,100; transportation: $2,000; personal expenses: $2,000. **Financial aid:** Priority filing date for institution's financial aid form: March 1. In 2009-2010, 74% of undergraduates applied for financial aid. Of those, 46% were determined to have financial need; 95% had their need fully met. Average financial aid package (proportion receiving): $20,165 (46%). Average amount of gift aid, such as scholarships or grants (proportion receiving): $9,814 (45%). Average amount of self-help aid, such as work study or loans (proportion receiving): $3,189 (39%). Average need-based loan (excluding PLUS or other private loans): $4,793. Among students who received need-based aid, the average percentage of need met: 77%. Among students who received aid based on merit, the average award (and the proportion receiving): $5,408 (27%). Average amount of debt of borrowers graduating in 2009: $22,977. Proportion who borrowed: 58%.

CAMPUS LIFE AND EXTRACURRICULAR ACTIVITIES

Campus housing available (% using): women's dorms (47%), men's dorms (43%), apartments for married students (8%), apartment for single students (2%). Students who live in college-owned, operated, or affiliated housing: 65%. **Student employment:** During the 2009-2010 academic year, 50% of undergraduates worked on campus. Average per-year earnings: $3,000. **Clubs and organizations:** Number of student organizations: 38. Activities include: campus ministries, choral groups, concert band, drama/theater, international student organization, jazz band, music ensembles, radio station, student government, student newspaper, student film society, symphony orchestra, television station, yearbook. Number of fraternities: 0; sororities: 0. Average proportion of students who stay on campus on weekends: 40%.

SERVICES AND FACILITIES

Basic services: nonremedial tutoring, placement service, health service, health insurance. **Remedial assistance:** reading, math, writing, study skills. **Counseling services:** career, personal, academic, psychological, religious. **For learning-disabled students:** School does not offer a structured program with separate admission and additional fees. Services include: remedial math, remedial English, reading machines, tape recorders, diagnostic testing service, note-taking services, oral tests, learning center, readers, extended time for tests, tutors, priority seating, texts on tape, other testing accommodations. **Library:** Number of titles: 166,905; number of current serial subscriptions: 40,304. **Information technology resources:** Students are not required to lease or own a computer. Number of campus computers available to all students: 150. School has a wireless network. Approximate number of users that can be accommodated: 2,000. Proportion of college-owned housing units wired for high-speed internet access: 95%. **Campus safety:** Security services offered: 24-hour foot-and-vehicle patrols, late-night transport/escort service, 24-hour emergency telephones, lighted pathways/sidewalks, student patrols, controlled dormitory access (key, security card, etc).

TRANSFER AND INTERNATIONAL STUDENTS

Transfer students: May apply for admission for the following academic terms: Fall, Winter, Summer. Applicants need a minimum number of credits to apply. For fall 2009: Transfer applications received: 361. Transfer applicants offered admission: 278. Transfer applicants enrolled: 168. **International students:** Number of foreign undergraduates: 147 (6% of student body). Minimum TOEFL score required: 450 (paper); 133 (computer).

Tennessee State University

- **Address:** 3500 John Merritt Boulevard, Nashville, TN 37209-1561
- **Website:** http://www.tnstate.edu
- **Public**
- **Enrollment:** 5,458 full-time; 1,369 part-time

KEY STATS

✔ **U.S News College Ranking:** second tier, National Universities
✔ **ACT Score (25th/75th percentile):** 16-20
✔ **Tuition:** 2009-2010: $5,474 in state, $17,552 out of state
  Selectivity: Less selective   **Room/board:** $5,610
  Acceptance rate: 65%   **Average debt:** N/A
  Student/faculty ratio: 16/1   **Proportion who borrowed:** 80%

UNDERGRADUATE STUDENT BODY STATS

2009-2010 enrollment: 5,458 full-time; 1,369 part-time. Men: 37%; women: 63%. **Ethnic makeup:** African American: 85%; Asian American: 1%; Hispanic: 1%; White: 12%.

ADMISSIONS FACTS AND FIGURES

Phone: (615) 963-5101. **Email:** jcade@tnstate.edu. **Website:** http://www.tnstate.edu. **Application deadlines for fall 2011:** Regular decision: July 1. Early decision: Not offered. Early action: Not offered. Admission cannot be deferred. **Application fee:** $25. **To apply online, go to:** http://lander.tnstate.edu:9000/pls/PROD/bwskalog.P_DispLoginNon. **Admissions requirements/recommendations:** High school units required (recommended): English: 4 (4); Mathematics: 3 (4); Science: 2 (2); Foreign language: 2 (2); Social studies: 1 (1); History: 1 (1); Academic electives: 1 (1); Total units: 14 (17). Tests: The college uses SAT or ACT scores in admissions decisions. Either SAT or ACT required. Campus visit: Recommended. Admissions interview: Neither required nor recommended. Off-campus interview: May be arranged. **Factors that count in admissions decisions:** *Academic:* Secondary school record: Very Important. Class rank: Important. Letters of recommendation: Important. Standardized test scores: Important. Essay: Not Considered. *Nonacademic:* Interview: Not Considered. Extracurricular activities: Not Considered. Talent/ability: Not Considered. Character/personal qualities: Not Considered. Alumni/ae relationship: Important. Geographical residence: Not Considered. State residency: Important. Religious affiliation/commitment: Not Considered. Minority status: Not Considered. Volunteer work: Not Considered. Work experience: Not Considered. **Other schools with the greatest overlap in applicants:** Alabama State University; Austin Peay State University; Dillard University; Lipscomb University; Middle Tennessee State University. **Admissions statistics for the fall 2009 entering class:** Total applicants: 4,828. Total accepted: 3,136. Freshmen enrolled: 1,338; 33% were from out of state. Overall acceptance rate: 65%. **Average high school grade point average:** 2.9. **First-year students who submitted SAT scores:** 10%. **First-year students submitting ACT scores:** 89%. Scores (25/75 percentile): English: 15-20, Math: 15-19, Composite: 16-20.

ACADEMICS

Year founded: 1912. **Academic calendar:** Semester. **Degrees offered:** certificate, associate, bachelor's, master's, doctorate. **Most popular majors:** 13% nursing/registered nurse training (R.N., A.S.N., B.S.N., M.S.N.), 11% liberal arts and sciences/liberal studies, 10% business administration and management, 8% psychology, 7% special education and teaching. **Major fields of study:** agriculture, agriculture operations, and related sciences; area, ethnic, cultural, and gender studies; biological and biomedical sciences; business, management, marketing, and related support services; computer and information sciences and support services; education; engineering; engineering technologies/technicians; English language and literature/letters; family and consumer sciences/human sciences; foreign languages, literatures, and linguistics; health professions and related clinical sciences; history; liberal arts and sciences studies, and humanities; mathematics and statistics;

parks, recreation, leisure, and fitness studies; physical sciences; psychology; public administration and social service professions; security and protective services; social sciences; visual and performing arts. **Areas of required coursework:** arts/fine arts, humanities, mathematics, English (including composition), philosophy, foreign languages, sciences (biological or physical), history, social science. **Pre-professional programs:** pre-medicine. **Special academic programs (% participation):** cooperative (work-study plan) program (12%), cross-registration (2%), distance learning (5%), double major (3%), exchange student program (domestic) (3%), honors program (18%), independent study (1%), internships (14%), teacher certificate program (17%). **Teacher certification offered in:** early childhood, special education, elementary, adult education, secondary. **Cooperative education programs:** business, computer science, engineering. **Reserve Officers Training Corps (ROTC):** Air Force ROTC: Offered on campus. **Faculty and instruction (2009-2010):** Total instructional faculty: 454 full-time, 110 part-time (52% men; 48% women; 61% minorities). Full-time faculty with Ph.D. or other terminal degree: 83%. Student/faculty ratio: 16/1. Classes of fewer than 20 students: 52%; of 20 to 49 students: 45%; of 50 or more students: 2%. **Advanced Placement and International Baccalaureate credit:** AP tests may be used for: Credit only. Freshmen returning for sophomore year: 68%. **Graduation rates:** Four-year: 13%; five-year: 30%; six-year: 40%. **Graduate study:** 6% of students pursue further study immediately upon graduation; 5% within one year; 4% within five years. Fields in which graduates pursue further study: Master of Business Administration (MBA), 12%; law, 2%; medicine, 4%; engineering, 5%; education, 8%; arts and sciences, 6%; veterinary medicine, 1%.

COSTS AND FINANCIAL AID

Financial aid office: (615) 963-5701. **Expenses (2009-2010):** Tuition and fees 2009-2010: $5,474 in state, $17,552 out of state; room/board: $5,610. Estimated books and supplies: $1,250; transportation: $1,832; personal expenses: $1,500. **Financial aid:** Priority filing date for institution's financial aid form: April 1; deadline: August 1. In 2009-2010, 93% of undergraduates applied for financial aid. Of those, 85% were determined to have financial need; 19% had their need fully met. Average financial aid package (proportion receiving): $8,464 (85%). Average amount of gift aid, such as scholarships or grants (proportion receiving): $3,995 (0%). Average amount of self-help aid, such as work study or loans (proportion receiving): $4,197 (85%). Average need-based loan (excluding PLUS or other private loans): $4,197. Among students who received need-based aid, the average percentage of need met: 70%. Proportion who borrowed: 80%.

CAMPUS LIFE AND EXTRACURRICULAR ACTIVITIES

Campus housing available (% using): coed dorms (23%), women's dorms (37%), men's dorms (28%), apartment for single students (12%). Students who live in college-owned, operated, or affiliated housing: 38%. **Student employment:** During the 2009-2010 academic year, 34% of undergraduates worked on campus. Average per-year earnings: $3,000. **Clubs and organizations:** Number of student organizations: 124. Activities include: campus ministries, choral groups, concert band, dance, drama/theater, international student organization, jazz band, marching band, music ensembles, musical theater, pep band, radio station, student government, student newspaper, television station, yearbook. Number of fraternities: 13; sororities: 12. Average proportion of students who stay on campus on weekends: 31%. **Sports program (2009-2010):** Member of NCAA I. *Men's intercollegiate varsity sports:* basketball, cross country, football, golf, tennis, track and field (indoor), track and field (outdoor). *Women's intercollegiate varsity sports:* basketball, cross country, golf, softball, tennis, track and field (indoor), track and field (outdoor), volleyball.

SERVICES AND FACILITIES

Basic services: nonremedial tutoring, placement service, day care, health service. **Remedial assistance:** reading, math, writing, study skills. **Counseling services:** minority student, career, military, veteran student, academic, older student, psychological. **For learning-disabled students:** School does not offer a structured program with separate admission and additional fees. Services include: remedial math, remedial English, remedial reading, tape recorders, diagnostic testing service, oral tests, learning center, extended time for tests, tutors, other testing accommodations. **Library:** Number of titles: 402,587; number of current serial subscriptions: 1,656. **Information technology resources:** Students are not required to lease or own a computer. Number of campus computers available to all students: 1,200. School has a wireless network. Proportion of college-owned housing units wired for high-speed internet access: 100%. **Campus safety:** Security services offered: 24-hour foot-and-vehicle patrols, late-night transport/escort service, 24-hour emergency telephones, lighted pathways/sidewalks, controlled dormitory access (key, security card, etc).

TRANSFER AND INTERNATIONAL STUDENTS

Transfer students: May apply for admission for the following academic terms: Fall, Winter, Spring, Summer. Applicants need a minimum number of credits to apply. For fall 2009: Transfer applications received: 1,885. Transfer applicants offered admission: 1,137. Transfer applicants enrolled: 580. **International students:** Number of foreign undergraduates: 24. Minimum TOEFL score required: 500 (paper). Average TOEFL score: 525 (paper).

Tennessee Technological University

- **Address:** Campus Box 5006 USPS 077-460, Cookeville, TN 38505
- **Website:** http://www.tntech.edu
- **Public**
- **Enrollment:** 8,017 full-time; 901 part-time

KEY STATS

✔ **U.S News College Ranking:** 29, Regional Universities (South)
✔ **ACT Score (25th/75th percentile):** 20-26
✔ **Tuition:** 2010-2011: $5,800 in state, $17,980 out of state
  Selectivity: Selective   **Room/board:** $7,680
  Acceptance rate: 84%   **Average debt:** $14,691
  Student/faculty ratio: 21/1   **Proportion who borrowed:** 44%

UNDERGRADUATE STUDENT BODY STATS

2009-2010 enrollment: 8,017 full-time; 901 part-time. Men: 53%; women: 47%. **Ethnic makeup:** African American: 4%; Asian American: 1%; Hispanic: 2%; White: 90%; International: 2%.

ADMISSIONS FACTS AND FIGURES

Phone: (800) 255-8881. **Email:** admissions@tntech.edu. **Website:** http://www.tntech.edu. **Application deadlines for fall 2011:** Regular decision: August 1. Early decision: Not offered. Early action: Not offered. Admission can be deferred. **Application fee:** $15. **To apply online, go to:** http://www.tntech.edu/admissions/apply_online.html. **Admissions requirements/recommendations:** High school units required (recommended): English: 4; Mathematics: 3 (4); Science: 2 (3); Foreign language: 2; Social studies: 1; History: 1; Total units: 14. Tests: The college uses SAT or ACT scores in admissions decisions. Either SAT or ACT required. For admission to the fall 2011 entering class, the school will accept: ACT with or without writing accepted. Campus visit: Recommended. Admissions interview: Recommended. Off-campus interview: May be arranged. **Factors that count in admissions decisions:** *Academic:* Secondary school record: Very Important. Class rank: Important. Letters of recommendation: Considered. Standardized test scores: Very Important. Essay: Not Considered. *Nonacademic:* Interview: Not Considered. Extracurricular activities: Not Considered. Talent/ability: Not Considered. Character/personal qualities: Not Considered. Alumni/ae relationship: Not Considered. Geographical residence: Not Considered. State residency: Considered. Religious affiliation/commitment: Not Considered. Minority status: Not Considered. Volunteer work: Not Considered. Work experience: Not Considered. **Other schools with the greatest overlap in applicants:** Austin Peay State University; East Tennessee State University; Middle Tennessee State University; University of Tennessee; University of Tennessee–Chattanooga. **Admissions statistics for the fall 2009 entering class:** Total applicants: 4,486. Total accepted: 3,786. Freshmen enrolled: 1,893; 4% were from out of state. Overall acceptance rate: 84%. **Credentials of fall 2009 freshmen:** 25% ranked in the top 10 percent of their high school class; 53% were in the top 25 percent; 84% were in the top half. (Proportion submitting class standing: 74%.) **Average high school grade point average:** 3.4. **First-year students who submitted SAT scores:** 8%. Scores (25/75 percentile): Critical Reading: 470-610, Math: 490-640, Combined: 960-1250. **First-year students submitting ACT scores:** 97%. Scores (25/75 percentile): English: 20-26, Math: 19-25, Composite: 20-26.

ACADEMICS

Year founded: 1915. **Academic calendar:** Semester. **Degrees offered:** bachelor's, post-bachelor's certificate, master's, doctorate. **Most popular majors:** 17% multi/interdisciplinary studies, 7% business administration and management, 6% mechanical engineering, 5% liberal arts and sciences/liberal studies, 4% nursing/registered nurse training (R.N., A.S.N., B.S.N., M.S.N.). **Major fields of study:** agriculture, agriculture operations, and related sciences; area, ethnic, cultural, and gender studies; biological and biomedical sciences; business, management, marketing, and related support services; communication, journalism, and related programs; computer and information sciences and support services; education; engineering; engineering technologies/technicians; English language and literature/letters; family and consumer sciences/human sciences; foreign languages, literatures, and linguistics; health professions and related clinical sciences; history; mathematics and statistics; multi/interdisciplinary studies; natural resources and conservation; parks, recreation, leisure, and fitness studies; physical sciences; psychology; social sciences; visual and performing arts. **Areas of required coursework:** arts/fine arts, humanities, computer literacy, mathematics, English (including composition), foreign languages, sciences (biological or physical), history, social science, other. **Pre-professional programs:** pre-law, pre-dentistry, pre-medicine, pre-veterinary science, pre-optometry, pre-pharmacy, other. **Special academic programs (% participation):** cooperative (work-study plan) program (15%), distance learning (15%), double major (3%), dual enrollment (3%), English as a Second Language (ESL) (0%), exchange student program (domestic) (0%), honors program (4%), independent study (5%), internships (19%), liberal arts/career combination (.8%), study abroad (.9%), teacher certificate program (8%). **Teacher certification offered in:** early childhood, special education, elementary, vo-tech, middle/junior high, secondary, bilingual/bicultural. **Cooperative education programs:** agriculture, business, computer science, education, engineering, home economics. **Reserve Officers Training Corps (ROTC):** Army ROTC: Offered on campus; Air Force ROTC: Offered at cooperating institution (Tennessee State University). **Faculty and instruction (2009-2010):** Total instructional faculty: 385 full-time, 248 part-time (52% men; 48% women; 10% minorities). Full-time faculty with Ph.D. or other terminal degree: 78%. Student/faculty ratio: 21/1. Classes of fewer than 20 students: 37%; of 20 to 49 students: 53%; of 50 or more students: 10%. **Advanced Placement and International Baccalaureate credit:** AP tests may be used for: Credit only. Scores accepted: 4, 5. International Baccalaureate exams may be used for: Credit only. **Freshmen returning for sophomore year:** 73%. **Graduation rates:** Four-year: 22%; five-year: 45%; six-year: 48%. **Graduate study:** 25% of students pursue further study immediately upon graduation.

COSTS AND FINANCIAL AID
Financial aid office: (931) 372-3073. **Expenses (2010-2011):** Tuition and fees 2010-2011: $5,800 in state, $17,980 out of state; room/board: $7,680. Estimated books and supplies: $1,700; transportation: $1,720; personal expenses: $1,580. **Financial aid:** Priority filing date for institution's financial aid form: March 15. In 2009-2010, 91% of undergraduates applied for financial aid. Of those, 54% were determined to have financial need; 32% had their need fully met. Average financial aid package (proportion receiving): $7,954 (55%). Average amount of gift aid, such as scholarships or grants (proportion receiving): $4,182 (30%). Average amount of self-help aid, such as work study or loans (proportion receiving): $1,968 (26%). Average need-based loan (excluding PLUS or other private loans): $1,804. Among students who received need-based aid, the average percentage of need met: 82%. Among students who received aid based on merit, the average award (and the proportion receiving): $5,647 (29%). The average athletic scholarship (and the proportion receiving): $12,666 (8%). Average amount of debt of borrowers graduating in 2009: $14,691. Proportion who borrowed: 44%.

CAMPUS LIFE AND EXTRACURRICULAR ACTIVITIES
Campus housing available (% using): coed dorms (22%), women's dorms (10%), men's dorms (11%), apartments for married students (7%), apartment for single students (6%), special housing for disabled students (1%), special housing for international students (4%). Students who live in college-owned, operated, or affiliated housing: 24%. **Student employment:** During the 2009-2010 academic year, 10% of undergraduates worked on campus. Average per-year earnings: $3,160. **Clubs and organizations:** Number of student organizations: 219. Activities include: choral groups, concert band, dance, drama/theater, jazz band, marching band, music ensembles, musical theater, pep band, radio station, student government, student newspaper, symphony orchestra, television station, yearbook. Number of fraternities: 13; sororities: 7. Proportion of men in fraternities: 10%; of women in sororities: 10%. Average proportion of students who stay on campus on weekends: 30%. **Sports program (2009-2010):** Member of NCAA I. *Men's intercollegiate varsity sports:* baseball, basketball, cross country, football, golf, tennis. *Women's intercollegiate varsity sports:* basketball, cross country, golf, soccer, softball, track and field (indoor), track and field (outdoor), volleyball.

SERVICES AND FACILITIES
Basic services: nonremedial tutoring, women's center, placement service, day care, health service, health insurance. **Remedial assistance:** reading, math, writing, study skills. **Counseling services:** minority student, career, military, personal, veteran student, academic, older student, psychological, birth control. **For learning-disabled students:** School does not offer a structured program with separate admission and additional fees. Services include: reading machines, tape recorders, videotaped classes, note-taking services, oral tests, learning center, readers, extended time for tests, priority registration, priority seating, texts on tape, typist/scribe, exams on tape or computer, other testing accommodations, other. **Library:** Number of titles: 676,414; number of current serial subscriptions: 2,141. **Information technology resources:** Students are not required to lease or own a computer. Number of campus computers available to all students: 1,114. School has a wireless network. Proportion of college-owned housing units wired for high-speed internet access: 100%. **Campus safety:** Security services offered: 24-hour foot-and-vehicle patrols, late-night transport/escort service, 24-hour emergency telephones, lighted pathways/sidewalks, controlled dormitory access (key, security card, etc.).

TRANSFER AND INTERNATIONAL STUDENTS
Transfer students: May apply for admission for the following academic terms: Fall, Spring, Summer. Applicants need a minimum number of credits to apply. For fall 2009: Transfer applications received: 2,117. Transfer applicants offered admission: 1,339. Transfer applicants enrolled: 725. **International students:** Number of foreign undergraduates: 209 (2% of student body). Number of countries represented: 47. Minimum TOEFL score required: 490 (paper); 57 (computer). Average TOEFL score: 525 (paper).

Tennessee Wesleyan College

- **Address:** PO Box 40, Athens, TN 37371-0040
- **Website:** http://www.twcnet.edu
- **Private; Religious affiliation:** United Methodist
- **Enrollment:** 935 full-time; 135 part-time

KEY STATS
✔ **U.S News College Ranking:** 29, Regional Colleges (South)
✔ **ACT Score (25th/75th percentile):** 19-24
✔ **Tuition:** 2009-2010: $18,600

Selectivity: Selective	**Room/board:** $6,100
Acceptance rate: 84%	**Average debt:** N/A
Student/faculty ratio: 15/1	**Proportion who borrowed:** N/A

UNDERGRADUATE STUDENT BODY STATS
2009-2010 enrollment: 935 full-time; 135 part-time. Men: 36%; women: 64%. **Ethnic makeup:** African American: 4%; Asian American: 1%; Hispanic: 1%; White: 92%; International: 2%. **Religious preference:** Roman Catholic: 3%; Protestant: 36%; Jewish: 1%; Unknown: 49%; United Methodist: 11%.

ADMISSIONS FACTS AND FIGURES
Phone: (423) 746-5286. **Email:** admissions@twcnet.edu. **Website:** http://www.twcnet.edu. **Application deadlines for fall 2011:** Regular decision: August 31. Early decision: Not offered. Early action: Not offered. Admission can be deferred. **Application fee:** $25. **To apply online, go to:** http://www.collegefortn.org/applications/TN_Common_App/apply.html?application_id=2771. **Admissions requirements/recommendations:** High school units required (recommended): English: (4); Mathematics: (2); Science: (2); Social studies: (1); History: (1); Total units: (10). Tests: The college uses SAT or ACT scores in admissions decisions. Either SAT or ACT required. For admission to the fall 2011 entering class, the school will accept: ACT with or without writing accepted. Campus visit: Recommended. Admissions interview: Recommended. Off-campus interview: May be arranged. **Factors that count in admissions decisions:** *Academic:* Secondary school record: Very Important. Class rank: Important. Letters of recommendation: Very Important. Standardized test scores: Very Important. Essay: Important. *Nonacademic:* Interview: Important. Extracurricular activities: Important. Talent/ability: Important. Character/personal qualities: Considered. Alumni/ae relationship: Considered. Geographical residence: Not Considered. State residency: Not Considered. Religious affiliation/commitment: Not Considered. Minority status: Not Considered. Volunteer work: Considered. Work experience: Not Considered. **Other schools with the great-**

est overlap in applicants: Carson-Newman College; Lee University; Maryville College; University of Tennessee; University of Tennessee–Chattanooga. **Admissions statistics for the fall 2009 entering class:** Total applicants: 699. Total accepted: 585. Freshmen enrolled: 249; 11% were from out of state. Overall acceptance rate: 84%. **Credentials of fall 2009 freshmen:** 29% ranked in the top 10 percent of their high school class; 55% were in the top 25 percent; 84% were in the top half. (Proportion submitting class standing: 76%.) **Average high school grade point average:** 3.3. **First-year students who submitted SAT scores:** 14%. Scores (25/75 percentile): Critical Reading: 400-530, Math: 400-510, Combined: 800-1040. **First-year students submitting ACT scores:** 91%. Scores (25/75 percentile): English: 19-26, Math: 17-24, Composite: 19-24.

ACADEMICS

Year founded: 1857. **Academic calendar:** Semester. **Degrees offered:** bachelor's. **Most popular majors:** 24% nursing/registered nurse training (R.N., A.S.N., B.S.N., M.S.N.), 10% business administration and management, 9% accounting, 8% teacher education, 6% health and physical education. **Major fields of study:** area, ethnic, cultural, and gender studies; biological and biomedical sciences; business, management, marketing, and related support services; computer and information sciences and support services; education; English language and literature/letters; health professions and related clinical sciences; history; mathematics and statistics; multi/interdisciplinary studies; natural resources and conservation; parks, recreation, leisure, and fitness studies; philosophy and religious studies; physical sciences; psychology; public administration and social service professions; theology and religious vocations; visual and performing arts. **Areas of required coursework:** arts/fine arts, humanities, computer literacy, mathematics, English (including composition), foreign languages, sciences (biological or physical), history, social science, other. **Pre-professional programs:** pre-dentistry, pre-medicine, pre-theology, pre-veterinary science, pre-pharmacy, other. **Special academic programs:** accelerated program, double major, honors program, independent study, internships, student-designed major, study abroad, teacher certificate program. **Teacher certification offered in:** early childhood, elementary, middle/junior high, secondary. **Faculty and instruction (2009-2010):** Total instructional faculty: 53 full-time, 34 part-time (56% men; 44% women; 3% minorities). Full-time faculty with Ph.D. or other terminal degree: 68%. Student/faculty ratio: 15/1. Classes of fewer than 20 students: 52%; of 20 to 49 students: 46%; of 50 or more students: 3%. **Advanced Placement and International Baccalaureate credit:** AP tests may be used for: Credit only. Scores accepted: 3, 4, 5. International Baccalaureate exams may be used for: Credit only. **Freshmen returning for sophomore year:** 62%. **Graduation rates:** Four-year: 33%; five-year: 52%; six-year: 44%. **Graduate study:** 19% of students pursue further study immediately upon graduation; 42% within one year; 50% within five years. Fields in which graduates pursue further study: Master of Business Administration (MBA), 13%; law, 2%; medicine, 5%; engineering, 2%; theology (or the seminary), 11%; education, 38%; arts and sciences, 29%.

COSTS AND FINANCIAL AID

Financial aid office: (423) 746-5209. **Expenses (2009-2010):** Tuition and fees 2009-2010: $18,600; room/board: $6,100.

CAMPUS LIFE AND EXTRACURRICULAR ACTIVITIES

Campus housing available (% using): women's dorms (29%), men's dorms (31%), apartment for single students (40%). Students who live in college-owned, operated, or affiliated housing: 32%. **Clubs and organizations:** Number of student organizations: 24. Activities include: choral groups, drama/theater, jazz band, literary magazine, music ensembles, musical theater, student government, student newspaper, yearbook. Number of fraternities: 1; sororities: 2. Proportion of men in fraternities: 7%; of women in sororities: 6%. Average proportion of students who stay on campus on weekends: 40%. **Sports program (2009-2010):** Member of NAIA. *Men's intercollegiate varsity sports:* baseball, basketball, cross country, golf, lacrosse, soccer. *Women's intercollegiate varsity sports:* basketball, cross country, golf, lacrosse, soccer, softball, volleyball.

SERVICES AND FACILITIES

Basic services: nonremedial tutoring. **Remedial assistance:** reading, math, writing, study skills. **Counseling services:** career, personal, veteran student, academic, psychological, religious. **For learning-disabled students:** School does not offer a structured program with separate admission and additional fees. Services include: remedial math, remedial English, tape recorders, untimed tests, note-taking services, oral tests, learning center, readers, extended time for tests, tutors. **Information technology resources:** Students are not required to lease or own a computer. Number of campus computers

available to all students: 150. School has a wireless network. Proportion of college-owned housing units wired for high-speed internet access: 100%. **Campus safety:** Security services offered: 24-hour foot-and-vehicle patrols, late-night transport/escort service, lighted pathways/sidewalks, controlled dormitory access (key, security card, etc).

TRANSFER AND INTERNATIONAL STUDENTS

Transfer students: May apply for admission for the following academic terms: Fall, Spring, Summer. Applicants need a minimum number of credits to apply. For fall 2009: Transfer applications received: 313. Transfer applicants offered admission: 256. Transfer applicants enrolled: 148. **International students:** Number of foreign undergraduates: 23 (2% of student body). Number of countries represented: 13. Minimum TOEFL score required: 550 (paper); 213 (computer).

Trevecca Nazarene University

- **Address:** 333 Murfreesboro Road, Nashville, TN 37210
- **Website:** http://www.trevecca.edu
- **Private; Religious affiliation:** Nazarene
- **Enrollment:** 1,153 full-time; 145 part-time

KEY STATS

✔ **U.S News College Ranking:** second tier, National Universities
✔ **ACT Score (25th/75th percentile):** 19-25
✔ **Tuition:** 2010-2011: $18,418

Selectivity: Selective	**Room/board:** $7,734
Acceptance rate: 69%	**Average debt:** N/A
Student/faculty ratio: 12/1	**Proportion who borrowed:** N/A

UNDERGRADUATE STUDENT BODY STATS

2009-2010 enrollment: 1,153 full-time; 145 part-time. Men: 44%; women: 56%. **Ethnic makeup:** African American: 7%; Asian American: 1%; Hispanic: 3%; White: 87%; International: 1%. **Religious preference:** Roman Catholic: 2%; Protestant: 38%; Muslim: 1%; No preference: 1%; Unknown: 4%; Nazarene: 54%.

ADMISSIONS FACTS AND FIGURES

Phone: (615) 248-1320. **Email:** admissions_und@trevecca.edu. **Website:** http://www.trevecca.edu. **Application deadlines for fall 2011:** Regular decision: August 1. Early decision: Not offered. Early action: Not offered. Admission can be deferred. **Application fee:** $25. **To apply online, go to:** https://www.trevecca.edu/site/hTtyiQ/application.html. **Admissions requirements/recommendations:** High school units required (recommended): English: (4); Mathematics: (2); Science: (1); Foreign language: (2); Social studies: (1); History: (1); Academic electives: (4); Total units: (15). Tests: The college uses SAT or ACT scores in admissions decisions. Either SAT or ACT required. For admission to the fall 2011 entering class, the school will accept: ACT with or without writing accepted. Campus visit: Recommended. Admissions interview: Recommended. Off-campus interview: May be arranged. **Factors that count in admissions decisions:** *Academic:* Secondary school record: Not Considered. Class rank: Considered. Letters of recommendation: Considered. Standardized test scores: Very Important. Essay: Considered. *Nonacademic:* Interview: Considered. Extracurricular activities: Considered. Talent/ability: Considered. Character/personal qualities: Very Important. Alumni/ae relationship: Not Considered. Geographical residence: Not Considered. State residency: Not Considered. Religious affiliation/commitment: Not Considered. Minority status: Not Considered. Volunteer work: Not Considered. Work experience: Not Considered. **Admissions statistics for the fall 2009 entering class:** Total applicants: 899. Total accepted: 623. Freshmen enrolled: 244; 39% were from out of state. Overall acceptance rate: 69%. **Credentials of fall 2009 freshmen:** 17% ranked in the top 10 percent of their high school class; 39% were in the top 25 percent; 68% were in the top half. (Proportion submitting class standing: 62%.) **Average high school grade point average:** 3.2. **First-year students who submitted SAT scores:** 25%. Scores (25/75 percentile): Critical Reading: 440-570, Math: 420-570, Combined: 860-1140. **First-year students submitting ACT scores:** 92%. Scores (25/75 percentile): English: 19-26, Math: 17-25, Composite: 19-25.

ACADEMICS

Year founded: 1901. **Academic calendar:** Semester. **Degrees offered:** associate, bachelor's, master's, doctorate. **Most popular majors:** 57% business, management, marketing, and related support services, 7% education, 7% philosophy and religious studies, 4% visual and performing arts, 3% biological and biomedical sciences. **Major fields of study:** biological and biomedical sciences; business, management, marketing, and related support services; communication, journalism, and related programs; computer and information sciences and support services; education; English language and literature/letters; health professions and related clinical sciences; history; mathematics and statistics; multi/interdisciplinary studies; parks, recreation, leisure, and fitness studies; philosophy and religious studies; physical sciences; psychology; public administration and social service professions; social sciences; theology and religious vocations; visual and performing arts. **Areas of required coursework:** arts/fine arts, humanities, computer literacy, mathematics, English (including composition), philosophy, foreign languages, sciences (biological or physical), history, social science, other. **Special academic programs:** double major, internships, study abroad, teacher certificate program, other. **Teacher certification offered in:** early childhood, elementary, middle/junior high, secondary. **Reserve Officers Training Corps (ROTC):** Army ROTC: Offered at cooperating institution (Vanderbilt University). **Faculty and instruction (2009-2010):** Total instructional faculty: 87 full-time, 135 part-time (61% men; 39% women; 5% minorities). Full-time faculty with Ph.D. or other terminal degree: 83%. Student/faculty ratio: 12/1. Classes of fewer than 20 students: 72%; of 20 to 49 students: 26%; of 50 or more students: 2%. **Advanced Placement and International Baccalaureate credit:** AP tests may be used for: Credit only. **Freshmen returning for sophomore year:** 71%. **Graduation rates:** Four-year: 37%; five-year: 47%; six-year: 47%.

COSTS AND FINANCIAL AID
Financial aid office: (615) 248-1242. **Expenses (2010-2011):** Tuition and fees 2010-2011: $18,418; room/board: $7,734. Estimated books and supplies: $1,100; transportation: $833; personal expenses: $405. **Financial aid:** Priority filing date for institution's financial aid form: February 25; deadline: July 30.

CAMPUS LIFE AND EXTRACURRICULAR ACTIVITIES
Campus housing available: women's dorms, men's dorms, apartments for married students, apartment for single students. Students who live in college-owned, operated, or affiliated housing: 61%. Activities include: campus ministries, choral groups, concert band, drama/theater, international student organization, jazz band, literary magazine, marching band, music ensembles, musical theater, pep band, radio station, student government, student newspaper, symphony orchestra, television station, yearbook. Number of fraternities: 0; sororities: 0. **Sports program (2009-2010):** Member of NAIA. *Men's intercollegiate varsity sports:* baseball, basketball, golf, soccer. *Women's intercollegiate varsity sports:* basketball, golf, soccer, softball, volleyball.

SERVICES AND FACILITIES
Basic services: health service. **Remedial assistance:** reading, math, writing, study skills. **Counseling services:** minority student, career, personal, veteran student, academic, older student, psychological, religious. **For learning-disabled students:** School does not offer a structured program with separate admission and additional fees. Total undergraduates in learning-disabled program or receiving services: 14. Services include: remedial math, remedial English, reading machines, remedial reading, tape recorders, note-taking services, oral tests, learning center, readers, extended time for tests, tutors, priority seating, texts on tape, typist/scribe, other testing accommodations. **Library:** Number of titles: 85,792; number of current serial subscriptions: 688. **Information technology resources:** Students are not required to lease or own a computer. Number of campus computers available to all students: 200. School has a wireless network. Approximate number of users that can be accommodated: 1,900. Proportion of college-owned housing units wired for high-speed internet access: 100%. **Campus safety:** Security services offered: 24-hour foot-and-vehicle patrols, late-night transport/escort service, lighted pathways/sidewalks, controlled dormitory access (key, security card, etc).

TRANSFER AND INTERNATIONAL STUDENTS
Transfer students: May apply for admission for the following academic terms: Fall, Spring, Summer. Applicants need a minimum number of credits to apply. For fall 2009: Transfer applications received: 250. Transfer applicants offered admission: 149. Transfer applicants enrolled: 77. **International students:** Number of foreign undergraduates: 16 (1% of student body). Number of countries represented: 10. Minimum TOEFL score required: 500 (paper); 173 (computer).

Tusculum College

■ **Address:** PO Box 5035, Greeneville, TN 37743
■ **Website:** http://www.tusculum.edu
■ **Private; Religious affiliation:** Presbyterian Church (USA)
■ **Enrollment:** N/A

KEY STATS
✔ **U.S News College Ranking:** second tier, Regional Universities (South)
✔ **SAT or ACT Score (25th/75th percentile):** N/A
✔ **Tuition:** 2009-2010: $19,530

Selectivity: Less selective	**Room/board:** $7,735
Acceptance rate: N/A	**Average debt:** N/A
Student/faculty ratio: N/A	**Proportion who borrowed:** N/A

Union University

■ **Address:** 1050 Union University Drive, Jackson, TN 38305
■ **Website:** http://www.uu.edu
■ **Private; Religious affiliation:** Baptist
■ **Enrollment:** 2,186 full-time; 594 part-time

KEY STATS
✔ **U.S News College Ranking:** 15, Regional Universities (South)
✔ **ACT Score (25th/75th percentile):** 23-30
✔ **Tuition:** 2010-2011: $22,390

Selectivity: More selective	**Room/board:** $7,460
Acceptance rate: 84%	**Average debt:** $24,253
Student/faculty ratio: 12/1	**Proportion who borrowed:** 58%

UNDERGRADUATE STUDENT BODY STATS
2009-2010 enrollment: 2,186 full-time; 594 part-time. Men: 41%; women: 59%. **Ethnic makeup:** African American: 11%; Asian American: 1%; Hispanic: 1%; White: 85%; International: 2%. **Religious preference:** Roman Catholic: 1%; Protestant: 16%; Baptist: 61%; Other: 22%.

ADMISSIONS FACTS AND FIGURES
Phone: (800) 338-6466. **Email:** info@uu.edu. **Website:** http://www.uu.edu. **Application deadlines for fall 2011:** Regular decision: August 15. Early decision: Not offered. Early action: Not offered. Admission can be deferred. **Application fee:** $35. **To apply online, go to:** http://www.uu.edu/union/admiss/apps.htm. **Admissions requirements/recommendations:** High school units required (recommended): English: 4 (4); Mathematics: 3 (4); Science: 3 (4); Foreign language: 1 (2); Social studies: 2 (2); History: 1 (2); Academic electives: 1 (4); Total units: 15 (22). Tests: The college uses SAT or ACT scores in admissions decisions. Either SAT or ACT required. For admission to the fall 2011 entering class, the school will accept: ACT with or without writing accepted. Campus visit: Recommended. Admissions interview: Recommended. Off-campus interview: May be arranged. **Factors that count in admissions decisions:** *Academic:* Secondary school record: Very Important. Class rank: Important. Letters of recommendation: Important. Standardized test scores: Considered. Essay: Considered. *Nonacademic:* Interview: Important. Extracurricular activities: Important. Talent/ability: Important. Character/personal qualities: Very Important. Alumni/ae relationship: Considered. Geographical residence: Not Considered. State residency: Not Considered. Religious affiliation/commitment: Important. Minority status: Not Considered. Volunteer work: Considered. Work experience: Considered. **Other schools with the greatest overlap in applicants:** Belmont University; Carson-Newman College; Samford University; University of Tennessee; Wheaton College. **Admissions statistics for the fall 2009 entering class:** Total applicants: 1,526. Total accepted: 1,278. Freshmen enrolled: 532; Overall acceptance rate: 84%. **Credentials of fall 2009 freshmen:** 35% ranked in the top 10 percent of their high school class; 63% were in the top 25 percent; 90% were in the top half. (Proportion submitting class standing: 67%.) **First-year students who submitted SAT scores:** 20%. Scores (25/75 percentile): Critical Reading: 510-660, Math: 510-630, Combined: 1020-1290. **First-year students submitting ACT scores:** 93%. Scores (25/75 percentile): English: 21-28, Math: 23-32, Composite: 23-30.

ACADEMICS

Year founded: 1823. **Academic calendar:** 4-1-4. **Degrees offered:** certificate, diploma, associate, bachelor's, master's, post-master's certificate, doctorate. **Major fields of study:** area, ethnic, cultural, and gender studies; biological and biomedical sciences; business, management, marketing, and related support services; communication, journalism, and related programs; computer and information sciences and support services; education; engineering; English language and literature/letters; family and consumer sciences/human sciences; foreign languages, literatures, and linguistics; health professions and related clinical sciences; history; mathematics and statistics; parks, recreation, leisure, and fitness studies; philosophy and religious studies; physical sciences; psychology; public administration and social service professions; social sciences; theology and religious vocations; visual and performing arts. **Areas of required coursework:** arts/fine arts, humanities, computer literacy, mathematics, English (including composition), sciences (biological or physical), history, social science, other. **Pre-professional programs:** pre-law, pre-dentistry, pre-medicine, pre-theology, pre-veterinary science, pre-optometry, pre-pharmacy, other. **Special academic programs (% participation):** accelerated program, cooperative (work-study plan) program, cross-registration, distance learning, double major (7%), dual enrollment, English as a Second Language (ESL), exchange student program (domestic), honors program (1%), independent study, internships, study abroad, teacher certificate program (11%). **Teacher certification offered in:** early childhood, special education, elementary, middle/junior high, secondary. **Cooperative education programs:** business, education. **Faculty and instruction (2009-2010):** Total instructional faculty: 210 full-time, 5 part-time (52% men; 48% women; 7% minorities). Full-time faculty with Ph.D. or other terminal degree: 80%. Student/faculty ratio: 12/1. Classes of fewer than 20 students: 68%; of 20 to 49 students: 31%; of 50 or more students: 1%. **Advanced Placement and International Baccalaureate credit:** AP tests may be used for: Credit only. Scores accepted: 3, 4, 5. International Baccalaureate exams may be used for: Credit only. **Freshmen returning for sophomore year:** 88%. **Graduation rates:** Six-year: 62%. **Graduate study:** 11% of students pursue further study immediately upon graduation; 19% within one year; 24% within five years. Fields in which graduates pursue further study: Master of Business Administration (MBA), 8%; law, 7%; medicine, 8%; dentistry, 1%; engineering, 1%; theology (or the seminary), 16%; education, 12%; arts and sciences, 47%.

COSTS AND FINANCIAL AID

Financial aid office: (731) 661-5015. **Expenses (2010-2011):** Tuition and fees 2010-2011: $22,390; room/board: $7,460. Estimated books and supplies: $1,200; transportation: $2,200; personal expenses: $3,700. **Financial aid:** Priority filing date for institution's financial aid form: February 1. In 2009-2010, 86% of undergraduates applied for financial aid. Of those, 72% were determined to have financial need; 25% had their need fully met. Average financial aid package (proportion receiving): $19,643 (72%). Average amount of gift aid, such as scholarships or grants (proportion receiving): $5,479 (51%). Average amount of self-help aid, such as work study or loans (proportion receiving): $4,508 (45%). Average need-based loan (excluding PLUS or other private loans): $4,453. Among students who received need-based aid, the average percentage of met need: 69%. Among students who received aid based on merit, the average award (and the proportion receiving): $7,432 (11%). The average athletic scholarship (and the proportion receiving): $10,243 (10%). Average amount of debt of borrowers graduating in 2009: $24,253. Proportion who borrowed: 58%.

CAMPUS LIFE AND EXTRACURRICULAR ACTIVITIES

Campus housing available (% using): women's dorms (61%), men's dorms (31%), apartments for married students (4%), special housing for disabled students (4%). Students who live in college-owned, operated, or affiliated housing: 55%. **Student employment:** During the 2009-2010 academic year, 26% of undergraduates worked on campus. Average per-year earnings: $800. **Clubs and organizations:** Number of student organizations: 47. Activities include: campus ministries, choral groups, concert band, drama/theater, jazz band, literary magazine, music ensembles, musical theater, opera, pep band, student government, student newspaper, student film society, symphony orchestra, television station, yearbook. Number of fraternities: 3; sororities: 3. Proportion of men in fraternities: 8%; of women in sororities: 12%. Average proportion of students who stay on campus on weekends: 65%. **Sports program (2009-2010):** Member of NAIA.

SERVICES AND FACILITIES

Basic services: nonremedial tutoring, placement service, health service, health insurance. **Remedial assistance:** study skills. **Counseling services:** minority student, career, personal, veteran student, academic, psychological,

religious. **For learning-disabled students:** School does not offer a structured program with separate admission and additional fees. Services include: tape recorders, other special classes, diagnostic testing service, untimed tests, note-taking services, oral tests, learning center, extended time for tests, tutors, priority seating. **Library:** Number of titles: 135,096; number of current serial subscriptions: 1,139. **Information technology resources:** Students are not required to lease or own a computer. Number of campus computers available to all students: 200. School has a wireless network. Proportion of college-owned housing units wired for high-speed internet access: 100%. **Campus safety:** Security services offered: 24-hour foot-and-vehicle patrols, late-night transport/escort service, 24-hour emergency telephones, lighted pathways/sidewalks, student patrols, controlled dormitory access (key, security card, etc).

TRANSFER AND INTERNATIONAL STUDENTS

Transfer students: May apply for admission for the following academic terms: Fall, Winter, Spring, Summer. Applicants need a minimum number of credits to apply. For fall 2009: Transfer applications received: 305. Transfer applicants offered admission: 188. Transfer applicants enrolled: 103. **International students:** Number of foreign undergraduates: 43 (2% of student body). Number of countries represented: 40. Minimum TOEFL score required: 500 (paper); 173 (computer). Average TOEFL score: 545 (paper).

University of Memphis

- **Address:** Memphis, TN 38152
- **Website:** http://www.memphis.edu
- **Public**
- **Enrollment:** 12,517 full-time; 4,200 part-time

KEY STATS
- ✔ **U.S News College Ranking:** second tier, National Universities
- ✔ **ACT Score (25th/75th percentile):** 19-24
- ✔ **Tuition:** 2009-2010: $6,458 in state, $13,874 out of state
  - **Selectivity:** Selective   **Room/board:** $7,350
  - **Acceptance rate:** 61%   **Average debt:** $23,342
  - **Student/faculty ratio:** 15/1   **Proportion who borrowed:** 29%

UNDERGRADUATE STUDENT BODY STATS

2009-2010 enrollment: 12,517 full-time; 4,200 part-time. Men: 39%; women: 61%. **Ethnic makeup:** African American: 39%; Asian American: 3%; Hispanic: 2%; White: 55%; International: 1%.

ADMISSIONS FACTS AND FIGURES

Phone: (901) 678-2111. **Email:** recruitment@memphis.edu. **Website:** http://www.memphis.edu. **Application deadlines for fall 2011:** Regular decision: July 1. Early decision: Not offered. Early action: Not offered. Admission cannot be deferred. **Application fee:** $25. **To apply online, go to:** http://www.memphis.edu/admissions/apply.php. **Admissions requirements/recommendations:** High school units required (recommended): English: 4; Mathematics: 3; Science: 2; Foreign language: 2; Social studies: 1; History: 1; Academic electives: 0; Total units: 14. Tests: The college uses SAT or ACT scores in admissions decisions. Either SAT or ACT required. For admission to the fall 2011 entering class, the school will accept: ACT with or without writing accepted. Campus visit: Recommended. Admissions interview: Recommended. Off-campus interview: Not available. **Factors that count in admissions decisions:** *Academic:* Secondary school record: Very Important. Class rank: Not Considered. Letters of recommendation: Not Considered. Standardized test scores: Very Important. Essay: Not Considered. *Nonacademic:* Interview: Not Considered. Extracurricular activities: Not Considered. Talent/ability: Considered. Character/personal qualities: Considered. Alumni/ae relationship: Not Considered. Geographical residence: Not Considered. State residency: Not Considered. Religious affiliation/commitment: Not Considered. Minority status: Not Considered. Volunteer work: Not Considered. Work experience: Considered. **Other schools with the greatest overlap in applicants:** Christian Brothers University; Middle Tennessee State University; Tennessee State University; University of Mississippi; University of Tennessee. **Admissions statistics for the fall 2009 entering class:** Total applicants: 6,107. Total accepted: 3,726. Freshmen enrolled: 2,256; 10% were from out of state. Overall acceptance rate: 61%. **Credentials of fall 2009 freshmen:** 15% ranked in the top 10 percent of their high school class; 42% were in the top 25 percent; 78% were in the top half. (Proportion submitting class standing: 66%.) **Average high school grade point average:** 3.2. **First-year students who submitted SAT scores:** 6%. Scores (25/75 percentile): Critical Reading: 440-570, Math: 450-560, Combined: 890-1130. **First-year students submitting ACT scores:** 94%. Scores (25/75 percentile): English: 17-23, Math: 19-25, Composite: 19-24.

ACADEMICS

Year founded: 1912. **Academic calendar:** Semester. **Degrees offered:** certificate, bachelor's, post-bachelor's certificate, master's, post-master's certificate, doctorate. **Most popular majors:** 20% business, management, marketing, and related support services, 13% multi/interdisciplinary studies, 9% education, 7% health professions and related clinical sciences, 7% liberal arts and sciences studies, and humanities. **Major fields of study:** agriculture, agriculture operations, and related sciences; architecture and related services; area, ethnic, cultural, and gender studies; biological and biomedical sciences; business, management, marketing, and related support services; communication, journalism, and related programs; computer and information sciences and support services; education; engineering; engineering technologies/technicians; English language and literature/letters; foreign languages, literatures, and linguistics; health professions and related clinical sciences; history; liberal arts and sciences studies, and humanities; mathematics and statistics; multi/interdisciplinary studies; parks, recreation, leisure, and fitness studies; philosophy and religious studies; physical sciences; psychology; public administration and social service professions; security and protective services; social sciences; visual and performing arts. **Areas of required coursework:** arts/fine arts, humanities, computer literacy, mathematics, English (including composition), philosophy, foreign languages, sciences (biological or physical), history, social science. **Preprofessional programs:** pre-law, pre-dentistry, pre-medicine, pre-veterinary science, pre-optometry, pre-pharmacy, other. **Special academic programs (% participation):** accelerated program (1%), cooperative (work-study plan) program (1%), cross-registration (3%), distance learning (12%), double major (1%), dual enrollment (1%), English as a Second Language (ESL) (.5%), exchange student program (domestic) (1%), honors program (10%), independent study (12%), internships (55%), student-designed major (4%), study abroad (8%), teacher certificate program (9%). **Teacher certification offered in:** early childhood, special education, elementary, middle/junior high, secondary. **Cooperative education programs:** engineering, technologies. **Reserve Officers Training Corps (ROTC):** Army ROTC: Offered on campus; Navy ROTC: Offered on campus; Air Force ROTC: Offered on campus. **Faculty and instruction (2009-2010):** Total instructional faculty: 840 full-time, 495 part-time (55% men; 45% women; 22% minorities). Full-time faculty with Ph.D. or other terminal degree: 78%. Student/faculty ratio: 15/1. Classes of fewer than 20 students: 38%; of 20 to 49 students: 51%; of 50 or more students: 11%. **Advanced Placement and International Baccalaureate credit:** AP tests may be used for: Credit only. Scores accepted: 3, 4, 5. International Baccalaureate exams may be used for: Credit only. **Freshmen returning for sophomore year:** 74%. **Graduation rates:** Four-year: 14%; five-year: 30%; six-year: 39%. **Graduate study:** 48% of students pursue further study immediately upon graduation; 26% within five years. Fields in which graduates pursue further study: Master of Business Administration (MBA), 7%; law, 3%; medicine, 3%; engineering, 6%; education, 9%; arts and sciences, 4%.

COSTS AND FINANCIAL AID

Financial aid office: (901) 678-4825. **Expenses (2009-2010):** Tuition and fees 2009-2010: $6,458 in state, $13,874 out of state; room/board: $7,350. Estimated books and supplies: $1,200; transportation: $1,902; personal expenses: $2,499. **Financial aid:** Priority filing date for institution's financial aid form: March 1; deadline: June 1. In 2009-2010, 89% of undergraduates applied for financial aid. Of those, 71% were determined to have financial need; 8% had their need fully met. Average financial aid package (proportion receiving): $9,005 (63%). Average amount of gift aid, such as scholarships or grants (proportion receiving): $5,942 (50%). Average amount of self-help aid, such as work study or loans (proportion receiving): $4,373 (57%). Average need-based loan (excluding PLUS or other private loans): $4,360. Among students who received need-based aid, the average percentage of need met: 70%. Among students who received aid based on merit, the average award (and the proportion receiving): $7,945 (16%). The average athletic scholarship (and the proportion receiving): $13,944 (2%). Average amount of debt of borrowers graduating in 2009: $23,342. Proportion who borrowed: 29%.

CAMPUS LIFE AND EXTRACURRICULAR ACTIVITIES

Campus housing available (% using): women's dorms (44%), men's dorms (27%), sorority housing (2%), fraternity housing (1%), apartments for married students (6%), apartment for single students (20%), special housing

for disabled students (0%). Students who live in college-owned, operated, or affiliated housing: 13%. **Student employment:** During the 2009-2010 academic year, 10% of undergraduates worked on campus. Average per-year earnings: $3,435. **Clubs and organizations:** Number of student organizations: 206. Activities include: campus ministries, choral groups, concert band, dance, drama/theater, international student organization, jazz band, literary magazine, marching band, music ensembles, musical theater, opera, pep band, radio station, student government, student newspaper, student film society, symphony orchestra. Number of fraternities: 15; sororities: 12. Proportion of men in fraternities: 7%; of women in sororities: 5%. Average proportion of students who stay on campus on weekends: 25%. **Sports program (2009-2010):** Member of NCAA I. *Men's intercollegiate varsity sports:* baseball, basketball, cross country, football, golf, rifle, soccer, tennis, track and field (indoor), track and field (outdoor). *Women's intercollegiate varsity sports:* basketball, cross country, golf, rifle, soccer, softball, tennis, track and field (indoor), track and field (outdoor), volleyball.

SERVICES AND FACILITIES

Basic services: nonremedial tutoring, women's center, placement service, day care, health service, health insurance. **Remedial assistance:** reading, math, writing, study skills. **Counseling services:** minority student, career, military, personal, veteran student, academic, older student, psychological, birth control, religious. **For learning-disabled students:** School does not offer a structured program with separate admission and additional fees. Total undergraduates in learning-disabled program or receiving services: 385. Services include: remedial math, remedial English, reading machines, remedial reading, tape recorders, diagnostic testing service, note-taking services, oral tests, learning center, readers, extended time for tests, tutors, early syllabus, priority registration, priority seating, substitution of courses, texts on tape, exams on tape or computer, other testing accommodations, other. **Library:** Number of titles: 2,055,029; number of current serial subscriptions: 7,065. **Information technology resources:** Students are not required to lease or own a computer. Number of campus computers available to all students: 5,000. School has a wireless network. Approximate number of users that can be accommodated: 32,075. Proportion of college-owned housing units wired for high-speed internet access: 100%. **Campus safety:** Security services offered: 24-hour foot-and-vehicle patrols, late-night transport/escort service, 24-hour emergency telephones, lighted pathways/sidewalks, student patrols, controlled dormitory access (key, security card, etc).

TRANSFER AND INTERNATIONAL STUDENTS

Transfer students: May apply for admission for the following academic terms: Fall, Spring, Summer. Applicants need a minimum number of credits to apply. For fall 2009: Transfer applications received: 3,437. Transfer applicants offered admission: 2,073. Transfer applicants enrolled: 1,452. **International students:** Number of foreign undergraduates: 229 (1% of student body). Number of countries represented: 77. Minimum TOEFL score required: 500 (paper); 173 (computer). Average TOEFL score: 571 (paper).

University of Tennessee

- **Address:** 527 Andy Holt Tower, Knoxville, TN 37996
- **Website:** http://admissions.utk.edu
- **Public**
- **Enrollment:** 19,774 full-time; 1,408 part-time

KEY STATS

✔ **U.S News College Ranking:** 104, National Universities
✔ **ACT Score (25th/75th percentile):** 24-29
✔ **Tuition:** 2009-2010: $6,850 in state, $20,646 out of state
   Selectivity: More selective   **Room/board:** $6,652
   Acceptance rate: 73%   **Average debt:** $24,593
   Student/faculty ratio: 16/1   **Proportion who borrowed:** 47%

UNDERGRADUATE STUDENT BODY STATS

2009-2010 enrollment: 19,774 full-time; 1,408 part-time. Men: 51%; women: 49%. **Ethnic makeup:** African American: 8%; American-Indian: 1%; Asian American: 3%; Hispanic: 2%; White: 85%; International: 1%.

ADMISSIONS FACTS AND FIGURES

Phone: (865) 974-2184. **Email:** admissions@utk.edu. **Website:** http://admissions.utk.edu. **Application deadlines for fall 2011:** Regular decision:

December 1; decision sent by March 15. Early decision: Not offered. Early action: Not offered. Admission cannot be deferred. **Application fee:** $30. **To apply online, go to:** https://www.applyweb.com/apply/utk/index.html. **Admissions requirements/recommendations:** High school units required (recommended): English: 4; Mathematics: 3; Science: 2; Foreign language: 2; Social studies: 1; History: 1; Total units: 14. Tests: The college uses SAT or ACT scores in admissions decisions. Either SAT or ACT required. For admission to the fall 2011 entering class, the school will accept: ACT with or without writing accepted. Campus visit: Recommended. Admissions interview: Neither required nor recommended. Off-campus interview: Not available. **Factors that count in admissions decisions:** *Academic:* Secondary school record: Very Important. Class rank: Considered. Letters of recommendation: Considered. Standardized test scores: Very Important. Essay: Considered. *Nonacademic:* Interview: Not Considered. Extracurricular activities: Considered. Talent/ability: Considered. Character/personal qualities: Considered. Alumni/ae relationship: Considered. Geographical residence: Considered. State residency: Considered. Religious affiliation/commitment: Not Considered. Minority status: Considered. Volunteer work: Considered. Work experience: Considered. **Other schools with the greatest overlap in applicants:** Middle Tennessee State University; Tennessee Technological University; University of Georgia; University of Memphis; University of Tennessee–Chattanooga. **Admissions statistics for the fall 2009 entering class:** Total applicants: 12,234. Total accepted: 8,892. Freshmen enrolled: 3,717; 10% were from out of state. Overall acceptance rate: 73%. **Credentials of fall 2009 freshmen:** 39% ranked in the top 10 percent of their high school class; 70% were in the top 25 percent; 92% were in the top half. (Proportion submitting class standing: 42%.) **Average high school grade point average:** 3.8. **First-year students who submitted SAT scores:** 28%. Scores (25/75 percentile): Critical Reading: 510-640, Math: 530-650, Combined: 1040-1290. **First-year students submitting ACT scores:** 94%. Scores (25/75 percentile): English: 24-30, Math: 23-28, Composite: 24-29.

ACADEMICS

Year founded: 1794. **Academic calendar:** Semester. **Degrees offered:** bachelor's, post-bachelor's certificate, master's, post-master's certificate, doctorate. **Most popular majors:** 18% business administration and management, 10% journalism, 10% psychology, 9% social sciences, 8% engineering. **Major fields of study:** agriculture, agriculture operations, and related sciences; architecture and related services; area, ethnic, cultural, and gender studies; biological and biomedical sciences; business, management, marketing, and related support services; communication, journalism, and related programs; computer and information sciences and support services; education; engineering; English language and literature/letters; family and consumer sciences/human sciences; foreign languages, literatures, and linguistics; health professions and related clinical sciences; history; mathematics and statistics; multi/interdisciplinary studies; natural resources and conservation; parks, recreation, leisure, and fitness studies; philosophy and religious studies; physical sciences; psychology; public administration and social service professions; social sciences; visual and performing arts. **Areas of required coursework:** humanities, mathematics, English (including composition), sciences (biological or physical), social science, other. **Pre-professional programs:** pre-law, pre-dentistry, pre-medicine, pre-veterinary science, pre-pharmacy. **Special academic programs:** accelerated program, cooperative (work-study plan) program, cross-registration, distance learning, double major, dual enrollment, English as a Second Language (ESL), exchange student program (domestic), external degree program, honors program, independent study, internships, liberal arts/career combination, student-designed major, study abroad, teacher certificate program. **Teacher certification offered in:** early childhood, special education, elementary, middle/junior high, secondary. **Cooperative education programs:** business, engineering. **Reserve Officers Training Corps (ROTC):** Army ROTC: Offered on campus; Air Force ROTC: Offered on campus. **Faculty and instruction (2009-2010):** Total instructional faculty: 1,536 full-time, 84 part-time (61% men; 39% women; 16% minorities). Full-time faculty with Ph.D. or other terminal degree: 82%. Student/faculty ratio: 16/1. Classes of fewer than 20 students: 31%; of 20 to 49 students: 60%; of 50 or more students: 9%. **Advanced Placement and International Baccalaureate credit:** AP tests may be used for: Credit and/or placement. Scores accepted: 4, 5. International Baccalaureate exams may be used for: Credit and/or placement. **Freshmen returning for sophomore year:** 84%. **Graduation rates:** Four-year: 31%; five-year: 55%; six-year: 61%. **Graduate study:** 15% of students pursue further study immediately upon graduation; 18% within one year.

COSTS AND FINANCIAL AID

Financial aid office: (865) 974-3131. **Expenses (2009-2010):** Tuition and fees 2009-2010: $6,850 in state, $20,646 out of state; room/board: $6,652.

Estimated books and supplies: $1,366; transportation: $2,052; personal expenses: $3,260. **Financial aid:** Priority filing date for institution's financial aid form: March 1. In 2009-2010, 87% of undergraduates applied for financial aid. Of those, 51% were determined to have financial need; 28% had their need fully met. Average financial aid package (proportion receiving): $10,679 (50%). Average amount of gift aid, such as scholarships or grants (proportion receiving): $3,104 (44%). Average amount of self-help aid, such as work study or loans (proportion receiving): $4,177 (31%). Average need-based loan (excluding PLUS or other private loans): $4,304. Among students who received need-based aid, the average percentage of need met: 73%. Among students who received aid based on merit, the average award (and the proportion receiving): $2,461 (12%). The average athletic scholarship (and the proportion receiving): $16,985 (2%). Average amount of debt of borrowers graduating in 2009: $24,593. Proportion who borrowed: 47%.

CAMPUS LIFE AND EXTRACURRICULAR ACTIVITIES

Campus housing available (% using): coed dorms (52%), women's dorms (28%), men's dorms (16%), fraternity housing, apartments for married students (4%). Students who live in college-owned, operated, or affiliated housing: 26%. **Student employment:** During the 2009-2010 academic year, 15% of undergraduates worked on campus. Average per-year earnings: $7,063. **Clubs and organizations:** Number of student organizations: 260. Activities include: campus ministries, choral groups, concert band, dance, drama/theater, international student organization, jazz band, literary magazine, marching band, music ensembles, musical theater, opera, pep band, radio station, student government, student newspaper, student film society, symphony orchestra, television station, yearbook. Number of fraternities: 23; sororities: 18. Proportion of men in fraternities: 14%; of women in sororities: 24%. **Sports program (2009-2010):** Member of NCAA I. *Men's intercollegiate varsity sports:* baseball, basketball, cross country, football, golf, swimming, tennis, track and field (indoor), track and field (outdoor). *Women's intercollegiate varsity sports:* basketball, crew (heavyweight), cross country, golf, crew (lightweight), soccer, softball, swimming, tennis, track and field (indoor), track and field (outdoor), volleyball.

SERVICES AND FACILITIES

Basic services: nonremedial tutoring, women's center, placement service, health service, health insurance. **Remedial assistance:** study skills. **Counseling services:** minority student, career, military, personal, veteran student, academic, older student, psychological, birth control. **For learning-disabled students:** School does not offer a structured program with separate admission and additional fees. Total undergraduates in learning-disabled program or receiving services: 367. Services include: reading machines, tape recorders, diagnostic testing service, note-taking services, oral tests, learning center, readers, extended time for tests, tutors, priority registration, priority seating, substitution of courses, texts on tape, typist/scribe, exams on tape or computer, other testing accommodations. **Library:** Number of titles: 3,332,418; number of current serial subscriptions: 58,377. **Information technology resources:** Students are not required to lease or own a computer. Number of campus computers available to all students: 1,700. School has a wireless network. Approximate number of users that can be accommodated: 15,000. Proportion of college-owned housing units wired for high-speed internet access: 100%. **Campus safety:** Security services offered: 24-hour foot-and-vehicle patrols, late-night transport/escort service, 24-hour emergency telephones, lighted pathways/sidewalks, controlled dormitory access (key, security card, etc).

TRANSFER AND INTERNATIONAL STUDENTS

Transfer students: May apply for admission for the following academic terms: Fall, Spring, Summer. Applicants need a minimum number of credits to apply. For fall 2009: Transfer applications received: 2,938. Transfer applicants offered admission: 1,937. Transfer applicants enrolled: 1,326. **International students:** Number of foreign undergraduates: 228 (1% of student body). Number of countries represented: 47. Minimum TOEFL score required: 523 (paper); 70 (computer).

University of Tennessee–Chattanooga

- **Address:** 615 McCallie Avenue, Chattanooga, TN 37403
- **Website:** http://www.utc.edu
- **Public**
- **Enrollment:** 8,009 full-time; 1,030 part-time

KEY STATS

✔ **U.S News College Ranking:** 47, Regional Universities (South)
✔ **ACT Score (25th/75th percentile):** 20-25
✔ **Tuition:** 2009-2010: $5,656 in state, $16,954 out of state

Selectivity: Selective	**Room/board:** $6,890
Acceptance rate: 79%	**Average debt:** $19,456
Student/faculty ratio: 18/1	**Proportion who borrowed:** 65%

UNDERGRADUATE STUDENT BODY STATS

2009-2010 enrollment: 8,009 full-time; 1,030 part-time. Men: 44%; women: 56%. **Ethnic makeup:** African American: 16%; American-Indian: 1%; Asian American: 2%; Hispanic: 2%; White: 79%; International: 1%.

ADMISSIONS FACTS AND FIGURES

Phone: (423) 425-4662. **Email:** utcmocs@utc.edu. **Website:** http://www.utc.edu. **Application deadlines for fall 2011:** Regular decision: August 1. Early decision: Not offered. Early action: Not offered. Admission can be deferred. **Application fee:** $30. **To apply online, go to:** https://secure.utc.edu/admissions/secure/. **Admissions requirements/recommendations:** High school units required (recommended): English: 4; Mathematics: 3; Science: 2; Foreign language: 2; Social studies: 1; History: 1; Total units: 14. Tests: The college uses SAT or ACT scores in admissions decisions. Either SAT or ACT required. For admission to the fall 2011 entering class, the school will accept: ACT with or without writing accepted. Campus visit: Neither required nor recommended. Admissions interview: Neither required nor recommended. Off-campus interview: May be arranged. **Factors that count in admissions decisions:** *Academic:* Secondary school record: Very Important. Class rank: Not Considered. Letters of recommendation: Considered. Standardized test scores: Very Important. Essay: Considered. *Nonacademic:* Interview: Not Considered. Extracurricular activities: Considered. Talent/ability: Considered. Character/personal qualities: Important. Alumni/ae relationship: Not Considered. Geographical residence: Not Considered. State residency: Not Considered. Religious affiliation/commitment: Not Considered. Minority status: Not Considered. Volunteer work: Considered. Work experience: Considered. **Other schools with the greatest overlap in applicants:** East Tennessee State University; Middle Tennessee State University; Tennessee State University; Tennessee Technological University; University of Tennessee. **Admissions statistics for the fall 2009 entering class:** Total applicants: 6,700. Total accepted: 5,302. Freshmen enrolled: 2,209; 4% were from out of state. Overall acceptance rate: 79%. **Credentials of fall 2009 freshmen:** 43% ranked in the top 25 percent of their high school class; 84% were in the top half. (Proportion submitting class standing: 86%.) **Average high school grade point average:** 3.3. **First-year students who submitted SAT scores:** 5%. Scores (25/75 percentile): Critical Reading: 490-610, Math: 470-580, Combined: 960-1190. **First-year students submitting ACT scores:** 95%. Scores (25/75 percentile): English: 20-26, Math: 18-24, Composite: 20-25.

ACADEMICS

Year founded: 1886. **Academic calendar:** Semester. **Degrees offered:** bachelor's, post-bachelor's certificate, master's, post-master's certificate, doctorate. **Most popular majors:** 27% business administration and management, 7% early childhood education and teaching, 7% kinesiology and exercise science, 7% psychology, 6% nursing/registered nurse training (R.N., A.S.N., B.S.N., M.S.N.). **Major fields of study:** biological and biomedical sciences; business, management, marketing, and related support services; communication, journalism, and related programs; computer and information sciences and support services; education; engineering; English language and literature/letters; family and consumer sciences/human sciences; foreign languages, literatures, and linguistics; health professions and related clinical sciences; history; legal professions and studies; liberal arts and sciences studies, and humanities; mathematics and statistics; natural resources and conservation; parks, recreation, leisure, and fitness studies; philosophy and religious studies; physical sciences; psychology; public administration and social service professions; security and protective services; social sciences; visual and performing arts. **Areas of required coursework:** arts/fine arts, humanities, computer literacy, mathematics, English (including compo-

sition), sciences (biological or physical), social science. **Pre-professional programs:** pre-law, pre-dentistry, pre-medicine, pre-veterinary science, pre-pharmacy, other. **Special academic programs:** cooperative (work-study plan) program, cross-registration, distance learning, double major, dual enrollment, English as a Second Language (ESL), honors program, independent study, internships, study abroad, teacher certificate program. **Teacher certification offered in:** early childhood, special education, elementary, middle/junior high, secondary, bilingual/bicultural. **Cooperative education programs:** business, engineering, health professions, social/behavioral science. **Reserve Officers Training Corps (ROTC):** Army ROTC: Offered on campus. **Faculty and instruction (2009-2010):** Total instructional faculty: 411 full-time, 285 part-time (55% men; 45% women; 11% minorities). Full-time faculty with Ph.D. or other terminal degree: 73%. Student/faculty ratio: 18/1. Classes of fewer than 20 students: 38%; of 20 to 49 students: 59%; of 50 or more students: 4%. **Advanced Placement and International Baccalaureate credit:** AP tests may be used for: Credit only. Scores accepted: 3. **Freshmen returning for sophomore year:** 64%. **Graduation rates:** Four-year: 16%; five-year: 37%; six-year: 42%. **Graduate study:** 25% of students pursue further study within one year. Fields in which graduates pursue further study: Master of Business Administration (MBA), 18%; law, 11%; medicine, 27%; engineering, 7%; education, 9%; arts and sciences, 35%.

COSTS AND FINANCIAL AID

Financial aid office: (423) 425-4677. **Expenses (2009-2010):** Tuition and fees 2009-2010: $5,656 in state, $16,954 out of state; room/board: $6,890. Estimated books and supplies: $1,000; transportation: $1,662; personal expenses: $1,430. **Financial aid:** Priority filing date for institution's financial aid form: April 1. In 2009-2010, 87% of undergraduates applied for financial aid. Of those, 60% were determined to have financial need; 70% had their need fully met. Average financial aid package (proportion receiving): $9,853 (59%). Average amount of gift aid, such as scholarships or grants (proportion receiving): $4,320 (52%). Average amount of self-help aid, such as work study or loans (proportion receiving): $7,234 (59%). Average need-based loan (excluding PLUS or other private loans): $4,310. Among students who received need-based aid, the average percentage of need met: 83%. Among students who received aid based on merit, the average award (and the proportion receiving): $2,720 (13%). The average athletic scholarship (and the proportion receiving): $13,109 (3%). Average amount of debt of borrowers graduating in 2009: $19,456. Proportion who borrowed: 65%.

CAMPUS LIFE AND EXTRACURRICULAR ACTIVITIES

Campus housing available (% using): coed dorms (100%), apartments for married students, apartment for single students. Students who live in college-owned, operated, or affiliated housing: 34%. **Student employment:** During the 2009-2010 academic year, 15% of undergraduates worked on campus. Average per-year earnings: $5,500. **Clubs and organizations:** Number of student organizations: 130. Activities include: campus ministries, choral groups, concert band, dance, drama/theater, international student organization, jazz band, literary magazine, marching band, model UN, music ensembles, musical theater, opera, pep band, radio station, student government, student newspaper, student film society, symphony orchestra. Number of fraternities: 9; sororities: 6. Proportion of men in fraternities: 6%; of women in sororities: 8%. Average proportion of students who stay on campus on weekends: 10%. **Sports program (2009-2010):** Member of NCAA I. *Men's intercollegiate varsity sports:* basketball, cross country, football, golf, tennis, track and field (outdoor), wrestling. *Women's intercollegiate varsity sports:* basketball, cross country, golf, soccer, softball, tennis, track and field (outdoor), volleyball.

SERVICES AND FACILITIES

Basic services: nonremedial tutoring, women's center, placement service, day care, health service, health insurance. **Remedial assistance:** reading, math, writing, study skills. **Counseling services:** career, personal, academic, older student, psychological. **For learning-disabled students:** School does not offer a structured program with separate admission and additional fees. Total undergraduates in learning-disabled program or receiving services: 575. Services include: remedial math, remedial English, tape recorders, untimed tests, note-taking services, oral tests, readers, extended time for tests, tutors. **Library:** Number of titles: 596,000; number of current serial subscriptions: 2,718. **Information technology resources:** Students are not required to lease or own a computer. Number of campus computers available to all students: 965. School has a wireless network. Approximate number of users that can be accommodated: 3,150. Proportion of college-owned housing units wired for high-speed internet access: 100%. **Campus safety:** Security services offered: 24-hour foot-and-vehicle patrols, late-night transport/escort service, 24-hour emergency telephones, lighted pathways/sidewalks, controlled dormitory access (key, security card, etc).

TRANSFER AND INTERNATIONAL STUDENTS

Transfer students: May apply for admission for the following academic terms: Fall, Spring, Summer. Applicants need a minimum number of credits to apply. For fall 2009: Transfer applications received: 1,546. Transfer applicants offered admission: 963. Transfer applicants enrolled: 695. **International students:** Number of foreign undergraduates: 63 (1% of student body). Number of countries represented: 45. Minimum TOEFL score required: 500 (paper); 173 (computer). Average TOEFL score: 512 (paper).

University of Tennessee–Martin

■ **Address:** University Street, Martin, TN 38238
■ **Website:** http://www.utm.edu
■ **Public**
■ **Enrollment:** 5,856 full-time; 1,730 part-time

KEY STATS
✔ **U.S News College Ranking:** 47, Regional Universities (South)
✔ **ACT Score (25th/75th percentile):** 20-25
✔ **Tuition:** 2010-2011: $6,034 in state, $18,104 out of state

Selectivity: Selective	**Room/board:** $5,973
Acceptance rate: 75%	**Average debt:** $20,997
Student/faculty ratio: 19/1	**Proportion who borrowed:** 71%

UNDERGRADUATE STUDENT BODY STATS

2009-2010 enrollment: 5,856 full-time; 1,730 part-time. Men: 43%; women: 57%. **Ethnic makeup:** African American: 16%; Asian American: 1%; Hispanic: 1%; White: 80%; International: 2%.

ADMISSIONS FACTS AND FIGURES

Phone: (800) 829-8861. **Email:** admitme@utm.edu. **Website:** http://www.utm.edu. **Application deadlines for fall 2011:** Regular decision: August 1. Early decision: Not offered. Early action: Not offered. Admission can be deferred. **Application fee:** $30. **To apply online, go to:** https://banner.utm.edu/prod/twbkwbis.P_GenMenu?name=homepage. **Admissions requirements/recommendations:** High school units required (recommended): English: 4; Mathematics: 3; Science: 2; Foreign language: 2; Social studies: 0; History: 2; Academic electives: 0; Total units: 14. Tests: The college uses SAT or ACT scores in admissions decisions. Either SAT or ACT required. For admission to the fall 2011 entering class, the school will accept: ACT with or without writing accepted. Campus visit: Neither required nor recommended. Admissions interview: Neither required nor recommended. Off-campus interview: Not available. **Factors that count in admissions decisions:** *Academic:* Secondary school record: Very Important. Class rank: Not Considered. Letters of recommendation: Not Considered. Standardized test scores: Very Important. Essay: Not Considered. *Nonacademic:* Interview: Not Considered. Extracurricular activities: Not Considered. Talent/ability: Not Considered. Character/personal qualities: Not Considered. Alumni/ae relationship: Not Considered. Geographical residence: Not Considered. State residency: Not Considered. Religious affiliation/commitment: Not Considered. Minority status: Not Considered. Volunteer work: Not Considered. Work experience: Not Considered. **Other schools with the greatest overlap in applicants:** Austin Peay State University; Middle Tennessee State University; Murray State University; University of Tennessee; University of Tennessee–Chattanooga. **Admissions statistics for the fall 2009 entering class:** Total applicants: 3,625. Total accepted: 2,701. Freshmen enrolled: 1,394; 3% were from out of state. Overall acceptance rate: 75%. **Credentials of fall 2009 freshmen:** 20% ranked in the top 10 percent of their high school class; 50% were in the top 25 percent; 88% were in the top half. (Proportion submitting class standing: 82%.) **Average high school grade point average:** 3.4. **First-year students submitting ACT scores:** 89%. Scores (25/75 percentile): English: 18-24, Math: 20-25, Composite: 20-25.

ACADEMICS

Year founded: 1900. **Academic calendar:** Semester. **Degrees offered:** bachelor's, master's. **Most popular majors:** 17% marketing/marketing management, 11% multi/interdisciplinary studies, 10% multi/interdisciplinary studies, 7% agriculture, 7% biology/biological sciences. **Major fields of study:** agriculture, agriculture operations, and related sciences; biological

and biomedical sciences; business, management, marketing, and related support services; communication, journalism, and related programs; computer and information sciences and support services; education; engineering; engineering technologies/technicians; English language and literature/letters; family and consumer sciences/human sciences; foreign languages, literatures, and linguistics; health professions and related clinical sciences; history; mathematics and statistics; multi/interdisciplinary studies; natural resources and conservation; parks, recreation, leisure, and fitness studies; philosophy and religious studies; physical sciences; psychology; public administration and social service professions; security and protective services; social sciences; visual and performing arts. **Areas of required coursework:** arts/fine arts, humanities, mathematics, English (including composition), sciences (biological or physical), social science, other. **Special academic programs (% participation):** accelerated program, cooperative (work-study plan) program (28.9%), distance learning (35.6%), double major (.8%), dual enrollment (8.6%), English as a Second Language (ESL), honors program (7.4%), independent study (5.9%), internships (35.8%), student-designed major (10.9%), study abroad (.2%), teacher certificate program (14%). **Teacher certification offered in:** early childhood, special education, elementary, middle/junior high, secondary. **Cooperative education programs:** agriculture, business. **Reserve Officers Training Corps (ROTC):** Army ROTC: Offered on campus. **Faculty and instruction (2009-2010):** Total instructional faculty: 270 full-time, 263 part-time (53% men; 47% women; 8% minorities). Full-time faculty with Ph.D. or other terminal degree: 75%. Student/faculty ratio: 19/1. Classes of fewer than 20 students: 51%; of 20 to 49 students: 43%; of 50 or more students: 7%. **Advanced Placement and International Baccalaureate credit:** AP tests may be used for: Credit only. Scores accepted: 3, 4, 5. **Freshmen returning for sophomore year:** 71%. **Graduation rates:** Four-year: 24%; five-year: 43%; six-year: 46%. **Graduate study:** 18% of students pursue further study immediately upon graduation.

COSTS AND FINANCIAL AID

Financial aid office: (731) 587-7040. **Expenses (2010-2011):** Tuition and fees 2010-2011: $6,034 in state, $18,104 out of state; room/board: $5,973. Estimated books and supplies: $1,500; transportation: $1,140; personal expenses: $2,368. **Financial aid:** Priority filing date for institution's financial aid form: March 1. In 2009-2010, 96% of undergraduates applied for financial aid. Of those, 71% were determined to have financial need; 31% had their need fully met. Average financial aid package (proportion receiving): $11,491 (70%). Average amount of gift aid, such as scholarships or grants (proportion receiving): $5,687 (47%). Average amount of self-help aid, such as work study or loans (proportion receiving): $4,016 (45%). Average need-based loan (excluding PLUS or other private loans): $3,886. Among students who received need-based aid, the average percentage of need met: 78%. Among students who received aid based on merit, the average award (and the proportion receiving): $5,229 (20%). The average athletic scholarship (and the proportion receiving): $8,486 (5%). Average amount of debt of borrowers graduating in 2009: $20,997. Proportion who borrowed: 71%.

CAMPUS LIFE AND EXTRACURRICULAR ACTIVITIES

Campus housing available (% using): women's dorms (25%), men's dorms (27%), apartments for married students (9%), apartment for single students (39%), special housing for disabled students. Students who live in college-owned, operated, or affiliated housing: 39%. **Student employment:** During the 2009-2010 academic year, 16% of undergraduates worked on campus. Average per-year earnings: $2,110. **Clubs and organizations:** Number of student organizations: 125. Activities include: choral groups, concert band, dance, drama/theater, jazz band, literary magazine, marching band, music ensembles, opera, pep band, radio station, student government, student newspaper, television station, yearbook. Number of fraternities: 11; sororities: 8. Proportion of men in fraternities: 14%; of women in sororities: 9%. Average proportion of students who stay on campus on weekends: 56%. **Sports program (2009-2010):** Member of NCAA I. *Men's intercollegiate varsity sports:* baseball, basketball, cross country, football, golf, rifle. *Women's intercollegiate varsity sports:* basketball, cross country, equestrian, rifle, soccer, softball, tennis, volleyball.

SERVICES AND FACILITIES

Basic services: nonremedial tutoring, placement service, day care, health service, health insurance. **Remedial assistance:** reading, math, study skills. **Counseling services:** minority student, career, personal, veteran student, academic, older student, psychological, birth control. **For learning-disabled students:** School does not offer a structured program with separate admission and additional fees. Services include: remedial math, remedial English, reading machines, tape recorders, note-taking services, oral tests, learning center, readers, extended time for tests, tutors, priority seating, texts on tape, exams on tape or computer, other testing accommodations, other. **Library:** Number of titles: 534,802; number of current serial subscriptions: 1,132. **Information technology resources:** Students are not required to lease or own a computer. Number of campus computers available to all students: 234. School has a wireless network. Approximate number of users that can be accommodated: 2,000. Proportion of college-owned housing units wired for high-speed internet access: 100%. **Campus safety:** Security services offered: 24-hour foot-and-vehicle patrols, 24-hour emergency telephones, lighted pathways/sidewalks, controlled dormitory access (key, security card, etc).

TRANSFER AND INTERNATIONAL STUDENTS

Transfer students: May apply for admission for the following academic terms: Fall, Spring, Summer. Applicants need a minimum number of credits to apply. For fall 2009: Transfer applications received: 1,162. Transfer applicants offered admission: 781. Transfer applicants enrolled: 555. **International students:** Number of foreign undergraduates: 133 (2% of student body). Number of countries represented: 24. Minimum TOEFL score required: 500 (paper); 173 (computer). Average TOEFL score: 520 (paper).

Vanderbilt University

- **Address:** Nashville, TN 37240
- **Website:** http://www.vanderbilt.edu
- **Private**
- **Enrollment:** 6,738 full-time; 56 part-time

KEY STATS

✔ **U.S News College Ranking:** 17, National Universities
✔ **ACT Score (25th/75th percentile):** 30-34
✔ **Tuition:** 2010-2011: $39,932

Selectivity: Most selective	**Room/board:** $13,068
Acceptance rate: 20%	**Average debt:** $19,563
Student/faculty ratio: 8/1	**Proportion who borrowed:** 40%

UNDERGRADUATE STUDENT BODY STATS

2009-2010 enrollment: 6,738 full-time; 56 part-time. Men: 48%; women: 52%. **Ethnic makeup:** African American: 9%; American-Indian: 1%; Asian American: 8%; Hispanic: 6%; White: 73%; International: 4%.

ADMISSIONS FACTS AND FIGURES

Phone: (800) 288-0432. **Email:** admissions@vanderbilt.edu. **Website:** http://www.vanderbilt.edu. **Application deadlines for fall 2011:** Regular decision: January 3; decision sent by April 1. Early decision: Send application by: November 1; Decision sent by: December 15. Early action: Not offered. Admission can be deferred. **Application fee:** $50. **To apply online, go to:** http://www.vanderbilt.edu/admissions. **Admissions requirements/recommendations:** High school units required (recommended): English: 4 (4); Mathematics: 3 (4); Science: 3 (4); Foreign language: 2 (2); Social studies: 2 (3); History: 1 (1); Academic electives: 3 (3); Total units: 18 (21). **Tests:** The college uses SAT or ACT scores in admissions decisions. Either SAT or ACT required. For admission to the fall 2011 entering class, the school will accept: ACT with writing required. Campus visit: Recommended. Admissions interview: Neither required nor recommended. Off-campus interview: May not be arranged. **Factors that count in admissions decisions:** *Academic:* Secondary school record: Very Important. Class rank: Very Important. Letters of recommendation: Important. Standardized test scores: Very Important. Essay: Very Important. *Nonacademic:* Interview: Considered. Extracurricular activities: Very Important. Talent/ability: Important. Character/personal qualities: Very Important. Alumni/ae relationship: Considered. Geographical residence: Considered. State residency: Considered. Religious affiliation/commitment: Not Considered. Minority status: Considered. Volunteer work: Considered. Work experience: Considered. **Other schools with the greatest overlap in applicants:** Duke University; Harvard University; Princeton University; Washington University in St. Louis; Yale University. **Admissions statistics for the fall 2009 entering class:** Total applicants: 19,353. Total accepted: 3,899. Freshmen enrolled: 1,599; 84% were from out of state. Overall acceptance rate: 20%. Non-early acceptance rate: 20%. **Size of waiting list:** 4036 applicants; enrolled from waiting list: 117. **Credentials of fall 2009 freshmen:** 86% ranked in the top 10 percent of their high school class; 97% were in the top 25 percent; 100% were in the top half. (Proportion submitting class standing: 41%.) **Average high school grade point average:** 3.7. **First-year students**

who submitted SAT scores: 55%. Scores (25/75 percentile): Critical Reading: 660-750, Math: 690-770, Combined: 1350-1520. **First-year students submitting ACT scores:** 58%. Scores (25/75 percentile): English: 31-35, Math: 19-34, Composite: 30-34.

ACADEMICS

Year founded: 1873. **Academic calendar:** Semester. **Degrees offered:** bachelor's, master's, doctorate. **Most popular majors:** 31% social sciences, 13% engineering, 7% multi/interdisciplinary studies, 6% foreign languages, literatures, and linguistics, 6% psychology. **Major fields of study:** area, ethnic, cultural, and gender studies; biological and biomedical sciences; communication, journalism, and related programs; computer and information sciences and support services; education; engineering; English language and literature/letters; foreign languages, literatures, and linguistics; history; mathematics and statistics; multi/interdisciplinary studies; philosophy and religious studies; physical sciences; psychology; social sciences; visual and performing arts. **Areas of required coursework:** humanities, mathematics, English (including composition), foreign languages, sciences (biological or physical), social science. **Pre-professional programs:** pre-law, pre-dentistry, pre-medicine, other. **Special academic programs:** accelerated program, cooperative (work-study plan) program, cross-registration, distance learning, double major, dual enrollment, English as a Second Language (ESL), honors program, independent study, internships, student-designed major, study abroad, teacher certificate program. **Teacher certification offered in:** early childhood, special education, elementary, middle/junior high, secondary. **Reserve Officers Training Corps (ROTC):** Army ROTC: Offered on campus; Navy ROTC: Offered on campus; Air Force ROTC: Offered at cooperating institution (Tennessee State University). **Faculty and instruction (2009-2010):** Total instructional faculty: 902 full-time, 212 part-time. Full-time faculty with Ph.D. or other terminal degree: 97%. Student/faculty ratio: 8/1. Classes of fewer than 20 students: 65%; of 20 to 49 students: 28%; of 50 or more students: 8%. **Freshmen returning for sophomore year:** 96%. **Graduation rates:** Four-year: 84%; five-year: 90%; six-year: 91%. **Graduate study:** 48% of students pursue further study immediately upon graduation. Fields in which graduates pursue further study: Master of Business Administration (MBA), 24%; law, 21%; medicine, 15%; engineering, 9%; theology (or the seminary), 1%; education, 10%; arts and sciences, 37%.

COSTS AND FINANCIAL AID

Financial aid office: (615) 322-3591. **Expenses (2010-2011):** Tuition and fees 2010-2011: $39,932; room/board: $13,068. Estimated books and supplies: $1,344 personal expenses: $2,290. **Financial aid:** Priority filing date for institution's financial aid form: February 1. In 2009-2010, 54% of undergraduates applied for financial aid. Of those, 46% were determined to have financial need; 99% had their need fully met. Average financial aid package (proportion receiving): $41,954 (46%). Average amount of gift aid, such as scholarships or grants (proportion receiving): $34,715 (42%). Average amount of self-help aid, such as work study or loans (proportion receiving): $2,471 (25%). Average need-based loan (excluding PLUS or other private loans): $526. Among students who received need-based aid, the average percentage of need met: 99%. Among students who received aid based on merit, the average award (and the proportion receiving): $20,506 (9%). The average athletic scholarship (and the proportion receiving): $38,495 (4%). Average amount of debt of borrowers graduating in 2009: $19,563. Proportion who borrowed: 40%.

CAMPUS LIFE AND EXTRACURRICULAR ACTIVITIES

Campus housing available: coed dorms, women's dorms, men's dorms, apartments for married students, apartment for single students, special housing for disabled students, special housing for international students, other housing options. Students who live in college-owned, operated, or affiliated housing: 90%. **Clubs and organizations:** Number of student organizations: 300. Activities include: campus ministries, choral groups, concert band, dance, drama/theater, international student organization, jazz band, literary magazine, marching band, model UN, music ensembles, musical theater, opera, pep band, radio station, student government, student newspaper, student film society, symphony orchestra, television station, yearbook. Number of fraternities: 16; sororities: 14. Proportion of men in fraternities: 35%; of women in sororities: 50%. Average proportion of students who stay on campus on weekends: 90%. **Sports program (2009-2010):** Member of NCAA I. *Men's intercollegiate varsity sports:* baseball, basketball, cross country, football, golf, tennis. *Women's intercollegiate varsity sports:* basketball, bowling, cross country, golf, lacrosse, soccer, tennis, track and field (outdoor).

SERVICES AND FACILITIES

Basic services: nonremedial tutoring, women's center, placement service, day care, health service, health insurance. **Remedial assistance:** writing, study skills. **Counseling services:** minority student, career, military, personal, veteran student, academic, older student, psychological, birth control, religious. **For learning-disabled students:** School does not offer a structured program with separate admission and additional fees. Total undergraduates in learning-disabled program or receiving services: 211. Services include: reading machines, tape recorders, diagnostic testing service, note-taking services, oral tests, learning center, readers, extended time for tests, tutors, priority registration, priority seating, substitution of courses, texts on tape, typist/scribe, exams on tape or computer, other testing accommodations, waiver of foreign language degree requirement, waiver of math degree requirement. **Library:** Number of titles: 3,467,542; number of current serial subscriptions: 55,260. **Information technology resources:** Students are not required to lease or own a computer. Number of campus computers available to all students: 500. School has a wireless network. Approximate number of users that can be accommodated: 10,000. Proportion of college-owned housing units wired for high-speed internet access: 100%. **Campus safety:** Security services offered: 24-hour foot-and-vehicle patrols, late-night transport/escort service, 24-hour emergency telephones, lighted pathways/sidewalks, student patrols, controlled dormitory access (key, security card, etc).

TRANSFER AND INTERNATIONAL STUDENTS

Transfer students: May apply for admission for the following academic terms: Fall. Applicants need a minimum number of credits to apply. For fall 2009: Transfer applications received: 757. Transfer applicants offered admission: 388. Transfer applicants enrolled: 240. **International students:** Number of foreign undergraduates: 262 (4% of student body). Number of countries represented: 34. Minimum TOEFL score required: 570 (paper); 230 (computer).

Victory University

- ■ **Address:** 255 N. Highland, Memphis, TN 38111-1375
- ■ **Website:** http://www.victory.edu
- ■ **Religious affiliation:** Christian nondenominational
- ■ **Enrollment:** 487 full-time; 188 part-time

KEY STATS

- ✔ **U.S News College Ranking:** second tier, Regional Colleges (South)
- ✔ **ACT Score (25th/75th percentile):** 14-18
- ✔ **Tuition:** 2009-2010: $0 in state, $0 out of state

Selectivity: Less selective	**Room/board:** $9,664
Acceptance rate: 15%	**Average debt:** $21,505
Student/faculty ratio: 18/1	**Proportion who borrowed:** 58%

UNDERGRADUATE STUDENT BODY STATS

2009-2010 enrollment: 487 full-time; 188 part-time. Men: 25%; women: 75%. **Ethnic makeup:** African American: 79%; Asian American: 1%; Hispanic: 1%; White: 18%; International: 1%.

ADMISSIONS FACTS AND FIGURES

Phone: (901) 320-9797. **Email:** admissions@victory.edu. **Website:** http://www.victory.edu. **Application deadlines for fall 2011:** Regular decision: August 21. Early decision: Not offered. Early action: Not offered. Admission can be deferred. **Application fee:** $25. **To apply online, go to:** http://www.victory.edu/app_lander.aspx. **Admissions requirements/recommendations:** High school units required (recommended): English: 4; Mathematics: 3; Science: 3; Social studies: 3; Academic electives: 1; Total units: 14. Tests: The college uses SAT or ACT scores in admissions decisions. Either SAT or ACT required. For admission to the fall 2011 entering class, the school will accept: ACT with or without writing accepted. Campus visit: Recommended. Admissions interview: Recommended. Off-campus interview: May be arranged. **Factors that count in admissions decisions:** *Academic:* Secondary school record: Important. Class rank: Considered. Letters of recommendation: Considered. Standardized test scores: Very Important. Essay: Considered. *Nonacademic:* Interview: Considered. Extracurricular activities: Considered. Talent/ability: Considered. Character/personal qualities: Considered. Alumni/ae relationship: Not Considered. Geographical residence: Not Considered. State residency: Not Considered. Religious affiliation/commitment: Not Considered. Minority status: Not

Considered. Volunteer work: Considered. Work experience: Not Considered. **Other schools with the greatest overlap in applicants:** Bethel College; Christian Brothers University; LeMoyne-Owen College; Union University; University of Memphis. **Admissions statistics for the fall 2009 entering class:** Freshmen enrolled: 19; 11% were from out of state. Overall acceptance rate: 15%. **Average high school grade point average:** 2.2. **First-year students who submitted SAT scores:** 5%. **First-year students submitting ACT scores:** 47%. Scores (25/75 percentile): English: N/A, Math: N/A, Composite: 14-18.

ACADEMICS

Year founded: 1941. **Academic calendar:** Semester. **Degrees offered:** certificate, associate, bachelor's, post-bachelor's certificate. **Most popular majors:** 29% business, management, marketing, and related support services, 29% education, 13% psychology, 12% theology and religious vocations, 9% liberal arts and sciences studies, and humanities. **Major fields of study:** biological and biomedical sciences; business, management, marketing, and related support services; education; English language and literature/letters; history; legal professions and studies; liberal arts and sciences studies, and humanities; psychology; theology and religious vocations. **Areas of required coursework:** arts/fine arts, humanities, computer literacy, mathematics, English (including composition), sciences (biological or physical), history, social science, other. **Pre-professional programs:** pre-law, pre-theology, other. **Special academic programs:** accelerated program, distance learning, double major, dual enrollment, independent study, internships, liberal arts/career combination, student-designed major, study abroad, teacher certificate program, other. **Teacher certification offered in:** elementary, middle/junior high, secondary. **Faculty and instruction (2009-2010):** Total instructional faculty: 23 full-time, 35 part-time (52% men; 48% women; 38% minorities). Full-time faculty with Ph.D. or other terminal degree: 52%. Student/faculty ratio: 18/1. Classes of fewer than 20 students: 64%; of 20 to 49 students: 36%. **Advanced Placement and International Baccalaureate credit:** AP tests may be used for: Credit and/or placement. Scores accepted: 3, 4, 5. International Baccalaureate exams may be used for: Credit only. **Freshmen returning for sophomore year:** 45%. **Graduation rates:** Four-year: 16%; five-year: 19%; six-year: 18%.

COSTS AND FINANCIAL AID

Financial aid office: (901) 320-9787. **Expenses (2009-2010):** Tuition and fees 2009-2010: $0 in state, $0 out of state; room/board: $9,664. Estimated books and supplies: $1,600. **Financial aid:** Priority filing date for institution's financial aid form: February 15. In 2009-2010, 95% of undergraduates applied for financial aid. Of those, 88% were determined to have financial need; 2% had their need fully met. Average financial aid package (proportion receiving): $4,709 (88%). Average amount of gift aid, such as scholarships or grants (proportion receiving): $3,146 (73%). Average amount of self-help aid, such as work study or loans (proportion receiving): $2,283 (73%). Average need-based loan (excluding PLUS or other private loans): $2,226. Among students who received need-based aid, the average percentage of need met: 47%. Among students who received aid based on merit, the average award (and the proportion receiving): $0 (0%). The average athletic scholarship (and the proportion receiving): $0 (0%). Average amount of debt of borrowers graduating in 2009: $21,505. Proportion who borrowed: 58%.

CAMPUS LIFE AND EXTRACURRICULAR ACTIVITIES

Students who live in college-owned, operated, or affiliated housing: 0%. **Student employment:** During the 2009-2010 academic year, 1% of undergraduates worked on campus. Average per-year earnings: $7,540. **Clubs and organizations:** Number of student organizations: 8. Activities include: choral groups, drama/theater, student government. Number of fraternities: 0; sororities: 0.

SERVICES AND FACILITIES

Basic services: nonremedial tutoring, health insurance. **Remedial assistance:** reading, math, writing, study skills. **Counseling services:** career, academic, religious, other. **For learning-disabled students:** School does not offer a structured program with separate admission and additional fees. Services include: remedial math, remedial English, remedial reading, tape recorders, diagnostic testing service, untimed tests, note-taking services, oral tests, learning center, readers, extended time for tests, tutors, other. **Library:** Number of titles: 50,053; number of current serial subscriptions: 1,477. **Information technology resources:** Students are not required to lease or own a computer. Number of campus computers available to all students: 31. School has a wireless network. Approximate number of users that can be accommodated: 1,000. Proportion of college-owned housing units wired for high-speed internet access: 0%. **Campus safety:** Security services offered: 24-hour foot-and-vehicle patrols, lighted pathways/sidewalks.

TRANSFER AND INTERNATIONAL STUDENTS
Transfer students: May apply for admission for the following academic terms: Fall, Spring, Summer. Applicants need a minimum number of cred-

its to apply. For fall 2009: Transfer applicants enrolled: 98. **International students:** Number of foreign undergraduates: 4 (1% of student body). Number of countries represented: 14. Minimum TOEFL score required: 500 (paper); 175 (computer).

Texas

Abilene Christian University

- **Address:** ACU Box 29100, Abilene, TX 79699-9000
- **Website:** http://www.acu.edu
- **Private; Religious affiliation:** Church of Christ
- **Enrollment:** 3,591 full-time; 325 part-time

KEY STATS

✔ **U.S News College Ranking:** 19, Regional Universities (West)
✔ **SAT Score (25th/75th percentile):** 970-1220
✔ **Tuition:** 2010-2011: $22,760

Selectivity: Selective	**Room/board:** $7,884
Acceptance rate: 49%	**Average debt:** $35,453
Student/faculty ratio: 15/1	**Proportion who borrowed:** 71%

UNDERGRADUATE STUDENT BODY STATS

2009-2010 enrollment: 3,591 full-time; 325 part-time. Men: 46%; women: 54%. **Ethnic makeup:** African American: 8%; American-Indian: 1%; Asian American: 1%; Hispanic: 8%; White: 79%; International: 3%. **Religious preference:** Roman Catholic: 4%; Protestant: 22%; Unknown: 4%; Church of Christ: 52%; Baptist: 14%; Other: 4%.

ADMISSIONS FACTS AND FIGURES

Phone: (800) 460-6228. **Email:** info@admissions.acu.edu. **Website:** http://www.acu.edu. **Application deadlines for fall 2011:** Regular decision: February 15; decision sent by March 15. Early decision: Not offered. Early action: Send application by: November 1; Decision sent by: November 19. Admission cannot be deferred. **Application fee:** $50. **To apply online, go to:** http://www.acu.edu/admissions/ugrad/applyonline.html. **Admissions requirements/recommendations:** High school units required (recommended): English: (4); Mathematics: (3); Science: (3); Foreign language: (2); Total units: (12). Tests: The college uses SAT or ACT scores in admissions decisions. Either SAT or ACT required. For admission to the fall 2011 entering class, the school will accept: ACT with or without writing accepted. Campus visit: Recommended. Admissions interview: Neither required nor recommended. Off-campus interview: Not available. **Factors that count in admissions decisions:** *Academic:* Secondary school record: Very Important. Class rank: Very Important. Letters of recommendation: Considered. Standardized test scores: Very Important. Essay: Very Important. *Nonacademic:* Interview: Not Considered. Extracurricular activities: Considered. Talent/ability: Important. Character/personal qualities: Important. Alumni/ae relationship: Considered. Geographical residence: Not Considered. State residency: Not Considered. Religious affiliation/commitment: Not Considered. Minority status: Not Considered. Volunteer work: Considered. Work experience: Considered. **Other schools with the greatest overlap in applicants:** Baylor University; Hardin-Simmons University; Harding University; Texas A&M University–College Station; Texas Tech University. **Admissions statistics for the fall 2009 entering class:** Total applicants: 3,712. Total accepted: 1,823. Freshmen enrolled: 983; 14% were from out of state. Overall acceptance rate: 49%. Non-early acceptance rate: 49%. **Size of waiting list:** 0 applicants; enrolled from waiting list: N/A. **Credentials of fall 2009 freshmen:** 23% ranked in the top 10 percent of their high school class; 49% were in the top 25 percent; 78% were in the top half. (Proportion submitting class standing: 68%.) **Average high school grade point average:** 3.5. **First-year students who submitted SAT scores:** 55%. Scores (25/75 percentile): Critical Reading: 480-600, Math: 490-620, Combined: 970-1220. **First-year students submitting ACT scores:** 45%. Scores (25/75 percentile): English: 20-26, Math: 20-28, Composite: 21-27.

ACADEMICS

Year founded: 1906. **Academic calendar:** Semester. **Degrees offered:** certificate, associate, bachelor's, post-bachelor's certificate, master's, post-master's certificate. **Most popular majors:** 7% business administration and management, 6% accounting, 6% elementary education and teaching, 6% multi/interdisciplinary studies, 6% psychology. **Major fields of study:** agriculture, agriculture operations, and related sciences; biological and biomedical sci-

ences; business, management, marketing, and related support services; communication, journalism, and related programs; computer and information sciences and support services; education; engineering; English language and literature/letters; family and consumer sciences/human sciences; foreign languages, literatures, and linguistics; health professions and related clinical sciences; history; legal professions and studies; liberal arts and sciences studies, and humanities; mathematics and statistics; multi/interdisciplinary studies; natural resources and conservation; parks, recreation, leisure, and fitness studies; physical sciences; psychology; public administration and social service professions; social sciences; theology and religious vocations; visual and performing arts. **Areas of required coursework:** arts/fine arts, humanities, mathematics, English (including composition), foreign languages, sciences (biological or physical), history, social science, other. **Pre-professional programs:** pre-law, pre-dentistry, pre-medicine, pre-theology, pre-veterinary science, pre-optometry, pre-pharmacy, other. **Special academic programs (% participation):** cross-registration (14%), distance learning (37%), double major (3%), dual enrollment, English as a Second Language (ESL) (1%), honors program (16%), independent study (4%), internships (51%), student-designed major (5%), study abroad (24%), teacher certificate program (12%). **Teacher certification offered in:** early childhood, special education, elementary, middle/junior high, secondary. **Cooperative education programs:** engineering, natural science. **Faculty and instruction (2009-2010):** Total instructional faculty: 236 full-time, 135 part-time (63% men; 37% women; 8% minorities). Full-time faculty with Ph.D. or other terminal degree: 82%. Student/faculty ratio: 15/1. Classes of fewer than 20 students: 47%; of 20 to 49 students: 47%; of 50 or more students: 6%. **Advanced Placement and International Baccalaureate credit:** AP tests may be used for: Credit only. Scores accepted: 3, 4, 5. International Baccalaureate exams may be used for: Credit only. **Freshmen returning for sophomore year:** 75%. **Graduation rates:** Four-year: 41%; five-year: 59%; six-year: 58%. **Graduate study:** 32% of students pursue further study immediately upon graduation; 38% within one year. Fields in which graduates pursue further study: Master of Business Administration (MBA), 16%; medicine, 11%; theology (or the seminary), 8%; education, 8%; arts and sciences, 52%.

COSTS AND FINANCIAL AID

Financial aid office: (325) 674-2643. **Expenses (2010-2011):** Tuition and fees 2010-2011: $22,760; room/board: $7,884. Estimated books and supplies: $1,250; transportation: $1,490; personal expenses: $1,916. **Financial aid:** Priority filing date for institution's financial aid form: March 1. In 2009-2010, 83% of undergraduates applied for financial aid. Of those, 67% were determined to have financial need; 18% had their need fully met. Average financial aid package (proportion receiving): $13,841 (67%). Average amount of gift aid, such as scholarships or grants (proportion receiving): $10,152 (65%). Average amount of self-help aid, such as work study or loans (proportion receiving): $4,984 (52%). Average need-based loan (excluding PLUS or other private loans): $4,228. Among students who received need-based aid, the average percentage of need met: 67%. Among students who received aid based on merit, the average award (and the proportion receiving): $6,690 (14%). The average athletic scholarship (and the proportion receiving): $13,071 (7%). Average amount of debt of borrowers graduating in 2009: $35,453. Proportion who borrowed: 71%.

CAMPUS LIFE AND EXTRACURRICULAR ACTIVITIES

Campus housing available (% using): women's dorms (54%), men's dorms (45%), apartments for married students (1%), special housing for disabled students. Students who live in college-owned, operated, or affiliated housing: 42%. **Student employment:** During the 2009-2010 academic year, 14% of undergraduates worked on campus. Average per-year earnings: $4,300. **Clubs and organizations:** Number of student organizations: 100. Activities include: campus ministries, choral groups, concert band, drama/theater, international student organization, jazz band, literary magazine, marching band, model UN, music ensembles, musical theater, opera, radio station, student government, student newspaper, symphony orchestra, television station. Number of fraternities: 6; sororities: 5. Proportion of men in fraternities: 19%; of women in sororities: 19%. Average proportion of students who stay on campus on weekends: 25%. **Sports program (2009-2010):**

Member of NCAA II. **Men's intercollegiate varsity sports:** baseball, basketball, cross country, football, tennis, track and field (indoor), track and field (outdoor). **Women's intercollegiate varsity sports:** basketball, cross country, soccer, softball, tennis, track and field (indoor), track and field (outdoor), volleyball.

SERVICES AND FACILITIES

Basic services: nonremedial tutoring, placement service, health service, health insurance, other. **Remedial assistance:** reading, math, study skills. **Counseling services:** minority student, career, military, personal, veteran student, academic, older student, psychological, religious. **For learning-disabled students:** School does not offer a structured program with separate admission and additional fees. Total undergraduates in learning-disabled program or receiving services: 187. Services include: remedial math, remedial English, reading machines, remedial reading, tape recorders, diagnostic testing service, note-taking services, oral tests, learning center, readers, extended time for tests, tutors, priority seating, texts on tape, other testing accommodations, other. **Library:** Number of titles: 542,615; number of current serial subscriptions: 1,123. **Information technology resources:** Students are not required to lease or own a computer. Number of campus computers available to all students: 700. School has a wireless network. Approximate number of users that can be accommodated: 10,050. Proportion of college-owned housing units wired for high-speed internet access: 100%. **Campus safety:** Security services offered: 24-hour foot-and-vehicle patrols, late-night transport/escort service, 24-hour emergency telephones, lighted pathways/sidewalks, student patrols, controlled dormitory access (key, security card, etc).

TRANSFER AND INTERNATIONAL STUDENTS

Transfer students: May apply for admission for the following academic terms: Fall, Spring, Summer. Applicants do not need a minimum number of credits to apply. For fall 2009: Transfer applications received: 538. Transfer applicants offered admission: 262. Transfer applicants enrolled: 184. **International students:** Number of foreign undergraduates: 116 (3% of student body). Number of countries represented: 59. Minimum TOEFL score required: 525 (paper); 197 (computer).

Angelo State University

- **Address:** 2601 W. Avenue N, San Angelo, TX 76909
- **Website:** http://www.angelo.edu
- **Public**
- **Enrollment:** 4,899 full-time; 960 part-time

KEY STATS

✔ **U.S News College Ranking:** second tier, Regional Universities (West)
✔ **ACT Score (25th/75th percentile):** 18-23
✔ **Tuition:** 2010-2011: $6,138 in state, $14,568 out of state

Selectivity: Selective	**Room/board:** $7,256
Acceptance rate: 92%	**Average debt:** $16,372
Student/faculty ratio: 19/1	**Proportion who borrowed:** 37%

UNDERGRADUATE STUDENT BODY STATS

2009-2010 enrollment: 4,899 full-time; 960 part-time. Men: 45%; women: 55%. **Ethnic makeup:** African American: 7%; American-Indian: 1%; Asian American: 2%; Hispanic: 24%; White: 65%; International: 1%.

ADMISSIONS FACTS AND FIGURES

Phone: (325) 942-2041. **Email:** admissions@angelo.edu. **Website:** http://www.angelo.edu. **Application deadlines for fall 2011:** Regular decision: August 15. Early decision: Not offered. Early action: Not offered. Admission can be deferred. **Application fee:** $25. **To apply online, go to:** https://www.applytexas.org. **Admissions requirements/recommendations:** High school units required (recommended): English: 4 (4); Mathematics: 3 (3); Science: 3 (3); Foreign language: 2 (2); Social studies: 3 (3); History: 0 (0); Academic electives: 0 (1); Total units: 23 (23). Tests: The college uses SAT or ACT scores in admissions decisions. Either SAT or ACT required. For admission to the fall 2011 entering class, the school will accept: ACT with or without writing accepted. Campus visit: Recommended. Admissions interview: Neither required nor recommended. Off-campus interview: Not available. **Factors that count in admissions decisions:** *Academic:* Secondary school record: Very Important. Class rank: Very Important. Letters of recommendation: Not Considered. Standardized test scores: Very Important. Essay:

Not Considered. *Nonacademic:* Interview: Not Considered. Extracurricular activities: Not Considered. Talent/ability: Not Considered. Character/personal qualities: Not Considered. Alumni/ae relationship: Not Considered. Geographical residence: Not Considered. State residency: Not Considered. Religious affiliation/commitment: Not Considered. Minority status: Not Considered. Volunteer work: Not Considered. Work experience: Not Considered. **Other schools with the greatest overlap in applicants:** Texas A&M University–College Station; Texas State University–San Marcos; Texas Tech University; University of Texas–Austin. **Admissions statistics for the fall 2009 entering class:** Total applicants: 2,920. Total accepted: 2,674. Freshmen enrolled: 1,474; 1% were from out of state. Overall acceptance rate: 92%. **Credentials of fall 2009 freshmen:** 15% ranked in the top 10 percent of their high school class; 31% were in the top 25 percent; 74% were in the top half. (Proportion submitting class standing: 93%.) **First-year students who submitted SAT scores:** 62%. Scores (25/75 percentile): Critical Reading: 410-520, Math: 430-540, Combined: 840-1060. **First-year students submitting ACT scores:** 67%. Scores (25/75 percentile): English: 18-24, Math: 18-24, Composite: 18-23.

ACADEMICS

Year founded: 1928. **Academic calendar:** Semester. **Degrees offered:** associate, bachelor's, master's, doctorate. **Most popular majors:** 23% business administration and management, 13% health and physical education, 12% multi/interdisciplinary studies, 7% communication studies/speech communication and rhetoric, 7% psychology. **Major fields of study:** agriculture, agriculture operations, and related sciences; biological and biomedical sciences; business, management, marketing, and related support services; communication, journalism, and related programs; computer and information sciences and support services; English language and literature/letters; foreign languages, literatures, and linguistics; health professions and related clinical sciences; history; liberal arts and sciences studies, and humanities; mathematics and statistics; multi/interdisciplinary studies; natural resources and conservation; parks, recreation, leisure, and fitness studies; physical sciences; psychology; security and protective services; social sciences; visual and performing arts. **Areas of required coursework:** arts/fine arts, computer literacy, mathematics, English (including composition), sciences (biological or physical), history, social science, other. **Pre-professional programs:** other. **Special academic programs:** distance learning, double major, dual enrollment, English as a Second Language (ESL), honors program, independent study, internships, study abroad, teacher certificate program. **Teacher certification offered in:** early childhood, special education, elementary, middle/junior high, secondary. **Reserve Officers Training Corps (ROTC):** Air Force ROTC: Offered on campus. **Faculty and instruction (2009-2010):** Total instructional faculty: 247 full-time, 74 part-time (55% men; 45% women; 13% minorities). Full-time faculty with Ph.D. or other terminal degree: 72%. Student/faculty ratio: 19/1. Classes of fewer than 20 students: 28%; of 20 to 49 students: 63%; of 50 or more students: 9%. **Advanced Placement and International Baccalaureate credit:** AP tests may be used for: Credit only. Scores accepted: 3, 4, 5. **Freshmen returning for sophomore year:** 58%. **Graduation rates:** Four-year: 15%; five-year: 25%; six-year: 33%. **Graduate study:** 19% of students pursue further study within one year.

COSTS AND FINANCIAL AID

Financial aid office: (325) 942-2246. **Expenses (2010-2011):** Tuition and fees 2010-2011: $6,138 in state, $14,568 out of state; room/board: $7,256. Estimated books and supplies: $1,000; transportation: $1,000; personal expenses: $700. **Financial aid:** Priority filing date for institution's financial aid form: April 1. In 2009-2010, 76% of undergraduates applied for financial aid. Of those, 62% were determined to have financial need; 30% had their need fully met. Average financial aid package (proportion receiving): $7,016 (62%). Average amount of gift aid, such as scholarships or grants (proportion receiving): $4,534 (50%). Average amount of self-help aid, such as work study or loans (proportion receiving): $3,713 (43%). Average need-based loan (excluding PLUS or other private loans): $3,655. Among students who received need-based aid, the average percentage of need met: 45%. Among students who received aid based on merit, the average award (and the proportion receiving): $3,648 (14%). The average athletic scholarship (and the proportion receiving): $4,512 (2%). Average amount of debt of borrowers graduating in 2009: $16,372. Proportion who borrowed: 37%.

CAMPUS LIFE AND EXTRACURRICULAR ACTIVITIES

Campus housing available (% using): coed dorms (82%), women's dorms (5%), apartment for single students (8%), special housing for disabled students, other housing options (5%). Students who live in college-owned, operated, or affiliated housing: 38%. **Student employment:** During the 2009-2010 academic year, 10% of undergraduates worked on campus.

Average per-year earnings: $7,200. **Clubs and organizations:** Number of student organizations: 100. Activities include: campus ministries, choral groups, concert band, drama/theater, international student organization, jazz band, literary magazine, marching band, music ensembles, musical theater, pep band, radio station, student government, student newspaper, student film society, television station. Number of fraternities: 4; sororities: 2. Proportion of men in fraternities: 3%; of women in sororities: 4%. Average proportion of students who stay on campus on weekends: 20%. **Sports program (2009-2010):** Member of NCAA II. *Men's intercollegiate varsity sports:* baseball, basketball, cross country, football, track and field (outdoor). *Women's intercollegiate varsity sports:* basketball, cross country, golf, soccer, softball, track and field (outdoor), volleyball.

SERVICES AND FACILITIES

Basic services: nonremedial tutoring, placement service, health service, health insurance. **Remedial assistance:** reading, math, writing. **Counseling services:** career, personal, veteran student, academic, psychological. **For learning-disabled students:** School does not offer a structured program with separate admission and additional fees. Services include: remedial math, remedial English, remedial reading, tape recorders, diagnostic testing service, note-taking services, oral tests, learning center, extended time for tests. **Library:** Number of titles: 521,253; number of current serial subscriptions: 1,628. **Information technology resources:** Students are not required to lease or own a computer. Number of campus computers available to all students: 700. School has a wireless network. Proportion of college-owned housing units wired for high-speed internet access: 100%. **Campus safety:** Security services offered: 24-hour foot-and-vehicle patrols, late-night transport/escort service, 24-hour emergency telephones, lighted pathways/sidewalks, controlled dormitory access (key, security card, etc).

TRANSFER AND INTERNATIONAL STUDENTS

Transfer students: May apply for admission for the following academic terms: Fall, Spring, Summer. Applicants need a minimum number of credits to apply. For fall 2009: Transfer applications received: 601. Transfer applicants offered admission: 568. Transfer applicants enrolled: 472. **International students:** Number of foreign undergraduates: 48 (1% of student body). Number of countries represented: 21. Minimum TOEFL score required: 550 (paper); 213 (computer).

Austin College

- **Address:** 900 N. Grand Avenue, Sherman, TX 75090-4400
- **Website:** http://www.austincollege.edu
- **Private; Religious affiliation:** Presbyterian
- **Enrollment:** 1,325 full-time; 10 part-time

KEY STATS

✔ **U.S News College Ranking:** 81, National Liberal Arts Colleges
✔ **SAT Score (25th/75th percentile):** 1130-1350
✔ **Tuition:** 2010-2011: $27,850

Selectivity: More selective	**Room/board:** N/A
Acceptance rate: 80%	**Average debt:** N/A
Student/faculty ratio: 14/1	**Proportion who borrowed:** N/A

UNDERGRADUATE STUDENT BODY STATS

2009-2010 enrollment: 1,325 full-time; 10 part-time. Men: 46%; women: 54%. **Ethnic makeup:** African American: 3%; American-Indian: 1%; Asian American: 15%; Hispanic: 10%; White: 69%; International: 2%. **Religious preference:** Roman Catholic: 16%; Protestant: 41%; Jewish: 1%; Muslim: 3%; Hindu: 4%; Buddhist: 1%; No preference: 1%; Unknown: 20%; Presbyterian: 8%.

ADMISSIONS FACTS AND FIGURES

Phone: (800) 442-5363. **Email:** admission@austincollege.edu. **Website:** http://www.austincollege.edu. **Application deadlines for fall 2011:** Regular decision: May 1. Early decision: Not offered. Early action: Send application by: January 15; Decision sent by: March 1. Admission can be deferred. **Application fee:** $35. **To apply online, go to:** http://austincollege.edu/Category.asp?712. **Admissions requirements/recommendations:** High school units required (recommended): English: 4 (4); Mathematics: 3 (4); Science: 3 (4); Foreign language: 2 (3); Social studies: 2 (3); Academic electives: 1. Tests: The college uses SAT or ACT scores in admissions decisions. Either SAT or ACT required. For admission to the fall 2011

entering class, the school will accept: ACT with writing required. Campus visit: Recommended. Admissions interview: Recommended. Off-campus interview: May be arranged. **Factors that count in admissions decisions:** *Academic:* Secondary school record: Very Important. Class rank: Important. Letters of recommendation: Important. Standardized test scores: Important. Essay: Important. *Nonacademic:* Interview: Considered. Extracurricular activities: Important. Talent/ability: Important. Character/personal qualities: Important. Alumni/ae relationship: Considered. Geographical residence: Considered. State residency: Considered. Religious affiliation/commitment: Considered. Minority status: Considered. Volunteer work: Considered. Work experience: Considered. **Other schools with the greatest overlap in applicants:** Baylor University; Southern Methodist University; Southwestern University; Texas A&M University–College Station; Trinity University. **Admissions statistics for the fall 2009 entering class:** Total applicants: 1,750. Total accepted: 1,394. Freshmen enrolled: 413; 8% were from out of state. Accepted through early-decision or early-action plans: 42%. Overall acceptance rate: 80%. Non-early acceptance rate: 79%. **Size of waiting list:** 22 applicants; enrolled from waiting list: 7. **Credentials of fall 2009 freshmen:** 41% ranked in the top 10 percent of their high school class; 70% were in the top 25 percent; 92% were in the top half. (Proportion submitting class standing: 60%.) **Average high school grade point average:** 3.6. **First-year students who submitted SAT scores:** 69%. Scores (25/75 percentile): Critical Reading: 560-680, Math: 570-670, Combined: 1130-1350. **First-year students submitting ACT scores:** 49%. Scores (25/75 percentile): English: N/A, Math: N/A, Composite: 24-26.

ACADEMICS

Year founded: 1849. **Academic calendar:** 4-1-4. **Degrees offered:** bachelor's, master's. **Most popular majors:** 20% social sciences, 15% psychology, 13% business, management, marketing, and related support services, 8% biological and biomedical sciences, 8% multi/interdisciplinary studies. **Major fields of study:** area, ethnic, cultural, and gender studies; biological and biomedical sciences; business, management, marketing, and related support services; communication, journalism, and related programs; computer and information sciences and support services; education; English language and literature/letters; foreign languages, literatures, and linguistics; history; mathematics and statistics; multi/interdisciplinary studies; natural resources and conservation; philosophy and religious studies; physical sciences; psychology; social sciences; visual and performing arts. **Areas of required coursework:** humanities, mathematics, English (including composition), foreign languages, sciences (biological or physical), social science. **Pre-professional programs:** pre-law, pre-dentistry, pre-medicine, pre-theology, other. **Special academic programs (% participation):** double major (28.6%), exchange student program (domestic) (0%), honors program (5.8%), independent study (50%), internships (4.6%), student-designed major (8.4%), study abroad (75.8%), teacher certificate program (6.9%), other. **Teacher certification offered in:** early childhood, elementary, middle/junior high, secondary. **Cooperative education programs:** engineering. **Faculty and instruction (2009-2010):** Total instructional faculty: 91 full-time, 28 part-time (66% men; 34% women; 10% minorities). Full-time faculty with Ph.D. or other terminal degree: 93%. Student/faculty ratio: 14/1. Classes of fewer than 20 students: 59%; of 20 to 49 students: 38%; of 50 or more students: 3%. **Advanced Placement and International Baccalaureate credit:** AP tests may be used for: Placement only. Scores accepted: 4, 5. International Baccalaureate exams may be used for: Placement only. **Freshmen returning for sophomore year:** 83%. **Graduation rates:** Four-year: 67%; five-year: 72%; six-year: 74%. **Graduate study:** 44% of students pursue further study immediately upon graduation; 22% within one year. Fields in which graduates pursue further study: Master of Business Administration (MBA), 6%; law, 7%; medicine, 19%; engineering, 3%; theology (or the seminary), 3%; education, 22%; arts and sciences, 40%.

COSTS AND FINANCIAL AID

Financial aid office: (903) 813-2900. **Expenses (2010-2011):** Tuition and fees 2010-2011: $27,850. Estimated books and supplies: $1,200; transportation: $500; personal expenses: $800. **Financial aid:** Priority filing date for institution's financial aid form: April 1. In 2009-2010, 73% of undergraduates applied for financial aid. Of those, 61% were determined to have financial need; 95% had their need fully met. Average financial aid package (proportion receiving): $26,331 (61%). Average amount of gift aid, such as scholarships or grants (proportion receiving): $19,001 (61%). Average amount of self-help aid, such as work study or loans (proportion receiving): $7,087 (48%). Average need-based loan (excluding PLUS or other private loans): $6,200. Among students who received need-based aid, the average percentage of need met: 95%. Among students who received aid based on merit, the average award (and the proportion receiving): $12,949 (22%). The average athletic scholarship (and the proportion receiving): $0 (0%).

CAMPUS LIFE AND EXTRACURRICULAR ACTIVITIES

Campus housing available (% using): coed dorms (25%), women's dorms (31%), men's dorms (16%), apartment for single students (23%), special housing for international students, other housing options (5%). Students who live in college-owned, operated, or affiliated housing: 70%. **Student employment:** During the 2009-2010 academic year, 35% of undergraduates worked on campus. Average per-year earnings: $1,127. **Clubs and organizations:** Number of student organizations: 4. Activities include: campus ministries, choral groups, dance, drama/theater, international student organization, jazz band, literary magazine, model UN, music ensembles, musical theater, pep band, student government, student newspaper, symphony orchestra, yearbook. Number of fraternities: 6; sororities: 7. Proportion of men in fraternities: 27%; of women in sororities: 28%. Average proportion of students who stay on campus on weekends: 60%. **Sports program (2009-2010):** Member of NCAA III. *Men's intercollegiate varsity sports:* baseball, basketball, football, soccer, swimming, tennis. *Women's intercollegiate varsity sports:* basketball, soccer, softball, swimming, tennis, volleyball.

SERVICES AND FACILITIES

Basic services: nonremedial tutoring, health service, health insurance, other. **Remedial assistance:** other. **Counseling services:** minority student, career, military, personal, veteran student, academic, older student, psychological, birth control, religious, other. **For learning-disabled students:** School does not offer a structured program with separate admission and additional fees. Total undergraduates in learning-disabled program or receiving services: 50. Services include: reading machines, tape recorders, note-taking services, learning center, extended time for tests, tutors, texts on tape, other. **Library:** Number of titles: 230,222; number of current serial subscriptions: 10,352. **Information technology resources:** Students are not required to lease or own a computer. Number of campus computers available to all students: 104. School has a wireless network. Approximate number of users that can be accommodated: 4,590. Proportion of college-owned housing units wired for high-speed internet access: 100%. **Campus safety:** Security services offered: 24-hour foot-and-vehicle patrols, late-night transport/escort service, 24-hour emergency telephones, lighted pathways/sidewalks, controlled dormitory access (key, security card, etc).

TRANSFER AND INTERNATIONAL STUDENTS

Transfer students: May apply for admission for the following academic terms: Fall, Spring, Summer. Applicants do not need a minimum number of credits to apply. For fall 2009: Transfer applications received: 125. Transfer applicants offered admission: 78. Transfer applicants enrolled: 33. **International students:** Number of foreign undergraduates: 24 (2% of student body). Number of countries represented: 22. Minimum TOEFL score required: 550 (paper); 80 (computer). Average TOEFL score: 600 (paper).

Baylor University

- **Address:** 1 Bear Place, Waco, TX 76798
- **Website:** http://www.baylor.edu
- **Private; Religious affiliation:** Baptist
- **Enrollment:** 11,905 full-time; 244 part-time

KEY STATS
✔ **U.S News College Ranking:** 79, National Universities
✔ **SAT Score (25th/75th percentile):** 1080-1290
✔ **Tuition:** 2010-2011: $29,754

Selectivity: More selective	**Room/board:** $8,331
Acceptance rate: 50%	**Average debt:** N/A
Student/faculty ratio: 15/1	**Proportion who borrowed:** N/A

UNDERGRADUATE STUDENT BODY STATS

2009-2010 enrollment: 11,905 full-time; 244 part-time. Men: 41%; women: 59%. **Ethnic makeup:** African American: 8%; American-Indian: 1%; Asian American: 7%; Hispanic: 11%; White: 71%; International: 2%. **Religious preference:** Roman Catholic: 14%; Protestant: 39%; Muslim: 1%; Hindu: 1%; Buddhist: 1%; No preference: 3%; Baptist: 38%.

ADMISSIONS FACTS AND FIGURES

Phone: (800) 229-5678. **Email:** Admissions@Baylor.edu. **Website:** http://www.baylor.edu. **Application deadlines for fall 2011:** Regular decision: Rolling. Early decision: Not offered. Early action: Send application by: November 1; Decision sent by: January 15. Admission cannot be deferred. **Application fee:** $50. **To apply online, go to:** http://www.baylor.edu/admissions/index.php?id=56249. **Admissions requirements/recommendations:** High school units required (recommended): English: 4; Mathematics: 4; Science: 4; Foreign language: 2; Social studies: 2; History: 1; Total units: 17. Tests: The college uses SAT or ACT scores in admissions decisions. Either SAT or ACT required. For admission to the fall 2011 entering class, the school will accept: ACT with writing required. Campus visit: Recommended. **Factors that count in admissions decisions:** *Academic:* Secondary school record: Very Important. Class rank: Very Important. Letters of recommendation: Considered. Standardized test scores: Very Important. Essay: Considered. *Nonacademic:* Interview: Considered. Extracurricular activities: Considered. Talent/ability: Considered. Character/personal qualities: Considered. Alumni/ae relationship: Considered. Geographical residence: Not Considered. State residency: Not Considered. Religious affiliation/commitment: Considered. Minority status: Not Considered. Volunteer work: Considered. Work experience: Not Considered. **Other schools with the greatest overlap in applicants:** Texas A&M University–College Station; Texas Christian University; Texas Tech University; University of North Texas; University of Texas–Austin. **Admissions statistics for the fall 2009 entering class:** Total applicants: 31,440. Total accepted: 15,699. Freshmen enrolled: 3,098; 19% were from out of state. Overall acceptance rate: 50%. Non-early acceptance rate: 50%. **Credentials of fall 2009 freshmen:** 40% ranked in the top 10 percent of their high school class; 73% were in the top 25 percent; 95% were in the top half. (Proportion submitting class standing: 86%.) **First-year students who submitted SAT scores:** 58%. Scores (25/75 percentile): Critical Reading: 530-640, Math: 550-650, Combined: 1080-1290. **First-year students submitting ACT scores:** 42%. Scores (25/75 percentile): English: 23-29, Math: 23-28, Composite: 23-29.

ACADEMICS

Year founded: 1845. **Academic calendar:** Semester. **Degrees offered:** bachelor's, master's, post-master's certificate, doctorate. **Most popular majors:** 8% biology/biological sciences, 6% psychology, 4% finance, 4% marketing/marketing management, 4% nursing/registered nurse training (R.N., A.S.N., B.S.N., M.S.N.). **Major fields of study:** architecture and related services; area, ethnic, cultural, and gender studies; biological and biomedical sciences; business, management, marketing, and related support services; communication, journalism, and related programs; computer and information sciences and support services; education; engineering; English language and literature/letters; family and consumer sciences/human sciences; foreign languages, literatures, and linguistics; health professions and related clinical sciences; history; liberal arts and sciences studies, and humanities; mathematics and statistics; multi/interdisciplinary studies; natural resources and conservation; parks, recreation, leisure, and fitness studies; philosophy and religious studies; physical sciences; psychology; public administration and social service professions; security and protective services; social sciences; theology and religious vocations; transportation and materials moving; visual and performing arts. **Areas of required coursework:** arts/fine arts, humanities, mathematics, English (including composition), foreign languages, sciences (biological or physical), history, social science, other. **Pre-professional programs:** pre-law, pre-dentistry, pre-medicine, pre-veterinary science, pre-optometry, pre-pharmacy, other. **Special academic programs:** accelerated program, double major, honors program, internships, student-designed major, study abroad, teacher certificate program. **Teacher certification offered in:** early childhood, special education, elementary, middle/junior high, secondary. **Cooperative education programs:** health professions. **Reserve Officers Training Corps (ROTC):** Army ROTC: Offered on campus; Air Force ROTC: Offered on campus. **Faculty and instruction (2009-2010):** Total instructional faculty: 859 full-time, 287 part-time (59% men; 41% women; 10% minorities). Full-time faculty with Ph.D. or other terminal degree: 81%. Student/faculty ratio: 15/1. Classes of fewer than 20 students: 48%; of 20 to 49 students: 44%; of 50 or more students: 9%. **Advanced Placement and International Baccalaureate credit:** AP tests may be used for: Credit and/or placement. Scores accepted: 4, 5. International Baccalaureate exams may be used for: Credit and/or placement. **Freshmen returning for sophomore year:** 85%. **Graduation rates:** Four-year: 47%; five-year: 67%; six-year: 70%.

COSTS AND FINANCIAL AID

Financial aid office: (254) 710-2611. **Expenses (2010-2011):** Tuition and fees 2010-2011: $29,754; room/board: $8,331. Estimated books and supplies: $1,398; transportation: $1,992; personal expenses: $1,890. **Financial aid:** Priority filing date for institution's financial aid form: March 1. In 2009-2010, 64% of undergraduates applied for financial aid. Of those, 55% were determined to have financial need; 17% had their need fully met. Average financial aid package (proportion receiving): $20,452 (55%). Average amount of gift aid, such as scholarships or grants (proportion receiving): $15,180 (52%). Average amount of self-help aid, such as work study or loans (proportion receiving): $6,210 (45%). Average need-based loan (excluding PLUS or other private loans): $3,169. Among students who received need-based aid, the average percentage of need met: 67%. Among students who received aid based on merit, the average award (and the proportion receiving): $8,805 (31%). The average athletic scholarship (and the proportion receiving): $24,437 (3%).

CAMPUS LIFE AND EXTRACURRICULAR ACTIVITIES

Campus housing available: women's dorms, men's dorms, apartments for married students, apartment for single students, special housing for disabled students. Students who live in college-owned, operated, or affiliated housing: 39%. **Student employment:** During the 2009-2010 academic year, 14% of undergraduates worked on campus. Average per-year earnings: $1,405. **Clubs and organizations:** Number of student organizations: 272. Activities include: campus ministries, choral groups, concert band, dance, drama/theater, international student organization, jazz band, literary magazine, marching band, model UN, music ensembles, musical theater, opera, pep band, radio station, student government, student newspaper, student film society, symphony orchestra, television station, yearbook. Number of fraternities: 21; sororities: 18. Proportion of men in fraternities: 10%; of women in sororities: 18%. **Sports program (2009-2010):** Member of NCAA I. *Men's intercollegiate varsity sports:* baseball, basketball, cross country, football, golf, tennis, track and field (indoor), track and field (outdoor). *Women's intercollegiate varsity sports:* basketball, cross country, equestrian, golf, soccer, softball, tennis, track and field (indoor), track and field (outdoor), volleyball.

SERVICES AND FACILITIES

Basic services: nonremedial tutoring, health service, health insurance, other. **Remedial assistance:** math, writing, study skills. **Counseling services:** career, personal, academic, psychological, religious. **For learning-disabled students:** School does not offer a structured program with separate admission and additional fees. Total undergraduates in learning-disabled program or receiving services: 199. Services include: reading machines, tape recorders, note-taking services, oral tests, readers, extended time for tests, tutors, priority registration, priority seating, substitution of courses, texts on tape, typist/scribe, exams on tape or computer, other testing accommodations. **Library:** Number of titles: 2,446,201; number of current serial subscriptions: 60,348. **Information technology resources:** Students are not required to lease or own a computer. Number of campus computers available to all students: 1,710. School has a wireless network. Approximate number of users that can be accommodated: 10,000. Proportion of college-owned housing units wired for high-speed internet access: 100%. **Campus safety:** Security services offered: 24-hour foot-and-vehicle patrols, late-night transport/escort service, 24-hour emergency telephones, lighted pathways/sidewalks, controlled dormitory access (key, security card, etc).

TRANSFER AND INTERNATIONAL STUDENTS

Transfer students: May apply for admission for the following academic terms: Fall, Spring, Summer. Applicants need a minimum number of credits to apply. For fall 2009: Transfer applications received: 2,311. Transfer applicants offered admission: 877. Transfer applicants enrolled: 422. **International students:** Number of foreign undergraduates: 206 (2% of student body). Number of countries represented: 72. Minimum TOEFL score required: 540 (paper); 76 (computer).

College of St. Thomas More

- **Address:** 3020 Lubbock Avenue, Fort Worth, TX 76109-2323
- **Website:** http://www.cstm.edu/
- **Private; Religious affiliation:** Roman Catholic
- **Enrollment:** N/A

KEY STATS

✔ **U.S News College Ranking:** Unranked, National Liberal Arts Colleges
✔ **SAT or ACT Score (25th/75th percentile):** N/A
✔ **Tuition:** 2009-2010: $12,550

Selectivity: N/A	Room/board: $3,690
Acceptance rate: N/A	Average debt: N/A
Student/faculty ratio: N/A	Proportion who borrowed: N/A

Concordia University Texas

- **Address:** 11400 Concordia University Drive, Austin, TX 78726
- **Website:** http://www.concordia.edu
- **Private; Religious affiliation:** Lutheran Church-Missouri Synod
- **Enrollment:** 861 full-time; 249 part-time

KEY STATS

✔ **U.S News College Ranking:** 18, Regional Colleges (West)
✔ **SAT Score (25th/75th percentile):** 890-1140
✔ **Tuition:** 2010-2011: $21,700

Selectivity: Selective	Room/board: $8,160
Acceptance rate: 53%	Average debt: $30,000
Student/faculty ratio: 10/1	Proportion who borrowed: 65%

UNDERGRADUATE STUDENT BODY STATS

2009-2010 enrollment: 861 full-time; 249 part-time. Men: 42%; women: 58%. **Ethnic makeup:** African American: 11%; American-Indian: 1%; Asian American: 2%; Hispanic: 18%; White: 68%. **Religious preference:** Roman Catholic: 25%; Protestant: 20%; No preference: 10%; Unknown: 10%; Lutheran Church-Missouri Synod: 35%.

ADMISSIONS FACTS AND FIGURES

Phone: (800) 865-4282. **Email:** admissions@concordia.edu. **Website:** http://www.concordia.edu. **Application deadlines for fall 2011:** Regular decision: Rolling. Early decision: Not offered. Early action: Not offered. Admission can be deferred. **Application fee:** $25. **To apply online, go to:** https://www.applyweb.com/apply/ctx/. **Admissions requirements/recommendations:** High school units required (recommended): English: 4 (4); Mathematics: 3 (3); Science: 3 (3); Total units: 10 (10). Tests: The college uses SAT or ACT scores in admissions decisions. Either SAT or ACT required. For admission to the fall 2011 entering class, the school will accept: ACT with or without writing accepted. Campus visit: Recommended. Admissions interview: Recommended. Off-campus interview: May be arranged. **Factors that count in admissions decisions:** *Academic:* Secondary school record: Very Important. Class rank: Important. Letters of recommendation: Considered. Standardized test scores: Very Important. Essay: Considered. *Nonacademic:* Interview: Not Considered. Extracurricular activities: Not Considered. Talent/ability: Not Considered. Geographical residence: Not Considered. State residency: Not Considered. Religious affiliation/commitment: Not Considered. Minority status: Not Considered. Volunteer work: Not Considered. Work experience: Not Considered. **Other schools with the greatest overlap in applicants:** St. Edward's University; Texas State University–San Marcos; University of Houston; University of Mary Hardin-Baylor. **Admissions statistics for the fall 2009 entering class:** Total applicants: 1,023. Total accepted: 543. Freshmen enrolled: 222; Overall acceptance rate: 53%. **Credentials of fall 2009 freshmen:** 7% ranked in the top 10 percent of their high school class; 50% were in the top 25 percent; 69% were in the top half. (Proportion submitting class standing: 72%.) **Average high school grade point average:** 3.4. **First-year students who submitted SAT scores:** 82%. Scores (25/75 percentile): Critical Reading: 440-560, Math: 450-580, Combined: 890-1140. **First-year students submitting ACT scores:** 46%. Scores (25/75 percentile): English: 18-24, Math: 17-24, Composite: 19-24.

ACADEMICS

Year founded: 1926. **Academic calendar:** Semester. **Degrees offered:** certificate, associate, bachelor's, post-bachelor's certificate, master's. **Most popular majors:** 41% business, management, marketing, and related support services, 12% social sciences, 11% education, 8% parks, recreation, leisure, and fitness studies, 8% theology and religious vocations. **Major fields of study:** biological and biomedical sciences; business, management, marketing, and related support services; communication, journalism, and related programs; computer and information sciences and support services; education; English language and literature/letters; history; liberal arts and sciences studies, and humanities; mathematics and statistics; natural resources and conservation; parks, recreation, leisure, and fitness studies; security and protective services; social sciences; theology and religious vocations. **Areas of required coursework:** arts/fine arts, humanities, computer literacy, mathematics, English (including composition), sciences (biological or physical), history, social science, other. **Pre-professional programs:** pre-law, pre-dentistry, pre-medicine, pre-theology, pre-veterinary science. **Special academic programs:** accelerated program, double major, dual enrollment, exchange student program (domestic), independent study, internships, teacher certificate program. **Teacher certification offered in:** early childhood, elementary, middle/junior high, secondary. **Reserve Officers Training Corps (ROTC):** Army ROTC: Offered at cooperating institution (University of Texas–Austin); Air Force ROTC: Offered at cooperating institution (University of Texas–Austin). **Faculty and instruction (2009-2010):** Total instructional faculty: 55 full-time, 226 part-time (62% men; 38% women; 14% minorities). Full-time faculty with Ph.D. or other terminal degree: 84%. Student/faculty ratio: 10/1. Classes of fewer than 20 students: 80%; of 20 to 49 students: 20%; of 50 or more students: 0%. **Advanced Placement and International Baccalaureate credit:** AP tests may be used for: Credit only. Scores accepted: 3. International Baccalaureate exams may be used for: Credit only. **Freshmen returning for sophomore year:** 54%. **Graduation rates:** Four-year: 18%; five-year: 32%; six-year: 33%.

COSTS AND FINANCIAL AID

Financial aid office: (512) 486-1283. **Expenses (2010-2011):** Tuition and fees 2010-2011: $21,700; room/board: $8,160. Estimated books and supplies: $1,320; transportation: $810; personal expenses: $1,320. **Financial aid:** Priority filing date for institution's financial aid form: May 1. In 2009-2010, 92% of undergraduates applied for financial aid. Of those, 72% were determined to have financial need; 33% had their need fully met. Average financial aid package (proportion receiving): $20,951 (72%). Average amount of gift aid, such as scholarships or grants (proportion receiving): $7,765 (54%). Average amount of self-help aid, such as work study or loans (proportion receiving): $9,527 (55%). Average need-based loan (excluding PLUS or other private loans): $3,934. Among students who received need-based aid, the average percentage of need met: 82%. Among students who received aid based on merit, the average award (and the proportion receiving): $8,386 (12%). The average athletic scholarship (and the proportion receiving): $0 (0%). Average amount of debt of borrowers graduating in 2009: $30,000. Proportion who borrowed: 65%.

CAMPUS LIFE AND EXTRACURRICULAR ACTIVITIES

Campus housing available: coed dorms, special housing for disabled students. Students who live in college-owned, operated, or affiliated housing: 20%. Activities include: campus ministries, choral groups, drama/theater, literary magazine, music ensembles, radio station, student government, student newspaper, yearbook. Number of fraternities: 0; sororities: 0. **Sports program (2009-2010):** Member of NCAA III. *Men's intercollegiate varsity sports:* baseball, basketball, cross country, golf, soccer. *Women's intercollegiate varsity sports:* basketball, cross country, golf, soccer, softball, volleyball.

SERVICES AND FACILITIES

Basic services: nonremedial tutoring. **Remedial assistance:** reading, math, writing, study skills. **Counseling services:** career, personal, academic, psychological, religious. **For learning-disabled students:** School does not offer a structured program with separate admission and additional fees. Services include: remedial math, remedial English, untimed tests, extended time for tests, tutors, priority seating, waiver of math degree requirement, other. **Information technology resources:** Students are not required to lease or own a computer. School has a wireless network. **Campus safety:** Security services offered: 24-hour foot-and-vehicle patrols, lighted pathways/sidewalks, controlled dormitory access (key, security card, etc).

TRANSFER AND INTERNATIONAL STUDENTS

Transfer students: May apply for admission for the following academic terms: Fall, Spring, Summer. Applicants need a minimum number of credits to apply. For fall 2009: Transfer applications received: 502. Transfer applicants offered admission: 184. Transfer applicants enrolled: 98. **International students:** Number of foreign undergraduates: 1. Minimum TOEFL score required: 550 (paper).

Dallas Baptist University

■ **Address:** 3000 Mountain Creek Parkway, Dallas, TX 75211-9299
■ **Website:** http://www.dbu.edu
■ **Private; Religious affiliation:** Baptist
■ **Enrollment:** 2,214 full-time; 1,319 part-time

KEY STATS

✔ **U.S News College Ranking:** 51, Regional Universities (West)
✔ **ACT Score (25th/75th percentile):** 18-26
✔ **Tuition:** 2010-2011: $18,690

Selectivity: Selective	**Room/board:** $5,868
Acceptance rate: 46%	**Average debt:** $17,214
Student/faculty ratio: 14/1	**Proportion who borrowed:** 79%

UNDERGRADUATE STUDENT BODY STATS

2009-2010 enrollment: 2,214 full-time; 1,319 part-time. Men: 41%; women: 59%. **Ethnic makeup:** African American: 19%; American-Indian: 1%; Asian American: 2%; Hispanic: 9%; White: 62%; International: 8%. **Religious preference:** Roman Catholic: 3%; Protestant: 22%; No preference: 4%; Unknown: 6%; Baptist : 48%; Non-Denominational: 14%; Other: 3%.

ADMISSIONS FACTS AND FIGURES

Phone: (214) 333-5360. **Email:** admiss@dbu.edu. **Website:** http://www.dbu.edu. **Application deadlines for fall 2011:** Regular decision: Rolling. Early decision: Not offered. Early action: Not offered. Admission can be deferred. **Application fee:** $25. **To apply online, go to:** http://www.dbu.edu/applications.asp. **Admissions requirements/recommendations:** High school units required (recommended): English: (4); Mathematics: (3); Science: (2); Foreign language: (2); Social studies: (3); History: (2); Total units: (16). Tests: The college uses SAT or ACT scores in admissions decisions. Either SAT or ACT required. For admission to the fall 2011 entering class, the school will accept: ACT with writing required. Campus visit: Recommended. Admissions interview: Recommended. Off-campus interview: May be arranged. **Factors that count in admissions decisions:** *Academic:* Secondary school record: Very Important. Class rank: Very Important. Letters of recommendation: Considered. Standardized test scores: Very Important. Essay: Very Important. *Nonacademic:* Interview: Considered. Extracurricular activities: Considered. Talent/ability: Important. Character/personal qualities: Very Important. Alumni/ae relationship: Considered. Geographical residence: Not Considered. State residency: Not Considered. Religious affiliation/commitment: Important. Minority status: Not Considered. Volunteer work: Considered. Work experience: Considered. **Other schools with the greatest overlap in applicants:** Abilene Christian University; Baylor University; Texas A&M University–College Station; Texas Christian University; University of North Texas. **Admissions statistics for the fall 2009 entering class:** Total applicants: 1,601. Total accepted: 730. Freshmen enrolled: 351; 8% were from out of state. Overall acceptance rate: 46%. **Credentials of fall 2009 freshmen:** 19% ranked in the top 10 percent of their high school class; 39% were in the top 25 percent; 61% were in the top half. (Proportion submitting class standing: 77%.) **Average high school grade point average:** 3.5. **First-year students who submitted SAT scores:** 46%. Scores (25/75 percentile): Critical Reading: 478-643, Math: 499-637, Combined: 977-1280. **First-year students submitting ACT scores:** 54%. Scores (25/75 percentile): English: N/A, Math: N/A, Composite: 18-26.

ACADEMICS

Year founded: 1898. **Academic calendar:** 4-1-4. **Degrees offered:** certificate, associate, transfer-associate, bachelor's, post-bachelor's certificate, master's, post-master's certificate, doctorate. **Most popular majors:** 21% business administration and management, 14% general studies, 13% psychology, 8% communication studies/speech communication and rhetoric, 6% marketing/marketing management. **Major fields of study:** biological and biomedical sciences; business, management, marketing, and related support services; communication, journalism, and related programs; computer and information sciences and support services; education; English language and literature/letters; health professions and related clinical sciences; liberal arts and sciences studies, and humanities; mathematics and statistics; multi/

interdisciplinary studies; philosophy and religious studies; psychology; public administration and social service professions; security and protective services; social sciences; theology and religious vocations; visual and performing arts. **Areas of required coursework:** arts/fine arts, humanities, computer literacy, mathematics, English (including composition), foreign languages, sciences (biological or physical), history, social science, other. **Pre-professional programs:** pre-law, pre-dentistry, pre-medicine, pre-theology, pre-veterinary science, pre-optometry, pre-pharmacy, other. **Special academic programs:** accelerated program, distance learning, double major, dual enrollment, English as a Second Language (ESL), honors program, independent study, internships, study abroad, teacher certificate program, weekend college. **Teacher certification offered in:** early childhood, special education, elementary, middle/junior high, secondary. **Reserve Officers Training Corps (ROTC):** Army ROTC: Offered at cooperating institution (University of Texas–Arlington); Air Force ROTC: Offered at cooperating institution (Texas Christian University). **Faculty and instruction (2009-2010):** Total instructional faculty: 123 full-time, 409 part-time (57% men; 43% women; 9% minorities). Full-time faculty with Ph.D. or other terminal degree: 72%. Student/faculty ratio: 14/1. Classes of fewer than 20 students: 66%; of 20 to 49 students: 32%; of 50 or more students: 2%. **Advanced Placement and International Baccalaureate credit:** AP tests may be used for: Credit only. Scores accepted: 3, 4. International Baccalaureate exams may be used for: Credit only. **Freshmen returning for sophomore year:** 71%. **Graduation rates:** Four-year: 38%; five-year: 49%; six-year: 52%.

COSTS AND FINANCIAL AID

Financial aid office: (214) 333-5460. **Expenses (2010-2011):** Tuition and fees 2010-2011: $18,690; room/board: $5,868. Estimated books and supplies: $2,040; transportation: $792; personal expenses: $1,764. **Financial aid:** Priority filing date for institution's financial aid form: March 15. In 2009-2010, 87% of undergraduates applied for financial aid. Of those, 63% were determined to have financial need; 46% had their need fully met. Average financial aid package (proportion receiving): $13,557 (61%). Average amount of gift aid, such as scholarships or grants (proportion receiving): $3,624 (42%). Average amount of self-help aid, such as work study or loans (proportion receiving): $3,738 (47%). Average need-based loan (excluding PLUS or other private loans): $3,991. Among students who received need-based aid, the average percentage of need met: 64%. Among students who received aid based on merit, the average award (and the proportion receiving): $7,088 (18%). The average athletic scholarship (and the proportion receiving): $11,973 (5%). Average amount of debt of borrowers graduating in 2009: $17,214. Proportion who borrowed: 79%.

CAMPUS LIFE AND EXTRACURRICULAR ACTIVITIES

Campus housing available (% using): women's dorms (31%), men's dorms (20%), apartments for married students (0%), apartment for single students (49%), special housing for disabled students (0%). Students who live in college-owned, operated, or affiliated housing: 42%. **Student employment:** During the 2009-2010 academic year, 27% of undergraduates worked on campus. Average per-year earnings: $3,200. **Clubs and organizations:** Number of student organizations: 50. Activities include: campus ministries, choral groups, drama/theater, international student organization, music ensembles, musical theater, opera, student government, yearbook. Number of fraternities: 2; sororities: 4. Proportion of men in fraternities: 1%; of women in sororities: 3%. Average proportion of students who stay on campus on weekends: 80%. **Sports program (2009-2010):** Member of NCAA II. *Men's intercollegiate varsity sports:* baseball, basketball, cross country, golf, tennis, track and field (indoor), track and field (outdoor). *Women's intercollegiate varsity sports:* cross country, golf, soccer, tennis, track and field (indoor), track and field (outdoor), volleyball.

SERVICES AND FACILITIES

Basic services: nonremedial tutoring, placement service, health service, health insurance. **Remedial assistance:** reading, math, writing, study skills, other. **Counseling services:** minority student, career, military, personal, veteran student, academic, older student, psychological, religious. **For learning-disabled students:** School does not offer a structured program with separate admission and additional fees. Total undergraduates in learning-disabled program or receiving services: 69. Services include: remedial math, reading machines, tape recorders, videotaped classes, untimed tests, note-taking services, oral tests, learning center, readers, extended time for tests, tutors, priority seating, texts on tape, typist/scribe, other testing accommodations. **Library:** Number of titles: 315,195; number of current serial subscriptions: 374. **Information technology resources:** Students are not required to lease or own a computer. Number of campus computers available to all students: 208. School has a wireless network. Approximate number of users that can

be accommodated: 2,750. Proportion of college-owned housing units wired for high-speed internet access: 100%. **Campus safety:** Security services offered: 24-hour foot-and-vehicle patrols, late-night transport/escort service, 24-hour emergency telephones, lighted pathways/sidewalks, controlled dormitory access (key, security card, etc).

TRANSFER AND INTERNATIONAL STUDENTS

Transfer students: May apply for admission for the following academic terms: Fall, Winter, Spring, Summer. Applicants do not need a minimum number of credits to apply. For fall 2009: Transfer applications received: 547. Transfer applicants offered admission: 306. Transfer applicants enrolled: 222. **International students:** Number of foreign undergraduates: 270 (8% of student body). Number of countries represented: 45. Minimum TOEFL score required: 525 (paper); 71 (computer). Average TOEFL score: 525 (paper).

East Texas Baptist University

- **Address:** 1209 N. Grove, Marshall, TX 75670
- **Website:** http://www.etbu.edu
- **Private; Religious affiliation:** Baptist
- **Enrollment:** 1,082 full-time; 97 part-time

KEY STATS

✔ **U.S News College Ranking:** 18, Regional Colleges (West)
✔ **SAT Score (25th/75th percentile):** 840-1050
✔ **Tuition:** 2010-2011: $19,550

Selectivity: Selective	**Room/board:** $5,436
Acceptance rate: 53%	**Average debt:** $21,380
Student/faculty ratio: 15/1	**Proportion who borrowed:** 77%

UNDERGRADUATE STUDENT BODY STATS

2009-2010 enrollment: 1,082 full-time; 97 part-time. Men: 49%; women: 51%. **Ethnic makeup:** African American: 15%; American-Indian: 2%; Asian American: 1%; Hispanic: 8%; White: 73%; International: 1%. **Religious preference:** Roman Catholic: 3%; Protestant: 10%; No preference: 17%; Baptist: 63%; Church of Christ: 3%; Other: 4%.

ADMISSIONS FACTS AND FIGURES

Phone: (800) 804-3828. **Email:** admissions@etbu.edu. **Website:** http://www.etbu.edu. **Application deadlines for fall 2011:** Regular decision: August 17. Early decision: Not offered. Early action: Not offered. Admission can be deferred. **Application fee:** $25. **To apply online, go to:** https://www.etbu.edu/php/admissions/application_form.php. **Admissions requirements/recommendations:** Tests: The college uses SAT or ACT scores in admissions decisions. Either SAT or ACT required. For admission to the fall 2011 entering class, the school will accept: ACT with or without writing accepted. Campus visit: Recommended. Admissions interview: Neither required nor recommended. Off-campus interview: May be arranged. **Factors that count in admissions decisions:** *Academic:* Secondary school record: Not Considered. Class rank: Very Important. Letters of recommendation: Not Considered. Standardized test scores: Very Important. Essay: Not Considered. *Nonacademic:* Interview: Not Considered. Extracurricular activities: Not Considered. Talent/ability: Not Considered. Character/personal qualities: Considered. Alumni/ae relationship: Not Considered. Geographical residence: Not Considered. State residency: Not Considered. Religious affiliation/commitment: Not Considered. Minority status: Not Considered. Volunteer work: Not Considered. Work experience: Not Considered. **Other schools with the greatest overlap in applicants:** Baylor University; Dallas Baptist University; Stephen F. Austin State University; University of Texas–Tyler. **Admissions statistics for the fall 2009 entering class:** Total applicants: 1,038. Total accepted: 546. Freshmen enrolled: 279; 10% were from out of state. Overall acceptance rate: 53%. **Credentials of fall 2009 freshmen:** 13% ranked in the top 10 percent of their high school class; 45% were in the top 25 percent; 81% were in the top half. (Proportion submitting class standing: 91%.) **Average high school grade point average:** 3.3. **First-year students who submitted SAT scores:** 67%. Scores (25/75 percentile): Critical Reading: 420-510, Math: 420-540, Combined: 840-1050. **First-year students submitting ACT scores:** 61%. Scores (25/75 percentile): English: 17-23, Math: 17-24, Composite: 19-23.

ACADEMICS

Year founded: 1912. **Academic calendar:** Semester. **Degrees offered:** certificate, bachelor's. **Most popular majors:** 19% education, 15% multi/interdisciplinary studies, 13% business, management, marketing, and related support services, 13% health professions and related clinical sciences, 7% theology and religious vocations. **Major fields of study:** biological and biomedical sciences; business, management, marketing, and related support services; communication, journalism, and related programs; education; English language and literature/letters; foreign languages, literatures, and linguistics; health professions and related clinical sciences; history; liberal arts and sciences studies, and humanities; mathematics and statistics; parks, recreation, leisure, and fitness studies; philosophy and religious studies; physical sciences; psychology; social sciences; theology and religious vocations; visual and performing arts. **Areas of required coursework:** arts/fine arts, humanities, mathematics, English (including composition), sciences (biological or physical), history, social science, other. **Pre-professional programs:** pre-law, pre-dentistry, pre-medicine, pre-theology, pre-veterinary science, pre-optometry, pre-pharmacy. **Special academic programs:** accelerated program, cross-registration, distance learning, double major, dual enrollment, exchange student program (domestic), honors program, independent study, internships, liberal arts/career combination, student-designed major, study abroad, teacher certificate program. **Teacher certification offered in:** early childhood, elementary, middle/junior high, secondary. **Faculty and instruction (2009-2010):** Total instructional faculty: 64 full-time, 36 part-time (61% men; 39% women; 8% minorities). Full-time faculty with Ph.D. or other terminal degree: 89%. Student/faculty ratio: 15/1. Classes of fewer than 20 students: 58%; of 20 to 49 students: 42%; of 50 or more students: 1%. **Advanced Placement and International Baccalaureate credit:** AP tests may be used for: Credit only. Scores accepted: 3, 4, 5. International Baccalaureate exams may be used for: Credit and/or placement. **Freshmen returning for sophomore year:** 58%. **Graduation rates:** Four-year: 27%; five-year: 40%; six-year: 37%. **Graduate study:** 48% of students pursue further study within five years.

COSTS AND FINANCIAL AID

Financial aid office: (903) 923-2137. **Expenses (2010-2011):** Tuition and fees 2010-2011: $19,550; room/board: $5,436. Estimated books and supplies: $892; transportation: $848; personal expenses: $1,448. **Financial aid:** Priority filing date for institution's financial aid form: June 1. In 2009-2010, 95% of undergraduates applied for financial aid. Of those, 83% were determined to have financial need; 20% had their need fully met. Average financial aid package (proportion receiving): $14,327 (83%). Average amount of gift aid, such as scholarships or grants (proportion receiving): $6,247 (65%). Average amount of self-help aid, such as work study or loans (proportion receiving): $3,809 (61%). Average need-based loan (excluding PLUS or other private loans): $3,634. Among students who received need-based aid, the average percentage of need met: 48%. Among students who received aid based on merit, the average award (and the proportion receiving): $6,692 (17%). Average amount of debt of borrowers graduating in 2009: $21,380. Proportion who borrowed: 77%.

CAMPUS LIFE AND EXTRACURRICULAR ACTIVITIES

Campus housing available (% using): women's dorms (17%), men's dorms (14%), apartments for married students (2%), apartment for single students (65%), other housing options (2%). Students who live in college-owned, operated, or affiliated housing: 81%. **Student employment:** During the 2009-2010 academic year, 4% of undergraduates worked on campus. Average per-year earnings: $4,800. **Clubs and organizations:** Number of student organizations: 38. Activities include: campus ministries, choral groups, concert band, drama/theater, international student organization, jazz band, literary magazine, marching band, model UN, music ensembles, musical theater, pep band, radio station, student government, student newspaper, symphony orchestra, yearbook. Number of fraternities: 2; sororities: 2. Proportion of men in fraternities: 5%; of women in sororities: 14%. Average proportion of students who stay on campus on weekends: 35%. **Sports program (2009-2010):** Member of NCAA III. *Men's intercollegiate varsity sports:* baseball, basketball, cross country, football, soccer. *Women's intercollegiate varsity sports:* basketball, cross country, soccer, softball, volleyball.

SERVICES AND FACILITIES

Basic services: nonremedial tutoring, placement service, health service, health insurance. **Remedial assistance:** study skills. **Counseling services:** career, personal, academic, psychological, religious. **For learning-disabled students:** School does not offer a structured program with separate admission and additional fees. Total undergraduates in learning-disabled program or receiving services: 33. Services include: reading machines, tape recorders, note-taking services, oral tests, extended time for tests, tutors, priority seating, texts on tape, other testing accommodations. **Library:** Number of titles: 121,757; number of current serial subscriptions: 150. **Information technology resources:** Students are not required to lease or own a computer. Number of campus computers available to all students: 206. School has a wireless network. Approximate number of users that can be accommodated: 2,000. Proportion of college-owned housing units wired for high-speed internet access: 100%. **Campus safety:** Security services offered: 24-hour foot-and-vehicle patrols, late-night transport/escort service, 24-hour emergency telephones, lighted pathways/sidewalks, controlled dormitory access (key, security card, etc).

TRANSFER AND INTERNATIONAL STUDENTS

Transfer students: May apply for admission for the following academic terms: Fall, Spring, Summer. Applicants need a minimum number of credits to apply. For fall 2009: Transfer applications received: 295. Transfer applicants offered admission: 164. Transfer applicants enrolled: 109. **International students:** Number of foreign undergraduates: 16 (1% of student body). Number of countries represented: 19. Minimum TOEFL score required: 500 (paper); 173 (computer).

Hardin-Simmons University

- **Address:** 2200 Hickory, Abilene, TX 79698-1000
- **Website:** http://www.hsutx.edu/
- **Private; Religious affiliation:** Baptist
- **Enrollment:** 1,730 full-time; 176 part-time

KEY STATS

✔ **U.S News College Ranking:** 32, Regional Universities (West)
✔ **SAT Score (25th/75th percentile):** 930-1160
✔ **Tuition:** 2010-2011: $20,990

Selectivity: Selective	**Room/board:** $6,282
Acceptance rate: 38%	**Average debt:** $35,429
Student/faculty ratio: 13/1	**Proportion who borrowed:** 73%

UNDERGRADUATE STUDENT BODY STATS

2009-2010 enrollment: 1,730 full-time; 176 part-time. Men: 44%; women: 56%. **Ethnic makeup:** African American: 6%; American-Indian: 1%; Asian American: 1%; Hispanic: 10%; White: 81%; International: 1%. **Religious preference:** Roman Catholic: 6%; Protestant: 14%; Jewish: 1%; No preference: 3%; Unknown: 8%; Baptist: 53%; Non denominational : 12%; Other: 3%.

ADMISSIONS FACTS AND FIGURES

Phone: (325) 670-1206. **Email:** enroll@hsutx.edu. **Website:** http://www.hsutx.edu/. **Application deadlines for fall 2011:** Regular decision: Rolling. Early decision: Not offered. Early action: Not offered. Admission can be deferred. **Application fee:** $50. **To apply online, go to:** http://www.hsutx.edu/admissions/apply/. **Admissions requirements/recommendations:** High school units required (recommended): English: 3; Mathematics: 2; Science: 2; Social studies: 2; Academic electives: 7; Total units: 16. Tests: The college uses SAT or ACT scores in admissions decisions. Either SAT or ACT required. For admission to the fall 2011 entering class, the school will accept: ACT with writing required. Campus visit: Recommended. Admissions interview: Neither required nor recommended. Off-campus interview: Not available. **Factors that count in admissions decisions:** *Academic:* Secondary school record: Important. Class rank: Very Important. Letters of recommendation: Important. Standardized test scores: Very Important. Essay: Not Considered. *Nonacademic:* Interview: Not Considered. Extracurricular activities: Considered. Talent/ability: Important. Character/personal qualities: Important. Alumni/ae relationship: Considered. Geographical residence: Not Considered. State residency: Not Considered. Religious affiliation/commitment: Considered. Minority status: Not Considered. Volunteer work: Not Considered. Work experience: Not Considered. **Other schools with the greatest overlap in applicants:** Abilene Christian University; Baylor University; Texas A&M University–College Station; Texas Tech University; University of Mary Hardin-Baylor. **Admissions statistics for the fall 2009 entering class:** Total applicants: 1,677. Total accepted: 634. Freshmen enrolled: 409; 5% were from out of state. Overall acceptance rate: 38%. **Credentials of fall 2009 freshmen:** 27% ranked in the top 10 percent of their high school class; 59% were in the top 25 percent; 85% were in the top half. (Proportion submitting class standing:

91%.) **Average high school grade point average:** 3.6. **First-year students who submitted SAT scores:** 76%. Scores (25/75 percentile): Critical Reading: 450-560, Math: 480-600, Combined: 930-1160. **First-year students submitting ACT scores:** 71%. Scores (25/75 percentile): English: 19-25, Math: 19-25, Composite: 20-25.

ACADEMICS

Year founded: 1891. **Academic calendar:** Semester. **Degrees offered:** bachelor's, post-bachelor's certificate, master's, doctorate. **Most popular majors:** 17% education, 15% business, management, marketing, and related support services, 12% health professions and related clinical sciences, 10% biological and biomedical sciences, 10% parks, recreation, leisure, and fitness studies. **Major fields of study:** agriculture, agriculture operations, and related sciences; biological and biomedical sciences; business, management, marketing, and related support services; communication, journalism, and related programs; computer and information sciences and support services; education; English language and literature/letters; foreign languages, literatures, and linguistics; health professions and related clinical sciences; history; legal professions and studies; mathematics and statistics; natural resources and conservation; parks, recreation, leisure, and fitness studies; philosophy and religious studies; physical sciences; psychology; public administration and social service professions; security and protective services; social sciences; theology and religious vocations; visual and performing arts. **Areas of required coursework:** arts/fine arts, humanities, computer literacy, mathematics, English (including composition), sciences (biological or physical), history, social science, other. **Pre-professional programs:** pre-law, pre-dentistry, pre-medicine, pre-theology, pre-pharmacy, other. **Special academic programs (% participation):** accelerated program (1.5%), cross-registration (13.5%), distance learning (0%), double major (4%), dual enrollment (0%), honors program (0%), independent study (3.5%), internships (21.8%), study abroad (3.9%), teacher certificate program (13.9%). **Teacher certification offered in:** early childhood, special education, elementary, middle/junior high, secondary. **Faculty and instruction (2009-2010):** Total instructional faculty: 136 full-time, 72 part-time (60% men; 40% women; 5% minorities). Full-time faculty with Ph.D. or other terminal degree: 89%. Student/faculty ratio: 13/1. Classes of fewer than 20 students: 63%; of 20 to 49 students: 36%; of 50 or more students: 1%. **Advanced Placement and International Baccalaureate credit:** AP tests may be used for: Credit only. Scores accepted: 3, 4, 5. **Freshmen returning for sophomore year:** 66%. **Graduation rates:** Four-year: 29%; five-year: 46%; six-year: 49%. **Graduate study:** 40% of students pursue further study immediately upon graduation; 10% within one year; 5% within five years. Fields in which graduates pursue further study: Master of Business Administration (MBA), 7%; law, 1%; medicine, 3%; theology (or the seminary), 5%; education, 10%; arts and sciences, 25%.

COSTS AND FINANCIAL AID

Financial aid office: (325) 670-5891. **Expenses (2010-2011):** Tuition and fees 2010-2011: $20,990; room/board: $6,282. Estimated books and supplies: $800; transportation: $1,098; personal expenses: $1,476. **Financial aid:** Priority filing date for institution's financial aid form: March 15. In 2009-2010, 98% of undergraduates applied for financial aid. Of those, 71% were determined to have financial need; 22% had their need fully met. Average financial aid package (proportion receiving): $16,930 (71%). Average amount of gift aid, such as scholarships or grants (proportion receiving): $6,349 (51%). Average amount of self-help aid, such as work study or loans (proportion receiving): $4,542 (63%). Average need-based loan (excluding PLUS or other private loans): $4,113. Among students who received need-based aid, the average percentage of need met: 69%. Among students who received aid based on merit, the average award (and the proportion receiving): $6,983 (28%). The average athletic scholarship (and the proportion receiving): $0 (0%). Average amount of debt of borrowers graduating in 2009: $35,429. Proportion who borrowed: 73%.

CAMPUS LIFE AND EXTRACURRICULAR ACTIVITIES

Campus housing available (% using): women's dorms (41%), men's dorms (41%), apartments for married students (0%), apartment for single students (11%), other housing options (7%). Students who live in college-owned, operated, or affiliated housing: 44%. **Student employment:** During the 2009-2010 academic year, 0% of undergraduates worked on campus. Average per-year earnings: $0. **Clubs and organizations:** Number of student organizations: 0. Activities include: campus ministries, choral groups, concert band, dance, drama/theater, jazz band, literary magazine, marching band, model UN, music ensembles, musical theater, opera, student government, student newspaper, symphony orchestra, yearbook. Number of fraternities: 5; sororities: 4. Proportion of men in fraternities: 3%; of women in sororities: 9%. Average proportion of students who stay on campus on

weekends: 50%. **Sports program (2009-2010):** Member of NCAA III. **Men's intercollegiate varsity sports:** baseball, basketball, cross country, football, golf, soccer, tennis, track and field (indoor), track and field (outdoor). **Women's intercollegiate varsity sports:** basketball, cross country, golf, soccer, softball, tennis, track and field (indoor), track and field (outdoor), volleyball.

SERVICES AND FACILITIES

Basic services: nonremedial tutoring, placement service, health service. **Remedial assistance:** reading, math, writing, study skills, other. **Counseling services:** minority student, career, military, personal, veteran student, academic, older student, psychological, religious. **For learning-disabled students:** School does not offer a structured program with separate admission and additional fees. Total undergraduates in learning-disabled program or receiving services: 35. Services include: remedial math, remedial English, remedial reading, tape recorders, untimed tests, note-taking services, oral tests, readers, extended time for tests, tutors, priority seating, other testing accommodations, other. **Library:** Number of titles: 326,490; number of current serial subscriptions: 609. **Information technology resources:** Students are not required to lease or own a computer. Number of campus computers available to all students: 234. School has a wireless network. Approximate number of users that can be accommodated: 1,300. Proportion of college-owned housing units wired for high-speed internet access: 100%. **Campus safety:** Security services offered: 24-hour foot-and-vehicle patrols, late-night transport/escort service, 24-hour emergency telephones, lighted pathways/sidewalks, controlled dormitory access (key, security card, etc).

TRANSFER AND INTERNATIONAL STUDENTS

Transfer students: May apply for admission for the following academic terms: Fall, Spring, Summer. Applicants need a minimum number of credits to apply. For fall 2009: Transfer applications received: 445. Transfer applicants offered admission: 197. Transfer applicants enrolled: 138. **International students:** Number of foreign undergraduates: 26 (1% of student body). Number of countries represented: 9. Minimum TOEFL score required: 550 (paper); 213 (computer). Average TOEFL score: 570 (paper).

Houston Baptist University

- **Address:** 7502 Fondren Road, Houston, TX 77074-3298
- **Website:** http://www.hbu.edu
- **Private; Religious affiliation:** Baptist
- **Enrollment:** 2,005 full-time; 328 part-time

KEY STATS
✔ **U.S News College Ranking:** 50, Regional Universities (West)
✔ **SAT Score (25th/75th percentile):** 930-1160
✔ **Tuition:** 2010-2011: $23,180

Selectivity: Selective	**Room/board:** $6,975
Acceptance rate: 42%	**Average debt:** N/A
Student/faculty ratio: 15/1	**Proportion who borrowed:** N/A

UNDERGRADUATE STUDENT BODY STATS

2009-2010 enrollment: 2,005 full-time; 328 part-time. Men: 35%; women: 65%. **Ethnic makeup:** African American: 20%; Asian American: 14%; Hispanic: 25%; White: 37%; International: 4%.

ADMISSIONS FACTS AND FIGURES

Phone: (281) 649-3211. **Email:** admissions@hbu.edu. **Website:** http://www.hbu.edu. **Application deadlines for fall 2011:** Regular decision: Rolling. Early decision: Not offered. Early action: Not offered. Admission cannot be deferred. **To apply online, go to:** http://www.hbu.edu/apply. **Admissions requirements/recommendations:** High school units required (recommended): English: 4 (4); Mathematics: 3 (3); Science: 3 (3); Foreign language: 0 (2); Social studies: 4 (4); History: 0 (2); Academic electives: 0 (4); Total units: 14 (24). Tests: The college uses SAT or ACT scores in admissions decisions. Either SAT or ACT required. For admission to the fall 2011 entering class, the school will accept: ACT with writing recommended. Campus visit: Recommended. Admissions interview: Recommended. Off-campus interview: May be arranged. **Factors that count in admissions decisions:** *Academic:* Secondary school record: Important. Class rank: Very Important. Letters of recommendation: Considered. Standardized test scores: Very Important. Essay: Considered. *Nonacademic:* Interview: Considered. Extracurricular activities: Considered. Talent/ability: Considered. Character/personal qualities: Important. Alumni/ae relationship: Considered. Geographical residence: Not Considered. State residency: Not Considered. Religious affiliation/commitment: Not Considered. Minority status: Not Considered. Volunteer work: Considered. Work experience: Considered. **Other schools with the greatest overlap in applicants:** Baylor University; Texas A&M University–College Station; Texas State University–San Marcos; University of Houston–Downtown; University of Texas–Austin. **Admissions statistics for the fall 2009 entering class:** Total applicants: 8,119. Total accepted: 3,431. Freshmen enrolled: 554; 4% were from out of state. Overall acceptance rate: 42%. **Credentials of fall 2009 freshmen:** 23% ranked in the top 10 percent of their high school class; 51% were in the top 25 percent; 77% were in the top half. (Proportion submitting class standing: 79%.) **First-year students who submitted SAT scores:** 91%. Scores (25/75 percentile): Critical Reading: 460-570, Math: 470-590, Combined: 930-1160. **First-year students submitting ACT scores:** 35%. Scores (25/75 percentile): English: 19-24, Math: 18-24, Composite: 20-25.

ACADEMICS

Year founded: 1960. **Academic calendar:** Semester. **Degrees offered:** bachelor's, master's. **Major fields of study:** biological and biomedical sciences; business, management, marketing, and related support services; communication, journalism, and related programs; education; English language and literature/letters; family and consumer sciences/human sciences; foreign languages, literatures, and linguistics; health professions and related clinical sciences; history; liberal arts and sciences studies, and humanities; mathematics and statistics; multi/interdisciplinary studies; parks, recreation, leisure, and fitness studies; philosophy and religious studies; physical sciences; psychology; social sciences; visual and performing arts. **Areas of required coursework:** arts/fine arts, humanities, computer literacy, mathematics, English (including composition), foreign languages, sciences (biological or physical), social science, other. **Pre-professional programs:** pre-law, pre-dentistry, pre-medicine, pre-optometry, pre-pharmacy, other. **Special academic programs:** accelerated program, double major, honors program, internships, study abroad, teacher certificate program. **Teacher certification offered in:** early childhood, special education, elementary, middle/junior high, secondary, bilingual/bicultural. **Reserve Officers Training Corps (ROTC):** Army ROTC: Offered at cooperating institution (University of Houston–Downtown); Navy ROTC: Offered at cooperating institution (Rice University); Air Force ROTC: Offered at cooperating institution (University of Houston–Downtown). **Faculty and instruction (2009-2010):** Total instructional faculty: 115 full-time, 131 part-time (46% men; 54% women; 20% minorities). Full-time faculty with Ph.D. or other terminal degree: 84%. Student/faculty ratio: 15/1. Classes of fewer than 20 students: 63%; of 20 to 49 students: 36%; of 50 or more students: 1%. **Advanced Placement and International Baccalaureate credit:** AP tests may be used for: Credit only. Scores accepted: 3, 4, 5. International Baccalaureate exams may be used for: Placement only. **Freshmen returning for sophomore year:** 71%. **Graduation rates:** Four-year: 24%; five-year: 42%; six-year: 48%.

COSTS AND FINANCIAL AID

Financial aid office: (281) 649-3389. **Expenses (2010-2011):** Tuition and fees 2010-2011: $23,180; room/board: $6,975. Estimated books and supplies: $1,350; transportation: $1,260; personal expenses: $1,900. **Financial aid:** Priority filing date for institution's financial aid form: March 1; deadline: April 15. In 2009-2010, 76% of undergraduates applied for financial aid. Of those, 69% were determined to have financial need; 30% had their need fully met. Average financial aid package (proportion receiving): $17,712 (68%). Average amount of gift aid, such as scholarships or grants (proportion receiving): $7,266 (58%). Average amount of self-help aid, such as work study or loans (proportion receiving): $8,875 (60%). Average need-based loan (excluding PLUS or other private loans): $1,263. Among students who received need-based aid, the average percentage of need met: 83%. Among students who received aid based on merit, the average award (and the proportion receiving): $3,749 (5%). The average athletic scholarship (and the proportion receiving): $7,381 (5%).

CAMPUS LIFE AND EXTRACURRICULAR ACTIVITIES

Campus housing available (% using): coed dorms (33%), women's dorms (20%), men's dorms (11%), apartment for single students (36%). Students who live in college-owned, operated, or affiliated housing: 34%. **Student employment:** During the 2009-2010 academic year, 8% of undergraduates worked on campus. Average per-year earnings: $867. **Clubs and organizations:** Number of student organizations: 45. Activities include: campus ministries, choral groups, concert band, dance, drama/theater, international student organization, jazz band, music ensembles, opera, pep band, student government, student newspaper, symphony orchestra, yearbook. Number of fraternities: 3; sororities: 2. Proportion of men in fraternities: 10%; of

women in sororities: 10%. Average proportion of students who stay on campus on weekends: 50%. **Sports program (2009-2010):** Member of NCAA I. **Men's intercollegiate varsity sports:** baseball, basketball, cross country, golf, soccer, track and field (indoor), track and field (outdoor). **Women's intercollegiate varsity sports:** basketball, cross country, golf, soccer, softball, track and field (indoor), track and field (outdoor), volleyball.

SERVICES AND FACILITIES

Basic services: nonremedial tutoring, placement service, health service. **Remedial assistance:** study skills. **Counseling services:** minority student, career, personal, academic, older student, psychological, religious. **For learning-disabled students:** School does not offer a structured program with separate admission and additional fees. Services include: remedial math, remedial English, remedial reading, diagnostic testing service, untimed tests, oral tests, learning center, extended time for tests. **Library:** Number of titles: 226,418; number of current serial subscriptions: 59,718. **Information technology resources:** Students are not required to lease or own a computer. Number of campus computers available to all students: 100. School has a wireless network. Approximate number of users that can be accommodated: 200. Proportion of college-owned housing units wired for high-speed internet access: 100%. **Campus safety:** Security services offered: 24-hour foot-and-vehicle patrols, late-night transport/escort service, 24-hour emergency telephones, lighted pathways/sidewalks, controlled dormitory access (key, security card, etc).

TRANSFER AND INTERNATIONAL STUDENTS

Transfer students: May apply for admission for the following academic terms: Fall, Spring, Summer. Applicants need a minimum number of credits to apply. For fall 2009: Transfer applications received: 1,540. Transfer applicants offered admission: 775. Transfer applicants enrolled: 236. **International students:** Number of foreign undergraduates: 98 (4% of student body). Number of countries represented: 35. Minimum TOEFL score required: 550 (paper); 213 (computer).

Howard Payne University

- **Address:** 1000 Fisk Avenue, Brownwood, TX 76801
- **Website:** http://www.hputx.edu
- **Private; Religious affiliation:** Baptist
- **Enrollment:** 939 full-time; 278 part-time

KEY STATS
- ✔ **U.S News College Ranking:** 16, Regional Colleges (West)
- ✔ **SAT Score (25th/75th percentile):** 850-1120
- ✔ **Tuition:** 2010-2011: $17,598

Selectivity: Selective	**Room/board:** $5,875
Acceptance rate: 59%	**Average debt:** $28,400
Student/faculty ratio: 11/1	**Proportion who borrowed:** 75%

UNDERGRADUATE STUDENT BODY STATS

2009-2010 enrollment: 939 full-time; 278 part-time. Men: 52%; women: 48%. **Ethnic makeup:** African American: 7%; American-Indian: 1%; Asian American: 1%; Hispanic: 16%; White: 75%; International: 1%. **Religious preference:** Roman Catholic: 4%; No preference: 2%; Unknown: 6%; Baptist: 45%; Christian: 22%; Other: 21%.

ADMISSIONS FACTS AND FIGURES

Phone: (325) 649-8020. **Email:** enroll@hputx.edu. **Website:** http://www.hputx.edu. **Application deadlines for fall 2011:** Regular decision: Rolling. Early decision: Not offered. Early action: Not offered. Admission cannot be deferred. **Admissions requirements/recommendations:** High school units required (recommended): English: (4); Mathematics: (3); Science: (3); Foreign language: (2); Social studies: (4); Total units: (16). Tests: The college uses SAT or ACT scores in admissions decisions. Either SAT or ACT required. For admission to the fall 2011 entering class, the school will accept: ACT with writing required. Campus visit: Recommended. Admissions interview: Required. Off-campus interview: May be arranged. **Factors that count in admissions decisions: Academic:** Secondary school record: Important. Class rank: Important. Letters of recommendation: Important. Standardized test scores: Very Important. Essay: Considered. **Nonacademic:** Interview: Considered. Extracurricular activities: Considered. Talent/ability: Considered. Character/personal qualities: Important. Alumni/ae relationship: Considered. Geographical residence: Considered.

State residency: Not Considered. Religious affiliation/commitment: Considered. Minority status: Considered. Volunteer work: Considered. Work experience: Considered. **Other schools with the greatest overlap in applicants:** Baylor University; Hardin-Simmons University; Texas A&M University–College Station; Texas Tech University; University of Texas–Austin. **Admissions statistics for the fall 2009 entering class:** Total applicants: 907. Total accepted: 535. Freshmen enrolled: 218; 1% were from out of state. Overall acceptance rate: 59%. **Credentials of fall 2009 freshmen:** 11% ranked in the top 10 percent of their high school class; 30% were in the top 25 percent; 77% were in the top half. (Proportion submitting class standing: 86%.) **Average high school grade point average:** 3.4. **First-year students who submitted SAT scores:** 68%. Scores (25/75 percentile): Critical Reading: 410-570, Math: 440-550, Combined: 850-1120. **First-year students submitting ACT scores:** 55%. Scores (25/75 percentile): English: 18-25, Math: 18-25, Composite: 18-24.

ACADEMICS

Year founded: 1889. **Academic calendar:** Semester. **Degrees offered:** certificate, associate, bachelor's, master's. **Most popular majors:** 15% business, management, marketing, and related support services, 15% education, 12% theology and religious vocations, 11% communication, journalism, and related programs, 8% social sciences. **Major fields of study:** biological and biomedical sciences; business, management, marketing, and related support services; communication, journalism, and related programs; computer and information sciences and support services; education; English language and literature/letters; foreign languages, literatures, and linguistics; health professions and related clinical sciences; history; legal professions and studies; liberal arts and sciences studies, and humanities; mathematics and statistics; parks, recreation, leisure, and fitness studies; philosophy and religious studies; physical sciences; psychology; social sciences; theology and religious vocations; visual and performing arts. **Areas of required coursework:** arts/fine arts, humanities, computer literacy, mathematics, English (including composition), foreign languages, sciences (biological or physical), history, social science, other. **Pre-professional programs:** pre-law, pre-dentistry, pre-medicine, pre-theology, pre-veterinary science, pre-pharmacy. **Special academic programs:** cooperative (work-study plan) program, distance learning, double major, dual enrollment, honors program, independent study, internships, study abroad, teacher certificate program. **Teacher certification offered in:** elementary, middle/junior high, secondary, bilingual/bicultural. **Faculty and instruction (2009-2010):** Total instructional faculty: 77 full-time, 45 part-time (63% men; 37% women; 3% minorities). Full-time faculty with Ph.D. or other terminal degree: 62%. Student/faculty ratio: 11/1. Classes of fewer than 20 students: 74%; of 20 to 49 students: 26%; of 50 or more students: 1%. **Advanced Placement and International Baccalaureate credit:** AP tests may be used for: Credit only. Scores accepted: 3, 4, 5. International Baccalaureate exams may be used for: Credit only. **Freshmen returning for sophomore year:** 61%. **Graduation rates:** Four-year: 26%; five-year: 37%; six-year: 38%.

COSTS AND FINANCIAL AID

Financial aid office: (325) 649-8014. **Expenses (2010-2011):** Tuition and fees 2010-2011: $17,598; room/board: $5,875. Estimated books and supplies: $1,200; transportation: $875; personal expenses: $1,575. **Financial aid:** Priority filing date for institution's financial aid form: March 15. In 2009-2010, 88% of undergraduates applied for financial aid. Of those, 78% were determined to have financial need; 35% had their need fully met. Average financial aid package (proportion receiving): $15,273 (78%). Average amount of gift aid, such as scholarships or grants (proportion receiving): $10,858 (77%). Average amount of self-help aid, such as work study or loans (proportion receiving): $5,795 (55%). Average need-based loan (excluding PLUS or other private loans): $3,927. Among students who received need-based aid, the average percentage of need met: 86%. Among students who received aid based on merit, the average award (and the proportion receiving): $6,166 (18%). The average athletic scholarship (and the proportion receiving): $0 (0%). Average amount of debt of borrowers graduating in 2009: $28,400. Proportion who borrowed: 75%.

CAMPUS LIFE AND EXTRACURRICULAR ACTIVITIES

Campus housing available (% using): women's dorms (37%), men's dorms (45%), apartment for single students (18%). Students who live in college-owned, operated, or affiliated housing: 45%. **Student employment:** During the 2009-2010 academic year, 14% of undergraduates worked on campus. Average per-year earnings: $2,000. **Clubs and organizations:** Number of student organizations: 30. Activities include: campus ministries, choral groups, concert band, drama/theater, jazz band, literary magazine, marching band, model UN, music ensembles, musical theater, student government, stu-

dent newspaper, symphony orchestra, yearbook. Number of fraternities: 4; sororities: 4. Proportion of men in fraternities: 16%; of women in sororities: 16%. Average proportion of students who stay on campus on weekends: 50%. **Sports program (2009-2010):** Member of NCAA III. *Men's intercollegiate varsity sports:* baseball, basketball, football, soccer, tennis. *Women's intercollegiate varsity sports:* basketball, soccer, softball, tennis, volleyball.

SERVICES AND FACILITIES

Basic services: nonremedial tutoring, health service. **Remedial assistance:** reading, math, writing, study skills. **Counseling services:** career, personal, academic, older student, religious. **For learning-disabled students:** School does not offer a structured program with separate admission and additional fees. Services include: remedial math, remedial English, remedial reading, tape recorders, videotaped classes, diagnostic testing service, untimed tests, note-taking services, oral tests, extended time for tests, tutors, early syllabus, priority seating, texts on tape, exams on tape or computer, other testing accommodations. **Library:** Number of titles: 125,488; number of current serial subscriptions: 31,109. **Information technology resources:** Students are not required to lease or own a computer. Number of campus computers available to all students: 246. School has a wireless network. Approximate number of users that can be accommodated: 400. Proportion of college-owned housing units wired for high-speed internet access: 100%. **Campus safety:** Security services offered: 24-hour foot-and-vehicle patrols, late-night transport/escort service, 24-hour emergency telephones, lighted pathways/sidewalks, controlled dormitory access (key, security card, etc).

TRANSFER AND INTERNATIONAL STUDENTS

Transfer students: May apply for admission for the following academic terms: Fall, Spring, Summer. Applicants need a minimum number of credits to apply. For fall 2009: Transfer applications received: 151. Transfer applicants offered admission: 86. Transfer applicants enrolled: 89. **International students:** Number of foreign undergraduates: 11 (1% of student body). Number of countries represented: 0. Minimum TOEFL score required: 550 (paper); 213 (computer). Average TOEFL score: 550 (paper).

Huston-Tillotson University

- **Address:** 900 Chicon Street, Austin, TX 78702
- **Website:** http://www.htu.edu/
- **Private; Religious affiliation:** United Church of Christ/Methodist
- **Enrollment:** N/A

KEY STATS

✔ **U.S News College Ranking:** second tier, National Liberal Arts Colleges
✔ **SAT or ACT Score (25th/75th percentile):** N/A
✔ **Tuition:** 2009-2010: $11,434

Selectivity: Selective	**Room/board:** $6,690
Acceptance rate: N/A	**Average debt:** N/A
Student/faculty ratio: N/A	**Proportion who borrowed:** N/A

Jarvis Christian College

- **Address:** PO Box 1470, Hawkins, TX 75765-1470
- **Website:** http://www.jarvis.edu
- **Private; Religious affiliation:** Christian Church (Disciples of Christ)
- **Enrollment:** 614 full-time; 14 part-time

KEY STATS

✔ **U.S News College Ranking:** second tier, National Liberal Arts Colleges
✔ **SAT Score (25th/75th percentile):** 660-800
✔ **Tuition:** 2010-2011: $11,146

Selectivity: Least selective	**Room/board:** $7,788
Acceptance rate: 23%	**Average debt:** $18,550
Student/faculty ratio: 13/1	**Proportion who borrowed:** 83%

UNDERGRADUATE STUDENT BODY STATS

2009-2010 enrollment: 614 full-time; 14 part-time. Men: 45%; women: 55%. **Ethnic makeup:** African American: 93%; Hispanic: 3%; White: 3%; International: 1%. **Religious preference:** Roman Catholic: 1%; Protestant: 68%; No preference: 27%; Christian Church (Disciples of Christ): 4%.

ADMISSIONS FACTS AND FIGURES

Phone: (903) 769-5730. **Email:** Recruitment@jarvis.edu. **Website:** http://www.jarvis.edu. **Application deadlines for fall 2011:** Regular decision: August 1. Early decision: Not offered. Early action: Not offered. Admission can be deferred. **Application fee:** $50. **To apply online, go to:** http://jccjics1.jarvis.edu/ics/Admissions/. **Admissions requirements/recommendations:** High school units required (recommended): English: 3 (3); Mathematics: 2 (2); Science: 1 (1); Foreign language: 0 (0); Social studies: 3 (3); History: 0 (0); Academic electives: 7 (7); Total units: 16 (16). Tests: The college uses SAT or ACT scores in admissions decisions. ACT required. For admission to the fall 2011 entering class, the school will accept: ACT with or without writing accepted. Campus visit: Recommended. Admissions interview: Recommended. Off-campus interview: May be arranged. **Factors that count in admissions decisions:** *Academic:* Secondary school record: Important. Class rank: Considered. Letters of recommendation: Considered. Standardized test scores: Important. Essay: Not Considered. *Nonacademic:* Interview: Not Considered. Extracurricular activities: Considered. Talent/ability: Considered. Character/personal qualities: Considered. Alumni/ae relationship: Not Considered. Geographical residence: Not Considered. State residency: Not Considered. Religious affiliation/commitment: Not Considered. Minority status: Not Considered. Volunteer work: Not Considered. Work experience: Not Considered. **Other schools with the greatest overlap in applicants:** Huston-Tillotson University; Paul Quinn College; Texas College; Wiley College. **Admissions statistics for the fall 2009 entering class:** Total applicants: 525. Total accepted: 119. Freshmen enrolled: 119; 2% were from out of state. Overall acceptance rate: 23%. **Size of waiting list:** 0 applicants; enrolled from waiting list: 0. **Credentials of fall 2009 freshmen:** 2% ranked in the top 10 percent of their high school class; 6% were in the top 25 percent; 30% were in the top half. (Proportion submitting class standing: 74%.) **Average high school grade point average:** 2.5. **First-year students who submitted SAT scores:** 30%. Scores (25/75 percentile): Critical Reading: 350-400, Math: 310-400, Combined: 660-800. **First-year students submitting ACT scores:** 19%. Scores (25/75 percentile): English: N/A, Math: N/A, Composite: 17-18.

ACADEMICS

Year founded: 1912. **Academic calendar:** Semester. **Degrees offered:** bachelor's. **Major fields of study:** biological and biomedical sciences; business, management, marketing, and related support services; computer and information sciences and support services; education; English language and literature/letters; health professions and related clinical sciences; history; mathematics and statistics; philosophy and religious studies; physical sciences; social sciences. **Areas of required coursework:** arts/fine arts, humanities, computer literacy, mathematics, English (including composition), foreign languages, sciences (biological or physical), history, social science, other. **Pre-professional programs:** pre-law, pre-medicine. **Special academic programs (% participation):** cooperative (work-study plan) program (85%), cross-registration (1%), distance learning (15%), double major (1%), dual enrollment, English as a Second Language (ESL), honors program, internships (11%), liberal arts/career combination, student-designed major (14%), study abroad, teacher certificate program (9%). **Teacher certification offered in:** special education, elementary, middle/junior high, secondary. **Cooperative education programs:** business, health professions, social/behavioral science. **Faculty and instruction (2009-2010):** Total instructional faculty: 35 (51% men; 49% women). Full-time faculty with Ph.D. or other terminal degree: 49%. Student/faculty ratio: 13/1. Classes of fewer than 20 students: 60%; of 20 to 49 students: 39%; of 50 or more students: 1%. **Advanced Placement and International Baccalaureate credit:** AP tests may be used for: Placement only. International Baccalaureate exams may be used for: Placement only. **Freshmen returning for sophomore year:** 59%. **Graduation rates:** Four-year: 9%; five-year: 15%; six-year: 16%. **Graduate study:** 1% of students pursue further study immediately upon graduation; 2% within one year; 4% within five years. Fields in which graduates pursue further study: Master of Business Administration (MBA), 1%; law, 1%; medicine, 1%; theology (or the seminary), 1%; education, 7%.

COSTS AND FINANCIAL AID

Financial aid office: (903) 769-5740. **Expenses (2010-2011):** Tuition and fees 2010-2011: $11,146; room/board: $7,788. Estimated books and supplies: $1,300; transportation: $1,200; personal expenses: $1,800. **Financial aid:** Priority filing date for institution's financial aid form: April 15; deadline: April 15. In 2009-2010, 100% of undergraduates applied for financial aid. Of those, 100% were determined to have financial need; 11% had their need fully met. Average financial aid package (proportion receiving): $11,020 (100%). Average amount of gift aid, such as scholarships or grants (proportion receiving): $6,957 (100%). Average amount of self-help aid,

such as work study or loans (proportion receiving): $4,047 (87%). Average need-based loan (excluding PLUS or other private loans): $3,604. Among students who received need-based aid, the average percentage of need met: 82%. Among students who received aid based on merit, the average award (and the proportion receiving): $0 (0%). The average athletic scholarship (and the proportion receiving): $7,322 (8%). Average amount of debt of borrowers graduating in 2009: $18,550. Proportion who borrowed: 83%.

CAMPUS LIFE AND EXTRACURRICULAR ACTIVITIES

Campus housing available (% using): women's dorms (18%), men's dorms (18%), apartments for married students (2%), apartment for single students (2%). Students who live in college-owned, operated, or affiliated housing: 2%. **Student employment:** During the 2009-2010 academic year, 2% of undergraduates worked on campus. Average per-year earnings: $4,320. **Clubs and organizations:** Number of student organizations: 33. Activities include: choral groups, drama/theater, international student organization, music ensembles, pep band, student government. Number of fraternities: 4; sororities: 4. Proportion of men in fraternities: 6%; of women in sororities: 10%. Average proportion of students who stay on campus on weekends: 70%. **Sports program (2009-2010):** Member of NAIA. *Men's intercollegiate varsity sports:* baseball, basketball. *Women's intercollegiate varsity sports:* basketball, volleyball.

SERVICES AND FACILITIES

Basic services: nonremedial tutoring, placement service, health service, health insurance. **Remedial assistance:** reading, math, writing, study skills. **Counseling services:** minority student, career, personal, veteran student, academic, older student, psychological, birth control, religious. **For learning-disabled students:** School does not offer a structured program with separate admission and additional fees. Services include: remedial math, remedial English, remedial reading, tape recorders, videotaped classes, diagnostic testing service, oral tests, extended time for tests, tutors. **Library:** Number of titles: 55,020; number of current serial subscriptions: 136. **Information technology resources:** Students are not required to lease or own a computer. Number of campus computers available to all students: 318. School has a wireless network. Approximate number of users that can be accommodated: 1,000. Proportion of college-owned housing units wired for high-speed internet access: 90%. **Campus safety:** Security services offered: 24-hour foot-and-vehicle patrols, 24-hour emergency telephones, lighted pathways/sidewalks, student patrols, controlled dormitory access (key, security card, etc).

TRANSFER AND INTERNATIONAL STUDENTS

Transfer students: May apply for admission for the following academic terms: Fall, Spring. Applicants do not need a minimum number of credits to apply. **International students:** Number of foreign undergraduates: 3 (1% of student body). Number of countries represented: 1. Minimum TOEFL score required: 500 (paper); 173 (computer). Average TOEFL score: 535 (paper).

Lamar University

- **Address:** Lamar Station, Box 10001, Beaumont, TX 77710
- **Website:** http://www.lamar.edu
- **Public**
- **Enrollment:** 6,864 full-time; 2,741 part-time

KEY STATS

✔ **U.S News College Ranking:** second tier, Regional Universities (West)
✔ **SAT Score (25th/75th percentile):** 830-1040
✔ **Tuition:** 2010-2011: $6,944 in state, $16,244 out of state

Selectivity: Less selective	**Room/board:** $6,900
Acceptance rate: 59%	**Average debt:** $12,003
Student/faculty ratio: 20/1	**Proportion who borrowed:** 61%

UNDERGRADUATE STUDENT BODY STATS

2009-2010 enrollment: 6,864 full-time; 2,741 part-time. Men: 40%; women: 60%. **Ethnic makeup:** African American: 32%; Asian American: 4%; Hispanic: 8%; White: 56%; International: 1%.

ADMISSIONS FACTS AND FIGURES

Phone: (409) 880-8888. **Email:** admissions@lamar.edu. **Website:** http://www.lamar.edu. **Application deadlines for fall 2011:** Regular decision: August 1. Early decision: Not offered. Early action: Not offered. Admission can be deferred. **Application fee:** $25. **To apply online, go to:** http://www.lamar.edu/admissions/1366_5552.htm. **Admissions requirements/recommendations:** High school units required (recommended): English: 4; Mathematics: 3; Science: 2; Foreign language: 0 (2); Social studies: 3; History: 0; Academic electives: 3; Total units: 15. Tests: The college uses SAT or ACT scores in admissions decisions. Either SAT or ACT required. For admission to the fall 2011 entering class, the school will accept: ACT with writing required. Campus visit: Recommended. Admissions interview: Neither required nor recommended. Off-campus interview: Not available. **Factors that count in admissions decisions:** *Academic:* Secondary school record: Important. Class rank: Very Important. Letters of recommendation: Not Considered. Standardized test scores: Not Considered. Essay: Not Considered. *Nonacademic:* Interview: Not Considered. Extracurricular activities: Considered. Talent/ability: Considered. Character/personal qualities: Not Considered. Alumni/ae relationship: Not Considered. Geographical residence: Not Considered. State residency: Not Considered. Religious affiliation/commitment: Not Considered. Minority status: Not Considered. Volunteer work: Not Considered. Work experience: Not Considered. **Admissions statistics for the fall 2009 entering class:** Total applicants: 5,766. Total accepted: 3,394. Freshmen enrolled: 1,485; 2% were from out of state. Overall acceptance rate: 59%. **Credentials of fall 2009 freshmen:** 13% ranked in the top 10 percent of their high school class; 37% were in the top 25 percent; 75% were in the top half. (Proportion submitting class standing: 93%.) **First-year students who submitted SAT scores:** 82%. Scores (25/75 percentile): Critical Reading: 410-510, Math: 420-530, Combined: 830-1040. **First-year students submitting ACT scores:** 18%. Scores (25/75 percentile): English: N/A, Math: N/A, Composite: 16-22.

ACADEMICS

Year founded: 1923. **Academic calendar:** Semester. **Degrees offered:** associate, bachelor's, master's, doctorate. **Most popular majors:** 20% business, management, marketing, and related support services, 17% multi/interdisciplinary studies, 10% general studies, 9% engineering, 7% nursing/registered nurse training (R.N., A.S.N., B.S.N., M.S.N.). **Major fields of study:** biological and biomedical sciences; business, management, marketing, and related support services; communication, journalism, and related programs; computer and information sciences and support services; education; engineering; engineering technologies/technicians; English language and literature/letters; foreign languages, literatures, and linguistics; health professions and related clinical sciences; history; mathematics and statistics; natural resources and conservation; physical sciences; psychology; security and protective services; social sciences; visual and performing arts. **Areas of required coursework:** arts/fine arts, humanities, mathematics, English (including composition), philosophy, sciences (biological or physical), history, social science, other. **Pre-professional programs:** pre-law, pre-dentistry, pre-medicine, pre-veterinary science, pre-optometry, pre-pharmacy. **Teacher certification offered in:** early childhood, special education, elementary, secondary. **Cooperative education programs:** computer science, education, natural science. **Faculty and instruction (2009-2010):** Total instructional faculty: 417 full-time, 166 part-time (57% men; 43% women; 19% minorities). Full-time faculty with Ph.D. or other terminal degree: 70%. Student/faculty ratio: 20/1. Classes of fewer than 20 students: 34%; of 20 to 49 students: 57%; of 50 or more students: 8%. **Advanced Placement and International Baccalaureate credit:** AP tests may be used for: Placement only. International Baccalaureate exams may be used for: Placement only. **Freshmen returning for sophomore year:** 64%. **Graduation rates:** Four-year: 9%; five-year: 23%; six-year: 33%.

COSTS AND FINANCIAL AID

Financial aid office: (409) 880-8450. **Expenses (2010-2011):** Tuition and fees 2010-2011: $6,944 in state, $16,244 out of state; room/board: $6,900. Estimated transportation: $2,276; personal expenses: $2,138. **Financial aid:** Priority filing date for institution's financial aid form: April 1. In 2009-2010, 74% of undergraduates applied for financial aid. Of those, 54% were determined to have financial need; 6% had their need fully met. Average financial aid package (proportion receiving): $10,723 (54%). Average amount of gift aid, such as scholarships or grants (proportion receiving): N/A (45%). Average amount of self-help aid, such as work study or loans (proportion receiving): N/A (54%). Among students who received need-based aid, the average percentage of need met: 54%. Average amount of debt of borrowers graduating in 2009: $12,003. Proportion who borrowed: 61%.

CAMPUS LIFE AND EXTRACURRICULAR ACTIVITIES

Campus housing available (% using): coed dorms (100%). Students who live in college-owned, operated, or affiliated housing: 19%. **Clubs and organiza-**

tions: Number of student organizations: 119. Activities include: campus ministries, choral groups, concert band, dance, drama/theater, international student organization, jazz band, literary magazine, marching band, music ensembles, musical theater, opera, pep band, radio station, student government, student newspaper, student film society, symphony orchestra, television station. Number of fraternities: 9; sororities: 7. Proportion of men in fraternities: 2%; of women in sororities: 1%. **Sports program (2009-2010):** Member of NCAA I. *Men's intercollegiate varsity sports:* baseball, basketball, cross country, football, golf, track and field (indoor), track and field (outdoor). *Women's intercollegiate varsity sports:* basketball, cross country, golf, soccer, tennis, track and field (indoor), track and field (outdoor), volleyball.

SERVICES AND FACILITIES

Basic services: nonremedial tutoring, placement service, health service, health insurance. **Remedial assistance:** reading, math, writing, study skills. **Counseling services:** minority student, career, veteran student, academic. **For learning-disabled students:** School does not offer a structured program with separate admission and additional fees. Total undergraduates in learning-disabled program or receiving services: 49. Services include: remedial math, remedial English, reading machines, remedial reading, tape recorders, note-taking services, oral tests, readers, extended time for tests, tutors, early syllabus, priority registration, priority seating, texts on tape, exams on tape or computer, other. **Library:** Number of titles: 526,180; number of current serial subscriptions: 26,618. **Information technology resources:** Students are not required to lease or own a computer. School has a wireless network. Proportion of college-owned housing units wired for high-speed internet access: 100%. **Campus safety:** Security services offered: 24-hour foot-and-vehicle patrols, late-night transport/escort service, 24-hour emergency telephones, lighted pathways/sidewalks, controlled dormitory access (key, security card, etc).

TRANSFER AND INTERNATIONAL STUDENTS

Transfer students: May apply for admission for the following academic terms: Fall, Spring, Summer. Applicants need a minimum number of credits to apply. For fall 2009: Transfer applications received: 1,704. Transfer applicants offered admission: 1,089. Transfer applicants enrolled: 631. **International students:** Number of foreign undergraduates: 94 (1% of student body). Minimum TOEFL score required: 500 (paper); 61 (computer). Average TOEFL score: 541 (paper).

LeTourneau University

- **Address:** PO Box 7001, Longview, TX 75607-7001
- **Website:** http://www.letu.edu
- **Private; Religious affiliation:** Christian interdenominational
- **Enrollment:** 2,899 full-time; 199 part-time

KEY STATS

✔ **U.S News College Ranking:** 35, Regional Universities (West)
✔ **SAT Score (25th/75th percentile):** 1060-1293
✔ **Tuition:** 2010-2011: $21,980

Selectivity: More selective	**Room/board:** $8,390
Acceptance rate: 70%	**Average debt:** N/A
Student/faculty ratio: 23/1	**Proportion who borrowed:** N/A

UNDERGRADUATE STUDENT BODY STATS

2009-2010 enrollment: 2,899 full-time; 199 part-time. Men: 45%; women: 55%. **Ethnic makeup:** African American: 20%; Asian American: 1%; Hispanic: 7%; White: 70%; International: 2%. **Religious preference:** Roman Catholic: 2%; Protestant: 93%; Unknown: 3%; Other: 2%.

ADMISSIONS FACTS AND FIGURES

Phone: (903) 233-4300. **Email:** admissions@letu.edu. **Website:** http://www.letu.edu. **Application deadlines for fall 2011:** Regular decision: Rolling; decision sent by August 26. Early decision: Not offered. Early action: Not offered. Admission can be deferred. **Application fee:** $25. **To apply online, go to:** http://www.letu.edu/opencms/opencms/_Admissions/apply.html. **Admissions requirements/recommendations:** High school units required (recommended): English: 4 (0); Mathematics: 3 (0); Science: 3 (0); Foreign language: 0 (1); Social studies: 2 (0); History: 1 (0); Academic electives: 0 (2); Total units: 16 (3). Tests: The college uses SAT or ACT scores in admissions decisions. Either SAT or ACT required. For admission to the fall 2011 entering class, the school will accept: ACT with or without writing accepted.

Campus visit: Recommended. Admissions interview: Neither required nor recommended. Off-campus interview: May be arranged. **Factors that count in admissions decisions:** *Academic:* Secondary school record: Very Important. Class rank: Important. Letters of recommendation: Considered. Standardized test scores: Very Important. Essay: Important. *Nonacademic:* Interview: Considered. Extracurricular activities: Considered. Talent/ability: Considered. Character/personal qualities: Important. Alumni/ae relationship: Considered. Geographical residence: Not Considered. State residency: Not Considered. Religious affiliation/commitment: Important. Minority status: Considered. Volunteer work: Considered. Work experience: Not Considered. **Other schools with the greatest overlap in applicants:** Baylor University; Texas A&M University–College Station; University of Texas–Tyler. **Admissions statistics for the fall 2009 entering class:** Total applicants: 986. Total accepted: 688. Freshmen enrolled: 346; 45% were from out of state. Overall acceptance rate: 70%. **Credentials of fall 2009 freshmen:** 41% ranked in the top 10 percent of their high school class; 67% were in the top 25 percent; 90% were in the top half. (Proportion submitting class standing: 57%.) **Average high school grade point average:** 3.6. **First-year students who submitted SAT scores:** 66%. Scores (25/75 percentile): Critical Reading: 510-640, Math: 550-653, Combined: 1060-1293. **First-year students submitting ACT scores:** 52%. Scores (25/75 percentile): English: 21-29, Math: 22-29, Composite: 22-29.

ACADEMICS

Year founded: 1946. **Academic calendar:** Semester. **Degrees offered:** associate, bachelor's, master's. **Most popular majors:** 25% engineering, 16% transportation and materials moving, 15% business, management, marketing, and related support services. **Major fields of study:** biological and biomedical sciences; business, management, marketing, and related support services; communication, journalism, and related programs; computer and information sciences and support services; education; engineering; engineering technologies/technicians; English language and literature/letters; history; mathematics and statistics; multi/interdisciplinary studies; parks, recreation, leisure, and fitness studies; physical sciences; psychology; social sciences; theology and religious vocations; transportation and materials moving. **Areas of required coursework:** humanities, mathematics, English (including composition), sciences (biological or physical), history, social science, other. **Pre-professional programs:** pre-law, pre-dentistry, pre-medicine, pre-theology, pre-veterinary science, pre-optometry, pre-pharmacy. **Special academic programs:** accelerated program, cooperative (work-study plan) program, distance learning, double major, dual enrollment, English as a Second Language (ESL), honors program, independent study, internships, study abroad, teacher certificate program, weekend college. **Teacher certification offered in:** early childhood, special education, elementary, vo-tech, middle/junior high, secondary. **Cooperative education programs:** business, computer science, education, engineering, technologies, other. **Faculty and instruction (2009-2010):** Total instructional faculty: 70 full-time, 184 part-time (65% men; 35% women; 12% minorities). Full-time faculty with Ph.D. or other terminal degree: 74%. Student/faculty ratio: 23/1. Classes of fewer than 20 students: 73%; of 20 to 49 students: 27%; of 50 or more students: 0%. **Advanced Placement and International Baccalaureate credit:** AP tests may be used for: Credit only. Scores accepted: 3, 4, 5. International Baccalaureate exams may be used for: Credit only. **Freshmen returning for sophomore year:** 74%. **Graduation rates:** Four-year: 29%; five-year: 45%; six-year: 49%.

COSTS AND FINANCIAL AID

Financial aid office: (903) 233-3430. **Expenses (2010-2011):** Tuition and fees 2010-2011: $21,980; room/board: $8,390. Estimated books and supplies: $1,390; transportation: $1,220; personal expenses: $1,130. **Financial aid:** Priority filing date for institution's financial aid form: February 15. In 2009-2010, 87% of undergraduates applied for financial aid. Of those, 78% were determined to have financial need; 7% had their need fully met. Average financial aid package (proportion receiving): $10,706 (77%). Average amount of gift aid, such as scholarships or grants (proportion receiving): $8,618 (56%). Average amount of self-help aid, such as work study or loans (proportion receiving): $5,214 (67%). Average need-based loan (excluding PLUS or other private loans): $5,206. Among students who received need-based aid, the average percentage of need met: 43%. Among students who received aid based on merit, the average award (and the proportion receiving): $5,862 (6%). The average athletic scholarship (and the proportion receiving): $0 (0%).

CAMPUS LIFE AND EXTRACURRICULAR ACTIVITIES

Campus housing available (% using): women's dorms (21%), men's dorms (58%), apartments for married students (5%), apartment for single students

(11%), special housing for disabled students (2%), other housing options (3%). Students who live in college-owned, operated, or affiliated housing: 75%. **Student employment:** During the 2009-2010 academic year, 27% of undergraduates worked on campus. Average per-year earnings: $1,375. **Clubs and organizations:** Number of student organizations: 22. Activities include: campus ministries, choral groups, drama/theater, international student organization, jazz band, literary magazine, music ensembles, musical theater, student government, student newspaper, student film society, yearbook. Number of fraternities: 0; sororities: 0. Average proportion of students who stay on campus on weekends: 75%. **Sports program (2009-2010):** Member of NCAA III. *Men's intercollegiate varsity sports:* baseball, basketball, golf, soccer, tennis. *Women's intercollegiate varsity sports:* basketball, golf, soccer, softball, tennis, volleyball.

SERVICES AND FACILITIES

Basic services: nonremedial tutoring, placement service, health service, health insurance. **Remedial assistance:** reading, math, writing, study skills. **Counseling services:** career, personal, academic, psychological, religious. **Library:** Number of titles: 116,019; number of current serial subscriptions: 332. **Information technology resources:** Students are not required to lease or own a computer. Number of campus computers available to all students: 210. School has a wireless network. Approximate number of users that can be accommodated: 2,300. Proportion of college-owned housing units wired for high-speed internet access: 100%. **Campus safety:** Security services offered: 24-hour foot-and-vehicle patrols, late-night transport/escort service, 24-hour emergency telephones, lighted pathways/sidewalks, student patrols, controlled dormitory access (key, security card, etc).

TRANSFER AND INTERNATIONAL STUDENTS

Transfer students: May apply for admission for the following academic terms: Fall, Spring, Summer. Applicants do not need a minimum number of credits to apply. For fall 2009: Transfer applications received: 434. Transfer applicants offered admission: 350. Transfer applicants enrolled: 285. **International students:** Number of foreign undergraduates: 57 (2% of student body). Number of countries represented: 20. Minimum TOEFL score required: 500 (paper); 173 (computer).

Lubbock Christian University

- **Address:** 5601 19th Street, Lubbock, TX 79407
- **Website:** http://www.lcu.edu
- **Private; Religious affiliation:** Church of Christ
- **Enrollment:** 1,278 full-time; 263 part-time

KEY STATS

✔ **U.S News College Ranking:** second tier, Regional Universities (West)
✔ **ACT Score (25th/75th percentile):** 18-24
✔ **Tuition:** 2010-2011: $16,180

Selectivity: Selective	**Room/board:** $5,146
Acceptance rate: 66%	**Average debt:** $26,320
Student/faculty ratio: 12/1	**Proportion who borrowed:** 79%

UNDERGRADUATE STUDENT BODY STATS

2009-2010 enrollment: 1,278 full-time; 263 part-time. Men: 41%; women: 59%. **Ethnic makeup:** African American: 6%; Asian American: 1%; Hispanic: 16%; White: 76%; International: 1%. **Religious preference:** Roman Catholic: 9%; Protestant: 45%; Unknown: 1%; Church of Christ: 42%.

ADMISSIONS FACTS AND FIGURES

Phone: (806) 720-7151. **Email:** admissions@lcu.edu. **Website:** http://www.lcu.edu. **Application deadlines for fall 2011:** Regular decision: August 15. Early decision: Not offered. Early action: Not offered. Admission cannot be deferred. **Application fee:** $25. **Admissions requirements/recommendations:** High school units required (recommended): English: (4); Mathematics: (3); Science: (3); Foreign language: (2); Social studies: (1); History: (2); Academic electives: (2); Total units: (21). Tests: The college uses SAT or ACT scores in admissions decisions. Either SAT or ACT required. For admission to the fall 2011 entering class, the school will accept: ACT with writing recommended. Campus visit: Recommended. Admissions interview: Neither required nor recommended. Off-campus interview: May not be arranged. **Factors that count in admissions decisions:** *Academic:* Secondary school record: Considered. Class rank: Considered. Letters of recommendation: Considered. Standardized test scores: Important. Essay: Not Considered.

Nonacademic: Interview: Not Considered. Extracurricular activities: Considered. Talent/ability: Considered. Character/personal qualities: Important. Alumni/ae relationship: Considered. Geographical residence: Not Considered. State residency: Not Considered. Religious affiliation/commitment: Not Considered. Minority status: Not Considered. Volunteer work: Considered. Work experience: Not Considered. **Other schools with the greatest overlap in applicants:** Abilene Christian University; Harding University; Oklahoma Christian University; Texas Tech University; West Texas A&M University. **Admissions statistics for the fall 2009 entering class:** Total applicants: 1,044. Total accepted: 684. Freshmen enrolled: 252; 18% were from out of state. Overall acceptance rate: 66%. **Credentials of fall 2009 freshmen:** 17% ranked in the top 10 percent of their high school class; 45% were in the top 25 percent; 75% were in the top half. (Proportion submitting class standing: 73%.) **Average high school grade point average:** 3.5. **First-year students who submitted SAT scores:** 52%. Scores (25/75 percentile): Critical Reading: 430-560, Math: 440-540, Combined: 870-1100. **First-year students submitting ACT scores:** 73%. Scores (25/75 percentile): English: 17-24, Math: 18-24, Composite: 18-24.

ACADEMICS

Year founded: 1957. **Academic calendar:** Semester. **Degrees offered:** associate, bachelor's, master's. **Most popular majors:** 30% business, management, marketing, and related support services, 20% education, 12% health professions and related clinical sciences, 6% parks, recreation, leisure, and fitness studies, 5% public administration and social service professions. **Major fields of study:** agriculture, agriculture operations, and related sciences; biological and biomedical sciences; business, management, marketing, and related support services; communication, journalism, and related programs; computer and information sciences and support services; education; engineering; English language and literature/letters; family and consumer sciences/human sciences; foreign languages, literatures, and linguistics; health professions and related clinical sciences; history; liberal arts and sciences studies, and humanities; mathematics and statistics; parks, recreation, leisure, and fitness studies; physical sciences; psychology; public administration and social service professions; security and protective services; theology and religious vocations; visual and performing arts. **Areas of required coursework:** arts/fine arts, humanities, mathematics, English (including composition), sciences (biological or physical), history, social science, other. **Pre-professional programs:** pre-law, pre-dentistry, pre-medicine, pre-veterinary science, pre-pharmacy. **Special academic programs (% participation):** distance learning (59%), double major (1%), English as a Second Language (ESL) (2%), honors program (1%), internships (22%), liberal arts/career combination (5%), student-designed major (5%), study abroad (1%), teacher certificate program (19%). **Teacher certification offered in:** early childhood, special education, elementary, middle/junior high, secondary, bilingual/bicultural. **Cooperative education programs:** agriculture, engineering, health professions, other. **Reserve Officers Training Corps (ROTC):** Army ROTC: Offered at cooperating institution (Texas Tech University Health Sciences Center); Air Force ROTC: Offered at cooperating institution (Texas Tech University). **Faculty and instruction (2009-2010):** Total instructional faculty: 85 full-time, 86 part-time (59% men; 41% women; 8% minorities). Full-time faculty with Ph.D. or other terminal degree: 69%. Student/faculty ratio: 12/1. Classes of fewer than 20 students: 67%; of 20 to 49 students: 31%; of 50 or more students: 3%. **Advanced Placement and International Baccalaureate credit:** AP tests may be used for: Credit only. Scores accepted: 3, 4. International Baccalaureate exams may be used for: Credit only. **Freshmen returning for sophomore year:** 66%. **Graduation rates:** Four-year: 28%; five-year: 39%; six-year: 42%. **Graduate study:** 23% of students pursue further study immediately upon graduation.

COSTS AND FINANCIAL AID

Financial aid office: (800) 933-7601. **Expenses (2010-2011):** Tuition and fees 2010-2011: $16,180; room/board: $5,146. Estimated books and supplies: $1,150; transportation: $1,928; personal expenses: $2,158. **Financial aid:** Priority filing date for institution's financial aid form: June 1. In 2009-2010, 86% of undergraduates applied for financial aid. Of those, 73% were determined to have financial need; 7% had their need fully met. Average financial aid package (proportion receiving): $13,010 (73%). Average amount of gift aid, such as scholarships or grants (proportion receiving): $9,089 (67%). Average amount of self-help aid, such as work study or loans (proportion receiving): $4,976 (68%). Average need-based loan (excluding PLUS or other private loans): $4,124. Among students who received need-based aid, the average percentage of need met: 67%. Among students who received aid based on merit, the average award (and the proportion receiving): $3,839 (15%). The average athletic scholarship (and the proportion

receiving): $7,817 (7%). Average amount of debt of borrowers graduating in 2009: $26,320. Proportion who borrowed: 79%.

CAMPUS LIFE AND EXTRACURRICULAR ACTIVITIES

Campus housing available (% using): women's dorms (46%), men's dorms (35%), apartments for married students (3%), apartment for single students (16%). Students who live in college-owned, operated, or affiliated housing: 28%. **Student employment:** During the 2009-2010 academic year, 17% of undergraduates worked on campus. Average per-year earnings: $2,000. **Clubs and organizations:** Number of student organizations: 17. Activities include: campus ministries, choral groups, concert band, drama/theater, jazz band, music ensembles, musical theater, pep band, student government, student newspaper, yearbook. Number of fraternities: 4; sororities: 4. Proportion of men in fraternities: 14%; of women in sororities: 14%. Average proportion of students who stay on campus on weekends: 28%. **Sports program (2009-2010):** Member of NAIA. *Men's intercollegiate varsity sports:* baseball, basketball, cross country, golf, soccer, track and field (indoor), track and field (outdoor). *Women's intercollegiate varsity sports:* basketball, cross country, golf, soccer, softball, track and field (indoor), track and field (outdoor), volleyball.

SERVICES AND FACILITIES

Basic services: nonremedial tutoring, placement service, health service. **Remedial assistance:** reading, math, writing, study skills. **Counseling services:** minority student, career, personal, veteran student, academic, older student, psychological, religious. **For learning-disabled students:** School does not offer a structured program with separate admission and additional fees. Total undergraduates in learning-disabled program or receiving services: 57. Services include: remedial math, remedial English, reading machines, remedial reading, tape recorders, untimed tests, note-taking services, oral tests, learning center, readers, extended time for tests, tutors, early syllabus, priority registration, priority seating, texts on tape, typist/scribe, exams on tape or computer, other testing accommodations. **Library:** Number of titles: 121,889; number of current serial subscriptions: 43. **Information technology resources:** Students are not required to lease or own a computer. Number of campus computers available to all students: 169. School has a wireless network. Approximate number of users that can be accommodated: 1,000. Proportion of college-owned housing units wired for high-speed internet access: 100%. **Campus safety:** Security services offered: 24-hour foot-and-vehicle patrols, late-night transport/escort service, lighted pathways/sidewalks, controlled dormitory access (key, security card, etc).

TRANSFER AND INTERNATIONAL STUDENTS

Transfer students: May apply for admission for the following academic terms: Fall, Spring, Summer. Applicants need a minimum number of credits to apply. For fall 2009: Transfer applications received: 540. Transfer applicants offered admission: 352. Transfer applicants enrolled: 256. **International students:** Number of foreign undergraduates: 9 (1% of student body). Number of countries represented: 15. Minimum TOEFL score required: 525 (paper); 196 (computer).

McMurry University

- **Address:** S. 14th and Sayles Boulevard, Abilene, TX 79697
- **Website:** http://www.mcm.edu
- **Private; Religious affiliation:** Methodist
- **Enrollment:** 1,216 full-time; 293 part-time

KEY STATS

✔ **U.S News College Ranking:** 14, Regional Colleges (West)
✔ **SAT Score (25th/75th percentile):** 850-1090
✔ **Tuition:** 2010-2011: $20,680

Selectivity: Selective	**Room/board:** $6,976
Acceptance rate: 57%	**Average debt:** $27,935
Student/faculty ratio: 14/1	**Proportion who borrowed:** 77%

UNDERGRADUATE STUDENT BODY STATS

2009-2010 enrollment: 1,216 full-time; 293 part-time. Men: 49%; women: 51%. **Ethnic makeup:** African American: 16%; American-Indian: 1%; Asian American: 1%; Hispanic: 15%; White: 66%; International: 1%. **Religious preference:** Roman Catholic: 10%; Protestant: 32%; Unknown: 31%; Methodist: 16%; Other: 11%.

ADMISSIONS FACTS AND FIGURES

Phone: (325) 793-4700. **Email:** admissions@mcm.edu. **Website:** http://www.mcm.edu. **Application deadlines for fall 2011:** Regular decision: August 15. Early decision: Not offered. Early action: Not offered. Admission can be deferred. **Application fee:** $20. **To apply online, go to:** http://www.mcm.edu/newsite/web/enrollment/apply.htm. **Admissions requirements/recommendations:** High school units required (recommended): English: 4 (4); Mathematics: 3 (3); Science: 3 (3); Foreign language: (2); Social studies: 4 (4); Total units: 14 (16). Tests: The college uses SAT or ACT scores in admissions decisions. Either SAT or ACT required. For admission to the fall 2011 entering class, the school will accept: ACT with writing recommended. Campus visit: Recommended. Admissions interview: Neither required nor recommended. Off-campus interview: May be arranged. **Factors that count in admissions decisions:** *Academic:* Secondary school record. Very Important. Class rank: Very Important. Letters of recommendation: Considered. Standardized test scores: Very Important. Essay: Important. *Nonacademic:* Interview: Considered. Extracurricular activities: Important. Talent/ability: Important. Character/personal qualities: Important. Alumni/ae relationship: Considered. Geographical residence: Considered. State residency: Considered. Religious affiliation/commitment: Considered. Minority status: Not Considered. Volunteer work: Important. Work experience: Considered. **Admissions statistics for the fall 2009 entering class:** Total applicants: 1,574. Total accepted: 896. Freshmen enrolled: 320; 3% were from out of state. Overall acceptance rate: 57%. **Credentials of fall 2009 freshmen:** 15% ranked in the top 10 percent of their high school class; 36% were in the top 25 percent; 71% were in the top half. (Proportion submitting class standing: 95%.) **Average high school grade point average:** 3.3. **First-year students who submitted SAT scores:** 64%. Scores (25/75 percentile): Critical Reading: 410-540, Math: 440-550, Combined: 850-1090. **First-year students submitting ACT scores:** 61%. Scores (25/75 percentile): English: 15-23, Math: 17-24, Composite: 17-24.

ACADEMICS

Year founded: 1923. **Academic calendar:** Semester. **Degrees offered:** bachelor's. **Most popular majors:** 26% business, management, marketing, and related support services, 24% education, 12% health professions and related clinical sciences, 9% visual and performing arts, 6% social sciences. **Major fields of study:** biological and biomedical sciences; business, management, marketing, and related support services; computer and information sciences and support services; education; English language and literature/letters; foreign languages, literatures, and linguistics; health professions and related clinical sciences; history; mathematics and statistics; philosophy and religious studies; physical sciences; psychology; social sciences; visual and performing arts. **Areas of required coursework:** arts/fine arts, humanities, computer literacy, mathematics, English (including composition), philosophy, foreign languages, sciences (biological or physical), history, social science. **Pre-professional programs:** pre-law, pre-dentistry, pre-medicine, pre-theology, pre-veterinary science, pre-pharmacy, other. **Special academic programs:** accelerated program, cross-registration, double major, dual enrollment, honors program, independent study, internships, liberal arts/career combination, student-designed major, teacher certificate program. **Teacher certification offered in:** early childhood, elementary, middle/junior high, secondary, bilingual/bicultural. **Faculty and instruction (2009-2010):** Total instructional faculty: 77 full-time, 68 part-time (57% men; 43% women; 5% minorities). Full-time faculty with Ph.D. or other terminal degree: 79%. Student/faculty ratio: 14/1. Classes of fewer than 20 students: 67%; of 20 to 49 students: 32%; of 50 or more students: 1%. **Advanced Placement and International Baccalaureate credit:** AP tests may be used for: Credit and/or placement. Scores accepted: 3, 4, 5. International Baccalaureate exams may be used for: Credit and/or placement. **Freshmen returning for sophomore year:** 57%. **Graduation rates:** Four-year: 26%; five-year: 36%; six-year: 42%. **Graduate study:** 38% of students pursue further study immediately upon graduation. Fields in which graduates pursue further study: Master of Business Administration (MBA), 18%; law, 8%; dentistry, 8%; engineering, 2%; theology (or the seminary), 4%; education, 11%; arts and sciences, 49%.

COSTS AND FINANCIAL AID

Financial aid office: (325) 793-4709. **Expenses (2010-2011):** Tuition and fees 2010-2011: $20,680; room/board: $6,976. Estimated books and supplies: $1,200; transportation: $1,050; personal expenses: $1,963. **Financial aid:** Priority filing date for institution's financial aid form: March 15. In 2009-2010, 91% of undergraduates applied for financial aid. Of those, 84% were determined to have financial need; 14% had their need fully met. Average financial aid package (proportion receiving): $17,424 (84%). Average amount of gift aid, such as scholarships or grants (proportion receiving):

$9,646 (78%). Average amount of self-help aid, such as work study or loans (proportion receiving): $4,826 (72%). Average need-based loan (excluding PLUS or other private loans): $4,252. Among students who received need-based aid, the average percentage of need met: 84%. Among students who received aid based on merit, the average award (and the proportion receiving): $5,458 (6%). The average athletic scholarship (and the proportion receiving): $0 (0%). Average amount of debt of borrowers graduating in 2009: $27,935. Proportion who borrowed: 77%.

CAMPUS LIFE AND EXTRACURRICULAR ACTIVITIES

Campus housing available (% using): coed dorms (22%), women's dorms (22%), men's dorms (41%), apartment for single students (15%), special housing for disabled students (0%). Students who live in college-owned, operated, or affiliated housing: 48%. **Student employment:** During the 2009-2010 academic year, 6% of undergraduates worked on campus. Average per-year earnings: $2,320. **Clubs and organizations:** Number of student organizations: 45. Activities include: campus ministries, choral groups, concert band, drama/theater, international student organization, jazz band, literary magazine, marching band, model UN, music ensembles, musical theater, student government, student newspaper, yearbook. Number of fraternities: 5; sororities: 6. Proportion of men in fraternities: 5%; of women in sororities: 9%. Average proportion of students who stay on campus on weekends: 50%. **Sports program (2009-2010):** Member of NCAA III. *Men's intercollegiate varsity sports:* baseball, basketball, cross country, football, golf, soccer, swimming, tennis, track and field (indoor), track and field (outdoor). *Women's intercollegiate varsity sports:* basketball, cross country, golf, soccer, swimming, tennis, track and field (indoor), track and field (outdoor), volleyball.

SERVICES AND FACILITIES

Basic services: nonremedial tutoring, placement service, health service, other. **Remedial assistance:** reading, math, writing, study skills. **Counseling services:** minority student, career, military, personal, veteran student, academic, older student, psychological, birth control, religious, other. **For learning-disabled students:** School does not offer a structured program with separate admission and additional fees. Services include: tape recorders, oral tests, learning center, extended time for tests, priority seating, other testing accommodations, other. **Library:** Number of titles: 151,507; number of current serial subscriptions: 300. **Information technology resources:** Students are required to lease or own a computer. Number of campus computers available to all students: 248. School has a wireless network. Approximate number of users that can be accommodated: 1,600. Proportion of college-owned housing units wired for high-speed internet access: 100%. **Campus safety:** Security services offered: 24-hour foot-and-vehicle patrols, late-night transport/escort service, lighted pathways/sidewalks, controlled dormitory access (key, security card, etc).

TRANSFER AND INTERNATIONAL STUDENTS

Transfer students: May apply for admission for the following academic terms: Fall, Spring, Summer. Applicants need a minimum number of credits to apply. For fall 2009: Transfer applications received: 481. Transfer applicants offered admission: 281. Transfer applicants enrolled: 201. **International students:** Number of foreign undergraduates: 9 (1% of student body). Number of countries represented: 9. Minimum TOEFL score required: 550 (paper); 213 (computer).

Midwestern State University

- **Address:** 3410 Taft Boulevard, Wichita Falls, TX 76308-2099
- **Website:** http://www.mwsu.edu
- **Public**
- **Enrollment:** 4,168 full-time; 1,438 part-time

KEY STATS

✔ **U.S News College Ranking:** second tier, Regional Universities (West)
✔ **SAT Score (25th/75th percentile):** 910-1120
✔ **Tuition:** 2010-2011: $6,720 in state, $7,620 out of state

Selectivity: Selective	**Room/board:** $5,940
Acceptance rate: 88%	**Average debt:** $19,049
Student/faculty ratio: 18/1	**Proportion who borrowed:** 52%

UNDERGRADUATE STUDENT BODY STATS

2009-2010 enrollment: 4,168 full-time; 1,438 part-time. Men: 42%; women: 58%. **Ethnic makeup:** African American: 13%; American-Indian: 1%; Asian American: 4%; Hispanic: 11%; White: 65%; International: 7%.

ADMISSIONS FACTS AND FIGURES

Phone: (800) 842-1922. **Email:** admissions@mwsu.edu. **Website:** http://www.mwsu.edu. **Application deadlines for fall 2011:** Regular decision: August 7. Early decision: Not offered. Early action: Send application by: August 7; Decision sent by: N/A. Admission cannot be deferred. **Application fee:** $25. **To apply online, go to:** http://admissions.mwsu.edu/apply.asp. **Admissions requirements/recommendations:** High school units required (recommended): English: 4 (4); Mathematics: 3 (3); Science: 2 (2); Academic electives: 6 (6); Total units: 15 (15). Tests: The college uses SAT or ACT scores in admissions decisions. Either SAT or ACT required. For admission to the fall 2011 entering class, the school will accept: ACT with writing required. Campus visit: Recommended. Admissions interview: Recommended. Off-campus interview: Not available. **Factors that count in admissions decisions:** *Academic:* Secondary school record: Very Important. Class rank: Very Important. Letters of recommendation: Not Considered. Standardized test scores: Very Important. Essay: Considered. *Nonacademic:* Interview: Important. Extracurricular activities: Important. Talent/ability: Important. Character/personal qualities: Considered. Alumni/ae relationship: Considered. Geographical residence: Considered. State residency: Considered. Religious affiliation/commitment: Not Considered. Minority status: Not Considered. Volunteer work: Important. Work experience: Important. **Other schools with the greatest overlap in applicants:** Texas A&M University–College Station; Texas State University–San Marcos; Texas Tech University; University of North Texas; University of Texas–Austin. **Admissions statistics for the fall 2009 entering class:** Total applicants: 2,225. Total accepted: 1,956. Freshmen enrolled: 715; 3% were from out of state. Overall acceptance rate: 88%. Non-early acceptance rate: 88%. **Credentials of fall 2009 freshmen:** 15% ranked in the top 10 percent of their high school class; 41% were in the top 25 percent; 74% were in the top half. (Proportion submitting class standing: 93%.) **Average high school grade point average:** 3.5. **First-year students who submitted SAT scores:** 79%. Scores (25/75 percentile): Critical Reading: 450-550, Math: 460-570, Combined: 910-1120. **First-year students submitting ACT scores:** 57%. Scores (25/75 percentile): English: 18-24, Math: 18-24, Composite: 18-23.

ACADEMICS

Year founded: 1922. **Academic calendar:** Semester. **Degrees offered:** associate, bachelor's, post-bachelor's certificate, master's. **Most popular majors:** 6% education, 2% communication, journalism, and related programs, 2% engineering, 1% computer and information sciences and support services, 1% natural resources and conservation. **Major fields of study:** biological and biomedical sciences; business, management, marketing, and related support services; communication, journalism, and related programs; computer and information sciences and support services; education; engineering; engineering technologies/technicians; English language and literature/letters; foreign languages, literatures, and linguistics; health professions and related clinical sciences; history; legal professions and studies; liberal arts and sciences studies, and humanities; mathematics and statistics; multi/interdisciplinary studies; natural resources and conservation; parks, recreation, leisure, and fitness studies; physical sciences; psychology; public administration and social service professions; security and protective services; social sciences; visual and performing arts. **Areas of required coursework:** arts/fine arts, humanities, computer literacy, mathematics, English (including composition), philosophy, foreign languages, sciences (biological or physical), history, social science. **Pre-professional programs:** pre-law, pre-dentistry, pre-medicine, pre-veterinary science, pre-optometry, pre-pharmacy, other. **Special academic programs:** distance learning, double major, dual enrollment, English as a Second Language (ESL), honors program, independent study, internships, liberal arts/career combination, study abroad, teacher certificate program. **Teacher certification offered in:** early childhood, special education, elementary, middle/junior high, secondary, bilingual/bicultural. **Cooperative education programs:** business, education, health professions. **Reserve Officers Training Corps (ROTC):** Air Force ROTC: Offered at cooperating institution (University of North Texas). **Faculty and instruction (2009-2010):** Total instructional faculty: 241 full-time, 94 part-time (52% men; 48% women; 11% minorities). Full-time faculty with Ph.D. or other terminal degree: 71%. Student/faculty ratio: 18/1. Classes of fewer than 20 students: 31%; of 20 to 49 students: 58%; of 50 or more students: 11%. **Advanced Placement and International Baccalaureate credit:** AP tests may be used for: Credit and/or placement. Scores accepted: 3, 4, 5. International Baccalaureate exams may be used for: Credit and/or

placement. **Freshmen returning for sophomore year:** 71%. **Graduation rates:** Four-year: 10%; five-year: 25%; six-year: 31%.

COSTS AND FINANCIAL AID

Financial aid office: (940) 397-4214. **Expenses (2010-2011):** Tuition and fees 2010-2011: $6,720 in state, $7,620 out of state; room/board: $5,940. Estimated books and supplies: $1,500; transportation: $1,402; personal expenses: $1,506. **Financial aid:** Priority filing date for institution's financial aid form: March 1. In 2009-2010, 58% of undergraduates applied for financial aid. Of those, 51% were determined to have financial need; 17% had their need fully met. Average financial aid package (proportion receiving): $8,459 (51%). Average amount of gift aid, such as scholarships or grants (proportion receiving): $5,885 (42%). Average amount of self-help aid, such as work study or loans (proportion receiving): $7,205 (38%). Average need-based loan (excluding PLUS or other private loans): $7,136. Among students who received need-based aid, the average percentage of need met: 70%. Among students who received aid based on merit, the average award (and the proportion receiving): $2,096 (18%). The average athletic scholarship (and the proportion receiving): $5,792 (1%). Average amount of debt of borrowers graduating in 2009: $19,049. Proportion who borrowed: 52%.

CAMPUS LIFE AND EXTRACURRICULAR ACTIVITIES

Campus housing available (% using): coed dorms (14%), women's dorms (27%), men's dorms (20%), apartments for married students, apartment for single students (37%), special housing for disabled students, other housing options (2%). Students who live in college-owned, operated, or affiliated housing: 22%. **Student employment:** During the 2009-2010 academic year, 10% of undergraduates worked on campus. Average per-year earnings: $3,771. **Clubs and organizations:** Number of student organizations: 136. Activities include: campus ministries, choral groups, concert band, dance, drama/theater, international student organization, jazz band, literary magazine, marching band, music ensembles, pep band, student government, student newspaper, student film society, television station, yearbook. Number of fraternities: 8; sororities: 8. Average proportion of students who stay on campus on weekends: 20%. **Sports program (2009-2010):** Member of NCAA II. *Men's intercollegiate varsity sports:* basketball, football, golf, soccer, tennis. *Women's intercollegiate varsity sports:* basketball, cross country, soccer, softball, tennis, volleyball.

SERVICES AND FACILITIES

Basic services: nonremedial tutoring, placement service, health service, health insurance. **Remedial assistance:** reading, math, writing, study skills. **Counseling services:** minority student, career, military, personal, veteran student, academic, older student, psychological, birth control. **For learning-disabled students:** School does not offer a structured program with separate admission and additional fees. Total undergraduates in learning-disabled program or receiving services: 47. Services include: remedial math, remedial English, reading machines, remedial reading, tape recorders, note-taking services, oral tests, learning center, readers, extended time for tests, tutors, early syllabus, priority registration, priority seating, substitution of courses, texts on tape, typist/scribe, exams on tape or computer, other testing accommodations. **Library:** Number of titles: 392,484; number of current serial subscriptions: 400. **Information technology resources:** Students are not required to lease or own a computer. Number of campus computers available to all students: 405. School has a wireless network. Approximate number of users that can be accommodated: 1,800. Proportion of college-owned housing units wired for high-speed internet access: 100%. **Campus safety:** Security services offered: 24-hour foot-and-vehicle patrols, late-night transport/escort service, 24-hour emergency telephones, lighted pathways/sidewalks, controlled dormitory access (key, security card, etc).

TRANSFER AND INTERNATIONAL STUDENTS

Transfer students: May apply for admission for the following academic terms: Fall, Spring, Summer. Applicants need a minimum number of credits to apply. For fall 2009: Transfer applications received: 1,402. Transfer applicants offered admission: 974. Transfer applicants enrolled: 662. **International students:** Number of foreign undergraduates: 366 (7% of student body). Number of countries represented: 38. Minimum TOEFL score required: 550 (paper); 213 (computer).

Our Lady of the Lake University

- **Address:** 411 S.W. 24th Street, San Antonio, TX 78207-4689
- **Website:** http://www.ollusa.edu
- **Private; Religious affiliation:** Roman Catholic
- **Enrollment:** 1,180 full-time; 415 part-time

KEY STATS

- ✔ **U.S News College Ranking:** 62, Regional Universities (West)
- ✔ **SAT Score (25th/75th percentile):** 820-1010
- ✔ **Tuition:** 2010-2011: $21,900

Selectivity: Selective	**Room/board:** $6,838
Acceptance rate: 63%	**Average debt:** $22,133
Student/faculty ratio: 11/1	**Proportion who borrowed:** 81%

UNDERGRADUATE STUDENT BODY STATS

2009-2010 enrollment: 1,180 full-time; 415 part-time. Men: 28%; women: 72%. **Ethnic makeup:** African American: 8%; Asian American: 1%; Hispanic: 71%; White: 20%; International: 1%. **Religious preference:** Jewish: 1%; No preference: 7%; Roman Catholic: 70%; Church of Christ: 3%; Other: 19%.

ADMISSIONS FACTS AND FIGURES

Phone: (800) 436-6558. **Email:** admission@lake.ollusa.edu. **Website:** http://www.ollusa.edu. **Application deadlines for fall 2011:** Regular decision: July 15. Early decision: Not offered. Early action: Not offered. Admission can be deferred. **Application fee:** $25. **To apply online, go to:** http://admissions.ollusa.edu/s/346/ollu.aspx?sid=346&gid=1&pgid=257. **Admissions requirements/recommendations:** High school units required (recommended): English: 4; Mathematics: 3 (3); Science: 2; Foreign language: 2; Social studies: 3; Total units: 16. Tests: The college uses SAT or ACT scores in admissions decisions. Either SAT or ACT required. For admission to the fall 2011 entering class, the school will accept: ACT with or without writing accepted. Campus visit: Recommended. Admissions interview: Neither required nor recommended. Off-campus interview: May be arranged. **Factors that count in admissions decisions:** *Academic:* Secondary school record: Important. Class rank: Important. Letters of recommendation: Important. Standardized test scores: Important. Essay: Considered. *Nonacademic:* Interview: Not Considered. Extracurricular activities: Considered. Talent/ability: Considered. Character/personal qualities: Not Considered. Alumni/ae relationship: Not Considered. Geographical residence: Considered. State residency: Considered. Religious affiliation/commitment: Not Considered. Minority status: Considered. Volunteer work: Considered. Work experience: Considered. **Other schools with the greatest overlap in applicants:** St. Mary's University of San Antonio; University of the Incarnate Word. **Admissions statistics for the fall 2009 entering class:** Total applicants: 1,232. Total accepted: 781. Freshmen enrolled: 252; 4% were from out of state. Overall acceptance rate: 63%. **Credentials of fall 2009 freshmen:** 18% ranked in the top 10 percent of their high school class; 49% were in the top 25 percent; 74% were in the top half. (Proportion submitting class standing: 72%.) **Average high school grade point average:** 3.2. **First-year students who submitted SAT scores:** 86%. Scores (25/75 percentile): Critical Reading: 410-500, Math: 410-510, Combined: 820-1010. **First-year students submitting ACT scores:** 46%. Scores (25/75 percentile): English: 14-20, Math: 16-22, Composite: 16-21.

ACADEMICS

Year founded: 1895. **Academic calendar:** Semester. **Degrees offered:** certificate, bachelor's, post-bachelor's certificate, master's, post-master's certificate, doctorate. **Most popular majors:** 19% business, management, marketing, and related support services, 19% education, 11% psychology, 9% public administration and social service professions, 8% social sciences. **Major fields of study:** area, ethnic, cultural, and gender studies; biological and biomedical sciences; business, management, marketing, and related support services; communication, journalism, and related programs; computer and information sciences and support services; education; English language and literature/letters; family and consumer sciences/human sciences; foreign languages, literatures, and linguistics; health professions and related clinical sciences; history; liberal arts and sciences studies, and humanities; library science; mathematics and statistics; multi/interdisciplinary studies; philosophy and religious studies; physical sciences; psychology; public administration and social service professions; security and protective services; social sciences; visual and performing arts. **Areas of required coursework:** arts/fine arts, mathematics, English

(including composition), philosophy, foreign languages, sciences (biological or physical), history, social science, other. **Special academic programs (% participation):** accelerated program (4%), cooperative (work-study plan) program (26%), cross-registration (15%), distance learning (27%), double major (16%), honors program (3%), independent study (12%), internships (4%), study abroad (1%), teacher certificate program (9%), weekend college (36%). **Teacher certification offered in:** early childhood, special education, elementary, middle/junior high, secondary, bilingual/bicultural. **Reserve Officers Training Corps (ROTC):** Army ROTC: Offered at cooperating institution (St. Mary's University of San Antonio); Air Force ROTC: Offered at cooperating institution (St. Mary's University of San Antonio). **Faculty and instruction (2009-2010):** Total instructional faculty: 108 full-time, 120 part-time (51% men; 49% women; 43% minorities). Full-time faculty with Ph.D. or other terminal degree: 73%. Student/faculty ratio: 11/1. Classes of fewer than 20 students: 70%; of 20 to 49 students: 30%. **Advanced Placement and International Baccalaureate credit:** AP tests may be used for: Credit only. Scores accepted: 3, 4, 5. International Baccalaureate exams may be used for: Credit only. **Freshmen returning for sophomore year:** 59%. **Graduation rates:** Four-year: 19%; five-year: 33%; six-year: 37%. **Graduate study:** 37% of students pursue further study immediately upon graduation. Fields in which graduates pursue further study: Master of Business Administration (MBA), 20%; law, 2%; medicine, 2%; engineering, 1%; theology (or the seminary), 1%; education, 10%; arts and sciences, 55%; veterinary medicine, 1%.

COSTS AND FINANCIAL AID

Financial aid office: (210) 434-6711. **Expenses (2010-2011):** Tuition and fees 2010-2011: $21,900; room/board: $6,838. Estimated books and supplies: $1,200; transportation: $1,450; personal expenses: $1,850. **Financial aid:** Priority filing date for institution's financial aid form: May 1. In 2009-2010, 100% of undergraduates applied for financial aid. Of those, 100% were determined to have financial need; 30% had their need fully met. Average financial aid package (proportion receiving): $22,500 (100%). Average amount of gift aid, such as scholarships or grants (proportion receiving): $3,143 (95%). Average amount of self-help aid, such as work study or loans (proportion receiving): $3,990 (86%). Average need-based loan (excluding PLUS or other private loans): $3,300. Among students who received need-based aid, the average percentage of need met: 82%. Among students who received aid based on merit, the average award (and the proportion receiving): $17,180 (4%). The average athletic scholarship (and the proportion receiving): $4,165 (6%). Average amount of debt of borrowers graduating in 2009: $22,133. Proportion who borrowed: 81%.

CAMPUS LIFE AND EXTRACURRICULAR ACTIVITIES

Campus housing available (% using): coed dorms (80%), women's dorms (20%). Students who live in college-owned, operated, or affiliated housing: 41%. **Student employment:** During the 2009-2010 academic year, 34% of undergraduates worked on campus. Average per-year earnings: $2,000. **Clubs and organizations:** Number of student organizations: 67. Activities include: campus ministries, choral groups, dance, drama/theater, international student organization, jazz band, literary magazine, music ensembles, musical theater, student government, student newspaper, symphony orchestra, television station. Number of fraternities: 0; sororities: 0. Average proportion of students who stay on campus on weekends: 50%. **Sports program (2009-2010):** Member of NAIA. *Men's intercollegiate varsity sports:* basketball, golf, soccer, tennis. *Women's intercollegiate varsity sports:* basketball, cross country, golf, soccer, softball, tennis, volleyball.

SERVICES AND FACILITIES

Basic services: women's center, placement service, health service, health insurance. **Remedial assistance:** reading, math, writing, study skills. **Counseling services:** career, personal, veteran student, academic, psychological, religious, other. **For learning-disabled students:** School does not offer a structured program with separate admission and additional fees. Services include: remedial math, remedial English, reading machines, remedial reading, tape recorders, note-taking services, oral tests, learning center, extended time for tests, tutors, early syllabus, priority seating, substitution of courses, texts on tape, exams on tape or computer, other testing accommodations. **Library:** Number of titles: 179,448; number of current serial subscriptions: 153,201. **Information technology resources:** Students are not required to lease or own a computer. Number of campus computers available to all students: 236. School has a wireless network. Approximate number of users that can be accommodated: 1,650. Proportion of college-owned housing units wired for high-speed internet access: 100%. **Campus safety:** Security services offered: 24-hour foot-and-vehicle patrols, late-night transport/escort service, 24-hour emergency telephones, lighted pathways/sidewalks, controlled dormitory access (key, security card, etc.).

TRANSFER AND INTERNATIONAL STUDENTS

Transfer students: May apply for admission for the following academic terms: Fall, Winter, Spring, Summer. Applicants do not need a minimum number of credits to apply. For fall 2009: Transfer applications received: 675. Transfer applicants offered admission: 332. Transfer applicants enrolled: 178. **International students:** Number of foreign undergraduates: 14 (1% of student body). Number of countries represented: 12. Minimum TOEFL score required: 525 (paper); 71 (computer). Average TOEFL score: 540 (paper).

Prairie View A&M University

- **Address:** PO Box 188, Prairie View, TX 77446
- **Website:** http://www.pvamu.edu
- **Public; Religious affiliation:**
- **Enrollment:** 6,080 full-time; 537 part-time

KEY STATS

✔ **U.S News College Ranking:** second tier, Regional Universities (West)
✔ **SAT Score (25th/75th percentile):** 750-940
✔ **Tuition:** 2010-2011: $6,664 in state, $14,974 out of state

Selectivity: Less selective	**Room/board:** $6,738
Acceptance rate: 41%	**Average debt:** $7,890
Student/faculty ratio: 18/1	**Proportion who borrowed:** 78%

UNDERGRADUATE STUDENT BODY STATS

2009-2010 enrollment: 6,080 full-time; 537 part-time. Men: 42%; women: 58%. **Ethnic makeup:** African American: 88%; Asian American: 2%; Hispanic: 4%; White: 4%; International: 1%.

ADMISSIONS FACTS AND FIGURES

Phone: (936) 857-2626. **Email:** admissions@pvamu.edu. **Website:** http://www.pvamu.edu. **Application deadlines for fall 2011:** Regular decision: June 1. Early decision: Not offered. Early action: Not offered. Admission can be deferred. **Application fee:** $25. **To apply online, go to:** https://www.apply-texas.org/adappc/gen/c_start.WBX?s_logon_msg=Y. **Admissions requirements/recommendations:** High school units required (recommended): English: 4 (4); Mathematics: 4 (4); Science: 3 (3); Foreign language: 2 (2); Social studies: 4 (4); Academic electives: (4); Total units: 18 (22). Tests: The college uses SAT or ACT scores in admissions decisions. Either SAT or ACT required. For admission to the fall 2011 entering class, the school will accept: ACT with or without writing accepted. Campus visit: Recommended. Admissions interview: Neither required nor recommended. Off-campus interview: Not available. **Factors that count in admissions decisions:** *Academic:* Secondary school record: Very Important. Class rank: Important. Letters of recommendation: Considered. Standardized test scores: Very Important. Essay: Not Considered. *Nonacademic:* Interview: Not Considered. Extracurricular activities: Considered. Talent/ability: Not Considered. Character/personal qualities: Not Considered. Alumni/ae relationship: Not Considered. Geographical residence: Not Considered. State residency: Not Considered. Religious affiliation/commitment: Not Considered. Minority status: Not Considered. Volunteer work: Not Considered. Work experience: Not Considered. **Admissions statistics for the fall 2009 entering class:** Total applicants: 7,318. Total accepted: 3,021. Freshmen enrolled: 1,589; Overall acceptance rate: 41%. **Credentials of fall 2009 freshmen:** 6% ranked in the top 10 percent of their high school class; 23% were in the top 25 percent; 60% were in the top half. (Proportion submitting class standing: 100%.) **Average high school grade point average:** 2.9. **First-year students who submitted SAT scores:** 78%. Scores (25/75 percentile): Critical Reading: 370-460, Math: 380-480, Combined: 750-940. **First-year students submitting ACT scores:** 44%. Scores (25/75 percentile): English: N/A, Math: N/A, Composite: 15-19.

ACADEMICS

Year founded: 1876. **Academic calendar:** Semester. **Degrees offered:** bachelor's, master's, doctorate. **Most popular majors:** 14% student counseling and personnel services, 13% educational administration and supervision, 8% nursing, 4% multi/interdisciplinary studies, 2% communication and media studies. **Major fields of study:** agriculture, agriculture operations, and related sciences; architecture and related services; biological and biomedical sciences; business, management, marketing, and related support services; communication, journalism, and related programs; computer and information sciences and support services; engineering; engineering technologies/

technicians; English language and literature/letters; family and consumer sciences/human sciences; foreign languages, literatures, and linguistics; health professions and related clinical sciences; history; mathematics and statistics; multi/interdisciplinary studies; parks, recreation, leisure, and fitness studies; physical sciences; psychology; public administration and social service professions; security and protective services; social sciences; visual and performing arts. **Areas of required coursework:** arts/fine arts, humanities, computer literacy, mathematics, English (including composition), philosophy, sciences (biological or physical), history, social science. **Preprofessional programs:** pre-law, pre-dentistry, pre-medicine, pre-veterinary science, pre-pharmacy. **Special academic programs:** accelerated program, cooperative (work-study plan) program, distance learning, double major, dual enrollment, English as a Second Language (ESL), independent study, internships, liberal arts/career combination, study abroad, teacher certificate program. **Teacher certification offered in:** early childhood, special education, elementary, vo-tech, middle/junior high, adult education, secondary, bilingual/bicultural. **Cooperative education programs:** agriculture, business, computer science, education, engineering, natural science, social/behavioral science, technologies. **Reserve Officers Training Corps (ROTC):** Army ROTC: Offered on campus; Navy ROTC: Offered on campus. **Faculty and instruction (2009-2010):** Total instructional faculty: 352 full-time, 151 part-time (58% men; 42% women; 87% minorities). Full-time faculty with Ph.D. or other terminal degree: 63%. Student/faculty ratio: 18/1. Classes of fewer than 20 students: 16%; of 20 to 49 students: 22%; of 50 or more students: 62%. **Advanced Placement and International Baccalaureate credit:** AP tests may be used for: Credit only. Scores accepted: 3, 4, 5. International Baccalaureate exams may be used for: Credit only. **Freshmen returning for sophomore year:** 72%. **Graduation rates:** Four-year: 8%; five-year: 16%; six-year: 35%.

COSTS AND FINANCIAL AID

Financial aid office: (936) 857-2424. **Expenses (2010-2011):** Tuition and fees 2010-2011: $6,664 in state, $14,974 out of state; room/board: $6,738. Estimated books and supplies: $1,000; transportation: $1,500; personal expenses: $1,500. **Financial aid:** Priority filing date for institution's financial aid form: March 1; deadline: March 1. In 2009-2010, 86% of undergraduates applied for financial aid. Of those, 86% were determined to have financial need; Average financial aid package (proportion receiving): N/A (86%). Average amount of gift aid, such as scholarships or grants (proportion receiving): N/A (86%). Average amount of debt of borrowers graduating in 2009: $7,890. Proportion who borrowed: 78%.

CAMPUS LIFE AND EXTRACURRICULAR ACTIVITIES

Campus housing available (% using): coed dorms (39%), women's dorms, men's dorms, apartment for single students (61%). Students who live in college-owned, operated, or affiliated housing: 68%. Average per-year earnings: $1,120. **Clubs and organizations:** Number of student organizations: 82. Activities include: campus ministries, choral groups, concert band, drama/theater, international student organization, jazz band, music ensembles, radio station, student government, student newspaper, yearbook. Number of fraternities: 10; sororities: 10. Proportion of men in fraternities: 4%; of women in sororities: 3%. Average proportion of students who stay on campus on weekends: 80%. **Sports program (2009-2010):** Member of NCAA I. **Men's intercollegiate varsity sports:** baseball, basketball, cross country, football, golf, tennis, track and field (indoor), track and field (outdoor). **Women's intercollegiate varsity sports:** basketball, cross country, golf, soccer, softball, tennis, track and field (indoor), track and field (outdoor), volleyball.

SERVICES AND FACILITIES

Basic services: nonremedial tutoring, placement service, health service, health insurance. **Remedial assistance:** reading, math, writing, study skills. **Counseling services:** minority student, career, military, personal, veteran student, academic, psychological. **For learning-disabled students:** School does not offer a structured program with separate admission and additional fees. Total undergraduates in learning-disabled program or receiving services: 94. Services include: remedial math, remedial English, remedial reading, tape recorders, diagnostic testing service, untimed tests, note-taking services, learning center, readers, extended time for tests, tutors, priority registration, priority seating, typist/scribe, exams on tape or computer, other testing accommodations, other. **Library:** Number of titles: 1,143,080; number of current serial subscriptions: 39,724. **Information technology resources:** Students are not required to lease or own a computer. Number of campus computers available to all students: 3,000. School has a wireless network. Proportion of college-owned housing units wired for high-speed internet access: 100%. **Campus safety:** Security services offered: 24-hour foot-and-vehicle patrols, late-night transport/escort service, 24-hour emergency telephones, lighted pathways/sidewalks, controlled dormitory access (key, security card, etc).

TRANSFER AND INTERNATIONAL STUDENTS

Transfer students: May apply for admission for the following academic terms: Fall, Spring, Summer. Applicants do not need a minimum number of credits to apply. For fall 2009: Transfer applications received: 1,589. Transfer applicants offered admission: 611. Transfer applicants enrolled: 345. **International students:** Number of foreign undergraduates: 62 (1% of student body). Number of countries represented: 16. Minimum TOEFL score required: 500 (paper); 173 (computer). Average TOEFL score: 500 (paper).

Rice University

- **Address:** PO Box 1892, Houston, TX 77251-1892
- **Website:** http://www.rice.edu
- **Private**
- **Enrollment:** 3,262 full-time; 57 part-time

KEY STATS

✔ **U.S News College Ranking:** 17, National Universities
✔ **SAT Score (25th/75th percentile):** 1320-1530
✔ **Tuition:** 2010-2011: $33,771
  Selectivity: Most selective   **Room/board:** $11,750
  Acceptance rate: 22%   **Average debt:** $16,716
  Student/faculty ratio: 6/1   **Proportion who borrowed:** 31%

UNDERGRADUATE STUDENT BODY STATS

2009-2010 enrollment: 3,262 full-time; 57 part-time. Men: 52%; women: 48%. **Ethnic makeup:** African American: 7%; Asian American: 21%; Hispanic: 12%; White: 50%; International: 9%. **Religious preference:** Roman Catholic: 18%; Protestant: 34%; Jewish: 4%; Muslim: 1%; Hindu: 4%; Buddhist: 2%; No preference: 32%; Other: 2%.

ADMISSIONS FACTS AND FIGURES

Phone: (713) 348-7423. **Email:** admission@rice.edu. **Website:** http://www.rice.edu. **Application deadlines for fall 2011:** Regular decision: January 2; decision sent by April 1. Early decision: Send application by: November 1; Decision sent by: December 15. Early action: Not offered. Admission can be deferred. **Application fee:** $65. **To apply online, go to:** http://www.commonapp.org. **Admissions requirements/recommendations:** High school units required (recommended): English: 4 (4); Mathematics: 3 (4); Science: 2 (4); Foreign language: 2 (4); Social studies: 2 (2); Academic electives: 3 (3); Total units: 16 (20). Tests: The college uses SAT or ACT scores in admissions decisions. Either SAT or ACT required. For admission to the fall 2011 entering class, the school will accept: ACT with writing required. Campus visit: Recommended. Admissions interview: Recommended. Off-campus interview: May be arranged. **Factors that count in admissions decisions: Academic:** Secondary school record: Very Important. Class rank: Very Important. Letters of recommendation: Very Important. Standardized test scores: Very Important. Essay: Very Important. **Nonacademic:** Interview: Considered. Extracurricular activities: Very Important. Talent/ability: Very Important. Character/personal qualities: Very Important. Alumni/ae relationship: Considered. Geographical residence: Considered. State residency: Considered. Religious affiliation/commitment: Not Considered. Minority status: Considered. Volunteer work: Considered. Work experience: Considered. **Other schools with the greatest overlap in applicants:** Duke University; Harvard University; Stanford University; University of Texas–Austin; Washington University in St. Louis. **Admissions statistics for the fall 2009 entering class:** Total applicants: 11,172. Total accepted: 2,495. Freshmen enrolled: 894; 46% were from out of state. Accepted through early-decision or early-action plans: 26%. Overall acceptance rate: 22%. Early-decision acceptance rate: 35%. Non-early acceptance rate: 21%. **Size of waiting list:** 2301 applicants; enrolled from waiting list: 2. **Credentials of fall 2009 freshmen:** 84% ranked in the top 10 percent of their high school class; 94% were in the top 25 percent; 99% were in the top half. (Proportion submitting class standing: 61%.) **First-year students who submitted SAT scores:** 89%. Scores (25/75 percentile): Critical Reading: 640-750, Math: 680-780, Combined: 1320-1530. **First-year students submitting ACT scores:** 44%. Scores (25/75 percentile): English: N/A, Math: N/A, Composite: 30-34.

ACADEMICS

Year founded: 1912. **Academic calendar:** Semester. **Degrees offered:** bachelor's, master's, doctorate. **Most popular majors:** 6% English language and literature, 6% political science and government, 6% psychology, 5% biochemistry, 5% economics. **Major fields of study:** architecture and related services; area, ethnic, cultural, and gender studies; biological and biomedical sciences; business, management, marketing, and related support services; computer and information sciences and support services; engineering; English language and literature/letters; foreign languages, literatures, and linguistics; history; mathematics and statistics; multi/interdisciplinary studies; parks, recreation, leisure, and fitness studies; philosophy and religious studies; physical sciences; psychology; public administration and social service professions; social sciences; visual and performing arts. **Areas of required coursework:** English (including composition), other. **Pre-professional programs:** pre-law, pre-dentistry, pre-medicine, other. **Special academic programs (% participation):** cross-registration, double major (30%), dual enrollment, English as a Second Language (ESL), exchange student program (domestic), honors program, independent study, internships, liberal arts/career combination, student-designed major (0%), study abroad (40%), teacher certificate program, other. **Teacher certification offered in:** secondary. **Reserve Officers Training Corps (ROTC):** Army ROTC: Offered at cooperating institution (University of Houston); Navy ROTC: Offered on campus; Air Force ROTC: Offered at cooperating institution (University of Houston). **Faculty and instruction (2009-2010):** Total instructional faculty: 615 full-time, 122 part-time (69% men; 31% women; 17% minorities). Full-time faculty with Ph.D. or other terminal degree: 97%. Student/faculty ratio: 6/1. Classes of fewer than 20 students: 65%; of 20 to 49 students: 27%; of 50 or more students: 8%. **Advanced Placement and International Baccalaureate credit:** AP tests may be used for: Credit and/or placement. Scores accepted: 4, 5. International Baccalaureate exams may be used for: Credit and/or placement. **Freshmen returning for sophomore year:** 97%. **Graduation rates:** Four-year: 83%; five-year: 92%; six-year: 93%. **Graduate study:** 37% of students pursue further study within one year; 90% within five years. Fields in which graduates pursue further study: Master of Business Administration (MBA), 12%; law, 16%; medicine, 15%; engineering, 10%; theology (or the seminary), 2%; education, 3%; arts and sciences, 14%.

COSTS AND FINANCIAL AID

Financial aid office: (713) 348-4958. **Expenses (2010-2011):** Tuition and fees 2010-2011: $33,771; room/board: $11,750. Estimated books and supplies: $800; transportation: $250; personal expenses: $1,550. **Financial aid:** Priority filing date for institution's financial aid form: March 1. In 2009-2010, 53% of undergraduates applied for financial aid. Of those, 41% were determined to have financial need; 100% had their need fully met. Average financial aid package (proportion receiving): $25,819 (41%). Average amount of gift aid, such as scholarships or grants (proportion receiving): $23,558 (41%). Average amount of self-help aid, such as work study or loans (proportion receiving): $3,650 (38%). Average need-based loan (excluding PLUS or other private loans): $3,722. Among students who received need-based aid, the average percentage of need met: 100%. Among students who received aid based on merit, the average award (and the proportion receiving): $16,015 (12%). The average athletic scholarship (and the proportion receiving): $31,256 (9%). Average amount of debt of borrowers graduating in 2009: $16,716. Proportion who borrowed: 31%.

CAMPUS LIFE AND EXTRACURRICULAR ACTIVITIES

Campus housing available (% using): coed dorms (100%), special housing for disabled students. Students who live in college-owned, operated, or affiliated housing: 83%. **Student employment:** During the 2009-2010 academic year, 37% of undergraduates worked on campus. Average per-year earnings: $5,800. **Clubs and organizations:** Number of student organizations: 218. Activities include: campus ministries, choral groups, concert band, dance, drama/theater, international student organization, jazz band, literary magazine, marching band, model UN, music ensembles, musical theater, opera, pep band, radio station, student government, student newspaper, student film society, symphony orchestra, television station, yearbook. Number of fraternities: 0; sororities: 0. Average proportion of students who stay on campus on weekends: 90%. **Sports program (2009-2010):** Member of NCAA I. **Men's intercollegiate varsity sports:** baseball, basketball, cross country, football, golf, tennis, track and field (indoor), track and field (outdoor). **Women's intercollegiate varsity sports:** basketball, cross country, soccer, swimming, tennis, track and field (indoor), track and field (outdoor), volleyball.

SERVICES AND FACILITIES

Basic services: nonremedial tutoring, women's center, placement service, day care, health service, health insurance. **Remedial assistance:** reading, math, writing, study skills, other. **Counseling services:** minority student, career, personal, academic, psychological, birth control, other. **For learning-disabled students:** School does not offer a structured program with separate admission and additional fees. Total undergraduates in learning-disabled program or receiving services: 45. Services include: reading machines, tape recorders, note-taking services, extended time for tests, tutors, early syllabus, priority registration, priority seating, texts on tape, exams on tape or computer, other testing accommodations, other. **Library:** Number of titles: 2,620,342; number of current serial subscriptions: 81,789. **Information technology resources:** Students are not required to lease or own a computer. Number of campus computers available to all students: 543. School has a wireless network. Approximate number of users that can be accommodated: 5,000. Proportion of college-owned housing units wired for high-speed internet access: 100%. **Campus safety:** Security services offered: 24-hour foot-and-vehicle patrols, late-night transport/escort service, 24-hour emergency telephones, lighted pathways/sidewalks, controlled dormitory access (key, security card, etc).

TRANSFER AND INTERNATIONAL STUDENTS

Transfer students: May apply for admission for the following academic terms: Fall. Applicants need a minimum number of credits to apply. For fall 2009: Transfer applications received: 447. Transfer applicants offered admission: 113. Transfer applicants enrolled: 69. **International students:** Number of foreign undergraduates: 283 (9% of student body). Number of countries represented: 47. Minimum TOEFL score required: 600 (paper); 250 (computer).

Sam Houston State University

- **Address:** 1803 Avenue I, Huntsville, TX 77341
- **Website:** http://www.shsu.edu
- **Public**
- **Enrollment:** 12,223 full-time; 2,346 part-time

KEY STATS
- ✔ **U.S News College Ranking:** second tier, Regional Universities (West)
- ✔ **SAT Score (25th/75th percentile):** 900-1090
- ✔ **Tuition:** 2010-2011: $6,515 in state, $14,825 out of state

Selectivity: Selective	**Room/board:** $6,744
Acceptance rate: 72%	**Average debt:** $6,195
Student/faculty ratio: 20/1	**Proportion who borrowed:** 55%

UNDERGRADUATE STUDENT BODY STATS

2009-2010 enrollment: 12,223 full-time; 2,346 part-time. Men: 44%; women: 56%. **Ethnic makeup:** African American: 16%; American-Indian: 1%; Asian American: 2%; Hispanic: 14%; White: 67%; International: 1%.

ADMISSIONS FACTS AND FIGURES

Phone: (936) 294-1828. **Email:** admissions@shsu.edu. **Website:** http://www.shsu.edu. **Application deadlines for fall 2011:** Regular decision: August 1. Early decision: Not offered. Early action: Not offered. Admission cannot be deferred. **Application fee:** $40. **To apply online, go to:** http://www.Applytexas.org. **Admissions requirements/recommendations:** High school units required (recommended): English: 4 (4); Mathematics: 3 (4); Science: 2 (4); Foreign language: 0 (2); Social studies: 3 (4); History: 3 (4); Academic electives: 1 (0); Total units: 22 (26). Tests: The college uses SAT or ACT scores in admissions decisions. Either SAT or ACT required. For admission to the fall 2011 entering class, the school will accept: ACT with or without writing accepted. Campus visit: Recommended. Admissions interview: Neither required nor recommended. Off-campus interview: Not available. **Factors that count in admissions decisions:** *Academic:* Secondary school record: Important. Class rank: Very Important. Letters of recommendation: Considered. Standardized test scores: Very Important. Essay: Considered. *Nonacademic:* Interview: Not Considered. Extracurricular activities: Considered. Talent/ability: Considered. Character/personal qualities: Considered. Alumni/ae relationship: Not Considered. Geographical residence: Not Considered. State residency: Not Considered. Religious affiliation/commitment: Not Considered. Minority status: Not Considered. Volunteer work: Considered. Work experience: Considered. **Admissions statistics for the fall 2009 entering class:** Total applicants: 7,258. Total accepted:

5,210. Freshmen enrolled: 2,170; 3% were from out of state. Overall acceptance rate: 72%. **Credentials of fall 2009 freshmen:** 15% ranked in the top 10 percent of their high school class; 45% were in the top 25 percent; 84% were in the top half. (Proportion submitting class standing: 89%.) **First-year students who submitted SAT scores:** 83%. Scores (25/75 percentile): Critical Reading: 440-540, Math: 460-550, Combined: 900-1090. **First-year students submitting ACT scores:** 45%. Scores (25/75 percentile): English: 17-22, Math: 18-23, Composite: 18-22.

ACADEMICS

Year founded: 1879. **Academic calendar:** Semester. **Degrees offered:** certificate, diploma, bachelor's, post-bachelor's certificate, master's, doctorate. **Most popular majors:** 26% business, management, marketing, and related support services, 17% security and protective services, 12% multi/interdisciplinary studies, 6% psychology, 6% visual and performing arts. **Major fields of study:** agriculture, agriculture operations, and related sciences; architecture and related services; biological and biomedical sciences; business, management, marketing, and related support services; communication, journalism, and related programs; education; engineering technologies/technicians; English language and literature/letters; family and consumer sciences/human sciences; foreign languages, literatures, and linguistics; health professions and related clinical sciences; history; mathematics and statistics; multi/interdisciplinary studies; natural resources and conservation; parks, recreation, leisure, and fitness studies; philosophy and religious studies; physical sciences; psychology; security and protective services; social sciences; visual and performing arts. **Areas of required coursework:** arts/fine arts, humanities, computer literacy, mathematics, English (including composition), philosophy, foreign languages, sciences (biological or physical), history, social science, other. **Pre-professional programs:** pre-law, pre-dentistry, pre-medicine, pre-veterinary science, pre-pharmacy. **Special academic programs:** distance learning, double major, dual enrollment, English as a Second Language (ESL), honors program, independent study, internships, teacher certificate program. **Teacher certification offered in:** early childhood, special education, elementary, middle/junior high, secondary, bilingual/bicultural. **Cooperative education programs:** agriculture, art, computer science, home economics. **Reserve Officers Training Corps (ROTC):** Army ROTC: Offered on campus. **Faculty and instruction (2009-2010):** Total instructional faculty: 658 full-time, 169 part-time (52% men; 48% women; 9% minorities). Full-time faculty with Ph.D. or other terminal degree: 81%. Student/faculty ratio: 20/1. Classes of fewer than 20 students: 22%; of 20 to 49 students: 64%; of 50 or more students: 14%. **Advanced Placement and International Baccalaureate credit:** AP tests may be used for: Credit only. Scores accepted: 3. **Freshmen returning for sophomore year:** 72%. **Graduation rates:** Four-year: 21%; five-year: 39%; six-year: 44%.

COSTS AND FINANCIAL AID

Financial aid office: (936) 294-1774. **Expenses (2010-2011):** Tuition and fees 2010-2011: $6,515 in state, $14,825 out of state; room/board: $6,744. Estimated books and supplies: $1,084; transportation: $1,658; personal expenses: $1,822. **Financial aid:** Priority filing date for institution's financial aid form: April 1. In 2009-2010, 67% of undergraduates applied for financial aid. Of those, 31% were determined to have financial need; Average financial aid package (proportion receiving): $4,340 (26%). Average amount of gift aid, such as scholarships or grants (proportion receiving): $906 (14%). Average amount of self-help aid, such as work study or loans (proportion receiving): $758 (16%). Average need-based loan (excluding PLUS or other private loans): $189. Among students who received need-based aid, the average percentage of need met: 31%. Among students who received aid based on merit, the average award (and the proportion receiving): $321 (6%). Average amount of debt of borrowers graduating in 2009: $6,195. Proportion who borrowed: 55%.

CAMPUS LIFE AND EXTRACURRICULAR ACTIVITIES

Campus housing available (% using): coed dorms (49%), women's dorms (22%), men's dorms (8%), sorority housing (4%), fraternity housing (0%), apartment for single students (17%). Students who live in college-owned, operated, or affiliated housing: 22%. **Student employment:** During the 2009-2010 academic year, 8% of undergraduates worked on campus. Average per-year earnings: $3,700. **Clubs and organizations:** Number of student organizations: 208. Activities include: campus ministries, choral groups, concert band, dance, drama/theater, international student organization, jazz band, marching band, music ensembles, musical theater, pep band, radio station, student government, student newspaper, symphony orchestra, television station, yearbook. Number of fraternities: 16; sororities: 12. **Sports program (2009-2010):** Member of NCAA I. *Men's intercollegiate varsity sports:* baseball, basketball, football, golf, track and field (indoor), track and field (outdoor). **Women's intercollegiate varsity sports:** basketball, bowling, golf, soccer, softball, tennis, track and field (indoor), track and field (outdoor), volleyball.

SERVICES AND FACILITIES

Basic services: placement service, health service, health insurance. **Remedial assistance:** reading, math, writing, study skills. **Counseling services:** minority student, career, personal, academic, older student, psychological. **For learning-disabled students:** School does not offer a structured program with separate admission and additional fees. Services include: remedial math, remedial English, reading machines, remedial reading, tape recorders, note-taking services, oral tests, learning center, extended time for tests, texts on tape. **Library:** Number of titles: 1,296,696; number of current serial subscriptions: 13,946. **Information technology resources:** Students are not required to lease or own a computer. Number of campus computers available to all students: 616. School has a wireless network. Approximate number of users that can be accommodated: 1,800. Proportion of college-owned housing units wired for high-speed internet access: 0%. **Campus safety:** Security services offered: late-night transport/escort service, 24-hour emergency telephones, lighted pathways/sidewalks, controlled dormitory access (key, security card, etc).

TRANSFER AND INTERNATIONAL STUDENTS

Transfer students: May apply for admission for the following academic terms: Fall, Spring, Summer. Applicants need a minimum number of credits to apply. For fall 2009: Transfer applications received: 3,170. Transfer applicants offered admission: 2,989. Transfer applicants enrolled: 2,050. **International students:** Number of foreign undergraduates: 132 (1% of student body). Number of countries represented: 42. Minimum TOEFL score required: 550 (paper); 213 (computer).

Schreiner University

- ■ **Address:** 2100 Memorial Boulevard, Kerrville, TX 78028
- ■ **Website:** http://www.schreiner.edu
- ■ **Private; Religious affiliation:** Presbyterian
- ■ **Enrollment:** 977 full-time; 51 part-time

KEY STATS

✔ **U.S News College Ranking:** 20, Regional Colleges (West)
✔ **SAT Score (25th/75th percentile):** 880-1120
✔ **Tuition:** 2010-2011: $19,547

Selectivity: Selective	**Room/board:** $9,390
Acceptance rate: 62%	**Average debt:** N/A
Student/faculty ratio: 14/1	**Proportion who borrowed:** N/A

UNDERGRADUATE STUDENT BODY STATS

2009-2010 enrollment: 977 full-time; 51 part-time. Men: 44%; women: 56%. **Ethnic makeup:** African American: 4%; American-Indian: 2%; Hispanic: 22%; White: 72%. **Religious preference:** Roman Catholic: 23%; Protestant: 1%; Jewish: 1%; No preference: 8%; Unknown: 1%; Presbyterian: 6%; Baptist: 12%; Other: 48%.

ADMISSIONS FACTS AND FIGURES

Phone: (800) 343-4919. **Email:** admissions@schreiner.edu. **Website:** http://www.schreiner.edu. **Application deadlines for fall 2011:** Regular decision: August 1. Early decision: Not offered. Early action: Not offered. Admission can be deferred. **Application fee:** $25. **To apply online, go to:** http://www.schreiner.edu/admission/apply.html#undergraduate. **Admissions requirements/recommendations:** High school units required (recommended): English: 4 (4); Mathematics: 3 (3); Science: 3 (3); Foreign language: 2 (2); Social studies: 2 (2); History: 2 (2); Academic electives: 4 (0); Total units: 24 (24). Tests: The college uses SAT or ACT scores in admissions decisions. Either SAT or ACT required. For admission to the fall 2011 entering class, the school will accept: ACT with writing required. Campus visit: Recommended. Admissions interview: Recommended. Off-campus interview: May be arranged. **Factors that count in admissions decisions: *Academic:*** Secondary school record: Important. Class rank: Important. Letters of recommendation: Considered. Standardized test scores: Important. Essay: Important. ***Nonacademic:*** Interview: Important. Extracurricular activities: Considered. Talent/ability: Considered. Character/personal qualities: Important. Alumni/ae relationship: Not Considered. Geographical residence: Not Considered. State residency: Not Considered.

Religious affiliation/commitment: Not Considered. Minority status: Not Considered. Volunteer work: Considered. Work experience: Considered. **Other schools with the greatest overlap in applicants:** Austin College; Baylor University; Texas A&M University–College Station; Texas Lutheran University; Texas State University–San Marcos. **Admissions statistics for the fall 2009 entering class:** Total applicants: 991. Total accepted: 613. Freshmen enrolled: 290; 0% were from out of state. Overall acceptance rate: 62%. **Credentials of fall 2009 freshmen:** 16% ranked in the top 10 percent of their high school class; 43% were in the top 25 percent; 79% were in the top half. (Proportion submitting class standing: 91%.) **Average high school grade point average:** 3.5. **First-year students who submitted SAT scores:** 86%. Scores (25/75 percentile): Critical Reading: 440-550, Math: 440-570, Combined: 880-1120. **First-year students submitting ACT scores:** 48%. Scores (25/75 percentile): English: 16-23, Math: 17-24, Composite: 18-23.

ACADEMICS

Year founded: 1923. **Academic calendar:** Semester. **Degrees offered:** certificate, associate, bachelor's, post-bachelor's certificate, master's. **Most popular majors:** 24% business, management, marketing, and related support services, 18% parks, recreation, leisure, and fitness studies, 14% biological and biomedical sciences, 11% psychology, 9% visual and performing arts. **Major fields of study:** biological and biomedical sciences; business, management, marketing, and related support services; education; engineering; English language and literature/letters; history; legal professions and studies; liberal arts and sciences studies, and humanities; mathematics and statistics; multi/interdisciplinary studies; parks, recreation, leisure, and fitness studies; philosophy and religious studies; physical sciences; psychology; social sciences; visual and performing arts. **Areas of required coursework:** arts/fine arts, humanities, computer literacy, mathematics, English (including composition), philosophy, foreign languages, sciences (biological or physical), history, social science, other. **Pre-professional programs:** pre-law, pre-dentistry, pre-medicine, pre-theology, pre-veterinary science, pre-optometry, pre-pharmacy. **Special academic programs:** accelerated program, double major, dual enrollment, honors program, independent study, internships, liberal arts/career combination, student-designed major, study abroad, teacher certificate program. **Teacher certification offered in:** early childhood, elementary, middle/junior high, secondary. **Faculty and instruction (2009-2010):** Total instructional faculty: 61 full-time, 31 part-time (50% men; 50% women; 10% minorities). Full-time faculty with Ph.D. or other terminal degree: 69%. Student/faculty ratio: 14/1. Classes of fewer than 20 students: 48%; of 20 to 49 students: 52%; of 50 or more students: 0%. **Advanced Placement and International Baccalaureate credit:** AP tests may be used for: Credit only. International Baccalaureate exams may be used for: Credit only. **Freshmen returning for sophomore year:** 65%. **Graduation rates:** Four-year: 26%; five-year: 40%; six-year: 43%. **Graduate study:** 24% of students pursue further study immediately upon graduation; 35% within one year. Fields in which graduates pursue further study: Master of Business Administration (MBA), 14%; law, 4%; theology (or the seminary), 8%; education, 22%; arts and sciences, 52%; veterinary medicine, 4%.

COSTS AND FINANCIAL AID

Financial aid office: (830) 792-7217. **Expenses (2010-2011):** Tuition and fees 2010-2011: $19,547; room/board: $9,390. Estimated books and supplies: $1,200; transportation: $500; personal expenses: $1,000. **Financial aid:** Priority filing date for institution's financial aid form: April 1; deadline: August 1. In 2009-2010, 89% of undergraduates applied for financial aid. Of those, 80% were determined to have financial need; 16% had their need fully met. Average financial aid package (proportion receiving): $15,360 (80%). Average amount of gift aid, such as scholarships or grants (proportion receiving): $11,946 (79%). Average amount of self-help aid, such as work study or loans (proportion receiving): $4,068 (68%). Average need-based loan (excluding PLUS or other private loans): $3,409. Among students who received need-based aid, the average percentage of need met: 74%. Among students who received aid based on merit, the average award (and the proportion receiving): $7,041 (18%). The average athletic scholarship (and the proportion receiving): $0 (0%).

CAMPUS LIFE AND EXTRACURRICULAR ACTIVITIES

Campus housing available (% using): coed dorms (64%), apartments for married students (1%), apartment for single students (34%), special housing for disabled students (1%). Students who live in college-owned, operated, or affiliated housing: 69%. **Student employment:** During the 2009-2010 academic year, 10% of undergraduates worked on campus. Average per-year earnings: $1,500. **Clubs and organizations:** Number of student organizations: 38. Activities include: campus ministries, choral groups, concert band, dance, drama/theater, literary magazine, music ensembles, musical theater, pep band, student government, student newspaper, symphony orchestra. Number of fraternities: 2; sororities: 2. Proportion of men in fraternities: 7%; of women in sororities: 15%. Average proportion of students who stay on campus on weekends: 55%. **Sports program (2009-2010):** Member of NCAA III. **Men's intercollegiate varsity sports:** baseball, basketball, cross country, golf, soccer, tennis. **Women's intercollegiate varsity sports:** basketball, cross country, golf, soccer, softball, tennis, volleyball.

SERVICES AND FACILITIES

Basic services: nonremedial tutoring, placement service, health service, health insurance. **Remedial assistance:** writing. **Counseling services:** career, personal, academic, older student, psychological, birth control, religious. **For learning-disabled students:** School does not offer a structured program with separate admission and additional fees. Services include: remedial math, remedial English, reading machines, untimed tests, note-taking services, oral tests, learning center, readers, extended time for tests, tutors, texts on tape, other testing accommodations. **Library:** Number of titles: 83,100; number of current serial subscriptions: 225. **Information technology resources:** Students are not required to lease or own a computer. Number of campus computers available to all students: 120. School has a wireless network. Approximate number of users that can be accommodated: 800. Proportion of college-owned housing units wired for high-speed internet access: 100%. **Campus safety:** Security services offered: 24-hour foot-and-vehicle patrols, late-night transport/escort service, 24-hour emergency telephones, lighted pathways/sidewalks, controlled dormitory access (key, security card, etc).

TRANSFER AND INTERNATIONAL STUDENTS

Transfer students: May apply for admission for the following academic terms: Fall, Spring, Summer. Applicants need a minimum number of credits to apply. For fall 2009: Transfer applications received: 217. Transfer applicants offered admission: 135. Transfer applicants enrolled: 66. **International students:** Number of foreign undergraduates: 4. Number of countries represented: 3. Minimum TOEFL score required: 550 (paper); 213 (computer). Average TOEFL score: 584 (paper).

Southern Methodist University

- **Address:** PO Box 750181, Dallas, TX 75275-0181
- **Website:** http://www.smu.edu
- **Private; Religious affiliation:** United Methodist
- **Enrollment:** 5,921 full-time; 307 part-time

KEY STATS

✔ **U.S News College Ranking:** 56, National Universities
✔ **SAT Score (25th/75th percentile):** 1140-1340
✔ **Tuition:** 2009-2010: $35,160

Selectivity: More selective	**Room/board:** $12,446
Acceptance rate: 53%	**Average debt:** $20,146
Student/faculty ratio: 11/1	**Proportion who borrowed:** 32%

UNDERGRADUATE STUDENT BODY STATS

2009-2010 enrollment: 5,921 full-time; 307 part-time. Men: 47%; women: 53%. **Ethnic makeup:** African American: 5%; American-Indian: 1%; Asian American: 6%; Hispanic: 8%; White: 74%; International: 6%. **Religious preference:** Roman Catholic: 18%; Protestant: 19%; Jewish: 1%; Muslim: 2%; Hindu: 1%; No preference: 38%; United Methodist: 11%; Non-Denominational, Christian: 8%; Other: 2%.

ADMISSIONS FACTS AND FIGURES

Phone: (800) 323-0672. **Email:** ugadmission@smu.edu. **Website:** http://www.smu.edu. **Application deadlines for fall 2011:** Regular decision: March 15. Early decision: Not offered. Early action: Send application by: November 1; Decision sent by: December 31. Admission can be deferred. **Application fee:** $60. **To apply online, go to:** http://www.smu.edu/apply. **Admissions requirements/recommendations:** High school units required (recommended): English: 4 (4); Mathematics: 3 (4); Science: 3 (4); Foreign language: 2 (3); Social studies: 1 (2); History: 2 (3); Total units: 15. Tests: The college uses SAT or ACT scores in admissions decisions. Either SAT or ACT required. For admission to the fall 2011 entering class, the school will accept: ACT with or without writing accepted. Campus visit: Recommended. Admissions interview: Neither required nor recommended. Off-campus interview: May be arranged. **Factors that count in admissions**

decisions: *Academic:* Secondary school record: Very Important. Class rank: Very Important. Letters of recommendation: Very Important. Standardized test scores: Very Important. Essay: Very Important. *Nonacademic:* Interview: Considered. Extracurricular activities: Important. Talent/ability: Important. Character/personal qualities: Important. Alumni/ae relationship: Considered. Geographical residence: Not Considered. State residency: Not Considered. Religious affiliation/commitment: Not Considered. Minority status: Not Considered. Volunteer work: Important. Work experience: Important. **Other schools with the greatest overlap in applicants:** Texas A&M University–College Station; Texas Christian University; University of Southern California; University of Texas–Austin; Vanderbilt University. **Admissions statistics for the fall 2009 entering class:** Total applicants: 8,356. Total accepted: 4,467. Freshmen enrolled: 1,329; 47% were from out of state. Overall acceptance rate: 53%. Non-early acceptance rate: 53%. **Size of waiting list:** 735 applicants; enrolled from waiting list: 183. **Credentials of fall 2009 freshmen:** 43% ranked in the top 10 percent of their high school class; 73% were in the top 25 percent; 93% were in the top half. (Proportion submitting class standing: 46%.) **Average high school grade point average:** 3.6. **First-year students who submitted SAT scores:** 73%. Scores (25/75 percentile): Critical Reading: 560-660, Math: 580-680, Combined: 1140-1340. **First-year students submitting ACT scores:** 53%. Scores (25/75 percentile): English: 25-32, Math: 25-30, Composite: 25-30.

ACADEMICS

Year founded: 1911. **Academic calendar:** Semester. **Degrees offered:** certificate, bachelor's, post-bachelor's certificate, master's, doctorate. **Most popular majors:** 26% business, management, marketing, and related support services, 17% social sciences, 13% communication, journalism, and related programs, 7% visual and performing arts, 6% engineering. **Major fields of study:** area, ethnic, cultural, and gender studies; biological and biomedical sciences; business, management, marketing, and related support services; communication, journalism, and related programs; computer and information sciences and support services; education; engineering; English language and literature/letters; foreign languages, literatures, and linguistics; health professions and related clinical sciences; history; liberal arts and sciences studies, and humanities; mathematics and statistics; multi/interdisciplinary studies; natural resources and conservation; philosophy and religious studies; physical sciences; psychology; public administration and social service professions; social sciences; visual and performing arts. **Areas of required coursework:** arts/fine arts, humanities, computer literacy, mathematics, English (including composition), philosophy, sciences (biological or physical), history, social science. **Pre-professional programs:** pre-law, predentistry, pre-medicine, pre-theology, pre-optometry, pre-pharmacy. **Special academic programs:** accelerated program, cooperative (work-study plan) program, distance learning, double major, English as a Second Language (ESL), exchange student program (domestic), honors program, independent study, internships, student-designed major, study abroad, teacher certificate program. **Teacher certification offered in:** elementary, secondary, bilingual/bicultural. **Cooperative education programs:** business, engineering. **Reserve Officers Training Corps (ROTC):** Army ROTC: Offered on campus; Air Force ROTC: Offered at cooperating institution (University of North Texas). **Faculty and instruction (2009-2010):** Total instructional faculty: 660 full-time, 386 part-time (62% men; 38% women; 13% minorities). Full-time faculty with Ph.D. or other terminal degree: 84%. Student/faculty ratio: 11/1. Classes of fewer than 20 students: 59%; of 20 to 49 students: 32%; of 50 or more students: 9%. **Advanced Placement and International Baccalaureate credit:** AP tests may be used for: Credit and/or placement. Scores accepted: 4, 5. International Baccalaureate exams may be used for: Credit only. **Freshmen returning for sophomore year:** 88%. **Graduation rates:** Four-year: 62%; five-year: 75%; six-year: 77%.

COSTS AND FINANCIAL AID

Financial aid office: (214) 768-3016. **Expenses (2009-2010):** Tuition and fees 2009-2010: $35,160; room/board: $12,446. Estimated books and supplies: $800; transportation: $500; personal expenses: $1,100. **Financial aid:** Priority filing date for institution's financial aid form: March 1. In 2009-2010, 43% of undergraduates applied for financial aid. Of those, 36% were determined to have financial need; 35% had their need fully met. Average financial aid package (proportion receiving): $30,985 (36%). Average amount of gift aid, such as scholarships or grants (proportion receiving): $17,879 (30%). Average amount of self-help aid, such as work study or loans (proportion receiving): $5,905 (33%). Average need-based loan (excluding PLUS or other private loans): $3,433. Among students who received need-based aid, the average percentage of need met: 88%. Among students who received aid based on merit, the average award (and the proportion receiving): $14,240 (35%). The average athletic scholarship (and the

proportion receiving): $39,142 (5%). Average amount of debt of borrowers graduating in 2009: $20,146. Proportion who borrowed: 32%.

CAMPUS LIFE AND EXTRACURRICULAR ACTIVITIES

Campus housing available (% using): coed dorms (31%), sorority housing (11%), fraternity housing (11%), apartments for married students (2%), apartment for single students (8%). Students who live in college-owned, operated, or affiliated housing: 33%. Average per-year earnings: $2,500. **Clubs and organizations:** Number of student organizations: 200. Activities include: campus ministries, choral groups, concert band, dance, drama/theater, international student organization, jazz band, literary magazine, marching band, model UN, music ensembles, musical theater, opera, pep band, radio station, student government, student newspaper, student film society, symphony orchestra, television station, yearbook. Number of fraternities: 13; sororities: 14. Proportion of men in fraternities: 25%; of women in sororities: 32%. Average proportion of students who stay on campus on weekends: 85%. **Sports program (2009-2010):** Member of NCAA I. *Men's intercollegiate varsity sports:* basketball, football, golf, soccer, swimming, tennis. *Women's intercollegiate varsity sports:* basketball, crew (heavyweight), cross country, equestrian, golf, soccer, swimming, tennis,track and field (indoor), track and field (outdoor), volleyball.

SERVICES AND FACILITIES

Basic services: nonremedial tutoring, women's center, placement service, health service, health insurance. **Remedial assistance:** reading, math, writing, study skills. **Counseling services:** minority student, career, personal, academic, older student, psychological, birth control, religious. **For learning-disabled students:** School does not offer a structured program with separate admission and additional fees. Total undergraduates in learning-disabled program or receiving services: 356. Services include: reading machines, note-taking services, learning center, readers, extended time for tests, tutors, priority registration, substitution of courses, texts on tape, typist/scribe, exams on tape or computer, other testing accommodations, other. **Library:** Number of titles: 2,978,640; number of current serial subscriptions: 16,132. **Information technology resources:** Students are not required to lease or own a computer. Number of campus computers available to all students: 409. School has a wireless network. Approximate number of users that can be accommodated: 4,000. Proportion of college-owned housing units wired for high-speed internet access: 95%. **Campus safety:** Security services offered: 24-hour foot-and-vehicle patrols, late-night transport/escort service, 24-hour emergency telephones, lighted pathways/sidewalks, controlled dormitory access (key, security card, etc).

TRANSFER AND INTERNATIONAL STUDENTS

Transfer students: May apply for admission for the following academic terms: Fall, Spring, Summer. Applicants do not need a minimum number of credits to apply. For fall 2009: Transfer applications received: 823. Transfer applicants offered admission: 560. Transfer applicants enrolled: 306. **International students:** Number of foreign undergraduates: 362 (6% of student body). Number of countries represented: 80. Minimum TOEFL score required: 550 (paper); 80 (computer).

Southwestern Adventist University

- **Address:** PO Box 567, Keene, TX 76059
- **Website:** http://www.swau.edu
- **Private; Religious affiliation:** Seventh-day Adventist
- **Enrollment:** N/A

KEY STATS

✔ **U.S News College Ranking:** second tier, Regional Colleges (West)
✔ **SAT or ACT Score (25th/75th percentile):** N/A
✔ **Tuition:** 2009-2010: $16,216

Selectivity: Less selective	Room/board: $7,148
Acceptance rate: N/A	Average debt: N/A
Student/faculty ratio: N/A	Proportion who borrowed: N/A

Southwestern Assemblies of God Univ.

- **Address:** 1200 Sycamore Street, Waxahachie, TX 75165
- **Website:** http://www.sagu.edu/
- **Private; Religious affiliation:** Assemblies of God
- **Enrollment:** 1,402 full-time; 306 part-time

KEY STATS

✔ **U.S News College Ranking:** second tier, Regional Colleges (West)
✔ **SAT or ACT Score (25th/75th percentile):** N/A
✔ **Tuition:** 2010-2011: $13,950

Selectivity: Less selective	Room/board: N/A
Acceptance rate: 37%	Average debt: N/A
Student/faculty ratio: 13/1	Proportion who borrowed: N/A

UNDERGRADUATE STUDENT BODY STATS

2009-2010 enrollment: 1,402 full-time; 306 part-time. Men: 50%; women: 50%. **Ethnic makeup:** African American: 9%; American-Indian: 1%; Asian American: 2%; Hispanic: 18%; White: 70%; International: 1%. **Religious preference:** Protestant: 27%; Assemblies of God: 73%.

ADMISSIONS FACTS AND FIGURES

Phone: (888) 937-7248. **Email:** admissions@sagu.edu. **Website:** http://www.sagu.edu/. **Application deadlines for fall 2011:** Regular decision: Rolling. Early decision: Not offered. Early action: Not offered. Admission can be deferred. **Application fee:** $35. **To apply online, go to:** https://www.applyweb.com/apply/sagu/menu.html. **Admissions requirements/recommendations:** High school units required (recommended): English: 4 (4); Mathematics: 2 (2); Science: 2 (2); Foreign language: 0 (0); Social studies: 2 (2); History: 2 (2); Academic electives: 0 (0). Tests: The college uses SAT or ACT scores in admissions decisions. Either SAT or ACT required. For admission to the fall 2011 entering class, the school will accept: ACT with writing recommended. Campus visit: Recommended. Admissions interview: Neither required nor recommended. Off-campus interview: Not available. **Factors that count in admissions decisions:** *Academic:* Secondary school record: Important. Class rank: Considered. Letters of recommendation: Very Important. Standardized test scores: Very Important. Essay: Important. *Nonacademic:* Interview: Not Considered. Extracurricular activities: Not Considered. Talent/ability: Not Considered. Character/personal qualities: Very Important. Alumni/ae relationship: Considered. Geographical residence: Not Considered. State residency: Not Considered. Religious affiliation/commitment: Very Important. Minority status: Not Considered. Volunteer work: Not Considered. Work experience: Not Considered. **Admissions statistics for the fall 2009 entering class:** Total applicants: 1,037. Total accepted: 381. Freshmen enrolled: 343; Overall acceptance rate: 37%.

ACADEMICS

Year founded: 1927. **Academic calendar:** Semester. **Degrees offered:** associate, bachelor's, master's. **Most popular majors:** 41% theology and religious vocations, 15% liberal arts and sciences studies, and humanities, 12% business, management, marketing, and related support services, 12% education, 5% psychology. **Major fields of study:** business, management, marketing, and related support services; communication, journalism, and related programs; education; history; liberal arts and sciences studies, and humanities; psychology; social sciences; theology and religious vocations; visual and performing arts. **Areas of required coursework:** arts/fine arts, computer literacy, mathematics, English (including composition), sciences (biological or physical), history, social science. **Special academic programs:** double major, dual enrollment, internships, student-designed major, teacher certificate program. **Teacher certification offered in:** early childhood, elementary, middle/junior high, secondary. **Reserve Officers Training Corps (ROTC):** Air Force ROTC: Offered at cooperating institution. **Faculty and instruction (2009-2010):** Total instructional faculty: 65 full-time, 48 part-time (65% men; 35% women; 9% minorities). Full-time faculty with Ph.D. or other terminal degree: 54%. Student/faculty ratio: 13/1. **Advanced Placement and International Baccalaureate credit:** International Baccalaureate exams may be used for: Credit only. **Freshmen returning for sophomore year:** 63%. **Graduation rates:** Four-year: 29%; five-year: 42%; six-year: 35%. **Graduate study:** 29% of students pursue further study immediately upon graduation; 71% within five years. Fields in which graduates pursue further study: Master of Business Administration (MBA), 8%; theology (or the seminary), 41%; education, 21%; arts and sciences, 30%.

COSTS AND FINANCIAL AID

Expenses (2010-2011): Tuition and fees 2010-2011: $13,950. Estimated books and supplies: $1,228; transportation: $2,828; personal expenses: $2,564. **Financial aid:** Priority filing date for institution's financial aid form: March 15; deadline: May 1. In 2009-2010, 100% of undergraduates applied for financial aid. Of those, 93% were determined to have financial need; 8% had their need fully met. Average financial aid package (proportion receiving): $11,363 (93%). Average amount of gift aid, such as scholarships or grants (proportion receiving): $7,475 (86%). Average amount of self-help aid, such as work study or loans (proportion receiving): $4,690 (88%). Average need-based loan (excluding PLUS or other private loans): $4,423. Among students who received need-based aid, the average percentage of need met: 50%. Among students who received aid based on merit, the average award (and the proportion receiving): $2,697 (5%). The average athletic scholarship (and the proportion receiving): $3,674 (1%).

CAMPUS LIFE AND EXTRACURRICULAR ACTIVITIES

Campus housing available (% using): coed dorms (84%), women's dorms (10%), men's dorms, apartments for married students (4%), apartment for single students (2%), special housing for disabled students (0%). **Student employment:** During the 2009-2010 academic year, 1% of undergraduates worked on campus. Average per-year earnings: $730. **Clubs and organizations:** Number of student organizations: 18. Activities include: choral groups, concert band, drama/theater, jazz band, literary magazine, music ensembles, student government, student newspaper, yearbook. Number of fraternities: 0; sororities: 0. Average proportion of students who stay on campus on weekends: 40%. **Sports program (2009-2010):** Member of NAIA. **Men's intercollegiate varsity sports:** baseball, basketball, football, soccer. **Women's intercollegiate varsity sports:** basketball, soccer, volleyball.

SERVICES AND FACILITIES

Basic services: placement service, health service. **Remedial assistance:** reading, math, writing, study skills. **Counseling services:** minority student, career, personal, veteran student, academic, older student, psychological, religious. **For learning-disabled students:** School does not offer a structured program with separate admission and additional fees. Services include: remedial math, remedial English, remedial reading, diagnostic testing service, untimed tests, oral tests, learning center, extended time for tests, priority registration, priority seating, texts on tape. **Information technology resources:** Students are not required to lease or own a computer. Number of campus computers available to all students: 74. School has a wireless network. **Campus safety:** Security services offered: 24-hour foot-and-vehicle patrols, late-night transport/escort service, 24-hour emergency telephones, lighted pathways/sidewalks, student patrols, controlled dormitory access (key, security card, etc).

TRANSFER AND INTERNATIONAL STUDENTS

Transfer students: May apply for admission for the following academic terms: Fall, Spring, Summer. Applicants need a minimum number of credits to apply. For fall 2009: Transfer applicants enrolled: 229. **International students:** Number of foreign undergraduates: 16 (1% of student body). Number of countries represented: 23. Minimum TOEFL score required: 525 (paper); 197 (computer).

Southwestern Christian College

- **Address:** PO Box 10, Terrell, TX 75160
- **Website:** http://www.swcc.edu
- **Private**
- **Enrollment:** N/A

....

KEY STATS

✔ **U.S News College Ranking:** Unranked, Regional Colleges (West)
✔ **SAT or ACT Score (25th/75th percentile):** N/A
✔ **Tuition:** 2009-2010: $6,185

Selectivity: N/A	Room/board: $4,325
Acceptance rate: N/A	Average debt: N/A
Student/faculty ratio: N/A	Proportion who borrowed: N/A

Southwestern University

- **Address:** PO Box 770, Georgetown, TX 78627-0770
- **Website:** http://www.southwestern.edu
- **Private; Religious affiliation:** United Methodist
- **Enrollment:** 1,280 full-time; 21 part-time

....

KEY STATS

✔ **U.S News College Ranking:** 62, National Liberal Arts Colleges
✔ **SAT Score (25th/75th percentile):** 1140-1350
✔ **Tuition:** 2010-2011: $31,630

Selectivity: More selective	Room/board: $9,770
Acceptance rate: 63%	Average debt: $24,036
Student/faculty ratio: 10/1	Proportion who borrowed: 61%

UNDERGRADUATE STUDENT BODY STATS

2009-2010 enrollment: 1,280 full-time; 21 part-time. Men: 38%; women: 62%. **Ethnic makeup:** African American: 3%; American-Indian: 1%; Asian American: 4%; Hispanic: 15%; White: 77%. **Religious preference:** Roman Catholic: 16%; Protestant: 26%; Jewish: 2%; Buddhist: 1%; No preference: 1%; United Methodist: 16%; Not reported: 35%; Other: 3%.

ADMISSIONS FACTS AND FIGURES

Phone: (800) 252-3166. **Email:** admission@southwestern.edu. **Website:** http://www.southwestern.edu. **Application deadlines for fall 2011:** Regular decision: Rolling. Early decision: Send application by: November 1; Decision sent by: December 15. Early action: Send application by: December 1; Decision sent by: February 1. Admission can be deferred. **Application fee:** $40. **To apply online, go to:** http://www.southwestern.edu/admission/apply/application.php. **Admissions requirements/recommendations:** High school units required (recommended): English: 4 (4); Mathematics: 4 (4); Science: 3 (4); Foreign language: 2 (3); Social studies: 2 (3); History: 1 (2); Academic electives: 1; Total units: 17 (20). Tests: The college uses SAT or ACT scores in admissions decisions. Either SAT or ACT required. For admission to the fall 2011 entering class, the school will accept: ACT with writing required. Campus visit: Recommended. Admissions interview: Recommended. Off-campus interview: May be arranged. **Factors that count in admissions decisions:** *Academic:* Secondary school record: Very Important. Class rank: Very Important. Letters of recommendation: Very Important. Standardized test scores: Very Important. Essay: Very Important. *Nonacademic:* Interview: Important. Extracurricular activities: Important. Talent/ability: Important. Character/personal qualities: Important. Alumni/ae relationship: Important. Geographical residence: Important. State residency: Not Considered. Religious affiliation/commitment: Not Considered. Minority status: Important. Volunteer work: Important. Work experience: Important. **Other schools with the greatest overlap in applicants:** Austin College; Baylor University; Texas A&M University–College Station; Trinity University; University of Texas–Austin. **Admissions statistics for the fall 2009 entering class:** Total applicants: 2,490. Total accepted: 1,579. Freshmen enrolled: 375; 9% were from out of state. Overall acceptance rate: 63%. Early-decision acceptance rate: 79%. Non-early acceptance rate: 63%. **Size of waiting list:** 57 applicants; enrolled from waiting list: 6. **Credentials of fall 2009 freshmen:** 49% ranked in the top 10 percent of their high school class; 84% were in the top 25 percent; 98% were in the top half. (Proportion submitting class standing: 98%.) **First-year students who submitted SAT scores:** 91%. Scores (25/75 percentile): Critical Reading: 570-680, Math: 570-670, Combined: 1140-1350. **First-year students submitting ACT scores:** 58%. Scores (25/75 percentile): English: N/A, Math: N/A, Composite: 25-30.

ACADEMICS

Year founded: 1840. **Academic calendar:** Semester. **Degrees offered:** bachelor's. **Most popular majors:** 14% business, management, marketing, and related support services, 14% social sciences, 11% biological and biomedical sciences, 9% communication, journalism, and related programs, 9% visual and performing arts. **Major fields of study:** agriculture, agriculture operations, and related sciences; area, ethnic, cultural, and gender studies; biological and biomedical sciences; business, management, marketing, and related support services; communication, journalism, and related programs; computer and information sciences and support services; education; English language and literature/letters; foreign languages, literatures, and linguistics; health professions and related clinical sciences; history; liberal arts and sciences studies, and humanities; mathematics and statistics; multi/interdisciplinary studies; philosophy and religious studies; physical sciences; psychology; social sciences; visual and performing arts. **Areas**

of required coursework: arts/fine arts, humanities, mathematics, English (including composition), foreign languages, sciences (biological or physical), social science, other. **Pre-professional programs:** pre-law, pre-medicine, other. **Special academic programs (% participation):** double major (10%), honors program (5%), independent study (25%), internships (37%), liberal arts/career combination, student-designed major (1%), study abroad (48%), teacher certificate program (7%). **Teacher certification offered in:** early childhood, special education, elementary, middle/junior high, secondary. **Faculty and instruction (2009-2010):** Total instructional faculty: 122 full-time, 44 part-time (52% men; 48% women; 14% minorities). Full-time faculty with Ph.D. or other terminal degree: 100%. Student/faculty ratio: 10/1. Classes of fewer than 20 students: 80%; of 20 to 49 students: 20%; of 50 or more students: 0%. **Advanced Placement and International Baccalaureate credit:** AP tests may be used for: Credit only. Scores accepted: 4, 5. International Baccalaureate exams may be used for: Credit and/or placement. **Freshmen returning for sophomore year:** 84%. **Graduation rates:** Four-year: 64%; five-year: 76%; six-year: 77%. **Graduate study:** 26% of students pursue further study immediately upon graduation. Fields in which graduates pursue further study: law, 18%; medicine, 3%; dentistry, 1%; engineering, 4%; theology (or the seminary), 4%; arts and sciences, 49%.

COSTS AND FINANCIAL AID

Financial aid office: (512) 863-1259. **Expenses (2010-2011):** Tuition and fees 2010-2011: $31,630; room/board: $9,770. Estimated books and supplies: $1,000; transportation: $320; personal expenses: $900. **Financial aid:** Priority filing date for institution's financial aid form: March 1; deadline: March 1. In 2009-2010, 67% of undergraduates applied for financial aid. Of those, 57% were determined to have financial need; 34% had their need fully met. Average financial aid package (proportion receiving): $26,810 (57%). Average amount of gift aid, such as scholarships or grants (proportion receiving): $20,735 (57%). Average amount of self-help aid, such as work study or loans (proportion receiving): $6,104 (48%). Average need-based loan (excluding PLUS or other private loans): $5,728. Among students who received need-based aid, the average percentage of need met: 90%. Among students who received aid based on merit, the average award (and the proportion receiving): $12,688 (32%). The average athletic scholarship (and the proportion receiving): $0 (0%). Average amount of debt of borrowers graduating in 2009: $24,036. Proportion who borrowed: 61%.

CAMPUS LIFE AND EXTRACURRICULAR ACTIVITIES

Campus housing available (% using): coed dorms (34%), women's dorms (16%), men's dorms (6%), sorority housing, fraternity housing (7%), apartments for married students, apartment for single students (37%), special housing for disabled students, special housing for international students. Students who live in college-owned, operated, or affiliated housing: 82%. **Student employment:** During the 2009-2010 academic year, 41% of undergraduates worked on campus. Average per-year earnings: $1,400. **Clubs and organizations:** Number of student organizations: 96. Activities include: choral groups, concert band, dance, drama/theater, jazz band, literary magazine, music ensembles, musical theater, radio station, student government, student newspaper, student film society. Number of fraternities: 4; sororities: 4. Proportion of men in fraternities: 29%; of women in sororities: 30%. Average proportion of students who stay on campus on weekends: 75%. **Sports program (2009-2010):** Member of NCAA III. *Men's intercollegiate varsity sports:* baseball, basketball, cross country, golf, lacrosse, soccer, swimming, tennis, track and field (outdoor). *Women's intercollegiate varsity sports:* basketball, cross country, golf, soccer, softball, swimming, tennis, track and field (outdoor), volleyball.

SERVICES AND FACILITIES

Basic services: nonremedial tutoring, placement service, health service, health insurance. **Remedial assistance:** writing, study skills, other. **Counseling services:** minority student, career, personal, academic, psychological, birth control, religious. **For learning-disabled students:** School does not offer a structured program with separate admission and additional fees. Total undergraduates in learning-disabled program or receiving services: 73. Services include: tape recorders, note-taking services, oral tests, readers, extended time for tests, tutors, priority registration, priority seating, texts on tape, typist/scribe, other testing accommodations, other. **Library:** Number of titles: 378,865; number of current serial subscriptions: 1,112. **Information technology resources:** Students are not required to lease or own a computer. Number of campus computers available to all students: 290. School has a wireless network. Approximate number of users that can be accommodated: 3,000. Proportion of college-owned housing units wired for high-speed internet access: 100%. **Campus safety:** Security services offered: 24-hour foot-and-vehicle patrols, late-night transport/escort service, 24-hour emer-

gency telephones, lighted pathways/sidewalks, controlled dormitory access (key, security card, etc).

TRANSFER AND INTERNATIONAL STUDENTS

Transfer students: May apply for admission for the following academic terms: Fall, Spring. Applicants do not need a minimum number of credits to apply. For fall 2009: Transfer applications received: 89. Transfer applicants offered admission: 53. Transfer applicants enrolled: 25. **International students:** Number of foreign undergraduates: 3. Number of countries represented: 4. Minimum TOEFL score required: 570 (paper); 230 (computer).

St. Edward's University

- ■ **Address:** 3001 S. Congress Avenue, Austin, TX 78704
- ■ **Website:** http://www.gotostedwards.com
- ■ **Private; Religious affiliation:** Roman Catholic
- ■ **Enrollment:** 3,463 full-time; 905 part-time

KEY STATS

✔ **U.S News College Ranking:** 21, Regional Universities (West)
✔ **SAT Score (25th/75th percentile):** 1030-1235
✔ **Tuition:** 2010-2011: $26,484

Selectivity: Selective	**Room/board:** $9,036
Acceptance rate: 66%	**Average debt:** $29,810
Student/faculty ratio: 15/1	**Proportion who borrowed:** 79%

UNDERGRADUATE STUDENT BODY STATS

2009-2010 enrollment: 3,463 full-time; 905 part-time. Men: 41%; women: 59%. **Ethnic makeup:** African American: 5%; American-Indian: 1%; Asian American: 3%; Hispanic: 30%; White: 58%; International: 3%. **Religious preference:** Protestant: 16%; Jewish: 2%; Muslim: 1%; No preference: 5%; Roman Catholic: 53%; Christian: 13%; Other: 10%.

ADMISSIONS FACTS AND FIGURES

Phone: (512) 448-8500. **Email:** seu.admit@stedwards.edu. **Website:** http://www.gotostedwards.com. **Application deadlines for fall 2011:** Regular decision: May 1. Early decision: Not offered. Early action: Not offered. Admission can be deferred. **Application fee:** $45. **To apply online, go to:** http://www.gotostedwards.com/applynow.xml. **Admissions requirements/recommendations:** High school units required (recommended): English: 4 (4); Mathematics: 3 (4); Science: 2 (3); Foreign language: 2 (3); Social studies: 1 (1); History: 2 (3); Academic electives: 0 (1); Total units: 14 (20). **Tests:** The college uses SAT or ACT scores in admissions decisions. Either SAT or ACT required. For admission to the fall 2011 entering class, the school will accept: ACT with writing required. Campus visit: Recommended. Admissions interview: Recommended. Off-campus interview: Not available. **Factors that count in admissions decisions:** *Academic:* Secondary school record: Very Important. Class rank: Important. Letters of recommendation: Important. Standardized test scores: Very Important. Essay: Very Important. *Nonacademic:* Interview: Considered. Extracurricular activities: Important. Talent/ability: Considered. Character/personal qualities: Considered. Alumni/ae relationship: Considered. Geographical residence: Considered. State residency: Not Considered. Religious affiliation/commitment: Considered. Minority status: Considered. Volunteer work: Important. Work experience: Considered. **Other schools with the greatest overlap in applicants:** Baylor University; Texas A&M University–College Station; Texas State University–San Marcos; University of Texas–Austin; University of Texas–San Antonio. **Admissions statistics for the fall 2009 entering class:** Total applicants: 2,981. Total accepted: 1,970. Freshmen enrolled: 757; 8% were from out of state. Overall acceptance rate: 66%. **Size of waiting list:** 332 applicants; enrolled from waiting list: 73. **Credentials of fall 2009 freshmen:** 19% ranked in the top 10 percent of their high school class; 54% were in the top 25 percent; 88% were in the top half. (Proportion submitting class standing: 78%.) **First-year students who submitted SAT scores:** 71%. Scores (25/75 percentile): Critical Reading: 520-625, Math: 510-610, Combined: 1030-1235. **First-year students submitting ACT scores:** 27%. Scores (25/75 percentile): English: 21-28, Math: 21-26, Composite: 22-27.

ACADEMICS

Year founded: 1885. **Academic calendar:** Semester. **Degrees offered:** bachelor's, post-bachelor's certificate, master's. **Most popular majors:** 10% business administration and management, 10% psychology, 9% communication and media studies, 5% marketing/marketing management, 4% English composition. **Major fields of study:** area, ethnic, cultural, and gender studies; biological and biomedical sciences; business, management, marketing, and related support services; communication, journalism, and related programs; computer and information sciences and support services; education; English language and literature/letters; foreign languages, literatures, and linguistics; history; liberal arts and sciences studies, and humanities; mathematics and statistics; multi/interdisciplinary studies; natural resources and conservation; parks, recreation, leisure, and fitness studies; philosophy and religious studies; physical sciences; psychology; public administration and social service professions; security and protective services; social sciences; theology and religious vocations; visual and performing arts. **Areas of required coursework:** arts/fine arts, humanities, computer literacy, mathematics, English (including composition), philosophy, foreign languages, sciences (biological or physical), history, social science. **Pre-professional programs:** pre-law, pre-dentistry, pre-medicine, other. **Special academic programs (% participation):** double major, honors program, internships, study abroad (33%), teacher certificate program. **Teacher certification offered in:** early childhood, elementary, middle/junior high, secondary, bilingual/bicultural. **Cooperative education programs:** business, education, health professions, humanities, natural science, social/behavioral science, technologies. **Reserve Officers Training Corps (ROTC):** Army ROTC: Offered at cooperating institution (University of Texas–Austin); Air Force ROTC: Offered at cooperating institution (University of Texas–Austin). **Faculty and instruction (2009-2010):** Total instructional faculty: 184 full-time, 295 part-time (53% men; 47% women; 13% minorities). Full-time faculty with Ph.D. or other terminal degree: 90%. Student/faculty ratio: 15/1. Classes of fewer than 20 students: 50%; of 20 to 49 students: 50%. **Advanced Placement and International Baccalaureate credit:** AP tests may be used for: Credit only. Scores accepted: 3, 4, 5. International Baccalaureate exams may be used for: Credit only. **Freshmen returning for sophomore year:** 84%. **Graduation rates:** Four-year: 44%; five-year: 62%; six-year: 59%.

COSTS AND FINANCIAL AID

Financial aid office: (512) 448-8520. **Expenses (2010-2011):** Tuition and fees 2010-2011: $26,484; room/board: $9,036. Estimated books and supplies: $1,100; transportation: $870; personal expenses: $2,310. **Financial aid:** Priority filing date for institution's financial aid form: March 1; deadline: April 15. In 2009-2010, 74% of undergraduates applied for financial aid. Of those, 64% were determined to have financial need; 13% had their need fully met. Average financial aid package (proportion receiving): $20,039 (64%). Average amount of gift aid, such as scholarships or grants (proportion receiving): $11,815 (58%). Average amount of self-help aid, such as work study or loans (proportion receiving): $4,559 (47%). Average need-based loan (excluding PLUS or other private loans): $4,360. Among students who received need-based aid, the average percentage of need met: 67%. Among students who received aid based on merit, the average award (and the proportion receiving): $8,167 (7%). The average athletic scholarship (and the proportion receiving): $16,211 (4%). Average amount of debt of borrowers graduating in 2009: $29,810. Proportion who borrowed: 79%.

CAMPUS LIFE AND EXTRACURRICULAR ACTIVITIES

Campus housing available (% using): coed dorms (66%), women's dorms (8%), apartment for single students (26%), special housing for disabled students, other housing options. Students who live in college-owned, operated, or affiliated housing: 38%. **Student employment:** During the 2009-2010 academic year, 18% of undergraduates worked on campus. Average per-year earnings: $2,000. **Clubs and organizations:** Number of student organizations: 94. Activities include: campus ministries, choral groups, dance, drama/theater, international student organization, literary magazine, music ensembles, musical theater, student government, student newspaper, student film society, symphony orchestra, television station. Number of fraternities: 0; sororities: 0. Average proportion of students who stay on campus on weekends: 50%. **Sports program (2009-2010):** Member of NCAA II. **Men's intercollegiate varsity sports:** baseball, basketball, golf, soccer, tennis. **Women's intercollegiate varsity sports:** basketball, golf, soccer, softball, tennis, volleyball.

SERVICES AND FACILITIES

Basic services: nonremedial tutoring, health service, health insurance. **Remedial assistance:** reading, math, writing, study skills. **Counseling services:** minority student, career, personal, academic, psychological, religious. **For learning-disabled students:** School does not offer a structured program with separate admission and additional fees. Total undergraduates in learning-disabled program or receiving services: 71. Services include: remedial math, remedial English, reading machines, remedial reading, tape recorders, other special classes, note-taking services, oral tests, learning center, readers, extended time for tests, tutors, priority seating, substitution of courses, texts on tape, typist/scribe, exams on tape or computer, other testing accommodations, waiver of foreign language degree requirement, waiver of math degree requirement, other. **Library:** Number of titles: 149,204; number of current serial subscriptions: 25,609. **Information technology resources:** Students are not required to lease or own a computer. Number of campus computers available to all students: 748. School has a wireless network. Approximate number of users that can be accommodated: 1,500. Proportion of college-owned housing units wired for high-speed internet access: 100%. **Campus safety:** Security services offered: 24-hour foot-and-vehicle patrols, late-night transport/escort service, 24-hour emergency telephones, lighted pathways/sidewalks, controlled dormitory access (key, security card; etc).

TRANSFER AND INTERNATIONAL STUDENTS

Transfer students: May apply for admission for the following academic terms: Fall, Spring, Summer. Applicants do not need a minimum number of credits to apply. For fall 2009: Transfer applications received: 552. Transfer applicants offered admission: 349. Transfer applicants enrolled: 239. **International students:** Number of foreign undergraduates: 113 (3% of student body). Number of countries represented: 28. Minimum TOEFL score required: 500 (paper); 61 (computer).

Stephen F. Austin State University

- **Address:** SFA Station 13051, Nacogdoches, TX 75962
- **Website:** http://www.sfasu.edu
- **Public**
- **Enrollment:** 9,663 full-time; 1,481 part-time

KEY STATS

- ✔ **U.S News College Ranking:** 71, Regional Universities (West)
- ✔ **SAT Score (25th/75th percentile):** 860-1070
- ✔ **Tuition:** 2009-2010: $6,528 in state, $14,958 out of state

Selectivity: Selective	**Room/board:** $7,377
Acceptance rate: 73%	**Average debt:** N/A
Student/faculty ratio: 21/1	**Proportion who borrowed:** N/A

UNDERGRADUATE STUDENT BODY STATS

2009-2010 enrollment: 9,663 full-time; 1,481 part-time. Men: 39%; women: 61%. **Ethnic makeup:** African American: 23%; American-Indian: 1%; Asian American: 1%; Hispanic: 10%; White: 64%; International: 1%.

ADMISSIONS FACTS AND FIGURES

Phone: (936) 468-2504. **Email:** admissions@sfasu.edu. **Website:** http://www.sfasu.edu. **Application deadlines for fall 2011:** Regular decision: Rolling. Early decision: Not offered. Early action: Not offered. Admission cannot be deferred. **Application fee:** $35. To apply online, go to: http://www.sfasu.edu/admissions. **Admissions requirements/recommendations:** High school units required (recommended): English: 4; Mathematics: 3; Science: 3; Foreign language: 2; Social studies: (3); Total units: 12 (18). Tests: The college uses SAT or ACT scores in admissions decisions. Either SAT or ACT required. For admission to the fall 2011 entering class, the school will accept: ACT with writing required. Campus visit: Recommended. Admissions interview: Neither required nor recommended. Off-campus interview: Not available. **Factors that count in admissions decisions:** *Academic:* Secondary school record: Very Important. Class rank: Very Important. Letters of recommendation: Not Considered. Standardized test scores: Very Important. Essay: Not Considered. *Nonacademic:* Interview: Not Considered. Extracurricular activities: Considered. Talent/ability: Considered. Character/personal qualities: Not Considered. Alumni/ae relationship: Not Considered. Geographical residence: Considered. State residency: Not Considered. Religious affiliation/commitment: Not Considered. Minority status: Not Considered. Volunteer work: Considered. Work experience: Considered. **Other schools with the greatest overlap in applicants:** Sam Houston State University; Texas A&M University–College Station; Texas State University–San Marcos; University of Houston; University of Texas–Austin. **Admissions statistics for the fall 2009 entering class:** Total applicants: 8,960. Total accepted: 6,511. Freshmen enrolled: 2,396; 2% were from out of state. Overall acceptance rate: 73%. **Credentials of fall 2009 freshmen:** 13% ranked in the top 10 percent of their high school class; 40% were in the top 25 percent; 78% were in the top half. (Proportion submitting class standing: 95%.) **First-year students who submitted SAT scores:**

82%. Scores (25/75 percentile): Critical Reading: 420-530, Math: 440-540, Combined: 860-1070. **First-year students submitting ACT scores:** 46%. Scores (25/75 percentile): English: 16-23, Math: 17-23, Composite: 18-23.

ACADEMICS

Year founded: 1923. **Academic calendar:** Semester. **Degrees offered:** bachelor's, master's, doctorate. **Most popular majors:** 13% multi/interdisciplinary studies, 6% health and physical education, 6% nursing/registered nurse training (R.N., A.S.N., B.S.N., M.S.N.), 5% business/commerce, 4% psychology. **Major fields of study:** agriculture, agriculture operations, and related sciences; architecture and related services; biological and biomedical sciences; business, management, marketing, and related support services; communication, journalism, and related programs; computer and information sciences and support services; English language and literature/letters; family and consumer sciences/human sciences; foreign languages, literatures, and linguistics; health professions and related clinical sciences; history; legal professions and studies; liberal arts and sciences studies, and humanities; mathematics and statistics; multi/interdisciplinary studies; natural resources and conservation; parks, recreation, leisure, and fitness studies; philosophy and religious studies; physical sciences; psychology; public administration and social service professions; security and protective services; social sciences; visual and performing arts. **Areas of required coursework:** arts/fine arts, humanities, mathematics, English (including composition), sciences (biological or physical), history, social science, other. **Pre-professional programs:** pre-law, pre-dentistry, pre-medicine, pre-theology, pre-veterinary science, pre-optometry, pre-pharmacy, other. **Special academic programs:** accelerated program, distance learning, double major, dual enrollment, honors program, independent study, internships, liberal arts/career combination, student-designed major, study abroad, teacher certificate program. **Teacher certification offered in:** early childhood, special education, elementary, middle/junior high, secondary, bilingual/bicultural. **Reserve Officers Training Corps (ROTC):** Army ROTC: Offered on campus. **Faculty and instruction (2009-2010):** Total instructional faculty: 485 full-time, 172 part-time (49% men; 51% women; 8% minorities). Full-time faculty with Ph.D. or other terminal degree: 74%. Student/faculty ratio: 21/1. Classes of fewer than 20 students: 25%; of 20 to 49 students: 64%; of 50 or more students: 10%. **Advanced Placement and International Baccalaureate credit:** AP tests may be used for: Credit only. Scores accepted: 3, 4, 5. International Baccalaureate exams may be used for: Credit only. **Freshmen returning for sophomore year:** 64%. **Graduation rates:** Four-year: 18%; five-year: 37%; six-year: 40%. **Graduate study:** 5% of students pursue further study within one year.

COSTS AND FINANCIAL AID

Financial aid office: (936) 468-2403. **Expenses (2009-2010):** Tuition and fees 2009-2010: $6,528 in state, $14,958 out of state; room/board: $7,377. Estimated books and supplies: $1,072; transportation: $2,711; personal expenses: $1,720. **Financial aid:** Priority filing date for institution's financial aid form: April 1.

CAMPUS LIFE AND EXTRACURRICULAR ACTIVITIES

Campus housing available (% using): coed dorms (61%), women's dorms (26%), men's dorms (12%), sorority housing, fraternity housing, apartments for married students, apartment for single students (1%), special housing for disabled students, other housing options. Students who live in college-owned, operated, or affiliated housing: 44%. **Clubs and organizations:** Number of student organizations: 211. Activities include: campus ministries, choral groups, concert band, dance, drama/theater, international student organization, jazz band, literary magazine, marching band, music ensembles, musical theater, opera, pep band, radio station, student government, student newspaper, student film society, symphony orchestra, television station, yearbook. Number of fraternities: 25; sororities: 14. Proportion of men in fraternities: 15%; of women in sororities: 9%. **Sports program (2009-2010):** Member of NCAA I. **Men's intercollegiate varsity sports:** baseball, basketball, cross country, football, golf, track and field (indoor), track and field (outdoor). **Women's intercollegiate varsity sports:** basketball, bowling, cross country, golf, soccer, softball, tennis, track and field (indoor), track and field (outdoor), volleyball.

SERVICES AND FACILITIES

Basic services: placement service, health service. **Remedial assistance:** reading, math, writing, study skills. **Counseling services:** minority student, career, military, personal, veteran student, academic, older student, psychological. **For learning-disabled students:** School does not offer a structured program with separate admission and additional fees. Services include: remedial math, remedial English, reading machines, remedial reading,

tape recorders, other special classes, diagnostic testing service, note-taking services, oral tests, learning center, readers, extended time for tests, tutors, other. **Library:** Number of titles: 982,129; number of current serial subscriptions: 1,378. **Information technology resources:** Students are not required to lease or own a computer. Number of campus computers available to all students: 1,000. School has a wireless network. Proportion of college-owned housing units wired for high-speed internet access: 100%. **Campus safety:** Security services offered: 24-hour foot-and-vehicle patrols, late-night transport/escort service, 24-hour emergency telephones, lighted pathways/sidewalks, controlled dormitory access (key, security card, etc).

TRANSFER AND INTERNATIONAL STUDENTS

Transfer students: May apply for admission for the following academic terms: Fall, Spring, Summer. Applicants need a minimum number of credits to apply. For fall 2009: Transfer applications received: 1,939. Transfer applicants offered admission: 1,514. Transfer applicants enrolled: 934. **International students:** Number of foreign undergraduates: 110 (1% of student body). Number of countries represented: 34. Minimum TOEFL score required: 550 (paper); 213 (computer). Average TOEFL score: 602 (paper).

St. Mary's University of San Antonio

- **Address:** 1 Camino Santa Maria, San Antonio, TX 78228
- **Website:** http://www.stmarytx.edu
- **Private; Religious affiliation:** Roman Catholic
- **Enrollment:** 2,212 full-time; 160 part-time

KEY STATS

✔ **U.S News College Ranking:** 19, Regional Universities (West)
✔ **SAT Score (25th/75th percentile):** 940-1160
✔ **Tuition:** 2010-2011: $22,556

Selectivity: Selective	**Room/board:** $7,550
Acceptance rate: 76%	**Average debt:** $22,592
Student/faculty ratio: 13/1	**Proportion who borrowed:** 79%

UNDERGRADUATE STUDENT BODY STATS

2009-2010 enrollment: 2,212 full-time; 160 part-time. Men: 40%; women: 60%. **Ethnic makeup:** African American: 4%; Asian American: 3%; Hispanic: 70%; White: 20%; International: 3%. **Religious preference:** Protestant: 1%; Muslim: 1%; No preference: 6%; Unknown: 31%; Roman Catholic: 45%; Other: 13%.

ADMISSIONS FACTS AND FIGURES

Phone: (210) 436-3126. **Email:** uadm@stmarytx.edu. **Website:** http://www.stmarytx.edu. **Application deadlines for fall 2011:** Regular decision: Rolling. Early decision: Not offered. Early action: Not offered. Admission can be deferred. **Application fee:** $30. **To apply online, go to:** https://www.stmarytx.edu/admission/apply/. **Admissions requirements/recommendations:** High school units required (recommended): English: 4 (4); Mathematics: 3 (4); Science: 3 (4); Foreign language: 2 (4); Social studies: 3 (4); Academic electives: 1; Total units: 16 (20). Tests: The college uses SAT or ACT scores in admissions decisions. Either SAT or ACT required. For admission to the fall 2011 entering class, the school will accept: ACT with writing recommended. Campus visit: Recommended. Admissions interview: Recommended. Off-campus interview: May be arranged. **Factors that count in admissions decisions:** *Academic:* Secondary school record: Very Important. Class rank: Important. Letters of recommendation: Considered. Standardized test scores: Important. Essay: Considered. *Nonacademic:* Interview: Considered. Extracurricular activities: Considered. Talent/ability: Considered. Character/personal qualities: Considered. Alumni/ae relationship: Considered. Geographical residence: Considered. State residency: Not Considered. Religious affiliation/commitment: Not Considered. Minority status: Not Considered. Volunteer work: Considered. Work experience: Considered. **Other schools with the greatest overlap in applicants:** Baylor University; St. Edward's University; University of Texas–Austin; University of Texas–San Antonio; University of the Incarnate Word. **Admissions statistics for the fall 2009 entering class:** Total applicants: 2,462. Total accepted: 1,871. Freshmen enrolled: 531; 6% were from out of state. Overall acceptance rate: 76%. **Credentials of fall 2009 freshmen:** 33% ranked in the top 10 percent of their high school class; 66% were in the top 25 percent; 87% were in the top half. (Proportion submitting class standing: 87%.) **Average high school grade point average:** 3.4. **First-year students who submitted SAT scores:** 85%. Scores (25/75 percentile): Critical Reading: 470-570, Math:

470-590, Combined: 940-1160. **First-year students submitting ACT scores:** 38%. Scores (25/75 percentile): English: 19-25, Math: 19-25, Composite: 20-25.

ACADEMICS

Year founded: 1852. **Academic calendar:** Semester. **Degrees offered:** bachelor's, master's, doctorate. **Most popular majors:** 27% business/commerce, 15% social sciences, 14% biology/biological sciences, 7% communication studies/speech communication and rhetoric, 7% psychology. **Major fields of study:** biological and biomedical sciences; business, management, marketing, and related support services; communication, journalism, and related programs; computer and information sciences and support services; education; engineering; English language and literature/letters; foreign languages, literatures, and linguistics; history; mathematics and statistics; multi/interdisciplinary studies; parks, recreation, leisure, and fitness studies; philosophy and religious studies; physical sciences; psychology; public administration and social service professions; social sciences; theology and religious vocations; visual and performing arts. **Areas of required coursework:** arts/fine arts, humanities, computer literacy, mathematics, English (including composition), philosophy, foreign languages, sciences (biological or physical), history, social science, other. **Pre-professional programs:** pre-law, pre-dentistry, pre-medicine, pre-optometry, pre-pharmacy, other. **Special academic programs (% participation):** cross-registration (.1%), distance learning, double major (12%), dual enrollment, exchange student program (domestic), honors program (5%), independent study (23%), internships (18%), study abroad (24%), teacher certificate program (3%), other. **Teacher certification offered in:** early childhood, elementary, middle/junior high, secondary. **Reserve Officers Training Corps (ROTC):** Army ROTC: Offered on campus; Air Force ROTC: Offered at cooperating institution (University of Texas–San Antonio). **Faculty and instruction (2009-2010):** Total instructional faculty: 197 full-time, 143 part-time (62% men; 38% women; 25% minorities). Full-time faculty with Ph.D. or other terminal degree: 92%. Student/faculty ratio: 13/1. Classes of fewer than 20 students: 41%; of 20 to 49 students: 58%; of 50 or more students: 1%. **Advanced Placement and International Baccalaureate credit:** AP tests may be used for: Credit and/or placement. Scores accepted: 3, 4, 5. International Baccalaureate exams may be used for: Credit and/or placement. **Freshmen returning for sophomore year:** 79%. **Graduation rates:** Four-year: 31%; five-year: 52%; six-year: 58%. **Graduate study:** 22% of students pursue further study immediately upon graduation; 39% within one year. Fields in which graduates pursue further study: Master of Business Administration (MBA), 17%; law, 13%; medicine, 10%; dentistry, 1%; engineering, 2%; theology (or the seminary), 1%; education, 5%; arts and sciences, 50%; veterinary medicine, 1%.

COSTS AND FINANCIAL AID

Financial aid office: (210) 436-3141. **Expenses (2010-2011):** Tuition and fees 2010-2011: $22,556; room/board: $7,550. Estimated books and supplies: $1,300; transportation: $1,100; personal expenses: $3,174. **Financial aid:** Priority filing date for institution's financial aid form: March 31. In 2009-2010, 85% of undergraduates applied for financial aid. Of those, 79% were determined to have financial need; 25% had their need fully met. Average financial aid package (proportion receiving): $20,138 (79%). Average amount of gift aid, such as scholarships or grants (proportion receiving): $14,206 (77%). Average amount of self-help aid, such as work study or loans (proportion receiving): $4,700 (74%). Average need-based loan (excluding PLUS or other private loans): $6,124. Among students who received need-based aid, the average percentage of need met: 76%. Among students who received aid based on merit, the average award (and the proportion receiving): $7,292 (25%). The average athletic scholarship (and the proportion receiving): $12,612 (3%). Average amount of debt of borrowers graduating in 2009: $22,592. Proportion who borrowed: 79%.

CAMPUS LIFE AND EXTRACURRICULAR ACTIVITIES

Campus housing available (% using): coed dorms (82%), women's dorms (8%), special housing for disabled students (1%). Students who live in college-owned, operated, or affiliated housing: 55%. **Student employment:** During the 2009-2010 academic year, 12% of undergraduates worked on campus. Average per-year earnings: $2,200. **Clubs and organizations:** Number of student organizations: 48. Activities include: campus ministries, choral groups, concert band, dance, drama/theater, international student organization, jazz band, literary magazine, music ensembles, musical theater, pep band, student government, student newspaper. Number of fraternities: 5; sororities: 6. Proportion of men in fraternities: 22%; of women in sororities: 16%. Average proportion of students who stay on campus on weekends: 80%. **Sports program (2009-2010):** Member of NCAA II.

Men's intercollegiate varsity sports: baseball, basketball, golf, soccer, tennis. **Women's intercollegiate varsity sports:** basketball, cross country, golf, soccer, softball, tennis, volleyball.

SERVICES AND FACILITIES

Basic services: nonremedial tutoring, placement service, health service, health insurance. **Remedial assistance:** reading, math, writing, study skills. **Counseling services:** minority student, career, military, personal, veteran student, academic, older student, psychological, religious, other. **For learning-disabled students:** School does not offer a structured program with separate admission and additional fees. Total undergraduates in learning-disabled program or receiving services: 40. Services include: reading machines, diagnostic testing service, note-taking services, oral tests, learning center, readers, extended time for tests, tutors, early syllabus, priority registration, priority seating, texts on tape, exams on tape or computer, other testing accommodations. **Library:** Number of titles: 595,259; number of current serial subscriptions: 415. **Information technology resources:** Students are required to lease or own a computer. Number of campus computers available to all students: 100. School has a wireless network. Approximate number of users that can be accommodated: 5,950. Proportion of college-owned housing units wired for high-speed internet access: 100%. **Campus safety:** Security services offered: 24-hour foot-and-vehicle patrols, late-night transport/escort service, 24-hour emergency telephones, lighted pathways/sidewalks, controlled dormitory access (key, security card, etc).

TRANSFER AND INTERNATIONAL STUDENTS

Transfer students: May apply for admission for the following academic terms: Fall, Spring, Summer. Applicants do not need a minimum number of credits to apply. For fall 2009: Transfer applications received: 529. Transfer applicants offered admission: 282. Transfer applicants enrolled: 125. **International students:** Number of foreign undergraduates: 62 (3% of student body). Number of countries represented: 41. Minimum TOEFL score required: 550 (paper); 213 (computer). Average TOEFL score: 663 (paper).

Sul Ross State University

- ■ **Address:** PO Box C-114, Alpine, TX 79832
- ■ **Website:** http://www.sulross.edu
- ■ **Public**
- ■ **Enrollment:** 1,409 full-time; 758 part-time

KEY STATS

✔ **U.S News College Ranking:** second tier, Regional Universities (West)
✔ **SAT or ACT Score (25th/75th percentile):** N/A
✔ **Tuition:** 2010-2011: $4,396 in state, $11,044 out of state

Selectivity: Less selective	**Room/board:** $6,370
Acceptance rate: 97%	**Average debt:** N/A
Student/faculty ratio: N/A	**Proportion who borrowed:** N/A

UNDERGRADUATE STUDENT BODY STATS

2009-2010 enrollment: 1,409 full-time; 758 part-time. Men: 45%; women: 55%. **Ethnic makeup:** African American: 7%; Hispanic: 61%; White: 29%; International: 2%.

ADMISSIONS FACTS AND FIGURES

Phone: (432) 837-8050. **Email:** admissions@sulross.edu. **Website:** http://www.sulross.edu. **Application deadlines for fall 2011:** Regular decision: Rolling. Early decision: Not offered. Early action: Not offered. Admission can be deferred. **Application fee:** $25. **To apply online, go to:** http://www.applytexas.org. **Admissions requirements/recommendations:** High school units required (recommended): English: 4 (4); Mathematics: 3 (4); Science: 2 (4); Foreign language: 0 (3); Social studies: 0 (0); History: 1 (2); Academic electives: 0 (3); Total units: 15 (31). Tests: The college uses SAT or ACT scores in admissions decisions. Either SAT or ACT required. For admission to the fall 2011 entering class, the school will accept: ACT with or without writing accepted. Campus visit: Recommended. Admissions interview: Recommended. Off-campus interview: May be arranged. **Factors that count in admissions decisions:** *Academic:* Secondary school record: Considered. Class rank: Considered. Letters of recommendation: Considered. Standardized test scores: Considered. Essay: Not Considered. *Nonacademic:* Interview: Not Considered. Extracurricular activities: Not Considered. Talent/ability: Considered. Character/personal qualities: Not Considered.

Alumni/ae relationship; Not Considered. Geographical residence: Not Considered. State residency: Not Considered. Religious affiliation/commitment: Not Considered. Minority status: Not Considered. Volunteer work: Not Considered. Work experience: Not Considered. **Admissions statistics for the fall 2009 entering class:** Total applicants: 956. Total accepted: 932. Freshmen enrolled: 386; 3% were from out of state. Overall acceptance rate: 97%. **Credentials of fall 2009 freshmen:** 4% ranked in the top 10 percent of their high school class; 13% were in the top 25 percent; 48% were in the top half. (Proportion submitting class standing: 92%.) **Average high school grade point average:** 3.5.

ACADEMICS

Year founded: 1917. **Academic calendar:** Semester. **Degrees offered:** certificate, associate, bachelor's, post-bachelor's certificate, master's. **Major fields of study:** agriculture, agriculture operations, and related sciences; area, ethnic, cultural, and gender studies; biological and biomedical sciences; business, management, marketing, and related support services; computer and information sciences and support services; engineering technologies/technicians; English language and literature/letters; foreign languages, literatures, and linguistics; mathematics and statistics; multi/interdisciplinary studies; natural resources and conservation; parks, recreation, leisure, and fitness studies; physical sciences; psychology; security and protective services; social sciences; visual and performing arts. **Areas of required coursework:** arts/fine arts, humanities, mathematics, English (including composition), sciences (biological or physical), history, social science, other. **Pre-professional programs:** pre-law, pre-dentistry, pre-medicine, pre-veterinary science, pre-optometry, pre-pharmacy. **Special academic programs (% participation):** cross-registration, distance learning (10%), double major, dual enrollment, honors program (3%), independent study, internships (10%), liberal arts/career combination, teacher certificate program (30%). **Teacher certification offered in:** early childhood, elementary, vo-tech, middle/junior high, secondary. **Faculty and instruction (2009-2010):** Total instructional faculty: N/A. Classes of fewer than 20 students: 66%; of 20 to 49 students: 32%; of 50 or more students: 2%. **Advanced Placement and International Baccalaureate credit:** AP tests may be used for: Credit only. Scores accepted: 3, 4. **Graduation rates:** Six-year: 20%.

COSTS AND FINANCIAL AID

Financial aid office: (432) 837-8059. **Expenses (2010-2011):** Tuition and fees 2010-2011: $4,396 in state, $11,044 out of state; room/board: $6,370. **Financial aid:** Priority filing date for institution's financial aid form: March 1; deadline: April 1.

CAMPUS LIFE AND EXTRACURRICULAR ACTIVITIES

Campus housing available: coed dorms, apartments for married students, other housing options. **Student employment:** During the 2009-2010 academic year, 9% of undergraduates worked on campus. Average per-year earnings: $4,944. **Clubs and organizations:** Number of student organizations: 48. Activities include: campus ministries, choral groups, concert band, dance, drama/theater, jazz band, music ensembles, musical theater, pep band, radio station, student government, student newspaper, yearbook. Number of fraternities: 0; sororities: 0. Average proportion of students who stay on campus on weekends: 45%. **Sports program (2009-2010):** Member of NCAA III.

SERVICES AND FACILITIES

Basic services: nonremedial tutoring, placement service, day care, health service, health insurance. **Remedial assistance:** reading, math, writing, study skills. **Counseling services:** minority student, career, personal, academic, older student, psychological, birth control. **For learning-disabled students:** Services include: remedial math, remedial English, reading machines, remedial reading, tape recorders, videotaped classes, diagnostic testing service, note-taking services, oral tests, readers, extended time for tests, tutors, other. **Information technology resources:** Students are not required to lease or own a computer. Number of campus computers available to all students: 230. **Campus safety:** Security services offered: 24-hour foot-and-vehicle patrols, late-night transport/escort service, 24-hour emergency telephones, lighted pathways/sidewalks, controlled dormitory access (key, security card, etc).

TRANSFER AND INTERNATIONAL STUDENTS

Transfer students: May apply for admission for the following academic terms: Fall, Winter, Spring, Summer. Applicants need a minimum number of credits to apply. For fall 2009: Transfer applications received: 422. Transfer applicants offered admission: 399. Transfer applicants enrolled: 349. **International students:** Number of foreign undergraduates: 51 (2% of

student body). Minimum TOEFL score required: 520 (paper); 190 (computer).

Tarleton State University

- **Address:** Box T 0001, Tarleton Station, Stephenville, TX 76402
- **Website:** http://www.tarleton.edu
- **Public**
- **Enrollment:** N/A

KEY STATS

✔ **U.S News College Ranking:** second tier, Regional Universities (West)
✔ **SAT or ACT Score (25th/75th percentile):** N/A
✔ **Tuition:** 2009-2010: $4,909 in state, $11,557 out of state
  Selectivity: Less selective **Room/board:** $6,591
  Acceptance rate: N/A **Average debt:** N/A
  Student/faculty ratio: N/A **Proportion who borrowed:** N/A

Texas A&M International University

- **Address:** 5201 University Boulevard, Laredo, TX 78041-1900
- **Website:** http://www.tamiu.edu
- **Public**
- **Enrollment:** 3,349 full-time; 1,966 part-time

KEY STATS

✔ **U.S News College Ranking:** 71, Regional Universities (West)
✔ **SAT Score (25th/75th percentile):** 800-990
✔ **Tuition:** 2010-2011: $6,093 in state, $15,393 out of state
  Selectivity: Selective **Room/board:** $6,918
  Acceptance rate: 53% **Average debt:** $13,746
  Student/faculty ratio: 20/1 **Proportion who borrowed:** 68%

UNDERGRADUATE STUDENT BODY STATS

2009-2010 enrollment: 3,349 full-time; 1,966 part-time. Men: 40%; women: 60%. **Ethnic makeup:** African American: 1%; Asian American: 1%; Hispanic: 94%; White: 2%; International: 2%.

ADMISSIONS FACTS AND FIGURES

Phone: (956) 326-2200. **Email:** enroll@tamiu.edu. **Website:** http://www.tamiu.edu. **Application deadlines for fall 2011:** Regular decision: July 1. Early decision: Not offered. Early action: Not offered. Admission can be deferred. **To apply online, go to:** https://www.applytexas.org/adappc/gen/c_start. WBX. **Admissions requirements/recommendations:** High school units required (recommended): English: 4; Mathematics: 3; Science: 2; Foreign language: (2); Social studies: 3; Total units: 13 (3). Tests: The college uses SAT or ACT scores in admissions decisions. Either SAT or ACT required. For admission to the fall 2011 entering class, the school will accept: ACT with or without writing accepted. Campus visit: Neither required nor recommended. Admissions interview: Neither required nor recommended. Off-campus interview: May be arranged. **Factors that count in admissions decisions:** *Academic:* Secondary school record: Very Important. Class rank: Very Important. Letters of recommendation: Not Considered. Standardized test scores: Very Important. Essay: Not Considered. *Nonacademic:* Interview: Not Considered. Extracurricular activities: Not Considered. Talent/ability: Not Considered. Character/personal qualities: Not Considered. Alumni/ae relationship: Not Considered. Geographical residence: Not Considered. State residency: Not Considered. Religious affiliation/commitment: Not Considered. Minority status: Not Considered. Volunteer work: Not Considered. Work experience: Not Considered. **Other schools with the greatest overlap in applicants:** Texas A&M University–College Station; Texas A&M University–Kingsville; Texas State University–San Marcos; University of Texas–Austin; University of Texas–San Antonio. **Admissions statistics for the fall 2009 entering class:** Total applicants: 3,176. Total accepted: 1,673. Freshmen enrolled: 720; 0% were from out of state. Overall acceptance rate: 53%. **Credentials of fall 2009 freshmen:** 21% ranked in the top 10 percent of their high school class; 50% were in the top 25 percent; 84% were in the top half. (Proportion submitting class standing: 98%.) **Average high school grade point average:** 3.6. **First-year students who submitted SAT scores:** 81%. Scores (25/75 percentile): Critical Reading:

390-480, Math: 410-510, Combined: 800-990. **First-year students submitting ACT scores:** 37%. Scores (25/75 percentile): English: 14-20, Math: 16-21, Composite: 15-20.

ACADEMICS

Year founded: 1970. **Academic calendar:** Semester. **Degrees offered:** bachelor's, master's, doctorate. **Most popular majors:** 18% multi/interdisciplinary studies, 15% business administration and management, 7% management information systems, 6% accounting, 6% criminal justice/police science. **Major fields of study:** area, ethnic, cultural, and gender studies; biological and biomedical sciences; business, management, marketing, and related support services; communication, journalism, and related programs; computer and information sciences and support services; English language and literature/letters; foreign languages, literatures, and linguistics; health professions and related clinical sciences; history; mathematics and statistics; multi/interdisciplinary studies; natural resources and conservation; parks, recreation, leisure, and fitness studies; physical sciences; psychology; public administration and social service professions; security and protective services; social sciences; visual and performing arts. **Areas of required coursework:** arts/fine arts, mathematics, English (including composition), sciences (biological or physical), history, social science. **Pre-professional programs:** pre-law, pre-dentistry, pre-medicine. **Special academic programs (% participation):** distance learning (2%), double major (5%), dual enrollment (4%), honors program (3%), independent study (3%), internships (3%), study abroad (1%), teacher certificate program (23%). **Teacher certification offered in:** early childhood, special education, elementary, middle/junior high, secondary, bilingual/bicultural. **Reserve Officers Training Corps (ROTC):** Army ROTC: Offered on campus. **Faculty and instruction (2009-2010):** Total instructional faculty: 162 full-time, 141 part-time (55% men; 45% women; 50% minorities). Full-time faculty with Ph.D. or other terminal degree: 51%. Student/faculty ratio: 20/1. Classes of fewer than 20 students: 33%; of 20 to 49 students: 55%; of 50 or more students: 12%. **Advanced Placement and International Baccalaureate credit:** AP tests may be used for: Credit only. Scores accepted: 3, 4, 5. **Freshmen returning for sophomore year:** 66%. **Graduation rates:** Four-year: 19%; five-year: 32%; six-year: 36%. **Graduate study:** 27% of students pursue further study within one year. Fields in which graduates pursue further study: Master of Business Administration (MBA), 4%; medicine, 1%; education, 2%; arts and sciences, 1%.

COSTS AND FINANCIAL AID

Financial aid office: (956) 326-2225. **Expenses (2010-2011):** Tuition and fees 2010-2011: $6,093 in state, $15,393 out of state; room/board: $6,918. Estimated books and supplies: $1,750; transportation: $1,052; personal expenses: $2,260. **Financial aid:** Priority filing date for institution's financial aid form: March 15. In 2009-2010, 94% of undergraduates applied for financial aid. Of those, 86% were determined to have financial need; 9% had their need fully met. Average financial aid package (proportion receiving): $9,248 (85%). Average amount of gift aid, such as scholarships or grants (proportion receiving): $5,740 (84%). Average amount of self-help aid, such as work study or loans (proportion receiving): $3,932 (49%). Average need-based loan (excluding PLUS or other private loans): $4,014. Among students who received need-based aid, the average percentage of need met: 70%. Among students who received aid based on merit, the average award (and the proportion receiving): $3,450 (4%). The average athletic scholarship (and the proportion receiving): $2,865 (4%). Average amount of debt of borrowers graduating in 2009: $13,746. Proportion who borrowed: 68%.

CAMPUS LIFE AND EXTRACURRICULAR ACTIVITIES

Campus housing available (% using): coed dorms (64%), apartments for married students (0%), apartment for single students (35%), special housing for disabled students (1%), other housing options. **Student employment:** During the 2009-2010 academic year, 4% of undergraduates worked on campus. Average per-year earnings: $6,225. **Clubs and organizations:** Number of student organizations: 55. Activities include: campus ministries, choral groups, concert band, dance, international student organization, marching band, model UN, music ensembles, pep band, student government, student newspaper. Number of fraternities: 4; sororities: 2. Average proportion of students who stay on campus on weekends: 10%. **Sports program (2009-2010):** Member of NCAA II. **Men's intercollegiate varsity sports:** baseball, basketball, cross country, golf, soccer. **Women's intercollegiate varsity sports:** basketball, cross country, golf, soccer, softball, volleyball.

SERVICES AND FACILITIES

Basic services: nonremedial tutoring, placement service, health service. **Remedial assistance:** reading, math, writing, study skills. **Counseling ser-**

vices: minority student, career, personal, veteran student, academic. **For learning-disabled students:** School does not offer a structured program with separate admission and additional fees. Services include: remedial math, remedial English, reading machines, remedial reading, tape recorders, other special classes, videotaped classes, untimed tests, note-taking services, special bookstore section, oral tests, readers, extended time for tests, tutors, priority seating, texts on tape, typist/scribe, exams on tape or computer, other testing accommodations. **Library:** Number of titles: 316,587; number of current serial subscriptions: 32,689. **Information technology resources:** Students are not required to lease or own a computer. Number of campus computers available to all students: 460. School has a wireless network. Approximate number of users that can be accommodated: 3,076. Proportion of college-owned housing units wired for high-speed internet access: 100%. **Campus safety:** Security services offered: 24-hour foot-and-vehicle patrols, late-night transport/escort service, 24-hour emergency telephones, lighted pathways/sidewalks, student patrols, controlled dormitory access (key, security card, etc).

TRANSFER AND INTERNATIONAL STUDENTS

Transfer students: May apply for admission for the following academic terms: Fall, Spring, Summer. Applicants need a minimum number of credits to apply. For fall 2009: Transfer applications received: 857. Transfer applicants offered admission: 644. Transfer applicants enrolled: 437. **International students:** Number of foreign undergraduates: 131 (2% of student body). Number of countries represented: 18. Minimum TOEFL score required: 550 (paper); 213 (computer). Average TOEFL score: 567 (paper).

Texas A&M University—College Station

- **Address:** College Station, TX 77843
- **Website:** http://www.tamu.edu
- **Public**
- **Enrollment:** 35,401 full-time; 3,409 part-time

....

KEY STATS

✔ **U.S News College Ranking:** 63, National Universities
✔ **SAT Score (25th/75th percentile):** 1100-1310
✔ **Tuition:** 2009-2010: $8,176 in state, $22,666 out of state
   Selectivity: More selective   **Room/board:** $8,039
   Acceptance rate: 67%   **Average debt:** $21,276
   Student/faculty ratio: 18/1   **Proportion who borrowed:** 54%

UNDERGRADUATE STUDENT BODY STATS

2009-2010 enrollment: 35,401 full-time; 3,409 part-time. Men: 52%; women: 48%. **Ethnic makeup:** African American: 3%; American-Indian: 1%; Asian American: 5%; Hispanic: 14%; White: 75%; International: 1%.

ADMISSIONS FACTS AND FIGURES

Phone: (979) 845-3741. **Email:** admissions@tamu.edu. **Website:** http://www.tamu.edu. **Application deadlines for fall 2011:** Regular decision: January 15. Early decision: Not offered. Early action: Not offered. Admission cannot be deferred. **Application fee:** $60. **To apply online, go to:** http://www.tamu.edu/admissions. **Admissions requirements/recommendations:** High school units required (recommended): English: 4 (4); Mathematics: 4 (4); Science: 3 (3); Foreign language: 2 (2); Social studies: 2 (2); History: 1 (1); Total units: 18 (19). Tests: The college uses SAT or ACT scores in admissions decisions. Either SAT or ACT required. For admission to the fall 2011 entering class, the school will accept: ACT with writing required. Campus visit: Recommended. Admissions interview: Neither required nor recommended. Off-campus interview: Not available. **Factors that count in admissions decisions:** *Academic:* Secondary school record: Very Important. Class rank: Very Important. Letters of recommendation: Considered. Standardized test scores: Very Important. Essay: Important. *Nonacademic:* Interview: Not Considered. Extracurricular activities: Very Important. Talent/ability: Very Important. Character/personal qualities: Considered. Alumni/ae relationship: Not Considered. Geographical residence: Important. State residency: Important. Religious affiliation/commitment: Not Considered. Minority status: Not Considered. Volunteer work: Important. Work experience: Important. **Other schools with the greatest overlap in applicants:** Baylor University; Rice University; Texas State University—San Marcos; Texas Tech University; University of Texas—Austin. **Admissions statistics for the fall 2009 entering class:** Total applicants: 22,757. Total accepted: 15,158. Freshmen enrolled: 8,071; 4% were from out of state. Overall acceptance rate: 67%. **Size of waiting list:** 5869 applicants; enrolled from waiting list: 119. **Credentials of fall 2009 freshmen:** 50% ranked in the top 10 percent of their high school class; 89% were in the top 25 percent; 99% were in the top half. (Proportion submitting class standing: 99%.) **First-year students who submitted SAT scores:** 75%. Scores (25/75 percentile): Critical Reading: 530-640, Math: 570-670, Combined: 1100-1310. **First-year students submitting ACT scores:** 25%. Scores (25/75 percentile): English: 23-30, Math: 24-29, Composite: 24-30.

ACADEMICS

Year founded: 1876. **Academic calendar:** Semester. **Degrees offered:** bachelor's, post-bachelor's certificate, master's, doctorate. **Most popular majors:** 18% business, management, marketing, and related support services, 12% agriculture, agriculture operations, and related sciences, 12% engineering, 9% biological and biomedical sciences, 8% multi/interdisciplinary studies. **Major fields of study:** agriculture, agriculture operations, and related sciences; architecture and related services; area, ethnic, cultural, and gender studies; biological and biomedical sciences; business, management, marketing, and related support services; communication, journalism, and related programs; communications technologies/technicians and support services; computer and information sciences and support services; education; engineering; engineering technologies/technicians; English language and literature/letters; family and consumer sciences/human sciences; foreign languages, literatures, and linguistics; health professions and related clinical sciences; history; mathematics and statistics; multi/interdisciplinary studies; natural resources and conservation; parks, recreation, leisure, and fitness studies; philosophy and religious studies; physical sciences; psychology; social sciences; visual and performing arts. **Areas of required coursework:** arts/fine arts, humanities, computer literacy, mathematics, English (including composition), foreign languages, sciences (biological or physical), history, social science, other. **Pre-professional programs:** pre-law, pre-dentistry, pre-medicine, pre-veterinary science, pre-optometry, pre-pharmacy. **Special academic programs (% participation):** accelerated program, cooperative (work-study plan) program (2%), cross-registration, distance learning, double major, dual enrollment, English as a Second Language (ESL), exchange student program (domestic), honors program (24%), independent study, internships (28.9%), liberal arts/career combination, study abroad (12.8%), teacher certificate program (7.52%), other. **Teacher certification offered in:** early childhood, special education, elementary, middle/junior high, secondary, bilingual/bicultural. **Cooperative education programs:** agriculture, business, computer science, engineering, health professions, humanities, natural science, social/behavioral science, technologies. **Reserve Officers Training Corps (ROTC):** Army ROTC: Offered on campus; Navy ROTC: Offered on campus; Air Force ROTC: Offered on campus. **Faculty and instruction (2009-2010):** Total instructional faculty: 2,317 full-time, 501 part-time (69% men; 31% women; 22% minorities). Full-time faculty with Ph.D. or other terminal degree: 93%. Student/faculty ratio: 18/1. Classes of fewer than 20 students: 22%; of 20 to 49 students: 56%; of 50 or more students: 22%. **Advanced Placement and International Baccalaureate credit:** AP tests may be used for: Credit only. Scores accepted: 3, 4, 5. International Baccalaureate exams may be used for: Credit and/or placement. **Freshmen returning for sophomore year:** 92%. **Graduation rates:** Four-year: 45%; five-year: 75%; six-year: 80%. **Graduate study:** 22% of students pursue further study immediately upon graduation.

COSTS AND FINANCIAL AID

Financial aid office: (979) 845-3236. **Expenses (2009-2010):** Tuition and fees 2009-2010: $8,176 in state, $22,606 out of state; room/board: $8,039. Estimated books and supplies: $1,278; transportation: $600; personal expenses: $2,223. **Financial aid:** Priority filing date for institution's financial aid form: March 31. In 2009-2010, 55% of undergraduates applied for financial aid. Of those, 38% were determined to have financial need; 47% had their need fully met. Average financial aid package (proportion receiving): $14,658 (37%). Average amount of gift aid, such as scholarships or grants (proportion receiving): $8,953 (33%). Average amount of self-help aid, such as work study or loans (proportion receiving): $6,293 (24%). Average need-based loan (excluding PLUS or other private loans): $6,070. Among students who received need-based aid, the average percentage of need met: 71%. Among students who received aid based on merit, the average award (and the proportion receiving): $3,441 (5%). The average athletic scholarship (and the proportion receiving): $8,069 (0%). Average amount of debt of borrowers graduating in 2009: $21,276. Proportion who borrowed: 54%.

CAMPUS LIFE AND EXTRACURRICULAR ACTIVITIES

Campus housing available (% using): coed dorms (46%), women's dorms (18%), men's dorms (34%), apartment for single students, special housing for disabled students, special housing for international students, other housing options (2%). Students who live in college-owned, operated, or affiliated housing: 24%. **Student employment:** During the 2009-2010 academic year, 23% of undergraduates worked on campus. Average per-year earnings: $2,625. **Clubs and organizations:** Number of student organizations: 700. Activities include: campus ministries, choral groups, concert band, dance, drama/theater, international student organization, jazz band, literary magazine, marching band, music ensembles, musical theater, pep band, radio station, student government, student newspaper, student film society, symphony orchestra, television station, yearbook. Number of fraternities: 35; sororities: 25. Proportion of men in fraternities: 5%; of women in sororities: 12%. **Sports program (2009-2010):** Member of NCAA I. *Men's intercollegiate varsity sports:* baseball, basketball, cross country, football, golf, swimming, tennis, track and field (indoor), track and field (outdoor). *Women's intercollegiate varsity sports:* basketball, cross country, equestrian, golf, soccer, softball, swimming, tennis, track and field (indoor), track and field (outdoor), volleyball.

SERVICES AND FACILITIES

Basic services: women's center, placement service, day care, health service. **Remedial assistance:** study skills. **Counseling services:** minority student, career, personal, academic, older student, psychological. **For learning-disabled students:** School does not offer a structured program with separate admission and additional fees. Total undergraduates in learning-disabled program or receiving services: 713. Services include: reading machines, tape recorders, note-taking services, extended time for tests, priority registration, priority seating, substitution of courses, texts on tape, other. **Library:** Number of titles: 4,088,969; number of current serial subscriptions: 91,580. **Information technology resources:** Students are not required to lease or own a computer. Number of campus computers available to all students: 1,630. School has a wireless network. Approximate number of users that can be accommodated: 5,000. Proportion of college-owned housing units wired for high-speed internet access: 100%. **Campus safety:** Security services offered: 24-hour foot-and-vehicle patrols, late-night transport/escort service, 24-hour emergency telephones, lighted pathways/sidewalks, controlled dormitory access (key, security card, etc).

TRANSFER AND INTERNATIONAL STUDENTS

Transfer students: May apply for admission for the following academic terms: Fall, Spring, Summer. Applicants need a minimum number of credits to apply. For fall 2009: Transfer applications received: 4,273. Transfer applicants offered admission: 2,225. Transfer applicants enrolled: 1,533. **International students:** Number of foreign undergraduates: 574 (1% of student body). Number of countries represented: 125. Minimum TOEFL score required: 550 (paper); 80 (computer). Average TOEFL score: 633 (paper).

Texas A&M University–Commerce

- **Address:** PO Box 3011, Commerce, TX 75429
- **Website:** http://www.tamu-commerce.edu
- **Public**
- **Enrollment:** 4,096 full-time; 1,250 part-time

KEY STATS

✔ **U.S News College Ranking:** second tier, National Universities
✔ **SAT Score (25th/75th percentile):** 860-1090
✔ **Tuition:** 2010-2011: $5,500 in state, $14,040 out of state

Selectivity: Selective	**Room/board:** $7,232
Acceptance rate: 71%	**Average debt:** $21,881
Student/faculty ratio: 12/1	**Proportion who borrowed:** 74%

UNDERGRADUATE STUDENT BODY STATS

2009-2010 enrollment: 4,096 full-time; 1,250 part-time. Men: 38%; women: 62%. **Ethnic makeup:** African American: 19%; American-Indian: 1%; Asian American: 2%; Hispanic: 10%; White: 67%; International: 1%.

ADMISSIONS FACTS AND FIGURES

Phone: (903) 886-5106. **Email:** Admissions@tamu-commerce.edu. **Website:** http://www.tamu-commerce.edu. **Application deadlines for fall 2011:** Regular decision: August 1. Early decision: Not offered. Early action: Not offered.

Admission can be deferred. **Application fee:** $25. **To apply online, go to:** http://www7.tamu-commerce.edu/future_students.asp. **Admissions requirements/recommendations:** High school units required (recommended): English: 4; Mathematics: 3; Science: 2; Foreign language: (2); Social studies: 2; History: 2; Total units: 12. Tests: The college uses SAT or ACT scores in admissions decisions. Either SAT or ACT required. For admission to the fall 2011 entering class, the school will accept: ACT with or without writing accepted. Campus visit: Neither required nor recommended. Admissions interview: Neither required nor recommended. Off-campus interview: Not available. **Factors that count in admissions decisions:** *Academic:* Secondary school record: Very Important. Class rank: Very Important. Letters of recommendation: Not Considered. Standardized test scores: Very Important. Essay: Not Considered. *Nonacademic:* Interview: Not Considered. Extracurricular activities: Not Considered. Talent/ability: Not Considered. Character/personal qualities: Not Considered. Alumni/ae relationship: Not Considered. Geographical residence: Not Considered. State residency: Not Considered. Religious affiliation/commitment: Not Considered. Minority status: Not Considered. Volunteer work: Not Considered. Work experience: Considered. **Admissions statistics for the fall 2009 entering class:** Total applicants: 2,179. Total accepted: 1,547. Freshmen enrolled: 574; 5% were from out of state. Overall acceptance rate: 71%. **Credentials of fall 2009 freshmen:** 23% ranked in the top 10 percent of their high school class; 42% were in the top 25 percent; 69% were in the top half. (Proportion submitting class standing: 90%.) **Average high school grade point average:** 3.0. **First-year students who submitted SAT scores:** 70%. Scores (25/75 percentile): Critical Reading: 420-540, Math: 440-550, Combined: 860-1090. **First-year students submitting ACT scores:** 51%. Scores (25/75 percentile): English: 16-23, Math: 17-24, Composite: 18-24.

ACADEMICS

Year founded: 1889. **Academic calendar:** Semester. **Degrees offered:** bachelor's, master's, doctorate. **Major fields of study:** agriculture, agriculture operations, and related sciences; biological and biomedical sciences; business, management, marketing, and related support services; communication, journalism, and related programs; communications technologies/technicians and support services; computer and information sciences and support services; engineering technologies/technicians; English language and literature/letters; health professions and related clinical sciences; history; legal professions and studies; mathematics and statistics; multi/interdisciplinary studies; parks, recreation, leisure, and fitness studies; physical sciences; psychology; public administration and social service professions; security and protective services; social sciences; visual and performing arts. **Areas of required coursework:** humanities, mathematics, English (including composition), sciences (biological or physical), history. **Special academic programs:** cooperative (work-study plan) program, distance learning, double major, dual enrollment, honors program, independent study, internships, study abroad, teacher certificate program, weekend college, other. **Teacher certification offered in:** early childhood, special education, elementary, secondary. **Cooperative education programs:** agriculture, art, business, computer science, education, engineering, humanities, natural science, social/behavioral science, technologies. **Faculty and instruction (2009-2010):** Total instructional faculty: 329 full-time, 361 part-time (49% men; 51% women; 13% minorities). Student/faculty ratio: 12/1. Classes of fewer than 20 students: 67%; of 20 to 49 students: 28%; of 50 or more students: 5%. **Advanced Placement and International Baccalaureate credit:** AP tests may be used for: Credit and/or placement. Scores accepted: 3, 4, 5. International Baccalaureate exams may be used for: Placement only. **Freshmen returning for sophomore year:** 59%. **Graduation rates:** Four-year: 22%; five-year: 34%; six-year: 43%.

COSTS AND FINANCIAL AID

Financial aid office: (903) 886-5096. **Expenses (2010-2011):** Tuition and fees 2010-2011: $5,500 in state, $14,040 out of state; room/board: $7,232. Estimated books and supplies: $1,400; transportation: $1,500; personal expenses: $1,867. **Financial aid:** Priority filing date for institution's financial aid form: April 15. In 2009-2010, 82% of undergraduates applied for financial aid. Of those, 70% were determined to have financial need; 31% had their need fully met. Average financial aid package (proportion receiving): $9,608 (69%). Average amount of gift aid, such as scholarships or grants (proportion receiving): $7,113 (61%). Average amount of self-help aid, such as work study or loans (proportion receiving): $4,340 (55%). Average need-based loan (excluding PLUS or other private loans): $4,097. Among students who received need-based aid, the average percentage of need met: 64%. Among students who received aid based on merit, the average award (and the proportion receiving): $2,581 (7%). The average athletic scholarship (and the proportion receiving): $5,074 (2%). Average amount of debt of borrowers graduating in 2009: $21,881. Proportion who borrowed: 74%.

CAMPUS LIFE AND EXTRACURRICULAR ACTIVITIES

Campus housing available: coed dorms, women's dorms, men's dorms, sorority housing, fraternity housing, apartments for married students, special housing for international students. Students who live in college-owned, operated, or affiliated housing: 27%. Activities include: choral groups, concert band, dance, drama/theater, marching band, music ensembles, musical theater, pep band, radio station, student government, student newspaper. **Sports program (2009-2010):** Member of NCAA II.

SERVICES AND FACILITIES

Basic services: nonremedial tutoring, women's center, placement service, day care, health service, health insurance. **Remedial assistance:** reading, math, writing, study skills. **Counseling services:** career, personal, veteran student, academic, psychological. **For learning-disabled students:** School does not offer a structured program with separate admission and additional fees. Services include: remedial English, remedial reading, tape recorders, diagnostic testing service, untimed tests, tutors. **Information technology resources:** Students are not required to lease or own a computer. School has a wireless network. **Campus safety:** Security services offered: 24-hour foot-and-vehicle patrols, 24-hour emergency telephones, lighted pathways/sidewalks, controlled dormitory access (key, security card, etc).

TRANSFER AND INTERNATIONAL STUDENTS

Transfer students: May apply for admission for the following academic terms: Fall, Winter, Spring, Summer. Applicants need a minimum number of credits to apply. For fall 2009: Transfer applications received: 1,470. Transfer applicants offered admission: 1,330. Transfer applicants enrolled: 835. **International students:** Number of foreign undergraduates: 51 (1% of student body). Minimum TOEFL score required: 500 (paper); 175 (computer). Average TOEFL score: 550 (paper).

Texas A&M University–Corpus Christi

- **Address:** 6300 Ocean Drive, Corpus Christi, TX 78412-5503
- **Website:** http://www.tamucc.edu
- **Public**
- **Enrollment:** 5,826 full-time; 1,765 part-time

KEY STATS

✔ **U.S News College Ranking:** 59, Regional Universities (West)
✔ **SAT Score (25th/75th percentile):** 870-1090
✔ **Tuition:** 2010-2011: $6,514 in state, $15,814 out of state

Selectivity: Less selective	**Room/board:** $9,283
Acceptance rate: 85%	**Average debt:** $19,000
Student/faculty ratio: 19/1	**Proportion who borrowed:** 58%

UNDERGRADUATE STUDENT BODY STATS

2009-2010 enrollment: 5,826 full-time; 1,765 part-time. Men: 41%; women: 59%. **Ethnic makeup:** African American: 5%; American-Indian: 1%; Asian American: 3%; Hispanic: 41%; White: 48%; International: 3%.

ADMISSIONS FACTS AND FIGURES

Phone: (361) 825-2624. **Email:** admiss@tamucc.edu. **Website:** http://www.tamucc.edu. **Application deadlines for fall 2011:** Regular decision: July 1. Early decision: Not offered. Early action: Not offered. Admission cannot be deferred. **Application fee:** $25. **To apply online, go to:** http://www.apply-texas.org. **Admissions requirements/recommendations:** High school units required (recommended): English: 4; Mathematics: 3; Science: 3; Foreign language: 2; Social studies: 3; Total units: 15. Tests: The college uses SAT or ACT scores in admissions decisions. Either SAT or ACT required. For admission to the fall 2011 entering class, the school will accept: ACT with or without writing accepted. Campus visit: Recommended. Admissions interview: Neither required nor recommended. Off-campus interview: Not available. **Factors that count in admissions decisions:** *Academic:* Secondary school record: Very Important. Class rank: Very Important. Letters of recommendation: Considered. Standardized test scores: Important. Essay: Not Considered. *Nonacademic:* Interview: Not Considered. Extracurricular activities: Considered. Talent/ability: Considered. Character/personal qualities: Considered. Alumni/ae relationship: Not Considered. Geographical residence: Not Considered. State residency: Not Considered. Religious affiliation/commitment: Not Considered. Minority status: Not Considered. Volunteer work: Considered. Work experience: Considered. **Other schools with the greatest overlap in applicants:** Texas A&M University–College Station; Texas State University–San Marcos; University of Texas–Austin; University of Texas–San Antonio. **Admissions statistics for the fall 2009 entering class:** Total applicants: 4,744. Total accepted: 4,015. Freshmen enrolled: 1,308; 3% were from out of state. Overall acceptance rate: 85%. **Credentials of fall 2009 freshmen:** 14% ranked in the top 10 percent of their high school class; 45% were in the top 25 percent; 84% were in the top half. (Proportion submitting class standing: 98%.) **Average high school grade point average:** 3.3. **First-year students who submitted SAT scores:** 81%. Scores (25/75 percentile): Critical Reading: 430-540, Math: 440-550, Combined: 870-1090. **First-year students submitting ACT scores:** 50%. Scores (25/75 percentile): English: 16-22, Math: 17-23, Composite: 17-22.

ACADEMICS
Year founded: 1947. **Academic calendar:** Semester. **Degrees offered:** bachelor's, post-bachelor's certificate, master's, doctorate. **Most popular majors:** 13% multi/interdisciplinary studies, 10% nursing/registered nurse training (R.N., A.S.N., B.S.N., M.S.N.), 8% psychology, 7% communication studies/speech communication and rhetoric, 5% health and physical education. **Major fields of study:** biological and biomedical sciences; business, management, marketing, and related support services; communication, journalism, and related programs; computer and information sciences and support services; engineering technologies/technicians; English language and literature/letters; foreign languages, literatures, and linguistics; health professions and related clinical sciences; history; mathematics and statistics; multi/interdisciplinary studies; natural resources and conservation; parks, recreation, leisure, and fitness studies; physical sciences; psychology; security and protective services; social sciences; visual and performing arts. **Areas of required coursework:** arts/fine arts, computer literacy, mathematics, English (including composition), philosophy, foreign languages, sciences (biological or physical), history, social science. **Pre-professional programs:** pre-law, pre-dentistry, pre-medicine, pre-veterinary science, pre-optometry, pre-pharmacy. **Special academic programs (% participation):** cooperative (work-study plan) program (5%), distance learning (53%), double major (2%), dual enrollment (0%), honors program (1%), independent study (8%), internships (2%), study abroad (0%), teacher certificate program (21%). **Teacher certification offered in:** early childhood, special education, elementary, vo-tech, middle/junior high, secondary, bilingual/bicultural. **Cooperative education programs:** education, health professions. **Reserve Officers Training Corps (ROTC):** Army ROTC: Offered on campus. **Faculty and instruction (2009-2010):** Total instructional faculty: 328 full-time, 200 part-time (50% men; 50% women; 19% minorities). Full-time faculty with Ph.D. or other terminal degree: 81%. Student/faculty ratio: 19/1. Classes of fewer than 20 students: 23%; of 20 to 49 students: 65%; of 50 or more students: 11%. **Advanced Placement and International Baccalaureate credit:** AP tests may be used for: Credit only. Scores accepted: 3, 4, 5. **Freshmen returning for sophomore year:** 60%. **Graduation rates:** Four-year: 19%; five-year: 34%; six-year: 39%. **Graduate study:** 13% of students pursue further study immediately upon graduation; 18% within one year; 24% within five years. Fields in which graduates pursue further study: Master of Business Administration (MBA), 13%; education, 43%; arts and sciences, 21%.

COSTS AND FINANCIAL AID
Financial aid office: (361) 825-2338. **Expenses (2010-2011):** Tuition and fees 2010-2011: $6,514 in state, $15,814 out of state; room/board: $9,283. Estimated books and supplies: $1,185; transportation: $909; personal expenses: $1,408. **Financial aid:** Priority filing date for institution's financial aid form: March 31. In 2009-2010, 66% of undergraduates applied for financial aid. Of those, 55% were determined to have financial need; 11% had their need fully met. Average financial aid package (proportion receiving): $9,277 (53%). Average amount of gift aid, such as scholarships or grants (proportion receiving): $5,981 (42%). Average amount of self-help aid, such as work study or loans (proportion receiving): $4,509 (41%). Average need-based loan (excluding PLUS or other private loans): $4,280. Among students who received need-based aid, the average percentage of need met: 60%. Among students who received aid based on merit, the average award (and the proportion receiving): $2,173 (3%). The average athletic scholarship (and the proportion receiving): $7,726 (3%). Average amount of debt of borrowers graduating in 2009: $19,000. Proportion who borrowed: 58%.

CAMPUS LIFE AND EXTRACURRICULAR ACTIVITIES
Campus housing available (% using): coed dorms (44%), apartment for single students (54%), special housing for disabled students (2%). Students

who live in college-owned, operated, or affiliated housing: 18%. **Student employment:** During the 2009-2010 academic year, 12% of undergraduates worked on campus. Average per-year earnings: $5,500. **Clubs and organizations:** Number of student organizations: 130. Activities include: campus ministries, choral groups, concert band, dance, drama/theater, international student organization, jazz band, literary magazine, music ensembles, musical theater, opera, pep band, student government, student newspaper, symphony orchestra. Number of fraternities: 6; sororities: 5. Proportion of men in fraternities: 4%; of women in sororities: 5%. Average proportion of students who stay on campus on weekends: 40%. **Sports program (2009-2010):** Member of NCAA I. *Men's intercollegiate varsity sports:* baseball, basketball, cross country, tennis, track and field (indoor), track and field (outdoor). *Women's intercollegiate varsity sports:* basketball, cross country, golf, softball, tennis, track and field (indoor), track and field (outdoor), volleyball.

SERVICES AND FACILITIES
Basic services: nonremedial tutoring, women's center, placement service, health service. **Remedial assistance:** reading, math, writing, study skills. **Counseling services:** minority student, career, personal, veteran student, academic, psychological. **For learning-disabled students:** School does not offer a structured program with separate admission and additional fees. Services include: remedial math, remedial English, remedial reading, tape recorders, videotaped classes, note-taking services, oral tests, learning center, readers, extended time for tests, tutors, texts on tape. **Library:** Number of titles: 474,085; number of current serial subscriptions: 1,809. **Information technology resources:** Students are not required to lease or own a computer. Number of campus computers available to all students: 1,085. School has a wireless network. Approximate number of users that can be accommodated: 10,000. Proportion of college-owned housing units wired for high-speed internet access: 100%. **Campus safety:** Security services offered: 24-hour foot-and-vehicle patrols, late-night transport/escort service, 24-hour emergency telephones, lighted pathways/sidewalks, controlled dormitory access (key, security card, etc).

TRANSFER AND INTERNATIONAL STUDENTS
Transfer students: May apply for admission for the following academic terms: Fall, Spring, Summer. Applicants need a minimum number of credits to apply. For fall 2009: Transfer applications received: 1,735. Transfer applicants offered admission: 1,600. Transfer applicants enrolled: 906. **International students:** Number of foreign undergraduates: 237 (3% of student body). Number of countries represented: 27. Minimum TOEFL score required: 550 (paper); 213 (computer). Average TOEFL score: 584 (paper).

Texas A&M University–Kingsville

- **Address:** MSC 128, Kingsville, TX 78363
- **Website:** http://www.tamuk.edu
- **Public**
- **Enrollment:** 4,592 full-time; 1,690 part-time

KEY STATS
✔ **U.S News College Ranking:** second tier, National Universities
✔ **SAT or ACT Score (25th/75th percentile):** N/A
✔ **Tuition:** 2009-2010: $5,981 in state, $14,292 out of state
Selectivity: Selective   **Room/board:** $5,900
Acceptance rate: 86%   **Average debt:** N/A
Student/faculty ratio: N/A   **Proportion who borrowed:** N/A

UNDERGRADUATE STUDENT BODY STATS
2009-2010 enrollment: 4,592 full-time; 1,690 part-time. Men: 49%; women: 51%.

ADMISSIONS FACTS AND FIGURES
Phone: (361) 593-2315. **Email:** admissions@tamuk.edu. **Website:** http://www.tamuk.edu. **Application deadlines for fall 2011:** Regular decision: Rolling. Early decision: Not offered. Early action: Not offered. Admission can be deferred. **Application fee:** $15. **To apply online, go to:** http://www.tamuk.edu/general/applyonline.html. **Admissions requirements/recommendations:** High school units required (recommended): English: 4 (4); Mathematics: 3 (3); Science: 3 (3); Foreign language: 3 (3); Social studies: 4 (4); History: 3 (3); Academic electives: 3 (3); Total units: 24 (24). Tests: The college uses SAT or ACT scores in admissions decisions. Either SAT or ACT required. For admission to the fall 2011 entering class, the school will accept: ACT

with or without writing accepted. Campus visit: Recommended. Admissions interview: Neither required nor recommended. Off-campus interview: May be arranged. **Factors that count in admissions decisions:** *Academic:* Secondary school record: Considered. Class rank: Considered. Letters of recommendation: Not Considered. Standardized test scores: Important. Essay: Not Considered. *Nonacademic:* Interview: Not Considered. Extracurricular activities: Not Considered. Talent/ability: Not Considered. Character/personal qualities: Not Considered. Alumni/ae relationship: Not Considered. Geographical residence: Not Considered. State residency: Not Considered. Religious affiliation/commitment: Not Considered. Minority status: Not Considered. Volunteer work: Not Considered. Work experience: Not Considered. **Other schools with the greatest overlap in applicants:** Texas A&M University–College Station; Texas A&M University–Corpus Christi; Texas State University–San Marcos; University of Texas–Pan American. **Admissions statistics for the fall 2009 entering class:** Freshmen enrolled: 1,086; 2% were from out of state. Overall acceptance rate: 86%. **Credentials of fall 2009 freshmen:** 9% ranked in the top 10 percent of their high school class; 40% were in the top 25 percent.

ACADEMICS

Year founded: 1925. **Academic calendar:** Semester. **Degrees offered:** bachelor's, post-bachelor's certificate, master's, post-master's certificate, doctorate. **Major fields of study:** agriculture, agriculture operations, and related sciences; biological and biomedical sciences; business, management, marketing, and related support services; communication, journalism, and related programs; computer and information sciences and support services; education; engineering; engineering technologies/technicians; English language and literature/letters; family and consumer sciences/human sciences; foreign languages, literatures, and linguistics; health professions and related clinical sciences; history; mathematics and statistics; multi/interdisciplinary studies; natural resources and conservation; parks, recreation, leisure, and fitness studies; personal and culinary services; physical sciences; psychology; public administration and social service professions; security and protective services; social sciences; visual and performing arts. **Areas of required coursework:** arts/fine arts, humanities, computer literacy, mathematics, English (including composition), foreign languages, sciences (biological or physical), history, social science. **Pre-professional programs:** pre-law, pre-dentistry, pre-medicine, pre-veterinary science, pre-optometry, pre-pharmacy, other. **Special academic programs (% participation):** accelerated program (2%), cooperative (work-study plan) program (15%), cross-registration (2%), distance learning (1%), double major (2%), dual enrollment (2%), English as a Second Language (ESL) (1%), honors program (1%), internships (22%), liberal arts/career combination (4%), study abroad (1%), teacher certificate program (20%). **Teacher certification offered in:** early childhood, special education, elementary, middle/junior high, adult education, secondary, bilingual/bicultural. **Cooperative education programs:** agriculture, business, education, engineering, home economics. **Reserve Officers Training Corps (ROTC):** Army ROTC: Offered on campus. **Advanced Placement and International Baccalaureate credit:** AP tests may be used for: Credit only. Scores accepted: 3, 4, 5. International Baccalaureate exams may be used for: Credit only. **Freshmen returning for sophomore year:** 61%. **Graduation rates:** Four-year: 8%; five-year: 20%; six-year: 30%. **Graduate study:** 50% of students pursue further study immediately upon graduation; 55% within one year; 65% within five years.

COSTS AND FINANCIAL AID

Financial aid office: (361) 593-2173. **Expenses (2009-2010):** Tuition and fees 2009-2010: $5,981 in state, $14,292 out of state; room/board: $5,900. Estimated books and supplies: $1,200; transportation: $1,848; personal expenses: $2,636. **Financial aid:** Priority filing date for institution's financial aid form: April 15.

CAMPUS LIFE AND EXTRACURRICULAR ACTIVITIES

Campus housing available (% using): coed dorms (80%), women's dorms (10%), men's dorms (5%), apartment for single students (5%). Students who live in college-owned, operated, or affiliated housing: 40%. **Student employment:** During the 2009-2010 academic year, 18% of undergraduates worked on campus. Average per-year earnings: $1,752. **Clubs and organizations:** Number of student organizations: 200. Activities include: choral groups, concert band, dance, drama/theater, jazz band, literary magazine, marching band, music ensembles, musical theater, opera, pep band, radio station, student government, student newspaper, television station. Number of fraternities: 5; sororities: 5. Proportion of men in fraternities: 2%; of women in sororities: 2%. Average proportion of students who stay on campus on weekends: 10%. **Sports program (2009-2010):** Member of NCAA II.

SERVICES AND FACILITIES

Basic services: nonremedial tutoring, women's center, placement service, day care, health service, health insurance. **Remedial assistance:** reading, math, writing, study skills. **Counseling services:** minority student, career, military, personal, veteran student, academic, older student, psychological, birth control. **For learning-disabled students:** School does not offer a structured program with separate admission and additional fees. Services include: remedial math, remedial English, reading machines, remedial reading, tape recorders, other special classes, videotaped classes, diagnostic testing service, note-taking services, oral tests, learning center, readers, extended time for tests, tutors, other testing accommodations. **Library:** Number of titles: 750,000; number of current serial subscriptions: 44,000. **Information technology resources:** Students are not required to lease or own a computer. Number of campus computers available to all students: 600. School has a wireless network. Proportion of college-owned housing units wired for high-speed internet access: 99%. **Campus safety:** Security services offered: 24-hour foot-and-vehicle patrols, late-night transport/escort service, 24-hour emergency telephones, lighted pathways/sidewalks, controlled dormitory access (key, security card, etc).

TRANSFER AND INTERNATIONAL STUDENTS

Transfer students: May apply for admission for the following academic terms: Fall, Spring, Summer. Applicants need a minimum number of credits to apply. For fall 2009: Transfer applicants enrolled: 1,023. **International students:** Number of countries represented: 18. Minimum TOEFL score required: 500 (paper). Average TOEFL score: 567 (paper).

Texas Christian University

- **Address:** 2800 S. University Drive, Fort Worth, TX 76129
- **Website:** http://www.tcu.edu
- **Private; Religious affiliation:** Christian Church (Disciples of Christ)
- **Enrollment:** 7,326 full-time; 314 part-time

KEY STATS

✔ **U.S News College Ranking:** 99, National Universities
✔ **SAT Score (25th/75th percentile):** 1050-1280
✔ **Tuition:** 2010-2011: $30,048

Selectivity: More selective	**Room/board:** $10,010
Acceptance rate: 59%	**Average debt:** $32,357
Student/faculty ratio: 13/1	**Proportion who borrowed:** 43%

UNDERGRADUATE STUDENT BODY STATS

2009-2010 enrollment: 7,326 full-time; 314 part-time. Men: 41%; women: 59%. **Ethnic makeup:** African American: 5%; American-Indian: 1%; Asian American: 3%; Hispanic: 10%; White: 77%; International: 5%. **Religious preference:** Roman Catholic: 14%; Protestant: 1%; Jewish: 1%; Muslim: 1%; Hindu: 1%; Buddhist: 1%; No preference: 30%; Unknown: 1%; Christian Church (Disciples of Christ): 4%; Other: 46%.

ADMISSIONS FACTS AND FIGURES

Phone: (817) 257-7490. **Email:** frogmail@tcu.edu. **Website:** http://www.tcu.edu. **Application deadlines for fall 2011:** Regular decision: February 15; decision sent by April 1. Early decision: Not offered. Early action: Send application by: November 1; Decision sent by: January 1. Admission can be deferred. **Application fee:** $40. **To apply online, go to:** http://www.admissions.tcu.edu/apply/. **Admissions requirements/recommendations:** High school units required (recommended): English: 4 (4); Mathematics: 3 (4); Science: 3 (4); Foreign language: 2 (4); Social studies: 3 (4); Academic electives: 2 (0); Total units: 17 (20). Tests: The college uses SAT or ACT scores in admissions decisions. Either SAT or ACT required. For admission to the fall 2011 entering class, the school will accept ACT with writing recommended. Campus visit: Recommended. Admissions interview: Recommended. Off-campus interview: May be arranged. **Factors that count in admissions decisions:** *Academic:* Secondary school record: Very Important. Class rank: Very Important. Letters of recommendation: Very Important. Standardized test scores: Very Important. Essay: Very Important. *Nonacademic:* Interview: Considered. Extracurricular activities: Important. Talent/ability: Important. Character/personal qualities: Very Important. Alumni/ae relationship: Considered. Geographical residence: Important. State residency: Not Considered. Religious affiliation/commitment: Important. Minority status: Important. Volunteer work: Important. Work experience: Important. **Other schools with the greatest overlap in applicants:**

Baylor University; Southern Methodist University; Texas A&M University–College Station; Trinity University; University of Texas–Austin. **Admissions statistics for the fall 2009 entering class:** Total applicants: 11,953. Total accepted: 7,083. Freshmen enrolled: 1,823; 27% were from out of state. Overall acceptance rate: 59%. Non-early acceptance rate: 59%. **Size of waiting list:** 481 applicants; enrolled from waiting list: 152. **Credentials of fall 2009 freshmen:** 30% ranked in the top 10 percent of their high school class; 61% were in the top 25 percent; 90% were in the top half. (Proportion submitting class standing: 62%.) **First-year students who submitted SAT scores:** 59%. Scores (25/75 percentile): Critical Reading: 520-630, Math: 530-650, Combined: 1050-1280. **First-year students submitting ACT scores:** 41%. Scores (25/75 percentile): English: N/A, Math: N/A, Composite: 23-28.

ACADEMICS

Year founded: 1873. **Academic calendar:** Semester. **Degrees offered:** certificate, diploma, bachelor's, post-bachelor's certificate, master's, doctorate. **Most popular majors:** 25% business, management, marketing, and related support services, 19% communication, journalism, and related programs, 12% health professions and related clinical sciences, 8% education, 7% social sciences. **Major fields of study:** agriculture, agriculture operations, and related sciences; area, ethnic, cultural, and gender studies; biological and biomedical sciences; business, management, marketing, and related support services; communication, journalism, and related programs; computer and information sciences and support services; education; engineering; English language and literature/letters; foreign languages, literatures, and linguistics; health professions and related clinical sciences; history; liberal arts and sciences studies, and humanities; mathematics and statistics; multi/interdisciplinary studies; natural resources and conservation; parks, recreation, leisure, and fitness studies; philosophy and religious studies; physical sciences; psychology; public administration and social service professions; security and protective services; social sciences; theology and religious vocations; visual and performing arts. **Areas of required coursework:** arts/fine arts, humanities, mathematics, English (including composition), sciences (biological or physical), history, social science, other. **Pre-professional programs:** pre-law, pre-dentistry, pre-medicine, pre-veterinary science, pre-optometry, other. **Special academic programs:** accelerated program, cross-registration, distance learning, double major, dual enrollment, English as a Second Language (ESL), honors program, independent study, internships, liberal arts/career combination, study abroad, teacher certificate program. **Teacher certification offered in:** early childhood, special education, elementary, middle/junior high, secondary, bilingual/bicultural. **Reserve Officers Training Corps (ROTC):** Army ROTC: Offered on campus; Air Force ROTC: Offered on campus. **Faculty and instruction (2009-2010):** Total instructional faculty: 523 full-time, 276 part-time (55% men; 45% women; 10% minorities). Full-time faculty with Ph.D. or other terminal degree: 84%. Student/faculty ratio: 13/1. Classes of fewer than 20 students: 42%; of 20 to 49 students: 50%; of 50 or more students: 8%. **Advanced Placement and International Baccalaureate credit:** AP tests may be used for: Credit only. Scores accepted: 3, 4, 5. International Baccalaureate exams may be used for: Credit only. **Freshmen returning for sophomore year:** 85%. **Graduation rates:** Four-year: 55%; five-year: 71%; six-year: 74%. **Graduate study:** 27% of students pursue further study within one year. Fields in which graduates pursue further study: Master of Business Administration (MBA), 16%; law, 9%; medicine, 14%; dentistry, 1%; engineering, 2%; theology (or the seminary), 1%; education, 13%; arts and sciences, 10%.

COSTS AND FINANCIAL AID

Financial aid office: (817) 257-7858. **Expenses (2010-2011):** Tuition and fees 2010-2011: $30,048; room/board: $10,010. Estimated books and supplies: $1,000; transportation: $450; personal expenses: $1,500. **Financial aid:** Priority filing date for institution's financial aid form: May 1; deadline: May 1. In 2009-2010, 52% of undergraduates applied for financial aid. Of those, 42% were determined to have financial need; 29% had their need fully met. Average financial aid package (proportion receiving): $20,647 (42%). Average amount of gift aid, such as scholarships or grants (proportion receiving): $17,440 (39%). Average amount of self-help aid, such as work study or loans (proportion receiving): $5,660 (33%). Average need-based loan (excluding PLUS or other private loans): $4,368. Among students who received need-based aid, the average percentage of need met: 71%. Among students who received aid based on merit, the average award (and the proportion receiving): $10,715 (25%). The average athletic scholarship (and the proportion receiving): $22,842 (3%). Average amount of debt of borrowers graduating in 2009: $32,357. Proportion who borrowed: 43%.

CAMPUS LIFE AND EXTRACURRICULAR ACTIVITIES

Campus housing available: coed dorms, women's dorms, men's dorms, sorority housing, fraternity housing, apartment for single students, special housing for disabled students, other housing options. Students who live in college-owned, operated, or affiliated housing: 47%. **Clubs and organizations:** Number of student organizations: 207. Activities include: campus ministries, choral groups, concert band, dance, drama/theater, international student organization, jazz band, literary magazine, marching band, model UN, music ensembles, musical theater, opera, pep band, radio station, student government, student newspaper, television station, yearbook. Number of fraternities: 15; sororities: 18. Proportion of men in fraternities: 38%; of women in sororities: 42%. Average proportion of students who stay on campus on weekends: 67%. **Sports program (2009-2010):** Member of NCAA I. **Men's intercollegiate varsity sports:** baseball, basketball, cross country, football, golf, swimming, tennis, track and field (indoor), track and field (outdoor). **Women's intercollegiate varsity sports:** basketball, cross country, equestrian, golf, rifle, soccer, swimming, tennis, track and field (indoor), track and field (outdoor), volleyball.

SERVICES AND FACILITIES

Basic services: nonremedial tutoring, women's center, health service, health insurance. **Counseling services:** minority student, career, military, personal, veteran student, academic, older student, psychological, birth control, religious. **For learning-disabled students:** School does not offer a structured program with separate admission and additional fees. Total undergraduates in learning-disabled program or receiving services: 101. Services include: tape recorders, extended time for tests, priority seating, other. **Library:** Number of titles: 1,415,044; number of current serial subscriptions: 68,131. **Information technology resources:** Students are not required to lease or own a computer. Number of campus computers available to all students: 1,400. School has a wireless network. Approximate number of users that can be accommodated: 10,000. Proportion of college-owned housing units wired for high-speed internet access: 100%. **Campus safety:** Security services offered: 24-hour foot-and-vehicle patrols, late-night transport/escort service, 24-hour emergency telephones, lighted pathways/sidewalks, student patrols, controlled dormitory access (key, security card, etc).

TRANSFER AND INTERNATIONAL STUDENTS

Transfer students: May apply for admission for the following academic terms: Fall, Spring, Summer. Applicants do not need a minimum number of credits to apply. For fall 2009: Transfer applications received: 1,553. Transfer applicants offered admission: 796. Transfer applicants enrolled: 407. **International students:** Number of foreign undergraduates: 380 (5% of student body). Number of countries represented: 73. Minimum TOEFL score required: 550 (paper); 213 (computer).

Texas College

- **Address:** 2404 N. Grand Avenue, Tyler, TX 75702
- **Website:** http://www.texascollege.edu
- **Private; Religious affiliation:** Christian Methodist Episcopal Church
- **Enrollment:** 910 full-time; 26 part-time

KEY STATS

✔ **U.S News College Ranking:** Unranked, Regional Colleges (West)
✔ **ACT Score:** 16
✔ **Tuition:** 2010-2011: $9,490

Selectivity: N/A	Room/board: $6,600
Acceptance rate: N/A	Average debt: $18,735
Student/faculty ratio: 24/1	Proportion who borrowed: 92%

UNDERGRADUATE STUDENT BODY STATS

2009-2010 enrollment: 910 full-time; 26 part-time. Men: 55%; women: 45%. **Ethnic makeup:** African American: 83%; Hispanic: 12%; White: 3%; International: 1%. **Religious preference:** Roman Catholic: 8%; Protestant: 42%; Muslim: 1%; No preference: 9%; Unknown: 37%; Christian Methodist Episcopal Church: 3%.

ADMISSIONS FACTS AND FIGURES

Phone: (903) 593-8311. **Email:** cmarshall-biggins@texascollege.edu. **Website:** http://www.texascollege.edu. **Application deadlines for fall 2011:** Regular decision: Rolling. Early decision: Not offered. Early action: Not offered. Admission cannot be deferred. **Application fee:** $20. **Admissions require-**

ments/recommendations: High school units required (recommended): English: 4 (4); Mathematics: 2 (2); Science: 2 (2); Foreign language: 0 (0); Social studies: 2 (2); History: 0 (0); Academic electives: 6 (6); Total units: 16 (16). Tests: The college does not use SAT or ACT scores in admissions decisions. Neither SAT nor ACT required. Campus visit: Recommended. Admissions interview: Recommended. Off-campus interview: May be arranged. **Factors that count in admissions decisions:** *Academic:* Secondary school record: Not Considered. Class rank: Not Considered. Letters of recommendation: Not Considered. Standardized test scores: Not Considered. Essay: Not Considered. *Nonacademic:* Interview: Not Considered. Extracurricular activities: Not Considered. Talent/ability: Not Considered. Character/personal qualities: Not Considered. Alumni/ae relationship: Not Considered. Geographical residence: Not Considered. State residency: Not Considered. Religious affiliation/commitment: Not Considered. Minority status: Not Considered. Volunteer work: Not Considered. Work experience: Not Considered. **Admissions statistics for the fall 2009 entering class:** Freshmen enrolled: 224; 14% were from out of state. **Average high school grade point average:** 2.9. **First-year students who submitted SAT scores:** 34%. **First-year students submitting ACT scores:** 39%. Scores (25/75 percentile): English: N/A, Math: N/A, Composite: N/A.

ACADEMICS

Year founded: 1894. **Academic calendar:** Semester. **Degrees offered:** associate, bachelor's, post-bachelor's certificate. **Most popular majors:** 56% business administration and management, 15% health and physical education, 12% biology, 4% social work, 4% sociology. **Major fields of study:** biological and biomedical sciences; business, management, marketing, and related support services; computer and information sciences and support services; education; English language and literature/letters; history; liberal arts and sciences studies, and humanities; mathematics and statistics; parks, recreation, leisure, and fitness studies; philosophy and religious studies; public administration and social service professions; social sciences; visual and performing arts. **Areas of required coursework:** arts/fine arts, computer literacy, mathematics, English (including composition), foreign languages, sciences (biological or physical), history, social science, other. **Special academic programs:** accelerated program, distance learning, double major, dual enrollment, independent study, internships, teacher certificate program. **Teacher certification offered in:** early childhood, elementary, middle/junior high, secondary. **Faculty and instruction (2009-2010):** Total instructional faculty: 34 full-time, 17 part-time (57% men; 43% women; 76% minorities). Full-time faculty with Ph.D. or other terminal degree: 35%. Student/faculty ratio: 24/1. Classes of fewer than 20 students: 60%; of 20 to 49 students: 23%; of 50 or more students: 17%. **Advanced Placement and International Baccalaureate credit:** AP tests may be used for: Credit only. Scores accepted: 3. **Freshmen returning for sophomore year:** 47%. **Graduation rates:** Four-year: 2%; five-year: 6%; six-year: 20%. **Graduate study:** Fields in which graduates pursue further study: Master of Business Administration (MBA), 25%; law, 1%.

COSTS AND FINANCIAL AID

Financial aid office: (903) 593-8311. **Expenses (2010-2011):** Tuition and fees 2010-2011: $9,490; room/board: $6,600. Estimated books and supplies: $2,300; transportation: $650; personal expenses: $0. **Financial aid:** Priority filing date for institution's financial aid form: June 1. In 2009-2010, 89% of undergraduates applied for financial aid. Of those, 87% were determined to have financial need; 4% had their need fully met. Average financial aid package (proportion receiving): $9,402 (86%). Average amount of gift aid, such as scholarships or grants (proportion receiving): $6,375 (82%). Average amount of self-help aid, such as work study or loans (proportion receiving): $3,590 (79%). Average need-based loan (excluding PLUS or other private loans): $3,304. Among students who received need-based aid, the average percentage of need met: 58%. Among students who received aid based on merit, the average award (and the proportion receiving): $3,099 (3%). The average athletic scholarship (and the proportion receiving): $0 (0%). Average amount of debt of borrowers graduating in 2009: $18,735. Proportion who borrowed: 92%.

CAMPUS LIFE AND EXTRACURRICULAR ACTIVITIES

Campus housing available: women's dorms, men's dorms. **Student employment:** During the 2009-2010 academic year, 0% of undergraduates worked on campus. Activities include: campus ministries, choral groups, concert band, marching band, music ensembles, student government, yearbook. Number of fraternities: 4; sororities: 3. Proportion of men in fraternities: 5%; of women in sororities: 4%. Average proportion of students who stay on campus on weekends: 20%. **Sports program (2009-2010):** Member of NAIA. *Men's intercollegiate varsity sports:* baseball, basketball, football, soccer, track and field (outdoor). *Women's intercollegiate varsity sports:* basketball, soccer, softball, track and field (outdoor), volleyball.

SERVICES AND FACILITIES

Basic services: nonremedial tutoring, health service, health insurance. **Remedial assistance:** reading, math, writing, study skills. **Counseling services:** career, personal, academic, religious. **For learning-disabled students:** School does not offer a structured program with separate admission and additional fees. Total undergraduates in learning-disabled program or receiving services: 1. Services include: remedial math, remedial English, remedial reading, diagnostic testing service, untimed tests, oral tests, learning center, extended time for tests, tutors, take home exams. **Library:** Number of titles: 80,500; number of current serial subscriptions: 71. **Information technology resources:** Students are not required to lease or own a computer. Number of campus computers available to all students: 108. School has a wireless network. Proportion of college-owned housing units wired for high-speed internet access: 100%. **Campus safety:** Security services offered: 24-hour foot-and-vehicle patrols, 24-hour emergency telephones, lighted pathways/sidewalks.

TRANSFER AND INTERNATIONAL STUDENTS

Transfer students: May apply for admission for the following academic terms: Fall, Spring, Summer. Applicants do not need a minimum number of credits to apply. For fall 2009: Transfer applicants enrolled: 167. **International students:** Number of foreign undergraduates: 9 (1% of student body). Minimum TOEFL score required: 500 (paper).

Texas Lutheran University

- **Address:** 1000 W. Court, Seguin, TX 78155-5999
- **Website:** http://www.tlu.edu
- **Private; Religious affiliation:** Evangelical Lutheran Church in America
- **Enrollment:** 1,305 full-time; 82 part-time

KEY STATS

✔ **U.S News College Ranking:** second tier, National Liberal Arts Colleges
✔ **SAT Score (25th/75th percentile):** 900-1120
✔ **Tuition:** 2010-2011: $22,890

Selectivity: Selective	**Room/board:** $7,540	
Acceptance rate: 66%	**Average debt:** $29,200	
Student/faculty ratio: 15/1	**Proportion who borrowed:** 63%	

UNDERGRADUATE STUDENT BODY STATS

2009-2010 enrollment: 1,305 full-time; 82 part-time. Men: 48%; women: 52%. **Ethnic makeup:** African American: 10%; Asian American: 1%; Hispanic: 23%; White: 64%; International: 1%. **Religious preference:** Roman Catholic: 19%; Protestant: 28%; No preference: 1%; Unknown: 23%; Evangelical Lutheran Church in America: 19%.

ADMISSIONS FACTS AND FIGURES

Phone: (800) 771-8521. **Email:** admissions@tlu.edu. **Website:** http://www.tlu.edu. **Application deadlines for fall 2011:** Regular decision: Rolling. Early decision: Not offered. Early action: Not offered. Admission can be deferred. **Application fee:** $25. **To apply online, go to:** http://www.tlu.edu/apply. **Admissions requirements/recommendations:** High school units required (recommended): English: 4 (4); Mathematics: 3 (4); Science: 3 (4); Foreign language: 2 (3); Social studies: 3 (4); History: 0 (0); Academic electives: 0 (0); Total units: 17 (23). Tests: The college uses SAT or ACT scores in admissions decisions. Either SAT or ACT required. For admission to the fall 2011 entering class, the school will accept: ACT with or without writing accepted. Campus visit: Recommended. Admissions interview: Recommended. Off-campus interview: May be arranged. **Factors that count in admissions decisions:** *Academic:* Secondary school record: Very Important. Class rank: Very Important. Letters of recommendation: Very Important. Standardized test scores: Very Important. Essay: Very Important. *Nonacademic:* Interview: Important. Extracurricular activities: Considered. Talent/ability: Important. Character/personal qualities: Important. Alumni/ae relationship: Not Considered. Geographical residence: Not Considered. State residency: Not Considered. Religious affiliation/commitment: Not Considered. Minority status: Not Considered. Volunteer work: Important. Work experience: Considered. **Other schools with the greatest overlap in applicants:** Baylor University; Texas A&M University–College Station; Texas State University–San Marcos; University of Texas–Austin; University of

Texas–San Antonio. **Admissions statistics for the fall 2009 entering class:** Total applicants: 1,070. Total accepted: 711. Freshmen enrolled: 346; 3% were from out of state. Overall acceptance rate: 66%. **Size of waiting list:** 0 applicants; enrolled from waiting list: 0. **Credentials of fall 2009 freshmen:** 22% ranked in the top 10 percent of their high school class; 52% were in the top 25 percent; 84% were in the top half. (Proportion submitting class standing: 92%.) **Average high school grade point average:** 3.5. **First-year students who submitted SAT scores:** 88%. Scores (25/75 percentile): Critical Reading: 440-550, Math: 460-570, Combined: 900-1120. **First-year students submitting ACT scores:** 48%. Scores (25/75 percentile): English: N/A, Math: N/A, Composite: 18-23.

ACADEMICS

Year founded: 1891. **Academic calendar:** Semester. **Degrees offered:** bachelor's. **Most popular majors:** 31% business, management, marketing, and related support services, 16% parks, recreation, leisure, and fitness studies, 8% biological and biomedical sciences, 8% education. **Major fields of study:** biological and biomedical sciences; business, management, marketing, and related support services; communication, journalism, and related programs; computer and information sciences and support services; education; English language and literature/letters; foreign languages, literatures, and linguistics; health professions and related clinical sciences; history; mathematics and statistics; parks, recreation, leisure, and fitness studies; philosophy and religious studies; physical sciences; psychology; social sciences; theology and religious vocations; visual and performing arts. **Areas of required coursework:** arts/fine arts, humanities, computer literacy, mathematics, English (including composition), philosophy, foreign languages, sciences (biological or physical), history, social science, other. **Pre-professional programs:** pre-law, pre-dentistry, pre-medicine, pre-theology, pre-veterinary science, pre-pharmacy, other. **Special academic programs (% participation):** double major (16%), dual enrollment, honors program (9%), independent study (13%), internships (26%), study abroad (21%), teacher certificate program (10%). **Teacher certification offered in:** elementary, middle/junior high, secondary. **Reserve Officers Training Corps (ROTC):** Army ROTC: Offered at cooperating institution (Texas State University–San Marcos); Air Force ROTC: Offered at cooperating institution (Texas State University–San Marcos). **Faculty and instruction (2009-2010):** Total instructional faculty: 68 full-time, 66 part-time (54% men; 46% women; 13% minorities). Full-time faculty with Ph.D. or other terminal degree: 79%. Student/faculty ratio: 15/1. Classes of fewer than 20 students: 55%; of 20 to 49 students: 43%; of 50 or more students: 1%. **Advanced Placement and International Baccalaureate credit:** AP tests may be used for: Placement only. Scores accepted: 3, 4, 5. International Baccalaureate exams may be used for: Placement only. **Freshmen returning for sophomore year:** 68%. **Graduation rates:** Four-year: 31%; five-year: 47%; six-year: 49%.

COSTS AND FINANCIAL AID

Financial aid office: (830) 372-8075. **Expenses (2010-2011):** Tuition and fees 2010-2011: $22,890; room/board: $7,540. Estimated books and supplies: $950; transportation: $1,300; personal expenses: $960. **Financial aid:** Priority filing date for institution's financial aid form: March 1. In 2009-2010, 83% of undergraduates applied for financial aid. Of those, 73% were determined to have financial need; 37% had their need fully met. Average financial aid package (proportion receiving): $18,482 (73%). Average amount of gift aid, such as scholarships or grants (proportion receiving): $13,472 (72%). Average amount of self-help aid, such as work study or loans (proportion receiving): $8,957 (59%). Average need-based loan (excluding PLUS or other private loans): $4,844. Among students who received need-based aid, the average percentage of need met: 37%. Among students who received aid based on merit, the average award (and the proportion receiving): $8,785 (20%). The average athletic scholarship (and the proportion receiving): $0 (0%). Average amount of debt of borrowers graduating in 2009: $29,200. Proportion who borrowed: 63%.

CAMPUS LIFE AND EXTRACURRICULAR ACTIVITIES

Campus housing available (% using): coed dorms (30%), women's dorms (26%), men's dorms (21%), apartments for married students (1%), apartment for single students (22%). Students who live in college-owned, operated, or affiliated housing: 62%. **Student employment:** During the 2009-2010 academic year, 25% of undergraduates worked on campus. Average per-year earnings: $3,304. **Clubs and organizations:** Number of student organizations: 50. Activities include: campus ministries, choral groups, concert band, dance, drama/theater, international student organization, jazz band, literary magazine, music ensembles, musical theater, pep band, student government, student newspaper. Number of fraternities: 4; sororities: 4. Proportion of men in fraternities: 10%; of women in sororities: 14%.

Average proportion of students who stay on campus on weekends: 40%. **Sports program (2009-2010):** Member of NCAA III. *Men's intercollegiate varsity sports:* baseball, basketball, football, golf, soccer, tennis. *Women's intercollegiate varsity sports:* basketball, cross country, golf, soccer, softball, tennis, track and field (indoor), track and field (outdoor), volleyball.

SERVICES AND FACILITIES

Basic services: nonremedial tutoring, women's center, placement service, health service, other. **Remedial assistance:** reading, math, writing, study skills, other. **Counseling services:** career, personal, veteran student, academic, psychological, birth control, religious. **For learning-disabled students:** School does not offer a structured program with separate admission and additional fees. Total undergraduates in learning-disabled program or receiving services: 12. Services include: reading machines, tape recorders, note-taking services, oral tests, extended time for tests, tutors, priority registration, priority seating, other testing accommodations. **Library:** Number of titles: 172,147; number of current serial subscriptions: 543. **Information technology resources:** Students are not required to lease or own a computer. Number of campus computers available to all students: 222. School has a wireless network. Approximate number of users that can be accommodated: 600. Proportion of college-owned housing units wired for high-speed internet access: 100%. **Campus safety:** Security services offered: 24-hour foot-and-vehicle patrols, late-night transport/escort service, 24-hour emergency telephones, lighted pathways/sidewalks, controlled dormitory access (key, security card, etc).

TRANSFER AND INTERNATIONAL STUDENTS

Transfer students: May apply for admission for the following academic terms: Fall, Spring, Summer. Applicants do not need a minimum number of credits to apply. For fall 2009: Transfer applications received: 185. Transfer applicants offered admission: 118. Transfer applicants enrolled: 82. **International students:** Number of foreign undergraduates: 19 (1% of student body). Number of countries represented: 8. Minimum TOEFL score required: 550 (paper); 213 (computer). Average TOEFL score: 585 (paper).

Texas Southern University

- **Address:** 3100 Cleburne, Houston, TX 77004
- **Website:** http://www.tsu.edu
- **Public**
- **Enrollment:** N/A

KEY STATS
✔ **U.S News College Ranking:** Unranked, Regional Universities (West)
✔ **SAT or ACT Score (25th/75th percentile):** N/A
✔ **Tuition:** 2009-2010: $6,401 in state, $14,711 out of state

Selectivity: N/A	Room/board: $8,706
Acceptance rate: N/A	Average debt: $35,304
Student/faculty ratio: N/A	Proportion who borrowed: 39%

Texas State University–San Marcos

- **Address:** 601 University Drive, San Marcos, TX 78666
- **Website:** http://www.txstate.edu
- **Public**
- **Enrollment:** 21,215 full-time; 4,787 part-time

KEY STATS
✔ **U.S News College Ranking:** 40, Regional Universities (West)
✔ **SAT Score (25th/75th percentile):** 970-1160
✔ **Tuition:** 2010-2011: $7,838 in state, $17,138 out of state

Selectivity: Selective	Room/board: $6,810
Acceptance rate: 76%	Average debt: $19,757
Student/faculty ratio: 20/1	Proportion who borrowed: 58%

UNDERGRADUATE STUDENT BODY STATS
2009-2010 enrollment: 21,215 full-time; 4,787 part-time. Men: 45%; women: 55%. **Ethnic makeup:** African American: 6%; American-Indian: 1%; Asian American: 2%; Hispanic: 24%; White: 66%; International: 1%. **Religious preference:** Roman Catholic: 34%; Protestant: 64%; Other: 2%.

ADMISSIONS FACTS AND FIGURES

Phone: (512) 245-2364. **Email:** admissions@txstate.edu. **Website:** http://www.txstate.edu. **Application deadlines for fall 2011:** Regular decision: May 1. Early decision: Not offered. Early action: Not offered. Admission can be deferred. **Application fee:** $60. **To apply online, go to:** http://www.admission.txstate.edu/index.htm. **Admissions requirements/recommendations:** High school units required (recommended): English: 4 (4); Mathematics: 3 (4); Science: 3 (4); Foreign language: 2 (3); Social studies: 4 (4); Academic electives: 4 (3); Total units: 24 (26). Tests: The college uses SAT or ACT scores in admissions decisions. Either SAT or ACT required. For admission to the fall 2011 entering class, the school will accept: ACT with writing required. Campus visit: Required. Admissions interview: Neither required nor recommended. Off-campus interview: Not available. **Factors that count in admissions decisions:** *Academic:* Secondary school record: Considered. Class rank: Very Important. Letters of recommendation: Not Considered. Standardized test scores: Very Important. Essay: Considered. *Nonacademic:* Interview: Not Considered. Extracurricular activities: Not Considered. Talent/ability: Considered. Character/personal qualities: Not Considered. Alumni/ae relationship: Not Considered. Geographical residence: Not Considered. State residency: Not Considered. Religious affiliation/commitment: Not Considered. Minority status: Not Considered. Volunteer work: Not Considered. Work experience: Not Considered. **Other schools with the greatest overlap in applicants:** Texas A&M University–College Station; Texas Tech University; University of North Texas; University of Texas–Austin; University of Texas–San Antonio. **Admissions statistics for the fall 2009 entering class:** Total applicants: 12,172. Total accepted: 9,211. Freshmen enrolled: 3,667; 2% were from out of state. Overall acceptance rate: 76%. **Credentials of fall 2009 freshmen:** 14% ranked in the top 10 percent of their high school class; 52% were in the top 25 percent; 92% were in the top half. (Proportion submitting class standing: 98%.) **First-year students who submitted SAT scores:** 74%. Scores (25/75 percentile): Critical Reading: 480-570, Math: 490-590, Combined: 970-1160. **First-year students submitting ACT scores:** 25%. Scores (25/75 percentile): English: 20-25, Math: 20-25, Composite: 21-25.

ACADEMICS

Year founded: 1899. **Academic calendar:** Semester. **Degrees offered:** bachelor's, post-bachelor's certificate, master's, doctorate. **Most popular majors:** 9% multi/interdisciplinary studies, 6% business administration and management, 6% psychology, 5% health and physical education, 5% marketing/marketing management. **Major fields of study:** agriculture, agriculture operations, and related sciences; architecture and related services; area, ethnic, cultural, and gender studies; biological and biomedical sciences; business, management, marketing, and related support services; communication, journalism, and related programs; communications technologies/technicians and support services; computer and information sciences and support services; engineering; engineering technologies/technicians; English language and literature/letters; family and consumer sciences/human sciences; foreign languages, literatures, and linguistics; health professions and related clinical sciences; history; mathematics and statistics; multi/interdisciplinary studies; natural resources and conservation; parks, recreation, leisure, and fitness studies; philosophy and religious studies; physical sciences; psychology; public administration and social service professions; security and protective services; social sciences; visual and performing arts. **Areas of required coursework:** humanities, mathematics, English (including composition), philosophy, sciences (biological or physical), history, social science, other. **Pre-professional programs:** pre-law, pre-dentistry, pre-medicine, pre-veterinary science, pre-pharmacy, other. **Special academic programs (% participation):** cross-registration, distance learning (18%), double major (2%), dual enrollment (.056%), English as a Second Language (ESL) (.4%), exchange student program (domestic), honors program (1%), independent study, internships, study abroad (3.2%), teacher certificate program (16%), weekend college. **Teacher certification offered in:** early childhood, special education, elementary, vo-tech, secondary, bilingual/bicultural. **Cooperative education programs:** agriculture, home economics, technologies, vocational arts. **Reserve Officers Training Corps (ROTC):** Army ROTC: Offered on campus; Air Force ROTC: Offered on campus. **Faculty and instruction (2009-2010):** Total instructional faculty: 1,017 full-time, 454 part-time (53% men; 47% women; 17% minorities). Full-time faculty with Ph.D. or other terminal degree: 77%. Student/faculty ratio: 20/1. Classes of fewer than 20 students: 18%; of 20 to 49 students: 64%; of 50 or more students: 18%. **Advanced Placement and International Baccalaureate credit:** AP tests may be used for: Credit only. International Baccalaureate exams may be used for: Credit only. **Freshmen returning for sophomore year:** 77%. **Graduation rates:** Four-year: 24%; five-year: 48%; six-year: 55%. **Graduate study:** 26% of students pursue further study within one year. Fields in which graduates pursue further study: Master of Business Administration (MBA), 17%; law, 5%; medicine, 9%; dentistry, 1%; engineering, 1%; theology (or the seminary), 1%; education, 15%; arts and sciences, 27%; veterinary medicine, 1%.

COSTS AND FINANCIAL AID

Financial aid office: (512) 245-2315. **Expenses (2010-2011):** Tuition and fees 2010-2011: $7,838 in state, $17,138 out of state; room/board: $6,810. Estimated books and supplies: $1,050; transportation: $950; personal expenses: $2,670. **Financial aid:** Priority filing date for institution's financial aid form: April 1. In 2009-2010, 69% of undergraduates applied for financial aid. Of those, 54% were determined to have financial need; 6% had their need fully met. Average financial aid package (proportion receiving): $13,634 (52%). Average amount of gift aid, such as scholarships or grants (proportion receiving): $6,374 (39%). Average amount of self-help aid, such as work study or loans (proportion receiving): $4,042 (43%). Average need-based loan (excluding PLUS or other private loans): $4,438. Among students who received need-based aid, the average percentage of need met: 65%. Among students who received aid based on merit, the average award (and the proportion receiving): $2,611 (2%). The average athletic scholarship (and the proportion receiving): $5,189 (1%). Average amount of debt of borrowers graduating in 2009: $19,757. Proportion who borrowed: 58%.

CAMPUS LIFE AND EXTRACURRICULAR ACTIVITIES

Campus housing available (% using): coed dorms (75%), women's dorms (14%), men's dorms (1%), sorority housing, fraternity housing, apartments for married students (1%), apartment for single students (9%), special housing for disabled students. Students who live in college-owned, operated, or affiliated housing: 24%. **Student employment:** During the 2009-2010 academic year, 7% of undergraduates worked on campus. Average per-year earnings: $5,272. **Clubs and organizations:** Number of student organizations: 307. Activities include: choral groups, concert band, dance, drama/theater, jazz band, literary magazine, marching band, music ensembles, musical theater, opera, pep band, radio station, student government, student newspaper, student film society, symphony orchestra, yearbook. Number of fraternities: 13; sororities: 7. Proportion of men in fraternities: 5%; of women in sororities: 5%. **Sports program (2009-2010):** Member of NCAA I. *Men's intercollegiate varsity sports:* baseball, basketball, cross country, football, golf, track and field (indoor), track and field (outdoor). *Women's intercollegiate varsity sports:* basketball, cross country, golf, soccer, softball, tennis, track and field (indoor), track and field (outdoor), volleyball.

SERVICES AND FACILITIES

Basic services: nonremedial tutoring, women's center, placement service, health service, health insurance. **Remedial assistance:** reading, math, writing, study skills. **Counseling services:** minority student, career, military, personal, veteran student, academic, psychological, birth control. **For learning-disabled students:** School does not offer a structured program with separate admission and additional fees. Services include: remedial math, remedial English, reading machines, remedial reading, tape recorders, diagnostic testing service, untimed tests, note-taking services, oral tests, learning center, readers, extended time for tests, tutors. **Library:** Number of titles: 1,543,562; number of current serial subscriptions: 14,764. **Information technology resources:** Students are not required to lease or own a computer. Number of campus computers available to all students: 1,792. School has a wireless network. Approximate number of users that can be accommodated: 6,000. Proportion of college-owned housing units wired for high-speed internet access: 100%. **Campus safety:** Security services offered: 24-hour foot-and-vehicle patrols, late-night transport/escort service, 24-hour emergency telephones, lighted pathways/sidewalks, student patrols, controlled dormitory access (key, security card, etc).

TRANSFER AND INTERNATIONAL STUDENTS

Transfer students: May apply for admission for the following academic terms: Fall, Spring, Summer. Applicants need a minimum number of credits to apply. For fall 2009: Transfer applications received: 4,983. Transfer applicants offered admission: 4,441. Transfer applicants enrolled: 3,299. **International students:** Number of foreign undergraduates: 159 (1% of student body). Number of countries represented: 41. Minimum TOEFL score required: 550 (paper); 213 (computer).

Texas Tech University

- **Address:** Box 45005, Lubbock, TX 79409
- **Website:** http://www.ttu.edu
- **Public**
- **Enrollment:** 22,061 full-time; 2,175 part-time

KEY STATS

✔ **U.S News College Ranking:** 159, National Universities
✔ **SAT Score (25th/75th percentile):** 990-1200
✔ **Tuition:** 2009-2010: $7,485 in state, $15,795 out of state

Selectivity: Selective	**Room/board:** $7,527
Acceptance rate: 68%	**Average debt:** $21,001
Student/faculty ratio: 23/1	**Proportion who borrowed:** 67%

UNDERGRADUATE STUDENT BODY STATS

2009-2010 enrollment: 22,061 full-time; 2,175 part-time. Men: 56%; women: 44%. **Ethnic makeup:** African American: 5%; American-Indian: 1%; Asian American: 3%; Hispanic: 14%; White: 75%; International: 3%.

ADMISSIONS FACTS AND FIGURES

Phone: (806) 742-1480. **Email:** admissions@ttu.edu. **Website:** http://www.ttu.edu. **Application deadlines for fall 2011:** Regular decision: August 1. Early decision: Not offered. Early action: Not offered. Admission cannot be deferred. **Application fee:** $50. **To apply online, go to:** http://www.gototexastech.com. **Admissions requirements/recommendations:** High school units required (recommended): English: 4; Mathematics: 3; Science: 2; Foreign language: 2; Social studies: 0; History: 0; Academic electives: 0; Total units: 11. Tests: The college uses SAT or ACT scores in admissions decisions. Either SAT or ACT required. For admission to the fall 2011 entering class, the school will accept: ACT with writing required. Campus visit: Recommended. Admissions interview: Neither required nor recommended. Off-campus interview: Not available. **Factors that count in admissions decisions:** *Academic:* Secondary school record: Very Important. Class rank: Very Important. Letters of recommendation: Considered. Standardized test scores: Very Important. Essay: Important. *Nonacademic:* Interview: Not Considered. Extracurricular activities: Important. Talent/ability: Important. Character/personal qualities: Important. Alumni/ae relationship: Important. Geographical residence: Not Considered. State residency: Not Considered. Religious affiliation/commitment: Not Considered. Minority status: Considered. Volunteer work: Important. Work experience: Important. **Other schools with the greatest overlap in applicants:** Texas A&M University–College Station; Texas State University–San Marcos; University of North Texas; University of Texas–Austin; University of Texas–San Antonio. **Admissions statistics for the fall 2009 entering class:** Total applicants: 16,541. Total accepted: 11,242. Freshmen enrolled: 4,586; 5% were from out of state. Overall acceptance rate: 68%. **Credentials of fall 2009 freshmen:** 21% ranked in the top 10 percent of their high school class; 53% were in the top 25 percent; 86% were in the top half. (Proportion submitting class standing: 100%.) **First-year students who submitted SAT scores:** 63%. Scores (25/75 percentile): Critical Reading: 480-580, Math: 510-620, Combined: 990-1200. **First-year students submitting ACT scores:** 37%. Scores (25/75 percentile): English: 20-26, Math: 21-27, Composite: 21-26.

ACADEMICS

Year founded: 1923. **Academic calendar:** Semester. **Degrees offered:** bachelor's, post-bachelor's certificate, master's, doctorate. **Most popular majors:** 25% business, management, marketing, and related support services, 10% engineering, 9% family and consumer sciences/human sciences, 6% communication, journalism, and related programs, 6% social sciences. **Major fields of study:** agriculture, agriculture operations, and related sciences; architecture and related services; area, ethnic, cultural, and gender studies; biological and biomedical sciences; business, management, marketing, and related support services; communication, journalism, and related programs; computer and information sciences and support services; engineering; engineering technologies/technicians; English language and literature/letters; family and consumer sciences/human sciences; foreign languages, literatures, and linguistics; health professions and related clinical sciences; history; liberal arts and sciences studies, and humanities; mathematics and statistics; multi/interdisciplinary studies; natural resources and conservation; parks, recreation, leisure, and fitness studies; philosophy and religious studies; physical sciences; psychology; public administration and social service professions; social sciences; visual and performing arts. **Areas**

of required coursework: arts/fine arts, humanities, mathematics, English (including composition), philosophy, foreign languages, sciences (biological or physical), history, social science, other. **Pre-professional programs:** pre-law, pre-dentistry, pre-medicine, pre-veterinary science, pre-optometry, pre-pharmacy, other. **Special academic programs (% participation):** accelerated program, cooperative (work-study plan) program, distance learning, double major (5%), dual enrollment, English as a Second Language (ESL), external degree program, honors program (3%), independent study (26%), internships, student-designed major (2%), study abroad, teacher certificate program (8%). **Teacher certification offered in:** early childhood, special education, elementary, middle/junior high, secondary, bilingual/bicultural. **Cooperative education programs:** agriculture, art, business, computer science, education, engineering, health professions, home economics, humanities, natural science, social/behavioral science, technologies, other. **Reserve Officers Training Corps (ROTC):** Army ROTC: Offered on campus; Air Force ROTC: Offered on campus. **Faculty and instruction (2009-2010):** Total instructional faculty: 1,148 full-time, 102 part-time (63% men; 37% women; 20% minorities). Full-time faculty with Ph.D. or other terminal degree: 90%. Student/faculty ratio: 23/1. Classes of fewer than 20 students: 22%; of 20 to 49 students: 56%; of 50 or more students: 22%. **Advanced Placement and International Baccalaureate credit:** AP tests may be used for: Credit only. Scores accepted: 3, 4, 5. International Baccalaureate exams may be used for: Credit only. **Freshmen returning for sophomore year:** 82%. **Graduation rates:** Four-year: 32%; five-year: 54%; six-year: 60%. **Graduate study:** 30% of students pursue further study immediately upon graduation; 30% within one year. Fields in which graduates pursue further study: Master of Business Administration (MBA), 24%; law, 7%; medicine, 6%; dentistry, 1%; engineering, 4%; theology (or the seminary), 1%; education, 11%; arts and sciences, 23%.

COSTS AND FINANCIAL AID

Financial aid office: (806) 742-3681. **Expenses (2009-2010):** Tuition and fees 2009-2010: $7,485 in state, $15,795 out of state; room/board: $7,527. Estimated books and supplies: $1,000; transportation: $1,500; personal expenses: $1,890. **Financial aid:** Priority filing date for institution's financial aid form: April 15. In 2009-2010, 61% of undergraduates applied for financial aid. Of those, 42% were determined to have financial need; 17% had their need fully met. Average financial aid package (proportion receiving): $10,578 (41%). Average amount of gift aid, such as scholarships or grants (proportion receiving): $9,519 (34%). Average amount of self-help aid, such as work study or loans (proportion receiving): $5,394 (31%). Average need-based loan (excluding PLUS or other private loans): $5,394. Among students who received need-based aid, the average percentage of need met: 59%. Among students who received aid based on merit, the average award (and the proportion receiving): $4,973 (18%). The average athletic scholarship (and the proportion receiving): $15,309 (1%). Average amount of debt of borrowers graduating in 2009: $21,001. Proportion who borrowed: 67%.

CAMPUS LIFE AND EXTRACURRICULAR ACTIVITIES

Campus housing available (% using): coed dorms (41%), women's dorms (26%), men's dorms (26%), apartment for single students (6%), special housing for disabled students (1%). Students who live in college-owned, operated, or affiliated housing: 25%. **Student employment:** During the 2009-2010 academic year, 11% of undergraduates worked on campus. Average per-year earnings: $8,316. **Clubs and organizations:** Number of student organizations: 453. Activities include: campus ministries, choral groups, concert band, dance, drama/theater, international student organization, jazz band, literary magazine, marching band, model UN, music ensembles, musical theater, pep band, student government, student newspaper, symphony orchestra, yearbook. Number of fraternities: 28; sororities: 18. Proportion of men in fraternities: 13%; of women in sororities: 18%. Average proportion of students who stay on campus on weekends: 67%. **Sports program (2009-2010):** Member of NCAA I. *Men's intercollegiate varsity sports:* baseball, basketball, cross country, football, golf, tennis, track and field (indoor), track and field (outdoor). *Women's intercollegiate varsity sports:* basketball, cross country, golf, soccer, softball, tennis, track and field (indoor), track and field (outdoor), volleyball.

SERVICES AND FACILITIES

Basic services: nonremedial tutoring, placement service, health service, health insurance. **Remedial assistance:** reading, math, writing, study skills, other. **Counseling services:** minority student, career, personal, academic, psychological, other. **For learning-disabled students:** School does not offer a structured program with separate admission and additional fees. Total undergraduates in learning-disabled program or receiving services: 884. Services include: remedial math, remedial English, remedial reading, tape recorders, note-taking services, learning center, readers, extended time for tests, tutors, priority registration, priority seating, texts on tape. **Library:** Number of titles: 2,639,325; number of current serial subscriptions: 55,413. **Information technology resources:** Students are not required to lease or own a computer. Number of campus computers available to all students: 2,000. School has a wireless network. Approximate number of users that can be accommodated: 19,600. Proportion of college-owned housing units wired for high-speed internet access: 100%. **Campus safety:** Security services offered: 24-hour foot-and-vehicle patrols, late-night transport/escort service, 24-hour emergency telephones, lighted pathways/sidewalks, controlled dormitory access (key, security card, etc).

TRANSFER AND INTERNATIONAL STUDENTS

Transfer students: May apply for admission for the following academic terms: Fall, Spring, Summer. Applicants need a minimum number of credits to apply. For fall 2009: Transfer applications received: 4,713. Transfer applicants offered admission: 3,793. Transfer applicants enrolled: 2,437. **International students:** Number of foreign undergraduates: 653 (3% of student body). Number of countries represented: 120. Minimum TOEFL score required: 550 (paper); 79 (computer).

Texas Wesleyan University

- **Address:** 1201 Wesleyan, Fort Worth, TX 76105-1536
- **Website:** http://www.txwesleyan.edu
- **Private; Religious affiliation:** Methodist
- **Enrollment:** 1,171 full-time; 631 part-time

KEY STATS

✔ **U.S News College Ranking:** 71, Regional Universities (West)
✔ **SAT Score (25th/75th percentile):** 870-1080
✔ **Tuition:** 2009-2010: $17,760

Selectivity: Less selective	**Room/board:** $6,656
Acceptance rate: 61%	**Average debt:** N/A
Student/faculty ratio: 12/1	**Proportion who borrowed:** N/A

UNDERGRADUATE STUDENT BODY STATS

2009-2010 enrollment: 1,171 full-time; 631 part-time. Men: 35%; women: 65%. **Ethnic makeup:** African American: 20%; American-Indian: 1%; Asian American: 2%; Hispanic: 23%; White: 52%; International: 2%. **Religious preference:** Roman Catholic: 11%; Protestant: 13%; No preference: 17%; Unknown: 28%; Methodist: 8%; Other: 3%.

ADMISSIONS FACTS AND FIGURES

Phone: (817) 531-4458. **Email:** freshman@txwesleyan.edu. **Website:** http://www.txwesleyan.edu. **Application deadlines for fall 2011:** Regular decision: Rolling. Early decision: Not offered. Early action: Not offered. Admission can be deferred. **Application fee:** $25. **To apply online, go to:** http://www.txwesleyan.edu/admission/AdmissionApplications.htm. **Admissions requirements/recommendations:** High school units required (recommended): English: (4); Mathematics: (4); Science: (3); Foreign language: (1); Social studies: (3); Academic electives: (7); Total units: (20). Tests: The college uses SAT or ACT scores in admissions decisions. Either SAT or ACT required. For admission to the fall 2011 entering class, the school will accept: ACT with or without writing accepted. Campus visit: Neither required nor recommended. Admissions interview: Recommended. Off-campus interview: May be arranged. **Factors that count in admissions decisions: Academic:** Secondary school record: Very Important. Class rank: Important. Letters of recommendation: Considered. Standardized test scores: Very Important. Essay: Considered. **Nonacademic:** Interview: Not Considered. Extracurricular activities: Considered. Talent/ability: Not Considered. Character/personal qualities: Not Considered. Alumni/ae relationship: Considered. Geographical residence: Not Considered. State residency: Not Considered. Religious affiliation/commitment: Not Considered. Minority status: Not Considered. Volunteer work: Considered. Work experience: Considered. **Other schools with the greatest overlap in applicants:** Dallas Baptist University; University of Dallas; University of St. Mary; University of Texas–Arlington; University of Texas–Dallas. **Admissions statistics for the fall 2009 entering class:** Total applicants: 631. Total accepted: 388. Freshmen enrolled: 188; 2% were from out of state. Overall acceptance rate: 61%. **Size of waiting list:** 0 applicants; enrolled from waiting list: 0. **Credentials of fall 2009 freshmen:** 11% ranked in the top 10 percent of their high school class; 17% were in the top 25 percent; 33% were in the top

half. (Proportion submitting class standing: 72%.) **First-year students who submitted SAT scores:** 66%. Scores (25/75 percentile): Critical Reading: 440-530, Math: 430-550, Combined: 870-1080. **First-year students submitting ACT scores:** 29%. Scores (25/75 percentile): English: 16-21, Math: 16-21, Composite: 18-21.

ACADEMICS

Year founded: 1890. **Academic calendar:** Semester. **Degrees offered:** bachelor's, master's. **Most popular majors:** 20% education, 13% business, management, marketing, and related support services, 12% multi/interdisciplinary studies, 8% psychology, 7% legal professions and studies. **Major fields of study:** biological and biomedical sciences; business, management, marketing, and related support services; communication, journalism, and related programs; computer and information sciences and support services; education; English language and literature/letters; foreign languages, literatures, and linguistics; health professions and related clinical sciences; legal professions and studies; mathematics and statistics; multi/interdisciplinary studies; parks, recreation, leisure, and fitness studies; philosophy and religious studies; physical sciences; psychology; science technologies/technicians; security and protective services; social sciences; theology and religious vocations; visual and performing arts. **Areas of required coursework:** arts/fine arts, humanities, computer literacy, mathematics, English (including composition), sciences (biological or physical), history, social science. **Pre-professional programs:** pre-law, pre-medicine, pre-theology. **Special academic programs:** accelerated program, distance learning, double major, dual enrollment, English as a Second Language (ESL), exchange student program (domestic), independent study, internships, liberal arts/career combination, study abroad, teacher certificate program, weekend college. **Teacher certification offered in:** early childhood, elementary, middle/junior high, bilingual/bicultural. **Reserve Officers Training Corps (ROTC):** Army ROTC: Offered on campus; Air Force ROTC: Offered at cooperating institution (Texas Christian University). **Faculty and instruction (2009-2010):** Total instructional faculty: 165 full-time, 94 part-time (51% men; 49% women; 10% minorities). Full-time faculty with Ph.D. or other terminal degree: 92%. Student/faculty ratio: 12/1. Classes of fewer than 20 students: 66%; of 20 to 49 students: 34%; of 50 or more students: 0%. **Advanced Placement and International Baccalaureate credit:** International Baccalaureate exams may be used for: Credit and/or placement. **Freshmen returning for sophomore year:** 62%. **Graduation rates:** Four-year: 10%; five-year: 26%; six-year: 28%.

COSTS AND FINANCIAL AID

Financial aid office: (817) 531-4420. **Expenses (2009-2010):** Tuition and fees 2009-2010: $17,760; room/board: $6,656. Estimated books and supplies: $1,020. **Financial aid:** Priority filing date for institution's financial aid form: March 15.

CAMPUS LIFE AND EXTRACURRICULAR ACTIVITIES

Campus housing available: coed dorms, women's dorms, men's dorms, apartments for married students. Students who live in college-owned, operated, or affiliated housing: 19%. **Student employment:** During the 2009-2010 academic year, 1% of undergraduates worked on campus. Average per-year earnings: $5,678. **Clubs and organizations:** Number of student organizations: 34. Activities include: choral groups, concert band, drama/theater, literary magazine, music ensembles, musical theater, opera, student government, student newspaper. Number of fraternities: 4; sororities: 4. Proportion of men in fraternities: 2%; of women in sororities: 2%. Average proportion of students who stay on campus on weekends: 70%. **Sports program (2009-2010):** Member of NAIA. **Men's intercollegiate varsity sports:** baseball, basketball, golf, soccer, tennis. **Women's intercollegiate varsity sports:** basketball, soccer, softball, tennis, volleyball.

SERVICES AND FACILITIES

Basic services: nonremedial tutoring, placement service, health service. **Remedial assistance:** reading, math, writing, study skills. **Counseling services:** minority student, personal, academic, older student, psychological, religious. **For learning-disabled students:** School does not offer a structured program with separate admission and additional fees. Services include: remedial math, remedial English. **Library:** Number of titles: 194,616; number of current serial subscriptions: 555. **Information technology resources:** Students are not required to lease or own a computer. Number of campus computers available to all students: 150. School has a wireless network. Proportion of college-owned housing units wired for high-speed internet access: 100%. **Campus safety:** Security services offered: 24-hour foot-and-vehicle patrols, late-night transport/escort service, 24-hour emergency telephones, lighted pathways/sidewalks, controlled dormitory access (key, security card, etc).

TRANSFER AND INTERNATIONAL STUDENTS

Transfer students: May apply for admission for the following academic terms: Fall, Spring, Summer. Applicants need a minimum number of credits to apply. For fall 2009: Transfer applications received: 638. Transfer applicants offered admission: 427. Transfer applicants enrolled: 264. **International students:** Number of foreign undergraduates: 32 (2% of student body). Number of countries represented: 22. Minimum TOEFL score required: 520 (paper); 190 (computer).

Texas Woman's University

- **Address:** Box 425619, Denton, TX 76204-5587
- **Website:** http://www.twu.edu
- **Public**
- **Enrollment:** 5,327 full-time; 2,409 part-time

KEY STATS

✔ **U.S News College Ranking:** second tier, National Universities
✔ **SAT Score (25th/75th percentile):** 890-1110
✔ **Tuition:** 2010-2011: $6,960 in state, $16,260 out of state

Selectivity: Selective	**Room/board:** $6,549
Acceptance rate: 83%	**Average debt:** $22,293
Student/faculty ratio: 17/1	**Proportion who borrowed:** 57%

UNDERGRADUATE STUDENT BODY STATS

2009-2010 enrollment: 5,327 full-time; 2,409 part-time. Men: 8%; women: 92%. **Ethnic makeup:** African American: 21%; American-Indian: 1%; Asian American: 8%; Hispanic: 19%; White: 50%; International: 2%.

ADMISSIONS FACTS AND FIGURES

Phone: (940) 898-3188. **Email:** admissions@twu.edu. **Website:** http://www. twu.edu. **Application deadlines for fall 2011:** Regular decision: July 15. Early decision: Not offered. Early action: Not offered. Admission can be deferred. **Application fee:** $30. **To apply online, go to:** http://www.twu.edu/admissions/forms.asp. **Admissions requirements/recommendations:** High school units required (recommended): English: 4; Mathematics: 3; Science: 2; Foreign language: 0; Social studies: 2; Academic electives: 3; Total units: 22. Tests: The college uses SAT or ACT scores in admissions decisions. Neither SAT nor ACT required. For admission to the fall 2011 entering class, the school will accept: ACT with or without writing accepted. Campus visit: Recommended. Admissions interview: Neither required nor recommended. Off-campus interview: Not available. **Factors that count in admissions decisions:** *Academic:* Secondary school record: Very Important. Class rank: Very Important. Letters of recommendation: Not Considered. Standardized test scores: Very Important. Essay: Not Considered. *Nonacademic:* Interview: Not Considered. Extracurricular activities: Not Considered. Talent/ability: Not Considered. Character/personal qualities: Not Considered. Alumni/ae relationship: Not Considered. Geographical residence: Not Considered. State residency: Not Considered. Religious affiliation/commitment: Not Considered. Minority status: Not Considered. Volunteer work: Not Considered. Work experience: Not Considered. **Other schools with the greatest overlap in applicants:** University of North Texas; University of Texas–Arlington; University of Texas–Dallas. **Admissions statistics for the fall 2009 entering class:** Total applicants: 2,405. Total accepted: 1,988. Freshmen enrolled: 742; 1% were from out of state. Overall acceptance rate: 83%. **Credentials of fall 2009 freshmen:** 21% ranked in the top 10 percent of their high school class; 50% were in the top 25 percent; 80% were in the top half. (Proportion submitting class standing: 92%.) **First-year students who submitted SAT scores:** 73%. Scores (25/75 percentile): Critical Reading: 440-550, Math: 450-560, Combined: 890-1110. **First-year students submitting ACT scores:** 24%. Scores (25/75 percentile): English: N/A, Math: N/A, Composite: 19-24.

ACADEMICS

Year founded: 1901. **Academic calendar:** Semester. **Degrees offered:** bachelor's, post-bachelor's certificate, master's, post-master's certificate, doctorate. **Most popular majors:** 27% nursing/registered nurse training (R.N., A.S.N., B.S.N., M.S.N.), 13% multi/interdisciplinary studies, 12% general studies, 6% psychology, 4% child development. **Major fields of study:** biological and biomedical sciences; business, management, marketing, and related

support services; computer and information sciences and support services; English language and literature/letters; family and consumer sciences/human sciences; health professions and related clinical sciences; history; legal professions and studies; liberal arts and sciences studies, and humanities; mathematics and statistics; multi/interdisciplinary studies; parks, recreation, leisure, and fitness studies; physical sciences; psychology; public administration and social service professions; security and protective services; social sciences; visual and performing arts. **Areas of required coursework:** arts/fine arts, humanities, computer literacy, mathematics, English (including composition), sciences (biological or physical), history, social science, other. **Pre-professional programs:** pre-law, pre-dentistry, pre-medicine, other. **Special academic programs (% participation):** accelerated program, cooperative (work-study plan) program (6%), cross-registration (1%), distance learning (87%), double major (5%), dual enrollment (0%), honors program (2%), independent study (19%), internships (33%), liberal arts/career combination, study abroad, teacher certificate program (17%). **Teacher certification offered in:** early childhood, special education, elementary, middle/junior high, secondary, bilingual/bicultural. **Cooperative education programs:** art, business, computer science, health professions, humanities, social/behavioral science. **Reserve Officers Training Corps (ROTC):** Army ROTC: Offered at cooperating institution (University of Texas–Arlington); Air Force ROTC: Offered at cooperating institution (University of North Texas). **Faculty and instruction (2009-2010):** Total instructional faculty: 453 full-time, 370 part-time (26% men; 74% women; 14% minorities). Student/faculty ratio: 17/1. Classes of fewer than 20 students: 42%; of 20 to 49 students: 51%; of 50 or more students: 7%. **Advanced Placement and International Baccalaureate credit:** AP tests may be used for: Placement only. Scores accepted: 3, 4, 5. International Baccalaureate exams may be used for: Placement only. **Freshmen returning for sophomore year:** 71%. **Graduation rates:** Four-year: 22%; five-year: 36%; six-year: 44%. **Graduate study:** 5% of students pursue further study within one year. Fields in which graduates pursue further study: Master of Business Administration (MBA), 15%; law, 1%; medicine, 1%; dentistry, 1%; engineering, 1%; theology (or the seminary), 1%; education, 8%; arts and sciences, 3%; veterinary medicine, 1%.

COSTS AND FINANCIAL AID

Financial aid office: (940) 898-3050. **Expenses (2010-2011):** Tuition and fees 2010-2011: $6,960 in state, $16,260 out of state; room/board: $6,549. Estimated books and supplies: $1,020; transportation: $834; personal expenses: $1,964. **Financial aid:** Priority filing date for institution's financial aid form: March 1. In 2009-2010, 79% of undergraduates applied for financial aid. Of those, 64% were determined to have financial need; 35% had their need fully met. Average financial aid package (proportion receiving): $7,813 (62%). Average amount of gift aid, such as scholarships or grants (proportion receiving): $7,592 (62%). Average amount of self-help aid, such as work study or loans (proportion receiving): $3,900 (52%). Average need-based loan (excluding PLUS or other private loans): $3,703. Among students who received need-based aid, the average percentage of need met: 88%. Among students who received aid based on merit, the average award (and the proportion receiving): $3,000 (11%). The average athletic scholarship (and the proportion receiving): $5,409 (3%). Average amount of debt of borrowers graduating in 2009: $22,293. Proportion who borrowed: 57%.

CAMPUS LIFE AND EXTRACURRICULAR ACTIVITIES

Campus housing available (% using): coed dorms (29%), women's dorms (31%), sorority housing (2%), apartments for married students (4%), apartment for single students (15%), special housing for disabled students (2%), special housing for international students (2%), other housing options (15%). Students who live in college-owned, operated, or affiliated housing: 11%. **Student employment:** During the 2009-2010 academic year, 18% of undergraduates worked on campus. Average per-year earnings: $4,430. **Clubs and organizations:** Number of student organizations: 135. Activities include: campus ministries, choral groups, dance, drama/theater, international student organization, jazz band, music ensembles, musical theater, opera, student government, student newspaper. Number of fraternities: 1; sororities: 9. of women in sororities: 1%. Average proportion of students who stay on campus on weekends: 35%. **Sports program (2009-2010):** Member of NCAA II. *Women's intercollegiate varsity sports:* basketball, gymnastics, soccer, softball, volleyball.

SERVICES AND FACILITIES

Basic services: nonremedial tutoring, placement service, health service, health insurance. **Remedial assistance:** reading, math, writing, study skills, other. **Counseling services:** minority student, career, personal, veteran student, academic, older student, psychological, birth control. **For learning-disabled students:** School does not offer a structured program with separate admission and additional fees. Services include: remedial math, remedial English, tape recorders, note-taking services, oral tests, learning center, readers, extended time for tests, priority registration, priority seating, texts on tape, other testing accommodations. **Library:** Number of titles: 530,011; number of current serial subscriptions: 35,625. **Information technology resources:** Students are not required to lease or own a computer. Number of campus computers available to all students: 1,500. School has a wireless network. Approximate number of users that can be accommodated: 3,000. Proportion of college-owned housing units wired for high-speed internet access: 100%. **Campus safety:** Security services offered: 24-hour foot-and-vehicle patrols, late-night transport/escort service, 24-hour emergency telephones, lighted pathways/sidewalks, controlled dormitory access (key, security card, etc).

TRANSFER AND INTERNATIONAL STUDENTS

Transfer students: May apply for admission for the following academic terms: Fall, Spring, Summer. Applicants need a minimum number of credits to apply. For fall 2009: Transfer applications received: 2,923. Transfer applicants offered admission: 2,771. Transfer applicants enrolled: 1,170. **International students:** Number of foreign undergraduates: 129 (2% of student body). Number of countries represented: 41. Minimum TOEFL score required: 550 (paper); 213 (computer). Average TOEFL score: 575 (paper).

Trinity University

- **Address:** 1 Trinity Place, San Antonio, TX 78212-7200
- **Website:** http://www.trinity.edu
- **Private; Religious affiliation:** Presbyterian
- **Enrollment:** 2,435 full-time; 52 part-time

KEY STATS

✔ **U.S News College Ranking:** 1, Regional Universities (West)
✔ **SAT Score (25th/75th percentile):** 1200-1390
✔ **Tuition:** 2010-2011: $30,012

Selectivity: More selective	**Room/board:** $10,312
Acceptance rate: 59%	**Average debt:** N/A
Student/faculty ratio: 10/1	**Proportion who borrowed:** N/A

UNDERGRADUATE STUDENT BODY STATS

2009-2010 enrollment: 2,435 full-time; 52 part-time. Men: 46%; women: 54%. **Ethnic makeup:** African American: 4%; American-Indian: 1%; Asian American: 7%; Hispanic: 11%; White: 71%; International: 7%. **Religious preference:** Roman Catholic: 20%; Protestant: 40%; Jewish: 3%; Muslim: 1%; Hindu: 1%; Buddhist: 1%; No preference: 23%; Presbyterian: 5%.

ADMISSIONS FACTS AND FIGURES

Phone: (800) 874-6489. **Email:** admissions@trinity.edu. **Website:** http://www.trinity.edu. **Application deadlines for fall 2011:** Regular decision: February 1; decision sent by April 1. Early decision: Send application by: November 1; Decision sent by: December 1. Early action: Send application by: December 1; Decision sent by: February 1. Admission can be deferred. **Application fee:** $50. **To apply online, go to:** http://www.trinity.edu/departments/admissions/apply3.htm. **Admissions requirements/recommendations:** High school units required (recommended): English: 4 (4); Mathematics: 3 (3); Science: 3 (3); Foreign language: 2 (3); Social studies: 3 (3); Academic electives: 0 (3); Total units: 15 (19). Tests: The college uses SAT or ACT scores in admissions decisions. Either SAT or ACT required. For admission to the fall 2011 entering class, the school will accept: ACT with or without writing accepted. Campus visit: Recommended. Admissions interview: Recommended. Off-campus interview: May be arranged. **Factors that count in admissions decisions:** *Academic:* Secondary school record: Very Important. Class rank: Very Important. Letters of recommendation: Important. Standardized test scores: Important. Essay: Important. *Nonacademic:* Interview: Important. Extracurricular activities: Important. Talent/ability: Important. Character/personal qualities: Important. Alumni/ae relationship: Considered. Geographical residence: Considered. State residency: Not Considered. Religious affiliation/commitment: Not Considered. Minority status: Considered. Volunteer work: Considered. Work experience: Considered. **Other schools with the greatest overlap in applicants:** Baylor University; Rice University; Southwestern University; Texas A&M University–College Station; University of Texas–Austin. **Admissions statistics for the fall 2009 entering class:** Total applicants: 4,209. Total accepted: 2,489. Freshmen enrolled: 642; 30% were from out of state. Overall acceptance rate: 59%. Non-early acceptance rate: 59%. **Size of waiting list:** 360 applicants; enrolled from waiting list: 24. **Credentials of fall 2009 freshmen:** 55% ranked in the top 10 percent of their high school class; 86% were in the top 25 percent; 98% were in the top half. (Proportion submitting class standing: 58%.) **Average high school grade point average:** 3.6. **First-year students who submitted SAT scores:** 62%. Scores (25/75 percentile): Critical Reading: 590-700, Math: 610-690, Combined: 1200-1390. **First-year students submitting ACT scores:** 35%. Scores (25/75 percentile): English: 27-33, Math: 26-31, Composite: 27-31.

ACADEMICS

Year founded: 1869. **Academic calendar:** Semester. **Degrees offered:** bachelor's, master's. **Most popular majors:** 28% business, management, marketing, and related support services, 16% social sciences, 7% English language and literature/letters, 7% communication, journalism, and related programs, 6% visual and performing arts. **Major fields of study:** area, ethnic, cultural, and gender studies; biological and biomedical sciences; business, management, marketing, and related support services; communication, journalism, and related programs; communications technologies/technicians and support services; computer and information sciences and support services; education; engineering; engineering technologies/technicians; English language and literature/letters; foreign languages, literatures, and linguistics; health professions and related clinical sciences; history; philosophy and religious studies; physical sciences; psychology; public administration and social service professions; social sciences; theology and religious vocations; visual and performing arts. **Areas of required coursework:** arts/fine arts, humanities, computer literacy, English (including composition), philosophy, foreign languages, sciences (biological or physical), social science, other. **Pre-professional programs:** pre-law, pre-dentistry, pre-medicine. **Special academic programs:** distance learning, double major, honors program, independent study, internships, student-designed major, study abroad, teacher certificate program. **Teacher certification offered in:** early childhood, special education, elementary, middle/junior high, secondary, bilingual/bicultural. **Reserve Officers Training Corps (ROTC):** Air Force ROTC: Offered at cooperating institution (University of Texas–San Antonio). **Faculty and instruction (2009-2010):** Total instructional faculty: 243 full-time, 81 part-time (59% men; 41% women; 13% minorities). Full-time faculty with Ph.D. or other terminal degree: 98%. Student/faculty ratio: 10/1. Classes of fewer than 20 students: 61%; of 20 to 49 students: 38%; of 50 or more students: 2%. **Advanced Placement and International Baccalaureate credit:** AP tests may be used for: Credit and/or placement. Scores accepted: 4, 5. International Baccalaureate exams may be used for: Credit and/or placement. **Freshmen returning for sophomore year:** 89%. **Graduation rates:** Four-year: 68%; five-year: 77%; six-year: 79%. **Graduate study:** 34% of students pursue further study immediately upon graduation. Fields in which graduates pursue further study: Master of Business Administration (MBA), 25%; law, 13%; medicine, 17%; engineering, 14%; education, 20%.

COSTS AND FINANCIAL AID

Financial aid office: (210) 999-8315. **Expenses (2010-2011):** Tuition and fees 2010-2011: $30,012; room/board: $10,312. Estimated books and supplies: $950 personal expenses: $1,050. **Financial aid:** Priority filing date for institution's financial aid form: February 15; deadline: April 1. In 2009-2010, 51% of undergraduates applied for financial aid. Of those, 39% were determined to have financial need; 46% had their need fully met. Average financial aid package (proportion receiving): $23,645 (39%). Average amount of gift aid, such as scholarships or grants (proportion receiving): $16,619 (38%). Average amount of self-help aid, such as work study or loans (proportion receiving): $8,120 (33%). Average need-based loan (excluding PLUS or other private loans): $6,658. Among students who received need-based aid, the average percentage of need met: 90%. Among students who received aid based on merit, the average award (and the proportion receiving): $12,112 (44%). The average athletic scholarship (and the proportion receiving): $0 (0%).

CAMPUS LIFE AND EXTRACURRICULAR ACTIVITIES

Campus housing available (% using): coed dorms (87%), special housing for disabled students, other housing options (8%). Students who live in college-owned, operated, or affiliated housing: 73%. **Student employment:** During the 2009-2010 academic year, 30% of undergraduates worked on campus. Average per-year earnings: $1,800. **Clubs and organizations:** Number of student organizations: 84. Activities include: campus ministries, choral groups, concert band, dance, drama/theater, international student organization, jazz band, literary magazine, model UN, music ensembles, musical theater, opera, radio station, student government, student newspaper, student film society, symphony orchestra, television station, yearbook. Number of fraternities: 7; sororities: 7. Proportion of men in fraternities: 20%; of women in sororities: 27%. **Sports program (2009-2010):** Member of NCAA III. *Men's intercollegiate varsity sports:* baseball, basketball, cross country, football, golf, soccer, swimming, tennis, track and field (outdoor). *Women's intercollegiate varsity sports:* basketball, cross country, golf, soccer, softball, swimming, tennis, track and field (outdoor), volleyball.

SERVICES AND FACILITIES

Basic services: women's center, health service. **Counseling services:** career, personal, academic, psychological. **For learning-disabled students:** School does not offer a structured program with separate admission and additional fees. Services include: reading machines, tape recorders, note-taking services, oral tests, readers, extended time for tests, priority registration, priority seating, substitution of courses, texts on tape, typist/scribe, exams on tape or computer, other testing accommodations. **Library:** Number of titles: 916,994; number of current serial subscriptions: 31,518. **Information technology resources:** Students are not required to lease or own a computer. Number of campus computers available to all students: 500. School has a wireless network. Approximate number of users that can be accommodated: 5,000. Proportion of college-owned housing units wired for high-speed internet access: 100%. **Campus safety:** Security services offered: 24-hour foot-and-vehicle patrols, late-night transport/escort service, 24-hour emergency telephones, lighted pathways/sidewalks, controlled dormitory access (key, security card, etc).

TRANSFER AND INTERNATIONAL STUDENTS

Transfer students: May apply for admission for the following academic terms: Fall, Spring. Applicants do not need a minimum number of credits to apply. For fall 2009: Transfer applications received: 131. Transfer applicants offered admission: 60. Transfer applicants enrolled: 28. **International students:** Number of foreign undergraduates: 169 (7% of student body). Number of countries represented: 44. Minimum TOEFL score required: 600 (paper); 250 (computer). Average TOEFL score: 605 (paper).

University of Dallas

- **Address:** 1845 E. Northgate Drive, Irving, TX 75062-4736
- **Website:** http://www.udallas.edu
- **Private; Religious affiliation:** Roman Catholic
- **Enrollment:** 1,279 full-time; 23 part-time

KEY STATS

✔ **U.S News College Ranking:** 15, Regional Universities (West)
✔ **SAT Score (25th/75th percentile):** 1090-1350
✔ **Tuition:** 2010-2011: $27,815

Selectivity: More selective	**Room/board:** $8,650
Acceptance rate: 92%	**Average debt:** $24,624
Student/faculty ratio: 13/1	**Proportion who borrowed:** 57%

UNDERGRADUATE STUDENT BODY STATS

2009-2010 enrollment: 1,279 full-time; 23 part-time. Men: 49%; women: 51%. **Ethnic makeup:** African American: 1%; Asian American: 5%; Hispanic: 15%; White: 76%; International: 3%. **Religious preference:** Protestant: 7%; Unknown: 10%; Roman Catholic: 82%; Other: 1%.

ADMISSIONS FACTS AND FIGURES

Phone: (972) 721-5266. **Email:** ugadmis@udallas.edu. **Website:** http://www.udallas.edu. **Application deadlines for fall 2011:** Regular decision: July 1. Early decision: Not offered. Early action: Send application by: December 1; Decision sent by: January 15. Admission can be deferred. **Application fee:** $40. **To apply online, go to:** http://www.udallas.edu/futurestudents/admiss. **Admissions requirements/recommendations:** High school units required (recommended): English: 4 (4); Mathematics: 3 (4); Science: 3 (3); Foreign language: 2 (3); Social studies: 3 (4); History: 3 (4); Academic electives: 4 (4); Total units: 24 (28). Tests: The college uses SAT or ACT scores in admissions decisions. Either SAT or ACT required. For admission to the fall 2011 entering class, the school will accept: ACT with writing required. Campus visit: Recommended. Admissions interview: Recommended. Off-campus interview: May be arranged. **Factors that count in admissions decisions:** *Academic:* Secondary school record: Very Important. Class rank: Important. Letters of recommendation: Very Important. Standardized test scores: Very Important. Essay: Very Important. *Nonacademic:* Interview:

Considered. Extracurricular activities: Considered. Talent/ability: Important. Character/personal qualities: Very Important. Alumni/ae relationship: Considered. Geographical residence: Not Considered. State residency: Not Considered. Religious affiliation/commitment: Not Considered. Minority status: Not Considered. Volunteer work: Considered. Work experience: Considered. **Other schools with the greatest overlap in applicants:** Southern Methodist University; Texas A&M University–College Station; University of Notre Dame; University of Texas–Arlington; University of Texas–Austin. **Admissions statistics for the fall 2009 entering class:** Total applicants: 1,056. Total accepted: 972. Freshmen enrolled: 320; 55% were from out of state. Accepted through early-decision or early-action plans: 37%. Overall acceptance rate: 92%. Non-early acceptance rate: 90%. **Size of waiting list:** 0 applicants; enrolled from waiting list: 0. **Credentials of fall 2009 freshmen:** 36% ranked in the top 10 percent of their high school class; 58% were in the top 25 percent; 87% were in the top half. (Proportion submitting class standing: 44%.) **Average high school grade point average:** 3.7. **First-year students who submitted SAT scores:** 77%. Scores (25/75 percentile): Critical Reading: 560-700, Math: 530-650, Combined: 1090-1350. **First-year students submitting ACT scores:** 51%. Scores (25/75 percentile): English: 22-29, Math: 23-32, Composite: 23-30.

ACADEMICS

Year founded: 1956. **Academic calendar:** Semester. **Degrees offered:** bachelor's, post-bachelor's certificate, master's, post-master's certificate, doctorate. **Most popular majors:** 17% English language and literature, 11% biology/biological sciences, 11% business administration and management, 9% history, 7% psychology. **Major fields of study:** architecture and related services; biological and biomedical sciences; business, management, marketing, and related support services; education; engineering; English language and literature/letters; foreign languages, literatures, and linguistics; health professions and related clinical sciences; history; legal professions and studies; mathematics and statistics; multi/interdisciplinary studies; philosophy and religious studies; physical sciences; psychology; social sciences; theology and religious vocations; visual and performing arts. **Areas of required coursework:** arts/fine arts, humanities, mathematics, English (including composition), philosophy, foreign languages, sciences (biological or physical), history, social science, other. **Pre-professional programs:** pre-law, pre-dentistry, pre-medicine, pre-theology, pre-veterinary science, other. **Special academic programs (% participation):** double major (5%), dual enrollment, independent study (5%), internships (15%), liberal arts/career combination (20%), student-designed major (1%), study abroad (74%), teacher certificate program (8%). **Teacher certification offered in:** early childhood, elementary, middle/junior high, secondary. **Reserve Officers Training Corps (ROTC):** Army ROTC: Offered at cooperating institution (University of Texas–Arlington); Air Force ROTC: Offered at cooperating institution (University of North Texas). **Faculty and instruction (2009-2010):** Total instructional faculty: 125 full-time, 108 part-time (69% men; 31% women; 8% minorities). Full-time faculty with Ph.D. or other terminal degree: 93%. Student/faculty ratio: 13/1. Classes of fewer than 20 students: 49%; of 20 to 49 students: 48%; of 50 or more students: 3%. **Advanced Placement and International Baccalaureate credit:** AP tests may be used for: Credit and/or placement. Scores accepted: 3, 4. International Baccalaureate exams may be used for: Credit and/or placement. **Freshmen returning for sophomore year:** 82%. **Graduation rates:** Four-year: 62%; five-year: 71%; six-year: 65%. **Graduate study:** 23% of students pursue further study immediately upon graduation; 35% within one year. Fields in which graduates pursue further study: Master of Business Administration (MBA), 8%; law, 5%; medicine, 26%; theology (or the seminary), 14%; education, 10%; arts and sciences, 37%.

COSTS AND FINANCIAL AID

Financial aid office: (972) 721-5266. **Expenses (2010-2011):** Tuition and fees 2010-2011: $27,815; room/board: $8,650. Estimated books and supplies: $1,700; transportation: $3,000; personal expenses: $1,900. **Financial aid:** Priority filing date for institution's financial aid form: January 15; deadline: March 1. In 2009-2010, 62% of undergraduates applied for financial aid. Of those, 62% were determined to have financial need; 18% had their need fully met. Average financial aid package (proportion receiving): $20,940 (62%). Average amount of gift aid, such as scholarships or grants (proportion receiving): $16,235 (61%). Average amount of self-help aid, such as work study or loans (proportion receiving): $5,440 (52%). Average need-based loan (excluding PLUS or other private loans): $5,110. Among students who received need-based aid, the average percentage of need met: 73%. Among students who received aid based on merit, the average award (and the proportion receiving): $11,400 (34%). The average athletic scholarship (and the proportion receiving): $0 (0%). Average amount of debt of borrowers graduating in 2009: $24,624. Proportion who borrowed: 57%.

CAMPUS LIFE AND EXTRACURRICULAR ACTIVITIES

Campus housing available (% using): coed dorms (6%), women's dorms (44%), men's dorms (32%), apartment for single students (18%). Students who live in college-owned, operated, or affiliated housing: 57%. **Student employment:** During the 2009-2010 academic year, 28% of undergraduates worked on campus. Average per-year earnings: $2,080. **Clubs and organizations:** Number of student organizations: 35. Activities include: campus ministries, choral groups, dance, drama/theater, international student organization, literary magazine, music ensembles, musical theater, student government, student newspaper, student film society, yearbook. Number of fraternities: 0; sororities: 0. Average proportion of students who stay on campus on weekends: 80%. **Sports program (2009-2010):** Member of NCAA III. **Men's intercollegiate varsity sports:** baseball, basketball, cross country, golf, lacrosse, soccer, track and field (outdoor). **Women's intercollegiate varsity sports:** basketball, cross country, lacrosse, soccer, softball, track and field (outdoor), volleyball.

SERVICES AND FACILITIES

Basic services: nonremedial tutoring, health service, health insurance, other. **Remedial assistance:** other. **Counseling services:** career, personal, academic, religious. **For learning-disabled students:** School does not offer a structured program with separate admission and additional fees. Services include: reading machines. **Library:** Number of titles: 245,228; number of current serial subscriptions: 1,310. **Information technology resources:** Students are not required to lease or own a computer. Number of campus computers available to all students: 125. School has a wireless network. Proportion of college-owned housing units wired for high-speed internet access: 100%. **Campus safety:** Security services offered: 24-hour foot-and-vehicle patrols, late-night transport/escort service, 24-hour emergency telephones, lighted pathways/sidewalks, controlled dormitory access (key, security card, etc).

TRANSFER AND INTERNATIONAL STUDENTS

Transfer students: May apply for admission for the following academic terms: Fall, Spring. Applicants need a minimum number of credits to apply. For fall 2009: Transfer applications received: 96. Transfer applicants offered admission: 86. Transfer applicants enrolled: 50. **International students:** Number of foreign undergraduates: 33 (3% of student body). Number of countries represented: 13. Minimum TOEFL score required: 550 (paper); 213 (computer).

University of Houston

- **Address:** 4800 Calhoun Road, Houston, TX 77204
- **Website:** http://www.uh.edu
- **Public**
- **Enrollment:** 21,096 full-time; 8,202 part-time

KEY STATS

✔ **U.S News College Ranking:** second tier, National Universities
✔ **SAT Score (25th/75th percentile):** 970-1190
✔ **Tuition:** 2010-2011: $8,997 in state, $18,297 out of state

Selectivity: Selective	**Room/board:** N/A
Acceptance rate: 70%	**Average debt:** N/A
Student/faculty ratio: 22/1	**Proportion who borrowed:** N/A

UNDERGRADUATE STUDENT BODY STATS

2009-2010 enrollment: 21,096 full-time; 8,202 part-time. Men: 50%; women: 50%. **Ethnic makeup:** African American: 15%; Asian American: 22%; Hispanic: 24%; White: 34%; International: 4%.

ADMISSIONS FACTS AND FIGURES

Phone: (713) 743-1010. **Email:** admissions@uh.edu. **Website:** http://www.uh.edu. **Application deadlines for fall 2011:** Regular decision: April 1. Early decision: Not offered. Early action: Not offered. Admission cannot be deferred. **Application fee:** $50. **To apply online, go to:** http://www.uh.edu/enroll/admis. **Admissions requirements/recommendations:** High school units required (recommended): English: (4); Mathematics: (3); Science: (2); Foreign language: (2); Social studies: (3). Tests: The college uses SAT or ACT scores in admissions decisions. Either SAT or ACT required. For admission to the fall 2011 entering class, the school will accept: ACT with or without writing accepted. Campus visit: Recommended. Admissions interview: Neither required nor recommended. Off-campus interview: Not available. **Factors that count in admissions decisions:** *Academic:* Secondary school record: Very Important. Class rank: Very Important. Letters of recommendation: Considered. Standardized test scores: Important. Essay: Not Considered. *Nonacademic:* Interview: Not Considered. Extracurricular activities: Considered. Talent/ability: Considered. Character/personal qualities: Considered. Alumni/ae relationship: Not Considered. Geographical residence: Not Considered. State residency: Not Considered. Religious affiliation/commitment: Not Considered. Minority status: Not Considered. Volunteer work: Considered. Work experience: Considered. **Other schools with the greatest overlap in applicants:** Sam Houston State University; Texas A&M University–College Station; Texas State University–San Marcos; University of Texas–Austin; University of Texas–San Antonio. **Admissions statistics for the fall 2009 entering class:** Total applicants: 11,393. Total accepted: 7,941. Freshmen enrolled: 3,295; 3% were from out of state. Overall acceptance rate: 70%. **Credentials of fall 2009 freshmen:** 24% ranked in the top 10 percent of their high school class; 60% were in the top 25 percent; 88% were in the top half. (Proportion submitting class standing: 92%.) **Average high school grade point average:** 3.6. **First-year students who submitted SAT scores:** 91%. Scores (25/75 percentile): Critical Reading: 470-570, Math: 500-620, Combined: 970-1190. **First-year students submitting ACT scores:** 30%. Scores (25/75 percentile): English: 19-25, Math: 19-26, Composite: 20-25.

ACADEMICS

Year founded: 1927. **Academic calendar:** Semester. **Degrees offered:** bachelor's, master's, doctorate. **Most popular majors:** 40% business, management, marketing, and related support services, 8% psychology, 8% social sciences, 6% biological and biomedical sciences, 6% communication, journalism, and related programs. **Major fields of study:** architecture and related services; area, ethnic, cultural, and gender studies; biological and biomedical sciences; business, management, marketing, and related support services; communication, journalism, and related programs; computer and information sciences and support services; engineering; engineering technologies/technicians; English language and literature/letters; family and consumer sciences/human sciences; foreign languages, literatures, and linguistics; health professions and related clinical sciences; history; mathematics and statistics; multi/interdisciplinary studies; natural resources and conservation; parks, recreation, leisure, and fitness studies; philosophy and religious studies; physical sciences; psychology; social sciences; visual and performing arts. **Areas of required coursework:** arts/fine arts, humanities, mathematics, English (including composition), sciences (biological or physical), history, social science. **Pre-professional programs:** pre-law, pre-dentistry, pre-medicine, pre-veterinary science, pre-optometry, pre-pharmacy. **Special academic programs (% participation):** cooperative (work-study plan) program (1%), cross-registration, distance learning (62%), double major (6%), dual enrollment, English as a Second Language (ESL), exchange student program (domestic), honors program (5.2%), independent study (6%), internships (10%), study abroad, teacher certificate program (9%), weekend college. **Teacher certification offered in:** early childhood, special education, elementary, vo-tech, middle/junior high, secondary, bilingual/bicultural. **Cooperative education programs:** art, business, computer science, education, engineering, health professions, home economics, humanities, natural science, social/behavioral science, technologies, other. **Reserve Officers Training Corps (ROTC):** Army ROTC: Offered on campus; Navy ROTC: Offered at cooperating institution (Rice University); Air Force ROTC: Offered on campus. **Faculty and instruction (2009-2010):** Total instructional faculty: 1,256 full-time, 524 part-time (64% men; 36% women; 22% minorities). Full-time faculty with Ph.D. or other terminal degree: 88%. Student/faculty ratio: 22/1. Classes of fewer than 20 students: 30%; of 20 to 49 students: 47%; of 50 or more students: 23%. **Advanced Placement and International Baccalaureate credit:** AP tests may be used for: Credit only. Scores accepted: 3, 4. International Baccalaureate exams may be used for: Credit only. **Freshmen returning for sophomore year:** 78%. **Graduation rates:** Four-year: 12%; five-year: 32%; six-year: 41%.

COSTS AND FINANCIAL AID

Financial aid office: (713) 743-1010. **Expenses (2010-2011):** Tuition and fees 2010-2011: $8,997 in state, $18,297 out of state. Estimated books and supplies: $1,100. **Financial aid:** Priority filing date for institution's financial aid form: April 1. In 2009-2010, 66% of undergraduates applied for financial aid. Of those, 58% were determined to have financial need; 25% had their need fully met. Average financial aid package (proportion receiving): $12,018 (56%). Average amount of gift aid, such as scholarships or grants (proportion receiving): $6,649 (50%). Average amount of self-help aid, such as work study or loans (proportion receiving): $7,098 (47%). Average need-based loan (excluding PLUS or other private loans): $6,908. Among students who received need-based aid, the average percentage of need met:

76%. Among students who received aid based on merit, the average award (and the proportion receiving): $4,544 (2%). The average athletic scholarship (and the proportion receiving): $4,161 (1%).

CAMPUS LIFE AND EXTRACURRICULAR ACTIVITIES

Campus housing available (% using): coed dorms (32%), sorority housing (2%), fraternity housing (3%), apartments for married students (1%), apartment for single students (46%), special housing for disabled students (2%). Students who live in college-owned, operated, or affiliated housing: 13%. **Student employment:** During the 2009-2010 academic year, 20% of undergraduates worked on campus. Average per-year earnings: $6,890. **Clubs and organizations:** Number of student organizations: 518. Activities include: campus ministries, choral groups, concert band, dance, drama/theater, international student organization, jazz band, literary magazine, marching band, music ensembles, musical theater, opera, pep band, radio station, student government, student newspaper, student film society, symphony orchestra, television station, yearbook. Number of fraternities: 26; sororities: 18. Proportion of men in fraternities: 2%; of women in sororities: 3%. **Sports program (2009-2010):** Member of NCAA I. *Men's intercollegiate varsity sports:* baseball, basketball, cross country, football, golf, track and field (indoor), track and field (outdoor). *Women's intercollegiate varsity sports:* basketball, cross country, soccer, softball, swimming, tennis, track and field (indoor), track and field (outdoor), volleyball.

SERVICES AND FACILITIES

Basic services: nonremedial tutoring, women's center, placement service, day care, health service, health insurance. **Remedial assistance:** reading, math, writing, study skills. **Counseling services:** minority student, career, military, personal, veteran student, academic, older student, psychological, birth control, religious. **For learning-disabled students:** School does not offer a structured program with separate admission and additional fees. Services include: remedial math, remedial English, reading machines, remedial reading, tape recorders, videotaped classes, diagnostic testing service, note-taking services, oral tests, learning center, readers, extended time for tests, tutors, priority registration, priority seating, proofreading services, texts on tape, exams on tape or computer, other testing accommodations, waiver of foreign language degree requirement, other. **Library:** Number of titles: 2,666,072; number of current serial subscriptions: 77,788. **Information technology resources:** Students are not required to lease or own a computer. Number of campus computers available to all students: 505. School has a wireless network. Approximate number of users that can be accommodated: 35,000. Proportion of college-owned housing units wired for high-speed internet access: 100%. **Campus safety:** Security services offered: 24-hour foot-and-vehicle patrols, late-night transport/escort service, 24-hour emergency telephones, lighted pathways/sidewalks, controlled dormitory access (key, security card, etc).

TRANSFER AND INTERNATIONAL STUDENTS

Transfer students: May apply for admission for the following academic terms: Fall, Spring, Summer. Applicants need a minimum number of credits to apply. For fall 2009: Transfer applications received: 5,177. Transfer applicants offered admission: 4,647. Transfer applicants enrolled: 3,020. **International students:** Number of foreign undergraduates 1231 (4% of student body). Number of countries represented: 111. Minimum TOEFL score required: 550 (paper); 79 (computer). Average TOEFL score: 550 (paper).

University of Houston–Downtown

- ■ **Address:** 1 Main Street, Houston, TX 77002
- ■ **Website:** http://www.uhd.edu
- ■ **Public**
- ■ **Enrollment:** 6,091 full-time; 6,488 part-time

KEY STATS

✔ **U.S News College Ranking:** Unranked, Regional Colleges (West)
✔ **SAT or ACT Score (25th/75th percentile):** N/A
✔ **Tuition:** 2010-2011: $5,492 in state, $14,792 out of state
  Selectivity: N/A   **Room/board:** $4,300
  Acceptance rate: 100%   **Average debt:** $16,204
  Student/faculty ratio: 20/1   **Proportion who borrowed:** 75%

UNDERGRADUATE STUDENT BODY STATS

2009-2010 enrollment: 6,091 full-time; 6,488 part-time. Men: 38%; women: 62%. **Ethnic makeup:** African American: 28%; Asian American: 10%; Hispanic: 35%; White: 22%; International: 5%.

ADMISSIONS FACTS AND FIGURES

Phone: (713) 221-8522. **Email:** uhdadmit@uhd.edu. **Website:** http://www.uhd.edu. **Application deadlines for fall 2011:** Regular decision: June 1. Early decision: Not offered. Early action: Not offered. Admission cannot be deferred. **Application fee:** $35. **To apply online, go to:** http://www.uhd.edu/admissions/forms.html. **Admissions requirements/recommendations:** High school units required (recommended): English: (4); Mathematics: (3); Science: (3); Foreign language: (3); Social studies: (2); History: (2); Academic electives: (1); Total units: (28). Tests: The college does not use SAT or ACT scores in admissions decisions. Neither SAT nor ACT required. Campus visit: Recommended. Admissions interview: Neither required nor recommended. Off-campus interview: Not available. **Factors that count in admissions decisions:** *Academic:* Secondary school record: Not Considered. Class rank: Not Considered. Letters of recommendation: Not Considered. Standardized test scores: Not Considered. Essay: Not Considered. *Nonacademic:* Interview: Not Considered. Extracurricular activities: Not Considered. Talent/ability: Not Considered. Character/personal qualities: Not Considered. Alumni/ae relationship: Not Considered. Geographical residence: Not Considered. State residency: Not Considered. Religious affiliation/commitment: Not Considered. Minority status: Not Considered. Volunteer work: Not Considered. Work experience: Not Considered. **Admissions statistics for the fall 2009 entering class:** Total applicants: 2,442. Total accepted: 2,434. Freshmen enrolled: 1,071; 2% were from out of state. Overall acceptance rate: 100%.

ACADEMICS

Year founded: 1974. **Academic calendar:** Semester. **Degrees offered:** bachelor's, master's. **Most popular majors:** 40% business, management, marketing, and related support services, 18% liberal arts and sciences studies, and humanities, 10% multi/interdisciplinary studies, 7% psychology, 7% security and protective services. **Major fields of study:** biological and biomedical sciences; business, management, marketing, and related support services; computer and information sciences and support services; engineering technologies/technicians; English language and literature/letters; foreign languages, literatures, and linguistics; history; liberal arts and sciences studies, and humanities; mathematics and statistics; multi/interdisciplinary studies; philosophy and religious studies; physical sciences; psychology; security and protective services; social sciences. **Areas of required coursework:** arts/fine arts, humanities, computer literacy, mathematics, English (including composition), sciences (biological or physical), history, social science, other. **Pre-professional programs:** pre-dentistry, pre-medicine, pre-veterinary science, pre-optometry, pre-pharmacy, other. **Special academic programs:** distance learning, dual enrollment, English as a Second Language (ESL), honors program, independent study, internships, study abroad, teacher certificate program, weekend college. **Teacher certification offered in:** early childhood, elementary, middle/junior high, secondary, bilingual/bicultural. **Reserve Officers Training Corps (ROTC):** Army ROTC: Offered at cooperating institution (University of Houston); Air Force ROTC: Offered at cooperating institution (University of Houston). **Faculty and instruction (2009-2010):** Total instructional faculty: 316 full-time, 278 part-time (52% men; 48% women; 36% minorities). Full-time faculty with Ph.D. or other terminal degree: 81%. Student/faculty ratio: 20/1. Classes of fewer than 20 students: 26%; of 20 to 49 students: 68%; of 50 or more students: 6%. **Advanced Placement and International Baccalaureate credit:** AP tests may be used for: Credit only. Scores accepted: 3, 4, 5. **Freshmen returning for sophomore year:** 57%. **Graduation rates:** Four-year: 2%; five-year: 6%; six-year: 14%.

COSTS AND FINANCIAL AID

Financial aid office: (713) 221-8041. **Expenses (2010-2011):** Tuition and fees 2010-2011: $5,492 in state, $14,792 out of state; room/board: $4,300. **Financial aid:** Priority filing date for institution's financial aid form: April 1. In 2009-2010, 80% of undergraduates applied for financial aid. Of those, 80% were determined to have financial need; 4% had their need fully met. Average financial aid package (proportion receiving): $8,126 (77%). Average amount of gift aid, such as scholarships or grants (proportion receiving): $5,465 (67%). Average amount of self-help aid, such as work study or loans (proportion receiving): $4,094 (64%). Average need-based loan (excluding PLUS or other private loans): $3,819. Among students who received need-based aid, the average percentage of need met: 49%. Among students who received aid based on merit, the average award (and the proportion receiving): $2,669 (2%). The average athletic scholarship (and the proportion

receiving): $0 (0%). Average amount of debt of borrowers graduating in 2009: $16,204. Proportion who borrowed: 75%.

CAMPUS LIFE AND EXTRACURRICULAR ACTIVITIES
Students who live in college-owned, operated, or affiliated housing: 0%. **Student employment:** During the 2009-2010 academic year, 4% of undergraduates worked on campus. Average per-year earnings: $9,259. **Clubs and organizations:** Number of student organizations: 52. Activities include: campus ministries, drama/theater, international student organization, jazz band, literary magazine, model UN, student government, student newspaper. Number of fraternities: 2; sororities: 6. Proportion of men in fraternities: 1%; of women in sororities: 1%.

SERVICES AND FACILITIES
Basic services: nonremedial tutoring, placement service, health service, health insurance, other. **Remedial assistance:** reading, math, writing, study skills. **Counseling services:** minority student, career, military, personal, veteran student, academic, older student, psychological, birth control, religious. **For learning-disabled students:** School does not offer a structured program with separate admission and additional fees. Total undergraduates in learning-disabled program or receiving services: 69. Services include: remedial math, remedial English, reading machines, remedial reading, tape recorders, note-taking services, learning center, extended time for tests, tutors, priority registration, priority seating, other testing accommodations. **Library:** Number of titles: 322,786; number of current serial subscriptions: 5,585. **Information technology resources:** Students are not required to lease or own a computer. Number of campus computers available to all students: 1,650. School has a wireless network. Approximate number of users that can be accommodated: 400. **Campus safety:** Security services offered: 24-hour foot-and-vehicle patrols, late-night transport/escort service, 24-hour emergency telephones, lighted pathways/sidewalks.

TRANSFER AND INTERNATIONAL STUDENTS
Transfer students: May apply for admission for the following academic terms: Fall, Spring, Summer. Applicants need a minimum number of credits to apply. For fall 2009: Transfer applications received: 3,185. Transfer applicants offered admission: 3,185. Transfer applicants enrolled: 2,127. **International students:** Number of foreign undergraduates: 611 (5% of student body). Number of countries represented: 76. Minimum TOEFL score required: 550 (paper); 213 (computer).

University of Mary Hardin-Baylor

- **Address:** 900 College Street, UMHB Box 8425, Belton, TX 76513
- **Website:** http://www.umhb.edu
- **Private; Religious affiliation:** Baptist
- **Enrollment:** 2,302 full-time; 245 part-time

KEY STATS
✔ **U.S News College Ranking:** 30, Regional Universities (West)
✔ **ACT Score (25th/75th percentile):** 19-28
✔ **Tuition:** 2010-2011: $21,700

Selectivity: Selective	**Room/board:** $6,040
Acceptance rate: 42%	**Average debt:** N/A
Student/faculty ratio: 11/1	**Proportion who borrowed:** 85%

UNDERGRADUATE STUDENT BODY STATS
2009-2010 enrollment: 2,302 full-time; 245 part-time. Men: 39%; women: 61%. **Ethnic makeup:** African American: 13%; American-Indian: 1%; Asian American: 2%; Hispanic: 14%; White: 69%; International: 1%. **Religious preference:** Roman Catholic: 13%; Protestant: 29%; No preference: 10%; Unknown: 2%; Baptist: 45%; Other: 1%.

ADMISSIONS FACTS AND FIGURES
Phone: (254) 295-4520. **Email:** admission@umhb.edu. **Website:** http://www.umhb.edu. **Application deadlines for fall 2011:** Regular decision: Rolling. Early decision: Not offered. Early action: Not offered. Admission can be deferred. **Application fee:** $35. **To apply online, go to:** http://www.umhb.edu/prospective/apps_and_forms.html. **Admissions requirements/recommendations:** High school units required (recommended): English: 4 (4); Mathematics: 3 (3); Social studies: 2 (2); Total units: 22 (22). Tests: The college uses SAT or ACT scores in admissions decisions. Either SAT or ACT required. For admission to the fall 2011 entering class, the school

will accept: ACT with writing required. Campus visit: Recommended. Admissions interview: Recommended. Off-campus interview: May be arranged. **Factors that count in admissions decisions:** *Academic:* Secondary school record: Considered. Class rank: Important. Letters of recommendation: Considered. Standardized test scores: Very Important. Essay: Considered. *Nonacademic:* Interview: Considered. Extracurricular activities: Considered. Talent/ability: Considered. Character/personal qualities: Considered. Alumni/ae relationship: Considered. Geographical residence: Considered. State residency: Considered. Religious affiliation/commitment: Considered. Minority status: Considered. Volunteer work: Considered. Work experience: Considered. **Admissions statistics for the fall 2009 entering class:** Total applicants: 5,379. Total accepted: 2,276. Freshmen enrolled: 479; 1% were from out of state. Overall acceptance rate: 42%. **Credentials of fall 2009 freshmen:** 18% ranked in the top 10 percent of their high school class; 48% were in the top 25 percent; 80% were in the top half. (Proportion submitting class standing: 85%.) **First-year students who submitted SAT scores:** 44%. Scores (25/75 percentile): Critical Reading: 415-619, Math: 440-598, Combined: 855-1217. **First-year students submitting ACT scores:** 45%. Scores (25/75 percentile): English: 18-26, Math: 17-26, Composite: 19-28.

ACADEMICS
Year founded: 1845. **Academic calendar:** Semester. **Degrees offered:** bachelor's, master's, doctorate. **Most popular majors:** 15% business, management, marketing, and related support services, 15% education, 13% nursing/registered nurse training (R.N., A.S.N., B.S.N., M.S.N.), 10% liberal arts and sciences studies, and humanities, 7% psychology. **Major fields of study:** area, ethnic, cultural, and gender studies; biological and biomedical sciences; business, management, marketing, and related support services; communication, journalism, and related programs; computer and information sciences and support services; education; English language and literature/letters; foreign languages, literatures, and linguistics; health professions and related clinical sciences; history; liberal arts and sciences studies, and humanities; mathematics and statistics; parks, recreation, leisure, and fitness studies; philosophy and religious studies; physical sciences; psychology; public administration and social service professions; security and protective services; social sciences; theology and religious vocations; visual and performing arts. **Areas of required coursework:** mathematics, English (including composition), foreign languages, sciences (biological or physical), social science, other. **Pre-professional programs:** pre-law, pre-dentistry, pre-medicine, pre-theology, pre-veterinary science, pre-optometry, pre-pharmacy, other. **Special academic programs:** accelerated program, double major, dual enrollment, English as a Second Language (ESL), honors program, independent study, internships, student-designed major, study abroad, teacher certificate program, other. **Teacher certification offered in:** early childhood, special education, elementary, middle/junior high, secondary. **Reserve Officers Training Corps (ROTC):** Army ROTC: Offered on campus; Air Force ROTC: Offered at cooperating institution (Baylor University). **Faculty and instruction (2009-2010):** Total instructional faculty: 133 full-time, 125 part-time (47% men; 53% women; 16% minorities). Student/faculty ratio: 11/1. Classes of fewer than 20 students: 55%; of 20 to 49 students: 45%; of 50 or more students: 0%. **Advanced Placement and International Baccalaureate credit:** AP tests may be used for: Credit only. Scores accepted: 4, 5. Freshmen returning for sophomore year: 62%. **Graduation rates:** Four-year: 30%; five-year: 46%; six-year: 44%.

COSTS AND FINANCIAL AID
Financial aid office: (254) 295-4517. **Expenses (2010-2011):** Tuition and fees 2010-2011: $21,700; room/board: $6,040. Estimated books and supplies: $1,200; transportation: $1,848; personal expenses: $1,812. **Financial aid:** Priority filing date for institution's financial aid form: March 1. In 2009-2010, 93% of undergraduates applied for financial aid. Of those, 83% were determined to have financial need; 23% had their need fully met. Average financial aid package (proportion receiving): $15,535 (83%). Average amount of gift aid, such as scholarships or grants (proportion receiving): $7,863 (77%). Average amount of self-help aid, such as work study or loans (proportion receiving): $4,657 (67%). Average need-based loan (excluding PLUS or other private loans): $4,203. Among students who received need-based aid, the average percentage of need met: 62%. Among students who received aid based on merit, the average award (and the proportion receiving): $4,686 (9%). Proportion who borrowed: 85%.

CAMPUS LIFE AND EXTRACURRICULAR ACTIVITIES
Campus housing available (% using): women's dorms (36%), men's dorms (20%), apartment for single students (44%), special housing for disabled students (0%). Students who live in college-owned, operated, or affiliated

housing: 50%. **Student employment:** During the 2009-2010 academic year, 23% of undergraduates worked on campus. Average per-year earnings: $2,425. **Clubs and organizations:** Number of student organizations: 54. Activities include: choral groups, concert band, drama/theater, international student organization, jazz band, literary magazine, marching band, music ensembles, musical theater, opera, pep band, student government, student newspaper, symphony orchestra, yearbook. Number of fraternities: 0; sororities: 0. Average proportion of students who stay on campus on weekends: 60%. **Sports program (2009-2010):** Member of NCAA III. *Men's intercollegiate varsity sports:* baseball, basketball, football, golf, soccer, tennis. *Women's intercollegiate varsity sports:* basketball, golf, soccer, softball, tennis, volleyball.

SERVICES AND FACILITIES

Basic services: nonremedial tutoring, health service. **Remedial assistance:** reading, math, writing, study skills. **Counseling services:** minority student, career, military, personal, veteran student, academic, older student, psychological, religious. **For learning-disabled students:** School does not offer a structured program with separate admission and additional fees. Total undergraduates in learning-disabled program or receiving services: 60. Services include: remedial math, remedial English, remedial reading, tape recorders, other special classes, diagnostic testing service, untimed tests, note-taking services, oral tests, learning center, readers, extended time for tests, tutors, priority registration, priority seating, texts on tape, other testing accommodations. **Library:** Number of titles: 203,748; number of current serial subscriptions: 907. **Information technology resources:** Students are not required to lease or own a computer. Number of campus computers available to all students: 275. School has a wireless network. Proportion of college-owned housing units wired for high-speed internet access: 100%. **Campus safety:** Security services offered: 24-hour foot-and-vehicle patrols, 24-hour emergency telephones, lighted pathways/sidewalks, controlled dormitory access (key, security card, etc).

TRANSFER AND INTERNATIONAL STUDENTS

Transfer students: May apply for admission for the following academic terms: Fall, Spring, Summer. Applicants need a minimum number of credits to apply. For fall 2009: Transfer applications received: 604. Transfer applicants offered admission: 500. Transfer applicants enrolled: 278. **International students:** Number of foreign undergraduates: 34 (1% of student body). Number of countries represented: 21.

University of North Texas

- **Address:** 1155 Union Circle #311425, Denton, TX 76203
- **Website:** http://www.unt.edu
- **Public**
- **Enrollment:** 22,140 full-time; 6,334 part-time

....

KEY STATS

✔ **U.S News College Ranking:** second tier, National Universities
✔ **SAT Score (25th/75th percentile):** 980-1210
✔ **Tuition:** 2010-2011: $7,600 in state, $16,900 out of state

Selectivity: Selective	**Room/board:** $6,716
Acceptance rate: 64%	**Average debt:** $0
Student/faculty ratio: 23/1	**Proportion who borrowed:** 0%

UNDERGRADUATE STUDENT BODY STATS

2009-2010 enrollment: 22,140 full-time; 6,334 part-time. Men: 46%; women: 54%. **Ethnic makeup:** African American: 14%; American-Indian: 1%; Asian American: 6%; Hispanic: 14%; White: 63%; International: 2%.

ADMISSIONS FACTS AND FIGURES

Phone: (940) 565-2681. **Email:** undergrad@unt.edu. **Website:** http://www.unt.edu. **Application deadlines for fall 2011:** Regular decision: August 1. Early decision: Not offered. Early action: Not offered. Admission can be deferred. **Application fee:** $60. **To apply online, go to:** https://www.applytexas.org/adappc/gen/c_start.WBX. **Admissions requirements/recommendations:** High school units required (recommended): English: 4 (4); Mathematics: 4 (4); Science: 4 (4); Foreign language: 2 (3); Social studies: 2 (2); History: 2 (2); Academic electives: 4 (4); Total units: 26 (27). Tests: The college uses SAT or ACT scores in admissions decisions. Either SAT or ACT required. For admission to the fall 2011 entering class, the school will accept: ACT with writing required. Campus visit: Recommended. Admissions interview:

Neither required nor recommended. Off-campus interview: Not available. **Factors that count in admissions decisions:** *Academic:* Secondary school record: Very Important. Class rank: Very Important. Letters of recommendation: Important. Standardized test scores: Very Important. Essay: Important. *Nonacademic:* Interview: Considered. Extracurricular activities: Considered. Talent/ability: Considered. Character/personal qualities: Considered. Alumni/ae relationship: Not Considered. Geographical residence: Considered. State residency: Not Considered. Religious affiliation/commitment: Not Considered. Minority status: Not Considered. Volunteer work: Considered. Work experience: Considered. **Other schools with the greatest overlap in applicants:** Texas A&M University–College Station; Texas State University–San Marcos; Texas Tech University; Texas Woman's University; University of Texas–Arlington. **Admissions statistics for the fall 2009 entering class:** Total applicants: 12,883. Total accepted: 8,218. Freshmen enrolled: 3,327; 3% were from out of state. Overall acceptance rate: 64%. **Credentials of fall 2009 freshmen:** 21% ranked in the top 10 percent of their high school class; 51% were in the top 25 percent; 89% were in the top half. (Proportion submitting class standing: 97%.) **First-year students who submitted SAT scores:** 86%. Scores (25/75 percentile): Critical Reading: 480-600, Math: 500-610, Combined: 980-1210. **First-year students submitting ACT scores:** 39%. Scores (25/75 percentile): English: 19-25, Math: 19-25, Composite: 20-25.

ACADEMICS

Year founded: 1890. **Academic calendar:** Semester. **Degrees offered:** bachelor's, post-bachelor's certificate, master's, doctorate. **Most popular majors:** 21% business, management, marketing, and related support services, 17% multi/interdisciplinary studies, 11% visual and performing arts, 8% communication, journalism, and related programs, 5% English language and literature/letters. **Major fields of study:** architecture and related services; biological and biomedical sciences; business, management, marketing, and related support services; communication, journalism, and related programs; computer and information sciences and support services; engineering; engineering technologies/technicians; English language and literature/letters; family and consumer sciences/human sciences; foreign languages, literatures, and linguistics; health professions and related clinical sciences; history; liberal arts and sciences studies, and humanities; mathematics and statistics; multi/interdisciplinary studies; parks, recreation, leisure, and fitness studies; philosophy and religious studies; physical sciences; psychology; public administration and social service professions; science technologies/technicians; security and protective services; social sciences; visual and performing arts. **Areas of required coursework:** arts/fine arts, humanities, computer literacy, mathematics, English (including composition), philosophy, foreign languages, sciences (biological or physical), history, social science, other. **Pre-professional programs:** pre-law, pre-dentistry, pre-medicine, pre-veterinary science, pre-optometry, pre-pharmacy, other. **Special academic programs (% participation):** accelerated program (10.6%), cooperative (work-study plan) program (9.2%), cross-registration (5.4%), distance learning (28.4%), double major (8.05%), dual enrollment (10.8%), English as a Second Language (ESL) (4.2%), exchange student program (domestic) (3.5%), honors program (5.9%), independent study (6.7%), internships (19.3%), study abroad (8.7%), teacher certificate program (8%). **Teacher certification offered in:** early childhood, special education, elementary, vo-tech, middle/junior high, secondary, bilingual/bicultural. **Cooperative education programs:** art, business, computer science, engineering, humanities, natural science, social/behavioral science, technologies. **Reserve Officers Training Corps (ROTC):** Army ROTC: Offered on campus; Air Force ROTC: Offered on campus. **Faculty and instruction (2009-2010):** Total instructional faculty: 1,035 full-time, 487 part-time (55% men; 45% women; 20% minorities). Full-time faculty with Ph.D. or other terminal degree: 89%. Student/faculty ratio: 23/1. Classes of fewer than 20 students: 29%; of 20 to 49 students: 52%; of 50 or more students: 19%. **Advanced Placement and International Baccalaureate credit:** AP tests may be used for: Credit only. Scores accepted: 3, 4, 5. International Baccalaureate exams may be used for: Credit only. **Freshmen returning for sophomore year:** 76%. **Graduation rates:** Four-year: 19%; five-year: 39%; six-year: 47%. **Graduate study:** 14% of students pursue further study immediately upon graduation. Fields in which graduates pursue further study: Master of Business Administration (MBA), 7%; law, 9%; medicine, 16%; dentistry, 1%; engineering, 4%; theology (or the seminary), 1%; education, 19%; arts and sciences, 41%; veterinary medicine, 2%.

COSTS AND FINANCIAL AID

Financial aid office: (940) 565-2302. **Expenses (2010-2011):** Tuition and fees 2010-2011: $7,600 in state, $16,900 out of state; room/board: $6,716. Estimated books and supplies: $1,050; transportation: $1,540; personal expenses: $1,240. **Financial aid:** Priority filing date for institution's financial aid form: March 31. In 2009-2010, 67% of undergraduates applied for financial aid. Of those, 52% were determined to have financial need; 29% had their need fully met. Average financial aid package (proportion receiving): $10,811 (50%). Average amount of gift aid, such as scholarships or grants (proportion receiving): $6,245 (41%). Average amount of self-help aid, such as work study or loans (proportion receiving): $5,074 (43%). Average need-based loan (excluding PLUS or other private loans): $4,286. Among students who received need-based aid, the average percentage of need met: 71%. Among students who received aid based on merit, the average award (and the proportion receiving): $4,843 (10%). The average athletic scholarship (and the proportion receiving): $11,849 (1%). Average amount of debt of borrowers graduating in 2009: $0.

CAMPUS LIFE AND EXTRACURRICULAR ACTIVITIES

Campus housing available (% using): coed dorms (87%), women's dorms (4%), sorority housing (2%), fraternity housing (3%), apartments for married students (0%), apartment for single students (0%), special housing for disabled students (1%), cooperative housing (0%). Students who live in college-owned, operated, or affiliated housing: 17%. **Student employment:** During the 2009-2010 academic year, 13% of undergraduates worked on campus. Average per-year earnings: $9,100. **Clubs and organizations:** Number of student organizations: 330. Activities include: campus ministries, choral groups, concert band, dance, drama/theater, international student organization, jazz band, literary magazine, marching band, music ensembles, musical theater, opera, pep band, radio station, student government, student newspaper, student film society, symphony orchestra, television station. Number of fraternities: 22; sororities: 16. Proportion of men in fraternities: 5%; of women in sororities: 5%. Average proportion of students who stay on campus on weekends: 60%. **Sports program (2009-2010):** Member of NCAA I. *Men's intercollegiate varsity sports:* basketball, cross country, football, golf, track and field (indoor), track and field (outdoor). *Women's intercollegiate varsity sports:* basketball, cross country, golf, soccer, softball, swimming, tennis, track and field (indoor), track and field (outdoor), volleyball.

SERVICES AND FACILITIES

Basic services: nonremedial tutoring, women's center, placement service, health service, health insurance. **Remedial assistance:** reading, math, writing, study skills. **Counseling services:** minority student, career, military, personal, veteran student, academic, older student, psychological, birth control. **For learning-disabled students:** School does not offer a structured program with separate admission and additional fees. Services include: reading machines, diagnostic testing service, note-taking services, oral tests, learning center, readers, extended time for tests, early syllabus, priority seating, exams on tape or computer, other testing accommodations. **Library:** Number of titles: 2,249,500; number of current serial subscriptions: 40,376. **Information technology resources:** Students are not required to lease or own a computer. Number of campus computers available to all students: 740. School has a wireless network. Approximate number of users that can be accommodated: 3,000. Proportion of college-owned housing units wired for high-speed internet access: 100%. **Campus safety:** Security services offered: 24-hour foot-and-vehicle patrols, late-night transport/escort service, 24-hour emergency telephones, lighted pathways/sidewalks, controlled dormitory access (key, security card, etc).

TRANSFER AND INTERNATIONAL STUDENTS

Transfer students: May apply for admission for the following academic terms: Fall, Spring, Summer. Applicants need a minimum number of credits to apply. For fall 2009: Transfer applications received: 9,684. Transfer applicants offered admission: 5,673. Transfer applicants enrolled: 4,012. **International students:** Number of foreign undergraduates: 703 (2% of student body). Number of countries represented: 128. Minimum TOEFL score required: 550 (paper); 213 (computer). Average TOEFL score: 569 (paper).

University of St. Thomas

■ **Address:** 3800 Montrose Boulevard, Houston, TX 77006-4696
■ **Website:** http://www.stthom.edu
■ **Private; Religious affiliation:** Roman Catholic
■ **Enrollment:** 1,313 full-time; 479 part-time

KEY STATS

✔ **U.S News College Ranking:** 27, Regional Universities (West)
✔ **SAT Score (25th/75th percentile):** 1020-1250
✔ **Tuition:** 2010-2011: $23,500

Selectivity: Selective	**Room/board:** $7,900
Acceptance rate: 80%	**Average debt:** $22,857
Student/faculty ratio: 12/1	**Proportion who borrowed:** 71%

UNDERGRADUATE STUDENT BODY STATS

2009-2010 enrollment: 1,313 full-time; 479 part-time. Men: 40%; women: 60%. **Ethnic makeup:** African American: 5%; American-Indian: 1%; Asian American: 12%; Hispanic: 34%; White: 44%; International: 4%. **Religious preference:** Protestant: 12%; Jewish: 1%; Muslim: 3%; Hindu: 1%; Buddhist: 1%; Unknown: 25%; Roman Catholic: 51%; Orthodox: 1%; Other: 5%.

ADMISSIONS FACTS AND FIGURES

Phone: (713) 525-3500. **Email:** admissions@stthom.edu. **Website:** http://www.stthom.edu. **Application deadlines for fall 2011:** Regular decision: May 1. Early decision: Not offered. Early action: Send application by: November 1; Decision sent by: December 15. Admission can be deferred. **Application fee:** $25. **To apply online, go to:** http://www.applyweb.com/apply/stthom_undergrad/. **Admissions requirements/recommendations:** High school units required (recommended): English: 4 (4); Mathematics: 3 (3); Science: 3 (3); Foreign language: 2 (2); Social studies: 2 (2); History: 1 (1); Total units: 18 (18). Tests: The college uses SAT or ACT scores in admissions decisions. Either SAT or ACT required. For admission to the fall 2011 entering class, the school will accept: ACT with writing required. Campus visit: Recommended. Admissions interview: Recommended. Off-campus interview: May be arranged. **Factors that count in admissions decisions: Academic:** Secondary school record: Very Important. Class rank: Very Important. Letters of recommendation: Considered. Standardized test scores: Very Important. Essay: Very Important. **Nonacademic:** Interview: Considered. Extracurricular activities: Considered. Talent/ability: Considered. Character/personal qualities: Considered. Alumni/ae relationship: Not Considered. Geographical residence: Not Considered. State residency: Not Considered. Religious affiliation/commitment: Not Considered. Minority status: Not Considered. Volunteer work: Considered. Work experience: Considered. **Admissions statistics for the fall 2009 entering class:** Total applicants: 866. Total accepted: 692. Freshmen enrolled: 287; 5% were from out of state. Overall acceptance rate: 80%. Non-early acceptance rate: 80%. **Credentials of fall 2009 freshmen:** 28% ranked in the top 10 percent of their high school class; 58% were in the top 25 percent; 83% were in the top half. (Proportion submitting class standing: 78%.) **Average high school grade point average:** 3.4. **First-year students who submitted SAT scores:** 74%. Scores (25/75 percentile): Critical Reading: 510-620, Math: 510-630, Combined: 1020-1250. **First-year students submitting ACT scores:** 23%. Scores (25/75 percentile): English: 22-28, Math: 21-27, Composite: 23-27.

ACADEMICS

Year founded: 1947. **Academic calendar:** Semester. **Degrees offered:** diploma, bachelor's, master's, doctorate. **Most popular majors:** 24% business, management, marketing, and related support services, 19% liberal arts and sciences studies, and humanities, 7% biological and biomedical sciences, 7% education, 7% psychology. **Major fields of study:** biological and biomedical sciences; business, management, marketing, and related support services; communication, journalism, and related programs; education; English language and literature/letters; foreign languages, literatures, and linguistics; history; liberal arts and sciences studies, and humanities; mathematics and statistics; natural resources and conservation; philosophy and religious studies; physical sciences; psychology; social sciences; theology and religious vocations; visual and performing arts. **Areas of required coursework:** arts/fine arts, mathematics, English (including composition), philosophy, foreign languages, sciences (biological or physical), history, social science, other. **Pre-professional programs:** pre-law, pre-dentistry, pre-medicine, pre-veterinary science, pre-optometry, pre-pharmacy, other. **Special academic programs:** accelerated program, distance learning, double major, dual enrollment, honors program, independent study, internships, liberal arts/career combination, student-designed major, study abroad, teacher certificate program, weekend college. **Teacher certification offered in:** early childhood, special education, elementary, middle/junior high, secondary, bilingual/bicultural. **Reserve Officers Training Corps (ROTC):** Army ROTC: Offered at cooperating institution (University of Houston); Air Force ROTC: Offered at cooperating institution (University of Houston). **Faculty and instruction (2009-2010):** Total instructional faculty: 125 full-time, 137 part-time (58% men; 42% women; 16% minorities). Full-time faculty with Ph.D. or other terminal degree: 92%. Student/faculty ratio: 12/1. Classes of fewer than 20 students: 57%; of 20 to 49 students: 43%; of 50 or more students: 0%. **Advanced Placement and International Baccalaureate credit:** AP tests may be used for: Credit only. Scores accepted: 3, 4, 5. International Baccalaureate exams may be used for: Credit only. **Freshmen returning for sophomore year:** 69%. **Graduation rates:** Four-year: 30%; five-year: 44%; six-year: 50%.

COSTS AND FINANCIAL AID

Financial aid office: (713) 942-3465. **Expenses (2010-2011):** Tuition and fees 2010-2011: $23,500; room/board: $7,900. Estimated books and supplies: $1,030; transportation: $1,726; personal expenses: $1,944. **Financial aid:** Priority filing date for institution's financial aid form: April 15. In 2009-2010, 68% of undergraduates applied for financial aid. Of those, 60% were determined to have financial need; 11% had their need fully met. Average financial aid package (proportion receiving): $15,107 (59%). Average amount of gift aid, such as scholarships or grants (proportion receiving): $11,859 (57%). Average amount of self-help aid, such as work study or loans (proportion receiving): $4,629 (42%). Average need-based loan (excluding PLUS or other private loans): $4,684. Among students who received need-based aid, the average percentage of need met: 65%. Among students who received aid based on merit, the average award (and the proportion receiving): $7,987 (24%). The average athletic scholarship (and the proportion receiving): $5,322 (1%). Average amount of debt of borrowers graduating in 2009: $22,857. Proportion who borrowed: 71%.

CAMPUS LIFE AND EXTRACURRICULAR ACTIVITIES

Campus housing available (% using): coed dorms (85%), apartment for single students (15%), other housing options. Students who live in college-owned, operated, or affiliated housing: 18%. Average per-year earnings: $6,240. **Clubs and organizations:** Number of student organizations: 67. Activities include: campus ministries, choral groups, dance, drama/theater, international student organization, jazz band, literary magazine, music ensembles, musical theater, student government, student newspaper. Number of fraternities: 0; sororities: 0. Average proportion of students who stay on campus on weekends: 50%. **Sports program (2009-2010):** Member of NAIA. *Men's intercollegiate varsity sports:* basketball, soccer. *Women's intercollegiate varsity sports:* volleyball.

SERVICES AND FACILITIES

Basic services: nonremedial tutoring, placement service, health service, other. **Remedial assistance:** reading, math, writing, study skills, other. **Counseling services:** career, military, personal, veteran student, academic, psychological, religious. **For learning-disabled students:** School does not offer a structured program with separate admission and additional fees. Total undergraduates in learning-disabled program or receiving services: 31. Services include: remedial math, remedial English, note-taking services, oral tests, learning center, extended time for tests, early syllabus, priority registration, texts on tape, exams on tape or computer, other testing accommodations. **Library:** Number of titles: 237,456; number of current serial subscriptions: 46,107. **Information technology resources:** Students are not required to lease or own a computer. Number of campus computers available to all students: 290. School has a wireless network. Approximate number of users that can be accommodated: 1,960. Proportion of college-owned housing units wired for high-speed internet access: 90%. **Campus safety:** Security services offered: 24-hour foot-and-vehicle patrols, late-night transport/escort service, 24-hour emergency telephones, lighted pathways/sidewalks, controlled dormitory access (key, security card, etc).

TRANSFER AND INTERNATIONAL STUDENTS

Transfer students: May apply for admission for the following academic terms: Fall, Spring, Summer. Applicants need a minimum number of credits to apply. For fall 2009: Transfer applications received: 299. Transfer applicants offered admission: 263. Transfer applicants enrolled: 152. **International students:** Number of foreign undergraduates: 73 (4% of student body). Number of countries represented: 57. Minimum TOEFL score required: 550 (paper); 79 (computer). Average TOEFL score: 610 (paper).

University of Texas–Arlington

- ■ **Address:** 701 S. Nedderman Drive, Arlington, TX 76019-0111
- ■ **Website:** http://www.uta.edu
- ■ **Public**
- ■ **Enrollment:** 14,293 full-time; 7,077 part-time

KEY STATS

✔ **U.S News College Ranking:** second tier, National Universities
✔ **SAT Score (25th/75th percentile):** 950-1190
✔ **Tuition:** 2009-2010: $8,186 in state, $16,496 out of state

Selectivity: Selective	**Room/board:** $6,097
Acceptance rate: 74%	**Average debt:** $15,171
Student/faculty ratio: 23/1	**Proportion who borrowed:** 53%

UNDERGRADUATE STUDENT BODY STATS

2009-2010 enrollment: 14,293 full-time; 7,077 part-time. Men: 46%; women: 54%. **Ethnic makeup:** African American: 16%; American-Indian: 1%; Asian American: 12%; Hispanic: 19%; White: 49%; International: 4%.

ADMISSIONS FACTS AND FIGURES

Phone: (817) 272-6287. **Email:** admissions@uta.edu. **Website:** http://www.uta.edu. **Application deadlines for fall 2011:** Regular decision: Rolling. Early decision: Not offered. Early action: Not offered. Admission can be deferred. **Application fee:** $35. **To apply online, go to:** http://www.applytexas.org. **Admissions requirements/recommendations:** High school units required (recommended): English: 4 (4); Mathematics: 3 (3); Science: 3 (3); Foreign language: 2 (3); Social studies: 3 (4); History: 0 (0); Academic electives: 5 (5); Total units: 20. Tests: The college uses SAT or ACT scores in admissions decisions. Either SAT or ACT required. For admission to the fall 2011 entering class, the school will accept: ACT with writing required. Campus visit: Recommended. Admissions interview: Neither required nor recommended. Off-campus interview: Not available. **Factors that count in admissions decisions: Academic:** Secondary school record: Important. Class rank: Very Important. Letters of recommendation: Considered. Standardized test scores: Very Important. Essay: Considered. **Nonacademic:** Interview: Not Considered. Extracurricular activities: Considered. Talent/ability: Considered. Character/personal qualities: Considered. Alumni/ae relationship: Not Considered. Geographical residence: Not Considered. State residency: Not Considered. Religious affiliation/commitment: Not Considered. Minority status: Not Considered. Volunteer work: Considered. Work experience: Considered. **Admissions statistics for the fall 2009 entering class:** Total applicants: 6,784. Total accepted: 4,990. Freshmen enrolled: 2,319; 2% were from out of state. Overall acceptance rate: 74%. **Credentials of fall 2009 freshmen:** 24% ranked in the top 10 percent of their high school class; 66% were in the top 25 percent; 91% were in the top half. (Proportion submitting class standing: 92%.) **First-year students who submitted SAT scores:** 89%. Scores (25/75 percentile): Critical Reading: 460-580, Math: 490-610, Combined: 950-1190. **First-year students submitting ACT scores:** 36%. Scores (25/75 percentile): English: 19-26, Math: 18-25, Composite: 20-25.

ACADEMICS

Year founded: 1895. **Academic calendar:** Other. **Degrees offered:** bachelor's, post-bachelor's certificate, master's, post-master's certificate, doctorate. **Most popular majors:** 23% business, management, marketing, and related support services, 15% multi/interdisciplinary studies, 8% biological and biomedical sciences, 8% health professions and related clinical sciences, 6% engineering. **Major fields of study:** architecture and related services; biological and biomedical sciences; business, management, marketing, and related support services; communication, journalism, and related programs; computer and information sciences and support services; engineering; English language and literature/letters; family and consumer sciences/human sciences; foreign languages, literatures, and linguistics; health professions and related clinical sciences; history; mathematics and statistics; multi/interdisciplinary studies; parks, recreation, leisure, and fitness studies; philosophy and religious studies; physical sciences; psychology; public administration and social service professions; security and protective services; social sciences; visual and performing arts. **Areas of required coursework:** arts/fine arts, humanities, computer literacy, mathematics, English (including composition), foreign languages, sciences (biological or physical), history, social science, other. **Pre-professional programs:** pre-law, pre-dentistry, pre-medicine, pre-pharmacy. **Special academic programs:** cross-registration, distance learning, double major, dual enrollment, English as a Second Language (ESL), honors program, independent study, internships, student-designed major, study abroad, teacher certificate program. **Teacher certification offered in:** early childhood, elementary, middle/junior high, secondary, bilingual/bicultural. **Cooperative education programs:** business, engineering, other. **Reserve Officers Training Corps (ROTC):** Army ROTC: Offered on campus; Air Force ROTC: Offered at cooperating institution (Texas Christian University). **Faculty and instruction (2009-2010):** Total instructional faculty: 823 full-time, 328 part-time (60% men; 40% women; 19% minorities). Full-time faculty with Ph.D. or other terminal degree: 82%. Student/faculty ratio: 23/1. Classes of fewer than 20 students: 27%; of 20 to 49 students: 47%; of 50 or more students: 26%. **Advanced Placement and International Baccalaureate credit:** AP tests may be used for: Credit only. Scores accepted: 3, 4, 5. International Baccalaureate exams may be used for: Credit only. **Freshmen returning for sophomore year:** 64%. **Graduation rates:** Four-year: 17%; five-year: 35%; six-year: 43%.

COSTS AND FINANCIAL AID
Financial aid office: (817) 272-3568. **Expenses (2009-2010):** Tuition and fees 2009-2010: $8,186 in state, $16,496 out of state; room/board: $6,097. Estimated books and supplies: $908; transportation: $2,500; personal expenses: $1,490. **Financial aid:** Priority filing date for institution's financial aid form: May 15. In 2009-2010, 73% of undergraduates applied for financial aid. Of those, 64% were determined to have financial need; 9% had their need fully met. Average financial aid package (proportion receiving): $9,939 (64%). Average amount of gift aid, such as scholarships or grants (proportion receiving): $6,493 (51%). Average amount of self-help aid, such as work study or loans (proportion receiving): $4,730 (61%). Average need-based loan (excluding PLUS or other private loans): $4,162. Among students who received need-based aid, the average percentage of need met: 73%. Among students who received aid based on merit, the average award (and the proportion receiving): $5,050 (2%). The average athletic scholarship (and the proportion receiving): $3,989 (0%). Average amount of debt of borrowers graduating in 2009: $15,171. Proportion who borrowed: 53%.

CAMPUS LIFE AND EXTRACURRICULAR ACTIVITIES
Campus housing available: coed dorms, women's dorms, men's dorms, sorority housing, fraternity housing, apartments for married students, apartment for single students, other housing options. Students who live in college-owned, operated, or affiliated housing: 16%. **Clubs and organizations:** Number of student organizations: 260. Activities include: campus ministries, choral groups, concert band, dance, drama/theater, international student organization, jazz band, literary magazine, marching band, music ensembles, opera, radio station, student government, student newspaper, student film society, symphony orchestra. Number of fraternities: 17; sororities: 15. Proportion of men in fraternities: 6%; of women in sororities: 3%. Average proportion of students who stay on campus on weekends: 60%. **Sports program (2009-2010):** Member of NCAA I. *Men's intercollegiate varsity sports:* baseball, basketball, cross country, golf, tennis, track and field (outdoor). *Women's intercollegiate varsity sports:* basketball, cross country, softball, tennis, track and field (outdoor), volleyball.

SERVICES AND FACILITIES
Basic services: nonremedial tutoring, placement service, day care, health service, health insurance. **Remedial assistance:** reading, math, writing, study skills. **Counseling services:** minority student, career, military, personal, veteran student, academic, older student, psychological, birth control. **For learning-disabled students:** School does not offer a structured program with separate admission and additional fees. Total undergraduates in learning-disabled program or receiving services: 99. Services include: remedial math, remedial English, tape recorders, diagnostic testing service, note-taking services, readers, extended time for tests, tutors, priority seating, substitution of courses, typist/scribe. **Library:** Number of titles: 1,194,412; number of current serial subscriptions: 42,675. **Information technology resources:** Students are not required to lease or own a computer. Number of campus computers available to all students: 600. School has a wireless network. Approximate number of users that can be accommodated: 10,000. Proportion of college-owned housing units wired for high-speed internet access: 90%. **Campus safety:** Security services offered: 24-hour foot-and-vehicle patrols, late-night transport/escort service, 24-hour emergency telephones, lighted pathways/sidewalks, controlled dormitory access (key, security card, etc).

TRANSFER AND INTERNATIONAL STUDENTS
Transfer students: May apply for admission for the following academic terms: Fall, Winter, Spring, Summer. Applicants need a minimum number of credits to apply. For fall 2009: Transfer applications received: 6,662. Transfer applicants offered admission: 6,125. Transfer applicants enrolled:

3,944. **International students:** Number of foreign undergraduates: 820 (4% of student body). Number of countries represented: 81. Minimum TOEFL score required: 550 (paper); 213 (computer).

University of Texas–Austin

- **Address:** Austin, TX 78712-1111
- **Website:** http://www.utexas.edu
- **Public**
- **Enrollment:** 35,364 full-time; 2,804 part-time

KEY STATS
✔ **U.S News College Ranking:** 45, National Universities
✔ **SAT Score (25th/75th percentile):** 1100-1360
✔ **Tuition:** 2010-2011: $9,418 in state, $31,218 out of state

Selectivity: More selective	**Room/board:** $10,112
Acceptance rate: 45%	**Average debt:** $22,102
Student/faculty ratio: 17/1	**Proportion who borrowed:** 50%

UNDERGRADUATE STUDENT BODY STATS
2009-2010 enrollment: 35,364 full-time; 2,804 part-time. Men: 49%; women: 51%. **Ethnic makeup:** African American: 5%; Asian American: 18%; Hispanic: 19%; White: 53%; International: 4%.

ADMISSIONS FACTS AND FIGURES
Phone: (512) 475-7440. **Email:** askadmit@uts.cc.utexas.edu. **Website:** http://www.utexas.edu. **Application deadlines for fall 2011:** Regular decision: December 1. Early decision: Not offered. Early action: Not offered. Admission can be deferred. **Application fee:** $60. **To apply online, go to:** http://bealonghorn.utexas.edu/freshmen/admission/requirements/. **Admissions requirements/recommendations:** High school units required (recommended): English: 4 (4); Mathematics: 3 (4); Science: 3 (4); Foreign language: 2 (2); Social studies: 4 (4); Academic electives: 5 (6); Total units: 21 (26). **Tests:** The college uses SAT or ACT scores in admissions decisions. Either SAT or ACT required. For admission to the fall 2011 entering class, the school will accept: ACT with writing required. Campus visit: Recommended. Admissions interview: Neither required nor recommended. Off-campus interview: Not available. **Factors that count in admissions decisions:** *Academic:* Secondary school record: Very Important. Class rank: Very Important. Letters of recommendation: Considered. Standardized test scores: Important. Essay: Important. *Nonacademic:* Interview: Not Considered. Extracurricular activities: Important. Talent/ability: Important. Character/personal qualities: Considered. Alumni/ae relationship: Not Considered. Geographical residence: Not Considered. State residency: Considered. Religious affiliation/commitment: Not Considered. Minority status: Considered. Volunteer work: Important. Work experience: Important. **Other schools with the greatest overlap in applicants:** Baylor University; Rice University; Texas A&M University–College Station; Texas State University–San Marcos; Texas Tech University. **Admissions statistics for the fall 2009 entering class:** Total applicants: 31,362. Total accepted: 14,213. Freshmen enrolled: 7,243; 8% were from out of state. Overall acceptance rate: 45%. **Size of waiting list:** 253 applicants; enrolled from waiting list: 165. **Credentials of fall 2009 freshmen:** 77% ranked in the top 10 percent of their high school class; 94% were in the top 25 percent; 99% were in the top half. (Proportion submitting class standing: 99%.) **First-year students who submitted SAT scores:** 92%. Scores (25/75 percentile): Critical Reading: 530-660, Math: 570-700, Combined: 1100-1360. **First-year students submitting ACT scores:** 44%. Scores (25/75 percentile): English: 25-32, Math: 23-31, Composite: 24-30.

ACADEMICS
Year founded: 1883. **Academic calendar:** Semester. **Degrees offered:** bachelor's, master's, doctorate. **Most popular majors:** 14% communication, journalism, and related programs, 13% social sciences, 12% business, management, marketing, and related support services, 11% engineering, 8% biological and biomedical sciences. **Major fields of study:** architecture and related services; area, ethnic, cultural, and gender studies; biological and biomedical sciences; business, management, marketing, and related support services; communication, journalism, and related programs; computer and information sciences and support services; engineering; English language and literature/letters; family and consumer sciences/human sciences; foreign languages, literatures, and linguistics; health professions and related clinical sciences; history; liberal arts and sciences studies, and

humanities; mathematics and statistics; multi/interdisciplinary studies; parks, recreation, leisure, and fitness studies; philosophy and religious studies; physical sciences; psychology; public administration and social service professions; social sciences; visual and performing arts. **Areas of required coursework:** arts/fine arts, humanities, mathematics, English (including composition), foreign languages, sciences (biological or physical), history, social science. **Pre-professional programs:** pre-pharmacy. **Special academic programs:** accelerated program, cooperative (work-study plan) program, distance learning, double major, dual enrollment, English as a Second Language (ESL), honors program, independent study, internships, liberal arts/career combination, student-designed major, study abroad, teacher certificate program. **Teacher certification offered in:** early childhood, special education, elementary, middle/junior high, secondary, bilingual/bicultural. **Cooperative education programs:** engineering. **Reserve Officers Training Corps (ROTC):** Army ROTC: Offered on campus; Navy ROTC: Offered on campus; Air Force ROTC: Offered on campus. **Faculty and instruction (2009-2010):** Total instructional faculty: 2,770 full-time, 269 part-time (62% men; 38% women; 19% minorities). Full-time faculty with Ph.D. or other terminal degree: 92%. Student/faculty ratio: 17/1. Classes of fewer than 20 students: 36%; of 20 to 49 students: 40%; of 50 or more students: 23%. **Advanced Placement and International Baccalaureate credit:** AP tests may be used for: Credit only. Scores accepted: 2, 3, 4, 5. International Baccalaureate exams may be used for: Credit only. **Freshmen returning for sophomore year:** 92%. **Graduation rates:** Four-year: 51%; five-year: 77%; six-year: 81%.

COSTS AND FINANCIAL AID

Financial aid office: (512) 475-6203. **Expenses (2010-2011):** Tuition and fees 2010-2011: $9,418 in state, $31,218 out of state; room/board: $10,112. Estimated books and supplies: $874; transportation: $1,200; personal expenses: $2,424. **Financial aid:** Priority filing date for institution's financial aid form: April 1. In 2009-2010, 61% of undergraduates applied for financial aid. Of those, 44% were determined to have financial need; 24% had their need fully met. Average financial aid package (proportion receiving): $12,388 (44%). Average amount of gift aid, such as scholarships or grants (proportion receiving): $8,822 (36%). Average amount of self-help aid, such as work study or loans (proportion receiving): $4,419 (34%). Average need-based loan (excluding PLUS or other private loans): $4,204. Among students who received need-based aid, the average percentage of need met: 75%. Among students who received aid based on merit, the average award (and the proportion receiving): N/A (5%). Average amount of debt of borrowers graduating in 2009: $22,102. Proportion who borrowed: 50%.

CAMPUS LIFE AND EXTRACURRICULAR ACTIVITIES

Campus housing available (% using): coed dorms (84%), women's dorms (13%), men's dorms (3%), apartments for married students (0%), apartment for single students (0%), other housing options. Students who live in college-owned, operated, or affiliated housing: 20%. **Clubs and organizations:** Number of student organizations: 900. Activities include: campus ministries, choral groups, concert band, dance, drama/theater, international student organization, jazz band, literary magazine, marching band, music ensembles, musical theater, opera, pep band, radio station, student government, student newspaper, student film society, symphony orchestra, television station, yearbook. Number of fraternities: 35; sororities: 27. Proportion of men in fraternities: 10%; of women in sororities: 12%. **Sports program (2009-2010):** Member of NCAA I. *Men's intercollegiate varsity sports:* baseball, basketball, cross country, football, golf, swimming, tennis, track and field (indoor), track and field (outdoor). *Women's intercollegiate varsity sports:* basketball, crew (heavyweight), cross country, golf, crew (lightweight), soccer, softball, swimming, tennis, track and field (indoor), track and field (outdoor), volleyball.

SERVICES AND FACILITIES

Basic services: nonremedial tutoring, women's center, placement service, day care, health service, health insurance. **Remedial assistance:** reading, math, writing, study skills. **Counseling services:** minority student, career, personal, academic, older student, psychological, birth control. **For learning-disabled students:** School does not offer a structured program with separate admission and additional fees. Total undergraduates in learning-disabled program or receiving services: 172. Services include: reading machines, tape recorders, videotaped classes, note-taking services, oral tests, learning center, readers, extended time for tests, tutors, priority registration, priority seating, substitution of courses, texts on tape, typist/scribe, exams on tape or computer, other testing accommodations, other. **Library:** Number of titles: 9,853,414; number of current serial subscriptions: 97,191. **Information technology resources:** Students are not required to lease or own a computer. Number of campus computers available to all students: 3,000. School has a wireless network. Approximate number of users that can be accommodated: 25,000. Proportion of college-owned housing units wired for high-speed internet access: 100%. **Campus safety:** Security services offered: 24-hour foot-and-vehicle patrols, late-night transport/escort service, 24-hour emergency telephones, lighted pathways/sidewalks, controlled dormitory access (key, security card, etc).

TRANSFER AND INTERNATIONAL STUDENTS

Transfer students: May apply for admission for the following academic terms: Fall, Spring, Summer. Applicants need a minimum number of credits to apply. For fall 2009: Transfer applications received: 7,432. Transfer applicants offered admission: 3,209. Transfer applicants enrolled: 2,419. **International students:** Number of foreign undergraduates: 1616 (4% of student body). Number of countries represented: 117. Minimum TOEFL score required: 550 (paper); 79 (computer).

University of Texas—Brownsville

- **Address:** 80 Fort Brown, Brownsville, TX 78520
- **Website:** http://www.utb.edu
- **Public**
- **Enrollment:** 6,086 full-time; 10,173 part-time

KEY STATS

✔ **U.S News College Ranking:** Unranked, Regional Universities (West)
✔ **SAT or ACT Score (25th/75th percentile):** N/A
✔ **Tuition:** 2009-2010: $4,872 in state, $12,074 out of state
   Selectivity: N/A   **Room/board:** $5,782
   Acceptance rate: 100%   **Average debt:** N/A
   Student/faculty ratio: 20/1 **Proportion who borrowed:** N/A

UNDERGRADUATE STUDENT BODY STATS

2009-2010 enrollment: 6,086 full-time; 10,173 part-time. Men: 41%; women: 59%. **Ethnic makeup:** African American: 1%; Hispanic: 90%; White: 5%; International: 5%.

ADMISSIONS FACTS AND FIGURES

Phone: (956) 882-8295. **Email:** admissions@utb.edu. **Website:** http://www.utb.edu. **Application deadlines for fall 2011:** Regular decision: July 1; decision sent by July 1. Early decision: Not offered. Early action: Not offered. Admission can be deferred. **To apply online, go to:** http://www.utb.edu/em/Pages/future_p_apply.aspx. **Admissions requirements/recommendations:** High school units required (recommended): English: 4 (4); Mathematics: 2 (4); Science: 2 (3); Foreign language: 3 (3); Social studies: 4 (4); History: 2 (2); Academic electives: 1 (4); Total units: 19 (25). Tests: The college does not use SAT or ACT scores in admissions decisions. Neither SAT nor ACT required. Campus visit: Neither required nor recommended. Admissions interview: Neither required nor recommended. Off-campus interview: Not available. **Factors that count in admissions decisions:** *Academic:* Secondary school record: Not Considered. Class rank: Not Considered. Letters of recommendation: Not Considered. Standardized test scores: Not Considered. Essay: Not Considered. *Nonacademic:* Interview: Not Considered. Extracurricular activities: Not Considered. Talent/ability: Not Considered. Character/personal qualities: Not Considered. Alumni/ae relationship: Not Considered. Geographical residence: Not Considered. State residency: Not Considered. Religious affiliation/commitment: Not Considered. Minority status: Not Considered. Volunteer work: Not Considered. Work experience: Not Considered. **Admissions statistics for the fall 2009 entering class:** Total applicants: 3,526. Total accepted: 3,526. Freshmen enrolled: 2,060; 1% were from out of state. Overall acceptance rate: 100%. **Credentials of fall 2009 freshmen:** 9% ranked in the top 10 percent of their high school class; 27% were in the top 25 percent; 57% were in the top half. (Proportion submitting class standing: 79%.) **Average high school grade point average:** 2.7.

ACADEMICS

Year founded: 1926. **Academic calendar:** Semester. **Degrees offered:** certificate, associate, transfer-associate, terminal-associate, bachelor's, master's, doctorate. **Most popular majors:** 26% multi/interdisciplinary studies, 7% biology/biological sciences, 6% psychology, 5% business/commerce, 4% criminal justice/law enforcement administration. **Major fields of study:** biological and biomedical sciences; business, management, marketing, and related support services; communication, journalism, and related programs; computer and information sciences and support services; engineering; engineering technologies/technicians; English language and literature/letters; foreign languages, literatures, and linguistics; health professions and related clinical sciences; history; mathematics and statistics; multi/interdisciplinary studies; natural resources and conservation; parks, recreation, leisure, and fitness studies; physical sciences; psychology; security and protective services; social sciences; visual and performing arts. **Areas of required coursework:** arts/fine arts, humanities, computer literacy, mathematics, English (including composition), philosophy, foreign languages, sciences (biological or physical), history, social science. **Special academic programs:** cooperative (work-study plan) program, distance learning, double major, dual enrollment, English as a Second Language (ESL), independent study, internships, study abroad, teacher certificate program. **Teacher certification offered in:** early childhood, special education, elementary, vo-tech, middle/junior high, adult education, secondary, bilingual/bicultural. **Cooperative education programs:** business, computer science, engineering, health professions, social/behavioral science, technologies, vocational arts. **Faculty and instruction (2009-2010):** Total instructional faculty: 369 full-time, 351 part-time (54% men; 46% women; 56% minorities). Full-time faculty with Ph.D. or other terminal degree: 63%. Student/faculty ratio: 20/1. Classes of fewer than 20 students: 62%; of 20 to 49 students: 34%; of 50 or more students: 4%. **Advanced Placement and International Baccalaureate credit:** AP tests may be used for: Credit only. Scores accepted: 3, 4, 5. International Baccalaureate exams may be used for: Credit only. **Freshmen returning for sophomore year:** 64%. **Graduation rates:** Four-year: 4%; five-year: 10%; six-year: 17%.

COSTS AND FINANCIAL AID

Financial aid office: (956) 882-8277. **Expenses (2009-2010):** Tuition and fees 2009-2010: $4,872 in state, $12,074 out of state; room/board: $5,782. Estimated books and supplies: $646; transportation: $1,657; personal expenses: $2,651. **Financial aid:** Priority filing date for institution's financial aid form: March 1. In 2009-2010, 86% of undergraduates applied for financial aid. Of those, 81% were determined to have financial need; Average financial aid package (proportion receiving): $8,685 (81%). Average amount of gift aid, such as scholarships or grants (proportion receiving): $7,045 (74%). Average amount of self-help aid, such as work study or loans (proportion receiving): $4,078 (42%). Average need-based loan (excluding PLUS or other private loans): $3,845. Among students who received need-based aid, the average percentage of need met: 59%. Among students who received aid based on merit, the average award (and the proportion receiving): $3,577 (2%). The average athletic scholarship (and the proportion receiving): $4,105 (2%).

CAMPUS LIFE AND EXTRACURRICULAR ACTIVITIES

Campus housing available: coed dorms, women's dorms, men's dorms, special housing for disabled students, cooperative housing. Students who live in college-owned, operated, or affiliated housing: 1%. **Clubs and organizations:** Number of student organizations: 56. Activities include: choral groups, concert band, dance, drama/theater, jazz band, music ensembles, opera, radio station, student government, student newspaper, symphony orchestra. Average proportion of students who stay on campus on weekends: 5%. **Sports program (2009-2010):** Member of NAIA. *Men's intercollegiate varsity sports:* baseball, golf, soccer. *Women's intercollegiate varsity sports:* golf, soccer, volleyball.

SERVICES AND FACILITIES

Basic services: nonremedial tutoring, placement service, day care, health service, health insurance. **Remedial assistance:** reading, math, writing, study skills. **Counseling services:** minority student, career, military, personal, veteran student, academic, older student, psychological, birth control. **For learning-disabled students:** School does not offer a structured program with separate admission and additional fees. **Information technology resources:** Students are not required to lease or own a computer. Number of campus computers available to all students: 650. School has a wireless network. Proportion of college-owned housing units wired for high-speed internet access: 100%. **Campus safety:** Security services offered: 24-hour foot-and-vehicle patrols, late-night transport/escort service, 24-hour emergency telephones, lighted pathways/sidewalks, controlled dormitory access (key, security card, etc).

TRANSFER AND INTERNATIONAL STUDENTS

Transfer students: May apply for admission for the following academic terms: Fall, Spring, Summer. Applicants need a minimum number of credits to apply. For fall 2009: Transfer applications received: 558. Transfer applicants offered admission: 558. Transfer applicants enrolled: 286. **International students:** Number of foreign undergraduates: 500 (5% of student body). Number of countries represented: 21.

University of Texas–Dallas

- **Address:** 800 W. Campbell Road, Richardson, TX 75080-3021
- **Website:** http://www.utdallas.edu
- **Public**
- **Enrollment:** 7,326 full-time; 2,475 part-time

KEY STATS
✔ **U.S News College Ranking:** 143, National Universities
✔ **SAT Score (25th/75th percentile):** 1080-1350
✔ **Tuition:** 2009-2010: $10,340 in state, $23,730 out of state
  Selectivity: More selective   **Room/board:** $7,733
  Acceptance rate: 52%   **Average debt:** N/A
  Student/faculty ratio: 20/1   **Proportion who borrowed:** N/A

UNDERGRADUATE STUDENT BODY STATS

2009-2010 enrollment: 7,326 full-time; 2,475 part-time. Men: 55%; women: 45%. **Ethnic makeup:** African American: 7%; American-Indian: 1%; Asian American: 22%; Hispanic: 12%; White: 54%; International: 4%.

ADMISSIONS FACTS AND FIGURES

Phone: (972) 883-2270. **Email:** interest@utdallas.edu. **Website:** http://www.utdallas.edu. **Application deadlines for fall 2011:** Regular decision: July 1. Early decision: Not offered. Early action: Not offered. Admission can be deferred. **Application fee:** $50. **To apply online, go to:** http://www.utdallas.edu/enroll/apply/index.php. **Admissions requirements/recommendations:** High school units required (recommended): English: 4 (4); Mathematics: 4 (4); Science: 3 (3); Foreign language: 2 (3); Social studies: 3 (4); Academic electives: 2 (3); Total units: 18 (24). Tests: The college uses SAT or ACT scores in admissions decisions. Either SAT or ACT required. For admission to the fall 2011 entering class, the school will accept: ACT with writing required. Campus visit: Recommended. Admissions interview: Neither required nor recommended. Off-campus interview: Not available. **Factors that count in admissions decisions:** *Academic:* Secondary school record: Very Important. Class rank: Very Important. Letters of recommendation: Considered. Standardized test scores: Very Important. Essay: Important. *Nonacademic:* Interview: Not Considered. Extracurricular activities: Important. Talent/ability: Considered. Character/personal qualities: Considered. Alumni/ae relationship: Not Considered. Geographical residence: Considered. State residency: Considered. Religious affiliation/commitment: Not Considered. Minority status: Not Considered. Volunteer work: Considered. Work experience: Considered. **Other schools with the greatest overlap in applicants:** Texas A&M University–College Station; University of North Texas; University of Oklahoma; University of Texas–Arlington; University of Texas–Austin. **Admissions statistics for the fall 2009 entering class:** Total applicants: 5,554. Total accepted: 2,870. Freshmen enrolled: 1,343; 5% were from out of state. Overall acceptance rate: 52%. **Credentials of fall 2009 freshmen:** 36% ranked in the top 10 percent of their high school class; 70% were in the top 25 percent; 92% were in the top half. (Proportion submitting class standing: 80%.) **Average high school grade point average:** 3.6. **First-year students who submitted SAT scores:** 94%. Scores (25/75 percentile): Critical Reading: 520-660, Math: 560-690, Combined: 1080-1350. **First-year students submitting ACT scores:** 46%. Scores (25/75 percentile): English: 25-31, Math: 23-30, Composite: 24-30.

ACADEMICS

Year founded: 1969. **Academic calendar:** Semester. **Degrees offered:** bachelor's, post-bachelor's certificate, master's, doctorate. **Most popular majors:** 32% business, management, marketing, and related support services; 13% multi/interdisciplinary studies, 10% psychology, 8% biological and biomedical sciences, 8% social sciences. **Major fields of study:** area, ethnic, cultural, and gender studies; biological and biomedical sciences; business, management, marketing, and related support services; computer and information sciences and support services; engineering; health professions and related clinical sciences; liberal arts and sciences studies, and humanities; mathematics and statistics; multi/interdisciplinary studies; physical sciences; psychology; public administration and social service professions; social sciences; visual and performing arts. **Areas of required coursework:** arts/fine arts, humanities, computer literacy, mathematics, English (including composition), sciences (biological or physical), history, social science. **Preprofessional programs:** pre-law, pre-dentistry, pre-medicine, pre-veterinary science, pre-optometry, pre-pharmacy, other. **Special academic programs:** accelerated program, cooperative (work-study plan) program, cross-registration, distance learning, double major, dual enrollment, English as a Second

Language (ESL), honors program, independent study, internships, liberal arts/career combination, student-designed major, study abroad, teacher certificate program, other. **Teacher certification offered in:** early childhood, elementary, middle/junior high, secondary. **Cooperative education programs:** computer science, engineering, other. **Reserve Officers Training Corps (ROTC):** Army ROTC: Offered at cooperating institution (University of Texas–Arlington); Air Force ROTC: Offered at cooperating institution (University of North Texas). **Faculty and instruction (2009-2010):** Total instructional faculty: 533 full-time, 261 part-time (67% men; 33% women; 22% minorities). Full-time faculty with Ph.D. or other terminal degree: 92%. Student/faculty ratio: 20/1. Classes of fewer than 20 students: 30%; of 20 to 49 students: 45%; of 50 or more students: 25%. **Advanced Placement and International Baccalaureate credit:** AP tests may be used for: Credit only. Scores accepted: 3, 4, 5. International Baccalaureate exams may be used for: Credit only. **Freshmen returning for sophomore year:** 82%. **Graduation rates:** Four-year: 43%; five-year: 59%; six-year: 63%. **Graduate study:** 21% of students pursue further study immediately upon graduation. Fields in which graduates pursue further study: Master of Business Administration (MBA), 43%; law, 10%; medicine, 20%; dentistry, 1%; engineering, 10%; education, 3%; arts and sciences, 13%.

COSTS AND FINANCIAL AID

Financial aid office: (972) 883-2941. **Expenses (2009-2010):** Tuition and fees 2009-2010: $10,340 in state, $23,730 out of state; room/board: $7,733. Estimated books and supplies: $1,200; transportation: $1,400; personal expenses: $1,929. **Financial aid:** Priority filing date for institution's financial aid form: March 31; deadline: March 31.

CAMPUS LIFE AND EXTRACURRICULAR ACTIVITIES

Campus housing available (% using): coed dorms (19%), other housing options (81%). Students who live in college-owned, operated, or affiliated housing: 24%. **Student employment:** During the 2009-2010 academic year, 11% of undergraduates worked on campus. Average per-year earnings: $3,910. **Clubs and organizations:** Number of student organizations: 147. Activities include: choral groups, concert band, dance, drama/theater, international student organization, jazz band, literary magazine, music ensembles, musical theater, pep band, radio station, student government, student newspaper, student film society, symphony orchestra, television station. Number of fraternities: 9; sororities: 7. Proportion of men in fraternities: 4%; of women in sororities: 4%. Average proportion of students who stay on campus on weekends: 65%. **Sports program (2009-2010):** Member of NCAA III. *Men's intercollegiate varsity sports:* baseball, basketball, cross country, golf, soccer, tennis. *Women's intercollegiate varsity sports:* basketball, cross country, golf, soccer, softball, tennis, volleyball.

SERVICES AND FACILITIES

Basic services: nonremedial tutoring, women's center, health service, health insurance, other. **Remedial assistance:** reading, math, writing, study skills. **Counseling services:** minority student, career, personal, veteran student, academic, older student, psychological, birth control. **For learning-disabled students:** School does not offer a structured program with separate admission and additional fees. Total undergraduates in learning-disabled program or receiving services: 110. Services include: remedial math, remedial English, reading machines, remedial reading, tape recorders, other special classes, note-taking services, oral tests, learning center, readers, extended time for tests, tutors, priority seating, other testing accommodations, other. **Library:** Number of titles: 1,668,979; number of current serial subscriptions: 37,567. **Information technology resources:** Students are not required to lease or own a computer. Number of campus computers available to all students: 520. School has a wireless network. Approximate number of users that can be accommodated: 5,000. Proportion of college-owned housing units wired for high-speed internet access: 0%. **Campus safety:** Security services offered: 24-hour foot-and-vehicle patrols, late-night transport/escort service, 24-hour emergency telephones, lighted pathways/sidewalks.

TRANSFER AND INTERNATIONAL STUDENTS

Transfer students: May apply for admission for the following academic terms: Fall, Spring, Summer. Applicants do not need a minimum number of credits to apply. For fall 2009: Transfer applications received: 3,700. Transfer applicants offered admission: 2,497. Transfer applicants enrolled: 1,705. **International students:** Number of foreign undergraduates: 339 (4% of student body). Number of countries represented: 85. Minimum TOEFL score required: 550 (paper); 80 (computer). Average TOEFL score: 594 (paper).

University of Texas–El Paso

- **Address:** 500 W. University Avenue, El Paso, TX 79968
- **Website:** http://www.utep.edu
- **Public**
- **Enrollment:** 11,434 full-time; 5,771 part-time

KEY STATS

✔ **U.S News College Ranking:** second tier, National Universities
✔ **SAT Score (25th/75th percentile):** 800-1020
✔ **Tuition:** 2010-2011: $6,504 in state, $15,804 out of state

Selectivity: Less selective	**Room/board:** $8,426
Acceptance rate: 99%	**Average debt:** $17,346
Student/faculty ratio: 20/1	**Proportion who borrowed:** 64%

UNDERGRADUATE STUDENT BODY STATS

2009-2010 enrollment: 11,434 full-time; 5,771 part-time. Men: 45%; women: 55%. **Ethnic makeup:** African American: 3%; Asian American: 1%; Hispanic: 80%; White: 9%; International: 7%.

ADMISSIONS FACTS AND FIGURES

Phone: (915) 747-5890. **Email:** futureminer@utep.edu. **Website:** http://www.utep.edu. **Application deadlines for fall 2011:** Regular decision: Rolling. Early decision: Not offered. Early action: Not offered. Admission can be deferred. **To apply online, go to:** https://www.applytexas.org/adappc/commonapp.WBX. **Admissions requirements/recommendations:** High school units required (recommended): English: 4; Mathematics: 3; Science: 3; Foreign language: 2; Social studies: 2; History: 2; Academic electives: 6; Total units: 24. Tests: The college uses SAT or ACT scores in admissions decisions. Neither SAT nor ACT required. For admission to the fall 2011 entering class, the school will accept: ACT with or without writing accepted. Campus visit: Recommended. Admissions interview: Neither required nor recommended. Off-campus interview: Not available. **Factors that count in admissions decisions:** *Academic:* Secondary school record: Very Important. Class rank: Very Important. Letters of recommendation: Considered. Standardized test scores: Important. Essay: Not Considered. *Nonacademic:* Interview: Considered. Extracurricular activities: Considered. Talent/ability: Considered. Character/personal qualities: Considered. Alumni/ae relationship: Not Considered. Geographical residence: Considered. State residency: Important. Religious affiliation/commitment: Not Considered. Minority status: Not Considered. Volunteer work: Considered. Work experience: Considered. **Admissions statistics for the fall 2009 entering class:** Total applicants: 5,809. Total accepted: 5,742. Freshmen enrolled: 2,516; Overall acceptance rate: 99%. **Credentials of fall 2009 freshmen:** 20% ranked in the top 10 percent of their high school class; 43% were in the top 25 percent; 72% were in the top half. (Proportion submitting class standing: 88%.) **Average high school grade point average:** 3.1. **First-year students who submitted SAT scores:** 81%. Scores (25/75 percentile): Critical Reading: 390-500, Math: 410-520, Combined: 800-1020. **First-year students submitting ACT scores:** 20%. Scores (25/75 percentile): English: 13-20, Math: 16-22, Composite: 15-21.

ACADEMICS

Year founded: 1913. **Academic calendar:** Semester. **Degrees offered:** bachelor's, master's, doctorate. **Most popular majors:** 18% business, management, marketing, and related support services, 16% education, 10% health professions and related clinical sciences, 9% multi/interdisciplinary studies, 8% engineering. **Major fields of study:** area, ethnic, cultural, and gender studies; biological and biomedical sciences; business, management, marketing, and related support services; communication, journalism, and related programs; computer and information sciences and support services; engineering; English language and literature/letters; foreign languages, literatures, and linguistics; health professions and related clinical sciences; history; mathematics and statistics; multi/interdisciplinary studies; natural resources and conservation; parks, recreation, leisure, and fitness studies; philosophy and religious studies; physical sciences; psychology; public administration and social service professions; security and protective services; social sciences; visual and performing arts. **Areas of required coursework:** arts/fine arts, humanities, computer literacy, mathematics, English (including composition), foreign languages, sciences (biological or physical), history, social science, other. **Pre-professional programs:** pre-law, pre-dentistry, pre-medicine, pre-veterinary science, pre-optometry, pre-pharmacy, other. **Special academic programs:** accelerated program, cooperative (work-study plan) program, cross-registration, distance learning, double major, dual enrollment,

English as a Second Language (ESL), exchange student program (domestic), honors program, independent study, internships, study abroad, teacher certificate program, weekend college. **Teacher certification offered in:** early childhood, special education, elementary, vo-tech, middle/junior high, secondary, bilingual/bicultural. **Cooperative education programs:** health professions, other. **Reserve Officers Training Corps (ROTC):** Army ROTC: Offered on campus; Air Force ROTC: Offered on campus. **Faculty and instruction (2009-2010):** Total instructional faculty: 695 full-time, 463 part-time (57% men; 43% women; 41% minorities). Student/faculty ratio: 20/1. Classes of fewer than 20 students: 35%; of 20 to 49 students: 55%; of 50 or more students: 11%. **Advanced Placement and International Baccalaureate credit:** AP tests may be used for: Credit only. Scores accepted: 3, 4, 5. International Baccalaureate exams may be used for: Credit only. **Freshmen returning for sophomore year:** 69%. **Graduation rates:** Four-year: 5%; five-year: 20%; six-year: 32%.

COSTS AND FINANCIAL AID

Financial aid office: (915) 747-5204. **Expenses (2010-2011):** Tuition and fees 2010-2011: $6,504 in state, $15,804 out of state; room/board: $8,426. Estimated books and supplies: $1,335; transportation: $1,972; personal expenses: $1,616. **Financial aid:** Priority filing date for institution's financial aid form: March 15. 41% had their need fully met. Average financial aid package (proportion receiving): $12,125 (N/A). Average amount of gift aid, such as scholarships or grants (proportion receiving): $7,139 (N/A). Average amount of self-help aid, such as work study or loans (proportion receiving): $6,827 (N/A). Average need-based loan (excluding PLUS or other private loans): $6,549. Among students who received need-based aid, the average percentage of need met: 84%. Among students who received aid based on merit, the average award (and the proportion receiving): $2,396 (N/A). The average athletic scholarship (and the proportion receiving): $6,606 (N/A). Average amount of debt of borrowers graduating in 2009: $17,346. Proportion who borrowed: 64%.

CAMPUS LIFE AND EXTRACURRICULAR ACTIVITIES

Campus housing available (% using): apartment for single students (70%), special housing for disabled students (5%), special housing for international students (5%), other housing options (5%). **Student employment:** During the 2009-2010 academic year, 10% of undergraduates worked on campus. Average per-year earnings: $6,000. **Clubs and organizations:** Number of student organizations: 155. Activities include: choral groups, concert band, dance, drama/theater, jazz band, literary magazine, marching band, music ensembles, musical theater, opera, pep band, radio station, student government, student newspaper, student film society, symphony orchestra. Number of fraternities: 6; sororities: 8. Average proportion of students who stay on campus on weekends: 75%. **Sports program (2009-2010):** Member of NCAA I. *Men's intercollegiate varsity sports:* basketball, cross country, football, golf, track and field (indoor), track and field (outdoor). *Women's intercollegiate varsity sports:* basketball, cross country, golf, rifle, soccer, softball, squash, tennis, track and field (indoor), track and field (outdoor), volleyball.

SERVICES AND FACILITIES

Basic services: nonremedial tutoring, women's center, day care, health service, health insurance. **Remedial assistance:** reading, math, writing, study skills. **Counseling services:** minority student, career, personal, older student, psychological. **For learning-disabled students:** School does not offer a structured program with separate admission and additional fees. Total undergraduates in learning-disabled program or receiving services: 60. Services include: reading machines, tape recorders, note-taking services, oral tests, learning center, readers, extended time for tests, priority registration, priority seating, substitution of courses, texts on tape, typist/scribe, exams on tape or computer, other testing accommodations. **Library:** Number of titles: 1,420,646; number of current serial subscriptions: 34,812. **Information technology resources:** Students are not required to lease or own a computer. Number of campus computers available to all students: 1,408. School has a wireless network. Approximate number of users that can be accommodated: 4,000. Proportion of college-owned housing units wired for high-speed internet access: 100%. **Campus safety:** Security services offered: 24-hour foot-and-vehicle patrols, late-night transport/escort service, 24-hour emergency telephones, lighted pathways/sidewalks, student patrols, controlled dormitory access (key, security card, etc).

TRANSFER AND INTERNATIONAL STUDENTS

Transfer students: May apply for admission for the following academic terms: Fall, Spring, Summer. Applicants do not need a minimum number of credits to apply. For fall 2009: Transfer applications received: 3,145. Transfer applicants offered admission: 3,037. Transfer applicants enrolled:

1,829. **International students:** Number of foreign undergraduates: 1152 (7% of student body). Number of countries represented: 74. Minimum TOEFL score required: 500 (paper); 61 (computer).

University of Texas of the Permian Basin

- ■ **Address:** 4901 E. University Boulevard, Odessa, TX 79762-0001
- ■ **Website:** http://www.utpb.edu
- ■ **Public**
- ■ **Enrollment:** 1,927 full-time; 812 part-time

KEY STATS
✔ **U.S News College Ranking:** 84, Regional Universities (West)
✔ **SAT Score (25th/75th percentile):** 905-1095
✔ **Tuition:** 2010-2011: $6,229 in state, $14,539 out of state

Selectivity: Selective	**Room/board:** $6,964
Acceptance rate: 85%	**Average debt:** $18,507
Student/faculty ratio: 17/1	**Proportion who borrowed:** 64%

UNDERGRADUATE STUDENT BODY STATS

2009-2010 enrollment: 1,927 full-time; 812 part-time. Men: 41%; women: 59%. **Ethnic makeup:** African American: 5%; American-Indian: 1%; Asian American: 1%; Hispanic: 43%; White: 49%; International: 1%.

ADMISSIONS FACTS AND FIGURES

Phone: (432) 552-2605. **Email:** admissions@utpb.edu. **Website:** http://www.utpb.edu. **Application deadlines for fall 2011:** Regular decision: July 15. Early decision: Not offered. Early action: Not offered. Admission can be deferred. **Application fee:** None. **To apply online, go to:** http://ss.utpb.edu/admissions/apply-now/. **Admissions requirements/recommendations:** High school units required (recommended): English: 4 (0); Mathematics: 3; Science: 3; Foreign language: 2 (0); Social studies: 4 (0); History: 0 (0); Academic electives: 4 (0); Total units: 24 (0). Tests: The college uses SAT or ACT scores in admissions decisions. Either SAT or ACT required. For admission to the fall 2011 entering class, the school will accept: ACT with or without writing accepted. Campus visit: Recommended. Admissions interview: Neither required nor recommended. Off-campus interview: Not available. **Factors that count in admissions decisions:** *Academic:* Secondary school record: Considered. Class rank: Very Important. Letters of recommendation: Considered. Standardized test scores: Very Important. Essay: Not Considered. *Nonacademic:* Interview: Considered. Extracurricular activities: Considered. Talent/ability: Considered. Character/personal qualities: Considered. Alumni/ae relationship: Not Considered. Geographical residence: Not Considered. State residency: Not Considered. Religious affiliation/commitment: Not Considered. Minority status: Not Considered. Volunteer work: Considered. Work experience: Considered. **Other schools with the greatest overlap in applicants:** Angelo State University; Sul Ross State University; Texas A&M University–College Station; Texas Tech University; University of Texas–Austin. **Admissions statistics for the fall 2009 entering class:** Total applicants: 884. Total accepted: 747. Freshmen enrolled: 398; 3% were from out of state. Overall acceptance rate: 85%. **Credentials of fall 2009 freshmen:** 23% ranked in the top 10 percent of their high school class; 53% were in the top 25 percent; 86% were in the top half. (Proportion submitting class standing: 98%.) **First-year students who submitted SAT scores:** 70%. Scores (25/75 percentile): Critical Reading: 445-540, Math: 460-555, Combined: 905-1095. **First-year students submitting ACT scores:** 37%. Scores (25/75 percentile): English: 17-22, Math: 18-24, Composite: 19-23.

ACADEMICS

Year founded: 1969. **Academic calendar:** Semester. **Degrees offered:** bachelor's, master's. **Most popular majors:** 22% business, management, marketing, and related support services, 12% family and consumer sciences/human sciences, 9% psychology, 8% social sciences, 8% parks, recreation, leisure, and fitness studies. **Major fields of study:** biological and biomedical sciences; business, management, marketing, and related support services; communication, journalism, and related programs; computer and information sciences and support services; engineering technologies/technicians; English language and literature/letters; family and consumer sciences/human sciences; foreign languages, literatures, and linguistics; history; liberal arts and sciences studies, and humanities; mathematics and statistics; multi/interdisciplinary studies; natural resources and conservation; parks, recreation, leisure, and fitness studies; physical sciences; psychology;

public administration and social service professions; security and protective services; social sciences; visual and performing arts. **Areas of required coursework:** arts/fine arts, humanities, computer literacy, mathematics, English (including composition), sciences (biological or physical), history, social science, other. **Special academic programs:** cooperative (work-study) program, distance learning, double major, dual enrollment, English as a Second Language (ESL), honors program, independent study, internships, liberal arts/career combination, study abroad, teacher certificate program. **Teacher certification offered in:** early childhood, special education, elementary, middle/junior high, secondary, bilingual/bicultural. **Cooperative education programs:** business, computer science. **Faculty and instruction (2009-2010):** Total instructional faculty: 119 full-time, 101 part-time (48% men; 52% women; 20% minorities). Full-time faculty with Ph.D. or other terminal degree: 82%. Student/faculty ratio: 17/1. Classes of fewer than 20 students: 35%; of 20 to 49 students: 53%; of 50 or more students: 12%. **Advanced Placement and International Baccalaureate credit:** AP tests may be used for: Credit and/or placement. Scores accepted: 4, 5. International Baccalaureate exams may be used for: Credit and/or placement. **Freshmen returning for sophomore year:** 59%. **Graduation rates:** Four-year: 18%; five-year: 27%; six-year: 32%. **Graduate study:** 24% of students pursue further study immediately upon graduation. Fields in which graduates pursue further study: Master of Business Administration (MBA), 22%; law, 3%; medicine, 8%; engineering, 3%; education, 20%; arts and sciences, 44%.

COSTS AND FINANCIAL AID

Financial aid office: (432) 552-2620. **Expenses (2010-2011):** Tuition and fees 2010-2011: $6,229 in state, $14,539 out of state; room/board: $6,964. Estimated books and supplies: $915; transportation: $779; personal expenses: $1,817. **Financial aid:** Priority filing date for institution's financial aid form: March 1. In 2009-2010, 71% of undergraduates applied for financial aid. Of those, 57% were determined to have financial need; 23% had their need fully met. Average financial aid package (proportion receiving): $7,384 (57%). Average amount of gift aid, such as scholarships or grants (proportion receiving): $6,842 (40%). Average amount of self-help aid, such as work study or loans (proportion receiving): $3,598 (32%). Average need-based loan (excluding PLUS or other private loans): $3,540. Among students who received need-based aid, the average percentage of need met: 81%. Among students who received aid based on merit, the average award (and the proportion receiving): $2,460 (13%). The average athletic scholarship (and the proportion receiving): $3,072 (3%). Average amount of debt of borrowers graduating in 2009: $18,507. Proportion who borrowed: 64%.

CAMPUS LIFE AND EXTRACURRICULAR ACTIVITIES

Campus housing available (% using): coed dorms, apartment for single students (90%), special housing for disabled students (4%), other housing options (6%). Students who live in college-owned, operated, or affiliated housing: 19%. Average per-year earnings: $4,500. **Clubs and organizations:** Number of student organizations: 47. Activities include: campus ministries, choral groups, concert band, dance, drama/theater, international student organization, jazz band, literary magazine, music ensembles, pep band, student government, student newspaper, symphony orchestra. Number of fraternities: 0; sororities: 0. Average proportion of students who stay on campus on weekends: 10%. **Sports program (2009-2010):** Member of NCAA II. *Men's intercollegiate varsity sports:* baseball, basketball, cross country, soccer, swimming. *Women's intercollegiate varsity sports:* basketball, cross country, soccer, softball, swimming, volleyball.

SERVICES AND FACILITIES

Basic services: nonremedial tutoring, placement service, health service, health insurance, other. **Remedial assistance:** reading, math, writing, study skills, other. **Counseling services:** minority student, career, personal, academic, psychological, other. **For learning-disabled students:** School does not offer a structured program with separate admission and additional fees. Total undergraduates in learning-disabled program or receiving services: 20. Services include: remedial math, remedial English, reading machines, remedial reading, tape recorders, videotaped classes, diagnostic testing service, untimed tests, note-taking services, special bookstore section, oral tests, learning center, readers, extended time for tests, tutors, priority registration, priority seating, texts on tape, other testing accommodations, other. **Library:** Number of titles: 286,608; number of current serial subscriptions: 40,040. **Information technology resources:** Students are not required to lease or own a computer. Number of campus computers available to all students: 250. School has a wireless network. Approximate number of users that can be accommodated: 400. Proportion of college-owned housing units wired for high-speed internet access: 100%. **Campus safety:** Security services offered: 24-hour foot-and-vehicle patrols, late-night transport/escort service, 24-hour emergency telephones, lighted pathways/sidewalks, student patrols, controlled dormitory access (key, security card, etc).

TRANSFER AND INTERNATIONAL STUDENTS

Transfer students: May apply for admission for the following academic terms: Fall, Spring, Summer. Applicants need a minimum number of credits to apply. For fall 2009: Transfer applications received: 740. Transfer applicants offered admission: 685. Transfer applicants enrolled: 463. **International students:** Number of foreign undergraduates: 15 (1% of student body). Number of countries represented: 20. Minimum TOEFL score required: 550 (paper); 213 (computer).

University of Texas—Pan American

- **Address:** 1201 W. University Drive, Edinburg, TX 78539
- **Website:** http://www.utpa.edu
- **Public**
- **Enrollment:** 11,786 full-time; 4,161 part-time

KEY STATS

✔ **U.S News College Ranking:** second tier, Regional Universities (West)
✔ **ACT Score (25th/75th percentile):** 17-21
✔ **Tuition:** 2010-2011: $5,425 in state, $13,735 out of state

Selectivity: Selective	**Room/board:** $5,294
Acceptance rate: 68%	**Average debt:** $13,088
Student/faculty ratio: 21/1	**Proportion who borrowed:** 64%

UNDERGRADUATE STUDENT BODY STATS

2009-2010 enrollment: 11,786 full-time; 4,161 part-time. Men: 43%; women: 57%. **Ethnic makeup:** African American: 1%; Asian American: 1%; Hispanic: 90%; White: 5%; International: 3%.

ADMISSIONS FACTS AND FIGURES

Phone: (956) 381-2206. **Email:** admissions@utpa.edu. **Website:** http://www.utpa.edu. **Application deadlines for fall 2011:** Regular decision: August 11. Early decision: Not offered. Early action: Not offered. Admission cannot be deferred. **To apply online, go to:** http://admissions.panam.edu. **Admissions requirements/recommendations:** High school units required (recommended): English: 4; Mathematics: 3; Science: 3; Foreign language: 2; Social studies: 4; Academic electives: 4; Total units: 24. Tests: The college uses SAT or ACT scores in admissions decisions. Either SAT or ACT required. For admission to the fall 2011 entering class, the school will accept: ACT with or without writing accepted. Campus visit: Recommended. Admissions interview: Neither required nor recommended. Off-campus interview: Not available. **Factors that count in admissions decisions:** *Academic:* Secondary school record: Important. Class rank: Important. Letters of recommendation: Not Considered. Standardized test scores: Very Important. Essay: Not Considered. *Nonacademic:* Interview: Not Considered. Extracurricular activities: Not Considered. Talent/ability: Not Considered. Character/personal qualities: Not Considered. Alumni/ae relationship: Not Considered. Geographical residence: Not Considered. State residency: Not Considered. Religious affiliation/commitment: Not Considered. Minority status: Not Considered. Volunteer work: Not Considered. Work experience: Not Considered. **Admissions statistics for the fall 2009 entering class:** Total applicants: 6,531. Total accepted: 4,433. Freshmen enrolled: 2,882; 2% were from out of state. Overall acceptance rate: 68%. **Credentials of fall 2009 freshmen:** 17% ranked in the top 10 percent of their high school class; 45% were in the top 25 percent; 77% were in the top half. (Proportion submitting class standing: 95%.) **First-year students who submitted SAT scores:** 42%. Scores (25/75 percentile): Critical Reading: 410-510, Math: 430-530, Combined: 840-1040. **First-year students submitting ACT scores:** 81%. Scores (25/75 percentile): English: 17-21, Math: 15-20, Composite: 17-21.

ACADEMICS

Year founded: 1927. **Academic calendar:** Semester. **Degrees offered:** bachelor's, master's, doctorate. **Most popular majors:** 18% business, management, marketing, and related support services, 14% multi/interdisciplinary studies, 12% health professions and related clinical sciences, 7% mathematics and statistics, 6% English language and literature/letters. **Major fields of study:** area, ethnic, cultural, and gender studies; biological and biomedical sciences; business, management, marketing, and related support services; communication, journalism, and related programs; computer and information sciences and support services; engineering; English language and literature/letters; foreign languages, literatures, and linguistics; health professions and related clinical sciences; history; liberal arts and sciences studies, and humanities; mathematics and statistics; multi/interdisciplinary studies; parks, recreation, leisure, and fitness studies; philosophy and religious studies; physical sciences; psychology; public administration and social service professions; security and protective services; social sciences; visual and performing arts. **Areas of required coursework:** arts/fine arts, humanities, computer literacy, mathematics, English (including composition), philosophy, foreign languages, sciences (biological or physical), history, social science. **Pre-professional programs:** pre-law, pre-dentistry, pre-medicine, pre-optometry, pre-pharmacy. **Special academic programs:** accelerated program, cooperative (work-study plan) program, distance learning, double major, dual enrollment, English as a Second Language (ESL), exchange student program (domestic), honors program, independent study, internships, study abroad, teacher certificate program, weekend college. **Teacher certification offered in:** early childhood, special education, elementary, middle/junior high, secondary, bilingual/bicultural. **Cooperative education programs:** health professions. **Reserve Officers Training Corps (ROTC):** Army ROTC: Offered on campus. **Faculty and instruction (2009-2010):** Total instructional faculty: 653 full-time, 162 part-time (61% men; 39% women; 47% minorities). Full-time faculty with Ph.D. or other terminal degree: 81%. Student/faculty ratio: 21/1. Classes of fewer than 20 students: 17%; of 20 to 49 students: 63%; of 50 or more students: 20%. **Advanced Placement and International Baccalaureate credit:** AP tests may be used for: Credit and/or placement. Scores accepted: 3, 4, 5. International Baccalaureate exams may be used for: Placement only. **Freshmen returning for sophomore year:** 72%. **Graduation rates:** Four-year: 14%; five-year: 28%; six-year: 35%. **Graduate study:** 3% of students pursue further study immediately upon graduation; 15% within one year; 5% within five years. Fields in which graduates pursue further study: Master of Business Administration (MBA), 10%; law, 15%; medicine, 10%; dentistry, 5%; engineering, 5%; education, 20%; arts and sciences, 10%.

COSTS AND FINANCIAL AID
Financial aid office: (956) 381-2501. **Expenses (2010-2011):** Tuition and fees 2010-2011: $5,425 in state, $13,735 out of state; room/board: $5,294. Estimated books and supplies: $1,000. **Financial aid:** Priority filing date for institution's financial aid form: April 1. Average amount of debt of borrowers graduating in 2009: $13,088. Proportion who borrowed: 64%.

CAMPUS LIFE AND EXTRACURRICULAR ACTIVITIES
Campus housing available: coed dorms, women's dorms, men's dorms, apartments for married students, apartment for single students. Students who live in college-owned, operated, or affiliated housing: 4%. Average per-year earnings: $5,602. **Clubs and organizations:** Number of student organizations: 102. Activities include: campus ministries, choral groups, concert band, dance, drama/theater, international student organization, jazz band, music ensembles, musical theater, pep band, student government, student newspaper, symphony orchestra. Number of fraternities: 7; sororities: 6. **Sports program (2009-2010):** Member of NCAA I. *Men's intercollegiate varsity sports:* baseball, basketball, cross country, golf, tennis, track and field (outdoor). *Women's intercollegiate varsity sports:* basketball, cross country, golf, softball, tennis, track and field (outdoor), volleyball.

SERVICES AND FACILITIES
Basic services: nonremedial tutoring, placement service, day care, health service, health insurance. **Remedial assistance:** reading, math, writing. **Counseling services:** minority student, career, personal, veteran student, academic, psychological. **For learning-disabled students:** School does not offer a structured program with separate admission and additional fees. Services include: remedial math, reading machines, remedial reading, tape recorders, videotaped classes, diagnostic testing service, untimed tests, note-taking services, oral tests, learning center, readers, extended time for tests, tutors, priority registration, priority seating, other testing accommodations, other. **Library:** Number of titles: 598,008; number of current serial subscriptions: 35,004. **Information technology resources:** Students are not required to lease or own a computer. Number of campus computers available to all students: 900. School has a wireless network. Proportion of college-owned housing units wired for high-speed internet access: 100%. **Campus safety:** Security services offered: 24-hour foot-and-vehicle patrols, late-night transport/escort service, 24-hour emergency telephones, lighted pathways/sidewalks, controlled dormitory access (key, security card, etc).

TRANSFER AND INTERNATIONAL STUDENTS
Transfer students: May apply for admission for the following academic terms: Fall, Spring, Summer. Applicants need a minimum number of cred-

its to apply. For fall 2009: Transfer applications received: 1,518. Transfer applicants offered admission: 1,395. Transfer applicants enrolled: 923. **International students:** Number of foreign undergraduates: 537 (3% of student body). Number of countries represented: 33. Minimum TOEFL score required: 500 (paper); 173 (computer). Average TOEFL score: 542 (paper).

University of Texas–San Antonio

- **Address:** 1 UTSA Circle, San Antonio, TX 78249
- **Website:** http://www.utsa.edu
- **Public**
- **Enrollment:** 19,773 full-time; 5,233 part-time

KEY STATS
✔ **U.S News College Ranking:** 62, Regional Universities (West)
✔ **SAT Score (25th/75th percentile):** 920-1140
✔ **Tuition:** 2010-2011: $7,891 in state, $17,191 out of state

Selectivity: Selective	**Room/board:** $9,141
Acceptance rate: 87%	**Average debt:** $23,145
Student/faculty ratio: 23/1	**Proportion who borrowed:** 64%

UNDERGRADUATE STUDENT BODY STATS
2009-2010 enrollment: 19,773 full-time; 5,233 part-time. Men: 50%; women: 50%. **Ethnic makeup:** African American: 9%; Asian American: 7%; Hispanic: 44%; White: 37%; International: 2%.

ADMISSIONS FACTS AND FIGURES
Phone: (800) 669-0919. **Email:** prospects@utsa.edu. **Website:** http://www.utsa.edu. **Application deadlines for fall 2011:** Regular decision: July 1; decision sent by September 1. Early decision: Not offered. Early action: Not offered. Admission cannot be deferred. **Application fee:** $40. **To apply online, go to:** http://admissions.utsa.edu/. **Admissions requirements/recommendations:** High school units required (recommended): English: 4 (4); Mathematics: 3 (3); Science: 3 (3); Foreign language: 2 (2); Social studies: 4 (4); Total units: 17 (17). **Tests:** The college uses SAT or ACT scores in admissions decisions. Either SAT or ACT required. For admission to the fall 2011 entering class, the school will accept: ACT with writing required. Campus visit: Recommended. Admissions interview: Neither required nor recommended. Off-campus interview: May be arranged. **Factors that count in admissions decisions:** *Academic:* Secondary school record: Not Considered. Class rank: Very Important. Letters of recommendation: Considered. Standardized test scores: Very Important. Essay: Not Considered. *Nonacademic:* Interview: Not Considered. Extracurricular activities: Not Considered. Talent/ability: Not Considered. Character/personal qualities: Not Considered. Alumni/ae relationship: Not Considered. Geographical residence: Not Considered. State residency: Not Considered. Religious affiliation/commitment: Not Considered. Minority status: Not Considered. Volunteer work: Not Considered. Work experience: Not Considered. **Other schools with the greatest overlap in applicants:** Texas A&M University–College Station; Texas State University–San Marcos; Texas Tech University; University of Houston; University of Texas–Austin. **Admissions statistics for the fall 2009 entering class:** Total applicants: 11,993. Total accepted: 10,426. Freshmen enrolled: 4,883; 1% were from out of state. Overall acceptance rate: 87%. **Credentials of fall 2009 freshmen:** 10% ranked in the top 10 percent of their high school class; 38% were in the top 25 percent; 74% were in the top half. (Proportion submitting class standing: 92%.) **First-year students who submitted SAT scores:** 84%. Scores (25/75 percentile): Critical Reading: 450-560, Math: 470-580, Combined: 920-1140. **First-year students submitting ACT scores:** 32%. Scores (25/75 percentile): English: 18-25, Math: 18-24, Composite: 19-24.

ACADEMICS
Year founded: 1969. **Academic calendar:** Semester. **Degrees offered:** bachelor's, master's, doctorate. **Most popular majors:** 27% business, management, marketing, and related support services, 11% multi/interdisciplinary studies, 10% biological and biomedical sciences, 7% psychology, 6% social sciences. **Major fields of study:** architecture and related services; area, ethnic, cultural, and gender studies; biological and biomedical sciences; business, management, marketing, and related support services; communication, journalism, and related programs; computer and information sciences and support services; engineering; English language and literature/letters; foreign languages, literatures, and linguistics; health professions and related clinical sciences; history; liberal arts and sciences studies, and humani-

ties; mathematics and statistics; multi/interdisciplinary studies; natural resources and conservation; parks, recreation, leisure, and fitness studies; philosophy and religious studies; physical sciences; psychology; security and protective services; social sciences; visual and performing arts. **Areas of required coursework:** arts/fine arts, humanities, mathematics, English (including composition), sciences (biological or physical), history, social science, other. **Pre-professional programs:** pre-law, pre-dentistry, pre-medicine. **Special academic programs:** accelerated program, cooperative (work-study plan) program, distance learning, double major, dual enrollment, English as a Second Language (ESL), exchange student program (domestic), honors program, independent study, internships, study abroad, teacher certificate program, other. **Teacher certification offered in:** early childhood, special education, elementary, middle/junior high, adult education, secondary, bilingual/bicultural. **Reserve Officers Training Corps (ROTC):** Army ROTC: Offered on campus; Air Force ROTC: Offered on campus. **Faculty and instruction (2009-2010):** Total instructional faculty: 966 full-time, 255 part-time (56% men; 44% women; 36% minorities). Full-time faculty with Ph.D. or other terminal degree: 73%. Student/faculty ratio: 23/1. Classes of fewer than 20 students: 25%; of 20 to 49 students: 53%; of 50 or more students: 22%. **Advanced Placement and International Baccalaureate credit:** AP tests may be used for: Credit only. Scores accepted: 3. International Baccalaureate exams may be used for: Placement only. **Freshmen returning for sophomore year:** 58%. **Graduation rates:** Four-year: 8%; five-year: 19%; six-year: 28%. **Graduate study:** 9% of students pursue further study immediately upon graduation; 13% within one year. Fields in which graduates pursue further study: Master of Business Administration (MBA), 12%; law, 6%; medicine, 5%; dentistry, 1%; engineering, 3%; education, 9%; arts and sciences, 12%.

COSTS AND FINANCIAL AID

Financial aid office: (210) 458-8000. **Expenses (2010-2011):** Tuition and fees 2010-2011: $7,891 in state, $17,191 out of state; room/board: $9,141. Estimated books and supplies: $1,000; transportation: $880; personal expenses: $1,785. **Financial aid:** Priority filing date for institution's financial aid form: March 31. In 2009-2010, 73% of undergraduates applied for financial aid. Of those, 61% were determined to have financial need; 20% had their need fully met. Average financial aid package (proportion receiving): $8,412 (59%). Average amount of gift aid, such as scholarships or grants (proportion receiving): $5,416 (50%). Average amount of self-help aid, such as work study or loans (proportion receiving): $4,140 (49%). Average need-based loan (excluding PLUS or other private loans): $4,027. Among students who received need-based aid, the average percentage of need met: 53%. Among students who received aid based on merit, the average award (and the proportion receiving): $1,742 (4%). The average athletic scholarship (and the proportion receiving): $8,506 (1%). Average amount of debt of borrowers graduating in 2009: $23,145. Proportion who borrowed: 64%.

CAMPUS LIFE AND EXTRACURRICULAR ACTIVITIES

Campus housing available (% using): coed dorms (14%), apartment for single students (80%), special housing for disabled students (3%), special housing for international students (3%). Students who live in college-owned, operated, or affiliated housing: 12%. **Student employment:** During the 2009-2010 academic year, 4% of undergraduates worked on campus. Average per-year earnings: $6,929. **Clubs and organizations:** Number of student organizations: 235. Activities include: campus ministries, choral groups, concert band, dance, drama/theater, jazz band, literary magazine, music ensembles, opera, pep band, student government, student newspaper, symphony orchestra, yearbook. Number of fraternities: 11; sororities: 12. Proportion of men in fraternities: 3%; of women in sororities: 2%. Average proportion of students who stay on campus on weekends: 65%. **Sports program (2009-2010):** Member of NCAA I. **Men's intercollegiate varsity sports:** baseball, basketball, cross country, golf, tennis, track and field (indoor), track and field (outdoor). **Women's intercollegiate varsity sports:** basketball, cross country, golf, soccer, softball, tennis, track and field (indoor), track and field (outdoor), volleyball.

SERVICES AND FACILITIES

Basic services: nonremedial tutoring, women's center, placement service, health service, health insurance, other. **Remedial assistance:** reading, math, writing, study skills. **Counseling services:** minority student, career, military, personal, veteran student, academic, older student, psychological, birth control. **For learning-disabled students:** School does not offer a structured program with separate admission and additional fees. Total undergraduates in learning-disabled program or receiving services: 200. Services include: remedial math, remedial English, reading machines, remedial reading, tape recorders, note-taking services, learning center, readers, extended time

for tests, tutors, substitution of courses, texts on tape. **Library:** Number of titles: 795,438; number of current serial subscriptions: 35,264. **Information technology resources:** Students are not required to lease or own a computer. Number of campus computers available to all students: 800. School has a wireless network. Approximate number of users that can be accommodated: 2,500. Proportion of college-owned housing units wired for high-speed internet access: 100%. **Campus safety:** Security services offered: 24-hour foot-and-vehicle patrols, late-night transport/escort service, 24-hour emergency telephones, lighted pathways/sidewalks, controlled dormitory access (key, security card, etc).

TRANSFER AND INTERNATIONAL STUDENTS

Transfer students: May apply for admission for the following academic terms: Fall, Spring, Summer. Applicants need a minimum number of credits to apply. For fall 2009: Transfer applications received: 4,514. Transfer applicants offered admission: 4,221. Transfer applicants enrolled: 2,743. **International students:** Number of foreign undergraduates: 542 (2% of student body). Number of countries represented: 51. Minimum TOEFL score required: 500 (paper). Average TOEFL score: 500 (paper).

University of Texas–Tyler

- **Address:** 3900 University Boulevard, Tyler, TX 75799
- **Website:** http://www.uttyler.edu
- **Public**
- **Enrollment:** 3,862 full-time; 1,189 part-time

KEY STATS

✔ **U.S News College Ranking:** 71, Regional Universities (West)
✔ **SAT Score (25th/75th percentile):** 950-1170
✔ **Tuition:** 2009-2010: $6,042 in state, $14,352 out of state

Selectivity: Selective	**Room/board:** $7,340
Acceptance rate: 86%	**Average debt:** N/A
Student/faculty ratio: 16/1	**Proportion who borrowed:** N/A

UNDERGRADUATE STUDENT BODY STATS

2009-2010 enrollment: 3,862 full-time; 1,189 part-time. Men: 42%; women: 58%. **Ethnic makeup:** African American: 10%; American-Indian: 1%; Asian American: 2%; Hispanic: 8%; White: 78%; International: 1%.

ADMISSIONS FACTS AND FIGURES

Phone: (903) 566-7202. **Email:** admissions@uttyler.edu. **Website:** http://www.uttyler.edu. **Application deadlines for fall 2011:** Regular decision: Rolling. Early decision: Not offered. Early action: Not offered. Admission can be deferred. **Application fee:** $25. **To apply online, go to:** http://www.go2uttyler.com/apply.html. **Admissions requirements/recommendations:** High school units required (recommended): English: 4; Mathematics: 3 (4); Science: 3; Foreign language: 2; Social studies: 3. Tests: The college uses SAT or ACT scores in admissions decisions. Either SAT or ACT required. For admission to the fall 2011 entering class, the school will accept: ACT with writing recommended. Campus visit: Recommended. Admissions interview: Neither required nor recommended. Off-campus interview: Not available. **Factors that count in admissions decisions:** *Academic:* Secondary school record: Very Important. Class rank: Very Important. Letters of recommendation: Not Considered. Standardized test scores: Very Important. Essay: Not Considered. *Nonacademic:* Interview: Not Considered. Extracurricular activities: Important. Talent/ability: Important. Character/personal qualities: Important. Alumni/ae relationship: Not Considered. Geographical residence: Not Considered. State residency: Not Considered. Religious affiliation/commitment: Not Considered. Minority status: Not Considered. Volunteer work: Important. Work experience: Considered. **Other schools with the greatest overlap in applicants:** Stephen F. Austin State University; Texas A&M University–College Station; Texas Tech University; University of North Texas; University of Texas–Austin. **Admissions statistics for the fall 2009 entering class:** Total applicants: 1,568. Total accepted: 1,347. Freshmen enrolled: 596; 2% were from out of state. Overall acceptance rate: 86%. **Credentials of fall 2009 freshmen:** 19% ranked in the top 10 percent of their high school class; 56% were in the top 25 percent; 85% were in the top half. (Proportion submitting class standing: 48%.) **First-year students who submitted SAT scores:** 78%. Scores (25/75 percentile): Critical Reading: 460-580, Math: 490-590, Combined: 950-1170. **First-year students submitting ACT scores:** 62%. Scores (25/75 percentile): English: 19-25, Math: 20-25, Composite: 20-25.

ACADEMICS

Year founded: 1971. **Academic calendar:** Semester. **Degrees offered:** bachelor's, post-bachelor's certificate, master's, doctorate. **Most popular majors:** 23% business, management, marketing, and related support services, 19% health professions and related clinical sciences, 15% multi/interdisciplinary studies, 7% psychology, 6% parks, recreation, leisure, and fitness studies. **Major fields of study:** biological and biomedical sciences; business, management, marketing, and related support services; communication, journalism, and related programs; computer and information sciences and support services; engineering; engineering technologies/technicians; English language and literature/letters; foreign languages, literatures, and linguistics; health professions and related clinical sciences; history; liberal arts and sciences studies, and humanities; mathematics and statistics; multi/interdisciplinary studies; parks, recreation, leisure, and fitness studies; physical sciences; psychology; security and protective services; social sciences; visual and performing arts. **Areas of required coursework:** arts/fine arts, humanities, mathematics, English (including composition), sciences (biological or physical), history, social science. **Pre-professional programs:** pre-law, pre-dentistry, pre-medicine, pre-theology. **Special academic programs:** cooperative (work-study plan) program, distance learning, double major, honors program, independent study, internships, student-designed major, study abroad, teacher certificate program. **Teacher certification offered in:** early childhood, special education, elementary, vo-tech, middle/junior high, secondary, bilingual/bicultural. **Faculty and instruction (2009-2010):** Total instructional faculty: 261 full-time, 126 part-time (47% men; 53% women; 10% minorities). Full-time faculty with Ph.D. or other terminal degree: 75%. Student/faculty ratio: 16/1. Classes of fewer than 20 students: 33%; of 20 to 49 students: 55%; of 50 or more students: 12%. **Advanced Placement and International Baccalaureate credit:** AP tests may be used for: Credit only. Scores accepted: 3, 4, 5. International Baccalaureate exams may be used for: Credit only. **Freshmen returning for sophomore year:** 64%. **Graduation rates:** Four-year: 15%; five-year: 28%; six-year: 36%. **Graduate study:** 10% of students pursue further study within one year.

COSTS AND FINANCIAL AID

Financial aid office: (903) 566-7180. **Expenses (2009-2010):** Tuition and fees 2009-2010: $6,042 in state, $14,352 out of state; room/board: $7,340. **Financial aid:** Priority filing date for institution's financial aid form: April 1.

CAMPUS LIFE AND EXTRACURRICULAR ACTIVITIES

Campus housing available: coed dorms. Students who live in college-owned, operated, or affiliated housing: 14%. **Student employment:** During the 2009-2010 academic year, 6% of undergraduates worked on campus. Average per-year earnings: $3,803. **Clubs and organizations:** Number of student organizations: 70. Activities include: campus ministries, choral groups, concert band, international student organization, jazz band, literary magazine, model UN, music ensembles, musical theater, opera, pep band, student government, student newspaper. Number of fraternities: 2; sororities: 4. Proportion of men in fraternities: 1%; of women in sororities: 2%. Average proportion of students who stay on campus on weekends: 40%. **Sports program (2009-2010):** Member of NCAA III. *Men's intercollegiate varsity sports:* baseball, basketball, cross country, golf, soccer, tennis, track and field (outdoor). *Women's intercollegiate varsity sports:* basketball, cross country, golf, soccer, softball, tennis, track and field (outdoor), volleyball.

SERVICES AND FACILITIES

Basic services: nonremedial tutoring, placement service, health service, health insurance. **Remedial assistance:** writing, study skills. **Counseling services:** minority student, career, military, personal, veteran student, academic, older student, psychological, birth control. **For learning-disabled students:** School does not offer a structured program with separate admission and additional fees. Services include: reading machines, tape recorders, videotaped classes, note-taking services, oral tests, readers, extended time for tests, priority seating, other testing accommodations. **Library:** Number of titles: 299,270; number of current serial subscriptions: 525. **Information technology resources:** Students are not required to lease or own a computer. Number of campus computers available to all students: 192. School has a wireless network. Approximate number of users that can be accommodated: 1,000. Proportion of college-owned housing units wired for high-speed internet access: 100%. **Campus safety:** Security services offered: 24-hour foot-and-vehicle patrols, late-night transport/escort service, 24-hour emergency telephones, lighted pathways/sidewalks, controlled dormitory access (key, security card, etc).

TRANSFER AND INTERNATIONAL STUDENTS

Transfer students: May apply for admission for the following academic terms: Fall, Spring, Summer. Applicants need a minimum number of credits to apply. For fall 2009: Transfer applications received: 1,444. Transfer applicants offered admission: 1,387. Transfer applicants enrolled: 823. **International students:** Number of foreign undergraduates: 48 (1% of student body). Number of countries represented: 44. Minimum TOEFL score required: 550 (paper); 213 (computer).

University of the Incarnate Word

- **Address:** 4301 Broadway, San Antonio, TX 78209-6397
- **Website:** http://www.uiw.edu
- **Private; Religious affiliation:** Roman Catholic
- **Enrollment:** 3,373 full-time; 1,846 part-time

KEY STATS
✔ **U.S News College Ranking:** 59, Regional Universities (West)
✔ **SAT Score (25th/75th percentile):** 870-1110
✔ **Tuition:** 2010-2011: $21,890

Selectivity: Selective	**Room/board:** $9,220
Acceptance rate: 66%	**Average debt:** N/A
Student/faculty ratio: 15/1	**Proportion who borrowed:** N/A

UNDERGRADUATE STUDENT BODY STATS

2009-2010 enrollment: 3,373 full-time; 1,846 part-time. Men: 35%; women: 65%. **Ethnic makeup:** African American: 7%; Asian American: 3%; Hispanic: 57%; White: 30%; International: 3%. **Religious preference:** Protestant: 1%; Muslim: 1%; No preference: 15%; Unknown: 7%; Roman Catholic: 49%; Christian: 10%; Other: 17%.

ADMISSIONS FACTS AND FIGURES

Phone: (210) 829-6005. **Email:** admis@uiwtx.edu. **Website:** http://www.uiw.edu. **Application deadlines for fall 2011:** Regular decision: Rolling. Early decision: Not offered. Early action: Not offered. Admission can be deferred. **Application fee:** $20. **To apply online, go to:** http://www.uiw.edu/admissions/apply.html. **Admissions requirements/recommendations:** High school units required (recommended): English: 4 (4); Mathematics: 3 (4); Science: 3 (3); Foreign language: 2 (2); Social studies: 3 (4); History: 0 (0); Academic electives: 0 (0); Total units: 16 (18). Tests: The college uses SAT or ACT scores in admissions decisions. Either SAT or ACT required. For admission to the fall 2011 entering class, the school will accept: ACT with or without writing accepted. Campus visit: Recommended. Admissions interview: Recommended. Off-campus interview: May be arranged. **Factors that count in admissions decisions:** *Academic:* Secondary school record: Very Important. Class rank: Important. Letters of recommendation: Considered. Standardized test scores: Important. Essay: Considered. *Nonacademic:* Interview: Considered. Extracurricular activities: Considered. Talent/ability: Considered. Character/personal qualities: Considered. Alumni/ae relationship: Considered. Geographical residence: Considered. State residency: Not Considered. Religious affiliation/commitment: Not Considered. Minority status: Not Considered. Volunteer work: Considered. Work experience: Considered. **Other schools with the greatest overlap in applicants:** St. Mary's University of San Antonio; Texas Lutheran University; Texas State University–San Marcos; University of Texas–San Antonio. **Admissions statistics for the fall 2009 entering class:** Total applicants: 3,519. Total accepted: 2,311. Freshmen enrolled: 744; 3% were from out of state. Overall acceptance rate: 66%. **Credentials of fall 2009 freshmen:** 23% ranked in the top 10 percent of their high school class; 52% were in the top 25 percent; 82% were in the top half. (Proportion submitting class standing: 74%.) **Average high school grade point average:** 3.5. **First-year students who submitted SAT scores:** 88%. Scores (25/75 percentile): Critical Reading: 430-550, Math: 440-560, Combined: 870-1110. **First-year students submitting ACT scores:** 39%. Scores (25/75 percentile): English: 17-24, Math: 16-23, Composite: 18-23.

ACADEMICS

Year founded: 1881. **Academic calendar:** Semester. **Degrees offered:** associate, bachelor's, post-bachelor's certificate, master's, post-master's certificate, doctorate. **Most popular majors:** 43% business, management, marketing, and related support services, 10% health professions and related clinical sciences, 8% education, 7% visual and performing arts, 6% psychology. **Major fields of study:** area, ethnic, cultural, and gender studies; biological and biomedical sciences; business, management, marketing, and related support services; communication, journalism, and related programs; computer and information sciences and support services; education; engineering; English language and literature/letters; family and consumer sciences/human sciences; foreign languages, literatures, and linguistics; health professions and related clinical sciences; history; mathematics and statistics; multi/interdisciplinary studies; natural resources and conservation; parks, recreation, leisure, and fitness studies; philosophy and religious studies; physical sciences; psychology; social sciences; visual and performing arts. **Areas of required coursework:** arts/fine arts, computer literacy, mathematics, English (including composition), philosophy, foreign languages, sciences (biological or physical), history, social science, other. **Pre-professional programs:** pre-law, pre-dentistry, pre-medicine, pre-optometry, pre-pharmacy, other. **Special academic programs:** accelerated program, cross-registration, distance learning, double major, dual enrollment, English as a Second Language (ESL), honors program, independent study, internships, student-designed major, study abroad, teacher certificate program, weekend college. **Teacher certification offered in:** early childhood, elementary, secondary. **Reserve Officers Training Corps (ROTC):** Army ROTC: Offered at cooperating institution (St. Mary's University of San Antonio); Air Force ROTC: Offered at cooperating institution (University of Texas–San Antonio). **Faculty and instruction (2009-2010):** Total instructional faculty: 219 full-time, 349 part-time (44% men; 56% women; 36% minorities). Full-time faculty with Ph.D. or other terminal degree: 79%. Student/faculty ratio: 15/1. Classes of fewer than 20 students: 55%; of 20 to 49 students: 45%; of 50 or more students: 1%. **Advanced Placement and International Baccalaureate credit:** AP tests may be used for: Credit only. Scores accepted: 3, 4, 5. International Baccalaureate exams may be used for: Credit only. **Freshmen returning for sophomore year:** 66%. **Graduation rates:** Four-year: 18%; five-year: 36%; six-year: 42%.

COSTS AND FINANCIAL AID

Financial aid office: (210) 829-6008. **Expenses (2010-2011):** Tuition and fees 2010-2011: $21,890; room/board: $9,220. Estimated books and supplies: $1,200; transportation: $946; personal expenses: $1,620. **Financial aid:** Priority filing date for institution's financial aid form: April 1. In 2009-2010, 94% of undergraduates applied for financial aid. Of those, 87% were determined to have financial need; 22% had their need fully met. Average financial aid package (proportion receiving): $15,618 (87%). Average amount of gift aid, such as scholarships or grants (proportion receiving): $10,754 (80%). Average amount of self-help aid, such as work study or loans (proportion receiving): $4,800 (72%). Average need-based loan (excluding PLUS or other private loans): $4,576. Among students who received need-based aid, the average percentage of need met: 64%. Among students who received aid based on merit, the average award (and the proportion receiving): $6,908 (5%). The average athletic scholarship (and the proportion receiving): $12,989 (1%).

CAMPUS LIFE AND EXTRACURRICULAR ACTIVITIES

Campus housing available (% using): coed dorms (49%), women's dorms (11%), men's dorms (8%), apartment for single students (32%), special housing for disabled students. Students who live in college-owned, operated, or affiliated housing: 13%. **Student employment:** During the 2009-2010 academic year, 17% of undergraduates worked on campus. Average per-year earnings: $4,000. **Clubs and organizations:** Number of student organizations: 81. Activities include: campus ministries, choral groups, concert band, dance, drama/theater, international student organization, jazz band, literary magazine, music ensembles, musical theater, radio station, student government, student newspaper, television station. Number of fraternities: 4; sororities: 4. Proportion of men in fraternities: 1%; of women in sororities: 1%. **Sports program (2009-2010):** Member of NCAA II. **Men's intercollegiate varsity sports:** baseball, basketball, cross country, football, golf, soccer, swimming, tennis, track and field (outdoor). **Women's intercollegiate varsity sports:** basketball, cross country, golf, soccer, softball, swimming, sync swimming, tennis, track and field (outdoor), volleyball.

SERVICES AND FACILITIES

Basic services: nonremedial tutoring, placement service, health service, health insurance. **Remedial assistance:** reading, math, writing, study skills. **Counseling services:** minority student, career, military, personal, veteran student, academic, older student, psychological, religious. **For learning-disabled students:** School does not offer a structured program with separate admission and additional fees. Total undergraduates in learning-disabled program or receiving services: 174. Services include: remedial math, remedial English, remedial reading, tape recorders, note-taking services, oral tests, learning center, readers, extended time for tests, tutors, early syl-

labus, priority seating, substitution of courses, texts on tape, typist/scribe, exams on tape or computer, other testing accommodations, other. **Library:** Number of titles: 271,657; number of current serial subscriptions: 46,637. **Information technology resources:** Students are required to lease or own a computer. Number of campus computers available to all students: 250. School has a wireless network. Approximate number of users that can be accommodated: 4,000. Proportion of college-owned housing units wired for high-speed internet access: 100%. **Campus safety:** Security services offered: 24-hour foot-and-vehicle patrols, late-night transport/escort service, 24-hour emergency telephones, lighted pathways/sidewalks, controlled dormitory access (key, security card, etc).

TRANSFER AND INTERNATIONAL STUDENTS

Transfer students: May apply for admission for the following academic terms: Fall, Spring, Summer. Applicants do not need a minimum number of credits to apply. For fall 2009: Transfer applications received: 1,640. Transfer applicants offered admission: 1,215. Transfer applicants enrolled: 607. **International students:** Number of foreign undergraduates: 141 (3% of student body). Number of countries represented: 58. Minimum TOEFL score required: 550 (paper); 79 (computer).

Wayland Baptist University

- **Address:** 1900 W. Seventh Street, Plainview, TX 79072
- **Website:** http://www.wbu.edu
- **Private; Religious affiliation:** Southern Baptist Convention
- **Enrollment:** 748 full-time; 227 part-time

KEY STATS

✔ **U.S News College Ranking:** 62, Regional Universities (West)
✔ **ACT Score (25th/75th percentile):** 18-23
✔ **Tuition:** 2010-2011: $13,340

Selectivity: Selective	**Room/board:** $4,068
Acceptance rate: 99%	**Average debt:** $25,387
Student/faculty ratio: 8/1	**Proportion who borrowed:** 78%

UNDERGRADUATE STUDENT BODY STATS

2009-2010 enrollment: 748 full-time; 227 part-time. Men: 47%; women: 53%. **Ethnic makeup:** African American: 6%; American-Indian: 1%; Asian American: 1%; Hispanic: 23%; White: 66%; International: 3%. **Religious preference:** Roman Catholic: 11%; Protestant: 9%; No preference: 1%; Unknown: 14%; Southern Baptist Convention: 27%; Other Baptist: 19%; Other: 19%.

ADMISSIONS FACTS AND FIGURES

Phone: (806) 291-3500. **Email:** admityou@wbu.edu. **Website:** http://www.wbu.edu. **Application deadlines for fall 2011:** Regular decision: Rolling. Early decision: Not offered. Early action: Not offered. Admission cannot be deferred. **Application fee:** $35. To apply online, go to: https://apply.wbu.edu/. **Admissions requirements/recommendations:** High school units required (recommended): English: 3; Mathematics: 2 (3); Science: 2 (3); History: 2; Total units: 9 (6). Tests: The college uses SAT or ACT scores in admissions decisions. Either SAT or ACT required. For admission to the fall 2011 entering class, the school will accept: ACT with or without writing accepted. Campus visit: Recommended. Admissions interview: Recommended. Off-campus interview: May be arranged. **Factors that count in admissions decisions:** *Academic:* Secondary school record: Important. Class rank: Very Important. Letters of recommendation: Not Considered. Standardized test scores: Very Important. Essay: Not Considered. *Nonacademic:* Interview: Not Considered. Extracurricular activities: Not Considered. Talent/ability: Not Considered. Character/personal qualities: Not Considered. Alumni/ae relationship: Not Considered. Geographical residence: Not Considered. State residency: Not Considered. Religious affiliation/commitment: Not Considered. Minority status: Not Considered. Volunteer work: Not Considered. Work experience: Not Considered. **Other schools with the greatest overlap in applicants:** Hardin-Simmons University; Lubbock Christian University; Texas Tech University; West Texas A&M University. **Admissions statistics for the fall 2009 entering class:** Total applicants: 351. Total accepted: 347. Freshmen enrolled: 219; 14% were from out of state. Overall acceptance rate: 99%. **Credentials of fall 2009 freshmen:** 18% ranked in the top 10 percent of their high school class; 41% were in the top 25 percent; 72% were in the top half. (Proportion submitting class standing: 83%.) **Average high school grade point average:** 3.6. **First-year students who**

submitted SAT scores: 40%. Scores (25/75 percentile): Critical Reading: 410-540, Math: 430-570, Combined: 840-1110. First-year students submitting ACT scores: 71%. Scores (25/75 percentile): English: 17-24, Math: 16-23, Composite: 18-23.

ACADEMICS

Year founded: 1908. Academic calendar: Semester. Degrees offered: associate, transfer-associate, bachelor's, master's. Most popular majors: 22% business administration and management, 22% education, 8% biology/biological sciences, 7% criminal justice/law enforcement administration, 7% music. Major fields of study: biological and biomedical sciences; business, management, marketing, and related support services; communication, journalism, and related programs; education; English language and literature/letters; foreign languages, literatures, and linguistics; history; mathematics and statistics; philosophy and religious studies; physical sciences; psychology; security and protective services; social sciences; theology and religious vocations; visual and performing arts. Areas of required coursework: arts/fine arts, humanities, computer literacy, mathematics, English (including composition), foreign languages, sciences (biological or physical), history, social science. Special academic programs: accelerated program, distance learning, double major, dual enrollment, external degree program, honors program, internships, teacher certificate program. Teacher certification offered in: early childhood, special education, elementary, vo-tech, middle/junior high, secondary. Cooperative education programs: computer science, engineering. Reserve Officers Training Corps (ROTC): Army ROTC: Offered at cooperating institution; Air Force ROTC: Offered at cooperating institution. Faculty and instruction (2009-2010): Total instructional faculty: 92 full-time, 33 part-time (69% men; 31% women; 4% minorities). Full-time faculty with Ph.D. or other terminal degree: 71%. Student/faculty ratio: 8/1. Classes of fewer than 20 students: 81%; of 20 to 49 students: 19%; of 50 or more students: 0%. Advanced Placement and International Baccalaureate credit: AP tests may be used for: Credit only. Scores accepted: 3, 4, 5. International Baccalaureate exams may be used for: Credit only. Freshmen returning for sophomore year: 64%. Graduation rates: Four-year: 20%; five-year: 34%; six-year: 38%.

COSTS AND FINANCIAL AID

Financial aid office: (806) 291-3520. Expenses (2010-2011): Tuition and fees 2010-2011: $13,340; room/board: $4,068. Estimated books and supplies: $1,300; transportation: $1,070; personal expenses: $1,900. Financial aid: Priority filing date for institution's financial aid form: May 1. In 2009-2010, 87% of undergraduates applied for financial aid. Of those, 72% were determined to have financial need; 21% had their need fully met. Average financial aid package (proportion receiving): $11,850 (71%). Average amount of gift aid, such as scholarships or grants (proportion receiving): $9,044 (70%). Average amount of self-help aid, such as work study or loans (proportion receiving): $3,986 (52%). Average need-based loan (excluding PLUS or other private loans): $3,665. Among students who received need-based aid, the average percentage of need met: 73%. Among students who received aid based on merit, the average award (and the proportion receiving): $7,202 (20%). Average amount of debt of borrowers graduating in 2009: $25,387. Proportion who borrowed: 78%.

CAMPUS LIFE AND EXTRACURRICULAR ACTIVITIES

Campus housing available (% using): women's dorms (45%), men's dorms (47%), apartments for married students (8%). Students who live in college-owned, operated, or affiliated housing: 60%. Clubs and organizations: Number of student organizations: 29. Activities include: campus ministries, choral groups, concert band, drama/theater, marching band, music ensembles, musical theater, pep band, radio station, student government, student newspaper, television station, yearbook. Number of fraternities: 1; sororities: 1. Proportion of men in fraternities: 2%; of women in sororities: 1%. Sports program (2009-2010): Member of NAIA. Men's intercollegiate varsity sports: baseball, basketball, cross country, golf, soccer, track and field (indoor), track and field (outdoor). Women's intercollegiate varsity sports: basketball, cross country, golf, soccer, track and field (indoor), track and field (outdoor), volleyball.

SERVICES AND FACILITIES

Basic services: nonremedial tutoring, placement service, health service. Remedial assistance: reading, math, writing, study skills. Counseling services: career, personal, academic, psychological, religious. For learning-disabled students: School does not offer a structured program with separate admission and additional fees. Services include: remedial math, remedial English, remedial reading, tutors. Library: Number of titles: 128,786; number of current serial subscriptions: 497. Information technology resources:

Students are not required to lease or own a computer. Number of campus computers available to all students: 241. School has a wireless network. Approximate number of users that can be accommodated: 10,000. Campus safety: Security services offered: 24-hour emergency telephones, lighted pathways/sidewalks, controlled dormitory access (key, security card, etc).

TRANSFER AND INTERNATIONAL STUDENTS

Transfer students: May apply for admission for the following academic terms: Fall, Winter, Spring, Summer. Applicants need a minimum number of credits to apply. For fall 2009: Transfer applications received: 93. Transfer applicants offered admission: 92. Transfer applicants enrolled: 62. International students: Number of foreign undergraduates: 27 (3% of student body). Number of countries represented: 14. Minimum TOEFL score required: 500 (paper); 173 (computer).

West Texas A&M University

- Address: 2501 Fourth Avenue, Canyon, TX 79016-0001
- Website: http://www.wtamu.edu
- Public
- Enrollment: 4,869 full-time; 1,379 part-time

KEY STATS

✔ U.S News College Ranking: 77, Regional Universities (West)
✔ ACT Score (25th/75th percentile): 18-23
✔ Tuition: 2010-2011: $6,208 in state, $15,508 out of state

Selectivity: Selective	Room/board: $5,762
Acceptance rate: 55%	Average debt: N/A
Student/faculty ratio: N/A	Proportion who borrowed: N/A

UNDERGRADUATE STUDENT BODY STATS

2009-2010 enrollment: 4,869 full-time; 1,379 part-time. Men: 45%; women: 55%. Ethnic makeup: African American: 6%; American-Indian: 1%; Asian American: 1%; Hispanic: 21%; White: 69%; International: 2%.

ADMISSIONS FACTS AND FIGURES

Phone: (806) 651-2020. Email: admissions@mail.wtamu.edu. Website: http://www.wtamu.edu. Application deadlines for fall 2011: Regular decision: Rolling; decision sent by September 1. Early decision: Not offered. Early action: Not offered. Admission can be deferred. Application fee: $25. To apply online, go to: http://www.applytexas.org. Admissions requirements/recommendations: High school units required (recommended): English: 4 (4); Mathematics: 3 (4); Science: 3 (4); Foreign language: 2 (3); Social studies: 4 (4); Total units: 24 (24). Tests: The college uses SAT or ACT scores in admissions decisions. Either SAT or ACT required. For admission to the fall 2011 entering class, the school will accept: ACT with or without writing accepted. Campus visit: Recommended. Admissions interview: Neither required nor recommended. Off-campus interview: Not available. Factors that count in admissions decisions: Academic: Secondary school record: Very Important. Class rank: Very Important. Letters of recommendation: Considered. Standardized test scores: Very Important. Essay: Not Considered. Nonacademic: Interview: Not Considered. Extracurricular activities: Not Considered. Talent/ability: Not Considered. Character/personal qualities: Not Considered. Alumni/ae relationship: Not Considered. Geographical residence: Not Considered. State residency: Not Considered. Religious affiliation/commitment: Not Considered. Minority status: Not Considered. Volunteer work: Not Considered. Work experience: Not Considered. Other schools with the greatest overlap in applicants: Angelo State University; Midwestern State University; Tarleton State University; Texas Tech University. Admissions statistics for the fall 2009 entering class: Total applicants: 3,581. Total accepted: 1,962. Freshmen enrolled: 1,202; Overall acceptance rate: 55%. Credentials of fall 2009 freshmen: 15% ranked in the top 10 percent of their high school class; 40% were in the top 25 percent; 73% were in the top half. (Proportion submitting class standing: 95%.) First-year students who submitted SAT scores: 45%. Scores (25/75 percentile): Critical Reading: 430-550, Math: 450-560, Combined: 880-1110. First-year students submitting ACT scores: 77%. Scores (25/75 percentile): English: 16-23, Math: 17-24, Composite: 18-23.

ACADEMICS

Year founded: 1910. Academic calendar: Semester. Degrees offered: bachelor's, master's, doctorate. Most popular majors: 19% business, management, marketing, and related support services, 12% liberal arts and sciences studies, and humanities, 12% multi/interdisciplinary studies, 11% health professions and related clinical sciences, 6% education. **Major fields of study:** agriculture, agriculture operations, and related sciences; biological and biomedical sciences; business, management, marketing, and related support services; communication, journalism, and related programs; computer and information sciences and support services; engineering; engineering technologies/technicians; English language and literature/letters; foreign languages, literatures, and linguistics; health professions and related clinical sciences; legal professions and studies; liberal arts and sciences studies, and humanities; mathematics and statistics; multi/interdisciplinary studies; natural resources and conservation; parks, recreation, leisure, and fitness studies; physical sciences; psychology; public administration and social service professions; security and protective services; social sciences; visual and performing arts. **Areas of required coursework:** arts/fine arts, humanities, mathematics, English (including composition), sciences (biological or physical), history, social science, other. **Pre-professional programs:** pre-dentistry, pre-medicine, pre-veterinary science. **Special academic programs (% participation):** cooperative (work-study plan) program, distance learning (81.78%), double major, dual enrollment, English as a Second Language (ESL) (1.37%), honors program (1.8%), independent study (10.99%), internships, liberal arts/career combination, study abroad, teacher certificate program (14.47%). **Teacher certification offered in:** early childhood, special education, elementary, middle/junior high, secondary, bilingual/bicultural. **Cooperative education programs:** agriculture, business, computer science, engineering, health professions, humanities, natural science, social/behavioral science, technologies. **Advanced Placement and International Baccalaureate credit:** AP tests may be used for: Credit only. Scores accepted: 3, 4, 5. International Baccalaureate exams may be used for: Credit only. **Freshmen returning for sophomore year:** 65%. **Graduation rates:** Six-year: 38%.

COSTS AND FINANCIAL AID
Financial aid office: (806) 651-2055. **Expenses (2010-2011):** Tuition and fees 2010-2011: $6,208 in state, $15,508 out of state; room/board: $5,762. Estimated books and supplies: $1,200; transportation: $1,500; personal expenses: $1,950. **Financial aid:** Priority filing date for institution's financial aid form: May 1. In 2009-2010, 75% of undergraduates applied for financial aid. Of those, 60% were determined to have financial need; 12% had their need fully met. Average financial aid package (proportion receiving): $8,425 (53%). Average amount of gift aid, such as scholarships or grants (proportion receiving): $5,623 (38%). Average amount of self-help aid, such as work study or loans (proportion receiving): $4,471 (38%). Average need-based loan (excluding PLUS or other private loans): $4,204. Among students who received need-based aid, the average percentage of need met: 58%. Among students who received aid based on merit, the average award (and the proportion receiving): $2,308 (7%). The average athletic scholarship (and the proportion receiving): $2,147 (7%).

CAMPUS LIFE AND EXTRACURRICULAR ACTIVITIES
Campus housing available (% using): coed dorms (22%), women's dorms (42%), men's dorms (30%), sorority housing (3%), special housing for disabled students, other housing options (3%). **Student employment:** During the 2009-2010 academic year, 16% of undergraduates worked on campus. Average per-year earnings: $5,520. **Clubs and organizations:** Number of student organizations: 110. Activities include: campus ministries, choral groups, concert band, dance, drama/theater, international student organization, jazz band, literary magazine, marching band, music ensembles, musical theater, opera, radio station, student government, student newspaper, symphony orchestra, television station, yearbook. Number of fraternities: 5; sororities: 5. Average proportion of students who stay on campus on weekends: 12%. **Sports program (2009-2010):** Member of NCAA II. *Men's intercollegiate varsity sports:* baseball, basketball, cross country, football, golf, soccer. *Women's intercollegiate varsity sports:* basketball, cross country, fencing, golf, soccer, softball, volleyball.

SERVICES AND FACILITIES
Basic services: nonremedial tutoring, placement service, day care, health service, health insurance. **Remedial assistance:** reading, math, writing, study skills. **Counseling services:** minority student, career, military, personal, veteran student, academic, older student, psychological, birth control. **For learning-disabled students:** School does not offer a structured program with separate admission and additional fees. Services include: remedial math, remedial English, remedial reading, tape recorders, diagnostic testing service, untimed tests, note-taking services, oral tests, readers, extended time for tests, tutors, priority registration, texts on tape, other testing accommodations, other. **Library:** Number of titles: 1,105,750; number of current serial subscriptions: 19,638. **Information technology resources:** Students are

not required to lease or own a computer. Number of campus computers available to all students: 560. School has a wireless network. Approximate number of users that can be accommodated: 50. Proportion of college-owned housing units wired for high-speed internet access: 90%. **Campus safety:** Security services offered: 24-hour foot-and-vehicle patrols, late-night transport/escort service, 24-hour emergency telephones, lighted pathways/sidewalks, controlled dormitory access (key, security card, etc).

TRANSFER AND INTERNATIONAL STUDENTS
Transfer students: May apply for admission for the following academic terms: Fall, Winter, Spring, Summer. Applicants need a minimum number of credits to apply. **International students:** Number of foreign undergraduates: 90 (2% of student body). Minimum TOEFL score required: 525 (paper); 197 (computer). Average TOEFL score: 525 (paper).

Wiley College

- **Address:** 711 Wiley Avenue, Marshall, TX 75670
- **Website:** http://www.wileyc.edu
- **Private; Religious affiliation:** United Methodist
- **Enrollment:** 1,170 full-time; 67 part-time

KEY STATS
✔ **U.S News College Ranking:** second tier, Regional Colleges (West)
✔ **ACT Score (25th/75th percentile):** 13-18
✔ **Tuition:** 2010-2011: $10,522

Selectivity: Least selective	**Room/board:** $5,842
Acceptance rate: 98%	**Average debt:** $24,906
Student/faculty ratio: 19/1	**Proportion who borrowed:** 89%

UNDERGRADUATE STUDENT BODY STATS
2009-2010 enrollment: 1,170 full-time; 67 part-time. Men: 38%; women: 62%. **Ethnic makeup:** African American: 92%; Hispanic: 4%; White: 2%; International: 2%. **Religious preference:** Roman Catholic: 3%; Protestant: 85%; No preference: 4%; United Methodist: 8%.

ADMISSIONS FACTS AND FIGURES
Phone: (800) 658-6889. **Email:** admissions@wileyc.edu. **Website:** http://www.wileyc.edu. **Application deadlines for fall 2011:** Regular decision: September 3. Early decision: Not offered. Early action: Not offered. Admission can be deferred. **Application fee:** $25. **To apply online, go to:** http://www.wileyc.edu/apply/. **Admissions requirements/recommendations:** High school units required (recommended): English: 4 (4); Mathematics: 2 (2); Science: 2; Social studies: 2 (2); Academic electives: 6 (6); Total units: 16 (16). Tests: The college uses SAT or ACT scores in admissions decisions. Neither SAT nor ACT required. For admission to the fall 2011 entering class, the school will accept: ACT with or without writing accepted. Campus visit: Recommended. Admissions interview: Neither required nor recommended. Off-campus interview: May be arranged. **Factors that count in admissions decisions:** *Academic:* Secondary school record: Considered. Class rank: Considered. Letters of recommendation: Important. Standardized test scores: Important. Essay: Considered. ***Nonacademic:*** Interview: Considered. Extracurricular activities: Important. Talent/ability: Very Important. Character/personal qualities: Very Important. Alumni/ae relationship: Not Considered. Geographical residence: Considered. State residency: Not Considered. Religious affiliation/commitment: Not Considered. Minority status: Not Considered. Volunteer work: Not Considered. Work experience: Considered. **Admissions statistics for the fall 2009 entering class:** Total applicants: 1,816. Total accepted: 1,788. Freshmen enrolled: 312; 30% were from out of state. Overall acceptance rate: 98%. **Size of waiting list:** 0 applicants; enrolled from waiting list: 0. **Credentials of fall 2009 freshmen:** 3% ranked in the top 10 percent of their high school class; 9% were in the top 25 percent; 39% were in the top half. (Proportion submitting class standing: 30%.) **Average high school grade point average:** 2.6. **First-year students who submitted SAT scores:** 51%. Scores (25/75 percentile): Critical Reading: 320-420, Math: 330-430, Combined: 650-850. **First-year students submitting ACT scores:** 73%. Scores (25/75 percentile): English: 11-18, Math: 15-17, Composite: 13-18.

ACADEMICS
Year founded: 1873. **Academic calendar:** Semester. **Degrees offered:** associate, bachelor's. **Most popular majors:** 46% business administration, management, and operations, 19% criminal justice and corrections, 16%

early childhood education and teaching, 6% biology/biological sciences, 5% sociology. **Major fields of study:** biological and biomedical sciences; business, management, marketing, and related support services; communication, journalism, and related programs; computer and information sciences and support services; education; English language and literature/letters; history; mathematics and statistics; physical sciences; security and protective services; social sciences; visual and performing arts. **Areas of required coursework:** humanities, computer literacy, mathematics, English (including composition), foreign languages, sciences (biological or physical), history, social science, other. **Pre-professional programs:** pre-medicine, other. **Special academic programs (% participation):** distance learning (10%), double major (1%), independent study (2%), internships (2%), study abroad (1%), teacher certificate program (10%), weekend college (3%). **Teacher certification offered in:** early childhood, secondary. **Faculty and instruction (2009-2010):** Total instructional faculty: 56 full-time, 24 part-time (56% men; 44% women; 89% minorities). Full-time faculty with Ph.D. or other terminal degree: 68%. Student/faculty ratio: 19/1. Classes of fewer than 20 students: 60%; of 20 to 49 students: 38%; of 50 or more students: 2%. **Freshmen returning for sophomore year:** 56%. **Graduation rates:** Four-year: 12%; five-year: 17%; six-year: 26%. **Graduate study:** 8% of students pursue further study immediately upon graduation; 12% within one year; 17% within five years. Fields in which graduates pursue further study: Master of Business Administration (MBA), 3%; law, 5%; medicine, 20%; dentistry, 5%; theology (or the seminary), 10%; education, 50%; arts and sciences, 7%.

COSTS AND FINANCIAL AID

Financial aid office: (903) 927-3210. **Expenses (2010-2011):** Tuition and fees 2010-2011: $10,522; room/board: $5,842. Estimated books and supplies: $400; transportation: $540; personal expenses: $1,060. **Financial aid:** Priority filing date for institution's financial aid form: April 15; deadline: April 15. In 2009-2010, 98% of undergraduates applied for financial aid. Of those, 95% were determined to have financial need; 85% had their need fully met. Average financial aid package (proportion receiving): $14,701 (95%). Average amount of gift aid, such as scholarships or grants (proportion receiving): $6,900 (78%). Average amount of self-help aid, such as work study or loans (proportion receiving): $9,122 (90%). Average need-based loan (excluding PLUS or other private loans): $7,500. Among students who received need-based aid, the average percentage of need met: 95%. Among students who received aid based on merit, the average award (and the proportion receiving): $9,015 (4%). The average athletic scholarship (and the proportion receiving): $4,738 (3%). Average amount of debt of borrowers graduating in 2009: $24,906. Proportion who borrowed: 89%.

CAMPUS LIFE AND EXTRACURRICULAR ACTIVITIES

Campus housing available (% using): women's dorms (57%), men's dorms (43%). Students who live in college-owned, operated, or affiliated housing: 52%. **Student employment:** During the 2009-2010 academic year, 34% of undergraduates worked on campus. Average per-year earnings: $1,846. **Clubs and organizations:** Number of student organizations: 25. Activities include: choral groups, drama/theater, music ensembles, radio station, student government, student newspaper, yearbook. Number of fraternities: 4; sororities: 4. Average proportion of students who stay on campus on weekends: 40%. **Sports program (2009-2010):** Member of NAIA. *Men's intercollegiate varsity sports:* baseball, basketball, cross country, track and field (outdoor). *Women's intercollegiate varsity sports:* basketball, cross country, softball, track and field (outdoor), volleyball.

SERVICES AND FACILITIES

Basic services: placement service, health service, health insurance. **Remedial assistance:** reading, math, writing. **Counseling services:** career, personal, academic, religious. **For learning-disabled students:** School does not offer a structured program with separate admission and additional fees. Total undergraduates in learning-disabled program or receiving services: 7. Services include: remedial math, remedial English, remedial reading, diagnostic testing service, untimed tests, learning center, extended time for tests, tutors. **Library:** Number of titles: 85,286; number of current serial subscriptions: 352. **Information technology resources:** Students are required to lease or own a computer. Number of campus computers available to all students: 206. School has a wireless network. Approximate number of users that can be accommodated: 85. Proportion of college-owned housing units wired for high-speed internet access: 100%. **Campus safety:** Security services offered: 24-hour foot-and-vehicle patrols, 24-hour emergency telephones, controlled dormitory access (key, security card, etc).

TRANSFER AND INTERNATIONAL STUDENTS

Transfer students: May apply for admission for the following academic terms: Fall, Spring, Summer. Applicants do not need a minimum number of credits to apply. For fall 2009: Transfer applications received: 436. Transfer applicants offered admission: 431. Transfer applicants enrolled: 148. **International students:** Number of foreign undergraduates: 25 (2% of student body). Number of countries represented: 8. Minimum TOEFL score required: 500 (paper); 200 (computer).

Utah

Brigham Young University—Provo

- **Address:** A-209 ASB, Provo, UT 84602
- **Website:** http://www.byu.edu
- **Private; Religious affiliation:** Church of Jesus Christ of Latter-day Saints
- **Enrollment:** 28,048 full-time; 2,697 part-time

KEY STATS
✔ **U.S News College Ranking:** 75, National Universities
✔ **ACT Score (25th/75th percentile):** 25-30
✔ **Tuition:** 2010-2011: $4,420

Selectivity: More selective	**Room/board:** $7,120
Acceptance rate: 69%	**Average debt:** $10,730
Student/faculty ratio: 21/1	**Proportion who borrowed:** 24%

UNDERGRADUATE STUDENT BODY STATS
2009-2010 enrollment: 28,048 full-time; 2,697 part-time. Men: 51%; women: 49%. **Ethnic makeup:** Asian American: 4%; Hispanic: 4%; White: 88%; International: 3%. **Religious preference:** No preference: 1%; Church of Jesus Christ of Latter-day Saints: 98%; Other: 1%.

ADMISSIONS FACTS AND FIGURES
Phone: (801) 422-2507. **Email:** admissions@byu.edu. **Website:** http://www.byu.edu. **Application deadlines for fall 2011:** Regular decision: February 1. Early decision: Not offered. Early action: Not offered. Admission can be deferred. **Application fee:** $30. **To apply online, go to:** http://besmart.com/apply.honorcode.php. **Admissions requirements/recommendations:** High school units required (recommended): English: 4 (4); Mathematics: 3 (4); Science: 2 (3); Foreign language: 2 (4); History: 2. Tests: The college uses SAT or ACT scores in admissions decisions. Either SAT or ACT required. For admission to the fall 2011 entering class, the school will accept: ACT with writing recommended. Campus visit: Neither required nor recommended. Admissions interview: Neither required nor recommended. Off-campus interview: Not available. **Factors that count in admissions decisions:** *Academic:* Secondary school record: Very Important. Class rank: Not Considered. Letters of recommendation: Important. Standardized test scores: Very Important. Essay: Important. *Nonacademic:* Interview: Very Important. Extracurricular activities: Important. Talent/ability: Considered. Character/personal qualities: Very Important. Alumni/ae relationship: Not Considered. Geographical residence: Not Considered. State residency: Not Considered. Religious affiliation/commitment: Very Important. Minority status: Important. Volunteer work: Important. Work experience: Considered. **Other schools with the greatest overlap in applicants:** Brigham Young University–Hawaii; Brigham Young University–Idaho; University of Utah; Utah State University; Utah Valley University. **Admissions statistics for the fall 2009 entering class:** Total applicants: 10,212. Total accepted: 7,049. Freshmen enrolled: 5,421; 67% were from out of state. Overall acceptance rate: 69%. **Credentials of fall 2009 freshmen:** 51% ranked in the top 10 percent of their high school class; 83% were in the top 25 percent; 98% were in the top half. (Proportion submitting class standing: 78%.) **Average high school grade point average:** 3.8. **First-year students who submitted SAT scores:** 33%. Scores (25/75 percentile): Critical Reading: 560-670, Math: 570-680, Combined: 1130-1350. **First-year students submitting ACT scores:** 94%. Scores (25/75 percentile): English: 25-32, Math: 25-30, Composite: 25-30.

ACADEMICS
Year founded: 1875. **Academic calendar:** Semester. **Degrees offered:** bachelor's, post-bachelor's certificate, master's, doctorate. **Most popular majors:** 15% business, management, marketing, and related support services, 10% biological and biomedical sciences, 9% education, 9% social sciences, 7% family and consumer sciences/human sciences. **Major fields of study:** agriculture, agriculture operations, and related sciences; area, ethnic, cultural, and gender studies; biological and biomedical sciences; business, management, marketing, and related support services; communication, journalism, and related programs; communications technologies/technicians and support services; computer and information sciences and support services; education; engineering; English language and literature/letters; family and consumer sciences/human sciences; foreign languages, literatures, and linguistics; health professions and related clinical sciences; history; liberal arts and sciences studies, and humanities; mathematics and statistics; multi/interdisciplinary studies; natural resources and conservation; parks, recreation, leisure, and fitness studies; philosophy and religious studies; physical sciences; psychology; public administration and social service professions; social sciences; visual and performing arts. **Areas of required coursework:** arts/fine arts, humanities, mathematics, English (including composition), foreign languages, sciences (biological or physical), history, social science, other. **Special academic programs (% participation):** accelerated program, cooperative (work-study plan) program, cross-registration, distance learning, double major (2.3%), English as a Second Language (ESL), external degree program (2.2%), honors program (1.4%), independent study (32.2%), internships, liberal arts/career combination, study abroad (13.5%), teacher certificate program (9.3%). **Teacher certification offered in:** early childhood, special education, elementary, middle/junior high, secondary, bilingual/bicultural. **Reserve Officers Training Corps (ROTC):** Army ROTC: Offered on campus; Air Force ROTC: Offered on campus. **Faculty and instruction (2009-2010):** Total instructional faculty: 1,283 full-time, 403 part-time (69% men; 31% women; 6% minorities). Full-time faculty with Ph.D. or other terminal degree: 86%. Student/faculty ratio: 21/1. Classes of fewer than 20 students: 47%; of 20 to 49 students: 42%; of 50 or more students: 11%. **Advanced Placement and International Baccalaureate credit:** AP tests may be used for: Placement only. Scores accepted: 3, 4, 5. International Baccalaureate exams may be used for: Credit and/or placement. **Freshmen returning for sophomore year:** 84%. **Graduation rates:** Four-year: 30%; five-year: 52%; six-year: 77%.

COSTS AND FINANCIAL AID
Financial aid office: (801) 422-4104. **Expenses (2010-2011):** Tuition and fees 2010-2011: $4,420; room/board: $7,120. Estimated books and supplies: $900; transportation: $2,250; personal expenses: $1,720. **Financial aid:** Priority filing date for institution's financial aid form: April 15. In 2009-2010, 47% of undergraduates applied for financial aid. Of those, 39% were determined to have financial need; 3% had their need fully met. Average financial aid package (proportion receiving): $6,656 (36%). Average amount of gift aid, such as scholarships or grants (proportion receiving): $4,252 (29%). Average amount of self-help aid, such as work study or loans (proportion receiving): $4,374 (15%). Average need-based loan (excluding PLUS or other private loans): $4,374. Among students who received need-based aid, the average percentage of need met: 44%. Among students who received aid based on merit, the average award (and the proportion receiving): $3,188 (27%). The average athletic scholarship (and the proportion receiving): $6,527 (2%). Average amount of debt of borrowers graduating in 2009: $10,730. Proportion who borrowed: 24%.

CAMPUS LIFE AND EXTRACURRICULAR ACTIVITIES
Campus housing available (% using): women's dorms (16%), men's dorms (16%), apartments for married students (15%), apartment for single students (49%), special housing for disabled students (1%), other housing options (3%). Students who live in college-owned, operated, or affiliated housing: 18%. **Student employment:** During the 2009-2010 academic year, 43% of undergraduates worked on campus. Average per-year earnings: $5,760. **Clubs and organizations:** Number of student organizations: 390. Activities include: choral groups, concert band, dance, drama/theater, international student organization, jazz band, literary magazine, marching band, model UN, music ensembles, musical theater, opera, pep band, radio station, student government, student newspaper, student film society, symphony orchestra, television station. Number of fraternities: 0; sororities: 0. **Sports program (2009-2010):** Member of NCAA I. *Men's intercollegiate varsity sports:* baseball, basketball, cross country, football, golf, swimming, tennis, track and field (indoor), track and field (outdoor), volleyball. *Women's intercollegiate varsity sports:* basketball, cross country, golf, gymnastics, soccer, softball, swimming, tennis, track and field (indoor), track and field (outdoor), volleyball.

SERVICES AND FACILITIES

Basic services: nonremedial tutoring, women's center, placement service, health service, health insurance, other. **Remedial assistance:** reading, math, writing, study skills, other. **Counseling services:** minority student, career, military, personal, veteran student, academic, older student, psychological, religious. **For learning-disabled students:** School does not offer a structured program with separate admission and additional fees. Total undergraduates in learning-disabled program or receiving services: 110. Services include: reading machines, tape recorders, other special classes, diagnostic testing service, note-taking services, oral tests, learning center, readers, extended time for tests, tutors, priority registration, priority seating, substitution of courses, texts on tape, typist/scribe, exams on tape or computer, other testing accommodations, other. **Library:** Number of titles: 4,168,102; number of current serial subscriptions: 77,646. **Information technology resources:** Students are not required to lease or own a computer. Number of campus computers available to all students: 3,800. School has a wireless network. Approximate number of users that can be accommodated: 5,000. Proportion of college-owned housing units wired for high-speed internet access: 100%. **Campus safety:** Security services offered: 24-hour foot-and-vehicle patrols, late-night transport/escort service, 24-hour emergency telephones, lighted pathways/sidewalks, student patrols, controlled dormitory access (key, security card, etc).

TRANSFER AND INTERNATIONAL STUDENTS

Transfer students: May apply for admission for the following academic terms: Fall, Winter, Spring, Summer. Applicants need a minimum number of credits to apply. For fall 2009: Transfer applications received: 2,189. Transfer applicants offered admission: 883. Transfer applicants enrolled: 695. **International students:** Number of foreign undergraduates: 842 (3% of student body). Number of countries represented: 118. Minimum TOEFL score required: 550 (paper).

Dixie State College of Utah

- **Address:** 225 S. 700 E, Saint George, UT 84770-2876
- **Website:** http://www.dixie.edu
- **Public**
- **Enrollment:** 4,520 full-time; 3,188 part-time

KEY STATS

- ✔ **U.S News College Ranking:** Unranked, Regional Colleges (West)
- ✔ **ACT Score (25th/75th percentile):** 18-23
- ✔ **Tuition:** 2010-2011: $3,490 in state, $12,118 out of state

Selectivity: N/A	**Room/board:** $4,100
Acceptance rate: 66%	**Average debt:** N/A
Student/faculty ratio: 21/1	**Proportion who borrowed:** N/A

UNDERGRADUATE STUDENT BODY STATS

2009-2010 enrollment: 4,520 full-time; 3,188 part-time. Men: 49%; women: 51%. **Ethnic makeup:** African American: 2%; American-Indian: 1%; Asian American: 3%; Hispanic: 5%; White: 89%.

ADMISSIONS FACTS AND FIGURES

Phone: (435) 652-7702. **Email:** admit@dixie.edu. **Website:** http://www.dixie.edu. **Application deadlines for fall 2011:** Regular decision: Rolling. Early decision: Not offered. Early action: Not offered. Admission can be deferred. **Application fee:** $35. **To apply online, go to:** https://bannersec.dixie.edu/proddad/bwskalog.P_DispLoginNon. **Admissions requirements/recommendations:** High school units required (recommended): English: (4); Mathematics: (4); Science: (2); Foreign language: (2); History: (3); Total units: (16). Tests: The college does not use SAT or ACT scores in admissions decisions. Neither SAT nor ACT required. Campus visit: Recommended. Admissions interview: Neither required nor recommended. **Factors that count in admissions decisions:** *Academic:* Secondary school record: Not Considered. Class rank: Not Considered. Letters of recommendation: Not Considered. Standardized test scores: Not Considered. Essay: Not Considered. *Nonacademic:* Interview: Not Considered. Extracurricular activities: Not Considered. Talent/ability: Not Considered. Character/personal qualities: Not Considered. Alumni/ae relationship: Not Considered. Geographical residence: Not Considered. State residency: Not Considered. Religious affiliation/commitment: Not Considered. Minority status: Not Considered. Volunteer work: Not Considered. Work experience: Not Considered. **Admissions statistics for the fall 2009 entering class:** Total

applicants: 4,215. Total accepted: 2,774. Freshmen enrolled: 1,743; 13% were from out of state. Overall acceptance rate: 66%. **Credentials of fall 2009 freshmen:** 7% ranked in the top 10 percent of their high school class; 24% were in the top 25 percent; 56% were in the top half. (Proportion submitting class standing: 72%.) **Average high school grade point average:** 3.1.

ACADEMICS

Year founded: 1911. **Academic calendar:** Semester. **Degrees offered:** certificate, associate, transfer-associate, terminal-associate, bachelor's. **Most popular majors:** 36% business administration and management, 17% elementary education and teaching, 12% digital communication and media/multimedia, 10% English language and literature, 10% computer and information sciences. **Major fields of study:** biological and biomedical sciences; business, management, marketing, and related support services; communication, journalism, and related programs; computer and information sciences and support services; education; English language and literature/letters; health professions and related clinical sciences. **Areas of required coursework:** arts/fine arts, humanities, computer literacy, mathematics, English (including composition), sciences (biological or physical), history, social science. **Special academic programs:** accelerated program, cooperative (work-study plan) program, distance learning, double major, dual enrollment, English as a Second Language (ESL), honors program, independent study, internships, student-designed major, study abroad, teacher certificate program. **Teacher certification offered in:** elementary, secondary. **Cooperative education programs:** art, business, computer science, education, engineering, health professions, natural science, social/behavioral science, technologies, other. **Reserve Officers Training Corps (ROTC):** Army ROTC: Offered on campus. **Faculty and instruction (2009-2010):** Total instructional faculty: 131 full-time, 303 part-time (51% men; 49% women; 4% minorities). Full-time faculty with Ph.D. or other terminal degree: 54%. Student/faculty ratio: 21/1. Classes of fewer than 20 students: 31%; of 20 to 49 students: 65%; of 50 or more students: 4%. **Advanced Placement and International Baccalaureate credit:** AP tests may be used for: Credit and/or placement. Scores accepted: 3, 4, 5. **Freshmen returning for sophomore year:** 53%. **Graduation rates:** Four-year: 28%; five-year: 29%; six-year: 31%.

COSTS AND FINANCIAL AID

Financial aid office: (435) 652-7575. **Expenses (2010-2011):** Tuition and fees 2010-2011: $3,490 in state, $12,118 out of state; room/board: $4,100. Estimated books and supplies: $1,150; transportation: $3,250; personal expenses: $6,140. **Financial aid:** Priority filing date for institution's financial aid form: March 1.

CAMPUS LIFE AND EXTRACURRICULAR ACTIVITIES

Campus housing available: coed dorms, men's dorms, apartments for married students, apartment for single students. Students who live in college-owned, operated, or affiliated housing: 4%. Activities include: campus ministries, choral groups, concert band, dance, drama/theater, international student organization, jazz band, literary magazine, marching band, music ensembles, musical theater, pep band, radio station, student government, student newspaper, symphony orchestra, television station. Number of fraternities: 0; sororities: 0. **Sports program (2009-2010):** Member of NCAA II. **Men's intercollegiate varsity sports:** baseball, basketball, football, golf, soccer. **Women's intercollegiate varsity sports:** basketball, soccer, softball, tennis, volleyball.

SERVICES AND FACILITIES

Basic services: nonremedial tutoring, health service. **Remedial assistance:** reading, math, writing, study skills. **Counseling services:** minority student, career, academic, older student. **For learning-disabled students:** School does not offer a structured program with separate admission and additional fees. Total undergraduates in learning-disabled program or receiving services: 73. Services include: remedial math, remedial English, reading machines, remedial reading, tape recorders, other special classes, untimed tests, note-taking services, oral tests, learning center, readers, extended time for tests, priority registration, priority seating, texts on tape, typist/scribe, other testing accommodations. **Library:** Number of titles: 153,051; number of current serial subscriptions: 203. **Information technology resources:** Students are not required to lease or own a computer. Number of campus computers available to all students: 400. School has a wireless network. Proportion of college-owned housing units wired for high-speed internet access: 100%. **Campus safety:** Security services offered: 24-hour foot-and-vehicle patrols, lighted pathways/sidewalks.

TRANSFER AND INTERNATIONAL STUDENTS

Transfer students: May apply for admission for the following academic terms: Fall, Spring, Summer. Applicants need a minimum number of credits to apply. For fall 2009: Transfer applications received: 913. Transfer applicants offered admission: 705. Transfer applicants enrolled: 512. **International students:** Number of foreign undergraduates: 19. Number of countries represented: 11. Minimum TOEFL score required: 500 (paper); 173 (computer). Average TOEFL score: 500 (paper).

Southern Utah University

- ■ **Address:** 351 W. Center Street, Cedar City, UT 84720
- ■ **Website:** http://www.suu.edu
- ■ **Public**
- ■ **Enrollment:** 5,467 full-time; 1,762 part-time

KEY STATS

✔ **U.S News College Ranking:** 75, Regional Universities (West)
✔ **ACT Score (25th/75th percentile):** 19-25
✔ **Tuition:** 2009-2010: $4,269 in state, $12,847 out of state
   Selectivity: Selective   **Room/board:** $5,300
   Acceptance rate: N/A   **Average debt:** N/A
   Student/faculty ratio: 26/1   **Proportion who borrowed:** N/A

UNDERGRADUATE STUDENT BODY STATS

2009-2010 enrollment: 5,467 full-time; 1,762 part-time. Men: 42%; women: 58%. **Ethnic makeup:** African American: 1%; American-Indian: 2%; Asian American: 2%; Hispanic: 4%; White: 88%; International: 2%.

ADMISSIONS FACTS AND FIGURES

Phone: (435) 586-7740. **Email:** adminfo@suu.edu. **Website:** http://www.suu.edu. **Application deadlines for fall 2011:** Regular decision: August 1. Early decision: Not offered. Early action: Send application by: N/A; Decision sent by: N/A. Admission can be deferred. **Application fee:** $40. **To apply online, go to:** https://bannersec.suu.edu/pls/proddad/bwskalog.p_disploginnon. **Admissions requirements/recommendations:** High school units required (recommended): English: (4); Mathematics: (3); Science: (3); Foreign language: (2); Social studies: (3). Tests: The college uses SAT or ACT scores in admissions decisions. Either SAT or ACT required. For admission to the fall 2011 entering class, the school will accept: ACT with or without writing accepted. Campus visit: Recommended. Admissions interview: Neither required nor recommended. Off-campus interview: Not available. **Factors that count in admissions decisions: *Academic:*** Secondary school record: Not Considered. Class rank: Not Considered. Letters of recommendation: Not Considered. Standardized test scores: Very Important. Essay: Not Considered. ***Nonacademic:*** Interview: Not Considered. Extracurricular activities: Not Considered. Talent/ability: Not Considered. Character/personal qualities: Not Considered. Alumni/ae relationship: Not Considered. Geographical residence: Not Considered. State residency: Not Considered. Religious affiliation/commitment: Not Considered. Minority status: Considered. Volunteer work: Not Considered. Work experience: Not Considered. **Admissions statistics for the fall 2009 entering class:** Freshmen enrolled: 1,316; 18% were from out of state. **Credentials of fall 2009 freshmen:** 26% ranked in the top 10 percent of their high school class; 51% were in the top 25 percent; 80% were in the top half. (Proportion submitting class standing: 74%.) **Average high school grade point average:** 3.4. **First-year students who submitted SAT scores:** 12%. Scores (25/75 percentile): Critical Reading: 450-580, Math: 450-570, Combined: 900-1150. **First-year students submitting ACT scores:** 88%. Scores (25/75 percentile): English: 18-25, Math: 18-24, Composite: 19-25.

ACADEMICS

Year founded: 1897. **Academic calendar:** Semester. **Degrees offered:** certificate, diploma, associate, transfer-associate, terminal-associate, bachelor's, master's. **Most popular majors:** 20% education, 15% business, management, marketing, and related support services, 9% health professions and related clinical sciences, 8% biological and biomedical sciences, 7% psychology. **Major fields of study:** agriculture, agriculture operations, and related sciences; biological and biomedical sciences; business, management, marketing, and related support services; communication, journalism, and related programs; computer and information sciences and support services; construction trades; education; engineering; engineering technologies/technicians; English language and literature/letters; family and consumer sciences/human sciences; foreign languages, literatures, and linguistics; health professions and related clinical sciences; history; mathematics and statistics; multi/interdisciplinary studies; physical sciences; psychology; security and protective services; social sciences; visual and performing arts. **Areas of required coursework:** arts/fine arts, humanities, computer literacy, mathematics, English (including composition), philosophy, sciences (biological or physical), history, social science. **Pre-professional programs:** pre-law, pre-dentistry, pre-medicine, pre-veterinary science, pre-optometry, pre-pharmacy. **Special academic programs:** cooperative (work-study plan) program, distance learning, double major, English as a Second Language (ESL), honors program, independent study, internships, liberal arts/career combination, teacher certificate program, weekend college. **Teacher certification offered in:** early childhood, special education, elementary, secondary. **Reserve Officers Training Corps (ROTC):** Army ROTC: Offered on campus. **Faculty and instruction (2009-2010):** Total instructional faculty: 216 full-time, 110 part-time (63% men; 37% women; 14% minorities). Full-time faculty with Ph.D. or other terminal degree: 75%. Student/faculty ratio: 26/1. Classes of fewer than 20 students: 40%; of 20 to 49 students: 50%; of 50 or more students: 10%. **Freshmen returning for sophomore year:** 64%. **Graduation rates:** Four-year: 23%; five-year: 35%; six-year: 41%.

COSTS AND FINANCIAL AID

Financial aid office: (435) 586-7735. **Expenses (2009-2010):** Tuition and fees 2009-2010: $4,269 in state, $12,847 out of state; room/board: $5,300.

CAMPUS LIFE AND EXTRACURRICULAR ACTIVITIES

Campus housing available: coed dorms, women's dorms, men's dorms, sorority housing, fraternity housing, apartment for single students, special housing for disabled students, special housing for international students. Students who live in college-owned, operated, or affiliated housing: 13%. Activities include: choral groups, concert band, dance, drama/theater, jazz band, literary magazine, marching band, music ensembles, musical theater, opera, pep band, radio station, student government, student newspaper, symphony orchestra, television station, yearbook. Number of fraternities: 2; sororities: 1. Proportion of men in fraternities: 4%; of women in sororities: 4%. **Sports program (2009-2010):** Member of NCAA I. *Men's intercollegiate varsity sports:* baseball, basketball, cross country, football, golf, track and field (indoor), track and field (outdoor). *Women's intercollegiate varsity sports:* basketball, cross country, golf, gymnastics, soccer, tennis, track and field (indoor), track and field (outdoor).

SERVICES AND FACILITIES

Basic services: placement service, health service, health insurance. **Remedial assistance:** reading, math, writing, study skills. **Counseling services:** career, personal, veteran student, academic, older student, psychological. **For learning-disabled students:** Services include: remedial math, remedial English, tape recorders, diagnostic testing service, note-taking services, oral tests, learning center, readers, extended time for tests, tutors. **Information technology resources:** Students are not required to lease or own a computer. Number of campus computers available to all students: 771. School has a wireless network. Proportion of college-owned housing units wired for high-speed internet access: 100%. **Campus safety:** Security services offered: 24-hour emergency telephones, lighted pathways/sidewalks.

TRANSFER AND INTERNATIONAL STUDENTS

Transfer students: May apply for admission for the following academic terms: Fall. Applicants do not need a minimum number of credits to apply. For fall 2009: Transfer applications received: 928. Transfer applicants offered admission: 655. Transfer applicants enrolled: 426. **International students:** Number of foreign undergraduates: 97 (2% of student body). Minimum TOEFL score required: 500 (paper); 173 (computer). Average TOEFL score: 510 (paper).

University of Utah

- **Address:** 201 S. Presidents Circle, Salt Lake City, UT 84112
- **Website:** http://www.utah.edu
- **Public**
- **Enrollment:** 15,189 full-time; 6,960 part-time

KEY STATS

✔ **U.S News College Ranking:** 129, National Universities
✔ **ACT Score (25th/75th percentile):** 21-27
✔ **Tuition:** 2010-2011: $6,274 in state, $19,842 out of state

Selectivity: Selective	**Room/board:** N/A
Acceptance rate: 80%	**Average debt:** $15,201
Student/faculty ratio: 15/1	**Proportion who borrowed:** 40%

UNDERGRADUATE STUDENT BODY STATS

2009-2010 enrollment: 15,189 full-time; 6,960 part-time. Men: 55%; women: 45%. **Ethnic makeup:** African American: 1%; American-Indian: 1%; Asian American: 6%; Hispanic: 6%; White: 84%; International: 3%.

ADMISSIONS FACTS AND FIGURES

Phone: (801) 581-7281. **Email:** Admissions@sa.utah.edu. **Website:** http://www.utah.edu. **Application deadlines for fall 2011:** Regular decision: April 1. Early decision: Not offered. Early action: Not offered. Admission cannot be deferred. **Application fee:** $45. **To apply online, go to:** http://www.sa.utah.edu/admiss/appdownload/. **Admissions requirements/recommendations:** High school units required (recommended): English: 4 (4); Mathematics: 2 (2); Science: 3 (3); Foreign language: 2 (2); Social studies: 0 (0); History: 1 (1); Academic electives: 4 (4); Total units: 16 (16). Tests: The college uses SAT or ACT scores in admissions decisions. Either SAT or ACT required. For admission to the fall 2011 entering class, the school will accept: ACT with or without writing accepted. Campus visit: Recommended. Admissions interview: Neither required nor recommended. Off-campus interview: May be arranged. **Factors that count in admissions decisions:** *Academic:* Secondary school record: Very Important. Class rank: Considered. Letters of recommendation: Considered. Standardized test scores: Very Important. Essay: Not Considered. *Nonacademic:* Interview: Considered. Extracurricular activities: Considered. Talent/ability: Important. Character/personal qualities: Not Considered. Alumni/ae relationship: Not Considered. Geographical residence: Not Considered. State residency: Not Considered. Religious affiliation/commitment: Not Considered. Minority status: Considered. Volunteer work: Not Considered. Work experience: Not Considered. **Other schools with the greatest overlap in applicants:** Brigham Young University–Provo; Utah State University; Utah Valley University; Weber State University; Westminster College. **Admissions statistics for the fall 2009 entering class:** Total applicants: 7,890. Total accepted: 6,318. Freshmen enrolled: 2,867; 18% were from out of state. Overall acceptance rate: 80%. **Credentials of fall 2009 freshmen:** 23% ranked in the top 10 percent of their high school class; 48% were in the top 25 percent; 82% were in the top half. (Proportion submitting class standing: 66%.) **Average high school grade point average:** 3.5. **First-year students who submitted SAT scores:** 24%. Scores (25/75 percentile): Critical Reading: 490-630, Math: 500-630, Combined: 990-1260. **First-year students submitting ACT scores:** 90%. Scores (25/75 percentile): English: 21-27, Math: 20-26, Composite: 21-27.

ACADEMICS

Year founded: 1850. **Academic calendar:** Semester. **Degrees offered:** certificate, bachelor's, post-bachelor's certificate, master's, post-master's certificate, doctorate. **Most popular majors:** 17% social sciences, 13% business, management, marketing, and related support services, 8% communication, journalism, and related programs, 7% engineering, 7% health professions and related clinical sciences. **Major fields of study:** architecture and related services; area, ethnic, cultural, and gender studies; biological and biomedical sciences; business, management, marketing, and related support services; communication, journalism, and related programs; computer and information sciences and support services; education; engineering; English language and literature/letters; family and consumer sciences/human sciences; foreign languages, literatures, and linguistics; health professions and related clinical sciences; history; liberal arts and sciences studies, and humanities; mathematics and statistics; multi/interdisciplinary studies; natural resources and conservation; parks, recreation, leisure, and fitness studies; philosophy and religious studies; physical sciences; psychology; public administration and social service professions; social sciences; visual and performing arts. **Areas of required coursework:** arts/fine arts, humanities, mathematics, English (including composition), foreign languages, sciences (biological or physical), history, social science. **Pre-professional programs:** pre-law, pre-dentistry, pre-medicine, pre-veterinary science, pre-optometry, pre-pharmacy. **Special academic programs (% participation):** accelerated program (13%), distance learning (57%), double major (6%), dual enrollment (.4%), English as a Second Language (ESL) (2.3%), exchange student program (domestic) (.2%), honors program (8%), independent study (14%), internships (34%), student-designed major (.3%), study abroad (6.29%), teacher certificate program (2%). **Teacher certification offered in:** early childhood, special education, elementary, middle/junior high, secondary, bilingual/bicultural. **Cooperative education programs:** art, business, computer science, education, engineering, health professions, humanities, natural science, social/behavioral science, technologies. **Reserve Officers Training Corps (ROTC):** Army ROTC: Offered on campus; Navy ROTC: Offered on campus; Air Force ROTC: Offered on campus. **Faculty and instruction (2009-2010):** Total instructional faculty: 1,269 full-time, 620 part-time (59% men; 41% women; 9% minorities). Full-time faculty with Ph.D. or other terminal degree: 82%. Student/faculty ratio: 15/1. Classes of fewer than 20 students: 43%; of 20 to 49 students: 41%; of 50 or more students: 15%. **Advanced Placement and International Baccalaureate credit:** AP tests may be used for: Credit only. Scores accepted: 3, 4, 5. International Baccalaureate exams may be used for: Placement only. **Freshmen returning for sophomore year:** 81%. **Graduation rates:** Four-year: 22%; five-year: 44%; six-year: 58%. **Graduate study:** 15% of students pursue further study immediately upon graduation; 26% within one year; 34% within five years. Fields in which graduates pursue further study: Master of Business Administration (MBA), 9%; law, 2%; engineering, 18%; education, 6%; arts and sciences, 28%.

COSTS AND FINANCIAL AID

Financial aid office: (801) 581-8788. **Expenses (2010-2011):** Tuition and fees 2010-2011: $6,274 in state, $19,842 out of state. Estimated books and supplies: $1,090; transportation: $1,332; personal expenses: $4,500. **Financial aid:** Priority filing date for institution's financial aid form: April 1. In 2009-2010, 48% of undergraduates applied for financial aid. Of those, 42% were determined to have financial need; 16% had their need fully met. Average financial aid package (proportion receiving): $10,944 (41%). Average amount of gift aid, such as scholarships or grants (proportion receiving): $5,317 (33%). Average amount of self-help aid, such as work study or loans (proportion receiving): $7,312 (30%). Average need-based loan (excluding PLUS or other private loans): $4,820. Among students who received need-based aid, the average percentage of need met: 63%. Among students who received aid based on merit, the average award (and the proportion receiving): $4,688 (5%). The average athletic scholarship (and the proportion receiving): $7,479 (1%). Average amount of debt of borrowers graduating in 2009: $15,201. Proportion who borrowed: 40%.

CAMPUS LIFE AND EXTRACURRICULAR ACTIVITIES

Campus housing available (% using): coed dorms (59%), sorority housing (4%), fraternity housing (4%), apartments for married students (14%), special housing for disabled students (1%), special housing for international students (4%). Students who live in college-owned, operated, or affiliated housing: 12%. **Student employment:** During the 2009-2010 academic year, 11% of undergraduates worked on campus. Average per-year earnings: $2,000. **Clubs and organizations:** Number of student organizations: 238. Activities include: campus ministries, choral groups, concert band, dance, drama/theater, international student organization, jazz band, literary magazine, marching band, model UN, music ensembles, musical theater, opera, pep band, radio station, student government, student newspaper, student film society, symphony orchestra, television station. Number of fraternities: 7; sororities: 6. Proportion of men in fraternities: 3%; of women in sororities: 4%. Average proportion of students who stay on campus on weekends: 20%. **Sports program (2009-2010):** Member of NCAA I. *Men's intercollegiate varsity sports:* baseball, basketball, football, golf, skiing (nordic), skiing (alpine), swimming, tennis, track and field (indoor), track and field (outdoor). *Women's intercollegiate varsity sports:* basketball, cross country, gymnastics, skiing (nordic), skiing (alpine), soccer, softball, swimming, tennis, track and field (indoor), track and field (outdoor), volleyball.

SERVICES AND FACILITIES

Basic services: nonremedial tutoring, women's center, placement service, day care, health service, health insurance. **Remedial assistance:** math. **Counseling services:** minority student, career, military, personal, veteran student, academic, older student, psychological, birth control. **For learning-disabled students:** School does not offer a structured program with separate admission and additional fees. Total undergraduates in learning-disabled program or receiving services: 241. Services include: reading machines, tape recorders, note-taking services, oral tests, readers, extended time for tests, tutors, priority registration, priority seating, texts on tape, other testing accommodations, other. **Library:** Number of titles: 3,373,141; number of current serial subscriptions: 48,777. **Information technology resources:** Students are not required to lease or own a computer. Number of campus computers available to all students: 3,000. School has a wireless network. Approximate number of users that can be accommodated: 51,000. Proportion of college-owned housing units wired for high-speed internet access: 100%. **Campus safety:** Security services offered: 24-hour foot-and-vehicle patrols, late-night transport/escort service, 24-hour emergency telephones, lighted pathways/sidewalks, controlled dormitory access (key, security card, etc).

TRANSFER AND INTERNATIONAL STUDENTS

Transfer students: May apply for admission for the following academic terms: Fall, Spring, Summer. Applicants need a minimum number of credits to apply. For fall 2009: Transfer applications received: 3,324. Transfer applicants offered admission: 2,592. Transfer applicants enrolled: 1,965. **International students:** Number of foreign undergraduates: 583 (3% of student body). Number of countries represented: 113. Minimum TOEFL score required: 500 (paper); 61 (computer). Average TOEFL score: 566 (paper).

Utah State University

- **Address:** Old Main Hill, Logan, UT 84322
- **Website:** http://www.usu.edu
- **Public**
- **Enrollment:** 11,632 full-time; 2,177 part-time

KEY STATS

✔ **U.S News College Ranking:** 170, National Universities
✔ **ACT Score (25th/75th percentile):** 21-27
✔ **Tuition:** 2010-2011: $5,150 in state, $14,797 out of state

Selectivity: Selective	**Room/board:** $5,070
Acceptance rate: 98%	**Average debt:** N/A
Student/faculty ratio: 18/1	**Proportion who borrowed:** N/A

UNDERGRADUATE STUDENT BODY STATS

2009-2010 enrollment: 11,632 full-time; 2,177 part-time. Men: 51%; women: 49%. **Ethnic makeup:** African American: 1%; American-Indian: 1%; Asian American: 2%; Hispanic: 3%; White: 91%; International: 4%.

ADMISSIONS FACTS AND FIGURES

Phone: (435) 797-1079. **Email:** admit@usu.edu. **Website:** http://www. usu.edu. **Application deadlines for fall 2011:** Regular decision: Rolling. Early decision: Not offered. Early action: Not offered. Admission can be deferred. **Application fee:** $40. **To apply online, go to:** http://www.usu.edu/admissions/. **Admissions requirements/recommendations:** High school units required (recommended): English: 4; Mathematics: 3; Science: 3; Foreign language: (2); History: 1; Academic electives: 4; Total units: 15 (2). Tests: The college uses SAT or ACT scores in admissions decisions. Either SAT or ACT required. For admission to the fall 2011 entering class, the school will accept: ACT with or without writing accepted. Campus visit: Recommended. Admissions interview: Neither required nor recommended. Off-campus interview: Not available. **Factors that count in admissions decisions:** *Academic:* Secondary school record: Important. Class rank: Considered. Letters of recommendation: Considered. Standardized test scores: Very Important. Essay: Not Considered. *Nonacademic:* Interview: Not Considered. Extracurricular activities: Not Considered. Talent/ability: Not Considered. Character/personal qualities: Not Considered. Alumni/ae relationship: Not Considered. Geographical residence: Not Considered. State residency: Not Considered. Religious affiliation/commitment: Not Considered. Minority status: Not Considered. Volunteer work: Not Considered. Work experience: Not Considered. **Other schools with the greatest overlap in applicants:** Brigham Young University–Provo; University of Utah. **Admissions statistics for the fall 2009 entering class:** Total applicants: 6,438. Total accepted: 6,289. Freshmen enrolled: 2,839; 22% were from out of state. Overall acceptance rate: 98%. **Credentials of fall 2009 freshmen:** 24% ranked in the top 10 percent of their high school class; 49% were in the top 25 percent; 82% were in the top half. (Proportion submitting class standing: 79%.) **Average high school grade point average:** 3.5. **First-year students who submitted SAT scores:** 8%. Scores (25/75 percentile): Critical Reading: 470-630, Math: 460-630, Combined: 930-1260. **First-year**

students submitting ACT scores: 95%. Scores (25/75 percentile): English: 20-28, Math: 20-27, Composite: 21-27.

ACADEMICS

Year founded: 1888. **Academic calendar:** Semester. **Degrees offered:** certificate, associate, transfer-associate, terminal-associate, bachelor's, post-bachelor's certificate, master's, post-master's certificate, doctorate. **Most popular majors:** 7% multi/interdisciplinary studies, 6% elementary education and teaching, 4% business administration and management, 4% economics, 4% physical education teaching and coaching. **Major fields of study:** agriculture, agriculture operations, and related sciences; architecture and related services; area, ethnic, cultural, and gender studies; biological and biomedical sciences; business, management, marketing, and related support services; communication, journalism, and related programs; computer and information sciences and support services; education; engineering; engineering technologies/technicians; English language and literature/letters; family and consumer sciences/human sciences; foreign languages, literatures, and linguistics; health professions and related clinical sciences; legal professions and studies; liberal arts and sciences studies, and humanities; mathematics and statistics; mechanic and repair technologies/technicians; multi/interdisciplinary studies; natural resources and conservation; parks, recreation, leisure, and fitness studies; philosophy and religious studies; physical sciences; precision production; psychology; public administration and social service professions; social sciences; transportation and materials moving; visual and performing arts. **Areas of required coursework:** arts/fine arts, humanities, computer literacy, mathematics, English (including composition), sciences (biological or physical), history, social science, other. **Pre-professional programs:** pre-law, pre-dentistry, pre-medicine, pre-veterinary science. **Special academic programs:** accelerated program, cooperative (work-study plan) program, cross-registration, distance learning, double major, dual enrollment, English as a Second Language (ESL), honors program, independent study, internships, liberal arts/career combination, student-designed major, study abroad, teacher certificate program, weekend college. **Teacher certification offered in:** early childhood, special education, elementary, vo-tech, middle/junior high, secondary, bilingual/bicultural. **Cooperative education programs:** agriculture, business, computer science, education, engineering, home economics, humanities, natural science, social/behavioral science. **Reserve Officers Training Corps (ROTC):** Army ROTC: Offered on campus; Air Force ROTC: Offered on campus. **Faculty and instruction (2009-2010):** Total instructional faculty: 708 full-time, 169 part-time (64% men; 36% women; 6% minorities). Full-time faculty with Ph.D. or other terminal degree: 86%. Student/faculty ratio: 18/1. Classes of fewer than 20 students: 34%; of 20 to 49 students: 49%; of 50 or more students: 17%. **Advanced Placement and International Baccalaureate credit:** AP tests may be used for: Credit and/or placement. Scores accepted: 3, 4, 5. International Baccalaureate exams may be used for: Credit only. **Freshmen returning for sophomore year:** 74%. **Graduation rates:** Four-year: 27%; five-year: 42%; six-year: 56%. **Graduate study:** 32% of students pursue further study within one year. Fields in which graduates pursue further study: law, 7%; medicine, 8%.

COSTS AND FINANCIAL AID

Financial aid office: (435) 797-0173. **Expenses (2010-2011):** Tuition and fees 2010-2011: $5,150 in state, $14,797 out of state; room/board: $5,070. Estimated books and supplies: $1,170; transportation: $1,470; personal expenses: $2,140. **Financial aid:** In 2009-2010, 60% of undergraduates applied for financial aid. Of those, 52% were determined to have financial need; 10% had their need fully met. Average financial aid package (proportion receiving): $7,300 (51%). Average amount of gift aid, such as scholarships or grants (proportion receiving): $4,959 (37%). Average amount of self-help aid, such as work study or loans (proportion receiving): $4,192 (27%). Average need-based loan (excluding PLUS or other private loans): $4,080. Among students who received need-based aid, the average percentage of need met: 63%. Among students who received aid based on merit, the average award (and the proportion receiving): $2,500 (3%). The average athletic scholarship (and the proportion receiving): $8,030 (0%).

CAMPUS LIFE AND EXTRACURRICULAR ACTIVITIES

Campus housing available: coed dorms, women's dorms, men's dorms, sorority housing, fraternity housing, apartments for married students, apartment for single students, special housing for disabled students, special housing for international students, other housing options. **Student employment:** During the 2009-2010 academic year, 22% of undergraduates worked on campus. Average per-year earnings: $6,000. **Clubs and organizations:** Number of student organizations: 200. Activities include: campus ministries, choral groups, concert band, dance, drama/theater, international student organization, jazz band, marching band, music ensembles, musical theater, opera, pep band, radio station, student government, student newspaper, student film society, symphony orchestra, television station. Number of fraternities: 6; sororities: 4. Proportion of men in fraternities: 2%; of women in sororities: 2%. **Sports program (2009-2010):** Member of NCAA I. **Men's intercollegiate varsity sports:** basketball, cross country, football, golf, tennis, track and field (indoor), track and field (outdoor). **Women's intercollegiate varsity sports:** basketball, cross country, gymnastics, soccer, softball, tennis, track and field (indoor), track and field (outdoor), volleyball.

SERVICES AND FACILITIES

Basic services: nonremedial tutoring, women's center, placement service, day care, health service, health insurance, other. **Remedial assistance:** reading, math, writing, study skills. **Counseling services:** minority student, career, military, personal, veteran student, academic, older student, psychological, birth control, religious. **For learning-disabled students:** Services include: reading machines, tape recorders, note-taking services, readers, extended time for tests, other. **Library:** Number of titles: 1,647,042; number of current serial subscriptions: 10,749. **Information technology resources:** Students are not required to lease or own a computer. Number of campus computers available to all students: 925. School has a wireless network. Approximate number of users that can be accommodated: 15,000. Proportion of college-owned housing units wired for high-speed internet access: 100%. **Campus safety:** Security services offered: 24-hour foot-and-vehicle patrols, late-night transport/escort service, 24-hour emergency telephones, lighted pathways/sidewalks.

TRANSFER AND INTERNATIONAL STUDENTS

Transfer students: May apply for admission for the following academic terms: Fall, Spring, Summer. Applicants need a minimum number of credits to apply. For fall 2009: Transfer applications received: 2,174. Transfer applicants offered admission: 2,081. Transfer applicants enrolled: 1,022. **International students:** Number of foreign undergraduates: 483 (4% of student body). Number of countries represented: 78. Minimum TOEFL score required: 525 (paper); 71 (computer). Average TOEFL score: 525 (paper).

Utah Valley University

- **Address:** 800 W. University Parkway, Orem, UT 84058-5999
- **Website:** http://www.uvu.edu/
- **Public**
- **Enrollment:** N/A

KEY STATS

✔ **U.S News College Ranking:** Unranked, Regional Colleges (West)
✔ **SAT or ACT Score (25th/75th percentile):** N/A
✔ **Tuition:** 2009-2010: $4,048 in state, $11,888 out of state

Selectivity: N/A	Room/board: $8,670
Acceptance rate: N/A	Average debt: N/A
Student/faculty ratio: N/A	Proportion who borrowed: N/A

Weber State University

- **Address:** 1103 University Circle, Ogden, UT 84408-1103
- **Website:** http://weber.edu
- **Public**
- **Enrollment:** 10,570 full-time; 11,811 part-time

KEY STATS

✔ **U.S News College Ranking:** 56, Regional Universities (West)
✔ **ACT Score (25th/75th percentile):** 19-24
✔ **Tuition:** 2009-2010: $4,081 in state, $11,547 out of state

Selectivity: Selective	Room/board: $4,259
Acceptance rate: 100%	Average debt: N/A
Student/faculty ratio: 22/1	Proportion who borrowed: N/A

UNDERGRADUATE STUDENT BODY STATS

2009-2010 enrollment: 10,570 full-time; 11,811 part-time. Men: 48%; women: 52%. **Ethnic makeup:** African American: 1%; American-Indian: 1%; Asian American: 2%; Hispanic: 5%; White: 91%; International: 1%.

Religious preference: Roman Catholic: 4%; Protestant: 6%; Jewish: 1%; No preference: 5%; Unknown: 24%; LDS(The Church of Jesus Christ of Later Day Saints): 59%; Other: 1%.

ADMISSIONS FACTS AND FIGURES

Phone: (801) 626-6744. **Email:** admissions@weber.edu. **Website:** http://weber.edu. **Application deadlines for fall 2011:** Regular decision: Rolling. Early decision: Not offered. Early action: Not offered. Admission can be deferred. **Application fee:** $30. **To apply online, go to:** http://www.weber.edu/admissions/studentapplication.html. **Admissions requirements/recommendations:** High school units required (recommended): English: (4); Mathematics: (2); Science: (2); Foreign language: (2); History: (1); Academic electives: (4); Total units: (15). Tests: The college uses SAT or ACT scores in admissions decisions. Neither SAT nor ACT required. For admission to the fall 2011 entering class, the school will accept: ACT with or without writing accepted. Campus visit: Recommended. Admissions interview: Neither required nor recommended. Off-campus interview: Not available. **Factors that count in admissions decisions:** *Academic:* Secondary school record: Important. Class rank: Not Considered. Letters of recommendation: Not Considered. Standardized test scores: Important. Essay: Not Considered. *Nonacademic:* Interview: Considered. Extracurricular activities: Considered. Talent/ability: Not Considered. Character/personal qualities: Considered. Alumni/ae relationship: Not Considered. Geographical residence: Not Considered. State residency: Not Considered. Religious affiliation/commitment: Not Considered. Minority status: Not Considered. Volunteer work: Not Considered. Work experience: Not Considered. **Other schools with the greatest overlap in applicants:** Brigham Young University–Provo; University of Utah; Utah State University; Utah Valley University. **Admissions statistics for the fall 2009 entering class:** Freshmen enrolled: 2,377; 14% were from out of state. Overall acceptance rate: 100%. **Average high school grade point average:** 3.3. **First-year students submitting ACT scores:** 69%. Scores (25/75 percentile): English: 18-25, Math: 17-24, Composite: 19-24.

ACADEMICS

Year founded: 1889. **Academic calendar:** Semester. **Degrees offered:** certificate, associate, transfer-associate, terminal-associate, bachelor's, post-bachelor's certificate, master's. **Most popular majors:** 7% orthoptics/orthoptist, 5% nursing/registered nurse training (R.N., A.S.N., B.S.N., M.S.N.), 4% accounting, 4% medical radiologic technology/science-radiation therapist, 4% psychology. **Major fields of study:** biological and biomedical sciences; business, management, marketing, and related support services; communication, journalism, and related programs; computer and information sciences and support services; construction trades; education; engineering; engineering technologies/technicians; English language and literature/letters; family and consumer sciences/human sciences; foreign languages, literatures, and linguistics; health professions and related clinical sciences; mathematics and statistics; physical sciences; psychology; public administration and social service professions; security and protective services; social sciences; visual and performing arts. **Areas of required coursework:** arts/fine arts, humanities, computer literacy, mathematics, English (including composition), sciences (biological or physical), history, social science. **Preprofessional programs:** pre-law, pre-dentistry, pre-medicine, pre-pharmacy. **Special academic programs:** accelerated program, cooperative (work-study plan) program, distance learning, double major, dual enrollment, English as a Second Language (ESL), exchange student program (domestic), external degree program, honors program, independent study, internships, student-designed major, study abroad, teacher certificate program. **Teacher certification offered in:** early childhood, special education, elementary, middle/junior high, secondary. **Cooperative education programs:** health professions, social/behavioral science, technologies. **Reserve Officers Training Corps (ROTC):** Army ROTC: Offered on campus; Navy ROTC: Offered on campus; Air Force ROTC: Offered on campus. **Faculty and instruction (2009-2010):** Total instructional faculty: 481 full-time, 385 part-time (55% men; 45% women; 9% minorities). Full-time faculty with Ph.D. or other terminal degree: 87%. Student/faculty ratio: 22/1. Classes of fewer than 20 students: 46%; of 20 to 49 students: 50%; of 50 or more students: 5%. **Advanced Placement and International Baccalaureate credit:** AP tests may be used for: Credit and/or placement. International Baccalaureate exams may be used for: Credit and/or placement. **Freshmen returning for sophomore year:** 71%. **Graduation rates:** Four-year: 12%; five-year: 29%; six-year: 42%. **Graduate study:** 51% of students pursue further study immediately upon graduation. Fields in which graduates pursue further study: law, 8%; medicine, 11%; dentistry, 7%; education, 8%.

COSTS AND FINANCIAL AID

Financial aid office: (801) 626-7569. **Expenses (2009-2010):** Tuition and fees 2009-2010: $4,081 in state, $11,547 out of state; room/board: $4,259. Estimated books and supplies: $1,200; transportation: $1,520; personal expenses: $1,486. **Financial aid:** Priority filing date for institution's financial aid form: March 1.

CAMPUS LIFE AND EXTRACURRICULAR ACTIVITIES

Campus housing available (% using): women's dorms (4%), men's dorms (7%), apartments for married students (11%), apartment for single students (77%), special housing for disabled students (1%). Students who live in college-owned, operated, or affiliated housing: 4%. **Student employment:** During the 2009-2010 academic year, 5% of undergraduates worked on campus. Average per-year earnings: $7,500. **Clubs and organizations:** Number of student organizations: 138. Activities include: choral groups, concert band, dance, drama/theater, jazz band, literary magazine, marching band, music ensembles, musical theater, opera, pep band, radio station, student government, student newspaper, student film society, symphony orchestra, television station. Number of fraternities: 0; sororities: 0. Average proportion of students who stay on campus on weekends: 4%. **Sports program (2009-2010):** Member of NCAA I. *Men's intercollegiate varsity sports:* basketball, cross country, football, golf, tennis, track and field (indoor), track and field (outdoor). *Women's intercollegiate varsity sports:* basketball, cross country, golf, soccer, softball, tennis, track and field (indoor), track and field (outdoor), volleyball.

SERVICES AND FACILITIES

Basic services: nonremedial tutoring, women's center, placement service, day care, health service, health insurance. **Remedial assistance:** math, other. **Counseling services:** minority student, career, military, personal, veteran student, academic, older student, psychological, birth control, religious. **For learning-disabled students:** School does not offer a structured program with separate admission and additional fees. Services include: remedial math, remedial English, reading machines, remedial reading, tape recorders, other special classes, videotaped classes, untimed tests, note-taking services, oral tests, learning center, readers, extended time for tests, tutors, priority registration, texts on tape, other testing accommodations. **Library:** Number of titles: 547,753; number of current serial subscriptions: 1,544. **Information technology resources:** Students are not required to lease or own a computer. Number of campus computers available to all students: 600. School has a wireless network. Approximate number of users that can be accommodated: 60,000. Proportion of college-owned housing units wired for high-speed internet access: 75%. **Campus safety:** Security services offered: 24-hour foot-and-vehicle patrols, late-night transport/escort service, 24-hour emergency telephones, lighted pathways/sidewalks, controlled dormitory access (key, security card, etc).

TRANSFER AND INTERNATIONAL STUDENTS

Transfer students: May apply for admission for the following academic terms: Fall, Spring, Summer. Applicants need a minimum number of credits to apply. For fall 2009: Transfer applicants enrolled: 1,008. **International students:** Number of foreign undergraduates: 191 (1% of student body). Number of countries represented: 35.

Western Governors University

- **Address:** 4001 S. 700 E Suite 700, Salt Lake City, UT 84107-2533
- **Website:** http://www.wgu.edu/
- **Private**
- **Enrollment:** 13,228 full-time

KEY STATS

✔ **U.S News College Ranking:** Unranked, Regional Colleges (West)
✔ **SAT or ACT Score (25th/75th percentile):** N/A
✔ **Tuition:** 2009-2010: $5,870

Selectivity: N/A	Room/board: $12,600
Acceptance rate: N/A	Average debt: N/A
Student/faculty ratio: N/A	Proportion who borrowed: N/A

UNDERGRADUATE STUDENT BODY STATS

2009-2010 enrollment: 13,228 full-time. Men: 41%; women: 59%.

ADMISSIONS FACTS AND FIGURES

Phone: (866) 225-5948. **Email:** info@wgu.edu. **Website:** http://www.wgu.edu/. **Application deadlines for fall 2011:** Regular decision: Rolling. Early decision: Not offered. Early action: Not offered. Admission can be deferred. **Application fee:** $65. **To apply online, go to:** https://www.wgu.edu/wgu/app/app_step0.asp. **Admissions requirements/recommendations:** Tests: The college does not use SAT or ACT scores in admissions decisions. Neither SAT nor ACT required. Campus visit: Neither required nor recommended. Admissions interview: Required. Off-campus interview: May be arranged. **Factors that count in admissions decisions:** *Academic:* Secondary school record: Not Considered. Class rank: Not Considered. Letters of recommendation: Not Considered. Standardized test scores: Not Considered. Essay: Not Considered. *Nonacademic:* Interview: Important. Extracurricular activities: Not Considered. Talent/ability: Not Considered. Character/personal qualities: Not Considered. Alumni/ae relationship: Not Considered. Geographical residence: Not Considered. State residency: Not Considered. Religious affiliation/commitment: Not Considered. Minority status: Not Considered. Volunteer work: Not Considered. Work experience: Not Considered.

ACADEMICS

Year founded: 1996. **Academic calendar:** Continuous. **Degrees offered:** bachelor's, post-bachelor's certificate, master's. **Major fields of study:** business, management, marketing, and related support services; computer and information sciences and support services; education. **Areas of required coursework:** arts/fine arts, mathematics, English (including composition), sciences (biological or physical), social science, other. **Special academic programs:** accelerated program, distance learning, teacher certificate program. **Teacher certification offered in:** early childhood, special education, elementary, middle/junior high, secondary. **Cooperative education programs:** education.

COSTS AND FINANCIAL AID

Financial aid office: (801) 327-8104. **Expenses (2009-2010):** Tuition and fees 2009-2010: $5,870; room/board: $12,600. Estimated books and supplies: $1,640.

SERVICES AND FACILITIES

Basic services: nonremedial tutoring, placement service, other. **Remedial assistance:** other. **Counseling services:** academic, other. **For learning-disabled students:** School does not offer a structured program with separate admission and additional fees. **Information technology resources:** Students are required to lease or own a computer. School does not have a wireless network.

TRANSFER AND INTERNATIONAL STUDENTS

Transfer students: May apply for admission for the following academic terms: Fall, Winter, Spring, Summer. Applicants do not need a minimum number of credits to apply.

Westminster College

- **Address:** 1840 S. 1300 E, Salt Lake City, UT 84105-3697
- **Website:** http://www.westminstercollege.edu
- **Private**
- **Enrollment:** 2,035 full-time; 137 part-time

KEY STATS

✔ **U.S News College Ranking:** 23, Regional Universities (West)
✔ **ACT Score (25th/75th percentile):** 22-27
✔ **Tuition:** 2010-2011: $25,980

Selectivity: More selective	Room/board: $7,274
Acceptance rate: 82%	Average debt: $20,251
Student/faculty ratio: 10/1	Proportion who borrowed: 54%

UNDERGRADUATE STUDENT BODY STATS

2009-2010 enrollment: 2,035 full-time; 137 part-time. Men: 45%; women: 55%. **Ethnic makeup:** African American: 1%; American-Indian: 1%; Asian American: 3%; Hispanic: 6%; White: 86%; International: 2%. **Religious preference:** Roman Catholic: 6%; Jewish: 1%; No preference: 3%; Unknown: 72%; Church of Jesus Christ of Latter-day Saints: 12%; Other: 6%.

ADMISSIONS FACTS AND FIGURES

Phone: (801) 832-2200. **Email:** admission@westminstercollege.edu. **Website:** http://www.westminstercollege.edu. **Application deadlines for fall 2011:** Regular decision: Rolling. Early decision: Not offered. Early action: Not offered. Admission can be deferred. **Application fee:** $40. **To apply online, go to:** http://www.westminstercollege.edu/admissions_freshmen/index.cfm?parent=2935&detail=2941. **Admissions requirements/recommendations:** High school units required (recommended): English: 4 (4); Mathematics: 2 (3); Science: 3 (3); Foreign language: 2 (3); Social studies: 2 (2); History: 1 (1); Academic electives: 2 (3); Total units: 16 (19). Tests: The college uses SAT or ACT scores in admissions decisions. Either SAT or ACT required. For admission to the fall 2011 entering class, the school will accept: ACT with writing recommended. Campus visit: Recommended. Admissions interview: Recommended. Off-campus interview: May be arranged. **Factors that count in admissions decisions:** *Academic:* Secondary school record: Very Important. Class rank: Important. Letters of recommendation: Considered. Standardized test scores: Important. Essay: Important. *Nonacademic:* Interview: Important. Extracurricular activities: Considered. Talent/ability: Considered. Character/personal qualities: Considered. Alumni/ae relationship: Considered. Geographical residence: Considered. State residency: Not Considered. Religious affiliation/commitment: Not Considered. Minority status: Not Considered. Volunteer work: Not Considered. Work experience: Not Considered. **Other schools with the greatest overlap in applicants:** Brigham Young University–Provo; Colorado College; University of Colorado–Boulder; University of Utah; Utah State University. **Admissions statistics for the fall 2009 entering class:** Total applicants: 1,625. Total accepted: 1,329. Freshmen enrolled: 469; 41% were from out of state. Overall acceptance rate: 82%. **Credentials of fall 2009 freshmen:** 29% ranked in the top 10 percent of their high school class; 60% were in the top 25 percent; 85% were in the top half. (Proportion submitting class standing: 75%.) **Average high school grade point average:** 3.5. **First-year students who submitted SAT scores:** 41%. Scores (25/75 percentile): Critical Reading: 510-620, Math: 500-630, Combined: 1010-1250. **First-year students submitting ACT scores:** 78%. Scores (25/75 percentile): English: 21-26, Math: 21-27, Composite: 22-27.

ACADEMICS

Year founded: 1875. **Academic calendar:** 4-1-4. **Degrees offered:** bachelor's, post-bachelor's certificate, master's. **Most popular majors:** 32% business, management, marketing, and related support services, 20% health professions and related clinical sciences, 7% social sciences, 5% psychology, 5% transportation and materials moving. **Major fields of study:** biological and biomedical sciences; business, management, marketing, and related support services; communication, journalism, and related programs; computer and information sciences and support services; education; English language and literature/letters; health professions and related clinical sciences; history; legal professions and studies; mathematics and statistics; philosophy and religious studies; physical sciences; psychology; social sciences; transportation and materials moving; visual and performing arts. **Areas of required coursework:** arts/fine arts, humanities, computer literacy, mathematics, English (including composition), philosophy, foreign languages, sciences (biological or physical), history, social science, other. **Pre-professional programs:** pre-law, pre-dentistry, pre-medicine. **Special academic programs (% participation):** cross-registration (3%), double major (3%), exchange student program (domestic) (1%), honors program (7%), independent study (17%), internships (47%), student-designed major (1%), study abroad (4%), teacher certificate program (1%). **Teacher certification offered in:** early childhood, special education, elementary, middle/junior high, secondary, bilingual/bicultural. **Cooperative education programs:** other. **Reserve Officers Training Corps (ROTC):** Army ROTC: Offered at cooperating institution (University of Utah); Navy ROTC: Offered at cooperating institution (University of Utah); Air Force ROTC: Offered at cooperating institution (University of Utah). **Faculty and instruction (2009-2010):** Total instructional faculty: 136 full-time, 191 part-time (50% men; 50% women; 3% minorities). Full-time faculty with Ph.D. or other terminal degree: 94%. Student/faculty ratio: 10/1. Classes of fewer than 20 students: 59%; of 20 to 49 students: 41%; of 50 or more students: 0%. **Advanced Placement and International Baccalaureate credit:** AP tests may be used for: Placement only. Scores accepted: 3, 4, 5. International Baccalaureate exams may be used for: Credit and/or placement. **Freshmen returning for sophomore year:** 78%. **Graduation rates:** Four-year: 42%; five-year: 53%; six-year: 56%. **Graduate study:** 16% of students pursue further study immediately upon graduation; 16% within one year. Fields in which graduates pursue further study: Master of Business Administration (MBA), 32%; law, 1%; medicine, 1%; education, 1%; arts and sciences, 65%.

COSTS AND FINANCIAL AID

Financial aid office: (801) 832-2500. **Expenses (2010-2011):** Tuition and fees 2010-2011: $25,980; room/board: $7,274. Estimated books and supplies: $1,000; transportation: $1,100; personal expenses: $1,301. **Financial aid:** Priority filing date for institution's financial aid form: April 15. In 2009-2010, 70% of undergraduates applied for financial aid. Of those, 60% were determined to have financial need; 34% had their need fully met. Average financial aid package (proportion receiving): $18,640 (60%). Average amount of gift aid, such as scholarships or grants (proportion receiving): $13,657 (60%). Average amount of self-help aid, such as work study or loans (proportion receiving): $5,749 (52%). Average need-based loan (excluding PLUS or other private loans): $4,980. Among students who received need-based aid, the average percentage of need met: 78%. Among students who received aid based on merit, the average award (and the proportion receiving): $10,995 (33%). The average athletic scholarship (and the proportion receiving): $4,920 (1%). Average amount of debt of borrowers graduating in 2009: $20,251. Proportion who borrowed: 54%.

CAMPUS LIFE AND EXTRACURRICULAR ACTIVITIES

Campus housing available (% using): women's dorms (13%), men's dorms (13%), apartment for single students (60%), special housing for disabled students (5%), other housing options (9%). Students who live in college-owned, operated, or affiliated housing: 28%. **Student employment:** During the 2009-2010 academic year, 20% of undergraduates worked on campus. Average per-year earnings: $3,058. **Clubs and organizations:** Number of student organizations: 76. Activities include: campus ministries, choral groups, dance, drama/theater, international student organization, jazz band, literary magazine, music ensembles, musical theater, student government, student newspaper, student film society, symphony orchestra. Number of fraternities: 0; sororities: 0. Average proportion of students who stay on campus on weekends: 80%. **Sports program (2009-2010):** Member of NAIA. *Men's intercollegiate varsity sports:* basketball, cross country, golf, soccer. *Women's intercollegiate varsity sports:* basketball, cross country, golf, soccer, volleyball.

SERVICES AND FACILITIES

Basic services: nonremedial tutoring, women's center, placement service, health service, health insurance. **Remedial assistance:** math, writing. **Counseling services:** minority student, career, military, personal, veteran student, academic, older student, psychological, birth control, religious. **For learning-disabled students:** School does not offer a structured program with separate admission and additional fees. Total undergraduates in learning-disabled program or receiving services: 74. Services include: reading machines, tape recorders, untimed tests, note-taking services, readers, extended time for tests, tutors, priority registration, priority seating, texts on tape, typist/scribe, exams on tape or computer, other testing accommodations. **Library:** Number of titles: 187,585; number of current serial subscriptions: 12,139. **Information technology resources:** Students are not required to lease or own a computer. Number of campus computers available to all students: 587. School has a wireless network. Approximate number of users that can be accommodated: 3,500. Proportion of college-owned housing units wired for high-speed internet access: 100%. **Campus safety:** Security services offered: 24-hour foot-and-vehicle patrols, late-night transport/escort service, 24-hour emergency telephones, lighted pathways/sidewalks, controlled dormitory access (key, security card, etc).

TRANSFER AND INTERNATIONAL STUDENTS

Transfer students: May apply for admission for the following academic terms: Fall, Winter, Spring, Summer. Applicants do not need a minimum number of credits to apply. For fall 2009: Transfer applications received: 574. Transfer applicants offered admission: 441. Transfer applicants enrolled: 212. **International students:** Number of foreign undergraduates: 45 (2% of student body). Number of countries represented: 27. Minimum TOEFL score required: 550 (paper); 100 (computer). Average TOEFL score: 523 (paper).

Vermont

Bennington College

- **Address:** 1 College Drive, Bennington, VT 05201
- **Website:** http://www.bennington.edu
- **Private**
- **Enrollment:** 660 full-time; 4 part-time

KEY STATS
- ✔ **U.S News College Ranking:** 122, National Liberal Arts Colleges
- ✔ **SAT Score (25th/75th percentile):** 1180-1360
- ✔ **Tuition:** 2010-2011: $41,350

Selectivity: More selective	**Room/board:** $11,550
Acceptance rate: 66%	**Average debt:** $22,402
Student/faculty ratio: 9/1	**Proportion who borrowed:** 70%

UNDERGRADUATE STUDENT BODY STATS
2009-2010 enrollment: 660 full-time; 4 part-time. Men: 33%; women: 67%. **Ethnic makeup:** African American: 2%; Asian American: 2%; Hispanic: 2%; White: 88%; International: 6%.

ADMISSIONS FACTS AND FIGURES
Phone: (800) 833-6845. **Email:** admissions@bennington.edu. **Website:** http://www.bennington.edu. **Application deadlines for fall 2011:** Regular decision: January 3; decision sent by April 1. Early decision: Send application by: November 15; Decision sent by: December 20. Early action: Send application by: December 1; Decision sent by: February 1. Admission can be deferred. **Application fee:** $60. **To apply online, go to:** http://www.bennington.edu/go/admissions/applying-to-bennington. **Admissions requirements/ recommendations:** High school units required (recommended): English: (4); Mathematics: (4); Science: (3); Foreign language: (2); Social studies: (4); History: (4); Total units: (21). Tests: The college uses SAT or ACT scores in admissions decisions. Neither SAT nor ACT required. For admission to the fall 2011 entering class, the school will accept: ACT with or without writing accepted. Campus visit: Recommended. Admissions interview: Required. Off-campus interview: May be arranged. **Factors that count in admissions decisions:** *Academic:* Secondary school record: Very Important. Class rank: Very Important. Letters of recommendation: Very Important. Standardized test scores: Considered. Essay: Very Important. *Nonacademic:* Interview: Very Important. Extracurricular activities: Very Important. Talent/ability: Very Important. Character/personal qualities: Very Important. Alumni/ae relationship: Considered. Geographical residence: Considered. State residency: Not Considered. Religious affiliation/commitment: Not Considered. Minority status: Considered. Volunteer work: Considered. Work experience: Considered. **Other schools with the greatest overlap in applicants:** Bard College; Hampshire College; Marlboro College; Sarah Lawrence College; University of Vermont. **Admissions statistics for the fall 2009 entering class:** Total applicants: 1,054. Total accepted: 696. Freshmen enrolled: 197; 96% were from out of state. Accepted through early-decision or early-action plans: 21%. Overall acceptance rate: 66%. Early-decision acceptance rate: 47%. Non-early acceptance rate: 68%. **Size of waiting list:** 78 applicants; enrolled from waiting list: 14. **Credentials of fall 2009 freshmen:** 31% ranked in the top 10 percent of their high school class; 63% were in the top 25 percent; 85% were in the top half. (Proportion submitting class standing: 27%.) **Average high school grade point average:** 3.5. **First-year students who submitted SAT scores:** 41%. Scores (25/75 percentile): Critical Reading: 620-720, Math: 560-640, Combined: 1180-1360. **First-year students submitting ACT scores:** 15%. Scores (25/75 percentile): English: N/A, Math: N/A, Composite: 26-31.

ACADEMICS
Year founded: 1925. **Academic calendar:** Semester. **Degrees offered:** bachelor's, post-bachelor's certificate, master's. **Most popular majors:** 19% visual and performing arts, 14% English language and literature, 9% drama and dramatics/theater arts, 9% music. **Major fields of study:** architecture and related services; area, ethnic, cultural, and gender studies; biological and biomedical sciences; communication, journalism, and related programs; communications technologies/technicians and support services; computer and information sciences and support services; education; English language and literature/letters; family and consumer sciences/human sciences; foreign languages, literatures, and linguistics; health professions and related clinical sciences; history; legal professions and studies; liberal arts and sciences studies, and humanities; mathematics and statistics; multi/interdisciplinary studies; natural resources and conservation; philosophy and religious studies; physical sciences; psychology; social sciences; visual and performing arts. **Pre-professional programs:** pre-law, pre-medicine, pre-veterinary science, other. **Special academic programs (% participation):** accelerated program (0%), cross-registration (6%), double major (39%), English as a Second Language (ESL) (0%), exchange student program (domestic) (1%), independent study (75%), internships (100%), student-designed major (100%), study abroad (26%), teacher certificate program (3%). **Teacher certification offered in:** early childhood, elementary, middle/junior high, secondary, bilingual/bicultural. **Cooperative education programs:** other. **Faculty and instruction (2009-2010):** Total instructional faculty: 62 full-time, 32 part-time (53% men; 47% women; 13% minorities). Full-time faculty with Ph.D. or other terminal degree: 73%. Student/faculty ratio: 9/1. Classes of fewer than 20 students: 79%; of 20 to 49 students: 21%; of 50 or more students: 0%. **Advanced Placement and International Baccalaureate credit:** International Baccalaureate exams may be used for: Credit only. **Freshmen returning for sophomore year:** 86%. **Graduation rates:** Four-year: 49%; five-year: 58%; six-year: 58%. **Graduate study:** 8% of students pursue further study immediately upon graduation; 14% within one year; 38% within five years. Fields in which graduates pursue further study: Master of Business Administration (MBA), 6%; law, 2%; medicine, 6%; education, 20%; arts and sciences, 66%.

COSTS AND FINANCIAL AID
Financial aid office: (802) 440-4325. **Expenses (2010-2011):** Tuition and fees 2010-2011: $41,350; room/board: $11,550. Estimated books and supplies: $800; transportation: $450; personal expenses: $2,000. **Financial aid:** Priority filing date for institution's financial aid form: February 1; deadline: February 15. In 2009-2010, 75% of undergraduates applied for financial aid. Of those, 70% were determined to have financial need; 13% had their need fully met. Average financial aid package (proportion receiving): $32,970 (69%). Average amount of gift aid, such as scholarships or grants (proportion receiving): $28,738 (67%). Average amount of self-help aid, such as work study or loans (proportion receiving): $5,345 (63%). Average need-based loan (excluding PLUS or other private loans): $3,977. Among students who received need-based aid, the average percentage of need met: 81%. Among students who received aid based on merit, the average award (and the proportion receiving): $13,744 (9%). The average athletic scholarship (and the proportion receiving): $0 (0%). Average amount of debt of borrowers graduating in 2009: $22,402. Proportion who borrowed: 70%.

CAMPUS LIFE AND EXTRACURRICULAR ACTIVITIES
Campus housing available (% using): coed dorms (96%), special housing for disabled students (0%), cooperative housing (2%), other housing options (2%). Students who live in college-owned, operated, or affiliated housing: 96%. **Student employment:** During the 2009-2010 academic year, 23% of undergraduates worked on campus. Average per-year earnings: $2,131. **Clubs and organizations:** Number of student organizations: 42. Activities include: choral groups, dance, drama/theater, international student organization, literary magazine, music ensembles, musical theater, radio station, student government, student newspaper. Number of fraternities: 0; sororities: 0. Average proportion of students who stay on campus on weekends: 70%.

SERVICES AND FACILITIES
Basic services: nonremedial tutoring, health service, health insurance. **Counseling services:** minority student, career, personal, academic, psychological, birth control. **For learning-disabled students:** School does not offer a structured program with separate admission and additional fees. Total undergraduates in learning-disabled program or receiving services: 43. **Library:** Number of titles: 126,463; number of current serial subscriptions: 14,375. **Information technology resources:** Students are not required

to lease or own a computer. Number of campus computers available to all students: 90. School has a wireless network. Approximate number of users that can be accommodated: 600. Proportion of college-owned housing units wired for high-speed internet access: 95%. **Campus safety:** Security services offered: 24-hour foot-and-vehicle patrols, late-night transport/escort service, 24-hour emergency telephones, lighted pathways/sidewalks.

TRANSFER AND INTERNATIONAL STUDENTS
Transfer students: May apply for admission for the following academic terms: Fall, Spring. Applicants do not need a minimum number of credits to apply. For fall 2009: Transfer applications received: 81. Transfer applicants offered admission: 44. Transfer applicants enrolled: 17. **International students:** Number of foreign undergraduates: 38 (6% of student body). Number of countries represented: 20. Minimum TOEFL score required: 577 (paper); 233 (computer).

Burlington College

- **Address:** 95 North Avenue, Burlington, VT 05401
- **Website:** http://www.burlington.edu
- **Private**
- **Enrollment:** 120 full-time; 55 part-time

KEY STATS
- ✔ **U.S News College Ranking:** Unranked, National Liberal Arts Colleges
- ✔ **SAT or ACT Score (25th/75th percentile):** N/A
- ✔ **Tuition:** 2010-2011: $21,340

Selectivity: N/A	**Room/board:** $8,100
Acceptance rate: 83%	**Average debt:** $38,198
Student/faculty ratio: 6/1	**Proportion who borrowed:** 80%

UNDERGRADUATE STUDENT BODY STATS
2009-2010 enrollment: 120 full-time; 55 part-time. Men: 55%; women: 45%. **Ethnic makeup:** African American: 2%; Asian American: 2%; Hispanic: 2%; White: 92%; International: 1%.

ADMISSIONS FACTS AND FIGURES
Phone: (802) 862-9616. **Email:** admissions@burlington.edu. **Website:** http://www.burlington.edu. **Application deadlines for fall 2011:** Regular decision: August 15. Early decision: Not offered. Early action: Send application by: N/A; Decision sent by: N/A. Admission can be deferred. **Application fee:** $50. **To apply online, go to:** http://burlington.edu/admissions/forms/APP_CAMPUS.PDF. **Admissions requirements/recommendations:** High school units required (recommended): English: 0 (4); Mathematics: 0 (3); Science: 0 (3); Foreign language: 0 (2); Social studies: 0 (4); History: 0 (3); Academic electives: 0 (4); Total units: 0 (24). Tests: The college does not use SAT or ACT scores in admissions decisions. Neither SAT nor ACT required. For admission to the fall 2011 entering class, the school will accept: ACT with or without writing accepted. Campus visit: Recommended. Admissions interview: Recommended. Off-campus interview: May be arranged. **Factors that count in admissions decisions:** *Academic:* Secondary school record: Considered. Class rank: Not Considered. Letters of recommendation: Important. Standardized test scores: Considered. Essay: Very Important. *Nonacademic:* Interview: Very Important. Extracurricular activities: Considered. Talent/ability: Important. Character/personal qualities: Very Important. Alumni/ae relationship: Considered. Geographical residence: Not Considered. State residency: Not Considered. Religious affiliation/commitment: Not Considered. Minority status: Not Considered. Volunteer work: Important. Work experience: Considered. **Other schools with the greatest overlap in applicants:** Champlain College; Fitchburg State College; Marlboro College; New York University; University of Vermont. **Admissions statistics for the fall 2009 entering class:** Total applicants: 126. Total accepted: 104. Freshmen enrolled: 24; 57% were from out of state. Overall acceptance rate: 83%. Non-early acceptance rate: 83%. **Credentials of fall 2009 freshmen:** (Proportion submitting class standing: 23%.) **First-year students who submitted SAT scores:** 50%. **First-year students submitting ACT scores:** 18%. Scores (25/75 percentile): English: N/A, Math: N/A, Composite: N/A.

ACADEMICS
Year founded: 1972. **Academic calendar:** Semester. **Degrees offered:** certificate, associate, bachelor's. **Most popular majors:** 47% multi/interdisciplinary studies, 16% psychology, 13% film/cinema studies, 5% human services, 5% photography. **Major fields of study:** area, ethnic, cultural, and gender

studies; English language and literature/letters; health professions and related clinical sciences; legal professions and studies; liberal arts and sciences studies, and humanities; multi/interdisciplinary studies; psychology; public administration and social service professions; social sciences; visual and performing arts. **Areas of required coursework:** arts/fine arts, humanities, computer literacy, mathematics, English (including composition), philosophy, sciences (biological or physical), history, social science, other. **Pre-professional programs:** pre-law, other. **Special academic programs (% participation):** cross-registration (22%), distance learning (24%), double major (8%), dual enrollment (0%), external degree program (24%), independent study (92%), internships (62%), liberal arts/career combination (0%), student-designed major (30%), study abroad (5%). **Faculty and instruction (2009-2010):** Total instructional faculty: 6 full-time, 55 part-time (43% men; 57% women). Full-time faculty with Ph.D. or other terminal degree: 33%. Student/faculty ratio: 6/1. Classes of fewer than 20 students: 99%; of 20 to 49 students: 1%; of 50 or more students: 0%. **Advanced Placement and International Baccalaureate credit:** AP tests may be used for: Credit and/or placement. Scores accepted: 3, 4, 5. International Baccalaureate exams may be used for: Credit and/or placement. **Freshmen returning for sophomore year:** 61%. **Graduation rates:** Four-year: 20%; five-year: 30%; six-year: 27%. **Graduate study:** 0% of students pursue further study immediately upon graduation; 42% within one year; 60% within five years. Fields in which graduates pursue further study: law, 5%; theology (or the seminary), 1%; education, 5%; arts and sciences, 89%.

COSTS AND FINANCIAL AID
Financial aid office: (802) 862-9616. **Expenses (2010-2011):** Tuition and fees 2010-2011: $21,340; room/board: $8,100. Estimated books and supplies: $1,140; transportation: $1,800; personal expenses: $1,800. **Financial aid:** Priority filing date for institution's financial aid form: April 15. In 2009-2010, 78% of undergraduates applied for financial aid. Of those, 68% were determined to have financial need; 1% had their need fully met. Average financial aid package (proportion receiving): $12,910 (68%). Average amount of gift aid, such as scholarships or grants (proportion receiving): $7,443 (61%). Average amount of self-help aid, such as work study or loans (proportion receiving): $6,283 (68%). Average need-based loan (excluding PLUS or other private loans): $5,518. Among students who received need-based aid, the average percentage of need met: 52%. Among students who received aid based on merit, the average award (and the proportion receiving): $0 (0%). The average athletic scholarship (and the proportion receiving): $0 (0%). Average amount of debt of borrowers graduating in 2009: $38,198. Proportion who borrowed: 80%.

CAMPUS LIFE AND EXTRACURRICULAR ACTIVITIES
Campus housing available (% using): apartment for single students (50%), cooperative housing (50%). Students who live in college-owned, operated, or affiliated housing: 11%. **Student employment:** During the 2009-2010 academic year, 0% of undergraduates worked on campus. Average per-year earnings: $0. **Clubs and organizations:** Number of student organizations: 1. Activities include: literary magazine, student government, student film society. Number of fraternities: 0; sororities: 0. Average proportion of students who stay on campus on weekends: 10%.

SERVICES AND FACILITIES
Basic services: nonremedial tutoring. **Counseling services:** career, academic. **For learning-disabled students:** School does not offer a structured program with separate admission and additional fees. Total undergraduates in learning-disabled program or receiving services: 5. Services include: tape recorders, diagnostic testing service, untimed tests, oral tests, readers, extended time for tests, tutors, priority seating, proofreading services. **Library:** Number of titles: 14,591; number of current serial subscriptions: 1,471. **Information technology resources:** Students are not required to lease or own a computer. Number of campus computers available to all students: 20. School has a wireless network. Approximate number of users that can be accommodated: 20. Proportion of college-owned housing units wired for high-speed internet access: 100%. **Campus safety:** Security services offered: lighted pathways/sidewalks, student patrols, controlled dormitory access (key, security card, etc).

TRANSFER AND INTERNATIONAL STUDENTS
Transfer students: May apply for admission for the following academic terms: Fall, Spring, Summer. Applicants need a minimum number of credits to apply. For fall 2009: Transfer applications received: 44. Transfer applicants offered admission: 44. Transfer applicants enrolled: 42. **International students:** Number of foreign undergraduates: 2 (1% of stu-

dent body). Number of countries represented: 0. Minimum TOEFL score required: 550 (paper); 213 (computer).

Castleton State College

- **Address:** Castleton, VT 05735
- **Website:** http://www.castleton.edu
- **Public**
- **Enrollment:** 1,813 full-time; 221 part-time

KEY STATS

✔ **U.S News College Ranking:** second tier, Regional Universities (North)
✔ **SAT Score (25th/75th percentile):** 860-1070
✔ **Tuition:** 2010-2011: $9,096 in state, $19,656 out of state

Selectivity: Less selective	**Room/board:** $8,120
Acceptance rate: 71%	**Average debt:** N/A
Student/faculty ratio: 14/1	**Proportion who borrowed:** N/A

UNDERGRADUATE STUDENT BODY STATS

2009-2010 enrollment: 1,813 full-time; 221 part-time. Men: 46%; women: 54%. **Ethnic makeup:** African American: 1%; American-Indian: 1%; Asian American: 1%; Hispanic: 2%; White: 95%; International: 1%.

ADMISSIONS FACTS AND FIGURES

Phone: (800) 639-8521. **Email:** info@castleton.edu. **Website:** http://www.castleton.edu. **Application deadlines for fall 2011:** Regular decision: Rolling. Early decision: Not offered. Early action: Not offered. Admission can be deferred. **Application fee:** $35. **To apply online, go to:** https://www.applyweb.com/aw?castle. **Admissions requirements/recommendations:** High school units required (recommended): English: 4; Mathematics: 3 (4); Science: 3 (4); Foreign language: (2); Social studies: 3 (4); History: 3; Total units: 14 (2). Tests: The college uses SAT or ACT scores in admissions decisions. Either SAT or ACT required. For admission to the fall 2011 entering class, the school will accept: ACT with writing required. Campus visit: Recommended. Admissions interview: Recommended. Off-campus interview: May be arranged. **Factors that count in admissions decisions:** *Academic:* Secondary school record: Very Important. Class rank: Very Important. Letters of recommendation: Very Important. Standardized test scores: Important. Essay: Very Important. *Nonacademic:* Interview: Considered. Extracurricular activities: Considered. Talent/ability: Considered. Character/personal qualities: Very Important. Alumni/ae relationship: Not Considered. Geographical residence: Not Considered. State residency: Not Considered. Religious affiliation/commitment: Not Considered. Minority status: Not Considered. Volunteer work: Considered. Work experience: Considered. **Other schools with the greatest overlap in applicants:** Keene State College; Plymouth State University; University of Vermont. **Admissions statistics for the fall 2009 entering class:** Total applicants: 2,338. Total accepted: 1,657. Freshmen enrolled: 515; 37% were from out of state. Overall acceptance rate: 71%. **Credentials of fall 2009 freshmen:** 5% ranked in the top 10 percent of their high school class; 22% were in the top 25 percent; 63% were in the top half. (Proportion submitting class standing: 67%.) **Average high school grade point average:** 2.9. **First-year students who submitted SAT scores:** 95%. Scores (25/75 percentile): Critical Reading: 430-530, Math: 430-540, Combined: 860-1070. **First-year students submitting ACT scores:** 17%. Scores (25/75 percentile): English: N/A, Math: N/A, Composite: 17-21.

ACADEMICS

Year founded: 1787. **Academic calendar:** Semester. **Degrees offered:** certificate, associate, bachelor's, post-bachelor's certificate, master's. **Most popular majors:** 21% business, management, marketing, and related support services, 10% parks, recreation, leisure, and fitness studies, 9% multi/interdisciplinary studies, 8% mathematics and statistics, 8% visual and performing arts. **Major fields of study:** biological and biomedical sciences; business, management, marketing, and related support services; communication, journalism, and related programs; computer and information sciences and support services; education; English language and literature/letters; foreign languages, literatures, and linguistics; history; mathematics and statistics; parks, recreation, leisure, and fitness studies; physical sciences; psychology; public administration and social service professions; security and protective services; social sciences; visual and performing arts. **Areas of required coursework:** arts/fine arts, humanities, computer literacy, mathematics, English (including composition), sciences (biological or phys-

ical), social science. **Special academic programs:** cooperative (work-study plan) program, double major, dual enrollment, honors program, independent study, internships, liberal arts/career combination, study abroad, teacher certificate program. **Teacher certification offered in:** elementary, middle/junior high, secondary. **Reserve Officers Training Corps (ROTC):** Army ROTC: Offered at cooperating institution (University of Vermont). **Faculty and instruction (2009-2010):** Total instructional faculty: 90 full-time, 132 part-time (56% men; 44% women; 3% minorities). Full-time faculty with Ph.D. or other terminal degree: 96%. Student/faculty ratio: 14/1. Classes of fewer than 20 students: 73%; of 20 to 49 students: 25%; of 50 or more students: 1%. **Advanced Placement and International Baccalaureate credit:** AP tests may be used for: Credit only. Scores accepted: 3. **Freshmen returning for sophomore year:** 69%. **Graduation rates:** Four-year: 30%; five-year: 45%; six-year: 43%.

COSTS AND FINANCIAL AID

Financial aid office: (802) 468-1292. **Expenses (2010-2011):** Tuition and fees 2010-2011: $9,096 in state, $19,656 out of state; room/board: $8,120. **Financial aid:** Priority filing date for institution's financial aid form: April 1.

CAMPUS LIFE AND EXTRACURRICULAR ACTIVITIES

Campus housing available (% using): coed dorms (100%). Students who live in college-owned, operated, or affiliated housing: 49%. **Clubs and organizations:** Number of student organizations: 40. Activities include: choral groups, concert band, dance, drama/theater, jazz band, literary magazine, marching band, music ensembles, musical theater, pep band, radio station, student government, student newspaper, student film society, television station. Number of fraternities: 0; sororities: 0. Average proportion of students who stay on campus on weekends: 67%. **Sports program (2009-2010):** Member of NCAA III. *Men's intercollegiate varsity sports:* baseball, basketball, cross country, football, golf, ice hockey, skiing (alpine), soccer, tennis. *Women's intercollegiate varsity sports:* basketball, cross country, field hockey, ice hockey, skiing (alpine), soccer, softball, tennis, volleyball.

SERVICES AND FACILITIES

Basic services: health service, health insurance. **Remedial assistance:** math, writing, study skills. **Counseling services:** career, military, academic, birth control. **For learning-disabled students:** School does not offer a structured program with separate admission and additional fees. Services include: remedial math, remedial English, reading machines, tape recorders, note-taking services, oral tests, learning center, extended time for tests, tutors, early syllabus, priority seating, texts on tape, exams on tape or computer, other testing accommodations. **Library:** Number of titles: 190,313; number of current serial subscriptions: 665. **Information technology resources:** Students are not required to lease or own a computer. Number of campus computers available to all students: 225. School has a wireless network. Proportion of college-owned housing units wired for high-speed internet access: 100%. **Campus safety:** Security services offered: 24-hour foot-and-vehicle patrols, late-night transport/escort service, 24-hour emergency telephones, lighted pathways/sidewalks, controlled dormitory access (key, security card, etc).

TRANSFER AND INTERNATIONAL STUDENTS

Transfer students: May apply for admission for the following academic terms: Fall, Spring. Applicants do not need a minimum number of credits to apply. For fall 2009: Transfer applications received: 397. Transfer applicants offered admission: 261. Transfer applicants enrolled: 159. **International students:** Number of foreign undergraduates: 21 (1% of student body). Minimum TOEFL score required: 500 (paper); 173 (computer).

Champlain College

- **Address:** 163 S. Willard Street, Burlington, VT 05401
- **Website:** http://www.champlain.edu
- **Private**
- **Enrollment:** 2,084 full-time; 589 part-time

KEY STATS

✔ **U.S News College Ranking:** 17, Regional Colleges (North)
✔ **SAT Score (25th/75th percentile):** 1020-1210
✔ **Tuition:** 2010-2011: $27,180

Selectivity: Selective	**Room/board:** $12,130
Acceptance rate: 78%	**Average debt:** $18,000
Student/faculty ratio: 17/1	**Proportion who borrowed:** N/A

UNDERGRADUATE STUDENT BODY STATS

2009-2010 enrollment: 2,084 full-time; 589 part-time. Men: 58%; women: 42%. **Ethnic makeup:** African American: 1%; Asian American: 1%; Hispanic: 1%; White: 95%.

ADMISSIONS FACTS AND FIGURES

Phone: (800) 570-5858. **Email:** admission@champlain.edu. **Website:** http://www.champlain.edu. **Application deadlines for fall 2011:** Regular decision: January 31; decision sent by March 25. Early decision: Send application by: November 15; Decision sent by: December 15. Early action: Not offered. Admission can be deferred. **Application fee:** $50. **To apply online, go to:** https://www.applyweb.com/apply/champln/indexa.html. **Admissions requirements/recommendations:** High school units required (recommended): English: 4; Mathematics: 3 (4); Science: 3 (4); Foreign language: (2); Social studies: (2); History: 4; Academic electives: 4; Total units: 20. Tests: The college uses SAT or ACT scores in admissions decisions. Either SAT or ACT required. For admission to the fall 2011 entering class, the school will accept: ACT with or without writing accepted. Campus visit: Recommended. Admissions interview: Recommended. Off-campus interview: May be arranged. **Factors that count in admissions decisions:** *Academic:* Secondary school record: Very Important. Class rank: Important. Letters of recommendation: Important. Standardized test scores: Important. Essay: Very Important. *Nonacademic:* Interview: Important. Extracurricular activities: Important. Talent/ability: Considered. Character/personal qualities: Considered. Alumni/ae relationship: Considered. Geographical residence: Considered. State residency: Not Considered. Religious affiliation/commitment: Not Considered. Minority status: Not Considered. Volunteer work: Considered. Work experience: Considered. **Other schools with the greatest overlap in applicants:** Quinnipiac University; Rochester Institute of Technology; St. Michael's College; University of Maine; University of Vermont. **Admissions statistics for the fall 2009 entering class:** Total applicants: 2,929. Total accepted: 2,270. Freshmen enrolled: 545; 77% were from out of state. Accepted through early-decision or early-action plans: 39%. Overall acceptance rate: 78%. Early-decision acceptance rate: 70%. Non-early acceptance rate: 79%. **Size of waiting list:** 0 applicants; enrolled from waiting list: 0. **Credentials of fall 2009 freshmen:** 10% ranked in the top 10 percent of their high school class; 15% were in the top 25 percent; 85% were in the top half. (Proportion submitting class standing: 78%.) **First-year students who submitted SAT scores:** 91%. Scores (25/75 percentile): Critical Reading: 510-610, Math: 510-600, Combined: 1020-1210. **First-year students submitting ACT scores:** 19%. Scores (25/75 percentile): English: N/A, Math: N/A, Composite: 21-26.

ACADEMICS

Year founded: 1878. **Academic calendar:** Semester. **Degrees offered:** certificate, associate, bachelor's, master's. **Most popular majors:** 36% business administration and management, 20% computer and information sciences and support services, 10% intermedia/multimedia, 7% computer and information sciences and support services, 5% accounting. **Major fields of study:** business, management, marketing, and related support services; communication, journalism, and related programs; computer and information sciences and support services; education; engineering; health professions and related clinical sciences; legal professions and studies; liberal arts and sciences studies, and humanities; psychology; public administration and social service professions; security and protective services; visual and performing arts. **Areas of required coursework:** arts/fine arts, humanities, computer literacy, mathematics, English (including composition), philosophy, sciences (biological or physical), history, social science, other. **Pre-professional programs:** pre-law. **Special academic programs (% participa-**

tion): accelerated program (5.4%), cross-registration (.3%), distance learning (70%), double major (1.5%), independent study (.3%), internships (47.8%), liberal arts/career combination (100%), student-designed major (0%), study abroad (10%). **Teacher certification offered in:** elementary, middle/junior high, secondary. **Reserve Officers Training Corps (ROTC):** Army ROTC: Offered at cooperating institution. **Faculty and instruction (2009-2010):** Total instructional faculty: 90 full-time, 244 part-time (58% men; 42% women; 2% minorities). Full-time faculty with Ph.D. or other terminal degree: 52%. Student/faculty ratio: 17/1. Classes of fewer than 20 students: 60%; of 20 to 49 students: 40%. **Advanced Placement and International Baccalaureate credit:** AP tests may be used for: Placement only. Scores accepted: 3. International Baccalaureate exams may be used for: Placement only. **Freshmen returning for sophomore year:** 78%. **Graduation rates:** Four-year: 52%; five-year: 57%; six-year: 66%. **Graduate study:** 10% of students pursue further study immediately upon graduation. Fields in which graduates pursue further study: Master of Business Administration (MBA), 16%; education, 22%; arts and sciences, 33%.

COSTS AND FINANCIAL AID

Financial aid office: (800) 570-5858. **Expenses (2010-2011):** Tuition and fees 2010-2011: $27,180; room/board: $12,130. Estimated books and supplies: $600. **Financial aid:** Priority filing date for institution's financial aid form: March 1; deadline: March 1. In 2009-2010, 73% of undergraduates applied for financial aid. Of those, 61% were determined to have financial need; 16% had their need fully met. Average financial aid package (proportion receiving): $15,071 (61%). Average amount of gift aid, such as scholarships or grants (proportion receiving): $7,691 (49%). Average amount of self-help aid, such as work study or loans (proportion receiving): $6,395 (57%). Average need-based loan (excluding PLUS or other private loans): $4,687. Among students who received need-based aid, the average percentage of need met: 70%. Among students who received aid based on merit, the average award (and the proportion receiving): $3,060 (8%). The average athletic scholarship (and the proportion receiving): $0 (0%). Average amount of debt of borrowers graduating in 2009: $18,000.

CAMPUS LIFE AND EXTRACURRICULAR ACTIVITIES

Campus housing available (% using): coed dorms (95%), women's dorms (1%), special housing for international students (4%). Students who live in college-owned, operated, or affiliated housing: 40%. **Student employment:** During the 2009-2010 academic year, 7% of undergraduates worked on campus. Average per-year earnings: $2,100. **Clubs and organizations:** Number of student organizations: 35. Activities include: choral groups, dance, drama/theater, international student organization, literary magazine, music ensembles, musical theater, radio station, student government, student newspaper. Number of fraternities: 0; sororities: 0. Average proportion of students who stay on campus on weekends: 82%.

SERVICES AND FACILITIES

Basic services: nonremedial tutoring, women's center, health service, health insurance. **Remedial assistance:** other. **Counseling services:** career, personal, academic, older student, other. **For learning-disabled students:** School does not offer a structured program with separate admission and additional fees. Services include: reading machines, tape recorders, untimed tests, note-taking services, readers, extended time for tests, tutors, priority seating, other testing accommodations. **Library:** Number of titles: 40,620; number of current serial subscriptions: 34,915. **Information technology resources:** Students are not required to lease or own a computer. Number of campus computers available to all students: 380. School has a wireless network. Approximate number of users that can be accommodated: 1,380. Proportion of college-owned housing units wired for high-speed internet access: 100%. **Campus safety:** Security services offered: 24-hour foot-and-vehicle patrols, late-night transport/escort service, 24-hour emergency telephones, lighted pathways/sidewalks, controlled dormitory access (key, security card, etc).

TRANSFER AND INTERNATIONAL STUDENTS

Transfer students: May apply for admission for the following academic terms: Fall, Spring. Applicants do not need a minimum number of credits to apply. For fall 2009: Transfer applications received: 368. Transfer applicants offered admission: 246. Transfer applicants enrolled: 106. **International students:** Number of foreign undergraduates: 4. Number of countries represented: 19. Minimum TOEFL score required: 500 (paper); 173 (computer). Average TOEFL score: 525 (paper).

College of St. Joseph

- **Address:** 71 Clement Road, Rutland, VT 05701
- **Website:** http://www.csj.edu
- **Private; Religious affiliation:** Roman Catholic
- **Enrollment:** 175 full-time; 67 part-time

....

KEY STATS

✔ **U.S News College Ranking:** second tier, Regional Universities (North)
✔ **SAT Score (25th/75th percentile):** 770-970
✔ **Tuition:** 2010-2011: $18,300

Selectivity: Least selective	**Room/board:** $8,600
Acceptance rate: 78%	**Average debt:** $30,579
Student/faculty ratio: 9/1	**Proportion who borrowed:** 100%

UNDERGRADUATE STUDENT BODY STATS

2009-2010 enrollment: 175 full-time; 67 part-time. Men: 38%; women: 62%. **Ethnic makeup:** African American: 6%; American-Indian: 1%; Hispanic: 1%; White: 91%.

ADMISSIONS FACTS AND FIGURES

Phone: (802) 773-5286. **Email:** admissions@csj.edu. **Website:** http://www.csj.edu. **Application deadlines for fall 2011:** Regular decision: Rolling. Early decision: Not offered. Early action: Not offered. Admission can be deferred. **Application fee:** $25. **To apply online, go to:** http://www.csj.edu/undergraduate-admission-application/. **Admissions requirements/recommendations:** High school units required (recommended): English: 4 (0); Mathematics: 3 (0); Science: 2 (0); Foreign language: 0 (2); Social studies: 0 (0); History: 3 (0); Academic electives: 5 (0); Total units: 16 (0). Tests: The college uses SAT or ACT scores in admissions decisions. Either SAT or ACT required. For admission to the fall 2011 entering class, the school will accept: ACT with or without writing accepted. Campus visit: Recommended. Admissions interview: Recommended. Off-campus interview: May be arranged. **Factors that count in admissions decisions:** *Academic:* Secondary school record: Very Important. Class rank: Not Considered. Letters of recommendation: Very Important. Standardized test scores: Important. Essay: Important. *Nonacademic:* Interview: Important. Extracurricular activities: Considered. Talent/ability: Important. Character/personal qualities: Considered. Alumni/ae relationship: Considered. Geographical residence: Not Considered. State residency: Not Considered. Religious affiliation/commitment: Not Considered. Minority status: Not Considered. Volunteer work: Considered. Work experience: Not Considered. **Other schools with the greatest overlap in applicants:** Castleton State College; Johnson State College; Lyndon State College; University of Vermont. **Admissions statistics for the fall 2009 entering class:** Total applicants: 130. Total accepted: 101. Freshmen enrolled: 48; 33% were from out of state. Overall acceptance rate: 78%. **Credentials of fall 2009 freshmen:** 11% ranked in the top 25 percent of their high school class; 50% were in the top half. (Proportion submitting class standing: 86%.) **First-year students who submitted SAT scores:** 87%. Scores (25/75 percentile): Critical Reading: 380-480, Math: 390-490, Combined: 770-970. **First-year students submitting ACT scores:** 13%. Scores (25/75 percentile): English: N/A, Math: N/A, Composite: 15-20.

ACADEMICS

Year founded: 1956. **Academic calendar:** Semester. **Degrees offered:** associate, bachelor's, post-bachelor's certificate, master's. **Most popular majors:** 37% business administration and management, 12% accounting, 12% psychology, 7% human services, 7% liberal arts and sciences/liberal studies. **Major fields of study:** business, management, marketing, and related support services; communication, journalism, and related programs; computer and information sciences and support services; education; English language and literature/letters; liberal arts and sciences studies, and humanities; parks, recreation, leisure, and fitness studies; psychology; public administration and social service professions. **Areas of required coursework:** arts/fine arts, computer literacy, mathematics, English (including composition), philosophy, sciences (biological or physical), history, social science, other. **Special academic programs (% participation):** accelerated program (19%), double major (7%), internships (24%), teacher certificate program (15%). **Teacher certification offered in:** elementary, secondary. **Faculty and instruction (2009-2010):** Total instructional faculty: 13 full-time, 52 part-time (55% men; 45% women; 3% minorities). Full-time faculty with Ph.D. or other terminal degree: 62%. Student/faculty ratio: 9/1. Classes of fewer than 20 students: 97%; of 20 to 49 students: 3%; of 50 or more students: 0%. **Advanced Placement and International Baccalaureate credit:** AP tests may be

used for: Placement only. Scores accepted: 4, 5. International Baccalaureate exams may be used for: Credit and/or placement. **Freshmen returning for sophomore year:** 70%. **Graduation rates:** Four-year: 27%; five-year: 38%; six-year: 40%. **Graduate study:** 20% of students pursue further study immediately upon graduation.

COSTS AND FINANCIAL AID

Financial aid office: (802) 773-5900. **Expenses (2010-2011):** Tuition and fees 2010-2011: $18,300; room/board: $8,600. Estimated books and supplies: $1,000; transportation: $650; personal expenses: $1,350. **Financial aid:** Priority filing date for institution's financial aid form: March 1. In 2009-2010, 97% of undergraduates applied for financial aid. Of those, 93% were determined to have financial need; 4% had their need fully met. Average financial aid package (proportion receiving): $17,669 (93%). Average amount of gift aid, such as scholarships or grants (proportion receiving): $9,982 (86%). Average amount of self-help aid, such as work study or loans (proportion receiving): $4,504 (82%). Average need-based loan (excluding PLUS or other private loans): $4,212. Among students who received need-based aid, the average percentage of need met: 83%. Among students who received aid based on merit, the average award (and the proportion receiving): $2,406 (5%). The average athletic scholarship (and the proportion receiving): $0 (0%). Average amount of debt of borrowers graduating in 2009: $30,579. Proportion who borrowed: 100%.

CAMPUS LIFE AND EXTRACURRICULAR ACTIVITIES

Campus housing available (% using): women's dorms (53%), men's dorms (47%). Students who live in college-owned, operated, or affiliated housing: 39%. **Student employment:** During the 2009-2010 academic year, 0% of undergraduates worked on campus. Average per-year earnings: $0. **Clubs and organizations:** Number of student organizations: 21. Activities include: campus ministries, choral groups, dance, literary magazine, student government, yearbook. Number of fraternities: 0; sororities: 0. Average proportion of students who stay on campus on weekends: 40%. **Sports program (2009-2010):** Member of NAIA. *Men's intercollegiate varsity sports:* baseball, basketball, soccer. *Women's intercollegiate varsity sports:* basketball, soccer.

SERVICES AND FACILITIES

Basic services: nonremedial tutoring, placement service, health insurance. **Remedial assistance:** reading, math, writing, study skills, other. **Counseling services:** career, personal, veteran student, academic, psychological, religious. **For learning-disabled students:** School does not offer a structured program with separate admission and additional fees. Services include: remedial math, remedial English, untimed tests, note-taking services, oral tests, learning center, extended time for tests, tutors, priority seating. **Library:** Number of titles: 59,208; number of current serial subscriptions: 35,505. **Information technology resources:** Students are not required to lease or own a computer. Number of campus computers available to all students: 30. School has a wireless network. Approximate number of users that can be accommodated: 50. Proportion of college-owned housing units wired for high-speed internet access: 100%. **Campus safety:** Security services offered: 24-hour emergency telephones, lighted pathways/sidewalks, controlled dormitory access (key, security card, etc).

TRANSFER AND INTERNATIONAL STUDENTS

Transfer students: May apply for admission for the following academic terms: Fall, Spring, Summer. Applicants do not need a minimum number of credits to apply. For fall 2009: Transfer applications received: 32. Transfer applicants offered admission: 29. Transfer applicants enrolled: 27. **International students:** Number of countries represented: 0. Minimum TOEFL score required: 550 (paper); 213 (computer).

Goddard College

- **Address:** 123 Pitkin Road, Plainfield, VT 05667
- **Website:** http://www.goddard.edu
- **Private**
- **Enrollment:** 275 full-time

KEY STATS

- ✔ **U.S News College Ranking:** Unranked, Regional Universities (North)
- ✔ **SAT or ACT Score (25th/75th percentile):** N/A
- ✔ **Tuition:** 2010-2011: $13,022

Selectivity: N/A	**Room/board:** $1,152
Acceptance rate: 83%	**Average debt:** $21,700
Student/faculty ratio: N/A	**Proportion who borrowed:** 82%

UNDERGRADUATE STUDENT BODY STATS

2009-2010 enrollment: 275 full-time. Men: 37%; women: 63%. **Ethnic makeup:** African American: 5%; American-Indian: 1%; Asian American: 1%; Hispanic: 6%; White: 87%.

ADMISSIONS FACTS AND FIGURES

Phone: (800) 906-8312. **Email:** admissions@goddard.edu. **Website:** http://www.goddard.edu. **Application deadlines for fall 2011:** Regular decision: Rolling. Early decision: Not offered. Early action: Not offered. Admission can be deferred. **Application fee:** $40. **Admissions requirements/recommendations:** Tests: The college does not use SAT or ACT scores in admissions decisions. Neither SAT nor ACT required. Campus visit: Neither required nor recommended. Admissions interview: Required. Off-campus interview: Not available. **Factors that count in admissions decisions:** *Academic:* Secondary school record: Important. Class rank: Important. Letters of recommendation: Very Important. Standardized test scores: Not Considered. Essay: Very Important. *Nonacademic:* Interview: Very Important. Extracurricular activities: Considered. Talent/ability: Important. Character/personal qualities: Very Important. Alumni/ae relationship: Considered. Geographical residence: Not Considered. State residency: Not Considered. Religious affiliation/commitment: Not Considered. Minority status: Not Considered. Volunteer work: Considered. Work experience: Considered. **Other schools with the greatest overlap in applicants:** Antioch College; Evergreen State College; Lesley University; Prescott College; Union Institute and University. **Admissions statistics for the fall 2009 entering class:** Total applicants: 12. Total accepted: 10. Freshmen enrolled: 10; Overall acceptance rate: 83%.

ACADEMICS

Year founded: 1863. **Academic calendar:** Semester. **Degrees offered:** bachelor's, post-bachelor's certificate, master's. **Major fields of study:** education; English language and literature/letters; health professions and related clinical sciences; liberal arts and sciences studies, and humanities; multi/interdisciplinary studies; psychology. **Areas of required coursework:** arts/fine arts, humanities, mathematics, English (including composition), sciences (biological or physical), social science. **Special academic programs (% participation):** distance learning (100%), external degree program (100%), independent study (100%), liberal arts/career combination (100%), student-designed major (100%), teacher certificate program. **Teacher certification offered in:** early childhood, elementary, middle/junior high, adult education, secondary. **Faculty and instruction (2009-2010):** Total instructional faculty: 6 full-time, 124 part-time (28% men; 72% women). Full-time faculty with Ph.D. or other terminal degree: 83%. **Advanced Placement and International Baccalaureate credit:** AP tests may be used for: Credit only. Scores accepted: 3, 4, 5. International Baccalaureate exams may be used for: Credit only.

COSTS AND FINANCIAL AID

Financial aid office: (800) 468-4888. **Expenses (2010-2011):** Tuition and fees 2010-2011: $13,022; room/board: $1,152. Estimated books and supplies: $250; transportation: $775. **Financial aid:** In 2009-2010, 78% of undergraduates applied for financial aid. Of those, 62% were determined to have financial need; 2% had their need fully met. Average financial aid package (proportion receiving): $7,791 (61%). Average amount of gift aid, such as scholarships or grants (proportion receiving): $4,590 (47%). Average amount of self-help aid, such as work study or loans (proportion receiving): $4,485 (58%). Average need-based loan (excluding PLUS or other private loans): $4,485. Among students who received need-based aid, the average percentage of need met: 37%. Among students who received aid based on merit, the average award (and the proportion receiving): $0 (0%). The aver-

age athletic scholarship (and the proportion receiving): $0 (0%). Average amount of debt of borrowers graduating in 2009: $21,700. Proportion who borrowed: 82%.

CAMPUS LIFE AND EXTRACURRICULAR ACTIVITIES

Campus housing available: coed dorms, women's dorms, men's dorms, special housing for disabled students. Students who live in college-owned, operated, or affiliated housing: 0%. Activities include: radio station, student government. Number of fraternities: 0; sororities: 0.

SERVICES AND FACILITIES

Remedial assistance: study skills. **For learning-disabled students:** School does not offer a structured program with separate admission and additional fees. Services include: tape recorders, note-taking services, readers, priority seating, texts on tape, typist/scribe, other. **Information technology resources:** Students are required to lease or own a computer. Number of campus computers available to all students: 60. School has a wireless network. **Campus safety:** Security services offered: lighted pathways/sidewalks.

TRANSFER AND INTERNATIONAL STUDENTS

Transfer students: May apply for admission for the following academic terms: Fall, Spring. Applicants do not need a minimum number of credits to apply. **International students:** Number of foreign undergraduates: 0. Minimum TOEFL score required: 550 (paper).

Green Mountain College

- **Address:** 1 College Circle, Poultney, VT 05764-1199
- **Website:** http://www.greenmtn.edu
- **Private; Religious affiliation:** United Methodist
- **Enrollment:** 736 full-time; 25 part-time

KEY STATS

- ✔ **U.S News College Ranking:** second tier, National Liberal Arts Colleges
- ✔ **SAT Score (25th/75th percentile):** 950-1180
- ✔ **Tuition:** 2010-2011: $27,948

Selectivity: Selective	**Room/board:** $10,142
Acceptance rate: 62%	**Average debt:** $39,862
Student/faculty ratio: 14/1	**Proportion who borrowed:** 82%

UNDERGRADUATE STUDENT BODY STATS

2009-2010 enrollment: 736 full-time; 25 part-time. Men: 45%; women: 55%. **Ethnic makeup:** African American: 3%; American-Indian: 1%; Asian American: 1%; Hispanic: 3%; White: 92%. **Religious preference:** Roman Catholic: 15%; Protestant: 1%; Jewish: 2%; No preference: 6%; Unknown: 64%; United Methodist: 3%; Christian: 2%; Other: 7%.

ADMISSIONS FACTS AND FIGURES

Phone: (802) 287-8208. **Email:** admiss@greenmtn.edu. **Website:** http://www.greenmtn.edu. **Application deadlines for fall 2011:** Regular decision: Rolling. Early decision: Not offered. Early action: Not offered. Admission can be deferred. **Application fee:** $30. **To apply online, go to:** https://campus.greenmtn.edu/admissions05/app2005.htm. **Admissions requirements/recommendations:** High school units required (recommended): English: 4; Mathematics: 3 (4); Science: 3 (4); Foreign language: 2 (3); Social studies: 3; History: 1 (2); Academic electives: 5; Total units: 21. Tests: The college uses SAT or ACT scores in admissions decisions. Neither SAT nor ACT required. For admission to the fall 2011 entering class, the school will accept: ACT with or without writing accepted. Campus visit: Recommended. Admissions interview: Recommended. Off-campus interview: Not available. **Factors that count in admissions decisions:** *Academic:* Secondary school record: Important. Class rank: Important. Letters of recommendation: Very Important. Standardized test scores: Important. Essay: Important. *Nonacademic:* Interview: Important. Extracurricular activities: Important. Talent/ability: Considered. Character/personal qualities: Considered. Alumni/ae relationship: Considered. Geographical residence: Not Considered. State residency: Not Considered. Religious affiliation/commitment: Considered. Minority status: Considered. Volunteer work: Important. Work experience: Considered. **Other schools with the greatest overlap in applicants:** Colby-Sawyer College; Franklin Pierce University; St. Michael's College; Unity College; University of Vermont. **Admissions statistics for the fall 2009 entering class:** Total applicants: 1,496. Total accepted: 923. Freshmen enrolled: 221; 92% were from out of state. Overall acceptance rate: 62%. **First-year students who submitted SAT scores:** 73%. Scores (25/75 percentile): Critical Reading: 490-610, Math: 460-570, Combined: 950-1180.

ACADEMICS

Year founded: 1834. **Academic calendar:** Semester. **Degrees offered:** certificate, bachelor's, master's. **Major fields of study:** biological and biomedical sciences; business, management, marketing, and related support services; communication, journalism, and related programs; education; English language and literature/letters; health professions and related clinical sciences; history; liberal arts and sciences studies, and humanities; multi/interdisciplinary studies; natural resources and conservation; parks, recreation, leisure, and fitness studies; philosophy and religious studies; psychology; social sciences; visual and performing arts. **Areas of required coursework:** arts/fine arts, humanities, mathematics, English (including composition), philosophy, sciences (biological or physical), history, social science, other. **Pre-professional programs:** pre-law, pre-medicine, pre-veterinary science. **Special academic programs (% participation):** double major (1%), exchange student program (domestic), honors program, independent study (10%), internships (10%), student-designed major (.5%). **Teacher certification offered in:** special education, elementary, secondary. **Faculty and instruction (2009-2010):** Total instructional faculty: N/A. Student/faculty ratio: 14/1. Classes of fewer than 20 students: 54%; of 20 to 49 students: 46%. **Advanced Placement and International Baccalaureate credit:** AP tests may be used for: Credit only. Scores accepted: 3, 4, 5. International Baccalaureate exams may be used for: Credit only. **Freshmen returning for sophomore year:** 66%. **Graduation rates:** Four-year: 28%; five-year: 42%; six-year: 44%.

COSTS AND FINANCIAL AID

Financial aid office: (802) 287-8210. **Expenses (2010-2011):** Tuition and fees 2010-2011: $27,948; room/board: $10,142. Estimated books and supplies: $1,100; transportation: $800; personal expenses: $590. **Financial aid:** Priority filing date for institution's financial aid form: March 1. In 2009-2010, 89% of undergraduates applied for financial aid. Of those, 81% were determined to have financial need; 13% had their need fully met. Average financial aid package (proportion receiving): $19,464 (79%). Average amount of gift aid, such as scholarships or grants (proportion receiving): $15,201 (78%). Average amount of self-help aid, such as work study or loans (proportion receiving): $5,161 (71%). Average need-based loan (excluding PLUS or other private loans): $4,512. Among students who received need-based aid, the average percentage of need met: 65%. Among students who received aid based on merit, the average award (and the proportion receiving): $11,488 (16%). The average athletic scholarship (and the proportion receiving): $0 (0%). Average amount of debt of borrowers graduating in 2009: $39,862. Proportion who borrowed: 82%.

CAMPUS LIFE AND EXTRACURRICULAR ACTIVITIES

Campus housing available (% using): coed dorms (88%), cooperative housing (3%), other housing options (9%). Students who live in college-owned, operated, or affiliated housing: 84%. **Clubs and organizations:** Number of student organizations: 37. Activities include: choral groups, concert band, drama/theater, international student organization, jazz band, literary magazine, music ensembles, radio station, student government, student newspaper, yearbook. Number of fraternities: 0; sororities: 0. Average proportion of students who stay on campus on weekends: 75%. **Sports program (2009-2010):** Member of NCAA III. *Men's intercollegiate varsity sports:* basketball, cross country, golf, lacrosse, skiing (alpine), soccer, tennis. *Women's intercollegiate varsity sports:* basketball, cross country, lacrosse, skiing (alpine), soccer, softball, tennis, volleyball.

SERVICES AND FACILITIES

Basic services: nonremedial tutoring, health service, health insurance. **Remedial assistance:** reading, math, writing, study skills. **Counseling services:** minority student, career, personal, academic, psychological, birth control, religious. **For learning-disabled students:** School does not offer a structured program with separate admission and additional fees. Total undergraduates in learning-disabled program or receiving services: 62. Services include: remedial math, reading machines, tape recorders, note-taking services, oral tests, learning center, readers, extended time for tests, tutors, priority seating, texts on tape, other. **Library:** Number of titles: 69,000; number of current serial subscriptions: 298. **Information technology resources:** Students are not required to lease or own a computer. Number of campus computers available to all students: 115. School has a wireless network. Approximate number of users that can be accommodated: 700. Proportion of college-owned housing units wired for high-speed internet access: 100%. **Campus safety:** Security services offered: 24-hour foot-

and-vehicle patrols, late-night transport/escort service, lighted pathways/sidewalks, controlled dormitory access (key, security card, etc.).

TRANSFER AND INTERNATIONAL STUDENTS

Transfer students: May apply for admission for the following academic terms: Fall, Spring. Applicants need a minimum number of credits to apply. For fall 2009: Transfer applications received: 147. Transfer applicants offered admission: 91. Transfer applicants enrolled: 39. **International students:** Number of foreign undergraduates: 0. Number of countries represented: 14. Minimum TOEFL score required: 500 (paper); 173 (computer). Average TOEFL score: 526 (paper).

Johnson State College

- ■ **Address:** 337 College Hill, Johnson, VT 05656-9405
- ■ **Website:** http://www.jsc.edu
- ■ **Public**
- ■ **Enrollment:** N/A

KEY STATS

✔ **U.S News College Ranking:** second tier, Regional Universities (North)
✔ **SAT or ACT Score (25th/75th percentile):** N/A
✔ **Tuition:** 2009-2010: $8,716 in state, $17,956 out of state
    Selectivity: Less selective   **Room/board:** $7,808
    Acceptance rate: N/A   **Average debt:** N/A
    Student/faculty ratio: N/A   **Proportion who borrowed:** N/A

Lyndon State College

- ■ **Address:** PO Box 919, Lyndonville, VT 05851
- ■ **Website:** http://www.lyndonstate.edu
- ■ **Public**
- ■ **Enrollment:** N/A

KEY STATS

✔ **U.S News College Ranking:** second tier, Regional Colleges (North)
✔ **SAT or ACT Score (25th/75th percentile):** N/A
✔ **Tuition:** 2009-2010: $8,820 in state, $18,060 out of state
    Selectivity: Less selective   **Room/board:** $7,808
    Acceptance rate: N/A   **Average debt:** N/A
    Student/faculty ratio: N/A   **Proportion who borrowed:** N/A

Marlboro College

- ■ **Address:** PO Box A, 2582 South Road, Marlboro, VT 05344-0300
- ■ **Website:** http://www.marlboro.edu
- ■ **Private**
- ■ **Enrollment:** N/A

KEY STATS

✔ **U.S News College Ranking:** second tier, National Liberal Arts Colleges
✔ **SAT or ACT Score (25th/75th percentile):** N/A
✔ **Tuition:** 2009-2010: $33,660
    Selectivity: Selective   **Room/board:** $9,220
    Acceptance rate: N/A   **Average debt:** N/A
    Student/faculty ratio: N/A   **Proportion who borrowed:** N/A

Middlebury College

- **Address:** Middlebury, VT 05753
- **Website:** http://www.middlebury.edu
- **Private**
- **Enrollment:** 2,456 full-time; 26 part-time

KEY STATS

✔ **U.S News College Ranking:** 4, National Liberal Arts Colleges
✔ **SAT Score (25th/75th percentile):** 1288-1470
✔ **Tuition:** N/A

Selectivity: Most selective   **Room/board:** N/A
Acceptance rate: 20%   **Average debt:** $21,458
Student/faculty ratio: 9/1   **Proportion who borrowed:** 44%

UNDERGRADUATE STUDENT BODY STATS

2009-2010 enrollment: 2,456 full-time; 26 part-time. Men: 49%; women: 51%. **Ethnic makeup:** African American: 4%; Asian American: 9%; Hispanic: 5%; White: 71%; International: 10%.

ADMISSIONS FACTS AND FIGURES

Phone: (802) 443-3000. **Email:** admissions@middlebury.edu. **Website:** http://www.middlebury.edu. **Application deadlines for fall 2011:** Regular decision: January 1; decision sent by April 1. Early decision: Send application by: November 1; Decision sent by: December 15. Early action: Not offered. Admission can be deferred. **Application fee:** $65. **To apply online, go to:** http://www.middlebury.edu/admissions/applying/. **Admissions requirements/recommendations:** High school units required (recommended): English: (4); Mathematics: (4); Science: (3); Foreign language: (4); Social studies: (3). Tests: The college uses SAT or ACT scores in admissions decisions. Either SAT or ACT required. For admission to the fall 2011 entering class, the school will accept: ACT with or without writing accepted. Campus visit: Recommended. Admissions interview: Neither required nor recommended. Off-campus interview: May be arranged. **Factors that count in admissions decisions:** *Academic:* Secondary school record: Very Important. Class rank: Very Important. Letters of recommendation: Important. Standardized test scores: Important. Essay: Important. *Nonacademic:* Interview: Considered. Extracurricular activities: Very Important. Talent/ability: Very Important. Character/personal qualities: Very Important. Alumni/ae relationship: Considered. Geographical residence: Considered. State residency: Considered. Religious affiliation/commitment: Not Considered. Minority status: Important. Volunteer work: Considered. Work experience: Considered. **Admissions statistics for the fall 2009 entering class:** Total applicants: 6,904. Total accepted: 1,413. Freshmen enrolled: 603; 95% were from out of state. Overall acceptance rate: 20%. Non-early acceptance rate: 20%. **Size of waiting list:** 1527 applicants; enrolled from waiting list: 42. **Credentials of fall 2009 freshmen:** 87% ranked in the top 10 percent of their high school class; 94% were in the top 25 percent; 100% were in the top half. (Proportion submitting class standing: 49%.) **First-year students who submitted SAT scores:** 87%. Scores (25/75 percentile): Critical Reading: 638-730, Math: 650-740, Combined: 1288-1470. **First-year students submitting ACT scores:** 36%. Scores (25/75 percentile): English: 29-33, Math: 30-35, Composite: 30-33.

ACADEMICS

Year founded: 1800. **Academic calendar:** 4-1-4. **Degrees offered:** bachelor's, master's, doctorate. **Most popular majors:** 10% economics, 7% area, ethnic, cultural, and gender studies, 6% English language and literature/letters, 6% environmental studies, 6% political science and government. **Major fields of study:** area, ethnic, cultural, and gender studies; biological and biomedical sciences; computer and information sciences and support services; English language and literature/letters; foreign languages, literatures, and linguistics; history; liberal arts and sciences studies, and humanities; mathematics and statistics; multi/interdisciplinary studies; natural resources and conservation; philosophy and religious studies; physical sciences; psychology; social sciences; visual and performing arts. **Areas of required coursework:** arts/fine arts, English (including composition), philosophy, foreign languages, sciences (biological or physical), history, social science, other. **Pre-professional programs:** pre-law, pre-dentistry, pre-medicine, other. **Special academic programs (% participation):** accelerated program, double major (23%), exchange student program (domestic) (2%), honors program, independent study, internships (50%), student-designed major, study abroad (60%), teacher certificate program (1%), other. **Teacher certification offered in:** elementary, secondary. **Reserve Officers Training Corps (ROTC):** Army

ROTC: Offered at cooperating institution (Norwich University). **Faculty and instruction (2009-2010):** Total instructional faculty: 260 full-time, 51 part-time (59% men; 41% women; 9% minorities). Full-time faculty with Ph.D. or other terminal degree: 95%. Student/faculty ratio: 9/1. Classes of fewer than 20 students: 69%; of 20 to 49 students: 29%; of 50 or more students: 3%. **Advanced Placement and International Baccalaureate credit:** AP tests may be used for: Placement only. Scores accepted: 4, 5. International Baccalaureate exams may be used for: Placement only. **Freshmen returning for sophomore year:** 96%. **Graduation rates:** Four-year: 83%; five-year: 91%; six-year: 92%.

COSTS AND FINANCIAL AID

Financial aid office: (802) 443-5158. **Financial aid:** Priority filing date for institution's financial aid form: November 15; deadline: February 1. In 2009-2010, 54% of undergraduates applied for financial aid. Of those, 49% were determined to have financial need; 100% had their need fully met. Average financial aid package (proportion receiving): $33,345 (49%). Average amount of gift aid, such as scholarships or grants (proportion receiving): $29,918 (49%). Average amount of self-help aid, such as work study or loans (proportion receiving): $4,633 (42%). Average need-based loan (excluding PLUS or other private loans): $3,659. Among students who received need-based aid, the average percentage of need met: 100%. Among students who received aid based on merit, the average award (and the proportion receiving): $0 (0%). The average athletic scholarship (and the proportion receiving): $0 (0%). Average amount of debt of borrowers graduating in 2009: $21,458. Proportion who borrowed: 44%.

CAMPUS LIFE AND EXTRACURRICULAR ACTIVITIES

Campus housing available: coed dorms, apartment for single students, special housing for disabled students, other housing options. Students who live in college-owned, operated, or affiliated housing: 97%. **Student employment:** During the 2009-2010 academic year, 30% of undergraduates worked on campus. Average per-year earnings: $2,600. **Clubs and organizations:** Number of student organizations: 120. Activities include: choral groups, dance, drama/theater, jazz band, literary magazine, music ensembles, musical theater, radio station, student government, student newspaper, student film society, symphony orchestra, yearbook. Number of fraternities: 0; sororities: 0. Average proportion of students who stay on campus on weekends: 98%. **Sports program (2009-2010):** Member of NCAA III. *Men's intercollegiate varsity sports:* baseball, basketball, cross country, football, golf, ice hockey, lacrosse, skiing (nordic), skiing (alpine), soccer, swimming, tennis, track and field (indoor), track and field (outdoor). *Women's intercollegiate varsity sports:* basketball, cross country, field hockey, golf, ice hockey, lacrosse, skiing (nordic), skiing (alpine), soccer, softball, squash, swimming, tennis, track and field (indoor), track and field (outdoor), volleyball.

SERVICES AND FACILITIES

Basic services: nonremedial tutoring, health service, health insurance, other. **For learning-disabled students:** School does not offer a structured program with separate admission and additional fees. Services include: reading machines, tape recorders, diagnostic testing service, note-taking services, oral tests, learning center, readers, extended time for tests, tutors, other. **Library:** Number of titles: 716,328; number of current serial subscriptions: 42,443. **Information technology resources:** Students are not required to lease or own a computer. Number of campus computers available to all students: 494. School has a wireless network. Approximate number of users that can be accommodated: 6,072. Proportion of college-owned housing units wired for high-speed internet access: 100%. **Campus safety:** Security services offered: late-night transport/escort service, 24-hour emergency telephones, lighted pathways/sidewalks, controlled dormitory access (key, security card, etc).

TRANSFER AND INTERNATIONAL STUDENTS

Transfer students: May apply for admission for the following academic terms: Fall, Spring. Applicants do not need a minimum number of credits to apply. For fall 2009: Transfer applications received: 219. Transfer applicants offered admission: 28. Transfer applicants enrolled: 15. **International students:** Number of foreign undergraduates: 257 (10% of student body). Number of countries represented: 233. Average TOEFL score: 627 (paper).

Norwich University

- **Address:** 158 Harmon Drive, Northfield, VT 05663
- **Website:** http://www.norwich.edu
- **Private**
- **Enrollment:** 2,088 full-time; 69 part-time

KEY STATS

✔ **U.S News College Ranking:** 51, Regional Universities (North)
✔ **SAT Score (25th/75th percentile):** 950-1170
✔ **Tuition:** 2010-2011: $28,738

Selectivity: Selective	**Room/board:** $9,958
Acceptance rate: 65%	**Average debt:** $29,473
Student/faculty ratio: N/A	**Proportion who borrowed:** 87%

UNDERGRADUATE STUDENT BODY STATS

2009-2010 enrollment: 2,088 full-time; 69 part-time. Men: 72%; women: 28%. **Ethnic makeup:** African American: 3%; Asian American: 2%; Hispanic: 5%; White: 89%.

ADMISSIONS FACTS AND FIGURES

Phone: (800) 468-6679. **Email:** nuadm@norwich.edu. **Website:** http://www.norwich.edu. **Application deadlines for fall 2011:** Regular decision: Rolling. Early decision: Not offered. Early action: Not offered. Admission cannot be deferred. **Application fee:** $35. **To apply online, go to:** http://norwich.gotoextinguisher.com/application/login/. **Admissions requirements/recommendations:** High school units required (recommended): English: (4); Mathematics: (3); Science: (3); Foreign language: (2); Social studies: (0); History: 0 (3); Academic electives: (0); Total units: (12). Tests: The college uses SAT or ACT scores in admissions decisions. Either SAT or ACT required. For admission to the fall 2011 entering class, the school will accept: ACT with writing recommended. Campus visit: Recommended. Admissions interview: Recommended. Off-campus interview: May be arranged. **Factors that count in admissions decisions:** *Academic:* Secondary school record: Very Important. Class rank: Important. Letters of recommendation: Important. Standardized test scores: Important. Essay: Important. *Nonacademic:* Interview: Important. Extracurricular activities: Very Important. Talent/ability: Very Important. Character/personal qualities: Very Important. Alumni/ae relationship: Important. Geographical residence: Considered. State residency: Not Considered. Religious affiliation/commitment: Not Considered. Minority status: Considered. Volunteer work: Important. Work experience: Considered. **Other schools with the greatest overlap in applicants:** Clarkson University; Pennsylvania State University–University Park; The Citadel; United States Military Academy; Virginia Military Institute. **Admissions statistics for the fall 2009 entering class:** Total applicants: 3,322. Total accepted: 2,171. Freshmen enrolled: 684; 90% were from out of state. Overall acceptance rate: 65%. **Credentials of fall 2009 freshmen:** 10% ranked in the top 10 percent of their high school class; 33% were in the top 25 percent; 68% were in the top half. (Proportion submitting class standing: 71%.) **Average high school grade point average:** 3.0. **First-year students who submitted SAT scores:** 95%. Scores (25/75 percentile): Critical Reading: 470-580, Math: 480-590, Combined: 950-1170. **First-year students submitting ACT scores:** 36%. Scores (25/75 percentile): English: 19-24, Math: 19-26, Composite: 20-25.

ACADEMICS

Year founded: 1819. **Academic calendar:** Semester. **Degrees offered:** certificate, bachelor's, master's, post-master's certificate. **Most popular majors:** 24% criminal justice/law enforcement administration, 12% nursing/registered nurse training (R.N., A.S.N., B.S.N., M.S.N.), 8% history, 6% architecture, 5% management science. **Major fields of study:** architecture and related services; area, ethnic, cultural, and gender studies; biological and biomedical sciences; business, management, marketing, and related support services; communication, journalism, and related programs; computer and information sciences and support services; engineering; English language and literature/letters; health professions and related clinical sciences; history; mathematics and statistics; physical sciences; psychology; social sciences. **Areas of required coursework:** humanities, mathematics, English (including composition), sciences (biological or physical), history, social science, other. **Pre-professional programs:** pre-law, pre-dentistry, pre-medicine, other. **Special academic programs (% participation):** cooperative (work-study plan) program (25%), distance learning (10%), double major (4%), English as a Second Language (ESL) (.2%), independent study (4%), internships (2%), study abroad (9%), teacher certificate program (.5%). **Teacher certi-**

fication offered in: elementary, secondary. **Reserve Officers Training Corps (ROTC):** Army ROTC: Offered on campus; Navy ROTC: Offered on campus; Air Force ROTC: Offered on campus. **Faculty and instruction (2009-2010):** Total instructional faculty: 117 full-time, 179 part-time (67% men; 33% women; 7% minorities). Full-time faculty with Ph.D. or other terminal degree: 92%. Classes of fewer than 20 students: 51%; of 20 to 49 students: 48%; of 50 or more students: 1%. **Advanced Placement and International Baccalaureate credit:** AP tests may be used for: Placement only. Scores accepted: 3, 4, 5. **Freshmen returning for sophomore year:** 76%. **Graduation rates:** Four-year: 39%; five-year: 50%; six-year: 51%. **Graduate study:** 23% of students pursue further study immediately upon graduation. Fields in which graduates pursue further study: Master of Business Administration (MBA), 2%; law, 4%; medicine, 2%; dentistry, 2%; engineering, 4%; education, 6%; arts and sciences, 79%.

COSTS AND FINANCIAL AID

Financial aid office: (802) 485-2015. **Expenses (2010-2011):** Tuition and fees 2010-2011: $28,738; room/board: $9,958. Estimated books and supplies: $1,000; transportation: $1,200. **Financial aid:** Priority filing date for institution's financial aid form: March 1. In 2009-2010, 81% of undergraduates applied for financial aid. Of those, 73% were determined to have financial need; 29% had their need fully met. Average financial aid package (proportion receiving): $22,182 (73%). Average amount of gift aid, such as scholarships or grants (proportion receiving): $18,150 (73%). Average amount of self-help aid, such as work study or loans (proportion receiving): $5,505 (53%). Average need-based loan (excluding PLUS or other private loans): $4,725. Among students who received need-based aid, the average percentage of need met: 75%. Among students who received aid based on merit, the average award (and the proportion receiving): $12,342 (24%). The average athletic scholarship (and the proportion receiving): $0 (0%). Average amount of debt of borrowers graduating in 2009: $29,473. Proportion who borrowed: 87%.

CAMPUS LIFE AND EXTRACURRICULAR ACTIVITIES

Campus housing available (% using): coed dorms (99%), other housing options (1%). Students who live in college-owned, operated, or affiliated housing: 83%. **Student employment:** During the 2009-2010 academic year, 45% of undergraduates worked on campus. Average per-year earnings: $2,000. **Clubs and organizations:** Number of student organizations: 39. Activities include: choral groups, concert band, drama/theater, jazz band, literary magazine, marching band, music ensembles, pep band, radio station, student government, student newspaper, yearbook. Number of fraternities: 0; sororities: 0. Average proportion of students who stay on campus on weekends: 60%. **Sports program (2009-2010):** Member of NCAA III. *Men's intercollegiate varsity sports:* baseball, basketball, cross country, football, ice hockey, lacrosse, soccer, swimming, tennis, wrestling. *Women's intercollegiate varsity sports:* basketball, cross country, ice hockey, lacrosse, soccer, softball, swimming, volleyball.

SERVICES AND FACILITIES

Basic services: nonremedial tutoring, placement service, health service, health insurance. **Remedial assistance:** reading, math, writing, study skills. **Counseling services:** career, military, personal, veteran student, academic, psychological, religious. **For learning-disabled students:** School does not offer a structured program with separate admission and additional fees. Total undergraduates in learning-disabled program or receiving services: 82. Services include: remedial math, remedial English, diagnostic testing service, oral tests, learning center, readers, extended time for tests, tutors, priority seating, texts on tape, other testing accommodations, other. **Library:** Number of titles: 138,202; number of current serial subscriptions: 43,000. **Information technology resources:** Students are not required to lease or own a computer. Number of campus computers available to all students: 305. School has a wireless network. Approximate number of users that can be accommodated: 2,000. Proportion of college-owned housing units wired for high-speed internet access: 100%. **Campus safety:** Security services offered: 24-hour foot-and-vehicle patrols, 24-hour emergency telephones, lighted pathways/sidewalks.

TRANSFER AND INTERNATIONAL STUDENTS

Transfer students: May apply for admission for the following academic terms: Fall, Spring. Applicants need a minimum number of credits to apply. For fall 2009: Transfer applications received: 271. Transfer applicants offered admission: 152. Transfer applicants enrolled: 76. **International students:** Number of foreign undergraduates: 0. Number of countries represented: 20. Minimum TOEFL score required: 550 (paper); 173 (computer). Average TOEFL score: 550 (paper).

Southern Vermont College

- **Address:** 982 Mansion Drive, Bennington, VT 05201
- **Website:** http://www.svc.edu
- **Private**
- **Enrollment:** 427 full-time; 54 part-time

KEY STATS

- ✔ **U.S News College Ranking:** second tier, Regional Colleges (North)
- ✔ **ACT Score (25th/75th percentile):** 19-24
- ✔ **Tuition:** 2009-2010: $18,880

Selectivity: Selective	**Room/board:** $8,840
Acceptance rate: 93%	**Average debt:** N/A
Student/faculty ratio: N/A	**Proportion who borrowed:** N/A

UNDERGRADUATE STUDENT BODY STATS

2009-2010 enrollment: 427 full-time; 54 part-time. Men: 36%; women: 64%. **Ethnic makeup:** African American: 7%; Asian American: 2%; Hispanic: 2%; White: 88%; International: 1%.

ADMISSIONS FACTS AND FIGURES

Phone: (802) 447-6304. **Email:** admis@svc.edu. **Website:** http://www.svc.edu. **Application deadlines for fall 2011:** Regular decision: Rolling. Early decision: Not offered. Early action: Not offered. Admission can be deferred. **Application fee:** $30. **To apply online, go to:** http://collegeapply.com. **Admissions requirements/recommendations:** High school units required (recommended): English: (4); Mathematics: (4); Science: (4); Foreign language: (2); Social studies: (4); History: (2); Total units: (22). Tests: The college uses SAT or ACT scores in admissions decisions. Neither SAT nor ACT required. For admission to the fall 2011 entering class, the school will accept: ACT with writing recommended. Campus visit: Recommended. Admissions interview: Recommended. Off-campus interview: May be arranged. **Factors that count in admissions decisions:** *Academic:* Secondary school record: Considered. Class rank: Considered. Letters of recommendation: Considered. Standardized test scores: Considered. Essay: Considered. *Nonacademic:* Interview: Considered. Extracurricular activities: Considered. Talent/ability: Considered. Character/personal qualities: Considered. Alumni/ae relationship: Considered. Geographical residence: Not Considered. State residency: Not Considered. Religious affiliation/commitment: Not Considered. Minority status: Not Considered. Volunteer work: Considered. Work experience: Not Considered. **Other schools with the greatest overlap in applicants:** Keene State College; Massachusetts College of Liberal Arts; University at Albany–SUNY. **Admissions statistics for the fall 2009 entering class:** Overall acceptance rate: 93%.

ACADEMICS

Year founded: 1926. **Academic calendar:** Semester. **Degrees offered:** associate, bachelor's. **Major fields of study:** business, management, marketing, and related support services; communication, journalism, and related programs; English language and literature/letters; health professions and related clinical sciences; history; liberal arts and sciences studies, and humanities; psychology; security and protective services. **Areas of required coursework:** humanities, computer literacy, mathematics, English (including composition), philosophy, sciences (biological or physical), history, social science. **Advanced Placement and International Baccalaureate credit:** AP tests may be used for: Credit and/or placement. Scores accepted: 4, 5. **Freshmen returning for sophomore year:** 58%. **Graduation rates:** Four-year: 33%; five-year: 38%; six-year: 42%.

COSTS AND FINANCIAL AID

Financial aid office: (877) 563-6076. **Expenses (2009-2010):** Tuition and fees 2009-2010: $18,880; room/board: $8,840. Estimated books and supplies: $1,300. **Financial aid:** Priority filing date for institution's financial aid form: March 1; deadline: March 1.

CAMPUS LIFE AND EXTRACURRICULAR ACTIVITIES

Clubs and organizations: Number of student organizations: 14. Activities include: concert band, drama/theater, student government, yearbook. Number of fraternities: 0; sororities: 0. **Sports program (2009-2010):** Member of NCAA III.

SERVICES AND FACILITIES

Basic services: nonremedial tutoring, placement service. **Remedial assistance:** writing, study skills. **Counseling services:** career, veteran student, aca-

demic, psychological. **For learning-disabled students:** School does not offer a structured program with separate admission and additional fees. Services include: learning center, extended time for tests, tutors. **Information technology resources:** Students are not required to lease or own a computer. Number of campus computers available to all students: 100. School has a wireless network. Proportion of college-owned housing units wired for high-speed internet access: 100%. **Campus safety:** Security services offered: 24-hour foot-and-vehicle patrols, late-night transport/escort service.

TRANSFER AND INTERNATIONAL STUDENTS

Transfer students: May apply for admission for the following academic terms: Fall, Spring, Summer. Applicants need a minimum number of credits to apply. **International students:** Number of foreign undergraduates: 4 (1% of student body). Number of countries represented: 6. Average TOEFL score: 500 (paper).

St. Michael's College

- **Address:** 1 Winooski Park, Colchester, VT 05439
- **Website:** http://www.smcvt.edu
- **Private; Religious affiliation:** Roman Catholic
- **Enrollment:** 1,900 full-time; 50 part-time

KEY STATS

- ✔ **U.S News College Ranking:** 93, National Liberal Arts Colleges
- ✔ **SAT Score (25th/75th percentile):** 1040-1250
- ✔ **Tuition:** 2010-2011: $34,845

Selectivity: Selective	**Room/board:** $8,685
Acceptance rate: 81%	**Average debt:** $30,742
Student/faculty ratio: 11/1	**Proportion who borrowed:** 76%

UNDERGRADUATE STUDENT BODY STATS

2009-2010 enrollment: 1,900 full-time; 50 part-time. Men: 48%; women: 52%. **Ethnic makeup:** African American: 1%; Asian American: 1%; Hispanic: 2%; White: 94%; International: 2%.

ADMISSIONS FACTS AND FIGURES

Phone: (800) 762-8000. **Email:** admission@smcvt.edu. **Website:** http://www.smcvt.edu. **Application deadlines for fall 2011:** Regular decision: February 1; decision sent by April 1. Early decision: Not offered. Early action: Send application by: November 1; Decision sent by: January 1. Admission can be deferred. **Application fee:** $50. **To apply online, go to:** http://www.smcvt.edu/admissions. **Admissions requirements/recommendations:** High school units required (recommended): English: 4 (4); Mathematics: 3 (4); Science: 3 (4); Foreign language: 3 (4); Social studies: 3 (4); Total units: 16 (20). Tests: The college uses SAT or ACT scores in admissions decisions. Neither SAT nor ACT required. For admission to the fall 2011 entering class, the school will accept: ACT with or without writing accepted. Campus visit: Recommended. Admissions interview: Recommended. Off-campus interview: May be arranged. **Factors that count in admissions decisions:** *Academic:* Secondary school record: Very Important. Class rank: Very Important. Letters of recommendation: Important. Standardized test scores: Considered. Essay: Important. *Nonacademic:* Interview: Not Considered. Extracurricular activities: Important. Talent/ability: Important. Character/personal qualities: Important. Alumni/ae relationship: Considered. Geographical residence: Considered. State residency: Considered. Religious affiliation/commitment: Not Considered. Minority status: Considered. Volunteer work: Considered. Work experience: Considered. **Other schools with the greatest overlap in applicants:** Boston College; Fairfield University; Providence College; St. Anselm College; Stonehill College. **Admissions statistics for the fall 2009 entering class:** Total applicants: 3,228. Total accepted: 2,613. Freshmen enrolled: 475; 86% were from out of state. Accepted through early-decision or early-action plans: 45%. Overall acceptance rate: 81%. Non-early acceptance rate: 85%. **Size of waiting list:** 321 applicants; enrolled from waiting list: 94. **Credentials of fall 2009 freshmen:** 25% ranked in the top 10 percent of their high school class; 54% were in the top 25 percent; 81% were in the top half. (Proportion submitting class standing: 70%.) **Average high school grade point average:** 3.4. **First-year students who submitted SAT scores:** 99%. Scores (25/75 percentile): Critical Reading: 520-630, Math: 520-620, Combined: 1040-1250. **First-year students submitting ACT scores:** 25%. Scores (25/75 percentile): English: N/A, Math: N/A, Composite: 22-27.

ACADEMICS

Year founded: 1904. **Academic calendar:** Semester. **Degrees offered:** bachelor's, post-bachelor's certificate, master's, post-master's certificate. **Most popular majors:** 23% business, management, marketing, and related support services, 14% social sciences, 13% psychology, 9% biological and biomedical sciences, 8% English language and literature/letters. **Major fields of study:** area, ethnic, cultural, and gender studies; biological and biomedical sciences; business, management, marketing, and related support services; communication, journalism, and related programs; computer and information sciences and support services; education; engineering; English language and literature/letters; foreign languages, literatures, and linguistics; history; mathematics and statistics; natural resources and conservation; physical sciences; psychology; social sciences; visual and performing arts. **Areas of required coursework:** arts/fine arts, humanities, mathematics, English (including composition), philosophy, foreign languages, sciences (biological or physical), history, social science, other. **Preprofessional programs:** pre-law, pre-dentistry, pre-medicine, pre-veterinary science, pre-optometry, pre-pharmacy. **Special academic programs (% participation):** cross-registration (1%), double major (14%), dual enrollment (2%), English as a Second Language (ESL) (1%), honors program (17%), independent study (16%), internships (43%), liberal arts/career combination (1%), student-designed major (1%), study abroad (35%), teacher certificate program (14%). **Teacher certification offered in:** elementary, middle/junior high, secondary. **Cooperative education programs:** education. **Reserve Officers Training Corps (ROTC):** Army ROTC: Offered at cooperating institution (University of Vermont); Air Force ROTC: Offered at cooperating institution (Norwich University). **Faculty and instruction (2009-2010):** Total instructional faculty: 151 full-time, 57 part-time (53% men; 47% women; 7% minorities). Full-time faculty with Ph.D. or other terminal degree: 87%. Student/faculty ratio: 11/1. Classes of fewer than 20 students: 59%; of 20 to 49 students: 40%; of 50 or more students: 1%. **Advanced Placement and International Baccalaureate credit:** AP tests may be used for: Placement only. Scores accepted: 3, 4, 5. International Baccalaureate exams may be used for: Placement only. **Freshmen returning for sophomore year:** 89%. **Graduation rates:** Four-year: 71%; five-year: 76%; six-year: 77%. **Graduate study:** 17% of students pursue further study immediately upon graduation; 21% within one year; 46% within five years. Fields in which graduates pursue further study: Master of Business Administration (MBA), 14%; law, 7%; medicine, 5%; dentistry, 2%; engineering, 2%; education, 35%; arts and sciences, 35%.

COSTS AND FINANCIAL AID

Financial aid office: (802) 654-3243. **Expenses (2010-2011):** Tuition and fees 2010-2011: $34,845; room/board: $8,685. Estimated books and supplies: $1,400; transportation: $500; personal expenses: $200. **Financial aid:** Priority filing date for institution's financial aid form: February 15. In 2009-2010, 74% of undergraduates applied for financial aid. Of those, 62% were determined to have financial need; 23% had their need fully met. Average financial aid package (proportion receiving): $21,928 (62%). Average amount of gift aid, such as scholarships or grants (proportion receiving): $16,539 (60%). Average amount of self-help aid, such as work study or loans (proportion receiving): $6,255 (52%). Average need-based loan (excluding PLUS or other private loans): $5,270. Among students who received need-based aid, the average percentage of need met: 77%. Among students who received aid based on merit, the average award (and the proportion receiving): $8,180 (28%). The average athletic scholarship (and the proportion receiving): $41,495 (1%). Average amount of debt of borrowers graduating in 2009: $30,742. Proportion who borrowed: 76%.

CAMPUS LIFE AND EXTRACURRICULAR ACTIVITIES

Campus housing available (% using): coed dorms (52%), women's dorms (0%), apartment for single students (47%), special housing for disabled students (1%), other housing options. Students who live in college-owned, operated, or affiliated housing: 98%. **Student employment:** During the 2009-2010 academic year, 17% of undergraduates worked on campus. Average per-year earnings: $1,261. **Clubs and organizations:** Number of student organizations: 50. Activities include: campus ministries, choral groups, concert band, dance, drama/theater, jazz band, literary magazine, music ensembles, musical theater, radio station, student government, student newspaper, yearbook. Number of fraternities: 0; sororities: 0. Average proportion of students who stay on campus on weekends: 90%. **Sports program (2009-2010):** Member of NCAA II. *Men's intercollegiate varsity sports:* baseball, basketball, cross country, golf, ice hockey, lacrosse, skiing (nordic), skiing (alpine), soccer, swimming, tennis. *Women's intercollegiate varsity sports:* basketball, cross country, field hockey, ice hockey, lacrosse, skiing (nordic), skiing (alpine), soccer, softball, swimming, tennis, volleyball.

SERVICES AND FACILITIES

Basic services: nonremedial tutoring, women's center, placement service, health service, health insurance. **Remedial assistance:** writing, study skills. **Counseling services:** minority student, career, personal, academic, psychological, religious. **For learning-disabled students:** School does not offer a structured program with separate admission and additional fees. Total undergraduates in learning-disabled program or receiving services: 184. Services include: reading machines, tape recorders, note-taking services, readers, extended time for tests, tutors, texts on tape, other. **Library:** Number of titles: 244,278; number of current serial subscriptions: 7,575. **Information technology resources:** Students are not required to lease or own a computer. Number of campus computers available to all students: 375. School has a wireless network. Approximate number of users that can be accommodated: 9,000. Proportion of college-owned housing units wired for high-speed internet access: 100%. **Campus safety:** Security services offered: 24-hour foot-and-vehicle patrols, late-night transport/escort service, 24-hour emergency telephones, lighted pathways/sidewalks, student patrols, controlled dormitory access (key, security card, etc).

TRANSFER AND INTERNATIONAL STUDENTS

Transfer students: May apply for admission for the following academic terms: Fall, Spring. Applicants do not need a minimum number of credits to apply. For fall 2009: Transfer applications received: 127. Transfer applicants offered admission: 77. Transfer applicants enrolled: 51. **International students:** Number of foreign undergraduates: 30 (2% of student body). Number of countries represented: 12. Minimum TOEFL score required: 550 (paper); 213 (computer).

University of Vermont

- **Address:** 194 S. Prospect Street, Burlington, VT 05405-0160
- **Website:** http://www.uvm.edu
- **Public**
- **Enrollment:** 10,212 full-time; 1,170 part-time

KEY STATS

✔ **U.S News College Ranking:** 94, National Universities
✔ **SAT Score (25th/75th percentile):** 1090-1280
✔ **Tuition:** 2010-2011: $14,132 in state, $32,840 out of state

Selectivity: More selective	**Room/board:** $9,382
Acceptance rate: 71%	**Average debt:** $27,696
Student/faculty ratio: 17/1	**Proportion who borrowed:** 63%

UNDERGRADUATE STUDENT BODY STATS

2009-2010 enrollment: 10,212 full-time; 1,170 part-time. Men: 44%; women: 56%. **Ethnic makeup:** African American: 1%; Asian American: 2%; Hispanic: 2%; White: 93%; International: 1%.

ADMISSIONS FACTS AND FIGURES

Phone: (802) 656-3370. **Email:** admissions@uvm.edu. **Website:** http://www.uvm.edu. **Application deadlines for fall 2011:** Regular decision: January 15; decision sent by March 31. Early decision: Not offered. Early action: Send application by: November 1; Decision sent by: December 15. Admission can be deferred. **Application fee:** $55. **To apply online, go to:** http://www.uvm.edu/admissions/undergraduate/applying/?Page=application.html. **Admissions requirements/recommendations:** High school units required (recommended): English: 4; Mathematics: 3; Science: 2; Foreign language: 2; Social studies: 3; Total units: 16. Tests: The college uses SAT or ACT scores in admissions decisions. Either SAT or ACT required. For admission to the fall 2011 entering class, the school will accept: ACT with writing required. Campus visit: Recommended. Admissions interview: Neither required nor recommended. Off-campus interview: May be arranged. **Factors that count in admissions decisions:** *Academic:* Secondary school record: Very Important. Class rank: Important. Letters of recommendation: Considered. Standardized test scores: Important. Essay: Important. *Nonacademic:* Interview: Considered. Extracurricular activities: Considered. Talent/ability: Considered. Character/personal qualities: Important. Alumni/ae relationship: Considered. Geographical residence: Considered. State residency: Important. Religious affiliation/commitment: Not Considered. Minority status: Considered. Volunteer work: Considered. Work experience: Considered. **Other schools with the greatest overlap in applicants:** Boston University; Northeastern University; University of Connecticut; University of Massachusetts–Amherst; University of New

Hampshire. **Admissions statistics for the fall 2009 entering class:** Total applicants: 22,365. Total accepted: 15,856. Freshmen enrolled: 2,619; 75% were from out of state. Accepted through early-decision or early-action plans: 41%. Overall acceptance rate: 71%. Non-early acceptance rate: 74%. **Size of waiting list:** 3456 applicants; enrolled from waiting list: 218. **Credentials of fall 2009 freshmen:** 29% ranked in the top 10 percent of their high school class; 66% were in the top 25 percent; 96% were in the top half. (Proportion submitting class standing: 52%.) **First-year students who submitted SAT scores:** 93%. Scores (25/75 percentile): Critical Reading: 540-640, Math: 550-640, Combined: 1090-1280. **First-year students submitting ACT scores:** 29%. Scores (25/75 percentile): English: N/A, Math: N/A, Composite: 24-28.

ACADEMICS

Year founded: 1791. **Academic calendar:** Semester. **Degrees offered:** bachelor's, post-bachelor's certificate, master's, post-master's certificate, doctorate. **Most popular majors:** 9% business administration and management, 8% psychology, 7% English language and literature, 6% political science and government, 4% history. **Major fields of study:** agriculture, agriculture operations, and related sciences; area, ethnic, cultural, and gender studies; biological and biomedical sciences; business, management, marketing, and related support services; communication, journalism, and related programs; computer and information sciences and support services; education; engineering; English language and literature/letters; family and consumer sciences/human sciences; foreign languages, literatures, and linguistics; health professions and related clinical sciences; history; liberal arts and sciences studies, and humanities; mathematics and statistics; multi/interdisciplinary studies; natural resources and conservation; parks, recreation, leisure, and fitness studies; philosophy and religious studies; physical sciences; psychology; public administration and social service professions; social sciences; visual and performing arts. **Areas of required coursework:** arts/fine arts, humanities, mathematics, English (including composition), sciences (biological or physical), social science, other. **Pre-professional programs:** pre-law, pre-dentistry, pre-medicine, pre-veterinary science, other. **Special academic programs (% participation):** cooperative (work-study plan) program (1%), cross-registration, distance learning (29%), double major (8%), dual enrollment, exchange student program (domestic) (1%), honors program (10%), independent study (25%), internships (10%), liberal arts/career combination (1%), student-designed major (1%), study abroad (20%), teacher certificate program (8%), other. **Teacher certification offered in:** early childhood, special education, elementary, middle/junior high, secondary. **Cooperative education programs:** business, computer science, engineering. **Reserve Officers Training Corps (ROTC):** Army ROTC: Offered on campus; Air Force ROTC: Offered at cooperating institution (Norwich University). **Faculty and instruction (2009-2010):** Total instructional faculty: 597 full-time, 155 part-time (55% men; 45% women; 12% minorities). Full-time faculty with Ph.D. or other terminal degree: 86%. Student/faculty ratio: 17/1. Classes of fewer than 20 students: 46%; of 20 to 49 students: 41%; of 50 or more students: 13%. **Advanced Placement and International Baccalaureate credit:** AP tests may be used for: Credit only. Scores accepted: 4, 5. International Baccalaureate exams may be used for: Credit only. **Freshmen returning for sophomore year:** 85%. **Graduation rates:** Four-year: 57%; five-year: 71%; six-year: 73%. **Graduate study:** 25% of students pursue further study within one year. Fields in which graduates pursue further study: Master of Business Administration (MBA), 4%; law, 8%; medicine, 7%; dentistry, 3%; engineering, 6%; education, 28%; arts and sciences, 28%; veterinary medicine, 3%.

COSTS AND FINANCIAL AID

Financial aid office: (802) 656-5700. **Expenses (2010-2011):** Tuition and fees 2010-2011: $14,132 in state, $32,840 out of state; room/board: $9,382. Estimated books and supplies: $1,200; transportation: $200; personal expenses: $1,456. **Financial aid:** Priority filing date for institution's financial aid form: February 10. In 2009-2010, 71% of undergraduates applied for financial aid. Of those, 59% were determined to have financial need; 20% had their need fully met. Average financial aid package (proportion receiving): $18,364 (59%). Average amount of gift aid, such as scholarships or grants (proportion receiving): $14,576 (50%). Average amount of self-help aid, such as work study or loans (proportion receiving): $7,260 (49%). Average need-based loan (excluding PLUS or other private loans): $6,413. Among students who received need-based aid, the average percentage of need met: 71%. Among students who received aid based on merit, the average award (and the proportion receiving): $2,426 (18%). The average athletic scholarship (and the proportion receiving): $22,910 (2%). Average amount of debt of borrowers graduating in 2009: $27,696. Proportion who borrowed: 63%.

CAMPUS LIFE AND EXTRACURRICULAR ACTIVITIES

Campus housing available (% using): coed dorms (84%), sorority housing (1%), fraternity housing (3%), apartments for married students (2%), apartment for single students (10%). Students who live in college-owned, operated, or affiliated housing: 51%. **Student employment:** During the 2009-2010 academic year, 10% of undergraduates worked on campus. Average per-year earnings: $1,800. **Clubs and organizations:** Number of student organizations: 171. Activities include: campus ministries, choral groups, concert band, dance, drama/theater, international student organization, jazz band, literary magazine, music ensembles, musical theater, pep band, radio station, student government, student newspaper, student film society, symphony orchestra, television station. Number of fraternities: 10; sororities: 7. Proportion of men in fraternities: 6%; of women in sororities: 5%. Average proportion of students who stay on campus on weekends: 85%. **Sports program (2009-2010):** Member of NCAA I. *Men's intercollegiate varsity sports:* basketball, cross country, ice hockey, skiing (nordic), skiing (alpine), soccer, track and field (indoor), track and field (outdoor). *Women's intercollegiate varsity sports:* basketball, cross country, field hockey, ice hockey, skiing (nordic), skiing (alpine), soccer, swimming, track and field (indoor), track and field (outdoor).

SERVICES AND FACILITIES

Basic services: nonremedial tutoring, women's center, placement service, health service, health insurance. **Remedial assistance:** reading, math, writing, study skills. **Counseling services:** minority student, career, personal, veteran student, academic, older student, psychological, birth control, religious. **For learning-disabled students:** School does not offer a structured program with separate admission and additional fees. Total undergraduates in learning-disabled program or receiving services: 247. Services include: reading machines, tape recorders, other special classes, note-taking services, oral tests, learning center, readers, extended time for tests, tutors, priority registration, priority seating, texts on tape, typist/scribe, exams on tape or computer, other testing accommodations, other. **Library:** Number of titles: 2,647,610; number of current serial subscriptions: 20,093. **Information technology resources:** Students are not required to lease or own a computer. Number of campus computers available to all students: 470. School has a wireless network. Approximate number of users that can be accommodated: 5,000. Proportion of college-owned housing units wired for high-speed internet access: 96%. **Campus safety:** Security services offered: 24-hour foot-and-vehicle patrols, late-night transport/escort service, 24-hour emergency telephones, lighted pathways/sidewalks, controlled dormitory access (key, security card, etc).

TRANSFER AND INTERNATIONAL STUDENTS

Transfer students: May apply for admission for the following academic terms: Fall, Spring. Applicants do not need a minimum number of credits to apply. For fall 2009: Transfer applications received: 1,250. Transfer applicants offered admission: 880. Transfer applicants enrolled: 467. **International students:** Number of foreign undergraduates: 73 (1% of student body). Number of countries represented: 20. Minimum TOEFL score required: 550 (paper); 213 (computer). Average TOEFL score: 600 (paper).

Vermont Technical College

- **Address:** PO Box 500, Randolph Center, VT 05061
- **Website:** http://www.vtc.edu
- **Public**
- **Enrollment:** 1,264 full-time; 399 part-time

KEY STATS

- ✔ **U.S News College Ranking:** 31, Regional Colleges (North)
- ✔ **SAT Score (25th/75th percentile):** 870-1080
- ✔ **Tuition:** 2010-2011: $11,004 in state, $20,340 out of state

Selectivity: Less selective	**Room/board:** $8,120
Acceptance rate: 63%	**Average debt:** $26,000
Student/faculty ratio: 11/1	**Proportion who borrowed:** 80%

UNDERGRADUATE STUDENT BODY STATS

2009-2010 enrollment: 1,264 full-time; 399 part-time. Men: 57%; women: 43%. **Ethnic makeup:** African American: 1%; Asian American: 1%; Hispanic: 1%; White: 96%.

ADMISSIONS FACTS AND FIGURES

Phone: (802) 728-1244. **Email:** admissions@vtc.edu. **Website:** http://www.vtc.edu. **Application deadlines for fall 2011:** Regular decision: Rolling. Early decision: Not offered. Early action: Send application by: November 1; Decision sent by: December 1. Admission can be deferred. **Application fee:** $38. **To apply online, go to:** http://www.vtc.edu/section_admissions/admissions_applyonline.html. **Admissions requirements/recommendations:** High school units required (recommended): English: 4; Mathematics: 3 (4); Science: 2 (3); Foreign language: 0 (2); Social studies: 2; History: 2; Academic electives: 2; Total units: 16. Tests: The college uses SAT or ACT scores in admissions decisions. Neither SAT nor ACT required. Campus visit: Recommended. Admissions interview: Recommended. Off-campus interview: May be arranged. **Factors that count in admissions decisions:** *Academic:* Secondary school record: Very Important. Class rank: Important. Letters of recommendation: Important. Standardized test scores: Very Important. Essay: Considered. *Nonacademic:* Interview: Important. Extracurricular activities: Considered. Talent/ability: Not Considered. Character/personal qualities: Important. Alumni/ae relationship: Not Considered. Geographical residence: Not Considered. State residency: Not Considered. Religious affiliation/commitment: Not Considered. Minority status: Not Considered. Volunteer work: Considered. Work experience: Considered. **Other schools with the greatest overlap in applicants:** Clarkson University; Norwich University; Rochester Institute of Technology; University of Vermont; Wentworth Institute of Technology. **Admissions statistics for the fall 2009 entering class:** Total applicants: 844. Total accepted: 534. Freshmen enrolled: 254; Overall acceptance rate: 63%. Non-early acceptance rate: 63%. **Size of waiting list:** 240 applicants; enrolled from waiting list: 129. **Credentials of fall 2009 freshmen:** 4% ranked in the top 10 percent of their high school class; 15% were in the top 25 percent; 55% were in the top half. (Proportion submitting class standing: 58%.) **Average high school grade point average:** 0.9. **First-year students who submitted SAT scores:** 67%. Scores (25/75 percentile): Critical Reading: 420-540, Math: 450-540, Combined: 870-1080. **First-year students submitting ACT scores:** 11%. Scores (25/75 percentile): English: N/A, Math: N/A, Composite: N/A.

ACADEMICS

Year founded: 1866. **Academic calendar:** Semester. **Degrees offered:** certificate, associate, bachelor's. **Major fields of study:** agriculture, agriculture operations, and related sciences; architecture and related services; business, management, marketing, and related support services; computer and information sciences and support services; construction trades; engineering technologies/technicians; health professions and related clinical sciences. **Areas of required coursework:** arts/fine arts, humanities, computer literacy, mathematics, English (including composition), sciences (biological or physical), social science. **Special academic programs:** double major, dual enrollment, internships, study abroad, other. **Cooperative education programs:** health professions. **Faculty and instruction (2009-2010):** Total instructional faculty: 79 full-time, 150 part-time (49% men; 51% women; 1% minorities). Full-time faculty with Ph.D. or other terminal degree: 23%. Student/faculty ratio: 11/1. Classes of fewer than 20 students: 63%; of 20 to 49 students: 37%; of 50 or more students: 0%. **Advanced Placement and International Baccalaureate credit:** International Baccalaureate exams may be used for: Credit only. **Freshmen returning for sophomore year:** 70%. **Graduation rates:** Four-year: 24%; five-year: 57%; six-year: 53%. **Graduate study:** 1% of students pursue further study immediately upon graduation; 1% within one year. Fields in which graduates pursue further study: Master of Business Administration (MBA), 50%; engineering, 50%.

COSTS AND FINANCIAL AID

Financial aid office: (800) 965-8790. **Expenses (2010-2011):** Tuition and fees 2010-2011: $11,004 in state, $20,340 out of state; room/board: $8,120. Estimated books and supplies: $1,000; transportation: $1. **Financial aid:** Priority filing date for institution's financial aid form: March 1. In 2009-2010, 84% of undergraduates applied for financial aid. Of those, 72% were determined to have financial need; 13% had their need fully met. Average financial aid package (proportion receiving): $8,152 (71%). Average amount of gift aid, such as scholarships or grants (proportion receiving): $5,272 (55%). Average amount of self-help aid, such as work study or loans (proportion receiving): $3,652 (69%). Average need-based loan (excluding PLUS or other private loans): $3,484. Among students who received need-based aid, the average percentage of need met: 68%. Among students who received aid based on merit, the average award (and the proportion receiving): $4,632 (2%). The average athletic scholarship (and the proportion receiving): $0 (0%). Average amount of debt of borrowers graduating in 2009: $26,000. Proportion who borrowed: 80%.

CAMPUS LIFE AND EXTRACURRICULAR ACTIVITIES

Campus housing available (% using): coed dorms (100%), special housing for disabled students. **Student employment:** During the 2009-2010 academic year, 20% of undergraduates worked on campus. Average per-year earnings: $850. **Clubs and organizations:** Number of student organizations: 6. Activities include: radio station, student government, television station, yearbook. Number of fraternities: 0; sororities: 0. Average proportion of students who stay on campus on weekends: 35%. **Sports program (2009-2010):** Member of NAIA. *Men's intercollegiate varsity sports:* baseball, basketball, cross country, golf, soccer. *Women's intercollegiate varsity sports:* basketball, cross country, golf, soccer, softball.

SERVICES AND FACILITIES

Basic services: nonremedial tutoring, placement service, health service, health insurance. **Remedial assistance:** reading, math, writing, study skills. **Counseling services:** minority student, career, personal, veteran student, academic, older student, other. **For learning-disabled students:** School does not offer a structured program with separate admission and additional fees. Services include: remedial math, remedial English, reading machines, remedial reading, tape recorders, diagnostic testing service, untimed tests, note-taking services, oral tests, learning center, readers, extended time for tests, tutors. **Library:** Number of titles: 59,480; number of current serial subscriptions: 1,156. **Information technology resources:** Students are not required to lease or own a computer. Number of campus computers available to all students: 400. School has a wireless network. Proportion of college-owned housing units wired for high-speed internet access: 100%. **Campus safety:** Security services offered: 24-hour foot-and-vehicle patrols, 24-hour emergency telephones, lighted pathways/sidewalks, controlled dormitory access (key, security card, etc).

TRANSFER AND INTERNATIONAL STUDENTS

Transfer students: May apply for admission for the following academic terms: Fall, Spring. Applicants do not need a minimum number of credits to apply. For fall 2009: Transfer applications received: 933. Transfer applicants offered admission: 448. Transfer applicants enrolled: 327. **International students:** Number of foreign undergraduates: 3. Minimum TOEFL score required: 500 (paper); 61 (computer). Average TOEFL score: 525 (paper).

Virginia

Averett University

- **Address:** 420 W. Main Street, Danville, VA 24541
- **Website:** http://www.averett.edu
- **Private**
- **Enrollment:** 714 full-time; 73 part-time

KEY STATS

✔ **U.S News College Ranking:** 35, Regional Colleges (South)
✔ **SAT Score (25th/75th percentile):** 830-1035
✔ **Tuition:** 2010-2011: $22,956

Selectivity: Less selective	**Room/board:** $8,274
Acceptance rate: 91%	**Average debt:** $30,943
Student/faculty ratio: 12/1	**Proportion who borrowed:** 67%

UNDERGRADUATE STUDENT BODY STATS

2009-2010 enrollment: 714 full-time; 73 part-time. Men: 52%; women: 48%. **Ethnic makeup:** African American: 32%; American-Indian: 1%; Asian American: 1%; Hispanic: 3%; White: 59%; International: 4%. **Religious preference:** Roman Catholic: 7%; Protestant: 58%; Jewish: 1%; Muslim: 1%; No preference: 6%; Unknown: 27%.

ADMISSIONS FACTS AND FIGURES

Phone: (800) 283-7388. **Email:** admit@averett.edu. **Website:** http://www.averett.edu. **Application deadlines for fall 2011:** Regular decision: July 15. Early decision: Not offered. Early action: Not offered. Admission can be deferred. **Application fee:** None. **To apply online, go to:** http://www.averett.edu/admissions/form/apply.html. **Admissions requirements/recommendations:** High school units required (recommended): English: 4 (4); Mathematics: 3 (4); Science: 3 (4); Foreign language: 0 (3); Social studies: 3 (4); History: 3 (3); Academic electives: 3 (0); Total units: 16 (25). Tests: The college uses SAT or ACT scores in admissions decisions. Either SAT or ACT required. For admission to the fall 2011 entering class, the school will accept: ACT with or without writing accepted. Campus visit: Recommended. Admissions interview: Recommended. Off-campus interview: May be arranged. **Factors that count in admissions decisions:** *Academic:* Secondary school record: Very Important. Class rank: Not Considered. Letters of recommendation: Important. Standardized test scores: Important. Essay: Important. *Nonacademic:* Interview: Important. Extracurricular activities: Important. Talent/ability: Considered. Character/personal qualities: Not Considered. Alumni/ae relationship: Considered. Geographical residence: Considered. State residency: Considered. Religious affiliation/commitment: Not Considered. Minority status: Not Considered. Volunteer work: Considered. Work experience: Considered. **Other schools with the greatest overlap in applicants:** Appalachian State University; Christopher Newport University; East Carolina University; James Madison University; Virginia Tech. **Admissions statistics for the fall 2009 entering class:** Total applicants: 1,159. Total accepted: 1,056. Freshmen enrolled: 227; Overall acceptance rate: 91%. **Size of waiting list:** 0 applicants; enrolled from waiting list: 0. **Credentials of fall 2009 freshmen:** 5% ranked in the top 10 percent of their high school class; 29% were in the top 25 percent; 62% were in the top half. (Proportion submitting class standing: 11%.) **Average high school grade point average:** 3.0. **First-year students who submitted SAT scores:** 88%. Scores (25/75 percentile): Critical Reading: 410-510, Math: 420-525, Combined: 830-1035. **First-year students submitting ACT scores:** 24%. Scores (25/75 percentile): English: N/A, Math: N/A, Composite: 17-21.

ACADEMICS

Year founded: 1859. **Academic calendar:** Semester. **Degrees offered:** associate, transfer-associate, bachelor's, master's. **Major fields of study:** agriculture, agriculture operations, and related sciences; biological and biomedical sciences; business, management, marketing, and related support services; communication, journalism, and related programs; computer and information sciences and support services; education; English language and literature/letters; health professions and related clinical sciences; history; liberal arts and sciences studies, and humanities; mathematics and statistics; multi/interdisciplinary studies; natural resources and conservation; parks, recreation, leisure, and fitness studies; philosophy and religious studies; physical sciences; psychology; security and protective services; social sciences; transportation and materials moving; visual and performing arts. **Areas of required coursework:** arts/fine arts, humanities, computer literacy, mathematics, English (including composition), sciences (biological or physical), history, social science, other. **Pre-professional programs:** pre-law, pre-dentistry, pre-medicine, pre-theology, pre-pharmacy, other. **Special academic programs (% participation):** accelerated program, cooperative (work-study plan) program (17%), cross-registration (0%), distance learning (12%), double major (4%), dual enrollment (5%), exchange student program (domestic) (0%), external degree program (7%), honors program (4%), independent study (15%), internships (10%), student-designed major (0%), study abroad (5%), teacher certificate program (16%), other (0%). **Teacher certification offered in:** early childhood, elementary, middle/junior high, secondary. **Cooperative education programs:** business, computer science, education, health professions, humanities, natural science, social/behavioral science, technologies, other. **Faculty and instruction (2009-2010):** Total instructional faculty: 52 full-time, 33 part-time (53% men; 47% women; 6% minorities). Full-time faculty with Ph.D. or other terminal degree: 71%. Student/faculty ratio: 12/1. **Advanced Placement and International Baccalaureate credit:** AP tests may be used for: Placement only. Scores accepted: 3, 4, 5. International Baccalaureate exams may be used for: Placement only. **Freshmen returning for sophomore year:** 59%. **Graduation rates:** Four-year: 34%; five-year: 44%; six-year: 41%.

COSTS AND FINANCIAL AID

Financial aid office: (434) 791-5646. **Expenses (2010-2011):** Tuition and fees 2010-2011: $22,956; room/board: $8,274. Estimated books and supplies: $1,000; transportation: $700; personal expenses: $1,400. **Financial aid:** Priority filing date for institution's financial aid form: April 1. In 2009-2010, 94% of undergraduates applied for financial aid. Of those, 85% were determined to have financial need; 21% had their need fully met. Average financial aid package (proportion receiving): $15,682 (85%). Average amount of gift aid, such as scholarships or grants (proportion receiving): $12,492 (84%). Average amount of self-help aid, such as work study or loans (proportion receiving): $3,935 (71%). Average need-based loan (excluding PLUS or other private loans): $3,747. Among students who received need-based aid, the average percentage of need met: 75%. Among students who received aid based on merit, the average award (and the proportion receiving): $7,934 (14%). The average athletic scholarship (and the proportion receiving): $0 (0%). Average amount of debt of borrowers graduating in 2009: $30,943. Proportion who borrowed: 67%.

CAMPUS LIFE AND EXTRACURRICULAR ACTIVITIES

Campus housing available (% using): coed dorms (50%), women's dorms (15%), men's dorms (20%), apartment for single students (15%). Students who live in college-owned, operated, or affiliated housing: 51%. **Student employment:** During the 2009-2010 academic year, 10% of undergraduates worked on campus. Average per-year earnings: $1,200. **Clubs and organizations:** Number of student organizations: 32. Activities include: choral groups, drama/theater, literary magazine, musical theater, student government, student newspaper. Number of fraternities: 2; sororities: 1. Proportion of men in fraternities: 2%; of women in sororities: 2%. Average proportion of students who stay on campus on weekends: 75%. **Sports program (2009-2010):** Member of NCAA III. *Men's intercollegiate varsity sports:* baseball, basketball, cross country, football, golf, soccer, tennis. *Women's intercollegiate varsity sports:* basketball, cross country, equestrian, lacrosse, soccer, tennis, volleyball.

SERVICES AND FACILITIES

Basic services: nonremedial tutoring, placement service, health insurance, other. **Remedial assistance:** reading, math, writing, study skills. **Counseling services:** minority student, career, personal, veteran student, academic, older student, psychological, religious, other. **For learning-disabled students:** School does not offer a structured program with separate admission and additional fees. Services include: remedial math, remedial English, tape recorders, untimed tests, note-taking services, oral tests, learning center, readers, extended time for tests, tutors, priority seating, texts on tape. **Library:** Number of titles: 127,041; number of current serial subscriptions: 258. **Information technology resources:** Students are not required to lease or own a computer. Number of campus computers available to all students: 260. School has a wireless network. Approximate number of users that can be accommodated: 60. Proportion of college-owned housing units wired for high-speed internet access: 100%. **Campus safety:** Security services offered: 24-hour foot-and-vehicle patrols, late-night transport/escort service, 24-hour emergency telephones, lighted pathways/sidewalks, controlled dormitory access (key, security card, etc).

TRANSFER AND INTERNATIONAL STUDENTS
Transfer students: May apply for admission for the following academic terms: Fall, Spring, Summer. Applicants need a minimum number of credits to apply. For fall 2009: Transfer applications received: 195. Transfer applicants offered admission: 191. Transfer applicants enrolled: 88. **International students:** Number of foreign undergraduates: 34 (4% of student body). Number of countries represented: 16. Minimum TOEFL score required: 500 (paper); 173 (computer). Average TOEFL score: 585 (paper).

Bluefield College

- **Address:** 3000 College Drive, Bluefield, VA 24605
- **Website:** http://www.bluefield.edu
- **Private; Religious affiliation:** Baptist
- **Enrollment:** 643 full-time; 95 part-time

KEY STATS
✔ **U.S News College Ranking:** 39, Regional Colleges (South)
✔ **SAT Score (25th/75th percentile):** 790-1130
✔ **Tuition:** 2010-2011: $18,800

Selectivity: Less selective	**Room/board:** $7,150
Acceptance rate: 47%	**Average debt:** $19,675
Student/faculty ratio: 8/1	**Proportion who borrowed:** 87%

UNDERGRADUATE STUDENT BODY STATS
2009-2010 enrollment: 643 full-time; 95 part-time. Men: 41%; women: 59%. **Ethnic makeup:** African American: 20%; Asian American: 1%; Hispanic: 2%; White: 75%; International: 2%. **Religious preference:** Roman Catholic: 2%; Protestant: 32%; Jewish: 1%; No preference: 10%; Unknown: 1%; Baptist: 54%.

ADMISSIONS FACTS AND FIGURES
Phone: (276) 326-4272. **Email:** admissions@bluefield.edu. **Website:** http://www.bluefield.edu. **Application deadlines for fall 2011:** Regular decision: Rolling. Early decision: Not offered. Early action: Not offered. Admission can be deferred. **Application fee:** $30. **To apply online, go to:** http://www.bluefield.edu/templates/System/details.asp?id=30250&PID=260348. **Admissions requirements/recommendations:** High school units required (recommended): English: 4; Mathematics: 3; Science: 3; Social studies: 3; Academic electives: 6; Total units: 22. Tests: The college uses SAT or ACT scores in admissions decisions. Either SAT or ACT required. For admission to the fall 2011 entering class, the school will accept: ACT with or without writing accepted. Campus visit: Recommended. Admissions interview: Recommended. Off-campus interview: May be arranged. **Factors that count in admissions decisions:** *Academic:* Secondary school record: Important. Class rank: Not Considered. Letters of recommendation: Important. Standardized test scores: Very Important. Essay: Considered. *Nonacademic:* Interview: Important. Extracurricular activities: Considered. Talent/ability: Considered. Character/personal qualities: Important. Alumni/ae relationship: Considered. Geographical residence: Not Considered. State residency: Not Considered. Religious affiliation/commitment: Considered. Minority status: Not Considered. Volunteer work: Considered. Work experience: Considered. **Other schools with the greatest overlap in applicants:** Concord University; Ferrum College; Liberty University; Radford University; University of Virginia–Wise. **Admissions statistics for the fall 2009 entering class:** Total applicants: 716. Total accepted: 340. Overall acceptance rate: 47%. **Credentials of fall 2009 freshmen:** 16% ranked in the top 10 percent of their high school class; 30% were in the top 25 percent; 50% were in the top half. (Proportion submitting class standing: 73%.) **Average high school grade point average:** 3.1. **First-year students who submitted SAT scores:** 80%. Scores (25/75 percentile): Critical Reading: 400-560, Math: 390-570,

Combined: 790-1130. **First-year students submitting ACT scores:** 20%. Scores (25/75 percentile): English: N/A, Math: N/A, Composite: 17-20.

ACADEMICS
Year founded: 1922. **Academic calendar:** Semester. **Degrees offered:** bachelor's. **Most popular majors:** 37% human resources management/personnel administration, 24% psychology, 12% criminal justice/safety studies. **Major fields of study:** biological and biomedical sciences; business, management, marketing, and related support services; communication, journalism, and related programs; education; English language and literature/letters; history; mathematics and statistics; parks, recreation, leisure, and fitness studies; philosophy and religious studies; physical sciences; psychology; security and protective services; social sciences; theology and religious vocations; visual and performing arts. **Areas of required coursework:** arts/fine arts, humanities, mathematics, English (including composition), philosophy, sciences (biological or physical), history, social science, other. **Pre-professional programs:** pre-law, pre-dentistry, pre-medicine, pre-theology, pre-veterinary science, pre-optometry, pre-pharmacy. **Special academic programs (% participation):** accelerated program (73%), double major (0%), dual enrollment (0%), honors program (2%), internships (0%), student-designed major (1%), study abroad (2%), teacher certificate program (14%). **Teacher certification offered in:** elementary, middle/junior high, secondary. **Faculty and instruction (2009-2010):** Total instructional faculty: 37 full-time, 58 part-time (58% men; 42% women; 7% minorities). Full-time faculty with Ph.D. or other terminal degree: 57%. Student/faculty ratio: 8/1. Classes of fewer than 20 students: 87%; of 20 to 49 students: 13%; of 50 or more students: 0%. **Advanced Placement and International Baccalaureate credit:** AP tests may be used for: Credit and/or placement. Scores accepted: 3, 4, 5. International Baccalaureate exams may be used for: Credit and/or placement. **Freshmen returning for sophomore year:** 65%. **Graduation rates:** Four-year: 39%; five-year: 39%; six-year: 38%. **Graduate study:** 22% of students pursue further study immediately upon graduation; 17% within one year. Fields in which graduates pursue further study: Master of Business Administration (MBA), 10%; law, 1%; medicine, 2%; theology (or the seminary), 15%; education, 4%; arts and sciences, 5%.

COSTS AND FINANCIAL AID
Financial aid office: (276) 326-4215. **Expenses (2010-2011):** Tuition and fees 2010-2011: $18,800; room/board: $7,150. Estimated books and supplies: $1,200; transportation: $1,454; personal expenses: $1,500. **Financial aid:** Priority filing date for institution's financial aid form: March 15. In 2009-2010, 92% of undergraduates applied for financial aid. Of those, 85% were determined to have financial need; 17% had their need fully met. Average financial aid package (proportion receiving): $13,338 (85%). Average amount of gift aid, such as scholarships or grants (proportion receiving): $9,042 (82%). Average amount of self-help aid, such as work study or loans (proportion receiving): $5,323 (73%). Average need-based loan (excluding PLUS or other private loans): $5,151. Among students who received need-based aid, the average percentage of need met: 63%. Among students who received aid based on merit, the average award (and the proportion receiving): $3,788 (10%). The average athletic scholarship (and the proportion receiving): $5,043 (7%). Average amount of debt of borrowers graduating in 2009: $19,675. Proportion who borrowed: 87%.

CAMPUS LIFE AND EXTRACURRICULAR ACTIVITIES
Campus housing available (% using): coed dorms (16%), women's dorms (45%), men's dorms (38%), apartments for married students (0%), other housing options (1%). **Student employment:** During the 2009-2010 academic year, 2% of undergraduates worked on campus. Average per-year earnings: $1,300. **Clubs and organizations:** Number of student organizations: 10. Activities include: campus ministries, choral groups, concert band, drama/theater, jazz band, literary magazine, music ensembles, student government, student newspaper. Number of fraternities: 3; sororities: 2. Average proportion of students who stay on campus on weekends: 60%. **Sports program (2009-2010):** Member of NAIA. *Men's intercollegiate varsity sports:* baseball, basketball, cross country, golf, soccer, tennis. *Women's intercollegiate varsity sports:* basketball, cross country, soccer, softball, tennis, volleyball.

SERVICES AND FACILITIES
Basic services: nonremedial tutoring, health service, health insurance, other. **Remedial assistance:** math, writing, study skills. **Counseling services:** career, academic, other. **For learning-disabled students:** School does not offer a structured program with separate admission and additional fees. Total undergraduates in learning-disabled program or receiving services: 14. Services include: remedial math, remedial English, tape recorders, untimed

tests, note-taking services, oral tests, extended time for tests, tutors, priority seating, texts on tape, other testing accommodations. **Library:** Number of titles: 88,100; number of current serial subscriptions: 17,700. **Information technology resources:** Students are not required to lease or own a computer. Number of campus computers available to all students: 100. School has a wireless network. Approximate number of users that can be accommodated: 10,254. Proportion of college-owned housing units wired for high-speed internet access: 100%. **Campus safety:** Security services offered: late-night transport/escort service, lighted pathways/sidewalks, student patrols, controlled dormitory access (key, security card, etc).

TRANSFER AND INTERNATIONAL STUDENTS

Transfer students: May apply for admission for the following academic terms: Fall, Spring, Summer. Applicants need a minimum number of credits to apply. For fall 2009: Transfer applications received: 185. Transfer applicants offered admission: 107. Transfer applicants enrolled: 42. **International students:** Number of foreign undergraduates: 10 (2% of student body). Number of countries represented: 2. Minimum TOEFL score required: 500 (paper); 173 (computer). Average TOEFL score: 510 (paper).

Bridgewater College

- **Address:** 402 E. College Street, Bridgewater, VA 22812-1599
- **Website:** http://www.bridgewater.edu
- **Private; Religious affiliation:** Church of the Brethren
- **Enrollment:** 1,576 full-time; 14 part-time

KEY STATS

✔ **U.S News College Ranking:** 187, National Liberal Arts Colleges
✔ **SAT Score (25th/75th percentile):** 910-1110
✔ **Tuition:** 2010-2011: $25,500

Selectivity: Selective	**Room/board:** $10,350
Acceptance rate: 86%	**Average debt:** $29,331
Student/faculty ratio: 14/1	**Proportion who borrowed:** 74%

UNDERGRADUATE STUDENT BODY STATS

2009-2010 enrollment: 1,576 full-time; 14 part-time. Men: 41%; women: 59%. **Ethnic makeup:** African American: 7%; Asian American: 1%; Hispanic: 2%; White: 89%; International: 1%. **Religious preference:** Roman Catholic: 12%; Protestant: 59%; No preference: 6%; Unknown: 10%; Church of the Brethren: 8%; Other: 5%.

ADMISSIONS FACTS AND FIGURES

Phone: (800) 759-8328. **Email:** admissions@bridgewater.edu. **Website:** http://www.bridgewater.edu. **Application deadlines for fall 2011:** Regular decision: Rolling. Early decision: Not offered. Early action: Not offered. Admission can be deferred. **Application fee:** $30. **To apply online, go to:** http://www.bridgewater.edu/Admissions/StepsToApply. **Admissions requirements/recommendations:** High school units required (recommended): English: 4 (4); Mathematics: 3 (4); Science: 2 (4); Foreign language: 0 (3); Academic electives: 4 (4); Total units: 15 (22). Tests: The college uses SAT or ACT scores in admissions decisions. Either SAT or ACT required. For admission to the fall 2011 entering class, the school will accept: ACT with or without writing accepted. Campus visit: Recommended. Admissions interview: Recommended. Off-campus interview: May be arranged. **Factors that count in admissions decisions:** *Academic:* Secondary school record: Very Important. Class rank: Important. Letters of recommendation: Important. Standardized test scores: Very Important. Essay: Not Considered. *Nonacademic:* Interview: Important. Extracurricular activities: Important. Talent/ability: Important. Character/personal qualities: Important. Alumni/ae relationship: Not Considered. Geographical residence: Considered. State residency: Considered. Religious affiliation/commitment: Not Considered. Minority status: Not Considered. Volunteer work: Considered. Work experience: Considered. **Other schools with the greatest overlap in applicants:** James Madison University; Radford University; Virginia Tech. **Admissions statistics for the fall 2009 entering class:** Total applicants: 3,186. Total accepted: 2,726. Freshmen enrolled: 497; 20% were from out of state. Overall acceptance rate: 86%. **Credentials of fall 2009 freshmen:** 20% ranked in the top 10 percent of their high school class; 47% were in the top 25 percent; 84% were in the top half. (Proportion submitting class standing: 84%.) **Average high school grade point average:** 3.4. **First-year students who submitted SAT scores:** 89%. Scores (25/75 percentile): Critical Reading: 450-550, Math: 460-560, Combined: 910-1110.

First-year students submitting ACT scores: 29%. Scores (25/75 percentile): English: 17-24, Math: 17-23, Composite: 18-23.

ACADEMICS

Year founded: 1880. **Academic calendar:** 4-1-4. **Degrees offered:** bachelor's. **Most popular majors:** 16% business administration and management, 12% biology/biological sciences, 8% psychology, 6% mass communication/media studies, 5% kinesiology and exercise science. **Major fields of study:** agriculture, agriculture operations, and related sciences; biological and biomedical sciences; business, management, marketing, and related support services; communication, journalism, and related programs; computer and information sciences and support services; education; English language and literature/letters; family and consumer sciences/human sciences; foreign languages, literatures, and linguistics; health professions and related clinical sciences; history; liberal arts and sciences studies, and humanities; mathematics and statistics; natural resources and conservation; parks, recreation, leisure, and fitness studies; philosophy and religious studies; physical sciences; psychology; social sciences; visual and performing arts. **Areas of required coursework:** arts/fine arts, humanities, computer literacy, mathematics, English (including composition), philosophy, sciences (biological or physical), history, social science, other. **Pre-professional programs:** pre-law, pre-dentistry, pre-medicine, pre-veterinary science, pre-pharmacy, other. **Special academic programs (% participation):** double major (11%), honors program (11%), independent study (8%), internships (.5%), study abroad (4%), teacher certificate program (14%). **Teacher certification offered in:** elementary, secondary. **Faculty and instruction (2009-2010):** Total instructional faculty: 101 full-time, 35 part-time (53% men; 47% women; 4% minorities). Full-time faculty with Ph.D. or other terminal degree: 79%. Student/faculty ratio: 14/1. Classes of fewer than 20 students: 54%; of 20 to 49 students: 45%; of 50 or more students: 1%. **Advanced Placement and International Baccalaureate credit:** AP tests may be used for: Credit and/or placement. Scores accepted: 3, 4, 5. International Baccalaureate exams may be used for: Credit only. **Freshmen returning for sophomore year:** 74%. **Graduation rates:** Four-year: 54%; five-year: 57%; six-year: 57%. **Graduate study:** 26% of students pursue further study within one year.

COSTS AND FINANCIAL AID

Financial aid office: (540) 828-5376. **Expenses (2010-2011):** Tuition and fees 2010-2011: $25,500; room/board: $10,350. Estimated books and supplies: $1,100; transportation: $1,200; personal expenses: $1,080. **Financial aid:** Priority filing date for institution's financial aid form: March 1. In 2009-2010, 86% of undergraduates applied for financial aid. Of those, 76% were determined to have financial need; 14% had their need fully met. Average financial aid package (proportion receiving): $21,596 (76%). Average amount of gift aid, such as scholarships or grants (proportion receiving): $17,183 (76%). Average amount of self-help aid, such as work study or loans (proportion receiving): $5,181 (58%). Average need-based loan (excluding PLUS or other private loans): $4,923. Among students who received need-based aid, the average percentage of need met: 79%. Among students who received aid based on merit, the average award (and the proportion receiving): $9,887 (24%). Average amount of debt of borrowers graduating in 2009: $29,331. Proportion who borrowed: 74%.

CAMPUS LIFE AND EXTRACURRICULAR ACTIVITIES

Campus housing available (% using): coed dorms (24%), women's dorms (34%), men's dorms (21%), apartment for single students (16%), special housing for disabled students, other housing options (5%). Students who live in college-owned, operated, or affiliated housing: 84%. **Student employment:** During the 2009-2010 academic year, 10% of undergraduates worked on campus. Average per-year earnings: $458. **Clubs and organizations:** Number of student organizations: 74. Activities include: campus ministries, choral groups, concert band, dance, drama/theater, international student organization, jazz band, literary magazine, music ensembles, musical theater, pep band, radio station, student government, student newspaper, yearbook. Number of fraternities: 0; sororities: 0. Average proportion of students who stay on campus on weekends: 60%. **Sports program (2009-2010):** Member of NCAA III. **Men's intercollegiate varsity sports:** baseball, basketball, cross country, football, golf, soccer, tennis, track and field (indoor), track and field (outdoor). **Women's intercollegiate varsity sports:** basketball, cross country, equestrian, field hockey, lacrosse, soccer, softball, swimming, tennis, track and field (indoor), track and field (outdoor), volleyball.

SERVICES AND FACILITIES

Basic services: nonremedial tutoring, placement service, health service, health insurance, other. **Counseling services:** minority student, career, personal, academic, psychological, birth control, religious. **For learning-disabled**

students: School does not offer a structured program with separate admission and additional fees. Total undergraduates in learning-disabled program or receiving services: 100. Services include: tape recorders, untimed tests, note-taking services, special bookstore section, readers, extended time for tests, tutors, priority seating, texts on tape. **Library:** Number of titles: 177,520; number of current serial subscriptions: 32,465. **Information technology resources:** Students are not required to lease or own a computer. Number of campus computers available to all students: 193. School has a wireless network. Approximate number of users that can be accommodated: 450. Proportion of college-owned housing units wired for high-speed internet access: 100%. **Campus safety:** Security services offered: 24-hour foot-and-vehicle patrols, 24-hour emergency telephones, lighted pathways/sidewalks, controlled dormitory access (key, security card, etc).

TRANSFER AND INTERNATIONAL STUDENTS

Transfer students: May apply for admission for the following academic terms: Fall, Winter, Spring, Summer. Applicants do not need a minimum number of credits to apply. For fall 2009: Transfer applications received: 105. Transfer applicants offered admission: 95. Transfer applicants enrolled: 55. **International students:** Number of foreign undergraduates: 9 (1% of student body). Number of countries represented: 10. Minimum TOEFL score required: 500 (paper); 173 (computer).

Christopher Newport University

- **Address:** 1 University Place, Newport News, VA 23606
- **Website:** http://www.cnu.edu
- **Public**
- **Enrollment:** 4,620 full-time; 166 part-time

KEY STATS

✔ **U.S News College Ranking:** second tier, National Liberal Arts Colleges
✔ **SAT Score (25th/75th percentile):** 1120-1280
✔ **Tuition:** 2010-2011: $9,250 in state, $17,632 out of state
  Selectivity: More selective   **Room/board:** $9,340
  Acceptance rate: 60%   **Average debt:** $18,285
  Student/faculty ratio: 18/1   **Proportion who borrowed:** 55%

UNDERGRADUATE STUDENT BODY STATS

2009-2010 enrollment: 4,620 full-time; 166 part-time. Men: 44%; women: 56%. **Ethnic makeup:** African American: 8%; American-Indian: 1%; Asian American: 3%; Hispanic: 3%; White: 84%.

ADMISSIONS FACTS AND FIGURES

Phone: (757) 594-7015. **Email:** admit@cnu.edu. **Website:** http://www.cnu.edu. **Application deadlines for fall 2011:** Regular decision: March 1. Early decision: Not offered. Early action: Send application by: December 1; Decision sent by: January 1. Admission can be deferred. **Application fee:** $50. **To apply online, go to:** http://admissions.cnu.edu. **Admissions requirements/recommendations:** High school units required (recommended): English: 4 (4); Mathematics: 4 (4); Science: 3 (4); Foreign language: 3 (4); History: 3 (4); Academic electives: (4); Total units: 23 (23). Tests: The college uses SAT or ACT scores in admissions decisions. Neither SAT nor ACT required. For admission to the fall 2011 entering class, the school will accept: ACT with or without writing accepted. Campus visit: Recommended. Admissions interview: Neither required nor recommended. Off-campus interview: May be arranged. **Factors that count in admissions decisions:** *Academic:* Secondary school record: Very Important. Class rank: Not Considered. Letters of recommendation: Important. Standardized test scores: Considered. Essay: Considered. *Nonacademic:* Interview: Not Considered. Extracurricular activities: Considered. Talent/ability: Considered. Character/personal qualities: Considered. Alumni/ae relationship: Important. Geographical residence: Not Considered. State residency: Not Considered. Religious affiliation/commitment: Not Considered. Minority status: Not Considered. Volunteer work: Considered. Work experience: Considered. **Other schools with the greatest overlap in applicants:** George Mason University; James Madison University; University of Mary Washington; University of Virginia; Virginia Tech. **Admissions statistics for the fall 2009 entering class:** Total applicants: 7,317. Total accepted: 4,422. Freshmen enrolled: 1,213; 9% were from out of state. Overall acceptance rate: 60%. Non-early acceptance rate: 60%. **Size of waiting list:** 750 applicants; enrolled from waiting list: 0. **Credentials of fall 2009 freshmen:** 19% ranked in the top 10 percent of their high school class; 57% were in the top

25 percent; 95% were in the top half. (Proportion submitting class standing: 66%.) **Average high school grade point average:** 3.6. **First-year students who submitted SAT scores:** 64%. Scores (25/75 percentile): Critical Reading: 560-640, Math: 560-640, Combined: 1120-1280. **First-year students submitting ACT scores:** 21%. Scores (25/75 percentile): English: N/A, Math: N/A, Composite: 22-27.

ACADEMICS

Year founded: 1960. **Academic calendar:** Semester. **Degrees offered:** bachelor's, master's. **Most popular majors:** 19% business administration and management, 12% biology/biological sciences, 11% communication studies/speech communication and rhetoric, 10% psychology, 9% political science and government. **Major fields of study:** agriculture, agriculture operations, and related sciences; biological and biomedical sciences; business, management, marketing, and related support services; communication, journalism, and related programs; computer and information sciences and support services; engineering; English language and literature/letters; foreign languages, literatures, and linguistics; history; mathematics and statistics; multi/interdisciplinary studies; natural resources and conservation; philosophy and religious studies; physical sciences; psychology; public administration and social service professions; social sciences; visual and performing arts. **Areas of required coursework:** arts/fine arts, humanities, mathematics, English (including composition), philosophy, foreign languages, sciences (biological or physical), history, social science. **Pre-professional programs:** pre-law, pre-dentistry, pre-medicine, pre-theology, pre-veterinary science, pre-pharmacy, other. **Special academic programs:** cross-registration, double major, dual enrollment, honors program, independent study, internships, student-designed major, study abroad. **Reserve Officers Training Corps (ROTC):** Army ROTC: Offered on campus. **Faculty and instruction (2009-2010):** Total instructional faculty: 236 full-time, 93 part-time (57% men; 43% women; 10% minorities). Full-time faculty with Ph.D. or other terminal degree: 86%. Student/faculty ratio: 18/1. Classes of fewer than 20 students: 23%; of 20 to 49 students: 69%; of 50 or more students: 8%. **Advanced Placement and International Baccalaureate credit:** AP tests may be used for: Credit only. Scores accepted: 3, 4, 5. International Baccalaureate exams may be used for: Credit only. **Freshmen returning for sophomore year:** 80%. **Graduation rates:** Four-year: 39%; five-year: 55%; six-year: 58%. **Graduate study:** 28% of students pursue further study immediately upon graduation.

COSTS AND FINANCIAL AID

Financial aid office: (757) 594-7170. **Expenses (2010-2011):** Tuition and fees 2010-2011: $9,250 in state, $17,632 out of state; room/board: $9,340. Estimated books and supplies: $988; transportation: $1,141; personal expenses: $1,903. **Financial aid:** Priority filing date for institution's financial aid form: March 1. In 2009-2010, 65% of undergraduates applied for financial aid. Of those, 42% were determined to have financial need; 11% had their need fully met. Average financial aid package (proportion receiving): $7,937 (40%). Average amount of gift aid, such as scholarships or grants (proportion receiving): $4,719 (33%). Average amount of self-help aid, such as work study or loans (proportion receiving): $3,928 (35%). Average need-based loan (excluding PLUS or other private loans): $3,849. Among students who received need-based aid, the average percentage of need met: 72%. Among students who received aid based on merit, the average award (and the proportion receiving): $961 (6%). The average athletic scholarship (and the proportion receiving): $0 (0%). Average amount of debt of borrowers graduating in 2009: $18,285. Proportion who borrowed: 55%.

CAMPUS LIFE AND EXTRACURRICULAR ACTIVITIES

Campus housing available (% using): coed dorms (66%), sorority housing (1%), fraternity housing (2%), apartment for single students (27%), special housing for disabled students (1%), other housing options (2%). Students who live in college-owned, operated, or affiliated housing: 61%. **Student employment:** During the 2009-2010 academic year, 20% of undergraduates worked on campus. **Clubs and organizations:** Number of student organizations: 158. Activities include: campus ministries, choral groups, concert band, dance, drama/theater, international student organization, jazz band, literary magazine, marching band, model UN, music ensembles, musical theater, pep band, radio station, student government, student newspaper, student film society, symphony orchestra. Number of fraternities: 7; sororities: 7. Proportion of men in fraternities: 12%; of women in sororities: 15%. Average proportion of students who stay on campus on weekends: 70%. **Sports program (2009-2010):** Member of NCAA III. *Men's intercollegiate varsity sports:* baseball, basketball, cross country, football, golf, lacrosse, soccer, tennis, track and field (indoor), track and field (outdoor). *Women's intercollegiate varsity sports:* basketball, cross country, field hockey, lacrosse, soccer, softball, tennis, track and field (indoor), track and field (outdoor), volleyball.

SERVICES AND FACILITIES

Basic services: health service, other. **Counseling services:** minority student, career, personal, veteran student, academic, religious. **For learning-disabled students:** School does not offer a structured program with separate admission and additional fees. Services include: tape recorders, untimed tests, note-taking services, oral tests, readers, extended time for tests, priority registration. **Library:** Number of titles: 196,638; number of current serial subscriptions: 33,337. **Information technology resources:** Students are not required to lease or own a computer. Number of campus computers available to all students: 414. School has a wireless network. Approximate number of users that can be accommodated: 3,000. Proportion of college-owned housing units wired for high-speed internet access: 100%. **Campus safety:** Security services offered: 24-hour foot-and-vehicle patrols, late-night transport/escort service, 24-hour emergency telephones, lighted pathways/sidewalks, student patrols, controlled dormitory access (key, security card, etc).

TRANSFER AND INTERNATIONAL STUDENTS

Transfer students: May apply for admission for the following academic terms: Fall, Spring. Applicants need a minimum number of credits to apply. For fall 2009: Transfer applications received: 617. Transfer applicants offered admission: 341. Transfer applicants enrolled: 172. **International students:** Number of foreign undergraduates: 18. Number of countries represented: 9. Minimum TOEFL score required: 530 (paper); 71 (computer).

College of William and Mary

- **Address:** PO Box 8795, Williamsburg, VA 23187-8795
- **Website:** http://www.wm.edu
- **Public**
- **Enrollment:** 5,760 full-time; 76 part-time

KEY STATS

✔ **U.S News College Ranking:** 31, National Universities
✔ **SAT Score (25th/75th percentile):** 1240-1450
✔ **Tuition:** 2009-2010: $11,100 in state, $30,902 out of state

Selectivity: Most selective	**Room/board:** $8,502
Acceptance rate: 34%	**Average debt:** $21,544
Student/faculty ratio: 12/1	**Proportion who borrowed:** 38%

UNDERGRADUATE STUDENT BODY STATS

2009-2010 enrollment: 5,760 full-time; 76 part-time. Men: 46%; women: 54%. **Ethnic makeup:** African American: 7%; American-Indian: 1%; Asian American: 8%; Hispanic: 7%; White: 74%; International: 3%.

ADMISSIONS FACTS AND FIGURES

Phone: (757) 221-4223. **Email:** admission@wm.edu. **Website:** http://www.wm.edu. **Application deadlines for fall 2011:** Regular decision: January 1; decision sent by April 1. Early decision: Send application by: November 1; Decision sent by: December 1. Early action: Not offered. Admission can be deferred. **Application fee:** $60. **To apply online, go to:** http://www.wm.edu/admission/application. **Admissions requirements/recommendations:** High school units required (recommended): English: (4); Mathematics: (4); Science: (4); Foreign language: (4); Social studies: (4). Tests: The college uses SAT or ACT scores in admissions decisions. Either SAT or ACT required. For admission to the fall 2011 entering class, the school will accept: ACT with or without writing accepted. Campus visit: Recommended. Admissions interview: Neither required nor recommended. Off-campus interview: Not available. **Factors that count in admissions decisions:** *Academic:* Secondary school record: Very Important. Class rank: Very Important. Letters of recommendation: Very Important. Standardized test scores: Very Important. Essay: Very Important. *Nonacademic:* Interview: Considered. Extracurricular activities: Very Important. Talent/ability: Very Important. Character/personal qualities: Very Important. Alumni/ae relationship: Considered. Geographical residence: Considered. State residency: Very Important. Religious affiliation/commitment: Not Considered. Minority status: Considered. Volunteer work: Very Important. Work experience: Very Important. **Other schools with the greatest overlap in applicants:** Duke University; Georgetown University; University of North Carolina–Chapel Hill; University of Virginia; Virginia Tech. **Admissions statistics for the fall 2009 entering class:** Total applicants: 12,109. Total accepted: 4,058.

Freshmen enrolled: 1,395; 35% were from out of state. Accepted through early-decision or early-action plans: 36%. Overall acceptance rate: 34%. Early-decision acceptance rate: 53%. Non-early acceptance rate: 32%. **Size of waiting list:** 2748 applicants; enrolled from waiting list: 17. **Credentials of fall 2009 freshmen:** 79% ranked in the top 10 percent of their high school class; 98% were in the top 25 percent; 100% were in the top half. (Proportion submitting class standing: 46%.) **Average high school grade point average:** 4.0. **First-year students who submitted SAT scores:** 94%. Scores (25/75 percentile): Critical Reading: 620-730, Math: 620-720, Combined: 1240-1450. **First-year students submitting ACT scores:** 29%. Scores (25/75 percentile): English: 26-32, Math: 28-34, Composite: 27-32.

ACADEMICS

Year founded: 1693. **Academic calendar:** Semester. **Degrees offered:** bachelor's, master's, post-master's certificate, doctorate. **Most popular majors:** 23% social sciences, 12% business administration and management, 10% multi/interdisciplinary studies, 9% psychology, 8% English language and literature. **Major fields of study:** area, ethnic, cultural, and gender studies; biological and biomedical sciences; business, management, marketing, and related support services; computer and information sciences and support services; English language and literature/letters; foreign languages, literatures, and linguistics; history; legal professions and studies; mathematics and statistics; multi/interdisciplinary studies; parks, recreation, leisure, and fitness studies; philosophy and religious studies; physical sciences; psychology; public administration and social service professions; social sciences; visual and performing arts. **Areas of required coursework:** arts/fine arts, humanities, computer literacy, mathematics, English (including composition), philosophy, foreign languages, sciences (biological or physical), history, social science. **Pre-professional programs:** pre-law, pre-medicine, pre-veterinary science, pre-pharmacy, other. **Special academic programs:** accelerated program, double major, dual enrollment, honors program, independent study, internships, student-designed major, study abroad, teacher certificate program. **Teacher certification offered in:** special education, elementary, middle/junior high, secondary. **Reserve Officers Training Corps (ROTC):** Army ROTC: Offered on campus. **Faculty and instruction (2009-2010):** Total instructional faculty: 572 full-time, 224 part-time (61% men; 39% women; 11% minorities). Full-time faculty with Ph.D. or other terminal degree: 94%. Student/faculty ratio: 12/1. Classes of fewer than 20 students: 48%; of 20 to 49 students: 45%; of 50 or more students: 7%. **Advanced Placement and International Baccalaureate credit:** AP tests may be used for: Credit and/or placement. Scores accepted: 3, 4, 5. International Baccalaureate exams may be used for: Credit and/or placement. **Freshmen returning for sophomore year:** 95%. **Graduation rates:** Four-year: 83%; five-year: 90%; six-year: 91%. **Graduate study:** 29% of students pursue further study immediately upon graduation. Fields in which graduates pursue further study: Master of Business Administration (MBA), 7%; law, 16%; medicine, 17%; dentistry, 2%; engineering, 1%; theology (or the seminary), 1%; education, 9%; arts and sciences, 28%; veterinary medicine, 1%.

COSTS AND FINANCIAL AID

Financial aid office: (757) 221-2420. **Expenses (2009-2010):** Tuition and fees 2009-2010: $11,100 in state, $30,902 out of state; room/board: $8,502. Estimated books and supplies: $1,050; transportation: $500; personal expenses: $1,200. **Financial aid:** Priority filing date for institution's financial aid form: March 15; deadline: March 15. In 2009-2010, 52% of undergraduates applied for financial aid. Of those, 33% were determined to have financial need; 17% had their need fully met. Average financial aid package (proportion receiving): $14,220 (33%). Average amount of gift aid, such as scholarships or grants (proportion receiving): N/A (25%). Average amount of self-help aid, such as work study or loans (proportion receiving): $3,682 (27%). Average need-based loan (excluding PLUS or other private loans): $3,275. Among students who received need-based aid, the average percentage of need met: 78%. Among students who received aid based on merit, the average award (and the proportion receiving): $6,221 (5%). The average athletic scholarship (and the proportion receiving): $18,909 (5%). Average amount of debt of borrowers graduating in 2009: $21,544. Proportion who borrowed: 38%.

CAMPUS LIFE AND EXTRACURRICULAR ACTIVITIES

Campus housing available (% using): coed dorms (80%), sorority housing (4%), fraternity housing (5%), apartment for single students (11%), special housing for disabled students, special housing for international students. Students who live in college-owned, operated, or affiliated housing: 74%. **Clubs and organizations:** Number of student organizations: 400. Activities include: campus ministries, choral groups, concert band, dance, drama/theater, international student organization, jazz band, literary magazine, model

UN, music ensembles, musical theater, opera, pep band, radio station, student government, student newspaper, student film society, symphony orchestra, television station, yearbook. Number of fraternities: 18; sororities: 11. Proportion of men in fraternities: 25%; of women in sororities: 29%. Average proportion of students who stay on campus on weekends: 85%. **Sports program (2009-2010):** Member of NCAA I. **Men's intercollegiate varsity sports:** baseball, basketball, cross country, football, golf, gymnastics, soccer, swimming, tennis, track and field (indoor), track and field (outdoor). **Women's intercollegiate varsity sports:** basketball, cross country, field hockey, golf, gymnastics, lacrosse, soccer, swimming, tennis, track and field (indoor), track and field (outdoor), volleyball.

SERVICES AND FACILITIES

Basic services: nonremedial tutoring, placement service, day care, health service, health insurance. **Counseling services:** minority student, career, military, personal, veteran student, academic, older student, psychological, birth control. **For learning-disabled students:** School does not offer a structured program with separate admission and additional fees. Total undergraduates in learning-disabled program or receiving services: 69. Services include: tape recorders, note-taking services, readers, extended time for tests, texts on tape. **Library:** Number of titles: 3,876,585; number of current serial subscriptions: 85,071. **Information technology resources:** Students are required to lease or own a computer. Number of campus computers available to all students: 400. School has a wireless network. Approximate number of users that can be accommodated: 12,000. Proportion of college-owned housing units wired for high-speed internet access: 100%. **Campus safety:** Security services offered: 24-hour foot-and-vehicle patrols, late-night transport/escort service, 24-hour emergency telephones, lighted pathways/sidewalks, student patrols, controlled dormitory access (key, security card, etc).

TRANSFER AND INTERNATIONAL STUDENTS

Transfer students: May apply for admission for the following academic terms: Fall, Spring. Applicants need a minimum number of credits to apply. For fall 2009: Transfer applications received: 776. Transfer applicants offered admission: 339. Transfer applicants enrolled: 174. **International students:** Number of foreign undergraduates: 153 (3% of student body). Number of countries represented: 43. Minimum TOEFL score required: 600 (paper); 100 (computer). Average TOEFL score: 596 (paper).

Eastern Mennonite University

■ **Address:** 1200 Park Road, Harrisonburg, VA 22802-2462
■ **Website:** http://www.emu.edu
■ **Private; Religious affiliation:** Mennonite Church USA
■ **Enrollment:** 994 full-time; 79 part-time

KEY STATS

✔ **U.S News College Ranking:** 181, National Liberal Arts Colleges
✔ **SAT Score (25th/75th percentile):** 930-1220
✔ **Tuition:** 2009-2010: $25,200

Selectivity: Selective	**Room/board:** $8,040
Acceptance rate: 42%	**Average debt:** N/A
Student/faculty ratio: 10/1	**Proportion who borrowed:** N/A

UNDERGRADUATE STUDENT BODY STATS

2009-2010 enrollment: 994 full-time; 79 part-time. Men: 37%; women: 63%. **Ethnic makeup:** African American: 7%; Asian American: 1%; Hispanic: 4%; White: 86%; International: 2%. **Religious preference:** Roman Catholic: 3%; Protestant: 10%; No preference: 10%; Mennonite Church USA: 51%; Baptist: 13%; Other: 13%.

ADMISSIONS FACTS AND FIGURES

Phone: (800) 368-2665. **Email:** admiss@emu.edu. **Website:** http://www.emu.edu. **Application deadlines for fall 2011:** Regular decision: Rolling. Early decision: Not offered. Early action: Not offered. Admission can be deferred. **Application fee:** $25. **To apply online, go to:** http://www.emu.edu/admissions/apply/. **Admissions requirements/recommendations:** High school units required (recommended): English: (4); Mathematics: (3); Science: (3); Foreign language: (2); Social studies: (3); Academic electives: (6); Total units: (21). Tests: The college uses SAT or ACT scores in admissions decisions. Either SAT or ACT required. For admission to the fall 2011 entering class, the school will accept: ACT with writing required. Campus

visit: Recommended. Admissions interview: Recommended. Off-campus interview: May be arranged. **Factors that count in admissions decisions:** *Academic:* Secondary school record: Important. Class rank: Not Considered. Letters of recommendation: Very Important. Standardized test scores: Very Important. Essay: Not Considered. *Nonacademic:* Interview: Considered. Extracurricular activities: Considered. Talent/ability: Considered. Character/personal qualities: Considered. Alumni/ae relationship: Considered. Geographical residence: Not Considered. State residency: Not Considered. Religious affiliation/commitment: Not Considered. Minority status: Not Considered. Volunteer work: Considered. Work experience: Not Considered. **Other schools with the greatest overlap in applicants:** Bridgewater College; Goshen College; Messiah College. **Admissions statistics for the fall 2009 entering class:** Total applicants: 1,318. Total accepted: 549. Freshmen enrolled: 219; 49% were from out of state. Overall acceptance rate: 42%. **Credentials of fall 2009 freshmen:** 17% ranked in the top 10 percent of their high school class; 39% were in the top 25 percent. **Average high school grade point average:** 3.5. **First-year students who submitted SAT scores:** 76%. Scores (25/75 percentile): Critical Reading: 460-600, Math: 470-620, Combined: 930-1220. **First-year students submitting ACT scores:** 23%. Scores (25/75 percentile): English: 21-28, Math: 20-28, Composite: 22-28.

ACADEMICS

Year founded: 1917. **Academic calendar:** Semester. **Degrees offered:** certificate, associate, terminal-associate, bachelor's, post-bachelor's certificate, master's. **Most popular majors:** 15% health professions and related clinical sciences, 10% liberal arts and sciences studies, and humanities, 9% public administration and social service professions, 8% education, 7% business, management, marketing, and related support services. **Major fields of study:** agriculture, agriculture operations, and related sciences; biological and biomedical sciences; business, management, marketing, and related support services; communication, journalism, and related programs; computer and information sciences and support services; education; English language and literature/letters; foreign languages, literatures, and linguistics; health professions and related clinical sciences; history; liberal arts and sciences studies, and humanities; mathematics and statistics; multi/interdisciplinary studies; natural resources and conservation; parks, recreation, leisure, and fitness studies; philosophy and religious studies; physical sciences; psychology; public administration and social service professions; social sciences; theology and religious vocations; visual and performing arts. **Areas of required coursework:** humanities, mathematics, English (including composition), foreign languages, sciences (biological or physical), social science, other. **Pre-professional programs:** pre-law, pre-dentistry, pre-medicine, pre-theology, pre-veterinary science, pre-optometry, pre-pharmacy, other. **Special academic programs (% participation):** distance learning (6%), double major, English as a Second Language (ESL) (1%), honors program (6%), independent study (17%), internships (47%), study abroad (72%), teacher certificate program (13%). **Teacher certification offered in:** early childhood, special education, elementary, middle/junior high, secondary, bilingual/bicultural. **Faculty and instruction (2009-2010):** Total instructional faculty: 97 full-time, 91 part-time (51% men; 49% women; 4% minorities). Full-time faculty with Ph.D. or other terminal degree: 52%. Student/faculty ratio: 10/1. Classes of fewer than 20 students: 70%; of 20 to 49 students: 29%; of 50 or more students: 2%. **Advanced Placement and International Baccalaureate credit:** AP tests may be used for: Credit and/or placement. Scores accepted: 3, 4, 5. International Baccalaureate exams may be used for: Credit and/or placement. **Freshmen returning for sophomore year:** 79%. **Graduation rates:** Four-year: 48%; five-year: 59%; six-year: 62%. **Graduate study:** 6% of students pursue further study immediately upon graduation. Fields in which graduates pursue further study: Master of Business Administration (MBA), 6%; law, 1%; medicine, 9%; theology (or the seminary), 15%; education, 8%; arts and sciences, 61%.

COSTS AND FINANCIAL AID

Financial aid office: (540) 432-4139. **Expenses (2009-2010):** Tuition and fees 2009-2010: $25,200; room/board: $8,040. Estimated books and supplies: $1,000; transportation: $630; personal expenses: $1,000. **Financial aid:** Priority filing date for institution's financial aid form: April 15.

CAMPUS LIFE AND EXTRACURRICULAR ACTIVITIES

Campus housing available (% using): coed dorms (75%), women's dorms (0%), apartments for married students (0%), apartment for single students (24%), special housing for disabled students (0%), other housing options (1%). Students who live in college-owned, operated, or affiliated housing: 69%. **Student employment:** During the 2009-2010 academic year, 6% of undergraduates worked on campus. Average per-year earnings: $1,457. **Clubs and organizations:** Number of student organizations: 35. Activities include: campus ministries, choral groups, dance, drama/theater, international student organization, jazz band, literary magazine, music ensembles, musical theater, student government, student newspaper, student film society, symphony orchestra, yearbook. Number of fraternities: 0; sororities: 0. Average proportion of students who stay on campus on weekends: 80%. **Sports program (2009-2010):** Member of NCAA III. *Men's intercollegiate varsity sports:* baseball, basketball, cross country, soccer, track and field (indoor), track and field (outdoor), volleyball. *Women's intercollegiate varsity sports:* basketball, cross country, field hockey, soccer, softball, track and field (indoor), track and field (outdoor), volleyball.

SERVICES AND FACILITIES

Basic services: nonremedial tutoring, health service. **Remedial assistance:** reading, math, writing, study skills. **Counseling services:** minority student, career, personal, veteran student, academic, older student, psychological, birth control, religious, other. **For learning-disabled students:** School does not offer a structured program with separate admission and additional fees. Services include: remedial English, reading machines, remedial reading, tape recorders, other special classes, videotaped classes, untimed tests, note-taking services, oral tests, learning center, readers, extended time for tests, tutors, priority registration, priority seating, texts on tape, other testing accommodations, other. **Library:** Number of titles: 166,154; number of current serial subscriptions: 861. **Information technology resources:** Students are not required to lease or own a computer. Number of campus computers available to all students: 100. School has a wireless network. Proportion of college-owned housing units wired for high-speed internet access: 100%. **Campus safety:** Security services offered: late-night transport/escort service, 24-hour emergency telephones, lighted pathways/sidewalks, controlled dormitory access (key, security card, etc).

TRANSFER AND INTERNATIONAL STUDENTS

Transfer students: May apply for admission for the following academic terms: Fall, Spring, Summer. Applicants need a minimum number of credits to apply. For fall 2009: Transfer applications received: 203. Transfer applicants offered admission: 130. Transfer applicants enrolled: 73. **International students:** Number of foreign undergraduates: 23 (2% of student body). Number of countries represented: 20. Minimum TOEFL score required: 550 (paper); 79 (computer).

Emory and Henry College

- **Address:** PO Box 947, Emory, VA 24327
- **Website:** http://www.ehc.edu
- **Private; Religious affiliation:** United Methodist
- **Enrollment:** 899 full-time; 73 part-time

KEY STATS

✔ **U.S News College Ranking:** 144, National Liberal Arts Colleges
✔ **SAT Score (25th/75th percentile):** 910-1140
✔ **Tuition:** 2010-2011: $26,000

Selectivity: Selective	**Room/board:** $8,560
Acceptance rate: 70%	**Average debt:** $19,168
Student/faculty ratio: 10/1	**Proportion who borrowed:** 65%

UNDERGRADUATE STUDENT BODY STATS

2009-2010 enrollment: 899 full-time; 73 part-time. Men: 52%; women: 48%. **Ethnic makeup:** African American: 8%; American-Indian: 1%; Hispanic: 1%; White: 88%; International: 1%.

ADMISSIONS FACTS AND FIGURES

Phone: (800) 848-5493. **Email:** ehadmiss@ehc.edu. **Website:** http://www.ehc.edu. **Application deadlines for fall 2011:** Regular decision: Rolling. Early decision: Not offered. Early action: Send application by: December 1; Decision sent by: January 1. Admission can be deferred. **To apply online, go to:** http://www.ehc.edu/admissions/howtoapply.html. **Admissions requirements/recommendations:** High school units required (recommended): English: 4; Mathematics: 3; Science: 2; Foreign language: 2; Social studies: 2; Total units: 15 (1). Tests: The college uses SAT or ACT scores in admissions decisions. Either SAT or ACT required. For admission to the fall 2011 entering class, the school will accept: ACT with writing recommended. Campus visit: Recommended. Admissions interview: Recommended. Off-campus interview: May be arranged. **Factors that count in admissions decisions:** *Academic:* Secondary school record: Very Important. Class rank:

Considered. Letters of recommendation: Very Important. Standardized test scores: Important. Essay: Important. *Nonacademic:* Interview: Very Important. Extracurricular activities: Important. Talent/ability: Important. Character/personal qualities: Very Important. Alumni/ae relationship: Considered. Geographical residence: Important. State residency: Important. Religious affiliation/commitment: Considered. Minority status: Considered. Volunteer work: Important. Work experience: Considered. **Other schools with the greatest overlap in applicants:** East Tennessee State University; Radford University; Roanoke College; University of Virginia–Wise; Virginia Tech. **Admissions statistics for the fall 2009 entering class:** Total applicants: 1,328. Total accepted: 932. Freshmen enrolled: 291; 43% were from out of state. Overall acceptance rate: 70%. Non-early acceptance rate: 70%. **Credentials of fall 2009 freshmen:** 20% ranked in the top 10 percent of their high school class; 43% were in the top 25 percent; 79% were in the top half. (Proportion submitting class standing: 73%.) **Average high school grade point average:** 3.4. **First-year students who submitted SAT scores:** 73%. Scores (25/75 percentile): Critical Reading: 450-570, Math: 460-570, Combined: 910-1140. **First-year students submitting ACT scores:** 27%. Scores (25/75 percentile): English: 18-25, Math: 16-25, Composite: 18-25.

ACADEMICS

Year founded: 1836. **Academic calendar:** Semester. **Degrees offered:** bachelor's, master's. **Most popular majors:** 15% social sciences, 13% business, management, marketing, and related support services, 9% biological and biomedical sciences, 9% visual and performing arts, 8% education. **Major fields of study:** area, ethnic, cultural, and gender studies; biological and biomedical sciences; business, management, marketing, and related support services; communication, journalism, and related programs; computer and information sciences and support services; education; English language and literature/letters; foreign languages, literatures, and linguistics; health professions and related clinical sciences; history; mathematics and statistics; natural resources and conservation; parks, recreation, leisure, and fitness studies; philosophy and religious studies; physical sciences; psychology; public administration and social service professions; social sciences; visual and performing arts. **Areas of required coursework:** arts/fine arts, humanities, computer literacy, mathematics, English (including composition), foreign languages, sciences (biological or physical), history, social science, other. **Pre-professional programs:** pre-law, pre-dentistry, pre-medicine, pre-theology, pre-veterinary science, pre-pharmacy, other. **Special academic programs (% participation):** cooperative (work-study plan) program, distance learning, double major, dual enrollment, honors program, independent study, internships, liberal arts/career combination, student-designed major, study abroad (21%), teacher certificate program. **Teacher certification offered in:** early childhood, elementary, middle/junior high, secondary. **Faculty and instruction (2009-2010):** Total instructional faculty: 75 full-time, 56 part-time (57% men; 43% women; 3% minorities). Full-time faculty with Ph.D. or other terminal degree: 85%. Student/faculty ratio: 10/1. Classes of fewer than 20 students: 75%; of 20 to 49 students: 25%. **Advanced Placement and International Baccalaureate credit:** International Baccalaureate exams may be used for: Credit only. **Freshmen returning for sophomore year:** 67%. **Graduation rates:** Four-year: 47%; five-year: 55%; six-year: 57%. **Graduate study:** 30% of students pursue further study immediately upon graduation. Fields in which graduates pursue further study: Master of Business Administration (MBA), 20%; law, 10%; medicine, 10%; dentistry, 5%; theology (or the seminary), 10%; education, 25%; arts and sciences, 20%.

COSTS AND FINANCIAL AID

Financial aid office: (276) 944-6229. **Expenses (2010-2011):** Tuition and fees 2010-2011: $26,000; room/board: $8,560. Estimated books and supplies: $1,000; transportation: $1,350; personal expenses: $1,300. **Financial aid:** Priority filing date for institution's financial aid form: April 15. In 2009-2010, 92% of undergraduates applied for financial aid. Of those, 82% were determined to have financial need; 27% had their need fully met. Average financial aid package (proportion receiving): $23,244 (82%). Average amount of gift aid, such as scholarships or grants (proportion receiving): $20,989 (65%). Average amount of self-help aid, such as work study or loans (proportion receiving): $4,553 (65%). Average need-based loan (excluding PLUS or other private loans): $4,283. Among students who received need-based aid, the average percentage of need met: 86%. Among students who received aid based on merit, the average award (and the proportion receiving): $11,497 (19%). The average athletic scholarship (and the proportion receiving): $0 (0%). Average amount of debt of borrowers graduating in 2009: $19,168. Proportion who borrowed: 65%.

CAMPUS LIFE AND EXTRACURRICULAR ACTIVITIES

Campus housing available: coed dorms, women's dorms, men's dorms, special housing for disabled students, other housing options. Students who live in college-owned, operated, or affiliated housing: 76%. **Clubs and organizations:** Number of student organizations: 70. Activities include: campus ministries, choral groups, dance, drama/theater, international student organization, jazz band, literary magazine, music ensembles, musical theater, opera, pep band, radio station, student government, student newspaper, television station, yearbook. Number of fraternities: 7; sororities: 6. Proportion of men in fraternities: 14%; of women in sororities: 21%. Average proportion of students who stay on campus on weekends: 65%. **Sports program (2009-2010):** Member of NCAA III. *Men's intercollegiate varsity sports:* baseball, basketball, cross country, football, golf, soccer, tennis. *Women's intercollegiate varsity sports:* basketball, cross country, soccer, softball, swimming, tennis, volleyball.

SERVICES AND FACILITIES

Basic services: nonremedial tutoring, day care, health service, health insurance. **Remedial assistance:** reading, math, writing, study skills. **Counseling services:** minority student, career, military, personal, veteran student, academic, older student, psychological, birth control, religious. **For learning-disabled students:** School does not offer a structured program with separate admission and additional fees. Services include: remedial English, reading machines, tape recorders, untimed tests, note-taking services, oral tests, readers, extended time for tests, tutors, texts on tape, other testing accommodations. **Library:** Number of titles: 251,192; number of current serial subscriptions: 74,890. **Information technology resources:** Students are not required to lease or own a computer. Number of campus computers available to all students: 250. School has a wireless network. Approximate number of users that can be accommodated: 150. Proportion of college-owned housing units wired for high-speed internet access: 100%. **Campus safety:** Security services offered: 24-hour foot-and-vehicle patrols, late-night transport/escort service, 24-hour emergency telephones, lighted pathways/sidewalks, controlled dormitory access (key, security card, etc).

TRANSFER AND INTERNATIONAL STUDENTS

Transfer students: May apply for admission for the following academic terms: Fall, Spring, Summer. Applicants need a minimum number of credits to apply. For fall 2009: Transfer applications received: 154. Transfer applicants offered admission: 84. Transfer applicants enrolled: 51. **International students:** Number of foreign undergraduates: 13 (1% of student body). Number of countries represented: 3. Minimum TOEFL score required: 550 (paper); 213 (computer).

Ferrum College

- **Address:** 215 Ferrum Mountain Road, Ferrum, VA 24088
- **Website:** http://www.ferrum.edu
- **Private; Religious affiliation:** United Methodist
- **Enrollment:** 1,388 full-time; 38 part-time

KEY STATS

✔ **U.S News College Ranking:** second tier, National Liberal Arts Colleges
✔ **SAT Score (25th/75th percentile):** 790-990
✔ **Tuition:** 2010-2011: $24,945

Selectivity: Less selective	**Room/board:** $8,080
Acceptance rate: 80%	**Average debt:** $29,040
Student/faculty ratio: 16/1	**Proportion who borrowed:** 82%

UNDERGRADUATE STUDENT BODY STATS

2009-2010 enrollment: 1,388 full-time; 38 part-time. Men: 51%; women: 49%. **Ethnic makeup:** African American: 31%; American-Indian: 1%; Asian American: 1%; Hispanic: 3%; White: 64%; International: 1%. **Religious preference:** Roman Catholic: 8%; Protestant: 55%; No preference: 2%; United Methodist: 10%; Orthodox: 0%; Other: 25%.

ADMISSIONS FACTS AND FIGURES

Phone: (800) 868-9797. **Email:** admissions@ferrum.edu. **Website:** http://www.ferrum.edu. **Application deadlines for fall 2011:** Regular decision: Rolling. Early decision: Not offered. Early action: Not offered. Admission can be deferred. **Application fee:** $25. **To apply online, go to:** http://www.ferrum.edu/admissions/apply/. **Admissions requirements/recommendations:** High school units required (recommended): English: 4 (4); Mathematics: 3

(3); Science: 2 (2); Foreign language: 0 (2); Social studies: 3 (3); Academic electives: 2 (2); Total units: 22 (24). Tests: The college uses SAT or ACT scores in admissions decisions. Either SAT or ACT required. For admission to the fall 2011 entering class, the school will accept: ACT with or without writing accepted. Campus visit: Recommended. Admissions interview: Recommended. Off-campus interview: May not be arranged. **Factors that count in admissions decisions:** *Academic:* Secondary school record: Considered. Class rank: Considered. Letters of recommendation: Considered. Standardized test scores: Very Important. Essay: Considered. *Nonacademic:* Interview: Considered. Extracurricular activities: Considered. Talent/ability: Considered. Character/personal qualities: Considered. Alumni/ae relationship: Not Considered. Geographical residence: Not Considered. State residency: Not Considered. Religious affiliation/commitment: Not Considered. Minority status: Not Considered. Volunteer work: Considered. Work experience: Considered. **Other schools with the greatest overlap in applicants:** Bridgewater College; Lynchburg College; Radford University; Roanoke College; Virginia Tech. **Admissions statistics for the fall 2009 entering class:** Total applicants: 2,427. Total accepted: 1,932. Freshmen enrolled: 546; 16% were from out of state. Overall acceptance rate: 80%. **Size of waiting list:** 0 applicants; enrolled from waiting list: 0. **Credentials of fall 2009 freshmen:** 4% ranked in the top 10 percent of their high school class; 18% were in the top 25 percent; 49% were in the top half. (Proportion submitting class standing: 78%.) **Average high school grade point average:** 2.8. **First-year students who submitted SAT scores:** 85%. Scores (25/75 percentile): Critical Reading: 390-500, Math: 400-490, Combined: 790-990. **First-year students submitting ACT scores:** 12%. Scores (25/75 percentile): English: N/A, Math: N/A, Composite: 16-21.

ACADEMICS

Year founded: 1913. **Academic calendar:** Semester. **Degrees offered:** bachelor's. **Most popular majors:** 31% health professions and related clinical sciences, 14% business, management, marketing, and related support services, 10% liberal arts and sciences studies, and humanities, 6% security and protective services, 5% parks, recreation, leisure, and fitness studies. **Major fields of study:** agriculture, agriculture operations, and related sciences; biological and biomedical sciences; business, management, marketing, and related support services; computer and information sciences and support services; English language and literature/letters; foreign languages, literatures, and linguistics; health professions and related clinical sciences; history; liberal arts and sciences studies, and humanities; mathematics and statistics; natural resources and conservation; parks, recreation, leisure, and fitness studies; philosophy and religious studies; physical sciences; psychology; public administration and social service professions; security and protective services; social sciences; visual and performing arts. **Areas of required coursework:** arts/fine arts, mathematics, English (including composition), philosophy, sciences (biological or physical), history, social science, other. **Pre-professional programs:** other. **Special academic programs:** double major, dual enrollment, exchange student program (domestic), honors program, independent study, internships, liberal arts/career combination, student-designed major, study abroad, teacher certificate program. **Teacher certification offered in:** special education, elementary, middle/junior high, secondary. **Faculty and instruction (2009-2010):** Total instructional faculty: 69 full-time, 40 part-time (50% men; 50% women; 8% minorities). Full-time faculty with Ph.D. or other terminal degree: 70%. Student/faculty ratio: 16/1. Classes of fewer than 20 students: 60%; of 20 to 49 students: 40%; of 50 or more students: 0%. **Freshmen returning for sophomore year:** 55%. **Graduation rates:** Four-year: 23%; five-year: 34%; six-year: 35%. **Graduate study:** 12% of students pursue further study immediately upon graduation. Fields in which graduates pursue further study: medicine, 38%; engineering, 25%; theology (or the seminary), 12%; education, 12%; arts and sciences, 12%.

COSTS AND FINANCIAL AID

Financial aid office: (540) 365-4282. **Expenses (2010-2011):** Tuition and fees 2010-2011: $24,945; room/board: $8,080. Estimated books and supplies: $900; transportation: $489; personal expenses: $1,200. **Financial aid:** Priority filing date for institution's financial aid form: March 1. In 2009-2010, 95% of undergraduates applied for financial aid. Of those, 88% were determined to have financial need. Average financial aid package (proportion receiving): $19,884 (88%). Average amount of gift aid, such as scholarships or grants (proportion receiving): $14,425 (88%). Average amount of self-help aid, such as work study or loans (proportion receiving): $4,993 (79%). Average need-based loan (excluding PLUS or other private loans): $3,674. Among students who received need-based aid, the average percentage of need met: 88%. Among students who received aid based on merit, the average award (and the proportion receiving): $7,151 (12%). The average athletic scholarship (and the proportion receiving): $0 (0%). Average amount of debt of borrowers graduating in 2009: $29,040. Proportion who borrowed: 82%.

CAMPUS LIFE AND EXTRACURRICULAR ACTIVITIES

Campus housing available (% using): coed dorms (63%), women's dorms (7%), apartments for married students (1%), apartment for single students (13%), special housing for disabled students (1%). Students who live in college-owned, operated, or affiliated housing: 86%. **Student employment:** During the 2009-2010 academic year, 20% of undergraduates worked on campus. Average per-year earnings: $1,000. Activities include: campus ministries, choral groups, concert band, dance, drama/theater, international student organization, jazz band, literary magazine, model UN, music ensembles, musical theater, radio station, student government, student newspaper. Number of fraternities: 4; sororities: 4. Average proportion of students who stay on campus on weekends: 75%. **Sports program (2009-2010):** Member of NCAA III. *Men's intercollegiate varsity sports:* baseball, basketball, cross country, football, golf, soccer, tennis. *Women's intercollegiate varsity sports:* basketball, cross country, lacrosse, soccer, softball, tennis, volleyball.

SERVICES AND FACILITIES

Basic services: nonremedial tutoring, placement service, health service, health insurance. **Remedial assistance:** reading, math, writing, study skills. **Counseling services:** minority student, career, personal, veteran student, academic, psychological, birth control, religious. **For learning-disabled students:** School does not offer a structured program with separate admission and additional fees. Services include: remedial math, remedial English, reading machines, note-taking services, oral tests, learning center, readers, extended time for tests, tutors, texts on tape, typist/scribe, exams on tape or computer, other. **Library:** Number of titles: 114,875; number of current serial subscriptions: 27,695. **Information technology resources:** Students are not required to lease or own a computer. School has a wireless network. Approximate number of users that can be accommodated: 2,000. Proportion of college-owned housing units wired for high-speed internet access: 100%. **Campus safety:** Security services offered: 24-hour foot-and-vehicle patrols, late-night transport/escort service, 24-hour emergency telephones, lighted pathways/sidewalks, controlled dormitory access (key, security card, etc).

TRANSFER AND INTERNATIONAL STUDENTS

Transfer students: May apply for admission for the following academic terms: Fall, Spring. Applicants do not need a minimum number of credits to apply. For fall 2009: Transfer applications received: 245. Transfer applicants offered admission: 122. Transfer applicants enrolled: 61. **International students:** Number of foreign undergraduates: 11 (1% of student body). Number of countries represented: 7. Minimum TOEFL score required: 550 (paper).

George Mason University

- **Address:** 4400 University Drive, Fairfax, VA 22030
- **Website:** http://www.gmu.edu
- **Public**
- **Enrollment:** 15,189 full-time; 4,513 part-time

KEY STATS

✔ **U.S News College Ranking:** 143, National Universities
✔ **SAT Score (25th/75th percentile):** 1030-1250
✔ **Tuition:** 2010-2011: $8,684 in state, $25,448 out of state
  Selectivity: Selective   Room/board: $8,320
  Acceptance rate: 63%   Average debt: $19,528
  Student/faculty ratio: 16/1   Proportion who borrowed: 52%

UNDERGRADUATE STUDENT BODY STATS

2009-2010 enrollment: 15,189 full-time; 4,513 part-time. Men: 47%; women: 53%. **Ethnic makeup:** African American: 8%; Asian American: 16%; Hispanic: 9%; White: 63%; International: 3%.

ADMISSIONS FACTS AND FIGURES

Phone: (703) 993-2400. **Email:** admissions@gmu.edu. **Website:** http://www.gmu.edu. **Application deadlines for fall 2011:** Regular decision: January 15; decision sent by April 1. Early decision: Not offered. Early action: Send application by: November 1; Decision sent by: December 15. Admission can be deferred. **Application fee:** $75. **To apply online, go to:** http://admissions.gmu.edu. **Admissions requirements/recommendations:** High school units required (recommended): English: 4 (4); Mathematics: 3 (4); Science: 3 (4); Foreign language: 2 (3); Social studies: 3 (4); Academic electives: 3 (5); Total units: 18 (23). **Tests:** The college uses SAT or ACT scores in admissions decisions. Neither SAT nor ACT required. For admission to the fall 2011 entering class, the school will accept: ACT with or without writing accepted. Campus visit: Recommended. Admissions interview: Neither required nor recommended. Off-campus interview: Not available. **Factors that count in admissions decisions:** *Academic:* Secondary school record: Very Important. Class rank: Important. Letters of recommendation: Important. Standardized test scores: Considered. Essay: Important. *Nonacademic:* Interview: Not Considered. Extracurricular activities: Considered. Talent/ability: Important. Character/personal qualities: Important. Alumni/ae relationship: Important. Geographical residence: Not Considered. State residency: Not Considered. Religious affiliation/commitment: Not Considered. Minority status: Not Considered. Volunteer work: Considered. Work experience: Considered. **Other schools with the greatest overlap in applicants:** George Washington University; James Madison University; University of Maryland–College Park; University of Virginia; Virginia Tech. **Admissions statistics for the fall 2009 entering class:** Total applicants: 13,732. Total accepted: 8,691. Freshmen enrolled: 2,656; 21% were from out of state. Accepted through early-decision or early-action plans: 27%. Overall acceptance rate: 63%. Non-early acceptance rate: 60%. **Size of waiting list:** 1032 applicants; enrolled from waiting list: 103. **Credentials of fall 2009 freshmen:** 21% ranked in the top 10 percent of their high school class; 57% were in the top 25 percent; 93% were in the top half. (Proportion submitting class standing: 53%.) **Average high school grade point average:** 3.6. **First-year students who submitted SAT scores:** 78%. Scores (25/75 percentile): Critical Reading: 510-620, Math: 520-630, Combined: 1030-1250. **First-year students submitting ACT scores:** 9%. Scores (25/75 percentile): English: 22-28, Math: 21-26, Composite: 23-27.

ACADEMICS

Year founded: 1972. **Academic calendar:** Semester. **Degrees offered:** bachelor's, post-bachelor's certificate, master's, doctorate. **Most popular majors:** 7% psychology, 6% accounting, 6% nursing/registered nurse training (R.N., A.S.N., B.S.N., M.S.N.), 6% political science and government, 6% speech and rhetorical studies. **Major fields of study:** area, ethnic, cultural, and gender studies; biological and biomedical sciences; business, management, marketing, and related support services; communication, journalism, and related programs; computer and information sciences and support services; education; engineering; English language and literature/letters; foreign languages, literatures, and linguistics; health professions and related clinical sciences; history; liberal arts and sciences studies, and humanities; mathematics and statistics; multi/interdisciplinary studies; parks, recreation, leisure, and fitness studies; philosophy and religious studies; physical sciences; psychology; public administration and social service professions; security and protective services; social sciences; visual and performing arts. **Areas of required coursework:** arts/fine arts, humanities, computer literacy, mathematics, English (including composition), philosophy, foreign languages, sciences (biological or physical), history, social science, other. **Pre-professional programs:** pre-law, pre-dentistry, pre-medicine, pre-theology, pre-veterinary science, pre-optometry, pre-pharmacy, other. **Special academic programs:** accelerated program, cooperative (work-study plan) program, cross-registration, distance learning, double major, dual enrollment, English as a Second Language (ESL), external degree program, honors program, independent study, internships, liberal arts/career combination, student-designed major, study abroad, teacher certificate program, other. **Teacher certification offered in:** early childhood, special education, elementary, middle/junior high, adult education, secondary, bilingual/bicultural. **Cooperative education programs:** art, business, computer science, education, engineering, health professions, humanities, natural science, social/behavioral science, technologies. **Reserve Officers Training Corps (ROTC):** Army ROTC: Offered on campus; Air Force ROTC: Offered at cooperating institution (University of Maryland–College Park). **Faculty and instruction (2009-2010):** Total instructional faculty: 1,128 full-time, 1,072 part-time (55% men; 45% women; 17% minorities). Full-time faculty with Ph.D. or other terminal degree: 91%. Student/faculty ratio: 16/1. Classes of fewer than 20 students: 29%; of 20 to 49 students: 54%; of 50 or more students: 17%. **Advanced Placement and International Baccalaureate credit:** AP tests may be used for: Credit and/or placement. Scores accepted: 4, 5. International Baccalaureate exams may be used for: Credit and/or placement. **Freshmen returning for sophomore year:** 85%. **Graduation rates:** Four-year: 39%; five-year: 58%; six-year: 63%.

COSTS AND FINANCIAL AID

Financial aid office: (703) 993-2353. **Expenses (2010-2011):** Tuition and fees 2010-2011: $8,684 in state, $25,448 out of state; room/board: $8,320. Estimated books and supplies: $900; transportation: $1,300; personal expenses: $1,440. **Financial aid:** Priority filing date for institution's financial aid form: March 1. In 2009-2010, 62% of undergraduates applied for financial aid. Of those, 46% were determined to have financial need; 10% had their need fully met. Average financial aid package (proportion receiving): $11,449 (45%). Average amount of gift aid, such as scholarships or grants (proportion receiving): $6,685 (36%). Average amount of self-help aid, such as work study or loans (proportion receiving): $4,722 (37%). Average need-based loan (excluding PLUS or other private loans): $4,454. Among students who received need-based aid, the average percentage of need met: 71%. Among students who received aid based on merit, the average award (and the proportion receiving): $6,171 (2%). The average athletic scholarship (and the proportion receiving): $15,344 (2%). Average amount of debt of borrowers graduating in 2009: $19,528. Proportion who borrowed: 52%.

CAMPUS LIFE AND EXTRACURRICULAR ACTIVITIES

Campus housing available (% using): coed dorms (80%), apartment for single students (19%), special housing for disabled students (0%), other housing options (1%). Students who live in college-owned, operated, or affiliated housing: 26%. Average per-year earnings: $3,825. **Clubs and organizations:** Number of student organizations: 255. Activities include: campus ministries, choral groups, concert band, dance, drama/theater, international student organization, jazz band, literary magazine, model UN, music ensembles, musical theater, opera, pep band, radio station, student government, student newspaper, student film society, symphony orchestra, television station, yearbook. Number of fraternities: 23; sororities: 15. Proportion of men in fraternities: 7%; of women in sororities: 6%. Average proportion of students who stay on campus on weekends: 97%. **Sports program (2009-2010):** Member of NCAA I. *Men's intercollegiate varsity sports:* baseball, basketball, cross country, golf, soccer, swimming, tennis, track and field (indoor), track and field (outdoor), volleyball, wrestling. *Women's intercollegiate varsity sports:* basketball, crew (heavyweight), cross country, lacrosse, soccer, softball, swimming, tennis, track and field (indoor), track and field (outdoor), volleyball.

SERVICES AND FACILITIES

Basic services: nonremedial tutoring, women's center, placement service, day care, health service, health insurance, other. **Remedial assistance:** reading, math, writing, study skills, other. **Counseling services:** minority student, career, military, personal, veteran student, academic, older student, psychological, birth control, religious, other. **For learning-disabled students:** School does not offer a structured program with separate admission and additional fees. Services include: reading machines, tape recorders, note-taking services, oral tests, learning center, readers, extended time for tests, priority registration, priority seating, texts on tape, typist/scribe, exams on tape or computer, other testing accommodations, other. **Library:** Number of titles: 1,867,357; number of current serial subscriptions: 56,433. **Information technology resources:** Students are not required to lease or own a computer. Number of campus computers available to all students: 1,437. School has a wireless network. Approximate number of users that can be accommodated: 25,000. Proportion of college-owned housing units wired for high-speed internet access: 100%. **Campus safety:** Security services offered: 24-hour foot-and-vehicle patrols, late-night transport/escort service, 24-hour emergency telephones, lighted pathways/sidewalks, student patrols, controlled dormitory access (key, security card, etc.).

TRANSFER AND INTERNATIONAL STUDENTS

Transfer students: May apply for admission for the following academic terms: Fall, Spring, Summer. Applicants need a minimum number of credits to apply. For fall 2009: Transfer applications received: 6,199. Transfer applicants offered admission: 4,068. Transfer applicants enrolled: 2,600. **International students:** Number of foreign undergraduates: 589 (3% of student body). Number of countries represented: 94. Minimum TOEFL score required: 570 (paper); 230 (computer).

Hampden-Sydney College

- **Address:** PO Box 667, Hampden-Sydney, VA 23943
- **Website:** http://www.hsc.edu
- **Private; Religious affiliation:** Presbyterian
- **Enrollment:** 1,068 full-time

KEY STATS

✔ **U.S News College Ranking:** 111, National Liberal Arts Colleges
✔ **SAT Score (25th/75th percentile):** 1000-1210
✔ **Tuition:** 2010-2011: $32,364

Selectivity: Selective	**Room/board:** $10,126
Acceptance rate: 56%	**Average debt:** $23,822
Student/faculty ratio: 9/1	**Proportion who borrowed:** 54%

UNDERGRADUATE STUDENT BODY STATS

2009-2010 enrollment: 1,068 full-time. Men: 100%; women: 0%. **Ethnic makeup:** African American: 5%; Asian American: 1%; Hispanic: 1%; White: 91%; International: 2%. **Religious preference:** Roman Catholic: 13%; Protestant: 25%; Jewish: 1%; No preference: 1%; Unknown: 25%; Presbyterian: 11%; Other: 24%.

ADMISSIONS FACTS AND FIGURES

Phone: (800) 755-0733. **Email:** hsapp@hsc.edu. **Website:** http://www.hsc.edu. **Application deadlines for fall 2011:** Regular decision: March 1; decision sent by April 15. Early decision: Send application by: November 15; Decision sent by: December 15. Early action: Send application by: January 15; Decision sent by: February 15. Admission cannot be deferred. **Application fee:** $30. **To apply online, go to:** http://www.hsc.edu/admissions/apply/. **Admissions requirements/recommendations:** High school units required (recommended): English: 4; Mathematics: 3 (4); Science: 2 (3); Foreign language: 2 (3); Social studies: 1; History: 1; Academic electives: 3; Total units: 16. Tests: The college uses SAT or ACT scores in admissions decisions. Either SAT or ACT required. For admission to the fall 2011 entering class, the school will accept: ACT with or without writing accepted. Campus visit: Recommended. Admissions interview: Recommended. Off-campus interview: Not available. **Factors that count in admissions decisions:** *Academic:* Secondary school record: Very Important. Class rank: Important. Letters of recommendation: Very Important. Standardized test scores: Very Important. Essay: Very Important. *Nonacademic:* Interview: Considered. Extracurricular activities: Important. Talent/ability: Considered. Character/personal qualities: Very Important. Alumni/ae relationship: Not Considered. Geographical residence: Not Considered. State residency: Not Considered. Religious affiliation/commitment: Not Considered. Minority status: Not Considered. Volunteer work: Considered. Work experience: Considered. **Other schools with the greatest overlap in applicants:** James Madison University; Randolph-Macon College; University of North Carolina–Chapel Hill; University of Virginia; Virginia Tech. **Admissions statistics for the fall 2009 entering class:** Total applicants: 2,270. Total accepted: 1,272. Freshmen enrolled: 295; 36% were from out of state. Overall acceptance rate: 56%. Non-early acceptance rate: 56%. **Credentials of fall 2009 freshmen:** 15% ranked in the top 10 percent of their high school class; 35% were in the top 25 percent; 63% were in the top half. (Proportion submitting class standing: 73%.) **Average high school grade point average:** 3.2. **First-year students who submitted SAT scores:** 100%. Scores (25/75 percentile): Critical Reading: 500-600, Math: 500-610, Combined: 1000-1210. **First-year students submitting ACT scores:** 10%. Scores (25/75 percentile): English: 20-26, Math: 19-26, Composite: 21-26.

ACADEMICS

Year founded: 1775. **Academic calendar:** Semester. **Degrees offered:** bachelor's. **Major fields of study:** biological and biomedical sciences; business, management, marketing, and related support services; computer and information sciences and support services; English language and literature/letters; foreign languages, literatures, and linguistics; history; liberal arts and sciences studies, and humanities; mathematics and statistics; multi/interdisciplinary studies; philosophy and religious studies; physical sciences; psychology; social sciences; visual and performing arts. **Areas of required coursework:** arts/fine arts, humanities, mathematics, English (including composition), philosophy, foreign languages, sciences (biological or physical), history, social science, other. **Special academic programs (% participation):** cooperative (work-study plan) program (45%), cross-registration (1%), double major (14%), exchange student program (domestic) (1%), honors program (18%), independent study (7%), internships (24%), study abroad

(9%). **Cooperative education programs:** other. **Reserve Officers Training Corps (ROTC):** Army ROTC: Offered at cooperating institution (Longwood University). **Faculty and instruction (2009-2010):** Total instructional faculty: 98 full-time, 21 part-time (71% men; 29% women; 8% minorities). Full-time faculty with Ph.D. or other terminal degree: 87%. Student/faculty ratio: 9/1. Classes of fewer than 20 students: 70%; of 20 to 49 students: 30%; of 50 or more students: 0%. **Advanced Placement and International Baccalaureate credit:** AP tests may be used for: Credit only. Scores accepted: 4. International Baccalaureate exams may be used for: Credit only. **Freshmen returning for sophomore year:** 79%. **Graduation rates:** Four-year: 61%; five-year: 66%; six-year: 66%. **Graduate study:** 21% of students pursue further study immediately upon graduation; 25% within one year; 40% within five years. Fields in which graduates pursue further study: Master of Business Administration (MBA), 22%; law, 24%; medicine, 13%; dentistry, 2%; engineering, 2%; theology (or the seminary), 4%; education, 6%; arts and sciences, 35%; veterinary medicine, 2%.

COSTS AND FINANCIAL AID

Financial aid office: (434) 223-6119. **Expenses (2010-2011):** Tuition and fees 2010-2011: $32,364; room/board: $10,126. Estimated books and supplies: $1,200; transportation: $1,200; personal expenses: $1,100. **Financial aid:** Priority filing date for institution's financial aid form: March 1; deadline: May 1. In 2009-2010, 64% of undergraduates applied for financial aid. Of those, 52% were determined to have financial need; 26% had their need fully met. Average financial aid package (proportion receiving): $23,772 (52%). Average amount of gift aid, such as scholarships or grants (proportion receiving): $18,945 (52%). Average amount of self-help aid, such as work study or loans (proportion receiving): $6,000 (42%). Average need-based loan (excluding PLUS or other private loans): $4,725. Among students who received need-based aid, the average percentage of need met: 80%. Among students who received aid based on merit, the average award (and the proportion receiving): $9,413 (44%). The average athletic scholarship (and the proportion receiving): $0 (0%). Average amount of debt of borrowers graduating in 2009: $23,822. Proportion who borrowed: 54%.

CAMPUS LIFE AND EXTRACURRICULAR ACTIVITIES

Campus housing available (% using): men's dorms (64%), fraternity housing (12%), apartments for married students (1%), apartment for single students (10%), special housing for international students (1%), other housing options (12%). Students who live in college-owned, operated, or affiliated housing: 95%. **Student employment:** During the 2009-2010 academic year, 33% of undergraduates worked on campus. Average per-year earnings: $1,600. **Clubs and organizations:** Number of student organizations: 54. Activities include: campus ministries, choral groups, drama/theater, international student organization, literary magazine, music ensembles, pep band, radio station, student government, student newspaper, yearbook. Number of fraternities: 10; sororities: 0. Proportion of men in fraternities: 34%; Average proportion of students who stay on campus on weekends: 70%. **Sports program (2009-2010):** Member of NCAA III.

SERVICES AND FACILITIES

Basic services: nonremedial tutoring, health service. **Remedial assistance:** math, writing, study skills. **Counseling services:** minority student, career, military, personal, veteran student, academic, older student, psychological, religious. **For learning-disabled students:** School does not offer a structured program with separate admission and additional fees. Services include: reading machines, tape recorders, videotaped classes, note-taking services, oral tests, learning center, extended time for tests, tutors, early syllabus, exams on tape or computer, other. **Library:** Number of titles: 262,890; number of current serial subscriptions: 19,004. **Information technology resources:** Students are not required to lease or own a computer. Number of campus computers available to all students: 160. School has a wireless network. Approximate number of users that can be accommodated: 10,000. Proportion of college-owned housing units wired for high-speed internet access: 98%. **Campus safety:** Security services offered: 24-hour foot-and-vehicle patrols, 24-hour emergency telephones, lighted pathways/sidewalks.

TRANSFER AND INTERNATIONAL STUDENTS

Transfer students: May apply for admission for the following academic terms: Fall, Spring. Applicants need a minimum number of credits to apply. For fall 2009: Transfer applications received: 51. Transfer applicants offered admission: 25. Transfer applicants enrolled: 15. **International students:** Number of foreign undergraduates: 15 (2% of student body). Number of countries represented: 18. Minimum TOEFL score required: 570 (paper); 230 (computer). Average TOEFL score: 590 (paper).

Hampton University

- **Address:** Tyler Street, Hampton, VA 23668
- **Website:** http://www.hamptonu.edu
- **Private**
- **Enrollment:** 4,236 full-time; 329 part-time

KEY STATS

✔ **U.S News College Ranking:** 32, Regional Universities (South)
✔ **SAT Score (25th/75th percentile):** 959-1182
✔ **Tuition:** 2010-2011: $18,074

Selectivity: Selective	**Room/board:** $8,048
Acceptance rate: 47%	**Average debt:** N/A
Student/faculty ratio: 12/1	**Proportion who borrowed:** N/A

UNDERGRADUATE STUDENT BODY STATS

2009-2010 enrollment: 4,236 full-time; 329 part-time. Men: 36%; women: 64%. **Ethnic makeup:** African American: 96%; Hispanic: 1%; White: 2%; International: 1%. **Religious preference:** Roman Catholic: 8%; Protestant: 75%; Muslim: 8%; No preference: 8%; Other: 1%.

ADMISSIONS FACTS AND FIGURES

Phone: (757) 727-5328. **Email:** admissions@hamptonu.edu. **Website:** http://www.hamptonu.edu. **Application deadlines for fall 2011:** Regular decision: March 1. Early decision: Not offered. Early action: Send application by: December 1; Decision sent by: December 15. Admission can be deferred. **Application fee:** $35. **To apply online, go to:** http://www.hamptonu.edu/studentservices/admissions/apply.htm. **Admissions requirements/recommendations:** High school units required (recommended): English: 4 (4); Mathematics: 3 (3); Science: 2 (2); Foreign language: (2); Social studies: 2 (2); Academic electives: 6 (6); Total units: 17 (17). Tests: The college uses SAT or ACT scores in admissions decisions. Either SAT or ACT required. For admission to the fall 2011 entering class, the school will accept: ACT with or without writing accepted. Campus visit: Recommended. Admissions interview: Neither required nor recommended. Off-campus interview: May be arranged. **Factors that count in admissions decisions:** *Academic:* Secondary school record: Very Important. Class rank: Important. Letters of recommendation: Important. Standardized test scores: Very Important. Essay: Very Important. *Nonacademic:* Interview: Considered. Extracurricular activities: Considered. Talent/ability: Considered. Character/personal qualities: Very Important. Alumni/ae relationship: Not Considered. Geographical residence: Not Considered. State residency: Not Considered. Religious affiliation/commitment: Not Considered. Minority status: Not Considered. Volunteer work: Considered. Work experience: Considered. **Other schools with the greatest overlap in applicants:** Howard University; Norfolk State University; North Carolina A&T State University; Old Dominion University; University of Virginia. **Admissions statistics for the fall 2009 entering class:** Total applicants: 8,119. Total accepted: 3,789. Freshmen enrolled: 1,039; 54% were from out of state. Accepted through early-decision or early-action plans: 22%. Overall acceptance rate: 47%. Non-early acceptance rate: 54%. **Credentials of fall 2009 freshmen:** 5% ranked in the top 10 percent of their high school class; 27% were in the top 25 percent; 56% were in the top half. (Proportion submitting class standing: 89%.) **Average high school grade point average:** 3.3. **First-year students who submitted SAT scores:** 61%. Scores (25/75 percentile): Critical Reading: 482-614, Math: 477-568, Combined: 959-1182. **First-year students submitting ACT scores:** 39%. Scores (25/75 percentile): English: 15-29, Math: 17-27, Composite: 16-28.

ACADEMICS

Year founded: 1868. **Academic calendar:** Semester. **Degrees offered:** associate, bachelor's, master's, doctorate. **Most popular majors:** 1% biological and biomedical sciences, 1% business, management, marketing, and related support services, 0% health professions and related clinical sciences, 0% psychology. **Major fields of study:** architecture and related services; biological and biomedical sciences; business, management, marketing, and related support services; communication, journalism, and related programs; communications technologies/technicians and support services; computer and information sciences and support services; engineering; English language and literature/letters; foreign languages, literatures, and linguistics; health professions and related clinical sciences; history; mathematics and statistics; mechanic and repair technologies/technicians; natural resources and conservation; parks, recreation, leisure, and fitness studies; physical sciences; psychology; public administration and social service professions; social sciences; transportation and materials moving; visual and performing arts.

Areas of required coursework: arts/fine arts, humanities, computer literacy, mathematics, English (including composition), foreign languages, sciences (biological or physical), history, social science, other. **Pre-professional programs:** pre-law, pre-medicine, pre-pharmacy. **Special academic programs (% participation):** accelerated program (25%), cooperative (work-study plan) program (33%), cross-registration, distance learning (12%), double major (15%), dual enrollment (8%), honors program (29%), independent study (76%), internships (88%), study abroad, teacher certificate program. **Teacher certification offered in:** early childhood, special education, elementary, middle/junior high. **Cooperative education programs:** art, business, computer science, education, engineering, health professions, humanities, natural science, social/behavioral science, technologies, other. **Reserve Officers Training Corps (ROTC):** Army ROTC: Offered on campus; Navy ROTC: Offered on campus. **Faculty and instruction (2009-2010):** Total instructional faculty: 347 full-time, 119 part-time (55% men; 45% women; 78% minorities). Full-time faculty with Ph.D. or other terminal degree: 81%. Student/faculty ratio: 12/1. Classes of fewer than 20 students: 51%; of 20 to 49 students: 44%; of 50 or more students: 5%. **Advanced Placement and International Baccalaureate credit:** AP tests may be used for: Credit and/or placement. Scores accepted: 3, 4, 5. International Baccalaureate exams may be used for: Placement only. **Freshmen returning for sophomore year:** 78%. **Graduation rates:** Four-year: 38%; five-year: 51%; six-year: 54%. **Graduate study:** 48% of students pursue further study immediately upon graduation; 10% within one year; 42% within five years. Fields in which graduates pursue further study: Master of Business Administration (MBA), 30%; law, 5%; medicine, 10%; engineering, 2%; education, 20%.

COSTS AND FINANCIAL AID

Financial aid office: (800) 624-3341. **Expenses (2010-2011):** Tuition and fees 2010-2011: $18,074; room/board: $8,048. Estimated books and supplies: $1,025; transportation: $1,750; personal expenses: $1,423. **Financial aid:** Priority filing date for institution's financial aid form: March 1; deadline: April 30. In 2009-2010, 54% of undergraduates applied for financial aid. Of those, 45% were determined to have financial need; 35% had their need fully met. Average financial aid package (proportion receiving): $4,545 (41%). Average amount of gift aid, such as scholarships or grants (proportion receiving): $3,349 (38%). Average amount of self-help aid, such as work study or loans (proportion receiving): $3,212 (34%). Average need-based loan (excluding PLUS or other private loans): $3,214. Among students who received need-based aid, the average percentage of need met: 41%. Among students who received aid based on merit, the average award (and the proportion receiving): $8,442 (3%). The average athletic scholarship (and the proportion receiving): $17,572 (2%).

CAMPUS LIFE AND EXTRACURRICULAR ACTIVITIES

Campus housing available (% using): coed dorms (6%), women's dorms (63%), men's dorms (31%). Students who live in college-owned, operated, or affiliated housing: 68%. **Student employment:** During the 2009-2010 academic year, 1% of undergraduates worked on campus. Average per-year earnings: $1,500. **Clubs and organizations:** Number of student organizations: 96. Activities include: campus ministries, choral groups, concert band, dance, drama/theater, international student organization, jazz band, literary magazine, marching band, model UN, music ensembles, musical theater, opera, pep band, radio station, student government, student newspaper, student film society, symphony orchestra, television station, yearbook. Number of fraternities: 6; sororities: 3. Proportion of men in fraternities: 5%; of women in sororities: 4%. Average proportion of students who stay on campus on weekends: 68%. **Sports program (2009-2010):** Member of NCAA I. *Men's intercollegiate varsity sports:* basketball, cross country, football, golf, tennis, track and field (indoor), track and field (outdoor). *Women's intercollegiate varsity sports:* basketball, bowling, cross country, golf, softball, tennis, track and field (indoor), track and field (outdoor), volleyball.

SERVICES AND FACILITIES

Basic services: nonremedial tutoring, placement service, day care, health service, health insurance. **Remedial assistance:** reading, math, writing, study skills. **Counseling services:** career, military, personal, veteran student, academic, older student, psychological, religious. **For learning-disabled students:** School does not offer a structured program with separate admission and additional fees. Total undergraduates in learning-disabled program or receiving services: 45. Services include: remedial math, remedial English, remedial reading, tape recorders, untimed tests, note-taking services, oral tests, readers, extended time for tests, tutors, early syllabus, priority registration, priority seating, substitution of courses, other testing accommodations, waiver of foreign language degree requirement, waiver of math degree

requirement, other. **Library:** Number of titles: 265,000; number of current serial subscriptions: 1,100. **Information technology resources:** Students are not required to lease or own a computer. Number of campus computers available to all students: 1,500. School has a wireless network. Approximate number of users that can be accommodated: 2,500. Proportion of college-owned housing units wired for high-speed internet access: 100%. **Campus safety:** Security services offered: 24-hour foot-and-vehicle patrols, 24-hour emergency telephones, lighted pathways/sidewalks, controlled dormitory access (key, security card, etc).

TRANSFER AND INTERNATIONAL STUDENTS

Transfer students: May apply for admission for the following academic terms: Fall, Spring. Applicants need a minimum number of credits to apply. For fall 2009: Transfer applications received: 1,127. Transfer applicants offered admission: 384. Transfer applicants enrolled: 186. **International students:** Number of foreign undergraduates: 40 (1% of student body). Minimum TOEFL score required: 550 (paper). Average TOEFL score: 575 (paper).

Hollins University

- **Address:** PO Box 9707, Roanoke, VA 24020
- **Website:** http://www.hollins.edu
- **Private**
- **Enrollment:** 763 full-time; 33 part-time

KEY STATS

✔ **U.S News College Ranking:** 105, National Liberal Arts Colleges
✔ **SAT Score (25th/75th percentile):** 960-1230
✔ **Tuition:** 2010-2011: $29,475

Selectivity: Selective	**Room/board:** $10,200
Acceptance rate: 90%	**Average debt:** $24,002
Student/faculty ratio: 11/1	**Proportion who borrowed:** 83%

UNDERGRADUATE STUDENT BODY STATS

2009-2010 enrollment: 763 full-time; 33 part-time. Men: 1%; women: 99%. **Ethnic makeup:** African American: 8%; American-Indian: 1%; Asian American: 2%; Hispanic: 4%; White: 82%; International: 4%. **Religious preference:** Roman Catholic: 14%; Protestant: 29%; Jewish: 2%; Muslim: 1%; Hindu: 1%; Buddhist: 2%; No preference: 16%; Non-Denominational: 21%; Other: 14%.

ADMISSIONS FACTS AND FIGURES

Phone: (800) 456-9595. **Email:** huadm@hollins.edu. **Website:** http://www.hollins.edu. **Application deadlines for fall 2011:** Regular decision: Rolling. Early decision: Send application by: December 1; Decision sent by: December 15. Early action: Not offered. Admission can be deferred. **Application fee:** $40. **To apply online, go to:** http://www.hollins.edu/admissions/apply/apply.htm. **Admissions requirements/recommendations:** High school units required (recommended): English: 4 (4); Mathematics: 3 (3); Science: 3 (3); Foreign language: 3 (3); Social studies: 3 (3); History: 0 (3); Academic electives: 0; Total units: 16. Tests: The college uses SAT or ACT scores in admissions decisions. Either SAT or ACT required. For admission to the fall 2011 entering class, the school will accept: ACT with or without writing accepted. Campus visit: Recommended. Admissions interview: Recommended. Off-campus interview: May be arranged. **Factors that count in admissions decisions:** *Academic:* Secondary school record: Considered. Class rank: Considered. Letters of recommendation: Important. Standardized test scores: Very Important. Essay: Important. *Nonacademic:* Interview: Considered. Extracurricular activities: Considered. Talent/ability: Important. Character/personal qualities: Considered. Alumni/ae relationship: Considered. Geographical residence: Not Considered. State residency: Not Considered. Religious affiliation/commitment: Not Considered. Minority status: Not Considered. Volunteer work: Considered. Work experience: Considered. **Other schools with the greatest overlap in applicants:** James Madison University; Randolph College; Roanoke College; Sweet Briar College; University of Mary Washington. **Admissions statistics for the fall 2009 entering class:** Total applicants: 693. Total accepted: 625. Freshmen enrolled: 198; 48% were from out of state. Accepted through early-decision or early-action plans: 16%. Overall acceptance rate: 90%. Early-decision acceptance rate: 66%. Non-early acceptance rate: 93%. **Size of waiting list:** 26 applicants; enrolled from waiting list: 0. **Credentials of fall 2009 freshmen:** 23% ranked in the top 10 percent of their high school class; 55% were in the top 25 percent; 83% were in the top half. (Proportion submitting class standing: 73%.) **Average high school grade point average:** 3.5. **First-year students who submitted SAT scores:** 77%. Scores (25/75 percentile): Critical Reading: 510-660, Math: 450-570, Combined: 960-1230. **First-year students submitting ACT scores:** 35%. Scores (25/75 percentile): English: N/A, Math: N/A, Composite: 22-28.

ACADEMICS

Year founded: 1842. **Academic calendar:** 4-1-4. **Degrees offered:** bachelor's, master's, post-master's certificate. **Most popular majors:** 19% English language and literature/letters, 16% visual and performing arts, 14% social sciences, 11% psychology, 8% business, management, marketing, and related support services. **Major fields of study:** area, ethnic, cultural, and gender studies; biological and biomedical sciences; business, management, marketing, and related support services; communication, journalism, and related programs; English language and literature/letters; foreign languages, literatures, and linguistics; history; mathematics and statistics; multi/interdisciplinary studies; natural resources and conservation; philosophy and religious studies; physical sciences; psychology; social sciences; visual and performing arts. **Areas of required coursework:** computer literacy, mathematics, English (including composition), foreign languages, sciences (biological or physical). **Pre-professional programs:** pre-law, pre-medicine, pre-veterinary science. **Special academic programs (% participation):** accelerated program (1%), cross-registration (2%), double major (13%), dual enrollment, exchange student program (domestic), independent study (63%), internships (69%), student-designed major (1%), study abroad (27%), teacher certificate program. **Teacher certification offered in:** elementary, middle/junior high, secondary. **Faculty and instruction (2009-2010):** Total instructional faculty: 72 full-time, 26 part-time (49% men; 51% women; 8% minorities). Full-time faculty with Ph.D. or other terminal degree: 97%. Student/faculty ratio: 11/1. Classes of fewer than 20 students: 86%; of 20 to 49 students: 14%. **Advanced Placement and International Baccalaureate credit:** AP tests may be used for: Credit only. Scores accepted: 4, 5. International Baccalaureate exams may be used for: Credit and/or placement. **Freshmen returning for sophomore year:** 73%. **Graduation rates:** Four-year: 60%; five-year: 64%; six-year: 65%. **Graduate study:** 34% of students pursue further study within one year. Fields in which graduates pursue further study: law, 2%; medicine, 7%; theology (or the seminary), 2%; education, 10%; arts and sciences, 2%; veterinary medicine, 5%.

COSTS AND FINANCIAL AID

Financial aid office: (540) 362-6332. **Expenses (2010-2011):** Tuition and fees 2010-2011: $29,475; room/board: $10,200. Estimated books and supplies: $1,000; transportation: $1,000; personal expenses: $1,000. **Financial aid:** Priority filing date for institution's financial aid form: February 15. In 2009-2010, 89% of undergraduates applied for financial aid. Of those, 79% were determined to have financial need; 13% had their need fully met. Average financial aid package (proportion receiving): $22,059 (79%). Average amount of gift aid, such as scholarships or grants (proportion receiving): $16,471 (79%). Average amount of self-help aid, such as work study or loans (proportion receiving): $6,603 (66%). Average need-based loan (excluding PLUS or other private loans): $5,240. Among students who received need-based aid, the average percentage of need met: 84%. Among students who received aid based on merit, the average award (and the proportion receiving): $11,994 (21%). The average athletic scholarship (and the proportion receiving): $0 (0%). Average amount of debt of borrowers graduating in 2009: $24,002. Proportion who borrowed: 83%.

CAMPUS LIFE AND EXTRACURRICULAR ACTIVITIES

Campus housing available (% using): women's dorms (62%), apartment for single students (16%), special housing for disabled students, special housing for international students (4%), other housing options (5%). Students who live in college-owned, operated, or affiliated housing: 78%. **Clubs and organizations:** Number of student organizations: 32. Activities include: campus ministries, choral groups, dance, drama/theater, international student organization, literary magazine, model UN, music ensembles, musical theater, student government, student newspaper, student film society, television station, yearbook. Number of fraternities: 0; sororities: 0. Average proportion of students who stay on campus on weekends: 40%. **Sports program (2009-2010):** Member of NCAA III. *Women's intercollegiate varsity sports:* basketball, equestrian, golf, lacrosse, soccer, swimming, tennis, volleyball.

SERVICES AND FACILITIES

Basic services: nonremedial tutoring, placement service, health service, health insurance. **Remedial assistance:** reading, math, writing, study skills.

Counseling services: minority student, career, personal, academic, older student, psychological, birth control, religious. **For learning-disabled students:** School does not offer a structured program with separate admission and additional fees. Total undergraduates in learning-disabled program or receiving services: 23. Services include: tape recorders, untimed tests, note-taking services, oral tests, learning center, readers, extended time for tests, tutors, texts on tape, other testing accommodations, other. **Library:** Number of titles: 236,427; number of current serial subscriptions: 31,032. **Information technology resources:** Students are not required to lease or own a computer. Number of campus computers available to all students: 113. School has a wireless network. Approximate number of users that can be accommodated: 400. Proportion of college-owned housing units wired for high-speed internet access: 100%. **Campus safety:** Security services offered: 24-hour foot-and-vehicle patrols, late-night transport/escort service, 24-hour emergency telephones, lighted pathways/sidewalks, controlled dormitory access (key, security card, etc).

TRANSFER AND INTERNATIONAL STUDENTS

Transfer students: May apply for admission for the following academic terms: Fall, Spring. Applicants do not need a minimum number of credits to apply. For fall 2009: Transfer applications received: 67. Transfer applicants offered admission: 48. Transfer applicants enrolled: 25. **International students:** Number of foreign undergraduates: 31 (4% of student body). Number of countries represented: 11. Minimum TOEFL score required: 550 (paper); 213 (computer). Average TOEFL score: 567 (paper).

James Madison University

- **Address:** 800 S. Main Street, Harrisonburg, VA 22807
- **Website:** http://www.jmu.edu
- **Public**
- **Enrollment:** 16,489 full-time; 792 part-time

KEY STATS

✔ **U.S News College Ranking:** 3, Regional Universities (South)
✔ **SAT Score (25th/75th percentile):** 1050-1240
✔ **Tuition:** 2010-2011: $7,860 in state, $20,624 out of state
  Selectivity: More selective **Room/board:** $8,020
  Acceptance rate: 61% **Average debt:** $18,183
  Student/faculty ratio: 16/1 **Proportion who borrowed:** 51%

UNDERGRADUATE STUDENT BODY STATS

2009-2010 enrollment: 16,489 full-time; 792 part-time. Men: 40%; women: 60%. **Ethnic makeup:** African American: 4%; Asian American: 5%; Hispanic: 3%; White: 87%; International: 1%. **Religious preference:** Roman Catholic: 32%; Protestant: 26%; Jewish: 2%; No preference: 23%; Unknown: 4%; Other: 13%.

ADMISSIONS FACTS AND FIGURES

Phone: (540) 568-5681. **Email:** admissions@jmu.edu. **Website:** http://www.jmu.edu. **Application deadlines for fall 2011:** Regular decision: January 15; decision sent by April 1. Early decision: Not offered. Early action: Send application by: November 1; Decision sent by: January 15. Admission can be deferred. **Application fee:** $50. **To apply online, go to:** http://www.jmu.edu/admissions. **Admissions requirements/recommendations:** High school units required (recommended): English: 4 (4); Mathematics: 4 (4); Science: 3 (4); Foreign language: 2 (3); Social studies: 3 (4). Tests: The college uses SAT or ACT scores in admissions decisions. Either SAT or ACT required. For admission to the fall 2011 entering class, the school will accept: ACT with or without writing accepted. Campus visit: Neither required nor recommended. Admissions interview: Neither required nor recommended. Off-campus interview: Not available. **Factors that count in admissions decisions:** *Academic:* Secondary school record: Very Important. Class rank: Considered. Letters of recommendation: Considered. Standardized test scores: Important. Essay: Considered. *Nonacademic:* Interview: Not Considered. Extracurricular activities: Considered. Talent/ability: Considered. Character/personal qualities: Considered. Alumni/ae relationship: Considered. Geographical residence: Considered. State residency: Considered. Religious affiliation/commitment: Not Considered. Minority status: Not Considered. Volunteer work: Considered. Work experience: Considered. **Other schools with the greatest overlap in applicants:** George Mason University; Pennsylvania State University–University Park; University of Delaware; University of Virginia; Virginia Tech. **Admissions**

statistics for the fall 2009 entering class: Total applicants: 20,963. Total accepted: 12,872. Freshmen enrolled: 3,952; 33% were from out of state. Overall acceptance rate: 61%. Non-early acceptance rate: 61%. **Size of waiting list:** 2867 applicants; enrolled from waiting list: 498. **Credentials of fall 2009 freshmen:** 28% ranked in the top 10 percent of their high school class; 72% were in the top 25 percent; 98% were in the top half. (Proportion submitting class standing: 57%.) **Average high school grade point average:** 3.8. **First-year students who submitted SAT scores:** 97%. Scores (25/75 percentile): Critical Reading: 520-610, Math: 530-630, Combined: 1050-1240. **First-year students submitting ACT scores:** 31%. Scores (25/75 percentile): English: N/A, Math: N/A, Composite: 22-27.

ACADEMICS

Year founded: 1908. **Academic calendar:** Semester. **Degrees offered:** bachelor's, master's, post-master's certificate, doctorate. **Most popular majors:** 21% business, management, marketing, and related support services, 13% health professions and related clinical sciences, 9% communication, journalism, and related programs, 9% social sciences, 6% liberal arts and sciences studies, and humanities. **Major fields of study:** biological and biomedical sciences; business, management, marketing, and related support services; communication, journalism, and related programs; computer and information sciences and support services; education; English language and literature/letters; family and consumer sciences/human sciences; foreign languages, literatures, and linguistics; health professions and related clinical sciences; history; legal professions and studies; liberal arts and sciences studies, and humanities; mathematics and statistics; multi/interdisciplinary studies; parks, recreation, leisure, and fitness studies; philosophy and religious studies; physical sciences; psychology; public administration and social service professions; social sciences; visual and performing arts. **Areas of required coursework:** arts/fine arts, humanities, mathematics, English (including composition), philosophy, sciences (biological or physical), history, social science, other. **Pre-professional programs:** pre-law, predentistry, pre-medicine, pre-theology, pre-veterinary science, pre-optometry, pre-pharmacy, other. **Special academic programs:** accelerated program, distance learning, double major, English as a Second Language (ESL), honors program, independent study, internships, study abroad, teacher certificate program, other. **Teacher certification offered in:** early childhood, special education, elementary, middle/junior high, secondary. **Cooperative education programs:** other. **Reserve Officers Training Corps (ROTC):** Army ROTC: Offered on campus; Air Force ROTC: Offered at cooperating institution (University of Virginia). **Faculty and instruction (2009-2010):** Total instructional faculty: 906 full-time, 434 part-time (52% men; 48% women; 6% minorities). Full-time faculty with Ph.D. or other terminal degree: 78%. Student/faculty ratio: 16/1. Classes of fewer than 20 students: 29%; of 20 to 49 students: 57%; of 50 or more students: 14%. **Advanced Placement and International Baccalaureate credit:** International Baccalaureate exams may be used for: Credit only. **Freshmen returning for sophomore year:** 92%. **Graduation rates:** Four-year: 64%; five-year: 79%; six-year: 81%. **Graduate study:** 27% of students pursue further study immediately upon graduation. Fields in which graduates pursue further study: Master of Business Administration (MBA), 13%; law, 5%; medicine, 2%; dentistry, 1%; engineering, 1%; education, 29%; arts and sciences, 50%.

COSTS AND FINANCIAL AID

Financial aid office: (540) 568-7820. **Expenses (2010-2011):** Tuition and fees 2010-2011: $7,860 in state, $20,624 out of state; room/board: $8,020. Estimated books and supplies: $876; transportation: $1,942; personal expenses: $1,854. **Financial aid:** Priority filing date for institution's financial aid form: March 1. In 2009-2010, 92% of undergraduates applied for financial aid. Of those, 40% were determined to have financial need; 62% had their need fully met. Average financial aid package (proportion receiving): $7,885 (34%). Average amount of gift aid, such as scholarships or grants (proportion receiving): $7,055 (15%). Average amount of self-help aid, such as work study or loans (proportion receiving): $4,255 (27%). Average need-based loan (excluding PLUS or other private loans): $4,189. Among students who received need-based aid, the average percentage of need met: 51%. Among students who received aid based on merit, the average award (and the proportion receiving): $3,056 (1%). The average athletic scholarship (and the proportion receiving): $14,938 (2%). Average amount of debt of borrowers graduating in 2009: $18,183. Proportion who borrowed: 51%.

CAMPUS LIFE AND EXTRACURRICULAR ACTIVITIES

Campus housing available (% using): coed dorms (87%), sorority housing (4%), fraternity housing, apartment for single students (1%), other housing options (8%). Students who live in college-owned, operated, or affiliated housing: 37%. **Student employment:** During the 2009-2010 academic year,

20% of undergraduates worked on campus. Average per-year earnings: $2,160. **Clubs and organizations:** Number of student organizations: 298. Activities include: campus ministries, choral groups, concert band, dance, drama/theater, international student organization, jazz band, literary magazine, marching band, music ensembles, musical theater, opera, pep band, radio station, student government, student newspaper, student film society, symphony orchestra, yearbook. Number of fraternities: 15; sororities: 9. Proportion of men in fraternities: 10%; of women in sororities: 12%. Average proportion of students who stay on campus on weekends: 72%. **Sports program (2009-2010):** Member of NCAA I. *Men's intercollegiate varsity sports:* baseball, basketball, football, golf, soccer, tennis. *Women's intercollegiate varsity sports:* basketball, cross country, field hockey, golf, lacrosse, soccer, softball, swimming, tennis, track and field (indoor), track and field (outdoor), volleyball.

SERVICES AND FACILITIES

Basic services: nonremedial tutoring, women's center, placement service, health service, health insurance, other. **Counseling services:** minority student, career, personal, veteran student, academic, older student, psychological, other. **For learning-disabled students:** School does not offer a structured program with separate admission and additional fees. Total undergraduates in learning-disabled program or receiving services: 200. **Library:** Number of titles: 645,741; number of current serial subscriptions: 12,830. **Information technology resources:** Students are not required to lease or own a computer. Number of campus computers available to all students: 1,738. School has a wireless network. Approximate number of users that can be accommodated: 1,500. Proportion of college-owned housing units wired for high-speed internet access: 100%. **Campus safety:** Security services offered: 24-hour foot-and-vehicle patrols, late-night transport/escort service, 24-hour emergency telephones, lighted pathways/sidewalks, student patrols, controlled dormitory access (key, security card, etc).

TRANSFER AND INTERNATIONAL STUDENTS

Transfer students: May apply for admission for the following academic terms: Fall, Spring, Summer. Applicants need a minimum number of credits to apply. For fall 2009: Transfer applications received: 2,178. Transfer applicants offered admission: 1,144. Transfer applicants enrolled: 683. **International students:** Number of foreign undergraduates: 207 (1% of student body). Number of countries represented: 60. Minimum TOEFL score required: 550 (paper); 213 (computer).

Liberty University

- **Address:** 1971 University Boulevard, Lynchburg, VA 24502-2269
- **Website:** http://www.liberty.edu
- **Private; Religious affiliation:** Southern Baptist
- **Enrollment:** 18,405 full-time; 10,581 part-time

KEY STATS

✔ **U.S News College Ranking:** second tier, Regional Universities (South)
✔ **SAT Score (25th/75th percentile):** 880-1130
✔ **Tuition:** 2009-2010: $17,742

Selectivity: Selective	**Room/board:** $5,996
Acceptance rate: 20%	**Average debt:** N/A
Student/faculty ratio: 44/1	**Proportion who borrowed:** N/A

UNDERGRADUATE STUDENT BODY STATS

2009-2010 enrollment: 18,405 full-time; 10,581 part-time. Men: 46%; women: 54%. **Ethnic makeup:** African American: 14%; Asian American: 1%; Hispanic: 3%; White: 78%; International: 4%. **Religious preference:** No preference: 6%; Southern Baptist: 34%; Other: 52%.

ADMISSIONS FACTS AND FIGURES

Phone: (800) 543-5317. **Email:** admissions@liberty.edu. **Website:** http://www.liberty.edu. **Application deadlines for fall 2011:** Regular decision: Rolling. Early decision: Not offered. Early action: Not offered. Admission can be deferred. **Application fee:** $40. **To apply online, go to:** http://www.liberty.edu/apply. **Admissions requirements/recommendations:** High school units required (recommended): English: 4 (4); Mathematics: 3 (3); Science: 2 (2); Foreign language: 2 (2); Social studies: 2 (2); Academic electives: 4 (4); Total units: 17 (17). Tests: The college uses SAT or ACT scores in admissions decisions. Either SAT or ACT required. For admission to the fall 2011 entering class, the school will accept: ACT with or without writing accepted.

Campus visit: Recommended. Admissions interview: Neither required nor recommended. Off-campus interview: May be arranged. **Factors that count in admissions decisions:** *Academic:* Secondary school record: Very Important. Class rank: Considered. Letters of recommendation: Considered. Standardized test scores: Very Important. Essay: Important. *Nonacademic:* Interview: Not Considered. Extracurricular activities: Considered. Talent/ability: Considered. Character/personal qualities: Considered. Alumni/ae relationship: Not Considered. Geographical residence: Not Considered. State residency: Not Considered. Religious affiliation/commitment: Not Considered. Minority status: Not Considered. Volunteer work: Not Considered. Work experience: Not Considered. **Admissions statistics for the fall 2009 entering class:** Total applicants: 37,362. Total accepted: 7,428. Freshmen enrolled: 5,005; Overall acceptance rate: 20%. **Credentials of fall 2009 freshmen:** 15% ranked in the top 10 percent of their high school class; 35% were in the top 25 percent; 65% were in the top half. (Proportion submitting class standing: 43%.) **Average high school grade point average:** 3.2. **First-year students who submitted SAT scores:** 71%. Scores (25/75 percentile): Critical Reading: 450-570, Math: 430-560, Combined: 880-1130. **First-year students submitting ACT scores:** 29%. Scores (25/75 percentile): English: 17-24, Math: 18-24, Composite: 18-24.

ACADEMICS

Year founded: 1971. **Academic calendar:** Semester. **Degrees offered:** certificate, diploma, associate, terminal-associate, bachelor's, master's, post-master's certificate, doctorate. **Most popular majors:** 18% philosophy and religious studies, 17% multi/interdisciplinary studies, 16% business, management, marketing, and related support services, 12% psychology, 6% health professions and related clinical sciences. **Major fields of study:** biological and biomedical sciences; business, management, marketing, and related support services; communication, journalism, and related programs; communications technologies/technicians and support services; computer and information sciences and support services; education; English language and literature/letters; family and consumer sciences/human sciences; foreign languages, literatures, and linguistics; health professions and related clinical sciences; history; legal professions and studies; liberal arts and sciences studies, and humanities; mathematics and statistics; multi/interdisciplinary studies; parks, recreation, leisure, and fitness studies; philosophy and religious studies; psychology; security and protective services; social sciences; theology and religious vocations; transportation and materials moving; visual and performing arts. **Areas of required coursework:** humanities, computer literacy, mathematics, English (including composition), philosophy, sciences (biological or physical), history, social science, other. **Pre-professional programs:** pre-law, pre-theology. **Special academic programs:** accelerated program, cooperative (work-study plan) program, distance learning, double major, dual enrollment, English as a Second Language (ESL), external degree program, honors program, independent study, internships, student-designed major, teacher certificate program, weekend college. **Teacher certification offered in:** early childhood, special education, elementary, middle/junior high, secondary. **Reserve Officers Training Corps (ROTC):** Army ROTC: Offered on campus; Air Force ROTC: Offered at cooperating institution (University of Virginia). **Faculty and instruction (2009-2010):** Total instructional faculty: 379 full-time, 1,040 part-time (62% men; 38% women). Student/faculty ratio: 44/1. Classes of fewer than 20 students: 29%; of 20 to 49 students: 67%; of 50 or more students: 4%. **Advanced Placement and International Baccalaureate credit:** AP tests may be used for: Credit and/or placement. Scores accepted: 3, 4, 5. International Baccalaureate exams may be used for: Credit and/or placement. **Freshmen returning for sophomore year:** 74%. **Graduation rates:** Four-year: 28%; five-year: 39%; six-year: 48%.

COSTS AND FINANCIAL AID

Financial aid office: (434) 582-2270. **Expenses (2009-2010):** Tuition and fees 2009-2010: $17,742; room/board: $5,996. Estimated books and supplies: $1,400; transportation: $2,000; personal expenses: $1,400. **Financial aid:** Priority filing date for institution's financial aid form: March 1; deadline: March 1.

CAMPUS LIFE AND EXTRACURRICULAR ACTIVITIES

Campus housing available: women's dorms, men's dorms, apartment for single students, special housing for disabled students. **Student employment:** During the 2009-2010 academic year, 12% of undergraduates worked on campus. **Clubs and organizations:** Number of student organizations: 30. Activities include: choral groups, concert band, drama/theater, marching band, music ensembles, musical theater, pep band, radio station, student government, student newspaper, television station, yearbook. Number of fraternities: 0; sororities: 0. Average proportion of students who stay on

campus on weekends: 85%. **Sports program (2009-2010):** Member of NCAA I.

SERVICES AND FACILITIES

Basic services: nonremedial tutoring, women's center, placement service, health service. **Remedial assistance:** reading, math, writing, study skills. **Counseling services:** minority student, career, military, personal, veteran student, academic, religious. **For learning-disabled students:** School does not offer a structured program with separate admission and additional fees. Services include: remedial math, remedial English, remedial reading, oral tests, learning center, extended time for tests, tutors. **Library:** Number of titles: 314,642; number of current serial subscriptions: 56,187. **Information technology resources:** Students are not required to lease or own a computer. Number of campus computers available to all students: 1,200. School has a wireless network. Proportion of college-owned housing units wired for high-speed internet access: 100%. **Campus safety:** Security services offered: 24-hour foot-and-vehicle patrols, late-night transport/escort service, lighted pathways/sidewalks, controlled dormitory access (key, security card, etc).

TRANSFER AND INTERNATIONAL STUDENTS

Transfer students: May apply for admission for the following academic terms: Fall, Winter, Spring, Summer. Applicants do not need a minimum number of credits to apply. For fall 2009: Transfer applications received: 4,973. Transfer applicants offered admission: 4,058. Transfer applicants enrolled: 3,202. **International students:** Number of foreign undergraduates: 1019 (4% of student body). Number of countries represented: 72. Minimum TOEFL score required: 500 (paper); 173 (computer). Average TOEFL score: 557 (paper).

Longwood University

- **Address:** 201 High Street, Farmville, VA 23909
- **Website:** http://www.whylongwood.com
- **Public**
- **Enrollment:** 3,868 full-time; 218 part-time

KEY STATS

✔ **U.S News College Ranking:** 27, Regional Universities (South)
✔ **SAT Score (25th/75th percentile):** 960-1120
✔ **Tuition:** 2010-2011: $9,855 in state, $20,085 out of state

Selectivity: Selective	**Room/board:** $8,114
Acceptance rate: 70%	**Average debt:** $20,855
Student/faculty ratio: 18/1	**Proportion who borrowed:** 62%

UNDERGRADUATE STUDENT BODY STATS

2009-2010 enrollment: 3,868 full-time; 218 part-time. Men: 35%; women: 65%. **Ethnic makeup:** African American: 6%; American-Indian: 1%; Asian American: 1%; Hispanic: 2%; White: 89%.

ADMISSIONS FACTS AND FIGURES

Phone: (434) 395-2060. **Email:** admissions@longwood.edu. **Website:** http://www.whylongwood.com. **Application deadlines for fall 2011:** Regular decision: Rolling. Early decision: Not offered. Early action: Send application by: December 1; Decision sent by: January 1. Admission can be deferred. **Application fee:** $40. **To apply online, go to:** http://www.whylongwood.com/applynow/applyonline.htm. **Admissions requirements/recommendations:** High school units required (recommended): English: 4 (4); Mathematics: 3 (4); Science: 3 (4); Foreign language: 2 (4); Social studies: 2 (2); History: 2 (2); Total units: 24 (24). Tests: The college uses SAT or ACT scores in admissions decisions. Either SAT or ACT required. For admission to the fall 2011 entering class, the school will accept: ACT with or without writing accepted. Campus visit: Recommended. Admissions interview: Neither required nor recommended. Off-campus interview: Not available. **Factors that count in admissions decisions:** *Academic:* Secondary school record: Very Important. Class rank: Important. Letters of recommendation: Considered. Standardized test scores: Very Important. Essay: Very Important. *Nonacademic:* Interview: Not Considered. Extracurricular activities: Important. Talent/ability: Important. Character/personal qualities: Important. Alumni/ae relationship: Important. Geographical residence: Important. State residency: Considered. Religious affiliation/commitment: Not Considered. Minority status: Important. Volunteer work: Important. Work experience: Not Considered. **Other schools with the greatest overlap in applicants:** Christopher Newport University; James Madison University;

Radford University; Virginia Tech. **Admissions statistics for the fall 2009 entering class:** Total applicants: 4,301. Total accepted: 2,995. Freshmen enrolled: 1,010; 4% were from out of state. Accepted through early-decision or early-action plans: 24%. Overall acceptance rate: 70%. Non-early acceptance rate: 89%. **Size of waiting list:** 0 applicants; enrolled from waiting list: 0. **Credentials of fall 2009 freshmen:** 12% ranked in the top 10 percent of their high school class; 40% were in the top 25 percent; 84% were in the top half. (Proportion submitting class standing: 79%.) **Average high school grade point average:** 3.4. **First-year students who submitted SAT scores:** 87%. Scores (25/75 percentile): Critical Reading: 480-560, Math: 480-560, Combined: 960-1120. **First-year students submitting ACT scores:** 13%. Scores (25/75 percentile): English: N/A, Math: N/A, Composite: 20-24.

ACADEMICS

Year founded: 1839. **Academic calendar:** Semester. **Degrees offered:** bachelor's, post-bachelor's certificate, master's, post-master's certificate. **Most popular majors:** 22% liberal arts and sciences/liberal studies, 17% business administration and management, 9% social sciences, 7% history, 6% visual and performing arts. **Major fields of study:** biological and biomedical sciences; business, management, marketing, and related support services; communication, journalism, and related programs; computer and information sciences and support services; education; English language and literature/letters; foreign languages, literatures, and linguistics; health professions and related clinical sciences; history; liberal arts and sciences studies, and humanities; mathematics and statistics; parks, recreation, leisure, and fitness studies; physical sciences; psychology; public administration and social service professions; security and protective services; social sciences; visual and performing arts. **Areas of required coursework:** arts/fine arts, humanities, computer literacy, mathematics, English (including composition), philosophy, foreign languages, sciences (biological or physical), history, social science, other. **Pre-professional programs:** pre-law, pre-dentistry, pre-medicine, pre-veterinary science, pre-pharmacy, other. **Special academic programs (% participation):** accelerated program (5%), cross-registration (5%), distance learning (5%), double major (1%), dual enrollment (5%), exchange student program (domestic) (5%), honors program (5%), independent study (5%), internships (100%), study abroad (5%), teacher certificate program (23%). **Teacher certification offered in:** early childhood, special education, elementary, middle/junior high, secondary. **Reserve Officers Training Corps (ROTC):** Army ROTC: Offered on campus. **Faculty and instruction (2009-2010):** Total instructional faculty: 207 full-time, 72 part-time (48% men; 52% women; 9% minorities). Full-time faculty with Ph.D. or other terminal degree: 85%. Student/faculty ratio: 18/1. Classes of fewer than 20 students: 44%; of 20 to 49 students: 54%; of 50 or more students: 1%. **Advanced Placement and International Baccalaureate credit:** AP tests may be used for: Credit only. Scores accepted: 3, 4, 5. International Baccalaureate exams may be used for: Credit only. **Freshmen returning for sophomore year:** 77%. **Graduation rates:** Four-year: 49%; five-year: 57%; six-year: 63%. **Graduate study:** 14% of students pursue further study immediately upon graduation. Fields in which graduates pursue further study: Master of Business Administration (MBA), 9%; law, 1%; medicine, 1%; dentistry, 1%; theology (or the seminary), 1%; education, 38%; arts and sciences, 48%; veterinary medicine, 1%.

COSTS AND FINANCIAL AID

Financial aid office: (434) 395-2077. **Expenses (2010-2011):** Tuition and fees 2010-2011: $9,855 in state, $20,085 out of state; room/board: $8,114. Estimated books and supplies: $1,000; transportation: $1,000; personal expenses: $1,500. **Financial aid:** Priority filing date for institution's financial aid form: March 1. In 2009-2010, 65% of undergraduates applied for financial aid. Of those, 43% were determined to have financial need; 55% had their need fully met. Average financial aid package (proportion receiving): $10,118 (42%). Average amount of gift aid, such as scholarships or grants (proportion receiving): $5,380 (40%). Average amount of self-help aid, such as work study or loans (proportion receiving): $5,297 (35%). Average need-based loan (excluding PLUS or other private loans): $5,504. Among students who received need-based aid, the average percentage of need met: 85%. Among students who received aid based on merit, the average award (and the proportion receiving): $3,941 (6%). The average athletic scholarship (and the proportion receiving): $9,773 (3%). Average amount of debt of borrowers graduating in 2009: $20,855. Proportion who borrowed: 62%.

CAMPUS LIFE AND EXTRACURRICULAR ACTIVITIES

Campus housing available (% using): coed dorms (54%), women's dorms (10%), sorority housing (1%), fraternity housing (1%), apartment for single students (1%), special housing for disabled students (1%), special housing for international students (1%), other housing options (31%). Students who live in college-owned, operated, or affiliated housing: 75%. **Student employment:** During the 2009-2010 academic year, 18% of undergraduates worked on campus. Average per-year earnings: $2,300. **Clubs and organizations:** Number of student organizations: 125. Activities include: campus ministries, choral groups, concert band, dance, drama/theater, international student organization, jazz band, literary magazine, music ensembles, musical theater, opera, pep band, radio station, student government, student newspaper, symphony orchestra, yearbook. Number of fraternities: 9; sororities: 13. Proportion of men in fraternities: 15%; of women in sororities: 19%. Average proportion of students who stay on campus on weekends: 65%. **Sports program (2009-2010):** Member of NCAA I. *Men's intercollegiate varsity sports:* baseball, basketball, cross country, golf, soccer, tennis. *Women's intercollegiate varsity sports:* basketball, cross country, field hockey, golf, lacrosse, soccer, softball, tennis.

SERVICES AND FACILITIES

Basic services: nonremedial tutoring, placement service, health service, health insurance. **Remedial assistance:** reading, math, writing, study skills, other. **Counseling services:** minority student, career, personal, veteran student, academic, psychological, birth control, religious. **For learning-disabled students:** School does not offer a structured program with separate admission and additional fees. Total undergraduates in learning-disabled program or receiving services: 191. Services include: reading machines, tape recorders, note-taking services, learning center, readers, extended time for tests, tutors, priority registration, texts on tape, other testing accommodations, other. **Library:** Number of titles: 344,567; number of current serial subscriptions: 2,303. **Information technology resources:** Students are required to lease or own a computer. Number of campus computers available to all students: 350. School has a wireless network. Approximate number of users that can be accommodated: 3,000. Proportion of college-owned housing units wired for high-speed internet access: 100%. **Campus safety:** Security services offered: 24-hour foot-and-vehicle patrols, late-night transport/escort service, 24-hour emergency telephones, lighted pathways/sidewalks, student patrols, controlled dormitory access (key, security card, etc.).

TRANSFER AND INTERNATIONAL STUDENTS

Transfer students: May apply for admission for the following academic terms: Fall, Spring, Summer. Applicants need a minimum number of credits to apply. For fall 2009: Transfer applications received: 540. Transfer applicants offered admission: 295. Transfer applicants enrolled: 178. **International students:** Number of foreign undergraduates: 15. Number of countries represented: 10. Minimum TOEFL score required: 550 (paper); 213 (computer).

Lynchburg College

- **Address:** 1501 Lakeside Drive, Lynchburg, VA 24501
- **Website:** http://www.lynchburg.edu
- **Private; Religious affiliation:** Christian Church (Disciples of Christ)
- **Enrollment:** 2,110 full-time; 89 part-time

KEY STATS

✔ **U.S News College Ranking:** 40, Regional Universities (South)
✔ **SAT Score (25th/75th percentile):** 915-1130
✔ **Tuition:** 2010-2011: $29,905

Selectivity: Selective	**Room/board:** $8,020
Acceptance rate: 66%	**Average debt:** $30,954
Student/faculty ratio: 12/1	**Proportion who borrowed:** 67%

UNDERGRADUATE STUDENT BODY STATS

2009-2010 enrollment: 2,110 full-time; 89 part-time. Men: 40%; women: 60%. **Ethnic makeup:** African American: 8%; American-Indian: 1%; Asian American: 1%; Hispanic: 2%; White: 87%. **Religious preference:** Roman Catholic: 19%; Protestant: 21%; Jewish: 1%; No preference: 8%; Unknown: 20%; Christian Church (Disciples of Christ): 12%; Baptist: 14%; Other: 5%.

ADMISSIONS FACTS AND FIGURES

Phone: (434) 544-8300. **Email:** admissions@lynchburg.edu. **Website:** http://www.lynchburg.edu. **Application deadlines for fall 2011:** Regular decision: Rolling. Early decision: Send application by: November 15; Decision sent by: December 15. Early action: Not offered. Admission can be deferred. **Application fee:** $30. **To apply online, go to:** http://www.lynchburg.edu/applying.xml. **Admissions requirements/recommendations:** High school units required (recommended): English: 4 (4); Mathematics: 3 (4); Science: 3 (4); Foreign language: 2 (3); Social studies: 2 (2); History: 2 (2); Academic electives: 0 (1); Total units: 16 (20). Tests: The college uses SAT or ACT scores in admissions decisions. Either SAT or ACT required. For admission to the fall 2011 entering class, the school will accept: ACT with or without writing accepted. Campus visit: Recommended. Admissions interview: Recommended. Off-campus interview: May be arranged. **Factors that count in admissions decisions:** *Academic:* Secondary school record: Very Important. Class rank: Important. Letters of recommendation: Considered. Standardized test scores: Very Important. Essay: Considered. *Nonacademic:* Interview: Important. Extracurricular activities: Considered. Talent/ability: Considered. Character/personal qualities: Considered. Alumni/ae relationship: Not Considered. Geographical residence: Not Considered. State residency: Not Considered. Religious affiliation/commitment: Not Considered. Minority status: Not Considered. Volunteer work: Considered. Work experience: Considered. **Other schools with the greatest overlap in applicants:** James Madison University; Longwood University; Radford University; Roanoke College; Virginia Commonwealth University. **Admissions statistics for the fall 2009 entering class:** Total applicants: 4,571. Total accepted: 3,011. Freshmen enrolled: 593; 40% were from out of state. Overall acceptance rate: 66%. Early-decision acceptance rate: 51%. Non-early acceptance rate: 66%. **Credentials of fall 2009 freshmen:** 12% ranked in the top 10 percent of their high school class; 40% were in the top 25 percent; 77% were in the top half. (Proportion submitting class standing: 60%.) **Average high school grade point average:** 3.2. **First-year students who submitted SAT scores:** 93%. Scores (25/75 percentile): Critical Reading: 460-560, Math: 455-570, Combined: 915-1130. **First-year students submitting ACT scores:** 32%. Scores (25/75 percentile): English: N/A, Math: N/A, Composite: 19-24.

ACADEMICS

Year founded: 1903. **Academic calendar:** Semester. **Degrees offered:** bachelor's, master's, post-master's certificate. **Most popular majors:** 14% health professions and related clinical sciences, 12% education, 11% business, management, marketing, and related support services, 11% communication, journalism, and related programs, 9% biological and biomedical sciences. **Major fields of study:** biological and biomedical sciences; business, management, marketing, and related support services; communication, journalism, and related programs; computer and information sciences and support services; education; English language and literature/letters; foreign languages, literatures, and linguistics; health professions and related clinical sciences; history; mathematics and statistics; natural resources and conservation; parks, recreation, leisure, and fitness studies; philosophy and religious studies; physical sciences; psychology; social sciences; visual and performing arts. **Areas of required coursework:** arts/fine arts, humanities, mathematics, English (including composition), philosophy, foreign languages, sciences (biological or physical), history, social science, other. **Pre-professional programs:** pre-law, pre-dentistry, pre-medicine, pre-theology, pre-veterinary science, pre-optometry, pre-pharmacy, other. **Special academic programs:** accelerated program, cross-registration, double major, dual enrollment, honors program, independent study, internships, study abroad, teacher certificate program. **Teacher certification offered in:** early childhood, special education, elementary, middle/junior high, secondary, bilingual/bicultural. **Faculty and instruction (2009-2010):** Total instructional faculty: 155 full-time, 104 part-time (49% men; 51% women; 7% minorities). Full-time faculty with Ph.D. or other terminal degree: 74%. Student/faculty ratio: 12/1. Classes of fewer than 20 students: 59%; of 20 to 49 students: 41%; of 50 or more students: 0%. **Advanced Placement and International Baccalaureate credit:** AP tests may be used for: Credit and/or placement. Scores accepted: 3, 4, 5. International Baccalaureate exams may be used for: Credit and/or placement. **Freshmen returning for sophomore year:** 72%. **Graduation rates:** Four-year: 54%; five-year: 61%; six-year: 56%. **Graduate study:** 17% of students pursue further study within one year.

COSTS AND FINANCIAL AID

Financial aid office: (434) 544-8228. **Expenses (2010-2011):** Tuition and fees 2010-2011: $29,905; room/board: $8,020. Estimated books and supplies: $1,000; transportation: $400; personal expenses: $200. **Financial aid:** Priority filing date for institution's financial aid form: March 1. In 2009-2010, 82% of undergraduates applied for financial aid. Of those, 70% were determined to have financial need; 22% had their need fully met. Average financial aid package (proportion receiving): $20,193 (69%). Average amount of gift aid, such as scholarships or grants (proportion receiving): $16,607 (69%). Average amount of self-help aid, such as work study or loans (proportion receiving): $4,388 (58%). Average need-based loan (excluding PLUS or other private loans): $3,526. Among students who received need-based aid, the average percentage of need met: 78%. Among students who received aid based on merit, the average award (and the proportion receiving): $9,958 (27%). The average athletic scholarship (and the proportion receiving): $0 (0%). Average amount of debt of borrowers graduating in 2009: $30,954. Proportion who borrowed: 67%.

CAMPUS LIFE AND EXTRACURRICULAR ACTIVITIES

Campus housing available (% using): coed dorms (62%), sorority housing (2%), fraternity housing (1%), apartment for single students (16%), special housing for disabled students (2%), special housing for international students (1%), other housing options (16%). Students who live in college-owned, operated, or affiliated housing: 78%. **Student employment:** During the 2009-2010 academic year, 33% of undergraduates worked on campus. Average per-year earnings: $1,800. **Clubs and organizations:** Number of student organizations: 100. Activities include: campus ministries, choral groups, concert band, dance, drama/theater, international student organization, jazz band, literary magazine, model UN, music ensembles, musical theater, pep band, student government, student newspaper, student film society, symphony orchestra, yearbook. Number of fraternities: 4; sororities: 6. Proportion of men in fraternities: 8%; of women in sororities: 10%. Average proportion of students who stay on campus on weekends: 90%. **Sports program (2009-2010):** Member of NCAA III. *Men's intercollegiate varsity sports:* baseball, basketball, cross country, golf, lacrosse, soccer, tennis, track and field (indoor), track and field (outdoor). *Women's intercollegiate varsity sports:* basketball, cross country, equestrian, field hockey, lacrosse, soccer, softball, tennis, track and field (indoor), track and field (outdoor), volleyball.

SERVICES AND FACILITIES

Basic services: nonremedial tutoring, health service, health insurance, other. **Counseling services:** minority student, career, personal, veteran student, academic, older student, psychological, birth control, religious. **For learning-disabled students:** School does not offer a structured program with separate admission and additional fees. Total undergraduates in learning-disabled program or receiving services: 218. Services include: reading machines, tape recorders, untimed tests, note-taking services, oral tests, learning center, readers, extended time for tests, tutors, priority registration, priority seating, substitution of courses, texts on tape, typist/scribe, other testing accommodations, other. **Library:** Number of titles: 234,310; number of current serial subscriptions: 254. **Information technology resources:** Students are not required to lease or own a computer. Number of campus computers available to all students: 450. School has a wireless network. Approximate number of users that can be accommodated: 1,000. Proportion of college-owned housing units wired for high-speed internet access: 100%. **Campus safety:** Security services offered: 24-hour foot-and-vehicle patrols, late-night transport/escort service, 24-hour emergency telephones, lighted pathways/sidewalks, controlled dormitory access (key, security card, etc).

TRANSFER AND INTERNATIONAL STUDENTS

Transfer students: May apply for admission for the following academic terms: Fall, Spring, Summer. Applicants need a minimum number of credits to apply. For fall 2009: Transfer applications received: 629. Transfer applicants offered admission: 201. Transfer applicants enrolled: 114. **International students:** Number of foreign undergraduates: 3. Number of countries represented: 6. Minimum TOEFL score required: 525 (paper); 197 (computer).

Mary Baldwin College

- **Address:** New and Frederick Streets, Staunton, VA 24401
- **Website:** http://www.mbc.edu
- **Private; Religious affiliation:** Presbyterian
- **Enrollment:** 969 full-time; 604 part-time

KEY STATS

✔ **U.S News College Ranking:** 27, Regional Universities (South)
✔ **SAT Score (25th/75th percentile):** 870-1100
✔ **Tuition:** 2010-2011: $25,655

Selectivity: Selective	Room/board: $7,420
Acceptance rate: 62%	Average debt: $25,665
Student/faculty ratio: 10/1	Proportion who borrowed: 74%

UNDERGRADUATE STUDENT BODY STATS

2009-2010 enrollment: 969 full-time; 604 part-time. Men: 9%; women: 91%. **Ethnic makeup:** African American: 18%; Asian American: 2%; Hispanic: 4%; White: 75%; International: 1%. **Religious preference:** Roman Catholic: 12%; Protestant: 40%; Jewish: 1%; No preference: 2%; Unknown: 17%; Presbyterian: 4%; Other: 24%.

ADMISSIONS FACTS AND FIGURES

Phone: (800) 468-2262. **Email:** admit@mbc.edu. **Website:** http://www.mbc.edu. **Application deadlines for fall 2011:** Regular decision: Rolling. Early decision: Send application by: November 15; Decision sent by: December 1. Early action: Not offered. Admission can be deferred. **Application fee:** $35. **To apply online, go to:** http://www.mbc.edu/admission/. **Admissions requirements/recommendations:** High school units required (recommended): English: 4; Mathematics: 3; Science: 2; Foreign language: 2 (3); Social studies: 3; Academic electives: (2). Tests: The college uses SAT or ACT scores in admissions decisions. Either SAT or ACT required. For admission to the fall 2011 entering class, the school will accept: ACT with or without writing accepted. Campus visit: Recommended. Admissions interview: Recommended. Off-campus interview: May be arranged. **Factors that count in admissions decisions:** *Academic:* Secondary school record: Very Important. Class rank: Considered. Letters of recommendation: Considered. Standardized test scores: Very Important. Essay: Considered. *Nonacademic:* Interview: Important. Extracurricular activities: Important. Talent/ability: Considered. Character/personal qualities: Important. Alumni/ae relationship: Considered. Geographical residence: Not Considered. State residency: Not Considered. Religious affiliation/commitment: Not Considered. Minority status: Not Considered. Volunteer work: Considered. Work experience: Considered. **Other schools with the greatest overlap in applicants:** Hollins University; James Madison University; Randolph College; University of Mary Washington; University of Virginia. **Admissions statistics for the fall 2009 entering class:** Total applicants: 2,147. Total accepted: 1,332. Freshmen enrolled: 227; 29% were from out of state. Overall acceptance rate: 62%. Non-early acceptance rate: 62%. **Credentials of fall 2009 freshmen:** 13% ranked in the top 10 percent of their high school class; 39% were in the top 25 percent; 75% were in the top half. (Proportion submitting class standing: 52%.) **Average high school grade point average:** 3.3. **First-year students who submitted SAT scores:** 90%. Scores (25/75 percentile): Critical Reading: 440-560, Math: 430-540, Combined: 870-1100. **First-year students submitting ACT scores:** 28%. Scores (25/75 percentile): English: N/A, Math: N/A, Composite: 17-23.

ACADEMICS

Year founded: 1842. **Academic calendar:** 4-1-4. **Degrees offered:** certificate, bachelor's, master's. **Most popular majors:** 15% business, management, marketing, and related support services; 15% social sciences; 15% visual and performing arts; 14% history; 11% psychology. **Major fields of study:** area, ethnic, cultural, and gender studies; biological and biomedical sciences; business, management, marketing, and related support services; communication, journalism, and related programs; computer and information sciences and support services; English language and literature/letters; foreign languages, literatures, and linguistics; health professions and related clinical sciences; history; mathematics and statistics; multi/interdisciplinary studies; philosophy and religious studies; physical sciences; psychology; public administration and social service professions; social sciences; visual and performing arts. **Areas of required coursework:** arts/fine arts, humanities, computer literacy, mathematics, English (including composition), philosophy, sciences (biological or physical), history, social science, other. **Pre-professional programs:** pre-law, pre-medicine. **Special academic programs (% participation):** accelerated program (15%), cross-registration (15%), distance learning (40%), double major (4%), dual enrollment (8%), English as a Second Language (ESL) (3%), exchange student program (domestic) (1%), external degree program (40%), honors program (10%), independent study (20%), internships (75%), liberal arts/career combination (100%), student-designed major (2%), study abroad (40%), teacher certificate program (21%), other. **Teacher certification offered in:** early childhood, special education, elementary, middle/junior high, secondary. **Cooperative education programs:** computer science, engineering, other. **Reserve Officers Training Corps (ROTC):** Army ROTC: Offered on campus; Navy ROTC: Offered at cooperating institution (Virginia Military Institute); Air Force ROTC: Offered on campus. **Faculty and instruction (2009-2010):** Total instructional faculty: 76 full-time, 60 part-time (43% men; 57% women; 15% minorities). Full-time faculty with Ph.D. or other terminal degree: 99%. Student/faculty ratio: 10/1. Classes of fewer than 20 students: 61%; of 20 to 49 students: 39%; of 50 or more students: 0%. **Advanced Placement and International Baccalaureate credit:** AP tests may be used for: Credit only. Scores accepted:

4, 5. International Baccalaureate exams may be used for: Placement only. **Freshmen returning for sophomore year:** 65%. **Graduation rates:** Four-year: 44%; five-year: 49%; six-year: 48%. **Graduate study:** 25% of students pursue further study immediately upon graduation; 25% within one year; 45% within five years. Fields in which graduates pursue further study: Master of Business Administration (MBA), 15%; law, 15%; medicine, 10%; dentistry, 2%; theology (or the seminary), 5%; education, 35%; arts and sciences, 15%; veterinary medicine, 3%.

COSTS AND FINANCIAL AID

Financial aid office: (540) 887-7022. **Expenses (2010-2011):** Tuition and fees 2010-2011: $25,655; room/board: $7,420. Estimated books and supplies: $900; transportation: $400; personal expenses: $1,000. **Financial aid:** Priority filing date for institution's financial aid form: March 15. In 2009-2010, 90% of undergraduates applied for financial aid. Of those, 82% were determined to have financial need; 14% had their need fully met. Average financial aid package (proportion receiving): $19,749 (81%). Average amount of gift aid, such as scholarships or grants (proportion receiving): $15,304 (78%). Average amount of self-help aid, such as work study or loans (proportion receiving): $5,732 (69%). Average need-based loan (excluding PLUS or other private loans): $4,885. Among students who received need-based aid, the average percentage of need met: 77%. Among students who received aid based on merit, the average award (and the proportion receiving): $10,768 (6%). The average athletic scholarship (and the proportion receiving): $0 (0%). Average amount of debt of borrowers graduating in 2009: $25,665. Proportion who borrowed: 74%.

CAMPUS LIFE AND EXTRACURRICULAR ACTIVITIES

Campus housing available (% using): women's dorms (83%), other housing options (17%). Students who live in college-owned, operated, or affiliated housing: 62%. **Student employment:** During the 2009-2010 academic year, 16% of undergraduates worked on campus. Average per-year earnings: $1,326. **Clubs and organizations:** Number of student organizations: 34. Activities include: choral groups, dance, drama/theater, literary magazine, marching band, music ensembles, musical theater, radio station, student government, student newspaper, student film society, television station, yearbook. Number of fraternities: 0; sororities: 0. Average proportion of students who stay on campus on weekends: 40%. **Sports program (2009-2010):** Member of NCAA III. *Women's intercollegiate varsity sports:* basketball, cross country, soccer, softball, tennis, volleyball.

SERVICES AND FACILITIES

Basic services: women's center, health service. **Remedial assistance:** reading, math, writing, study skills. **Counseling services:** minority student, career, military, personal, academic, psychological, birth control, religious. **For learning-disabled students:** School does not offer a structured program with separate admission and additional fees. Total undergraduates in learning-disabled program or receiving services: 50. Services include: tape recorders, videotaped classes, untimed tests, note-taking services, oral tests, learning center, readers, extended time for tests, tutors. **Library:** Number of titles: 151,915; number of current serial subscriptions: 23,091. **Information technology resources:** Students are not required to lease or own a computer. Number of campus computers available to all students: 227. School has a wireless network. Approximate number of users that can be accommodated: 890. Proportion of college-owned housing units wired for high-speed internet access: 100%. **Campus safety:** Security services offered: 24-hour foot-and-vehicle patrols, late-night transport/escort service, 24-hour emergency telephones, lighted pathways/sidewalks, controlled dormitory access (key, security card, etc).

TRANSFER AND INTERNATIONAL STUDENTS

Transfer students: May apply for admission for the following academic terms: Fall, Spring. Applicants need a minimum number of credits to apply. For fall 2009: Transfer applications received: 138. Transfer applicants offered admission: 74. Transfer applicants enrolled: 55. **International students:** Number of foreign undergraduates: 13 (1% of student body). Number of countries represented: 8. Minimum TOEFL score required: 500 (paper); 177 (computer). Average TOEFL score: 500 (paper).

Marymount University

- **Address:** 2807 N. Glebe Road, Arlington, VA 22207
- **Website:** http://www.marymount.edu
- **Private; Religious affiliation:** Roman Catholic
- **Enrollment:** 1,899 full-time; 325 part-time

KEY STATS

✔ **U.S News College Ranking:** 40, Regional Universities (South)
✔ **SAT Score (25th/75th percentile):** 860-1070
✔ **Tuition:** 2010-2011: $23,426

Selectivity: Selective	**Room/board:** $10,325
Acceptance rate: 83%	**Average debt:** $22,946
Student/faculty ratio: 14/1	**Proportion who borrowed:** 76%

UNDERGRADUATE STUDENT BODY STATS

2009-2010 enrollment: 1,899 full-time; 325 part-time. Men: 28%; women: 72%. **Ethnic makeup:** African American: 15%; Asian American: 8%; Hispanic: 13%; White: 55%; International: 9%. **Religious preference:** Protestant: 8%; Jewish: 1%; Muslim: 5%; Buddhist: 1%; Unknown: 39%; Roman Catholic: 33%; Christian: 10%; Other: 3%.

ADMISSIONS FACTS AND FIGURES

Phone: (703) 284-1500. **Email:** admissions@marymount.edu. **Website:** http://www.marymount.edu. **Application deadlines for fall 2011:** Regular decision: Rolling. Early decision: Not offered. Early action: Not offered. Admission can be deferred. **Application fee:** $40. **To apply online, go to:** http://www.marymount.edu/application/. **Admissions requirements/recommendations:** High school units required (recommended): English: (4); Mathematics: (3); Science: (2); Foreign language: (3); Social studies: (3); Total units: 15. Tests: The college uses SAT or ACT scores in admissions decisions. Either SAT or ACT required. For admission to the fall 2011 entering class, the school will accept: ACT with or without writing accepted. Campus visit: Recommended. Admissions interview: Recommended. Off-campus interview: May be arranged. **Factors that count in admissions decisions:** *Academic:* Secondary school record: Very Important. Class rank: Considered. Letters of recommendation: Important. Standardized test scores: Very Important. Essay: Considered. *Nonacademic:* Interview: Important. Extracurricular activities: Considered. Talent/ability: Important. Character/personal qualities: Considered. Alumni/ae relationship: Considered. Geographical residence: Not Considered. State residency: Not Considered. Religious affiliation/commitment: Not Considered. Minority status: Not Considered. Volunteer work: Considered. Work experience: Considered. **Admissions statistics for the fall 2009 entering class:** Total applicants: 1,809. Total accepted: 1,495. Freshmen enrolled: 390; 45% were from out of state. Overall acceptance rate: 83%. **Credentials of fall 2009 freshmen:** 9% ranked in the top 10 percent of their high school class; 34% were in the top 25 percent; 70% were in the top half. (Proportion submitting class standing: 16%.) **Average high school grade point average:** 3.1. **First-year students who submitted SAT scores:** 93%. Scores (25/75 percentile): Critical Reading: 440-540, Math: 420-530, Combined: 860-1070. **First-year students submitting ACT scores:** 24%. Scores (25/75 percentile): English: 17-22, Math: 16-22, Composite: 18-22.

ACADEMICS

Year founded: 1950. **Academic calendar:** Semester. **Degrees offered:** certificate, bachelor's, post-bachelor's certificate, master's, post-master's certificate. **Most popular majors:** 19% nursing/registered nurse training (R.N., A.S.N., B.S.N., M.S.N.), 13% business administration and management, 6% interior design, 6% liberal arts and sciences/liberal studies, 6% psychology. **Major fields of study:** biological and biomedical sciences; business, management, marketing, and related support services; communication, journalism, and related programs; computer and information sciences and support services; English language and literature/letters; health professions and related clinical sciences; history; legal professions and studies; liberal arts and sciences studies, and humanities; mathematics and statistics; natural resources and conservation; parks, recreation, leisure, and fitness studies; philosophy and religious studies; psychology; security and protective services; social sciences; visual and performing arts. **Areas of required coursework:** humanities, mathematics, English (including composition), philosophy, sciences (biological or physical), history, social science, other. **Pre-professional programs:** pre-law, pre-medicine, other. **Special academic programs (% participation):** accelerated program (21%), cross-registration (4%), distance learning (27%), double major (4%), honors program (3%),

independent study (7%), internships (92%), student-designed major (7%), study abroad (8%), teacher certificate program (6%). **Teacher certification offered in:** early childhood, special education, elementary, secondary. **Reserve Officers Training Corps (ROTC):** Army ROTC: Offered at cooperating institution (Georgetown University). **Faculty and instruction (2009-2010):** Total instructional faculty: 141 full-time, 178 part-time (35% men; 65% women; 5% minorities). Full-time faculty with Ph.D. or other terminal degree: 87%. Student/faculty ratio: 14/1. Classes of fewer than 20 students: 49%; of 20 to 49 students: 50%; of 50 or more students: 1%. **Advanced Placement and International Baccalaureate credit:** AP tests may be used for: Credit and/or placement. Scores accepted: 3, 4, 5. International Baccalaureate exams may be used for: Credit and/or placement. **Freshmen returning for sophomore year:** 71%. **Graduation rates:** Four-year: 42%; five-year: 54%; six-year: 51%. **Graduate study:** 35% of students pursue further study within one year; 45% within five years. Fields in which graduates pursue further study: Master of Business Administration (MBA), 19%; law, 4%; medicine, 7%; engineering, 6%; education, 9%; arts and sciences, 43%.

COSTS AND FINANCIAL AID

Financial aid office: (703) 284-1530. **Expenses (2010-2011):** Tuition and fees 2010-2011: $23,426; room/board: $10,325. Estimated books and supplies: $800; transportation: $470; personal expenses: $900. **Financial aid:** Priority filing date for institution's financial aid form: March 1. In 2009-2010, 72% of undergraduates applied for financial aid. Of those, 60% were determined to have financial need; 14% had their need fully met. Average financial aid package (proportion receiving): $15,574 (60%). Average amount of gift aid, such as scholarships or grants (proportion receiving): $6,427 (39%). Average amount of self-help aid, such as work study or loans (proportion receiving): $5,443 (51%). Average need-based loan (excluding PLUS or other private loans): $4,337. Among students who received need-based aid, the average percentage of need met: 67%. Among students who received aid based on merit, the average award (and the proportion receiving): $9,553 (20%). Average amount of debt of borrowers graduating in 2009: $22,946. Proportion who borrowed: 76%.

CAMPUS LIFE AND EXTRACURRICULAR ACTIVITIES

Campus housing available (% using): coed dorms (52%), women's dorms (35%), men's dorms (11%), apartment for single students (2%), other housing options. Students who live in college-owned, operated, or affiliated housing: 32%. **Student employment:** During the 2009-2010 academic year, 10% of undergraduates worked on campus. Average per-year earnings: $1,800. **Clubs and organizations:** Number of student organizations: 37. Activities include: campus ministries, choral groups, dance, drama/theater, international student organization, literary magazine, student government, student newspaper, yearbook. Number of fraternities: 0; sororities: 0. Average proportion of students who stay on campus on weekends: 60%. **Sports program (2009-2010):** Member of NCAA III. *Men's intercollegiate varsity sports:* basketball, cross country, golf, lacrosse, soccer, swimming. *Women's intercollegiate varsity sports:* basketball, cross country, lacrosse, soccer, swimming, volleyball.

SERVICES AND FACILITIES

Basic services: nonremedial tutoring, health service, health insurance. **Remedial assistance:** math, writing, study skills. **Counseling services:** career, personal, academic, psychological, religious. **For learning-disabled students:** School does not offer a structured program with separate admission and additional fees. Total undergraduates in learning-disabled program or receiving services: 70. Services include: reading machines, tape recorders, note-taking services, oral tests, learning center, extended time for tests, tutors, early syllabus, proofreading services, texts on tape, exams on tape or computer, other testing accommodations, other. **Library:** Number of titles: 233,286; number of current serial subscriptions: 6,988. **Information technology resources:** Students are not required to lease or own a computer. Number of campus computers available to all students: 280. School has a wireless network. Approximate number of users that can be accommodated: 500. Proportion of college-owned housing units wired for high-speed internet access: 100%. **Campus safety:** Security services offered: 24-hour foot-and-vehicle patrols, late-night transport/escort service, 24-hour emergency telephones, lighted pathways/sidewalks, controlled dormitory access (key, security card, etc).

TRANSFER AND INTERNATIONAL STUDENTS

Transfer students: May apply for admission for the following academic terms: Fall, Spring, Summer. Applicants need a minimum number of credits to apply. For fall 2009: Transfer applications received: 715. Transfer applicants offered admission: 560. Transfer applicants enrolled: 253.

International students: Number of foreign undergraduates: 191 (9% of student body). Number of countries represented: 62. Minimum TOEFL score required: 550 (paper); 79 (computer).

Norfolk State University

- **Address:** 700 Park Avenue, Norfolk, VA 23504
- **Website:** http://www.nsu.edu
- **Public**
- **Enrollment:** N/A

....

KEY STATS

✔ **U.S News College Ranking:** second tier, Regional Universities (South)
✔ **SAT or ACT Score (25th/75th percentile):** N/A
✔ **Tuition:** 2009-2010: $5,872 in state, $17,931 out of state

Selectivity: Less selective	**Room/board:** $8,376
Acceptance rate: N/A	**Average debt:** N/A
Student/faculty ratio: N/A	**Proportion who borrowed:** N/A

Old Dominion University

- **Address:** 5115 Hampton Boulevard, Norfolk, VA 23529
- **Website:** http://www.odu.edu
- **Public**
- **Enrollment:** 13,776 full-time; 4,477 part-time

....

KEY STATS

✔ **U.S News College Ranking:** second tier, National Universities
✔ **SAT Score (25th/75th percentile):** 960-1150
✔ **Tuition:** 2009-2010: $7,318 in state, $19,768 out of state

Selectivity: Selective	**Room/board:** $7,868
Acceptance rate: 72%	**Average debt:** $17,250
Student/faculty ratio: 21/1	**Proportion who borrowed:** 81%

UNDERGRADUATE STUDENT BODY STATS

2009-2010 enrollment: 13,776 full-time; 4,477 part-time. Men: 45%; women: 55%. **Ethnic makeup:** African American: 24%; American-Indian: 1%; Asian American: 5%; Hispanic: 4%; White: 65%; International: 1%.

ADMISSIONS FACTS AND FIGURES

Phone: (757) 683-3685. **Email:** admit@odu.edu. **Website:** http://www.odu.edu. **Application deadlines for fall 2011:** Regular decision: February 1. Early decision: Not offered. Early action: Send application by: December 1; Decision sent by: January 15. Admission can be deferred. **Application fee:** $50. **To apply online, go to:** http://admissions.odu.edu/undergraduate.php. **Admissions requirements/recommendations:** High school units required (recommended): English: 4 (4); Mathematics: 3 (3); Science: 3 (3); Foreign language: 3 (3); Social studies: 3 (3); Total units: 16 (16). Tests: The college uses SAT or ACT scores in admissions decisions. Either SAT or ACT required. For admission to the fall 2011 entering class, the school will accept ACT with writing recommended. Campus visit: Recommended. Admissions interview: Neither required nor recommended. Off-campus interview: Not available. **Factors that count in admissions decisions:** *Academic:* Secondary school record: Very Important. Class rank: Important. Letters of recommendation: Important. Standardized test scores: Very Important. Essay: Important. *Nonacademic:* Interview: Considered. Extracurricular activities: Very Important. Talent/ability: Considered. Character/personal qualities: Considered. Alumni/ae relationship: Considered. Geographical residence: Not Considered. State residency: Not Considered. Religious affiliation/commitment: Not Considered. Minority status: Not Considered. Volunteer work: Important. Work experience: Important. **Other schools with the greatest overlap in applicants:** Christopher Newport University; College of William and Mary; James Madison University; University of Virginia; Virginia Tech. **Admissions statistics for the fall 2009 entering class:** Total applicants: 9,878. Total accepted: 7,125. Freshmen enrolled: 2,755; 8% were from out of state. Accepted through early-decision or early-action plans: 56%. Overall acceptance rate: 72%. Non-early acceptance rate: 69%. **Credentials of fall 2009 freshmen:** 11% ranked in the top 10 percent of their high school class; 39% were in the top 25 percent; 82% were in the top half. (Proportion submit-

ting class standing: 66%.) **Average high school grade point average:** 3.3. **First-year students who submitted SAT scores:** 81%. Scores (25/75 percentile): Critical Reading: 480-570, Math: 480-580, Combined: 960-1150. **First-year students submitting ACT scores:** 25%. Scores (25/75 percentile): English: 18-23, Math: 17-23, Composite: 18-23.

ACADEMICS

Year founded: 1930. **Academic calendar:** Semester. **Degrees offered:** bachelor's, master's, post-master's certificate, doctorate. **Most popular majors:** 19% business, management, marketing, and related support services, 16% health professions and related clinical sciences, 11% social sciences, 8% education, 6% multi/interdisciplinary studies. **Major fields of study:** area, ethnic, cultural, and gender studies; biological and biomedical sciences; business, management, marketing, and related support services; computer and information sciences and support services; education; engineering; engineering technologies/technicians; English language and literature/letters; foreign languages, literatures, and linguistics; health professions and related clinical sciences; history; mathematics and statistics; multi/interdisciplinary studies; parks, recreation, leisure, and fitness studies; philosophy and religious studies; physical sciences; psychology; social sciences; visual and performing arts. **Areas of required coursework:** arts/fine arts, humanities, computer literacy, mathematics, English (including composition), philosophy, foreign languages, sciences (biological or physical), history, social science, other. **Pre-professional programs:** pre-law, pre-dentistry, pre-medicine, pre-veterinary science, pre-optometry, pre-pharmacy. **Special academic programs:** accelerated program, cooperative (work-study plan) program, cross-registration, distance learning, double major, dual enrollment, English as a Second Language (ESL), exchange student program (domestic), honors program, independent study, internships, liberal arts/career combination, student-designed major, study abroad, teacher certificate program, other. **Teacher certification offered in:** early childhood, special education, elementary, vo-tech, middle/junior high, secondary. **Cooperative education programs:** art, business, computer science, education, engineering, health professions, humanities, natural science, social/behavioral science, technologies, vocational arts. **Reserve Officers Training Corps (ROTC):** Army ROTC: Offered on campus; Navy ROTC: Offered on campus. **Faculty and instruction (2009-2010):** Total instructional faculty: 696 full-time, 461 part-time (52% men; 48% women; 19% minorities). Full-time faculty with Ph.D. or other terminal degree: 79%. Student/faculty ratio: 21/1. Classes of fewer than 20 students: 36%; of 20 to 49 students: 54%; of 50 or more students: 10%. **Advanced Placement and International Baccalaureate credit:** AP tests may be used for: Credit and/or placement. Scores accepted: 3, 4, 5. International Baccalaureate exams may be used for: Credit only. **Freshmen returning for sophomore year:** 77%. **Graduation rates:** Four-year: 23%; five-year: 43%; six-year: 51%.

COSTS AND FINANCIAL AID

Financial aid office: (757) 683-3683. **Expenses (2009-2010):** Tuition and fees 2009-2010: $7,318 in state, $19,768 out of state; room/board: $7,868. Estimated books and supplies: $1,000; transportation: $1,000; personal expenses: $1,875. **Financial aid:** Priority filing date for institution's financial aid form: February 15; deadline: March 15. In 2009-2010, 76% of undergraduates applied for financial aid. Of those, 58% were determined to have financial need; 46% had their need fully met. Average financial aid package (proportion receiving): $7,701 (54%). Average amount of gift aid, such as scholarships or grants (proportion receiving): $4,483 (27%). Average amount of self-help aid, such as work study or loans (proportion receiving): $4,171 (33%). Average need-based loan (excluding PLUS or other private loans): $4,063. Among students who received need-based aid, the average percentage of need met: 74%. Among students who received aid based on merit, the average award (and the proportion receiving): $3,441 (2%). The average athletic scholarship (and the proportion receiving): $14,193 (2%). Average amount of debt of borrowers graduating in 2009: $17,250. Proportion who borrowed: 81%.

CAMPUS LIFE AND EXTRACURRICULAR ACTIVITIES

Campus housing available (% using): coed dorms (55%), apartment for single students (41%), special housing for disabled students (2%), special housing for international students (2%). Students who live in college-owned, operated, or affiliated housing: 25%. **Student employment:** During the 2009-2010 academic year, 7% of undergraduates worked on campus. Average per-year earnings: $4,500. **Clubs and organizations:** Number of student organizations: 155. Activities include: campus ministries, choral groups, concert band, dance, drama/theater, international student organization, jazz band, marching band, model UN, music ensembles, musical theater, pep band, radio station, student government, student newspaper, student film society, symphony orchestra, television station. Number of fraternities: 14; sororities: 10. Proportion of men in fraternities: 4%; of women in sororities: 4%. **Sports program (2009-2010):** Member of NCAA I. *Men's intercollegiate varsity sports:* baseball, basketball, football, golf, soccer, swimming, tennis, wrestling. *Women's intercollegiate varsity sports:* basketball, crew (heavyweight), field hockey, golf, lacrosse, crew (lightweight), soccer, swimming, tennis.

SERVICES AND FACILITIES

Basic services: nonremedial tutoring, women's center, placement service, day care, health service, health insurance. **Counseling services:** minority student, career, military, personal, veteran student, academic, older student, psychological, birth control, religious, other. **For learning-disabled students:** School does not offer a structured program with separate admission and additional fees. Total undergraduates in learning-disabled program or receiving services: 216. Services include: reading machines, tape recorders, other special classes, note-taking services, readers, extended time for tests, priority registration, priority seating, substitution of courses, texts on tape, typist/scribe, exams on tape or computer, other testing accommodations, other. **Library:** Number of titles: 1,183,464; number of current serial subscriptions: 10,495. **Information technology resources:** Students are not required to lease or own a computer. Number of campus computers available to all students: 2,035. School has a wireless network. Approximate number of users that can be accommodated: 15,000. Proportion of college-owned housing units wired for high-speed internet access: 100%. **Campus safety:** Security services offered: 24-hour foot-and-vehicle patrols, late-night transport/escort service, 24-hour emergency telephones, lighted pathways/sidewalks, student patrols, controlled dormitory access (key, security card, etc).

TRANSFER AND INTERNATIONAL STUDENTS

Transfer students: May apply for admission for the following academic terms: Fall, Spring, Summer. Applicants need a minimum number of credits to apply. For fall 2009: Transfer applications received: 3,522. Transfer applicants offered admission: 3,293. Transfer applicants enrolled: 2,174. **International students:** Number of foreign undergraduates: 260 (1% of student body). Number of countries represented: 118. Minimum TOEFL score required: 550 (paper); 213 (computer).

Radford University

■ **Address:** PO Box 6890, Radford, VA 24142
■ **Website:** http://www.radford.edu
■ **Public**
■ **Enrollment:** 7,440 full-time; 333 part-time

KEY STATS

✔ **U.S News College Ranking:** 38, Regional Universities (South)
✔ **SAT Score (25th/75th percentile):** 920-1100
✔ **Tuition:** 2009-2010: $6,904 in state, $16,568 out of state
  Selectivity: Selective   **Room/board:** $6,970
  Acceptance rate: 71%   **Average debt:** $18,817
  Student/faculty ratio: 19/1   **Proportion who borrowed:** 59%

UNDERGRADUATE STUDENT BODY STATS

2009-2010 enrollment: 7,440 full-time; 333 part-time. Men: 43%; women: 57%. **Ethnic makeup:** African American: 6%; Asian American: 2%; Hispanic: 3%; White: 88%; International: 1%.

ADMISSIONS FACTS AND FIGURES

Phone: (540) 831-5371. **Email:** admissions@radford.edu. **Website:** http://www.radford.edu. **Application deadlines for fall 2011:** Early decision: Not offered. Early action: Send application by: December 15; Decision sent by: January 15. Admission can be deferred. **Application fee:** $50. **To apply online, go to:** https://www.applyweb.com/apply/runet/menu.html. **Admissions requirements/recommendations:** High school units required (recommended): English: 4 (4); Mathematics: 4 (4); Science: 4 (4); Foreign language: 3 (3); Social studies: 2 (2); History: 2 (2); Academic electives: 5 (5); Total units: 24 (24). Tests: The college uses SAT or ACT scores in admissions decisions. Either SAT or ACT required. For admission to the fall 2011 entering class, the school will accept: ACT with or without writing accepted. Campus visit: Recommended. Admissions interview: Recommended. Off-campus interview: May be arranged. **Factors that**

count in admissions decisions: *Academic:* Secondary school record: Very Important. Class rank: Important. Letters of recommendation: Considered. Standardized test scores: Considered. Essay: Considered. *Nonacademic:* Interview: Considered. Extracurricular activities: Considered. Talent/ability: Considered. Character/personal qualities: Considered. Alumni/ae relationship: Considered. Geographical residence: Considered. State residency: Considered. Religious affiliation/commitment: Not Considered. Minority status: Considered. Volunteer work: Considered. Work experience: Considered. **Other schools with the greatest overlap in applicants:** James Madison University; Longwood University; Old Dominion University; Virginia Commonwealth University; Virginia Tech. **Admissions statistics for the fall 2009 entering class:** Total applicants: 6,166. Total accepted: 4,384. Freshmen enrolled: 1,447; 7% were from out of state. Overall acceptance rate: 71%. Non-early acceptance rate: 71%. **Size of waiting list:** 43 applicants; enrolled from waiting list: 41. **Credentials of fall 2009 freshmen:** 9% ranked in the top 10 percent of their high school class; 25% were in the top 25 percent; 71% were in the top half. (Proportion submitting class standing: 69%.) **Average high school grade point average:** 3.2. **First-year students who submitted SAT scores:** 88%. Scores (25/75 percentile): Critical Reading: 460-550, Math: 460-550, Combined: 920-1100. **First-year students submitting ACT scores:** 12%. Scores (25/75 percentile): English: N/A, Math: N/A, Composite: 19-23.

ACADEMICS

Year founded: 1910. **Academic calendar:** Semester. **Degrees offered:** bachelor's, post-bachelor's certificate, master's, post-master's certificate, doctorate. **Most popular majors:** 12% multi/interdisciplinary studies, 9% business administration and management, 7% criminal justice/safety studies, 7% physical education teaching and coaching, 5% nursing/registered nurse training (R.N., A.S.N., B.S.N., M.S.N.). **Major fields of study:** biological and biomedical sciences; business, management, marketing, and related support services; communication, journalism, and related programs; computer and information sciences and support services; education; English language and literature/letters; family and consumer sciences/human sciences; foreign languages, literatures, and linguistics; health professions and related clinical sciences; history; mathematics and statistics; multi/interdisciplinary studies; parks, recreation, leisure, and fitness studies; philosophy and religious studies; physical sciences; psychology; public administration and social service professions; security and protective services; social sciences; visual and performing arts. **Areas of required coursework:** arts/fine arts, humanities, mathematics, English (including composition), philosophy, sciences (biological or physical), history, social science. **Pre-professional programs:** pre-law, pre-dentistry, pre-medicine, pre-veterinary science, pre-pharmacy. **Special academic programs (% participation):** accelerated program (.1%), cross-registration, distance learning (4.1%), double major (4.7%), dual enrollment, honors program (2.2%), independent study (13.5%), internships (23.4%), student-designed major, study abroad (3.7%), teacher certificate program (11.9%). **Teacher certification offered in:** early childhood, special education, elementary, middle/junior high, secondary. **Reserve Officers Training Corps (ROTC):** Army ROTC: Offered on campus. **Faculty and instruction (2009-2010):** Total instructional faculty: 387 full-time, 140 part-time (49% men; 51% women; 9% minorities). Full-time faculty with Ph.D. or other terminal degree: 83%. Student/faculty ratio: 19/1. Classes of fewer than 20 students: 33%; of 20 to 49 students: 60%; of 50 or more students: 6%. **Advanced Placement and International Baccalaureate credit:** AP tests may be used for: Placement only. Scores accepted: 3, 4, 5. International Baccalaureate exams may be used for: Credit only. **Freshmen returning for sophomore year:** 77%. **Graduation rates:** Four-year: 40%; five-year: 55%; six-year: 57%. **Graduate study:** 3% of students pursue further study immediately upon graduation; 11% within one year; 22% within five years. Fields in which graduates pursue further study: Master of Business Administration (MBA), 15%; law, 1%; education, 14%; arts and sciences, 33%.

COSTS AND FINANCIAL AID

Financial aid office: (540) 831-5408. **Expenses (2009-2010):** Tuition and fees 2009-2010: $6,904 in state, $16,568 out of state; room/board: $6,970. Estimated books and supplies: $877; transportation: $1,300; personal expenses: $1,600. **Financial aid:** Priority filing date for institution's financial aid form: February 15. In 2009-2010, 65% of undergraduates applied for financial aid. Of those, 46% were determined to have financial need; 27% had their need fully met. Average financial aid package (proportion receiving): $9,394 (44%). Average amount of gift aid, such as scholarships or grants (proportion receiving): $7,661 (29%). Average amount of self-help aid, such as work study or loans (proportion receiving): $3,953 (37%). Average need-based loan (excluding PLUS or other private loans): $3,694. Among students who received need-based aid, the average percentage of need met: 83%. Among students who received aid based on merit, the average award (and the proportion receiving): $3,895 (2%). The average athletic scholarship (and the proportion receiving): $4,513 (0%). Average amount of debt of borrowers graduating in 2009: $18,817. Proportion who borrowed: 59%.

CAMPUS LIFE AND EXTRACURRICULAR ACTIVITIES

Campus housing available (% using): coed dorms (99%), apartment for single students (1%), special housing for disabled students. Students who live in college-owned, operated, or affiliated housing: 34%. **Student employment:** During the 2009-2010 academic year, 11% of undergraduates worked on campus. Average per-year earnings: $2,263. **Clubs and organizations:** Number of student organizations: 237. Activities include: campus ministries, choral groups, concert band, dance, drama/theater, international student organization, jazz band, literary magazine, music ensembles, musical theater, pep band, radio station, student government, student newspaper, television station, yearbook. Number of fraternities: 15; sororities: 12. Proportion of men in fraternities: 9%; of women in sororities: 11%. Average proportion of students who stay on campus on weekends: 53%. **Sports program (2009-2010):** Member of NCAA I. *Men's intercollegiate varsity sports:* baseball, basketball, cross country, golf, soccer, tennis, track and field (indoor), track and field (outdoor). *Women's intercollegiate varsity sports:* basketball, cross country, field hockey, golf, soccer, softball, swimming, tennis, track and field (indoor), track and field (outdoor), volleyball.

SERVICES AND FACILITIES

Basic services: nonremedial tutoring, placement service, health service, health insurance. **Remedial assistance:** reading, math, writing, study skills, other. **Counseling services:** minority student, career, military, personal, veteran student, academic, older student, psychological, birth control, other. **For learning-disabled students:** School does not offer a structured program with separate admission and additional fees. Services include: reading machines, tape recorders, note-taking services, oral tests, learning center, readers, extended time for tests, tutors, priority registration, priority seating, texts on tape, typist/scribe, exams on tape or computer, other testing accommodations, other. **Library:** Number of titles: 382,048; number of current serial subscriptions: 11,069. **Information technology resources:** Students are not required to lease or own a computer. Number of campus computers available to all students: 731. School has a wireless network. Approximate number of users that can be accommodated: 4,000. Proportion of college-owned housing units wired for high-speed internet access: 100%. **Campus safety:** Security services offered: 24-hour foot-and-vehicle patrols, late-night transport/escort service, 24-hour emergency telephones, lighted pathways/sidewalks, controlled dormitory access (key, security card, etc).

TRANSFER AND INTERNATIONAL STUDENTS

Transfer students: May apply for admission for the following academic terms: Fall, Spring, Summer. Applicants do not need a minimum number of credits to apply. For fall 2009: Transfer applications received: 1,474. Transfer applicants offered admission: 976. Transfer applicants enrolled: 624. **International students:** Number of foreign undergraduates: 45 (1% of student body). Number of countries represented: 31. Minimum TOEFL score required: 520 (paper); 190 (computer). Average TOEFL score: 470 (paper).

Randolph College

- ■ **Address:** 2500 Rivermont Avenue, Lynchburg, VA 24503-1555
- ■ **Website:** http://www.randolphcollege.edu/
- ■ **Private; Religious affiliation:** United Methodist
- ■ **Enrollment:** 472 full-time; 16 part-time

KEY STATS

✔ **U.S News College Ranking:** 114, National Liberal Arts Colleges
✔ **SAT Score (25th/75th percentile):** 1000-1220
✔ **Tuition:** 2009-2010: $28,430

Selectivity: Selective	**Room/board:** $9,715
Acceptance rate: 81%	**Average debt:** N/A
Student/faculty ratio: 7/1	**Proportion who borrowed:** N/A

UNDERGRADUATE STUDENT BODY STATS

2009-2010 enrollment: 472 full-time; 16 part-time. **Men:** 27%; **women:** 73%. **Ethnic makeup:** African American: 11%; American-Indian: 1%; Asian

American: 2%; Hispanic: 6%; White: 68%; International: 12%. **Religious preference:** Roman Catholic: 18%; Protestant: 45%; Jewish: 2%; Muslim: 3%; Hindu: 2%; Buddhist: 1%; No preference: 6%; Unknown: 11%; United Methodist: 9%; Other: 3%.

ADMISSIONS FACTS AND FIGURES

Phone: (800) 745-7692. **Email:** admissions@randolphcollege.edu. **Website:** http://www.randolphcollege.edu/. **Application deadlines for fall 2011:** Regular decision: April 1; decision sent by April 15. Early decision: Not offered. Early action: Send application by: February 1; Decision sent by: February 15. Admission can be deferred. **Application fee:** $35. **To apply online, go to:** http://www.randolphcollege.edu/x195.xml. **Admissions requirements/recommendations:** High school units required (recommended): English: 4 (4); Mathematics: 3 (4); Science: 3 (3); Foreign language: 3 (4); Social studies: 0 (0); History: 2 (2); Academic electives: 1 (2); Total units: 16 (19). Tests: The college uses SAT or ACT scores in admissions decisions. Either SAT or ACT required. For admission to the fall 2011 entering class, the school will accept: ACT with or without writing accepted. Campus visit: Recommended. Admissions interview: Recommended. Off-campus interview: May be arranged. **Factors that count in admissions decisions:** *Academic:* Secondary school record: Very Important. Class rank: Important. Letters of recommendation: Important. Standardized test scores: Important. Essay: Important. *Nonacademic:* Interview: Considered. Extracurricular activities: Important. Talent/ability: Considered. Character/personal qualities: Very Important. Alumni/ae relationship: Considered. Geographical residence: Not Considered. State residency: Not Considered. Religious affiliation/commitment: Not Considered. Minority status: Not Considered. Volunteer work: Considered. Work experience: Considered. **Other schools with the greatest overlap in applicants:** College of William and Mary; Hollins University; Sweet Briar College; University of Mary Washington; University of Virginia. **Admissions statistics for the fall 2009 entering class:** Total applicants: 1,068. Total accepted: 865. Freshmen enrolled: 135; 56% were from out of state. Overall acceptance rate: 81%. Non-early acceptance rate: 81%. **Size of waiting list:** 0 applicants; enrolled from waiting list: 0. **Credentials of fall 2009 freshmen:** 25% ranked in the top 10 percent of their high school class; 53% were in the top 25 percent; 86% were in the top half. (Proportion submitting class standing: 51%.) **Average high school grade point average:** 3.5. **First-year students who submitted SAT scores:** 91%. Scores (25/75 percentile): Critical Reading: 500-620, Math: 500-600, Combined: 1000-1220. **First-year students submitting ACT scores:** 25%. Scores (25/75 percentile): English: N/A, Math: N/A, Composite: N/A.

ACADEMICS

Year founded: 1891. **Academic calendar:** Semester. **Degrees offered:** bachelor's, master's. **Most popular majors:** 13% political science and government, 10% biology, 10% history, 9% English language and literature, 9% economics. **Major fields of study:** area, ethnic, cultural, and gender studies; biological and biomedical sciences; business, management, marketing, and related support services; communication, journalism, and related programs; education; engineering; English language and literature/letters; foreign languages, literatures, and linguistics; history; mathematics and statistics; multi/interdisciplinary studies; natural resources and conservation; parks, recreation, leisure, and fitness studies; philosophy and religious studies; physical sciences; psychology; social sciences; visual and performing arts. **Areas of required coursework:** arts/fine arts, humanities, mathematics, English (including composition), philosophy, foreign languages, sciences (biological or physical), history, social science, other. **Pre-professional programs:** pre-law, pre-medicine, pre-veterinary science. **Special academic programs (% participation):** accelerated program (5%), cross-registration (9%), double major (16%), dual enrollment (0%), exchange student program (domestic) (1%), honors program (8%), independent study (7%), internships (34%), liberal arts/career combination (1%), student-designed major (3%), study abroad (42%), teacher certificate program (5%), other (0%). **Teacher certification offered in:** early childhood, special education, elementary, secondary. **Faculty and instruction (2009-2010):** Total instructional faculty: 65 full-time, 21 part-time (43% men; 57% women; 7% minorities). Full-time faculty with Ph.D. or other terminal degree: 94%. Student/faculty ratio: 7/1. Classes of fewer than 20 students: 92%; of 20 to 49 students: 8%. **Advanced Placement and International Baccalaureate credit:** AP tests may be used for: Credit and/or placement. Scores accepted: 3, 4, 5. International Baccalaureate exams may be used for: Credit and/or placement. **Freshmen returning for sophomore year:** 72%. **Graduation rates:** Four-year: 62%; five-year: 64%; six-year: 64%. **Graduate study:** 25% of students pursue further study immediately upon graduation; 60% within five years. Fields in which graduates pursue further study: Master of Business Administration (MBA),

2%; law, 12%; medicine, 5%; engineering, 1%; theology (or the seminary), 2%; education, 20%; arts and sciences, 52%; veterinary medicine, 5%.

COSTS AND FINANCIAL AID
Financial aid office: (434) 947-8128. **Expenses (2009-2010):** Tuition and fees 2009-2010: $28,430; room/board: $9,715. Estimated books and supplies: $800; transportation: $500; personal expenses: $1,000. **Financial aid:** Priority filing date for institution's financial aid form: March 1.

CAMPUS LIFE AND EXTRACURRICULAR ACTIVITIES
Campus housing available: coed dorms, women's dorms, other housing options. Students who live in college-owned, operated, or affiliated housing: 90%. **Student employment:** During the 2009-2010 academic year, 65% of undergraduates worked on campus. Average per-year earnings: $1,860. **Clubs and organizations:** Number of student organizations: 40. Activities include: choral groups, dance, drama/theater, international student organization, literary magazine, model UN, music ensembles, pep band, radio station, student government, student newspaper, student film society, yearbook. Number of fraternities: 0; sororities: 0. Average proportion of students who stay on campus on weekends: 60%. **Sports program (2009-2010):** Member of NCAA III. *Men's intercollegiate varsity sports:* basketball, cross country, lacrosse, soccer, tennis. *Women's intercollegiate varsity sports:* basketball, cross country, equestrian, soccer, softball, swimming, tennis, volleyball.

SERVICES AND FACILITIES
Basic services: nonremedial tutoring, health service, health insurance. **Remedial assistance:** writing, study skills. **Counseling services:** minority student, career, personal, academic, older student, psychological, birth control. **For learning-disabled students:** School does not offer a structured program with separate admission and additional fees. Services include: reading machines, tape recorders, other special classes, note-taking services, oral tests, learning center, readers, extended time for tests, tutors, priority registration, priority seating, texts on tape, other testing accommodations, other. **Library:** Number of titles: 198,000; number of current serial subscriptions: 520. **Information technology resources:** Students are not required to lease or own a computer. Number of campus computers available to all students: 150. School has a wireless network. Proportion of college-owned housing units wired for high-speed internet access: 100%. **Campus safety:** Security services offered: 24-hour foot-and-vehicle patrols, late-night transport/escort service, 24-hour emergency telephones, lighted pathways/sidewalks, controlled dormitory access (key, security card, etc).

TRANSFER AND INTERNATIONAL STUDENTS
Transfer students: May apply for admission for the following academic terms: Fall, Spring. Applicants do not need a minimum number of credits to apply. For fall 2009: Transfer applications received: 42. Transfer applicants offered admission: 30. Transfer applicants enrolled: 19. **International students:** Number of foreign undergraduates: 56 (12% of student body). Number of countries represented: 33. Minimum TOEFL score required: 550 (paper); 79 (computer). Average TOEFL score: 600 (paper).

Randolph-Macon College

- **Address:** PO Box 5005, Ashland, VA 23005-5505
- **Website:** http://www.rmc.edu
- **Private; Religious affiliation:** United Methodist
- **Enrollment:** 1,218 full-time; 28 part-time

KEY STATS
✔ **U.S News College Ranking:** 131, National Liberal Arts Colleges
✔ **SAT Score (25th/75th percentile):** 980-1160
✔ **Tuition:** 2010-2011: $30,608

Selectivity: Selective	**Room/board:** $9,391
Acceptance rate: 58%	**Average debt:** $26,763
Student/faculty ratio: 11/1	**Proportion who borrowed:** 72%

UNDERGRADUATE STUDENT BODY STATS
2009-2010 enrollment: 1,218 full-time; 28 part-time. Men: 47%; women: 53%. **Ethnic makeup:** African American: 11%; American-Indian: 1%; Asian American: 2%; Hispanic: 2%; White: 81%; International: 2%. **Religious preference:** Roman Catholic: 13%; Protestant: 1%; Jewish: 1%; Buddhist: 1%;

No preference: 2%; Unknown: 38%; United Methodist: 10%; Baptist: 12%; Other: 22%.

ADMISSIONS FACTS AND FIGURES
Phone: (800) 888-1762. **Email:** admissions@rmc.edu. **Website:** http://www.rmc.edu. **Application deadlines for fall 2011:** Regular decision: March 1; decision sent by April 1. Early decision: Not offered. Early action: Send application by: November 15; Decision sent by: January 1. Admission can be deferred. **Application fee:** $30. **To apply online, go to:** http://www.rmc.edu/apply/. **Admissions requirements/recommendations:** High school units required (recommended): English: 4 (4); Mathematics: 3 (4); Science: 3 (4); Foreign language: 2 (4); Social studies: 1 (2); History: 2 (2); Academic electives: 1 (2); Total units: 16 (22). Tests: The college uses SAT or ACT scores in admissions decisions. Either SAT or ACT required. For admission to the fall 2011 entering class, the school will accept: ACT with writing recommended. Campus visit: Recommended. Admissions interview: Recommended. Off-campus interview: May be arranged. **Factors that count in admissions decisions:** *Academic:* Secondary school record: Very Important. Class rank: Important. Letters of recommendation: Important. Standardized test scores: Important. Essay: Important. *Nonacademic:* Interview: Considered. Extracurricular activities: Considered. Talent/ability: Considered. Character/personal qualities: Considered. Alumni/ae relationship: Considered. Geographical residence: Not Considered. State residency: Not Considered. Religious affiliation/commitment: Not Considered. Minority status: Considered. Volunteer work: Considered. Work experience: Considered. **Other schools with the greatest overlap in applicants:** James Madison University; University of Mary Washington; University of Virginia; Virginia Commonwealth University; Virginia Tech. **Admissions statistics for the fall 2009 entering class:** Total applicants: 4,308. Total accepted: 2,507. Freshmen enrolled: 362; 32% were from out of state. Accepted through early-decision or early-action plans: 68%. Overall acceptance rate: 58%. Non-early acceptance rate: 65%. **Size of waiting list:** 362 applicants; enrolled from waiting list: 76. **Credentials of fall 2009 freshmen:** 16% ranked in the top 10 percent of their high school class; 40% were in the top 25 percent; 79% were in the top half. (Proportion submitting class standing: 67%.) **Average high school grade point average:** 3.3. **First-year students who submitted SAT scores:** 85%. Scores (25/75 percentile): Critical Reading: 490-580, Math: 490-580, Combined: 980-1160.

ACADEMICS
Year founded: 1830. **Academic calendar:** 4-1-4. **Degrees offered:** bachelor's. **Most popular majors:** 14% economics, 13% history, 12% sociology, 9% accounting, 9% biology/biological sciences. **Major fields of study:** area, ethnic, cultural, and gender studies; biological and biomedical sciences; business, management, marketing, and related support services; computer and information sciences and support services; English language and literature/letters; foreign languages, literatures, and linguistics; history; mathematics and statistics; multi/interdisciplinary studies; natural resources and conservation; philosophy and religious studies; physical sciences; psychology; social sciences; visual and performing arts. **Areas of required coursework:** arts/fine arts, humanities, computer literacy, mathematics, English (including composition), foreign languages, sciences (biological or physical), history, social science, other. **Pre-professional programs:** pre-law, pre-dentistry, pre-medicine, pre-theology, pre-veterinary science, pre-optometry, pre-pharmacy, other. **Special academic programs (% participation):** accelerated program (2%), cross-registration (0%), double major (11%), exchange student program (domestic) (0%), honors program (9%), independent study (1%), internships (43%), study abroad (67%), teacher certificate program (5%). **Teacher certification offered in:** elementary, middle/junior high, secondary. **Reserve Officers Training Corps (ROTC):** Army ROTC: Offered at cooperating institution (University of Richmond). **Faculty and instruction (2009-2010):** Total instructional faculty: 91 full-time, 52 part-time (56% men; 44% women; 6% minorities). Full-time faculty with Ph.D. or other terminal degree: 98%. Student/faculty ratio: 11/1. Classes of fewer than 20 students: 67%; of 20 to 49 students: 33%; of 50 or more students: 0%. **Advanced Placement and International Baccalaureate credit:** AP tests may be used for: Credit and/or placement. Scores accepted: 4, 5. International Baccalaureate exams may be used for: Credit and/or placement. **Freshmen returning for sophomore year:** 75%. **Graduation rates:** Four-year: 56%; five-year: 63%; six-year: 63%. **Graduate study:** 36% of students pursue further study immediately upon graduation; 40% within one year; 47% within five years. Fields in which graduates pursue further study: Master of Business Administration (MBA), 24%; law, 6%; medicine, 4%; engineering, 1%; theology (or the seminary), 4%; education, 14%; arts and sciences, 17%.

COSTS AND FINANCIAL AID

Financial aid office: (804) 752-7259. **Expenses (2010-2011):** Tuition and fees 2010-2011: $30,608; room/board: $9,391. Estimated books and supplies: $1,000; transportation: $780; personal expenses: $720. **Financial aid:** Priority filing date for institution's financial aid form: February 1; deadline: March 1. In 2009-2010, 77% of undergraduates applied for financial aid. Of those, 65% were determined to have financial need; 26% had their need fully met. Average financial aid package (proportion receiving): $21,777 (65%). Average amount of gift aid, such as scholarships or grants (proportion receiving): $17,689 (65%). Average amount of self-help aid, such as work study or loans (proportion receiving): $5,234 (52%). Average need-based loan (excluding PLUS or other private loans): $4,627. Among students who received need-based aid, the average percentage of need met: 79%. Among students who received aid based on merit, the average award (and the proportion receiving): $10,726 (33%). The average athletic scholarship (and the proportion receiving): $0 (0%). Average amount of debt of borrowers graduating in 2009: $26,763. Proportion who borrowed: 72%.

CAMPUS LIFE AND EXTRACURRICULAR ACTIVITIES

Campus housing available (% using): coed dorms (57%), women's dorms (15%), men's dorms (15%), sorority housing (4%), fraternity housing (7%), apartment for single students, special housing for disabled students (1%), special housing for international students (1%), other housing options. Students who live in college-owned, operated, or affiliated housing: 82%. **Student employment:** During the 2009-2010 academic year, 40% of undergraduates worked on campus. Average per-year earnings: $1,500. **Clubs and organizations:** Number of student organizations: 104. Activities include: campus ministries, choral groups, dance, drama/theater, international student organization, jazz band, literary magazine, music ensembles, musical theater, pep band, radio station, student government, student newspaper, student film society, television station, yearbook. Number of fraternities: 6; sororities: 5. Proportion of men in fraternities: 34%; of women in sororities: 35%. Average proportion of students who stay on campus on weekends: 80%. **Sports program (2009-2010):** Member of NCAA III. *Men's intercollegiate varsity sports:* baseball, basketball, football, golf, lacrosse, soccer, tennis. *Women's intercollegiate varsity sports:* basketball, field hockey, lacrosse, soccer, softball, tennis, volleyball.

SERVICES AND FACILITIES

Basic services: nonremedial tutoring, women's center, placement service, health service. **Remedial assistance:** reading, math, writing, study skills. **Counseling services:** minority student, career, personal, academic, psychological, religious. **For learning-disabled students:** School does not offer a structured program with separate admission and additional fees. Services include: reading machines, tape recorders, note-taking services, learning center, extended time for tests, tutors, texts on tape. **Library:** Number of titles: 220,161; number of current serial subscriptions: 3,641. **Information technology resources:** Students are not required to lease or own a computer. Number of campus computers available to all students: 356. School has a wireless network. Approximate number of users that can be accommodated: 50. Proportion of college-owned housing units wired for high-speed internet access: 100%. **Campus safety:** Security services offered: 24-hour foot-and-vehicle patrols, late-night transport/escort service, 24-hour emergency telephones, lighted pathways/sidewalks, controlled dormitory access (key, security card, etc).

TRANSFER AND INTERNATIONAL STUDENTS

Transfer students: May apply for admission for the following academic terms: Fall, Spring. Applicants do not need a minimum number of credits to apply. For fall 2009: Transfer applications received: 137. Transfer applicants offered admission: 64. Transfer applicants enrolled: 33. **International students:** Number of foreign undergraduates: 24 (2% of student body). Number of countries represented: 17. Minimum TOEFL score required: 550 (paper); 80 (computer). Average TOEFL score: 605 (paper).

Regent University

- **Address:** 1000 Regent University Drive, Virginia Beach, VA 23464-5037
- **Website:** http://www.regent.edu
- **Private; Religious affiliation:** non-denominational
- **Enrollment:** 1,050 full-time; 868 part-time

KEY STATS

✔ **U.S News College Ranking:** second tier, National Universities
✔ **SAT Score (25th/75th percentile):** 880-1180
✔ **Tuition:** 2010-2011: $15,300

Selectivity: Selective	**Room/board:** $8,600
Acceptance rate: 64%	**Average debt:** N/A
Student/faculty ratio: 16/1	**Proportion who borrowed:** N/A

UNDERGRADUATE STUDENT BODY STATS

2009-2010 enrollment: 1,050 full-time; 868 part-time. Men: 34%; women: 66%. **Ethnic makeup:** African American: 26%; American-Indian: 1%; Asian American: 2%; Hispanic: 6%; White: 64%; International: 1%. **Religious preference:** Roman Catholic: 2%; Protestant: 58%; Unknown: 12%; non-denominational: 28%.

ADMISSIONS FACTS AND FIGURES

Phone: (888) 718-1222. **Email:** admissions@regent.edu. **Website:** http://www.regent.edu. **Application deadlines for fall 2011:** Regular decision: August 3; decision sent by July 31. Early decision: Not offered. Early action: Not offered. Admission can be deferred. **Application fee:** $50. **To apply online, go to:** http://www.regent.edu/admissions/application.html. **Admissions requirements/recommendations:** High school units required (recommended): English: 4 (4); Mathematics: 3 (3); Science: 3 (3); Foreign language: 3 (3); Social studies: 3 (3). Tests: The college uses SAT or ACT scores in admissions decisions. Either SAT or ACT required. For admission to the fall 2011 entering class, the school will accept: ACT with or without writing accepted. Campus visit: Recommended. Admissions interview: Recommended. Off-campus interview: May be arranged. **Factors that count in admissions decisions:** *Academic:* Secondary school record: Considered. Class rank: Not Considered. Letters of recommendation: Considered. Standardized test scores: Very Important. Essay: Important. *Nonacademic:* Interview: Not Considered. Extracurricular activities: Considered. Talent/ability: Considered. Character/personal qualities: Considered. Alumni/ae relationship: Not Considered. Geographical residence: Not Considered. State residency: Not Considered. Religious affiliation/commitment: Not Considered. Minority status: Not Considered. Volunteer work: Considered. Work experience: Considered. **Other schools with the greatest overlap in applicants:** Liberty University; Old Dominion University; Strayer University; University of Maryland–University College; University of Phoenix. **Admissions statistics for the fall 2009 entering class:** Total applicants: 223. Total accepted: 143. Freshmen enrolled: 106; 62% were from out of state. Overall acceptance rate: 64%. **Average high school grade point average:** 3.0. **First-year students who submitted SAT scores:** 55%. Scores (25/75 percentile): Critical Reading: 460-600, Math: 420-580, Combined: 880-1180. **First-year students submitting ACT scores:** 13%. Scores (25/75 percentile): English: 17-24, Math: 16-22, Composite: 16-22.

ACADEMICS

Year founded: 1977. **Academic calendar:** Semester. **Degrees offered:** certificate, associate, bachelor's, post-bachelor's certificate, master's, post-master's certificate, doctorate. **Most popular majors:** 30% psychology, 29% organizational behavior studies, 16% communication studies/speech communication and rhetoric, 11% divinity/ministry (B.D., M.Div.), 9% teacher education and professional development. **Major fields of study:** business, management, marketing, and related support services; communication, journalism, and related programs; education; English language and literature/letters; psychology; social sciences; theology and religious vocations. **Areas of required coursework:** arts/fine arts, humanities, computer literacy, mathematics, English (including composition), foreign languages, sciences (biological or physical), history, social science, other. **Pre-professional programs:** pre-law, pre-theology. **Special academic programs (% participation):** distance learning (96%), double major, dual enrollment, internships, study abroad, teacher certificate program. **Teacher certification offered in:** elementary. **Reserve Officers Training Corps (ROTC):** Army ROTC: Offered at cooperating institution (Old Dominion University). **Faculty and instruction (2009-2010):** Total instructional faculty: 178 full-time, 378 part-time (59% men; 41% women; 17% minorities). Full-time faculty with Ph.D. or other terminal degree: 85%. Student/faculty ratio: 16/1. Classes of fewer than 20 students: 55%; of 20 to 49 students: 45%. **Advanced Placement and International Baccalaureate credit:** International Baccalaureate exams may be used for: Credit only. **Freshmen returning for sophomore year:** 69%.

COSTS AND FINANCIAL AID
Financial aid office: (757) 226-4125. **Expenses (2010-2011):** Tuition and fees 2010-2011: $15,300; room/board: $8,600. Estimated books and supplies: $780; transportation: $2,700; personal expenses: $5,850. **Financial aid:** Priority filing date for institution's financial aid form: March 15.

CAMPUS LIFE AND EXTRACURRICULAR ACTIVITIES
Campus housing available (% using): apartments for married students (50%), apartment for single students (50%). Students who live in college-owned, operated, or affiliated housing: 6%. **Clubs and organizations:** Number of student organizations: 40. Activities include: campus ministries, choral groups, concert band, dance, drama/theater, international student organization, student government, student newspaper. Number of fraternities: 0; sororities: 0.

SERVICES AND FACILITIES
Basic services: health insurance. **Remedial assistance:** math, writing. **Counseling services:** career, military, personal, veteran student, academic, older student, psychological, religious. **For learning-disabled students:** School does not offer a structured program with separate admission and additional fees. Services include: reading machines, readers. **Library:** Number of titles: 295,314; number of current serial subscriptions: 3,329. **Information technology resources:** Students are not required to lease or own a computer. Number of campus computers available to all students: 200. School has a wireless network. Approximate number of users that can be accommodated: 3,000. Proportion of college-owned housing units wired for high-speed internet access: 100%. **Campus safety:** Security services offered: 24-hour foot-and-vehicle patrols, late-night transport/escort service, 24-hour emergency telephones, lighted pathways/sidewalks, controlled dormitory access (key, security card, etc).

TRANSFER AND INTERNATIONAL STUDENTS
Transfer students: May apply for admission for the following academic terms: Fall, Spring, Summer. Applicants need a minimum number of credits to apply. For fall 2009: Transfer applications received: 1,247. Transfer applicants offered admission: 936. Transfer applicants enrolled: 598. **International students:** Number of foreign undergraduates: 11 (1% of student body). Number of countries represented: 7. Minimum TOEFL score required: 577 (paper); 233 (computer).

Roanoke College

- **Address:** 221 College Lane, Salem, VA 24153-3794
- **Website:** http://www.roanoke.edu
- **Private; Religious affiliation:** Lutheran
- **Enrollment:** 1,934 full-time; 110 part-time

KEY STATS
✔ **U.S News College Ranking:** 158, National Liberal Arts Colleges
✔ **SAT Score (25th/75th percentile):** 990-1190
✔ **Tuition:** 2010-2011: $31,214

Selectivity: Selective	**Room/board:** $10,308
Acceptance rate: 68%	**Average debt:** $25,932
Student/faculty ratio: 13/1	**Proportion who borrowed:** 66%

UNDERGRADUATE STUDENT BODY STATS
2009-2010 enrollment: 1,934 full-time; 110 part-time. Men: 44%; women: 56%. **Ethnic makeup:** African American: 4%; American-Indian: 1%; Asian American: 1%; Hispanic: 3%; White: 90%; International: 1%. **Religious preference:** Roman Catholic: 19%; Protestant: 42%; Jewish: 2%; No preference: 13%; Unknown: 11%; Lutheran: 9%; Other: 4%.

ADMISSIONS FACTS AND FIGURES
Phone: (540) 375-2270. **Email:** admissions@roanoke.edu. **Website:** http://www.roanoke.edu. **Application deadlines for fall 2011:** Regular decision: March 15; decision sent by April 1. Early decision: Send application by: N/A; Decision sent by: N/A. Early action: Not offered. Admission can be deferred. **Application fee:** $33. **To apply online, go to:** http://roanoke.edu/

Apply_to_Roanoke.htm. **Admissions requirements/recommendations:** High school units required (recommended): English: 4; Mathematics: 3; Science: 2; Foreign language: (4); Social studies: 2; Academic electives: 5; Total units: 18. Tests: The college uses SAT or ACT scores in admissions decisions. Either SAT or ACT required. For admission to the fall 2011 entering class, the school will accept: ACT with or without writing accepted. Campus visit: Recommended. Admissions interview: Recommended. Off-campus interview: May be arranged. **Factors that count in admissions decisions:** *Academic:* Secondary school record: Very Important. Class rank: Very Important. Letters of recommendation: Important. Standardized test scores: Very Important. Essay: Considered. *Nonacademic:* Interview: Important. Extracurricular activities: Important. Talent/ability: Considered. Character/personal qualities: Very Important. Alumni/ae relationship: Considered. Geographical residence: Not Considered. State residency: Not Considered. Religious affiliation/commitment: Not Considered. Minority status: Considered. Volunteer work: Considered. Work experience: Considered. **Admissions statistics for the fall 2009 entering class:** Total applicants: 4,169. Total accepted: 2,853. Freshmen enrolled: 560; 51% were from out of state. Overall acceptance rate: 68%. Early-decision acceptance rate: 33%. Non-early acceptance rate: 70%. **Size of waiting list:** 428 applicants; enrolled from waiting list: 34. **Credentials of fall 2009 freshmen:** 21% ranked in the top 10 percent of their high school class; 47% were in the top 25 percent; 84% were in the top half. (Proportion submitting class standing: 51%.) **Average high school grade point average:** 3.3. **First-year students who submitted SAT scores:** 76%. Scores (25/75 percentile): Critical Reading: 500-600, Math: 490-590, Combined: 990-1190. **First-year students submitting ACT scores:** 31%. Scores (25/75 percentile): English: N/A, Math: N/A, Composite: N/A.

ACADEMICS
Year founded: 1842. **Academic calendar:** Semester. **Degrees offered:** bachelor's. **Most popular majors:** 23% business administration and management, 10% psychology, 10% sociology, 9% English language and literature, 8% history. **Major fields of study:** biological and biomedical sciences; business, management, marketing, and related support services; computer and information sciences and support services; English language and literature/letters; foreign languages, literatures, and linguistics; health professions and related clinical sciences; history; mathematics and statistics; natural resources and conservation; parks, recreation, leisure, and fitness studies; philosophy and religious studies; physical sciences; psychology; security and protective services; social sciences; theology and religious vocations; visual and performing arts. **Areas of required coursework:** arts/fine arts, humanities, computer literacy, mathematics, English (including composition), philosophy, foreign languages, sciences (biological or physical), history, social science, other. **Pre-professional programs:** pre-law, pre-dentistry, pre-medicine, pre-theology, pre-veterinary science, pre-pharmacy. **Special academic programs:** accelerated program, cross-registration, double major, dual enrollment, English as a Second Language (ESL), external degree program, honors program, independent study, internships, liberal arts/career combination, study abroad, teacher certificate program. **Teacher certification offered in:** elementary, secondary. **Faculty and instruction (2009-2010):** Total instructional faculty: 166 full-time, 42 part-time (53% men; 47% women; 8% minorities). Full-time faculty with Ph.D. or other terminal degree: 82%. Student/faculty ratio: 13/1. Classes of fewer than 20 students: 54%; of 20 to 49 students: 46%; of 50 or more students: 0%. **Advanced Placement and International Baccalaureate credit:** AP tests may be used for: Credit and/or placement. Scores accepted: 3, 4, 5. International Baccalaureate exams may be used for: Placement only. **Freshmen returning for sophomore year:** 76%. **Graduation rates:** Four-year: 58%; five-year: 63%; six-year: 64%.

COSTS AND FINANCIAL AID
Financial aid office: (540) 375-2235. **Expenses (2010-2011):** Tuition and fees 2010-2011: $31,214; room/board: $10,308. Estimated books and supplies: $1,000; transportation: $1,250; personal expenses: $1,000. **Financial aid:** Priority filing date for institution's financial aid form: March 1. In 2009-2010, 82% of undergraduates applied for financial aid. Of those, 67% were determined to have financial need; 32% had their need fully met. Average financial aid package (proportion receiving): $24,772 (67%). Average amount of gift aid, such as scholarships or grants (proportion receiving): $19,058 (66%). Average amount of self-help aid, such as work study or loans (proportion receiving): $5,527 (51%). Average need-based loan (excluding PLUS or other private loans): $4,558. Among students who received need-based aid, the average percentage of need met: 87%. Among students who received aid based on merit, the average award (and the proportion receiving): $10,405 (31%). The average athletic scholarship (and the proportion receiving): $0 (0%). Average amount of debt of borrowers graduating in 2009: $25,932. Proportion who borrowed: 66%.

CAMPUS LIFE AND EXTRACURRICULAR ACTIVITIES

Campus housing available: coed dorms, women's dorms, men's dorms, sorority housing, fraternity housing, apartment for single students, other housing options. Students who live in college-owned, operated, or affiliated housing: 63%. **Student employment:** During the 2009-2010 academic year, 30% of undergraduates worked on campus. Average per-year earnings: $2,000. **Clubs and organizations:** Number of student organizations: 90. Activities include: campus ministries, choral groups, concert band, dance, drama/theater, international student organization, jazz band, literary magazine, model UN, music ensembles, musical theater, pep band, radio station, student government, student newspaper, student film society, yearbook. Number of fraternities: 4; sororities: 4. Proportion of men in fraternities: 22%; of women in sororities: 25%. **Sports program (2009-2010):** Member of NCAA III.

SERVICES AND FACILITIES

Basic services: nonremedial tutoring, placement service, health service. **Remedial assistance:** writing, study skills. **Counseling services:** minority student, career, personal, academic, older student, psychological, birth control, religious. **For learning-disabled students:** School does not offer a structured program with separate admission and additional fees. Services include: tape recorders, untimed tests, note-taking services, oral tests, learning center, extended time for tests, tutors, other testing accommodations. **Library:** Number of titles: 214,724; number of current serial subscriptions: 15,839. **Information technology resources:** Students are not required to lease or own a computer. Number of campus computers available to all students: 200. School has a wireless network. Approximate number of users that can be accommodated: 1,000. Proportion of college-owned housing units wired for high-speed internet access: 100%. **Campus safety:** Security services offered: 24-hour foot-and-vehicle patrols, late-night transport/escort service, 24-hour emergency telephones, lighted pathways/sidewalks, controlled dormitory access (key, security card, etc).

TRANSFER AND INTERNATIONAL STUDENTS

Transfer students: May apply for admission for the following academic terms: Fall, Spring, Summer. Applicants need a minimum number of credits to apply. For fall 2009: Transfer applications received: 368. Transfer applicants offered admission: 180. Transfer applicants enrolled: 82. **International students:** Number of foreign undergraduates: 28 (1% of student body). Number of countries represented: 25. Minimum TOEFL score required: 520 (paper); 190 (computer).

Shenandoah University

- **Address:** 1460 University Drive, Winchester, VA 22601
- **Website:** http://www.su.edu
- **Private; Religious affiliation:** United Methodist
- **Enrollment:** 1,673 full-time; 94 part-time

KEY STATS

✔ **U.S News College Ranking:** 32, Regional Universities (South)
✔ **SAT Score (25th/75th percentile):** 880-1130
✔ **Tuition:** 2010-2011: $25,080

Selectivity: Selective	**Room/board:** $8,870
Acceptance rate: 84%	**Average debt:** N/A
Student/faculty ratio: 9/1	**Proportion who borrowed:** 88%

UNDERGRADUATE STUDENT BODY STATS

2009-2010 enrollment: 1,673 full-time; 94 part-time. Men: 43%; women: 57%. **Ethnic makeup:** African American: 12%; Asian American: 2%; Hispanic: 3%; White: 80%; International: 3%. **Religious preference:** Roman Catholic: 19%; Protestant: 29%; Jewish: 1%; Muslim: 2%; Hindu: 1%; Buddhist: 1%; No preference: 15%; Unknown: 3%; United Methodist: 11%; Baptist: 8%; Other: 10%.

ADMISSIONS FACTS AND FIGURES

Phone: (540) 665-4581. **Email:** admit@su.edu. **Website:** http://www.su.edu. **Application deadlines for fall 2011:** Regular decision: August 1. Early decision: Not offered. Early action: Not offered. Admission can be deferred. **Application fee:** $30. **To apply online, go to:** https://www.applyweb.com/apply/su/index.html. **Admissions requirements/recommendations:** High school units required (recommended): English: 4; Mathematics: 3 (4); Science: 2 (4); Foreign language: 2 (3); Social studies: 2 (4); History: (4);

Academic electives: 2 (4); Total units: 15. Tests: The college uses SAT or ACT scores in admissions decisions. Either SAT or ACT required. For admission to the fall 2011 entering class, the school will accept: ACT with or without writing accepted. Campus visit: Recommended. Admissions interview: Recommended. Off-campus interview: May be arranged. **Factors that count in admissions decisions:** *Academic:* Secondary school record: Very Important. Class rank: Not Considered. Letters of recommendation: Important. Standardized test scores: Very Important. Essay: Not Considered. *Nonacademic:* Interview: Not Considered. Extracurricular activities: Important. Talent/ability: Important. Character/personal qualities: Not Considered. Alumni/ae relationship: Not Considered. Geographical residence: Not Considered. State residency: Not Considered. Religious affiliation/commitment: Not Considered. Minority status: Not Considered. Volunteer work: Considered. Work experience: Considered. **Other schools with the greatest overlap in applicants:** Bridgewater College; Christopher Newport University; James Madison University; Radford University; Virginia Commonwealth University. **Admissions statistics for the fall 2009 entering class:** Total applicants: 1,466. Total accepted: 1,236. Freshmen enrolled: 435; 34% were from out of state. Overall acceptance rate: 84%. **Size of waiting list:** N/A applicants; enrolled from waiting list: 0. **Credentials of fall 2009 freshmen:** 14% ranked in the top 10 percent of their high school class; 41% were in the top 25 percent; 75% were in the top half. (Proportion submitting class standing: 43%.) **Average high school grade point average:** 3.2. **First-year students who submitted SAT scores:** 96%. Scores (25/75 percentile): Critical Reading: 440-570, Math: 440-560, Combined: 880-1130. **First-year students submitting ACT scores:** 23%. Scores (25/75 percentile): English: N/A, Math: N/A, Composite: 18-23.

ACADEMICS

Year founded: 1875. **Academic calendar:** Semester. **Degrees offered:** certificate, bachelor's, post-bachelor's certificate, master's, post-master's certificate, doctorate. **Most popular majors:** 25% nursing/registered nurse training (R.N., A.S.N., B.S.N., M.S.N.), 14% business administration and management, 8% drama and dramatics/theater arts, 7% respiratory care therapy/therapist, 6% biology/biological sciences. **Major fields of study:** area, ethnic, cultural, and gender studies; biological and biomedical sciences; business, management, marketing, and related support services; communication, journalism, and related programs; education; English language and literature/letters; foreign languages, literatures, and linguistics; health professions and related clinical sciences; history; liberal arts and sciences studies, and humanities; mathematics and statistics; natural resources and conservation; philosophy and religious studies; physical sciences; psychology; public administration and social service professions; security and protective services; social sciences; visual and performing arts. **Areas of required coursework:** arts/fine arts, humanities, computer literacy, mathematics, English (including composition), philosophy, sciences (biological or physical), history, social science, other. **Pre-professional programs:** pre-law, pre-dentistry, pre-medicine, pre-theology, pre-pharmacy, other. **Special academic programs:** accelerated program, distance learning, double major, dual enrollment, English as a Second Language (ESL), internships, study abroad, teacher certificate program, weekend college. **Teacher certification offered in:** special education, elementary, middle/junior high, secondary. **Cooperative education programs:** health professions. **Faculty and instruction (2009-2010):** Total instructional faculty: 215 full-time, 236 part-time (38% men; 62% women; 10% minorities). Full-time faculty with Ph.D. or other terminal degree: 80%. Student/faculty ratio: 9/1. Classes of fewer than 20 students: 78%; of 20 to 49 students: 21%; of 50 or more students: 1%. **Advanced Placement and International Baccalaureate credit:** AP tests may be used for: Credit only. Scores accepted: 3, 4, 5. International Baccalaureate exams may be used for: Credit only. **Freshmen returning for sophomore year:** 69%. **Graduation rates:** Four-year: 33%; five-year: 48%; six-year: 48%. **Graduate study:** 20% of students pursue further study immediately upon graduation; 35% within one year; 45% within five years. Fields in which graduates pursue further study: Master of Business Administration (MBA), 13%; law, 1%; medicine, 1%; theology (or the seminary), 1%; education, 25%; arts and sciences, 24%.

COSTS AND FINANCIAL AID

Financial aid office: (540) 665-4538. **Expenses (2010-2011):** Tuition and fees 2010-2011: $25,080; room/board: $8,870. Estimated books and supplies: $1,500; transportation: $600; personal expenses: $2,000. **Financial aid:** In 2009-2010, 70% of undergraduates applied for financial aid. Of those, 67% were determined to have financial need; 18% had their need fully met. Average financial aid package (proportion receiving): $15,545 (67%). Average amount of gift aid, such as scholarships or grants (proportion receiving): $5,000 (54%). Average amount of self-help aid, such as work study or loans (proportion receiving): $6,500 (64%). Average need-based loan (excluding PLUS or other private loans): $4,500. Among students who received need-based aid, the average percentage of need met: 92%. Among students who received aid based on merit, the average award (and the proportion receiving): $4,000 (7%). The average athletic scholarship (and the proportion receiving): $4,500 (0%). Proportion who borrowed: 88%.

CAMPUS LIFE AND EXTRACURRICULAR ACTIVITIES

Campus housing available (% using): coed dorms (99%), special housing for disabled students (1%). Students who live in college-owned, operated, or affiliated housing: 49%. **Student employment:** During the 2009-2010 academic year, 50% of undergraduates worked on campus. Average per-year earnings: $1,500. **Clubs and organizations:** Number of student organizations: 49. Activities include: choral groups, concert band, dance, drama/theater, international student organization, jazz band, literary magazine, music ensembles, musical theater, opera, pep band, student government, student newspaper, symphony orchestra, television station. Number of fraternities: 0; sororities: 0. Average proportion of students who stay on campus on weekends: 60%. **Sports program (2009-2010):** Member of NCAA III. *Men's intercollegiate varsity sports:* baseball, basketball, cross country, football, golf, lacrosse, soccer, tennis, track and field (indoor), track and field (outdoor). *Women's intercollegiate varsity sports:* basketball, cross country, field hockey, lacrosse, soccer, softball, tennis, track and field (indoor), track and field (outdoor), volleyball.

SERVICES AND FACILITIES

Basic services: nonremedial tutoring, placement service, day care, health service, health insurance. **Remedial assistance:** reading, math, writing, study skills. **Counseling services:** minority student, career, military, personal, veteran student, academic, older student, psychological, birth control, religious. **For learning-disabled students:** School does not offer a structured program with separate admission and additional fees. Total undergraduates in learning-disabled program or receiving services: 68. Services include: remedial math, reading machines, tape recorders, note-taking services, oral tests, learning center, readers, extended time for tests, tutors, priority registration, priority seating, texts on tape, other testing accommodations, other. **Library:** Number of titles: 131,174; number of current serial subscriptions: 19,479. **Information technology resources:** Students are not required to lease or own a computer. Number of campus computers available to all students: 175. School has a wireless network. Approximate number of users that can be accommodated: 3,500. Proportion of college-owned housing units wired for high-speed internet access: 100%. **Campus safety:** Security services offered: 24-hour foot-and-vehicle patrols, late-night transport/escort service, 24-hour emergency telephones, lighted pathways/sidewalks, student patrols, controlled dormitory access (key, security card, etc).

TRANSFER AND INTERNATIONAL STUDENTS

Transfer students: May apply for admission for the following academic terms: Fall, Spring. Applicants do not need a minimum number of credits to apply. For fall 2009: Transfer applications received: 423. Transfer applicants offered admission: 371. Transfer applicants enrolled: 213. **International students:** Number of foreign undergraduates: 50 (3% of student body). Number of countries represented: 69. Minimum TOEFL score required: 527 (paper); 71 (computer). Average TOEFL score: 525 (paper).

St. Paul's College

- **Address:** 115 College Drive, Lawrenceville, VA 23868
- **Website:** http://www.saintpauls.edu
- **Private; Religious affiliation:** Episcopal
- **Enrollment:** 566 full-time; 18 part-time

KEY STATS
✔ **U.S News College Ranking:** second tier, Regional Colleges (South)
✔ **SAT Score (25th/75th percentile):** 570-840
✔ **Tuition:** 2010-2011: $13,130

Selectivity: Least selective	**Room/board:** $6,640
Acceptance rate: 99%	**Average debt:** $21,917
Student/faculty ratio: 17/1	**Proportion who borrowed:** 19%

UNDERGRADUATE STUDENT BODY STATS
2009-2010 enrollment: 566 full-time; 18 part-time. Men: 50%; women: 50%.
Ethnic makeup: African American: 97%; Hispanic: 1%; White: 2%.

ADMISSIONS FACTS AND FIGURES

Phone: (434) 848-1856. **Email:** admissions@saintpauls.edu. **Website:** http://www.saintpauls.edu. **Application deadlines for fall 2011:** Regular decision: Rolling. Early decision: Not offered. Early action: Not offered. Admission can be deferred. **Application fee:** $20. **Admissions requirements/recommendations:** High school units required (recommended): English: 4; Mathematics: 2; Science: 2; Foreign language: 1; Social studies: 2. Tests: The college uses SAT or ACT scores in admissions decisions. Either SAT or ACT required. For admission to the fall 2011 entering class, the school will accept: ACT with or without writing accepted. Campus visit: Recommended. Admissions interview: Neither required nor recommended. Off-campus interview: May be arranged. **Factors that count in admissions decisions: *Academic:*** Secondary school record: Very Important. Class rank: Very Important. Letters of recommendation: Very Important. Standardized test scores: Very Important. Essay: Very Important. *Nonacademic:* Interview: Important. Extracurricular activities: Considered. Talent/ability: Considered. Character/personal qualities: Important. Alumni/ae relationship: Considered. Geographical residence: Not Considered. State residency: Not Considered. Religious affiliation/commitment: Not Considered. Minority status: Considered. Volunteer work: Not Considered. Work experience: Considered. **Admissions statistics for the fall 2009 entering class:** Total applicants: 403. Total accepted: 398. Freshmen enrolled: 157; 1% were from out of state. Overall acceptance rate: 99%. **Credentials of fall 2009 freshmen:** 1% ranked in the top 10 percent of their high school class; 2% were in the top 25 percent; 32% were in the top half. (Proportion submitting class standing: 70%.) **Average high school grade point average:** 2.2. **First-year students who submitted SAT scores:** 83%. Scores (25/75 percentile): Critical Reading: 250-420, Math: 320-420, Combined: 570-840. **First-year students submitting ACT scores:** 21%. Scores (25/75 percentile): English: 14-16, Math: 9-16, Composite: 13-16.

ACADEMICS

Year founded: 1888. **Academic calendar:** Semester. **Degrees offered:** bachelor's. **Most popular majors:** 71% business, management, marketing, and related support services, 11% security and protective services, 6% social sciences, 4% biological and biomedical sciences, 4% liberal arts and sciences studies, and humanities. **Major fields of study:** business, management, marketing, and related support services; English language and literature/letters; liberal arts and sciences studies, and humanities; philosophy and religious studies; security and protective services. **Areas of required coursework:** arts/fine arts, computer literacy, mathematics, English (including composition), sciences (biological or physical), history. **Special academic programs (% participation):** accelerated program (77%), double major (2%), honors program (11%), independent study (7%), internships (25%), liberal arts/career combination, teacher certificate program (8%), other. **Teacher certification offered in:** early childhood, special education, elementary, secondary. **Reserve Officers Training Corps (ROTC):** Army ROTC: Offered at cooperating institution (Virginia State University). **Faculty and instruction (2009-2010):** Total instructional faculty: 28 full-time, 18 part-time (52% men; 48% women; 83% minorities). Full-time faculty with Ph.D. or other terminal degree: 57%. Student/faculty ratio: 17/1. Classes of fewer than 20 students: 73%; of 20 to 49 students: 26%; of 50 or more students: 1%. **Freshmen returning for sophomore year:** 44%. **Graduation rates:** Six-year: 18%. **Graduate study:** Fields in which graduates pursue further study: Master of Business Administration (MBA), 10%; law, 2%; medicine, 3%; theology (or the seminary), 2%; education, 10%; arts and sciences, 5%.

COSTS AND FINANCIAL AID

Financial aid office: (434) 848-6497. **Expenses (2010-2011):** Tuition and fees 2010-2011: $13,130; room/board: $6,640. Estimated books and supplies: $1,500; transportation: $1,800; personal expenses: $1,400. **Financial aid:** In 2009-2010, 98% of undergraduates applied for financial aid. Of those, 96% were determined to have financial need; 11% had their need fully met. Average financial aid package (proportion receiving): $8,147 (96%). Average amount of gift aid, such as scholarships or grants (proportion receiving): $4,508 (70%). Average amount of self-help aid, such as work study or loans (proportion receiving): $4,324 (83%). Average need-based loan (excluding PLUS or other private loans): $1,337. Among students who received need-based aid, the average percentage of need met: 57%. Among students who received aid based on merit, the average award (and the proportion receiving): $0 (0%). The average athletic scholarship (and the proportion receiving): $9,459 (21%). Average amount of debt of borrowers graduating in 2009: $21,917. Proportion who borrowed: 19%.

CAMPUS LIFE AND EXTRACURRICULAR ACTIVITIES

Campus housing available: women's dorms, men's dorms, sorority housing, fraternity housing, other housing options. Students who live in college-owned, operated, or affiliated housing: 78%. **Student employment:** During the 2009-2010 academic year, 2% of undergraduates worked on campus. Average per-year earnings: $3,200. **Clubs and organizations:** Number of student organizations: 28. Activities include: campus ministries, choral groups, student government. Number of fraternities: 5; sororities: 3. Proportion of men in fraternities: 2%; of women in sororities: 3%. Average proportion of students who stay on campus on weekends: 50%. **Sports program (2009-2010):** Member of NCAA II. *Men's intercollegiate varsity sports:* baseball, basketball, cross country, football, golf, tennis, track and field (indoor), track and field (outdoor). *Women's intercollegiate varsity sports:* basketball, bowling, cross country, golf, softball, tennis, track and field (indoor), track and field (outdoor), volleyball.

SERVICES AND FACILITIES

Basic services: nonremedial tutoring, placement service, day care, health insurance. **Remedial assistance:** reading, math, writing, study skills. **Counseling services:** career, personal, academic, older student, psychological, religious. **For learning-disabled students:** School does not offer a structured program with separate admission and additional fees. Services include: remedial math, remedial English, remedial reading, tape recorders, diagnostic testing service, untimed tests, note-taking services, learning center, extended time for tests, tutors, other testing accommodations. **Library:** Number of titles: 55,100; number of current serial subscriptions: 167. **Information technology resources:** Students are not required to lease or own a computer. Number of campus computers available to all students: 100. School has a wireless network. Proportion of college-owned housing units wired for high-speed internet access: 90%. **Campus safety:** Security services offered: 24-hour foot-and-vehicle patrols, 24-hour emergency telephones, lighted pathways/sidewalks, controlled dormitory access (key, security card, etc).

TRANSFER AND INTERNATIONAL STUDENTS

Transfer students: May apply for admission for the following academic terms: Fall, Spring. Applicants need a minimum number of credits to apply. For fall 2009: Transfer applications received: 114. Transfer applicants offered admission: 97. Transfer applicants enrolled: 83. **International students:** Number of foreign undergraduates: 2.

Sweet Briar College

- **Address:** 134 Chapel Road, Sweet Briar, VA 24595
- **Website:** http://www.sbc.edu
- **Private**
- **Enrollment:** 709 full-time; 36 part-time

KEY STATS

- ✔ **U.S News College Ranking:** 101, National Liberal Arts Colleges
- ✔ **SAT Score (25th/75th percentile):** 940-1148
- ✔ **Tuition:** 2010-2011: $30,195

Selectivity: Selective	**Room/board:** $10,780
Acceptance rate: 82%	**Average debt:** $25,372
Student/faculty ratio: 8/1	**Proportion who borrowed:** 52%

UNDERGRADUATE STUDENT BODY STATS

2009-2010 enrollment: 709 full-time; 36 part-time. Men: 3%; women: 97%. **Ethnic makeup:** African American: 4%; Asian American: 1%; Hispanic: 4%; White: 89%; International: 2%.

ADMISSIONS FACTS AND FIGURES

Phone: (800) 381-6142. **Email:** admissions@sbc.edu. **Website:** http://www.sbc.edu. **Application deadlines for fall 2011:** Regular decision: February 1; decision sent by March 15. Early decision: Not offered. Early action: Not offered. Admission can be deferred. **Application fee:** $40. **To apply online, go to:** http://www.admissions.sbc.edu/apply/. **Admissions requirements/recommendations:** High school units required (recommended): English: 4 (4); Mathematics: 3 (4); Science: 3 (4); Foreign language: 2 (4); Social studies: 3 (4); Total units: 16 (20). Tests: The college uses SAT or ACT scores in admissions decisions. Either SAT or ACT required. For admission to the fall 2011 entering class, the school will accept: ACT with or without writing accepted. Campus visit: Recommended. Admissions interview:

Recommended. Off-campus interview: May be arranged. **Factors that count in admissions decisions:** *Academic:* Secondary school record: Very Important. Class rank: Considered. Letters of recommendation: Important. Standardized test scores: Important. Essay: Important. *Nonacademic:* Interview: Important. Extracurricular activities: Considered. Talent/ability: Considered. Character/personal qualities: Considered. Alumni/ae relationship: Considered. Geographical residence: Not Considered. State residency: Not Considered. Religious affiliation/commitment: Not Considered. Minority status: Considered. Volunteer work: Considered. Work experience: Considered. **Other schools with the greatest overlap in applicants:** College of William and Mary; Hollins University; Mount Holyoke College; Randolph College; University of Virginia. **Admissions statistics for the fall 2009 entering class:** Total applicants: 572. Total accepted: 471. Freshmen enrolled: 157; 58% were from out of state. Overall acceptance rate: 82%. **Credentials of fall 2009 freshmen:** 22% ranked in the top 10 percent of their high school class; 45% were in the top 25 percent; 78% were in the top half. (Proportion submitting class standing: 62%.) **Average high school grade point average:** 3.4. **First-year students who submitted SAT scores:** 90%. Scores (25/75 percentile): Critical Reading: 480-628, Math: 460-520, Combined: 940-1148. **First-year students submitting ACT scores:** 33%. Scores (25/75 percentile): English: 18-26, Math: 20-27, Composite: 20-27.

ACADEMICS

Year founded: 1901. **Academic calendar:** Semester. **Degrees offered:** bachelor's, master's. **Most popular majors:** 17% business, management, marketing, and related support services, 13% engineering technologies/technicians, 7% history. **Major fields of study:** biological and biomedical sciences; business, management, marketing, and related support services; English language and literature/letters; social sciences; visual and performing arts. **Areas of required coursework:** arts/fine arts, humanities, English (including composition), foreign languages, sciences (biological or physical), social science, other. **Special academic programs (% participation):** accelerated program (5%), cross-registration (5%), double major (15%), dual enrollment (15%), exchange student program (domestic) (5%), honors program (35%), independent study (25%), internships (25%), liberal arts/career combination (0%), student-designed major (2%), study abroad (31%), teacher certificate program (7%). **Teacher certification offered in:** elementary, secondary. **Faculty and instruction (2009-2010):** Total instructional faculty: 76 full-time, 55 part-time (47% men; 53% women; 7% minorities). Full-time faculty with Ph.D. or other terminal degree: 95%. Student/faculty ratio: 8/1. Classes of fewer than 20 students: 91%; of 20 to 49 students: 9%. **Advanced Placement and International Baccalaureate credit:** AP tests may be used for: Placement only. Scores accepted: 4, 5. International Baccalaureate exams may be used for: Placement only. **Freshmen returning for sophomore year:** 76%. **Graduation rates:** Four-year: 59%; five-year: 59%; six-year: 60%. **Graduate study:** 24% of students pursue further study immediately upon graduation; 50% within five years. Fields in which graduates pursue further study: Master of Business Administration (MBA), 6%; law, 4%; medicine, 21%; education, 10%; arts and sciences, 54%; veterinary medicine, 5%.

COSTS AND FINANCIAL AID

Financial aid office: (434) 381-6156. **Expenses (2010-2011):** Tuition and fees 2010-2011: $30,195; room/board: $10,780. Estimated books and supplies: $900; transportation: $300; personal expenses: $950. **Financial aid:** Priority filing date for institution's financial aid form: March 1. In 2009-2010, 68% of undergraduates applied for financial aid. Of those, 68% were determined to have financial need; 83% had their need fully met. Average financial aid package (proportion receiving): $18,064 (67%). Average amount of gift aid, such as scholarships or grants (proportion receiving): $15,960 (53%). Average amount of self-help aid, such as work study or loans (proportion receiving): $5,010 (53%). Average need-based loan (excluding PLUS or other private loans): $4,515. Among students who received need-based aid, the average percentage of need met: 29%. Among students who received aid based on merit, the average award (and the proportion receiving): $11,705 (40%). Average amount of debt of borrowers graduating in 2009: $25,372. Proportion who borrowed: 52%.

CAMPUS LIFE AND EXTRACURRICULAR ACTIVITIES

Campus housing available (% using): women's dorms (79%), special housing for disabled students (1%), special housing for international students (5%), other housing options (5%). Students who live in college-owned, operated, or affiliated housing: 92%. **Student employment:** During the 2009-2010 academic year, 69% of undergraduates worked on campus. Average per-year earnings: $1,000. **Clubs and organizations:** Number of student organizations: 61. Activities include: campus ministries, choral groups, dance, drama/theater, literary magazine, model UN, music ensembles, musical theater, radio station, student government, student newspaper, student film society, symphony orchestra, yearbook. Number of fraternities: 0; sororities: 0. Average proportion of students who stay on campus on weekends: 65%. **Sports program (2009-2010):** Member of NCAA III. *Women's intercollegiate varsity sports:* field hockey, lacrosse, soccer, softball, swimming, tennis, volleyball.

SERVICES AND FACILITIES

Basic services: nonremedial tutoring, placement service, health service, health insurance. **Counseling services:** career, personal, academic, psychological, birth control, religious. **For learning-disabled students:** School does not offer a structured program with separate admission and additional fees. Services include: tape recorders, note-taking services, learning center, readers, extended time for tests, tutors, priority seating, substitution of courses. **Library:** Number of titles: 297,073; number of current serial subscriptions: 720. **Information technology resources:** Students are not required to lease or own a computer. Number of campus computers available to all students: 70. School has a wireless network. Approximate number of users that can be accommodated: 600. Proportion of college-owned housing units wired for high-speed internet access: 99%. **Campus safety:** Security services offered: 24-hour foot-and-vehicle patrols, late-night transport/escort service, 24-hour emergency telephones, lighted pathways/sidewalks, student patrols, controlled dormitory access (key, security card, etc).

TRANSFER AND INTERNATIONAL STUDENTS

Transfer students: May apply for admission for the following academic terms: Fall, Spring. Applicants need a minimum number of credits to apply. For fall 2009: Transfer applications received: 50. Transfer applicants offered admission: 35. Transfer applicants enrolled: 19. **International students:** Number of foreign undergraduates: 10 (2% of student body). Number of countries represented: 7. Minimum TOEFL score required: 550 (paper); 213 (computer).

University of Mary Washington

■ **Address:** 1301 College Avenue, Fredericksburg, VA 22401
■ **Website:** http://www.umw.edu
■ **Public**
■ **Enrollment:** 3,751 full-time; 646 part-time

KEY STATS
✔ **U.S News College Ranking:** 13, Regional Universities (South)
✔ **SAT Score (25th/75th percentile):** 1060-1270
✔ **Tuition:** 2010-2011: $7,862 in state, $19,590 out of state
  Selectivity: Selective   **Room/board:** $8,116
  Acceptance rate: 74%   **Average debt:** $16,000
  Student/faculty ratio: 16/1   **Proportion who borrowed:** 57%

UNDERGRADUATE STUDENT BODY STATS

2009-2010 enrollment: 3,751 full-time; 646 part-time. Men: 35%; women: 65%. **Ethnic makeup:** African American: 5%; Asian American: 5%; Hispanic: 4%; White: 86%.

ADMISSIONS FACTS AND FIGURES

Phone: (540) 654-2000. **Email:** admit@umw.edu. **Website:** http://www.umw.edu. **Application deadlines for fall 2011:** Regular decision: February 1; decision sent by April 1. Early decision: Not offered. Early action: Not offered. Admission can be deferred. **Application fee:** $50. **To apply online, go to:** https://www.applyweb.com/apply/umw. **Admissions requirements/recommendations:** High school units required (recommended): English: 4 (4); Mathematics: 3 (4); Science: 3 (4); Foreign language: 2 (4); Social studies: 2 (2); History: 1 (2); Academic electives: 0 (0); Total units: 15 (20). Tests: The college uses SAT or ACT scores in admissions decisions. Either SAT or ACT required. For admission to the fall 2011 entering class, the school will accept: ACT with or without writing accepted. Campus visit: Recommended. Admissions interview: Neither required nor recommended. Off-campus interview: Not available. **Factors that count in admissions decisions:** *Academic:* Secondary school record: Very Important. Class rank: Important. Letters of recommendation: Important. Standardized test scores: Important. Essay: Important. *Nonacademic:* Interview: Not Considered. Extracurricular activities: Important. Talent/ability: Considered. Character/personal qualities: Considered. Alumni/ae relationship: Considered. Geographical residence: Considered. State residency: Considered. Religious

affiliation/commitment: Not Considered. Minority status: Considered. Volunteer work: Considered. Work experience: Considered. **Other schools with the greatest overlap in applicants:** College of William and Mary; James Madison University; University of Richmond; University of Virginia; Virginia Tech. **Admissions statistics for the fall 2009 entering class:** Total applicants: 4,761. Total accepted: 3,541. Freshmen enrolled: 963; 20% were from out of state. Overall acceptance rate: 74%. **Size of waiting list:** 549 applicants; enrolled from waiting list: 117. **Average high school grade point average:** 3.6. **First-year students who submitted SAT scores:** 91%. Scores (25/75 percentile): Critical Reading: 540-650, Math: 520-620, Combined: 1060-1270. **First-year students submitting ACT scores:** 23%. Scores (25/75 percentile): English: N/A, Math: N/A, Composite: 24-28.

ACADEMICS

Year founded: 1908. **Academic calendar:** Semester. **Degrees offered:** certificate, bachelor's, post-bachelor's certificate, master's. **Most popular majors:** 16% social sciences, 13% business, management, marketing, and related support services, 12% psychology, 10% English language and literature/letters, 10% multi/interdisciplinary studies. **Major fields of study:** area, ethnic, cultural, and gender studies; biological and biomedical sciences; business, management, marketing, and related support services; computer and information sciences and support services; English language and literature/letters; foreign languages, literatures, and linguistics; liberal arts and sciences studies, and humanities; mathematics and statistics; multi/interdisciplinary studies; philosophy and religious studies; physical sciences; psychology; social sciences; visual and performing arts. **Areas of required coursework:** arts/fine arts, humanities, computer literacy, mathematics, English (including composition), philosophy, foreign languages, sciences (biological or physical), history, social science. **Pre-professional programs:** pre-law, pre-dentistry, pre-medicine, pre-veterinary science, pre-pharmacy. **Special academic programs:** accelerated program, distance learning, double major, independent study, internships, student-designed major, study abroad, teacher certificate program. **Teacher certification offered in:** special education, elementary, middle/junior high, secondary, bilingual/bicultural. **Reserve Officers Training Corps (ROTC):** Army ROTC: Offered at cooperating institution (George Mason University). **Faculty and instruction (2009-2010):** Total instructional faculty: 242 full-time, 128 part-time (49% men; 51% women; 11% minorities). Full-time faculty with Ph.D. or other terminal degree: 90%. Student/faculty ratio: 16/1. Classes of fewer than 20 students: 42%; of 20 to 49 students: 54%; of 50 or more students: 4%. **Advanced Placement and International Baccalaureate credit:** AP tests may be used for: Credit only. Scores accepted: 3, 4, 5. International Baccalaureate exams may be used for: Credit and/or placement. **Freshmen returning for sophomore year:** 84%. **Graduation rates:** Four-year: 67%; five-year: 75%; six-year: 76%. **Graduate study:** 24% of students pursue further study immediately upon graduation; 24% within one year. Fields in which graduates pursue further study: Master of Business Administration (MBA), 1%; law, 5%; medicine, 1%; education, 33%; arts and sciences, 60%.

COSTS AND FINANCIAL AID

Financial aid office: (540) 654-2468. **Expenses (2010-2011):** Tuition and fees 2010-2011: $7,862 in state, $19,590 out of state; room/board: $8,116. Estimated books and supplies: $1,000; transportation: $1,152; personal expenses: $1,600. **Financial aid:** Priority filing date for institution's financial aid form: March 1; deadline: May 15. In 2009-2010, 52% of undergraduates applied for financial aid. Of those, 28% were determined to have financial need; 19% had their need fully met. Average financial aid package (proportion receiving): $9,800 (27%). Average amount of gift aid, such as scholarships or grants (proportion receiving): $6,200 (13%). Average amount of self-help aid, such as work study or loans (proportion receiving): $8,900 (18%). Average need-based loan (excluding PLUS or other private loans): $4,200. Among students who received need-based aid, the average percentage of need met: 56%. Among students who received aid based on merit, the average award (and the proportion receiving): $1,750 (11%). The average athletic scholarship (and the proportion receiving): $0 (0%). Average amount of debt of borrowers graduating in 2009: $16,000. Proportion who borrowed: 57%.

CAMPUS LIFE AND EXTRACURRICULAR ACTIVITIES

Campus housing available (% using): coed dorms (42%), women's dorms (10%), men's dorms (0%), apartment for single students (47%), special housing for disabled students, special housing for international students, other housing options (1%). Students who live in college-owned, operated, or affiliated housing: 57%. **Student employment:** During the 2009-2010 academic year, 18% of undergraduates worked on campus. Average per-year earnings: $1,630. **Clubs and organizations:** Number of student organizations: 130. Activities include: campus ministries, choral groups, concert band, dance, drama/theater, international student organization, jazz band, literary magazine, model UN, music ensembles, musical theater, opera, radio station, student government, student newspaper, student film society, symphony orchestra, yearbook. Number of fraternities: 0; sororities: 0. Average proportion of students who stay on campus on weekends: 60%. **Sports program (2009-2010):** Member of NCAA III. *Men's intercollegiate varsity sports:* baseball, basketball, cross country, lacrosse, soccer, swimming, tennis, track and field (indoor), track and field (outdoor). *Women's intercollegiate varsity sports:* basketball, crew (heavyweight), cross country, equestrian, field hockey, lacrosse, crew (lightweight), soccer, softball, swimming, tennis, track and field (indoor), track and field (outdoor), volleyball.

SERVICES AND FACILITIES

Basic services: nonremedial tutoring, health service, health insurance, other. **Counseling services:** minority student, career, personal, academic, older student, psychological, birth control. **For learning-disabled students:** School does not offer a structured program with separate admission and additional fees. Total undergraduates in learning-disabled program or receiving services: 90. Services include: reading machines, tape recorders, note-taking services, extended time for tests, priority seating, substitution of courses, texts on tape, exams on tape or computer, other testing accommodations, other. **Library:** Number of titles: 418,240; number of current serial subscriptions: 39,866. **Information technology resources:** Students are not required to lease or own a computer. Number of campus computers available to all students: 350. School has a wireless network. Approximate number of users that can be accommodated: 11,700. Proportion of college-owned housing units wired for high-speed internet access: 100%. **Campus safety:** Security services offered: 24-hour foot-and-vehicle patrols, late-night transport/escort service, 24-hour emergency telephones, lighted pathways/sidewalks, student patrols, controlled dormitory access (key, security card, etc).

TRANSFER AND INTERNATIONAL STUDENTS

Transfer students: May apply for admission for the following academic terms: Fall, Spring. Applicants do not need a minimum number of credits to apply. For fall 2009: Transfer applications received: 541. Transfer applicants offered admission: 356. Transfer applicants enrolled: 219. **International students:** Number of foreign undergraduates: 20. Number of countries represented: 28. Minimum TOEFL score required: 580 (paper); 88 (computer). Average TOEFL score: 570 (paper).

University of Richmond

- **Address:** 28 Westhampton Way, Univ. of Richmond, VA 23173
- **Website:** http://www.richmond.edu
- **Private**
- **Enrollment:** 2,872 full-time; 53 part-time

KEY STATS

✔ **U.S News College Ranking:** 32, National Liberal Arts Colleges
✔ **SAT Score (25th/75th percentile):** 1170-1350
✔ **Tuition:** 2010-2011: $41,610

Selectivity: More selective	**Room/board:** $8,810
Acceptance rate: 39%	**Average debt:** $21,555
Student/faculty ratio: 8/1	**Proportion who borrowed:** 42%

UNDERGRADUATE STUDENT BODY STATS

2009-2010 enrollment: 2,872 full-time; 53 part-time. Men: 47%; women: 53%. **Ethnic makeup:** African American: 8%; Asian American: 5%; Hispanic: 4%; White: 78%; International: 5%.

ADMISSIONS FACTS AND FIGURES

Phone: (804) 289-8640. **Email:** admissions@richmond.edu. **Website:** http://www.richmond.edu. **Application deadlines for fall 2011:** Regular decision: January 15; decision sent by April 1. Early decision: Send application by: November 15; Decision sent by: December 15. Early action: Not offered. Admission can be deferred. **Application fee:** $50. **To apply online, go to:** http://admissions.richmond.edu/apply/index.html. **Admissions requirements/recommendations:** High school units required (recommended): English: 4; Mathematics: 3 (4); Science: 2 (4); Foreign language: 2 (4); History: 2 (4); Total units: 16 (20). Tests: The college uses SAT or ACT scores in admissions decisions. Either SAT or ACT required. For admission to the fall 2011 entering class, the school will accept: ACT with or without

writing accepted. Campus visit: Recommended. Admissions interview: Neither required nor recommended. Off-campus interview: Not available. **Factors that count in admissions decisions:** *Academic:* Secondary school record: Very Important. Class rank: Important. Letters of recommendation: Considered. Standardized test scores: Important. Essay: Important. *Nonacademic:* Interview: Considered. Extracurricular activities: Considered. Talent/ability: Important. Character/personal qualities: Important. Alumni/ae relationship: Considered. Geographical residence: Considered. State residency: Considered. Religious affiliation/commitment: Not Considered. Minority status: Considered. Volunteer work: Considered. Work experience; Considered. **Other schools with the greatest overlap in applicants:** Boston College; College of William and Mary; Georgetown University; University of Virginia; Wake Forest University. **Admissions statistics for the fall 2009 entering class:** Total applicants: 7,880. Total accepted: 3,093. Freshmen enrolled: 918; 79% were from out of state. Accepted through early-decision or early-action plans: 27%. Overall acceptance rate: 39%. Early-decision acceptance rate: 66%. Non-early acceptance rate: 38%. **Size of waiting list:** 2161 applicants; enrolled from waiting list: 11. **Credentials of fall 2009 freshmen:** 58% ranked in the top 10 percent of their high school class; 87% were in the top 25 percent; 98% were in the top half. (Proportion submitting class standing: 35%.) **First-year students who submitted SAT scores:** 87%. Scores (25/75 percentile): Critical Reading: 580-670, Math: 590-680, Combined: 1170-1350. **First-year students submitting ACT scores:** 37%. Scores (25/75 percentile): English: N/A, Math: N/A, Composite: 26-30.

ACADEMICS

Year founded: 1830. **Academic calendar:** Semester. **Degrees offered:** certificate, diploma, associate, bachelor's, post-bachelor's certificate, master's, post-master's certificate. **Most popular majors:** 29% business, management, marketing, and related support services, 17% social sciences, 8% English language and literature/letters, 7% foreign languages, literatures, and linguistics, 6% psychology. **Major fields of study:** area, ethnic, cultural, and gender studies; biological and biomedical sciences; business, management, marketing, and related support services; communication, journalism, and related programs; computer and information sciences and support services; English language and literature/letters; foreign languages, literatures, and linguistics; history; liberal arts and sciences studies, and humanities; mathematics and statistics; multi/interdisciplinary studies; natural resources and conservation; philosophy and religious studies; physical sciences; psychology; security and protective services; social sciences; visual and performing arts. **Areas of required coursework:** arts/fine arts, humanities, mathematics, English (including composition), foreign languages, sciences (biological or physical), history, social science, other. **Pre-professional programs:** pre-law, pre-dentistry, pre-medicine, pre-veterinary science, pre-optometry, pre-pharmacy. **Special academic programs:** accelerated program, cross-registration, double major, English as a Second Language (ESL), exchange student program (domestic), honors program, independent study, internships, student-designed major, study abroad, teacher certificate program. **Teacher certification offered in:** elementary, secondary. **Reserve Officers Training Corps (ROTC):** Army ROTC: Offered on campus. **Faculty and instruction (2009-2010):** Total instructional faculty: 320 full-time, 103 part-time (61% men; 39% women; 9% minorities). Full-time faculty with Ph.D. or other terminal degree: 80%. Student/faculty ratio: 8/1. Classes of fewer than 20 students: 66%; of 20 to 49 students: 34%; of 50 or more students: 0%. **Advanced Placement and International Baccalaureate credit:** AP tests may be used for: Credit only. Scores accepted: 4, 5. International Baccalaureate exams may be used for: Credit only. **Freshmen returning for sophomore year:** 91%. **Graduation rates:** Four-year: 82%; five-year: 86%; six-year: 86%. **Graduate study:** 44% of students pursue further study immediately upon graduation; 40% within one year; 52% within five years. Fields in which graduates pursue further study: Master of Business Administration (MBA), 18%; law, 21%; medicine, 11%; dentistry, 1%; engineering, 1%; theology (or the seminary), 3%; education, 6%; arts and sciences, 35%; veterinary medicine, 1%.

COSTS AND FINANCIAL AID

Financial aid office: (804) 289-8438. **Expenses (2010-2011):** Tuition and fees 2010-2011: $41,610; room/board: $8,810. Estimated books and supplies: $1,050 personal expenses: $990. **Financial aid:** In 2009-2010, 55% of undergraduates applied for financial aid. Of those, 46% were determined to have financial need; 93% had their need fully met. Average financial aid package (proportion receiving): $36,857 (46%). Average amount of gift aid, such as scholarships or grants (proportion receiving): $33,404 (46%). Average amount of self-help aid, such as work study or loans (proportion receiving): $3,190 (39%). Average need-based loan (excluding PLUS or other private loans): $3,032. Among students who received need-based aid, the average percentage of need met: 100%. Among students who received aid based on merit, the average award (and the proportion receiving): $19,879 (14%). The average athletic scholarship (and the proportion receiving): $31,319 (6%). Average amount of debt of borrowers graduating in 2009: $21,555. Proportion who borrowed: 42%.

CAMPUS LIFE AND EXTRACURRICULAR ACTIVITIES

Campus housing available (% using): coed dorms (12%), women's dorms (34%), men's dorms (25%), apartment for single students (23%), special housing for disabled students (1%), other housing options (5%). Students who live in college-owned, operated, or affiliated housing: 91%. **Student employment:** During the 2009-2010 academic year, 39% of undergraduates worked on campus. Average per-year earnings: $1,464. **Clubs and organizations:** Number of student organizations: 208. Activities include: campus ministries, choral groups, concert band, dance, drama/theater, international student organization, jazz band, literary magazine, model UN, music ensembles, musical theater, pep band, radio station, student government, student newspaper, student film society, symphony orchestra. Number of fraternities: 6; sororities: 8. Proportion of men in fraternities: 17%; of women in sororities: 25%. Average proportion of students who stay on campus on weekends: 91%. **Sports program (2009-2010):** Member of NCAA I. *Men's intercollegiate varsity sports:* baseball, basketball, cross country, football, golf, soccer, tennis, track and field (indoor), track and field (outdoor). *Women's intercollegiate varsity sports:* basketball, cross country, field hockey, golf, lacrosse, soccer, swimming, tennis, track and field (indoor), track and field (outdoor).

SERVICES AND FACILITIES

Basic services: nonremedial tutoring, placement service, health service, other. **Counseling services:** minority student, career, military, personal, academic, psychological, birth control, religious. **For learning-disabled students:** School does not offer a structured program with separate admission and additional fees. Total undergraduates in learning-disabled program or receiving serial services: 112. **Library:** Number of titles: 857,897; number of current serial subscriptions: 30,118. **Information technology resources:** Students are not required to lease or own a computer. Number of campus computers available to all students: 1,000. School has a wireless network. Approximate number of users that can be accommodated: 10,000. Proportion of college-owned housing units wired for high-speed internet access: 100%. **Campus safety:** Security services offered: 24-hour foot-and-vehicle patrols, late-night transport/escort service, 24-hour emergency telephones, lighted pathways/sidewalks, controlled dormitory access (key, security card, etc).

TRANSFER AND INTERNATIONAL STUDENTS

Transfer students: May apply for admission for the following academic terms: Fall, Spring. Applicants need a minimum number of credits to apply. For fall 2009: Transfer applications received: 305. Transfer applicants offered admission: 99. Transfer applicants enrolled: 54. **International students:** Number of foreign undergraduates: 153 (5% of student body). Number of countries represented: 72. Minimum TOEFL score required: 550 (paper); 80 (computer).

University of Virginia

- **Address:** Charlottesville, VA 22904
- **Website:** http://www.virginia.edu
- **Public**
- **Enrollment:** 14,696 full-time; 780 part-time

KEY STATS

✔ **U.S News College Ranking:** 25, National Universities
✔ **SAT Score (25th/75th percentile):** 1230-1440
✔ **Tuition:** 2010-2011: $10,628 in state, $33,574 out of state

Selectivity: Most selective	**Room/board:** $8,652
Acceptance rate: 32%	**Average debt:** $19,939
Student/faculty ratio: 16/1	**Proportion who borrowed:** 34%

UNDERGRADUATE STUDENT BODY STATS

2009-2010 enrollment: 14,696 full-time; 780 part-time. Men: 44%; women: 56%. **Ethnic makeup:** African American: 8%; Asian American: 12%; Hispanic: 5%; White: 69%; International: 5%.

ADMISSIONS FACTS AND FIGURES

Phone: (434) 982-3200. **Email:** undergradadmission@virginia.edu. **Website:** http://www.virginia.edu. **Application deadlines for fall 2011:** Regular decision: January 1; decision sent by April 1. Early decision: Not offered. Early action: Not offered. Admission can be deferred. **Application fee:** $60. **To apply online, go to:** https://www.commonapp.org/CommonApp/default.aspx. **Admissions requirements/recommendations:** High school units required (recommended): English: 4; Mathematics: 4 (5); Science: 2 (4); Foreign language: 2 (5); Social studies: 1 (4); Total units: 16. Tests: The college uses SAT or ACT scores in admissions decisions. Either SAT or ACT required. For admission to the fall 2011 entering class, the school will accept: ACT with writing required. Campus visit: Recommended. Admissions interview: Neither required nor recommended. Off-campus interview: Not available. **Factors that count in admissions decisions:** *Academic:* Secondary school record: Very Important. Class rank: Very Important. Letters of recommendation: Very Important. Standardized test scores: Important. Essay: Important. *Nonacademic:* Interview: Not Considered. Extracurricular activities: Important. Talent/ability: Important. Character/personal qualities: Important. Alumni/ae relationship: Very Important. Geographical residence: Considered. State residency: Very Important. Religious affiliation/commitment: Not Considered. Minority status: Very Important. Volunteer work: Considered. Work experience: Considered. **Other schools with the greatest overlap in applicants:** College of William and Mary; Cornell University; Duke University; University of North Carolina–Chapel Hill; Virginia Tech. **Admissions statistics for the fall 2009 entering class:** Total applicants: 21,108. Total accepted: 6,768. Freshmen enrolled: 3,246; 28% were from out of state. Overall acceptance rate: 32%. **Size of waiting list:** 4522 applicants; enrolled from waiting list: 420. **Credentials of fall 2009 freshmen:** 89% ranked in the top 10 percent of their high school class; 97% were in the top 25 percent; 99% were in the top half. (Proportion submitting class standing: 48%.) **Average high school grade point average:** 4.0. **First-year students who submitted SAT scores:** 97%. Scores (25/75 percentile): Critical Reading: 600-710, Math: 630-730, Combined: 1230-1440. **First-year students submitting ACT scores:** 26%. Scores (25/75 percentile): English: 27-34, Math: 27-33, Composite: 27-32.

ACADEMICS

Year founded: 1819. **Academic calendar:** Semester. **Degrees offered:** certificate, bachelor's, post-bachelor's certificate, master's, post-master's certificate, doctorate. **Most popular majors:** 9% business/commerce, 9% economics, 8% history, 8% psychology, 7% biology/biological sciences. **Major fields of study:** architecture and related services; area, ethnic, cultural, and gender studies; biological and biomedical sciences; business, management, marketing, and related support services; computer and information sciences and support services; education; engineering; English language and literature/letters; foreign languages, literatures, and linguistics; health professions and related clinical sciences; history; liberal arts and sciences studies, and humanities; mathematics and statistics; multi/interdisciplinary studies; natural resources and conservation; philosophy and religious studies; physical sciences; psychology; social sciences; visual and performing arts. **Areas of required coursework:** humanities, mathematics, English (including composition), foreign languages, sciences (biological or physical), history, social science, other. **Pre-professional programs:** pre-law, pre-medicine. **Special academic programs:** accelerated program, cooperative (work-study plan) program, double major, English as a Second Language (ESL), exchange student program (domestic), honors program, independent study, internships, liberal arts/career combination, student-designed major, study abroad, teacher certificate program. **Teacher certification offered in:** special education, elementary, middle/junior high, secondary. **Cooperative education programs:** engineering, health professions. **Reserve Officers Training Corps (ROTC):** Army ROTC: Offered on campus; Navy ROTC: Offered on campus; Air Force ROTC: Offered on campus. **Faculty and instruction (2009-2010):** Total instructional faculty: 1,220 full-time, 104 part-time (66% men; 34% women; 12% minorities). Full-time faculty with Ph.D. or other terminal degree: 92%. Student/faculty ratio: 16/1. Classes of fewer than 20 students: 52%; of 20 to 49 students: 33%; of 50 or more students: 15%. **Advanced Placement and International Baccalaureate credit:** AP tests may be used for: Credit and/or placement. Scores accepted: 3, 4, 5. International Baccalaureate exams may be used for: Credit and/or placement. **Freshmen returning for sophomore year:** 97%. **Graduation rates:** Four-year: 84%; five-year: 92%; six-year: 93%.

COSTS AND FINANCIAL AID

Financial aid office: (434) 982-6000. **Expenses (2010-2011):** Tuition and fees 2010-2011: $10,628 in state, $33,574 out of state; room/board: $8,652. Estimated books and supplies: $1,167 personal expenses: $2,270. **Financial**

aid: Priority filing date for institution's financial aid form: March 1. In 2009-2010, 57% of undergraduates applied for financial aid. Of those, 30% were determined to have financial need; 100% had their need fully met. Average financial aid package (proportion receiving): $20,202 (30%). Average amount of gift aid, such as scholarships or grants (proportion receiving): $14,772 (26%). Average amount of self-help aid, such as work study or loans (proportion receiving): $6,070 (19%). Average need-based loan (excluding PLUS or other private loans): $5,468. Among students who received need-based aid, the average percentage of need met: 100%. Among students who received aid based on merit, the average award (and the proportion receiving): $9,858 (11%). The average athletic scholarship (and the proportion receiving): $20,349 (3%). Average amount of debt of borrowers graduating in 2009: $19,939. Proportion who borrowed: 34%.

CAMPUS LIFE AND EXTRACURRICULAR ACTIVITIES

Campus housing available: coed dorms, sorority housing, fraternity housing, apartments for married students, apartment for single students, special housing for international students, cooperative housing. Students who live in college-owned, operated, or affiliated housing: 43%. **Clubs and organizations:** Number of student organizations: 530. Activities include: campus ministries, choral groups, concert band, dance, drama/theater, international student organization, jazz band, literary magazine, marching band, model UN, music ensembles, musical theater, opera, pep band, radio station, student government, student newspaper, student film society, symphony orchestra, television station, yearbook. Number of fraternities: 32; sororities: 22. Proportion of men in fraternities: 30%; of women in sororities: 30%. **Sports program (2009-2010):** Member of NCAA I. *Men's intercollegiate varsity sports:* baseball, basketball, cross country, football, golf, lacrosse, soccer, swimming, tennis, track and field (indoor), track and field (outdoor), wrestling. *Women's intercollegiate varsity sports:* basketball, crew (heavyweight), cross country, field hockey, golf, lacrosse, soccer, softball, swimming, tennis, track and field (indoor), track and field (outdoor), volleyball.

SERVICES AND FACILITIES

Basic services: nonremedial tutoring, women's center, placement service, day care, health service, health insurance. **Remedial assistance:** reading, math, writing, study skills. **Counseling services:** minority student, career, military, personal, veteran student, academic, older student, psychological, birth control. **For learning-disabled students:** School does not offer a structured program with separate admission and additional fees. Services include: tape recorders, diagnostic testing service, untimed tests, note-taking services, oral tests, learning center, readers, extended time for tests, tutors. **Library:** Number of titles: 5,053,162; number of current serial subscriptions: 52,802. **Information technology resources:** Students are not required to lease or own a computer. Number of campus computers available to all students: 1,859. School has a wireless network. Proportion of college-owned housing units wired for high-speed internet access: 100%. **Campus safety:** Security services offered: 24-hour foot-and-vehicle patrols, late-night transport/escort service, 24-hour emergency telephones, lighted pathways/sidewalks, controlled dormitory access (key, security card, etc).

TRANSFER AND INTERNATIONAL STUDENTS

Transfer students: May apply for admission for the following academic terms: Fall, Spring. Applicants need a minimum number of credits to apply. For fall 2009: Transfer applications received: 2,434. Transfer applicants offered admission: 958. Transfer applicants enrolled: 640. **International students:** Number of foreign undergraduates: 748 (5% of student body). Number of countries represented: 109. Minimum TOEFL score required: 550 (paper); 213 (computer). Average TOEFL score: 620 (paper).

University of Virginia—Wise

- **Address:** 1 College Avenue, Wise, VA 24293
- **Website:** http://www.uvawise.edu
- **Public**
- **Enrollment:** 1,495 full-time; 520 part-time

KEY STATS

✔ **U.S News College Ranking:** second tier, National Liberal Arts Colleges
✔ **SAT Score (25th/75th percentile):** 840-1060
✔ **Tuition:** 2010-2011: $7,194 in state, $19,734 out of state
  Selectivity: Less selective   **Room/board:** $8,559
  Acceptance rate: 89%   **Average debt:** $12,120
  Student/faculty ratio: 15/1   **Proportion who borrowed:** 58%

UNDERGRADUATE STUDENT BODY STATS

2009-2010 enrollment: 1,495 full-time; 520 part-time. Men: 47%; women: 53%. **Ethnic makeup:** African American: 11%; Asian American: 1%; Hispanic: 2%; White: 85%.

ADMISSIONS FACTS AND FIGURES

Phone: (888) 282-9324. **Email:** admissions@uvawise.edu. **Website:** http://www.uvawise.edu. **Application deadlines for fall 2011:** Regular decision: August 15. Early decision: Not offered. Early action: Send application by: December 1; Decision sent by: December 15. Admission can be deferred. **Application fee:** $25. **To apply online, go to:** https://www.applyweb.com/apply/uvawise/menu.html. **Admissions requirements/recommendations:** High school units required (recommended): English: 4; Mathematics: 3; Science: 2; Foreign language: 2; Social studies: 1; History: 1; Academic electives: 5; Total units: 18. Tests: The college uses SAT or ACT scores in admissions decisions. Either SAT or ACT required. For admission to the fall 2011 entering class, the school will accept: ACT with writing recommended. Campus visit: Recommended. Admissions interview: Recommended. Off-campus interview: May be arranged. **Factors that count in admissions decisions:** *Academic:* Secondary school record: Very Important. Class rank: Very Important. Letters of recommendation: Considered. Standardized test scores: Important. Essay: Considered. *Nonacademic:* Interview: Considered. Extracurricular activities: Considered. Talent/ability: Important. Character/personal qualities: Considered. Alumni/ae relationship: Not Considered. Geographical residence: Not Considered. State residency: Not Considered. Religious affiliation/commitment: Not Considered. Minority status: Considered. Volunteer work: Considered. Work experience: Considered. **Admissions statistics for the fall 2009 entering class:** Total applicants: 1,068. Total accepted: 952. Freshmen enrolled: 406; 6% were from out of state. Overall acceptance rate: 89%. Non-early acceptance rate: 89%. **Credentials of fall 2009 freshmen:** 12% ranked in the top 10 percent of their high school class; 38% were in the top 25 percent; 75% were in the top half. (Proportion submitting class standing: 78%.) **Average high school grade point average:** 3.2. **First-year students who submitted SAT scores:** 90%. Scores (25/75 percentile): Critical Reading: 420-530, Math: 420-530, Combined: 840-1060. **First-year students submitting ACT scores:** 27%. Scores (25/75 percentile): English: 15-21, Math: 16-22, Composite: 16-22.

ACADEMICS

Year founded: 1954. **Academic calendar:** Semester. **Degrees offered:** bachelor's. **Most popular majors:** 25% business/commerce, 22% liberal arts and sciences/liberal studies, 20% social sciences, 9% English language and literature, 9% biological and physical sciences. **Major fields of study:** biological and biomedical sciences; business, management, marketing, and related support services; communication, journalism, and related programs; computer and information sciences and support services; engineering; English language and literature/letters; foreign languages, literatures, and linguistics; history; liberal arts and sciences studies, and humanities; mathematics and statistics; multi/interdisciplinary studies; physical sciences; psychology; science technologies/technicians; social sciences; visual and performing arts. **Areas of required coursework:** arts/fine arts, humanities, computer literacy, mathematics, English (including composition), foreign languages, sciences (biological or physical), history, social science. **Pre-professional programs:** pre-law, pre-dentistry, pre-medicine, pre-veterinary science, pre-pharmacy. **Special academic programs (% participation):** accelerated program (.5%), cooperative (work-study plan) program (2%), distance learning (1%), double major (3%), dual enrollment (8%), honors program (1%), independent study (4%), internships (2%), liberal arts/career combination (10%), student-designed major (0%), study abroad (0%), teacher certificate program (5%). **Teacher certification offered in:** early childhood, special education, elementary, middle/junior high, secondary. **Cooperative education programs:** other. **Reserve Officers Training Corps (ROTC):** Army ROTC: Offered on campus. **Faculty and instruction (2009-2010):** Total instructional faculty: 93 full-time, 72 part-time (52% men; 48% women; 4% minorities). Full-time faculty with Ph.D. or other terminal degree: 70%. Student/faculty ratio: 15/1. Classes of fewer than 20 students: 65%; of 20 to 49 students: 34%; of 50 or more students: 1%. **Advanced Placement and International Baccalaureate credit:** AP tests may be used for: Placement only. Scores accepted: 3, 4, 5. International Baccalaureate exams may be used for: Placement only. **Freshmen returning for sophomore year:** 67%. **Graduation rates:** Four-year: 31%; five-year: 43%; six-year: 46%. **Graduate study:** 15% of students pursue further study immediately upon graduation; 20% within one year.

COSTS AND FINANCIAL AID

Financial aid office: (276) 328-0103. **Expenses (2010-2011):** Tuition and fees 2010-2011: $7,194 in state, $19,734 out of state; room/board: $8,559. Estimated books and supplies: $700; transportation: $850; personal expenses: $1,240. **Financial aid:** Priority filing date for institution's financial aid form: April 1; deadline: April 1. In 2009-2010, 90% of undergraduates applied for financial aid. Of those, 76% were determined to have financial need; 73% had their need fully met. Average financial aid package (proportion receiving): $9,212 (75%). Average amount of gift aid, such as scholarships or grants (proportion receiving): $5,474 (65%). Average amount of self-help aid, such as work study or loans (proportion receiving): $3,346 (49%). Average need-based loan (excluding PLUS or other private loans): $3,168. Among students who received need-based aid, the average percentage of need met: 74%. Among students who received aid based on merit, the average award (and the proportion receiving): $3,456 (8%). The average athletic scholarship (and the proportion receiving): $3,225 (9%). Average amount of debt of borrowers graduating in 2009: $12,120. Proportion who borrowed: 58%.

CAMPUS LIFE AND EXTRACURRICULAR ACTIVITIES

Campus housing available (% using): coed dorms (99%), special housing for disabled students (1%). Students who live in college-owned, operated, or affiliated housing: 35%. **Clubs and organizations:** Number of student organizations: 51. Activities include: choral groups, concert band, dance, drama/theater, jazz band, literary magazine, marching band, music ensembles, musical theater, pep band, radio station, student government, student newspaper, television station. Number of fraternities: 4; sororities: 3. Proportion of men in fraternities: 11%; of women in sororities: 9%. Average proportion of students who stay on campus on weekends: 44%. **Sports program (2009-2010):** Member of NAIA. *Men's intercollegiate varsity sports:* baseball, basketball, cross country, football, golf, tennis. *Women's intercollegiate varsity sports:* basketball, cross country, golf, softball, tennis, volleyball.

SERVICES AND FACILITIES

Basic services: nonremedial tutoring, placement service, health service. **Remedial assistance:** reading, math, writing, study skills. **Counseling services:** career, personal, academic, older student, psychological. **For learning-disabled students:** School does not offer a structured program with separate admission and additional fees. Total undergraduates in learning-disabled program or receiving services: 68. Services include: remedial math, remedial English, reading machines, remedial reading, tape recorders, learning center, readers, extended time for tests, tutors, priority seating, other testing accommodations, other. **Library:** Number of titles: 157,245; number of current serial subscriptions: 6,617. **Information technology resources:** Students are not required to lease or own a computer. Number of campus computers available to all students: 173. School does not have a wireless network. Proportion of college-owned housing units wired for high-speed internet access: 100%. **Campus safety:** Security services offered: 24-hour foot-and-vehicle patrols, late-night transport/escort service, 24-hour emergency telephones, lighted pathways/sidewalks.

TRANSFER AND INTERNATIONAL STUDENTS

Transfer students: May apply for admission for the following academic terms: Fall, Spring, Summer. Applicants need a minimum number of credits to apply. For fall 2009: Transfer applications received: 247. Transfer applicants offered admission: 189. Transfer applicants enrolled: 136. **International students:** Number of foreign undergraduates: 0. Number of countries represented: 7. Minimum TOEFL score required: 550 (paper); 234 (computer). Average TOEFL score: 560 (paper).

Virginia Commonwealth University

- **Address:** Box 842527, Richmond, VA 23284
- **Website:** http://www.vcu.edu
- **Public**
- **Enrollment:** 19,181 full-time; 3,968 part-time

KEY STATS

✔ **U.S News College Ranking:** 167, National Universities
✔ **SAT Score (25th/75th percentile):** 980-1190
✔ **Tuition:** 2009-2010: $7,254 in state, $20,926 out of state

Selectivity: Selective	Room/board: $10,492
Acceptance rate: 59%	Average debt: $22,864
Student/faculty ratio: 18/1	Proportion who borrowed: 61%

UNDERGRADUATE STUDENT BODY STATS

2009-2010 enrollment: 19,181 full-time; 3,968 part-time. Men: 43%; women: 57%. **Ethnic makeup:** African American: 20%; American-Indian: 1%; Asian American: 12%; Hispanic: 4%; White: 61%; International: 3%.

ADMISSIONS FACTS AND FIGURES

Phone: (800) 841-3638. **Email:** ugrad@vcu.edu. **Website:** http://www.vcu.edu. **Application deadlines for fall 2011:** Regular decision: Rolling. Early decision: Not offered. Early action: Not offered. Admission can be deferred. **Application fee:** $40. **To apply online, go to:** http://www.vcu.edu/ugrad. **Admissions requirements/recommendations:** High school units required (recommended): English: 4 (4); Mathematics: 3 (4); Science: 3 (4); Foreign language: 2 (3); Social studies: 1 (1); History: 2 (3); Total units: 20 (24). Tests: The college uses SAT or ACT scores in admissions decisions. Either SAT or ACT required. For admission to the fall 2011 entering class, the school will accept: ACT with or without writing accepted. Campus visit: Recommended. Admissions interview: Neither required nor recommended. Off-campus interview: Not available. **Factors that count in admissions decisions:** *Academic:* Secondary school record: Very Important. Class rank: Considered. Letters of recommendation: Considered. Standardized test scores: Important. Essay: Considered. *Nonacademic:* Interview: Not Considered. Extracurricular activities: Considered. Talent/ability: Important. Character/personal qualities: Not Considered. Alumni/ae relationship: Not Considered. Geographical residence: Not Considered. State residency: Not Considered. Religious affiliation/commitment: Not Considered. Minority status: Not Considered. Volunteer work: Considered. Work experience: Considered. **Other schools with the greatest overlap in applicants:** George Mason University; James Madison University; Old Dominion University; University of Virginia; Virginia Tech. **Admissions statistics for the fall 2009 entering class:** Total applicants: 16,915. Total accepted: 10,055. Freshmen enrolled: 3,665; 9% were from out of state. Overall acceptance rate: 59%. **Size of waiting list:** 1001 applicants; enrolled from waiting list: 34. **Credentials of fall 2009 freshmen:** 16% ranked in the top 10 percent of their high school class; 47% were in the top 25 percent; 87% were in the top half. (Proportion submitting class standing: 69%.) **Average high school grade point average:** 3.4. **First-year students who submitted SAT scores:** 93%. Scores (25/75 percentile): Critical Reading: 490-600, Math: 490-590, Combined: 980-1190. **First-year students submitting ACT scores:** 20%. Scores (25/75 percentile): English: 20-26, Math: 18-25, Composite: 20-25.

ACADEMICS

Year founded: 1838. **Academic calendar:** Semester. **Degrees offered:** certificate, bachelor's, post-bachelor's certificate, master's, post-master's certificate, doctorate. **Most popular majors:** 14% business, management, marketing, and related support services, 13% visual and performing arts, 11% health professions and related clinical sciences, 9% psychology, 8% security and protective services. **Major fields of study:** area, ethnic, cultural, and gender studies; biological and biomedical sciences; business, management, marketing, and related support services; communication, journalism, and related programs; computer and information sciences and support services; education; engineering; English language and literature/letters; foreign languages, literatures, and linguistics; health professions and related clinical sciences; history; mathematics and statistics; multi/interdisciplinary studies; natural resources and conservation; parks, recreation, leisure, and fitness studies; philosophy and religious studies; physical sciences; psychology; public administration and social service professions; security and protective services; social sciences; visual and performing arts. **Areas of required coursework:** arts/fine arts, humanities, mathematics, English (including composition), sciences (biological or physical), social science. **Pre-professional programs:** pre-law, pre-dentistry, pre-medicine, pre-veterinary science, pre-optometry, pre-pharmacy, other. **Special academic programs:** accelerated program, cooperative (work-study plan) program, distance learning, double major, English as a Second Language (ESL), exchange student program (domestic), honors program, independent study, internships, liberal arts/career combination, student-designed major, study abroad, teacher certificate program. **Teacher certification offered in:** early childhood, special education, elementary, middle/junior high, adult education, secondary. **Cooperative education programs:** agriculture, art, business, computer science, education, engineering, humanities, natural science, social/behavioral science, technologies. **Reserve Officers Training Corps (ROTC):** Army ROTC: Offered at cooperating institution (University of Richmond). **Faculty and instruction (2009-2010):** Total instructional faculty: 1,919 full-time, 1,128 part-time (55% men; 45% women; 18% minorities). Student/faculty ratio: 18/1. Classes of fewer than 20 students: 38%; of 20 to 49 students: 46%; of 50 or more students: 16%. **Advanced Placement and International Baccalaureate credit:** AP tests may be used for: Credit only. Scores accepted: 3, 4, 5. International Baccalaureate exams may be used for: Credit only. **Freshmen returning for sophomore year:** 83%. **Graduation rates:** Four-year: 25%; five-year: 44%; six-year: 51%.

COSTS AND FINANCIAL AID

Financial aid office: (804) 828-6669. **Expenses (2009-2010):** Tuition and fees 2009-2010: $7,254 in state, $20,926 out of state; room/board: $10,492. Estimated books and supplies: $1,250; transportation: $1,620; personal expenses: $1,500. **Financial aid:** Priority filing date for institution's financial aid form: March 1. In 2009-2010, 63% of undergraduates applied for financial aid. Of those, 51% were determined to have financial need; 11% had their need fully met. Average financial aid package (proportion receiving): $9,365 (50%). Average amount of gift aid, such as scholarships or grants (proportion receiving): $5,603 (38%). Average amount of self-help aid, such as work study or loans (proportion receiving): $4,528 (44%). Average need-based loan (excluding PLUS or other private loans): $4,414. Among students who received need-based aid, the average percentage of need met: 60%. Among students who received aid based on merit, the average award (and the proportion receiving): $6,229 (4%). The average athletic scholarship (and the proportion receiving): $18,296 (1%). Average amount of debt of borrowers graduating in 2009: $22,864. Proportion who borrowed: 61%.

CAMPUS LIFE AND EXTRACURRICULAR ACTIVITIES

Campus housing available (% using): coed dorms (98%), women's dorms (1%), men's dorms (1%), apartments for married students, apartment for single students, special housing for disabled students, special housing for international students, other housing options. Students who live in college-owned, operated, or affiliated housing: 22%. **Clubs and organizations:** Number of student organizations: 380. Activities include: campus ministries, choral groups, dance, drama/theater, international student organization, literary magazine, musical theater, pep band, radio station, student government, student newspaper, television station, yearbook. Number of fraternities: 17; sororities: 15. Proportion of men in fraternities: 6%; of women in sororities: 5%. Average proportion of students who stay on campus on weekends: 70%. **Sports program (2009-2010):** Member of NCAA I. *Men's intercollegiate varsity sports:* baseball, basketball, cross country, golf, soccer, tennis, track and field (indoor), track and field (outdoor). *Women's intercollegiate varsity sports:* basketball, cross country, field hockey, soccer, tennis, track and field (indoor), track and field (outdoor), volleyball.

SERVICES AND FACILITIES

Basic services: nonremedial tutoring, day care, health service. **Remedial assistance:** reading, math, writing, other. **Counseling services:** career, personal, academic, psychological, birth control, other. **For learning-disabled students:** School does not offer a structured program with separate admission and additional fees. Total undergraduates in learning-disabled program or receiving services: 300. Services include: note-taking services, oral tests, learning center, readers, extended time for tests, tutors, priority registration, priority seating, substitution of courses, typist/scribe, exams on tape or computer, other testing accommodations. **Library:** Number of titles: 2,130,683; number of current serial subscriptions: 50,646. **Information technology resources:** Students are required to lease or own a computer. Number of campus computers available to all students: 1,400. School has a wireless network. Approximate number of users that can be accommodated: 16,300. Proportion of college-owned housing units wired for high-speed internet access: 100%. **Campus safety:** Security services offered: 24-hour foot-and-vehicle patrols, late-night transport/escort service, 24-hour emer-

gency telephones, lighted pathways/sidewalks, student patrols, controlled dormitory access (key, security card, etc).

TRANSFER AND INTERNATIONAL STUDENTS

Transfer students: May apply for admission for the following academic terms: Fall, Spring. Applicants do not need a minimum number of credits to apply. For fall 2009: Transfer applications received: 4,936. Transfer applicants offered admission: 2,996. Transfer applicants enrolled: 2,043. **International students:** Number of foreign undergraduates: 640 (3% of student body). Number of countries represented: 85. Minimum TOEFL score required: 550 (paper); 80 (computer). Average TOEFL score: 579 (paper).

Virginia Intermont College

- **Address:** 1013 Moore Street, Bristol, VA 24201
- **Website:** http://www.vic.edu
- **Private; Religious affiliation:** Baptist
- **Enrollment:** N/A

KEY STATS
✔ **U.S News College Ranking:** second tier, Regional Colleges (South)
✔ **SAT or ACT Score (25th/75th percentile):** N/A
✔ **Tuition:** 2010-2011: $24,542

Selectivity: Less selective	Room/board: $7,690
Acceptance rate: 69%	Average debt: $16,337
Student/faculty ratio: N/A	Proportion who borrowed: 76%

Virginia Military Institute

- **Address:** VMI Parade, Lexington, VA 24450-0304
- **Website:** http://www.vmi.edu
- **Public**
- **Enrollment:** 1,500 full-time

KEY STATS
✔ **U.S News College Ranking:** 62, National Liberal Arts Colleges
✔ **SAT Score (25th/75th percentile):** 1050-1220
✔ **Tuition:** 2010-2011: $12,328 in state, $30,320 out of state

Selectivity: Selective	Room/board: $7,132
Acceptance rate: 56%	Average debt: $19,046
Student/faculty ratio: 11/1	Proportion who borrowed: 34%

UNDERGRADUATE STUDENT BODY STATS

2009-2010 enrollment: 1,500 full-time. Men: 92%; women: 8%. **Ethnic makeup:** African American: 6%; Asian American: 4%; Hispanic: 4%; White: 84%; International: 2%. **Religious preference:** Roman Catholic: 29%; Protestant: 61%; Jewish: 1%; Muslim: 1%; Buddhist: 1%; No preference: 4%; Other: 1%.

ADMISSIONS FACTS AND FIGURES

Phone: (800) 767-4207. **Email:** admissions@vmi.edu. **Website:** http://www.vmi.edu. **Application deadlines for fall 2011:** Regular decision: February 1. Early decision: Send application by: November 15; Decision sent by: December 15. Early action: Not offered. Admission cannot be deferred. **Application fee:** $40. **To apply online, go to:** http://www.vmi.edu/admissions. **Admissions requirements/recommendations:** High school units required (recommended): English: 4 (4); Mathematics: 3 (4); Science: 3 (4); Foreign language: 3 (4); Social studies: 2 (2); History: 1 (1); Total units: 16 (19). Tests: The college uses SAT or ACT scores in admissions decisions. Either SAT or ACT required. For admission to the fall 2011 entering class, the school will accept: ACT with or without writing accepted. Campus visit: Recommended. Admissions interview: Recommended. Off-campus interview: May be arranged. **Factors that count in admissions decisions:** *Academic:* Secondary school record: Very Important. Class rank: Very Important. Letters of recommendation: Considered. Standardized test scores: Very Important. Essay: Considered. *Nonacademic:* Interview: Important. Extracurricular activities: Important. Talent/ability: Considered. Character/personal qualities: Very Important. Alumni/ae relationship: Considered. Geographical residence: Considered. State residency: Important. Religious affiliation/commitment: Not Considered. Minority status: Important. Volunteer work: Important. Work experience: Considered. **Other schools with the greatest overlap in applicants:** The Citadel; United States Air Force Academy; United States Military Academy; United States Naval Academy. **Admissions statistics for the fall 2009 entering class:** Total applicants: 1,598. Total accepted: 889. Freshmen enrolled: 455; 44% were from out of state. Accepted through early-decision or early-action plans: 33%. Overall acceptance rate: 56%. Early-decision acceptance rate: 68%. Non-early acceptance rate: 53%. **Size of waiting list:** 253 applicants; enrolled from waiting list: 4. **Credentials of fall 2009 freshmen:** 12% ranked in the top 10 percent of their high school class; 48% were in the top 25 percent; 84% were in the top half. (Proportion submitting class standing: 65%.) **Average high school grade point average:** 3.4. **First-year students who submitted SAT scores:** 89%. Scores (25/75 percentile): Critical Reading: 520-610, Math: 530-610, Combined: 1050-1220. **First-year students submitting ACT scores:** 40%. Scores (25/75 percentile): English: 21-27, Math: 21-26, Composite: 22-27.

ACADEMICS

Year founded: 1839. **Academic calendar:** Semester. **Degrees offered:** bachelor's. **Most popular majors:** 27% social sciences, 26% engineering, 15% history, 11% psychology, 6% physical sciences. **Major fields of study:** biological and biomedical sciences; computer and information sciences and support services; engineering; English language and literature/letters; foreign languages, literatures, and linguistics; history; mathematics and statistics; physical sciences; psychology; social sciences. **Areas of required coursework:** humanities, mathematics, English (including composition), foreign languages, sciences (biological or physical), history, other. **Special academic programs (% participation):** double major (7.93%), exchange student program (domestic), honors program (5.51%), independent study (40.7%), internships (3.1%), study abroad (14.8%), teacher certificate program (.68%), other (13.8%). **Teacher certification offered in:** secondary. **Reserve Officers Training Corps (ROTC):** Army ROTC: Offered on campus; Navy ROTC: Offered on campus; Air Force ROTC: Offered on campus. **Faculty and instruction (2009-2010):** Total instructional faculty: 122 full-time, 50 part-time (78% men; 22% women; 9% minorities). Full-time faculty with Ph.D. or other terminal degree: 96%. Student/faculty ratio: 11/1. Classes of fewer than 20 students: 71%; of 20 to 49 students: 29%. **Advanced Placement and International Baccalaureate credit:** AP tests may be used for: Credit and/or placement. Scores accepted: 3, 4, 5. International Baccalaureate exams may be used for: Placement only. **Freshmen returning for sophomore year:** 82%. **Graduation rates:** Four-year: 64%; five-year: 70%; six-year: 73%. **Graduate study:** 5% of students pursue further study immediately upon graduation. Fields in which graduates pursue further study: law, 20%; medicine, 7%; engineering, 33%; arts and sciences, 40%.

COSTS AND FINANCIAL AID

Financial aid office: (540) 464-7208. **Expenses (2010-2011):** Tuition and fees 2010-2011: $12,328 in state, $30,320 out of state; room/board: $7,132. Estimated books and supplies: $775; transportation: $400; personal expenses: $1,750. **Financial aid:** Priority filing date for institution's financial aid form: March 1; deadline: March 1. In 2009-2010, 61% of undergraduates applied for financial aid. Of those, 45% were determined to have financial need; 49% had their need fully met. Average financial aid package (proportion receiving): $19,078 (45%). Average amount of gift aid, such as scholarships or grants (proportion receiving): $16,888 (43%). Average amount of self-help aid, such as work study or loans (proportion receiving): $3,942 (27%). Average need-based loan (excluding PLUS or other private loans): $3,935. Among students who received need-based aid, the average percentage of need met: 90%. Among students who received aid based on merit, the average award (and the proportion receiving): $15,850 (28%). The average athletic scholarship (and the proportion receiving): $15,878 (8%). Average amount of debt of borrowers graduating in 2009: $19,046. Proportion who borrowed: 34%.

CAMPUS LIFE AND EXTRACURRICULAR ACTIVITIES

Campus housing available (% using): other housing options (100%). Students who live in college-owned, operated, or affiliated housing: 100%. **Student employment:** During the 2009-2010 academic year, 10% of undergraduates worked on campus. Average per-year earnings: $3,045. **Clubs and organizations:** Number of student organizations: 43. Activities include: campus ministries, choral groups, concert band, drama/theater, international student organization, jazz band, literary magazine, marching band, music ensembles, musical theater, pep band, student government, student newspaper, yearbook. Number of fraternities: 0; sororities: 0. Average proportion of students who stay on campus on weekends: 70%. **Sports program (2009-2010):** Member of NCAA I. **Men's intercollegiate varsity sports:** baseball,

basketball, cross country, football, lacrosse, rifle, soccer, swimming, track and field (indoor), track and field (outdoor), wrestling. **Women's intercollegiate varsity sports:** cross country, rifle, soccer, swimming, track and field (indoor), track and field (outdoor), water polo.

SERVICES AND FACILITIES

Basic services: nonremedial tutoring, health service. **Remedial assistance:** reading, math, writing, study skills. **Counseling services:** career, military, personal, veteran student, academic, psychological, birth control, religious, other. **For learning-disabled students:** School does not offer a structured program with separate admission and additional fees. Total undergraduates in learning-disabled program or receiving services: 105. Services include: reading machines, tape recorders, note-taking services, oral tests, learning center, extended time for tests, tutors, priority seating, substitution of courses, texts on tape, other testing accommodations, other. **Library:** Number of titles: 453,550; number of current serial subscriptions: 66,311. **Information technology resources:** Students are not required to lease or own a computer. Number of campus computers available to all students: 400. School has a wireless network. Approximate number of users that can be accommodated: 2,000. Proportion of college-owned housing units wired for high-speed internet access: 100%. **Campus safety:** Security services offered: 24-hour foot-and-vehicle patrols, late-night transport/escort service, 24-hour emergency telephones, lighted pathways/sidewalks, student patrols, controlled dormitory access (key, security card, etc).

TRANSFER AND INTERNATIONAL STUDENTS

Transfer students: May apply for admission for the following academic terms: Fall. Applicants do not need a minimum number of credits to apply. For fall 2009: Transfer applications received: 127. Transfer applicants offered admission: 50. Transfer applicants enrolled: 33. **International students:** Number of foreign undergraduates: 26 (2% of student body). Number of countries represented: 15. Minimum TOEFL score required: 500 (paper); 173 (computer). Average TOEFL score: 565 (paper).

Virginia State University

- **Address:** 1 Hayden Drive, Petersburg, VA 23806
- **Website:** http://www.vsu.edu
- **Public**
- **Enrollment:** 4,547 full-time; 324 part-time

KEY STATS

✔ **U.S News College Ranking:** 74, Regional Universities (South)
✔ **SAT Score (25th/75th percentile):** 790-950
✔ **Tuition:** 2009-2010: $6,174 in state, $14,508 out of state
   Selectivity: Less selective   **Room/board:** $8,050
   Acceptance rate: 67%   **Average debt:** N/A
   Student/faculty ratio: 17/1   **Proportion who borrowed:** N/A

UNDERGRADUATE STUDENT BODY STATS

2009-2010 enrollment: 4,547 full-time; 324 part-time. Men: 38%; women: 62%. **Ethnic makeup:** African American: 93%; Hispanic: 1%; White: 5%.

ADMISSIONS FACTS AND FIGURES

Phone: (804) 524-5902. **Email:** admiss@vsu.edu. **Website:** http://www.vsu.edu. **Application deadlines for fall 2011:** Regular decision: May 1. Early decision: Not offered. Early action: Not offered. Admission cannot be deferred. **Application fee:** $25. **To apply online, go to:** http://www.vsu.edu/pages/107.asp. **Admissions requirements/recommendations:** High school units required (recommended): English: 4; Mathematics: 3; Science: 2; Foreign language: (2); Social studies: 2; Total units: 11. Tests: The college uses SAT or ACT scores in admissions decisions. Either SAT or ACT required. For admission to the fall 2011 entering class, the school will accept: ACT with or without writing accepted. Campus visit: Recommended. Admissions interview: Neither required nor recommended. Off-campus interview: Not available. **Factors that count in admissions decisions:** **Academic:** Secondary school record: Very Important. Class rank: Considered. Letters of recommendation: Very Important. Standardized test scores: Very Important. Essay: Very Important. **Nonacademic:** Interview: Not Considered. Extracurricular activities: Considered. Talent/ability: Considered. Character/personal qualities: Considered. Alumni/ae relationship: Considered. Geographical residence: Considered. State residency: Considered. Religious affiliation/commitment: Not Considered. Minority status: Not Considered.

Volunteer work: Considered. Work experience: Considered. **Admissions statistics for the fall 2009 entering class:** Total applicants: 6,341. Total accepted: 4,225. Freshmen enrolled: 1,204; 40% were from out of state. Overall acceptance rate: 67%. **Credentials of fall 2009 freshmen:** 7% ranked in the top 10 percent of their high school class; 24% were in the top 25 percent; 62% were in the top half. (Proportion submitting class standing: 82%.) **Average high school grade point average:** 2.9. **First-year students who submitted SAT scores:** 92%. Scores (25/75 percentile): Critical Reading: 400-480, Math: 390-470, Combined: 790-950. **First-year students submitting ACT scores:** 19%. Scores (25/75 percentile): English: N/A, Math: N/A, Composite: 18-20.

ACADEMICS

Year founded: 1882. **Academic calendar:** Semester. **Degrees offered:** associate, bachelor's, post-bachelor's certificate, master's, post-master's certificate, doctorate. **Most popular majors:** 11% physical education teaching and coaching, 10% criminal justice/safety studies, 9% mass communication/media studies, 9% psychology, 8% business administration and management. **Major fields of study:** agriculture, agriculture operations, and related sciences; biological and biomedical sciences; business, management, marketing, and related support services; communication, journalism, and related programs; computer and information sciences and support services; education; engineering; engineering technologies/technicians; English language and literature/letters; family and consumer sciences/human sciences; health professions and related clinical sciences; history; liberal arts and sciences studies, and humanities; mathematics and statistics; multi/interdisciplinary studies; physical sciences; psychology; public administration and social service professions; security and protective services; social sciences; visual and performing arts. **Areas of required coursework:** arts/fine arts, humanities, computer literacy, mathematics, English (including composition), philosophy, foreign languages, sciences (biological or physical), history, social science. **Pre-professional programs:** other. **Special academic programs:** cooperative (work-study plan) program, double major, dual enrollment, exchange student program (domestic), honors program, independent study, internships, teacher certificate program. **Teacher certification offered in:** early childhood, special education, elementary, middle/junior high, secondary. **Cooperative education programs:** agriculture, art, business, computer science, education, engineering, home economics, humanities, natural science, social/behavioral science, technologies, vocational arts. **Reserve Officers Training Corps (ROTC):** Army ROTC: Offered on campus. **Faculty and instruction (2009-2010):** Total instructional faculty: 247 full-time, 103 part-time (55% men; 45% women). Student/faculty ratio: 17/1. Classes of fewer than 20 students: 37%; of 20 to 49 students: 53%; of 50 or more students: 10%. **Advanced Placement and International Baccalaureate credit:** AP tests may be used for: Credit only. Scores accepted: 3. **Freshmen returning for sophomore year:** 71%. **Graduation rates:** Four-year: 25%; five-year: 41%; six-year: 42%. **Graduate study:** 19% of students pursue further study immediately upon graduation; 12% within one year; 31% within five years.

COSTS AND FINANCIAL AID

Financial aid office: (804) 524-5992. **Expenses (2009-2010):** Tuition and fees 2009-2010: $6,174 in state, $14,508 out of state; room/board: $8,050. Estimated books and supplies: $900; transportation: $1,000; personal expenses: $775. **Financial aid:** Priority filing date for institution's financial aid form: March 31; deadline: May 1.

CAMPUS LIFE AND EXTRACURRICULAR ACTIVITIES

Campus housing available (% using): coed dorms (14%), women's dorms (40%), men's dorms (21%), apartment for single students (15%). Students who live in college-owned, operated, or affiliated housing: 62%. **Clubs and organizations:** Number of student organizations: 70. Activities include: campus ministries, choral groups, concert band, dance, drama/theater, jazz band, literary magazine, marching band, music ensembles, pep band, radio station, student government, student newspaper, television station, yearbook. Number of fraternities: 5; sororities: 4. Proportion of men in fraternities: 2%; of women in sororities: 5%. **Sports program (2009-2010):** Member of NCAA II. *Men's intercollegiate varsity sports:* baseball, basketball, cross country, football, golf, tennis, track and field (indoor), track and field (outdoor). *Women's intercollegiate varsity sports:* basketball, cross country, golf, softball, tennis, track and field (outdoor), volleyball.

SERVICES AND FACILITIES

Basic services: nonremedial tutoring, placement service, health service. **Counseling services:** veteran student, academic, psychological. **For learning-disabled students:** School does not offer a structured program with separate admission and additional fees. Services include: reading machines, tape

recorders, untimed tests, note-taking services, special bookstore section, oral tests, learning center, readers, extended time for tests, tutors, priority registration, priority seating, texts on tape, other testing accommodations. **Library:** Number of titles: 312,154; number of current serial subscriptions: 2,632. **Information technology resources:** Students are not required to lease or own a computer. Number of campus computers available to all students: 750. School has a wireless network. Approximate number of users that can be accommodated: 1,200. Proportion of college-owned housing units wired for high-speed internet access: 100%. **Campus safety:** Security services offered: late-night transport/escort service, 24-hour emergency telephones, lighted pathways/sidewalks, controlled dormitory access (key, security card, etc).

TRANSFER AND INTERNATIONAL STUDENTS

Transfer students: May apply for admission for the following academic terms: Fall, Spring, Summer. Applicants need a minimum number of credits to apply. For fall 2009: Transfer applicants enrolled: 227. **International students:** Number of foreign undergraduates: 17. Number of countries represented: 32. Minimum TOEFL score required: 500 (paper); 173 (computer).

Virginia Tech

- **Address:** Blacksburg, VA 24061
- **Website:** http://www.vt.edu
- **Public**
- **Enrollment:** 23,104 full-time; 454 part-time

KEY STATS

- ✔ **U.S News College Ranking:** 69, National Universities
- ✔ **SAT Score (25th/75th percentile):** 1110-1310
- ✔ **Tuition:** 2009-2010: $8,605 in state, $21,878 out of state
  Selectivity: More selective **Room/board:** $6,580
  Acceptance rate: 67% **Average debt:** $22,070
  Student/faculty ratio: 16/1 **Proportion who borrowed:** 52%

UNDERGRADUATE STUDENT BODY STATS

2009-2010 enrollment: 23,104 full-time; 454 part-time. Men: 57%; women: 43%. **Ethnic makeup:** African American: 4%; Asian American: 8%; Hispanic: 3%; White: 82%; International: 2%. **Religious preference:** Roman Catholic: 27%; Protestant: 58%; Jewish: 2%; Muslim: 1%; Hindu: 1%; Buddhist: 1%; No preference: 8%; Other: 2%.

ADMISSIONS FACTS AND FIGURES

Phone: (540) 231-6267. **Email:** vtadmiss@vt.edu. **Website:** http://www.vt.edu. **Application deadlines for fall 2011:** Regular decision: January 15; decision sent by April 1. Early decision: Send application by: November 1; decision sent by: December 15. Early action: Not offered. Admission can be deferred. **Application fee:** $60. **To apply online, go to:** http://www.admiss.vt.edu/apply/apply_online.php. **Admissions requirements/recommendations:** High school units required (recommended): English: 4; Mathematics: 3 (4); Science: 2 (3); Foreign language: (3); Social studies: 1; History: 1; Academic electives: 4; Total units: 18. Tests: The college uses SAT or ACT scores in admissions decisions. Either SAT or ACT required. For admission to the fall 2011 entering class, the school will accept: ACT with writing required. Campus visit: Recommended. Admissions interview: Neither required nor recommended. **Factors that count in admissions decisions:** *Academic:* Secondary school record: Very Important. Class rank: Not Considered. Letters of recommendation: Considered. Standardized test scores: Very Important. Essay: Not Considered. *Nonacademic:* Interview: Not Considered. Extracurricular activities: Considered. Talent/ability: Considered. Character/personal qualities: Considered. Alumni/ae relationship: Considered. Geographical residence: Considered. State residency: Considered. Religious affiliation/commitment: Not Considered. Minority status: Considered. Volunteer work: Considered. Work experience: Considered. **Other schools with the greatest overlap in applicants:** College of William and Mary; James Madison University; University of North Carolina–Chapel Hill; University of Virginia. **Admissions statistics for the fall 2009 entering class:** Total applicants: 21,053. Total accepted: 14,040. Freshmen enrolled: 5,050; 27% were from out of state. Accepted through early-decision or early-action plans: 23%. Overall acceptance rate: 67%. Early-decision acceptance rate: 52%. Non-early acceptance rate: 69%. **Size of waiting list:** 2919 applicants; enrolled from waiting list: 859. **Credentials of fall 2009 freshmen:** 44% ranked in the top 10 percent of their high school class; 85% were in the top 25 percent; 99% were in the top half. (Proportion submitting class standing: 62%.) **First-year students who submitted SAT scores:** 96%. Scores (25/75 percentile): Critical Reading: 540-640, Math: 570-670, Combined: 1110-1310.

ACADEMICS

Year founded: 1872. **Academic calendar:** Semester. **Degrees offered:** certificate, associate, bachelor's, master's, post-master's certificate, doctorate. **Most popular majors:** 22% business, management, marketing, and related support services, 20% engineering, 9% social sciences, 8% family and consumer sciences/human sciences, 7% biological and biomedical sciences. **Major fields of study:** agriculture, agriculture operations, and related sciences; architecture and related services; biological and biomedical sciences; business, management, marketing, and related support services; communication, journalism, and related programs; computer and information sciences and support services; education; engineering; engineering technologies/technicians; English language and literature/letters; family and consumer sciences/human sciences; foreign languages, literatures, and linguistics; history; liberal arts and sciences studies, and humanities; mathematics and statistics; natural resources and conservation; philosophy and religious studies; physical sciences; psychology; public administration and social service professions; social sciences; visual and performing arts. **Areas of required coursework:** arts/fine arts, humanities, computer literacy, mathematics, English (including composition), foreign languages, sciences (biological or physical), history, social science. **Pre-professional programs:** pre-law, pre-dentistry, pre-medicine, pre-veterinary science, pre-optometry, pre-pharmacy, other. **Special academic programs:** accelerated program, cooperative (work-study plan) program, distance learning, double major, dual enrollment, English as a Second Language (ESL), honors program, independent study, internships, study abroad, teacher certificate program. **Teacher certification offered in:** early childhood, elementary, vo-tech, middle/junior high, secondary. **Cooperative education programs:** agriculture, business, computer science, education, engineering, natural science. **Reserve Officers Training Corps (ROTC):** Army ROTC: Offered on campus; Navy ROTC: Offered on campus; Air Force ROTC: Offered on campus. **Faculty and instruction (2009-2010):** Total instructional faculty: 1,364 full-time, 224 part-time (67% men; 33% women; 15% minorities). Full-time faculty with Ph.D. or other terminal degree: 90%. Student/faculty ratio: 16/1. Classes of fewer than 20 students: 24%; of 20 to 49 students: 55%; of 50 or more students: 21%. **Advanced Placement and International Baccalaureate credit:** AP tests may be used for: Credit and/or placement. Scores accepted: 3, 4, 5. International Baccalaureate exams may be used for: Credit and/or placement. Freshmen returning for sophomore year: 91%. **Graduation rates:** Four-year: 53%; five-year: 77%; six-year: 80%. **Graduate study:** 21% of students pursue further study immediately upon graduation.

COSTS AND FINANCIAL AID

Financial aid office: (540) 231-5179. **Expenses (2009-2010):** Tuition and fees 2009-2010: $8,605 in state, $21,878 out of state; room/board: $6,580. Estimated books and supplies: $1,080; transportation: $1,600; personal expenses: $1,700. **Financial aid:** Priority filing date for institution's financial aid form: March 1; deadline: March 1. In 2009-2010, 65% of undergraduates applied for financial aid. Of those, 41% were determined to have financial need; 26% had their need fully met. Average financial aid package (proportion receiving): $11,642 (40%). Average amount of gift aid, such as scholarships or grants (proportion receiving): $6,329 (29%). Average amount of self-help aid, such as work study or loans (proportion receiving): $4,478 (31%). Average need-based loan (excluding PLUS or other private loans): $4,248. Among students who received need-based aid, the average percentage of need met: 71%. Among students who received aid based on merit, the average award (and the proportion receiving): $2,564 (8%). The average athletic scholarship (and the proportion receiving): $15,571 (2%). Average amount of debt of borrowers graduating in 2009: $22,070. Proportion who borrowed: 52%.

CAMPUS LIFE AND EXTRACURRICULAR ACTIVITIES

Campus housing available (% using): coed dorms (57%), women's dorms (6%), men's dorms (8%), sorority housing (5%), fraternity housing (2%), special housing for international students, other housing options (8%). Students who live in college-owned, operated, or affiliated housing: 37%. **Clubs and organizations:** Number of student organizations: 698. Activities include: campus ministries, choral groups, concert band, dance, drama/theater, international student organization, jazz band, literary magazine, marching band, model UN, music ensembles, musical theater, opera, pep band, radio station, student government, student newspaper, student film society, television station, yearbook. Number of fraternities: 33; sororities:

22. Average proportion of students who stay on campus on weekends: 75%. **Sports program (2009-2010):** Member of NCAA I. *Men's intercollegiate varsity sports:* baseball, basketball, cross country, football, golf, soccer, swimming, tennis, track and field (indoor), wrestling. *Women's intercollegiate varsity sports:* basketball, cross country, lacrosse, soccer, softball, swimming, tennis, track and field (indoor), volleyball.

SERVICES AND FACILITIES

Basic services: nonremedial tutoring, women's center, placement service, health service, health insurance. **Counseling services:** minority student, career, military, personal, academic, older student, psychological, birth control, religious. **For learning-disabled students:** School does not offer a structured program with separate admission and additional fees. Services include: reading machines, tape recorders, note-taking services, oral tests, learning center, readers, extended time for tests, tutors, priority registration, priority seating, texts on tape, other testing accommodations. **Library:** Number of titles: 2,385,815; number of current serial subscriptions: 27,150. **Information technology resources:** Students are required to lease or own a computer. School has a wireless network. Approximate number of users that can be accommodated: 8,000. Proportion of college-owned housing units wired for high-speed internet access: 100%. **Campus safety:** Security services offered: 24-hour foot-and-vehicle patrols, late-night transport/escort service, 24-hour emergency telephones, lighted pathways/sidewalks, controlled dormitory access (key, security card, etc).

TRANSFER AND INTERNATIONAL STUDENTS

Transfer students: May apply for admission for the following academic terms: Fall, Spring, Summer. Applicants need a minimum number of credits to apply. **International students:** Number of foreign undergraduates: 411 (2% of student body). Number of countries represented: 75. Minimum TOEFL score required: 550 (paper); 207 (computer).

Virginia Union University

- **Address:** 1500 N. Lombardy Street, Richmond, VA 23220
- **Website:** http://www.vuu.edu/
- **Private; Religious affiliation:** Baptist
- **Enrollment:** 1,270 full-time; 37 part-time

KEY STATS
✔ **U.S News College Ranking:** 64, Regional Colleges (South)
✔ **SAT Score (25th/75th percentile):** 680-840
✔ **Tuition:** 2010-2011: $14,630

Selectivity: Least selective	**Room/board:** $6,830
Acceptance rate: 81%	**Average debt:** N/A
Student/faculty ratio: N/A	**Proportion who borrowed:** N/A

UNDERGRADUATE STUDENT BODY STATS
2009-2010 enrollment: 1,270 full-time; 37 part-time. Men: 45%; women: 55%. **Ethnic makeup:** African American: 98%; White: 2%.

ADMISSIONS FACTS AND FIGURES
Phone: (804) 257-5600. **Email:** admissions@vuu.edu. **Website:** http://www.vuu.edu/. **Application deadlines for fall 2011:** Regular decision: August 9; decision sent by April 1. Early decision: Not offered. Early action: Not offered. Admission cannot be deferred. **Application fee:** $25. **To apply online, go to:** http://www.vuu.edu/admissions/apply.htm. **Admissions requirements/recommendations:** High school units required (recommended): English: 4 (4); Mathematics: 3 (3); Science: 2 (2); Foreign language: 2 (2); Social studies: 1 (1); History: 1 (1); Academic electives: 3 (3); Total units: 18 (18). Tests: The college uses SAT or ACT scores in admissions decisions. Either SAT or ACT required. For admission to the fall 2011 entering class, the school will accept: ACT with or without writing accepted. Campus visit: Neither required nor recommended. Admissions interview: Neither required nor recommended. Off-campus interview: May be arranged. **Factors that count in admissions decisions:** *Academic:* Secondary school record: Important. Class rank: Considered. Letters of recommendation: Considered. Standardized test scores: Important. Essay: Important. *Nonacademic:* Interview: Considered. Extracurricular activities: Considered. Talent/ability: Considered. Character/personal qualities: Considered. Alumni/ae relationship: Considered. Geographical residence: Considered. State residency: Not Considered. Religious affiliation/commitment: Not Considered. Minority status: Not Considered. Volunteer work: Considered.

Work experience: Not Considered. **Other schools with the greatest overlap in applicants:** Randolph-Macon College; Shaw University; St. Paul's College; Virginia State University. **Admissions statistics for the fall 2009 entering class:** Total applicants: 5,260. Total accepted: 4,257. Freshmen enrolled: 560; Overall acceptance rate: 81%. **Size of waiting list:** 4 applicants; enrolled from waiting list: 0. **Average high school grade point average:** 2.3. **First-year students who submitted SAT scores:** 100%.

ACADEMICS
Year founded: 1865. **Academic calendar:** Semester. **Degrees offered:** certificate, bachelor's, master's, doctorate. **Major fields of study:** biological and biomedical sciences; business, management, marketing, and related support services; communication, journalism, and related programs; computer and information sciences and support services; education; philosophy and religious studies; psychology; public administration and social service professions; security and protective services; social sciences. **Areas of required coursework:** arts/fine arts, humanities, computer literacy, mathematics, English (including composition), foreign languages, sciences (biological or physical), history, social science. **Pre-professional programs:** pre-medicine, pre-theology. **Special academic programs (% participation):** double major, honors program (1%), independent study, internships (15%), teacher certificate program (10%), weekend college (12%). **Teacher certification offered in:** early childhood, special education, elementary, adult education, secondary. **Advanced Placement and International Baccalaureate credit:** Scores accepted: 4, 5. International Baccalaureate exams may be used for: Placement only. **Freshmen returning for sophomore year:** 56%. **Graduation rates:** Six-year: 28%.

COSTS AND FINANCIAL AID
Financial aid office: (804) 257-5882. **Expenses (2010-2011):** Tuition and fees 2010-2011: $14,630; room/board: $6,830. **Financial aid:** Priority filing date for institution's financial aid form: March 1. In 2009-2010, 90% of undergraduates applied for financial aid. Of those, 85% were determined to have financial need; Average financial aid package (proportion receiving): $10,921 (84%). Average amount of gift aid, such as scholarships or grants (proportion receiving): $5,371 (65%). Average amount of self-help aid, such as work study or loans (proportion receiving): $4,249 (71%). Average need-based loan (excluding PLUS or other private loans): $3,894.

CAMPUS LIFE AND EXTRACURRICULAR ACTIVITIES
Campus housing available (% using): coed dorms (17%), women's dorms (53%), men's dorms (30%). **Student employment:** During the 2009-2010 academic year, 27% of undergraduates worked on campus. Average per-year earnings: $2,000. **Clubs and organizations:** Number of student organizations: 24. Activities include: campus ministries, choral groups, dance, drama/theater, international student organization, model UN, music ensembles, pep band, radio station, student government, student newspaper, yearbook. Number of fraternities: 4; sororities: 3. Average proportion of students who stay on campus on weekends: 80%. **Sports program (2009-2010):** Member of NCAA II. *Men's intercollegiate varsity sports:* basketball, cross country, football, track and field (indoor), track and field (outdoor). *Women's intercollegiate varsity sports:* basketball, cross country, softball, tennis, track and field (indoor), track and field (outdoor), volleyball.

SERVICES AND FACILITIES
Basic services: placement service, health service, health insurance. **Remedial assistance:** reading, math, writing, study skills. **Counseling services:** career, personal, academic, psychological, religious. **For learning-disabled students:** School does not offer a structured program with separate admission and additional fees. Services include: remedial math, remedial English, reading machines, remedial reading, learning center, tutors. **Information technology resources:** Students are not required to lease or own a computer. Number of campus computers available to all students: 300. School has a wireless network. Approximate number of users that can be accommodated: 2,000. Proportion of college-owned housing units wired for high-speed internet access: 100%. **Campus safety:** Security services offered: 24-hour foot-and-vehicle patrols, late-night transport/escort service, 24-hour emergency telephones, lighted pathways/sidewalks, controlled dormitory access (key, security card, etc).

TRANSFER AND INTERNATIONAL STUDENTS
Transfer students: May apply for admission for the following academic terms: Fall, Winter, Summer. Applicants do not need a minimum number of credits to apply. For fall 2009: Transfer applicants enrolled: 39. **International students:** Number of foreign undergraduates: 0.

Virginia Wesleyan College

- **Address:** 1584 Wesleyan Drive, Norfolk, VA 23502-5599
- **Website:** http://www.vwc.edu
- **Private; Religious affiliation:** United Methodist
- **Enrollment:** 1,143 full-time; 193 part-time

KEY STATS
- ✔ **U.S News College Ranking:** second tier, National Liberal Arts Colleges
- ✔ **SAT Score (25th/75th percentile):** 880-1070
- ✔ **Tuition:** 2010-2011: $28,556

Selectivity: Less selective	**Room/board:** $7,680
Acceptance rate: 75%	**Average debt:** $27,658
Student/faculty ratio: 11/1	**Proportion who borrowed:** 80%

UNDERGRADUATE STUDENT BODY STATS
2009-2010 enrollment: 1,143 full-time; 193 part-time. Men: 37%; women: 63%. **Ethnic makeup:** African American: 21%; Asian American: 2%; Hispanic: 4%; White: 73%; International: 1%. **Religious preference:** Roman Catholic: 16%; Protestant: 2%; Jewish: 1%; No preference: 1%; Unknown: 27%; United Methodist: 13%; Baptist: 12%; Other: 28%.

ADMISSIONS FACTS AND FIGURES
Phone: (800) 737-8684. **Email:** admissions@vwc.edu. **Website:** http://www.vwc.edu. **Application deadlines for fall 2011:** Regular decision: Rolling. Early decision: Not offered. Early action: Not offered. Admission cannot be deferred. **Application fee:** $40. **To apply online, go to:** http://www.vwc.edu/admissions/. **Admissions requirements/recommendations:** High school units required (recommended): English: 4 (4); Mathematics: 3 (3); Science: 2 (2); Foreign language: 2 (2); Social studies: 0 (0); History: 1 (1); Academic electives: 0 (4); Total units: 12 (16). Tests: The college uses SAT or ACT scores in admissions decisions. Either SAT or ACT required. For admission to the fall 2011 entering class, the school will accept: ACT with or without writing accepted. Campus visit: Recommended. Admissions interview: Recommended. Off-campus interview: May be arranged. **Factors that count in admissions decisions:** *Academic:* Secondary school record: Very Important. Class rank: Not Considered. Letters of recommendation: Important. Standardized test scores: Important. Essay: Important. *Nonacademic:* Interview: Considered. Extracurricular activities: Important. Talent/ability: Considered. Character/personal qualities: Considered. Alumni/ae relationship: Considered. Geographical residence: Not Considered. State residency: Not Considered. Religious affiliation/commitment: Not Considered. Minority status: Not Considered. Volunteer work: Considered. Work experience: Considered. **Other schools with the greatest overlap in applicants:** Christopher Newport University; College of William and Mary; Lynchburg College; Old Dominion University; Randolph-Macon College. **Admissions statistics for the fall 2009 entering class:** Total applicants: 1,372. Total accepted: 1,033. Freshmen accepted: 319; 27% were from out of state. Overall acceptance rate: 75%. **Credentials of fall 2009 freshmen:** 10% ranked in the top 10 percent of their high school class; 34% were in the top 25 percent; 70% were in the top half. (Proportion submitting class standing: 79%.) **Average high school grade point average:** 3.1. **First-year students who submitted SAT scores:** 83%. Scores (25/75 percentile): Critical Reading: 440-530, Math: 440-540, Combined: 880-1070. **First-year students submitting ACT scores:** 17%. Scores (25/75 percentile): English: 17-23, Math: 18-23, Composite: 18-23.

ACADEMICS
Year founded: 1961. **Academic calendar:** 4-1-4. **Degrees offered:** bachelor's. **Most popular majors:** 19% business administration and management, 10% criminal justice/safety studies, 9% mass communication/media studies, 8% parks, recreation, and leisure studies, 8% social sciences. **Major fields of study:** area, ethnic, cultural, and gender studies; biological and biomedical sciences; business, management, marketing, and related support services; communication, journalism, and related programs; computer and information sciences and support services; education; English language and literature/letters; foreign languages, literatures, and linguistics; history; liberal arts and sciences studies, and humanities; mathematics and statistics; multi/interdisciplinary studies; natural resources and conservation; parks, recreation, leisure, and fitness studies; philosophy and religious studies; physical sciences; psychology; public administration and social service professions; social sciences; visual and performing arts. **Areas of required coursework:** arts/fine arts, humanities, mathematics, English (including composition), foreign languages, sciences (biological or physical), history,

social science, other. **Pre-professional programs:** pre-law, pre-dentistry, pre-medicine, pre-theology, pre-veterinary science, pre-pharmacy, other. **Special academic programs (% participation):** cross-registration (1%), double major (8%), honors program (4%), independent study (15%), internships (55%), liberal arts/career combination (33%), student-designed major (1%), study abroad (1%), teacher certificate program (9%), other. **Teacher certification offered in:** early childhood, special education, elementary, middle/junior high, secondary. **Reserve Officers Training Corps (ROTC):** Army ROTC: Offered at cooperating institution (Old Dominion University). **Faculty and instruction (2009-2010):** Total instructional faculty: 84 full-time, 45 part-time (53% men; 47% women; 10% minorities). Full-time faculty with Ph.D. or other terminal degree: 89%. Student/faculty ratio: 11/1. Classes of fewer than 20 students: 75%; of 20 to 49 students: 25%. **Advanced Placement and International Baccalaureate credit:** AP tests may be used for: Credit only. Scores accepted: 4, 5. International Baccalaureate exams may be used for: Placement only. **Freshmen returning for sophomore year:** 67%. **Graduation rates:** Four-year: 35%; five-year: 43%; six-year: 45%. **Graduate study:** 25% of students pursue further study immediately upon graduation. Fields in which graduates pursue further study: law, 14%; medicine, 14%; theology (or the seminary), 5%; education, 19%; arts and sciences, 48%.

COSTS AND FINANCIAL AID

Financial aid office: (757) 455-3345. **Expenses (2010-2011):** Tuition and fees 2010-2011: $28,556; room/board: $7,680. Estimated books and supplies: $1,000; transportation: $1,800; personal expenses: $1,800. **Financial aid:** Priority filing date for institution's financial aid form: March 1. In 2009-2010, 87% of undergraduates applied for financial aid. Of those, 74% were determined to have financial need; 11% had their need fully met. Average financial aid package (proportion receiving): $17,752 (73%). Average amount of gift aid, such as scholarships or grants (proportion receiving): $13,507 (73%). Average amount of self-help aid, such as work study or loans (proportion receiving): $9,255 (61%). Average need-based loan (excluding PLUS or other private loans): $7,228. Among students who received need-based aid, the average percentage of need met: 68%. Among students who received aid based on merit, the average award (and the proportion receiving): $7,171 (18%). Average amount of debt of borrowers graduating in 2009: $27,658. Proportion who borrowed: 80%.

CAMPUS LIFE AND EXTRACURRICULAR ACTIVITIES

Campus housing available (% using): coed dorms (39%), women's dorms (7%), sorority housing (4%), fraternity housing (4%), apartment for single students (28%), special housing for disabled students (1%), special housing for international students (6%), other housing options (11%). Students who live in college-owned, operated, or affiliated housing: 69%. **Student employment:** During the 2009-2010 academic year, 10% of undergraduates worked on campus. Average per-year earnings: $2,000. **Clubs and organizations:** Number of student organizations: 70. Activities include: campus ministries, choral groups, dance, drama/theater, international student organization, literary magazine, model UN, musical theater, radio station, student government, student newspaper, yearbook. Number of fraternities: 3; sororities: 4. Proportion of men in fraternities: 7%; of women in sororities: 3%. Average proportion of students who stay on campus on weekends: 70%. **Sports program (2009-2010):** Member of NCAA III. *Men's intercollegiate varsity sports:* baseball, basketball, cross country, golf, lacrosse, soccer, tennis, track and field (indoor), track and field (outdoor). *Women's intercollegiate varsity sports:* basketball, cross country, field hockey, lacrosse, soccer, softball, tennis, track and field (indoor), track and field (outdoor), volleyball.

SERVICES AND FACILITIES

Basic services: nonremedial tutoring, women's center, health service, health insurance, other. **Remedial assistance:** reading, math, writing, study skills. **Counseling services:** minority student, career, military, personal, veteran student, academic, older student, psychological, birth control, religious. **For learning-disabled students:** School does not offer a structured program with separate admission and additional fees. Total undergraduates in learning-disabled program or receiving services: 60. Services include: remedial math, remedial English, tape recorders, other special classes, untimed tests, note-taking services, oral tests, learning center, readers, extended time for tests, tutors, early syllabus, priority registration, priority seating, proofreading services, texts on tape, typist/scribe, exams on tape or computer, other testing accommodations, other. **Library:** Number of titles: 129,000; number of current serial subscriptions: 800. **Information technology resources:** Students are not required to lease or own a computer. Number of campus computers available to all students: 118. School has a wireless network. Approximate number of users that can be accommodated: 600. Proportion of college-owned housing units wired for high-speed internet access: 100%.

Campus safety: Security services offered: 24-hour foot-and-vehicle patrols, late-night transport/escort service, 24-hour emergency telephones, lighted pathways/sidewalks, controlled dormitory access (key, security card, etc).

TRANSFER AND INTERNATIONAL STUDENTS

Transfer students: May apply for admission for the following academic terms: Fall, Spring, Summer. Applicants need a minimum number of credits to apply. For fall 2009: Transfer applications received: 182. Transfer applicants offered admission: 135. Transfer applicants enrolled: 84. **International students:** Number of foreign undergraduates: 7 (1% of student body). Number of countries represented: 8. Minimum TOEFL score required: 550 (paper); 213 (computer).

Washington and Lee University

- **Address:** 204 W. Washington Street, Lexington, VA 24450-2116
- **Website:** http://www.wlu.edu
- **Private**
- **Enrollment:** 1,758 full-time; 1 part-time

KEY STATS

✔ **U.S News College Ranking:** 14, National Liberal Arts Colleges
✔ **SAT Score (25th/75th percentile):** 1320-1470
✔ **Tuition:** 2010-2011: $40,387

Selectivity: Most selective	**Room/board:** $10,243
Acceptance rate: 19%	**Average debt:** $23,615
Student/faculty ratio: 9/1	**Proportion who borrowed:** 31%

UNDERGRADUATE STUDENT BODY STATS

2009-2010 enrollment: 1,758 full-time; 1 part-time. Men: 50%; women: 50%. **Ethnic makeup:** African American: 4%; Asian American: 4%; Hispanic: 2%; White: 86%; International: 5%. **Religious preference:** Roman Catholic: 18%; Protestant: 38%; Jewish: 3%; No preference: 38%; Other: 3%.

ADMISSIONS FACTS AND FIGURES

Phone: (540) 463-8710. **Email:** admissions@wlu.edu. **Website:** http://www.wlu.edu. **Application deadlines for fall 2011:** Regular decision: January 15; decision sent by April 1. Early decision: Send application by: November 16; Decision sent by: December 21. Early action: Not offered. Admission can be deferred. **Application fee:** $50. **To apply online, go to:** http://www.wlu.edu/x19502.xml. **Admissions requirements/recommendations:** High school units required (recommended): English: 4; Mathematics: 3 (4); Science: 1 (3); Foreign language: 3 (4); Social studies: 1; History: 1 (2); Academic electives: 4; Total units: 17. Tests: The college uses SAT or ACT scores in admissions decisions. Either SAT or ACT required. For admission to the fall 2011 entering class, the school will accept: ACT with writing required. Campus visit: Recommended. Admissions interview: Recommended. Off-campus interview: May be arranged. **Factors that count in admissions decisions:** *Academic:* Secondary school record: Very Important. Class rank: Very Important. Letters of recommendation: Important. Standardized test scores: Very Important. Essay: Considered. *Nonacademic:* Interview: Considered. Extracurricular activities: Very Important. Talent/ability: Considered. Character/personal qualities: Very Important. Alumni/ae relationship: Considered. Geographical residence: Considered. State residency: Considered. Religious affiliation/commitment: Not Considered. Minority status: Considered. Volunteer work: Considered. Work experience: Considered. **Other schools with the greatest overlap in applicants:** College of William and Mary; Princeton University; University of Virginia; Vanderbilt University; Wake Forest University. **Admissions statistics for the fall 2009 entering class:** Total applicants: 6,222. Total accepted: 1,181. Freshmen enrolled: 472; 86% were from out of state. Accepted through early-decision or early-action plans: 46%. Overall acceptance rate: 19%. Early-decision acceptance rate: 43%. Non-early acceptance rate: 17%. **Size of waiting list:** 1870 applicants; enrolled from waiting list: 97. **Credentials of fall 2009 freshmen:** 81% ranked in the top 10 percent of their high school class; 94% were in the top 25 percent; 99% were in the top half. (Proportion submitting class standing: 48%.) **First-year students who submitted SAT scores:** 61%. Scores (25/75 percentile): Critical Reading: 660-740, Math: 660-730, Combined: 1320-1470. **First-year students submitting ACT scores:** 37%. Scores (25/75 percentile): English: N/A, Math: N/A, Composite: 29-32.

ACADEMICS

Year founded: 1749. **Academic calendar:** Other. **Degrees offered:** bachelor's, master's. **Most popular majors:** 14% business administration and management, 11% political science and government, 8% history, 7% accounting and business/management, 6% economics. **Major fields of study:** area, ethnic, cultural, and gender studies; biological and biomedical sciences; business, management, marketing, and related support services; communication, journalism, and related programs; computer and information sciences and support services; engineering; English language and literature/letters; foreign languages, literatures, and linguistics; history; mathematics and statistics; multi/interdisciplinary studies; natural resources and conservation; philosophy and religious studies; physical sciences; psychology; public administration and social service professions; social sciences; visual and performing arts. **Areas of required coursework:** humanities, mathematics, English (including composition), foreign languages, sciences (biological or physical), social science, other. **Pre-professional programs:** other. **Special academic programs (% participation):** accelerated program (1%), double major (28%), exchange student program (domestic), honors program (10%), independent study (1%), internships, liberal arts/career combination, student-designed major (1%), study abroad (53%), teacher certificate program (5%). **Teacher certification offered in:** elementary, middle/junior high, secondary. **Cooperative education programs:** education. **Reserve Officers Training Corps (ROTC):** Army ROTC: Offered at cooperating institution (Virginia Military Institute). **Faculty and instruction (2009-2010):** Total instructional faculty: 225 full-time, 56 part-time (66% men; 34% women; 8% minorities). Full-time faculty with Ph.D. or other terminal degree: 96%. Student/faculty ratio: 9/1. Classes of fewer than 20 students: 72%; of 20 to 49 students: 28%; of 50 or more students: 0%. **Advanced Placement and International Baccalaureate credit:** AP tests may be used for: Credit only. Scores accepted: 4, 5. International Baccalaureate exams may be used for: Credit only. **Freshmen returning for sophomore year:** 94%. **Graduation rates:** Four-year: 88%; five-year: 90%; six-year: 91%. **Graduate study:** 25% of students pursue further study immediately upon graduation. Fields in which graduates pursue further study: Master of Business Administration (MBA), 7%; law, 37%; medicine, 26%; dentistry, 3%; engineering, 3%; theology (or the seminary), 1%; arts and sciences, 23%.

COSTS AND FINANCIAL AID

Financial aid office: (540) 458-8717. **Expenses (2010-2011):** Tuition and fees 2010-2011: $40,387; room/board: $10,243. Estimated books and supplies: $1,700 personal expenses: $1,890. **Financial aid:** Priority filing date for institution's financial aid form: February 1; deadline: March 1. In 2009-2010, 40% of undergraduates applied for financial aid. Of those, 35% were determined to have financial need; 100% had their need fully met. Average financial aid package (proportion receiving): $37,052 (35%). Average amount of gift aid, such as scholarships or grants (proportion receiving): $31,111 (33%). Average amount of self-help aid, such as work study or loans (proportion receiving): $4,515 (13%). Average need-based loan (excluding PLUS or other private loans): $3,700. Among students who received need-based aid, the average percentage of need met: 100%. Among students who received aid based on merit, the average award (and the proportion receiving): $27,499 (9%). The average athletic scholarship (and the proportion receiving): $0 (0%). Average amount of debt of borrowers graduating in 2009: $23,615. Proportion who borrowed: 31%.

CAMPUS LIFE AND EXTRACURRICULAR ACTIVITIES

Campus housing available (% using): coed dorms (57%), sorority housing (9%), fraternity housing (21%), apartment for single students (11%), special housing for disabled students, special housing for international students (1%), other housing options (1%). Students who live in college-owned, operated, or affiliated housing: 60%. **Student employment:** During the 2009-2010 academic year, 19% of undergraduates worked on campus. Average per-year earnings: $905. **Clubs and organizations:** Number of student organizations: 168. Activities include: campus ministries, choral groups, concert band, dance, drama/theater, international student organization, jazz band, literary magazine, model UN, music ensembles, pep band, radio station, student government, student newspaper, student film society, symphony orchestra, television station, yearbook. Number of fraternities: 16; sororities: 8. Proportion of men in fraternities: 81%; of women in sororities: 79%. Average proportion of students who stay on campus on weekends: 95%. **Sports program (2009-2010):** Member of NCAA III. *Men's intercollegiate varsity sports:* baseball, basketball, cross country, football, golf, lacrosse, soccer, swimming, tennis, track and field (outdoor), wrestling. *Women's intercollegiate varsity sports:* basketball, cross country, equestrian, field hockey, lacrosse, soccer, swimming, tennis, track and field (outdoor), volleyball.

SERVICES AND FACILITIES

Basic services: nonremedial tutoring, placement service, health service, health insurance. **Counseling services:** minority student, career, personal, veteran student, academic, older student, psychological, birth control, religious. **For learning-disabled students:** School does not offer a structured program with separate admission and additional fees. Total undergraduates in learning-disabled program or receiving services: 55. Services include: reading machines, tape recorders, untimed tests, note-taking services, oral tests, readers, extended time for tests, tutors, priority registration, texts on tape, other. **Library:** Number of titles: 956,354; number of current serial subscriptions: 10,362. **Information technology resources:** Students are not required to lease or own a computer. Number of campus computers available to all students: 300. School has a wireless network. Approximate number of users that can be accommodated: 2,000. Proportion of college-owned housing units wired for high-speed internet access: 100%. **Campus safety:** Security services offered: 24-hour foot-and-vehicle patrols, late-night transport/escort service, 24-hour emergency telephones, lighted pathways/sidewalks, controlled dormitory access (key, security card, etc).

TRANSFER AND INTERNATIONAL STUDENTS

Transfer students: May apply for admission for the following academic terms: Fall, Winter. Applicants need a minimum number of credits to apply. For fall 2009: Transfer applications received: 92. Transfer applicants offered admission: 17. Transfer applicants enrolled: 11. **International students:** Number of foreign undergraduates: 80 (5% of student body). Number of countries represented: 41. Minimum TOEFL score required: 600 (paper); 250 (computer).

Washington

Central Washington University

- ■ **Address:** 400 E. University Way, Ellensburg, WA 98926-7501
- ■ **Website:** http://www.cwu.edu
- ■ **Public**
- ■ **Enrollment:** 9,315 full-time; 1,450 part-time

....

KEY STATS

✔ **U.S News College Ranking:** 40, Regional Universities (West)

✔ **SAT Score (25th/75th percentile):** 880-1100

✔ **Tuition:** 2010-2011: $7,113 in state, $17,754 out of state

Selectivity: Selective	**Room/board:** $8,901
Acceptance rate: 83%	**Average debt:** $16,507
Student/faculty ratio: 21/1	**Proportion who borrowed:** 55%

UNDERGRADUATE STUDENT BODY STATS

2009-2010 enrollment: 9,315 full-time; 1,450 part-time. Men: 49%; women: 51%. **Ethnic makeup:** African American: 3%; American-Indian: 3%; Asian American: 6%; Hispanic: 8%; White: 78%; International: 2%.

ADMISSIONS FACTS AND FIGURES

Phone: (866) 298-4968. **Email:** cwuadmis@cwu.edu. **Website:** http://www.cwu.edu. **Application deadlines for fall 2011:** Regular decision: April 1. Early decision: Not offered. Early action: Not offered. Admission cannot be deferred. **Application fee:** $55. **To apply online, go to:** http://www.cwu.edu/~cwuadmis/. **Admissions requirements/recommendations:** High school units required (recommended): English: 4 (4); Mathematics: 3 (4); Science: 2 (3); Foreign language: 2 (2); Social studies: 3 (3); Total units: 15 (18). Tests: The college uses SAT or ACT scores in admissions decisions. Either SAT or ACT required. For admission to the fall 2011 entering class, the school will accept: ACT with or without writing accepted. Campus visit: Recommended. Admissions interview: Recommended. Off-campus interview: Not available. **Factors that count in admissions decisions:** *Academic:* Secondary school record: Very Important. Class rank: Not Considered. Letters of recommendation: Considered. Standardized test scores: Important. Essay: Considered. *Nonacademic:* Interview: Considered. Extracurricular activities: Considered. Talent/ability: Considered. Character/personal qualities: Considered. Alumni/ae relationship: Not Considered. Geographical residence: Not Considered. State residency: Not Considered. Religious affiliation/commitment: Not Considered. Minority status: Not Considered. Volunteer work: Considered. Work experience: Considered. **Other schools with the greatest overlap in applicants:** Eastern Washington University; Pacific Lutheran University; University of Washington; Washington State University; Western Washington University. **Admissions statistics for the fall 2009 entering class:** Total applicants: 4,960. Total accepted: 4,098. Freshmen enrolled: 1,660; 5% were from out of state. Overall acceptance rate: 83%. **Size of waiting list:** 0 applicants; enrolled from waiting list: N/A. **Average high school grade point average:** 3.1. **First-year students who submitted SAT scores:** 88%. Scores (25/75 percentile): Critical Reading: 440-550, Math: 440-550, Combined: 880-1100. **First-year students submitting ACT scores:** 23%. Scores (25/75 percentile): English: 17-23, Math: 17-23, Composite: 18-23.

ACADEMICS

Year founded: 1891. **Academic calendar:** Quarter. **Degrees offered:** certificate, bachelor's, post-bachelor's certificate, master's. **Most popular majors:** 26% business, management, marketing, and related support services, 19% education, 11% social sciences, 7% security and protective services, 4% parks, recreation, leisure, and fitness studies. **Major fields of study:** area, ethnic, cultural, and gender studies; biological and biomedical sciences; business, management, marketing, and related support services; communication, journalism, and related programs; computer and information sciences and support services; education; engineering; engineering technologies/technicians; English language and literature/letters; family and consumer sciences/human sciences; foreign languages, literatures, and linguistics; health professions and related clinical sciences; history; liberal arts and sciences

studies, and humanities; mathematics and statistics; multi/interdisciplinary studies; parks, recreation, leisure, and fitness studies; philosophy and religious studies; physical sciences; psychology; public administration and social service professions; security and protective services; social sciences; transportation and materials moving; visual and performing arts. **Areas of required coursework:** arts/fine arts, humanities, computer literacy, mathematics, English (including composition), philosophy, foreign languages, sciences (biological or physical), history, social science. **Pre-professional programs:** pre-law, pre-dentistry, pre-medicine, pre-veterinary science, pre-optometry, pre-pharmacy, other. **Special academic programs (% participation):** cooperative (work-study plan) program (22%), distance learning (55%), double major (8%), dual enrollment (1%), English as a Second Language (ESL) (1%), exchange student program (domestic) (.3%), honors program (1%), independent study (13%), internships (28%), student-designed major (6%), study abroad (4%), teacher certificate program (17%). **Teacher certification offered in:** early childhood, special education, elementary, vo-tech, middle/junior high, secondary, bilingual/bicultural. **Cooperative education programs:** art, business, computer science, education, health professions, home economics, humanities, natural science, social/behavioral science, technologies, vocational arts, other. **Reserve Officers Training Corps (ROTC):** Army ROTC: Offered on campus; Air Force ROTC: Offered on campus. **Faculty and instruction (2009-2010):** Total instructional faculty: 432 full-time, 173 part-time (58% men; 42% women; 11% minorities). Full-time faculty with Ph.D. or other terminal degree: 87%. Student/faculty ratio: 21/1. Classes of fewer than 20 students: 39%; of 20 to 49 students: 55%; of 50 or more students: 6%. **Advanced Placement and International Baccalaureate credit:** AP tests may be used for: Placement only. Scores accepted: 3, 4, 5. International Baccalaureate exams may be used for: Placement only. **Freshmen returning for sophomore year:** 77%. **Graduation rates:** Four-year: 28%; five-year: 50%; six-year: 54%. **Graduate study:** 17% of students pursue further study within one year; 32% within five years.

COSTS AND FINANCIAL AID

Financial aid office: (509) 963-1611. **Expenses (2010-2011):** Tuition and fees 2010-2011: $7,113 in state, $17,754 out of state; room/board: $8,901. Estimated books and supplies: $972; transportation: $1,176; personal expenses: $2,040. **Financial aid:** Priority filing date for institution's financial aid form: March 1. In 2009-2010, 69% of undergraduates applied for financial aid. Of those, 53% were determined to have financial need; 53% had their need fully met. Average financial aid package (proportion receiving): $8,993 (52%). Average amount of gift aid, such as scholarships or grants (proportion receiving): $6,201 (44%). Average amount of self-help aid, such as work study or loans (proportion receiving): $4,248 (43%). Average need-based loan (excluding PLUS or other private loans): $4,052. Among students who received need-based aid, the average percentage of need met: 70%. Among students who received aid based on merit, the average award (and the proportion receiving): $710 (0%). The average athletic scholarship (and the proportion receiving): $1,000 (0%). Average amount of debt of borrowers graduating in 2009: $16,507. Proportion who borrowed: 55%.

CAMPUS LIFE AND EXTRACURRICULAR ACTIVITIES

Campus housing available (% using): coed dorms (77%), women's dorms (1%), apartments for married students (4%), apartment for single students (17%), special housing for disabled students (1%), special housing for international students, other housing options. Students who live in college-owned, operated, or affiliated housing: 34%. **Student employment:** During the 2009-2010 academic year, 27% of undergraduates worked on campus. Average per-year earnings: $3,000. **Clubs and organizations:** Number of student organizations: 138. Activities include: choral groups, concert band, dance, drama/theater, jazz band, literary magazine, marching band, music ensembles, musical theater, opera, pep band, radio station, student government, student newspaper, student film society, symphony orchestra, television station. Number of fraternities: 0; sororities: 0. Average proportion of students who stay on campus on weekends: 40%. **Sports program (2009-2010):** Member of NCAA II. *Men's intercollegiate varsity sports:* baseball, basketball, cross country, football, track and field (outdoor). *Women's intercollegiate varsity sports:* basketball, cross country, soccer, softball, track and field (outdoor), volleyball.

SERVICES AND FACILITIES

Basic services: nonremedial tutoring, placement service, day care, health service, health insurance. **Remedial assistance:** reading, math, writing. **Counseling services:** minority student, career, military, personal, veteran student, academic, older student, psychological, birth control, other. **For learning-disabled students:** School does not offer a structured program with separate admission and additional fees. Services include: remedial math, remedial English, reading machines, remedial reading, tape recorders, other special classes, note-taking services, oral tests, readers, extended time for tests, early syllabus, priority registration, priority seating, substitution of courses, texts on tape, typist/scribe, exams on tape or computer, other testing accommodations, other. **Library:** Number of titles: 698,571; number of current serial subscriptions: 21,687. **Information technology resources:** Students are not required to lease or own a computer. Number of campus computers available to all students: 769. School has a wireless network. Approximate number of users that can be accommodated: 3,500. Proportion of college-owned housing units wired for high-speed internet access: 84%. **Campus safety:** Security services offered: 24-hour foot-and-vehicle patrols, late-night transport/escort service, 24-hour emergency telephones, lighted pathways/sidewalks, controlled dormitory access (key, security card, etc).

TRANSFER AND INTERNATIONAL STUDENTS

Transfer students: May apply for admission for the following academic terms: Fall, Winter, Spring, Summer. Applicants need a minimum number of credits to apply. For fall 2009: Transfer applications received: 2,409. Transfer applicants offered admission: 2,086. Transfer applicants enrolled: 1,509. **International students:** Number of foreign undergraduates: 228 (2% of student body). Number of countries represented: 51. Minimum TOEFL score required: 525 (paper); 195 (computer). Average TOEFL score: 565 (paper).

City University

- **Address:** 11900 N.E. First Street, Bellevue, WA 98005
- **Website:** http://www.cityu.edu
- **Private**
- **Enrollment:** N/A

KEY STATS

✔ **U.S News College Ranking:** Unranked, Regional Universities (West)
✔ **SAT or ACT Score (25th/75th percentile):** N/A
✔ **Tuition:** 2009-2010: $13,880

Selectivity: N/A	**Room/board:** $11,015
Acceptance rate: N/A	**Average debt:** N/A
Student/faculty ratio: N/A	**Proportion who borrowed:** N/A

Cornish College of the Arts

- **Address:** 1000 Lenora Street, Seattle, WA 98121
- **Website:** http://www.cornish.edu
- **Private**
- **Enrollment:** 775 full-time; 19 part-time

KEY STATS

✔ **U.S News College Ranking:** Unranked Specialty School–Fine Arts
✔ **SAT or ACT Score (25th/75th percentile):** N/A
✔ **Tuition:** 2009-2010: $27,750

Selectivity: N/A	**Room/board:** $9,500
Acceptance rate: 67%	**Average debt:** $35,569
Student/faculty ratio: 8/1	**Proportion who borrowed:** 91%

UNDERGRADUATE STUDENT BODY STATS

2009-2010 enrollment: 775 full-time; 19 part-time. Men: 37%; women: 63%. **Ethnic makeup:** African American: 3%; American-Indian: 1%; Asian American: 6%; Hispanic: 3%; White: 85%; International: 2%.

ADMISSIONS FACTS AND FIGURES

Phone: (800) 726-2787. **Email:** admission@cornish.edu. **Website:** http://www.cornish.edu. **Application deadlines for fall 2011:** Regular decision: August 15. Early decision: Not offered. Early action: Not offered. Admission can be deferred. **Application fee:** $35. **To apply online, go to:** https://www.applyweb.com/apply/cornish/. **Admissions requirements/recommendations:** High school units required (recommended): English: 4 (4); Mathematics: 2 (2); Science: 2 (2); Foreign language: 2 (2); Social studies: 2 (2); History: 2 (2); Academic electives: 0 (0); Total units: 18 (18). Tests: The college uses SAT or ACT scores in admissions decisions. Neither SAT nor ACT required. Campus visit: Recommended. Admissions interview: Recommended. Off-campus interview: May be arranged. **Factors that count in admissions decisions:** *Academic:* Secondary school record: Important. Class rank: Not Considered. Letters of recommendation: Very Important. Standardized test scores: Considered. Essay: Very Important. *Nonacademic:* Interview: Important. Extracurricular activities: Important. Talent/ability: Very Important. Character/personal qualities: Important. Alumni/ae relationship: Important. Geographical residence: Not Considered. State residency: Not Considered. Religious affiliation/commitment: Not Considered. Minority status: Considered. Volunteer work: Not Considered. Work experience: Not Considered. **Other schools with the greatest overlap in applicants:** California College of the Arts; California Institute of the Arts; Pacific Northwest College of Art; University of the Arts; Western Washington University. **Admissions statistics for the fall 2009 entering class:** Total applicants: 1,099. Total accepted: 740. Freshmen enrolled: 190; 39% were from out of state. Overall acceptance rate: 67%. **Size of waiting list:** 0 applicants; enrolled from waiting list: 0.

ACADEMICS

Year founded: 1914. **Academic calendar:** Semester. **Degrees offered:** bachelor's. **Most popular majors:** 32% drama and dramatics/theater arts, 20% design and visual communications, 18% fine/studio arts, 18% music performance, 12% dance. **Major fields of study:** visual and performing arts. **Areas of required coursework:** arts/fine arts, humanities, English (including composition), sciences (biological or physical), history, social science, other. **Special academic programs (% participation):** independent study (27%), internships (32%), study abroad (3%). **Faculty and instruction (2009-2010):** Total instructional faculty: 59 full-time, 115 part-time (48% men; 52% women; 14% minorities). Student/faculty ratio: 8/1. Classes of fewer than 20 students: 92%; of 20 to 49 students: 8%. **Advanced Placement and International Baccalaureate credit:** AP tests may be used for: Credit only. Scores accepted: 3, 4, 5. International Baccalaureate exams may be used for: Credit only. **Freshmen returning for sophomore year:** 67%. **Graduation rates:** Four-year: 49%; five-year: 56%; six-year: 47%.

COSTS AND FINANCIAL AID

Financial aid office: (206) 726-5014. **Expenses (2009-2010):** Tuition and fees 2009-2010: $27,750; room/board: $9,500. Estimated books and supplies: $1,800; transportation: $800; personal expenses: $2,000. **Financial aid:** Priority filing date for institution's financial aid form: March 1. In 2009-2010, 91% of undergraduates applied for financial aid. Of those, 80% were determined to have financial need; 9% had their need fully met. Average financial aid package (proportion receiving): $15,561 (80%). Average amount of gift aid, such as scholarships or grants (proportion receiving): $9,373 (73%). Average amount of self-help aid, such as work study or loans (proportion receiving): $7,243 (77%). Average need-based loan (excluding PLUS or other private loans): $4,544. Among students who received need-based aid, the average percentage of need met: 53%. Among students who received aid based on merit, the average award (and the proportion receiving): $4,498 (18%). The average athletic scholarship (and the proportion receiving): $0 (0%). Average amount of debt of borrowers graduating in 2009: $35,569. Proportion who borrowed: 91%.

CAMPUS LIFE AND EXTRACURRICULAR ACTIVITIES

Campus housing available (% using): coed dorms (100%), special housing for disabled students (0%). Students who live in college-owned, operated, or affiliated housing: 23%. **Student employment:** During the 2009-2010 academic year, 26% of undergraduates worked on campus. Average per-year earnings: $1,090. **Clubs and organizations:** Number of student organizations: 14. Activities include: choral groups, concert band, dance, drama/theater, international student organization, jazz band, literary magazine, music ensembles, musical theater, opera, student government, student film society, symphony orchestra. Number of fraternities: 0; sororities: 0. Average proportion of students who stay on campus on weekends: 45%.

SERVICES AND FACILITIES

Basic services: nonremedial tutoring, health insurance, other. **Remedial assistance:** writing. **Counseling services:** minority student, career, personal, academic, older student, psychological, birth control. **For learning-disabled students:** School does not offer a structured program with separate admission and additional fees. Total undergraduates in learning-disabled program or receiving services: 10. Services include: reading machines, tape recorders, untimed tests, note-taking services, oral tests, readers, extended time for tests, priority registration, texts on tape, other testing accommodations, other. **Library:** Number of titles: 29,961; number of current serial subscriptions: 188. **Information technology resources:** Students are not required to lease or own a computer. Number of campus computers available to all students: 50. School has a wireless network. Approximate number of users that can be accommodated: 400. Proportion of college-owned housing units wired for high-speed internet access: 100%. **Campus safety:** Security services offered: 24-hour foot-and-vehicle patrols, late-night transport/escort service, 24-hour emergency telephones, lighted pathways/sidewalks, controlled dormitory access (key, security card, etc).

TRANSFER AND INTERNATIONAL STUDENTS

Transfer students: May apply for admission for the following academic terms: Fall, Spring. Applicants do not need a minimum number of credits to apply. **International students:** Number of foreign undergraduates: 13 (2% of student body). Number of countries represented: 11. Minimum TOEFL score required: 525 (paper); 195 (computer).

Eastern Washington University

- **Address:** 526 Fifth Street, Cheney, WA 99004
- **Website:** http://www.ewu.edu
- **Public**
- **Enrollment:** 8,631 full-time; 1,288 part-time

KEY STATS
- ✔ **U.S News College Ranking:** 56, Regional Universities (West)
- ✔ **SAT Score (25th/75th percentile):** 850-1070
- ✔ **Tuition:** 2010-2011: $6,620 in state, $15,293 out of state
  - **Selectivity:** Less selective
  - **Acceptance rate:** 82%
  - **Student/faculty ratio:** 21/1
  - **Room/board:** $7,350
  - **Average debt:** $18,435
  - **Proportion who borrowed:** 68%

UNDERGRADUATE STUDENT BODY STATS
2009-2010 enrollment: 8,631 full-time; 1,288 part-time. Men: 45%; women: 55%. **Ethnic makeup:** African American: 4%; American-Indian: 2%; Asian American: 4%; Hispanic: 9%; White: 80%; International: 2%.

ADMISSIONS FACTS AND FIGURES
Phone: (509) 359-2397. **Email:** admissions@mail.ewu.edu. **Website:** http://www.ewu.edu. **Application deadlines for fall 2011:** Regular decision: August 15. Early decision: Not offered. Early action: Not offered. Admission can be deferred. **Application fee:** $50. **To apply online, go to:** http://www.ewu.edu/undergradadmissions. **Admissions requirements/recommendations:** High school units required (recommended): English: 4; Mathematics: 3; Science: 2; Foreign language: 2; Social studies: 3; Total units: 15. Tests: The college uses SAT or ACT scores in admissions decisions. Either SAT or ACT required. For admission to the fall 2011 entering class, the school will accept: ACT with writing required. Campus visit: Recommended. Admissions interview: Neither required nor recommended. Off-campus interview: Not available. **Factors that count in admissions decisions:** *Academic:* Secondary school record: Important. Class rank: Not Considered. Letters of recommendation: Not Considered. Standardized test scores: Very Important. Essay: Important. *Nonacademic:* Interview: Considered. Extracurricular activities: Considered. Talent/ability: Considered. Character/personal qualities: Considered. Alumni/ae relationship: Not Considered. Geographical residence: Not Considered. State residency: Not Considered. Religious affiliation/commitment: Not Considered. Minority status: Not Considered. Volunteer work: Considered. Work experience: Considered. **Other schools with the greatest overlap in applicants:** Central Washington University; University of Washington; Washington State University; Western Washington University. **Admissions statistics for the fall 2009 entering class:** Total applicants: 3,728. Total accepted: 3,069. Freshmen enrolled: 1,469; 7% were from out of state. Overall acceptance rate: 82%. **Average high school grade point average:** 3.2. **First-year students who submitted SAT scores:** 89%. Scores (25/75 percentile): Critical Reading: 420-530, Math: 430-540, Combined: 850-1070. **First-year students submitting ACT scores:** 22%. Scores (25/75 percentile): English: 15-22, Math: 17-23, Composite: 17-23.

ACADEMICS
Year founded: 1882. **Academic calendar:** Quarter. **Degrees offered:** certificate, bachelor's, master's, post-master's certificate. **Most popular majors:** 23% business, management, marketing, and related support services; 11% education, 9% health professions and related clinical sciences, 9% social sciences, 7% multi/interdisciplinary studies. **Major fields of study:** architecture and related services; area, ethnic, cultural, and gender studies; biological and biomedical sciences; business, management, marketing, and related support services; communication, journalism, and related programs; communications technologies/technicians and support services; computer and information sciences and support services; education; engineering; engineering technologies/technicians; English language and literature/letters; family and consumer sciences/human sciences; foreign languages, literatures, and linguistics; health professions and related clinical sciences; history; liberal arts and sciences studies, and humanities; mathematics and statistics; military technologies; multi/interdisciplinary studies; natural resources and conservation; parks, recreation, leisure, and fitness studies; philosophy and religious studies; physical sciences; psychology; public administration and social service professions; social sciences; visual and performing arts. **Areas of required coursework:** arts/fine arts, humanities, computer literacy, mathematics, English (including composition), philosophy, foreign languages, sciences (biological or physical), history, social science, other. **Pre-professional programs:** pre-law, pre-dentistry, pre-medicine, pre-veterinary science. **Special academic programs:** distance learning, double major, English as a Second Language (ESL), honors program, independent study, internships, student-designed major, study abroad, teacher certificate program, other. **Teacher certification offered in:** special education, elementary, middle/junior high, secondary. **Reserve Officers Training Corps (ROTC):** Army ROTC: Offered on campus. **Faculty and instruction (2009-2010):** Total instructional faculty: 412 full-time, 207 part-time (51% men; 49% women; 10% minorities). Full-time faculty with Ph.D. or other terminal degree: 97%. Student/faculty ratio: 21/1. Classes of fewer than 20 students: 32%; of 20 to 49 students: 56%; of 50 or more students: 12%. **Advanced Placement and International Baccalaureate credit:** AP tests may be used for: Placement only. Scores accepted: 3, 4, 5. International Baccalaureate exams may be used for: Credit only. **Freshmen returning for sophomore year:** 74%. **Graduation rates:** Four-year: 21%; five-year: 40%; six-year: 48%.

COSTS AND FINANCIAL AID
Financial aid office: (509) 359-2314. **Expenses (2010-2011):** Tuition and fees 2010-2011: $6,620 in state, $15,293 out of state; room/board: $7,350. Estimated books and supplies: $1,035; transportation: $1,545; personal expenses: $2,163. **Financial aid:** Priority filing date for institution's financial aid form: February 15. In 2009-2010, 73% of undergraduates applied for financial aid. Of those, 56% were determined to have financial need; 33% had their need fully met. Average financial aid package (proportion receiving): $11,043 (55%). Average amount of gift aid, such as scholarships or grants (proportion receiving): $5,875 (45%). Average amount of self-help aid, such as work study or loans (proportion receiving): $3,577 (44%). Average need-based loan (excluding PLUS or other private loans): $3,217. Among students who received need-based aid, the average percentage of need met: 71%. Among students who received aid based on merit, the average award (and the proportion receiving): $2,908 (5%). The average athletic scholarship (and the proportion receiving): $8,015 (2%). Average amount of debt of borrowers graduating in 2009: $18,435. Proportion who borrowed: 68%.

CAMPUS LIFE AND EXTRACURRICULAR ACTIVITIES
Campus housing available (% using): coed dorms (90%), sorority housing (1%), fraternity housing (1%), apartments for married students (3%), apartment for single students (2%), special housing for disabled students. Students who live in college-owned, operated, or affiliated housing: 16%. **Student employment:** During the 2009-2010 academic year, 12% of undergraduates worked on campus. Average per-year earnings: $3,200. **Clubs and organizations:** Number of student organizations: 109. Activities include: campus ministries, choral groups, concert band, dance, drama/theater, international student organization, jazz band, literary magazine, marching band, model UN, music ensembles, musical theater, pep band, radio station, student government, student newspaper, student film society, symphony orchestra. Number of fraternities: 9; sororities: 8. Proportion of men in fraternities: 5%; of women in sororities: 6%. **Sports program (2009-2010):** Member of NCAA I. *Men's intercollegiate varsity sports:* basketball, cross country, football, tennis, track and field (indoor), track and field (outdoor). *Women's intercollegiate varsity sports:* basketball, cross country, golf, soccer, tennis, track and field (indoor), track and field (outdoor), volleyball.

SERVICES AND FACILITIES

Basic services: women's center, placement service, day care, health service, health insurance. **Remedial assistance:** math, writing, study skills, other. **Counseling services:** minority student, career, military, personal, veteran student, academic, older student, psychological. **For learning-disabled students:** School does not offer a structured program with separate admission and additional fees. Total undergraduates in learning-disabled program or receiving services: 359. Services include: remedial math, reading machines, tape recorders, videotaped classes, diagnostic testing service, untimed tests, note-taking services, oral tests, learning center, readers, extended time for tests, tutors, priority registration, priority seating, substitution of courses, texts on tape, typist/scribe, exams on tape or computer, other testing accommodations, other. **Library:** Number of titles: 803,569; number of current serial subscriptions: 1,072. **Information technology resources:** Students are not required to lease or own a computer. Number of campus computers available to all students: 812. School has a wireless network. Approximate number of users that can be accommodated: 750. Proportion of college-owned housing units wired for high-speed internet access: 100%. **Campus safety:** Security services offered: late-night transport/escort service, 24-hour emergency telephones, lighted pathways/sidewalks, controlled dormitory access (key, security card, etc).

TRANSFER AND INTERNATIONAL STUDENTS

Transfer students: May apply for admission for the following academic terms: Fall, Winter, Spring, Summer. Applicants need a minimum number of credits to apply. For fall 2009: Transfer applications received: 2,112. Transfer applicants offered admission: 1,843. Transfer applicants enrolled: 1,293. **International students:** Number of foreign undergraduates: 184 (2% of student body). Number of countries represented: 33. Minimum TOEFL score required: 525 (paper); 71 (computer). Average TOEFL score: 490 (paper).

Evergreen State College

- **Address:** 2700 Evergreen Parkway NW, Olympia, WA 98505
- **Website:** http://www.evergreen.edu
- **Public**
- **Enrollment:** 4,119 full-time; 432 part-time

KEY STATS

✔ **U.S News College Ranking:** 29, Regional Universities (West)
✔ **SAT Score (25th/75th percentile):** 960-1230
✔ **Tuition:** 2010-2011: $6,681 in state, $17,808 out of state

Selectivity: Selective	**Room/board:** $8,460
Acceptance rate: 95%	**Average debt:** $14,310
Student/faculty ratio: 23/1	**Proportion who borrowed:** 51%

UNDERGRADUATE STUDENT BODY STATS

2009-2010 enrollment: 4,119 full-time; 432 part-time. Men: 46%; women: 54%. **Ethnic makeup:** African American: 5%; American-Indian: 4%; Asian American: 5%; Hispanic: 5%; White: 81%; International: 1%.

ADMISSIONS FACTS AND FIGURES

Phone: (360) 867-6170. **Email:** admissions@evergreen.edu. **Website:** http://www.evergreen.edu. **Application deadlines for fall 2011:** Regular decision: Rolling. Early decision: Not offered. Early action: Not offered. Admission can be deferred. **Application fee:** $50. **To apply online, go to:** http://www.evergreen.edu/admissions/apply.htm. **Admissions requirements/recommendations:** High school units required (recommended): English: 4; Mathematics: 3; Science: 2; Foreign language: 2; Social studies: 3; History: 0; Academic electives: 0; Total units: 15. Tests: The college uses SAT or ACT scores in admissions decisions. Either SAT or ACT required. For admission to the fall 2011 entering class, the school will accept: ACT with or without writing accepted. Campus visit: Recommended. Admissions interview: Neither required nor recommended. Off-campus interview: May be arranged. **Factors that count in admissions decisions:** *Academic:* Secondary school record: Very Important. Class rank: Not Considered. Letters of recommendation: Considered. Standardized test scores: Important. Essay: Very Important. *Nonacademic:* Interview: Considered. Extracurricular activities: Considered. Talent/ability: Not Considered. Character/personal qualities: Not Considered. Alumni/ae relationship: Not Considered. Geographical residence: Not Considered. State residency: Not Considered. Religious affiliation/commitment: Not Considered. Minority status: Not

Considered. Volunteer work: Considered. Work experience: Considered. **Other schools with the greatest overlap in applicants:** Central Washington University; University of Oregon; University of Washington; Washington State University; Western Washington University. **Admissions statistics for the fall 2009 entering class:** Total applicants: 1,769. Total accepted: 1,687. Freshmen enrolled: 578; 43% were from out of state. Overall acceptance rate: 95%. **Credentials of fall 2009 freshmen:** 12% ranked in the top 10 percent of their high school class; 29% were in the top 25 percent; 62% were in the top half. (Proportion submitting class standing: 19%.) **Average high school grade point average:** 3.0. **First-year students who submitted SAT scores:** 78%. Scores (25/75 percentile): Critical Reading: 500-640, Math: 460-590, Combined: 960-1230. **First-year students submitting ACT scores:** 30%. Scores (25/75 percentile): English: 20-27, Math: 18-25, Composite: 20-26.

ACADEMICS

Year founded: 1967. **Academic calendar:** Quarter. **Degrees offered:** bachelor's, master's. **Most popular majors:** 23% humanities/humanistic studies, 23% social sciences, 12% visual and performing arts, 11% environmental studies, 10% natural sciences. **Major fields of study:** agriculture, agriculture operations, and related sciences; area, ethnic, cultural, and gender studies; biological and biomedical sciences; business, management, marketing, and related support services; communication, journalism, and related programs; computer and information sciences and support services; English language and literature/letters; foreign languages, literatures, and linguistics; health professions and related clinical sciences; liberal arts and sciences studies, and humanities; mathematics and statistics; multi/interdisciplinary studies; natural resources and conservation; physical sciences; psychology; social sciences; visual and performing arts. **Special academic programs (% participation):** accelerated program, double major (5%), exchange student program (domestic), independent study (79%), internships (72%), student-designed major (100%), study abroad (35%), weekend college (1%), other. **Faculty and instruction (2009-2010):** Total instructional faculty: 169 full-time, 74 part-time (49% men; 51% women; 26% minorities). Full-time faculty with Ph.D. or other terminal degree: 86%. Student/faculty ratio: 23/1. Classes of fewer than 20 students: 36%; of 20 to 49 students: 56%; of 50 or more students: 8%. **Advanced Placement and International Baccalaureate credit:** AP tests may be used for: Credit only. Scores accepted: 3, 4, 5. International Baccalaureate exams may be used for: Credit only. **Freshmen returning for sophomore year:** 70%. **Graduation rates:** Four-year: 43%; five-year: 57%; six-year: 59%. **Graduate study:** 24% of students pursue further study within one year; 51% within five years. Fields in which graduates pursue further study: Master of Business Administration (MBA), 3%; law, 4%; medicine, 8%; education, 14%; arts and sciences, 71%.

COSTS AND FINANCIAL AID

Financial aid office: (360) 867-6205. **Expenses (2010-2011):** Tuition and fees 2010-2011: $6,681 in state, $17,808 out of state; room/board: $8,460. Estimated books and supplies: $972; transportation: $1,176; personal expenses: $2,040. **Financial aid:** Priority filing date for institution's financial aid form: March 15. In 2009-2010, 71% of undergraduates applied for financial aid. Of those, 60% were determined to have financial need; 36% had their need fully met. Average financial aid package (proportion receiving): $10,554 (56%). Average amount of gift aid, such as scholarships or grants (proportion receiving): $7,978 (44%). Average amount of self-help aid, such as work study or loans (proportion receiving): $4,029 (43%). Average need-based loan (excluding PLUS or other private loans): $3,952. Among students who received need-based aid, the average percentage of need met: 79%. Among students who received aid based on merit, the average award (and the proportion receiving): $4,128 (1%). The average athletic scholarship (and the proportion receiving): $1,646 (0%). Average amount of debt of borrowers graduating in 2009: $14,310. Proportion who borrowed: 51%.

CAMPUS LIFE AND EXTRACURRICULAR ACTIVITIES

Campus housing available (% using): coed dorms (42%), apartments for married students (1%), apartment for single students (28%), special housing for disabled students (1%), special housing for international students (3%), other housing options (16%). Students who live in college-owned, operated, or affiliated housing: 21%. **Student employment:** During the 2009-2010 academic year, 29% of undergraduates worked on campus. Average per-year earnings: $4,338. **Clubs and organizations:** Number of student organizations: 83. Activities include: campus ministries, choral groups, dance, drama/theater, literary magazine, model UN, music ensembles, pep band, radio station, student government, student newspaper, student film society, television station. Number of fraternities: 0; sororities: 0. Average proportion of students who stay on campus on weekends: 80%. **Sports program (2009-2010):** Member of NAIA. *Men's intercollegiate varsity sports:* basketball, cross country, soccer, track and field (indoor), track and field (outdoor). *Women's intercollegiate varsity sports:* basketball, cross country, soccer, track and field (indoor), track and field (outdoor), volleyball.

SERVICES AND FACILITIES

Basic services: nonremedial tutoring, women's center, placement service, day care, health service. **Counseling services:** minority student, career, personal, veteran student, academic, psychological, birth control, other. **For learning-disabled students:** School does not offer a structured program with separate admission and additional fees. Services include: reading machines, tape recorders, note-taking services, learning center, extended time for tests, tutors, priority registration, priority seating, texts on tape, other testing accommodations, other. **Library:** Number of titles: 480,716; number of current serial subscriptions: 25,855. **Information technology resources:** Students are not required to lease or own a computer. Number of campus computers available to all students: 408. School has a wireless network. Approximate number of users that can be accommodated: 5,000. Proportion of college-owned housing units wired for high-speed internet access: 100%. **Campus safety:** Security services offered: 24-hour foot-and-vehicle patrols, late-night transport/escort service, 24-hour emergency telephones, lighted pathways/sidewalks, student patrols, controlled dormitory access (key, security card, etc).

TRANSFER AND INTERNATIONAL STUDENTS

Transfer students: May apply for admission for the following academic terms: Fall, Winter, Spring. Applicants need a minimum number of credits to apply. For fall 2009: Transfer applications received: 1,326. Transfer applicants offered admission: 1,280. Transfer applicants enrolled: 780. **International students:** Number of foreign undergraduates: 26 (1% of student body). Number of countries represented: 14. Minimum TOEFL score required: 550 (paper); 213 (computer).

Gonzaga University

- **Address:** 502 E. Boone Avenue, Spokane, WA 99258-0001
- **Website:** http://www.gonzaga.edu
- **Private; Religious affiliation:** Roman Catholic
- **Enrollment:** 4,604 full-time; 125 part-time

KEY STATS

✔ **U.S News College Ranking:** 4, Regional Universities (West)
✔ **SAT Score (25th/75th percentile):** 1080-1290
✔ **Tuition:** 2010-2011: $30,925

Selectivity: More selective	**Room/board:** $8,300
Acceptance rate: 78%	**Average debt:** $24,883
Student/faculty ratio: 10/1	**Proportion who borrowed:** 70%

UNDERGRADUATE STUDENT BODY STATS

2009-2010 enrollment: 4,604 full-time; 125 part-time. Men: 47%; women: 53%. **Ethnic makeup:** African American: 1%; American-Indian: 1%; Asian American: 5%; Hispanic: 5%; White: 86%; International: 2%. **Religious preference:** Protestant: 25%; Jewish: 1%; Muslim: 1%; No preference: 23%; Roman Catholic: 49%.

ADMISSIONS FACTS AND FIGURES

Phone: (800) 322-2584. **Email:** mcculloh@gu.gonzaga.edu. **Website:** http://www.gonzaga.edu. **Application deadlines for fall 2011:** Regular decision: February 1; decision sent by March 15. Early decision: Not offered. Early action: Send application by: November 15; Decision sent by: January 15. Admission can be deferred. **Application fee:** $50. **To apply online, go to:** http://www.gonzaga.edu/Admissions/Undergraduate-Admissions/default.asp. **Admissions requirements/recommendations:** High school units required (recommended): English: 4 (4); Mathematics: 3 (4); Science: 3 (4); Foreign language: 3 (4); Social studies: 2 (3); History: 2 (3); Academic electives: 3 (3); Total units: 20 (25). Tests: The college uses SAT or ACT scores in admissions decisions. Either SAT or ACT required. For admission to the fall 2011 entering class, the school will accept: ACT with or without writing accepted. Campus visit: Recommended. Admissions interview: Recommended. Off-campus interview: May be arranged. **Factors that count in admissions decisions:** *Academic:* Secondary school record: Very Important. Class rank: Important. Letters of recommendation: Important.

Standardized test scores: Important. Essay: Important. *Nonacademic:* Interview: Considered. Extracurricular activities: Important. Talent/ability: Important. Character/personal qualities: Very Important. Alumni/ae relationship: Considered. Geographical residence: Not Considered. State residency: Not Considered. Religious affiliation/commitment: Not Considered. Minority status: Considered. Volunteer work: Considered. Work experience: Considered. **Other schools with the greatest overlap in applicants:** Santa Clara University; Seattle University; University of Portland; University of Washington; Washington State University. **Admissions statistics for the fall 2009 entering class:** Total applicants: 5,042. Total accepted: 3,952. Freshmen enrolled: 1,239; 53% were from out of state. Overall acceptance rate: 78%. Non-early acceptance rate: 78%. **Size of waiting list:** 162 applicants; enrolled from waiting list: 0. **Credentials of fall 2009 freshmen:** 38% ranked in the top 10 percent of their high school class; 72% were in the top 25 percent; 93% were in the top half. (Proportion submitting class standing: 55%.) **Average high school grade point average:** 3.7. **First-year students who submitted SAT scores:** 87%. Scores (25/75 percentile): Critical Reading: 530-640, Math: 550-650, Combined: 1080-1290. **First-year students submitting ACT scores:** 51%. Scores (25/75 percentile): English: N/A, Math: N/A, Composite: 24-29.

ACADEMICS

Year founded: 1887. **Academic calendar:** Semester. **Degrees offered:** bachelor's, master's, doctorate. **Most popular majors:** 27% business, management, marketing, and related support services, 11% communication, journalism, and related programs, 10% social sciences, 9% engineering, 8% psychology. **Major fields of study:** area, ethnic, cultural, and gender studies; biological and biomedical sciences; business, management, marketing, and related support services; communication, journalism, and related programs; communications technologies/technicians and support services; computer and information sciences and support services; education; engineering; English language and literature/letters; foreign languages, literatures, and linguistics; health professions and related clinical sciences; history; liberal arts and sciences studies, and humanities; mathematics and statistics; multi/interdisciplinary studies; philosophy and religious studies; physical sciences; psychology; security and protective services; social sciences; visual and performing arts. **Areas of required coursework:** arts/fine arts, humanities, mathematics, English (including composition), philosophy, foreign languages, sciences (biological or physical), history, social science. **Pre-professional programs:** pre-law, pre-dentistry, pre-medicine. **Special academic programs (% participation):** double major (13%), dual enrollment (1%), English as a Second Language (ESL), honors program (4%), internships, study abroad (28%), teacher certificate program (11%). **Teacher certification offered in:** special education, elementary, middle/junior high, secondary. **Reserve Officers Training Corps (ROTC):** Army ROTC: Offered on campus. **Faculty and instruction (2009-2010):** Total instructional faculty: 397 full-time, 334 part-time (59% men; 41% women; 8% minorities). Full-time faculty with Ph.D. or other terminal degree: 83%. Student/faculty ratio: 10/1. Classes of fewer than 20 students: 46%; of 20 to 49 students: 53%; of 50 or more students: 1%. **Advanced Placement and International Baccalaureate credit:** AP tests may be used for: Placement only. Scores accepted: 4, 5. International Baccalaureate exams may be used for: Credit only. **Freshmen returning for sophomore year:** 92%. **Graduation rates:** Four-year: 68%; five-year: 81%; six-year: 81%.

COSTS AND FINANCIAL AID

Financial aid office: (509) 323-4049. **Expenses (2010-2011):** Tuition and fees 2010-2011: $30,925; room/board: $8,300. Estimated books and supplies: $1,000; transportation: $1,350; personal expenses: $1,700. **Financial aid:** Priority filing date for institution's financial aid form: February 1. In 2009-2010, 85% of undergraduates applied for financial aid. Of those, 58% were determined to have financial need; 28% had their need fully met. Average financial aid package (proportion receiving): $22,922 (58%). Average amount of gift aid, such as scholarships or grants (proportion receiving): $16,522 (57%). Average amount of self-help aid, such as work study or loans (proportion receiving): $7,027 (42%). Average need-based loan (excluding PLUS or other private loans): $5,312. Among students who received need-based aid, the average percentage of need met: 83%. Among students who received aid based on merit, the average award (and the proportion receiving): $10,029 (37%). The average athletic scholarship (and the proportion receiving): $21,648 (3%). Average amount of debt of borrowers graduating in 2009: $24,883. Proportion who borrowed: 70%.

CAMPUS LIFE AND EXTRACURRICULAR ACTIVITIES

Campus housing available (% using): coed dorms (45%), women's dorms (8%), men's dorms (8%), apartment for single students (28%), other housing options (5%). Students who live in college-owned, operated, or affiliated housing: 60%. **Student employment:** During the 2009-2010 academic year, 18% of undergraduates worked on campus. Average per-year earnings: $3,078. **Clubs and organizations:** Number of student organizations: 102. Activities include: choral groups, concert band, dance, drama/theater, jazz band, literary magazine, music ensembles, pep band, radio station, student government, student newspaper, symphony orchestra, television station, yearbook. Number of fraternities: 0; sororities: 0. Average proportion of students who stay on campus on weekends: 75%. **Sports program (2009-2010):** Member of NCAA I. *Men's intercollegiate varsity sports:* baseball, basketball, cross country, golf, soccer, tennis. *Women's intercollegiate varsity sports:* basketball, crew (heavyweight), cross country, golf, crew (lightweight), soccer, tennis, volleyball.

SERVICES AND FACILITIES

Basic services: health service, health insurance. **Remedial assistance:** writing. **Counseling services:** minority student, career, military, personal, veteran student, academic, older student, psychological, religious. **For learning-disabled students:** School does not offer a structured program with separate admission and additional fees. Total undergraduates in learning-disabled program or receiving services: 65. Services include: reading machines, tape recorders, note-taking services, oral tests, readers, extended time for tests, early syllabus, priority registration, priority seating, substitution of courses, texts on tape, typist/scribe, exams on tape or computer, other testing accommodations, other. **Library:** Number of titles: 311,198; number of current serial subscriptions: 53,506. **Information technology resources:** Students are not required to lease or own a computer. Number of campus computers available to all students: 500. School has a wireless network. Approximate number of users that can be accommodated: 2,500. Proportion of college-owned housing units wired for high-speed internet access: 99%. **Campus safety:** Security services offered: 24-hour foot-and-vehicle patrols, late-night transport/escort service, 24-hour emergency telephones, lighted pathways/sidewalks, student patrols, controlled dormitory access (key, security card, etc).

TRANSFER AND INTERNATIONAL STUDENTS

Transfer students: May apply for admission for the following academic terms: Fall, Spring. Applicants need a minimum number of credits to apply. For fall 2009: Transfer applications received: 450. Transfer applicants offered admission: 338. Transfer applicants enrolled: 172. **International students:** Number of foreign undergraduates: 86 (2% of student body). Number of countries represented: 18. Minimum TOEFL score required: 550 (paper); 213 (computer). Average TOEFL score: 582 (paper).

Heritage University

- **Address:** 3240 Fort Road, Toppenish, WA 98948
- **Website:** http://www.heritage.edu
- **Private**
- **Enrollment:** N/A

KEY STATS
✔ **U.S News College Ranking:** Unranked, Regional Universities (West)
✔ **SAT or ACT Score (25th/75th percentile):** N/A
✔ **Tuition:** 2009-2010: $11,220

Selectivity: N/A	Room/board: $8,460
Acceptance rate: N/A	Average debt: N/A
Student/faculty ratio: N/A	Proportion who borrowed: N/A

Northwest University

- **Address:** 5520 108th Avenue NE, Kirkland, WA 98033
- **Website:** http://www.northwestu.edu
- **Private; Religious affiliation:** Assemblies of God
- **Enrollment:** 972 full-time; 174 part-time

KEY STATS
✔ **U.S News College Ranking:** 12, Regional Colleges (West)
✔ **SAT Score (25th/75th percentile):** 880-1060
✔ **Tuition:** 2010-2011: $22,650

Selectivity: Less selective	Room/board: $6,724
Acceptance rate: 74%	Average debt: $23,965
Student/faculty ratio: N/A	Proportion who borrowed: 76%

UNDERGRADUATE STUDENT BODY STATS

2009-2010 enrollment: 972 full-time; 174 part-time. Men: 40%; women: 60%. **Ethnic makeup:** African American: 4%; American-Indian: 1%; Asian American: 7%; Hispanic: 6%; White: 80%; International: 2%. **Religious preference:** Roman Catholic: 1%; Assemblies of God: 34%; Non-A/G Protestant: 65%.

ADMISSIONS FACTS AND FIGURES

Phone: (425) 889-5231. **Email:** admissions@northwestu.edu. **Website:** http://www.northwestu.edu. **Application deadlines for fall 2011:** Regular decision: July 15. Early decision: Not offered. Early action: Not offered. Admission can be deferred. **Application fee:** $30. **To apply online, go to:** http://www.washingtonmentor.org/applications/northwest_university/apply.html. **Admissions requirements/recommendations:** High school units required (recommended): English: (4); Mathematics: (3); Science: (2); Foreign language: (2); Social studies: (2); History: (2); Academic electives: (3); Total units: (16). Tests: The college uses SAT or ACT scores in admissions decisions. Either SAT or ACT required. For admission to the fall 2011 entering class, the school will accept: ACT with or without writing accepted. Campus visit: Recommended. Admissions interview: Neither required nor recommended. Off-campus interview: May be arranged. **Factors that count in admissions decisions:** *Academic:* Secondary school record: Very Important. Class rank: Important. Letters of recommendation: Very Important. Standardized test scores: Important. Essay: Very Important. *Nonacademic:* Interview: Considered. Extracurricular activities: Important. Talent/ability: Considered. Character/personal qualities: Very Important. Alumni/ae relationship: Considered. Geographical residence: Not Considered. State residency: Not Considered. Religious affiliation/commitment: Very Important. Minority status: Not Considered. Volunteer work: Considered. Work experience: Not Considered. **Other schools with the greatest overlap in applicants:** Pacific Lutheran University; Seattle Pacific University; University of Washington; Western Washington University; Whitworth University. **Admissions statistics for the fall 2009 entering class:** Total applicants: 471. Total accepted: 349. Overall acceptance rate: 74%. Size of waiting list: 0 applicants; enrolled from waiting list: 0. **Average high school grade point average:** 3.3. **First-year students who submitted SAT scores:** 84%. Scores (25/75 percentile): Critical Reading: 450-580, Math: 430-480, Combined: 880-1060. **First-year students submitting ACT scores:** 30%. Scores (25/75 percentile): English: N/A, Math: N/A, Composite: 17-24.

ACADEMICS

Year founded: 1934. **Academic calendar:** Semester. **Degrees offered:** certificate, diploma, associate, transfer-associate, terminal-associate, bachelor's, master's. **Major fields of study:** business, management, marketing, and related support services; communication, journalism, and related programs; education; English language and literature/letters; health professions and related clinical sciences; history; liberal arts and sciences studies, and humanities; mathematics and statistics; multi/interdisciplinary studies; natural resources and conservation; philosophy and religious studies; psychology; social sciences; theology and religious vocations. **Areas of required coursework:** arts/fine arts, humanities, mathematics, English (including composition), sciences (biological or physical), history, social science, other. **Pre-professional programs:** pre-law, pre-dentistry, pre-medicine, pre-theology. **Special academic programs:** double major, English as a Second Language (ESL), independent study, internships, study abroad, teacher certificate program. **Teacher certification offered in:** elementary, secondary. **Reserve Officers Training Corps (ROTC):** Army ROTC: Offered at cooperating institution. **Faculty and instruction (2009-2010):** Total instructional faculty: 56 full-time, 54 part-time (54% men; 46% women). Full-time faculty with Ph.D. or other terminal degree: 61%. **Advanced Placement and International Baccalaureate credit:** AP tests may be used for: Placement only. International Baccalaureate exams may be used for: Credit and/or placement. **Freshmen returning for sophomore year:** 69%. **Graduation rates:** Four-year: 43%; five-year: 48%; six-year: 49%.

COSTS AND FINANCIAL AID

Financial aid office: (425) 889-5336. **Expenses (2010-2011):** Tuition and fees 2010-2011: $22,650; room/board: $6,724. Estimated books and supplies: $1,000; transportation: $400; personal expenses: $1,650. **Financial aid:** Priority filing date for institution's financial aid form: February 15. In 2009-2010, 87% of undergraduates applied for financial aid. Of those, 77% were determined to have financial need; 14% had their need fully met. Average financial aid package (proportion receiving): $15,580 (77%). Average amount of gift aid, such as scholarships or grants (proportion receiving): $11,427 (76%). Average amount of self-help aid, such as work study or loans (proportion receiving): $4,939 (66%). Average need-based loan (excluding PLUS or other private loans): $3,791. Among students who received need-based aid, the average percentage of need met: 71%. Among students who received aid based on merit, the average award (and the proportion receiving): $6,632 (15%). The average athletic scholarship (and the proportion receiving): $8,397 (2%). Average amount of debt of borrowers graduating in 2009: $23,965. Proportion who borrowed: 76%.

CAMPUS LIFE AND EXTRACURRICULAR ACTIVITIES

Campus housing available (% using): women's dorms (43%), men's dorms (21%), apartments for married students (13%), apartment for single students (23%). **Student employment:** During the 2009-2010 academic year, 14% of undergraduates worked on campus. Average per-year earnings: $5,130. Activities include: campus ministries, choral groups, concert band, drama/theater, jazz band, music ensembles, radio station, student government, student newspaper, yearbook. Number of fraternities: 0; sororities: 0. Average proportion of students who stay on campus on weekends: 50%. **Sports program (2009-2010):** Member of NAIA. *Men's intercollegiate varsity sports:* basketball, cross country, soccer, track and field (indoor). *Women's intercollegiate varsity sports:* basketball, cross country, soccer, track and field (indoor), volleyball.

SERVICES AND FACILITIES

Basic services: nonremedial tutoring, placement service, health service, health insurance. **Remedial assistance:** reading, math, writing, study skills. **Counseling services:** career, personal, academic, psychological, religious, other. **For learning-disabled students:** School does not offer a structured program with separate admission and additional fees. Services include: tape recorders, other special classes, untimed tests, note-taking services, oral tests, learning center, readers, extended time for tests, tutors, priority registration, priority seating, texts on tape, other testing accommodations, other. **Library:** Number of titles: 100,356; number of current serial subscriptions: 13,443. **Information technology resources:** Students are not required to lease or own a computer. Number of campus computers available to all students: 135. School has a wireless network. Approximate number of users that can be accommodated: 900. Proportion of college-owned housing units wired for high-speed internet access: 100%. **Campus safety:** Security services offered: 24-hour foot-and-vehicle patrols, late-night transport/escort service, 24-hour emergency telephones, lighted pathways/sidewalks, controlled dormitory access (key, security card, etc).

TRANSFER AND INTERNATIONAL STUDENTS

Transfer students: May apply for admission for the following academic terms: Fall, Spring, Summer. Applicants do not need a minimum number of credits to apply. **International students:** Number of foreign undergraduates: 24 (2% of student body). Number of countries represented: 15. Minimum TOEFL score required: 500 (paper); 173 (computer). Average TOEFL score: 575 (paper).

Pacific Lutheran University

- **Address:** 12180 Park Street S, Tacoma, WA 98447
- **Website:** http://www.plu.edu
- **Private; Religious affiliation:** Lutheran
- **Enrollment:** 3,139 full-time; 166 part-time

KEY STATS

✔ **U.S News College Ranking:** 13, Regional Universities (West)
✔ **SAT Score (25th/75th percentile):** 980-1220
✔ **Tuition:** 2010-2011: $29,200

Selectivity: Selective	**Room/board:** $8,800
Acceptance rate: 78%	**Average debt:** $24,639
Student/faculty ratio: 15/1	**Proportion who borrowed:** 72%

UNDERGRADUATE STUDENT BODY STATS

2009-2010 enrollment: 3,139 full-time; 166 part-time. Men: 38%; women: 62%. **Ethnic makeup:** African American: 3%; American-Indian: 1%; Asian American: 6%; Hispanic: 3%; White: 83%; International: 5%. **Religious preference:** Roman Catholic: 10%; Protestant: 38%; Buddhist: 1%; No preference: 10%; Unknown: 15%; Lutheran: 23%; Other: 3%.

ADMISSIONS FACTS AND FIGURES

Phone: (800) 274-6758. **Email:** admission@plu.edu. **Website:** http://www.plu.edu. **Application deadlines for fall 2011:** Regular decision: Rolling. Early decision: Not offered. Early action: Not offered. Admission can be deferred. **Application fee:** $40. **To apply online, go to:** https://www.applyweb.com/apply/plu/menu.html. **Admissions requirements/recommendations:** High school units required (recommended): English: (4); Mathematics: 2 (3); Science: (2); Foreign language: 2 (2); Social studies: (2); Academic electives: (3); Total units: (17). Tests: The college uses SAT or ACT scores in admissions decisions. Either SAT or ACT required. For admission to the fall 2011 entering class, the school will accept: ACT with writing recommended. Campus visit: Recommended. Admissions interview: Recommended. Off-campus interview: May be arranged. **Factors that count in admissions decisions:** *Academic:* Secondary school record: Very Important. Class rank: Important. Letters of recommendation: Important. Standardized test scores: Important. Essay: Very Important. *Nonacademic:* Interview: Considered. Extracurricular activities: Important. Talent/ability: Important. Character/personal qualities: Important. Alumni/ae relationship: Not Considered. Geographical residence: Not Considered. State residency: Not Considered. Religious affiliation/commitment: Not Considered. Minority status: Not Considered. Volunteer work: Important. Work experience: Considered. **Other schools with the greatest overlap in applicants:** Central Washington University; Linfield College; University of Washington; Washington State University; Western Washington University. **Admissions statistics for the fall 2009 entering class:** Total applicants: 2,571. Total accepted: 2,014. Freshmen enrolled: 716; 25% were from out of state. Overall acceptance rate: 78%. **Credentials of fall 2009 freshmen:** 33% ranked in the top 10 percent of their high school class; 65% were in the top 25 percent; 87% were in the top half. (Proportion submitting class standing: 25%.) **Average high school grade point average:** 3.6. **First-year students who submitted SAT scores:** 77%. Scores (25/75 percentile): Critical Reading: 480-610, Math: 500-610, Combined: 980-1220. **First-year students submitting ACT scores:** 23%. Scores (25/75 percentile): English: 23-29, Math: 22-27, Composite: 23-28.

ACADEMICS

Year founded: 1890. **Academic calendar:** 4-1-4. **Degrees offered:** bachelor's, post-bachelor's certificate, master's, post-master's certificate. **Most popular majors:** 15% business, management, marketing, and related support services, 11% social sciences, 9% health professions and related clinical sciences, 8% communication, journalism, and related programs, 7% education. **Major fields of study:** area, ethnic, cultural, and gender studies; biological and biomedical sciences; business, management, marketing, and related support services; communication, journalism, and related programs; computer and information sciences and support services; education; engineering; English language and literature/letters; foreign languages, literatures, and linguistics; health professions and related clinical sciences; history; legal professions and studies; mathematics and statistics; multi/interdisciplinary studies; natural resources and conservation; parks, recreation, leisure, and fitness studies; philosophy and religious studies; physical sciences; psychology; public administration and social service professions; social sciences; visual and performing arts. **Areas of required coursework:**

arts/fine arts, humanities, mathematics, English (including composition), philosophy, foreign languages, sciences (biological or physical), history, social science, other. **Pre-professional programs:** pre-dentistry, pre-medicine, pre-theology, pre-veterinary science, pre-optometry, pre-pharmacy, other. **Special academic programs:** cooperative (work-study plan) program, double major, English as a Second Language (ESL), honors program, independent study, internships, liberal arts/career combination, student-designed major, study abroad, teacher certificate program. **Teacher certification offered in:** early childhood, special education, elementary, middle/junior high, secondary. **Cooperative education programs:** art, business, computer science, education, humanities, natural science, social/behavioral science. **Reserve Officers Training Corps (ROTC):** Army ROTC: Offered on campus. **Faculty and instruction (2009-2010):** Total instructional faculty: 206 full-time, 72 part-time (48% men; 52% women; 9% minorities). Full-time faculty with Ph.D. or other terminal degree: 90%. Student/faculty ratio: 15/1. Classes of fewer than 20 students: 46%; of 20 to 49 students: 53%; of 50 or more students: 2%. **Advanced Placement and International Baccalaureate credit:** AP tests may be used for: Credit and/or placement. Scores accepted: 3, 4, 5. International Baccalaureate exams may be used for: Credit only. **Freshmen returning for sophomore year:** 83%. **Graduation rates:** Four-year: 59%; five-year: 68%; six-year: 68%. **Graduate study:** 15% of students pursue further study within one year. Fields in which graduates pursue further study: law, 13%; medicine, 13%; dentistry, 3%; engineering, 3%; theology (or the seminary), 6%; education, 22%; arts and sciences, 40%.

COSTS AND FINANCIAL AID

Financial aid office: (253) 535-7134. **Expenses (2010-2011):** Tuition and fees 2010-2011: $29,200; room/board: $8,800. Estimated books and supplies: $972; transportation: $567; personal expenses: $2,040. **Financial aid:** Priority filing date for institution's financial aid form: January 31. In 2009-2010, 82% of undergraduates applied for financial aid. Of those, 71% were determined to have financial need; 30% had their need fully met. Average financial aid package (proportion receiving): $27,906 (71%). Average amount of gift aid, such as scholarships or grants (proportion receiving): $15,898 (70%). Average amount of self-help aid, such as work study or loans (proportion receiving): $11,085 (64%). Average need-based loan (excluding PLUS or other private loans): $9,067. Among students who received need-based aid, the average percentage of need met: 86%. Among students who received aid based on merit, the average award (and the proportion receiving): $11,635 (24%). The average athletic scholarship (and the proportion receiving): $0 (0%). Average amount of debt of borrowers graduating in 2009: $24,639. Proportion who borrowed: 72%.

CAMPUS LIFE AND EXTRACURRICULAR ACTIVITIES

Campus housing available (% using): coed dorms (75%), women's dorms (11%), apartments for married students (0%), apartment for single students (14%), special housing for disabled students (0%). Students who live in college-owned, operated, or affiliated housing: 49%. **Student employment:** During the 2009-2010 academic year, 40% of undergraduates worked on campus. Average per-year earnings: $4,000. **Clubs and organizations:** Number of student organizations: 89. Activities include: campus ministries, choral groups, concert band, dance, drama/theater, international student organization, jazz band, literary magazine, music ensembles, musical theater, opera, pep band, radio station, student government, student newspaper, symphony orchestra, television station. Number of fraternities: 0; sororities: 0. Average proportion of students who stay on campus on weekends: 75%. **Sports program (2009-2010):** Member of NCAA III. *Men's intercollegiate varsity sports:* baseball, basketball, cross country, football, golf, soccer, swimming, tennis, track and field (indoor), track and field (outdoor). *Women's intercollegiate varsity sports:* basketball, crew (heavyweight), cross country, crew (lightweight), soccer, softball, swimming, tennis, track and field (indoor), track and field (outdoor), volleyball.

SERVICES AND FACILITIES

Basic services: nonremedial tutoring, women's center, placement service, health service, health insurance. **Counseling services:** minority student, career, military, personal, veteran student, academic, psychological, birth control, religious. **For learning-disabled students:** School does not offer a structured program with separate admission and additional fees. Services include: reading machines, tape recorders, other special classes, videotaped classes, untimed tests, note-taking services, oral tests, learning center, readers, extended time for tests, tutors, priority registration, priority seating, texts on tape, other. **Library:** Number of titles: 338,470; number of current serial subscriptions: 6,071. **Information technology resources:** Students are not required to lease or own a computer. Number of campus computers available to all students: 435. School has a wireless network. Approximate

number of users that can be accommodated: 1,500. Proportion of college-owned housing units wired for high-speed internet access: 100%. **Campus safety:** Security services offered: 24-hour foot-and-vehicle patrols, late-night transport/escort service, 24-hour emergency telephones, lighted pathways/sidewalks, student patrols, controlled dormitory access (key, security card, etc).

TRANSFER AND INTERNATIONAL STUDENTS

Transfer students: May apply for admission for the following academic terms: Fall, Spring. Applicants do not need a minimum number of credits to apply. For fall 2009: Transfer applications received: 790. Transfer applicants offered admission: 497. Transfer applicants enrolled: 210. **International students:** Number of foreign undergraduates: 151 (5% of student body). Number of countries represented: 25. Minimum TOEFL score required: 550 (paper); 213 (computer). Average TOEFL score: 583 (paper).

Seattle Pacific University

- **Address:** 3307 Third Avenue W, Seattle, WA 98119-1997
- **Website:** http://www.spu.edu
- **Private; Religious affiliation:** Free Methodist
- **Enrollment:** 2,891 full-time; 125 part-time

KEY STATS

✔ **U.S News College Ranking:** 14, Regional Universities (West)
✔ **SAT Score (25th/75th percentile):** 990-1250
✔ **Tuition:** 2010-2011: $28,965

Selectivity: Selective	**Room/board:** $8,817
Acceptance rate: 93%	**Average debt:** $25,799
Student/faculty ratio: 14/1	**Proportion who borrowed:** 70%

UNDERGRADUATE STUDENT BODY STATS

2009-2010 enrollment: 2,891 full-time; 125 part-time. Men: 33%; women: 67%. **Ethnic makeup:** African American: 3%; American-Indian: 1%; Asian American: 9%; Hispanic: 4%; White: 82%; International: 1%. **Religious preference:** Roman Catholic: 4%; No preference: 1%; Unknown: 19%; Free Methodist: 3%; Other: 69%.

ADMISSIONS FACTS AND FIGURES

Phone: (800) 366-3344. **Email:** admissions@spu.edu. **Website:** http://www.spu.edu. **Application deadlines for fall 2011:** Regular decision: February 1; decision sent by March 1. Early decision: Not offered. Early action: Send application by: November 15; Decision sent by: January 5. Admission cannot be deferred. **Application fee:** $45. **To apply online, go to:** https://app.applyyourself.com/?id=spu-u. **Admissions requirements/recommendations:** High school units required (recommended): English: (4); Mathematics: (3); Science: (3); Foreign language: (3); History: (2). Tests: The college uses SAT or ACT scores in admissions decisions. Either SAT or ACT required. For admission to the fall 2011 entering class, the school will accept: ACT with or without writing accepted. Campus visit: Recommended. Admissions interview: Recommended. Off-campus interview: May be arranged. **Factors that count in admissions decisions:** *Academic:* Secondary school record: Very Important. Class rank: Considered. Letters of recommendation: Very Important. Standardized test scores: Very Important. Essay: Very Important. *Nonacademic:* Interview: Important. Extracurricular activities: Important. Talent/ability: Important. Character/personal qualities: Important. Alumni/ae relationship: Considered. Geographical residence: Considered. State residency: Not Considered. Religious affiliation/commitment: Important. Minority status: Important. Volunteer work: Important. Work experience: Important. **Other schools with the greatest overlap in applicants:** Azusa Pacific University; Pacific Lutheran University; University of Washington; Western Washington University; Whitworth University. **Admissions statistics for the fall 2009 entering class:** Total applicants: 1,973. Total accepted: 1,830. Freshmen enrolled: 682; 43% were from out of state. Overall acceptance rate: 93%. Non-early acceptance rate: 93%. **Size of waiting list:** 210 applicants; enrolled from waiting list: 128. **Credentials of fall 2009 freshmen:** 32% ranked in the top 10 percent of their high school class; 63% were in the top 25 percent. **Average high school grade point average:** 3.6. **First-year students who submitted SAT scores:** 90%. Scores (25/75 percentile): Critical Reading: 500-630, Math: 490-620, Combined: 990-1250. **First-year students submitting ACT scores:** 42%. Scores (25/75 percentile): English: 21-28, Math: 20-28, Composite: 21-28.

ACADEMICS

Year founded: 1891. **Academic calendar:** Quarter. **Degrees offered:** certificate, diploma, bachelor's, master's, post-master's certificate, doctorate. **Most popular majors:** 12% business, management, marketing, and related support services, 9% health professions and related clinical sciences, 7% communication, journalism, and related programs, 6% psychology, 6% social sciences. **Major fields of study:** area, ethnic, cultural, and gender studies; biological and biomedical sciences; business, management, marketing, and related support services; communication, journalism, and related programs; computer and information sciences and support services; education; engineering; English language and literature/letters; family and consumer sciences/human sciences; foreign languages, literatures, and linguistics; health professions and related clinical sciences; history; liberal arts and sciences studies, and humanities; mathematics and statistics; parks, recreation, leisure, and fitness studies; philosophy and religious studies; physical sciences; psychology; social sciences; theology and religious vocations; visual and performing arts. **Areas of required coursework:** arts/fine arts, humanities, mathematics, English (including composition), philosophy, foreign languages, sciences (biological or physical), history, social science, other. **Pre-professional programs:** pre-law, pre-dentistry, pre-medicine, pre-optometry. **Special academic programs:** distance learning, double major, exchange student program (domestic), external degree program, honors program, independent study, internships, liberal arts/career combination, student-designed major, study abroad, teacher certificate program. **Teacher certification offered in:** special education, elementary, secondary. **Reserve Officers Training Corps (ROTC):** Army ROTC: Offered at cooperating institution (University of Washington); Navy ROTC: Offered at cooperating institution (University of Washington); Air Force ROTC: Offered at cooperating institution (University of Washington). **Faculty and instruction (2009-2010):** Total instructional faculty: 191 full-time, 160 part-time (52% men; 48% women; 7% minorities). Full-time faculty with Ph.D. or other terminal degree: 86%. Student/faculty ratio: 14/1. Classes of fewer than 20 students: 47%; of 20 to 49 students: 48%; of 50 or more students: 5%. **Advanced Placement and International Baccalaureate credit:** AP tests may be used for: Credit only. International Baccalaureate exams may be used for: Credit only. **Freshmen returning for sophomore year:** 86%. **Graduation rates:** Four-year: 60%; five-year: 71%; six-year: 67%.

COSTS AND FINANCIAL AID

Financial aid office: (206) 281-2061. **Expenses (2010-2011):** Tuition and fees 2010-2011: $28,965; room/board: $8,817. Estimated books and supplies: $942; transportation: $978; personal expenses: $1,785. **Financial aid:** Priority filing date for institution's financial aid form: February 1. In 2009-2010, 78% of undergraduates applied for financial aid. Of those, 68% were determined to have financial need; 6% had their need fully met. Average financial aid package (proportion receiving): $24,734 (68%). Average amount of gift aid, such as scholarships or grants (proportion receiving): $20,131 (67%). Average amount of self-help aid, such as work study or loans (proportion receiving): $7,750 (63%). Average need-based loan (excluding PLUS or other private loans): $5,108. Among students who received need-based aid, the average percentage of need met: 83%. Among students who received aid based on merit, the average award (and the proportion receiving): $13,592 (25%). The average athletic scholarship (and the proportion receiving): $15,881 (2%). Average amount of debt of borrowers graduating in 2009: $25,799. Proportion who borrowed: 70%.

CAMPUS LIFE AND EXTRACURRICULAR ACTIVITIES

Campus housing available (% using): coed dorms (80%), apartments for married students (2%), apartment for single students (17%). Students who live in college-owned, operated, or affiliated housing: 54%. Average per-year earnings: $2,067. Activities include: campus ministries, choral groups, drama/theater, jazz band, literary magazine, music ensembles, musical theater, pep band, radio station, student government, student newspaper, symphony orchestra, yearbook. Number of fraternities: 0; sororities: 0. **Sports program (2009-2010):** Member of NCAA II. *Men's intercollegiate varsity sports:* basketball, cross country, soccer, track and field (indoor). *Women's intercollegiate varsity sports:* basketball, cross country, soccer, track and field (indoor), volleyball.

SERVICES AND FACILITIES

Basic services: health service, health insurance. **Remedial assistance:** reading, math, writing, study skills. **Counseling services:** career, academic, psychological, religious. **For learning-disabled students:** School does not offer a structured program with separate admission and additional fees. Services include: reading machines, tape recorders, note-taking services, oral tests, learning center, readers, extended time for tests, tutors, early syllabus, prior-

ity registration, priority seating, proofreading services, texts on tape, typist/scribe, exams on tape or computer, other testing accommodations. **Library:** Number of titles: 204,519; number of current serial subscriptions: 3,204. **Information technology resources:** Students are not required to lease or own a computer. Number of campus computers available to all students: 475. School has a wireless network. Approximate number of users that can be accommodated: 5,000. Proportion of college-owned housing units wired for high-speed internet access: 100%. **Campus safety:** Security services offered: 24-hour foot-and-vehicle patrols, late-night transport/escort service, 24-hour emergency telephones, lighted pathways/sidewalks, controlled dormitory access (key, security card, etc).

TRANSFER AND INTERNATIONAL STUDENTS

Transfer students: May apply for admission for the following academic terms: Fall, Winter, Spring, Summer. Applicants do not need a minimum number of credits to apply. For fall 2009: Transfer applications received: 495. Transfer applicants offered admission: 368. Transfer applicants enrolled: 239. **International students:** Number of foreign undergraduates: 25 (1% of student body). Minimum TOEFL score required: 550 (paper); 80 (computer). Average TOEFL score: 582 (paper).

Seattle University

- **Address:** 901 12th Avenue, Seattle, WA 98122-1090
- **Website:** http://www.seattleu.edu
- **Private; Religious affiliation:** Roman Catholic (Jesuit)
- **Enrollment:** 4,062 full-time; 244 part-time

KEY STATS

✔ **U.S News College Ranking:** 6, Regional Universities (West)
✔ **SAT Score (25th/75th percentile):** 1040-1280
✔ **Tuition:** 2010-2011: $30,825

Selectivity: More selective	**Room/board:** $9,315
Acceptance rate: 66%	**Average debt:** $26,665
Student/faculty ratio: 13/1	**Proportion who borrowed:** 79%

UNDERGRADUATE STUDENT BODY STATS

2009-2010 enrollment: 4,062 full-time; 244 part-time. Men: 40%; women: 60%. **Ethnic makeup:** African American: 5%; American-Indian: 1%; Asian American: 19%; Hispanic: 8%; White: 57%; International: 10%. **Religious preference:** Roman Catholic: 33%; Protestant: 24%; Non-Christian: 6%; Other: 37%.

ADMISSIONS FACTS AND FIGURES

Phone: (206) 296-2000. **Email:** admissions@seattleu.edu. **Website:** http://www.seattleu.edu. **Application deadlines for fall 2011:** Regular decision: Rolling. Early decision: Not offered. Early action: Send application by: November 15; Decision sent by: December 22. Admission can be deferred. **Application fee:** $50. **To apply online, go to:** http://www.seattleu.edu/home/prospective_students/freshmen/how_to_apply/application_instructions/. **Admissions requirements/recommendations:** High school units required (recommended): English: 4 (4); Mathematics: 3 (3); Science: 2 (2); Foreign language: 2 (2); Social studies: 2 (2); History: 1 (1); Academic electives: 2 (2); Total units: 16 (16). Tests: The college uses SAT or ACT scores in admissions decisions. Either SAT or ACT required. For admission to the fall 2011 entering class, the school will accept: ACT with or without writing accepted. Campus visit: Recommended. Admissions interview: Neither required nor recommended. Off-campus interview: May be arranged. **Factors that count in admissions decisions:** *Academic:* Secondary school record: Very Important. Class rank: Considered. Letters of recommendation: Important. Standardized test scores: Very Important. Essay: Important. *Nonacademic:* Interview: Considered. Extracurricular activities: Important. Talent/ability: Considered. Character/personal qualities: Very Important. Alumni/ae relationship: Considered. Geographical residence: Considered. State residency: Not Considered. Religious affiliation/commitment: Considered. Minority status: Considered. Volunteer work: Considered. Work experience: Considered. **Other schools with the greatest overlap in applicants:** Gonzaga University; University of Oregon; University of Portland; University of Washington; Western Washington University. **Admissions statistics for the fall 2009 entering class:** Total applicants: 5,578. Total accepted: 3,692. Freshmen enrolled: 734; 51% were from out of state. Accepted through early-decision or early-action plans: 42%. Overall acceptance rate: 66%. Non-early acceptance rate: 61%. **Size of waiting list:** 416 applicants; enrolled from waiting list: 33. **Credentials of fall 2009 freshmen:** 30% ranked in the top 10 percent of their high school class; 61% were in the top 25 percent; 93% were in the top half. (Proportion submitting class standing: 53%.) **Average high school grade point average:** 3.6. **First-year students who submitted SAT scores:** 87%. Scores (25/75 percentile): Critical Reading: 520-640, Math: 520-640, Combined: 1040-1280. **First-year students submitting ACT scores:** 43%. Scores (25/75 percentile): English: 23-30, Math: 23-28, Composite: 23-29.

ACADEMICS

Year founded: 1891. **Academic calendar:** Quarter. **Degrees offered:** bachelor's, post-bachelor's certificate, master's, post-master's certificate, doctorate. **Most popular majors:** 29% business/commerce, 19% nursing, 6% social sciences, 5% creative writing, 5% journalism. **Major fields of study:** area, ethnic, cultural, and gender studies; biological and biomedical sciences; business, management, marketing, and related support services; communication, journalism, and related programs; computer and information sciences and support services; engineering; English language and literature/letters; foreign languages, literatures, and linguistics; health professions and related clinical sciences; history; liberal arts and sciences studies, and humanities; mathematics and statistics; multi/interdisciplinary studies; natural resources and conservation; philosophy and religious studies; physical sciences; psychology; public administration and social service professions; security and protective services; social sciences; visual and performing arts. **Areas of required coursework:** arts/fine arts, mathematics, English (including composition), philosophy, sciences (biological or physical), history, social science, other. **Pre-professional programs:** pre-law, pre-medicine. **Special academic programs (% participation):** cooperative (work-study plan) program, cross-registration, double major, honors program (2%), independent study (24%), internships (10%), liberal arts/career combination, student-designed major (1%), study abroad (2%). **Teacher certification offered in:** special education, elementary, middle/junior high, secondary. **Reserve Officers Training Corps (ROTC):** Army ROTC: Offered on campus; Navy ROTC: Offered at cooperating institution (University of Washington); Air Force ROTC: Offered at cooperating institution (University of Washington). **Faculty and instruction (2009-2010):** Total instructional faculty: 435 full-time, 243 part-time (51% men; 49% women; 6% minorities). Full-time faculty with Ph.D. or other terminal degree: 79%. Student/faculty ratio: 13/1. Classes of fewer than 20 students: 53%; of 20 to 49 students: 46%; of 50 or more students: 1%. **Advanced Placement and International Baccalaureate credit:** AP tests may be used for: Credit and/or placement. Scores accepted: 3, 4, 5. International Baccalaureate exams may be used for: Credit and/or placement. **Freshmen returning for sophomore year:** 88%. **Graduation rates:** Four-year: 52%; five-year: 71%; six-year: 71%.

COSTS AND FINANCIAL AID

Financial aid office: (206) 296-2000. **Expenses (2010-2011):** Tuition and fees 2010-2011: $30,825; room/board: $9,315. Estimated books and supplies: $1,440; transportation: $1,605; personal expenses: $2,253. **Financial aid:** Priority filing date for institution's financial aid form: February 1. In 2009-2010, 82% of undergraduates applied for financial aid. Of those, 64% were determined to have financial need; 22% had their need fully met. Average financial aid package (proportion receiving): $28,428 (63%). Average amount of gift aid, such as scholarships or grants (proportion receiving): $16,432 (60%). Average amount of self-help aid, such as work study or loans (proportion receiving): $8,583 (52%). Average need-based loan (excluding PLUS or other private loans): $4,766. Among students who received need-based aid, the average percentage of need met: 77%. Among students who received aid based on merit, the average award (and the proportion receiving): $5,402 (0%). The average athletic scholarship (and the proportion receiving): $16,311 (1%). Average amount of debt of borrowers graduating in 2009: $26,665. Proportion who borrowed: 79%.

CAMPUS LIFE AND EXTRACURRICULAR ACTIVITIES

Campus housing available (% using): coed dorms (79%), apartment for single students (18%), special housing for disabled students. Students who live in college-owned, operated, or affiliated housing: 41%. **Student employment:** During the 2009-2010 academic year, 27% of undergraduates worked on campus. Average per-year earnings: $2,900. **Clubs and organizations:** Number of student organizations: 108. Activities include: campus ministries, choral groups, drama/theater, international student organization, jazz band, literary magazine, music ensembles, pep band, radio station, student government, student newspaper. Number of fraternities: 0; sororities: 0. **Sports program (2009-2010):** Member of NCAA I. *Men's intercollegiate varsity sports:* baseball, basketball, cross country, golf, soccer, swimming, tennis, track and field (indoor), track and field (outdoor). *Women's intercol-*

legiate varsity sports: basketball, cross country, golf, soccer, softball, swimming, tennis, track and field (indoor), track and field (outdoor), volleyball.

SERVICES AND FACILITIES

Basic services: nonremedial tutoring, health service, health insurance. **Counseling services:** minority student, career, military, personal, veteran student, academic, older student, psychological, birth control, religious. **For learning-disabled students:** School does not offer a structured program with separate admission and additional fees. Services include: reading machines, tape recorders, note-taking services, oral tests, learning center, readers, extended time for tests, tutors, priority registration, priority seating, substitution of courses, texts on tape, other testing accommodations, other. **Library:** Number of titles: 245,069; number of current serial subscriptions: 1,802. **Information technology resources:** Students are not required to lease or own a computer. Number of campus computers available to all students: 300. School has a wireless network. Approximate number of users that can be accommodated: 4,000. Proportion of college-owned housing units wired for high-speed internet access: 100%. **Campus safety:** Security services offered: 24-hour foot-and-vehicle patrols, late-night transport/escort service, 24-hour emergency telephones, lighted pathways/sidewalks, controlled dormitory access (key, security card, etc).

TRANSFER AND INTERNATIONAL STUDENTS

Transfer students: May apply for admission for the following academic terms: Fall, Winter, Spring, Summer. Applicants need a minimum number of credits to apply. For fall 2009: Transfer applications received: 1,360. Transfer applicants offered admission: 769. Transfer applicants enrolled: 431. **International students:** Number of foreign undergraduates: 418 (10% of student body). Number of countries represented: 55. Minimum TOEFL score required: 520 (paper). Average TOEFL score: 567 (paper).

St. Martin's University

- **Address:** 5300 Pacific Avenue SE, Lacey, WA 98503
- **Website:** http://www.stmartin.edu
- **Private; Religious affiliation:** Roman Catholic (Benedictine)
- **Enrollment:** 1,053 full-time; 306 part-time

KEY STATS

✔ **U.S News College Ranking:** 51, Regional Universities (West)
✔ **SAT Score (25th/75th percentile):** 870-1110
✔ **Tuition:** 2010-2011: $26,402

Selectivity: Selective	**Room/board:** $8,660
Acceptance rate: 78%	**Average debt:** $28,518
Student/faculty ratio: 12/1	**Proportion who borrowed:** 78%

UNDERGRADUATE STUDENT BODY STATS

2009-2010 enrollment: 1,053 full-time; 306 part-time. Men: 45%; women: 55%. **Ethnic makeup:** African American: 8%; American-Indian: 2%; Asian American: 10%; Hispanic: 9%; White: 66%; International: 6%. **Religious preference:** Protestant: 10%; Muslim: 1%; Buddhist: 1%; No preference: 51%; Roman Catholic (Benedictine): 27%; Listed as Christian: 10%.

ADMISSIONS FACTS AND FIGURES

Phone: (800) 368-8803. **Email:** admissions@stmartin.edu. **Website:** http://www.stmartin.edu. **Application deadlines for fall 2011:** Regular decision: Rolling. Early decision: Not offered. Early action: Not offered. Admission cannot be deferred. **Application fee:** $35. **To apply online, go to:** http://www.stmartin.edu/apply/. **Admissions requirements/recommendations:** High school units required (recommended): English: (4); Mathematics: (3); Science: (3); Foreign language: (2); Social studies: (2); History: (0); Academic electives: (3); Total units: (17). Tests: The college uses SAT or ACT scores in admissions decisions. Either SAT or ACT required. For admission to the fall 2011 entering class, the school will accept: ACT with writing required. Campus visit: Recommended. Admissions interview: Recommended. Off-campus interview: May be arranged. **Factors that count in admissions decisions:** *Academic:* Secondary school record: Very Important. Class rank: Considered. Letters of recommendation: Important. Standardized test scores: Important. Essay: Important. *Nonacademic:* Interview: Considered. Extracurricular activities: Important. Talent/ability: Considered. Character/personal qualities: Important. Alumni/ae relationship: Considered. Geographical residence: Not Considered. State residency: Not Considered. Religious affiliation/commitment: Not

Considered. Minority status: Not Considered. Volunteer work: Important. Work experience: Considered. **Other schools with the greatest overlap in applicants:** Central Washington University; Evergreen State College; Gonzaga University; Pacific Lutheran University; University of Portland. **Admissions statistics for the fall 2009 entering class:** Total applicants: 734. Total accepted: 575. Freshmen enrolled: 180; 24% were from out of state. Overall acceptance rate: 78%. **Credentials of fall 2009 freshmen:** 19% ranked in the top 10 percent of their high school class; 50% were in the top 25 percent; 82% were in the top half. (Proportion submitting class standing: 35%.) **Average high school grade point average:** 3.2. **First-year students who submitted SAT scores:** 90%. Scores (25/75 percentile): Critical Reading: 430-550, Math: 440-560, Combined: 870-1110. **First-year students submitting ACT scores:** 26%. Scores (25/75 percentile): English: N/A, Math: N/A, Composite: 16-24.

ACADEMICS

Year founded: 1895. **Academic calendar:** Semester. **Degrees offered:** bachelor's, post-bachelor's certificate, master's, post-master's certificate. **Most popular majors:** 32% business, management, marketing, and related support services, 15% psychology, 10% education, 8% engineering, 8% security and protective services. **Major fields of study:** biological and biomedical sciences; business, management, marketing, and related support services; computer and information sciences and support services; education; engineering; English language and literature/letters; history; liberal arts and sciences studies, and humanities; mathematics and statistics; philosophy and religious studies; physical sciences; psychology; public administration and social service professions; social sciences; visual and performing arts. **Areas of required coursework:** arts/fine arts, humanities, computer literacy, mathematics, English (including composition), philosophy, foreign languages, sciences (biological or physical), history, social science, other. **Preprofessional programs:** pre-law, pre-dentistry, pre-medicine, pre-veterinary science, pre-optometry, pre-pharmacy. **Special academic programs:** distance learning, double major, English as a Second Language (ESL), exchange student program (domestic), independent study, internships, study abroad, teacher certificate program. **Teacher certification offered in:** special education, elementary, middle/junior high, secondary, bilingual/bicultural. **Reserve Officers Training Corps (ROTC):** Army ROTC: Offered at cooperating institution (Pacific Lutheran University); Air Force ROTC: Offered at cooperating institution (University of Washington). **Faculty and instruction (2009-2010):** Total instructional faculty: 78 full-time, 116 part-time (60% men; 40% women; 11% minorities). Full-time faculty with Ph.D. or other terminal degree: 78%. Student/faculty ratio: 12/1. Classes of fewer than 20 students: 63%; of 20 to 49 students: 32%; of 50 or more students: 6%. **Advanced Placement and International Baccalaureate credit:** AP tests may be used for: Credit only. Scores accepted: 3, 4, 5. International Baccalaureate exams may be used for: Credit only. **Freshmen returning for sophomore year:** 74%. **Graduation rates:** Four-year: 35%; five-year: 50%; six-year: 52%. **Graduate study:** 5% of students pursue further study immediately upon graduation; 29% within one year.

COSTS AND FINANCIAL AID

Financial aid office: (360) 438-4397. **Expenses (2010-2011):** Tuition and fees 2010-2011: $26,402; room/board: $8,660. Estimated books and supplies: $1,000; transportation: $2,000; personal expenses: $1,000. **Financial aid:** Priority filing date for institution's financial aid form: April 15. In 2009-2010, 91% of undergraduates applied for financial aid. Of those, 81% were determined to have financial need; 25% had their need fully met. Average financial aid package (proportion receiving): $18,279 (81%). Average amount of gift aid, such as scholarships or grants (proportion receiving): $13,848 (79%). Average amount of self-help aid, such as work study or loans (proportion receiving): $5,604 (67%). Average need-based loan (excluding PLUS or other private loans): $3,883. Among students who received need-based aid, the average percentage of need met: 77%. Among students who received aid based on merit, the average award (and the proportion receiving): $6,990 (17%). The average athletic scholarship (and the proportion receiving): $7,925 (8%). Average amount of debt of borrowers graduating in 2009: $28,518. Proportion who borrowed: 78%.

CAMPUS LIFE AND EXTRACURRICULAR ACTIVITIES

Campus housing available (% using): coed dorms (98%), apartment for single students (2%), special housing for disabled students (0%). Students who live in college-owned, operated, or affiliated housing: 31%. **Student employment:** During the 2009-2010 academic year, 13% of undergraduates worked on campus. Average per-year earnings: $1,500. **Clubs and organizations:** Number of student organizations: 23. Activities include: campus ministries, choral groups, concert band, dance, drama/theater, international

student organization, jazz band, model UN, musical theater, pep band, student government, student newspaper. Number of fraternities: 0; sororities: 0. Average proportion of students who stay on campus on weekends: 40%. **Sports program (2009-2010):** Member of NCAA II. **Men's intercollegiate varsity sports:** baseball, basketball, cross country, golf, soccer, track and field (indoor), track and field (outdoor). **Women's intercollegiate varsity sports:** basketball, cross country, golf, soccer, softball, track and field (indoor), track and field (outdoor), volleyball.

SERVICES AND FACILITIES

Basic services: nonremedial tutoring, placement service, health insurance. **Remedial assistance:** study skills, other. **Counseling services:** career, personal, veteran student, academic, older student, psychological, religious. **For learning-disabled students:** School does not offer a structured program with separate admission and additional fees. Services include: tape recorders, untimed tests, note-taking services, oral tests, learning center, readers, extended time for tests, tutors, texts on tape, other testing accommodations, other. **Library:** Number of titles: 95,053; number of current serial subscriptions: 2,570. **Information technology resources:** Students are not required to lease or own a computer. Number of campus computers available to all students: 153. School has a wireless network. Approximate number of users that can be accommodated: 100. Proportion of college-owned housing units wired for high-speed internet access: 100%. **Campus safety:** Security services offered: 24-hour foot-and-vehicle patrols, late-night transport/escort service, lighted pathways/sidewalks, student patrols, controlled dormitory access (key, security card, etc).

TRANSFER AND INTERNATIONAL STUDENTS

Transfer students: May apply for admission for the following academic terms: Fall, Spring, Summer. Applicants need a minimum number of credits to apply. For fall 2009: Transfer applications received: 443. Transfer applicants offered admission: 341. Transfer applicants enrolled: 323. **International students:** Number of foreign undergraduates: 79 (6% of student body). Number of countries represented: 14. Minimum TOEFL score required: 525 (paper); 197 (computer). Average TOEFL score: 550 (paper).

University of Puget Sound

- ■ **Address:** 1500 N. Warner Street, Tacoma, WA 98416
- ■ **Website:** http://www.pugetsound.edu
- ■ **Private**
- ■ **Enrollment:** 2,585 full-time; 22 part-time

KEY STATS
- ✔ **U.S News College Ranking:** 81, National Liberal Arts Colleges
- ✔ **SAT Score (25th/75th percentile):** 1130-1340
- ✔ **Tuition:** 2010-2011: $37,390

Selectivity: More selective	**Room/board:** $9,650
Acceptance rate: 63%	**Average debt:** $29,514
Student/faculty ratio: 12/1	**Proportion who borrowed:** 63%

UNDERGRADUATE STUDENT BODY STATS

2009-2010 enrollment: 2,585 full-time; 22 part-time. Men: 41%; women: 59%. **Ethnic makeup:** African American: 3%; American-Indian: 2%; Asian American: 10%; Hispanic: 4%; White: 81%; International: 1%. **Religious preference:** Roman Catholic: 8%; Protestant: 25%; Jewish: 8%; Buddhist: 3%; No preference: 50%; Other: 6%.

ADMISSIONS FACTS AND FIGURES

Phone: (253) 879-3211. **Email:** admission@pugetsound.edu. **Website:** http://www.pugetsound.edu. **Application deadlines for fall 2011:** Regular decision: January 15; decision sent by April 1. Early decision: Send application by: November 15; Decision sent by: December 15. Early action: Not offered. Admission can be deferred. **Application fee:** $50. **To apply online, go to:** https://app.commonapp.org/application/applicantlogin. aspx?d=1219862357301. **Admissions requirements/recommendations:** High school units required (recommended): English: 0 (4); Mathematics: 0 (4); Science: 0 (4); Foreign language: 0 (3); Social studies: 0 (3); History: 0 (3); Academic electives: 0 (0); Total units: 0 (19). Tests: The college uses SAT or ACT scores in admissions decisions. Either SAT or ACT required. For admission to the fall 2011 entering class, the school will accept: ACT with writing recommended. Campus visit: Recommended. Admissions interview: Recommended. Off-campus interview: May be arranged. **Factors that**

count in admissions decisions: *Academic:* Secondary school record: Very Important. Class rank: Considered. Letters of recommendation: Important. Standardized test scores: Important. Essay: Very Important. *Nonacademic:* Interview: Considered. Extracurricular activities: Important. Talent/ability: Important. Character/personal qualities: Important. Alumni/ae relationship: Important. Geographical residence: Not Considered. State residency: Not Considered. Religious affiliation/commitment: Not Considered. Minority status: Important. Volunteer work: Considered. Work experience: Considered. **Other schools with the greatest overlap in applicants:** Colorado College; Lewis & Clark College; University of Washington; Whitman College; Willamette University. **Admissions statistics for the fall 2009 entering class:** Total applicants: 5,561. Total accepted: 3,526. Freshmen enrolled: 721; 76% were from out of state. Accepted through early-decision or early-action plans: 14%. Overall acceptance rate: 63%. Early-decision acceptance rate: 92%. Non-early acceptance rate: 63%. **Size of waiting list:** 311 applicants; enrolled from waiting list: 15. **Credentials of fall 2009 freshmen:** 31% ranked in the top 10 percent of their high school class; 68% were in the top 25 percent; 93% were in the top half. (Proportion submitting class standing: 58%.) **Average high school grade point average:** 3.5. **First-year students who submitted SAT scores:** 84%. Scores (25/75 percentile): Critical Reading: 570-680, Math: 560-660, Combined: 1130-1340. **First-year students submitting ACT scores:** 52%. Scores (25/75 percentile): English: 25-32, Math: 24-29, Composite: 25-30.

ACADEMICS

Year founded: 1888. **Academic calendar:** Semester. **Degrees offered:** bachelor's, master's, post-master's certificate. **Most popular majors:** 15% business administration and management, 10% English language and literature, 8% economics, 6% biology/biological sciences, 6% psychology. **Major fields of study:** area, ethnic, cultural, and gender studies; biological and biomedical sciences; business, management, marketing, and related support services; communication, journalism, and related programs; computer and information sciences and support services; education; English language and literature/letters; foreign languages, literatures, and linguistics; history; mathematics and statistics; multi/interdisciplinary studies; parks, recreation, leisure, and fitness studies; philosophy and religious studies; physical sciences; psychology; social sciences; visual and performing arts. **Areas of required coursework:** arts/fine arts, humanities, mathematics, English (including composition), foreign languages, sciences (biological or physical), history, social science, other. **Pre-professional programs:** pre-law, pre-dentistry, pre-medicine, pre-veterinary science, other. **Special academic programs (% participation):** cooperative (work-study plan) program (1%), double major (14%), honors program (5%), independent study (9%), internships (13%), student-designed major (0%), study abroad (38%), teacher certificate program (0%). **Teacher certification offered in:** elementary, middle/junior high, secondary. **Cooperative education programs:** art, business, computer science, health professions, humanities, natural science, social/behavioral science. **Reserve Officers Training Corps (ROTC):** Army ROTC: Offered at cooperating institution (Pacific Lutheran University). **Faculty and instruction (2009-2010):** Total instructional faculty: 226 full-time, 51 part-time (53% men; 47% women; 7% minorities). Full-time faculty with Ph.D. or other terminal degree: 87%. Student/faculty ratio: 12/1. Classes of fewer than 20 students: 54%; of 20 to 49 students: 46%; of 50 or more students: 0%. **Advanced Placement and International Baccalaureate credit:** AP tests may be used for: Credit and/or placement. Scores accepted: 4, 5. International Baccalaureate exams may be used for: Credit and/or placement. **Freshmen returning for sophomore year:** 85%. **Graduation rates:** Four-year: 68%; five-year: 77%; six-year: 78%. **Graduate study:** 24% of students pursue further study immediately upon graduation; 25% within one year; 38% within five years. Fields in which graduates pursue further study: Master of Business Administration (MBA), 8%; law, 10%; medicine, 6%; dentistry, 1%; engineering, 1%; education, 19%; arts and sciences, 38%; veterinary medicine, 1%.

COSTS AND FINANCIAL AID

Financial aid office: (800) 396-7192. **Expenses (2010-2011):** Tuition and fees 2010-2011: $37,390; room/board: $9,650. Estimated books and supplies: $1,000; transportation: $500; personal expenses: $1,800. **Financial aid:** Priority filing date for institution's financial aid form: February 1. In 2009-2010, 71% of undergraduates applied for financial aid. Of those, 64% were determined to have financial need; 23% had their need fully met. Average financial aid package (proportion receiving): $27,595 (64%). Average amount of gift aid, such as scholarships or grants (proportion receiving): $22,319 (63%). Average amount of self-help aid, such as work study or loans (proportion receiving): $6,967 (50%). Average need-based loan (excluding PLUS or other private loans): $5,357. Among students who received need-based aid, the average percentage of need met: 82%. Among students who received aid based on merit, the average award (and the proportion receiving): $8,809 (25%). The average athletic scholarship (and the proportion receiving): $0 (0%). Average amount of debt of borrowers graduating in 2009: $29,514. Proportion who borrowed: 63%.

CAMPUS LIFE AND EXTRACURRICULAR ACTIVITIES

Campus housing available (% using): coed dorms (57%), women's dorms (0%), sorority housing (8%), fraternity housing (6%), special housing for disabled students (1%), other housing options (11%). Students who live in college-owned, operated, or affiliated housing: 59%. **Student employment:** During the 2009-2010 academic year, 47% of undergraduates worked on campus. Average per-year earnings: $2,000. **Clubs and organizations:** Number of student organizations: 63. Activities include: campus ministries, choral groups, concert band, dance, drama/theater, jazz band, literary magazine, model UN, music ensembles, musical theater, opera, pep band, radio station, student government, student newspaper, student film society, symphony orchestra, yearbook. Number of fraternities: 3; sororities: 4. Proportion of men in fraternities: 18%; of women in sororities: 21%. Average proportion of students who stay on campus on weekends: 90%. **Sports program (2009-2010):** Member of NCAA III. *Men's intercollegiate varsity sports:* baseball, basketball, cross country, football, golf, soccer, swimming, tennis, track and field (indoor), track and field (outdoor). *Women's intercollegiate varsity sports:* basketball, crew (heavyweight), cross country, golf, lacrosse, crew (lightweight), soccer, softball, swimming, tennis, track and field (indoor), track and field (outdoor), volleyball.

SERVICES AND FACILITIES

Basic services: nonremedial tutoring, health service, health insurance, other. **Counseling services:** minority student, career, personal, veteran student, academic, older student, psychological, birth control, religious. **For learning-disabled students:** School does not offer a structured program with separate admission and additional fees. Total undergraduates in learning-disabled program or receiving services: 177. Services include: reading machines, note-taking services, learning center, readers, extended time for tests, tutors, proofreading services, substitution of courses, typist/scribe, exams on tape or computer, other testing accommodations, waiver of foreign language degree requirement. **Library:** Number of titles: 471,611; number of current serial subscriptions: 16,623. **Information technology resources:** Students are not required to lease or own a computer. Number of campus computers available to all students: 350. School has a wireless network. Approximate number of users that can be accommodated: 1,500. Proportion of college-owned housing units wired for high-speed internet access: 100%. **Campus safety:** Security services offered: 24-hour foot-and-vehicle patrols, late-night transport/escort service, 24-hour emergency telephones, lighted pathways/sidewalks, student patrols, controlled dormitory access (key, security card, etc).

TRANSFER AND INTERNATIONAL STUDENTS

Transfer students: May apply for admission for the following academic terms: Fall, Spring. Applicants need a minimum number of credits to apply. For fall 2009: Transfer applications received: 256. Transfer applicants offered admission: 148. Transfer applicants enrolled: 58. **International students:** Number of foreign undergraduates: 13 (1% of student body). Number of countries represented: 11. Minimum TOEFL score required: 550 (paper); 213 (computer). Average TOEFL score: 598 (paper).

University of Washington

- **Address:** Seattle, WA 98195
- **Website:** http://www.washington.edu
- **Public**
- **Enrollment:** 26,365 full-time; 3,209 part-time

KEY STATS

✔ **U.S News College Ranking:** 41, National Universities
✔ **SAT Score (25th/75th percentile):** 1100-1330
✔ **Tuition:** 2009-2010: $7,692 in state, $24,367 out of state
Selectivity: More selective   **Room/board:** $8,949
Acceptance rate: 58%   **Average debt:** $17,800
Student/faculty ratio: 12/1   **Proportion who borrowed:** 49%

UNDERGRADUATE STUDENT BODY STATS

2009-2010 enrollment: 26,365 full-time; 3,209 part-time. Men: 48%; women: 52%. **Ethnic makeup:** African American: 3%; American-Indian: 1%; Asian American: 28%; Hispanic: 6%; White: 55%; International: 6%.

ADMISSIONS FACTS AND FIGURES

Phone: (206) 543-9686. **Email:** askuwadm@u.washington.edu. **Website:** http://www.washington.edu. **Application deadlines for fall 2011:** Regular decision: January 15; decision sent by April 15. Early decision: Not offered. Early action: Not offered. Admission cannot be deferred. **Application fee:** $60. **To apply online, go to:** http://www.washington.edu/students/uga/. **Admissions requirements/recommendations:** High school units required (recommended): English: 4 (4); Mathematics: 3 (4); Science: 2 (3); Foreign language: 2 (3); Social studies: 3 (4); History: 0 (1); Academic electives: 0 (0); Total units: 15 (20). Tests: The college uses SAT or ACT scores in admissions decisions. Either SAT or ACT required. For admission to the fall 2011 entering class, the school will accept: ACT with writing required. Campus visit: Neither required nor recommended. Admissions interview: Neither required nor recommended. Off-campus interview: Not available. **Factors that count in admissions decisions:** *Academic:* Secondary school record: Very Important. Class rank: Not Considered. Letters of recommendation: Not Considered. Standardized test scores: Important. Essay: Very Important. *Nonacademic:* Interview: Not Considered. Extracurricular activities: Important. Talent/ability: Important. Character/personal qualities: Not Considered. Alumni/ae relationship: Not Considered. Geographical residence: Not Considered. State residency: Considered. Religious affiliation/commitment: Not Considered. Minority status: Not Considered. Volunteer work: Important. Work experience: Important. **Other schools with the greatest overlap in applicants:** University of California–Berkeley; University of California–Los Angeles; University of Oregon; Washington State University; Western Washington University. **Admissions statistics for the fall 2009 entering class:** Total applicants: 21,268. Total accepted: 12,264. Freshmen enrolled: 5,338; 16% were from out of state. Overall acceptance rate: 58%. **Size of waiting list:** 2866 applicants; enrolled from waiting list: 1002. **Credentials of fall 2009 freshmen:** 86% ranked in the top 10 percent of their high school class; 97% were in the top 25 percent; 100% were in the top half. (Proportion submitting class standing: 50%.) **Average high school grade point average:** 3.7. **First-year students who submitted SAT scores:** 90%. Scores (25/75 percentile): Critical Reading: 530-650, Math: 570-680, Combined: 1100-1330. **First-year students submitting ACT scores:** 28%. Scores (25/75 percentile): English: 22-30, Math: 24-30, Composite: 24-30.

ACADEMICS

Year founded: 1861. **Academic calendar:** Quarter. **Degrees offered:** bachelor's, master's, post-master's certificate, doctorate. **Most popular majors:** 17% social sciences, 11% business, management, marketing, and related support services, 10% biological and biomedical sciences, 9% engineering, 5% psychology. **Major fields of study:** architecture and related services; area, ethnic, cultural, and gender studies; biological and biomedical sciences; business, management, marketing, and related support services; communication, journalism, and related programs; computer and information sciences and support services; engineering; English language and literature/letters; foreign languages, literatures, and linguistics; health professions and related clinical sciences; history; liberal arts and sciences studies, and humanities; library science; mathematics and statistics; multi/interdisciplinary studies; natural resources and conservation; philosophy and religious studies; physical sciences; psychology; public administration and social service professions; security and protective services; social sciences; theology and religious vocations; visual and performing arts. **Areas of required coursework:** humanities, mathematics, English (including composition), foreign languages, sciences (biological or physical), social science, other. **Preprofessional programs:** pre-law, pre-dentistry, pre-medicine, pre-veterinary science, pre-optometry, pre-pharmacy. **Special academic programs:** accelerated program, cooperative (work-study plan) program, distance learning, double major, English as a Second Language (ESL), exchange student program (domestic), honors program, independent study, internships, student-designed major, study abroad, teacher certificate program, other. **Teacher certification offered in:** special education, elementary, middle/junior high, secondary, bilingual/bicultural. **Cooperative education programs:** business, engineering. **Reserve Officers Training Corps (ROTC):** Army ROTC: Offered on campus; Navy ROTC: Offered on campus; Air Force ROTC: Offered on campus. **Faculty and instruction (2009-2010):** Total instructional faculty: 3,046 full-time, 706 part-time (60% men; 40% women; 20% minorities). Full-time faculty with Ph.D. or other terminal degree: 90%. Student/faculty ratio: 12/1. Classes of fewer than 20 students: 33%; of 20 to 49 students: 49%; of 50 or more students: 18%. **Advanced Placement and International**

Baccalaureate credit: AP tests may be used for: Credit only. Scores accepted: 4, 5. International Baccalaureate exams may be used for: Placement only. **Freshmen returning for sophomore year:** 93%. **Graduation rates:** Four-year: 54%; five-year: 76%; six-year: 81%. **Graduate study:** 18% of students pursue further study within one year.

COSTS AND FINANCIAL AID

Financial aid office: (206) 543-6101. **Expenses (2009-2010):** Tuition and fees 2009-2010: $7,692 in state, $24,367 out of state; room/board: $8,949. Estimated books and supplies: $1,035; transportation: $504; personal expenses: $2,265. **Financial aid:** Priority filing date for institution's financial aid form: February 28. In 2009-2010, 54% of undergraduates applied for financial aid. Of those, 39% were determined to have financial need; 33% had their need fully met. Average financial aid package (proportion receiving): $11,550 (37%). Average amount of gift aid, such as scholarships or grants (proportion receiving): $8,720 (29%). Average amount of self-help aid, such as work study or loans (proportion receiving): $3,140 (24%). Average need-based loan (excluding PLUS or other private loans): $2,850. Among students who received need-based aid, the average percentage of need met: 79%. Among students who received aid based on merit, the average award (and the proportion receiving): $4,430 (3%). The average athletic scholarship (and the proportion receiving): $14,890 (1%). Average amount of debt of borrowers graduating in 2009: $17,800. Proportion who borrowed: 49%.

CAMPUS LIFE AND EXTRACURRICULAR ACTIVITIES

Campus housing available (% using): coed dorms (60%), sorority housing, fraternity housing, apartments for married students (4%), apartment for single students (12%), special housing for disabled students. Students who live in college-owned, operated, or affiliated housing: 23%. Average per-year earnings: $3,600. **Clubs and organizations:** Number of student organizations: 500. Activities include: campus ministries, choral groups, concert band, dance, drama/theater, international student organization, jazz band, literary magazine, marching band, model UN, music ensembles, musical theater, opera, pep band, radio station, student government, student newspaper, student film society, symphony orchestra, television station. Number of fraternities: 34; sororities: 16. Proportion of men in fraternities: 6%; of women in sororities: 5%. **Sports program (2009-2010):** Member of NCAA I. *Men's intercollegiate varsity sports:* baseball, basketball, cross country, football, golf, soccer, swimming, tennis, track and field (indoor), track and field (outdoor). *Women's intercollegiate varsity sports:* basketball, crew (heavyweight), cross country, golf, gymnastics, crew (lightweight), soccer, softball, swimming, tennis, track and field (indoor), track and field (outdoor), volleyball.

SERVICES AND FACILITIES

Basic services: nonremedial tutoring, women's center, placement service, day care, health service, health insurance. **Remedial assistance:** reading, math, writing, study skills. **Counseling services:** minority student, career, military, personal, veteran student, academic, older student, psychological, birth control. **For learning-disabled students:** School does not offer a structured program with separate admission and additional fees. Total undergraduates in learning-disabled program or receiving services: 329. Services include: reading machines, tape recorders, note-taking services, oral tests, learning center, readers, extended time for tests, early syllabus, priority registration, priority seating, texts on tape, exams on tape or computer, other testing accommodations. **Library:** Number of titles: 6,953,813; number of current serial subscriptions: 63,295. **Information technology resources:** Students are not required to lease or own a computer. Number of campus computers available to all students: 5,000. School has a wireless network. Approximate number of users that can be accommodated: 80,000. Proportion of college-owned housing units wired for high-speed internet access: 100%. **Campus safety:** Security services offered: 24-hour foot-and-vehicle patrols, late-night transport/escort service, 24-hour emergency telephones, lighted pathways/sidewalks, controlled dormitory access (key, security card, etc).

TRANSFER AND INTERNATIONAL STUDENTS

Transfer students: May apply for admission for the following academic terms: Fall, Winter, Spring, Summer. Applicants do not need a minimum number of credits to apply. For fall 2009: Transfer applications received: 4,541. Transfer applicants offered admission: 2,119. Transfer applicants enrolled: 1,600. **International students:** Number of foreign undergraduates: 1610 (6% of student body). Number of countries represented: 83. Minimum TOEFL score required: 540 (paper); 207 (computer). Average TOEFL score: 590 (paper).

Walla Walla University

- **Address:** 204 S. College Avenue, College Place, WA 99324-1198
- **Website:** http://www.wallawalla.edu
- **Private; Religious affiliation:** Seventh-day Adventist
- **Enrollment:** 1,459 full-time; 111 part-time

....

KEY STATS

✔ **U.S News College Ranking:** 55, Regional Universities (West)
✔ **ACT Score (25th/75th percentile):** 21-27
✔ **Tuition:** 2009-2010: $21,936

Selectivity: Selective	**Room/board:** $4,320
Acceptance rate: 98%	**Average debt:** N/A
Student/faculty ratio: 14/1	**Proportion who borrowed:** N/A

UNDERGRADUATE STUDENT BODY STATS

2009-2010 enrollment: 1,459 full-time; 111 part-time. Men: 49%; women: 51%. **Ethnic makeup:** African American: 4%; American-Indian: 1%; Asian American: 7%; Hispanic: 10%; White: 77%; International: 1%.

ADMISSIONS FACTS AND FIGURES

Phone: (509) 527-2327. **Email:** info@wallawalla.edu. **Website:** http://www.wallawalla.edu. **Application deadlines for fall 2011:** Regular decision: Rolling. Early decision: Send application by: N/A; Decision sent by: N/A. Early action: Not offered. Admission can be deferred. **Application fee:** $40. **To apply online, go to:** http://www.wallawalla.edu/enrollment/requirements/. **Admissions requirements/recommendations:** High school units required (recommended): English: 4 (4); Mathematics: 3 (4); Science: 2 (3); Foreign language: (2); Social studies: (1); History: 2 (2); Total units: 11 (16). Tests: The college uses SAT or ACT scores in admissions decisions. Either SAT or ACT required. For admission to the fall 2011 entering class, the school will accept: ACT with or without writing accepted. Campus visit: Neither required nor recommended. Admissions interview: Neither required nor recommended. Off-campus interview: Not available. **Factors that count in admissions decisions:** *Academic:* Secondary school record: Very Important. Class rank: Considered. Letters of recommendation: Very Important. Standardized test scores: Considered. Essay: Not Considered. *Nonacademic:* Interview: Not Considered. Extracurricular activities: Considered. Talent/ability: Considered. Character/personal qualities: Important. Alumni/ae relationship: Not Considered. Geographical residence: Not Considered. State residency: Not Considered. Religious affiliation/commitment: Not Considered. Minority status: Not Considered. Volunteer work: Not Considered. Work experience: Not Considered. **Other schools with the greatest overlap in applicants:** Andrews University; La Sierra University; Pacific Union College; Southern Adventist University; Southwestern Adventist University. **Admissions statistics for the fall 2009 entering class:** Total applicants: 505. Total accepted: 496. Freshmen enrolled: 311; 61% were from out of state. Overall acceptance rate: 98%. Non-early acceptance rate: 98%. **Size of waiting list:** 0 applicants; enrolled from waiting list: 0. **Credentials of fall 2009 freshmen:** 2% ranked in the top 10 percent of their high school class; 5% were in the top 25 percent; 20% were in the top half. (Proportion submitting class standing: 99%.) **First-year students submitting ACT scores:** 38%. Scores (25/75 percentile): English: 19-26, Math: 21-28, Composite: 21-27.

ACADEMICS

Year founded: 1892. **Academic calendar:** Quarter. **Degrees offered:** diploma, associate, bachelor's, master's. **Most popular majors:** 19% business, management, marketing, and related support services, 18% health professions and related clinical sciences, 12% engineering, 5% biological and biomedical sciences, 5% communication, journalism, and related programs. **Major fields of study:** biological and biomedical sciences; business, management, marketing, and related support services; communication, journalism, and related programs; communications technologies/technicians and support services; computer and information sciences and support services; education; engineering; English language and literature/letters; foreign languages, literatures, and linguistics; health professions and related clinical sciences; history; liberal arts and sciences studies, and humanities; mathematics and statistics; mechanic and repair technologies/technicians; natural resources and conservation; parks, recreation, leisure, and fitness studies; philosophy and religious studies; physical sciences; psychology; theology and religious vocations; visual and performing arts. **Areas of required coursework:** humanities, mathematics, English (including composition), philosophy, sciences (biological or physical), history, social science,

other. **Pre-professional programs:** pre-law, pre-dentistry, pre-medicine, pre-veterinary science, other. **Special academic programs:** cooperative (work-study plan) program, distance learning, double major, honors program, independent study, internships, liberal arts/career combination, study abroad, teacher certificate program. **Teacher certification offered in:** elementary, secondary. **Faculty and instruction (2009-2010):** Total instructional faculty: 111 full-time, 75 part-time (53% men; 47% women; 5% minorities). Student/faculty ratio: 14/1. Classes of fewer than 20 students: 63%; of 20 to 49 students: 33%; of 50 or more students: 4%. **Advanced Placement and International Baccalaureate credit:** AP tests may be used for: Placement only. Scores accepted: 3, 4. International Baccalaureate exams may be used for: Placement only. **Freshmen returning for sophomore year:** 73%. **Graduation rates:** Four-year: 21%; five-year: 40%; six-year: 49%.

COSTS AND FINANCIAL AID

Financial aid office: (800) 656-2815. **Expenses (2009-2010):** Tuition and fees 2009-2010: $21,936; room/board: $4,320. **Financial aid:** Priority filing date for institution's financial aid form: April 30.

CAMPUS LIFE AND EXTRACURRICULAR ACTIVITIES

Campus housing available: women's dorms, men's dorms, apartments for married students, apartment for single students, special housing for disabled students. Students who live in college-owned, operated, or affiliated housing: 63%. Activities include: campus ministries, choral groups, concert band, drama/theater, international student organization, jazz band, literary magazine, music ensembles, radio station, student government, student newspaper, symphony orchestra, television station, yearbook. Number of fraternities: 0; sororities: 0. **Sports program (2009-2010):** Member of NAIA. *Men's intercollegiate varsity sports:* basketball, golf, ice hockey, soccer, volleyball. *Women's intercollegiate varsity sports:* basketball, softball, volleyball.

SERVICES AND FACILITIES

Basic services: nonremedial tutoring, health service, health insurance. **Remedial assistance:** reading, math, writing, study skills. **Counseling services:** minority student, career, personal, academic, older student, psychological, birth control, religious. **For learning-disabled students:** School does not offer a structured program with separate admission and additional fees. Services include: remedial math, remedial English, remedial reading, tape recorders, other special classes, videotaped classes, untimed tests, note-taking services, oral tests, learning center, readers, extended time for tests, tutors, priority registration, priority seating, texts on tape, other testing accommodations, other. **Library:** Number of titles: 273,266; number of current serial subscriptions: 3,727. **Information technology resources:** Students are not required to lease or own a computer. Number of campus computers available to all students: 150. School has a wireless network. Proportion of college-owned housing units wired for high-speed internet access: 70%. **Campus safety:** Security services offered: 24-hour foot-and-vehicle patrols, late-night transport/escort service, 24-hour emergency telephones, lighted pathways/sidewalks, student patrols.

TRANSFER AND INTERNATIONAL STUDENTS

Transfer students: May apply for admission for the following academic terms: Fall, Winter, Spring, Summer. Applicants need a minimum number of credits to apply. For fall 2009: Transfer applications received: 196. Transfer applicants offered admission: 191. Transfer applicants enrolled: 136. **International students:** Number of foreign undergraduates: 11 (1% of student body). Number of countries represented: 17. Minimum TOEFL score required: 550 (paper); 213 (computer).

Washington State University

- **Address:** French Administration Building, Pullman, WA 99164
- **Website:** http://www.wsu.edu
- **Public**
- **Enrollment:** 18,712 full-time; 3,014 part-time

KEY STATS

✔ **U.S News College Ranking:** 111, National Universities
✔ **SAT Score (25th/75th percentile):** 970-1200
✔ **Tuition:** 2010-2011: $9,488 in state, $20,530 out of state
  - Selectivity: Selective
  - Acceptance rate: 76%
  - Student/faculty ratio: 15/1
  - Room/board: $9,664
  - Average debt: N/A
  - Proportion who borrowed: N/A

UNDERGRADUATE STUDENT BODY STATS

2009-2010 enrollment: 18,712 full-time; 3,014 part-time. Men: 48%; women: 52%. **Ethnic makeup:** African American: 2%; American-Indian: 1%; Asian American: 6%; Hispanic: 7%; White: 81%; International: 3%.

ADMISSIONS FACTS AND FIGURES

Phone: (888) 468-6978. **Email:** admiss2@wsu.edu. **Website:** http://www.wsu.edu. **Application deadlines for fall 2011:** Regular decision: Rolling. Early decision: Not offered. Early action: Not offered. Admission cannot be deferred. **Application fee:** $50. **To apply online, go to:** http://about.wsu.edu/admission. **Admissions requirements/recommendations:** High school units required (recommended): English: 4 (4); Mathematics: 3 (4); Science: 2 (2); Foreign language: 2 (2); Social studies: 3 (3); History: 0 (0); Academic electives: 0 (0); Total units: 15 (16). Tests: The college uses SAT or ACT scores in admissions decisions. Either SAT or ACT required. For admission to the fall 2011 entering class, the school will accept: ACT with or without writing accepted. Campus visit: Recommended. Admissions interview: Neither required nor recommended. Off-campus interview: Not available. **Factors that count in admissions decisions:** *Academic:* Secondary school record: Important. Class rank: Important. Letters of recommendation: Considered. Standardized test scores: Very Important. Essay: Important. *Nonacademic:* Interview: Not Considered. Extracurricular activities: Considered. Talent/ability: Considered. Character/personal qualities: Considered. Alumni/ae relationship: Not Considered. Geographical residence: Not Considered. State residency: Not Considered. Religious affiliation/commitment: Not Considered. Minority status: Not Considered. Volunteer work: Considered. Work experience: Considered. **Other schools with the greatest overlap in applicants:** Central Washington University; Eastern Washington University; Gonzaga University; University of Washington; Western Washington University. **Admissions statistics for the fall 2009 entering class:** Total applicants: 12,478. Total accepted: 9,489. Freshmen enrolled: 3,668; 11% were from out of state. Overall acceptance rate: 76%. **Size of waiting list:** 775 applicants; enrolled from waiting list: 348. **Credentials of fall 2009 freshmen:** 30% ranked in the top 10 percent of their high school class; 55% were in the top 25 percent; 86% were in the top half. (Proportion submitting class standing: 51%.) **Average high school grade point average:** 3.4. **First-year students who submitted SAT scores:** 92%. Scores (25/75 percentile): Critical Reading: 480-590, Math: 490-610, Combined: 970-1200. **First-year students submitting ACT scores:** 26%. Scores (25/75 percentile): English: N/A, Math: N/A, Composite: 21-26.

ACADEMICS

Year founded: 1890. **Academic calendar:** Semester. **Degrees offered:** certificate, bachelor's, post-bachelor's certificate, master's, post-master's certificate, doctorate. **Most popular majors:** 17% business, management, marketing, and related support services, 15% social sciences, 9% communication, journalism, and related programs, 9% health professions and related clinical sciences, 7% engineering. **Major fields of study:** agriculture, agriculture operations, and related sciences; architecture and related services; area, ethnic, cultural, and gender studies; biological and biomedical sciences; business, management, marketing, and related support services; communication, journalism, and related programs; computer and information sciences and support services; education; engineering; engineering technologies/technicians; English language and literature/letters; family and consumer sciences/human sciences; foreign languages, literatures, and linguistics; health professions and related clinical sciences; history; liberal arts and sciences studies, and humanities; mathematics and statistics; multi/interdisciplinary studies; natural resources and conservation; parks, recreation, leisure, and fitness studies; philosophy and religious studies;

physical sciences; psychology; public administration and social service professions; security and protective services; social sciences; visual and performing arts. **Areas of required coursework:** arts/fine arts, humanities, mathematics, English (including composition), sciences (biological or physical), history, social science, other. **Pre-professional programs:** pre-law, predentistry, pre-medicine, pre-veterinary science. **Special academic programs:** cooperative (work-study plan) program, cross-registration, distance learning, double major, dual enrollment, English as a Second Language (ESL), exchange student program (domestic), external degree program, honors program, independent study, internships, liberal arts/career combination, student-designed major, study abroad, teacher certificate program. **Teacher certification offered in:** early childhood, special education, elementary, middle/junior high, secondary, bilingual/bicultural. **Cooperative education programs:** health professions. **Reserve Officers Training Corps (ROTC):** Army ROTC: Offered on campus; Navy ROTC: Offered at cooperating institution (University of Idaho); Air Force ROTC: Offered on campus. **Faculty and instruction (2009-2010):** Total instructional faculty: 1,151 full-time, 475 part-time (59% men; 41% women; 12% minorities). Full-time faculty with Ph.D. or other terminal degree: 90%. Student/faculty ratio: 15/1. Classes of fewer than 20 students: 39%; of 20 to 49 students: 41%; of 50 or more students: 20%. **Advanced Placement and International Baccalaureate credit:** AP tests may be used for: Credit and/or placement. Scores accepted: 3, 4, 5. International Baccalaureate exams may be used for: Credit only. **Freshmen returning for sophomore year:** 83%. **Graduation rates:** Four-year: 40%; five-year: 64%; six-year: 69%.

COSTS AND FINANCIAL AID

Financial aid office: (509) 335-9711. **Expenses (2010-2011):** Tuition and fees 2010-2011: $9,488 in state, $20,530 out of state; room/board: $9,664. Estimated books and supplies: $936; transportation: $1,434; personal expenses: $2,108. **Financial aid:** Priority filing date for institution's financial aid form: February 15. In 2009-2010, 69% of undergraduates applied for financial aid. Of those, 53% were determined to have financial need; 26% had their need fully met. Average financial aid package (proportion receiving): $11,018 (52%). Average amount of gift aid, such as scholarships or grants (proportion receiving): $8,197 (38%). Average amount of self-help aid, such as work study or loans (proportion receiving): $4,304 (41%). Average need-based loan (excluding PLUS or other private loans): $4,211. Among students who received need-based aid, the average percentage of need met: 81%. Among students who received aid based on merit, the average award (and the proportion receiving): $3,387 (12%). The average athletic scholarship (and the proportion receiving): $17,766 (2%).

CAMPUS LIFE AND EXTRACURRICULAR ACTIVITIES

Campus housing available (% using): coed dorms (22%), women's dorms (9%), men's dorms (4%), sorority housing (10%), fraternity housing (12%), apartments for married students (5%), apartment for single students (10%), special housing for disabled students (1%), special housing for international students (1%), other housing options. Students who live in college-owned, operated, or affiliated housing: 35%. **Student employment:** During the 2009-2010 academic year, 25% of undergraduates worked on campus. Average per-year earnings: $3,213. **Clubs and organizations:** Number of student organizations: 300. Activities include: campus ministries, choral groups, concert band, dance, drama/theater, international student organization, jazz band, literary magazine, marching band, model UN, music ensembles, musical theater, opera, pep band, radio station, student government, student newspaper, student film society, symphony orchestra, television station, yearbook. Number of fraternities: 25; sororities: 13. Proportion of men in fraternities: 15%; of women in sororities: 26%. Average proportion of students who stay on campus on weekends: 75%. **Sports program (2009-2010):** Member of NCAA I. *Men's intercollegiate varsity sports:* baseball, basketball, cross country, football, golf, track and field (indoor), track and field (outdoor). *Women's intercollegiate varsity sports:* basketball, cross country, golf, crew (lightweight), soccer, swimming, tennis, track and field (indoor), track and field (outdoor), volleyball.

SERVICES AND FACILITIES

Basic services: nonremedial tutoring, women's center, placement service, day care, health service, health insurance. **Counseling services:** minority student, career, military, personal, veteran student, academic, older student, psychological, birth control. **For learning-disabled students:** School does not offer a structured program with separate admission and additional fees. Total undergraduates in learning-disabled program or receiving services: 610. **Library:** Number of titles: 2,382,839; number of current serial subscriptions: 35,609. **Information technology resources:** Students are not required to lease or own a computer. Number of campus computers available to all students: 2,500. School has a wireless network. Approximate number of users that can be accommodated: 10,000. Proportion of college-owned housing units wired for high-speed internet access: 100%. **Campus safety:** Security services offered: 24-hour foot-and-vehicle patrols, late-night transport/escort service, 24-hour emergency telephones, lighted pathways/sidewalks, student patrols, controlled dormitory access (key, security card, etc).

TRANSFER AND INTERNATIONAL STUDENTS
Transfer students: May apply for admission for the following academic terms: Fall, Spring, Summer. Applicants need a minimum number of credits to apply. For fall 2009: Transfer applications received: 4,855. Transfer applicants offered admission: 3,728. Transfer applicants enrolled: 2,606. **International students:** Number of foreign undergraduates: 677 (3% of student body). Number of countries represented: 99. Minimum TOEFL score required: 520 (paper); 68 (computer).

Western Washington University

- **Address:** 516 High Street, Bellingham, WA 98225
- **Website:** http://www.wwu.edu
- **Public**
- **Enrollment:** 12,313 full-time; 1,083 part-time

KEY STATS
✔ **U.S News College Ranking:** 21, Regional Universities (West)
✔ **SAT Score (25th/75th percentile):** 1010-1230
✔ **Tuition:** 2009-2010: $6,159 in state, $17,190 out of state

Selectivity: Selective	**Room/board:** $8,393
Acceptance rate: 73%	**Average debt:** $15,929
Student/faculty ratio: 19/1	**Proportion who borrowed:** 50%

UNDERGRADUATE STUDENT BODY STATS
2009-2010 enrollment: 12,313 full-time; 1,083 part-time. Men: 45%; women: 55%. **Ethnic makeup:** African American: 3%; American-Indian: 3%; Asian American: 9%; Hispanic: 5%; White: 80%; International: 1%.

ADMISSIONS FACTS AND FIGURES
Phone: (360) 650-3440. **Email:** admit@cc.wwu.edu. **Website:** http://www.wwu.edu. **Application deadlines for fall 2011:** Regular decision: March 1. Early decision: Not offered. Early action: Not offered. Admission can be deferred. **Application fee:** $50. **To apply online, go to:** http://www.ac.wwu.edu/~admit/applynow.html. **Admissions requirements/recommendations:** High school units required (recommended): English: 4; Mathematics: 3; Science: 2; Foreign language: 2; Social studies: 3; Academic electives: 1; Total units: 16. Tests: The college uses SAT or ACT scores in admissions decisions. Either SAT or ACT required. For admission to the fall 2011 entering class, the school will accept: ACT with or without writing accepted. Campus visit: Recommended. Admissions interview: Neither required nor recommended. Off-campus interview: Not available. **Factors that count in admissions decisions:** *Academic:* Secondary school record: Very Important. Class rank: Considered. Letters of recommendation: Considered. Standardized test scores: Important. Essay: Important. *Nonacademic:* Interview: Not Considered. Extracurricular activities: Considered. Talent/ability: Considered. Character/personal qualities: Considered. Alumni/ae relationship: Not Considered. Geographical residence: Considered. State residency: Considered. Religious affiliation/commitment: Not Considered. Minority status: Not Considered. Volunteer work: Considered. Work experience: Considered. **Other schools with the greatest overlap in applicants:** Gonzaga University; Pacific Lutheran University; Seattle University; University of Washington; Washington State University. **Admissions statistics for the fall 2009 entering class:** Total applicants: 9,620. Total accepted: 6,990. Freshmen enrolled: 2,688; 9% were from out of state. Overall acceptance rate: 73%. **Size of waiting list:** 774 applicants; enrolled from waiting list: 354. **Credentials of fall 2009 freshmen:** 24% ranked in the top 10 percent of their high school class; 58% were in the top 25 percent; 92% were in the top half. (Proportion submitting class standing: 56%.) **Average high school grade point average:** 3.5. **First-year students who submitted SAT scores:** 94%. Scores (25/75 percentile): Critical Reading: 500-620, Math: 510-610, Combined: 1010-1230. **First-year students submitting ACT scores:** 25%. Scores (25/75 percentile): English: 21-28, Math: 21-27, Composite: 21-27.

ACADEMICS
Year founded: 1893. **Academic calendar:** Quarter. **Degrees offered:** bachelor's, post-bachelor's certificate, master's, post-master's certificate. **Most popular majors:** 15% business, management, marketing, and related support services, 13% social sciences, 7% visual and performing arts, 6% communication, journalism, and related programs, 6% psychology. **Major fields of study:** area, ethnic, cultural, and gender studies; biological and biomedical sciences; business, management, marketing, and related support services; communication, journalism, and related programs; computer and information sciences and support services; education; engineering technologies/technicians; English language and literature/letters; family and consumer sciences/human sciences; foreign languages, literatures, and linguistics; health professions and related clinical sciences; history; liberal arts and sciences studies, and humanities; mathematics and statistics; multi/interdisciplinary studies; natural resources and conservation; parks, recreation, leisure, and fitness studies; philosophy and religious studies; physical sciences; psychology; public administration and social service professions; social sciences; visual and performing arts. **Areas of required coursework:** humanities, mathematics, English (including composition), sciences (biological or physical), social science, other. **Pre-professional programs:** pre-law, pre-dentistry, pre-medicine, pre-veterinary science, pre-optometry, pre-pharmacy, other. **Special academic programs (% participation):** distance learning (19.2%), double major (4.8%), English as a Second Language (ESL) (.7%), honors program (2.9%), independent study (26.5%), internships (21.2%), student-designed major (7.6%), study abroad (8.7%), teacher certificate program (5%). **Teacher certification offered in:** early childhood, special education, elementary, secondary. **Cooperative education programs:** education, health professions, humanities. **Faculty and instruction (2009-2010):** Total instructional faculty: 498 full-time, 232 part-time (53% men; 47% women; 14% minorities). Full-time faculty with Ph.D. or other terminal degree: 85%. Student/faculty ratio: 19/1. Classes of fewer than 20 students: 36%; of 20 to 49 students: 52%; of 50 or more students: 13%. **Advanced Placement and International Baccalaureate credit:** AP tests may be used for: Placement only. Scores accepted: 3, 4, 5. **Freshmen returning for sophomore year:** 85%. **Graduation rates:** Four-year: 35%; five-year: 63%; six-year: 67%. **Graduate study:** 16% of students pursue further study within one year.

COSTS AND FINANCIAL AID
Financial aid office: (360) 650-3470. **Expenses (2009-2010):** Tuition and fees 2009-2010: $6,159 in state, $17,190 out of state; room/board: $8,393. Estimated books and supplies: $1,020; transportation: $1,293; personal expenses: $2,052. **Financial aid:** Priority filing date for institution's financial aid form: February 15. In 2009-2010, 63% of undergraduates applied for financial aid. Of those, 43% were determined to have financial need; 23% had their need fully met. Average financial aid package (proportion receiving): $11,001 (41%). Average amount of gift aid, such as scholarships or grants (proportion receiving): $7,788 (31%). Average amount of self-help aid, such as work study or loans (proportion receiving): $4,697 (34%). Average need-based loan (excluding PLUS or other private loans): $4,326. Among students who received need-based aid, the average percentage of need met: 85%. Among students who received aid based on merit, the average award (and the proportion receiving): $1,510 (2%). The average athletic scholarship (and the proportion receiving): $5,187 (1%). Average amount of debt of borrowers graduating in 2009: $15,929. Proportion who borrowed: 50%.

CAMPUS LIFE AND EXTRACURRICULAR ACTIVITIES
Students who live in college-owned, operated, or affiliated housing: 29%. **Student employment:** During the 2009-2010 academic year, 12% of undergraduates worked on campus. Average per-year earnings: $2,626. **Clubs and organizations:** Number of student organizations: 221. Activities include: campus ministries, concert band, dance, drama/theater, international student organization, jazz band, literary magazine, music ensembles, musical theater, opera, pep band, radio station, student government, student newspaper, student film society, symphony orchestra, television station. Number of fraternities: 0; sororities: 0. Average proportion of students who stay on campus on weekends: 65%. **Sports program (2009-2010):** Member of NCAA II. *Men's intercollegiate varsity sports:* basketball, cross country, golf. *Women's intercollegiate varsity sports:* basketball, crew (heavyweight), cross country.

SERVICES AND FACILITIES
Basic services: nonremedial tutoring, women's center, placement service, day care, health service, health insurance. **Remedial assistance:** math, writing, study skills. **Counseling services:** minority student, career, personal, veteran student, academic, psychological, birth control. **For learning-disabled**

students: School does not offer a structured program with separate admission and additional fees. Total undergraduates in learning-disabled program or receiving services: 226. Services include: note-taking services, readers, extended time for tests, priority registration, substitution of courses, texts on tape, typist/scribe, exams on tape or computer, other testing accommodations. **Library:** Number of titles: 1,413,611; number of current serial subscriptions: 16,821. **Information technology resources:** Students are not required to lease or own a computer. Number of campus computers available to all students: 2,317. School has a wireless network. Approximate number of users that can be accommodated: 3,000. Proportion of college-owned housing units wired for high-speed internet access: 100%. **Campus safety:** Security services offered: 24-hour foot-and-vehicle patrols, late-night transport/escort service, 24-hour emergency telephones, lighted pathways/sidewalks, student patrols, controlled dormitory access (key, security card, etc).

TRANSFER AND INTERNATIONAL STUDENTS

Transfer students: May apply for admission for the following academic terms: Fall, Winter, Spring, Summer. Applicants do not need a minimum number of credits to apply. For fall 2009: Transfer applications received: 2,226. Transfer applicants offered admission: 1,290. Transfer applicants enrolled: 791. **International students:** Number of foreign undergraduates: 139 (1% of student body). Number of countries represented: 34. Minimum TOEFL score required: 550 (paper); 80 (computer).

Whitman College

- ■ **Address:** 345 Boyer Avenue, Walla Walla, WA 99362-2083
- ■ **Website:** http://www.whitman.edu
- ■ **Private**
- ■ **Enrollment:** 1,483 full-time; 32 part-time

KEY STATS

- ✔ **U.S News College Ranking:** 38, National Liberal Arts Colleges
- ✔ **SAT Score (25th/75th percentile):** 1240-1430
- ✔ **Tuition:** 2010-2011: $38,770

Selectivity: Most selective	**Room/board:** $9,720
Acceptance rate: 44%	**Average debt:** $17,955
Student/faculty ratio: 10/1	**Proportion who borrowed:** 49%

UNDERGRADUATE STUDENT BODY STATS

2009-2010 enrollment: 1,483 full-time; 32 part-time. Men: 42%; women: 58%. **Ethnic makeup:** African American: 2%; American-Indian: 1%; Asian American: 11%; Hispanic: 6%; White: 78%; International: 2%.

ADMISSIONS FACTS AND FIGURES

Phone: (509) 527-5176. **Email:** admission@whitman.edu. **Website:** http://www.whitman.edu. **Application deadlines for fall 2011:** Regular decision: January 15; decision sent by April 1. Early decision: Send application by: November 15; Decision sent by: December 31. Early action: Not offered. Admission can be deferred. **Application fee:** $50. **To apply online, go to:** https://www.commonapp.org/CommonApp/default.aspx. **Admissions requirements/recommendations:** High school units required (recommended): English: (4); Mathematics: (4); Science: (3); Foreign language: (2); Social studies: (2); History: (2); Academic electives: (0); Total units: (18). Tests: The college uses SAT or ACT scores in admissions decisions. Either SAT or ACT required. For admission to the fall 2011 entering class, the school will accept: ACT with or without writing accepted. Campus visit: Recommended. Admissions interview: Recommended. Off-campus interview: May be arranged. **Factors that count in admissions decisions:** *Academic:* Secondary school record: Very Important. Class rank: Considered. Letters of recommendation: Important. Standardized test scores: Important. Essay: Very Important. *Nonacademic:* Interview: Considered. Extracurricular activities: Important. Talent/ability: Important. Character/personal qualities: Very Important. Alumni/ae relationship: Considered. Geographical residence: Considered. State residency: Considered. Religious affiliation/commitment: Not Considered. Minority status: Important. Volunteer work: Considered. Work experience: Considered. **Other schools with the greatest overlap in applicants:** Lewis & Clark College; Pomona College; University of Puget Sound; University of Washington; Willamette University. **Admissions statistics for the fall 2009 entering class:** Total applicants: 3,290. Total accepted: 1,442. Freshmen enrolled: 396; 38% were from out of state. Accepted through early-decision

or early-action plans: 30%. Overall acceptance rate: 44%. Early-decision acceptance rate: 72%. Non-early acceptance rate: 42%. **Size of waiting list:** 551 applicants; enrolled from waiting list: 10. **Credentials of fall 2009 freshmen:** 67% ranked in the top 10 percent of their high school class; 90% were in the top 25 percent; 100% were in the top half. (Proportion submitting class standing: 62%.) **Average high school grade point average:** 3.8. **First-year students who submitted SAT scores:** 74%. Scores (25/75 percentile): Critical Reading: 630-730, Math: 610-700, Combined: 1240-1430. **First-year students submitting ACT scores:** 26%. Scores (25/75 percentile): English: N/A, Math: N/A, Composite: 28-32.

ACADEMICS

Year founded: 1883. **Academic calendar:** Semester. **Degrees offered:** bachelor's. **Most popular majors:** 9% biology/biological sciences, 9% psychology, 7% political science and government, 6% English language and literature, 6% philosophy. **Major fields of study:** area, ethnic, cultural, and gender studies; biological and biomedical sciences; communication, journalism, and related programs; English language and literature/letters; foreign languages, literatures, and linguistics; history; mathematics and statistics; multi/interdisciplinary studies; philosophy and religious studies; physical sciences; psychology; social sciences; visual and performing arts. **Areas of required coursework:** arts/fine arts, humanities, sciences (biological or physical), social science, other. **Pre-professional programs:** pre-law, pre-dentistry, pre-medicine, pre-theology, pre-veterinary science. **Special academic programs (% participation):** accelerated program, cooperative (work-study plan) program, cross-registration, double major, dual enrollment, exchange student program (domestic), honors program, independent study, liberal arts/career combination, student-designed major, study abroad (45%), other. **Cooperative education programs:** computer science, education, engineering, natural science, social/behavioral science. **Faculty and instruction (2009-2010):** Total instructional faculty: 130 full-time, 56 part-time (56% men; 44% women; 13% minorities). Full-time faculty with Ph.D. or other terminal degree: 95%. Student/faculty ratio: 10/1. Classes of fewer than 20 students: 67%; of 20 to 49 students: 32%; of 50 or more students: 1%. **Advanced Placement and International Baccalaureate credit:** AP tests may be used for: Credit and/or placement. Scores accepted: 4, 5. International Baccalaureate exams may be used for: Credit and/or placement. **Freshmen returning for sophomore year:** 94%. **Graduation rates:** Four-year: 81%; five-year: 88%; six-year: 89%.

COSTS AND FINANCIAL AID

Financial aid office: (509) 527-5178. **Expenses (2010-2011):** Tuition and fees 2010-2011: $38,770; room/board: $9,720. Estimated books and supplies: $1,400. **Financial aid:** Priority filing date for institution's financial aid form: November 15; deadline: February 1. In 2009-2010, 55% of undergraduates applied for financial aid. Of those, 44% were determined to have financial need; 76% had their need fully met. Average financial aid package (proportion receiving): $29,197 (44%). Average amount of gift aid, such as scholarships or grants (proportion receiving): $24,366 (44%). Average amount of self-help aid, such as work study or loans (proportion receiving): $5,886 (37%). Average need-based loan (excluding PLUS or other private loans): $4,361. Among students who received need-based aid, the average percentage of need met: 94%. Among students who received aid based on merit, the average award (and the proportion receiving): $10,686 (29%). The average athletic scholarship (and the proportion receiving): $0 (0%). Average amount of debt of borrowers graduating in 2009: $17,955. Proportion who borrowed: 49%.

CAMPUS LIFE AND EXTRACURRICULAR ACTIVITIES

Campus housing available: coed dorms, women's dorms, sorority housing, fraternity housing, apartment for single students, other housing options. Students who live in college-owned, operated, or affiliated housing: 62%. **Student employment:** During the 2009-2010 academic year, 55% of undergraduates worked on campus. Average per-year earnings: $1,200. **Clubs and organizations:** Number of student organizations: 81. Activities include: campus ministries, choral groups, concert band, dance, drama/theater, international student organization, jazz band, literary magazine, music ensembles, musical theater, radio station, student government, student newspaper, student film society, symphony orchestra. Number of fraternities: 4; sororities: 3. Proportion of men in fraternities: 39%; of women in sororities: 30%. Average proportion of students who stay on campus on weekends: 95%. **Sports program (2009-2010):** Member of NCAA III. *Men's intercollegiate varsity sports:* baseball, basketball, cross country, golf, skiing (nordic), skiing (alpine), soccer, swimming. *Women's intercollegiate varsity sports:* basketball, cross country, golf, skiing (nordic), skiing (alpine), soccer, swimming, volleyball.

SERVICES AND FACILITIES

Basic services: nonremedial tutoring, health service, health insurance. **Remedial assistance:** reading, math, writing, study skills. **Counseling services:** minority student, career, military, personal, veteran student, academic, older student, psychological, birth control, religious. **For learning-disabled students:** School does not offer a structured program with separate admission and additional fees. Total undergraduates in learning-disabled program or receiving services: 84. Services include: reading machines, tape recorders, videotaped classes, diagnostic testing service, note-taking services, oral tests, learning center, extended time for tests, tutors, early syllabus, priority seating, proofreading services, texts on tape, typist/scribe, exams on tape or computer, other testing accommodations, other. **Library:** Number of titles: 537,317; number of current serial subscriptions: 30,027. **Information technology resources:** Students are not required to lease or own a computer. Number of campus computers available to all students: 140. School has a wireless network. Approximate number of users that can be accommodated: 1,200. Proportion of college-owned housing units wired for high-speed internet access: 100%. **Campus safety:** Security services offered: 24-hour foot-and-vehicle patrols, late-night transport/escort service, 24-hour emergency telephones, lighted pathways/sidewalks, student patrols, controlled dormitory access (key, security card, etc).

TRANSFER AND INTERNATIONAL STUDENTS

Transfer students: May apply for admission for the following academic terms: Fall, Spring. Applicants do not need a minimum number of credits to apply. For fall 2009: Transfer applications received: 118. Transfer applicants offered admission: 64. Transfer applicants enrolled: 21. **International students:** Number of foreign undergraduates: 35 (2% of student body). Number of countries represented: 33. Minimum TOEFL score required: 560 (paper); 85 (computer). Average TOEFL score: 600 (paper).

Whitworth University

- **Address:** 300 W. Hawthorne, Spokane, WA 99251
- **Website:** http://www.whitworth.edu
- **Private; Religious affiliation:** Presbyterian Church (USA)
- **Enrollment:** 2,301 full-time; 149 part-time

KEY STATS

- ✔ **U.S News College Ranking:** 9, Regional Universities (West)
- ✔ **SAT Score (25th/75th percentile):** 1080-1290
- ✔ **Tuition:** 2010-2011: $30,204

Selectivity: Selective	**Room/board:** $8,450
Acceptance rate: 53%	**Average debt:** $18,801
Student/faculty ratio: 12/1	**Proportion who borrowed:** 68%

UNDERGRADUATE STUDENT BODY STATS

2009-2010 enrollment: 2,301 full-time; 149 part-time. Men: 42%; women: 58%. **Ethnic makeup:** African American: 2%; American-Indian: 1%; Asian American: 4%; Hispanic: 3%; White: 88%; International: 1%. **Religious preference:** Roman Catholic: 10%; Protestant: 80%; No preference: 10%.

ADMISSIONS FACTS AND FIGURES

Phone: (800) 533-4668. **Email:** admissions@whitworth.edu. **Website:** http://www.whitworth.edu. **Application deadlines for fall 2011:** Regular decision: March 1; decision sent by April 1. Early decision: Not offered. Early action: Send application by: November 30; Decision sent by: December 20. Admission can be deferred. **To apply online, go to:** http://www.whitworth.edu/Administration/Admissions/Apply/Index.htm. **Admissions requirements/recommendations:** High school units required (recommended): English: (4); Mathematics: (3); Science: (3); Foreign language: (2); Social studies: (3); History: (3); Total units: (18). Tests: The college uses SAT or ACT scores in admissions decisions. Neither SAT nor ACT required. For admission to the fall 2011 entering class, the school will accept: ACT with or without writing accepted. Campus visit: Recommended. Admissions interview: Recommended. Off-campus interview: May be arranged. **Factors that count in admissions decisions:** *Academic:* Secondary school record: Very Important. Class rank: Not Considered. Letters of recommendation: Very Important. Standardized test scores: Important. Essay: Very Important. *Nonacademic:* Interview: Important. Extracurricular activities: Important. Talent/ability: Important. Character/personal qualities: Important. Alumni/ae relationship: Important. Geographical residence: Important. State residency: Important. Religious affiliation/commitment: Important. Minority

status: Important. Volunteer work: Important. Work experience: Important. **Other schools with the greatest overlap in applicants:** Gonzaga University; Pacific Lutheran University; Seattle Pacific University; University of Washington; Washington State University. **Admissions statistics for the fall 2009 entering class:** Total applicants: 5,862. Total accepted: 3,129. Freshmen enrolled: 555; 45% were from out of state. Accepted through early-decision or early-action plans: 47%. Overall acceptance rate: 53%. Non-early acceptance rate: 50%. **Size of waiting list:** 665 applicants; enrolled from waiting list: 608. **Average high school grade point average:** 3.7. **First-year students who submitted SAT scores:** 75%. Scores (25/75 percentile): Critical Reading: 540-650, Math: 540-640, Combined: 1080-1290. **First-year students submitting ACT scores:** 36%. Scores (25/75 percentile): English: N/A, Math: N/A, Composite: 24-29.

ACADEMICS

Year founded: 1890. **Academic calendar:** 4-1-4. **Degrees offered:** bachelor's, master's. **Most popular majors:** 16% business, management, marketing, and related support services, 9% education, 9% social sciences, 7% health professions and related clinical sciences, 6% communication, journalism, and related programs. **Major fields of study:** area, ethnic, cultural, and gender studies; biological and biomedical sciences; business, management, marketing, and related support services; communication, journalism, and related programs; computer and information sciences and support services; education; English language and literature/letters; foreign languages, literatures, and linguistics; health professions and related clinical sciences; history; liberal arts and sciences studies, and humanities; mathematics and statistics; multi/interdisciplinary studies; philosophy and religious studies; physical sciences; psychology; social sciences; visual and performing arts. **Areas of required coursework:** arts/fine arts, humanities, mathematics, English (including composition), foreign languages, sciences (biological or physical), social science, other. **Pre-professional programs:** pre-law, pre-dentistry, pre-medicine, pre-theology, pre-veterinary science, pre-pharmacy. **Special academic programs (% participation):** double major (15%), dual enrollment, English as a Second Language (ESL) (1%), exchange student program (domestic), independent study (39%), internships (25%), student-designed major (1%), study abroad (43%), teacher certificate program (14%). **Teacher certification offered in:** special education, elementary, middle/junior high, secondary. **Reserve Officers Training Corps (ROTC):** Army ROTC: Offered at cooperating institution (Gonzaga University). **Faculty and instruction (2009-2010):** Total instructional faculty: 156 full-time, 166 part-time (52% men; 48% women; 10% minorities). Full-time faculty with Ph.D. or other terminal degree: 78%. Student/faculty ratio: 12/1. Classes of fewer than 20 students: 59%; of 20 to 49 students: 38%; of 50 or more students: 4%. **Advanced Placement and International Baccalaureate credit:** AP tests may be used for: Credit and/or placement. Scores accepted: 3, 4, 5. International Baccalaureate exams may be used for: Credit and/or placement. **Freshmen returning for sophomore year:** 87%. **Graduation rates:** Four-year: 61%; five-year: 72%; six-year: 75%. **Graduate study:** 17% of students pursue further study immediately upon graduation; 43% within five years.

COSTS AND FINANCIAL AID

Financial aid office: (800) 533-4668. **Expenses (2010-2011):** Tuition and fees 2010-2011: $30,204; room/board: $8,450. Estimated books and supplies: $816; transportation: $672; personal expenses: $1,008. **Financial aid:** Priority filing date for institution's financial aid form: March 1. In 2009-2010, 79% of undergraduates applied for financial aid. Of those, 71% were determined to have financial need; 19% had their need fully met. Average financial aid package (proportion receiving): $23,442 (71%). Average amount of gift aid, such as scholarships or grants (proportion receiving): $16,353 (68%). Average amount of self-help aid, such as work study or loans (proportion receiving): $6,577 (60%). Average need-based loan (excluding PLUS or other private loans): $4,818. Among students who received need-based aid, the average percentage of need met: 81%. Among students who received aid based on merit, the average award (and the proportion receiving): $10,424 (22%). The average athletic scholarship (and the proportion receiving): $0 (0%). Average amount of debt of borrowers graduating in 2009: $18,801. Proportion who borrowed: 68%.

CAMPUS LIFE AND EXTRACURRICULAR ACTIVITIES

Campus housing available (% using): coed dorms (82%), women's dorms (5%), men's dorms (6%), other housing options (7%). Students who live in college-owned, operated, or affiliated housing: 64%. **Student employment:** During the 2009-2010 academic year, 43% of undergraduates worked on campus. Average per-year earnings: $3,000. **Clubs and organizations:** Number of student organizations: 53. Activities include: campus ministries, choral groups, concert band, dance, drama/theater, international student organization, jazz band, literary magazine, music ensembles, musical theater, radio station, student government, student newspaper, symphony orchestra, yearbook. Number of fraternities: 0; sororities: 0. Average proportion of students who stay on campus on weekends: 78%. **Sports program (2009-2010):** Member of NCAA III. *Men's intercollegiate varsity sports:* baseball, basketball, cross country, football, golf, soccer, swimming, tennis, track and field (outdoor). *Women's intercollegiate varsity sports:* basketball, cross country, golf, soccer, softball, swimming, tennis, track and field (outdoor), volleyball.

SERVICES AND FACILITIES
Basic services: nonremedial tutoring, placement service, health service, health insurance. **Counseling services:** minority student, career, personal, academic, older student, psychological, birth control, religious. **For learning-disabled students:** School does not offer a structured program with separate admission and additional fees. Services include: remedial math, remedial English, tape recorders, videotaped classes, untimed tests, note-taking services, oral tests, readers, extended time for tests, tutors, priority registration, priority seating, texts on tape, other testing accommodations. **Library:**

Number of titles: 194,294; number of current serial subscriptions: 2,687. **Information technology resources:** Students are not required to lease or own a computer. Number of campus computers available to all students: 250. School has a wireless network. Approximate number of users that can be accommodated: 1,000. Proportion of college-owned housing units wired for high-speed internet access: 100%. **Campus safety:** Security services offered: 24-hour foot-and-vehicle patrols, late-night transport/escort service, 24-hour emergency telephones, lighted pathways/sidewalks, student patrols, controlled dormitory access (key, security card, etc).

TRANSFER AND INTERNATIONAL STUDENTS
Transfer students: May apply for admission for the following academic terms: Fall, Winter, Spring, Summer. Applicants do not need a minimum number of credits to apply. For fall 2009: Transfer applications received: 243. Transfer applicants offered admission: 157. Transfer applicants enrolled: 92. **International students:** Number of foreign undergraduates: 31 (1% of student body). Number of countries represented: 21. Minimum TOEFL score required: 550 (paper); 79 (computer). Average TOEFL score: 570 (paper).

West Virginia

Alderson-Broaddus College

- **Address:** 101 College Hill Drive, Philippi, WV 26416
- **Website:** http://www.ab.edu
- **Private; Religious affiliation:** American Baptist
- **Enrollment:** 566 full-time; 26 part-time

KEY STATS
✔ **U.S News College Ranking:** 22, Regional Colleges (South)
✔ **ACT Score (25th/75th percentile):** 19-23
✔ **Tuition:** 2010-2011: $22,204

Selectivity: Selective	**Room/board:** $7,222
Acceptance rate: 74%	**Average debt:** $29,613
Student/faculty ratio: 10/1	**Proportion who borrowed:** 98%

UNDERGRADUATE STUDENT BODY STATS
2009-2010 enrollment: 566 full-time; 26 part-time. Men: 34%; women: 66%. **Ethnic makeup:** African American: 4%; Asian American: 1%; Hispanic: 2%; White: 90%; International: 2%. **Religious preference:** Roman Catholic: 6%; Protestant: 1%; No preference: 4%; Unknown: 9%; American Baptist: 4%; Baptist: 20%; Other: 56%.

ADMISSIONS FACTS AND FIGURES
Phone: (800) 263-1549. **Email:** admissions@ab.edu. **Website:** http://www.ab.edu. **Application deadlines for fall 2011:** Regular decision: August 25. Early decision: Not offered. Early action: Not offered. Admission can be deferred. **Application fee:** $25. **To apply online, go to:** http://www.wvmentor.org/applications/wv_common_app/apply/alderson_broaddus.html. **Admissions requirements/recommendations:** High school units required (recommended): English: 4 (4); Mathematics: 3 (3); Science: 3 (3); Foreign language: 0 (1); Social studies: 1 (3); Total units: 11 (14). Tests: The college uses SAT or ACT scores in admissions decisions. Either SAT or ACT required. For admission to the fall 2011 entering class, the school will accept: ACT with or without writing accepted. Campus visit: Recommended. Admissions interview: Recommended. Off-campus interview: May be arranged. **Factors that count in admissions decisions:** *Academic:* Secondary school record: Very Important. Class rank: Not Considered. Letters of recommendation: Considered. Standardized test scores: Very Important. Essay: Important. *Nonacademic:* Interview: Considered. Extracurricular activities: Not Considered. Talent/ability: Considered. Character/personal qualities: Not Considered. Alumni/ae relationship: Considered. Geographical residence: Not Considered. State residency: Not Considered. Religious affiliation/commitment: Not Considered. Minority status: Not Considered. Volunteer work: Not Considered. Work experience: Not Considered. **Other schools with the greatest overlap in applicants:** Davis and Elkins College; Fairmont State University; West Virginia University; West Virginia University–Parkersburg; West Virginia Wesleyan College. **Admissions statistics for the fall 2009 entering class:** Total applicants: 597. Total accepted: 441. Freshmen enrolled: 162; 18% were from out of state. Overall acceptance rate: 74%. **Credentials of fall 2009 freshmen:** 21% ranked in the top 10 percent of their high school class; 41% were in the top 25 percent; 81% were in the top half. (Proportion submitting class standing: 69%.) **Average high school grade point average:** 3.3. **First-year students who submitted SAT scores:** 35%. Scores (25/75 percentile): Critical Reading: 440-530, Math: 420-510, Combined: 860-1040. **First-year students submitting ACT scores:** 85%. Scores (25/75 percentile): English: 19-24, Math: 17-24, Composite: 19-23.

ACADEMICS
Year founded: 1871. **Academic calendar:** Semester. **Degrees offered:** certificate, associate, bachelor's, master's. **Most popular majors:** 27% nursing/registered nurse training (R.N., A.S.N., B.S.N., M.S.N.), 15% health services/allied health/health sciences, 8% biology/biological sciences, 8% business administration and management, 5% computer science. **Major fields of study:** biological and biomedical sciences; business, management, marketing, and related support services; communication, journalism, and related programs; computer and information sciences and support services; education; English language and literature/letters; family and consumer sciences/human sciences; health professions and related clinical sciences; history; liberal arts and sciences studies, and humanities; mathematics and statistics; natural resources and conservation; parks, recreation, leisure, and fitness studies; philosophy and religious studies; physical sciences; psychology; social sciences; visual and performing arts. **Areas of required coursework:** arts/fine arts, humanities, computer literacy, mathematics, English (including composition), philosophy, sciences (biological or physical), history, social science, other. **Pre-professional programs:** pre-law, pre-dentistry, pre-medicine, pre-theology, pre-veterinary science, pre-pharmacy, other. **Special academic programs (% participation):** double major (10%), honors program (1%), independent study (23%), internships (8%), study abroad (5%), teacher certificate program (13%), weekend college (4%). **Teacher certification offered in:** special education, elementary, middle/junior high, secondary. **Faculty and instruction (2009-2010):** Total instructional faculty: 59 full-time, 30 part-time (47% men; 53% women; 8% minorities). Full-time faculty with Ph.D. or other terminal degree: 46%. Student/faculty ratio: 10/1. Classes of fewer than 20 students: 79%; of 20 to 49 students: 19%; of 50 or more students: 2%. **Advanced Placement and International Baccalaureate credit:** AP tests may be used for: Placement only. Scores accepted: 5. **Freshmen returning for sophomore year:** 68%. **Graduation rates:** Four-year: 28%; five-year: 37%; six-year: 46%. **Graduate study:** 15% of students pursue further study immediately upon graduation; 18% within one year; 29% within five years. Fields in which graduates pursue further study: Master of Business Administration (MBA), 7%; law, 4%; medicine, 11%; dentistry, 4%; theology (or the seminary), 4%; education, 48%; arts and sciences, 19%; veterinary medicine, 4%.

COSTS AND FINANCIAL AID
Financial aid office: (304) 457-6354. **Expenses (2010-2011):** Tuition and fees 2010-2011: $22,204; room/board: $7,222. Estimated books and supplies: $800; transportation: $900; personal expenses: $1,620. **Financial aid:** Priority filing date for institution's financial aid form: March 1. In 2009-2010, 99% of undergraduates applied for financial aid. Of those, 92% were determined to have financial need; 27% had their need fully met. Average financial aid package (proportion receiving): $20,942 (92%). Average amount of gift aid, such as scholarships or grants (proportion receiving): $16,092 (91%). Average amount of self-help aid, such as work study or loans (proportion receiving): $5,431 (74%). Average need-based loan (excluding PLUS or other private loans): $4,981. Among students who received need-based aid, the average percentage of need met: 81%. Among students who received aid based on merit, the average award (and the proportion receiving): $8,196 (7%). The average athletic scholarship (and the proportion receiving): $12,251 (5%). Average amount of debt of borrowers graduating in 2009: $29,613. Proportion who borrowed: 98%.

CAMPUS LIFE AND EXTRACURRICULAR ACTIVITIES
Campus housing available (% using): coed dorms (83%), women's dorms (8%), apartments for married students (1%), apartment for single students (8%). Students who live in college-owned, operated, or affiliated housing: 64%. **Clubs and organizations:** Number of student organizations: 52. Activities include: campus ministries, choral groups, concert band, drama/theater, jazz band, literary magazine, music ensembles, musical theater, radio station, student government, student newspaper, television station, yearbook. Number of fraternities: 2; sororities: 3. Proportion of men in fraternities: 9%; of women in sororities: 6%. Average proportion of students who stay on campus on weekends: 25%. **Sports program (2009-2010):** Member of NCAA II. *Men's intercollegiate varsity sports:* baseball, basketball, cross country, soccer, track and field (indoor), track and field (outdoor). *Women's intercollegiate varsity sports:* basketball, cross country, soccer, softball, track and field (indoor), track and field (outdoor), volleyball.

SERVICES AND FACILITIES
Basic services: nonremedial tutoring, placement service, day care, health service, health insurance. **Remedial assistance:** reading, math, writing, study skills. **Counseling services:** minority student, career, military, personal, veteran student, academic, older student, psychological, birth control, reli-

gious. **For learning-disabled students:** School does not offer a structured program with separate admission and additional fees. Services include: remedial math, remedial English, remedial reading, tape recorders, other special classes, note-taking services, oral tests, learning center, readers, extended time for tests, tutors, priority seating, other testing accommodations. **Library:** Number of titles: 60,000; number of current serial subscriptions: 11,000. **Information technology resources:** Students are not required to lease or own a computer. Number of campus computers available to all students: 100. School has a wireless network. Approximate number of users that can be accommodated: 500. Proportion of college-owned housing units wired for high-speed internet access: 100%. **Campus safety:** Security services offered: late-night transport/escort service, 24-hour emergency telephones, lighted pathways/sidewalks, controlled dormitory access (key, security card, etc).

TRANSFER AND INTERNATIONAL STUDENTS

Transfer students: May apply for admission for the following academic terms: Fall, Spring, Summer. Applicants do not need a minimum number of credits to apply. For fall 2009: Transfer applications received: 119. Transfer applicants offered admission: 68. Transfer applicants enrolled: 30. **International students:** Number of foreign undergraduates: 14 (2% of student body). Number of countries represented: 6. Minimum TOEFL score required: 500 (paper); 173 (computer).

Bethany College

- **Address:** PO Box 419, Bethany, WV 26032
- **Website:** http://www.bethanywv.edu
- **Private; Religious affiliation:** Christian Church (Disciples of Christ)
- **Enrollment:** 820 full-time; 10 part-time

KEY STATS
✔ **U.S News College Ranking:** 162, National Liberal Arts Colleges
✔ **ACT Score (25th/75th percentile):** 17-24
✔ **Tuition:** 2010-2011: $22,596

Selectivity: Selective	**Room/board:** $9,255
Acceptance rate: 78%	**Average debt:** $25,000
Student/faculty ratio: 14/1	**Proportion who borrowed:** 90%

UNDERGRADUATE STUDENT BODY STATS

2009-2010 enrollment: 820 full-time; 10 part-time. Men: 53%; women: 47%. **Ethnic makeup:** African American: 10%; Asian American: 1%; Hispanic: 2%; White: 85%; International: 1%. **Religious preference:** Roman Catholic: 23%; Protestant: 21%; No preference: 7%; Unknown: 46%; Christian Church (Disciples of Christ): 3%.

ADMISSIONS FACTS AND FIGURES

Phone: (304) 829-7611. **Email:** admission@bethanywv.edu. **Website:** http://www.bethanywv.edu. **Application deadlines for fall 2011:** Regular decision: Rolling. Early decision: Not offered. Early action: Not offered. Admission can be deferred. **To apply online, go to:** http://www.wvmentor.org/applications/bethany_college/apply.html. **Admissions requirements/recommendations:** High school units required (recommended): English: 4 (0); Mathematics: 3 (0); Science: 3 (0); Foreign language: 2 (0); Social studies: 3 (0); History: 0 (0); Academic electives: 0 (0); Total units: 15 (0). Tests: The college uses SAT or ACT scores in admissions decisions. Either SAT or ACT required. For admission to the fall 2011 entering class, the school will accept: ACT with or without writing accepted. Campus visit: Recommended. Admissions interview: Recommended. Off-campus interview: May be arranged. **Factors that count in admissions decisions:** *Academic:* Secondary school record: Very Important. Class rank: Very Important. Letters of recommendation: Very Important. Standardized test scores: Very Important. Essay: Very Important. *Nonacademic:* Interview: Important. Extracurricular activities: Important. Talent/ability: Considered. Character/personal qualities: Important. Alumni/ae relationship: Considered. Geographical residence: Not Considered. State residency: Not Considered. Religious affiliation/commitment: Not Considered. Minority status: Not Considered. Volunteer work: Considered. Work experience: Considered. **Other schools with the greatest overlap in applicants:** Muskingum University; Thiel College; Washington and Jefferson College; Waynesburg University; West Liberty University. **Admissions statistics for the fall 2009 entering class:** Total applicants: 1,378. Total accepted: 1,076. Freshmen enrolled: 283; 76% were from out of state. Overall acceptance rate: 78%. **Credentials of fall 2009**

freshmen: 7% ranked in the top 10 percent of their high school class; 26% were in the top 25 percent. **First-year students who submitted SAT scores:** 52%. Scores (25/75 percentile): Critical Reading: 470-520, Math: 450-500, Combined: 920-1020. **First-year students submitting ACT scores:** 58%. Scores (25/75 percentile): English: 16-23, Math: 17-23, Composite: 17-24.

ACADEMICS

Year founded: 1840. **Academic calendar:** 4-1-4. **Degrees offered:** bachelor's. **Most popular majors:** 18% education, 12% communication, journalism, and related programs, 10% social sciences, 7% biological and biomedical sciences, 7% parks, recreation, leisure, and fitness studies. **Major fields of study:** agriculture, agriculture operations, and related sciences; biological and biomedical sciences; business, management, marketing, and related support services; communication, journalism, and related programs; computer and information sciences and support services; education; English language and literature/letters; foreign languages, literatures, and linguistics; history; mathematics and statistics; multi/interdisciplinary studies; natural resources and conservation; philosophy and religious studies; physical sciences; psychology; public administration and social service professions; social sciences; visual and performing arts. **Areas of required coursework:** arts/fine arts, humanities, mathematics, English (including composition), philosophy, foreign languages, sciences (biological or physical), history, social science. **Pre-professional programs:** pre-law, pre-dentistry, pre-medicine, pre-veterinary science. **Special academic programs (% participation):** double major (3%), independent study (13%), internships (40%), student-designed major (6%), study abroad (1%), teacher certificate program (14%), other (10%). **Teacher certification offered in:** special education, elementary, middle/junior high, secondary. **Faculty and instruction (2009-2010):** Total instructional faculty: 49 full-time, 23 part-time (54% men; 46% women; 7% minorities). Full-time faculty with Ph.D. or other terminal degree: 78%. Student/faculty ratio: 14/1. Classes of fewer than 20 students: 73%; of 20 to 49 students: 26%; of 50 or more students: 1%. **Advanced Placement and International Baccalaureate credit:** AP tests may be used for: Credit only. Scores accepted: 3, 4, 5. International Baccalaureate exams may be used for: Placement only. **Freshmen returning for sophomore year:** 68%. **Graduation rates:** Four-year: 58%; five-year: 69%; six-year: 69%. **Graduate study:** 42% of students pursue further study within one year; 60% within five years. Fields in which graduates pursue further study: Master of Business Administration (MBA), 5%; law, 5%; medicine, 10%; dentistry, 5%; theology (or the seminary), 2%; education, 15%; arts and sciences, 41%.

COSTS AND FINANCIAL AID

Financial aid office: (304) 829-7141. **Expenses (2010-2011):** Tuition and fees 2010-2011: $22,596; room/board: $9,255. Estimated books and supplies: $1,300; transportation: $1,300; personal expenses: $1,300. **Financial aid:** Priority filing date for institution's financial aid form: March 1; deadline: August 1. In 2009-2010, 95% of undergraduates applied for financial aid. Of those, 85% were determined to have financial need; Average financial aid package (proportion receiving): N/A (85%). Average amount of gift aid, such as scholarships or grants (proportion receiving): $9,824 (77%). Average amount of self-help aid, such as work study or loans (proportion receiving): $7,258 (85%). Average need-based loan (excluding PLUS or other private loans): $7,258. Among students who received need-based aid, the average percentage of need met: 49%. Among students who received aid based on merit, the average award (and the proportion receiving): $7,189 (7%). The average athletic scholarship (and the proportion receiving): $0 (0%). Average amount of debt of borrowers graduating in 2009: $25,000. Proportion who borrowed: 90%.

CAMPUS LIFE AND EXTRACURRICULAR ACTIVITIES

Campus housing available (% using): coed dorms (64%), women's dorms (10%), men's dorms (7%), sorority housing (10%), fraternity housing (9%), special housing for disabled students (0%). Students who live in college-owned, operated, or affiliated housing: 90%. **Student employment:** During the 2009-2010 academic year, 65% of undergraduates worked on campus. Average per-year earnings: $1,600. **Clubs and organizations:** Number of student organizations: 65. Activities include: choral groups, concert band, dance, drama/theater, international student organization, jazz band, literary magazine, model UN, music ensembles, musical theater, pep band, radio station, student government, student newspaper, student film society, television station, yearbook. Number of fraternities: 6; sororities: 4. Proportion of men in fraternities: 34%; of women in sororities: 45%. Average proportion of students who stay on campus on weekends: 65%. **Sports program (2009-2010):** Member of NCAA III. *Men's intercollegiate varsity sports:* baseball, basketball, cross country, football, golf, soccer, swimming, tennis, track and field (indoor), track and field (outdoor). *Women's intercollegiate varsity*

sports: basketball, cross country, golf, soccer, softball, swimming, tennis, track and field (indoor), track and field (outdoor), volleyball.

SERVICES AND FACILITIES

Basic services: nonremedial tutoring, placement service, health service, health insurance. **Remedial assistance:** reading, math, writing, study skills, other. **Counseling services:** minority student, career, personal, academic, psychological, religious. **For learning-disabled students:** School does not offer a structured program with separate admission and additional fees. Total undergraduates in learning-disabled program or receiving services: 54. Services include: remedial math, remedial English, remedial reading, tape recorders, other special classes, diagnostic testing service, untimed tests, note-taking services, oral tests, learning center, readers, extended time for tests, tutors, priority seating, other testing accommodations, other. **Library:** Number of titles: 130,696; number of current serial subscriptions: 91. **Information technology resources:** Students are not required to lease or own a computer. Number of campus computers available to all students: 150. School has a wireless network. Approximate number of users that can be accommodated: 224. Proportion of college-owned housing units wired for high-speed internet access: 100%. **Campus safety:** Security services offered: 24-hour foot-and-vehicle patrols, late-night transport/escort service, 24-hour emergency telephones, lighted pathways/sidewalks, student patrols, controlled dormitory access (key, security card, etc).

TRANSFER AND INTERNATIONAL STUDENTS

Transfer students: May apply for admission for the following academic terms: Fall, Spring. Applicants need a minimum number of credits to apply. For fall 2009: Transfer applications received: 137. Transfer applicants offered admission: 79. Transfer applicants enrolled: 37. **International students:** Number of foreign undergraduates: 6 (1% of student body). Number of countries represented: 9. Minimum TOEFL score required: 550 (paper); 173 (computer). Average TOEFL score: 600 (paper).

Bluefield State College

- **Address:** 219 Rock Street, Bluefield, WV 24701
- **Website:** http://www.bluefieldstate.edu
- **Public**
- **Enrollment:** 1,599 full-time; 390 part-time

KEY STATS

✔ **U.S News College Ranking:** second tier, Regional Colleges (South)
✔ **ACT Score (25th/75th percentile):** 16-21
✔ **Tuition:** 2009-2010: $4,596 in state, $9,000 out of state

Selectivity: Less selective	**Room/board:** N/A
Acceptance rate: 79%	**Average debt:** $19,500
Student/faculty ratio: 17/1	**Proportion who borrowed:** 50%

UNDERGRADUATE STUDENT BODY STATS

2009-2010 enrollment: 1,599 full-time; 390 part-time. Men: 39%; women: 61%. **Ethnic makeup:** African American: 13%; Hispanic: 1%; White: 82%; International: 3%.

ADMISSIONS FACTS AND FIGURES

Phone: (304) 327-4065. **Email:** bscadmit@bluefieldstate.edu. **Website:** http://www.bluefieldstate.edu. **Application deadlines for fall 2011:** Regular decision: Rolling. Early decision: Not offered. Early action: Not offered. Admission can be deferred. **To apply online, go to:** http://www.wvmentor.org/applications/wv_common_app/apply/bluefield.html. **Admissions requirements/recommendations:** High school units required (recommended): English: 4 (4); Mathematics: 4 (4); Science: 3 (3); Foreign language: 2 (2); Social studies: 3 (3); Total units: 17 (17). Tests: The college uses SAT or ACT scores in admissions decisions. Either SAT or ACT required. For admission to the fall 2011 entering class, the school will accept: ACT with or without writing accepted. Campus visit: Neither required nor recommended. Admissions interview: Neither required nor recommended. Off-campus interview: May be arranged. **Factors that count in admissions decisions:** *Academic:* Secondary school record: Not Considered. Class rank: Not Considered. Letters of recommendation: Not Considered. Standardized test scores: Important. Essay: Not Considered. *Nonacademic:* Interview: Not Considered. Extracurricular activities: Not Considered. Talent/ability: Not Considered. Character/personal qualities: Not Considered. Alumni/ae relationship: Not Considered. Geographical

residence: Not Considered. State residency: Not Considered. Religious affiliation/commitment: Not Considered. Minority status: Not Considered. Volunteer work: Not Considered. Work experience: Not Considered. **Other schools with the greatest overlap in applicants:** Concord University; Marshall University; Mountain State University; West Virginia University; West Virginia University Institute of Technology. **Admissions statistics for the fall 2009 entering class:** Total applicants: 546. Total accepted: 434. Freshmen enrolled: 319; 10% were from out of state. Overall acceptance rate: 79%. **Average high school grade point average:** 3.4. **First-year students who submitted SAT scores:** 8%. Scores (25/75 percentile): Critical Reading: 400-500, Math: 380-530, Combined: 780-1030. **First-year students submitting ACT scores:** 72%. Scores (25/75 percentile): English: 16-20, Math: 15-21, Composite: 16-21.

ACADEMICS

Year founded: 1895. **Academic calendar:** Semester. **Degrees offered:** associate, bachelor's. **Most popular majors:** 20% general studies, 12% elementary education and teaching, 11% accounting, 10% criminal justice/safety studies, 9% nursing. **Major fields of study:** business, management, marketing, and related support services; computer and information sciences and support services; education; engineering technologies/technicians; health professions and related clinical sciences; liberal arts and sciences studies, and humanities; multi/interdisciplinary studies; security and protective services; social sciences. **Areas of required coursework:** arts/fine arts, humanities, computer literacy, mathematics, English (including composition), sciences (biological or physical), history, social science. **Pre-professional programs:** pre-law, pre-dentistry, pre-medicine, pre-veterinary science, pre-pharmacy. **Special academic programs (% participation):** distance learning (12%), double major (1%), dual enrollment (1%), honors program (1%), independent study (1%), internships (1%), teacher certificate program (12%). **Teacher certification offered in:** elementary, middle/junior high. **Faculty and instruction (2009-2010):** Total instructional faculty: 79 full-time, 70 part-time (49% men; 51% women; 6% minorities). Full-time faculty with Ph.D. or other terminal degree: 54%. Student/faculty ratio: 17/1. Classes of fewer than 20 students: 46%; of 20 to 49 students: 53%; of 50 or more students: 1%. **Advanced Placement and International Baccalaureate credit:** AP tests may be used for: Credit only. Scores accepted: 3, 4, 5. International Baccalaureate exams may be used for: Credit only. **Freshmen returning for sophomore year:** 62%. **Graduation rates:** Four-year: 11%; five-year: 20%; six-year: 23%. **Graduate study:** 5% of students pursue further study immediately upon graduation; 10% within one year; 12% within five years. Fields in which graduates pursue further study: Master of Business Administration (MBA), 18%; law, 10%; medicine, 10%; dentistry, 1%; engineering, 25%; education, 15%; arts and sciences, 15%.

COSTS AND FINANCIAL AID

Financial aid office: (304) 327-4020. **Expenses (2009-2010):** Tuition and fees 2009-2010: $4,596 in state, $9,000 out of state. Estimated books and supplies: $1,600; transportation: $2,000; personal expenses: $1,100. **Financial aid:** Priority filing date for institution's financial aid form: March 1. In 2009-2010, 78% of undergraduates applied for financial aid. Of those, 67% were determined to have financial need; 40% had their need fully met. Average financial aid package (proportion receiving): $6,200 (67%). Average amount of gift aid, such as scholarships or grants (proportion receiving): $3,500 (67%). Average amount of self-help aid, such as work study or loans (proportion receiving): $4,700 (54%). Average need-based loan (excluding PLUS or other private loans): $3,600. Among students who received need-based aid, the average percentage of need met: 70%. Among students who received aid based on merit, the average award (and the proportion receiving): $1,400 (26%). The average athletic scholarship (and the proportion receiving): $3,100 (3%). Average amount of debt of borrowers graduating in 2009: $19,500. Proportion who borrowed: 50%.

CAMPUS LIFE AND EXTRACURRICULAR ACTIVITIES

Students who live in college-owned, operated, or affiliated housing: 0%. **Student employment:** During the 2009-2010 academic year, 5% of undergraduates worked on campus. Average per-year earnings: $4,000. **Clubs and organizations:** Number of student organizations: 49. Activities include: choral groups, drama/theater, radio station, student government, student newspaper, yearbook. Number of fraternities: 4; sororities: 5. Proportion of men in fraternities: 5%; of women in sororities: 4%. **Sports program (2009-2010):** Member of NCAA II. *Men's intercollegiate varsity sports:* baseball, basketball, cross country, golf, tennis. *Women's intercollegiate varsity sports:* basketball, cross country, softball, tennis, volleyball.

SERVICES AND FACILITIES

Basic services: nonremedial tutoring, placement service, health service, health insurance. **Remedial assistance:** reading, math, writing, study skills. **Counseling services:** minority student, career, military, personal, veteran student, academic, older student, psychological, birth control. **For learning-disabled students:** School does not offer a structured program with separate admission and additional fees. Services include: remedial math, remedial English, reading machines, remedial reading, tape recorders, untimed tests, note-taking services, oral tests, readers, extended time for tests, tutors. **Library:** Number of titles: 73,652; number of current serial subscriptions: 22,292. **Information technology resources:** Students are not required to lease or own a computer. Number of campus computers available to all students: 250. School has a wireless network. Approximate number of users that can be accommodated: 500. **Campus safety:** Security services offered: late-night transport/escort service, lighted pathways/sidewalks, student patrols.

TRANSFER AND INTERNATIONAL STUDENTS

Transfer students: May apply for admission for the following academic terms: Fall, Spring, Summer. Applicants do not need a minimum number of credits to apply. For fall 2009: Transfer applications received: 369. Transfer applicants offered admission: 262. Transfer applicants enrolled: 207. **International students:** Number of foreign undergraduates: 65 (3% of student body). Number of countries represented: 19. Minimum TOEFL score required: 500 (paper); 500 (computer). Average TOEFL score: 525 (paper).

Concord University

- **Address:** Vermillion Street, Athens, WV 24712
- **Website:** http://www.concord.edu
- **Public**
- **Enrollment:** 2,346 full-time; 466 part-time

KEY STATS

- ✔ **U.S News College Ranking:** 39, Regional Colleges (South)
- ✔ **ACT Score (25th/75th percentile):** 18-23
- ✔ **Tuition:** 2010-2011: $4,976 in state, $11,052 out of state

Selectivity: Selective	**Room/board:** $6,766
Acceptance rate: 68%	**Average debt:** $14,030
Student/faculty ratio: 18/1	**Proportion who borrowed:** 86%

UNDERGRADUATE STUDENT BODY STATS

2009-2010 enrollment: 2,346 full-time; 466 part-time. Men: 42%; women: 58%. **Ethnic makeup:** African American: 5%; Asian American: 2%; Hispanic: 1%; White: 92%.

ADMISSIONS FACTS AND FIGURES

Phone: (304) 384-5249. **Email:** admissions@concord.edu. **Website:** http://www.concord.edu. **Application deadlines for fall 2011:** Regular decision: Rolling. Early decision: Not offered. Early action: Not offered. Admission can be deferred. **To apply online, go to:** http://www.concord.edu/admissions/apply. **Admissions requirements/recommendations:** High school units required (recommended): English: 4; Mathematics: 4; Science: 3; Foreign language: 2; Social studies: 3; History: 1; Academic electives: 0; Total units: 13. Tests: The college uses SAT or ACT scores in admissions decisions. Either SAT or ACT required. For admission to the fall 2011 entering class, the school will accept: ACT with or without writing accepted. Campus visit: Recommended. Admissions interview: Neither required nor recommended. Off-campus interview: May be arranged. **Factors that count in admissions decisions:** *Academic:* Secondary school record: Very Important. Class rank: Considered. Letters of recommendation: Considered. Standardized test scores: Very Important. Essay: Considered. *Nonacademic:* Interview: Considered. Extracurricular activities: Considered. Talent/ability: Considered. Character/personal qualities: Considered. Alumni/ae relationship: Considered. Geographical residence: Considered. State residency: Considered. Religious affiliation/commitment: Considered. Minority status: Considered. Volunteer work: Considered. Work experience: Considered. **Other schools with the greatest overlap in applicants:** Bluefield State College; Marshall University; West Virginia University. **Admissions statistics for the fall 2009 entering class:** Total applicants: 2,986. Total accepted: 2,027. Freshmen enrolled: 611; 23% were from out of state. Overall acceptance rate: 68%. **Credentials of fall 2009 freshmen:** 18% ranked in the top 10 percent of their high school class; 43% were in the top 25 percent; 80%

were in the top half. (Proportion submitting class standing: 98%.) **Average high school grade point average:** 3.2. **First-year students who submitted SAT scores:** 35%. Scores (25/75 percentile): Critical Reading: 420-520, Math: 430-530, Combined: 850-1050. **First-year students submitting ACT scores:** 81%. Scores (25/75 percentile): English: N/A, Math: N/A, Composite: 18-23.

ACADEMICS

Year founded: 1872. **Academic calendar:** Semester. **Degrees offered:** associate, bachelor's, master's. **Most popular majors:** 21% business, management, marketing, and related support services, 18% education, 9% biological and biomedical sciences, 8% social sciences, 7% liberal arts and sciences studies, and humanities. **Major fields of study:** biological and biomedical sciences; business, management, marketing, and related support services; communication, journalism, and related programs; computer and information sciences and support services; education; English language and literature/letters; health professions and related clinical sciences; history; liberal arts and sciences studies, and humanities; mathematics and statistics; multi/interdisciplinary studies; physical sciences; psychology; public administration and social service professions; social sciences; visual and performing arts. **Areas of required coursework:** arts/fine arts, computer literacy, mathematics, English (including composition), foreign languages, sciences (biological or physical), history, social science. **Pre-professional programs:** pre-law, pre-dentistry, pre-medicine, pre-veterinary science, pre-pharmacy. **Special academic programs:** cross-registration, distance learning, double major, dual enrollment, English as a Second Language (ESL), honors program, independent study, internships, student-designed major, teacher certificate program. **Teacher certification offered in:** early childhood, special education, elementary, secondary. **Faculty and instruction (2009-2010):** Total instructional faculty: 117 full-time, 89 part-time (52% men; 48% women; 5% minorities). Full-time faculty with Ph.D. or other terminal degree: 63%. Student/faculty ratio: 18/1. Classes of fewer than 20 students: 65%; of 20 to 49 students: 33%; of 50 or more students: 2%. **Advanced Placement and International Baccalaureate credit:** AP tests may be used for: Credit only. **Freshmen returning for sophomore year:** 66%. **Graduation rates:** Four-year: 19%; five-year: 31%; six-year: 35%.

COSTS AND FINANCIAL AID

Financial aid office: (304) 384-6069. **Expenses (2010-2011):** Tuition and fees 2010-2011: $4,976 in state, $11,052 out of state; room/board: $6,766. Estimated books and supplies: $1,100; transportation: $1,306; personal expenses: $1,610. **Financial aid:** Priority filing date for institution's financial aid form: April 15. In 2009-2010, 89% of undergraduates applied for financial aid. Of those, 69% were determined to have financial need; 39% had their need fully met. Average financial aid package (proportion receiving): $9,562 (69%). Average amount of gift aid, such as scholarships or grants (proportion receiving): $5,604 (55%). Average amount of self-help aid, such as work study or loans (proportion receiving): $3,792 (51%). Average need-based loan (excluding PLUS or other private loans): $3,604. Among students who received need-based aid, the average percentage of need met: 99%. Among students who received aid based on merit, the average award (and the proportion receiving): $3,345 (8%). The average athletic scholarship (and the proportion receiving): $5,082 (4%). Average amount of debt of borrowers graduating in 2009: $14,030. Proportion who borrowed: 86%.

CAMPUS LIFE AND EXTRACURRICULAR ACTIVITIES

Campus housing available (% using): coed dorms (8%), women's dorms (46%), men's dorms (46%), special housing for disabled students. Students who live in college-owned, operated, or affiliated housing: 39%. **Student employment:** During the 2009-2010 academic year, 27% of undergraduates worked on campus. Average per-year earnings: $1,156. **Clubs and organizations:** Number of student organizations: 62. Activities include: choral groups, concert band, dance, drama/theater, jazz band, literary magazine, marching band, music ensembles, musical theater, pep band, radio station, student government, student newspaper, student film society, television station, yearbook. Number of fraternities: 5; sororities: 4. Proportion of men in fraternities: 20%; of women in sororities: 25%. Average proportion of students who stay on campus on weekends: 30%. **Sports program (2009-2010):** Member of NCAA II. *Men's intercollegiate varsity sports:* baseball, basketball, cross country, football, golf, soccer, tennis, track and field (indoor), track and field (outdoor). *Women's intercollegiate varsity sports:* basketball, cross country, golf, soccer, softball, tennis, track and field (indoor), track and field (outdoor), volleyball.

SERVICES AND FACILITIES

Basic services: nonremedial tutoring, placement service, day care, health service. **Remedial assistance:** reading, math, writing, study skills. **Counseling**

services: minority student, career, military, personal, veteran student, academic, older student, psychological, birth control. **For learning-disabled students:** School does not offer a structured program with separate admission and additional fees. Services include: remedial math, remedial English, remedial reading, tape recorders, untimed tests, note-taking services, oral tests, readers, extended time for tests, tutors, texts on tape, other testing accommodations. **Library:** Number of titles: 156,000; number of current serial subscriptions: 227. **Information technology resources:** Students are not required to lease or own a computer. Number of campus computers available to all students: 350. School has a wireless network. Approximate number of users that can be accommodated: 500. Proportion of college-owned housing units wired for high-speed internet access: 100%. **Campus safety:** Security services offered: 24-hour foot-and-vehicle patrols, late-night transport/escort service, 24-hour emergency telephones, lighted pathways/sidewalks, controlled dormitory access (key, security card, etc).

TRANSFER AND INTERNATIONAL STUDENTS
Transfer students: May apply for admission for the following academic terms: Fall, Winter, Spring, Summer. Applicants do not need a minimum number of credits to apply. **International students:** Number of foreign undergraduates: 0. Number of countries represented: 19. Minimum TOEFL score required: 500 (paper); 173 (computer). Average TOEFL score: 562 (paper).

Davis and Elkins College

- **Address:** 100 Campus Drive, Elkins, WV 26241
- **Website:** http://www.davisandelkins.edu
- **Private; Religious affiliation:** Presbyterian
- **Enrollment:** 626 full-time; 84 part-time

KEY STATS
✔ **U.S News College Ranking:** 27, Regional Colleges (South)
✔ **ACT Score (25th/75th percentile):** 17-22
✔ **Tuition:** 2010-2011: $21,120

Selectivity: Selective	**Room/board:** $7,750
Acceptance rate: 68%	**Average debt:** $27,583
Student/faculty ratio: 13/1	**Proportion who borrowed:** 80%

UNDERGRADUATE STUDENT BODY STATS
2009-2010 enrollment: 626 full-time; 84 part-time. Men: 40%; women: 60%. **Ethnic makeup:** African American: 4%; American-Indian: 1%; Hispanic: 1%; White: 88%; International: 6%.

ADMISSIONS FACTS AND FIGURES
Phone: (304) 637-1230. **Email:** admiss@davisandelkins.edu. **Website:** http://www.davisandelkins.edu. **Application deadlines for fall 2011:** Regular decision: Rolling. Early decision: Not offered. Early action: Not offered. Admission can be deferred. **To apply online, go to:** http://www.davisandelkins.edu/admission/application_online.cfm. **Admissions requirements/recommendations:** High school units required (recommended): English: 4 (4); Mathematics: 3 (4); Science: 3 (4); Foreign language: 1 (2); Social studies: 3 (4); History: 0 (0); Academic electives: 0 (4); Total units: 15 (24). Tests: The college uses SAT or ACT scores in admissions decisions. Either SAT or ACT required. For admission to the fall 2011 entering class, the school will accept: ACT with or without writing accepted. Campus visit: Recommended. Admissions interview: Recommended. Off-campus interview: May be arranged. **Factors that count in admissions decisions:** *Academic:* Secondary school record: Very Important. Class rank: Important. Letters of recommendation: Important. Standardized test scores: Very Important. Essay: Considered. *Nonacademic:* Interview: Considered. Extracurricular activities: Important. Talent/ability: Important. Character/personal qualities: Considered. Alumni/ae relationship: Considered. Geographical residence: Not Considered. State residency: Not Considered. Religious affiliation/commitment: Not Considered. Minority status: Not Considered. Volunteer work: Considered. Work experience: Considered. **Other schools with the greatest overlap in applicants:** Alderson-Broaddus College; Fairmont State University; Glenville State College; West Virginia University; West Virginia Wesleyan College. **Admissions statistics for the fall 2009 entering class:** Total applicants: 1,141. Total accepted: 775. Freshmen enrolled: 235; 35% were from out of state. Overall acceptance rate: 68%. **Credentials of fall 2009 freshmen:** 16% ranked in the top 10 percent of their high school class; 29% were in the top 25 percent; 69% were in the top half. (Proportion

submitting class standing: 66%.) **Average high school grade point average:** 3.0. **First-year students who submitted SAT scores:** 36%. Scores (25/75 percentile): Critical Reading: 410-540, Math: 420-550, Combined: 830-1090. **First-year students submitting ACT scores:** 60%. Scores (25/75 percentile): English: 16-23, Math: 19-21, Composite: 17-22.

ACADEMICS
Year founded: 1904. **Academic calendar:** 4-1-4. **Degrees offered:** associate, bachelor's. **Most popular majors:** 20% marketing/marketing management, 20% political science and government, 16% elementary education and teaching, 11% parks, recreation, and leisure studies, 9% psychology. **Major fields of study:** biological and biomedical sciences; business, management, marketing, and related support services; communication, journalism, and related programs; computer and information sciences and support services; education; engineering technologies/technicians; English language and literature/letters; foreign languages, literatures, and linguistics; history; mathematics and statistics; natural resources and conservation; parks, recreation, leisure, and fitness studies; philosophy and religious studies; physical sciences; psychology; social sciences; theology and religious vocations; visual and performing arts. **Areas of required coursework:** arts/fine arts, humanities, computer literacy, mathematics, English (including composition), philosophy, sciences (biological or physical), history, social science, other. **Pre-professional programs:** pre-law, pre-dentistry, pre-medicine, pre-theology, pre-veterinary science, pre-pharmacy. **Special academic programs (% participation):** double major (17%), honors program (9%), independent study (16%), internships (78%), student-designed major (2%), study abroad (5%), teacher certificate program (17%). **Teacher certification offered in:** elementary, middle/junior high, secondary. **Cooperative education programs:** other. **Faculty and instruction (2009-2010):** Total instructional faculty: 39 full-time, 31 part-time (51% men; 49% women; 7% minorities). Full-time faculty with Ph.D. or other terminal degree: 69%. Student/faculty ratio: 13/1. Classes of fewer than 20 students: 70%; of 20 to 49 students: 29%; of 50 or more students: 2%. **Advanced Placement and International Baccalaureate credit:** AP tests may be used for: Credit and/or placement. Scores accepted: 3, 4, 5. International Baccalaureate exams may be used for: Credit and/or placement. **Freshmen returning for sophomore year:** 63%. **Graduation rates:** Four-year: 35%; five-year: 54%; six-year: 48%. **Graduate study:** Fields in which graduates pursue further study: Master of Business Administration (MBA), 11%; law, 6%; education, 44%; arts and sciences, 39%.

COSTS AND FINANCIAL AID
Financial aid office: (304) 637-1373. **Expenses (2010-2011):** Tuition and fees 2010-2011: $21,120; room/board: $7,750. Estimated books and supplies: $1,200; transportation: $0; personal expenses: $1,500. **Financial aid:** Priority filing date for institution's financial aid form: March 1. In 2009-2010, 100% of undergraduates applied for financial aid. Of those, 79% were determined to have financial need; 36% had their need fully met. Average financial aid package (proportion receiving): $19,574 (79%). Average amount of gift aid, such as scholarships or grants (proportion receiving): $4,797 (44%). Average amount of self-help aid, such as work study or loans (proportion receiving): $6,328 (67%). Average need-based loan (excluding PLUS or other private loans): $5,523. Among students who received need-based aid, the average percentage of need met: 84%. Among students who received aid based on merit, the average award (and the proportion receiving): $11,606 (21%). The average athletic scholarship (and the proportion receiving): $5,748 (28%). Average amount of debt of borrowers graduating in 2009: $27,583. Proportion who borrowed: 80%.

CAMPUS LIFE AND EXTRACURRICULAR ACTIVITIES
Campus housing available (% using): coed dorms (38%), women's dorms (32%), men's dorms (30%). Students who live in college-owned, operated, or affiliated housing: 54%. **Student employment:** During the 2009-2010 academic year, 6% of undergraduates worked on campus. Average per-year earnings: $1,500. **Clubs and organizations:** Number of student organizations: 25. Activities include: choral groups, concert band, drama/theater, jazz band, literary magazine, music ensembles, musical theater, radio station, student government, student newspaper, yearbook. Number of fraternities: 1; sororities: 1. Proportion of men in fraternities: 4%; of women in sororities: 5%. Average proportion of students who stay on campus on weekends: 60%. **Sports program (2009-2010):** Member of NCAA II. *Men's intercollegiate varsity sports:* baseball, basketball, cross country, golf, soccer, tennis, track and field (indoor). *Women's intercollegiate varsity sports:* basketball, cross country, soccer, softball, tennis, track and field (indoor), volleyball.

SERVICES AND FACILITIES

Basic services: nonremedial tutoring, placement service, health service, health insurance. **Remedial assistance:** reading, math, writing, study skills. **Counseling services:** minority student, career, personal, veteran student, academic, older student, psychological, birth control. **For learning-disabled students:** School does not offer a structured program with separate admission and additional fees. Total undergraduates in learning-disabled program or receiving services: 52. Services include: remedial math, remedial English, reading machines, remedial reading, untimed tests, note-taking services, oral tests, learning center, readers, extended time for tests, tutors, proofreading services, texts on tape, typist/scribe. **Library:** Number of titles: 126,722; number of current serial subscriptions: 951. **Information technology resources:** Students are not required to lease or own a computer. Number of campus computers available to all students: 81. School has a wireless network. Approximate number of users that can be accommodated: 1,500. Proportion of college-owned housing units wired for high-speed internet access: 100%. **Campus safety:** Security services offered: 24-hour foot-and-vehicle patrols, late-night transport/escort service, 24-hour emergency telephones, lighted pathways/sidewalks, controlled dormitory access (key, security card, etc).

TRANSFER AND INTERNATIONAL STUDENTS

Transfer students: May apply for admission for the following academic terms: Fall, Winter, Spring, Summer. Applicants do not need a minimum number of credits to apply. For fall 2009: Transfer applications received: 248. Transfer applicants offered admission: 120. Transfer applicants enrolled: 75. **International students:** Number of foreign undergraduates: 41 (6% of student body). Number of countries represented: 21. Minimum TOEFL score required: 500 (paper); 173 (computer).

Fairmont State University

- **Address:** 1201 Locust Avenue, Fairmont, WV 26554
- **Website:** http://www.fairmontstate.edu
- **Public**
- **Enrollment:** 3,652 full-time; 571 part-time

KEY STATS

- ✔ **U.S News College Ranking:** 44, Regional Colleges (South)
- ✔ **ACT Score (25th/75th percentile):** 18-23
- ✔ **Tuition:** 2009-2010: $4,952 in state, $10,684 out of state
  - **Selectivity:** Selective   **Room/board:** $6,400
  - **Acceptance rate:** 61%   **Average debt:** N/A
  - **Student/faculty ratio:** 17/1   **Proportion who borrowed:** N/A

UNDERGRADUATE STUDENT BODY STATS

2009-2010 enrollment: 3,652 full-time; 571 part-time. Men: 44%; women: 56%. **Ethnic makeup:** African American: 4%; Asian American: 1%; Hispanic: 1%; White: 92%; International: 1%.

ADMISSIONS FACTS AND FIGURES

Phone: (304) 367-4892. **Email:** admit@fairmontstate.edu. **Website:** http://www.fairmontstate.edu. **Application deadlines for fall 2011:** Regular decision: Rolling. Early decision: Not offered. Early action: Not offered. Admission cannot be deferred. **Application fee:** None. **To apply online, go to:** http://www.fairmontstate.edu/admissions/undergraduate/applying.asp. **Admissions requirements/recommendations:** High school units required (recommended): English: 4; Mathematics: 4; Science: 3; Foreign language: 2; Social studies: 2; History: 1; Academic electives: 8; Total units: 26. Tests: The college uses SAT or ACT scores in admissions decisions. Either SAT or ACT required. For admission to the fall 2011 entering class, the school will accept: ACT with writing recommended. Campus visit: Recommended. Admissions interview: Recommended. Off-campus interview: Not available. **Factors that count in admissions decisions:** *Academic:* Secondary school record: Not Considered. Class rank: Not Considered. Letters of recommendation: Not Considered. Standardized test scores: Very Important. Essay: Not Considered. *Nonacademic:* Interview: Not Considered. Extracurricular activities: Not Considered. Talent/ability: Not Considered. Character/personal qualities: Not Considered. Alumni/ae relationship: Not Considered. Geographical residence: Not Considered. State residency: Not Considered. Religious affiliation/commitment: Not Considered. Minority status: Not Considered. Volunteer work: Not Considered. Work experience: Not Considered. **Other schools with the greatest overlap in applicants:** Glenville State College; Marshall University; Shepherd University; West Virginia University; West Virginia Wesleyan College. **Admissions statistics for the fall 2009 entering class:** Total applicants: 3,079. Total accepted: 1,892. Freshmen enrolled: 820; 9% were from out of state. Overall acceptance rate: 61%. **Credentials of fall 2009 freshmen:** 10% ranked in the top 10 percent of their high school class; 30% were in the top 25 percent; 70% were in the top half. (Proportion submitting class standing: 75%.) **Average high school grade point average:** 3.1. **First-year students who submitted SAT scores:** 7%. Scores (25/75 percentile): Critical Reading: 410-490, Math: 410-520, Combined: 820-1010. **First-year students submitting ACT scores:** 87%. Scores (25/75 percentile): English: 17-23, Math: 16-22, Composite: 18-23.

ACADEMICS

Year founded: 1865. **Academic calendar:** Semester. **Degrees offered:** associate, bachelor's, master's. **Most popular majors:** 25% business, management, marketing, and related support services, 12% education, 10% security and protective services, 9% engineering technologies/technicians, 7% liberal arts and sciences studies, and humanities. **Major fields of study:** biological and biomedical sciences; business, management, marketing, and related support services; communication, journalism, and related programs; communications technologies/technicians and support services; computer and information sciences and support services; education; engineering technologies/technicians; English language and literature/letters; family and consumer sciences/human sciences; health professions and related clinical sciences; history; mathematics and statistics; multi/interdisciplinary studies; physical sciences; psychology; security and protective services; social sciences; visual and performing arts. **Areas of required coursework:** arts/fine arts, humanities, computer literacy, mathematics, English (including composition), foreign languages, sciences (biological or physical), history, social science. **Pre-professional programs:** pre-law, pre-dentistry, pre-medicine, pre-pharmacy, other. **Special academic programs:** accelerated program, cooperative (work-study plan) program, cross-registration, distance learning, double major, English as a Second Language (ESL), honors program, independent study, internships, liberal arts/career combination, study abroad, teacher certificate program, weekend college. **Teacher certification offered in:** early childhood, special education, elementary, middle/junior high, secondary. **Cooperative education programs:** education, health professions. **Reserve Officers Training Corps (ROTC):** Army ROTC: Offered at cooperating institution (West Virginia University); Air Force ROTC: Offered at cooperating institution. **Faculty and instruction (2009-2010):** Total instructional faculty: 165 full-time, 169 part-time (49% men; 51% women; 9% minorities). Full-time faculty with Ph.D. or other terminal degree: 72%. Student/faculty ratio: 17/1. Classes of fewer than 20 students: 48%; of 20 to 49 students: 45%; of 50 or more students: 7%. **Advanced Placement and International Baccalaureate credit:** AP tests may be used for: Placement only. Scores accepted: 3, 4, 5. International Baccalaureate exams may be used for: Placement only. **Freshmen returning for sophomore year:** 68%. **Graduation rates:** Four-year: 14%; five-year: 30%; six-year: 42%. **Graduate study:** 35% of students pursue further study immediately upon graduation.

COSTS AND FINANCIAL AID

Financial aid office: (304) 367-4213. **Expenses (2009-2010):** Tuition and fees 2009-2010: $4,952 in state, $10,684 out of state; room/board: $6,400. **Financial aid:** Priority filing date for institution's financial aid form: March 1. In 2009-2010, 82% of undergraduates applied for financial aid. Of those, 67% were determined to have financial need; 14% had their need fully met. Average financial aid package (proportion receiving): $7,654 (67%). Average amount of gift aid, such as scholarships or grants (proportion receiving): N/A (52%). Average amount of self-help aid, such as work study or loans (proportion receiving): $8,269 (50%). Average need-based loan (excluding PLUS or other private loans): $3,635. Among students who received aid based on merit, the average award (and the proportion receiving): $1,109 (11%).

CAMPUS LIFE AND EXTRACURRICULAR ACTIVITIES

Campus housing available (% using): coed dorms (90%), apartment for single students (10%). Students who live in college-owned, operated, or affiliated housing: 20%. **Student employment:** During the 2009-2010 academic year, 10% of undergraduates worked on campus. Average per-year earnings: $2,000. **Clubs and organizations:** Number of student organizations: 81. Activities include: campus ministries, choral groups, concert band, dance, drama/theater, international student organization, jazz band, literary magazine, marching band, music ensembles, musical theater, student government, student newspaper, symphony orchestra, yearbook. Number of fraternities: 5; sororities: 4. Proportion of men in fraternities: 2%; of women in sororities: 2%. Average proportion of students who stay on campus on weekends: 20%. **Sports program (2009-2010):** Member of NCAA II.

SERVICES AND FACILITIES
Basic services: nonremedial tutoring, placement service, health service. **Remedial assistance:** reading, math, writing, study skills. **Counseling services:** minority student, career, military, personal, veteran student, academic, psychological. **For learning-disabled students:** School offers a structured program with separate admission and additional fees. Services include: remedial math, remedial English, reading machines, remedial reading, tape recorders, diagnostic testing service, note-taking services, special bookstore section, oral tests, learning center, readers, extended time for tests, tutors, priority registration, priority seating, other testing accommodations. **Library:** Number of titles: 224,122; number of current serial subscriptions: 27,267. **Information technology resources:** Students are not required to lease or own a computer. Number of campus computers available to all students: 1,100. School has a wireless network. Approximate number of users that can be accommodated: 5,000. Proportion of college-owned housing units wired for high-speed internet access: 100%. **Campus safety:** Security services offered: 24-hour foot-and-vehicle patrols, late-night transport/escort service, 24-hour emergency telephones, lighted pathways/sidewalks, student patrols, controlled dormitory access (key, security card, etc).

TRANSFER AND INTERNATIONAL STUDENTS
Transfer students: May apply for admission for the following academic terms: Fall, Spring, Summer. Applicants need a minimum number of credits to apply. For fall 2009: Transfer applications received: 1,153. Transfer applicants offered admission: 639. Transfer applicants enrolled: 467. **International students:** Number of foreign undergraduates: 56 (1% of student body). Number of countries represented: 19. Minimum TOEFL score required: 500 (paper); 173 (computer).

Glenville State College

- **Address:** 200 High Street, Glenville, WV 26351
- **Website:** http://www.glenville.edu
- **Public**
- **Enrollment:** 1,118 full-time; 559 part-time

KEY STATS
✔ **U.S News College Ranking:** 68, Regional Colleges (South)
✔ **ACT Score (25th/75th percentile):** 17-21
✔ **Tuition:** 2009-2010: $4,888 in state, $11,702 out of state

Selectivity: Less selective	**Room/board:** $6,460
Acceptance rate: 100%	**Average debt:** $19,722
Student/faculty ratio: 18/1	**Proportion who borrowed:** 77%

UNDERGRADUATE STUDENT BODY STATS
2009-2010 enrollment: 1,118 full-time; 559 part-time. Men: 57%; women: 43%. **Ethnic makeup:** African American: 9%; American-Indian: 1%; Hispanic: 1%; White: 89%.

ADMISSIONS FACTS AND FIGURES
Phone: (304) 462-4128. **Email:** admissions@glenville.edu. **Website:** http://www.glenville.edu. **Application deadlines for fall 2011:** Regular decision: Rolling. Early decision: Not offered. Early action: Not offered. Admission cannot be deferred. **Application fee:** $10. **To apply online, go to:** https://www.glenville.edu/applicant_information.asp. **Admissions requirements/recommendations:** High school units required (recommended): English: 4 (0); Mathematics: 4 (0); Science: 3 (0); Foreign language: 2 (0); Social studies: 3 (0); History: 0 (0); Academic electives: 15 (0); Total units: 32 (0). Tests: The college uses SAT or ACT scores in admissions decisions. Either SAT or ACT required. For admission to the fall 2011 entering class, the school will accept: ACT with or without writing accepted. Campus visit: Recommended. Admissions interview: Neither required nor recommended. Off-campus interview: May be arranged. **Factors that count in admissions decisions:** *Academic:* Secondary school record: Very Important. Class rank: Considered. Letters of recommendation: Not Considered. Standardized test scores: Very Important. Essay: Not Considered. *Nonacademic:* Interview: Not Considered. Extracurricular activities: Not Considered. Talent/ability: Important. Character/personal qualities: Not Considered. Alumni/ae relationship: Not Considered. Geographical residence: Not Considered. State residency: Not Considered. Religious affili-

ation/commitment: Not Considered. Minority status: Not Considered. Volunteer work: Not Considered. Work experience: Not Considered. **Other schools with the greatest overlap in applicants:** Fairmont State University; Marshall University; West Virginia University; West Virginia University–Parkersburg. **Admissions statistics for the fall 2009 entering class:** Total applicants: 927. Total accepted: 926. Freshmen enrolled: 325; 15% were from out of state. Overall acceptance rate: 100%. **Size of waiting list:** 0 applicants; enrolled from waiting list: 0. **Credentials of fall 2009 freshmen:** 12% ranked in the top 10 percent of their high school class; 30% were in the top 25 percent; 90% were in the top half. (Proportion submitting class standing: 85%.) **Average high school grade point average:** 2.9. **First-year students who submitted SAT scores:** 17%. Scores (25/75 percentile): Critical Reading: 370-480, Math: 370-470, Combined: 740-950. **First-year students submitting ACT scores:** 83%. Scores (25/75 percentile): English: 15-22, Math: 16-20, Composite: 17-21.

ACADEMICS
Year founded: 1872. **Academic calendar:** Semester. **Degrees offered:** associate, bachelor's. **Most popular majors:** 24% education, 22% social sciences, 20% business, management, marketing, and related support services, 12% natural resources and conservation, 9% liberal arts and sciences studies, and humanities. **Major fields of study:** biological and biomedical sciences; business, management, marketing, and related support services; education; English language and literature/letters; health professions and related clinical sciences; history; liberal arts and sciences studies, and humanities; multi/interdisciplinary studies; natural resources and conservation; physical sciences; social sciences. **Areas of required coursework:** arts/fine arts, computer literacy, mathematics, English (including composition), sciences (biological or physical), history, social science, other. **Special academic programs:** cooperative (work-study plan) program, distance learning, double major, dual enrollment, internships, student-designed major, study abroad, teacher certificate program. **Teacher certification offered in:** early childhood, special education, elementary, middle/junior high, secondary. **Cooperative education programs:** health professions. **Faculty and instruction (2009-2010):** Total instructional faculty: 61 full-time, 41 part-time (56% men; 44% women; 3% minorities). Full-time faculty with Ph.D. or other terminal degree: 54%. Student/faculty ratio: 18/1. Classes of fewer than 20 students: 55%; of 20 to 49 students: 44%; of 50 or more students: 1%. **Advanced Placement and International Baccalaureate credit:** AP tests may be used for: Credit only. Scores accepted: 3, 4, 5. **Freshmen returning for sophomore year:** 65%. **Graduation rates:** Four-year: 16%; five-year: 33%; six-year: 38%. **Graduate study:** 11% of students pursue further study immediately upon graduation; 53% within one year; 42% within five years. Fields in which graduates pursue further study: Master of Business Administration (MBA), 16%; education, 63%.

COSTS AND FINANCIAL AID
Financial aid office: (304) 462-4103. **Expenses (2009-2010):** Tuition and fees 2009-2010: $4,888 in state, $11,702 out of state; room/board: $6,460. Estimated books and supplies: $1,100; transportation: $2,250; personal expenses: $2,260. **Financial aid:** Priority filing date for institution's financial aid form: February 1. In 2009-2010, 92% of undergraduates applied for financial aid. Of those, 83% were determined to have financial need; 26% had their need fully met. Average financial aid package (proportion receiving): $11,448 (82%). Average amount of gift aid, such as scholarships or grants (proportion receiving): $5,650 (63%). Average amount of self-help aid, such as work study or loans (proportion receiving): $3,761 (65%). Average need-based loan (excluding PLUS or other private loans): $3,663. Among students who received need-based aid, the average percentage of need met: 76%. Among students who received aid based on merit, the average award (and the proportion receiving): $2,089 (4%). The average athletic scholarship (and the proportion receiving): $3,329 (4%). Average amount of debt of borrowers graduating in 2009: $19,722. Proportion who borrowed: 77%.

CAMPUS LIFE AND EXTRACURRICULAR ACTIVITIES
Campus housing available (% using): women's dorms (41%), men's dorms (58%), apartments for married students (1%), special housing for disabled students (0%). Students who live in college-owned, operated, or affiliated housing: 33%. **Student employment:** During the 2009-2010 academic year, 15% of undergraduates worked on campus. Average per-year earnings: $314. **Clubs and organizations:** Number of student organizations: 46. Activities include: choral groups, concert band, dance, drama/theater, jazz band, literary magazine, marching band, music ensembles, pep band, student government, student newspaper. Number of fraternities: 1; sororities: 3. Proportion of men in fraternities: 1%; of women in sororities: 4%. Average proportion

of students who stay on campus on weekends: 30%. **Sports program (2009-2010):** Member of NCAA II. *Men's intercollegiate varsity sports:* basketball, cross country, football, golf, track and field (outdoor). *Women's intercollegiate varsity sports:* basketball, cross country, golf, softball, track and field (outdoor), volleyball.

SERVICES AND FACILITIES

Basic services: nonremedial tutoring, placement service, health service. **Remedial assistance:** math, writing, study skills. **Counseling services:** career, personal, academic, psychological, birth control, other. **For learning-disabled students:** School does not offer a structured program with separate admission and additional fees. Total undergraduates in learning-disabled program or receiving services: 22. Services include: remedial math, remedial English, tape recorders, videotaped classes, untimed tests, note-taking services, oral tests, readers, extended time for tests, tutors, early syllabus, priority seating, proofreading services, texts on tape, exams on tape or computer. **Library:** Number of titles: 116,220; number of current serial subscriptions: 22,835. **Information technology resources:** Students are not required to lease or own a computer. Number of campus computers available to all students: 183. School has a wireless network. Approximate number of users that can be accommodated: 900. Proportion of college-owned housing units wired for high-speed internet access: 100%. **Campus safety:** Security services offered: late-night transport/escort service, 24-hour emergency telephones, lighted pathways/sidewalks, student patrols, controlled dormitory access (key, security card, etc).

TRANSFER AND INTERNATIONAL STUDENTS

Transfer students: May apply for admission for the following academic terms: Fall, Spring, Summer. Applicants need a minimum number of credits to apply. For fall 2009: Transfer applications received: 165. Transfer applicants offered admission: 165. Transfer applicants enrolled: 83. **International students:** Number of foreign undergraduates: 0. Number of countries represented: 1. Minimum TOEFL score required: 550 (paper); 213 (computer).

Marshall University

- **Address:** 1 John Marshall Drive, Huntington, WV 25755
- **Website:** http://www.marshall.edu
- **Public**
- **Enrollment:** 8,043 full-time; 1,649 part-time

KEY STATS

✔ **U.S News College Ranking:** 47, Regional Universities (South)
✔ **ACT Score (25th/75th percentile):** 19-25
✔ **Tuition:** 2009-2010: $5,236 in state, $12,482 out of state

Selectivity: Selective	**Room/board:** $7,556
Acceptance rate: 86%	**Average debt:** $19,562
Student/faculty ratio: 19/1	**Proportion who borrowed:** 62%

UNDERGRADUATE STUDENT BODY STATS

2009-2010 enrollment: 8,043 full-time; 1,649 part-time. Men: 44%; women: 56%. **Ethnic makeup:** African American: 6%; Asian American: 1%; Hispanic: 1%; White: 90%; International: 1%.

ADMISSIONS FACTS AND FIGURES

Phone: (800) 642-3499. **Email:** admissions@marshall.edu. **Website:** http://www.marshall.edu. **Application deadlines for fall 2011:** Regular decision: Rolling. Early decision: Not offered. Early action: Not offered. Admission can be deferred. **Application fee:** $30. **To apply online, go to:** http://www.marshall.edu/admissions/apply.asp. **Admissions requirements/recommendations:** High school units required (recommended): English: 4; Mathematics: 4; Science: 3; Foreign language: 2; Social studies: 3; Total units: 20. Tests: The college uses SAT or ACT scores in admissions decisions. Either SAT or ACT required. For admission to the fall 2011 entering class, the school will accept: ACT with or without writing accepted. Campus visit: Recommended. Admissions interview: Neither required nor recommended. Off-campus interview: Not available. **Factors that count in admissions decisions:** *Academic:* Secondary school record: Considered. Class rank: Not Considered. Letters of recommendation: Not Considered. Standardized test scores: Very Important. Essay: Not Considered. *Nonacademic:* Interview: Not Considered. Extracurricular activities: Not Considered. Talent/ability: Not Considered. Character/personal qualities:

Not Considered. Alumni/ae relationship: Not Considered. Geographical residence: Not Considered. State residency: Not Considered. Religious affiliation/commitment: Not Considered. Minority status: Not Considered. Volunteer work: Not Considered. Work experience: Not Considered. **Admissions statistics for the fall 2009 entering class:** Total applicants: 2,577. Total accepted: 2,208. Freshmen enrolled: 1,882; 25% were from out of state. Overall acceptance rate: 86%. **Average high school grade point average:** 3.3. **First-year students who submitted SAT scores:** 26%. Scores (25/75 percentile): Critical Reading: 440-560, Math: 430-550, Combined: 870-1110. **First-year students submitting ACT scores:** 89%. Scores (25/75 percentile): English: 17-24, Math: 20-26, Composite: 19-25.

ACADEMICS

Year founded: 1837. **Academic calendar:** Semester. **Degrees offered:** certificate, associate, bachelor's, post-bachelor's certificate, master's, post-master's certificate, doctorate. **Major fields of study:** biological and biomedical sciences; business, management, marketing, and related support services; communication, journalism, and related programs; computer and information sciences and support services; education; engineering technologies/technicians; English language and literature/letters; family and consumer sciences/human sciences; foreign languages, literatures, and linguistics; health professions and related clinical sciences; history; liberal arts and sciences studies, and humanities; mathematics and statistics; multi/interdisciplinary studies; natural resources and conservation; parks, recreation, leisure, and fitness studies; physical sciences; psychology; public administration and social service professions; security and protective services; social sciences; visual and performing arts. **Areas of required coursework:** arts/fine arts, humanities, computer literacy, mathematics, English (including composition), foreign languages, sciences (biological or physical), social science. **Pre-professional programs:** pre-law, pre-dentistry, pre-medicine, pre-veterinary science, pre-pharmacy. **Special academic programs:** accelerated program, cooperative (work-study plan) program, cross-registration, distance learning, double major, dual enrollment, English as a Second Language (ESL), exchange student program (domestic), honors program, independent study, internships, study abroad, teacher certificate program. **Teacher certification offered in:** early childhood, special education, elementary, middle/junior high, secondary. **Cooperative education programs:** education, other. **Reserve Officers Training Corps (ROTC):** Army ROTC: Offered on campus. **Faculty and instruction (2009-2010):** Total instructional faculty: 478 full-time, 269 part-time (55% men; 45% women; 10% minorities). Full-time faculty with Ph.D. or other terminal degree: 80%. Student/faculty ratio: 19/1. Classes of fewer than 20 students: 40%; of 20 to 49 students: 55%; of 50 or more students: 5%. **Advanced Placement and International Baccalaureate credit:** AP tests may be used for: Credit and/or placement. Scores accepted: 3, 4, 5. International Baccalaureate exams may be used for: Credit only. **Freshmen returning for sophomore year:** 72%. **Graduation rates:** Four-year: 21%; five-year: 40%; six-year: 44%.

COSTS AND FINANCIAL AID

Financial aid office: (304) 696-3162. **Expenses (2009-2010):** Tuition and fees 2009-2010: $5,236 in state, $12,482 out of state; room/board: $7,556. Estimated books and supplies: $1,100 personal expenses: $2,230. **Financial aid:** Priority filing date for institution's financial aid form: March 1. In 2009-2010, 73% of undergraduates applied for financial aid. Of those, 57% were determined to have financial need; 30% had their need fully met. Average financial aid package (proportion receiving): $9,498 (56%). Average amount of gift aid, such as scholarships or grants (proportion receiving): $6,177 (39%). Average amount of self-help aid, such as work study or loans (proportion receiving): $6,923 (43%). Average need-based loan (excluding PLUS or other private loans): $6,871. Among students who received need-based aid, the average percentage of need met: 58%. Among students who received aid based on merit, the average award (and the proportion receiving): $6,063 (16%). The average athletic scholarship (and the proportion receiving): $11,995 (5%). Average amount of debt of borrowers graduating in 2009: $19,562. Proportion who borrowed: 62%.

CAMPUS LIFE AND EXTRACURRICULAR ACTIVITIES

Campus housing available: coed dorms, women's dorms, special housing for disabled students. **Student employment:** During the 2009-2010 academic year, 4% of undergraduates worked on campus. Average per-year earnings: $2,306. **Clubs and organizations:** Number of student organizations: 192. Activities include: campus ministries, choral groups, concert band, dance, drama/theater, international student organization, jazz band, literary magazine, marching band, music ensembles, musical theater, opera, pep band, radio station, student government, student newspaper, symphony orchestra, television station, yearbook. Number of fraternities: 13;

sororities: 8. **Sports program (2009-2010):** Member of NCAA I. *Men's inter-collegiate varsity sports:* baseball, basketball, cross country, football, golf, soccer. *Women's intercollegiate varsity sports:* basketball, cross country, golf, soccer, softball, swimming, tennis, track and field (indoor), track and field (outdoor), volleyball.

SERVICES AND FACILITIES
Basic services: nonremedial tutoring, women's center, placement service, day care, health service, health insurance. **Remedial assistance:** reading, math, writing, study skills. **Counseling services:** minority student, career, personal, veteran student, academic, older student, psychological, birth control, religious. **For learning-disabled students:** School does not offer a structured program with separate admission and additional fees. Services include: remedial math, remedial English, reading machines, remedial reading, tape recorders, diagnostic testing service, untimed tests, note-taking services, oral tests, learning center, readers, extended time for tests, tutors, priority registration, texts on tape, other testing accommodations, other. **Library:** Number of titles: 1,616,398; number of current serial subscriptions: 21,447. **Information technology resources:** Students are not required to lease or own a computer. Number of campus computers available to all students: 1,865. School has a wireless network. Approximate number of users that can be accommodated: 7,500. Proportion of college-owned housing units wired for high-speed internet access: 100%. **Campus safety:** Security services offered: 24-hour foot-and-vehicle patrols, late-night transport/escort service, 24-hour emergency telephones, lighted pathways/sidewalks, controlled dormitory access (key, security card, etc).

TRANSFER AND INTERNATIONAL STUDENTS
Transfer students: May apply for admission for the following academic terms: Fall, Spring, Summer. Applicants do not need a minimum number of credits to apply. For fall 2009: Transfer applications received: 1,018. Transfer applicants offered admission: 984. Transfer applicants enrolled: 839. **International students:** Number of foreign undergraduates: 110 (1% of student body). Number of countries represented: 50. Minimum TOEFL score required: 500 (paper); 173 (computer).

Mountain State University

- **Address:** 609 S. Kanawha Street, Beckley, WV 25802
- **Website:** http://www.mountainstate.edu
- **Private**
- **Enrollment:** 3,753 full-time; 1,490 part-time

KEY STATS
✔ **U.S News College Ranking:** second tier, Regional Universities (South)
✔ **ACT Score (25th/75th percentile):** 17-23
✔ **Tuition:** 2010-2011: $9,000

Selectivity: Less selective	**Room/board:** $6,366
Acceptance rate: 100%	**Average debt:** $33,218
Student/faculty ratio: 14/1	**Proportion who borrowed:** 81%

UNDERGRADUATE STUDENT BODY STATS
2009-2010 enrollment: 3,753 full-time; 1,490 part-time. Men: 33%; women: 67%. **Ethnic makeup:** African American: 15%; American-Indian: 1%; Asian American: 2%; Hispanic: 2%; White: 76%; International: 5%.

ADMISSIONS FACTS AND FIGURES
Phone: (304) 929-4636. **Email:** gomsu@mountainstate.edu. **Website:** http://www.mountainstate.edu. **Application deadlines for fall 2011:** Regular decision: Rolling. Early decision: Not offered. Early action: Not offered. Admission can be deferred. **Application fee:** $25. **To apply online, go to:** http://www.mountainstate.edu/prospective/enrollment/apply/apply_freshmen.aspx. **Admissions requirements/recommendations:** High school units required (recommended): English: 4 (4); Mathematics: 2 (2); Science: 2 (2); Foreign language: 0 (0); Social studies: 3 (3); History: 0 (2); Academic electives: 0 (0); Total units: 13 (15). **Tests:** The college uses SAT or ACT scores in admissions decisions. Neither SAT nor ACT required. For admission to the fall 2011 entering class, the school will accept: ACT with or without writing accepted. Campus visit: Recommended. Admissions interview: Recommended. Off-campus interview: May be arranged. **Factors that count in admissions decisions:** *Academic:* Secondary school record: Very Important. Class rank: Very Important. Letters of recommendation: Very Important. Standardized test scores: Very Important. Essay: Very Important.

Nonacademic: Interview: Very Important. Extracurricular activities: Very Important. Talent/ability: Very Important. Character/personal qualities: Very Important. Alumni/ae relationship: Very Important. Geographical residence: Very Important. State residency: Very Important. Religious affiliation/commitment: Very Important. Minority status: Very Important. Volunteer work: Very Important. Work experience: Very Important. **Other schools with the greatest overlap in applicants:** Bluefield State College; Concord University; Marshall University; West Virginia University; West Virginia University Institute of Technology. **Admissions statistics for the fall 2009 entering class:** Total applicants: 1,780. Total accepted: 1,780. Freshmen enrolled: 762; 39% were from out of state. Overall acceptance rate: 100%. **Credentials of fall 2009 freshmen:** 2% ranked in the top 10 percent of their high school class; 14% were in the top 25 percent; 41% were in the top half. (Proportion submitting class standing: 16%.) **Average high school grade point average:** 3.0. **First-year students submitting ACT scores:** 7%. Scores (25/75 percentile): English: 17-23, Math: 17-23, Composite: 17-23.

ACADEMICS
Year founded: 1933. **Academic calendar:** Semester. **Degrees offered:** certificate, associate, transfer-associate, terminal-associate, bachelor's, post-bachelor's certificate, master's, post-master's certificate. **Most popular majors:** 37% health professions and related clinical sciences, 31% business, management, marketing, and related support services, 15% security and protective services, 8% multi/interdisciplinary studies, 4% biological and biomedical sciences. **Major fields of study:** biological and biomedical sciences; business, management, marketing, and related support services; computer and information sciences and support services; education; engineering technologies/technicians; health professions and related clinical sciences; legal professions and studies; liberal arts and sciences studies, and humanities; library science; multi/interdisciplinary studies; parks, recreation, leisure, and fitness studies; personal and culinary services; psychology; public administration and social service professions; security and protective services; theology and religious vocations; visual and performing arts. **Areas of required coursework:** arts/fine arts, humanities, computer literacy, mathematics, English (including composition), sciences (biological or physical), social science, other. **Pre-professional programs:** pre-law, pre-medicine. **Special academic programs (% participation):** accelerated program (38%), distance learning (63%), double major (.6%), dual enrollment (.6%), English as a Second Language (ESL) (.3%), independent study (63%), internships (88%), liberal arts/career combination (.2%), student-designed major (.9%), weekend college (9%). **Cooperative education programs:** business, computer science, engineering, health professions, natural science, social/behavioral science, technologies. **Faculty and instruction (2009-2010):** Total instructional faculty: 97 full-time, 335 part-time (43% men; 57% women; 61% minorities). Full-time faculty with Ph.D. or other terminal degree: 29%. Student/faculty ratio: 14/1. Classes of fewer than 20 students: 66%; of 20 to 49 students: 33%; of 50 or more students: 1%. **Advanced Placement and International Baccalaureate credit:** AP tests may be used for: Credit only. Scores accepted: 3. International Baccalaureate exams may be used for: Credit only. **Freshmen returning for sophomore year:** 45%. **Graduation rates:** Four-year: 3%; five-year: 5%; six-year: 13%. **Graduate study:** 20% of students pursue further study immediately upon graduation; 40% within one year; 20% within five years. Fields in which graduates pursue further study: Master of Business Administration (MBA), 5%; law, 3%; medicine, 3%; education, 10%.

COSTS AND FINANCIAL AID
Financial aid office: (304) 929-1595. **Expenses (2010-2011):** Tuition and fees 2010-2011: $9,000; room/board: $6,366. Estimated books and supplies: $1,300; transportation: $600; personal expenses: $600. **Financial aid:** Priority filing date for institution's financial aid form: March 1. In 2009-2010, 50% of undergraduates applied for financial aid. Of those, 50% were determined to have financial need; 4% had their need fully met. Average financial aid package (proportion receiving): $7,033 (50%). Average amount of gift aid, such as scholarships or grants (proportion receiving): $4,211 (35%). Average amount of self-help aid, such as work study or loans (proportion receiving): $4,647 (46%). Average need-based loan (excluding PLUS or other private loans): $4,592. Among students who received need-based aid, the average percentage of need met: 48%. Among students who received aid based on merit, the average award (and the proportion receiving): $4,214 (0%). The average athletic scholarship (and the proportion receiving): $5,329 (2%). Average amount of debt of borrowers graduating in 2009: $33,218. Proportion who borrowed: 81%.

CAMPUS LIFE AND EXTRACURRICULAR ACTIVITIES

Campus housing available (% using): coed dorms (5%), other housing options (95%). Students who live in college-owned, operated, or affiliated housing: 4%. **Student employment:** During the 2009-2010 academic year, 4% of undergraduates worked on campus. Average per-year earnings: $1,800. **Clubs and organizations:** Number of student organizations: 19. Activities include: campus ministries, choral groups, concert band, drama/theater, international student organization, literary magazine, music ensembles, pep band, student government. Number of fraternities: 1; sororities: 1. Average proportion of students who stay on campus on weekends: 80%. **Sports program (2009-2010):** Member of NAIA. *Men's intercollegiate varsity sports:* basketball, cross country, soccer, track and field (indoor). *Women's intercollegiate varsity sports:* cross country, track and field (indoor), volleyball.

SERVICES AND FACILITIES

Basic services: placement service. **Remedial assistance:** reading, math, writing, study skills. **Counseling services:** career, veteran student, academic. **For learning-disabled students:** School does not offer a structured program with separate admission and additional fees. Services include: remedial math, remedial English, reading machines, remedial reading, tape recorders, videotaped classes, diagnostic testing service, untimed tests, note-taking services, oral tests, learning center, readers, extended time for tests, tutors. **Library:** Number of titles: 118,195; number of current serial subscriptions: 173. **Information technology resources:** Students are not required to lease or own a computer. Number of campus computers available to all students: 167. School has a wireless network. Approximate number of users that can be accommodated: 1,000. Proportion of college-owned housing units wired for high-speed internet access: 100%. **Campus safety:** Security services offered: 24-hour foot-and-vehicle patrols, lighted pathways/sidewalks, student patrols, controlled dormitory access (key, security card, etc).

TRANSFER AND INTERNATIONAL STUDENTS

Transfer students: May apply for admission for the following academic terms: Fall, Winter, Spring, Summer. Applicants do not need a minimum number of credits to apply. For fall 2009: Transfer applications received: 1,845. Transfer applicants offered admission: 1,845. Transfer applicants enrolled: 839. **International students:** Number of foreign undergraduates: 244 (5% of student body). Number of countries represented: 44. Minimum TOEFL score required: 500 (paper); 173 (computer). Average TOEFL score: 520 (paper).

Ohio Valley University

- **Address:** 1 Campus View Drive, Vienna, WV 26105-8000
- **Website:** http://www.ovu.edu
- **Private; Religious affiliation:** Church of Christ
- **Enrollment:** 415 full-time; 64 part-time

KEY STATS

✔ **U.S News College Ranking:** 46, Regional Colleges (South)
✔ **ACT Score (25th/75th percentile):** 19-23
✔ **Tuition:** 2010-2011: $16,960

Selectivity: Selective	**Room/board:** N/A
Acceptance rate: 57%	**Average debt:** $14,976
Student/faculty ratio: 11/1	**Proportion who borrowed:** 93%

UNDERGRADUATE STUDENT BODY STATS

2009-2010 enrollment: 415 full-time; 64 part-time. Men: 47%; women: 53%. **Ethnic makeup:** African American: 5%; Hispanic: 4%; White: 85%; International: 7%. **Religious preference:** Church of Christ: 51%; Other: 49%.

ADMISSIONS FACTS AND FIGURES

Phone: (877) 446-8668. **Email:** admissions@ovu.edu. **Website:** http://www.ovu.edu. **Application deadlines for fall 2011:** Regular decision: July 31. Early decision: Not offered. Early action: Not offered. Admission can be deferred. **Application fee:** $20. **To apply online, go to:** http://www.ovu.edu/site.cfm/onlineapplication.cfm. **Admissions requirements/recommendations:** High school units required (recommended): English: 3 (3); Mathematics: 3 (3); Science: 3 (3); Foreign language: (0); Social studies: 2 (2); History: 1 (1); Academic electives: (0); Total units: 12 (3). Tests: The college uses SAT or ACT scores in admissions decisions. Either SAT or ACT required. For admission to the fall 2011 entering class, the school will accept: ACT with or without writing accepted. Campus visit: Recommended. Admissions interview: Neither required nor recommended. Off-campus interview: May be arranged. **Factors that count in admissions decisions:** *Academic:* Secondary school record: Very Important. Class rank: Important. Letters of recommendation: Considered. Standardized test scores: Very Important. Essay: Considered. *Nonacademic:* Interview: Considered. Extracurricular activities: Not Considered. Talent/ability: Not Considered. Character/personal qualities: Very Important. Alumni/ae relationship: Considered. Geographical residence: Not Considered. State residency: Not Considered. Religious affiliation/commitment: Considered. Minority status: Not Considered. Volunteer work: Not Considered. Work experience: Not Considered. **Other schools with the greatest overlap in applicants:** Freed-Hardeman University; Harding University; Lipscomb University; Marshall University; West Virginia University–Parkersburg. **Admissions statistics for the fall 2009 entering class:** Total applicants: 437. Total accepted: 251. Freshmen enrolled: 90; 12% were from out of state. Overall acceptance rate: 57%. **Size of waiting list:** 0 applicants; enrolled from waiting list: 0. **Credentials of fall 2009 freshmen:** 16% ranked in the top 10 percent of their high school class; 26% were in the top 25 percent; 56% were in the top half. (Proportion submitting class standing: 71%.) **Average high school grade point average:** 3.0. **First-year students who submitted SAT scores:** 26%. Scores (25/75 percentile): Critical Reading: 430-510, Math: 440-500, Combined: 870-1010. **First-year students submitting ACT scores:** 86%. Scores (25/75 percentile): English: 18-24, Math: 17-23, Composite: 19-23.

ACADEMICS

Year founded: 1958. **Academic calendar:** Semester. **Degrees offered:** certificate, associate, bachelor's, master's. **Most popular majors:** 53% business/commerce, 16% elementary education and teaching, 13% psychology, 8% Bible/biblical studies. **Major fields of study:** business, management, marketing, and related support services; education; liberal arts and sciences studies, and humanities; psychology; theology and religious vocations. **Areas of required coursework:** arts/fine arts, humanities, computer literacy, mathematics, English (including composition), sciences (biological or physical), history, social science, other. **Pre-professional programs:** pre-law. **Special academic programs (% participation):** accelerated program, distance learning (78%), double major (.5%), English as a Second Language (ESL) (0%), honors program, independent study, internships (32%), study abroad (20%), teacher certificate program (32%), weekend college. **Teacher certification offered in:** special education, elementary, middle/junior high, secondary. **Faculty and instruction (2009-2010):** Total instructional faculty: 23 full-time, 50 part-time (62% men; 38% women; 4% minorities). Full-time faculty with Ph.D. or other terminal degree: 65%. Student/faculty ratio: 11/1. Classes of fewer than 20 students: 78%; of 20 to 49 students: 22%. **Advanced Placement and International Baccalaureate credit:** AP tests may be used for: Placement only. Scores accepted: 3, 4, 5. International Baccalaureate exams may be used for: Credit only. **Freshmen returning for sophomore year:** 64%. **Graduation rates:** Four-year: 46%; five-year: 46%; six-year: 49%.

COSTS AND FINANCIAL AID

Financial aid office: (304) 865-6075. **Expenses (2010-2011):** Tuition and fees 2010-2011: $16,960. Estimated books and supplies: $1,000; transportation: $1,200; personal expenses: $800. **Financial aid:** Priority filing date for institution's financial aid form: March 1; deadline: March 1. In 2009-2010, 90% of undergraduates applied for financial aid. Of those, 78% were determined to have financial need; 17% had their need fully met. Average financial aid package (proportion receiving): $12,250 (76%). Average amount of gift aid, such as scholarships or grants (proportion receiving): $9,162 (69%). Average amount of self-help aid, such as work study or loans (proportion receiving): $4,610 (65%). Average need-based loan (excluding PLUS or other private loans): $4,202. Among students who received need-based aid, the average percentage of need met: 68%. Among students who received aid based on merit, the average award (and the proportion receiving): $6,447 (10%). The average athletic scholarship (and the proportion receiving): $8,302 (12%). Average amount of debt of borrowers graduating in 2009: $14,976. Proportion who borrowed: 93%.

CAMPUS LIFE AND EXTRACURRICULAR ACTIVITIES

Campus housing available (% using): women's dorms (47%), men's dorms (44%), apartments for married students (9%). Students who live in college-owned, operated, or affiliated housing: 55%. **Student employment:** During the 2009-2010 academic year, 17% of undergraduates worked on campus. Average per-year earnings: $1,000. **Clubs and organizations:** Number of student organizations: 2. Activities include: choral groups, concert band, drama/theater, jazz band, literary magazine, music ensembles, musical theater, pep band, student government, student newspaper, symphony orchestra. Number of fraternities: 4; sororities: 4. Average proportion of students who stay on campus on weekends: 60%. **Sports program (2009-2010):** Member of NCAA II. *Men's intercollegiate varsity sports:* baseball, basketball, cross country, golf, soccer. *Women's intercollegiate varsity sports:* basketball, cross country, golf, soccer, softball, volleyball.

SERVICES AND FACILITIES

Basic services: nonremedial tutoring, placement service, health service, health insurance. **Remedial assistance:** reading, math, writing, study skills, other. **Counseling services:** minority student, career, personal, academic, older student, psychological, religious. **For learning-disabled students:** School does not offer a structured program with separate admission and additional fees. Services include: remedial math, remedial English, remedial reading, tape recorders, other special classes, untimed tests, note-taking services, oral tests, learning center, readers, extended time for tests, tutors, priority seating, other testing accommodations. **Library:** Number of titles: 36,000; number of current serial subscriptions: 145. **Information technology resources:** Students are not required to lease or own a computer. Number of campus computers available to all students: 75. School has a wireless network. Approximate number of users that can be accommodated: 200. Proportion of college-owned housing units wired for high-speed internet access: 100%. **Campus safety:** Security services offered: 24-hour emergency telephones, lighted pathways/sidewalks, controlled dormitory access (key, security card, etc).

TRANSFER AND INTERNATIONAL STUDENTS

Transfer students: May apply for admission for the following academic terms: Fall, Spring. Applicants need a minimum number of credits to apply. For fall 2009: Transfer applications received: 137. Transfer applicants offered admission: 79. Transfer applicants enrolled: 42. **International students:** Number of foreign undergraduates: 29 (7% of student body). Number of countries represented: 8. Minimum TOEFL score required: 500 (paper); 173 (computer). Average TOEFL score: 500 (paper).

Shepherd University

- **Address:** PO Box 3210, Shepherdstown, WV 25443-3210
- **Website:** http://www.shepherd.edu
- **Public**
- **Enrollment:** 3,301 full-time; 801 part-time

KEY STATS

✔ **U.S News College Ranking:** 44, Regional Colleges (South)
✔ **ACT Score (25th/75th percentile):** 20-24
✔ **Tuition:** 2009-2010: $5,234 in state, $13,574 out of state

Selectivity: Selective	Room/board: $7,522
Acceptance rate: 94%	Average debt: $20,053
Student/faculty ratio: 19/1	Proportion who borrowed: 65%

UNDERGRADUATE STUDENT BODY STATS

2009-2010 enrollment: 3,301 full-time; 801 part-time. Men: 43%; women: 57%. **Ethnic makeup:** African American: 5%; Asian American: 2%; Hispanic: 2%; White: 90%.

ADMISSIONS FACTS AND FIGURES

Phone: (304) 876-5212. **Email:** admissions@shepherd.edu. **Website:** http://www.shepherd.edu. **Application deadlines for fall 2011:** Regular decision: Rolling. Early decision: Not offered. Early action: Send application by: November 15; Decision sent by: December 15. Admission can be deferred. **Application fee:** $45. **To apply online, go to:** http://www.shepherd.edu/admweb/. **Admissions requirements/recommendations:** High school units required (recommended): English: 4; Mathematics: 4; Science: 3; Foreign language: 2; Social studies: 2; History: 1; Academic electives: 7; Total units: 23. Tests: The college uses SAT or ACT scores in admissions decisions. Either SAT or ACT required. For admission to the fall 2011 entering class, the school will accept: ACT with or without writing accepted. Campus visit: Recommended. Admissions interview: Recommended. Off-campus interview: Not available. **Factors that count in admissions decisions:** *Academic:* Secondary school record: Very Important. Class rank: Considered. Letters of recommendation: Considered. Standardized test scores: Very Important. Essay: Considered. *Nonacademic:* Interview: Considered. Extracurricular activities: Considered. Talent/ability: Considered. Character/personal qualities: Considered. Alumni/ae relationship: Not Considered. Geographical

residence: Not Considered. State residency: Not Considered. Religious affiliation/commitment: Not Considered. Minority status: Not Considered. Volunteer work: Considered. Work experience: Considered. **Other schools with the greatest overlap in applicants:** Bridgewater College; Frostburg State University; Radford University; Salisbury University; West Virginia University. **Admissions statistics for the fall 2009 entering class:** Total applicants: 1,768. Total accepted: 1,657. Freshmen enrolled: 801; 38% were from out of state. Overall acceptance rate: 94%. Non-early acceptance rate: 94%. **Average high school grade point average:** 3.2. **First-year students who submitted SAT scores:** 40%. Scores (25/75 percentile): Critical Reading: 450-560, Math: 450-550, Combined: 900-1110. **First-year students submitting ACT scores:** 56%. Scores (25/75 percentile): English: 17-23, Math: 20-25, Composite: 20-24.

ACADEMICS

Year founded: 1871. **Academic calendar:** Semester. **Degrees offered:** bachelor's, master's. **Most popular majors:** 18% business, management, marketing, and related support services, 15% education, 14% liberal arts and sciences studies, and humanities, 8% health professions and related clinical sciences, 8% visual and performing arts. **Major fields of study:** biological and biomedical sciences; business, management, marketing, and related support services; communication, journalism, and related programs; computer and information sciences and support services; education; English language and literature/letters; family and consumer sciences/human sciences; foreign languages, literatures, and linguistics; health professions and related clinical sciences; history; mathematics and statistics; natural resources and conservation; parks, recreation, leisure, and fitness studies; physical sciences; psychology; public administration and social service professions; social sciences; visual and performing arts. **Areas of required coursework:** arts/fine arts, humanities, computer literacy, mathematics, English (including composition), sciences (biological or physical), history, social science, other. **Pre-professional programs:** pre-law, pre-dentistry, pre-medicine, pre-veterinary science. **Special academic programs (% participation):** cooperative (work-study plan) program, distance learning (5%), double major (3%), honors program (5%), independent study (5%), internships (13%), study abroad (5%), teacher certificate program (13%). **Teacher certification offered in:** early childhood, elementary, middle/junior high, secondary. **Cooperative education programs:** art, business, computer science, education, engineering, health professions, home economics, humanities, natural science, social/behavioral science. **Reserve Officers Training Corps (ROTC):** Air Force ROTC: Offered at cooperating institution (University of Maryland–College Park). **Faculty and instruction (2009-2010):** Total instructional faculty: 124 full-time, 210 part-time (53% men; 47% women; 14% minorities). Full-time faculty with Ph.D. or other terminal degree: 81%. Student/faculty ratio: 19/1. Classes of fewer than 20 students: 40%; of 20 to 49 students: 59%; of 50 or more students: 1%. **Advanced Placement and International Baccalaureate credit:** AP tests may be used for: Credit only. Scores accepted: 3, 4, 5. International Baccalaureate exams may be used for: Credit only. **Freshmen returning for sophomore year:** 67%. **Graduation rates:** Four-year: 21%; five-year: 38%; six-year: 40%. **Graduate study:** 43% of students pursue further study immediately upon graduation; 43% within one year. Fields in which graduates pursue further study: Master of Business Administration (MBA), 28%; law, 4%; theology (or the seminary), 4%; education, 16%; arts and sciences, 48%.

COSTS AND FINANCIAL AID

Financial aid office: (304) 876-5470. **Expenses (2009-2010):** Tuition and fees 2009-2010: $5,234 in state, $13,574 out of state; room/board: $7,522. Estimated books and supplies: $1,100; transportation: $1,125; personal expenses: $1,000. **Financial aid:** Priority filing date for institution's financial aid form: March 1. In 2009-2010, 86% of undergraduates applied for financial aid. Of those, 51% were determined to have financial need; 23% had their need fully met. Average financial aid package (proportion receiving): $10,791 (50%). Average amount of gift aid, such as scholarships or grants (proportion receiving): $4,145 (33%). Average amount of self-help aid, such as work study or loans (proportion receiving): $3,941 (41%). Average need-based loan (excluding PLUS or other private loans): $3,888. Among students who received need-based aid, the average percentage of need met: 84%. Among students who received aid based on merit, the average award (and the proportion receiving): $8,775 (23%). The average athletic scholarship (and the proportion receiving): $5,910 (5%). Average amount of debt of borrowers graduating in 2009: $20,053. Proportion who borrowed: 65%.

CAMPUS LIFE AND EXTRACURRICULAR ACTIVITIES

Campus housing available (% using): coed dorms (55%), apartment for single students (23%), other housing options (22%). Students who live in college-owned, operated, or affiliated housing: 34%. **Student employment:** During the 2009-2010 academic year, 15% of undergraduates worked on campus. Average per-year earnings: $1,700. **Clubs and organizations:** Number of student organizations: 58. Activities include: choral groups, concert band, dance, drama/theater, jazz band, literary magazine, marching band, music ensembles, musical theater, pep band, radio station, student government, student newspaper, student film society, symphony orchestra. Number of fraternities: 4; sororities: 3. Proportion of men in fraternities: 3%; of women in sororities: 4%. Average proportion of students who stay on campus on weekends: 40%. **Sports program (2009-2010):** Member of NCAA II. *Men's intercollegiate varsity sports:* baseball, basketball, football, golf, soccer, tennis. *Women's intercollegiate varsity sports:* basketball, lacrosse, soccer, softball, tennis, volleyball.

SERVICES AND FACILITIES

Basic services: health service, other. **Remedial assistance:** reading, math, writing, study skills, other. **Counseling services:** minority student, career, military, personal, veteran student, academic, older student, psychological, birth control. **For learning-disabled students:** School does not offer a structured program with separate admission and additional fees. Total undergraduates in learning-disabled program or receiving services: 146. Services include: tape recorders, videotaped classes, note-taking services, oral tests, learning center, readers, extended time for tests, tutors, priority registration, priority seating, proofreading services, texts on tape, typist/scribe, other testing accommodations, other. **Library:** Number of titles: 183,219; number of current serial subscriptions: 495. **Information technology resources:** Students are not required to lease or own a computer. Number of campus computers available to all students: 380. School has a wireless network. Approximate number of users that can be accommodated: 1,000. Proportion of college-owned housing units wired for high-speed internet access: 100%. **Campus safety:** Security services offered: 24-hour foot-and-vehicle patrols, late-night transport/escort service, 24-hour emergency telephones, lighted pathways/sidewalks, student patrols, controlled dormitory access (key, security card, etc).

TRANSFER AND INTERNATIONAL STUDENTS

Transfer students: May apply for admission for the following academic terms: Fall, Spring, Summer. Applicants need a minimum number of credits to apply. For fall 2009: Transfer applications received: 613. Transfer applicants offered admission: 589. Transfer applicants enrolled: 354. **International students:** Number of foreign undergraduates: 17. Number of countries represented: 15. Minimum TOEFL score required: 550 (paper); 79 (computer).

University of Charleston

- **Address:** 2300 MacCorkle Avenue SE, Charleston, WV 25304
- **Website:** http://www.ucwv.edu
- **Private**
- **Enrollment:** 981 full-time; 31 part-time

KEY STATS

✔ **U.S News College Ranking:** 11, Regional Colleges (South)
✔ **ACT Score (25th/75th percentile):** 19-24
✔ **Tuition:** 2010-2011: $24,700

Selectivity: Selective	**Room/board:** $8,700
Acceptance rate: 79%	**Average debt:** N/A
Student/faculty ratio: 14/1	**Proportion who borrowed:** N/A

UNDERGRADUATE STUDENT BODY STATS

2009-2010 enrollment: 981 full-time; 31 part-time. Men: 41%; women: 59%. **Ethnic makeup:** African American: 8%; Asian American: 1%; Hispanic: 1%; White: 80%; International: 10%.

ADMISSIONS FACTS AND FIGURES

Phone: (800) 995-4682. **Email:** admissions@ucwv.edu. **Website:** http://www.ucwv.edu. **Application deadlines for fall 2011:** Regular decision: Rolling. Early decision: Not offered. Early action: Not offered. Admission can be deferred. **Application fee:** $25. **To apply online, go to:** http://www.ucwv.edu/admissions/online_application.aspx. **Admissions requirements/recommendations:** High school units required (recommended): English: (4); Mathematics: (3); Science: (3); Foreign language: (1); Social studies: (3); History: (2); Total units: (16). Tests: The college uses SAT or ACT

scores in admissions decisions. Either SAT or ACT required. For admission to the fall 2011 entering class, the school will accept: ACT with or without writing accepted. Campus visit: Recommended. Admissions interview: Recommended. Off-campus interview: May be arranged. **Factors that count in admissions decisions: Academic:** Secondary school record: Important. Class rank: Important. Letters of recommendation: Considered. Standardized test scores: Very Important. Essay: Considered. **Nonacademic:** Interview: Considered. Extracurricular activities: Important. Talent/ability: Considered. Character/personal qualities: Considered. Alumni/ae relationship: Important. Geographical residence: Not Considered. State residency: Not Considered. Religious affiliation/commitment: Not Considered. Minority status: Not Considered. Volunteer work: Considered. Work experience: Considered. **Other schools with the greatest overlap in applicants:** Marshall University; West Virginia State University; West Virginia University; West Virginia Wesleyan College. **Admissions statistics for the fall 2009 entering class:** Total applicants: 1,225. Total accepted: 970. Freshmen enrolled: 273; 46% were from out of state. Overall acceptance rate: 79%. **Credentials of fall 2009 freshmen:** 20% ranked in the top 10 percent of their high school class; 44% were in the top 25 percent; 74% were in the top half. (Proportion submitting class standing: 58%.) **Average high school grade point average:** 3.3. **First-year students who submitted SAT scores:** 33%. Scores (25/75 percentile): Critical Reading: 440-530, Math: 430-520, Combined: 870-1050. **First-year students submitting ACT scores:** 68%. Scores (25/75 percentile): English: 18-25, Math: 17-24, Composite: 19-24.

ACADEMICS

Year founded: 1888. **Academic calendar:** Semester. **Degrees offered:** associate, terminal-associate, bachelor's, master's. **Most popular majors:** 22% business, management, marketing, and related support services, 18% health professions and related clinical sciences, 15% biological and biomedical sciences, 7% visual and performing arts, 6% communication, journalism, and related programs. **Major fields of study:** biological and biomedical sciences; business, management, marketing, and related support services; computer and information sciences and support services; education; English language and literature/letters; health professions and related clinical sciences; history; liberal arts and sciences studies, and humanities; natural resources and conservation; parks, recreation, leisure, and fitness studies; physical sciences; psychology; social sciences; visual and performing arts. **Areas of required coursework:** humanities, computer literacy, mathematics, English (including composition), sciences (biological or physical), history, social science, other. **Pre-professional programs:** pre-pharmacy. **Special academic programs:** cooperative (work-study plan) program, double major, dual enrollment, English as a Second Language (ESL), honors program, independent study, internships, liberal arts/career combination, student-designed major, study abroad. **Teacher certification offered in:** special education, elementary, middle/junior high, secondary. **Reserve Officers Training Corps (ROTC):** Army ROTC: Offered on campus. **Faculty and instruction (2009-2010):** Total instructional faculty: 86 full-time, 34 part-time (41% men; 59% women; 8% minorities). Full-time faculty with Ph.D. or other terminal degree: 59%. Student/faculty ratio: 14/1. Classes of fewer than 20 students: 82%; of 20 to 49 students: 17%; of 50 or more students: 2%. **Advanced Placement and International Baccalaureate credit:** AP tests may be used for: Credit only. Scores accepted: 3, 4, 5. **Freshmen returning for sophomore year:** 67%. **Graduation rates:** Four-year: 38%; five-year: 43%; six-year: 43%. **Graduate study:** 42% of students pursue further study immediately upon graduation. Fields in which graduates pursue further study: Master of Business Administration (MBA), 21%; law, 6%; medicine, 2%; dentistry, 2%; theology (or the seminary), 2%; education, 6%; arts and sciences, 62%.

COSTS AND FINANCIAL AID

Financial aid office: (304) 357-4759. **Expenses (2010-2011):** Tuition and fees 2010-2011: $24,700; room/board: $8,700. Estimated books and supplies: $1,500; transportation: $750; personal expenses: $250. **Financial aid:** Priority filing date for institution's financial aid form: March 1; deadline: August 15.

CAMPUS LIFE AND EXTRACURRICULAR ACTIVITIES

Campus housing available (% using): coed dorms (80%), other housing options (20%). Students who live in college-owned, operated, or affiliated housing: 59%. **Student employment:** During the 2009-2010 academic year, 14% of undergraduates worked on campus. Average per-year earnings: $1,000. **Clubs and organizations:** Number of student organizations: 42. Activities include: campus ministries, choral groups, dance, drama/theater, model UN, music ensembles, pep band, student government, student newspaper, yearbook. Number of fraternities: 2; sororities: 3. Proportion of men in fraternities: 2%; of women in sororities: 4%. Average proportion of students who stay on campus on weekends: 70%. **Sports program (2009-2010):** Member of NCAA II.

SERVICES AND FACILITIES
Basic services: nonremedial tutoring, placement service. **Remedial assistance:** reading, math, writing, study skills. **Counseling services:** career, personal, academic, psychological. **For learning-disabled students:** School does not offer a structured program with separate admission and additional fees. Services include: remedial English, reading machines, remedial reading, tape recorders, other special classes, untimed tests, note-taking services, oral tests, learning center, readers, extended time for tests, tutors, priority seating, texts on tape, other. **Library:** Number of titles: 164,457; number of current serial subscriptions: 14,192. **Information technology resources:** Students are not required to lease or own a computer. Number of campus computers available to all students: 200. School has a wireless network. Approximate number of users that can be accommodated: 2,000. Proportion of college-owned housing units wired for high-speed internet access: 100%. **Campus safety:** Security services offered: 24-hour foot-and-vehicle patrols, late-night transport/escort service, 24-hour emergency telephones, lighted pathways/sidewalks, controlled dormitory access (key, security card, etc).

TRANSFER AND INTERNATIONAL STUDENTS
Transfer students: May apply for admission for the following academic terms: Fall, Spring, Summer. Applicants need a minimum number of credits to apply. **International students:** Number of foreign undergraduates: 96 (10% of student body). Number of countries represented: 15. Minimum TOEFL score required: 550 (paper); 79 (computer).

West Liberty University

- **Address:** Route 88, PO Box 295, West Liberty, WV 26074-0295
- **Website:** http://www.westliberty.edu
- **Public**
- **Enrollment:** 2,266 full-time; 331 part-time

KEY STATS
✔ **U.S News College Ranking:** 49, Regional Colleges (South)
✔ **ACT Score (25th/75th percentile):** 18-23
✔ **Tuition:** 2009-2010: $4,880 in state, $11,950 out of state
  Selectivity: Selective   **Room/board:** $6,870
  Acceptance rate: 79%   **Average debt:** $18,910
  Student/faculty ratio: 17/1   **Proportion who borrowed:** 82%

UNDERGRADUATE STUDENT BODY STATS
2009-2010 enrollment: 2,266 full-time; 331 part-time. Men: 44%; women: 56%. **Ethnic makeup:** African American: 3%; Asian American: 1%; Hispanic: 1%; White: 94%; International: 1%.

ADMISSIONS FACTS AND FIGURES
Phone: (304) 336-8076. **Email:** admissions@westliberty.edu. **Website:** http://www.westliberty.edu. **Application deadlines for fall 2011:** Regular decision: Rolling. Early decision: Not offered. Early action: Not offered. Admission cannot be deferred. **To apply online, go to:** http://www.westliberty.edu/students/admissions/?id=684. **Admissions requirements/recommendations:** High school units required (recommended): English: 4; Mathematics: 4; Science: 3; Foreign language: 2; Social studies: 2; History: 1. Tests: The college uses SAT or ACT scores in admissions decisions. Either SAT or ACT required. For admission to the fall 2011 entering class, the school will accept: ACT with writing required. Campus visit: Recommended. Admissions interview: Recommended. Off-campus interview: May be arranged. **Factors that count in admissions decisions:** *Academic:* Secondary school record: Very Important. Class rank: Not Considered. Letters of recommendation: Considered. Standardized test scores: Very Important. Essay: Not Considered. *Nonacademic:* Interview: Not Considered. Extracurricular activities: Not Considered. Talent/ability: Considered. Character/personal qualities: Not Considered. Alumni/ae relationship: Not Considered. Geographical residence: Not Considered. State residency: Not Considered. Religious affiliation/commitment: Not Considered. Minority status: Not Considered. Volunteer work: Not Considered. Work experience: Not Considered. **Other schools with the greatest overlap in applicants:** Bethany University; Fairmont State University; Ohio University; West Virginia University; Wheeling Jesuit University. **Admissions statistics for the fall 2009 entering class:** Total applicants: 1,773. Total accepted: 1,392. Freshmen

enrolled: 578; 32% were from out of state. Overall acceptance rate: 79%. **Credentials of fall 2009 freshmen:** 10% ranked in the top 10 percent of their high school class; 30% were in the top 25 percent; 65% were in the top half. (Proportion submitting class standing: 78%.) **Average high school grade point average:** 3.2. **First-year students who submitted SAT scores:** 12%. Scores (25/75 percentile): Critical Reading: 390-490, Math: 380-490, Combined: 770-980. **First-year students submitting ACT scores:** 88%. Scores (25/75 percentile): English: 17-23, Math: 16-22, Composite: 18-23.

ACADEMICS
Year founded: 1837. **Academic calendar:** Semester. **Degrees offered:** associate, bachelor's. **Most popular majors:** 23% business, management, marketing, and related support services, 22% education, 15% health professions and related clinical sciences, 8% liberal arts and sciences studies, and humanities, 7% security and protective services. **Major fields of study:** biological and biomedical sciences; business, management, marketing, and related support services; communication, journalism, and related programs; education; English language and literature/letters; health professions and related clinical sciences; history; liberal arts and sciences studies, and humanities; mathematics and statistics; multi/interdisciplinary studies; parks, recreation, leisure, and fitness studies; physical sciences; psychology; security and protective services; social sciences; visual and performing arts. **Areas of required coursework:** arts/fine arts, humanities, computer literacy, mathematics, English (including composition), philosophy, sciences (biological or physical), history, social science, other. **Pre-professional programs:** pre-law, pre-dentistry, pre-medicine, pre-veterinary science, pre-optometry, pre-pharmacy, other. **Special academic programs:** accelerated program, cooperative (work-study plan) program, distance learning, double major, dual enrollment, honors program, independent study, internships, liberal arts/career combination, student-designed major, study abroad, teacher certificate program, weekend college, other. **Teacher certification offered in:** early childhood, special education, elementary, middle/junior high, secondary. **Reserve Officers Training Corps (ROTC):** Army ROTC: Offered at cooperating institution (Franciscan University of Steubenville). **Faculty and instruction (2009-2010):** Total instructional faculty: 114 full-time, 88 part-time (51% men; 49% women; 3% minorities). Full-time faculty with Ph.D. or other terminal degree: 49%. Student/faculty ratio: 17/1. Classes of fewer than 20 students: 45%; of 20 to 49 students: 54%; of 50 or more students: 0%. **Advanced Placement and International Baccalaureate credit:** AP tests may be used for: Credit only. **Freshmen returning for sophomore year:** 69%. **Graduation rates:** Six-year: 45%. **Graduate study:** 20% of students pursue further study immediately upon graduation; 25% within one year; 33% within five years. Fields in which graduates pursue further study: Master of Business Administration (MBA), 22%; law, 7%; medicine, 3%; dentistry, 2%; engineering, 3%; theology (or the seminary), 1%; education, 49%; arts and sciences, 12%; veterinary medicine, 1%.

COSTS AND FINANCIAL AID
Financial aid office: (304) 336-8016. **Expenses (2009-2010):** Tuition and fees 2009-2010: $4,880 in state, $11,950 out of state; room/board: $6,870. **Financial aid:** Priority filing date for institution's financial aid form: March 1. In 2009-2010, 88% of undergraduates applied for financial aid. Of those, 67% were determined to have financial need; Average financial aid package (proportion receiving): $8,023 (85%). Average amount of gift aid, such as scholarships or grants (proportion receiving): $5,177 (47%). Average amount of self-help aid, such as work study or loans (proportion receiving): $4,483 (55%). Average need-based loan (excluding PLUS or other private loans): $4,311. Average amount of debt of borrowers graduating in 2009: $18,910. Proportion who borrowed: 82%.

CAMPUS LIFE AND EXTRACURRICULAR ACTIVITIES
Campus housing available (% using): coed dorms (68%), women's dorms (14%), men's dorms (14%), sorority housing (1%), fraternity housing (1%), apartments for married students (0%), apartment for single students (0%), special housing for disabled students (2%). Students who live in college-owned, operated, or affiliated housing: 37%. **Clubs and organizations:** Number of student organizations: 32. Activities include: choral groups, concert band, dance, drama/theater, jazz band, literary magazine, music ensembles, musical theater, pep band, radio station, student government, student newspaper, television station. Number of fraternities: 9; sororities: 4. Average proportion of students who stay on campus on weekends: 20%. **Sports program (2009-2010):** Member of NCAA II. *Men's intercollegiate varsity sports:* baseball, basketball, cross country, football, golf, track and field (indoor), track and field (outdoor), wrestling. *Women's intercollegiate varsity sports:* basketball, cross country, golf, softball, track and field (indoor), track and field (outdoor), volleyball.

SERVICES AND FACILITIES

Basic services: nonremedial tutoring, placement service, health service. **Remedial assistance:** math, writing. **Counseling services:** minority student, career, personal, veteran student, academic, older student, psychological, birth control, religious. **For learning-disabled students:** School does not offer a structured program with separate admission and additional fees. Total undergraduates in learning-disabled program or receiving services: 107. Services include: remedial math, remedial English, tape recorders, untimed tests, note-taking services, oral tests, learning center, readers, extended time for tests, tutors, priority registration, priority seating, texts on tape. **Library:** Number of titles: 193,538; number of current serial subscriptions: 420. **Information technology resources:** Students are not required to lease or own a computer. Number of campus computers available to all students: 500. School has a wireless network. Approximate number of users that can be accommodated: 200. Proportion of college-owned housing units wired for high-speed internet access: 100%. **Campus safety:** Security services offered: 24-hour foot-and-vehicle patrols, late-night transport/escort service, 24-hour emergency telephones, lighted pathways/sidewalks, controlled dormitory access (key, security card, etc).

TRANSFER AND INTERNATIONAL STUDENTS

Transfer students: May apply for admission for the following academic terms: Fall, Spring, Summer. Applicants need a minimum number of credits to apply. For fall 2009: Transfer applications received: 776. Transfer applicants offered admission: 580. Transfer applicants enrolled: 233. **International students:** Number of foreign undergraduates: 16 (1% of student body). Number of countries represented: 9. Minimum TOEFL score required: 500 (paper); 173 (computer). Average TOEFL score: 510 (paper).

West Virginia State University

- **Address:** PO Box 1000, Institute, WV 25112
- **Website:** http://www.wvstateu.edu
- **Public**
- **Enrollment:** N/A

KEY STATS

✔ **U.S News College Ranking:** second tier, National Liberal Arts Colleges
✔ **SAT or ACT Score (25th/75th percentile):** N/A
✔ **Tuition:** 2009-2010: $4,524 in state, $10,764 out of state

Selectivity: Selective	**Room/board:** $6,070
Acceptance rate: N/A	**Average debt:** N/A
Student/faculty ratio: N/A	**Proportion who borrowed:** N/A

West Virginia University

- **Address:** PO Box 6201, Morgantown, WV 26506-6201
- **Website:** http://www.wvu.edu
- **Public**
- **Enrollment:** 20,260 full-time; 1,460 part-time

KEY STATS

✔ **U.S News College Ranking:** 176, National Universities
✔ **ACT Score (25th/75th percentile):** 20-26
✔ **Tuition:** 2009-2010: $5,304 in state, $16,402 out of state

Selectivity: Selective	**Room/board:** $7,528
Acceptance rate: 88%	**Average debt:** $17,321
Student/faculty ratio: 23/1	**Proportion who borrowed:** N/A

UNDERGRADUATE STUDENT BODY STATS

2009-2010 enrollment: 20,260 full-time; 1,460 part-time. Men: 55%; women: 45%. **Ethnic makeup:** African American: 3%; Asian American: 2%; Hispanic: 3%; White: 91%; International: 2%.

ADMISSIONS FACTS AND FIGURES

Phone: (800) 344-9881. **Email:** go2wvu@mail.wvu.edu. **Website:** http://www.wvu.edu. **Application deadlines for fall 2011:** Regular decision: August 1. Early decision: Not offered. Early action: Not offered. Admission can be deferred. **Application fee:** $25. **To apply online, go to:** http://www.arc.wvu.edu/admissions/applications.html. **Admissions requirements/rec-**

ommendations: High school units required (recommended): English: 4; Mathematics: 4; Science: 3; Foreign language: 2; Social studies: 3; Total units: 17. Tests: The college uses SAT or ACT scores in admissions decisions. Either SAT or ACT required. For admission to the fall 2011 entering class, the school will accept: ACT with or without writing accepted. Campus visit: Recommended. Admissions interview: Neither required nor recommended. Off-campus interview: Not available. **Factors that count in admissions decisions:** *Academic:* Secondary school record: Important. Class rank: Not Considered. Letters of recommendation: Considered. Standardized test scores: Very Important. Essay: Not Considered. *Nonacademic:* Interview: Not Considered. Extracurricular activities: Considered. Talent/ability: Considered. Character/personal qualities: Not Considered. Alumni/ae relationship: Not Considered. Geographical residence: Not Considered. State residency: Important. Religious affiliation/commitment: Not Considered. Minority status: Not Considered. Volunteer work: Considered. Work experience: Not Considered. **Other schools with the greatest overlap in applicants:** James Madison University; Marshall University; Pennsylvania State University–University Park; University of Pittsburgh; Virginia Tech. **Admissions statistics for the fall 2009 entering class:** Total applicants: 14,229. Total accepted: 12,496. Freshmen enrolled: 4,589; 51% were from out of state. Overall acceptance rate: 88%. **Credentials of fall 2009 freshmen:** 19% ranked in the top 10 percent of their high school class; 45% were in the top 25 percent; 77% were in the top half. (Proportion submitting class standing: 65%.) **Average high school grade point average:** 3.3. **First-year students who submitted SAT scores:** 46%. Scores (25/75 percentile): Critical Reading: 460-560, Math: 480-580, Combined: 940-1140. **First-year students submitting ACT scores:** 55%. Scores (25/75 percentile): English: 18-25, Math: 19-26, Composite: 20-26.

ACADEMICS

Year founded: 1867. **Academic calendar:** Semester. **Degrees offered:** bachelor's, master's, doctorate. **Most popular majors:** 13% business, management, marketing, and related support services, 10% communication, journalism, and related programs, 9% engineering, 9% health professions and related clinical sciences, 8% multi/interdisciplinary studies. **Major fields of study:** agriculture, agriculture operations, and related sciences; architecture and related services; biological and biomedical sciences; business, management, marketing, and related support services; communication, journalism, and related programs; computer and information sciences and support services; education; engineering; English language and literature/letters; family and consumer sciences/human sciences; foreign languages, literatures, and linguistics; health professions and related clinical sciences; history; liberal arts and sciences studies, and humanities; mathematics and statistics; multi/interdisciplinary studies; natural resources and conservation; parks, recreation, leisure, and fitness studies; philosophy and religious studies; physical sciences; psychology; public administration and social service professions; security and protective services; social sciences; visual and performing arts. **Areas of required coursework:** humanities, mathematics, English (including composition), sciences (biological or physical), social science. **Pre-professional programs:** pre-pharmacy. **Special academic programs:** accelerated program, cooperative (work-study plan) program, distance learning, double major, English as a Second Language (ESL), exchange student program (domestic), external degree program, honors program, independent study, internships, student-designed major, study abroad, teacher certificate program, weekend college. **Teacher certification offered in:** early childhood, special education, elementary, middle/junior high, secondary. **Cooperative education programs:** engineering. **Reserve Officers Training Corps (ROTC):** Army ROTC: Offered on campus; Air Force ROTC: Offered on campus. **Faculty and instruction (2009-2010):** Total instructional faculty: 935 full-time, 300 part-time (57% men; 43% women; 11% minorities). Full-time faculty with Ph.D. or other terminal degree: 80%. Student/faculty ratio: 23/1. Classes of fewer than 20 students: 33%; of 20 to 49 students: 47%; of 50 or more students: 20%. **Advanced Placement and International Baccalaureate credit:** AP tests may be used for: Placement only. Scores accepted: 3, 4, 5. International Baccalaureate exams may be used for: Credit only. **Freshmen returning for sophomore year:** 80%. **Graduation rates:** Four-year: 32%; five-year: 53%; six-year: 58%.

COSTS AND FINANCIAL AID

Financial aid office: (800) 344-9881. **Expenses (2009-2010):** Tuition and fees 2009-2010: $5,304 in state, $16,402 out of state; room/board: $7,528. Estimated books and supplies: $1,178; transportation: $909; personal expenses: $873. **Financial aid:** In 2009-2010, 80% of undergraduates applied for financial aid. Of those, 62% were determined to have financial need; 24% had their need fully met. Average financial aid package (proportion receiving): $6,959 (49%). Average amount of gift aid, such as scholarships or grants (proportion receiving): $5,266 (34%). Average amount of self-help aid, such as work study or loans (proportion receiving): $4,479 (41%). Average need-based loan (excluding PLUS or other private loans): $4,433. Among students who received need-based aid, the average percentage of need met: 75%. Among students who received aid based on merit, the average award (and the proportion receiving): $1,912 (16%). The average athletic scholarship (and the proportion receiving): $17,432 (1%). Average amount of debt of borrowers graduating in 2009: $17,321.

CAMPUS LIFE AND EXTRACURRICULAR ACTIVITIES

Campus housing available: coed dorms, women's dorms, men's dorms, sorority housing, fraternity housing, apartments for married students, apartment for single students, special housing for disabled students, special housing for international students, other housing options. Students who live in college-owned, operated, or affiliated housing: 26%. **Student employment:** During the 2009-2010 academic year, 7% of undergraduates worked on campus. Average per-year earnings: $1,336. **Clubs and organizations:** Number of student organizations: 370. Activities include: choral groups, concert band, dance, drama/theater, jazz band, literary magazine, marching band, music ensembles, musical theater, pep band, radio station, student government, student newspaper, symphony orchestra, television station, yearbook. Number of fraternities: 16; sororities: 10. Proportion of men in fraternities: 7%; of women in sororities: 7%. Average proportion of students who stay on campus on weekends: 90%. **Sports program (2009-2010):** Member of NCAA I. *Men's intercollegiate varsity sports:* baseball, basketball, football, rifle, soccer, swimming, wrestling. *Women's intercollegiate varsity sports:* basketball, cross country, gymnastics, crew (lightweight), rifle, soccer, swimming, tennis, track and field (indoor), track and field (outdoor), volleyball.

SERVICES AND FACILITIES

Basic services: nonremedial tutoring, women's center, placement service, health service, health insurance. **Remedial assistance:** reading, math, writing, study skills. **Counseling services:** minority student, career, military, personal, veteran student, academic, older student, psychological, birth control, religious. **For learning-disabled students:** School does not offer a structured program with separate admission and additional fees. Services include: remedial math, reading machines, tape recorders, diagnostic testing service, untimed tests, note-taking services, oral tests, learning center, readers, extended time for tests, tutors, priority registration, priority seating, substitution of courses, texts on tape, typist/scribe, exams on tape or computer, other testing accommodations. **Library:** Number of titles: 1,622,266; number of current serial subscriptions: 44,866. **Information technology resources:** Students are not required to lease or own a computer. Number of campus computers available to all students: 3,500. School has a wireless network. Approximate number of users that can be accommodated: 7,100. Proportion of college-owned housing units wired for high-speed internet access: 100%. **Campus safety:** Security services offered: 24-hour foot-and-vehicle patrols, late-night transport/escort service, 24-hour emergency telephones, lighted pathways/sidewalks, controlled dormitory access (key, security card, etc).

TRANSFER AND INTERNATIONAL STUDENTS

Transfer students: May apply for admission for the following academic terms: Fall, Spring, Summer. Applicants need a minimum number of credits to apply. For fall 2009: Transfer applications received: 2,242. Transfer applicants offered admission: 1,569. Transfer applicants enrolled: 960. **International students:** Number of foreign undergraduates: 398 (2% of student body). Number of countries represented: 68. Minimum TOEFL score required: 500 (paper); 173 (computer).

West Virginia Univ. Institute of Technology

- **Address:** 405 Fayette Pike, Montgomery, WV 25136
- **Website:** http://www.wvutech.edu
- **Public**
- **Enrollment:** N/A

KEY STATS

✔ **U.S News College Ranking:** 71, Regional Colleges (South)
✔ **SAT or ACT Score (25th/75th percentile):** N/A
✔ **Tuition:** 2009-2010: $5,164 in state, $13,264 out of state

Selectivity: Less selective	**Room/board:** $7,720
Acceptance rate: N/A	**Average debt:** N/A
Student/faculty ratio: N/A	**Proportion who borrowed:** N/A

West Virginia University—Parkersburg

- **Address:** 300 Campus Drive, Parkersburg, WV 26101-9577
- **Website:** http://www.wvup.edu
- **Public**
- **Enrollment:** N/A

KEY STATS

✔ **U.S News College Ranking:** Unranked, Regional Colleges (South)
✔ **ACT Score (25th/75th percentile):** 16-21
✔ **Tuition:** 2009-2010: $2,844 in state, $7,512 out of state

Selectivity: N/A	**Room/board:** N/A
Acceptance rate: 100%	**Average debt:** N/A
Student/faculty ratio: N/A	**Proportion who borrowed:** N/A

West Virginia Wesleyan College

- **Address:** 59 College Avenue, Buckhannon, WV 26201
- **Website:** http://www.wvwc.edu
- **Private; Religious affiliation:** United Methodist
- **Enrollment:** 1,321 full-time; 35 part-time

KEY STATS

✔ **U.S News College Ranking:** second tier, National Liberal Arts Colleges
✔ **ACT Score (25th/75th percentile):** 19-25
✔ **Tuition:** 2010-2011: $23,980

Selectivity: Selective	**Room/board:** $7,140
Acceptance rate: 81%	**Average debt:** $21,502
Student/faculty ratio: 13/1	**Proportion who borrowed:** 71%

UNDERGRADUATE STUDENT BODY STATS

2009-2010 enrollment: 1,321 full-time; 35 part-time. Men: 46%; women: 54%. **Ethnic makeup:** African American: 8%; American-Indian: 1%; Asian American: 1%; Hispanic: 3%; White: 83%; International: 4%.

ADMISSIONS FACTS AND FIGURES

Phone: (800) 722-9933. **Email:** admissions@wvwc.edu. **Website:** http://www.wvwc.edu. **Application deadlines for fall 2011:** Regular decision: Rolling. Early decision: Not offered. Early action: Not offered. Admission can be deferred. **Application fee:** $35. **To apply online, go to:** http://www.applyweb.com/apply/wvwc/. **Admissions requirements/recommendations:** High school units required (recommended): English: 4; Mathematics: 3; Science: 3; Foreign language: (2); Social studies: 3; Total units: 15. Tests: The college uses SAT or ACT scores in admissions decisions. Either SAT or ACT required. For admission to the fall 2011 entering class, the school will accept: ACT with or without writing accepted. Campus visit: Recommended. Admissions interview: Recommended. Off-campus interview: May be arranged. **Factors that count in admissions decisions:** *Academic:* Secondary school record: Very Important. Class rank: Important. Letters of recommendation: Considered. Standardized test scores: Important. Essay: Considered. *Nonacademic:* Interview: Important. Extracurricular activities: Important. Talent/ability: Important. Character/personal qualities: Important. Alumni/ae relationship: Important. Geographical residence: Considered. State residency: Considered. Religious affiliation/commitment: Considered. Minority status: Not Considered. Volunteer work: Important. Work experience: Considered. **Other schools with the greatest overlap in applicants:** Marietta College; Marshall University; University of Charleston; West Virginia University; Westminster College. **Admissions statistics for the fall 2009 entering class:** Total applicants: 1,353. Total accepted: 1,096. Freshmen enrolled: 399; 44% were from out of state. Overall acceptance rate: 81%. **Credentials of fall 2009 freshmen:** 28% ranked in the top 10 percent of their high school class; 59% were in the top 25 percent; 81% were in the top half. (Proportion submitting class standing: 81%.) **Average high school grade point average:** 3.3. **First-year students who submitted SAT scores:** 50%. Scores (25/75 percentile): Critical Reading: 420-540, Math: 440-568, Combined: 860-1108. **First-year students submitting ACT scores:** 70%. Scores (25/75 percentile): English: 18-25, Math: 19-25, Composite: 19-25.

ACADEMICS

Year founded: 1890. **Academic calendar:** Semester. **Degrees offered:** bachelor's, master's. **Most popular majors:** 20% business, management, marketing, and related support services, 13% education, 10% parks, recreation, leisure, and fitness studies, 10% psychology, 7% biological and biomedical sciences. **Major fields of study:** biological and biomedical sciences; business, management, marketing, and related support services; communication, journalism, and related programs; computer and information sciences and support services; education; English language and literature/letters; health professions and related clinical sciences; history; legal professions and studies; natural resources and conservation; parks, recreation, leisure, and fitness studies; philosophy and religious studies; physical sciences; psychology; security and protective services; social sciences; theology and religious vocations; visual and performing arts. **Areas of required coursework:** arts/fine arts, humanities, mathematics, English (including composition), philosophy, sciences (biological or physical), history, social science. **Preprofessional programs:** pre-law, pre-dentistry, pre-medicine, pre-theology, pre-veterinary science, pre-optometry, pre-pharmacy. **Special academic programs (% participation):** double major (11%), English as a Second Language (ESL), exchange student program (domestic), honors program, independent study, internships, student-designed major, study abroad, teacher certificate program. **Teacher certification offered in:** early childhood, special education, elementary, middle/junior high, secondary. **Cooperative education programs:** engineering. **Faculty and instruction (2009-2010):** Total instructional faculty: 75 full-time, 81 part-time (49% men; 51% women; 2% minorities). Full-time faculty with Ph.D. or other terminal degree: 76%. Student/faculty ratio: 13/1. Classes of fewer than 20 students: 52%; of 20 to 49 students: 47%; of 50 or more students: 1%. **Advanced Placement and International Baccalaureate credit:** AP tests may be used for: Credit only. Scores accepted: 3. **Freshmen returning for sophomore year:** 74%. **Graduation rates:** Four-year: 43%; five-year: 52%; six-year: 53%. **Graduate study:** 27% of students pursue further study immediately upon graduation; 36% within one year. Fields in which graduates pursue further study: Master of Business Administration (MBA), 13%; law, 5%; medicine, 14%; theology (or the seminary), 5%; education, 5%; arts and sciences, 58%.

COSTS AND FINANCIAL AID

Financial aid office: (304) 473-8080. **Expenses (2010-2011):** Tuition and fees 2010-2011: $23,980; room/board: $7,140. Estimated books and supplies: $2,500; transportation: $1,000; personal expenses: $2,500. **Financial aid:** Priority filing date for institution's financial aid form: February 15. In 2009-2010, 99% of undergraduates applied for financial aid. Of those, 77% were determined to have financial need; 33% had their need fully met. Average financial aid package (proportion receiving): $23,785 (76%). Average amount of gift aid, such as scholarships or grants (proportion receiving): $18,591 (76%). Average amount of self-help aid, such as work study or loans (proportion receiving): $4,514 (56%). Average need-based loan (excluding PLUS or other private loans): $4,189. Among students who received need-based aid, the average percentage of need met: 78%. Among students who received aid based on merit, the average award (and the proportion receiving): $12,053 (20%). The average athletic scholarship (and the proportion receiving): $16,779 (14%). Average amount of debt of borrowers graduating in 2009: $21,502. Proportion who borrowed: 71%.

CAMPUS LIFE AND EXTRACURRICULAR ACTIVITIES

Campus housing available: coed dorms, women's dorms, men's dorms, sorority housing, fraternity housing, special housing for disabled students. Students who live in college-owned, operated, or affiliated housing: 79%. Average per-year earnings: $1,000. Activities include: campus ministries, choral groups, dance, drama/theater, international student organization, jazz band, literary magazine, music ensembles, musical theater, opera,

radio station, student government, student newspaper, yearbook. Number of fraternities: 5; sororities: 4. Proportion of men in fraternities: 25%; of women in sororities: 25%. Average proportion of students who stay on campus on weekends: 50%. **Sports program (2009-2010):** Member of NCAA II. **Men's intercollegiate varsity sports:** baseball, basketball, cross country, football, golf, soccer, swimming, tennis, track and field (indoor), track and field (outdoor). **Women's intercollegiate varsity sports:** basketball, cross country, golf, soccer, softball, swimming, tennis, track and field (indoor), track and field (outdoor), volleyball.

SERVICES AND FACILITIES

Basic services: nonremedial tutoring, placement service, health service, health insurance. **Remedial assistance:** reading, math, writing, study skills. **Counseling services:** minority student, career, personal, academic, older student, psychological, religious. **For learning-disabled students:** School does not offer a structured program with separate admission and additional fees. Services include: remedial math, remedial English, reading machines, remedial reading, tape recorders, other special classes, diagnostic testing service, untimed tests, note-taking services, oral tests, learning center, readers, extended time for tests, tutors, priority registration, priority seating, texts on tape, other testing accommodations, other. **Library:** Number of titles: 130,000; number of current serial subscriptions: 15,177. **Information technology resources:** Students are required to lease or own a computer. School has a wireless network. Proportion of college-owned housing units wired for high-speed internet access: 100%. **Campus safety:** Security services offered: 24-hour foot-and-vehicle patrols, late-night transport/escort service, 24-hour emergency telephones, lighted pathways/sidewalks, student patrols, controlled dormitory access (key, security card, etc).

TRANSFER AND INTERNATIONAL STUDENTS

Transfer students: May apply for admission for the following academic terms: Fall, Spring, Summer. Applicants need a minimum number of credits to apply. For fall 2009: Transfer applications received: 147. Transfer applicants offered admission: 111. Transfer applicants enrolled: 60. **International students:** Number of foreign undergraduates: 54 (4% of student body). Minimum TOEFL score required: 500 (paper).

Wheeling Jesuit University

- **Address:** 316 Washington Avenue, Wheeling, WV 26003
- **Website:** http://www.wju.edu
- **Private; Religious affiliation:** Roman Catholic
- **Enrollment:** 900 full-time; 186 part-time

KEY STATS

✔ **U.S News College Ranking:** 22, Regional Universities (South)
✔ **ACT Score (25th/75th percentile):** 20-25
✔ **Tuition:** 2010-2011: $25,010

Selectivity: Selective	**Room/board:** $8,828
Acceptance rate: 74%	**Average debt:** $26,334
Student/faculty ratio: 11/1	**Proportion who borrowed:** 89%

UNDERGRADUATE STUDENT BODY STATS

2009-2010 enrollment: 900 full-time; 186 part-time. Men: 41%; women: 59%. **Ethnic makeup:** African American: 2%; Asian American: 1%; Hispanic: 2%; White: 91%; International: 3%. **Religious preference:** Roman Catholic: 64%; Other: 36%.

ADMISSIONS FACTS AND FIGURES

Phone: (800) 624-6992. **Email:** admiss@wju.edu. **Website:** http://www.wju.edu. **Application deadlines for fall 2011:** Regular decision: Rolling; decision sent by August 15. Early decision: Not offered. Early action: Not offered. Admission can be deferred. **Application fee:** $25. **To apply online, go to:** http://www.wju.edu/admissions/adm_apply.asp. **Admissions requirements/recommendations:** High school units required (recommended): English: 4 (4); Mathematics: 2 (2); Science: 1 (1); Foreign language: (2); Social studies: 2 (2); History: 2; Academic electives: 6 (6); Total units: 15 (15). Tests: The college uses SAT or ACT scores in admissions decisions. Either SAT or ACT required. For admission to the fall 2011 entering class, the school will accept: ACT with or without writing accepted. Campus visit: Recommended. Admissions interview: Recommended. Off-campus interview: May be arranged. **Factors that count in admissions decisions:** *Academic:* Secondary school record: Important. Class rank: Not Considered.

Letters of recommendation: Considered. Standardized test scores: Very Important. Essay: Important. *Nonacademic:* Interview: Important. Extracurricular activities: Considered. Talent/ability: Considered. Character/personal qualities: Considered. Alumni/ae relationship: Not Considered. Geographical residence: Not Considered. State residency: Not Considered. Religious affiliation/commitment: Not Considered. Minority status: Not Considered. Volunteer work: Considered. Work experience: Considered. **Other schools with the greatest overlap in applicants:** Bethany College; Duquesne University; Ohio State University–Columbus; Ohio University; West Virginia University. **Admissions statistics for the fall 2009 entering class:** Total applicants: 1,299. Total accepted: 966. Freshmen enrolled: 264; 60% were from out of state. Overall acceptance rate: 74%. **Credentials of fall 2009 freshmen:** 22% ranked in the top 10 percent of their high school class; 50% were in the top 25 percent; 85% were in the top half. (Proportion submitting class standing: 76%.) **Average high school grade point average:** 3.5. **First-year students who submitted SAT scores:** 52%. Scores (25/75 percentile): Critical Reading: 470-560, Math: 460-560, Combined: 930-1120. **First-year students submitting ACT scores:** 79%. Scores (25/75 percentile): English: 19-25, Math: 18-24, Composite: 20-25.

ACADEMICS

Year founded: 1954. **Academic calendar:** Semester. **Degrees offered:** bachelor's, master's, doctorate. **Most popular majors:** 24% health professions and related clinical sciences, 15% business, management, marketing, and related support services, 14% psychology, 13% social sciences, 10% physical sciences. **Major fields of study:** biological and biomedical sciences; business, management, marketing, and related support services; computer and information sciences and support services; education; English language and literature/letters; foreign languages, literatures, and linguistics; health professions and related clinical sciences; history; liberal arts and sciences studies, and humanities; mathematics and statistics; multi/interdisciplinary studies; philosophy and religious studies; physical sciences; psychology; security and protective services; social sciences; theology and religious vocations. **Areas of required coursework:** arts/fine arts, humanities, mathematics, English (including composition), philosophy, foreign languages, sciences (biological or physical), history, social science, other. **Pre-professional programs:** pre-law, pre-dentistry, pre-medicine, pre-veterinary science, pre-pharmacy, other. **Special academic programs (% participation):** distance learning (11%), double major (4%), English as a Second Language (ESL), exchange student program (domestic), honors program (6%), independent study (28%), internships (33%), liberal arts/career combination (30%), student-designed major (2%), study abroad (1%), teacher certificate program (11%), other. **Teacher certification offered in:** special education, elementary, secondary. **Faculty and instruction (2009-2010):** Total instructional faculty: 72 full-time, 73 part-time (55% men; 45% women; 6% minorities). Full-time faculty with Ph.D. or other terminal degree: 65%. Student/faculty ratio: 11/1. Classes of fewer than 20 students: 66%; of 20 to 49 students: 34%; of 50 or more students: 0%. **Advanced Placement and International Baccalaureate credit:** AP tests may be used for: Credit only. Scores accepted: 3, 4, 5. **Freshmen returning for sophomore year:** 74%. **Graduation rates:** Four-year: 49%; five-year: 54%; six-year: 57%. **Graduate study:** 10% of students pursue further study immediately upon graduation; 30% within one year. Fields in which graduates pursue further study: Master of Business Administration (MBA), 5%; law, 3%; medicine, 10%; dentistry, 5%; engineering, 6%; theology (or the seminary), 3%; education, 5%; arts and sciences, 8%; veterinary medicine, 1%.

COSTS AND FINANCIAL AID

Financial aid office: (304) 243-2304. **Expenses (2010-2011):** Tuition and fees 2010-2011: $25,010; room/board: $8,828. Estimated books and supplies: $1,000; transportation: $600; personal expenses: $600. **Financial aid:** Priority filing date for institution's financial aid form: February 15. In 2009-2010, 91% of undergraduates applied for financial aid. Of those, 80% were determined to have financial need; 35% had their need fully met. Average financial aid package (proportion receiving): $21,466 (80%). Average amount of gift aid, such as scholarships or grants (proportion receiving): $6,559 (53%). Average amount of self-help aid, such as work study or loans (proportion receiving): $5,295 (60%). Average need-based loan (excluding PLUS or other private loans): $4,767. Among students who received need-based aid, the average percentage of need met: 86%. Among students who received aid based on merit, the average award (and the proportion receiving): $10,869 (20%). The average athletic scholarship (and the proportion receiving): $4,854 (5%). Average amount of debt of borrowers graduating in 2009: $26,334. Proportion who borrowed: 89%.

CAMPUS LIFE AND EXTRACURRICULAR ACTIVITIES

Campus housing available (% using): coed dorms (54%), women's dorms (20%), men's dorms (17%), apartments for married students (3%), apartment for single students (5%), special housing for disabled students (1%). Students who live in college-owned, operated, or affiliated housing: 78%. **Student employment:** During the 2009-2010 academic year, 21% of undergraduates worked on campus. Average per-year earnings: $1,550. **Clubs and organizations:** Number of student organizations: 40. Activities include: campus ministries, choral groups, dance, drama/theater, international student organization, literary magazine, musical theater, pep band, radio station, student government, student newspaper, television station, yearbook. Number of fraternities: 0; sororities: 0. Average proportion of students who stay on campus on weekends: 70%. **Sports program (2009-2010):** Member of NCAA II. *Men's intercollegiate varsity sports:* baseball, basketball, cross country, golf, lacrosse, soccer, swimming, track and field (indoor), track and field (outdoor). *Women's intercollegiate varsity sports:* basketball, cross country, golf, soccer, softball, swimming, track and field (indoor), track and field (outdoor), volleyball.

SERVICES AND FACILITIES

Basic services: nonremedial tutoring, women's center, placement service, health service, health insurance. **Remedial assistance:** reading, math, writing, study skills. **Counseling services:** minority student, career, personal, academic, older student, psychological, religious. **For learning-disabled students:** School does not offer a structured program with separate admission and additional fees. Total undergraduates in learning-disabled program or receiving services: 44. Services include: remedial math, remedial English, remedial reading, untimed tests, note-taking services, oral tests, learning center, readers, extended time for tests, tutors, priority seating, substitution of courses, texts on tape. **Library:** Number of titles: 148,117; number of current serial subscriptions: 432. **Information technology resources:** Students are not required to lease or own a computer. Number of campus computers available to all students: 325. School has a wireless network. Approximate number of users that can be accommodated: 200. Proportion of college-owned housing units wired for high-speed internet access: 100%. **Campus safety:** Security services offered: 24-hour foot-and-vehicle patrols, late-night transport/escort service, 24-hour emergency telephones, lighted pathways/sidewalks, student patrols, controlled dormitory access (key, security card, etc).

TRANSFER AND INTERNATIONAL STUDENTS

Transfer students: May apply for admission for the following academic terms: Fall, Spring. Applicants need a minimum number of credits to apply. For fall 2009: Transfer applications received: 127. Transfer applicants offered admission: 86. Transfer applicants enrolled: 38. **International students:** Number of foreign undergraduates: 34 (3% of student body). Number of countries represented: 21. Minimum TOEFL score required: 550 (paper); 213 (computer). Average TOEFL score: 585 (paper).

Wisconsin

Alverno College

■ **Address:** 3400 S. 43rd Street, PO Box 343922, Milwaukee, WI 53234-3922
■ **Website:** http://www.alverno.edu
■ **Private; Religious affiliation:** Roman Catholic
■ **Enrollment:** 1,720 full-time; 667 part-time

....

KEY STATS

✔ **U.S News College Ranking:** 61, Regional Universities (Midwest)
✔ **ACT Score (25th/75th percentile):** 17-22
✔ **Tuition:** 2010-2011: $20,060

Selectivity: Selective	**Room/board:** $6,780
Acceptance rate: 85%	**Average debt:** $32,142
Student/faculty ratio: 13/1	**Proportion who borrowed:** 83%

UNDERGRADUATE STUDENT BODY STATS

2009-2010 enrollment: 1,720 full-time; 667 part-time. Men: 0%; women: 100%. **Ethnic makeup:** African American: 18%; American-Indian: 1%; Asian American: 5%; Hispanic: 13%; White: 62%; International: 1%. **Religious preference:** Protestant: 19%; Muslim: 1%; Buddhist: 1%; No preference: 18%; Unknown: 9%; Roman Catholic: 32%; Other: 20%.

ADMISSIONS FACTS AND FIGURES

Phone: (414) 382-6100. **Email:** admissions@alverno.edu. **Website:** http://www.alverno.edu. **Application deadlines for fall 2011:** Regular decision: Rolling. Early decision: Not offered. Early action: Not offered. Admission can be deferred. **Application fee:** $20. **To apply online, go to:** http://www.alverno.edu/prospective_students/application_page.html. **Admissions requirements/recommendations:** High school units required (recommended): English: 4; Mathematics: 3; Science: 3; Foreign language: (2); Social studies: 3; Academic electives: 4; Total units: 17. Tests: The college uses SAT or ACT scores in admissions decisions. Either SAT or ACT required. For admission to the fall 2011 entering class, the school will accept: ACT with or without writing accepted. Campus visit: Recommended. Admissions interview: Recommended. Off-campus interview: May be arranged. **Factors that count in admissions decisions:** *Academic:* Secondary school record: Important. Class rank: Not Considered. Letters of recommendation: Considered. Standardized test scores: Very Important. Essay: Important. *Nonacademic:* Interview: Considered. Extracurricular activities: Considered. Talent/ability: Considered. Character/personal qualities: Considered. Alumni/ae relationship: Not Considered. Geographical residence: Not Considered. State residency: Not Considered. Religious affiliation/commitment: Not Considered. Minority status: Not Considered. Volunteer work: Considered. Work experience: Considered. **Other schools with the greatest overlap in applicants:** Carroll University; Marian University; Mount Mary College; University of Wisconsin–Milwaukee; University of Wisconsin–Parkside. **Admissions statistics for the fall 2009 entering class:** Total applicants: 525. Total accepted: 446. Freshmen enrolled: 244; 7% were from out of state. Overall acceptance rate: 85%. **Credentials of fall 2009 freshmen:** 10% ranked in the top 10 percent of their high school class; 29% were in the top 25 percent; 63% were in the top half. (Proportion submitting class standing: 83%.) **Average high school grade point average:** 2.9. **First-year students who submitted SAT scores:** 1%. **First-year students submitting ACT scores:** 99%. Scores (25/75 percentile): English: N/A, Math: N/A, Composite: 17-22.

ACADEMICS

Year founded: 1887. **Academic calendar:** Semester. **Degrees offered:** associate, bachelor's, post-bachelor's certificate, master's, post-master's certificate. **Most popular majors:** 37% health professions and related clinical sciences, 19% business, management, marketing, and related support services, 9% education, 8% psychology, 7% communication, journalism, and related programs. **Major fields of study:** biological and biomedical sciences; business, management, marketing, and related support services; communication, journalism, and related programs; communications technologies/technicians and support services; computer and information sciences and support services; education; English language and literature/letters; health professions and related clinical sciences; history; liberal arts and sciences studies, and humanities; mathematics and statistics; multi/interdisciplinary studies; natural resources and conservation; philosophy and religious studies; physical sciences; psychology; public administration and social service professions; social sciences; visual and performing arts. **Areas of required coursework:** arts/fine arts, humanities, computer literacy, mathematics, English (including composition), sciences (biological or physical), social science, other. **Pre-professional programs:** pre-law, pre-dentistry, pre-medicine, pre-veterinary science, pre-optometry, pre-pharmacy, other. **Special academic programs (% participation):** double major (2.7%), independent study (19.3%), internships (56.3%), student-designed major (0%), study abroad (3.6%), teacher certificate program (9.94%), weekend college (28.3%), other (10.8%). **Teacher certification offered in:** early childhood, elementary, middle/junior high, secondary. **Reserve Officers Training Corps (ROTC):** Army ROTC: Offered at cooperating institution (Marquette University); Air Force ROTC: Offered at cooperating institution (Marquette University). **Faculty and instruction (2009-2010):** Total instructional faculty: 118 full-time, 137 part-time (22% men; 78% women; 9% minorities). Full-time faculty with Ph.D. or other terminal degree: 92%. Student/faculty ratio: 13/1. Classes of fewer than 20 students: 46%; of 20 to 49 students: 53%; of 50 or more students: 0%. **Advanced Placement and International Baccalaureate credit:** AP tests may be used for: Placement only. Scores accepted: 3, 4, 5. International Baccalaureate exams may be used for: Credit only. **Freshmen returning for sophomore year:** 73%. **Graduation rates:** Four-year: 17%; five-year: 33%; six-year: 39%. **Graduate study:** 11% of students pursue further study immediately upon graduation. Fields in which graduates pursue further study: Master of Business Administration (MBA), 22%; law, 3%; medicine, 6%; education, 22%; arts and sciences, 14%.

COSTS AND FINANCIAL AID

Financial aid office: (414) 382-6046. **Expenses (2010-2011):** Tuition and fees 2010-2011: $20,060; room/board: $6,780. Estimated books and supplies: $1,056; transportation: $1,200; personal expenses: $1,760. **Financial aid:** Priority filing date for institution's financial aid form: March 15. In 2009-2010, 92% of undergraduates applied for financial aid. Of those, 83% were determined to have financial need; Average financial aid package (proportion receiving): $14,191 (83%). Average amount of gift aid, such as scholarships or grants (proportion receiving): $10,651 (71%). Average amount of self-help aid, such as work study or loans (proportion receiving): $4,418 (78%). Average need-based loan (excluding PLUS or other private loans): $4,088. Among students who received aid based on merit, the average award (and the proportion receiving): $5,195 (12%). The average athletic scholarship (and the proportion receiving): $0 (0%). Average amount of debt of borrowers graduating in 2009: $32,142. Proportion who borrowed: 83%.

CAMPUS LIFE AND EXTRACURRICULAR ACTIVITIES

Campus housing available (% using): women's dorms (100%). Students who live in college-owned, operated, or affiliated housing: 9%. **Student employment:** During the 2009-2010 academic year, 11% of undergraduates worked on campus. Average per-year earnings: $3,500. **Clubs and organizations:** Number of student organizations: 41. Activities include: campus ministries, choral groups, dance, drama/theater, international student organization, literary magazine, model UN, music ensembles, radio station, student government, student newspaper. Number of fraternities: 0; sororities: 5. of women in sororities: 2%. Average proportion of students who stay on campus on weekends: 40%. **Sports program (2009-2010):** Member of NCAA III. *Women's intercollegiate varsity sports:* basketball, cross country, soccer, softball, tennis, volleyball.

SERVICES AND FACILITIES

Basic services: nonremedial tutoring, day care, health service, health insurance. **Remedial assistance:** reading, math, writing, study skills. **Counseling services:** career, personal, academic, psychological, religious. **For learning-disabled students:** School does not offer a structured program with separate admission and additional fees. Total undergraduates in learning-disabled program or receiving services: 42. Services include: remedial math, remedial English, reading machines, remedial reading, tape recorders, note-taking services, learning center, extended time for tests, tutors, texts on tape. **Library:** Number of titles: 95,197; number of current serial subscriptions: 40,428. **Information technology resources:** Students are not required to lease or own a computer. Number of campus computers available to all students: 580. School has a wireless network. Approximate number of users that can be accommodated: 1,200. Proportion of college-owned housing units wired for high-speed internet access: 100%. **Campus safety:** Security services offered: 24-hour foot-and-vehicle patrols, late-night transport/escort service, 24-hour emergency telephones, lighted pathways/sidewalks, controlled dormitory access (key, security card, etc).

TRANSFER AND INTERNATIONAL STUDENTS
Transfer students: May apply for admission for the following academic terms: Fall, Spring. Applicants need a minimum number of credits to apply. For fall 2009: Transfer applications received: 425. Transfer applicants offered admission: 391. Transfer applicants enrolled: 265. **International students:** Number of foreign undergraduates: 15 (1% of student body). Number of countries represented: 12. Minimum TOEFL score required: 520 (paper); 190 (computer).

Beloit College

- **Address:** 700 College Avenue, Beloit, WI 53511
- **Website:** http://www.beloit.edu
- **Private**
- **Enrollment:** 1,346 full-time; 61 part-time

KEY STATS
✔ **U.S News College Ranking:** 55, National Liberal Arts Colleges
✔ **ACT Score (25th/75th percentile):** 25-30
✔ **Tuition:** 2010-2011: $35,038
  Selectivity: More selective   **Room/board:** $7,164
  Acceptance rate: 73%   **Average debt:** $17,909
  Student/faculty ratio: 11/1   **Proportion who borrowed:** 69%

UNDERGRADUATE STUDENT BODY STATS
2009-2010 enrollment: 1,346 full-time; 61 part-time. Men: 43%; women: 57%. **Ethnic makeup:** African American: 4%; American-Indian: 1%; Asian American: 3%; Hispanic: 4%; White: 82%; International: 6%.

ADMISSIONS FACTS AND FIGURES
Phone: (608) 363-2500. **Email:** admiss@beloit.edu. **Website:** http://www.beloit.edu. **Application deadlines for fall 2011:** Regular decision: January 15. Early decision: Not offered. Early action: Send application by: December 1; Decision sent by: January 15. Admission can be deferred. **Application fee:** $35. **To apply online, go to:** http://www.beloit.edu/apply. **Admissions requirements/recommendations:** High school units required (recommended): English: (4); Mathematics: (4); Science: (3); Foreign language: (2); Social studies: (4). Tests: The college uses SAT or ACT scores in admissions decisions. Either SAT or ACT required. For admission to the fall 2011 entering class, the school will accept: ACT with or without writing accepted. Campus visit: Recommended. Admissions interview: Recommended. Off-campus interview: May be arranged. **Factors that count in admissions decisions:** *Academic:* Secondary school record: Very Important. Class rank: Important. Letters of recommendation: Very Important. Standardized test scores: Important. Essay: Very Important. *Nonacademic:* Interview: Important. Extracurricular activities: Considered. Talent/ability: Considered. Character/personal qualities: Considered. Alumni/ae relationship: Considered. Geographical residence: Not Considered. State residency: Not Considered. Religious affiliation/commitment: Not Considered. Minority status: Not Considered. Volunteer work: Considered. Work experience: Considered. **Other schools with the greatest overlap in applicants:** Grinnell College; Kalamazoo College; Knox College; Lawrence University; Macalester College. **Admissions statistics for the fall 2009 entering class:** Total applicants: 1,962. Total accepted: 1,429. Freshmen enrolled: 332; 79% were from out of state. Accepted through early-decision or early-action plans: 42%. Overall acceptance rate: 73%. Non-early acceptance rate: 64%. **Size of waiting list:** 52 applicants; enrolled from waiting list: 8. **Credentials of fall 2009 freshmen:** 32% ranked in the top 10 percent of their high school class; 69% were in the top 25 percent; 93% were in the top half. (Proportion submitting class standing: 64%.) **Average high school grade point average:** 3.4. **First-year**

students who submitted SAT scores: 45%. Scores (25/75 percentile): Critical Reading: 575-710, Math: 560-670, Combined: 1135-1380. **First-year students submitting ACT scores:** 66%. Scores (25/75 percentile): English: 24-32, Math: 22-28, Composite: 25-30.

ACADEMICS
Year founded: 1846. **Academic calendar:** Semester. **Degrees offered:** bachelor's. **Most popular majors:** 7% anthropology, 7% international relations and affairs, 7% political science and government, 7% sociology, 6% psychology. **Major fields of study:** area, ethnic, cultural, and gender studies; biological and biomedical sciences; business, management, marketing, and related support services; computer and information sciences and support services; education; engineering; English language and literature/letters; foreign languages, literatures, and linguistics; history; mathematics and statistics; multi/interdisciplinary studies; natural resources and conservation; philosophy and religious studies; physical sciences; psychology; social sciences; visual and performing arts. **Areas of required coursework:** humanities, English (including composition), sciences (biological or physical), social science, other. **Pre-professional programs:** pre-law, pre-dentistry, pre-medicine, pre-veterinary science. **Special academic programs (% participation):** double major (23%), English as a Second Language (ESL) (1%), exchange student program (domestic) (4%), independent study (59%), internships (64%), student-designed major (1%), study abroad (48%), teacher certificate program (3%). **Teacher certification offered in:** elementary, middle/junior high, secondary, bilingual/bicultural. **Cooperative education programs:** engineering, health professions, other. **Faculty and instruction (2009-2010):** Total instructional faculty: 123 full-time, 12 part-time (53% men; 47% women; 11% minorities). Full-time faculty with Ph.D. or other terminal degree: 93%. Student/faculty ratio: 11/1. Classes of fewer than 20 students: 70%; of 20 to 49 students: 30%; of 50 or more students: 0%. **Advanced Placement and International Baccalaureate credit:** AP tests may be used for: Credit only. Scores accepted: 4, 5. International Baccalaureate exams may be used for: Credit only. **Freshmen returning for sophomore year:** 89%. **Graduation rates:** Four-year: 74%; five-year: 83%; six-year: 85%. **Graduate study:** 15% of students pursue further study immediately upon graduation; 34% within one year; 65% within five years. Fields in which graduates pursue further study: Master of Business Administration (MBA), 12%; law, 10%; medicine, 9%; engineering, 3%; education, 6%; arts and sciences, 60%.

COSTS AND FINANCIAL AID
Financial aid office: (608) 363-2663. **Expenses (2010-2011):** Tuition and fees 2010-2011: $35,038; room/board: $7,164. Estimated books and supplies: $600 personal expenses: $900. **Financial aid:** Priority filing date for institution's financial aid form: March 1; deadline: March 1. In 2009-2010, 75% of undergraduates applied for financial aid. Of those, 64% were determined to have financial need; 39% had their need fully met. Average financial aid package (proportion receiving): $28,203 (64%). Average amount of gift aid, such as scholarships or grants (proportion receiving): $21,235 (63%). Average amount of self-help aid, such as work study or loans (proportion receiving): $1,867 (61%). Average need-based loan (excluding PLUS or other private loans): $5,101. Among students who received need-based aid, the average percentage of need met: 94%. Among students who received aid based on merit, the average award (and the proportion receiving): $13,583 (27%). The average athletic scholarship (and the proportion receiving): $0 (0%). Average amount of debt of borrowers graduating in 2009: $17,909. Proportion who borrowed: 69%.

CAMPUS LIFE AND EXTRACURRICULAR ACTIVITIES
Campus housing available (% using): coed dorms (70%), women's dorms (4%), sorority housing (2%), fraternity housing (7%), apartment for single students (6%), other housing options (11%). Students who live in college-owned, operated, or affiliated housing: 96%. **Student employment:** During the 2009-2010 academic year, 30% of undergraduates worked on campus. Average per-year earnings: $1,550. **Clubs and organizations:** Number of student organizations: 60. Activities include: choral groups, dance, drama/theater, international student organization, jazz band, literary magazine, music ensembles, musical theater, radio station, student government, student newspaper, student film society, symphony orchestra, television station, yearbook. Number of fraternities: 3; sororities: 3. Proportion of men in fraternities: 8%; of women in sororities: 6%. Average proportion of students who stay on campus on weekends: 98%. **Sports program (2009-2010):** Member of NCAA III. *Men's intercollegiate varsity sports:* baseball, basketball, cross country, football, golf, soccer, swimming, tennis, track and field (indoor), track and field (outdoor). *Women's intercollegiate varsity sports:* basketball, cross country, soccer, softball, swimming, tennis, track and field (indoor), track and field (outdoor), volleyball.

SERVICES AND FACILITIES

Basic services: nonremedial tutoring, women's center, health service, health insurance. **Remedial assistance:** study skills. **Counseling services:** minority student, career, personal, academic, psychological, birth control, other. **For learning-disabled students:** School does not offer a structured program with separate admission and additional fees. Total undergraduates in learning-disabled program or receiving services: 55. Services include: reading machines, tape recorders, untimed tests, note-taking services, oral tests, learning center, readers, extended time for tests, tutors, texts on tape, typist/scribe, other testing accommodations, other. **Library:** Number of titles: 631,140; number of current serial subscriptions: 23,017. **Information technology resources:** Students are not required to lease or own a computer. Number of campus computers available to all students: 302. School has a wireless network. Approximate number of users that can be accommodated: 700. Proportion of college-owned housing units wired for high-speed internet access: 100%. **Campus safety:** Security services offered: 24-hour foot-and-vehicle patrols, late-night transport/escort service, 24-hour emergency telephones, lighted pathways/sidewalks, student patrols, controlled dormitory access (key, security card, etc).

TRANSFER AND INTERNATIONAL STUDENTS

Transfer students: May apply for admission for the following academic terms: Fall, Spring. Applicants do not need a minimum number of credits to apply. For fall 2009: Transfer applications received: 93. Transfer applicants offered admission: 57. Transfer applicants enrolled: 26. **International students:** Number of foreign undergraduates: 85 (6% of student body). Number of countries represented: 32. Minimum TOEFL score required: 550 (paper); 80 (computer). Average TOEFL score: 592 (paper).

Cardinal Stritch University

- **Address:** 6801 N. Yates Road, Milwaukee, WI 53217
- **Website:** http://www.stritch.edu
- **Private; Religious affiliation:** Roman Catholic
- **Enrollment:** 2,857 full-time; 189 part-time

KEY STATS

- ✔ **U.S News College Ranking:** 66, Regional Universities (Midwest)
- ✔ **ACT Score (25th/75th percentile):** 20-25
- ✔ **Tuition:** 2009-2010: $21,790

Selectivity: Selective	**Room/board:** $6,600
Acceptance rate: 41%	**Average debt:** N/A
Student/faculty ratio: N/A	**Proportion who borrowed:** N/A

UNDERGRADUATE STUDENT BODY STATS

2009-2010 enrollment: 2,857 full-time; 189 part-time. Men: 34%; women: 66%. **Ethnic makeup:** African American: 24%; American-Indian: 1%; Asian American: 2%; Hispanic: 4%; White: 66%; International: 3%. **Religious preference:** Roman Catholic: 16%; Protestant: 17%; Jewish: 1%; Unknown: 64%; Other: 2%.

ADMISSIONS FACTS AND FIGURES

Phone: (414) 410-4040. **Email:** admityou@stritch.edu. **Website:** http://www.stritch.edu. **Application deadlines for fall 2011:** Regular decision: August 1. Early decision: Not offered. Early action: Not offered. Admission cannot be deferred. **Application fee:** $25. **To apply online, go to:** https://secure.stritch.edu/OnlineApplication/index.php. **Admissions requirements/recommendations:** High school units required (recommended): English: 4 (4); Mathematics: 2 (2); Science: 2 (2); Social studies: 2 (2); Academic electives: 6 (6); Total units: 16 (16). Tests: The college uses SAT or ACT scores in admissions decisions. Either SAT or ACT required. For admission to the fall 2011 entering class, the school will accept: ACT with or without writing accepted. Campus visit: Recommended. Admissions interview: Recommended. Off-campus interview: May be arranged. **Factors that count in admissions decisions:** *Academic:* Secondary school record: Not Considered. Class rank: Not Considered. Letters of recommendation: Not Considered. Standardized test scores: Very Important. Essay: Not Considered. *Nonacademic:* Interview: Very Important. Extracurricular activities: Not Considered. Talent/ability: Not Considered. Character/personal qualities: Not Considered. Alumni/ae relationship: Not Considered. Geographical residence: Not Considered. State residency: Not Considered. Religious affiliation/commitment: Not Considered. Minority status: Not Considered. Volunteer work: Not Considered. Work experience: Not

Considered. **Admissions statistics for the fall 2009 entering class:** Total applicants: 1,033. Total accepted: 421. Freshmen enrolled: 267; Overall acceptance rate: 41%. **Credentials of fall 2009 freshmen:** 12% ranked in the top 10 percent of their high school class; 35% were in the top 25 percent. **First-year students who submitted SAT scores:** 8%. Scores (25/75 percentile): Critical Reading: 453-553, Math: 463-518, Combined: 916-1071. **First-year students submitting ACT scores:** 88%. Scores (25/75 percentile): English: 19-25, Math: 18-25, Composite: 20-25.

ACADEMICS

Year founded: 1937. **Academic calendar:** Semester. **Degrees offered:** certificate, associate, bachelor's, post-bachelor's certificate, master's, doctorate. **Major fields of study:** biological and biomedical sciences; business, management, marketing, and related support services; communication, journalism, and related programs; computer and information sciences and support services; education; English language and literature/letters; foreign languages, literatures, and linguistics; mathematics and statistics; philosophy and religious studies; physical sciences; psychology; social sciences; visual and performing arts. **Areas of required coursework:** arts/fine arts, humanities, mathematics, English (including composition), philosophy, foreign languages, sciences (biological or physical), history, social science. **Preprofessional programs:** pre-law, pre-dentistry, pre-medicine, pre-veterinary science, pre-optometry, pre-pharmacy, other. **Special academic programs:** accelerated program, distance learning, double major, English as a Second Language (ESL), honors program, independent study, internships, study abroad, teacher certificate program. **Teacher certification offered in:** early childhood, special education, elementary, middle/junior high, secondary. **Faculty and instruction (2009-2010):** Total instructional faculty: 103 full-time, 350 part-time (52% men; 48% women; 12% minorities). **Freshmen returning for sophomore year:** 81%. **Graduation rates:** Six-year: 62%.

COSTS AND FINANCIAL AID

Financial aid office: (414) 410-4048. **Expenses (2009-2010):** Tuition and fees 2009-2010: $21,790; room/board: $6,600. Estimated books and supplies: $700 personal expenses: $6,042. **Financial aid:** Priority filing date for institution's financial aid form: April 15.

CAMPUS LIFE AND EXTRACURRICULAR ACTIVITIES

Campus housing available (% using): coed dorms (90%), apartment for single students (10%). **Clubs and organizations:** Number of student organizations: 20. Activities include: choral groups, concert band, drama/theater, jazz band, music ensembles, musical theater, radio station, student government, student newspaper. Number of fraternities: 0; sororities: 0. **Sports program (2009-2010):** Member of NAIA. *Men's intercollegiate varsity sports:* baseball, basketball, cross country, soccer, volleyball. *Women's intercollegiate varsity sports:* basketball, cross country, soccer, softball.

SERVICES AND FACILITIES

Basic services: nonremedial tutoring, placement service, health service, health insurance. **Remedial assistance:** reading, math, writing, study skills. **Counseling services:** career, personal, veteran student, academic, religious. **Library:** Number of titles: 132,775; number of current serial subscriptions: 3,533. **Information technology resources:** Students are not required to lease or own a computer. Number of campus computers available to all students: 275. School has a wireless network. Proportion of college-owned housing units wired for high-speed internet access: 100%. **Campus safety:** Security services offered: 24-hour foot-and-vehicle patrols, late-night transport/escort service, 24-hour emergency telephones, lighted pathways/sidewalks, controlled dormitory access (key, security card, etc).

TRANSFER AND INTERNATIONAL STUDENTS

Transfer students: May apply for admission for the following academic terms: Fall, Spring. Applicants need a minimum number of credits to apply. **International students:** Number of foreign undergraduates: 96 (3% of student body). Number of countries represented: 17. Minimum TOEFL score required: 550 (paper); 213 (computer). Average TOEFL score: 525 (paper).

Carroll University

■ **Address:** 100 N. East Avenue, Waukesha, WI 53186
■ **Website:** http://www.carrollu.edu/
■ **Private; Religious affiliation:** Presbyterian Church (USA)
■ **Enrollment:** 2,632 full-time; 486 part-time

....

KEY STATS

✔ **U.S News College Ranking:** 40, Regional Universities (Midwest)
✔ **ACT Score (25th/75th percentile):** 20-25
✔ **Tuition:** 2010-2011: $24,065

Selectivity: Selective	**Room/board:** $7,371
Acceptance rate: 78%	**Average debt:** $27,066
Student/faculty ratio: 16/1	**Proportion who borrowed:** 78%

UNDERGRADUATE STUDENT BODY STATS

2009-2010 enrollment: 2,632 full-time; 486 part-time. Men: 34%; women: 66%. **Ethnic makeup:** African American: 1%; Asian American: 1%; Hispanic: 4%; White: 92%; International: 1%. **Religious preference:** Roman Catholic: 14%; Protestant: 7%; Unknown: 70%; Presbyterian Church (USA): 1%; Lutheran: 8%.

ADMISSIONS FACTS AND FIGURES

Phone: (262) 524-7220. **Email:** ccinfo@carrollu.edu. **Website:** http://www.carrollu.edu/. **Application deadlines for fall 2011:** Regular decision: Rolling. Early decision: Not offered. Early action: Not offered. Admission can be deferred. **To apply online, go to:** https://my.carrollu.edu/ics/Admissions/Visitor.jnz?portlet=Apply_Online. **Admissions requirements/recommendations:** High school units required (recommended): English: (4); Mathematics: (4); Science: (3); Foreign language: (0); Social studies: (3); History: (3); Total units: (17). Tests: The college uses SAT or ACT scores in admissions decisions. Either SAT or ACT required. For admission to the fall 2011 entering class, the school will accept: ACT with or without writing accepted. Campus visit: Recommended. Admissions interview: Recommended. Off-campus interview: Not available. **Factors that count in admissions decisions:** *Academic:* Secondary school record: Very Important. Class rank: Very Important. Letters of recommendation: Considered. Standardized test scores: Important. Essay: Considered. *Nonacademic:* Interview: Considered. Extracurricular activities: Considered. Talent/ability: Considered. Character/personal qualities: Considered. Alumni/ae relationship: Considered. Geographical residence: Considered. State residency: Considered. Religious affiliation/commitment: Not Considered. Minority status: Considered. Volunteer work: Not Considered. Work experience: Considered. **Other schools with the greatest overlap in applicants:** Carthage College; Marquette University; University of Wisconsin–Madison; University of Wisconsin–Milwaukee; University of Wisconsin–Whitewater. **Admissions statistics for the fall 2009 entering class:** Total applicants: 2,620. Total accepted: 2,039. Freshmen enrolled: 1,486; 24% were from out of state. Overall acceptance rate: 78%. **Credentials of fall 2009 freshmen:** 21% ranked in the top 10 percent of their high school class; 50% were in the top 25 percent; 85% were in the top half. (Proportion submitting class standing: 85%.) **Average high school grade point average:** 3.3. **First-year students who submitted SAT scores:** 2%. **First-year students submitting ACT scores:** 98%. Scores (25/75 percentile): English: 20-25, Math: 20-25, Composite: 20-25.

ACADEMICS

Year founded: 1846. **Academic calendar:** Semester. **Degrees offered:** bachelor's, master's. **Most popular majors:** 13% nursing/registered nurse training (R.N., A.S.N., B.S.N., M.S.N.), 12% business administration and management, 10% psychology, 8% elementary education and teaching, 6% kinesiology and exercise science. **Major fields of study:** area, ethnic, cultural, and gender studies; biological and biomedical sciences; business, management, marketing, and related support services; communication, journalism, and related programs; communications technologies/technicians and support services; computer and information sciences and support services; education; engineering; English language and literature/letters; foreign languages, literatures, and linguistics; health professions and related clinical sciences; history; mathematics and statistics; natural resources and conservation; parks, recreation, leisure, and fitness studies; philosophy and religious studies; physical sciences; psychology; security and protective services; social sciences; visual and performing arts. **Areas of required coursework:** arts/fine arts, humanities, computer literacy, mathematics, English (including composition), sciences (biological or physical), social

science. **Pre-professional programs:** pre-law, pre-dentistry, pre-medicine, pre-theology, pre-veterinary science, pre-optometry, pre-pharmacy. **Special academic programs (% participation):** distance learning (23%), double major (5%), exchange student program (domestic) (0%), honors program (4%), independent study (2%), internships (33%), liberal arts/career combination (2%), student-designed major, study abroad (1%), teacher certificate program (13%). **Teacher certification offered in:** early childhood, elementary, middle/junior high, secondary. **Reserve Officers Training Corps (ROTC):** Army ROTC: Offered at cooperating institution (Marquette University); Air Force ROTC: Offered at cooperating institution (Marquette University). **Faculty and instruction (2009-2010):** Total instructional faculty: 118 full-time, 203 part-time (40% men; 60% women; 2% minorities). Full-time faculty with Ph.D. or other terminal degree: 68%. Student/faculty ratio: 16/1. Classes of fewer than 20 students: 60%; of 20 to 49 students: 38%; of 50 or more students: 2%. **Advanced Placement and International Baccalaureate credit:** AP tests may be used for: Credit and/or placement. Scores accepted: 3, 4, 5. International Baccalaureate exams may be used for: Credit and/or placement. **Freshmen returning for sophomore year:** 76%. **Graduation rates:** Six-year: 57%. **Graduate study:** 51% of students pursue further study within five years.

COSTS AND FINANCIAL AID

Financial aid office: (262) 524-7296. **Expenses (2010-2011):** Tuition and fees 2010-2011: $24,065; room/board: $7,371. Estimated books and supplies: $1,120; transportation: $1,022; personal expenses: $1,427. **Financial aid:** In 2009-2010, 89% of undergraduates applied for financial aid. Of those, 80% were determined to have financial need; 29% had their need fully met. Average financial aid package (proportion receiving): $17,231 (80%). Average amount of gift aid, such as scholarships or grants (proportion receiving): $12,726 (80%). Average amount of self-help aid, such as work study or loans (proportion receiving): $4,505 (62%). Average need-based loan (excluding PLUS or other private loans): $3,170. Among students who received need-based aid, the average percentage of need met: 80%. Among students who received aid based on merit, the average award (and the proportion receiving): $9,370 (22%). The average athletic scholarship (and the proportion receiving): $0 (0%). Average amount of debt of borrowers graduating in 2009: $27,066. Proportion who borrowed: 78%.

CAMPUS LIFE AND EXTRACURRICULAR ACTIVITIES

Campus housing available (% using): coed dorms (78%), women's dorms (9%), apartment for single students (13%). Students who live in college-owned, operated, or affiliated housing: 52%. **Student employment:** During the 2009-2010 academic year, 24% of undergraduates worked on campus. Average per-year earnings: $1,670. **Clubs and organizations:** Number of student organizations: 48. Activities include: choral groups, concert band, dance, drama/theater, international student organization, jazz band, literary magazine, music ensembles, pep band, radio station, student government, student newspaper. Number of fraternities: 2; sororities: 3. Proportion of men in fraternities: 5%; of women in sororities: 6%. Average proportion of students who stay on campus on weekends: 40%. **Sports program (2009-2010):** Member of NCAA III. *Men's intercollegiate varsity sports:* baseball, basketball, cross country, football, golf, soccer, swimming, tennis, track and field (indoor), track and field (outdoor). *Women's intercollegiate varsity sports:* basketball, cross country, golf, soccer, swimming, tennis, track and field (indoor), track and field (outdoor), volleyball.

SERVICES AND FACILITIES

Basic services: nonremedial tutoring, placement service, health service, health insurance. **Remedial assistance:** math, writing, study skills. **Counseling services:** minority student, career, personal, academic, religious. **For learning-disabled students:** School does not offer a structured program with separate admission and additional fees. Services include: remedial math, remedial English, reading machines, note-taking services, oral tests, learning center, extended time for tests, tutors, substitution of courses, typist/scribe, exams on tape or computer, other testing accommodations. **Library:** Number of titles: 150,000; number of current serial subscriptions: 20,200. **Information technology resources:** Students are not required to lease or own a computer. Number of campus computers available to all students: 250. School has a wireless network. Approximate number of users that can be accommodated: 320. Proportion of college-owned housing units wired for high-speed internet access: 100%. **Campus safety:** Security services offered: 24-hour foot-and-vehicle patrols, late-night transport/escort service, 24-hour emergency telephones, lighted pathways/sidewalks, student patrols, controlled dormitory access (key, security card, etc).

TRANSFER AND INTERNATIONAL STUDENTS

Transfer students: May apply for admission for the following academic terms: Fall, Winter, Spring, Summer. Applicants need a minimum number of credits to apply. **International students:** Number of foreign undergraduates: 38 (1% of student body). Number of countries represented: 25. Minimum TOEFL score required: 550 (paper); 213 (computer). Average TOEFL score: 578 (paper).

Carthage College

- **Address:** 2001 Alford Park Drive, Kenosha, WI 53140
- **Website:** http://www.carthage.edu
- **Private; Religious affiliation:** Evangelical Lutheran Church in America
- **Enrollment:** 2,475 full-time; 556 part-time

KEY STATS

✔ **U.S News College Ranking:** 11, Regional Colleges (Midwest)
✔ **ACT Score (25th/75th percentile):** 21-26
✔ **Tuition:** 2010-2011: $29,750

Selectivity: Selective	**Room/board:** $8,150
Acceptance rate: 75%	**Average debt:** $29,075
Student/faculty ratio: 14/1	**Proportion who borrowed:** 80%

UNDERGRADUATE STUDENT BODY STATS

2009-2010 enrollment: 2,475 full-time; 556 part-time. Men: 43%; women: 57%. **Ethnic makeup:** African American: 4%; Asian American: 2%; Hispanic: 5%; White: 89%. **Religious preference:** Roman Catholic: 31%; Protestant: 5%; Jewish: 1%; Hindu: 1%; Buddhist: 1%; Unknown: 43%; Evangelical Lutheran Church in America: 18%.

ADMISSIONS FACTS AND FIGURES

Phone: (262) 551-6000. **Email:** admissions@carthage.edu. **Website:** http://www.carthage.edu. **Application deadlines for fall 2011:** Regular decision: Rolling. Early decision: Not offered. Early action: Send application by: July 19; Decision sent by: September 15. Admission can be deferred. **Application fee:** $35. **To apply online, go to:** http://www.carthage.edu/apply. **Admissions requirements/recommendations:** High school units required (recommended): English: (4); Mathematics: (3); Science: (3); Foreign language: (2); Social studies: (3); History: (0); Academic electives: (3); Total units: (18). Tests: The college uses SAT or ACT scores in admissions decisions. Either SAT or ACT required. For admission to the fall 2011 entering class, the school will accept: ACT with or without writing accepted. Campus visit: Recommended. Admissions interview: Recommended. Off-campus interview: May be arranged. **Factors that count in admissions decisions:** *Academic:* Secondary school record: Very Important. Class rank: Considered. Letters of recommendation: Considered. Standardized test scores: Very Important. Essay: Considered. *Nonacademic:* Interview: Considered. Extracurricular activities: Considered. Talent/ability: Considered. Character/personal qualities: Considered. Alumni/ae relationship: Not Considered. Geographical residence: Not Considered. State residency: Not Considered. Religious affiliation/commitment: Not Considered. Minority status: Not Considered. Volunteer work: Considered. Work experience: Considered. **Other schools with the greatest overlap in applicants:** Augustana College; Marquette University; Northern Illinois University; University of Illinois–Urbana-Champaign; University of Wisconsin–Madison. **Admissions statistics for the fall 2009 entering class:** Total applicants: 6,338. Total accepted: 4,757. Freshmen enrolled: 722; Accepted through early-decision or early-action plans: 22%. Overall acceptance rate: 75%. Non-early acceptance rate: 76%. **Credentials of fall 2009 freshmen:** 20% ranked in the top 10 percent of their high school class; 46% were in the top 25 percent; 75% were in the top half. (Proportion submitting class standing: 80%.) **Average high school grade point average:** 3.2. **First-year students who submitted SAT scores:** 7%. Scores (25/75 percentile): Critical Reading: 490-600, Math: 500-600, Combined: 990-1200. **First-year students submitting ACT scores:** 96%. Scores (25/75 percentile): English: 21-27, Math: 21-27, Composite: 21-26.

ACADEMICS

Year founded: 1847. **Academic calendar:** 4-1-4. **Degrees offered:** bachelor's, master's. **Major fields of study:** area, ethnic, cultural, and gender studies; biological and biomedical sciences; business, management, marketing, and related support services; communication, journalism, and related programs; communications technologies/technicians and support services; computer and information sciences and support services; education; English language and literature/letters; foreign languages, literatures, and linguistics; health professions and related clinical sciences; history; liberal arts and sciences studies, and humanities; mathematics and statistics; multi/interdisciplinary studies; natural resources and conservation; parks, recreation, leisure, and fitness studies; philosophy and religious studies; physical sciences; psychology; public administration and social service professions; security and protective services; social sciences; theology and religious vocations; visual and performing arts. **Areas of required coursework:** arts/fine arts, humanities, mathematics, English (including composition), foreign languages, sciences (biological or physical), social science, other. **Pre-professional programs:** pre-law, pre-dentistry, pre-medicine, pre-theology, pre-veterinary science, pre-optometry, pre-pharmacy, other. **Special academic programs (% participation):** accelerated program (5%), cross-registration (1%), double major (27%), honors program (3%), independent study (1%), internships (5%), student-designed major (1%), study abroad (4%), teacher certificate program (21%). **Teacher certification offered in:** special education, elementary, middle/junior high, secondary. **Cooperative education programs:** engineering, health professions. **Reserve Officers Training Corps (ROTC):** Army ROTC: Offered at cooperating institution (Marquette University); Air Force ROTC: Offered at cooperating institution (Marquette University). **Faculty and instruction (2009-2010):** Total instructional faculty: N/A. Student/faculty ratio: 14/1. Classes of fewer than 20 students: 58%; of 20 to 49 students: 42%; of 50 or more students: 0%. **Advanced Placement and International Baccalaureate credit:** AP tests may be used for: Placement only. Scores accepted: 3, 4, 5. International Baccalaureate exams may be used for: Credit only. **Freshmen returning for sophomore year:** 76%. **Graduation rates:** Four-year: 51%; five-year: 57%; six-year: 56%. **Graduate study:** 15% of students pursue further study immediately upon graduation; 15% within one year; 20% within five years. Fields in which graduates pursue further study: Master of Business Administration (MBA), 25%; law, 10%; medicine, 5%; dentistry, 1%; theology (or the seminary), 1%; education, 35%; arts and sciences, 15%; veterinary medicine, 1%.

COSTS AND FINANCIAL AID

Financial aid office: (262) 551-6001. **Expenses (2010-2011):** Tuition and fees 2010-2011: $29,750; room/board: $8,150. Estimated books and supplies: $1,600; transportation: $1,200; personal expenses: $1,900. **Financial aid:** Priority filing date for institution's financial aid form: February 15. In 2009-2010, 88% of undergraduates applied for financial aid. Of those, 75% were determined to have financial need; 14% had their need fully met. Average financial aid package (proportion receiving): $18,268 (75%). Average amount of gift aid, such as scholarships or grants (proportion receiving): $13,416 (75%). Average amount of self-help aid, such as work study or loans (proportion receiving): $5,784 (63%). Average need-based loan (excluding PLUS or other private loans): $4,266. Among students who received need-based aid, the average percentage of need met: 65%. Among students who received aid based on merit, the average award (and the proportion receiving): $9,564 (23%). The average athletic scholarship (and the proportion receiving): $0 (0%). Average amount of debt of borrowers graduating in 2009: $29,075. Proportion who borrowed: 80%.

CAMPUS LIFE AND EXTRACURRICULAR ACTIVITIES

Campus housing available (% using): coed dorms (63%), women's dorms (15%), men's dorms (2%), sorority housing (6%), fraternity housing (5%), apartment for single students (2%), special housing for disabled students (1%), other housing options (6%). **Student employment:** During the 2009-2010 academic year, 52% of undergraduates worked on campus. Average per-year earnings: $2,000. **Clubs and organizations:** Number of student organizations: 90. Activities include: campus ministries, choral groups, concert band, dance, drama/theater, international student organization, jazz band, literary magazine, model UN, music ensembles, musical theater, opera, pep band, radio station, student government, student newspaper, student film society, symphony orchestra, yearbook. Number of fraternities: 8; sororities: 7. Average proportion of students who stay on campus on weekends: 80%. **Sports program (2009-2010):** Member of NCAA III. *Men's intercollegiate varsity sports:* baseball, basketball, cross country, football, golf, lacrosse, soccer, swimming, tennis, track and field (indoor), track and field (outdoor), volleyball. *Women's intercollegiate varsity sports:* basketball, cross country, golf, lacrosse, soccer, softball, swimming, tennis, track and field (indoor), track and field (outdoor), volleyball, water polo.

SERVICES AND FACILITIES

Basic services: nonremedial tutoring, placement service, health service. **Remedial assistance:** writing, study skills. **Counseling services:** career, personal, academic, older student, psychological, religious. **For learning-**

disabled students: School does not offer a structured program with separate admission and additional fees. Services include: reading machines, tape recorders, diagnostic testing service, untimed tests, note-taking services, oral tests, readers, extended time for tests, tutors. **Library:** Number of titles: 125,488; number of current serial subscriptions: 425. **Information technology resources:** Students are not required to lease or own a computer. Number of campus computers available to all students: 250. School has a wireless network. Approximate number of users that can be accommodated: 3,000. Proportion of college-owned housing units wired for high-speed internet access: 96%. **Campus safety:** Security services offered: 24-hour foot-and-vehicle patrols, late-night transport/escort service, 24-hour emergency telephones, lighted pathways/sidewalks, student patrols, controlled dormitory access (key, security card, etc).

TRANSFER AND INTERNATIONAL STUDENTS

Transfer students: May apply for admission for the following academic terms: Fall, Winter, Spring, Summer. Applicants do not need a minimum number of credits to apply. For fall 2009: Transfer applications received: 334. Transfer applicants offered admission: 215. Transfer applicants enrolled: 72. **International students:** Number of foreign undergraduates: 13. Number of countries represented: 16. Minimum TOEFL score required: 500 (paper); 173 (computer).

Concordia University Wisconsin

- **Address:** 12800 N. Lake Shore Drive, Mequon, WI 53097
- **Website:** http://www.cuw.edu
- **Private; Religious affiliation:** Lutheran Church Missouri Synod
- **Enrollment:** 2,330 full-time; 1,757 part-time

KEY STATS

✔ **U.S News College Ranking:** 72, Regional Universities (Midwest)
✔ **ACT Score (25th/75th percentile):** 19-25
✔ **Tuition:** 2010-2011: $22,150

Selectivity: Selective	Room/board: $8,310
Acceptance rate: 64%	Average debt: $25,169
Student/faculty ratio: 12/1	Proportion who borrowed: 76%

UNDERGRADUATE STUDENT BODY STATS

2009-2010 enrollment: 2,330 full-time; 1,757 part-time. Men: 36%; women: 64%. **Ethnic makeup:** African American: 14%; American-Indian: 1%; Asian American: 1%; Hispanic: 2%; White: 80%; International: 1%. **Religious preference:** Roman Catholic: 19%; Protestant: 15%; Lutheran Church Missouri Synod: 65%.

ADMISSIONS FACTS AND FIGURES

Phone: (262) 243-4300. **Email:** admissions@cuw.edu. **Website:** http://www.cuw.edu. **Application deadlines for fall 2011:** Regular decision: August 1. Early decision: Not offered. Early action: Not offered. Admission cannot be deferred. **Application fee:** $35. **To apply online, go to:** https://www.cuw.edu/Academics/enrollment/. **Admissions requirements/recommendations:** High school units required (recommended): English: 3 (4); Mathematics: 2 (3); Science: 2; Foreign language: (2); Social studies: 2; Total units: 16. Tests: The college uses SAT or ACT scores in admissions decisions. ACT required. For admission to the fall 2011 entering class, the school will accept: ACT with or without writing accepted. Campus visit: Recommended. Admissions interview: Recommended. Off-campus interview: May be arranged. **Factors that count in admissions decisions:** *Academic:* Secondary school record: Very Important. Class rank: Considered. Letters of recommendation: Considered. Standardized test scores: Very Important. Essay: Considered. *Nonacademic:* Interview: Considered. Extracurricular activities: Considered. Talent/ability: Considered. Character/personal qualities: Important. Alumni/ae relationship: Considered. Geographical residence: Not Considered. State residency: Considered. Religious affiliation/commitment: Considered. Minority status: Considered. Volunteer work: Considered. Work experience: Important. **Admissions statistics for the fall 2009 entering class:** Total applicants: 2,538. Total accepted: 1,616. Freshmen enrolled: 471; 29% were from out of state. Overall acceptance rate: 64%. **Credentials of fall 2009 freshmen:** 15% ranked in the top 10 percent of their high school class; 39% were in the top 25 percent; 71% were in the top half. (Proportion submitting class standing: 81%.) **Average high school grade point average:** 3.4. **First-year students submitting ACT scores:** 96%. Scores (25/75 percentile): English: 19-25, Math: 19-25, Composite: 19-25.

ACADEMICS

Year founded: 1881. **Academic calendar:** 4-1-4. **Degrees offered:** certificate, associate, bachelor's, post-bachelor's certificate, master's. **Most popular majors:** 37% business, management, marketing, and related support services, 17% health professions and related clinical sciences, 12% education, 7% security and protective services, 6% biological and biomedical sciences. **Major fields of study:** biological and biomedical sciences; business, management, marketing, and related support services; communication, journalism, and related programs; computer and information sciences and support services; education; English language and literature/letters; foreign languages, literatures, and linguistics; health professions and related clinical sciences; liberal arts and sciences studies, and humanities; mathematics and statistics; natural resources and conservation; parks, recreation, leisure, and fitness studies; psychology; public administration and social service professions; social sciences; theology and religious vocations; visual and performing arts. **Areas of required coursework:** arts/fine arts, humanities, computer literacy, mathematics, English (including composition), philosophy, foreign languages, sciences (biological or physical), history, social science, other. **Pre-professional programs:** pre-law, pre-medicine. **Special academic programs (% participation):** accelerated program (40%), cooperative (work-study plan) program (1%), distance learning, double major (7%), dual enrollment (.05%), English as a Second Language (ESL) (1%), exchange student program (domestic) (1%), honors program, independent study (1%), internships (1%), liberal arts/career combination (3%), student-designed major (1%), study abroad (1%), teacher certificate program (1%). **Teacher certification offered in:** early childhood, special education, elementary, middle/junior high, secondary. **Cooperative education programs:** other. **Faculty and instruction (2009-2010):** Total instructional faculty: 109 full-time, 150 part-time (46% men; 54% women; 6% minorities). Full-time faculty with Ph.D. or other terminal degree: 68%. Student/faculty ratio: 12/1. Classes of fewer than 20 students: 51%; of 20 to 49 students: 47%; of 50 or more students: 2%. **Advanced Placement and International Baccalaureate credit:** AP tests may be used for: Credit only. **Freshmen returning for sophomore year:** 79%. **Graduation rates:** Four-year: 32%; five-year: 49%; six-year: 62%. **Graduate study:** 21% of students pursue further study immediately upon graduation; 29% within one year. Fields in which graduates pursue further study: Master of Business Administration (MBA), 25%; medicine, 25%; theology (or the seminary), 18%; education, 16%.

COSTS AND FINANCIAL AID

Financial aid office: (262) 243-4569. **Expenses (2010-2011):** Tuition and fees 2010-2011: $22,150; room/board: $8,310. Estimated books and supplies: $1,270; transportation: $370; personal expenses: $1,930. **Financial aid:** Priority filing date for institution's financial aid form: April 1; deadline: April 1. In 2009-2010, 93% of undergraduates applied for financial aid. Of those, 81% were determined to have financial need; 28% had their need fully met. Average financial aid package (proportion receiving): $21,364 (81%). Average amount of gift aid, such as scholarships or grants (proportion receiving): $10,948 (75%). Average amount of self-help aid, such as work study or loans (proportion receiving): $6,256 (75%). Average need-based loan (excluding PLUS or other private loans): $5,939. Among students who received need-based aid, the average percentage of need met: 73%. Among students who received aid based on merit, the average award (and the proportion receiving): $8,308 (15%). The average athletic scholarship (and the proportion receiving): $0 (0%). Average amount of debt of borrowers graduating in 2009: $25,169. Proportion who borrowed: 76%.

CAMPUS LIFE AND EXTRACURRICULAR ACTIVITIES

Campus housing available (% using): women's dorms (56%), men's dorms (44%). Students who live in college-owned, operated, or affiliated housing: 63%. **Student employment:** During the 2009-2010 academic year, 38% of undergraduates worked on campus. Average per-year earnings: $2,500. Activities include: campus ministries, choral groups, concert band, drama/theater, international student organization, jazz band, marching band, music ensembles, musical theater, pep band, radio station, student government, student newspaper. Number of fraternities: 0; sororities: 0. Average proportion of students who stay on campus on weekends: 60%. **Sports program (2009-2010):** Member of NCAA III. *Men's intercollegiate varsity sports:* baseball, basketball, cross country, football, golf, ice hockey, soccer, tennis, track and field (indoor), track and field (outdoor), wrestling. *Women's intercollegiate varsity sports:* basketball, cross country, golf, ice hockey, soccer, softball, tennis, track and field (indoor), track and field (outdoor), volleyball.

SERVICES AND FACILITIES

Basic services: nonremedial tutoring, placement service, health service. **Remedial assistance:** reading, writing, study skills. **Counseling services:** minority student, career, personal, academic, older student, psychological, religious. **Library:** Number of titles: 85,414; number of current serial subscriptions: 969. **Information technology resources:** Students are not required to lease or own a computer. Number of campus computers available to all students: 200. School has a wireless network. Approximate number of users that can be accommodated: 250. Proportion of college-owned housing units wired for high-speed internet access: 100%. **Campus safety:** Security services offered: 24-hour emergency telephones, lighted pathways/sidewalks, controlled dormitory access (key, security card, etc).

TRANSFER AND INTERNATIONAL STUDENTS

Transfer students: May apply for admission for the following academic terms: Fall, Winter, Spring, Summer. Applicants do not need a minimum number of credits to apply. For fall 2009: Transfer applications received: 484. Transfer applicants offered admission: 245. Transfer applicants enrolled: 136. **International students:** Number of foreign undergraduates: 23 (1% of student body). Minimum TOEFL score required: 500 (paper); 173 (computer). Average TOEFL score: 509 (paper).

Edgewood College

- **Address:** 1000 Edgewood College Drive, Madison, WI 53711-1997
- **Website:** http://www.edgewood.edu
- **Private; Religious affiliation:** Roman Catholic
- **Enrollment:** 1,514 full-time; 374 part-time

KEY STATS

- ✔ **U.S News College Ranking:** 52, Regional Universities (Midwest)
- ✔ **ACT Score (25th/75th percentile):** 20-25
- ✔ **Tuition:** 2010-2011: $21,988

Selectivity: Selective	**Room/board:** $7,384
Acceptance rate: 72%	**Average debt:** $31,327
Student/faculty ratio: 11/1	**Proportion who borrowed:** 70%

UNDERGRADUATE STUDENT BODY STATS

2009-2010 enrollment: 1,514 full-time; 374 part-time. Men: 29%; women: 71%. **Ethnic makeup:** African American: 4%; American-Indian: 1%; Asian American: 2%; Hispanic: 4%; White: 88%; International: 2%. **Religious preference:** Protestant: 1%; Jewish: 1%; Muslim: 1%; Hindu: 1%; Buddhist: 1%; No preference: 3%; Unknown: 29%; Roman Catholic: 30%; Christian: 14%; Other: 19%.

ADMISSIONS FACTS AND FIGURES

Phone: (608) 663-2294. **Email:** admissions@edgewood.edu. **Website:** http://www.edgewood.edu. **Application deadlines for fall 2011:** Regular decision: August 14. Early decision: Not offered. Early action: Not offered. Admission can be deferred. **Application fee:** $25. **To apply online, go to:** http://www.applyweb.com/aw?edgewd. **Admissions requirements/recommendations:** High school units required (recommended): English: 4 (4); Mathematics: 2 (2); Science: 2 (2); Foreign language: 2 (2); Social studies: 2 (2); History: 1 (1); Total units: 16 (16). **Tests:** The college uses SAT or ACT scores in admissions decisions. Either SAT or ACT required. For admission to the fall 2011 entering class, the school will accept: ACT with or without writing accepted. Campus visit: Recommended. Admissions interview: Neither required nor recommended. Off-campus interview: Not available. **Factors that count in admissions decisions:** *Academic:* Secondary school record: Not Considered. Class rank: Very Important. Letters of recommendation: Considered. Standardized test scores: Very Important. Essay: Considered. *Nonacademic:* Interview: Not Considered. Extracurricular activities: Not Considered. Talent/ability: Not Considered. Character/personal qualities: Not Considered. Alumni/ae relationship: Not Considered. Geographical residence: Not Considered. State residency: Not Considered. Religious affiliation/commitment: Not Considered. Minority status: Not Considered. Volunteer work: Not Considered. Work experience: Not Considered. **Other schools with the greatest overlap in applicants:** University of Wisconsin–Eau Claire; University of Wisconsin–La Crosse; University of Wisconsin–Madison; University of Wisconsin–Milwaukee; University of Wisconsin–Whitewater. **Admissions statistics for the fall 2009 entering class:** Total applicants: 1,210. Total accepted: 876. Freshmen enrolled: 287; 9% were from out of state. Overall acceptance rate: 72%. **Credentials of fall**

2009 freshmen: 12% ranked in the top 10 percent of their high school class; 36% were in the top 25 percent; 79% were in the top half. (Proportion submitting class standing: 71%.) **Average high school grade point average:** 3.3. **First-year students who submitted SAT scores:** 2%. Scores (25/75 percentile): Critical Reading: 440-570, Math: 430-580, Combined: 870-1150. **First-year students submitting ACT scores:** 98%. Scores (25/75 percentile): English: 19-25, Math: 19-25, Composite: 20-25.

ACADEMICS

Year founded: 1927. **Academic calendar:** Semester. **Degrees offered:** associate, bachelor's, master's. **Most popular majors:** 18% nursing/registered nurse training (R.N., A.S.N., B.S.N., M.S.N.), 15% business/commerce, 11% psychology, 7% communication studies/speech communication and rhetoric, 7% elementary education and teaching. **Major fields of study:** biological and biomedical sciences; business, management, marketing, and related support services; communication, journalism, and related programs; computer and information sciences and support services; education; English language and literature/letters; foreign languages, literatures, and linguistics; health professions and related clinical sciences; history; mathematics and statistics; multi/interdisciplinary studies; philosophy and religious studies; physical sciences; psychology; security and protective services; social sciences; visual and performing arts. **Areas of required coursework:** arts/fine arts, humanities, computer literacy, mathematics, English (including composition), philosophy, foreign languages, sciences (biological or physical), history, social science, other. **Special academic programs:** accelerated program, double major, dual enrollment, honors program, independent study, internships, liberal arts/career combination, student-designed major, study abroad, teacher certificate program. **Teacher certification offered in:** early childhood, special education, elementary, middle/junior high, secondary, bilingual/bicultural. **Reserve Officers Training Corps (ROTC):** Army ROTC: Offered at cooperating institution (University of Wisconsin–Madison). **Faculty and instruction (2009-2010):** Total instructional faculty: 108 full-time, 197 part-time (49% men; 51% women; 10% minorities). Full-time faculty with Ph.D. or other terminal degree: 89%. Student/faculty ratio: 11/1. Classes of fewer than 20 students: 77%; of 20 to 49 students: 22%; of 50 or more students: 1%. **Advanced Placement and International Baccalaureate credit:** AP tests may be used for: Credit and/or placement. Scores accepted: 3, 4, 5. International Baccalaureate exams may be used for: Credit and/or placement. **Freshmen returning for sophomore year:** 72%. **Graduation rates:** Four-year: 27%; five-year: 48%; six-year: 50%. **Graduate study:** 17% of students pursue further study immediately upon graduation. Fields in which graduates pursue further study: Master of Business Administration (MBA), 21%; law, 5%; medicine, 4%; theology (or the seminary), 3%; education, 13%; arts and sciences, 9%.

COSTS AND FINANCIAL AID

Financial aid office: (608) 663-2305. **Expenses (2010-2011):** Tuition and fees 2010-2011: $21,988; room/board: $7,384. Estimated books and supplies: $800; transportation: $515; personal expenses: $2,392. **Financial aid:** Priority filing date for institution's financial aid form: March 1. In 2009-2010, 84% of undergraduates applied for financial aid. Of those, 76% were determined to have financial need; 13% had their need fully met. Average financial aid package (proportion receiving): $16,399 (76%). Average amount of gift aid, such as scholarships or grants (proportion receiving): $10,575 (69%). Average amount of self-help aid, such as work study or loans (proportion receiving): $6,683 (72%). Average need-based loan (excluding PLUS or other private loans): $5,296. Among students who received need-based aid, the average percentage of need met: 53%. Among students who received aid based on merit, the average award (and the proportion receiving): $3,910 (15%). The average athletic scholarship (and the proportion receiving): $0 (0%). Average amount of debt of borrowers graduating in 2009: $31,327. Proportion who borrowed: 70%.

CAMPUS LIFE AND EXTRACURRICULAR ACTIVITIES

Campus housing available (% using): coed dorms (43%), women's dorms (40%), apartment for single students (11%), special housing for disabled students (6%). Students who live in college-owned, operated, or affiliated housing: 31%. Average per-year earnings: $1,800. **Clubs and organizations:** Number of student organizations: 40. Activities include: campus ministries, choral groups, concert band, dance, drama/theater, international student organization, jazz band, literary magazine, marching band, music ensembles, musical theater, pep band, student government, student newspaper, symphony orchestra. Number of fraternities: 0; sororities: 0. Average proportion of students who stay on campus on weekends: 31%. **Sports program (2009-2010):** Member of NCAA III. *Men's intercollegiate varsity sports:* baseball, basketball, cross country, golf, soccer, track and field (indoor), track and field (outdoor). **Women's intercollegiate varsity sports:** basketball, cross country, golf, soccer, softball, tennis, track and field (indoor), track and field (outdoor), volleyball.

SERVICES AND FACILITIES

Basic services: nonremedial tutoring, placement service, health service, health insurance. **Remedial assistance:** reading, math, writing, study skills. **Counseling services:** minority student, career, military, personal, veteran student, academic, older student, psychological, religious. **For learning-disabled students:** School does not offer a structured program with separate admission and additional fees. Total undergraduates in learning-disabled program or receiving services: 166. Services include: remedial math, remedial English, reading machines, tape recorders, note-taking services, oral tests, learning center, readers, extended time for tests, tutors, priority registration, priority seating, substitution of courses, texts on tape, typist/scribe, exams on tape or computer, other testing accommodations, waiver of foreign language degree requirement, waiver of math degree requirement, other. **Library:** Number of titles: 107,873; number of current serial subscriptions: 164. **Information technology resources:** Students are not required to lease or own a computer. Number of campus computers available to all students: 146. School has a wireless network. Approximate number of users that can be accommodated: 2,000. Proportion of college-owned housing units wired for high-speed internet access: 100%. **Campus safety:** Security services offered: 24-hour foot-and-vehicle patrols, late-night transport/escort service, 24-hour emergency telephones, lighted pathways/sidewalks, student patrols, controlled dormitory access (key, security card, etc).

TRANSFER AND INTERNATIONAL STUDENTS

Transfer students: May apply for admission for the following academic terms: Fall, Winter, Spring, Summer. Applicants need a minimum number of credits to apply. For fall 2009: Transfer applications received: 409. Transfer applicants offered admission: 251. Transfer applicants enrolled: 157. **International students:** Number of foreign undergraduates: 31 (2% of student body). Number of countries represented: 22. Minimum TOEFL score required: 525 (paper); 72 (computer).

Lakeland College

- **Address:** W3711 South Drive, Plymouth, WI 53073
- **Website:** http://www.lakeland.edu
- **Private; Religious affiliation:** United Church of Christ
- **Enrollment:** N/A

KEY STATS

✔ **U.S News College Ranking:** second tier, Regional Universities (Midwest)
✔ **ACT Score (25th/75th percentile):** 17-23
✔ **Tuition:** 2009-2010: $18,970

Selectivity: Selective	**Room/board:** $6,778
Acceptance rate: 89%	**Average debt:** N/A
Student/faculty ratio: N/A	**Proportion who borrowed:** N/A

Lawrence University

- **Address:** PO Box 599, Appleton, WI 54912
- **Website:** http://www.lawrence.edu
- **Private**
- **Enrollment:** 1,433 full-time; 62 part-time

KEY STATS

✔ **U.S News College Ranking:** 67, National Liberal Arts Colleges
✔ **ACT Score (25th/75th percentile):** 27-31
✔ **Tuition:** 2010-2011: $36,312

Selectivity: More selective	**Room/board:** $7,407
Acceptance rate: 69%	**Average debt:** $25,049
Student/faculty ratio: 9/1	**Proportion who borrowed:** 76%

UNDERGRADUATE STUDENT BODY STATS

2009-2010 enrollment: 1,433 full-time; 62 part-time. Men: 46%; women: 54%. **Ethnic makeup:** African American: 3%; Asian American: 3%; Hispanic: 2%; White: 84%; International: 8%. **Religious preference:** Roman

Catholic: 10%; Protestant: 12%; Jewish: 3%; No preference: 8%; Unknown: 55%; Other: 12%.

ADMISSIONS FACTS AND FIGURES

Phone: (800) 227-0982. **Email:** excel@lawrence.edu. **Website:** http://www.lawrence.edu. **Application deadlines for fall 2011:** Regular decision: January 15; decision sent by April 1. Early decision: Send application by: November 15; Decision sent by: December 1. Early action: Send application by: December 1; Decision sent by: January 15. Admission can be deferred. **Application fee:** $40. **To apply online, go to:** http://www.lawrence.edu/admissions/apply/. **Admissions requirements/recommendations:** High school units required (recommended): English: 4; Mathematics: (3); Science: (3); Foreign language: (2); Total units: 16. Tests: The college uses SAT or ACT scores in admissions decisions. Neither SAT nor ACT required. For admission to the fall 2011 entering class, the school will accept: ACT with or without writing accepted. Campus visit: Recommended. Admissions interview: Recommended. Off-campus interview: May be arranged. **Factors that count in admissions decisions:** *Academic:* Secondary school record: Very Important. Class rank: Very Important. Letters of recommendation: Important. Standardized test scores: Considered. Essay: Important. *Nonacademic:* Interview: Considered. Extracurricular activities: Important. Talent/ability: Important. Character/personal qualities: Important. Alumni/ae relationship: Considered. Geographical residence: Not Considered. State residency: Not Considered. Religious affiliation/commitment: Not Considered. Minority status: Considered. Volunteer work: Considered. Work experience: Considered. **Other schools with the greatest overlap in applicants:** Beloit College; Carleton College; Macalester College; St. Olaf College; University of Wisconsin–Madison. **Admissions statistics for the fall 2009 entering class:** Total applicants: 2,516. Total accepted: 1,739. Freshmen enrolled: 352; 65% were from out of state. Accepted through early-decision or early-action plans: 36%. Overall acceptance rate: 69%. Early-decision acceptance rate: 86%. Non-early acceptance rate: 62%. **Size of waiting list:** 175 applicants; enrolled from waiting list: 27. **Credentials of fall 2009 freshmen:** 38% ranked in the top 10 percent of their high school class; 70% were in the top 25 percent; 97% were in the top half. (Proportion submitting class standing: 60%.) **Average high school grade point average:** 3.6. **First-year students who submitted SAT scores:** 34%. Scores (25/75 percentile): Critical Reading: 590-730, Math: 600-710, Combined: 1190-1440. **First-year students submitting ACT scores:** 55%. Scores (25/75 percentile): English: 27-33, Math: 25-30, Composite: 27-31.

ACADEMICS

Year founded: 1847. **Academic calendar:** Trimester. **Degrees offered:** bachelor's. **Most popular majors:** 23% visual and performing arts, 13% social sciences, 10% psychology, 9% mathematics, 8% English language and literature. **Major fields of study:** area, ethnic, cultural, and gender studies; biological and biomedical sciences; computer and information sciences and support services; education; English language and literature/letters; foreign languages, literatures, and linguistics; history; legal professions and studies; liberal arts and sciences studies, and humanities; mathematics and statistics; multi/interdisciplinary studies; natural resources and conservation; philosophy and religious studies; physical sciences; psychology; social sciences; visual and performing arts. **Areas of required coursework:** arts/fine arts, humanities, foreign languages, sciences (biological or physical), social science, other. **Pre-professional programs:** pre-law, pre-dentistry, pre-medicine, pre-veterinary science, pre-optometry, pre-pharmacy. **Special academic programs (% participation):** double major (27.8%), independent study (50%), internships (5.6%), student-designed major (2%), study abroad (37%), teacher certificate program (4.2%). **Teacher certification offered in:** middle/junior high, secondary. **Cooperative education programs:** engineering, other. **Faculty and instruction (2009-2010):** Total instructional faculty: 157 full-time, 32 part-time (61% men; 39% women; 11% minorities). Full-time faculty with Ph.D. or other terminal degree: 89%. Student/faculty ratio: 9/1. Classes of fewer than 20 students: 75%; of 20 to 49 students: 23%; of 50 or more students: 2%. **Advanced Placement and International Baccalaureate credit:** AP tests may be used for: Credit and/or placement. Scores accepted: 4, 5. International Baccalaureate exams may be used for: Credit and/or placement. **Freshmen returning for sophomore year:** 90%. **Graduation rates:** Four-year: 60%; five-year: 75%; six-year: 76%. **Graduate study:** 18% of students pursue further study immediately upon graduation; 20% within one year; 1% within five years. Fields in which graduates pursue further study: law, 2%; medicine, 2%; arts and sciences, 15%.

COSTS AND FINANCIAL AID

Financial aid office: (920) 832-6583. **Expenses (2010-2011):** Tuition and fees 2010-2011: $36,312; room/board: $7,407. Estimated books and supplies:

$750; transportation: $300; personal expenses: $900. **Financial aid:** Priority filing date for institution's financial aid form: March 1. In 2009-2010, 73% of undergraduates applied for financial aid. Of those, 61% were determined to have financial need; 77% had their need fully met. Average financial aid package (proportion receiving): $26,155 (60%). Average amount of gift aid, such as scholarships or grants (proportion receiving): $18,952 (60%). Average amount of self-help aid, such as work study or loans (proportion receiving): $7,203 (55%). Average need-based loan (excluding PLUS or other private loans): $5,540. Among students who received need-based aid, the average percentage of need met: 92%. Among students who received aid based on merit, the average award (and the proportion receiving): $12,417 (31%). The average athletic scholarship (and the proportion receiving): $0 (0%). Average amount of debt of borrowers graduating in 2009: $25,049. Proportion who borrowed: 76%.

CAMPUS LIFE AND EXTRACURRICULAR ACTIVITIES
Campus housing available (% using): coed dorms (79%), women's dorms (2%), other housing options (19%). Students who live in college-owned, operated, or affiliated housing: 98%. **Student employment:** During the 2009-2010 academic year, 18% of undergraduates worked on campus. Average per-year earnings: $1,500. **Clubs and organizations:** Number of student organizations: 100. Activities include: campus ministries, choral groups, concert band, dance, drama/theater, international student organization, jazz band, literary magazine, model UN, music ensembles, musical theater, opera, pep band, radio station, student government, student newspaper, student film society, symphony orchestra, yearbook. Number of fraternities: 5; sororities: 3. Proportion of men in fraternities: 17%; of women in sororities: 10%. Average proportion of students who stay on campus on weekends: 90%. **Sports program (2009-2010):** Member of NCAA III. *Men's intercollegiate varsity sports:* baseball, basketball, cross country, fencing, football, golf, ice hockey, soccer, swimming, tennis, track and field (indoor), track and field (outdoor). *Women's intercollegiate varsity sports:* basketball, cross country, fencing, soccer, softball, swimming, tennis, track and field (indoor), track and field (outdoor), volleyball.

SERVICES AND FACILITIES
Basic services: nonremedial tutoring, placement service, health service, health insurance. **Remedial assistance:** other. **Counseling services:** minority student, career, personal, academic, older student, psychological, birth control. **For learning-disabled students:** School does not offer a structured program with separate admission and additional fees. Total undergraduates in learning-disabled program or receiving services: 38. Services include: tape recorders, untimed tests, note-taking services, oral tests, learning center, readers, extended time for tests, tutors, other testing accommodations, other. **Library:** Number of titles: 674,194; number of current serial subscriptions: 35,069. **Information technology resources:** Students are not required to lease or own a computer. Number of campus computers available to all students: 354. School has a wireless network. Approximate number of users that can be accommodated: 500. Proportion of college-owned housing units wired for high-speed internet access: 100%. **Campus safety:** Security services offered: 24-hour foot-and-vehicle patrols, late-night transport/escort service, 24-hour emergency telephones, lighted pathways/sidewalks, controlled dormitory access (key, security card, etc).

TRANSFER AND INTERNATIONAL STUDENTS
Transfer students: May apply for admission for the following academic terms: Fall, Winter, Spring. Applicants do not need a minimum number of credits to apply. For fall 2009: Transfer applications received: 114. Transfer applicants offered admission: 72. Transfer applicants enrolled: 33. **International students:** Number of foreign undergraduates: 113 (8% of student body). Number of countries represented: 50. Minimum TOEFL score required: 577 (paper); 233 (computer).

Maranatha Baptist Bible College

- **Address:** 745 W. Main Street, Watertown, WI 53094
- **Website:** http://www.mbbc.edu
- **Private; Religious affiliation:** Baptist
- **Enrollment:** 737 full-time; 52 part-time

KEY STATS
✔ **U.S News College Ranking:** 71, Regional Colleges (Midwest)
✔ **ACT Score:** 23
✔ **Tuition:** 2009-2010: $11,000

Selectivity: Selective	**Room/board:** $5,990
Acceptance rate: 51%	**Average debt:** N/A
Student/faculty ratio: 14/1	**Proportion who borrowed:** N/A

UNDERGRADUATE STUDENT BODY STATS
2009-2010 enrollment: 737 full-time; 52 part-time. Men: 43%; women: 57%. **Ethnic makeup:** African American: 1%; Asian American: 1%; Hispanic: 1%; White: 97%. **Religious preference:** Baptist: 90%; Other: 10%.

ADMISSIONS FACTS AND FIGURES
Phone: (920) 206-2327. **Email:** admissions@mbbc.edu. **Website:** http://www.mbbc.edu. **Application deadlines for fall 2011:** Regular decision: Rolling. Early decision: Not offered. Early action: Not offered. Admission can be deferred. **Application fee:** $50. **To apply online, go to:** https://apply.mbbc.edu/. **Admissions requirements/recommendations:** High school units required (recommended): English: 4 (4); Mathematics: 3 (3); Science: 3 (3); Foreign language: 2 (2); Social studies: 3 (3); History: 3 (3); Academic electives: (0); Total units: 18 (18). Tests: The college uses SAT or ACT scores in admissions decisions. Either SAT or ACT required. For admission to the fall 2011 entering class, the school will accept: ACT with or without writing accepted. Campus visit: Recommended. Admissions interview: Neither required nor recommended. **Factors that count in admissions decisions:** *Academic:* Secondary school record: Important. Class rank: Considered. Letters of recommendation: Very Important. Standardized test scores: Important. Essay: Very Important. *Nonacademic:* Interview: Considered. Extracurricular activities: Considered. Talent/ability: Considered. Character/personal qualities: Very Important. Alumni/ae relationship: Not Considered. Geographical residence: Not Considered. State residency: Not Considered. Religious affiliation/commitment: Very Important. Minority status: Not Considered. Volunteer work: Not Considered. Work experience: Not Considered. **Other schools with the greatest overlap in applicants:** Cedarville University; Clearwater Christian College; Northland College. **Admissions statistics for the fall 2009 entering class:** Total applicants: 406. Total accepted: 207. Freshmen enrolled: 198; 75% were from out of state. Overall acceptance rate: 51%. **Size of waiting list:** 0 applicants; enrolled from waiting list: 0. **Credentials of fall 2009 freshmen:** 20% ranked in the top 10 percent of their high school class; 31% were in the top 25 percent; 58% were in the top half. (Proportion submitting class standing: 55%.) **Average high school grade point average:** 3.4. **First-year students who submitted SAT scores:** 10%. **First-year students submitting ACT scores:** 90%. Scores (25/75 percentile): English: N/A, Math: N/A, Composite: N/A.

ACADEMICS
Year founded: 1968. **Academic calendar:** Semester. **Degrees offered:** certificate, associate, bachelor's, master's. **Most popular majors:** 18% humanities/humanistic studies, 16% nursing/registered nurse training (R.N., A.S.N., B.S.N., M.S.N.), 13% Bible/biblical studies, 12% business administration and management, 12% elementary education and teaching. **Major fields of study:** biological and biomedical sciences; business, management, marketing, and related support services; education; English language and literature/letters; health professions and related clinical sciences; liberal arts and sciences studies, and humanities; theology and religious vocations; visual and performing arts. **Areas of required coursework:** arts/fine arts, humanities, mathematics, English (including composition), sciences (biological or physical), history, other. **Pre-professional programs:** pre-medicine. **Special academic programs (% participation):** distance learning (4%), double major (1%), independent study (1%), internships (3%), study abroad (1%). **Teacher certification offered in:** early childhood, elementary, middle/junior high, secondary. **Reserve Officers Training Corps (ROTC):** Army ROTC: Offered on campus; Air Force ROTC: Offered at cooperating institution (University of Wisconsin–Whitewater). **Faculty and instruction (2009-2010):** Total instructional faculty: 45 full-time, 34 part-time (63% men; 37% women; 5% minorities). Full-time faculty with Ph.D. or other terminal degree: 33%.

Student/faculty ratio: 14/1. Classes of fewer than 20 students: 62%; of 20 to 49 students: 31%; of 50 or more students: 8%. **Advanced Placement and International Baccalaureate credit:** AP tests may be used for: Credit and/or placement. Scores accepted: 3, 4, 5. **Freshmen returning for sophomore year:** 73%. **Graduation rates:** Four-year: 32%; five-year: 45%; six-year: 50%. **Graduate study:** 21% of students pursue further study immediately upon graduation; 15% within one year. Fields in which graduates pursue further study: Master of Business Administration (MBA), 25%; theology (or the seminary), 40%; education, 35%; arts and sciences, 10%.

COSTS AND FINANCIAL AID
Financial aid office: (920) 206-2319. **Expenses (2009-2010):** Tuition and fees 2009-2010: $11,000; room/board: $5,990. Estimated books and supplies: $980; transportation: $1,470; personal expenses: $2,230. **Financial aid:**

CAMPUS LIFE AND EXTRACURRICULAR ACTIVITIES
Campus housing available (% using): women's dorms (60%), men's dorms (40%). Students who live in college-owned, operated, or affiliated housing: 68%. **Student employment:** During the 2009-2010 academic year, 37% of undergraduates worked on campus. Average per-year earnings: $3,900. Activities include: campus ministries, choral groups, concert band, drama/theater, music ensembles, pep band, student government, symphony orchestra, yearbook. Number of fraternities: 0; sororities: 0. **Sports program (2009-2010):** Member of NCAA III. *Men's intercollegiate varsity sports:* baseball, basketball, cross country, football, soccer, wrestling. *Women's intercollegiate varsity sports:* basketball, cross country, soccer, softball, volleyball.

SERVICES AND FACILITIES
Basic services: nonremedial tutoring, placement service. **Remedial assistance:** writing, study skills. **Counseling services:** personal, academic, religious. **For learning-disabled students:** School does not offer a structured program with separate admission and additional fees. Total undergraduates in learning-disabled program or receiving services: 52. Services include: remedial English, untimed tests, oral tests, readers, extended time for tests, tutors, priority seating, proofreading services, texts on tape. **Library:** Number of titles: 100,553; number of current serial subscriptions: 19,180. **Information technology resources:** Students are not required to lease or own a computer. Number of campus computers available to all students: 150. School has a wireless network. Approximate number of users that can be accommodated: 500. Proportion of college-owned housing units wired for high-speed internet access: 100%. **Campus safety:** Security services offered: late-night transport/escort service, lighted pathways/sidewalks, student patrols, controlled dormitory access (key, security card, etc).

TRANSFER AND INTERNATIONAL STUDENTS
Transfer students: May apply for admission for the following academic terms: Fall, Spring. Applicants need a minimum number of credits to apply. For fall 2009: Transfer applications received: 84. Transfer applicants offered admission: 53. Transfer applicants enrolled: 34. **International students:** Number of foreign undergraduates: 2. Number of countries represented: 10. Minimum TOEFL score required: 500 (paper); 171 (computer).

Marian University

- **Address:** 45 S. National Avenue, Fond du Lac, WI 54935
- **Website:** http://www.marianuniversity.edu
- **Private; Religious affiliation:** Roman Catholic
- **Enrollment:** 1,492 full-time; 493 part-time

KEY STATS
✔ **U.S News College Ranking:** 99, Regional Universities (Midwest)
✔ **ACT Score (25th/75th percentile):** 18-22
✔ **Tuition:** 2010-2011: $21,490

Selectivity: Less selective	Room/board: $5,700
Acceptance rate: 83%	Average debt: $24,595
Student/faculty ratio: 14/1	Proportion who borrowed: 96%

UNDERGRADUATE STUDENT BODY STATS
2009-2010 enrollment: 1,492 full-time; 493 part-time. Men: 27%; women: 73%. **Ethnic makeup:** African American: 7%; American-Indian: 1%; Asian American: 2%; Hispanic: 3%; White: 86%; International: 1%. **Religious preference:** Protestant: 30%; Unknown: 29%; Roman Catholic: 35%; Other: 6%.

Phone: (920) 923-7650. **Email:** admissions@marianuniversity.edu. **Website:** http://www.marianuniversity.edu. **Application deadlines for fall 2011:** Regular decision: Rolling. Early decision: Not offered. Early action: Not offered. Admission can be deferred. **Application fee:** $20. **To apply online, go to:** http://www.marianuniversity.edu/interior.aspx?id=128. **Admissions requirements/recommendations:** High school units required (recommended): English: 4; Mathematics: 2 (3); Science: 1 (2); Foreign language: (2); History: 1; Total units: 17. Tests: The college uses SAT or ACT scores in admissions decisions. Either SAT or ACT required. For admission to the fall 2011 entering class, the school will accept: ACT with writing recommended. Campus visit: Recommended. Admissions interview: Recommended. Off-campus interview: May be arranged. **Factors that count in admissions decisions:** *Academic:* Secondary school record: Very Important. Class rank: Very Important. Letters of recommendation: Considered. Standardized test scores: Very Important. Essay: Considered. *Nonacademic:* Interview: Important. Extracurricular activities: Considered. Talent/ability: Considered. Character/personal qualities: Important. Alumni/ae relationship: Considered. Geographical residence: Not Considered. State residency: Not Considered. Religious affiliation/commitment: Not Considered. Minority status: Not Considered. Volunteer work: Considered. Work experience: Considered. **Other schools with the greatest overlap in applicants:** Carroll College; Ripon College; University of Wisconsin–Milwaukee; University of Wisconsin–Oshkosh. **Admissions statistics for the fall 2009 entering class:** Total applicants: 1,016. Total accepted: 844. Freshmen enrolled: 319; 9% were from out of state. Overall acceptance rate: 83%. **Credentials of fall 2009 freshmen:** 8% ranked in the top 10 percent of their high school class; 31% were in the top 25 percent; 66% were in the top half. (Proportion submitting class standing: 87%.) **Average high school grade point average:** 2.9. **First-year students submitting ACT scores:** 95%. Scores (25/75 percentile): English: 16-22, Math: 17-23, Composite: 18-22.

ACADEMICS
Year founded: 1936. **Academic calendar:** Semester. **Degrees offered:** bachelor's, post-bachelor's certificate, master's, doctorate. **Most popular majors:** 39% nursing, 23% business, management, marketing, and related support services, 13% criminal justice/law enforcement administration, 9% education, 4% psychology. **Major fields of study:** biological and biomedical sciences; business, management, marketing, and related support services; communication, journalism, and related programs; computer and information sciences and support services; education; English language and literature/letters; foreign languages, literatures, and linguistics; health professions and related clinical sciences; history; liberal arts and sciences studies, and humanities; mathematics and statistics; multi/interdisciplinary studies; parks, recreation, leisure, and fitness studies; physical sciences; psychology; public administration and social service professions; security and protective services; visual and performing arts. **Areas of required coursework:** arts/fine arts, humanities, mathematics, English (including composition), philosophy, sciences (biological or physical), history, social science. **Pre-professional programs:** pre-law, pre-dentistry, pre-medicine, pre-veterinary science, other. **Special academic programs:** accelerated program, cooperative (work-study plan) program, distance learning, double major, dual enrollment, honors program, independent study, internships, liberal arts/career combination, student-designed major, study abroad, teacher certificate program, weekend college. **Teacher certification offered in:** early childhood, elementary, middle/junior high, secondary. **Cooperative education programs:** business, computer science, education, health professions, social/behavioral science, other. **Reserve Officers Training Corps (ROTC):** Army ROTC: Offered on campus. **Faculty and instruction (2009-2010):** Total instructional faculty: 84 full-time, 202 part-time (44% men; 56% women; 7% minorities). Full-time faculty with Ph.D. or other terminal degree: 60%. Student/faculty ratio: 14/1. Classes of fewer than 20 students: 67%; of 20 to 49 students: 32%; of 50 or more students: 2%. **Advanced Placement and International Baccalaureate credit:** AP tests may be used for: Credit only. Scores accepted: 3, 4, 5. **Freshmen returning for sophomore year:** 75%. **Graduation rates:** Four-year: 29%; five-year: 41%; six-year: 47%. **Graduate study:** 12% of students pursue further study within one year.

COSTS AND FINANCIAL AID
Financial aid office: (920) 923-7614. **Expenses (2010-2011):** Tuition and fees 2010-2011: $21,490; room/board: $5,700. Estimated books and supplies: $700; transportation: $2,000; personal expenses: $1,454. **Financial aid:** Priority filing date for institution's financial aid form: March 1. In 2009-2010, 96% of undergraduates applied for financial aid. Of those, 84% were determined to have financial need; 46% had their need fully

met. Average financial aid package (proportion receiving): $19,560 (84%). Average amount of gift aid, such as scholarships or grants (proportion receiving): $10,669 (82%). Average amount of self-help aid, such as work study or loans (proportion receiving): $7,550 (78%). Average need-based loan (excluding PLUS or other private loans): $6,758. Among students who received need-based aid, the average percentage of need met: 91%. Among students who received aid based on merit, the average award (and the proportion receiving): $4,931 (11%). The average athletic scholarship (and the proportion receiving): $0 (0%). Average amount of debt of borrowers graduating in 2009: $24,595. Proportion who borrowed: 96%.

CAMPUS LIFE AND EXTRACURRICULAR ACTIVITIES

Campus housing available: coed dorms, sorority housing, fraternity housing, apartment for single students, special housing for disabled students. Students who live in college-owned, operated, or affiliated housing: 32%. **Student employment:** During the 2009-2010 academic year, 25% of undergraduates worked on campus. Average per-year earnings: $1,400. **Clubs and organizations:** Number of student organizations: 41. Activities include: campus ministries, choral groups, concert band, dance, drama/theater, jazz band, literary magazine, model UN, music ensembles, student government, student newspaper, symphony orchestra. Number of fraternities: 1; sororities: 3. Proportion of men in fraternities: 6%; of women in sororities: 7%. Average proportion of students who stay on campus on weekends: 33%. **Sports program (2009-2010):** Member of NCAA III.

SERVICES AND FACILITIES

Basic services: nonremedial tutoring, placement service, day care, health service, health insurance. **Remedial assistance:** reading, math, writing, study skills, other. **Counseling services:** minority student, career, military, personal, veteran student, academic, older student, psychological, religious. **For learning-disabled students:** School does not offer a structured program with separate admission and additional fees. Total undergraduates in learning-disabled program or receiving services: 19. Services include: remedial math, remedial English, reading machines, remedial reading, tape recorders, other special classes, note-taking services, oral tests, learning center, readers, extended time for tests, tutors, priority registration, priority seating, texts on tape, other testing accommodations, other. **Library:** Number of titles: 116,270; number of current serial subscriptions: 1,464. **Information technology resources:** Students are not required to lease or own a computer. Number of campus computers available to all students: 450. School has a wireless network. Proportion of college-owned housing units wired for high-speed internet access: 100%. **Campus safety:** Security services offered: 24-hour foot-and-vehicle patrols, late-night transport/escort service, 24-hour emergency telephones, lighted pathways/sidewalks, student patrols, controlled dormitory access (key, security card, etc).

TRANSFER AND INTERNATIONAL STUDENTS

Transfer students: May apply for admission for the following academic terms: Fall, Winter, Spring, Summer. Applicants do not need a minimum number of credits to apply. For fall 2009: Transfer applications received: 341. Transfer applicants offered admission: 254. Transfer applicants enrolled: 128. **International students:** Number of foreign undergraduates: 22 (1% of student body). Number of countries represented: 11. Minimum TOEFL score required: 525 (paper); 193 (computer). Average TOEFL score: 700 (paper).

Marquette University

- **Address:** PO Box 1881, Milwaukee, WI 53201-1881
- **Website:** http://www.marquette.edu
- **Private; Religious affiliation:** Roman Catholic (Jesuit)
- **Enrollment:** 7,693 full-time; 388 part-time

....

KEY STATS

✔ **U.S News College Ranking:** 75, National Universities
✔ **ACT Score (25th/75th percentile):** 24-29
✔ **Tuition:** 2010-2011: $30,462

Selectivity: More selective	**Room/board:** $9,890
Acceptance rate: 66%	**Average debt:** $31,469
Student/faculty ratio: 14/1	**Proportion who borrowed:** 65%

UNDERGRADUATE STUDENT BODY STATS

2009-2010 enrollment: 7,693 full-time; 388 part-time. Men: 48%; women: 52%. **Ethnic makeup:** African American: 5%; Asian American: 4%; Hispanic: 6%; White: 83%; International: 2%. **Religious preference:** Protestant 14%; Muslim: 1%; No preference: 29%; Roman Catholic (Jesuit): 55%; Eastern Orthodox, Jewish: 1%.

ADMISSIONS FACTS AND FIGURES

Phone: (800) 222-6544. **Email:** admissions@marquette.edu. **Website:** http://www.marquette.edu. **Application deadlines for fall 2011:** Regular decision: December 1; decision sent by January 31. Early decision: Not offered. Early action: Not offered. Admission can be deferred. **Application fee:** $30. **To apply online, go to:** http://www.marquette.edu/student/ugrad/applytoday.shtml. **Admissions requirements/recommendations:** High school units required (recommended): English: 4 (4); Mathematics: 2 (3); Science: 2 (3); Foreign language: 0 (2); Social studies: 2 (3); History: 0 (0); Academic electives: 2 (4); Total units: 16 (22). Tests: The college uses SAT or ACT scores in admissions decisions. Either SAT or ACT required. For admission to the fall 2011 entering class, the school will accept: ACT with writing recommended. Campus visit: Recommended. Admissions interview: Neither required nor recommended. Off-campus interview: Not available. **Factors that count in admissions decisions:** *Academic:* Secondary school record: Very Important. Class rank: Important. Letters of recommendation: Important. Standardized test scores: Important. Essay: Important. *Nonacademic:* Interview: Not Considered. Extracurricular activities: Considered. Talent/ability: Considered. Character/personal qualities: Considered. Alumni/ae relationship: Considered. Geographical residence: Considered. State residency: Considered. Religious affiliation/commitment: Not Considered. Minority status: Considered. Volunteer work: Considered. Work experience: Not Considered. **Other schools with the greatest overlap in applicants:** Loyola University Chicago; St. Louis University; University of Illinois–Urbana-Champaign; University of Wisconsin–Madison; University of Wisconsin–Milwaukee. **Admissions statistics for the fall 2009 entering class:** Total applicants: 17,825. Total accepted: 11,682. Freshmen enrolled: 1,952; 65% were from out of state. Overall acceptance rate: 66%. **Size of waiting list:** 2461 applicants; enrolled from waiting list: 558. **Credentials of fall 2009 freshmen:** 33% ranked in the top 10 percent of their high school class; 65% were in the top 25 percent; 92% were in the top half. (Proportion submitting class standing: 56%.) **First-year students who submitted SAT scores:** 24%. Scores (25/75 percentile): Critical Reading: 540-640, Math: 540-660, Combined: 1080-1300. **First-year students submitting ACT scores:** 92%. Scores (25/75 percentile): English: 24-29, Math: 24-31, Composite: 24-29.

ACADEMICS

Year founded: 1881. **Academic calendar:** Semester. **Degrees offered:** bachelor's, post-bachelor's certificate, master's, post-master's certificate, doctorate. **Most popular majors:** 25% business, management, marketing, and related support services, 11% communication, journalism, and related programs, 10% social sciences, 9% engineering, 9% health professions and related clinical sciences. **Major fields of study:** biological and biomedical sciences; business, management, marketing, and related support services; communication, journalism, and related programs; computer and information sciences and support services; education; engineering; engineering technologies/technicians; English language and literature/letters; foreign languages, literatures, and linguistics; health professions and related clinical sciences; history; mathematics and statistics; multi/interdisciplinary studies; philosophy and religious studies; physical sciences; psychology; public administration and social service professions; social sciences; theology and religious vocations; visual and performing arts. **Areas of required coursework:** arts/fine arts, humanities, mathematics, English (including composition), philosophy, foreign languages, sciences (biological or physical), history, social science, other. **Pre-professional programs:** pre-law, pre-dentistry, pre-medicine. **Special academic programs (% participation):** accelerated program (1%), cooperative (work-study plan) program (5%), cross-registration (1%), distance learning, double major (31%), dual enrollment, English as a Second Language (ESL) (4%), honors program (5%), independent study (25%), internships, liberal arts/career combination, study abroad (22%), teacher certificate program (5%), weekend college (2%). **Teacher certification offered in:** elementary, middle/junior high, secondary. **Cooperative education programs:** business, engineering. **Reserve Officers Training Corps (ROTC):** Army ROTC: Offered on campus; Navy ROTC: Offered on campus; Air Force ROTC: Offered on campus. **Faculty and instruction (2009-2010):** Total instructional faculty: 627 full-time, 483 part-time (58% men; 42% women; 11% minorities). Full-time faculty with Ph.D. or other terminal degree: 90%. Student/faculty ratio: 14/1. Classes of fewer than 20 students: 39%; of 20 to 49 students: 50%; of 50 or more students: 11%. **Advanced Placement and International Baccalaureate credit:** AP tests may be used for: Credit and/or placement. Scores accepted: 3, 4, 5. International Baccalaureate exams may be used for: Credit and/or placement. **Freshmen returning for sophomore year:** 90%. **Graduation rates:** Four-year: 60%; five-year: 79%; six-year: 80%. **Graduate study:** 33% of students pursue further study within one year; 42% within five years. Fields in which graduates pursue further study: Master of Business Administration (MBA), 11%; law, 13%; medicine, 7%; dentistry, 2%; engineering, 7%; education, 10%.

COSTS AND FINANCIAL AID

Financial aid office: (414) 288-0200. **Expenses (2010-2011):** Tuition and fees 2010-2011: $30,462; room/board: $9,890. Estimated books and supplies: $900; transportation: $200; personal expenses: $1,800. **Financial aid:** Priority filing date for institution's financial aid form: March 1. In 2009-2010, 73% of undergraduates applied for financial aid. Of those, 60% were determined to have financial need; 28% had their need fully met. Average financial aid package (proportion receiving): $21,428 (60%). Average amount of gift aid, such as scholarships or grants (proportion receiving): $14,614 (58%). Average amount of self-help aid, such as work study or loans (proportion receiving): $6,991 (52%). Average need-based loan (excluding PLUS or other private loans): $5,440. Among students who received need-based aid, the average percentage of need met: 78%. Among students who received aid based on merit, the average award (and the proportion receiving): $8,138 (24%). The average athletic scholarship (and the proportion receiving): $23,938 (1%). Average amount of debt of borrowers graduating in 2009: $31,469. Proportion who borrowed: 65%.

CAMPUS LIFE AND EXTRACURRICULAR ACTIVITIES

Campus housing available (% using): coed dorms (59%), women's dorms (8%), men's dorms (8%), sorority housing, fraternity housing (1%), apartments for married students, apartment for single students (16%), special housing for disabled students, special housing for international students (0%), other housing options. Students who live in college-owned, operated, or affiliated housing: 54%. **Student employment:** During the 2009-2010 academic year, 25% of undergraduates worked on campus. Average per-year earnings: $3,000. **Clubs and organizations:** Number of student organizations: 240. Activities include: campus ministries, choral groups, concert band, dance, drama/theater, international student organization, jazz band, literary magazine, model UN, music ensembles, musical theater, pep band, radio station, student government, student newspaper, symphony orchestra, television station, yearbook. Number of fraternities: 10; sororities: 12. Proportion of men in fraternities: 8%; of women in sororities: 12%. Average proportion of students who stay on campus on weekends: 90%. **Sports program (2009-2010):** Member of NCAA I. *Men's intercollegiate varsity sports:* basketball, cross country, golf, soccer, tennis, track and field (indoor), track and field (outdoor). *Women's intercollegiate varsity sports:* basketball, cross country, soccer, tennis, track and field (indoor), track and field (outdoor), volleyball.

SERVICES AND FACILITIES

Basic services: nonremedial tutoring, placement service, day care, health service, health insurance, other. **Counseling services:** minority student, career, military, personal, veteran student, academic, older student, psychological, religious. **For learning-disabled students:** School does not offer a structured program with separate admission and additional fees. Services include: reading machines, tape recorders, note-taking services, oral tests, readers, extended time for tests, tutors, texts on tape, other testing accommodations, other. **Library:** Number of titles: 1,597,164; number of current serial subscriptions: 27,425. **Information technology resources:** Students are not required to lease or own a computer. Number of campus computers available to all students: 1,129. School has a wireless network. Approximate number of users that can be accommodated: 8,000. Proportion of college-owned housing units wired for high-speed internet access: 100%. **Campus safety:** Security services offered: 24-hour foot-and-vehicle patrols, late-night transport/escort service, 24-hour emergency telephones, lighted pathways/sidewalks, student patrols, controlled dormitory access (key, security card, etc).

TRANSFER AND INTERNATIONAL STUDENTS

Transfer students: May apply for admission for the following academic terms: Fall, Spring, Summer. Applicants do not need a minimum number of credits to apply. For fall 2009: Transfer applications received: 641. Transfer applicants offered admission: 350. Transfer applicants enrolled: 160. **International students:** Number of foreign undergraduates: 141 (2%

of student body). Number of countries represented: 41. Minimum TOEFL score required: 550 (paper); 78 (computer). Average TOEFL score: 582 (paper).

Milwaukee Institute of Art and Design

- **Address:** 273 E. Erie Street, Milwaukee, WI 53202
- **Website:** http://www.miad.edu
- **Private**
- **Enrollment:** 648 full-time; 32 part-time

KEY STATS

✔ **U.S News College Ranking:** Unranked Specialty School–Fine Arts
✔ **SAT or ACT Score (25th/75th percentile):** N/A
✔ **Tuition:** 2010-2011: $27,302

Selectivity: N/A	Room/board: $8,130
Acceptance rate: 71%	Average debt: $24,900
Student/faculty ratio: 11/1	Proportion who borrowed: 76%

UNDERGRADUATE STUDENT BODY STATS

2009-2010 enrollment: 648 full-time; 32 part-time. Men: 44%; women: 56%. **Ethnic makeup:** African American: 4%; American-Indian: 1%; Asian American: 3%; Hispanic: 9%; White: 81%; International: 2%.

ADMISSIONS FACTS AND FIGURES

Phone: (414) 291-8070. **Email:** admissions@miad.edu. **Website:** http://www.miad.edu. **Application deadlines for fall 2011:** Regular decision: Rolling. Early decision: Not offered. Early action: Send application by: November 15; Decision sent by: December 1. Admission can be deferred. **Application fee:** $25. **To apply online, go to:** http://www.miad.edu/content/view/207/82/. **Admissions requirements/recommendations:** High school units required (recommended): English: 0 (0); Mathematics: 0 (0); Science: 0 (0); Foreign language: 0 (0); Social studies: 0 (0); History: 0 (0); Academic electives: 0 (0); Total units: 0 (0). Tests: The college uses SAT or ACT scores in admissions decisions. Neither SAT nor ACT required. For admission to the fall 2011 entering class, the school will accept: ACT with or without writing accepted. Campus visit: Recommended. Admissions interview: Recommended. Off-campus interview: Not available. **Factors that count in admissions decisions: *Academic:*** Secondary school record: Considered. Class rank: Considered. Letters of recommendation: Considered. Standardized test scores: Considered. Essay: Very Important. ***Nonacademic:*** Interview: Very Important. Extracurricular activities: Considered. Talent/ability: Very Important. Character/personal qualities: Very Important. Alumni/ae relationship: Not Considered. Geographical residence: Not Considered. State residency: Not Considered. Religious affiliation/commitment: Not Considered. Minority status: Not Considered. Volunteer work: Considered. Work experience: Considered. **Other schools with the greatest overlap in applicants:** Kansas City Art Institute; Maryland Institute College of Art; Maryland Institute College of Art; Minneapolis College of Art and Design; Minneapolis College of Art and Design; University of Wisconsin–Milwaukee; University of Wisconsin–Milwaukee; University of Wisconsin–Stout; University of Wisconsin–Stout. **Admissions statistics for the fall 2009 entering class:** Total applicants: 442. Total accepted: 312. Freshmen enrolled: 177; 37% were from out of state. Accepted through early-decision or early-action plans: 6%. Overall acceptance rate: 71%. Non-early acceptance rate: 82%. **Credentials of fall 2009 freshmen:** 8% ranked in the top 10 percent of their high school class; 31% were in the top 25 percent; 61% were in the top half. (Proportion submitting class standing: 75%.) **Average high school grade point average:** 3.0. **First-year students who submitted SAT scores:** 1%. **First-year students submitting ACT scores:** 41%. Scores (25/75 percentile): English: N/A, Math: N/A, Composite: N/A.

ACADEMICS

Year founded: 1974. **Academic calendar:** Semester. **Degrees offered:** bachelor's. **Major fields of study:** visual and performing arts. **Areas of required coursework:** arts/fine arts, humanities, computer literacy, English (including composition), sciences (biological or physical), history, social science. **Special academic programs:** cross-registration, double major, exchange student program (domestic), independent study, internships, study abroad. **Faculty and instruction (2009-2010):** Total instructional faculty: 40 full-time, 71 part-time (59% men; 41% women; 9% minorities). Full-time faculty with Ph.D. or other terminal degree: 78%. Student/faculty ratio: 11/1. Classes of fewer than 20 students: 73%; of 20 to 49 students: 27%; of 50 or more students: 0%. **Advanced Placement and International Baccalaureate credit:** AP tests may be used for: Credit only. Scores accepted: 3, 4, 5. International Baccalaureate exams may be used for: Credit only. **Freshmen returning for sophomore year:** 72%. **Graduation rates:** Four-year: 43%; five-year: 54%; six-year: 49%. **Graduate study:** 3% of students pursue further study immediately upon graduation. Fields in which graduates pursue further study: arts and sciences, 100%.

COSTS AND FINANCIAL AID

Financial aid office: (414) 291-3272. **Expenses (2010-2011):** Tuition and fees 2010-2011: $27,302; room/board: $8,130. Estimated books and supplies: $1,980; transportation: $1,798; personal expenses: $1,798. **Financial aid:** Priority filing date for institution's financial aid form: February 15. In 2009-2010, 92% of undergraduates applied for financial aid. Of those, 86% were determined to have financial need; 11% had their need fully met. Average financial aid package (proportion receiving): $19,455 (86%). Average amount of gift aid, such as scholarships or grants (proportion receiving): $12,888 (86%). Average amount of self-help aid, such as work study or loans (proportion receiving): $7,108 (80%). Average need-based loan (excluding PLUS or other private loans): $6,236. Among students who received need-based aid, the average percentage of need met: 69%. Among students who received aid based on merit, the average award (and the proportion receiving): $9,611 (13%). The average athletic scholarship (and the proportion receiving): $0 (0%). Average amount of debt of borrowers graduating in 2009: $24,900. Proportion who borrowed: 76%.

CAMPUS LIFE AND EXTRACURRICULAR ACTIVITIES

Campus housing available (% using): coed dorms (100%). Students who live in college-owned, operated, or affiliated housing: 25%. **Student employment:** During the 2009-2010 academic year, 20% of undergraduates worked on campus. Average per-year earnings: $1,500. **Clubs and organizations:** Number of student organizations: 12. Activities include: international student organization, student government, student newspaper. Number of fraternities: 0; sororities: 0. Average proportion of students who stay on campus on weekends: 85%.

SERVICES AND FACILITIES

Basic services: nonremedial tutoring, placement service, health service, health insurance. **Remedial assistance:** reading, writing, study skills. **Counseling services:** minority student, career, personal, academic, psychological, birth control. **For learning-disabled students:** School does not offer a structured program with separate admission and additional fees. Total undergraduates in learning-disabled program or receiving services: 29. Services include: remedial English, remedial reading, oral tests, learning center, readers, extended time for tests, tutors, early syllabus, priority registration, priority seating, substitution of courses, texts on tape, exams on tape or computer, other testing accommodations. **Library:** Number of titles: 34,844; number of current serial subscriptions: 24,292. **Information technology resources:** Students are not required to lease or own a computer. Number of campus computers available to all students: 253. School has a wireless network. Approximate number of users that can be accommodated: 500. Proportion of college-owned housing units wired for high-speed internet access: 100%. **Campus safety:** Security services offered: 24-hour foot-and-vehicle patrols, 24-hour emergency telephones, lighted pathways/sidewalks, controlled dormitory access (key, security card, etc).

TRANSFER AND INTERNATIONAL STUDENTS

Transfer students: May apply for admission for the following academic terms: Fall, Spring, Summer. Applicants do not need a minimum number of credits to apply. For fall 2009: Transfer applications received: 112. Transfer applicants offered admission: 84. Transfer applicants enrolled: 48. **International students:** Number of foreign undergraduates: 13 (2% of student body). Number of countries represented: 6. Minimum TOEFL score required: 550 (paper); 213 (computer).

Milwaukee School of Engineering

- **Address:** 1025 N. Broadway, Milwaukee, WI 53202-3109
- **Website:** http://www.msoe.edu
- **Private**
- **Enrollment:** 2,246 full-time; 192 part-time

KEY STATS

✔ **U.S News College Ranking:** 11, Regional Colleges (Midwest)
✔ **ACT Score (25th/75th percentile):** 24-29
✔ **Tuition:** 2010-2011: $29,520

Selectivity: Selective	**Room/board:** $7,431
Acceptance rate: 67%	**Average debt:** $35,722
Student/faculty ratio: 14/1	**Proportion who borrowed:** 94%

UNDERGRADUATE STUDENT BODY STATS

2009-2010 enrollment: 2,246 full-time; 192 part-time. Men: 81%; women: 19%. **Ethnic makeup:** African American: 3%; American-Indian: 1%; Asian American: 3%; Hispanic: 3%; White: 87%; International: 3%.

ADMISSIONS FACTS AND FIGURES

Phone: (800) 332-6763. **Email:** explore@msoe.edu. **Website:** http://www.msoe.edu. **Application deadlines for fall 2011:** Regular decision: Rolling. Early decision: Not offered. Early action: Not offered. Admission can be deferred. **Application fee:** $25. **To apply online, go to:** http://www.msoe.edu/admission. **Admissions requirements/recommendations:** High school units required (recommended): English: 4 (4); Mathematics: 4 (4); Science: 2 (2); Foreign language: 0 (0); Social studies: 0 (0); History: 0 (0); Academic electives: 0 (0); Total units: 10 (12). Tests: The college uses SAT or ACT scores in admissions decisions. Either SAT or ACT required. For admission to the fall 2011 entering class, the school will accept: ACT with or without writing accepted. Campus visit: Recommended. Admissions interview: Neither required nor recommended. Off-campus interview: May be arranged. **Factors that count in admissions decisions:** *Academic:* Secondary school record: Very Important. Class rank: Not Considered. Letters of recommendation: Considered. Standardized test scores: Very Important. Essay: Not Considered. *Nonacademic:* Interview: Not Considered. Extracurricular activities: Considered. Talent/ability: Not Considered. Character/personal qualities: Considered. Alumni/ae relationship: Not Considered. Geographical residence: Not Considered. State residency: Not Considered. Religious affiliation/commitment: Not Considered. Minority status: Not Considered. Volunteer work: Considered. Work experience: Considered. **Other schools with the greatest overlap in applicants:** Marquette University; Michigan Technological University; University of Wisconsin–Madison; University of Wisconsin–Milwaukee; University of Wisconsin–Platteville. **Admissions statistics for the fall 2009 entering class:** Total applicants: 2,126. Total accepted: 1,427. Freshmen enrolled: 534; 37% were from out of state. Overall acceptance rate: 67%. **Average high school grade point average:** 3.5. **First-year students who submitted SAT scores:** 3%. Scores (25/75 percentile): Critical Reading: 500-640, Math: 530-590, Combined: 1030-1230. **First-year students submitting ACT scores:** 97%. Scores (25/75 percentile): English: 22-29, Math: 25-30, Composite: 24-29.

ACADEMICS

Year founded: 1903. **Academic calendar:** Quarter. **Degrees offered:** bachelor's, master's. **Most popular majors:** 63% engineering, 17% business, management, marketing, and related support services, 11% engineering technologies/technicians, 8% health professions and related clinical sciences, 1% communication, journalism, and related programs. **Major fields of study:** business, management, marketing, and related support services; communication, journalism, and related programs; engineering; engineering technologies/technicians; health professions and related clinical sciences. **Areas of required coursework:** humanities, computer literacy, mathematics, English (including composition), sciences (biological or physical), social science, other. **Special academic programs (% participation):** distance learning (4%), double major (4%), dual enrollment (1%), English as a Second Language (ESL) (1%), independent study (92%), internships (84%), study abroad (2%). **Reserve Officers Training Corps (ROTC):** Army ROTC: Offered at cooperating institution (Marquette University); Navy ROTC: Offered at cooperating institution (Marquette University); Air Force ROTC: Offered at cooperating institution (Marquette University). **Faculty and instruction (2009-2010):** Total instructional faculty: 132 full-time, 119 part-time (71% men; 29% women; 11% minorities). Full-time faculty with Ph.D. or other terminal degree: 73%. Student/faculty ratio: 14/1. Classes of fewer than 20 students: 41%; of 20 to 49 students: 59%; of 50 or more students: 0%. **Advanced Placement and International Baccalaureate credit:** AP tests may be used for: Credit and/or placement. Scores accepted: 4, 5. International Baccalaureate exams may be used for: Placement only. **Freshmen returning for sophomore year:** 75%. **Graduation rates:** Four-year: 39%; five-year: 52%; six-year: 55%. **Graduate study:** 10% of students pursue further study immediately upon graduation; 12% within one year. Fields in which graduates pursue further study: Master of Business Administration (MBA), 15%; law, 2%; medicine, 3%; engineering, 69%; arts and sciences, 11%.

COSTS AND FINANCIAL AID

Financial aid office: (414) 277-7511. **Expenses (2010-2011):** Tuition and fees 2010-2011: $29,520; room/board: $7,431. Estimated books and supplies: $2,640; transportation: $2,000; personal expenses: $2,000. **Financial aid:** Priority filing date for institution's financial aid form: March 15. In 2009-2010, 92% of undergraduates applied for financial aid. Of those, 83% were determined to have financial need; 14% had their need fully met. Average financial aid package (proportion receiving): $17,687 (83%). Average amount of gift aid, such as scholarships or grants (proportion receiving): $14,730 (82%). Average amount of self-help aid, such as work study or loans (proportion receiving): $3,440 (74%). Average need-based loan (excluding PLUS or other private loans): $3,246. Among students who received need-based aid, the average percentage of need met: 67%. Among students who received aid based on merit, the average award (and the proportion receiving): $9,724 (17%). The average athletic scholarship (and the proportion receiving): $0 (0%). Average amount of debt of borrowers graduating in 2009: $35,722. Proportion who borrowed: 94%.

CAMPUS LIFE AND EXTRACURRICULAR ACTIVITIES

Campus housing available (% using): coed dorms (99%), special housing for disabled students (1%). Students who live in college-owned, operated, or affiliated housing: 40%. **Student employment:** During the 2009-2010 academic year, 9% of undergraduates worked on campus. Average per-year earnings: $1,800. **Clubs and organizations:** Number of student organizations: 61. Activities include: campus ministries, dance, drama/theater, international student organization, jazz band, literary magazine, pep band, radio station, student government, symphony orchestra. Number of fraternities: 3; sororities: 3. Proportion of men in fraternities: 8%; of women in sororities: 13%. Average proportion of students who stay on campus on weekends: 70%. **Sports program (2009-2010):** Member of NCAA III. *Men's intercollegiate varsity sports:* baseball, basketball, cross country, golf, ice hockey, lacrosse, soccer, tennis, track and field (indoor), track and field (outdoor), volleyball, wrestling. *Women's intercollegiate varsity sports:* basketball, crew (heavyweight), cross country, golf, crew (lightweight), soccer, softball, tennis, track and field (indoor), track and field (outdoor), volleyball.

SERVICES AND FACILITIES

Basic services: nonremedial tutoring, women's center, placement service, health service, health insurance, other. **Remedial assistance:** reading, math, writing, study skills, other. **Counseling services:** minority student, career, military, personal, veteran student, academic, older student, psychological. **For learning-disabled students:** School does not offer a structured program with separate admission and additional fees. Services include: remedial math, reading machines, tape recorders, videotaped classes, diagnostic testing service, untimed tests, note-taking services, oral tests, learning center, readers, extended time for tests, tutors, early syllabus, priority registration, priority seating, texts on tape, typist/scribe, exams on tape or computer, take home exams, other testing accommodations, waiver of foreign language degree requirement. **Library:** Number of titles: 49,527; number of current serial subscriptions: 389. **Information technology resources:** Students are required to lease or own a computer. Number of campus computers available to all students: 250. School has a wireless network. Approximate number of users that can be accommodated: 5,500. Proportion of college-owned housing units wired for high-speed internet access: 100%. **Campus safety:** Security services offered: 24-hour foot-and-vehicle patrols, late-night transport/escort service, 24-hour emergency telephones, lighted pathways/sidewalks, controlled dormitory access (key, security card, etc).

TRANSFER AND INTERNATIONAL STUDENTS

Transfer students: May apply for admission for the following academic terms: Fall, Winter, Spring, Summer. Applicants need a minimum number of credits to apply. For fall 2009: Transfer applications received: 393. Transfer applicants offered admission: 220. Transfer applicants enrolled: 146. **International students:** Number of foreign undergraduates: 66 (3%

of student body). Number of countries represented: 15. Minimum TOEFL score required: 550 (paper); 213 (computer).

Mount Mary College

- ■ **Address:** 2900 N. Menomonee River Parkway, Milwaukee, WI 53222
- ■ **Website:** http://www.mtmary.edu
- ■ **Private; Religious affiliation:** Roman Catholic
- ■ **Enrollment:** 921 full-time; 520 part-time

KEY STATS

✔ **U.S News College Ranking:** second tier, Regional Universities (Midwest)
✔ **ACT Score (25th/75th percentile):** 16-22
✔ **Tuition:** 2010-2011: $22,118

Selectivity: Selective	**Room/board:** $7,498
Acceptance rate: 50%	**Average debt:** $21,414
Student/faculty ratio: 13/1	**Proportion who borrowed:** 86%

UNDERGRADUATE STUDENT BODY STATS

2009-2010 enrollment: 921 full-time; 520 part-time. Men: 4%; women: 96%. **Ethnic makeup:** African American: 22%; American-Indian: 1%; Asian American: 4%; Hispanic: 8%; White: 65%; International: 1%. **Religious preference:** Roman Catholic: 35%; Protestant: 13%; No preference: 48%; Other: 4%.

ADMISSIONS FACTS AND FIGURES

Phone: (800) 321-6265. **Email:** admiss@mtmary.edu. **Website:** http://www.mtmary.edu. **Application deadlines for fall 2011:** Regular decision: Rolling. Early decision: Not offered. Early action: Not offered. Admission can be deferred. **Application fee:** $25. **To apply online, go to:** http://www.mtmary.edu/apply.htm. **Admissions requirements/recommendations:** High school units required (recommended): English: 4 (4); Mathematics: 2 (3); Science: 2 (2); Foreign language: 0 (2); Social studies: 2 (2); History: 2 (2); Academic electives: 2 (2); Total units: 16 (16). Tests: The college uses SAT or ACT scores in admissions decisions. Either SAT or ACT required. For admission to the fall 2011 entering class, the school will accept: ACT with or without writing accepted. Campus visit: Recommended. Admissions interview: Recommended. Off-campus interview: May be arranged. **Factors that count in admissions decisions:** *Academic:* Secondary school record: Very Important. Class rank: Important. Letters of recommendation: Considered. Standardized test scores: Important. Essay: Considered. *Nonacademic:* Interview: Considered. Extracurricular activities: Considered. Talent/ability: Important. Character/personal qualities: Important. Alumni/ae relationship: Not Considered. Geographical residence: Not Considered. State residency: Not Considered. Religious affiliation/commitment: Not Considered. Minority status: Not Considered. Volunteer work: Considered. Work experience: Considered. **Other schools with the greatest overlap in applicants:** Alverno College. **Admissions statistics for the fall 2009 entering class:** Total applicants: 808. Total accepted: 404. Freshmen enrolled: 161; 1% were from out of state. Overall acceptance rate: 50%. **Credentials of fall 2009 freshmen:** 16% ranked in the top 10 percent of their high school class; 41% were in the top 25 percent; 70% were in the top half. (Proportion submitting class standing: 81%.) **Average high school grade point average:** 2.9. **First-year students submitting ACT scores:** 89%. Scores (25/75 percentile): English: 14-24, Math: 15-23, Composite: 16-22.

ACADEMICS

Year founded: 1913. **Academic calendar:** Semester. **Degrees offered:** bachelor's, post-bachelor's certificate, master's, post-master's certificate. **Most popular majors:** 33% health professions and related clinical sciences, 17% business, management, marketing, and related support services, 16% visual and performing arts, 6% psychology, 5% English language and literature/letters. **Major fields of study:** biological and biomedical sciences; business, management, marketing, and related support services; communication, journalism, and related programs; computer and information sciences and support services; education; English language and literature/letters; foreign languages, literatures, and linguistics; health professions and related clinical sciences; history; legal professions and studies; liberal arts and sciences studies, and humanities; mathematics and statistics; multi/interdisciplinary studies; philosophy and religious studies; physical sciences; psychology; public administration and social service professions; security and protective services; social sciences; theology and religious vocations; visual and performing arts. **Areas of required coursework:** arts/fine arts, humanities, mathematics, English (including composition), philosophy, sciences (biological or physical), history, social science, other. **Pre-professional programs:** pre-law, pre-dentistry, pre-medicine, pre-veterinary science, pre-pharmacy. **Special academic programs (% participation):** accelerated program (6%), distance learning, double major (5%), dual enrollment, honors program (5%), independent study (16%), internships (22%), liberal arts/career combination (49%), student-designed major (1%), study abroad (22%). **Teacher certification offered in:** early childhood, elementary, middle/junior high, secondary, bilingual/bicultural. **Cooperative education programs:** health professions. **Reserve Officers Training Corps (ROTC):** Army ROTC: Offered at cooperating institution (Marquette University); Air Force ROTC: Offered at cooperating institution (Marquette University). **Faculty and instruction (2009-2010):** Total instructional faculty: 66 full-time, 141 part-time (20% men; 80% women). Full-time faculty with Ph.D. or other terminal degree: 62%. Student/faculty ratio: 13/1. Classes of fewer than 20 students: 81%; of 20 to 49 students: 18%; of 50 or more students: 1%. **Advanced Placement and International Baccalaureate credit:** AP tests may be used for: Credit and/or placement. Scores accepted: 3, 4, 5. International Baccalaureate exams may be used for: Credit and/or placement. **Freshmen returning for sophomore year:** 69%. **Graduation rates:** Four-year: 20%; five-year: 32%; six-year: 40%.

COSTS AND FINANCIAL AID
Financial aid office: (414) 256-1258. **Expenses (2010-2011):** Tuition and fees 2010-2011: $22,118; room/board: $7,498. Estimated books and supplies: $1,200; transportation: $1,420; personal expenses: $1,604. **Financial aid:** Priority filing date for institution's financial aid form: March 1. In 2009-2010, 93% of undergraduates applied for financial aid. Of those, 85% were determined to have financial need; 8% had their need fully met. Average financial aid package (proportion receiving): $16,132 (85%). Average amount of gift aid, such as scholarships or grants (proportion receiving): $11,547 (85%). Average amount of self-help aid, such as work study or loans (proportion receiving): $4,934 (81%). Average need-based loan (excluding PLUS or other private loans): $4,493. Among students who received need-based aid, the average percentage of need met: 68%. Among students who received aid based on merit, the average award (and the proportion receiving): $5,355 (13%). The average athletic scholarship (and the proportion receiving): $0 (0%). Average amount of debt of borrowers graduating in 2009: $21,414. Proportion who borrowed: 86%.

CAMPUS LIFE AND EXTRACURRICULAR ACTIVITIES
Campus housing available (% using): women's dorms (100%). Students who live in college-owned, operated, or affiliated housing: 15%. **Student employment:** During the 2009-2010 academic year, 17% of undergraduates worked on campus. Average per-year earnings: $2,000. **Clubs and organizations:** Number of student organizations: 42. Activities include: campus ministries, choral groups, dance, international student organization, literary magazine, model UN, music ensembles, student government, student newspaper. Number of fraternities: 0; sororities: 0. Average proportion of students who stay on campus on weekends: 20%. **Sports program (2009-2010):** Member of NCAA III. **Women's intercollegiate varsity sports:** basketball, cross country, soccer, softball, tennis, volleyball.

SERVICES AND FACILITIES
Basic services: nonremedial tutoring, women's center, placement service, day care, health insurance. **Remedial assistance:** reading, math, writing, study skills. **Counseling services:** minority student, career, personal, academic, older student, psychological, religious. **For learning-disabled students:** School does not offer a structured program with separate admission and additional fees. Total undergraduates in learning-disabled program or receiving services: 34. Services include: remedial math, remedial English, reading machines, remedial reading, tape recorders, other special classes, untimed tests, note-taking services, special bookstore section, oral tests, learning center, readers, extended time for tests, tutors, priority registration, priority seating, texts on tape, typist/scribe, other testing accommodations, other. **Library:** Number of titles: 692,734; number of current serial subscriptions: 29,755. **Information technology resources:** Students are not required to lease or own a computer. Number of campus computers available to all students: 188. School has a wireless network. Approximate number of users that can be accommodated: 200. Proportion of college-owned housing units wired for high-speed internet access: 100%. **Campus safety:** Security services offered: 24-hour foot-and-vehicle patrols, late-night transport/escort service, 24-hour emergency telephones, lighted pathways/sidewalks, controlled dormitory access (key, security card, etc).

TRANSFER AND INTERNATIONAL STUDENTS
Transfer students: May apply for admission for the following academic terms: Fall, Spring, Summer. Applicants do not need a minimum number of credits to apply. For fall 2009: Transfer applications received: 506. Transfer applicants offered admission: 268. Transfer applicants enrolled: 155. **International students:** Number of foreign undergraduates: 10 (1% of student body). Number of countries represented: 13. Minimum TOEFL score required: 500 (paper); 173 (computer). Average TOEFL score: 550 (paper).

Northland College

- **Address:** 1411 Ellis Avenue, Ashland, WI 54806
- **Website:** http://www.northland.edu
- **Private; Religious affiliation:** United Church of Christ
- **Enrollment:** 565 full-time; 37 part-time

KEY STATS
✔ **U.S News College Ranking:** 183, National Liberal Arts Colleges
✔ **ACT Score (25th/75th percentile):** 20-26
✔ **Tuition:** 2009-2010: $24,021

Selectivity: Selective	**Room/board:** $6,765
Acceptance rate: 79%	**Average debt:** N/A
Student/faculty ratio: 12/1	**Proportion who borrowed:** N/A

UNDERGRADUATE STUDENT BODY STATS
2009-2010 enrollment: 565 full-time; 37 part-time. Men: 45%; women: 55%. **Ethnic makeup:** American-Indian: 3%; Asian American: 1%; Hispanic: 2%; White: 90%; International: 3%.

ADMISSIONS FACTS AND FIGURES
Phone: (715) 682-1224. **Email:** admit@northland.edu. **Website:** http://www.northland.edu. **Application deadlines for fall 2011:** Regular decision: Rolling. Early decision: Not offered. Early action: Not offered. Admission can be deferred. **To apply online, go to:** http://www.wisconsinmentor.org/applications/northland_college/apply.html. **Admissions requirements/recommendations:** High school units required (recommended): English: 4 (4); Mathematics: 3 (3); Science: 3 (3); Foreign language: 0 (2); Social studies: 3 (3); History: 0 (0); Academic electives: 3 (4); Total units: 18 (21). Tests: The college uses SAT or ACT scores in admissions decisions. Either SAT or ACT required. For admission to the fall 2011 entering class, the school will accept: ACT with or without writing accepted. Campus visit: Recommended. Admissions interview: Recommended. Off-campus interview: May be arranged. **Factors that count in admissions decisions:** *Academic:* Secondary school record: Very Important. Class rank: Important. Letters of recommendation: Important. Standardized test scores: Important. Essay: Important. *Nonacademic:* Interview: Considered. Extracurricular activities: Considered. Talent/ability: Considered. Character/personal qualities: Considered. Alumni/ae relationship: Considered. Geographical residence: Considered. State residency: Not Considered. Religious affiliation/commitment: Not Considered. Minority status: Not Considered. Volunteer work: Considered. Work experience: Considered. **Other schools with the greatest overlap in applicants:** College of the Atlantic; Green Mountain College; University of Minnesota–Twin Cities; University of Wisconsin–Madison; University of Wisconsin–Stevens Point. **Admissions statistics for the fall 2009 entering class:** Total applicants: 582. Total accepted: 457. Freshmen enrolled: 135; 59% were from out of state. Overall acceptance rate: 79%. **Credentials of fall 2009 freshmen:** 25% ranked in the top 10 percent of their high school class; 48% were in the top 25 percent; 74% were in the top half. (Proportion submitting class standing: 77%.) **Average high school grade point average:** 3.3. **First-year students who submitted SAT scores:** 16%. Scores (25/75 percentile): Critical Reading: 510-670, Math: 500-640, Combined: 1010-1310. **First-year students submitting ACT scores:** 93%. Scores (25/75 percentile): English: 20-27, Math: 18-26, Composite: 20-26.

ACADEMICS
Year founded: 1892. **Academic calendar:** 4-1-4. **Degrees offered:** bachelor's. **Most popular majors:** 19% education, 9% English language and literature/letters, 9% biological and biomedical sciences, 9% health professions and related clinical sciences, 9% physical sciences. **Major fields of study:** biological and biomedical sciences; business, management, marketing, and related support services; education; history; liberal arts and sciences studies, and humanities; mathematics and statistics; natural resources and con-

servation; philosophy and religious studies; physical sciences; psychology; social sciences; visual and performing arts. **Areas of required coursework:** arts/fine arts, humanities, mathematics, English (including composition), philosophy, sciences (biological or physical), history, social science. **Pre-professional programs:** pre-law, pre-dentistry, pre-medicine, pre-theology, pre-veterinary science. **Special academic programs (% participation):** double major (10%), honors program (20%), independent study (60%), internships (50%), student-designed major (10%), study abroad (2%), teacher certificate program (30%). **Teacher certification offered in:** elementary, middle/junior high, secondary. **Cooperative education programs:** engineering. **Faculty and instruction (2009-2010):** Total instructional faculty: 39 full-time, 35 part-time (62% men; 38% women). Full-time faculty with Ph.D. or other terminal degree: 82%. Student/faculty ratio: 12/1. Classes of fewer than 20 students: 61%; of 20 to 49 students: 39%. **Advanced Placement and International Baccalaureate credit:** AP tests may be used for: Placement only. International Baccalaureate exams may be used for: Credit and/or placement. **Freshmen returning for sophomore year:** 72%. **Graduation rates:** Four-year: 50%; five-year: 59%; six-year: 60%. **Graduate study:** 23% of students pursue further study immediately upon graduation.

COSTS AND FINANCIAL AID
Financial aid office: (715) 682-1255. **Expenses (2009-2010):** Tuition and fees 2009-2010: $24,021; room/board: $6,765. Estimated books and supplies: $800; transportation: $1,000; personal expenses: $1,650. **Financial aid:** Priority filing date for institution's financial aid form: April 15.

CAMPUS LIFE AND EXTRACURRICULAR ACTIVITIES
Campus housing available (% using): coed dorms (85%), women's dorms (15%), apartment for single students (0%), cooperative housing (0%), other housing options. Students who live in college-owned, operated, or affiliated housing: 64%. **Student employment:** During the 2009-2010 academic year, 85% of undergraduates worked on campus. Average per-year earnings: $1,152. **Clubs and organizations:** Number of student organizations: 36. Activities include: choral groups, concert band, dance, drama/theater, jazz band, music ensembles, radio station, student government, student newspaper, symphony orchestra, yearbook. Number of fraternities: 0; sororities: 0. Average proportion of students who stay on campus on weekends: 90%. **Sports program (2009-2010):** Member of NCAA III. **Men's intercollegiate varsity sports:** baseball, basketball, cross country, ice hockey, soccer. **Women's intercollegiate varsity sports:** basketball, cross country, soccer, softball, volleyball.

SERVICES AND FACILITIES
Basic services: nonremedial tutoring, women's center, placement service, health service, health insurance. **Remedial assistance:** math, study skills. **Counseling services:** minority student, career, personal, veteran student, academic, psychological, birth control, religious. **For learning-disabled students:** School does not offer a structured program with separate admission and additional fees. Services include: tape recorders, note-taking services, oral tests, readers, extended time for tests, tutors, priority seating, other testing accommodations. **Library:** Number of titles: 77,000; number of current serial subscriptions: 245. **Information technology resources:** Students are not required to lease or own a computer. Number of campus computers available to all students: 89. School has a wireless network. Proportion of college-owned housing units wired for high-speed internet access: 100%. **Campus safety:** Security services offered: 24-hour foot-and-vehicle patrols, late-night transport/escort service, 24-hour emergency telephones, lighted pathways/sidewalks, student patrols, controlled dormitory access (key, security card, etc).

TRANSFER AND INTERNATIONAL STUDENTS
Transfer students: May apply for admission for the following academic terms: Fall, Winter. Applicants do not need a minimum number of credits to apply. For fall 2009: Transfer applications received: 152. Transfer applicants offered admission: 99. Transfer applicants enrolled: 48. **International students:** Number of foreign undergraduates: 18 (3% of student body). Number of countries represented: 5. Minimum TOEFL score required: 525 (paper); 193 (computer). Average TOEFL score: 600 (paper).

Ripon College

- **Address:** 300 Seward Street, Ripon, WI 54971-0248
- **Website:** http://www.ripon.edu
- **Private**
- **Enrollment:** 1,046 full-time; 18 part-time

KEY STATS
✔ **U.S News College Ranking:** 105, National Liberal Arts Colleges
✔ **ACT Score (25th/75th percentile):** 22-27
✔ **Tuition:** 2010-2011: $27,081
Selectivity: More selective   **Room/board:** $7,770
Acceptance rate: 79%   **Average debt:** $26,073
Student/faculty ratio: 15/1   **Proportion who borrowed:** 76%

UNDERGRADUATE STUDENT BODY STATS
2009-2010 enrollment: 1,046 full-time; 18 part-time. Men: 48%; women: 52%. **Ethnic makeup:** African American: 1%; American-Indian: 1%; Asian American: 1%; Hispanic: 3%; White: 91%; International: 3%.

ADMISSIONS FACTS AND FIGURES
Phone: (920) 748-8337. **Email:** adminfo@ripon.edu. **Website:** http://www.ripon.edu. **Application deadlines for fall 2011:** Regular decision: Rolling. Early decision: Not offered. Early action: Not offered. Admission can be deferred. **Application fee:** $30. **To apply online, go to:** http://www.ripon.edu/admission/apply/index.html. **Admissions requirements/recommendations:** High school units required (recommended): English: 4 (4); Mathematics: 3 (4); Science: 3 (4); Foreign language: (1); Social studies: 3 (4); Academic electives: 4; Total units: 17 (17). Tests: The college uses SAT or ACT scores in admissions decisions. Either SAT or ACT required. For admission to the fall 2011 entering class, the school will accept: ACT with or without writing accepted. Campus visit: Recommended. Admissions interview: Recommended. Off-campus interview: May be arranged. **Factors that count in admissions decisions:** *Academic:* Secondary school record: Very Important. Class rank: Important. Letters of recommendation: Important. Standardized test scores: Very Important. Essay: Important. *Nonacademic:* Interview: Important. Extracurricular activities: Important. Talent/ability: Important. Character/personal qualities: Very Important. Alumni/ae relationship: Considered. Geographical residence: Not Considered. State residency: Not Considered. Religious affiliation/commitment: Not Considered. Minority status: Considered. Volunteer work: Very Important. Work experience: Considered. **Other schools with the greatest overlap in applicants:** Carthage College; Marquette University; St. Norbert College; University of Wisconsin–La Crosse; University of Wisconsin–Madison. **Admissions statistics for the fall 2009 entering class:** Total applicants: 1,064. Total accepted: 845. Freshmen enrolled: 249; 71% were from out of state. Overall acceptance rate: 79%. **Credentials of fall 2009 freshmen:** 28% ranked in the top 10 percent of their high school class; 61% were in the top 25 percent; 89% were in the top half. (Proportion submitting class standing: 87%.) **Average high school grade point average:** 3.4. **First-year students who submitted SAT scores:** 12%. Scores (25/75 percentile): Critical Reading: 490-640, Math: 500-640, Combined: 990-1280. **First-year students submitting ACT scores:** 86%. Scores (25/75 percentile): English: N/A, Math: N/A, Composite: 22-27.

ACADEMICS
Year founded: 1851. **Academic calendar:** Semester. **Degrees offered:** bachelor's. **Most popular majors:** 20% business, management, marketing, and related support services, 14% history, 13% psychology, 9% political science and government, 8% biological and biomedical sciences. **Major fields of study:** area, ethnic, cultural, and gender studies; biological and biomedical sciences; business, management, marketing, and related support services; communication, journalism, and related programs; computer and information sciences and support services; education; English language and literature/letters; foreign languages, literatures, and linguistics; history; mathematics and statistics; natural resources and conservation; parks, recreation, leisure, and fitness studies; philosophy and religious studies; physical sciences; psychology; social sciences; visual and performing arts. **Areas of required coursework:** arts/fine arts, humanities, English (including composition), sciences (biological or physical), social science, other. **Pre-professional programs:** pre-law, pre-dentistry, pre-medicine, pre-theology, pre-veterinary science, pre-optometry, pre-pharmacy. **Special academic programs (% participation):** accelerated program (1%), double major (35%), exchange student program (domestic) (10%), independent study (25%),

internships (10%), student-designed major (3%), study abroad (20%), teacher certificate program (8%). **Teacher certification offered in:** early childhood, elementary, middle/junior high, secondary, bilingual/bicultural. **Reserve Officers Training Corps (ROTC):** Army ROTC: Offered on campus. **Faculty and instruction (2009-2010):** Total instructional faculty: 62 full-time, 27 part-time (58% men; 42% women; 4% minorities). Full-time faculty with Ph.D. or other terminal degree: 95%. Student/faculty ratio: 15/1. Classes of fewer than 20 students: 59%; of 20 to 49 students: 39%; of 50 or more students: 2%. **Advanced Placement and International Baccalaureate credit:** AP tests may be used for: Credit and/or placement. Scores accepted: 4, 5. International Baccalaureate exams may be used for: Credit and/or placement. **Freshmen returning for sophomore year:** 86%. **Graduation rates:** Four-year: 60%; five-year: 76%; six-year: 76%. **Graduate study:** 27% of students pursue further study immediately upon graduation; 55% within five years. Fields in which graduates pursue further study: Master of Business Administration (MBA), 13%; law, 21%; medicine, 37%; engineering, 3%; theology (or the seminary), 3%; education, 5%; arts and sciences, 21%.

COSTS AND FINANCIAL AID
Financial aid office: (920) 748-8101. **Expenses (2010-2011):** Tuition and fees 2010-2011: $27,081; room/board: $7,770. Estimated books and supplies: $1,000; transportation: $500; personal expenses: $1,000. **Financial aid:** Priority filing date for institution's financial aid form: March 1. In 2009-2010, 93% of undergraduates applied for financial aid. Of those, 85% were determined to have financial need; 31% had their need fully met. Average financial aid package (proportion receiving): $22,365 (85%). Average amount of gift aid, such as scholarships or grants (proportion receiving): $17,850 (84%). Average amount of self-help aid, such as work study or loans (proportion receiving): $5,525 (81%). Average need-based loan (excluding PLUS or other private loans): $4,378. Among students who received need-based aid, the average percentage of need met: 89%. Among students who received aid based on merit, the average award (and the proportion receiving): $10,587 (17%). The average athletic scholarship (and the proportion receiving): $0 (0%). Average amount of debt of borrowers graduating in 2009: $26,073. Proportion who borrowed: 76%.

CAMPUS LIFE AND EXTRACURRICULAR ACTIVITIES
Campus housing available (% using): coed dorms (38%), women's dorms (4%), men's dorms (4%), sorority housing (21%), fraternity housing (26%), apartment for single students (5%). Students who live in college-owned, operated, or affiliated housing: 90%. **Student employment:** During the 2009-2010 academic year, 21% of undergraduates worked on campus. Average per-year earnings: $794. **Clubs and organizations:** Number of student organizations: 58. Activities include: campus ministries, choral groups, concert band, dance, drama/theater, international student organization, jazz band, literary magazine, music ensembles, musical theater, radio station, student government, student newspaper, student film society, symphony orchestra, yearbook. Number of fraternities: 5; sororities: 3. Proportion of men in fraternities: 35%; of women in sororities: 29%. Average proportion of students who stay on campus on weekends: 87%. **Sports program (2009-2010):** Member of NCAA III. *Men's intercollegiate varsity sports:* baseball, basketball, cross country, football, golf, soccer, swimming, tennis, track and field (indoor), track and field (outdoor). *Women's intercollegiate varsity sports:* basketball, cross country, golf, soccer, softball, swimming, tennis, track and field (indoor), track and field (outdoor), volleyball.

SERVICES AND FACILITIES
Basic services: nonremedial tutoring, placement service, health service, health insurance. **Remedial assistance:** reading, writing, study skills. **Counseling services:** minority student, career, military, personal, academic, birth control. **For learning-disabled students:** School does not offer a structured program with separate admission and additional fees. Services include: tape recorders, untimed tests, note-taking services, oral tests, readers, extended time for tests, tutors, texts on tape, other. **Library:** Number of titles: 185,000; number of current serial subscriptions: 341. **Information technology resources:** Students are not required to lease or own a computer. Number of campus computers available to all students: 150. School has a wireless network. Approximate number of users that can be accommodated: 1,000. Proportion of college-owned housing units wired for high-speed internet access: 100%. **Campus safety:** Security services offered: late-night transport/escort service, 24-hour emergency telephones, lighted pathways/sidewalks, controlled dormitory access (key, security card, etc).

TRANSFER AND INTERNATIONAL STUDENTS
Transfer students: May apply for admission for the following academic terms: Fall, Spring. Applicants need a minimum number of credits to apply. For fall 2009: Transfer applications received: 61. Transfer applicants offered admission: 48. Transfer applicants enrolled: 29. **International students:** Number of foreign undergraduates: 30 (3% of student body). Number of countries represented: 14. Minimum TOEFL score required: 550 (paper); 213 (computer). Average TOEFL score: 570 (paper).

Silver Lake College

■ **Address:** 2406 S. Alverno Road, Manitowoc, WI 54220
■ **Website:** http://www.sl.edu
■ **Private; Religious affiliation:** Roman Catholic
■ **Enrollment:** 190 full-time; 317 part-time

KEY STATS
✔ **U.S News College Ranking:** 99, Regional Universities (Midwest)
✔ **ACT Score (25th/75th percentile):** 16-23
✔ **Tuition:** 2010-2011: $21,170

Selectivity: Less selective	**Room/board:** $7,295
Acceptance rate: 74%	**Average debt:** $18,706
Student/faculty ratio: 6/1	**Proportion who borrowed:** 88%

UNDERGRADUATE STUDENT BODY STATS
2009-2010 enrollment: 190 full-time; 317 part-time. Men: 32%; women: 68%. **Ethnic makeup:** African American: 4%; American-Indian: 4%; Asian American: 1%; Hispanic: 1%; White: 88%; International: 1%. **Religious preference:** No preference: 2%; Unknown: 51%; Roman Catholic: 23%; Lutheran: 9%; Other: 15%.

ADMISSIONS FACTS AND FIGURES
Phone: (920) 686-6175. **Email:** admslc@silver.sl.edu. **Website:** http://www.sl.edu. **Application deadlines for fall 2011:** Regular decision: Rolling. Early decision: Not offered. Early action: Not offered. Admission can be deferred. **Application fee:** $50. **To apply online, go to:** http://www.wisconsinmentor.org/Applications/Silver_Lake_College/apply.html. **Admissions requirements/recommendations:** High school units required (recommended): English: 4; Mathematics: 3; Science: 3; Foreign language: (1); Social studies: (2); History: (2); Academic electives: (8); Total units: 21. Tests: The college uses SAT or ACT scores in admissions decisions. Either SAT or ACT required. For admission to the fall 2011 entering class, the school will accept: ACT with or without writing accepted. Campus visit: Recommended. Admissions interview: Recommended. Off-campus interview: May be arranged. **Factors that count in admissions decisions:** *Academic:* Secondary school record: Important. Class rank: Not Considered. Letters of recommendation: Considered. Standardized test scores: Very Important. Essay: Considered. *Nonacademic:* Interview: Not Considered. Extracurricular activities: Considered. Talent/ability: Considered. Character/personal qualities: Considered. Alumni/ae relationship: Considered. Geographical residence: Not Considered. State residency: Not Considered. Religious affiliation/commitment: Not Considered. Minority status: Not Considered. Volunteer work: Considered. Work experience: Considered. **Other schools with the greatest overlap in applicants:** Lakeland College; Marian University; St. Norbert College; University of Wisconsin–Stevens Point. **Admissions statistics for the fall 2009 entering class:** Total applicants: 152. Total accepted: 112. Freshmen enrolled: 30; 13% were from out of state. Overall acceptance rate: 74%. **Credentials of fall 2009 freshmen:** 4% ranked in the top 10 percent of their high school class; 17% were in the top 25 percent; 33% were in the top half. (Proportion submitting class standing: 77%.) **Average high school grade point average:** 2.9. **First-year students submitting ACT scores:** 87%. Scores (25/75 percentile): English: 15-22, Math: 17-24, Composite: 16-23.

ACADEMICS
Year founded: 1935. **Academic calendar:** Semester. **Degrees offered:** certificate, associate, bachelor's, post-bachelor's certificate, master's. **Major fields of study:** biological and biomedical sciences; business, management, marketing, and related support services; computer and information sciences and support services; education; English language and literature/letters; health professions and related clinical sciences; history; mathematics and statistics; psychology; public administration and social service professions; theology and religious vocations; visual and performing arts. **Areas of required coursework:** arts/fine arts, humanities, computer literacy, mathematics, English (including composition), philosophy, sciences (biological or physical), history, social science, other. **Pre-professional programs:** pre-dentistry, pre-medicine, pre-theology, pre-veterinary science, other.

Special academic programs: accelerated program, double major, internships, student-designed major, teacher certificate program. **Teacher certification offered in:** early childhood, special education, elementary, middle/junior high, secondary. **Faculty and instruction (2009-2010):** Total instructional faculty: 39 full-time, 78 part-time (21% men; 79% women; 3% minorities). Full-time faculty with Ph.D. or other terminal degree: 49%. Student/faculty ratio: 6/1. Classes of fewer than 20 students: 97%; of 20 to 49 students: 3%. **Advanced Placement and International Baccalaureate credit:** AP tests may be used for: Credit only. Scores accepted: 3, 4, 5. **Freshmen returning for sophomore year:** 65%. **Graduation rates:** Four-year: 20%; five-year: 44%; six-year: 50%.

COSTS AND FINANCIAL AID

Financial aid office: (920) 686-6122. **Expenses (2010-2011):** Tuition and fees 2010-2011: $21,170; room/board: $7,295. Estimated books and supplies: $1,050; transportation: $1,100; personal expenses: $1,500. **Financial aid:** Priority filing date for institution's financial aid form: March 15. In 2009-2010, 87% of undergraduates applied for financial aid. Of those, 85% were determined to have financial need; 15% had their need fully met. Average financial aid package (proportion receiving): $16,479 (85%). Average amount of gift aid, such as scholarships or grants (proportion receiving): $9,146 (81%). Average amount of self-help aid, such as work study or loans (proportion receiving): $4,857 (76%). Average need-based loan (excluding PLUS or other private loans): $4,388. Among students who received need-based aid, the average percentage of need met: 66%. Among students who received aid based on merit, the average award (and the proportion receiving): $6,602 (5%). The average athletic scholarship (and the proportion receiving): $3,000 (1%). Average amount of debt of borrowers graduating in 2009: $18,706. Proportion who borrowed: 88%.

CAMPUS LIFE AND EXTRACURRICULAR ACTIVITIES

Campus housing available (% using): coed dorms (100%). Students who live in college-owned, operated, or affiliated housing: 20%. **Student employment:** During the 2009-2010 academic year, 0% of undergraduates worked on campus. Average per-year earnings: $0. **Clubs and organizations:** Number of student organizations: 13. Activities include: campus ministries, choral groups, dance, jazz band, literary magazine, music ensembles, student government, student newspaper. Number of fraternities: 0; sororities: 0. Average proportion of students who stay on campus on weekends: 50%.

SERVICES AND FACILITIES

Basic services: nonremedial tutoring, placement service, health service, health insurance. **Remedial assistance:** reading, math, writing, study skills. **Counseling services:** career, personal, academic, religious. **For learning-disabled students:** School does not offer a structured program with separate admission and additional fees. Services include: remedial math, remedial English, remedial reading, tape recorders, untimed tests, learning center, readers, extended time for tests, tutors, proofreading services, other. **Library:** Number of titles: 62,531; number of current serial subscriptions: 251. **Information technology resources:** Students are not required to lease or own a computer. Number of campus computers available to all students: 70. School has a wireless network. Approximate number of users that can be accommodated: 100. **Campus safety:** Security services offered: 24-hour emergency telephones, lighted pathways/sidewalks, controlled dormitory access (key, security card, etc).

TRANSFER AND INTERNATIONAL STUDENTS

Transfer students: May apply for admission for the following academic terms: Fall, Spring, Summer. Applicants need a minimum number of credits to apply. For fall 2009: Transfer applications received: 152. Transfer applicants offered admission: 112. Transfer applicants enrolled: 30. **International students:** Number of foreign undergraduates: 5 (1% of student body). Minimum TOEFL score required: 550 (paper); 213 (computer).

St. Norbert College

■ **Address:** 100 Grant Street, De Pere, WI 54115-2099
■ **Website:** http://www.snc.edu
■ **Private; Religious affiliation:** Roman Catholic
■ **Enrollment:** 2,041 full-time; 72 part-time

KEY STATS
✔ **U.S News College Ranking:** 127, National Liberal Arts Colleges
✔ **ACT Score (25th/75th percentile):** 21-26
✔ **Tuition:** 2010-2011: $28,043
   Selectivity: Selective   **Room/board:** $7,349
   Acceptance rate: 83%   **Average debt:** $30,001
   Student/faculty ratio: 14/1   **Proportion who borrowed:** 72%

UNDERGRADUATE STUDENT BODY STATS

2009-2010 enrollment: 2,041 full-time; 72 part-time. Men: 42%; women: 58%. **Ethnic makeup:** African American: 1%; Asian American: 1%; Hispanic: 2%; White: 92%; International: 4%. **Religious preference:** Protestant: 22%; Muslim: 1%; No preference: 1%; Unknown: 19%; Roman Catholic: 55%; Other: 2%.

ADMISSIONS FACTS AND FIGURES

Phone: (800) 236-4878. **Email:** admit@snc.edu. **Website:** http://www.snc.edu. **Application deadlines for fall 2011:** Regular decision: Rolling. Early decision: Not offered. Early action: Not offered. Admission can be deferred. **Application fee:** $25. **To apply online, go to:** http://www.snc.edu/futurestudents/apply. **Admissions requirements/recommendations:** High school units required (recommended): English: (4); Mathematics: (3); Science: (3); Foreign language: (2); Social studies: (2); History: (2); Total units: (16). Tests: The college uses SAT or ACT scores in admissions decisions. Either SAT or ACT required. For admission to the fall 2011 entering class, the school will accept: ACT with or without writing accepted. Campus visit: Recommended. Admissions interview: Recommended. Off-campus interview: May be arranged. **Factors that count in admissions decisions:** *Academic:* Secondary school record: Important. Class rank: Considered. Letters of recommendation: Considered. Standardized test scores: Very Important. Essay: Considered. *Nonacademic:* Interview: Considered. Extracurricular activities: Considered. Talent/ability: Considered. Character/personal qualities: Considered. Alumni/ae relationship: Considered. Geographical residence: Considered. State residency: Considered. Religious affiliation/commitment: Considered. Minority status: Considered. Volunteer work: Considered. Work experience: Considered. **Other schools with the greatest overlap in applicants:** Marquette University; University of Wisconsin–Eau Claire; University of Wisconsin–Green Bay; University of Wisconsin–Madison; University of Wisconsin–Oshkosh. **Admissions statistics for the fall 2009 entering class:** Total applicants: 2,024. Total accepted: 1,686. Freshmen enrolled: 545; 27% were from out of state. Overall acceptance rate: 83%. **Credentials of fall 2009 freshmen:** 24% ranked in the top 10 percent of their high school class; 53% were in the top 25 percent; 86% were in the top half. (Proportion submitting class standing: 74%.) **Average high school grade point average:** 3.4. **First-year students submitting ACT scores:** 95%. Scores (25/75 percentile): English: 21-27, Math: 20-26, Composite: 21-26.

ACADEMICS

Year founded: 1898. **Academic calendar:** Semester. **Degrees offered:** bachelor's, master's. **Most popular majors:** 22% business/commerce, 15% elementary education and teaching, 11% communication studies/speech communication and rhetoric, 6% biology/biological sciences, 5% English language and literature. **Major fields of study:** biological and biomedical sciences; business, management, marketing, and related support services; communication, journalism, and related programs; computer and information sciences and support services; education; English language and literature/letters; foreign languages, literatures, and linguistics; history; liberal arts and sciences studies, and humanities; mathematics and statistics; multi/interdisciplinary studies; natural resources and conservation; philosophy and religious studies; physical sciences; psychology; social sciences; visual and performing arts. **Areas of required coursework:** arts/fine arts, humanities, mathematics, English (including composition), philosophy, sciences (biological or physical), history, social science, other. **Pre-professional programs:** pre-law, pre-dentistry, pre-medicine, pre-veterinary science, pre-pharmacy. **Special academic programs (% participation):** distance learning, double major (13%), dual enrollment, English as a Second Language (ESL)

(1%), honors program (13%), independent study, internships (36%), student-designed major, study abroad (32%), teacher certificate program (18%), other. **Teacher certification offered in:** early childhood, elementary, middle/junior high, secondary, bilingual/bicultural. **Reserve Officers Training Corps (ROTC):** Army ROTC: Offered on campus. **Faculty and instruction (2009-2010):** Total instructional faculty: 134 full-time, 49 part-time (58% men; 42% women; 5% minorities). Full-time faculty with Ph.D. or other terminal degree: 87%. Student/faculty ratio: 14/1. Classes of fewer than 20 students: 45%; of 20 to 49 students: 55%; of 50 or more students: 1%. **Advanced Placement and International Baccalaureate credit:** AP tests may be used for: Credit only. Scores accepted: 3, 4, 5. International Baccalaureate exams may be used for: Credit and/or placement. **Freshmen returning for sophomore year:** 82%. **Graduation rates:** Four-year: 64%; five-year: 70%; six-year: 71%. **Graduate study:** 19% of students pursue further study immediately upon graduation.

COSTS AND FINANCIAL AID

Financial aid office: (920) 403-3071. **Expenses (2010-2011):** Tuition and fees 2010-2011: $28,043; room/board: $7,349. Estimated books and supplies: $900; transportation: $350; personal expenses: $750. **Financial aid:** Priority filing date for institution's financial aid form: March 1. In 2009-2010, 80% of undergraduates applied for financial aid. Of those, 68% were determined to have financial need; 40% had their need fully met. Average financial aid package (proportion receiving): $24,799 (68%). Average amount of gift aid, such as scholarships or grants (proportion receiving): $19,152 (66%). Average amount of self-help aid, such as work study or loans (proportion receiving): $5,226 (56%). Average need-based loan (excluding PLUS or other private loans): $4,566. Among students who received need-based aid, the average percentage of need met: 94%. Among students who received aid based on merit, the average award (and the proportion receiving): $8,957 (29%). The average athletic scholarship (and the proportion receiving): $0 (0%). Average amount of debt of borrowers graduating in 2009: $30,001. Proportion who borrowed: 72%.

CAMPUS LIFE AND EXTRACURRICULAR ACTIVITIES

Campus housing available (% using): coed dorms (60%), women's dorms (11%), apartment for single students (15%), special housing for disabled students (1%), special housing for international students (2%), other housing options (11%). Students who live in college-owned, operated, or affiliated housing: 76%. **Student employment:** During the 2009-2010 academic year, 47% of undergraduates worked on campus. Average per-year earnings: $1,588. **Clubs and organizations:** Number of student organizations: 63. Activities include: campus ministries, choral groups, concert band, drama/theater, international student organization, jazz band, literary magazine, music ensembles, musical theater, pep band, radio station, student government, student newspaper, student film society, television station. Number of fraternities: 3; sororities: 4. Proportion of men in fraternities: 7%; of women in sororities: 7%. Average proportion of students who stay on campus on weekends: 80%. **Sports program (2009-2010):** Member of NCAA III. *Men's intercollegiate varsity sports:* baseball, basketball, cross country, football, golf, ice hockey, soccer, tennis, track and field (indoor), track and field (outdoor). *Women's intercollegiate varsity sports:* basketball, cross country, golf, ice hockey, soccer, softball, tennis, track and field (indoor), track and field (outdoor), volleyball.

SERVICES AND FACILITIES

Basic services: nonremedial tutoring, women's center, placement service, day care, health service, health insurance. **Remedial assistance:** reading, math, writing, study skills. **Counseling services:** minority student, career, military, personal, veteran student, academic, older student, psychological, religious. **For learning-disabled students:** School does not offer a structured program with separate admission and additional fees. Services include: remedial math, remedial English, reading machines, remedial reading, tape recorders, diagnostic testing service, note-taking services, learning center, readers, extended time for tests, tutors, priority registration, priority seating, substitution of courses, texts on tape, typist/scribe, exams on tape or computer, other testing accommodations. **Library:** Number of titles: 230,595; number of current serial subscriptions: 377. **Information technology resources:** Students are not required to lease or own a computer. Number of campus computers available to all students: 202. School has a wireless network. Approximate number of users that can be accommodated: 2,000. Proportion of college-owned housing units wired for high-speed internet access: 99%. **Campus safety:** Security services offered: 24-hour foot-and-vehicle patrols, late-night transport/escort service, 24-hour emergency telephones, lighted pathways/sidewalks, student patrols, controlled dormitory access (key, security card, etc).

TRANSFER AND INTERNATIONAL STUDENTS

Transfer students: May apply for admission for the following academic terms: Fall, Winter, Spring, Summer. Applicants do not need a minimum number of credits to apply. For fall 2009: Transfer applications received: 108. Transfer applicants offered admission: 74. Transfer applicants enrolled: 48. **International students:** Number of foreign undergraduates: 86 (4% of student body). Number of countries represented: 32. Minimum TOEFL score required: 550 (paper); 80 (computer). Average TOEFL score: 620 (paper).

University of Wisconsin–Eau Claire

- **Address:** 105 Garfield Avenue, Eau Claire, WI 54701
- **Website:** http://www.uwec.edu
- **Public**
- **Enrollment:** 9,802 full-time; 685 part-time

KEY STATS

✔ **U.S News College Ranking:** 24, Regional Universities (Midwest)
✔ **ACT Score (25th/75th percentile):** 23-26
✔ **Tuition:** 2009-2010: $6,633 in state, $14,206 out of state
Selectivity: More selective **Room/board:** $5,630
Acceptance rate: 67% **Average debt:** $19,687
Student/faculty ratio: 21/1 **Proportion who borrowed:** 68%

UNDERGRADUATE STUDENT BODY STATS

2009-2010 enrollment: 9,802 full-time; 685 part-time. Men: 42%; women: 58%. **Ethnic makeup:** African American: 1%; American-Indian: 1%; Asian American: 3%; Hispanic: 1%; White: 93%; International: 1%.

ADMISSIONS FACTS AND FIGURES

Phone: (715) 836-5415. **Email:** admissions@uwec.edu. **Website:** http://www.uwec.edu. **Application deadlines for fall 2011:** Regular decision: Rolling. Early decision: Not offered. Early action: Not offered. Admission cannot be deferred. **Application fee:** $44. **To apply online, go to:** http://www.uwec.edu/admissions. **Admissions requirements/recommendations:** High school units required (recommended): English: 4; Mathematics: 3; Science: 3; Foreign language: 2; Social studies: 3; Academic electives: 2; Total units: 17. Tests: The college uses SAT or ACT scores in admissions decisions. Either SAT or ACT required. For admission to the fall 2011 entering class, the school will accept: ACT with or without writing accepted. Campus visit: Recommended. Admissions interview: Neither required nor recommended. Off-campus interview: Not available. **Factors that count in admissions decisions:** *Academic:* Secondary school record: Very Important. Class rank: Very Important. Letters of recommendation: Considered. Standardized test scores: Important. Essay: Considered. *Nonacademic:* Interview: Considered. Extracurricular activities: Considered. Talent/ability: Considered. Character/personal qualities: Considered. Alumni/ae relationship: Not Considered. Geographical residence: Not Considered. State residency: Not Considered. Religious affiliation/commitment: Not Considered. Minority status: Considered. Volunteer work: Considered. Work experience: Considered. **Other schools with the greatest overlap in applicants:** University of Minnesota–Twin Cities; University of Wisconsin–La Crosse; University of Wisconsin–Madison; University of Wisconsin–Milwaukee; University of Wisconsin–Stevens Point. **Admissions statistics for the fall 2009 entering class:** Total applicants: 7,414. Total accepted: 4,993. Freshmen enrolled: 2,013; 27% were from out of state. Overall acceptance rate: 67%. **Size of waiting list:** 0 applicants; enrolled from waiting list: 0. **Credentials of fall 2009 freshmen:** 29% ranked in the top 10 percent of their high school class; 61% were in the top 25 percent; 98% were in the top half. (Proportion submitting class standing: 87%.) **First-year students who submitted SAT scores:** 2%. Scores (25/75 percentile): Critical Reading: 520-640, Math: 520-670, Combined: 1040-1310. **First-year students submitting ACT scores:** 98%. Scores (25/75 percentile): English: 21-26, Math: 22-26, Composite: 23-26.

ACADEMICS

Year founded: 1916. **Academic calendar:** Semester. **Degrees offered:** certificate, associate, transfer-associate, terminal-associate, bachelor's, post-bachelor's certificate, master's, post-master's certificate. **Most popular majors:** 23% business, management, marketing, and related support services, 11% health professions and related clinical sciences, 8% communication, journalism, and related programs, 8% education, 7% security and protective services. **Major fields of study:** area, ethnic, cultural, and gender studies;

biological and biomedical sciences; business, management, marketing, and related support services; communication, journalism, and related programs; computer and information sciences and support services; education; English language and literature/letters; family and consumer sciences/human sciences; foreign languages, literatures, and linguistics; health professions and related clinical sciences; history; mathematics and statistics; parks, recreation, leisure, and fitness studies; philosophy and religious studies; physical sciences; psychology; public administration and social service professions; security and protective services; social sciences; visual and performing arts. **Areas of required coursework:** arts/fine arts, humanities, computer literacy, mathematics, English (including composition), philosophy, foreign languages, sciences (biological or physical), history, social science, other. **Pre-professional programs:** pre-law, pre-dentistry, pre-medicine, pre-theology, pre-veterinary science, pre-optometry, pre-pharmacy, other. **Special academic programs (% participation):** accelerated program (3%), cooperative (work-study plan) program (1%), distance learning (3%), double major (8%), dual enrollment (2%), English as a Second Language (ESL) (1%), exchange student program (domestic) (1%), honors program (6%), independent study (14%), internships (53%), liberal arts/career combination (9%), student-designed major (0%), study abroad (18%), teacher certificate program (12%). **Teacher certification offered in:** early childhood, special education, elementary, middle/junior high, secondary, bilingual/bicultural. **Cooperative education programs:** art, business, computer science, education, engineering, health professions, humanities, natural science, social/behavioral science, technologies, vocational arts. **Reserve Officers Training Corps (ROTC):** Army ROTC: Offered on campus. **Faculty and instruction (2009-2010):** Total instructional faculty: 410 full-time, 95 part-time (50% men; 50% women; 10% minorities). Full-time faculty with Ph.D. or other terminal degree: 81%. Student/faculty ratio: 21/1. Classes of fewer than 20 students: 25%; of 20 to 49 students: 62%; of 50 or more students: 13%. **Advanced Placement and International Baccalaureate credit:** AP tests may be used for: Credit only. Scores accepted: 3, 4, 5. International Baccalaureate exams may be used for: Credit only. **Freshmen returning for sophomore year:** 83%. **Graduation rates:** Four-year: 25%; five-year: 57%; six-year: 61%. **Graduate study:** 15% of students pursue further study within one year.

COSTS AND FINANCIAL AID

Financial aid office: (715) 836-3373. **Expenses (2009-2010):** Tuition and fees 2009-2010: $6,633 in state, $14,206 out of state; room/board: $5,630. Estimated books and supplies: $460; transportation: $900; personal expenses: $1,800. **Financial aid:** Priority filing date for institution's financial aid form: April 15. In 2009-2010, 71% of undergraduates applied for financial aid. Of those, 48% were determined to have financial need; 59% had their need fully met. Average financial aid package (proportion receiving): $8,587 (47%). Average amount of gift aid, such as scholarships or grants (proportion receiving): $5,368 (30%). Average amount of self-help aid, such as work study or loans (proportion receiving): $5,937 (44%). Average need-based loan (excluding PLUS or other private loans): $4,604. Among students who received need-based aid, the average percentage of need met: 90%. Among students who received aid based on merit, the average award (and the proportion receiving): $1,834 (7%). Average amount of debt of borrowers graduating in 2009: $19,687. Proportion who borrowed: 68%.

CAMPUS LIFE AND EXTRACURRICULAR ACTIVITIES

Campus housing available (% using): coed dorms (77%), women's dorms (9%), men's dorms (5%), apartment for single students (9%). Students who live in college-owned, operated, or affiliated housing: 38%. **Student employment:** During the 2009-2010 academic year, 21% of undergraduates worked on campus. Average per-year earnings: $1,144. **Clubs and organizations:** Number of student organizations: 239. Activities include: campus ministries, choral groups, concert band, dance, drama/theater, international student organization, jazz band, literary magazine, marching band, model UN, music ensembles, musical theater, opera, pep band, radio station, student government, student newspaper, student film society, symphony orchestra, television station. Number of fraternities: 2; sororities: 3. Average proportion of students who stay on campus on weekends: 70%. **Sports program (2009-2010):** Member of NCAA III. *Men's intercollegiate varsity sports:* basketball, cross country, football, golf, ice hockey, swimming, tennis, track and field (indoor), track and field (outdoor), wrestling. *Women's intercollegiate varsity sports:* basketball, cross country, golf, gymnastics, ice hockey, soccer, softball, swimming, tennis, track and field (indoor), track and field (outdoor), volleyball.

SERVICES AND FACILITIES

Basic services: nonremedial tutoring, women's center, placement service, day care, health service, health insurance, other. **Remedial assistance:** read-

ing, math, writing, study skills. **Counseling services:** minority student, career, military, personal, veteran student, academic, older student, psychological, birth control. **For learning-disabled students:** School does not offer a structured program with separate admission and additional fees. Total undergraduates in learning-disabled program or receiving services: 46. Services include: reading machines, learning center, tutors, priority registration. **Library:** Number of titles: 944,303; number of current serial subscriptions: 18,382. **Information technology resources:** Students are not required to lease or own a computer. Number of campus computers available to all students: 1,200. School has a wireless network. Approximate number of users that can be accommodated: 4,500. Proportion of college-owned housing units wired for high-speed internet access: 100%. **Campus safety:** Security services offered: 24-hour foot-and-vehicle patrols, late-night transport/escort service, 24-hour emergency telephones, lighted pathways/sidewalks, student patrols, controlled dormitory access (key, security card, etc).

TRANSFER AND INTERNATIONAL STUDENTS

Transfer students: May apply for admission for the following academic terms: Fall, Winter, Spring, Summer. Applicants do not need a minimum number of credits to apply. For fall 2009: Transfer applications received: 1,439. Transfer applicants offered admission: 946. Transfer applicants enrolled: 563. **International students:** Number of foreign undergraduates: 136 (1% of student body). Number of countries represented: 39. Minimum TOEFL score required: 550 (paper); 213 (computer).

University of Wisconsin–Green Bay

- **Address:** 2420 Nicolet Drive, Green Bay, WI 54311
- **Website:** http://www.uwgb.edu
- **Public**
- **Enrollment:** 4,991 full-time; 1,390 part-time

KEY STATS

- ✔ **U.S News College Ranking:** second tier, National Liberal Arts Colleges
- ✔ **ACT Score (25th/75th percentile):** 20-24
- ✔ **Tuition:** 2009-2010: $6,614 in state, $14,187 out of state

Selectivity: Selective	**Room/board:** $5,000
Acceptance rate: 70%	**Average debt:** $19,636
Student/faculty ratio: 25/1	**Proportion who borrowed:** 71%

UNDERGRADUATE STUDENT BODY STATS

2009-2010 enrollment: 4,991 full-time; 1,390 part-time. Men: 36%; women: 64%. **Ethnic makeup:** African American: 1%; American-Indian: 2%; Asian American: 3%; Hispanic: 1%; White: 92%; International: 1%. **Religious preference:** Roman Catholic: 35%; Protestant: 40%; Jewish: 1%; Muslim: 1%; Hindu: 1%; Buddhist: 1%; No preference: 10%; Other: 11%.

ADMISSIONS FACTS AND FIGURES

Phone: (920) 465-2111. **Email:** uwgb@uwgb.edu. **Website:** http://www.uwgb.edu. **Application deadlines for fall 2011:** Regular decision: Rolling. Early decision: Not offered. Early action: Not offered. Admission can be deferred. **Application fee:** $44. **To apply online, go to:** http://apply.wisconsin.edu. **Admissions requirements/recommendations:** High school units required (recommended): English: 4 (4); Mathematics: 3 (3); Science: 3 (3); Foreign language: 0 (2); Social studies: 3 (3); History: 0 (0); Academic electives: 2 (2); Total units: 17 (19). Tests: The college uses SAT or ACT scores in admissions decisions. Either SAT or ACT required. For admission to the fall 2011 entering class, the school will accept: ACT with or without writing accepted. Campus visit: Recommended. Admissions interview: Neither required nor recommended. Off-campus interview: May be arranged. **Factors that count in admissions decisions:** *Academic:* Secondary school record: Very Important. Class rank: Considered. Letters of recommendation: Considered. Standardized test scores: Very Important. Essay: Considered. *Nonacademic:* Interview: Considered. Extracurricular activities: Very Important. Talent/ability: Important. Character/personal qualities: Considered. Alumni/ae relationship: Not Considered. Geographical residence: Not Considered. State residency: Considered. Religious affiliation/commitment: Not Considered. Minority status: Considered. Volunteer work: Considered. Work experience: Considered. **Other schools with the greatest overlap in applicants:** University of Wisconsin–Eau Claire; University of Wisconsin–Madison; University of Wisconsin–Milwaukee; University of Wisconsin–Oshkosh; University of Wisconsin–Stevens Point. **Admissions statistics for the fall 2009 entering class:** Total applicants: 3,563.

Total accepted: 2,487. Freshmen enrolled: 1,046; 5% were from out of state. Overall acceptance rate: 70%. **Size of waiting list:** 124 applicants; enrolled from waiting list: 99. **Average high school grade point average:** 3.3. **First-year students who submitted SAT scores:** 2%. **First-year students submitting ACT scores:** 98%. Scores (25/75 percentile): English: 20-24, Math: 19-25, Composite: 20-24.

ACADEMICS

Year founded: 1965. **Academic calendar:** Semester. **Degrees offered:** certificate, associate, bachelor's, post-bachelor's certificate, master's. **Most popular majors:** 13% business administration and management, 10% psychology, 9% biomedical sciences, 8% developmental and child psychology, 6% communication, journalism, and related programs. **Major fields of study:** biological and biomedical sciences; business, management, marketing, and related support services; communication, journalism, and related programs; computer and information sciences and support services; education; English language and literature/letters; foreign languages, literatures, and linguistics; health professions and related clinical sciences; history; liberal arts and sciences studies, and humanities; mathematics and statistics; multi/interdisciplinary studies; natural resources and conservation; philosophy and religious studies; physical sciences; psychology; social sciences; visual and performing arts. **Areas of required coursework:** arts/fine arts, humanities, mathematics, English (including composition), sciences (biological or physical), social science, other. **Pre-professional programs:** pre-law, pre-dentistry, pre-medicine, pre-veterinary science, pre-optometry, pre-pharmacy. **Special academic programs (% participation):** cross-registration (1%), distance learning (5%), double major (30%), dual enrollment (1%), English as a Second Language (ESL) (1%), exchange student program (domestic) (1%), external degree program (2%), independent study (30%), internships (60%), liberal arts/career combination (5%), student-designed major (1%), study abroad (15%), teacher certificate program (10%). **Teacher certification offered in:** early childhood, elementary, middle/junior high, secondary, bilingual/bicultural. **Reserve Officers Training Corps (ROTC):** Army ROTC: Offered at cooperating institution (St. Norbert College). **Faculty and instruction (2009-2010):** Total instructional faculty: 189 full-time, 133 part-time (49% men; 51% women; 10% minorities). Full-time faculty with Ph.D. or other terminal degree: 85%. Student/faculty ratio: 25/1. Classes of fewer than 20 students: 26%; of 20 to 49 students: 60%; of 50 or more students: 14%. **Advanced Placement and International Baccalaureate credit:** AP tests may be used for: Credit and/or placement. Scores accepted: 3, 4, 5. International Baccalaureate exams may be used for: Placement only. **Freshmen returning for sophomore year:** 75%. **Graduation rates:** Four-year: 25%; five-year: 48%; six-year: 52%. **Graduate study:** 20% of students pursue further study immediately upon graduation; 30% within one year; 40% within five years. Fields in which graduates pursue further study: Master of Business Administration (MBA), 20%; law, 5%; medicine, 10%; education, 20%; arts and sciences, 45%.

COSTS AND FINANCIAL AID

Financial aid office: (920) 465-2075. **Expenses (2009-2010):** Tuition and fees 2009-2010: $6,614 in state, $14,187 out of state; room/board: $5,000. Estimated books and supplies: $800; transportation: $660; personal expenses: $2,000. **Financial aid:** Priority filing date for institution's financial aid form: April 15. In 2009-2010, 82% of undergraduates applied for financial aid. Of those, 64% were determined to have financial need; 44% had their need fully met. Average financial aid package (proportion receiving): $10,169 (61%). Average amount of gift aid, such as scholarships or grants (proportion receiving): $6,129 (35%). Average amount of self-help aid, such as work study or loans (proportion receiving): $5,224 (48%). Average need-based loan (excluding PLUS or other private loans): $5,117. Among students who received need-based aid, the average percentage of need met: 86%. Among students who received aid based on merit, the average award (and the proportion receiving): $2,255 (1%). The average athletic scholarship (and the proportion receiving): $7,795 (2%). Average amount of debt of borrowers graduating in 2009: $19,636. Proportion who borrowed: 71%.

CAMPUS LIFE AND EXTRACURRICULAR ACTIVITIES

Campus housing available (% using): coed dorms (40%), apartment for single students (60%). Students who live in college-owned, operated, or affiliated housing: 31%. **Student employment:** During the 2009-2010 academic year, 20% of undergraduates worked on campus. Average per-year earnings: $1,000. **Clubs and organizations:** Number of student organizations: 120. Activities include: choral groups, concert band, dance, drama/theater, jazz band, literary magazine, music ensembles, musical theater, opera, pep band, radio station, student government, student newspaper, student film society, symphony orchestra, television station. Number of fraternities: 1;

sororities: 1. Proportion of men in fraternities: 1%; of women in sororities: 1%. Average proportion of students who stay on campus on weekends: 35%. **Sports program (2009-2010):** Member of NCAA I. *Men's intercollegiate varsity sports:* basketball, cross country, golf, skiing (nordic), soccer, swimming, tennis. *Women's intercollegiate varsity sports:* basketball, cross country, golf, skiing (nordic), soccer, softball, swimming, tennis, volleyball.

SERVICES AND FACILITIES

Basic services: nonremedial tutoring, placement service, health service, health insurance. **Remedial assistance:** math, writing. **Counseling services:** minority student, career, personal, veteran student, academic, psychological, birth control, religious. **For learning-disabled students:** School does not offer a structured program with separate admission and additional fees. Services include: remedial math, remedial English, tape recorders, untimed tests, note-taking services, readers, extended time for tests, priority registration, priority seating, texts on tape. **Library:** Number of titles: 348,590; number of current serial subscriptions: 4,825. **Information technology resources:** Students are not required to lease or own a computer. Number of campus computers available to all students: 550. School has a wireless network. Proportion of college-owned housing units wired for high-speed internet access: 100%. **Campus safety:** Security services offered: 24-hour foot-and-vehicle patrols, late-night transport/escort service, 24-hour emergency telephones, lighted pathways/sidewalks, student patrols, controlled dormitory access (key, security card, etc).

TRANSFER AND INTERNATIONAL STUDENTS

Transfer students: May apply for admission for the following academic terms: Fall, Spring, Summer. Applicants need a minimum number of credits to apply. For fall 2009: Transfer applications received: 1,574. Transfer applicants offered admission: 1,169. Transfer applicants enrolled: 800. **International students:** Number of foreign undergraduates: 53 (1% of student body). Number of countries represented: 27. Minimum TOEFL score required: 500 (paper).

University of Wisconsin—La Crosse

- **Address:** 1725 State Street, La Crosse, WI 54601
- **Website:** http://www.uwlax.edu
- **Public**
- **Enrollment:** 8,307 full-time; 451 part-time

....

KEY STATS

✔ **U.S News College Ranking:** 14, Regional Universities (Midwest)
✔ **ACT Score (25th/75th percentile):** 23-27
✔ **Tuition:** 2009-2010: $7,509 in state, $15,082 out of state
  Selectivity: More selective   **Room/board:** $5,630
  Acceptance rate: 69%   **Average debt:** $21,998
  Student/faculty ratio: 21/1   **Proportion who borrowed:** 65%

UNDERGRADUATE STUDENT BODY STATS

2009-2010 enrollment: 8,307 full-time; 451 part-time. Men: 43%; women: 57%. **Ethnic makeup:** African American: 1%; Asian American: 3%; Hispanic: 2%; White: 91%; International: 2%.

ADMISSIONS FACTS AND FIGURES

Phone: (608) 785-8939. **Email:** admissions@uwlax.edu. **Website:** http://www.uwlax.edu. **Application deadlines for fall 2011:** Regular decision: Rolling. Early decision: Not offered. Early action: Not offered. Admission cannot be deferred. **Application fee:** $44. **To apply online, go to:** http://www.apply.wisconsin.edu. **Admissions requirements/recommendations:** High school units required (recommended): English: 4 (4); Mathematics: 3 (4); Science: 3 (4); Foreign language: 0 (3); Social studies: 3 (4); History: 0; Academic electives: 4 (4); Total units: 17 (23). Tests: The college uses SAT or ACT scores in admissions decisions. Either SAT or ACT required. For admission to the fall 2011 entering class, the school will accept: ACT with or without writing accepted. Campus visit: Recommended. Admissions interview: Neither required nor recommended. Off-campus interview: Not available. **Factors that count in admissions decisions:** *Academic:* Secondary school record: Very Important. Class rank: Very Important. Letters of recommendation: Considered. Standardized test scores: Very Important. Essay: Important. *Nonacademic:* Interview: Considered. Extracurricular activities: Important. Talent/ability: Considered. Character/personal qualities: Considered. Alumni/ae relationship: Considered. Geographical residence:

Considered. State residency: Considered. Religious affiliation/commitment: Not Considered. Minority status: Considered. Volunteer work: Important. Work experience: Considered. **Other schools with the greatest overlap in applicants:** Marquette University; University of Minnesota–Twin Cities; University of Wisconsin–Eau Claire; University of Wisconsin–Madison. **Admissions statistics for the fall 2009 entering class:** Total applicants: 6,504. Total accepted: 4,492. Freshmen enrolled: 1,778; 17% were from out of state. Overall acceptance rate: 69%. **Size of waiting list:** 20 applicants; enrolled from waiting list: 14. **Credentials of fall 2009 freshmen:** 30% ranked in the top 10 percent of their high school class; 79% were in the top 25 percent; 98% were in the top half. (Proportion submitting class standing: 85%.) **Average high school grade point average:** 3.6. **First-year students who submitted SAT scores:** 2%. Scores (25/75 percentile): Critical Reading: 510-650, Math: 530-660, Combined: 1040-1310. **First-year students submitting ACT scores:** 97%. Scores (25/75 percentile): English: 22-27, Math: 23-27, Composite: 23-27.

ACADEMICS

Year founded: 1909. **Academic calendar:** Semester. **Degrees offered:** certificate, associate, bachelor's, post-bachelor's certificate, master's. **Most popular majors:** 23% business, management, marketing, and related support services, 15% education, 11% biological and biomedical sciences, 10% social sciences, 8% health professions and related clinical sciences. **Major fields of study:** biological and biomedical sciences; business, management, marketing, and related support services; communication, journalism, and related programs; computer and information sciences and support services; education; English language and literature/letters; foreign languages, literatures, and linguistics; health professions and related clinical sciences; history; mathematics and statistics; parks, recreation, leisure, and fitness studies; philosophy and religious studies; physical sciences; psychology; public administration and social service professions; social sciences; visual and performing arts. **Areas of required coursework:** arts/fine arts, humanities, mathematics, English (including composition), sciences (biological or physical), history, social science, other. **Pre-professional programs:** pre-law, pre-dentistry, pre-medicine, pre-veterinary science, pre-optometry, pre-pharmacy, other. **Special academic programs:** cooperative (work-study plan) program, cross-registration, distance learning, double major, dual enrollment, English as a Second Language (ESL), honors program, independent study, internships, liberal arts/career combination, study abroad, teacher certificate program. **Teacher certification offered in:** early childhood, special education, elementary, middle/junior high, secondary. **Reserve Officers Training Corps (ROTC):** Army ROTC: Offered on campus. **Faculty and instruction (2009-2010):** Total instructional faculty: 376 full-time, 155 part-time (53% men; 47% women; 13% minorities). Full-time faculty with Ph.D. or other terminal degree: 75%. Student/faculty ratio: 21/1. Classes of fewer than 20 students: 42%; of 20 to 49 students: 51%; of 50 or more students: 7%. **Advanced Placement and International Baccalaureate credit:** AP tests may be used for: Credit and/or placement. Scores accepted: 3, 4, 5. International Baccalaureate exams may be used for: Credit only. **Freshmen returning for sophomore year:** 87%. **Graduation rates:** Four-year: 34%; five-year: 65%; six-year: 66%. **Graduate study:** 28% of students pursue further study immediately upon graduation.

COSTS AND FINANCIAL AID

Financial aid office: (608) 785-8604. **Expenses (2009-2010):** Tuition and fees 2009-2010: $7,509 in state, $15,082 out of state; room/board: $5,630. Estimated books and supplies: $300; transportation: $775; personal expenses: $2,000. **Financial aid:** Priority filing date for institution's financial aid form: March 15. In 2009-2010, 67% of undergraduates applied for financial aid. Of those, 42% were determined to have financial need; 29% had their need fully met. Average financial aid package (proportion receiving): $6,397 (40%). Average amount of gift aid, such as scholarships or grants (proportion receiving): $5,523 (18%). Average amount of self-help aid, such as work study or loans (proportion receiving): $4,008 (37%). Average need-based loan (excluding PLUS or other private loans): $3,817. Among students who received need-based aid, the average percentage of need met: 81%. Among students who received aid based on merit, the average award (and the proportion receiving): $1,524 (2%). The average athletic scholarship (and the proportion receiving): $0 (0%). Average amount of debt of borrowers graduating in 2009: $21,998. Proportion who borrowed: 65%.

CAMPUS LIFE AND EXTRACURRICULAR ACTIVITIES

Campus housing available (% using): coed dorms (64%), apartment for single students, special housing for disabled students (1%), special housing for international students (4%). Students who live in college-owned, operated, or affiliated housing: 34%. **Student employment:** During the 2009-

2010 academic year, 20% of undergraduates worked on campus. Average per-year earnings: $2,037. **Clubs and organizations:** Number of student organizations: 182. Activities include: campus ministries, choral groups, concert band, dance, drama/theater, international student organization, jazz band, literary magazine, marching band, music ensembles, pep band, radio station, student government, student newspaper, symphony orchestra. Number of fraternities: 3; sororities: 2. Proportion of men in fraternities: 1%; of women in sororities: 1%. Average proportion of students who stay on campus on weekends: 65%. **Sports program (2009-2010):** Member of NCAA III. **Men's intercollegiate varsity sports:** baseball, basketball, cross country, football, swimming, tennis, track and field (indoor), track and field (outdoor), wrestling. **Women's intercollegiate varsity sports:** basketball, cross country, gymnastics, soccer, softball, swimming, tennis, track and field (indoor), track and field (outdoor), volleyball.

SERVICES AND FACILITIES

Basic services: women's center, placement service, day care, health service, health insurance. **Remedial assistance:** reading, math, writing, study skills. **Counseling services:** minority student, career, personal, veteran student, academic, older student, psychological. **For learning-disabled students:** School does not offer a structured program with separate admission and additional fees. Total undergraduates in learning-disabled program or receiving services: 70. Services include: reading machines, tape recorders, note-taking services, oral tests, readers, extended time for tests, priority registration, texts on tape, other testing accommodations. **Library:** Number of titles: 546,766; number of current serial subscriptions: 8,120. **Information technology resources:** Students are not required to lease or own a computer. Number of campus computers available to all students: 575. School has a wireless network. Approximate number of users that can be accommodated: 9,000. Proportion of college-owned housing units wired for high-speed internet access: 100%. **Campus safety:** Security services offered: 24-hour foot-and-vehicle patrols, late-night transport/escort service, 24-hour emergency telephones, lighted pathways/sidewalks, controlled dormitory access (key, security card, etc).

TRANSFER AND INTERNATIONAL STUDENTS

Transfer students: May apply for admission for the following academic terms: Fall, Winter, Spring, Summer. Applicants need a minimum number of credits to apply. For fall 2009: Transfer applications received: 808. Transfer applicants offered admission: 656. Transfer applicants enrolled: 398. **International students:** Number of foreign undergraduates: 191 (2% of student body). Number of countries represented: 42. Minimum TOEFL score required: 550 (paper); 73 (computer).

University of Wisconsin–Madison

- **Address:** 500 Lincoln Drive, Madison, WI 53706
- **Website:** http://www.wisc.edu
- **Public**
- **Enrollment:** 27,803 full-time; 2,540 part-time

KEY STATS

✔ **U.S News College Ranking:** 45, National Universities
✔ **ACT Score (25th/75th percentile):** 26-30
✔ **Tuition:** 2009-2010: $8,314 in state, $23,063 out of state
  Selectivity: More selective   **Room/board:** $8,040
  Acceptance rate: 57%   **Average debt:** $21,552
  Student/faculty ratio: 17/1   **Proportion who borrowed:** 50%

UNDERGRADUATE STUDENT BODY STATS

2009-2010 enrollment: 27,803 full-time; 2,540 part-time. Men: 48%; women: 52%. **Ethnic makeup:** African American: 3%; American-Indian: 1%; Asian American: 6%; Hispanic: 4%; White: 81%; International: 5%.

ADMISSIONS FACTS AND FIGURES

Phone: (608) 262-3961. **Email:** onwisconsin@admissions.wisc.edu. **Website:** http://www.wisc.edu. **Application deadlines for fall 2011:** Regular decision: February 1. Early decision: Not offered. Early action: Not offered. Admission can be deferred. **Application fee:** $44. **To apply online, go to:** http://www.apply.wisconsin.edu. **Admissions requirements/recommendations:** High school units required (recommended): English: 4 (4); Mathematics: 3 (4); Science: 3 (4); Foreign language: 2 (4); Social studies: 3 (4); Academic electives: 2 (2); Total units: 17 (20). Tests: The college uses SAT or ACT scores in admissions decisions. Either SAT or ACT required. For admission to the fall 2011 entering class, the school will accept: ACT with writing required. Campus visit: Recommended. Admissions interview: Neither required nor recommended. Off-campus interview: Not available. **Factors that count in admissions decisions:** *Academic:* Secondary school record: Very Important. Class rank: Very Important. Letters of recommendation: Considered. Standardized test scores: Important. Essay: Important. *Nonacademic:* Interview: Not Considered. Extracurricular activities: Considered. Talent/ability: Considered. Character/personal qualities: Considered. Alumni/ae relationship: Considered. Geographical residence: Not Considered. State residency: Important. Religious affiliation/commitment: Not Considered. Minority status: Considered. Volunteer work: Considered. Work experience: Considered. **Other schools with the greatest overlap in applicants:** Marquette University; University of Illinois–Urbana-Champaign; University of Minnesota–Twin Cities; University of Wisconsin–Eau Claire; University of Wisconsin–La Crosse. **Admissions statistics for the fall 2009 entering class:** Total applicants: 24,855. Total accepted: 14,228. Freshmen enrolled: 5,680; 36% were from out of state. Overall acceptance rate: 57%. **Credentials of fall 2009 freshmen:** 57% ranked in the top 10 percent of their high school class; 91% were in the top 25 percent; 99% were in the top half. (Proportion submitting class standing: 71%.) **Average high school grade point average:** 3.7. **First-year students who submitted SAT scores:** 22%. Scores (25/75 percentile): Critical Reading: 550-670, Math: 620-720, Combined: 1170-1390. **First-year students submitting ACT scores:** 89%. Scores (25/75 percentile): English: 25-31, Math: 26-31, Composite: 26-30.

ACADEMICS

Year founded: 1848. **Academic calendar:** Semester. **Degrees offered:** bachelor's, master's, post-master's certificate, doctorate. **Most popular majors:** 5% biology/biological sciences, 5% economics, 5% political science and government, 4% communication studies/speech communication and rhetoric, 4% psychology. **Major fields of study:** agriculture, agriculture operations, and related sciences; architecture and related services; area, ethnic, cultural, and gender studies; biological and biomedical sciences; business, management, marketing, and related support services; communication, journalism, and related programs; computer and information sciences and support services; education; engineering; English language and literature/letters; family and consumer sciences/human sciences; foreign languages, literatures, and linguistics; health professions and related clinical sciences; history; legal professions and studies; mathematics and statistics; multi/interdisciplinary studies; natural resources and conservation; parks, recreation, leisure, and fitness studies; philosophy and religious studies; physical sciences; psychology; public administration and social service professions; social sciences; visual and performing arts. **Areas of required coursework:** humanities, mathematics, English (including composition), foreign languages, sciences (biological or physical), social science, other. **Special academic programs (% participation):** accelerated program (6%), cooperative (work-study plan) program (4%), distance learning, double major (26%), dual enrollment (1%), English as a Second Language (ESL) (1%), honors program (4%), independent study (40%), internships (23%), liberal arts/career combination (0%), student-designed major (1%), study abroad (21%), teacher certificate program (5%). **Teacher certification offered in:** early childhood, special education, elementary, middle/junior high, secondary, bilingual/bicultural. **Cooperative education programs:** agriculture, engineering. **Reserve Officers Training Corps (ROTC):** Army ROTC: Offered on campus; Navy ROTC: Offered on campus; Air Force ROTC: Offered on campus. **Faculty and instruction (2009-2010):** Total instructional faculty: 2,397 full-time, 441 part-time (62% men; 38% women; 15% minorities). Full-time faculty with Ph.D. or other terminal degree: 91%. Student/faculty ratio: 17/1. Classes of fewer than 20 students: 44%; of 20 to 49 students: 37%; of 50 or more students: 19%. **Advanced Placement and International Baccalaureate credit:** AP tests may be used for: Credit only. Scores accepted: 3, 4, 5. International Baccalaureate exams may be used for: Credit only. **Freshmen returning for sophomore year:** 94%. **Graduation rates:** Four-year: 50%; five-year: 79%; six-year: 82%. **Graduate study:** 20% of students pursue further study immediately upon graduation; 30% within one year; 42% within five years.

COSTS AND FINANCIAL AID

Financial aid office: (608) 262-3060. **Expenses (2009-2010):** Tuition and fees 2009-2010: $8,314 in state, $23,063 out of state; room/board: $8,040. Estimated books and supplies: $1,040; transportation: $580; personal expenses: $2,310. **Financial aid:** In 2009-2010, 55% of undergraduates applied for financial aid. Of those, 36% were determined to have financial need; 20% had their need fully met. Average financial aid package (proportion receiving): $11,141 (36%). Average amount of gift aid, such as scholarships or grants (proportion receiving): $5,850 (23%). Average amount of

self-help aid, such as work study or loans (proportion receiving): $5,557 (31%). Average need-based loan (excluding PLUS or other private loans): $4,896. Among students who received need-based aid, the average percentage of need met: 76%. Among students who received aid based on merit, the average award (and the proportion receiving): $3,234 (10%). The average athletic scholarship (and the proportion receiving): $20,815 (2%). Average amount of debt of borrowers graduating in 2009: $21,552. Proportion who borrowed: 50%.

CAMPUS LIFE AND EXTRACURRICULAR ACTIVITIES

Campus housing available: coed dorms, women's dorms, men's dorms, apartments for married students, apartment for single students, other housing options. Students who live in college-owned, operated, or affiliated housing: 25%. **Clubs and organizations:** Number of student organizations: 635. Activities include: choral groups, concert band, dance, drama/theater, international student organization, jazz band, literary magazine, marching band, music ensembles, musical theater, opera, pep band, radio station, student government, student newspaper, student film society, symphony orchestra, television station, yearbook. Number of fraternities: 26; sororities: 11. Proportion of men in fraternities: 9%; of women in sororities: 8%. **Sports program (2009-2010):** Member of NCAA I. *Men's intercollegiate varsity sports:* basketball, cross country, football, golf, ice hockey, soccer, swimming, tennis, track and field (indoor), track and field (outdoor), wrestling. *Women's intercollegiate varsity sports:* basketball, crew (heavyweight), cross country, golf, ice hockey, crew (lightweight), soccer, softball, swimming, tennis, track and field (indoor), track and field (outdoor), volleyball.

SERVICES AND FACILITIES

Basic services: nonremedial tutoring, women's center, placement service, day care, health service, health insurance. **Counseling services:** minority student, career, military, personal, veteran student, academic, older student, psychological, birth control. **For learning-disabled students:** School does not offer a structured program with separate admission and additional fees. Services include: untimed tests, note-taking services, oral tests, learning center, readers, extended time for tests, tutors, priority registration, priority seating, texts on tape, other testing accommodations. **Information technology resources:** Students are not required to lease or own a computer. School has a wireless network. Proportion of college-owned housing units wired for high-speed internet access: 100%. **Campus safety:** Security services offered: 24-hour foot-and-vehicle patrols, late-night transport/escort service, 24-hour emergency telephones, lighted pathways/sidewalks, student patrols, controlled dormitory access (key, security card, etc).

TRANSFER AND INTERNATIONAL STUDENTS

Transfer students: May apply for admission for the following academic terms: Fall, Spring, Summer. Applicants need a minimum number of credits to apply. For fall 2009: Transfer applications received: 4,217. Transfer applicants offered admission: 1,943. Transfer applicants enrolled: 1,170. **International students:** Number of foreign undergraduates: 1433 (5% of student body). Number of countries represented: 91. Minimum TOEFL score required: 550 (paper); 80 (computer).

University of Wisconsin–Milwaukee

- **Address:** PO Box 413, Milwaukee, WI 53201
- **Website:** http://www.uwm.edu
- **Public**
- **Enrollment:** 21,005 full-time; 4,199 part-time

KEY STATS

✔ **U.S News College Ranking:** second tier, National Universities
✔ **ACT Score (25th/75th percentile):** 19-24
✔ **Tuition:** 2010-2011: $8,284 in state, $18,012 out of state

Selectivity: Selective	**Room/board:** $8,900
Acceptance rate: 77%	**Average debt:** $19,830
Student/faculty ratio: 21/1	**Proportion who borrowed:** 67%

UNDERGRADUATE STUDENT BODY STATS

2009-2010 enrollment: 21,005 full-time; 4,199 part-time. Men: 49%; women: 51%. **Ethnic makeup:** African American: 7%; American-Indian: 1%; Asian American: 5%; Hispanic: 5%; White: 81%; International: 1%.

ADMISSIONS FACTS AND FIGURES

Phone: (414) 229-2222. **Email:** uwmlook@uwm.edu. **Website:** http://www.uwm.edu. **Application deadlines for fall 2011:** Regular decision: July 1. Early decision: Not offered. Early action: Not offered. Admission can be deferred. **Application fee:** $44. **To apply online, go to:** http://www.apply.wisconsin.edu. **Admissions requirements/recommendations:** High school units required (recommended): English: 4 (4); Mathematics: 3 (4); Science: 3 (3); Foreign language: 0 (2); Social studies: 3 (3); Academic electives: 2 (2); Total units: 17 (20). Tests: The college uses SAT or ACT scores in admissions decisions. Either SAT or ACT required. For admission to the fall 2011 entering class, the school will accept: ACT with or without writing accepted. Campus visit: Recommended. Admissions interview: Neither required nor recommended. Off-campus interview: Not available. **Factors that count in admissions decisions:** *Academic:* Secondary school record: Very Important. Class rank: Very Important. Letters of recommendation: Considered. Standardized test scores: Important. Essay: Considered. *Nonacademic:* Interview: Considered. Extracurricular activities: Considered. Talent/ability: Important. Character/personal qualities: Considered. Alumni/ae relationship: Not Considered. Geographical residence: Considered. State residency: Considered. Religious affiliation/commitment: Not Considered. Minority status: Considered. Volunteer work: Considered. Work experience: Considered. **Admissions statistics for the fall 2009 entering class:** Total applicants: 11,469. Total accepted: 8,841. Freshmen enrolled: 4,100; 3% were from out of state. Overall acceptance rate: 77%. **Credentials of fall 2009 freshmen:** 8% ranked in the top 10 percent of their high school class; 26% were in the top 25 percent; 63% were in the top half. (Proportion submitting class standing: 85%.) **Average high school grade point average:** 3.1. **First-year students who submitted SAT scores:** 3%. Scores (25/75 percentile): Critical Reading: 470-600, Math: 490-620, Combined: 960-1220. **First-year students submitting ACT scores:** 97%. Scores (25/75 percentile): English: 18-25, Math: 18-24, Composite: 19-24.

ACADEMICS

Year founded: 1956. **Academic calendar:** Semester. **Degrees offered:** certificate, bachelor's, post-bachelor's certificate, master's, post-master's certificate, doctorate. **Most popular majors:** 26% business, management, marketing, and related support services, 9% education, 9% health professions and related clinical sciences, 8% visual and performing arts, 7% communication, journalism, and related programs. **Major fields of study:** architecture and related services; area, ethnic, cultural, and gender studies; biological and biomedical sciences; business, management, marketing, and related support services; communication, journalism, and related programs; computer and information sciences and support services; education; engineering; English language and literature/letters; foreign languages, literatures, and linguistics; health professions and related clinical sciences; history; liberal arts and sciences studies, and humanities; mathematics and statistics; multi/interdisciplinary studies; natural resources and conservation; parks, recreation, leisure, and fitness studies; philosophy and religious studies; physical sciences; psychology; public administration and social service professions; security and protective services; social sciences; visual and performing arts. **Areas of required coursework:** arts/fine arts, humanities, mathematics, English (including composition), foreign languages, sciences (biological or physical), history, social science, other. **Pre-professional programs:** pre-law, pre-dentistry, pre-medicine, pre-pharmacy. **Special academic programs:** accelerated program, cooperative (work-study plan) program, cross-registration, distance learning, double major, dual enrollment, English as a Second Language (ESL), external degree program, honors program, independent study, internships, liberal arts/career combination, student-designed major, study abroad, teacher certificate program. **Teacher certification offered in:** early childhood, special education, elementary, middle/junior high, secondary, bilingual/bicultural. **Cooperative education programs:** business, computer science, engineering, health professions, humanities, natural science, social/behavioral science. **Reserve Officers Training Corps (ROTC):** Army ROTC: Offered at cooperating institution (Marquette University); Air Force ROTC: Offered at cooperating institution (Marquette University). **Faculty and instruction (2009-2010):** Total instructional faculty: 1,050 full-time, 557 part-time (52% men; 48% women; 21% minorities). Full-time faculty with Ph.D. or other terminal degree: 78%. Student/faculty ratio: 21/1. Classes of fewer than 20 students: 35%; of 20 to 49 students: 48%; of 50 or more students: 16%. **Advanced Placement and International Baccalaureate credit:** AP tests may be used for: Credit and/or placement. Scores accepted: 3, 4, 5. International Baccalaureate exams may be used for: Credit and/or placement. **Freshmen returning for sophomore year:** 72%. **Graduation rates:** Four-year: 15%; five-year: 35%; six-year: 43%.

COSTS AND FINANCIAL AID

Financial aid office: (414) 229-6300. **Expenses (2010-2011):** Tuition and fees 2010-2011: $8,284 in state, $18,012 out of state; room/board: $8,900. Estimated books and supplies: $1,000; transportation: $2,328; personal expenses: $1,600. **Financial aid:** Priority filing date for institution's financial aid form: March 1. In 2009-2010, 88% of undergraduates applied for financial aid. Of those, 74% were determined to have financial need; 22% had their need fully met. Average financial aid package (proportion receiving): $7,800 (61%). Average amount of gift aid, such as scholarships or grants (proportion receiving): $6,834 (29%). Average amount of self-help aid, such as work study or loans (proportion receiving): $4,499 (50%). Average need-based loan (excluding PLUS or other private loans): $4,348. Among students who received need-based aid, the average percentage of need met: 52%. Among students who received aid based on merit, the average award (and the proportion receiving): $3,217 (0%). The average athletic scholarship (and the proportion receiving): $425 (0%). Average amount of debt of borrowers graduating in 2009: $19,830. Proportion who borrowed: 67%.

CAMPUS LIFE AND EXTRACURRICULAR ACTIVITIES

Campus housing available (% using): coed dorms (74%), apartments for married students (3%), apartment for single students (17%), special housing for disabled students (6%), other housing options. Students who live in college-owned, operated, or affiliated housing: 15%. **Clubs and organizations:** Number of student organizations: 290. Activities include: campus ministries, choral groups, concert band, dance, drama/theater, international student organization, jazz band, literary magazine, music ensembles, musical theater, pep band, radio station, student government, student newspaper, student film society, symphony orchestra. **Sports program (2009-2010):** Member of NCAA I. *Men's intercollegiate varsity sports:* baseball, basketball, soccer, swimming, track and field (indoor), track and field (outdoor). *Women's intercollegiate varsity sports:* basketball, soccer, swimming, tennis, track and field (indoor), track and field (outdoor), volleyball.

SERVICES AND FACILITIES

Basic services: nonremedial tutoring, women's center, placement service, day care, health service, health insurance, other. **Remedial assistance:** reading, math, writing, study skills. **Counseling services:** minority student, career, military, personal, veteran student, academic, older student, psychological, birth control. **For learning-disabled students:** School does not offer a structured program with separate admission and additional fees. Total undergraduates in learning-disabled program or receiving services: 360. Services include: remedial math, remedial English, reading machines, remedial reading, tape recorders, diagnostic testing service, note-taking services, oral tests, learning center, readers, extended time for tests, tutors, texts on tape, typist/scribe, exams on tape or computer, other testing accommodations, other. **Library:** Number of titles: 2,213,354; number of current serial subscriptions: 57,270. **Information technology resources:** Students are not required to lease or own a computer. Number of campus computers available to all students: 1,000. School has a wireless network. Approximate number of users that can be accommodated: 8,000. Proportion of college-owned housing units wired for high-speed internet access: 100%. **Campus safety:** Security services offered: 24-hour foot-and-vehicle patrols, late-night transport/escort service, 24-hour emergency telephones, lighted pathways/sidewalks, student patrols, controlled dormitory access (key, security card, etc).

TRANSFER AND INTERNATIONAL STUDENTS

Transfer students: May apply for admission for the following academic terms: Fall, Winter, Spring, Summer. Applicants need a minimum number of credits to apply. For fall 2009: Transfer applications received: 4,344. Transfer applicants offered admission: 2,593. Transfer applicants enrolled: 1,556. **International students:** Number of foreign undergraduates: 294 (1% of student body). Number of countries represented: 58. Minimum TOEFL score required: 520 (paper); 190 (computer). Average TOEFL score: 550 (paper).

University of Wisconsin–Oshkosh

- **Address:** 800 Algoma Boulevard, Oshkosh, WI 54901
- **Website:** http://www.uwosh.edu
- **Public**
- **Enrollment:** 9,242 full-time; 2,363 part-time

KEY STATS

✔ **U.S News College Ranking:** 76, Regional Universities (Midwest)
✔ **ACT Score (25th/75th percentile):** 20-24
✔ **Tuition:** 2010-2011: $6,682 in state, $14,670 out of state

Selectivity: Selective	**Room/board:** $6,922
Acceptance rate: 85%	**Average debt:** $21,000
Student/faculty ratio: 21/1	**Proportion who borrowed:** 64%

UNDERGRADUATE STUDENT BODY STATS

2009-2010 enrollment: 9,242 full-time; 2,363 part-time. Men: 41%; women: 59%. **Ethnic makeup:** African American: 2%; American-Indian: 1%; Asian American: 3%; Hispanic: 2%; White: 91%; International: 1%.

ADMISSIONS FACTS AND FIGURES

Phone: (920) 424-0202. **Email:** oshadmuw@uwosh.edu. **Website:** http://www.uwosh.edu. **Application deadlines for fall 2011:** Regular decision: Rolling. Early decision: Not offered. Early action: Not offered. Admission cannot be deferred. **Application fee:** $44. **To apply online, go to:** http://apply.wisconsin.edu. **Admissions requirements/recommendations:** High school units required (recommended): English: 4 (4); Mathematics: 3 (4); Science: 3 (4); Foreign language: 0 (2); Social studies: 3 (3); History: 0 (1); Academic electives: 4; Total units: 17. Tests: The college uses SAT or ACT scores in admissions decisions. Either SAT or ACT required. For admission to the fall 2011 entering class, the school will accept: ACT with or without writing accepted. Campus visit: Recommended. Admissions interview: Neither required nor recommended. Off-campus interview: Not available. **Factors that count in admissions decisions:** *Academic:* Secondary school record: Very Important. Class rank: Important. Letters of recommendation: Considered. Standardized test scores: Important. Essay: Considered. *Nonacademic:* Interview: Not Considered. Extracurricular activities: Considered. Talent/ability: Considered. Character/personal qualities: Considered. Alumni/ae relationship: Not Considered. Geographical residence: Not Considered. State residency: Not Considered. Religious affiliation/commitment: Not Considered. Minority status: Considered. Volunteer work: Considered. Work experience: Considered. **Other schools with the greatest overlap in applicants:** University of Wisconsin–Eau Claire; University of Wisconsin–La Crosse; University of Wisconsin–Stevens Point; University of Wisconsin–Whitewater. **Admissions statistics for the fall 2009 entering class:** Total applicants: 4,901. Total accepted: 4,172. Freshmen enrolled: 1,898; 2% were from out of state. Overall acceptance rate: 85%. **Credentials of fall 2009 freshmen:** 10% ranked in the top 10 percent of their high school class; 35% were in the top 25 percent; 85% were in the top half. (Proportion submitting class standing: 84%.) **Average high school grade point average:** 3.2. **First-year students submitting ACT scores:** 96%. Scores (25/75 percentile): English: 19-24, Math: 19-25, Composite: 20-24.

ACADEMICS

Year founded: 1871. **Academic calendar:** Semester. **Degrees offered:** certificate, associate, bachelor's, master's. **Most popular majors:** 19% business, management, marketing, and related support services, 17% education, 12% health professions and related clinical sciences, 8% communication, journalism, and related programs, 8% social sciences. **Major fields of study:** biological and biomedical sciences; business, management, marketing, and related support services; communication, journalism, and related programs; computer and information sciences and support services; education; health professions and related clinical sciences; history; mathematics and statistics; philosophy and religious studies; psychology; public administration and social service professions; social sciences. **Areas of required coursework:** arts/fine arts, humanities, mathematics, English (including composition), sciences (biological or physical), social science. **Pre-professional programs:** pre-law, pre-dentistry, pre-medicine, pre-veterinary science, pre-optometry, pre-pharmacy. **Special academic programs:** accelerated program, cooperative (work-study plan) program, distance learning, double major, English as a Second Language (ESL), exchange student program (domestic), honors program, independent study, internships, liberal arts/career combination, student-designed major, study abroad, teacher certificate program, weekend college. **Teacher certification offered in:** early childhood, special education, elementary, middle/junior high, adult education, secondary, bilingual/bicultural. **Reserve Officers Training Corps (ROTC):** Army ROTC: Offered on campus. **Faculty and instruction (2009-2010):** Total instructional faculty: 413 full-time, 195 part-time (48% men; 52% women; 10% minorities). Full-time faculty with Ph.D. or other terminal degree: 81%. Student/faculty ratio: 21/1. Classes of fewer than 20 students: 35%; of 20 to 49 students: 56%; of 50 or more students: 9%. **Advanced Placement and International Baccalaureate credit:** International Baccalaureate exams may be used for: Credit and/or placement. **Freshmen returning for sophomore year:** 75%. **Graduation rates:** Four-year: 15%; five-year: 42%; six-year: 48%. **Graduate study:** 12% of students pursue further study within one year. Fields in which graduates pursue further study: Master of Business Administration (MBA), 8%; education, 8%; arts and sciences, 84%.

COSTS AND FINANCIAL AID

Financial aid office: (920) 424-3377. **Expenses (2010-2011):** Tuition and fees 2010-2011: $6,682 in state, $14,670 out of state; room/board: $6,922. Estimated books and supplies: $500; transportation: $350; personal expenses: $1,000. **Financial aid:** Priority filing date for institution's financial aid form: March 15. In 2009-2010, 80% of undergraduates applied for financial aid. Of those, 48% were determined to have financial need; 15% had their need fully met. Average financial aid package (proportion receiving): $5,350 (48%). Average amount of gift aid, such as scholarships or grants (proportion receiving): $2,200 (34%). Average amount of self-help aid, such as work study or loans (proportion receiving): $3,500 (34%). Average need-based loan (excluding PLUS or other private loans): $3,750. Among students who received need-based aid, the average percentage of need met: 33%. Among students who received aid based on merit, the average award (and the proportion receiving): $390 (5%). The average athletic scholarship (and the proportion receiving): $0 (0%). Average amount of debt of borrowers graduating in 2009: $21,000. Proportion who borrowed: 64%.

CAMPUS LIFE AND EXTRACURRICULAR ACTIVITIES

Campus housing available (% using): coed dorms (98%), women's dorms, men's dorms, sorority housing (1%), fraternity housing (1%), special housing for disabled students. Students who live in college-owned, operated, or affiliated housing: 35%. **Student employment:** During the 2009-2010 academic year, 14% of undergraduates worked on campus. Average per-year earnings: $2,500. **Clubs and organizations:** Number of student organizations: 152. Activities include: campus ministries, choral groups, concert band, dance, drama/theater, international student organization, jazz band, literary magazine, model UN, music ensembles, musical theater, pep band, radio station, student government, student newspaper, student film society, television station. Number of fraternities: 7; sororities: 7. Average proportion of students who stay on campus on weekends: 60%. **Sports program (2009-2010):** Member of NCAA III. *Men's intercollegiate varsity sports:* baseball, basketball, cross country, football, golf, soccer, swimming, tennis, track and field (indoor), track and field (outdoor), volleyball, wrestling. *Women's intercollegiate varsity sports:* basketball, cross country, golf, gymnastics, soccer, softball, swimming, tennis, track and field (indoor), track and field (outdoor), volleyball.

SERVICES AND FACILITIES

Basic services: nonremedial tutoring, women's center, placement service, day care, health service, health insurance. **Remedial assistance:** reading, math, writing, study skills. **Counseling services:** minority student, career, military, personal, veteran student, academic, older student, psychological, birth control. **For learning-disabled students:** School does not offer a structured program with separate admission and additional fees. Services include: remedial math, remedial English, reading machines, remedial reading, tape recorders, videotaped classes, untimed tests, note-taking services, oral tests, learning center, readers, extended time for tests, tutors, texts on tape, other testing accommodations. **Library:** Number of titles: 612,843; number of current serial subscriptions: 2,983. **Information technology resources:** Students are not required to lease or own a computer. Number of campus computers available to all students: 500. School has a wireless network. Approximate number of users that can be accommodated: 111. Proportion of college-owned housing units wired for high-speed internet access: 100%. **Campus safety:** Security services offered: 24-hour foot-and-vehicle patrols, late-night transport/escort service, 24-hour emergency telephones, lighted pathways/sidewalks, student patrols, controlled dormitory access (key, security card, etc.).

TRANSFER AND INTERNATIONAL STUDENTS

Transfer students: May apply for admission for the following academic terms: Fall, Spring, Summer. Applicants do not need a minimum number of credits to apply. For fall 2009: Transfer applications received: 2,226. Transfer applicants offered admission: 1,593. Transfer applicants enrolled: 1,016. **International students:** Number of foreign undergraduates: 80 (1% of student body). Minimum TOEFL score required: 523 (paper); 193 (computer). Average TOEFL score: 550 (paper).

University of Wisconsin–Parkside

- **Address:** 900 Wood Road, Kenosha, WI 53141-2000
- **Website:** http://www.uwp.edu
- **Public**
- **Enrollment:** 3,688 full-time; 1,465 part-time

KEY STATS

✔ **U.S News College Ranking:** second tier, National Liberal Arts Colleges
✔ **ACT Score (25th/75th percentile):** 18-23
✔ **Tuition:** 2009-2010: $6,280 in state, $13,853 out of state

Selectivity: Selective	**Room/board:** $6,252
Acceptance rate: 63%	**Average debt:** N/A
Student/faculty ratio: 20/1	**Proportion who borrowed:** N/A

UNDERGRADUATE STUDENT BODY STATS

2009-2010 enrollment: 3,688 full-time; 1,465 part-time. Men: 45%; women: 55%. **Ethnic makeup:** African American: 10%; Asian American: 3%; Hispanic: 9%; White: 76%; International: 1%.

ADMISSIONS FACTS AND FIGURES

Phone: (262) 595-2355. **Email:** admissions@uwp.edu. **Website:** http://www.uwp.edu. **Application deadlines for fall 2011:** Regular decision: August 1. Early decision: Not offered. Early action: Not offered. Admission can be deferred. **Application fee:** $44. **To apply online, go to:** http://www.apply.wisconsin.edu. **Admissions requirements/recommendations:** High school units required (recommended): English: 4 (4); Mathematics: 3 (4); Science: 3 (4); Foreign language: 0 (2); Social studies: 3 (4); History: 0 (0); Academic electives: 3 (2); Total units: 17 (22). Tests: The college uses SAT or ACT scores in admissions decisions. Neither SAT nor ACT required. For admission to the fall 2011 entering class, the school will accept: ACT with or without writing accepted. Campus visit: Neither required nor recommended. Admissions interview: Neither required nor recommended. Off-campus interview: Not available. **Factors that count in admissions decisions:** *Academic:* Secondary school record: Very Important. Class rank: Very Important. Letters of recommendation: Considered. Standardized test scores: Important. Essay: Considered. *Nonacademic:* Interview: Not Considered. Extracurricular activities: Considered. Talent/ability: Considered. Character/personal qualities: Considered. Alumni/ae relationship: Considered. Geographical residence: Considered. State residency: Not Considered. Religious affiliation/commitment: Not Considered. Minority status: Considered. Volunteer work: Considered. Work experience: Considered. **Other schools with the greatest overlap in applicants:** University of Wisconsin–Milwaukee; University of Wisconsin–Stevens Point. **Admissions statistics for the fall 2009 entering class:** Total applicants: 2,287. Total accepted: 1,452. Freshmen enrolled: 890; 8% were from out of state. Overall acceptance rate: 63%. **Credentials of fall 2009 freshmen:** 11% ranked in the top 10 percent of their high school class; 29% were in the top 25 percent; 66% were in the top half. (Proportion submitting class standing: 95%.) **First-year students submitting ACT scores:** 92%. Scores (25/75 percentile): English: 17-23, Math: 17-23, Composite: 18-23.

ACADEMICS

Year founded: 1968. **Academic calendar:** Semester. **Degrees offered:** certificate, bachelor's, master's. **Most popular majors:** 22% business, management, marketing, and related support services, 9% social sciences, 8% visual and performing arts, 7% communication, journalism, and related programs, 7% psychology. **Major fields of study:** biological and biomedical sciences; business, management, marketing, and related support services; communication, journalism, and related programs; computer and information sciences and support services; English language and literature/letters; foreign languages, literatures, and linguistics; health professions and related clinical sciences; history; liberal arts and sciences studies, and humanities; mathematics and statistics; parks, recreation, leisure, and fitness studies;

philosophy and religious studies; physical sciences; psychology; security and protective services; social sciences; visual and performing arts. **Areas of required coursework:** arts/fine arts, humanities, mathematics, English (including composition), foreign languages, sciences (biological or physical), social science, other. **Pre-professional programs:** pre-law, pre-dentistry, pre-medicine, pre-veterinary science, pre-optometry, pre-pharmacy, other. **Special academic programs:** accelerated program, distance learning, double major, dual enrollment, exchange student program (domestic), honors program, independent study, internships, liberal arts/career combination, study abroad, teacher certificate program, weekend college, other. **Teacher certification offered in:** early childhood, elementary, middle/junior high, secondary. **Reserve Officers Training Corps (ROTC):** Army ROTC: Offered at cooperating institution (University of Wisconsin–Milwaukee). **Faculty and instruction (2009-2010):** Total instructional faculty: 175 full-time, 106 part-time (53% men; 47% women; 20% minorities). Full-time faculty with Ph.D. or other terminal degree: 78%. Student/faculty ratio: 20/1. Classes of fewer than 20 students: 46%; of 20 to 49 students: 46%; of 50 or more students: 8%. **Advanced Placement and International Baccalaureate credit:** AP tests may be used for: Credit and/or placement. Scores accepted: 3, 4, 5. International Baccalaureate exams may be used for: Placement only. **Freshmen returning for sophomore year:** 63%. **Graduation rates:** Four-year: 8%; five-year: 22%; six-year: 27%.

COSTS AND FINANCIAL AID

Financial aid office: (262) 595-2004. **Expenses (2009-2010):** Tuition and fees 2009-2010: $6,280 in state, $13,853 out of state; room/board: $6,252. **Financial aid:** Priority filing date for institution's financial aid form: November 15. In 2009-2010, 78% of undergraduates applied for financial aid. Of those, 63% were determined to have financial need; Average financial aid package (proportion receiving): N/A (61%). Average amount of gift aid, such as scholarships or grants (proportion receiving): $6,315 (34%). Average amount of self-help aid, such as work study or loans (proportion receiving): $3,676 (42%).

CAMPUS LIFE AND EXTRACURRICULAR ACTIVITIES

Campus housing available (% using): coed dorms (55%), apartment for single students (44%), special housing for disabled students (0%), special housing for international students (1%). Students who live in college-owned, operated, or affiliated housing: 17%. **Clubs and organizations:** Number of student organizations: 71. Activities include: choral groups, concert band, dance, drama/theater, jazz band, literary magazine, music ensembles, musical theater, pep band, radio station, student government, student newspaper, symphony orchestra. Proportion of men in fraternities: 1%; of women in sororities: 1%. Average proportion of students who stay on campus on weekends: 50%. **Sports program (2009-2010):** Member of NCAA II. *Men's intercollegiate varsity sports:* baseball, basketball, cross country, golf, soccer, track and field (outdoor), wrestling. *Women's intercollegiate varsity sports:* basketball, cross country, soccer, softball, track and field (outdoor), volleyball.

SERVICES AND FACILITIES

Basic services: nonremedial tutoring, women's center, placement service, day care, health service, health insurance. **Remedial assistance:** reading, math, writing, study skills. **Counseling services:** minority student, military, personal, veteran student, academic, psychological, birth control, other. **For learning-disabled students:** School does not offer a structured program with separate admission and additional fees. Services include: remedial math, remedial English, reading machines, remedial reading, untimed tests, note-taking services, learning center, extended time for tests, other. **Library:** Number of titles: 393,425; number of current serial subscriptions: 3,965. **Information technology resources:** Students are not required to lease or own a computer. School has a wireless network. Proportion of college-owned housing units wired for high-speed internet access: 100%. **Campus safety:** Security services offered: 24-hour foot-and-vehicle patrols, late-night transport/escort service, 24-hour emergency telephones, lighted pathways/sidewalks, student patrols, controlled dormitory access (key, security card, etc).

TRANSFER AND INTERNATIONAL STUDENTS

Transfer students: May apply for admission for the following academic terms: Fall, Winter, Spring, Summer. Applicants need a minimum number of credits to apply. For fall 2009: Transfer applications received: 1,045. Transfer applicants offered admission: 655. Transfer applicants enrolled: 358. **International students:** Number of foreign undergraduates: 50 (1% of student body). Number of countries represented: 24. Minimum TOEFL score required: 525 (paper).

University of Wisconsin–Platteville

- **Address:** 1 University Plaza, Platteville, WI 53818
- **Website:** http://www.uwplatt.edu
- **Public**
- **Enrollment:** 6,235 full-time; 621 part-time

KEY STATS

✔ **U.S News College Ranking:** 84, Regional Universities (Midwest)
✔ **ACT Score (25th/75th percentile):** 20-25
✔ **Tuition:** 2009-2010: $6,450 in state, $14,400 out of state

Selectivity: Selective	Room/board: $5,550
Acceptance rate: 80%	Average debt: N/A
Student/faculty ratio: N/A	Proportion who borrowed: N/A

UNDERGRADUATE STUDENT BODY STATS

2009-2010 enrollment: 6,235 full-time; 621 part-time. Men: 64%; women: 36%. **Ethnic makeup:** African American: 2%; American-Indian: 1%; Asian American: 1%; Hispanic: 1%; White: 95%.

ADMISSIONS FACTS AND FIGURES

Phone: (715) 608-1125. **Email:** admit@uwplatt.edu. **Website:** http://www.uwplatt.edu. **Application deadlines for fall 2011:** Regular decision: Rolling. Early decision: Not offered. Early action: Not offered. Admission can be deferred. **Application fee:** $44. **To apply online, go to:** http://www.apply.wisconsin.edu/. **Admissions requirements/recommendations:** High school units required (recommended): English: 4; Mathematics: 3; Science: 3; Social studies: 3; Total units: 17. Tests: The college uses SAT or ACT scores in admissions decisions. Either SAT or ACT required. For admission to the fall 2011 entering class, the school will accept: ACT with or without writing accepted. Campus visit: Recommended. Admissions interview: Neither required nor recommended. Off-campus interview: May be arranged. **Factors that count in admissions decisions:** *Academic:* Secondary school record: Very Important. Class rank: Very Important. Letters of recommendation: Considered. Standardized test scores: Very Important. Essay: Very Important. *Nonacademic:* Interview: Considered. Extracurricular activities: Important. Talent/ability: Considered. Character/personal qualities: Very Important. Alumni/ae relationship: Important. Geographical residence: Considered. State residency: Not Considered. Religious affiliation/commitment: Not Considered. Minority status: Considered. Volunteer work: Important. Work experience: Considered. **Other schools with the greatest overlap in applicants:** University of Wisconsin–La Crosse; University of Wisconsin–Madison; University of Wisconsin–Milwaukee; University of Wisconsin–Stevens Point; University of Wisconsin–Whitewater. **Admissions statistics for the fall 2009 entering class:** Total applicants: 3,661. Total accepted: 2,936. Freshmen enrolled: 1,518; 20% were from out of state. Overall acceptance rate: 80%. **Credentials of fall 2009 freshmen:** 9% ranked in the top 10 percent of their high school class; 34% were in the top 25 percent; 75% were in the top half. (Proportion submitting class standing: 91%.) **First-year students submitting ACT scores:** 95%. Scores (25/75 percentile): English: 18-24, Math: 20-26, Composite: 20-25.

ACADEMICS

Year founded: 1866. **Academic calendar:** Semester. **Degrees offered:** associate, bachelor's, post-bachelor's certificate, master's. **Most popular majors:** 21% engineering, 16% business, management, marketing, and related support services, 9% education, 9% engineering technologies/technicians, 9% security and protective services. **Major fields of study:** agriculture, agriculture operations, and related sciences; biological and biomedical sciences; business, management, marketing, and related support services; communication, journalism, and related programs; communications technologies/ technicians and support services; computer and information sciences and support services; education; engineering; engineering technologies/technicians; English language and literature/letters; foreign languages, literatures, and linguistics; history; mathematics and statistics; multi/interdisciplinary studies; natural resources and conservation; philosophy and religious studies; physical sciences; psychology; security and protective services; social sciences; visual and performing arts. **Areas of required coursework:** arts/fine arts, humanities, mathematics, English (including composition), foreign languages, sciences (biological or physical), history, social science, other. **Pre-professional programs:** pre-law, pre-dentistry, pre-medicine, pre-veterinary science, pre-optometry, pre-pharmacy, other. **Special academic programs:** cooperative (work-study plan) program, distance learning, double major, dual enrollment, English as a Second Language (ESL), exchange student program (domestic), external degree program, honors program, independent study, internships, liberal arts/career combination, student-designed major, study abroad, teacher certificate program. **Teacher certification offered in:** early childhood, elementary, middle/junior high, adult education, secondary, bilingual/bicultural. **Cooperative education programs:** agriculture, art, business, computer science, education, engineering, humanities, technologies, vocational arts, other. **Reserve Officers Training Corps (ROTC):** Army ROTC: Offered at cooperating institution (University of Dubuque). **Faculty and instruction (2009-2010):** Total instructional faculty: N/A. Classes of fewer than 20 students: 26%; of 20 to 49 students: 69%; of 50 or more students: 5%. **Advanced Placement and International Baccalaureate credit:** AP tests may be used for: Credit only. Scores accepted: 2, 3, 4, 5. **Freshmen returning for sophomore year:** 75%. **Graduation rates:** Four-year: 18%; five-year: 48%; six-year: 53%.

COSTS AND FINANCIAL AID

Financial aid office: (608) 342-1836. **Expenses (2009-2010):** Tuition and fees 2009-2010: $6,450 in state, $14,400 out of state; room/board: $5,550. Estimated books and supplies: $350; transportation: $1,100; personal expenses: $2,650. **Financial aid:** Priority filing date for institution's financial aid form: March 15.

CAMPUS LIFE AND EXTRACURRICULAR ACTIVITIES

Campus housing available: coed dorms, women's dorms, men's dorms, sorority housing, fraternity housing, special housing for disabled students, other housing options. Students who live in college-owned, operated, or affiliated housing: 40%. **Student employment:** During the 2009-2010 academic year, 27% of undergraduates worked on campus. **Clubs and organizations:** Number of student organizations: 200. Activities include: campus ministries, choral groups, concert band, drama/theater, international student organization, jazz band, literary magazine, marching band, music ensembles, musical theater, pep band, radio station, student government, student newspaper, symphony orchestra, television station. Number of fraternities: 8; sororities: 5. Proportion of men in fraternities: 6%; of women in sororities: 6%. **Sports program (2009-2010):** Member of NCAA III. *Men's intercollegiate varsity sports:* baseball, basketball, cross country, football, soccer, track and field (indoor), track and field (outdoor), wrestling. *Women's intercollegiate varsity sports:* basketball, cross country, golf, soccer, softball, track and field (indoor), track and field (outdoor), volleyball.

SERVICES AND FACILITIES

Basic services: nonremedial tutoring, women's center, placement service, day care, health service, health insurance. **Remedial assistance:** math, writing, study skills, other. **Counseling services:** minority student, career, military, personal, veteran student, academic, older student, psychological, birth control, other. **For learning-disabled students:** School does not offer a structured program with separate admission and additional fees. Total undergraduates in learning-disabled program or receiving services: 110. Services include: remedial math, remedial English, reading machines, tape recorders, note-taking services, extended time for tests, tutors, priority registration, priority seating, substitution of courses, texts on tape, exams on tape or computer, other testing accommodations. **Library:** Number of titles: 241,869; number of current serial subscriptions: 1,038. **Information technology resources:** Students are not required to lease or own a computer. Number of campus computers available to all students: 1,200. School has a wireless network. Approximate number of users that can be accommodated: 1,000. Proportion of college-owned housing units wired for high-speed internet access: 100%. **Campus safety:** Security services offered: 24-hour foot-and-vehicle patrols, 24-hour emergency telephones, lighted pathways/ sidewalks, controlled dormitory access (key, security card, etc).

TRANSFER AND INTERNATIONAL STUDENTS

Transfer students: May apply for admission for the following academic terms: Fall, Spring. Applicants need a minimum number of credits to apply. For fall 2009: Transfer applications received: 741. Transfer applicants offered admission: 523. Transfer applicants enrolled: 377. **International students:** Number of foreign undergraduates: 12. Number of countries represented: 14. Minimum TOEFL score required: 500 (paper); 63 (computer).

University of Wisconsin–River Falls

- **Address:** 410 S. Third Street, River Falls, WI 54022
- **Website:** http://www.uwrf.edu
- **Public**
- **Enrollment:** 5,762 full-time; 460 part-time

KEY STATS

- ✔ **U.S News College Ranking:** 72, Regional Universities (Midwest)
- ✔ **ACT Score (25th/75th percentile):** 20-24
- ✔ **Tuition:** 2010-2011: $6,890 in state, $14,550 out of state

Selectivity: Selective	**Room/board:** $5,574
Acceptance rate: 76%	**Average debt:** N/A
Student/faculty ratio: 23/1	**Proportion who borrowed:** 72%

UNDERGRADUATE STUDENT BODY STATS

2009-2010 enrollment: 5,762 full-time; 460 part-time. Men: 41%; women: 59%. **Ethnic makeup:** African American: 1%; Asian American: 2%; Hispanic: 1%; White: 94%; International: 1%.

ADMISSIONS FACTS AND FIGURES

Phone: (715) 425-3500. **Email:** admit@uwrf.edu. **Website:** http://www.uwrf.edu. **Application deadlines for fall 2011:** Regular decision: Rolling. Early decision: Not offered. Early action: Not offered. Admission can be deferred. **Application fee:** $44. **To apply online, go to:** http://apply.wisconsin.edu. **Admissions requirements/recommendations:** High school units required (recommended): English: 4 (4); Mathematics: 3 (4); Science: 3 (4); Foreign language: 0 (2); Social studies: 3 (4); History: 0 (0); Academic electives: 4 (3); Total units: 17 (22). Tests: The college uses SAT or ACT scores in admissions decisions. Either SAT or ACT required. For admission to the fall 2011 entering class, the school will accept: ACT with or without writing accepted. Campus visit: Recommended. Admissions interview: Recommended. Off-campus interview: May be arranged. **Factors that count in admissions decisions:** *Academic:* Secondary school record: Very Important. Class rank: Very Important. Letters of recommendation: Considered. Standardized test scores: Very Important. Essay: Important. *Nonacademic:* Interview: Not Considered. Extracurricular activities: Considered. Talent/ability: Considered. Character/personal qualities: Considered. Alumni/ae relationship: Not Considered. Geographical residence: Not Considered. State residency: Not Considered. Religious affiliation/commitment: Not Considered. Minority status: Considered. Volunteer work: Considered. Work experience: Considered. **Other schools with the greatest overlap in applicants:** University of Minnesota–Duluth; University of Minnesota–Twin Cities; University of Wisconsin–Eau Claire; University of Wisconsin–La Crosse; University of Wisconsin–Madison. **Admissions statistics for the fall 2009 entering class:** Total applicants: 3,358. Total accepted: 2,566. Freshmen enrolled: 1,337; 48% were from out of state. Overall acceptance rate: 76%. **Credentials of fall 2009 freshmen:** 12% ranked in the top 10 percent of their high school class; 35% were in the top 25 percent; 76% were in the top half. (Proportion submitting class standing: 3%.) **First-year students who submitted SAT scores:** 2%. Scores (25/75 percentile): Critical Reading: 440-520, Math: 470-590, Combined: 910-1110. **First-year students submitting ACT scores:** 97%. Scores (25/75 percentile): English: 19-25, Math: 19-24, Composite: 20-24.

ACADEMICS

Year founded: 1874. **Academic calendar:** Semester. **Degrees offered:** certificate, bachelor's, post-bachelor's certificate, master's, post-master's certificate. **Most popular majors:** 12% business administration and management, 8% public relations, advertising, and applied communication, 7% biology/biological sciences, 7% elementary education and teaching, 6% animal sciences. **Major fields of study:** agriculture, agriculture operations, and related sciences; biological and biomedical sciences; business, management, marketing, and related support services; communication, journalism, and related programs; computer and information sciences and support services; education; English language and literature/letters; foreign languages, literatures, and linguistics; health professions and related clinical sciences; history; liberal arts and sciences studies, and humanities; mathematics and statistics; multi/interdisciplinary studies; natural resources and conservation; physical sciences; psychology; public administration and social service professions; social sciences; visual and performing arts. **Areas of required coursework:** arts/fine arts, humanities, mathematics, English (including composition), sciences (biological or physical), social science, other. **Pre-professional programs:** pre-law, pre-dentistry, pre-medicine, pre-

veterinary science, pre-optometry, pre-pharmacy, other. **Special academic programs:** accelerated program, cooperative (work-study plan) program, cross-registration, distance learning, double major, dual enrollment, English as a Second Language (ESL), exchange student program (domestic), honors program, independent study, internships, student-designed major, study abroad, teacher certificate program. **Teacher certification offered in:** early childhood, special education, elementary, middle/junior high, secondary, bilingual/bicultural. **Cooperative education programs:** agriculture, business, education. **Reserve Officers Training Corps (ROTC):** Army ROTC: Offered on campus. **Faculty and instruction (2009-2010):** Total instructional faculty: 236 full-time, 112 part-time (56% men; 44% women; 7% minorities). Full-time faculty with Ph.D. or other terminal degree: 72%. Student/faculty ratio: 23/1. Classes of fewer than 20 students: 37%; of 20 to 49 students: 58%; of 50 or more students: 6%. **Advanced Placement and International Baccalaureate credit:** AP tests may be used for: Credit and/or placement. Scores accepted: 3, 4, 5. International Baccalaureate exams may be used for: Credit and/or placement. **Freshmen returning for sophomore year:** 73%. **Graduation rates:** Four-year: 24%; five-year: 49%; six-year: 55%.

COSTS AND FINANCIAL AID

Financial aid office: (715) 425-3141. **Expenses (2010-2011):** Tuition and fees 2010-2011: $6,890 in state, $14,550 out of state; room/board: $5,574. Estimated books and supplies: $330; transportation: $1,100; personal expenses: $1,900. **Financial aid:** In 2009-2010, 82% of undergraduates applied for financial aid. Of those, 60% were determined to have financial need; 19% had their need fully met. Average financial aid package (proportion receiving): $9,099 (56%). Average amount of gift aid, such as scholarships or grants (proportion receiving): $1,934 (34%). Average amount of self-help aid, such as work study or loans (proportion receiving): $3,485 (25%). Average need-based loan (excluding PLUS or other private loans): $3,645. Among students who received need-based aid, the average percentage of need met: 84%. Among students who received aid based on merit, the average award (and the proportion receiving): $1,151 (1%). The average athletic scholarship (and the proportion receiving): $0 (0%). Proportion who borrowed: 72%.

CAMPUS LIFE AND EXTRACURRICULAR ACTIVITIES

Campus housing available (% using): coed dorms (90%), women's dorms (10%), special housing for disabled students. Students who live in college-owned, operated, or affiliated housing: 38%. **Student employment:** During the 2009-2010 academic year, 15% of undergraduates worked on campus. Average per-year earnings: $3,200. **Clubs and organizations:** Number of student organizations: 185. Activities include: choral groups, concert band, dance, drama/theater, international student organization, jazz band, literary magazine, model UN, music ensembles, musical theater, pep band, radio station, student government, student newspaper, symphony orchestra, television station. Number of fraternities: 3; sororities: 3. Proportion of men in fraternities: 2%; of women in sororities: 2%. Average proportion of students who stay on campus on weekends: 70%. **Sports program (2009-2010):** Member of NCAA III. *Men's intercollegiate varsity sports:* basketball, cross country, football, ice hockey, swimming, track and field (indoor), track and field (outdoor). *Women's intercollegiate varsity sports:* basketball, cross country, golf, ice hockey, soccer, softball, swimming, tennis, track and field (indoor), track and field (outdoor), volleyball.

SERVICES AND FACILITIES

Basic services: nonremedial tutoring, placement service, day care, health service, health insurance. **Remedial assistance:** reading, math, writing, study skills. **Counseling services:** minority student, career, military, personal, veteran student, academic, psychological, birth control. **For learning-disabled students:** School does not offer a structured program with separate admission and additional fees. Total undergraduates in learning-disabled program or receiving services: 72. Services include: remedial math, reading machines, note-taking services, oral tests, extended time for tests, tutors, priority registration, priority seating, texts on tape, exams on tape or computer, other testing accommodations, other. **Library:** Number of titles: 287,248; number of current serial subscriptions: 3,834. **Information technology resources:** Students are not required to lease or own a computer. Number of campus computers available to all students: 770. School has a wireless network. Approximate number of users that can be accommodated: 800. Proportion of college-owned housing units wired for high-speed internet access: 100%. **Campus safety:** Security services offered: 24-hour foot-and-vehicle patrols, late-night transport/escort service, 24-hour emergency telephones, lighted pathways/sidewalks, controlled dormitory access (key, security card, etc).

TRANSFER AND INTERNATIONAL STUDENTS

Transfer students: May apply for admission for the following academic terms: Fall, Winter, Spring, Summer. Applicants do not need a minimum number of credits to apply. For fall 2009: Transfer applications received: 878. Transfer applicants offered admission: 646. Transfer applicants enrolled: 448. **International students:** Number of foreign undergraduates: 55 (1% of student body). Number of countries represented: 16. Minimum TOEFL score required: 550 (paper); 80 (computer).

University of Wisconsin–Stevens Point

- **Address:** 2100 Main Street, Stevens Point, WI 54481
- **Website:** http://www.uwsp.edu
- **Public**
- **Enrollment:** 8,216 full-time; 488 part-time

KEY STATS

- ✔ **U.S News College Ranking:** 43, Regional Universities (Midwest)
- ✔ **ACT Score (25th/75th percentile):** 21-25
- ✔ **Tuition:** 2010-2011: $6,850 in state, $14,423 out of state

Selectivity: Selective	**Room/board:** $5,860
Acceptance rate: 73%	**Average debt:** $22,650
Student/faculty ratio: 20/1	**Proportion who borrowed:** 71%

UNDERGRADUATE STUDENT BODY STATS

2009-2010 enrollment: 8,216 full-time; 488 part-time. Men: 48%; women: 52%. **Ethnic makeup:** African American: 1%; American-Indian: 1%; Asian American: 3%; Hispanic: 1%; White: 92%; International: 2%.

ADMISSIONS FACTS AND FIGURES

Phone: (715) 346-2441. **Email:** admiss@uwsp.edu. **Website:** http://www. uwsp.edu. **Application deadlines for fall 2011:** Regular decision: Rolling. Early decision: Not offered. Early action: Not offered. Admission cannot be deferred. **Application fee:** $44. **To apply online, go to:** http://apply. wisconsin.edu. **Admissions requirements/recommendations:** High school units required (recommended): English: 4 (4); Mathematics: 3 (4); Science: 3 (4); Foreign language: 0 (3); Social studies: 3 (4); Total units: 17 (22). Tests: The college uses SAT or ACT scores in admissions decisions. Either SAT or ACT required. For admission to the fall 2011 entering class, the school will accept: ACT with or without writing accepted. Campus visit: Recommended. Admissions interview: Neither required nor recommended. Off-campus interview: Not available. **Factors that count in admissions decisions: _Academic:_** Secondary school record: Very Important. Class rank: Very Important. Letters of recommendation: Important. Standardized test scores: Very Important. Essay: Important. **_Nonacademic:_** Interview: Not Considered. Extracurricular activities: Considered. Talent/ability: Considered. Character/personal qualities: Considered. Alumni/ae relationship: Not Considered. Geographical residence: Not Considered. State residency: Not Considered. Religious affiliation/commitment: Not Considered. Minority status: Considered. Volunteer work: Considered. Work experience: Considered. **Other schools with the greatest overlap in applicants:** University of Wisconsin–Eau Claire; University of Wisconsin–La Crosse; University of Wisconsin–Madison; University of Wisconsin–Milwaukee; University of Wisconsin–Oshkosh. **Admissions statistics for the fall 2009 entering class:** Total applicants: 5,178. Total accepted: 3,767. Freshmen enrolled: 1,640; 9% were from out of state. Overall acceptance rate: 73%. **Size of waiting list:** 462 applicants; enrolled from waiting list: 0. **Credentials of fall 2009 freshmen:** 15% ranked in the top 10 percent of their high school class; 46% were in the top 25 percent; 93% were in the top half. (Proportion submitting class standing: 87%.) **Average high school grade point average:** 3.4. **First-year students who submitted SAT scores:** 1%. Scores (25/75 percentile): Critical Reading: 515-655, Math: 490-652, Combined: 1005-1307. **First-year students submitting ACT scores:** 96%. Scores (25/75 percentile): English: 19-26, Math: 19-25, Composite: 21-25.

ACADEMICS

Year founded: 1894. **Academic calendar:** Semester. **Degrees offered:** certificate, associate, bachelor's, master's, doctorate. **Most popular majors:** 14% social sciences, 13% natural resources/conservation, 12% education, 8% business/commerce, 7% biological and biomedical sciences. **Major fields of study:** area, ethnic, cultural, and gender studies; biological and biomedical sciences; business, management, marketing, and related support services; communication, journalism, and related programs; computer and information sciences and support services; education; English language and literature/letters; foreign languages, literatures, and linguistics; health professions and related clinical sciences; history; liberal arts and sciences studies, and humanities; mathematics and statistics; multi/interdisciplinary studies; natural resources and conservation; parks, recreation, leisure, and fitness studies; philosophy and religious studies; physical sciences; psychology; public administration and social service professions; social sciences; visual and performing arts. **Areas of required coursework:** arts/ fine arts, humanities, mathematics, English (including composition), sciences (biological or physical), history, social science, other. **Pre-professional programs:** pre-law, pre-dentistry, pre-medicine, pre-veterinary science, pre-optometry, pre-pharmacy, other. **Special academic programs (% participation):** accelerated program, cooperative (work-study plan) program, distance learning, double major, dual enrollment, English as a Second Language (ESL), independent study (18%), internships (56%), student-designed major, study abroad (23%), teacher certificate program. **Teacher certification offered in:** early childhood, special education, elementary, secondary. **Cooperative education programs:** agriculture, art, business, computer science, education, engineering, health professions, home economics, humanities, natural science, social/behavioral science, technologies, vocational arts. **Reserve Officers Training Corps (ROTC)** Army ROTC: Offered on campus. **Faculty and instruction (2009-2010):** Total instructional faculty: 398 full-time, 85 part-time (56% men; 44% women; 8% minorities). Full-time faculty with Ph.D. or other terminal degree: 78%. Student/faculty ratio: 20/1. Classes of fewer than 20 students: 31%; of 20 to 49 students: 63%; of 50 or more students: 7%. **Advanced Placement and International Baccalaureate credit:** AP tests may be used for: Credit and/or placement. Scores accepted: 3, 4, 5. International Baccalaureate exams may be used for: Credit and/or placement. **Freshmen returning for sophomore year:** 77%. **Graduation rates:** Four-year: 20%; five-year: 53%; six-year: 60%. **Graduate study:** 16% of students pursue further study immediately upon graduation. Fields in which graduates pursue further study: Master of Business Administration (MBA), 5%; medicine, 1%; education, 5%; arts and sciences, 19%; veterinary medicine, 1%.

COSTS AND FINANCIAL AID

Financial aid office: (715) 346-4771. **Expenses (2010-2011):** Tuition and fees 2010-2011: $6,850 in state, $14,423 out of state; room/board: $5,860. Estimated books and supplies: $500; transportation: $344; personal expenses: $1,830. **Financial aid:** Priority filing date for institution's financial aid form: May 15. In 2009-2010, 77% of undergraduates applied for financial aid. Of those, 56% were determined to have financial need; 72% had their need fully met. Average financial aid package (proportion receiving): $8,284 (54%). Average amount of gift aid, such as scholarships or grants (proportion receiving): $6,568 (29%). Average amount of self-help aid, such as work study or loans (proportion receiving): $5,114 (50%). Average need-based loan (excluding PLUS or other private loans): $4,682. Among students who received need-based aid, the average percentage of need met: 76%. Among students who received aid based on merit, the average award (and the proportion receiving): $2,072 (6%). The average athletic scholarship (and the proportion receiving): $0 (0%). Average amount of debt of borrowers graduating in 2009: $22,650. Proportion who borrowed: 71%.

CAMPUS LIFE AND EXTRACURRICULAR ACTIVITIES

Campus housing available (% using): coed dorms (62%), women's dorms (5%), men's dorms (6%), special housing for disabled students, special housing for international students. Students who live in college-owned, operated, or affiliated housing: 36%. **Student employment:** During the 2009-2010 academic year, 21% of undergraduates worked on campus. Average per-year earnings: $1,784. **Clubs and organizations:** Number of student organizations: 192. Activities include: campus ministries, choral groups, concert band, dance, drama/theater, international student organization, jazz band, literary magazine, model UN, music ensembles, musical theater, opera, pep band, radio station, student government, student newspaper, student film society, symphony orchestra, television station. Number of fraternities: 5; sororities: 3. Proportion of men in fraternities: 2%; of women in sororities: 1%. Average proportion of students who stay on campus on weekends: 60%. **Sports program (2009-2010):** Member of NCAA III. **_Men's intercollegiate varsity sports:_** baseball, basketball, cross country, football, ice hockey, swimming, track and field (indoor), track and field (outdoor), wrestling. **_Women's intercollegiate varsity sports:_** basketball, cross country, golf, ice hockey, soccer, softball, swimming, tennis, track and field (indoor), track and field (outdoor), volleyball.

SERVICES AND FACILITIES

Basic services: nonremedial tutoring, women's center, placement service, day care, health service, other. **Remedial assistance:** reading, math, writing, study skills. **Counseling services:** minority student, career, military, personal, veteran student, academic, older student, psychological, birth control, religious. **For learning-disabled students:** School does not offer a structured program with separate admission and additional fees. Total undergraduates in learning-disabled program or receiving services: 117. Services include: remedial math, remedial English, reading machines, other special classes, untimed tests, note-taking services, oral tests, extended time for tests, tutors, priority registration, priority seating, substitution of courses, texts on tape, exams on tape or computer, other testing accommodations. **Library:** Number of titles: 1,010,315; number of current serial subscriptions: 44,504. **Information technology resources:** Students are not required to lease or own a computer. Number of campus computers available to all students: 1,217. School has a wireless network. Approximate number of users that can be accommodated: 25,600. Proportion of college-owned housing units wired for high-speed internet access: 100%. **Campus safety:** Security services offered: 24-hour foot-and-vehicle patrols, late-night transport/escort service, 24-hour emergency telephones, lighted pathways/sidewalks, student patrols, controlled dormitory access (key, security card, etc).

TRANSFER AND INTERNATIONAL STUDENTS

Transfer students: May apply for admission for the following academic terms: Fall, Spring, Summer. Applicants need a minimum number of credits to apply. For fall 2009: Transfer applications received: 1,248. Transfer applicants offered admission: 857. Transfer applicants enrolled: 635. **International students:** Number of foreign undergraduates: 176 (2% of student body). Number of countries represented: 24. Minimum TOEFL score required: 525 (paper); 70 (computer). Average TOEFL score: 540 (paper).

University of Wisconsin–Stout

- ■ **Address:** 1 Clock Tower Plaza, Menomonie, WI 54751
- ■ **Website:** http://www.uwstout.edu
- ■ **Public**
- ■ **Enrollment:** 6,802 full-time; 1,169 part-time

KEY STATS

- ✔ **U.S News College Ranking:** 66, Regional Universities (Midwest)
- ✔ **ACT Score (25th/75th percentile):** 19-23
- ✔ **Tuition:** 2009-2010: $7,658 in state, $15,403 out of state

Selectivity: Selective	**Room/board:** $5,196
Acceptance rate: 77%	**Average debt:** $25,134
Student/faculty ratio: 20/1	**Proportion who borrowed:** 78%

UNDERGRADUATE STUDENT BODY STATS

2009-2010 enrollment: 6,802 full-time; 1,169 part-time. Men: 52%; women: 48%. **Ethnic makeup:** African American: 1%; American-Indian: 1%; Asian American: 3%; Hispanic: 1%; White: 94%; International: 1%.

ADMISSIONS FACTS AND FIGURES

Phone: (715) 232-1411. **Email:** admissions@uwstout.edu. **Website:** http://www.uwstout.edu. **Application deadlines for fall 2011:** Regular decision: Rolling. Early decision: Not offered. Early action: Not offered. Admission cannot be deferred. **Application fee:** $44. **To apply online, go to:** http://www.apply.wisconsin.edu. **Admissions requirements/recommendations:** High school units required (recommended): English: 4 (4); Mathematics: 3 (3); Science: 3 (3); Foreign language: 0 (2); Social studies: 3 (3); History: 0 (0); Academic electives: 4 (4); Total units: 17 (19). Tests: The college uses SAT or ACT scores in admissions decisions. Either SAT or ACT required. For admission to the fall 2011 entering class, the school will accept: ACT with or without writing accepted. Campus visit: Recommended. Admissions interview: Recommended. Off-campus interview: May be arranged. **Factors that count in admissions decisions:** *Academic:* Secondary school record: Important. Class rank: Very Important. Letters of recommendation: Considered. Standardized test scores: Very Important. Essay: Important. *Nonacademic:* Interview: Considered. Extracurricular activities: Considered. Talent/ability: Considered. Character/personal qualities: Considered. Alumni/ae relationship: Considered. Geographical residence: Not Considered. State residency: Not Considered. Religious affiliation/commitment: Not Considered. Minority status: Considered. Volunteer work: Considered. Work experience: Considered. **Other schools with the greatest overlap in applicants:** University of Minnesota–Twin Cities; University of Wisconsin–Eau Claire; University of Wisconsin–River Falls; University of Wisconsin–Stevens Point; Winona State University. **Admissions statistics for the fall 2009 entering class:** Total applicants: 3,817. Total accepted: 2,930. Freshmen enrolled: 1,526; 34% were from out of state. Overall acceptance rate: 77%. **Credentials of fall 2009 freshmen:** 7% ranked in the top 10 percent of their high school class; 26% were in the top 25 percent; 73% were in the top half. (Proportion submitting class standing: 91%.) **First-year students submitting ACT scores:** 98%. Scores (25/75 percentile): English: 18-24, Math: 17-23, Composite: 19-23.

ACADEMICS

Year founded: 1891. **Academic calendar:** 4-1-4. **Degrees offered:** certificate, bachelor's, post-bachelor's certificate, master's, post-master's certificate. **Most popular majors:** 13% business administration and management, 8% hospitality administration/management, 8% design and applied arts, 6% construction engineering technology/technician, 5% sales, distribution, and marketing operations. **Major fields of study:** business, management, marketing, and related support services; communications technologies/technicians and support services; computer and information sciences and support services; education; engineering; engineering technologies/technicians; English language and literature/letters; family and consumer sciences/human sciences; health professions and related clinical sciences; mathematics and statistics; psychology; science technologies/technicians; visual and performing arts. **Areas of required coursework:** arts/fine arts, humanities, mathematics, English (including composition), philosophy, sciences (biological or physical), history, social science. **Pre-professional programs:** pre-law, other. **Special academic programs:** accelerated program, cooperative (work-study plan) program, cross-registration, distance learning, double major, dual enrollment, exchange student program (domestic), external degree program, honors program, independent study, internships, study abroad, teacher certificate program. **Teacher certification offered in:** early childhood, special education, elementary, vo-tech, secondary. **Cooperative education programs:** art, business, computer science, education, engineering, home economics, humanities, natural science, social/behavioral science, technologies, vocational arts. **Reserve Officers Training Corps (ROTC):** Army ROTC: Offered on campus; Air Force ROTC: Offered at cooperating institution (University of St. Thomas). **Faculty and instruction (2009-2010):** Total instructional faculty: 346 full-time, 68 part-time (57% men; 43% women; 11% minorities). Full-time faculty with Ph.D. or other terminal degree: 79%. Student/faculty ratio: 20/1. Classes of fewer than 20 students: 33%; of 20 to 49 students: 64%; of 50 or more students: 4%. **Advanced Placement and International Baccalaureate credit:** AP tests may be used for: Credit only. Scores accepted: 3, 4, 5. **Freshmen returning for sophomore year:** 71%. **Graduation rates:** Four-year: 19%; five-year: 48%; six-year: 52%. **Graduate study:** 11% of students pursue further study within one year.

COSTS AND FINANCIAL AID

Financial aid office: (715) 232-1363. **Expenses (2009-2010):** Tuition and fees 2009-2010: $7,658 in state, $15,403 out of state; room/board: $5,196. Estimated books and supplies: $356; transportation: $1,056; personal expenses: $1,882. **Financial aid:** Priority filing date for institution's financial aid form: March 15. In 2009-2010, 79% of undergraduates applied for financial aid. Of those, 56% were determined to have financial need; 54% had their need fully met. Average financial aid package (proportion receiving): $9,291 (56%). Average amount of gift aid, such as scholarships or grants (proportion receiving): $5,346 (31%). Average amount of self-help aid, such as work study or loans (proportion receiving): $4,728 (53%). Average need-based loan (excluding PLUS or other private loans): $4,207. Among students who received need-based aid, the average percentage of need met: 90%. Among students who received aid based on merit, the average award (and the proportion receiving): $1,707 (3%). The average athletic scholarship (and the proportion receiving): $0 (0%). Average amount of debt of borrowers graduating in 2009: $25,134. Proportion who borrowed: 78%.

CAMPUS LIFE AND EXTRACURRICULAR ACTIVITIES

Campus housing available (% using): coed dorms (91%), apartment for single students (9%), special housing for disabled students. Students who live in college-owned, operated, or affiliated housing: 40%. **Student employment:** During the 2009-2010 academic year, 27% of undergraduates worked on campus. Average per-year earnings: $1,537. **Clubs and organizations:** Number of student organizations: 120. Activities include: campus ministries, choral groups, concert band, dance, drama/theater, international student organization, jazz band, literary magazine, marching band, model UN, music ensembles, musical theater, pep band, radio station, student government, student newspaper, student film society. Number of fraternities: 5; sororities: 3. Proportion of men in fraternities: 2%; of women in sororities: 3%. Average proportion of students who stay on campus on weekends: 60%. **Sports program (2009-2010):** Member of NCAA III.

SERVICES AND FACILITIES

Basic services: nonremedial tutoring, women's center, placement service, day care, health service. **Remedial assistance:** reading, math, writing, study skills. **Counseling services:** minority student, career, personal, veteran student, academic, older student, psychological, birth control. **For learning-disabled students:** School does not offer a structured program with separate admission and additional fees. Services include: remedial math, remedial English, reading machines, tape recorders, diagnostic testing service, note-taking services, oral tests, extended time for tests, tutors, early syllabus, priority registration, texts on tape, exams on tape or computer, other testing accommodations, other. **Library:** Number of titles: 224,716; number of current serial subscriptions: 44,943. **Information technology resources:** Students are required to lease or own a computer. Number of campus computers available to all students: 875. School has a wireless network. Approximate number of users that can be accommodated: 4,500. Proportion of college-owned housing units wired for high-speed internet access: 100%. **Campus safety:** Security services offered: 24-hour foot-and-vehicle patrols, 24-hour emergency telephones, lighted pathways/sidewalks, controlled dormitory access (key, security card, etc).

TRANSFER AND INTERNATIONAL STUDENTS

Transfer students: May apply for admission for the following academic terms: Fall, Spring, Summer. Applicants do not need a minimum number of credits to apply. For fall 2009: Transfer applications received: 1,307. Transfer applicants offered admission: 966. Transfer applicants enrolled: 690. **International students:** Number of foreign undergraduates: 71 (1% of student body). Number of countries represented: 33. Minimum TOEFL score required: 500 (paper); 173 (computer). Average TOEFL score: 525 (paper).

University of Wisconsin–Superior

- ■ **Address:** Belknap and Catlin, PO Box 2000, Superior, WI 54880-4500
- ■ **Website:** http://www.uwsuper.edu
- ■ **Public**
- ■ **Enrollment:** 2,083 full-time; 492 part-time

KEY STATS

✔ **U.S News College Ranking:** 84, Regional Universities (Midwest)
✔ **ACT Score (25th/75th percentile):** 19-24
✔ **Tuition:** 2009-2010: $6,736 in state, $14,309 out of state

Selectivity: Selective	**Room/board:** $5,285
Acceptance rate: 68%	**Average debt:** $22,516
Student/faculty ratio: 18/1	**Proportion who borrowed:** 75%

UNDERGRADUATE STUDENT BODY STATS

2009-2010 enrollment: 2,083 full-time; 492 part-time. Men: 43%; women: 57%. **Ethnic makeup:** African American: 2%; American-Indian: 3%; Asian American: 1%; Hispanic: 1%; White: 87%; International: 6%.

ADMISSIONS FACTS AND FIGURES

Phone: (715) 394-8230. **Email:** admissions@uwsuper.edu. **Website:** http://www.uwsuper.edu. **Application deadlines for fall 2011:** Regular decision: Rolling. Early decision: Not offered. Early action: Not offered. Admission can be deferred. **Application fee:** $44. **To apply online, go to:** http://www.apply.wisconsin.edu. **Admissions requirements/recommendations:** High school units required (recommended): English: 4; Mathematics: 3; Science: 3; Foreign language: 0; Social studies: 3; Academic electives: 4; Total units: 17. Tests: The college uses SAT or ACT scores in admissions decisions. Either SAT or ACT required. For admission to the fall 2011 entering class, the school will accept: ACT with or without writing accepted. Campus visit: Recommended. Admissions interview: Recommended. Off-campus interview: May be arranged. **Factors that count in admissions decisions:** *Academic:* Secondary school record: Very Important. Class rank: Important. Letters of recommendation: Considered. Standardized test scores: Important. Essay: Considered. *Nonacademic:* Interview: Considered. Extracurricular activities: Considered. Talent/ability: Considered. Character/personal qualities: Considered. Alumni/ae relationship: Considered. Geographical residence: Considered. State residency: Not Considered.

Religious affiliation/commitment: Not Considered. Minority status: Considered. Volunteer work: Considered. Work experience: Considered. **Other schools with the greatest overlap in applicants:** University of Minnesota–Duluth; University of Minnesota–Twin Cities; University of Wisconsin–Eau Claire; University of Wisconsin–Madison; University of Wisconsin–River Falls. **Admissions statistics for the fall 2009 entering class:** Total applicants: 965. Total accepted: 655. Freshmen enrolled: 369; 44% were from out of state. Overall acceptance rate: 68%. **Credentials of fall 2009 freshmen:** 11% ranked in the top 10 percent of their high school class; 33% were in the top 25 percent; 75% were in the top half. (Proportion submitting class standing: 81%.) **First-year students who submitted SAT scores:** 6%. **First-year students submitting ACT scores:** 85%. Scores (25/75 percentile): English: 19-24, Math: 18-25, Composite: 19-24.

ACADEMICS

Year founded: 1893. **Academic calendar:** Semester. **Degrees offered:** certificate, associate, bachelor's, master's, post-master's certificate. **Most popular majors:** 18% business, management, marketing, and related support services, 14% education, 11% communication, journalism, and related programs, 9% multi/interdisciplinary studies, 9% social sciences. **Major fields of study:** agriculture, agriculture operations, and related sciences; biological and biomedical sciences; business, management, marketing, and related support services; communication, journalism, and related programs; computer and information sciences and support services; education; English language and literature/letters; health professions and related clinical sciences; history; legal professions and studies; liberal arts and sciences studies, and humanities; mathematics and statistics; multi/interdisciplinary studies; physical sciences; psychology; public administration and social service professions; security and protective services; social sciences; transportation and materials moving; visual and performing arts. **Areas of required coursework:** arts/fine arts, humanities, computer literacy, mathematics, English (including composition), philosophy, sciences (biological or physical), history, social science, other. **Pre-professional programs:** pre-law, pre-medicine, pre-veterinary science, pre-optometry, pre-pharmacy. **Special academic programs:** cooperative (work-study plan) program, cross-registration, distance learning, double major, dual enrollment, English as a Second Language (ESL), exchange student program (domestic), external degree program, independent study, internships, liberal arts/career combination, student-designed major, study abroad, teacher certificate program. **Teacher certification offered in:** early childhood, special education, elementary, middle/junior high, secondary. **Cooperative education programs:** engineering, natural science. **Reserve Officers Training Corps (ROTC):** Air Force ROTC: Offered at cooperating institution (University of Minnesota–Duluth). **Faculty and instruction (2009-2010):** Total instructional faculty: 112 full-time, 56 part-time (53% men; 47% women; 10% minorities). Full-time faculty with Ph.D. or other terminal degree: 73%. Student/faculty ratio: 18/1. Classes of fewer than 20 students: 57%; of 20 to 49 students: 39%; of 50 or more students: 3%. **Advanced Placement and International Baccalaureate credit:** AP tests may be used for: Credit and/or placement. Scores accepted: 3, 4, 5. International Baccalaureate exams may be used for: Credit only. **Freshmen returning for sophomore year:** 68%. **Graduation rates:** Four-year: 20%; five-year: 35%; six-year: 39%. **Graduate study:** 13% of students pursue further study immediately upon graduation.

COSTS AND FINANCIAL AID

Financial aid office: (715) 394-8200. **Expenses (2009-2010):** Tuition and fees 2009-2010: $6,736 in state, $14,309 out of state; room/board: $5,285. Estimated books and supplies: $750; transportation: $1,300; personal expenses: $2,070. **Financial aid:** Priority filing date for institution's financial aid form: April 1. In 2009-2010, 70% of undergraduates applied for financial aid. Of those, 58% were determined to have financial need; 24% had their need fully met. Average financial aid package (proportion receiving): N/A (58%). Average amount of gift aid, such as scholarships or grants (proportion receiving): $5,452 (37%). Average amount of self-help aid, such as work study or loans (proportion receiving): $4,760 (53%). Average need-based loan (excluding PLUS or other private loans): $3,811. Among students who received aid based on merit, the average award (and the proportion receiving): $1,769 (2%). The average athletic scholarship (and the proportion receiving): $0 (0%). Average amount of debt of borrowers graduating in 2009: $22,516. Proportion who borrowed: 75%.

CAMPUS LIFE AND EXTRACURRICULAR ACTIVITIES

Campus housing available (% using): coed dorms (98%), special housing for disabled students (1%), other housing options (1%). Students who live in college-owned, operated, or affiliated housing: 25%. **Student employment:** During the 2009-2010 academic year, 15% of undergraduates worked on campus. Average per-year earnings: $2,000. **Clubs and organizations:** Number of student organizations: 60. Activities include: campus ministries, choral groups, concert band, dance, drama/theater, international student organization, jazz band, music ensembles, musical theater, pep band, radio station, student government, student newspaper, symphony orchestra. Number of fraternities: 0; sororities: 1. Average proportion of students who stay on campus on weekends: 40%. **Sports program (2009-2010):** Member of NCAA III.

SERVICES AND FACILITIES

Basic services: nonremedial tutoring, women's center, placement service, day care, health service, health insurance. **Remedial assistance:** reading, math, writing, study skills. **Counseling services:** minority student, career, military, personal, veteran student, academic, older student, psychological, birth control, religious. **For learning-disabled students:** School does not offer a structured program with separate admission and additional fees. Total undergraduates in learning-disabled program or receiving services: 15. Services include: remedial math, remedial English, tape recorders, learning center, extended time for tests, tutors, texts on tape, other. **Library:** Number of titles: 190,757; number of current serial subscriptions: 785. **Information technology resources:** Students are not required to lease or own a computer. Number of campus computers available to all students: 325. School has a wireless network. Approximate number of users that can be accommodated: 700. Proportion of college-owned housing units wired for high-speed internet access: 100%. **Campus safety:** Security services offered: 24-hour foot-and-vehicle patrols, late-night transport/escort service, 24-hour emergency telephones, lighted pathways/sidewalks, controlled dormitory access (key, security card, etc).

TRANSFER AND INTERNATIONAL STUDENTS

Transfer students: May apply for admission for the following academic terms: Fall, Spring, Summer. Applicants do not need a minimum number of credits to apply. For fall 2009: Transfer applications received: 634. Transfer applicants offered admission: 481. Transfer applicants enrolled: 329. **International students:** Number of foreign undergraduates: 151 (6% of student body). Number of countries represented: 32. Minimum TOEFL score required: 525 (paper); 197 (computer). Average TOEFL score: 540 (paper).

University of Wisconsin–Whitewater

- **Address:** 800 W. Main Street, Whitewater, WI 53190
- **Website:** http://www.uww.edu
- **Public**
- **Enrollment:** 9,117 full-time; 613 part-time

KEY STATS

✔ **U.S News College Ranking:** 49, Regional Universities (Midwest)
✔ **ACT Score (25th/75th percentile):** 20-24
✔ **Tuition:** 2009-2010: $6,495 in state, $14,068 out of state

Selectivity: Selective	**Room/board:** $5,028
Acceptance rate: 69%	**Average debt:** $20,715
Student/faculty ratio: 23/1	**Proportion who borrowed:** 67%

UNDERGRADUATE STUDENT BODY STATS

2009-2010 enrollment: 9,117 full-time; 613 part-time. Men: 50%; women: 50%. **Ethnic makeup:** African American: 5%; Asian American: 2%; Hispanic: 3%; White: 90%; International: 1%.

ADMISSIONS FACTS AND FIGURES

Phone: (262) 472-1440. **Email:** uwwadmit@mail.uww.edu. **Website:** http://www.uww.edu. **Application deadlines for fall 2011:** Regular decision: August 1. Early decision: Not offered. Early action: Not offered. Admission can be deferred. **Application fee:** $44. **To apply online, go to:** http://www.uww.edu/apply/index.php. **Admissions requirements/recommendations:** High school units required (recommended): English: 4 (4); Mathematics: 3 (4); Science: 3 (4); Foreign language: 0 (2); Social studies: 3 (4); Academic electives: 4; Total units: 17 (20). Tests: The college uses SAT or ACT scores in admissions decisions. Neither SAT nor ACT required. For admission to the fall 2011 entering class, the school will accept: ACT with or without writing accepted. Campus visit: Recommended. Admissions interview: Neither required nor recommended. Off-campus interview: Not available. **Factors that count in admissions decisions:** *Academic:* Secondary school

record: Very Important. Class rank: Very Important. Letters of recommendation: Considered. Standardized test scores: Very Important. Essay: Important. *Nonacademic:* Interview: Considered. Extracurricular activities: Considered. Talent/ability: Considered. Character/personal qualities: Considered. Alumni/ae relationship: Considered. Geographical residence: Considered. State residency: Considered. Religious affiliation/commitment: Not Considered. Minority status: Important. Volunteer work: Considered. Work experience: Considered. **Other schools with the greatest overlap in applicants:** University of Wisconsin–Eau Claire; University of Wisconsin–La Crosse; University of Wisconsin–Madison; University of Wisconsin–Milwaukee; University of Wisconsin–Oshkosh. **Admissions statistics for the fall 2009 entering class:** Total applicants: 6,496. Total accepted: 4,460. Freshmen enrolled: 1,953; 10% were from out of state. Overall acceptance rate: 69%. **Credentials of fall 2009 freshmen:** 9% ranked in the top 10 percent of their high school class; 31% were in the top 25 percent; 77% were in the top half. (Proportion submitting class standing: 91%.) **First-year students who submitted SAT scores:** 3%. Scores (25/75 percentile): Critical Reading: 433-540, Math: 450-605, Combined: 883-1145. **First-year students submitting ACT scores:** 98%. Scores (25/75 percentile): English: 19-24, Math: 19-25, Composite: 20-24.

ACADEMICS

Year founded: 1868. **Academic calendar:** Semester. **Degrees offered:** associate, bachelor's, master's. **Most popular majors:** 32% business, management, marketing, and related support services, 15% education, 11% communication, journalism, and related programs, 9% social sciences, 6% public administration and social service professions. **Major fields of study:** area, ethnic, cultural, and gender studies; biological and biomedical sciences; business, management, marketing, and related support services; communication, journalism, and related programs; computer and information sciences and support services; education; engineering technologies/technicians; English language and literature/letters; foreign languages, literatures, and linguistics; health professions and related clinical sciences; history; liberal arts and sciences studies, and humanities; mathematics and statistics; multi/interdisciplinary studies; physical sciences; psychology; public administration and social service professions; social sciences; visual and performing arts. **Areas of required coursework:** arts/fine arts, humanities, mathematics, English (including composition), sciences (biological or physical), history, social science. **Pre-professional programs:** pre-law, pre-dentistry, pre-medicine, pre-veterinary science, pre-optometry, pre-pharmacy, other. **Special academic programs:** accelerated program, cooperative (work-study plan) program, cross-registration, distance learning, double major, dual enrollment, English as a Second Language (ESL), exchange student program (domestic), external degree program, honors program, independent study, internships, student-designed major, study abroad, teacher certificate program, weekend college. **Teacher certification offered in:** early childhood, special education, elementary, middle/junior high, secondary, bilingual/bicultural. **Reserve Officers Training Corps (ROTC):** Army ROTC: Offered on campus; Air Force ROTC: Offered on campus. **Faculty and instruction (2009-2010):** Total instructional faculty: 406 full-time, 120 part-time (54% men; 46% women; 16% minorities). Full-time faculty with Ph.D. or other terminal degree: 83%. Student/faculty ratio: 23/1. Classes of fewer than 20 students: 42%; of 20 to 49 students: 52%; of 50 or more students: 5%. **Advanced Placement and International Baccalaureate credit:** AP tests may be used for: Credit only. Scores accepted: 3, 4, 5. International Baccalaureate exams may be used for: Credit only. **Freshmen returning for sophomore year:** 76%. **Graduation rates:** Four-year: 25%; five-year: 49%; six-year: 54%. **Graduate study:** 17% of students pursue further study immediately upon graduation.

COSTS AND FINANCIAL AID

Financial aid office: (262) 472-1130. **Expenses (2009-2010):** Tuition and fees 2009-2010: $6,495 in state, $14,068 out of state; room/board: $5,028. Estimated books and supplies: $640; transportation: $850; personal expenses: $1,500. **Financial aid:** Priority filing date for institution's financial aid form: March 15. In 2009-2010, 79% of undergraduates applied for financial aid. Of those, 55% were determined to have financial need; 61% had their need fully met. Average financial aid package (proportion receiving): $7,957 (53%). Average amount of gift aid, such as scholarships or grants (proportion receiving): $5,220 (32%). Average amount of self-help aid, such as work study or loans (proportion receiving): $4,135 (48%). Average need-based loan (excluding PLUS or other private loans): $3,984. Among students who received need-based aid, the average percentage of need met: 73%. Among students who received aid based on merit, the average award (and the proportion receiving): $1,424 (4%). The average athletic scholarship (and the proportion receiving): $0 (0%). Average amount of debt of borrowers graduating in 2009: $20,715. Proportion who borrowed: 67%.

CAMPUS LIFE AND EXTRACURRICULAR ACTIVITIES

Campus housing available (% using): coed dorms (80%), women's dorms (10%), men's dorms (10%), special housing for disabled students. Students who live in college-owned, operated, or affiliated housing: 38%. **Student employment:** During the 2009-2010 academic year, 23% of undergraduates worked on campus. Average per-year earnings: $1,904. **Clubs and organizations:** Number of student organizations: 170. Activities include: choral groups, concert band, dance, drama/theater, jazz band, literary magazine, marching band, music ensembles, musical theater, pep band, radio station, student government, student newspaper, symphony orchestra, television station. Number of fraternities: 9; sororities: 9. Proportion of men in fraternities: 2%; of women in sororities: 5%. Average proportion of students who stay on campus on weekends: 40%. **Sports program (2009-2010):** Member of NCAA III. *Men's intercollegiate varsity sports:* baseball, basketball, cross country, football, soccer, swimming, tennis, track and field (indoor), track and field (outdoor), wrestling. *Women's intercollegiate varsity sports:* basketball, bowling, cross country, golf, gymnastics, soccer, softball, swimming, tennis, track and field (indoor), track and field (outdoor), volleyball.

SERVICES AND FACILITIES

Basic services: nonremedial tutoring, women's center, placement service, day care, health service, health insurance, other. **Remedial assistance:** reading, math, writing, study skills, other. **Counseling services:** minority student, career, military, personal, veteran student, academic, older student, psychological, birth control, other. **For learning-disabled students:** School does not offer a structured program with separate admission and additional fees. Total undergraduates in learning-disabled program or receiving services: 80. Services include: remedial math, remedial English, remedial reading, tape recorders, other special classes, note-taking services, learning center, readers, extended time for tests, tutors, priority registration, substitution of courses, texts on tape, typist/scribe, exams on tape or computer, other testing accommodations, other. **Library:** Number of titles: 683,705; number of current serial subscriptions: 6,647. **Information technology resources:** Students are not required to lease or own a computer. Number of campus computers available to all students: 1,300. School has a wireless network. Approximate number of users that can be accommodated: 10,000. Proportion of college-owned housing units wired for high-speed internet access: 100%. **Campus safety:** Security services offered: 24-hour foot-and-vehicle patrols, late-night transport/escort service, 24-hour emergency telephones, lighted pathways/sidewalks, controlled dormitory access (key, security card, etc).

TRANSFER AND INTERNATIONAL STUDENTS

Transfer students: May apply for admission for the following academic terms: Fall, Winter, Spring, Summer. Applicants need a minimum number of credits to apply. For fall 2009: Transfer applications received: 1,561. Transfer applicants offered admission: 947. Transfer applicants enrolled: 781. **International students:** Number of foreign undergraduates: 75 (1% of student body). Number of countries represented: 37. Minimum TOEFL score required: 500 (paper); 173 (computer).

Viterbo University

- **Address:** 900 Viterbo Drive, La Crosse, WI 54601
- **Website:** http://www.viterbo.edu
- **Private; Religious affiliation:** Roman Catholic
- **Enrollment:** N/A

KEY STATS

✔ **U.S News College Ranking:** second tier, Regional Universities (Midwest)
✔ **SAT or ACT Score (25th/75th percentile):** N/A
✔ **Tuition:** 2009-2010: $20,160

Selectivity: Selective	**Room/board:** $6,710
Acceptance rate: N/A	**Average debt:** N/A
Student/faculty ratio: N/A	**Proportion who borrowed:** N/A

Wisconsin Lutheran College

- **Address:** 8800 W. Bluemound Road, Milwaukee, WI 53226
- **Website:** http://www.wlc.edu
- **Private; Religious affiliation:** Lutheran
- **Enrollment:** 724 full-time; 52 part-time

KEY STATS

✔ **U.S News College Ranking:** 183, National Liberal Arts Colleges
✔ **ACT Score (25th/75th percentile):** 21-26
✔ **Tuition:** 2010-2011: $21,960

Selectivity: Selective	**Room/board:** $7,810
Acceptance rate: 73%	**Average debt:** $20,340
Student/faculty ratio: 10/1	**Proportion who borrowed:** 73%

UNDERGRADUATE STUDENT BODY STATS

2009-2010 enrollment: 724 full-time; 52 part-time. Men: 46%; women: 54%. **Ethnic makeup:** African American: 4%; American-Indian: 1%; Asian American: 1%; Hispanic: 3%; White: 89%; International: 2%. **Religious preference:** Roman Catholic: 7%; Protestant: 10%; No preference: 5%; Unknown: 2%; Lutheran: 62%; other Lutheran (non-WELS/ELS): 10%; Other: 4%.

ADMISSIONS FACTS AND FIGURES

Phone: (414) 443-8811. **Email:** admissions@wlc.edu. **Website:** http://www.wlc.edu. **Application deadlines for fall 2011:** Regular decision: Rolling. Early decision: Not offered. Early action: Not offered. Admission can be deferred. **Application fee:** $20. **To apply online, go to:** http://www.wlc.edu/admissions/. **Admissions requirements/recommendations:** High school units required (recommended): English: (4); Mathematics: (4); Science: (3); Foreign language: (3); Social studies: (3); Total units: (17). Tests: The college uses SAT or ACT scores in admissions decisions. Either SAT or ACT required. For admission to the fall 2011 entering class, the school will accept: ACT with or without writing accepted. Campus visit: Recommended. Admissions interview: Recommended. Off-campus interview: May be arranged. **Factors that count in admissions decisions:** *Academic:* Secondary school record: Important. Class rank: Important. Letters of recommendation: Important. Standardized test scores: Important. Essay: Considered. *Nonacademic:* Interview: Considered. Extracurricular activities: Considered. Talent/ability: Considered. Character/personal qualities: Important. Alumni/ae relationship: Considered. Geographical residence: Not Considered. State residency: Not Considered. Religious affiliation/commitment: Considered. Minority status: Considered. Volunteer work: Considered. Work experience: Considered. **Admissions statistics for the fall 2009 entering class:** Total applicants: 693. Total accepted: 505. Freshmen enrolled: 202; 25% were from out of state. Overall acceptance rate: 73%. **Credentials of fall 2009 freshmen:** 24% ranked in the top 10 percent of their high school class; 46% were in the top 25 percent; 80% were in the top half. (Proportion submitting class standing: 85%.) **Average high school grade point average:** 3.4. **First-year students who submitted SAT scores:** 11%. **First-year students submitting ACT scores:** 96%. Scores (25/75 percentile): English: 20-27, Math: 19-27, Composite: 21-26.

ACADEMICS

Year founded: 1973. **Academic calendar:** Semester. **Degrees offered:** bachelor's. **Most popular majors:** 17% education, 13% communication studies/speech communication and rhetoric, 11% biology/biological sciences, 11% psychology, 7% business administration and management. **Major fields of study:** biological and biomedical sciences; business, management, marketing, and related support services; communication, journalism, and related programs; education; English language and literature/letters; foreign languages, literatures, and linguistics; history; mathematics and statistics; multi/interdisciplinary studies; philosophy and religious studies; physical sciences; psychology; social sciences; theology and religious vocations; visual and performing arts. **Areas of required coursework:** arts/fine arts, humanities, mathematics, English (including composition), foreign languages, sciences (biological or physical), history, social science, other. **Pre-professional programs:** pre-law, pre-dentistry, pre-medicine, pre-veterinary science, pre-pharmacy, other. **Special academic programs:** double major, dual enrollment, English as a Second Language (ESL), independent study, internships, student-designed major, study abroad, teacher certificate program. **Teacher certification offered in:** early childhood, elementary, middle/junior high, secondary. **Reserve Officers Training Corps (ROTC):** Army ROTC: Offered at cooperating institution (Marquette University); Navy

ROTC: Offered at cooperating institution (Marquette University); Air Force ROTC: Offered at cooperating institution (Marquette University). **Faculty and instruction (2009-2010):** Total instructional faculty: 55 full-time, 35 part-time (61% men; 39% women). Full-time faculty with Ph.D. or other terminal degree: 69%. Student/faculty ratio: 10/1. Classes of fewer than 20 students: 64%; of 20 to 49 students: 35%; of 50 or more students: 1%. **Advanced Placement and International Baccalaureate credit:** AP tests may be used for: Placement only. Scores accepted: 3, 4, 5. **Freshmen returning for sophomore year:** 76%. **Graduation rates:** Four-year: 53%; five-year: 61%; six-year: 64%.

COSTS AND FINANCIAL AID

Financial aid office: (414) 443-8856. **Expenses (2010-2011):** Tuition and fees 2010-2011: $21,960; room/board: $7,810. Estimated books and supplies: $700; transportation: $300; personal expenses: $1,530. **Financial aid:** Priority filing date for institution's financial aid form: March 1. In 2009-2010, 86% of undergraduates applied for financial aid. Of those, 79% were determined to have financial need; 22% had their need fully met. Average financial aid package (proportion receiving): $17,521 (79%). Average amount of gift aid, such as scholarships or grants (proportion receiving): $13,061 (78%). Average amount of self-help aid, such as work study or loans (proportion receiving): $5,060 (71%). Average need-based loan (excluding PLUS or other private loans): $4,070. Among students who received need-based aid, the average percentage of need met: 83%. Among students who received aid based on merit, the average award (and the proportion receiving): $8,774 (18%). The average athletic scholarship (and the proportion receiving): $0 (0%). Average amount of debt of borrowers graduating in 2009: $20,340. Proportion who borrowed: 73%.

CAMPUS LIFE AND EXTRACURRICULAR ACTIVITIES

Campus housing available: women's dorms, men's dorms, apartment for single students. Students who live in college-owned, operated, or affiliated housing: 72%. **Student employment:** During the 2009-2010 academic year, 34% of undergraduates worked on campus. Average per-year earnings: $1,820. Activities include: campus ministries, choral groups, concert band, dance, international student organization, jazz band, music ensembles, pep band, student government, student newspaper. Number of fraternities: 0; sororities: 0. **Sports program (2009-2010):** Member of NCAA III. *Men's intercollegiate varsity sports:* baseball, basketball, cross country, football, golf, soccer, tennis, track and field (indoor), track and field (outdoor). *Women's intercollegiate varsity sports:* basketball, cross country, golf, soccer, softball, tennis, track and field (indoor), track and field (outdoor), volleyball.

SERVICES AND FACILITIES

Basic services: nonremedial tutoring, placement service, health service, health insurance. **Counseling services:** minority student, career, personal, veteran student, academic, older student, psychological, birth control, religious. **For learning-disabled students:** School does not offer a structured program with separate admission and additional fees. Total undergraduates in learning-disabled program or receiving services: 58. Services include: tape recorders, videotaped classes, untimed tests, note-taking services, learning center, extended time for tests, tutors, other. **Library:** Number of titles: 78,107; number of current serial subscriptions: 310. **Information technology resources:** Students are not required to lease or own a computer. Number of campus computers available to all students: 350. School has a wireless network. Proportion of college-owned housing units wired for high-speed internet access: 100%. **Campus safety:** Security services offered: 24-hour foot-and-vehicle patrols, late-night transport/escort service, lighted pathways/sidewalks, controlled dormitory access (key, security card, etc).

TRANSFER AND INTERNATIONAL STUDENTS

Transfer students: May apply for admission for the following academic terms: Fall, Spring, Summer. Applicants need a minimum number of credits to apply. For fall 2009: Transfer applications received: 103. Transfer applicants offered admission: 56. Transfer applicants enrolled: 34. **International students:** Number of foreign undergraduates: 17 (2% of student body). Number of countries represented: 8. Minimum TOEFL score required: 550 (paper); 213 (computer).

Wyoming

University of Wyoming

- **Address:** 1000 E. University Avenue, Laramie, WY 82071
- **Website:** http://www.uwyo.edu
- **Public**
- **Enrollment:** 8,128 full-time; 1,620 part-time

KEY STATS

✔ **U.S News College Ranking:** 153, National Universities
✔ **ACT Score (25th/75th percentile):** 21-27
✔ **Tuition:** 2010-2011: $3,726 in state, $11,646 out of state
  Selectivity: Selective   **Room/board:** $8,360
  Acceptance rate: 96%   **Average debt:** $17,084
  Student/faculty ratio: 14/1   **Proportion who borrowed:** 50%

UNDERGRADUATE STUDENT BODY STATS

2009-2010 enrollment: 8,128 full-time; 1,620 part-time. Men: 47%; women: 53%. **Ethnic makeup:** African American: 1%; American-Indian: 1%; Asian American: 1%; Hispanic: 4%; White: 90%; International: 3%.

ADMISSIONS FACTS AND FIGURES

Phone: (307) 766-5160. **Email:** Why-wyo@uwyo.edu. **Website:** http://www.uwyo.edu. **Application deadlines for fall 2011:** Regular decision: August 10. Early decision: Not offered. Early action: Not offered. Admission can be deferred. **Application fee:** $40. **To apply online, go to:** http://www.uwyo.edu/admissions/apply. **Admissions requirements/recommendations:** High school units required (recommended): English: 4 (4); Mathematics: 3 (4); Science: 3 (4); Foreign language: (2); Total units: 13 (19). Tests: The college uses SAT or ACT scores in admissions decisions. Either SAT or ACT required. For admission to the fall 2011 entering class, the school will accept: ACT with or without writing accepted. Campus visit: Recommended. Admissions interview: Neither required nor recommended. Off-campus interview: May be arranged. **Factors that count in admissions decisions: Academic:** Secondary school record: Very Important. Class rank: Not Considered. Letters of recommendation: Considered. Standardized test scores: Very Important. Essay: Considered. **Nonacademic:** Interview: Considered. Extracurricular activities: Considered. Talent/ability: Considered. Character/personal qualities: Considered. Alumni/ae relationship: Not Considered. Geographical residence: Not Considered. State residency: Considered. Religious affiliation/commitment: Not Considered. Minority status: Not Considered. Volunteer work: Not Considered. Work experience: Not Considered. **Admissions statistics for the fall 2009 entering class:** Total applicants: 3,709. Total accepted: 3,557. Freshmen enrolled: 1,594; 47% were from out of state. Overall acceptance rate: 96%. **Credentials of fall 2009 freshmen:** 22% ranked in the top 10 percent of their high school class; 49% were in the top 25 percent; 81% were in the top half. (Proportion submitting class standing: 76%.) **Average high school grade point average:** 3.4. **First-year students who submitted SAT scores:** 18%. Scores (25/75 percentile): Critical Reading: 480-600, Math: 490-620, Combined: 970-1220. **First-year students submitting ACT scores:** 92%. Scores (25/75 percentile): English: 20-26, Math: 20-26, Composite: 21-27.

ACADEMICS

Year founded: 1886. **Academic calendar:** Semester. **Degrees offered:** certificate, bachelor's, post-bachelor's certificate, master's, post-master's certificate, doctorate. **Most popular majors:** 8% elementary education and teaching, 6% business administration and management, 6% nursing/registered nurse training (R.N., A.S.N., B.S.N., M.S.N.), 5% psychology, 4% secondary education and teaching. **Major fields of study:** agriculture, agriculture operations, and related sciences; area, ethnic, cultural, and gender studies; biological and biomedical sciences; business, management, marketing, and related support services; communication, journalism, and related programs; computer and information sciences and support services; education; engineering; English language and literature/letters; family and consumer sciences/human sciences; foreign languages, literatures, and linguistics; health professions and related clinical sciences; history; liberal arts and sciences studies, and humanities; mathematics and statistics; multi/interdisciplinary studies; natural resources and conservation; parks, recreation, leisure, and fitness studies; philosophy and religious studies; physical sciences; psychology; public administration and social service professions; security and protective services; social sciences; visual and performing arts. **Areas of required coursework:** arts/fine arts, humanities, mathematics, English (including composition), sciences (biological or physical), social science, other. **Pre-professional programs:** pre-law, pre-dentistry, pre-medicine, pre-veterinary science, pre-optometry, pre-pharmacy, other. **Special academic programs:** accelerated program, distance learning, double major, English as a Second Language (ESL), exchange student program (domestic), external degree program, honors program, independent study, internships, student-designed major, study abroad. **Teacher certification offered in:** special education, elementary, vo-tech, middle/junior high, secondary. **Cooperative education programs:** agriculture, business, education, health professions, home economics, humanities, natural science, social/behavioral science, technologies, vocational arts. **Reserve Officers Training Corps (ROTC):** Army ROTC: Offered on campus; Air Force ROTC: Offered on campus. **Faculty and instruction (2009-2010):** Total instructional faculty: 730 full-time, 53 part-time (63% men; 37% women; 9% minorities). Full-time faculty with Ph.D. or other terminal degree: 85%. Student/faculty ratio: 14/1. Classes of fewer than 20 students: 39%; of 20 to 49 students: 52%; of 50 or more students: 9%. **Advanced Placement and International Baccalaureate credit:** AP tests may be used for: Credit and/or placement. Scores accepted: 3, 4, 5. International Baccalaureate exams may be used for: Credit only. **Freshmen returning for sophomore year:** 74%. **Graduation rates:** Four-year: 22%; five-year: 45%; six-year: 55%. **Graduate study:** 18% of students pursue further study immediately upon graduation.

COSTS AND FINANCIAL AID

Financial aid office: (307) 766-2116. **Expenses (2010-2011):** Tuition and fees 2010-2011: $3,726 in state, $11,646 out of state; room/board: $8,360. Estimated books and supplies: $1,200; transportation: $889; personal expenses: $2,200. **Financial aid:** Priority filing date for institution's financial aid form: February 1. In 2009-2010, 63% of undergraduates applied for financial aid. Of those, 44% were determined to have financial need; 22% had their need fully met. Average financial aid package (proportion receiving): $9,332 (44%). Average amount of gift aid, such as scholarships or grants (proportion receiving): $4,660 (27%). Average amount of self-help aid, such as work study or loans (proportion receiving): $3,641 (37%). Average need-based loan (excluding PLUS or other private loans): $3,446. Among students who received need-based aid, the average percentage of need met: 44%. Among students who received aid based on merit, the average award (and the proportion receiving): $4,751 (40%). The average athletic scholarship (and the proportion receiving): $9,842 (3%). Average amount of debt of borrowers graduating in 2009: $17,084. Proportion who borrowed: 50%.

CAMPUS LIFE AND EXTRACURRICULAR ACTIVITIES

Campus housing available: coed dorms, sorority housing, fraternity housing, apartments for married students, apartment for single students, special housing for disabled students. Students who live in college-owned, operated, or affiliated housing: 23%. **Student employment:** During the 2009-2010 academic year, 27% of undergraduates worked on campus. Average per-year earnings: $2,480. **Clubs and organizations:** Number of student organizations: 239. Activities include: campus ministries, choral groups, concert band, dance, drama/theater, international student organization, jazz band, literary magazine, marching band, model UN, music ensembles, musical theater, opera, pep band, radio station, student government, student newspaper, student film society, symphony orchestra, television station. Number of fraternities: 9; sororities: 6. Proportion of men in fraternities: 5%; of women in sororities: 5%. Average proportion of students who stay on campus on weekends: 70%. **Sports program (2009-2010):** Member of NCAA I. **Men's intercollegiate varsity sports:** basketball, cross country, football, golf, swimming, track and field (outdoor), wrestling. **Women's intercollegiate varsity sports:** basketball, cross country, golf, soccer, swimming, tennis, track and field (outdoor), volleyball.

SERVICES AND FACILITIES

Basic services: nonremedial tutoring, women's center, placement service, day care, health service, health insurance. **Counseling services:** minority student, career, military, personal, veteran student, academic, older student, psychological, birth control. **For learning-disabled students:** School does not offer a structured program with separate admission and additional fees. Total undergraduates in learning-disabled program or receiving services: 109. Services include: reading machines, tape recorders, note-taking services, oral tests, learning center, readers, extended time for tests, tutors, priority registration, substitution of courses, texts on tape, typist/scribe, exams on tape or computer, other testing accommodations, other. **Library:** Number of titles: 2,971,418; number of current serial subscriptions: 75,864. **Information technology resources:** Students are not required to lease or own a computer. Number of campus computers available to all students: 1,302. School has a wireless network. Proportion of college-owned housing units wired for high-speed internet access: 100%. **Campus safety:** Security services offered: 24-hour foot-and-vehicle patrols, late-night transport/escort service, 24-hour emergency telephones, lighted pathways/sidewalks, controlled dormitory access (key, security card, etc).

TRANSFER AND INTERNATIONAL STUDENTS

Transfer students: May apply for admission for the following academic terms: Fall, Spring, Summer. Applicants need a minimum number of credits to apply. For fall 2009: Transfer applications received: 1,895. Transfer applicants offered admission: 1,802. Transfer applicants enrolled: 1,095. **International students:** Number of foreign undergraduates: 300 (3% of student body). Number of countries represented: 56. Minimum TOEFL score required: 525 (paper); 197 (computer). Average TOEFL score: 582 (paper).

Index of Schools

A

Abilene Christian Univ., 1524
Adams State College, 461
Adelphi Univ., 1080
Adrian College, 884
Agnes Scott College, 548
Alabama Agricultural and Mechanical Univ., 330
Alabama State Univ., 331
Alaska Pacific Univ., 353
Albany State Univ., 549
Albertus Magnus College, 478
Albion College, 885
Albright College, 1343
Alcorn State Univ., 954
Alderson-Broaddus College, 1667
Alfred Univ., 1081
Alice Lloyd College, 741
Allegheny College, 1344
Allen Univ., 1451
Alma College, 886
Alvernia Univ., 1345
Alverno College, 1684
American Indian College of the Assemblies of God, 357
American International College, 823
American Jewish Univ., 378
American Univ., 504
Amherst College, 824
Anderson Univ. (IN), 652
Anderson Univ. (SC), 1452
Andrews Univ., 887
Angelo State Univ., 1525
Anna Maria College, 825
Appalachian State Univ., 1192
Aquinas College (MI), 888
Aquinas College (TN), 1489
Arcadia Univ., 1346
Arizona State Univ., 357
Arkansas Baptist College, 361
Arkansas State Univ.–Jonesboro, 361
Arkansas Tech Univ., 362
Armstrong Atlantic State Univ., 550
Art Academy of Cincinnati, 1246
Art Center College of Design, 379
Asbury Univ., 742
Ashland Univ., 1246
Assumption College, 825
Atlanta Christian College, 551
Atlantic Union College, 826
Auburn Univ., 331
Auburn Univ.–Montgomery, 333
Augsburg College, 921
Augusta State Univ., 551
Augustana College (IL), 598
Augustana College (SD), 1478
Aurora Univ., 599
Austin College, 1526
Austin Peay State Univ., 1489
Averett Univ., 1608
Avila Univ., 970
Azusa Pacific Univ., 379

B

Babson College, 827
Bacone College, 1303
Baker College of Flint, 889
Baker Univ., 722
Baldwin-Wallace College, 1247
Ball State Univ., 653
Baptist Bible College, 971
Baptist Bible College and Seminary, 1347
Bard College, 1081
Bard College at Simon's Rock, 828
Barnard College, 1082
Barry Univ., 512
Barton College, 1193
Bates College, 784
Bay Path College, 829
Baylor Univ., 1527
Beacon College, 513
Becker College, 830
Belhaven Univ., 955
Bellarmine Univ., 743
Bellevue Univ., 1013
Belmont Abbey College, 1194
Belmont Univ., 1490
Beloit College, 1685
Bemidji State Univ., 922
Benedict College, 1453
Benedictine College, 723
Benedictine Univ., 599
Bennett College, 1195
Bennington College, 1595
Bentley Univ., 830
Berea College, 744
Berklee College of Music, 832
Berry College, 551
Bethany College (KS), 724
Bethany College (WV), 1668
Bethany Lutheran College, 923
Bethany Univ., 380
Bethel College (IN), 654
Bethel College (KS), 725
Bethel College (TN), 1491
Bethel Univ., 923
Bethune-Cookman Univ., 513
Binghamton Univ.–SUNY, 1083
Biola Univ., 380
Birmingham-Southern College, 334
Black Hills State Univ., 1479
Blackburn College, 600
Bloomfield College, 1046
Bloomsburg Univ. of Pennsylvania, 1347
Blue Mountain College, 956
Bluefield College, 1609
Bluefield State College, 1669
Bluffton Univ., 1248
Boise State Univ., 591
Boricua College, 1084
Boston Architectural College, 832
Boston College, 833
Boston Conservatory, 834
Boston Univ., 835

Bowdoin College, 785
Bowie State Univ., 799
Bowling Green State Univ., 1249
Bradley Univ., 601
Brandeis Univ., 835
Brenau Univ., 553
Brescia Univ., 745
Brevard College, 1196
Brewton-Parker College, 554
Briar Cliff Univ., 695
Bridgewater College, 1610
Bridgewater State College, 836
Brigham Young Univ.–Hawaii, 587
Brigham Young Univ.–Idaho, 592
Brigham Young Univ.–Provo, 1587
Brown Univ., 1441
Bryan College, 1492
Bryant Univ., 1442
Bryn Athyn College of the New Church, 1348
Bryn Mawr College, 1349
Bucknell Univ., 1350
Buena Vista Univ., 696
Buffalo State College–SUNY, 1084
Burlington College, 1596
Butler Univ., 655

C

Cabrini College, 1351
Caldwell College, 1047
California Baptist Univ., 382
California College of the Arts, 383
California Institute of Technology, 384
California Institute of the Arts, 385
California Lutheran Univ., 385
California Maritime Academy, 387
California Polytechnic State Univ.–San Luis Obispo, 387
California State Polytechnic Univ.–Pomona, 388
California State Univ.–Bakersfield, 389
California State Univ.–Chico, 390
California State Univ.–Dominguez Hills, 391
California State Univ.–East Bay, 392
California State Univ.–Fresno, 393
California State Univ.–Fullerton, 394
California State Univ.–Long Beach, 396
California State Univ.–Los Angeles, 397
California State Univ.–Monterey Bay, 398
California State Univ.–Northridge, 399
California State Univ.–Sacramento, 399
California State Univ.–San Bernardino, 400
California State Univ.–San Marcos, 402
California State Univ.–Stanislaus, 402
California Univ. of Pennsylvania, 1352
Calumet College of St. Joseph, 656
Calvin College, 889
Cambridge College, 837
Cameron Univ., 1303

Campbell Univ., 1197
Campbellsville Univ., 746
Canisius College, 1085
Capital Univ., 1250
Cardinal Stritch Univ., 1686
Carleton College, 924
Carlow Univ., 1353
Carnegie Mellon Univ., 1353
Carroll College, 1005
Carroll Univ., 1687
Carson-Newman College, 1493
Carthage College, 1688
Case Western Reserve Univ., 1251
Castleton State College, 1597
Catawba College, 1198
Catholic Univ. of America, 505
Cazenovia College, 1086
Cedar Crest College, 1355
Cedarville Univ., 1253
Centenary College, 1048
Centenary College of Louisiana, 766
Central Baptist College, 363
Central Christian College, 726
Central College, 697
Central Connecticut State Univ., 479
Central Methodist Univ., 971
Central Michigan Univ., 890
Central State Univ., 1254
Central Washington Univ., 1648
Centre College, 747
Chadron State College, 1013
Chaminade Univ. of Honolulu, 587
Champlain College, 1598
Chancellor Univ., 1255
Chapman Univ., 403
Charleston Southern Univ., 1453
Chatham Univ., 1356
Chester College of New England, 1034
Chestnut Hill College, 1357
Cheyney Univ. of Pennsylvania, 1358
Chicago State Univ., 602
Chowan Univ., 1199
Christian Brothers Univ., 1494
Christopher Newport Univ., 1611
The Citadel, 1454
City Univ., 1649
Claflin Univ., 1455
Claremont McKenna College, 405
Clarion Univ. of Pennsylvania, 1359
Clark Atlanta Univ., 554
Clark Univ., 838
Clarke Univ., 698
Clarkson Univ., 1087
Clayton State Univ., 555
Clearwater Christian College, 514
Cleary Univ., 891
Clemson Univ., 1456
Cleveland Institute of Art, 1255
Cleveland Institute of Music, 1256
Cleveland State Univ., 1256
Coastal Carolina Univ., 1457
Coe College, 699

Cogswell Polytechnical College, 406
Coker College, 1458
Colby College, 786
Colby-Sawyer College, 1034
Colgate Univ., 1088
College at Brockport–SUNY, 1089
College for Creative Studies, 892
College of Charleston, 1459
College of Idaho, 592
College of Mount St. Joseph, 1257
College of Mount St. Vincent, 1091
College of New Jersey, 1049
College of New Rochelle, 1092
College of Notre Dame of Maryland, 800
College of Our Lady of the Elms, 839
College of Santa Fe, 1073
College of St. Benedict, 925
College of St. Elizabeth, 1050
College of St. Joseph, 1599
College of St. Mary, 1014
College of St. Rose, 1092
College of St. Scholastica, 926
College of St. Thomas More, 1528
College of the Atlantic, 787
College of the Holy Cross, 839
College of the Ozarks, 972
College of Visual Arts, 927
College of William and Mary, 1612
College of Wooster, 1258
Colorado Christian Univ., 461
Colorado College, 461
Colorado School of Mines, 462
Colorado State Univ., 463
Colorado State Univ.–Pueblo, 464
Columbia College (IL), 602
Columbia College (MO), 973
Columbia College (SC), 1460
Columbia Univ., 1093
Columbus College of Art and Design, 1259
Columbus State Univ., 556
Concord Univ., 1670
Concordia College (AL), 335
Concordia College (NY), 1094
Concordia College–Moorhead, 928
Concordia Univ. (CA), 406
Concordia Univ. (MI), 892
Concordia Univ. (NE), 1015
Concordia Univ. (OR), 1324
Concordia Univ. Chicago, 602
Concordia Univ. Texas, 1528
Concordia Univ. Wisconsin, 1689
Concordia Univ.–St. Paul, 929
Connecticut College, 480
Converse College, 1461
Cooper Union, 1094
Coppin State Univ., 801
Corban Univ., 1324
Corcoran College of Art and Design, 506
Cornell College, 700
Cornell Univ., 1095
Cornerstone Univ., 892
Cornish College of the Arts, 1649
Covenant College, 557
Creighton Univ., 1016
Crown College, 930

Culver-Stockton College, 974
Cumberland Univ., 1495
CUNY–Baruch College, 1096
CUNY–Brooklyn College, 1097
CUNY–City College, 1098
CUNY–College of Staten Island, 1099
CUNY–Hunter College, 1100
CUNY–John Jay College of Criminal Justice, 1101
CUNY–Lehman College, 1102
CUNY–Medgar Evers College, 1103
CUNY–New York City College of Technology, 1104
CUNY–Queens College, 1105
CUNY–York College, 1106
Curry College, 840
Curtis Institute of Music, 1360

D

D'Youville College, 1109
Daemen College, 1106
Dakota State Univ., 1480
Dakota Wesleyan Univ., 1481
Dallas Baptist Univ., 1529
Dalton State College, 558
Dana College, 1017
Daniel Webster College, 1034
Dartmouth College, 1034
Davenport Univ., 894
Davidson College, 1200
Davis and Elkins College, 1671
Defiance College, 1260
Delaware State Univ., 499
Delaware Valley College, 1360
Delta State Univ., 957
Denison Univ., 1261
DePaul Univ., 603
DePauw Univ., 657
DeSales Univ., 1361
Dickinson College, 1362
Dickinson State Univ., 1237
Dillard Univ., 766
Dixie State College of Utah, 1588
Doane College, 1018
Dominican College, 1107
Dominican Univ., 604
Dominican Univ. of California, 407
Dordt College, 701
Dowling College, 1108
Drake Univ., 702
Drew Univ., 1050
Drexel Univ., 1364
Drury Univ., 975
Duke Univ., 1201
Duquesne Univ., 1365

E

Earlham College, 658
East Carolina Univ., 1202
East Central Univ., 1304
East Stroudsburg Univ. of Pennsylvania, 1367
East Tennessee State Univ., 1496
East Texas Baptist Univ., 1530
Eastern Connecticut State Univ., 481
Eastern Illinois Univ., 605
Eastern Kentucky Univ., 748
Eastern Mennonite Univ., 1613

Eastern Michigan Univ., 894
Eastern Nazarene College, 841
Eastern New Mexico Univ., 1074
Eastern Oregon Univ., 1325
Eastern Univ., 1366
Eastern Washington Univ., 1650
East-West Univ., 606
Eckerd College, 515
Edgewood College, 1690
Edinboro Univ. of Pennsylvania, 1368
Edward Waters College, 516
Elizabeth City State Univ., 1202
Elizabethtown College, 1369
Elmhurst College, 607
Elmira College, 1110
Elon Univ., 1203
Embry-Riddle Aeronautical Univ., 516
Emerson College, 842
Emmanuel College (GA), 558
Emmanuel College (MA), 843
Emory and Henry College, 1614
Emory Univ., 559
Emporia State Univ., 727
Endicott College, 844
Erskine College, 1462
Eureka College, 608
Evangel Univ., 976
Evergreen State College, 1651
Excelsior College, 1111

F

Fairfield Univ., 482
Fairleigh Dickinson Univ., 1051
Fairmont State Univ., 1672
Farmingdale State College–SUNY, 1111
Fashion Institute of Technology, 1112
Faulkner Univ., 335
Fayetteville State Univ., 1204
Felician College, 1052
Ferris State Univ., 896
Ferrum College, 1615
Finlandia Univ., 897
Fisher College, 845
Fisk Univ., 1497
Fitchburg State College, 845
Flagler College, 517
Florida A&M Univ., 518
Florida Atlantic Univ., 520
Florida Gulf Coast Univ., 521
Florida Institute of Technology, 522
Florida International Univ., 523
Florida Memorial Univ., 524
Florida Southern College, 524
Florida State Univ., 525
Fontbonne Univ., 977
Fordham Univ., 1113
Fort Hays State Univ., 728
Fort Lewis College, 465
Fort Valley State Univ., 560
Framingham State College, 846
Francis Marion Univ., 1463
Franciscan Univ. of Steubenville, 1262
Franklin and Marshall College, 1370
Franklin College, 659
Franklin Pierce Univ., 1035
Franklin Univ., 1263
Free Will Baptist Bible College, 1499
Freed-Hardeman Univ., 1498

Fresno Pacific Univ., 408
Friends Univ., 728
Frostburg State Univ., 802
Furman Univ., 1464

G

Gallaudet Univ., 507
Gannon Univ., 1371
Gardner-Webb Univ., 1205
Geneva College, 1372
George Fox Univ., 1326
George Mason Univ., 1616
George Washington Univ., 508
Georgetown College, 749
Georgetown Univ., 507
Georgia College & State Univ., 561
Georgia Institute of Technology, 562
Georgia Southern Univ., 563
Georgia Southwestern State Univ., 564
Georgia State Univ., 565
Georgian Court Univ., 1053
Gettysburg College, 1372
Glenville State College, 1673
Goddard College, 1600
Golden Gate Univ., 409
Goldey Beacom College, 500
Gonzaga Univ., 1652
Gordon College, 847
Goshen College, 660
Goucher College, 803
Grace Bible College, 897
Grace College and Seminary, 661
Graceland Univ., 703
Grambling State Univ., 767
Grand Valley State Univ., 897
Grand View Univ., 704
Granite State College, 1036
Gratz College, 1373
Great Basin College, 1030
Green Mountain College, 1600
Greensboro College, 1206
Greenville College, 609
Grinnell College, 705
Grove City College, 1373
Guilford College, 1206
Gustavus Adolphus College, 931
Gwynedd-Mercy College, 1374

H

Hamilton College, 1114
Hamline Univ., 932
Hampden-Sydney College, 1617
Hampshire College, 848
Hampton Univ., 1618
Hannibal-LaGrange College, 978
Hanover College, 662
Harding Univ., 363
Hardin-Simmons Univ., 1531
Harris-Stowe State Univ., 979
Hartwick College, 1115
Harvard Univ., 849
Harvey Mudd College, 410
Hastings College, 1019
Haverford College, 1375
Hawaii Pacific Univ., 588
Heidelberg Univ., 1263
Henderson State Univ., 364
Hendrix College, 365

Moore College of Art and Design, 1399
Moravian College, 1399
Morehead State Univ., 754
Morehouse College, 570
Morgan State Univ., 809
Morningside College, 710
Morris College, 1466
Mount Aloysius College, 1400
Mount Holyoke College, 858
Mount Ida College, 859
Mount Marty College, 1482
Mount Mary College, 1697
Mount Mercy College, 711
Mount Olive College, 1215
Mount St. Mary College ((NY), 1133
Mount St. Mary's College (CA), 420
Mount St. Mary's Univ., 810
Mount Vernon Nazarene Univ., 1274
Mountain State Univ., 1675
Muhlenberg College, 1401
Murray State Univ., 755
Muskingum Univ., 1275

N

Naropa Univ., 468
National Hispanic Univ., 421
National Univ., 421
National-Louis Univ., 625
Nazareth College, 1134
Nebraska Wesleyan Univ., 1021
Neumann Univ., 1402
New College of Florida, 529
New England College, 1038
New England Conservatory of Music, 860
New Jersey City Univ., 1057
New Jersey Institute of Technology, 1058
New Mexico Highlands Univ., 1074
New Mexico Institute of Mining and Technology, 1075
New Mexico State Univ., 1075
New School, 1135
New York Institute of Technology, 1136
New York Univ., 1137
Newberry College, 1466
Newbury College, 860
Newman Univ., 731
Niagara Univ., 1138
Nicholls State Univ., 774
Nichols College, 860
Norfolk State Univ., 1627
North Carolina A&T State Univ., 1215
North Carolina Central Univ., 1216
North Carolina State Univ.–Raleigh, 1217
North Carolina Wesleyan College, 1218
North Central College, 625
North Central Univ., 938
North Dakota State Univ., 1241
North Georgia College and State Univ., 571
North Greenville Univ., 1468
North Park Univ., 629
Northeastern Illinois Univ., 627
Northeastern State Univ., 1305
Northeastern Univ., 861
Northern Illinois Univ., 628
Northern Kentucky Univ., 756

Northern Michigan Univ., 907
Northern State Univ., 1483
Northland College, 1698
Northwest Christian Univ., 1330
Northwest Missouri State Univ., 988
Northwest Nazarene Univ., 595
Northwest Univ., 1653
Northwestern College (IA), 712
Northwestern College (MN), 939
Northwestern Oklahoma State Univ., 1306
Northwestern State Univ. of Louisiana, 775
Northwestern Univ., 630
Northwood Univ., 908
Norwich Univ., 1603
Notre Dame College of Ohio, 1276
Notre Dame de Namur Univ., 421
Nova Southeastern Univ., 530
Nyack College, 1139

O

Oakland City Univ., 677
Oakland Univ., 909
Oakwood Univ., 339
Oberlin College, 1277
Occidental College, 422
Oglethorpe Univ., 572
Ohio Dominican Univ., 1278
Ohio Northern Univ., 1279
Ohio State Univ.–Columbus, 1280
Ohio Univ., 1281
Ohio Valley Univ., 1676
Ohio Wesleyan Univ., 1283
Oklahoma Baptist Univ., 1307
Oklahoma Christian Univ., 1308
Oklahoma City Univ., 1309
Oklahoma Panhandle State Univ., 1311
Oklahoma State Univ., 1311
Oklahoma Wesleyan Univ., 1312
Old Dominion Univ., 1627
Olivet College, 910
Olivet Nazarene Univ., 631
Oral Roberts Univ., 1313
Oregon Institute of Technology, 1331
Oregon State Univ., 1332
Otis College of Art and Design, 423
Ottawa Univ., 732
Otterbein College, 1284
Ouachita Baptist Univ., 368
Our Lady of Holy Cross College, 776
Our Lady of the Lake Univ., 1541

P

Pace Univ., 1139
Pacific Lutheran Univ., 1654
Pacific Northwest College of Art, 1333
Pacific Union College, 424
Pacific Univ., 1333
Paine College, 573
Palm Beach Atlantic Univ., 531
Park Univ., 988
Patten Univ., 425
Paul Smith's College, 1140
Peace College, 1219
Peirce College, 1403
Pennsylvania College of Technology, 1404

Pennsylvania State Univ.–Univ. Park, 1405
Pepperdine Univ., 425
Peru State College, 1022
Pfeiffer Univ., 1220
Philadelphia Biblical Univ., 1406
Philadelphia Univ., 1407
Philander Smith College, 370
Piedmont College, 574
Pikeville College, 757
Pine Manor College, 862
Pittsburg State Univ., 732
Pitzer College, 426
Plymouth State Univ., 1039
Point Loma Nazarene Univ., 427
Point Park Univ., 1408
Polytechnic Institute of New York Univ., 1140
Pomona College, 428
Portland State Univ., 1334
Post Univ., 484
Prairie View A&M Univ., 1542
Pratt Institute, 1141
Presbyterian College, 1469
Prescott College, 358
Princeton Univ., 1059
Principia College, 632
Providence College, 1444
Purchase College–SUNY, 1142
Purdue Univ.–Calumet, 678
Purdue Univ.–North Central, 679
Purdue Univ.–West Lafayette, 680

Q

Queens Univ. of Charlotte, 1221
Quincy Univ., 633
Quinnipiac Univ., 485

R

Radford Univ., 1628
Ramapo College of New Jersey, 1060
Randolph College, 1629
Randolph-Macon College, 1630
Reed College, 1335
Regent Univ., 1631
Regis College, 863
Regis Univ., 469
Reinhardt Univ., 575
Rensselaer Polytechnic Institute, 1143
Rhode Island College, 1445
Rhode Island School of Design, 1446
Rhodes College, 1508
Rice Univ., 1543
Richard Stockton College of New Jersey, 1061
Rider Univ., 1062
Ringling College of Art and Design, 532
Ripon College, 1699
Rivier College, 1040
Roanoke College, 1632
Robert Morris Univ. (IL), 634
Robert Morris Univ. (PA), 1409
Roberts Wesleyan College, 1144
Rochester College, 911
Rochester Institute of Technology, 1145
Rockford College, 635
Rockhurst Univ., 989
Rocky Mountain College, 1008

Roger Williams Univ., 1447
Rogers State Univ., 1315
Rollins College, 532
Roosevelt Univ., 636
Rose-Hulman Institute of Technology, 681
Rosemont College, 1410
Rowan Univ., 1063
Russell Sage College, 1147
Rust College, 964
Rutgers, the State Univ. of New Jersey–Camden, 1065
Rutgers, the State Univ. of New Jersey–New Brunswick, 1067
Rutgers, the State Univ. of New Jersey–Newark, 1066

S

Sacred Heart Univ., 486
Sage Colleges–Albany, 1148
Saginaw Valley State Univ., 912
Salem College, 1222
Salem State College, 863
Salisbury Univ., 811
Salve Regina Univ., 1448
Sam Houston State Univ., 1544
Samford Univ., 339
San Diego State Univ., 429
San Francisco Art Institute, 430
San Francisco Conservatory of Music, 430
San Francisco State Univ., 431
San Jose State Univ., 432
Santa Clara Univ., 433
Sarah Lawrence College, 1149
Savannah College of Art and Design, 576
Savannah State Univ., 577
School of the Art Institute of Chicago, 637
Schreiner Univ., 1545
Scripps College, 434
Seattle Pacific Univ., 1655
Seattle Univ., 1656
Seton Hall Univ., 1068
Seton Hill Univ., 1411
Sewanee–Univ. of the South, 1509
Shaw Univ., 1222
Shawnee State Univ., 1285
Shenandoah Univ., 1633
Shepherd Univ., 1677
Shimer College, 638
Shippensburg Univ. of Pennsylvania, 1412
Shorter College, 578
Siena College, 1149
Siena Heights Univ., 912
Sierra Nevada College, 1030
Silver Lake College, 1700
Simmons College, 864
Simpson College, 713
Simpson Univ., 435
Skidmore College, 1150
Slippery Rock Univ. of Pennsylvania, 1413
Smith College, 865
Sojourner-Douglass College, 812
Sonoma State Univ., 436

South Carolina State Univ., 1470
South Dakota School of Mines and Technology, 1484
South Dakota State Univ., 1485
Southeast Missouri State Univ., 990
Southeastern Louisiana Univ., 777
Southeastern Oklahoma State Univ., 1316
Southeastern Univ., 534
Southern Adventist Univ., 1510
Southern Arkansas Univ., 370
Southern California Institute of Architecture, 437
Southern Connecticut State Univ., 487
Southern Illinois Univ.–Carbondale, 638
Southern Illinois Univ.–Edwardsville, 639
Southern Methodist Univ., 1546
Southern Nazarene Univ., 1317
Southern New Hampshire Univ., 1041
Southern Oregon Univ., 1336
Southern Polytechnic State Univ., 579
Southern Univ. and A&M College, 778
Southern Univ.–New Orleans, 778
Southern Utah Univ., 1589
Southern Vermont College, 1604
Southern Wesleyan Univ., 1471
Southwest Baptist Univ., 991
Southwest Minnesota State Univ., 940
Southwestern Adventist Univ., 1547
Southwestern Assemblies of God Univ., 1547
Southwestern Christian College, 1548
Southwestern College, 733
Southwestern Oklahoma State Univ., 1318
Southwestern Univ., 1548
Spalding Univ., 758
Spelman College, 580
Spring Arbor Univ., 912
Spring Hill College, 340
Springfield College, 866
St. Ambrose Univ., 714
St. Andrews Presbyterian College, 1223
St. Anselm College, 1042
St. Augustine's College, 1224
St. Bonaventure Univ., 1152
St. Catherine Univ., 941
St. Cloud State Univ., 942
St. Edward's Univ., 1549
St. Francis College, 1153
St. Francis Univ., 1414
St. Gregory's Univ., 1319
St. John Fisher College, 1154
St. John's College (MD), 813
St. John's College (NM), 1077
St. John's Univ. (MN), 943
St. John's Univ. (NY), 1155
St. Joseph College (CT), 488
St. Joseph's College (IN), 682
St. Joseph's College (ME), 791
St. Joseph's College New York, 1156
St. Joseph's Univ., 1415
St. Lawrence Univ., 1157
St. Leo Univ., 536
St. Louis Univ., 992
St. Martin's Univ., 1657
St. Mary's College, 684

St. Mary's College of California, 439
St. Mary's College of Maryland, 813
St. Mary's Univ. of Minnesota, 944
St. Mary's Univ. of San Antonio, 1551
St. Mary-of-the-Woods College, 683
St. Michael's College, 1604
St. Norbert College, 1701
St. Olaf College, 945
St. Paul's College, 1634
St. Peter's College, 1070
St. Thomas Aquinas College, 1158
St. Thomas Univ., 537
St. Vincent College, 1416
St. Xavier Univ., 640
Stanford Univ., 438
Stephen F. Austin State Univ., 1550
Stephens College, 991
Sterling College, 734
Stetson Univ., 535
Stevens Institute of Technology, 1069
Stevenson Univ., 812
Stillman College, 341
Stonehill College, 867
Suffolk Univ., 868
Sul Ross State Univ., 1552
SUNY College of Agriculture and Technology–Cobleskill, 1160
SUNY College of Environmental Science and Forestry, 1161
SUNY College of Technology–Alfred, 1162
SUNY College of Technology–Delhi, 1163
SUNY College–Cortland, 1159
SUNY College–Old Westbury, 1164
SUNY College–Oneonta, 1165
SUNY College–Potsdam, 1166
SUNY Empire State College, 1167
SUNY Institute of Technology–Utica/Rome, 1170
SUNY Maritime College, 1171
SUNY–Fredonia, 1168
SUNY–Geneseo, 1169
SUNY–New Paltz, 1172
SUNY–Oswego, 1173
SUNY–Plattsburgh, 1174
SUNY–Stony Brook, 1175
Susquehanna Univ., 1417
Swarthmore College, 1418
Sweet Briar College, 1635
Syracuse Univ., 1176

T

Tabor College, 735
Talladega College, 342
Tarleton State Univ., 1553
Taylor Univ., 685
Temple Univ., 1419
Tennessee State Univ., 1511
Tennessee Technological Univ., 1512
Tennessee Wesleyan College, 1513
Texas A&M International Univ., 1553
Texas A&M Univ.–College Station, 1554
Texas A&M Univ.–Commerce, 1555
Texas A&M Univ.–Corpus Christi, 1556
Texas A&M Univ.–Kingsville, 1557
Texas Christian Univ., 1558
Texas College, 1559

Texas Lutheran Univ., 1560
Texas Southern Univ., 1561
Texas State Univ.–San Marcos, 1561
Texas Tech Univ., 1563
Texas Wesleyan Univ., 1564
Texas Woman's Univ., 1565
The Citadel, 1454
Thiel College, 1421
Thomas Aquinas College, 440
Thomas College, 791
Thomas Edison State College, 1071
Thomas More College, 758
Thomas More College of Liberal Arts, 1043
Thomas Univ., 581
Tiffin Univ., 1286
Toccoa Falls College, 581
Tougaloo College, 964
Touro College, 1177
Towson Univ., 814
Transylvania Univ., 759
Trevecca Nazarene Univ., 1514
Trine Univ., 687
Trinity Christian College, 641
Trinity College, 489
Trinity International Univ., 642
Trinity Univ. (DC), 510
Trinity Univ. (TX), 1566
Troy Univ., 342
Truman State Univ., 993
Tufts Univ., 870
Tulane Univ., 778
Tusculum College, 1515
Tuskegee Univ., 343

U

Union College (KY), 760
Union College (NE), 1023
Union College (NY), 1178
Union Institute and Univ., 1287
Union Univ., 1515
United States Air Force Academy, 470
United States Coast Guard Academy, 490
United States Merchant Marine Academy, 1179
United States Military Academy, 1180
United States Naval Academy, 815
Unity College, 791
Univ. at Albany–SUNY, 1181
Univ. at Buffalo–SUNY, 1182
Univ. of Akron, 1287
Univ. of Alabama, 344
Univ. of Alabama–Birmingham, 345
Univ. of Alabama–Huntsville, 346
Univ. of Alaska–Anchorage, 354
Univ. of Alaska–Fairbanks, 355
Univ. of Alaska–Southeast, 356
Univ. of Arizona, 359
Univ. of Arkansas, 371
Univ. of Arkansas–Fort Smith, 373
Univ. of Arkansas–Little Rock, 373
Univ. of Arkansas–Monticello, 373
Univ. of Arkansas–Pine Bluff, 374
Univ. of Baltimore, 816
Univ. of Bridgeport, 491
Univ. of California–Berkeley, 441
Univ. of California–Davis, 442

Univ. of California–Irvine, 443
Univ. of California–Los Angeles, 444
Univ. of California–Riverside, 445
Univ. of California–San Diego, 446
Univ. of California–Santa Barbara, 447
Univ. of California–Santa Cruz, 448
Univ. of Central Arkansas, 374
Univ. of Central Florida, 538
Univ. of Central Missouri, 994
Univ. of Central Oklahoma, 1319
Univ. of Charleston, 1678
Univ. of Chicago, 643
Univ. of Cincinnati, 1288
Univ. of Colorado–Boulder, 471
Univ. of Colorado–Colorado Springs, 472
Univ. of Colorado–Denver, 473
Univ. of Connecticut, 492
Univ. of Dallas, 1567
Univ. of Dayton, 1289
Univ. of Delaware, 500
Univ. of Denver, 474
Univ. of Detroit Mercy, 914
Univ. of Dubuque, 715
Univ. of Evansville, 688
Univ. of Findlay, 1291
Univ. of Florida, 539
Univ. of Georgia, 582
Univ. of Great Falls, 1009
Univ. of Hartford, 493
Univ. of Hawaii–Hilo, 589
Univ. of Hawaii–Manoa, 589
Univ. of Hawaii–West Oahu, 590
Univ. of Houston, 1568
Univ. of Houston–Downtown, 1569
Univ. of Idaho, 596
Univ. of Illinois–Chicago, 644
Univ. of Illinois–Springfield, 645
Univ. of Illinois–Urbana-Champaign, 646
Univ. of Indianapolis, 689
Univ. of Iowa, 716
Univ. of Kansas, 736
Univ. of Kentucky, 761
Univ. of La Verne, 449
Univ. of Louisiana–Lafayette, 779
Univ. of Louisiana–Monroe, 780
Univ. of Louisville, 762
Univ. of Maine, 791
Univ. of Maine–Augusta, 792
Univ. of Maine–Farmington, 793
Univ. of Maine–Fort Kent, 794
Univ. of Maine–Machias, 795
Univ. of Maine–Presque Isle, 796
Univ. of Mary, 1242
Univ. of Mary Hardin-Baylor, 1570
Univ. of Mary Washington, 1636
Univ. of Maryland–Baltimore County, 816
Univ. of Maryland–College Park, 818
Univ. of Maryland–Eastern Shore, 819
Univ. of Maryland–Univ. College, 820
Univ. of Massachusetts–Amherst, 871
Univ. of Massachusetts–Boston, 872
Univ. of Massachusetts–Dartmouth, 873
Univ. of Massachusetts–Lowell, 874
Univ. of Memphis, 1516

About the Authors and Editors

Founded in 1933, Washington, D.C.-based *U.S.News & World Report* delivers a unique brand of journalism to millions of monthly magazine readers and visitors to usnews.com. In 1983, *U.S. News* began its exclusive annual rankings of American colleges and universities. The *U.S. News* education franchise is second to none. Its annual college and graduate school rankings are among the most eagerly anticipated magazine issues in the country.

Anne McGrath, the book's editor, is managing editor of the publications division at *U.S.News & World Report*, which is responsible for the monthly magazine, the annual "Best Colleges" and "Best Graduate Schools" guidebooks, and several special newsstand publications each year. Previously, she covered higher education and primary and secondary education for the magazine and managed the website's health channel.

Robert J. Morse is the director of data research at *U.S.News & World Report*. He is in charge of research, data collection, methodologies, and survey design for the annual "Best Colleges" and "Best Graduate Schools" rankings. He is also responsible for the yearly "Best High Schools" and "World's Best Universities" rankings.

Samuel Flanigan is the deputy director of data research at *U.S.News & World Report*. Besides playing a key role in the design and execution of the "Best Colleges" and "Best Graduate Schools" rankings, he has primary responsibility for producing the *U.S. News Ultimate College Guide*'s directory and Insider's Index.

Margaret Mannix is the executive editor of *U.S.News & World Report*. She oversees the publications division, *U.S. News Weekly* digital magazine, and the website's Politics & Policy channel. She is the editor of the *U.S. News* books *What College Really Costs* (Sourcebooks, 2005) and *Paying for College* (2003).

Brian Kelly is the editor of U.S. News Media Group, overseeing the weekly magazine, the website, newsstand books, and new business ventures. He is a former editor at the *Washington Post* and the author of four books.

Notes

Notes

Notes

Notes

Notes

Notes

Notes

Notes

Notes

Notes

Notes

Notes

Notes

Notes

Notes

Notes

Notes

Notes

Notes

Notes

Notes

Notes

Notes

Notes

Notes

Notes

Notes

Notes

Notes

Notes

Notes

Notes

Notes

Notes

Notes

Notes

Notes

Notes

Notes